D1499704

# NIV & AMPLIFIED
# SIDE-BY-SIDE
# BIBLE

NIV & AMPLIFIED
SIDE-BY-SIDE
BIBLE

NEW INTERNATIONAL VERSION
AMPLIFIED BIBLE

# NIV & AMPLIFIED
# SIDE-BY-SIDE
# BIBLE

**ZONDERVAN®**

*NIV & Amplified Side-by-Side Bible*
Published by Zondervan
Grand Rapids, Michigan 49530, USA

www.zondervan.com

Library of Congress Catalog Card Number 2012940485

*Printed in China*

N110910

12 13 14 15 16 17 18 19 20 /CTC/ 15 14 13 12 11 10 9 8 7 6 5 4 3 2 1

A portion of the purchase price of your NIV® Bible is provided to Biblica so together we can support the mission of *Transforming lives through God's Word.*

Biblica provides God's Word to people through translation, publishing and Bible engagement in Africa, Asia Pacific, Europe, Latin America, Middle East, and North America. Through its worldwide reach, Biblica engages people with God's Word so that their lives are transformed through a relationship with Jesus Christ.

# Table of Contents

THE
## Old Testament

THE
## New Testament

# Table of Contents

## The
## Old Testament

## The
## New Testament

# Preface

## TO THE

## NEW INTERNATIONAL VERSION

The goal of the New International Version (NIV) is to enable English-speaking people from around the world to read and hear God's eternal Word in their own language. Our work as translators is motivated by our conviction that the Bible is God's Word in written form. We believe that the Bible contains the divine answer to the deepest needs of humanity, sheds unique light on our path in a dark world and sets forth the way to our eternal well-being. Out of these deep convictions, we have sought to recreate as far as possible the experience of the original audience—blending transparency to the original text with accessibility for the millions of English speakers around the world. We have prioritized accuracy, clarity and literary quality with the goal of creating a translation suitable for public and private reading, evangelism, teaching, preaching, memorizing and liturgical use. We have also sought to preserve a measure of continuity with the long tradition of translating the Scriptures into English.

The complete NIV Bible was first published in 1978. It was a completely new translation made by over a hundred scholars working directly from the best available Hebrew, Aramaic and Greek texts. The translators came from the United States, Great Britain, Canada, Australia and New Zealand, giving the translation an international scope. They were from many denominations and churches—including Anglican, Assemblies of God, Baptist, Brethren, Christian Reformed, Church of Christ, Evangelical Covenant, Evangelical Free, Lutheran, Mennonite, Methodist, Nazarene, Presbyterian, Wesleyan and others. This breadth of denominational and theological perspective helped to safeguard the translation from sectarian bias. For these reasons, and by the grace of God, the NIV has gained a wide readership in all parts of the English-speaking world.

The work of translating the Bible is never finished. As good as they are, English translations must be regularly updated so that they will continue to communicate accurately the meaning of God's Word. Updates are needed in order to reflect the latest developments in our understanding of the biblical world and its languages and to keep pace with changes in English usage. Recognizing, then, that the NIV would retain its ability to communicate God's Word accurately only if it were regularly updated, the original translators established The Committee on Bible Translation (CBT). The committee is a self-perpetuating group of biblical scholars charged with keeping abreast of advances in biblical scholarship and changes in English and issuing periodic updates to the NIV. CBT is an independent, self-governing body and has sole responsibility for the NIV text. The committee mirrors the original group of translators in its diverse international and denominational makeup and in its unifying commitment to the Bible as God's inspired Word.

In obedience to its mandate, the committee has issued periodic updates to the NIV. An initial revision was released in 1984. A more thorough revision process was completed in 2005, resulting in the separately published Today's New International Version (TNIV). The updated NIV you now have in your hands builds on both the original NIV and the TNIV and represents the latest effort of the committee to articulate God's unchanging Word in the way the original authors might have said it had they been speaking in English to the global English-speaking audience today.

The first concern of the translators has continued to be the accuracy of the translation and its faithfulness to the intended meaning of the biblical writers. This has moved the translators to go beyond a formal word-for-word rendering of the original texts. Because thought patterns and syntax differ from language to language, accurate communication of the meaning of the biblical authors demands constant regard for varied contextual uses of words and idioms and for frequent modifications in sentence structures.

As an aid to the reader, sectional headings have been inserted. They are not to be regarded as part of the biblical text and are not intended for oral reading. It is the committee's hope that these headings may prove more helpful to the reader than the traditional chapter divisions, which were introduced long after the Bible was written.

For the Old Testament the standard Hebrew text, the Masoretic Text as published in the latest edition of *Biblia Hebraica,* has been used throughout. The Masoretic Text tradition contains marginal notations that offer variant readings. These have sometimes been followed instead of the text itself. Because such instances involve variants within the Masoretic tradition, they have not been indicated in the textual notes. In a few cases, words in the basic consonantal text have been divided differently than in the Masoretic Text. Such cases are usually indicated in the textual footnotes. The Dead Sea Scrolls contain biblical texts that represent an earlier stage of the transmission of the Hebrew text. They have been consulted, as have been the Samaritan Pentateuch and the ancient scribal traditions concerning deliberate textual changes. The translators also consulted the more important early versions—the Greek Septuagint, Aquila, Symmachus and Theodotion, the Latin Vulgate, the Syriac Peshitta, the Aramaic Targums and, for the Psalms, the *Juxta Hebraica* of Jerome. Readings from these versions, the Dead Sea Scrolls and the scribal traditions were occasionally followed where the Masoretic Text seemed doubtful and where accepted principles of textual criticism showed that one or more of these textual witnesses appeared to provide the correct reading. In rare cases, the committee has emended the Hebrew text where it appears to have become corrupted at an even earlier stage of its transmission. These departures from the Masoretic Text are also indicated in the textual footnotes. Sometimes the vowel indicators (which are later additions to the basic consonantal text) found in the Masoretic Text did not, in the judgment of the committee, represent the correct vowels for the original text. Accordingly, some words have been read with a different set of vowels. These instances are usually not indicated in the footnotes.

The Greek text used in translating the New Testament is an eclectic one, based on the latest editions of the Nestle-Aland/United Bible Societies' Greek New Testament. The committee has made its choices among the variant readings in accordance with widely accepted principles of New Testament textual criticism. Footnotes call attention to places where uncertainty remains.

The New Testament authors, writing in Greek, often quote the Old Testament from its ancient Greek version, the Septuagint. This is one reason why some of the Old Testament quotations in the NIV New Testament are not identical to the corresponding passages in the NIV Old Testament. Such quotations in the New Testament are indicated with the footnote "(see Septuagint)."

Other footnotes in this version are of several kinds, most of which need no explanation. Those giving alternative translations begin with "Or" and generally introduce the alternative with the last word preceding it in the text, except when it is a single-word alternative. When poetry is quoted in a footnote, a slash mark indicates a line division.

It should be noted that references to diseases, minerals, flora and fauna, architectural details, clothing, jewelry, musical instruments and other articles cannot always be identified with precision. Also, linear measurements and measures of capacity can only be approximated (see the Table of Weights and Measures). Although *Selah,* used mainly in the Psalms, is probably a musical term, its meaning is uncertain. Since it may interrupt reading and distract the reader, this word has not been kept in the English text, but every occurrence has been signaled by a footnote.

One of the main reasons the task of Bible translation is never finished is the change in our own language, English. Although a basic core of the language remains relatively stable, many diverse and complex linguistic factors continue to bring about subtle shifts in the meanings and/or connotations of even old, well-established words and phrases. One of the shifts that creates particular challenges to writers and translators alike is the manner in which gender is presented. The original NIV (1978) was published in a time when "a man" would naturally be understood, in many contexts, to be referring to a person, whether male or female. But most English speakers today tend to hear a distinctly male connotation in this word. In recognition of this change in English, this edition of the NIV, along with almost all other recent English translations, substitutes other expressions when the original text intends to refer generically to men and women equally. Thus, for instance, the NIV (1984) rendering of 1 Corinthians 8:3, "But the man who loves God is known by God" becomes in this edition "But whoever loves God is known by God." On the other hand, "man" and "mankind," as ways of denoting the human race, are still widely used. This edition of the NIV therefore continues to use these words, along with other expressions, in this way.

A related shift in English creates a greater challenge for modern translations: the move away from using the third-person masculine singular pronouns—"he/him/his"—to refer to men and women equally. This usage does persist at a low level in some forms of English, and this revision therefore occasionally uses these pronouns in a generic sense. But the tendency, recognized in day-to-day usage and confirmed by extensive research, is away from the generic use of "he," "him" and "his." In recognition of this shift in language and in an effort to translate into the "common" English that people are actually using, this revision of the NIV generally uses other constructions when the biblical text is plainly addressed to men and women equally. The reader will frequently encounter a "they," "them" or "their" to express a generic singular idea. Thus, for instance, Mark 8:36 reads: "What good is it for someone to gain the whole world, yet forfeit their soul?" This generic use of the "indefinite" or "singular" "they/them/their" has a venerable place in English idiom and has quickly become established as standard English, spoken and written, all over the world. Where an individual emphasis is deemed to be present, "anyone" or "everyone" or some other equivalent is generally used as the antecedent of such pronouns.

Sometimes the chapter and/or verse numbering in English translations of the Old Testament differs from that found in published Hebrew texts. This is particularly the case in the Psalms, where the traditional titles are often included in the Hebrew verse numbering. Such differences are indicated in the footnotes at the bottom of the page. In the New Testament, verse numbers that marked off portions of the traditional English text not supported by the best Greek manuscripts now appear in brackets, with a footnote indicating the text that has been omitted (see, for example, Matthew 17:[21]).

Mark 16:9–20 and John 7:53–8:11, although long accorded virtually equal status with the rest of the Gospels in which they stand, have a very questionable—and confused—standing in the textual history of the New Testament, as noted in the bracketed annotations with which they are set off. A different typeface has been chosen for these passages to indicate even more clearly their uncertain status.

Basic formatting of the text, such as lining the poetry, paragraphing (both prose and poetry), setting up of (administrative-like) lists, indenting letters and lengthy prayers within narratives and the insertion of sectional headings, has been the work of the committee. However, the choice between single-column and double-column formats has been left to the publishers. Also the issuing of "red-letter" editions is a publisher's choice—one the committee does not endorse.

The committee has again been reminded that every human effort is flawed—including this revision of the NIV. We trust, however, that many will find in it an improved representation of the Word of God, through which they hear his call to faith in our Lord Jesus Christ and to service in his kingdom. We offer this version of the Bible to him in whose name and for whose glory it has been made.

The Committee on Bible Translation
*September 2010*

# Preface

## TO THE
## AMPLIFIED BIBLE

In 1958 The Lockman Foundation and Zondervan Publishing House issued the first edition of The Amplified New Testament after more than 20,000 hours of research and prayerful study. Some four years later the first of two Old Testament volumes appeared (The Amplified Old Testament, Part Two—Job to Malachi), followed in 1964 by the publication of The Amplified Old Testament, Part One—Genesis to Esther. The next year (1965) The Amplified Bible came out in one volume.

Now, twenty-two years later, Zondervan Bible Publishers and The Lockman Foundation are pleased to present The Amplified Bible, Expanded Edition. The purpose of all the characters in the story of the making of The Amplified Bible is still relevant today: to communicate the Word of God to people and to exalt Jesus Christ. This has been the fourfold aim of The Lockman Foundation from the beginning:

1. That it should be true to the original Hebrew and Greek.
2. That it should be grammatically correct.
3. That it should be understandable to the masses.
4. That it should give the Lord Jesus Christ His proper place, the place which the Word gives Him.

From the days of John Wycliffe (1329-1384) and the first English Bible to the present, translators have worked diligently on English versions designed to faithfully present the Scriptures in contemporary language. The Amplified Bible is not an attempt to duplicate what has already been achieved, nor is it intended to be a substitute for other translations. Its genius lies in its rigorous attempt to go beyond the traditional "word-for-word" concept of translation to bring out the richness of the Hebrew and Greek languages. Its purpose is to reveal, together with the single English word equivalent to each key Hebrew and Greek word, any other clarifying meanings that may be concealed by the traditional translation method. Perhaps for the first time in an English version of the Bible, the full meaning of the key words in the original text is available for the reader. In a sense, the creative use of the amplification merely helps the reader comprehend what the Hebrew and Greek listener instinctively understood (as a matter of course).

Take as an example the Greek word *pisteuo*, which the vast majority of versions render "believe." That simple translation, however hardly does justice to the many meanings contained in the Greek *pisteuo*: "to adhere to, cleave to; to trust, to have faith in; to rely on, to depend on." Consequently, the reader gains understanding through the use of amplification, as in John 11:25: "Jesus said to her, I am [Myself] the Resurrection and the Life. Whoever believes in (adheres to, trusts in, and relies on) Me, although he may die, yet he shall live."

In the words of the apostle Paul, "And we are setting these truths forth in words not taught by human wisdom but taught by the [Holy] Spirit. . . [that His glory may be both manifested and recognized]" (1 Cor 2:13; Phil 1:11).

## INTRODUCTION TO THE AMPLIFIED BIBLE

### ABOUT THE AMPLIFIED BIBLE

The story of the Amplified Bible is a remarkable story of faith, hope, and love. It's the story of a woman, a foundation, a committee, and a publisher. Commitment, energy, enthusiasm, giftedness—these are the words that paint the picture, the picture of the making of a translation.

Frances Siewert (Litt. B., B.D., M.A., Litt. D.) was a woman with an intense dedication to the study of the Bible. It was Mrs. Siewert (1881-1967) who laid the foundation of the Amplified Bible, devoting her life to a familiarity with the Bible, with the Hebrew and Greek languages, and with the cultural and archaeological background of Biblical times, which would result in the publication of this unique translation.

Every vision need visionaries willing to follow the cause. The story of this dream is no different. Mrs. Siewert's vision was seen by a California non-profit foundation called The Lockman Foundation, made up of Christian men and women who through their commitment, their expertise, and their financial support undergirded Mrs. Siewert's monumental translation project. The Lockman Foundation's purpose remains today what is was then: to promote Bible translation, Christian evangelism, education, and benevolence.

Commitment, energy, enthusiasm, giftedness—the things visions are made of—describes the efforts of the committee appointed by The Lockman Foundation to carefully review the impressive work of Mrs. Siewert. This Editorial Board, made up of dedicated people, lent credibility and organization to this unprecedented attempt to bring out the richness of the Hebrew and Greek languages within the English text itself.

One chapter yet remained to bring the vision into reality. A publishing house in Grand Rapids, Michigan, on its way to becoming a major religious publishing firm, seized the opportunity to participate in a project which all visionaries involved strongly believed would be used by God to change lives. The Zondervan Publishing House joined the team, and the dream became reality with the publication of The Amplified New Testament in 1958, followed by the two-volume Amplified Old Testament in 1962 and 1964, and the one-volume Amplified Bible in 1965.

## FEATURES OF THE AMPLIFIED BIBLE

The Amplified Bible, Expanded Edition, features the text of The Amplified Bible, with explanatory and devotional footnotes; a reference system contained within the text; a comprehensive bibliography of original sources cited in the footnotes.

## THE TEXT OF THE AMPLIFIED BIBLE

The text of the Amplified Bible is easy to understand, and is made even easier to understand by the inclusion of informative footnotes which often alert readers to different textual readings and give insight into Greek grammar and translation. Numerous Bible translations are among the sources cited in the footnotes, as well as some of the greatest lexicographers of all time and some of the best of Bible commentators.

To help readers achieve the greatest possible clarity and understanding in their reading of the text of The Amplified Bible, some explanation of the various markings within the text is necessary:

Parentheses ( ) signify additional phases of meaning included in the original word, phrase, or clause of the original language.

Brackets [ ] contained justified clarifying words or comments not actually expressed in the immediate original text, as well as definitions of Hebrew and Greek names.

Italics point out:

1. certain familiar passages now recognized as not adequately supported by the original manuscripts. This is the primary use of italics in the New Testament, so that, upon encountering italics, the reader is alerted to a matter of textual readings. Often these will be accompanied by a footnote. See as an example Matthew 16:2-3.

2. conjunctions such as "and," "or," and the like, not in the original text, but used to connect additional English words indicated in the same original word. In this use, the reader, upon encountering a conjunction in italics, is alerted to the addition of an amplified word or phrase. See as an example Acts 24:3.

3. words which are not found in the original Hebrew or Greek but implied by it.

Capitals are used:

1. in names and personal pronouns referring to the Deity. See as an example Psalm 94.

2. in proper names of persons, places, specific feasts, topographical names, personifications, and the like. See as an example Proverbs 1:2; John 7:2.

Abbreviations may on occasion be encountered in either the text or in the footnotes.

| | |
|---|---|
| cf., | compare, confer |
| ch., chs. | chapter, chapters |
| e.g. | for example |

| etc. | and so on |
| i.e., | that is |
| v., vv. | verse, verses |
| ff. | following |
| ft. | foot |
| c. | about |
| KJV | King James Version |
| RV | Revised Version |
| ASV | American Standard Version |

## THE REFERENCE SYSTEM

The reference system of the Amplified Bible is contained within the text. The Scripture references are placed within brackets at the end of a verse, and are intended to cover any part of the preceding verse to which they apply. If a verse contains more than one Scripture reference, the list of references is in Biblical order. A sensitivity to the prophecy-fulfillment motif is indicated by such references as [Fulfilled in. . . ]; [Foretold in. . . ].

# THE
# Old Testament

# Genesis

# Genesis

## The Beginning

**1** In the beginning God created the heavens and the earth. ²Now the earth was formless and empty, darkness was over the surface of the deep, and the Spirit of God was hovering over the waters.

³And God said, "Let there be light," and there was light. ⁴God saw that the light was good, and he separated the light from the darkness. ⁵God called the light "day," and the darkness he called "night." And there was evening, and there was morning—the first day. ⁶And God said, "Let there be a vault between the waters to separate water from water." ⁷So God made the vault and separated the water under the vault from the water above it. And it was so. ⁸God called the vault "sky." And there was evening, and there was morning—the second day.

⁹And God said, "Let the water under the sky be gathered to one place, and let dry ground appear." And it was so. ¹⁰God called the dry ground "land," and the gathered waters he called "seas." And God saw that it was good.

¹¹Then God said, "Let the land produce vegetation: seed-bearing plants and trees on the land that bear fruit with seed in it, according to their various kinds." And it was so. ¹²The land produced vegetation: plants bearing seed according to their kinds and trees bearing fruit with seed in it according to their kinds. And God saw that it was good. ¹³And there was evening, and there was morning—the third day.

¹⁴And God said, "Let there be lights in the vault of the sky to separate the day from the night, and let them serve as signs to mark sacred times, and days and years, ¹⁵and let them be lights in the vault of the sky to give light on the earth." And it was so. ¹⁶God made two great lights—the greater light to govern the day and the lesser light to govern the night. He also made the stars. ¹⁷God set them in the vault of the sky to give light on the earth, ¹⁸to govern the day and the night, and to separate light from darkness. And God saw that it was good. ¹⁹And there was evening, and there was morning—the fourth day.

²⁰And God said, "Let the water teem with living creatures, and let birds fly above the earth across the vault of the sky." ²¹So God created the great creatures of the sea and every living thing with which the water teems and that moves about in it, according to their kinds, and every winged bird according to its kind. And God saw that it was good. ²²God blessed them and said, "Be fruitful and increase in number and fill the water in the seas, and let the birds increase on the earth." ²³And there was evening, and there was morning—the fifth day.

**1** In the beginning God (prepared, formed, fashioned, and) created the heavens and the earth. [Heb. 11:3.]

²The earth was without form and an empty waste, and darkness was upon the face of the very great deep. The Spirit of God was moving (hovering, brooding) over the face of the waters.

³And God said, Let there be light; and there was light. ⁴And God saw that the light was good (suitable, pleasant) *and* He approved it; and God separated the light from the darkness. [II Cor. 4:6.]

⁵And God called the light Day, and the darkness He called Night. And there was evening and there was morning, one day.

⁶And God said, Let there be a firmament [the expanse of the sky] in the midst of the waters, and let it separate the waters [below] from the waters [above].

⁷And God made the firmament [the expanse] and separated the waters which were under the expanse from the waters which were above the expanse. And it was so.

⁸And God called the firmament Heavens. And there was evening and there was morning, a second day.

⁹And God said, Let the waters under the heavens be collected into one place [of standing], and let the dry land appear. And it was so.

¹⁰God called the dry land Earth, and the accumulated waters He called Seas. And God saw that this was good (fitting, admirable) *and* He approved it.

¹¹And God said, Let the earth put forth [tender] vegetation: plants yielding seed and fruit trees yielding fruit whose seed is in itself, each according to its kind, upon the earth. And it was so.

¹²The earth brought forth vegetation: plants yielding seed according to their own kinds and trees bearing fruit in which was their seed, each according to its kind. And God saw that it was good (suitable, admirable) *and* He approved it.

¹³And there was evening and there was morning, a third day.

¹⁴And God said, Let there be lights in the expanse of the heavens to separate the day from the night, and let them be signs *and* tokens [of God's provident care], and [to mark] seasons, days, and years, [Gen. 8:22.]

¹⁵And let them be lights in the expanse of the sky to give light upon the earth. And it was so.

¹⁶And God made the two great lights—the greater light (the sun) to rule the day and the lesser light (the moon) to rule the night. He also made the stars.

¹⁷And God set them in the expanse of the heavens to give light upon the earth,

¹⁸To rule over the day and over the night, and to separate the light from the darkness. And God saw that it was good (fitting, pleasant) *and* He approved it.

¹⁹And there was evening and there was morning, a fourth day.

²⁰And God said, Let the waters bring forth abundantly *and* swarm with living creatures, and let birds fly over the earth in the open expanse of the heavens.

²¹God created the great sea monsters and every living creature that moves, which the waters brought forth abundantly, according to their kinds, and every winged bird according to its kind. And God saw that it was good (suitable, admirable) *and* He approved it.

²²And God blessed them, saying, Be fruitful, multiply, and fill the waters in the seas, and let the fowl multiply in the earth.

²³And there was evening and there was morning, a fifth day.

## New International Version

24And God said, "Let the land produce living creatures according to their kinds: the livestock, the creatures that move along the ground, and the wild animals, each according to its kind." And it was so. 25God made the wild animals according to their kinds, the livestock according to their kinds, and all the creatures that move along the ground according to their kinds. And God saw that it was good.
26Then God said, "Let us make mankind in our image, in our likeness, so that they may rule over the fish in the sea and the birds in the sky, over the livestock and all the wild animals,[a] and over all the creatures that move along the ground."

27So God created mankind in his own image,
    in the image of God he created them;
    male and female he created them.

28God blessed them and said to them, "Be fruitful and increase in number; fill the earth and subdue it. Rule over the fish in the sea and the birds in the sky and over every living creature that moves on the ground."
29Then God said, "I give you every seed-bearing plant on the face of the whole earth and every tree that has fruit with seed in it. They will be yours for food. 30And to all the beasts of the earth and all the birds in the sky and all the creatures that move along the ground—everything that has the breath of life in it—I give every green plant for food." And it was so. 31God saw all that he had made, and it was very good. And there was evening, and there was morning—the sixth day.

**2** Thus the heavens and the earth were completed in all their vast array.

2By the seventh day God had finished the work he had been doing; so on the seventh day he rested from all his work. 3Then God blessed the seventh day and made it holy, because on it he rested from all the work of creating that he had done.

### Adam and Eve

4This is the account of the heavens and the earth when they were created, when the LORD God made the earth and the heavens.

5Now no shrub had yet appeared on the earth[b] and no plant had yet sprung up, for the LORD God had not sent rain on the earth and there was no one to work the ground, 6but streams[c] came up from the earth and watered the whole surface of the ground. 7Then the LORD God formed a man[d] from the dust of the ground and breathed into his nostrils the breath of life, and the man became a living being.
8Now the LORD God had planted a garden in the east, in Eden; and there he put the man he had formed. 9The LORD God made all kinds of trees grow out of the ground—trees that were pleasing to the eye and good for food. In the middle of the garden were the tree of life and the tree of the knowledge of good and evil.
10A river watering the garden flowed from Eden; from there it was separated into four headwaters. 11The name of the first is the Pishon; it winds through the entire land of Havilah, where there is gold. 12(The gold of that land

a 26 Probable reading of the original Hebrew text (see Syriac); Masoretic Text the earth    b 5 Or land; also in verse 6    c 6 Or mist    d 7 The Hebrew for man (adam) sounds like and may be related to the Hebrew for ground (adamah); it is also the name Adam (see verse 20).

## Amplified Bible

24And God said, Let the earth bring forth living creatures according to their kinds: livestock, creeping things, and [wild] beasts of the earth according to their kinds. And it was so.
25And God made the [wild] beasts of the earth according to their kinds, and domestic animals according to their kinds, and everything that creeps upon the earth according to its kind. And God saw that it was good (fitting, pleasant) and He approved it.
26God said, Let Us [Father, Son, and Holy Spirit] make mankind in Our image, after Our likeness, and let them have complete authority over the fish of the sea, the birds of the air, the [tame] beasts, and over all of the earth, and over everything that creeps upon the earth. [Ps. 104:30; Heb. 1:2; 11:3.]
27So God created man in His own image, in the image and likeness of God He created him; male and female He created them. [Col. 3:9, 10; James 3:8, 9.]
28And God blessed them and said to them, Be fruitful, multiply, and fill the earth, and subdue it [using all its vast resources in the service of God and man]; and have dominion over the fish of the sea, the birds of the air, and over every living creature that moves upon the earth.
29And God said, See, I have given you every plant yielding seed that is on the face of all the land and every tree with seed in its fruit; you shall have them for food.
30And to all the animals on the earth and to every bird of the air and to everything that creeps on the ground—to everything in which there is the breath of life—I have given every green plant for food. And it was so.
31And God saw everything that He had made, and behold, it was very good (suitable, pleasant) and He approved it completely. And there was evening and there was morning, a sixth day.

**2** Thus the heavens and the earth were finished, and all the host of them.

2And on the seventh day God ended His work which He had done; and He rested on the seventh day from all His work which He had done. [Heb. 4:9, 10.]
3And God blessed (spoke good of) the seventh day, set it apart as His own, and hallowed it, because on it God rested from all His work which He had created and done. [Exod. 20:11.]
4This is the history of the heavens and of the earth when they were created. In the day that the Lord God made the earth and the heavens—
5When no plant of the field was yet in the earth and no herb of the field had yet sprung up, for the Lord God had not [yet] caused it to rain upon the earth and there was no man to till the ground,
6But there went up a mist (fog, vapor) from the land and watered the whole surface of the ground—
7Then the Lord God formed man from the [a]dust of the ground and breathed into his nostrils the breath or spirit of life, and man became a living being. [I Cor. 15:45-49.]
8And the Lord God planted a garden toward the east, in Eden [delight]; and there He put the man whom He had formed (framed, constituted).
9And out of the ground the Lord God made to grow every tree that is pleasant to the sight or to be desired—good (suitable, pleasant) for food; the tree of life also in the center of the garden, and the tree of the knowledge of [the difference between] good and evil and blessing and calamity. [Rev. 2:7; 22:14, 19.]
10Now a river went out of Eden to water the garden; and from there it divided and became four [river] heads.
11The first is named Pishon; it is the one flowing around the whole land of Havilah, where there is gold.

a The same essential chemical elements are found in man and animal life that are in the soil. This scientific fact was not known to man until recent times, but God was displaying it here.

## New International Version

is good; aromatic resin[a] and onyx are also there.) [13]The name of the second river is the Gihon; it winds through the entire land of Cush.[b] [14]The name of the third river is the Tigris; it runs along the east side of Ashur. And the fourth river is the Euphrates.

[15]The LORD God took the man and put him in the Garden of Eden to work it and take care of it. [16]And the LORD God commanded the man, "You are free to eat from any tree in the garden; [17]but you must not eat from the tree of the knowledge of good and evil, for when you eat from it you will certainly die."

[18]The LORD God said, "It is not good for the man to be alone. I will make a helper suitable for him."

[19]Now the LORD God had formed out of the ground all the wild animals and all the birds in the sky. He brought them to the man to see what he would name them; and whatever the man called each living creature, that was its name. [20]So the man gave names to all the livestock, the birds in the sky and all the wild animals.

But for Adam[c] no suitable helper was found. [21]So the LORD God caused the man to fall into a deep sleep; and while he was sleeping, he took one of the man's ribs[d] and then closed up the place with flesh. [22]Then the LORD God made a woman from the rib[e] he had taken out of the man, and he brought her to the man.

[23]The man said,

"This is now bone of my bones
    and flesh of my flesh;
she shall be called 'woman,'
    for she was taken out of man."

[24]That is why a man leaves his father and mother and is united to his wife, and they become one flesh.

[25]Adam and his wife were both naked, and they felt no shame.

### The Fall

**3** Now the serpent was more crafty than any of the wild animals the LORD God had made. He said to the woman, "Did God really say, 'You must not eat from any tree in the garden'?"

[2]The woman said to the serpent, "We may eat fruit from the trees in the garden, [3]but God did say, 'You must not eat fruit from the tree that is in the middle of the garden, and you must not touch it, or you will die.'"

[4]"You will not certainly die," the serpent said to the woman. [5]"For God knows that when you eat from it your eyes will be opened, and you will be like God, knowing good and evil."

[6]When the woman saw that the fruit of the tree was good for food and pleasing to the eye, and also desirable for gaining wisdom, she took some and ate it. She also gave some to her husband, who was with her, and he ate it. [7]Then the eyes of both of them were opened, and they realized they were naked; so they sewed fig leaves together and made coverings for themselves.

[8]Then the man and his wife heard the sound of the LORD God as he was walking in the garden in the cool of the day, and they hid from the LORD God among the trees of the garden. [9]But the LORD God called to the man, "Where are you?"

## Amplified Bible

[12]The gold of that land is of high quality; bdellium (pearl?) and onyx stone are there.

[13]The second river is named Gihon; it is the one flowing around the whole land of Cush.

[14]The third river is named Hiddekel [the Tigris]; it is the one flowing east of Assyria. And the fourth river is the Euphrates.

[15]And the Lord God took the man and put him in the Garden of Eden to tend and guard *and* keep it.

[16]And the Lord God commanded the man, saying, You may freely eat of every tree of the garden;

[17]But of the tree of the knowledge of good and evil *and* blessing and calamity you shall not eat, for in the day that you eat of it you shall surely die.

[18]Now the Lord God said, It is not good (sufficient, satisfactory) that the man should be alone; I will make him a helper meet (suitable, adapted, complementary) for him.

[19]And out of the ground the Lord God formed every [wild] beast *and* living creature of the field and every bird of the air and brought them to Adam to see what he would call them; and whatever Adam called every living creature, that was its name.

[20]And Adam gave names to all the livestock and to the birds of the air and to every [wild] beast of the field; but for Adam there was not found a helper meet (suitable, adapted, complementary) for him.

[21]And the Lord God caused a deep sleep to fall upon Adam; and while he slept, He took one of his ribs *or* a part of his side and closed up the [place with] flesh.

[22]And the rib *or* part of his side which the Lord God had taken from the man He built up *and* made into a woman, and He brought her to the man.

[23]Then Adam said, This [creature] is now bone of my bones and flesh of my flesh; she shall be called Woman, because she was taken out of a man.

[24]Therefore a man shall leave his father and his mother and shall become united *and* cleave to his wife, and they shall become one flesh. [Matt. 19:5; I Cor. 6:16; Eph. 5:31-33.]

[25]And the man and his wife were both naked and were not embarrassed *or* ashamed in each other's presence.

**3** Now the serpent was more subtle *and* crafty than any living creature of the field which the Lord God had made. And he [Satan] said to the woman, Can it really be that God has said, You shall not eat from every tree of the garden? [Rev. 12:9-11.]

[2]And the woman said to the serpent, We may eat the fruit from the trees of the garden,

[3]Except the fruit from the tree which is in the middle of the garden. God has said, You shall not eat of it, neither shall you touch it, lest you die.

[4]But the serpent said to the woman, You shall not surely die, [II Cor. 11:3.]

[5]For God knows that in the day you eat of it your eyes will be opened, and you will be like God, knowing the difference between good and evil *and* blessing and calamity.

[6]And when the woman saw that the tree was good (suitable, pleasant) for food and that it was delightful to look at, and a tree to be desired in order to make one wise, she took of its fruit and ate; and she gave some also to her husband, and he ate.

[7]Then the eyes of them both were opened, and they knew that they were naked; and they sewed fig leaves together and made themselves apronlike girdles.

[8]And they heard the sound of the Lord God walking in the garden in the cool of the day, and Adam and his wife hid themselves from the presence of the Lord God among the trees of the garden.

[9]But the Lord God called to Adam and said to him, Where are you?

---

[a] 12 Or *good; pearls*    [b] 13 Possibly southeast Mesopotamia
[c] 20 Or *the man*    [d] 21 Or *took part of the man's side*    [e] 22 Or *part*

## New International Version

[10]He answered, "I heard you in the garden, and I was afraid because I was naked; so I hid."

[11]And he said, "Who told you that you were naked? Have you eaten from the tree that I commanded you not to eat from?"

[12]The man said, "The woman you put here with me—she gave me some fruit from the tree, and I ate it."

[13]Then the LORD God said to the woman, "What is this you have done?"

The woman said, "The serpent deceived me, and I ate."

[14]So the LORD God said to the serpent, "Because you have done this,

"Cursed are you above all livestock
    and all wild animals!
You will crawl on your belly
    and you will eat dust
    all the days of your life.
[15]And I will put enmity
    between you and the woman,
    and between your offspring[a] and hers;
he will crush[b] your head,
    and you will strike his heel."

[16]To the woman he said,

"I will make your pains in childbearing very severe;
    with painful labor you will give birth to children.
Your desire will be for your husband,
    and he will rule over you."

[17]To Adam he said, "Because you listened to your wife and ate fruit from the tree about which I commanded you, 'You must not eat from it,'

"Cursed is the ground because of you;
    through painful toil you will eat food from it
    all the days of your life.
[18]It will produce thorns and thistles for you,
    and you will eat the plants of the field.
[19]By the sweat of your brow
    you will eat your food
until you return to the ground,
    since from it you were taken;
for dust you are
    and to dust you will return."

[20]Adam[c] named his wife Eve,[d] because she would become the mother of all the living.

[21]The LORD God made garments of skin for Adam and his wife and clothed them. [22]And the LORD God said, "The man has now become like one of us, knowing good and evil. He must not be allowed to reach out his hand and take also from the tree of life and eat, and live forever." [23]So the LORD God banished him from the Garden of Eden to work the ground from which he had been taken. [24]After he drove the man out, he placed on the east side[e] of the Garden of Eden cherubim and a flaming sword flashing back and forth to guard the way to the tree of life.

### Cain and Abel

**4** Adam[c] made love to his wife Eve, and she became pregnant and gave birth to Cain.[f] She said, "With the help of the LORD I have brought forth[g] a man." [2]Later she gave birth to his brother Abel.

Now Abel kept flocks, and Cain worked the soil. [3]In the course of time Cain brought some of the fruits of the

## Amplified Bible

[10]He said, I heard the sound of You [walking] in the garden, and I was afraid because I was naked; and I hid myself.

[11]And He said, Who told you that you were naked? Have you eaten of the tree of which I commanded you that you should not eat?

[12]And the man said, The woman whom You gave to be with me—she gave me [fruit] from the tree, and I ate.

[13]And the Lord God said to the woman, What is this you have done? And the woman said, The serpent beguiled (cheated, outwitted, and deceived) me, and I ate.

[14]And the Lord God said to the serpent, Because you have done this, you are cursed above all [domestic] animals and above every [wild] living thing of the field; upon your belly you shall go, and you shall eat dust [and what it contains] all the days of your life.

[15]And I will put enmity between you and the woman, and between your offspring and her [a]Offspring; He will bruise and tread your head underfoot, and you will lie in wait and bruise His heel. [Gal. 4:4.]

[16]To the woman He said, I will greatly multiply your grief and your suffering in pregnancy and the pangs of childbearing; with spasms of distress you will bring forth children. Yet your desire and craving will be for your husband, and he will rule over you.

[17]And to Adam He said, Because you have listened and given heed to the voice of your wife and have eaten of the tree of which I commanded you, saying, You shall not eat of it, the ground is under a curse because of you; in sorrow and toil shall you eat [of the fruits] of it all the days of your life.

[18]Thorns also and thistles shall it bring forth for you, and you shall eat the plants of the field.

[19]In the sweat of your face shall you eat bread until you return to the ground, for out of it you were taken; for dust you are and to dust you shall return.

[20]The man called his wife's name Eve [life spring], because she was the mother of all the living.

[21]For Adam also and for his wife the Lord God made long coats (tunics) of skins and clothed them.

[22]And the Lord God said, Behold, the man has become like one of Us [the Father, Son, and Holy Spirit], to know [how to distinguish between] good and evil and blessing and calamity; and now, lest he put forth his hand and take also from the tree of life and eat, and live [b]forever—

[23]Therefore the Lord God sent him forth from the Garden of Eden to till the ground from which he was taken.

[24]So [God] drove out the man; and He placed at the east of the Garden of Eden the [c]cherubim and a flaming sword which turned every way, to keep and guard the way to the tree of life. [Rev. 2:7; 22:2, 14, 19.]

**4** And Adam knew Eve as his wife, and she became pregnant and bore Cain; and she said, I have gotten and gained a man with the help of the Lord.

[2]And [next] she gave birth to his brother Abel. Now Abel was a keeper of sheep, but Cain was a tiller of the ground.

[3]And in the course of time Cain brought to the Lord an offering of the fruit of the ground.

---

[a] Christ fulfills through his victory over Satan the wonderful promise here spoken. See also Isa. 9:6; Matt. 1:23; Luke 1:31; Rom. 16:20; Gal. 4:4; Rev. 12:17. [b] This sentence is left unfinished, as if to hasten to avert the tragedy suggested of men living on forever in their now fallen state. [c] Cherubim are ministering spirits manifesting God's invisible presence and symbolizing His action (E. F. Harrison et al., eds., *Baker's Dictionary of Theology*).

---

[a] 15 Or *seed*   [b] 15 Or *strike*   [c] 20,1 Or *The man*   [d] 20 *Eve* probably means *living.*   [e] 24 Or *placed in front*   [f] 1 *Cain* sounds like the Hebrew for *brought forth* or *acquired.*   [g] 1 Or *have acquired*

## New International Version

soil as an offering to the LORD. 4And Abel also brought an offering—fat portions from some of the firstborn of his flock. The LORD looked with favor on Abel and his offering, 5but on Cain and his offering he did not look with favor. So Cain was very angry, and his face was downcast.

6Then the LORD said to Cain, "Why are you angry? Why is your face downcast? 7If you do what is right, will you not be accepted? But if you do not do what is right, sin is crouching at your door; it desires to have you, but you must rule over it."

8Now Cain said to his brother Abel, "Let's go out to the field."a While they were in the field, Cain attacked his brother Abel and killed him.

9Then the LORD said to Cain, "Where is your brother Abel?"

"I don't know," he replied. "Am I my brother's keeper?"

10The LORD said, "What have you done? Listen! Your brother's blood cries out to me from the ground. 11Now you are under a curse and driven from the ground, which opened its mouth to receive your brother's blood from your hand. 12When you work the ground, it will no longer yield its crops for you. You will be a restless wanderer on the earth."

13Cain said to the LORD, "My punishment is more than I can bear. 14Today you are driving me from the land, and I will be hidden from your presence; I will be a restless wanderer on the earth, and whoever finds me will kill me."

15But the LORD said to him, "Not sob; anyone who kills Cain will suffer vengeance seven times over." Then the LORD put a mark on Cain so that no one who found him would kill him. 16So Cain went out from the LORD's presence and lived in the land of Nod,c east of Eden.

17Cain made love to his wife, and she became pregnant and gave birth to Enoch. Cain was then building a city, and he named it after his son Enoch. 18To Enoch was born Irad, and Irad was the father of Mehujael, and Mehujael was the father of Methushael, and Methushael was the father of Lamech.

19Lamech married two women, one named Adah and the other Zillah. 20Adah gave birth to Jabal; he was the father of those who live in tents and raise livestock. 21His brother's name was Jubal; he was the father of all who play stringed instruments and pipes. 22Zillah also had a son, Tubal-Cain, who forged all kinds of tools out ofd bronze and iron. Tubal-Cain's sister was Naamah.

23Lamech said to his wives,

"Adah and Zillah, listen to me;
     wives of Lamech, hear my words.
I have killed a man for wounding me,
     a young man for injuring me.
24If Cain is avenged seven times,
     then Lamech seventy-seven times."

## Amplified Bible

4And Abel brought of the firstborn of his flock and of the fat portions. And the Lord had respect and regard for Abel and for his offering, [Heb. 11:4.]

5But for aCain and his offering He had no respect or regard. So Cain was exceedingly angry and indignant, and he looked sad and depressed.

6And the Lord said to Cain, Why are you angry? And why do you look sad and depressed and dejected?

7If you do well, will you not be accepted? And if you do not do well, sin crouches at your door; its desire is for you, but you must master it.

8And Cain said to his brother, bLet us go out to the field. And when they were in the field, Cain rose up against Abel his brother and killed him. [I John 3:12.]

9And the Lord said to Cain, Where is Abel your brother? And he said, I do not know. Am I my brother's keeper?

10And [the Lord] said, What have you done? The voice of your brother's blood is crying to Me from the ground.

11And now you are cursed by reason of the earth, which has opened its mouth to receive your brother's [shed] blood from your hand.

12When you till the ground, it shall no longer yield to you its strength; you shall be a fugitive and a vagabond on the earth [in perpetual exile, a degraded outcast].

13Then Cain said to the Lord, My punishment is cgreater than I can bear.

14Behold, You have driven me out this day from the face of the land, and from Your face I will be hidden; and I will be a fugitive and a vagabond and a wanderer on the earth, and whoever finds me will kill me.

15And the Lord said to him, dTherefore, if anyone kills Cain, vengeance shall be taken on him sevenfold. And the Lord set a emark or sign upon Cain, lest anyone finding him should kill him.

16So Cain went away from the presence of the Lord and dwelt in the land of Nod [wandering], east of Eden.

17And Cain's wife [one of Adam's offspring] became pregnant and bore Enoch; and Cain built a fcity and named it after his son Enoch.

18To Enoch was born Irad, and Irad was the father of Mehujael, and Mehujael the father of Methusael, and Methusael the father of Lamech.

19And Lamech took two wives; the name of the one was Adah and of the other was Zillah.

20Adah bore Jabal; he was the father of those who dwell in tents and have cattle and purchase possessions.

21His brother's name was Jubal; he was the father of all those who play the lyre and pipe.

22Zillah bore Tubal-cain; he was the forger of all [cutting] instruments of bronze and iron. The sister of Tubal-cain was Naamah.

23Lamech said to his wives, Adah and Zillah, Hear my voice; you wives of Lamech, listen to what I say; for I have slain a man [merely] for wounding me, and a young man [only] for striking and bruising me.

24If Cain is avenged sevenfold, truly Lamech [will be avenged] seventy-sevenfold.

a In bringing the offering he did, Cain denied that he was a sinful creature under the sentence of divine condemnation. He insisted on approaching God on the ground of personal worthiness. Instead of accepting God's way, he offered to God the fruits of the ground **which God had cursed.** He presented the product of his own toil, the work of his own hands, and God refused to receive it (Arthur W. Pink, *Gleanings in Genesis*). b The Hebrew omits this clause, but various other texts show that it was originally included. c Some ancient versions read, "too great to be forgiven!" d Some versions read, "Not so!" e Many commentators believe this sign not to have been like a brand on the forehead, but something awesome about Cain's appearance that made people dread and avoid him. f C. H. Dodd (cited by Adam Clarke, *The Holy Bible with A Commentary*) shows that it would have been possible for Adam and Eve, in the more than 100 years he estimates may have elapsed since their union, to have had over 32,000 descendants at the time Cain went to Nod, all of them having sprung from Cain and Abel, who married their sisters.

a 8 Samaritan Pentateuch, Septuagint, Vulgate and Syriac; Masoretic Text does not have *"Let's go out to the field."*   b 15 Septuagint, Vulgate and Syriac; Hebrew *Very well*   c 16 *Nod* means *wandering* (see verses 12 and 14).   d 22 Or *who instructed all who work in*

## New International Version

25Adam made love to his wife again, and she gave birth to a son and named him Seth,ᵃ saying, "God has granted me another child in place of Abel, since Cain killed him." 26Seth also had a son, and he named him Enosh.

At that time people began to call onᵇ the name of the LORD.

### From Adam to Noah

5 This is the written account of Adam's family line.

When God created mankind, he made them in the likeness of God. 2He created them male and female and blessed them. And he named them "Mankind"ᶜ when they were created.

3When Adam had lived 130 years, he had a son in his own likeness, in his own image; and he named him Seth. 4After Seth was born, Adam lived 800 years and had other sons and daughters. 5Altogether, Adam lived a total of 930 years, and then he died.

6When Seth had lived 105 years, he became the fatherᵈ of Enosh. 7After he became the father of Enosh, Seth lived 807 years and had other sons and daughters. 8Altogether, Seth lived a total of 912 years, and then he died.

9When Enosh had lived 90 years, he became the father of Kenan. 10After he became the father of Kenan, Enosh lived 815 years and had other sons and daughters. 11Altogether, Enosh lived a total of 905 years, and then he died.

12When Kenan had lived 70 years, he became the father of Mahalalel. 13After he became the father of Mahalalel, Kenan lived 840 years and had other sons and daughters. 14Altogether, Kenan lived a total of 910 years, and then he died.

15When Mahalalel had lived 65 years, he became the father of Jared. 16After he became the father of Jared, Mahalalel lived 830 years and had other sons and daughters. 17Altogether, Mahalalel lived a total of 895 years, and then he died.

18When Jared had lived 162 years, he became the father of Enoch. 19After he became the father of Enoch, Jared lived 800 years and had other sons and daughters. 20Altogether, Jared lived a total of 962 years, and then he died.

21When Enoch had lived 65 years, he became the father of Methuselah. 22After he became the father of Methuselah, Enoch walked faithfully with God 300 years and had other sons and daughters. 23Altogether, Enoch lived a total of 365 years. 24Enoch walked faithfully with God; then he was no more, because God took him away.

25When Methuselah had lived 187 years, he became the father of Lamech. 26After he became the father of Lamech, Methuselah lived 782 years and had other sons and daugh-

## Amplified Bible

25And Adam's wife again became pregnant, and she bore a son and called his name Seth. For God, she said, has appointed for me another child instead of Abel, for Cain slew him.

26And to Seth also a son was born, whom he named Enosh. At that time men began to call [upon God] by the name of the Lord.

5 This is the book (the written record, the history) of the generations of the offspring of Adam. When God created man, He made him in the likeness of God.

2He created them male and female and blessed them and named them [both] Adam [Man] at the time they were created.

3When Adam had lived 130 years, he had a son in his own likeness, after his image; and he named him Seth.

4After he had Seth, Adam lived 800 years and had other sons and daughters.

5So altogether Adam lived 930 years, and he died.

6When Seth had lived 105 years, Enosh was born.

7Seth lived after the birth of Enosh 807 years and had other sons and daughters.

8So Seth lived 912 years, and he died.

9When Enosh had lived 90 years, Kenan was born to him.

10Enosh lived after the birth of Kenan 815 years and had other sons and daughters.

11So Enosh lived 905 years, and he died.

12When Kenan was 70 years old, Mahalalel was born.

13Kenan lived after the birth of Mahalalel 840 years and had other sons and daughters.

14So Kenan lived 910 years, and he died.

15When Mahalalel was 65 years old, Jared was born.

16Mahalalel lived after the birth of Jared 830 years and had other sons and daughters.

17So Mahalalel lived 895 years, and he died.

18When Jared was 162 years old, Enoch was born.

19Jared lived after the birth of Enoch 800 years and had other sons and daughters.

20So Jared lived 962 years, and he died.

21When Enoch was 65 years old, Methuselah was born.

22Enoch walked [in habitual fellowship] with God after the birth of Methuselah 300 years and had other sons and daughters.

23So all the days of Enoch were 365 years.

24And Enoch walked [in habitual fellowship] with God; and he was not, for God took him [home with Him]. [Heb. 11:5.]

25When Methuselah was 187 years old, Lamech was born to him.

26Methuselah lived after the birth of Lamech 782 years and had other sons and daughters.

---

ᵃ 25 Seth probably means granted.    ᵇ 26 Or to proclaim
ᶜ 2 Hebrew adam    ᵈ 6 Father may mean ancestor; also in verses 7-26.

## New International Version

ters. 27Altogether, Methuselah lived a total of 969 years, and then he died.

28When Lamech had lived 182 years, he had a son. 29He named him Noah[a] and said, "He will comfort us in the labor and painful toil of our hands caused by the ground the LORD has cursed." 30After Noah was born, Lamech lived 595 years and had other sons and daughters. 31Altogether, Lamech lived a total of 777 years, and then he died.

32After Noah was 500 years old, he became the father of Shem, Ham and Japheth.

### Wickedness in the World

**6** When human beings began to increase in number on the earth and daughters were born to them, 2the sons of God saw that the daughters of humans were beautiful, and they married any of them they chose. 3Then the LORD said, "My Spirit will not contend with[b] humans forever, for they are mortal[c]; their days will be a hundred and twenty years."

4The Nephilim were on the earth in those days—and also afterward—when the sons of God went to the daughters of humans and had children by them. They were the heroes of old, men of renown.

5The LORD saw how great the wickedness of the human race had become on the earth, and that every inclination of the thoughts of the human heart was only evil all the time. 6The LORD regretted that he had made human beings on the earth, and his heart was deeply troubled. 7So the LORD said, "I will wipe from the face of the earth the human race I have created—and with them the animals, the birds and the creatures that move along the ground—for I regret that I have made them." 8But Noah found favor in the eyes of the LORD.

### Noah and the Flood

9This is the account of Noah and his family.

Noah was a righteous man, blameless among the people of his time, and he walked faithfully with God. 10Noah had three sons: Shem, Ham and Japheth.

11Now the earth was corrupt in God's sight and was full of violence. 12God saw how corrupt the earth had become, for all the people on earth had corrupted their ways. 13So God said to Noah, "I am going to put an end to all people, for the earth is filled with violence because of them. I am surely going to destroy both them and the earth. 14So make yourself an ark of cypress[d] wood; make rooms in it and coat it with pitch inside and out. 15This is how you are to build it: The ark is to be three hundred cubits long, fifty cubits wide and thirty cubits high.[e] 16Make a roof for it, leaving below the roof an opening one cubit[f] high all

## Amplified Bible

27So Methuselah lived 969 years, and he died.
28When Lamech was 182 years old, a son was born.
29He named him Noah, saying, This one shall bring us relief and comfort from our work and the [grievous] toil of our hands due to the ground being cursed by the Lord.
30Lamech lived after the birth of Noah 595 years and had other sons and daughters.
31So all the days of [a]Lamech were 777 years, and he died.
32After Noah was 500 years old, he became the father of Shem, Ham, and Japheth.

**6** When men began to multiply on the face of the land and daughters were born to them,
2The sons of God saw that the daughters of men were fair, and they took wives of all they desired and chose.
3Then the Lord said, My Spirit shall not forever dwell and strive with man, for he also is flesh; but his days shall yet be 120 years.
4There were giants on the earth in those days—and also afterward—when the sons of God lived with the daughters of men, and they bore children to them. These were the mighty men who were of old, men of renown.
5The Lord saw that the wickedness of man was great in the earth, and that every imagination and intention of all human thinking was only evil continually.
6And the Lord regretted that He had made man on the earth, and He was grieved at heart.
7So the Lord said, I will destroy, blot out, and wipe away mankind, whom I have created from the face of the ground—not only man, [but] the beasts and the creeping things and the birds of the air—for it grieves Me and makes Me regretful that I have made them.
8But Noah found grace (favor) in the eyes of the Lord.
9This is the history of the generations of Noah. Noah was a just and righteous man, blameless in his [evil] generation; Noah walked [in habitual fellowship] with God.
10And Noah became the father of three sons: Shem, Ham, and Japheth.
11The earth was depraved and putrid in God's sight, and the land was filled with violence (desecration, infringement, outrage, assault, and lust for power).
12And God looked upon the world and saw how degenerate, debased, and vicious it was, for all humanity had corrupted their way upon the earth and lost their true direction.
13God said to Noah, I intend to make an end of all flesh, for through men the land is filled with violence; and behold, I will [b]destroy them and the land.
14Make yourself an ark of gopher or cypress wood; make in it rooms (stalls, pens, coops, nests, cages, and compartments) and cover it inside and out with pitch (bitumen).
15And this is the way you are to make it: the length of the ark shall be 300 cubits, its breadth 50 cubits, and its height 30 cubits [that is, 450 ft. x 75 ft. x 45 ft.].
16You shall make a roof or [c]window [a place for light] for

---

[a] It is now well known that the age of mankind cannot be reckoned in years from the facts listed in genealogies, for there are numerous known intentional gaps in them. For example, as B. B. Warfield (*Studies in Theology*) points out, the genealogy in Matt. 1:1-17 omits the three kings, Ahaziah, Jehoash, and Amaziah, and indicates that Joram (Matt. 1:8) begat Uzziah, who was his great-great-grandson. The mistaking of compressed genealogies as bases for chronology has been very misleading. So far, the dates in years of very early Old Testament events are altogether speculative and relative, and the tendency is to put them farther and farther back into antiquity. [b] Enoch had warned these people (Jude 14, 15); Noah had preached righteousness to them (II Pet. 2:5); God's Spirit had been striving with them (Gen. 6:3). Yet they had rejected God and were without excuse. [c] Noah's ark possibly had a window area large enough to admit light and provide ventilation.

---

[a] 29 Noah sounds like the Hebrew for comfort.   [b] 3 Or My spirit will not remain in   [c] 3 Or corrupt   [d] 14 The meaning of the Hebrew for this word is uncertain.   [e] 15 That is, about 450 feet long, 75 feet wide and 45 feet high or about 135 meters long, 23 meters wide and 14 meters high   [f] 16 That is, about 18 inches or about 45 centimeters

## New International Version

around.ᵃ Put a door in the side of the ark and make lower, middle and upper decks. ¹⁷I am going to bring floodwaters on the earth to destroy all life under the heavens, every creature that has the breath of life in it. Everything on earth will perish. ¹⁸But I will establish my covenant with you, and you will enter the ark—you and your sons and your wife and your sons' wives with you. ¹⁹You are to bring into the ark two of all living creatures, male and female, to keep them alive with you. ²⁰Two of every kind of bird, of every kind of animal and of every kind of creature that moves along the ground will come to you to be kept alive. ²¹You are to take every kind of food that is to be eaten and store it away as food for you and for them."

²²Noah did everything just as God commanded him.

**7** The LORD then said to Noah, "Go into the ark, you and your whole family, because I have found you righteous in this generation. ²Take with you seven pairs of every kind of clean animal, a male and its mate, and one pair of every kind of unclean animal, a male and its mate, ³also seven pairs of every kind of bird, male and female, to keep their various kinds alive throughout the earth. ⁴Seven days from now I will send rain on the earth for forty days and forty nights, and I will wipe from the face of the earth every living creature I have made."

⁵And Noah did all that the LORD commanded him.

⁶Noah was six hundred years old when the floodwaters came on the earth. ⁷And Noah and his sons and his wife and his sons' wives entered the ark to escape the waters of the flood. ⁸Pairs of clean and unclean animals, of birds and of all creatures that move along the ground, ⁹male and female, came to Noah and entered the ark, as God had commanded Noah. ¹⁰And after the seven days the floodwaters came on the earth.

¹¹In the six hundredth year of Noah's life, on the seventeenth day of the second month—on that day all the springs of the great deep burst forth, and the floodgates of the heavens were opened. ¹²And rain fell on the earth forty days and forty nights.

¹³On that very day Noah and his sons, Shem, Ham and Japheth, together with his wife and the wives of his three sons, entered the ark. ¹⁴They had with them every wild animal according to its kind, all livestock according to their kinds, every creature that moves along the ground according to its kind and every bird according to its kind,

## Amplified Bible

the ark and finish it to a cubit [at least 18 inches] above—and the ᵃdoor of the ark you shall put in the side of it; and you shall make it with lower, second, and third stories.

¹⁷For behold, I, even I, will bring a flood of waters upon the earth to destroy *and* make putrid all flesh under the heavens in which are the breath *and* spirit of life; everything that is on the land shall die.

¹⁸But I will establish My covenant (promise, pledge) with you, and you shall come into the ark—you and your sons and your wife and your sons' wives with you.

¹⁹And of every living thing of all flesh [found on land], you shall bring two of every sort into the ark, to keep them alive with you; they shall be male and female.

²⁰Of fowls *and* birds according to their kinds, of beasts according to their kinds, of every creeping thing of the ground according to its kind—two of every sort shall come in with you, that they may be kept alive.

²¹Also take with you every sort of food that is eaten, and you shall collect *and* store it up, and it shall serve as food for you and for them.

²²Noah did this; he did all that God commanded him.

**7** And the Lord said to Noah, Come with all your household into the ark, for I have seen you to be righteous (upright and in right standing) before Me in this generation. [Ps. 27:5; 33:18, 19; II Pet. 2:9.]

²Of every clean beast you shall receive *and* take with you seven pairs, the male and his mate, and of beasts that are not clean a pair of each kind, the male and his mate, [Lev. 11.]

³Also of the birds of the air seven pairs, the male and the female, to keep seed [their kind] alive over all the earth *or* land.

⁴For in seven days I will cause it to rain upon the earth forty days and forty nights, and every living substance *and* thing that I have made I will destroy, blot out, *and* wipe away from the face of the earth.

⁵And Noah did all that the Lord commanded him. [Heb. 11:7.]

⁶Noah was 600 years old when the flood of waters came upon the earth *or* land.

⁷And Noah and his sons and his wife and his sons' wives with him went into the ark because of the waters of the flood. [Matt. 24:38; Luke 17:27.]

⁸Of ᵇclean animals and of animals that are not clean, and of birds *and* fowls, and of everything that creeps on the ground,

⁹There went in two and two with Noah into the ark, the male and the female, as God had commanded Noah.

¹⁰And after the seven days the floodwaters came upon the earth *or* land.

¹¹In the year 600 of Noah's life, in the seventeenth day of the second month, that same day all the fountains of the great deep were broken up *and* burst forth, and the windows *and* floodgates of the heavens were opened.

¹²And it rained upon the earth forty days and forty nights.

¹³On the very same day Noah and Shem, Ham, and Japheth, the sons of Noah, and Noah's wife and the three wives of his sons with them, went into the ark,

¹⁴They and every [wild] beast according to its kind, all the livestock according to their kinds, every moving thing that creeps on the land according to its kind, and every fowl according to its kind, every winged thing of every sort.

---

ᵃ "Here can only be meant an entrance which was afterward closed, and only opened again at the end of the flood. And since there were three stories of the ark, the word is to be understood, perhaps, of three entrances capable of being closed, and to which there would have been constructed a way of access from the outside" (J. P. Lange, *A Commentary on the Holy Scriptures*). ᵇ Noah had many years in which to interest travelers in securing these animals for him. The five extra pairs of clean animals were for food, and for sacrifice later.

---

ᵃ 16 The meaning of the Hebrew for this clause is uncertain.

## New International Version

everything with wings. <sup>15</sup>Pairs of all creatures that have the breath of life in them came to Noah and entered the ark. <sup>16</sup>The animals going in were male and female of every living thing, as God had commanded Noah. Then the LORD shut him in.

<sup>17</sup>For forty days the flood kept coming on the earth, and as the waters increased they lifted the ark high above the earth. <sup>18</sup>The waters rose and increased greatly on the earth, and the ark floated on the surface of the water. <sup>19</sup>They rose greatly on the earth, and all the high mountains under the entire heavens were covered. <sup>20</sup>The waters rose and covered the mountains to a depth of more than fifteen cubits.<sup>a,b</sup> <sup>21</sup>Every living thing that moved on land perished—birds, livestock, wild animals, all the creatures that swarm over the earth, and all mankind. <sup>22</sup>Everything on dry land that had the breath of life in its nostrils died. <sup>23</sup>Every living thing on the face of the earth was wiped out; people and animals and the creatures that move along the ground and the birds were wiped from the earth. Only Noah was left, and those with him in the ark.

<sup>24</sup>The waters flooded the earth for a hundred and fifty days.

**8** But God remembered Noah and all the wild animals and the livestock that were with him in the ark, and he sent a wind over the earth, and the waters receded. <sup>2</sup>Now the springs of the deep and the floodgates of the heavens had been closed, and the rain had stopped falling from the sky. <sup>3</sup>The water receded steadily from the earth. At the end of the hundred and fifty days the water had gone down, <sup>4</sup>and on the seventeenth day of the seventh month the ark came to rest on the mountains of Ararat. <sup>5</sup>The waters continued to recede until the tenth month, and on the first day of the tenth month the tops of the mountains became visible.

<sup>6</sup>After forty days Noah opened a window he had made in the ark <sup>7</sup>and sent out a raven, and it kept flying back and forth until the water had dried up from the earth. <sup>8</sup>Then he sent out a dove to see if the water had receded from the surface of the ground. <sup>9</sup>But the dove could find nowhere to perch because there was water over all the surface of the earth; so it returned to Noah in the ark. He reached out his hand and took the dove and brought it back to himself in the ark. <sup>10</sup>He waited seven more days and again sent out the dove from the ark. <sup>11</sup>When the dove returned to him in the evening, there in its beak was a freshly plucked olive leaf! Then Noah knew that the water had receded from the earth. <sup>12</sup>He waited seven more days and sent the dove out again, but this time it did not return to him.

<sup>13</sup>By the first day of the first month of Noah's six hundred and first year, the water had dried up from the earth.

## Amplified Bible

<sup>15</sup>And they went into the ark with Noah, two and two of all flesh in which there were the breath *and* spirit of life.

<sup>16</sup>And they that entered, male and female of all flesh, went in as God had commanded [Noah]; and the Lord shut him in *and* closed [the door] round about him.

<sup>17</sup>The flood [that is, the downpour of rain] was forty days upon the earth; and the waters increased and bore up the ark, and it was lifted [high] above the land.

<sup>18</sup>And the waters became mighty and increased greatly upon the land, and the ark went [gently floating] upon the surface of the waters.

<sup>19</sup>And the waters prevailed so exceedingly *and* were so mighty upon the earth that all the high hills under the whole sky were covered.

<sup>20</sup>[In fact] the waters became fifteen cubits higher, as the high hills were covered.

<sup>21</sup>And all flesh ceased to breathe that moved upon the earth—fowls *and* birds, [tame] animals, [wild] beasts, all swarming *and* creeping things that swarm *and* creep upon the land, and all mankind.

<sup>22</sup>Everything on the dry land in whose nostrils were the breath *and* spirit of life died.

<sup>23</sup>God destroyed (blotted out) every living thing that was upon the face of the earth; man and animals and the creeping things and the birds of the heavens were destroyed (blotted out) from the land. Only Noah remained alive, and those who were with him in the ark. [Matt. 24:37-44.]

<sup>24</sup>And the waters prevailed [mightily] upon the earth *or* land 150 days (five months).

**8** And God [earnestly] remembered Noah and every living thing and all the animals that were with him in the ark; and God made a wind blow over the land, and the waters sank down *and* abated.

<sup>2</sup>Also the fountains of the deep and the windows of the heavens were closed, the gushing rain from the sky was checked,

<sup>3</sup>And the waters receded from the land continually. At the end of 150 days the waters had diminished.

<sup>4</sup>On the seventeenth day of the seventh month the ark came to rest on the mountains of Ararat [in Armenia].

<sup>5</sup>And the waters continued to diminish until the tenth month; on the first day of the tenth month the tops of the high hills were seen.

<sup>6</sup>At the end of [another] forty days Noah opened *a* window of the ark which he had made

<sup>7</sup>And sent forth a raven, which kept going to and fro until the waters were dried up from the land.

<sup>8</sup>Then he sent forth a dove to see if the waters had decreased from the surface of the ground.

<sup>9</sup>But the dove found no resting-place on which to roost, and she returned to him to the ark, for the waters were [yet] on the face of the whole land. So he put forth his hand and drew her to him into the ark.

<sup>10</sup>He waited another seven days and again sent forth the dove out of the ark.

<sup>11</sup>And the dove came back to him in the evening, and behold, in her mouth was a newly sprouted *and* freshly plucked olive leaf! So Noah knew that the waters had subsided from the land.

<sup>12</sup>Then he waited another seven days and sent forth the dove, but she did not return to him any more.

<sup>13</sup>In the year 601 [of Noah's life], on the first day of the first month, the waters were drying up from the land. And

---

<sup>a</sup> 20 That is, about 23 feet or about 6.8 meters    <sup>b</sup> 20 Or *rose more than fifteen cubits, and the mountains were covered*

## New International Version

Noah then removed the covering from the ark and saw that the surface of the ground was dry. [14]By the twenty-seventh day of the second month the earth was completely dry.

[15]Then God said to Noah, [16]"Come out of the ark, you and your wife and your sons and their wives. [17]Bring out every kind of living creature that is with you—the birds, the animals, and all the creatures that move along the ground—so they can multiply on the earth and be fruitful and increase in number on it."

[18]So Noah came out, together with his sons and his wife and his sons' wives. [19]All the animals and all the creatures that move along the ground and all the birds—everything that moves on land—came out of the ark, one kind after another.

[20]Then Noah built an altar to the LORD and, taking some of all the clean animals and clean birds, he sacrificed burnt offerings on it. [21]The LORD smelled the pleasing aroma and said in his heart: "Never again will I curse the ground because of humans, even though[a] every inclination of the human heart is evil from childhood. And never again will I destroy all living creatures, as I have done.

[22]"As long as the earth endures,
　seedtime and harvest,
　cold and heat,
　summer and winter,
　day and night
　will never cease."

### God's Covenant With Noah

**9** Then God blessed Noah and his sons, saying to them, "Be fruitful and increase in number and fill the earth. [2]The fear and dread of you will fall on all the beasts of the earth, and on all the birds in the sky, on every creature that moves along the ground, and on all the fish in the sea; they are given into your hands. [3]Everything that lives and moves about will be food for you. Just as I gave you the green plants, I now give you everything.

[4]"But you must not eat meat that has its lifeblood still in it. [5]And for your lifeblood I will surely demand an accounting. I will demand an accounting from every animal. And from each human being, too, I will demand an accounting for the life of another human being.

[6]"Whoever sheds human blood,
　by humans shall their blood be shed;
for in the image of God
　has God made mankind.

[7]As for you, be fruitful and increase in number; multiply on the earth and increase upon it."

[8]Then God said to Noah and to his sons with him: [9]"I now establish my covenant with you and with your descendants after you [10]and with every living creature that was

---

## Amplified Bible

Noah [a]removed the covering of the ark and looked, and behold, the surface of the ground was drying.

[14]And on the twenty-seventh day of the second month the land was entirely dry.

[15]And God spoke to Noah, saying,

[16]Go forth from the ark, you and your wife and your sons and their wives with you.

[17]Bring forth every living thing that is with you of all flesh—birds and beasts and every creeping thing that creeps on the ground—that they may breed abundantly on the land and be fruitful and multiply upon the earth.

[18]And Noah went forth, and his wife and his sons and their wives with him [after being in the ark one year and ten days].

[19]Every beast, every creeping thing, every bird—and whatever moves on the land—went forth by families out of the ark.

[20]And Noah built an altar to the Lord and took of every clean [four-footed] animal and of every clean fowl *or* bird and offered burnt offerings on the altar.

[21]When the Lord smelled the pleasing odor [a scent of satisfaction to His heart], the Lord said to Himself, I will never again curse the ground because of man, for the imagination (the strong desire) of man's heart is evil *and* wicked from his youth; neither will I ever again smite *and* destroy every living thing, as I have done.

[22]While the earth remains, seedtime and harvest, cold and heat, summer and winter, and day and night shall not cease.

**9** And God pronounced a blessing upon Noah and his sons and said to them, Be fruitful and multiply and fill the earth.

[2]And the fear of you and the dread *and* terror of you shall be upon every beast of the land, every bird of the air, all that creeps upon the ground, and upon all the fish of the sea; they are delivered into your hand.

[3]Every moving thing that lives shall be food for you; and as I gave you the green vegetables *and* plants, I give you everything.

[4]But you shall not eat flesh with the life of it, which is its blood.

[5]And surely for your lifeblood I will require an accounting; from every beast I will require it; and from man, from every man [who spills another's lifeblood] I will require a reckoning.

[6]Whoever sheds man's blood, by man shall his blood be shed; for in the image of God He made man.

[7]And you, be fruitful and multiply; bring forth abundantly on the earth and multiply on it.

[8]Then God spoke to Noah and to his sons with him, saying,

[9]Behold, I establish My covenant *or* pledge with you and with your descendants after you

[10]And with every living creature that is with you—

---

a Possibly overhanging eaves which prevented the rain from coming through the perforated window space had also prevented Noah from seeing the mountaintops. It is well to remember that the Architect of Noah's ark was the omniscient Scientist He Whose "ways are past finding out," though men have learned much from them through the centuries. Nothing was lacking in Noah's ark to keep it from being suited for all that was required of it. The comfortable, light, well-ventilated, watertight, perfectly planned boat, large enough to accommodate all the original land animals intelligently and to permit the four human couples to live separately and in peace, needs no apology today. "In 1609 at Hoorn, in Holland, the Netherlandish Mennonite, P. Jansen, produced a vessel after the pattern of the ark, only smaller, whereby he proved it was well adapted for floating, and would carry a cargo greater by one-third than any other form of like cubical content" (J. P. Lange, *A Commentary*). It revolutionized shipbuilding. By 1900 every large vessel on the high seas was definitely inclined toward the proportions of Noah's ark (as verified by "Lloyd's Register of Shipping," *The World Almanac*). Later, ships were built longer for speed, a matter of no concern to Noah.

## New International Version

with you—the birds, the livestock and all the wild animals, all those that came out of the ark with you—every living creature on earth. ¹¹I establish my covenant with you: Never again will all life be destroyed by the waters of a flood; never again will there be a flood to destroy the earth."

¹²And God said, "This is the sign of the covenant I am making between me and you and every living creature with you, a covenant for all generations to come: ¹³I have set my rainbow in the clouds, and it will be the sign of the covenant between me and the earth. ¹⁴Whenever I bring clouds over the earth and the rainbow appears in the clouds, ¹⁵I will remember my covenant between me and you and all living creatures of every kind. Never again will the waters become a flood to destroy all life. ¹⁶Whenever the rainbow appears in the clouds, I will see it and remember the everlasting covenant between God and all living creatures of every kind on the earth."

¹⁷So God said to Noah, "This is the sign of the covenant I have established between me and all life on the earth."

### The Sons of Noah

¹⁸The sons of Noah who came out of the ark were Shem, Ham and Japheth. (Ham was the father of Canaan.) ¹⁹These were the three sons of Noah, and from them came the people who were scattered over the whole earth.

²⁰Noah, a man of the soil, proceeded[a] to plant a vineyard. ²¹When he drank some of its wine, he became drunk and lay uncovered inside his tent. ²²Ham, the father of Canaan, saw his father naked and told his two brothers outside. ²³But Shem and Japheth took a garment and laid it across their shoulders; then they walked in backward and covered their father's naked body. Their faces were turned the other way so that they would not see their father naked.

²⁴When Noah awoke from his wine and found out what his youngest son had done to him, ²⁵he said,

"Cursed be Canaan!
    The lowest of slaves
    will he be to his brothers."

²⁶He also said,

"Praise be to the LORD, the God of Shem!
    May Canaan be the slave of Shem.
²⁷May God extend Japheth's[b] territory;
    may Japheth live in the tents of Shem,
    and may Canaan be the slave of Japheth."

²⁸After the flood Noah lived 350 years. ²⁹Noah lived a total of 950 years, and then he died.

### The Table of Nations

**10** This is the account of Shem, Ham and Japheth, Noah's sons, who themselves had sons after the flood.

*The Japhethites*
²The sons[c] of Japheth:
    Gomer, Magog, Madai, Javan, Tubal, Meshek and Tiras.
³The sons of Gomer:
    Ashkenaz, Riphath and Togarmah.

---

[a] 20 Or *soil, was the first*   [b] 27 *Japheth* sounds like the Hebrew for *extend.*   [c] 2 *Sons* may mean *descendants* or *successors* or *nations*; also in verses 3, 4, 6, 7, 20-23, 29 and 31.

## Amplified Bible

whether the birds, the livestock, or the wild beasts of the earth along with you, as many as came out of the ark—every animal of the earth.

¹¹I will establish My covenant *or* pledge with you: Never again shall all flesh be cut off by the waters of a flood; neither shall there ever again be a flood to destroy the earth *and* make it corrupt.

¹²And God said, This is the token of the covenant (solemn pledge) which I am making between Me and you and every living creature that is with you, for all future generations:

¹³I set My bow [rainbow] in the cloud, and it shall be a token *or* sign of a covenant *or* solemn pledge between Me and the earth.

¹⁴And it shall be that when I bring clouds over the earth and the bow [rainbow] is seen in the clouds,

¹⁵I will [earnestly] remember My covenant *or* solemn pledge which is between Me and you and every living creature of all flesh; and the waters will no more become a flood to destroy *and* make all flesh corrupt.

¹⁶When the bow [rainbow] is in the clouds and I look upon it, I will [earnestly] remember the everlasting covenant *or* pledge between God and every living creature of all flesh that is upon the earth.

¹⁷And God said to Noah, This [rainbow] is the token *or* sign of the covenant *or* solemn pledge which I have established between Me and all flesh upon the earth.

¹⁸The sons of Noah who went forth from the ark were Shem, Ham, and Japheth. Ham was the father of Canaan [born later].

¹⁹These are the three sons of Noah, and from them the whole earth was overspread *and* stocked with inhabitants.

²⁰And Noah began to cultivate the ground, and he planted a vineyard.

²¹And he drank of the wine and became drunk, and he was uncovered *and* lay naked in his tent.

²²And Ham, the father of Canaan, glanced at *and* saw the nakedness of his father and told his two brothers outside.

²³So Shem and Japheth took a garment, laid it upon the shoulders of both, and went backward and covered the nakedness of their father; and their faces were backward, and they did not see their father's nakedness.

²⁴When Noah awoke from his wine, and knew the thing which his youngest son had done to him,

²⁵He exclaimed, Cursed be Canaan! He shall be the [a]servant of servants to his brethren! [Deut. 27:16.]

²⁶He also said, Blessed be the Lord, the God of Shem! *And* blessed by the Lord my God be Shem! And let Canaan be his servant.

²⁷May God enlarge Japheth; and let him dwell in the tents of Shem, and let Canaan be his servant.

²⁸And Noah lived after the flood 350 years.

²⁹All the days of Noah were 950 years, and he died.

**10** This is the history of the generations (descendants) of the sons of Noah, Shem, Ham, and Japheth. The sons born to them after the flood *were:*

²The sons of Japheth: Gomer, Magog, Madai, Javan, Tubal, Meshech, and Tiras.

³The sons of Gomer: Ashkenaz, Riphath, and Togarmah.

---

[a] The language of Noah here is an actual prophecy and not merely an expression of personal feeling. That Noah placed a curse on his youngest grandchild, Canaan, who would naturally be his favorite, can only be explained on the ground that in the prophetic spirit he saw into the future of the Canaanites. God Himself found the delinquency of the Canaanites insufferable and ultimately drove them out or subdued them and put the descendants of Shem in their place. But Noah's foresight did not yet include the extermination of the Canaanite peoples, for then he would have expressed it differently. He would not merely have called them "the servant of servants" if he had foreseen their destruction. The form of the expression, therefore, testifies to the great age of the prophecy (J. P. Lange, *A Commentary*).

## New International Version

<sup>4</sup>The sons of Javan:
Elishah, Tarshish, the Kittites and the Rodanites.<sup>a</sup>
<sup>5</sup>(From these the maritime peoples spread out into their territories by their clans within their nations, each with its own language.)

*The Hamites*
<sup>6</sup>The sons of Ham:
Cush, Egypt, Put and Canaan.
<sup>7</sup>The sons of Cush:
Seba, Havilah, Sabtah, Raamah and Sabteka.
The sons of Raamah:
Sheba and Dedan.

<sup>8</sup>Cush was the father<sup>b</sup> of Nimrod, who became a mighty warrior on the earth. <sup>9</sup>He was a mighty hunter before the LORD; that is why it is said, "Like Nimrod, a mighty hunter before the LORD." <sup>10</sup>The first centers of his kingdom were Babylon, Uruk, Akkad and Kalneh, in<sup>c</sup> Shinar.<sup>d</sup> <sup>11</sup>From that land he went to Assyria, where he built Nineveh, Rehoboth Ir,<sup>e</sup> Calah <sup>12</sup>and Resen, which is between Nineveh and Calah—which is the great city.

<sup>13</sup>Egypt was the father of
the Ludites, Anamites, Lehabites, Naphtuhites, <sup>14</sup>Pathrusites, Kasluhites (from whom the Philistines came) and Caphtorites.
<sup>15</sup>Canaan was the father of
Sidon his firstborn,<sup>f</sup> and of the Hittites, <sup>16</sup>Jebusites, Amorites, Girgashites, <sup>17</sup>Hivites, Arkites, Sinites, <sup>18</sup>Arvadites, Zemarites and Hamathites.

Later the Canaanite clans scattered <sup>19</sup>and the borders of Canaan reached from Sidon toward Gerar as far as Gaza, and then toward Sodom, Gomorrah, Admah and Zeboyim, as far as Lasha.
<sup>20</sup>These are the sons of Ham by their clans and languages, in their territories and nations.

*The Semites*
<sup>21</sup>Sons were also born to Shem, whose older brother was<sup>g</sup> Japheth; Shem was the ancestor of all the sons of Eber.

<sup>22</sup>The sons of Shem:
Elam, Ashur, Arphaxad, Lud and Aram.
<sup>23</sup>The sons of Aram:
Uz, Hul, Gether and Meshek.<sup>h</sup>
<sup>24</sup>Arphaxad was the father of<sup>i</sup> Shelah,
and Shelah the father of Eber.
<sup>25</sup>Two sons were born to Eber:
One was named Peleg,<sup>j</sup> because in his time the earth was divided; his brother was named Joktan.
<sup>26</sup>Joktan was the father of
Almodad, Sheleph, Hazarmaveth, Jerah, <sup>27</sup>Hadoram, Uzal, Diklah, <sup>28</sup>Obal, Abimael, Sheba, <sup>29</sup>Ophir, Havilah and Jobab. All these were sons of Joktan.

<sup>30</sup>The region where they lived stretched from Mesha toward Sephar, in the eastern hill country.
<sup>31</sup>These are the sons of Shem by their clans and languages, in their territories and nations.

<sup>32</sup>These are the clans of Noah's sons, according to their lines of descent, within their nations. From these the nations spread out over the earth after the flood.

## Amplified Bible

<sup>4</sup>The sons of Javan: Elishah, Tarshish, Kittim, and Dodanim.
<sup>5</sup>From these the coastland peoples spread. [These are the sons of Japheth] in their lands, each with his own language, by their families within their nations.
<sup>6</sup>The sons of Ham: Cush, Egypt [Mizraim], Put, and Canaan.
<sup>7</sup>The sons of Cush: Seba, Havilah, Sabtah, Raamah, and Sabteca; and the sons of Raamah: Sheba and Dedan.
<sup>8</sup>Cush became the father of Nimrod; he was the first to be a mighty man on the earth.
<sup>9</sup>He was a mighty hunter before the Lord; therefore it is said, Like Nimrod, a mighty hunter before the Lord.
<sup>10</sup>The beginning of his kingdom was Babel, Erech, Accad, and Calneh, in the land of Shinar [in Babylonia].
<sup>11</sup>Out of the land he [Nimrod] went forth into Assyria and built Nineveh, Rehoboth-Ir, Calah,
<sup>12</sup>And Resen, which is between Nineveh and Calah; all these [suburbs combined to form] the great city.
<sup>13</sup>And Egypt [Mizraim] became the father of Ludim, Anamim, Lehabim, Naphtuhim,
<sup>14</sup>Pathrusim, Casluhim (from whom came the Philistines), and Caphtorim.
<sup>15</sup>Canaan became the father of Sidon his firstborn, Heth [the Hittites],
<sup>16</sup>The Jebusites, the Amorites, the Girgashites,
<sup>17</sup>The Hivites, the Arkites, the Sinites,
<sup>18</sup>The Arvadites, the Zemarites and the Hamathites. Afterward the families of the Canaanites spread abroad
<sup>19</sup>And the territory of the Canaanites extended from Sidon as one goes to Gerar as far as Gaza, and as one goes to <sup>a</sup>Sodom, Gomorrah, Admah, and Zeboiim, as far as Lasha.
<sup>20</sup>These are the sons of Ham by their families, their languages, their lands, and their nations.
<sup>21</sup>To Shem also, the younger brother of Japheth and the ancestor of all the children of Eber [including the Hebrews], children were born.
<sup>22</sup>The sons of Shem: Elam, Asshur, Arpachshad, Lud, and Aram.
<sup>23</sup>The sons of Aram: Uz, Hul, Gether, and Mash.
<sup>24</sup>Arpachshad became the father of Shelah; and Shelah became the father of Eber.
<sup>25</sup>To Eber were born two sons: the name of one was Peleg [division], because [the inhabitants of] the earth were divided up in his days; and his brother's name was Joktan.
<sup>26</sup>Joktan became the father of Almodad, Sheleph, Hazarmaveth, Jerah,
<sup>27</sup>Hadoram, Uzal, Diklah,
<sup>28</sup>Obal, Abimael, Sheba,
<sup>29</sup>Ophir, Havilah, and Jobab; all these were the sons of Joktan.
<sup>30</sup>The territory in which they lived extended from Mesha as one goes toward Sephar to the hill country of the east.
<sup>31</sup>These are Shem's descendants by their families, their languages, their lands, and their nations.
<sup>32</sup>These are the families of the sons of Noah, according to their generations, within their nations; and from these the nations spread abroad on the earth after the flood. [Acts 17:26.]

---

<sup>a</sup> 4 Some manuscripts of the Masoretic Text and Samaritan Pentateuch (see also Septuagint and 1 Chron. 1:7); most manuscripts of the Masoretic Text *Dodanites*   <sup>b</sup> 8 *Father* may mean *ancestor* or *predecessor* or *founder*; also in verses 13, 15, 24 and 26.   <sup>c</sup> 10 Or *Uruk and Akkad—all of them in*   <sup>d</sup> 10 That is, Babylonia   <sup>e</sup> 11 Or *Nineveh with its city squares*   <sup>f</sup> 15 Or *of the Sidonians, the foremost*   <sup>g</sup> 21 Or *Shem, the older brother of*   <sup>h</sup> 23 See Septuagint and 1 Chron. 1:17; Hebrew *Mash.*   <sup>i</sup> 24 Hebrew; Septuagint *father of Cainan, and Cainan was the father of*   <sup>j</sup> 25 *Peleg* means *division*.

---

<sup>a</sup> Surely no greater proof is needed of the great antiquity of this portion of Genesis than the fact that it mentions as still standing these four cities of the plain which were utterly destroyed in Abraham's time (Gen. 19:27-29; Deut. 29:23).

## New International Version

### The Tower of Babel

**11** Now the whole world had one language and a common speech. [2]As people moved eastward,[a] they found a plain in Shinar[b] and settled there.

[3]They said to each other, "Come, let's make bricks and bake them thoroughly." They used brick instead of stone, and tar for mortar. [4]Then they said, "Come, let us build ourselves a city, with a tower that reaches to the heavens, so that we may make a name for ourselves; otherwise we will be scattered over the face of the whole earth."

[5]But the LORD came down to see the city and the tower the people were building. [6]The LORD said, "If as one people speaking the same language they have begun to do this, then nothing they plan to do will be impossible for them. [7]Come, let us go down and confuse their language so they will not understand each other."

[8]So the LORD scattered them from there over all the earth, and they stopped building the city. [9]That is why it was called Babel[c]—because there the LORD confused the language of the whole world. From there the LORD scattered them over the face of the whole earth.

### From Shem to Abram

[10]This is the account of Shem's family line.

Two years after the flood, when Shem was 100 years old, he became the father[d] of Arphaxad. [11]And after he became the father of Arphaxad, Shem lived 500 years and had other sons and daughters.

[12]When Arphaxad had lived 35 years, he became the father of Shelah. [13]And after he became the father of Shelah, Arphaxad lived 403 years and had other sons and daughters.[e]

[14]When Shelah had lived 30 years, he became the father of Eber. [15]And after he became the father of Eber, Shelah lived 403 years and had other sons and daughters.

[16]When Eber had lived 34 years, he became the father of Peleg. [17]And after he became the father of Peleg, Eber lived 430 years and had other sons and daughters.

[18]When Peleg had lived 30 years, he became the father of Reu. [19]And after he became the father of Reu, Peleg lived 209 years and had other sons and daughters.

[20]When Reu had lived 32 years, he became the father of Serug. [21]And after he became the father of Serug, Reu lived 207 years and had other sons and daughters.

[22]When Serug had lived 30 years, he became the father of Nahor. [23]And after he became the father of Nahor, Serug lived 200 years and had other sons and daughters.

[24]When Nahor had lived 29 years, he became the father of Terah. [25]And after he became the father of Terah, Nahor lived 119 years and had other sons and daughters.

## Amplified Bible

**11** And the whole earth was of one language and of one accent *and* mode of expression.

[2]And as they journeyed eastward, they found a plain (valley) in the land of Shinar, and they settled *and* dwelt there.

[3]And they said one to another, Come, let us make bricks and burn them thoroughly. So they had brick for stone, and slime (bitumen) for mortar.

[4]And they said, Come, let us build us a city and a tower whose top reaches into the sky, and let us make a name for ourselves, lest we be scattered over the whole earth.

[5]And the Lord came down to see the city and the tower which the sons of men had built.

[6]And the Lord said, Behold, they are one people and they have [a]all one language; and this is only the beginning of what they will do, and now nothing they have imagined they can do will be impossible for them.

[7]Come, let Us go down and there confound (mix up, confuse) their language, that they may not understand one another's speech.

[8]So the Lord scattered them abroad from that place upon the face of the whole earth, and they gave up building the city.

[9]Therefore the name of it was called Babel—because there the Lord confounded the language of all the earth; and from that place the Lord scattered them abroad upon the face of the whole earth.

[10]This is the history of the generations of Shem. Shem was 100 years old when he became the father of Arpachshad, two years after the flood.

[11]And Shem lived after Arpachshad was born 500 years and had other sons and daughters.

[12]When Arpachshad had lived 35 years, he became the father of Shelah.

[13]Arpachshad lived after Shelah was born 403 years and had other sons and daughters.

[14]When Shelah had lived 30 years, he became the father of Eber.

[15]Shelah lived after Eber was born 403 years and had other sons and daughters.

[16]When Eber had lived 34 years, he became the father of Peleg.

[17]And Eber lived after Peleg was born 430 years and had other sons and daughters.

[18]When Peleg had lived 30 years, he became the father of Reu.

[19]And Peleg lived after Reu was born 209 years and had other sons and daughters.

[20]When Reu had lived 32 years, he became the father of Serug.

[21]And Reu lived after Serug was born 207 years and had other sons and daughters.

[22]When Serug had lived 30 years, he became the father of Nahor.

[23]And Serug lived after Nahor was born 200 years and had other sons and daughters.

[24]When Nahor had lived 29 years, he became the father of Terah.

[25]And Nahor lived after Terah was born 119 years and had other sons and daughters.

---

*a 2* Or *from the east*; or *in the east*   *b 2* That is, Babylonia   *c 9* That is, Babylon; *Babel* sounds like the Hebrew for *confused*.   *d 10* Father may mean *ancestor*; also in verses 11-25.   *e 12,13* Hebrew; Septuagint (see also Luke 3:35, 36 and note at Gen. 10:24) *35 years, he became the father of Cainan.* 13And after he became the father of Cainan, Arphaxad lived 430 years and had other sons and daughters, and then he died. When Cainan had lived 130 years, he became the father of Shelah. And after he became the father of Shelah, Cainan lived 330 years and had other sons and daughters

*a Some noted philologists have declared that a common origin of all languages cannot be denied. One, Max Mueller (*The Science of Language*), said "We have examined all possible forms which language can assume, and now we ask, can we reconcile with these three distinct forms, the radical, the terminational, the inflectional, the admission of one common origin of human speech? I answer decidedly, 'Yes'." *The New Bible Commentary* says, "The original unity of human language, though still far from demonstrable, becomes increasingly probable."

## New International Version

26After Terah had lived 70 years, he became the father of Abram, Nahor and Haran.

### Abram's Family
27This is the account of Terah's family line.

Terah became the father of Abram, Nahor and Haran. And Haran became the father of Lot. 28While his father Terah was still alive, Haran died in Ur of the Chaldeans, in the land of his birth. 29Abram and Nahor both married. The name of Abram's wife was Sarai, and the name of Nahor's wife was Milkah; she was the daughter of Haran, the father of both Milkah and Iskah. 30Now Sarai was childless because she was not able to conceive.

31Terah took his son Abram, his grandson Lot son of Haran, and his daughter-in-law Sarai, the wife of his son Abram, and together they set out from Ur of the Chaldeans to go to Canaan. But when they came to Harran, they settled there.

32Terah lived 205 years, and he died in Harran.

### The Call of Abram
**12** The LORD had said to Abram, "Go from your country, your people and your father's household to the land I will show you.

2 "I will make you into a great nation,
    and I will bless you;
I will make your name great,
    and you will be a blessing.a
3 I will bless those who bless you,
    and whoever curses you I will curse;
and all peoples on earth
    will be blessed through you."b

4So Abram went, as the LORD had told him; and Lot went with him. Abram was seventy-five years old when he set out from Harran. 5He took his wife Sarai, his nephew Lot, all the possessions they had accumulated and the people they had acquired in Harran, and they set out for the land of Canaan, and they arrived there.

6Abram traveled through the land as far as the site of the great tree of Moreh at Shechem. At that time the Canaanites were in the land. 7The LORD appeared to Abram and said, "To your offspringc I will give this land." So he built an altar there to the LORD, who had appeared to him.

8From there he went on toward the hills east of Bethel and pitched his tent, with Bethel on the west and Ai on the east. There he built an altar to the LORD and called on the name of the LORD.

## Amplified Bible

26After Terah had lived 70 years, he became the father of [at different times], aAbram and Nahor and Haran, [his firstborn].

27Now this is the history of the descendants of Terah. Terah was the father of Abram, Nahor, and Haran; and Haran was the father of Lot.

28Haran died before his father Terah [died] in the land of his birth, in bUr of the Chaldees.

29And Abram and Nahor took wives. The name of Abram's wife was Sarai, and the name of Nahor's wife was Milcah, the daughter of Haran the father of Milcah and Iscah.

30But Sarai was barren; she had no child.

31And Terah took Abram his son, Lot the son of Haran, his grandson, and Sarai his daughter-in-law, his son Abram's wife, and they went forth together to go from Ur of the Chaldees into the land of Canaan; but when they came to Haran, they settled there.

32And Terah lived 205 years; and Terah died in Haran.

**12** Now [in Haran] the Lord said to Abram, Go for yourself [for your own advantage] away from your country, from your relatives and your father's house, to the land that I will show you. [Heb. 11:8-10.]

2And I will make of you a great nation, and I will bless you [with abundant increase of favors] and make your name famous and distinguished, and you will be a blessing [dispensing good to others].

3And I will bless those who bless you [who confer prosperity or happiness upon you] and ccurse him who curses or uses insolent language toward you; in you will all the families and kindred of the earth be blessed [and by you they will bless themselves]. [Gal. 3:8.]

4So Abram departed, as the Lord had directed him; and Lot [his nephew] went with him. Abram was seventy-five years old when he left Haran.

5Abram took Sarai his wife, and Lot his brother's son, and all their possessions that they had gathered, and the persons [servants] that they had acquired in Haran, and they went forth to go to the land of Canaan. When they came to the land of Canaan,

6Abram passed through the land to the locality of Shechem, to the oak or terebinth tree of Moreh. And the Canaanite was then in the land.

7Then the Lord appeared to Abram and said, I will give this land to your posterity. So Abram built an altar there to the Lord, Who had appeared to him.

8From there he pulled up [his tent pegs] and departed to the mountain on the east of Bethel and pitched his tent, with Bethel on the west and Ai on the east; and there he built an altar to the Lord and called upon the name of the Lord.

a Abram is only mentioned first by way of dignity. Noah's sons also are given as "Shem, Ham, and Japheth" in Gen. 5:32, although Shem was not the oldest, but for dignity is named first, as is Abram here (Adam Clarke, *The Holy Bible with A Commentary*). b Abram's home town was Ur of the Chaldees. As the result of extensive archaeological excavations there by C. Leonard Woolley in 1922-34, a great deal is known about Abram's background. Space will not permit more than a glimpse at excavated Ur, but a few items will show the high state of civilization. The entire house of the average middle-class person had from ten to twenty rooms and measured forty to fifty-two feet; the lower floor was for servants, the upper floor for the family, with five rooms for their use; additionally, there was a guest chamber and a lavatory reserved for visitors, and a private chapel. A school was found and what the students studied was shown by the clay tablets discovered there. In the days of Abram the pupils had reading, writing, and arithmetic as today. They learned the multiplication and division tables and even worked at square and cube root. A bill of lading of about 2040 B.C. (about the era in which Abram is believed to have lived) showed that the commerce of that time was far-reaching. Even the name "Abraham" has been found on the excavated clay tablets (J. P. Free, *Archaeology and Bible History*). c To look with disfavor on the Jews was to invite God's displeasure; to treat the Jews offensively was to incur His wrath. But to befriend the Jews was to bring down upon one's head the rewards of a promise that could not be broken.

## New International Version

9Then Abram set out and continued toward the Negev.

### Abram in Egypt

10Now there was a famine in the land, and Abram went down to Egypt to live there for a while because the famine was severe. 11As he was about to enter Egypt, he said to his wife Sarai, "I know what a beautiful woman you are. 12When the Egyptians see you, they will say, 'This is his wife.' Then they will kill me but will let you live. 13Say you are my sister, so that I will be treated well for your sake and my life will be spared because of you."

14When Abram came to Egypt, the Egyptians saw that Sarai was a very beautiful woman. 15And when Pharaoh's officials saw her, they praised her to Pharaoh, and she was taken into his palace. 16He treated Abram well for her sake, and Abram acquired sheep and cattle, male and female donkeys, male and female servants, and camels.

17But the LORD inflicted serious diseases on Pharaoh and his household because of Abram's wife Sarai. 18So Pharaoh summoned Abram. "What have you done to me?" he said. "Why didn't you tell me she was your wife? 19Why did you say, 'She is my sister,' so that I took her to be my wife? Now then, here is your wife. Take her and go!" 20Then Pharaoh gave orders about Abram to his men, and they sent him on his way, with his wife and everything he had.

### Abram and Lot Separate

**13** So Abram went up from Egypt to the Negev, with his wife and everything he had, and Lot went with him. 2Abram had become very wealthy in livestock and in silver and gold. 3From the Negev he went from place to place until he came to Bethel, to the place between Bethel and Ai where his tent had been earlier 4and where he had first built an altar. There Abram called on the name of the LORD.

5Now Lot, who was moving about with Abram, also had flocks and herds and tents. 6But the land could not support them while they stayed together, for their possessions were so great that they were not able to stay together. 7And quarreling arose between Abram's herders and Lot's. The Canaanites and Perizzites were also living in the land at that time.

8So Abram said to Lot, "Let's not have any quarreling between you and me, or between your herders and mine, for we are close relatives. 9Is not the whole land before

## Amplified Bible

9Abram journeyed on, still going toward the South (the Negeb).

10Now there was a famine in the land, and Abram *a*went down into Egypt to live temporarily, for the famine in the land was oppressive (intense and grievous). 11And when he was about to enter into Egypt, he said to Sarai his wife, I know that you are beautiful to behold. 12So when the Egyptians see you, they will say, This is his wife; and they will kill me, but they will let you live. 13Say, I beg of you, that you are *b*my sister, so that it may go well with me for your sake and my life will be spared because of you.

14And when Abram came into Egypt, the Egyptians saw that the woman was very beautiful. 15The princes of Pharaoh also saw her and commended her to Pharaoh, and she was taken into Pharaoh's house [harem].

16And he treated Abram well for her sake; he acquired sheep, oxen, he-donkeys, menservants, maidservants, she-donkeys, and *c*camels.

17But the Lord scourged Pharaoh and his household with serious plagues because of Sarai, Abram's wife.

18And Pharaoh called Abram and said, What is this that you have done to me? Why did you not tell me that she was your wife?

19Why did you say, She is my sister, so that I took her to be my wife? Now then, here is your wife; take her and get away [from here]!

20And Pharaoh commanded his men concerning him, and they brought him on his way with his wife and all that he had.

**13** So Abram went up out of Egypt, he and his wife and all that he had, and Lot with him, into the South [country of Judah, the Negeb].

2Now Abram was extremely rich in livestock and in silver and in gold.

3And he journeyed on from the South [country of Judah, the Negeb] as far as Bethel, to the place where his tent had been at the beginning, between Bethel and Ai,

4Where he had built an altar at first; and there Abram called on the name of the Lord. [Gal. 3:6-9.]

5But Lot, who went with Abram, also had flocks and herds and tents.

6Now the land was not able to nourish *and* support them so they could dwell together, for their possessions were too great for them to live together.

7And there was strife between the herdsmen of Abram's cattle and the herdsmen of Lot's cattle. And the Canaanite and the Perizzite were dwelling then in the land [making fodder more difficult to obtain].

8So Abram said to Lot, Let there be no strife, I beg of you, between you and me, or between your herdsmen and my herdsmen, for we are relatives.

9Is not the whole land before you? Separate yourself, I beg of you, from me. If you take the left hand, then I will

*a* Some books on archaeology frequently allude to the critical view that strangers could not have come into Egypt in earlier times, quoting Strabo and Diodorus to that effect; but later archaeological discoveries show that people from the region of Palestine and Syria were coming to Egypt in the period of Abraham. This is clearly indicated by a tomb painting at Beni Hassan, dating a little after 2000 B.C. It shows Asiatic Semites who had come to Egypt. Furthermore, the archaeological and historical indications of the coming of the Hyksos into Egypt around 1900 B.C. provided another piece of evidence that strangers could come into that land (J. P. Free, *Abraham in Egypt*). *b* Sarai was Abraham's half sister. They had the same father, but different mothers (Gen. 20:12). *c* Critics have set aside the statement that Abraham had camels in Egypt as an error. But archaeological evidence, including some twenty objects ranging from the seventh century B.C. to the period before 3000 B.C., proves the authenticity of the Bible record concerning Abraham. It includes not only statuettes, plaques, rock carvings, and drawings representing camels, but also "camel bones, a camel skull, and a camel hair rope" (J. P. Free, *Archaeology and Bible History*).

## New International Version

you? Let's part company. If you go to the left, I'll go to the right; if you go to the right, I'll go to the left."

¹⁰Lot looked around and saw that the whole plain of the Jordan toward Zoar was well watered, like the garden of the LORD, like the land of Egypt. (This was before the LORD destroyed Sodom and Gomorrah.) ¹¹So Lot chose for himself the whole plain of the Jordan and set out toward the east. The two men parted company: ¹²Abram lived in the land of Canaan, while Lot lived among the cities of the plain and pitched his tents near Sodom. ¹³Now the people of Sodom were wicked and were sinning greatly against the LORD.

¹⁴The LORD said to Abram after Lot had parted from him, "Look around from where you are, to the north and south, to the east and west. ¹⁵All the land that you see I will give to you and your offspringᵃ forever. ¹⁶I will make your offspring like the dust of the earth, so that if anyone could count the dust, then your offspring could be counted. ¹⁷Go, walk through the length and breadth of the land, for I am giving it to you."

¹⁸So Abram went to live near the great trees of Mamre at Hebron, where he pitched his tents. There he built an altar to the LORD.

### Abram Rescues Lot

**14** At the time when Amraphel was king of Shinar,ᵇ Arioch king of Ellasar, Kedorlaomer king of Elam and Tidal king of Goyim, ²these kings went to war against Bera king of Sodom, Birsha king of Gomorrah, Shinab king of Admah, Shemeber king of Zeboyim, and the king of Bela (that is, Zoar). ³All these latter kings joined forces in the Valley of Siddim (that is, the Dead Sea Valley). ⁴For twelve years they had been subject to Kedorlaomer, but in the thirteenth year they rebelled.

⁵In the fourteenth year, Kedorlaomer and the kings allied with him went out and defeated the Rephaites in Ashteroth Karnaim, the Zuzites in Ham, the Emites in Shaveh Kiriathaim ⁶and the Horites in the hill country of Seir, as far as El Paran near the desert. ⁷Then they turned back and went to En Mishpat (that is, Kadesh), and they conquered the whole territory of the Amalekites, as well as the Amorites who were living in Hazezon Tamar.

⁸Then the king of Sodom, the king of Gomorrah, the king of Admah, the king of Zeboyim and the king of Bela (that is, Zoar) marched out and drew up their battle lines in the Valley of Siddim ⁹against Kedorlaomer king of Elam, Tidal king of Goyim, Amraphel king of Shinar and Arioch king of Ellasar—four kings against five. ¹⁰Now the Valley of Siddim was full of tar pits, and when the kings of Sodom and Gomorrah fled, some of the men fell into them and the rest fled to the hills. ¹¹The four kings seized all the goods of Sodom and Gomorrah and all their food; then they went away. ¹²They also carried off Abram's nephew Lot and his possessions, since he was living in Sodom.

¹³A man who had escaped came and reported this to Abram the Hebrew. Now Abram was living near the great

## Amplified Bible

go to the right; or if you choose the right hand, then I will go to the left.

¹⁰And Lot looked and saw that everywhere the Jordan Valley was well watered. Before the Lord destroyed Sodom and Gomorrah, [it was all] like the garden of the Lord, like the land of Egypt, as you go to Zoar.

¹¹Then Lot chose for himself all the Jordan Valley and [he] traveled east. So they separated.

¹²Abram dwelt in the land of Canaan, and Lot dwelt in the cities of the [Jordan] Valley and moved his tent as far as Sodom *and* dwelt there.

¹³But the men of Sodom were wicked and exceedingly great sinners against the Lord.

¹⁴The Lord said to Abram after Lot had left him, Lift up now your eyes and look from the place where you are, northward and southward and eastward and westward;

¹⁵For all the land which you see I will give to you and to your posterity forever. [Acts 7:5.]

¹⁶And I will make your descendants like the dust of the earth, so that if a man could count the dust of the earth, then could your descendants also be counted. [Gen. 28:14.]

¹⁷Arise, walk through the land, the length of it and the breadth of it, for I will give it to you.

¹⁸Then Abram moved his tent and came and dwelt among the oaks *or* terebinths of Mamre, which are at Hebron, and built there an altar to the Lord.

**14** In the days of the kings Amraphel of Shinar, Arioch of Ellasar, Chedorlaomer of Elam, and Tidal of Goiim,

²They made war on the kings Bera of Sodom, Birsha of Gomorrah, Shinab of Admah, Shemeber of Zeboiim, and the king of Bela, ᵃthat is, Zoar.

³The latter kings joined together [as allies] in the Valley of Siddim, which is [now] the [Dead] Sea of Salt.

⁴Twelve years they had served Chedorlaomer, but in the thirteenth year they rebelled.

⁵And in the fourteenth year, Chedorlaomer and the kings who were with him attacked *and* subdued the Rephaim in Ashteroth-karnaim, the Zuzim in Ham, and the Emim in Shaveh-kiriathaim,

⁶And the Horites in their Mount Seir as far as El-paran, which is on the border of the wilderness.

⁷Then they turned back and came to En-mishpat, which [now] is Kadesh, and subdued all the country of the Amalekites, and also the Amorites who dwelt in Hazazon-tamar.

⁸Then the kings of Sodom, Gomorrah, Admah, Zeboiim, and Bela, that is, Zoar, went out and [together] they joined battle [with those kings] in the Valley of Siddim,

⁹With the kings Chedorlaomer of Elam, Tidal of Goiim, Amraphel of Shinar, and Arioch of Ellasar—four kings against five.

¹⁰Now the Valley of Siddim was full of slime *or* bitumen pits, and as the kings of Sodom and Gomorrah fled, they fell (were overthrown) there and the remainder [of the kings] fled to the mountain.

¹¹[The victors] took all the wealth of Sodom and Gomorrah and all the supply of provisions and departed.

¹²And they also took Lot, Abram's brother's son, who dwelt in Sodom, and his goods away with them.

¹³Then one who had escaped came and told Abram the Hebrew [one from the other side], who was living by the

---

ᵃ One of the notable proofs of the antiquity of the early sections of Genesis is that many of the original names of places about which they speak were so old that Moses, the writer, had to add an explanation in order to identify these ancient names so that the Israelites returning from Egypt might recognize them. Chapter 14 alone contains six such explanatory notes (Gen. 14:2, 3, 7, 8, 15, and 17).

## New International Version

trees of Mamre the Amorite, a brother*a* of Eshkol and Aner, all of whom were allied with Abram. ¹⁴When Abram heard that his relative had been taken captive, he called out the 318 trained men born in his household and went in pursuit as far as Dan. ¹⁵During the night Abram divided his men to attack them and he routed them, pursuing them as far as Hobah, north of Damascus. ¹⁶He recovered all the goods and brought back his relative Lot and his possessions, together with the women and the other people.

¹⁷After Abram returned from defeating Kedorlaomer and the kings allied with him, the king of Sodom came out to meet him in the Valley of Shaveh (that is, the King's Valley).

¹⁸Then Melchizedek king of Salem brought out bread and wine. He was priest of God Most High, ¹⁹and he blessed Abram, saying,

"Blessed be Abram by God Most High,
    Creator of heaven and earth.
²⁰And praise be to God Most High,
    who delivered your enemies into your hand."

Then Abram gave him a tenth of everything.

²¹The king of Sodom said to Abram, "Give me the people and keep the goods for yourself."

²²But Abram said to the king of Sodom, "With raised hand I have sworn an oath to the LORD, God Most High, Creator of heaven and earth, ²³that I will accept nothing belonging to you, not even a thread or the strap of a sandal, so that you will never be able to say, 'I made Abram rich.' ²⁴I will accept nothing but what my men have eaten and the share that belongs to the men who went with me—to Aner, Eshkol and Mamre. Let them have their share."

### The LORD's Covenant With Abram

**15** After this, the word of the LORD came to Abram in a vision:

"Do not be afraid, Abram.
    I am your shield,*b*
    your very great reward.*c*"

²But Abram said, "Sovereign LORD, what can you give me since I remain childless and the one who will inherit*d* my estate is Eliezer of Damascus?" ³And Abram said, "You have given me no children; so a servant in my household will be my heir." ⁴Then the word of the LORD came to him: "This man will not be your heir, but a son who is your own flesh and blood will be your heir." ⁵He took him outside and said, "Look up at the sky and count the stars—if indeed you can count them." Then he said to him, "So shall your offspring*e* be." ⁶Abram believed the LORD, and he credited it to him as righteousness.

⁷He also said to him, "I am the LORD, who brought you out of Ur of the Chaldeans to give you this land to take possession of it."

⁸But Abram said, "Sovereign LORD, how can I know that I will gain possession of it?"

⁹So the LORD said to him, "Bring me a heifer, a goat and a ram, each three years old, along with a dove and a young pigeon."

¹⁰Abram brought all these to him, cut them in two and arranged the halves opposite each other; the birds, howev-

## Amplified Bible

oaks *or* terebinths of Mamre the Amorite, a brother of Eshcol and of Aner—these were allies of Abram.

¹⁴When Abram heard that [his nephew] had been captured, he armed (led forth) the 318 trained servants born in his own house and pursued the enemy as far as Dan.

¹⁵He divided his forces against them by night, he and his servants, and attacked *and* routed them, and pursued them as far as Hobah, which is north of Damascus.

¹⁶And he brought back all the goods and also brought back his kinsman Lot and his possessions, the women also and the people.

¹⁷After his [Abram's] return from the defeat *and* slaying of Chedorlaomer and the kings who were with him, the king of Sodom went out to meet him at the Valley of Shaveh, that is, the King's Valley.

¹⁸Melchizedek king of Salem [later called Jerusalem] brought out bread and wine [for their nourishment]; he was the priest of God Most High,

¹⁹And he blessed him and said, Blessed (favored with blessings, made blissful, joyful) be Abram by God Most High, Possessor *and* Maker of heaven and earth,

²⁰And blessed, praised, *and* glorified be God Most High, Who has given your foes into your hand! And [Abram] gave him a tenth of all [he had taken]. [Heb. 7:1-10.]

²¹And the king of Sodom said to Abram, Give me the persons and keep the goods for yourself.

²²But Abram said to the king of Sodom, I have lifted up my hand *and* sworn to the Lord, God Most High, the Possessor *and* Maker of heaven and earth,

²³That I would not take a thread or a shoelace or anything that is yours, lest you should say, I have made Abram rich.

²⁴[Take all] except only what my young men have eaten and the share of the men [allies] who went with me—Aner, Eshcol, and Mamre; let them take their portion.

**15** After these things, the word of the Lord came to Abram in a vision, saying, Fear not, Abram, I am your *a*Shield, your abundant compensation, *and* your reward shall be exceedingly great.

²And Abram said, Lord God, what can You give me, since I am going on [from this world] childless and he who shall be the owner *and* heir of my house is this [steward] Eliezer of Damascus?

³And Abram continued, Look, You have given me no child; and [a servant] born in my house is my heir.

⁴And behold, the word of the Lord came to him, saying, This man shall not be your heir, but he who shall come from your own body shall be your heir.

⁵And He brought him outside [his tent into the starlight] and said, Look now toward the heavens and count the stars—if you are able to number them. Then He said to him, So shall your descendants be. [Heb. 11:12.]

⁶And he [Abram] believed in (trusted in, relied on, remained steadfast to) the Lord, and He counted it to him as righteousness (right standing with God). [Rom. 4:3, 18-22; Gal. 3:6; James 2:23.]

⁷And He said to him, I am the [same] Lord, Who brought you out of Ur of the Chaldees to give you this land as an inheritance.

⁸But he [Abram] said, Lord God, by what shall I know that I shall inherit it?

⁹And He said to him, Bring to Me a heifer three years old, a she-goat three years old, a ram three years old, a turtledove, and a young pigeon.

¹⁰And he brought Him all these and cut them down the middle [into halves] and laid each half opposite the other; but the birds he did not divide.

---

*a* 13 Or *a relative*; or *an ally*    *b* 1 Or *sovereign*    *c* 1 Or *shield; / your reward will be very great*    *d* 2 The meaning of the Hebrew for this phrase is uncertain.    *e* 5 Or *seed*

*a* The reference is to the Lord as Abram's King.

## New International Version

er, he did not cut in half. [11]Then birds of prey came down on the carcasses, but Abram drove them away.

[12]As the sun was setting, Abram fell into a deep sleep, and a thick and dreadful darkness came over him. [13]Then the LORD said to him, "Know for certain that for four hundred years your descendants will be strangers in a country not their own and that they will be enslaved and mistreated there. [14]But I will punish the nation they serve as slaves, and afterward they will come out with great possessions. [15]You, however, will go to your ancestors in peace and be buried at a good old age. [16]In the fourth generation your descendants will come back here, for the sin of the Amorites has not yet reached its full measure."

[17]When the sun had set and darkness had fallen, a smoking firepot with a blazing torch appeared and passed between the pieces. [18]On that day the LORD made a covenant with Abram and said, "To your descendants I give this land, from the Wadi[a] of Egypt to the great river, the Euphrates— [19]the land of the Kenites, Kenizzites, Kadmonites, [20]Hittites, Perizzites, Rephaites, [21]Amorites, Canaanites, Girgashites and Jebusites."

### Hagar and Ishmael

**16** Now Sarai, Abram's wife, had borne him no children. But she had an Egyptian slave named Hagar; [2]so she said to Abram, "The LORD has kept me from having children. Go, sleep with my slave; perhaps I can build a family through her."

Abram agreed to what Sarai said. [3]So after Abram had been living in Canaan ten years, Sarai his wife took her Egyptian slave Hagar and gave her to her husband to be his wife. [4]He slept with Hagar, and she conceived.

When she knew she was pregnant, she began to despise her mistress. [5]Then Sarai said to Abram, "You are responsible for the wrong I am suffering. I put my slave in your arms, and now that she knows she is pregnant, she despises me. May the LORD judge between you and me."

[6]"Your slave is in your hands," Abram said. "Do with her whatever you think best." Then Sarai mistreated Hagar; so she fled from her.

[7]The angel of the LORD found Hagar near a spring in the desert; it was the spring that is beside the road to Shur.

## Amplified Bible

[11]And when the birds of prey swooped down upon the carcasses, Abram drove them away.

[12]When the sun was setting, a deep sleep overcame Abram, and a horror (a terror, a shuddering fear) of great darkness assailed *and* oppressed him.

[13]And [God] said to Abram, Know positively that your descendants will be strangers dwelling as temporary residents in a land that is not theirs [Egypt], and they will be slaves there and will be afflicted *and* oppressed for 400 years. [Fulfilled in Exod. 12:40.]

[14]But I will bring judgment on that nation whom they will serve, and afterward they will come out with great possessions. [Acts 7:6, 7.]

[15]And you shall go to your fathers in peace; you shall be buried at a good old (hoary) age.

[16]And in the [a]fourth generation they [your descendants] shall come back here, for the iniquity of the [b]Amorites is not yet full *and* complete. [Josh. 24:15.]

[17]When the sun had gone down and a [thick] darkness had come on, behold, a smoking oven and a flaming torch passed between those pieces.

[18]On the same day the Lord made a covenant (promise, pledge) with Abram, saying, To your descendants I have given this land, from the river of Egypt to the great river Euphrates—the land of

[19]The Kenites, the Kenizzites, the Kadmonites,

[20]The Hittites, the Perizzites, the Rephaim,

[21]The Amorites, the Canaanites, the Girgashites, and the Jebusites.

**16** Now Sarai, Abram's wife, had borne him no children. She had an Egyptian maid whose name was Hagar.

[2]And Sarai said to Abram, See here, the Lord has restrained me from bearing [children]. I am asking you to have intercourse with my maid; it may be that I can obtain children by her. And Abram listened to *and* heeded what Sarai said.

[3]So Sarai, Abram's wife, took Hagar her Egyptian maid, after Abram had dwelt ten years in the land of Canaan, and gave her to her husband Abram to be his [secondary] wife.

[4]And he had intercourse with Hagar, and she became pregnant; and when she saw that she was with child, she looked with contempt upon her mistress *and* despised her.

[5]Then Sarai said to Abram, May [the responsibility for] my wrong *and* deprivation of rights be upon you! I gave my maid into your bosom, and when she saw that she was with child, I was contemptible *and* despised in her eyes. May the Lord be the judge between you and me.

[6]But Abram said to Sarai, See here, your maid is in your hands *and* power; do as you please with her. And when Sarai dealt severely with her, humbling *and* afflicting her, she [Hagar] fled from her.

[7]But [c]the Angel of the Lord found her by a spring of water in the wilderness on the road to Shur.

[a] This prophecy was literally fulfilled. Moses, for example, who led the Israelites back to Canaan after their 400 years in Egypt, was "in the fourth generation" from Jacob—Levi, Kohath, Amram, Moses. [b] The most important and powerful group of that region. The name "Amorite" later became virtually synonymous with that of the inhabitants of Canaan generally. [c] "The Angel of the Lord" or "of God," or "of His presence" is readily identified with the Lord God (Gen. 16:11, 13; 22:11, 12; 31:11, 13; Exod. 3:1-6 and other passages). But it is obvious that the "Angel of the Lord" is a distinct person in Himself from God the Father (Gen. 24:7; Exod. 23:20; Zech. 1:12, 13 and other passages). Nor does the "Angel of the Lord" appear again after Christ came in human form. He must of necessity be One of the "three-in-one" Godhead. The "Angel of the Lord" is the visible Lord God of the Old Testament, as Jesus Christ is of the New Testament. Thus His deity is clearly portrayed in the Old Testament. *The Cambridge Bible* observes, "There is a fascinating forecast of the coming Messiah, breaking through the dimness with amazing consistency, at intervals from Genesis to Malachi. Abraham, Moses, the slave girl Hagar, the impoverished farmer Gideon, even the humble parents of Samson, had seen and talked with Him centuries before the herald angels proclaimed His birth in Bethlehem."

## New International Version

8And he said, "Hagar, slave of Sarai, where have you come from, and where are you going?"

"I'm running away from my mistress Sarai," she answered.

9Then the angel of the LORD told her, "Go back to your mistress and submit to her." 10The angel added, "I will increase your descendants so much that they will be too numerous to count."

11The angel of the LORD also said to her:

"You are now pregnant
and you will give birth to a son.
You shall name him Ishmael,*a*
for the LORD has heard of your misery.
12He will be a wild donkey of a man;
his hand will be against everyone
and everyone's hand against him,
and he will live in hostility
toward*b* all his brothers."

13She gave this name to the LORD who spoke to her: "You are the God who sees me," for she said, "I have now seen*c* the One who sees me." 14That is why the well was called Beer Lahai Roi*d*; it is still there, between Kadesh and Bered.

15So Hagar bore Abram a son, and Abram gave the name Ishmael to the son she had borne. 16Abram was eighty-six years old when Hagar bore him Ishmael.

### The Covenant of Circumcision

**17** When Abram was ninety-nine years old, the LORD appeared to him and said, "I am God Almighty*e*; walk before me faithfully and be blameless. 2Then I will make my covenant between me and you and will greatly increase your numbers."

3Abram fell facedown, and God said to him, 4"As for me, this is my covenant with you: You will be the father of many nations. 5No longer will you be called Abram*f*; your name will be Abraham,*g* for I have made you a father of many nations. 6I will make you very fruitful; I will make nations of you, and kings will come from you. 7I will establish my covenant as an everlasting covenant between me and you and your descendants after you for the generations to come, to be your God and the God of your descendants after you. 8The whole land of Canaan, where you now reside as a foreigner, I will give as an everlasting possession to you and your descendants after you; and I will be their God."

9Then God said to Abraham, "As for you, you must keep my covenant, you and your descendants after you for the generations to come. 10This is my covenant with you and your descendants after you, the covenant you are to keep: Every male among you shall be circumcised. 11You are

## Amplified Bible

8And He said, Hagar, Sarai's maid, where did you come from, and where are you intending to go? And she said, I am running away from my mistress Sarai.

9The Angel of the Lord said to her, Go back to your mistress and [humbly] submit to her control.

10Also the Angel of the Lord said to her, I will multiply your descendants exceedingly, so that they shall not be numbered for multitude.

11And the Angel of the Lord continued, See now, you are with child and shall bear a son, and shall call his name Ishmael [God hears], because the Lord has heard *and* paid attention to your affliction.

12And he [Ishmael] will be as a *a*wild ass among men; his hand will be against every man and every man's hand against him, and he will live to the east *and* on the borders of all his kinsmen.

13So she called the name of the Lord Who spoke to her, You are a God of seeing, for she said, Have I [not] even here [in the wilderness] looked upon Him Who sees me [and lived]? *Or* have I here also seen [the future purposes or designs of] Him Who sees me?

14Therefore the well was called Beer-lahai-roi [A well to the Living One Who sees me]; it is *b*between Kadesh and Bered.

15And Hagar bore Abram a son, and Abram called the name of his son whom Hagar bore *c*Ishmael.

16Abram was eighty-six years old when Hagar bore Ishmael.

**17** When Abram was ninety-nine years old, the Lord appeared to him and said, I am the Almighty God; walk *and* live habitually before Me and be perfect (blameless, wholehearted, complete).

2And I will make My covenant (solemn pledge) between Me and you and will multiply you exceedingly.

3Then Abram fell on his face, and God said to him,

4As for Me, behold, My covenant (solemn pledge) is with you, and you shall be the father of many nations.

5Nor shall your name any longer be Abram [high, exalted father]; but your name shall be Abraham [father of a multitude], for I have made you the father of many nations.

6And I will make you exceedingly fruitful and I will make nations of you, and *d*kings will come from you.

7And I will establish My covenant between Me and you and your descendants after you throughout their generations for an everlasting, solemn pledge, to be a God to you and to your posterity after you. [Gal. 3:16.]

8And I will give to you and to your posterity after you the land in which you are a stranger [going from place to place], all the land of Canaan, for an everlasting possession; and I will be their God. [Acts 7:5.]

9And God said to Abraham, As for you, you shall therefore keep My covenant, you and your descendants after you throughout their generations.

10This is My covenant, which you shall keep, between Me and you and your posterity after you: Every male among you shall be circumcised.

*a* "Nothing can be more descriptive of the wandering, lawless, freebooting life of the Arabs than this. From the beginning to the present they have kept their independence, and God preserves them as a lasting monument of His providential care and an incontestable argument of the truth of divine revelation. Had the books of Moses no other proof of their divine origin, the account of Ishmael and the prophecy concerning his descendants during a period of nearly 4,000 years would be sufficient. To attempt to refute it would be a most ridiculous presumption and folly" (Adam Clarke, *The Holy Bible with A Commentary*). *b* This, "it is between Kadesh and Bered," is further proof of the antiquity of the original names, since the place had to be identified to the reader in the time of Moses. *c* Ishmael was the first person whom God named before his birth (Gen. 16:11). Others were: Isaac (Gen. 17:19); Josiah (I Kings 13:2); Solomon (I Chron. 22:9); Jesus (Matt. 1:21); and John the Baptist (Luke 1:13). *d* This prophecy and promise has been literally fulfilled countless times—for example, by all of the kings of Israel and Judah.

*a* 11 *Ishmael* means *God hears.*    *b* 12 Or *live to the east / of*    *c* 13 Or *seen the back of*    *d* 14 *Beer Lahai Roi* means *well of the Living One who sees me.*    *e* 1 Hebrew *El-Shaddai*    *f* 5 *Abram* means *exalted father.*    *g* 5 *Abraham* probably means *father of many.*

## New International Version

to undergo circumcision, and it will be the sign of the covenant between me and you. ¹²For the generations to come every male among you who is eight days old must be circumcised, including those born in your household or bought with money from a foreigner—those who are not your offspring. ¹³Whether born in your household or bought with your money, they must be circumcised. My covenant in your flesh is to be an everlasting covenant. ¹⁴Any uncircumcised male, who has not been circumcised in the flesh, will be cut off from his people; he has broken my covenant."

¹⁵God also said to Abraham, "As for Sarai your wife, you are no longer to call her Sarai; her name will be Sarah. ¹⁶I will bless her and will surely give you a son by her. I will bless her so that she will be the mother of nations; kings of peoples will come from her."

¹⁷Abraham fell facedown; he laughed and said to himself, "Will a son be born to a man a hundred years old? Will Sarah bear a child at the age of ninety?" ¹⁸And Abraham said to God, "If only Ishmael might live under your blessing!"

¹⁹Then God said, "Yes, but your wife Sarah will bear you a son, and you will call him Isaac.ᵃ I will establish my covenant with him as an everlasting covenant for his descendants after him. ²⁰And as for Ishmael, I have heard you: I will surely bless him; I will make him fruitful and will greatly increase his numbers. He will be the father of twelve rulers, and I will make him into a great nation. ²¹But my covenant I will establish with Isaac, whom Sarah will bear to you by this time next year." ²²When he had finished speaking with Abraham, God went up from him.

²³On that very day Abraham took his son Ishmael and all those born in his household or bought with his money, every male in his household, and circumcised them, as God told him. ²⁴Abraham was ninety-nine years old when he was circumcised, ²⁵and his son Ishmael was thirteen; ²⁶Abraham and his son Ishmael were both circumcised on that very day. ²⁷And every male in Abraham's household, including those born in his household or bought from a foreigner, was circumcised with him.

### The Three Visitors

**18** The LORD appeared to Abraham near the great trees of Mamre while he was sitting at the entrance to his tent in the heat of the day. ²Abraham looked up and saw three men standing nearby. When he saw them, he hurried from the entrance of his tent to meet them and bowed low to the ground.

³He said, "If I have found favor in your eyes, my lord,ᵇ do not pass your servant by. ⁴Let a little water be brought, and then you may all wash your feet and rest under this tree. ⁵Let me get you something to eat, so you can be refreshed and then go on your way—now that you have come to your servant."

"Very well," they answered, "do as you say."

⁶So Abraham hurried into the tent to Sarah. "Quick," he said, "get three seahsᶜ of the finest flour and knead it and bake some bread."

⁷Then he ran to the herd and selected a choice, tender

ᵃ 19 Isaac means he laughs.   ᵇ 3 Or eyes, Lord   ᶜ 6 That is, probably about 36 pounds or about 16 kilograms

## Amplified Bible

¹¹And you shall circumcise the flesh of your foreskin, and it shall be a token or sign of the covenant (the promise or pledge) between Me and you.

¹²He who is eight days old among you shall be circumcised, every male throughout your generations, whether born in [your] house or bought with [your] money from any foreigner not of your offspring.

¹³He that is born in your house and he that is bought with your money must be circumcised; and My covenant shall be in your flesh for an everlasting covenant.

¹⁴And the male who is not circumcised, that soul shall be cut off from his people; he has broken My covenant.

¹⁵And God said to Abraham, As for Sarai your wife, you shall not call her name Sarai; but Sarah [Princess] her name shall be.

¹⁶And I will bless her and give you a son also by her. Yes, I will bless her, and she shall be a mother of nations; kings of peoples shall come from her.

¹⁷Then Abraham fell on his face and laughed and said in his heart, Shall a child be born to a man who is a hundred years old? And shall Sarah, who is ninety years old, bear a son?

¹⁸And [he] said to God, Oh, that Ishmael might live before You!

¹⁹But God said, Sarah your wife shall bear you a son indeed, and you shall call his name Isaac [laughter]; and I will establish My covenant or solemn pledge with him for an everlasting covenant and with his posterity after him.

²⁰And as for Ishmael, I have heard and heeded you: behold, I will bless him and will make him fruitful and will multiply him exceedingly; He will be the father of twelve princes, and I will make him a great nation. [Fulfilled in Gen. 25:12-18.]

²¹But My covenant, My promise and pledge, I will establish with Isaac, whom Sarah will bear to you at this season next year.

²²And God stopped talking with him and went up from Abraham.

²³And Abraham took Ishmael his son and all who were born in his house and all who were bought with his money, every male among [those] of Abraham's house, and circumcised [them] the very same day, as God had said to him.

²⁴And Abraham was ninety-nine years old when he was circumcised.

²⁵And Ishmael his son was thirteen years old when he was circumcised.

²⁶On the very same day Abraham was circumcised, and Ishmael his son as well.

²⁷And all the men of his house, both those born in the house and those bought with money from a foreigner, were circumcised along with him.

**18** Now the Lord appeared to Abraham by the oaks or terebinths of Mamre; as he sat at the door of his tent in the heat of the day,

²He lifted up his eyes and looked, and behold, three men stood at a little distance from him. He ran from the tent door to meet them and bowed himself to the ground

³And said, My lord, if now I have found favor in your sight, do not pass by your servant, I beg of you.

⁴Let a little water be brought, and you may wash your feet and recline and rest yourselves under the tree.

⁵And I will bring a morsel (mouthful) of bread to refresh and sustain your hearts before you go on further— for that is why you have come to your servant. And they replied, Do as you have said.

⁶So Abraham hastened into the tent to Sarah and said, Quickly get ready three measures of fine meal, knead it, and bake cakes.

⁷And Abraham ran to the herd and brought a calf tender

## New International Version

calf and gave it to a servant, who hurried to prepare it. [8]He then brought some curds and milk and the calf that had been prepared, and set these before them. While they ate, he stood near them under a tree.

[9]"Where is your wife Sarah?" they asked him.

"There, in the tent," he said.

[10]Then one of them said, "I will surely return to you about this time next year, and Sarah your wife will have a son."

Now Sarah was listening at the entrance to the tent, which was behind him. [11]Abraham and Sarah were already very old, and Sarah was past the age of childbearing. [12]So Sarah laughed to herself as she thought, "After I am worn out and my lord is old, will I now have this pleasure?"

[13]Then the LORD said to Abraham, "Why did Sarah laugh and say, 'Will I really have a child, now that I am old?' [14]Is anything too hard for the LORD? I will return to you at the appointed time next year, and Sarah will have a son."

[15]Sarah was afraid, so she lied and said, "I did not laugh."

But he said, "Yes, you did laugh."

### Abraham Pleads for Sodom

[16]When the men got up to leave, they looked down toward Sodom, and Abraham walked along with them to see them on their way. [17]Then the LORD said, "Shall I hide from Abraham what I am about to do? [18]Abraham will surely become a great and powerful nation, and all nations on earth will be blessed through him.[a] [19]For I have chosen him, so that he will direct his children and his household after him to keep the way of the LORD by doing what is right and just, so that the LORD will bring about for Abraham what he has promised him."

[20]Then the LORD said, "The outcry against Sodom and Gomorrah is so great and their sin so grievous [21]that I will go down and see if what they have done is as bad as the outcry that has reached me. If not, I will know."

[22]The men turned away and went toward Sodom, but Abraham remained standing before the LORD.[b] [23]Then Abraham approached him and said: "Will you sweep away the righteous with the wicked? [24]What if there are fifty righteous people in the city? Will you really sweep it away and not spare[c] the place for the sake of the fifty righteous people in it? [25]Far be it from you to do such a thing—to kill the righteous with the wicked, treating the righteous and the wicked alike. Far be it from you! Will not the Judge of all the earth do right?"

[26]The LORD said, "If I find fifty righteous people in the city of Sodom, I will spare the whole place for their sake."

[27]Then Abraham spoke up again: "Now that I have been so bold as to speak to the Lord, though I am nothing but dust and ashes, [28]what if the number of the righteous is five less than fifty? Will you destroy the whole city for lack of five people?"

"If I find forty-five there," he said, "I will not destroy it."

[29]Once again he spoke to him, "What if only forty are found there?"

## Amplified Bible

and good and gave it to the young man [to butcher]; then he [Abraham] hastened to prepare it.

[8]And he took curds and milk and the calf which he had made ready, and set it before [the men]; and he stood by them under the tree while they ate.

[9]And they said to him, Where is Sarah your wife? And he said, [She is here] in the tent.

[10][a] [The Lord] said, I will surely return to you when the season comes round, and behold, Sarah your wife will have a son. And Sarah was listening *and* heard it at the tent door which was behind Him. [Rom. 9:9-12.]

[11]Now Abraham and Sarah were old, well advanced in years; it had ceased to be with Sarah as with [young] women. [She was past the age of childbearing].

[12]Therefore Sarah laughed to herself, saying, After I have become aged shall I have pleasure *and* delight, my lord (husband), being old also? [I Pet. 3:6.]

[13]And the Lord asked Abraham, Why did Sarah laugh, saying, Shall I really bear a child when I am so old?

[14]Is anything too hard *or* too wonderful for the Lord? At the appointed time, when the season [for her delivery] comes around, I will return to you and Sarah shall have borne a son. [Matt. 19:26.]

[15]Then Sarah denied it, saying, I did not laugh; for she was afraid. And He said, No, but you did laugh.

[16]The men rose up from there and faced toward Sodom, and Abraham went with them to bring them on the way.

[17]And the Lord said, Shall I hide from Abraham [My friend and servant] what I am going to do, [Gal. 3:8.]

[18]Since Abraham shall surely become a great and mighty nation, and all the nations of the earth shall be blessed through him *and* shall bless themselves by him? [Gen. 12:2-3.]

[19]For I have known (chosen, acknowledged) him [as My own], so that he may teach *and* command his children and the sons of his house after him to keep the way of the Lord and to do what is just and righteous, so that the Lord may bring Abraham what He has promised him.

[20]And the Lord said, Because the shriek [of the sins] of Sodom and Gomorrah is great and their sin is exceedingly grievous,

[21]I will go down now and see whether they have done altogether [as vilely and wickedly] as is the cry of it which has come to Me; and if not, I will know.

[22]Now the [two] men turned from there and went toward Sodom, but Abraham still stood before the Lord.

[23]And Abraham came close and said, Will You destroy the righteous (those upright and in right standing with God) together with the wicked?

[24]Suppose there are in the city fifty righteous; will You destroy the place and not spare it for [the sake of] the fifty righteous in it?

[25]Far be it from You to do such a thing—to slay the righteous with the wicked, so that the righteous fare as do the wicked! Far be it from You! Shall not the Judge of all the earth execute judgment *and* do righteously?

[26]And the Lord said, If I find in the city of Sodom fifty righteous (upright and in right standing with God), I will spare the whole place for their sake.

[27]Abraham answered, Behold now, I who am but dust and ashes have taken upon myself to speak to the Lord.

[28]If five of the fifty righteous should be lacking—will You destroy the whole city for lack of five? He said, If I find forty-five, I will not destroy it.

[29]And [Abraham] spoke to Him yet again, and said, Sup-

---

[a] One of the three guests was the Lord, and since God the Father was never seen in bodily form (John 1:18), only the "Angel of the covenant," Christ Himself, can be meant here; see especially Gen. 18:22 and also the footnote on Gen. 16:7. [b] The word "Lord" as applied to God is obviously the most important word in the Bible, for it occurs oftener than any other important word—by actual count more than 5,000 times. **Nothing** is "too hard *or* too wonderful" for Him when He is truly made Lord.

---

[a] *18* Or *will use his name in blessings* (see 48:20)    [b] *22* Masoretic Text; an ancient Hebrew scribal tradition *but the LORD remained standing before Abraham*    [c] *24* Or *forgive*; also in verse 26

## New International Version

He said, "For the sake of forty, I will not do it."
30Then he said, "May the Lord not be angry, but let me speak. What if only thirty can be found there?"
He answered, "I will not do it if I find thirty there."
31Abraham said, "Now that I have been so bold as to speak to the Lord, what if only twenty can be found there?"
He said, "For the sake of twenty, I will not destroy it."
32Then he said, "May the Lord not be angry, but let me speak just once more. What if only ten can be found there?"
He answered, "For the sake of ten, I will not destroy it."
33When the LORD had finished speaking with Abraham, he left, and Abraham returned home.

### Sodom and Gomorrah Destroyed

**19** The two angels arrived at Sodom in the evening, and Lot was sitting in the gateway of the city. When he saw them, he got up to meet them and bowed down with his face to the ground. 2"My lords," he said, "please turn aside to your servant's house. You can wash your feet and spend the night and then go on your way early in the morning."

"No," they answered, "we will spend the night in the square."

3But he insisted so strongly that they did go with him and entered his house. He prepared a meal for them, baking bread without yeast, and they ate. 4Before they had gone to bed, all the men from every part of the city of Sodom—both young and old—surrounded the house. 5They called to Lot, "Where are the men who came to you tonight? Bring them out to us so that we can have sex with them."

6Lot went outside to meet them and shut the door behind him 7and said, "No, my friends. Don't do this wicked thing. 8Look, I have two daughters who have never slept with a man. Let me bring them out to you, and you can do what you like with them. But don't do anything to these men, for they have come under the protection of my roof."

9"Get out of our way," they replied. "This fellow came here as a foreigner, and now he wants to play the judge! We'll treat you worse than them." They kept bringing pressure on Lot and moved forward to break down the door.

10But the men inside reached out and pulled Lot back into the house and shut the door. 11Then they struck the men who were at the door of the house, young and old, with blindness so that they could not find the door.

12The two men said to Lot, "Do you have anyone else here—sons-in-law, sons or daughters, or anyone else in the city who belongs to you? Get them out of here, 13because we are going to destroy this place. The outcry to the LORD against its people is so great that he has sent us to destroy it."

14So Lot went out and spoke to his sons-in-law, who were pledged to marry*a* his daughters. He said, "Hurry and get out of this place, because the LORD is about to destroy the city!" But his sons-in-law thought he was joking.

15With the coming of dawn, the angels urged Lot, saying, "Hurry! Take your wife and your two daughters who are here, or you will be swept away when the city is punished."

16When he hesitated, the men grasped his hand and the hands of his wife and of his two daughters and led them safely out of the city, for the LORD was merciful to them.

a 14 Or were married to

## Amplified Bible

pose [only] forty shall be found there. And He said, I will not do it for forty's sake.
30Then [Abraham] said to Him, Oh, let not the Lord be angry, and I will speak [again]. Suppose [only] thirty shall be found there. And He answered, I will not do it if I find thirty there.
31And [Abraham] said, Behold now, I have taken upon myself to speak [again] to the Lord. Suppose [only] twenty shall be found there. And [the Lord] replied, I will not destroy it for twenty's sake.
32And he said, Oh, let not the Lord be angry, and I will speak again only this once. Suppose ten [righteous people] shall be found there. And [the Lord] said, I will not destroy it for ten's sake.
33And the Lord went His way when He had finished speaking with Abraham, and Abraham returned to his place.

**19** It was evening when the two angels came to Sodom. Lot was sitting at Sodom's [city] gate. Seeing them, Lot rose up to meet them and bowed to the ground.

2And he said, My lords, turn aside, I beg of you, into your servant's house and spend the night and bathe your feet. Then you can arise early and go on your way. But they said, No, we will spend the night in the square.

3[Lot] entreated *and* urged them greatly until they yielded and [with him] entered his house. And he made them a dinner [with drinking] and had unleavened bread which he baked, and they ate.

4But before they lay down, the men of the city of Sodom, both young and old, all the men from every quarter, surrounded the house.

5And they called to Lot and said, Where are the men who came to you tonight? Bring them out to us, that we may know (be intimate with) them.

6And Lot went out of the door to the men and shut the door after him

7And said, I beg of you, my brothers, do not behave so wickedly.

8Look now, I have two daughters who are virgins; let me, I beg of you, bring them out to you, and you can do as you please with them. But only do nothing to these men, for they have come under the protection of my roof.

9But they said, Stand back! And they said, This fellow came in to live here temporarily, and now he presumes to be [our] judge! Now we will deal worse with you than with them. So they rushed at *and* pressed violently against Lot and came close to breaking down the door.

10But the men [the angels] reached out and pulled Lot into the house to them and shut the door after him.

11And they struck the men who were at the door of the house with blindness [which dazzled them], from the youths to the old men, so that they wearied themselves [groping] to find the door.

12And the [two] men asked Lot, Have you any others here—sons-in-law or your sons or your daughters? Whomever you have in the city, bring them out of this place,

13For we will spoil *and* destroy [Sodom]; for the outcry *and* shriek against its people has grown great before the Lord, and He has sent us to destroy it.

14And Lot went out and spoke to his sons-in-law, who were to marry his daughters, and said, Up, get out of this place, for the Lord will spoil *and* destroy this city! But he seemed to his sons-in-law to be [only] joking.

15When morning came, the angels urged Lot to hurry, saying, Arise, take your wife and two daughters who are here [and be off], lest you [too] be consumed *and* swept away in the iniquity *and* punishment of the city.

16But while he lingered, the men seized him and his wife and his two daughters by the hand, for the Lord was merciful to him; and they brought him forth and set him outside the city and left him there.

## New International Version

<sup>17</sup>As soon as they had brought them out, one of them said, "Flee for your lives! Don't look back, and don't stop anywhere in the plain! Flee to the mountains or you will be swept away!"

<sup>18</sup>But Lot said to them, "No, my lords,ᵃ please! <sup>19</sup>Yourᵇ servant has found favor in yourᵇ eyes, and youᵇ have shown great kindness to me in sparing my life. But I can't flee to the mountains; this disaster will overtake me, and I'll die. <sup>20</sup>Look, here is a town near enough to run to, and it is small. Let me flee to it—it is very small, isn't it? Then my life will be spared."

<sup>21</sup>He said to him, "Very well, I will grant this request too; I will not overthrow the town you speak of. <sup>22</sup>But flee there quickly, because I cannot do anything until you reach it." (That is why the town was called Zoar.ᶜ)

<sup>23</sup>By the time Lot reached Zoar, the sun had risen over the land. <sup>24</sup>Then the LORD rained down burning sulfur on Sodom and Gomorrah—from the LORD out of the heavens. <sup>25</sup>Thus he overthrew those cities and the entire plain, destroying all those living in the cities—and also the vegetation in the land. <sup>26</sup>But Lot's wife looked back, and she became a pillar of salt.

<sup>27</sup>Early the next morning Abraham got up and returned to the place where he had stood before the LORD. <sup>28</sup>He looked down toward Sodom and Gomorrah, toward all the land of the plain, and he saw dense smoke rising from the land, like smoke from a furnace.

<sup>29</sup>So when God destroyed the cities of the plain, he remembered Abraham, and he brought Lot out of the catastrophe that overthrew the cities where Lot had lived.

### Lot and His Daughters

<sup>30</sup>Lot and his two daughters left Zoar and settled in the mountains, for he was afraid to stay in Zoar. He and his two daughters lived in a cave. <sup>31</sup>One day the older daughter said to the younger, "Our father is old, and there is no man around here to give us children—as is the custom all over the earth. <sup>32</sup>Let's get our father to drink wine and then sleep with him and preserve our family line through our father."

<sup>33</sup>That night they got their father to drink wine, and the older daughter went in and slept with him. He was not aware of it when she lay down or when she got up.

<sup>34</sup>The next day the older daughter said to the younger, "Last night I slept with my father. Let's get him to drink wine again tonight, and you go in and sleep with him so we can preserve our family line through our father." <sup>35</sup>So they got their father to drink wine that night also, and the younger daughter went in and slept with him. Again he was not aware of it when she lay down or when she got up.

<sup>36</sup>So both of Lot's daughters became pregnant by their

## Amplified Bible

<sup>17</sup>And when they had brought them forth, they said, Escape for your life! Do not look behind you or stop anywhere in ᵃthe whole valley; escape to the mountains [of Moab], lest you be consumed.

<sup>18</sup>And Lot said to them, Oh, not that, my lords!

<sup>19</sup>Behold now, your servant has found favor in your sight, and you have magnified your kindness and mercy to me in saving my life; but I cannot escape to the mountains, lest the evil overtake me, and I die.

<sup>20</sup>See now yonder city; it is near enough to flee to, and it is a little one. Oh, let me escape to it! Is it not a little one? And my life will be saved!

<sup>21</sup>And [the angel] said to him, See, I have yielded to your entreaty concerning this thing also; I will not destroy this city of which you have spoken.

<sup>22</sup>Make haste and take refuge there, for I cannot do anything until you arrive there. Therefore the name of the city was called Zoar [little].

<sup>23</sup>The sun had risen over the earth when Lot entered Zoar.

<sup>24</sup>Then the Lord rained on Sodom and on Gomorrah brimstone and fire from the Lord out of the heavens.

<sup>25</sup>He overthrew, destroyed, *and* ended those cities, and all the valley and all the inhabitants of the cities, and what grew on the ground.

<sup>26</sup>But [Lot's] wife looked back from behind him, and she ᵇbecame a pillar of salt.

<sup>27</sup>Abraham went up early the next morning to the place where he [only the day before] had stood before the Lord.

<sup>28</sup>And he looked toward Sodom and Gomorrah, and toward all the land of the valley, and saw, and behold, smoke of ᶜthe country went up like the smoke of a furnace.

<sup>29</sup>When God ravaged *and* destroyed the cities of the plain [of Siddim], He [earnestly] remembered Abraham [imprinted and fixed him indelibly on His mind], and He sent Lot out of the midst of the overthrow when He overthrew the cities where Lot lived.

<sup>30</sup>And Lot went up out of Zoar and dwelt in the mountain, and his two daughters with him, for he feared to dwell in Zoar; and he lived in a cave, he and his two daughters.

<sup>31</sup>The elder said to the younger, Our father is aging, and there is not a man on earth to live with us in the customary way.

<sup>32</sup>Come, let us make our father drunk with wine, and we will lie with him, so that we may preserve offspring (our race) through our father.

<sup>33</sup>And they made their father drunk with wine that night, and the older went in and lay with her father; and he was not aware of it when she lay down or when she arose.

<sup>34</sup>Then the next day the firstborn said to the younger, See here, I lay last night with my father; let us make him drunk with wine tonight also, and then you go in and lie with him, so that we may preserve offspring (our race) through our father.

<sup>35</sup>And they made their father drunk with wine again that night, and the younger arose and lay with him; and he was not aware of it when she lay down or when she arose.

<sup>36</sup>Thus both the daughters of Lot were with child by their father.

ᵃ The valley which Lot had once so much coveted (Gen. 13:10, 11).
ᵇ Lot's wife not only "looked back" to where her heart's interests were, but she lingered behind; and probably overtaken by the fire and brimstone, her dead body became incrusted with salt, which, in that salt-packed area now the Dead Sea, grew larger with more incrustations—a veritable "pillar of salt." In fact, at the southern end of the Dead Sea there is a mountain of table salt called Jebel Usdum, "Mount of Sodom." It is about six miles long, three miles wide, and 1,000 feet high. It is covered with a crust of earth several feet thick, but the rest of the mountain is said to be solid salt (George T. B. Davis, *Rebuilding Palestine According to Prophecy*). Somewhere in this area Lot's wife looked back to where her treasures and her heart were, and "she became a pillar of salt." Jesus said, "Remember Lot's wife" (Luke 17:32). ᶜ Not only were Sodom and Gomorrah blazing ruins, but also Admah and Zeboiim (Deut. 29:23; Hos. 11:8), as well as all the towns in the Valley of Siddim; Zoar was the lone exception.

---

ᵃ 18 Or *No, Lord*; or *No, my lord*    ᵇ 19 The Hebrew is singular.
ᶜ 22 *Zoar* means *small*.

## New International Version

father. ³⁷The older daughter had a son, and she named him Moabᵃ; he is the father of the Moabites of today. ³⁸The younger daughter also had a son, and she named him Ben-Ammiᵇ; he is the father of the Ammonitesᶜ of today.

### Abraham and Abimelek

**20** Now Abraham moved on from there into the region of the Negev and lived between Kadesh and Shur. For a while he stayed in Gerar, ²and there Abraham said of his wife Sarah, "She is my sister." Then Abimelek king of Gerar sent for Sarah and took her.

³But God came to Abimelek in a dream one night and said to him, "You are as good as dead because of the woman you have taken; she is a married woman."

⁴Now Abimelek had not gone near her, so he said, "Lord, will you destroy an innocent nation? ⁵Did he not say to me, 'She is my sister,' and didn't she also say, 'He is my brother'? I have done this with a clear conscience and clean hands."

⁶Then God said to him in the dream, "Yes, I know you did this with a clear conscience, and so I have kept you from sinning against me. That is why I did not let you touch her. ⁷Now return the man's wife, for he is a prophet, and he will pray for you and you will live. But if you do not return her, you may be sure that you and all who belong to you will die."

⁸Early the next morning Abimelek summoned all his officials, and when he told them all that had happened, they were very much afraid. ⁹Then Abimelek called Abraham in and said, "What have you done to us? How have I wronged you that you have brought such great guilt upon me and my kingdom? You have done things to me that should never be done." ¹⁰And Abimelek asked Abraham, "What was your reason for doing this?"

¹¹Abraham replied, "I said to myself, 'There is surely no fear of God in this place, and they will kill me because of my wife.' ¹²Besides, she really is my sister, the daughter of my father though not of my mother; and she became my wife. ¹³And when God had me wander from my father's household, I said to her, 'This is how you can show your love to me: Everywhere we go, say of me, "He is my brother."'"

¹⁴Then Abimelek brought sheep and cattle and male and female slaves and gave them to Abraham, and he returned Sarah his wife to him. ¹⁵And Abimelek said, "My land is before you; live wherever you like."

¹⁶To Sarah he said, "I am giving your brother a thousand shekelsᵈ of silver. This is to cover the offense against you before all who are with you; you are completely vindicated."

¹⁷Then Abraham prayed to God, and God healed Abimelek, his wife and his female slaves so they could have children again, ¹⁸for the LORD had kept all the women in Abimelek's household from conceiving because of Abraham's wife Sarah.

### The Birth of Isaac

**21** Now the LORD was gracious to Sarah as he had said, and the LORD did for Sarah what he had prom-

## Amplified Bible

³⁷The older bore a son, and named him Moab [of a father]; he is the father of the Moabites to this day. ³⁸The younger also bore a son and named him Ben-ammi [son of my people]; he is the father of the Ammonites to this day.

**20** Now Abraham journeyed from there toward the ᵃSouth country (the Negeb) and dwelt between Kadesh and Shur; and he lived temporarily in Gerar. ²And Abraham said of Sarah his wife, She is my sister. And Abimelech king of Gerar sent and took Sarah [into his harem].

³But God came to Abimelech in a dream by night and said, Behold, you are a dead man because of the woman whom you have taken [as your own], for she is a man's wife.

⁴But Abimelech had not come near her, so he said, Lord, will you slay a people who are just *and* innocent?

⁵Did not the man tell me, She is my sister? And she herself said, He is my brother. In integrity of heart and innocency of hands I have done this.

⁶Then God said to him in the dream, Yes, I know you did this in the integrity of your heart, for it was I Who kept you back *and* spared you from sinning against Me; therefore I did not give you occasion to touch her.

⁷So now restore to the man his wife, for he is a prophet, and he will pray for you and you will live. But if you do not restore her [to him], know that you shall surely die, you and all who are yours.

⁸So Abimelech rose early in the morning and called all his servants and told them all these things; and the men were exceedingly filled with reverence *and* fear.

⁹Then Abimelech called Abraham and said to him, What have you done to us? And how have I offended you that you have brought on me and my kingdom a great sin? You have done to me what ought not to be done [to anyone].

¹⁰And Abimelech said to Abraham, What did you see [in us] that [justified] you in doing such a thing as this?

¹¹And Abraham said, Because I thought, Surely there is no reverence *or* fear of God at all in this place, and they will slay me because of my wife.

¹²But truly, she is my sister; she is the daughter of my father but not of my mother; and she became my wife.

¹³When God caused me to wander from my father's house, I said to her, This kindness you can show me: at every place we stop, say of me, He is my brother.

¹⁴Then Abimelech took sheep and oxen and male and female slaves and gave them to Abraham and restored to him Sarah his wife.

¹⁵And Abimelech said, Behold, my land is before you; dwell wherever it pleases you.

¹⁶And to Sarah he said, Behold, I have given this brother of yours a thousand pieces of silver; see, it is to compensate you [for all that has occurred] and to vindicate your honor before all who are with you; before all men you are cleared *and* compensated.

¹⁷So Abraham prayed to God, and God healed Abimelech and his wife and his female slaves, and they bore children,

¹⁸For the Lord had closed fast the wombs of all in Abimelech's household because of Sarah, Abraham's wife.

**21** The Lord visited Sarah as He had said, and the Lord did for her as He had promised.

ᵃ "Primitive geographic expressions such as 'the South country (the Negeb)' (Gen. 12:9; 13:1, 3; 20:1; 24:62) and 'the east country' (Gen. 25:6) are used in the time of Abraham . . . After the time of Genesis they have well-known and well-defined names; I submit that they were written down in early days, and that no writer after Moses could have used such archaic expressions as these" (P. J. Wiseman, *New Discoveries in Babylonia About Genesis*).

---

ᵃ 37 *Moab* sounds like the Hebrew for *from father.* ᵇ 38 *Ben-Ammi* means *son of my father's people.* ᶜ 38 Hebrew *Bene-Ammon* ᵈ 16 That is, about 25 pounds or about 12 kilograms

## New International Version

ised. ²Sarah became pregnant and bore a son to Abraham in his old age, at the very time God had promised him. ³Abraham gave the name Isaac*a* to the son Sarah bore him. ⁴When his son Isaac was eight days old, Abraham circumcised him, as God commanded him. ⁵Abraham was a hundred years old when his son Isaac was born to him.

⁶Sarah said, "God has brought me laughter, and everyone who hears about this will laugh with me." ⁷And she added, "Who would have said to Abraham that Sarah would nurse children? Yet I have borne him a son in his old age."

### Hagar and Ishmael Sent Away

⁸The child grew and was weaned, and on the day Isaac was weaned Abraham held a great feast. ⁹But Sarah saw that the son whom Hagar the Egyptian had borne to Abraham was mocking, ¹⁰and she said to Abraham, "Get rid of that slave woman and her son, for that woman's son will never share in the inheritance with my son Isaac."

¹¹The matter distressed Abraham greatly because it concerned his son. ¹²But God said to him, "Do not be so distressed about the boy and your slave woman. Listen to whatever Sarah tells you, because it is through Isaac that your offspring*b* will be reckoned. ¹³I will make the son of the slave into a nation also, because he is your offspring."

¹⁴Early the next morning Abraham took some food and a skin of water and gave them to Hagar. He set them on her shoulders and then sent her off with the boy. She went on her way and wandered in the Desert of Beersheba.

¹⁵When the water in the skin was gone, she put the boy under one of the bushes. ¹⁶Then she went off and sat down about a bowshot away, for she thought, "I cannot watch the boy die." And as she sat there, she*c* began to sob.

¹⁷God heard the boy crying, and the angel of God called to Hagar from heaven and said to her, "What is the matter, Hagar? Do not be afraid; God has heard the boy crying as he lies there. ¹⁸Lift the boy up and take him by the hand, for I will make him into a great nation."

¹⁹Then God opened her eyes and she saw a well of water. So she went and filled the skin with water and gave the boy a drink.

²⁰God was with the boy as he grew up. He lived in the desert and became an archer. ²¹While he was living in the Desert of Paran, his mother got a wife for him from Egypt.

### The Treaty at Beersheba

²²At that time Abimelek and Phicol the commander of his forces said to Abraham, "God is with you in everything you do. ²³Now swear to me here before God that you will not deal falsely with me or my children or my descendants. Show to me and the country where you now reside as a foreigner the same kindness I have shown to you."

²⁴Abraham said, "I swear it."

²⁵Then Abraham complained to Abimelek about a well of water that Abimelek's servants had seized. ²⁶But Abim-

## Amplified Bible

²For Sarah became pregnant and bore Abraham a son in his old age, at the set time God had told him. ³Abraham *a*named his son whom Sarah bore to him Isaac [laughter].

⁴And Abraham circumcised his son Isaac when he was eight days old, as God had commanded him.

⁵Abraham was a hundred years old when Isaac was born.

⁶And Sarah said, God has made me to laugh; all who hear will laugh with me.

⁷And she said, Who would have said to Abraham that Sarah would nurse children at the breast? For I have borne him a son in his old age! [Heb. 11:12.]

⁸And the child grew and was *b*weaned, and Abraham made a great feast the same day that Isaac was weaned.

⁹Now Sarah saw the son of Hagar the Egyptian, whom she had borne to Abraham, mocking [Isaac].

¹⁰Therefore she said to Abraham, Cast out this bondwoman and her son, for the son of this bondwoman shall not be an heir with my son Isaac. [Gal. 4:28-31.]

¹¹And the thing was very grievous (serious, evil) in Abraham's sight on account of his son [Ishmael].

¹²God said to Abraham, Do not let it seem grievous *and* evil to you because of the youth and your bondwoman; in all that Sarah has said to you, do what she asks, for in Isaac shall your posterity be called. [Rom. 9:7.]

¹³And I will make a nation of the son of the bondwoman also, because he is your offspring.

¹⁴So Abraham rose early in the morning and took bread and a bottle of water and gave them to Hagar, putting them on her shoulders, and he sent her and the *c*youth away. And she wandered on [aimlessly] and lost her way in the wilderness of Beersheba.

¹⁵When the water in the bottle was all gone, Hagar caused the youth to lie down under one of the shrubs.

¹⁶Then she went and sat down opposite him a good way off, about a bowshot, for she said, Let me not see the death of the lad. And as she sat down opposite him, *d*he lifted up his voice and wept *and* she raised her voice and wept.

¹⁷And God heard the voice of the youth, and the angel of God called to Hagar out of heaven and said to her, What troubles you, Hagar? Fear not, for God has heard the voice of the youth where he is.

¹⁸Arise, raise up the youth and support him with your hand, for I intend to make him a great nation.

¹⁹Then God opened her eyes and she saw a well of water; and she went and filled the [empty] bottle with water and caused the youth to drink.

²⁰And God was with the youth, and he developed; and he dwelt in the wilderness and became an archer.

²¹He dwelt in the Wilderness of Paran; and his mother took a wife for him out of the land of Egypt.

²²At that time Abimelech and Phicol the commander of his army said to Abraham, God is with you in everything you do.

²³So now, swear to me here by God that you will not deal falsely with me or with my son or with my posterity; but as I have dealt with you kindly, you will do the same with me and with the land in which you have sojourned.

²⁴And Abraham said, I will swear.

²⁵When Abraham complained to *and* reasoned with Abimelech about a well of water [Abimelech's] servants had violently seized,

---

*a* See footnote on Gen. 16:15. *b* This was probably when the child was about three years of age. Samuel served in the sanctuary from the time that he was weaned (I Sam. 1:22-28). A Hebrew mother is quoted in II Maccabees 7:27 as saying to her son that she gave him "suck three years." *c* Ishmael was born when Abraham was eighty-six years old (Gen. 16:16), so Ishmael was fourteen when Isaac was born. Isaac was weaned (Gen. 21:8) at least three years later probably (II Chron. 31:16; II Maccabees 7:27). *d* The Hebrew says, "she lifted up her voice." *The Septuagint* (Greek translation of the Old Testament) says "he . . ."—which the next verse seems to support. The circumstances allow either.

---

*a* 3 *Isaac* means *he laughs.*   *b* 12 Or *seed*   *c* 16 Hebrew; Septuagint *the child*

## New International Version

elek said, "I don't know who has done this. You did not tell me, and I heard about it only today."

27So Abraham brought sheep and cattle and gave them to Abimelek, and the two men made a treaty. 28Abraham set apart seven ewe lambs from the flock, 29and Abimelek asked Abraham, "What is the meaning of these seven ewe lambs you have set apart by themselves?"

30He replied, "Accept these seven lambs from my hand as a witness that I dug this well."

31So that place was called Beersheba,a because the two men swore an oath there.

32After the treaty had been made at Beersheba, Abimelek and Phicol the commander of his forces returned to the land of the Philistines. 33Abraham planted a tamarisk tree in Beersheba, and there he called on the name of the LORD, the Eternal God. 34And Abraham stayed in the land of the Philistines for a long time.

### Abraham Tested

**22** Some time later God tested Abraham. He said to him, "Abraham!"

"Here I am," he replied.

2Then God said, "Take your son, your only son, whom you love—Isaac—and go to the region of Moriah. Sacrifice him there as a burnt offering on a mountain I will show you."

3Early the next morning Abraham got up and loaded his donkey. He took with him two of his servants and his son Isaac. When he had cut enough wood for the burnt offering, he set out for the place God had told him about. 4On the third day Abraham looked up and saw the place in the distance. 5He said to his servants, "Stay here with the donkey while I and the boy go over there. We will worship and then we will come back to you."

6Abraham took the wood for the burnt offering and placed it on his son Isaac, and he himself carried the fire and the knife. As the two of them went on together, 7Isaac spoke up and said to his father Abraham, "Father?"

"Yes, my son?" Abraham replied.

"The fire and wood are here," Isaac said, "but where is the lamb for the burnt offering?"

8Abraham answered, "God himself will provide the lamb for the burnt offering, my son." And the two of them went on together.

9When they reached the place God had told him about, Abraham built an altar there and arranged the wood on it. He bound his son Isaac and laid him on the altar, on top of the wood. 10Then he reached out his hand and took the knife to slay his son. 11But the angel of the LORD called out to him from heaven, "Abraham! Abraham!"

"Here I am," he replied.

12"Do not lay a hand on the boy," he said. "Do not do anything to him. Now I know that you fear God, because you have not withheld from me your son, your only son."

## Amplified Bible

26Abimelech said, I know not who did this thing; you did not tell me, and I did not hear of it until today.

27So Abraham took sheep and oxen and gave them to Abimelech, and the two men made a league or covenant.

28Abraham set apart seven ewe lambs of the flock,

29And Abimelech said to Abraham, What do these seven ewe lambs which you have set apart mean?

30He said, You are to accept these seven ewe lambs from me as a witness for me that I dug this well.

31Therefore that place was called Beersheba [well of the oath], because there both parties swore an oath.

32Thus they made a covenant at Beersheba; then Abimelech and Phicol the commander of his army returned to the land of the Philistines.

33Abraham planted a tamarisk tree in Beersheba and called there on the name of the Lord, the Eternal God.

34And Abraham sojourned in Philistia many days.

**22** After these events, God tested and proved Abraham and said to him, Abraham! And he said, Here I am.

2[God] said, Take now your son, your only son Isaac, whom you love, and go to the region of Moriah; and offer him there as a burnt offering upon one of the mountains of which I will tell you.

3So Abraham rose early in the morning, saddled his donkey, and took two of his young men with him and his son Isaac; and he split the wood for the burnt offering, and then began the trip to the place of which God had told him.

4On the third day Abraham looked up and saw the place in the distance.

5And Abraham said to his servants, Settle down and stay here with the donkey, and I and the young man will go yonder and worship and acome again to you.

6Then Abraham took the wood for the burnt offering and laid it on [the shoulders of] Isaac his son, and he took the fire (the firepot) in his own hand, and a knife; and the two of them went on together.

7And Isaac said to Abraham, My father! And he said, Here I am, my son. [Isaac] said, See, here are the fire and the wood, but where is the lamb for the burnt sacrifice?

8Abraham said, My son, bGod Himself will provide a lamb for the burnt offering. So the two went on together.

9When they came to the place of which God had told him, Abraham built an altar there; then he laid the wood in order and cbound Isaac his son and laid him on the altar on the wood. [Matt. 10:37.]

10And Abraham stretched forth his hand and took hold of the knife to slay his son. [Heb. 11:17-19.]

11But the dAngel of the Lord called to him from heaven and said, Abraham, Abraham! He answered, Here I am.

12And He said, Do not lay your hand on the lad or do anything to him; for now I know that you fear and revere God, since you have not held back from Me or begrudged giving Me your son, your only son.

---

a Abraham was not lying to his servants or trying to deceive them. He believed God, Who had promised him that this young man's posterity was to inherit the promises made to Abraham (Gen. 12:2, 3). b We must not suppose that this was the language merely of faith and obedience. Abraham spoke prophetically, and referred to that Lamb of God which He had provided for Himself, Who in the fullness of time would take away the sin of the world, and of Whom Isaac was a most expressive type (Adam Clarke, *The Holy Bible with A Commentary*). For Abraham was a prophet (Gen. 20:7). Jesus said Abraham hoped for "My day [My incarnation]; and he did see it and was delighted" (John 8:56). c Isaac, who was perhaps twenty-five years old (according to the ancient historian Josephus), shared his father's confidence in God's promise. Was not his very existence the result of God keeping His word? (Gen. 17:15-17.) d See footnote on Gen. 16:7.

---

a 31 *Beersheba* can mean *well of seven* and *well of the oath.*

## New International Version

<sup>13</sup>Abraham looked up and there in a thicket he saw a ram*a* caught by its horns. He went over and took the ram and sacrificed it as a burnt offering instead of his son. <sup>14</sup>So Abraham called that place The LORD Will Provide. And to this day it is said, "On the mountain of the LORD it will be provided."

<sup>15</sup>The angel of the LORD called to Abraham from heaven a second time <sup>16</sup>and said, "I swear by myself, declares the LORD, that because you have done this and have not withheld your son, your only son, <sup>17</sup>I will surely bless you and make your descendants as numerous as the stars in the sky and as the sand on the seashore. Your descendants will take possession of the cities of their enemies, <sup>18</sup>and through your offspring*b* all nations on earth will be blessed,*c* because you have obeyed me."

<sup>19</sup>Then Abraham returned to his servants, and they set off together for Beersheba. And Abraham stayed in Beersheba.

### Nahor's Sons

<sup>20</sup>Some time later Abraham was told, "Milkah is also a mother; she has borne sons to your brother Nahor: <sup>21</sup>Uz the firstborn, Buz his brother, Kemuel (the father of Aram), <sup>22</sup>Kesed, Hazo, Pildash, Jidlaph and Bethuel." <sup>23</sup>Bethuel became the father of Rebekah. Milkah bore these eight sons to Abraham's brother Nahor. <sup>24</sup>His concubine, whose name was Reumah, also had sons: Tebah, Gaham, Tahash and Maakah.

### The Death of Sarah

**23** Sarah lived to be a hundred and twenty-seven years old. <sup>2</sup>She died at Kiriath Arba (that is, Hebron) in the land of Canaan, and Abraham went to mourn for Sarah and to weep over her.

<sup>3</sup>Then Abraham rose from beside his dead wife and spoke to the Hittites.*d* He said, <sup>4</sup>"I am a foreigner and stranger among you. Sell me some property for a burial site here so I can bury my dead."

<sup>5</sup>The Hittites replied to Abraham, <sup>6</sup>"Sir, listen to us. You are a mighty prince among us. Bury your dead in the choicest of our tombs. None of us will refuse you his tomb for burying your dead."

<sup>7</sup>Then Abraham rose and bowed down before the people of the land, the Hittites. <sup>8</sup>He said to them, "If you are willing to let me bury my dead, then listen to me and intercede with Ephron son of Zohar on my behalf <sup>9</sup>so he will sell me the cave of Machpelah, which belongs to him and is at the end of his field. Ask him to sell it to me for the full price as a burial site among you."

<sup>10</sup>Ephron the Hittite was sitting among his people and he replied to Abraham in the hearing of all the Hittites who had come to the gate of his city. <sup>11</sup>"No, my lord," he

## Amplified Bible

<sup>13</sup>Then Abraham looked up *and* glanced around, and behold, behind him was a ram caught in a thicket by his horns. And Abraham went and took the ram and offered it up for a burnt offering *and* an ascending sacrifice instead of his son!

<sup>14</sup>So Abraham called the name of that place The Lord Will Provide. And it is said to this day, On the mount of the Lord it will be provided.

<sup>15</sup>The Angel of the Lord called to Abraham from heaven a second time

<sup>16</sup>And said, I have sworn by Myself, says the Lord, that since you have done this and have not withheld [from Me] *or* begrudged [giving Me] your son, your only son,

<sup>17</sup>In blessing I will bless you and in multiplying I will multiply your descendants like the stars of the heavens and like the sand on the seashore. And your Seed (Heir) will possess the gate of His enemies, [Heb. 6:13, 14; 11:12.]

<sup>18</sup>And in your Seed [*a*Christ] shall all the nations of the earth be blessed *and* [by Him] bless themselves, because you have heard *and* obeyed My voice. [Gen. 12:2-3; 13:16; 22:18; 26:4; 28:14; Acts 3:25, 26; Gal. 3:16.]

<sup>19</sup>So Abraham returned to his servants, and they rose up and went with him to Beersheba; there Abraham lived.

<sup>20</sup>Now after these things, it was told Abraham, Milcah has also borne children to your brother Nahor:

<sup>21</sup>Uz the firstborn, Buz his brother, Kemuel the father of Aram,

<sup>22</sup>Chesed, Hazo, Pildash, Jidlaph, and Bethuel.

<sup>23</sup>Bethuel became the father of Rebekah. These eight Milcah bore to Nahor, Abraham's brother.

<sup>24</sup>And his concubine, whose name was Reumah, bore Tebah, Gaham, Tahash, and Maacah.

**23** Sarah lived 127 years; this was the length of the life of Sarah.

<sup>2</sup>And Sarah died in Kiriath-arba, *b*that is, Hebron, in the land of Canaan. And Abraham went to mourn for Sarah and to weep for her.

<sup>3</sup>And Abraham stood up from before his dead and said to the sons of Heth,

<sup>4</sup>I am a stranger and a sojourner with you; give me property for a burial place among you, that I may bury my dead out of my sight.

<sup>5</sup>And the Hittites replied to Abraham,

<sup>6</sup>Listen to us, my lord; you are a mighty prince among us. Bury your dead in any tomb *or* grave of ours that you choose; none of us will withhold from you his tomb or hinder you from burying your dead.

<sup>7</sup>And Abraham stood up and bowed himself to the people of the land, the Hittites.

<sup>8</sup>And he said to them, If you are willing to grant my dead a burial out of my sight, listen to me and ask Ephron son of Zohar for me,

<sup>9</sup>That he may give me the cave of Machpelah, which he owns—it is at the end of his field. For the full price let him give it to me here in your presence as a burial place to which I may hold fast among you.

<sup>10</sup>Now Ephron was present there among the sons of Heth; so, in the hearing of all who went in at the gate of his city, Ephron the Hittite answered Abraham, saying,

*a* We have the authority of the apostle Paul (Gal. 3:8, 16, 18) to restrict this promise to our blessed Lord, Who was the Seed through Whom alone all God's blessings of providence, mercy, grace, and glory should be conveyed to the nations of the earth (Adam Clarke, *The Holy Bible with A Commentary*). *b* Surely this indicates that this detail was written at a very early date—before Israel had entered the land. No one in later times would need to be told where Hebron was. Not only was its location conspicuous in Joshua's and Caleb's day, but it became a "city of refuge." Besides all this, David was king in Hebron for seven years. Obviously the Israelites had not yet entered Canaan and had to be told not only the name of the place where Abraham and Isaac had lived and were buried, but also its location (P. J. Wiseman, *New Discoveries in Babylonia About Genesis*).

*a* 13 Many manuscripts of the Masoretic Text, Samaritan Pentateuch, Septuagint and Syriac; most manuscripts of the Masoretic Text *a ram behind him*   *b* 18 Or *seed*   *c* 18 Or *and all nations on earth will use the name of your offspring in blessings* (see 48:20)   *d* 3 Or *the descendants of Heth*; also in verses 5, 7, 10, 16, 18 and 20

## New International Version

said. "Listen to me; I give[a] you the field, and I give[a] you the cave that is in it. I give[a] it to you in the presence of my people. Bury your dead."

[12]Again Abraham bowed down before the people of the land [13]and he said to Ephron in their hearing, "Listen to me, if you will. I will pay the price of the field. Accept it from me so I can bury my dead there."

[14]Ephron answered Abraham, [15]"Listen to me, my lord; the land is worth four hundred shekels[b] of silver, but what is that between you and me? Bury your dead."

[16]Abraham agreed to Ephron's terms and weighed out for him the price he had named in the hearing of the Hittites: four hundred shekels of silver, according to the weight current among the merchants.

[17]So Ephron's field in Machpelah near Mamre—both the field and the cave in it, and all the trees within the borders of the field—was deeded [18]to Abraham as his property in the presence of all the Hittites who had come to the gate of the city. [19]Afterward Abraham buried his wife Sarah in the cave in the field of Machpelah near Mamre (which is at Hebron) in the land of Canaan. [20]So the field and the cave in it were deeded to Abraham by the Hittites as a burial site.

### Isaac and Rebekah

**24** Abraham was now very old, and the LORD had blessed him in every way. [2]He said to the senior servant in his household, the one in charge of all that he had, "Put your hand under my thigh. [3]I want you to swear by the LORD, the God of heaven and the God of earth, that you will not get a wife for my son from the daughters of the Canaanites, among whom I am living, [4]but will go to my country and my own relatives and get a wife for my son Isaac."

[5]The servant asked him, "What if the woman is unwilling to come back with me to this land? Shall I then take your son back to the country you came from?"

[6]"Make sure that you do not take my son back there," Abraham said. [7]"The LORD, the God of heaven, who brought me out of my father's household and my native land and who spoke to me and promised me on oath, saying, 'To your offspring[c] I will give this land'—he will send his angel before you so that you can get a wife for my son from there. [8]If the woman is unwilling to come back with you, then you will be released from this oath of mine. Only do not take my son back there." [9]So the servant put his hand under the thigh of his master Abraham and swore an oath to him concerning this matter.

[10]Then the servant left, taking with him ten of his master's camels loaded with all kinds of good things from his master. He set out for Aram Naharaim[d] and made his way to the town of Nahor. [11]He had the camels kneel down near

## Amplified Bible

[11]No, my lord, hear me; I give you the field, and the cave that is in it I give you. In the presence of the sons of my people I give it to you. Bury your dead.

[12]Then Abraham bowed himself down before the people of the land.

[13]And he said to Ephron in the presence of the people of the land, But if you will give it, I beg of you, hear me. I will give you the price of the field; accept it from me, and I will bury my dead there.

[14]Ephron replied to Abraham, saying,

[15]My lord, listen to me. The land is worth 400 shekels of silver; what is that between you and me? So bury your dead.

[16]So Abraham listened to what Ephron said *and* acted upon it. He weighed to Ephron the silver which he had named in the hearing of the Hittites: 400 shekels of silver, according to the weights current among the merchants.

[17]So the field of Ephron in Machpelah, which was to the east of Mamre [Hebron]—the field and the cave which was in it, and all the trees that were in the field and in all its borders round about—was made over

[18]As a possession to Abraham in the presence of the Hittites, before all who went in at his city gate.

[19]After this, Abraham buried Sarah his wife in the cave of the field of [a]Machpelah to the east of Mamre, that is, Hebron, in the land of Canaan.

[20]The field and the cave in it were conveyed to Abraham for a permanent burial place by the sons of Heth.

**24** Now Abraham was old, well advanced in years, and the Lord had blessed Abraham in all things.

[2]And Abraham said to the eldest servant of his house [Eliezer of Damascus], who ruled over all that he had, I beg of you, put your hand under my thigh; [Gen. 15:2.]

[3]And you shall swear by the Lord, the God of heaven and earth, that you will not take a wife for my son from the daughters of the Canaanites, among whom I have settled,

[4]But you shall go to my country and to my relatives and take [b]a wife for my son Isaac.

[5]The servant said to him, But perhaps the woman will not be willing to come along after me to this country. Must I take your son to the country from which you came?

[6]Abraham said to him, See to it that you do not take my son back there.

[7]The Lord, the God of heaven, Who took me from my father's house, from the land of my family *and* my birth, Who spoke to me and swore to me, saying, To your offspring I will give this land—He will send His [c]Angel before you, and you will take a wife from there for my son.

[8]And if the woman should [d]not be willing to go along after you, then you will be clear from this oath; only you must not take my son back there.

[9]So the servant put his hand under the thigh of Abraham his master and swore to him concerning this matter.

[10]And the servant took ten of his master's camels and departed, taking some of all his master's treasures with him; thus he journeyed to Mesopotamia [between the Tigris and the Euphrates], to the city of Nahor [Abraham's brother].

[11]And he made his camels to kneel down outside the

---

[a] Here were buried Abraham and Sarah, Isaac and Rebekah, and Jacob and Leah (Gen. 49:31; 50:13). [b] This chapter is highly illustrative of God the Father, Who sends forth His Holy Spirit to win the consent of the individual soul to become the bride of His Son. Keep these resemblances constantly in mind as you read and see how the story unfolds. First meet the Father and note His concern about His Son's bride. Then get acquainted with the Holy Spirit's great, selfless heart, Whose one purpose is to win the girl for His Master's Son. Then meet the Son and note His tenderness as He claims His bride. The longest chapter in Genesis is devoted to this important story. [c] See footnote on Gen. 16:7. [d] The Holy Spirit does not win unwilling souls, only "whosoever will."

[a] 11 Or *sell*   [b] 15 That is, about 10 pounds or about 4.6 kilograms   [c] 7 Or *seed*   [d] 10 That is, Northwest Mesopotamia

## New International Version

the well outside the town; it was toward evening, the time the women go out to draw water.

¹²Then he prayed, "Lᴏʀᴅ, God of my master Abraham, make me successful today, and show kindness to my master Abraham. ¹³See, I am standing beside this spring, and the daughters of the townspeople are coming out to draw water. ¹⁴May it be that when I say to a young woman, 'Please let down your jar that I may have a drink,' and she says, 'Drink, and I'll water your camels too'—let her be the one you have chosen for your servant Isaac. By this I will know that you have shown kindness to my master."

¹⁵Before he had finished praying, Rebekah came out with her jar on her shoulder. She was the daughter of Bethuel son of Milkah, who was the wife of Abraham's brother Nahor. ¹⁶The woman was very beautiful, a virgin; no man had ever slept with her. She went down to the spring, filled her jar and came up again.

¹⁷The servant hurried to meet her and said, "Please give me a little water from your jar."

¹⁸"Drink, my lord," she said, and quickly lowered the jar to her hands and gave him a drink.

¹⁹After she had given him a drink, she said, "I'll draw water for your camels too, until they have had enough to drink." ²⁰So she quickly emptied her jar into the trough, ran back to the well to draw more water, and drew enough for all his camels. ²¹Without saying a word, the man watched her closely to learn whether or not the Lᴏʀᴅ had made his journey successful.

²²When the camels had finished drinking, the man took out a gold nose ring weighing a beka*ᵃ* and two gold bracelets weighing ten shekels.*ᵇ* ²³Then he asked, "Whose daughter are you? Please tell me, is there room in your father's house for us to spend the night?"

²⁴She answered him, "I am the daughter of Bethuel, the son that Milkah bore to Nahor." ²⁵And she added, "We have plenty of straw and fodder, as well as room for you to spend the night."

²⁶Then the man bowed down and worshiped the Lᴏʀᴅ, ²⁷saying, "Praise be to the Lᴏʀᴅ, the God of my master Abraham, who has not abandoned his kindness and faithfulness to my master. As for me, the Lᴏʀᴅ has led me on the journey to the house of my master's relatives."

²⁸The young woman ran and told her mother's household about these things. ²⁹Now Rebekah had a brother named Laban, and he hurried out to the man at the spring. ³⁰As soon as he had seen the nose ring, and the bracelets on his sister's arms, and had heard Rebekah tell what the man said to her, he went out to the man and found him standing by the camels near the spring. ³¹"Come, you who are blessed by the Lᴏʀᴅ," he said. "Why are you standing out here? I have prepared the house and a place for the camels."

³²So the man went to the house, and the camels were unloaded. Straw and fodder were brought for the camels, and water for him and his men to wash their feet. ³³Then food was set before him, but he said, "I will not eat until I have told you what I have to say."

"Then tell us," Laban said.

³⁴So he said, "I am Abraham's servant. ³⁵The Lᴏʀᴅ

## Amplified Bible

city by a well of water at the time of the evening when women go out to draw water.

¹²And he said, O Lord, God of my master Abraham, I pray You, cause me to meet with good success today, and show kindness to my master Abraham.

¹³See, I stand here by the well of water, and the daughters of the men of the city are coming to draw water.

¹⁴And let it so be that the girl to whom I say, I pray you, let down your jar that I may drink, and she replies, Drink, and I will give your camels drink also—let her be the one whom You have selected *and* appointed *and* indicated for Your servant Isaac [to be a wife to him]; and by it I shall know that You have shown kindness *and* faithfulness to my master.

¹⁵Before he had finished speaking, behold, out came Rebekah, who was the daughter of Bethuel son of Milcah, who was the wife of Nahor the brother of Abraham, with her water jar on her shoulder.

¹⁶And the girl was very beautiful *and* attractive, chaste *and* modest, and unmarried. And she went down to the well, filled her water jar, and came up.

¹⁷And the servant ran to meet her, and said, I pray you, let me drink a little water from your water jar.

¹⁸And she said, Drink, my lord; and she quickly let down her jar onto her hand and gave him a drink.

¹⁹When she had given him a drink, she said, I will draw water for your camels also, until they finish drinking.

²⁰So she quickly emptied her jar into the trough and ran again to the well and drew water for all his camels.

²¹The man stood gazing at her in silence, waiting to know if the Lord had made his trip prosperous.

²²And when the camels had finished drinking, the man took a gold earring *or* nose ring of half a shekel in weight, and for her hands two bracelets of ten shekels in weight in gold,

²³And said, Whose daughter are you? I pray you, tell me: Is there room in your father's house for us to lodge there?

²⁴And she said to him, I am the daughter of Bethuel son of Milcah and [her husband] Nahor.

²⁵She said also to him, We have both straw and provender (fodder) enough, and also room in which to lodge.

²⁶The man bowed down his head and worshiped the Lord

²⁷And said, Blessed be the Lord, the God of my master Abraham, Who has not left my master bereft *and* destitute of His loving-kindness and steadfastness. As for me, going on the way [of obedience and faith] the Lord led me to the house of my master's kinsmen.

²⁸The girl related to her mother's household what had happened.

²⁹Now Rebekah had a brother whose name was Laban, and Laban ran out to the man at the well.

³⁰For when he saw the earring *or* nose ring, and the bracelets on his sister's arms, and when he heard Rebekah his sister saying, The man said this to me, he went to the man and found him standing by the camels at the well.

³¹He cried, Come in, you blessed of the Lord! Why do you stand outside? For I have made the house ready *and* have prepared a place for the camels.

³²So the man came into the house; and [Laban] ungirded his camels and gave straw and provender for the camels and water to bathe his feet and the feet of the men who were with him.

³³A meal was set before him, but he said, *ᵃ*I will not eat until I have told you of my errand. And [Laban] said, Speak on.

³⁴And he said, I am Abraham's servant.

---

*ᵃ* The characteristics of a model servant of God are pictured here: 1. He is dependable and trustworthy (Gen. 24:2); 2. He is a praying person (Gen. 24:12); 3. He is so in earnest that he refuses to eat before attending to his Master's business (Gen. 24:33); 4. He never speaks his own name but is always speaking about his Master (Gen. 24:35ff.); 5. He gives God all the glory (Gen. 24:48).

---

*ᵃ 22* That is, about 1/5 ounce or about 5.7 grams    *ᵇ 22* That is, about 4 ounces or about 115 grams

## New International Version

has blessed my master abundantly, and he has become wealthy. He has given him sheep and cattle, silver and gold, male and female servants, and camels and donkeys. <sup>36</sup>My master's wife Sarah has borne him a son in her old age, and he has given him everything he owns. <sup>37</sup>And my master made me swear an oath, and said, 'You must not get a wife for my son from the daughters of the Canaanites, in whose land I live, <sup>38</sup>but go to my father's family and to my own clan, and get a wife for my son.'

<sup>39</sup>"Then I asked my master, 'What if the woman will not come back with me?'

<sup>40</sup>"He replied, 'The Lord, before whom I have walked faithfully, will send his angel with you and make your journey a success, so that you can get a wife for my son from my own clan and from my father's family. <sup>41</sup>You will be released from my oath if, when you go to my clan, they refuse to give her to you—then you will be released from my oath.'

<sup>42</sup>"When I came to the spring today, I said, 'Lord, God of my master Abraham, if you will, please grant success to the journey on which I have come. <sup>43</sup>See, I am standing beside this spring. If a young woman comes out to draw water and I say to her, "Please let me drink a little water from your jar," <sup>44</sup>and if she says to me, "Drink, and I'll draw water for your camels too," let her be the one the Lord has chosen for my master's son.'

<sup>45</sup>"Before I finished praying in my heart, Rebekah came out, with her jar on her shoulder. She went down to the spring and drew water, and I said to her, 'Please give me a drink.'

<sup>46</sup>"She quickly lowered her jar from her shoulder and said, 'Drink, and I'll water your camels too.' So I drank, and she watered the camels also.

<sup>47</sup>"I asked her, 'Whose daughter are you?'

"She said, 'The daughter of Bethuel son of Nahor, whom Milkah bore to him.'

"Then I put the ring in her nose and the bracelets on her arms, <sup>48</sup>and I bowed down and worshiped the Lord. I praised the Lord, the God of my master Abraham, who had led me on the right road to get the granddaughter of my master's brother for his son. <sup>49</sup>Now if you will show kindness and faithfulness to my master, tell me; and if not, tell me, so I may know which way to turn."

<sup>50</sup>Laban and Bethuel answered, "This is from the Lord; we can say nothing to you one way or the other. <sup>51</sup>Here is Rebekah; take her and go, and let her become the wife of your master's son, as the Lord has directed."

<sup>52</sup>When Abraham's servant heard what they said, he bowed down to the ground before the Lord. <sup>53</sup>Then the servant brought out gold and silver jewelry and articles of clothing and gave them to Rebekah; he also gave costly gifts to her brother and to her mother. <sup>54</sup>Then he and the men who were with him ate and drank and spent the night there.

When they got up the next morning, he said, "Send me on my way to my master."

<sup>55</sup>But her brother and her mother replied, "Let the young woman remain with us ten days or so; then you<sup>a</sup> may go."

<sup>56</sup>But he said to them, "Do not detain me, now that the Lord has granted success to my journey. Send me on my way so I may go to my master."

<sup>57</sup>Then they said, "Let's call the young woman and ask

## Amplified Bible

<sup>35</sup>And the Lord has blessed my master mightily, and he has become great; and He has given him flocks, herds, silver, gold, menservants, maidservants, camels, and asses. <sup>36</sup>And Sarah my master's wife bore a son to my master when she was old, and to him he has given all that he has.

<sup>37</sup>And my master made me swear, saying, You must not take a wife for my son from the daughters of the Canaanites, in whose land I dwell,

<sup>38</sup>But you shall go to my father's house and to my family and take a wife for my son.

<sup>39</sup>And I said to my master, But suppose the woman will not follow me.

<sup>40</sup>And he said to me, The Lord, in Whose presence I walk [habitually], will send His <sup>a</sup>Angel with you and prosper your way, and you will take a wife for my son from my kindred and from my father's house.

<sup>41</sup>Then you shall be clear from my oath, when you come to my kindred; and if they do not give her to you, you shall be free *and* innocent of my oath.

<sup>42</sup>I came today to the well and said, O Lord, God of my master Abraham, if You are now causing me to go on my way prosperously—

<sup>43</sup>See, I am standing by the well of water; now let it be that when the maiden comes out to draw water and I say to her, I pray you, give me a little water from your [water] jar to drink,

<sup>44</sup>And if she says to me, You drink, and I will draw water for your camels also, let that same woman be the one whom the Lord has selected *and* indicated for my master's son.

<sup>45</sup>And before I had finished praying in my heart, behold, Rebekah came out with her [water] jar on her shoulder, and she went down to the well and drew water. And I said to her, I pray you, let me have a drink.

<sup>46</sup>And she quickly let down her [water] jar from her shoulder and said, Drink, and I will water your camels also. So I drank, and she gave the camels drink also.

<sup>47</sup>I asked her, Whose daughter are you? She said, The daughter of Bethuel, Nahor's son, whom Milcah bore to him. And I put the earring *or* nose ring on her face and the bracelets on her arms.

<sup>48</sup>And I bowed down my head and worshiped the Lord and blessed the Lord, the God of my master Abraham, Who had led me in the right way to take my master's brother's daughter to his son.

<sup>49</sup>And now if you will deal kindly and truly with my master [showing faithfulness to him], tell me; and if not, tell me, that I may turn to the right or to the left.

<sup>50</sup>Then Laban and Bethuel answered, The thing comes forth from the Lord; we cannot speak bad or good to you.

<sup>51</sup>Rebekah is before you; take her and go, and let her be the wife of your master's son, as the Lord has said.

<sup>52</sup>And when Abraham's servant heard their words, he bowed himself to the ground before the Lord.

<sup>53</sup>And the servant brought out jewels of silver, jewels of gold, and garments and gave them to Rebekah; he also gave precious things to her brother and her mother.

<sup>54</sup>Then they ate and drank, he and the men who were with him, and stayed there all night. And in the morning they arose, and he said. Send me away to my master.

<sup>55</sup>But [Rebekah's] brother and mother said, Let the girl stay with us a few days—at least ten; then she may go.

<sup>56</sup>But [the servant] said to them, Do not hinder *and* delay me, seeing that the Lord has caused me to go prosperously on my way. Send me away, that I may go to my master.

<sup>57</sup>And they said, We will call the girl and ask her [what is] her desire.

## New International Version

her about it." ⁵⁸So they called Rebekah and asked her, "Will you go with this man?"

"I will go," she said.

⁵⁹So they sent their sister Rebekah on her way, along with her nurse and Abraham's servant and his men. ⁶⁰And they blessed Rebekah and said to her,

"Our sister, may you increase
   to thousands upon thousands;
may your offspring possess
   the cities of their enemies."

⁶¹Then Rebekah and her attendants got ready and mounted the camels and went back with the man. So the servant took Rebekah and left.

⁶²Now Isaac had come from Beer Lahai Roi, for he was living in the Negev. ⁶³He went out to the field one evening to meditate,ᵃ and as he looked up, he saw camels approaching. ⁶⁴Rebekah also looked up and saw Isaac. She got down from her camel ⁶⁵and asked the servant, "Who is that man in the field coming to meet us?"

"He is my master," the servant answered. So she took her veil and covered herself.

⁶⁶Then the servant told Isaac all he had done. ⁶⁷Isaac brought her into the tent of his mother Sarah, and he married Rebekah. So she became his wife, and he loved her; and Isaac was comforted after his mother's death.

### The Death of Abraham

**25** Abraham had taken another wife, whose name was Keturah. ²She bore him Zimran, Jokshan, Medan, Midian, Ishbak and Shuah. ³Jokshan was the father of Sheba and Dedan; the descendants of Dedan were the Ashurites, the Letushites and the Leummites. ⁴The sons of Midian were Ephah, Epher, Hanok, Abida and Eldaah. All these were descendants of Keturah.

⁵Abraham left everything he owned to Isaac. ⁶But while he was still living, he gave gifts to the sons of his concubines and sent them away from his son Isaac to the land of the east.

⁷Abraham lived a hundred and seventy-five years. ⁸Then Abraham breathed his last and died at a good old age, an old man and full of years; and he was gathered to his people. ⁹His sons Isaac and Ishmael buried him in the cave of Machpelah near Mamre, in the field of Ephron son of Zohar the Hittite, ¹⁰the field Abraham had bought from the Hittites.ᵇ There Abraham was buried with his wife Sarah. ¹¹After Abraham's death, God blessed his son Isaac, who then lived near Beer Lahai Roi.

### Ishmael's Sons

¹²This is the account of the family line of Abraham's son Ishmael, whom Sarah's slave, Hagar the Egyptian, bore to Abraham.

¹³These are the names of the sons of Ishmael, listed in the order of their birth: Nebaioth the firstborn of Ishmael, Kedar, Adbeel, Mibsam, ¹⁴Mishma, Dumah, Massa, ¹⁵Hadad, Tema, Jetur, Naphish and Kedemah. ¹⁶These were the sons of Ishmael, and these are the names of the twelve tribal rulers according to their settlements and

ᵃ 63 The meaning of the Hebrew for this word is uncertain.
ᵇ 10 Or the descendants of Heth

## Amplified Bible

⁵⁸So they called Rebekah and said to her, Will you go with this man? And she said, I will go.

⁵⁹So they sent away Rebekah their sister and her nurse [Deborah] and Abraham's servant and his men.

⁶⁰And they blessed Rebekah and said to her, You are our sister; may you become the mother of thousands of ten thousands, and let your posterity possess the gate of their enemies.

⁶¹And Rebekah and her maids arose and followed the man upon their camels. Thus the servant took Rebekah and went on his way.

⁶²Now Isaac had returned from going to the well Beer-lahai-roi [A well to the Living One Who sees me], for he [now] dwelt in the South country (the Negeb).

⁶³And Isaac went out to meditate *and* bow down [in prayer] in the open country in the evening; and he looked up and saw that, behold, the camels were coming.

⁶⁴And Rebekah looked up, and when she saw Isaac, she dismounted from the camel.

⁶⁵For she [had] said to the servant, Who is that man walking across the field to meet us? And the servant [had] said, He is my master. So she took a veil and concealed herself with it.

⁶⁶And the servant told Isaac everything that he had done.

⁶⁷And Isaac brought her into his mother Sarah's tent, and he took Rebekah and she became his wife, and he loved her; thus Isaac was comforted after his mother's death.

**25** Abraham took another wife, and her name was Keturah.

²And she bore him Zimran, Jokshan, Medan, Midian, Ishbak, and Shuah.

³Jokshan was the father of Sheba and Dedan. The sons of Dedan were Asshurim, Letushim, and Leummim.

⁴The sons of Midian were Ephah, Epher, Hanoch, Abida, and Eldaah. All these were the children of Keturah.

⁵And Abraham gave all that he had to Isaac.

⁶But to the sons of his concubines [Hagar and Keturah] Abraham gave gifts, and while he was still living he sent them to the east country, away from Isaac his son [of promise].

⁷The days of Abraham's life were 175 years.

⁸Then Abraham's spirit was released, and he died at a good (ample, full) old age, an old man, satisfied *and* satiated, and ᵃwas gathered to his people. [Gen. 15:15.]

⁹And his sons ᵇIsaac and Ishmael buried him in the cave of Machpelah, in the field of Ephron the son of Zohar the Hittite, which is east of Mamre,

¹⁰The field which Abraham purchased from the Hittites. There Abraham was buried with Sarah his wife.

¹¹After the death of Abraham, God blessed his son Isaac, and Isaac dwelt at Beer-lahai-roi [A well to the Living One Who sees me].

¹²Now this is the history of the descendants of Ishmael, Abraham's son, whom Hagar the Egyptian, Sarah's handmaid, bore to Abraham.

¹³These are the names of the sons of Ishmael, named in the order of their births: Nebaioth, the firstborn of Ishmael, and Kedar, Adbeel, Mibsam,

¹⁴Mishma, Dumah, Massa,

¹⁵Hadad, Tema, Jetur, Naphish, and Kedemah.

¹⁶These are the sons of Ishmael, and these are their names, by their villages and by their encampments (sheepfolds)—twelve princes according to their tribes. [Foretold in Gen. 17:20.]

ᵃ This often repeated expression forms a remarkable testimony to the Old Testament belief in a life beyond the grave and to our recognition and fellowship with our loved ones there. ᵇ Isaac was seventy-five and Ishmael nearly ninety years of age when their father died. Jacob and Esau were fifteen, and may have been present.

## New International Version

camps. [17] Ishmael lived a hundred and thirty-seven years. He breathed his last and died, and he was gathered to his people. [18] His descendants settled in the area from Havilah to Shur, near the eastern border of Egypt, as you go toward Ashur. And they lived in hostility toward[a] all the tribes related to them.

### Jacob and Esau

[19] This is the account of the family line of Abraham's son Isaac.

Abraham became the father of Isaac, [20] and Isaac was forty years old when he married Rebekah daughter of Bethuel the Aramean from Paddan Aram[b] and sister of Laban the Aramean.

[21] Isaac prayed to the LORD on behalf of his wife, because she was childless. The LORD answered his prayer, and his wife Rebekah became pregnant. [22] The babies jostled each other within her, and she said, "Why is this happening to me?" So she went to inquire of the LORD.

[23] The LORD said to her,

"Two nations are in your womb,
    and two peoples from within you will be separated;
one people will be stronger than the other,
    and the older will serve the younger."

[24] When the time came for her to give birth, there were twin boys in her womb. [25] The first to come out was red, and his whole body was like a hairy garment; so they named him Esau.[c] [26] After this, his brother came out, with his hand grasping Esau's heel; so he was named Jacob.[d] Isaac was sixty years old when Rebekah gave birth to them.

[27] The boys grew up, and Esau became a skillful hunter, a man of the open country, while Jacob was content to stay at home among the tents. [28] Isaac, who had a taste for wild game, loved Esau, but Rebekah loved Jacob.

[29] Once when Jacob was cooking some stew, Esau came in from the open country, famished. [30] He said to Jacob, "Quick, let me have some of that red stew! I'm famished!" (That is why he was also called Edom.[e])

[31] Jacob replied, "First sell me your birthright."

[32] "Look, I am about to die," Esau said. "What good is the birthright to me?"

[33] But Jacob said, "Swear to me first." So he swore an oath to him, selling his birthright to Jacob.

[34] Then Jacob gave Esau some bread and some lentil stew. He ate and drank, and then got up and left.

So Esau despised his birthright.

### Isaac and Abimelek

**26** Now there was a famine in the land—besides the previous famine in Abraham's time—and Isaac went to Abimelek king of the Philistines in Gerar. [2] The LORD appeared to Isaac and said, "Do not go down to Egypt; live in the land where I tell you to live. [3] Stay in this land for a while, and I will be with you and will bless you. For to you and your descendants I will give all these lands and will confirm the oath I swore to your father Abraham. [4] I will make your descendants as numerous as the stars in the sky and will give them all these lands, and through your offspring[f] all nations on earth will be blessed,[g] [5] because Abraham obeyed me and did everything I required of him, keeping my commands, my decrees and my instructions." [6] So Isaac stayed in Gerar.

[7] When the men of that place asked him about his wife, he said, "She is my sister," because he was afraid to say,

---

[a] 18 Or lived to the east of    [b] 20 That is, Northwest Mesopotamia
[c] 25 Esau may mean hairy.    [d] 26 Jacob means he grasps the heel, a
Hebrew idiom for he deceives.    [e] 30 Edom means red.    [f] 4 Or seed
[g] 4 Or and all nations on earth will use the name of your offspring in
blessings (see 48:20)

## Amplified Bible

[17] And Ishmael lived 137 years; then his spirit left him, and he died and was gathered to his kindred. [18] And [Ishmael's sons] dwelt from Havilah to Shur, which is before Egypt in the direction of Assyria. [Ishmael] dwelt close [to the lands] of all his brethren.

[19] And this is the history of the descendants of Isaac, Abraham's son: Abraham was the father of Isaac. [20] Isaac was forty years old when he married Rebekah, the daughter of Bethuel the Aramean of Padan-aram, the sister of Laban the Aramean.

[21] And Isaac prayed much to the Lord for his wife because she was unable to bear children; and the Lord granted his prayer, and Rebekah his wife became pregnant. [22] [Two] children struggled together within her; and she said, If it is so [that the Lord has heard our prayer], why am I like this? And she went to inquire of the Lord. [23] The Lord said to her, [The founders of] two nations are in your womb, and the separation of two peoples has begun in your body; the one people shall be stronger than the other, and the elder shall serve the younger.

[24] When her days to be delivered were fulfilled, behold, there were twins in her womb. [25] The first came out red all over like a hairy garment, and they named him Esau [hairy]. [26] Afterward his brother came forth, and his hand grasped Esau's heel; so he was named Jacob [supplanter]. Isaac was sixty years old when she gave birth to them.

[27] When the boys grew up, Esau was a cunning *and* skilled hunter, a man of the outdoors; but Jacob was a plain *and* quiet man, dwelling in tents. [28] And Isaac loved [and was partial to] Esau, because he ate of Esau's game; but Rebekah loved Jacob. [29] Jacob was boiling pottage (lentil stew) one day, when Esau came from the field and was faint [with hunger]. [30] And Esau said to Jacob, I beg of you, let me have some of that red lentil stew to eat, for I am faint *and* famished! That is why his name was called Edom [red]. [31] Jacob answered, Then sell me today your birthright (the rights of a firstborn). [32] Esau said, See here, I am at the point of death; what good can this birthright do me? [33] Jacob said, Swear to me today [that you are selling it to me]; and he swore to [Jacob] and sold him his birthright. [34] Then Jacob gave Esau bread and stew of lentils, and he ate and drank and rose up and went his way. Thus Esau scorned his birthright as beneath his notice.

**26** And there was a famine in the land, other than the former famine that was in the days of Abraham. And Isaac went to Gerar, to Abimelech king of the Philistines.

[2] And the Lord appeared to him and said, Do not go down to Egypt; live in the land of which I will tell you. [3] Dwell temporarily in this land, and I will be with you and will favor you with blessings; for to you and to your descendants I will give all these lands, and I will perform the oath which I swore to Abraham your father. [4] And I will make your descendants to multiply as the stars of the heavens, and will give to your posterity all these lands (kingdoms); and by your Offspring shall all the nations of the earth be blessed, *or* by Him bless themselves, [Gen. 22:18; Acts 3:25, 26; Gal. 3:16.] [5] For Abraham listened to *and* obeyed My voice and kept My charge, My commands, My statutes, and My laws. [6] So Isaac stayed in Gerar.

[7] And the men of the place asked him about his wife, and he said, She is my sister; for he was afraid to say, She is

## New International Version

"She is my wife." He thought, "The men of this place might kill me on account of Rebekah, because she is beautiful."

⁸When Isaac had been there a long time, Abimelek king of the Philistines looked down from a window and saw Isaac caressing his wife Rebekah. ⁹So Abimelek summoned Isaac and said, "She is really your wife! Why did you say, 'She is my sister'?"

Isaac answered him, "Because I thought I might lose my life on account of her."

¹⁰Then Abimelek said, "What is this you have done to us? One of the men might well have slept with your wife, and you would have brought guilt upon us."

¹¹So Abimelek gave orders to all the people: "Anyone who harms this man or his wife shall surely be put to death."

¹²Isaac planted crops in that land and the same year reaped a hundredfold, because the LORD blessed him. ¹³The man became rich, and his wealth continued to grow until he became very wealthy. ¹⁴He had so many flocks and herds and servants that the Philistines envied him. ¹⁵So all the wells that his father's servants had dug in the time of his father Abraham, the Philistines stopped up, filling them with earth.

¹⁶Then Abimelek said to Isaac, "Move away from us; you have become too powerful for us."

¹⁷So Isaac moved away from there and encamped in the Valley of Gerar, where he settled. ¹⁸Isaac reopened the wells that had been dug in the time of his father Abraham, which the Philistines had stopped up after Abraham died, and he gave them the same names his father had given them.

¹⁹Isaac's servants dug in the valley and discovered a well of fresh water there. ²⁰But the herders of Gerar quarreled with those of Isaac and said, "The water is ours!" So he named the well Esek,ᵃ because they disputed with him. ²¹Then they dug another well, but they quarreled over that one also; so he named it Sitnah.ᵇ ²²He moved on from there and dug another well, and no one quarreled over it. He named it Rehoboth,ᶜ saying, "Now the LORD has given us room and we will flourish in the land."

²³From there he went up to Beersheba. ²⁴That night the LORD appeared to him and said, "I am the God of your father Abraham. Do not be afraid, for I am with you; I will bless you and will increase the number of your descendants for the sake of my servant Abraham."

²⁵Isaac built an altar there and called on the name of the LORD. There he pitched his tent, and there his servants dug a well.

²⁶Meanwhile, Abimelek had come to him from Gerar, with Ahuzzath his personal adviser and Phicol the commander of his forces. ²⁷Isaac asked them, "Why have you come to me, since you were hostile to me and sent me away?"

²⁸They answered, "We saw clearly that the LORD was with you; so we said, 'There ought to be a sworn agreement between us'—between us and you. Let us make a treaty with you ²⁹that you will do us no harm, just as we did not harm you but always treated you well and sent you away peacefully. And now you are blessed by the LORD."

³⁰Isaac then made a feast for them, and they ate and drank. ³¹Early the next morning the men swore an oath to

## Amplified Bible

my wife—[thinking], Lest the men of the place should kill me for Rebekah, because she is attractive *and* is beautiful to look upon.

⁸When he had been there a long time, Abimelech king of the Philistines looked out of a window and saw Isaac caressing Rebekah his wife.

⁹And Abimelech called Isaac and said, See here, she is certainly your wife! How did you [dare] say to me, She is my sister? And Isaac said to him, Because I thought, Lest I die on account of her.

¹⁰And Abimelech said, What is this you have done to us? One of the men might easily have lain with your wife, and you would have brought guilt *and* sin upon us.

¹¹Then Abimelech charged all his people, He who touches this man or his wife shall surely be put to death.

¹²Then Isaac sowed seed in that land and received in the same year a hundred times as much as he had planted, and the Lord favored him with blessings.

¹³And the man became great and gained more and more until he became very wealthy *and* distinguished;

¹⁴He owned flocks, herds, and a great supply of servants, and the Philistines envied him.

¹⁵Now all the wells which his father's servants had dug in the days of Abraham his father, the Philistines had closed and filled with earth.

¹⁶And Abimelech said to Isaac, Go away from us, for you are much mightier than we are.

¹⁷So Isaac went away from there and pitched his tent in the Valley of Gerar, and dwelt there.

¹⁸And Isaac dug again the wells of water which had been dug in the days of Abraham his father, for the Philistines had stopped them after the death of Abraham; and he gave them the names by which his father had called them.

¹⁹Now Isaac's servants dug in the valley and found there a well of living [spring] water.

²⁰And the herdsmen of Gerar quarreled with Isaac's herdsmen, saying, The water is ours. And he named the well Esek [contention] because they quarreled with him.

²¹Then [his servants] dug another well, and they quarreled over that also; so he named it Sitnah [enmity].

²²And he moved away from there and dug another well, and for that one they did not quarrel. He named it Rehoboth [room], saying, For now the Lord has made room for us, and we shall be fruitful in the land.

²³Now he went up from there to Beersheba.

²⁴And the Lord appeared to him the same night and said, I am the God of Abraham your father. Fear not, for I am with you and will favor you with blessings and multiply your descendants for the sake of My servant Abraham.

²⁵And [Isaac] ᵃbuilt an altar there and called on the name of the Lord and pitched his tent there; and there Isaac's servants were digging a well.

²⁶Then Abimelech went to him from Gerar with Ahuzzah, one of his friends, and Phicol, his army's commander.

²⁷And Isaac said to them, Why have you come to me, seeing that you hate me and have sent me away from you?

²⁸They said, We saw that the Lord was certainly with you; so we said, Let there be now an oath between us [carrying a curse with it to befall the one who breaks it], even between you and us, and let us make a covenant with you

²⁹That you will do us no harm, inasmuch as we have not touched you and have done to you nothing but good and have sent you away in peace. You are now the blessed *or* favored of the Lord!

³⁰And he made them a [formal] dinner, and they ate and drank.

³¹And they rose up early in the morning and took oaths

---

ᵃ *20 Esek* means *dispute.*     ᵇ *21 Sitnah* means *opposition.*
ᶜ *22 Rehoboth* means *room.*

ᵃ With Isaac God came first. Before doing anything else in the new place, he built an altar and then waited there to call upon the Lord. Second came his home; he pitched his tent. Third came his business; his servants dug a well.

## New International Version

each other. Then Isaac sent them on their way, and they went away peacefully.

<sup>32</sup>That day Isaac's servants came and told him about the well they had dug. They said, "We've found water!" <sup>33</sup>He called it Shibah,<sup>a</sup> and to this day the name of the town has been Beersheba.<sup>b</sup>

### Jacob Takes Esau's Blessing

<sup>34</sup>When Esau was forty years old, he married Judith daughter of Beeri the Hittite, and also Basemath daughter of Elon the Hittite. <sup>35</sup>They were a source of grief to Isaac and Rebekah.

**27** When Isaac was old and his eyes were so weak that he could no longer see, he called for Esau his older son and said to him, "My son."

"Here I am," he answered.

<sup>2</sup>Isaac said, "I am now an old man and don't know the day of my death. <sup>3</sup>Now then, get your equipment—your quiver and bow—and go out to the open country to hunt some wild game for me. <sup>4</sup>Prepare me the kind of tasty food I like and bring it to me to eat, so that I may give you my blessing before I die."

<sup>5</sup>Now Rebekah was listening as Isaac spoke to his son Esau. When Esau left for the open country to hunt game and bring it back, <sup>6</sup>Rebekah said to her son Jacob, "Look, I overheard your father say to your brother Esau, <sup>7</sup>'Bring me some game and prepare me some tasty food to eat, so that I may give you my blessing in the presence of the LORD before I die.' <sup>8</sup>Now, my son, listen carefully and do what I tell you: <sup>9</sup>Go out to the flock and bring me two choice young goats, so I can prepare some tasty food for your father, just the way he likes it. <sup>10</sup>Then take it to your father to eat, so that he may give you his blessing before he dies."

<sup>11</sup>Jacob said to Rebekah his mother, "But my brother Esau is a hairy man while I have smooth skin. <sup>12</sup>What if my father touches me? I would appear to be tricking him and would bring down a curse on myself rather than a blessing."

<sup>13</sup>His mother said to him, "My son, let the curse fall on me. Just do what I say; go and get them for me."

<sup>14</sup>So he went and got them and brought them to his mother, and she prepared some tasty food, just the way his father liked it. <sup>15</sup>Then Rebekah took the best clothes of Esau her older son, which she had in the house, and put them on her younger son Jacob. <sup>16</sup>She also covered his hands and the smooth part of his neck with the goatskins. <sup>17</sup>Then she handed to her son Jacob the tasty food and the bread she had made.

<sup>18</sup>He went to his father and said, "My father."

"Yes, my son," he answered. "Who is it?"

<sup>19</sup>Jacob said to his father, "I am Esau your firstborn. I have done as you told me. Please sit up and eat some of my game, so that you may give me your blessing."

<sup>20</sup>Isaac asked his son, "How did you find it so quickly, my son?"

"The LORD your God gave me success," he replied.

<sup>21</sup>Then Isaac said to Jacob, "Come near so I can touch you, my son, to know whether you really are my son Esau or not."

<sup>22</sup>Jacob went close to his father Isaac, who touched him and said, "The voice is the voice of Jacob, but the hands

## Amplified Bible

[with a curse] with one another; and Isaac sent them on their way and they departed from him in peace.

<sup>32</sup>That same day Isaac's servants came and told him about the well they had dug, saying, We have found water!

<sup>33</sup>And he named [the well] Shibah; therefore the name of the city is Beersheba [well of the oath] to this day. [Gen. 21:31.]

<sup>34</sup>Now Esau was 40 years old when he took as wife Judith the daughter of Beeri the Hittite, and Basemath the daughter of Elon the Hittite.

<sup>35</sup>And they made life bitter *and* a grief of mind *and* spirit for Isaac and Rebekah [their parents-in-law].

**27** When Isaac was old and his eyes were dim so that he could not see, he called Esau his elder son, and said to him, My son! And he answered him, Here I am.

<sup>2</sup>He said, See here now; I am old, I do not know when I may die.

<sup>3</sup>So now, I pray you, take your weapons, your [arrows in a] quiver and your bow, and go out into the open country and hunt game for me,

<sup>4</sup>And prepare me appetizing meat, such as I love, and bring it to me, that I may eat of it, [preparatory] to giving you my blessing [as my firstborn] before I die.

<sup>5</sup>But Rebekah heard what Isaac said to Esau his son; and when Esau had gone to the open country to hunt for game that he might bring it,

<sup>6</sup>Rebekah said to Jacob her younger son, See here, I heard your father say to Esau your brother,

<sup>7</sup>Bring me game and make me appetizing meat, so that I may eat and declare my blessing upon you before the Lord before my death.

<sup>8</sup>So now, my son, do exactly as I command you.

<sup>9</sup>Go now to the flock, and from it bring me two good *and* suitable kids; and I will make them into appetizing meat for your father, such as he loves.

<sup>10</sup>And you shall bring it to your father, that he may eat and declare his blessing upon you before his death.

<sup>11</sup>But Jacob said to Rebekah his mother, Listen, Esau my brother is a hairy man and I am a smooth man.

<sup>12</sup>Suppose my father feels me; I will seem to him to be a cheat *and* an imposter, and I will bring [his] curse on me and not [his] blessing.

<sup>13</sup>But his mother said to him, On me be your curse, my son; only obey my word and go, fetch them to me.

<sup>14</sup>So [Jacob] went, got [the kids], and brought them to his mother; and his mother prepared appetizing meat with a delightful odor, such as his father loved.

<sup>15</sup>Then Rebekah took her elder son Esau's best clothes which were with her in the house, and put them on Jacob her younger son.

<sup>16</sup>And she put the skins of the kids on his hands and on the smooth part of his neck.

<sup>17</sup>And she gave the savory meat and the bread which she had prepared into the hand of her son Jacob.

<sup>18</sup>So he went to his father and said, My father. And he said, Here am I; who are you, my son?

<sup>19</sup>And Jacob said to his father, I am Esau your firstborn; I have done what you told me to do. Now sit up and eat of my game, so that you may proceed to bless me.

<sup>20</sup>And Isaac said to his son, How is it that you have found the game so quickly, my son? And he said, Because the Lord your God caused it to come to me.

<sup>21</sup>But Isaac said to Jacob, Come close to me, I beg of you, that I may feel you, my son, *and* know whether you really are my son Esau or not.

<sup>22</sup>So Jacob went near to Isaac, and his father felt him and said, The voice is Jacob's voice, but the hands are the hands of Esau.

---

<sup>a</sup> 33 *Shibah* can mean *oath* or *seven.*   <sup>b</sup> 33 *Beersheba* can mean *well of the oath* and *well of seven.*

## New International Version

are the hands of Esau." 23He did not recognize him, for his hands were hairy like those of his brother Esau; so he proceeded to bless him. 24"Are you really my son Esau?" he asked.

"I am," he replied.

25Then he said, "My son, bring me some of your game to eat, so that I may give you my blessing."

Jacob brought it to him and he ate; and he brought some wine and he drank. 26Then his father Isaac said to him, "Come here, my son, and kiss me."

27So he went to him and kissed him. When Isaac caught the smell of his clothes, he blessed him and said,

"Ah, the smell of my son
is like the smell of a field
that the LORD has blessed.
28 May God give you heaven's dew
and earth's richness—
an abundance of grain and new wine.
29 May nations serve you
and peoples bow down to you.
Be lord over your brothers,
and may the sons of your mother bow down to you.
May those who curse you be cursed
and those who bless you be blessed."

30After Isaac finished blessing him, and Jacob had scarcely left his father's presence, his brother Esau came in from hunting. 31He too prepared some tasty food and brought it to his father. Then he said to him, "My father, please sit up and eat some of my game, so that you may give me your blessing."

32His father Isaac asked him, "Who are you?"

"I am your son," he answered, "your firstborn, Esau."

33Isaac trembled violently and said, "Who was it, then, that hunted game and brought it to me? I ate it just before you came and I blessed him—and indeed he will be blessed!"

34When Esau heard his father's words, he burst out with a loud and bitter cry and said to his father, "Bless me—me too, my father!"

35But he said, "Your brother came deceitfully and took your blessing."

36Esau said, "Isn't he rightly named Jacob*a*? This is the second time he has taken advantage of me: He took my birthright, and now he's taken my blessing!" Then he asked, "Haven't you reserved any blessing for me?"

37Isaac answered Esau, "I have made him lord over you and have made all his relatives his servants, and I have sustained him with grain and new wine. So what can I possibly do for you, my son?"

38Esau said to his father, "Do you have only one blessing, my father? Bless me too, my father!" Then Esau wept aloud.

39His father Isaac answered him,

"Your dwelling will be
away from the earth's richness,
away from the dew of heaven above.
40 You will live by the sword
and you will serve your brother.
But when you grow restless,
you will throw his yoke
from off your neck."

41Esau held a grudge against Jacob because of the blessing his father had given him. He said to himself, "The days of mourning for my father are near; then I will kill my brother Jacob."

42When Rebekah was told what her older son Esau had said, she sent for her younger son Jacob and said to him, "Your brother Esau is planning to avenge himself by kill-

*a 36 Jacob means he grasps the heel, a Hebrew idiom for he takes advantage of or he deceives.*

## Amplified Bible

23He could not identify him, because his hands were hairy like his brother Esau's hands; so he blessed him. 24But he said, Are you really my son Esau? He answered, I am.

25Then [Isaac] said, Bring it to me and I will eat of my son's game, that I may bless you. He brought it to him and he ate; and he brought him wine and he drank.

26Then his father Isaac said, Come near and kiss me, my son.

27So he came near and kissed him; and [Isaac] smelled his clothing and blessed him and said, The scent of my son is as the odor of a field which the Lord has blessed.

28And may God give you of the dew of the heavens and of the fatness of the earth and abundance of grain and [new] wine;

29Let peoples serve you and nations bow down to you; be master over your brothers, and let your mother's sons bow down to you. Let everyone be cursed who curses you and favored with blessings who blesses you.

30As soon as Isaac had finished blessing Jacob and Jacob was scarcely gone out from the presence of Isaac his father, Esau his brother came in from his hunting.

31Esau had also prepared savory food and brought it to his father and said to him, Let my father arise and eat of his son's game, that you may bless me.

32And Isaac his father said to him, Who are you? And he replied, I am your son, your firstborn, Esau.

33Then Isaac trembled *and* shook violently, and he said, Who? Where is he who has hunted game and brought it to me, and I ate of it all before you came and I have blessed him? Yes, and he shall be blessed.

34When Esau heard the words of his father, he cried out with a great and bitter cry and said to his father, Bless me, even me also, O my father! [Heb. 12:16, 17.]

35[Isaac] said, Your brother came with crafty cunning *and* treacherous deceit and has taken your blessing.

36[Esau] replied, Is he not rightly named Jacob [the supplanter]? For he has supplanted me these two times: he took away my birthright, and now he has taken away my blessing! Have you not still a blessing reserved for me?

37And Isaac answered Esau, Behold, I have made [Jacob] your lord and master; I have given all his brethren to him for servants, and with corn and [new] wine have I sustained him. What then can I do for you, my son?

38Esau said to his father, Have you only one blessing, my father? Bless me, even me also, O my father! And Esau lifted up [could not control] his voice and wept aloud.

39Then Isaac his father answered, Your [blessing and] dwelling shall all come from the fruitfulness of the earth and from the dew of the heavens above;

40By your sword you shall live and serve your brother. But [the time shall come] when you will grow restive *and* break loose, and you shall tear his yoke from off your neck.

41And Esau hated Jacob because of the blessing with which his father blessed him; and Esau said in his heart, The days of mourning for my father are very near. When [he is gone] I will *a*kill my brother Jacob.

42These words of Esau her elder son were repeated to Rebekah. She sent for Jacob her younger son and said to him, See here, your brother Esau comforts himself concerning you [by intending] to kill you.

*a Here began a feud that was to cost countless lives throughout succeeding centuries. Esau's descendants, the Amalekites, were the first enemies to obstruct the flight of Jacob's descendants from Egypt (Exod. 17:8); and the Edomites even refused to let their uncle Jacob's children pass through their land (Num. 20:17-20). Doeg, an Edomite, all but caused the death of Christ's chosen ancestor David (I Sam. 21, 22). Bloody battles were fought between the two nations in the centuries that followed. It was Herod, of Esau's race (Josephus, Antiquities of the Jews 14:1, Section 3), who had the male infants of Bethlehem slain in an effort to destroy the Christ Child (Matt. 2:16). Satan needs no better medium for his evil plans than a family feud, a "mere quarrel" between two brothers.*

## New International Version

ing you. 43Now then, my son, do what I say: Flee at once to my brother Laban in Harran. 44Stay with him for a while until your brother's fury subsides. 45When your brother is no longer angry with you and forgets what you did to him, I'll send word for you to come back from there. Why should I lose both of you in one day?"

46Then Rebekah said to Isaac, "I'm disgusted with living because of these Hittite women. If Jacob takes a wife from among the women of this land, from Hittite women like these, my life will not be worth living."

**28** So Isaac called for Jacob and blessed him. Then he commanded him: "Do not marry a Canaanite woman. 2Go at once to Paddan Aram,*a* to the house of your mother's father Bethuel. Take a wife for yourself there, from among the daughters of Laban, your mother's brother. 3May God Almighty*b* bless you and make you fruitful and increase your numbers until you become a community of peoples. 4May he give you and your descendants the blessing given to Abraham, so that you may take possession of the land where you now reside as a foreigner, the land God gave to Abraham." 5Then Isaac sent Jacob on his way, and he went to Paddan Aram, to Laban son of Bethuel the Aramean, the brother of Rebekah, who was the mother of Jacob and Esau.

6Now Esau learned that Isaac had blessed Jacob and had sent him to Paddan Aram to take a wife from there, and that when he blessed him he commanded him, "Do not marry a Canaanite woman," 7and that Jacob had obeyed his father and mother and had gone to Paddan Aram. 8Esau then realized how displeasing the Canaanite women were to his father Isaac; 9so he went to Ishmael and married Mahalath, the sister of Nebaioth and daughter of Ishmael son of Abraham, in addition to the wives he already had.

### Jacob's Dream at Bethel

10Jacob left Beersheba and set out for Harran. 11When he reached a certain place, he stopped for the night because the sun had set. Taking one of the stones there, he put it under his head and lay down to sleep. 12He had a dream in which he saw a stairway resting on the earth, with its top reaching to heaven, and the angels of God were ascending and descending on it. 13There above it*c* stood the LORD, and he said: "I am the LORD, the God of your father Abraham and the God of Isaac. I will give you and your descendants the land on which you are lying. 14Your descendants will be like the dust of the earth, and you will spread out to the west and to the east, to the north and to the south. All peoples on earth will be blessed through you and your offspring.*d* 15I am with you and will watch over you wherever you go, and I will bring you back to this land. I will not leave you until I have done what I have promised you."

16When Jacob awoke from his sleep, he thought, "Surely the LORD is in this place, and I was not aware of it." 17He was afraid and said, "How awesome is this place! This is none other than the house of God; this is the gate of heaven."

*a 2* That is, Northwest Mesopotamia; also in verses 5, 6 and 7
*b 3* Hebrew *El-Shaddai*   *c 13* Or *There beside him*   *d 14* Or *will use your name and the name of your offspring in blessings* (see 48:20)

## Amplified Bible

43So now, my son, do what I tell you; arise, flee to my brother Laban in Haran;

44Linger and dwell with him for a while until your brother's fury is spent.

45When your brother's anger is diverted from you, he will forget [the wrong] that you have done him. Then *a*I will send and bring you back from there. Why should I be deprived of both of you in one day?

46Then Rebekah said to Isaac, I am weary of my life because of the daughters of Heth [these wives of Esau]! If Jacob takes a wife of the daughters of Heth such as these Hittite girls around here, what good will my life be to me?

**28** So Isaac called Jacob and blessed him and commanded him, You shall not marry one of the women of Canaan.

2Arise, go to Padan-aram, to the house of Bethuel your mother's father, and take from there as a wife one of the daughters of Laban your mother's brother.

3May God Almighty bless you and make you fruitful and multiply you until you become a group of peoples.

4May He give the blessing [He gave to] Abraham to you and your descendants with you, that you may inherit the land He gave to Abraham, in which you are a sojourner.

5Thus Isaac sent Jacob away. He went to Padan-aram, to Laban son of Bethuel the Aramean, the brother of Rebekah, Jacob and Esau's mother.

6Now Esau saw that Isaac had blessed Jacob and sent him to Padan-aram to take him a wife from there, and that as he blessed him, he gave him a charge, saying, You shall not take a wife of the daughters of Canaan;

7And that Jacob obeyed his father and his mother and had gone to Padan-aram.

8Also Esau saw that the daughters of Canaan did not please Isaac his father.

9So Esau went to Ishmael and took to be his wife, [in addition] to the wives he [already] had, Mahalath daughter of Ishmael, Abraham's son, the sister of Nebaioth.

10And Jacob left Beersheba and went toward Haran.

11And he came to a certain place and stayed there overnight, because the sun was set. Taking one of the stones of the place, he put it under his head and lay down there to sleep.

12And he dreamed that there was a ladder set up on the earth, and the top of it reached to heaven; and the angels of God were ascending and descending on it!

13And behold, the Lord stood over *and* beside him and said, I am the Lord, the God of Abraham your father [forefather] and the God of Isaac; I will give to you and to your descendants the land on which you are lying.

14And your offspring shall be as [countless as] the dust or sand of the ground, and you shall spread abroad to the west and the east and the north and the south; and by you and your Offspring shall all the families of the earth be blessed *and* bless themselves. [Gen. 12:2-3; 13:16; 22:18; 26:4; Acts 3:25-26; Gal. 3:8, 16.]

15And behold, I am with you and will keep (watch over you with care, take notice of) you wherever you may go, and I will bring you back to this land; for I will not leave you until I have done all of which I have told you.

16And Jacob awoke from his sleep and he said, Surely the Lord is in this place and I did not know it.

17He was afraid and said, How to be feared *and* reverenced is this place! This is none other than the house of God, and *b*this is the gateway to heaven!

*a* But Rebekah never saw her son Jacob again. He was well over 40 and probably 57 years old when he fled from Esau to Haran, and he stayed there at least 20 years.   *b* "There is an open way between heaven and earth for each of us. The movement of the tide and the circulation of the blood are not more regular than the intercommunication between heaven and earth. Jacob may have thought that God was local; now he found Him to be omnipresent. Every lonely spot was His house, filled with angels" (F. B. Meyer, *Through the Bible Day by Day*). When Jacob found God in his own heart, he found Him everywhere.

## New International Version

[18]Early the next morning Jacob took the stone he had placed under his head and set it up as a pillar and poured oil on top of it. [19]He called that place Bethel,[a] though the city used to be called Luz.

[20]Then Jacob made a vow, saying, "If God will be with me and will watch over me on this journey I am taking and will give me food to eat and clothes to wear [21]so that I return safely to my father's household, then the LORD[b] will be my God [22]and[c] this stone that I have set up as a pillar will be God's house, and of all that you give me I will give you a tenth."

### Jacob Arrives in Paddan Aram

**29** Then Jacob continued on his journey and came to the land of the eastern peoples. [2]There he saw a well in the open country, with three flocks of sheep lying near it because the flocks were watered from that well. The stone over the mouth of the well was large. [3]When all the flocks were gathered there, the shepherds would roll the stone away from the well's mouth and water the sheep. Then they would return the stone to its place over the mouth of the well.

[4]Jacob asked the shepherds, "My brothers, where are you from?"

"We're from Harran," they replied.

[5]He said to them, "Do you know Laban, Nahor's grandson?"

"Yes, we know him," they answered.

[6]Then Jacob asked them, "Is he well?"

"Yes, he is," they said, "and here comes his daughter Rachel with the sheep."

[7]"Look," he said, "the sun is still high; it is not time for the flocks to be gathered. Water the sheep and take them back to pasture."

[8]"We can't," they replied, "until all the flocks are gathered and the stone has been rolled away from the mouth of the well. Then we will water the sheep."

[9]While he was still talking with them, Rachel came with her father's sheep, for she was a shepherd. [10]When Jacob saw Rachel daughter of his uncle Laban, and Laban's sheep, he went over and rolled the stone away from the mouth of the well and watered his uncle's sheep. [11]Then Jacob kissed Rachel and began to weep aloud. [12]He had told Rachel that he was a relative of her father and a son of Rebekah. So she ran and told her father.

[13]As soon as Laban heard the news about Jacob, his sister's son, he hurried to meet him. He embraced him and kissed him and brought him to his home, and there Jacob told him all these things. [14]Then Laban said to him, "You are my own flesh and blood."

### Jacob Marries Leah and Rachel

After Jacob had stayed with him for a whole month, [15]Laban said to him, "Just because you are a relative of mine, should you work for me for nothing? Tell me what your wages should be."

[16]Now Laban had two daughters; the name of the older was Leah, and the name of the younger was Rachel. [17]Leah had weak[d] eyes, but Rachel had a lovely figure and was beautiful. [18]Jacob was in love with Rachel and said, "I'll work for you seven years in return for your younger daughter Rachel."

[19]Laban said, "It's better that I give her to you than to some other man. Stay here with me." [20]So Jacob served seven years to get Rachel, but they seemed like only a few days to him because of his love for her.

## Amplified Bible

[18]And Jacob rose early in the morning and took the stone he had put under his head, and he set it up for a pillar (a monument to the vision in his dream), and he poured oil on its top [in dedication].

[19]And he named that place Bethel [the house of God]; but the name of that city was Luz at first.

[20]Then Jacob made a vow, saying, If God will be with me and will keep me in this way that I go and will give me food to eat and clothing to wear,

[21]So that I may come again to my father's house in peace, then the Lord shall be my God;

[22]And this stone which I have set up as a pillar (monument) shall be God's house [a sacred place to me], and of all [the increase of possessions] that You give me I will give the tenth to You.

**29** Then Jacob went [briskly and cheerfully] on his way [400 miles] and came to the land of the people of the East.

[2]As he looked, he saw a well in the field; and behold, there were three flocks of sheep lying by it, for out of that well the flocks were watered. The stone on the well's mouth was a big one,

[3]And when all the flocks were gathered there, [the shepherds] would roll the stone from the well's mouth, water the sheep, and replace the stone on the well's mouth.

[4]And Jacob said to them, My brothers, where are you from? And they said, We are from Haran.

[5][Jacob] said to them, Do you know Laban the grandson of Nahor? And they said, We know him.

[6]He said to them, Is it well with him? And they said, He is doing well; and behold, here comes his daughter Rachel with [his] sheep!

[7]He said, The sun is still high; it is a long time yet before the flocks need be gathered [in their folds]. [Why not] water the sheep and return them to their pasture?

[8]But they said, We cannot until all the flocks are gathered together; then [the shepherds] roll the stone from the well's mouth and we water the sheep.

[9]While he was still talking with them, Rachel came with her father's sheep, for she shepherded them.

[10]When Jacob saw Rachel daughter of Laban, his mother's brother, and the sheep of Laban his uncle, Jacob went near and rolled the stone from the well's mouth and watered the flock of his uncle Laban.

[11]Then Jacob kissed Rachel and he wept aloud.

[12]Jacob told Rachel he was her father's relative, Rebekah's son; and she ran and told her father.

[13]When Laban heard of the arrival of Jacob his sister's son, he ran to meet him, and embraced and kissed him and brought him to his house. And [Jacob] told Laban all these things.

[14]Then Laban said to him, Surely you are my bone and my flesh. And [Jacob] stayed with him a month.

[15]Then Laban said to Jacob, Just because you are my relative, should you work for me for nothing? Tell me, what shall your wages be?

[16]Now Laban had two daughters; the name of the elder was Leah and the name of the younger was Rachel.

[17]Leah's eyes were weak *and* dull looking, but Rachel was beautiful and attractive.

[18]And Jacob loved Rachel; so he said, I will work for you for seven years for Rachel your younger daughter.

[19]And Laban said, It is better that I give her to you than to another man. Stay *and* live with me.

[20]And Jacob served seven years for Rachel; and they seemed to him but a few days because of the love he had for her.

---

[a] 19 *Bethel* means *house of God.*    [b] 20,21 Or *Since God . . . father's household, the* LORD    [c] 21,22 Or *household, and the* LORD *will be my God,* [22]*then*    [d] 17 Or *delicate*

## New International Version

²¹Then Jacob said to Laban, "Give me my wife. My time is completed, and I want to make love to her."

²²So Laban brought together all the people of the place and gave a feast. ²³But when evening came, he took his daughter Leah and brought her to Jacob, and Jacob made love to her. ²⁴And Laban gave his servant Zilpah to his daughter as her attendant.

²⁵When morning came, there was Leah! So Jacob said to Laban, "What is this you have done to me? I served you for Rachel, didn't I? Why have you deceived me?"

²⁶Laban replied, "It is not our custom here to give the younger daughter in marriage before the older one. ²⁷Finish this daughter's bridal week; then we will give you the younger one also, in return for another seven years of work."

²⁸And Jacob did so. He finished the week with Leah, and then Laban gave him his daughter Rachel to be his wife. ²⁹Laban gave his servant Bilhah to his daughter Rachel as her attendant. ³⁰Jacob made love to Rachel also, and his love for Rachel was greater than his love for Leah. And he worked for Laban another seven years.

### Jacob's Children

³¹When the Lᴏʀᴅ saw that Leah was not loved, he enabled her to conceive, but Rachel remained childless. ³²Leah became pregnant and gave birth to a son. She named him Reuben,ᵃ for she said, "It is because the Lᴏʀᴅ has seen my misery. Surely my husband will love me now."

³³She conceived again, and when she gave birth to a son she said, "Because the Lᴏʀᴅ heard that I am not loved, he gave me this one too." So she named him Simeon.ᵇ

³⁴Again she conceived, and when she gave birth to a son she said, "Now at last my husband will become attached to me, because I have borne him three sons." So he was named Levi.ᶜ

³⁵She conceived again, and when she gave birth to a son she said, "This time I will praise the Lᴏʀᴅ." So she named him Judah.ᵈ Then she stopped having children.

**30** When Rachel saw that she was not bearing Jacob any children, she became jealous of her sister. So she said to Jacob, "Give me children, or I'll die!"

²Jacob became angry with her and said, "Am I in the place of God, who has kept you from having children?"

³Then she said, "Here is Bilhah, my servant. Sleep with her so that she can bear children for me and I too can build a family through her."

⁴So she gave him her servant Bilhah as a wife. Jacob slept with her, ⁵and she became pregnant and bore him a son. ⁶Then Rachel said, "God has vindicated me; he has listened to my plea and given me a son." Because of this she named him Dan.ᵉ

⁷Rachel's servant Bilhah conceived again and bore Jacob a second son. ⁸Then Rachel said, "I have had a great struggle with my sister, and I have won." So she named him Naphtali.ᶠ

⁹When Leah saw that she had stopped having children, she took her servant Zilpah and gave her to Jacob as a wife. ¹⁰Leah's servant Zilpah bore Jacob a son. ¹¹Then Leah said, "What good fortune!"ᵍ So she named him Gad.ʰ

¹²Leah's servant Zilpah bore Jacob a second son. ¹³Then

---

ᵃ 32 Reuben sounds like the Hebrew for he has seen my misery; the name means see, a son.    ᵇ 33 Simeon probably means one who hears.    ᶜ 34 Levi sounds like and may be derived from the Hebrew for attached.    ᵈ 35 Judah sounds like and may be derived from the Hebrew for praise.    ᵉ 6 Dan here means he has vindicated.    ᶠ 8 Naphtali means my struggle.    ᵍ 11 Or "A troop is coming!"    ʰ 11 Gad can mean good fortune or a troop.

## Amplified Bible

²¹Finally, Jacob said to Laban, Give me my wife, for my time is completed, so that I may take her to me.

²²And Laban gathered together all the men of the place and made a feast [with drinking].

²³But when night came, he took Leah his daughter and brought her to [Jacob], who had intercourse with her.

²⁴And Laban gave Zilpah his maid to his daughter Leah to be her maid.

²⁵But in the morning [Jacob saw his wife, and] behold, it was Leah! And he said to Laban, What is this you have done to me? Did I not work for you [all those seven years] for Rachel? Why then have you deceived and cheated and thrown me down [like this]?

²⁶And Laban said, It is not permitted in our country to give the younger [in marriage] before the elder.

²⁷Finish the [wedding feast] week [for Leah]; then we will give you [Rachel] also, and you shall work for me yet seven more years in return.

²⁸So Jacob complied and fulfilled [Leah's] week; then [Laban] gave him Rachel his daughter as his wife.

²⁹ (And Laban gave Bilhah his maid to Rachel his daughter to be her maid.)

³⁰And Jacob lived with Rachel also as his wife, and he loved Rachel more than Leah and served [Laban] another seven years [for her].

³¹And when the Lord saw that Leah was despised, He made her able to bear children, but Rachel was barren.

³²And Leah became pregnant and bore a son and named him Reuben [See, a son!]; for she said, Because the Lord has seen my humiliation and affliction; now my husband will love me.

³³ [Leah] became pregnant again and bore a son and said, Because the Lord heard that I am despised, He has given me this son also; and she named him Simeon [God hears].

³⁴And she became pregnant again and bore a son and said, Now this time will my husband be a companion to me, for I have borne him three sons. Therefore he was named Levi [companion].

³⁵Again she conceived and bore a son, and she said, Now will I praise the Lord! So she called his name Judah [praise]; then [for a time] she ceased bearing.

**30** When Rachel saw that she bore Jacob no children, she envied her sister, and said to Jacob, Give me children, or else I will die!

²And Jacob became very angry with Rachel and he said, Am I in God's stead, Who has denied you children?

³And she said, See here, take my maid Bilhah and have intercourse with her; and [when the baby comes] she shall deliver it upon my knees, that I by her may also have children.

⁴And she gave him Bilhah her maid as a [secondary] wife, and Jacob had intercourse with her.

⁵And Bilhah became pregnant and bore Jacob a son.

⁶And Rachel said, God has judged and vindicated me, and has heard my plea and has given me a son; so she named him Dan [judged].

⁷And Bilhah, Rachel's maid, conceived again and bore Jacob a second son.

⁸And Rachel said, With mighty wrestlings [in prayer to God] I have struggled with my sister and have prevailed; so she named him [this second son Bilhah bore] Naphtali [struggled].

⁹When Leah saw that she had ceased to bear, she gave Zilpah her maid to Jacob as a [secondary] wife.

¹⁰And Zilpah, Leah's maid, bore Jacob a son.

¹¹Then Leah said, Victory and good fortune have come; and she named him Gad [fortune].

¹²Zilpah, Leah's maid, bore Jacob [her] second son.

## New International Version

Leah said, "How happy I am! The women will call me happy." So she named him Asher.[a]

[14]During wheat harvest, Reuben went out into the fields and found some mandrake plants, which he brought to his mother Leah. Rachel said to Leah, "Please give me some of your son's mandrakes."

[15]But she said to her, "Wasn't it enough that you took away my husband? Will you take my son's mandrakes too?"

"Very well," Rachel said, "he can sleep with you tonight in return for your son's mandrakes."

[16]So when Jacob came in from the fields that evening, Leah went out to meet him. "You must sleep with me," she said. "I have hired you with my son's mandrakes." So she slept with her that night.

[17]God listened to Leah, and she became pregnant and bore Jacob a fifth son. [18]Then Leah said, "God has rewarded me for giving my servant to my husband." So she named him Issachar.[b]

[19]Leah conceived again and bore Jacob a sixth son. [20]Then Leah said, "God has presented me with a precious gift. This time my husband will treat me with honor, because I have borne him six sons." So she named him Zebulun.[c]

[21]Some time later she gave birth to a daughter and named her Dinah.

[22]Then God remembered Rachel; he listened to her and enabled her to conceive. [23]She became pregnant and gave birth to a son and said, "God has taken away my disgrace." [24]She named him Joseph,[d] and said, "May the LORD add to me another son."

### Jacob's Flocks Increase

[25]After Rachel gave birth to Joseph, Jacob said to Laban, "Send me on my way so I can go back to my own homeland. [26]Give me my wives and children, for whom I have served you, and I will be on my way. You know how much work I've done for you."

[27]But Laban said to him, "If I have found favor in your eyes, please stay. I have learned by divination that the LORD has blessed me because of you." [28]He added, "Name your wages, and I will pay them."

[29]Jacob said to him, "You know how I have worked for you and how your livestock has fared under my care. [30]The little you had before I came has increased greatly, and the LORD has blessed you wherever I have been. But now, when may I do something for my own household?"

[31]"What shall I give you?" he asked.

"Don't give me anything," Jacob replied. "But if you will do this one thing for me, I will go on tending your flocks and watching over them: [32]Let me go through all your flocks today and remove from them every speckled or spotted sheep, every dark-colored lamb and every spotted or speckled goat. They will be my wages. [33]And my honesty will testify for me in the future, whenever you check on the wages you have paid me. Any goat in my possession that is not speckled or spotted, or any lamb that is not dark-colored, will be considered stolen."

[34]"Agreed," said Laban. "Let it be as you have said." [35]That same day he removed all the male goats that were streaked or spotted, and all the speckled or spotted female goats (all that had white on them) and all the dark-colored lambs, and he placed them in the care of his sons. [36]Then

## Amplified Bible

[13]And Leah said, I am happy, for women will call me blessed (happy, fortunate, to be envied); and she named him Asher [happy].

[14]Now Reuben went at the time of wheat harvest and found some mandrakes (love apples) in the field and brought them to his mother Leah. Then Rachel said to Leah, Give me, I pray you, some of your son's mandrakes.

[15]But [Leah] answered, Is it not enough that you have taken my husband without your taking away my son's [a]mandrakes also? And Rachel said, Jacob shall sleep with you tonight [in exchange] for your son's mandrakes.

[16]And Jacob came out of the field in the evening, and Leah went out to meet him and said, You must sleep with me [tonight], for I have certainly paid your hire with my son's mandrakes. So he slept with her that night.

[17]And God heeded Leah's [prayer], and she conceived and bore Jacob [her] fifth son.

[18]Leah said, God has given me my hire, because I have given my maid to my husband; and she called his name Issachar [hired].

[19]And Leah became pregnant again and bore Jacob [her] sixth son.

[20]Then Leah said, God has endowed me with a good marriage gift [for my husband]; now will he dwell with me [and regard me as his wife in reality], because I have borne him six sons; and she named him Zebulun [dwelling].

[21]Afterwards she bore a daughter and called her Dinah.

[22]Then God remembered Rachel and answered her pleading and made it possible for her to have children.

[23]And [now for the first time] she became pregnant and bore a son; and she said, God has taken away my reproach, disgrace, *and* humiliation.

[24]And she called his name Joseph [may he add] and said, May the Lord add to me another son.

[25]When Rachel had borne Joseph, Jacob said to Laban, Send me away, that I may go to my own place and country.

[26]Give me my wives and my children, for whom I have served you, and let me go; for you know the work which I have done for you.

[27]And Laban said to him, If I have found favor in your sight, I pray you [do not go]; for I have learned by experience *and* from the omens in divination that the Lord has favored me with blessings on your account.

[28]He said, State your salary and I will give it.

[29]Jacob answered him, You know how I have served you, and how your possessions, your cattle *and* sheep *and* goats, have fared with me.

[30]For you had little before I came, and it has increased *and* multiplied abundantly; and the Lord has favored you with blessings wherever I turned. But now, when shall I provide for my own house also?

[31][Laban] said, What shall I give you? And Jacob said, You shall not give me anything, if you will do this one thing for me [of which I am about to tell you], and I will again feed *and* take care of your flock.

[32]Let me pass through all your flock today, removing from it every speckled and spotted animal and every black one among the sheep, and the spotted and speckled among the goats; and such shall be my wages.

[33]So later when the matter of my wages is brought before you, my fair dealing will be evident *and* answer for me. Every one that is not speckled and spotted among the goats and black among the sheep, if found with me, shall be counted as stolen.

[34]And Laban said, Good; let it be done as you say.

[35]But that same day [Laban] removed the he-goats that were streaked and spotted and all the she-goats that were speckled and spotted, every one that had white on it, and every black lamb, and put them in charge of his sons.

## New International Version

he put a three-day journey between himself and Jacob, while Jacob continued to tend the rest of Laban's flocks.
³⁷Jacob, however, took fresh-cut branches from poplar, almond and plane trees and made white stripes on them by peeling the bark and exposing the inner wood of the branches. ³⁸Then he placed the peeled branches in all the watering troughs, so that they would be directly in front of the flocks when they came to drink. When the flocks were in heat and came to drink, ³⁹they mated in front of the branches. And they bore young that were streaked or speckled or spotted. ⁴⁰Jacob set apart the young of the flock by themselves, but made the rest face the streaked and dark-colored animals that belonged to Laban. Thus he made separate flocks for himself and did not put them with Laban's animals. ⁴¹Whenever the stronger females were in heat, Jacob would place the branches in the troughs in front of the animals so they would mate near the branches, ⁴²but if the animals were weak, he would not place them there. So the weak animals went to Laban and the strong ones to Jacob. ⁴³In this way the man grew exceedingly prosperous and came to own large flocks, and female and male servants, and camels and donkeys.

### Jacob Flees From Laban

**31** Jacob heard that Laban's sons were saying, "Jacob has taken everything our father owned and has gained all this wealth from what belonged to our father." ²And Jacob noticed that Laban's attitude toward him was not what it had been.

³Then the LORD said to Jacob, "Go back to the land of your fathers and to your relatives, and I will be with you."

⁴So Jacob sent word to Rachel and Leah to come out to the fields where his flocks were. ⁵He said to them, "I see that your father's attitude toward me is not what it was before, but the God of my father has been with me. ⁶You know that I've worked for your father with all my strength, ⁷yet your father has cheated me by changing my wages ten times. However, God has not allowed him to harm me. ⁸If he said, 'The speckled ones will be your wages,' then all the flocks gave birth to speckled young; and if he said, 'The streaked ones will be your wages,' then all the flocks bore streaked young. ⁹So God has taken away your father's livestock and has given them to me.

¹⁰"In breeding season I once had a dream in which I looked up and saw that the male goats mating with the flock were streaked, speckled or spotted. ¹¹The angel of God said to me in the dream, 'Jacob.' I answered, 'Here I am.' ¹²And he said, 'Look up and see that all the male goats mating with the flock are streaked, speckled or spotted, for I have seen all that Laban has been doing to you. ¹³I am the God of Bethel, where you anointed a pillar and where you made a vow to me. Now leave this land at once and go back to your native land.'"

¹⁴Then Rachel and Leah replied, "Do we still have any share in the inheritance of our father's estate? ¹⁵Does he not regard us as foreigners? Not only has he sold us, but he has used up what was paid for us. ¹⁶Surely all the wealth

## Amplified Bible

³⁶And he set [a distance of] three days' journey between himself and Jacob; and Jacob was then left in care of the rest of Laban's flock.

³⁷But Jacob took fresh rods of poplar and almond and plane trees and peeled white streaks in them, exposing the white in the rods.

³⁸Then he set the rods which he had peeled in front of the flocks in the watering troughs where the flocks came to drink. And since they bred *and* conceived when they came to drink,

³⁹The flocks bred *and* conceived in sight of the rods and brought forth lambs *and* kids streaked, speckled, and spotted.

⁴⁰Jacob separated the lambs, and [as he had done with the peeled rods] he also set the faces of the flocks toward the streaked and all the dark in the [new] flock of Laban; and he put his own droves by themselves and did not let them breed with Laban's flock.

⁴¹And whenever the stronger animals were breeding, Jacob laid the rods in the watering troughs before the eyes of the flock, that they might breed *and* conceive among the rods.

⁴²But when the sheep *and* goats were feeble, he omitted putting the rods there; so the feebler animals were Laban's and the stronger Jacob's.

⁴³Thus the man increased *and* became exceedingly rich, and had many sheep *and* goats, and maidservants, menservants, camels, and donkeys.

**31** Jacob heard Laban's sons complaining, Jacob has taken away all that was our father's; he has acquired all this wealth *and* honor from what belonged to our father.

²And Jacob noticed that Laban looked at him less favorably than before.

³Then the Lord said to Jacob, Return to the land of your fathers and to your people, and I will be with you.

⁴So Jacob sent and called Rachel and Leah to the field to his flock,

⁵And he said to them, I see how your father looks at me, that he is not [friendly] toward me as before; but the God of my father has been with me.

⁶You know that I have served your father with all my might *and* power.

⁷But your father has deceived me and changed my wages ten times, but God did not allow him to hurt me.

⁸If he said, The speckled shall be your wages, then all the flock bore speckled; and if he said, The streaked shall be your hire, then all the flock bore streaked.

⁹Thus God has taken away the flocks of your father and given them to me.

¹⁰And I had a ᵃdream at the time the flock conceived. I looked up and saw that the rams which mated with the she-goats were streaked, speckled, and spotted.

¹¹And the ᵇAngel of God said to me in the dream, Jacob. And I said, Here am I.

¹²And He said, Look up and see, all the rams which mate with the flock are streaked, speckled, and mottled; for I have seen all that Laban does to you.

¹³I am the God of Bethel, where you anointed the pillar and where you vowed a vow to Me. Now arise, get out from this land and return to your native land.

¹⁴And Rachel and Leah answered him, Is there any portion or inheritance for us in our father's house?

¹⁵Are we not counted by him as strangers? For he sold us and has also quite devoured our money [the price you paid for us].

ᵃ We naturally wonder why we have not heard of this dream before and are tempted to question Jacob's truthfulness; but the Samaritan text removes all such doubt by recording the whole dream in the previous chapter (Gen. 30), right after Gen. 30:36 (Adam Clarke, *The Holy Bible with A Commentary*). ᵇ See footnote on Gen. 16:7. Note especially Gen. 31:13, where the Angel says, "I am the God of Bethel."

## New International Version

that God took away from our father belongs to us and our children. So do whatever God has told you."

<sup>17</sup>Then Jacob put his children and his wives on camels, <sup>18</sup>and he drove all his livestock ahead of him, along with all the goods he had accumulated in Paddan Aram,*a* to go to his father Isaac in the land of Canaan.

<sup>19</sup>When Laban had gone to shear his sheep, Rachel stole her father's household gods. <sup>20</sup>Moreover, Jacob deceived Laban the Aramean by not telling him he was running away. <sup>21</sup>So he fled with all he had, crossed the Euphrates River, and headed for the hill country of Gilead.

### Laban Pursues Jacob

<sup>22</sup>On the third day Laban was told that Jacob had fled. <sup>23</sup>Taking his relatives with him, he pursued Jacob for seven days and caught up with him in the hill country of Gilead. <sup>24</sup>Then God came to Laban the Aramean in a dream at night and said to him, "Be careful not to say anything to Jacob, either good or bad."

<sup>25</sup>Jacob had pitched his tent in the hill country of Gilead when Laban overtook him, and Laban and his relatives camped there too. <sup>26</sup>Then Laban said to Jacob, "What have you done? You've deceived me, and you've carried off my daughters like captives in war. <sup>27</sup>Why did you run off secretly and deceive me? Why didn't you tell me, so I could send you away with joy and singing to the music of timbrels and harps? <sup>28</sup>You didn't even let me kiss my grandchildren and my daughters goodbye. You have done a foolish thing. <sup>29</sup>I have the power to harm you; but last night the God of your father said to me, 'Be careful not to say anything to Jacob, either good or bad.' <sup>30</sup>Now you have gone off because you longed to return to your father's household. But why did you steal my gods?"

<sup>31</sup>Jacob answered Laban, "I was afraid, because I thought you would take your daughters away from me by force. <sup>32</sup>But if you find anyone who has your gods, that person shall not live. In the presence of our relatives, see for yourself whether there is anything of yours here with me; and if so, take it." Now Jacob did not know that Rachel had stolen the gods.

<sup>33</sup>So Laban went into Jacob's tent and into Leah's tent and into the tent of the two female servants, but he found nothing. After he came out of Leah's tent, he entered Rachel's tent. <sup>34</sup>Now Rachel had taken the household gods and put them inside her camel's saddle and was sitting on them. Laban searched through everything in the tent but found nothing.

## Amplified Bible

<sup>16</sup>For all the riches which God has taken from our father are ours and our children's. Now then, whatever God has said to you, do it.

<sup>17</sup>Then Jacob rose up and set his sons and his wives upon the camels;

<sup>18</sup>And he drove away all his livestock and all his gain which he had gotten, the livestock he had obtained *and* accumulated in Padan-aram, to go to Isaac his father in the land of Canaan.

<sup>19</sup>Now Laban had gone to shear his sheep [possibly to the feast of sheepshearing], and Rachel stole her father's household gods.

<sup>20</sup>And Jacob outwitted Laban the Syrian [Aramean] in that he did not tell him that he [intended] to flee *and* slip away secretly.

<sup>21</sup>So he fled with all that he had, and arose and crossed the river [Euphrates] and set his face toward the hill country of Gilead.

<sup>22</sup>But on the third day Laban was told that Jacob had fled.

<sup>23</sup>So he took his kinsmen with him and pursued after [Jacob] for seven days, and they overtook him in the hill country of Gilead.

<sup>24</sup>But God came to Laban the Syrian [Aramean] in a dream by night and said to him, Be careful that you do not speak from good to bad to Jacob [peaceably, then violently].

<sup>25</sup>Then Laban overtook Jacob. Now Jacob had pitched his tent on the hill, and Laban coming with his kinsmen pitched [his tents] on the same hill of Gilead.

<sup>26</sup>And Laban said to Jacob, What do you mean stealing away *and* leaving like this without my knowing it, and carrying off my daughters as if captives of the sword?

<sup>27</sup>Why did you flee secretly and cheat me and did not tell me, so that I might have sent you away with joy *and* gladness and with singing, with tambourine and lyre?

<sup>28</sup>And why did you not permit me to kiss my sons [grandchildren] and my daughters good-bye? Now you have done foolishly [in behaving like this].

<sup>29</sup>It is in my power to do you harm; but the God of your father spoke to me last night, saying, Be careful that you do not speak from good to bad to Jacob [peaceably, then violently].

<sup>30</sup>And now you felt you must go because you were homesick for your father's house, but why did you steal my [household] *a* gods?

<sup>31</sup>Jacob answered Laban, Because I was afraid; for I thought, Suppose you would take your daughters from me by force.

<sup>32</sup>The one with whom you find those gods of yours, let him not live. Here before our kinsmen [search my possessions and] take whatever you find that belongs to you. For Jacob did not know that Rachel had stolen [the images].

<sup>33</sup>So Laban went into Jacob's tent and into Leah's tent and the tent of the two maids, but he did not find them. Then he went from Leah's tent into Rachel's tent.

<sup>34</sup>Now Rachel had taken the images (gods) and put them in the camel's saddle and sat on them. Laban searched *and* felt through all the tent, but did not find them.

*a* Why was Laban making such a great commotion about some small idols? It had never been satisfactorily explained until the answer was found in the excavated Nuzi tablets (J. P. Free, *Archaeology Illuminates the Bible*), which showed that possession of the father's household gods played an important role in inheritance (W. F. Albright, "Recent Discoveries in Bible Lands," in *Young's Analytical Concordance to the Bible*). One of the Nuzi tablets indicated that in the region where Laban lived, a son-in-law who possessed the family images could appear in court and make claim to the estate of his father-in-law (various authors cited by Allan A. MacRae, "The Relation of Archaeology to the Bible," in American Scientific Affiliation, *Modern Science and Christian Faith*). Since Jacob's possession of the images implied the right to inheritance of Laban's wealth, one can understand why Laban organized his hurried expedition to recover the images (J. P. Free, *Archaeology and Bible History*).

*a 18* That is, Northwest Mesopotamia

## New International Version

35Rachel said to her father, "Don't be angry, my lord, that I cannot stand up in your presence; I'm having my period." So he searched but could not find the household gods.

36Jacob was angry and took Laban to task. "What is my crime?" he asked Laban. "How have I wronged you that you hunt me down? 37Now that you have searched through all my goods, what have you found that belongs to your household? Put it here in front of your relatives and mine, and let them judge between the two of us.

38"I have been with you for twenty years now. Your sheep and goats have not miscarried, nor have I eaten rams from your flocks. 39I did not bring you animals torn by wild beasts; I bore the loss myself. And you demanded payment from me for whatever was stolen by day or night. 40This was my situation: The heat consumed me in the daytime and the cold at night, and sleep fled from my eyes. 41It was like this for the twenty years I was in your household. I worked for you fourteen years for your two daughters and six years for your flocks, and you changed my wages ten times. 42If the God of my father, the God of Abraham and the Fear of Isaac, had not been with me, you would surely have sent me away empty-handed. But God has seen my hardship and the toil of my hands, and last night he rebuked you."

43Laban answered Jacob, "The women are my daughters, the children are my children, and the flocks are my flocks. All you see is mine. Yet what can I do today about these daughters of mine, or about the children they have borne? 44Come now, let's make a covenant, you and I, and let it serve as a witness between us."

45So Jacob took a stone and set it up as a pillar. 46He said to his relatives, "Gather some stones." So they took stones and piled them in a heap, and they ate there by the heap. 47Laban called it Jegar Sahadutha, and Jacob called it Galeed.a

48Laban said, "This heap is a witness between you and me today." That is why it was called Galeed. 49It was also called Mizpah,b because he said, "May the LORD keep watch between you and me when we are away from each other. 50If you mistreat my daughters or if you take any wives besides my daughters, even though no one is with us, remember that God is a witness between you and me."

51Laban also said to Jacob, "Here is this heap, and here is this pillar I have set up between you and me. 52This heap is a witness, and this pillar is a witness, that I will not go past this heap to your side to harm you and that you will not go past this heap and pillar to my side to harm me. 53May the God of Abraham and the God of Nahor, the God of their father, judge between us."

So Jacob took an oath in the name of the Fear of his father Isaac. 54He offered a sacrifice there in the hill country and invited his relatives to a meal. After they had eaten, they spent the night there.

55Early the next morning Laban kissed his grandchildren and his daughters and blessed them. Then he left and returned home.c

## Amplified Bible

35And [Rachel] said to her father, Do not be displeased, my lord, that I cannot rise up before you, for the period of women is upon me and I am unwell. And he searched, but did not find the gods.

36Then Jacob became angry and reproached and argued with Laban. And Jacob said to Laban, What is my fault? What is my sin, that you so hotly pursued me?

37Although you have searched and felt through all my household possessions, what have you found of all your household goods? Put it here before my brethren and yours, that they may judge and decide between us.

38These twenty years I have been with you; your ewes and your she-goats have not lost their young, and the rams of your flock have not been eaten by me.

39I did not bring you [the carcasses of the animals] torn by wild beasts; I bore the loss of it; you required of me [to make good] all that was stolen, whether it occurred by day or by night.

40This was [my lot]; by day the heat consumed me and by night the cold, and I could not sleep.

41I have been twenty years in your house. I served you fourteen years for your two daughters and six years for your flocks; and you have changed my wages ten times.

42And if the God of my father, the God of Abraham and the Dread [lest he should fall] and Fear [lest he offend] of Isaac, had not been with me, surely you would have sent me away now empty-handed. God has seen my affliction and humiliation and the [wearying] labor of my hands and rebuked you last night.

43Laban answered Jacob, These daughters are my daughters, these children are my children, these flocks are my flocks, and all that you see is mine. But what can I do today to these my daughters or to their children whom they have borne?

44So come now, let us make a covenant or league, you and I, and let it be for a witness between you and me.

45So Jacob set up a stone for a pillar or monument.

46And Jacob said to his brethren, Gather stones; and they took stones and made a heap, and they ate [together] there upon the heap. [Prov. 16:7.]

47Laban called it Jegar-sahadutha [witness heap, in Aramaic], but Jacob called it Galeed [awitness heap, in Hebrew.]

48Laban said, This heap is a witness today between you and me. Therefore it was named Galeed.

49And [the pillar or monument was called] Mizpah [watchpost], for he [Laban] said, May the Lord watch between you and me when we are absent and hidden one from another.

50If you should afflict, humiliate, or lower [divorce] my daughters, or if you should take other wives beside my daughters, although no man is with us [to witness], see (remember), God is witness between you and me.

51Laban said to Jacob, See this heap and this pillar, which I have set up between you and me.

52This heap is a witness and this pillar is a witness, that I will not pass by this heap to you, and that you will not pass by this heap and this pillar to me, for harm.

53The God of Abraham and the God of Nahor, and the god [the object of worship] of their father [Terah, an idolator], judge between us. But Jacob swore [only] by [the one true God] the Dread and Fear of his father Isaac. [Josh. 24:2.]

54Then Jacob offered a sacrifice on the mountain and called his brethren to eat food; and they ate food and lingered all night on the mountain.

55And early in the morning Laban rose up and kissed his grandchildren and his daughters and pronounced a blessing [asking God's favor] on them. Then Laban departed and returned to his home.

---

a 47 The Aramaic *Jegar Sahadutha* and the Hebrew *Galeed* both mean *witness heap.*    b 49 *Mizpah* means *watchtower.*    c 55 In Hebrew texts this verse (31:55) is numbered 32:1.

a *The Latin Vulgate* adds, "Each according to the idiom of his own tongue"—i.e., Laban in Aramaic and Jacob in Hebrew.

## New International Version

### Jacob Prepares to Meet Esau

**32**[a] Jacob also went on his way, and the angels of God met him. [2]When Jacob saw them, he said, "This is the camp of God!" So he named that place Mahanaim.[b]

[3]Jacob sent messengers ahead of him to his brother Esau in the land of Seir, the country of Edom. [4]He instructed them: "This is what you are to say to my lord Esau: 'Your servant Jacob says, I have been staying with Laban and have remained there till now. [5]I have cattle and donkeys, sheep and goats, male and female servants. Now I am sending this message to my lord, that I may find favor in your eyes.'"

[6]When the messengers returned to Jacob, they said, "We went to your brother Esau, and now he is coming to meet you, and four hundred men are with him."

[7]In great fear and distress Jacob divided the people who were with him into two groups,[c] and the flocks and herds and camels as well. [8]He thought, "If Esau comes and attacks one group,[d] the group[d] that is left may escape."

[9]Then Jacob prayed, "O God of my father Abraham, God of my father Isaac, LORD, you who said to me, 'Go back to your country and your relatives, and I will make you prosper,' [10]I am unworthy of all the kindness and faithfulness you have shown your servant. I had only my staff when I crossed this Jordan, but now I have become two camps. [11]Save me, I pray, from the hand of my brother Esau, for I am afraid he will come and attack me, and also the mothers with their children. [12]But you have said, 'I will surely make you prosper and will make your descendants like the sand of the sea, which cannot be counted.'"

[13]He spent the night there, and from what he had with him he selected a gift for his brother Esau: [14]two hundred female goats and twenty male goats, two hundred ewes and twenty rams, [15]thirty female camels with their young, forty cows and ten bulls, and twenty female donkeys and ten male donkeys. [16]He put them in the care of his servants, each herd by itself, and said to his servants, "Go ahead of me, and keep some space between the herds."

[17]He instructed the one in the lead: "When my brother Esau meets you and asks, 'Who do you belong to, and where are you going, and who owns all these animals in front of you?' [18]then you are to say, 'They belong to your servant Jacob. They are a gift sent to my lord Esau, and he is coming behind us.'"

[19]He also instructed the second, the third and all the others who followed the herds: "You are to say the same thing to Esau when you meet him. [20]And be sure to say, 'Your servant Jacob is coming behind us.'" For he thought, "I will pacify him with these gifts I am sending on ahead; later, when I see him, perhaps he will receive me." [21]So Jacob's gifts went on ahead of him, but he himself spent the night in the camp.

### Jacob Wrestles With God

[22]That night Jacob got up and took his two wives, his two female servants and his eleven sons and crossed the ford of the Jabbok. [23]After he had sent them across the stream, he sent over all his possessions. [24]So Jacob was left alone, and a man wrestled with him till daybreak. [25]When the man saw that he could not overpower him, he touched the socket of Jacob's hip so that his hip was

## Amplified Bible

**32** Then Jacob went on his way, and God's angels met him.

[2]When Jacob saw them, he said, This is God's army! So he named that place Mahanaim [two armies]. [Gen. 32:7, 10.]

[3]And Jacob sent messengers before him to Esau his brother in the land of Seir, the country of Edom.

[4]And he commanded them, Say this to my lord Esau: Your servant Jacob says this: I have been living temporarily with Laban and have stayed there till now.

[5]And I have oxen, donkeys, flocks, menservants, and women servants; and I have sent to tell my lord, that I may find mercy *and* kindness in your sight.

[6]And the messengers returned to Jacob, saying, We came to your brother Esau; and now he is [on the way] to meet you, and four hundred men are with him.

[7]Then Jacob was greatly afraid and distressed; and he divided the people who were with him, and the flocks and herds and camels, into two groups,

[8]Thinking, If Esau comes to the one group and smites it, then the other group which is left will escape.

[9]Jacob said, O God of my father Abraham and God of my father Isaac, the Lord Who said to me, Return to your country and to your people and I will do you good,

[10]I am not worthy of the least of all the mercy *and* loving-kindness and all the faithfulness which You have shown to Your servant, for with [only] my staff I passed over this Jordan [long ago], and now I have become two companies.

[11]Deliver me, I pray You, from the hand of my brother, from the hand of Esau; for I fear him, lest he come and smite [us all], the mothers with the children.

[12]And You said, I will surely do you good and make your descendants as the sand of the sea, which cannot be numbered for multitude.

[13]And Jacob lodged there that night and took from what he had with him as a present for his brother Esau:

[14]Two hundred she-goats, 20 he-goats, 200 ewes, 20 rams,

[15]Thirty milk camels with their colts, 40 cows, 10 bulls, 20 she-donkeys, and 10 [donkey] colts.

[16]And he put them into the charge of his servants, every drove by itself, and said to his servants, Pass over before me and put a space between drove and drove.

[17]And he commanded the first, When Esau my brother meets you and asks to whom you belong, where you are going, and whose are the animals before you,

[18]Then you shall say, They are your servant Jacob's; it is a present sent to my lord Esau; and moreover, he is behind us.

[19]And so he commanded the second and the third and all that followed the droves, saying, This is what you are to say to Esau when you meet him.

[20]And say, Moreover, your servant Jacob is behind us. For he said, I will appease him with the present that goes before me, and afterward I will see his face; perhaps he will accept me.

[21]So the present went on before him, and he himself lodged that night in the camp.

[22]But he rose up that [same] night and took his two wives, his two women servants, and his eleven sons and passed over the ford [of the] Jabbok.

[23]And he took them and sent them across the brook; also he sent over all that he had.

[24]And Jacob was left alone, and a Man wrestled with him until daybreak.

[25]And when [the [a]Man] saw that He did not prevail against [Jacob], He touched the hollow of his thigh; and Jacob's thigh was put out of joint as he wrestled with Him.

---

## New International Version

wrenched as he wrestled with the man. 26Then the man said, "Let me go, for it is daybreak."

But Jacob replied, "I will not let you go unless you bless me."

27The man asked him, "What is your name?"

"Jacob," he answered.

28Then the man said, "Your name will no longer be Jacob, but Israel,*a* because you have struggled with God and with humans and have overcome."

29Jacob said, "Please tell me your name."

But he replied, "Why do you ask my name?" Then he blessed him there.

30So Jacob called the place Peniel,*b* saying, "It is because I saw God face to face, and yet my life was spared."

31The sun rose above him as he passed Peniel,*c* and he was limping because of his hip. 32Therefore to this day the Israelites do not eat the tendon attached to the socket of the hip, because the socket of Jacob's hip was touched near the tendon.

### Jacob Meets Esau

**33** Jacob looked up and there was Esau, coming with his four hundred men; so he divided the children among Leah, Rachel and the two female servants. 2He put the female servants and their children in front, Leah and her children next, and Rachel and Joseph in the rear. 3He himself went on ahead and bowed down to the ground seven times as he approached his brother.

4But Esau ran to meet Jacob and embraced him; he threw his arms around his neck and kissed him. And they wept. 5Then Esau looked up and saw the women and children. "Who are these with you?" he asked.

Jacob answered, "They are the children God has graciously given your servant."

6Then the female servants and their children approached and bowed down. 7Next, Leah and her children came and bowed down. Last of all came Joseph and Rachel, and they too bowed down.

8Esau asked, "What's the meaning of all these flocks and herds I met?"

"To find favor in your eyes, my lord," he said.

9But Esau said, "I already have plenty, my brother. Keep what you have for yourself."

10"No, please!" said Jacob. "If I have found favor in your eyes, accept this gift from me. For to see your face is like seeing the face of God, now that you have received me favorably. 11Please accept the present that was brought to you, for God has been gracious to me and I have all I need." And because Jacob insisted, Esau accepted it.

12Then Esau said, "Let us be on our way; I'll accompany you."

13But Jacob said to him, "My lord knows that the children are tender and that I must care for the ewes and cows that are nursing their young. If they are driven hard just one day, all the animals will die. 14So let my lord go on ahead of his servant, while I move along slowly at the pace of the flocks and herds before me and the pace of the children, until I come to my lord in Seir."

## Amplified Bible

26Then He said, Let Me go, for day is breaking. But [Jacob] said, I will not let You go unless You declare a blessing upon me.

27[The Man] asked him, What is your name? And [in shock of realization, whispering] he said, Jacob [supplanter, schemer, trickster, swindler]!

28And He said, Your name shall be called no more Jacob [supplanter], but Israel [contender with God]; for you have contended *and* have power with God and with men and have prevailed. [Hos. 12:3-4.]

29Then Jacob asked Him, Tell me, I pray You, what [in contrast] is Your name? But He said, Why is it that you ask My name? And *a* [the Angel of God declared] a blessing on [Jacob] there.

30And Jacob called the name of the place Peniel [the face of God], saying, For I have seen God face to face, and my life is spared *and* not snatched away.

31And as he passed Penuel [Peniel], the sun rose upon him, and he was limping because of his thigh.

32That is why to this day the Israelites do not eat the sinew of the hip which is on the hollow of the thigh, because [the Angel of the Lord] touched the hollow of Jacob's thigh on the sinew of the hip.

**33** And Jacob raised his eyes and looked, and behold, Esau was coming and with him 400 men. So he divided the children to Leah and to Rachel and to the two maids.

2And he put the maids and their children in front, Leah and her children after them, and Rachel and Joseph last of all.

3Then Jacob went over [the stream] before them and bowed himself to the ground seven times, until he came near to his brother.

4But Esau ran to meet him, and embraced him and fell on his neck and kissed him, and they wept. [Luke 15:20.]

5[Esau] looked up and saw the women and the children and said, Who are these with you? And [Jacob] replied, They are the children whom God has graciously given your servant.

6Then the maids came near, they and their children, and they bowed themselves.

7And Leah also with her children came near, and they bowed themselves. After them Joseph and Rachel came near, and they bowed themselves.

8Esau said, What do you mean by all this company which I met? And he said, These are that I might find favor in the sight of my lord.

9And Esau said, I have plenty, my brother; keep what you have for yourself.

10But Jacob replied, No, I beg of you, if now I have found favor in your sight, receive my gift that I am presenting; for truly to see your face is to me as if I had seen the face of God, and you have received me favorably.

11Accept, I beg of you, my blessing *and* gift that I have brought to you; for God has dealt graciously with me and I have everything. And he kept urging him and he accepted it.

12Then [Esau] said, Let us get started on our journey, and I will go before you.

13But Jacob replied, You know, my lord, that the children are tender *and* delicate *and* need gentle care, and the flocks and herds with young are of concern to me; for if the men should overdrive them for a single day, the whole of the flocks would die.

14Let my lord, I pray you, pass over before his servant; and I will lead on slowly, governed by [consideration for] the livestock that set the pace before me and the endurance of the children, *b*until I come to my lord in Seir.

---

*a 28 Israel* probably means *he struggles with God.*    *b 30 Peniel* means *face of God.*    *c 31* Hebrew *Penuel*, a variant of *Peniel*

*a* This is God Himself (as Jacob eventually realizes in Gen. 32:30) in the form of an angel. See footnote on Gen. 16:7, as well as Hos. 12:3-4.
*b* Ever the deceiver, Jacob had no intention of following Esau to Seir. In fact, he heads in the opposite direction.

## New International Version

[15]Esau said, "Then let me leave some of my men with you."

"But why do that?" Jacob asked. "Just let me find favor in the eyes of my lord."

[16]So that day Esau started on his way back to Seir. [17]Jacob, however, went to Sukkoth, where he built a place for himself and made shelters for his livestock. That is why the place is called Sukkoth.[a]

[18]After Jacob came from Paddan Aram,[b] he arrived safely at the city of Shechem in Canaan and camped within sight of the city. [19]For a hundred pieces of silver,[c] he bought from the sons of Hamor, the father of Shechem, the plot of ground where he pitched his tent. [20]There he set up an altar and called it El Elohe Israel.[d]

### Dinah and the Shechemites

**34** Now Dinah, the daughter Leah had borne to Jacob, went out to visit the women of the land. [2]When Shechem son of Hamor the Hivite, the ruler of that area, saw her, he took her and raped her. [3]His heart was drawn to Dinah daughter of Jacob; he loved the young woman and spoke tenderly to her. [4]And Shechem said to his father Hamor, "Get me this girl as my wife."

[5]When Jacob heard that his daughter Dinah had been defiled, his sons were in the fields with his livestock; so he did nothing about it until they came home.

[6]Then Shechem's father Hamor went out to talk with Jacob. [7]Meanwhile, Jacob's sons had come in from the fields as soon as they heard what had happened. They were shocked and furious, because Shechem had done an outrageous thing in[e] Israel by sleeping with Jacob's daughter—a thing that should not be done.

[8]But Hamor said to them, "My son Shechem has his heart set on your daughter. Please give her to him as his wife. [9]Intermarry with us; give us your daughters and take our daughters for yourselves. [10]You can settle among us; the land is open to you. Live in it, trade[f] in it, and acquire property in it."

[11]Then Shechem said to Dinah's father and brothers, "Let me find favor in your eyes, and I will give you whatever you ask. [12]Make the price for the bride and the gift I am to bring as great as you like, and I'll pay whatever you ask me. Only give me the young woman as my wife."

[13]Because their sister Dinah had been defiled, Jacob's sons replied deceitfully as they spoke to Shechem and his father Hamor. [14]They said to them, "We can't do such a thing; we can't give our sister to a man who is not circumcised. That would be a disgrace to us. [15]We will enter into an agreement with you on one condition only: that you become like us by circumcising all your males. [16]Then we will give you our daughters and take your daughters for ourselves. We'll settle among you and become one people with you. [17]But if you will not agree to be circumcised, we'll take our sister and go."

[18]Their proposal seemed good to Hamor and his son Shechem. [19]The young man, who was the most honored of all his father's family, lost no time in doing what they said, because he was delighted with Jacob's daughter. [20]So

## Amplified Bible

[15]Then Esau said, Let me now leave with you some of the people who are with me. But [Jacob] said, What need is there for it? Let me find favor in the sight of my lord.

[16]So Esau turned back that day on his way to Seir.

[17]But Jacob journeyed to Succoth and built himself a house and made booths or places of shelter for his livestock; so the name of the place is called Succoth [booths].

[18]When Jacob came from Padan-aram, he arrived safely and in peace at the town of Shechem, in the land of Canaan, and pitched his tents before the [enclosed] town.

[19]Then he bought the piece of land on which he had encamped from the sons of Hamor, Shechem's father, for a hundred pieces of money.

[20]There he erected an altar and called it El-Elohe-Israel [God, the God of Israel].

**34** Now Dinah daughter of Leah, whom she bore to Jacob, went out [unattended] to see the girls of the place.

[2]And when Shechem son of Hamor the Hivite, prince of the country, saw her, he seized her, lay with her, and humbled, defiled, and disgraced her.

[3]But his soul longed for and clung to Dinah daughter of Jacob, and he loved the girl and spoke comfortingly to her young heart's wishes.

[4]And Shechem said to his father Hamor, Get me this girl to be my wife.

[5]Jacob heard that [Shechem] had defiled Dinah his daughter. Now his sons were with his livestock in the field. So Jacob held his peace until they came.

[6]But Hamor father of Shechem went out to Jacob to have a talk with him.

[7]When Jacob's sons heard it, they came from the field; and they were distressed and grieved and very angry, for [Shechem] had done a vile thing to Israel in lying with Jacob's daughter, which ought not to be done.

[8]And Hamor conferred with them, saying, The soul of my son Shechem craves your daughter [and sister]. I beg of you give her to him to be his wife.

[9]And make marriages with us and give your daughters to us and take our daughters to you.

[10]You shall dwell with us; the country will be open to you; live and trade and get your possessions in it.

[11]And Shechem said to [Dinah's] father and to her brothers, Let me find favor in your eyes, and I will give you whatever you ask of me.

[12]Ask me ever so much dowry and [marriage] gift, and I will give according to what you tell me; only give me the girl to be my wife.

[13]The sons of Jacob answered Shechem and Hamor his father deceitfully, [justifying their intended action by saying, in effect, we are going to do this] because Shechem had defiled and disgraced their sister Dinah.

[14]They said to them, We cannot do this thing and give our sister to one who is not circumcised, for that would be a reproach and disgrace to us.

[15]But we do consent to do this: if you will become as we are and every male among you be circumcised,

[16]Then we will give our daughters to you and we will take your daughters to us, and we will dwell with you and become one people.

[17]But if you will not listen to us and consent to be circumcised, then we will take our daughter and go.

[18]Their words pleased Hamor and his son Shechem.

[19]And the young man did not delay to do the thing, for he delighted in Jacob's daughter. He was honored above all his family [so, ranking first, he acted first].

---

[a] 17 *Sukkoth* means *shelters*.    [b] 18 That is, Northwest Mesopotamia
[c] 19 Hebrew *hundred kesitahs*; a kesitah was a unit of money of unknown weight and value.    [d] 20 *El Elohe Israel* can mean *El is the God of Israel* or *mighty is the God of Israel.*    [e] 7 Or *against*    [f] 10 Or *move about freely*; also in verse 21

## New International Version

Hamor and his son Shechem went to the gate of their city to speak to the men of their city. 21"These men are friendly toward us," they said. "Let them live in our land and trade in it; the land has plenty of room for them. We can marry their daughters and they can marry ours. 22But the men will agree to live with us as one people only on the condition that our males be circumcised, as they themselves are. 23Won't their livestock, their property and all their other animals become ours? So let us agree to their terms, and they will settle among us."

24All the men who went out of the city gate agreed with Hamor and his son Shechem, and every male in the city was circumcised.

25Three days later, while all of them were still in pain, two of Jacob's sons, Simeon and Levi, Dinah's brothers, took their swords and attacked the unsuspecting city, killing every male. 26They put Hamor and his son Shechem to the sword and took Dinah from Shechem's house and left. 27The sons of Jacob came upon the dead bodies and looted the city where*a* their sister had been defiled. 28They seized their flocks and herds and donkeys and everything else of theirs in the city and out in the fields. 29They carried off all their wealth and all their women and children, taking as plunder everything in the houses.

30Then Jacob said to Simeon and Levi, "You have brought trouble on me by making me obnoxious to the Canaanites and Perizzites, the people living in this land. We are few in number, and if they join forces against me and attack me, I and my household will be destroyed."

31But they replied, "Should he have treated our sister like a prostitute?"

### Jacob Returns to Bethel

**35** Then God said to Jacob, "Go up to Bethel and settle there, and build an altar there to God, who appeared to you when you were fleeing from your brother Esau."

2So Jacob said to his household and to all who were with him, "Get rid of the foreign gods you have with you, and purify yourselves and change your clothes. 3Then come, let us go up to Bethel, where I will build an altar to God, who answered me in the day of my distress and who has been with me wherever I have gone." 4So they gave Jacob all the foreign gods they had and the rings in their ears, and Jacob buried them under the oak at Shechem. 5Then they set out, and the terror of God fell on the towns all around them so that no one pursued them.

6Jacob and all the people with him came to Luz (that is, Bethel) in the land of Canaan. 7There he built an altar, and he called the place El Bethel,*b* because it was there that God revealed himself to him when he was fleeing from his brother.

8Now Deborah, Rebekah's nurse, died and was buried under the oak outside Bethel. So it was named Allon Bakuth.*c*

9After Jacob returned from Paddan Aram,*d* God appeared to him again and blessed him. 10God said to him,

## Amplified Bible

20Then Hamor and Shechem his son came to the gate of their [enclosed] town and discussed the matter with the citizens, saying,

21These men are peaceable with us; so let them dwell in the land and trade in it; for the land is large enough [for us and] for them; let us take their daughters for wives and let us give them our daughters.

22But the men will consent to our request that they live among us and be one people only on condition that every male among us be circumcised, as they are.

23Shall not their cattle and their possessions and all their beasts be ours? Only let us consent to them, and they will dwell here with us.

24And all the people who went out of the town gate listened *and* heeded what Hamor and Shechem said; and every male was circumcised who was a resident of that town.

25But on the third day [after the circumcision] when [all the men] were sore, two of the sons of Jacob, Simeon and Levi, Dinah's [full] brothers, took their swords, boldly entered the city [without danger], and slew all the males.

26And they killed Hamor and Shechem his son with the edge of the sword and took Dinah out of Shechem's house [where she had been all this time] and departed.

27[Then the rest of] Jacob's [eleven] sons came upon the slain and plundered the town, because there their sister had been defiled *and* disgraced.

28They took their flocks, their herds, their donkeys, and whatever was in the town and in the field;

29All their wealth and all their little ones and their wives they took captive, making spoil even of all [they found] in the houses.

30And Jacob said to Simeon and Levi, You have ruined me, making me infamous *and* embroiling me with the inhabitants of the land, the Canaanites and the Perizzites! And we are few in number, and they will gather together against me and attack me; and I shall be destroyed, I and my household.

31And they said, Should he [be permitted to] deal with our sister as with a harlot?

**35** And God said to Jacob, Arise, go up to Bethel and dwell there. And make there an altar to God Who appeared to you [in a distinct manifestation] when you fled from the presence of Esau your brother. [Gen. 28:11-22.]

2Then Jacob said to his household and to all who were with him, Put away the [images of] strange gods that are among you, and purify yourselves and change [into fresh] garments;

3Then let us arise and go up to Bethel, and I will make there an altar to God Who answered me in the day of my distress and was with me wherever I went.

4So they [both young men and women] gave to Jacob all the strange gods they had and their earrings which were [worn as charms against evil] in their ears; and Jacob buried *and* hid them under the oak near Shechem.

5And they journeyed and a terror from God fell on the towns round about them, and they did not pursue the sons of Jacob.

6So Jacob came to Luz, that is, Bethel, which is in the land of Canaan, he and all the people with him.

7There he built an altar, and called the place El-bethel [God of Bethel], for there God revealed Himself to him when he fled from the presence of his brother.

8But Deborah, Rebekah's nurse, died and was buried below Bethel under an oak; and the name of it was called Allon-bacuth [oak of weeping].

9And God [in a distinctly visible manifestation] appeared to Jacob again when he came out of Padan-aram, and declared a blessing on him. [Gen. 32:28.]

10Again God said to him, Your name is Jacob [supplant-

*a* 27 Or *because*    *b* 7 *El Bethel* means *God of Bethel.*    *c* 8 *Allon Bakuth* means *oak of weeping.*    *d* 9 That is, Northwest Mesopotamia; also in verse 26

## New International Version

"Your name is Jacob,*a* but you will no longer be called Jacob; your name will be Israel.*b*" So he named him Israel.

[11]And God said to him, "I am God Almighty*c*; be fruitful and increase in number. A nation and a community of nations will come from you, and kings will be among your descendants. [12]The land I gave to Abraham and Isaac I also give to you, and I will give this land to your descendants after you." [13]Then God went up from him at the place where he had talked with him.

[14]Jacob set up a stone pillar at the place where God had talked with him, and he poured out a drink offering on it; he also poured oil on it. [15]Jacob called the place where God had talked with him Bethel.*d*

### The Deaths of Rachel and Isaac

[16]Then they moved on from Bethel. While they were still some distance from Ephrath, Rachel began to give birth and had great difficulty. [17]And as she was having great difficulty in childbirth, the midwife said to her, "Don't despair, for you have another son." [18]As she breathed her last—for she was dying—she named her son Ben-Oni.*e* But his father named him Benjamin.*f*

[19]So Rachel died and was buried on the way to Ephrath (that is, Bethlehem). [20]Over her tomb Jacob set up a pillar, and to this day that pillar marks Rachel's tomb.

[21]Israel moved on again and pitched his tent beyond Migdal Eder. [22]While Israel was living in that region, Reuben went in and slept with his father's concubine Bilhah, and Israel heard of it.

Jacob had twelve sons:
[23]The sons of Leah:
  Reuben the firstborn of Jacob,
  Simeon, Levi, Judah, Issachar and Zebulun.
[24]The sons of Rachel:
  Joseph and Benjamin.
[25]The sons of Rachel's servant Bilhah:
  Dan and Naphtali.
[26]The sons of Leah's servant Zilpah:
  Gad and Asher.
  These were the sons of Jacob, who were born to him in Paddan Aram.

[27]Jacob came home to his father Isaac in Mamre, near Kiriath Arba (that is, Hebron), where Abraham and Isaac had stayed. [28]Isaac lived a hundred and eighty years. [29]Then he breathed his last and died and was gathered to his people, old and full of years. And his sons Esau and Jacob buried him.

### Esau's Descendants

**36** This is the account of the family line of Esau (that is, Edom).

[2]Esau took his wives from the women of Canaan: Adah daughter of Elon the Hittite, and Oholibamah daughter of Anah and granddaughter of Zibeon the Hivite— [3]also Basemath daughter of Ishmael and sister of Nebaioth.

[4]Adah bore Eliphaz to Esau, Basemath bore Reuel, [5]and Oholibamah bore Jeush, Jalam and Korah. These were the sons of Esau, who were born to him in Canaan.

## Amplified Bible

er]; you shall not be called Jacob any longer, but Israel shall be your name. So He called him Israel [contender with God].

[11]And God said to him, I am God Almighty. Be fruitful and multiply; a nation and a company of nations shall come from you and kings shall be born of your stock;

[12]The land which I gave Abraham and Isaac I will give to you, and to your descendants after you I will give the land.

[13]Then God ascended from him in the place where He talked with him.

[14]And Jacob set up a pillar (monument) in the place where he talked with [God], a pillar of stone; and he poured a drink offering on it and he poured oil on it.

[15]And Jacob called the name of the place where God had talked with him Bethel [house of God].

[16]And they journeyed from Bethel and had but a little way to go to Ephrath [Bethlehem] when Rachel suffered the pangs of childbirth and had hard labor.

[17]When she was in hard labor, the midwife said to her, Do not be afraid; you shall have this son also.

[18]And as her soul was departing, for she died, she called his name Ben-oni [son of my sorrow]; but his father called him Benjamin [son of the right hand].

[19]So Rachel died and was buried on the way to Ephrath, that is, Bethlehem.

[20]And Jacob set a pillar (monument) on her grave; that is the pillar of Rachel's grave to this day.

[21]Then Israel journeyed on and spread his tent on the other side of the tower of Edar.

[22]When Israel dwelt there, Reuben [his eldest son] went and lay with Bilhah his father's concubine; and Israel heard about it. Now Jacob's sons were twelve.

[23]The sons of Leah: Reuben, Jacob's firstborn, Simeon, Levi, Judah, Issachar, and Zebulun.

[24]The sons of Rachel: Joseph and Benjamin.

[25]The sons of Bilhah, Rachel's maid: Dan and Naphtali.

[26]And the sons of Zilpah, Leah's maid: Gad and Asher. These are the sons of Jacob born to him in Padan-aram.

[27]And Jacob came to Isaac his father at Mamre or Kiriath-arba, that is, Hebron, where Abraham and Isaac had sojourned.

[28]Now the days of Isaac were 180 years.

[29]And Isaac's spirit departed; he died and was gathered to his people, being an old man, satisfied *and* satiated with days; his sons Esau and Jacob buried him.

**36** Now this is the history of the descendants of Esau, that is, Edom.

[2]Esau took his wives from the women of Canaan: Adah daughter of Elon the Hittite, and Oholibamah daughter of Anah, the son of Zibeon the Hivite,

[3]And Basemath, Ishmael's daughter, sister of Nebaioth.

[4]Adah bore to Esau, Eliphaz; Basemath bore Reuel;

[5]And Oholibamah bore Jeush, Jalam, and Korah. These are the sons of Esau born to him in Canaan.

---

*a 10 Jacob* means *he grasps the heel,* a Hebrew idiom for *he deceives.*
*b 10 Israel* probably means *he struggles with God.*   *c 11* Hebrew
*El-Shaddai*   *d 15 Bethel* means *house of God.*   *e 18 Ben-Oni* means
*son of my trouble.*   *f 18 Benjamin* means *son of my right hand.*

## New International Version

⁶Esau took his wives and sons and daughters and all the members of his household, as well as his livestock and all his other animals and all the goods he had acquired in Canaan, and moved to a land some distance from his brother Jacob. ⁷Their possessions were too great for them to remain together; the land where they were staying could not support them both because of their livestock. ⁸So Esau (that is, Edom) settled in the hill country of Seir.

⁹This is the account of the family line of Esau the father of the Edomites in the hill country of Seir.

¹⁰These are the names of Esau's sons:
Eliphaz, the son of Esau's wife Adah, and Reuel, the son of Esau's wife Basemath.
¹¹The sons of Eliphaz:
Teman, Omar, Zepho, Gatam and Kenaz.
¹²Esau's son Eliphaz also had a concubine named Timna, who bore him Amalek. These were grandsons of Esau's wife Adah.
¹³The sons of Reuel:
Nahath, Zerah, Shammah and Mizzah. These were grandsons of Esau's wife Basemath.
¹⁴The sons of Esau's wife Oholibamah daughter of Anah and granddaughter of Zibeon, whom she bore to Esau:
Jeush, Jalam and Korah.

¹⁵These were the chiefs among Esau's descendants:
The sons of Eliphaz the firstborn of Esau:
Chiefs Teman, Omar, Zepho, Kenaz, ¹⁶Korah,ᵃ Gatam and Amalek. These were the chiefs descended from Eliphaz in Edom; they were grandsons of Adah.
¹⁷The sons of Esau's son Reuel:
Chiefs Nahath, Zerah, Shammah and Mizzah. These were the chiefs descended from Reuel in Edom; they were grandsons of Esau's wife Basemath.
¹⁸The sons of Esau's wife Oholibamah:
Chiefs Jeush, Jalam and Korah. These were the chiefs descended from Esau's wife Oholibamah daughter of Anah.
¹⁹These were the sons of Esau (that is, Edom), and these were their chiefs.

²⁰These were the sons of Seir the Horite, who were living in the region:
Lotan, Shobal, Zibeon, Anah, ²¹Dishon, Ezer and Dishan. These sons of Seir in Edom were Horite chiefs.
²²The sons of Lotan:
Hori and Homam.ᵇ Timna was Lotan's sister.
²³The sons of Shobal:
Alvan, Manahath, Ebal, Shepho and Onam.
²⁴The sons of Zibeon:
Aiah and Anah. This is the Anah who discovered the hot springsᶜ in the desert while he was grazing the donkeys of his father Zibeon.
²⁵The children of Anah:
Dishon and Oholibamah daughter of Anah.
²⁶The sons of Dishonᵈ:
Hemdan, Eshban, Ithran and Keran.
²⁷The sons of Ezer:
Bilhan, Zaavan and Akan.
²⁸The sons of Dishan:
Uz and Aran.
²⁹These were the Horite chiefs:
Lotan, Shobal, Zibeon, Anah, ³⁰Dishon, Ezer and

ᵃ 16 Masoretic Text; Samaritan Pentateuch (also verse 11 and 1 Chron. 1:36) does not have *Korah*.   ᵇ 22 Hebrew *Hemam*, a variant of *Homam* (see 1 Chron. 1:39)   ᶜ 24 Vulgate; Syriac *discovered water;* the meaning of the Hebrew for this word is uncertain.   ᵈ 26 Hebrew *Dishan*, a variant of *Dishon*

## Amplified Bible

⁶Now Esau took his wives, his sons, his daughters, and all the members of his household, his cattle, all his beasts, and all his possessions which he had obtained in the land of Canaan, and he went into a land away from his brother Jacob.

⁷For their great flocks *and* herds *and* possessions [which they had collected] made it impossible for them to dwell together; the land in which they were strangers could not support them because of their livestock.

⁸So Esau dwelt in the hill country of Seir; Esau is Edom.

⁹And this is the history of the descendants of Esau the father of the Edomites in the hill country of Seir.

¹⁰These are the names of Esau's sons: Eliphaz, the son of Adah, Esau's wife, and Reuel, the son of Basemath, Esau's wife.

¹¹And the sons of Eliphaz were Teman, Omar, Zepho, Gatam, and Kenaz.

¹²And Timna was a concubine of Eliphaz, Esau's son; and she bore Amalek to Eliphaz. These are the sons of Adah, Esau's wife.

¹³These are the sons of Reuel: Nahath, Zerah, Shammah, and Mizzah. These are the sons of Basemath, Esau's wife.

¹⁴And these are the sons of Oholibamah daughter of Anah, the son of Zibeon, Esau's wife. She bore to Esau: Jeush, Jalam, and Korah.

¹⁵These are the chiefs of the sons of Esau: The sons of Eliphaz the firstborn of Esau: Chiefs Teman, Omar, Zepho, Kenaz,

¹⁶Korah, Gatam, and Amalek. These are the chiefs of Eliphaz in the land of Edom; they are the sons of Adah.

¹⁷These are the sons of Reuel, Esau's son: Chiefs Nahath, Zerah, Shammah, Mizzah. These are the chiefs of Reuel in the land of Edom; they are the sons of Basemath, Esau's wife.

¹⁸These are the sons of Oholibamah, Esau's wife: Chiefs Jeush, Jalam, and Korah. These are the chiefs born of Oholibamah daughter of Anah, Esau's wife.

¹⁹These are the sons of Esau, that is, Edom, and these are their chiefs.

²⁰These are the sons of Seir the Horite, the inhabitants of the land: Lotan, Shobal, Zibeon, Anah,

²¹Dishon, Ezer, and Dishan. These are the chiefs of the ᵃHorites, the sons of Seir in the land of Edom.

²²The sons of Lotan are Hori and Hemam; and Lotan's sister is Timna.

²³The sons of Shobal are these: Alvan, Manahath, Ebal, Shepho, and Onam.

²⁴These are the sons of Zibeon: Aiah and Anah. This is the Anah who found the hot springs in the wilderness as he pastured the donkeys of Zibeon his father.

²⁵The children of Anah are these: Dishon and Oholibamah daughter of Anah [Esau's wife].

²⁶These are the sons of Dishon: Hemdan, Eshban, Ithran, and Cheran.

²⁷Ezer's sons are these: Bilhan, Zaavan, and Akan.

²⁸The sons of Dishan are these: Uz and Aran.

²⁹The Horite chiefs are these: Lotan, Shobal, Zibeon, Anah,

ᵃ Because of the similarity of the word 'Horites' to a Hebrew word for "cave," the term Horite was formerly interpreted as "cave dweller." But later archaeological discoveries have shown that the Horites are not to be explained as cave dwellers, but are to be identified with an important group in the Near East in patriarchal times (J. P. Free, *Archaeology and Bible History*). In fact, neither the Bible nor archaeology has any proof of aboriginal "cavemen." Cities of great antiquity have been unearthed with ever-increasing evidence that "when civilization appears it is already fully grown," and "pre-Semitic culture springs into view ready-made" (Hall, *History of the Near East*).

## New International Version

Dishan. These were the Horite chiefs, according to their divisions, in the land of Seir.

### The Rulers of Edom

[31]These were the kings who reigned in Edom before any Israelite king reigned:
[32]Bela son of Beor became king of Edom. His city was named Dinhabah.
[33]When Bela died, Jobab son of Zerah from Bozrah succeeded him as king.
[34]When Jobab died, Husham from the land of the Temanites succeeded him as king.
[35]When Husham died, Hadad son of Bedad, who defeated Midian in the country of Moab, succeeded him as king. His city was named Avith.
[36]When Hadad died, Samlah from Masrekah succeeded him as king.
[37]When Samlah died, Shaul from Rehoboth on the river succeeded him as king.
[38]When Shaul died, Baal-Hanan son of Akbor succeeded him as king.
[39]When Baal-Hanan son of Akbor died, Hadad[a] succeeded him as king. His city was named Pau, and his wife's name was Mehetabel daughter of Matred, the daughter of Me-Zahab.

[40]These were the chiefs descended from Esau, by name, according to their clans and regions:
Timna, Alvah, Jetheth, [41]Oholibamah, Elah, Pinon, [42]Kenaz, Teman, Mibzar, [43]Magdiel and Iram. These were the chiefs of Edom, according to their settlements in the land they occupied.

This is the family line of Esau, the father of the Edomites.

### Joseph's Dreams

**37** Jacob lived in the land where his father had stayed, the land of Canaan.

[2]This is the account of Jacob's family line.

Joseph, a young man of seventeen, was tending the flocks with his brothers, the sons of Bilhah and the sons of Zilpah, his father's wives, and he brought their father a bad report about them.
[3]Now Israel loved Joseph more than any of his other sons, because he had been born to him in his old age; and he made an ornate[b] robe for him. [4]When his brothers saw that their father loved him more than any of them, they hated him and could not speak a kind word to him.
[5]Joseph had a dream, and when he told it to his brothers, they hated him all the more. [6]He said to them, "Listen to this dream I had: [7]We were binding sheaves of grain out in the field when suddenly my sheaf rose and stood upright, while your sheaves gathered around mine and bowed down to it."
[8]His brothers said to him, "Do you intend to reign over us? Will you actually rule us?" And they hated him all the more because of his dream and what he had said.
[9]Then he had another dream, and he told it to his brothers. "Listen," he said, "I had another dream, and this time the sun and moon and eleven stars were bowing down to me."
[10]When he told his father as well as his brothers, his father rebuked him and said, "What is this dream you had?

## Amplified Bible

[30]Dishon, Ezer, Dishan. These are the Horite chiefs, according to their clans, in the land of Seir.
[31]And these are the kings who reigned in Edom before any king reigned over the Israelites:
[32]Bela son of Beor reigned in Edom. And the name of his city was Dinhabah.
[33]Now Bela died, and Jobab son of Zerah of Bozrah reigned in his stead.
[34]Then Jobab died, and Husham of the land of the Temanites reigned in his stead.
[35]And Husham died, and Hadad son of Bedad, who defeated Midian in the country of Moab, reigned in his stead. The name of his [enclosed] city was Avith.
[36]Hadad died, and Samlah of Masrekah succeeded him.
[37]Then Samlah died, and Shaul of Rehoboth on the river [Euphrates] reigned in his stead.
[38]And Shaul died, and Baal-hanan son of Achbor reigned in his stead.
[39]Baal-hanan son of Achbor died, and then Hadar reigned. His [enclosed] city was Pau; his wife's name was Mehetabel daughter of Matred, the daughter of Mezahab.
[40]And these are the names of the chiefs of Esau, according to their families and places of residence, by their names: Chiefs Timna, Alvah, Jetheth,
[41]Oholibamah, Elah, Pinon,
[42]Kenaz, Teman, Mibzar,
[43]Magdiel, and Iram. These are the chiefs of Edom [that is, of Esau the father of the Edomites], according to their dwelling places in their land.

**37** So Jacob dwelt in the land in which his father had been a stranger *and* sojourner, in the land of Canaan.
[2]This is the history of the descendants of Jacob *and* this is Jacob's line. Joseph, when he was seventeen years old, was shepherding the flock with his brothers; the lad was with the sons of Bilhah and Zilpah, his father's [secondary] wives; and Joseph brought to his father a bad report of them.
[3]Now Israel loved Joseph more than all his children because he was the son of his old age, and he made him a [distinctive] long tunic with sleeves.
[4]But when his brothers saw that their father loved [Joseph] more than all of his brothers, they hated him and could not say, Peace [in friendly greeting] to him *or* speak peaceably to him.
[5]Now Joseph had a dream and he told it to his brothers, and they hated him still more.
[6]And he said to them, Listen now *and* hear, I pray you, this dream that I have dreamed:
[7]We [brothers] were binding sheaves in the field, and behold, my sheaf arose and stood upright, and behold, your sheaves stood round about my sheaf and bowed down!
[8]His brothers said to him, Shall you indeed reign over us? Or are you going to have us as your subjects *and* dominate us? And they hated him all the more for his dreams and for what he said.
[9]But Joseph dreamed yet another dream and told it to his brothers [also]. He said, See here, I have dreamed again, and behold, [this time not only] eleven stars [but also] the sun and the moon bowed down *and* did reverence to me!
[10]And he told it to his father [as well as] his brethren. But his father rebuked him and said to him, What is the meaning of this dream that you have dreamed? Shall I and

*a 39* Many manuscripts of the Masoretic Text, Samaritan Pentateuch and Syriac (see also 1 Chron. 1:50); most manuscripts of the Masoretic Text *Hadar*    *b 3* The meaning of the Hebrew for this word is uncertain; also in verses 23 and 32.

## New International Version

Will your mother and I and your brothers actually come and bow down to the ground before you?" [11]His brothers were jealous of him, but his father kept the matter in mind.

### Joseph Sold by His Brothers
[12]Now his brothers had gone to graze their father's flocks near Shechem, [13]and Israel said to Joseph, "As you know, your brothers are grazing the flocks near Shechem. Come, I am going to send you to them."

"Very well," he replied.

[14]So he said to him, "Go and see if all is well with your brothers and with the flocks, and bring word back to me." Then he sent him off from the Valley of Hebron.

When Joseph arrived at Shechem, [15]a man found him wandering around in the fields and asked him, "What are you looking for?"

[16]He replied, "I'm looking for my brothers. Can you tell me where they are grazing their flocks?"

[17]"They have moved on from here," the man answered. "I heard them say, 'Let's go to Dothan.'"

So Joseph went after his brothers and found them near Dothan. [18]But they saw him in the distance, and before he reached them, they plotted to kill him.

[19]"Here comes that dreamer!" they said to each other. [20]"Come now, let's kill him and throw him into one of these cisterns and say that a ferocious animal devoured him. Then we'll see what comes of his dreams."

[21]When Reuben heard this, he tried to rescue him from their hands. "Let's not take his life," he said. [22]"Don't shed any blood. Throw him into this cistern here in the wilderness, but don't lay a hand on him." Reuben said this to rescue him from them and take him back to his father.

[23]So when Joseph came to his brothers, they stripped him of his robe—the ornate robe he was wearing— [24]and they took him and threw him into the cistern. The cistern was empty; there was no water in it.

[25]As they sat down to eat their meal, they looked up and saw a caravan of Ishmaelites coming from Gilead. Their camels were loaded with spices, balm and myrrh, and they were on their way to take them down to Egypt.

[26]Judah said to his brothers, "What will we gain if we kill our brother and cover up his blood? [27]Come, let's sell him to the Ishmaelites and not lay our hands on him; after all, he is our brother, our own flesh and blood." His brothers agreed.

[28]So when the Midianite merchants came by, his brothers pulled Joseph up out of the cistern and sold him for twenty shekels[a] of silver to the Ishmaelites, who took him to Egypt.

[29]When Reuben returned to the cistern and saw that Joseph was not there, he tore his clothes. [30]He went back to his brothers and said, "The boy isn't there! Where can I turn now?"

[31]Then they got Joseph's robe, slaughtered a goat and dipped the robe in the blood. [32]They took the ornate robe back to their father and said, "We found this. Examine it to see whether it is your son's robe."

[33]He recognized it and said, "It is my son's robe! Some ferocious animal has devoured him. Joseph has surely been torn to pieces."

[34]Then Jacob tore his clothes, put on sackcloth and mourned for his son many days. [35]All his sons and daugh-

## Amplified Bible

your mother and your brothers actually come to bow down ourselves to the earth *and* do homage to you?

[11]Joseph's brothers envied him *and* were jealous of him, but his father observed the saying *and* pondered over it.

[12]Joseph's brothers went to shepherd *and* feed their father's flock near Shechem.

[13][One day] Israel said to Joseph, Do not your brothers shepherd my flock at Shechem? Come, and I will send you to them. And he said, Here I am.

[14]And [Jacob] said to him, Go, I pray you, see whether everything is all right with your brothers and with the flock; then come back and bring me word. So he sent him out of the Hebron Valley, and he came to Shechem.

[15]And a certain man found him, and behold, he had lost his way *and* was wandering in the open country. The man asked him, What are you trying to find?

[16]And he said, I am looking for my brothers. Tell me, I pray you, where they are pasturing our flocks.

[17]But the man said, [They were here, but] they have gone. I heard them say, Let us go to Dothan. And Joseph went after his brothers and found them at Dothan.

[18]And when they saw him far off, even before he came near to them, they conspired to kill him.

[19]And they said one to another, See, here comes this dreamer *and* master of dreams.

[20]So come on now, let us kill him and throw his body into some pit; then we will say [to our father], Some wild *and* ferocious animal has devoured him; and we shall see what will become of his dreams!

[21]Now Reuben heard it and he delivered him out of their hands by saying, Let us not kill him.

[22]And Reuben said to them, Shed no blood, but cast him into this pit *or* well that is out here in the wilderness and lay no hand on him. He was trying to get Joseph out of their hands in order to rescue him *and* deliver him again to his father.

[23]When Joseph had come to his brothers, they stripped him of his [distinctive] long garment which he was wearing;

[24]Then they took him and cast him into the [well-like] pit which was empty; there was no water in it.

[25]Then they sat down to eat their lunch. When they looked up, behold, they saw a caravan of Ishmaelites [mixed Arabians] coming from Gilead, with their camels bearing gum [of the styrax tree], balm (balsam), and myrrh *or* ladanum, going on their way to carry them down to Egypt.

[26]And Judah said to his brothers, What do we gain if we slay our brother and conceal his blood?

[27]Come, let us sell him to the Ishmaelites [and Midianites, these mixed Arabians who are approaching], and let not our hand be upon him, for he is our brother and our flesh. And his brothers consented.

[28]Then as the Midianite [and Ishmaelite] merchants were passing by, the brothers pulled Joseph up and lifted him out of the well. And they sold him for twenty pieces of silver to the Ishmaelites, who took Joseph [captive] into Egypt.

[29]Then Reuben [who had not been there when the brothers plotted to sell the lad] returned to the pit; and behold, Joseph was not in the pit, and he rent his clothes.

[30]He rejoined his brothers and said, The boy is not there! And I, where shall I go [to hide from my father]?

[31]Then they took Joseph's [distinctive] long garment, killed a young goat, and dipped the garment in the blood;

[32]And they sent the garment to their father, saying, We have found this! Examine *and* decide whether it is your son's tunic or not.

[33]He said, My son's long garment! An evil [wild] beast has devoured him; Joseph is without doubt rent in pieces.

[34]And Jacob tore his clothes, put on sackcloth, and mourned many days for his son.

a 28 That is, about 8 ounces or about 230 grams

## New International Version

ters came to comfort him, but he refused to be comforted. "No," he said, "I will continue to mourn until I join my son in the grave." So his father wept for him.

³⁶Meanwhile, the Midianites[a] sold Joseph in Egypt to Potiphar, one of Pharaoh's officials, the captain of the guard.

### Judah and Tamar

**38** At that time, Judah left his brothers and went down to stay with a man of Adullam named Hirah. ²There Judah met the daughter of a Canaanite man named Shua. He married her and made love to her; ³she became pregnant and gave birth to a son, who was named Er. ⁴She conceived again and gave birth to a son and named him Onan. ⁵She gave birth to still another son and named him Shelah. It was at Kezib that she gave birth to him.

⁶Judah got a wife for Er, his firstborn, and her name was Tamar. ⁷But Er, Judah's firstborn, was wicked in the LORD's sight; so the LORD put him to death. ⁸Then Judah said to Onan, "Sleep with your brother's wife and fulfill your duty to her as a brother-in-law to raise up offspring for your brother." ⁹But Onan knew that the child would not be his; so whenever he slept with his brother's wife, he spilled his semen on the ground to keep from providing offspring for his brother. ¹⁰What he did was wicked in the LORD's sight; so the LORD put him to death also.

¹¹Judah then said to his daughter-in-law Tamar, "Live as a widow in your father's household until my son Shelah grows up." For he thought, "He may die too, just like his brothers." So Tamar went to live in her father's household.

¹²After a long time Judah's wife, the daughter of Shua, died. When Judah had recovered from his grief, he went up to Timnah, to the men who were shearing his sheep, and his friend Hirah the Adullamite went with him. ¹³When Tamar was told, "Your father-in-law is on his way to Timnah to shear his sheep," ¹⁴she took off her widow's clothes, covered herself with a veil to disguise herself, and then sat down at the entrance to Enaim, which is on the road to Timnah. For she saw that, though Shelah had now grown up, she had not been given to him as his wife.

¹⁵When Judah saw her, he thought she was a prostitute, for she had covered her face. ¹⁶Not realizing that she was his daughter-in-law, he went over to her by the roadside and said, "Come now, let me sleep with you."

"And what will you give me to sleep with you?" she asked.

¹⁷"I'll send you a young goat from my flock," he said.

"Will you give me something as a pledge until you send it?" she asked.

¹⁸He said, "What pledge should I give you?"

"Your seal and its cord, and the staff in your hand," she answered. So he gave them to her and slept with her, and she became pregnant by him. ¹⁹After she left, she took off her veil and put on her widow's clothes again.

²⁰Meanwhile Judah sent the young goat by his friend the Adullamite in order to get his pledge back from the woman, but he did not find her. ²¹He asked the men who lived there, "Where is the shrine prostitute who was beside the road at Enaim?"

"There hasn't been any shrine prostitute here," they said.

²²So he went back to Judah and said, "I didn't find her. Besides, the men who lived there said, 'There hasn't been any shrine prostitute here.'"

## Amplified Bible

³⁵And all his sons and daughters attempted to console him, but he refused to be comforted and said, I will go down to Sheol (the place of the dead) to my son mourning. And his father wept for him.

³⁶And the Midianites [and Ishmaelites] sold [Joseph] in Egypt to Potiphar, an officer of Pharaoh and the captain *and* chief executioner of the [royal] guard.

**38** At that time Judah withdrew from his brothers and went to [lodge with] a certain Adullamite named Hirah.

²There Judah saw *and* met a daughter of Shuah, a Canaanite; he took her as wife and lived with her.

³And she became pregnant and bore a son, and he called him Er.

⁴And she conceived again and bore a son and named him Onan.

⁵Again she conceived and bore a son and named him Shelah. [They were living] at Chezib when she bore him.

⁶Now Judah took a wife for Er, his firstborn; her name was Tamar.

⁷And Er, Judah's firstborn, was wicked in the sight of the Lord, and the Lord slew him.

⁸Then Judah told Onan, Marry your brother's widow; live with her and raise offspring for your brother.

⁹But Onan knew that the family would not be his, so when he cohabited with his brother's widow, he prevented conception, lest he should raise up a child for his brother.

¹⁰And the thing which he did displeased the Lord; therefore He slew him also.

¹¹Then Judah said to Tamar, his daughter-in-law, Remain a widow at your father's house till Shelah my [youngest] son is grown; for he thought, Lest perhaps [if Shelah should marry her] he would die also, as his brothers did. So Tamar went and lived in her father's house.

¹²But later Judah's wife, the daughter of Shuah, died; and when Judah was comforted, he went up to his sheepshearers at Timnath with his friend Hirah the Adullamite.

¹³Then it was told Tamar, Listen, your father-in-law is going up to Timnath to shear his sheep.

¹⁴So she put off her widow's garments and covered herself with a veil, wrapped herself up [in disguise], and sat in the entrance of Enaim, which is by the road to Timnath; for she saw that Shelah was grown and she was not given to him as his wife.

¹⁵When Judah saw her, he thought she was a harlot *or* devoted prostitute [under a vow to her goddess], for she had covered her face [as such women did].

¹⁶He turned to her by the road and said, Come, let me have intercourse with you; for he did not know that she was his daughter-in-law. And she said, What will you give me that you may have intercourse with me?

¹⁷He answered, I will send you a kid from the flock. And she said, Will you give me a pledge (deposit) until you send it?

¹⁸And he said, What pledge shall I give you? She said, Your signet [seal], your [signet] cord, and your staff that is in your hand. And he gave them to her and came in to her, and she became pregnant by him.

¹⁹And she arose and went away and laid aside her veil and put on the garments of her widowhood.

²⁰And Judah sent the kid by the hand of his friend the Adullamite, to receive his pledge from the woman's hand; but he was unable to find her.

²¹He asked the men of that place, Where is the harlot *or* cult prostitute who was openly by the roadside? They said, There was no harlot *or* temple prostitute here.

²²So he returned to Judah and said, I cannot find her; and also the local men said, There was no harlot *or* temple prostitute around here.

---

*a 36* Samaritan Pentateuch, Septuagint, Vulgate and Syriac (see also verse 28); Masoretic Text *Medanites*

## New International Version

²³Then Judah said, "Let her keep what she has, or we will become a laughingstock. After all, I did send her this young goat, but you didn't find her."

²⁴About three months later Judah was told, "Your daughter-in-law Tamar is guilty of prostitution, and as a result she is now pregnant."

Judah said, "Bring her out and have her burned to death!"

²⁵As she was being brought out, she sent a message to her father-in-law. "I am pregnant by the man who owns these," she said. And she added, "See if you recognize whose seal and cord and staff these are."

²⁶Judah recognized them and said, "She is more righteous than I, since I wouldn't give her to my son Shelah." And he did not sleep with her again.

²⁷When the time came for her to give birth, there were twin boys in her womb. ²⁸As she was giving birth, one of them put out his hand; so the midwife took a scarlet thread and tied it on his wrist and said, "This one came out first." ²⁹But when he drew back his hand, his brother came out, and she said, "So this is how you have broken out!" And he was named Perez.ᵃ ³⁰Then his brother, who had the scarlet thread on his wrist, came out. And he was named Zerah.ᵇ

### Joseph and Potiphar's Wife

**39** Now Joseph had been taken down to Egypt. Potiphar, an Egyptian who was one of Pharaoh's officials, the captain of the guard, bought him from the Ishmaelites who had taken him there.

²The LORD was with Joseph so that he prospered, and he lived in the house of his Egyptian master. ³When his master saw that the LORD was with him and that the LORD gave him success in everything he did, ⁴Joseph found favor in his eyes and became his attendant. Potiphar put him in charge of his household, and he entrusted to his care everything he owned. ⁵From the time he put him in charge of his household and of all that he owned, the LORD blessed the household of the Egyptian because of Joseph. The blessing of the LORD was on everything Potiphar had, both in the house and in the field. ⁶So Potiphar left everything he had in Joseph's care; with Joseph in charge, he did not concern himself with anything except the food he ate.

Now Joseph was well-built and handsome, ⁷and after a while his master's wife took notice of Joseph and said, "Come to bed with me!"

⁸But he refused. "With me in charge," he told her, "my master does not concern himself with anything in the house; everything he owns he has entrusted to my care. ⁹No one is greater in this house than I am. My master has withheld nothing from me except you, because you are his wife. How then could I do such a wicked thing and sin against God?" ¹⁰And though she spoke to Joseph day after day, he refused to go to bed with her or even be with her.

¹¹One day he went into the house to attend to his duties, and none of the household servants was inside. ¹²She caught him by his cloak and said, "Come to bed with me!" But he left his cloak in her hand and ran out of the house.

¹³When she saw that he had left his cloak in her hand and had run out of the house, ¹⁴she called her household

## Amplified Bible

²³And Judah said, Let her keep [the pledge articles] for herself, lest we be made ashamed. I sent this kid, but you have not found her.

²⁴But about three months later Judah was told, Tamar your daughter-in-law has played the harlot, and also she is with child by her lewdness. And Judah said, Bring her forth and let her be burned!

²⁵When she was brought forth, she [took the things he had given her in pledge and] sent [them] to her father-in-law, saying, I am with child by the man to whom these articles belong. Then she added, Make out clearly, I pray you, to whom these belong, the signet [seal], [signet] cord, and staff.

²⁶And Judah acknowledged them and said, She has been more righteous *and* just than I, because I did not give her to Shelah my son. And he did not cohabit with her again.

²⁷Now when the time came for her to be delivered, behold, there were twins in her womb.

²⁸And when she was in labor, one baby put out his hand; and the midwife took his hand and bound upon it a scarlet thread, saying, This baby was born first.

²⁹But he drew back his hand, and behold, his brother was born first. And she said, What a breaking forth you have made for yourself! Therefore his name was called Perez [breaking forth]. [Matt. 1:3.]

³⁰And afterward his brother who had the scarlet thread on his hand was born and was named Zerah [scarlet].

**39** And Joseph was brought down to Egypt; and Potiphar, an officer of Pharaoh, the captain *and* chief executioner of the [royal] guard, an Egyptian, bought him from the Ishmaelites who had brought him down there.

²But the Lord was with Joseph, and he [though a slave] was a successful *and* prosperous man; and he was in the house of his master the Egyptian.

³And his master saw that the Lord was with him and that the Lord made all that he did to flourish *and* succeed in his hand. [Gen. 21:22; 26:27, 28; 41:38, 39.]

⁴So Joseph pleased [Potiphar] *and* found favor in his sight, and he served him. And [his master] made him supervisor over his house and he put all that he had in his charge.

⁵From the time that he made him supervisor in his house and over all that he had, the Lord blessed the Egyptian's house for Joseph's sake; and the Lord's blessing was on all that he had in the house and in the field.

⁶And [Potiphar] left all that he had in Joseph's charge and paid no attention to anything he had except the food he ate. Now Joseph was an attractive person and fine-looking.

⁷Then after a time his master's wife cast her eyes upon Joseph, and she said, Lie with me.

⁸But he refused and said to his master's wife, See here, with me in the house my master has concern about nothing; he has put all that he has in my care.

⁹He is not greater in this house than I am; nor has he kept anything from me except you, for you are his wife. How then can I do this great evil and sin against God?

¹⁰She spoke to Joseph day after day, but he did not listen to her, to lie with her or to be with her.

¹¹Then it happened about this time that Joseph went into the house to attend to his duties, and none of the men of the house were indoors.

¹²And she caught him by his garment, saying, Lie with me! But he left his garment in her hand and fled and got out [of the house].

¹³And when she saw that he had left his garment in her hand and had fled away,

---

ᵃ 29 *Perez* means *breaking out.*   ᵇ 30 *Zerah* can mean *scarlet* or *brightness.*

## New International Version

servants. "Look," she said to them, "this Hebrew has been brought to us to make sport of us! He came in here to sleep with me, but I screamed. ¹⁵When he heard me scream for help, he left his cloak beside me and ran out of the house."

¹⁶She kept his cloak beside her until his master came home. ¹⁷Then she told him this story: "That Hebrew slave you brought us came to me to make sport of me. ¹⁸But as soon as I screamed for help, he left his cloak beside me and ran out of the house."

¹⁹When his master heard the story his wife told him, saying, "This is how your slave treated me," he burned with anger. ²⁰Joseph's master took him and put him in prison, the place where the king's prisoners were confined.

But while Joseph was there in the prison, ²¹the LORD was with him; he showed him kindness and granted him favor in the eyes of the prison warden. ²²So the warden put Joseph in charge of all those held in the prison, and he was made responsible for all that was done there. ²³The warden paid no attention to anything under Joseph's care, because the LORD was with Joseph and gave him success in whatever he did.

### The Cupbearer and the Baker

**40** Some time later, the cupbearer and the baker of the king of Egypt offended their master, the king of Egypt. ²Pharaoh was angry with his two officials, the chief cupbearer and the chief baker, ³and put them in custody in the house of the captain of the guard, in the same prison where Joseph was confined. ⁴The captain of the guard assigned them to Joseph, and he attended them.

After they had been in custody for some time, ⁵each of the two men—the cupbearer and the baker of the king of Egypt, who were being held in prison—had a dream the same night, and each dream had a meaning of its own.

⁶When Joseph came to them the next morning, he saw that they were dejected. ⁷So he asked Pharaoh's officials who were in custody with him in his master's house, "Why do you look so sad today?"

⁸"We both had dreams," they answered, "but there is no one to interpret them."

Then Joseph said to them, "Do not interpretations belong to God? Tell me your dreams."

⁹So the chief cupbearer told Joseph his dream. He said to him, "In my dream I saw a vine in front of me, ¹⁰and on the vine were three branches. As soon as it budded, it blossomed, and its clusters ripened into grapes. ¹¹Pharaoh's cup was in my hand, and I took the grapes, squeezed them into Pharaoh's cup and put the cup in his hand."

¹²"This is what it means," Joseph said to him. "The three branches are three days. ¹³Within three days Pharaoh will lift up your head and restore you to your position, and you will put Pharaoh's cup in his hand, just as you used to do when you were his cupbearer. ¹⁴But when all goes well with you, remember me and show me kindness; mention me to Pharaoh and get me out of this prison. ¹⁵I

## Amplified Bible

¹⁴She called to the men of her household and said to them, Behold, he [your master] has brought in a Hebrew to us to mock *and* insult us; he came in where I was to lie with me, and I screamed at the top of my voice.

¹⁵And when he heard me screaming and crying, he left his garment with me and fled and got out of the house.

¹⁶And she laid up his garment by her until his master came home.

¹⁷Then she told him the same story, saying, The Hebrew servant whom you brought among us came to me to mock *and* insult me.

¹⁸And when I screamed and cried, he left his garment with me and fled out [of the house].

¹⁹And when [Joseph's] master heard the words of his wife, saying to him, This is the way your servant treated me, his wrath was kindled.

²⁰And Joseph's master took him and put him in the prison, a place where the state prisoners were confined; so he was there in the prison.

²¹But the Lord was with Joseph, and showed him mercy *and* loving-kindness and gave him favor in the sight of the warden of the prison.

²²And the warden of the prison committed to Joseph's care all the prisoners who were in the prison; and whatsoever was done there, he was in charge of it.

²³The prison warden paid no attention to anything that was in [Joseph's] charge, for the Lord was with him and made whatever he did to prosper.

**40** Now some time later the butler and the baker of the king of Egypt offended their lord, Egypt's king.

²And Pharaoh was angry with his officers, the chief of the butlers and the chief of the bakers.

³He put them in custody in the house of the captain of the guard, in the prison where Joseph was confined.

⁴And the captain of the guard put them in Joseph's charge, and he served them; and they continued in custody for some time.

⁵And they both dreamed a dream in the same night, each man according to [the personal significance of] the interpretation of his dream—the butler and the baker of the king of Egypt, who were confined in the prison.

⁶When Joseph came to them in the morning and looked at them, he saw that they were sad *and* depressed.

⁷So he asked Pharaoh's officers who were in custody with him in his master's house, Why do you look so dejected *and* sad today?

⁸And they said to him, We have dreamed dreams, and there is no one to interpret them. And Joseph said to them, Do not interpretations belong to God? Tell me [your dreams], I pray you.

⁹And the chief butler told his dream to Joseph and said to him, In my dream I saw a vine before me,

¹⁰And on the vine were three branches. Then it was as though it budded; its blossoms burst forth and the clusters of them brought forth ripe grapes [almost all at once].

¹¹And Pharaoh's cup was in my hand, and I took the grapes and pressed them into Pharaoh's cup; then I gave the cup into Pharaoh's hand.

¹²And Joseph said to him, This is the interpretation of it: The three branches are three days.

¹³Within three days Pharaoh will lift up your head and restore you to your position, and you will again put Pharaoh's cup into his hand, as when you were his butler.

¹⁴But think of me when it shall be well with you and show kindness, I beg of you, to me, and mention me to Pharaoh and get me out of this house.

## New International Version

was forcibly carried off from the land of the Hebrews, and even here I have done nothing to deserve being put in a dungeon."

[16]When the chief baker saw that Joseph had given a favorable interpretation, he said to Joseph, "I too had a dream: On my head were three baskets of bread.[a] [17]In the top basket were all kinds of baked goods for Pharaoh, but the birds were eating them out of the basket on my head."

[18]"This is what it means," Joseph said. "The three baskets are three days. [19]Within three days Pharaoh will lift off your head and impale your body on a pole. And the birds will eat away your flesh."

[20]Now the third day was Pharaoh's birthday, and he gave a feast for all his officials. He lifted up the heads of the chief cupbearer and the chief baker in the presence of his officials: [21]He restored the chief cupbearer to his position, so that he once again put the cup into Pharaoh's hand— [22]but he impaled the chief baker, just as Joseph had said to them in his interpretation.

[23]The chief cupbearer, however, did not remember Joseph; he forgot him.

### Pharaoh's Dreams

**41** When two full years had passed, Pharaoh had a dream: He was standing by the Nile, [2]when out of the river there came up seven cows, sleek and fat, and they grazed among the reeds. [3]After them, seven other cows, ugly and gaunt, came up out of the Nile and stood beside those on the riverbank. [4]And the cows that were ugly and gaunt ate up the seven sleek, fat cows. Then Pharaoh woke up.

[5]He fell asleep again and had a second dream: Seven heads of grain, healthy and good, were growing on a single stalk. [6]After them, seven other heads of grain sprouted—thin and scorched by the east wind. [7]The thin heads of grain swallowed up the seven healthy, full heads. Then Pharaoh woke up; it had been a dream.

[8]In the morning his mind was troubled, so he sent for all the magicians and wise men of Egypt. Pharaoh told them his dreams, but no one could interpret them for him.

[9]Then the chief cupbearer said to Pharaoh, "Today I am reminded of my shortcomings. [10]Pharaoh was once angry with his servants, and he imprisoned me and the chief baker in the house of the captain of the guard. [11]Each of us had a dream the same night, and each dream had a meaning of its own. [12]Now a young Hebrew was there with us, a servant of the captain of the guard. We told him our dreams, and he interpreted them for us, giving each man the interpretation of his dream. [13]And things turned out exactly as he interpreted them to us: I was restored to my position, and the other man was impaled."

[14]So Pharaoh sent for Joseph, and he was quickly brought from the dungeon. When he had shaved and changed his clothes, he came before Pharaoh.

[15]Pharaoh said to Joseph, "I had a dream, and no one can interpret it. But I have heard it said of you that when you hear a dream you can interpret it."

## Amplified Bible

[15]For truly I was carried away from the land of the Hebrews by unlawful force, and here too I have done nothing for which they should put me into the dungeon.

[16]When the chief baker saw that the interpretation was good, he said to Joseph, I also dreamed, and behold, I had three cake baskets on my head.

[17]And in the uppermost basket were some of all kinds of baked food for Pharaoh, but the birds [of prey] were eating out of the basket on my head.

[18]And Joseph answered, This is the interpretation of it: The three baskets are three days.

[19]Within three days Pharaoh will lift up your head but will have you beheaded and hung on a tree, and [you will not so much as be given burial, but] the birds will eat your flesh.

[20]And on the third day, Pharaoh's birthday, he made a feast for all his servants; and he lifted up the heads of the chief butler and the chief baker [by inviting them also] among his servants.

[21]And he restored the chief butler to his butlership, and the butler gave the cup into Pharaoh's hand;

[22]But [Pharaoh] hanged the chief baker, as Joseph had interpreted to them.

[23]But [even after all that] the chief butler gave no thought to Joseph, but forgot [all about] him.

**41** After two full years, Pharaoh dreamed that he stood by the river [Nile].

[2]And behold, there came up out of the river [Nile] seven well-favored cows, sleek and handsome and fat; and they grazed in the reed grass [in a marshy pasture].

[3]And behold, seven other cows came up after them out of the river [Nile], ill favored and gaunt and ugly, and stood by the fat cows on the bank of the river [Nile].

[4]And the ill-favored, gaunt, and ugly cows ate up the seven well-favored and fat cows. Then Pharaoh awoke.

[5]But he slept and dreamed the second time; and behold, seven ears of grain came out on one stalk, plump and good.

[6]And behold, after them seven ears [of grain] sprouted, thin and blighted by the east wind.

[7]And the seven thin ears [of grain] devoured the seven plump and full ears. And Pharaoh awoke, and behold, it was a dream.

[8]So when morning came his spirit was troubled, and he sent and called for all the magicians and all the wise men of Egypt. And Pharaoh told them his dreams, but not one could interpret them to [him].

[9]Then the chief butler said to Pharaoh, I remember my faults today.

[10]When Pharaoh was angry with his servants and put me in custody in the captain of the guard's house, both me and the chief baker,

[11]We dreamed a dream in the same night, he and I; we dreamed each of us according to [the significance of] interpretation of his dream.

[12]And there was there with us a young man, a Hebrew, servant to the captain of the guard and chief executioner; and we told him our dreams, and he interpreted them to us, to each man according to the significance of his dream.

[13]And as he interpreted to us, so it came to pass; I was restored to my office [as chief butler], and the baker was hanged.

[14]Then Pharaoh sent and called Joseph, and they brought him hastily out of the dungeon. But Joseph [first] shaved himself, changed his clothes, and made himself presentable; then he came into Pharaoh's presence.

[15]And Pharaoh said to Joseph, I have dreamed a dream, and there is no one who can interpret it; and I have heard it said of you that you can understand a dream and interpret it.

[a] 16 Or three wicker baskets

## New International Version

16"I cannot do it," Joseph replied to Pharaoh, "but God will give Pharaoh the answer he desires."

17Then Pharaoh said to Joseph, "In my dream I was standing on the bank of the Nile, 18when out of the river there came up seven cows, fat and sleek, and they grazed among the reeds. 19After them, seven other cows came up—scrawny and very ugly and lean. I had never seen such ugly cows in all the land of Egypt. 20The lean, ugly cows ate up the seven fat cows that came up first. 21But even after they ate them, no one could tell that they had done so; they looked just as ugly as before. Then I woke up.

22"In my dream I saw seven heads of grain, full and good, growing on a single stalk. 23After them, seven other heads sprouted—withered and thin and scorched by the east wind. 24The thin heads of grain swallowed up the seven good heads. I told this to the magicians, but none of them could explain it to me."

25Then Joseph said to Pharaoh, "The dreams of Pharaoh are one and the same. God has revealed to Pharaoh what he is about to do. 26The seven good cows are seven years, and the seven good heads of grain are seven years; it is one and the same dream. 27The seven lean, ugly cows that came up afterward are seven years, and so are the seven worthless heads of grain scorched by the east wind: They are seven years of famine.

28"It is just as I said to Pharaoh: God has shown Pharaoh what he is about to do. 29Seven years of great abundance are coming throughout the land of Egypt, 30but seven years of famine will follow them. Then all the abundance in Egypt will be forgotten, and the famine will ravage the land. 31The abundance in the land will not be remembered, because the famine that follows it will be so severe. 32The reason the dream was given to Pharaoh in two forms is that the matter has been firmly decided by God, and God will do it soon.

33"And now let Pharaoh look for a discerning and wise man and put him in charge of the land of Egypt. 34Let Pharaoh appoint commissioners over the land to take a fifth of the harvest of Egypt during the seven years of abundance. 35They should collect all the food of these good years that are coming and store up the grain under the authority of Pharaoh, to be kept in the cities for food. 36This food should be held in reserve for the country, to be used during the seven years of famine that will come upon Egypt, so that the country may not be ruined by the famine."

37The plan seemed good to Pharaoh and to all his officials. 38So Pharaoh asked them, "Can we find anyone like this man, one in whom is the spirit of God*a*?" 39Then Pharaoh said to Joseph, "Since God has made all this known to you, there is no one so discerning and wise as you. 40You shall be in charge of my palace, and all my

*a 38 Or of the gods*

## Amplified Bible

16Joseph answered Pharaoh, It is not in me; God [not I] will give Pharaoh a [favorable] answer of peace.

17And Pharaoh said to Joseph, In my dream, behold, I stood on the bank of the river [Nile];

18And behold, there came up out of the river [Nile] seven fat, sleek, *and* handsome cows, and they grazed in the reed grass [of a marshy pasture].

19And behold, seven other cows came up after them, undernourished, gaunt, *and* ugly [just skin and bones; such emaciated animals] as I have never seen in all of Egypt.

20And the lean and ill favored cows ate up the seven fat cows that had come first.

21And when they had eaten them up, it could not be detected *and* known that they had eaten them, for they were still as thin *and* emaciated as at the beginning. Then I awoke. [But again I fell asleep and dreamed.]

22And I saw in my dream, and behold, seven ears [of grain] growing on one stalk, plump and good.

23And behold, seven [other] ears, withered, thin, and blighted by the east wind, sprouted after them.

24And the thin ears devoured the seven good ears. Now I told this to the magicians, but there was no one who could tell me what it meant.

25Then Joseph said to Pharaoh, The [two] dreams are one; God has shown Pharaoh what He is about to do.

26The seven good cows are seven years, and the seven good ears [of grain] are seven years; the [two] dreams are one [in their meaning].

27And the seven thin and ill favored cows that came up after them are seven years, and also the seven empty ears [of grain], blighted *and* shriveled by the east wind; they are seven years of hunger *and* famine.

28This is the message just as I have told Pharaoh: God has shown Pharaoh what He is about to do.

29Take note! Seven years of great plenty throughout all the land of Egypt are coming.

30Then there will come seven years of hunger *and* famine, and [there will be so much want that] all the great abundance of the previous years will be forgotten in the land of Egypt; and hunger (destitution, starvation) will exhaust (consume, finish) the land.

31And the plenty will become quite unknown in the land because of that following famine, for it will be very woefully severe.

32That the dream was sent twice to Pharaoh *and* in two forms indicates that this thing which God will very soon bring to pass is fully prepared *and* established by God.

33So now let Pharaoh seek out *and* provide a man discreet, understanding, proficient, *and* wise and set him over the land of Egypt [as governor].

34Let Pharaoh do this; then let him select and appoint officers over the land, and take one-fifth [of the produce] of the [whole] land of Egypt in the seven plenteous years [year by year].

35And let them gather all the food of these good years that are coming and lay up grain under the direction *and* authority of Pharaoh, and let them retain food [in fortified granaries] in the cities.

36And that food shall be put in store for the country against the seven years of hunger *and* famine that are to come upon the land of Egypt, so that the land may not be ruined *and* cut off by the famine.

37And the plan seemed good in the eyes of Pharaoh and in the eyes of all his servants.

38And Pharaoh said to his servants, Can we find this man's equal, a man in whom is the spirit of God?

39And Pharaoh said to Joseph, Forasmuch as [your] God has shown you all this, there is nobody as intelligent *and* discreet *and* understanding and wise as you are.

40You shall have charge over my house, and all my people shall be governed according to your word [with rever-

## New International Version

people are to submit to your orders. Only with respect to the throne will I be greater than you."

### Joseph in Charge of Egypt

⁴¹So Pharaoh said to Joseph, "I hereby put you in charge of the whole land of Egypt." ⁴²Then Pharaoh took his signet ring from his finger and put it on Joseph's finger. He dressed him in robes of fine linen and put a gold chain around his neck. ⁴³He had him ride in a chariot as his second-in-command,ᵃ and people shouted before him, "Make wayᵇ!" Thus he put him in charge of the whole land of Egypt.

⁴⁴Then Pharaoh said to Joseph, "I am Pharaoh, but without your word no one will lift hand or foot in all Egypt." ⁴⁵Pharaoh gave Joseph the name Zaphenath-Paneah and gave him Asenath daughter of Potiphera, priest of On,ᶜ to be his wife. And Joseph went throughout the land of Egypt.

⁴⁶Joseph was thirty years old when he entered the service of Pharaoh king of Egypt. And Joseph went out from Pharaoh's presence and traveled throughout Egypt. ⁴⁷During the seven years of abundance the land produced plentifully. ⁴⁸Joseph collected all the food produced in those seven years of abundance in Egypt and stored it in the cities. In each city he put the food grown in the fields surrounding it. ⁴⁹Joseph stored up huge quantities of grain, like the sand of the sea; it was so much that he stopped keeping records because it was beyond measure.

⁵⁰Before the years of famine came, two sons were born to Joseph by Asenath daughter of Potiphera, priest of On. ⁵¹Joseph named his firstborn Manassehᵈ and said, "It is because God has made me forget all my trouble and all my father's household." ⁵²The second son he named Ephraimᵉ and said, "It is because God has made me fruitful in the land of my suffering."

⁵³The seven years of abundance in Egypt came to an end, ⁵⁴and the seven years of famine began, just as Joseph had said. There was famine in all the other lands, but in the whole land of Egypt there was food. ⁵⁵When all Egypt began to feel the famine, the people cried to Pharaoh for food. Then Pharaoh told all the Egyptians, "Go to Joseph and do what he tells you."

⁵⁶When the famine had spread over the whole country, Joseph opened all the storehouses and sold grain to the Egyptians, for the famine was severe throughout Egypt. ⁵⁷And all the world came to Egypt to buy grain from Joseph, because the famine was severe everywhere.

### Joseph's Brothers Go to Egypt

**42** When Jacob learned that there was grain in Egypt, he said to his sons, "Why do you just keep looking at each other?" ²He continued, "I have heard that there is grain in Egypt. Go down there and buy some for us, so that we may live and not die."

³Then ten of Joseph's brothers went down to buy grain from Egypt. ⁴But Jacob did not send Benjamin, Joseph's brother, with the others, because he was afraid that harm

## Amplified Bible

ence, submission, and obedience]. Only in matters of the throne will I be greater than you are.

⁴¹Then Pharaoh said to Joseph, See, I have set you over all the land of Egypt.

⁴²And Pharaoh took off his [signet] ring from his hand and put it on Joseph's hand, and arrayed him in [official] vestments of fine linen and put a gold chain about his neck;

⁴³He made him to ride in the second chariot which he had, and [officials] cried before him, Bow the knee! And he set him over all the land of Egypt.

⁴⁴And Pharaoh said to Joseph, I am Pharaoh, and without you shall no man lift up his hand or foot in all the land of Egypt.

⁴⁵And Pharaoh called Joseph's name Zaphenath-paneah and he gave him Asenath daughter of Potiphera, priest of On, to be his wife. And Joseph made an [inspection] tour of all the land of Egypt.

⁴⁶Joseph [who had been in Egypt thirteen years] was thirty years old when he stood before Pharaoh king of Egypt. Joseph went out from the presence of Pharaoh and went [about his duties] through all the land of Egypt.

⁴⁷In the seven abundant years the earth brought forth by handfuls [for each seed planted].

⁴⁸And he gathered up all the [surplus] food of the seven [good] years in the land of Egypt and stored up the food in the cities; he stored away in each city the food from the fields around it.

⁴⁹And Joseph gathered grain as the sand of the sea, very much, until he stopped counting, for it could not be measured.

⁵⁰Now to Joseph were born two sons before the years of famine came, whom Asenath daughter of Potiphera, the priest of On, bore to him.

⁵¹And Joseph called the firstborn Manasseh [making to forget], For God, said he, has made me forget all my toil *and* hardship and all my father's house.

⁵²And the second he called Ephraim [to be fruitful], For [he said] God has caused me to be fruitful in the land of my affliction.

⁵³When the seven years of plenty were ended in the land of Egypt,

⁵⁴The seven years of scarcity *and* famine began to come, as Joseph had said they would; the famine was in all [the surrounding] lands, but in all of Egypt there was food.

⁵⁵But when all the land of Egypt was weakened with hunger, the people [there] cried to Pharaoh for food; and Pharaoh said to [them] all, Go to Joseph; what he says to you, do.

⁵⁶When the famine was over all the land, Joseph opened all the storehouses and sold to the Egyptians; for the famine grew extremely distressing in the land of Egypt.

⁵⁷And all countries came to Egypt to Joseph to buy grain, because the famine was severe over all [the known] earth.

**42** Now when Jacob learned that there was grain in Egypt, he said to his sons, Why do you look at one another?

²For, he said, I have heard that there is grain in Egypt; get down there and buy [grain] for us, that we may live and not die.

³So ten of Joseph's brethren went to buy grain in Egypt.

⁴But Benjamin, Joseph's [full] brother, Jacob did not send with his brothers; for he said, Lest perhaps some harm *or* injury should befall him.

---

ᵃ 43 Or *in the chariot of his second-in-command; or in his second chariot*   ᵇ 43 Or *Bow down*   ᶜ 45 That is, Heliopolis; also in verse 50
ᵈ 51 *Manasseh* sounds like and may be derived from the Hebrew for *forget*.   ᵉ 52 *Ephraim* sounds like the Hebrew for *twice fruitful*.

## New International Version

might come to him. 5So Israel's sons were among those who went to buy grain, for there was famine in the land of Canaan also.

6Now Joseph was the governor of the land, the person who sold grain to all its people. So when Joseph's brothers arrived, they bowed down to him with their faces to the ground. 7As soon as Joseph saw his brothers, he recognized them, but he pretended to be a stranger and spoke harshly to them. "Where do you come from?" he asked.

"From the land of Canaan," they replied, "to buy food."

8Although Joseph recognized his brothers, they did not recognize him. 9Then he remembered his dreams about them and said to them, "You are spies! You have come to see where our land is unprotected."

10"No, my lord," they answered. "Your servants have come to buy food. 11We are all the sons of one man. Your servants are honest men, not spies."

12"No!" he said to them. "You have come to see where our land is unprotected."

13But they replied, "Your servants were twelve brothers, the sons of one man, who lives in the land of Canaan. The youngest is now with our father, and one is no more."

14Joseph said to them, "It is just as I told you: You are spies! 15And this is how you will be tested: As surely as Pharaoh lives, you will not leave this place unless your youngest brother comes here. 16Send one of your number to get your brother; the rest of you will be kept in prison, so that your words may be tested to see if you are telling the truth. If you are not, then as surely as Pharaoh lives, you are spies!" 17And he put them all in custody for three days.

18On the third day, Joseph said to them, "Do this and you will live, for I fear God: 19If you are honest men, let one of your brothers stay here in prison, while the rest of you go and take grain back for your starving households. 20But you must bring your youngest brother to me, so that your words may be verified and that you may not die." This they proceeded to do.

21They said to one another, "Surely we are being punished because of our brother. We saw how distressed he was when he pleaded with us for his life, but we would not listen; that's why this distress has come on us."

22Reuben replied, "Didn't I tell you not to sin against the boy? But you wouldn't listen! Now we must give an accounting for his blood." 23They did not realize that Joseph could understand them, since he was using an interpreter.

24He turned away from them and began to weep, then came back and spoke to them again. He had Simeon taken from them and bound before their eyes.

25Joseph gave orders to fill their bags with grain, to put each man's silver back in his sack, and to give them provisions for their journey. After this was done for them, 26they loaded their grain on their donkeys and left.

27At the place where they stopped for the night one of them opened his sack to get feed for his donkey, and he saw his silver in the mouth of his sack. 28"My silver has been returned," he said to his brothers. "Here it is in my sack."

Their hearts sank and they turned to each other trembling and said, "What is this that God has done to us?"

29When they came to their father Jacob in the land of Canaan, they told him all that had happened to them. They

## Amplified Bible

5So the sons of Israel came to buy grain among those who came, for there was hunger *and* general lack of food in the land of Canaan.

6Now Joseph was the governor over the land, and he it was who sold to all the people of the land; and Joseph's [half] brothers came and bowed themselves down before him with their faces to the ground.

7Joseph saw his brethren and he recognized them, but he treated them as if he were a stranger to them and spoke roughly to them. He said, Where do you come from? And they replied, From the land of Canaan to buy food.

8Joseph knew his brethren, but they did not know him.

9And Joseph remembered the dreams he had dreamed about them and said to them, You are spies *and* with unfriendly purpose you have come to observe [secretly] the nakedness of the land.

10But they said to him, No, my lord, but your servants have come [only] to buy food.

11We are all one man's sons; we are true men; your servants are not spies.

12And he said to them, No, but you have come to see the nakedness of the land.

13But they said, Your servants are twelve brothers, the sons of one man in the land of Canaan; the youngest is today with our father, and one is not.

14And Joseph said to them, It is as I said to you, You are spies.

15You shall be proved by this test: by the life of Pharaoh, you shall not go away from here unless your youngest brother comes here.

16Send one of you and let him bring your brother, and you will be kept in prison, that your words may be proved whether there is any truth in you; or else by the life of Pharaoh you certainly are spies.

17Then he put them all in custody for three days.

18And Joseph said to them on the third day, Do this and live! I reverence *and* fear God.

19If you are true men, let one of your brothers be bound in your prison, but [the rest of] you go and carry grain for those weakened with hunger in your households.

20But bring your youngest brother to me, so your words will be verified and you shall live. And they did so.

21And they said one to another, We are truly guilty about our brother, for we saw the distress *and* anguish of his soul when he begged us [to let him go], and we would not hear. So this distress *and* difficulty has come upon us.

22Reuben answered them, Did I not tell you, Do not sin against the boy, and you would not hear? Therefore, behold, his blood is required [of us].

23But they did not know that Joseph understood them, for he spoke to them through an interpreter.

24And he turned away from them and wept; then he returned to them and talked with them, and took from them Simeon and bound him before their eyes.

25Then [privately] Joseph commanded that their sacks be filled with grain, every man's money be restored to his sack, and provisions be given to them for the journey. And this was done for them.

26They loaded their donkeys with grain and left.

27And as one of them opened his sack to give his donkey fodder at the lodging place, he caught sight of his money; for behold, it was in his sack's mouth.

28And he said to his brothers, My money is restored! Here it is in my sack! And their hearts failed them and they were afraid *and* turned trembling one to another, saying, What is this that God has done to us?

29When they came to Jacob their father in Canaan, they told him all that had befallen them, saying,

## New International Version

said, <sup>30</sup>"The man who is lord over the land spoke harshly to us and treated us as though we were spying on the land. <sup>31</sup>But we said to him, 'We are honest men; we are not spies. <sup>32</sup>We were twelve brothers, sons of one father. One is no more, and the youngest is now with our father in Canaan.' <sup>33</sup>"Then the man who is lord over the land said to us, 'This is how I will know whether you are honest men: Leave one of your brothers here with me, and take food for your starving households and go. <sup>34</sup>But bring your youngest brother to me so I will know that you are not spies but honest men. Then I will give your brother back to you, and you can trade<sup>a</sup> in the land.'"

<sup>35</sup>As they were emptying their sacks, there in each man's sack was his pouch of silver! When they and their father saw the money pouches, they were frightened. <sup>36</sup>Their father Jacob said to them, "You have deprived me of my children. Joseph is no more and Simeon is no more, and now you want to take Benjamin. Everything is against me!"

<sup>37</sup>Then Reuben said to his father, "You may put both of my sons to death if I do not bring him back to you. Entrust him to my care, and I will bring him back."

<sup>38</sup>But Jacob said, "My son will not go down there with you; his brother is dead and he is the only one left. If harm comes to him on the journey you are taking, you will bring my gray head down to the grave in sorrow."

### The Second Journey to Egypt

**43** Now the famine was still severe in the land. <sup>2</sup>So when they had eaten all the grain they had brought from Egypt, their father said to them, "Go back and buy us a little more food."

<sup>3</sup>But Judah said to him, "The man warned us solemnly, 'You will not see my face again unless your brother is with you.' <sup>4</sup>If you will send our brother along with us, we will go down and buy food for you. <sup>5</sup>But if you will not send him, we will not go down, because the man said to us, 'You will not see my face again unless your brother is with you.'"

<sup>6</sup>Israel asked, "Why did you bring this trouble on me by telling the man you had another brother?"

<sup>7</sup>They replied, "The man questioned us closely about ourselves and our family. 'Is your father still living?' he asked us. 'Do you have another brother?' We simply answered his questions. How were we to know he would say, 'Bring your brother down here'?"

<sup>8</sup>Then Judah said to Israel his father, "Send the boy along with me and we will go at once, so that we and you and our children may live and not die. <sup>9</sup>I myself will guarantee his safety; you can hold me personally responsible for him. If I do not bring him back to you and set him here before you, I will bear the blame before you all my life. <sup>10</sup>As it is, if we had not delayed, we could have gone and returned twice."

<sup>11</sup>Then their father Israel said to them, "If it must be, then do this: Put some of the best products of the land in your bags and take them down to the man as a gift—a little balm and a little honey, some spices and myrrh, some pistachio nuts and almonds. <sup>12</sup>Take double the amount of silver with you, for you must return the silver that was put back into the mouths of your sacks. Perhaps it was a mistake. <sup>13</sup>Take your brother also and go back to the man at once. <sup>14</sup>And may God Almighty<sup>b</sup> grant you mercy before

## Amplified Bible

<sup>30</sup>The man who is the lord of the land spoke roughly to us and took us for spies of the country.

<sup>31</sup>And we said to him, We are true men, not spies. <sup>32</sup>We are twelve brothers with the same father; one is no more, and the youngest is today with our father in the land of Canaan.

<sup>33</sup>And the man, the lord of the country, said to us, By this test I will know whether or not you are honest men: leave one of your brothers here with me and take grain for your famishing households and be gone.

<sup>34</sup>Bring your youngest brother to me; then I will know that you are not spies, but that you are honest men. And I will deliver to you your brother [whom I have kept bound in prison], and you may do business in the land.

<sup>35</sup>When they emptied their sacks, behold, every man's parcel of money was in his sack! When both they and their father saw the bundles of money, they were afraid.

<sup>36</sup>And Jacob their father said to them, You have bereaved me! Joseph is not, and Simeon is not, and you would take Benjamin from me. All these things are against me!

<sup>37</sup>And Reuben said to his father, Slay my two sons if I do not bring [Benjamin] back to you. Deliver him into my keeping, and I will bring him back to you.

<sup>38</sup>But [Jacob] said, My son shall not go down with you, for his brother is dead and he alone is left [of his mother's children]; if harm or accident should befall him on the journey you are to take, you would bring my hoary head down to Sheol (the place of the dead) with grief.

**43** But the hunger *and* destitution *and* starvation were very severe *and* extremely distressing in the land [Canaan].

<sup>2</sup>And when [the families of Jacob's sons] had eaten up the grain which the men had brought from Egypt, their father said to them, Go again; buy us a little food.

<sup>3</sup>But Judah said to him, The man solemnly *and* sternly warned us, saying, You shall not see my face again unless your brother is with you.

<sup>4</sup>If you will send our brother with us, we will go down [to Egypt] and buy you food;

<sup>5</sup>But if you will not send him, we will not go down; for the man said to us, You shall not see my face unless your brother is with you.

<sup>6</sup>And Israel said, Why did you do me such a wrong *and* suffer this evil to come upon me by telling the man that you had another brother?

<sup>7</sup>And they said, The man asked us straightforward questions about ourselves and our relatives. He said, Is your father still alive? Have you another brother? And we answered him accordingly. How could we know that he would say, Bring your brother down here?

<sup>8</sup>And Judah said to Israel his father, Send the lad with me and we will arise and go, that we may live and not die, both we and you and also our little ones.

<sup>9</sup>I will be security for him; you shall require him of me [personally]; if I do not bring him back to you and put him before you, then let me bear the blame forever.

<sup>10</sup>For if we had not lingered like this, surely by now we would have returned the second time.

<sup>11</sup>And their father Israel said to them, If it must be so, now do this; take of the choicest products in the land in your sacks and carry down a present to the man, a little balm (balsam) and a little honey, aromatic spices and gum (of rock rose) *or* ladanum, pistachio nuts, and almonds.

<sup>12</sup>And take double the [grain] money with you; and the money that was put back in the mouth of your sacks, carry it again with you; there is a possibility that [its being in your sacks] was an oversight.

<sup>13</sup>Take your brother and arise and return to the man;

<sup>14</sup>May God Almighty give you mercy *and* favor before

## New International Version

the man so that he will let your other brother and Benjamin come back with you. As for me, if I am bereaved, I am bereaved."

15So the men took the gifts and double the amount of silver, and Benjamin also. They hurried down to Egypt and presented themselves to Joseph. 16When Joseph saw Benjamin with them, he said to the steward of his house, "Take these men to my house, slaughter an animal and prepare a meal; they are to eat with me at noon." 17The man did as Joseph told him and took the men to Joseph's house. 18Now the men were frightened when they were taken to his house. They thought, "We were brought here because of the silver that was put back into our sacks the first time. He wants to attack us and overpower us and seize us as slaves and take our donkeys."

19So they went up to Joseph's steward and spoke to him at the entrance to the house. 20"We beg your pardon, our lord," they said, "we came down here the first time to buy food. 21But at the place where we stopped for the night we opened our sacks and each of us found his silver—the exact weight—in the mouth of his sack. So we have brought it back with us. 22We have also brought additional silver with us to buy food. We don't know who put our silver in our sacks."

23"It's all right," he said. "Don't be afraid. Your God, the God of your father, has given you treasure in your sacks; I received your silver." Then he brought Simeon out to them.

24The steward took the men into Joseph's house, gave them water to wash their feet and provided fodder for their donkeys. 25They prepared their gifts for Joseph's arrival at noon, because they had heard that they were to eat there.

26When Joseph came home, they presented to him the gifts they had brought into the house, and they bowed down before him to the ground. 27He asked them how they were, and then he said, "How is your aged father you told me about? Is he still living?"

28They replied, "Your servant our father is still alive and well." And they bowed down, prostrating themselves before him.

29As he looked about and saw his brother Benjamin, his own mother's son, he asked, "Is this your youngest brother, the one you told me about?" And he said, "God be gracious to you, my son." 30Deeply moved at the sight of his brother, Joseph hurried out and looked for a place to weep. He went into his private room and wept there.

31After he had washed his face, he came out and, controlling himself, said, "Serve the food."

32They served him by himself, the brothers by themselves, and the Egyptians who ate with him by themselves, because Egyptians could not eat with Hebrews, for that is detestable to Egyptians. 33The men had been seated before him in the order of their ages, from the firstborn to the youngest; and they looked at each other in astonishment. 34When portions were served to them from Joseph's table, Benjamin's portion was five times as much as anyone else's. So they feasted and drank freely with him.

### A Silver Cup in a Sack

**44** Now Joseph gave these instructions to the steward of his house: "Fill the men's sacks with as much food as they can carry, and put each man's silver in the

## Amplified Bible

the man, that he may release to you your other brother and Benjamin. If I am bereaved [of my sons], I am bereaved.

15Then the men took the present, and they took double the [grain] money with them, and Benjamin; and they arose and went down to Egypt and stood before Joseph.

16And when Joseph saw Benjamin with them, he said to the steward of his house, Bring the men into the house and kill an animal and make ready, for the men will dine with me at noon.

17And the man did as Joseph ordered and brought the men to Joseph's house.

18The men were afraid because they were brought to Joseph's house; and they said, We are brought in because of the money that was returned in our sacks the first time we came, so that he may find occasion to accuse and assail us, take us for slaves, and seize our donkeys.

19So they came near to the steward of Joseph's house and talked with him at the door of the house,

20And said, O sir, we came down truly the first time to buy food;

21And when we came to the inn, we opened our sacks and there was each man's money, full weight, returned in the mouth of his sack. Now we have brought it back again.

22And we have brought down with us other money to buy food; we do not know who put our money in our sacks.

23But [the steward] said, Peace be to you, fear not; your God and the God of your father has given you treasure in your sacks. I received your money. And he brought Simeon out to them.

24And the man brought the men into Joseph's house and gave them water, and they washed their feet; and he gave their donkeys provender.

25And they made ready the present they had brought for Joseph before his coming at noon, for they heard that they were to dine there.

26And when Joseph came home, they brought into the house to him the present which they had with them, and bowed themselves to him to the ground.

27He asked them of their welfare and said, Is your old father well, of whom you spoke? Is he still alive?

28And they answered, Your servant our father is in good health; he is still alive. And they bowed down their heads and made obeisance.

29And he looked up and saw his [full] brother Benjamin, his mother's [only other] son, and said, Is this your youngest brother, of whom you spoke to me? And he said, God be gracious to you, my son!

30And Joseph hurried from the room, for his heart yearned for his brother, and he sought privacy to weep; so he entered his chamber and wept there.

31And he washed his face and went out, and, restraining himself, said, Let dinner be served.

32And [the servants] set out [the food] for [Joseph] by himself, and for [his brothers] by themselves, and for those Egyptians who ate with him by themselves, according to the Egyptian custom not to eat food with the Hebrews; for that is an abomination to the Egyptians.

33And [Joseph's brothers] were given seats before him—the eldest according to his birthright and the youngest according to his youth; and the men looked at one another amazed [that so much was known about them].

34[Joseph] took and sent helpings to them from before him, but Benjamin's portion was five times as much as any of theirs. And they drank freely and were merry with him.

**44** And he commanded the steward of his house, saying, Fill the men's sacks with food, as much as they can carry, and put every man's money in his sack's mouth.

## New International Version

mouth of his sack. ²Then put my cup, the silver one, in the mouth of the youngest one's sack, along with the silver for his grain." And he did as Joseph said.

³As morning dawned, the men were sent on their way with their donkeys. ⁴They had not gone far from the city when Joseph said to his steward, "Go after those men at once, and when you catch up with them, say to them, 'Why have you repaid good with evil? ⁵Isn't this the cup my master drinks from and also uses for divination? This is a wicked thing you have done.'"

⁶When he caught up with them, he repeated these words to them. ⁷But they said to him, "Why does my lord say such things? Far be it from your servants to do anything like that! ⁸We even brought back to you from the land of Canaan the silver we found inside the mouths of our sacks. So why would we steal silver or gold from your master's house? ⁹If any of your servants is found to have it, he will die; and the rest of us will become my lord's slaves."

¹⁰"Very well, then," he said, "let it be as you say. Whoever is found to have it will become my slave; the rest of you will be free from blame."

¹¹Each of them quickly lowered his sack to the ground and opened it. ¹²Then the steward proceeded to search, beginning with the oldest and ending with the youngest. And the cup was found in Benjamin's sack. ¹³At this, they tore their clothes. Then they all loaded their donkeys and returned to the city.

¹⁴Joseph was still in the house when Judah and his brothers came in, and they threw themselves to the ground before him. ¹⁵Joseph said to them, "What is this you have done? Don't you know that a man like me can find things out by divination?"

¹⁶"What can we say to my lord?" Judah replied. "What can we say? How can we prove our innocence? God has uncovered your servants' guilt. We are now my lord's slaves—we ourselves and the one who was found to have the cup."

¹⁷But Joseph said, "Far be it from me to do such a thing! Only the man who was found to have the cup will become my slave. The rest of you, go back to your father in peace."

¹⁸Then Judah went up to him and said: "Pardon your servant, my lord, let me speak a word to my lord. Do not be angry with your servant, though you are equal to Pharaoh himself. ¹⁹My lord asked his servants, 'Do you have a father or a brother?' ²⁰And we answered, 'We have an aged father, and there is a young son born to him in his old age. His brother is dead, and he is the only one of his mother's sons left, and his father loves him.'

²¹"Then you said to your servants, 'Bring him down to me so I can see him for myself.' ²²And we said to my lord, 'The boy cannot leave his father; if he leaves him, his father will die.' ²³But you told your servants, 'Unless your youngest brother comes down with you, you will not see my face again.' ²⁴When we went back to your servant my father, we told him what my lord had said.

²⁵"Then our father said, 'Go back and buy a little more food.' ²⁶But we said, 'We cannot go down. Only if our youngest brother is with us will we go. We cannot see the man's face unless our youngest brother is with us.'

## Amplified Bible

²And put my cup, the silver cup, in the sack's mouth of the youngest, with his grain money. And [the steward] did according to what Joseph had said.

³As soon as the morning was light, the men were sent away, they and their donkeys.

⁴When they had left the city and were not yet far away, Joseph said to his steward, Up, follow after the men; and when you overtake them, say to them, Why have you rewarded evil for good? [Why have you stolen the silver cup?]

⁵Is it not my master's drinking cup with which he divines [the future]? You have done wrong in doing this.

⁶And the steward overtook them, and he said to them these same words.

⁷They said to him, Why does my lord say these things? Far be it from your servants to do such a thing!

⁸Note that the money which we found in the mouths of our sacks we brought back to you from the land of Canaan. Is it likely then that we would steal from your master's house silver or gold?

⁹With whomever of your servants [your master's cup] is found, not only let that one die, but the rest of us will be my lord's slaves.

¹⁰And the steward said, Now let it be as you say: he with whom [the cup] is found shall be my slave, but [the rest of] you shall be blameless.

¹¹Then quickly every man lowered his sack to the ground and every man opened his sack.

¹²And [the steward] searched, beginning with the eldest and stopping with the youngest; and the cup was found in Benjamin's sack.

¹³Then they rent their clothes; and after each man had loaded his donkey again, they returned to the city.

¹⁴Judah and his brethren came to Joseph's house, for he was still there; and they fell prostrate before him.

¹⁵Joseph said to them, What is this thing that you have done? Do you not realize that such a man as I can certainly detect *and* know by divination [everything you do without other knowledge of it]?

¹⁶And Judah said, What shall we say to my lord? What shall we reply? Or how shall we clear ourselves, since God has found out *and* exposed the iniquity of your servants? Behold, we are my lord's slaves, the rest of us as well as he with whom the cup is found.

¹⁷But [Joseph] said, God forbid that I should do that; but the man in whose hand the cup is found, he shall be my servant; and as for [the rest of] you, arise *and* go in peace to your father.

¹⁸Then Judah came close to [Joseph] and said, O my lord, let your servant, I pray you, speak a word to you in private, and let not your anger blaze against your servant, for you are as Pharaoh [so I will speak as if directly to him].

¹⁹My lord asked his servants, saying, Have you a father or a brother?

²⁰And we said to my lord, We have a father—an old man—and a young [brother, the] child of his old age; and his brother is dead, and he alone is left of his mother's [offspring], and his father loves him.

²¹And you said to your servants, Bring him down to me, that I may set my eyes on him.

²²And we said to my lord, The lad cannot leave his father; for if he should do so, his father would die.

²³And you told your servants, Unless your youngest brother comes with you, you shall not see my face again.

²⁴And when we went back to your servant my father, we told him what my lord had said.

²⁵And our father said, Go again and buy us a little food.

²⁶But we said, We cannot go down. If our youngest brother is with us, then we will go down; for we may not see the man's face except our youngest brother is with us.

## New International Version

27"Your servant my father said to us, 'You know that my wife bore me two sons. 28One of them went away from me, and I said, "He has surely been torn to pieces." And I have not seen him since. 29If you take this one from me too and harm comes to him, you will bring my gray head down to the grave in misery.'

30"So now, if the boy is not with us when I go back to your servant my father, and if my father, whose life is closely bound up with the boy's life, 31sees that the boy isn't there, he will die. Your servants will bring the gray head of our father down to the grave in sorrow. 32Your servant guaranteed the boy's safety to my father. I said, 'If I do not bring him back to you, I will bear the blame before you, my father, all my life!'

33"Now then, please let your servant remain here as my lord's slave in place of the boy, and let the boy return with his brothers. 34How can I go back to my father if the boy is not with me? No! Do not let me see the misery that would come on my father."

### Joseph Makes Himself Known

**45** Then Joseph could no longer control himself before all his attendants, and he cried out, "Have everyone leave my presence!" So there was no one with Joseph when he made himself known to his brothers. 2And he wept so loudly that the Egyptians heard him, and Pharaoh's household heard about it.

3Joseph said to his brothers, "I am Joseph! Is my father still living?" But his brothers were not able to answer him, because they were terrified at his presence.

4Then Joseph said to his brothers, "Come close to me." When they had done so, he said, "I am your brother Joseph, the one you sold into Egypt! 5And now, do not be distressed and do not be angry with yourselves for selling me here, because it was to save lives that God sent me ahead of you. 6For two years now there has been famine in the land, and for the next five years there will be no plowing and reaping. 7But God sent me ahead of you to preserve for you a remnant on earth and to save your lives by a great deliverance.[a]

8"So then, it was not you who sent me here, but God. He made me father to Pharaoh, lord of his entire household and ruler of all Egypt. 9Now hurry back to my father and say to him, 'This is what your son Joseph says: God has made me lord of all Egypt. Come down to me; don't delay. 10You shall live in the region of Goshen and be near me—you, your children and grandchildren, your flocks and herds, and all you have. 11I will provide for you there, because five years of famine are still to come. Otherwise you and your household and all who belong to you will become destitute.'

12"You can see for yourselves, and so can my brother Benjamin, that it is really I who am speaking to you. 13Tell my father about all the honor accorded me in Egypt and about everything you have seen. And bring my father down here quickly."

14Then he threw his arms around his brother Benjamin and wept, and Benjamin embraced him, weeping. 15And he kissed all his brothers and wept over them. Afterward his brothers talked with him.

16When the news reached Pharaoh's palace that Jo-

## Amplified Bible

27And your servant my father said to us, You know that [Rachel] my wife bore me two sons:

28And the one went out from me, and I said, Surely he is torn to pieces, and I have never seen him since.

29And if you take this son also from me, and harm or accident should befall him, you will bring down my gray hairs with sorrow and evil to Sheol (the place of the dead).

30Now therefore, when I come to your servant my father and the lad is not with us, since his life is bound up in the lad's life and his soul knit with the lad's soul,

31When he sees that the lad is not with us, he will die; and your servants will be responsible for his death and will bring down the gray hairs of your servant our father with sorrow to Sheol.

32For your servant became security for the lad to my father, saying, If I do not bring him to you, then I will bear the blame to my father forever.

33Now therefore, I pray you, let your servant remain instead of the youth [to be] a slave to my lord, and let the young man go home with his [half] brothers.

34For how can I go up to my father if the lad is not with me?—lest I witness the woe and the evil that will come upon my father.

**45** Then Joseph could not restrain himself [any longer] before all those who stood by him, and he called out, Cause every man to go out from me! So no one stood there with Joseph while he made himself known to his brothers.

2And he wept and sobbed aloud, and the Egyptians [who had just left him] heard it, and the household of Pharaoh heard about it.

3And Joseph said to his brothers, I am Joseph! Is my father still alive? And his brothers could not reply, for they were distressingly disturbed and dismayed at [the startling realization that they were in] his presence.

4And Joseph said to his brothers, Come near to me, I pray you. And they did so. And he said, I am Joseph your brother, whom you sold into Egypt!

5But now, do not be distressed and disheartened or vexed and angry with yourselves because you sold me here, for God sent me ahead of you to preserve life.

6For these two years the famine has been in the land, and there are still five years more in which there will be neither plowing nor harvest.

7God sent me before you to preserve for you a posterity and to continue a remnant on the earth, to save your lives by a great escape and save for you many survivors.

8So now it was not you who sent me here, but God; and He has made me a father to Pharaoh and lord of all his house and ruler over all the land of Egypt.

9Hurry and go up to my father and tell him, Your son Joseph says this to you: God has put me in charge of all Egypt. Come down to me; do not delay.

10You will live in the land of Goshen, and you will be close to me—you and your children and your grandchildren, your flocks, your herds, and all you have.

11And there I will sustain and provide for you, so that you and your household and all that are yours may not come to poverty and want, for there are yet five [more] years of [the scarcity, hunger, and starvation of] famine.

12Now notice! Your own eyes and the eyes of my brother Benjamin can see that I am talking to you personally [in your language and not through an interpreter].

13And you shall tell my father of all my glory in Egypt and of all that you have seen; and you shall hurry and bring my father down here.

14And he fell on his brother Benjamin's neck and wept, and Benjamin wept on his neck.

15Moreover, he kissed all his brothers and wept upon them; and after that his brothers conversed with him.

16When the report was heard in Pharaoh's house that

## New International Version

seph's brothers had come, Pharaoh and all his officials were pleased. [17]Pharaoh said to Joseph, "Tell your brothers, 'Do this: Load your animals and return to the land of Canaan, [18]and bring your father and your families back to me. I will give you the best of the land of Egypt and you can enjoy the fat of the land.'

[19]"You are also directed to tell them, 'Do this: Take some carts from Egypt for your children and your wives, and get your father and come. [20]Never mind about your belongings, because the best of all Egypt will be yours.'"

[21]So the sons of Israel did this. Joseph gave them carts, as Pharaoh had commanded, and he also gave them provisions for their journey. [22]To each of them he gave new clothing, but to Benjamin he gave three hundred shekels[a] of silver and five sets of clothes. [23]And this is what he sent to his father: ten donkeys loaded with the best things of Egypt, and ten female donkeys loaded with grain and bread and other provisions for his journey. [24]Then he sent his brothers away, and as they were leaving he said to them, "Don't quarrel on the way!"

[25]So they went up out of Egypt and came to their father Jacob in the land of Canaan. [26]They told him, "Joseph is still alive! In fact, he is ruler of all Egypt." Jacob was stunned; he did not believe them. [27]But when they told him everything Joseph had said to them, and when he saw the carts Joseph had sent to carry him back, the spirit of their father Jacob revived. [28]And Israel said, "I'm convinced! My son Joseph is still alive. I will go and see him before I die."

### Jacob Goes to Egypt

**46** So Israel set out with all that was his, and when he reached Beersheba, he offered sacrifices to the God of his father Isaac.

[2]And God spoke to Israel in a vision at night and said, "Jacob! Jacob!"

"Here I am," he replied.

[3]"I am God, the God of your father," he said. "Do not be afraid to go down to Egypt, for I will make you into a great nation there. [4]I will go down to Egypt with you, and I will surely bring you back again. And Joseph's own hand will close your eyes."

[5]Then Jacob left Beersheba, and Israel's sons took their father Jacob and their children and their wives in the carts that Pharaoh had sent to transport him. [6]So Jacob and all his offspring went to Egypt, taking with them their livestock and the possessions they had acquired in Canaan. [7]Jacob brought with him to Egypt his sons and grandsons and his daughters and granddaughters—all his offspring.

[8]These are the names of the sons of Israel (Jacob and his descendants) who went to Egypt:

Reuben the firstborn of Jacob.
[9]The sons of Reuben:
   Hanok, Pallu, Hezron and Karmi.
[10]The sons of Simeon:
   Jemuel, Jamin, Ohad, Jakin, Zohar and Shaul the son of a Canaanite woman.
[11]The sons of Levi:
   Gershon, Kohath and Merari.
[12]The sons of Judah:
   Er, Onan, Shelah, Perez and Zerah (but Er and Onan had died in the land of Canaan).
   The sons of Perez:
   Hezron and Hamul.

## Amplified Bible

Joseph's brothers had come, it pleased Pharaoh and his servants well.

[17]And Pharaoh said to Joseph, Tell your brothers this: Load your animals and return to the land of Canaan,

[18]And get your father and your households and come to me. And I will give you the best in the land of Egypt and you will live on the fat of the land.

[19]You therefore command them, saying, You do this: take wagons from the land of Egypt for your little ones and for your wives, and bring your father and come.

[20]Also do not look with regret or concern upon your goods, for the best of all the land of Egypt is yours.

[21]And the sons of Israel did so; and Joseph gave them wagons, as the order of Pharaoh permitted, and gave them provisions for the journey.

[22]To each of them he gave changes of raiment, but to Benjamin he gave 300 pieces of silver and five changes of raiment.

[23]And to his father he sent as follows: ten donkeys loaded with the good things of Egypt, and ten she-donkeys laden with grain, bread, and nourishing food and provision for his father [to supply all who were with him] on the way.

[24]So he sent his brothers away, and they departed, and he said to them, See that you do not disagree (get excited, quarrel) along the road.

[25]So they went up out of Egypt and came into the land of Canaan to Jacob their father,

[26]And they said to him, Joseph is still alive! And he is governor over all the land of Egypt! And Jacob's heart began to stop beating and [he almost] fainted, for he did not believe them.

[27]But when they told him all the words of Joseph which he had said to them, and when he saw the wagons which Joseph had sent to carry him, the spirit of Jacob their father revived [and warmth and life returned].

[28]And Israel said, It is enough! Joseph my son is still alive. I will go and see him before I die.

**46** So Israel made his journey with all that he had and came to Beersheba [a place hallowed by sacred memories] and offered sacrifices to the God of his father Isaac. [Gen. 21:33; 26:23-25.]

[2]And God spoke to Israel in visions of the night, and said, Jacob! Jacob! And he said, Here am I.

[3]And He said, I am God, the God of your father; do not be afraid to go down to Egypt, for I will there make of you a great nation.

[4]I will go down with you to Egypt, and I will also surely bring you [your people Israel] up again; and Joseph will put his hand upon your eyes [when they are about to close in death].

[5]So Jacob arose and set out from Beersheba, and Israel's sons conveyed their father, their little ones, and their wives in the wagons that Pharaoh had sent to carry him.

[6]And they took their cattle and the gains which they had acquired in the land of Canaan and came into Egypt, Jacob and all his offspring with him:

[7]His sons and his sons' sons with him, his daughters and his sons' daughters—all his offspring he brought with him into Egypt.

[8]And these are the names of the descendants of Israel who came into Egypt, Jacob and his sons: Reuben, Jacob's firstborn.

[9]And the sons of Reuben: Hanoch, Pallu, Hezron, and Carmi.

[10]The sons of Simeon: Jemuel, Jamin, Ohad, Jachin, Zohar, and Shaul the son of a Canaanite woman.

[11]The sons of Levi: Gershon, Kohath, and Merari.

[12]The sons of Judah: Er, Onan, Shelah, Perez, and Zerah; but Er and Onan died in the land of Canaan. And the sons of Perez were Hezron and Hamul.

---

[a] 22 That is, about 7 1/2 pounds or about 3.5 kilograms

## New International Version

13 The sons of Issachar:
Tola, Puah,[a] Jashub[b] and Shimron.
14 The sons of Zebulun:
Sered, Elon and Jahleel.
15 These were the sons Leah bore to Jacob in Paddan Aram,[c] besides his daughter Dinah. These sons and daughters of his were thirty-three in all.
16 The sons of Gad:
Zephon,[d] Haggi, Shuni, Ezbon, Eri, Arodi and Areli.
17 The sons of Asher:
Imnah, Ishvah, Ishvi and Beriah.
Their sister was Serah.
The sons of Beriah:
Heber and Malkiel.
18 These were the children born to Jacob by Zilpah, whom Laban had given to his daughter Leah—sixteen in all.
19 The sons of Jacob's wife Rachel:
Joseph and Benjamin. 20 In Egypt, Manasseh and Ephraim were born to Joseph by Asenath daughter of Potiphera, priest of On.[e]
21 The sons of Benjamin:
Bela, Beker, Ashbel, Gera, Naaman, Ehi, Rosh, Muppim, Huppim and Ard.
22 These were the sons of Rachel who were born to Jacob—fourteen in all.
23 The son of Dan:
Hushim.
24 The sons of Naphtali:
Jahziel, Guni, Jezer and Shillem.
25 These were the sons born to Jacob by Bilhah, whom Laban had given to his daughter Rachel—seven in all.

26 All those who went to Egypt with Jacob—those who were his direct descendants, not counting his sons' wives—numbered sixty-six persons. 27 With the two sons[f] who had been born to Joseph in Egypt, the members of Jacob's family, which went to Egypt, were seventy[g] in all.

28 Now Jacob sent Judah ahead of him to Joseph to get directions to Goshen. When they arrived in the region of Goshen, 29 Joseph had his chariot made ready and went to Goshen to meet his father Israel. As soon as Joseph appeared before him, he threw his arms around his father[h] and wept for a long time.
30 Israel said to Joseph, "Now I am ready to die, since I have seen for myself that you are still alive."
31 Then Joseph said to his brothers and to his father's household, "I will go up and speak to Pharaoh and will say to him, 'My brothers and my father's household, who were living in the land of Canaan, have come to me. 32 The men are shepherds; they tend livestock, and they have brought along their flocks and herds and everything they own.' 33 When Pharaoh calls you in and asks, 'What is your occupation?' 34 you should answer, 'Your servants have tended livestock from our boyhood on, just as our fathers did.' Then you will be allowed to settle in the region of Goshen, for all shepherds are detestable to the Egyptians."

**47** Joseph went and told Pharaoh, "My father and brothers, with their flocks and herds and everything they own, have come from the land of Canaan and are now in Goshen." 2 He chose five of his brothers and presented them before Pharaoh.

---

*a 13* Samaritan Pentateuch and Syriac (see also 1 Chron. 7:1); Masoretic Text *Puvah*   *b 13* Samaritan Pentateuch and some Septuagint manuscripts (see also Num. 26:24 and 1 Chron. 7:1); Masoretic Text *Iob*   *c 15* That is, Northwest Mesopotamia   *d 16* Samaritan Pentateuch and Septuagint (see also Num. 26:15); Masoretic Text *Ziphion*   *e 20* That is, Heliopolis   *f 27* Hebrew; Septuagint *the nine children*   *g 27* Hebrew (see also Exodus 1:5 and note); Septuagint (see also Acts 7:14) *seventy-five*   *h 29* Hebrew *around him*

## Amplified Bible

13 The sons of Issachar: Tola, Puvah, Iob, and Shimron.
14 The sons of Zebulun: Sered, Elon, and Jahleel.
15 These are the sons of Leah, whom she bore to Jacob in Padan-aram, together with his daughter Dinah. All of his sons and his daughters numbered thirty-three.
16 The sons of Gad: Ziphion, Haggi, Shuni, Ezbon, Eri, Arodi, and Areli.
17 The sons of Asher: Imnah, Ishvah, Ishvi, Beriah, and Serah their sister. And the sons of Beriah: Heber and Malchiel.
18 These are the sons of Zilpah, [the maid] whom Laban gave to Leah his daughter. And these she bore to Jacob—sixteen persons all told.
19 The sons of Rachel, Jacob's wife: Joseph and Benjamin.
20 And to Joseph in the land of Egypt were born Manasseh and Ephraim, whom Asenath daughter of Potiphera, priest of On, bore to him.
21 And the sons of [a]Benjamin: Bela, Becher, Ashbel, Gera, Naaman, Ehi, Rosh, Muppim, Huppim, and Ard.
22 These are the sons of Rachel, who were born to Jacob—fourteen persons in all.
23 The son of Dan: Hushim.
24 The sons of Naphtali: Jahzeel, Guni, Jezer, and Shillem.
25 These are the sons of Bilhah, [the maid] whom Laban gave to Rachel his daughter. And she bore these to Jacob—seven persons in all.
26 All the persons who came with Jacob into Egypt—who were his own offspring, not counting the wives of Jacob's sons—were sixty-six persons all told.
27 And the sons of Joseph, who were born to him in Egypt, were two persons. All the persons of the house of Jacob [including Joseph and Jacob himself], who came into Egypt, were seventy.
28 And he sent Judah before him to Joseph, to direct him to Goshen *and* meet him there; and they came into the land of Goshen.
29 Then Joseph made ready his chariot and went up to meet Israel his father in Goshen; and he presented himself *and* gave distinct evidence of himself to him [that he was Joseph], and [each] fell on the [other's] neck and wept on his neck a good while.
30 And Israel said to Joseph, Now let me die, since I have seen your face [and know] that you are still alive.
31 Joseph said to his brothers and to his father's household, I will go up and tell Pharaoh and say to him, My brothers and my father's household, who were in the land of Canaan, have come to me.
32 And the men are shepherds, for their occupation has been keeping livestock, and they have brought their flocks and their herds and all that they have.
33 When Pharaoh calls you and says, What is your occupation?
34 You shall say, Your servants' occupation has been as keepers of livestock from our youth until now, both we and our fathers before us—in order that you may live in the land of Goshen, for every shepherd is an abomination to the Egyptians.

**47** Then Joseph came and told Pharaoh, My father and my brothers, with their flocks and their herds and all that they own, have come from the land of Canaan, and they are in the land of Goshen.
2 And from among his brothers he took five men and presented them to Pharaoh.

---

*a* Benjamin, whom uninformed artists have frequently pictured as a mere youth when he met Joseph in Egypt, was in fact the father of 10 sons at this time. Joseph was 17 when his brothers sold him; he was in prison 13 years; he had been governor of Egypt during the 7 good years and through 2 years of the famine. So Joseph was 39 years of age at this time, and Benjamin was only a few years younger.

## New International Version

3Pharaoh asked the brothers, "What is your occupation?"

"Your servants are shepherds," they replied to Pharaoh, "just as our fathers were." 4They also said to him, "We have come to live here for a while, because the famine is severe in Canaan and your servants' flocks have no pasture. So now, please let your servants settle in Goshen."

5Pharaoh said to Joseph, "Your father and your brothers have come to you, 6and the land of Egypt is before you; settle your father and your brothers in the best part of the land. Let them live in Goshen. And if you know of any among them with special ability, put them in charge of my own livestock."

7Then Joseph brought his father Jacob in and presented him before Pharaoh. After Jacob blessed*a* Pharaoh, 8Pharaoh asked him, "How old are you?"

9And Jacob said to Pharaoh, "The years of my pilgrimage are a hundred and thirty. My years have been few and difficult, and they do not equal the years of the pilgrimage of my fathers." 10Then Jacob blessed*b* Pharaoh and went out from his presence.

11So Joseph settled his father and his brothers in Egypt and gave them property in the best part of the land, the district of Rameses, as Pharaoh directed. 12Joseph also provided his father and his brothers and all his father's household with food, according to the number of their children.

### Joseph and the Famine

13There was no food, however, in the whole region because the famine was severe; both Egypt and Canaan wasted away because of the famine. 14Joseph collected all the money that was to be found in Egypt and Canaan in payment for the grain they were buying, and he brought it to Pharaoh's palace. 15When the money of the people of Egypt and Canaan was gone, all Egypt came to Joseph and said, "Give us food. Why should we die before your eyes? Our money is all gone."

16"Then bring your livestock," said Joseph. "I will sell you food in exchange for your livestock, since your money is gone." 17So they brought their livestock to Joseph, and he gave them food in exchange for their horses, their sheep and goats, their cattle and donkeys. And he brought them through that year with food in exchange for all their livestock.

18When that year was over, they came to him the following year and said, "We cannot hide from our lord the fact that since our money is gone and our livestock belongs to you, there is nothing left for our lord except our bodies and our land. 19Why should we perish before your eyes—we and our land as well? Buy us and our land in exchange for food, and we with our land will be in bondage to Pharaoh. Give us seed so that we may live and not die, and that the land may not become desolate."

20So Joseph bought all the land in Egypt for Pharaoh. The Egyptians, one and all, sold their land, because the famine was too severe for them. The land became Pharaoh's, 21and Joseph reduced the people to servitude,*c* from one end of Egypt to the other. 22However, he did not buy the land of the priests, because they received a regular allotment from Pharaoh and had food enough from the allotment Pharaoh gave them. That is why they did not sell their land.

## Amplified Bible

3And Pharaoh said to his brothers, What is your occupation? And they said to Pharaoh, Your servants are shepherds, both we and our fathers before us.

4Moreover, they said to Pharaoh, We have come to sojourn in the land, for your servants have no pasture for our flocks, for the famine is very severe in Canaan. So now, we pray you, let your servants dwell in the land of Goshen.

5And Pharaoh spoke to Joseph, saying, Your father and your brothers have come to you.

6The land of Egypt is before you; make your father and your brothers dwell in the best of the land. Let them live in the land of Goshen. And if you know of any men of ability among them, put them in charge of my cattle.

7Then Joseph brought in Jacob his father and presented him before Pharaoh; and Jacob blessed Pharaoh.

8And Pharaoh asked Jacob, How old are you?

9Jacob said to Pharaoh, The days of the years of my pilgrimage are 130 years; few and evil have the days of the years of my life been, and they have *a*not attained to those of the life of my fathers in their pilgrimage.

10And Jacob blessed Pharaoh and went out from his presence.

11Joseph settled his father and brethren and gave them a possession in Egypt in the best of the land, in the land of Rameses (Goshen), as Pharaoh commanded.

12And Joseph supplied his father and his brethren and all his father's household with food, according to [the needs of] their families.

13[In the course of time] there was no food in all the land, for the famine was distressingly severe, so that the land of Egypt and all the land of Canaan hung in doubt and wavered by reason of the hunger (destitution, starvation) of the famine.

14And Joseph gathered up all the money that was found in the land of Egypt and in the land of Canaan [in payment] for the grain which they bought, and Joseph brought the money into Pharaoh's house.

15And when the money was exhausted in the land of Egypt and in the land of Canaan, all the Egyptians came to Joseph and said, Give us food! Why should we die before your very eyes? For we have no money left.

16Joseph said, Give up your livestock, and I will give you food in exchange for [them] if your money is gone.

17So they brought their livestock to Joseph, and [he] gave them food in exchange for the horses, flocks, cattle of the herds, and the donkeys; and he supplied them with food in exchange for all their livestock that year.

18When that year was ended, they came to [Joseph] the second year and said to him, We will not hide from my lord [the fact] that our money is spent; my lord also has our herds of livestock; there is nothing left in the sight of my lord but our bodies and our lands.

19Why should we perish before your eyes, both we and our land? Buy us and our land in exchange for food, and we and our land will be servants to Pharaoh. And give us seed [to plant], that we may live and not die, and that the land may not be desolate.

20And Joseph bought all the land of Egypt for Pharaoh; for the Egyptians sold every man his field because of the overwhelming severity of the famine upon them. The land became Pharaoh's,

21And as for the people, he removed them to cities *and* practically made slaves of them [at their own request], from one end of the borders of Egypt to the other.

22Only the priests' land he did not buy, for the priests had a fixed pension from Pharaoh and lived on the amount Pharaoh gave them. So they did not sell their land.

---

*a* 7 Or *greeted*   *b* 10 Or *said farewell to*   *c* 21 Samaritan Pentateuch and Septuagint (see also Vulgate); Masoretic Text *and he moved the people into the cities*

*a* Abraham, Jacob's grandfather, had lived to be 175 years old; Isaac, his father, lived to be 180. Jacob lived seventeen years after making this statement to Pharaoh, in which time he had an opportunity to get a much more optimistic view of God's treatment of him. He died at 147, having said, "The redeeming Angel . . . has redeemed me continually from every evil" (Gen. 48:16).

## New International Version

<sup>23</sup>Joseph said to the people, "Now that I have bought you and your land today for Pharaoh, here is seed for you so you can plant the ground. <sup>24</sup>But when the crop comes in, give a fifth of it to Pharaoh. The other four-fifths you may keep as seed for the fields and as food for yourselves and your households and your children."

<sup>25</sup>"You have saved our lives," they said. "May we find favor in the eyes of our lord; we will be in bondage to Pharaoh."

<sup>26</sup>So Joseph established it as a law concerning land in Egypt—still in force today—that a fifth of the produce belongs to Pharaoh. It was only the land of the priests that did not become Pharaoh's.

<sup>27</sup>Now the Israelites settled in Egypt in the region of Goshen. They acquired property there and were fruitful and increased greatly in number.

<sup>28</sup>Jacob lived in Egypt seventeen years, and the years of his life were a hundred and forty-seven. <sup>29</sup>When the time drew near for Israel to die, he called for his son Joseph and said to him, "If I have found favor in your eyes, put your hand under my thigh and promise that you will show me kindness and faithfulness. Do not bury me in Egypt, <sup>30</sup>but when I rest with my fathers, carry me out of Egypt and bury me where they are buried."

"I will do as you say," he said.

<sup>31</sup>"Swear to me," he said. Then Joseph swore to him, and Israel worshiped as he leaned on the top of his staff.<sup>a</sup>

### Manasseh and Ephraim

**48** Some time later Joseph was told, "Your father is ill." So he took his two sons Manasseh and Ephraim along with him. <sup>2</sup>When Jacob was told, "Your son Joseph has come to you," Israel rallied his strength and sat up on the bed.

<sup>3</sup>Jacob said to Joseph, "God Almighty<sup>b</sup> appeared to me at Luz in the land of Canaan, and there he blessed me <sup>4</sup>and said to me, 'I am going to make you fruitful and increase your numbers. I will make you a community of peoples, and I will give this land as an everlasting possession to your descendants after you.'

<sup>5</sup>"Now then, your two sons born to you in Egypt before I came to you here will be reckoned as mine; Ephraim and Manasseh will be mine, just as Reuben and Simeon are mine. <sup>6</sup>Any children born to you after them will be yours; in the territory they inherit they will be reckoned under the names of their brothers. <sup>7</sup>As I was returning from Paddan,<sup>c</sup> to my sorrow Rachel died in the land of Canaan while we were still on the way, a little distance from Ephrath. So I buried her there beside the road to Ephrath" (that is, Bethlehem).

<sup>8</sup>When Israel saw the sons of Joseph, he asked, "Who are these?"

<sup>9</sup>"They are the sons God has given me here," Joseph said to his father.

Then Israel said, "Bring them to me so I may bless them."

<sup>10</sup>Now Israel's eyes were failing because of old age, and he could hardly see. So Joseph brought his sons close to him, and his father kissed them and embraced them.

<sup>11</sup>Israel said to Joseph, "I never expected to see your face again, and now God has allowed me to see your children too."

<sup>12</sup>Then Joseph removed them from Israel's knees and bowed down with his face to the ground. <sup>13</sup>And Joseph

## Amplified Bible

<sup>23</sup>Then Joseph said to the people, Behold, I have today bought you and your land for Pharaoh. Now here is seed for you, and you shall sow the land.

<sup>24</sup>At [harvest time when you reap] the increase, you shall give one-fifth of it to Pharaoh, and four-fifths shall be your own to use for seed for the field and as food for you and those of your households and for your little ones.

<sup>25</sup>And they said, You have saved our lives! Let us find favor in the sight of my lord; and we will be Pharaoh's servants.

<sup>26</sup>And Joseph made it a law over the land of Egypt—to this day—that Pharaoh should have the fifth part [of the crops]; it was the priests' land only which did not become Pharaoh's.

<sup>27</sup>And Israel dwelt in the land of Egypt, in the country of Goshen; and they gained possessions there and grew and multiplied exceedingly.

<sup>28</sup>And Jacob lived in the land of Egypt seventeen years; so Jacob reached the age of 147 years.

<sup>29</sup>When the time drew near that Israel must die, he called his son Joseph and said to him, If now I have found favor in your sight, <sup>a</sup>put your hand under my thigh and [promise to] deal loyally and faithfully with me. Do not bury me, I beg of you, in Egypt,

<sup>30</sup>But let me lie with my fathers; you shall carry me out of Egypt and bury me in their burying place. And [Joseph] said, I will do as you have directed.

<sup>31</sup>Then Jacob said, Swear to me [that you will do it]. And he swore to him. And Israel bowed himself upon the head of the bed.

**48** Some time after these things occurred, someone told Joseph, Behold, your father is sick. And he took with him his two sons Manasseh and Ephraim [and went to Goshen].

<sup>2</sup>When Jacob was told, Your son Joseph has come to you, Israel collected his strength and sat up on the bed.

<sup>3</sup>And Jacob said to Joseph, God Almighty appeared to me at Luz [Bethel] in the land of Canaan and blessed me

<sup>4</sup>And said to me, Behold, I will make you fruitful and multiply you, and I will make you a multitude of people and will give this land to your descendants after you as an everlasting possession. [Gen. 28:13-22; 35:6-15.]

<sup>5</sup>And now your two sons, [Ephraim and Manasseh], who were born to you in the land of Egypt before I came to you in Egypt, are mine. [I am adopting them, and now] as Reuben and Simeon, [they] shall be mine.

<sup>6</sup>But other sons who may be born after them shall be your own; and they shall be called after the names of these [two] brothers *and* reckoned as belonging to them [when they come] into their inheritance.

<sup>7</sup>And as for me, when I came from Padan, Rachel died at my side in the land of Canaan on the way, when yet there was but a little way to come to Ephrath; and I buried her there on the way to Ephrath, that is, Bethlehem.

<sup>8</sup>When Israel [almost blind] saw Joseph's sons, he said, Who are these?

<sup>9</sup>And Joseph said to his father, They are my sons, whom God has given me in this place. And he said, Bring them to me, I pray you, that I may bless them.

<sup>10</sup>Now Israel's eyes were dim from age, so that he could not see. And Joseph brought them near to him, and he kissed and embraced them.

<sup>11</sup>Israel said to Joseph, I had not thought that I would see your face, but see, God has shown me your offspring also.

<sup>12</sup>Then Joseph took [the boys] from [his father's embrace] and he bowed [before him] with his face to the earth.

<sup>a</sup> This was a customary manner of taking a solemn oath. The gesture was a reference to the mark of circumcision, the sign of God's covenant, which is equivalent to our laying our hand upon the Bible. (Adam Clarke, *The Holy Bible with A Commentary*).

<sup>a</sup> 31 Or *Israel bowed down at the head of his bed*    <sup>b</sup> 3 Hebrew *El-Shaddai*    <sup>c</sup> 7 That is, Northwest Mesopotamia

## New International Version

took both of them, Ephraim on his right toward Israel's left hand and Manasseh on his left toward Israel's right hand, and brought them close to him. [14]But Israel reached out his right hand and put it on Ephraim's head, though he was the younger, and crossing his arms, he put his left hand on Manasseh's head, even though Manasseh was the firstborn.

[15]Then he blessed Joseph and said,

"May the God before whom my fathers
    Abraham and Isaac walked faithfully,
the God who has been my shepherd
    all my life to this day,
[16]the Angel who has delivered me from all harm
    —may he bless these boys.
May they be called by my name
    and the names of my fathers Abraham and Isaac,
and may they increase greatly
    on the earth."

[17]When Joseph saw his father placing his right hand on Ephraim's head he was displeased; so he took hold of his father's hand to move it from Ephraim's head to Manasseh's head. [18]Joseph said to him, "No, my father, this one is the firstborn; put your right hand on his head."

[19]But his father refused and said, "I know, my son, I know. He too will become a people, and he too will become great. Nevertheless, his younger brother will be greater than he, and his descendants will become a group of nations." [20]He blessed them that day and said,

"In your[a] name will Israel pronounce this blessing:
    'May God make you like Ephraim and Manasseh.'"

So he put Ephraim ahead of Manasseh.

[21]Then Israel said to Joseph, "I am about to die, but God will be with you[b] and take you[b] back to the land of your[b] fathers. [22]And to you I give one more ridge of land[c] than to your brothers, the ridge I took from the Amorites with my sword and my bow."

### Jacob Blesses His Sons

**49** Then Jacob called for his sons and said: "Gather around so I can tell you what will happen to you in days to come.

[2]"Assemble and listen, sons of Jacob;
    listen to your father Israel.

[3]"Reuben, you are my firstborn,
    my might, the first sign of my strength,
    excelling in honor, excelling in power.

## Amplified Bible

[13]Then Joseph took both [boys], Ephraim with his right hand toward Israel's left, and Manasseh with his left hand toward Israel's right, and brought them close to him. [14]And Israel reached out his right hand and laid it on the head of Ephraim, who was the younger, and his left hand on Manasseh's head, [a]crossing his hands intentionally, for Manasseh was the firstborn.

[15]Then [Jacob] blessed Joseph and said, God [Himself], before Whom my fathers Abraham and Isaac lived *and* walked habitually, God [Himself], Who has [been my Shepherd and has led and] fed me from the time I came into being until this day,

[16]The [b]redeeming Angel [that is, the Angel the Redeemer—not a created being but the Lord Himself] Who has redeemed me continually from every evil, bless the lads! And let my name be perpetuated in them [may they be worthy of having their names coupled with mine], and the names of my fathers Abraham and Isaac; and let them become a multitude in the midst of the earth.

[17]When Joseph saw that his father laid his right hand on Ephraim's head, it displeased him; and he held up his father's hand to move it to Manasseh's head.

[18]And Joseph said, Not so, my father, for this is the firstborn; put your right hand upon his head.

[19]But his father refused and said, I know, my son, I know. He also shall become a people and shall be great; but his younger brother shall be [c]greater than he, and his offspring shall become a multitude of nations.

[20]And he blessed them that day, saying, By you shall Israel bless [one another], saying, May God make you like Ephraim and like Manasseh. And he set Ephraim before Manasseh.

[21]And Israel said to Joseph, Behold, I [am about to] die, but God will be with you and bring you again to the land of your fathers.

[22]Moreover, I have given to you [Joseph] one portion [Shechem, one mountain slope] more than any of your brethren, which I took [reclaiming it] out of the hand of the Amorites with my sword and with my bow. [Gen. 33:18, 19; Josh. 24:32, 33; John 4:5.]

**49** And Jacob called for his sons and said, Gather yourselves together [around me], that I may tell you what shall befall you [d]in the latter *or* last days.

[2]Gather yourselves together and hear, you sons of Jacob; and hearken to Israel your father.

[3]Reuben, you are my [e]firstborn, my might, the beginning (the firstfruits) of my manly strength *and* vigor; [your birthright gave you] the preeminence in dignity and the preeminence in power.

---

[a] God acts independently of the claims of priority based on time of birth when He chooses men. He too "crossed His hands" in the case of Seth whom He chose over Cain; of Shem over Japheth; of Isaac over Ishmael; of Jacob over Esau; of Judah and Joseph over Reuben; of Moses over Aaron; of David over all his brothers; and of Mary over Martha. [b] The "Angel of the Lord" is here identified as Christ Himself. See also the footnote on Gen. 16:7. [c] This prophecy begins to be fulfilled "from the days of the judges onward, as the tribe of Ephraim in power and compass so increased that it became the head of the northern ten tribes, and its name became of like significance with that of Israel; although, in the time of Moses, Manasseh still outnumbered Ephraim by 20,000" (Karl F. Keil and F. Delitzsch, *Biblical Commentary on the Old Testament*). Joshua, whom Israel so long regarded as their ruler, was an Ephraimite. The ark of the covenant was placed in Shiloh in the territory of Ephraim, which increased the tribe's prestige. How could Jacob have prophesied Ephraim's supremacy so positively except by divine inspiration? [d] See Deut. 33, where Moses blesses the same tribes in a similar prophetic way. [e] Reuben was the eldest of Jacob's twelve sons and therefore entitled to the birthright, which would make him successor to his father as head of the family or tribe and inheritor of a double portion of his father's estate. But Reuben forfeited all this by his conduct with Bilhah, his father's concubine (Gen. 35:22). By adopting Joseph's two sons, Ephraim and Manasseh, and giving each of them a portion of the inheritance, Jacob virtually gave Joseph Reuben's extra portion of the land. And Judah became the tribal leader in Reuben's place (Gen. 49:8-10).

---

[a] 20 The Hebrew is singular.    [b] 21 The Hebrew is plural.
[c] 22 The Hebrew for *ridge of land* is identical with the place name Shechem.

## New International Version

4Turbulent as the waters, you will no longer excel,
  for you went up onto your father's bed,
  onto my couch and defiled it.

5"Simeon and Levi are brothers—
  their swords[a] are weapons of violence.
6Let me not enter their council,
  let me not join their assembly,
for they have killed men in their anger
  and hamstrung oxen as they pleased.
7Cursed be their anger, so fierce,
  and their fury, so cruel!
I will scatter them in Jacob
  and disperse them in Israel.

8"Judah,[b] your brothers will praise you;
  your hand will be on the neck of your enemies;
  your father's sons will bow down to you.
9You are a lion's cub, Judah;
  you return from the prey, my son.
Like a lion he crouches and lies down,
  like a lioness—who dares to rouse him?
10The scepter will not depart from Judah,
  nor the ruler's staff from between his feet,[c]
until he to whom it belongs[d] shall come
  and the obedience of the nations shall be his.
11He will tether his donkey to a vine,
  his colt to the choicest branch;
he will wash his garments in wine,
  his robes in the blood of grapes.
12His eyes will be darker than wine,
  his teeth whiter than milk.[e]

13"Zebulun will live by the seashore
  and become a haven for ships;
  his border will extend toward Sidon.

14"Issachar is a rawboned[f] donkey
  lying down among the sheep pens.[g]
15When he sees how good is his resting place
  and how pleasant is his land,
he will bend his shoulder to the burden
  and submit to forced labor.

16"Dan[h] will provide justice for his people
  as one of the tribes of Israel.
17Dan will be a snake by the roadside,
  a viper along the path,
that bites the horse's heels
  so that its rider tumbles backward.

18"I look for your deliverance, LORD.

19"Gad[i] will be attacked by a band of raiders,
  but he will attack them at their heels.

20"Asher's food will be rich;
  he will provide delicacies fit for a king.

21"Naphtali is a doe set free
  that bears beautiful fawns.[j]

22"Joseph is a fruitful vine,
  a fruitful vine near a spring,
  whose branches climb over a wall.[k]
23With bitterness archers attacked him;
  they shot at him with hostility.

## Amplified Bible

4But unstable *and* boiling over like water, you shall [a]not excel *and* have the preeminence [of the firstborn], because you went to your father's bed; you defiled it—he went to my couch! [Gen. 35:22.]
5Simeon and Levi are brothers [equally headstrong, deceitful, vindictive, and cruel]; their swords are weapons of violence. [Gen. 34:25-29.]
6O my soul, come not into their secret council; unto their assembly let not my honor be united [for I knew nothing of their plot], because in their anger they slew men [an honored man, Shechem, and the Shechemites], and in their self-will they disabled oxen.
7Cursed be their anger, for it was fierce, and their wrath, for it was cruel. I will divide them in Jacob and [b]scatter them in Israel.
8Judah, you are the one whom your brothers shall praise; your hand shall be on the neck of your enemies; your father's sons shall bow down to you.
9Judah, a lion's cub! With the prey, my son, you have gone high up [the mountain]. He stooped down, he crouched like a lion, and like a lioness—who dares provoke *and* rouse him? [Rev. 5:5.]
10The scepter *or* leadership shall not depart from Judah, nor the ruler's staff from between his feet, until Shiloh [the Messiah, the Peaceful One] comes to Whom it belongs, and to Him shall be the obedience of the people. [Num. 24:17; Ps. 60:7.]
11Binding His foal to the vine and His donkey's colt to the choice vine, He washes His garments in wine and His clothes in the blood of grapes. [Isa. 63:1-3; Zech. 9:9; Rev. 19:11-16.]
12His eyes are darker *and* more sparkling than wine, and His teeth whiter than milk.
13Zebulun shall live toward the seashore, and he shall be a haven *and* a landing place for ships; and his border shall be toward Sidon.
14Issachar is a strong-boned donkey crouching down between the sheepfolds.
15And he saw that rest was good and that the land was pleasant; and he bowed his shoulder to bear [his burdens] and became a servant to tribute [subjected to forced labor].
16Dan shall judge his people as one of the tribes of Israel.
17Dan shall be a serpent by the way, a horned snake in the path, that bites at the horse's heels, so that his rider falls backward.
18I wait for Your salvation, O Lord.
19Gad—a raiding troop shall raid him, but he shall raid at their heels *and* assault them [victoriously].
20Asher's food [supply] shall be rich *and* fat, and he shall yield *and* deliver royal delights.
21Naphtali is a hind let loose which yields lovely fawns.
22Joseph is a fruitful bough, a fruitful bough by a well (spring or fountain), whose branches run over the wall.
23Skilled archers have bitterly attacked *and* sorely worried him; they have shot at him and persecuted him.

---

[a] 5 The meaning of the Hebrew for this word is uncertain.   [b] 8 *Judah* sounds like and may be derived from the Hebrew for *praise*.
[c] 10 Or *from his descendants*   [d] 10 Or *to whom tribute belongs*; the meaning of the Hebrew for this phrase is uncertain.   [e] 12 Or *will be dull from wine, / his teeth white from milk*   [f] 14 Or *strong*
[g] 14 Or *the campfires*; or *the saddlebags*   [h] 16 *Dan* here means *he provides justice*.   [i] 19 *Gad* sounds like the Hebrew for *attack* and also for *band of raiders*.   [j] 21 Or *free; / he utters beautiful words*
[k] 22 Or *Joseph is a wild colt, / a wild colt near a spring, / a wild donkey on a terraced hill*

---

[a] The whole fertile territory once occupied by the tribe of Reuben has long since been deserted by its settled inhabitants and given up to the nomad tribes of the desert. Reuben did "not excel," and even before Jacob's death he had lost his "preeminence of the firstborn" (John D. Davis, *A Dictionary of the Bible*).   [b] This was literally fulfilled. Levi got no inheritance except 48 towns scattered throughout different parts of Canaan. As to Simeon, they were originally given only a few towns and villages in Judah's lot (Josh. 19:1). Afterward, needing more room, they formed colonies in districts which they conquered from the Idumeans and the Amalekites [I Chron. 4:39, 40]. (Adam Clarke, *The Holy Bible with A Commentary*).

## New International Version

24 But his bow remained steady,
  his strong arms stayed[a] limber,
because of the hand of the Mighty One of Jacob,
  because of the Shepherd, the Rock of Israel,
25 because of your father's God, who helps you,
  because of the Almighty,[b] who blesses you
with blessings of the skies above,
  blessings of the deep springs below,
  blessings of the breast and womb.
26 Your father's blessings are greater
  than the blessings of the ancient mountains,
  than[c] the bounty of the age-old hills.
Let all these rest on the head of Joseph,
  on the brow of the prince among[d] his brothers.

27 "Benjamin is a ravenous wolf;
  in the morning he devours the prey,
  in the evening he divides the plunder."

28 All these are the twelve tribes of Israel, and this is what their father said to them when he blessed them, giving each the blessing appropriate to him.

### The Death of Jacob

29 Then he gave them these instructions: "I am about to be gathered to my people. Bury me with my fathers in the cave in the field of Ephron the Hittite, 30 the cave in the field of Machpelah, near Mamre in Canaan, which Abraham bought along with the field as a burial place from Ephron the Hittite. 31 There Abraham and his wife Sarah were buried, there Isaac and his wife Rebekah were buried, and there I buried Leah. 32 The field and the cave in it were bought from the Hittites.[e]"

33 When Jacob had finished giving instructions to his sons, he drew his feet up into the bed, breathed his last and was gathered to his people.

**50** Joseph threw himself on his father and wept over him and kissed him. 2 Then Joseph directed the physicians in his service to embalm his father Israel. So the physicians embalmed him, 3 taking a full forty days, for that was the time required for embalming. And the Egyptians mourned for him seventy days.

4 When the days of mourning had passed, Joseph said to Pharaoh's court, "If I have found favor in your eyes, speak to Pharaoh for me. Tell him, 5 'My father made me swear an oath and said, "I am about to die; bury me in the tomb I dug for myself in the land of Canaan." Now let me go up and bury my father; then I will return.'"

6 Pharaoh said, "Go up and bury your father, as he made you swear to do."

7 So Joseph went up to bury his father. All Pharaoh's officials accompanied him—the dignitaries of his court and all the dignitaries of Egypt— 8 besides all the members of Joseph's household and his brothers and those belonging to his father's household. Only their children and their

## Amplified Bible

24 But his bow remained strong *and* steady *and* rested in the Strength that does not fail him, for the arms of his hands were made strong *and* active by the hands of the Mighty God of Jacob, by the name of the Shepherd, the Rock of Israel, [Gen. 48:15; Deut. 32:4; Isa. 9:6; 49:26.]
25 By the God of your father, Who will help you, and by the Almighty, Who will bless you with blessings of the heavens above, blessings lying in the deep beneath, blessings of the breasts and of the womb.
26 The blessings of your father [on you] are greater than the blessings of my forefathers [Abraham and Isaac on me] *and* are as lasting as the bounties of the eternal hills; they shall be on the head of Joseph, and on the crown of the head of him who was the consecrated one *and* the one separated from his brethren *and* [the one who] is prince among them.
27 Benjamin is a [a]ravenous wolf, in the morning devouring the prey and at night dividing the spoil.
28 All these are the twelve tribes of Israel, and this is what their father said to them as he blessed them, blessing each one according to the blessing suited to him.
29 He charged them and said to them, I am to be gathered to my [departed] people; bury me with my fathers in the cave that is in the field of Ephron the Hittite,
30 In the cave in the field at Machpelah, east of Mamre in the land of Canaan, that Abraham bought, along with the field of Ephron the Hittite, to possess as a cemetery. [Gen. 23:17-20.]
31 There they buried Abraham and Sarah his wife, there they buried Isaac and Rebekah his wife, and there I buried Leah.
32 The purchase of the field and the cave that is in it was from the sons of Heth.
33 When Jacob had finished commanding his sons, he drew his feet up into the bed and breathed his last and was gathered to his [departed] people.

**50** Then Joseph fell upon his father's face and wept over him and kissed him.

2 And Joseph ordered his servants the physicians to embalm his father. So the physicians embalmed Israel.
3 Then forty days were devoted [to this purpose] for him, for that is the customary number of days required for those who are embalmed. And the Egyptians wept and bemoaned him [as they would for royalty] for seventy days.
4 And when the days of weeping *and* deep grief were past, Joseph said to [the nobles of] the house of Pharaoh, If now I have found grace in your eyes, speak, I pray you, to Pharaoh [for Joseph was dressed in mourning and could not do so himself], saying,
5 My father made me swear, saying, I am about to die; in my tomb which I hewed out for myself in the land of Canaan, there you shall bury me. So now let me go up, I pray you, and bury my father, and I will come again.
6 And Pharaoh said, Go up and bury your father, as he made you swear.
7 And Joseph went up [to Canaan] to bury his father; and with him went all the officials of Pharaoh—the nobles of his court, *and* the elders of his house and all the nobles *and* elders of the land of Egypt—
8 And all the household of Joseph and his brethren and his father's household. Only their little ones and their flocks and herds they left in the land of Goshen.

a The tribe of Benjamin is fitly compared to a ravenous wolf because of the rude courage and ferocity which they invariably displayed, particularly in their war with the other tribes, in which they killed more men than all of their own numbers combined (Adam Clarke, *The Holy Bible with A Commentary*). The tribe was absorbed by the tribe of Judah and is not mentioned after the return from the Babylonian captivity, except in connection with its former land or as the source of some individual person. Ehud, Saul, Jonathan, and the apostle Paul were Benjamites.

a 23,24 Or *archers will attack . . . will shoot . . . will remain . . . will stay*   b 25 Hebrew *Shaddai*   c 26 Or *of my progenitors, / as great as*   d 26 Or *of the one separated from*   e 32 Or *the descendants of Heth*

## New International Version

flocks and herds were left in Goshen. [9]Chariots and horsemen[a] also went up with him. It was a very large company.

[10]When they reached the threshing floor of Atad, near the Jordan, they lamented loudly and bitterly; and there Joseph observed a seven-day period of mourning for his father. [11]When the Canaanites who lived there saw the mourning at the threshing floor of Atad, they said, "The Egyptians are holding a solemn ceremony of mourning." That is why that place near the Jordan is called Abel Mizraim.[b]

[12]So Jacob's sons did as he had commanded them: [13]They carried him to the land of Canaan and buried him in the cave in the field of Machpelah, near Mamre, which Abraham had bought along with the field as a burial place from Ephron the Hittite. [14]After burying his father, Joseph returned to Egypt, together with his brothers and all the others who had gone with him to bury his father.

### Joseph Reassures His Brothers

[15]When Joseph's brothers saw that their father was dead, they said, "What if Joseph holds a grudge against us and pays us back for all the wrongs we did to him?" [16]So they sent word to Joseph, saying, "Your father left these instructions before he died: [17]'This is what you are to say to Joseph: I ask you to forgive your brothers the sins and the wrongs they committed in treating you so badly.' Now please forgive the sins of the servants of the God of your father." When their message came to him, Joseph wept.

[18]His brothers then came and threw themselves down before him. "We are your slaves," they said.

[19]But Joseph said to them, "Don't be afraid. Am I in the place of God? [20]You intended to harm me, but God intended it for good to accomplish what is now being done, the saving of many lives. [21]So then, don't be afraid. I will provide for you and your children." And he reassured them and spoke kindly to them.

### The Death of Joseph

[22]Joseph stayed in Egypt, along with all his father's family. He lived a hundred and ten years [23]and saw the third generation of Ephraim's children. Also the children of Makir son of Manasseh were placed at birth on Joseph's knees.[c]

[24]Then Joseph said to his brothers, "I am about to die. But God will surely come to your aid and take you up out of this land to the land he promised on oath to Abraham, Isaac and Jacob." [25]And Joseph made the Israelites swear an oath and said, "God will surely come to your aid, and then you must carry my bones up from this place."

[26]So Joseph died at the age of a hundred and ten. And after they embalmed him, he was placed in a coffin in Egypt.

## Amplified Bible

[9]And there went with [Joseph] both chariots and horsemen; and it was a very great company.

[10]And they came to the threshing floor of Atad, which is beyond [west of] the Jordan, and there they mourned with a great lamentation and extreme demonstrations of sorrow [according to Egyptian custom]; and [Joseph] made a mourning for his father seven days.

[11]When the inhabitants of the land, the Canaanites, saw the mourning at the floor of Atad, they said, This is a grievous mourning for the Egyptians. Therefore the place was called Abel-mizraim [mourning of Egypt]; it is west of the Jordan.

[12]Thus [Jacob's] sons did for him as he had commanded them.

[13]For his sons carried him to the land of Canaan and buried him in the cave of the field of Machpelah, east of Mamre, which Abraham bought, along with the field, for a possession as a burying place from Ephron the Hittite.

[14]After he had buried his father, Joseph returned to Egypt, he and his brethren and all who had gone up with him.

[15]When Joseph's brethren saw that their father was dead, they said, Perhaps now Joseph will hate us and will pay us back for all the evil we did to him.

[16]And they sent a messenger to Joseph, saying, Your father commanded before he died, saying,

[17]So shall you say to Joseph: Forgive (take up and away all resentment and all claim to requital concerning), I pray you now, the trespass of your brothers and their sin, for they did evil to you. Now, we pray you, forgive the trespass of the servants of your father's God. And Joseph wept when they spoke thus to him.

[18]Then his brothers went and fell down before him, saying, See, we are your servants (your slaves)!

[19]And Joseph said to them, Fear not; for am I in the place of God? [Vengeance is His, not mine.]

[20]As for you, you thought evil against me, but God meant it for good, to bring about that many people should be kept alive, as they are this day.

[21]Now therefore, do not be afraid. I will provide for *and* support you and your little ones. And he comforted them [imparting cheer, hope, strength] and spoke to their hearts [kindly].

[22]Joseph dwelt in Egypt, he and his father's household. And Joseph lived 110 years.

[23]And Joseph saw Ephraim's children of the third generation; the children also of Machir son of Manasseh were brought up on Joseph's knees.

[24]And Joseph said to his brethren, I am going to die. But God will surely visit you and bring you out of this land to the land He swore to Abraham, to Isaac, and to Jacob [to give you].

[25]And Joseph took an oath from the sons of Israel, saying, God will surely visit you, and you will carry up my bones from here.

[26]So Joseph died, being 110 years old; and they embalmed him, and he was put [a]in a coffin in Egypt.

---

[a] Joseph's body remained in Egypt until the exodus to the promised land of Canaan about 200 years later. Its final resting-place was Shechem, near Samaria, "in the parcel of ground which Jacob bought from the sons of Hamor, the father of Shechem" (Josh. 24:32). Here each of his brothers was also buried (Acts 7:15, 16).

---

[a] 9 Or *charioteers*    [b] 11 *Abel Mizraim* means *mourning of the Egyptians.*    [c] 23 That is, were counted as his

# New International Version

## Exodus

### The Israelites Oppressed

**1** These are the names of the sons of Israel who went to Egypt with Jacob, each with his family: ²Reuben, Simeon, Levi and Judah; ³Issachar, Zebulun and Benjamin; ⁴Dan and Naphtali; Gad and Asher. ⁵The descendants of Jacob numbered seventy[a] in all; Joseph was already in Egypt.

⁶Now Joseph and all his brothers and all that generation died, ⁷but the Israelites were exceedingly fruitful; they multiplied greatly, increased in numbers and became so numerous that the land was filled with them.

⁸Then a new king, to whom Joseph meant nothing, came to power in Egypt. ⁹"Look," he said to his people, "the Israelites have become far too numerous for us. ¹⁰Come, we must deal shrewdly with them or they will become even more numerous and, if war breaks out, will join our enemies, fight against us and leave the country."

¹¹So they put slave masters over them to oppress them with forced labor, and they built Pithom and Rameses as store cities for Pharaoh. ¹²But the more they were oppressed, the more they multiplied and spread; so the Egyptians came to dread the Israelites ¹³and worked them ruthlessly. ¹⁴They made their lives bitter with harsh labor in brick and mortar and with all kinds of work in the fields; in all their harsh labor the Egyptians worked them ruthlessly.

¹⁵The king of Egypt said to the Hebrew midwives, whose names were Shiphrah and Puah, ¹⁶"When you are helping the Hebrew women during childbirth on the delivery stool, if you see that the baby is a boy, kill him; but if it is a girl, let her live." ¹⁷The midwives, however, feared God and did not do what the king of Egypt had told them to do; they let the boys live. ¹⁸Then the king of Egypt summoned the midwives and asked them, "Why have you done this? Why have you let the boys live?"

¹⁹The midwives answered Pharaoh, "Hebrew women are not like Egyptian women; they are vigorous and give birth before the midwives arrive."

²⁰So God was kind to the midwives and the people increased and became even more numerous. ²¹And because the midwives feared God, he gave them families of their own.

²²Then Pharaoh gave this order to all his people: "Every Hebrew boy that is born you must throw into the Nile, but let every girl live."

# Amplified Bible

## Exodus

**1** These are the names of the sons of Israel who came into Egypt with Jacob, each with his household:

²Reuben, Simeon, Levi, and Judah,

³Issachar, Zebulun, and Benjamin,

⁴Dan and Naphtali, Gad and Asher.

⁵All the offspring of Jacob were seventy persons; Joseph was already in Egypt.

⁶Then Joseph died, and all his brothers and all that generation.

⁷But the descendants of Israel were fruitful and increased abundantly; they multiplied and grew exceedingly strong, and the land was full of them.

⁸Now a new king arose over Egypt who did not know Joseph.

⁹He said to his people, Behold, the Israelites are too many and too mighty for us [and they [a]outnumber us both in people and in strength].

¹⁰Come, let us deal shrewdly with them, lest they multiply more and, should war befall us, they join our enemies, fight against us, and escape out of the land.

¹¹So they set over [the Israelites] taskmasters to afflict *and* oppress them with [increased] burdens. And [the Israelites] built Pithom and Rameses as store cities for Pharaoh.

¹²But the more [the Egyptians] oppressed them, the more they multiplied and expanded, so that [the Egyptians] were vexed *and* alarmed because of the Israelites.

¹³And the Egyptians reduced the Israelites to severe slavery.

¹⁴They made their lives bitter with hard service in mortar, brick, and all kinds of work in the field. All their service was with harshness *and* severity.

¹⁵Then the king of Egypt said to the Hebrew midwives, of whom one was named Shiprah and the other Puah,

¹⁶When you act as midwives to the Hebrew women and see them on the birthstool, if it is a son, you shall kill him; but if it is a daughter, she shall live.

¹⁷But the midwives feared God and did not do as the king of Egypt commanded, but let the male babies live.

¹⁸So the king of Egypt called for the midwives and said to them, Why have you done this thing and allowed the male children to live?

¹⁹The midwives answered Pharaoh, Because the Hebrew women are not like the Egyptian women; they are vigorous and quickly delivered; their babies are born before the midwife comes to them.

²⁰So God dealt well with the midwives and the people multiplied and became very strong.

²¹And because the midwives revered *and* feared God, He made them households [of their own].

²²Then Pharaoh charged all his people, saying, Every son born [to the Hebrews] you shall cast into the river [Nile], but every daughter you shall allow to live.

---

[a] Is there in all human history a more amazing spectacle than the exodus? A family of 70 immigrants grows into a people of slavery. Suddenly, according to God's detailed and preannounced plan, they are seen flinging away the shackles of generations of slavery and emigrating to a new country and a new life, with miraculous deliverances rescuing them from destruction again and again. The marvel of the exodus grows in wonder when, after more than 3,000 years, we see that same race, often persecuted almost to extinction, carrying out in startling detail God's predictions for their amazing national revitalization and prominence "in the last days" (adapted from many historians).

---

[a] 5 Masoretic Text (see also Gen. 46:27); Dead Sea Scrolls and Septuagint (see also Acts 7:14 and note at Gen. 46:27) *seventy-five*

## New International Version

### The Birth of Moses

**2** Now a man of the tribe of Levi married a Levite woman, [2]and she became pregnant and gave birth to a son. When she saw that he was a fine child, she hid him for three months. [3]But when she could hide him no longer, she got a papyrus basket[a] for him and coated it with tar and pitch. Then she placed the child in it and put it among the reeds along the bank of the Nile. [4]His sister stood at a distance to see what would happen to him.

[5]Then Pharaoh's daughter went down to the Nile to bathe, and her attendants were walking along the riverbank. She saw the basket among the reeds and sent her female slave to get it. [6]She opened it and saw the baby. He was crying, and she felt sorry for him. "This is one of the Hebrew babies," she said.

[7]Then his sister asked Pharaoh's daughter, "Shall I go and get one of the Hebrew women to nurse the baby for you?"

[8]"Yes, go," she answered. So the girl went and got the baby's mother. [9]Pharaoh's daughter said to her, "Take this baby and nurse him for me, and I will pay you." So the woman took the baby and nursed him. [10]When the child grew older, she took him to Pharaoh's daughter and he became her son. She named him Moses,[b] saying, "I drew him out of the water."

### Moses Flees to Midian

[11]One day, after Moses had grown up, he went out to where his own people were and watched them at their hard labor. He saw an Egyptian beating a Hebrew, one of his own people. [12]Looking this way and that and seeing no one, he killed the Egyptian and hid him in the sand. [13]The next day he went out and saw two Hebrews fighting. He asked the one in the wrong, "Why are you hitting your fellow Hebrew?"

[14]The man said, "Who made you ruler and judge over us? Are you thinking of killing me as you killed the Egyptian?" Then Moses was afraid and thought, "What I did must have become known."

[15]When Pharaoh heard of this, he tried to kill Moses, but Moses fled from Pharaoh and went to live in Midian, where he sat down by a well. [16]Now a priest of Midian had seven daughters, and they came to draw water and fill the troughs to water their father's flock. [17]Some shepherds came along and drove them away, but Moses got up and came to their rescue and watered their flock.

[18]When the girls returned to Reuel their father, he asked them, "Why have you returned so early today?"

[19]They answered, "An Egyptian rescued us from the shepherds. He even drew water for us and watered the flock."

[20]"And where is he?" Reuel asked his daughters. "Why did you leave him? Invite him to have something to eat."

[21]Moses agreed to stay with the man, who gave his daughter Zipporah to Moses in marriage. [22]Zipporah gave

## Amplified Bible

**2** Now [Amram] a man of the house of Levi [the priestly tribe] went and took as his wife [Jochebed] a daughter of Levi. [Exod. 6:18, 20; Num. 26:59.]

[2]And the woman became pregnant and bore a son; and when she saw that he was [exceedingly] beautiful, she hid him three months. [Acts 7:20; Heb. 11:23.]

[3]And when she could no longer hide him, she took for him an ark *or* basket made of bulrushes *or* papyrus [making it watertight by] daubing it with bitumen and pitch. Then she put the child in it and laid it among the rushes by the brink of the river [Nile].

[4]And his sister [Miriam] stood some distance away to [a]learn what would be done to him.

[5]Now the daughter of Pharaoh came down to bathe at the river, and her maidens walked along the bank; she saw the ark among the rushes and sent her maid to fetch it.

[6]When she opened it, she saw the child; and behold, the baby cried. And she took pity on him and said, This is one of the Hebrews' children!

[7]Then his sister said to Pharaoh's daughter, Shall I go and call a nurse of the Hebrew women to nurse the child for you?

[8]Pharaoh's daughter said to her, Go. And the girl went and called the child's mother.

[9]Then Pharaoh's daughter said to her, Take this child away and nurse it for me, and I will give you your wages. So the woman took the child and nursed it.

[10]And the child grew, and she brought him to Pharaoh's daughter and he became her son. And she called him Moses, for she said, Because I drew him out of the water.

[11]One day, after Moses was grown, it happened that he went out to his brethren and looked at their burdens; and he saw an Egyptian beating a Hebrew, one of [Moses'] brethren.

[12]He looked this way and that way, and when he saw no one, he killed the Egyptian and hid him in the sand.

[13]He went out the second day and saw two Hebrew men quarreling *and* fighting; and he said to the unjust aggressor, Why are you striking your comrade?

[14]And the man said, Who made you a prince and a judge over us? Do you intend to kill me as you killed the Egyptian? Then Moses was afraid and thought, Surely this thing is known.

[15]When Pharaoh heard of it, he sought to slay Moses. But Moses fled from Pharaoh's presence and [b]took refuge in the land of Midian, where he sat down by a well.

[16]Now the priest of Midian had seven daughters, and they came and drew water and filled the troughs to water their father's flock.

[17]The shepherds came and drove them away; but Moses stood up and helped them and watered their flock.

[18]And when they came to Reuel [Jethro] their father, he said, How is it that you have come so soon today?

[19]They said, An Egyptian delivered us from the shepherds; also he drew water for us and watered the flock.

[20]He said to his daughters, Where is he? Why have you left the man? Call him, that he may eat bread.

[21]And Moses was content to dwell with the man; and he gave Moses Zipporah his daughter.

---

[a] They launched the ark not only on the Nile but on God's providence. He would be Captain, Steersman, and Convoy of the tiny ark. Miriam stood to watch. There was no fear of fatal consequences, only the quiet expectancy that God would do something worthy of Himself. They reckoned on God's faithfulness and they were amply rewarded when the daughter of their greatest foe became the babe's patroness (F. B. Meyer, *Through the Bible Day by Day*). [b] "There was true heroism in the act, when Moses stepped down from Pharaoh's throne to share the lot of his brethren. But it would take many a long year of lonely waiting and trial before this strong and radiant nature could be broken down, shaped into a vessel meet for the Master's use, and prepared for every good work. . . . One blow struck when God's time is fulfilled is worth a thousand struck in premature eagerness" (F. B. Meyer, *Moses, the Servant of God*).

---

[a] 3 The Hebrew can also mean *ark*, as in Gen. 6:14.   [b] 10 *Moses* sounds like the Hebrew for *draw out*.

## New International Version

birth to a son, and Moses named him Gershom,[a] saying, "I have become a foreigner in a foreign land."

²³During that long period, the king of Egypt died. The Israelites groaned in their slavery and cried out, and their cry for help because of their slavery went up to God. ²⁴God heard their groaning and he remembered his covenant with Abraham, with Isaac and with Jacob. ²⁵So God looked on the Israelites and was concerned about them.

### Moses and the Burning Bush

**3** Now Moses was tending the flock of Jethro his father-in-law, the priest of Midian, and he led the flock to the far side of the wilderness and came to Horeb, the mountain of God. ²There the angel of the LORD appeared to him in flames of fire from within a bush. Moses saw that though the bush was on fire it did not burn up. ³So Moses thought, "I will go over and see this strange sight—why the bush does not burn up."

⁴When the LORD saw that he had gone over to look, God called to him from within the bush, "Moses! Moses!"

And Moses said, "Here I am."

⁵"Do not come any closer," God said. "Take off your sandals, for the place where you are standing is holy ground." ⁶Then he said, "I am the God of your father,[b] the God of Abraham, the God of Isaac and the God of Jacob." At this, Moses hid his face, because he was afraid to look at God.

⁷The LORD said, "I have indeed seen the misery of my people in Egypt. I have heard them crying out because of their slave drivers, and I am concerned about their suffering. ⁸So I have come down to rescue them from the hand of the Egyptians and to bring them up out of that land into a good and spacious land, a land flowing with milk and honey—the home of the Canaanites, Hittites, Amorites, Perizzites, Hivites and Jebusites. ⁹And now the cry of the Israelites has reached me, and I have seen the way the Egyptians are oppressing them. ¹⁰So now, go. I am sending you to Pharaoh to bring my people the Israelites out of Egypt."

¹¹But Moses said to God, "Who am I that I should go to Pharaoh and bring the Israelites out of Egypt?"

¹²And God said, "I will be with you. And this will be the sign to you that it is I who have sent you: When you have brought the people out of Egypt, you[c] will worship God on this mountain."

¹³Moses said to God, "Suppose I go to the Israelites and say to them, 'The God of your fathers has sent me to you,' and they ask me, 'What is his name?' Then what shall I tell them?"

¹⁴God said to Moses, "I AM WHO I AM.[d] This is what you are to say to the Israelites: 'I AM has sent me to you.'"

¹⁵God also said to Moses, "Say to the Israelites, 'The

## Amplified Bible

²²And she bore a son, and he called his name Gershom [expulsion, or a stranger there]; for he said, I have been a stranger *and* a sojourner in a foreign land.

²³However, after a long time [nearly forty years] the king of Egypt died; and the Israelites were sighing *and* groaning because of the bondage. They kept crying, and their cry because of slavery ascended to God.

²⁴And God heard their sighing *and* groaning and [earnestly] remembered His covenant with Abraham, with Isaac, and with Jacob.

²⁵God saw the Israelites and took knowledge of them *and* concerned Himself about them [knowing all, understanding, remembering all]. [Ps. 56:8, 9; 139:2.]

**3** Now Moses kept the flock of Jethro his father-in-law, the priest of Midian; and he led the flock to the back *or* west side of the wilderness and came to Horeb *or* Sinai, the mountain of God.

²The [a]Angel of the Lord appeared to him in a flame of fire out of the midst of a bush; and he looked, and behold, the bush burned with fire, yet was not consumed.

³And Moses said, I will now turn aside and see this great sight, why the bush is not burned.

⁴And when the Lord saw that he turned aside to see, God called to him out of the midst of the bush and said, Moses, Moses! And he said, Here am I.

⁵God said, Do not come near; put your shoes off your feet, for the place on which you stand is holy ground.

⁶Also He said, I am the God of your father, the God of Abraham, the God of Isaac, and the God of Jacob. And Moses hid his face, for he was afraid to look at God.

⁷And the Lord said, I have surely seen the affliction of My people who are in Egypt, and have heard their cry because of their taskmasters *and* oppressors; for I know their sorrows *and* sufferings *and* trials.

⁸And I have come down to deliver them out of the hand *and* power of the Egyptians and to bring them up out of that land to a land good and large, a land flowing with milk and honey [a land of plenty]—to the place of the Canaanite, the Hittite, the Amorite, the Perizzite, the Hivite, and the Jebusite.

⁹Now behold, the cry of the Israelites has come to Me, and I have also seen how the Egyptians oppress them.

¹⁰Come now therefore, and I will send you to Pharaoh, that you may bring forth My people, the Israelites, out of Egypt.

¹¹And Moses said to God, [b]Who am I, that I should go to Pharaoh and bring the Israelites out of Egypt?

¹²God said, I will surely be with you; and this shall be the sign to you that I have sent you: when you have brought the people out of Egypt, you shall serve God on this mountain [Horeb, or Sinai].

¹³And Moses said to God, Behold, when I come to the Israelites and say to them, The God of your fathers has sent me to you, and they say to me, What is His name? What shall I say to them?

¹⁴And God said to Moses, I AM WHO I AM *and* WHAT I AM, *and* I WILL BE WHAT I WILL BE; and He said, You shall say this to the Israelites: I AM has sent me to you!

¹⁵God said also to Moses, This shall you say to the Israelites: The Lord, the God of your fathers, of Abraham, of

---

[a] In this report of Moses and the burning bush, "the Angel of the Lord" is identified as the Lord Himself. See especially Exod. 3:4, 6. See also the footnote on Gen. 16:7.   [b] "There was something more than humility here; there was a tone of self-depreciation which was inconsistent with a true faith in God's selection and appointment. Surely it is God's business to choose His special instruments; and when we are persuaded that we are in the line of His purpose, we have no right to question the wisdom of His appointment. To do so is to depreciate His wisdom or to doubt His power and willingness to become **all that is necessary** to complete our need" (F. B. Meyer, *Moses, the Servant of God*).

---

[a] 22 *Gershom* sounds like the Hebrew for *a foreigner there*.
[b] 6 Masoretic Text; Samaritan Pentateuch (see Acts 7:32) *fathers*
[c] 12 The Hebrew is plural.   [d] 14 Or *I WILL BE WHAT I WILL BE*

## New International Version

LORD,[a] the God of your fathers—the God of Abraham, the God of Isaac and the God of Jacob—has sent me to you.'

"This is my name forever,
the name you shall call me
from generation to generation.

16"Go, assemble the elders of Israel and say to them, 'The LORD, the God of your fathers—the God of Abraham, Isaac and Jacob—appeared to me and said: I have watched over you and have seen what has been done to you in Egypt. 17And I have promised to bring you up out of your misery in Egypt into the land of the Canaanites, Hittites, Amorites, Perizzites, Hivites and Jebusites—a land flowing with milk and honey.'

18"The elders of Israel will listen to you. Then you and the elders are to go to the king of Egypt and say to him, 'The LORD, the God of the Hebrews, has met with us. Let us take a three-day journey into the wilderness to offer sacrifices to the LORD our God.' 19But I know that the king of Egypt will not let you go unless a mighty hand compels him. 20So I will stretch out my hand and strike the Egyptians with all the wonders that I will perform among them. After that, he will let you go.

21"And I will make the Egyptians favorably disposed toward this people, so that when you leave you will not go empty-handed. 22Every woman is to ask her neighbor and any woman living in her house for articles of silver and gold and for clothing, which you will put on your sons and daughters. And so you will plunder the Egyptians."

### Signs for Moses

4 Moses answered, "What if they do not believe me or listen to me and say, 'The LORD did not appear to you'?"

2Then the LORD said to him, "What is that in your hand?"

"A staff," he replied.

3The LORD said, "Throw it on the ground."

Moses threw it on the ground and it became a snake, and he ran from it. 4Then the LORD said to him, "Reach out your hand and take it by the tail." So Moses reached out and took hold of the snake and it turned back into a staff in his hand. 5"This," said the LORD, "is so that they may believe that the LORD, the God of their fathers—the God of Abraham, the God of Isaac and the God of Jacob—has appeared to you."

6Then the LORD said, "Put your hand inside your cloak." So Moses put his hand into his cloak, and when he took it out, the skin was leprous[b]—it had become as white as snow.

7"Now put it back into your cloak," he said. So Moses put his hand back into his cloak, and when he took it out, it was restored, like the rest of his flesh.

8Then the LORD said, "If they do not believe you or pay attention to the first sign, they may believe the second. 9But if they do not believe these two signs or listen to you, take some water from the Nile and pour it on the dry ground. The water you take from the river will become blood on the ground."

[a] 15 The Hebrew for LORD sounds like and may be related to the Hebrew for I AM in verse 14. [b] 6 The Hebrew word for leprous was used for various diseases affecting the skin.

## Amplified Bible

Isaac, and of Jacob, has sent me to you! This is My [a]name forever, and by this name I am to be remembered to all generations.

16Go, gather the elders of Israel together [the mature teachers and tribal leaders], and say to them, The Lord God of your fathers, the God of Abraham, of Isaac, and of Jacob, appeared to me, saying, I have surely visited you and seen that which is done to you in Egypt;

17And I have declared that I will bring you up out of the affliction of Egypt to the land of the Canaanite, the Hittite, the Amorite, the Perizzite, the Hivite, and the Jebusite, to a land flowing with milk and honey.

18And [the elders] shall believe and obey your voice; and you shall go, you and the elders of Israel, to the king of Egypt and you shall say to him, The Lord, the God of the Hebrews, has met with us; and now let us go, we beseech you, three days' journey into the wilderness, that we may sacrifice to the Lord our God.

19And I know that the king of Egypt will not let you go [unless forced to do so], no, not by a mighty hand.

20So I will stretch out My hand and smite Egypt with all My wonders which I will do in it; and after that he will let you go.

21And I will give this people favor and respect in the sight of the Egyptians; and it shall be that when you go, you shall not go empty-handed.

22But every woman shall [insistently] solicit of her neighbor and of her that may be residing at her house jewels and articles of silver and gold, and garments, which you shall put on your sons and daughters; and you shall strip the Egyptians [of belongings due to you].

4 And Moses answered, [b]But behold, they will not believe me or listen to and obey my voice; for they will say, The Lord has not appeared to you.

2And the Lord said to him, What is that in your hand? And he said, A rod.

3And He said, Cast it on the ground. And he did so and it became a serpent [the symbol of royal and divine power worn on the crown of the Pharaohs]; and Moses fled from before it.

4And the Lord said to Moses, Put forth your hand and take it by the tail. And he stretched out his hand and caught it, and it became a rod in his hand,

5[This you shall do, said the Lord] that the elders may believe that the Lord, the God of their fathers, of Abraham, of Isaac, and of Jacob, has indeed appeared to you.

6The Lord said also to him, Put your hand into your bosom. He put his hand into his bosom, and when he took it out, behold, his hand was leprous, as white as snow.

7[God] said, Put your hand into your bosom again. So he put his hand back into his bosom, and when he took it out, behold, it was restored as the rest of his flesh.

8[Then God said] If they will not believe you or heed the voice or the testimony of the first sign, they may believe the voice or the witness of the second sign.

9But if they will also not believe these two signs or heed your voice, you shall take some water of the river [Nile] and pour it upon the dry land; and the water which you take out of the river [Nile] shall become blood on the dry land.

[a] To know the name of God is to witness the manifestation of those attributes and apprehend that character which the name denotes (Exod. 6:3; I Kings 8:33ff.; Ps. 91:14; Isa. 52:6; 64:2; Jer. 16:21) (John D. Davis, A Dictionary of the Bible). God's name is His self-revelation (Charles Ellicott, A Bible Commentary). The name signifies the active presence of the person in the fullness of the revealed character (J. D. Douglas et al., eds., The New Bible Dictionary). [b] There need be no "buts" in our relationship to God's will. Nothing will take the Lord by surprise. The entire field has been surveyed and the preparations are complete. When the Lord says, "I will send thee," every provision has been made for the appointed task. "I will not fail thee." He who gives the command will also give the equipment (John Henry Jowett, My Daily Meditation).

## New International Version

[10]Moses said to the LORD, "Pardon your servant, Lord. I have never been eloquent, neither in the past nor since you have spoken to your servant. I am slow of speech and tongue."

[11]The LORD said to him, "Who gave human beings their mouths? Who makes them deaf or mute? Who gives them sight or makes them blind? Is it not I, the LORD? [12]Now go; I will help you speak and will teach you what to say."

[13]But Moses said, "Pardon your servant, Lord. Please send someone else."

[14]Then the LORD's anger burned against Moses and he said, "What about your brother, Aaron the Levite? I know he can speak well. He is already on his way to meet you, and he will be glad to see you. [15]You shall speak to him and put words in his mouth; I will help both of you speak and will teach you what to do. [16]He will speak to the people for you, and it will be as if he were your mouth and as if you were God to him. [17]But take this staff in your hand so you can perform the signs with it."

### Moses Returns to Egypt

[18]Then Moses went back to Jethro his father-in-law and said to him, "Let me return to my own people in Egypt to see if any of them are still alive."

Jethro said, "Go, and I wish you well."

[19]Now the LORD had said to Moses in Midian, "Go back to Egypt, for all those who wanted to kill you are dead." [20]So Moses took his wife and sons, put them on a donkey and started back to Egypt. And he took the staff of God in his hand.

[21]The LORD said to Moses, "When you return to Egypt, see that you perform before Pharaoh all the wonders I have given you the power to do. But I will harden his heart so that he will not let the people go. [22]Then say to Pharaoh, 'This is what the LORD says: Israel is my firstborn son, [23]and I told you, "Let my son go, so he may worship me." But you refused to let him go; so I will kill your firstborn son.'"

[24]At a lodging place on the way, the LORD met Moses[a] and was about to kill him. [25]But Zipporah took a flint knife, cut off her son's foreskin and touched Moses' feet with it.[b] "Surely you are a bridegroom of blood to me," she said. [26]So the LORD let him alone. (At that time she said "bridegroom of blood," referring to circumcision.)

[27]The LORD said to Aaron, "Go into the wilderness to meet Moses." So he met Moses at the mountain of God and kissed him. [28]Then Moses told Aaron everything the LORD had sent him to say, and also about all the signs he had commanded him to perform.

[29]Moses and Aaron brought together all the elders of the Israelites, [30]and Aaron told them everything the LORD had said to Moses. He also performed the signs before the people, [31]and they believed. And when they heard that the LORD was concerned about them and had seen their misery, they bowed down and worshiped.

## Amplified Bible

[10]And Moses said to the Lord, O Lord, I am not eloquent or a man of words, neither before nor since You have spoken to Your servant; for I am slow of speech and have a heavy and awkward tongue.

[11]And the Lord said to him, Who has made man's mouth? Or who makes the dumb, or the deaf, or the seeing, or the blind? Is it not I, the Lord?

[12]Now therefore go, and I will be with your mouth and will teach you what you shall say.

[13]And he said, Oh, my Lord, I pray You, send by the hand of [some other] whom You will [send].

[14]Then the anger of the Lord blazed against Moses; He said, Is there not Aaron your brother, the Levite? I know he can speak well. Also, he is coming out to meet you, and when he sees you, he will be overjoyed.

[15]You must speak to him and put the words in his mouth; and I will be with your mouth and with his mouth and will teach you what you shall do.

[16]He shall speak for you to the people, acting as a mouthpiece for you, and you shall be as God to him.

[17]And you shall take this rod in your hand with which you shall work the signs [that prove I sent you].

[18]And Moses went away and, returning to Jethro his father-in-law, said to him, Let me go back, I pray you, to my relatives in Egypt to see whether they are still alive. And Jethro said to Moses, Go in peace.

[19]The Lord said to Moses in Midian, Go back to Egypt; for all the men who were seeking your life [for killing the Egyptian] are dead. [Exod. 2:11, 12.]

[20]And Moses took his wife and his sons and set them on donkeys, and he returned to the land of Egypt; and Moses took the rod of God in his hand.

[21]And the Lord said to Moses, When you return into Egypt, see that you do before Pharaoh all those miracles and wonders which I have put in your hand; but I will make him stubborn and harden his heart, so that he will not let the people go.

[22]And you shall say to Pharaoh, Thus says the Lord, Israel is My son, even My firstborn.

[23]And I say to you, Let My son go, that he may serve Me; and if you refuse to let him go, behold, I will slay your son, your firstborn.

[24]Along the way at a [resting-] place, the Lord met [Moses] and sought to kill him [made him acutely and almost fatally ill].

[25][Now apparently he had [a]failed to circumcise one of his sons, his wife being opposed to it; but seeing his life in such danger] Zipporah took a flint knife and cut off the foreskin of her son and cast it to touch [Moses'] feet, and said, Surely a husband of blood you are to me!

[26]When He let [Moses] alone [to recover], Zipporah said, A husband of blood are you because of the circumcision.

[27]The Lord said to Aaron, Go into the wilderness to meet Moses. And he went, and met him in the mountain of God [Horeb, or Sinai] and kissed him.

[28]Moses told Aaron all the words of the Lord with which He had sent him, and all the signs with which He had charged him.

[29]Moses and Aaron went and gathered together [in Egypt] all the elders of the Israelites.

[30]Aaron spoke all the words which the Lord had spoken to Moses, and did the signs in the sight of the people.

[31]And the people believed; and when they heard that the Lord had visited the Israelites, and that He had looked [in compassion] upon their affliction, they bowed their heads and worshiped.

---

[a] He who is on his way to liberate the people of the circumcision has in Midian even neglected to circumcise his second son Eliezer (J. P. Lange, *A Commentary*). It was necessary that at this stage of Moses' experience he should learn that God is in earnest when He speaks, and will assuredly perform all that He has threatened (J. G. Murphy, *A Commentary on the Book of Exodus*).

---

[a] 24 Hebrew *him*    [b] 25 The meaning of the Hebrew for this clause is uncertain.

## New International Version

### Bricks Without Straw

**5** Afterward Moses and Aaron went to Pharaoh and said, "This is what the LORD, the God of Israel, says: 'Let my people go, so that they may hold a festival to me in the wilderness.'"

²Pharaoh said, "Who is the LORD, that I should obey him and let Israel go? I do not know the LORD and I will not let Israel go." ³Then they said, "The God of the Hebrews has met with us. Now let us take a three-day journey into the wilderness to offer sacrifices to the LORD our God, or he may strike us with plagues or with the sword."

⁴But the king of Egypt said, "Moses and Aaron, why are you taking the people away from their labor? Get back to your work!" ⁵Then Pharaoh said, "Look, the people of the land are now numerous, and you are stopping them from working."

⁶That same day Pharaoh gave this order to the slave drivers and overseers in charge of the people: ⁷"You are no longer to supply the people with straw for making bricks; let them go and gather their own straw. ⁸But require them to make the same number of bricks as before; don't reduce the quota. They are lazy; that is why they are crying out, 'Let us go and sacrifice to our God.' ⁹Make the work harder for the people so that they keep working and pay no attention to lies."

¹⁰Then the slave drivers and the overseers went out and said to the people, "This is what Pharaoh says: 'I will not give you any more straw. ¹¹Go and get your own straw wherever you can find it, but your work will not be reduced at all.'" ¹²So the people scattered all over Egypt to gather stubble to use for straw. ¹³The slave drivers kept pressing them, saying, "Complete the work required of you for each day, just as when you had straw." ¹⁴And Pharaoh's slave drivers beat the Israelite overseers they had appointed, demanding, "Why haven't you met your quota of bricks yesterday or today, as before?"

¹⁵Then the Israelite overseers went and appealed to Pharaoh: "Why have you treated your servants this way? ¹⁶Your servants are given no straw, yet we are told, 'Make bricks!' Your servants are being beaten, but the fault is with your own people."

¹⁷Pharaoh said, "Lazy, that's what you are—lazy! That is why you keep saying, 'Let us go and sacrifice to the LORD.' ¹⁸Now get to work. You will not be given any straw, yet you must produce your full quota of bricks."

¹⁹The Israelite overseers realized they were in trouble when they were told, "You are not to reduce the number of bricks required of you for each day." ²⁰When they left Pharaoh, they found Moses and Aaron waiting to meet them, ²¹and they said, "May the LORD look on you and judge you! You have made us obnoxious to Pharaoh and his officials and have put a sword in their hand to kill us."

### God Promises Deliverance

²²Moses returned to the LORD and said, "Why, Lord, why have you brought trouble on this people? Is this why

## Amplified Bible

**5** Afterward Moses and Aaron went in and told Pharaoh, Thus says the Lord, the God of Israel, Let My people go, that they may hold a feast to Me in the wilderness.

²But Pharaoh said, Who is the Lord, that I should obey His voice to let Israel go? I know not the Lord, neither will I let Israel go.

³And they said, The God of the Hebrews has met with us; let us go, we pray you, three days' journey into the desert and sacrifice to the Lord our God, lest He fall upon us with pestilence or with the sword.

⁴The king of Egypt said to Moses and Aaron, Why do you take the people from their jobs? Get to your burdens! ⁵Pharaoh said, Behold, the people of the land now are many, and you make them rest from their burdens!

⁶The very same day Pharaoh commanded the taskmasters of the people and their officers,

⁷You shall no more give the people straw to make brick; let them go and gather straw for themselves.

⁸But the number of the bricks which they made before you shall still require of them; you shall not diminish it in the least. For they are idle; that is why they cry, Let us go and sacrifice to our God.

⁹Let heavier work be laid upon the men that they may labor at it and pay no attention to lying words.

¹⁰The taskmasters of the people went out, and their officers, and they said to the people, Thus says Pharaoh, I will not give you straw.

¹¹Go, get *ᵃ*straw where you can find it; but your work shall not be diminished in the least.

¹²So the people were scattered through all the land of Egypt to gather the short stubble instead of straw.

¹³And the taskmasters were urgent, saying, Finish your work, your daily quotas, as when there was straw.

¹⁴And the Hebrew foremen, whom Pharaoh's taskmasters had set over them, were beaten and were asked, Why have you not fulfilled all your quota of making bricks yesterday and today, as before?

¹⁵Then the Hebrew foremen came to Pharaoh and cried, Why do you deal like this with your servants?

¹⁶No straw is given to your servants, yet they say to us, Make bricks! And behold, your servants are beaten, but the fault is in your own people.

¹⁷But [Pharaoh] said, You are idle, lazy *and* idle! That is why you say, Let us go and sacrifice to the Lord.

¹⁸Get out now and get to work; for no straw shall be given you, yet you shall deliver the full quota of bricks.

¹⁹And the Hebrew foremen saw that they were in an evil situation when it was said, You shall not diminish in the least your full daily quota of bricks.

²⁰And the foremen met Moses and Aaron, who were standing in the way as they came forth from Pharaoh.

²¹And the foremen said to them, The Lord look upon you and judge, because you have made us a rotten stench to be detested by Pharaoh and his servants and have put a sword in their hand to slay us.

²²Then Moses turned again to the Lord and said, O Lord, why have You dealt evil to this people? Why did You ever send me?

---

*ᵃ* Archaeologists became interested early in examining Egyptian bricks of Moses' time to see if they contained straw. They found that, while many did contain straw, many also did not, leaving the impression that the Bible was wrong. But as usual in such cases, sooner or later it is shown that "the testimony of the Lord is sure, making wise the simple" (Ps. 19:7)—who know no better than to doubt the truth of God's Word. It is now known that oat straw boiled in water, when added to clay, makes the clay much easier to handle. Without the organic material obtained from the straw, the difficulty of making bricks was greatly increased. The fact that brickmakers of Egypt found the use of straw essential, whether visible evidence remains or not, is fully borne out, as various writers have asserted. (See Allan A. MacRae's, "The Relation of Archaeology to the Bible" in *Modern Science and Christian Faith*.)

## New International Version

you sent me? <sup>23</sup>Ever since I went to Pharaoh to speak in your name, he has brought trouble on this people, and you have not rescued your people at all."

**6** Then the LORD said to Moses, "Now you will see what I will do to Pharaoh: Because of my mighty hand he will let them go; because of my mighty hand he will drive them out of his country."

<sup>2</sup>God also said to Moses, "I am the LORD. <sup>3</sup>I appeared to Abraham, to Isaac and to Jacob as God Almighty,<sup>a</sup> but by my name the LORD<sup>b</sup> I did not make myself fully known to them. <sup>4</sup>I also established my covenant with them to give them the land of Canaan, where they resided as foreigners. <sup>5</sup>Moreover, I have heard the groaning of the Israelites, whom the Egyptians are enslaving, and I have remembered my covenant.

<sup>6</sup>"Therefore, say to the Israelites: 'I am the LORD, and I will bring you out from under the yoke of the Egyptians. I will free you from being slaves to them, and I will redeem you with an outstretched arm and with mighty acts of judgment. <sup>7</sup>I will take you as my own people, and I will be your God. Then you will know that I am the LORD your God, who brought you out from under the yoke of the Egyptians. <sup>8</sup>And I will bring you to the land I swore with uplifted hand to give to Abraham, to Isaac and to Jacob. I will give it to you as a possession. I am the LORD.'"

<sup>9</sup>Moses reported this to the Israelites, but they did not listen to him because of their discouragement and harsh labor.

<sup>10</sup>Then the LORD said to Moses, <sup>11</sup>"Go, tell Pharaoh king of Egypt to let the Israelites go out of his country."

<sup>12</sup>But Moses said to the LORD, "If the Israelites will not listen to me, why would Pharaoh listen to me, since I speak with faltering lips<sup>c</sup>?"

### Family Record of Moses and Aaron

<sup>13</sup>Now the LORD spoke to Moses and Aaron about the Israelites and Pharaoh king of Egypt, and he commanded them to bring the Israelites out of Egypt.

<sup>14</sup>These were the heads of their families<sup>d</sup>:

The sons of Reuben the firstborn son of Israel were Hanok and Pallu, Hezron and Karmi. These were the clans of Reuben.

<sup>15</sup>The sons of Simeon were Jemuel, Jamin, Ohad, Jakin, Zohar and Shaul the son of a Canaanite woman. These were the clans of Simeon.

<sup>16</sup>These were the names of the sons of Levi according to their records: Gershon, Kohath and Merari. Levi lived 137 years.

<sup>17</sup>The sons of Gershon, by clans, were Libni and Shimei.

<sup>18</sup>The sons of Kohath were Amram, Izhar, Hebron and Uzziel. Kohath lived 133 years.

<sup>19</sup>The sons of Merari were Mahli and Mushi.

These were the clans of Levi according to their records.

<sup>20</sup>Amram married his father's sister Jochebed, who bore him Aaron and Moses. Amram lived 137 years.

<sup>21</sup>The sons of Izhar were Korah, Nepheg and Zikri.

<sup>22</sup>The sons of Uzziel were Mishael, Elzaphan and Sithri.

<sup>23</sup>Aaron married Elisheba, daughter of Ammina-

## Amplified Bible

<sup>23</sup>For since I came to Pharaoh to speak in Your name, he has done evil to this people, neither have You delivered Your people at all.

**6** Then the Lord said to Moses, Now you shall see what I will do to Pharaoh; for [compelled] by a strong hand he will [not only] let them go, but he will drive them out of his land with a strong hand.

<sup>2</sup>And God said to Moses, I am the Lord.

<sup>3</sup>I appeared to Abraham, to Isaac, and to Jacob as God Almighty [El-Shaddai], but by My <sup>a</sup>name the Lord [Yahweh—the redemptive name of God] I did not make Myself known to them [in acts and great miracles]. [Gen. 17:1.]

<sup>4</sup>I have also established My covenant with them to give them the land of Canaan, the land of their temporary residence in which they were strangers.

<sup>5</sup>I have also heard the groaning of the Israelites whom the Egyptians have enslaved; and I have [earnestly] remembered My covenant [with Abraham, Isaac, and Jacob].

<sup>6</sup>Accordingly, say to the Israelites, I am the Lord, and I will bring you out from under the burdens of the Egyptians, and I will free you from their bondage, and I will rescue you with an outstretched arm [with special and vigorous action] and by mighty acts of judgment.

<sup>7</sup>And I will take you to Me for a people, and I will be to you a God; and you shall know that it is I, the Lord your God, Who brings you out from under the burdens of the Egyptians.

<sup>8</sup>And I will bring you into the land concerning which I lifted up My hand *and* swore that I would give it to Abraham, Isaac, and Jacob; and I will give it to you for a heritage. I am the Lord [you have the pledge of My changeless omnipotence and faithfulness].

<sup>9</sup>Moses told this to the Israelites, but they refused to listen to Moses because of their impatience *and* anguish of spirit and because of their cruel bondage.

<sup>10</sup>The Lord said to Moses,

<sup>11</sup>Go in, tell Pharaoh king of Egypt to let the Israelites go out of his land.

<sup>12</sup>But Moses said to the Lord, Behold, [my own people] the Israelites have not listened to me; how then shall Pharaoh give heed to me, who am of deficient *and* impeded speech?

<sup>13</sup>But the Lord spoke to Moses and Aaron, and gave them a command for the Israelites and for Pharaoh king of Egypt, to bring the Israelites out of the land of Egypt.

<sup>14</sup>These are the heads of their clans. The sons of Reuben, Israel's firstborn: Hanoch, Pallu, Hezron, and Carmi; these are the families of Reuben.

<sup>15</sup>The sons of Simeon: Jemuel, Jamin, Ohad, Jachin, Zohar, and Shaul the son of a Canaanite woman; these are the families of Simeon.

<sup>16</sup>These are the names of the sons of Levi according to their births: Gershon, Kohath, and Merari; and Levi lived 137 years.

<sup>17</sup>The sons of Gershon: Libni and Shimi, by their families.

<sup>18</sup>The sons of Kohath: Amram, Izhar, Hebron, and Uzziel; and Kohath lived 133 years.

<sup>19</sup>The sons of Merari: Mahli and Mushi. These are the families of Levi according to their generations.

<sup>20</sup>Amram took Jochebed his father's sister as wife, and she bore him Aaron and Moses; and Amram lived 137 years.

<sup>21</sup>The sons of Izhar: Korah, Nepheg, and Zichri.

<sup>22</sup>The sons of Uzziel: Mishael, Elzaphan, and Sithri.

<sup>23</sup>Aaron took Elisheba, daughter of Amminadab and

---

<sup>a</sup> 3 Hebrew *El-Shaddai*   <sup>b</sup> 3 See note at 3:15.   <sup>c</sup> 12 Hebrew *I am uncircumcised of lips*; also in verse 30   <sup>d</sup> 14 The Hebrew for *families* here and in verse 25 refers to units larger than clans.

<sup>a</sup> See footnote on Exod. 3:15.

## New International Version

dab and sister of Nahshon, and she bore him Nadab and Abihu, Eleazar and Ithamar. 24The sons of Korah were Assir, Elkanah and Abiasaph. These were the Korahite clans. 25Eleazar son of Aaron married one of the daughters of Putiel, and she bore him Phinehas.

These were the heads of the Levite families, clan by clan.

26It was this Aaron and Moses to whom the LORD said, "Bring the Israelites out of Egypt by their divisions." 27They were the ones who spoke to Pharaoh king of Egypt about bringing the Israelites out of Egypt—this same Moses and Aaron.

### Aaron to Speak for Moses

28Now when the LORD spoke to Moses in Egypt, 29he said to him, "I am the LORD. Tell Pharaoh king of Egypt everything I tell you." 30But Moses said to the LORD, "Since I speak with faltering lips, why would Pharaoh listen to me?"

**7** Then the LORD said to Moses, "See, I have made you like God to Pharaoh, and your brother Aaron will be your prophet. 2You are to say everything I command you, and your brother Aaron is to tell Pharaoh to let the Israelites go out of his country. 3But I will harden Pharaoh's heart, and though I multiply my signs and wonders in Egypt, 4he will not listen to you. Then I will lay my hand on Egypt and with mighty acts of judgment I will bring out my divisions, my people the Israelites. 5And the Egyptians will know that I am the LORD when I stretch out my hand against Egypt and bring the Israelites out of it."

6Moses and Aaron did just as the LORD commanded them. 7Moses was eighty years old and Aaron eighty-three when they spoke to Pharaoh.

### Aaron's Staff Becomes a Snake

8The LORD said to Moses and Aaron, 9"When Pharaoh says to you, 'Perform a miracle,' then say to Aaron, 'Take your staff and throw it down before Pharaoh,' and it will become a snake."

10So Moses and Aaron went to Pharaoh and did just as the LORD commanded. Aaron threw his staff down in front of Pharaoh and his officials, and it became a snake. 11Pharaoh then summoned wise men and sorcerers, and the Egyptian magicians also did the same things by their secret arts: 12Each one threw down his staff and it became a snake. But Aaron's staff swallowed up their staffs. 13Yet Pharaoh's heart became hard and he would not listen to them, just as the LORD had said.

### The Plague of Blood

14Then the LORD said to Moses, "Pharaoh's heart is unyielding; he refuses to let the people go. 15Go to Pharaoh in the morning as he goes out to the river. Confront him on the bank of the Nile, and take in your hand the staff that was changed into a snake. 16Then say to him, 'The LORD, the God of the Hebrews, has sent me to say to you: Let my people go, so that they may worship me in the wilderness. But until now you have not listened. 17This is what the LORD says: By this you will know that I am the LORD:

## Amplified Bible

sister of Nahshon, as wife; she bore him Nadab, Abihu, Eleazar, and Ithamar. 24The sons of Korah: Assir, Elkanah, and Abiasaph. These are the families of the Korahites. 25Eleazar, Aaron's son, took one of the daughters of Putiel as wife; and she bore him Phinehas. These are the heads of the fathers' houses of the Levites by their families.

26These are the [same] Aaron and Moses to whom the Lord said, Bring out the Israelites from the land of Egypt by their hosts, 27And who spoke to [the] Pharaoh king of Egypt about bringing the Israelites out of Egypt; these are that Moses and Aaron.

28On the day when the Lord spoke to Moses in Egypt, 29The Lord said to Moses, I am the Lord; tell Pharaoh king of Egypt all that I say to you. 30But Moses said to the Lord, Behold, I am of deficient *and* impeded speech; how then shall Pharaoh listen to me?

**7** The Lord said to Moses, Behold, I make you as God to Pharaoh [to declare My will and purpose to him]; and Aaron your brother shall be your prophet. 2You shall speak all that I command you, and Aaron your brother shall tell Pharaoh to let the Israelites go out of his land. 3And I will make Pharaoh's heart stubborn *and* hard, and multiply My signs, My wonders, *and* miracles in the land of Egypt. 4But Pharaoh will not listen to you, and I will lay My hand upon Egypt and bring forth My hosts, My people the Israelites, out of the land of Egypt by great acts of judgment. 5The Egyptians shall know that I am the Lord when I stretch forth My hand upon Egypt and bring out the Israelites from among them. 6And Moses and Aaron did so, as the Lord commanded them. 7Now Moses was 80 years old and Aaron 83 years old when they spoke to Pharaoh.

8And the Lord said to Moses and Aaron, 9When Pharaoh says to you, Prove [your authority] by a miracle, then tell Aaron, Throw your rod down before Pharaoh, that it may become a serpent. 10So Moses and Aaron went to Pharaoh and did as the Lord had commanded; Aaron threw down his rod before Pharaoh and his servants, and it became a serpent. 11Then Pharaoh called for the wise men [skilled in magic and divination] and the sorcerers (wizards and jugglers). And they also, these magicians of Egypt, did similar things with their enchantments *and* secret arts. 12For they cast down every man his rod and they became serpents; but Aaron's rod swallowed up their rods. 13But Pharaoh's heart was hardened *and* stubborn and he would not listen to them, just as the Lord had said. 14Then the Lord said to Moses, Pharaoh's heart is hard *and* stubborn; he refuses to let the people go. 15Go to Pharaoh in the morning; he will be going out to the water; wait for him by the river's brink; and the rod which was turned to a serpent you shall take in your hand. 16And say to him, The Lord, the God of the Hebrews has sent me to you, saying, Let My people go, that they may serve Me in the wilderness; and behold, heretofore you have not listened. 17Thus says the Lord, In this you shall know, recognize,

## New International Version

With the staff that is in my hand I will strike the water of the Nile, and it will be changed into blood. ¹⁸The fish in the Nile will die, and the river will stink; the Egyptians will not be able to drink its water.'"

¹⁹The LORD said to Moses, "Tell Aaron, 'Take your staff and stretch out your hand over the waters of Egypt—over the streams and canals, over the ponds and all the reservoirs—and they will turn to blood.' Blood will be everywhere in Egypt, even in vessels*a* of wood and stone."

²⁰Moses and Aaron did just as the LORD had commanded. He raised his staff in the presence of Pharaoh and his officials and struck the water of the Nile, and all the water was changed into blood. ²¹The fish in the Nile died, and the river smelled so bad that the Egyptians could not drink its water. Blood was everywhere in Egypt.

²²But the Egyptian magicians did the same things by their secret arts, and Pharaoh's heart became hard; he would not listen to Moses and Aaron, just as the LORD had said. ²³Instead, he turned and went into his palace, and did not take even this to heart. ²⁴And all the Egyptians dug along the Nile to get drinking water, because they could not drink the water of the river.

### The Plague of Frogs

**8***b* ²⁵Seven days passed after the LORD struck the Nile. ¹Then the LORD said to Moses, "Go to Pharaoh and say to him, 'This is what the LORD says: Let my people go, so that they may worship me. ²If you refuse to let them go, I will send a plague of frogs on your whole country. ³The Nile will teem with frogs. They will come up into your palace and your bedroom and onto your bed, into the houses of your officials and on your people, and into your ovens and kneading troughs. ⁴The frogs will come up on you and your people and all your officials.'"

⁵Then the LORD said to Moses, "Tell Aaron, 'Stretch out your hand with your staff over the streams and canals and ponds, and make frogs come up on the land of Egypt.'"

⁶So Aaron stretched out his hand over the waters of Egypt, and the frogs came up and covered the land. ⁷But the magicians did the same things by their secret arts; they also made frogs come up on the land of Egypt.

⁸Pharaoh summoned Moses and Aaron and said, "Pray to the LORD to take the frogs away from me and my people, and I will let your people go to offer sacrifices to the LORD."

⁹Moses said to Pharaoh, "I leave to you the honor of setting the time for me to pray for you and your officials and your people that you and your houses may be rid of the frogs, except for those that remain in the Nile."

¹⁰"Tomorrow," Pharaoh said.

Moses replied, "It will be as you say, so that you may know there is no one like the LORD our God. ¹¹The frogs will leave you and your houses, your officials and your people; they will remain only in the Nile."

¹²After Moses and Aaron left Pharaoh, Moses cried out to the LORD about the frogs he had brought on Pharaoh.

## Amplified Bible

*and* understand that I am the Lord: behold, I will smite with the rod in my hand the waters in the [Nile] River, and they shall be turned to blood.

¹⁸The fish in the river shall die, the river shall become foul smelling, and the Egyptians shall loathe to drink from it.

¹⁹And the Lord said to Moses, Say to Aaron, Take your rod and stretch out your hand over the waters of Egypt, over their streams, rivers, pools, and ponds of water, that they may become blood; and there shall be blood throughout all the land of Egypt, in containers both of wood and of stone.

²⁰Moses and Aaron did as the Lord commanded; [Aaron] lifted up the rod and smote the waters in the river in the sight of Pharaoh and his servants, and all the waters in the river were turned to blood.

²¹And the fish in the river died; and the river became foul smelling, and the Egyptians could not drink its water, and there was blood throughout all the land of Egypt.

²²But the magicians of Egypt did the same by their enchantments *and* secret arts; and Pharaoh's heart was made hard *and* obstinate, and he did not listen to Moses and Aaron, just as the Lord had said.

²³And Pharaoh turned and went into his house; neither did he take even this to heart.

²⁴And all the Egyptians dug round about the river for water to drink, for they could not drink the water of the [Nile].

²⁵Seven days passed after the Lord had smitten the river.

**8** Then the Lord said to Moses, Go to Pharaoh and say to him, Thus says the Lord, Let My people go, that they may serve Me.

²And if you refuse to let them go, behold, I will smite your entire land with frogs;

³And the river shall swarm with frogs which shall go up and come into your house, into your bedchamber and on your bed, and into the houses of your servants and upon your people, and into your ovens, your kneading bowls, *and* your dough.

⁴And the frogs shall come up on you and on your people and all your servants.

⁵And the Lord said to Moses, Say to Aaron, Stretch out your hand with your rod over the rivers, the streams *and* canals, and over the pools, and cause frogs to come up on the land of Egypt.

⁶So Aaron stretched out his hand over the waters of Egypt, and the frogs came up and covered the land.

⁷But the magicians did the same thing with their enchantments *and* secret arts, and brought up [more] frogs upon the land of Egypt.

⁸Then Pharaoh called for Moses and Aaron, and said, Entreat the Lord, that He may take away the frogs from me and my people; and I will let the people go that they may sacrifice to the Lord.

⁹And Moses said to Pharaoh, Glory over me in this: dictate when I shall pray [to the Lord] for you, your servants, and your people, that the frogs may be destroyed from you and your houses and remain only in the river.

¹⁰And [Pharaoh] said, Tomorrow. [Moses] said, Let it be as you say, that you may know that there is no one like the Lord our God.

¹¹And the frogs shall depart from you and your houses and from your servants and your people; they shall remain in the river only.

¹²So Moses and Aaron went out from Pharaoh, and Moses cried to the Lord [as he had agreed with Pharaoh] concerning the frogs which He had brought against him.

---

*a* 19 Or *even on their idols*     *b* In Hebrew texts 8:1-4 is numbered 7:26-29, and 8:5-32 is numbered 8:1-28.

## New International Version

13And the LORD did what Moses asked. The frogs died in the houses, in the courtyards and in the fields. 14They were piled into heaps, and the land reeked of them. 15But when Pharaoh saw that there was relief, he hardened his heart and would not listen to Moses and Aaron, just as the LORD had said.

### The Plague of Gnats

16Then the LORD said to Moses, "Tell Aaron, 'Stretch out your staff and strike the dust of the ground,' and throughout the land of Egypt the dust will become gnats." 17They did this, and when Aaron stretched out his hand with the staff and struck the dust of the ground, gnats came on people and animals. All the dust throughout the land of Egypt became gnats. 18But when the magicians tried to produce gnats by their secret arts, they could not.

Since the gnats were on people and animals everywhere, 19the magicians said to Pharaoh, "This is the finger of God." But Pharaoh's heart was hard and he would not listen, just as the LORD had said.

### The Plague of Flies

20Then the LORD said to Moses, "Get up early in the morning and confront Pharaoh as he goes to the river and say to him, 'This is what the LORD says: Let my people go, so that they may worship me. 21If you do not let my people go, I will send swarms of flies on you and your officials, on your people and into your houses. The houses of the Egyptians will be full of flies; even the ground will be covered with them.

22"'But on that day I will deal differently with the land of Goshen, where my people live; no swarms of flies will be there, so that you will know that I, the LORD, am in this land. 23I will make a distinction[a] between my people and your people. This sign will occur tomorrow.'"

24And the LORD did this. Dense swarms of flies poured into Pharaoh's palace and into the houses of his officials; throughout Egypt the land was ruined by the flies. 25Then Pharaoh summoned Moses and Aaron and said, "Go, sacrifice to your God here in the land." 26But Moses said, "That would not be right. The sacrifices we offer the LORD our God would be detestable to the Egyptians. And if we offer sacrifices that are detestable in their eyes, will they not stone us? 27We must take a three-day journey into the wilderness to offer sacrifices to the LORD our God, as he commands us."

28Pharaoh said, "I will let you go to offer sacrifices to the LORD your God in the wilderness, but you must not go very far. Now pray for me."

29Moses answered, "As soon as I leave you, I will pray to the LORD, and tomorrow the flies will leave Pharaoh and his officials and his people. Only let Pharaoh be sure that he does not act deceitfully again by not letting the people go to offer sacrifices to the LORD."

30Then Moses left Pharaoh and prayed to the LORD, 31and the LORD did what Moses asked. The flies left Pharaoh and his officials and his people; not a fly remained. 32But this time also Pharaoh hardened his heart and would not let the people go.

## Amplified Bible

13And the Lord did according to the word of Moses, and the frogs died out of the houses, out of the courtyards *and* villages, and out of the fields. 14[The people] gathered them together in heaps, and the land was loathsome *and* stank. 15But when Pharaoh saw that there was temporary relief, he made his heart stubborn *and* hard and would not listen *or* heed them, just as the Lord had said.

16Then the Lord said to Moses, Say to Aaron, Stretch out your rod and strike the dust of the ground, that it may become biting gnats *or* mosquitoes throughout all the land of Egypt. 17And they did so; Aaron stretched out his hand with his rod and struck the dust of the earth, and there came biting gnats *or* mosquitoes on man and beast; all the dust of the land became biting gnats *or* mosquitoes throughout all the land of Egypt. 18The magicians tried by their enchantments *and* secret arts to bring forth gnats *or* mosquitoes, but they could not; and there were gnats *or* mosquitoes on man and beast. 19Then the magicians said to Pharaoh, This is the finger of God! But Pharaoh's heart was hardened *and* strong and he would not listen to them, just as the Lord had said.

20Then the Lord said to Moses, Rise up early in the morning and stand before Pharaoh as he comes forth to the water; and say to him, Thus says the Lord, Let My people go, that they may serve Me. 21Else, if you will not let My people go, behold, I will send swarms [of bloodsucking gadflies] upon you, your servants, and your people, and into your houses; and the houses of the Egyptians shall be full of swarms [of bloodsucking gadflies], and also the ground on which they stand. 22But on that day I will sever *and* set apart the land of Goshen in which My people dwell, that no swarms [of gadflies] shall be there, so that you may know that I am the Lord in the midst of the earth. 23And I will put a division *and* a sign of deliverance between My people and your people. By tomorrow shall this sign be in evidence. 24And the Lord did so; and there came heavy *and* oppressive swarms [of bloodsucking gadflies] into the house of Pharaoh and his servants' houses; and in all of Egypt the land was corrupted *and* ruined by reason of the great invasion [of gadflies].

25And Pharaoh called for Moses and Aaron, and said, Go, sacrifice to your God [here] in the land [of Egypt]. 26And Moses said, It is not suitable *or* right to do that; for the animals the Egyptians hold sacred and will not permit to be slain are those which we are accustomed to sacrifice to the Lord our God; if we did this before the eyes of the Egyptians, would they not stone us? 27We will go a three days' journey into the wilderness and sacrifice to the Lord our God, as He will command us. 28So Pharaoh said, I will let you go, that you may sacrifice to the Lord your God in the wilderness; only you shall not go very far away. Entreat [your God] for me. 29Moses said, I go out from you, and I will entreat the Lord that the swarms [of bloodsucking gadflies] may depart from Pharaoh, his servants, and his people tomorrow; only let not Pharaoh deal deceitfully any more in not letting the people go to sacrifice to the Lord. 30So Moses went out from Pharaoh and entreated the Lord. 31And the Lord did as Moses had spoken: He removed the swarms [of attacking gadflies] from Pharaoh, from his servants, and his people; there remained not one. 32But Pharaoh hardened his heart *and* made it stubborn this time also, nor would he let the people go.

---

a 23 Septuagint and Vulgate; Hebrew *will put a deliverance*

## New International Version

### The Plague on Livestock

**9** Then the LORD said to Moses, "Go to Pharaoh and say to him, 'This is what the LORD, the God of the Hebrews, says: "Let my people go, so that they may worship me." ²If you refuse to let them go and continue to hold them back, ³the hand of the LORD will bring a terrible plague on your livestock in the field—on your horses, donkeys and camels and on your cattle, sheep and goats. ⁴But the LORD will make a distinction between the livestock of Israel and that of Egypt, so that no animal belonging to the Israelites will die.'"

⁵The LORD set a time and said, "Tomorrow the LORD will do this in the land." ⁶And the next day the LORD did it: All the livestock of the Egyptians died, but not one animal belonging to the Israelites died. ⁷Pharaoh investigated and found that not even one of the animals of the Israelites had died. Yet his heart was unyielding and he would not let the people go.

### The Plague of Boils

⁸Then the LORD said to Moses and Aaron, "Take handfuls of soot from a furnace and have Moses toss it into the air in the presence of Pharaoh. ⁹It will become fine dust over the whole land of Egypt, and festering boils will break out on people and animals throughout the land."

¹⁰So they took soot from a furnace and stood before Pharaoh. Moses tossed it into the air, and festering boils broke out on people and animals. ¹¹The magicians could not stand before Moses because of the boils that were on them and on all the Egyptians. ¹²But the LORD hardened Pharaoh's heart and he would not listen to Moses and Aaron, just as the LORD had said to Moses.

### The Plague of Hail

¹³Then the LORD said to Moses, "Get up early in the morning, confront Pharaoh and say to him, 'This is what the LORD, the God of the Hebrews, says: Let my people go, so that they may worship me, ¹⁴or this time I will send the full force of my plagues against you and against your officials and your people, so you may know that there is no one like me in all the earth. ¹⁵For by now I could have stretched out my hand and struck you and your people with a plague that would have wiped you off the earth. ¹⁶But I have raised you up[a] for this very purpose, that I might show you my power and that my name might be proclaimed in all the earth. ¹⁷You still set yourself against my people and will not let them go. ¹⁸Therefore, at this time tomorrow I will send the worst hailstorm that has ever fallen on Egypt, from the day it was founded till now. ¹⁹Give an order now to bring your livestock and everything you have in the field to a place of shelter, because the hail will fall on every person and animal that has not been brought in and is still out in the field, and they will die.'"

²⁰Those officials of Pharaoh who feared the word of the LORD hurried to bring their slaves and their livestock inside. ²¹But those who ignored the word of the LORD left their slaves and livestock in the field.

²²Then the LORD said to Moses, "Stretch out your hand toward the sky so that hail will fall all over Egypt—on people and animals and on everything growing in the fields of Egypt." ²³When Moses stretched out his staff toward the sky, the LORD sent thunder and hail, and lightning flashed

## Amplified Bible

**9** Then the Lord said to Moses, Go to Pharaoh and tell him, Thus says the Lord God of the Hebrews: Let My people go, that they may serve Me.

²If you refuse to let them go and still hold them, ³Behold, the hand of the Lord [will fall] upon your livestock which are out in the field, upon the horses, the donkeys, the camels, the herds and the flocks; there shall be a very severe plague.

⁴But the Lord shall make a distinction between the livestock of Israel and the livestock of Egypt, and nothing shall die of all that belongs to the Israelites.

⁵And the Lord set a time, saying, Tomorrow the Lord will do this thing in the land.

⁶And the Lord did that the next day, and all [kinds of] the livestock of Egypt died; but of the livestock of the Israelites not one died.

⁷Pharaoh sent to find out, and behold, there was not one of the cattle of the Israelites dead. But the heart of Pharaoh was hardened [his mind was set] and he did not let the people go.

⁸The Lord said to Moses and Aaron, Take handfuls of ashes *or* soot from the brickkiln and let Moses sprinkle them toward the heavens in the sight of Pharaoh.

⁹And it shall become small dust over all the land of Egypt, and become boils breaking out in sores on man and beast in all the land [occupied by the Egyptians].

¹⁰So they took ashes *or* soot of the kiln and stood before Pharaoh; and Moses threw them toward the sky, and it became boils erupting in sores on man and beast.

¹¹And the magicians could not stand before Moses because of their boils; for the boils were on the magicians and all the Egyptians.

¹²But the Lord hardened the heart of Pharaoh, making it strong *and* obstinate, and he did not listen to them or heed them, just as the Lord had told Moses.

¹³Then the Lord said to Moses, Rise up early in the morning and stand before Pharaoh and say to him, Thus says the Lord, the God of the Hebrews, Let My people go, that they may serve Me.

¹⁴For this time I will send all My plagues upon your heart and upon your servants and your people, that you may recognize *and* know that there is none like Me in all the earth.

¹⁵For by now I could have put forth My hand and have struck you and your people with pestilence, and you would have been cut off from the earth.

¹⁶But for this very purpose have I let you live, that I might show you My power, and that My name may be declared throughout all the earth. [Rom. 9:17-24.]

¹⁷Since you are still exalting yourself [in haughty defiance] against My people by not letting them go,

¹⁸Behold, tomorrow about this time I will cause it to rain a very heavy *and* dreadful fall of hail, such as has not been in Egypt from its founding until now.

¹⁹Send therefore now and gather your cattle in hastily, and all that you have in the field; for every man and beast that is in the field and is not brought home shall be struck by the hail and shall die.

²⁰Then he who feared the word of the Lord among the servants of Pharaoh made his servants and his livestock flee into the houses *and* shelters.

²¹And he who ignored the word of the Lord left his servants and his livestock in the field.

²²The Lord said to Moses, Stretch forth your hand toward the heavens, that there may be hail in all the land of Egypt, upon man and beast, and upon all the vegetation of the field, throughout the land of Egypt.

²³Then Moses stretched forth his rod toward the heavens, and the Lord sent thunder and hail, and fire (light-

---

## New International Version

down to the ground. So the LORD rained hail on the land of Egypt; <sup>24</sup>hail fell and lightning flashed back and forth. It was the worst storm in all the land of Egypt since it had become a nation. <sup>25</sup>Throughout Egypt hail struck everything in the fields—both people and animals; it beat down everything growing in the fields and stripped every tree. <sup>26</sup>The only place it did not hail was the land of Goshen, where the Israelites were.

<sup>27</sup>Then Pharaoh summoned Moses and Aaron. "This time I have sinned," he said to them. "The LORD is in the right, and I and my people are in the wrong. <sup>28</sup>Pray to the LORD, for we have had enough thunder and hail. I will let you go; you don't have to stay any longer."

<sup>29</sup>Moses replied, "When I have gone out of the city, I will spread out my hands in prayer to the LORD. The thunder will stop and there will be no more hail, so you may know that the earth is the LORD's. <sup>30</sup>But I know that you and your officials still do not fear the LORD God."

<sup>31</sup>(The flax and barley were destroyed, since the barley had headed and the flax was in bloom. <sup>32</sup>The wheat and spelt, however, were not destroyed, because they ripen later.)

<sup>33</sup>Then Moses left Pharaoh and went out of the city. He spread out his hands toward the LORD; the thunder and hail stopped, and the rain no longer poured down on the land. <sup>34</sup>When Pharaoh saw that the rain and hail and thunder had stopped, he sinned again: He and his officials hardened their hearts. <sup>35</sup>So Pharaoh's heart was hard and he would not let the Israelites go, just as the LORD had said through Moses.

### The Plague of Locusts

**10** Then the LORD said to Moses, "Go to Pharaoh, for I have hardened his heart and the hearts of his officials so that I may perform these signs of mine among them <sup>2</sup>that you may tell your children and grandchildren how I dealt harshly with the Egyptians and how I performed my signs among them, and that you may know that I am the LORD."

<sup>3</sup>So Moses and Aaron went to Pharaoh and said to him, "This is what the LORD, the God of the Hebrews, says: 'How long will you refuse to humble yourself before me? Let my people go, so that they may worship me. <sup>4</sup>If you refuse to let them go, I will bring locusts into your country tomorrow. <sup>5</sup>They will cover the face of the ground so that it cannot be seen. They will devour what little you have left after the hail, including every tree that is growing in your fields. <sup>6</sup>They will fill your houses and those of all your officials and all the Egyptians—something neither your parents nor your ancestors have ever seen from the day they settled in this land till now.'" Then Moses turned and left Pharaoh.

<sup>7</sup>Pharaoh's officials said to him, "How long will this man be a snare to us? Let the people go, so that they may worship the LORD their God. Do you not yet realize that Egypt is ruined?"

<sup>8</sup>Then Moses and Aaron were brought back to Pharaoh. "Go, worship the LORD your God," he said. "But tell me who will be going."

<sup>9</sup>Moses answered, "We will go with our young and our old, with our sons and our daughters, and with our flocks and herds, because we are to celebrate a festival to the LORD."

## Amplified Bible

ning) ran down to *and* along the ground, and the Lord rained hail upon the land of Egypt.

<sup>24</sup>So there was hail and fire flashing continually in the midst of the weighty hail, such as had not been in all the land of Egypt since it became a nation.

<sup>25</sup>The hail struck down throughout all the land of Egypt everything that was in the field, both man and beast; and the hail beat down all the vegetation of the field and shattered every tree of the field.

<sup>26</sup>Only in the land of Goshen, where the Israelites were, was there no hail.

<sup>27</sup>And Pharaoh sent for Moses and Aaron, and said to them, I have sinned this time; the Lord is in the right and I and my people are in the wrong.

<sup>28</sup>Entreat the Lord, for there has been enough of these mighty thunderings and hail [these voices of God]; I will let you go; you shall stay here no longer.

<sup>29</sup>Moses said to him, As soon as I leave the city, I will stretch out my hands to the Lord; the thunder shall cease, neither shall there be any more hail, that you may know that the earth is the Lord's.

<sup>30</sup>But as for you and your servants, I know that you do not yet [reverently] fear the Lord God.

<sup>31</sup>The flax and the barley were smitten *and* ruined, for the barley was in the ear and the flax in bloom.

<sup>32</sup>But the wheat and spelt [another wheat] were not smitten, for they ripen late and were not grown up yet.

<sup>33</sup>So Moses left the city and Pharaoh, and stretched forth his hands to the Lord; and the thunder and hail ceased, and rain was no longer poured upon the earth.

<sup>34</sup>But when Pharaoh saw that the rain, the hail, and the thunder had ceased, he sinned yet more, and toughened *and* stiffened his hard heart, he and his servants.

<sup>35</sup>So Pharaoh's heart was strong *and* obstinate; he would not let the Israelites go, just as the Lord had said by Moses. [Exod. 4:21.]

**10** The Lord said to Moses, Go to Pharaoh, for I have made his heart hard, and his servants' hearts, that I might show these My signs [of divine power] before him,

<sup>2</sup>And that you may recount in the ears of your son and of your grandson what I have done in derision of the Egyptians *and* what things I have [repeatedly] done there—My signs [of divine power] done among them—that you may recognize *and* know that I am the Lord.

<sup>3</sup>So Moses and Aaron went to Pharaoh, and said to him, Thus says the Lord, the God of the Hebrews, How long will you refuse to humble yourself before Me? Let My people go, that they may serve Me.

<sup>4</sup>For if you refuse to let My people go, behold, tomorrow I will bring locusts into your country.

<sup>5</sup>And they shall cover the land so that one cannot see the ground; and they shall eat the remainder of what escaped and is left to you from the hail, and they shall eat every tree of yours that grows in the field;

<sup>6</sup>The locusts shall fill your houses and those of all your servants and of all the Egyptians, as neither your fathers nor your fathers' fathers have seen from their birth until this day. Then Moses departed from Pharaoh.

<sup>7</sup>And Pharaoh's servants said to him, How long shall this man be a snare to us? Let the men go, that they may serve the Lord their God; do you not yet understand *and* know that Egypt is destroyed?

<sup>8</sup>So Moses and Aaron were brought again to Pharaoh; and he said to them, Go, serve the Lord your God; but just who are to go?

<sup>9</sup>And Moses said, We will go with our young and our old, with our sons and our daughters, with our flocks and our herds [all of us and all we have], for we must hold a feast to the Lord.

## New International Version

[10]Pharaoh said, "The Lord be with you—if I let you go, along with your women and children! Clearly you are bent on evil.[a] [11]No! Have only the men go and worship the Lord, since that's what you have been asking for." Then Moses and Aaron were driven out of Pharaoh's presence.

[12]And the Lord said to Moses, "Stretch out your hand over Egypt so that locusts swarm over the land and devour everything growing in the fields, everything left by the hail."

[13]So Moses stretched out his staff over Egypt, and the Lord made an east wind blow across the land all that day and all that night. By morning the wind had brought the locusts; [14]they invaded all Egypt and settled down in every area of the country in great numbers. Never before had there been such a plague of locusts, nor will there ever be again. [15]They covered all the ground until it was black. They devoured all that was left after the hail—everything growing in the fields and the fruit on the trees. Nothing green remained on tree or plant in all the land of Egypt.

[16]Pharaoh quickly summoned Moses and Aaron and said, "I have sinned against the Lord your God and against you. [17]Now forgive my sin once more and pray to the Lord your God to take this deadly plague away from me."

[18]Moses then left Pharaoh and prayed to the Lord. [19]And the Lord changed the wind to a very strong west wind, which caught up the locusts and carried them into the Red Sea.[b] Not a locust was left anywhere in Egypt. [20]But the Lord hardened Pharaoh's heart, and he would not let the Israelites go.

### The Plague of Darkness

[21]Then the Lord said to Moses, "Stretch out your hand toward the sky so that darkness spreads over Egypt—darkness that can be felt." [22]So Moses stretched out his hand toward the sky, and total darkness covered all Egypt for three days. [23]No one could see anyone else or move about for three days. Yet all the Israelites had light in the places where they lived.

[24]Then Pharaoh summoned Moses and said, "Go, worship the Lord. Even your women and children may go with you; only leave your flocks and herds behind." [25]But Moses said, "You must allow us to have sacrifices and burnt offerings to present to the Lord our God. [26]Our livestock too must go with us; not a hoof is to be left behind. We have to use some of them in worshiping the Lord our God, and until we get there we will not know what we are to use to worship the Lord." [27]But the Lord hardened Pharaoh's heart, and he was not willing to let them go. [28]Pharaoh said to Moses, "Get out of my sight! Make sure you do not appear before me again! The day you see my face you will die." [29]"Just as you say," Moses replied. "I will never appear before you again."

### The Plague on the Firstborn

**11** Now the Lord had said to Moses, "I will bring one more plague on Pharaoh and on Egypt. After that, he will let you go from here, and when he does, he will drive you out completely. [2]Tell the people that men

## Amplified Bible

[10]Pharaoh said to them, Let the Lord be with you, if I ever let you go with your little ones! See, you have some evil purpose in mind.

[11]Not so! You that are men, [without your families] go and serve the Lord, for that is what you want. And [Moses and Aaron] were driven from Pharaoh's presence.

[12]Then the Lord said to Moses, Stretch out your hand over the land of Egypt for the locusts, that they may come up on the land of Egypt and eat all the vegetation of the land, all that the hail has left.

[13]And Moses stretched forth his rod over the land of Egypt, and the Lord brought an east wind upon the land all that day and all that night; when it was morning, the east wind brought the locusts.

[14]And the locusts came up over all the land of Egypt and settled down on the whole country of Egypt, a very dreadful mass of them; never before were there such locusts as these, nor will there ever be again.

[15]For they covered the whole land, so that the ground was darkened, and they ate every bit of vegetation of the land and all the fruit of the trees which the hail had left; there remained not a green thing of the trees or the plants of the field in all the land of Egypt.

[16]Then Pharaoh sent for Moses and Aaron in haste. He said, I have sinned against the Lord your God and you.

[17]Now therefore forgive my sin, I pray you, only this once, and entreat the Lord your God only that He may remove from me this [plague of] death.

[18]Then Moses left Pharaoh and entreated the Lord.

[19]And the Lord turned a violent west wind, which lifted the locusts and drove them into the Red Sea; not one locust remained in all the country of Egypt.

[20]But the Lord made Pharaoh's heart more strong *and* obstinate, and he would not let the Israelites go.

[21]And the Lord said to Moses, Stretch out your hand toward the heavens, that there may be darkness over the land of Egypt, a darkness which may be felt.

[22]So Moses stretched out his hand toward the sky, and for three days a thick darkness was all over the land of Egypt.

[23]The Egyptians could not see one another, nor did anyone rise from his place for three days; but all the Israelites had natural light in their dwellings.

[24]And Pharaoh called to Moses, and said, Go, serve the Lord; let your little ones also go with you; it is only your flocks and your herds that must not go.

[25]But Moses said, You must give into our hand also sacrifices and burnt offerings, that we may sacrifice to the Lord our God.

[26]Our livestock also shall go with us; there shall not a hoof be left behind; for of them must we take to serve the Lord our God, and we know not with what we must serve the Lord until we arrive there.

[27]But the Lord made Pharaoh's heart stronger *and* more stubborn, and he would not let them go.

[28]And Pharaoh said to Moses, Get away from me! See that you never enter my presence again, for the day you see my face again you shall die!

[29]And Moses said, You have spoken truly; I will never see your face again.

**11** Then the Lord said to Moses, Yet will I bring one plague more on Pharaoh and on Egypt; afterwards he will let you go. When he lets you go from here, he will thrust you out altogether.

[2]Speak now in the hearing of the people, and let every

---

[a] 10 Or *Be careful, trouble is in store for you!*  [b] 19 Or *the Sea of Reeds*

## New International Version

and women alike are to ask their neighbors for articles of silver and gold." ³(The LORD made the Egyptians favorably disposed toward the people, and Moses himself was highly regarded in Egypt by Pharaoh's officials and by the people.)

⁴So Moses said, "This is what the LORD says: 'About midnight I will go throughout Egypt. ⁵Every firstborn son in Egypt will die, from the firstborn son of Pharaoh, who sits on the throne, to the firstborn son of the female slave, who is at her hand mill, and all the firstborn of the cattle as well. ⁶There will be loud wailing throughout Egypt—worse than there has ever been or ever will be again. ⁷But among the Israelites not a dog will bark at any person or animal.' Then you will know that the LORD makes a distinction between Egypt and Israel. ⁸All these officials of yours will come to me, bowing down before me and saying, 'Go, you and all the people who follow you!' After that I will leave." Then Moses, hot with anger, left Pharaoh.

⁹The LORD had said to Moses, "Pharaoh will refuse to listen to you—so that my wonders may be multiplied in Egypt." ¹⁰Moses and Aaron performed all these wonders before Pharaoh, but the LORD hardened Pharaoh's heart, and he would not let the Israelites go out of his country.

### The Passover and the Festival of Unleavened Bread

**12** The LORD said to Moses and Aaron in Egypt, ²"This month is to be for you the first month, the first month of your year. ³Tell the whole community of Israel that on the tenth day of this month each man is to take a lamb[a] for his family, one for each household. ⁴If any household is too small for a whole lamb, they must share one with their nearest neighbor, having taken into account the number of people there are. You are to determine the amount of lamb needed in accordance with what each person will eat. ⁵The animals you choose must be year-old males without defect, and you may take them from the sheep or the goats. ⁶Take care of them until the fourteenth day of the month, when all the members of the community of Israel must slaughter them at twilight. ⁷Then they are to take some of the blood and put it on the sides and tops of the doorframes of the houses where they eat the lambs. ⁸That same night they are to eat the meat roasted over the fire, along with bitter herbs, and bread made without yeast. ⁹Do not eat the meat raw or boiled in water, but roast it over a fire—with the head, legs and internal organs. ¹⁰Do not leave any of it till morning; if some is left till morning, you must burn it. ¹¹This is how you are to eat it: with your cloak tucked into your belt, your sandals on your feet and your staff in your hand. Eat it in haste; it is the LORD's Passover.

¹²"On that same night I will pass through Egypt and strike down every firstborn of both people and animals, and I will bring judgment on all the gods of Egypt. I am the LORD. ¹³The blood will be a sign for you on the houses where you are, and when I see the blood, I will pass over

---

*a 3 The Hebrew word can mean lamb or kid; also in verse 4.*

## Amplified Bible

man solicit *and* ask of his neighbor, and every woman of her neighbor, jewels of silver and jewels of gold.

³And the Lord gave the people favor in the sight of the Egyptians. Moreover, the man Moses was exceedingly great in the land of Egypt, in the sight of Pharaoh's servants and of the people.

⁴And Moses said, Thus says the Lord, About midnight I will go out into the midst of Egypt;

⁵And all the firstborn in the land [the pride, hope, and joy] of Egypt shall die, from the firstborn of Pharaoh, who sits on his throne, even to the firstborn of the maidservant who is behind the hand mill, and all the firstborn of beasts.

⁶There shall be a great cry in all the land of Egypt, such as has never been nor ever shall be again.

⁷But against any of the Israelites shall not so much as a dog move his tongue against man or beast, that you may know that the Lord makes a distinction between the Egyptians and Israel.

⁸And all these your servants shall come down to me and bow down to me, saying, Get out, and all the people who follow you! And after that I will go out. And he went out from Pharaoh in great anger.

⁹Then the Lord said to Moses, Pharaoh will not listen to you, that My wonders *and* miracles may be multiplied in the land of Egypt.

¹⁰Moses and Aaron did all these wonders *and* miracles before Pharaoh; and the Lord hardened Pharaoh's stubborn heart, and he did not let the Israelites go out of his land.

**12** The Lord said to Moses and Aaron in the land of Egypt,

²This month shall be to you the beginning of months, the first month of the year to you.

³Tell all the congregation of Israel, On the tenth day of this month they shall take every man a lamb *or* kid, according to [the size of] the family of which he is the father, a lamb *or* kid for each house.

⁴And if the household is too small to consume the lamb, let him and his next door neighbor take it according to the number of persons, every man according to what each can eat shall make your count for the lamb.

⁵Your lamb *or* kid shall be without blemish, a male of the first year; you shall take it from the sheep or the goats. [I Pet. 1:19, 20.]

⁶And you shall keep it until the fourteenth day of the same month; and the whole assembly of the congregation of Israel shall [each] kill [his] lamb in the evening.

⁷They shall take of the blood and put it on the two side posts and on the lintel [above the door space] of the houses in which they shall eat [the Passover lamb]. [Matt. 26:28; John 1:29; Heb. 9:14.]

⁸They shall eat the flesh that night roasted; with unleavened bread and bitter herbs they shall eat it.

⁹Eat not of it raw nor boiled at all with water, but roasted—its head, its legs, and its inner parts.

¹⁰You shall let nothing of the meat remain until the morning; and the bones *and* unedible bits which remain of it until morning you shall burn with fire.

¹¹And you shall eat it thus: [as fully prepared for a journey] your loins girded, your shoes on your feet, and your staff in your hand; and you shall eat it in haste. It is the Lord's Passover.

¹²For I will pass through the land of Egypt this night and will smite all the firstborn in the land of Egypt, both man and beast; and against all the gods of Egypt I will execute judgment [proving their helplessness]. I am the Lord.

¹³The blood shall be for a token *or* sign to you upon [the doorposts of] the houses where you are, [that] when I see the blood, I will pass over you, and no plague shall be upon

## New International Version

you. No destructive plague will touch you when I strike Egypt.

¹⁴"This is a day you are to commemorate; for the generations to come you shall celebrate it as a festival to the LORD—a lasting ordinance. ¹⁵For seven days you are to eat bread made without yeast. On the first day remove the yeast from your houses, for whoever eats anything with yeast in it from the first day through the seventh must be cut off from Israel. ¹⁶On the first day hold a sacred assembly, and another one on the seventh day. Do no work at all on these days, except to prepare food for everyone to eat; that is all you may do.

¹⁷"Celebrate the Festival of Unleavened Bread, because it was on this very day that I brought your divisions out of Egypt. Celebrate this day as a lasting ordinance for the generations to come. ¹⁸In the first month you are to eat bread made without yeast, from the evening of the fourteenth day until the evening of the twenty-first day. ¹⁹For seven days no yeast is to be found in your houses. And anyone, whether foreigner or native-born, who eats anything with yeast in it must be cut off from the community of Israel. ²⁰Eat nothing made with yeast. Wherever you live, you must eat unleavened bread."

²¹Then Moses summoned all the elders of Israel and said to them, "Go at once and select the animals for your families and slaughter the Passover lamb. ²²Take a bunch of hyssop, dip it into the blood in the basin and put some of the blood on the top and on both sides of the doorframe. None of you shall go out of the door of your house until morning. ²³When the LORD goes through the land to strike down the Egyptians, he will see the blood on the top and sides of the doorframe and will pass over that doorway, and he will not permit the destroyer to enter your houses and strike you down.

²⁴"Obey these instructions as a lasting ordinance for you and your descendants. ²⁵When you enter the land that the LORD will give you as he promised, observe this ceremony. ²⁶And when your children ask you, 'What does this ceremony mean to you?' ²⁷then tell them, 'It is the Passover sacrifice to the LORD, who passed over the houses of the Israelites in Egypt and spared our homes when he struck down the Egyptians.'" Then the people bowed down and worshiped. ²⁸The Israelites did just what the LORD commanded Moses and Aaron.

²⁹At midnight the LORD struck down all the firstborn in Egypt, from the firstborn of Pharaoh, who sat on the throne, to the firstborn of the prisoner, who was in the dungeon, and the firstborn of all the livestock as well. ³⁰Pharaoh and all his officials and all the Egyptians got up during the night, and there was loud wailing in Egypt, for there was not a house without someone dead.

### The Exodus

³¹During the night Pharaoh summoned Moses and Aaron and said, "Up! Leave my people, you and the Israelites! Go, worship the LORD as you have requested. ³²Take your flocks and herds, as you have said, and go. And also bless me."

³³The Egyptians urged the people to hurry and leave the country. "For otherwise," they said, "we will all die!"

## Amplified Bible

you to destroy you when I smite the land of Egypt. [I Cor. 5:7; Heb. 11:28.]

¹⁴And this day shall be to you for a memorial. You shall keep it as a feast to the Lord throughout your generations, keep it as an ordinance forever.

¹⁵[In celebration of the Passover in future years] seven days shall you eat unleavened bread; even the first day you shall put away leaven [symbolic of corruption] out of your houses; for whoever eats leavened bread from the first day until the seventh day, that person shall be cut off from Israel.

¹⁶On the first day you shall hold a solemn *and* holy assembly, and on the seventh day there shall be a solemn *and* holy assembly; no kind of work shall be done in them, save [preparation of] that which every person must eat—that only may be done by you.

¹⁷And you shall observe the Feast of Unleavened Bread, for on this very day have I brought your hosts out of the land of Egypt; therefore shall you observe this day throughout your generations as an ordinance forever.

¹⁸In the first month, on the fourteenth day of the month at evening, you shall eat unleavened bread [and continue] until the twenty-first day of the month at evening.

¹⁹Seven days no leaven [symbolic of corruption] shall be found in your houses; whoever eats what is leavened shall be excluded from the congregation of Israel, whether a stranger or native-born. [I Cor. 5:6-8.]

²⁰You shall eat nothing leavened; in all your dwellings you shall eat unleavened bread [during that week].

²¹Then Moses called for all the elders of Israel, and said to them, Go forth, select and take a lamb according to your families and kill the Passover [lamb].

²²And you shall take a bunch of hyssop, dip it in the blood in the basin, and touch the lintel above the door and the two side posts with the blood; and none of you shall go out of his house until morning.

²³For the Lord will pass through to slay the Egyptians; and when He sees the blood upon the lintel and the two side posts, the Lord will pass over the door and will not allow the destroyer to come into your houses to slay you.

²⁴You shall observe this rite for an ordinance to you and to your sons forever.

²⁵When you come to the land which the Lord will give you, as He has promised, you shall keep this service.

²⁶When your children shall say to you, What do you mean by this service?

²⁷You shall say, It is the sacrifice of the Lord's Passover, for He passed over the houses of the Israelites in Egypt when He slew the Egyptians but spared our houses. And the people bowed their heads and worshiped.

²⁸The Israelites went and, as the Lord had commanded Moses and Aaron, so they did.

²⁹At midnight the Lord slew every firstborn in the land of Egypt, from the firstborn of Pharaoh who sat on his throne to the firstborn of the prisoner in the dungeon, and all the firstborn of the livestock.

³⁰Pharaoh rose up in the night, he, all his servants, and all the Egyptians; and there was a great cry in Egypt, for there was not a house where there was not one dead.

³¹He called for Moses and Aaron by night, and said, Rise up, get out from among my people, both you and the Israelites; and go, serve the Lord, as you said.

³²Also take your flocks and your herds, as you have said, and be gone! And [ask your God to] bless me also.

³³The Egyptians were urgent with the people to depart, that they might send them out of the land in haste; for they said, We are all dead men.

## New International Version

³⁴So the people took their dough before the yeast was added, and carried it on their shoulders in kneading troughs wrapped in clothing. ³⁵The Israelites did as Moses instructed and asked the Egyptians for articles of silver and gold and for clothing. ³⁶The LORD had made the Egyptians favorably disposed toward the people, and they gave them what they asked for; so they plundered the Egyptians.

³⁷The Israelites journeyed from Rameses to Sukkoth. There were about six hundred thousand men on foot, besides women and children. ³⁸Many other people went up with them, and also large droves of livestock, both flocks and herds. ³⁹With the dough the Israelites had brought from Egypt, they baked loaves of unleavened bread. The dough was without yeast because they had been driven out of Egypt and did not have time to prepare food for themselves.

⁴⁰Now the length of time the Israelite people lived in Egyptᵃ was 430 years. ⁴¹At the end of the 430 years, to the very day, all the LORD's divisions left Egypt. ⁴²Because the LORD kept vigil that night to bring them out of Egypt, on this night all the Israelites are to keep vigil to honor the LORD for the generations to come.

### Passover Restrictions

⁴³The LORD said to Moses and Aaron, "These are the regulations for the Passover meal:

"No foreigner may eat it. ⁴⁴Any slave you have bought may eat it after you have circumcised him, ⁴⁵but a temporary resident or a hired worker may not eat it.

⁴⁶"It must be eaten inside the house; take none of the meat outside the house. Do not break any of the bones. ⁴⁷The whole community of Israel must celebrate it.

⁴⁸"A foreigner residing among you who wants to celebrate the LORD's Passover must have all the males in his household circumcised; then he may take part like one born in the land. No uncircumcised male may eat it. ⁴⁹The same law applies both to the native-born and to the foreigner residing among you."

⁵⁰All the Israelites did just what the LORD had commanded Moses and Aaron. ⁵¹And on that very day the LORD brought the Israelites out of Egypt by their divisions.

### Consecration of the Firstborn

**13** The LORD said to Moses, ²"Consecrate to me every firstborn male. The first offspring of every womb among the Israelites belongs to me, whether human or animal."

³Then Moses said to the people, "Commemorate this day, the day you came out of Egypt, out of the land of slavery, because the LORD brought you out of it with a mighty hand. Eat nothing containing yeast. ⁴Today, in the month of Aviv, you are leaving. ⁵When the LORD brings you into the land of the Canaanites, Hittites, Amorites, Hivites and Jebusites—the land he swore to your ancestors to give you, a land flowing with milk and honey—you are to observe this ceremony in this month: ⁶For seven days eat bread made without yeast and on the seventh day hold a festival to the LORD. ⁷Eat unleavened bread during those seven days; nothing with yeast in it is to be seen among

## Amplified Bible

³⁴The people took their dough before it was leavened, their kneading bowls being bound up in their clothes on their shoulders.

³⁵The Israelites did according to the word of Moses; and they [urgently] asked of the Egyptians jewels of silver and of gold, and clothing.

³⁶The Lord gave the people favor in the sight of the Egyptians, so that they gave them what they asked. And they stripped the Egyptians [of those things].

³⁷The Israelites journeyed from Rameses to Succoth, about 600,000 men on foot, besides women and children.

³⁸And a mixed multitude went also with them, and very much livestock, both flocks and herds.

³⁹They baked unleavened cakes of the dough which they brought from Egypt; it was not leavened because they were driven from Egypt and could not delay, nor had they prepared for themselves any food.

⁴⁰Now the time the Israelites dwelt in Egypt was 430 years. [Gen. 15:13, 14.]

⁴¹At the end of the 430 years, even that very day, all the hosts of the Lord went out of Egypt.

⁴²It was a night of watching unto the Lord *and* to be much observed for bringing them out of Egypt; this same night of watching unto the Lord is to be observed by all the Israelites throughout their generations.

⁴³The Lord said to Moses and Aaron, This is the ordinance of the Passover: No foreigner shall eat of it;

⁴⁴But every man's servant who is bought for money, when you have circumcised him, then may he eat of it.

⁴⁵A foreigner or hired servant shall not eat of it.

⁴⁶In one house shall it be eaten [by one company]; you shall not carry any of the flesh outside the house; neither shall you break a bone of it. [John 19:33, 36.]

⁴⁷All the congregation of Israel shall keep it.

⁴⁸When a stranger sojourning with you wishes to keep the Passover to the Lord, let all his males be circumcised, and then let him come near and keep it; and he shall be as one that is born in the land. But no uncircumcised person shall eat of it.

⁴⁹There shall be one law for the native-born and for the stranger or foreigner who sojourns among you.

⁵⁰Thus did all the Israelites; as the Lord commanded Moses and Aaron, so did they.

⁵¹And on that very day the Lord brought the Israelites out of the land of Egypt by their hosts.

**13** The Lord said to Moses,
²Sanctify (consecrate, set apart) to Me all the firstborn [males]; whatever is first to open the womb among the Israelites, both of man and of beast, is Mine.

³And Moses said to the people, [Earnestly] remember this day in which you came out from Egypt, out of the house of bondage *and* bondmen, for by strength of hand the Lord brought you out from this place; no leavened bread shall be eaten.

⁴This day you go forth in the month Abib.

⁵And when the Lord brings you into the land of the Canaanites, Hittites, Amorites, Hivites, and Jebusites, which He promised *and* swore to your fathers to give you, a land flowing with milk and honey [a land of plenty], you shall keep this service in this month.

⁶Seven days you shall eat unleavened bread and the seventh day shall be a feast to the Lord.

⁷Unleavened bread shall be eaten for seven days; no

---

*ᵃ 40* Masoretic Text; Samaritan Pentateuch and Septuagint *Egypt and Canaan*

## New International Version

you, nor shall any yeast be seen anywhere within your borders. [8]On that day tell your son, 'I do this because of what the LORD did for me when I came out of Egypt.' [9]This observance will be for you like a sign on your hand and a reminder on your forehead that this law of the LORD is to be on your lips. For the LORD brought you out of Egypt with his mighty hand. [10]You must keep this ordinance at the appointed time year after year.

[11]"After the LORD brings you into the land of the Canaanites and gives it to you, as he promised on oath to you and your ancestors, [12]you are to give over to the LORD the first offspring of every womb. All the firstborn males of your livestock belong to the LORD. [13]Redeem with a lamb every firstborn donkey, but if you do not redeem it, break its neck. Redeem every firstborn among your sons.

[14]"In days to come, when your son asks you, 'What does this mean?' say to him, 'With a mighty hand the LORD brought us out of Egypt, out of the land of slavery. [15]When Pharaoh stubbornly refused to let us go, the LORD killed the firstborn of both people and animals in Egypt. This is why I sacrifice to the LORD the first male offspring of every womb and redeem each of my firstborn sons.' [16]And it will be like a sign on your hand and a symbol on your forehead that the LORD brought us out of Egypt with his mighty hand."

### Crossing the Sea

[17]When Pharaoh let the people go, God did not lead them on the road through the Philistine country, though that was shorter. For God said, "If they face war, they might change their minds and return to Egypt." [18]So God led the people around by the desert road toward the Red Sea.[a] The Israelites went up out of Egypt ready for battle.

[19]Moses took the bones of Joseph with him because Joseph had made the Israelites swear an oath. He had said, "God will surely come to your aid, and then you must carry my bones up with you from this place."[b]

[20]After leaving Sukkoth they camped at Etham on the edge of the desert. [21]By day the LORD went ahead of them in a pillar of cloud to guide them on their way and by night in a pillar of fire to give them light, so that they could travel by day or night. [22]Neither the pillar of cloud by day nor the pillar of fire by night left its place in front of the people.

**14** Then the LORD said to Moses, [2]"Tell the Israelites to turn back and encamp near Pi Hahiroth, between Migdol and the sea. They are to encamp by the sea, directly opposite Baal Zephon. [3]Pharaoh will think, 'The Israelites are wandering around the land in confusion, hemmed in by the desert.' [4]And I will harden Pharaoh's heart, and he will pursue them. But I will gain glory for myself through Pharaoh and all his army, and the Egyptians will know that I am the LORD." So the Israelites did this.

## Amplified Bible

leavened bread shall be seen with you, neither shall there be leaven in all your territory.

[8]You shall explain to your son on that day, This is done because of what the Lord did for me when I came out of Egypt.

[9]It shall be as a sign to you upon your hand and as a memorial between your eyes, that the law of the Lord may be in your mouth; for with a strong hand the Lord has brought you out of Egypt.

[10]You shall therefore keep this ordinance at this time from year to year.

[11]And when the Lord brings you into the land of the Canaanites, as He promised *and* swore to you and your fathers, and shall give it to you,

[12]You shall set apart to the Lord all that first opens the womb. All the firstlings of your livestock that are males shall be the Lord's.

[13]Every firstborn of a donkey you shall redeem by [substituting for it] a lamb, or if you will not redeem it, then you shall break its neck; and every firstborn among your sons shall you redeem.

[14]And when, in time to come, your son asks you, What does this mean? You shall say to him, By strength of hand the Lord brought us out from Egypt, from the house of bondage *and* bondmen.

[15]For when Pharaoh stubbornly refused to let us go, the Lord slew all the firstborn in the land of Egypt, both the firstborn of man and of livestock. Therefore I sacrifice to the Lord all the males that first open the womb; but all the firstborn of my sons I redeem.

[16]And it shall be as a reminder upon your hand or as frontlets between your eyes, for by a strong hand the Lord brought us out of Egypt.

[17]When Pharaoh let the people go, God led them not by way of the land of the Philistines, although that was nearer; for God said, Lest the people change their purpose when they see war and return to Egypt.

[18]But God led the people around by way of the wilderness toward the Red Sea. And the Israelites went up marshaled [in ranks] out of the land of Egypt.

[19]And Moses took the bones of Joseph with him, for [Joseph] had strictly sworn the Israelites, saying, Surely God will be with you, and you must carry my bones away from here with you. [Gen. 50:25.]

[20]They journeyed from Succoth and encamped at Etham on the edge of the wilderness.

[21]The Lord went before them by day in a pillar of cloud to lead them along the way and by night in a pillar of fire to give them light, that they might travel by day and by night.

[22]The pillar of cloud by day and the pillar of fire by night did not depart from before the people.

**14** And the Lord said to Moses, [2]Tell the Israelites to turn back and encamp before Pi-hahiroth, between Migdol and the [Red] Sea, before [a]Baal-zephon. You shall encamp opposite it by the sea.

[3]For Pharaoh will say of the Israelites, They are entangled in the land; the wilderness has shut them in.

[4]I will harden (make stubborn, strong) Pharaoh's heart, that he will pursue them, and I will gain honor *and* glory over Pharaoh and all his host, and the Egyptians shall know that I am the Lord. And they did so.

[a] Melvin Grove Kyle has said that travelers who follow the coast of the Red Sea along the line of the exodus need no other guidebook than the Bible. The whole topography corresponds to that mentioned in the Biblical account (Floyd E. Hamilton, *The Basis of Christian Faith*).

---

[a] 18 Or *the Sea of Reeds*   [b] 19 See Gen. 50:25.

## New International Version

⁵When the king of Egypt was told that the people had fled, Pharaoh and his officials changed their minds about them and said, "What have we done? We have let the Israelites go and have lost their services!" ⁶So he had his chariot made ready and took his army with him. ⁷He took six hundred of the best chariots, along with all the other chariots of Egypt, with officers over all of them. ⁸The LORD hardened the heart of Pharaoh king of Egypt, so that he pursued the Israelites, who were marching out boldly. ⁹The Egyptians—all Pharaoh's horses and chariots, horsemenᵃ and troops—pursued the Israelites and overtook them as they camped by the sea near Pi Hahiroth, opposite Baal Zephon.

¹⁰As Pharaoh approached, the Israelites looked up, and there were the Egyptians, marching after them. They were terrified and cried out to the LORD. ¹¹They said to Moses, "Was it because there were no graves in Egypt that you brought us to the desert to die? What have you done to us by bringing us out of Egypt? ¹²Didn't we say to you in Egypt, 'Leave us alone; let us serve the Egyptians'? It would have been better for us to serve the Egyptians than to die in the desert!"

¹³Moses answered the people, "Do not be afraid. Stand firm and you will see the deliverance the LORD will bring you today. The Egyptians you see today you will never see again. ¹⁴The LORD will fight for you; you need only to be still."

¹⁵Then the LORD said to Moses, "Why are you crying out to me? Tell the Israelites to move on. ¹⁶Raise your staff and stretch out your hand over the sea to divide the water so that the Israelites can go through the sea on dry ground. ¹⁷I will harden the hearts of the Egyptians so that they will go in after them. And I will gain glory through Pharaoh and all his army, through his chariots and his horsemen. ¹⁸The Egyptians will know that I am the LORD when I gain glory through Pharaoh, his chariots and his horsemen."

¹⁹Then the angel of God, who had been traveling in front of Israel's army, withdrew and went behind them. The pillar of cloud also moved from in front and stood behind them, ²⁰coming between the armies of Egypt and Israel. Throughout the night the cloud brought darkness to the one side and light to the other side; so neither went near the other all night long.

²¹Then Moses stretched out his hand over the sea, and all that night the LORD drove the sea back with a strong east wind and turned it into dry land. The waters were divided, ²²and the Israelites went through the sea on dry ground, with a wall of water on their right and on their left.

²³The Egyptians pursued them, and all Pharaoh's horses and chariots and horsemen followed them into the sea. ²⁴During the last watch of the night the LORD looked down from the pillar of fire and cloud at the Egyptian army and threw it into confusion. ²⁵He jammedᵇ the wheels of their chariots so that they had difficulty driving. And the Egyptians said, "Let's get away from the Israelites! The LORD is fighting for them against Egypt."

## Amplified Bible

⁵It was told the king of Egypt that the people had fled; and the heart of Pharaoh and of his servants was changed toward the people, and they said, What is this we have done? We have let Israel go from serving us!

⁶And he made ready his chariots and took his army, ⁷And took 600 chosen chariots and all the other chariots of Egypt, with officers over all of them.

⁸The Lord made hard *and* strong the heart of Pharaoh king of Egypt, and he pursued the Israelites, for [they] left proudly *and* defiantly. [Acts 13:17.]

⁹The Egyptians pursued them, all the horses and chariots of Pharaoh and his horsemen and his army, and overtook them encamped at the [Red] Sea by Pi-hahiroth, in front of Baal-zephon.

¹⁰When Pharaoh drew near, the Israelites looked up, and behold, the Egyptians were marching after them; and the Israelites were exceedingly frightened and cried out to the Lord.

¹¹And they said to Moses, Is it because there are no graves in Egypt that you have taken us away to die in the wilderness? Why have you treated us this way and brought us out of Egypt?

¹²Did we not tell you in Egypt, Let us alone; let us serve the Egyptians? For it would have been better for us to serve the Egyptians than to die in the wilderness.

¹³Moses told the people, Fear not; stand still (firm, confident, undismayed) and see the salvation of the Lord which He will work for you today. For the Egyptians you have seen today you shall never see again.

¹⁴The Lord will fight for you, and you shall hold your peace *and* remain at rest.

¹⁵The Lord said to Moses, Why do you cry to Me? Tell the people of Israel to go forward!

¹⁶Lift up your rod and stretch out your hand over the sea and divide it, and the Israelites shall go on dry ground through the midst of the sea.

¹⁷And I, behold, I will harden (make stubborn and strong) the hearts of the Egyptians, and they shall go [into the sea] after them; and I will gain honor over Pharaoh and all his host, his chariots, and horsemen.

¹⁸The Egyptians shall know *and* realize that I am the Lord when I have gained honor *and* glory over Pharaoh, his chariots, and his horsemen.

¹⁹And the ᵃAngel of God Who went before the host of Israel moved and went behind them; and the pillar of the cloud went from before them and stood behind them,

²⁰Coming between the camp of Egypt and the host of Israel. It was a cloud and darkness to the Egyptians, but it gave light by night to the Israelites; and the one host did not come near the other all night.

²¹Then Moses stretched out his hand over the sea, and the Lord caused the sea to go back by a strong east wind all that night and made the sea dry land; and the waters were divided.

²²And the Israelites went into the midst of the sea on dry ground, the waters being a wall to them on their right hand and on their left.

²³The Egyptians pursued and went in after them into the midst of the sea, even all Pharaoh's horses, his chariots, and his horsemen.

²⁴And in the morning watch the Lord through the pillar of fire and cloud looked down on the host of the Egyptians and discomfited [them],

²⁵And bound (clogged, took off) their chariot wheels, making them drive heavily; and the Egyptians said, Let us flee from the face of Israel, for the Lord fights for them against the Egyptians!

---

ᵃ 9 Or *charioteers*; also in verses 17, 18, 23, 26 and 28    ᵇ 25 See Samaritan Pentateuch, Septuagint and Syriac; Masoretic Text *removed*

ᵃ See footnote on Gen. 16:7; here the "Angel of God" is associated with the cloud (Exod. 13:21).

## New International Version

26Then the LORD said to Moses, "Stretch out your hand over the sea so that the waters may flow back over the Egyptians and their chariots and horsemen." 27Moses stretched out his hand over the sea, and at daybreak the sea went back to its place. The Egyptians were fleeing toward*a* it, and the LORD swept them into the sea. 28The water flowed back and covered the chariots and horsemen — the entire army of Pharaoh that had followed the Israelites into the sea. Not one of them survived.

29But the Israelites went through the sea on dry ground, with a wall of water on their right and on their left. 30That day the LORD saved Israel from the hands of the Egyptians, and Israel saw the Egyptians lying dead on the shore. 31And when the Israelites saw the mighty hand of the LORD displayed against the Egyptians, the people feared the LORD and put their trust in him and in Moses his servant.

### The Song of Moses and Miriam

**15** Then Moses and the Israelites sang this song to the LORD:

"I will sing to the LORD,
   for he is highly exalted.
Both horse and driver
   he has hurled into the sea.

2 "The LORD is my strength and my defense*b*;
   he has become my salvation.
He is my God, and I will praise him,
   my father's God, and I will exalt him.
3 The LORD is a warrior;
   the LORD is his name.
4 Pharaoh's chariots and his army
   he has hurled into the sea.
The best of Pharaoh's officers
   are drowned in the Red Sea.*c*
5 The deep waters have covered them;
   they sank to the depths like a stone.
6 Your right hand, LORD,
   was majestic in power.
Your right hand, LORD,
   shattered the enemy.

7 "In the greatness of your majesty
   you threw down those who opposed you.
You unleashed your burning anger;
   it consumed them like stubble.
8 By the blast of your nostrils
   the waters piled up.
The surging waters stood up like a wall;
   the deep waters congealed in the heart of the sea.
9 The enemy boasted,
   'I will pursue, I will overtake them.
I will divide the spoils;
   I will gorge myself on them.
I will draw my sword
   and my hand will destroy them.'
10 But you blew with your breath,
   and the sea covered them.
They sank like lead
   in the mighty waters.
11 Who among the gods
   is like you, LORD?
Who is like you —
   majestic in holiness,
awesome in glory,
   working wonders?

## Amplified Bible

26Then the Lord said to Moses, Stretch out your hand over the sea, that the waters may come again upon the Egyptians, upon their chariots and horsemen.
27So Moses stretched forth his hand over the sea, and the sea returned to its strength *and* normal flow when the morning appeared; and the Egyptians fled into it [being met by it]; and the Lord overthrew the Egyptians *and* shook them off into the midst of the sea.
28The waters returned and covered the chariots, the horsemen, and all the host of Pharaoh that pursued them; not even one of them remained.
29But the Israelites walked on dry ground in the midst of the sea, the waters being a wall to them on their right hand and on their left.
30Thus the Lord saved Israel that day from the hand of the Egyptians, and Israel saw the Egyptians dead upon the seashore.
31And Israel saw that great work which the Lord did against the Egyptians, and the people [reverently] feared the Lord and trusted in (relied on, remained steadfast to) the Lord and to His servant Moses.

**15** Then Moses and the Israelites sang this song to the Lord, saying, I will sing to the Lord, for He has triumphed gloriously; the horse and his rider *or* its chariot has He thrown into the sea.
2The Lord is my Strength and my Song, and He has become my Salvation; this is my God, and I will praise Him, my father's God, and I will exalt Him.
3The Lord is a Man of War; the Lord is His name.
4Pharaoh's chariots and his host has He cast into the sea; his chosen captains also are sunk in the Red Sea.
5The floods cover them; they sank in the depths [clad in mail] like a stone.
6Your right hand, O Lord, is glorious in power; Your right hand, O Lord, shatters the enemy.
7In the greatness of Your majesty You overthrow those rising against You. You send forth Your fury; it consumes them like stubble.
8With the blast of Your nostrils the waters piled up, the floods stood fixed in a heap, the deeps congealed in the heart of the sea.
9The enemy said, I will pursue, I will overtake, I will divide the spoil; my desire shall be satisfied upon them; I will draw my sword, my hand shall destroy them.
10You [Lord] blew with Your wind, the sea covered them; [clad in mail] they sank as lead in the mighty waters.
11Who is like You, O Lord, among the gods? Who is like You, glorious in holiness, awesome in splendor, doing wonders?

---

*a* 27 Or *from*   *b* 2 Or *song*   *c* 4 Or *the Sea of Reeds*; also in verse 22

## New International Version

<sup>12</sup>"You stretch out your right hand,
and the earth swallows your enemies.
<sup>13</sup>In your unfailing love you will lead
the people you have redeemed.
In your strength you will guide them
to your holy dwelling.
<sup>14</sup>The nations will hear and tremble;
anguish will grip the people of Philistia.
<sup>15</sup>The chiefs of Edom will be terrified,
the leaders of Moab will be seized with trembling,
the people[a] of Canaan will melt away;
<sup>16</sup>     terror and dread will fall on them.
By the power of your arm
they will be as still as a stone—
until your people pass by, LORD,
until the people you bought[b] pass by.
<sup>17</sup>You will bring them in and plant them
on the mountain of your inheritance—
the place, LORD, you made for your dwelling,
the sanctuary, Lord, your hands established.

<sup>18</sup>"The LORD reigns
for ever and ever."

<sup>19</sup>When Pharaoh's horses, chariots and horsemen[c] went
into the sea, the LORD brought the waters of the sea back
over them, but the Israelites walked through the sea on
dry ground. <sup>20</sup>Then Miriam the prophet, Aaron's sister,
took a timbrel in her hand, and all the women followed
her, with timbrels and dancing. <sup>21</sup>Miriam sang to them:

"Sing to the LORD,
for he is highly exalted.
Both horse and driver
he has hurled into the sea."

### The Waters of Marah and Elim

<sup>22</sup>Then Moses led Israel from the Red Sea and they went
into the Desert of Shur. For three days they traveled in the
desert without finding water. <sup>23</sup>When they came to Marah, they could not drink its water because it was bitter.
(That is why the place is called Marah.[d]) <sup>24</sup>So the people
grumbled against Moses, saying, "What are we to drink?"
<sup>25</sup>Then Moses cried out to the LORD, and the LORD
showed him a piece of wood. He threw it into the water,
and the water became fit to drink.
There the LORD issued a ruling and instruction for them
and put them to the test. <sup>26</sup>He said, "If you listen carefully
to the LORD your God and do what is right in his eyes, if
you pay attention to his commands and keep all his decrees, I will not bring on you any of the diseases I brought
on the Egyptians, for I am the LORD, who heals you."
<sup>27</sup>Then they came to Elim, where there were twelve
springs and seventy palm trees, and they camped there
near the water.

### Manna and Quail

**16** The whole Israelite community set out from Elim
and came to the Desert of Sin, which is between
Elim and Sinai, on the fifteenth day of the second month
after they had come out of Egypt. <sup>2</sup>In the desert the whole
community grumbled against Moses and Aaron. <sup>3</sup>The Israelites said to them, "If only we had died by the LORD's
hand in Egypt! There we sat around pots of meat and ate
all the food we wanted, but you have brought us out into
this desert to starve this entire assembly to death."

## Amplified Bible

<sup>12</sup>You stretched out Your right hand, the earth's [sea]
swallowed them.
<sup>13</sup>You in Your mercy *and* loving-kindness have led forth
the people whom You have redeemed; You have guided
them in Your strength to Your holy habitation.
<sup>14</sup>The peoples have heard of it; they tremble; pangs have
taken hold on the inhabitants of Philistia.
<sup>15</sup>Now the chiefs of Edom are dismayed; the mighty
men of Moab [renowned for strength], trembling takes
hold of them; all the inhabitants of Canaan have melted
away—little by little.
<sup>16</sup>Terror and dread fall upon them; because of the great-
ness of Your arm they are as still as a stone—till Your people pass by *and* over [into Canaan], O Lord, till the people
pass by whom You have purchased.
<sup>17</sup>You will bring them in [to the land] and plant them on
Your own mountain, the place, O Lord, You have made for
Your dwelling, the sanctuary, O Lord, which Your hands
have established.
<sup>18</sup>The Lord will reign forever and ever.
<sup>19</sup>For the horses of Pharaoh went with his chariots and
horsemen into the sea, and the Lord brought back the waters of the sea upon them, but the Israelites walked on dry
ground in the midst of the sea.
<sup>20</sup>Then Miriam the prophetess, the sister of Aaron, took
a timbrel in her hand, and all the women went out after her
with timbrels and dancing.
<sup>21</sup>And Miriam responded to them, Sing to the Lord, for
He has triumphed gloriously *and* is highly exalted; the
horse and his rider He has thrown into the sea.
<sup>22</sup>Then Moses led Israel onward from the Red Sea and
they went into the Wilderness of Shur; they went three
days [thirty-three miles] in the wilderness and found no
water.
<sup>23</sup>When they came to Marah, they could not drink its
waters for they were bitter; therefore it was named Marah
[bitterness].
<sup>24</sup>The people murmured against Moses, saying, What
shall we drink?
<sup>25</sup>And he cried to the Lord, and the Lord showed him
a tree which he cast into the waters, and the waters were
made sweet. There [the Lord] made for them a statute and
an ordinance, and there He proved them,
<sup>26</sup>Saying, If you will diligently hearken to the voice of
the Lord your God and will do what is right in His sight,
and will listen to *and* obey His commandments and keep
all His statutes, I will put none of the diseases upon you
which I brought upon the Egyptians, for I am the Lord
Who heals you.
<sup>27</sup>And they came to Elim, where there were twelve
springs of water and seventy palm trees; and they encamped there by the waters.

**16** They set out from Elim, and all the congregation
of Israel came to the Wilderness of Sin, which is
between Elim and Sinai, on the fifteenth day of the second
month after they left the land of Egypt.
<sup>2</sup>And the whole congregation of Israel murmured
against Moses and Aaron in the wilderness,
<sup>3</sup>And said to them, Would that we had died by the hand
of the Lord in the land of Egypt, when we sat by the flesh-
pots and ate bread to the full; for you have brought us out
into this wilderness to kill this whole assembly with hunger.

---

[a] 15 Or *rulers*     [b] 16 Or *created*     [c] 19 Or *charioteers*     [d] 23 *Marah*
means *bitter.*

## New International Version

[4]Then the LORD said to Moses, "I will rain down bread from heaven for you. The people are to go out each day and gather enough for that day. In this way I will test them and see whether they will follow my instructions. [5]On the sixth day they are to prepare what they bring in, and that is to be twice as much as they gather on the other days."

[6]So Moses and Aaron said to all the Israelites, "In the evening you will know that it was the LORD who brought you out of Egypt, [7]and in the morning you will see the glory of the LORD, because he has heard your grumbling against him. Who are we, that you should grumble against us?" [8]Moses also said, "You will know that it was the LORD when he gives you meat to eat in the evening and all the bread you want in the morning, because he has heard your grumbling against him. Who are we? You are not grumbling against us, but against the LORD."

[9]Then Moses told Aaron, "Say to the entire Israelite community, 'Come before the LORD, for he has heard your grumbling.'"

[10]While Aaron was speaking to the whole Israelite community, they looked toward the desert, and there was the glory of the LORD appearing in the cloud.

[11]The LORD said to Moses, [12]"I have heard the grumbling of the Israelites. Tell them, 'At twilight you will eat meat, and in the morning you will be filled with bread. Then you will know that I am the LORD your God.'"

[13]That evening quail came and covered the camp, and in the morning there was a layer of dew around the camp. [14]When the dew was gone, thin flakes like frost on the ground appeared on the desert floor. [15]When the Israelites saw it, they said to each other, "What is it?" For they did not know what it was.

Moses said to them, "It is the bread the LORD has given you to eat. [16]This is what the LORD has commanded: 'Everyone is to gather as much as they need. Take an omer[a] for each person you have in your tent.'"

[17]The Israelites did as they were told; some gathered much, some little. [18]And when they measured it by the omer, the one who gathered much did not have too much, and the one who gathered little did not have too little. Everyone had gathered just as much as they needed.

[19]Then Moses said to them, "No one is to keep any of it until morning."

[20]However, some of them paid no attention to Moses; they kept part of it until morning, but it was full of maggots and began to smell. So Moses was angry with them.

[21]Each morning everyone gathered as much as they needed, and when the sun grew hot, it melted away. [22]On the sixth day, they gathered twice as much—two omers[b] for each person—and the leaders of the community came and reported this to Moses. [23]He said to them, "This is what the LORD commanded: 'Tomorrow is to be a day of sabbath rest, a holy sabbath to the LORD. So bake what you want to bake and boil what you want to boil. Save whatever is left and keep it until morning.'"

[24]So they saved it until morning, as Moses commanded, and it did not stink or get maggots in it. [25]"Eat it today,"

## Amplified Bible

[4]Then the Lord said to Moses, Behold, I will rain bread from the heavens for you; and the people shall go out and gather a day's portion every day, that I may prove them, whether they will walk in My law or not.

[5]On the sixth day they shall prepare to bring in twice as much as they gather daily.

[6]So Moses and Aaron said to all Israel, At evening you shall know that the Lord has brought you out from the land of Egypt,

[7]And in the morning you shall see the glory of the Lord, for He hears your murmurings against the Lord. For what are we, that you murmur against us?

[8]And Moses said, [This will happen] when the Lord gives you in the evening flesh to eat and in the morning bread to the full, because the Lord has heard your grumblings which you murmur against Him; what are we? Your murmurings are not against us, but against the Lord.

[9]And Moses said to Aaron, Say to all the congregation of Israel, Come near before the Lord, for He has heard your murmurings.

[10]And as Aaron spoke to the whole congregation of Israel, they looked toward the wilderness, and behold, the glory of the Lord appeared in the cloud!

[11]The Lord said to Moses,

[12]I have heard the murmurings of the Israelites; speak to them, saying, At twilight you shall eat meat, and between the two evenings you shall be filled with bread; and you shall know that I am the Lord your God.

[13]In the evening quails came up and covered the camp; and in the morning the dew lay round about the camp.

[14]And when the dew had gone, behold, upon the face of the wilderness there lay a fine, round *and* flakelike thing, as fine as hoarfrost on the ground.

[15]When the Israelites saw it, they said one to another, Manna [What is it?]. For they did not know what it was. And Moses said to them, This is the bread which the Lord has given you to eat. [John 6:31, 33.]

[16]This is what the Lord has commanded: Let every man gather of it as much as he will need, an omer for each person, according to the number of your persons; take it, every man for those in his tent.

[17]The [people] did so, and gathered, some more, some less.

[18]When they measured it with an omer, he who gathered much had nothing over, and he who gathered little had no lack; each gathered according to his need.

[19]Moses said, Let none of it be left until morning.

[20]But they did not listen to Moses; some of them left of it until morning, and it bred worms, became foul, *and* stank; and Moses was angry with them.

[21]They gathered it every morning, each as much as he needed, for when the sun became hot it melted.

[22]And on the sixth day they gathered twice as much bread, two omers for each person; and all the leaders of the congregation came and told Moses.

[23]He said to them, The Lord has said, Tomorrow is a solemn rest, a holy Sabbath to the Lord; bake and boil what you will bake and boil today; and all that remains over put aside for you to keep until morning.

[24]They laid it aside till morning, as Moses told them; and it did not become foul, neither was it wormy.

---

[a] 16 That is, possibly about 3 pounds or about 1.4 kilograms; also in verses 18, 32, 33 and 36    [b] 22 That is, possibly about 6 pounds or about 2.8 kilograms

## New International Version

Moses said, "because today is a sabbath to the LORD. You will not find any of it on the ground today. 26Six days you are to gather it, but on the seventh day, the Sabbath, there will not be any."

27Nevertheless, some of the people went out on the seventh day to gather it, but they found none. 28Then the LORD said to Moses, "How long will you*a* refuse to keep my commands and my instructions? 29Bear in mind that the LORD has given you the Sabbath; that is why on the sixth day he gives you bread for two days. Everyone is to stay where they are on the seventh day; no one is to go out." 30So the people rested on the seventh day.

31The people of Israel called the bread manna.*b* It was white like coriander seed and tasted like wafers made with honey. 32Moses said, "This is what the LORD has commanded: 'Take an omer of manna and keep it for the generations to come, so they can see the bread I gave you to eat in the wilderness when I brought you out of Egypt.'"

33So Moses said to Aaron, "Take a jar and put an omer of manna in it. Then place it before the LORD to be kept for the generations to come."

34As the LORD commanded Moses, Aaron put the manna with the tablets of the covenant law, so that it might be preserved. 35The Israelites ate manna forty years, until they came to a land that was settled; they ate manna until they reached the border of Canaan.

36(An omer is one-tenth of an ephah.)

### Water From the Rock

**17** The whole Israelite community set out from the Desert of Sin, traveling from place to place as the LORD commanded. They camped at Rephidim, but there was no water for the people to drink. 2So they quarreled with Moses and said, "Give us water to drink."

Moses replied, "Why do you quarrel with me? Why do you put the LORD to the test?"

3But the people were thirsty for water there, and they grumbled against Moses. They said, "Why did you bring us up out of Egypt to make us and our children and livestock die of thirst?"

4Then Moses cried out to the LORD, "What am I to do with these people? They are almost ready to stone me."

5The LORD answered Moses, "Go out in front of the people. Take with you some of the elders of Israel and take in your hand the staff with which you struck the Nile, and go. 6I will stand there before you by the rock at Horeb. Strike the rock, and water will come out of it for the people to drink." So Moses did this in the sight of the elders of Israel. 7And he called the place Massah*c* and Meribah*d* because the Israelites quarreled and because they tested the LORD saying, "Is the LORD among us or not?"

### The Amalekites Defeated

8The Amalekites came and attacked the Israelites at Rephidim. 9Moses said to Joshua, "Choose some of our men and go out to fight the Amalekites. Tomorrow I will stand on top of the hill with the staff of God in my hands."

10So Joshua fought the Amalekites as Moses had ordered, and Moses, Aaron and Hur went to the top of the hill. 11As long as Moses held up his hands, the Israelites were winning, but whenever he lowered his hands, the Amalekites were winning. 12When Moses' hands grew tired, they took a stone and put it under him and he sat

## Amplified Bible

25Moses said, Eat that today, for today is a Sabbath to the Lord. Today you shall find none in the field. 26Six days you shall gather it, but on the seventh day, the Sabbath, there shall be none.

27On the seventh day some of the people went out to gather, but they found none.

28The Lord said to Moses, How long do you [people] refuse to keep My commandments and My laws?

29See, the Lord has given you the Sabbath; therefore He gives you on the sixth day the bread for two days; let every man remain in his place; let no man leave his place on the seventh day.

30So the people rested on the seventh day.

31The house of Israel called the bread manna; it was like coriander seed, white, and it tasted like wafers made with honey.

32Moses said, This is what the Lord commands, Take an omer of it to be kept throughout your generations, that they may see the bread with which I fed you in the wilderness when I brought you out of the land of Egypt.

33And Moses said to Aaron, Take a pot and put an omer of manna in it, and lay it up before the Lord, to be kept throughout your generations.

34As the Lord commanded Moses, Aaron laid it up before the Testimony to be kept [in the ark]. [Heb. 9:4.]

35And the Israelites ate manna forty years, until they came to a habitable land; they ate the manna until they came to the border of the land of Canaan.

36(Now an omer is the tenth of an ephah.)

**17** All the congregation of the Israelites moved on from the Wilderness of Sin by stages, according to the commandment of the Lord, and encamped at Rephidim; but there was no water for the people to drink.

2Therefore, the people contended with Moses, and said, Give us water that we may drink. And Moses said to them, Why do you find fault with me? Why do you tempt the Lord *and* try His patience?

3But the people thirsted there for water, and the people murmured against Moses, and said, Why did you bring us up out of Egypt to kill us and our children and livestock with thirst?

4So Moses cried to the Lord, What shall I do with this people? They are almost ready to stone me.

5And the Lord said to Moses, Pass on before the people, and take with you some of the elders of Israel; and take in your hand the rod with which you smote the river [Nile], and go.

6Behold, I will stand before you there on the rock at [Mount] Horeb; and you shall strike the rock, and water shall come out of it, that the people may drink. And Moses did so in the sight of the elders of Israel. [I Cor. 10:4.]

7He called the place Massah [proof] and Meribah [contention] because of the faultfinding of the Israelites and because they tempted *and* tried the patience of the Lord, saying, Is the Lord among us or not?

8Then came Amalek [descendants of Esau] and fought with Israel at Rephidim.

9And Moses said to Joshua, Choose us out men and go out, fight with Amalek. Tomorrow I will stand on the top of the hill with the rod of God in my hand.

10So Joshua did as Moses said and fought with Amalek; and Moses, Aaron, and Hur went up to the hilltop.

11When Moses held up his hand, Israel prevailed; and when he lowered his hand, Amalek prevailed.

12But Moses' hands were heavy *and* grew weary. So

---

*a 28* The Hebrew is plural. *b 31 Manna* sounds like the Hebrew for *What is it?* (see verse 15). *c 7 Massah* means *testing*. *d 7 Meribah* means *quarreling*.

## New International Version

on it. Aaron and Hur held his hands up—one on one side, one on the other—so that his hands remained steady till sunset. ¹³So Joshua overcame the Amalekite army with the sword.

¹⁴Then the LORD said to Moses, "Write this on a scroll as something to be remembered and make sure that Joshua hears it, because I will completely blot out the name of Amalek from under heaven."

¹⁵Moses built an altar and called it The LORD is my Banner. ¹⁶He said, "Because hands were lifted up against*a* the throne of the LORD,*b* the LORD will be at war against the Amalekites from generation to generation."

### Jethro Visits Moses

**18** Now Jethro, the priest of Midian and father-in-law of Moses, heard of everything God had done for Moses and for his people Israel, and how the LORD had brought Israel out of Egypt.

²After Moses had sent away his wife Zipporah, his father-in-law Jethro received her ³and her two sons. One son was named Gershom,*c* for Moses said, "I have become a foreigner in a foreign land"; ⁴and the other was named Eliezer,*d* for he said, "My father's God was my helper; he saved me from the sword of Pharaoh."

⁵Jethro, Moses' father-in-law, together with Moses' sons and wife, came to him in the wilderness, where he was camped near the mountain of God. ⁶Jethro had sent word to him, "I, your father-in-law Jethro, am coming to you with your wife and her two sons."

⁷So Moses went out to meet his father-in-law and bowed down and kissed him. They greeted each other and then went into the tent. ⁸Moses told his father-in-law about everything the LORD had done to Pharaoh and the Egyptians for Israel's sake and about all the hardships they had met along the way and how the LORD had saved them.

⁹Jethro was delighted to hear about all the good things the LORD had done for Israel in rescuing them from the hand of the Egyptians. ¹⁰He said, "Praise be to the LORD, who rescued you from the hand of the Egyptians and of Pharaoh, and who rescued the people from the hand of the Egyptians. ¹¹Now I know that the LORD is greater than all other gods, for he did this to those who had treated Israel arrogantly." ¹²Then Jethro, Moses' father-in-law, brought a burnt offering and other sacrifices to God, and Aaron came with all the elders of Israel to eat a meal with Moses' father-in-law in the presence of God.

¹³The next day Moses took his seat to serve as judge for the people, and they stood around him from morning till evening. ¹⁴When his father-in-law saw all that Moses was doing for the people, he said, "What is this you are doing for the people? Why do you alone sit as judge, while all these people stand around you from morning till evening?"

¹⁵Moses answered him, "Because the people come to me to seek God's will. ¹⁶Whenever they have a dispute, it is brought to me, and I decide between the parties and inform them of God's decrees and instructions."

¹⁷Moses' father-in-law replied, "What you are doing is not good. ¹⁸You and these people who come to you will only wear yourselves out. The work is too heavy for you;

## Amplified Bible

[the other men] took a stone and put it under him and he sat on it. Then Aaron and Hur held up his hands, one on one side and one on the other side; so his hands were steady until the going down of the sun.

¹³And Joshua mowed down *and* disabled Amalek and his people with the sword.

¹⁴And the Lord said to Moses, Write this for a memorial in the book and rehearse it in the ears of Joshua, that I will utterly blot out the remembrance of Amalek from under the heavens. [I Sam. 15:2-8.]

¹⁵And Moses built an altar and called the name of it, The Lord is my Banner;

¹⁶And he said, Because [theirs] is a hand against the throne of the Lord, the Lord will have war with Amalek from generation to generation.

**18** Now Jethro [Reuel], the priest of Midian, Moses' father-in-law, heard of all that God had done for Moses and for Israel His people, and that the Lord had brought Israel out of Egypt.

²Then Jethro, Moses' father-in-law, took Zipporah, Moses' wife, after Moses had sent her back [to her father],

³And her two sons, of whom the name of the one was Gershom [ expulsion, or a stranger there], for Moses said, I have been an alien in a strange land;

⁴And the name of the other was Eliezer [God is help], for the God of my father, said Moses, was my help, and delivered me from the sword of Pharaoh.

⁵And Jethro, Moses' father-in-law, came with Moses' sons and his wife to the wilderness where he was encamped at the mount of God [Horeb, or Sinai].

⁶And he said [in a message] to Moses, I, your father-in-law Jethro, am come to you and your wife and her two sons with her.

⁷And Moses went out to meet his father-in-law and bowed in homage and kissed him; and each asked the other of his welfare and they came into the tent.

⁸Moses told his father-in-law all the Lord had done to Pharaoh and the Egyptians for Israel's sake and all the hardships that had come upon them by the way and how the Lord delivered them.

⁹Jethro rejoiced for all the goodness the Lord had done to Israel in that He had delivered them out of the hand of the Egyptians.

¹⁰Jethro said, Blessed be the Lord, Who has delivered you out of the hand of the Egyptians and out of the hand of Pharaoh, Who has delivered the people [Israel] from under the hand of the Egyptians.

¹¹Now I know that the Lord is greater than all gods. Yes, in the [very] thing in which they dealt proudly [He showed Himself infinitely superior to all their gods].

¹²And Jethro, Moses' father-in-law, took a burnt offering and sacrifices [to offer] to God, and Aaron came with all the elders of Israel to eat bread with Moses' father-in-law before God.

¹³Next day Moses sat to judge the people, and the people stood around Moses from morning till evening.

¹⁴When Moses' father-in-law saw all that he was doing for the people, he said, What is this that you do for the people? Why do you sit alone, and all the people stand around you from morning till evening?

¹⁵Moses said to his father-in-law, Because the people come to me to inquire of God.

¹⁶When they have a dispute they come to me, and I judge between a man and his neighbor, and I make them know the statutes of God and His laws.

¹⁷Moses' father-in-law said to him, The thing that you are doing is not good.

¹⁸You will surely wear out both yourself and this people with you, for the thing is too heavy for you; you are not able to perform it all by yourself.

---

*a 16 Or to*   *b 16 The meaning of the Hebrew for this clause is uncertain.*   *c 3 Gershom sounds like the Hebrew for a foreigner there.*
*d 4 Eliezer means my God is helper.*

## New International Version

you cannot handle it alone. ¹⁹Listen now to me and I will give you some advice, and may God be with you. You must be the people's representative before God and bring their disputes to him. ²⁰Teach them his decrees and instructions, and show them the way they are to live and how they are to behave. ²¹But select capable men from all the people—men who fear God, trustworthy men who hate dishonest gain—and appoint them as officials over thousands, hundreds, fifties and tens. ²²Have them serve as judges for the people at all times, but have them bring every difficult case to you; the simple cases they can decide themselves. That will make your load lighter, because they will share it with you. ²³If you do this and God so commands, you will be able to stand the strain, and all these people will go home satisfied."

²⁴Moses listened to his father-in-law and did everything he said. ²⁵He chose capable men from all Israel and made them leaders of the people, officials over thousands, hundreds, fifties and tens. ²⁶They served as judges for the people at all times. The difficult cases they brought to Moses, but the simple ones they decided themselves.

²⁷Then Moses sent his father-in-law on his way, and Jethro returned to his own country.

### At Mount Sinai

**19** On the first day of the third month after the Israelites left Egypt—on that very day—they came to the Desert of Sinai. ²After they set out from Rephidim, they entered the Desert of Sinai, and Israel camped there in the desert in front of the mountain.

³Then Moses went up to God, and the LORD called to him from the mountain and said, "This is what you are to say to the descendants of Jacob and what you are to tell the people of Israel: ⁴'You yourselves have seen what I did to Egypt, and how I carried you on eagles' wings and brought you to myself. ⁵Now if you obey me fully and keep my covenant, then out of all nations you will be my treasured possession. Although the whole earth is mine, ⁶you*ᵃ* will be for me a kingdom of priests and a holy nation.' These are the words you are to speak to the Israelites."

⁷So Moses went back and summoned the elders of the people and set before them all the words the LORD had commanded him to speak. ⁸The people all responded together, "We will do everything the LORD has said." So Moses brought their answer back to the LORD.

⁹The LORD said to Moses, "I am going to come to you in a dense cloud, so that the people will hear me speaking with you and will always put their trust in you." Then Moses told the LORD what the people had said.

¹⁰And the LORD said to Moses, "Go to the people and consecrate them today and tomorrow. Have them wash their clothes ¹¹and be ready by the third day, because on that day the LORD will come down on Mount Sinai in the sight of all the people. ¹²Put limits for the people around the mountain and tell them, 'Be careful that you do not approach the mountain or touch the foot of it. Whoever touches the mountain is to be put to death. ¹³They are to be stoned or shot with arrows; not a hand is to be laid on them. No person or animal shall be permitted to live.' Only when the ram's horn sounds a long blast may they approach the mountain."

## Amplified Bible

¹⁹Listen now to [me]; I will counsel you, and God will be with you. You shall represent the people before God, bringing their cases *and* causes to Him,

²⁰Teaching them the decrees and laws, showing them the way they must walk and the work they must do.

²¹Moreover, you shall choose able men from all the people—God-fearing men of truth who hate unjust gain—and place them over thousands, hundreds, fifties, and tens, to be their rulers.

²²And let them judge the people at all times; every great matter they shall bring to you, but every small matter they shall judge. So it will be easier for you, and they will bear the burden with you.

²³If you will do this, and God so commands you, you will be able to endure [the strain], and all these people also will go to their [tents] in peace.

²⁴So Moses listened to *and* heeded the voice of his father-in-law and did all that he had said.

²⁵Moses chose able men out of all Israel and made them heads over the people, rulers of thousands, of hundreds, of fifties, and of tens.

²⁶And they judged the people at all times; the hard cases they brought to Moses, but every small matter they decided themselves.

²⁷Then Moses let his father-in-law depart, and he went his way into his own land.

**19** In the third month after the Israelites left the land of Egypt, the same day, they came into the Wilderness of Sinai.

²When they had departed from Rephidim and had come to the Wilderness of Sinai, they encamped there before the mountain.

³And Moses went up to God, and the Lord called to him out of the mountain, Say this to the house of Jacob and tell the Israelites:

⁴You have seen what I did to the Egyptians, and how I bore you on eagles' wings and brought you to Myself.

⁵Now therefore, if you will obey My voice in truth and keep My covenant, then you shall be My own peculiar possession *and* treasure from among *and* above all peoples; for all the earth is Mine.

⁶And you shall be to Me a kingdom of priests, a holy nation [consecrated, set apart to the worship of God]. These are the words you shall speak to the Israelites.

⁷So Moses called for the elders of the people and told them all these words which the Lord commanded him.

⁸And all the people answered together, and said, All that the Lord has spoken we will do. And Moses reported the words of the people to the Lord.

⁹And the Lord said to Moses, Behold, I come to you in a thick cloud, that the people may hear when I speak with you and believe you *and* remain steadfast forever. Then Moses told the words of the people to the Lord.

¹⁰And the Lord said to Moses, Go and sanctify the people [set them apart for God] today and tomorrow, and let them wash their clothes

¹¹And be ready by the third day, for the third day the Lord will come down upon Mount Sinai [in the cloud] in the sight of all the people.

¹²And you shall set bounds for the people round about, saying, Take heed that you go not up into the mountain or touch the border of it. Whoever touches the mountain shall surely be put to death.

¹³No hand shall touch it [or the offender], but he shall surely be stoned or shot [with arrows]; whether beast or man, he shall not live. When the trumpet sounds a long blast, they shall come up to the mountain. [Num. 24:8.]

*ᵃ 5,6* Or *possession, for the whole earth is mine.* *⁶You*

## New International Version

¹⁴After Moses had gone down the mountain to the people, he consecrated them, and they washed their clothes. ¹⁵Then he said to the people, "Prepare yourselves for the third day. Abstain from sexual relations."

¹⁶On the morning of the third day there was thunder and lightning, with a thick cloud over the mountain, and a very loud trumpet blast. Everyone in the camp trembled. ¹⁷Then Moses led the people out of the camp to meet with God, and they stood at the foot of the mountain. ¹⁸Mount Sinai was covered with smoke, because the LORD descended on it in fire. The smoke billowed up from it like smoke from a furnace, and the whole mountain*a* trembled violently. ¹⁹As the sound of the trumpet grew louder and louder, Moses spoke and the voice of God answered him.*b* ²⁰The LORD descended to the top of Mount Sinai and called Moses to the top of the mountain. So Moses went up ²¹and the LORD said to him, "Go down and warn the people so they do not force their way through to see the LORD and many of them perish. ²²Even the priests, who approach the LORD, must consecrate themselves, or the LORD will break out against them."

²³Moses said to the LORD, "The people cannot come up Mount Sinai, because you yourself warned us, 'Put limits around the mountain and set it apart as holy.'"

²⁴The LORD replied, "Go down and bring Aaron up with you. But the priests and the people must not force their way through to come up to the LORD, or he will break out against them."

²⁵So Moses went down to the people and told them.

### The Ten Commandments

**20** And God spoke all these words:

²"I am the LORD your God, who brought you out of Egypt, out of the land of slavery.

³"You shall have no other gods before*c* me.

⁴"You shall not make for yourself an image in the form of anything in heaven above or on the earth beneath or in the waters below. ⁵You shall not bow down to them or worship them; for I, the LORD your God, am a jealous God, punishing the children for the sin of the parents to the third and fourth generation of those who hate me, ⁶but showing love to a thousand generations of those who love me and keep my commandments.

⁷"You shall not misuse the name of the LORD your God, for the LORD will not hold anyone guiltless who misuses his name.

⁸"Remember the Sabbath day by keeping it holy. ⁹Six days you shall labor and do all your work, ¹⁰but the seventh day is a sabbath to the LORD your God. On it you shall not do any work, neither you, nor your son or daughter, nor your male or female servant, nor your animals, nor any foreigner residing in your towns. ¹¹For in six days the LORD made the heavens and the earth, the sea, and all that is in them, but he rested on the seventh day. Therefore the LORD blessed the Sabbath day and made it holy.

## Amplified Bible

¹⁴So Moses went down from the mountain to the people and sanctified them [set them apart for God], and they washed their clothes.

¹⁵And he said to the people, Be ready by the day after tomorrow; do not go near a woman.

¹⁶The third morning there were thunders and lightnings, and a thick cloud upon the mountain, and a very loud trumpet blast, so that all the people in the camp trembled.

¹⁷Then Moses brought the people from the camp to meet God, and they stood at the foot of the mountain.

¹⁸Mount Sinai was wrapped in smoke, for the Lord descended upon it in fire; its smoke ascended like that of a furnace, and the whole mountain quaked greatly.

¹⁹As the trumpet blast grew louder and louder, Moses spoke and God answered him with a voice. [Deut. 4:12.]

²⁰The Lord came down upon Mount Sinai to the top of the mountain, and the Lord called Moses to the top of the mountain, and Moses went up.

²¹The Lord said to Moses, Go down and warn the people, lest they break through to the Lord to gaze and many of them perish.

²²And also let the priests, who come near to the Lord, sanctify (set apart) themselves [for God], lest the Lord break forth against them.

²³And Moses said to the Lord, The people cannot come up to Mount Sinai, for You Yourself charged us, saying, Set bounds about the mountain and sanctify it [set it apart for God].

²⁴Then the Lord said to him, Go, get down and you shall come up, you and Aaron with you; but let not the priests and the people break through to come up to the Lord, lest He break forth against them.

²⁵So Moses went down to the people and told them.

**20** Then God spoke all these words:

²I am the Lord your God, Who has brought you out of the land of Egypt, out of the house of bondage.

³You shall have no other gods before or besides Me.

⁴You shall not make yourself any graven image [to worship it] or any likeness of anything that is in the heavens above, or that is in the earth beneath, or that is in the water under the earth;

⁵You shall not bow down yourself to them or serve them; for I the Lord your God am a jealous God, visiting the iniquity of the fathers upon the children to the third and fourth generation of those who hate Me, [Isa. 42:8; 48:11.]

⁶But showing mercy and steadfast love to a thousand generations of those who love Me and keep My commandments.

⁷You shall not use or repeat the name of the Lord your God in vain [that is, lightly or frivolously, in false affirmations or profanely]; for the Lord will not hold him guiltless who takes His name in vain.

⁸[Earnestly] remember the Sabbath day, to keep it holy (withdrawn from common employment and dedicated to God).

⁹Six days you shall labor and do all your work,

¹⁰But the seventh day is a Sabbath to the Lord your God; in it you shall not do any work, you, or your son, your daughter, your manservant, your maidservant, your domestic animals, or the sojourner within your gates.

¹¹For in six days the Lord made the heavens and the earth, the sea, and all that is in them, and rested the seventh day. That is why the Lord blessed the Sabbath day and hallowed it [set it apart for His purposes].

---

*a 18* Most Hebrew manuscripts; a few Hebrew manuscripts and Septuagint *and all the people*     *b 19* Or *and God answered him with thunder*     *c 3* Or *besides*

## New International Version

12 "Honor your father and your mother, so that you may live long in the land the LORD your God is giving you.
13 "You shall not murder.
14 "You shall not commit adultery.
15 "You shall not steal.
16 "You shall not give false testimony against your neighbor.
17 "You shall not covet your neighbor's house. You shall not covet your neighbor's wife, or his male or female servant, his ox or donkey, or anything that belongs to your neighbor."

18 When the people saw the thunder and lightning and heard the trumpet and saw the mountain in smoke, they trembled with fear. They stayed at a distance 19 and said to Moses, "Speak to us yourself and we will listen. But do not have God speak to us or we will die."
20 Moses said to the people, "Do not be afraid. God has come to test you, so that the fear of God will be with you to keep you from sinning."
21 The people remained at a distance, while Moses approached the thick darkness where God was.

### Idols and Altars

22 Then the LORD said to Moses, "Tell the Israelites this: 'You have seen for yourselves that I have spoken to you from heaven: 23 Do not make any gods to be alongside me; do not make for yourselves gods of silver or gods of gold.
24 "'Make an altar of earth for me and sacrifice on it your burnt offerings and fellowship offerings, your sheep and goats and your cattle. Wherever I cause my name to be honored, I will come to you and bless you. 25 If you make an altar of stones for me, do not build it with dressed stones, for you will defile it if you use a tool on it. 26 And do not go up to my altar on steps, or your private parts may be exposed.'

**21** "These are the laws you are to set before them:

### Hebrew Servants

2 "If you buy a Hebrew servant, he is to serve you for six years. But in the seventh year, he shall go free, without paying anything. 3 If he comes alone, he is to go free alone; but if he has a wife when he comes, she is to go with him. 4 If his master gives him a wife and she bears him sons or daughters, the woman and her children shall belong to her master, and only the man shall go free.
5 "But if the servant declares, 'I love my master and my wife and children and do not want to go free,' 6 then his master must take him before the judges.ᵃ He shall take him to the door or the doorpost and pierce his ear with an awl. Then he will be his servant for life.
7 "If a man sells his daughter as a servant, she is not to go free as male servants do. 8 If she does not please the master who has selected her for himself,ᵇ he must let her be redeemed. He has no right to sell her to foreigners, because he has broken faith with her. 9 If he selects her

## Amplified Bible

12 Regard (treat with honor, due obedience, and courtesy) your father and mother, that your days may be long in the land the Lord your God gives you.
13 You shall not commit murder.
14 You shall not commit ᵃadultery. [Prov. 6:25, 26; Matt. 5:28; Rom. 1:24; Eph. 5:3.]
15 You shall not steal. [Prov. 11:1; 16:8; 21:6; 22:16; Jer. 17:11; Mal. 3:8.]
16 You shall not witness falsely against your neighbor. [Exod. 23:1; Prov. 19:9; 24:28.]
17 You shall not covet your neighbor's house, your neighbor's wife, or his manservant, or his maidservant, or his ox, or his donkey, or anything that is your neighbor's. [Luke 12:15; Col. 3:5.]
18 Now all the people perceived the thunderings and the lightnings and the noise of the trumpet and the smoking mountain, and as [they] looked they trembled with fear and fell back and stood afar off.
19 And they said to Moses, You speak to us and we will listen, but let not God speak to us, lest we die.
20 And Moses said to the people, Fear not; for God has come to prove you, so that the [reverential] fear of Him may be before you, that you may not sin.
21 And the people stood afar off, but Moses drew near to the thick darkness where God was.
22 And the Lord said to Moses, Thus shall you say to the Israelites, You have seen for yourselves that I have talked with you from heaven.
23 You shall not make [gods to share] with Me [My glory and your worship]; gods of silver or gods of gold you shall not make for yourselves.
24 An altar of earth you shall make to Me and sacrifice on it your burnt offerings and your peace offerings, your sheep and your oxen. In every place where I record My name and cause it to be remembered I will come to you and bless you.
25 And if you will make Me an altar of stone, you shall not build it of hewn stone, for if you lift up a tool upon it you have polluted it.
26 Neither shall you go up by steps to My altar, that your nakedness be not exposed upon it.

**21** Now these are the ordinances you [Moses] shall set before [the Israelites].
2 If you buy a Hebrew servant [as the result of debt or theft], he shall serve six years, and in the seventh he shall go out free, paying nothing. [Lev. 25:39.]
3 If he came [to you] by himself, he shall go out by himself; if he came married, then his wife shall go out with him.
4 If his master has given him a wife and she has borne him sons or daughters, the wife and her children shall be her master's, and he shall go out [of your service] alone.
5 But if the servant shall plainly say, I love my master, my wife, and my children; I will not go free,
6 Then his master shall bring him to God [the judges as His agents]; he shall bring him to the door or doorpost and shall pierce his ear with an awl; and he shall serve him for life.
7 If a man sells his daughter to be a maidservant or bondwoman, she shall not go out [in six years] as menservants do.
8 If she does not please her master who has espoused her to himself, he shall let her be redeemed. To sell her to a foreign people he shall have no power, for he has dealt faithlessly with her.

---

ᵃ Observe here the expansion of the meaning of the seventh commandment in many catechisms to include whoredom in all its forms, as well as unchastity [premarital relations, sexual impurity, and lustful desire under whatever name] (J. P. Lange, *A Commentary*). Not only is adultery forbidden here, but also fornication and all kinds of mental and sensual uncleanness. All impure books, songs, pictures, etc., which tend to inflame and debauch the mind are against this law (Adam Clarke, *The Holy Bible with A Commentary*).

---

ᵃ 6 Or *before God*   ᵇ 8 Or *master so that he does not choose her*

## New International Version

for his son, he must grant her the rights of a daughter. ¹⁰If he marries another woman, he must not deprive the first one of her food, clothing and marital rights. ¹¹If he does not provide her with these three things, she is to go free, without any payment of money.

### Personal Injuries

¹²"Anyone who strikes a person with a fatal blow is to be put to death. ¹³However, if it is not done intentionally, but God lets it happen, they are to flee to a place I will designate. ¹⁴But if anyone schemes and kills someone deliberately, that person is to be taken from my altar and put to death.

¹⁵"Anyone who attacks*a* their father or mother is to be put to death.

¹⁶"Anyone who kidnaps someone is to be put to death, whether the victim has been sold or is still in the kidnapper's possession.

¹⁷"Anyone who curses their father or mother is to be put to death.

¹⁸"If people quarrel and one person hits another with a stone or with their fist*b* and the victim does not die but is confined to bed, ¹⁹the one who struck the blow will not be held liable if the other can get up and walk around outside with a staff; however, the guilty party must pay the injured person for any loss of time and see that the victim is completely healed.

²⁰"Anyone who beats their male or female slave with a rod must be punished if the slave dies as a direct result, ²¹but they are not to be punished if the slave recovers after a day or two, since the slave is their property.

²²"If people are fighting and hit a pregnant woman and she gives birth prematurely*c* but there is no serious injury, the offender must be fined whatever the woman's husband demands and the court allows. ²³But if there is serious injury, you are to take life for life, ²⁴eye for eye, tooth for tooth, hand for hand, foot for foot, ²⁵burn for burn, wound for wound, bruise for bruise.

²⁶"An owner who hits a male or female slave in the eye and destroys it must let the slave go free to compensate for the eye. ²⁷And an owner who knocks out the tooth of a male or female slave must let the slave go free to compensate for the tooth.

²⁸"If a bull gores a man or woman to death, the bull is to be stoned to death, and its meat must not be eaten. But the owner of the bull will not be held responsible. ²⁹If, however, the bull has had the habit of goring and the owner has been warned but has not kept it penned up and it kills a man or woman, the bull is to be stoned and its owner also is to be put to death. ³⁰However, if payment is demanded, the owner may redeem his life by the payment of whatever is demanded. ³¹This law also applies if the bull gores a son or daughter. ³²If the bull gores a male or female slave, the owner must pay thirty shekels*d* of silver to the master of the slave, and the bull is to be stoned to death.

³³"If anyone uncovers a pit or digs one and fails to cover it and an ox or a donkey falls into it, ³⁴the one who opened the pit must pay the owner for the loss and take the dead animal in exchange.

³⁵"If anyone's bull injures someone else's bull and it dies, the two parties are to sell the live one and divide both the money and the dead animal equally. ³⁶However,

## Amplified Bible

⁹And if he espouses her to his son, he shall deal with her as with a daughter.

¹⁰If he marries again, her food, clothing, and privilege as a wife shall he not diminish.

¹¹And if he does not do these three things for her, then shall she go out free, without payment of money.

¹²Whoever strikes a man so that he dies shall surely be put to death.

¹³But if he did not lie in wait for him, but God allowed him to fall into his hand, then I will appoint you a place to which he may flee [for protection until duly tried]. [Num. 35:22-28.]

¹⁴But if a man comes willfully upon another to slay him craftily, you shall take him from My altar [to which he may have fled for protection], that he may die.

¹⁵Whoever strikes his father or his mother shall surely be put to death.

¹⁶Whoever kidnaps a man, whether he sells him or is found with him in his possession, shall surely be put to death.

¹⁷Whoever curses his father or his mother shall surely be put to death.

¹⁸If men quarrel and one strikes another with a stone or with his fist and he does not die but keeps his bed,

¹⁹If he rises again and walks about leaning upon his staff, then he that struck him shall be clear, except he must pay for the loss of his time and shall cause him to be thoroughly healed.

²⁰And if a man strikes his servant or his maid with a rod and he [or she] dies under his hand, he shall surely be punished.

²¹But if the servant lives on for a day or two, the offender shall not be punished, for he [has injured] his own property.

²²If men contend with each other, and a pregnant woman [interfering] is hurt so that she has a miscarriage, yet no further damage follows, [the one who hurt her] shall surely be punished with a fine [paid] to the woman's husband, as much as the judges determine.

²³But if any damage follows, then you shall give life for life,

²⁴Eye for eye, tooth for tooth, hand for hand, foot for foot,

²⁵Burn for burn, wound for wound, and lash for lash.

²⁶And if a man hits the eye of his servant or the eye of his maid so that it is destroyed, he shall let him go free for his eye's sake.

²⁷And if he knocks out his manservant's tooth or his maidservant's tooth, he shall let him go free for his tooth's sake.

²⁸If an ox gores a man or a woman to death, then the ox shall surely be stoned, and its flesh shall not be eaten; but the owner of the ox shall be clear.

²⁹But if the ox has tried to gore before, and its owner has been warned but has not kept it closed in and it kills a man or a woman, the ox shall be stoned and its owner also put to death.

³⁰If a ransom is put on [the man's] life, then he shall give for the redemption of his life whatever is laid upon him.

³¹If the [man's ox] has gored another's son or daughter, he shall be dealt with according to this same rule.

³²If the ox gores a manservant or a maidservant, the owner shall give to their master thirty shekels of silver, and the ox shall be stoned.

³³If a man leaves a pit open or digs a pit and does not cover it and an ox or a donkey falls into it,

³⁴The owner of the pit shall make it good; he shall give money to the animal's owner, but the dead beast shall be his.

³⁵If one man's ox hurts another's so that it dies, they shall sell the live ox and divide the price of it; the dead ox also they shall divide between them.

---

*a 15* Or *kills*   *b 18* Or *with a tool*   *c 22* Or *she has a miscarriage*
*d 32* That is, about 12 ounces or about 345 grams

## New International Version

if it was known that the bull had the habit of goring, yet the owner did not keep it penned up, the owner must pay, animal for animal, and take the dead animal in exchange.

### Protection of Property

**22** [a] "Whoever steals an ox or a sheep and slaughters it or sells it must pay back five head of cattle for the ox and four sheep for the sheep.

[2]"If a thief is caught breaking in at night and is struck a fatal blow, the defender is not guilty of bloodshed; [3]but if it happens after sunrise, the defender is guilty of bloodshed.

"Anyone who steals must certainly make restitution, but if they have nothing, they must be sold to pay for their theft. [4]If the stolen animal is found alive in their possession—whether ox or donkey or sheep—they must pay back double.

[5]"If anyone grazes their livestock in a field or vineyard and lets them stray and they graze in someone else's field, the offender must make restitution from the best of their own field or vineyard.

[6]"If a fire breaks out and spreads into thornbushes so that it burns shocks of grain or standing grain or the whole field, the one who started the fire must make restitution.

[7]"If anyone gives a neighbor silver or goods for safekeeping and they are stolen from the neighbor's house, the thief, if caught, must pay back double. [8]But if the thief is not found, the owner of the house must appear before the judges, and they must[b] determine whether the owner of the house has laid hands on the other person's property. [9]In all cases of illegal possession of an ox, a donkey, a sheep, a garment, or any other lost property about which somebody says, 'This is mine,' both parties are to bring their cases before the judges.[c] The one whom the judges declare[d] guilty must pay back double to the other.

[10]"If anyone gives a donkey, an ox, a sheep or any other animal to their neighbor for safekeeping and it dies or is injured or is taken away while no one is looking, [11]the issue between them will be settled by the taking of an oath before the Lord that the neighbor did not lay hands on the other person's property. The owner is to accept this, and no restitution is required. [12]But if the animal was stolen from the neighbor, restitution must be made to the owner. [13]If it was torn to pieces by a wild animal, the neighbor shall bring in the remains as evidence and shall not be required to pay for the torn animal.

[14]"If anyone borrows an animal from their neighbor and it is injured or dies while the owner is not present, they must make restitution. [15]But if the owner is with the animal, the borrower will not have to pay. If the animal was hired, the money paid for the hire covers the loss.

### Social Responsibility

[16]"If a man seduces a virgin who is not pledged to be married and sleeps with her, he must pay the bride-price, and she shall be his wife. [17]If her father absolutely refuses to give her to him, he must still pay the bride-price for virgins.

[18]"Do not allow a sorceress to live.

[19]"Anyone who has sexual relations with an animal is to be put to death.

[20]"Whoever sacrifices to any god other than the Lord must be destroyed.[e]

[21]"Do not mistreat or oppress a foreigner, for you were foreigners in Egypt.

[22]"Do not take advantage of the widow or the fatherless. [23]If you do and they cry out to me, I will certainly hear their cry. [24]My anger will be aroused, and I will kill you

[a] In Hebrew texts 22:1 is numbered 21:37, and 22:2-31 is numbered 22:1-30.    [b] 8 Or before God, and he will    [c] 9 Or before God    [d] 9 Or whom God declares    [e] 20 The Hebrew term refers to the irrevocable giving over of things or persons to the Lord, often by totally destroying them.

## Amplified Bible

[36]Or if it is known that the ox has gored in the past, and its owner has not kept it closed in, he shall surely pay ox for ox, and the dead beast shall be his.

**22** If a man steals an ox or sheep and kills or sells it, he shall pay five oxen for an ox, or four sheep for a sheep.

[2]If a thief is found breaking in and is struck so that he dies, there shall be no blood shed for him.

[3]But if the sun has risen [so he can be seen], blood must be shed for slaying him. The thief [if he lives] must make full restitution; if he has nothing, then he shall be sold for his theft.

[4]If the beast which he stole is found in his possession alive, whether it is ox or ass or sheep, he shall restore double.

[5]If a man causes a field or vineyard to be grazed over or lets his beast loose and it feeds in another man's field, he shall make restitution of the best of his own field or his own vineyard.

[6]If fire breaks out and catches so that the stacked grain or standing grain or the field be consumed, he who kindled the fire shall make full restitution.

[7]If a man delivers to his neighbor money or goods to keep and it is stolen out of the neighbor's house, then, if the thief is found, he shall pay double.

[8]But if the thief is not found, the house owner shall appear before God [the judges as His agents] to find whether he stole his neighbor's goods.

[9]For every unlawful deed, whether it concerns ox, donkey, sheep, clothing, or any lost thing at all, which another identifies as his, the cause of both parties shall come before God [the judges]. Whomever [they] shall condemn shall pay his neighbor double.

[10]If a man delivers to his neighbor a donkey or an ox or a sheep or any beast to keep and it dies or is hurt or driven away, no man seeing it,

[11]Then an oath before the Lord shall be required between the two that the man has not taken his neighbor's property; and the owner of it shall accept his word and not require him to make good the loss.

[12]But if it is stolen when in his care, he shall make restitution to its owner.

[13]If it be torn in pieces [by some wild beast or by accident], let him bring [the mangled carcass] for witness; he shall not make good what was torn.

[14]And if a man borrows anything of his neighbor and it gets hurt or dies without its owner being with it, the borrower shall make full restitution.

[15]But if the owner is with it [when the damage is done], the borrower shall not make it good. If it is a hired thing, the damage is included in its hire.

[16]If a man seduces a virgin not betrothed and lies with her, he shall surely pay a dowry for her to become his wife.

[17]If her father utterly refuses to give her to him, he shall pay money equivalent to the dowry of virgins.

[18]You shall not allow a woman to live who practices sorcery.

[19]Whoever lies carnally with a beast shall surely be put to death.

[20]He who sacrifices to any god but the Lord only shall be utterly destroyed.

[21]You shall not wrong a stranger or oppress him; for you were strangers in the land of Egypt.

[22]You shall not afflict any widow or fatherless child.

[23]If you afflict them in any way and they cry at all to Me, I will surely hear their cry;

[24]And My wrath shall burn; I will kill you with the

## New International Version

with the sword; your wives will become widows and your children fatherless.

25 "If you lend money to one of my people among you who is needy, do not treat it like a business deal; charge no interest. 26 If you take your neighbor's cloak as a pledge, return it by sunset, 27 because that cloak is the only covering your neighbor has. What else can they sleep in? When they cry out to me, I will hear, for I am compassionate.

28 "Do not blaspheme God*a* or curse the ruler of your people.

29 "Do not hold back offerings from your granaries or your vats.*b*

"You must give me the firstborn of your sons. 30 Do the same with your cattle and your sheep. Let them stay with their mothers for seven days, but give them to me on the eighth day.

31 "You are to be my holy people. So do not eat the meat of an animal torn by wild beasts; throw it to the dogs.

### Laws of Justice and Mercy

**23** "Do not spread false reports. Do not help a guilty person by being a malicious witness.

2 "Do not follow the crowd in doing wrong. When you give testimony in a lawsuit, do not pervert justice by siding with the crowd, 3 and do not show favoritism to a poor person in a lawsuit.

4 "If you come across your enemy's ox or donkey wandering off, be sure to return it. 5 If you see the donkey of someone who hates you fallen down under its load, do not leave it there; be sure you help them with it.

6 "Do not deny justice to your poor people in their lawsuits. 7 Have nothing to do with a false charge and do not put an innocent or honest person to death, for I will not acquit the guilty.

8 "Do not accept a bribe, for a bribe blinds those who see and twists the words of the innocent.

9 "Do not oppress a foreigner; you yourselves know how it feels to be foreigners, because you were foreigners in Egypt.

### Sabbath Laws

10 "For six years you are to sow your fields and harvest the crops, 11 but during the seventh year let the land lie unplowed and unused. Then the poor among your people may get food from it, and the wild animals may eat what is left. Do the same with your vineyard and your olive grove.

12 "Six days do your work, but on the seventh day do not work, so that your ox and your donkey may rest, and so that the slave born in your household and the foreigner living among you may be refreshed.

13 "Be careful to do everything I have said to you. Do not invoke the names of other gods; do not let them be heard on your lips.

### The Three Annual Festivals

14 "Three times a year you are to celebrate a festival to me.

15 "Celebrate the Festival of Unleavened Bread; for seven days eat bread made without yeast, as I commanded you. Do this at the appointed time in the month of Aviv, for in that month you came out of Egypt.

"No one is to appear before me empty-handed.

16 "Celebrate the Festival of Harvest with the firstfruits of the crops you sow in your field.

"Celebrate the Festival of Ingathering at the end of the year, when you gather in your crops from the field.

*a 28* Or *Do not revile the judges*    *b 29* The meaning of the Hebrew for this phrase is uncertain.

## Amplified Bible

sword, and your wives shall be widows and your children fatherless.

25 If you lend money to any of My people with you who is poor, you shall not be to him as a creditor, neither shall you require interest from him.

26 If you ever take your neighbor's garment in pledge, you shall give it back to him before the sun goes down;

27 For that is his only covering, his clothing for his body. In what shall he sleep? When he cries to Me, I will hear, for I am gracious *and* merciful.

28 You shall not revile God [the judges as His agents] or esteem lightly *or* curse a ruler of your people.

29 You shall not delay to bring to Me from the fullness [of your harvested grain] and the outflow [of your grape juice *and* olive oil]; give Me the firstborn of your sons [or redeem them]. [Exod. 34:19, 20.]

30 Likewise shall you do with your oxen *and* your sheep. Seven days the firstborn [beast] shall be with its mother; on the eighth day you shall give it to Me.

31 And you shall be holy men [consecrated] to Me; therefore you shall not eat any flesh that is torn by beasts in the field; you shall throw it to the dogs.

**23** You shall not repeat *or* raise a false report; you shall not join with the wicked to be an unrighteous witness.

2 You shall not follow a crowd to do evil; nor shall you bear witness at a trial so as to side with a multitude to pervert justice.

3 Neither shall you be partial to a poor man in his trial [just because he is poor].

4 If you meet your enemy's ox or his donkey going astray, you shall surely bring it back to him again.

5 If you see the donkey of one who hates you lying [helpless] under his load, you shall refrain from leaving the man to cope with it alone; you shall help him to release the animal.

6 You shall not pervert the justice due to your poor in his cause.

7 Keep far from a false matter and [be very careful] not to condemn to death the innocent and the righteous, for I will not justify *and* acquit the wicked.

8 You shall take no bribe, for the bribe blinds those who have sight and perverts the testimony *and* the cause of the righteous.

9 Also you shall not oppress a temporary resident, for you know the heart of a stranger *and* sojourner, seeing you were strangers *and* sojourners in Egypt.

10 Six years you shall sow your land and reap its yield.

11 But the seventh year you shall release it *and* let it rest and lie fallow, that the poor of your people may eat [what the land voluntarily yields], and what they leave the wild beasts shall eat. In like manner you shall deal with your vineyard and olive grove.

12 Six days you shall do your work, but the seventh day you shall rest and keep Sabbath, that your ox and your donkey may rest, and the son of your bondwoman, and the alien, may be refreshed.

13 In all I have said to you take heed; do not mention the name of other gods [either in blessing or cursing]; do not let such speech be heard from your mouth.

14 Three times in the year you shall keep a feast to Me.

15 You shall keep the Feast of Unleavened Bread; seven days you shall eat unleavened bread as I commanded you, at the time appointed in the month of Abib, for in it you came out of Egypt. None shall appear before Me empty-handed.

16 Also you shall keep the Feast of Harvest [Pentecost], [acknowledging] the firstfruits of your toil, of what you sow in the field. And [third] you shall keep the Feast of Ingathering [Booths or Tabernacles] at the end of the year, when you gather in the fruit of your labors from the field.

## New International Version

¹⁷"Three times a year all the men are to appear before the Sovereign LORD.

¹⁸"Do not offer the blood of a sacrifice to me along with anything containing yeast.

"The fat of my festival offerings must not be kept until morning.

¹⁹"Bring the best of the firstfruits of your soil to the house of the LORD your God.

"Do not cook a young goat in its mother's milk.

### God's Angel to Prepare the Way

²⁰"See, I am sending an angel ahead of you to guard you along the way and to bring you to the place I have prepared. ²¹Pay attention to him and listen to what he says. Do not rebel against him; he will not forgive your rebellion, since my Name is in him. ²²If you listen carefully to what he says and do all that I say, I will be an enemy to your enemies and will oppose those who oppose you. ²³My angel will go ahead of you and bring you into the land of the Amorites, Hittites, Perizzites, Canaanites, Hivites and Jebusites, and I will wipe them out. ²⁴Do not bow down before their gods or worship them or follow their practices. You must demolish them and break their sacred stones to pieces. ²⁵Worship the LORD your God, and his blessing will be on your food and water. I will take away sickness from among you, ²⁶and none will miscarry or be barren in your land. I will give you a full life span.

²⁷"I will send my terror ahead of you and throw into confusion every nation you encounter. I will make all your enemies turn their backs and run. ²⁸I will send the hornet ahead of you to drive the Hivites, Canaanites and Hittites out of your way. ²⁹But I will not drive them out in a single year, because the land would become desolate and the wild animals too numerous for you. ³⁰Little by little I will drive them out before you, until you have increased enough to take possession of the land.

³¹"I will establish your borders from the Red Sea*ᵃ* to the Mediterranean Sea,*ᵇ* and from the desert to the Euphrates River. I will give into your hands the people who live in the land, and you will drive them out before you. ³²Do not make a covenant with them or with their gods. ³³Do not let them live in your land or they will cause you to sin against me, because the worship of their gods will certainly be a snare to you."

### The Covenant Confirmed

**24** Then the LORD said to Moses, "Come up to the LORD, you and Aaron, Nadab and Abihu, and seventy of the elders of Israel. You are to worship at a distance, ²but Moses alone is to approach the LORD; the others must not come near. And the people may not come up with him."

³When Moses went and told the people all the LORD's words and laws, they responded with one voice, "Everything the LORD has said we will do." ⁴Moses then wrote down everything the LORD had said.

He got up early the next morning and built an altar at

## Amplified Bible

¹⁷Three times in the year all your males shall appear before the Lord God.

¹⁸You shall not offer the blood of My sacrifice with leavened bread [but keep it unmixed], neither shall the fat of My feast remain all night until morning.

¹⁹The first of the firstfruits of your ground you shall bring into the house of the Lord your God. You shall not boil a kid in its mother's milk.

²⁰Behold, I send an ᵃAngel before you to keep *and* guard you on the way and to bring you to the place I have prepared.

²¹Give heed to Him, listen to *and* obey His voice; be not rebellious before Him *or* provoke Him, for He will not pardon your transgression; for My ᵇName is in Him. [Exod. 32:34; 33:14; Isa. 63:9.]

²²But if you will indeed listen to and obey His voice and all that I speak, then I will be an enemy to your enemies and an adversary to your adversaries.

²³When My Angel goes before you and brings you to the Amorites, the Hittites, the Perizzites, the Canaanites, the Hivites, and the Jebusites, and I reject them *and* blot them out,

²⁴You shall not bow down to their gods or serve them or do after their works; but you shall utterly overthrow them and break down their pillars *and* images.

²⁵You shall serve the Lord your God; He shall bless your bread and water, and I will take sickness from your midst.

²⁶None shall lose her young by miscarriage or be barren in your land; I will fulfill the number of your days.

²⁷I will send My terror before you and will throw into confusion all the people to whom you shall come, and I will make all your foes turn from you [in flight].

²⁸And I will send hornets before you which shall drive out the Hivite, Canaanite, and Hittite from before you.

²⁹I will not drive them out from before you in one year, lest the land become desolate [for lack of attention] and the wild beasts multiply against you.

³⁰Little by little I will drive them out from before you, until you have increased *and* are numerous enough to take possession of the land.

³¹I will set your borders from the Red Sea to the Sea of the Philistines, and from the wilderness to the river [Euphrates]; for I will deliver the inhabitants of the land into your hand and you shall drive them out before you.

³²You shall make no covenant with them or with their gods.

³³They shall not dwell in your land, lest they make you sin against Me; for if you serve their gods, it will surely be a snare to you.

**24** God said to Moses, Come up to the Lord, you and Aaron, Nadab and Abihu [Aaron's sons], and seventy of Israel's elders, and worship at a distance.

²Moses alone shall come near the Lord; the others shall not come near, and neither shall the people come up with him.

³Moses came and told the people all that the Lord had said and all the ordinances; and all the people answered with one voice, All that the Lord has spoken we will do.

⁴Moses ᶜwrote all the words of the Lord. He rose up early in the morning and built an altar at the foot of the

ᵃ See footnote on Gen. 16:7. ᵇ Representing God's presence. ᶜ The contemporary evidence, supplied by archaeology, that writing had long been in common use before the time of Moses now makes conjectures about the contents of the earlier books of the Old Testament being handed down **orally** look absurd. Not only is much of the misleading criticism of the Bible now recognized as unjustified, it is out of harmony with the scientific outlook of the present day (Sir Charles Marston, *New Bible Evidence*).

## New International Version

the foot of the mountain and set up twelve stone pillars representing the twelve tribes of Israel. ⁵Then he sent young Israelite men, and they offered burnt offerings and sacrificed young bulls as fellowship offerings to the LORD. ⁶Moses took half of the blood and put it in bowls, and the other half he splashed against the altar. ⁷Then he took the Book of the Covenant and read it to the people. They responded, "We will do everything the LORD has said; we will obey."

⁸Moses then took the blood, sprinkled it on the people and said, "This is the blood of the covenant that the LORD has made with you in accordance with all these words."

⁹Moses and Aaron, Nadab and Abihu, and the seventy elders of Israel went up ¹⁰and saw the God of Israel. Under his feet was something like a pavement made of lapis lazuli, as bright blue as the sky. ¹¹But God did not raise his hand against these leaders of the Israelites; they saw God, and they ate and drank.

¹²The LORD said to Moses, "Come up to me on the mountain and stay here, and I will give you the tablets of stone with the law and commandments I have written for their instruction."

¹³Then Moses set out with Joshua his aide, and Moses went up on the mountain of God. ¹⁴He said to the elders, "Wait here for us until we come back to you. Aaron and Hur are with you, and anyone involved in a dispute can go to them."

¹⁵When Moses went up on the mountain, the cloud covered it, ¹⁶and the glory of the LORD settled on Mount Sinai. For six days the cloud covered the mountain, and on the seventh day the LORD called to Moses from within the cloud. ¹⁷To the Israelites the glory of the LORD looked like a consuming fire on top of the mountain. ¹⁸Then Moses entered the cloud as he went on up the mountain. And he stayed on the mountain forty days and forty nights.

### Offerings for the Tabernacle

**25** The LORD said to Moses, ²"Tell the Israelites to bring me an offering. You are to receive the offering for me from everyone whose heart prompts them to give. ³These are the offerings you are to receive from them: gold, silver and bronze; ⁴blue, purple and scarlet yarn and fine linen; goat hair; ⁵ram skins dyed red and another type of durable leather*; acacia wood; ⁶olive oil for the light; spices for the anointing oil and for the fragrant incense; ⁷and onyx stones and other gems to be mounted on the ephod and breastpiece.

⁸"Then have them make a sanctuary for me, and I will dwell among them. ⁹Make this tabernacle and all its furnishings exactly like the pattern I will show you.

### The Ark

¹⁰"Have them make an ark*b* of acacia wood—two and a half cubits long, a cubit and a half wide, and a cubit and a half high.*c* ¹¹Overlay it with pure gold, both inside and out,

## Amplified Bible

mountain and set up twelve pillars representing Israel's twelve tribes.

⁵And he sent young Israelite men, who offered burnt offerings and sacrificed peace offerings of oxen to the Lord.

⁶And Moses took half of the blood and put it in basins, and half of the blood he dashed against the altar.

⁷Then he took the Book of the Covenant and read in the hearing of the people; and they said, All that the Lord has said we will do, and we will be obedient.

⁸And Moses took the [remaining half of] blood and sprinkled it on the people, and said, Behold the blood of the covenant which the Lord has made with you in accordance with all these words. [I Cor. 11:25; Heb. 8:6; 10:28, 29.]

⁹Then Moses, Aaron, Nadab, and Abihu, and seventy of the elders of Israel went up [the mountainside].

¹⁰And they saw the God of Israel [that is, a convincing manifestation of His presence], and under His feet it was like pavement of bright sapphire stone, like the very heavens in clearness. [Exod. 33:20-23; Deut. 4:12; Ezek. 28:14]

¹¹And upon the nobles of the Israelites He laid not His hand [to conceal Himself from them, to rebuke their daring, or to harm them]; but they saw [the manifestation of the presence of] God, and ate and drank. [Exod. 19:21.]

¹²And the Lord said to Moses, Come up to Me into the mountain and be there, and I will give you tables of stone, with the law and the commandments which *a*I have written that you may teach them. [II Cor. 3:2, 3.]

¹³So Moses rose up with Joshua his attendant; and Moses went up into the mountain of God.

¹⁴And he said to the elders, Tarry here for us until we come back to you; remember, Aaron and Hur are with you; whoever has a cause, let him go to them.

¹⁵Then Moses went up into the mountain, and the cloud covered the mountain.

¹⁶The glory of the Lord rested on Mount Sinai, and the cloud covered it for six days. On the seventh day [God] called to Moses out of the midst of the cloud.

¹⁷And the glory of the Lord appeared to the Israelites like devouring fire on the top of the mountain.

¹⁸Moses entered into the midst of the cloud and went up the mountain, and Moses was on the mountain forty days and nights.

**25** And the Lord said to Moses, ²Speak to the Israelites, that they take for Me an offering. From every man who gives it willingly *and* ungrudgingly with his heart you shall take My offering.

³This is the offering you shall receive from them: gold, silver, and bronze,

⁴Blue, purple, and scarlet [stuff] and fine twined linen and goats' hair,

⁵Rams' skins tanned red, goatskins, dolphin *or* porpoise skins, acacia wood,

⁶Oil for the light, spices for anointing oil and for sweet incense,

⁷Onyx stones, and stones for setting in the ephod and in the breastplate.

⁸Let them make Me a sanctuary, that I may dwell among them. [Heb. 8:1, 2; 10:1.]

⁹And you shall make it according to all that I show you, the pattern of the tabernacle *or* dwelling and the pattern of all the furniture of it.

¹⁰They shall make an ark of acacia wood: two and a half cubits long, a cubit and a half wide, and a cubit and a half high.

¹¹You shall overlay the ark with pure gold, inside and

---

*a* The two tables were "written with the finger of God" (Exod. 31:18), and "the tables were the work of God" (Exod. 32:16). A man may be said to write what a secretary writes at his dictation; but if he expressly states that certain things are written with his own hand, it is unreasonable to suppose that they were written by the hand of another (J. P. Lange, *A Commentary*).

---

*a 5* Possibly the hides of large aquatic mammals    *b 10* That is, a chest
*c 10* That is, about 3 3/4 feet long and 2 1/4 feet wide and high or about 1.1 meters long and 68 centimeters wide and high; similarly in verse 17

## New International Version

and make a gold molding around it. ¹²Cast four gold rings for it and fasten them to its four feet, with two rings on one side and two rings on the other. ¹³Then make poles of acacia wood and overlay them with gold. ¹⁴Insert the poles into the rings on the sides of the ark to carry it. ¹⁵The poles are to remain in the rings of this ark; they are not to be removed. ¹⁶Then put in the ark the tablets of the covenant law, which I will give you.

¹⁷"Make an atonement cover of pure gold—two and a half cubits long and a cubit and a half wide. ¹⁸And make two cherubim out of hammered gold at the ends of the cover. ¹⁹Make one cherub on one end and the second cherub on the other; make the cherubim of one piece with the cover, at the two ends. ²⁰The cherubim are to have their wings spread upward, overshadowing the cover with them. The cherubim are to face each other, looking toward the cover. ²¹Place the cover on top of the ark and put in the ark the tablets of the covenant law that I will give you. ²²There, above the cover between the two cherubim that are over the ark of the covenant law, I will meet with you and give you all my commands for the Israelites.

### The Table

²³"Make a table of acacia wood—two cubits long, a cubit wide and a cubit and a half high.ᵃ ²⁴Overlay it with pure gold and make a gold molding around it. ²⁵Also make around it a rim a handbreadthᵇ wide and put a gold molding on the rim. ²⁶Make four gold rings for the table and fasten them to the four corners, where the four legs are. ²⁷The rings are to be close to the rim to hold the poles used in carrying the table. ²⁸Make the poles of acacia wood, overlay them with gold and carry the table with them. ²⁹And make its plates and dishes of pure gold, as well as its pitchers and bowls for the pouring out of offerings. ³⁰Put the bread of the Presence on this table to be before me at all times.

### The Lampstand

³¹"Make a lampstand of pure gold. Hammer out its base and shaft, and make its flowerlike cups, buds and blossoms of one piece with them. ³²Six branches are to extend from the sides of the lampstand—three on one side and three on the other. ³³Three cups shaped like almond flowers with buds and blossoms are to be on one branch, three on the next branch, and the same for all six branches extending from the lampstand. ³⁴And on the lampstand there are to be four cups shaped like almond flowers with buds and blossoms. ³⁵One bud shall be under the first pair of branches extending from the lampstand, a second bud under the second pair, and a third bud under the third

## Amplified Bible

out, and make a gold crown, a rim *or* border, around its top.

¹²You shall cast four gold rings and attach them to the four lower corners of it, two rings on either side.

¹³You shall make poles of acacia wood and overlay them with gold,

¹⁴And put the poles through the rings on the ark's sides, by which to carry it.

¹⁵The poles shall remain in the rings of the ark; they shall not be removed from it [that the ark be not touched].

¹⁶And you shall put inside the ark the Testimony [the Ten Commandments] which I will give you.

¹⁷And you shall make a mercy seat (a covering) of pure gold, two cubits and a half long and a cubit and a half wide.

¹⁸And you shall make two cherubim (winged angelic figures) of [solid] hammered gold on the two ends of the mercy seat.

¹⁹Make one cherub on each end, making the cherubim of one piece with the mercy seat, on the two ends of it.

²⁰And the cherubim shall spread out their wings above, covering the mercy seat with their wings, facing each other and looking down toward the mercy seat.

²¹You shall put the mercy seat on the top of the ark, and in the ark you shall put the Testimony [the Ten Commandments] that I will give you.

²²There I will meet with you and, from above the mercy seat, from between the two cherubim that are upon the ark of the Testimony, I will speak intimately with you of all which I will give you in commandment to the Israelites.

²³Also, make a table of acacia wood, two cubits long, one cubit wide, and a cubit and a half high [for the showbread].

²⁴You shall overlay it with pure gold and make a crown, a rim *or* molding, of gold around the top of it;

²⁵And make a frame of a handbreadth around *and* below the top of it and put around it a gold molding as a border.

²⁶You shall make for it four rings of gold and fasten them at the four corners that are on the table's four legs.

²⁷Close against the frame shall the rings be as places for the poles to pass to carry the table [of showbread].

²⁸You shall make the poles of acacia wood and overlay them with gold, that the table may be carried with them.

²⁹And you shall make its plates [for showbread] and cups [for incense], and its flagons and bowls [for liquids in sacrifice]; make them of pure gold.

³⁰And you shall set the showbread (the bread of the Presence) on the table before Me always. [John 6:58.]

³¹You shall make a lampstand of pure gold. Of beaten *and* turned work shall the lampstand be made, both its base and its shaft; its cups, its knobs, and its flowers shall be of one piece with it.

³²Six branches shall come out of the sides of it; three branches of the lampstand out of the one side and three branches out of its other side;

³³Three cups made like almond blossoms, each with a knob and a flower on one branch, and three cups made like almond blossoms on the other branch with a knob and a flower; so for the six branches coming out of the lampstand;

³⁴And on the [center shaft] itself you shall [make] four cups like almond blossoms with their knobs and their flowers.

³⁵Also make a knob [on the shaft] under each pair of the six branches going out from the lampstand and one piece with it;

## New International Version

pair—six branches in all. ³⁶The buds and branches shall all be of one piece with the lampstand, hammered out of pure gold.

³⁷"Then make its seven lamps and set them up on it so that they light the space in front of it. ³⁸Its wick trimmers and trays are to be of pure gold. ³⁹A talent*a* of pure gold is to be used for the lampstand and all these accessories. ⁴⁰See that you make them according to the pattern shown you on the mountain.

### The Tabernacle

**26** "Make the tabernacle with ten curtains of finely twisted linen and blue, purple and scarlet yarn, with cherubim woven into them by a skilled worker. ²All the curtains are to be the same size—twenty-eight cubits long and four cubits wide.*b* ³Join five of the curtains together, and do the same with the other five. ⁴Make loops of blue material along the edge of the end curtain in one set, and do the same with the end curtain in the other set. ⁵Make fifty loops on one curtain and fifty loops on the end curtain of the other set, with the loops opposite each other. ⁶Then make fifty gold clasps and use them to fasten the curtains together so that the tabernacle is a unit.

⁷"Make curtains of goat hair for the tent over the tabernacle—eleven altogether. ⁸All eleven curtains are to be the same size—thirty cubits long and four cubits wide.*c* ⁹Join five of the curtains together into one set and the other six into another set. Fold the sixth curtain double at the front of the tent. ¹⁰Make fifty loops along the edge of the end curtain in one set and also along the edge of the end curtain in the other set. ¹¹Then make fifty bronze clasps and put them in the loops to fasten the tent together as a unit. ¹²As for the additional length of the tent curtains, the half curtain that is left over is to hang down at the rear of the tabernacle. ¹³The tent curtains will be a cubit*d* longer on both sides; what is left will hang over the sides of the tabernacle so as to cover it. ¹⁴Make for the tent a covering of ram skins dyed red, and over that a covering of the other durable leather.*e*

¹⁵"Make upright frames of acacia wood for the tabernacle. ¹⁶Each frame is to be ten cubits long and a cubit and a half wide,*f* ¹⁷with two projections set parallel to each other. Make all the frames of the tabernacle in this way. ¹⁸Make twenty frames for the south side of the tabernacle ¹⁹and make forty silver bases to go under them—two bases for

## Amplified Bible

³⁶Their knobs and their branches shall be of one piece with it; the whole of it one beaten work of pure gold.

³⁷And you shall make the lamps of the [lampstand] to include a *a*seventh one [at the top of the shaft]. [The priests] shall set up the [seven] lamps of it so they may give light in front of it.

³⁸Its snuffers and its ashtrays shall be of pure gold.

³⁹Use a talent of pure gold for it, including all these utensils.

⁴⁰And see to it that you copy [exactly] their pattern which was shown you on the mountain. [Heb. 8:5, 6.]

**26** Moreover, you shall make the tabernacle with ten curtains; of fine twined linen, and blue and purple and scarlet [stuff], with cherubim skillfully embroidered shall you make them.

²The length of one curtain shall be twenty-eight cubits and the breadth of one curtain four cubits; each of the curtains shall measure the same.

³The five curtains shall be coupled to one another, and the other five curtains shall be coupled to one another.

⁴And you shall make loops of blue on the edge of the last curtain in the first set, and likewise in the second set.

⁵Fifty loops you shall make on the one curtain and fifty loops on the edge of the last curtain that is in the second coupling *or* set, so that the loops on one correspond to the loops on the other.

⁶And you shall make fifty clasps of gold and fasten the curtains together with the clasps; then the tabernacle shall be one whole.

⁷And make curtains of goats' hair to be a [second] covering over the tabernacle; eleven curtains shall you make.

⁸One curtain shall be thirty cubits long and four cubits wide; and the eleven curtains shall all measure the same.

⁹You shall join together five curtains by themselves and six curtains by themselves, and shall double over the sixth curtain in the front of the tabernacle [to make a closed door].

¹⁰And make fifty loops on the edge of the outmost curtain in the one set and fifty loops on the edge of the outmost curtain in the second set.

¹¹You shall make fifty clasps of bronze and put the clasps into the loops and couple the tent together, that it may be one whole.

¹²The surplus that remains of the tent curtains, the half curtain that remains, shall hang over the back of the tabernacle.

¹³And the cubit on the one side and the cubit on the other side of what remains in the length of the curtains of the tent shall hang over the sides of the tabernacle, on this side and that side, to cover it.

¹⁴You shall make a [third] covering for the tent of rams' skins tanned red, and a [fourth] covering above that of dolphin *or* porpoise skins.

¹⁵And you shall make the upright frame for the tabernacle of boards of acacia wood.

¹⁶Ten cubits shall be the length of a board and a cubit and a half shall be the breadth of one board.

¹⁷Make two tenons in each board for dovetailing *and* fitting together; so shall you do for all the tabernacle boards.

¹⁸And make the boards for the tabernacle: twenty boards for the south side;

¹⁹And you shall make forty silver sockets under the

---

*a* 39 That is, about 75 pounds or about 34 kilograms    *b* 2 That is, about 42 feet long and 6 feet wide or about 13 meters long and 1.8 meters wide    *c* 8 That is, about 45 feet long and 6 feet wide or about 13.5 meters long and 1.8 meters wide    *d* 13 That is, about 18 inches or about 45 centimeters    *e* 14 Possibly the hides of large aquatic mammals (see 25:5)    *f* 16 That is, about 15 feet long and 2 1/4 feet wide or about 4.5 meters long and 68 centimeters wide

*a* Certain Biblical critics in the past doubted the existence of the tabernacle and asserted that the concept of a sevenfold lamp was unknown until hundreds of years later, in Babylonian times (600 B.C.). The first objective evidence to the contrary came to light in W. F. Albright's excavation of Tell Beit Mirsim, south of Jerusalem, where he found seven-sprouted lamps from about 1200 B.C. The seventh season at Dothan yielded three sevenfold lamps from the period 1200-1400 B.C., showing again that this was not a late idea (Joseph P. Free, *Near Eastern Archaeology*).

## New International Version

each frame, one under each projection. [20]For the other side, the north side of the tabernacle, make twenty frames [21]and forty silver bases—two under each frame. [22]Make six frames for the far end, that is, the west end of the tabernacle, [23]and make two frames for the corners at the far end. [24]At these two corners they must be double from the bottom all the way to the top and fitted into a single ring; both shall be like that. [25]So there will be eight frames and sixteen silver bases—two under each frame.

[26]"Also make crossbars of acacia wood: five for the frames on one side of the tabernacle, [27]five for those on the other side, and five for the frames on the west, at the far end of the tabernacle. [28]The center crossbar is to extend from end to end at the middle of the frames. [29]Overlay the frames with gold and make gold rings to hold the crossbars. Also overlay the crossbars with gold.

[30]"Set up the tabernacle according to the plan shown you on the mountain.

[31]"Make a curtain of blue, purple and scarlet yarn and finely twisted linen, with cherubim woven into it by a skilled worker. [32]Hang it with gold hooks on four posts of acacia wood overlaid with gold and standing on four silver bases. [33]Hang the curtain from the clasps and place the ark of the covenant law behind the curtain. The curtain will separate the Holy Place from the Most Holy Place. [34]Put the atonement cover on the ark of the covenant law in the Most Holy Place. [35]Place the table outside the curtain on the north side of the tabernacle and put the lampstand opposite it on the south side.

[36]"For the entrance to the tent make a curtain of blue, purple and scarlet yarn and finely twisted linen—the work of an embroiderer. [37]Make gold hooks for this curtain and five posts of acacia wood overlaid with gold. And cast five bronze bases for them.

## Amplified Bible

twenty boards, two sockets under each board for its two tenons.

[20]And for the north side of the tabernacle there shall be twenty boards

[21]And their forty silver sockets, two sockets under each board.

[22]For the back or west side of the tabernacle you shall make six boards.

[23]Make two boards for the corners of the tabernacle in the rear on both sides.

[24]They shall be coupled down below and coupled together on top with one ring. Thus shall it be for both of them; they shall form the two corners.

[25]And there shall be eight boards and their sockets of silver, sixteen sockets, two sockets under each board.

[26]And you shall make bars of acacia wood: five for the boards of one side,

[27]And five bars for the boards of the other side of the tabernacle, and five bars for the boards of the rear end of the tabernacle, for the back wall to the west.

[28]And the middle bar halfway up the boards shall pass through from end to end.

[29]You shall overlay the boards with gold and make their rings of gold to hold the bars and overlay the bars with gold.

[30]You shall erect the tabernacle after the plan of it shown you on the mountain.

[31]And make a veil of blue, purple, and scarlet [stuff] and fine twined linen, skillfully worked with cherubim on it.

[32]You shall hang it on four pillars of acacia wood overlaid with gold, with gold hooks, on four sockets of silver.

[33]And you shall hang the veil from the clasps and bring the ark of the Testimony into place within the veil; and the veil shall separate for you the Holy Place from the Most Holy Place.

[34]And you shall put the mercy seat on the ark of the Testimony in the Most Holy Place.

[35]And you shall set the table [for the showbread] outside the veil [in the Holy Place] on the north side and the lampstand opposite the table on the south side of the tabernacle.

[36]You shall make a hanging [to form a screen] for the door of the tent of blue, purple, and scarlet [stuff] and fine twined linen, embroidered. [John 10:9.]

[37]You shall make five pillars of acacia wood to support the hanging curtain and overlay them with gold; their hooks shall be of gold, and you shall cast five [base] sockets of bronze for them.

### The Altar of Burnt Offering

**27** "Build an altar of acacia wood, three cubits[a] high; it is to be square, five cubits long and five cubits wide.[b] [2]Make a horn at each of the four corners, so that the horns and the altar are of one piece, and overlay the altar with bronze. [3]Make all its utensils of bronze—its pots to remove the ashes, and its shovels, sprinkling bowls, meat forks and firepans. [4]Make a grating for it, a bronze network, and make a bronze ring at each of the four corners of the network. [5]Put it under the ledge of the altar so that it is halfway up the altar. [6]Make poles of acacia wood for the altar and overlay them with bronze. [7]The poles are to

**27** And make the altar of acacia wood, five cubits square and three cubits high [within reach of all].

[2]Make horns for it on its four corners; they shall be of one piece with it, and you shall overlay it with bronze.

[3]You shall make pots to take away its ashes, and shovels, basins, forks, and firepans; make all its utensils of bronze.

[4]Also make for it a grate, a network of bronze; and on the net you shall make four bronze rings at its four corners.

[5]And you shall put it under the ledge of the altar, so that the net will extend halfway down the altar.

[6]And make poles for the altar, poles of acacia wood overlaid with bronze.

---

[a] 1 That is, about 4 1/2 feet or about 1.4 meters    [b] 1 That is, about 7 1/2 feet or about 2.3 meters long and wide

# New International Version

be inserted into the rings so they will be on two sides of the altar when it is carried. [8]Make the altar hollow, out of boards. It is to be made just as you were shown on the mountain.

## The Courtyard

[9]"Make a courtyard for the tabernacle. The south side shall be a hundred cubits[a] long and is to have curtains of finely twisted linen, [10]with twenty posts and twenty bronze bases and with silver hooks and bands on the posts. [11]The north side shall also be a hundred cubits long and is to have curtains, with twenty posts and twenty bronze bases and with silver hooks and bands on the posts.

[12]"The west end of the courtyard shall be fifty cubits[b] wide and have curtains, with ten posts and ten bases. [13]On the east end, toward the sunrise, the courtyard shall also be fifty cubits wide. [14]Curtains fifteen cubits[c] long are to be on one side of the entrance, with three posts and three bases, [15]and curtains fifteen cubits long are to be on the other side, with three posts and three bases.

[16]"For the entrance to the courtyard, provide a curtain twenty cubits[d] long, of blue, purple and scarlet yarn and finely twisted linen—the work of an embroiderer—with four posts and four bases. [17]All the posts around the courtyard are to have silver bands and hooks, and bronze bases. [18]The courtyard shall be a hundred cubits long and fifty cubits wide,[e] with curtains of finely twisted linen five cubits[f] high, and with bronze bases. [19]All the other articles used in the service of the tabernacle, whatever their function, including all the tent pegs for it and those for the courtyard, are to be of bronze.

## Oil for the Lampstand

[20]"Command the Israelites to bring you clear oil of pressed olives for the light so that the lamps may be kept burning. [21]In the tent of meeting, outside the curtain that shields the ark of the covenant law, Aaron and his sons are to keep the lamps burning before the LORD from evening till morning. This is to be a lasting ordinance among the Israelites for the generations to come.

## The Priestly Garments

**28** "Have Aaron your brother brought to you from among the Israelites, along with his sons Nadab and Abihu, Eleazar and Ithamar, so they may serve me as priests. [2]Make sacred garments for your brother Aaron to give him dignity and honor. [3]Tell all the skilled workers to whom I have given wisdom in such matters that they are to make garments for Aaron, for his consecration, so he may serve me as priest. [4]These are the garments they are to make: a breastpiece, an ephod, a robe, a woven tunic, a turban and a sash. They are to make these sacred garments for your brother Aaron and his sons, so they may serve me as priests. [5]Have them use gold, and blue, purple and scarlet yarn, and fine linen.

## The Ephod

[6]"Make the ephod of gold, and of blue, purple and scarlet yarn, and of finely twisted linen—the work of skilled hands. [7]It is to have two shoulder pieces attached to two

---

[a] 9 That is, about 150 feet or about 45 meters; also in verse 11
[b] 12 That is, about 75 feet or about 23 meters; also in verse 13
[c] 14 That is, about 23 feet or about 6.8 meters; also in verse 15
[d] 16 That is, about 30 feet or about 9 meters    [e] 18 That is, about 150 feet long and 75 feet wide or about 45 meters long and 23 meters wide
[f] 18 That is, about 7 1/2 feet or about 2.3 meters

# Amplified Bible

[7]The poles shall be put through the rings on the two sides of the altar, with which to carry it. [Num. 4:14, 15.]

[8]You shall make [the altar] hollow with slabs or planks; as shown you on the mountain, so shall it be made.

[9]And you shall make the court of the tabernacle. On the south side the court shall have hangings of fine twined linen, a hundred cubits long for one side;

[10]Their pillars shall be twenty and their sockets twenty, of bronze, but the hooks of the pillars and their joinings shall be of silver;

[11]Likewise for the north side hangings, a hundred cubits long, and their twenty pillars and their twenty sockets of bronze, but the hooks of the pillars and their joinings shall be of silver.

[12]And for the breadth of the court on the west side there shall be hangings of fifty cubits, with ten pillars and ten sockets.

[13]The breadth of the court to the front, the east side, shall be fifty cubits.

[14]The hangings for one side of the gate shall be fifteen cubits, with three pillars and three sockets.

[15]On the other side the hangings shall be fifteen cubits, with three pillars and three sockets.

[16]And for the gate of the court there shall be a hanging [for a screen] twenty cubits long, of blue, purple, and scarlet [stuff] and fine twined linen, embroidered. It shall have four pillars and four sockets for them.

[17]All the pillars round about the court shall be joined together with silver rods; their hooks shall be of silver and their sockets of bronze.

[18]The length of the court shall be a hundred cubits and the breadth fifty and the height five cubits, [with hangings of] fine twined linen and sockets of bronze.

[19]All the tabernacle's utensils and instruments used in all its service, and all its pegs and all the pegs for the court, shall be of bronze.

[20]You shall command the Israelites to provide you with pure oil of crushed olives for the light, to cause it to burn continually [every night].

[21]In the Tent of Meeting [of God with His people], outside the veil which sets apart the Testimony, Aaron and his sons shall keep it burning from evening to morning before the Lord. It shall be a statute to be observed on behalf of the Israelites throughout their generations.

**28** From among the Israelites take your brother Aaron and his sons with him, that he may minister to Me in the priest's office, even Aaron, Nadab and Abihu, Eleazar and Ithamar, Aaron's sons.

[2]And you shall make for Aaron your brother sacred garments [appointed official dress set apart for special holy services] for honor and for beauty.

[3]Tell all who are expert, whom I have endowed with skill and good judgment, that they shall make Aaron's garments to sanctify him for My priesthood.

[4]They shall make these garments: a breastplate, an ephod [a distinctive vestment to which the breastplate was to be attached], a robe, long and sleeved tunic of checkerwork, a turban, and a sash or band. They shall make sacred garments for Aaron your brother and his sons to minister to Me in the priest's office.

[5]They shall receive [from the people] and use gold, and blue, purple, and scarlet [stuff], and fine linen.

[6]And they shall make the ephod of gold, of blue, purple, and scarlet [stuff], and fine twined linen, skillfully woven and worked.

[7]It shall have two shoulder straps to join the two [back and front] edges, that it may be held together.

## New International Version

of its corners, so it can be fastened. ⁸Its skillfully woven waistband is to be like it—of one piece with the ephod and made with gold, and with blue, purple and scarlet yarn, and with finely twisted linen.

⁹"Take two onyx stones and engrave on them the names of the sons of Israel ¹⁰in the order of their birth—six names on one stone and the remaining six on the other. ¹¹Engrave the names of the sons of Israel on the two stones the way a gem cutter engraves a seal. Then mount the stones in gold filigree settings ¹²and fasten them on the shoulder pieces of the ephod as memorial stones for the sons of Israel. Aaron is to bear the names on his shoulders as a memorial before the LORD. ¹³Make gold filigree settings ¹⁴and two braided chains of pure gold, like a rope, and attach the chains to the settings.

### The Breastpiece
¹⁵"Fashion a breastpiece for making decisions—the work of skilled hands. Make it like the ephod: of gold, and of blue, purple and scarlet yarn, and of finely twisted linen. ¹⁶It is to be square—a span*ᵃ* long and a span wide—and folded double. ¹⁷Then mount four rows of precious stones on it. The first row shall be carnelian, chrysolite and beryl; ¹⁸the second row shall be turquoise, lapis lazuli and emerald; ¹⁹the third row shall be jacinth, agate and amethyst; ²⁰the fourth row shall be topaz, onyx and jasper.*ᵇ* Mount them in gold filigree settings. ²¹There are to be twelve stones, one for each of the names of the sons of Israel, each engraved like a seal with the name of one of the twelve tribes.

²²"For the breastpiece make braided chains of pure gold, like a rope. ²³Make two gold rings for it and fasten them to two corners of the breastpiece. ²⁴Fasten the two gold chains to the rings at the corners of the breastpiece, ²⁵and the other ends of the chains to the two settings, attaching them to the shoulder pieces of the ephod at the front. ²⁶Make two gold rings and attach them to the other two corners of the breastpiece on the inside edge next to the ephod. ²⁷Make two more gold rings and attach them to the bottom of the shoulder pieces on the front of the ephod, close to the seam just above the waistband of the ephod. ²⁸The rings of the breastpiece are to be tied to the rings of the ephod with blue cord, connecting it to the waistband, so that the breastpiece will not swing out from the ephod.

²⁹"Whenever Aaron enters the Holy Place, he will bear the names of the sons of Israel over his heart on the breastpiece of decision as a continuing memorial before the LORD. ³⁰Also put the Urim and the Thummim in the breastpiece, so they may be over Aaron's heart whenever he enters the presence of the LORD. Thus Aaron will always bear the means of making decisions for the Israelites over his heart before the LORD.

### Other Priestly Garments
³¹"Make the robe of the ephod entirely of blue cloth, ³²with an opening for the head in its center. There shall

## Amplified Bible

⁸The skillfully woven girding band which is on the ephod shall be made of the same, of gold, blue, purple, and scarlet [stuff], and fine twined linen.

⁹And you shall take two onyx *or* beryl stones and engrave on them the names of the twelve sons of Israel;

¹⁰Six of their names on one stone and the six names of the rest on the other stone, arranged in order of their birth.

¹¹With the work of a stone engraver, like the engravings of a signet, you shall engrave the two stones according to the names of the sons of Israel. You shall have them set in sockets *or* rosettes of gold.

¹²And you shall put the two stones upon the [two] shoulder straps of the ephod [of the high priest] as memorial stones for Israel; and Aaron shall bear their names upon his two shoulders as a memorial before the Lord.

¹³And you shall make sockets *or* rosettes of gold for settings,

¹⁴And two chains of pure gold, like cords shall you twist them, and fasten the corded chains to the settings.

¹⁵You shall make a breastplate of judgment, in skilled work; like the workmanship of the ephod shall you make it, of gold, blue, purple, and scarlet [stuff], and of fine twined linen.

¹⁶The breastplate shall be square *and* doubled; a span [nine inches] shall be its length and a span shall be its breadth.

¹⁷You shall set in it four rows of stones: a sardius, a topaz, and a carbuncle shall be the first row;

¹⁸The second row an emerald, a sapphire, and a diamond [so called at that time];

¹⁹The third row a jacinth, an agate, and an amethyst;

²⁰And the fourth row a beryl, an onyx, and a jasper; they shall be set in gold filigree.

²¹And the stones shall be twelve, according to the names of the sons of Israel, like the engravings of a signet, each with its name for the twelve tribes.

²²You shall make for the breastplate chains of pure gold twisted like cords.

²³You shall make on the breastplate two rings of gold and put [them] on the two edges of the breastplate.

²⁴And you shall put the two twisted, cordlike chains of gold in the two rings which are on the edges of the breastplate.

²⁵The other two ends of the two twisted, cordlike chains you shall fasten in the two sockets *or* rosettes in front, putting them on the shoulder straps of the ephod;

²⁶And make two rings of gold and put them at the two ends of the breastplate on its inside edge next to the ephod.

²⁷Two gold rings you shall make and attach them to the lower part of the two shoulder pieces of the ephod in front, close by where they join, above the skillfully woven girdle *or* band of the ephod.

²⁸And they shall bind the breastplate by its rings to the rings of the ephod with a lace of blue, that it may be above the skillfully woven girding band of the ephod, and that the breastplate may not become loose from the ephod.

²⁹So Aaron shall bear the names of the sons of Israel in the breastplate of judgment upon his heart when he goes into the Holy Place, to bring them in continual remembrance before the Lord.

³⁰In the breastplate of judgment you shall put the Urim and the Thummim [unspecified articles used when the high priest asked God's counsel for all Israel]; they shall be upon Aaron's heart when he goes in before the Lord, and Aaron shall bear the judgment (rights, judicial decisions) of the Israelites upon his heart before the Lord continually.

³¹Make the robe [to be worn beneath] the ephod all of blue.

³²There shall be a hole in the center of it [to slip over

---

*ᵃ 16* That is, about 9 inches or about 23 centimeters   *ᵇ 20* The precise identification of some of these precious stones is uncertain.

## New International Version

be a woven edge like a collar[a] around this opening, so that it will not tear. 33Make pomegranates of blue, purple and scarlet yarn around the hem of the robe, with gold bells between them. 34The gold bells and the pomegranates are to alternate around the hem of the robe. 35Aaron must wear it when he ministers. The sound of the bells will be heard when he enters the Holy Place before the LORD and when he comes out, so that he will not die.

36"Make a plate of pure gold and engrave on it as on a seal: HOLY TO THE LORD. 37Fasten a blue cord to it to attach it to the turban; it is to be on the front of the turban. 38It will be on Aaron's forehead, and he will bear the guilt involved in the sacred gifts the Israelites consecrate, whatever their gifts may be. It will be on Aaron's forehead continually so that they will be acceptable to the LORD.

39"Weave the tunic of fine linen and make the turban of fine linen. The sash is to be the work of an embroiderer. 40Make tunics, sashes and caps for Aaron's sons to give them dignity and honor. 41After you put these clothes on your brother Aaron and his sons, anoint and ordain them. Consecrate them so they may serve me as priests.

42"Make linen undergarments as a covering for the body, reaching from the waist to the thigh. 43Aaron and his sons must wear them whenever they enter the tent of meeting or approach the altar to minister in the Holy Place, so that they will not incur guilt and die.

"This is to be a lasting ordinance for Aaron and his descendants.

### Consecration of the Priests

**29** "This is what you are to do to consecrate them, so they may serve me as priests: Take a young bull and two rams without defect. 2And from the finest wheat flour make round loaves without yeast, thick loaves without yeast and with olive oil mixed in, and thin loaves without yeast and brushed with olive oil. 3Put them in a basket and present them along with the bull and the two rams. 4Then bring Aaron and his sons to the entrance to the tent of meeting and wash them with water. 5Take the garments and dress Aaron with the tunic, the robe of the ephod, the ephod itself and the breastpiece. Fasten the ephod on him by its skillfully woven waistband. 6Put the turban on his head and attach the sacred emblem to the turban. 7Take the anointing oil and anoint him by pouring it on his head. 8Bring his sons and dress them in tunics 9and fasten caps on them. Then tie sashes on Aaron and his sons.[b] The priesthood is theirs by a lasting ordinance.

"Then you shall ordain Aaron and his sons.

10"Bring the bull to the front of the tent of meeting, and Aaron and his sons shall lay their hands on its head.

## Amplified Bible

the head], with a binding of woven work around the hole, like the opening in a coat of mail or a garment, that it may not fray or tear.

33And you shall make pomegranates of blue, purple, and scarlet [stuff] around about its skirts, with gold bells between them;

34A gold bell and a pomegranate, a gold bell and a pomegranate, round about on the skirts of the robe.

35Aaron shall wear the robe when he ministers, and its sound shall be heard when he goes [alone] into the Holy of Holies before the Lord and when he comes out, lest he die there.

36And you shall make a plate of pure gold and engrave on it, like the engravings of a signet, HOLY TO THE LORD. [Exod. 39:30.]

37You shall fasten it on the front of the turban with a blue cord.

38It shall be upon Aaron's forehead, that Aaron may take upon himself and bear [any] iniquity [connected with] the holy things which the Israelites shall give and dedicate; and it shall always be upon his forehead, that they may be accepted before the Lord [in the priest's person]. [Luke 24:44; Heb. 8:1, 2.]

39And you shall weave the long and sleeved tunic of checkerwork of fine linen or silk and make a turban of fine linen or silk; and you shall make a girdle, the work of the embroiderer.

40For Aaron's sons you shall make long and sleeved tunics and belts or sashes and caps, for glory and honor and beauty.

41And you shall put them on Aaron your brother and his sons with him, and shall anoint them and ordain and sanctify them [set them apart for God], that they may serve Me as priests.

42You shall make for them [white] linen trunks to cover their naked flesh, reaching from the waist to the thighs.

43And they shall be on Aaron and his sons when they go into the Tent of Meeting or when they come near to the altar to minister in the Holy Place, lest they bring iniquity upon themselves and die; it shall be a statute forever to Aaron and to his descendants after him.

**29** This is what you shall do to consecrate (set them apart) that they may serve Me as priests. Take one young bull and two rams, all without blemish,

2And unleavened bread and unleavened cakes mixed with oil and unleavened wafers spread with oil; of fine flour shall you make them.

3You shall put them in one basket and bring them in [it], and bring also the bull and the two rams;

4And bring Aaron and his sons to the door of the Tent of Meeting [out where the laver is] and wash them with water.

5Then take the garments and put on Aaron the long and sleeved tunic and the robe of the ephod and the ephod and the breastplate, and gird him with the skillfully woven girding band of the ephod.

6And you shall put the turban or miter upon his head and put the holy crown upon the turban.

7Then take the anointing oil and pour it on his head and anoint him.

8And bring his sons and put long and sleeved tunics on them.

9And you shall gird them with sashes or belts, Aaron and his sons, and bind caps on them; and the priest's office shall be theirs by a perpetual statute. Thus you shall ordain and consecrate Aaron and his sons.

10Then bring the bull before the Tent of Meeting, and Aaron and his sons shall lay their hands upon its head.

---

a 32 The meaning of the Hebrew for this word is uncertain.
b 9 Hebrew; Septuagint on them

## New International Version

[11]Slaughter it in the LORD's presence at the entrance to the tent of meeting. [12]Take some of the bull's blood and put it on the horns of the altar with your finger, and pour out the rest of it at the base of the altar. [13]Then take all the fat on the internal organs, the long lobe of the liver, and both kidneys with the fat on them, and burn them on the altar. [14]But burn the bull's flesh and its hide and its intestines outside the camp. It is a sin offering.[a]

[15]"Take one of the rams, and Aaron and his sons shall lay their hands on its head. [16]Slaughter it and take the blood and splash it against the sides of the altar. [17]Cut the ram into pieces and wash the internal organs and the legs, putting them with the head and the other pieces. [18]Then burn the entire ram on the altar. It is a burnt offering to the LORD, a pleasing aroma, a food offering presented to the LORD.

[19]"Take the other ram, and Aaron and his sons shall lay their hands on its head. [20]Slaughter it, take some of its blood and put it on the lobes of the right ears of Aaron and his sons, on the thumbs of their right hands, and on the big toes of their right feet. Then splash blood against the sides of the altar. [21]And take some blood from the altar and some of the anointing oil and sprinkle it on Aaron and his garments and on his sons and their garments. Then he and his sons and their garments will be consecrated.

[22]"Take from this ram the fat, the fat tail, the fat on the internal organs, the long lobe of the liver, both kidneys with the fat on them, and the right thigh. (This is the ram for the ordination.) [23]From the basket of bread made without yeast, which is before the LORD, take one round loaf, one thick loaf with olive oil mixed in, and one thin loaf. [24]Put all these in the hands of Aaron and his sons and have them wave them before the LORD as a wave offering. [25]Then take them from their hands and burn them on the altar along with the burnt offering for a pleasing aroma to the LORD, a food offering presented to the LORD. [26]After you take the breast of the ram for Aaron's ordination, wave it before the LORD as a wave offering, and it will be your share.

[27]"Consecrate those parts of the ordination ram that belong to Aaron and his sons: the breast that was waved and the thigh that was presented. [28]This is always to be the perpetual share from the Israelites for Aaron and his sons. It is the contribution the Israelites are to make to the LORD from their fellowship offerings.

[29]"Aaron's sacred garments will belong to his descendants so that they can be anointed and ordained in them. [30]The son who succeeds him as priest and comes to the tent of meeting to minister in the Holy Place is to wear them seven days.

[31]"Take the ram for the ordination and cook the meat

## Amplified Bible

[11]And you shall kill the bull before the Lord by the door of the Tent of Meeting.

[12]And you shall take of the blood of the bull and put it on the horns of the altar with your finger, and pour out all the blood at the base of the altar.

[13]And take all the fat that covers the entrails, and the appendage that is on the liver, and the two kidneys, and the fat that is on them, and burn them on the altar.

[14]But the flesh of the bull, its hide, and the contents of its entrails you shall burn with fire outside the camp; it is a sin offering. [Heb. 13:11-13.]

[15]You shall also take one of the rams, and Aaron and his sons shall lay their hands upon the head of the ram.

[16]And you shall kill the ram and you shall take its blood and throw it against the altar round about.

[17]And you shall cut the ram in pieces and wash its entrails and legs and put them with its pieces and its head,

[18]And you shall burn the whole ram upon the altar. It is a burnt offering to the Lord; it is a sweet *and* satisfying fragrance, an offering made by fire to the Lord.

[19]And you shall take the other ram, and Aaron and his sons shall lay their hands upon the head of the ram;

[20]Then you shall kill the ram and take part of its blood and put it on the tip of the right ears of Aaron and his sons and on the thumb of their right hands and on the great toe of their right feet, and dash the rest of the blood against the altar round about.

[21]Then you shall take part of the blood that is on the altar, and of the anointing oil, and sprinkle it upon Aaron and his garments and on his sons and their garments; and he and his garments and his sons and their garments shall be sanctified *and* made holy.

[22]Also you shall take the fat of the ram, the fat tail, the fat that covers the entrails, the appendage on the liver, the two kidneys with the fat that is on them, and the right thigh; for it is a ram of consecration *and* ordination.

[23]Take also one loaf of bread, and one cake of oiled bread, and one wafer out of the basket of the unleavened bread that is before the Lord.

[24]And put all these in the hands of Aaron and his sons and they shall wave them for a wave offering before the Lord.

[25]Then you shall take them from their hands, add them to the burnt offering, and burn them on the altar for a sweet *and* satisfying fragrance before the Lord; it is an offering made by fire to the Lord.

[26]And take the breast of the ram of Aaron's consecration *and* ordination and wave it for a wave offering before the Lord; and it shall be your portion [Moses].

[27]And you shall sanctify (set apart for God) the waved breast of the ram used in the ordination and the waved thigh of the priests' portion, since it is for Aaron and his sons.

[28]It shall be for Aaron and his sons as their due portion from the Israelites perpetually, an offering from the Israelites of their peace *and* thanksgiving sacrifices, their offering to the Lord.

[29]The holy garments of Aaron shall pass to his descendants who succeed him, to be anointed in them and to be consecrated *and* ordained in them.

[30]And that son who is [high] priest in his stead shall put them on [each day for] seven days when he comes into the Tent of Meeting to minister in the Holy Place.

[31]You shall take the ram of the consecration *and* ordination and boil its flesh in a holy *and* set-apart place.

*a* 14 Or *purification offering*; also in verse 36

## New International Version

in a sacred place. ³²At the entrance to the tent of meeting, Aaron and his sons are to eat the meat of the ram and the bread that is in the basket. ³³They are to eat these offerings by which atonement was made for their ordination and consecration. But no one else may eat them, because they are sacred. ³⁴And if any of the meat of the ordination ram or any bread is left over till morning, burn it up. It must not be eaten, because it is sacred.

³⁵"Do for Aaron and his sons everything I have commanded you, taking seven days to ordain them. ³⁶Sacrifice a bull each day as a sin offering to make atonement. Purify the altar by making atonement for it, and anoint it to consecrate it. ³⁷For seven days make atonement for the altar and consecrate it. Then the altar will be most holy, and whatever touches it will be holy.

³⁸"This is what you are to offer on the altar regularly each day: two lambs a year old. ³⁹Offer one in the morning and the other at twilight. ⁴⁰With the first lamb offer a tenth of an ephah*a* of the finest flour mixed with a quarter of a hin*b* of oil from pressed olives, and a quarter of a hin of wine as a drink offering. ⁴¹Sacrifice the other lamb at twilight with the same grain offering and its drink offering as in the morning—a pleasing aroma, a food offering presented to the LORD.

⁴²"For the generations to come this burnt offering is to be made regularly at the entrance to the tent of meeting, before the LORD. There I will meet you and speak to you; ⁴³there also I will meet with the Israelites, and the place will be consecrated by my glory.

⁴⁴"So I will consecrate the tent of meeting and the altar and will consecrate Aaron and his sons to serve me as priests. ⁴⁵Then I will dwell among the Israelites and be their God. ⁴⁶They will know that I am the LORD their God, who brought them out of Egypt so that I might dwell among them. I am the LORD their God.

### The Altar of Incense

**30** "Make an altar of acacia wood for burning incense. ²It is to be square, a cubit long and a cubit wide, and two cubits high*c*—its horns of one piece with it. ³Overlay the top and all the sides and the horns with pure gold, and make a gold molding around it. ⁴Make two gold rings for the altar below the molding—two on each of the opposite sides—to hold the poles used to carry it. ⁵Make the poles of acacia wood and overlay them with gold. ⁶Put the altar in front of the curtain that shields the ark of the covenant law—before the atonement cover that is over the tablets of the covenant law—where I will meet with you.

⁷"Aaron must burn fragrant incense on the altar every morning when he tends the lamps. ⁸He must burn incense again when he lights the lamps at twilight so incense will burn regularly before the LORD for the generations to

---

*a 40* That is, probably about 3 1/2 pounds or about 1.6 kilograms
*b 40* That is, probably about 1 quart or about 1 liter   *c 2* That is, about 1 1/2 feet long and wide and 3 feet high or about 45 centimeters long and wide and 90 centimeters high

## Amplified Bible

³²Aaron and his sons shall eat the flesh of the ram and the bread in the basket, at the door of the Tent of Meeting. ³³They shall eat those things with which atonement was made, to ordain and consecrate them; but a stranger (layman) shall not eat of them because they are holy (set apart to the worship of God).

³⁴And if any of the flesh or bread for the ordination remains until morning, you shall burn it with fire; it shall not be eaten, because it is holy (set apart to the worship of God).

³⁵Thus shall you do to Aaron and to his sons according to all I have commanded you; during seven days shall you ordain them.

³⁶You shall offer every day a bull as a sin offering for atonement. And you shall cleanse the altar by making atonement for it, and anoint it to consecrate it.

³⁷Seven days you shall make atonement for the altar and sanctify it [set it apart for God]; and the altar shall be most holy; whoever *or* whatever touches the altar must be holy (set apart for God's service).

³⁸Now this is what you shall offer on the altar: two lambs a year old shall be offered day by day continually.

³⁹One lamb you shall offer in the morning and the other lamb in the evening;

⁴⁰And with the one lamb a tenth measure of fine flour mixed with a fourth of a hin of beaten oil, and a fourth of a hin of wine for a drink offering [to be poured out].

⁴¹And the other lamb you shall offer at evening, and do with it as with the cereal offering of the morning and with the drink offering, for a sweet *and* satisfying fragrance, an offering made by fire to the Lord.

⁴²This shall be a continual burnt offering throughout your generations at the door of the Tent of Meeting before the Lord, where I will meet with you to speak there to you.

⁴³There I will meet with the Israelites, and the Tent of Meeting shall be sanctified by My glory [the Shekinah, God's visible presence].

⁴⁴And I will sanctify the Tent of Meeting and the altar; I will sanctify also both Aaron and his sons to minister to Me in the priest's office.

⁴⁵And I will dwell among the Israelites and be their God.

⁴⁶And they shall know [from personal experience] that I am the Lord their God, Who brought them forth out of the land of Egypt that I might dwell among them; I am the Lord their God.

**30** And you shall make an altar to burn incense upon; of acacia wood you shall make it. ²A cubit shall be its length and a cubit its breadth; its top shall be square and it shall be two cubits high. Its horns shall be of one piece with it.

³And you shall overlay it with pure gold, its top and its sides round about and its horns, and you shall make a crown (a rim or molding) of gold around it.

⁴You shall make two golden rings under the rim of it, on the two ribs on the two opposite sides of it; and they shall be holders for the poles with which to carry it.

⁵And you shall make the poles of acacia wood, overlaid with gold.

⁶You shall put the altar [of incense] in front *and* outside of the veil that screens the ark of the Testimony, before the mercy seat that is over the Testimony (the Law, the tables of stone), where I will meet with you.

⁷And Aaron shall burn on it incense of sweet spices; every morning when he trims *and* fills the lamps he shall burn it. [Ps. 141:2; Rev. 5:8; 8:3, 4.]

⁸And when Aaron lights the lamps in the evening, he shall burn it, a perpetual incense before the Lord throughout your generations.

## New International Version

come. ⁹Do not offer on this altar any other incense or any burnt offering or grain offering, and do not pour a drink offering on it. ¹⁰Once a year Aaron shall make atonement on its horns. This annual atonement must be made with the blood of the atoning sin offering*ᵃ* for the generations to come. It is most holy to the LORD."

### Atonement Money

¹¹Then the LORD said to Moses, ¹²"When you take a census of the Israelites to count them, each one must pay the LORD a ransom for his life at the time he is counted. Then no plague will come on them when you number them. ¹³Each one who crosses over to those already counted is to give a half shekel,*ᵇ* according to the sanctuary shekel, which weighs twenty gerahs. This half shekel is an offering to the LORD. ¹⁴All who cross over, those twenty years old or more, are to give an offering to the LORD. ¹⁵The rich are not to give more than a half shekel and the poor are not to give less when you make the offering to the LORD to atone for your lives. ¹⁶Receive the atonement money from the Israelites and use it for the service of the tent of meeting. It will be a memorial for the Israelites before the LORD, making atonement for your lives."

### Basin for Washing

¹⁷Then the LORD said to Moses, ¹⁸"Make a bronze basin, with its bronze stand, for washing. Place it between the tent of meeting and the altar, and put water in it. ¹⁹Aaron and his sons are to wash their hands and feet with water from it. ²⁰Whenever they enter the tent of meeting, they shall wash with water so that they will not die. Also, when they approach the altar to minister by presenting a food offering to the LORD, ²¹they shall wash their hands and feet so that they will not die. This is to be a lasting ordinance for Aaron and his descendants for the generations to come."

### Anointing Oil

²²Then the LORD said to Moses, ²³"Take the following fine spices: 500 shekels*ᶜ* of liquid myrrh, half as much (that is, 250 shekels) of fragrant cinnamon, 250 shekels*ᵈ* of fragrant calamus, ²⁴500 shekels of cassia—all according to the sanctuary shekel—and a hin*ᵉ* of olive oil. ²⁵Make these into a sacred anointing oil, a fragrant blend, the work of a perfumer. It will be the sacred anointing oil. ²⁶Then use it to anoint the tent of meeting, the ark of the covenant law, ²⁷the table and all its articles, the lampstand and its accessories, the altar of incense, ²⁸the altar of burnt offering and all its utensils, and the basin with its stand. ²⁹You shall consecrate them so they will be most holy, and whatever touches them will be holy.

³⁰"Anoint Aaron and his sons and consecrate them so they may serve me as priests. ³¹Say to the Israelites, 'This is to be my sacred anointing oil for the generations to come. ³²Do not pour it on anyone else's body and do not make any other oil using the same formula. It is sacred, and you are to consider it sacred. ³³Whoever makes perfume like it and puts it on anyone other than a priest must be cut off from their people.'"

## Amplified Bible

⁹You shall offer no unholy incense on the altar nor burnt sacrifice nor cereal offering; and you shall pour no libation (drink offering) on it.

¹⁰Aaron shall make atonement upon the horns of it once a year; with the blood of the sin offering of atonement once in the year shall he make atonement upon *and* for it throughout your generations. It is most holy to the Lord.

¹¹And the Lord said to Moses,

¹²When you take the census of the Israelites, every man shall give a ransom for himself to the Lord when you number them, that no plague may fall upon them when you number them. [Rom. 8:1-4.]

¹³This is what everyone shall give as he joins those already numbered: a half shekel, in terms of the sanctuary shekel, a shekel being twenty gerahs; a half shekel as an offering to the Lord.

¹⁴Everyone from twenty years old and upward, as he joins those already numbered, shall give this offering to the Lord. [Matt. 10:24; I Pet. 1:18, 19.]

¹⁵The rich shall not give more and the poor shall not give less than half a shekel when [you] give this offering to the Lord to make atonement for yourselves.

¹⁶And you shall take the atonement money of the Israelites and use it [exclusively] for the service of the Tent of Meeting, that it may bring the Israelites to remembrance before the Lord, to make atonement for yourselves.

¹⁷And the Lord said to Moses,

¹⁸You shall also make a laver *or* large basin of bronze, and its base of bronze, for washing; and you shall put it [outside in the court] between the Tent of Meeting and the altar [of burnt offering], and you shall put water in it;

¹⁹There Aaron and his sons shall wash their hands and their feet. [Tit. 3:5.]

²⁰When they go into the Tent of Meeting, they shall wash with water, that they die not; or when they come near to the altar to minister, to burn an offering made by fire to the Lord, [John 13:6-8.]

²¹So they shall wash their hands and their feet, lest they die; it shall be a perpetual statute for [Aaron] and his descendants throughout their generations.

²²Moreover, the Lord said to Moses,

²³Take the best spices: of liquid myrrh 500 shekels, of sweet-scented cinnamon half as much, 250 shekels, of fragrant calamus 250 shekels,

²⁴And of cassia 500 shekels, in terms of the sanctuary shekel, and of olive oil a hin.

²⁵And you shall make of these a holy anointing oil, a perfume compounded after the art of the perfumer; it shall be a sacred anointing oil.

²⁶And you shall anoint the Tent of Meeting with it, and the ark of the Testimony,

²⁷And the [showbread] table and all its utensils, and the lampstand and its utensils, and the altar of incense,

²⁸And the altar of burnt offering with all its utensils, and the laver [for cleansing] and its base.

²⁹You shall sanctify (separate) them, that they may be most holy; whoever *and* whatever touches them must be holy (set apart to God).

³⁰And you shall anoint Aaron and his sons and sanctify (separate) them, that they may minister to Me as priests.

³¹And say to the Israelites, This is a holy anointing oil [symbol of the Holy Spirit], sacred to Me alone throughout your generations. [Rom. 8:9; I Cor. 12:3.]

³²It shall not be poured upon a layman's body, nor shall you make any other like it in composition; it is holy, and you shall hold it sacred.

³³Whoever compounds any like it or puts any of it upon an outsider shall be cut off from his people.

---

*ᵃ* 10 Or *purification offering*   *ᵇ* 13 That is, about 1/5 ounce or about 5.8 grams; also in verse 15   *ᶜ* 23 That is, about 12 1/2 pounds or about 5.8 kilograms; also in verse 24   *ᵈ* 23 That is, about 6 1/4 pounds or about 2.9 kilograms   *ᵉ* 24 That is, probably about 1 gallon or about 3.8 liters

## New International Version

### Incense

³⁴Then the LORD said to Moses, "Take fragrant spices—gum resin, onycha and galbanum—and pure frankincense, all in equal amounts, ³⁵and make a fragrant blend of incense, the work of a perfumer. It is to be salted and pure and sacred. ³⁶Grind some of it to powder and place it in front of the ark of the covenant law in the tent of meeting, where I will meet with you. It shall be most holy to you. ³⁷Do not make any incense with this formula for yourselves; consider it holy to the LORD. ³⁸Whoever makes incense like it to enjoy its fragrance must be cut off from their people."

### Bezalel and Oholiab

**31** Then the LORD said to Moses, ²"See, I have chosen Bezalel son of Uri, the son of Hur, of the tribe of Judah, ³and I have filled him with the Spirit of God, with wisdom, with understanding, with knowledge and with all kinds of skills— ⁴to make artistic designs for work in gold, silver and bronze, ⁵to cut and set stones, to work in wood, and to engage in all kinds of crafts. ⁶Moreover, I have appointed Oholiab son of Ahisamak, of the tribe of Dan, to help him. Also I have given ability to all the skilled workers to make everything I have commanded you: ⁷the tent of meeting, the ark of the covenant law with the atonement cover on it, and all the other furnishings of the tent— ⁸the table and its articles, the pure gold lampstand and all its accessories, the altar of incense, ⁹the altar of burnt offering and all its utensils, the basin with its stand— ¹⁰and also the woven garments, both the sacred garments for Aaron the priest and the garments for his sons when they serve as priests, ¹¹and the anointing oil and fragrant incense for the Holy Place. They are to make them just as I commanded you."

### The Sabbath

¹²Then the LORD said to Moses, ¹³"Say to the Israelites, 'You must observe my Sabbaths. This will be a sign between me and you for the generations to come, so you may know that I am the LORD, who makes you holy.

¹⁴"'Observe the Sabbath, because it is holy to you. Anyone who desecrates it is to be put to death; those who do any work on that day must be cut off from their people. ¹⁵For six days work is to be done, but the seventh day is a day of sabbath rest, holy to the LORD. Whoever does any work on the Sabbath day is to be put to death. ¹⁶The Israelites are to observe the Sabbath, celebrating it for the generations to come as a lasting covenant. ¹⁷It will be a sign between me and the Israelites forever, for in six days the LORD made the heavens and the earth, and on the seventh day he rested and was refreshed.'"

¹⁸When the LORD finished speaking to Moses on Mount Sinai, he gave him the two tablets of the covenant law, the tablets of stone inscribed by the finger of God.

## Amplified Bible

³⁴Then the Lord said to Moses, Take sweet spices—stacte, onycha, and galbanum, sweet spices with pure frankincense, an equal amount of each— ³⁵And make of them incense, a perfume after the perfumer's art, seasoned with salt *and* mixed, pure and sacred. ³⁶You shall beat some of it very small and put some of it before the Testimony in the Tent of Meeting, where I will meet with you; it shall be to you most holy. ³⁷And the incense which you shall make according to its composition you shall not make for yourselves; it shall be to you holy to the Lord. ³⁸Whoever makes any like it for perfume shall be cut off from his people.

**31** And the Lord said to Moses, ²See, I have called by name Bezalel son of Uri, the son of Hur, of the tribe of Judah. ³And I have filled him with the Spirit of God, in wisdom *and* ability, in understanding *and* intelligence, and in knowledge, and in all kinds of craftsmanship, ⁴To devise skillful works, to work in gold, and in silver, and in bronze, ⁵And in cutting of stones for setting, and in carving of wood, to work in all kinds of craftsmanship. ⁶And behold, I have appointed with him Aholiab son of Ahisamach, of the tribe of Dan; and to all who are wisehearted I have given wisdom *and* ability to make all that I have commanded you: ⁷The Tent of Meeting, the ark of the Testimony, the mercy seat that is on it, all the furnishings of the tent— ⁸The table [of the showbread] and its utensils, the pure lampstand with all its utensils, the altar of incense, ⁹The altar of burnt offering with all its utensils, the laver and its base— ¹⁰The finely worked garments, the holy garments for Aaron the [high] priest and for his sons to minister as priests, ¹¹And the anointing oil and incense of sweet spices for the Holy Place. According to all that I have commanded you shall they do.

¹²And the Lord said to Moses, ¹³Say to the Israelites, Truly you shall keep My Sabbaths, for it is a sign between Me and you throughout your generations, that you may know that I, the Lord, sanctify you [set you apart for Myself].

¹⁴You shall keep the Sabbath therefore, for it is holy to you; everyone who profanes it shall surely be put to death; for whoever does work on the Sabbath shall be cut off from among his people. ¹⁵Six days may work be done, but the seventh is the Sabbath of rest, sacred to the Lord; whoever does work on the Sabbath day shall surely be put to death. ¹⁶Wherefore the Israelites shall keep the Sabbath to observe it throughout their generations, a perpetual covenant. ¹⁷It is a sign between Me and the Israelites forever; for in six days the Lord made the heavens and earth, and on the seventh day He ceased and was refreshed.

¹⁸And He gave to Moses, when He had ceased communing with him on Mount Sinai, the two tables of the Testimony, tables of stone, written with the finger of God.

## New International Version

### The Golden Calf

**32** When the people saw that Moses was so long in coming down from the mountain, they gathered around Aaron and said, "Come, make us gods[a] who will go before us. As for this fellow Moses who brought us up out of Egypt, we don't know what has happened to him."

2 Aaron answered them, "Take off the gold earrings that your wives, your sons and your daughters are wearing, and bring them to me." 3 So all the people took off their earrings and brought them to Aaron. 4 He took what they handed him and made it into an idol cast in the shape of a calf, fashioning it with a tool. Then they said, "These are your gods,[b] Israel, who brought you up out of Egypt."

5 When Aaron saw this, he built an altar in front of the calf and announced, "Tomorrow there will be a festival to the LORD." 6 So the next day the people rose early and sacrificed burnt offerings and presented fellowship offerings. Afterward they sat down to eat and drink and got up to indulge in revelry.

7 Then the LORD said to Moses, "Go down, because your people, whom you brought up out of Egypt, have become corrupt. 8 They have been quick to turn away from what I commanded them and have made themselves an idol cast in the shape of a calf. They have bowed down to it and sacrificed to it and have said, 'These are your gods, Israel, who brought you up out of Egypt.'

9 "I have seen these people," the LORD said to Moses, "and they are a stiff-necked people. 10 Now leave me alone so that my anger may burn against them and that I may destroy them. Then I will make you into a great nation."

11 But Moses sought the favor of the LORD his God. "LORD," he said, "why should your anger burn against your people, whom you brought out of Egypt with great power and a mighty hand? 12 Why should the Egyptians say, 'It was with evil intent that he brought them out, to kill them in the mountains and to wipe them off the face of the earth'? Turn from your fierce anger; relent and do not bring disaster on your people. 13 Remember your servants Abraham, Isaac and Israel, to whom you swore by your own self: 'I will make your descendants as numerous as the stars in the sky and I will give your descendants all this land I promised them, and it will be their inheritance forever.'" 14 Then the LORD relented and did not bring on his people the disaster he had threatened.

15 Moses turned and went down the mountain with the two tablets of the covenant law in his hands. They were inscribed on both sides, front and back. 16 The tablets were the work of God; the writing was the writing of God, engraved on the tablets.

17 When Joshua heard the noise of the people shouting, he said to Moses, "There is the sound of war in the camp."

18 Moses replied:

"It is not the sound of victory,
    it is not the sound of defeat;
    it is the sound of singing that I hear."

19 When Moses approached the camp and saw the calf and the dancing, his anger burned and he threw the tablets out of his hands, breaking them to pieces at the foot

## Amplified Bible

**32** When the people saw that Moses delayed to come down from the mountain, [they] gathered together to Aaron, and said to him, Up, make us gods to go before us; as for this Moses, the man who brought us up out of the land of Egypt, we do not know what has become of him.

2 So Aaron replied, Take the gold rings from the ears of your wives, your sons, and daughters, and bring them to me.

3 So all the people took the gold rings from their ears and brought them to Aaron.

4 And he received the gold at their hand and fashioned it with a graving tool and made it a molten calf; and they said, These are your gods, O Israel, which brought you up out of the land of Egypt!

5 And when Aaron saw the molten calf, he built an altar before it; and Aaron made proclamation, and said, Tomorrow shall be a feast to the Lord.

6 And they rose up early the next day and offered burnt offerings and brought peace offerings; and the people sat down to eat and drink and rose up to play.

7 The Lord said to Moses, Go down, for your people, whom you brought out of the land of Egypt, have corrupted themselves;

8 They have turned aside quickly out of the way which I commanded them; they have made them a molten calf and have worshiped it and sacrificed to it, and said, These are your gods, O Israel, that brought you up out of the land of Egypt!

9 And the Lord said to Moses, I have seen this people, and behold, it is a stiff-necked people;

10 Now therefore let Me alone, that My wrath may burn hot against them and that I may destroy them; but I will make of you a great nation.

11 But Moses besought the Lord his God, and said, Lord, why does Your wrath blaze hot against Your people, whom You have brought forth out of the land of Egypt with great power and a mighty hand?

12 Why should the Egyptians say, For evil He brought them forth, to slay them in the mountains and consume them from the face of the earth? Turn from Your fierce wrath, and change Your mind concerning this evil against Your people.

13 [Earnestly] remember Abraham, Isaac, and Israel, Your servants, to whom You swore by Your own self and said to them, I will multiply your seed as the stars of the heavens, and all this land that I have spoken of will I give to your seed, and they shall inherit it forever.

14 Then the Lord turned from the evil which He had thought to do to His people.

15 And Moses turned and went down from the mountain with the two tables of the Testimony in his hand, tables or tablets that were written on both sides.

16 The tables were the work of God; the writing was the writing of God, graven upon the tables.

17 And when Joshua heard the noise of the people as they shouted, he said to Moses, There is a noise of war in the camp.

18 But Moses said, It is not the sound of shouting for victory, neither is it the sound of the cry of the defeated, but the sound of singing that I hear.

19 And as soon as he came near to the camp he saw the calf and the dancing. And Moses' anger blazed hot and he cast the tables out of his hands and broke them at the foot of the mountain.

---

a 1 Or *a god*; also in verses 23 and 31    b 4 Or *This is your god*; also in verse 8

## New International Version

of the mountain. ²⁰And he took the calf the people had made and burned it in the fire; then he ground it to powder, scattered it on the water and made the Israelites drink it.

²¹He said to Aaron, "What did these people do to you, that you led them into such great sin?"

²²"Do not be angry, my lord," Aaron answered. "You know how prone these people are to evil. ²³They said to me, 'Make us gods who will go before us. As for this fellow Moses who brought us up out of Egypt, we don't know what has happened to him.' ²⁴So I told them, 'Whoever has any gold jewelry, take it off.' Then they gave me the gold, and I threw it into the fire, and out came this calf!"

²⁵Moses saw that the people were running wild and that Aaron had let them get out of control and so become a laughingstock to their enemies. ²⁶So he stood at the entrance to the camp and said, "Whoever is for the LORD, come to me." And all the Levites rallied to him.

²⁷Then he said to them, "This is what the LORD, the God of Israel, says: 'Each man strap a sword to his side. Go back and forth through the camp from one end to the other, each killing his brother and friend and neighbor.'" ²⁸The Levites did as Moses commanded, and that day about three thousand of the people died. ²⁹Then Moses said, "You have been set apart to the LORD today, for you were against your own sons and brothers, and he has blessed you this day."

³⁰The next day Moses said to the people, "You have committed a great sin. But now I will go up to the LORD; perhaps I can make atonement for your sin."

³¹So Moses went back to the LORD and said, "Oh, what a great sin these people have committed! They have made themselves gods of gold. ³²But now, please forgive their sin—but if not, then blot me out of the book you have written."

³³The LORD replied to Moses, "Whoever has sinned against me I will blot out of my book. ³⁴Now go, lead the people to the place I spoke of, and my angel will go before you. However, when the time comes for me to punish, I will punish them for their sin."

³⁵And the LORD struck the people with a plague because of what they did with the calf Aaron had made.

**33** Then the LORD said to Moses, "Leave this place, you and the people you brought up out of Egypt, and go up to the land I promised on oath to Abraham, Isaac and Jacob, saying, 'I will give it to your descendants.' ²I will send an angel before you and drive out the Canaanites, Amorites, Hittites, Perizzites, Hivites and Jebusites. ³Go up to the land flowing with milk and honey. But I will not go with you, because you are a stiff-necked people and I might destroy you on the way."

⁴When the people heard these distressing words, they began to mourn and no one put on any ornaments. ⁵For the LORD had said to Moses, "Tell the Israelites, 'You are a stiff-necked people. If I were to go with you even for a moment, I might destroy you. Now take off your ornaments and I will decide what to do with you.'" ⁶So the Israelites stripped off their ornaments at Mount Horeb.

## Amplified Bible

²⁰And he took the calf they had made and burned it in the fire, and ground it to powder and scattered it on the water and made the Israelites drink it.

²¹And Moses said to Aaron, What did this people do to you, that you have brought so great a sin upon them?

²²And Aaron said, Let not the anger of my lord blaze hot; you know the people, that they are set on evil.

²³For they said to me, Make us gods which shall go before us; as for this Moses, the man who brought us up out of the land of Egypt, we do not know what has become of him.

²⁴I said to them, Those who have any gold, let them take it off. So they gave it to me; then I cast it into the fire, and there came out this calf.

²⁵And when Moses saw that the people were unruly *and* unrestrained (for Aaron had let them get out of control, so that they were a derision *and* object of shame among their enemies),

²⁶Then Moses stood in the gate of the camp, and said, Whoever is on the Lord's side, let him come to me. And all the Levites [the priestly tribe] gathered together to him.

²⁷And he said to them, Thus says the Lord God of Israel, Every man put his sword on his side and go in and out from gate to gate throughout the camp and slay every man his brother, and every man his companion, and every man his neighbor.

²⁸And the sons of Levi did according to the word of Moses; and there fell of the people that day about 3000 men.

²⁹And Moses said [to the Levites, By your obedience to God's command] you have consecrated yourselves today [as priests] to the Lord, each man [at the cost of being] against his own son and his own brother, that the Lord may restore *and* bestow His blessing upon *you* this day.

³⁰The next day Moses said to the people, You have sinned a great sin. And now I will go up to the Lord; perhaps I can make atonement for your sin.

³¹So Moses returned to the Lord, and said, Oh, these people have sinned a great sin and have made themselves gods of gold!

³²Yet now, if You will forgive their sin—and if not, blot me, I pray You, out of Your book which You have written!

³³But the Lord said to Moses, Whoever has sinned against Me, I will blot him [not you] out of My book. [Dan. 12:1; Phil. 4:3; Rev. 3:5.]

³⁴But now go, lead the people to the place of which I have told you. Behold, My ªAngel shall go before you. Nevertheless, in the day when I punish I will visit their sin upon them! [Exod. 23:20; 33:2, 3.]

³⁵And the Lord sent a plague upon the people because they made the calf which Aaron fashioned for them.

**33** The Lord said to Moses, Depart, go up from here, you and the people whom you have brought from the land of Egypt, to the land which I swore to Abraham, Isaac, and Jacob, saying, To your descendants I will give it.

²I will send an ªAngel before you, and I will drive out the Canaanite, Amorite, Hittite, Perizzite, Hivite, and Jebusite. [Exod. 23:23; 34:11.]

³Go up to a land flowing with milk and honey; but I will not go up among you, for you are a stiff-necked people, lest I destroy you on the way.

⁴When the people heard these evil tidings, they mourned and no man put on his ornaments.

⁵For the Lord had said to Moses, Say to the Israelites, You are a stiff-necked people! If I should come among you for one moment, I would consume *and* destroy you. Now therefore [penitently] leave off your ornaments, that I may know what to do with you.

⁶And the Israelites left off all their ornaments, from Mount Horeb onward.

---

ª See footnote on Gen. 16:7.

## New International Version

### The Tent of Meeting
7Now Moses used to take a tent and pitch it outside the camp some distance away, calling it the "tent of meeting." Anyone inquiring of the LORD would go to the tent of meeting outside the camp. 8And whenever Moses went out to the tent, all the people rose and stood at the entrances to their tents, watching Moses until he entered the tent. 9As Moses went into the tent, the pillar of cloud would come down and stay at the entrance, while the LORD spoke with Moses. 10Whenever the people saw the pillar of cloud standing at the entrance to the tent, they all stood and worshiped, each at the entrance to their tent. 11The LORD would speak to Moses face to face, as one speaks to a friend. Then Moses would return to the camp, but his young aide Joshua son of Nun did not leave the tent.

### Moses and the Glory of the LORD
12Moses said to the LORD, "You have been telling me, 'Lead these people,' but you have not let me know whom you will send with me. You have said, 'I know you by name and you have found favor with me.' 13If you are pleased with me, teach me your ways so I may know you and continue to find favor with you. Remember that this nation is your people."

14The LORD replied, "My Presence will go with you, and I will give you rest."

15Then Moses said to him, "If your Presence does not go with us, do not send us up from here. 16How will anyone know that you are pleased with me and with your people unless you go with us? What else will distinguish me and your people from all the other people on the face of the earth?"

17And the LORD said to Moses, "I will do the very thing you have asked, because I am pleased with you and I know you by name."

18Then Moses said, "Now show me your glory."

19And the LORD said, "I will cause all my goodness to pass in front of you, and I will proclaim my name, the LORD, in your presence. I will have mercy on whom I will have mercy, and I will have compassion on whom I will have compassion. 20But," he said, "you cannot see my face, for no one may see me and live."

21Then the LORD said, "There is a place near me where you may stand on a rock. 22When my glory passes by, I will put you in a cleft in the rock and cover you with my hand until I have passed by. 23Then I will remove my hand and you will see my back; but my face must not be seen."

### The New Stone Tablets
**34** The LORD said to Moses, "Chisel out two stone tablets like the first ones, and I will write on them the words that were on the first tablets, which you broke. 2Be ready in the morning, and then come up on Mount Sinai. Present yourself to me there on top of the mountain. 3No one is to come with you or be seen anywhere on the mountain; not even the flocks and herds may graze in front of the mountain."

4So Moses chiseled out two stone tablets like the first ones and went up Mount Sinai early in the morning, as the

## Amplified Bible

7Now Moses used to take [his own] tent and pitch it outside the camp, far off from the camp, and he called it the tent of meeting [of God with His own people]. And everyone who sought the Lord went out to [that temporary] tent of meeting which was outside the camp.

8When Moses went out to the tent of meeting, all the people rose and stood, every man at his tent door, and looked after Moses until he had gone into the tent.

9When Moses entered the tent, the pillar of cloud would descend and stand at the door of the tent, and the Lord would talk with Moses.

10And all the people saw the pillar of cloud stand at the tent door, and all the people rose up and worshiped, every man at his tent door.

11And the Lord spoke to Moses face to face, as a man speaks to his friend. Moses returned to the camp, but his minister Joshua son of Nun, a young man, did not depart from the [temporary prayer] tent.

12Moses said to the Lord, See, You say to me, Bring up this people, but You have not let me know whom You will send with me. Yet You said, I know you by name and you have also found favor in My sight.

13Now therefore, I pray You, if I have found favor in Your sight, show me now Your way, that I may know You [progressively become more deeply and intimately acquainted with You, perceiving and recognizing and understanding more strongly and clearly] and that I may find favor in Your sight. And [Lord, do] consider that this nation is Your people.

14And the Lord said, My Presence shall go with you, and I will give you rest.

15And Moses said to the Lord, If Your Presence does not go with me, do not carry us up from here!

16For by what shall it be known that I and Your people have found favor in Your sight? Is it not in Your going with us so that we are distinguished, I and Your people, from all the other people upon the face of the earth?

17And the Lord said to Moses, I will do this thing also that you have asked, for you have found favor, loving-kindness, and mercy in My sight and I know you personally and by name. [Rev. 2:17.]

18And Moses said, I beseech You, show me Your glory.

19And God said, I will make all My goodness pass before you, and I will proclaim My name, THE LORD, before you; for I will be gracious to whom I will be gracious, and will show mercy and loving-kindness on whom I will show mercy and loving-kindness. [Rom. 9:15, 16.]

20But, He said, You can not see My face, for no man shall see Me and live.

21And the Lord said, Behold, there is a place beside Me, and you shall stand upon the rock,

22And while My glory passes by, I will put you in a cleft of the rock and cover you with My hand until I have passed by.

23Then I will take away My hand and you shall see My back; but My face shall not be seen.

**34** The Lord said to Moses, Cut two tables of stone like the first, and I will write upon these tables the words that were on the first tables, which you broke.

2Be ready and come up in the morning to Mount Sinai, and present yourself there to Me on the top of the mountain.

3And no man shall come up with you, neither let any man be seen throughout all the mountain; neither let flocks or herds feed before that mountain.

4So Moses cut two tables of stone like the first, and he rose up early in the morning and went up on Mount Sinai,

## New International Version

LORD had commanded him; and he carried the two stone tablets in his hands. ⁵Then the LORD came down in the cloud and stood there with him and proclaimed his name, the LORD. ⁶And he passed in front of Moses, proclaiming, "The LORD, the LORD, the compassionate and gracious God, slow to anger, abounding in love and faithfulness, ⁷maintaining love to thousands, and forgiving wickedness, rebellion and sin. Yet he does not leave the guilty unpunished; he punishes the children and their children for the sin of the parents to the third and fourth generation."

⁸Moses bowed to the ground at once and worshiped. ⁹"Lord," he said, "if I have found favor in your eyes, then let the Lord go with us. Although this is a stiff-necked people, forgive our wickedness and our sin, and take us as your inheritance."

¹⁰Then the LORD said: "I am making a covenant with you. Before all your people I will do wonders never before done in any nation in all the world. The people you live among will see how awesome is the work that I, the LORD, will do for you. ¹¹Obey what I command you today. I will drive out before you the Amorites, Canaanites, Hittites, Perizzites, Hivites and Jebusites. ¹²Be careful not to make a treaty with those who live in the land where you are going, or they will be a snare among you. ¹³Break down their altars, smash their sacred stones and cut down their Asherah poles.ᵃ ¹⁴Do not worship any other god, for the LORD, whose name is Jealous, is a jealous God.

¹⁵"Be careful not to make a treaty with those who live in the land; for when they prostitute themselves to their gods and sacrifice to them, they will invite you and you will eat their sacrifices. ¹⁶And when you choose some of their daughters as wives for your sons and those daughters prostitute themselves to their gods, they will lead your sons to do the same.

¹⁷"Do not make any idols.

¹⁸"Celebrate the Festival of Unleavened Bread. For seven days eat bread made without yeast, as I commanded you. Do this at the appointed time in the month of Aviv, for in that month you came out of Egypt.

¹⁹"The first offspring of every womb belongs to me, including all the firstborn males of your livestock, whether from herd or flock. ²⁰Redeem the firstborn donkey with a lamb, but if you do not redeem it, break its neck. Redeem all your firstborn sons.

"No one is to appear before me empty-handed.

²¹"Six days you shall labor, but on the seventh day you shall rest; even during the plowing season and harvest you must rest.

²²"Celebrate the Festival of Weeks with the firstfruits of the wheat harvest, and the Festival of Ingathering at the turn of the year.ᵇ ²³Three times a year all your men are to appear before the Sovereign LORD, the God of Israel. ²⁴I will drive out nations before you and enlarge your territory, and no one will covet your land when you go up three times each year to appear before the LORD your God.

## Amplified Bible

as the Lord had commanded him, and took ᵃin his hand two tables of stone.

⁵And the Lord descended in the cloud and stood with him there and proclaimed the name of the Lord.

⁶And the Lord passed by before him, and proclaimed, The Lord! the Lord! a God merciful and gracious, slow to anger, and abundant in loving-kindness and truth,

⁷Keeping mercy and loving-kindness for thousands, forgiving iniquity and transgression and sin, but Who will by no means clear the guilty, visiting the iniquity of the fathers upon the children and the children's children, to the third and fourth generation.

⁸And Moses made haste to bow his head toward the earth and worshiped.

⁹And he said, If now I have found favor and loving-kindness in Your sight, O Lord, let the Lord, I pray You, go in the midst of us, although it is a stiff-necked people, and pardon our iniquity and our sin, and take us for Your inheritance.

¹⁰And the Lord said, Behold, I lay down [afresh the terms of the mutual agreement between Israel and Me] a covenant. Before all your people I will do marvels (wonders, miracles) such as have not been wrought or created in all the earth or in any nation; and all the people among whom you are shall see the work of the Lord; for it is a terrible thing [fearful and full of awe] that I will do with you.

¹¹Observe what I command you this day. Behold, I drive out before you the Amorite, Canaanite, Hittite, Perizzite, Hivite, and Jebusite.

¹²Take heed to yourself, lest you make a covenant or mutual agreement with the inhabitants of the land to which you go, lest it become a snare in the midst of you.

¹³But you shall destroy their altars, dash in pieces their pillars (obelisks, images), and cut down their Asherim [symbols of the goddess Asherah];

¹⁴For you shall worship no other god; for the Lord, Whose name is Jealous, is a jealous (impassioned) God,

¹⁵Lest you make a covenant with the inhabitants of the land, and when they play the harlot after their gods and sacrifice to their gods and one invites you, you eat of his food sacrificed to idols,

¹⁶And you take of their daughters for your sons, and their daughters play the harlot after their gods and make your sons play the harlot after their gods.

¹⁷You shall make for yourselves no molten gods.

¹⁸The Feast of Unleavened Bread you shall keep. Seven days you shall eat unleavened bread, as I commanded you, in the time of the month of Abib; for in the month of Abib you came out of Egypt.

¹⁹All the males that first open the womb among your livestock are Mine, whether ox or sheep.

²⁰But the firstling of a donkey [an unclean beast] you shall redeem with a lamb or kid, and if you do not redeem it, then you shall break its neck. All the firstborn of your sons you shall redeem. And none of you shall appear before Me empty-handed.

²¹Six days you shall work, but on the seventh day you shall rest; even in plowing time and in harvest you shall rest [on the Sabbath].

²²You shall observe the Feast of Weeks, the firstfruits of the wheat harvest, and the Feast of Ingathering at the year's end.

²³Three times in the year shall all your males appear before the Lord God, the God of Israel.

²⁴For I will cast out the nations before you and enlarge your borders; neither shall any man desire [and molest] your land when you go up to appear before the Lord your God three times in the year.

ᵃ The two tables of stone are believed to have been pocket-size, easily carried in one hand. The pictures of Moses carrying tombstone-size tables are the result of the misconception of artists, and are not supported by the Bible.

ᵃ 13 That is, wooden symbols of the goddess Asherah   ᵇ 22 That is, in the autumn

## New International Version

25"Do not offer the blood of a sacrifice to me along with anything containing yeast, and do not let any of the sacrifice from the Passover Festival remain until morning.

26"Bring the best of the firstfruits of your soil to the house of the LORD your God.

"Do not cook a young goat in its mother's milk."

27Then the LORD said to Moses, "Write down these words, for in accordance with these words I have made a covenant with you and with Israel." 28Moses was there with the LORD forty days and forty nights without eating bread or drinking water. And he wrote on the tablets the words of the covenant—the Ten Commandments.

### The Radiant Face of Moses

29When Moses came down from Mount Sinai with the two tablets of the covenant law in his hands, he was not aware that his face was radiant because he had spoken with the LORD. 30When Aaron and all the Israelites saw Moses, his face was radiant, and they were afraid to come near him. 31But Moses called to them; so Aaron and all the leaders of the community came back to him, and he spoke to them. 32Afterward all the Israelites came near him, and he gave them all the commands the LORD had given him on Mount Sinai.

33When Moses finished speaking to them, he put a veil over his face. 34But whenever he entered the LORD's presence to speak with him, he removed the veil until he came out. And when he came out and told the Israelites what he had been commanded, 35they saw that his face was radiant. Then Moses would put the veil back over his face until he went in to speak with the LORD.

### Sabbath Regulations

**35** Moses assembled the whole Israelite community and said to them, "These are the things the LORD has commanded you to do: 2For six days, work is to be done, but the seventh day shall be your holy day, a day of sabbath rest to the LORD. Whoever does any work on it is to be put to death. 3Do not light a fire in any of your dwellings on the Sabbath day."

### Materials for the Tabernacle

4Moses said to the whole Israelite community, "This is what the LORD has commanded: 5From what you have, take an offering for the LORD. Everyone who is willing is to bring to the LORD an offering of gold, silver and bronze; 6blue, purple and scarlet yarn and fine linen; goat hair; 7ram skins dyed red and another type of durable leather[a]; acacia wood; 8olive oil for the light; spices for the anointing oil and for the fragrant incense; 9and onyx stones and other gems to be mounted on the ephod and breastpiece. 10"All who are skilled among you are to come and make everything the LORD has commanded: 11the tabernacle with its tent and its covering, clasps, frames, crossbars,

## Amplified Bible

25You shall not offer the blood of My sacrifice with leaven; neither shall the sacrifice of the Feast of the Passover be left until morning.

26The first of the firstfruits of your ground you shall bring to the house of the Lord your God. You shall not boil a kid in his mother's milk.

27And the Lord said to Moses, Write these words, for after the purpose and character of these words I have made a covenant with you and with Israel.

28Moses was there with the Lord forty days and forty nights; he ate no bread and drank no water. And he wrote upon the tables the words of the covenant, the Ten Commandments.

29When Moses came down from Mount Sinai with the two tables of the Testimony in his hand, he did not know that the skin of his face shone and sent forth beams by reason of his speaking with the Lord.

30When Aaron and all the Israelites saw Moses, behold, the skin of his face shone, and they feared to come near him.

31But Moses called to them; and Aaron and all the leaders of the congregation returned to him, and [he] talked with them.

32Afterward all the Israelites came near, and he gave them in commandment all the Lord had said to him in Mount Sinai.

33And when Moses had finished speaking with them, he put a veil on his face.

34But when Moses went in before the Lord to speak with Him, [a]he took the veil off until he came out. And he came out and told the Israelites what he was commanded.

35The Israelites saw the face of Moses, how the skin of it shone; and Moses put the veil on his face again until he went in to speak with God.

**35** Moses gathered all the congregation of the Israelites together and said to them, These are the things which the Lord has commanded that you do:

2Six days shall work be done, but the seventh day shall be to you a holy day, a Sabbath of rest to the Lord; whoever works [on that day] shall be put to death.

3You shall kindle no fire in all your dwellings on the Sabbath day.

4And Moses said to all the congregation of the Israelites, This is what the Lord commanded:

5Take from among you an offering to the Lord. Whoever is of a willing and generous heart, let him bring the Lord's offering: gold, silver, and bronze;

6Blue, purple, and scarlet [stuff], fine linen, goats' hair;

7And rams' skins tanned red, and skins of dolphins or porpoises; and acacia wood;

8And oil for the light; and spices for anointing oil and for fragrant incense;

9And onyx stones and other stones to be set for the ephod and the breastplate.

10And let every able and wisehearted man among you come and make all that the Lord has commanded:

11The tabernacle, its tent and its covering, its hooks, its boards, its bars, its pillars, and its sockets or bases;

---

a The apostle Paul expressly refers to this incident when he says that we all may, with unveiled faces, behold the glory of the Lord, and be transformed (II Cor. 3:13-18). That blessed vision, which of old was given only to the great leader of Israel, is now within reach of each individual believer. The Gospel has no fences to keep the crowd off the mount of vision; the lowliest and most unworthy of its children may pass upward where the shining glory is to be seen. "We all . . . are changed" (F. B. Meyer, Moses, the Servant of God).

---

a 7 Possibly the hides of large aquatic mammals; also in verse 23

## New International Version

posts and bases; [12]the ark with its poles and the atonement cover and the curtain that shields it; [13]the table with its poles and all its articles and the bread of the Presence; [14]the lampstand that is for light with its accessories, lamps and oil for the light; [15]the altar of incense with its poles, the anointing oil and the fragrant incense; the curtain for the doorway at the entrance to the tabernacle; [16]the altar of burnt offering with its bronze grating, its poles and all its utensils; the bronze basin with its stand; [17]the curtains of the courtyard with its posts and bases, and the curtain for the entrance to the courtyard; [18]the tent pegs for the tabernacle and for the courtyard, and their ropes; [19]the woven garments worn for ministering in the sanctuary—both the sacred garments for Aaron the priest and the garments for his sons when they serve as priests."

[20]Then the whole Israelite community withdrew from Moses' presence, [21]and everyone who was willing and whose heart moved them came and brought an offering to the LORD for the work on the tent of meeting, for all its service, and for the sacred garments. [22]All who were willing, men and women alike, came and brought gold jewelry of all kinds: brooches, earrings, rings and ornaments. They all presented their gold as a wave offering to the LORD. [23]Everyone who had blue, purple or scarlet yarn or fine linen, or goat hair, ram skins dyed red or the other durable leather brought them. [24]Those presenting an offering of silver or bronze brought it as an offering to the LORD, and everyone who had acacia wood for any part of the work brought it. [25]Every skilled woman spun with her hands and brought what she had spun—blue, purple or scarlet yarn or fine linen. [26]And all the women who were willing and had the skill spun the goat hair. [27]The leaders brought onyx stones and other gems to be mounted on the ephod and breastpiece. [28]They also brought spices and olive oil for the light and for the anointing oil and for the fragrant incense. [29]All the Israelite men and women who were willing brought to the LORD freewill offerings for all the work the LORD through Moses had commanded them to do.

### Bezalel and Oholiab

[30]Then Moses said to the Israelites, "See, the LORD has chosen Bezalel son of Uri, the son of Hur, of the tribe of Judah, [31]and he has filled him with the Spirit of God, with wisdom, with understanding, with knowledge and with all kinds of skills— [32]to make artistic designs for work in gold, silver and bronze, [33]to cut and set stones, to work in wood and to engage in all kinds of artistic crafts. [34]And he has given both him and Oholiab son of Ahisamak, of the tribe of Dan, the ability to teach others. [35]He has filled them with skill to do all kinds of work as engravers, designers, embroiderers in blue, purple and scarlet yarn and fine linen, and weavers—all of them skilled workers and designers.

**36** [1]So Bezalel, Oholiab and every skilled person to whom the LORD has given skill and ability to know

## Amplified Bible

[12]The ark and its poles, with the mercy seat, and the veil of the screen;

[13]The table and its poles and all its utensils, and the showbread (the bread of the Presence);

[14]The lampstand also for the light, and its utensils and its lamps, and the oil for the light;

[15]And the incense altar and its poles, the anointing oil and the fragrant incense, the hanging *or* screen for the door at the entrance of the tabernacle;

[16]The altar of burnt offering, with its bronze grating, its poles and all its utensils, the laver and its base;

[17]The court's hangings, its pillars and their sockets *or* bases, and the hanging *or* screen for the gate of the court;

[18]The pegs of the tabernacle and of the court, and their cords,

[19]The finely wrought garments for ministering in the Holy Place, the holy garments for Aaron the [high] priest and for his sons to minister as priests.

[20]Then all the congregation of the Israelites left Moses' presence.

[21]And they came, each one whose heart stirred him up and whose spirit made him willing, and brought the Lord's offering to be used for the [new] Tent of Meeting, for all its service, and the holy garments.

[22]They came, both men and women, all who were willinghearted, and brought brooches, earrings *or* nose rings, signet rings, and armlets *or* necklaces, all jewels of gold, everyone bringing an offering of gold to the Lord.

[23]And everyone with whom was found blue or purple or scarlet [stuff], or fine linen, or goats' hair, or rams' skins made red [in tanning], or dolphin *or* porpoise skins brought them.

[24]Everyone who could make an offering of silver or bronze brought it as the Lord's offering, and every man with whom was found any acacia wood for any work of the service brought it.

[25]All the women who had ability *and* were wisehearted spun with their hands and brought what they had spun of blue and purple and scarlet [stuff] and fine linen;

[26]And all the women who had ability *and* whose hearts stirred them up in wisdom spun the goats' hair.

[27]The leaders brought onyx stones and stones to be set for the ephod and for the breastplate,

[28]And spice, and oil for the light and for the anointing oil and for the fragrant incense.

[29]The Israelites brought a freewill offering to the Lord, all men and women whose hearts made them willing *and* moved them to bring anything for any of the work which the Lord had commanded by Moses to be done.

[30]And Moses said to the Israelites, See, the Lord called by name Bezalel son of Uri, the son of Hur, of the tribe of Judah;

[31]And He has filled him with the Spirit of God, with ability *and* wisdom, with intelligence *and* understanding, and with knowledge and all craftsmanship,

[32]To devise artistic designs, to work in gold, silver, and bronze,

[33]In cutting of stones for setting, and in carving of wood, for work in every skilled craft.

[34]And God has put in Bezalel's heart that he may teach, both he and Aholiab son of Ahisamach, of the tribe of Dan.

[35]He has filled them with wisdom of heart *and* ability to do all manner of craftsmanship, of the engraver, of the skillful workman, of the embroiderer in blue, purple, and scarlet [stuff] and in fine linen, and of the weaver, even of those who do or design any skilled work.

**36** Bezalel and Aholiab and every wisehearted man in whom the Lord has put wisdom and understand-

## New International Version

how to carry out all the work of constructing the sanctuary are to do the work just as the LORD has commanded."

²Then Moses summoned Bezalel and Oholiab and every skilled person to whom the LORD had given ability and who was willing to come and do the work. ³They received from Moses all the offerings the Israelites had brought to carry out the work of constructing the sanctuary. And the people continued to bring freewill offerings morning after morning. ⁴So all the skilled workers who were doing all the work on the sanctuary left what they were doing ⁵and said to Moses, "The people are bringing more than enough for doing the work the LORD commanded to be done."

⁶Then Moses gave an order and they sent this word throughout the camp: "No man or woman is to make anything else as an offering for the sanctuary." And so the people were restrained from bringing more, ⁷because what they already had was more than enough to do all the work.

### The Tabernacle

⁸All those who were skilled among the workers made the tabernacle with ten curtains of finely twisted linen and blue, purple and scarlet yarn, with cherubim woven into them by expert hands. ⁹All the curtains were the same size—twenty-eight cubits long and four cubits wide.ᵃ ¹⁰They joined five of the curtains together and did the same with the other five. ¹¹Then they made loops of blue material along the edge of the end curtain in one set, and the same was done with the end curtain in the other set. ¹²They also made fifty loops on one curtain and fifty loops on the end curtain of the other set, with the loops opposite each other. ¹³Then they made fifty gold clasps and used them to fasten the two sets of curtains together so that the tabernacle was a unit.

¹⁴They made curtains of goat hair for the tent over the tabernacle—eleven altogether. ¹⁵All eleven curtains were the same size—thirty cubits long and four cubits wide.ᵇ ¹⁶They joined five of the curtains into one set and the other six into another set. ¹⁷Then they made fifty loops along the edge of the end curtain in one set and also along the edge of the end curtain in the other set. ¹⁸They made fifty bronze clasps to fasten the tent together as a unit. ¹⁹Then they made for the tent a covering of ram skins dyed red, and over that a covering of the other durable leather.ᶜ

²⁰They made upright frames of acacia wood for the tabernacle. ²¹Each frame was ten cubits long and a cubit and a half wide,ᵈ ²²with two projections set parallel to each other. They made all the frames of the tabernacle in this way. ²³They made twenty frames for the south side of the tab-

## Amplified Bible

ing to know how to do all the work for the service of the sanctuary shall work according to all that the Lord has commanded.

²And Moses called Bezalel and Aholiab and every able *and* wisehearted man in whose mind the Lord had put wisdom *and* ability, everyone whose heart stirred him up to come to do the work;

³And they received from Moses all the freewill offerings which the Israelites had brought for doing the work of the sanctuary, to prepare it for service. And they continued to bring him freewill offerings every morning.

⁴And all the wise *and* able men who were doing the work on the sanctuary came, every man from the work he was doing,

⁵And they said to Moses, The people bring much more than enough for doing the work which the Lord commanded to do.

⁶So Moses commanded and it was proclaimed in all the camp, Let no man or woman do anything more for the sanctuary offering. So the people were restrained from bringing,

⁷For the stuff they had was sufficient to do all the work and more.

⁸And all the able *and* wisehearted men among them who did the work on the tabernacle made ten curtains of fine twined linen and blue, purple, and scarlet [stuff], with cherubim skillfully worked on them.

⁹The length of each curtain was twenty-eight cubits and its breadth four cubits; all the curtains were one size.

¹⁰[Bezalel] coupled five curtains one to another and the other five curtains he coupled one to another.

¹¹And he made loops of blue on the outer edge of the last curtain in the first set; this he did also on the inner edge of the first curtain in the second set.

¹²Fifty loops he made in the one curtain and fifty loops in the edge of the curtain which was the second set; the loops were opposite one another.

¹³And he made fifty clasps of gold and coupled the curtains together with the clasps so that the tabernacle became one unit.

¹⁴And he made eleven curtains of goats' hair for a tent over the tabernacle.

¹⁵The length of one curtain was thirty cubits and four cubits was the breadth; the eleven curtains were of equal size.

¹⁶And he coupled five curtains by themselves and the other six curtains by themselves.

¹⁷And he made fifty loops on the outmost edge of the curtain to be coupled and fifty loops he made on the inner edge of the second curtain to be coupled.

¹⁸He made fifty clasps of bronze to couple the tent together into one whole.

¹⁹He made a covering for the tent of ᵃrams' skins tanned red, and above it a covering of dolphin *or* porpoise skins.

²⁰He made boards of acacia wood for the upright framework of the tabernacle.

²¹The length of a board was ten cubits and the breadth one cubit and a half.

²²Each board had two tenons (projections) to fit into a mortise to form a clutch; he did this for all the boards of the tabernacle.

²³And he made thus the boards [for frames] for the tabernacle: twenty boards for the south side,

ᵃ The final coverings of the tabernacle tent are not to be confused with the second one of goats' hair (Exod. 36:14). There were **four distinct coverings** of the tabernacle tent: 1. A covering of fine twined linen woven with blue, purple, and scarlet, with figures of cherubim upon it. It was made of two long pieces, one running from north to south, the other from east to west [and overlapping for the ceiling] (Exod. 26:1, 6; 36:8ff.). 2. Over this a covering of woven goats' hair was thrown (Exod. 26:7; 36:14). 3. A third covering of rams' skins made red (Exod. 26:14; 36:19). 4. And "above it" another covering of dolphin or porpoise skins, weighing the others down and giving perfect protection from the weather (Exod. 26:14; 36:19).

ᵃ 9 That is, about 42 feet long and 6 feet wide or about 13 meters long and 1.8 meters wide    ᵇ 15 That is, about 45 feet long and 6 feet wide or about 14 meters long and 1.8 meters wide    ᶜ 19 Possibly the hides of large aquatic mammals (see 35:7)    ᵈ 21 That is, about 15 feet long and 2 1/4 feet wide or about 4.5 meters long and 68 centimeters wide

## New International Version

ernacle [24]and made forty silver bases to go under them—two bases for each frame, one under each projection. [25]For the other side, the north side of the tabernacle, they made twenty frames [26]and forty silver bases—two under each frame. [27]They made six frames for the far end, that is, the west end of the tabernacle, [28]and two frames were made for the corners of the tabernacle at the far end. [29]At these two corners the frames were double from the bottom all the way to the top and fitted into a single ring; both were made alike. [30]So there were eight frames and sixteen silver bases—two under each frame.

[31]They also made crossbars of acacia wood: five for the frames on one side of the tabernacle, [32]five for those on the other side, and five for the frames on the west, at the far end of the tabernacle. [33]They made the center crossbar so that it extended from end to end at the middle of the frames. [34]They overlaid the frames with gold and made gold rings to hold the crossbars. They also overlaid the crossbars with gold.

[35]They made the curtain of blue, purple and scarlet yarn and finely twisted linen, with cherubim woven into it by a skilled worker. [36]They made four posts of acacia wood for it and overlaid them with gold. They made gold hooks for them and cast their four silver bases. [37]For the entrance to the tent they made a curtain of blue, purple and scarlet yarn and finely twisted linen—the work of an embroiderer; [38]and they made five posts with hooks for them. They overlaid the tops of the posts and their bands with gold and made their five bases of bronze.

### The Ark

**37** Bezalel made the ark of acacia wood—two and a half cubits long, a cubit and a half wide, and a cubit and a half high.[a] [2]He overlaid it with pure gold, both inside and out, and made a gold molding around it. [3]He cast four gold rings for it and fastened them to its four feet, with two rings on one side and two rings on the other. [4]Then he made poles of acacia wood and overlaid them with gold. [5]And he inserted the poles into the rings at the sides of the ark to carry it.

[6]He made the atonement cover of pure gold—two and a half cubits long and a cubit and a half wide. [7]Then he made two cherubim out of hammered gold at the ends of the cover. [8]He made one cherub on one end and the second cherub on the other; at the two ends he made them of one piece with the cover. [9]The cherubim had their wings spread upward, overshadowing the cover with them. The cherubim faced each other, looking toward the cover.

### The Table

[10]They[b] made the table of acacia wood—two cubits long, a cubit wide and a cubit and a half high.[c] [11]Then they overlaid it with pure gold and made a gold molding around it. [12]They also made around it a rim a handbreadth[d] wide and put a gold molding on the rim. [13]They cast four gold

a 1 That is, about 3 3/4 feet long and 2 1/4 feet wide and high or about 1.1 meters long and 68 centimeters wide and high; similarly in verse 6 b 10 Or He; also in verses 11-29 c 10 That is, about 3 feet long, 1 1/2 feet wide and 2 1/4 feet high or about 90 centimeters long, 45 centimeters wide and 68 centimeters high d 12 That is, about 3 inches or about 7.5 centimeters

## Amplified Bible

[24]And he made under the twenty boards forty sockets or bases of silver, two sockets under one board for its two tenons or hands, and two sockets under another board for its two tenons.

[25]For the other side of the tabernacle, the north side, he made twenty boards

[26]And their forty sockets or bases of silver, two sockets under [the end of] each board.

[27]And for the rear or west side of the tabernacle he made six [frame] boards.

[28]And two boards he made for each corner of the tabernacle in the rear.

[29]They were separate below but linked together at the top with one ring; thus he made both of them in both corners.

[30]There were eight boards with sixteen sockets or bases of silver, and under [the end of] each board two sockets.

[31]He made bars of acacia wood, five for the [frame] boards of the one side of the tabernacle,

[32]And five bars for the boards of its other side, and five bars for the boards at the rear or west side.

[33]And he made the middle bar pass through halfway up the boards from one end to the other.

[34]He overlaid the boards and the bars with gold and made their rings of gold as places for the bars.

[35]And he made the veil of blue, purple, and scarlet [stuff] and fine twined linen, with cherubim skillfully worked. [Matt. 27:50, 51; Heb. 10:19-22.]

[36]For [the veil] he made four pillars of acacia [wood] and overlaid them with gold; their hooks were of gold, and he cast for them four sockets or bases of silver.

[37]And he made a screen for the tent door of blue, purple, and scarlet [stuff] and fine twined linen, embroidered,

[38]And he made the five pillars of it with their hooks, and overlaid their ornamental tops and joinings with gold, but their five sockets were of bronze.

**37** Bezalel made the ark of acacia wood—two cubits and a half was the length of it, a cubit and a half the breadth of it, and a cubit and a half the height of it.

[2]He overlaid it with pure gold within and without and made a molding or crown of gold to go around the top of it.

[3]He cast four rings of gold for its four corners, two rings on either side.

[4]He made poles of acacia wood and overlaid them with gold.

[5]He put the poles through the rings at the sides of the ark to carry it.

[6][Bezalel] made the mercy seat of pure gold, two cubits and a half its length and one cubit and a half its breadth.

[7]And he made two cherubim of beaten gold; on the two ends of the mercy seat he made them,

[8]One cherub at one end and one at the other end; of one piece with the mercy seat he made the cherubim at its two ends.

[9]And the cherubim spread out their wings on high, covering the mercy seat with their wings, with their faces to each other, looking down to the mercy seat. [Heb. 9:23-26.]

[10]Bezalel made the [showbread] table of acacia wood; it was two cubits long, a cubit wide, and a cubit and a half high.

[11]He overlaid it with pure gold and made a molding of gold around its top.

[12]And he made a border around it [just under the top] a handbreadth wide, and a molding of gold around the border.

## New International Version

rings for the table and fastened them to the four corners, where the four legs were. ¹⁴The rings were put close to the rim to hold the poles used in carrying the table. ¹⁵The poles for carrying the table were made of acacia wood and were overlaid with gold. ¹⁶And they made from pure gold the articles for the table—its plates and dishes and bowls and its pitchers for the pouring out of drink offerings.

### The Lampstand

¹⁷They made the lampstand of pure gold. They hammered out its base and shaft, and made its flowerlike cups, buds and blossoms of one piece with them. ¹⁸Six branches extended from the sides of the lampstand— three on one side and three on the other. ¹⁹Three cups shaped like almond flowers with buds and blossoms were on one branch, three on the next branch and the same for all six branches extending from the lampstand. ²⁰And on the lampstand were four cups shaped like almond flowers with buds and blossoms. ²¹One bud was under the first pair of branches extending from the lampstand, a second bud under the second pair, and a third bud under the third pair—six branches in all. ²²The buds and the branches were all of one piece with the lampstand, hammered out of pure gold.

²³They made its seven lamps, as well as its wick trimmers and trays, of pure gold. ²⁴They made the lampstand and all its accessories from one talentᵃ of pure gold.

### The Altar of Incense

²⁵They made the altar of incense out of acacia wood. It was square, a cubit long and a cubit wide and two cubits highᵇ—its horns of one piece with it. ²⁶They overlaid the top and all the sides and the horns with pure gold, and made a gold molding around it. ²⁷They made two gold rings below the molding—two on each of the opposite sides—to hold the poles used to carry it. ²⁸They made the poles of acacia wood and overlaid them with gold.

²⁹They also made the sacred anointing oil and the pure, fragrant incense—the work of a perfumer.

### The Altar of Burnt Offering

**38** Theyᶜ built the altar of burnt offering of acacia wood, three cubitsᵈ high; it was square, five cubits long and five cubits wide.ᵉ ²They made a horn at each of the four corners, so that the horns and the altar were of one piece, and they overlaid the altar with bronze. ³They made all its utensils of bronze—its pots, shovels, sprinkling bowls, meat forks and firepans. ⁴They made a grating for the altar, a bronze network, to be under its ledge, halfway up the altar. ⁵They cast bronze rings to hold the poles for the four corners of the bronze grating. ⁶They made the poles of acacia wood and overlaid them with bronze. ⁷They inserted the poles into the rings so they would be on the sides of the altar for carrying it. They made it hollow, out of boards.

### The Basin for Washing

⁸They made the bronze basin and its bronze stand from the mirrors of the women who served at the entrance to the tent of meeting.

## Amplified Bible

¹³And he cast for it four rings of gold and fastened the rings on the four corners that were at its four legs. ¹⁴Close to the border were the rings, the places for the poles to pass through to carry the [showbread] table.

¹⁵[Bezalel] made the poles of acacia wood to carry the [showbread] table and overlaid them with gold. ¹⁶He made of pure gold the vessels which were to be on the table, its plates and dishes [for bread], its bowls and flagons for pouring [liquid sacrifices].

¹⁷And he made the lampstand of pure gold; its base and shaft were made of hammered work; its cups, its knobs, and its flowers were of one piece with it. ¹⁸There were six branches going out of the sides of the lampstand, three branches out of one side of it and three branches out of the other side of it; ¹⁹Three cups made like almond blossoms in one branch, each with a [calyx] knob and a flower, and three cups made like almond blossoms in the [opposite] branch, each with a [calyx] knob and a flower; and so for the six branches going out of the lampstand. ²⁰On [the shaft of] the lampstand were four cups made like almond blossoms, with knobs and flowers [one at the top]. ²¹And a knob under each pair of branches, of one piece with the lampstand, for the six branches going out of it. ²²Their knobs and their branches were of one piece with it, all of it hammered work of pure gold. ²³And he made of pure gold its seven lamps, its snuffers, and its ashtrays. ²⁴Of a talent of pure gold he made the lampstand and all its utensils. [John 1:4, 5, 9; II Cor. 4:6.]

²⁵And [Bezalel] made the incense altar of acacia wood; its top was a cubit square and it was two cubits high; the horns were one piece with it. ²⁶He overlaid it with pure gold, its top, its sides round about, and its horns; also he made a rim around it of gold. ²⁷And he made two rings of gold for it under its rim, on its two opposite sides, as places for the poles [to pass through] to carry it. ²⁸And he made the poles of acacia wood and overlaid them with gold. ²⁹He also made the holy anointing oil [symbol of the Holy Spirit] and the pure, fragrant incense, after the perfumer's art.

**38** Bezalel made the burnt offering altar of acacia wood; its top was five cubits square and it was three cubits high. ²He made its horns on the four corners of it; the horns were of one piece with it, and he overlaid it with bronze. ³He made all the utensils *and* vessels of the altar, the pots, shovels, basins, forks *or* fleshhooks, and firepans; all its utensils *and* vessels he made of bronze. ⁴And he made for the altar a bronze grate of network under its ledge, extending halfway down it. ⁵He cast four rings for the four corners of the bronze grating to be places for the poles [with which to carry it]. ⁶And he made the poles of acacia wood and overlaid them with bronze. ⁷And he put the poles through the rings on the altar's sides with which to carry it; he made it hollow with planks. ⁸He made the laver and its base of bronze from the mirrors of the women who ministered at the door of the Tent of Meeting.

ᵃ 24 That is, about 75 pounds or about 34 kilograms    ᵇ 25 That is, about 1 1/2 feet long and wide and 3 feet high or about 45 centimeters long and wide and 90 centimeters high    ᶜ 1 Or *He*; also in verses 2-9  ᵈ 1 That is, about 4 1/2 feet or about 1.4 meters    ᵉ 1 That is, about 7 1/2 feet or about 2.3 meters long and wide

## New International Version

### The Courtyard

[9] Next they made the courtyard. The south side was a hundred cubits[a] long and had curtains of finely twisted linen, [10] with twenty posts and twenty bronze bases, and with silver hooks and bands on the posts. [11] The north side was also a hundred cubits long and had twenty posts and twenty bronze bases, with silver hooks and bands on the posts.

[12] The west end was fifty cubits[b] wide and had curtains, with ten posts and ten bases, with silver hooks and bands on the posts. [13] The east end, toward the sunrise, was also fifty cubits wide. [14] Curtains fifteen cubits[c] long were on one side of the entrance, with three posts and three bases, [15] and curtains fifteen cubits long were on the other side of the entrance to the courtyard, with three posts and three bases. [16] All the curtains around the courtyard were of finely twisted linen. [17] The bases for the posts were bronze. The hooks and bands on the posts were silver, and their tops were overlaid with silver; so all the posts of the courtyard had silver bands.

[18] The curtain for the entrance to the courtyard was made of blue, purple and scarlet yarn and finely twisted linen—the work of an embroiderer. It was twenty cubits[d] long and, like the curtains of the courtyard, five cubits[e] high, [19] with four posts and four bronze bases. Their hooks and bands were silver, and their tops were overlaid with silver. [20] All the tent pegs of the tabernacle and of the surrounding courtyard were bronze.

### The Materials Used

[21] These are the amounts of the materials used for the tabernacle, the tabernacle of the covenant law, which were recorded at Moses' command by the Levites under the direction of Ithamar son of Aaron, the priest. [22] (Bezalel son of Uri, the son of Hur, of the tribe of Judah, made everything the LORD commanded Moses; [23] with him was Oholiab son of Ahisamak, of the tribe of Dan—an engraver and designer, and an embroiderer in blue, purple and scarlet yarn and fine linen.) [24] The total amount of the gold from the wave offering used for all the work on the sanctuary was 29 talents and 730 shekels,[f] according to the sanctuary shekel.

[25] The silver obtained from those of the community who were counted in the census was 100 talents[g] and 1,775 shekels,[h] according to the sanctuary shekel— [26] one beka per person, that is, half a shekel,[i] according to the sanctuary shekel, from everyone who had crossed over to those counted, twenty years old or more, a total of 603,550 men. [27] The 100 talents of silver were used to cast the bases for the sanctuary and for the curtain—100 bases from the 100 talents, one talent for each base. [28] They used the 1,775 shekels to make the hooks for the posts, to overlay the tops of the posts, and to make their bands.

[29] The bronze from the wave offering was 70 talents and 2,400 shekels.[j] [30] They used it to make the bases for the entrance to the tent of meeting, the bronze altar with its bronze grating and all its utensils, [31] the bases for the surrounding courtyard and those for its entrance and all the tent pegs for the tabernacle and those for the surrounding courtyard.

## Amplified Bible

[9] And he made the court: for the south side the hangings of the court were of fine twined linen, a hundred cubits;

[10] Their pillars and their bronze sockets or bases were twenty; the hooks of the pillars and their joinings were silver.

[11] And for the north side the hangings were [also] a hundred cubits; their pillars and their sockets or bases of bronze were twenty; the hooks of the pillars and their joinings were of silver.

[12] But for the west side were hangings of fifty cubits; their pillars and their sockets or bases were ten; the hooks of the pillars and their joinings were of silver.

[13] And for the front, the east side, fifty cubits.

[14] The hangings for one side of the gate were fifteen cubits; their pillars three and their sockets or bases three.

[15] Also for the other side of the court gate, left and right, were hangings of fifteen cubits; their pillars three and their sockets or bases three.

[16] All the hangings around the court were of fine twined linen.

[17] The sockets for the pillars were of bronze, the hooks of the pillars and their joinings of silver, the overlaying of their tops of silver, and all the pillars of the court were joined with silver.

[18] The hanging or screen for the gate of the court was embroidered in blue, purple, and scarlet [stuff], and fine twined linen; the length was twenty cubits and the height in the breadth was five cubits, corresponding to the hangings of the court.

[19] Their pillars were four and their sockets of bronze four; their hooks were of silver, and the overlaying of their tops and their joinings were of silver.

[20] All the pegs for the tabernacle and around the court were of bronze.

[21] This is the sum of the things for the tabernacle of the Testimony, as counted at the command of Moses, for the work of the Levites under the direction of Ithamar son of Aaron, the [high] priest.

[22] Bezalel son of Uri, the son of Hur, of the tribe of Judah, made all that the Lord commanded Moses.

[23] With him was Aholiab son of Ahisamach, of the tribe of Dan, an engraver, a skillful craftsman, and embroiderer in blue, purple, and scarlet [stuff], and in fine linen.

[24] All the gold that was used for the work in all the building and furnishing of the sanctuary, the gold from the offering, was 29 talents and 730 shekels, by the shekel of the sanctuary.

[25] And the silver from those numbered of the congregation was 100 talents and 1,775 shekels, by sanctuary standards:

[26] A beka for each man, that is, half a shekel, by the sanctuary shekel, for everyone who was counted, from twenty years old and upward, for 603,550 men.

[27] The 100 talents of silver were for casting the sockets or bases of the sanctuary and of the veil; 100 sockets for the 100 talents, a talent for a socket.

[28] Of the 1,775 shekels he made hooks for the pillars, and overlaid their tops, and made joinings for them.

[29] The bronze of the offering was 70 talents and 2,400 shekels.

[30] With it Bezalel made the sockets for the door of the Tent of Meeting, and the bronze altar and the bronze grate for it, and all the utensils of the altar,

[31] The sockets of the court round about and of the court gate, and all the pegs of the tabernacle and around the court.

[a] 9 That is, about 150 feet or about 45 meters   [b] 12 That is, about 75 feet or about 23 meters   [c] 14 That is, about 22 feet or about 6.8 meters   [d] 18 That is, about 30 feet or about 9 meters   [e] 18 That is, about 7 1/2 feet or about 2.3 meters   [f] 24 The weight of the gold was a little over a ton or about 1 metric ton.   [g] 25 That is, about 3 3/4 tons or about 3.4 metric tons; also in verse 27   [h] 25 That is, about 44 pounds or about 20 kilograms; also in verse 28   [i] 26 That is, about 1/5 ounce or about 5.7 grams   [j] 29 The weight of the bronze was about 2 1/2 tons or about 2.4 metric tons.

## New International Version

### The Priestly Garments

**39** From the blue, purple and scarlet yarn they made woven garments for ministering in the sanctuary. They also made sacred garments for Aaron, as the LORD commanded Moses.

### The Ephod

2They*a* made the ephod of gold, and of blue, purple and scarlet yarn, and of finely twisted linen. 3They hammered out thin sheets of gold and cut strands to be worked into the blue, purple and scarlet yarn and fine linen—the work of skilled hands. 4They made shoulder pieces for the ephod, which were attached to two of its corners, so it could be fastened. 5Its skillfully woven waistband was like it—of one piece with the ephod and made with gold, and with blue, purple and scarlet yarn, and with finely twisted linen, as the LORD commanded Moses. 6They mounted the onyx stones in gold filigree settings and engraved them like a seal with the names of the sons of Israel. 7Then they fastened them on the shoulder pieces of the ephod as memorial stones for the sons of Israel, as the LORD commanded Moses.

### The Breastpiece

8They fashioned the breastpiece—the work of a skilled craftsman. They made it like the ephod: of gold, and of blue, purple and scarlet yarn, and of finely twisted linen. 9It was square—a span*b* long and a span wide—and folded double. 10Then they mounted four rows of precious stones on it. The first row was carnelian, chrysolite and beryl; 11the second row was turquoise, lapis lazuli and emerald; 12the third row was jacinth, agate and amethyst; 13the fourth row was topaz, onyx and jasper.*c* They were mounted in gold filigree settings. 14There were twelve stones, one for each of the names of the sons of Israel, each engraved like a seal with the name of one of the twelve tribes.

15For the breastpiece they made braided chains of pure gold, like a rope. 16They made two gold filigree settings and two gold rings, and fastened the rings to two of the corners of the breastpiece. 17They fastened the two gold chains to the rings at the corners of the breastpiece, 18and the other ends of the chains to the two settings, attaching them to the shoulder pieces of the ephod at the front. 19They made two gold rings and attached them to the other two corners of the breastpiece on the inside edge next to the ephod. 20Then they made two more gold rings and attached them to the bottom of the shoulder pieces on the front of the ephod, close to the seam just above the waistband of the ephod. 21They tied the rings of the breastpiece to the rings of the ephod with blue cord, connecting it to the waistband so that the breastpiece would not swing out from the ephod—as the LORD commanded Moses.

### Other Priestly Garments

22They made the robe of the ephod entirely of blue cloth—the work of a weaver— 23with an opening in the center of the robe like the opening of a collar,*d* and a band around this opening, so that it would not tear. 24They made pomegranates of blue, purple and scarlet yarn and finely twisted linen around the hem of the robe. 25And they made

## Amplified Bible

**39** And of the blue and purple and scarlet [stuff] they made finely wrought garments for serving in the Holy Place; they made the holy garments for Aaron, as the Lord had commanded Moses.

2And Bezalel made the ephod of gold, blue, purple, and scarlet [stuff], and fine twined linen.

3And they beat the gold into thin sheets and cut it into wires to work into the blue, purple, and scarlet [stuff] and the fine linen, in skilled design.

4They made shoulder pieces for the ephod, joined to it at its two edges.

5And the skillfully woven band on it, to gird it on, was of the same piece and workmanship with it, of gold, blue, purple, and scarlet [stuff], and fine twined linen, as the Lord had commanded Moses.

6And they prepared the onyx stones enclosed in settings of gold filigree and engraved as signets are engraved with the names of the sons of Israel.

7And he put them on the shoulder pieces of the ephod to be stones of memorial *or* remembrance for the Israelites, as the Lord had commanded Moses.

8And [Bezalel] made the breastplate skillfully, like the work of the ephod, of gold, blue, purple, and scarlet [stuff], and fine twined linen.

9The breastplate was a [hand's] span square when doubled over.

10And they set in it four rows of stones; a sardius, a topaz, and a carbuncle made the first row;

11The second row an emerald, a sapphire, and a diamond;

12The third row a jacinth, an agate, and an amethyst;

13And the fourth row a beryl, an onyx, and a jasper; they were enclosed in settings of gold filigree.

14There were twelve stones with their names according to those of the sons of Israel, engraved like a signet, each with its name, according to the twelve tribes.

15And they made [at the ends] of the breastplate twisted chains like cords, of pure gold.

16And they made two settings of gold filigree and two gold rings which they put on the two ends of the breastplate.

17And they put the two twisted cords *or* woven chains of gold in the two rings on the end edges of the breastplate.

18And the other two ends of the twisted cords *or* chains of gold they put on the two settings and put them on the shoulder pieces of the ephod, in front.

19They made two rings of gold and put them on the two ends of the breastplate, on the inside edge of it next to the ephod.

20And they made two [other] gold rings and attached them to the two shoulder pieces of the ephod underneath, in front, at its joining above the skillfully woven band of the ephod.

21They bound the breastplate by its rings to those of the ephod with a blue lace, that it might lie upon the skillfully woven band of the ephod and that the breastplate might not be loosed from the ephod, as the Lord commanded Moses.

22And he made the robe of the ephod of woven work all of blue.

23And there was an opening [for the head] in the middle of the robe like the hole in a coat of mail, with a binding around it, that it should not be torn.

24On the skirts of the robe they made pomegranates of blue and purple and scarlet [stuff] and twined linen.

---

*a 2* Or *He*; also in verses 7, 8 and 22  *b 9* That is, about 9 inches or about 23 centimeters  *c 13* The precise identification of some of these precious stones is uncertain.  *d 23* The meaning of the Hebrew for this word is uncertain.

## New International Version

bells of pure gold and attached them around the hem between the pomegranates. ²⁶The bells and pomegranates alternated around the hem of the robe to be worn for ministering, as the LORD commanded Moses.

²⁷For Aaron and his sons, they made tunics of fine linen—the work of a weaver— ²⁸and the turban of fine linen, the linen caps and the undergarments of finely twisted linen. ²⁹The sash was made of finely twisted linen and blue, purple and scarlet yarn—the work of an embroiderer—as the LORD commanded Moses.

³⁰They made the plate, the sacred emblem, out of pure gold and engraved on it, like an inscription on a seal: HOLY TO THE LORD. ³¹Then they fastened a blue cord to it to attach it to the turban, as the LORD commanded Moses.

### Moses Inspects the Tabernacle

³²So all the work on the tabernacle, the tent of meeting, was completed. The Israelites did everything just as the LORD commanded Moses. ³³Then they brought the tabernacle to Moses: the tent and all its furnishings, its clasps, frames, crossbars, posts and bases; ³⁴the covering of ram skins dyed red and the covering of another durable leatherᵃ and the shielding curtain; ³⁵the ark of the covenant law with its poles and the atonement cover; ³⁶the table with all its articles and the bread of the Presence; ³⁷the pure gold lampstand with its row of lamps and all its accessories, and the olive oil for the light; ³⁸the gold altar, the anointing oil, the fragrant incense, and the curtain for the entrance to the tent; ³⁹the bronze altar with its bronze grating, its poles and all its utensils; the basin with its stand; ⁴⁰the curtains of the courtyard with its posts and bases, and the curtain for the entrance to the courtyard; the ropes and tent pegs for the courtyard; all the furnishings for the tabernacle, the tent of meeting; ⁴¹and the woven garments worn for ministering in the sanctuary, both the sacred garments for Aaron the priest and the garments for his sons when serving as priests.

⁴²The Israelites had done all the work just as the LORD had commanded Moses. ⁴³Moses inspected the work and saw that they had done it just as the LORD had commanded. So Moses blessed them.

### Setting Up the Tabernacle

**40** Then the LORD said to Moses: ²"Set up the tabernacle, the tent of meeting, on the first day of the first month. ³Place the ark of the covenant law in it and shield the ark with the curtain. ⁴Bring in the table and set out what belongs on it. Then bring in the lampstand and set up its lamps. ⁵Place the gold altar of incense in front of the ark of the covenant law and put the curtain at the entrance to the tabernacle.

⁶"Place the altar of burnt offering in front of the entrance to the tabernacle, the tent of meeting; ⁷place the

## Amplified Bible

²⁵And they made bells of pure gold and put [them] between the pomegranates around the skirts of the robe;

²⁶A bell and a pomegranate, a bell and a pomegranate, round about on the skirts of the robe for ministering, as the Lord commanded Moses.

²⁷And they made the long *and* sleeved tunics woven of fine linen for Aaron and his sons,

²⁸And the turban, and the ornamental caps of fine linen, and the breeches of fine twined linen,

²⁹The girdle *or* sash of fine twined linen, and blue, purple, and scarlet embroidery, as the Lord commanded Moses.

³⁰And they made the plate of the holy crown of pure gold and wrote upon it an inscription, like the engravings of a signet, HOLY TO THE LORD. [Exod. 28:36.]

³¹They tied to it a lace of blue to fasten it on the turban above, as the Lord commanded Moses.

³²Thus all the work of the tabernacle of the Tent of Meeting was finished; according to all that the Lord commanded Moses, so the Israelites had done.

³³And they brought the tabernacle to Moses: the tent and all its furnishings, its clasps, its [frame] boards, its bars, its pillars, its sockets *or* bases;

³⁴And the covering of rams' skins made red, and the covering of dolphin *or* porpoise skins, and the veil of the screen;

³⁵The ark of the Testimony, its poles, and the mercy seat;

³⁶The table and all its utensils, and the showbread (bread of the Presence);

³⁷The pure [gold] lampstand and its lamps, with the lamps set in order, all its utensils, and the oil for the light;

³⁸The golden altar, the anointing oil, the fragrant incense, and the hanging for the door of the tent;

³⁹The bronze altar and its grate of bronze, its poles and all its utensils; the laver and its base;

⁴⁰The hangings of the court, its pillars and sockets *or* bases, and the screen for the court gate, its cords, and pegs, and all the utensils for the service of the tabernacle, for the Tent of Meeting [of God with His people]; [Exod. 29:42, 43.]

⁴¹The finely worked vestments for ministering in the Holy Place, the holy garments for Aaron the priest, and the garments of his sons to minister as priests.

⁴²According to all that the Lord had commanded Moses, so the Israelites had done all the work.

⁴³And Moses inspected all the work, and behold, they had done it; as the Lord had commanded, so had they done it. And Moses blessed them.

**40** And the Lord said to Moses,

²On the first day of the first month you shall set up the tabernacle of the Tent of Meeting [of God with you].

³And you shall put in it the ark of the Testimony and screen the ark [of God's Presence] with the veil. [Heb. 10:19-23.]

⁴You shall bring in the [showbread] table and set in order the things that are to be upon it; and you shall bring in the lampstand and set up *and* light its lamps. [Rev. 21:23-25.]

⁵You shall set the golden altar for the incense before the ark of the Testimony [outside the veil] and put the hanging *or* screen at the tabernacle door.

⁶You shall set the altar of the burnt offering before the door of the tabernacle of the Tent of Meeting.

---

ᵃ 34 Possibly the hides of large aquatic mammals

## New International Version

basin between the tent of meeting and the altar and put water in it. ⁸Set up the courtyard around it and put the curtain at the entrance to the courtyard.

⁹"Take the anointing oil and anoint the tabernacle and everything in it; consecrate it and all its furnishings, and it will be holy. ¹⁰Then anoint the altar of burnt offering and all its utensils; consecrate the altar, and it will be most holy. ¹¹Anoint the basin and its stand and consecrate them.

¹²"Bring Aaron and his sons to the entrance to the tent of meeting and wash them with water. ¹³Then dress Aaron in the sacred garments, anoint him and consecrate him so he may serve me as priest. ¹⁴Bring his sons and dress them in tunics. ¹⁵Anoint them just as you anointed their father, so they may serve me as priests. Their anointing will be to a priesthood that will continue throughout their generations." ¹⁶Moses did everything just as the LORD commanded him.

¹⁷So the tabernacle was set up on the first day of the first month in the second year. ¹⁸When Moses set up the tabernacle, he put the bases in place, erected the frames, inserted the crossbars and set up the posts. ¹⁹Then he spread the tent over the tabernacle and put the covering over the tent, as the LORD commanded him.

²⁰He took the tablets of the covenant law and placed them in the ark, attached the poles to the ark and put the atonement cover over it. ²¹Then he brought the ark into the tabernacle and hung the shielding curtain and shielded the ark of the covenant law, as the LORD commanded him.

²²Moses placed the table in the tent of meeting on the north side of the tabernacle outside the curtain ²³and set out the bread on it before the LORD, as the LORD commanded him.

²⁴He placed the lampstand in the tent of meeting opposite the table on the south side of the tabernacle ²⁵and set up the lamps before the LORD, as the LORD commanded him.

²⁶Moses placed the gold altar in the tent of meeting in front of the curtain ²⁷and burned fragrant incense on it, as the LORD commanded him.

²⁸Then he put up the curtain at the entrance to the tabernacle. ²⁹He set the altar of burnt offering near the entrance to the tabernacle, the tent of meeting, and offered on it burnt offerings and grain offerings, as the LORD commanded him.

³⁰He placed the basin between the tent of meeting and the altar and put water in it for washing, ³¹and Moses and

## Amplified Bible

⁷And you shall ᵃset the laver between the Tent of Meeting and the altar and put water in it.

⁸And you shall set up the court [curtains] round about and hang up the hanging *or* screen at the court gate.

⁹You shall take the anointing oil and anoint the tabernacle and all that is in it, and shall consecrate it and all its furniture, and it shall be holy.

¹⁰You shall anoint the altar of burnt offering and all its utensils; and consecrate (set apart for God) the altar, and the altar shall be most holy.

¹¹And you shall anoint the laver and its base and consecrate it.

¹²You shall bring Aaron and his sons to the door of the Tent of Meeting and wash them with water. [John 17:17-19.]

¹³You shall put on Aaron the holy garments, and anoint and consecrate him, so he may serve Me as priest.

¹⁴And you shall bring his sons and put long *and* sleeved tunics on them,

¹⁵And you shall anoint them as you anointed their father, that they may minister to Me as priests; for their anointing shall be to them for an everlasting priesthood throughout their generations.

¹⁶Thus did Moses; according to all that the Lord commanded him, so he did.

¹⁷And on the first day of the first month in the second year the tabernacle was erected.

¹⁸Moses set up the tabernacle, laid its sockets, set up its boards, put in its bars, and erected its pillars.

¹⁹[Moses] spread the tent over the tabernacle and put the covering of the tent over it, as the Lord had commanded him.

²⁰He took the Testimony [the Ten Commandments] and put it into the ark, and set the poles [in the rings] on the ark, and put the mercy seat on top of the ark.

²¹[Moses] brought the ark into the tabernacle and set up the veil of the screen and screened the ark of the Testimony, as the Lord had commanded him.

²²Moses put the table [of showbread] in the Tent of Meeting on the north side of the tabernacle outside the veil;

²³He set the bread [of the Presence] in order on it before the Lord, as the Lord had commanded him. [John 6:32-35.]

²⁴And he put the lampstand in the Tent of Meeting opposite the table on the south side of the tabernacle.

²⁵Moses set up *and* lighted the lamps before the Lord, as the Lord commanded him.

²⁶He put the golden altar [of incense] in the Tent of Meeting before the veil;

²⁷He burned sweet incense [symbol of prayer] upon it, as the Lord commanded him. [Ps. 141:2; Rev. 8:3.]

²⁸And he set up the hanging *or* screen at the door of the tabernacle.

²⁹[Moses] put the altar of burnt offering at the door of the tabernacle of the Tent of Meeting and offered on it the burnt offering and the cereal offering, as the Lord commanded him.

³⁰And Moses set the laver between the Tent of Meeting and the altar and put water in it for washing.

---

ᵃ Why was it necessary for one exact position for the laver to be demanded of Moses by God? Those who have published charts of the tabernacle furniture arrangement, with the laver off to one side or the other of the door into the sanctuary, have missed a point here. The laver was to be placed directly "between [the doors of] the Tent of Meeting and the altar [of burnt offering]," thus completing the "cross" made by the arrangement of the furniture, from the ark to the altar. It could have no significance to the Jews of that time, but the One Who planned it had those in mind to whom Christ would one day say, "And these [very Scriptures] testify about Me!" (John 5:39.) How fitting that at the foot of that "cross" there should be the altar, picturing our complete surrender, and then the laver, picturing our cleansing, that we may enter in through Him Who alone is "the Door" to the eternal Holy of Holies (John 10:1-9).

## New International Version

Aaron and his sons used it to wash their hands and feet. [32]They washed whenever they entered the tent of meeting or approached the altar, as the LORD commanded Moses.

[33]Then Moses set up the courtyard around the tabernacle and altar and put up the curtain at the entrance to the courtyard. And so Moses finished the work.

### The Glory of the LORD

[34]Then the cloud covered the tent of meeting, and the glory of the LORD filled the tabernacle. [35]Moses could not enter the tent of meeting because the cloud had settled on it, and the glory of the LORD filled the tabernacle.

[36]In all the travels of the Israelites, whenever the cloud lifted from above the tabernacle, they would set out; [37]but if the cloud did not lift, they did not set out—until the day it lifted. [38]So the cloud of the LORD was over the tabernacle by day, and fire was in the cloud by night, in the sight of all the Israelites during all their travels.

## Amplified Bible

[31]And Moses and Aaron and his sons washed their hands and their feet there.

[32]When they went into the Tent of Meeting or came near the altar, they washed, as the Lord commanded Moses.

[33]And he erected the court round about the tabernacle and the altar and set up the hanging or screen at the court gate. So Moses finished the work.

[34]Then the cloud [the Shekinah, God's visible presence] covered the Tent of Meeting, and the glory of the Lord filled the tabernacle! [Rev. 15:8.]

[35]And Moses was not able to enter the Tent of Meeting because the cloud remained upon it, and the glory of the Lord filled the tabernacle.

[36]In all their journeys, whenever the cloud was taken up from over the tabernacle, the Israelites went onward;

[37]But if the cloud was not taken up, they did not journey on till the day that it was taken up.

[38]For throughout all their journeys the cloud of the Lord was upon the tabernacle by day, and fire was in it by night, in the sight of all the house of Israel.

# Leviticus

# Leviticus

## New International Version

### The Burnt Offering

**1** The LORD called to Moses and spoke to him from the tent of meeting. He said, ²"Speak to the Israelites and say to them: 'When anyone among you brings an offering to the LORD, bring as your offering an animal from either the herd or the flock.

³"'If the offering is a burnt offering from the herd, you are to offer a male without defect. You must present it at the entrance to the tent of meeting so that it will be acceptable to the LORD. ⁴You are to lay your hand on the head of the burnt offering, and it will be accepted on your behalf to make atonement for you. ⁵You are to slaughter the young bull before the LORD, and then Aaron's sons the priests shall bring the blood and splash it against the sides of the altar at the entrance to the tent of meeting. ⁶You are to skin the burnt offering and cut it into pieces. ⁷The sons of Aaron the priest are to put fire on the altar and arrange wood on the fire. ⁸Then Aaron's sons the priests shall arrange the pieces, including the head and the fat, on the wood that is burning on the altar. ⁹You are to wash the internal organs and the legs with water, and the priest is to burn all of it on the altar. It is a burnt offering, a food offering, an aroma pleasing to the LORD.

¹⁰"'If the offering is a burnt offering from the flock, from either the sheep or the goats, you are to offer a male without defect. ¹¹You are to slaughter it at the north side of the altar before the LORD, and Aaron's sons the priests shall splash its blood against the sides of the altar. ¹²You are to cut it into pieces, and the priest shall arrange them, including the head and the fat, on the wood that is burning on the altar. ¹³You are to wash the internal organs and the legs with water, and the priest is to bring all of them and burn them on the altar. It is a burnt offering, a food offering, an aroma pleasing to the LORD.

¹⁴"'If the offering to the LORD is a burnt offering of birds, you are to offer a dove or a young pigeon. ¹⁵The priest shall bring it to the altar, wring off the head and burn it on the altar; its blood shall be drained out on the side of the altar. ¹⁶He is to remove the crop and the feathers[a] and throw them down east of the altar where the ashes are. ¹⁷He shall tear it open by the wings, not dividing it completely, and then the priest shall burn it on the wood

## Amplified Bible

**1** The Lord [a]called to Moses out of the Tent of Meeting, and said to him,

²Say to the Israelites, When any man of you brings an offering to the Lord, you shall bring your offering of [domestic] animals from the herd or from the flock.

³If his offering is a burnt offering from the herd, he shall offer a male without blemish; he shall offer it at the door of the Tent of Meeting, that he may be accepted before the Lord. [Rom. 12:1; Phil. 1:20.]

⁴And he shall lay [both] his hands upon the head of the burnt offering [transferring symbolically his guilt to the victim], and it shall be [b]an acceptable atonement for him. [Heb. 13:15, 16; I Pet. 1:2.]

⁵The man shall kill the young bull before the Lord, and the priests, Aaron's sons, shall present the blood and dash [it] round about upon the altar that is at the door of the Tent of Meeting.

⁶And he shall skin the burnt offering and cut it into pieces.

⁷And the sons of Aaron the priest shall put fire on the altar and lay wood in order on the fire;

⁸And Aaron's sons the priests shall lay the pieces, the head and the fat, in order on the wood on the fire on the altar.

⁹But its entrails and its legs he shall wash with water. And the priest shall burn all of it on the altar for a burnt offering, an offering by fire, a sweet *and* satisfying odor to the Lord. [Eph. 5:2; Phil. 4:18; I Pet. 2:5.]

¹⁰And if the man's offering is of the flock, from the sheep or the goats, for a burnt offering, he shall offer a male without blemish.

¹¹And he shall kill it on the north side of the altar before the Lord, and Aaron's sons the priests shall dash its blood round about against the altar.

¹²And [the man] shall cut it into pieces, with its head and its fat, and the priest shall lay them in order on the wood that is on the fire on the altar.

¹³But he shall wash the entrails and legs with water. The priest shall offer all of it and burn it on the altar; it is a burnt offering, an offering made by fire, a sweet *and* satisfying fragrance to the Lord.

¹⁴And if the offering to the Lord is a burnt offering of birds, then [the man] shall bring turtledoves or young pigeons.

¹⁵And the priest shall bring it to the altar, and wring off its head, and burn it on the altar; and its blood shall be drained out on the side of the altar.

¹⁶And he shall take away its crop with its feathers and cast it beside the altar on the east side, in the place for ashes.

¹⁷And he shall split it open [holding it] by its wings, but shall not cut it in two. And the priest shall burn it on the

---

a The first step toward understanding the message of Leviticus is to appreciate its viewpoint indicated here—"The Lord called to Moses out of the Tent of Meeting," and talked to him. Before this a forbidding God had spoken from the burning mountain. But now the tabernacle is erected according to the God-given pattern, and the God Who dwells among His people in fellowship with them talks with His servant Moses "out of the Tent of Meeting." The people, therefore, are not treated as sinners alienated from God, "but as being already brought into a new relationship, even that of fellowship, on the ground of a blood-sealed covenant" (J. Sidlow Baxter, *Explore the Book*).  b To render the self-sacrifice perfect, it was necessary that the offerer should spiritually die, sinking it as it were into the death of the sacrifice that had died for him, so that through the mediator of his salvation he should put his soul into a living fellowship with the Lord and bring his bodily members within the operations of the gracious Spirit of God. Thereby he would be renewed and sanctified [separated for holy use], both body and soul, and enter into union with God (Karl Keil and F. Delitzsch, *Biblical Commentary on the Old Testament*).

---

a 16 Or *crop with its contents*; the meaning of the Hebrew for this word is uncertain.

## New International Version

that is burning on the altar. It is a burnt offering, a food offering, an aroma pleasing to the LORD.

### The Grain Offering

**2** "'When anyone brings a grain offering to the LORD, their offering is to be of the finest flour. They are to pour olive oil on it, put incense on it ²and take it to Aaron's sons the priests. The priest shall take a handful of the flour and oil, together with all the incense, and burn this as a memorial*a* portion on the altar, a food offering, an aroma pleasing to the LORD. ³The rest of the grain offering belongs to Aaron and his sons; it is a most holy part of the food offerings presented to the LORD.

⁴"'If you bring a grain offering baked in an oven, it is to consist of the finest flour: either thick loaves made without yeast and with olive oil mixed in or thin loaves made without yeast and brushed with olive oil. ⁵If your grain offering is prepared on a griddle, it is to be made of the finest flour mixed with oil, and without yeast. ⁶Crumble it and pour oil on it; it is a grain offering. ⁷If your grain offering is cooked in a pan, it is to be made of the finest flour and some olive oil. ⁸Bring the grain offering made of these things to the LORD; present it to the priest, who shall take it to the altar. ⁹He shall take out the memorial portion from the grain offering and burn it on the altar as a food offering, an aroma pleasing to the LORD. ¹⁰The rest of the grain offering belongs to Aaron and his sons; it is a most holy part of the food offerings presented to the LORD.

¹¹"'Every grain offering you bring to the LORD must be made without yeast, for you are not to burn any yeast or honey in a food offering presented to the LORD. ¹²You may bring them to the LORD as an offering of the firstfruits, but they are not to be offered on the altar as a pleasing aroma. ¹³Season all your grain offerings with salt. Do not leave the salt of the covenant of your God out of your grain offerings; add salt to all your offerings.

¹⁴"'If you bring a grain offering of firstfruits to the LORD, offer crushed heads of new grain roasted in the fire. ¹⁵Put oil and incense on it; it is a grain offering. ¹⁶The priest shall burn the memorial portion of the crushed grain and the oil, together with all the incense, as a food offering presented to the LORD.

### The Fellowship Offering

**3** "'If your offering is a fellowship offering, and you offer an animal from the herd, whether male or female, you are to present before the LORD an animal without defect. ²You are to lay your hand on the head of your offering and slaughter it at the entrance to the tent of meeting. Then Aaron's sons the priests shall splash the blood against the sides of the altar. ³From the fellowship offering you are to bring a food offering to the LORD: the internal organs and all the fat that is connected to them, ⁴both kidneys with the fat on them near the loins, and the long lobe of the liver, which you will remove with the kidneys. ⁵Then Aaron's

*a 2 Or representative;* also in verses 9 and 16

## Amplified Bible

altar, on the wood that is on the fire; it is a burnt offering, an offering made by fire, a sweet *and* satisfying odor to the Lord.

**2** When anyone offers a cereal offering to the Lord, it shall be of fine flour; and he shall pour oil over it and lay frankincense on it.

²And he shall bring it to Aaron's sons the priests. Out of it he shall take a handful of the fine flour and oil, with all its frankincense, and the priest shall burn this on the altar as the memorial portion of it, an offering made by fire, of a sweet *and* satisfying fragrance to the Lord.

³What is left of the cereal offering shall be Aaron's and his sons'; it is a most holy part of the offerings made to the Lord by fire.

⁴When you bring as an offering cereal baked in the oven, it shall be unleavened cakes of fine flour mixed with oil, or unleavened wafers spread with oil.

⁵If your offering is cereal baked on a griddle, it shall be of fine flour unleavened, mixed with oil.

⁶You shall break it in pieces and pour oil on it; it is a cereal offering.

⁷And if your offering is cereal cooked in the frying pan, it shall be made of fine flour with oil.

⁸And you shall bring the cereal offering that is made of these things to the Lord; it shall be presented to the priest, and he shall bring it to the [bronze] altar.

⁹The priest shall take from the cereal offering its memorial portion and burn it on the altar, an offering made by fire, a sweet *and* satisfying fragrance to the Lord.

¹⁰What is left of the cereal offering shall be Aaron's and his sons'; it is a most holy part of the offerings made to the Lord by fire.

¹¹No cereal offering that you bring to the Lord shall be made with leaven, for you shall burn no leaven or honey in any offering made by fire to the Lord. [I Cor. 5:8.]

¹²As an offering of firstfruits you may offer leaven and honey to the Lord, but *a*they shall not be burned on the altar for a sweet odor [to the Lord, for their aid to fermentation is symbolic of corruption in the human heart].

¹³Every cereal offering you shall season with salt [symbol of preservation]; neither shall you allow the salt of the covenant of your God to be lacking from your cereal offering; with all your offerings you shall offer salt. [Mark 9:49, 50.]

¹⁴If you offer a cereal offering of your firstfruits to the Lord, you shall offer for it of your firstfruits grain in the ear parched with fire, bruised *and* crushed grain out of the fresh *and* fruitful ear.

¹⁵And you shall put oil on it and lay frankincense on it; it is a cereal offering.

¹⁶The priest shall burn as its memorial portion part of the bruised *and* crushed grain of it and part of the oil of it, with all its frankincense; it is an offering made by fire to the Lord.

**3** If a man's offering is a sacrifice of peace offering, if he offers an animal from the herd, whether male or female, he shall offer it without blemish before the Lord.

²He shall lay [both] his *b*hands upon the head of his offering and kill it at the door of the Tent of Meeting; and Aaron's sons the priests shall throw the blood against the altar round about.

³And from the sacrifice of the peace offering, an offering made by fire to the Lord, he shall offer the fat that covers and is upon the entrails,

⁴And the two kidneys with the fat that is on them at the loins, and the appendage of the liver which he shall take away with the kidneys.

*a There is to be no division between one's spiritual life and one's secular life, but the whole of one's life is to be of the nature of a sacrament (Col. 3:23, 24). b The Septuagint (Greek translation of the Old Testament) so reads.*

## New International Version

sons are to burn it on the altar on top of the burnt offering that is lying on the burning wood; it is a food offering, an aroma pleasing to the LORD.

6 "'If you offer an animal from the flock as a fellowship offering to the LORD, you are to offer a male or female without defect. 7 If you offer a lamb, you are to present it before the LORD, 8 lay your hand on its head and slaughter it in front of the tent of meeting. Then Aaron's sons shall splash its blood against the sides of the altar. 9 From the fellowship offering you are to bring a food offering to the LORD: its fat, the entire fat tail cut off close to the backbone, the internal organs and all the fat that is connected to them, 10 both kidneys with the fat on them near the loins, and the long lobe of the liver, which you will remove with the kidneys. 11 The priest shall burn them on the altar as a food offering presented to the LORD.

12 "'If your offering is a goat, you are to present it before the LORD, 13 lay your hand on its head and slaughter it in front of the tent of meeting. Then Aaron's sons shall splash its blood against the sides of the altar. 14 From what you offer you are to present this food offering to the LORD: the internal organs and all the fat that is connected to them, 15 both kidneys with the fat on them near the loins, and the long lobe of the liver, which you will remove with the kidneys. 16 The priest shall burn them on the altar as a food offering, a pleasing aroma. All the fat is the LORD's.

17 "'This is a lasting ordinance for the generations to come, wherever you live: You must not eat any fat or any blood.'"

### The Sin Offering

**4** The LORD said to Moses, 2 "Say to the Israelites: 'When anyone sins unintentionally and does what is forbidden in any of the LORD's commands—

3 "'If the anointed priest sins, bringing guilt on the people, he must bring to the LORD a young bull without defect as a sin offering[a] for the sin he has committed. 4 He is to present the bull at the entrance to the tent of meeting before the LORD. He is to lay his hand on its head and slaughter it there before the LORD. 5 Then the anointed priest shall take some of the bull's blood and carry it into the tent of meeting. 6 He is to dip his finger into the blood and sprinkle some of it seven times before the LORD, in front of the curtain of the sanctuary. 7 The priest shall then put some of the blood on the horns of the altar of fragrant incense that is before the LORD in the tent of meeting. The rest of the bull's blood he shall pour out at the base of the altar of burnt offering at the entrance to the tent of meeting. 8 He shall remove all the fat from the bull of the sin offering—all the fat that is connected to the internal organs, 9 both kidneys with the fat on them near the loins, and the long lobe of the liver, which he will remove with

## Amplified Bible

5 Aaron's sons shall burn it all on the altar upon the burnt offering which is on the wood on the fire, an offering made by fire, of a sweet *and* satisfying odor to the Lord.

6 If his peace offering to the Lord is an animal from the flock, male or female, he shall offer it without blemish.

7 If he offers a lamb, then he shall offer it before the Lord.

8 He shall lay [both] his hands on the head of his offering and kill it before the Tent of Meeting; and Aaron's sons shall throw its blood around against the altar.

9 And he shall offer from the peace offering as an offering made by fire to the Lord: the fat of it, the fat tail as a whole, taking it off close to the backbone, and the fat that covers and is upon the entrails,

10 And the two kidneys, and the fat on them at the loins, and the appendage of the liver, which he shall take away with the kidneys.

11 The priest shall burn it upon the altar, a food offering made by fire to the Lord.

12 If [a man's] offering is a goat, he shall offer it before the Lord,

13 And lay his hands upon its head, and kill it before the Tent of Meeting; and the sons of Aaron shall throw its blood against the altar round about.

14 Then he shall offer from it as his offering made by fire to the Lord: the fat that covers and is on the entrails,

15 And the two kidneys and the fat that is on them at the loins, and the appendage of the liver which he shall take away with the kidneys.

16 The priest shall burn them on the altar as food, offered by fire, for a sweet *and* satisfying fragrance. All the fat is the Lord's.

17 It shall be a perpetual statute for your generations in all your dwelling places, that you eat neither fat nor blood.

**4** And the Lord said to Moses, 2 Say to the Israelites, If anyone shall sin through error *or* unwittingly in any of the things which the Lord has commanded not to be done, and shall do any one of them—

3 If it is the anointed priest who sins, thus bringing guilt on the people, then let him offer for his sin which he has committed a young bull without blemish to the Lord as a sin offering. [Heb. 7:27, 28.]

4 He shall bring the bull to the door of the Tent of Meeting before the Lord, and shall lay [both] his hands on the bull's head and kill [it] before the Lord.

5 And the anointed priest shall take some of the bull's blood and bring it into the Tent of Meeting;

6 And the priest shall dip his finger in the blood and sprinkle some of [it] seven times before the Lord before the veil of the sanctuary.

7 And the priest shall put some of the blood on the horns of the altar of sweet incense before the Lord which is in the Tent of Meeting; and all the rest of the blood of the bull shall he pour out at the base of the altar of the burnt offering at the door of the Tent of Meeting.

8 And all the fat of the bull for the sin offering he shall take off of it—the fat that covers and is on the entrails,

9 And the two kidneys and the fat that is on the loins, and the appendage of the liver, which he shall take away with the kidneys—

---

a 3 Or *purification offering*; here and throughout this chapter

## New International Version

the kidneys— [10]just as the fat is removed from the ox[a] sacrificed as a fellowship offering. Then the priest shall burn them on the altar of burnt offering. [11]But the hide of the bull and all its flesh, as well as the head and legs, the internal organs and the intestines— [12]that is, all the rest of the bull—he must take outside the camp to a place ceremonially clean, where the ashes are thrown, and burn it there in a wood fire on the ash heap.

[13]"'If the whole Israelite community sins unintentionally and does what is forbidden in any of the LORD's commands, even though the community is unaware of the matter, when they realize their guilt [14]and the sin they committed becomes known, the assembly must bring a young bull as a sin offering and present it before the tent of meeting. [15]The elders of the community are to lay their hands on the bull's head before the LORD, and the bull shall be slaughtered before the LORD. [16]Then the anointed priest is to take some of the bull's blood into the tent of meeting. [17]He shall dip his finger into the blood and sprinkle it before the LORD seven times in front of the curtain. [18]He is to put some of the blood on the horns of the altar that is before the LORD in the tent of meeting. The rest of the blood he shall pour out at the base of the altar of burnt offering at the entrance to the tent of meeting. [19]He shall remove all the fat from it and burn it on the altar, [20]and do with this bull just as he did with the bull for the sin offering. In this way the priest will make atonement for the community, and they will be forgiven. [21]Then he shall take the bull outside the camp and burn it as he burned the first bull. This is the sin offering for the community.

[22]"'When a leader sins unintentionally and does what is forbidden in any of the commands of the LORD his God, when he realizes his guilt [23]and the sin he has committed becomes known, he must bring as his offering a male goat without defect. [24]He is to lay his hand on the goat's head and slaughter it at the place where the burnt offering is slaughtered before the LORD. It is a sin offering. [25]Then the priest shall take some of the blood of the sin offering with his finger and put it on the horns of the altar of burnt offering and pour out the rest of the blood at the base of the altar. [26]He shall burn all the fat on the altar as he burned the fat of the fellowship offering. In this way the priest will make atonement for the leader's sin, and he will be forgiven.

[27]"'If any member of the community sins unintentionally and does what is forbidden in any of the LORD's commands, when they realize their guilt [28]and the sin they have committed becomes known, they must bring as their offering for the sin they committed a female goat without defect. [29]They are to lay their hand on the head of the sin offering and slaughter it at the place of the burnt offering. [30]Then the priest is to take some of the blood with his finger and put it on the horns of the altar of burnt offering and pour out the rest of the blood at the base of the altar.

## Amplified Bible

[10]Just as these are taken off of the bull of the sacrifice of the peace offerings; and the priest shall burn them on the altar of burnt offering.

[11]But the hide of the bull and all its flesh, its head, its legs, its entrails, and its dung,

[12]Even the whole bull shall he carry forth without the camp to a clean place, where the ashes are poured out, and burn it on a fire of wood, there where the ashes are poured out. [Heb. 13:11-13.]

[13]If the whole congregation of Israel sins unintentionally, and it be hidden from the eyes of the assembly, and they have done what the Lord has commanded not to be done and are guilty,

[14]When the sin which they have committed becomes known, then the congregation shall offer a young bull for a sin offering and bring it before the Tent of Meeting.

[15]The elders of the congregation shall lay their hands upon the head of the bull before the Lord, and the bull shall be killed before the Lord.

[16]The anointed priest shall bring some of the bull's blood to the Tent of Meeting,

[17]And shall dip his finger in the blood, and sprinkle it seven times before the Lord, before the veil [which screens the ark of the covenant].

[18]He shall put some of the blood on the horns of the altar [of incense] which is before the Lord in the Tent of Meeting, and he shall pour out all the blood at the base of the altar of burnt offering near the door of the Tent of Meeting.

[19]And he shall take all its fat from the bull and burn it on the altar.

[20]Thus shall he do with the bull; as he did with the bull for a sin offering, so shall he do with this; and the priest shall make atonement for [the people], and they shall be forgiven.

[21]And he shall carry forth the bull outside the camp and burn it as he burned the first bull; it is the sin offering for the congregation.

[22]When a ruler or leader sins and unwittingly does any one of the things the Lord his God has forbidden, and is guilty,

[23]If his sin which he has committed be known to him, he shall bring as his offering a goat, a male without blemish.

[24]He shall lay his hand on the head of the goat and kill it in the place where they kill the burnt offering before the Lord; it is a sin offering.

[25]The priest shall take some of the blood of the sin offering with his finger and put it on the horns of the altar of burnt offering and pour the rest of its blood at the base of the altar of burnt offering.

[26]And he shall burn all its fat upon the altar like the fat of the sacrifice of peace offerings; so the priest shall make atonement for him for his sin, and it shall be forgiven him.

[27]If any one of the common people sins unwittingly in doing anything the Lord has commanded not to be done, and is guilty,

[28]When the sin which he has committed is made known to him, he shall bring for his offering a goat, a female without blemish, for his sin which he has committed.

[29]The offender shall lay his hand on the head of the sin offering and kill [it] at the place of the burnt offering.

[30]And the priest shall take some of its blood with his finger and put it on the horns of the altar of burnt offering and shall pour out the rest of its blood at the base of the altar.

---

[a] 10 The Hebrew word can refer to either male or female.

## New International Version

altar. [15]The priest is to take a handful of the finest flour and some olive oil, together with all the incense on the grain offering, and burn the memorial[a] portion on the altar as an aroma pleasing to the LORD. [16]Aaron and his sons shall eat the rest of it, but it is to be eaten without yeast in the sanctuary area; they are to eat it in the courtyard of the tent of meeting. [17]It must not be baked with yeast; I have given it as their share of the food offerings presented to me. Like the sin offering[b] and the guilt offering, it is most holy. [18]Any male descendant of Aaron may eat it. For all generations to come it is his perpetual share of the food offerings presented to the LORD. Whatever touches them will become holy.[c]'"

[19]The LORD also said to Moses, [20]"This is the offering Aaron and his sons are to bring to the LORD on the day he[d] is anointed: a tenth of an ephah[e] of the finest flour as a regular grain offering, half of it in the morning and half in the evening. [21]It must be prepared with oil on a griddle; bring it well-mixed and present the grain offering broken[f] in pieces as an aroma pleasing to the LORD. [22]The son who is to succeed him as anointed priest shall prepare it. It is the LORD's perpetual share and is to be burned completely; [23]Every grain offering of a priest shall be burned completely; it must not be eaten."

### The Sin Offering

[24]The LORD said to Moses, [25]"Say to Aaron and his sons: 'These are the regulations for the sin offering: The sin offering is to be slaughtered before the LORD in the place the burnt offering is slaughtered; it is most holy. [26]The priest who offers it shall eat it; it is to be eaten in the sanctuary area, in the courtyard of the tent of meeting. [27]Whatever touches any of the flesh will become holy, and if any of the blood is spattered on a garment, you must wash it in the sanctuary area. [28]The clay pot the meat is cooked in must be broken; but if it is cooked in a bronze pot, the pot is to be scoured and rinsed with water. [29]Any male in a priest's family may eat it; it is most holy. [30]But any sin offering whose blood is brought into the tent of meeting to make atonement in the Holy Place must not be eaten; it must be burned up.

### The Guilt Offering

**7** "'These are the regulations for the guilt offering, which is most holy: [2]The guilt offering is to be slaughtered in the place where the burnt offering is slaughtered, and its blood is to be splashed against the sides of the altar. [3]All its fat shall be offered: the fat tail and the fat that covers the internal organs, [4]both kidneys with the fat on them near the loins, and the long lobe of the liver, which is to be removed with the kidneys. [5]The priest shall burn them on the altar as a food offering presented to the LORD. It is a guilt offering. [6]Any male in a priest's family may eat it, but it must be eaten in the sanctuary area; it is most holy.

[7]"'The same law applies to both the sin offering[g] and the guilt offering: They belong to the priest who makes atonement with them. [8]The priest who offers a burnt of-

## Amplified Bible

[15]One of them shall take his handful of the fine flour of the cereal offering, the oil of it, and all the frankincense which is upon the cereal offering, and burn it on the altar as the memorial of it, a sweet *and* satisfying fragrance to the Lord. [16]And the remainder of it shall Aaron and his sons eat, without leaven in a holy place; in the court of the Tent of Meeting shall they eat it. [I Cor. 9:13, 14.] [17]It shall not be baked with leaven. I have given it as their portion of My offerings made by fire; it is most holy, like the sin offering and the guilt offering. [18]Every male among the children of Aaron may eat of it, as his portion forever throughout your generations, from the Lord's offerings made by fire; whoever touches them shall [first] be holy (consecrated and ceremonially clean).

[19]And the Lord said to Moses, [20]This is the offering which Aaron and his sons shall offer to the Lord on the day when one is anointed (and consecrated): the tenth of an ephah of fine flour for a regular cereal offering, half of it in the morning and half of it at night. [21]On a griddle *or* baking pan it shall be made with oil; and when it is fried you shall bring it in; in broken *and* fried pieces shall you offer the cereal offering as a sweet *and* satisfying odor to the Lord. [22]And the priest among Aaron's sons who is consecrated *and* anointed in his stead shall offer it; by a statute forever it shall be entirely burned to the Lord. [23]For every cereal offering of the priest shall be wholly burned, and not be eaten.

[24]And the Lord said to Moses, [25]Say to Aaron and his sons: This is the law of the sin offering: In the place where the burnt offering is killed shall the sin offering be killed before the Lord; it is most holy. [26]The priest who offers it for sin shall eat it; in a sacred place shall it be eaten, in the court of the Tent of Meeting. [27]Whoever *or* whatever touches its flesh shall [first] be dedicated and made clean, and when any of its blood is sprinkled on a garment, you shall wash that garment in a place set apart to God's worship. [28]But the earthen vessel in which it is boiled shall be broken, and if it is boiled in a bronze vessel, that vessel shall be scoured and rinsed in water. [29]Every male among the priests may eat of this offering; it is most holy. [30]But no sin offering shall be eaten of which any of the blood is brought into the Tent of Meeting to make atonement in the Holy Place; it shall be [wholly] burned with fire. [Heb. 13:11-13.]

**7** This is the law of the guilt *or* trespass offering; it is most holy *or* sacred: [2]In the place where they kill the burnt offering shall they kill the guilt *or* trespass offering; the blood of it shall the priest dash against the altar round about. [3]And he shall offer all its fat, the fat tail and the fat that covers the entrails, [4]And the two kidneys and the fat that is on them at the loins, and the lobe *or* appendage of the liver, which he shall take away with the kidneys. [5]And the priest shall burn them on the altar for an offering made by fire to the Lord; it is a guilt *or* trespass offering. [6]Every male among the priests may eat of it; it shall be eaten in a sacred place; it is most holy. [7]As is the sin offering, so is the guilt *or* trespass offering; there is one law for them: the priest who makes atonement with it shall have it. [8]And the priest who offers any man's burnt offering,

---

*a* 15 Or *representative*  *b* 17 Or *purification offering*; also in verses 25 and 30  *c* 18 Or *Whoever touches them must be holy*; similarly in verse 27  *d* 20 Or *each*  *e* 20 That is, probably about 3 1/2 pounds or about 1.6 kilograms  *f* 21 The meaning of the Hebrew for this word is uncertain.  *g* 7 Or *purification offering*; also in verse 37

## New International Version

fering for anyone may keep its hide for himself. ⁹Every grain offering baked in an oven or cooked in a pan or on a griddle belongs to the priest who offers it, ¹⁰and every grain offering, whether mixed with olive oil or dry, belongs equally to all the sons of Aaron.

### The Fellowship Offering

¹¹"'These are the regulations for the fellowship offering anyone may present to the LORD:

¹²"'If they offer it as an expression of thankfulness, then along with this thank offering they are to offer thick loaves made without yeast and with olive oil mixed in, thin loaves made without yeast and brushed with oil, and thick loaves of the finest flour well-kneaded and with oil mixed in. ¹³Along with their fellowship offering of thanksgiving they are to present an offering with thick loaves of bread made with yeast. ¹⁴They are to bring one of each kind as an offering, a contribution to the LORD; it belongs to the priest who splashes the blood of the fellowship offering against the altar. ¹⁵The meat of their fellowship offering of thanksgiving must be eaten on the day it is offered; they must leave none of it till morning.

¹⁶"'If, however, their offering is the result of a vow or is a freewill offering, the sacrifice shall be eaten on the day they offer it, but anything left over may be eaten on the next day. ¹⁷Any meat of the sacrifice left over till the third day must be burned up. ¹⁸If any meat of the fellowship offering is eaten on the third day, the one who offered it will not be accepted. It will not be reckoned to their credit, for it has become impure; the person who eats any of it will be held responsible.

¹⁹"'Meat that touches anything ceremonially unclean must not be eaten; it must be burned up. As for other meat, anyone ceremonially clean may eat it. ²⁰But if anyone who is unclean eats any meat of the fellowship offering belonging to the LORD, they must be cut off from their people. ²¹Anyone who touches something unclean—whether human uncleanness or an unclean animal or any unclean creature that moves along the ground[a]—and then eats any of the meat of the fellowship offering belonging to the LORD must be cut off from their people.'"

### Eating Fat and Blood Forbidden

²²The LORD said to Moses, ²³"Say to the Israelites: 'Do not eat any of the fat of cattle, sheep or goats. ²⁴The fat of an animal found dead or torn by wild animals may be used for any other purpose, but you must not eat it. ²⁵Anyone who eats the fat of an animal from which a food offering may be[b] presented to the LORD must be cut off from their people. ²⁶And wherever you live, you must not eat the blood of any bird or animal. ²⁷Anyone who eats blood must be cut off from their people.'"

### The Priests' Share

²⁸The LORD said to Moses, ²⁹"Say to the Israelites: 'Anyone who brings a fellowship offering to the LORD is to bring part of it as their sacrifice to the LORD. ³⁰With their own hands they are to present the food offering to the LORD; they are to bring the fat, together with the breast, and wave the breast before the LORD as a wave offering. ³¹The priest shall burn the fat on the altar, but the breast belongs to Aaron and his sons. ³²You are to give the right thigh of your fellowship offerings to the priest as a contri-

## Amplified Bible

that priest shall have for himself the hide of the burnt offering which he has offered.

⁹And every cereal offering that is baked in the oven and all that is prepared in a pan or on a griddle shall belong to the priest who offered it.

¹⁰And every cereal offering, mixed with oil or dry, all the sons of Aaron may have, one as well as another.

¹¹And this is the law of the sacrifice of peace offerings which shall be offered to the Lord:

¹²If one offers it for a thanksgiving, then he shall offer with the thank offering unleavened cakes mixed with oil, and unleavened wafers spread with oil, and cakes of fine flour mixed with oil.

¹³With cakes of leavened bread he shall offer his sacrifice of thanksgiving with the sacrifice of his peace offerings.

¹⁴And of it he shall offer one cake from each offering as an offering to the Lord; it shall belong to the priest who dashes the blood of the peace offerings.

¹⁵The flesh of the sacrifice of thanksgiving presented as a peace offering shall be eaten on the day that it is offered; none of it shall be left until morning.

¹⁶But if the sacrifice of the worshiper's offering is a vow or a freewill offering, it shall be eaten the same day that he offers his sacrifice, and on the morrow that which remains of it shall be eaten;

¹⁷But the remainder of the flesh of the sacrifice on the third day shall be [wholly] burned with fire.

¹⁸If any of the flesh of the sacrifice of his peace offerings be eaten at all on the third day, then the one who brought it shall not be credited with it; it shall not be accepted. It shall be an abomination *and* an abhorred thing; the one who eats of it shall bear his iniquity *and* answer for it.

¹⁹The flesh that comes in contact with anything that is not clean shall not be eaten; it shall be burned with fire. As for the meat, everyone who is clean [ceremonially] may eat of it.

²⁰But the one who eats of the flesh of the sacrifice of peace offerings that belong to the Lord when he is [ceremonially] unclean, that person shall be cut off from his people [deprived of the privileges of association with them].

²¹And if anyone touches any unclean thing—the uncleanness of man or an unclean beast or any unclean abomination—and then eats of the flesh of the sacrifice of the Lord's peace offerings, that person shall be cut off from his people.

²²And the Lord said to Moses,

²³Say to the Israelites, You shall eat no kind of fat, of ox, or sheep, or goat.

²⁴The fat of the beast that dies of itself and the fat of one that is torn with beasts may be put to any other use, but under no circumstances are you to eat of it.

²⁵For whoever eats the fat of the beast from which men offer an offering made by fire to the Lord, that person shall be cut off from his people.

²⁶Moreover, you shall eat no blood of any kind, whether of bird or of beast, in any of your dwellings.

²⁷Whoever eats any kind of blood, that person shall be cut off from his people.

²⁸And the Lord said to Moses,

²⁹Tell the Israelites, He who offers the sacrifice of his peace offerings to the Lord shall bring his offering to the Lord; from the sacrifice of his peace offerings

³⁰He shall bring with his own hands the offerings made by fire to the Lord; he shall bring the fat with the breast, that the breast may be waved as a wave offering before the Lord.

³¹The priest shall burn the fat on the altar, but the breast shall be for Aaron and his sons.

³²And the right thigh you shall give to the priest for an offering from the sacrifices of your peace offerings.

---

*a* 21 A few Hebrew manuscripts, Samaritan Pentateuch, Syriac and Targum (see 5:2); most Hebrew manuscripts *any unclean, detestable thing* *b* 25 Or *offering is*

## New International Version

bution. ³³The son of Aaron who offers the blood and the fat of the fellowship offering shall have the right thigh as his share. ³⁴From the fellowship offerings of the Israelites, I have taken the breast that is waved and the thigh that is presented and have given them to Aaron the priest and his sons as their perpetual share from the Israelites.'"

³⁵This is the portion of the food offerings presented to the LORD that were allotted to Aaron and his sons on the day they were presented to serve the LORD as priests. ³⁶On the day they were anointed, the LORD commanded that the Israelites give this to them as their perpetual share for the generations to come.

³⁷These, then, are the regulations for the burnt offering, the grain offering, the sin offering, the guilt offering, the ordination offering and the fellowship offering, ³⁸which the LORD gave Moses at Mount Sinai in the Desert of Sinai on the day he commanded the Israelites to bring their offerings to the LORD.

### The Ordination of Aaron and His Sons

**8** The LORD said to Moses, ²"Bring Aaron and his sons, their garments, the anointing oil, the bull for the sin offering,ᵃ the two rams and the basket containing bread made without yeast, ³and gather the entire assembly at the entrance to the tent of meeting." ⁴Moses did as the LORD commanded him, and the assembly gathered at the entrance to the tent of meeting.

⁵Moses said to the assembly, "This is what the LORD has commanded to be done." ⁶Then Moses brought Aaron and his sons forward and washed them with water. ⁷He put the tunic on Aaron, tied the sash around him, clothed him with the robe and put the ephod on him. He also fastened the ephod with a decorative waistband, which he tied around him. ⁸He placed the breastpiece on him and put the Urim and Thummim in the breastpiece. ⁹Then he placed the turban on Aaron's head and set the gold plate, the sacred emblem, on the front of it, as the LORD commanded Moses.

¹⁰Then Moses took the anointing oil and anointed the tabernacle and everything in it, and so consecrated them. ¹¹He sprinkled some of the oil on the altar seven times, anointing the altar and all its utensils and the basin with its stand, to consecrate them. ¹²He poured some of the anointing oil on Aaron's head and anointed him to consecrate him. ¹³Then he brought Aaron's sons forward, put tunics on them, tied sashes around them and fastened caps on them, as the LORD commanded Moses.

¹⁴He then presented the bull for the sin offering, and Aaron and his sons laid their hands on its head. ¹⁵Moses slaughtered the bull and took some of the blood, and with his finger he put it on all the horns of the altar to purify the altar. He poured out the rest of the blood at the base of the altar. So he consecrated it to make atonement for it. ¹⁶Moses also took all the fat around the internal organs, the long lobe of the liver, and both kidneys and their fat, and burned it on the altar. ¹⁷But the bull with its hide and its flesh and its intestines he burned up outside the camp, as the LORD commanded Moses.

## Amplified Bible

³³The son of Aaron who offers the blood of the peace offerings and the fat shall have the right thigh for his portion.

³⁴For I have taken the breast that was waved and the thigh that was offered from the Israelites, out of the sacrifices of their peace offerings, and have given them to Aaron the priest and to his sons as their perpetual due from the Israelites.

³⁵This is the anointing portion of Aaron and his sons out of the offerings to the Lord made by fire on the day when they were presented to minister to the Lord in the priest's office.

³⁶The Lord commanded this to be given them of the Israelites on the day when they were anointed. It is their portion perpetually throughout their generations.

³⁷This is the law of the burnt offering, the cereal offering, the sin offering, the guilt or trespass offering, the consecration offering, and the sacrifice of peace offerings,

³⁸Which the Lord ordered Moses on Mount Sinai on the day He commanded the Israelites to offer their sacrifices to the Lord, in the Wilderness of Sinai.

**8** And the Lord said to Moses, ²Take Aaron and his sons with him, and the garments [symbols of their office], and the anointing oil, and the bull of the sin offering, and the two rams, and the basket of unleavened bread;

³And assemble all the congregation at the door of the Tent of Meeting.

⁴Moses did as the Lord commanded him, and the congregation was assembled at the door of the Tent of Meeting.

⁵Moses told the congregation, This is what the Lord has commanded to be done.

⁶Moses brought Aaron and his sons and washed them with water.

⁷He put on Aaron the long undertunic, girded him with the long sash, clothed him with the robe, put the ephod (an upper vestment) upon him, and girded him with the skillfully woven cords attached to the ephod, binding it to him.

⁸And Moses put upon Aaron the breastplate; also he put in the breastplate the Urim and the Thummim [articles upon which the high priest put his hand when seeking the divine will concerning the nation].

⁹And he put the turban or miter on his head; on it, in front, Moses put the shining gold plate, the holy diadem, as the Lord commanded him.

¹⁰And Moses took the anointing oil and anointed the tabernacle and all that was in it, and consecrated them.

¹¹And he sprinkled some of the oil on the altar seven times and anointed the altar and all its utensils, and the laver and its base, to consecrate them.

¹²And he poured some of the anointing oil upon Aaron's head and anointed him to consecrate him.

¹³And Moses brought Aaron's sons and put undertunics on them and girded them with sashes and wound turbans on them, as the Lord commanded Moses.

¹⁴Then he brought the bull of the sin offering, and Aaron and his sons laid their hands on the head of the bull of the sin offering.

¹⁵Moses killed it and took the blood and put it on the horns of the altar round about with his finger and poured the blood at the base of the altar and purified and consecrated the altar to make atonement for it.

¹⁶He took all the fat that was on the entrails, and the lobe of the liver, and the two kidneys with their fat, and Moses burned them on the altar.

¹⁷But the bull [the sin offering] and its hide, its flesh, and its dung he burned with fire outside the camp, as the Lord commanded Moses.

ᵃ 2 Or *purification offering*; also in verse 14

## New International Version

18 He then presented the ram for the burnt offering, and Aaron and his sons laid their hands on its head. 19 Then Moses slaughtered the ram and splashed the blood against the sides of the altar. 20 He cut the ram into pieces and burned the head, the pieces and the fat. 21 He washed the internal organs and the legs with water and burned the whole ram on the altar. It was a burnt offering, a pleasing aroma, a food offering presented to the LORD, as the LORD commanded Moses.

22 He then presented the other ram, the ram for the ordination, and Aaron and his sons laid their hands on its head. 23 Moses slaughtered the ram and took some of its blood and put it on the lobe of Aaron's right ear, on the thumb of his right hand and on the big toe of his right foot. 24 Moses also brought Aaron's sons forward and put some of the blood on the lobes of their right ears, on the thumbs of their right hands and on the big toes of their right feet. Then he splashed blood against the sides of the altar. 25 After that, he took the fat, the fat tail, all the fat around the internal organs, the long lobe of the liver, both kidneys and their fat and the right thigh. 26 And from the basket of bread made without yeast, which was before the LORD, he took one thick loaf, one thick loaf with olive oil mixed in, and one thin loaf, and he put these on the fat portions and on the right thigh. 27 He put all these in the hands of Aaron and his sons, and they waved them before the LORD as a wave offering. 28 Then Moses took them from their hands and burned them on the altar on top of the burnt offering as an ordination offering, a pleasing aroma, a food offering presented to the LORD. 29 Moses also took the breast, which was his share of the ordination ram, and waved it before the LORD as a wave offering, as the LORD commanded Moses.

30 Then Moses took some of the anointing oil and some of the blood from the altar and sprinkled them on Aaron and his garments and on his sons and their garments. So he consecrated Aaron and his garments and his sons and their garments.

31 Moses then said to Aaron and his sons, "Cook the meat at the entrance to the tent of meeting and eat it there with the bread from the basket of ordination offerings, as I was commanded: 'Aaron and his sons are to eat it.' 32 Then burn up the rest of the meat and the bread, 33 Do not leave the entrance to the tent of meeting for seven days, until the days of your ordination are completed, for your ordination will last seven days. 34 What has been done today was commanded by the LORD to make atonement for you. 35 You must stay at the entrance to the tent of meeting day and night for seven days and do what the LORD requires, so you will not die; for that is what I have been commanded."

36 So Aaron and his sons did everything the LORD commanded through Moses.

## Amplified Bible

18 He brought the ram for the burnt offering, and Aaron and his sons laid their hands on the head of the ram. 19 And Moses killed it and dashed the blood upon the altar round about. 20 He cut the ram into pieces and Moses burned the head, the pieces, and the fat. 21 And he washed the entrails and the legs in water; then Moses burned the whole ram on the altar; it was a burnt sacrifice, for a sweet *and* satisfying fragrance, an offering made by fire to the Lord, as the Lord commanded Moses. 22 And he brought the other ram, the ram of consecration *and* ordination, and Aaron and his sons laid their hands upon the head of the ram. 23 And Moses killed it and took some of its blood and put it on the tip of Aaron's right ear, and on the thumb of his right hand, and on the great toe of his right foot. 24 And he brought Aaron's sons and Moses put some of the blood on the tips of their right ears, and the thumbs of their right hands, and the great toes of their right feet; and Moses dashed the blood upon the altar round about. 25 And he took the fat, the fat tail, all the fat that was on the entrails, the lobe of the liver, and the two kidneys and their fat, and the right thigh; 26 And out of the basket of unleavened bread, that was before the Lord, he took one unleavened cake, a cake of oiled bread, and one wafer and put them on the fat and on the right thigh; 27 And he put all these in Aaron's hands and his sons' hands and waved them for a wave offering before the Lord. 28 Then Moses took these things from their hands and burned them on the altar with the burnt offering as an ordination offering, for a sweet *and* satisfying fragrance, an offering made by fire to the Lord. 29 And Moses took the breast and waved it for a wave offering before the Lord; for of the ram of consecration *and* ordination it was Moses' portion, as the Lord commanded Moses. 30 And Moses took some of the anointing oil and some of the blood which was on the altar and sprinkled it on Aaron and his garments, and upon his sons and their garments also; so Moses consecrated Aaron and his garments, and his sons and his sons' garments. 31 And Moses said to Aaron and his sons, Boil the flesh at the door of the Tent of Meeting and there eat it with the bread that is in the basket of consecration *and* ordination, as I commanded, saying, Aaron and his sons shall eat it. 32 And what remains of the flesh and of the bread you shall burn with fire. 33 And you shall not go out of the door of the Tent of Meeting for seven days, until the days of your consecration *and* ordination are ended; for it will take seven days to consecrate *and* ordain you. 34 As has been done this day, so the Lord has commanded to do for your atonement. 35 At the door of the Tent of Meeting you shall remain day and night for seven days, [a] doing what the Lord has charged you to do, that you die not; for so I am commanded. 36 So Aaron and his sons did all the things which the Lord commanded through Moses.

---

[a] We have, every one of us, a charge to keep, an eternal God to glorify, an immortal soul to provide for, needful duty to be done, our generation to serve; and it must be our daily care to keep this charge, for it is the charge of the Lord our Master (Matthew Henry, *Commentary on the Holy Bible*). The laws contained in this book, for the most part ceremonial, had an important spiritual bearing, the study of which is highly instructive (Robert Jamieson, A. R. Fausset and David Brown, *A Commentary*). The Scripture references recorded within the text are intended to be a guide to its spiritual implications.

# New International Version

## The Priests Begin Their Ministry

**9** On the eighth day Moses summoned Aaron and his sons and the elders of Israel. [2]He said to Aaron, "Take a bull calf for your sin offering[a] and a ram for your burnt offering, both without defect, and present them before the LORD. [3]Then say to the Israelites: 'Take a male goat for a sin offering, a calf and a lamb—both a year old and without defect—for a burnt offering, [4]and an ox[b] and a ram for a fellowship offering to sacrifice before the LORD, together with a grain offering mixed with olive oil. For today the LORD will appear to you.'"

[5]They took the things Moses commanded to the front of the tent of meeting, and the entire assembly came near and stood before the LORD. [6]Then Moses said, "This is what the LORD has commanded you to do, so that the glory of the LORD may appear to you."

[7]Moses said to Aaron, "Come to the altar and sacrifice your sin offering and your burnt offering and make atonement for yourself and the people; sacrifice the offering that is for the people and make atonement for them, as the LORD has commanded."

[8]So Aaron came to the altar and slaughtered the calf as a sin offering for himself. [9]His sons brought the blood to him, and he dipped his finger into the blood and put it on the horns of the altar; the rest of the blood he poured out at the base of the altar. [10]On the altar he burned the fat, the kidneys and the long lobe of the liver from the sin offering, as the LORD commanded Moses; [11]the flesh and the hide he burned up outside the camp.

[12]Then he slaughtered the burnt offering. His sons handed him the blood, and he splashed it against the sides of the altar. [13]They handed him the burnt offering piece by piece, including the head, and he burned them on the altar. [14]He washed the internal organs and the legs and burned them on top of the burnt offering on the altar.

[15]Aaron then brought the offering that was for the people. He took the goat for the people's sin offering and slaughtered it and offered it for a sin offering as he did with the first one.

[16]He brought the burnt offering and offered it in the prescribed way. [17]He also brought the grain offering, took a handful of it and burned it on the altar in addition to the morning's burnt offering.

[18]He slaughtered the ox and the ram as the fellowship offering for the people. His sons handed him the blood, and he splashed it against the sides of the altar. [19]But the fat portions of the ox and the ram—the fat tail, the layer of fat, the kidneys and the long lobe of the liver— [20]these they laid on the breasts, and then Aaron burned the fat on the altar. [21]Aaron waved the breasts and the right thigh before the LORD as a wave offering, as Moses commanded.

[22]Then Aaron lifted his hands toward the people and blessed them. And having sacrificed the sin offering, the burnt offering and the fellowship offering, he stepped down.

[23]Moses and Aaron then went into the tent of meeting. When they came out, they blessed the people; and the glory of the LORD appeared to all the people. [24]Fire came out from the presence of the LORD and consumed the burnt offering and the fat portions on the altar. And when all the people saw it, they shouted for joy and fell facedown.

---

[a] 2 Or *purification offering*; here and throughout this chapter
[b] 4 The Hebrew word can refer to either male or female; also in verses 18 and 19.

# Amplified Bible

**9** On the eighth day Moses called Aaron and his sons and the elders of Israel; [2]And he said to Aaron, Take a young calf for a sin offering and a ram for a burnt offering, [each] without blemish, and offer them before the Lord. [Heb. 10:10-12.]

[3]And say to the Israelites, Take a male goat for a sin offering, and a calf and a lamb, both a year old, without blemish, for a burnt offering,

[4]Also a bull and a ram for peace offerings to sacrifice before the Lord, and a cereal offering mixed with oil, for today the Lord will appear to you.

[5]They brought before the Tent of Meeting what Moses [had] commanded; all the congregation drew near and stood before the Lord.

[6]And Moses said, This is the thing which the Lord commanded you to do, and the glory of the Lord will appear to you.

[7]And Moses said to Aaron, Draw near to the altar and offer your sin offering and your burnt offering and make atonement for yourself and for the people; and offer the offering of the people and make atonement for them, as the Lord commanded. [Heb. 5:1-5; 7:27.]

[8]So Aaron drew near to the altar and killed the calf of the sin offering, which was designated for himself.

[9]The sons of Aaron presented the blood to him; he dipped his finger in the blood and put it on the horns of the altar and poured out the blood at the altar's base;

[10]But the fat, the kidneys, and the lobe of the liver from the sin offering he burned on the altar, as the Lord had commanded Moses.

[11]And the flesh and the hide Aaron burned with fire outside the camp.

[12]He killed the burnt offering, and Aaron's sons delivered to him the blood, which he dashed round about upon the altar.

[13]And they brought the burnt offering to him piece by piece, and the head, and Aaron burned them upon the altar.

[14]And he washed the entrails and the legs and burned them with the burnt offering on the altar.

[15]Then Aaron presented the people's offering, and took the goat of the sin offering which was for the people and killed it and offered it for sin as he did the first sin offering. [Heb. 2:16, 17.]

[16]And he presented the burnt offering and offered it according to the ordinance.

[17]And Aaron presented the cereal offering and took a handful of it and burned it on the altar in addition to the burnt offering of the morning.

[18]He also killed the bull and the ram, the sacrifice of peace offerings, for the people; and Aaron's sons presented to him the blood, which he dashed upon the altar round about,

[19]And the fat of the bull and of the ram, the fat tail and that which covers the entrails, and the kidneys, and the lobe of the liver.

[20]And they put the fat upon the breasts, and Aaron burned the fat upon the altar;

[21]But the breasts and the right thigh Aaron waved for a wave offering before the Lord, as Moses commanded.

[22]Then Aaron lifted his hands toward the people and blessed them, and came down [from the altar] after offering the sin offering, the burnt offering, and the peace offerings.

[23]Moses and Aaron went into the Tent of Meeting, and when they came out they blessed the people, and the glory of the Lord [the Shekinah cloud] appeared to all the people [as promised]. [Lev. 9:6.]

[24]Then there came a fire out from before the Lord and consumed the burnt offering and the fat on the altar; and when all the people saw it, they shouted and fell on their faces.

## New International Version

### The Death of Nadab and Abihu

**10** Aaron's sons Nadab and Abihu took their censers, put fire in them and added incense; and they offered unauthorized fire before the LORD, contrary to his command. [2] So fire came out from the presence of the LORD and consumed them, and they died before the LORD. [3] Moses then said to Aaron, "This is what the LORD spoke of when he said:

"'Among those who approach me
   I will be proved holy;
in the sight of all the people
   I will be honored.'"

Aaron remained silent.

[4] Moses summoned Mishael and Elzaphan, sons of Aaron's uncle Uzziel, and said to them, "Come here; carry your cousins outside the camp, away from the front of the sanctuary." [5] So they came and carried them, still in their tunics, outside the camp, as Moses ordered.

[6] Then Moses said to Aaron and his sons Eleazar and Ithamar, "Do not let your hair become unkempt[a] and do not tear your clothes, or you will die and the LORD will be angry with the whole community. But your relatives, all the Israelites, may mourn for those the LORD has destroyed by fire. [7] Do not leave the entrance to the tent of meeting or you will die, because the LORD's anointing oil is on you." So they did as Moses said.

[8] Then the LORD said to Aaron, [9] "You and your sons are not to drink wine or other fermented drink whenever you go into the tent of meeting, or you will die. This is a lasting ordinance for the generations to come, [10] so that you can distinguish between the holy and the common, between the unclean and the clean, [11] and so you can teach the Israelites all the decrees the LORD has given them through Moses."

[12] Moses said to Aaron and his remaining sons, Eleazar and Ithamar, "Take the grain offering left over from the food offerings prepared without yeast and presented to the LORD and eat it beside the altar, for it is most holy. [13] Eat it in the sanctuary area, because it is your share and your sons' share of the food offerings presented to the LORD; for so I have been commanded. [14] But you and your sons and your daughters may eat the breast that was waved and the thigh that was presented. Eat them in a ceremonially clean place; they have been given to you and your children as your share of the Israelites' fellowship offerings. [15] The thigh that was presented and the breast that was waved must be brought with the fat portions of the food offerings, to be waved before the LORD as a wave offering. This will be the perpetual share for you and your children, as the LORD has commanded."

[16] When Moses inquired about the goat of the sin offer-

## Amplified Bible

**10** And Nadab and Abihu, the sons of Aaron, each took his censer and put fire in it, and put incense on it, and offered strange *and* unholy fire before the Lord, as He had not commanded them.

[2] And there came forth fire from before the Lord and killed them, and they died before the Lord.

[3] Then Moses said to Aaron, This is what the Lord meant when He said, I [a] [and My will, not their own] will be acknowledged as hallowed by those who come near Me, and before all the people I will be honored. And Aaron said nothing.

[4] Moses called Mishael and Elzaphan, sons of Uzziel uncle of Aaron, and said to them, Come near, carry your brethren from before the sanctuary out of the camp.

[5] So they drew near and carried them in their undertunics [stripped of their priestly vestments] out of the camp, as Moses had said.

[6] And Moses said to Aaron and Eleazar and Ithamar, his sons [the father and brothers of the two priests whom God had slain for offering false fire], Do not uncover your heads *or* let your hair go loose or tear your clothes, lest you die [also] and lest God's wrath should come upon all the congregation; but let your brethren, the whole house of Israel, bewail the burning which the Lord has kindled.

[7] And you shall not go out from the door of the Tent of Meeting, lest you die, for the Lord's anointing oil is upon you. And they did according to Moses' word.

[8] And the Lord said to Aaron,

[9] Do not drink wine or strong drink, you or your sons, when you go into the Tent of Meeting, lest you die; it shall be a statute forever in all your generations.

[10] You shall make a distinction *and* recognize a difference between the holy and the common *or* unholy, and between the unclean and the clean;

[11] And you are to teach the Israelites all the statutes which the Lord has spoken to them by Moses.

[12] And Moses said to Aaron and to Eleazar and Ithamar, his sons who were left, Take the cereal offering that remains of the offerings of the Lord made by fire and eat it without leaven beside the altar, for it is most holy.

[13] You shall eat it in a sacred place, because it is your due and your sons' due, from the offerings made by fire to the Lord; for so I am commanded.

[14] But the breast that is waved and the thigh that is offered you shall eat in a clean place, you and your sons and daughters with you; for they are your due and your sons' due, given out of the sacrifices of the peace offerings of the Israelites.

[15] The thigh that is offered and the breast that is waved they shall bring with the offerings made by fire of the fat, to wave for a wave offering before the Lord; and it shall be yours and your sons' with you as a portion *or* due perpetually, as the Lord has commanded.

[16] And Moses diligently tried to find [what had become

[a] Perhaps few believers have ever identified themselves with Nadab and Abihu, and yet few, if any, of us have not done exactly what they did in principle. Their sin, which God took so seriously and which proved fatal to them, was not a mere matter of failing to obey the letter of God's law for priests. Their inexcusable folly was in trying to please the Lord **their** way instead of **His** way. Who of us cannot recognize himself as the offerer of this prayer, with only the details lacking: "O Lord, make me rich! Then I will make large donations to Your interests!" Yet our very poverty may be the means to the end which He has in love and wisdom planned for us, the ultimate purpose of our creation, perhaps, which substitution of our will for His will would utterly defeat. No wonder God removed Nadab and Abihu from the earth! They, like ourselves, had acted like the child of a great painter who attempted to work on his father's priceless canvas instead of on the tablet assigned to him. They, like the child, were banished from the father's presence. And every believer does well to recognize the importance of being entirely surrendered to "God's will; nothing more; nothing less; nothing else; at any cost." And that does not mean first making an unholy alliance in marriage, or in business, or in thought, and then adjusting it to God's will. Remember Nadab and Abihu, who "offered strange *and* unholy fire before the Lord." It does not pay.

[a] 6 Or *Do not uncover your heads*

## New International Version

ing[a] and found that it had been burned up, he was angry with Eleazar and Ithamar, Aaron's remaining sons, and asked, [17]"Why didn't you eat the sin offering in the sanctuary area? It is most holy; it was given to you to take away the guilt of the community by making atonement for them before the LORD. [18]Since its blood was not taken into the Holy Place, you should have eaten the goat in the sanctuary area, as I commanded."

[19]Aaron replied to Moses, "Today they sacrificed their sin offering and their burnt offering before the LORD, but such things as this have happened to me. Would the LORD have been pleased if I had eaten the sin offering today?" [20]When Moses heard this, he was satisfied.

### Clean and Unclean Food

**11** The LORD said to Moses and Aaron, [2]"Say to the Israelites: 'Of all the animals that live on land, these are the ones you may eat: [3]You may eat any animal that has a divided hoof and that chews the cud.

[4]"'There are some that only chew the cud or only have a divided hoof, but you must not eat them. The camel, though it chews the cud, does not have a divided hoof; it is ceremonially unclean for you. [5]The hyrax, though it chews the cud, does not have a divided hoof; it is unclean for you. [6]The rabbit, though it chews the cud, does not have a divided hoof; it is unclean for you. [7]And the pig, though it has a divided hoof, does not chew the cud; it is unclean for you. [8]You must not eat their meat or touch their carcasses; they are unclean for you.

[9]"'Of all the creatures living in the water of the seas and the streams you may eat any that have fins and scales. [10]But all creatures in the seas or streams that do not have fins and scales—whether among all the swarming things or among all the other living creatures in the water—you are to regard as unclean. [11]And since you are to regard them as unclean, you must not eat their meat; you must regard their carcasses as unclean. [12]Anything living in the water that does not have fins and scales is to be regarded as unclean by you.

[13]"'These are the birds you are to regard as unclean and not eat because they are unclean: the eagle,[b] the vulture, the black vulture, [14]the red kite, any kind of black kite, [15]any kind of raven, [16]the horned owl, the screech owl, the gull, any kind of hawk, [17]the little owl, the cormorant, the

## Amplified Bible

of] the goat [that had been offered] for the sin offering, and behold, it was burned up [as waste]! And he was angry with Eleazar and Ithamar, the sons of Aaron who were left alive, and said,

[17]Why have you not eaten the sin offering in the Holy Place? It is most holy; and God has given it to you to bear *and* take away the iniquity of the congregation, to make atonement for them before the Lord.

[18]Behold, the blood of it was not brought within the Holy Place; you should indeed have eaten [the flesh of it] in the Holy Place, as I commanded.

[19]But Aaron said to Moses, Behold, this very day in which they have [obediently] offered their sin offering and their burnt offering before the Lord, such [terrible calamities] have befallen me [and them]! If I [and they] had eaten the most holy sin offering today [humbled as we have been by the sin of our kinsmen and God's judgment upon them], would it have been acceptable in the sight of the Lord? [Hos. 9:4.]

[20]And when Moses heard that, he was pacified.

**11** And the Lord said to Moses and Aaron, [2]Say to the Israelites: These are the animals [a]which you may eat among all the beasts that are on the earth. [Mark 7:15-19.]

[3]Whatever parts the hoof and is cloven-footed and chews the cud, any of these animals you may eat.

[4]Nevertheless these you shall not eat of those that chew the cud or divide the hoof: the camel, because it chews the cud but does not divide the hoof; it is unclean to you.

[5]And the coney *or* rock badger, because it chews the cud but does not divide the hoof; it is unclean to you.

[6]And the hare, because it chews the cud but does not divide the hoof; it is unclean to you.

[7]And the swine, because it divides the hoof and is cloven-footed but does not chew the cud; it is unclean to you.

[8]Of their flesh you shall not eat, and their carcasses you shall not touch; they are unclean to you.

[9]These you may eat of all that are in the waters: whatever has fins and scales in the waters, in the seas, and in the rivers, these you may eat;

[10]But all that have not fins and scales in the seas and in the rivers, of all the creeping things in the waters, and of all the living creatures which are in the waters, they are [to be considered] an abomination and abhorrence to you. [I Cor. 8:8-13.]

[11]They shall continue to be an abomination to you; you shall not eat of their flesh, but you shall detest their carcasses.

[12]Everything in the waters that has not fins or scales shall be abhorrent *and* detestable to you.

[13]These you shall have in abomination among the birds; they shall not be eaten, for they are detestable: the eagle, the ossifrage, the ospray,

[14]The kite, the whole species of falcon,

[15]Every kind of raven,

[16]The ostrich, the nighthawk, the sea gull, every species of hawk,

[17]The owl, the cormorant, the ibis,

---

[a] At first thought the laws given here seem only to have been made obsolete by Jesus. He taught that it is not what goes into the mouth but what comes out of it that defiles a man (Matt. 15:17-20), and Paul said that when the complete and perfect came, the incomplete and imperfect would become void and superseded (I Cor. 13:9, 10), for "there is nothing unclean of itself" (Rom. 14:14 KJV). But while all these specific laws have become void, we must not lose sight of the fact that they are "superseded" by the underlying spiritual principle, which is just as binding. Christ's teaching relates to the whole area of our living, including our eating and drinking, and is dominated by the principle, "Whatever you may do, do all for the honor *and* glory of God" (I Cor. 10:31). We do well to remember that it was Jesus Christ Himself who said, "Do not think that I have come to do away with *or* undo the Law . . .; I have not come to do away with *or* undo but to complete *and* fulfill" it (Matt. 5:17).

---

[a] 16 Or *purification offering*; also in verses 17 and 19   [b] 13 The precise identification of some of the birds, insects and animals in this chapter is uncertain.

## New International Version

great owl, 18the white owl, the desert owl, the osprey, 19the stork, any kind of heron, the hoopoe and the bat.

20"'All flying insects that walk on all fours are to be regarded as unclean by you. 21There are, however, some flying insects that walk on all fours that you may eat: those that have jointed legs for hopping on the ground. 22Of these you may eat any kind of locust, katydid, cricket or grasshopper. 23But all other flying insects that have four legs you are to regard as unclean.

24"'You will make yourselves unclean by these; whoever touches their carcasses will be unclean till evening. 25Whoever picks up one of their carcasses must wash their clothes, and they will be unclean till evening.

26"'Every animal that does not have a divided hoof or that does not chew the cud is unclean for you; whoever touches the carcass of any of them will be unclean. 27Of all the animals that walk on all fours, those that walk on their paws are unclean for you; whoever touches their carcasses will be unclean till evening. 28Anyone who picks up their carcasses must wash their clothes, and they will be unclean till evening. These animals are unclean for you.

29"'Of the animals that move along the ground, these are unclean for you: the weasel, the rat, any kind of great lizard, 30the gecko, the monitor lizard, the wall lizard, the skink and the chameleon. 31Of all those that move along the ground, these are unclean for you. Whoever touches them when they are dead will be unclean till evening. 32When one of them dies and falls on something, that article, whatever its use, will be unclean, whether it is made of wood, cloth, hide or sackcloth. Put it in water; it will be unclean till evening, and then it will be clean. 33If one of them falls into a clay pot, everything in it will be unclean, and you must break the pot. 34Any food you are allowed to eat that has come into contact with water from any such pot is unclean, and any liquid that is drunk from such a pot is unclean. 35Anything that one of their carcasses falls on becomes unclean; an oven or cooking pot must be broken up. They are unclean, and you are to regard them as unclean. 36A spring, however, or a cistern for collecting water remains clean, but anyone who touches one of these carcasses is unclean. 37If a carcass falls on any seeds that are to be planted, they remain clean. 38But if water has been put on the seed and a carcass falls on it, it is unclean for you.

39"'If an animal that you are allowed to eat dies, anyone who touches its carcass will be unclean till evening. 40Anyone who eats some of its carcass must wash their clothes, and they will be unclean till evening. Anyone who picks up the carcass must wash their clothes, and they will be unclean till evening.

41"'Every creature that moves along the ground is to be regarded as unclean; it is not to be eaten. 42You are not to eat any creature that moves along the ground, whether it moves on its belly or walks on all fours or on many feet; it

## Amplified Bible

18The swan, the pelican, the vulture,
19The stork, all kinds of heron, the hoopoe, and the bat.
20All winged insects that go upon all fours are to be an abomination to you;
21Yet of all winged insects that go upon all fours you may eat those which have legs above their feet with which to leap on the ground.
22Of these you may eat: the whole species of locust, of bald locust, of cricket, and of grasshopper. [Matt. 3:4.]
23But all other winged insects which have four feet shall be detestable to you.
24And by [contact with] these you shall become unclean; whoever touches the carcass of them shall be unclean until the evening,
25And whoever carries any part of their carcass shall wash his clothes and be unclean until the evening.
26Every beast which parts the hoof but is not cloven-footed or does not chew the cud is unclean to you; everyone who touches them shall be unclean.
27And all that go on their paws, among all kinds of four-footed beasts, are unclean to you; whoever touches their carcass shall be unclean until the evening,
28And he who carries their carcass shall wash his clothes and be unclean until the evening; they are unclean to you.
29These also are unclean to you among the creeping things [that multiply greatly] and creep upon the ground: the weasel, the mouse, any kind of great lizard,
30The gecko, the land crocodile, the lizard, the sand lizard, and the chameleon.
31These are unclean to you among all that creep; whoever touches them when they are dead shall be unclean until the evening.
32And upon whatever they may fall when they are dead, it shall be unclean, whether it is an article of wood or clothing or skin (bottle) or sack, any vessel in which work is done; it must be put in water, and it shall be unclean until the evening; so it shall be cleansed.
33And every earthen vessel into which any of these [creeping things] falls, whatever may be in it shall be unclean, and you shall break the vessel.
34Of all the food [in one of these unclean vessels] which may be eaten, that on which such water comes shall be unclean, and all drink that may be drunk from every such vessel shall be unclean.
35And everything upon which any part of their carcass falls shall be unclean; whether an oven, or pan with a lid, or hearth for pots, it shall be broken in pieces; they are unclean, and shall be unclean to you.
36Yet a spring or a cistern or reservoir of water shall be clean; but whoever touches their carcass shall be unclean.
37If a part of their carcass falls on seed which is to be sown, it shall be clean;
38But if any water be put on the seed and any part of their carcass falls on it, it shall be unclean to you.
39If any animal of which you may eat dies [unslaughtered], he who touches its carcass shall be unclean until the evening.
40And he who eats of its carcass [ignorantly] shall wash his clothes, and be unclean until the evening; he also who carries its carcass shall wash his clothes, and be unclean until the evening.
41And everything that creeps on the ground and [multiplies in] swarms shall be an abomination; it shall not be eaten.
42Whatever goes on its belly, and whatever goes on all fours, or whatever has more [than four] feet among all things that creep on the ground and swarm you shall not eat; for they are detestable.

## New International Version

is unclean. 43Do not defile yourselves by any of these creatures. Do not make yourselves unclean by means of them or be made unclean by them. 44I am the LORD your God; consecrate yourselves and be holy, because I am holy. Do not make yourselves unclean by any creature that moves along the ground. 45I am the LORD, who brought you up out of Egypt to be your God; therefore be holy, because I am holy.

46"'These are the regulations concerning animals, birds, every living thing that moves about in the water and every creature that moves along the ground. 47You must distinguish between the unclean and the clean, between living creatures that may be eaten and those that may not be eaten.'"

### Purification After Childbirth

**12** The LORD said to Moses, 2"Say to the Israelites: 'A woman who becomes pregnant and gives birth to a son will be ceremonially unclean for seven days, just as she is unclean during her monthly period. 3On the eighth day the boy is to be circumcised. 4Then the woman must wait thirty-three days to be purified from her bleeding. She must not touch anything sacred or go to the sanctuary until the days of her purification are over. 5If she gives birth to a daughter, for two weeks the woman will be unclean, as during her period. Then she must wait sixty-six days to be purified from her bleeding.

6"When the days of her purification for a son or daughter are over, she is to bring to the priest at the entrance to the tent of meeting a year-old lamb for a burnt offering and a young pigeon or a dove for a sin offering.*a* 7He shall offer them before the LORD to make atonement for her, and then she will be ceremonially clean from her flow of blood.

"'These are the regulations for the woman who gives birth to a boy or a girl. 8But if she cannot afford a lamb, she is to bring two doves or two young pigeons, one for a burnt offering and the other for a sin offering. In this way the priest will make atonement for her, and she will be clean.'"

### Regulations About Defiling Skin Diseases

**13** The LORD said to Moses and Aaron, 2"When anyone has a swelling or a rash or a shiny spot on their skin that may be a defiling skin disease,*b* they must be brought to Aaron the priest or to one of his sons*c* who is a priest. 3The priest is to examine the sore on the skin, and if the hair in the sore has turned white and the sore appears to be more than skin deep, it is a defiling skin disease. When the priest examines that person, he shall pronounce them ceremonially unclean. 4If the shiny spot on the skin is white but does not appear to be more than skin deep and the hair in it has not turned white, the priest is to isolate the affected person for seven days. 5On the seventh day the priest is to examine them, and if he sees that

## Amplified Bible

43You shall not make yourselves loathsome *and* abominable [by eating] any swarming thing that [multiplies by] swarms, neither shall you make yourselves unclean with them, that you should be defiled by them.

44For I am the Lord your God; so consecrate yourselves and be holy, for I am holy; neither defile yourselves with any manner of thing that multiplies in large numbers *or* swarms. [I Thess. 4:7, 8.]

45For I am the Lord Who brought you up out of the land of Egypt to be your God; therefore you shall be holy, for I am holy. [I Pet. 1:14-16.]

46This is the law of the beast, and of the bird, and of every living creature that moves in the waters, and creeps on the earth *and* multiplies in large numbers,

47To make a difference (a distinction) between the unclean and the clean, and between the animal that may be eaten and the animal that may not be eaten.

**12** And the Lord said to Moses,

2Say to the Israelites, If a woman conceives and bears a male child, she shall be unclean seven days, unclean as during her monthly discomfort.

3And on the eighth day the child shall be circumcised.

4Then she shall remain [separated] thirty-three days to be purified [from her loss] of blood; she shall touch no hallowed thing nor come into the [court of the] sanctuary until the days of her purifying are over.

5But if the child she bears is a girl, then she shall be unclean two weeks, as in her periodic impurity, and she shall remain separated sixty-six days to be purified [from her loss] of blood.

6When the days of her purifying are completed, whether for a son or for a daughter, she shall bring a lamb a year old for a burnt offering and a young pigeon or a turtledove for a sin offering to the door of the Tent of Meeting to the priest;

7And he shall offer it before the Lord and make atonement for her, and she shall be cleansed from the flow of her blood. This is the law for her who has borne a male or a female child.

8If she is unable to bring a lamb [for lack of means] then she shall bring two turtledoves or young pigeons, one for a burnt offering, the other for a sin offering; the priest shall make atonement for her, and she shall be clean. [Luke 2:22, 24.]

**13** And the Lord said to Moses and Aaron,

2When a man has a swelling on his skin, a scab, or a bright spot, and it becomes the disease of *a*leprosy in his skin, then he shall be brought to the priest, to Aaron or one of his sons.

3The priest shall look at the diseased spot on his skin, and if the hair in it has turned white and the disease appears depressed *and* deeper than his skin, it is a leprous disease; and the priest shall examine him, and pronounce him unclean.

4If the bright spot is white on his skin, not depressed, and the hair on it not turned white, the priest shall quarantine the person *or* bind up the spot for seven days.

5And the priest shall examine him on the seventh day,

---

*a* 6 Or *purification offering*; also in verse 8    *b* 2 The Hebrew word for *defiling skin disease*, traditionally translated "leprosy," was used for various diseases affecting the skin; here and throughout verses 3-46.    *c* 2 Or *descendants*

*a* Authorities are generally agreed that there certainly was true leprosy as it is known today in the Near East in New Testament times. But from the details of the disease in Lev. 13, it is believed that other very serious skin disorders were also included under the heading of "leprosy" in earlier times. Leprosy in the Old Testament, therefore, is not to be considered as confined to the traits by which it is known today, but rather defined by the symptoms, the treatment, and the history of individual cases as recorded in Leviticus and elsewhere. That it was worse than death is implied by the words of Aaron when his sister Miriam was stricken with it: "Alas, my lord [Moses], . . . Let her not be as one dead, of whom the flesh is half consumed when he cometh out of his mother's womb" (Num. 12:11, 12 KJV).

## New International Version

the sore is unchanged and has not spread in the skin, he is to isolate them for another seven days. [6]On the seventh day the priest is to examine them again, and if the sore has faded and has not spread in the skin, the priest shall pronounce them clean; it is only a rash. They must wash their clothes, and they will be clean. [7]But if the rash does spread in their skin after they have shown themselves to the priest to be pronounced clean, they must appear before the priest again. [8]The priest is to examine that person, and if the rash has spread in the skin, he shall pronounce them unclean; it is a defiling skin disease.

[9]"When anyone has a defiling skin disease, they must be brought to the priest. [10]The priest is to examine them, and if there is a white swelling in the skin that has turned the hair white and if there is raw flesh in the swelling, [11]it is a chronic skin disease and the priest shall pronounce them unclean. He is not to isolate them, because they are already unclean.

[12]"If the disease breaks out all over their skin and, so far as the priest can see, it covers all the skin of the affected person from head to foot, [13]the priest is to examine them, and if the disease has covered their whole body, he shall pronounce them clean. Since it has all turned white, they are clean. [14]But whenever raw flesh appears on them, they will be unclean. [15]When the priest sees the raw flesh, he shall pronounce them unclean. The raw flesh is unclean; they have a defiling disease. [16]If the raw flesh changes and turns white, they must go to the priest. [17]The priest is to examine them, and if the sores have turned white, the priest shall pronounce the affected person clean; then they will be clean.

[18]"When someone has a boil on their skin and it heals, [19]and in the place where the boil was, a white swelling or reddish-white spot appears, they must present themselves to the priest. [20]The priest is to examine it, and if it appears to be more than skin deep and the hair in it has turned white, the priest shall pronounce that person unclean. It is a defiling skin disease that has broken out where the boil was. [21]But if, when the priest examines it, there is no white hair in it and it is not more than skin deep and has faded, then the priest is to isolate them for seven days. [22]If it is spreading in the skin, the priest shall pronounce them unclean; it is a defiling disease. [23]But if the spot is unchanged and has not spread, it is only a scar from the boil, and the priest shall pronounce them clean.

[24]"When someone has a burn on their skin and a reddish-white or white spot appears in the raw flesh of the burn, [25]the priest is to examine the spot, and if the hair in it has turned white, and it appears to be more than skin deep, it is a defiling disease that has broken out in the burn. The priest shall pronounce them unclean; it is a defiling skin disease. [26]But if the priest examines it and there is no white hair in the spot and if it is not more than skin deep and has faded, then the priest is to isolate them for seven days. [27]On the seventh day the priest is to examine that person, and if it is spreading in the skin, the priest shall pronounce them unclean; it is a defiling skin disease. [28]If, however, the spot is unchanged and has not

## Amplified Bible

and if the disease in his estimation is at a standstill *and* has not spread in the skin, then the priest shall quarantine the person *or* bind up the spot seven more days.

[6]And the priest shall examine him again the seventh day, and if the diseased part has a more normal color and the disease has not spread in the skin, the priest shall pronounce him clean; it is only an eruption *or* a scab; and he shall wash his clothes and be clean.

[7]But if the eruption *or* scab spreads farther in the skin after he has shown himself to the priest for his cleansing, he shall be seen by the priest again.

[8]If the priest sees that the eruption *or* scab is spreading in the skin, then he shall pronounce him unclean; it is leprosy.

[9]When the disease of leprosy is in a man, he shall be brought to the priest;

[10]And the priest shall examine him, and if there is a white swelling in the skin and the hair on it has turned white and there is quick raw flesh in the swelling,

[11]It is a chronic leprosy in the skin of his body, and the priest shall pronounce him unclean; he shall not bind the spot up, for he is unclean.

[12]But if [supposed] leprosy breaks out in the skin, and it covers all the skin of him who has the disease from head to foot, wherever the priest looks,

[13]The priest shall examine him; if the [supposed] leprosy covers all his body, he shall pronounce him clean of the disease; it is all turned white, and he is clean.

[14]But when the raw flesh appears on him, he shall be unclean.

[15]And the priest shall examine the raw flesh and pronounce him unclean; for the raw flesh is unclean; it is leprosy.

[16]But if the raw flesh turns again and becomes white, he shall come to the priest,

[17]And the priest shall examine him, and if the diseased part is turned to white again, then the priest shall pronounce him clean who had the disease; he is clean.

[18]And when there is in the skin of the body [the scar of] a boil that is healed,

[19]And in the place of the boil there is a white swelling or a bright spot, reddish white, and it is shown to the priest,

[20]And if when the priest examines it it looks lower than the skin and the hair on it is turned white, the priest shall pronounce him unclean; it is the disease of leprosy; it has broken out in the boil.

[21]But if the priest examines it and finds no white hair in it and it is not lower than the skin but appears darker, then the priest shall bind it up for seven days.

[22]If it spreads in the skin, [he] shall pronounce him unclean; it is diseased.

[23]But if the bright spot does not spread, it is the scar of the boil, and the priest shall pronounce him clean.

[24]Or if there is any flesh in the skin of which there is a burn by fire and the quick flesh of the burn becomes a bright spot, reddish white or white,

[25]Then the priest shall examine it, and if the hair in the bright spot is turned white, and it appears deeper than the skin, it is leprosy broken out in the burn. Therefore the priest shall pronounce him unclean; it is the disease of leprosy.

[26]But if the priest examines it and there is no white hair in the bright spot and it is not lower than the rest of the skin but is darker, then the priest shall bind it up for seven days.

[27]And the priest shall examine him on the seventh day; if it is spreading in the skin, then the priest shall pronounce him unclean; it is leprosy.

[28]But if the bright spot has not spread but is darker, it is

## New International Version

spread in the skin but has faded, it is a swelling from the burn, and the priest shall pronounce them clean; it is only a scar from the burn.

29"If a man or woman has a sore on their head or chin, 30the priest is to examine the sore, and if it appears to be more than skin deep and the hair in it is yellow and thin, the priest shall pronounce them unclean; it is a defiling skin disease on the head or chin. 31But if, when the priest examines the sore, it does not seem to be more than skin deep and there is no black hair in it, then the priest is to isolate the affected person for seven days. 32On the seventh day the priest is to examine the sore, and if it has not spread and there is no yellow hair in it and it does not appear to be more than skin deep, 33then the man or woman must shave themselves, except for the affected area, and the priest is to keep them isolated another seven days. 34On the seventh day the priest is to examine the sore, and if it has not spread in the skin and appears to be no more than skin deep, the priest shall pronounce them clean. They must wash their clothes, and they will be clean. 35But if the sore does spread in the skin after they are pronounced clean, 36the priest is to examine them, and if he finds that the sore has spread in the skin, he does not need to look for yellow hair; they are unclean. 37If, however, the sore is unchanged so far as the priest can see, and if black hair has grown in it, the affected person is healed. They are clean, and the priest shall pronounce them clean.

38"When a man or woman has white spots on the skin, 39the priest is to examine them, and if the spots are dull white, it is a harmless rash that has broken out on the skin; they are clean.

40"A man who has lost his hair and is bald is clean. 41If he has lost his hair from the front of his scalp and has a bald forehead, he is clean. 42But if he has a reddish-white sore on his bald head or forehead, it is a defiling disease breaking out on his head or forehead. 43The priest is to examine him, and if the swollen sore on his head or forehead is reddish-white like a defiling skin disease, 44the man is diseased and is unclean. The priest shall pronounce him unclean because of the sore on his head.

45"Anyone with such a defiling disease must wear torn clothes, let their hair be unkempt,*a* cover the lower part of their face and cry out, 'Unclean! Unclean!' 46As long as they have the disease they remain unclean. They must live alone; they must live outside the camp.

### Regulations About Defiling Molds

47"As for any fabric that is spoiled with a defiling mold—any woolen or linen clothing, 48any woven or knitted material of linen or wool, any leather or anything made of leather— 49if the affected area in the fabric, the leather, the woven or knitted material, or any leather article, is greenish or reddish, it is a defiling mold and must be shown to the priest. 50The priest is to examine the affected area and isolate the article for seven days. 51On the seventh day he is to examine it, and if the mold has spread in the fabric, the woven or knitted material, or the leather, whatever its use, it is a persistent defiling mold; the article

## Amplified Bible

a swelling from the burn, and the priest shall pronounce him clean; for it is the scar of the burn.

29When a man or woman has a disease upon the head or in the beard,

30The priest shall examine the diseased place; if it appears to be deeper than the skin, with yellow, thin hair in it, the priest shall pronounce him unclean; it is a mangelike leprosy of the head or beard.

31If the priest examines the spot infected by the mangelike disease, and it does not appear deeper than the skin and there is no black hair in it, the priest shall bind up the spot for seven days.

32On the seventh day the priest shall examine the diseased spot; if the mange has not spread and has no yellow hair in it and does not look deeper than the skin,

33Then the patient shall be shaved, except the mangelike spot; and the priest shall bind up the spot seven days more.

34On the seventh day the priest shall look at the mangelike spot; if the mange has not spread and looks no deeper than the skin, he shall pronounce the patient clean; he shall wash his clothes and be clean.

35But if the mangelike spot spreads in the skin after his cleansing,

36Then the priest shall examine him, and if the mangelike spot is spread in the skin, the priest need not look for the yellow hair; the patient is unclean.

37But if in his estimation the mange is at a standstill and has black hair in it, the mangelike disease is healed; he is clean; the priest shall pronounce him clean.

38When a man or a woman has on the skin bright spots, even white bright spots,

39Then the priest shall look, and if the bright spots in the skin are a dull white, it is a harmless eruption; he is clean.

40If a man's hair has fallen from his head, he is bald, but he is clean.

41And if his hair has fallen out from the front of his head, he has baldness of the forehead, but he is clean.

42But if there is on the bald head or forehead a reddish white diseased spot, it is leprosy breaking out on his baldness.

43Then the priest shall examine him, and if the diseased swelling is reddish white on his bald head or forehead like the appearance of leprosy in the skin of the body,

44He is a leprous man; he is unclean; the priest shall surely pronounce him unclean; his disease is on his head.

45And the leper's clothes shall be rent, and the hair of his head shall hang loose, and he shall cover his upper lip and cry, Unclean, unclean!

46He shall remain unclean as long as the disease is in him; he is unclean; he shall live alone [and] his dwelling shall be outside the camp.

47The garment also that the disease of leprosy [symbolic of sin] is in, whether a wool or a linen garment, [Jude 23; Rev. 3:4.]

48Whether it be in woven or knitted stuff *or* in the warp or woof of linen or of wool, or in a skin or anything made of skin,

49If the disease is greenish or reddish in the garment, or in a skin or in the warp or woof or in anything made of skin, it is the plague of leprosy; show it to the priest.

50The priest shall examine the diseased article and shut it up for seven days.

51He shall examine the disease on the seventh day; if [it] is spread in the garment, or in the article, whatever service it may be used for, the disease is a rotting *or* corroding leprosy; it is unclean.

---

*a* 45 Or *clothes, uncover their head*

## New International Version

is unclean. [52] He must burn the fabric, the woven or knitted material of wool or linen, or any leather article that has been spoiled; because the defiling mold is persistent, the article must be burned.

[53] "But if, when the priest examines it, the mold has not spread in the fabric, the woven or knitted material, or the leather article, [54] he shall order that the spoiled article be washed. Then he is to isolate it for another seven days. [55] After the article has been washed, the priest is to examine it again, and if the mold has not changed its appearance, even though it has not spread, it is unclean. Burn it, no matter which side of the fabric has been spoiled. [56] If, when the priest examines it, the mold has faded after the article has been washed, he is to tear the spoiled part out of the fabric, the leather, or the woven or knitted material. [57] But if it reappears in the fabric, in the woven or knitted material, or in the leather article, it is a spreading mold; whatever has the mold must be burned. [58] Any fabric, woven or knitted material, or any leather article that has been washed and is rid of the mold, must be washed again. Then it will be clean."

[59] These are the regulations concerning defiling molds in woolen or linen clothing, woven or knitted material, or any leather article, for pronouncing them clean or unclean.

### Cleansing From Defiling Skin Diseases

**14** The LORD said to Moses, [2] "These are the regulations for any diseased person at the time of their ceremonial cleansing, when they are brought to the priest: [3] The priest is to go outside the camp and examine them. If they have been healed of their defiling skin disease,[a] [4] the priest shall order that two live clean birds and some cedar wood, scarlet yarn and hyssop be brought for the person to be cleansed. [5] Then the priest shall order that one of the birds be killed over fresh water in a clay pot. [6] He is then to take the live bird and dip it, together with the cedar wood, the scarlet yarn and the hyssop, into the blood of the bird that was killed over the fresh water. [7] Seven times he shall sprinkle the one to be cleansed of the defiling disease, and then pronounce them clean. After that, he is to release the live bird in the open fields.

[8] "The person to be cleansed must wash their clothes, shave off all their hair and bathe with water; then they will be ceremonially clean. After this they may come into the camp, but they must stay outside their tent for seven days. [9] On the seventh day they must shave off all their hair; they must shave their head, their beard, their eyebrows and the rest of their hair. They must wash their clothes and bathe themselves with water, and they will be clean.

[10] "On the eighth day they must bring two male lambs and one ewe lamb a year old, each without defect, along with three-tenths of an ephah[b] of the finest flour mixed with olive oil for a grain offering, and one log[c] of oil. [11] The priest who pronounces them clean shall present both the one to be cleansed and their offerings before the LORD at the entrance to the tent of meeting.

[12] "Then the priest is to take one of the male lambs and offer it as a guilt offering, along with the log of oil; he shall wave them before the LORD as a wave offering. [13] He is to slaughter the lamb in the sanctuary area where the sin offering[d] and the burnt offering are slaughtered. Like the

---

[a] 3 The Hebrew word for *defiling skin disease*, traditionally translated "leprosy," was used for various diseases affecting the skin; also in verses 7, 32, 54 and 57.   [b] 10 That is, probably about 11 pounds or about 5 kilograms   [c] 10 That is, about 1/3 quart or about 0.3 liter; also in verses 12, 15, 21 and 24   [d] 13 Or *purification offering*; also in verses 19, 22 and 31

## Amplified Bible

[52] He shall burn the garment, whether diseased in warp or woof, in wool or linen, or anything made of skin; for it is a rotting *or* corroding leprosy, to be burned in the fire.

[53] But if the priest finds the disease has not spread in the garment, in the warp or the woof, or in anything made of skin,

[54] Then the priest shall command that they wash the thing in which the plague is, and he shall shut it up seven days more.

[55] And the priest shall examine the diseased article after it has been washed, and if the diseased portion has not changed color, though the disease has not spread, it is unclean; you shall burn it in the fire; it is a rotting *or* corroding [disease], whether the leprous spot be inside or outside.

[56] If the priest looks and the diseased portion is less noticeable after it is washed, he shall tear it out of the garment, or the skin (leather), or out of the warp or woof.

[57] If it appears still in the garment, either in the warp or in the woof, or in anything made of skin, it is spreading; you shall burn the diseased part with fire.

[58] But the garment, or the woven or knitted stuff *or* warp or woof, or anything made of skin from which the disease departs when you have washed it, shall then be washed a second time, and be clean.

[59] This is the law for a leprous disease in a garment of wool or linen, either in the warp or woof, or in anything made of skin, to pronounce it clean or unclean.

**14** And the Lord said to Moses, [2] This shall be the law of the leper on the day when he is to be pronounced clean: he shall be brought to the priest [at a meeting place outside the camp];

[3] The priest shall go out of the camp [to meet him]; and [he] shall examine him, and if the disease is healed in the leper,

[4] Then the priest shall command to take for him who is to be cleansed two living clean birds and cedar wood and scarlet [material] and hyssop. [Heb. 9:19-22.]

[5] And the priest shall command to kill one of the birds in an earthen vessel over fresh, running water.

[6] As for the living bird, he shall take it, the cedar wood, and the scarlet [material], and the hyssop, and shall dip them and the living bird in the blood of the bird killed over the running water;

[7] And he shall sprinkle [the blood] on him who is to be cleansed from the leprosy seven times and shall pronounce him clean, and shall let go the living bird into the open field. [Heb. 9:13-15.]

[8] He who is to be cleansed shall wash his clothes, shave off all his hair, and bathe himself in water; and he shall be clean. After that he shall come into the camp, but stay outside his tent seven days.

[9] But on the seventh day he shall shave all his hair off his head, his beard, his eyebrows, and his [body]; and he shall wash his clothes and bathe his body in water, and be clean.

[10] On the eighth day he shall take two he-lambs without blemish and one ewe lamb a year old without blemish, and three-tenths of an ephah of fine flour for a cereal offering, mixed with oil, and one log of oil.

[11] And the priest who cleanses him shall set the man who is to be cleansed and these things before the Lord at the door of the Tent of Meeting;

[12] The priest shall take one of the male lambs and offer it for a guilt *or* trespass offering, and the log of oil, and wave them for a wave offering before the Lord.

[13] He shall kill the lamb in the place where they kill the sin offering and the burnt offering, in the sacred place

## New International Version

sin offering, the guilt offering belongs to the priest; it is most holy. [14]The priest is to take some of the blood of the guilt offering and put it on the lobe of the right ear of the one to be cleansed, on the thumb of their right hand and on the big toe of their right foot. [15]The priest shall then take some of the log of oil, pour it in the palm of his own left hand, [16]dip his right forefinger into the oil in his palm, and with his finger sprinkle some of it before the LORD seven times. [17]The priest is to put some of the oil remaining in his palm on the lobe of the right ear of the one to be cleansed, on the thumb of their right hand and on the big toe of their right foot, on top of the blood of the guilt offering. [18]The rest of the oil in his palm the priest shall put on the head of the one to be cleansed and make atonement for them before the LORD.

[19]"Then the priest is to sacrifice the sin offering and make atonement for the one to be cleansed from their uncleanness. After that, the priest shall slaughter the burnt offering [20]and offer it on the altar, together with the grain offering, and make atonement for them, and they will be clean. [21]"If, however, they are poor and cannot afford these, they must take one male lamb as a guilt offering to be waved to make atonement for them, together with a tenth of an ephah[a] of the finest flour mixed with olive oil for a grain offering, a log of oil, [22]and two doves or two young pigeons, such as they can afford, one for a sin offering and the other for a burnt offering.

[23]"On the eighth day they must bring them for their cleansing to the priest at the entrance to the tent of meeting, before the LORD. [24]The priest is to take the lamb for the guilt offering, together with the log of oil, and wave them before the LORD as a wave offering. [25]He shall slaughter the lamb for the guilt offering and take some of its blood and put it on the lobe of the right ear of the one to be cleansed, on the thumb of their right hand and on the big toe of their right foot. [26]The priest is to pour some of the oil into the palm of his own left hand, [27]and with his right forefinger sprinkle some of the oil from his palm seven times before the LORD. [28]Some of the oil in his palm he is to put on the same places he put the blood of the guilt offering—on the lobe of the right ear of the one to be cleansed, on the thumb of their right hand and on the big toe of their right foot. [29]The rest of the oil in his palm the priest shall put on the head of the one to be cleansed, to make atonement for them before the LORD. [30]Then he shall sacrifice the doves or the young pigeons, such as the person can afford, [31]one as a sin offering and the other as a burnt offering, together with the grain offering. In this way the priest will make atonement before the LORD on behalf of the one to be cleansed."

[32]These are the regulations for anyone who has a defiling skin disease and who cannot afford the regular offerings for their cleansing.

### Cleansing From Defiling Molds

[33]The LORD said to Moses and Aaron, [34]"When you enter the land of Canaan, which I am giving you as your possession, and I put a spreading mold in a house in that

## Amplified Bible

[the court of the tabernacle]; for as the sin offering is the priest's, so is the guilt or trespass offering; it is most holy; [14]And the priest shall take some of the blood of the guilt or trespass offering and put it on the tip of the right ear of him who is to be cleansed, and on the thumb of his right hand, and on the great toe of his right foot. [15]And the priest shall take some of the log of oil and pour it into the palm of his own left hand; [16]And the priest shall dip his right finger in the oil that is in his left hand and shall sprinkle some of the oil with his finger seven times before the Lord; [17]And of the rest of the oil that is in his hand shall the priest put some on the tip of the right ear of him who is to be cleansed, and on the thumb of his right hand, and on the great toe of his right foot, on the blood of the guilt or trespass offering [which he has previously placed in each of these places]. [18]And the rest of the oil that is in the priest's hand he shall pour upon the head of him who is to be cleansed and make atonement for him before the Lord.

[19]And the priest shall offer the sin offering and make atonement for him who is to be cleansed from his uncleanness, and afterward kill the burnt offering [victim]. [20]And the priest shall offer the burnt offering and the cereal offering on the altar; and he shall make atonement for him, and he shall be clean. [21]If the cleansed leper is poor and cannot afford so much, he shall take one lamb for a guilt or trespass offering to be waved to make atonement for him, and one tenth of an ephah of fine flour mixed with oil for a cereal offering, and a log of oil, [22]And two turtledoves or two young pigeons, such as he can afford, one for a sin offering, the other for a burnt offering.

[23]He shall bring them on the eighth day for his cleansing to the priest at the door of the Tent of Meeting, before the Lord. [24]And the priest shall take the lamb of the guilt or trespass offering, and the log of oil, and shall wave them for a wave offering before the Lord. [25]And he shall kill the lamb of the guilt or trespass offering, and the priest shall take some of the blood of the offering and put it on the tip of the right ear of him who is to be cleansed, and on the thumb of his right hand, and on the great toe of his right foot. [26]And the priest shall pour some of the oil into the palm of his own left hand, [27]And shall sprinkle with his right finger some of the oil that is in his left hand seven times before the Lord. [28]The priest shall put some of the oil in his hand on the tip of the right ear of the one to be cleansed, and on the thumb of his right hand, and on the great toe of his right foot, on the places where he has put the blood of the guilt offering. [29]The rest of the oil that is in the priest's hand he shall put on the head of the one to be cleansed, to make atonement for him before the Lord. [30]And he shall offer one of the turtledoves or of the young pigeons, such as he is able to get, [31]As he can afford, one for a sin offering and the other for a burnt offering, together with the cereal offering; and the priest shall make atonement for him who is to be cleansed before the Lord. [32]This is the law of him in whom is the plague of leprosy, who is not able to get what is required for his cleansing. [33]And the Lord said to Moses and Aaron, [34]When you have come into the land of Canaan, which I give to you for a possession, and I put the disease of leprosy in a house of the land of your possession,

## New International Version

land, ³⁵the owner of the house must go and tell the priest, 'I have seen something that looks like a defiling mold in my house.' ³⁶The priest is to order the house to be emptied before he goes in to examine the mold, so that nothing in the house will be pronounced unclean. After this the priest is to go in and inspect the house. ³⁷He is to examine the mold on the walls, and if it has greenish or reddish depressions that appear to be deeper than the surface of the wall, ³⁸the priest shall go out the doorway of the house and close it up for seven days. ³⁹On the seventh day the priest shall return to inspect the house. If the mold has spread on the walls, ⁴⁰he is to order that the contaminated stones be torn out and thrown into an unclean place outside the town. ⁴¹He must have all the inside walls of the house scraped and the material that is scraped off dumped into an unclean place outside the town. ⁴²Then they are to take other stones to replace these and take new clay and plaster the house.

⁴³"If the defiling mold reappears in the house after the stones have been torn out and the house scraped and plastered, ⁴⁴the priest is to go and examine it and, if the mold has spread in the house, it is a persistent defiling mold; the house is unclean. ⁴⁵It must be torn down—its stones, timbers and all the plaster—and taken out of the town to an unclean place.

⁴⁶"Anyone who goes into the house while it is closed up will be unclean till evening. ⁴⁷Anyone who sleeps or eats in the house must wash their clothes.

⁴⁸"But if the priest comes to examine it and the mold has not spread after the house has been plastered, he shall pronounce the house clean, because the defiling mold is gone. ⁴⁹To purify the house he is to take two birds and some cedar wood, scarlet yarn and hyssop. ⁵⁰He shall kill one of the birds over fresh water in a clay pot. ⁵¹Then he is to take the cedar wood, the hyssop, the scarlet yarn and the live bird, dip them into the blood of the dead bird and the fresh water, and sprinkle the house seven times. ⁵²He shall purify the house with the bird's blood, the fresh water, the live bird, the cedar wood, the hyssop and the scarlet yarn. ⁵³Then he is to release the live bird in the open fields outside the town. In this way he will make atonement for the house, and it will be clean."

⁵⁴These are the regulations for any defiling skin disease, for a sore, ⁵⁵for defiling molds in a house, ⁵⁶and for a swelling, a rash or a shiny spot, ⁵⁷to determine when something is clean or unclean.

These are the regulations for defiling skin diseases and defiling molds.

## Amplified Bible

³⁵Then he who owns the house shall come and tell the priest, It seems to me there is some sort of disease in my house.

³⁶Then the priest shall command that they empty the house before [he] goes in to examine the disease, so that all that is in the house may not be declared unclean; afterward [he] shall go in to see the house.

³⁷He shall examine the disease, and if it is in the walls of the house with depressed spots of dark green or dark red appearing beneath [the surface of] the wall,

³⁸Then the priest shall go out of the door and shut up the house seven days.

³⁹The priest shall come again on the seventh day and shall look; and if the disease has spread in the walls of the house,

⁴⁰He shall command that they take out the diseased stones and cast them into an unclean place outside the city.

⁴¹He shall cause the house to be scraped within round about and the plaster or mortar that is scraped off to be emptied out in an unclean place outside the city.

⁴²And they shall put other stones in the place of those stones, and he shall plaster the house with fresh mortar.

⁴³If the disease returns, breaking out in the house after he has removed the stones and has scraped and plastered the house,

⁴⁴Then the priest shall come and look, and if the disease is spreading in the house, it is a rotting or corroding leprosy in the house; it is unclean.

⁴⁵He shall tear down the house—its stones and its timber and all the plaster or mortar of the house—and shall carry them forth out of the city to an unclean place.

⁴⁶Moreover, he who enters the house during the whole time that it is shut up shall be unclean until the evening.

⁴⁷And he who lies down or eats in the house shall wash his clothes.

⁴⁸But if the priest inspects it and the disease has not spread after the house was plastered, he shall pronounce the house clean, because the disease is healed.

⁴⁹He shall take to cleanse the house two birds, cedar wood, scarlet [material], and hyssop;

⁵⁰And he shall kill one of the birds in an earthen vessel over running water,

⁵¹And he shall take the cedar wood, and the hyssop, and the scarlet [material], and the living bird, and dip them in the blood of the slain bird and in the running water, and sprinkle the house seven times.

⁵²And he shall cleanse the house with the blood of the bird, the running water, the living bird, the cedar wood, the hyssop, and the scarlet [material].

⁵³But he shall let the living bird go out of the city into the open field; so he shall make atonement for the house, and it shall be clean.

⁵⁴This is the law for all kinds of leprous diseases, and mangelike conditions,

⁵⁵For the leprosy of a garment or of a house,

⁵⁶And for a swelling or an eruption or a scab or a bright spot,

⁵⁷To teach when it is unclean and when it is clean. This is the law of leprosy.

### Discharges Causing Uncleanness

**15** The LORD said to Moses and Aaron, ²"Speak to the Israelites and say to them: 'When any man has an unusual bodily discharge, such a discharge is unclean.

**15** And the Lord said to Moses and Aaron, ²Say to the Israelites, When any man has a running discharge from his body, because of his discharge he is unclean.

## New International Version

³Whether it continues flowing from his body or is blocked, it will make him unclean. This is how his discharge will bring about uncleanness:

⁴"'Any bed the man with a discharge lies on will be unclean, and anything he sits on will be unclean. ⁵Anyone who touches his bed must wash their clothes and bathe with water, and they will be unclean till evening. ⁶Whoever sits on anything that the man with a discharge sat on must wash their clothes and bathe with water, and they will be unclean till evening.

⁷"'Whoever touches the man who has a discharge must wash their clothes and bathe with water, and they will be unclean till evening.

⁸"'If the man with the discharge spits on anyone who is clean, they must wash their clothes and bathe with water, and they will be unclean till evening.

⁹"'Everything the man sits on when riding will be unclean, ¹⁰and whoever touches any of the things that were under him will be unclean till evening; whoever picks up those things must wash their clothes and bathe with water, and they will be unclean till evening.

¹¹"'Anyone the man with a discharge touches without rinsing his hands with water must wash their clothes and bathe with water, and they will be unclean till evening.

¹²"'A clay pot that the man touches must be broken, and any wooden article is to be rinsed with water.

¹³"'When a man is cleansed from his discharge, he is to count off seven days for his ceremonial cleansing; he must wash his clothes and bathe himself with fresh water, and he will be clean. ¹⁴On the eighth day he must take two doves or two young pigeons and come before the LORD to the entrance to the tent of meeting and give them to the priest. ¹⁵The priest is to sacrifice them, the one for a sin offering*ᵃ* and the other for a burnt offering. In this way he will make atonement before the LORD for the man because of his discharge.

¹⁶"'When a man has an emission of semen, he must bathe his whole body with water, and he will be unclean till evening. ¹⁷Any clothing or leather that has semen on it must be washed with water, and it will be unclean till evening. ¹⁸When a man has sexual relations with a woman and there is an emission of semen, both of them must bathe with water, and they will be unclean till evening.

¹⁹"'When a woman has her regular flow of blood, the impurity of her monthly period will last seven days, and anyone who touches her will be unclean till evening.

²⁰"'Anything she lies on during her period will be unclean, and anything she sits on will be unclean. ²¹Anyone who touches her bed will be unclean; they must wash their clothes and bathe with water, and they will be unclean till evening. ²²Anyone who touches anything she sits on will be unclean; they must wash their clothes and bathe with water, and they will be unclean till evening. ²³Whether it is the bed or anything she was sitting on, when anyone touches it, they will be unclean till evening.

²⁴"'If a man has sexual relations with her and her monthly flow touches him, he will be unclean for seven days; any bed he lies on will be unclean.

²⁵"'When a woman has a discharge of blood for many

## Amplified Bible

³This shall be [the law concerning] his uncleanness in his discharge: whether his body runs with his discharge or has stopped [running], it is uncleanness in him.

⁴Every bed on which the one who has the discharge lies is unclean, and everything on which he sits shall be unclean.

⁵Whoever touches that person's bed shall wash his clothes, and bathe himself in water, and be unclean until the evening.

⁶And whoever sits on anything on which he who has the discharge has sat shall wash his clothes and bathe himself in water, and be unclean until the evening.

⁷And he who touches the flesh of him who has the discharge shall wash his clothes and bathe himself in water, and be unclean until the evening.

⁸And if he who has the discharge spits on him who is clean, then he shall wash his clothes and bathe himself in water, and be unclean until the evening.

⁹And any saddle on which he who has the discharge rides shall be unclean.

¹⁰Whoever touches anything that has been under him shall be unclean until evening; and he who carries those things shall wash his clothes and bathe himself in water, and be unclean until evening.

¹¹Whomever he who has the discharge touches without rinsing his hands in water shall wash his clothes and bathe himself in water, and be unclean until evening.

¹²The earthen vessel that he with the discharge touches shall be broken, and every vessel of wood shall be rinsed in water.

¹³When he who has a discharge is cleansed of it, he shall count seven days for his purification, then wash his clothes, bathe in running water, and be clean.

¹⁴On the eighth day he shall take two turtledoves or two young pigeons and come before the Lord to the door of the Tent of Meeting and give them to the priest;

¹⁵And the priest shall offer them, one for a sin offering and the other for a burnt offering; and [he] shall make atonement for the man before the Lord for his discharge.

¹⁶And if any man has a discharge of semen, he shall wash all his body in water, and be unclean until evening.

¹⁷And every garment and every skin on which the sperm comes shall be washed with water, and be unclean until evening.

¹⁸The woman also with whom a man with emission of semen shall lie, they shall both bathe themselves in water, and be unclean until evening.

¹⁹And if a woman has a discharge, her [regular] discharge of blood of her body, she shall be in her impurity *or* separation for seven days, and whoever touches her shall be unclean until evening.

²⁰And everything that she lies on in her separation shall be unclean; everything also that she sits on shall be unclean.

²¹And whoever touches her bed shall wash his clothes and bathe himself in water, and be unclean until evening.

²²Whoever touches anything she sat on shall wash his clothes and bathe himself in water, and be unclean until evening.

²³And if her flow has stained her bed or anything on which she sat, when he touches it, he shall be unclean until evening.

²⁴And if any man lie with her and her impurity be upon him, he shall be unclean seven days; and every bed on which he lies shall be unclean.

²⁵And if a woman has an issue of blood for many days,

---

*ᵃ 15* Or *purification offering*; also in verse 30

## New International Version

days at a time other than her monthly period or has a discharge that continues beyond her period, she will be unclean as long as she has the discharge, just as in the days of her period. 26 Any bed she lies on while her discharge continues will be unclean, as is her bed during her monthly period, and anything she sits on will be unclean, as during her period. 27 Anyone who touches them will be unclean; they must wash their clothes and bathe with water, and they will be unclean till evening.

28 "When she is cleansed from her discharge, she must count off seven days, and after that she will be ceremonially clean. 29 On the eighth day she must take two doves or two young pigeons and bring them to the priest at the entrance to the tent of meeting. 30 The priest is to sacrifice one for a sin offering and the other for a burnt offering. In this way he will make atonement for her before the LORD for the uncleanness of her discharge.

31 "You must keep the Israelites separate from things that make them unclean, so they will not die in their uncleanness for defiling my dwelling place,*a* which is among them.'"

32 These are the regulations for a man with a discharge, for anyone made unclean by an emission of semen, 33 for a woman in her monthly period, for a man or a woman with a discharge, and for a man who has sexual relations with a woman who is ceremonially unclean.

### The Day of Atonement

**16** The LORD spoke to Moses after the death of the two sons of Aaron who died when they approached the LORD. 2 The LORD said to Moses: "Tell your brother Aaron that he is not to come whenever he chooses into the Most Holy Place behind the curtain in front of the atonement cover on the ark, or else he will die. For I will appear in the cloud over the atonement cover.

3 "This is how Aaron is to enter the Most Holy Place: He must first bring a young bull for a sin offering*b* and a ram for a burnt offering. 4 He is to put on the sacred linen tunic, with linen undergarments next to his body; he is to tie the linen sash around him and put on the linen turban. These are sacred garments; so he must bathe himself with water before he puts them on. 5 From the Israelite community he is to take two male goats for a sin offering and a ram for a burnt offering.

6 "Aaron is to offer the bull for his own sin offering to make atonement for himself and his household. 7 Then he is to take the two goats and present them before the LORD at the entrance to the tent of meeting. 8 He is to cast lots for the two goats—one lot for the LORD and the other for the

## Amplified Bible

not during the time of her separation, or if she has a discharge beyond the time of her [regular] impurity, all the days of the issue of her uncleanness she shall be as in the days of her impurity; she shall be unclean. [Matt. 9:20.]

26 Every bed on which she lies all the days of her discharge shall be as the bed of her impurity, and whatever she sits on shall be unclean, as in her impurity.

27 And whoever touches those things shall be unclean, and shall wash his clothes and bathe himself in water, and be unclean until evening.

28 But if she is cleansed of her discharge, then she shall wait seven days, and after that she shall be clean.

29 And on the eighth day she shall take two turtledoves or two young pigeons and bring them to the priest at the door of the Tent of Meeting;

30 He shall offer one for a sin offering and the other for a burnt offering; and he shall make atonement for her before the Lord for her unclean discharge.

31 Thus you shall separate the Israelites from their uncleanness, lest they die in their uncleanness by defiling My tabernacle that is in the midst of them.

32 This is the law for him who has a discharge and for him who has emissions of sperm, being made unclean by it;

33 And for her who is sick with her impurity, and for any person who has a discharge, whether man or woman, and for him who lies with her who is unclean.

**16** After the death of Aaron's two sons, when they drew near before the Lord [offered false fire] and died, [Lev. 10:1, 2.]

2 The Lord said to Moses, Tell Aaron your brother he *a* must not come at all times into the Holy of Holies within the veil before the mercy seat upon the ark, lest he die; for I will appear in the cloud on the mercy seat. [Heb. 9:7-15, 25-28.]

3 But Aaron shall come into the holy enclosure in this way: with a young bull for a sin offering and a ram for a burnt offering.

4 He shall put on the holy linen undergarment, and he shall have the linen breeches upon his body, and be girded with the linen girdle *or* sash, and with the linen turban *or* miter shall he be attired; these are the holy garments; he shall bathe his body in water and then put them on.

5 He shall take [at the expense] of the congregation of the Israelites two male goats for a sin offering and one ram for a burnt offering.

6 And Aaron shall present the bull as the sin offering for himself and make atonement for himself and for his house [the other priests].

7 He shall take the two goats and present them before the Lord at the door of the Tent of Meeting.

8 Aaron shall cast lots on the two goats—one lot for the Lord, the other lot for Azazel *or* removal.

*a* Since the priests have been warned by the death of Nadab and Abihu to approach God with reverence and godly fear, directions are here given how the nearest approach might be made ... Within the veil none must ever come but the high priest only, and he but one day in the year. But see what a blessed change is made by the Gospel of Christ; all good Christians now have boldness to enter into the Holy of Holies, through the veil, every day (Heb. 10:19, 20); and we come **boldly** (not as Aaron must, with fear and trembling) to the throne of grace, or mercy seat (Heb. 4:16) ... Now therefore we are welcome to come at all times into the Holy Place "not made with hands." In the past Aaron could not come near "at all times," lest he die; we now must come near "at all times," that we may live. It is [keeping our] distance only that is our death (Matthew Henry, *A Commentary*).

## New International Version

scapegoat.*a* ⁹Aaron shall bring the goat whose lot falls to the LORD and sacrifice it for a sin offering. ¹⁰But the goat chosen by lot as the scapegoat shall be presented alive before the LORD to be used for making atonement by sending it into the wilderness as a scapegoat.

¹¹"Aaron shall bring the bull for his own sin offering to make atonement for himself and his household, and he is to slaughter the bull for his own sin offering. ¹²He is to take a censer full of burning coals from the altar before the LORD and two handfuls of finely ground fragrant incense and take them behind the curtain. ¹³He is to put the incense on the fire before the LORD, and the smoke of the incense will conceal the atonement cover above the tablets of the covenant law, so that he will not die. ¹⁴He is to take some of the bull's blood and with his finger sprinkle it on the front of the atonement cover; then he shall sprinkle some of it with his finger seven times before the atonement cover.

¹⁵"He shall then slaughter the goat for the sin offering for the people and take its blood behind the curtain and do with it as he did with the bull's blood: He shall sprinkle it on the atonement cover and in front of it. ¹⁶In this way he will make atonement for the Most Holy Place because of the uncleanness and rebellion of the Israelites, whatever their sins have been. He is to do the same for the tent of meeting, which is among them in the midst of their uncleanness. ¹⁷No one is to be in the tent of meeting from the time Aaron goes in to make atonement in the Most Holy Place until he comes out, having made atonement for himself, his household and the whole community of Israel.

¹⁸"Then he shall come out to the altar that is before the LORD and make atonement for it. He shall take some of the bull's blood and some of the goat's blood and put it on all the horns of the altar. ¹⁹He shall sprinkle some of the blood on it with his finger seven times to cleanse it and to consecrate it from the uncleanness of the Israelites.

²⁰"When Aaron has finished making atonement for the Most Holy Place, the tent of meeting and the altar, he shall bring forward the live goat. ²¹He is to lay both hands on the head of the live goat and confess over it all the wickedness and rebellion of the Israelites—all their sins—and put them on the goat's head. He shall send the goat away into the wilderness in the care of someone appointed for the task. ²²The goat will carry on itself all their sins to a remote place; and the man shall release it in the wilderness.

²³"Then Aaron is to go into the tent of meeting and take off the linen garments he put on before he entered the Most Holy Place, and he is to leave them there. ²⁴He shall bathe himself with water in the sanctuary area and put on his regular garments. Then he shall come out and sacrifice the burnt offering for himself and the burnt offering for the people, to make atonement for himself and for the people. ²⁵He shall also burn the fat of the sin offering on the altar.

²⁶"The man who releases the goat as a scapegoat must

## Amplified Bible

⁹And Aaron shall bring the goat on which the Lord's lot fell and offer him as a sin offering.

¹⁰But the goat on which the lot fell for Azazel *or* removal shall be presented alive before the Lord to make atonement over him, that he may be let go into the wilderness for Azazel (for dismissal).

¹¹Aaron shall present the bull as the sin offering for his own sins and shall make atonement for himself and for his house [the other priests], and shall kill the bull as the sin offering for himself.

¹²He shall take a censer full of burning coals of fire from off the [bronze] altar before the Lord, and his two hands full of sweet incense beaten small, and bring it within the veil [into the Holy of Holies],

¹³And put the incense on the fire [in the censer] before the Lord, that the cloud of the incense may cover the mercy seat that is upon [the ark of] the Testimony, lest he die.

¹⁴He shall take of the bull's blood and sprinkle it with his finger on the front [the east side] of the mercy seat, and before the mercy seat he shall sprinkle of the blood with his finger seven times.

¹⁵Then shall he kill the goat of the sin offering that is for [the sins of] the people and bring its blood within the veil [into the Holy of Holies] and do with that blood as he did with the blood of the bull, and sprinkle it on the mercy seat and before the mercy seat. [Heb. 2:17.]

¹⁶Thus he shall make atonement for the Holy Place because of the uncleanness of the Israelites and because of their transgressions, even all their sins; and so shall he do for the Tent of Meeting, that remains among them in the midst of their uncleanness. [Heb. 9:22-24.]

¹⁷There shall be no man in the Tent of Meeting when the high priest goes in to make atonement in the Holy of Holies [within the veil] until he comes out and has made atonement for his own sins and those of his house [the other priests] and of all the congregation of Israel.

¹⁸And he shall go out to the altar [of burnt offering in the court] which is before the Lord and make atonement for it, and shall take some of the blood of the bull and of the goat and put it on the horns of the altar round about.

¹⁹And he shall sprinkle some of the blood on it with his fingers seven times and cleanse it and hallow it from the uncleanness of the Israelites.

²⁰And when he has finished atoning for the Holy of Holies and the Tent of Meeting and the altar [of burnt offering], he shall present the live goat;

²¹And Aaron shall lay both his hands upon the head of the live goat and confess over him all the iniquities of the Israelites and all their transgressions, all their sins; and he shall put them upon the head of the goat [the sin-bearer], and send him away into the wilderness by the hand of a man *a* who is timely (ready, fit).

²²The goat shall bear upon himself all their iniquities, carrying them to a land cut off (a land of forgetfulness *and* separation, not inhabited)! And the man leading it shall let the goat go in the wilderness. [Ps. 103:12; Isa. 53:11, 12; John 1:29.]

²³Aaron shall come into the Tent of Meeting and put off the linen garments which he put on when he went into the Holy of Holies, and leave them there;

²⁴And he shall bathe his body with water in a sacred place and put on his garments, and come forth and offer his burnt offering and that of the people, and make atonement for himself and for them.

²⁵And the fat of the sin offering he shall burn upon the altar.

²⁶The man who led the sin-bearing goat out and let him

---

*a* This is suggestive of the part the personal worker has to play in showing the sinner that Christ the great Sin-bearer has made full substitution for him, if he will accept it. Notice the qualifications of this man, sent along to complete the picture of the transaction between the sinner and his only sin-bearer. He is to be a man, says the Hebrew, "timely (ready, fit)" to do such a task.

---

*a* 8 The meaning of the Hebrew for this word is uncertain; also in verses 10 and 26.

## New International Version

wash his clothes and bathe himself with water; afterward he may come into the camp. ²⁷The bull and the goat for the sin offerings, whose blood was brought into the Most Holy Place to make atonement, must be taken outside the camp; their hides, flesh and intestines are to be burned up. ²⁸The man who burns them must wash his clothes and bathe himself with water; afterward he may come into the camp.

²⁹"This is to be a lasting ordinance for you: On the tenth day of the seventh month you must deny yourselves*a* and not do any work—whether native-born or a foreigner residing among you— ³⁰because on this day atonement will be made for you, to cleanse you. Then, before the Lord, you will be clean from all your sins. ³¹It is a day of sabbath rest, and you must deny yourselves; it is a lasting ordinance. ³²The priest who is anointed and ordained to succeed his father as high priest is to make atonement. He is to put on the sacred linen garments ³³and make atonement for the Most Holy Place, for the tent of meeting and the altar, and for the priests and all the members of the community.

³⁴"This is to be a lasting ordinance for you: Atonement is to be made once a year for all the sins of the Israelites."

And it was done, as the Lord commanded Moses.

### Eating Blood Forbidden

**17** The Lord said to Moses, ²"Speak to Aaron and his sons and to all the Israelites and say to them: 'This is what the Lord has commanded: ³Any Israelite who sacrifices an ox,*b* a lamb or a goat in the camp or outside of it ⁴instead of bringing it to the entrance to the tent of meeting to present it as an offering to the Lord in front of the tabernacle of the Lord—that person shall be considered guilty of bloodshed; they have shed blood and must be cut off from their people. ⁵This is so the Israelites will bring to the Lord the sacrifices they are now making in the open fields. They must bring them to the priest, that is, to the Lord, at the entrance to the tent of meeting and sacrifice them as fellowship offerings. ⁶The priest is to splash the blood against the altar of the Lord at the entrance to the tent of meeting and burn the fat as an aroma pleasing to the Lord. ⁷They must no longer offer any of their sacrifices to the goat idols*c* to whom they prostitute themselves. This is to be a lasting ordinance for them and for the generations to come.'

⁸"Say to them: 'Any Israelite or any foreigner residing among them who offers a burnt offering or sacrifice ⁹and does not bring it to the entrance to the tent of meeting to sacrifice it to the Lord must be cut off from the people of Israel.

¹⁰"'I will set my face against any Israelite or any foreigner residing among them who eats blood, and I will cut them off from the people. ¹¹For the life of a creature is in the blood, and I have given it to you to make atone-

## Amplified Bible

go for Azazel *or* removal shall wash his clothes and bathe his body, and afterward he may come into the camp.

²⁷The bull and the goat for the sin offering, whose blood was brought in to make atonement in the Holy of Holies, shall be carried forth without the camp; their skins, their flesh, and their dung shall be burned with fire. [Heb. 13:11-13.]

²⁸And he who burns them shall wash his clothes and bathe his body in water, and afterward he may come into the camp.

²⁹It shall be a statute to you forever that in the seventh month [nearly October] on the tenth day of the month you shall afflict yourselves [by fasting with penitence and humiliation] and do no work at all, either the native-born or the stranger who dwells temporarily among you.

³⁰For on this day atonement shall be made for you, to cleanse you; from all your sins you shall be clean before the Lord. [Heb. 10:1, 2; I John 1:7, 9.]

³¹It is a sabbath of [solemn] rest to you, and you shall afflict yourselves [by fasting with penitence and humiliation]; it is a statute forever.

³²And the priest who shall be anointed and consecrated to minister in the priest's office in his father's stead shall make atonement, wearing the holy linen garments;

³³He shall make atonement for the Holy Sanctuary, for the Tent of Meeting, and for the altar [of burnt offering in the court], and shall make atonement for the priests and for all the people of the assembly.

³⁴This shall be an everlasting statute for you, that atonement may be made for the Israelites for all their sins once a year. And Moses did as the Lord commanded him.

**17** And the Lord said to Moses, ²Tell Aaron, his sons, and all the Israelites, This is what the Lord has commanded:

³If any man of the house of Israel kills an ox or lamb or goat in the camp or kills it outside the camp

⁴And does not bring it to the door of the Tent of Meeting to offer it as an offering to the Lord before the Lord's tabernacle, [guilt for shedding] *a*blood shall be imputed to that man; he has shed blood and shall be cut off from among his people.

⁵This is so that the Israelites, rather than offer their sacrifices [to idols] in the open field [where they slew them], may bring them to the Lord at the door of the Tent of Meeting, to the priest, to offer them as peace offerings to the Lord.

⁶And the priest shall dash the blood on the altar of the Lord at the door of the Tent of Meeting and burn the fat for a sweet *and* satisfying fragrance to the Lord.

⁷So they shall no more offer their sacrifices to goat-like gods *or* demons *or* field spirits after which they have played the harlot. This shall be a statute forever to them throughout their generations.

⁸And you shall say to them, Whoever of the house of Israel or of the strangers who dwell temporarily among you offers a burnt offering or sacrifice

⁹And does not bring it to the door of the Tent of Meeting to offer it to the Lord shall be cut off from among his people.

¹⁰Any one of the house of Israel or of the strangers who dwell temporarily among them who eats any kind of blood, against that person I will set My face and I will cut him off from among his people [that he may not be included in the atonement made for them]. [Ezek. 33:25.]

¹¹For the life (the animal soul) is in the blood, and I have

---

*a 29* Or *must fast;* also in verse 31   *b 3* The Hebrew word can refer to either male or female.   *c 7* Or *the demons*

*a* This requirement, that an animal to be killed was to be brought as an offering to the Lord, was no privation for the owner, for after offering it on the altar of burnt offering he received most of it back as a gift from God.

## New International Version

ment for yourselves on the altar; it is the blood that makes atonement for one's life.*  12Therefore I say to the Israelites, "None of you may eat blood, nor may any foreigner residing among you eat blood."

13"'Any Israelite or any foreigner residing among you who hunts any animal or bird that may be eaten must drain out the blood and cover it with earth,  14because the life of every creature is its blood. That is why I have said to the Israelites, "You must not eat the blood of any creature, because the life of every creature is its blood; anyone who eats it must be cut off."

15"'Anyone, whether native-born or foreigner, who eats anything found dead or torn by wild animals must wash their clothes and bathe with water, and they will be ceremonially unclean till evening; then they will be clean.  16But if they do not wash their clothes and bathe themselves, they will be held responsible.'"

### Unlawful Sexual Relations

**18** The LORD said to Moses,  2"Speak to the Israelites and say to them: 'I am the LORD your God.  3You must not do as they do in Egypt, where you used to live, and you must not do as they do in the land of Canaan, where I am bringing you. Do not follow their practices.  4You must obey my laws and be careful to follow my decrees. I am the LORD your God.  5Keep my decrees and laws, for the person who obeys them will live by them. I am the LORD.

6"'No one is to approach any close relative to have sexual relations. I am the LORD.

7"'Do not dishonor your father by having sexual relations with your mother. She is your mother; do not have relations with her.

8"'Do not have sexual relations with your father's wife; that would dishonor your father.

9"'Do not have sexual relations with your sister, either your father's daughter or your mother's daughter, whether she was born in the same home or elsewhere.

10"'Do not have sexual relations with your son's daughter or your daughter's daughter; that would dishonor you.

11"'Do not have sexual relations with the daughter of your father's wife, born to your father; she is your sister.

12"'Do not have sexual relations with your father's sister; she is your father's close relative.

13"'Do not have sexual relations with your mother's sister, because she is your mother's close relative.

14"'Do not dishonor your father's brother by approaching his wife to have sexual relations; she is your aunt.

15"'Do not have sexual relations with your daughter-in-law. She is your son's wife; do not have relations with her.

16"'Do not have sexual relations with your brother's wife; that would dishonor your brother.

17"'Do not have sexual relations with both a woman and her daughter. Do not have sexual relations with either her son's daughter or her daughter's daughter; they are her close relatives. That is wickedness.

18"'Do not take your wife's sister as a rival wife and have sexual relations with her while your wife is living.

19"'Do not approach a woman to have sexual relations during the uncleanness of her monthly period.

## Amplified Bible

given it for you upon the altar to make atonement for your souls; for it is the blood that makes atonement, by reason of the life [which it represents]. [Rom. 3:24-26.]

12Therefore I have said to the Israelites, No person among you shall eat blood, neither shall any stranger who dwells temporarily among you eat blood.

13And any of the Israelites or of the strangers who sojourn among them who takes in hunting any clean beast or bird shall pour out its blood and cover it with dust.

14As for the life of all flesh, the blood of it represents the life of it; therefore I said to the Israelites, You shall partake of the blood of no kind of flesh, for the life of all flesh is its blood. Whoever eats of it shall be cut off.

15And every person who eats what dies of itself or was torn by beasts, whether he is native-born or a temporary resident, shall wash his clothes and bathe himself in water, and be unclean until evening; then shall he be clean. [Acts 15:20.]

16But if he does not wash his clothes or bathe his body, he shall bear his own iniquity [for it shall not be borne by the sacrifice of atonement].

**18** And the Lord said to Moses,  2Say to the Israelites, I am the Lord your God.

3You shall not do as was done in the land of Egypt in which you dwelt, nor shall you do as is done in the land of Canaan to which I am bringing you; neither shall you walk in their statutes.

4You shall do My ordinances and keep My statutes and walk in them. I am the Lord your God.

5You shall therefore keep My statutes and My ordinances which, if a man does, he shall live by them. I am the Lord. [Luke 10:25-28; Rom. 10:4, 5; Gal. 3:12.]

6None of you shall approach anyone close of kin to him to have sexual relations. I am the Lord.

7The nakedness of your father, which is the nakedness of your mother, you shall not uncover; she is your mother; you shall not have intercourse with her.

8The nakedness of your father's wife you shall not uncover; it is your father's nakedness.

9You shall not have intercourse with *or* uncover the nakedness of your sister, the daughter of your father or of your mother, whether born at home or born abroad.

10You must not have sexual relations with your son's daughter or your daughter's daughter; their nakedness you shall not uncover, for they are your own flesh.

11You must not have intercourse with your father's wife's daughter; begotten by your father, she is your sister; you shall not uncover her nakedness.

12You shall not have intercourse with your father's sister; she is your father's near kinswoman.

13You shall not have sexual relations with your mother's sister, for she is your mother's near kinswoman.

14You shall not have intercourse with your father's brother's wife; you shall not approach his wife; she is your aunt.

15You shall not uncover the nakedness of your daughter-in-law; she is your son's wife; you shall not have intercourse with her.

16You shall not have intercourse with your brother's wife; she belongs to your brother.

17You shall not marry a woman and her daughter, nor shall you take her son's daughter or her daughter's daughter to have intercourse; they are [her] near kinswomen; it is wickedness *and* an outrageous offense.

18You must not marry a woman in addition to her sister, to be a rival to her, having sexual relations with the second sister when the first one is alive.

19Also you shall not have intercourse with a woman during her [menstrual period or similar] uncleanness.

---

*a* 11 Or *atonement by the life in the blood*

## New International Version

20"'Do not have sexual relations with your neighbor's wife and defile yourself with her.

21"'Do not give any of your children to be sacrificed to Molek, for you must not profane the name of your God. I am the LORD.

22"'Do not have sexual relations with a man as one does with a woman; that is detestable.

23"'Do not have sexual relations with an animal and defile yourself with it. A woman must not present herself to an animal to have sexual relations with it; that is a perversion.

24"'Do not defile yourselves in any of these ways, because this is how the nations that I am going to drive out before you became defiled. 25Even the land was defiled; so I punished it for its sin, and the land vomited out its inhabitants. 26But you must keep my decrees and my laws. The native-born and the foreigners residing among you must not do any of these detestable things, 27for all these things were done by the people who lived in the land before you, and the land became defiled. 28And if you defile the land, it will vomit you out as it vomited out the nations that were before you.

29"'Everyone who does any of these detestable things— such persons must be cut off from their people. 30Keep my requirements and do not follow any of the detestable customs that were practiced before you came and do not defile yourselves with them. I am the LORD your God.'"

### Various Laws

**19** The LORD said to Moses, 2"Speak to the entire assembly of Israel and say to them: 'Be holy because I, the LORD your God, am holy.

3"'Each of you must respect your mother and father, and you must observe my Sabbaths. I am the LORD your God.

4"'Do not turn to idols or make metal gods for yourselves. I am the LORD your God.

5"'When you sacrifice a fellowship offering to the LORD, sacrifice it in such a way that it will be accepted on your behalf. 6It shall be eaten on the day you sacrifice it or on the next day; anything left over until the third day must be burned up. 7If any of it is eaten on the third day, it is impure and will not be accepted. 8Whoever eats it will be held responsible because they have desecrated what is holy to the LORD; they must be cut off from their people.

9"'When you reap the harvest of your land, do not reap to the very edges of your field or gather the gleanings of your harvest. 10Do not go over your vineyard a second time or pick up the grapes that have fallen. Leave them for the poor and the foreigner. I am the LORD your God.

11"'Do not steal.

"'Do not lie.

"'Do not deceive one another.

12"'Do not swear falsely by my name and so profane the name of your God. I am the LORD.

13"'Do not defraud or rob your neighbor.

"'Do not hold back the wages of a hired worker overnight.

14"'Do not curse the deaf or put a stumbling block in front of the blind, but fear your God. I am the LORD.

15"'Do not pervert justice; do not show partiality to the

## Amplified Bible

20Moreover, you shall not lie carnally with your neighbor's wife, to defile yourself with her.

21You shall not give any of your children to pass through the fire *and* sacrifice them to Molech [the fire god], nor shall you profane the name of your God [by giving it to false gods]. I am the Lord.

22You shall not lie with a man as with a woman; it is an abomination. [I Cor. 6:9, 10.]

23Neither shall you lie with any beast and defile yourself with it; neither shall any woman yield herself to a beast to lie with it; it is confusion, perversion, *and* degradedly carnal.

24Do not defile yourselves in any of these ways, for in all these things the nations are defiled which I am casting out before you.

25And the land is defiled; therefore I visit the iniquity of it upon it, and the land itself vomits out her inhabitants.

26So you shall keep My statutes and My ordinances and shall not commit any of these abominations, neither the native-born nor any stranger who sojourns among you,

27For all these abominations have the men of the land done who were before you, and the land is defiled—

28[Do none of these things] lest the land spew you out when you defile it as it spewed out the nation that was before you.

29Whoever commits any of these abominations shall be cut off from among [his] people.

30So keep My charge: do not practice any of these abominable customs which were practiced before you and defile yourselves by them. I am the Lord your God.

**19** And the Lord said to Moses, 2Say to all the assembly of the Israelites, You shall be holy, for I the Lord your God am holy. [I Pet. 1:15.]

3Each of you shall give due respect to his mother and his father, and keep My Sabbaths holy. I the Lord am your God.

4Do not turn to idols *and* things of nought or make for yourselves molten gods. I the Lord am your God.

5And when you offer a sacrifice of peace offering to the Lord, you shall offer it so that you may be accepted.

6It shall be eaten the same day you offer it and on the day following; and if anything remains until the third day, it shall be burned in the fire.

7If it is eaten at all the third day, it is loathsome; it will not be accepted.

8But everyone who eats it shall bear his iniquity, for he has profaned a holy thing of the Lord; and that soul shall be cut off from his people [and not be included in the atonement made for them].

9And when you reap the harvest of your land, you shall not reap your field to its very corners, neither shall you gather the fallen ears *or* gleanings of your harvest.

10And you shall not glean your vineyard bare, neither shall you gather its fallen grapes; you shall leave them for the poor and the stranger. I am the Lord your God.

11You shall not steal, or deal falsely, or lie one to another. [Col. 3:9, 10.]

12And you shall not swear by My name falsely, neither shall you profane the name of your God. I am the Lord.

13You shall not defraud *or* oppress your neighbor or rob him; the wages of a hired servant shall not remain with you all night until morning.

14You shall not curse the deaf or put a stumbling block before the blind, but you shall [reverently] fear your God. I am the Lord.

15You shall do no injustice in judging a case; you shall

## New International Version

poor or favoritism to the great, but judge your neighbor fairly.

¹⁶"Do not go about spreading slander among your people.

"'Do not do anything that endangers your neighbor's life. I am the LORD.

¹⁷"Do not hate a fellow Israelite in your heart. Rebuke your neighbor frankly so you will not share in their guilt.

¹⁸"Do not seek revenge or bear a grudge against anyone among your people, but love your neighbor as yourself. I am the LORD.

¹⁹"Keep my decrees.

"'Do not mate different kinds of animals.

"'Do not plant your field with two kinds of seed.

"'Do not wear clothing woven of two kinds of material.

²⁰"If a man sleeps with a female slave who is promised to another man but who has not been ransomed or given her freedom, there must be due punishment.ᵃ Yet they are not to be put to death, because she had not been freed.

²¹The man, however, must bring a ram to the entrance to the tent of meeting for a guilt offering to the LORD. ²²With the ram of the guilt offering the priest is to make atonement for him before the LORD for the sin he has committed, and his sin will be forgiven.

²³"When you enter the land and plant any kind of fruit tree, regard its fruit as forbidden.ᵇ For three years you are to consider it forbiddenᵇ; it must not be eaten. ²⁴In the fourth year all its fruit will be holy, an offering of praise to the LORD. ²⁵But in the fifth year you may eat its fruit. In this way your harvest will be increased. I am the LORD your God.

²⁶"Do not eat any meat with the blood still in it.

"'Do not practice divination or seek omens.

²⁷"Do not cut the hair at the sides of your head or clip off the edges of your beard.

²⁸"Do not cut your bodies for the dead or put tattoo marks on yourselves. I am the LORD.

²⁹"Do not degrade your daughter by making her a prostitute, or the land will turn to prostitution and be filled with wickedness.

³⁰"Observe my Sabbaths and have reverence for my sanctuary. I am the LORD.

³¹"Do not turn to mediums or seek out spiritists, for you will be defiled by them. I am the LORD your God.

³²"Stand up in the presence of the aged, show respect for the elderly and revere your God. I am the LORD.

³³"When a foreigner resides among you in your land, do not mistreat them. ³⁴The foreigner residing among you must be treated as your native-born. Love them as yourself, for you were foreigners in Egypt. I am the LORD your God.

³⁵"Do not use dishonest standards when measuring length, weight or quantity. ³⁶Use honest scales and honest weights, an honest ephahᶜ and an honest hin.ᵈ I am the LORD your God, who brought you out of Egypt.

³⁷"Keep all my decrees and all my laws and follow them. I am the LORD.'"

## Amplified Bible

not be partial to the poor or show a preference for the mighty, but in righteousness *and* according to the merits of the case judge your neighbor.

¹⁶You shall not go up and down as a dispenser of gossip *and* scandal among your people, nor shall you [secure yourself by false testimony or by silence and] endanger the life of your neighbor. I am the Lord.

¹⁷You shall not hate your brother in your heart; but you shall surely rebuke your neighbor, lest you incur sin because of him. [Gal. 6:1; I John 2:9, 11; 3:15.]

¹⁸You shall not take revenge or bear any grudge against the sons of your people, but you shall love your neighbor as yourself. I am the Lord. [Matt. 5:43-46; Rom. 12:17, 19.]

¹⁹You shall keep My statutes. You shall not let your domestic animals breed with a different kind [of animal]; you shall not sow your field with mixed seed, neither wear a garment of linen mixed with wool.

²⁰And if a man lies carnally with a woman who is a slave betrothed to a husband and not yet ransomed or given her freedom, they shall be punished [after investigation]; they shall not be put to death, because she was not free;

²¹But he shall bring his guilt *or* trespass offering to the Lord to the door of the Tent of Meeting, a ram for a guilt *or* trespass offering.

²²The priest shall make atonement for him with the ram of the guilt *or* trespass offering before the Lord for his sin, and he shall be forgiven for committing the sin.

²³And when you come into the land and have planted all kinds of trees for food, then you shall count the fruit of them as inedible *and* forbidden to you for three years; it shall not be eaten.

²⁴In the fourth year all their fruit shall be holy for giving praise to the Lord.

²⁵But in the fifth year you may eat of the fruit [of the trees], that their produce may enrich you; I am the Lord your God.

²⁶You shall not eat anything with the blood; neither shall you use magic, omens, *or* witchcraft [or predict events by horoscope or signs and lucky days].

²⁷You shall not round the corners of the hair of your heads nor trim the corners of your beard [as some idolaters do].

²⁸You shall not make any cuttings in your flesh for the dead nor print *or* tattoo any marks upon you; I am the Lord.

²⁹Do not profane your daughter by causing her to be a harlot, lest the land fall into harlotry and become full of wickedness.

³⁰You shall keep My Sabbaths and reverence My sanctuary. I am the Lord.

³¹Turn not to those [mediums] who have familiar spirits or to wizards; do not seek them out to be defiled by them. I am the Lord your God.

³²You shall rise up before the hoary head and honor the face of the old man and [reverently] fear your God. I am the Lord.

³³And if a stranger dwells temporarily with you in your land, you shall not suppress *and* mistreat him.

³⁴But the stranger who dwells with you shall be to you as one born among you; and you shall love him as yourself, for you were strangers in the land of Egypt. I am the Lord your God.

³⁵You shall do no unrighteousness in judgment, in measures of length or weight or quantity.

³⁶You shall have accurate *and* just balances, just weights, just ephah and hin measures. I am the Lord your God, Who brought you out of the land of Egypt.

³⁷You shall observe all My statutes and ordinances and do them. I am the Lord.

---

ᵃ 20 Or *be an inquiry*   ᵇ 23 Hebrew *uncircumcised*   ᶜ 36 An ephah was a dry measure having the capacity of about 3/5 of a bushel or about 22 liters.   ᵈ 36 A hin was a liquid measure having the capacity of about 1 gallon or about 3.8 liters.

## New International Version

### Punishments for Sin

**20** The LORD said to Moses, [2]"Say to the Israelites: 'Any Israelite or any foreigner residing in Israel who sacrifices any of his children to Molek is to be put to death. The members of the community are to stone him. [3]I myself will set my face against him and will cut him off from his people; for by sacrificing his children to Molek, he has defiled my sanctuary and profaned my holy name. [4]If the members of the community close their eyes when that man sacrifices one of his children to Molek and if they fail to put him to death, [5]I myself will set my face against him and his family and will cut them off from their people together with all who follow him in prostituting themselves to Molek.

[6]"'I will set my face against anyone who turns to mediums and spiritists to prostitute themselves by following them, and I will cut them off from their people.

[7]"'Consecrate yourselves and be holy, because I am the LORD your God. [8]Keep my decrees and follow them. I am the LORD, who makes you holy.

[9]"'Anyone who curses their father or mother is to be put to death. Because they have cursed their father or mother, their blood will be on their own head.

[10]"'If a man commits adultery with another man's wife—with the wife of his neighbor—both the adulterer and the adulteress are to be put to death.

[11]"'If a man has sexual relations with his father's wife, he has dishonored his father. Both the man and the woman are to be put to death; their blood will be on their own heads.

[12]"'If a man has sexual relations with his daughter-in-law, both of them are to be put to death. What they have done is a perversion; their blood will be on their own heads.

[13]"'If a man has sexual relations with a man as one does with a woman, both of them have done what is detestable. They are to be put to death; their blood will be on their own heads.

[14]"'If a man marries both a woman and her mother, it is wicked. Both he and they must be burned in the fire, so that no wickedness will be among you.

[15]"'If a man has sexual relations with an animal, he is to be put to death, and you must kill the animal.

[16]"'If a woman approaches an animal to have sexual relations with it, kill both the woman and the animal. They are to be put to death; their blood will be on their own heads.

[17]"'If a man marries his sister, the daughter of either his father or his mother, and they have sexual relations, it is a disgrace. They are to be publicly removed from their people. He has dishonored his sister and will be held responsible.

[18]"'If a man has sexual relations with a woman during her monthly period, he has exposed the source of her flow, and she has also uncovered it. Both of them are to be cut off from their people.

[19]"'Do not have sexual relations with the sister of either your mother or your father, for that would dishonor a close relative; both of you would be held responsible.

[20]"'If a man has sexual relations with his aunt, he has

## Amplified Bible

**20** And the Lord said to Moses, [2]Moreover, you shall say to the Israelites, Any one of the Israelites or of the strangers that sojourn in Israel who gives any of his children to Molech [the fire god worshiped with human sacrifices] shall surely be put to death; the people of the land shall stone him with stones.

[3]I also will set My face against that man [opposing him, withdrawing My protection from him, and excluding him from My covenant] and will cut him off from among his people, because he has given of his children to Molech, defiling My sanctuary and profaning My holy name.

[4]And if the people of the land do at all hide their eyes from the man when he gives one of his children [as a burnt offering] to Molech [the fire god] *and* they overlook it *or* neglect to take legal action to punish him, winking at his sin, and do not kill him [as My law requires],

[5]Then I will set My face against that man and against his family and will cut him off from among their people, him and all who follow him to [unfaithfulness to Me, and thus] play the harlot after Molech.

[6]The person who turns to those who have familiar spirits and to wizards, [being unfaithful to Israel's Maker Who is her Husband, and thus] playing the harlot after them, I will set My face against that person and will cut him off from among his people [that he may not be included in the atonement made for them]. [Isa. 54:5.]

[7]Consecrate yourselves therefore, and be holy; for I am the Lord your God.

[8]And you shall keep My statutes and do them. I am the Lord Who sanctifies you.

[9]Everyone who curses his father or mother shall surely be put to death; he has cursed his father or mother; his bloodguilt is upon him.

[10]The man who commits adultery with another's wife, even his neighbor's wife, the adulterer and the adulteress shall surely be put to death. [John 8:4-11.]

[11]And the man who lies carnally with his father's wife has uncovered his father's nakedness; both of the guilty ones shall surely be put to death; their blood shall be upon their own heads.

[12]And if a man lies carnally with his daughter-in-law, both of them shall surely be put to death; they have wrought confusion, perversion, *and* defilement; their blood shall be upon their own heads.

[13]If a man lies with a male as if he were a woman, both men have committed an offense (something perverse, unnatural, abhorrent, and detestable); they shall surely be put to death; their blood shall be upon them.

[14]And if a man takes a wife and her mother, it is wickedness *and* an outrageous offense; all three shall be burned with fire, both he and they [after being stoned to death], that there be no wickedness among you. [Josh. 7:15, 25.]

[15]And if a man lies carnally with a beast, he shall surely be [stoned] to death, and you shall slay the beast.

[16]If a woman approaches any beast and lies carnally with it, you shall [stone] the woman and the beast; they shall surely be put to death; their blood is upon them.

[17]If a man takes his sister, his father's or his mother's daughter, and sees her nakedness and she sees his nakedness, it is a wicked *and* shameful thing; and they shall be cut off in the sight of their people; he has had sexual relations with his sister; he shall bear his iniquity.

[18]And if a man shall lie with a woman having her menstrual pains and shall uncover her nakedness, he has made naked her fountain, and she has uncovered the fountain of her blood; and both of them shall be cut off from among their people.

[19]You shall not uncover the nakedness of your mother's sister or of your father's sister, for that is to make naked his close kin; they shall bear their iniquity.

[20]And if a man shall lie carnally with his uncle's wife,

## New International Version

dishonored his uncle. They will be held responsible; they will die childless.

21 "'If a man marries his brother's wife, it is an act of impurity; he has dishonored his brother. They will be childless.

22 "'Keep all my decrees and laws and follow them, so that the land where I am bringing you to live may not vomit you out. 23 You must not live according to the customs of the nations I am going to drive out before you. Because they did all these things, I abhorred them. 24 But I said to you, "You will possess their land; I will give it to you as an inheritance, a land flowing with milk and honey." I am the LORD your God, who has set you apart from the nations.

25 "'You must therefore make a distinction between clean and unclean animals and between unclean and clean birds. Do not defile yourselves by any animal or bird or anything that moves along the ground—those that I have set apart as unclean for you. 26 You are to be holy to me because I, the LORD, am holy, and I have set you apart from the nations to be my own.

27 "'A man or woman who is a medium or spiritist among you must be put to death. You are to stone them; their blood will be on their own heads.'"

### Rules for Priests

**21** The LORD said to Moses, "Speak to the priests, the sons of Aaron, and say to them: 'A priest must not make himself ceremonially unclean for any of his people who die, 2 except for a close relative, such as his mother or father, his son or daughter, his brother, 3 or an unmarried sister who is dependent on him since she has no husband—for her he may make himself unclean. 4 He must not make himself unclean for people related to him by marriage,[a] and so defile himself.

5 "'Priests must not shave their heads or shave off the edges of their beards or cut their bodies. 6 They must be holy to their God and must not profane the name of their God. Because they present the food offerings to the LORD, the food of their God, they are to be holy.

7 "'They must not marry women defiled by prostitution or divorced from their husbands, because priests are holy to their God. 8 Regard them as holy, because they offer up the food of your God. Consider them holy, because I the LORD am holy—I who make you holy.

9 "'If a priest's daughter defiles herself by becoming a prostitute, she disgraces her father; she must be burned in the fire.

10 "'The high priest, the one among his brothers who has had the anointing oil poured on his head and who has been ordained to wear the priestly garments, must not let his hair become unkempt[b] or tear his clothes. 11 He must not enter a place where there is a dead body. He must not make himself unclean, even for his father or mother, 12 nor leave the sanctuary of his God or desecrate it, because he has been dedicated by the anointing oil of his God. I am the LORD.

13 "'The woman he marries must be a virgin. 14 He must not marry a widow, a divorced woman, or a woman defiled

---

## Amplified Bible

he has uncovered his uncle's nakedness; they shall bear their sin; they shall die childless [not literally, but in a legal sense].

21 And if a man shall take his brother's wife, it is impurity; he has uncovered his brother's nakedness; they shall be childless [not literally, but in a legal sense].

22 You shall therefore keep all My statutes and all My ordinances and do them, that the land where I am bringing you to dwell may not vomit you out [as it did those before you]. [Lev. 18:28.]

23 You shall not walk in the customs of the nation which I am casting out before you; for they did all these things, and therefore I was wearied *and* grieved by them.

24 But I have said to you, You shall inherit their land, and I will give it to you to possess, a land flowing with milk and honey. I am the Lord your God, Who has separated you from the peoples.

25 You shall therefore make a distinction between the clean beast and the unclean, and between the unclean fowl and the clean; and you shall not make yourselves detestable with beast or with bird or with anything with which the ground teems *or* that creeps, which I have set apart from you as unclean.

26 And you shall be holy to Me; for I the Lord am holy, and have separated you from the peoples, that you should be Mine.

27 A man or woman who is a medium *and* has a familiar spirit or is a wizard shall surely be put to death, be stoned with stones; their blood shall be upon them.

**21** The Lord said to Moses, Speak to the priests [exclusive of the high priest], the sons of Aaron, and say to them that none of them shall defile himself for the dead among his people [by touching a corpse or assisting in preparing it for burial],

2 Except for his near [blood] kin, for his mother, father, son, daughter, brother,

3 And for his sister, a virgin, who is near to him because she has had no husband; for her he may be defiled.

4 He shall not even defile himself, being a [bereaved] husband [his wife not being his blood kin] *or* being a chief man among his people, and so profane himself.

5 The priests [like the other Israelite men] shall not shave the crown of their heads or clip off the corners of their beard or make any cuttings in their flesh.

6 They shall be holy to their God and not profane the name of their God; for they offer the offerings made by fire to the Lord, the bread of their God; therefore they shall be holy.

7 They shall not take a wife who is a harlot or polluted *or* profane or divorced, for [the priest] is holy to his God.

8 You shall consecrate him therefore, for he offers the bread of your God; he shall be holy to you, for I the Lord Who sanctifies you am holy.

9 The daughter of any priest who profanes herself by playing the harlot profanes her father; she shall be burned with fire [after being stoned]. [Josh. 7:15, 25.]

10 But he who is the high priest among his brethren, upon whose head the anointing oil was poured and who is consecrated to put on the [sacred] garments, shall not let the hair of his head hang loose or rend his clothes [in mourning],

11 Neither shall he go in where any dead body lies nor defile himself [by doing so, even] for his father or for his mother;

12 Neither shall he go out of the sanctuary nor desecrate *or* make ceremonially unclean the sanctuary of his God, for the crown *or* consecration of the anointing oil of his God is upon him. I am the Lord.

13 He shall take a wife in her virginity.

14 A widow or a divorced woman or a woman who is polluted *or* profane or a harlot, these he shall not marry, but

---

*a 4 Or* unclean as a leader among his people    *b 10 Or* not uncover his head

## New International Version

by prostitution, but only a virgin from his own people, <sup>15</sup>so that he will not defile his offspring among his people. I am the LORD, who makes him holy.'"

<sup>16</sup>The LORD said to Moses, <sup>17</sup>"Say to Aaron: 'For the generations to come none of your descendants who has a defect may come near to offer the food of his God. <sup>18</sup>No man who has any defect may come near: no man who is blind or lame, disfigured or deformed; <sup>19</sup>no man with a crippled foot or hand, <sup>20</sup>or who is a hunchback or a dwarf, or who has any eye defect, or who has festering or running sores or damaged testicles. <sup>21</sup>No descendant of Aaron the priest who has any defect is to come near to present the food offerings to the LORD. He has a defect; he must not come near to offer the food of his God. <sup>22</sup>He may eat the most holy food of his God, as well as the holy food; <sup>23</sup>yet because of his defect, he must not go near the curtain or approach the altar, and so desecrate my sanctuary. I am the LORD, who makes them holy.'"

<sup>24</sup>So Moses told this to Aaron and his sons and to all the Israelites.

**22** The LORD said to Moses, <sup>2</sup>"Tell Aaron and his sons to treat with respect the sacred offerings the Israelites consecrate to me, so they will not profane my holy name. I am the LORD.

<sup>3</sup>"Say to them: 'For the generations to come, if any of your descendants is ceremonially unclean and yet comes near the sacred offerings that the Israelites consecrate to the LORD, that person must be cut off from my presence. I am the LORD.

<sup>4</sup>"'If a descendant of Aaron has a defiling skin disease<sup>a</sup> or a bodily discharge, he may not eat the sacred offerings until he is cleansed. He will also be unclean if he touches something defiled by a corpse or by anyone who has an emission of semen, <sup>5</sup>or if he touches any crawling thing that makes him unclean, or any person who makes him unclean, whatever the uncleanness may be. <sup>6</sup>The one who touches any such thing will be unclean till evening. He must not eat any of the sacred offerings unless he has bathed himself with water. <sup>7</sup>When the sun goes down, he will be clean, and after that he may eat the sacred offerings, for they are his food. <sup>8</sup>He must not eat anything found dead or torn by wild animals, and so become unclean through it. I am the LORD.

<sup>9</sup>"'The priests are to perform my service in such a way that they do not become guilty and die for treating it with contempt. I am the LORD, who makes them holy.

<sup>10</sup>"'No one outside a priest's family may eat the sacred offering, nor may the guest of a priest or his hired worker eat it. <sup>11</sup>But if a priest buys a slave with money, or if slaves are born in his household, they may eat his food. <sup>12</sup>If a priest's daughter marries anyone other than a priest, she may not eat any of the sacred contributions. <sup>13</sup>But if a priest's daughter becomes a widow or is divorced, yet has no children, and she returns to live in her father's household as in her youth, she may eat her father's food. No unauthorized person, however, may eat it.

<sup>a</sup> 4 The Hebrew word for *defiling skin disease*, traditionally translated "leprosy," was used for various diseases affecting the skin.

## Amplified Bible

he shall take as his wife a virgin of his own people, [I Tim. 3:2-7; Tit. 1:7-9.]

<sup>15</sup>That he may not profane *or* dishonor his children among his people; for I the Lord do sanctify the high priest.

<sup>16</sup>And the Lord said to Moses,

<sup>17</sup>Say to Aaron, Any one of your sons in their successive generations who has any blemish, let him not come near to offer the bread of his God.

<sup>18</sup>For no man who has a blemish shall approach [God's altar to serve as priest], a man blind or lame, or he who has a disfigured face or a limb too long,

<sup>19</sup>Or who has a fractured foot or hand,

<sup>20</sup>Or is a hunchback, or a dwarf, or has a defect in his eye, or has scurvy *or* itch, or scabs *or* skin trouble, or has damaged testicles.

<sup>21</sup>No man of the offspring of Aaron the priest who has a blemish *and* is disfigured *or* deformed shall come near [the altar] to offer the offerings of the Lord made by fire. He has a blemish; he shall not come near to offer the bread of his God.

<sup>22</sup>He may eat the bread of his God, both of the most holy and of the holy things,

<sup>23</sup>But he shall not come within the veil or come near the altar [of incense], because he has a blemish, that he may not desecrate *and* make unclean My sanctuaries *and* hallowed things; for I the Lord do sanctify them. [Heb. 7:28.]

<sup>24</sup>And Moses told it to Aaron and to his sons and to all the Israelites.

**22** And the Lord said to Moses, <sup>2</sup>Say to Aaron and his sons that they shall stay away from the holy things which the Israelites dedicate to Me, that they may not profane My holy name; I am the Lord.

<sup>3</sup>Tell them, Any one of your offspring throughout your generations who goes to the holy things which the Israelites dedicate to the Lord when he is unclean, that [priest] shall be cut off from My presence *and* excluded from the sanctuary; I am the Lord.

<sup>4</sup>No man of the offspring of Aaron who is a leper or has a discharge shall eat of the holy things [the offerings and the showbread] until he is clean. And whoever touches any person *or* thing made unclean by contact with a corpse or a man who has had a discharge of semen,

<sup>5</sup>Or whoever touches any dead creeping thing by which he may be made unclean, or a man from whom he may acquire uncleanness, whatever it may be, [Lev. 11:24-28.]

<sup>6</sup>The priest who has touched any such thing shall be unclean until evening and shall not eat of the holy things unless he has bathed with water. [Heb. 10:22.]

<sup>7</sup>When the sun is down, he shall be clean, and afterward may eat of the holy things, for they are his food.

<sup>8</sup>That which dies of itself or is torn by beasts he shall not eat, defiling himself with it. I am the Lord.

<sup>9</sup>The priests therefore shall observe My ordinance, lest they bear sin for it and die thereby if they profane it. I am the Lord, Who sanctifies them.

<sup>10</sup>No outsider [not of the family of Aaron] shall eat of the holy thing [which has been offered to God]; a sojourner with the priest or a hired servant shall not eat of the holy thing.

<sup>11</sup>But if a priest buys a slave with his money, the slave may eat of the holy thing, and he also who is born in the priest's house; they may eat of his food.

<sup>12</sup>If a priest's daughter is married to an outsider [not of the priestly tribe], she shall not eat of the offering of the holy things.

<sup>13</sup>But if a priest's daughter is a widow or divorced, and has no child, and returns to her father's house as in her youth, she shall eat of her father's food; but no stranger shall eat of it.

## New International Version

14 "'Anyone who eats a sacred offering by mistake must make restitution to the priest for the offering and add a fifth of the value to it. 15 The priests must not desecrate the sacred offerings the Israelites present to the LORD 16 by allowing them to eat the sacred offerings and so bring upon them guilt requiring payment. I am the LORD, who makes them holy.'"

### Unacceptable Sacrifices

17 The LORD said to Moses, 18 "Speak to Aaron and his sons and to all the Israelites and say to them: 'If any of you—whether an Israelite or a foreigner residing in Israel—presents a gift for a burnt offering to the LORD, either to fulfill a vow or as a freewill offering, 19 you must present a male without defect from the cattle, sheep or goats in order that it may be accepted on your behalf. 20 Do not bring anything with a defect, because it will not be accepted on your behalf. 21 When anyone brings from the herd or flock a fellowship offering to the LORD to fulfill a special vow or as a freewill offering, it must be without defect or blemish to be acceptable. 22 Do not offer to the LORD the blind, the injured or the maimed, or anything with warts or festering or running sores. Do not place any of these on the altar as a food offering presented to the LORD. 23 You may, however, present as a freewill offering an ox[a] or a sheep that is deformed or stunted, but it will not be accepted in fulfillment of a vow. 24 You must not offer to the LORD an animal whose testicles are bruised, crushed, torn or cut. You must not do this in your own land, 25 and you must not accept such animals from the hand of a foreigner and offer them as the food of your God. They will not be accepted on your behalf, because they are deformed and have defects.'"

26 The LORD said to Moses, 27 "When a calf, a lamb or a goat is born, it is to remain with its mother for seven days. From the eighth day on, it will be acceptable as a food offering presented to the LORD. 28 Do not slaughter a cow or a sheep and its young on the same day.

29 "When you sacrifice a thank offering to the LORD, sacrifice it in such a way that it will be accepted on your behalf. 30 It must be eaten that same day; leave none of it till morning. I am the LORD.

31 "Keep my commands and follow them. I am the LORD. 32 Do not profane my holy name, for I must be acknowledged as holy by the Israelites. I am the LORD, who made you holy 33 and who brought you out of Egypt to be your God. I am the LORD."

### The Appointed Festivals

**23** The LORD said to Moses, 2 "Speak to the Israelites and say to them: 'These are my appointed festivals, the appointed festivals of the LORD, which you are to proclaim as sacred assemblies.

### The Sabbath

3 "'There are six days when you may work, but the seventh day is a day of sabbath rest, a day of sacred assembly. You are not to do any work; wherever you live, it is a sabbath to the LORD.

### The Passover and the Festival of Unleavened Bread

4 "'These are the LORD's appointed festivals, the sacred assemblies you are to proclaim at their appointed times:

---

[a] 23 The Hebrew word can refer to either male or female.

## Amplified Bible

14 And if a man eats unknowingly of the holy thing [which has been offered to God], then he shall add one-fifth of its value to it and repay that amount to the priest for the holy thing.

15 The priests shall not profane the holy things the Israelites offer to the Lord,

16 And so cause them [by neglect of any essential observance] to bear the iniquity when they eat their holy things; for I the Lord sanctify them.

17 And the Lord said to Moses,

18 Say to Aaron and his sons and to all the Israelites, Whoever of the house of Israel and of the foreigners in Israel brings his offering, whether to pay a vow or as a freewill offering which is offered to the Lord for a burnt offering

19 That you may be accepted, you shall offer a male without blemish of the young bulls, the sheep, or the goats.

20 But you shall not offer anything which has a blemish, for it will not be acceptable for you. [I Pet. 1:19.]

21 And whoever offers a sacrifice of peace offering to the Lord to make a special vow to the Lord or for a freewill offering from the herd or from the flock must bring what is perfect to be accepted; there shall be no blemish in it.

22 Animals blind or made infirm and weak or maimed, or having sores or a wen or an itch or scabs, you shall not offer to the Lord or make an offering of them by fire upon the altar to the Lord.

23 For a freewill offering you may offer either a bull or a lamb which has some part too long or too short, but for [the payment of] a vow it shall not be accepted.

24 You shall not offer to the Lord any animal which has its testicles bruised or crushed or broken or cut, neither sacrifice it in your land.

25 Neither shall you offer as the bread of your God any such animals obtained from a foreigner [who may wish to pay respect to the true God], because their defects render them unfit; there is a blemish in them; they will not be accepted for you.

26 And the Lord said to Moses,

27 When a bull or a sheep or a goat is born, it shall remain for seven days with its mother; and from the eighth day on it shall be accepted for an offering made by fire to the Lord.

28 And whether [the mother] is a cow or a ewe, you shall not kill her and her young both in one day.

29 And when you sacrifice an offering of thanksgiving to the Lord, sacrifice it so that you may be accepted.

30 It shall be eaten on the same day; you shall leave none of it until the next day. I am the Lord.

31 So shall you heartily accept My commandments and conform your life and conduct to them. I am the Lord.

32 Neither shall you profane My holy name [applying it to an idol, or treating it with irreverence or contempt or as a byword]; but I will be hallowed among the Israelites. I am the Lord, Who consecrates and makes you holy,

33 Who brought you out of the land of Egypt to be your God. I am the Lord.

**23** The Lord said to Moses,

2 Say to the Israelites, The set feasts or appointed seasons of the Lord which you shall proclaim as holy convocations, even My set feasts, are these:

3 Six days shall work be done, but the seventh day is the Sabbath of rest, a holy convocation or assembly by summons. You shall do no work on that day; it is the Sabbath of the Lord in all your dwellings.

4 These are the set feasts or appointed seasons of the Lord, holy convocations you shall proclaim at their stated times:

## New International Version

[5]The LORD's Passover begins at twilight on the fourteenth day of the first month. [6]On the fifteenth day of that month the LORD's Festival of Unleavened Bread begins; for seven days you must eat bread made without yeast. [7]On the first day hold a sacred assembly and do no regular work. [8]For seven days present a food offering to the LORD. And on the seventh day hold a sacred assembly and do no regular work.'"

### Offering the Firstfruits
[9]The LORD said to Moses, [10]"Speak to the Israelites and say to them: 'When you enter the land I am going to give you and you reap its harvest, bring to the priest a sheaf of the first grain you harvest. [11]He is to wave the sheaf before the LORD so it will be accepted on your behalf; the priest is to wave it on the day after the Sabbath. [12]On the day you wave the sheaf, you must sacrifice as a burnt offering to the LORD a lamb a year old without defect, [13]together with its grain offering of two-tenths of an ephah[a] of the finest flour mixed with olive oil—a food offering presented to the LORD, a pleasing aroma—and its drink offering of a quarter of a hin[b] of wine. [14]You must not eat any bread, or roasted or new grain, until the very day you bring this offering to your God. This is to be a lasting ordinance for the generations to come, wherever you live.

### The Festival of Weeks
[15]"'From the day after the Sabbath, the day you brought the sheaf of the wave offering, count off seven full weeks. [16]Count off fifty days up to the day after the seventh Sabbath, and then present an offering of new grain to the LORD. [17]From wherever you live, bring two loaves made of two-tenths of an ephah of the finest flour, baked with yeast, as a wave offering of firstfruits to the LORD. [18]Present with this bread seven male lambs, each a year old and without defect, one young bull and two rams. They will be a burnt offering to the LORD, together with their grain offerings and drink offerings—a food offering, an aroma pleasing to the LORD. [19]Then sacrifice one male goat for a sin offering[c] and two lambs, each a year old, for a fellowship offering. [20]The priest is to wave the two lambs before the LORD as a wave offering, together with the bread of the firstfruits. They are a sacred offering to the LORD for the priest. [21]On that same day you are to proclaim a sacred assembly and do no regular work. This is to be a lasting ordinance for the generations to come, wherever you live.

[22]"'When you reap the harvest of your land, do not reap to the very edges of your field or gather the gleanings of your harvest. Leave them for the poor and for the foreigner residing among you. I am the LORD your God.'"

### The Festival of Trumpets
[23]The LORD said to Moses, [24]"Say to the Israelites: 'On the first day of the seventh month you are to have a day of sabbath rest, a sacred assembly commemorated with trumpet blasts. [25]Do no regular work, but present a food offering to the LORD.'"

### The Day of Atonement
[26]The LORD said to Moses, [27]"The tenth day of this seventh month is the Day of Atonement. Hold a sacred assembly and deny yourselves,[d] and present a food offering

## Amplified Bible

[5]On the fourteenth day of the first month at twilight is the Lord's Passover.

[6]On the fifteenth day of the same month is the Feast of Unleavened Bread to the Lord; for seven days you shall eat unleavened bread. [I Cor. 5:7, 8.]

[7]On the first day you shall have a holy "calling together;" you shall do no servile or laborious work on that day.

[8]But you shall offer an offering made by fire to the Lord for seven days; on the seventh day is a holy convocation; you shall do no servile or laborious work on that day.

[9]And the Lord said to Moses,

[10]Tell the Israelites, When you have come into the land I give you and you reap its harvest, you shall bring the sheaf of the firstfruits of your harvest to the priest.

[11]And he shall wave the sheaf before the Lord, that you may be accepted; on the next day after the Sabbath the priest shall wave it [before the Lord].

[12]You shall offer on the day when you wave the sheaf a male lamb a year old without blemish for a burnt offering to the Lord.

[13]Its cereal offering shall be two-tenths of an ephah of fine flour mixed with oil, an offering made by fire to the Lord for a sweet, pleasing, *and* satisfying fragrance; and the drink offering of it [to be poured out] shall be of wine, a fourth of a hin.

[14]And you shall eat neither bread nor parched grain nor green ears, until this same day when you have brought the offering of your God; it is a statute forever throughout your generations in all your houses.

[15]And you shall count from the day after the Sabbath, from the day that you brought the sheaf of the wave offering, seven Sabbaths; [seven full weeks] shall they be.

[16]Count fifty days to the day after the seventh Sabbath; then you shall present a cereal offering of new grain to the Lord.

[17]You shall bring from your dwellings two loaves of bread to be waved, made from two-tenths of an ephah of fine flour; they shall be baked with leaven, for firstfruits to the Lord.

[18]And you shall offer with the bread seven lambs, a year old and without blemish, and one young bull and two rams. They shall be a burnt offering to the Lord, with their cereal offering and their drink offerings, an offering made by fire, of a sweet *and* satisfying fragrance to the Lord.

[19]Then you shall sacrifice one he-goat for a sin offering and two he-lambs, a year old, for a sacrifice of peace offering.

[20]The priest shall wave the two lambs, together with the bread of the firstfruits, for a wave offering before the Lord. They shall be holy to the Lord for the priest.

[21]You shall make proclamation the same day, summoning a holy assembly; you shall do no servile work that day. It shall be a statute forever in all your dwellings throughout your generations.

[22]And when you reap the harvest of your land, you shall not wholly reap the corners of your field, neither shall you gather the gleanings of your harvest; you shall leave them for the poor and the stranger. I am the Lord your God.

[23]And the Lord said to Moses,

[24]Say to the Israelites, On the first day of the seventh month [almost October], you shall observe a day of solemn [sabbatical] rest, a memorial day announced by blowing of trumpets, a holy [called] assembly.

[25]You shall do no servile work on it, but you shall present an offering made by fire to the Lord.

[26]And the Lord said to Moses,

[27]Also the tenth day of this seventh month is the Day of Atonement; it shall be a holy [called] assembly, and you shall afflict yourselves [by fasting in penitence and humility] and present an offering made by fire to the Lord.

---

[a] 13 That is, probably about 7 pounds or about 3.2 kilograms; also in verse 17   [b] 13 That is, about 1 quart or about 1 liter   [c] 19 Or *purification offering*   [d] 27 Or *and fast*; similarly in verses 29 and 32

## New International Version

to the LORD. 28Do not do any work on that day, because it is the Day of Atonement, when atonement is made for you before the LORD your God. 29Those who do not deny themselves on that day must be cut off from their people. 30I will destroy from among their people anyone who does any work on that day. 31You shall do no work at all. This is to be a lasting ordinance for the generations to come, wherever you live. 32It is a day of sabbath rest for you, and you must deny yourselves. From the evening of the ninth day of the month until the following evening you are to observe your sabbath."

*The Festival of Tabernacles*
33The LORD said to Moses, 34"Say to the Israelites: 'On the fifteenth day of the seventh month the LORD's Festival of Tabernacles begins, and it lasts for seven days. 35The first day is a sacred assembly; do no regular work. 36For seven days present food offerings to the LORD, and on the eighth day hold a sacred assembly and present a food offering to the LORD. It is the closing special assembly; do no regular work.
37("These are the LORD's appointed festivals, which you are to proclaim as sacred assemblies for bringing food offerings to the LORD—the burnt offerings and grain offerings, sacrifices and drink offerings required for each day. 38These offerings are in addition to those for the LORD's Sabbaths and*a* in addition to your gifts and whatever you have vowed and all the freewill offerings you give to the LORD.)
39"'So beginning with the fifteenth day of the seventh month, after you have gathered the crops of the land, celebrate the festival to the LORD for seven days; the first day is a day of sabbath rest, and the eighth day also is a day of sabbath rest. 40On the first day you are to take branches from luxuriant trees—from palms, willows and other leafy trees—and rejoice before the LORD your God for seven days. 41Celebrate this as a festival to the LORD for seven days each year. This is to be a lasting ordinance for the generations to come; celebrate it in the seventh month. 42Live in temporary shelters for seven days: All native-born Israelites are to live in such shelters 43so your descendants will know that I had the Israelites live in temporary shelters when I brought them out of Egypt. I am the LORD your God.'"
44So Moses announced to the Israelites the appointed festivals of the LORD.

### Olive Oil and Bread Set Before the LORD

**24** The LORD said to Moses, 2"Command the Israelites to bring you clear oil of pressed olives for the light so that the lamps may be kept burning continually. 3Outside the curtain that shields the ark of the covenant law in the tent of meeting, Aaron is to tend the lamps before the LORD from evening till morning, continually. This is to be a lasting ordinance for the generations to come. 4The lamps on the pure gold lampstand before the LORD must be tended continually.
5"Take the finest flour and bake twelve loaves of bread, using two-tenths of an ephah*b* for each loaf. 6Arrange them in two stacks, six in each stack, on the table of pure gold before the LORD. 7By each stack put some pure in-

*a* 38 Or *These festivals are in addition to the* LORD's *Sabbaths, and these offerings are*   *b* 5 That is, probably about 7 pounds or about 3.2 kilograms

## Amplified Bible

28And you shall do no work on this day, for it is the Day of Atonement, to make atonement for you before the Lord your God.
29For whoever is not afflicted [by fasting in penitence and humility] on this day shall be cut off from among his people [that he may not be included in the atonement made for them].
30And whoever does any work on that same day I will destroy from among his people.
31You shall do no kind of work [on that day]. It is a statute forever throughout your generations in all your dwellings.
32It shall be to you a sabbath of rest, and you shall afflict yourselves [by fasting in penitence and humility]. On the ninth day of the month from evening to evening you shall keep your sabbath.
33And the Lord said to Moses,
34Say to the Israelites, The fifteenth day of this seventh month, and for seven days, is the Feast of Tabernacles *or* Booths to the Lord.
35On the first day shall be a holy convocation; you shall do no servile work on that day.
36For seven days you shall offer an offering made by fire to the Lord; on the eighth day shall be a holy convocation and you shall present an offering made by fire to the Lord. It is a solemn assembly; you shall do no laborious work on that day.
37These are the set feasts *or* appointed seasons of the Lord, which you shall proclaim to be holy convocations, to present an offering made by fire to the Lord, a burnt offering and a cereal offering, sacrifices and drink offerings, each on its own day.
38This is in addition to the Sabbaths of the Lord and besides your gifts and all your vowed offerings and all your freewill offerings which you give to the Lord.
39Also on the fifteenth day of the seventh month [nearly October], when you have gathered in the fruit of the land, you shall keep the feast of the Lord for seven days, the first day and the eighth day each a Sabbath.
40And on the first day you shall take the fruit of pleasing trees [and make booths of them], branches of palm trees, and boughs of thick (leafy) trees, and willows of the brook; and you shall rejoice before the Lord your God for seven days.
41You shall keep it as a feast to the Lord for seven days in the year, a statute forever throughout your generations; you shall keep it in the seventh month.
42You shall dwell in booths (shelters) for seven days: All native Israelites shall dwell in booths,
43That your generations may know that I made the Israelites dwell in booths when I brought them out of the land of Egypt. I am the Lord your God.
44Thus Moses declared to the Israelites the set *or* appointed feasts of the Lord.

**24** And the Lord said to Moses,
2Command the Israelites that they bring to you pure oil from beaten olives for the light [of the golden lampstand] to cause a lamp to burn continually.
3Outside the veil of the Testimony [between the Holy and the Most Holy Places] in the Tent of Meeting, Aaron shall keep it in order from evening to morning before the Lord continually; it shall be a statute forever throughout your generations.
4He shall keep the lamps in order upon the lampstand of pure gold before the Lord continually. [Rev. 1:12-18.]
5And you shall take fine flour and bake twelve cakes with it; two-tenths of an ephah shall be in each cake [of the showbread *or* bread of the Presence].
6And you shall set them in two rows, six in a row, upon the table of pure gold before the Lord.
7You shall put pure frankincense [in a bowl or spoon]

## New International Version

cense as a memorial[a] portion to represent the bread and to be a food offering presented to the LORD. [8]This bread is to be set out before the LORD regularly, Sabbath after Sabbath, on behalf of the Israelites, as a lasting covenant. [9]It belongs to Aaron and his sons, who are to eat it in the sanctuary area, because it is a most holy part of their perpetual share of the food offerings presented to the LORD."

### A Blasphemer Put to Death

[10]Now the son of an Israelite mother and an Egyptian father went out among the Israelites, and a fight broke out in the camp between him and an Israelite. [11]The son of the Israelite woman blasphemed the Name with a curse; so they brought him to Moses. (His mother's name was Shelomith, the daughter of Dibri the Danite.) [12]They put him in custody until the will of the LORD should be made clear to them.

[13]Then the LORD said to Moses: [14]"Take the blasphemer outside the camp. All those who heard him are to lay their hands on his head, and the entire assembly is to stone him. [15]Say to the Israelites: 'Anyone who curses their God will be held responsible; [16]anyone who blasphemes the name of the LORD is to be put to death. The entire assembly must stone them. Whether foreigner or native-born, when they blaspheme the Name they are to be put to death.

[17]"'Anyone who takes the life of a human being is to be put to death. [18]Anyone who takes the life of someone's animal must make restitution—life for life. [19]Anyone who injures their neighbor is to be injured in the same manner: [20]fracture for fracture, eye for eye, tooth for tooth. The one who has inflicted the injury must suffer the same injury. [21]Whoever kills an animal must make restitution, but whoever kills a human being is to be put to death. [22]You are to have the same law for the foreigner and the native-born. I am the LORD your God.'"

[23]Then Moses spoke to the Israelites, and they took the blasphemer outside the camp and stoned him. The Israelites did as the LORD commanded Moses.

### The Sabbath Year

**25** The LORD said to Moses at Mount Sinai, [2]"Speak to the Israelites and say to them: 'When you enter the land I am going to give you, the land itself must observe a sabbath to the LORD. [3]For six years sow your fields, and for six years prune your vineyards and gather their crops. [4]But in the seventh year the land is to have a year of sabbath rest, a sabbath to the LORD. Do not sow your fields or prune your vineyards. [5]Do not reap what grows of itself or harvest the grapes of your untended vines. The land is to have a year of rest. [6]Whatever the land yields during the sabbath year will be food for you—for yourself, your male and female servants, and the hired worker and temporary resident who live among you, [7]as well as for your livestock and the wild animals in your land. Whatever the land produces may be eaten.

### The Year of Jubilee

[8]"Count off seven sabbath years—seven times seven years—so that the seven sabbath years amount to a pe-

## Amplified Bible

beside each row, that it may be with the bread as a memorial portion, an offering to be made by fire to the Lord. [8]Every Sabbath day Aaron shall set the showbread in order before the Lord continually; it is on behalf of the Israelites, an everlasting covenant. [9]And the bread shall be for Aaron and his sons, and they shall eat it in a sacred place, for it is for [Aaron] a most holy portion of the offerings to the Lord made by fire, a perpetual due [to the high priest].

[10]Now the son of an Israelite woman, whose father was an Egyptian, went out among the Israelites, and he and a man of Israel quarreled *and* strove together in the camp. [11]The Israelite woman's son blasphemed the Name [of the Lord] and cursed. They brought him to Moses—his mother was Shelomith, the daughter of Dibri, of the tribe of Dan. [12]And they put him in custody until the will of the Lord might be declared to them. [13]And the Lord said to Moses, [14]Bring him who has cursed out of the camp, and let all who heard him lay their hands upon his head; then let all the congregation stone him. [15]And you shall say to the Israelites, Whoever curses his God shall bear his sin. [16]And he who blasphemes the Name of the Lord, he shall surely be put to death, and all the congregation shall certainly stone him; the stranger as well as he who was born in the land shall be put to death when he blasphemes the Name [of the Lord]. [17]And he who kills any man shall surely be put to death. [18]And he who kills a beast shall make it good, beast for beast. [19]And if a man causes a blemish *or* disfigurement on his neighbor, it shall be done to him as he has done: [20]Fracture for fracture, eye for eye, tooth for tooth; as he has caused a blemish *or* disfigurement on a man, so shall it be done to him. [Matt. 5:38-42; 7:2.] [21]He who kills a beast shall replace it; he who kills a man shall be put to death. [22]You shall have the same law for the sojourner among you as for one of your own nationality, for I am the Lord your God. [23]Moses spoke to the Israelites, and they brought him who had cursed out of the camp and stoned him with stones. Thus the Israelites did as the Lord commanded Moses.

**25** The Lord said to Moses on Mount Sinai, [2]Say to the Israelites, When you come into the land which I give you, then shall the land keep a sabbath to the Lord. [3]For six years you shall sow your field, and for six years you shall prune your vineyard and gather in its fruits. [4]But in the seventh year there shall be a sabbath of solemn rest for the land, a sabbath to the Lord; you shall neither sow your field nor prune your vineyard. [5]What grows of itself in your harvest you shall not reap and the grapes on your uncultivated vine you shall not gather, for it is a year of rest to the land. [6]And the sabbath rest of the [untilled] land shall [in its increase] furnish food for you, for your male and female slaves, your hired servant, and the temporary resident who lives with you, [7]For your domestic animals also and for the [wild] beasts in your land; all its yield shall be for food. [8]And you shall number seven sabbaths *or* weeks of years for you, seven times seven years, so the total time of the seven weeks of years shall be forty-nine years.

## New International Version

riod of forty-nine years. ⁹Then have the trumpet sounded everywhere on the tenth day of the seventh month; on the Day of Atonement sound the trumpet throughout your land. ¹⁰Consecrate the fiftieth year and proclaim liberty throughout the land to all its inhabitants. It shall be a jubilee for you; each of you is to return to your family property and to your own clan. ¹¹The fiftieth year shall be a jubilee for you; do not sow and do not reap what grows of itself or harvest the untended vines. ¹²For it is a jubilee and is to be holy for you; eat only what is taken directly from the fields.

¹³"'In this Year of Jubilee everyone is to return to their own property.

¹⁴"'If you sell land to any of your own people or buy land from them, do not take advantage of each other. ¹⁵You are to buy from your own people on the basis of the number of years since the Jubilee. And they are to sell to you on the basis of the number of years left for harvesting crops. ¹⁶When the years are many, you are to increase the price, and when the years are few, you are to decrease the price, because what is really being sold to you is the number of crops. ¹⁷Do not take advantage of each other, but fear your God. I am the LORD your God.

¹⁸"'Follow my decrees and be careful to obey my laws, and you will live safely in the land. ¹⁹Then the land will yield its fruit, and you will eat your fill and live there in safety. ²⁰You may ask, "What will we eat in the seventh year if we do not plant or harvest our crops?" ²¹I will send you such a blessing in the sixth year that the land will yield enough for three years. ²²While you plant during the eighth year, you will eat from the old crop and will continue to eat from it until the harvest of the ninth year comes in.

²³"'The land must not be sold permanently, because the land is mine and you reside in my land as foreigners and strangers. ²⁴Throughout the land that you hold as a possession, you must provide for the redemption of the land.

²⁵"'If one of your fellow Israelites becomes poor and sells some of their property, their nearest relative is to come and redeem what they have sold. ²⁶If, however, there is no one to redeem it for them but later on they prosper and acquire sufficient means to redeem it themselves, ²⁷they are to determine the value for the years since they sold it and refund the balance to the one to whom they sold it; they can then go back to their own property. ²⁸But if they do not acquire the means to repay, what was sold will remain in the possession of the buyer until the Year of Jubilee. It will be returned in the Jubilee, and they can then go back to their property.

²⁹"'Anyone who sells a house in a walled city retains the right of redemption a full year after its sale. During that time the seller may redeem it. ³⁰If it is not redeemed before a full year has passed, the house in the walled city shall belong permanently to the buyer and the buyer's descendants. It is not to be returned in the Jubilee. ³¹But houses in villages without walls around them are to be considered as belonging to the open country. They can be redeemed, and they are to be returned in the Jubilee.

³²"'The Levites always have the right to redeem their houses in the Levitical towns, which they possess. ³³So

## Amplified Bible

⁹Then you shall sound abroad the loud trumpet on the tenth day of the seventh month [almost October]; on the Day of Atonement blow the trumpet in all your land.

¹⁰And you shall hallow the fiftieth year and proclaim liberty throughout all the land to all its inhabitants. It shall be a jubilee for you; and each of you shall return to his ancestral possession [which through poverty was compelled to sell], and each of you shall return to his family [from whom he was separated in bond service].

¹¹That fiftieth year shall be a jubilee for you; in it you shall not sow, or reap and store what grows of itself, or gather the grapes of the uncultivated vines.

¹²For it is a jubilee; it shall be holy to you; you shall eat the [sufficient] increase of it out of the field.

¹³In this Year of Jubilee each of you shall return to his ancestral property.

¹⁴And if you sell anything to your neighbor or buy from your neighbor, you shall not wrong one another.

¹⁵According to the number of years after the Jubilee, you shall buy from your neighbor. And he shall sell to you according to the number of years [remaining in which you may gather] the crops [before you must restore the property to him].

¹⁶If the years [to the next Jubilee] are many, you may increase the price, and if the years remaining are few, you shall diminish the price, for the number of the crops is what he is selling to you.

¹⁷You shall not oppress *and* wrong one another, but you shall [reverently] fear your God. For I am the Lord your God.

¹⁸Therefore you shall do *and* give effect to My statutes and keep My ordinances and perform them, and you will dwell in the land in safety.

¹⁹The land shall yield its fruit; you shall eat your fill and dwell there in safety.

²⁰And if you say, What shall we eat in the seventh year if we are not to sow or gather in our increase?

²¹Then [this is My answer:] I will command My [special] blessings on you in the sixth year, so that it shall bring forth [sufficient] fruit for three years.

²²And you shall sow in the eighth year, but eat of the old store of produce; until the crops of the ninth year come in you shall eat of the old supply.

²³The land shall not be sold into perpetual ownership, for the land is Mine; for you are [only] strangers and temporary residents with Me. [Heb. 11:13; I Pet. 2:11-17.]

²⁴And in all the country you possess you shall grant a redemption for the land [in the Year of Jubilee].

²⁵If your brother has become poor and has sold some of his property, if any of his kin comes to redeem it, he shall [be allowed to] redeem what his brother has sold.

²⁶And if the man has no one to redeem his property, and he himself has become more prosperous *and* has enough to redeem it,

²⁷Then let him count the years since he sold it and restore the overpayment to the man to whom he sold it, and return to his ancestral possession. [I Kings 21:2, 3.]

²⁸But if he is unable to redeem it, it shall remain in the buyer's possession until the Year of Jubilee, when it shall be set free and he may return to it.

²⁹If a man sells a dwelling house in a fortified city, he may redeem it within a whole year after it is sold; for a full year he may have the right of redemption.

³⁰And if it is not redeemed within a full year, then the house that is in the fortified city shall be made sure, permanently *and* without limitations, for him who bought it, throughout his generations. It shall not go free in the Year of Jubilee.

³¹But the houses of the unwalled villages shall be counted with the fields of the country. They may be redeemed, and they shall go free in the Year of Jubilee.

³²Nevertheless, the cities of the Levites, the houses in the cities of their possession, the Levites may redeem at any time.

## New International Version

the property of the Levites is redeemable—that is, a house sold in any town they hold—and is to be returned in the Jubilee, because the houses in the towns of the Levites are their property among the Israelites. 34 But the pastureland belonging to their towns must not be sold; it is their permanent possession.

35 "If any of your fellow Israelites become poor and are unable to support themselves among you, help them as you would a foreigner and stranger, so they can continue to live among you. 36 Do not take interest or any profit from them, but fear your God, so that they may continue to live among you. 37 You must not lend them money at interest or sell them food at a profit. 38 I am the LORD your God, who brought you out of Egypt to give you the land of Canaan and to be your God.

39 "If any of your fellow Israelites become poor and sell themselves to you, do not make them work as slaves. 40 They are to be treated as hired workers or temporary residents among you; they are to work for you until the Year of Jubilee. 41 Then they and their children are to be released, and they will go back to their own clans and to the property of their ancestors. 42 Because the Israelites are my servants, whom I brought out of Egypt, they must not be sold as slaves. 43 Do not rule over them ruthlessly, but fear your God.

44 "Your male and female slaves are to come from the nations around you; from them you may buy slaves. 45 You may also buy some of the temporary residents living among you and members of their clans born in your country, and they will become your property. 46 You can bequeath them to your children as inherited property and can make them slaves for life, but you must not rule over your fellow Israelites ruthlessly.

47 "If a foreigner residing among you becomes rich and any of your fellow Israelites become poor and sell themselves to the foreigner or to a member of the foreigner's clan, 48 they retain the right of redemption after they have sold themselves. One of their relatives may redeem them: 49 An uncle or a cousin or any blood relative in their clan may redeem them. Or if they prosper, they may redeem themselves. 50 They and their buyer are to count the time from the year they sold themselves up to the Year of Jubilee. The price for their release is to be based on the rate paid to a hired worker for that number of years. 51 If many years remain, they must pay for their redemption a larger share of the price paid for them. 52 If only a few years remain until the Year of Jubilee, they are to compute that and pay for their redemption accordingly. 53 They are to be treated as workers hired from year to year; you must see to it that those to whom they owe service do not rule over them ruthlessly.

## Amplified Bible

33 But if a house is not redeemed by a Levite, the sold house in the city they possess shall go free in the Year of Jubilee, for the houses in the Levite cities are their ancestral possession among the Israelites. 34 But the field of unenclosed or pasture lands of their cities may not be sold; it is their perpetual possession.

35 And if your [Israelite] brother has become poor and his hand wavers [from poverty, sickness, or age and he is unable to support himself], then you shall uphold (strengthen, relieve) him, [treating him with the courtesy and consideration that you would] a stranger or a temporary resident with you [without property], so that he may live [along] with you. [I John 3:17.]

36 Charge him no interest or [portion of] increase, but fear your God, so your brother may [continue to] live along with you.

37 You shall not give him your money at interest nor lend him food at a profit.

38 I am the Lord your God, Who brought you forth out of the land of Egypt to give you the land of Canaan and to be your God.

39 And if your brother becomes poor beside you and sells himself to you, you shall not compel him to serve as a bondman (a slave not eligible for redemption),

40 But as a hired servant and as a temporary resident he shall be with you; he shall serve you till the Year of Jubilee,

41 And then he shall depart from you, he and his children with him, and shall go back to his own family and return to the possession of his fathers.

42 For the Israelites are My servants; I brought them out of the land of Egypt; they shall not be sold as bondmen. [I Cor. 7:23.]

43 You shall not rule over him with harshness (severity, oppression), but you shall [reverently] fear your God. [Eph. 6:9; Col. 4:1.]

44 As for your bondmen and your bondmaids whom you may have, they shall be from the nations round about you, of whom you may buy bondmen and bondmaids.

45 Moreover, of the children of the strangers who sojourn among you, of them you may buy and of their families that are with you which they have begotten in your land, and they shall be your possession.

46 And you shall make them an inheritance for your children after you, to hold for a possession; of them shall you take your bondmen always, but over your brethren the Israelites you shall not rule one over another with harshness (severity, oppression).

47 And if a sojourner or stranger with you becomes rich and your [Israelite] brother becomes poor beside him and sells himself to the stranger or sojourner with you or to a member of the stranger's family,

48 After he is sold he may be redeemed. One of his brethren may redeem him:

49 Either his uncle or his uncle's son may redeem him, or a near kinsman may redeem him; or if he has enough and is able, he may redeem himself.

50 And [the redeemer] shall reckon with the purchaser of the servant from the year when he sold himself to the purchaser to the Year of Jubilee, and the price of his release shall be adjusted according to the number of years. The time he was with his owner shall be counted as that of a hired servant.

51 If there remain many years [before the Year of Jubilee], in proportion to them he must refund [to the purchaser] for his release [the overpayment] for his acquisition.

52 And if little time remains until the Year of Jubilee, he shall count it over with him and he shall refund the proportionate amount for his release.

53 And as a servant hired year by year shall he deal with him; he shall not rule over him with harshness (severity, oppression) in your sight [make sure of that].

## New International Version

54 "'Even if someone is not redeemed in any of these ways, they and their children are to be released in the Year of Jubilee, 55 for the Israelites belong to me as servants. They are my servants, whom I brought out of Egypt. I am the LORD your God.

### Reward for Obedience

**26** "'Do not make idols or set up an image or a sacred stone for yourselves, and do not place a carved stone in your land to bow down before it. I am the LORD your God.

2 "'Observe my Sabbaths and have reverence for my sanctuary. I am the LORD.

3 "'If you follow my decrees and are careful to obey my commands, 4 I will send you rain in its season, and the ground will yield its crops and the trees their fruit. 5 Your threshing will continue until grape harvest and the grape harvest will continue until planting, and you will eat all the food you want and live in safety in your land.

6 "'I will grant peace in the land, and you will lie down and no one will make you afraid. I will remove wild beasts from the land, and the sword will not pass through your country. 7 You will pursue your enemies, and they will fall by the sword before you. 8 Five of you will chase a hundred, and a hundred of you will chase ten thousand, and your enemies will fall by the sword before you.

9 "'I will look on you with favor and make you fruitful and increase your numbers, and I will keep my covenant with you. 10 You will still be eating last year's harvest when you will have to move it out to make room for the new. 11 I will put my dwelling place[a] among you, and I will not abhor you. 12 I will walk among you and be your God, and you will be my people. 13 I am the LORD your God, who brought you out of Egypt so that you would no longer be slaves to the Egyptians; I broke the bars of your yoke and enabled you to walk with heads held high.

### Punishment for Disobedience

14 "'But if you will not listen to me and carry out all these commands, 15 and if you reject my decrees and abhor my laws and fail to carry out all my commands and so violate my covenant, 16 then I will do this to you: I will bring on you sudden terror, wasting diseases and fever that will destroy your sight and sap your strength. You will plant seed in vain, because your enemies will eat it. 17 I will set my face against you so that you will be defeated by your enemies; those who hate you will rule over you, and you will flee even when no one is pursuing you.

18 "'If after all this you will not listen to me, I will punish you for your sins seven times over. 19 I will break down your stubborn pride and make the sky above you like iron and the ground beneath you like bronze. 20 Your strength

## Amplified Bible

54 And if he is not redeemed during these years and by these means, then he shall go free in the Year of Jubilee, he and his children with him.

55 For to Me the Israelites are servants, My servants, whom I brought forth out of the land of Egypt. I am the Lord your God.

**26** You shall make for yourselves no idols nor shall you erect a graven image, pillar, or obelisk, nor shall you place any figured stone in your land to which or on which to bow down; for I am the Lord your God.

2 You shall keep My Sabbaths and reverence My sanctuary. I am the Lord.

3 If you walk in My statutes and keep My commandments and do them,

4 I will give you rain in due season, and the land shall yield her increase and the trees of the field yield their fruit.

5 And your threshing [time] shall reach to the vintage and the vintage [time] shall reach to the sowing time, and you shall eat your bread to the full and dwell in your land securely.

6 I will give peace in the land; you shall lie down and none shall fill you with dread or make you afraid; and I will clear ferocious (wild) beasts out of the land, and no sword shall go through your land.

7 And you shall chase your enemies, and they shall fall before you by the sword.

8 Five of you shall chase a hundred, and a hundred of you shall put ten thousand to flight; your enemies shall fall before you by the sword.

9 For I will be leaning toward you with favor and regard for you, rendering you fruitful, multiplying you, and establishing and ratifying My covenant with you. [II Kings 13:23.]

10 And you shall eat the [abundant] old store of produce long kept, and clear out the old [to make room] for the new.

11 I will set My dwelling in and among you, and My soul shall not despise or reject or separate itself from you.

12 And I will walk in and with and among you and will be your God, and you shall be My people.

13 I am the Lord your God, Who brought you forth out of the land of Egypt, that you should no more be slaves; and I have broken the bars of your yoke and made you walk erect [as free men].

14 But if you will not hearken to Me and will not do all these commandments,

15 And if you spurn and despise My statutes, and if your soul despises and rejects My ordinances, so that you will not do all My commandments, but break My covenant,

16 I will do this: I will appoint over you [sudden] terror (trembling, trouble), even consumption and fever that consume and waste the eyes and make the [physical] life pine away. You shall sow your seed in vain, for your enemies shall eat it.

17 I [the Lord] will set My face against you and [a] you shall be defeated and slain before your enemies; they who hate you shall rule over you; you shall flee when no one pursues you. [I Sam. 4:10; 31:1.]

18 And if in spite of all this you still will not listen and be obedient to Me, then I will chastise and discipline you seven times more for your sins.

19 And I will break and humble your pride in your power, and I will make your heavens as iron [yielding no answer, no blessing, no rain] and your earth [as sterile] as brass. [I Kings 17:1.]

*a This chapter abounds in prophecies of what God would do for, or against, His people if they did, or did not, meet His conditions. Each of these prophecies was literally fulfilled in the following centuries. The Scripture references indicate where these fulfillments are recorded; there are at least a dozen of them. Yet some people do not seem to have awakened to the fact that God **keeps His word,** whether for us or against us. It all depends on us.*

*a 11 Or my tabernacle*

## New International Version

will be spent in vain, because your soil will not yield its crops, nor will the trees of your land yield their fruit.

21 "'If you remain hostile toward me and refuse to listen to me, I will multiply your afflictions seven times over, as your sins deserve. 22 I will send wild animals against you, and they will rob you of your children, destroy your cattle and make you so few in number that your roads will be deserted.

23 "'If in spite of these things you do not accept my correction but continue to be hostile toward me, 24 I myself will be hostile toward you and will afflict you for your sins seven times over. 25 And I will bring the sword on you to avenge the breaking of the covenant. When you withdraw into your cities, I will send a plague among you, and you will be given into enemy hands. 26 When I cut off your supply of bread, ten women will be able to bake your bread in one oven, and they will dole out the bread by weight. You will eat, but you will not be satisfied.

27 "'If in spite of this you still do not listen to me but continue to be hostile toward me, 28 then in my anger I will be hostile toward you, and I myself will punish you for your sins seven times over. 29 You will eat the flesh of your sons and the flesh of your daughters. 30 I will destroy your high places, cut down your incense altars and pile your dead bodies[a] on the lifeless forms of your idols, and I will abhor you. 31 I will turn your cities into ruins and lay waste your sanctuaries, and I will take no delight in the pleasing aroma of your offerings. 32 I myself will lay waste the land, so that your enemies who live there will be appalled. 33 I will scatter you among the nations and will draw out my sword and pursue you. Your land will be laid waste, and your cities will lie in ruins. 34 Then the land will enjoy its sabbath years all the time that it lies desolate and you are in the country of your enemies; then the land will rest and enjoy its sabbaths. 35 All the time that it lies desolate, the land will have the rest it did not have during the sabbaths you lived in it.

36 "'As for those of you who are left, I will make their hearts so fearful in the lands of their enemies that the sound of a windblown leaf will put them to flight. They will run as though fleeing from the sword, and they will fall, even though no one is pursuing them. 37 They will stumble over one another as though fleeing from the sword, even though no one is pursuing them. So you will not be able to stand before your enemies. 38 You will perish among the nations; the land of your enemies will devour you. 39 Those of you who are left will waste away in the lands of their enemies because of their sins; also because of their ancestors' sins they will waste away.

40 "'But if they will confess their sins and the sins of their ancestors—their unfaithfulness and their hostility toward me, 41 which made me hostile toward them so that I sent them into the land of their enemies—then when their uncircumcised hearts are humbled and they pay for their sin, 42 I will remember my covenant with Jacob and

## Amplified Bible

20 And your strength shall be spent in vain, for your land shall not yield its increase, neither shall the trees of the land yield their fruit.

21 If you walk contrary to Me and will not heed Me, I will bring seven times more plagues upon you, according to your sins.

22 I will loose the wild beasts of the field among you, which shall rob you of your children, destroy your livestock, and make you few so that your roads shall be deserted and desolate. [II Kings 17:25, 26.]

23 If by these means you are not turned to Me but determine to walk contrary to Me,

24 I also will walk contrary to you, and I will smite you seven times for your sins.

25 And I will bring a sword upon you that shall execute the vengeance [for the breaking] of My covenant; and you shall be gathered together within your cities, and I will send the pestilence among you, and you shall be delivered into the hands of the enemy. [Num. 16:49; II Sam. 24:15.]

26 When I break your staff of bread and cut off your supply of food, ten women shall bake your bread in one oven, and they shall ration your bread and deliver it again by weight; and you shall eat, and not be satisfied. [Hag. 1:6.]

27 And if in spite of all this you will not listen and give heed to Me but walk contrary to Me,

28 Then I will walk contrary to you in wrath, and I also will chastise you seven times for your sins.

29 You shall eat the flesh of your sons and of your daughters. [II Kings 6:28, 29.]

30 And I will destroy your high places [devoted to idolatrous worship], and cut down your sun-images, and throw your dead bodies upon the [wrecked] bodies of your idols, and My soul shall abhor you [with deep and unutterable loathing]. [II Kings 23:8, 20.]

31 I will lay your cities waste, bring your sanctuaries to desolation, and I will not smell the fragrance of your sweet and soothing odors [of offerings made by fire]. [II Kings 25:4-10; II Chron. 36:19.]

32 And I will bring the land into desolation, and your enemies who dwell in it shall be astonished at it.

33 I will scatter you among the nations and draw out [your enemies'] sword after you; and your land shall be desolate and your cities a waste. [Ps. 44:11-14.]

34 Then shall the land [of Israel have the opportunity to] enjoy its sabbaths as long as it lies desolate and you are in your enemies' land; then shall the land rest, to enjoy and receive payments for its sabbaths [divinely ordained for it].

35 As long as it lies desolate and waste, it shall have rest, the rest it did not have in your sabbaths when you dwelt upon it. [II Chron. 36:21.]

36 As for those who are left of you, I will send dejection (lack of courage, a faintness) into their hearts in the lands of their enemies; the sound of a driven leaf shall put them to hasty and tumultuous flight, and they shall flee as if from the sword, and fall when no one pursues them.

37 They shall stumble over one another as if to escape a sword when no one pursues them; and you shall have no power to stand before your enemies.

38 You shall perish among the nations; the land of your enemies shall eat you up.

39 And those of you who are left shall pine away in their iniquity in your enemies' lands; also in the iniquities of their fathers shall they pine away like them.

40 But if they confess their own and their fathers' iniquity in their treachery which they committed against Me—and also that because they walked contrary to Me

41 I also walked contrary to them and brought them into the land of their enemies—if then their uncircumcised hearts are humbled and they then accept the punishment for their iniquity, [II Kings 24:10-14; Dan. 9:11-14.]

42 Then will I [earnestly] remember My covenant with Ja-

---

[a] 30 Or *your funeral offerings*

## New International Version

my covenant with Isaac and my covenant with Abraham, and I will remember the land. ⁴³For the land will be deserted by them and will enjoy its sabbaths while it lies desolate without them. They will pay for their sins because they rejected my laws and abhorred my decrees. ⁴⁴Yet in spite of this, when they are in the land of their enemies, I will not reject them or abhor them so as to destroy them completely, breaking my covenant with them. I am the Lᴏʀᴅ their God. ⁴⁵But for their sake I will remember the covenant with their ancestors whom I brought out of Egypt in the sight of the nations to be their God. I am the Lᴏʀᴅ.'"

⁴⁶These are the decrees, the laws and the regulations that the Lᴏʀᴅ established at Mount Sinai between himself and the Israelites through Moses.

### Redeeming What Is the Lᴏʀᴅ's

**27** The Lᴏʀᴅ said to Moses, ²"Speak to the Israelites and say to them: 'If anyone makes a special vow to dedicate a person to the Lᴏʀᴅ by giving the equivalent value, ³set the value of a male between the ages of twenty and sixty at fifty shekels*ᵃ* of silver, according to the sanctuary shekel*ᵇ*; ⁴for a female, set her value at thirty shekels*ᶜ*; ⁵for a person between the ages of five and twenty, set the value of a male at twenty shekels*ᵈ* and of a female at ten shekels*ᵉ*; ⁶for a person between one month and five years, set the value of a male at five shekels*ᶠ* of silver and that of a female at three shekels*ᵍ* of silver; ⁷for a person sixty years old or more, set the value of a male at fifteen shekels*ʰ* and of a female at ten shekels. ⁸If anyone making the vow is too poor to pay the specified amount, the person being dedicated is to be presented to the priest, who will set the value according to what the one making the vow can afford.

⁹"'If what they vowed is an animal that is acceptable as an offering to the Lᴏʀᴅ, such an animal given to the Lᴏʀᴅ becomes holy. ¹⁰They must not exchange it or substitute a good one for a bad one, or a bad one for a good one; if they should substitute one animal for another, both it and the substitute become holy. ¹¹If what they vowed is a ceremonially unclean animal—one that is not acceptable as an offering to the Lᴏʀᴅ—the animal must be presented to the priest, ¹²who will judge its quality as good or bad. Whatever value the priest then sets, that is what it will be. ¹³If the owner wishes to redeem the animal, a fifth must be added to its value.

¹⁴"'If anyone dedicates their house as something holy to the Lᴏʀᴅ, the priest will judge its quality as good or bad. Whatever value the priest then sets, so it will remain. ¹⁵If the one who dedicates their house wishes to redeem it, they must add a fifth to its value, and the house will again become theirs.

¹⁶"'If anyone dedicates to the Lᴏʀᴅ part of their family land, its value is to be set according to the amount of seed required for it—fifty shekels of silver to a homer*ⁱ* of barley

## Amplified Bible

cob, My covenant with Isaac, and My covenant with Abraham, and [earnestly] remember the land. [Ps. 106:44-46.]

⁴³But the land shall be left behind them and shall enjoy its sabbaths while it lies desolate without them; and they shall accept the punishment for their sins *and* make amends because they despised *and* rejected My ordinances and their soul scorned *and* rejected My statutes.

⁴⁴And *ᵃ*yet for all that, when they are in the land of their enemies, I will not spurn *and* cast them away, neither will I despise *and* abhor them to destroy them utterly and to break My covenant with them, for I am the Lord their God. [Deut. 4:31-35; Jer. 33:4, 5, 23-26; Rom. 11:2-5.]

⁴⁵But I will for their sake [earnestly] remember the covenant with their forefathers whom I brought forth out of the land of Egypt in the sight of the nations, that I might be their God. I am the Lord.

⁴⁶These are the statutes, ordinances, and laws which the Lord made between Him and the Israelites on Mount Sinai through Moses.

**27** And the Lord said to Moses, ²Say to the Israelites, When a man shall make a special vow of persons to the Lord at your valuation,

³Then your valuation of a male from twenty years old to sixty years old shall be fifty shekels of silver, according to the shekel of the sanctuary.

⁴And if the person is a female, your valuation shall be thirty shekels.

⁵And if the person is from five years old up to twenty years old, then your valuation shall be for the male twenty shekels and for the female ten shekels.

⁶And if a child is from a month to five years old, then your valuation shall be for the male five shekels of silver and for the female three shekels.

⁷And if the person is from sixty years old and above, if it be a male, then your valuation shall be fifteen shekels and for the female ten shekels.

⁸But if the man is too poor to pay your valuation, then he shall be set before the priest, and the priest shall value him; according to the ability of him who vowed shall the priest value him.

⁹If it is a beast of which men offer an offering to the Lord, all that any man gives of such to the Lord shall be holy.

¹⁰He shall not replace it or exchange it, a good for a bad, or a bad for a good; and if he makes any exchange of a beast for a beast, then both the original offering and that exchanged for it shall be holy.

¹¹If it is an unclean animal, such as is not offered as an offering to the Lord, he shall bring the animal before the priest,

¹²And the priest shall value it, whether it be good or bad; as you, the priest, value it, so shall it be.

¹³But if he wishes to redeem it, he shall add a fifth to your valuation.

¹⁴If a man dedicates his house to be sacred to the Lord, the priest shall appraise it, whether it be good or bad; as the priest appraises it, so shall it stand.

¹⁵If he who dedicates his house wants to redeem it, he shall add a fifth of your valuation to it, and it shall be his.

¹⁶And if a man shall dedicate to the Lord some part of a field of his possession, then your valuation shall be according to the seed [required] for it; [a sowing of] a homer of barley shall be valued at fifty shekels of silver.

---

*ᵃ 3* That is, about 1 1/4 pounds or about 575 grams; also in verse 16
*ᵇ 3* That is, about 2/5 ounce or about 12 grams; also in verse 25
*ᶜ 4* That is, about 12 ounces or about 345 grams    *ᵈ 5* That is, about 8 ounces or about 230 grams    *ᵉ 5* That is, about 4 ounces or about 115 grams; also in verse 7    *ᶠ 6* That is, about 2 ounces or about 58 grams    *ᵍ 6* That is, about 1 1/4 ounces or about 35 grams    *ʰ 7* That is, about 6 ounces or about 175 grams    *ⁱ 16* That is, probably about 300 pounds or about 135 kilograms

*ᵃ* No greater evidence that God keeps His word is available than the fact of the existence today of the Jews as a nation. Scattered for twenty-five centuries throughout the world with powerful forces determined to wipe them out, yet they are restored to their homeland because, in spite of all their sins against Him, God refuses to break His covenant with their forefathers and with them. The presence of even a small number of Jews in the world, after all the centuries of diabolical effort to exterminate them, would alone be sufficient assurance that God will keep His promises, whether good or bad, to individuals or to nations.

## New International Version

seed. [17] If they dedicate a field during the Year of Jubilee, the value that has been set remains. [18] But if they dedicate a field after the Jubilee, the priest will determine the value according to the number of years that remain until the next Year of Jubilee, and its set value will be reduced. [19] If the one who dedicates the field wishes to redeem it, they must add a fifth to its value, and the field will again become theirs. [20] If, however, they do not redeem the field, or if they have sold it to someone else, it can never be redeemed. [21] When the field is released in the Jubilee, it will become holy, like a field devoted to the LORD; it will become priestly property.

[22] "'If anyone dedicates to the LORD a field they have bought, which is not part of their family land, [23] the priest will determine its value up to the Year of Jubilee, and the owner must pay its value on that day as something holy to the LORD. [24] In the Year of Jubilee the field will revert to the person from whom it was bought, the one whose land it was. [25] Every value is to be set according to the sanctuary shekel, twenty gerahs to the shekel.

[26] "'No one, however, may dedicate the firstborn of an animal, since the firstborn already belongs to the LORD; whether an ox[a] or a sheep, it is the LORD's. [27] If it is one of the unclean animals, it may be bought back at its set value, adding a fifth of the value to it. If it is not redeemed, it is to be sold at its set value.

[28] "'But nothing that a person owns and devotes[b] to the LORD—whether a human being or an animal or family land—may be sold or redeemed; everything so devoted is most holy to the LORD.

[29] "'No person devoted to destruction[c] may be ransomed; they are to be put to death.

[30] "'A tithe of everything from the land, whether grain from the soil or fruit from the trees, belongs to the LORD; it is holy to the LORD. [31] Whoever would redeem any of their tithe must add a fifth of the value to it. [32] Every tithe of the herd and flock—every tenth animal that passes under the shepherd's rod—will be holy to the LORD. [33] No one may pick out the good from the bad or make any substitution. If anyone does make a substitution, both the animal and its substitute become holy and cannot be redeemed.'"

[34] These are the commands the LORD gave Moses at Mount Sinai for the Israelites.

## Amplified Bible

[17] If he dedicates his field during the Year of Jubilee, it shall stand according to your full valuation. [18] But if he dedicates his field after the Jubilee, then the priest shall count the money value in proportion to the years that remain until the Year of Jubilee, and it shall be deducted from your valuation. [19] If he who dedicates the field wishes to redeem it, then he shall add a fifth of the money of your appraisal to it, and it shall remain his. [20] But if he does not want to redeem the field, or if he has sold it to another man, it shall not be redeemed any more. [21] But the field, when it is released in the Jubilee, shall be holy to the Lord, as a field devoted [to God or destruction]; the priest shall have possession of it. [22] And if a man dedicates to the Lord a field he has bought, which is not of the fields of his [ancestral] possession, [23] The priest shall compute the amount of your valuation for it up to the Year of Jubilee; the man shall give that amount on that day as a holy thing to the Lord. [24] In the Year of Jubilee the field shall return to him of whom it was bought, to him to whom the land belonged [as his ancestral inheritance]. [25] And all your valuations shall be according to the sanctuary shekel; twenty gerahs shall make a shekel. [26] But the firstling of the animals, since a firstling belongs to the Lord, no man may dedicate, whether it be ox or sheep. It is the Lord's [already]. [27] If it be of an unclean animal, the owner may redeem it according to your valuation, and shall add a fifth to it; or if it is not redeemed, then it shall be sold according to your valuation. [28] But nothing that a man shall devote to the Lord of all that he has, whether of man or beast or of the field of his possession, shall be sold or redeemed; every devoted thing is most holy to the Lord. [29] No one doomed to death [under the claim of divine justice], who is to be completely destroyed from among men, shall be ransomed [from suffering the death penalty]; he shall surely be put to death. [30] And all the tithe of the land, whether of the seed of the land or of the fruit of the tree, is the Lord's; it is holy to the Lord. [I Cor. 9:11; Gal. 6:6.] [31] And if a man wants to redeem any of his tithe, he shall add a fifth to it. [32] And all the tithe of the herd or of the flock, whatever passes under the herdsman's staff [by means of which each tenth animal as it passes through a small door is selected and marked], the tenth shall be holy to the Lord. [II Cor. 9:7-9.] [33] The man shall not examine whether the animal is good or bad nor shall he exchange it. If he does exchange it, then both it and the animal substituted for it shall be holy; it shall not be redeemed. [34] These are the commandments which the Lord commanded Moses on Mount Sinai for the Israelites. [Rom. 10:4; Heb. 4:2; 12:18-29.]

---

[a] 26 The Hebrew word can refer to either male or female.
[b] 28 The Hebrew term refers to the irrevocable giving over of things or persons to the LORD.  [c] 29 The Hebrew term refers to the irrevocable giving over of things or persons to the LORD, often by totally destroying them.

# Numbers

# Numbers

## The Census

**1** The Lord spoke to Moses in the tent of meeting in the Desert of Sinai on the first day of the second month of the second year after the Israelites came out of Egypt. He said: ²"Take a census of the whole Israelite community by their clans and families, listing every man by name, one by one. ³You and Aaron are to count according to their divisions all the men in Israel who are twenty years old or more and able to serve in the army. ⁴One man from each tribe, each of them the head of his family, is to help you. ⁵These are the names of the men who are to assist you:

from Reuben, Elizur son of Shedeur;
⁶from Simeon, Shelumiel son of Zurishaddai;
⁷from Judah, Nahshon son of Amminadab;
⁸from Issachar, Nethanel son of Zuar;
⁹from Zebulun, Eliab son of Helon;
¹⁰from the sons of Joseph:
  from Ephraim, Elishama son of Ammihud;
  from Manasseh, Gamaliel son of Pedahzur;
¹¹from Benjamin, Abidan son of Gideoni;
¹²from Dan, Ahiezer son of Ammishaddai;
¹³from Asher, Pagiel son of Okran;
¹⁴from Gad, Eliasaph son of Deuel;
¹⁵from Naphtali, Ahira son of Enan."

¹⁶These were the men appointed from the community, the leaders of their ancestral tribes. They were the heads of the clans of Israel.

¹⁷Moses and Aaron took these men whose names had been specified, ¹⁸and they called the whole community together on the first day of the second month. The people registered their ancestry by their clans and families, and the men twenty years old or more were listed by name, one by one, ¹⁹as the Lord commanded Moses. And so he counted them in the Desert of Sinai:

²⁰From the descendants of Reuben the firstborn son of Israel:
All the men twenty years old or more who were able to serve in the army were listed by name, one by one, according to the records of their clans and families. ²¹The number from the tribe of Reuben was 46,500.

²²From the descendants of Simeon:
All the men twenty years old or more who were able to serve in the army were counted and listed by name, one by one, according to the records of their clans and families. ²³The number from the tribe of Simeon was 59,300.

²⁴From the descendants of Gad:
All the men twenty years old or more who were able to serve in the army were listed by name, according to the records of their clans and families. ²⁵The number from the tribe of Gad was 45,650.

²⁶From the descendants of Judah:
All the men twenty years old or more who were able to serve in the army were listed by name, according to the records of their clans and families. ²⁷The number from the tribe of Judah was 74,600.

²⁸From the descendants of Issachar:
All the men twenty years old or more who were

**1** The Lord spoke to Moses in the Wilderness of Sinai in the Tent of Meeting on the first day of the second month in the second year after they came out of the land of Egypt, saying,

²Take a census of all the males of the congregation of the Israelites by families, by their fathers' houses, according to the number of names, head by head.

³From twenty years old and upward, all in Israel who are able to go forth to war you and Aaron shall number, company by company.

⁴And with you there shall be a man [to assist you] from each tribe, each being the head of his father's house.

⁵And these are the names of the men who shall attend you: Of Reuben, Elizur son of Shedeur;
⁶Of Simeon, Shelumiel son of Zurishaddai;
⁷Of Judah, Nahshon son of Amminadab;
⁸Of Issachar, Nethanel son of Zuar;
⁹Of Zebulun, Eliab son of Helon;
¹⁰Of the sons of Joseph: of Ephraim, Elishama son of Ammihud; of Manasseh, Gamaliel son of Pedahzur;
¹¹Of Benjamin, Abidan son of Gideoni;
¹²Of Dan, Ahiezer son of Ammishaddai;
¹³Of Asher, Pagiel son of Ochran;
¹⁴Of Gad, Eliasaph son of Deuel;
¹⁵Of Naphtali, Ahira son of Enan.

¹⁶These were those chosen from the congregation, the leaders of their ancestral tribes, heads of thousands [the highest class of officers] in Israel.

¹⁷And Moses and Aaron took these men who have been named,

¹⁸And assembled all the congregation on the first day of the second month, and they declared their ancestry after their families, by their fathers' houses, according to the number of names from twenty years old and upward, head by head,

¹⁹As the Lord commanded Moses. So he numbered them in the Wilderness of Sinai.

²⁰The sons of Reuben, Israel's firstborn, their generations, by their families, by their fathers' houses, according to the number of names, head by head, every male from twenty years old and upward, all who were able to go to war:

²¹Those of the tribe of Reuben numbered 46,500.

²²Of the sons of Simeon, their generations, by their families, by their fathers' houses, those numbered of them according to the number of names, head by head, every male from twenty years old and upward, all who were able to go to war:

²³Those of the tribe of Simeon numbered 59,300.

²⁴Of the sons of Gad, their generations, by their families, by their fathers' houses, according to the number of names, from twenty years old and upward, all who were able to go to war:

²⁵Those of the tribe of Gad numbered 45,650.

²⁶Of the sons of Judah, their generations, by their families, by their fathers' houses, according to the number of names, from twenty years old and upward, all able to go to war:

²⁷Those of the tribe of Judah numbered 74,600.

²⁸Of the sons of Issachar, their generations, by their families, by their fathers' houses, according to the num-

## New International Version

able to serve in the army were listed by name, according to the records of their clans and families. [29]The number from the tribe of Issachar was 54,400.

[30]From the descendants of Zebulun:

All the men twenty years old or more who were able to serve in the army were listed by name, according to the records of their clans and families. [31]The number from the tribe of Zebulun was 57,400.

[32]From the sons of Joseph:

From the descendants of Ephraim:

All the men twenty years old or more who were able to serve in the army were listed by name, according to the records of their clans and families. [33]The number from the tribe of Ephraim was 40,500.

[34]From the descendants of Manasseh:

All the men twenty years old or more who were able to serve in the army were listed by name, according to the records of their clans and families. [35]The number from the tribe of Manasseh was 32,200.

[36]From the descendants of Benjamin:

All the men twenty years old or more who were able to serve in the army were listed by name, according to the records of their clans and families. [37]The number from the tribe of Benjamin was 35,400.

[38]From the descendants of Dan:

All the men twenty years old or more who were able to serve in the army were listed by name, according to the records of their clans and families. [39]The number from the tribe of Dan was 62,700.

[40]From the descendants of Asher:

All the men twenty years old or more who were able to serve in the army were listed by name, according to the records of their clans and families. [41]The number from the tribe of Asher was 41,500.

[42]From the descendants of Naphtali:

All the men twenty years old or more who were able to serve in the army were listed by name, according to the records of their clans and families. [43]The number from the tribe of Naphtali was 53,400.

[44]These were the men counted by Moses and Aaron and the twelve leaders of Israel, each one representing his family. [45]All the Israelites twenty years old or more who were able to serve in Israel's army were counted according to their families. [46]The total number was 603,550.

[47]The ancestral tribe of the Levites, however, was not counted along with the others. [48]The LORD had said to Moses: [49]"You must not count the tribe of Levi or include them in the census of the other Israelites. [50]Instead, appoint the Levites to be in charge of the tabernacle of the covenant law—over all its furnishings and everything belonging to it. They are to carry the tabernacle and all its furnishings; they are to take care of it and encamp around it. [51]Whenever the tabernacle is to move, the Levites are

## Amplified Bible

ber of names, from twenty years old and upward, all able to go to war:

[29]Those of the tribe of Issachar numbered 54,400.

[30]Of the sons of Zebulun, their generations, by their families, by their fathers' houses, according to the number of names, from twenty years old and upward, all able to go to war:

[31]Those of the tribe of Zebulun numbered 57,400.

[32]Of the sons of Joseph: the sons of Ephraim, their generations, by their families, by their fathers' houses, according to the number of names, from twenty years old and upward, all able to go to war:

[33]Those of the tribe of Ephraim numbered 40,500.

[34]Of the sons of Manasseh, their generations, by their families, by their fathers' houses, according to the number of names, from twenty years old and upward, all able to go to war:

[35]Those of the tribe of Manasseh numbered 32,200.

[36]Of the sons of Benjamin, their generations, by their families, by their fathers' houses, according to the number of names, from twenty years old and upward, all able to go to war:

[37]Those of the tribe of Benjamin numbered 35,400.

[38]Of the sons of Dan, their generations, by their families, by their fathers' houses, according to the number of names, from twenty years old and upward, all able to go to war:

[39]Those of the tribe of Dan numbered 62,700.

[40]Of the sons of Asher, their generations, by their families, by their fathers' houses, according to the number of names, from twenty years old and upward, all able to go to war:

[41]Those of the tribe of Asher numbered 41,500.

[42]Of the sons of Naphtali, their generations, by their families, by their fathers' houses, according to the number of names, from twenty years old and upward, all able to go to war:

[43]Those of the tribe of Naphtali numbered 53,400.

[44]These were numbered by Moses and Aaron, and the leaders of Israel, twelve men, each representing his father's house.

[45]So all those numbered of the Israelites, by their fathers' houses, from twenty years old and upward, able to go to war in Israel,

[46]All who were numbered were 603,550.

[47]But the Levites by their fathers' tribe were not numbered with them.

[48]For the Lord had said to Moses,

[49]Only the tribe of Levi you shall not number in the census of the Israelites.

[50]But appoint the Levites over the tabernacle of the Testimony, and over all its vessels and furnishings and all things that belong to it. They shall carry the tabernacle [when journeying] and all its furnishings, and they shall minister to it and encamp around it.

[51]When the tabernacle is to go forward, the Levites

## New International Version

to take it down, and whenever the tabernacle is to be set up, the Levites shall do it. Anyone else who approaches it is to be put to death. [52]The Israelites are to set up their tents by divisions, each of them in their own camp under their standard. [53]The Levites, however, are to set up their tents around the tabernacle of the covenant law so that my wrath will not fall on the Israelite community. The Levites are to be responsible for the care of the tabernacle of the covenant law."

[54]The Israelites did all this just as the LORD commanded Moses.

### The Arrangement of the Tribal Camps

**2** The LORD said to Moses and Aaron: [2]"The Israelites are to camp around the tent of meeting some distance from it, each of them under their standard and holding the banners of their family."

[3]On the east, toward the sunrise, the divisions of the camp of Judah are to encamp under their standard. The leader of the people of Judah is Nahshon son of Amminadab. [4]His division numbers 74,600.

[5]The tribe of Issachar will camp next to them. The leader of the people of Issachar is Nethanel son of Zuar. [6]His division numbers 54,400.

[7]The tribe of Zebulun will be next. The leader of the people of Zebulun is Eliab son of Helon. [8]His division numbers 57,400.

[9]All the men assigned to the camp of Judah, according to their divisions, number 186,400. They will set out first.

[10]On the south will be the divisions of the camp of Reuben under their standard. The leader of the people of Reuben is Elizur son of Shedeur. [11]His division numbers 46,500.

[12]The tribe of Simeon will camp next to them. The leader of the people of Simeon is Shelumiel son of Zurishaddai. [13]His division numbers 59,300.

[14]The tribe of Gad will be next. The leader of the people of Gad is Eliasaph son of Deuel.[a] [15]His division numbers 45,650.

[16]All the men assigned to the camp of Reuben, according to their divisions, number 151,450. They will set out second.

[17]Then the tent of meeting and the camp of the Levites will set out in the middle of the camps. They will set out in the same order as they encamp, each in their own place under their standard.

[18]On the west will be the divisions of the camp of Ephraim under their standard. The leader of the people of Ephraim is Elishama son of Ammihud. [19]His division numbers 40,500.

[20]The tribe of Manasseh will be next to them. The leader of the people of Manasseh is Gamaliel son of Pedahzur. [21]His division numbers 32,200.

## Amplified Bible

shall take it down, and when the tabernacle is to be pitched, the Levites shall set it up. And the excluded [any not of the tribe of Levi] who approach the tabernacle shall be put to death.

[52]The Israelites shall pitch their tents by their companies, every man by his own camp and every man by his own [tribal] standard.

[53]But the Levites shall encamp around the tabernacle of the Testimony, that there may be no wrath upon the congregation of the Israelites; and the Levites shall keep charge of the tabernacle of the Testimony.

[54]Thus did the Israelites; according to all that the Lord commanded Moses, so they did.

**2** The Lord said to Moses and Aaron,
[2]The Israelites shall encamp, each by his own [tribal] standard or banner with the ensign of his father's house, opposite the Tent of Meeting and facing it on every side.

[3]On the east side toward the sunrise shall they of the standard of the camp of Judah encamp by their companies; Nahshon son of Amminadab being the leader of the sons of Judah.

[4]Judah's host as numbered totaled 74,600.

[5]Next to Judah the tribe of Issachar shall encamp, Nethanel son of Zuar being the leader of the sons of Issachar.

[6]Issachar's host as numbered totaled 54,400.

[7]Then the tribe of Zebulun, Eliab son of Helon being the leader of the sons of Zebulun.

[8]Zebulun's host as numbered totaled 57,400.

[9]All these [three tribes] numbered in the camp of Judah totaled 186,400. They shall set forth first [on the march].

[10]On the south side shall be the standard of the camp of Reuben by their companies, the leader of the sons of Reuben being Elizur son of Shedeur.

[11]Reuben's host as numbered totaled 46,500.

[12]Those who encamp next to Reuben shall be the tribe of Simeon, the leader of the sons of Simeon being Shelumiel son of Zurishaddai.

[13]Simeon's host as numbered totaled 59,300.

[14]Then the tribe of Gad, the leader of the sons of Gad being Eliasaph son of Reuel (Deuel).

[15]Gad's host as numbered totaled 45,650.

[16]The whole number in [the three tribes of] the camp of Reuben was 151,450. They shall take second place [on the march].

[17]Then the Tent of Meeting shall set out, with the camp of the Levites in the midst of the camps; as they encamp so shall they set forward, every man in his place, standard after standard.

[18]On the west side shall be the standard of the camp of Ephraim by their companies, the leader of the sons of Ephraim being Elishama son of Ammihud.

[19]Ephraim's host as numbered totaled 40,500.

[20]Beside Ephraim shall be the tribe of Manasseh, the leader of the sons of Manasseh being Gamaliel son of Pedahzur.

[21]Manasseh's host as numbered totaled 32,200.

---

[a] 14 Many manuscripts of the Masoretic Text, Samaritan Pentateuch and Vulgate (see also 1:14); most manuscripts of the Masoretic Text *Reuel*

## New International Version

²²The tribe of Benjamin will be next. The leader of the people of Benjamin is Abidan son of Gideoni. ²³His division numbers 35,400.

²⁴All the men assigned to the camp of Ephraim, according to their divisions, number 108,100. They will set out third.

²⁵On the north will be the divisions of the camp of Dan under their standard. The leader of the people of Dan is Ahiezer son of Ammishaddai. ²⁶His division numbers 62,700.

²⁷The tribe of Asher will camp next to them. The leader of the people of Asher is Pagiel son of Okran. ²⁸His division numbers 41,500.

²⁹The tribe of Naphtali will be next. The leader of the people of Naphtali is Ahira son of Enan. ³⁰His division numbers 53,400.

³¹All the men assigned to the camp of Dan number 157,600. They will set out last, under their standards.

³²These are the Israelites, counted according to their families. All the men in the camps, by their divisions, number 603,550. ³³The Levites, however, were not counted along with the other Israelites, as the LORD commanded Moses.

³⁴So the Israelites did everything the LORD commanded Moses; that is the way they encamped under their standards, and that is the way they set out, each of them with their clan and family.

### The Levites

**3** This is the account of the family of Aaron and Moses at the time the LORD spoke to Moses at Mount Sinai.

²The names of the sons of Aaron were Nadab the first-born and Abihu, Eleazar and Ithamar. ³Those were the names of Aaron's sons, the anointed priests, who were ordained to serve as priests. ⁴Nadab and Abihu, however, died before the LORD when they made an offering with unauthorized fire before him in the Desert of Sinai. They had no sons, so Eleazar and Ithamar served as priests during the lifetime of their father Aaron.

⁵The LORD said to Moses, ⁶"Bring the tribe of Levi and present them to Aaron the priest to assist him. ⁷They are to perform duties for him and for the whole community at the tent of meeting by doing the work of the tabernacle. ⁸They are to take care of all the furnishings of the tent of meeting, fulfilling the obligations of the Israelites by doing the work of the tabernacle. ⁹Give the Levites to Aaron and his sons; they are the Israelites who are to be given wholly to him.ᵃ ¹⁰Appoint Aaron and his sons to serve as priests; anyone else who approaches the sanctuary is to be put to death."

¹¹The LORD also said to Moses, ¹²"I have taken the Levites from among the Israelites in place of the first male offspring of every Israelite woman. The Levites are mine, ¹³for all the firstborn are mine. When I struck down all the firstborn in Egypt, I set apart for myself every firstborn in

ᵃ 9 Most manuscripts of the Masoretic Text; some manuscripts of the Masoretic Text, Samaritan Pentateuch and Septuagint (see also 8:16) to me

## Amplified Bible

²²Then the tribe of Benjamin, the leader of the sons of Benjamin being Abidan son of Gideoni. ²³Benjamin's host as numbered totaled 35,400.

²⁴The whole number [of the three tribes] in the camp of Ephraim totaled 108,100. They shall go forward in third place.

²⁵The standard of the camp of Dan shall be on the north side [of the tabernacle] by their companies, the leader of the sons of Dan being Ahiezer son of Ammishaddai. ²⁶Dan's host as numbered totaled 62,700.

²⁷Encamped next to Dan shall be the tribe of Asher, the leader of the sons of Asher being Pagiel son of Ochran. ²⁸Asher's host as numbered totaled 41,500.

²⁹Then the tribe of Naphtali, the leader of the sons of Naphtali being Ahira son of Enan. ³⁰Naphtali's host as numbered totaled 53,400.

³¹The whole number [of the three tribes] in the camp of Dan totaled 157,600. They shall set out last, standard after standard.

³²These are the Israelites as numbered by their fathers' houses. All in the camps who were numbered by their companies were 603,550.

³³But the Levites were not numbered with the Israelites, for so the Lord commanded Moses.

³⁴Thus the Israelites did according to all the Lord commanded Moses; so they encamped by their standards, and so they set forward, everyone with his [tribal] families, according to his father's house.

**3** Now these are the generations of Aaron and Moses when the Lord spoke with Moses on Mount Sinai.

²These are the names of the sons of Aaron: Nadab the firstborn, Abihu, Eleazar, and Ithamar.

³These are the names of the sons of Aaron, the priests who were anointed, whom Aaron consecrated *and* ordained to minister in the priest's office.

⁴But Nadab and Abihu died before the Lord when they offered strange fire before the Lord in the Wilderness of Sinai; and they had no children. So Eleazar and Ithamar ministered in the priest's office in the presence *and* under the supervision of Aaron their father. [Lev. 10:1-4.]

⁵And the Lord said to Moses,

⁶Bring the tribe of Levi near and set them before Aaron the priest, that they may minister to him.

⁷And they shall carry out his instructions and the duties connected with the whole assembly before the Tent of Meeting, doing the service of the tabernacle.

⁸And they shall keep all the instruments *and* furnishings of the Tent of Meeting and take charge of [attending] the Israelites, to serve in the tabernacle.

⁹And you shall give the Levites [as servants and helpers] to Aaron and his sons; they are wholly given to him from among the Israelites.

¹⁰And you shall appoint Aaron and his sons, and they shall observe *and* attend to their priest's office; but the excluded [anyone daring to assume priestly duties or privileges who is not of the house of Aaron and called of God] who comes near [the holy things] shall be put to death.

¹¹And the Lord said to Moses,

¹²Behold, I have taken the Levites from among the Israelites instead of every firstborn who opens the womb among the Israelites; and the Levites shall be Mine,

¹³For all the firstborn are Mine. On the day that I slew all the firstborn in the land of Egypt, I consecrated for My-

## New International Version

Israel, whether human or animal. They are to be mine. I am the LORD."

¹⁴The LORD said to Moses in the Desert of Sinai, ¹⁵"Count the Levites by their families and clans. Count every male a month old or more." ¹⁶So Moses counted them, as he was commanded by the word of the LORD.

¹⁷These were the names of the sons of Levi:
Gershon, Kohath and Merari.
¹⁸These were the names of the Gershonite clans:
Libni and Shimei.
¹⁹The Kohathite clans:
Amram, Izhar, Hebron and Uzziel.
²⁰The Merarite clans:
Mahli and Mushi.
These were the Levite clans, according to their families.

²¹To Gershon belonged the clans of the Libnites and Shimeites; these were the Gershonite clans. ²²The number of all the males a month old or more who were counted was 7,500. ²³The Gershonite clans were to camp on the west, behind the tabernacle. ²⁴The leader of the families of the Gershonites was Eliasaph son of Lael. ²⁵At the tent of meeting the Gershonites were responsible for the care of the tabernacle and tent, its coverings, the curtain at the entrance to the tent of meeting, ²⁶the curtains of the courtyard, the curtain at the entrance to the courtyard surrounding the tabernacle and altar, and the ropes—and everything related to their use.

²⁷To Kohath belonged the clans of the Amramites, Izharites, Hebronites and Uzzielites; these were the Kohathite clans. ²⁸The number of all the males a month old or more was 8,600.ᵃ The Kohathites were responsible for the care of the sanctuary. ²⁹The Kohathite clans were to camp on the south side of the tabernacle. ³⁰The leader of the families of the Kohathite clans was Elizaphan son of Uzziel. ³¹They were responsible for the care of the ark, the table, the lampstand, the altars, the articles of the sanctuary used in ministering, the curtain, and everything related to their use. ³²The chief leader of the Levites was Eleazar son of Aaron, the priest. He was appointed over those who were responsible for the care of the sanctuary.

³³To Merari belonged the clans of the Mahlites and the Mushites; these were the Merarite clans. ³⁴The number of all the males a month old or more who were counted was 6,200. ³⁵The leader of the families of the Merarite clans was Zuriel son of Abihail; they were to camp on the north side of the tabernacle. ³⁶The Merarites were appointed to take care of the frames of the tabernacle, its crossbars, posts, bases, all its equipment, and everything related to their use, ³⁷as well as the posts of the surrounding courtyard with their bases, tent pegs and ropes.

³⁸Moses and Aaron and his sons were to camp to the east of the tabernacle, toward the sunrise, in front of the tent of meeting. They were responsible for the care of the

## Amplified Bible

self all the firstborn in Israel, both man and beast; Mine they shall be. I am the Lord.

¹⁴And the Lord said to Moses in the Wilderness of Sinai, ¹⁵Number the sons of Levi by their fathers' houses and by families. Every male from a month old and upward you shall number.

¹⁶So Moses numbered them as he was commanded by the word of the Lord.

¹⁷These were the sons of Levi by their names: Gershon, Kohath, and Merari.

¹⁸And these are the names of the sons of Gershon by their families: Libni and Shimei.

¹⁹The sons of Kohath by their families: Amram, Izhar, Hebron, and Uzziel.

²⁰The sons of Merari by their families: Mahli and Mushi. These are the families of the Levites by their fathers' houses.

²¹Of Gershon were the families of the Libnites and of the Shimeites. These are the families of the Gershonites.

²²The males who were numbered of them from a month old and upward totaled 7,500.

²³The families of the Gershonites were to encamp behind the tabernacle on the west,

²⁴The leader of the fathers' houses of the Gershonites being Eliasaph son of Lael.

²⁵And the responsibility of the sons of Gershon in the Tent of Meeting was to be the tabernacle, the tent, its covering, and the hangings for the door of the Tent of Meeting,

²⁶And the hangings of the court, the curtain for the door of the court which is around the tabernacle and the altar, its cords, and all the service pertaining to them.

²⁷Of Kohath were the families of the Amramites, the Izharites, the Hebronites, and the Uzzielites; these are the families of the Kohathites.

²⁸The number of all the males from a month old and upward totaled 8,600, attending to the duties of the sanctuary.

²⁹The families of the sons of Kohath were to encamp on the south side of the tabernacle,

³⁰The chief of the fathers' houses of the families of the Kohathites being Elizaphan son of Uzziel.

³¹Their charge was to be the ark, the table, the lampstand, the altars, and the utensils of the sanctuary with which the priests minister, and the screen, and all the service having to do with these.

³²Eleazar son of Aaron the priest was to be chief over the leaders of the Levites, and have the oversight of those who had charge of the sanctuary.

³³Of Merari were the families of the Mahlites and the Mushites; these are the families of Merari.

³⁴Their number of all the males from a month old and upward totaled 6,200.

³⁵And the head of the fathers' houses of the families of Merari was Zuriel son of Abihail; the Merarites were to encamp on the north side of the tabernacle.

³⁶And the appointed charge of the sons of Merari was the boards or frames of the tabernacle, and its bars, pillars, sockets or bases, and all the accessories or instruments of it, and all the work connected with them,

³⁷And the pillars of the surrounding court and their sockets or bases, with their pegs and their cords.

³⁸But those to encamp before the tabernacle toward the east, before the Tent of Meeting, toward the sunrise, were to be Moses and Aaron and his sons, keeping the full charge of the rites of the sanctuary in whatever was

---

ᵃ 28 Hebrew; some Septuagint manuscripts 8,300

## New International Version

sanctuary on behalf of the Israelites. Anyone else who approached the sanctuary was to be put to death.

<sup>39</sup>The total number of Levites counted at the LORD's command by Moses and Aaron according to their clans, including every male a month old or more, was 22,000.

<sup>40</sup>The LORD said to Moses, "Count all the firstborn Israelite males who are a month old or more and make a list of their names. <sup>41</sup>Take the Levites for me in place of all the firstborn of the Israelites, and the livestock of the Levites in place of all the firstborn of the livestock of the Israelites. I am the LORD."

<sup>42</sup>So Moses counted all the firstborn of the Israelites, as the LORD commanded him. <sup>43</sup>The total number of firstborn males a month old or more, listed by name, was 22,273.

<sup>44</sup>The LORD also said to Moses, <sup>45</sup>"Take the Levites in place of all the firstborn of Israel, and the livestock of the Levites in place of their livestock. The Levites are to be mine. I am the LORD. <sup>46</sup>To redeem the 273 firstborn Israelites who exceed the number of the Levites, <sup>47</sup>collect five shekels<sup>a</sup> for each one, according to the sanctuary shekel, which weighs twenty gerahs. <sup>48</sup>Give the money for the redemption of the additional Israelites to Aaron and his sons."

<sup>49</sup>So Moses collected the redemption money from those who exceeded the number redeemed by the Levites. <sup>50</sup>From the firstborn of the Israelites he collected silver weighing 1,365 shekels,<sup>b</sup> according to the sanctuary shekel. <sup>51</sup>Moses gave the redemption money to Aaron and his sons, as he was commanded by the word of the LORD.

### The Kohathites

4 The LORD said to Moses and Aaron: <sup>2</sup>"Take a census of the Kohathite branch of the Levites by their clans and families. <sup>3</sup>Count all the men from thirty to fifty years of age who come to serve in the work at the tent of meeting.

<sup>4</sup>"This is the work of the Kohathites at the tent of meeting: the care of the most holy things. <sup>5</sup>When the camp is to move, Aaron and his sons are to go in and take down the shielding curtain and put it over the ark of the covenant law. <sup>6</sup>Then they are to cover the curtain with a durable leather,<sup>c</sup> spread a cloth of solid blue over that and put the poles in place.

<sup>7</sup>"Over the table of the Presence they are to spread a blue cloth and put on it the plates, dishes and bowls, and

## Amplified Bible

required for the Israelites; and the <sup>a</sup>excluded [one not a descendant of Aaron and called of God] who came near [the sanctuary] was to be put to death.

<sup>39</sup>All the Levites whom Moses and Aaron numbered at the command of the Lord, by their families, all the males from a month old and upward, were 22,000.

<sup>40</sup>And the Lord said to Moses, Number all the firstborn of the males of the Israelites from a month old and upward, and take the number of their names.

<sup>41</sup>You shall take the Levites for Me instead of all the firstborn among the Israelites. I am the Lord; and you shall take the cattle of the Levites for Me instead of all the firstlings among the cattle of the Israelites.

<sup>42</sup>So Moses numbered, as the Lord commanded him, all the firstborn Israelites.

<sup>43</sup>But all the firstborn males from a month old and upward as numbered were 22,273 [273 more than the Levites].

<sup>44</sup>And the Lord said to Moses,

<sup>45</sup>Take the Levites [for Me] instead of all the firstborn Israelites, and the Levites' cattle instead of their cattle; and the Levites shall be Mine. I am the Lord.

<sup>46</sup>And for those 273 who are to be redeemed of the firstborn of the Israelites who outnumber the Levites,

<sup>47</sup>You shall take five shekels apiece, reckoning by the sanctuary shekel of twenty gerahs; you shall collect them,

<sup>48</sup>And you shall give the ransom silver from the excess number [over the Levites] to be redeemed to Aaron and his sons.

<sup>49</sup>So Moses took the redemption money from those who were left over from the number who were redeemed by the Levites.

<sup>50</sup>From the firstborn of the Israelites he took the money, 1,365 shekels, after the shekel of the sanctuary.

<sup>51</sup>And Moses gave the money from those who were ransomed to Aaron and his sons, as the Lord commanded Moses.

4 And the Lord said to Moses and Aaron,

<sup>2</sup>Take a census of the Kohathite division among the sons of Levi, by their families, by their fathers' houses,

<sup>3</sup>From thirty years old and up to fifty years old, all who can enter the service to do the work in the Tent of Meeting.

<sup>4</sup>This shall be the responsibility of the sons of Kohath in the Tent of Meeting: the most holy things.

<sup>5</sup>When the camp prepares to set forward, Aaron and his sons shall take down the veil [screening the Holy of Holies] and cover the ark of the Testimony with it,

<sup>6</sup>And shall put on it the covering of dolphin or porpoise skin, and shall spread over that a cloth wholly of blue, and shall put in place the poles of the ark.

<sup>7</sup>And upon the table of showbread they shall spread a cloth of blue and put on it the plates, the dishes for in-

---

<sup>a</sup> This ban against "the excluded" from coming near the sanctuary (the sacred tent, the tabernacle proper) is not to be construed as discrimination against people who were not Israelites. It included everyone except the ordained descendants of Levi of the house of Aaron. The tabernacle proper was made up of two small rooms which no one except the priest or priests who had the assignment was ever to enter. The congregation entered the outside enclosure only. This was true also of the later temples. Neither Jesus nor any of his disciples or Paul ever entered the sanctuary. When Jesus "taught in the temple" or "entered into the temple," the Greek word invariably indicates that He was in the temple enclosure (*hieron*) and not in the sanctuary (*naos*). (For more information, see Richard Trench, *Synonyms of The New Testament*). For a violation of this ban see II Chron. 26:16-21, which tells of King Uzziah, who attempted to enter the sanctuary to burn incense and while being forcibly put out by eighty priests became a leper—for the rest of his life.

<sup>a</sup> 47 That is, about 2 ounces or about 58 grams    <sup>b</sup> 50 That is, about 35 pounds or about 16 kilograms    <sup>c</sup> 6 Possibly the hides of large aquatic mammals; also in verses 8, 10, 11, 12, 14 and 25

## New International Version

the jars for drink offerings; the bread that is continually there is to remain on it. [8]They are to spread a scarlet cloth over them, cover that with the durable leather and put the poles in place.

[9]"They are to take a blue cloth and cover the lampstand that is for light, together with its lamps, its wick trimmers and trays, and all its jars for the olive oil used to supply it. [10]Then they are to wrap it and all its accessories in a covering of the durable leather and put it on a carrying frame.

[11]"Over the gold altar they are to spread a blue cloth and cover that with the durable leather and put the poles in place.

[12]"They are to take all the articles used for ministering in the sanctuary, wrap them in a blue cloth, cover that with the durable leather and put them on a carrying frame.

[13]"They are to remove the ashes from the bronze altar and spread a purple cloth over it. [14]Then they are to place on it all the utensils used for ministering at the altar, including the firepans, meat forks, shovels and sprinkling bowls. Over it they are to spread a covering of the durable leather and put the poles in place.

[15]"After Aaron and his sons have finished covering the holy furnishings and all the holy articles, and when the camp is ready to move, only then are the Kohathites to come and do the carrying. But they must not touch the holy things or they will die. The Kohathites are to carry those things that are in the tent of meeting.

[16]"Eleazar son of Aaron, the priest, is to have charge of the oil for the light, the fragrant incense, the regular grain offering and the anointing oil. He is to be in charge of the entire tabernacle and everything in it, including its holy furnishings and articles."

[17]The LORD said to Moses and Aaron, [18]"See that the Kohathite tribal clans are not destroyed from among the Levites. [19]So that they may live and not die when they come near the most holy things, do this for them: Aaron and his sons are to go into the sanctuary and assign to each man his work and what he is to carry. [20]But the Kohathites must not go in to look at the holy things, even for a moment, or they will die."

### The Gershonites

[21]The LORD said to Moses, [22]"Take a census also of the Gershonites by their families and clans. [23]Count all the men from thirty to fifty years of age who come to serve in the work at the tent of meeting.

[24]"This is the service of the Gershonite clans in their carrying and their other work: [25]They are to carry the curtains of the tabernacle, that is, the tent of meeting, its covering and its outer covering of durable leather, the curtains for the entrance to the tent of meeting, [26]the curtains of the courtyard surrounding the tabernacle and altar, the curtain for the entrance to the courtyard, the ropes and all the equipment used in the service of the tent. The Gershonites are to do all that needs to be done with these things. [27]All their service, whether carrying or doing other work, is to be done under the direction of Aaron and his sons. You shall assign to them as their responsibility all

## Amplified Bible

cense, the bowls, the flagons for the drink offering, and also the continual showbread.

[8]And they shall spread over them a cloth of scarlet, and put over that a covering of dolphin or porpoise skin, and put in place the poles [for carrying].

[9]And they shall take a cloth of blue and cover the lampstand for the light and its lamps, its snuffers, its ashtrays, and all the oil vessels from which it is supplied.

[10]And they shall put the lampstand and all its utensils within a covering of dolphin or porpoise skin and shall put it upon the frame [for carrying].

[11]And upon the golden [incense] altar they shall spread a cloth of blue, and cover it with a covering of dolphin or porpoise skin, and shall put in place its poles [for carrying].

[12]And they shall take all the utensils of the service with which they minister in the sanctuary, and put them in a cloth of blue, and cover them with a covering of dolphin or porpoise skin, and shall put them on the frame [for carrying].

[13]And they shall take away the ashes from the altar [of burnt offering] and spread a purple cloth over it.

[14]And they shall put upon it all its vessels and utensils with which they minister there, the firepans, the flesh-hooks or forks, the shovels, the basins, and all the vessels and utensils of the altar, and they shall spread over it all a covering of dolphin or porpoise skin, and shall put in its poles [for carrying].

[15]When Aaron and his sons have finished covering the sanctuary and all its furniture, as the camp sets out, after all that [is done but not before], the sons of Kohath shall come to carry them. But they shall not touch the holy things, lest they die. These are the things of the Tent of Meeting which the sons of Kohath are to carry.

[16]And Eleazar son of Aaron the priest shall have charge of the oil for the light, the fragrant incense, the continual cereal offering, and the anointing oil, with the oversight of all the tabernacle and of all that is in it, of the sanctuary and its utensils.

[17]And the Lord said to Moses and Aaron,

[18][Since] the tribe of the families of the Kohathites [are only Levites and not priests], do not [by exposing them to the sin of touching the most holy things] cut them off from among the Levites.

[19]But deal thus with them, that they may live and not die when they approach the most holy things: Aaron and his sons shall go in and appoint them each to his work and to his burden [to be carried on the march].

[20]But [the Kohathites] shall not go in to see the sanctuary [the Holy Place and the Holy of Holies] or its holy things, even for an instant, lest they die.

[21]And the Lord said to Moses,

[22]Take a census of the sons of Gershon, by their fathers' houses, by their families.

[23]From thirty years old and up to fifty years old you shall number them, all who enter for service to do the work in the Tent of Meeting.

[24]This is the service of the families of the Gershonites, in serving and in bearing burdens [when on the march]:

[25]And they shall carry the curtains of the tabernacle, and the Tent of Meeting, its covering, and the covering of dolphin or porpoise skin that is on top of it, and the hanging or screen for the door of the Tent of Meeting,

[26]And the hangings of the court, and the hanging or screen for the entrance of the gate of the court which is around the tabernacle and the altar [of burnt offering], and their cords, and all the equipment for their service; whatever needs to be done with them, that they shall do.

[27]Under the direction of Aaron and his sons shall be all the service of the sons of the Gershonites, in all they have to carry and in all they have to do; and you shall assign to their charge all that they are to carry [on the march].

## New International Version

they are to carry. <sup>28</sup>This is the service of the Gershonite clans at the tent of meeting. Their duties are to be under the direction of Ithamar son of Aaron, the priest.

### The Merarites

<sup>29</sup>"Count the Merarites by their clans and families. <sup>30</sup>Count all the men from thirty to fifty years of age who come to serve in the work at the tent of meeting. <sup>31</sup>As part of all their service at the tent, they are to carry the frames of the tabernacle, its crossbars, posts and bases, <sup>32</sup>as well as the posts of the surrounding courtyard with their bases, tent pegs, ropes, all their equipment and everything related to their use. Assign to each man the specific things he is to carry. <sup>33</sup>This is the service of the Merarite clans as they work at the tent of meeting under the direction of Ithamar son of Aaron, the priest."

### The Numbering of the Levite Clans

<sup>34</sup>Moses, Aaron and the leaders of the community counted the Kohathites by their clans and families. <sup>35</sup>All the men from thirty to fifty years of age who came to serve in the work at the tent of meeting, <sup>36</sup>counted by clans, were 2,750. <sup>37</sup>This was the total of all those in the Kohathite clans who served at the tent of meeting. Moses and Aaron counted them according to the LORD's command through Moses.

<sup>38</sup>The Gershonites were counted by their clans and families. <sup>39</sup>All the men from thirty to fifty years of age who came to serve in the work at the tent of meeting, <sup>40</sup>counted by their clans and families, were 2,630. <sup>41</sup>This was the total of those in the Gershonite clans who served at the tent of meeting. Moses and Aaron counted them according to the LORD's command.

<sup>42</sup>The Merarites were counted by their clans and families. <sup>43</sup>All the men from thirty to fifty years of age who came to serve in the work at the tent of meeting, <sup>44</sup>counted by their clans, were 3,200. <sup>45</sup>This was the total of those in the Merarite clans. Moses and Aaron counted them according to the LORD's command through Moses.

<sup>46</sup>So Moses, Aaron and the leaders of Israel counted all the Levites by their clans and families. <sup>47</sup>All the men from thirty to fifty years of age who came to do the work of serving and carrying the tent of meeting <sup>48</sup>numbered 8,580. <sup>49</sup>At the LORD's command through Moses, each was assigned his work and told what to carry.

Thus they were counted, as the LORD commanded Moses.

## Amplified Bible

<sup>28</sup>This is the service of the families of the sons of Gershon in the Tent of Meeting; and their work shall be under the direction of Ithamar son of Aaron, the [high] priest.

<sup>29</sup>As for the sons of Merari, you shall number them by their families and their fathers' houses;

<sup>30</sup>From thirty years old up to fifty years old you shall number them, everyone who enters the service to do the work of the Tent of Meeting.

<sup>31</sup>And this is what they are assigned to carry *and* to guard [on the march], according to all their service in the Tent of Meeting: the boards *or* frames of the tabernacle, and its bars, and its pillars, and its sockets *or* bases,

<sup>32</sup>And the pillars of the court round about with their sockets *or* bases, and pegs, and cords, with all their equipment and all their accessories for service; and you shall assign to them by name the articles which they are to carry [on the march].

<sup>33</sup>This is the work of the families of the sons of Merari, according to all their tasks in the Tent of Meeting, under the direction of Ithamar son of Aaron, the [high] priest.

<sup>34</sup>And Moses and Aaron and the leaders of the congregation numbered the sons of the Kohathites by their families and their fathers' houses,

<sup>35</sup>From thirty years old up to fifty years old, everyone who enters the service to do the work of the Tent of Meeting;

<sup>36</sup>And those who were numbered of them by their families were 2,750.

<sup>37</sup>These were numbered of the families of the Kohathites, all who did service in the Tent of Meeting, whom Moses and Aaron numbered according to the command of the Lord through Moses.

<sup>38</sup>And those that were numbered of the sons of Gershon, by their families, and by their fathers' houses,

<sup>39</sup>From thirty years old up to fifty years old, everyone who entered the service to do the work of the Tent of Meeting,

<sup>40</sup>Those who were enrolled of them, by their families, by their fathers' houses, were 2,630.

<sup>41</sup>These were numbered of the families of the sons of Gershon, all who served in the Tent of Meeting, whom Moses and Aaron numbered as the Lord commanded.

<sup>42</sup>And those numbered of the families of the sons of Merari, by their families, by their fathers' houses,

<sup>43</sup>From thirty years old up to fifty years old, everyone who entered into the service for work in the Tent of Meeting,

<sup>44</sup>Even those who were numbered of them by their families, were 3,200.

<sup>45</sup>These are those who were numbered of the families of the sons of Merari, whom Moses and Aaron numbered according to the command of the Lord by Moses.

<sup>46</sup>All those who were numbered of the Levites, whom Moses and Aaron and the leaders of Israel counted by their families and by their fathers' houses,

<sup>47</sup>From thirty years old up to fifty years old, everyone who could enter to do the work of service and of burden bearing in the Tent of Meeting,

<sup>48</sup>Those that were numbered of them were 8,580.

<sup>49</sup>According to the command of the Lord through Moses, they were assigned each to his work of serving and carrying. Thus they were numbered by him, as the Lord had commanded Moses.

## New International Version

### The Purity of the Camp

**5** The LORD said to Moses, [2]"Command the Israelites to send away from the camp anyone who has a defiling skin disease[a] or a discharge of any kind, or who is ceremonially unclean because of a dead body. [3]Send away male and female alike; send them outside the camp so they will not defile their camp, where I dwell among them." [4]The Israelites did so; they sent them outside the camp. They did just as the LORD had instructed Moses.

### Restitution for Wrongs

[5]The LORD said to Moses, [6]"Say to the Israelites: 'Any man or woman who wrongs another in any way[b] and so is unfaithful to the LORD is guilty [7]and must confess the sin they have committed. They must make full restitution for the wrong they have done, add a fifth of the value to it and give it all to the person they have wronged. [8]But if that person has no close relative to whom restitution can be made for the wrong, the restitution belongs to the LORD and must be given to the priest, along with the ram with which atonement is made for the wrongdoer. [9]All the sacred contributions the Israelites bring to a priest will belong to him. [10]Sacred things belong to their owners, but what they give to the priest will belong to the priest.'"

### The Test for an Unfaithful Wife

[11]Then the LORD said to Moses, [12]"Speak to the Israelites and say to them: 'If a man's wife goes astray and is unfaithful to him [13]so that another man has sexual relations with her, and this is hidden from her husband and her impurity is undetected (since there is no witness against her and she has not been caught in the act), [14]and if feelings of jealousy come over her husband and he suspects his wife and she is impure—or if he is jealous and suspects her even though she is not impure— [15]then he is to take his wife to the priest. He must also take an offering of a tenth of an ephah[c] of barley flour on her behalf. He must not pour olive oil on it or put incense on it, because it is a grain offering for jealousy, a reminder-offering to draw attention to wrongdoing.

[16]"The priest shall bring her and have her stand before the LORD. [17]Then he shall take some holy water in a clay jar and put some dust from the tabernacle floor into the water. [18]After the priest has had the woman stand before the LORD, he shall loosen her hair and place in her hands the reminder-offering, the grain offering for jealousy, while he himself holds the bitter water that brings a curse. [19]Then the priest shall put the woman under oath and say to her, "If no other man has had sexual relations with you and you have not gone astray and become impure while married to your husband, may this bitter water that brings a curse not harm you. [20]But if you have gone astray while married to your husband and you have made yourself impure by having sexual relations with a man other than your husband"— [21]here the priest is to put the woman under this curse—"may the LORD cause you to become a curse[d] among your people when he makes your womb miscarry and your abdomen swell. [22]May this water

## Amplified Bible

**5** The Lord said to Moses, [2]Command the Israelites that they put outside the camp every leper and everyone who has a discharge, and whoever is defiled by [coming in contact with] the dead.

[3]Both male and female you shall put out; without the camp you shall put them, that they may not defile their camp, in the midst of which I dwell.

[4]The Israelites did so, and put them outside the camp; as the Lord said to Moses, so the Israelites did.

[5]And the Lord said to Moses,

[6]Say to the Israelites, When a man or woman commits any sin that men commit by breaking faith with the Lord, and that person is guilty,

[7]Then he shall confess the sin which he has committed, and he shall make restitution for his wrong in full, and add a fifth to it, and give it to him whom he has wronged.

[8]But if the man [wronged] has no kinsman to whom the restitution may be made, let it be given to the Lord for the priest, besides the ram of atonement with which atonement shall be made for the offender.

[9]And every offering of all the holy things of the Israelites which they bring to the priest shall be his.

[10]And every man's hallowed things shall be the priest's; whatever any man gives the priest shall be his.

[11]And the Lord said to Moses,

[12]Say to the Israelites, If any man's wife goes astray and commits an offense of guilt against him,

[13]And a man lies with her carnally, and it is hidden from the eyes of her husband and it is kept secret though she is defiled, and there is no witness against her nor was she taken in the act,

[14]And if the spirit of jealousy comes upon him and he is jealous *and* suspicious of his wife who has defiled herself—or if the spirit of jealousy comes upon him and he is jealous *and* suspicious of his wife though she has not defiled herself—

[15]Then shall the man bring his wife to the priest, and he shall bring the offering required of her, a tenth of an ephah of barley meal; but he shall pour no oil upon it nor put frankincense on it [symbols of favor and joy], for it is a cereal offering of jealousy *and* suspicion, a memorial offering bringing iniquity to remembrance.

[16]And the priest shall bring her near and set her before the Lord.

[17]And the priest shall take holy water [probably from the sacred laver] in an earthen vessel and take some of the dust that is on the floor of the tabernacle and put it in the water.

[18]And the priest shall set the woman before the Lord, and let the hair of the woman's head hang loose, and put the meal offering of remembrance in her hands, which is the jealousy *and* suspicion offering. And the priest shall have in his hand the water of bitterness that brings the curse.

[19]Then the priest shall make her take an oath, and say to the woman, If no man has lain with you and if you have not gone astray to uncleanness with another instead of your husband, then be free from any effect of this water of bitterness which brings the curse.

[20]But if you have gone astray and you are defiled, some man having lain with you beside your husband,

[21]Then the priest shall make the woman take the oath of the curse, and say to the woman, The Lord make you a curse and an oath among your people when the Lord makes your thigh fall away and your body swell.

---

[a] 2 The Hebrew word for *defiling skin disease*, traditionally translated "leprosy," was used for various diseases affecting the skin.
[b] 6 Or *woman who commits any wrong common to mankind*    [c] 15 That is, probably about 3 1/2 pounds or about 1.6 kilograms    [d] 21 That is, may he cause your name to be used in cursing (see Jer. 29:22); or, may others see that you are cursed; similarly in verse 27.

## New International Version

that brings a curse enter your body so that your abdomen swells or your womb miscarries."

"'Then the woman is to say, "Amen. So be it."

23"'The priest is to write these curses on a scroll and then wash them off into the bitter water. 24He shall make the woman drink the bitter water that brings a curse, and this water that brings a curse and causes bitter suffering will enter her. 25The priest is to take from her hands the grain offering for jealousy, wave it before the Lord and bring it to the altar. 26The priest is then to take a handful of the grain offering as a memorial*a* offering and burn it on the altar; after that, he is to have the woman drink the water. 27If she has made herself impure and been unfaithful to her husband, this will be the result: When she is made to drink the water that brings a curse and causes bitter suffering, it will enter her, her abdomen will swell and her womb will miscarry, and she will become a curse. 28If, however, the woman has not made herself impure, but is clean, she will be cleared of guilt and will be able to have children.

29"'This, then, is the law of jealousy when a woman goes astray and makes herself impure while married to her husband, 30or when feelings of jealousy come over a man because he suspects his wife. The priest is to have her stand before the Lord and is to apply this entire law to her. 31The husband will be innocent of any wrongdoing, but the woman will bear the consequences of her sin.'"

### The Nazirite

**6** The Lord said to Moses, 2"Speak to the Israelites and say to them: 'If a man or woman wants to make a special vow, a vow of dedication to the Lord as a Nazirite, 3they must abstain from wine and other fermented drink and must not drink vinegar made from wine or other fermented drink. They must not drink grape juice or eat grapes or raisins. 4As long as they remain under their Nazirite vow, they must not eat anything that comes from the grapevine, not even the seeds or skins.

5"'During the entire period of their Nazirite vow, no razor may be used on their head. They must be holy until the period of their dedication to the Lord is over; they must let their hair grow long.

6"'Throughout the period of their dedication to the Lord, the Nazirite must not go near a dead body. 7Even if their own father or mother or brother or sister dies, they must not make themselves ceremonially unclean on account of them, because the symbol of their dedication to God is on their head. 8Throughout the period of their dedication, they are consecrated to the Lord.

9"'If someone dies suddenly in the Nazirite's presence, thus defiling the hair that symbolizes their dedication, they must shave their head on the seventh day—the day of their cleansing. 10Then on the eighth day they must bring two doves or two young pigeons to the priest at the entrance to the tent of meeting. 11The priest is to offer one as a sin offering*b* and the other as a burnt offering to make atonement for the Nazirite because they sinned by being in the presence of the dead body. That same day they are to consecrate their head again. 12They must rededicate themselves to the Lord for the same period of dedication and must bring a year-old male lamb as a guilt offering. The previous days do not count, because they became defiled during their period of dedication.

## Amplified Bible

22May this water that brings the curse go into your bowels and make your body swell and your thigh fall away. And the woman shall say, So let it be, so let it be.

23The priest shall then write these curses in a book and shall wash them off into the water of bitterness;

24And he shall cause the woman to drink the water of bitterness that brings the curse, and the water that brings the curse shall enter into her [to try her] bitterly.

25Then the priest shall take the cereal offering of jealousy *and* suspicion out of the woman's hand and shall wave the offering before the Lord and offer it upon the altar.

26And the priest shall take a handful of the cereal offering as the memorial portion of it and burn it on the altar, and afterward shall cause the woman to drink the water.

27And when he has made her drink the water, then if she is defiled and has committed a trespass against her husband, the curse water which she drank shall be bitterness and cause her body to swell and her thigh to fall away, and the woman shall be a curse among her people.

28But if the woman is not defiled and is clean, then she shall be free [from the curse] and be able to have children.

29This is the law of jealousy *and* suspicion when a wife goes aside to another instead of her husband and is defiled,

30Or when the spirit of jealousy *and* suspicion comes upon a man and he is jealous *and* suspicious of his wife; then shall he set the woman before the Lord, and the priest shall execute on her all this law.

31The [husband] shall be free from iniquity *and* guilt, and that woman [if guilty] shall bear her iniquity.

**6** And the Lord said to Moses, 2Say to the Israelites, When either a man or a woman shall make a special vow, the vow of a Nazirite, that is, one separated *and* consecrated to the Lord,

3He shall separate himself from wine and strong drink; he shall drink no vinegar of wine or of strong drink, and shall drink no grape juice, or eat grapes, fresh or dried. [Luke 1:15.]

4All the days of his separation he shall eat nothing produced from the grapevine, not even the seeds or the skins.

5All the days of the vow of his separation *and* abstinence there shall no razor come upon his head. Until the time is completed for which he separates himself to the Lord, he shall be holy, and shall let the locks of the hair of his head grow long.

6All the days that he separates himself to the Lord he shall not go near a dead body.

7He shall not make himself unclean for his father, mother, brother, or sister, when they die, because his separation *and* abstinence to his God is upon his head.

8All the days of his separation *and* abstinence he is holy to the Lord.

9And if any man dies very suddenly beside him, and he has defiled his consecrated head, then he shall shave his head on the day of his cleansing; on the seventh day shall he shave it.

10On the eighth day he shall bring two turtledoves or two young pigeons to the priest to the door of the Tent of Meeting,

11And the priest shall offer the one for a sin offering and the other for a burnt offering and make atonement for him because he sinned by reason of the dead body. He shall consecrate his head the same day,

12And he shall consecrate *and* separate himself to the Lord for the days of his separation and shall bring a male lamb a year old for a trespass *or* guilt offering; but the previous days shall be void *and* lost, because his separation was defiled.

---

*a* 26 Or *representative*   *b* 11 Or *purification offering*; also in verses 14 and 16

## New International Version

13"'Now this is the law of the Nazirite when the period of their dedication is over. They are to be brought to the entrance to the tent of meeting. 14There they are to present their offerings to the LORD: a year-old male lamb without defect for a burnt offering, a year-old ewe lamb without defect for a sin offering, a ram without defect for a fellowship offering, 15together with their grain offerings and drink offerings, and a basket of bread made with the finest flour and without yeast—thick loaves with olive oil mixed in, and thin loaves brushed with olive oil.

16"'The priest is to present all these before the LORD and make the sin offering and the burnt offering. 17He is to present the basket of unleavened bread and is to sacrifice the ram as a fellowship offering to the LORD, together with its grain offering and drink offering.

18"'Then at the entrance to the tent of meeting, the Nazirite must shave off the hair that symbolizes their dedication. They are to take the hair and put it in the fire that is under the sacrifice of the fellowship offering.

19"'After the Nazirite has shaved off the hair that symbolizes their dedication, the priest is to place in their hands a boiled shoulder of the ram, and one thick loaf and one thin loaf from the basket, both made without yeast. 20The priest shall then wave these before the LORD as a wave offering; they are holy and belong to the priest, together with the breast that was waved and the thigh that was presented. After that, the Nazirite may drink wine.

21"'This is the law of the Nazirite who vows offerings to the LORD in accordance with their dedication, in addition to whatever else they can afford. They must fulfill the vows they have made, according to the law of the Nazirite.'"

### The Priestly Blessing

22The LORD said to Moses, 23"Tell Aaron and his sons, 'This is how you are to bless the Israelites. Say to them:

24"'"The LORD bless you
   and keep you;
25the LORD make his face shine on you
   and be gracious to you;
26the LORD turn his face toward you
   and give you peace."'

27"So they will put my name on the Israelites, and I will bless them."

### Offerings at the Dedication of the Tabernacle

**7** When Moses finished setting up the tabernacle, he anointed and consecrated it and all its furnishings. He also anointed and consecrated the altar and all its utensils. 2Then the leaders of Israel, the heads of families who were the tribal leaders in charge of those who were counted, made offerings. 3They brought as their gifts before the LORD six covered carts and twelve oxen—an ox from each leader and a cart from every two. These they presented before the tabernacle.

4The LORD said to Moses, 5"Accept these from them, that they may be used in the work at the tent of meeting. Give them to the Levites as each man's work requires."

6So Moses took the carts and oxen and gave them to the Levites. 7He gave two carts and four oxen to the Gershonites, as their work required, 8and he gave four carts and eight oxen to the Merarites, as their work required. They were all under the direction of Ithamar son of Aaron, the priest. 9But Moses did not give any to the Kohathites,

## Amplified Bible

13And this is the law of the Nazirite when the days of his separation *and* abstinence are fulfilled. He shall be brought to the door of the Tent of Meeting,

14And he shall offer his gift to the Lord, one he-lamb a year old without blemish for a burnt offering, and one ewe lamb a year old without blemish for a sin offering, and one ram without blemish for a peace offering,

15And a basket of unleavened bread, cakes of fine flour mingled with oil, and wafers of unleavened bread spread with oil, and their cereal offering, and their drink offering.

16And the priest shall present them before the Lord and shall offer the person's sin offering and his burnt offering.

17And he shall offer the ram for a sacrifice of peace offering to the Lord, with the basket of unleavened bread; the priest shall offer also its cereal offering and its drink offering.

18And the Nazirite shall shave his consecrated head at the door of the Tent of Meeting, and shall take the hair and put it on the fire which is under the sacrifice of the peace offerings.

19And the priest shall take the boiled shoulder of the ram, and one unleavened cake out of the basket, and one unleavened wafer and shall put them upon the hands of the Nazirite, after he has shaven the hair of his separation *and* abstinence.

20And the priest shall wave them for a wave offering before the Lord; they are a holy portion for the priest, with the breast that is waved and the thigh *or* shoulder that is offered; and after that the Nazirite may drink wine.

21This is the law for the Nazirite who has made a vow. His offering to the Lord, besides what else he is able to afford, shall be according to the vow which he has vowed; so shall he do according to the law for his separation *and* abstinence [as a Nazirite]. [Acts 21:24, 26.]

22And the Lord said to Moses,

23Say to Aaron and his sons, This is the way you shall bless the Israelites. Say to them,

24The Lord bless you and watch, guard, *and* keep you;

25The Lord make His face to shine upon *and* enlighten you and be gracious (kind, merciful, and giving favor) to you;

26The Lord lift up His [approving] countenance upon you and give you peace (tranquility of heart and life continually).

27And they shall put My name upon the Israelites, and I will bless them.

**7** On the day that Moses had fully completed setting up the tabernacle and had anointed and consecrated it and all its furniture, and the altar and all its utensils, and had anointed and set them apart for holy use,

2The princes *or* leaders of Israel, heads of their fathers' houses, made offerings. These were the leaders of the tribes and were over those who were numbered.

3And they brought their offering before the Lord, six covered wagons and twelve oxen; a wagon for each two of the princes *or* leaders and an ox for each one; and they brought them before the tabernacle.

4Then the Lord said to Moses,

5Accept the things from them, that they may be used in doing the service of the Tent of Meeting, and give them to the Levites, to each man according to his service.

6So Moses took the wagons and the oxen and gave them to the Levites.

7Two wagons and four oxen he gave to the sons of Gershon, according to their service;

8And four wagons and eight oxen he gave to the sons of Merari, according to their service, under the supervision of Ithamar son of Aaron, the [high] priest.

9But to the sons of Kohath he gave none, because they

## New International Version

because they were to carry on their shoulders the holy things, for which they were responsible.

¹⁰When the altar was anointed, the leaders brought their offerings for its dedication and presented them before the altar. ¹¹For the LORD had said to Moses, "Each day one leader is to bring his offering for the dedication of the altar."

¹²The one who brought his offering on the first day was Nahshon son of Amminadab of the tribe of Judah.

¹³His offering was one silver plate weighing a hundred and thirty shekels[a] and one silver sprinkling bowl weighing seventy shekels,[b] both according to the sanctuary shekel, each filled with the finest flour mixed with olive oil as a grain offering; ¹⁴one gold dish weighing ten shekels,[c] filled with incense; ¹⁵one young bull, one ram and one male lamb a year old for a burnt offering; ¹⁶one male goat for a sin offering[d]; ¹⁷and two oxen, five rams, five male goats and five male lambs a year old to be sacrificed as a fellowship offering. This was the offering of Nahshon son of Amminadab.

¹⁸On the second day Nethanel son of Zuar, the leader of Issachar, brought his offering.

¹⁹The offering he brought was one silver plate weighing a hundred and thirty shekels and one silver sprinkling bowl weighing seventy shekels, both according to the sanctuary shekel, each filled with the finest flour mixed with olive oil as a grain offering; ²⁰one gold dish weighing ten shekels, filled with incense; ²¹one young bull, one ram and one male lamb a year old for a burnt offering; ²²one male goat for a sin offering; ²³and two oxen, five rams, five male goats and five male lambs a year old to be sacrificed as a fellowship offering. This was the offering of Nethanel son of Zuar.

²⁴On the third day, Eliab son of Helon, the leader of the people of Zebulun, brought his offering.

²⁵His offering was one silver plate weighing a hundred and thirty shekels and one silver sprinkling bowl weighing seventy shekels, both according to the sanctuary shekel, each filled with the finest flour mixed with olive oil as a grain offering; ²⁶one gold dish weighing ten shekels, filled with incense; ²⁷one young bull, one ram and one male lamb a year old for a burnt offering; ²⁸one male goat for a sin offering; ²⁹and two oxen, five rams, five male goats and five male lambs a year old to be sacrificed as a fellowship offering. This was the offering of Eliab son of Helon.

³⁰On the fourth day Elizur son of Shedeur, the leader of the people of Reuben, brought his offering.

³¹His offering was one silver plate weighing a hundred and thirty shekels and one silver sprinkling bowl weighing seventy shekels, both according to the sanctuary shekel, each filled with the finest flour mixed with olive oil as a grain offering; ³²one gold dish weighing ten shekels, filled with incense; ³³one

## Amplified Bible

were assigned the care of the sanctuary *and* the holy things which had to be carried on their shoulders.

¹⁰And the princes *or* leaders offered sacrifices for the dedication of the altar [of burnt offering] on the day that it was anointed; and they offered their sacrifice before the altar.

¹¹And the Lord said to Moses, They shall offer their offerings, each prince *or* leader on his day, for the dedication of the altar.

¹²He who offered his offering on the first day was Nahshon son of Amminadab, of the tribe of Judah.

¹³And his offering was one silver platter, the weight of which was 130 shekels, one silver basin of seventy shekels, according to the shekel of the sanctuary, both of them full of fine flour mixed with oil for a cereal offering;

¹⁴One golden bowl of ten shekels, full of incense;

¹⁵One young bull, one ram, one male lamb a year old, for a burnt offering;

¹⁶One male goat for a sin offering;

¹⁷And [a]for the sacrifice of peace offerings, two oxen, five rams, five male goats, five male lambs a year old. This was the offering of Nahshon son of Amminadab.

¹⁸The second day Nethanel son of Zuar, leader [of the tribe] of Issachar, offered.

¹⁹He gave for his offering one silver platter, the weight of which was 130 shekels, one silver basin of seventy shekels, after the shekel of the sanctuary, both of them full of fine flour mixed with oil for a cereal offering;

²⁰One golden bowl of ten shekels, full of incense;

²¹One young bull, one ram, one male lamb a year old, for a burnt offering;

²²One male goat for a sin offering;

²³And for the sacrifice of peace offerings, two oxen, five rams, five male goats, five male lambs a year old. This was the offering of Nethanel son of Zuar.

²⁴The third day Eliab son of Helon, leader of the sons of Zebulun, offered.

²⁵His offering was one silver platter, the weight of which was 130 shekels, one silver basin of seventy shekels, after the shekel of the sanctuary, both of them full of fine flour mixed with oil for a cereal offering;

²⁶One golden bowl of ten shekels, full of incense;

²⁷One young bull, one ram, one male lamb a year old, for a burnt offering;

²⁸One male goat for a sin offering;

²⁹And for the sacrifice of peace offerings, two oxen, five rams, five male goats, five male lambs a year old. This was the offering of Eliab son of Helon.

³⁰The fourth day Elizur son of Shedeur, leader of the sons of Reuben, offered.

³¹His offering was one silver platter of the weight of 130 shekels, one silver basin of seventy shekels, after the shekel of the sanctuary, both of them full of fine flour mixed with oil for a cereal offering;

³²One golden bowl of ten shekels, full of incense;

---

[a] Verses 12 to 17 give the detailed description of one tribe leader's offering. Then, instead of saying that the gifts of the other tribe leaders were exactly like this one and naming the leaders, the record goes on for **seventy** verses repeating what has already been said **eleven** more times! Why? These things "were written for our learning" (Rom. 15:4 KJV). Let us seek the answer. Other commentators give Matthew Henry credit for giving the correct view. He says that both in dictating that each tribal leader have a separate day for his gift and in giving the reports equal space, regardless of the contrast in the tribe's strength and rank in the camp, God had a definite purpose: "that an equal honor might thereby be put on each several tribe . . . Thus it was intimated that all the tribes of Israel had an equal share in the altar and an equal share in the sacrifices that were offered upon it. Though one tribe was posted more honorably in the camp than another, yet they and their services were all alike acceptable to God . . . Rich and poor meet together before God . . . He was letting us know that what is given is lent to the Lord, and He carefully records it, with everyone's name prefixed to his gift, because what is so given as a labor of love (Heb. 6:10 KJV) He will repay. Christ took particular notice of what was cast into the treasury (Mark 12:41)" (Matthew Henry, *A Commentary*).

---

[a] 13 That is, about 3 1/4 pounds or about 1.5 kilograms; also elsewhere in this chapter   [b] 13 That is, about 1 3/4 pounds or about 800 grams; also elsewhere in this chapter   [c] 14 That is, about 4 ounces or about 115 grams; also elsewhere in this chapter   [d] 16 Or *purification offering*; also elsewhere in this chapter

## New International Version

young bull, one ram and one male lamb a year old for a burnt offering; [34]one male goat for a sin offering; [35]and two oxen, five rams, five male goats and five male lambs a year old to be sacrificed as a fellowship offering. This was the offering of Elizur son of Shedeur.

[36]On the fifth day Shelumiel son of Zurishaddai, the leader of the people of Simeon, brought his offering.

[37]His offering was one silver plate weighing a hundred and thirty shekels and one silver sprinkling bowl weighing seventy shekels, both according to the sanctuary shekel, each filled with the finest flour mixed with olive oil as a grain offering; [38]one gold dish weighing ten shekels, filled with incense; [39]one young bull, one ram and one male lamb a year old for a burnt offering; [40]one male goat for a sin offering; [41]and two oxen, five rams, five male goats and five male lambs a year old to be sacrificed as a fellowship offering. This was the offering of Shelumiel son of Zurishaddai.

[42]On the sixth day Eliasaph son of Deuel, the leader of the people of Gad, brought his offering.

[43]His offering was one silver plate weighing a hundred and thirty shekels and one silver sprinkling bowl weighing seventy shekels, both according to the sanctuary shekel, each filled with the finest flour mixed with olive oil as a grain offering; [44]one gold dish weighing ten shekels, filled with incense; [45]one young bull, one ram and one male lamb a year old for a burnt offering; [46]one male goat for a sin offering; [47]and two oxen, five rams, five male goats and five male lambs a year old to be sacrificed as a fellowship offering. This was the offering of Eliasaph son of Deuel.

[48]On the seventh day Elishama son of Ammihud, the leader of the people of Ephraim, brought his offering.

[49]His offering was one silver plate weighing a hundred and thirty shekels and one silver sprinkling bowl weighing seventy shekels, both according to the sanctuary shekel, each filled with the finest flour mixed with olive oil as a grain offering; [50]one gold dish weighing ten shekels, filled with incense; [51]one young bull, one ram and one male lamb a year old for a burnt offering; [52]one male goat for a sin offering; [53]and two oxen, five rams, five male goats and five male lambs a year old to be sacrificed as a fellowship offering. This was the offering of Elishama son of Ammihud.

[54]On the eighth day Gamaliel son of Pedahzur, the leader of the people of Manasseh, brought his offering.

[55]His offering was one silver plate weighing a hundred and thirty shekels and one silver sprinkling bowl weighing seventy shekels, both according to the sanctuary shekel, each filled with the finest flour mixed with olive oil as a grain offering; [56]one gold dish weighing ten shekels, filled with incense; [57]one young bull, one ram and one male lamb a year old for a burnt offering; [58]one male goat for a sin offering; [59]and two oxen, five rams, five male goats and five male lambs a year old to be sacrificed as a fellowship offering. This was the offering of Gamaliel son of Pedahzur.

[60]On the ninth day Abidan son of Gideoni, the leader of the people of Benjamin, brought his offering.

[61]His offering was one silver plate weighing a hundred and thirty shekels and one silver sprinkling bowl weighing seventy shekels, both according to the sanctuary shekel, each filled with the finest flour mixed with olive oil as a grain offering; [62]one gold dish weighing ten shekels, filled with incense; [63]one

## Amplified Bible

[33]One young bull, one ram, one male lamb a year old, for a burnt offering;

[34]One male goat for a sin offering;

[35]And for the sacrifice of peace offerings, two oxen, five rams, five male goats, five male lambs a year old. This was the offering of Elizur son of Shedeur.

[36]The fifth day Shelumiel son of Zurishaddai, leader of the sons of Simeon, offered.

[37]His offering was one silver platter, the weight of which was 130 shekels, one silver basin of seventy shekels, after the shekel of the sanctuary, both of them full of fine flour mixed with oil for a cereal offering;

[38]One golden bowl of ten shekels, full of incense;

[39]One young bull, one ram, one male lamb a year old, for a burnt offering;

[40]One male goat for a sin offering;

[41]And for the sacrifice of peace offerings, two oxen, five rams, five male goats, five male lambs a year old. This was the offering of Shelumiel son of Zurishaddai.

[42]The sixth day Eliasaph son of Deuel, leader of the sons of Gad, offered.

[43]His offering was one silver platter of the weight of 130 shekels, a silver basin of seventy shekels, after the shekel of the sanctuary, both of them full of fine flour mixed with oil for a cereal offering;

[44]One golden bowl of ten shekels, full of incense;

[45]One young bull, one ram, one male lamb a year old, for a burnt offering;

[46]One male goat for a sin offering;

[47]And for the sacrifice of peace offerings, two oxen, five rams, five male goats, [and] five male lambs a year old. This was the offering of Eliasaph son of Deuel.

[48]The seventh day Elishama son of Ammihud, leader of the sons of Ephraim, offered.

[49]His offering was one silver platter, the weight of which was 130 shekels, one silver basin of seventy shekels, after the shekel of the sanctuary, both of them full of fine flour mixed with oil for a cereal offering;

[50]One golden bowl of ten shekels, full of incense;

[51]One young bull, one ram, one male lamb a year old, for a burnt offering;

[52]One male goat for a sin offering;

[53]And for the sacrifice of peace offerings, two oxen, five rams, five male goats, [and] five male lambs a year old. This was the offering of Elishama son of Ammihud.

[54]The eighth day Gamaliel son of Pedahzur, leader of the sons of Manasseh, offered.

[55]His offering was one silver platter of the weight of 130 shekels, one silver basin of seventy shekels, after the shekel of the sanctuary, both of them full of fine flour mixed with oil for a cereal offering;

[56]One golden bowl of ten shekels, full of incense;

[57]One young bull, one ram, one male lamb a year old, for a burnt offering;

[58]One male goat for a sin offering;

[59]And for the sacrifice of peace offerings, two oxen, five rams, five male goats, five male lambs a year old. This was the offering of Gamaliel son of Pedahzur.

[60]The ninth day Abidan son of Gideoni, prince *or* leader of the sons of Benjamin, offered.

[61]His offering was one silver platter, the weight of which was 130 shekels, one silver basin of seventy shekels, after the shekel of the sanctuary, both of them full of fine flour mixed with oil for a cereal offering;

[62]One golden bowl of ten shekels, full of incense;

## New International Version

young bull, one ram and one male lamb a year old for a burnt offering; <sup>64</sup>one male goat for a sin offering; <sup>65</sup>and two oxen, five rams, five male goats and five male lambs a year old to be sacrificed as a fellowship offering. This was the offering of Abidan son of Gideoni.

<sup>66</sup>On the tenth day Ahiezer son of Ammishaddai, the leader of the people of Dan, brought his offering. <sup>67</sup>His offering was one silver plate weighing a hundred and thirty shekels and one silver sprinkling bowl weighing seventy shekels, both according to the sanctuary shekel, each filled with the finest flour mixed with olive oil as a grain offering; <sup>68</sup>one gold dish weighing ten shekels, filled with incense; <sup>69</sup>one young bull, one ram and one male lamb a year old for a burnt offering; <sup>70</sup>one male goat for a sin offering; <sup>71</sup>and two oxen, five rams, five male goats and five male lambs a year old to be sacrificed as a fellowship offering. This was the offering of Ahiezer son of Ammishaddai.

<sup>72</sup>On the eleventh day Pagiel son of Okran, the leader of the people of Asher, brought his offering. <sup>73</sup>His offering was one silver plate weighing a hundred and thirty shekels and one silver sprinkling bowl weighing seventy shekels, both according to the sanctuary shekel, each filled with the finest flour mixed with olive oil as a grain offering; <sup>74</sup>one gold dish weighing ten shekels, filled with incense; <sup>75</sup>one young bull, one ram and one male lamb a year old for a burnt offering; <sup>76</sup>one male goat for a sin offering; <sup>77</sup>and two oxen, five rams, five male goats and five male lambs a year old to be sacrificed as a fellowship offering. This was the offering of Pagiel son of Okran.

<sup>78</sup>On the twelfth day Ahira son of Enan, the leader of the people of Naphtali, brought his offering. <sup>79</sup>His offering was one silver plate weighing a hundred and thirty shekels and one silver sprinkling bowl weighing seventy shekels, both according to the sanctuary shekel, each filled with the finest flour mixed with olive oil as a grain offering; <sup>80</sup>one gold dish weighing ten shekels, filled with incense; <sup>81</sup>one young bull, one ram and one male lamb a year old for a burnt offering; <sup>82</sup>one male goat for a sin offering; <sup>83</sup>and two oxen, five rams, five male goats and five male lambs a year old to be sacrificed as a fellowship offering. This was the offering of Ahira son of Enan.

<sup>84</sup>These were the offerings of the Israelite leaders for the dedication of the altar when it was anointed: twelve silver plates, twelve silver sprinkling bowls and twelve gold dishes. <sup>85</sup>Each silver plate weighed a hundred and thirty shekels, and each sprinkling bowl seventy shekels. Altogether, the silver dishes weighed two thousand four hundred shekels,[a] according to the sanctuary shekel. <sup>86</sup>The twelve gold dishes filled with incense weighed ten shekels each, according to the sanctuary shekel. Altogether, the gold dishes weighed a hundred and twenty shekels.[b] <sup>87</sup>The total number of animals for the burnt offering came to twelve young bulls, twelve rams and twelve male lambs a year old, together with their grain offering. Twelve male goats were used for the sin offering. <sup>88</sup>The total number of animals for the sacrifice of the fellowship offering came to twenty-four oxen, sixty rams, sixty male goats and sixty male lambs a year old. These were the offerings for the dedication of the altar after it was anointed.

<sup>89</sup>When Moses entered the tent of meeting to speak with the LORD, he heard the voice speaking to him from between the two cherubim above the atonement cover on the ark of the covenant law. In this way the LORD spoke to him.

## Amplified Bible

<sup>63</sup>One young bull, one ram, one male lamb a year old, for a burnt offering;

<sup>64</sup>One male goat for a sin offering;

<sup>65</sup>And for the sacrifice of peace offerings, two oxen, five rams, five male goats, five male lambs a year old. This was the offering of Abidan son of Gideoni.

<sup>66</sup>The tenth day Ahiezer son of Ammishaddai, leader of the sons of Dan, offered.

<sup>67</sup>His offering was one silver platter, the weight of which was 130 shekels, one silver basin of seventy shekels, after the shekel of the sanctuary, both of them full of fine flour mixed with oil for a cereal offering;

<sup>68</sup>One golden bowl of ten shekels, full of incense;

<sup>69</sup>One young bull, one ram, one male lamb a year old, for a burnt offering;

<sup>70</sup>One male goat for a sin offering;

<sup>71</sup>And for the sacrifice of peace offerings, two oxen, five rams, five male goats, five male lambs a year old. This was the offering of Ahiezer son of Ammishaddai.

<sup>72</sup>The eleventh day Pagiel son of Ochran, leader of the sons of Asher, offered.

<sup>73</sup>His offering was one silver platter, the weight of which was 130 shekels, one silver basin of seventy shekels, after the shekel of the sanctuary, both of them full of fine flour mixed with oil for a cereal offering;

<sup>74</sup>One golden bowl of ten shekels, full of incense;

<sup>75</sup>One young bull, one ram, one male lamb a year old, for a burnt offering;

<sup>76</sup>One male goat for a sin offering;

<sup>77</sup>And for the sacrifice of peace offerings, two oxen, five rams, five male goats, five male lambs a year old. This was the offering of Pagiel son of Ochran.

<sup>78</sup>The twelfth day Ahira son of Enan, leader of the sons of Naphtali, offered.

<sup>79</sup>His offering was one silver platter, the weight of which was 130 shekels, one silver basin of seventy shekels, after the shekel of the sanctuary, both of them full of fine flour mixed with oil for a cereal offering;

<sup>80</sup>One golden bowl of ten shekels, full of incense;

<sup>81</sup>One young bull, one ram, one male lamb a year old, for a burnt offering;

<sup>82</sup>One male goat for a sin offering;

<sup>83</sup>And for the sacrifice of peace offerings, two oxen, five rams, five male goats, five male lambs a year old. This was the offering of Ahira son of Enan.

<sup>84</sup>This was the dedication offering for the altar [of burnt offering] from the leaders of Israel on the day when it was anointed: twelve platters of silver, twelve silver basins, twelve golden bowls;

<sup>85</sup>Each platter of silver weighing 130 shekels, each basin seventy; all the silver vessels weighed 2,400 shekels, after the shekel of the sanctuary.

<sup>86</sup>The twelve golden bowls full of incense, weighing ten shekels apiece, after the shekel of the sanctuary, all the gold of the bowls being 120 shekels.

<sup>87</sup>All the oxen for the burnt offering were twelve bulls, the rams twelve, the male lambs a year old twelve, together with their cereal offering; and the male goats for a sin offering twelve.

<sup>88</sup>And all the oxen for the sacrifice of the peace offerings were twenty-four bulls, the rams sixty, the male goats sixty, the male lambs a year old sixty. This was the dedication of the altar [of burnt offering] after it was anointed.

<sup>89</sup>And when Moses went into the Tent of Meeting to speak with the Lord, he heard the voice speaking to him from above the mercy seat that was upon the ark of the Testimony from between the two cherubim; and He spoke to [Moses].

---

[a] 85 That is, about 60 pounds or about 28 kilograms   [b] 86 That is, about 3 pounds or about 1.4 kilograms

## New International Version

### Setting Up the Lamps

**8** The LORD said to Moses, [2]"Speak to Aaron and say to him, 'When you set up the lamps, see that all seven light up the area in front of the lampstand.'"

[3]Aaron did so; he set up the lamps so that they faced forward on the lampstand, just as the LORD commanded Moses. [4]This is how the lampstand was made: It was made of hammered gold—from its base to its blossoms. The lampstand was made exactly like the pattern the LORD had shown Moses.

### The Setting Apart of the Levites

[5]The LORD said to Moses: [6]"Take the Levites from among all the Israelites and make them ceremonially clean. [7]To purify them, do this: Sprinkle the water of cleansing on them; then have them shave their whole bodies and wash their clothes. And so they will purify themselves. [8]Have them take a young bull with its grain offering of the finest flour mixed with olive oil; then you are to take a second young bull for a sin offering.[a] [9]Bring the Levites to the front of the tent of meeting and assemble the whole Israelite community. [10]You are to bring the Levites before the LORD, and the Israelites are to lay their hands on them. [11]Aaron is to present the Levites before the LORD as a wave offering from the Israelites, so that they may be ready to do the work of the LORD.

[12]"Then the Levites are to lay their hands on the heads of the bulls, using one for a sin offering to the LORD and the other for a burnt offering, to make atonement for the Levites. [13]Have the Levites stand in front of Aaron and his sons and then present them as a wave offering to the LORD. [14]In this way you are to set the Levites apart from the other Israelites, and the Levites will be mine.

[15]"After you have purified the Levites and presented them as a wave offering, they are to come to do their work at the tent of meeting. [16]They are the Israelites who are to be given wholly to me. I have taken them as my own in place of the firstborn, the first male offspring from every Israelite woman. [17]Every firstborn male in Israel, whether human or animal, is mine. When I struck down all the firstborn in Egypt, I set them apart for myself. [18]And I have taken the Levites in place of all the firstborn sons in Israel. [19]From among all the Israelites, I have given the Levites as gifts to Aaron and his sons to do the work at the tent of meeting on behalf of the Israelites and to make atonement for them so that no plague will strike the Israelites when they go near the sanctuary."

[20]Moses, Aaron and the whole Israelite community did with the Levites just as the LORD commanded Moses. [21]The Levites purified themselves and washed their clothes. Then Aaron presented them as a wave offering

## Amplified Bible

**8** And the Lord said to Moses, [2]Say to Aaron, When you set up *and* light the lamps, the seven lamps shall be made to give light in front of the lampstand.

[3]And Aaron did so; he lighted the lamps of the lampstand to give light in front of it, as the Lord commanded Moses.

[4]And this was the workmanship of the candlestick: beaten *or* turned gold, beaten work [of gold] from its base to its flowers; according to the pattern which the Lord had shown Moses, so he made the lampstand.

[5]And the Lord said to Moses,

[6]Take the [a]Levites from among the Israelites and cleanse them.

[7]And thus you shall do to them to cleanse them: sprinkle the water of purification [water to be used in case of sin] upon them, and let them pass a razor over all their flesh and wash their clothes and cleanse themselves. [Num. 19:17, 18.]

[8]Then let them take a young bull and its cereal offering of fine flour mixed with oil, and another young bull you shall take for a sin offering.

[9]You shall present the Levites before the Tent of Meeting, and you shall assemble the whole Israelite congregation.

[10]And you shall present the Levites before the Lord, and the Israelites shall put their hands upon the Levites,

[11]And Aaron shall offer the Levites before the Lord as a wave offering from the Israelites *and* on their behalf, that they may do the service of the Lord.

[12]Then the Levites shall lay their hands upon the heads of the bulls, and you shall offer the one for a sin offering and the other for a burnt offering to the Lord, to make atonement for the Levites.

[13]And you shall present the Levites before Aaron and his sons and offer them as a wave offering to the Lord.

[14]Thus you shall separate the Levites from among the Israelites, and the Levites shall be Mine [in a very special sense].

[15]And after that the Levites shall go in to do service at the Tent of Meeting, when you have cleansed them and offered them as a wave offering.

[16]For they are wholly given to Me from among the Israelites; instead of all who open the womb, the firstborn of all the Israelites, I have taken the Levites for Myself.

[17]For all the firstborn of the Israelites are Mine, both of man and beast; on the day that I smote every firstborn in the land of Egypt [not of Israel], I consecrated them *and* set them apart for Myself.

[18]And I have taken the Levites instead of all the firstborn of the Israelites.

[19]And I have given the Levites as a gift to Aaron and to his sons from among the Israelites to do the service of the Israelites at the Tent of Meeting and to make atonement for them, that there may be no plague among the Israelites if they should come near the sanctuary.

[20]So Moses and Aaron and all the congregation of the Israelites did thus to the Levites; according to all that the Lord commanded Moses concerning [them], so did the Israelites to them.

[21]The Levites cleansed *and* purified themselves and they washed their clothes; and Aaron offered them as a

---

[a] There are many lessons for the Christian in this section (Num. 8:5-22). He sees here the importance of each member of God's family having his own particular task (I Cor. 12). It is necessary that special men be designated for particular duties in order that the work of God's kingdom shall be done in orderly fashion. Those who do the work of God must be cleansed from all defilement of flesh and spirit. No one is fit in himself to serve God. It is only as we see ourselves as guilty sinners saved through the sacrifice of the Lord Jesus Christ at Calvary that we can do anything that is worthwhile in God's sight. Apart from Him, "all our righteousnesses *are* as filthy rags" (Isa. 64:6 KJV). (F. Davidson, ed., *The New Bible Commentary*).

---

[a] 8 Or *purification offering*; also in verse 12

## New International Version

before the LORD and made atonement for them to purify them. 22After that, the Levites came to do their work at the tent of meeting under the supervision of Aaron and his sons. They did with the Levites just as the LORD commanded Moses.

23The LORD said to Moses, 24"This applies to the Levites: Men twenty-five years old or more shall come to take part in the work at the tent of meeting, 25but at the age of fifty, they must retire from their regular service and work no longer. 26They may assist their brothers in performing their duties at the tent of meeting, but they themselves must not do the work. This, then, is how you are to assign the responsibilities of the Levites."

### The Passover

**9** The LORD spoke to Moses in the Desert of Sinai in the first month of the second year after they came out of Egypt. He said, 2"Have the Israelites celebrate the Passover at the appointed time. 3Celebrate it at the appointed time, at twilight on the fourteenth day of this month, in accordance with all its rules and regulations."

4So Moses told the Israelites to celebrate the Passover, 5and they did so in the Desert of Sinai at twilight on the fourteenth day of the first month. The Israelites did everything just as the LORD commanded Moses.

6But some of them could not celebrate the Passover on that day because they were ceremonially unclean on account of a dead body. So they came to Moses and Aaron that same day 7and said to Moses, "We have become unclean because of a dead body, but why should we be kept from presenting the LORD's offering with the other Israelites at the appointed time?"

8Moses answered them, "Wait until I find out what the LORD commands concerning you."

9Then the LORD said to Moses, 10"Tell the Israelites: 'When any of you or your descendants are unclean because of a dead body or are away on a journey, they are still to celebrate the LORD's Passover, 11but they are to do it on the fourteenth day of the second month at twilight. They are to eat the lamb, together with unleavened bread and bitter herbs. 12They must not leave any of it till morning or break any of its bones. When they celebrate the Passover, they must follow all the regulations. 13But if anyone who is ceremonially clean and not on a journey fails to celebrate the Passover, they must be cut off from their people for not presenting the LORD's offering at the appointed time. They will bear the consequences of their sin.

14"'A foreigner residing among you is also to celebrate the LORD's Passover in accordance with its rules and regulations. You must have the same regulations for both the foreigner and the native-born.'"

### The Cloud Above the Tabernacle

15On the day the tabernacle, the tent of the covenant law, was set up, the cloud covered it. From evening till morning the cloud above the tabernacle looked like fire.

## Amplified Bible

wave offering before the Lord and Aaron made atonement for them to cleanse them.

22And after that the Levites went in to do their service in the Tent of Meeting with the attendance of Aaron and his sons; as the Lord had commanded Moses concerning the Levites, so did they to them.

23And the Lord said to Moses,

24This is what applies to the Levites: from twenty-five years old and upward they shall go in to perform the work of the service of the Tent of Meeting,

25And at the age of fifty years, they shall retire from the warfare of the service and serve no more,

26But shall help their brethren in the Tent of Meeting [attend to protecting the sacred things from being profaned], but shall do no regular *or* heavy service. Thus shall you direct the Levites in regard to their duties.

**9** The Lord said to Moses in the Wilderness of Sinai in the first month of the second year after they had come out of the land of Egypt,

2Let the Israelites keep the Passover at its appointed time.

3On the fourteenth day of this month in the evening, you shall keep it at its appointed time; according to all its statutes and ordinances you shall keep it.

4So Moses told the Israelites they should keep the Passover.

5And they kept the Passover on the fourteenth day of the first month in the evening in the Wilderness of Sinai; according to all that the Lord commanded Moses, so the Israelites did.

6And there were certain men who were defiled by touching the dead body of a man, so they could not keep the Passover on that day; and they came before Moses and Aaron on that day.

7Those men said to [Moses], We are defiled by touching the dead body. Why are we prevented from offering the Lord's offering at its appointed time among the Israelites?

8And Moses said to them, Stand still, and I will hear what the Lord will command concerning you.

9And the Lord said to Moses,

10Say to the Israelites, If any man of you or of your posterity shall be unclean by reason of touching a dead body or is far off on a journey, still he shall keep the Passover to the Lord.

11On the fourteenth day of the second month in the evening they shall keep it, and eat it with unleavened bread and bitter herbs.

12They shall leave none of it until the morning nor break any bone of it; according to all the statutes for the Passover they shall keep it. [John 19:36.]

13But the man who is clean and is not on a journey, yet does not keep the Passover, that person shall be cut off from among his people because he did not bring the Lord's offering at its appointed time; that man shall bear [the penalty of] his sin.

14And if a stranger sojourns among you and will keep the Passover to the Lord, according to [its] statutes and its ordinances, so shall he do; you shall have one statute both for the temporary resident and for him who was born in the land.

15And on the day that the tabernacle was erected, the cloud [of God's presence] covered the tabernacle, that is, the Tent of the Testimony; and at evening it was over the tabernacle, having the appearance of [a pillar of] fire until the morning. [Exod. 13:21.]

## New International Version

16That is how it continued to be; the cloud covered it, and at night it looked like fire. 17Whenever the cloud lifted from above the tent, the Israelites set out; wherever the cloud settled, the Israelites encamped. 18At the LORD's command the Israelites set out, and at his command they encamped. As long as the cloud stayed over the tabernacle, they remained in camp. 19When the cloud remained over the tabernacle a long time, the Israelites obeyed the LORD's order and did not set out. 20Sometimes the cloud was over the tabernacle only a few days; at the LORD's command they would encamp, and then at his command they would set out. 21Sometimes the cloud stayed only from evening till morning, and when it lifted in the morning, they set out. Whether by day or by night, whenever the cloud lifted, they set out. 22Whether the cloud stayed over the tabernacle for two days or a month or a year, the Israelites would remain in camp and not set out; but when it lifted, they would set out. 23At the LORD's command they encamped, and at the LORD's command they set out. They obeyed the LORD's order, in accordance with his command through Moses.

### The Silver Trumpets

**10** The LORD said to Moses: 2"Make two trumpets of hammered silver, and use them for calling the community together and for having the camps set out. 3When both are sounded, the whole community is to assemble before you at the entrance to the tent of meeting. 4If only one is sounded, the leaders—the heads of the clans of Israel—are to assemble before you. 5When a trumpet blast is sounded, the tribes camping on the east are to set out. 6At the sounding of a second blast, the camps on the south are to set out. The blast will be the signal for setting out. 7To gather the assembly, blow the trumpets, but not with the signal for setting out.

8"The sons of Aaron, the priests, are to blow the trumpets. This is to be a lasting ordinance for you and the generations to come. 9When you go into battle in your own land against an enemy who is oppressing you, sound a blast on the trumpets. Then you will be remembered by the LORD your God and rescued from your enemies. 10Also at your times of rejoicing—your appointed festivals and New Moon feasts—you are to sound the trumpets over your burnt offerings and fellowship offerings, and they will be a memorial for you before your God. I am the LORD your God."

### The Israelites Leave Sinai

11On the twentieth day of the second month of the second year, the cloud lifted from above the tabernacle of the covenant law. 12Then the Israelites set out from the Desert of Sinai and traveled from place to place until the cloud came to rest in the Desert of Paran. 13They set out, this first time, at the LORD's command through Moses.

14The divisions of the camp of Judah went first, under their standard. Nahshon son of Amminadab was in com-

## Amplified Bible

16So it was constantly; the cloud covered it by day, and the appearance of fire by night.

17Whenever the cloud was taken up from over the Tent, after that the Israelites journeyed; and in the place where the cloud rested, there the Israelites encamped.

18At the Lord's command the Israelites journeyed, and at [His] command they encamped. As long as the cloud rested upon the tabernacle they remained encamped.

19Even when the cloud tarried upon the tabernacle many days, the Israelites kept the Lord's charge and did not set out.

20And sometimes the cloud was only a few days upon the tabernacle, but according to the command of the Lord they remained encamped, and at His command they journeyed.

21And sometimes the cloud remained [over the tabernacle] from evening only until morning, but when the cloud was taken up, they journeyed; whether it was taken up by day or by night, they journeyed.

22Whether it was two days or a month or a longer time that the cloud tarried upon the tabernacle, dwelling on it, the Israelites remained encamped; but when it was taken up, they journeyed.

23At the command of the Lord they remained encamped, and at [His] command they journeyed; they kept the charge of the Lord, at the command of the Lord through Moses.

**10** And the Lord said to Moses, 2Make two trumpets of silver; of hammered or turned work you shall make them, that you may use them to call the congregation and for breaking camp.

3When they both are blown, all the congregation shall assemble before you at the door of the Tent of Meeting.

4And if one blast on a single trumpet is blown, then the princes or leaders, heads of the tribes of Israel, shall gather themselves to you.

5When you blow an alarm, the camps on the east side [of the tabernacle] shall set out.

6When you blow an alarm the second time, then the camps on the south side shall set out. An alarm shall be blown whenever they are to set out on their journeys.

7When the congregation is to be assembled, you shall blow [the trumpets in short, sharp tones], but not the blast of an alarm.

8And the sons of Aaron, the priests, shall blow the trumpets, and the trumpets shall be to you for a perpetual statute throughout your generations.

9When you go to war in your land against the enemy that oppresses you, then blow an alarm with the trumpets, that you may be remembered before the Lord your God, and you shall be saved from your enemies.

10Also in the day of rejoicing, and in your set feasts, and at the beginnings of your months, you shall blow the trumpets over your burnt offerings and your peace offerings; thus they may be a remembrance before your God. I am the Lord your God.

11On the twentieth day of the second month in the second year [since leaving Egypt], the cloud [of the Lord's presence] was taken up from over the tabernacle of the Testimony,

12And the Israelites took their journey by stages out of the Wilderness of Sinai, and the [guiding] cloud rested in the Wilderness of Paran.

13When the journey was to begin, at the command of the Lord through Moses,

14In the first place went the standard of the camp of the sons of Judah by their companies; and over their host was Nahshon son of Amminadab.

## New International Version

mand. ¹⁵Nethanel son of Zuar was over the division of the tribe of Issachar, ¹⁶and Eliab son of Helon was over the division of the tribe of Zebulun. ¹⁷Then the tabernacle was taken down, and the Gershonites and Merarites, who carried it, set out.

¹⁸The divisions of the camp of Reuben went next, under their standard. Elizur son of Shedeur was in command. ¹⁹Shelumiel son of Zurishaddai was over the division of the tribe of Simeon, ²⁰and Eliasaph son of Deuel was over the division of the tribe of Gad. ²¹Then the Kohathites set out, carrying the holy things. The tabernacle was to be set up before they arrived.

²²The divisions of the camp of Ephraim went next, under their standard. Elishama son of Ammihud was in command. ²³Gamaliel son of Pedahzur was over the division of the tribe of Manasseh, ²⁴and Abidan son of Gideoni was over the division of the tribe of Benjamin.

²⁵Finally, as the rear guard for all the units, the divisions of the camp of Dan set out under their standard. Ahiezer son of Ammishaddai was in command. ²⁶Pagiel son of Okran was over the division of the tribe of Asher, ²⁷and Ahira son of Enan was over the division of the tribe of Naphtali. ²⁸This was the order of march for the Israelite divisions as they set out.

²⁹Now Moses said to Hobab son of Reuel the Midianite, Moses' father-in-law, "We are setting out for the place about which the LORD said, 'I will give it to you.' Come with us and we will treat you well, for the LORD has promised good things to Israel."

³⁰He answered, "No, I will not go; I am going back to my own land and my own people."

³¹But Moses said, "Please do not leave us. You know where we should camp in the wilderness, and you can be our eyes. ³²If you come with us, we will share with you whatever good things the LORD gives us."

³³So they set out from the mountain of the LORD and traveled for three days. The ark of the covenant of the LORD went before them during those three days to find them a place to rest. ³⁴The cloud of the LORD was over them by day when they set out from the camp.

³⁵Whenever the ark set out, Moses said,

"Rise up, LORD!
May your enemies be scattered;
may your foes flee before you."

³⁶Whenever it came to rest, he said,

"Return, LORD,
to the countless thousands of Israel."

### Fire From the LORD

**11** Now the people complained about their hardships in the hearing of the LORD, and when he heard them his anger was aroused. Then fire from the LORD burned among them and consumed some of the outskirts of the camp. ²When the people cried out to Moses, he prayed to the LORD and the fire died down. ³So that

## Amplified Bible

¹⁵And over the host of the tribe of the sons of Issachar was Nethanel son of Zuar.

¹⁶And over the host of the tribe of the sons of Zebulun was Eliab son of Helon.

¹⁷When the tabernacle was taken down, the sons of Gershon and Merari, bearing [it] on their shoulders, set out.

¹⁸The standard of the camp of Reuben set forward by their companies; and over Reuben's host was Elizur son of Shedeur.

¹⁹And over the host of the tribe of the sons of Simeon was Shelumiel son of Zurishaddai.

²⁰And over the host of the tribe of the sons of Gad was Eliasaph son of Deuel.

²¹Then the Kohathites set forward, bearing the holy things, and the tabernacle was set up before they arrived.

²²And the standard of the camp of the sons of Ephraim set forward according to their companies; and over Ephraim's host was Elishama son of Ammihud.

²³Over the host of the tribe of the sons of Manasseh was Gamaliel son of Pedahzur.

²⁴And over the host of the tribe of the sons of Benjamin was Abidan son of Gideoni.

²⁵Then the standard of the camp of the sons of Dan, which was the rear guard of all the camps, set forward according to their companies; and over Dan's host was Ahiezer son of Ammishaddai.

²⁶And over the host of the tribe of the sons of Asher was Pagiel son of Ochran.

²⁷And over the host of the tribe of the sons of Naphtali was Ahira son of Enan.

²⁸This was the Israelites' order of march by their hosts when they set out.

²⁹And Moses said to Hobab son of Reuel the Midianite, Moses' father-in-law, We are journeying to the place of which the Lord said, I will give it to you. Come with us, and we will do you good, for the Lord has promised good concerning Israel.

³⁰And Hobab said to him, I will not go; I will depart to my own land and to my family.

³¹And Moses said, ªDo not leave us, I pray you; for you know how we are to encamp in the wilderness, and you will serve as eyes for us.

³²And if you will go with us, it shall be that whatever good the Lord does to us, the same we will do to you.

³³They departed from the mountain of the Lord [Mount Sinai] three days' journey; and the ark of the covenant of the Lord went before them during the three days' journey to seek out a resting-place for them.

³⁴The cloud of the Lord was over them by day when they went forward from the camp.

³⁵Whenever the ark set out, Moses said, Rise up, Lord; let Your enemies be scattered; and let those who hate You flee before You. [Ps. 68:1, 2.]

³⁶And when it rested, he said, Return, O Lord, to the ten thousand thousands in Israel.

**11** And the people grumbled *and* deplored their hardships, which was evil in the ears of the Lord, and when the Lord heard it, His anger was kindled; and the fire of the Lord burned among them and devoured those in the outlying parts of the camp.

²The people cried to Moses, and when Moses prayed to the Lord, the fire subsided.

---

ª The record does not say so, but Hobab seems to have remained with the Israelites, for later history shows that his descendants lived in Canaan (Judg. 1:16; I Sam. 15:6).

## New International Version

place was called Taberah,[a] because fire from the LORD had burned among them.

### Quail From the LORD

[4]The rabble with them began to crave other food, and again the Israelites started wailing and said, "If only we had meat to eat! [5]We remember the fish we ate in Egypt at no cost—also the cucumbers, melons, leeks, onions and garlic. [6]But now we have lost our appetite; we never see anything but this manna!"

[7]The manna was like coriander seed and looked like resin. [8]The people went around gathering it, and then ground it in a hand mill or crushed it in a mortar. They cooked it in a pot or made it into loaves. And it tasted something made with olive oil. [9]When the dew settled on the camp at night, the manna also came down.

[10]Moses heard the people of every family wailing at the entrance to their tents. The LORD became exceedingly angry, and Moses was troubled. [11]He asked the LORD, "Why have you brought this trouble on your servant? What have I done to displease you that you put the burden of all these people on me? [12]Did I conceive all these people? Did I give them birth? Why do you tell me to carry them in my arms, as a nurse carries an infant, to the land you promised on oath to their ancestors? [13]Where can I get meat for all these people? They keep wailing to me, 'Give us meat to eat!' [14]I cannot carry all these people by myself; the burden is too heavy for me. [15]If this is how you are going to treat me, please go ahead and kill me—if I have found favor in your eyes—and do not let me face my own ruin."

[16]The LORD said to Moses: "Bring me seventy of Israel's elders who are known to you as leaders and officials among the people. Have them come to the tent of meeting, that they may stand there with you. [17]I will come down and speak with you there, and I will take some of the power of the Spirit that is on you and put it on them. They will share the burden of the people with you so that you will not have to carry it alone.

[18]"Tell the people: 'Consecrate yourselves in preparation for tomorrow, when you will eat meat. The LORD heard you when you wailed, "If only we had meat to eat! We were better off in Egypt!" Now the LORD will give you meat, and you will eat it. [19]You will not eat it for just one day, or two days, or five, ten or twenty days, [20]but for a whole month—until it comes out of your nostrils and you loathe it—because you have rejected the LORD, who is among you, and have wailed before him, saying, "Why did we ever leave Egypt?" ' "

[21]But Moses said, "Here I am among six hundred thousand men on foot, and you say, 'I will give them meat to eat for a whole month!' [22]Would they have enough if flocks and herds were slaughtered for them? Would they have enough if all the fish in the sea were caught for them?"

[23]The LORD answered Moses, "Is the LORD's arm too short? Now you will see whether or not what I say will come true for you."

## Amplified Bible

[3]He called the name of the place Taberah [burning], because the fire of the Lord burned among them.

[4]And the mixed multitude among them [the rabble who followed Israel from Egypt] began to lust greatly [for familiar and dainty food], and the Israelites wept again and said, Who will give us meat to eat?

[5]We remember the fish we ate freely in Egypt *and* without cost, the cucumbers, melons, leeks, onions, and garlic.

[6]But now our soul (our strength) is dried up; there is nothing at all [in the way of food] to be seen but this manna.

[7]The manna was like coriander seed and its appearance was like that of bdellium [perhaps a precious stone].

[8]The people went about and gathered it, and ground it in mills or beat it in mortars, and boiled it in pots, and made cakes of it; and it tasted like cakes baked with fresh oil.

[9]And when the dew fell on the camp in the night, the manna fell with it.

[10]And Moses heard the people weeping throughout their families, every man at the door of his tent; and the anger of the Lord blazed hotly, and in the eyes of Moses it was evil.

[11]And Moses said to the Lord, Why have You dealt ill with Your servants? And why have I not found favor in Your sight, that You lay the burden of all this people on me?

[12]Have I conceived all this people? Have I brought them forth, that You should say to me, Carry them in your bosom, as a nursing father carries the sucking child, to the land which You swore to their fathers [to give them]?

[13]Where should I get meat to give to all these people? For they weep before me and say, Give us meat, that we may eat.

[14]I am not able to carry all these people alone, because the burden is too heavy for me.

[15]And if this is the way You deal with me, kill me, I pray You, at once, and be granting me a favor and let me not see my wretchedness [in the failure of all my efforts].

[16]And the Lord said to Moses, Gather for Me [a]seventy men of the elders of Israel whom you know to be the elders of the people and officers over them; and bring them to the Tent of Meeting and let them stand there with you.

[17]And I will come down and talk with you there; and I will take of the Spirit which is upon you and will put It upon them; and they shall bear the burden of the people with you, so that you may not have to bear it yourself alone.

[18]And say to the people, Consecrate yourselves for tomorrow, and you shall eat meat; for you have wept in the hearing of the Lord, saying, Who will give us meat to eat? For it was well with us in Egypt. Therefore the Lord will give you meat, and you shall eat.

[19]You shall not eat one day, or two, or five, or ten, or twenty days,

[20]But a whole month—until [you are satiated and vomit it up violently and] it comes out at your nostrils and is disgusting to you—because you have rejected *and* despised the Lord Who is among you, and have wept before Him, saying, Why did we come out of Egypt? [Ps. 106:13-15.]

[21]But Moses said, The people among whom I am are 600,000 footmen [besides all the women and children], and You have said, I will give them meat, that they may eat a whole month!

[22]Shall flocks and herds be killed to suffice them? Or shall all the fish of the sea be collected to satisfy them?

[23]The Lord said to Moses, Has the Lord's hand (His ability and power) become short (thwarted and inadequate)? You shall see now whether My word shall come to pass for you or not. [Isa. 50:2.]

[a] A council of seventy elders had existed the year before this (Exod. 24:9). It appears to be the source of the Sanhedrin, the highest Jewish assembly for government in the time of our Lord—usually translated "council."

## New International Version

24So Moses went out and told the people what the LORD had said. He brought together seventy of their elders and had them stand around the tent. 25Then the LORD came down in the cloud and spoke with him, and he took some of the power of the Spirit that was on him and put it on the seventy elders. When the Spirit rested on them, they prophesied—but did not do so again.

26However, two men, whose names were Eldad and Medad, had remained in the camp. They were listed among the elders, but did not go out to the tent. Yet the Spirit also rested on them, and they prophesied in the camp. 27A young man ran and told Moses, "Eldad and Medad are prophesying in the camp."

28Joshua son of Nun, who had been Moses' aide since youth, spoke up and said, "Moses, my lord, stop them!"

29But Moses replied, "Are you jealous for my sake? I wish that all the LORD's people were prophets and that the LORD would put his Spirit on them!" 30Then Moses and the elders of Israel returned to the camp.

31Now a wind went out from the LORD and drove quail in from the sea. It scattered them up to two cubits*a* deep all around the camp, as far as a day's walk in any direction. 32All that day and night and all the next day the people went out and gathered quail. No one gathered less than ten homers.*b* Then they spread them out all around the camp. 33But while the meat was still between their teeth and before it could be consumed, the anger of the LORD burned against the people, and he struck them with a severe plague. 34Therefore the place was named Kibroth Hattaavah,*c* because there they buried the people who had craved other food.

35From Kibroth Hattaavah the people traveled to Hazeroth and stayed there.

### Miriam and Aaron Oppose Moses

**12** Miriam and Aaron began to talk against Moses because of his Cushite wife, for he had married a Cushite. 2"Has the LORD spoken only through Moses?" they asked. "Hasn't he also spoken through us?" And the LORD heard this.

3 (Now Moses was a very humble man, more humble than anyone else on the face of the earth.)

4At once the LORD said to Moses, Aaron and Miriam, "Come out to the tent of meeting, all three of you." So the three of them went out. 5Then the LORD came down in a pillar of cloud; he stood at the entrance to the tent and summoned Aaron and Miriam. When the two of them stepped forward, 6he said, "Listen to my words:

"When there is a prophet among you,
  I, the LORD, reveal myself to them in visions,
  I speak to them in dreams.
7 But this is not true of my servant Moses;
  he is faithful in all my house.
8 With him I speak face to face,

## Amplified Bible

24So Moses went out and told the people the words of the Lord, and he gathered seventy men of the elders of the people and set them round about the Tent.

25And the Lord came down in the cloud and spoke to him, and took of the Spirit that was upon him and put It upon the seventy elders; and when the Spirit rested upon them, they prophesied [sounding forth the praises of God and declaring His will]. Then they did so no more. [Num. 11:29.]

26But there remained two men in the camp named Eldad and Medad. The Spirit rested upon them, and they were of those who were selected *and* listed, yet they did not go out to the Tent [as told to do], but they prophesied in the camp.

27And a young man ran to Moses and said, Eldad and Medad are prophesying [sounding forth the praises of God and declaring His will] in the camp.

28Joshua son of Nun, the minister of Moses, one of his chosen men, said, My lord Moses, forbid them!

29But Moses said to him, Are you *a*envious *or* jealous for my sake? Would that all the Lord's people were prophets and that the Lord would put His Spirit upon them! [Luke 9:49, 50.]

30And Moses went back into the camp, he and the elders of Israel.

31And there went forth a wind from the Lord and brought quails from the sea, and let them fall [so they flew low] beside the camp, about a day's journey on this side and on the other side, all around the camp, about two cubits above the ground.

32And the people rose all that day and all night and all the next day and caught *and* gathered the quails. He who gathered least gathered ten homers; and they spread them out for themselves round about the camp [to cure them by drying].

33While the meat was yet between their teeth, before it was consumed, the anger of the Lord was kindled against the people, and the Lord smote them with a very great plague.

34That place was called Kibroth-hattaavah [the graves of sensuous desire], because there they buried the people who lusted, whose physical appetite caused them to sin. [I Cor. 10:1-13.]

35The Israelites journeyed from Kibroth-hattaavah to Hazeroth, where they remained.

**12** Now Miriam and Aaron talked against Moses [their brother] because of his *b*Cushite wife, for he had married a Cushite woman.

2And they said, Has the Lord indeed spoken only by Moses? Has He not spoken also by us? And the Lord heard it.

3Now the man Moses was very meek (gentle, kind, and humble) *or* above all the men on the face of the earth.

4Suddenly the Lord said to Moses, Aaron, and Miriam, Come out, you three, to the Tent of Meeting. And the three of them came out.

5The Lord came down in a pillar of cloud, and stood at the Tent door and called Aaron and Miriam, and they came forward.

6And He said, Hear now My words: If there is a prophet among you, I the Lord make Myself known to him in a vision and speak to him in a dream.

7But not so with My servant Moses; he is entrusted *and* faithful in all My house. [Heb. 3:2, 5, 6.]

8With him I speak mouth to mouth [directly], clearly

---

*a* "Moses, the minister of God, rebukes our partial love, / Who envy at the gifts bestow'd on those we disapprove. / We do not our own spirit know, who wish to see suppressed, / The men that Jesus' spirit show, the men whom God hath blest" (Charles Wesley).  *b* Zipporah, Moses' wife, seems to have died some time before. Marriage with a Canaanite was forbidden, but not with an Egyptian or Cushite. Joseph's wife was an Egyptian (Gen. 41:45).

## New International Version

clearly and not in riddles;
he sees the form of the LORD.
Why then were you not afraid
to speak against my servant Moses?"

⁹The anger of the LORD burned against them, and he left them.

¹⁰When the cloud lifted from above the tent, Miriam's skin was leprous[a]—it became as white as snow. Aaron turned toward her and saw that she had a defiling skin disease, ¹¹and he said to Moses, "Please, my lord, I ask you not to hold against us the sin we have so foolishly committed. ¹²Do not let her be like a stillborn infant coming from its mother's womb with its flesh half eaten away."

¹³So Moses cried out to the LORD, "Please, God, heal her!"

¹⁴The LORD replied to Moses, "If her father had spit in her face, would she not have been in disgrace for seven days? Confine her outside the camp for seven days; after that she can be brought back." ¹⁵So Miriam was confined outside the camp for seven days, and the people did not move on till she was brought back.

¹⁶After that, the people left Hazeroth and encamped in the Desert of Paran.

### Exploring Canaan

**13** The LORD said to Moses, ²"Send some men to explore the land of Canaan, which I am giving to the Israelites. From each ancestral tribe send one of its leaders."

³So at the LORD's command Moses sent them out from the Desert of Paran. All of them were leaders of the Israelites. ⁴These are their names:

from the tribe of Reuben, Shammua son of Zakkur;
⁵from the tribe of Simeon, Shaphat son of Hori;
⁶from the tribe of Judah, Caleb son of Jephunneh;
⁷from the tribe of Issachar, Igal son of Joseph;
⁸from the tribe of Ephraim, Hoshea son of Nun;
⁹from the tribe of Benjamin, Palti son of Raphu;
¹⁰from the tribe of Zebulun, Gaddiel son of Sodi;
¹¹from the tribe of Manasseh (a tribe of Joseph), Gaddi son of Susi;
¹²from the tribe of Dan, Ammiel son of Gemalli;
¹³from the tribe of Asher, Sethur son of Michael;
¹⁴from the tribe of Naphtali, Nahbi son of Vophsi;
¹⁵from the tribe of Gad, Geuel son of Maki.

¹⁶These are the names of the men Moses sent to explore the land. (Moses gave Hoshea son of Nun the name Joshua.)

¹⁷When Moses sent them to explore Canaan, he said, "Go up through the Negev and on into the hill country. ¹⁸See what the land is like and whether the people who live there are strong or weak, few or many. ¹⁹What kind of land do they live in? Is it good or bad? What kind of towns do they live in? Are they unwalled or fortified? ²⁰How is the soil? Is it fertile or poor? Are there trees in it or not? Do your best to bring back some of the fruit of the land." (It was the season for the first ripe grapes.)

²¹So they went up and explored the land from the Desert of Zin as far as Rehob, toward Lebo Hamath. ²²They went up through the Negev and came to Hebron, where Ahiman, Sheshai and Talmai, the descendants of Anak, lived. (Hebron had been built seven years before Zoan in Egypt.) ²³When they reached the Valley of Eshkol,[b] they cut off a branch bearing a single cluster of grapes. Two of

---

## Amplified Bible

and not in dark speeches; and he beholds the form of the Lord. Why then were you not afraid to speak against My servant Moses?

⁹And the anger of the Lord was kindled against them, and He departed.

¹⁰And when the cloud departed from over the Tent, behold, Miriam was leprous, as white as snow. And Aaron looked at Miriam, and, behold, she was leprous!

¹¹And Aaron said to Moses, Oh, my lord, I plead with you, lay not the sin upon us in which we have done foolishly and in which we have sinned.

¹²Let her not be as one dead, already half decomposed when he comes out of his mother's womb.

¹³And Moses cried to the Lord, saying, Heal her now, O God, I beseech You!

¹⁴And the Lord said to Moses, If her father had but spit in her face, should she not be ashamed for seven days? Let her be shut up outside the camp for seven days, and after that let her be brought in again.

¹⁵So Miriam was shut up without the camp for seven days, and the people did not journey on until Miriam was brought in again.

¹⁶Afterward [they] removed from Hazeroth and encamped in the Wilderness of Paran.

**13** And the Lord said to Moses, ²Send men to explore and scout out [for yourselves] the land of Canaan, which I give to the Israelites. From each tribe of their fathers you shall send a man, every one a leader or head among them.

³So Moses by the command of the Lord sent scouts from the Wilderness of Paran, all of them men who were heads of the Israelites.

⁴These were their names: of the tribe of Reuben, Shammua son of Zaccur;
⁵Of the tribe of Simeon, Shaphat son of Hori;
⁶Of the tribe of Judah, Caleb son of Jephunneh;
⁷Of the tribe of Issachar, Igal son of Joseph;
⁸Of the tribe of Ephraim, Hoshea [that is, Joshua] son of Nun;
⁹Of the tribe of Benjamin, Palti son of Raphu;
¹⁰Of the tribe of Zebulun, Gaddiel son of Sodi;
¹¹Of the tribe of Joseph, that is, of the tribe of Manasseh, Gaddi son of Susi;
¹²Of the tribe of Dan, Ammiel son of Gemalli;
¹³Of the tribe of Asher, Sethur son of Michael;
¹⁴Of the tribe of Naphtali, Nahbi son of Vophsi;
¹⁵Of the tribe of Gad, Geuel son of Machi.

¹⁶These are the names of the men whom Moses sent to explore and scout out the land. And Moses called Hoshea son of Nun, Joshua.

¹⁷Moses sent them to scout out the land of Canaan, and said to them, Get up this way by the South (the Negeb) and go up into the hill country,

¹⁸And see what the land is and whether the people who dwell there are strong or weak, few or many,

¹⁹And whether the land they live in is good or bad, and whether the cities they dwell in are camps or strongholds,

²⁰And what the land is, whether it is fat or lean, whether there is timber on it or not. And be of good courage and bring some of the fruit of the land. Now the time was the time of the first ripe grapes.

²¹So they went up and scouted through the land from the Wilderness of Zin to Rehob, to the entrance of Hamath.

²²And then went up into the South (the Negeb) and came to Hebron; and Ahiman, Sheshai, and Talmai [probably three tribes of] the sons of Anak were there. (Hebron was built seven years before Zoan in Egypt.)

²³And they came to the Valley of Eshcol, and cut down from there a branch with one cluster of grapes, and they

---

[a] 10 The Hebrew for *leprous* was used for various diseases affecting the skin.  [b] 23 *Eshkol* means *cluster*; also in verse 24.

## New International Version

them carried it on a pole between them, along with some pomegranates and figs. ²⁴That place was called the Valley of Eshkol because of the cluster of grapes the Israelites cut off there. ²⁵At the end of forty days they returned from exploring the land.

### Report on the Exploration

²⁶They came back to Moses and Aaron and the whole Israelite community at Kadesh in the Desert of Paran. There they reported to them and to the whole assembly and showed them the fruit of the land. ²⁷They gave Moses this account: "We went into the land to which you sent us, and it does flow with milk and honey! Here is its fruit. ²⁸But the people who live there are powerful, and the cities are fortified and very large. We even saw descendants of Anak there. ²⁹The Amalekites live in the Negev; the Hittites, Jebusites and Amorites live in the hill country; and the Canaanites live near the sea and along the Jordan."

³⁰Then Caleb silenced the people before Moses and said, "We should go up and take possession of the land, for we can certainly do it."

³¹But the men who had gone up with him said, "We can't attack those people; they are stronger than we are." ³²And they spread among the Israelites a bad report about the land they had explored. They said, "The land we explored devours those living in it. All the people we saw there are of great size. ³³We saw the Nephilim there (the descendants of Anak come from the Nephilim). We seemed like grasshoppers in our own eyes, and we looked the same to them."

### The People Rebel

**14** That night all the members of the community raised their voices and wept aloud. ²All the Israelites grumbled against Moses and Aaron, and the whole assembly said to them, "If only we had died in Egypt! Or in this wilderness! ³Why is the LORD bringing us to this land only to let us fall by the sword? Our wives and children will be taken as plunder. Wouldn't it be better for us to go back to Egypt?" ⁴And they said to each other, "We should choose a leader and go back to Egypt."

⁵Then Moses and Aaron fell facedown in front of the whole Israelite assembly gathered there. ⁶Joshua son of Nun and Caleb son of Jephunneh, who were among those who had explored the land, tore their clothes ⁷and said to the entire Israelite assembly, "The land we passed through and explored is exceedingly good. ⁸If the LORD is pleased with us, he will lead us into that land, a land flowing with milk and honey, and will give it to us. ⁹Only do not rebel against the LORD. And do not be afraid of the people of the land, because we will devour them. Their protection is gone, but the LORD is with us. Do not be afraid of them."

¹⁰But the whole assembly talked about stoning them.

## Amplified Bible

carried it on a pole between two [of them]; they brought also some pomegranates and figs.

²⁴That place was called the Valley of Eshcol [cluster] because of the cluster which the Israelites cut down there.

²⁵And they returned from scouting out the land after forty days.

²⁶They came to Moses and Aaron and to all the Israelite congregation in the Wilderness of Paran at Kadesh, and brought them word, and showed them the land's fruit.

²⁷They told Moses, We came to the land to which you sent us; surely it flows with milk and honey. This is its fruit.

²⁸But the people who dwell there are strong, and the cities are ᵃfortified *and* very large; moreover, there we saw the sons of Anak [of great stature and courage].

²⁹Amalek dwells in the land of the South (the Negeb); the Hittite, the Jebusite, and the Amorite dwell in the hill country; and the Canaanite dwells by the sea and along by the side of the Jordan [River].

³⁰Caleb quieted the people before Moses, and said, Let us go up at once and possess it; we are well able to conquer it.

³¹But his fellow scouts said, We are not able to go up against the people [of Canaan], for they are stronger than we are.

³²So they brought the Israelites an evil report of the land which they had scouted out, saying, The land through which we went to spy it out is a land that devours its inhabitants. And all the people that we saw in it are men of great stature.

³³There we saw the Nephilim [or giants], the sons of Anak, who come from the giants; and we were in our own sight as grasshoppers, and so we were in their sight.

**14** And all the congregation cried out with a loud voice, and [they] wept that night.

²All the Israelites grumbled *and* deplored their situation, accusing Moses and Aaron, to whom the whole congregation said, Would that we had died in Egypt! Or that we had died in this wilderness!

³Why does the Lord bring us to this land to fall by the sword? Our wives and little ones will be a prey. Is it not better for us to return to Egypt? [Acts 7:37-39.]

⁴And they said one to another, Let us choose a captain and return to Egypt.

⁵Then Moses and Aaron fell on their faces before all the assembly of Israelites.

⁶And Joshua son of Nun and Caleb son of Jephunneh, who were among the scouts who had searched the land, rent their clothes,

⁷And they said to all the company of Israelites, The land through which we passed as scouts is an exceedingly good land.

⁸If the Lord delights in us, then He will bring us into this land and give it to us, a land flowing with milk and honey.

⁹Only do not rebel against the Lord, neither fear the people of the land, for they are bread for us. Their defense *and* the shadow [of protection] is removed from over them, but the Lord is with us. Fear them not.

¹⁰But all the congregation said to stone [Joshua and Ca-

---

ᵃ The scouts probably had not seen walled cities before, having lived their childhood in Goshen in Egypt. Those who forgot God's power to help them naturally found the situation formidable, as happens in the lives of most people. " 'But God' makes all the difference between cowards and Calebs."

## New International Version

Then the glory of the LORD appeared at the tent of meeting to all the Israelites. ¹¹The LORD said to Moses, "How long will these people treat me with contempt? How long will they refuse to believe in me, in spite of all the signs I have performed among them? ¹²I will strike them down with a plague and destroy them, but I will make you into a nation greater and stronger than they."

¹³Moses said to the LORD, "Then the Egyptians will hear about it! By your power you brought these people up from among them. ¹⁴And they will tell the inhabitants of this land about it. They have already heard that you, LORD, are with these people and that you, LORD, have been seen face to face, that your cloud stays over them, and that you go before them in a pillar of cloud by day and a pillar of fire by night. ¹⁵If you put all these people to death, leaving none alive, the nations who have heard this report about you will say, ¹⁶'The LORD was not able to bring these people into the land he promised them on oath, so he slaughtered them in the wilderness.'

¹⁷"Now may the Lord's strength be displayed, just as you have declared: ¹⁸'The LORD is slow to anger, abounding in love and forgiving sin and rebellion. Yet he does not leave the guilty unpunished; he punishes the children for the sin of the parents to the third and fourth generation.' ¹⁹In accordance with your great love, forgive the sin of these people, just as you have pardoned them from the time they left Egypt until now."

²⁰The LORD replied, "I have forgiven them, as you asked. ²¹Nevertheless, as surely as I live and as surely as the glory of the LORD fills the whole earth, ²²not one of those who saw my glory and the signs I performed in Egypt and in the wilderness but who disobeyed me and tested me ten times— ²³not one of them will ever see the land I promised on oath to their ancestors. No one who has treated me with contempt will ever see it. ²⁴But because my servant Caleb has a different spirit and follows me wholeheartedly, I will bring him into the land he went to, and his descendants will inherit it. ²⁵Since the Amalekites and the Canaanites are living in the valleys, turn back tomorrow and set out toward the desert along the route to the Red Sea.ᵃ"

²⁶The LORD said to Moses and Aaron: ²⁷"How long will this wicked community grumble against me? I have heard the complaints of these grumbling Israelites. ²⁸So tell them, 'As surely as I live, declares the LORD, I will do to you the very thing I heard you say: ²⁹In this wilderness your bodies will fall—every one of you twenty years old or more who was counted in the census and who has grumbled against me. ³⁰Not one of you will enter the land I swore with uplifted hand to make your home, except Caleb son of Jephunneh and Joshua son of Nun. ³¹As for your children that you said would be taken as plunder, I will bring them in to enjoy the land you have rejected. ³²But as for you, your bodies will fall in this wilderness. ³³Your children will be shepherds here for forty years, suffering

## Amplified Bible

leb] with stones. But the glory of the Lord appeared at the Tent of Meeting before all the Israelites.

¹¹And the Lord said to Moses, How long will this people provoke (spurn, despise) Me? And how long will it be before they believe Me [trusting in, relying on, clinging to Me], for all the signs which I have performed among them?

¹²I will smite them with the pestilence and disinherit them, and will make of you [Moses] a nation greater and mightier than they.

¹³But Moses said to the Lord, Then the Egyptians will hear of it, for You brought up this people in Your might from among them.

¹⁴And they will tell it to the inhabitants of this land. They have heard that You, Lord, are in the midst of this people [of Israel], that You, Lord, are seen face to face, and that Your cloud stands over them, and that You go before them in a pillar of cloud by day and in a pillar of fire by night.

¹⁵Now if You kill all this people as one man, then the nations that have heard Your fame will say,

¹⁶Because the Lord was not able to bring this people into the land which He swore to give to them, therefore He has slain them in the wilderness.

¹⁷And now, I pray You, let the power of my Lord be great, as You have promised, saying,

¹⁸The Lord is long-suffering *and* slow to anger, and abundant in mercy *and* loving-kindness, forgiving iniquity and transgression; but He will by no means clear the guilty, visiting the iniquity of the fathers upon the children, upon the third and fourth generation. [Exod. 34:6, 7.]

¹⁹Pardon, I pray You, the iniquity of this people according to the greatness of Your mercy *and* loving-kindness, just as You have forgiven [them] from Egypt until now.

²⁰And the Lord said, I have pardoned according to your word.

²¹But truly as I live and as all the earth shall be filled with the glory of the Lord, [Isa. 6:3; 11:9.]

²²Because all those men who have seen My glory and My [miraculous] signs which I performed in Egypt and in the wilderness, yet have tested *and* proved Me these ten times and have not heeded My voice,

²³Surely they shall not see the land which I swore to give to their fathers; nor shall any who provoked (spurned, despised) Me see it. [Heb. 6:4-11.]

²⁴But My servant Caleb, because he has a different spirit and has followed Me fully, I will bring him into the land into which he went, and his descendants shall possess it.

²⁵Now because the Amalekites and the Canaanites dwell in the valley, tomorrow turn and go into the wilderness by way of the Red Sea.

²⁶And the Lord said to Moses and Aaron,

²⁷How long will this evil congregation murmur against Me? I have heard the complaints the Israelites murmur against Me.

²⁸Tell them, As I live, says the Lord, what you have said in My hearing I will do to you:

²⁹Your dead bodies shall fall in this wilderness—of all who were numbered of you, from twenty years old and upward, who have murmured against Me, [Heb. 3:17-19.]

³⁰Surely none shall come into the land in which I swore to make you dwell, except Caleb son of Jephunneh and Joshua son of Nun.

³¹But your little ones whom you said would be a prey, them will I bring in and they shall know the land which you have despised *and* rejected.

³²But as for you, your dead bodies shall fall in this wilderness.

³³And your children shall be wanderers *and* shepherds in the wilderness for forty years and shall suffer for your

ᵃ 25 Or the Sea of Reeds

## New International Version

for your unfaithfulness, until the last of your bodies lies in the wilderness. 34For forty years—one year for each of the forty days you explored the land—you will suffer for your sins and know what it is like to have me against you.' 35I, the LORD, have spoken, and I will surely do these things to this whole wicked community, which has banded together against me. They will meet their end in this wilderness; here they will die."

36So the men Moses had sent to explore the land, who returned and made the whole community grumble against him by spreading a bad report about it— 37these men who were responsible for spreading the bad report about the land were struck down and died of a plague before the LORD. 38Of the men who went to explore the land, only Joshua son of Nun and Caleb son of Jephunneh survived.

39When Moses reported this to all the Israelites, they mourned bitterly. 40Early the next morning they set out for the highest point in the hill country, saying, "Now we are ready to go up to the land the LORD promised. Surely we have sinned!"

41But Moses said, "Why are you disobeying the LORD's command? This will not succeed! 42Do not go up, because the LORD is not with you. You will be defeated by your enemies, 43for the Amalekites and the Canaanites will face you there. Because you have turned away from the LORD, he will not be with you and you will fall by the sword."

44Nevertheless, in their presumption they went up toward the highest point in the hill country, though neither Moses nor the ark of the LORD's covenant moved from the camp. 45Then the Amalekites and the Canaanites who lived in that hill country came down and attacked them and beat them down all the way to Hormah.

### Supplementary Offerings

**15** The LORD said to Moses, 2"Speak to the Israelites and say to them: 'After you enter the land I am giving you as a home 3and you present to the LORD food offerings from the herd or the flock, as an aroma pleasing to the LORD—whether burnt offerings or sacrifices, for special vows or freewill offerings or festival offerings— 4then the person who brings an offering shall present to the LORD a grain offering of a tenth of an ephah[a] of the finest flour mixed with a quarter of a hin[b] of olive oil. 5With each lamb for the burnt offering or the sacrifice, prepare a quarter of a hin of wine as a drink offering.

6"'With a ram prepare a grain offering of two-tenths of an ephah[c] of the finest flour mixed with a third of a hin[d] of olive oil, 7and a third of a hin of wine as a drink offering. Offer it as an aroma pleasing to the LORD.

8"'When you prepare a young bull as a burnt offering or sacrifice, for a special vow or a fellowship offering to the LORD, 9bring with the bull a grain offering of three-tenths of an ephah[e] of the finest flour mixed with half a hin[f] of olive oil, 10and also bring half a hin of wine as a drink offering. This will be a food offering, an aroma pleasing to

## Amplified Bible

whoredoms (your infidelity to your espoused God), until your corpses are consumed in the wilderness. 34After the number of the days in which you spied out the land [of Canaan], even forty days, for each day a year shall you bear *and* suffer for your iniquities, even for forty years, and you shall know My displeasure [the revoking of My promise and My estrangement].

35I the Lord have spoken; surely this will I do to all this evil congregation who is gathered together against Me. In this wilderness they shall be consumed [by war, disease, plagues], and here they shall die. [I Cor. 10:10, 11.]

36And the men whom Moses sent to search the land, who returned and made all the congregation grumble *and* complain against him by bringing back a slanderous report of the land,

37Even those men who brought the evil report of the land died by a plague before the Lord. [Heb. 3:17-19; Jude 5-7.]

38But Joshua son of Nun and Caleb son of Jephunneh, who were among the men who went to search the land, lived still.

39Moses told [the Lord's] words to all the Israelites, and [they] mourned greatly.

40And they rose early in the morning and went up to the top of the mountain, saying, Behold, we are here, and we intend to go up to the place which the Lord has promised, for we have sinned.

41But Moses said, Why now do you transgress the command of the Lord [to turn back by way of the Red Sea], since it will not succeed?

42Go not up, for the Lord is not among you, that you be not struck down before your enemies.

43For the Amalekites and the Canaanites are there before you, and you shall fall by the sword. Because you have turned away from following after the Lord, therefore the Lord will not be with you.

44But they presumed to go up to the heights of the hill country; however, neither the ark of the covenant of the Lord nor Moses departed out of the camp.

45Then the Amalekites came down and the Canaanites who dwelt in that hill country and smote the Israelites and beat them back, even as far as Hormah.

**15** And the Lord said to Moses, 2Say to the Israelites, When you come into the land where you are to live, which I am giving you,

3And will make an offering by fire to the Lord from the herd or from the flock, a burnt offering or a sacrifice to fulfill a special vow or as a freewill offering or in your set feasts, to make a pleasant *and* soothing fragrance to the Lord,

4Then shall he who brings his offering to the Lord bring a cereal offering of a tenth of an ephah of fine flour mixed with a fourth of a hin of oil.

5And a fourth of a hin of wine for the drink offering you shall prepare with the burnt offering or for the sacrifice, for each lamb.

6Or for a ram you shall prepare for a cereal offering two tenths of an ephah of fine flour mixed with a third of a hin of oil.

7And for the drink offering you shall offer a third of a hin of wine, for a sweet *and* pleasing odor to the Lord.

8And when you prepare a bull for a burnt offering or for a sacrifice, in fulfilling a special vow or peace offering to the Lord,

9Then shall one offer with the bull a cereal offering of three tenths of an ephah of fine flour mixed with half a hin of oil.

10And you shall bring for the drink offering half a hin of wine for an offering made by fire, of a pleasant *and* soothing fragrance to the Lord.

---

*a* 4 That is, probably about 3 1/2 pounds or about 1.6 kilograms
*b* 4 That is, about 1 quart or about 1 liter; also in verse 5    *c* 6 That is, probably about 7 pounds or about 3.2 kilograms    *d* 6 That is, about 1 1/3 quarts or about 1.3 liters; also in verse 7    *e* 9 That is, probably about 11 pounds or about 5 kilograms    *f* 9 That is, about 2 quarts or about 1.9 liters; also in verse 10

## New International Version

the Lord. <sup>11</sup>Each bull or ram, each lamb or young goat, is to be prepared in this manner. <sup>12</sup>Do this for each one, for as many as you prepare.

<sup>13</sup>"'Everyone who is native-born must do these things in this way when they present a food offering as an aroma pleasing to the Lord. <sup>14</sup>For the generations to come, whenever a foreigner or anyone else living among you presents a food offering as an aroma pleasing to the Lord, they must do exactly as you do. <sup>15</sup>The community is to have the same rules for you and for the foreigner residing among you; this is a lasting ordinance for the generations to come. You and the foreigner shall be the same before the Lord: <sup>16</sup>The same laws and regulations will apply both to you and to the foreigner residing among you.'"

<sup>17</sup>The Lord said to Moses, <sup>18</sup>"Speak to the Israelites and say to them: 'When you enter the land to which I am taking you <sup>19</sup>and you eat the food of the land, present a portion as an offering to the Lord. <sup>20</sup>Present a loaf from the first of your ground meal and present it as an offering from the threshing floor. <sup>21</sup>Throughout the generations to come you are to give this offering to the Lord from the first of your ground meal.

### Offerings for Unintentional Sins

<sup>22</sup>"'Now if you as a community unintentionally fail to keep any of these commands the Lord gave Moses— <sup>23</sup>any of the Lord's commands to you through him, from the day the Lord gave them and continuing through the generations to come— <sup>24</sup>and if this is done unintentionally without the community being aware of it, then the whole community is to offer a young bull for a burnt offering as an aroma pleasing to the Lord, along with its prescribed grain offering and drink offering, and a male goat for a sin offering.[a] <sup>25</sup>The priest is to make atonement for the whole Israelite community, and they will be forgiven, for it was not intentional and they have presented to the Lord for their wrong a food offering and a sin offering. <sup>26</sup>The whole Israelite community and the foreigners residing among them will be forgiven, because all the people were involved in the unintentional wrong.

<sup>27</sup>"'But if just one person sins unintentionally, that person must bring a year-old female goat for a sin offering. <sup>28</sup>The priest is to make atonement before the Lord for the one who erred by sinning unintentionally, and when atonement has been made, that person will be forgiven. <sup>29</sup>One and the same law applies to everyone who sins unintentionally, whether a native-born Israelite or a foreigner residing among you.

<sup>30</sup>"'But anyone who sins defiantly, whether native-born or foreigner, blasphemes the Lord and must be cut off from the people of Israel. <sup>31</sup>Because they have despised the Lord's word and broken his commands, they must surely be cut off; their guilt remains on them.'"

### The Sabbath-Breaker Put to Death

<sup>32</sup>While the Israelites were in the wilderness, a man was found gathering wood on the Sabbath day. <sup>33</sup>Those who found him gathering wood brought him to Moses and Aaron and the whole assembly, <sup>34</sup>and they kept him in custody, because it was not clear what should be done to him.

[a] 24 Or *purification offering*; also in verses 25 and 27

## Amplified Bible

<sup>11</sup>Thus shall it be done for each bull or for each ram, or for each of the male lambs or of the kids.

<sup>12</sup>According to the number that you shall prepare, so shall you do to everyone according to their number.

<sup>13</sup>All who are native-born shall do these things in this way in bringing an offering made by fire of a sweet *and* pleasant odor to the Lord.

<sup>14</sup>And if a stranger sojourns with you or whoever may be among you throughout your generations, and he wishes to offer an offering made by fire, of a pleasing *and* soothing fragrance to the Lord, as you do, so shall he do.

<sup>15</sup>There shall be one [and the same] statute [both] for you [of the congregation] and for the stranger who is a temporary resident with you, a statute forever throughout your generations: as you are, so shall the stranger be before the Lord.

<sup>16</sup>One law and one ordinance shall be for you and for the stranger who sojourns with you.

<sup>17</sup>And the Lord said to Moses,

<sup>18</sup>Say to the Israelites, When you come into the land to which I am bringing you,

<sup>19</sup>Then, when you eat of the food of the land, you shall set apart a portion for a gift to the Lord [called a heave or taken-out offering].

<sup>20</sup>You shall set apart a cake made of the first of your coarse meal as a gift [to the Lord]; as an offering set apart from the threshing floor, so shall you lift it out *or* heave it.

<sup>21</sup>Of the first of your coarse meal you shall give to the Lord a portion for a gift throughout your generations [your heave or lifted-out offering].

<sup>22</sup>When you have erred and have not observed all these commandments which the Lord has spoken to Moses,

<sup>23</sup>Even all that the Lord has commanded you through Moses, from the day that the Lord gave commandment and onward throughout your generations,

<sup>24</sup>Then it shall be, if it was done unwittingly *or* in error without the knowledge of the congregation, that all the congregation shall offer one young bull for a burnt offering, for a pleasant *and* soothing fragrance to the Lord, with its cereal offering and its drink offering, according to the ordinance, and one male goat for a sin offering.

<sup>25</sup>And the priest shall make atonement for all the congregation of the Israelites, and they shall be forgiven, for it was an error and they have brought their offering, an offering made by fire to the Lord, and their sin offering before the Lord for their error.

<sup>26</sup>And all the congregation of the Israelites shall be forgiven and the stranger who lives temporarily among them, because all the people were involved in the error.

<sup>27</sup>And if any person sins unknowingly *or* unintentionally, he shall offer a female goat a year old for a sin offering.

<sup>28</sup>And the priest shall make atonement before the Lord for the person who commits an error when he sins unknowingly *or* unintentionally, to make atonement for him; and he shall be forgiven.

<sup>29</sup>You shall have one law for him who sins unknowingly *or* unintentionally, whether he is native born among the Israelites or a stranger who is sojourning among them.

<sup>30</sup>But the person who does anything [wrong] willfully *and* openly, whether he is native-born or a stranger, that one reproaches, reviles, *and* blasphemes the Lord, and that person shall be cut off from among his people [that the atonement made for them may not include him].

<sup>31</sup>Because he has despised and rejected the word of the Lord, and has broken His commandment, that person shall be utterly cut off; his iniquity shall be upon him.

<sup>32</sup>While the Israelites were in the wilderness, they found a man who was gathering sticks on the Sabbath day.

<sup>33</sup>Those who found him gathering sticks brought him to Moses and Aaron and to all the congregation.

<sup>34</sup>They put him in custody, because it was not certain *or* clear what should be done to him.

## New International Version

35Then the LORD said to Moses, "The man must die. The whole assembly must stone him outside the camp." 36So the assembly took him outside the camp and stoned him to death, as the LORD commanded Moses.

### Tassels on Garments

37The LORD said to Moses, 38"Speak to the Israelites and say to them: 'Throughout the generations to come you are to make tassels on the corners of your garments, with a blue cord on each tassel. 39You will have these tassels to look at and so you will remember all the commands of the LORD, that you may obey them and not prostitute yourselves by chasing after the lusts of your own hearts and eyes. 40Then you will remember to obey all my commands and will be consecrated to your God. 41I am the LORD your God, who brought you out of Egypt to be your God. I am the LORD your God.'"

### Korah, Dathan and Abiram

**16** Korah son of Izhar, the son of Kohath, the son of Levi, and certain Reubenites—Dathan and Abiram, sons of Eliab, and On son of Peleth—became insolent*a* 2and rose up against Moses. With them were 250 Israelite men, well-known community leaders who had been appointed members of the council. 3They came as a group to oppose Moses and Aaron and said to them, "You have gone too far! The whole community is holy, every one of them, and the LORD is with them. Why then do you set yourselves above the LORD's assembly?"

4When Moses heard this, he fell facedown. 5Then he said to Korah and all his followers: "In the morning the LORD will show who belongs to him and who is holy, and he will have that person come near him. The man he has chosen will he cause to come near him. 6You, Korah, and all your followers are to do this: Take censers 7and tomorrow put burning coals and incense in them before the LORD. The man the LORD chooses will be the one who is holy. You Levites have gone too far!"

8Moses also said to Korah, "Now listen, you Levites! 9Isn't it enough for you that the God of Israel has separated you from the rest of the Israelite community and brought you near himself to do the work at the LORD's tabernacle and to stand before the community and minister to them? 10He has brought you and all your fellow Levites near himself, but now you are trying to get the priesthood too. 11It is against the LORD that you and all your followers have banded together. Who is Aaron that you should grumble against him?"

12Then Moses summoned Dathan and Abiram, the sons of Eliab. But they said, "We will not come! 13Isn't it enough that you have brought us up out of a land flowing with milk and honey to kill us in the wilderness? And now you also want to lord it over us! 14Moreover, you haven't brought us into a land flowing with milk and honey or given us an inheritance of fields and vineyards. Do you want to treat these men like slaves*b*? No, we will not come!"

15Then Moses became very angry and said to the LORD, "Do not accept their offering. I have not taken so much as a donkey from them, nor have I wronged any of them."

## Amplified Bible

35And the Lord said to Moses, The man shall surely be put to death. All the congregation shall stone him with stones without the camp.

36And all the congregation brought him without the camp and stoned him to death with stones, as the Lord commanded Moses.

37And the Lord said to Moses,

38Speak to the Israelites and bid them make fringes or tassels on the corners in the borders of their garments throughout their generations, and put upon the fringe of the borders or upon the tassel of each corner a cord of blue.

39And it shall be to you a fringe or tassel that you may look upon and remember all the commandments of the Lord and do them, that you may not spy out and follow after [the desires of] your own heart and your own eyes, after which you used to follow and play the harlot [spiritually, if not physically],

40That you may remember and do all My commandments and be holy to your God.

41I am the Lord your God, Who brought you out of the land of Egypt to be your God. I am the Lord your God.

**16** Now Korah son of Izhar, the son of Kohath, the son of Levi, with Dathan and Abiram sons of Eliab, and On son of Peleth, sons of Reuben, took men,

2And they rose up before Moses, with certain of the Israelites, 250 princes or leaders of the congregation called to the assembly, men well known and of distinction.

3And they gathered together against Moses and Aaron, and said to them, [Enough of you!] You take too much upon yourselves, seeing that all the congregation is holy, every one of them, and the Lord is among them. Why then do you lift yourselves up above the assembly of the Lord?

4And when Moses heard it, he fell upon his face.

5And he said to Korah and all his company, In the morning the Lord will show who are His and who is holy, and will cause him to come near to Him; him whom He has chosen will He cause to come near to Him. [II Tim. 2:19.]

6Do this: Take censers, Korah and all your company,

7And put fire in them and put incense upon them before the Lord tomorrow; and the man whom the Lord chooses shall be holy. You take too much upon yourselves, you sons of Levi.

8And Moses said to Korah, Hear, I pray you, you sons of Levi:

9Does it seem but a small thing to you that the God of Israel has separated you from the congregation of Israel, to bring you near to Himself to do the service of the tabernacle of the Lord and to stand before the congregation to minister to them,

10And that He has brought you near to Him, and all your brethren the sons of Levi with you? Would you seek the priesthood also?

11Therefore you and all your company are gathered together against the Lord. And Aaron, what is he that you murmur against him?

12And Moses sent to call Dathan and Abiram, the sons of Eliab, and they said, We will not come up.

13Is it a small thing that you have brought us up out of a land flowing with milk and honey to kill us in the wilderness, but you must also make yourself a prince over us?

14Moreover, you have not brought us into a land that flows with milk and honey or given us an inheritance of fields and vineyards. Will you bore out the eyes of these men? We will not come up!

15And Moses was very angry and said to the Lord, Do not respect their offering! I have not taken one donkey from them, nor have I hurt one of them.

---

*a* 1 Or *Peleth—took men*   *b* 14 Or *to deceive these men*; Hebrew *Will you gouge out the eyes of these men*

## New International Version

[16] Moses said to Korah, "You and all your followers are to appear before the Lord tomorrow—you and they and Aaron. [17] Each man is to take his censer and put incense in it—250 censers in all—and present it before the Lord. You and Aaron are to present your censers also." [18] So each of them took his censer, put burning coals and incense in it, and stood with Moses and Aaron at the entrance to the tent of meeting. [19] When Korah had gathered all his followers in opposition to them at the entrance to the tent of meeting, the glory of the Lord appeared to the entire assembly. [20] The Lord said to Moses and Aaron, [21] "Separate yourselves from this assembly so I can put an end to them at once."

[22] But Moses and Aaron fell facedown and cried out, "O God, the God who gives breath to all living things, will you be angry with the entire assembly when only one man sins?"

[23] Then the Lord said to Moses, [24] "Say to the assembly, 'Move away from the tents of Korah, Dathan and Abiram.'"

[25] Moses got up and went to Dathan and Abiram, and the elders of Israel followed him. [26] He warned the assembly, "Move back from the tents of these wicked men! Do not touch anything belonging to them, or you will be swept away because of all their sins." [27] So they moved away from the tents of Korah, Dathan and Abiram. Dathan and Abiram had come out and were standing with their wives, children and little ones at the entrances to their tents.

[28] Then Moses said, "This is how you will know that the Lord has sent me to do all these things and that it was not my idea: [29] If these men die a natural death and suffer the fate of all mankind, then the Lord has not sent me. [30] But if the Lord brings about something totally new, and the earth opens its mouth and swallows them, with everything that belongs to them, and they go down alive into the realm of the dead, then you will know that these men have treated the Lord with contempt."

[31] As soon as he finished saying all this, the ground under them split apart [32] and the earth opened its mouth and swallowed them and their households, and all those associated with Korah, together with their possessions. [33] They went down alive into the realm of the dead, with everything they owned; the earth closed over them, and they perished and were gone from the community. [34] At their cries, all the Israelites around them fled, shouting, "The earth is going to swallow us too!"

[35] And fire came out from the Lord and consumed the 250 men who were offering the incense.

[36] The Lord said to Moses, [37] "Tell Eleazar son of Aaron, the priest, to remove the censers from the charred remains and scatter the coals some distance away, for the censers are holy— [38] the censers of the men who sinned at the cost of their lives. Hammer the censers into sheets to overlay the altar, for they were presented before the Lord and have become holy. Let them be a sign to the Israelites."

[39] So Eleazar the priest collected the bronze censers brought by those who had been burned to death, and he had them hammered out to overlay the altar, [40] as the Lord directed him through Moses. This was to remind the Israelites that no one except a descendant of Aaron should come to burn incense before the Lord, or he would become like Korah and his followers.

## Amplified Bible

[16] And Moses said to Korah, You and all your company be before the Lord tomorrow, you and they and Aaron.

[17] And let every man take his censer and put incense upon it and bring before the Lord every man his censer, 250 censers; you also and Aaron, each his censer.

[18] So they took every man his censer, and they put fire in them and laid incense upon it, and they stood at the entrance of the Tent of Meeting with Moses and Aaron.

[19] Then Korah assembled all the congregation against Moses and Aaron before the entrance of the Tent of Meeting, and the glory of the Lord appeared to all the congregation.

[20] And the Lord said to Moses and Aaron,

[21] Separate yourselves from among this congregation, that I may consume them in a moment.

[22] And they fell upon their faces, and said, O God, the God of the spirits of all flesh, shall one man sin and will You be angry with all the congregation?

[23] And the Lord said to Moses,

[24] Say to the congregation, Get away from around the tents of Korah, Dathan, and Abiram.

[25] Then Moses rose up and went to Dathan and Abiram, and the elders of Israel followed him.

[26] And he said to the congregation, Depart, I pray you, from the tents of these wicked men, and touch nothing of theirs, lest you be consumed in all their sins.

[27] So they got away from around the tents of Korah, Dathan, and Abiram. And Dathan and Abiram came out and stood in the door of their tents with their wives, and their sons, and their little ones.

[28] And Moses said, By this you shall know that the Lord has sent me to do all these works, for I do not act of my own accord.

[29] If these men die the common death of all men or if [only] what happens to everyone happens to them, then the Lord has not sent me.

[30] But if the Lord causes a new thing [to happen], and the earth opens its mouth and swallows them up, with all that belongs to them, and they go down alive into Sheol (the place of the dead), then you shall understand that these men have provoked (spurned, despised) the Lord!

[31] As soon as he stopped speaking, the ground under the offenders split apart

[32] And the earth opened its mouth and swallowed them and their households and [Korah and] all [his] men and all their possessions. [Num. 26:10, 11.]

[33] They and all that belonged to them went down alive into Sheol (the place of the dead); and the earth closed upon them, and they perished from among the assembly.

[34] And all Israel who were round about them fled at their cry, for they said, Lest the earth swallow us up also.

[35] And fire came forth from the Lord and devoured the 250 men who offered the incense.

[36] And the Lord said to Moses,

[37] Speak to Eleazar son of Aaron, the priest, that he take up the censers out of the burning and scatter the fire at a distance. For the censers are hallowed—

[38] The censers of these men who have sinned against themselves *and* at the cost of their own lives. Let the censers be made into hammered plates for a covering of the altar [of burnt offering], for they were used in offering before the Lord and therefore they are sacred. They shall be a sign [of warning] to the Israelites.

[39] Eleazar the priest took the bronze censers with which the Levites who were burned had offered incense, and they were hammered into broad sheets for a covering of the [brazen] altar [of burnt offering],

[40] To be a memorial [a warning forever] to the Israelites, so that no outsider, that is, no one not of the descendants of Aaron, should come near to offer incense before the Lord, lest he become as Korah and as his company, as the Lord said to Eleazar through Moses.

## New International Version

41The next day the whole Israelite community grumbled against Moses and Aaron. "You have killed the LORD's people," they said.

42But when the assembly gathered in opposition to Moses and Aaron and turned toward the tent of meeting, suddenly the cloud covered it and the glory of the LORD appeared. 43Then Moses and Aaron went to the front of the tent of meeting, 44and the LORD said to Moses, 45"Get away from this assembly so I can put an end to them at once." And they fell facedown.

46Then Moses said to Aaron, "Take your censer and put incense in it, along with burning coals from the altar, and hurry to the assembly to make atonement for them. Wrath has come out from the LORD; the plague has started." 47So Aaron did as Moses said, and ran into the midst of the assembly. The plague had already started among the people, but Aaron offered the incense and made atonement for them. 48He stood between the living and the dead, and the plague stopped. 49But 14,700 people died from the plague, in addition to those who had died because of Korah. 50Then Aaron returned to Moses at the entrance to the tent of meeting, for the plague had stopped.*a*

### The Budding of Aaron's Staff

**17**b The LORD said to Moses, 2"Speak to the Israelites and get twelve staffs from them, one from the leader of each of their ancestral tribes. Write the name of each man on his staff. 3On the staff of Levi write Aaron's name, for there must be one staff for the head of each ancestral tribe. 4Place them in the tent of meeting in front of the ark of the covenant law, where I meet with you. 5The staff belonging to the man I choose will sprout, and I will rid myself of this constant grumbling against you by the Israelites."

6So Moses spoke to the Israelites, and their leaders gave him twelve staffs, one for the leader of each of their ancestral tribes, and Aaron's staff was among them. 7Moses placed the staffs before the LORD in the tent of the covenant law.

8The next day Moses entered the tent and saw that Aaron's staff, which represented the tribe of Levi, had not only sprouted but had budded, blossomed and produced almonds. 9Then Moses brought out all the staffs from the LORD's presence to all the Israelites. They looked at them, and each of the leaders took his own staff.

10The LORD said to Moses, "Put back Aaron's staff in front of the ark of the covenant law, to be kept as a sign to the rebellious. This will put an end to their grumbling against me, so that they will not die." 11Moses did just as the LORD commanded him.

12The Israelites said to Moses, "We will die! We are lost, we are all lost! 13Anyone who even comes near the tabernacle of the LORD will die. Are we all going to die?"

## Amplified Bible

41But on the morrow all the congregation of the Israelites murmured against Moses and Aaron, saying, You have killed the people of the Lord.

42When the congregation was gathered against Moses and Aaron, they looked at the Tent of Meeting, and behold, the cloud covered it and they saw the Lord's glory.

43And Moses and Aaron came to the front of the Tent of Meeting.

44And the Lord said to Moses,

45Get away from among this congregation, that I may consume them in a moment. And Moses and Aaron fell on their faces.

46And Moses said to Aaron, Take a censer and put fire in it from off the altar and lay incense on it, and carry it quickly to the congregation and make atonement for them. For there is wrath gone out from the Lord; the plague has begun!

47So Aaron took the burning censer as Moses commanded, and ran into the midst of the congregation; and behold, the plague was begun among the people; and he put on the incense and made atonement for the people.

48And he stood between the dead and the living, and the plague was stayed.

49Now those who died in the plague were 14,700, besides those who died in the matter of Korah.

50And Aaron returned to Moses to the door of the Tent of Meeting, since the plague was stayed.

**17** And the Lord said to Moses, 2Speak to the Israelites and get from them rods *or* staves, one for each father's house, from all their leaders according to their father's houses, twelve rods. Write every man's name on his rod.

3And you shall write Aaron's name on the rod of Levi [his great-grandfather]. For there shall be one rod for the head of each father's house.

4You shall lay them up in the Tent of Meeting before [the ark of] the Testimony, where I meet with you.

5And the rod of the man whom I choose shall bud, and I will make to cease from Me the murmurings of the Israelites, which they murmur against you.

6And Moses spoke to the Israelites, and every one of their leaders gave him a rod *or* staff, one for each leader according to their fathers' houses, twelve rods, and the rod of Aaron was among their rods.

7And Moses deposited the rods before the Lord in the Tent of the Testimony.

8And the next day Moses went into the Tent of the Testimony, and behold, the rod of Aaron for the house of Levi had sprouted and brought forth buds and produced blossoms and yielded [ripe] almonds.

9Moses brought out all the rods from before the Lord to all the Israelites; and they looked, and each man took his rod.

10And the Lord told Moses, Put Aaron's rod back before the Testimony [in the ark], to be kept as a [warning] sign for the rebels; and you shall make an end of their murmurings against Me, lest they die.

11And Moses did so; as the Lord commanded him, so he did.

12The Israelites said to Moses, Behold, we perish, we are undone, all undone!

13Everyone who comes near, who comes near the tabernacle of the Lord, dies *or* shall die! Are we all to perish?

## New International Version

### Duties of Priests and Levites

**18** The LORD said to Aaron, "You, your sons and your family are to bear the responsibility for offenses connected with the sanctuary, and you and your sons alone are to bear the responsibility for offenses connected with the priesthood. ²Bring your fellow Levites from your ancestral tribe to join you and assist you when you and your sons minister before the tent of the covenant law. ³They are to be responsible to you and are to perform all the duties of the tent, but they must not go near the furnishings of the sanctuary or the altar. Otherwise both they and you will die. ⁴They are to join you and be responsible for the care of the tent of meeting—all the work at the tent—and no one else may come near where you are.

⁵"You are to be responsible for the care of the sanctuary and the altar, so that my wrath will not fall on the Israelites again. ⁶I myself have selected your fellow Levites from among the Israelites as a gift to you, dedicated to the LORD to do the work at the tent of meeting. ⁷But only you and your sons may serve as priests in connection with everything at the altar and inside the curtain. I am giving you the service of the priesthood as a gift. Anyone else who comes near the sanctuary is to be put to death."

### Offerings for Priests and Levites

⁸Then the LORD said to Aaron, "I myself have put you in charge of the offerings presented to me; all the holy offerings the Israelites give me I give to you and your sons as your portion, your perpetual share. ⁹You are to have the part of the most holy offerings that is kept from the fire. From all the gifts they bring me as most holy offerings, whether grain or sin*ᵃ* or guilt offerings, that part belongs to you and your sons. ¹⁰Eat it as something most holy; every male shall eat it. You must regard it as holy.

¹¹"This also is yours: whatever is set aside from the gifts of all the wave offerings of the Israelites. I give this to you and your sons and daughters as your perpetual share. Everyone in your household who is ceremonially clean may eat it.

¹²"I give you all the finest olive oil and all the finest new wine and grain they give the LORD as the firstfruits of their harvest. ¹³All the land's firstfruits that they bring to the LORD will be yours. Everyone in your household who is ceremonially clean may eat it.

¹⁴"Everything in Israel that is devoted*ᵇ* to the LORD is yours. ¹⁵The first offspring of every womb, both human and animal, that is offered to the LORD is yours. But you must redeem every firstborn son and every firstborn male of unclean animals. ¹⁶When they are a month old, you must

---

*ᵃ 9 Or purification*   *ᵇ 14 The Hebrew term refers to the irrevocable giving over of things or persons to the LORD.*

## Amplified Bible

**18** And the Lord said to Aaron, You and your sons and your father's house with you shall bear *and* remove the iniquity of the sanctuary [that is, the guilt for the offenses which the people unknowingly commit when brought into contact with the manifestations of God's presence]. And you and your sons with you shall bear *and* remove the iniquity of your priesthood [your own unintentional offenses].

²And your brethren also of the tribe of Levi, the tribe of your [fore]father, bring with you, that they may be joined to you and minister to you; but only you and your sons with you shall come before the Tent of the Testimony [into the Holy Place where only priests may go and into the Most Holy Place which only the high priest dares enter].

³And the Levites shall attend you [as servants] and attend to all the duties of the Tent; only they shall not come near the sacred vessels of the sanctuary or to the brazen altar, that they and also you [Aaron] die not.

⁴And they shall be joined to you and attend to the duties of the Tent of Meeting—all the [menial] service of the Tent—and no stranger [no layman, anyone who is not a Levite] shall come near you [Aaron and your sons].

⁵And you shall attend to the duties of the sanctuary and attend to the altar [of burnt offering and the altar of incense], that there be no wrath any more upon the Israelites [as in the incident of Korah, Dathan, and Abiram]. [Num. 16:42-50.]

⁶And I, behold, I have taken your brethren the Levites from among the Israelites; to you they are a gift, given to the Lord, to do the [menial] service of the Tent of Meeting.

⁷Therefore you and your sons with you shall attend to your priesthood for everything of the altar [of burnt offering and the altar of incense] and [of the Holy of Holies] within the veil, and you shall serve. I give you your priesthood as a service of gift. And the stranger [anyone other than Moses or your sons, Aaron] who comes near shall be put to death. [Exod. 40:18, 20, 26.]

⁸And the Lord said to Aaron, And I, behold, I have given you the charge of My heave offerings [whatever is taken out and kept of the offerings made to Me], all the dedicated *and* consecrated things of the Israelites; to you have I given them [as your portion] and to your sons as a continual allowance forever by reason of your anointing as priests. [Lev. 7:35.]

⁹This shall be yours of the most holy things, reserved from the fire: every offering of the people, every cereal offering and sin offering and trespass offering of theirs, which they shall render to Me, shall be most holy for you [Aaron] and for your sons.

¹⁰As the most holy thing *and* in a sacred place shall you eat of it; every male [of your house] shall eat of it. It shall be holy to you. [Lev. 22:10-16.]

¹¹And this also is yours: the heave offering of their gift, with all the wave offerings of the Israelites. I have given them to you and to your sons and to your daughters with you as a continual allowance forever; everyone in your house who is [ceremonially] clean may eat of it.

¹²All the best of the oil, and all the best of the [fresh] wine and of the grain, the firstfruits of what they give to the Lord, to you have I given them.

¹³Whatever is first ripe in the land, which they bring to the Lord, shall be yours. Everyone who is [ceremonially] clean in your house may eat of it.

¹⁴Every devoted thing in Israel [everything that has been vowed to the Lord] shall be yours.

¹⁵Everything that first opens the womb in all flesh, which they bring to the Lord, whether it be of men or beasts, shall be yours. Nevertheless the firstborn of man you shall surely redeem, and the firstling of unclean beasts you shall redeem.

¹⁶And those that are to be redeemed of them, from a

## New International Version

redeem them at the redemption price set at five shekels[a] of silver, according to the sanctuary shekel, which weighs twenty gerahs.

17"But you must not redeem the firstborn of a cow, a sheep or a goat; they are holy. Splash their blood against the altar and burn their fat as a food offering, an aroma pleasing to the LORD. 18Their meat is to be yours, just as the breast of the wave offering and the right thigh are yours. 19Whatever is set aside from the holy offerings the Israelites present to the LORD I give to you and your sons and daughters as your perpetual share. It is an everlasting covenant of salt before the LORD for both you and your offspring."

20The LORD said to Aaron, "You will have no inheritance in their land, nor will you have any share among them; I am your share and your inheritance among the Israelites.

21"I give to the Levites all the tithes in Israel as their inheritance in return for the work they do while serving at the tent of meeting. 22From now on the Israelites must not go near the tent of meeting, or they will bear the consequences of their sin and will die. 23It is the Levites who are to do the work at the tent of meeting and bear the responsibility for any offenses they commit against it. This is a lasting ordinance for the generations to come. They will receive no inheritance among the Israelites. 24Instead, I give to the Levites as their inheritance the tithes that the Israelites present as an offering to the LORD. That is why I said concerning them: 'They will have no inheritance among the Israelites.'"

25The LORD said to Moses, 26"Speak to the Levites and say to them: 'When you receive from the Israelites the tithe I give you as your inheritance, you must present a tenth of that tithe as the LORD's offering. 27Your offering will be reckoned to you as grain from the threshing floor or juice from the winepress. 28In this way you also will present an offering to the LORD from all the tithes you receive from the Israelites. From these tithes you must give the LORD's portion to Aaron the priest. 29You must present as the LORD's portion the best and holiest part of everything given to you.'

30"Say to the Levites: 'When you present the best part, it will be reckoned to you as the product of the threshing floor or the winepress. 31You and your households may eat the rest of it anywhere, for it is your wages for your work at the tent of meeting. 32By presenting the best part of it you will not be guilty in this matter; then you will not defile the holy offerings of the Israelites, and you will not die.'"

## Amplified Bible

month old shall you redeem, according to your estimate [of their age], for the fixed price of five shekels in silver, according to the shekel of the sanctuary, which is twenty gerahs.

17But the firstling of a cow or of a sheep or of a goat you shall not redeem. They [as the firstborn of clean beasts belong to God and] are holy. You shall sprinkle their blood upon the altar and shall burn their fat for an offering made by fire, for a sweet *and* soothing odor to the Lord.

18And the flesh of them shall be yours, as the wave breast and as the right shoulder are yours.

19All the heave offerings [the lifted-out and kept portions] of the holy things which the Israelites give to the Lord I give to you and to your sons and your daughters with you, as a continual debt forever. It is a covenant of salt [that cannot be dissolved or violated] forever before the Lord for you [Aaron] and for your posterity with you.

20And the Lord said to Aaron, You shall have no inheritance in the land [of the Israelites], neither shall you have any part among them. I am your portion and your inheritance among the Israelites.

21And, behold, I have given the Levites all the tithes in Israel for an inheritance in return for their service which they serve, the [menial] service of the Tent of Meeting.

22Henceforth the Israelites shall not come near the Tent of Meeting [the covered sanctuary, the Holy Place, and the Holy of Holies], lest they incur guilt and die.

23But the Levites shall do the [menial] service of the Tent of Meeting, and they shall bear and remove the iniquity of the people [that is, be answerable for the legal pollutions of the holy things and offer the necessary atonements for unintentional offenses in these matters]. It shall be a statute forever in all your generations, that among the Israelites the Levites have no inheritance [of land].

24But the tithes of the Israelites, which they present as an offering to the Lord, I have given to the Levites to inherit; therefore I have said to them, Among the Israelites they shall have no inheritance. [They have homes and cities and pasturage to use but not to possess as their personal inheritance.]

25And the Lord said to Moses,

26Moreover, you shall say to the Levites, When you take from the Israelites the tithe which I have given you from them for your inheritance, then you shall present an offering from it to the Lord, even a tenth of the tithe [paid by the people].

27And what you lift out and keep [your heave offering] shall be credited to you as though it were the grain of the threshing floor or as the fully ripe produce of the vine.

28Likewise you shall also present an offering to the Lord of all your tithes which you receive from the Israelites; and therefore you shall give this heave offering [lifted out and kept] for the Lord to Aaron the priest.

29Out of all the gifts to you, you shall present every offering due to the Lord, of all the best of it, even the hallowed part lifted out *and* held back out of it [for the Levites].

30Therefore you shall say to them, When you have lifted out *and* held back the best from it [and presented it to the Lord by giving it to yourselves, the Levites], then it shall be counted to [you] the Levites just as if it were the increase of the threshing floor or of the winepress.

31And you may eat it in every place, you and your households, for it is your reward for your service in the Tent of Meeting.

32And you shall be guilty of no sin by reason of it when you have lifted out *and* held back the best of it; neither shall you have polluted the holy things of the Israelites, neither shall you die [because of it].

---

[a] *16* That is, about 2 ounces or about 58 grams

## New International Version

### The Water of Cleansing

**19** The LORD said to Moses and Aaron: ²"This is a requirement of the law that the LORD has commanded: Tell the Israelites to bring you a red heifer without defect or blemish and that has never been under a yoke. ³Give it to Eleazar the priest; it is to be taken outside the camp and slaughtered in his presence. ⁴Then Eleazar the priest is to take some of its blood on his finger and sprinkle it seven times toward the front of the tent of meeting. ⁵While he watches, the heifer is to be burned—its hide, flesh, blood and intestines. ⁶The priest is to take some cedar wood, hyssop and scarlet wool and throw them onto the burning heifer. ⁷After that, the priest must wash his clothes and bathe himself with water. He may then come into the camp, but he will be ceremonially unclean till evening. ⁸The man who burns it must also wash his clothes and bathe with water, and he too will be unclean till evening.

⁹"A man who is clean shall gather up the ashes of the heifer and put them in a ceremonially clean place outside the camp. They are to be kept by the Israelite community for use in the water of cleansing; it is for purification from sin. ¹⁰The man who gathers up the ashes of the heifer must also wash his clothes, and he too will be unclean till evening. This will be a lasting ordinance both for the Israelites and for the foreigners residing among them.

¹¹"Whoever touches a human corpse will be unclean for seven days. ¹²They must purify themselves with the water on the third day and on the seventh day; then they will be clean. But if they do not purify themselves on the third and seventh days, they will not be clean. ¹³If they fail to purify themselves after touching a human corpse, they defile the LORD's tabernacle. They must be cut off from Israel. Because the water of cleansing has not been sprinkled on them, they are unclean; their uncleanness remains on them.

¹⁴"This is the law that applies when a person dies in a tent: Anyone who enters the tent and anyone who is in it will be unclean for seven days, ¹⁵and every open container without a lid fastened on it will be unclean.

¹⁶"Anyone out in the open who touches someone who has been killed with a sword or someone who has died a natural death, or anyone who touches a human bone or a grave, will be unclean for seven days.

¹⁷"For the unclean person, put some ashes from the burned purification offering into a jar and pour fresh water over them. ¹⁸Then a man who is ceremonially clean is to take some hyssop, dip it in the water and sprinkle the tent and all the furnishings and the people who were there. He must also sprinkle anyone who has touched a human bone or a grave or anyone who has been killed or anyone who has died a natural death. ¹⁹The man who is clean is to sprinkle those who are unclean on the third and seventh days, and on the seventh day he is to purify them. Those who are being cleansed must wash their clothes and bathe with water, and that evening they will be clean. ²⁰But if those who are unclean do not purify themselves, they must be cut off from the community, because they have defiled the sanctuary of the LORD. The water of cleansing has not been sprinkled on them, and they are unclean. ²¹This is a lasting ordinance for them.

"The man who sprinkles the water of cleansing must also wash his clothes, and anyone who touches the water of cleansing will be unclean till evening. ²²Anything that

## Amplified Bible

**19** And the Lord said to Moses and Aaron, ²This is the ritual of the law which the Lord has commanded: Tell the Israelites to bring you a red heifer without spot, in which is no blemish, upon which a yoke has never come.

³And you shall give her to Eleazar the priest, and he shall bring her outside the camp, and she shall be slaughtered before him.

⁴Eleazar the priest shall take some of her blood with his finger and sprinkle it toward the front of the Tent of Meeting seven times.

⁵The heifer shall be burned in his sight, her skin, flesh, blood, and dung.

⁶And the priest shall take cedar wood, and hyssop, and scarlet [stuff] and cast them into the midst of the burning heifer.

⁷Then the priest shall wash his clothes and bathe his body in water; afterward he shall come into the camp, but he shall be unclean until evening.

⁸He who burns the heifer shall wash his clothes and bathe his body in water, and shall be unclean until evening.

⁹And a man who is clean shall collect the ashes of the heifer and put them outside the camp in a clean place, and they shall be kept for the congregation of the Israelites for the water for impurity; it is a sin offering.

¹⁰And he who gathers the ashes of the heifer shall wash his clothes, and be unclean until evening. This shall be to the Israelites and to the stranger who sojourns among them a perpetual statute.

¹¹He who touches the dead body of any person shall be unclean for seven days.

¹²He shall purify himself with the water for impurity [made with the ashes of the burned heifer] on the third day, and on the seventh day he shall be clean. But if he does not purify himself the third day, then the seventh day he shall not be clean.

¹³Whoever touches the corpse of any who has died and does not purify himself defiles the tabernacle of the Lord, and that person shall be cut off from Israel. Because the water for impurity was not sprinkled upon him, he shall be unclean; his uncleanness is still upon him.

¹⁴This is the law when a man dies in a tent: all who come into the tent and all who are in the tent shall be unclean for seven days.

¹⁵And every open vessel, which has no covering fastened upon it, is unclean.

¹⁶And whoever in the open field touches one who is slain with a sword, or a dead body, or a bone of a dead man, or a grave, shall be unclean for seven days.

¹⁷And for the unclean, they shall take of the ashes of the burning of the sin offering, and the running water shall be put with it in a vessel.

¹⁸And a clean person shall take hyssop and dip it in the water and sprinkle it upon the tent, and upon all the vessels, and upon the persons who were there, and upon him who touched the bone, or the slain, or the naturally dead, or the grave.

¹⁹And the clean person shall sprinkle [the water for purification] upon the unclean person on the third day and on the seventh day, and on the seventh day the unclean man shall purify himself, and wash his clothes and bathe himself in water, and shall be clean at evening.

²⁰But the man who is unclean and does not purify himself, that person shall be cut off from among the congregation, because he has defiled the sanctuary of the Lord. The water for purification has not been sprinkled upon him; he is unclean.

²¹And it shall be a perpetual statute to them. He who sprinkles the water for impurity [upon another] shall wash his clothes, and he who touches the water for impurity shall be unclean until evening.

## New International Version

an unclean person touches becomes unclean, and anyone who touches it becomes unclean till evening."

### Water From the Rock

**20** In the first month the whole Israelite community arrived at the Desert of Zin, and they stayed at Kadesh. There Miriam died and was buried.

²Now there was no water for the community, and the people gathered in opposition to Moses and Aaron. ³They quarreled with Moses and said, "If only we had died when our brothers fell dead before the LORD! ⁴Why did you bring the LORD's community into this wilderness, that we and our livestock should die here? ⁵Why did you bring us up out of Egypt to this terrible place? It has no grain or figs, grapevines or pomegranates. And there is no water to drink!"

⁶Moses and Aaron went from the assembly to the entrance to the tent of meeting and fell facedown, and the glory of the LORD appeared to them. ⁷The LORD said to Moses, ⁸"Take the staff, and you and your brother Aaron gather the assembly together. Speak to that rock before their eyes and it will pour out its water. You will bring water out of the rock for the community so they and their livestock can drink."

⁹So Moses took the staff from the LORD's presence, just as he commanded him. ¹⁰He and Aaron gathered the assembly together in front of the rock and Moses said to them, "Listen, you rebels, must we bring you water out of this rock?" ¹¹Then Moses raised his arm and struck the rock twice with his staff. Water gushed out, and the community and their livestock drank.

¹²But the LORD said to Moses and Aaron, "Because you did not trust in me enough to honor me as holy in the sight of the Israelites, you will not bring this community into the land I give them."

¹³These were the waters of Meribah,ᵃ where the Israelites quarreled with the LORD and where he was proved holy among them.

### Edom Denies Israel Passage

¹⁴Moses sent messengers from Kadesh to the king of Edom, saying:

"This is what your brother Israel says: You know about all the hardships that have come on us. ¹⁵Our ancestors went down into Egypt, and we lived there many years. The Egyptians mistreated us and our ancestors, ¹⁶but when we cried out to the LORD, he heard our cry and sent an angel and brought us out of Egypt.

"Now we are here at Kadesh, a town on the edge of your territory. ¹⁷Please let us pass through your country. We will not go through any field or vineyard, or drink water from any well. We will travel along the King's Highway and not turn to the right or to the left until we have passed through your territory."

¹⁸But Edom answered:

"You may not pass through here; if you try, we will march out and attack you with the sword."

---

ᵃ 13 Meribah means *quarreling*.

## Amplified Bible

²²And whatever the unclean person touches shall be unclean, and anyone who touches it shall be unclean until evening.

**20** And the Israelites, the whole congregation, came into the Wilderness of Zin in the first month. And the people dwelt in Kadesh. Miriam died and was buried there.

²Now there was no water for the congregation, and they assembled together against Moses and Aaron.

³And the people contended with Moses, and said, Would that we had died when our brethren died [in the plague] before the Lord! [Num. 16:49.]

⁴And why have you brought up the congregation of the Lord into this wilderness, that we should die here, we and our livestock?

⁵And why have you made us come up out of Egypt to bring us into this evil place? It is no place of grain or of figs or of vines or of pomegranates. And there is no water to drink.

⁶Then Moses and Aaron went from the presence of the assembly to the door of the Tent of Meeting and fell on their faces. Then the glory of the Lord appeared to them.

⁷And the Lord said to Moses,

⁸Take the rod, and assemble the congregation, you and Aaron your brother, and tell the rock before their eyes to give forth its water, and you shall bring forth to them water out of the rock; so you shall give the congregation and their livestock drink.

⁹So Moses took the rod from before the Lord, as He commanded him.

¹⁰And Moses and Aaron assembled the congregation before the rock and Moses said to them, Hear now, you rebels; must we bring you water out of this rock?

¹¹And Moses lifted up his hand and with his rod he smote the rock ᵃtwice. And the water came out abundantly, and the congregation drank, and their livestock.

¹²And the Lord said to Moses and Aaron, Because you did not believe in (rely on, cling to) Me to sanctify Me in the eyes of the Israelites, you therefore ᵇshall not bring this congregation into the land which I have given them. [Ps. 106:32, 33.]

¹³These are the waters of Meribah [strife], where the Israelites contended with the Lord and He showed Himself holy among them.

¹⁴And Moses sent messengers from Kadesh to the king of Edom, saying, Thus says your kinsman Israel: You know all the adversity *and* birth pangs that have come upon us [as a nation]:

¹⁵How our fathers went down to Egypt; we dwelt there a long time, and the Egyptians dealt evilly with us and our fathers.

¹⁶But when we cried to the Lord, He heard us and sent an angel and brought us forth out of Egypt. Now behold, we are in Kadesh, a city on your country's edge.

¹⁷Let us pass, I pray you, through your country. We will not pass through field or vineyard, or drink of the water of the wells. We will go along the king's highway; we will not turn aside to the right hand or to the left until we have passed your borders.

¹⁸But Edom said to him, You shall not go through, lest I come out against you with the sword.

---

ᵃ "And the Rock was Christ," as I Cor. 10:4 explains. Once smitten at Rephidim (Exod. 17:6ff.), He did not need to be smitten, crucified, again. To smite the rock twice was to imply that Christ's death on the cross was not effectual or sufficient for time and eternity. ᵇ Possibly Moses was not aware of the significance of what he had been ordered to do, but nevertheless God held him responsible for not obeying Him exactly. Obedience to His will is vitally important, whether we understand His purpose or not. The motto "God's will: nothing more; nothing less; nothing else; at any cost" would have been priceless to Moses and Aaron that day, if they had only followed it.

## New International Version

### Amplified Bible

[NIV column]

¹⁹The Israelites replied:

"We will go along the main road, and if we or our livestock drink any of your water, we will pay for it. We only want to pass through on foot—nothing else."

²⁰Again they answered:

"You may not pass through."

Then Edom came out against them with a large and powerful army. ²¹Since Edom refused to let them go through their territory, Israel turned away from them.

#### The Death of Aaron

²²The whole Israelite community set out from Kadesh and came to Mount Hor. ²³At Mount Hor, near the border of Edom, the LORD said to Moses and Aaron, ²⁴"Aaron will be gathered to his people. He will not enter the land I give the Israelites, because both of you rebelled against my command at the waters of Meribah. ²⁵Get Aaron and his son Eleazar and take them up Mount Hor. ²⁶Remove Aaron's garments and put them on his son Eleazar, for Aaron will be gathered to his people; he will die there."

²⁷Moses did as the LORD commanded: They went up Mount Hor in the sight of the whole community. ²⁸Moses removed Aaron's garments and put them on his son Eleazar. And Aaron died there on top of the mountain. Then Moses and Eleazar came down from the mountain, ²⁹and when the whole community learned that Aaron had died, all the Israelites mourned for him thirty days.

#### Arad Destroyed

**21** When the Canaanite king of Arad, who lived in the Negev, heard that Israel was coming along the road to Atharim, he attacked the Israelites and captured some of them. ²Then Israel made this vow to the LORD: "If you will deliver these people into our hands, we will totally destroy[a] their cities." ³The LORD listened to Israel's plea and gave the Canaanites over to them. They completely destroyed them and their towns; so the place was named Hormah.[b]

#### The Bronze Snake

⁴They traveled from Mount Hor along the route to the Red Sea,[c] to go around Edom. But the people grew impatient on the way; ⁵they spoke against God and against Moses, and said, "Why have you brought us up out of Egypt to die in the wilderness? There is no bread! There is no water! And we detest this miserable food!"

⁶Then the LORD sent venomous snakes among them; they bit the people and many Israelites died. ⁷The people came to Moses and said, "We sinned when we spoke against the LORD and against you. Pray that the LORD will take the snakes away from us." So Moses prayed for the people.

⁸The LORD said to Moses, "Make a snake and put it up on a pole; anyone who is bitten can look at it and live."

[Amplified column]

¹⁹And the Israelites said to him, We will go by the highway, and if I and my livestock drink of your water, I will pay for it. Only let me pass through on foot, nothing else.

²⁰But Edom said, You shall not go through. And Edom came out against Israel with many people and a strong hand.

²¹Thus Edom refused to give Israel passage through his territory, [a]so Israel turned away from him.

²²They journeyed from Kadesh, and the Israelites, even the whole congregation, came to Mount Hor.

²³And the Lord said to Moses and Aaron at Mount Hor, on the border of the land of Edom,

²⁴Aaron shall be gathered to his people. For he shall not enter the land which I have given to the Israelites, because you both rebelled against My instructions at the waters of Meribah.

²⁵Take Aaron and Eleazar his son and bring them up to Mount Hor.

²⁶Strip Aaron of his vestments and put them on Eleazar his son, and Aaron shall be gathered to his people, and shall die there.

²⁷And Moses did as the Lord commanded; and they went up Mount Hor in the sight of all the congregation.

²⁸And Moses stripped Aaron of his [priestly] garments and put them on Eleazar his son. And Aaron died there on the mountain top; and Moses and Eleazar came down from the mountain.

²⁹When all the congregation saw that Aaron was dead, they wept and mourned for him thirty days, all the house of Israel.

**21** When the Canaanite king of Arad, who dwelt in the South (the Negeb), heard that Israel was coming by the way of Atharim [the route traveled by the spies sent out by Moses], he fought against Israel and took some of them captive.

²And Israel vowed a vow to the Lord, and said, If You will indeed deliver this people into my hand, then I will utterly destroy their cities.

³And the Lord hearkened to Israel and gave over the Canaanites. And they utterly destroyed them and their cities; and the name of the place was called Hormah [a banned or devoted thing].

⁴And they journeyed from Mount Hor by the way to the Red Sea, to go around the land of Edom, and the people became impatient (depressed, much discouraged), because [of the trials] of the way.

⁵And the people spoke against God and against Moses, Why have you brought us out of Egypt to die in the wilderness? For there is no bread, neither is there any water, and we loathe this light (contemptible, unsubstantial) manna.

⁶Then the Lord sent fiery (burning) serpents among the people; and they bit the people, and many Israelites died.

⁷And the people came to Moses, and said, We have sinned, for we have spoken against the Lord and against you; pray to the Lord, that He may take away the serpents from us. So Moses prayed for the people.

⁸And the Lord said to Moses, Make a fiery serpent [of bronze] and set it on a pole; and everyone who is bitten, when he looks at it, shall live.

---

[a] Israel (Jacob's offspring) did not fight Edom, the offspring of Jacob's brother Esau, because of the Lord's warning, later conveyed in definite instructions (Deut. 23:7). But what had begun as only a quarrel between twin brothers (Gen. 27:41) had now been passed on for generations and was to cost countless lives, extending throughout the Old Testament and into the New, where Herod, remotely related to Esau, tried to take the life of the Babe of Bethlehem, a descendant of Jacob. "See how much wood *or* how great a forest a tiny spark can set ablaze!" (James 3:5).

---

[a] 2 The Hebrew term refers to the irrevocable giving over of things or persons to the LORD, often by totally destroying them; also in verse 3.
[b] 3 *Hormah* means *destruction*.  [c] 4 Or *the Sea of Reeds*

# New International Version

9So Moses made a bronze snake and put it up on a pole. Then when anyone was bitten by a snake and looked at the bronze snake, they lived.

## The Journey to Moab

10The Israelites moved on and camped at Oboth. 11Then they set out from Oboth and camped in Iye Abarim, in the wilderness that faces Moab toward the sunrise. 12From there they moved on and camped in the Zered Valley. 13They set out from there and camped alongside the Arnon, which is in the wilderness extending into Amorite territory. The Arnon is the border of Moab, between Moab and the Amorites. 14That is why the Book of the Wars of the LORD says:

". . . Zahab*a* in Suphah and the ravines,
   the Arnon 15and*b* the slopes of the ravines
that lead to the settlement of Ar
   and lie along the border of Moab."

16From there they continued on to Beer, the well where the LORD said to Moses, "Gather the people together and I will give them water."

17Then Israel sang this song:

"Spring up, O well!
   Sing about it,
18about the well that the princes dug,
   that the nobles of the people sank—
   the nobles with scepters and staffs."

Then they went from the wilderness to Mattanah, 19from Mattanah to Nahaliel, from Nahaliel to Bamoth, 20and from Bamoth to the valley in Moab where the top of Pisgah overlooks the wasteland.

## Defeat of Sihon and Og

21Israel sent messengers to say to Sihon king of the Amorites:

22"Let us pass through your country. We will not turn aside into any field or vineyard, or drink water from any well. We will travel along the King's Highway until we have passed through your territory."

23But Sihon would not let Israel pass through his territory. He mustered his entire army and marched out into the wilderness against Israel. When he reached Jahaz, he fought with Israel. 24Israel, however, put him to the sword and took over his land from the Arnon to the Jabbok, but only as far as the Ammonites, because their border was fortified. 25Israel captured all the cities of the Amorites and occupied them, including Heshbon and all its surrounding settlements. 26Heshbon was the city of Sihon king of the Amorites, who had fought against the former king of Moab and had taken from him all his land as far as the Arnon.

27That is why the poets say:

"Come to Heshbon and let it be rebuilt;
   let Sihon's city be restored.

28"Fire went out from Heshbon,
   a blaze from the city of Sihon.
It consumed Ar of Moab,
   the citizens of Arnon's heights.
29Woe to you, Moab!
   You are destroyed, people of Chemosh!

# Amplified Bible

9And Moses made a serpent of bronze and put it on a pole, and if a serpent had bitten any man, when he looked to the serpent of bronze [*a*attentively, expectantly, with a steady and absorbing gaze], he lived.

10And the Israelites journeyed on and encamped at Oboth.

11They journeyed from Oboth and encamped at Iye-abarim, in the wilderness opposite Moab, toward the sunrise.

12From there they journeyed and encamped in the Valley of Zared.

13From there they journeyed and encamped on the other side of [the river] Arnon, which is in the desert *or* wilderness that extends from the frontier of the Amorites; for [the river] Arnon is the boundary of Moab, between Moab and the Amorites.

14That is why it is said in the Book of the Wars of the Lord: Waheb in Suphah, and the valleys of [the branches of] the Arnon [River],

15And the slope of the valleys that stretch toward the site of Ar and find support on the border of Moab.

16From there the Israelites went on to Beer [a well], the well of which the Lord had said to Moses, Assemble the people together and I will give them water. [John 7:37-39.]

17Then Israel sang this song, Spring up, O well! Let all sing to it, [Rom. 14:17.]

18The fountain that the princes opened, that the nobles of the people hollowed out from their staves. And from the wilderness *or* desert [Israel journeyed] to Mattanah,

19And from Mattanah to Nahaliel, and from Nahaliel to Bamoth,

20And from Bamoth to the valley that is in the field of Moab, to the top of Pisgah which looks down upon Jeshimon *and* the desert.

21And Israel sent messengers to Sihon king of the Amorites, saying,

22Let me pass through your land. We will not turn aside into field or vineyard; we will not drink the water of the wells. We will go by the king's highway until we have passed your border.

23But Sihon would not allow Israel to pass through his border. Instead Sihon gathered all his people together and went out against Israel into the wilderness, and came to Jahaz, and he fought against Israel.

24And Israel smote the king of the Amorites with the edge of the sword and possessed his land from the river Arnon to the river Jabbok, as far as the Ammonites, for the boundary of the Ammonites was strong.

25And Israel took all these cities and dwelt in all the cities of the Amorites, in Heshbon and in all its towns.

26For Heshbon was the city of Sihon king of the Amorites, who had fought against the former king of Moab and taken all his land out of his hand, as far as [the river] Arnon.

27That is why those who sing ballads say, Come to Heshbon, let the city of Sihon be built and established.

28For fire has gone out of Heshbon, a flame from the city of Sihon; it has devoured Ar of Moab and the lords of the heights of the Arnon.

29Woe to you, Moab! You are undone, O people of [the

---

*a* Jesus said that as Moses lifted up the serpent in the wilderness, so must the Son of Man be lifted up, "that everyone who believes in Him [who cleaves to Him, trusts Him and relies on Him] may *not perish, but* have eternal life *and* [actually] live forever!" (John 3:14, 15). Obviously this implies that the look that caused the victim of a fiery serpent to be healed was something far more than a casual glance. A "look" would save, but what kind of a look? The Hebrew text here means "look attentively, expectantly, with a steady and absorbing gaze." Or, as Jesus said in the last verse of the chapter quoted above (John 3:36), "He who believes in (has faith in, clings to, relies on) the Son has (now possesses) eternal life." But whoever does not so believe in, cling to, and rely on the Son "will never see . . . life." The look that saves is not just a fleeting glance; it is a God-honoring, God-answered, fixed, and absorbing gaze!

---

*a* 14 Septuagint; Hebrew *Waheb*   *b* 14,15 Or *"I have been given from Suphah and the ravines / of the Arnon* 15to

## New International Version

He has given up his sons as fugitives
and his daughters as captives
to Sihon king of the Amorites.

30 "But we have overthrown them;
Heshbon's dominion has been destroyed all the way
to Dibon.
We have demolished them as far as Nophah,
which extends to Medeba."

31 So Israel settled in the land of the Amorites. 32 After Moses had sent spies to Jazer, the Israelites captured its surrounding settlements and drove out the Amorites who were there. 33 Then they turned and went up along the road toward Bashan, and Og king of Bashan and his whole army marched out to meet them in battle at Edrei.

34 The Lord said to Moses, "Do not be afraid of him, for I have delivered him into your hands, along with his whole army and his land. Do to him what you did to Sihon king of the Amorites, who reigned in Heshbon."

35 So they struck him down, together with his sons and his whole army, leaving them no survivors. And they took possession of his land.

### Balak Summons Balaam

**22** Then the Israelites traveled to the plains of Moab and camped along the Jordan across from Jericho. 2 Now Balak son of Zippor saw all that Israel had done to the Amorites, 3 and Moab was terrified because there were so many people. Indeed, Moab was filled with dread because of the Israelites.

4 The Moabites said to the elders of Midian, "This horde is going to lick up everything around us, as an ox licks up the grass of the field."

So Balak son of Zippor, who was king of Moab at that time, 5 sent messengers to summon Balaam son of Beor, who was at Pethor, near the Euphrates River, in his native land. Balak said:

"A people has come out of Egypt; they cover the face of the land and have settled next to me. 6 Now come and put a curse on these people, because they are too powerful for me. Perhaps then I will be able to defeat them and drive them out of the land. For I know that whoever you bless is blessed, and whoever you curse is cursed."

7 The elders of Moab and Midian left, taking with them the fee for divination. When they came to Balaam, they told him what Balak had said.

8 "Spend the night here," Balaam said to them, "and I will report back to you with the answer the Lord gives me." So the Moabite officials stayed with him.

9 God came to Balaam and asked, "Who are these men with you?"

10 Balaam said to God, "Balak son of Zippor, king of Moab, sent me this message: 11 'A people that has come out of Egypt covers the face of the land. Now come and put a curse on them for me. Perhaps then I will be able to fight them and drive them away.'"

12 But God said to Balaam, "Do not go with them. You must not put a curse on those people, because they are blessed."

13 The next morning Balaam got up and said to Balak's officials, "Go back to your own country, for the Lord has refused to let me go with you."

14 So the Moabite officials returned to Balak and said, "Balaam refused to come with us."

15 Then Balak sent other officials, more numerous and more distinguished than the first. 16 They came to Balaam and said:

## Amplified Bible

god] Chemosh! Moab has given his sons as fugitives and his daughters into captivity to Sihon king of the Amorites.

30 We have shot them down; Heshbon has perished as far as Dibon, and we have laid them waste as far as Nophah, which reaches to Medeba.

31 Thus Israel dwelt in the land of the Amorites. 32 And Moses sent to spy out Jazer, and they took its villages and dispossessed the Amorites who were there.

33 Then they turned and went up by the way of Bashan; and Og the king of Bashan went out against them, he and all his people, to battle at Edrei.

34 But the Lord said to Moses, Do not fear him, for I have delivered him and all his people and his land into your hand; and you shall do to him as you did to Sihon king of the Amorites, who dwelt at Heshbon.

35 So the Israelites slew Og and his sons and all his people until there was not one left alive, And they possessed his land.

**22** The Israelites journeyed and encamped in the plains of Moab, on the east side of the Jordan [River] at Jericho.

2 And Balak [the king of Moab] son of Zippor saw all that Israel had done to the Amorites.

3 And Moab was terrified at the people *and* full of dread, because they were many. Moab was distressed *and* overcome with fear because of the Israelites.

4 And Moab said to the elders of Midian, Now will this multitude lick up all that is round about us, as the ox licks up the grass of the field. So Balak son of Zippor, the king of the Moabites at that time,

5 Sent messengers to Balaam [a foreteller of events] son of Beor at Pethor, which is by the [Euphrates] River, even to the land of the children of his people, to say to him, There is a people come out from Egypt; behold, they cover the face of the earth and they have settled down *and* dwell opposite me.

6 Now come, I beg of you, curse this people for me, for they are too powerful for me. Perhaps I may be able to defeat them and drive them out of the land, for I know that he whom you bless is blessed, and he whom you curse is cursed.

7 And the elders of Moab and of Midian departed with the rewards of foretelling in their hands; and they came to Balaam and told him the words of Balak.

8 And he said to them, Lodge here tonight and I will bring you word as the Lord may speak to me. And the princes of Moab abode with Balaam [that night].

9 And God came to Balaam, and said, What men are these with you?

10 And Balaam said to God, Balak son of Zippor, king of Moab, has sent to me, saying,

11 Behold, the people who came out of Egypt cover the face of the earth; come now, curse them for me. Perhaps I shall be able to fight against them and drive them out.

12 And God said to Balaam, You shall not go with them; you shall not curse the people, for they are blessed.

13 And Balaam rose up in the morning, and said to the princes of Balak, Go back to your own land, for the Lord refuses to permit me to go with you.

14 So the princes of Moab rose up and went to Balak, and said, Balaam refuses to come with us.

15 Then Balak again sent princes, more of them and more honorable than the first ones.

16 And they came to Balaam, and said to him, Thus says

## New International Version

"This is what Balak son of Zippor says: Do not let anything keep you from coming to me, [17]because I will reward you handsomely and do whatever you say. Come and put a curse on these people for me.'"

[18]But Balaam answered them, "Even if Balak gave me all the silver and gold in his palace, I could not do anything great or small to go beyond the command of the LORD my God. [19]Now spend the night here so that I can find out what else the LORD will tell me."

[20]That night God came to Balaam and said, "Since these men have come to summon you, go with them, but do only what I tell you."

### Balaam's Donkey

[21]Balaam got up in the morning, saddled his donkey and went with the Moabite officials. [22]But God was very angry when he went, and the angel of the LORD stood in the road to oppose him. Balaam was riding on his donkey, and his two servants were with him. [23]When the donkey saw the angel of the LORD standing in the road with a drawn sword in his hand, it turned off the road into a field. Balaam beat it to get it back on the road.

[24]Then the angel of the LORD stood in a narrow path through the vineyards, with walls on both sides. [25]When the donkey saw the angel of the LORD, it pressed close to the wall, crushing Balaam's foot against it. So he beat the donkey again.

[26]Then the angel of the LORD moved on ahead and stood in a narrow place where there was no room to turn, either to the right or to the left. [27]When the donkey saw the angel of the LORD, it lay down under Balaam, and he was angry and beat it with his staff. [28]Then the LORD opened the donkey's mouth, and it said to Balaam, "What have I done to you to make you beat me these three times?"

[29]Balaam answered the donkey, "You have made a fool of me! If only I had a sword in my hand, I would kill you right now."

[30]The donkey said to Balaam, "Am I not your own donkey, which you have always ridden, to this day? Have I been in the habit of doing this to you?"

"No," he said.

[31]Then the LORD opened Balaam's eyes, and he saw the angel of the LORD standing in the road with his sword drawn. So he bowed low and fell facedown.

[32]The angel of the LORD asked him, "Why have you beaten your donkey these three times? I have come here to oppose you because your path is a reckless one before me.[a] [33]The donkey saw me and turned away from me these three times. If it had not turned away, I would certainly have killed you by now, but I would have spared it."

[34]Balaam said to the angel of the LORD, "I have sinned. I did not realize you were standing in the road to oppose me. Now if you are displeased, I will go back."

[35]The angel of the LORD said to Balaam, "Go with the men, but speak only what I tell you." So Balaam went with Balak's officials.

[36]When Balak heard that Balaam was coming, he went out to meet him at the Moabite town on the Arnon border, at the edge of his territory. [37]Balak said to Balaam, "Did I not send you an urgent summons? Why didn't you come to me? Am I really not able to reward you?"

## Amplified Bible

Balak son of Zippor, I beg of you, let nothing hinder you from coming to me.

[17]For I will promote you to very great honor and I will do whatever you tell me; so come, I beg of you, curse this people for me.

[18]And Balaam answered the servants of Balak, If Balak would give me his house full of silver and gold, I cannot go beyond the word of the Lord my God, to do less or more.

[19]Now therefore, I pray you, tarry here again tonight that I may know what more the Lord will say to me.

[20]And God came to Balaam at night, and said to him, If the men come to call you, rise up and go with them, but still only what I tell you may you do.

[21]And Balaam rose up in the morning and saddled his donkey and went with the princes of Moab.

[22]And God's anger was kindled because he went, and the [a]Angel of the Lord stood in the way as an adversary against him. Now he was riding upon his donkey, and his two servants were with him.

[23]And the donkey saw the Angel of the Lord standing in the way and His sword drawn in His hand, and the donkey turned aside out of the way and went into the field. And Balaam struck the donkey to turn her into the way.

[24]But the Angel of the Lord stood in a path of the vineyards, a wall on this side and a wall on that side.

[25]And when the donkey saw the Angel of the Lord, she thrust herself against the wall and crushed Balaam's foot against it, and he struck her again.

[26]And the Angel of the Lord went further and stood in a narrow place where there was no room to turn, either to the right hand or to the left.

[27]And when the donkey saw the Angel of the Lord, she fell down under Balaam, and Balaam's anger was kindled and he struck the donkey with his staff.

[28]And the Lord opened the mouth of the donkey, and she said to Balaam, What have I done to you that you should strike me these three times?

[29]And Balaam said to the donkey, Because you have ridiculed *and* provoked me! I wish there were a sword in my hand, for now I would kill you!

[30]And the donkey said to Balaam, Am not I your donkey, upon which you have ridden all your life long until this day? Was I ever accustomed to do so to you? And he said, No.

[31]Then the Lord opened Balaam's eyes, and he saw the Angel of the Lord standing in the way with His sword drawn in His hand; and he bowed his head and fell on his face.

[32]And the Angel of the Lord said to him, Why have you struck your donkey these three times? See, I came out to stand against *and* resist you, for your behavior is willfully obstinate *and* contrary before Me.

[33]And the ass saw Me and turned from Me these three times. If she had not turned from Me, surely I would have slain you and saved her alive.

[34]Balaam said to the Angel of the Lord, I have sinned, for I did not know You stood in the way against me. But now, if my going displeases You, I will return.

[35]The Angel of the Lord said to Balaam, Go with the men, but you shall speak only what I tell you. So Balaam went with the princes of Balak.

[36]When Balak heard that Balaam had come, he went out to meet him at the city of Moab on the border formed by the Arnon [River], at the farthest end of the boundary.

[37]Balak said to Balaam, Did I not [earnestly] send to you to ask you [to come] to me? Why did you not come? Am not I able to promote you to honor?

---

[a] 32 The meaning of the Hebrew for this clause is uncertain.　　　　[a] See footnote on Gen. 16:7.

## New International Version

38"Well, I have come to you now," Balaam replied. "But I can't say whatever I please. I must speak only what God puts in my mouth."

39Then Balaam went with Balak to Kiriath Huzoth. 40Balak sacrificed cattle and sheep, and gave some to Balaam and the officials who were with him. 41The next morning Balak took Balaam up to Bamoth Baal, and from there he could see the outskirts of the Israelite camp.

### Balaam's First Message

**23** Balaam said, "Build me seven altars here, and prepare seven bulls and seven rams for me." 2Balak did as Balaam said, and the two of them offered a bull and a ram on each altar.

3Then Balaam said to Balak, "Stay here beside your offering while I go aside. Perhaps the LORD will come to meet with me. Whatever he reveals to me I will tell you." Then he went off to a barren height.

4God met with him, and Balaam said, "I have prepared seven altars, and on each altar I have offered a bull and a ram."

5The LORD put a word in Balaam's mouth and said, "Go back to Balak and give him this word."

6So he went back to him and found him standing beside his offering, with all the Moabite officials. 7Then Balaam spoke his message:

"Balak brought me from Aram,
    the king of Moab from the eastern mountains.
'Come,' he said, 'curse Jacob for me;
    come, denounce Israel.'
8How can I curse
    those whom God has not cursed?
How can I denounce
    those whom the LORD has not denounced?
9From the rocky peaks I see them,
    from the heights I view them.
I see a people who live apart
    and do not consider themselves one of the nations.
10Who can count the dust of Jacob
    or number even a fourth of Israel?
Let me die the death of the righteous,
    and may my final end be like theirs!"

11Balak said to Balaam, "What have you done to me? I brought you to curse my enemies, but you have done nothing but bless them!"

12He answered, "Must I not speak what the LORD puts in my mouth?"

### Balaam's Second Message

13Then Balak said to him, "Come with me to another place where you can see them; you will not see them all but only the outskirts of their camp. And from there, curse them for me." 14So he took him to the field of Zophim on the top of Pisgah, and there he built seven altars and offered a bull and a ram on each altar.

15Balaam said to Balak, "Stay here beside your offering while I meet with him over there."

16The LORD met with Balaam and put a word in his mouth and said, "Go back to Balak and give him this word."

17So he went to him and found him standing beside his offering, with the Moabite officials. Balak asked him, "What did the LORD say?"

18Then he spoke his message:

"Arise, Balak, and listen;
    hear me, son of Zippor.
19God is not human, that he should lie,
    not a human being, that he should change his mind.

## Amplified Bible

38And Balaam said to Balak, Indeed I have come to you, but do I now have any power at all to say anything? The word that God puts in my mouth, that shall I speak.

39And Balaam went with Balak, and they came to Kiriath-huzoth.

40And Balak offered oxen and sheep, and sent [portions] to Balaam and to the princes who were with him.

41And on the following day Balak took Balaam and brought him up into the high places of Bamoth-baal; from there he saw the nearest of the Israelites.

**23** And Balaam said to Balak, Build me here seven altars, and prepare me here seven oxen and seven rams.

2And Balak did as Balaam had spoken, and Balak and Balaam offered on each altar a bull and a ram.

3And Balaam said to Balak, Stand by your burnt offering and I will go. Perhaps the Lord will come to meet me; and whatever He shows me I will tell you. And he went to a bare height.

4God met Balaam, who said to Him, I have prepared seven altars, and I have offered on each altar a bull and a ram.

5And the Lord put a speech in Balaam's mouth, and said, Return to Balak and thus shall you speak.

6Balaam returned to Balak, who was standing by his burnt sacrifice, he and all the princes of Moab.

7Balaam took up his [figurative] speech and said: Balak, the king of Moab, has brought me from Aram, out of the mountains of the east, saying, Come, curse Jacob for me; and come, violently denounce Israel.

8How can I curse those God has not cursed? Or how can I [violently] denounce those the Lord has not denounced?

9For from the top of the rocks I see Israel, and from the hills I behold him. Behold, the people [of Israel] shall *a*dwell alone and shall not be reckoned *and* esteemed among the nations.

10Who can count the dust (the descendants) of Jacob and the number of the fourth part of Israel? Let me die the death of the righteous [those who are upright and in right standing with God], and let my last end be like theirs! [Ps. 37:37; Rev. 14:13.]

11And Balak said to Balaam, What have you done to me? I brought you to curse my enemies, and here you have [thoroughly] blessed them instead!

12And Balaam answered, Must I not be obedient *and* speak what the Lord has put in my mouth?

13Balak said to him, Come with me, I implore you, to another place from which you can see them, though you will see only the nearest and not all of them; and curse them for me from there.

14So he took Balaam into the field of Zophim to the top of [Mount] Pisgah, and built seven altars, and offered a bull and a ram on each altar.

15Balaam said to Balak, Stand here by your burnt offering while I go to meet the Lord yonder.

16And the Lord met Balaam and put a speech in his mouth, and said, Go again to Balak and speak thus.

17And when he returned to Balak, he was standing beside his burnt offering, and the princes of Moab with him. And Balak said to him, What has the Lord said?

18Balaam took up his [figurative] discourse and said: Rise up, Balak, and hear; listen [closely] to me, son of Zippor.

19God is not a man, that He should tell *or* act a lie, neither the son of man, that He should feel repentance *or*

---

*a* The literal fulfillment of this prophecy has been obvious during the more than thirty-four centuries since it was spoken. The Jews have always been separate as a nation from other peoples. Though conquered many times, they have never been absorbed by their conquerors or lost their identity. The prophecy had to become true, for "the Lord put [it] ... in Balaam's mouth" (Num. 23:5).

## New International Version

Does he speak and then not act?
    Does he promise and not fulfill?
20 I have received a command to bless;
    he has blessed, and I cannot change it.

21 "No misfortune is seen in Jacob,
    no misery observed[a] in Israel.
The LORD their God is with them;
    the shout of the King is among them.
22 God brought them out of Egypt;
    they have the strength of a wild ox.
23 There is no divination against[b] Jacob,
    no evil omens against[b] Israel.
It will now be said of Jacob
    and of Israel, 'See what God has done!'
24 The people rise like a lioness;
    they rouse themselves like a lion
that does not rest till it devours its prey
    and drinks the blood of its victims."

25 Then Balak said to Balaam, "Neither curse them at all
nor bless them at all!"

26 Balaam answered, "Did I not tell you I must do whatever the LORD says?"

### Balaam's Third Message

27 Then Balak said to Balaam, "Come, let me take you to
another place. Perhaps it will please God to let you curse
them for me from there." 28 And Balak took Balaam to the
top of Peor, overlooking the wasteland.
29 Balaam said, "Build me seven altars here, and prepare
seven bulls and seven rams for me." 30 Balak did as Balaam
had said, and offered a bull and a ram on each altar.

**24** Now when Balaam saw that it pleased the LORD
to bless Israel, he did not resort to divination as
at other times, but turned his face toward the wilderness.
2 When Balaam looked out and saw Israel encamped tribe
by tribe, the Spirit of God came on him 3 and he spoke his
message:

"The prophecy of Balaam son of Beor,
    the prophecy of one whose eye sees clearly,
4 the prophecy of one who hears the words of God,
    who sees a vision from the Almighty,[c]
    who falls prostrate, and whose eyes are opened:

5 "How beautiful are your tents, Jacob,
    your dwelling places, Israel!

6 "Like valleys they spread out,
    like gardens beside a river,
like aloes planted by the LORD,
    like cedars beside the waters.
7 Water will flow from their buckets;
    their seed will have abundant water.

"Their king will be greater than Agag;
    their kingdom will be exalted.

8 "God brought them out of Egypt;
    they have the strength of a wild ox.
They devour hostile nations
    and break their bones in pieces;
    with their arrows they pierce them.
9 Like a lion they crouch and lie down,
    like a lioness—who dares to rouse them?

"May those who bless you be blessed
    and those who curse you be cursed!"

10 Then Balak's anger burned against Balaam. He
struck his hands together and said to him, "I summoned

## Amplified Bible

compunction [for what He has promised]. Has He said
and shall He not do it? Or has He spoken and shall He not
make it good?
20 You see, I have received His command to bless Israel.
He has blessed, and I cannot reverse or qualify it.
21 [God] has not beheld iniquity in Jacob [for he is for-
given], neither has He seen mischief or perverseness in
Israel [for the same reason]. The Lord their God is with
Israel, and the shout of praise to their King is among the
people. [Rom. 4:7, 8; I John 3:1, 2.]
22 God brought them forth out of Egypt; they have as it
were the strength of a wild ox.
23 Surely there is no enchantment with or against Jacob,
neither is there any divination with or against Israel. [In
due season and even] now it shall be said of Jacob and of
Israel, What has God wrought!
24 Behold, a people! They rise up as a lioness and lift
themselves up as a lion; he shall not lie down until he devours the prey and drinks the blood of the slain.
25 And Balak said to Balaam, Neither curse them at all
nor bless them at all.
26 But Balaam answered Balak, Did I not say to you, All
the Lord speaks, that I must do?
27 And Balak said to Balaam, Come, I implore you; I will
take you to another place. Perhaps it will please God to let
you curse them for me from there.
28 So Balak brought Balaam to the top of [Mount] Peor,
that overlooks [the wilderness or desert] Jeshimon.
29 And Balaam said to Balak, Build me here seven altars,
and prepare me here seven bulls and seven rams.
30 And Balak did as Balaam had said, and offered a bull
and a ram on each altar.

**24** When Balaam saw that it pleased the Lord to bless
Israel, he did not go as he had done each time before [superstitiously] to meet with omens and signs in the
natural world, but he set his face toward the wilderness
or desert.
2 And Balaam lifted up his eyes and he saw Israel abiding in their tents according to their tribes. And the Spirit
of God came upon him
3 And he took up his [figurative] discourse and said:
Balaam son of Beor, the man whose eye is opened [at last,
to see clearly the purposes and will of God],
4 He [Balaam] who hears the words of God, who sees
the vision of the Almighty, falling down, but having his
eyes open and uncovered, he says:
5 How attractive and considerable are your tents, O Jacob, and your tabernacles, O Israel!
6 As valleys are they spread forth, as gardens by the
riverside, as [rare spice] of lignaloes which the Lord has
planted, and as cedar trees beside the waters. [Ps. 1:3.]
7 [Israel] shall pour water out of his own buckets [have
his own sources of rich blessing and plenty], and his offspring shall dwell by many waters, and his king shall be
higher than [a] Agag, and his kingdom shall be exalted.
8 God brought [Israel] forth out of Egypt; [Israel] has
strength like the wild ox; he shall eat up the nations, his
enemies, crushing their bones and piercing them through
with his arrows.
9 He couched, he lay down as a lion; and as a lioness, who
shall rouse him? Blessed [of God] is he who blesses you
[who prays for and contributes to your welfare] and cursed
[of God] is he who curses you [who in word, thought, or
deed would bring harm upon you]. [Matt. 25:40.]
10 Then Balak's anger was kindled against Balaam, and
he smote his hands together; and Balak said to Balaam,

---

[a] 21 Or He has not looked on Jacob's offenses / or on the wrongs found
[b] 23 Or in   [c] 4 Hebrew Shaddai; also in verse 16

[a] "Agag" was the title of the Amalekite kings, and it represents here the
kingdom of the Gentiles. The Amalekites at that time were the most
powerful of all the desert tribes (Num. 24:20).

## New International Version

you to curse my enemies, but you have blessed them these three times. [11]Now leave at once and go home! I said I would reward you handsomely, but the LORD has kept you from being rewarded."

[12]Balaam answered Balak, "Did I not tell the messengers you sent me, [13]'Even if Balak gave me all the silver and gold in his palace, I could not do anything of my own accord, good or bad, to go beyond the command of the LORD—and I must say only what the LORD says'? [14]Now I am going back to my people, but come, let me warn you of what this people will do to your people in days to come."

### Balaam's Fourth Message

[15]Then he spoke his message:

"The prophecy of Balaam son of Beor,
    the prophecy of one whose eye sees clearly,
[16]the prophecy of one who hears the words of God,
    who has knowledge from the Most High,
who sees a vision from the Almighty,
    who falls prostrate, and whose eyes are opened:

[17]"I see him, but not now;
    I behold him, but not near.
A star will come out of Jacob;
    a scepter will rise out of Israel.
He will crush the foreheads of Moab,
    the skulls[a] of[b] all the people of Sheth.[c]
[18]Edom will be conquered;
    Seir, his enemy, will be conquered,
    but Israel will grow strong.
[19]A ruler will come out of Jacob
    and destroy the survivors of the city."

### Balaam's Fifth Message

[20]Then Balaam saw Amalek and spoke his message:

"Amalek was first among the nations,
    but their end will be utter destruction."

### Balaam's Sixth Message

[21]Then he saw the Kenites and spoke his message:

"Your dwelling place is secure,
    your nest is set in a rock;
[22]yet you Kenites will be destroyed
    when Ashur takes you captive."

### Balaam's Seventh Message

[23]Then he spoke his message:

"Alas! Who can live when God does this?[d]
[24]    Ships will come from the shores of Cyprus;
they will subdue Ashur and Eber,
    but they too will come to ruin."

[25]Then Balaam got up and returned home, and Balak went his own way.

## Amplified Bible

I called you to curse my enemies, and, behold, you have done nothing but bless them these three times. [11]Therefore now go back where you belong *and* do it in a hurry! I had intended to promote you to great honor, but behold, the Lord has held you back from honor.

[12]Balaam said to Balak, Did I not say to your messengers whom you sent to me,

[13]If Balak would give me his house full of silver and gold, I cannot go beyond the command of the Lord, to do either good or bad of my own will, but what the Lord says, that will I speak?

[14]And now, behold, I am going to my people; come, I will tell you what this people [Israel] will do to your people [Moab] in the latter days.

[15]And he took up his [figurative] discourse, and said: Balaam son of Beor speaks, the man whose eye is opened speaks,

[16]He speaks, who heard the words of God and knew the knowledge of the Most High, who saw the vision of the Almighty, falling down, but having his eyes open *and* uncovered:

[17]I see Him, but not now; I behold Him, but He is not near. A [a]star (Star) shall come forth out of Jacob, and a scepter (Scepter) shall rise out of Israel and shall crush all the corners of Moab and break down all the sons of Sheth [Moab's sons of tumult]. [Matt. 2:2; Rom. 15:12.]

[18]And Edom shall be [taken as] a possession, [Mount] Seir also shall be dispossessed, who were Israel's enemies, while Israel does valiantly.

[19]Out of Jacob shall one (One) come having dominion and shall destroy the remnant from the city.

[20][Balaam] looked at Amalek and took up his [prophetic] utterance, and said: Amalek is the foremost of the [neighboring] nations, but in his latter end he shall [b]come to destruction.

[21]And he looked at the Kenites and took up his [prophetic] utterance, and said: Strong is your dwelling place, and you set your nest in the rock;

[22]Nevertheless the Kenites shall be wasted. How long shall Asshur (Assyria) take you away captive?

[23]And he took up his [prophetic] speech, and said: Alas, who shall live when God does this *and* establishes [Assyria]?

[24]But ships shall come from Kittim [Cyprus and the greater part of the Mediterranean's east coast] and shall afflict Assyria and Eber [the Hebrews, certain Arabs, and descendants of Nahor], and he [the victor] also shall come to destruction.

[25]And Balaam rose up, returned to his place, and Balak also went his way.

---

[a] "This imagery in the hieroglyphic language of the East denotes some eminent ruler—primarily David, but secondarily and preeminently the Messiah" (Robert Jamieson, A. R. Fausett and David Brown, *A Commentary*). Notice that the principal time for these events is set in the prophecy for "the latter days" (Num. 24:14). "The prophecy [concerning Moab] was partially, or typically, fulfilled in the time of David (II Sam. 8:2). Moab and Edom represented symbolically the enemies of Christ and His church, and as such will eventually be subdued by the King of kings (see Ps. 60:8)" (Charles J. Ellicott, *A Bible Commentary*). "The star which the wise men from the East saw, and which led them in the way to the newborn 'King of the Jews,' refers clearly to the prophecy of Balaam (Matt. 2:1, 2)" (J. P. Lange, *A Commentary*). [b] After the time of David (who was forced to rescue two of his wives from Amalekite bandits, I Sam. 30:18), the Amalekites are mentioned again only in Hezekiah's time (I Chron. 4:43), before "they disappear from the field of history . . . So that the word of God here also stood fast; and the first of the surrounding tribes who impiously sought to measure their strength with the cause and people of God were likewise the first to lose their national existence" (Patrick Fairbairn, ed., *The Imperial Bible-dictionary*).

---

[a] 17 Samaritan Pentateuch (see also Jer. 48:45); the meaning of the word in the Masoretic Text is uncertain.   [b] 17 Or possibly *Moab, / batter*   [c] 17 Or *all the noisy boasters*   [d] 23 Masoretic Text; with a different word division of the Hebrew *The people from the islands will gather from the north.*

## New International Version

### Moab Seduces Israel

**25** While Israel was staying in Shittim, the men began to indulge in sexual immorality with Moabite women, [2]who invited them to the sacrifices to their gods. The people ate the sacrificial meal and bowed down before these gods. [3]So Israel yoked themselves to the Baal of Peor. And the LORD's anger burned against them.

[4]The LORD said to Moses, "Take all the leaders of these people, kill them and expose them in broad daylight before the LORD, so that the LORD's fierce anger may turn away from Israel."

[5]So Moses said to Israel's judges, "Each of you must put to death those of your people who have yoked themselves to the Baal of Peor."

[6]Then an Israelite man brought into the camp a Midianite woman right before the eyes of Moses and the whole assembly of Israel while they were weeping at the entrance to the tent of meeting. [7]When Phinehas son of Eleazar, the son of Aaron, the priest, saw this, he left the assembly, took a spear in his hand [8]and followed the Israelite into the tent. He drove the spear into both of them, right through the Israelite man and into the woman's stomach. Then the plague against the Israelites was stopped; [9]but those who died in the plague numbered 24,000.

[10]The LORD said to Moses, [11]"Phinehas son of Eleazar, the son of Aaron, the priest, has turned my anger away from the Israelites. Since he was as zealous for my honor among them as I am, I did not put an end to them in my zeal. [12]Therefore tell him I am making my covenant of peace with him. [13]He and his descendants will have a covenant of a lasting priesthood, because he was zealous for the honor of his God and made atonement for the Israelites."

[14]The name of the Israelite who was killed with the Midianite woman was Zimri son of Salu, the leader of a Simeonite family. [15]And the name of the Midianite woman who was put to death was Kozbi daughter of Zur, a tribal chief of a Midianite family.

[16]The LORD said to Moses, [17]"Treat the Midianites as enemies and kill them. [18]They treated you as enemies when they deceived you in the Peor incident involving their sister Kozbi, the daughter of a Midianite leader, the woman who was killed when the plague came as a result of that incident."

### The Second Census

**26** After the plague the LORD said to Moses and Eleazar son of Aaron, the priest, [2]"Take a census of the whole Israelite community by families—all those twenty years old or more who are able to serve in the army of Israel." [3]So on the plains of Moab by the Jordan across from Jericho, Moses and Eleazar the priest spoke with them and said, [4]"Take a census of the men twenty years old or more, as the LORD commanded Moses."

These were the Israelites who came out of Egypt:

[5]The descendants of Reuben, the firstborn son of Israel, were:

through Hanok, the Hanokite clan;
through Pallu, the Palluite clan;
[6]through Hezron, the Hezronite clan;
through Karmi, the Karmite clan.

## Amplified Bible

**25** Israel settled down *and* remained in Shittim, and the people began to play the harlot with the daughters of Moab,

[2]Who invited the [Israelites] to the sacrifices of their gods, and [they] ate and bowed down to Moab's gods.

[3]So Israel joined himself to [the god] Baal of Peor. And the anger of the Lord was kindled against Israel.

[4]And the Lord said to Moses, Take all the leaders *or* chiefs of the people, and hang them before the Lord in the sun [after killing them], that the fierce anger of the Lord may turn away from Israel.

[5]And Moses said to the judges of Israel, Each one of you slay his men who joined themselves to Baal of Peor.

[6]And behold, one of the Israelites came and brought to his brethren a Midianite woman in the sight of Moses and of all the congregation of Israel while they were weeping at the door of the Tent of Meeting [over the divine judgment and the punishment].

[7]And when Phinehas son of Eleazar, the son of Aaron the priest, saw it, he rose up from the midst of the congregation and took a spear in his hand

[8]And went after the man of Israel into the inner room and thrust both of them through, the man of Israel and the woman through her body. Then the [smiting] plague was stayed from the Israelites.

[9]Nevertheless those who died in the [smiting] plague were 24,000.

[10]And the Lord said to Moses,

[11]Phinehas son of Eleazar, the son of Aaron the priest, has turned my wrath away from the Israelites, in that he was jealous with My jealousy among them, so that I did not consume the Israelites in My jealousy.

[12]Therefore say, Behold, I give to Phinehas the priest My covenant of peace.

[13]And he shall have it, and his descendants after him, the covenant of an everlasting priesthood, because he was jealous for his God and made atonement for the Israelites. [Ps. 106:28-31.]

[14]Now the man of Israel who was slain with the Midianite woman was Zimri son of Salu, a head of a father's house among the Simeonites.

[15]And the Midianite woman who was slain was Cozbi daughter of Zur; he was head of a father's house in Midian.

[16]And the Lord said to Moses,

[17]Provoke hostilities with the Midianites and attack them,

[18]For they harass you with their wiles with which they have beguiled you in the matter of Peor, and of Cozbi, the daughter of the prince of Midian, their sister, who was slain on the day of the plague in the matter of Peor.

**26** After the plague the Lord said to Moses and Eleazar son of Aaron, the priest,

[2]Take a census of all the [male] congregation of the Israelites from twenty years old and upward, by their fathers' houses, all in Israel able to go to war.

[3]And Moses and Eleazar the priest told [the people] in the plains of Moab by the Jordan at Jericho,

[4]A census of the people shall be taken from twenty years old and upward, as the Lord commanded Moses. And the Israelites who came forth out of the land of Egypt were:

[5]Reuben, the firstborn of Israel, the sons of Reuben: of Hanoch, the family of the Hanochites; of Pallu, the family of the Palluites;

[6]Of Hezron, the family of the Hezronites; of Carmi, the family of the Carmites.

## New International Version

[7] These were the clans of Reuben; those numbered were 43,730.

[8] The son of Pallu was Eliab, [9] and the sons of Eliab were Nemuel, Dathan and Abiram. The same Dathan and Abiram were the community officials who rebelled against Moses and Aaron and were among Korah's followers when they rebelled against the LORD. [10] The earth opened its mouth and swallowed them along with Korah, whose followers died when the fire devoured the 250 men. And they served as a warning sign. [11] The line of Korah, however, did not die out.

[12] The descendants of Simeon by their clans were:
through Nemuel, the Nemuelite clan;
through Jamin, the Jaminite clan;
through Jakin, the Jakinite clan;
[13] through Zerah, the Zerahite clan;
through Shaul, the Shaulite clan.
[14] These were the clans of Simeon; those numbered were 22,200.

[15] The descendants of Gad by their clans were:
through Zephon, the Zephonite clan;
through Haggi, the Haggite clan;
through Shuni, the Shunite clan;
[16] through Ozni, the Oznite clan;
through Eri, the Erite clan;
[17] through Arodi,[a] the Arodite clan;
through Areli, the Arelite clan.
[18] These were the clans of Gad; those numbered were 40,500.

[19] Er and Onan were sons of Judah, but they died in Canaan.
[20] The descendants of Judah by their clans were:
through Shelah, the Shelanite clan;
through Perez, the Perezite clan;
through Zerah, the Zerahite clan.
[21] The descendants of Perez were:
through Hezron, the Hezronite clan;
through Hamul, the Hamulite clan.
[22] These were the clans of Judah; those numbered were 76,500.

[23] The descendants of Issachar by their clans were:
through Tola, the Tolaite clan;
through Puah, the Puite[b] clan;
[24] through Jashub, the Jashubite clan;
through Shimron, the Shimronite clan.
[25] These were the clans of Issachar; those numbered were 64,300.

[26] The descendants of Zebulun by their clans were:
through Sered, the Seredite clan;
through Elon, the Elonite clan;
through Jahleel, the Jahleelite clan.
[27] These were the clans of Zebulun; those numbered were 60,500.

[28] The descendants of Joseph by their clans through Manasseh and Ephraim were:

[29] The descendants of Manasseh:
through Makir, the Makirite clan (Makir was the father of Gilead);
through Gilead, the Gileadite clan.
[30] These were the descendants of Gilead:
through Iezer, the Iezerite clan;
through Helek, the Helekite clan;
[31] through Asriel, the Asrielite clan;
through Shechem, the Shechemite clan;
[32] through Shemida, the Shemidaite clan;
through Hepher, the Hepherite clan.

## Amplified Bible

[7] These are the families of the Reubenites; and their number was 43,730.
[8] And the son of Pallu: Eliab.
[9] The sons of Eliab: Nemuel, Dathan, and Abiram. These are the Dathan and Abiram chosen from the congregation who contended against Moses and Aaron in the company of Korah when they contended against the Lord.
[10] And the earth opened its mouth and swallowed them up together with Korah, when that company died and the fire devoured 250 men; and they became a [warning] sign.
[11] But Korah's sons did not die.
[12] The sons of Simeon according to their families: of Nemuel, the family of the Nemuelites; of Jamin, the family of the Jaminites; of Jachin, the family of the Jachinites;
[13] Of Zerah, the family of the Zerahites; of Shaul, the family of the Shaulites.
[14] These are the families of the Simeonites, 22,200.
[15] The sons of Gad after their families: of Zephon, the family of the Zephonites; of Haggi, the family of the Haggites; of Shuni, the family of the Shunites;
[16] Of Ozni, the family of the Oznites; of Eri, the family of the Erites;
[17] Of Arod, the family of the Arodites; of Areli, the family of the Arelites.
[18] These, the families of the sons of Gad according to their numbering, totaled 40,500.
[19] The sons of Judah were Er and Onan, but Er and Onan died in the land of Canaan.
[20] And the sons of Judah according to their families were: of Shelah, the family of the Shelanites; of Perez, the family of the Perezites; of Zerah, the family of the Zerahites.
[21] And the sons of Perez were: of Hezron, the family of the Hezronites; of Hamul, the family of the Hamulites.
[22] These, the families of Judah according to their numbering, totaled 76,500.
[23] The sons of Issachar after their families: of Tola, the family of the Tolaites; of Puvah, the family of the Punites;
[24] Of Jashub, the family of the Jashubites; of Shimron, the family of the Shimronites.
[25] These, the families of Issachar according to their numbering, totaled 64,300.
[26] The sons of Zebulun after their families: of Sered, the family of the Seredites; of Elon, the family of the Elonites; of Jahleel, the family of the Jahleelites.
[27] These, the families of the Zebulunites according to their numbering, totaled 60,500.
[28] The sons of Joseph after their families were Manasseh and Ephraim.
[29] The sons of Manasseh: of Machir, the family of the Machirites (and Machir was the father of Gilead); of Gilead, the family of the Gileadites.
[30] These are the sons of Gilead: of Iezer, the family of the Iezerites; of Helek, the family of the Helekites;
[31] Of Asriel, the family of the Asrielites; of Shechem, the family of the Shechemites;
[32] Of Shemida, the family of the Shemidaites; and of Hepher, the family of the Hepherites.

---

[a] 17 Samaritan Pentateuch and Syriac (see also Gen. 46:16); Masoretic Text *Arod*   [b] 23 Samaritan Pentateuch, Septuagint, Vulgate and Syriac (see also 1 Chron. 7:1); Masoretic Text *through Puvah, the Punite*

## New International Version

33 (Zelophehad son of Hepher had no sons; he had only daughters, whose names were Mahlah, Noah, Hoglah, Milkah and Tirzah.)
34 These were the clans of Manasseh; those numbered were 52,700.

35 These were the descendants of Ephraim by their clans:
through Shuthelah, the Shuthelahite clan;
through Beker, the Bekerite clan;
through Tahan, the Tahanite clan.
36 These were the descendants of Shuthelah:
through Eran, the Eranite clan.
37 These were the clans of Ephraim; those numbered were 32,500.

These were the descendants of Joseph by their clans.

38 The descendants of Benjamin by their clans were:
through Bela, the Belaite clan;
through Ashbel, the Ashbelite clan;
through Ahiram, the Ahiramite clan;
39 through Shupham,[a] the Shuphamite clan;
through Hupham, the Huphamite clan.
40 The descendants of Bela through Ard and Naaman were:
through Ard,[b] the Ardite clan;
through Naaman, the Naamite clan.
41 These were the clans of Benjamin; those numbered were 45,600.

42 These were the descendants of Dan by their clans:
through Shuham, the Shuhamite clan.
These were the clans of Dan: 43 All of them were Shuhamite clans; and those numbered were 64,400.

44 The descendants of Asher by their clans were:
through Imnah, the Imnite clan;
through Ishvi, the Ishvite clan;
through Beriah, the Beriite clan;
45 and through the descendants of Beriah:
through Heber, the Heberite clan;
through Malkiel, the Malkielite clan.
46 (Asher had a daughter named Serah.)
47 These were the clans of Asher; those numbered were 53,400.

48 The descendants of Naphtali by their clans were:
through Jahzeel, the Jahzeelite clan;
through Guni, the Gunite clan;
49 through Jezer, the Jezerite clan;
through Shillem, the Shillemite clan.
50 These were the clans of Naphtali; those numbered were 45,400.

51 The total number of the men of Israel was 601,730.

52 The Lord said to Moses, 53 "The land is to be allotted to them as an inheritance based on the number of names. 54 To a larger group give a larger inheritance, and to a smaller group a smaller one; each is to receive its inheritance according to the number of those listed. 55 Be sure that the land is distributed by lot. What each group inherits will be according to the names for its ancestral tribe. 56 Each inheritance is to be distributed by lot among the larger and smaller groups."

57 These were the Levites who were counted by their clans:
through Gershon, the Gershonite clan;
through Kohath, the Kohathite clan;
through Merari, the Merarite clan.
58 These also were Levite clans:
the Libnite clan,

## Amplified Bible

33 Zelophehad son of Hepher had no sons, but only daughters, and their names were Mahlah, Noah, Hoglah, Milcah, and Tirzah.
34 These are the families of Manasseh, and their number was 52,700.
35 These are the sons of Ephraim according to their families: of Shuthelah, the family of the Shuthelahites; of Becher, the family of the Becherites; of Tahan, the family of the Tahanites.
36 And these are the sons of Shuthelah: of Eran, the family of the Eranites.
37 These, the families of the sons of Ephraim according to their number, totaled 32,500. These are the sons of Joseph after their families.
38 The sons of Benjamin according to their families: of Bela, the family of the Belaites; of Ashbel, the family of the Ashbelites; of Ahiram, the family of the Ahiramites;
39 Of Shephupham, the family of the Shuphamites; of Hupham, the family of the Huphamites.
40 And the sons of Bela were Ard and Naaman; of Ard, the family of the Ardites; of Naaman, the family of the Naamites.
41 These are the sons of Benjamin according to their families; and their number was 45,600.
42 These are the sons of Dan according to their families: of Shuham, the family of the Shuhamites. These are the families of Dan according to their families.
43 All the families of the Shuhamites according to their number were 64,400.
44 Of the sons of Asher according to their families: of Imnah, the family of the Imnites; of Ishvi, the family of the Ishvites; of Beriah, the family of the Beriites.
45 Of the sons of Beriah: of Heber, the family of the Heberites; of Malchiel, the family of the Malchielites.
46 And the name of the daughter of Asher was Serah.
47 These, the families of the sons of Asher according to their number, totaled 53,400.
48 Of the sons of Naphtali after their families: of Jahzeel, the family of the Jahzeelites; of Guni, the family of the Gunites;
49 Of Jezer, the family of the Jezerites; of Shillem, the family of the Shillemites.
50 These are the families of Naphtali according to their families; and their number totaled 45,400.
51 This was the number of the Israelites, 601,730.
52 And the Lord said to Moses,
53 To these the land shall be divided for inheritance according to the number of names.
54 To a larger tribe you shall give the greater inheritance, and to a small tribe the less inheritance; to each tribe shall its inheritance be given according to its numbers.
55 But the land shall be divided by lot; according to the names of the tribes of their fathers they shall inherit.
56 According to the lot shall their inheritance be divided between the larger and the smaller.
57 And these were numbered of the Levites according to their families: of Gershon, the family of the Gershonites; of Kohath, the family of the Kohathites; of Merari, the family of the Merarites.
58 These are the families of Levi: the family of the

---

a 39 A few manuscripts of the Masoretic Text, Samaritan Pentateuch, Vulgate and Syriac (see also Septuagint); most manuscripts of the Masoretic Text Shephupham    b 40 Samaritan Pentateuch and Vulgate (see also Septuagint); Masoretic Text does not have through Ard.

## New International Version

the Hebronite clan,
the Mahlite clan,
the Mushite clan,
the Korahite clan.
(Kohath was the forefather of Amram; 59the name of Amram's wife was Jochebed, a descendant of Levi, who was born to the Levites[a] in Egypt. To Amram she bore Aaron, Moses and their sister Miriam. 60Aaron was the father of Nadab and Abihu, Eleazar and Ithamar. 61But Nadab and Abihu died when they made an offering before the LORD with unauthorized fire.)

62All the male Levites a month old or more numbered 23,000. They were not counted along with the other Israelites because they received no inheritance among them.

63These are the ones counted by Moses and Eleazar the priest when they counted the Israelites on the plains of Moab by the Jordan across from Jericho. 64Not one of them was among those counted by Moses and Aaron the priest when they counted the Israelites in the Desert of Sinai. 65For the LORD had told those Israelites they would surely die in the wilderness, and not one of them was left except Caleb son of Jephunneh and Joshua son of Nun.

### Zelophehad's Daughters

**27** The daughters of Zelophehad son of Hepher, the son of Gilead, the son of Makir, the son of Manasseh, belonged to the clans of Manasseh son of Joseph. The names of the daughters were Mahlah, Noah, Hoglah, Milkah and Tirzah. They came forward 2and stood before Moses, Eleazar the priest, the leaders and the whole assembly at the entrance to the tent of meeting and said, 3"Our father died in the wilderness. He was not among Korah's followers, who banded together against the LORD, but he died for his own sin and left no sons. 4Why should our father's name disappear from his clan because he had no son? Give us property among our father's relatives."

5So Moses brought their case before the LORD, 6and the LORD said to him, 7"What Zelophehad's daughters are saying is right. You must certainly give them property as an inheritance among their father's relatives and give their father's inheritance to them.

8"Say to the Israelites, 'If a man dies and leaves no son, give his inheritance to his daughter. 9If he has no daughter, give his inheritance to his brothers. 10If he has no brothers, give his inheritance to his father's brothers. 11If his father had no brothers, give his inheritance to the nearest relative in his clan, that he may possess it. This is to have the force of law for the Israelites, as the LORD commanded Moses.'"

### Joshua to Succeed Moses

12Then the LORD said to Moses, "Go up this mountain in the Abarim Range and see the land I have given the Israelites. 13After you have seen it, you too will be gathered to your people, as your brother Aaron was, 14for when the community rebelled at the waters in the Desert of Zin, both of you disobeyed my command to honor me as holy before their eyes." (These were the waters of Meribah Kadesh, in the Desert of Zin.)

15Moses said to the LORD, 16"May the LORD, the God who gives breath to all living things, appoint someone

## Amplified Bible

Libnites, the family of the Hebronites, the family of the Mahlites, the family of the Mushites, the family of the Korahites. And Kohath was the father of Amram.

59Amram's wife was Jochebed daughter of Levi, who was born to Levi in Egypt; and she bore to Amram Aaron, Moses, and Miriam their sister.

60And to Aaron were born Nadab, Abihu, Eleazar, and Ithamar.

61But Nadab and Abihu died when they offered strange and unholy fire before the Lord.

62And those numbered of them were 23,000, every male from a month old and upward; for they were not numbered among the Israelites, because there was no inheritance given them among the Israelites.

63These were those numbered by Moses and Eleazar the priest, who numbered the Israelites in the plains of Moab by the Jordan at Jericho.

64But among these there was not a man of those numbered by Moses and Aaron the priest when they numbered the Israelites in the Wilderness of Sinai.

65For the Lord had said of them, They shall surely die in the wilderness. There was not left a man of them except Caleb son of Jephunneh and Joshua son of Nun.

**27** Then came the daughters of Zelophehad son of Hepher, the son of Gilead, the son of Machir, the son of Manasseh, from the families of Manasseh son of Joseph. The names of his daughters: Mahlah, Noah, Hoglah, Milcah, and Tirzah.

2They stood before Moses, Eleazar the priest, and the leaders, and all the congregation at the door of the Tent of Meeting, saying,

3Our father died in the wilderness. He was not among those who assembled together against the Lord in the company of Korah, but died for his own sin [as did all those who rebelled at Kadesh], and he had no sons. [Num. 14:26-35.]

4Why should the name of our father be removed from his family because he had no son? Give to us a possession among our father's brethren.

5Moses brought their case before the Lord.

6And the Lord said to Moses,

7The daughters of Zelophehad are justified and speak correctly. You shall surely give them an inheritance among their father's brethren, and you shall cause their father's inheritance to pass to them.

8And say to the Israelites, If a man dies and has no son, you shall cause his inheritance to pass to his daughter.

9If he has no daughter, you shall give his inheritance to his brethren.

10If he has no brethren, give his inheritance to his father's brethren.

11And if his father has no brethren, then give his inheritance to his next of kin, and he shall possess it. It shall be to the Israelites a statute and ordinance, as the Lord commanded Moses.

12And the Lord said to Moses, Go up into this mountain of Abarim and behold the land I have given to the Israelites.

13And when you have seen it, you also shall be gathered to your [departed] people as Aaron your brother was gathered,

14For you disobeyed My order in the Wilderness of Zin during the strife of the congregation to uphold My sanctity [by strict obedience to My authority] at the waters before their eyes. [These are the waters of Meribah in Kadesh in the Wilderness of Zin.] [Num. 20:10-12.]

15And Moses said to the Lord,

16Let the Lord, the God of the spirits of all flesh, set a man over the congregation

---

[a] 59 Or *Jochebed, a daughter of Levi, who was born to Levi*

## New International Version

over this community [17]to go out and come in before them, one who will lead them out and bring them in, so the LORD's people will not be like sheep without a shepherd."

[18]So the LORD said to Moses, "Take Joshua son of Nun, a man in whom is the spirit of leadership,[a] and lay your hand on him. [19]Have him stand before Eleazar the priest and the entire assembly and commission him in their presence. [20]Give him some of your authority so the whole Israelite community will obey him. [21]He is to stand before Eleazar the priest, who will obtain decisions for him by inquiring of the Urim before the LORD. At his command he and the entire community of the Israelites will go out, and at his command they will come in."

[22]Moses did as the LORD commanded him. He took Joshua and had him stand before Eleazar the priest and the whole assembly. [23]Then he laid his hands on him and commissioned him, as the LORD instructed through Moses.

### Daily Offerings

**28** The LORD said to Moses, [2]"Give this command to the Israelites and say to them: 'Make sure that you present to me at the appointed time my food offerings, as an aroma pleasing to me.' [3]Say to them: 'This is the food offering you are to present to the LORD: two lambs a year old without defect, as a regular burnt offering each day. [4]Offer one lamb in the morning and the other at twilight, [5]together with a grain offering of a tenth of an ephah[b] of the finest flour mixed with a quarter of a hin[c] of oil from pressed olives. [6]This is the regular burnt offering instituted at Mount Sinai as a pleasing aroma, a food offering presented to the LORD. [7]The accompanying drink offering is to be a quarter of a hin of fermented drink with each lamb. Pour out the drink offering to the LORD at the sanctuary. [8]Offer the second lamb at twilight, along with the same kind of grain offering and drink offering that you offer in the morning. This is a food offering, an aroma pleasing to the LORD.

### Sabbath Offerings

[9]"On the Sabbath day, make an offering of two lambs a year old without defect, together with its drink offering and a grain offering of two-tenths of an ephah[d] of the finest flour mixed with olive oil. [10]This is the burnt offering for every Sabbath, in addition to the regular burnt offering and its drink offering.

### Monthly Offerings

[11]"'On the first of every month, present to the LORD a burnt offering of two young bulls, one ram and seven male lambs a year old, all without defect. [12]With each bull there is to be a grain offering of three-tenths of an ephah[e] of the finest flour mixed with oil; with the ram, a grain offering of two-tenths of an ephah of the finest flour mixed with oil; [13]and with each lamb, a grain offering of a tenth of an ephah of the finest flour mixed with oil. This is for a burnt offering, a pleasing aroma, a food offering presented to the LORD. [14]With each bull there is to be a drink offering of half a hin[f] of wine; with the ram, a third of a hin[g]; and with each lamb, a quarter of a hin. This is the monthly burnt offering to be made at each new moon during the

## Amplified Bible

[17]Who shall go out and come in before them, leading them out and bringing them in, that the congregation of the Lord may not be as sheep which have no shepherd.

[18]The Lord said to Moses, Take Joshua son of Nun, a man in whom is the Spirit, and lay your hand upon him;

[19]And set him before Eleazar the priest and all the congregation and give him a charge in their sight.

[20]And put some of your honor *and* authority upon him, that all the congregation of the Israelites may obey him.

[21]He shall stand before Eleazar the priest, who shall inquire for him before the Lord by the judgment of the Urim [one of two articles in the priest's breastplate worn when asking counsel of the Lord for the people]. At Joshua's word the people shall go out and come in, both he and all the Israelite congregation with him.

[22]And Moses did as the Lord commanded him. He took Joshua and set him before Eleazar the priest and all the congregation,

[23]And he laid his hands upon him and commissioned him, as the Lord commanded through Moses.

**28** And the Lord said to Moses, [2]Command the Israelites, saying, My offering, My food for My offerings made by fire, My sweet *and* soothing odor you shall be careful to offer to Me at its proper time.

[3]And you shall say to the people, This is the offering made by fire which you shall offer to the Lord: two male lambs a year old without spot *or* blemish, two day by day, for a continual burnt offering.

[4]One lamb you shall offer in the morning and the other in the evening,

[5]Also a tenth of an ephah of flour for a cereal offering, mixed with a fourth of a hin of beaten oil.

[6]It is a continual burnt offering which was ordained in Mount Sinai for a sweet *and* soothing odor, an offering made by fire to the Lord.

[7]Its drink offering shall be a fourth of a hin for each lamb; in the Holy Place you shall pour out a fermented drink offering to the Lord.

[8]And the other lamb you shall offer in the evening; like the cereal offering of the morning and like its drink offering, you shall offer it, an offering made by fire, a sweet *and* soothing odor to the Lord.

[9]And on the Sabbath day two male lambs a year old without spot *or* blemish, and two-tenths of an ephah of flour for a cereal offering, mixed with oil, and its drink offering.

[10]This is the burnt offering of every Sabbath, besides the continual burnt offering and its drink offering.

[11]And at the beginning of your months you shall offer a burnt offering to the Lord: two young bulls, one ram, seven male lambs a year old without spot *or* blemish;

[12]And three-tenths of an ephah of fine flour for a cereal offering, mixed with oil, for each bull; and two-tenths of an ephah of fine flour for a cereal offering, mixed with oil, for the one ram.

[13]And a tenth part of fine flour mixed with oil as a cereal offering, for each lamb, for a burnt offering of a sweet *and* pleasant fragrance, an offering made by fire to the Lord.

[14]And their drink offerings shall be half a hin of wine for a bull, and a third of a hin for a ram, and a fourth of a hin for a lamb. This is the burnt offering of each month throughout the months of the year.

---

[a] 18 Or *the Spirit*    [b] 5 That is, probably about 3 1/2 pounds or about 1.6 kilograms; also in verses 13, 21 and 29    [c] 5 That is, about 1 quart or about 1 liter; also in verses 7 and 14    [d] 9 That is, probably about 7 pounds or about 3.2 kilograms; also in verses 12, 20 and 28    [e] 12 That is, probably about 11 pounds or about 5 kilograms; also in verses 20 and 28    [f] 14 That is, about 2 quarts or about 1.9 liters    [g] 14 That is, about 1 1/3 quarts or about 1.3 liters

## New International Version

year. [15] Besides the regular burnt offering with its drink offering, one male goat is to be presented to the LORD as a sin offering.[a]

### The Passover

[16] "'On the fourteenth day of the first month the LORD's Passover is to be held. [17] On the fifteenth day of this month there is to be a festival; for seven days eat bread made without yeast. [18] On the first day hold a sacred assembly and do no regular work. [19] Present to the LORD a food offering consisting of a burnt offering of two young bulls, one ram and seven male lambs a year old, all without defect. [20] With each bull offer a grain offering of three-tenths of an ephah of the finest flour mixed with oil; with the ram, two-tenths; [21] and with each of the seven lambs, one-tenth. [22] Include one male goat as a sin offering to make atonement for you. [23] Offer these in addition to the regular morning burnt offering. [24] In this way present the food offering every day for seven days as an aroma pleasing to the LORD; it is to be offered in addition to the regular burnt offering and its drink offering. [25] On the seventh day hold a sacred assembly and do no regular work.

### The Festival of Weeks

[26] "'On the day of firstfruits, when you present to the LORD an offering of new grain during the Festival of Weeks, hold a sacred assembly and do no regular work. [27] Present a burnt offering of two young bulls, one ram and seven male lambs a year old as an aroma pleasing to the LORD. [28] With each bull there is to be a grain offering of three-tenths of an ephah of the finest flour mixed with oil; with the ram, two-tenths; [29] and with each of the seven lambs, one-tenth. [30] Include one male goat to make atonement for you. [31] Offer these together with their drink offerings, in addition to the regular burnt offering and its grain offering. Be sure the animals are without defect.

### The Festival of Trumpets

**29** "'On the first day of the seventh month hold a sacred assembly and do no regular work. It is a day for you to sound the trumpets. [2] As an aroma pleasing to the LORD, offer a burnt offering of one young bull, one ram and seven male lambs a year old, all without defect. [3] With the bull offer a grain offering of three-tenths of an ephah[b] of the finest flour mixed with olive oil; with the ram, two-tenths[c]; [4] and with each of the seven lambs, one-tenth.[d] [5] Include one male goat as a sin offering[e] to make atonement for you. [6] These are in addition to the monthly and daily burnt offerings with their grain offerings and drink offerings as specified. They are food offerings presented to the LORD, a pleasing aroma.

### The Day of Atonement

[7] "'On the tenth day of this seventh month hold a sacred assembly. You must deny yourselves[f] and do no work. [8] Present as an aroma pleasing to the LORD a burnt offering

---

*a 15 Or purification offering; also in verse 22   b 3 That is, probably about 11 pounds or about 5 kilograms; also in verses 9 and 14   c 3 That is, probably about 7 pounds or about 3.2 kilograms; also in verses 9 and 14   d 4 That is, probably about 3 1/2 pounds or about 1.6 kilograms; also in verses 10 and 15   e 5 Or purification offering; also elsewhere in this chapter   f 7 Or must fast*

## Amplified Bible

[15] And one male goat for a sin offering to the Lord—it shall be offered in addition to the continual burnt offering and its drink offering.

[16] On the fourteenth day of the first month is the Lord's Passover.

[17] On the fifteenth day of this month is a feast; for seven days shall unleavened bread be eaten.

[18] On the first day there shall be a holy [summoned] assembly; you shall do no servile work that day.

[19] But you shall offer an offering made by fire, a burnt offering to the Lord: two young bulls, one ram, and seven male lambs a year old; they shall be without blemish to the best of your knowledge.

[20] And their cereal offering shall be of fine flour mixed with oil; three-tenths of an ephah shall you offer for a bull, and two-tenths for a ram;

[21] A tenth shall you offer for each of the seven male lambs,

[22] Also one male goat for a sin offering to make atonement for you.

[23] You shall offer these in addition to the burnt offering of the morning, which is for a continual burnt offering.

[24] In this way you shall offer daily for seven days the food of an offering made by fire, a sweet *and* soothing odor to the Lord; it shall be offered in addition to the continual burnt offering and its drink offering.

[25] And on the seventh day you shall have a holy [summoned] assembly; you shall do no work befitting a slave *or* a servant.

[26] Also in the day of the firstfruits, when you offer a cereal offering of new grain to the Lord at your Feast of Weeks, you shall have a holy [summoned] assembly; you shall do no servile work.

[27] But you shall offer the burnt offering for a sweet, pleasing, *and* soothing fragrance to the Lord: two young bulls, one ram, seven male lambs a year old,

[28] And their cereal offering of fine flour mixed with oil, three-tenths of an ephah for each bull, two-tenths for one ram,

[29] A tenth for each of the seven male lambs,

[30] And one male goat to make atonement for you.

[31] You shall offer them in addition to the continual burnt offering and its cereal offering and their drink offerings. See that they are without blemish.

**29** On the first day of the seventh month [on New Year's Day of the civil year], you shall have a holy [summoned] assembly; you shall do no servile work. It is a day of blowing of trumpets for you [everyone blowing who wishes, proclaiming that the glad New Year has come and that the great Day of Atonement and the Feast of Tabernacles are now approaching].

[2] And you shall offer a burnt offering for a sweet *and* pleasing odor to the Lord: one young bull, one ram, and seven male lambs a year old without blemish.

[3] Their cereal offering shall be of fine flour mixed with oil, three-tenths of an ephah for a bull, two-tenths for a ram,

[4] And one-tenth of an ephah for each of the seven lambs,

[5] And one male goat for a sin offering to make atonement for you.

[6] These are in addition to the burnt offering of the new moon and its cereal offering, and the daily burnt offering and its cereal offering, and their drink offerings, according to the ordinance for them, for a pleasant *and* soothing fragrance, an offering made by fire to the Lord.

[7] And you shall have on the tenth day of this seventh month a holy [summoned] assembly; [it is the great Day of Atonement, a day of humiliation] and you shall humble *and* abase yourselves; you shall not do any work in it.

[8] But you shall offer a burnt offering to the Lord for a

## New International Version

of one young bull, one ram and seven male lambs a year old, all without defect. [9]With the bull offer a grain offering of three-tenths of an ephah of the finest flour mixed with oil; with the ram, two-tenths; [10]and with each of the seven lambs, one-tenth. [11]Include one male goat as a sin offering, in addition to the sin offering for atonement and the regular burnt offering with its grain offering, and their drink offerings.

### The Festival of Tabernacles

[12]"'On the fifteenth day of the seventh month, hold a sacred assembly and do no regular work. Celebrate a festival to the LORD for seven days. [13]Present as an aroma pleasing to the LORD a food offering consisting of a burnt offering of thirteen young bulls, two rams and fourteen male lambs a year old, all without defect. [14]With each of the thirteen bulls offer a grain offering of three-tenths of an ephah of the finest flour mixed with oil; with each of the two rams, two-tenths; [15]and with each of the fourteen lambs, one-tenth. [16]Include one male goat as a sin offering, in addition to the regular burnt offering with its grain offering and drink offering.

[17]"'On the second day offer twelve young bulls, two rams and fourteen male lambs a year old, all without defect. [18]With the bulls, rams and lambs, offer their grain offerings and drink offerings according to the number specified. [19]Include one male goat as a sin offering, in addition to the regular burnt offering with its grain offering, and their drink offerings.

[20]"'On the third day offer eleven bulls, two rams and fourteen male lambs a year old, all without defect. [21]With the bulls, rams and lambs, offer their grain offerings and drink offerings according to the number specified. [22]Include one male goat as a sin offering, in addition to the regular burnt offering with its grain offering and drink offering.

[23]"'On the fourth day offer ten bulls, two rams and fourteen male lambs a year old, all without defect. [24]With the bulls, rams and lambs, offer their grain offerings and drink offerings according to the number specified. [25]Include one male goat as a sin offering, in addition to the regular burnt offering with its grain offering and drink offering.

[26]"'On the fifth day offer nine bulls, two rams and fourteen male lambs a year old, all without defect. [27]With the bulls, rams and lambs, offer their grain offerings and drink offerings according to the number specified. [28]Include one male goat as a sin offering, in addition to the regular burnt offering with its grain offering and drink offering.

[29]"'On the sixth day offer eight bulls, two rams and fourteen male lambs a year old, all without defect. [30]With the bulls, rams and lambs, offer their grain offerings and drink offerings according to the number specified. [31]Include one male goat as a sin offering, in addition to the regular burnt offering with its grain offering and drink offering.

[32]"'On the seventh day offer seven bulls, two rams and fourteen male lambs a year old, all without defect. [33]With the bulls, rams and lambs, offer their grain offerings and drink offerings according to the number specified. [34]In-

## Amplified Bible

sweet *and* soothing fragrance: one young bull, one ram, and seven male lambs a year old. See that they are without blemish.

[9]And their cereal offering shall be of fine flour mixed with oil, three-tenths of an ephah for the bull, two-tenths for the one ram,

[10]A tenth for each of the seven male lambs,

[11]One male goat for a sin offering, in addition to the sin offering of atonement, and the continual burnt offering and its cereal offering, and their drink offerings.

[12]And on the fifteenth day of the seventh month you shall have a holy [summoned] assembly; you shall do no servile work, and you shall keep a feast to the Lord for seven days.

[13]And you shall offer a burnt offering, an offering made by fire, of a sweet *and* pleasing fragrance to the Lord: thirteen young bulls, two rams, and fourteen male lambs a year old; they shall be without blemish.

[14]And their cereal offering shall be of fine flour mixed with oil, three-tenths of an ephah for each of the thirteen bulls, two-tenths for each of the two rams,

[15]And a tenth part for each of the fourteen male lambs,

[16]Also one male goat for a sin offering, in addition to the continual burnt offering, its cereal offering, and its drink offering.

[17]And on the second day you shall offer twelve young bulls, two rams, fourteen male lambs a year old without spot *or* blemish,

[18]With their cereal offering and the drink offerings for the bulls, the rams, and the lambs, by number according to the ordinance,

[19]Also one male goat for a sin offering, besides the continual burnt offering, its cereal offering, and their drink offerings.

[20]And on the third day eleven bulls, two rams, fourteen male lambs a year old without blemish,

[21]With their cereal offering and drink offerings for the bulls, the rams, and the lambs, by number according to the ordinance,

[22]And one male goat for a sin offering, besides the continual burnt offering, its cereal offering, and its drink offerings,

[23]On the fourth day ten bulls, two rams, and fourteen male lambs a year old without blemish,

[24]Their cereal offering and their drink offerings for the bulls, the rams, and the lambs shall be by number according to the ordinance,

[25]And one male goat for a sin offering, besides the continual burnt offering, its cereal offering, and its drink offerings,

[26]And on the fifth day nine bulls, two rams, and fourteen male lambs a year old without spot *or* blemish,

[27]And their cereal offering and drink offerings for the bulls, the rams, and the lambs, by number according to the ordinance,

[28]And one goat for a sin offering, besides the continual burnt offering, and its cereal offering, and its drink offerings.

[29]And on the sixth day eight bulls, two rams, and fourteen male lambs a year old without blemish,

[30]And their cereal offering and their drink offerings for the bulls, the rams, and the lambs, by number according to the ordinance,

[31]And one goat for a sin offering, besides the continual burnt offering, its cereal offering, and its drink offerings.

[32]And on the seventh day seven bulls, two rams, and fourteen male lambs a year old without blemish,

[33]And their cereal and drink offerings for the bulls, the rams, and the lambs, by number according to the ordinance.

## New International Version

clude one male goat as a sin offering, in addition to the regular burnt offering with its grain offering and drink offering. ³⁵"'On the eighth day hold a closing special assembly and do no regular work. ³⁶Present as an aroma pleasing to the LORD a food offering consisting of a burnt offering of one bull, one ram and seven male lambs a year old, all without defect. ³⁷With the bull, the ram and the lambs, offer their grain offerings and drink offerings according to the number specified. ³⁸Include one male goat as a sin offering, in addition to the regular burnt offering with its grain offering and drink offering.

³⁹"'In addition to what you vow and your freewill offerings, offer these to the LORD at your appointed festivals: your burnt offerings, grain offerings, drink offerings and fellowship offerings.'"

⁴⁰Moses told the Israelites all that the LORD commanded him.ᵃ

### Vows

**30** ᵇ Moses said to the heads of the tribes of Israel: ²"This is what the LORD commands: ²When a man makes a vow to the LORD or takes an oath to obligate himself by a pledge, he must not break his word but must do everything he said.

³"When a young woman still living in her father's household makes a vow to the LORD or obligates herself by a pledge ⁴and her father hears about her vow or pledge but says nothing to her, then all her vows and every pledge by which she obligated herself will stand. ⁵But if her father forbids her when he hears about it, none of her vows or the pledges by which she obligated herself will stand; the LORD will release her because her father has forbidden her.

⁶"If she marries after she makes a vow or after her lips utter a rash promise by which she obligates herself ⁷and her husband hears about it but says nothing to her, then her vows or the pledges by which she obligated herself will stand. ⁸But if her husband forbids her when he hears about it, he nullifies the vow that obligates her or the rash promise by which she obligates herself, and the LORD will release her.

⁹"Any vow or obligation taken by a widow or divorced woman will be binding on her.

¹⁰"If a woman living with her husband makes a vow or obligates herself by a pledge under oath ¹¹and her husband hears about it but says nothing to her and does not forbid her, then all her vows or the pledges by which she obligated herself will stand. ¹²But if her husband nullifies them when he hears about them, then none of the vows or pledges that came from her lips will stand. Her husband has nullified them, and the LORD will release her. ¹³Her husband may confirm or nullify any vow she makes or any sworn pledge to deny herself.ᶜ ¹⁴But if her husband says nothing to her about it from day to day, then he confirms all her vows or the pledges binding on her. He confirms them by saying nothing to her when he hears about them.

## Amplified Bible

³⁴And one male goat for a sin offering, besides the continual burnt offering, and its cereal offering, and its drink offerings.

³⁵On the eighth day you shall have a solemn assembly; you shall do no servile work.

³⁶You shall offer a burnt offering, an offering made by fire, of a sweet *and* pleasing fragrance to the Lord: one bull, one ram, seven male lambs a year old without blemish,

³⁷Their cereal offering and drink offerings for the bull, the ram, and the lambs shall be by number according to the ordinance,

³⁸And one male goat for a sin offering, besides the continual burnt offering, and its cereal offering, and its drink offerings.

³⁹These you shall offer to the Lord at your appointed feasts, besides the offerings you have vowed and your freewill offerings, for your burnt offerings, cereal offerings, drink offerings, and peace offerings.

⁴⁰And Moses told the Israelites all that the Lord commanded him.

**30** And Moses said to the heads *or* leaders of the tribes of Israel, This is the thing which the Lord has commanded:

²If a man vows a vow to the Lord or swears an oath to bind himself by a pledge, he shall not break *and* profane his word; he shall do according to all that proceeds out of his mouth.

³Also when a woman vows a vow to the Lord and binds herself by a pledge, being in her father's house in her youth,

⁴And her father hears her vow and her pledge with which she has bound herself and he offers no objection, then all her vows shall stand and every pledge with which she has bound herself shall stand.

⁵But if her father refuses to allow her [to carry out her vow] on the day that he hears about it, not any of her vows or of her pledges with which she has bound herself shall stand. And the Lord will forgive her because her father refused to let her [carry out her purpose].

⁶And if she is married to a husband while her vows are upon her or she has bound herself by a rash utterance

⁷And her husband hears of it and holds his peace concerning it on the day that he hears it, then her vows shall stand and her pledge with which she bound herself shall stand.

⁸But if her husband refuses to allow her [to keep her vow or pledge] on the day that he hears of it, then he shall make void *and* annul her vow which is upon her and the rash utterance of her lips by which she bound herself, and the Lord will forgive her.

⁹But the vow of a widow or of a divorced woman, with which she has bound herself, shall stand against her.

¹⁰And if she vowed in her husband's house or bound herself by a pledge with an oath

¹¹And her husband heard it and did not oppose or prohibit her, then all her vows and every pledge with which she bound herself shall stand.

¹²But if her husband positively made them void on the day he heard them, then whatever proceeded out of her lips concerning her vows or concerning her pledge of herself shall not stand. Her husband has annulled them, and the Lord will forgive her.

¹³Every vow and every binding oath to humble *or* afflict herself, her husband may establish it or her husband may annul it.

¹⁴But if her husband altogether holds his peace [concerning the matter] with her from day to day, then he establishes *and* confirms all her vows or all her pledges which are upon her. He establishes them because he said nothing to [restrain] her on the day he heard of them.

ᵃ 40 In Hebrew texts this verse (29:40) is numbered 30:1. ᵇ In Hebrew texts 30:1-16 is numbered 30:2-17. ᶜ 13 Or *to fast*

## New International Version

15If, however, he nullifies them some time after he hears about them, then he must bear the consequences of her wrongdoing."

16These are the regulations the LORD gave Moses concerning relationships between a man and his wife, and between a father and his young daughter still living at home.

### Vengeance on the Midianites

**31** The LORD said to Moses, 2"Take vengeance on the Midianites for the Israelites. After that, you will be gathered to your people."

3So Moses said to the people, "Arm some of your men to go to war against the Midianites so that they may carry out the LORD's vengeance on them. 4Send into battle a thousand men from each of the tribes of Israel." 5So twelve thousand men armed for battle, a thousand from each tribe, were supplied from the clans of Israel. 6Moses sent them into battle, a thousand from each tribe, along with Phinehas son of Eleazar, the priest, who took with him articles from the sanctuary and the trumpets for signaling.

7They fought against Midian, as the LORD commanded Moses, and killed every man. 8Among their victims were Evi, Rekem, Zur, Hur and Reba—the five kings of Midian. They also killed Balaam son of Beor with the sword. 9The Israelites captured the Midianite women and children and took all the Midianite herds, flocks and goods as plunder. 10They burned all the towns where the Midianites had settled, as well as all their camps. 11They took all the plunder and spoils, including the people and animals, 12and brought the captives, spoils and plunder to Moses and Eleazar the priest and the Israelite assembly at their camp on the plains of Moab, by the Jordan across from Jericho.

13Moses, Eleazar the priest and all the leaders of the community went to meet them outside the camp. 14Moses was angry with the officers of the army—the commanders of thousands and commanders of hundreds—who returned from the battle.

15"Have you allowed all the women to live?" he asked them. 16"They were the ones who followed Balaam's advice and enticed the Israelites to be unfaithful to the LORD in the Peor incident, so that a plague struck the LORD's people. 17Now kill all the boys. And kill every woman who has slept with a man, 18but save for yourselves every girl who has never slept with a man.

19"Anyone who has killed someone or touched someone who was killed must stay outside the camp seven days. On the third and seventh days you must purify yourselves and your captives. 20Purify every garment as well as everything made of leather, goat hair or wood."

21Then Eleazar the priest said to the soldiers who had gone into battle, "This is what is required by the law that the LORD gave Moses: 22Gold, silver, bronze, iron, tin, lead 23and anything else that can withstand fire must be put through the fire, and then it will be clean. But it must also be purified with the water of cleansing. And whatever cannot withstand fire must be put through that water. 24On

## Amplified Bible

15But if he shall nullify them after he hears of them, then he shall be responsible for *and* bear her iniquity.

16These are the statutes which the Lord commanded Moses, between a man and his wife, and between a father and his daughter while in her youth in her father's house.

**31** The Lord said to Moses, 2Avenge the Israelites on the Midianites; afterward you shall be gathered to your [departed] people.

3And Moses said to the people, Arm men from among you for the war, that they may go against Midian and execute the Lord's vengeance on Midian [for seducing Israel]. [Num. 25:16-18.]

4From each of the tribes of Israel you shall send 1,000 to the war.

5So there were provided out of the thousands of Israel 1,000 from each tribe, 12,000 armed for war.

6And Moses sent them to the war, 1,000 from each tribe, together with Phinehas son of Eleazar, the priest, with the [sacred] vessels of the sanctuary and the trumpets to blow the alarm in his hand.

7They fought with Midian, as the Lord commanded Moses, and slew every male,

8Including the five kings of Midian: Evi, Rekem, Zur, Hur, and Reba; also Balaam son of Beor they slew with the sword. [Num. 22:31-35; Neh. 13:1, 2.]

9And the Israelites took captive the women of Midian and their little ones, and all their cattle, their flocks, and their goods as booty.

10They burned all the cities in which they dwelt, and all their encampments.

11And they took all the spoil and all the prey, both of man and of beast.

12Then they brought the captives, the prey, and the spoil to Moses and Eleazar the priest and to the congregation of the Israelites at the camp on the plains of Moab by Jordan at Jericho.

13Moses and Eleazar the priest and all the princes *or* leaders of the congregation went to meet them outside the camp.

14But Moses was angry with the officers of the army, the commanders of thousands and of hundreds, who served in the war.

15And Moses said to them, Have you let all the women live?

16Behold, these caused the Israelites by the counsel of Balaam to trespass *and* act treacherously against the Lord in the matter of Peor, and so a [smiting] plague came among the congregation of the Lord. [Num. 25:1-9; 31:8.]

17Now therefore, kill every male among the little ones, and kill every woman who is not a virgin.

18But all the young girls who have not known man by lying with him keep alive for yourselves.

19Encamp outside the camp seven days; whoever has killed any person and whoever has touched any slain, purify yourselves and your captives on the third day and on the seventh day.

20You shall purify every garment, all that is made of skins, all work of goats' hair, and every article of wood.

21And Eleazar the priest said to the men of war who had gone to battle, This is the statute of the law which the Lord has commanded Moses:

22Only the gold, the silver, the bronze, the iron, the tin, and the lead,

23Everything that can stand fire, you shall make go through fire, and it shall be clean. Nevertheless it shall also be purified with the water of impurity; and all that cannot stand fire [such as fabrics] you shall pass through water.

## New International Version

the seventh day wash your clothes and you will be clean. Then you may come into the camp."

### Dividing the Spoils

25The Lord said to Moses, 26"You and Eleazar the priest and the family heads of the community are to count all the people and animals that were captured. 27Divide the spoils equally between the soldiers who took part in the battle and the rest of the community. 28From the soldiers who fought in the battle, set apart as tribute for the Lord one out of every five hundred, whether people, cattle, donkeys or sheep. 29Take this tribute from their half share and give it to Eleazar the priest as the Lord's part. 30From the Israelites' half, select one out of every fifty, whether people, cattle, donkeys, sheep or other animals. Give them to the Levites, who are responsible for the care of the Lord's tabernacle." 31So Moses and Eleazar the priest did as the Lord commanded Moses.

32The plunder remaining from the spoils that the soldiers took was 675,000 sheep, 3372,000 cattle, 3461,000 donkeys 35and 32,000 women who had never slept with a man.

36The half share of those who fought in the battle was:

337,500 sheep, 37of which the tribute for the Lord was 675;
3836,000 cattle, of which the tribute for the Lord was 72;
3930,500 donkeys, of which the tribute for the Lord was 61;
4016,000 people, of whom the tribute for the Lord was 32.

41Moses gave the tribute to Eleazar the priest as the Lord's part, as the Lord commanded Moses.

42The half belonging to the Israelites, which Moses set apart from that of the fighting men— 43the community's half—was 337,500 sheep, 4436,000 cattle, 4530,500 donkeys 46and 16,000 people. 47From the Israelites' half, Moses selected one out of every fifty people and animals, as the Lord commanded him, and gave them to the Levites, who were responsible for the care of the Lord's tabernacle.

48Then the officers who were over the units of the army—the commanders of thousands and commanders of hundreds—went to Moses 49and said to him, "Your servants have counted the soldiers under our command, and not one is missing. 50So we have brought as an offering to the Lord the gold articles each of us acquired—armlets, bracelets, signet rings, earrings and necklaces—to make atonement for ourselves before the Lord."

51Moses and Eleazar the priest accepted from them the gold—all the crafted articles. 52All the gold from the commanders of thousands and commanders of hundreds that Moses and Eleazar presented as a gift to the Lord

## Amplified Bible

24And you shall wash your clothes on the seventh day and you shall be clean; then you shall come into the camp. 25And the Lord said to Moses, 26Take the count of the prey that was taken, both of man and of beast, you and Eleazar the priest and the heads of the fathers' houses of the congregation.

27Divide the booty into two [equal] parts between the warriors who went out to battle and all the congregation. 28And levy a tribute to the Lord from the warriors who went to battle, one out of every 500 of the persons, the oxen, the donkeys, and the flocks. 29Take [this tribute] from the warriors' half and give it to Eleazar the priest as an offering to the Lord. 30And from the Israelites' half [of the booty] you shall take one out of every fifty of the persons, the oxen, the donkeys, the flocks, and of all livestock, and give them to the Levites who have charge of the tabernacle of the Lord. 31And Moses and Eleazar the priest did as the Lord commanded Moses.

32The prey, besides the booty which the men of war took, was 675,000 sheep, 33And 72,000 cattle, 34And 61,000 donkeys, 35And 32,000 persons in all, of the women who were virgins. 36And the half share, the portion of those who went to war, was: 337,500 sheep, 37And the Lord's tribute of the sheep was 675; 38The cattle were 36,000, of which the Lord's tribute was 72; 39The donkeys were 30,500, of which the Lord's tribute was 61; 40The persons were 16,000, of whom the Lord's tribute was 32 persons. 41And Moses gave the tribute which was the Lord's offering to Eleazar the priest, as the Lord commanded Moses. 42And the Israelites' half Moses separated from that of the warriors'—

43Now the congregation's half was 337,500 sheep, 44And 36,000 cattle, 45And 30,500 donkeys, 46And 16,000 persons— 47Even of the Israelites' half, Moses took one of every 50, both of persons and of beasts, and gave them to the Levites, who had charge of the tabernacle of the Lord, as the Lord commanded Moses. 48And the officers who were over the thousands of the army, the commanders of thousands and hundreds, came to Moses. 49They told [him], Your servants have counted the warriors under our command, and not one man of us is missing. 50We have brought as the Lord's offering what each man obtained—articles of gold, armlets, bracelets, signet rings, earrings, neck ornaments—to make atonement for ourselves before the Lord. 51Moses and Eleazar the priest took the gold from them, all the wrought articles. 52And all the gold of the offering that they offered to the Lord from the commanders of thousands and of hundreds was 16,750 shekels.

## New International Version

weighed 16,750 shekels.*ᵃ* ⁵³Each soldier had taken plunder for himself. ⁵⁴Moses and Eleazar the priest accepted the gold from the commanders of thousands and commanders of hundreds and brought it into the tent of meeting as a memorial for the Israelites before the LORD.

### The Transjordan Tribes

**32** The Reubenites and Gadites, who had very large herds and flocks, saw that the lands of Jazer and Gilead were suitable for livestock. ²So they came to Moses and Eleazar the priest and to the leaders of the community, and said, ³"Ataroth, Dibon, Jazer, Nimrah, Heshbon, Elealeh, Sebam, Nebo and Beon— ⁴the land the LORD subdued before the people of Israel—are suitable for livestock, and your servants have livestock. ⁵If we have found favor in your eyes," they said, "let this land be given to your servants as our possession. Do not make us cross the Jordan."

⁶Moses said to the Gadites and Reubenites, "Should your fellow Israelites go to war while you sit here? ⁷Why do you discourage the Israelites from crossing over into the land the LORD has given them? ⁸This is what your fathers did when I sent them from Kadesh Barnea to look over the land. ⁹After they went up to the Valley of Eshkol and viewed the land, they discouraged the Israelites from entering the land the LORD had given them. ¹⁰The LORD's anger was aroused that day and he swore this oath: ¹¹'Because they have not followed me wholeheartedly, not one of those who were twenty years old or more when they came up out of Egypt will see the land I promised on oath to Abraham, Isaac and Jacob— ¹²not one except Caleb son of Jephunneh the Kenizzite and Joshua son of Nun, for they followed the LORD wholeheartedly.' ¹³The LORD's anger burned against Israel and he made them wander in the wilderness forty years, until the whole generation of those who had done evil in his sight was gone.

¹⁴"And here you are, a brood of sinners, standing in the place of your fathers and making the LORD even more angry with Israel. ¹⁵If you turn away from following him, he will again leave all this people in the wilderness, and you will be the cause of their destruction."

¹⁶Then they came up to him and said, "We would like to build pens here for our livestock and cities for our women and children. ¹⁷But we will arm ourselves for battle*ᵇ* and go ahead of the Israelites until we have brought them to their place. Meanwhile our women and children will live in fortified cities, for protection from the inhabitants of the land. ¹⁸We will not return to our homes until each of the Israelites has received their inheritance. ¹⁹We will not receive any inheritance with them on the other side of the Jordan, because our inheritance has come to us on the east side of the Jordan."

²⁰Then Moses said to them, "If you will do this—if you will arm yourselves before the LORD for battle ²¹and if all of you who are armed cross over the Jordan before the LORD until he has driven his enemies out before him— ²²then when the land is subdued before the LORD, you may

## Amplified Bible

⁵³For the men of war had taken booty, every man for himself.

⁵⁴And Moses and Eleazar the priest received the gold from the commanders of thousands and of hundreds and brought it into the Tent of Meeting as a memorial for the Israelites before the Lord.

**32** Now the sons of Reuben and of Gad had a very great multitude of cattle, and they saw the land of Jazer and the land of Gilead [on the east side of the Jordan], and behold, the place was suitable for cattle.

²So the sons of Gad and of Reuben came and said to Moses, Eleazar the priest, and the leaders of the congregation,

³[The country around] Ataroth, Dibon, Jazer, Nimrah, Heshbon, Elealeh, Sebam, Nebo, and Beon,

⁴The land the Lord smote before the congregation of Israel, is a land for cattle, and your servants have cattle.

⁵And they said, If we have found favor in your sight, let this land be given to your servants for a possession. Do not take us over the Jordan.

⁶And Moses said to the sons of Gad and of Reuben, Shall your brethren go to war while you sit here?

⁷Why do you discourage the hearts of the Israelites from going over into the land which the Lord has given them?

⁸Thus your fathers did when I sent them from Kadesh-barnea to see the land!

⁹For when they went up to the Valley of Eshcol and saw the land, they discouraged the hearts of the Israelites from going into the land the Lord had given them.

¹⁰And the Lord's anger was kindled on that day and He swore, saying,

¹¹Surely none of the men who came up out of Egypt, from twenty years old and upward, shall see the land which I swore to Abraham, to Isaac, and to Jacob, because they have not wholly followed Me—

¹²Except Caleb son of Jephunneh the Kenizzite and Joshua son of Nun, for they have wholly followed the Lord.

¹³And the Lord's anger was kindled against Israel and He made them wander in the wilderness for forty years, until all the generation that had done evil in the sight of the Lord was consumed.

¹⁴And behold, you are risen up in your fathers' stead, a brood of sinful men, to increase still more the fierce anger of the Lord against Israel.

¹⁵For if you turn from following Him, He will again abandon them in the wilderness, and you will destroy all this people.

¹⁶But they came near to him and said, We will build sheepfolds here for our flocks and walled settlements for our little ones.

¹⁷But we will be armed and ready to go before the Israelites until we have brought them to their place. Our little ones shall dwell in the fortified settlements because of the people of the land.

¹⁸We will not return to our homes until the Israelites have inherited every man his inheritance.

¹⁹For we will not inherit with them on the [west] side of the Jordan and beyond, because our inheritance is fallen to us on this side of the Jordan eastward.

²⁰Moses replied, If you will do as you say, going armed before the Lord to war,

²¹And every armed man of you will pass over the Jordan before the Lord until He has driven out His enemies before Him

²²And the land is subdued before the Lord, then after-

---

*ᵃ 52* That is, about 420 pounds or about 190 kilograms
*ᵇ 17* Septuagint; Hebrew *will be quick to arm ourselves*

## New International Version

return and be free from your obligation to the Lord and to Israel. And this land will be your possession before the Lord.

²³"But if you fail to do this, you will be sinning against the Lord; and you may be sure that your sin will find you out. ²⁴Build cities for your women and children, and pens for your flocks, but do what you have promised."

²⁵The Gadites and Reubenites said to Moses, "We your servants will do as our lord commands. ²⁶Our children and wives, our flocks and herds will remain here in the cities of Gilead. ²⁷But your servants, every man who is armed for battle, will cross over to fight before the Lord, just as our lord says."

²⁸Then Moses gave orders about them to Eleazar the priest and Joshua son of Nun and to the family heads of the Israelite tribes. ²⁹He said to them, "If the Gadites and Reubenites, every man armed for battle, cross over the Jordan with you before the Lord, then when the land is subdued before you, you must give them the land of Gilead as their possession. ³⁰But if they do not cross over with you armed, they must accept their possession with you in Canaan."

³¹The Gadites and Reubenites answered, "Your servants will do what the Lord has said. ³²We will cross over before the Lord into Canaan armed, but the property we inherit will be on this side of the Jordan."

³³Then Moses gave to the Gadites, the Reubenites and the half-tribe of Manasseh son of Joseph the kingdom of Sihon king of the Amorites and the kingdom of Og king of Bashan—the whole land with its cities and the territory around them.

³⁴The Gadites built up Dibon, Ataroth, Aroer, ³⁵Atroth Shophan, Jazer, Jogbehah, ³⁶Beth Nimrah and Beth Haran as fortified cities, and built pens for their flocks. ³⁷And the Reubenites rebuilt Heshbon, Elealeh and Kiriathaim, ³⁸as well as Nebo and Baal Meon (these names were changed) and Sibmah. They gave names to the cities they rebuilt.

³⁹The descendants of Makir son of Manasseh went to Gilead, captured it and drove out the Amorites who were there. ⁴⁰So Moses gave Gilead to the Makirites, the descendants of Manasseh, and they settled there. ⁴¹Jair, a descendant of Manasseh, captured their settlements and called them Havvoth Jair.ᵃ ⁴²And Nobah captured Kenath and its surrounding settlements and called it Nobah after himself.

## Amplified Bible

ward you shall return and be guiltless [in this matter] before the Lord and before Israel, and this land shall be your possession before the Lord.

²³But if you will not do so, behold, you have sinned against the Lord; and be sure your sin will find you out. ²⁴Build settlements for your little ones, and folds for your sheep, and do that of which you have spoken.

²⁵And the sons of Gad and of Reuben said to Moses, Your servants will do as my lord commands.

²⁶Our little ones, our wives, our flocks, and all our cattle shall be there in the cities of Gilead.

²⁷But your servants will pass over, every man armed for war, before the Lord to battle, as my lord says.

²⁸So Moses gave command concerning them to Eleazar the priest and Joshua son of Nun and the heads of the fathers' houses of the tribes of Israel.

²⁹And Moses said to them, If the sons of Gad and Reuben will pass with you over the Jordan, every man armed to battle before the Lord, and the land shall be subdued before you, then you shall give them the land of Gilead for a possession.

³⁰But if they will not pass over with you armed, they shall have possessions among you in the land of Canaan.

³¹The sons of Gad and Reuben answered, As the Lord has said to your servants, so will we do.

³²We will pass over armed before the Lord into the land of Canaan, that the possession of our inheritance on this side of the Jordan may be ours.

³³Moses gave to them, to the sons of Gad and of Reuben and to half the tribe of Manasseh son of Joseph, the kingdom of Sihon king of the Amorites and the kingdom of Og king of Bashan—the land with its cities and their territories, even the cities round about the country.

³⁴And the sons of Gad built Dibon, Ataroth, Aroer,

³⁵Atroth-shophan, Jazer, Jogbehah,

³⁶Beth-nimrah, and Beth-haran, fortified cities, and folds for sheep.

³⁷And the sons of Reuben built Heshbon, Elealeh, Kiriathaim,

³⁸Nebo, and Baal-meon—their names were to be changed—and Shibmah; and they gave other names to the cities they built.

³⁹And the sons of Machir son of Manasseh went to Gilead and took it and dispossessed the Amorites who were in it.

⁴⁰And Moses gave Gilead to Machir son of Manasseh, and he settled in it.

⁴¹Jair son of Manasseh took their villages and called them Havvoth-jair.

⁴²And Nobah took Kenath and its villages and called it Nobah after his own name.

### Stages in Israel's Journey

**33** Here are the stages in the journey of the Israelites when they came out of Egypt by divisions under the leadership of Moses and Aaron. ²At the Lord's command Moses recorded the stages in their journey. This is their journey by stages:

³The Israelites set out from Rameses on the fifteenth day of the first month, the day after the Passover. They marched out defiantly in full view of all the Egyptians, ⁴who were burying all their firstborn, whom the Lord had struck down among them; for the Lord had brought judgment on their gods.

**33** These are the stages of the journeys of the Israelites by which they went out of the land of Egypt by their hosts under the leadership of Moses and Aaron.

²Moses recorded their starting places, as the Lord commanded, stage by stage; and these are their journeying stages from their starting places:

³They set out from Rameses on the fifteenth day of the first month; on the day after the Passover the Israelites went out [of Egypt] with a high hand *and* triumphantly in the sight of all the Egyptians,

⁴While the Egyptians were burying all their firstborn whom the Lord had struck down among them; upon their gods also the Lord executed judgments.

ᵃ 41 Or *them the settlements of Jair*

## New International Version

⁵The Israelites left Rameses and camped at Sukkoth.

⁶They left Sukkoth and camped at Etham, on the edge of the desert.

⁷They left Etham, turned back to Pi Hahiroth, to the east of Baal Zephon, and camped near Migdol.

⁸They left Pi Hahiroth*a* and passed through the sea into the desert, and when they had traveled for three days in the Desert of Etham, they camped at Marah.

⁹They left Marah and went to Elim, where there were twelve springs and seventy palm trees, and they camped there.

¹⁰They left Elim and camped by the Red Sea.*b*

¹¹They left the Red Sea and camped in the Desert of Sin.

¹²They left the Desert of Sin and camped at Dophkah.

¹³They left Dophkah and camped at Alush.

¹⁴They left Alush and camped at Rephidim, where there was no water for the people to drink.

¹⁵They left Rephidim and camped in the Desert of Sinai.

¹⁶They left the Desert of Sinai and camped at Kibroth Hattaavah.

¹⁷They left Kibroth Hattaavah and camped at Hazeroth.

¹⁸They left Hazeroth and camped at Rithmah.

¹⁹They left Rithmah and camped at Rimmon Perez.

²⁰They left Rimmon Perez and camped at Libnah.

²¹They left Libnah and camped at Rissah.

²²They left Rissah and camped at Kehelathah.

²³They left Kehelathah and camped at Mount Shepher.

²⁴They left Mount Shepher and camped at Haradah.

²⁵They left Haradah and camped at Makheloth.

²⁶They left Makheloth and camped at Tahath.

²⁷They left Tahath and camped at Terah.

²⁸They left Terah and camped at Mithkah.

²⁹They left Mithkah and camped at Hashmonah.

³⁰They left Hashmonah and camped at Moseroth.

³¹They left Moseroth and camped at Bene Jaakan.

³²They left Bene Jaakan and camped at Hor Haggidgad.

³³They left Hor Haggidgad and camped at Jotbathah.

³⁴They left Jotbathah and camped at Abronah.

³⁵They left Abronah and camped at Ezion Geber.

³⁶They left Ezion Geber and camped at Kadesh, in the Desert of Zin.

³⁷They left Kadesh and camped at Mount Hor, on the border of Edom. ³⁸At the Lord's command Aaron the priest went up Mount Hor, where he died on

## Amplified Bible

⁵The Israelites set out from Rameses and encamped in Succoth.

⁶And they departed from Succoth and encamped in Etham, which is at the edge of the wilderness.

⁷They set out from Etham and turned back to Pi-hahiroth, east of Baal-zephon, and they encamped before Migdol.

⁸And they journeyed from before Pi-hahiroth and passed through the midst of the [Red] Sea into the wilderness; and they went a three days' journey in the Wilderness of Etham and encamped at Marah.

⁹They journeyed from Marah and came to Elim; at Elim there were twelve springs of water and seventy palm trees, and they encamped there.

¹⁰They set out from Elim and encamped by the Red Sea.

¹¹They journeyed from the Red Sea and encamped in the Wilderness of Sin.

¹²And they traveled on from the Wilderness of Sin and encamped at Dophkah.

¹³And they departed from Dophkah and encamped at Alush.

¹⁴And they set out from Alush and encamped at Rephidim, where there was no water for the people to drink.

¹⁵And they departed from Rephidim and encamped in the Wilderness of Sinai.

¹⁶And they journeyed from the Wilderness of Sinai and encamped at Kibroth-hattaavah.

¹⁷And they traveled on from Kibroth-hattaavah and encamped at Hazeroth.

¹⁸And they journeyed from Hazeroth and encamped at Rithmah.

¹⁹And they departed from Rithmah and encamped at Rimmon-perez.

²⁰And they departed from Rimmon-perez and encamped at Libnah.

²¹And they removed from Libnah and encamped at Rissah.

²²And they journeyed from Rissah and encamped at Kehelathah.

²³And they went from Kehelathah and encamped at Mount Shepher.

²⁴And they removed from Mount Shepher and encamped at Haradah.

²⁵And they set out from Haradah and encamped at Makheloth.

²⁶And they removed from Makheloth and encamped at Tahath.

²⁷And they departed from Tahath and encamped at Terah.

²⁸And they removed from Terah and encamped at Mithkah.

²⁹And they set out from Mithkah and encamped at Hashmonah.

³⁰And they traveled on from Hashmonah and encamped at Moseroth.

³¹And they journeyed from Moseroth and pitched in Bene-jaakan.

³²And they set out from Bene-jaakan and encamped at Hor-haggidgad.

³³And they set out from Hor-haggidgad and encamped at Jotbathah.

³⁴And they journeyed from Jotbathah and encamped at Abronah.

³⁵And they traveled on from Abronah and encamped at Ezion-geber.

³⁶And they removed from Ezion-geber and encamped in the Wilderness of Zin, which is Kadesh.

³⁷And they removed from Kadesh and encamped at Mount Hor, on the edge of Edom.

³⁸Aaron the priest went up on Mount Hor at the command of the Lord, and died there in the fortieth year after

---

*a* 8 Many manuscripts of the Masoretic Text, Samaritan Pentateuch and Vulgate; most manuscripts of the Masoretic Text *left from before Hahiroth*    *b* 10 Or *the Sea of Reeds*; also in verse 11

## New International Version

the first day of the fifth month of the fortieth year after the Israelites came out of Egypt. <sup>39</sup>Aaron was a hundred and twenty-three years old when he died on Mount Hor.

<sup>40</sup>The Canaanite king of Arad, who lived in the Negev of Canaan, heard that the Israelites were coming.

<sup>41</sup>They left Mount Hor and camped at Zalmonah.

<sup>42</sup>They left Zalmonah and camped at Punon.

<sup>43</sup>They left Punon and camped at Oboth.

<sup>44</sup>They left Oboth and camped at Iye Abarim, on the border of Moab.

<sup>45</sup>They left Iye Abarim and camped at Dibon Gad.

<sup>46</sup>They left Dibon Gad and camped at Almon Diblathaim.

<sup>47</sup>They left Almon Diblathaim and camped in the mountains of Abarim, near Nebo.

<sup>48</sup>They left the mountains of Abarim and camped on the plains of Moab by the Jordan across from Jericho. <sup>49</sup>There on the plains of Moab they camped along the Jordan from Beth Jeshimoth to Abel Shittim.

<sup>50</sup>On the plains of Moab by the Jordan across from Jericho the LORD said to Moses, <sup>51</sup>"Speak to the Israelites and say to them: 'When you cross the Jordan into Canaan, <sup>52</sup>drive out all the inhabitants of the land before you. Destroy all their carved images and their cast idols, and demolish all their high places. <sup>53</sup>Take possession of the land and settle in it, for I have given you the land to possess. <sup>54</sup>Distribute the land by lot, according to your clans. To a larger group give a larger inheritance, and to a smaller group a smaller one. Whatever falls to them by lot will be theirs. Distribute it according to your ancestral tribes.

<sup>55</sup>"But if you do not drive out the inhabitants of the land, those you allow to remain will become barbs in your eyes and thorns in your sides. They will give you trouble in the land where you will live. <sup>56</sup>And then I will do to you what I plan to do to them.'"

### Boundaries of Canaan

**34** The LORD said to Moses, <sup>2</sup>"Command the Israelites and say to them: 'When you enter Canaan, the land that will be allotted to you as an inheritance is to have these boundaries:

<sup>3</sup>"'Your southern side will include some of the Desert of Zin along the border of Edom. Your southern boundary will start in the east from the southern end of the Dead Sea, <sup>4</sup>cross south of Scorpion Pass, continue on to Zin and go south of Kadesh Barnea. Then it will go to Hazar Addar and over to Azmon, <sup>5</sup>where it will turn, join the Wadi of Egypt and end at the Mediterranean Sea.

<sup>6</sup>"'Your western boundary will be the coast of the Mediterranean Sea. This will be your boundary on the west.

<sup>7</sup>"'For your northern boundary, run a line from the Mediterranean Sea to Mount Hor <sup>8</sup>and from Mount Hor to Lebo Hamath. Then the boundary will go to Zedad, <sup>9</sup>con-

## Amplified Bible

the Israelites came out of Egypt, the first day of the fifth month. [Num. 20:23-29.]

<sup>39</sup>Aaron was 123 years old when he died on Mount Hor.

<sup>40</sup>The Canaanite king of Arad, who lived in the South (the Negeb) in the land of Canaan, heard of the coming of the Israelites.

<sup>41</sup>They set out from Mount Hor and encamped at Zalmonah.

<sup>42</sup>And they set out from Zalmonah and encamped at Punon.

<sup>43</sup>And they set out from Punon and encamped at Oboth.

<sup>44</sup>And they traveled on from Oboth and encamped at Iye-abarim, on the border of Moab.

<sup>45</sup>And they departed from Iyim and encamped at Dibon-gad.

<sup>46</sup>And they set out from Dibon-gad and encamped in Almon-diblathaim.

<sup>47</sup>And they traveled on from Almon-diblathaim and encamped in the mountains of Abarim, before Nebo.

<sup>48</sup>And they departed from the mountains of Abarim and encamped in the plains of Moab by the Jordan at Jericho.

<sup>49</sup>And they encamped by the Jordan from Beth-jeshimoth as far as Abel-shittim in the plains of Moab.

<sup>50</sup>And the Lord said to Moses in the plains of Moab by the Jordan at Jericho,

<sup>51</sup>Tell the Israelites, When you have passed over the Jordan into the land of Canaan,

<sup>52</sup>Then you shall drive out all the inhabitants of the land before you and destroy all their figured stones and all their molten images and completely demolish all their [idolatrous] high places,

<sup>53</sup>And you shall take possession of the land and dwell in it, for to you I have given the land to possess it.

<sup>54</sup>You shall inherit the land by lot according to your families; to the large tribe you shall give a larger inheritance, and to the small tribe you shall give a smaller inheritance. Wherever the lot falls to any man, that shall be his. According to the tribes of your fathers you shall inherit.

<sup>55</sup>But if you will not drive out the inhabitants of the land from before you, then those you let remain of them shall be as pricks in your eyes and as thorns in your sides, and they shall vex you in the land in which you dwell.

<sup>56</sup>And as I thought to do to them, so will I do to you.

**34** And the Lord said to Moses,

<sup>2</sup>Command the Israelites, When you come into the land of Canaan (which is the land that shall be yours for an inheritance, the land of Canaan according to its boundaries),

<sup>3</sup>Your south side shall be from the Wilderness of Zin along the side of Edom, and your southern boundary from the end of the Salt [Dead] Sea eastward.

<sup>4</sup>Your boundary shall turn south of the ascent of Akrabbim, and pass on to Zin, and its end shall be south of Kadesh-barnea. Then it shall go on to Hazar-addar and pass on to Azmon.

<sup>5</sup>Then the boundary shall turn from Azmon to the Brook of Egypt, and it shall terminate at the [Mediterranean] Sea.

<sup>6</sup>For the western boundary you shall have the Great Sea and its coast.

<sup>7</sup>And this shall be your north border: from the Great Sea mark out your boundary line to Mount Hor;

<sup>8</sup>From Mount Hor you shall mark out your boundary to the entrance of Hamath, and its end shall be at Zedad;

## New International Version

tinue to Ziphron and end at Hazar Enan. This will be your boundary on the north.

¹⁰"'For your eastern boundary, run a line from Hazar Enan to Shepham. ¹¹The boundary will go down from Shepham to Riblah on the east side of Ain and continue along the slopes east of the Sea of Galilee.ᵃ ¹²Then the boundary will go down along the Jordan and end at the Dead Sea.

"'This will be your land, with its boundaries on every side.'"

¹³Moses commanded the Israelites: "Assign this land by lot as an inheritance. The LORD has ordered that it be given to the nine and a half tribes, ¹⁴because the families of the tribe of Reuben, the tribe of Gad and the half-tribe of Manasseh have received their inheritance. ¹⁵These two and a half tribes have received their inheritance east of the Jordan across from Jericho, toward the sunrise."

¹⁶The LORD said to Moses, ¹⁷"These are the names of the men who are to assign the land for you as an inheritance: Eleazar the priest and Joshua son of Nun. ¹⁸And appoint one leader from each tribe to help assign the land. ¹⁹These are their names:

Caleb son of Jephunneh,
  from the tribe of Judah;
²⁰Shemuel son of Ammihud,
  from the tribe of Simeon;
²¹Elidad son of Kislon,
  from the tribe of Benjamin;
²²Bukki son of Jogli,
  the leader from the tribe of Dan;
²³Hanniel son of Ephod,
  the leader from the tribe of Manasseh son of Joseph;
²⁴Kemuel son of Shiphtan,
  the leader from the tribe of Ephraim son of Joseph;
²⁵Elizaphan son of Parnak,
  the leader from the tribe of Zebulun;
²⁶Paltiel son of Azzan,
  the leader from the tribe of Issachar;
²⁷Ahihud son of Shelomi,
  the leader from the tribe of Asher;
²⁸Pedahel son of Ammihud,
  the leader from the tribe of Naphtali."

²⁹These are the men the LORD commanded to assign the inheritance to the Israelites in the land of Canaan.

## Amplified Bible

⁹Then the northern boundary shall go on to Ziphron, and the end of it shall be at Hazar-enan.

¹⁰You shall mark out your eastern boundary from Hazar-enan to Shepham;

¹¹The boundary shall go down from Shepham to Riblah on the east side of Ain and shall descend and reach to the shoulder of the Sea of Chinnereth [the Sea of Galilee] on the east;

¹²And the boundary shall go down to the Jordan, and the end shall be at the Salt Sea. This shall be your land with its boundaries all around.

¹³Moses commanded the Israelites, This is the land you shall inherit by lot, which the Lord has commanded to give to the nine tribes and the half-tribe [of Manasseh],

¹⁴For the tribes of the sons of Reuben and of Gad by their fathers' houses have received their inheritance, and also the half-tribe of Manasseh.

¹⁵The two and a half tribes have received their inheritance east of the Jordan at Jericho, toward the sunrise.

¹⁶And the Lord said to Moses,

¹⁷These are the men who shall divide the land to you for inheritance: Eleazar the priest and Joshua son of Nun.

¹⁸And [with them] you shall take one head or prince of each tribe to divide the land for inheritance.

¹⁹The names of the men are: Of the tribe of Judah, Caleb son of Jephunneh;

²⁰Of the tribe of the sons of Simeon, Shemuel son of Ammihud;

²¹Of the tribe of Benjamin, Elidad son of Chislon;

²²Of the tribe of the sons of Dan a leader, Bukki son of Jogli;

²³Of the sons of Joseph: of the tribe of the sons of Manasseh a leader, Hanniel son of Ephod;

²⁴And of the tribe of the sons of Ephraim a leader, Kemuel son of Shiphtan;

²⁵And of the tribe of the sons of Zebulun a leader, Elizaphan son of Parnach;

²⁶And of the tribe of the sons of Issachar a leader, Paltiel son of Azzan;

²⁷And of the tribe of the sons of Asher a leader, Ahihud son of Shelomi;

²⁸And of the tribe of the sons of Naphtali a leader, Pedahel son of Ammihud.

²⁹These are the men whom the Lord commanded to divide the inheritance to the Israelites in the land of Canaan.

### Towns for the Levites

**35** On the plains of Moab by the Jordan across from Jericho, the LORD said to Moses, ²"Command the Israelites to give the Levites towns to live in from the inheritance the Israelites will possess. And give them pasturelands around the towns. ³Then they will have towns to live in and pasturelands for the cattle they own and all their other animals.

⁴"The pasturelands around the towns that you give the Levites will extend a thousand cubitsᵇ from the town wall. ⁵Outside the town, measure two thousand cubitsᶜ on the east side, two thousand on the south side, two thousand on the west and two thousand on the north, with the town in the center. They will have this area as pastureland for the towns.

**35** And the Lord said to Moses in the plains of Moab by the Jordan at Jericho,

²Command the Israelites that they give to the Levites from the inheritance of their possession cities to dwell in; and [suburb] pasturelands round about the cities' walls you shall give to the Levites also.

³They shall have the cities to dwell in and their [suburb] pasturelands shall be for their cattle, for their wealth [in flocks], and for all their beasts.

⁴And the pasturelands of the cities which you shall give to the Levites shall reach from the wall of the city and outward 1,000 cubits round about.

⁵You shall measure from the wall of the city outward on the east, south, west, and north sides 2,000 cubits, the city being in the center. This shall belong to [the Levites] as [suburb] pasturelands for their cities.

ᵃ 11 Hebrew *Kinnereth*    ᵇ 4 That is, about 1,500 feet or about 450 meters    ᶜ 5 That is, about 3,000 feet or about 900 meters

## New International Version

### Cities of Refuge

⁶"Six of the towns you give the Levites will be cities of refuge, to which a person who has killed someone may flee. In addition, give them forty-two other towns. ⁷In all you must give the Levites forty-eight towns, together with their pasturelands. ⁸The towns you give the Levites from the land the Israelites possess are to be given in proportion to the inheritance of each tribe: Take many towns from a tribe that has many, but few from one that has few."

⁹Then the LORD said to Moses: ¹⁰"Speak to the Israelites and say to them: 'When you cross the Jordan into Canaan, ¹¹select some towns to be your cities of refuge, to which a person who has killed someone accidentally may flee. ¹²They will be places of refuge from the avenger, so that anyone accused of murder may not die before they stand trial before the assembly. ¹³These six towns you give will be your cities of refuge. ¹⁴Give three on this side of the Jordan and three in Canaan as cities of refuge. ¹⁵These six towns will be a place of refuge for Israelites and for foreigners residing among them, so that anyone who has killed another accidentally can flee there.

¹⁶"'If anyone strikes someone a fatal blow with an iron object, that person is a murderer; the murderer is to be put to death. ¹⁷Or if anyone is holding a stone and strikes someone a fatal blow with it, that person is a murderer; the murderer is to be put to death. ¹⁸Or if anyone is holding a wooden object and strikes someone a fatal blow with it, that person is a murderer; the murderer is to be put to death. ¹⁹The avenger of blood shall put the murderer to death; when the avenger comes upon the murderer, the avenger shall put the murderer to death. ²⁰If anyone with malice aforethought shoves another or throws something at them intentionally so that they die ²¹or if out of enmity one person hits another with their fist so that the other dies, that person is to be put to death; that person is a murderer. The avenger of blood shall put the murderer to death when they meet.

²²"'But if without enmity someone suddenly pushes another or throws something at them unintentionally ²³or, without seeing them, drops on them a stone heavy enough to kill them, and they die, then since that other person was not an enemy and no harm was intended, ²⁴the assembly must judge between the accused and the avenger of blood according to these regulations. ²⁵The assembly must protect the one accused of murder from the avenger of blood and send the accused back to the city of refuge to which they fled. The accused must stay there until the death of the high priest, who was anointed with the holy oil.

²⁶"'But if the accused ever goes outside the limits of the city of refuge to which they fled ²⁷and the avenger of blood finds them outside the city, the avenger of blood may kill the accused without being guilty of murder. ²⁸The accused must stay in the city of refuge until the death of the high priest; only after the death of the high priest may they return to their own property.

²⁹"'This is to have the force of law for you throughout the generations to come, wherever you live. ³⁰"'Anyone who kills a person is to be put to death as a

## Amplified Bible

⁶Of the cities which you shall give to the Levites there shall be the six cities of refuge, which you shall give for the manslayer to flee into; and in addition to them you shall give forty-two cities.

⁷So all the cities which you shall give to the Levites shall be forty-eight; you shall give them with their adjacent [suburb] pasturelands.

⁸As for the cities, you shall give from the possession of the Israelites, from the larger tribes you shall take many and from the smaller tribes few; each tribe shall give of its cities to the Levites in proportion to its inheritance.

⁹And the Lord said to Moses,

¹⁰Say to the Israelites, When you cross the Jordan into the land of Canaan,

¹¹Then you shall select cities to be cities of refuge for you, that the slayer who kills any person unintentionally *and* unawares may flee there.

¹²And the cities shall be to you for refuge from the avenger, that the manslayer may not die until he has had a fair trial before the congregation.

¹³And of the cities which you give there shall be your six cities for refuge.

¹⁴You shall give three cities on this [east] side of the Jordan and three cities in the land of Canaan, to be cities of refuge.

¹⁵These six cities shall be a refuge for the Israelites and for the stranger and the temporary resident among them; that anyone who kills any person unintentionally *and* unawares may flee there.

¹⁶But if he struck him down with an instrument of iron so that he died, he is a murderer; the murderer shall surely be put to death.

¹⁷And if he struck him down by throwing a stone, by which a person may die, and he died, he is a murderer; the murderer shall surely be put to death.

¹⁸Or if he struck him down with a weapon of wood in his hand, by which one may die, and he died, the offender is a murderer; he shall surely be put to death.

¹⁹The avenger of blood shall himself slay the murderer; when he meets him, he shall slay him.

²⁰But if he stabbed him through hatred or hurled at him by lying in wait so that he died

²¹Or in enmity struck him down with his hand so that he died, he that smote him shall surely be put to death; he is a murderer. The avenger of blood shall slay the murderer when he meets him.

²²But if he stabbed him suddenly without enmity or threw anything at *or* upon him without lying in wait

²³Or with any stone with which a man may be killed, not seeing him, and threw it at him so that he died, and was not his enemy nor sought to harm him,

²⁴Then the congregation shall judge between the slayer and the avenger of blood according to these ordinances.

²⁵And the congregation shall rescue the manslayer from the hand of the avenger of blood and restore him to his city of refuge to which he had fled; and he shall live in it until the high priest dies, who was anointed with the sacred oil.

²⁶But if the slayer shall at any time come outside the limits of his city of refuge to which he had fled

²⁷And the avenger of blood finds him outside the limits of his city of refuge and kills the manslayer, he shall not be guilty of blood

²⁸Because the manslayer should have remained in his city of refuge until the death of the high priest. But after the high priest's death the manslayer shall return to the land of his possession.

²⁹And these things shall be for a statute *and* ordinance to you throughout your generations in all your dwellings.

³⁰Whoever kills any person [intentionally], the mur-

## New International Version

murderer only on the testimony of witnesses. But no one is to be put to death on the testimony of only one witness.

³¹"'Do not accept a ransom for the life of a murderer, who deserves to die. They are to be put to death.

³²"'Do not accept a ransom for anyone who has fled to a city of refuge and so allow them to go back and live on their own land before the death of the high priest.

³³"'Do not pollute the land where you are. Bloodshed pollutes the land, and atonement cannot be made for the land on which blood has been shed, except by the blood of the one who shed it. ³⁴Do not defile the land where you live and where I dwell, for I, the LORD, dwell among the Israelites.'"

### Inheritance of Zelophehad's Daughters

**36** The family heads of the clan of Gilead son of Makir, the son of Manasseh, who were from the clans of the descendants of Joseph, came and spoke before Moses and the leaders, the heads of the Israelite families. ²They said, "When the LORD commanded my lord to give the land as an inheritance to the Israelites by lot, he ordered you to give the inheritance of our brother Zelophehad to his daughters. ³Now suppose they marry men from other Israelite tribes; then their inheritance will be taken from our ancestral inheritance and added to that of the tribe they marry into. And so part of the inheritance allotted to us will be taken away. ⁴When the Year of Jubilee for the Israelites comes, their inheritance will be added to that of the tribe into which they marry, and their property will be taken from the tribal inheritance of our ancestors."

⁵Then at the LORD's command Moses gave this order to the Israelites: "What the tribe of the descendants of Joseph is saying is right. ⁶This is what the LORD commands for Zelophehad's daughters: They may marry anyone they please as long as they marry within their father's tribal clan. ⁷No inheritance in Israel is to pass from one tribe to another, for every Israelite shall keep the tribal inheritance of their ancestors. ⁸Every daughter who inherits land in any Israelite tribe must marry someone in her father's tribal clan, so that every Israelite will possess the inheritance of their ancestors. ⁹No inheritance may pass from one tribe to another, for each Israelite tribe is to keep the land it inherits."

¹⁰So Zelophehad's daughters did as the LORD commanded Moses. ¹¹Zelophehad's daughters—Mahlah, Tirzah, Hoglah, Milkah and Noah—married their cousins on their father's side. ¹²They married within the clans of the descendants of Manasseh son of Joseph, and their inheritance remained in their father's tribe and clan.

¹³These are the commands and regulations the LORD gave through Moses to the Israelites on the plains of Moab by the Jordan across from Jericho.

## Amplified Bible

derer shall be put to death on the testimony of witnesses; but no one shall be put to death on the testimony of one witness.

³¹Moreover, you shall take no ransom for the life of a murderer guilty of death; but he shall surely be put to death.

³²And you shall accept no ransom for him who has fled to his city of refuge, so that he may return to dwell in the land before the death of the high priest.

³³So you shall not pollute the land in which you live; for blood pollutes the land, and no atonement can be made for the land for the blood shed in it, but by the blood of him who shed it.

³⁴And you shall not defile the land in which you live, in the midst of which I dwell, for I, the Lord, dwell in the midst of the people of Israel.

**36** The heads of the fathers' houses of the families of the sons of Gilead son of Machir, the son of Manasseh, of the fathers' houses of the sons of Joseph, came near and spoke before Moses and the leaders, the heads of the fathers' houses of the Israelites.

²They said, The Lord commanded [you] my lord to give the land for inheritance by lot to the Israelites; and my lord was commanded by the Lord to give the inheritance of Zelophehad our brother to his daughters.

³But if they are married to any of the sons of the other tribes of the Israelites, then their inheritance will be taken from that of our fathers and added to the inheritance of the tribe to which they are received *and* belong; so it will be taken out of the lot of our inheritance.

⁴And when the Jubilee of the Israelites comes, then their inheritance will be added to that of the tribe to which they are received *and* belong; so will their inheritance be taken away from that of the tribe of our fathers.

⁵And Moses commanded the Israelites according to the word of the Lord, saying, The tribe of the sons of Joseph is right.

⁶This is what the Lord commands concerning the daughters of Zelophehad: Let them marry whom they think best; only they shall marry within the family of the tribe of their father.

⁷So shall no inheritance of the Israelites be transferred from tribe to tribe, for every one of the Israelites shall cling to the inheritance of the tribe of his fathers.

⁸And every daughter who possesses an inheritance in any tribe of the Israelites shall be wife to one of the family of the tribe of her father, so that the Israelites may each one possess the inheritance of his fathers.

⁹So shall no inheritance be transferred from one tribe to another, but each of the tribes of the Israelites shall cling to its own inheritance.

¹⁰The daughters of Zelophehad did as the Lord commanded Moses.

¹¹For Mahlah, Tirzah, Hoglah, Milcah, and Noah, the daughters of Zelophehad, were married to sons of their father's brothers.

¹²They married into the families of the sons of Manasseh son of Joseph, and their inheritance remained in the tribe of the family of their father.

¹³These are the commandments and ordinances which the Lord commanded the Israelites through Moses in the plains of Moab by the Jordan [River] at Jericho.

# Deuteronomy

## The Command to Leave Horeb

**1** These are the words Moses spoke to all Israel in the wilderness east of the Jordan—that is, in the Arabah—opposite Suph, between Paran and Tophel, Laban, Hazeroth and Dizahab. ² (It takes eleven days to go from Horeb to Kadesh Barnea by the Mount Seir road.) ³In the fortieth year, on the first day of the eleventh month, Moses proclaimed to the Israelites all that the LORD had commanded him concerning them. ⁴This was after he had defeated Sihon king of the Amorites, who reigned in Heshbon, and at Edrei had defeated Og king of Bashan, who reigned in Ashtaroth.

⁵East of the Jordan in the territory of Moab, Moses began to expound this law, saying:

⁶The LORD our God said to us at Horeb, "You have stayed long enough at this mountain. ⁷Break camp and advance into the hill country of the Amorites; go to all the neighboring peoples in the Arabah, in the mountains, in the western foothills, in the Negev and along the coast, to the land of the Canaanites and to Lebanon, as far as the great river, the Euphrates. ⁸See, I have given you this land. Go in and take possession of the land the LORD swore he would give to your fathers—to Abraham, Isaac and Jacob—and to their descendants after them."

## The Appointment of Leaders

⁹At that time I said to you, "You are too heavy a burden for me to carry alone. ¹⁰The LORD your God has increased your numbers so that today you are as numerous as the stars in the sky. ¹¹May the LORD, the God of your ancestors, increase you a thousand times and bless you as he has promised! ¹²But how can I bear your problems and your burdens and your disputes all by myself? ¹³Choose some wise, understanding and respected men from each of your tribes, and I will set them over you."

¹⁴You answered me, "What you propose to do is good."

¹⁵So I took the leading men of your tribes, wise and respected men, and appointed them to have authority over you—as commanders of thousands, of hundreds, of fifties and of tens and as tribal officials. ¹⁶And I charged your judges at that time, "Hear the disputes between your people and judge fairly, whether the case is between two Israelites or between an Israelite and a foreigner residing among you. ¹⁷Do not show partiality in judging; hear both small and great alike. Do not be afraid of anyone, for judgment belongs to God. Bring me any case too hard for you, and I will hear it." ¹⁸And at that time I told you everything you were to do.

## Spies Sent Out

¹⁹Then, as the LORD our God commanded us, we set out from Horeb and went toward the hill country of the Amorites through all that vast and dreadful wilderness that you have seen, and so we reached Kadesh Barnea. ²⁰Then I said to you, "You have reached the hill country of the Amorites, which the LORD our God is giving us. ²¹See, the LORD your God has given you the land. Go up and take possession of it as the LORD, the God of your ancestors, told you. Do not be afraid; do not be discouraged."

# Deuteronomy

**1** These are the words which Moses spoke to all Israel [still] on the [east] side of the Jordan [River] in the wilderness, in the Arabah [the deep valley running north and south from the eastern arm of the Red Sea to beyond the Dead Sea], over near Suph, between Paran and Tophel, Laban, Hazeroth, and Dizahab.

²It is [only] eleven days' journey from Horeb by the way of Mount Seir to Kadesh-barnea [on Canaan's border; yet Israel took forty years to get beyond it].

³And in the fortieth year, on the first day of the eleventh month, Moses spoke to the Israelites according to all that the Lord had given him in commandment to them,

⁴After He had defeated Sihon king of the Amorites, who lived in Heshbon, and Og king of Bashan, who lived in Ashtaroth [and] Edrei.

⁵Beyond (east of) the Jordan in the land of Moab, Moses began to explain this law, saying,

⁶The Lord our God said to us in Horeb, You have dwelt long enough on this mountain.

⁷Turn and take up your journey and go to the hill country of the Amorites, and to all their neighbors in the Arabah, in the hill country, in the lowland, in the South (the Negeb), and on the coast, the land of the Canaanites, and Lebanon, as far as the great river, the river Euphrates.

⁸Behold, I have set the land before you; go in and take possession of the land which the Lord swore to your fathers, to Abraham, to Isaac, and to Jacob, to give to them and to their descendants after them.

⁹I said to you at that time, I am not able to bear you alone.

¹⁰The Lord your God has multiplied you, and behold, you are this day as the stars of the heavens for multitude.

¹¹May the Lord, the God of your fathers, make you a thousand times as many as you are and bless you as He has promised you!

¹²How can I bear alone the weariness *and* pressure and burden of you and your strife?

¹³Choose wise, understanding, experienced, *and* respected men according to your tribes, and I will make them heads over you.

¹⁴And you answered me, The thing which you have spoken is good for us to do.

¹⁵So I took the heads of your tribes, wise, experienced, *and* respected men, and made them heads over you, commanders of thousands, and hundreds, and fifties, and tens, and officers according to your tribes.

¹⁶And I charged your judges at that time: Hear the cases between your brethren and judge righteously between a man and his brother or the stranger *or* sojourner who is with him.

¹⁷You shall not be partial in judgment; but you shall hear the small as well as the great. You shall not be afraid of the face of man, for the judgment is God's. And the case that is too hard for you, you shall bring to me, and I will hear it.

¹⁸And I commanded you at that time all the things that you should do.

¹⁹And when we departed from Horeb, we went through all that great and terrible wilderness which you saw on the way to the hill country of the Amorites, as the Lord our God commanded us, and we came to Kadesh-barnea.

²⁰And I said to you, You have come to the hill country of the Amorites, which the Lord our God gives us.

²¹Behold, the Lord your God has set the land before you; go up and possess it, as the Lord, the God of your fathers, has said to you. Fear not, neither be dismayed.

## New International Version

²²Then all of you came to me and said, "Let us send men ahead to spy out the land for us and bring back a report about the route we are to take and the towns we will come to."

²³The idea seemed good to me; so I selected twelve of you, one man from each tribe. ²⁴They left and went up into the hill country, and came to the Valley of Eshkol and explored it. ²⁵Taking with them some of the fruit of the land, they brought it down to us and reported, "It is a good land that the LORD our God is giving us."

### Rebellion Against the LORD

²⁶But you were unwilling to go up; you rebelled against the command of the LORD your God. ²⁷You grumbled in your tents and said, "The LORD hates us; so he brought us out of Egypt to deliver us into the hands of the Amorites to destroy us. ²⁸Where can we go? Our brothers have made our hearts melt in fear. They say, 'The people are stronger and taller than we are; the cities are large, with walls up to the sky. We even saw the Anakites there.'"

²⁹Then I said to you, "Do not be terrified; do not be afraid of them. ³⁰The LORD your God, who is going before you, will fight for you, as he did for you in Egypt, before your very eyes, ³¹and in the wilderness. There you saw how the LORD your God carried you, as a father carries his son, all the way you went until you reached this place."

³²In spite of this, you did not trust in the LORD your God, ³³who went ahead of you on your journey, in fire by night and in a cloud by day, to search out places for you to camp and to show you the way you should go.

³⁴When the LORD heard what you said, he was angry and solemnly swore: ³⁵"No one from this evil generation shall see the good land I swore to give your ancestors, ³⁶except Caleb son of Jephunneh. He will see it, and I will give him and his descendants the land he set his feet on, because he followed the LORD wholeheartedly."

³⁷Because of you the LORD became angry with me also and said, "You shall not enter it, either. ³⁸But your assistant, Joshua son of Nun, will enter it. Encourage him, because he will lead Israel to inherit it. ³⁹And the little ones that you said would be taken captive, your children who do not yet know good from bad—they will enter the land. I will give it to them and they will take possession of it. ⁴⁰But as for you, turn around and set out toward the desert along the route to the Red Sea.ᵃ"

⁴¹Then you replied, "We have sinned against the LORD. We will go up and fight, as the LORD our God commanded us." So every one of you put on his weapons, thinking it easy to go up into the hill country.

⁴²But the LORD said to me, "Tell them, 'Do not go up and fight, because I will not be with you. You will be defeated by your enemies.'"

⁴³So I told you, but you would not listen. You rebelled against the LORD's command and in your arrogance you marched up into the hill country. ⁴⁴The Amorites who lived in those hills came out against you; they chased you like a swarm of bees and beat you down from Seir all the way to Hormah. ⁴⁵You came back and wept before the LORD, but he paid no attention to your weeping and turned a deaf ear to you. ⁴⁶And so you stayed in Kadesh many days—all the time you spent there.

## Amplified Bible

²²Then you all came near to me and said, Let us send men before us, that they may search out the land for us and bring us word again by what way we should go up and the cities into which we shall come.

²³The thing pleased me well, and I took twelve men of you, one for each tribe.

²⁴And they turned and went up into the hill country, and came to the Valley of Eshcol and spied it out.

²⁵And they took of the fruit of the land in their hands and brought it down to us and brought us word again, and said, It is a good land which the Lord our God gives us.

²⁶Yet you would not go up, but rebelled against the commandment of the Lord your God.

²⁷You were peevish *and* discontented in your tents, and said, Because the Lord hated us, He brought us forth out of the land of Egypt to deliver us into the hand of the Amorites to destroy us.

²⁸To what are we going up? Our brethren have made our hearts melt, saying, The people are bigger and taller than we are; the cities are great and fortified to the heavens. And moreover we have seen the [giantlike] sons of the Anakim there.

²⁹Then I said to you, Dread not, neither be afraid of them.

³⁰The Lord your God Who goes before you, He will fight for you just as He did for you in Egypt before your eyes,

³¹And in the wilderness, where you have seen how the Lord your God bore you, as a man carries his son, in all the way that you went until you came to this place.

³²Yet in spite of this word you did not believe (trust, rely on, and remain steadfast to) the Lord your God,

³³Who went in the way before you to search out a place to pitch your tents, in fire by night, to show you by what way you should go, and in the cloud by day.

³⁴And the Lord heard your words, and was angered and He swore,

³⁵Not one of these men of this evil generation shall see that good land which I swore to give to your fathers,

³⁶Except [Joshua, of course, and] Caleb son of Jephunneh; he shall see it, and to him and to his children I will give the land upon which he has walked, because he has wholly followed the Lord.

³⁷The Lord was angry with me also for your sakes, and said, You also shall not enter Canaan.

³⁸But Joshua son of Nun, who stands before you, he shall enter there. Encourage him, for he shall cause Israel to inherit it.

³⁹Moreover, your little ones whom you said would become a prey, and your children who at this time cannot discern between good and evil, they shall enter Canaan, and to them I will give it and they shall possess it.

⁴⁰But as for you, turn and journey into the wilderness by way of the Red Sea.

⁴¹Then you said to me, We have sinned against the Lord. We will go up and fight, as the Lord our God commanded us. And you girded on every man his battle weapons, and thought it a simple matter to go up into the hill country.

⁴²And the Lord said to me, Say to them, Do not go up or fight, for I am not among you—lest you be dangerously hurt by your enemies.

⁴³So I spoke to you, and you would not hear, but rebelled against the commandment of the Lord, and were presumptuous and went up into the hill country.

⁴⁴Then the Amorites who lived in that hill country came out against you and chased you as bees do and struck you down in Seir as far as Hormah.

⁴⁵And you returned and wept before the Lord, but the Lord would not heed your voice or listen to you.

⁴⁶So you remained in Kadesh; many days you remained there.

---

ᵃ 40 Or *the Sea of Reeds*

## New International Version

### Wanderings in the Wilderness

**2** Then we turned back and set out toward the wilderness along the route to the Red Sea,[a] as the LORD had directed me. For a long time we made our way around the hill country of Seir.

[2] Then the LORD said to me, [3] "You have made your way around this hill country long enough; now turn north. [4] Give the people these orders: 'You are about to pass through the territory of your relatives the descendants of Esau, who live in Seir. They will be afraid of you, but be very careful. [5] Do not provoke them to war, for I will not give you any of their land, not even enough to put your foot on. I have given Esau the hill country of Seir as his own. [6] You are to pay them in silver for the food you eat and the water you drink.'"

[7] The LORD your God has blessed you in all the work of your hands. He has watched over your journey through this vast wilderness. These forty years the LORD your God has been with you, and you have not lacked anything.

[8] So we went on past our relatives the descendants of Esau, who live in Seir. We turned from the Arabah road, which comes up from Elath and Ezion Geber, and traveled along the desert road of Moab.

[9] Then the LORD said to me, "Do not harass the Moabites or provoke them to war, for I will not give you any part of their land. I have given Ar to the descendants of Lot as a possession."

[10] (The Emites used to live there—a people strong and numerous, and as tall as the Anakites. [11] Like the Anakites, they too were considered Rephaites, but the Moabites called them Emites. [12] Horites used to live in Seir, but the descendants of Esau drove them out. They destroyed the Horites from before them and settled in their place, just as Israel did in the land the LORD gave them as their possession.)

[13] And the LORD said, "Now get up and cross the Zered Valley." So we crossed the valley.

[14] Thirty-eight years passed from the time we left Kadesh Barnea until we crossed the Zered Valley. By then, that entire generation of fighting men had perished from the camp, as the LORD had sworn to them. [15] The LORD's hand was against them until he had completely eliminated them from the camp.

[16] Now when the last of these fighting men among the people had died, [17] the LORD said to me, [18] "Today you are to pass by the region of Moab at Ar. [19] When you come to the Ammonites, do not harass them or provoke them to war, for I will not give you possession of any land belonging to the Ammonites. I have given it as a possession to the descendants of Lot."

[20] (That too was considered a land of the Rephaites, who used to live there; but the Ammonites called them Zamzummites. [21] They were a people strong and numerous, and as tall as the Anakites. The LORD destroyed them from before the Ammonites, who drove them out and settled in their place. [22] The LORD had done the same for the descendants of Esau, who lived in Seir, when he destroyed the Horites from before them. They drove them out and have lived in their place to this day. [23] And as for the Avvites who lived in villages as far as Gaza, the Caphtorites coming out from Caphtor[b] destroyed them and settled in their place.)

## Amplified Bible

**2** Then we turned, and took our journey into the wilderness by the way of the Red Sea, as the Lord directed me; and for many days we journeyed around Mount Seir.

[2] And the Lord spoke to me [Moses], saying,

[3] You have roamed around this mountain country long enough; turn northward.

[4] And command the Israelites, You are to pass through the territory of your kinsmen the sons of Esau, who live in Seir; and they will be afraid of you. So watch yourselves carefully.

[5] Do not provoke *or* stir them up, for I will not give you of their land, no, not enough for the sole of your foot to tread on, for I have given Mount Seir to Esau for a possession.

[6] You shall buy food from them for money, that you may eat, and you shall also buy water from them for money, that you may drink.

[7] For the Lord your God has blessed you in all the work of your hand. He knows your walking through this great wilderness. These forty years the Lord your God has been with you; you have lacked nothing.

[8] So we passed on from our brethren the sons of Esau, who dwelt in Seir, away from the Arabah (wilderness), and from Elath and from Ezion-geber. We turned and went by the way of the wilderness of Moab.

[9] And the Lord said to me, Do not trouble *or* assault Moab or contend with them in battle, for I will not give you any of their land for a possession, because I have given Ar to the sons of Lot for a possession.

[10] (The Emim dwelt there in times past, a people great and many, and tall as the Anakim.

[11] These also are known as Rephaim [of giant stature], as are the Anakim, but the Moabites call them Emim.

[12] The Horites also formerly lived in Seir, but the sons of Esau dispossessed them and destroyed them from before them and dwelt in their stead, as Israel did to the land of their possession which the Lord gave to them.)

[13] Now rise up and go over the brook Zered. So we went over the brook Zered.

[14] And the time from our leaving Kadesh-barnea until we had come over the brook Zered was thirty-eight years, until the whole generation of the men of war had perished from the camp, as the Lord had sworn to them.

[15] Moreover the hand of the Lord was against them to exterminate them from the midst of the camp, until they were all gone.

[16] So when all the men of war had died from among the people,

[17] The Lord spoke to me [Moses], saying,

[18] You are this day to pass through Ar, the border of Moab.

[19] But when you come near the territory of the sons of Ammon, do not trouble *or* assault them or provoke *or* stir them up, for I will not give you any of the land of the Ammonites for a possession, because I have given it to the sons of Lot for a possession.

[20] (That also is known as a land of Rephaim [of giant stature]; Rephaim dwelt there formerly, but the Ammonites call them Zamzummim,

[21] A people great and many, and tall as the Anakim. But the Lord destroyed them before [Ammon], and they dispossessed them and settled in their stead,

[22] As He did for the sons of Esau, who dwell in Seir, when He destroyed the Horites from before them, and they dispossessed them and settled in their stead even to this day.

[23] As for the Avvim who dwelt in villages as far as Gaza, the Caphtorim who came from Caphtor destroyed them and dwelt in their stead.)

---

[a] 1 Or *the Sea of Reeds*    [b] 23 That is, Crete

## New International Version

### Defeat of Sihon King of Heshbon

24 "Set out now and cross the Arnon Gorge. See, I have given into your hand Sihon the Amorite, king of Heshbon, and his country. Begin to take possession of it and engage him in battle. 25 This very day I will begin to put the terror and fear of you on all the nations under heaven. They will hear reports of you and will tremble and be in anguish because of you."

26 From the Desert of Kedemoth I sent messengers to Sihon king of Heshbon offering peace and saying, 27 "Let us pass through your country. We will stay on the main road; we will not turn aside to the right or to the left. 28 Sell us food to eat and water to drink for their price in silver. Only let us pass through on foot— 29 as the descendants of Esau, who live in Seir, and the Moabites, who live in Ar, did for us—until we cross the Jordan into the land the LORD our God is giving us." 30 But Sihon king of Heshbon refused to let us pass through. For the LORD your God had made his spirit stubborn and his heart obstinate in order to give him into your hands, as he has now done.

31 The LORD said to me, "See, I have begun to deliver Sihon and his country over to you. Now begin to conquer and possess his land."

32 When Sihon and all his army came out to meet us in battle at Jahaz, 33 the LORD our God delivered him over to us and we struck him down, together with his sons and his whole army. 34 At that time we took all his towns and completely destroyed[a] them—men, women and children. We left no survivors. 35 But the livestock and the plunder from the towns we had captured we carried off for ourselves. 36 From Aroer on the rim of the Arnon Gorge, and from the town in the gorge, even as far as Gilead, not one town was too strong for us. The LORD our God gave us all of them. 37 But in accordance with the command of the LORD our God, you did not encroach on any of the land of the Ammonites, neither the land along the course of the Jabbok nor that around the towns in the hills.

### Defeat of Og King of Bashan

**3** Next we turned and went up along the road toward Bashan, and Og king of Bashan with his whole army marched out to meet us in battle at Edrei. 2 The LORD said to me, "Do not be afraid of him, for I have delivered him into your hands, along with his whole army and his land. Do to him what you did to Sihon king of the Amorites, who reigned in Heshbon."

3 So the LORD our God also gave into our hands Og king of Bashan and all his army. We struck them down, leaving no survivors. 4 At that time we took all his cities. There was not one of the sixty cities that we did not take from them—the whole region of Argob, Og's kingdom in Bashan. 5 All these cities were fortified with high walls and with gates and bars, and there were also a great many unwalled villages. 6 We completely destroyed[a] them, as we had done with Sihon king of Heshbon, destroying[a] every city—men, women and children. 7 But all the livestock and the plunder from their cities we carried off for ourselves.

---

[a] 34,6 The Hebrew term refers to the irrevocable giving over of things or persons to the LORD, often by totally destroying them.

## Amplified Bible

24 Rise up, take your journey, and pass over the Valley of the Arnon. Behold, I have given into your hand Sihon the Amorite, king of Heshbon, and his land; begin to possess it and contend with him in battle.

25 This day will I begin to put the dread and fear of you upon the peoples who are under the whole heavens, who shall hear the report of you and shall tremble and be in anguish because of you.

26 So I sent messengers from the wilderness of Kedemoth to Sihon king of Heshbon with words of peace, saying,

27 Let me pass through your land. I will go only by the road, turning aside neither to the right nor to the left.

28 You shall sell me food to eat and sell me water to drink; only let me walk through,

29 As the sons of Esau, who dwell in Seir, and the Moabites, who dwell in Ar, [a] did for me, until I go over the Jordan into the land which the Lord our God gives us.

30 But Sihon king of Heshbon would not let us pass by him; for the Lord your God hardened his spirit and made his heart obstinate, that He might give him into your hand, as at this day.

31 And the Lord said to me [Moses], Behold, I have begun to give Sihon and his land over to you. Begin to take possession, that you may succeed him *and* occupy his land.

32 Then Sihon came out against us, he and all his people, to fight at Jahaz.

33 And the Lord our God gave him over to us, and we defeated him and his sons and all his people.

34 At the same time we took all his cities and utterly destroyed every city—men, women, and children. We left none to remain.

35 Only the cattle we took as booty for ourselves and the spoil of the cities which we had captured.

36 From Aroer, which is on the edge of the Arnon Valley, and from the city that is in the valley, as far as Gilead, there was no city too high *and* strong for us; the Lord our God delivered all to us.

37 Only you did not go near the land of the Ammonites, that is, to any bank of the river Jabbok and the cities of the hill country, and wherever the Lord our God had forbidden us.

**3** Then we turned and went up the road to Bashan, and Og king of Bashan came out against us, he and all his people, to battle at Edrei.

2 And the Lord said to me, Do not fear him, for I have given him and all his people and his land into your hand; and you shall do to him as you did to Sihon king of the Amorites, who lived at Heshbon.

3 So the Lord our God also gave into our hands Og king of Bashan and all his people, and we smote him until not one was left to him.

4 And we took all his cities at that time; there was not a city which we did not take from them, sixty cities, the whole region of Argob, the kingdom of Og in Bashan.

5 All these cities were fortified with high *and* haughty walls, gates, and bars, besides a great many unwalled villages.

6 And we utterly destroyed them, as we did to Sihon king of Heshbon, utterly destroying every city—men, women, and children.

7 But all the cattle and the spoil of the cities we took for booty for ourselves.

---

[a] All that is said here is that the Edomites and Moabites sold Israel bread and water. There is no denial, expressed or implied, of their hostility to Israel and their desire for her destruction. The passage is in entire harmony with Num. 20:17, 21, and Deut. 23:3, 4 (J. P. Lange, *A Commentary*).

## New International Version

8So at that time we took from these two kings of the Amorites the territory east of the Jordan, from the Arnon Gorge as far as Mount Hermon. 9(Hermon is called Sirion by the Sidonians; the Amorites call it Senir.) 10We took all the towns on the plateau, and all Gilead, and all Bashan as far as Salekah and Edrei, towns of Og's kingdom in Bashan. 11(Og king of Bashan was the last of the Rephaites. His bed was decorated with iron and was more than nine cubits long and four cubits wide.*a* It is still in Rabbah of the Ammonites.)

### Division of the Land

12Of the land that we took over at that time, I gave the Reubenites and the Gadites the territory north of Aroer by the Arnon Gorge, including half the hill country of Gilead, together with its towns. 13The rest of Gilead and also all of Bashan, the kingdom of Og, I gave to the half-tribe of Manasseh. (The whole region of Argob in Bashan used to be known as a land of the Rephaites. 14Jair, a descendant of Manasseh, took the whole region of Argob as far as the border of the Geshurites and the Maakathites; it was named after him, so that to this day Bashan is called Havvoth Jair.*b*) 15And I gave Gilead to Makir. 16But to the Reubenites and the Gadites I gave the territory extending from Gilead down to the Arnon Gorge (the middle of the gorge being the border) and out to the Jabbok River, which is the border of the Ammonites. 17Its western border was the Jordan in the Arabah, from Kinnereth to the Sea of the Arabah (that is, the Dead Sea), below the slopes of Pisgah.

18I commanded you at that time: "The LORD your God has given you this land to take possession of it. But all your able-bodied men, armed for battle, must cross over ahead of the other Israelites. 19However, your wives, your children and your livestock (I know you have much livestock) may stay in the towns I have given you, 20until the LORD gives rest to your fellow Israelites as he has to you, and they too have taken over the land that the LORD your God is giving them across the Jordan. After that, each of you may go back to the possession I have given you."

### Moses Forbidden to Cross the Jordan

21At that time I commanded Joshua: "You have seen with your own eyes all that the LORD your God has done to these two kings. The LORD will do the same to all the kingdoms over there where you are going. 22Do not be afraid of them; the LORD your God himself will fight for you."

23At that time I pleaded with the LORD: 24"Sovereign LORD, you have begun to show to your servant your greatness and your strong hand. For what god is there in heaven or on earth who can do the deeds and mighty works you do? 25Let me go over and see the good land beyond the Jordan—that fine hill country and Lebanon." 26But because of you the LORD was angry with me and would not listen to me. "That is enough," the LORD said. "Do not speak to me anymore about this matter. 27Go up to the top of Pisgah and look west and north and south and east. Look at the land with your own eyes, since you are not going to cross this Jordan. 28But commission Joshua, and encourage and strengthen him, for he will lead this people across and will cause them to inherit the land that you will see." 29So we stayed in the valley near Beth Peor.

## Amplified Bible

8So we took the land at that time out of the hand of the two kings of the Amorites who were beyond the Jordan, from the Valley of the Arnon to Mount Hermon 9(The Sidonians call Hermon, Sirion, and the Amorites call it Senir), 10All the cities of the plain, and all Gilead, and all Bashan as far as Salecah and Edrei, cities of the kingdom of Og in Bashan. 11For only Og king of Bashan remained of the remnant of the [gigantic] Rephaim. Behold, his bedstead was of iron; is it not in Rabbah of the Ammonites? Nine cubits was its length and four cubits its breadth, using the cubit of a man [the forearm to the end of the middle finger].

12When we took possession of this land, I gave to the Reubenites and the Gadites the territory from Aroer, which is on the edge of the Valley of the Arnon, and half the hill country of Gilead and its cities. 13The rest of Gilead and all of Bashan, the kingdom of Og, that is, all the region of Argob in Bashan, I gave to the half-tribe of Manasseh. It is called the land of Rephaim [of giant stature]. 14Jair son of Manasseh took all the region of Argob, that is, Bashan, as far as the border of the Geshurites and the Maacathites, and called it after his own name, Havvoth-jair, so called to this day. 15And I gave Gilead to Machir [son of Manasseh]. 16And to the Reubenites and Gadites I gave from Gilead even to the Valley of the Arnon, with the middle of the valley as the boundary of it, as far over as the river Jabbok, the boundary of the Ammonites, 17The Arabah also, with the Jordan as its boundary, from Chinnereth as far as the Sea of the Arabah, the Salt [Dead] Sea, under the cliffs [of the headlands] of Pisgah on the east.

18And I commanded you at that time, saying, The Lord your God has given you this land to possess it; you [Reuben, Gad, and the half-tribe of Manasseh] shall go over [the Jordan] armed before your brethren the other Israelites, all that are able for war. 19But your wives and your little ones and your cattle—I know that you have many cattle—shall remain in your cities which I have given you, 20Until the Lord has given rest to your brethren as to you, and until they also possess the land which the Lord your God has given them beyond the Jordan. Then shall you return every man to the possession which I have given you. 21And I commanded Joshua at that time, saying, Your *own* eyes have seen all that the Lord your God has done to these two kings [Sihon and Og]; so shall the Lord do to all the kingdoms into which you are going over [the Jordan]. 22You shall not fear them, for the Lord your God shall fight for you.

23And I besought the Lord at that time, saying, 24O Lord God, You have only begun to show Your servant Your greatness and Your mighty hand; for what god is there in heaven or on earth that can do according to Your works and according to Your might? 25I pray You, [will You not just] let me go over and see the good land that is beyond the Jordan, that goodly mountain country [with Hermon] and Lebanon? 26But the Lord was angry with me on your account and would not listen to me; and the Lord said to me, That is enough! Say no more to Me about it. 27Get up to the top of Pisgah and lift up your eyes westward and northward and southward and eastward, and behold it with your eyes, for you shall not go over this Jordan. 28But charge Joshua, and encourage and strengthen him, for he shall go over before this people and he shall cause them to possess the land which you shall see. 29So we remained in the valley opposite Beth-peor.

---

*a* 11 That is, about 14 feet long and 6 feet wide or about 4 meters long and 1.8 meters wide    *b* 14 Or *called the settlements of Jair*

## New International Version

### Obedience Commanded

4 Now, Israel, hear the decrees and laws I am about to teach you. Follow them so that you may live and may go in and take possession of the land the LORD, the God of your ancestors, is giving you. ²Do not add to what I command you and do not subtract from it, but keep the commands of the LORD your God that I give you.

³You saw with your own eyes what the LORD did at Baal Peor. The LORD your God destroyed from among you everyone who followed the Baal of Peor, ⁴but all of you who held fast to the LORD your God are still alive today.

⁵See, I have taught you decrees and laws as the LORD my God commanded me, so that you may follow them in the land you are entering to take possession of it. ⁶Observe them carefully, for this will show your wisdom and understanding to the nations, who will hear about all these decrees and say, "Surely this great nation is a wise and understanding people." ⁷What other nation is so great as to have their gods near them the way the LORD our God is near us whenever we pray to him? ⁸And what other nation is so great as to have such righteous decrees and laws as this body of laws I am setting before you today?

⁹Only be careful, and watch yourselves closely so that you do not forget the things your eyes have seen or let them fade from your heart as long as you live. Teach them to your children and to their children after them. ¹⁰Remember the day you stood before the LORD your God at Horeb, when he said to me, "Assemble the people before me to hear my words so that they may learn to revere me as long as they live in the land and may teach them to their children." ¹¹You came near and stood at the foot of the mountain while it blazed with fire to the very heavens, with black clouds and deep darkness. ¹²Then the LORD spoke to you out of the fire. You heard the sound of words but saw no form; there was only a voice. ¹³He declared to you his covenant, the Ten Commandments, which he commanded you to follow and then wrote them on two stone tablets. ¹⁴And the LORD directed me at that time to teach you the decrees and laws you are to follow in the land that you are crossing the Jordan to possess.

### Idolatry Forbidden

¹⁵You saw no form of any kind the day the LORD spoke to you at Horeb out of the fire. Therefore watch yourselves very carefully, ¹⁶so that you do not become corrupt and make for yourselves an idol, an image of any shape, whether formed like a man or a woman, ¹⁷or like any animal on earth or any bird that flies in the air, ¹⁸or like any creature that moves along the ground or any fish in the waters below. ¹⁹And when you look up to the sky and see the sun, the moon and the stars—all the heavenly array—do not be enticed into bowing down to them and worshiping things the LORD your God has apportioned to all the nations under heaven. ²⁰But as for you, the LORD took you and brought you out of the iron-smelting furnace, out of Egypt, to be the people of his inheritance, as you now are.

²¹The LORD was angry with me because of you, and he solemnly swore that I would not cross the Jordan and enter the good land the LORD your God is giving you as your

## Amplified Bible

4 Now listen and give heed, O Israel, to the statutes and ordinances which I teach you, and do them, that you may live and go in and possess the land which the Lord, the God of your fathers, gives you.

²You shall not add to the word which I command you, neither shall you diminish it, that you may keep the commandments of the Lord your God which I command you.

³Your eyes still see what the Lord did because of Baal-peor; for all the men who followed the Baal of Peor the Lord your God has destroyed from among you, [Num. 25:1-9.]

⁴But you who clung fast to the Lord your God are alive, every one of you, this day.

⁵Behold, I have taught you statutes and ordinances as the Lord my God commanded me, that you should do them in the land which you are entering to possess.

⁶So keep them and do them, for that is your wisdom and your understanding in the sight of the peoples who, when they hear all these statutes, will say, Surely this great nation is a wise and understanding people.

⁷For what great nation is there who has a god so near to them as the Lord our God is to us in all things for which we call upon Him?

⁸And what large and important nation has statutes and ordinances so upright and just as all this law which I set before you today?

⁹Only take heed, and guard your life diligently, lest you forget the things which your eyes have seen and lest they depart from your [mind and] heart all the days of your life. Teach them to your children and your children's children—

¹⁰Especially how on the day that you stood before the Lord your God in Horeb, the Lord said to me, Gather the people together to Me and I will make them hear My words, that they may learn [reverently] to fear Me all the days they live upon the earth and that they may teach their children.

¹¹And you came near and stood at the foot of the mountain, and the mountain burned with fire to the heart of heaven, with darkness, cloud, and thick gloom.

¹²And the Lord spoke to you out of the midst of the fire. You heard the voice of the words, but saw no form; there was only a voice.

¹³And He declared to you His covenant, which He commanded you to perform, the Ten Commandments, and He wrote them on two tables of stone.

¹⁴And the Lord commanded me at that time to teach you the statutes and precepts, that you might do them in the land which you are going over to possess.

¹⁵Therefore take good heed to yourselves, since you saw no form of Him on the day the Lord spoke to you on Horeb out of the midst of the fire,

¹⁶Beware lest you become corrupt by making for yourselves [to worship] a graven image in the form of any figure, the likeness of male or female,

¹⁷The likeness of any beast that is on the earth, or of any winged fowl that flies in the air,

¹⁸The likeness of anything that creeps on the ground, or of any fish that is in the waters beneath the earth.

¹⁹And beware lest you lift up your eyes to the heavens, and when you see the sun, moon, and stars, even all the host of the heavens, you be drawn away and worship them and serve them, things which the Lord your God has allotted to all nations under the whole heaven.

²⁰But the Lord has taken you and brought you forth out of the iron furnace, out of Egypt, to be to Him a people of His own possession, as you are this day.

²¹Furthermore the Lord was angry with me because of you, and He swore that I should not go over the Jordan and that I should not enter the good land which the Lord your God gives you for an inheritance.

## New International Version

inheritance. <sup>22</sup>I will die in this land; I will not cross the Jordan; but you are about to cross over and take possession of that good land. <sup>23</sup>Be careful not to forget the covenant of the LORD your God that he made with you; do not make for yourselves an idol in the form of anything the LORD your God has forbidden. <sup>24</sup>For the LORD your God is a consuming fire, a jealous God.

<sup>25</sup>After you have had children and grandchildren and have lived in the land a long time—if you then become corrupt and make any kind of idol, doing evil in the eyes of the LORD your God and arousing his anger, <sup>26</sup>I call the heavens and the earth as witnesses against you this day that you will quickly perish from the land that you are crossing the Jordan to possess. You will not live there long but will certainly be destroyed. <sup>27</sup>The LORD will scatter you among the peoples, and only a few of you will survive among the nations to which the LORD will drive you. <sup>28</sup>There you will worship man-made gods of wood and stone, which cannot see or hear or eat or smell. <sup>29</sup>But if from there you seek the LORD your God, you will find him if you seek him with all your heart and with all your soul. <sup>30</sup>When you are in distress and all these things have happened to you, then in later days you will return to the LORD your God and obey him. <sup>31</sup>For the LORD your God is a merciful God; he will not abandon or destroy you or forget the covenant with your ancestors, which he confirmed to them by oath.

### The LORD Is God

<sup>32</sup>Ask now about the former days, long before your time, from the day God created human beings on the earth; ask from one end of the heavens to the other. Has anything so great as this ever happened, or has anything like it ever been heard of? <sup>33</sup>Has any other people heard the voice of God[a] speaking out of fire, as you have, and lived? <sup>34</sup>Has any god ever tried to take for himself one nation out of another nation, by testings, by signs and wonders, by war, by a mighty hand and an outstretched arm, or by great and awesome deeds, like all the things the LORD your God did for you in Egypt before your very eyes?

<sup>35</sup>You were shown these things so that you might know that the LORD is God; besides him there is no other. <sup>36</sup>From heaven he made you hear his voice to discipline you. On earth he showed you his great fire, and you heard his words from out of the fire. <sup>37</sup>Because he loved your ancestors and chose their descendants after them, he brought you out of Egypt by his Presence and his great strength, <sup>38</sup>to drive out before you nations greater and stronger than you and to bring you into their land to give it to you for your inheritance, as it is today.

<sup>39</sup>Acknowledge and take to heart this day that the LORD is God in heaven above and on the earth below. There is no other. <sup>40</sup>Keep his decrees and commands, which I am giving you today, so that it may go well with you and your children after you and that you may live long in the land the LORD your God gives you for all time.

### Cities of Refuge

<sup>41</sup>Then Moses set aside three cities east of the Jordan, <sup>42</sup>to which anyone who had killed a person could flee if they had unintentionally killed a neighbor without malice aforethought. They could flee into one of these cities and

## Amplified Bible

<sup>22</sup>But I must die in this land; I must not cross the Jordan; but you shall go over and possess that good land.

<sup>23</sup>Take heed to yourselves, lest you forget the covenant of the Lord your God which He made with you, and make for yourselves a graven image in the form of anything which the Lord your God has forbidden you.

<sup>24</sup>For the Lord your God is a consuming fire, a jealous God.

<sup>25</sup>When children shall be born to you, and children's children, and you have grown old in the land, if you corrupt yourselves by making a graven image in the form of anything, and do evil in the sight of the Lord your God, provoking Him to anger,

<sup>26</sup>I call heaven and earth to witness against you this day that you shall soon utterly perish from the land which you are going over the Jordan to possess. You will not live long upon it but will be utterly destroyed.

<sup>27</sup>And the Lord will scatter you among the peoples, and you will be left few in number among the nations to which the Lord will drive you.

<sup>28</sup>There you will serve gods, the work of men's hands, wood and stone, which neither see nor hear nor eat nor smell.

<sup>29</sup>But if from there you will seek (inquire for and require as necessity) the Lord your God, you will find Him if you [truly] seek Him with all your heart [and mind] and soul and life.

<sup>30</sup>When you are in tribulation and all these things come upon you, in the latter days you will turn to the Lord your God and be obedient to His voice.

<sup>31</sup>For the Lord your God is a merciful God; He will not fail you or destroy you or forget the covenant of your fathers, which He swore to them.

<sup>32</sup>For ask now of the days that are past, which were before you, since the day that God created man upon the earth, and ask from one end of the heavens to the other, whether such a great thing as this has ever occurred or been heard of anywhere.

<sup>33</sup>Did ever people hear the voice of God speaking out of the midst of the fire, as you heard, and live?

<sup>34</sup>Or has God ever tried to go and take for Himself a nation from the midst of another nation, by trials, by signs, by wonders, by war, by a mighty hand, by an outstretched arm, and by great terrors, as the Lord your God did for you in Egypt before your eyes?

<sup>35</sup>To you it was shown, that you might realize and have personal knowledge that the Lord is God; there is no other besides Him.

<sup>36</sup>Out of heaven He made you hear His voice, that He might correct, discipline, and admonish you; and on earth He made you see His great fire, and you heard His words out of the midst of the fire.

<sup>37</sup>And because He loved your fathers, He chose their descendants after them, and brought you out from Egypt with His own Presence, by His mighty power,

<sup>38</sup>Driving out nations from before you, greater and mightier than yourselves, to bring you in, to give you their land for an inheritance, as it is this day;

<sup>39</sup>Know, recognize, and understand therefore this day and turn your [mind and] heart to it that the Lord is God in the heavens above and upon the earth beneath; there is no other.

<sup>40</sup>Therefore you shall keep His statutes and His commandments, which I command you this day, that it may go well with you and your children after you and that you may prolong your days in the land which the Lord your God gives you forever.

<sup>41</sup>Then Moses set apart three cities [of refuge] beyond the Jordan to the east,

<sup>42</sup>That the manslayer might flee there, who slew his neighbor unintentionally and had not previously been at enmity with him, that fleeing to one of these cities he might save his life:

<sup>a</sup> 33 Or of a god

## New International Version

save their life. [43]The cities were these: Bezer in the wilderness plateau, for the Reubenites; Ramoth in Gilead, for the Gadites; and Golan in Bashan, for the Manassites.

### Introduction to the Law

[44]This is the law Moses set before the Israelites. [45]These are the stipulations, decrees and laws Moses gave them when they came out of Egypt [46]and were in the valley near Beth Peor east of the Jordan, in the land of Sihon king of the Amorites, who reigned in Heshbon and was defeated by Moses and the Israelites as they came out of Egypt. [47]They took possession of his land and the land of Og king of Bashan, the two Amorite kings east of the Jordan. [48]This land extended from Aroer on the rim of the Arnon Gorge to Mount Sirion[a] (that is, Hermon), [49]and included all the Arabah east of the Jordan, as far as the Dead Sea,[b] below the slopes of Pisgah.

### The Ten Commandments

**5** Moses summoned all Israel and said:
Hear, Israel, the decrees and laws I declare in your hearing today. Learn them and be sure to follow them. [2]The Lord our God made a covenant with us at Horeb. [3]It was not with our ancestors[c] that the Lord made this covenant, but with us, with all of us who are alive here today. [4]The Lord spoke to you face to face out of the fire on the mountain. [5](At that time I stood between the Lord and you to declare to you the word of the Lord, because you were afraid of the fire and did not go up the mountain.) And he said:

[6]"I am the Lord your God, who brought you out of Egypt, out of the land of slavery.

[7]"You shall have no other gods before[d] me.

[8]"You shall not make for yourself an image in the form of anything in heaven above or on the earth beneath or in the waters below. You shall not bow down to them or worship them; for I, the Lord your God, am a jealous God, punishing the children for the sin of the parents to the third and fourth generation of those who hate me, [10]but showing love to a thousand generations of those who love me and keep my commandments.

[11]"You shall not misuse the name of the Lord your God, for the Lord will not hold anyone guiltless who misuses his name.

[12]"Observe the Sabbath day by keeping it holy, as the Lord your God has commanded you. [13]Six days you shall labor and do all your work, [14]but the seventh day is a sabbath to the Lord your God. On it you shall not do any work, neither you, nor your son or daughter, nor your male or female servant, nor your ox, your donkey or any of your animals, nor any foreigner residing in your towns, so that your male and female servants may rest, as you do. [15]Remember that you were slaves in Egypt and that the Lord your God brought you out of there with a mighty hand and an outstretched arm. Therefore the Lord your God has commanded you to observe the Sabbath day.

[16]"Honor your father and your mother, as the Lord your God has commanded you, so that you may live long and that it may go well with you in the land the Lord your God is giving you.

[17]"You shall not murder.

[18]"You shall not commit adultery.

## Amplified Bible

[43]Bezer in the wilderness on the tableland, for the Reubenites; and Ramoth in Gilead, for the Gadites; and Golan in Bashan, for the Manassites.

[44]This is the law which Moses set before the Israelites.

[45]These are the testimonies and the laws and the precepts which Moses spoke to the Israelites when they came out of Egypt,

[46]Beyond the Jordan in the valley opposite Beth-peor, in the land of Sihon king of the Amorites, who dwelt at Heshbon, whom Moses and the Israelites smote when they came out of Egypt.

[47]And they took possession of his land and the land of Og king of Bashan, the two kings of the Amorites, who lived beyond the Jordan to the east,

[48]From Aroer, which is on the edge of the Valley of the Arnon, as far as Mount Sirion (that is, Hermon),

[49]And all the Arabah (lowlands) beyond the Jordan eastward, as far as the Sea of the Arabah [the Dead Sea], under the slopes *and* springs of Pisgah.

**5** And Moses called all Israel, and said to them, Hear, O Israel, the statutes and ordinances which I speak in your hearing this day, that you may learn them and take heed and do them.

[2]The Lord our God made a covenant with us in Horeb.

[3]The Lord made this covenant not with our fathers, but with us, who are all of us here alive this day.

[4]The Lord spoke with you face to face at the mount out of the midst of the fire.

[5]I stood between the Lord and you at that time to show you the word of the Lord, for you were afraid because of the fire and went not up into the mount. He said,

[6]I am the Lord your God, Who brought you out of the land of Egypt, from the house of bondage.

[7]You shall have no other gods before Me *or* besides Me.

[8]You shall not make for yourself [to worship] a graven image or any likeness of anything that is in the heavens above or that is in the earth beneath or that is in the water under the earth.

[9]You shall not bow down to them or serve them; for I, the Lord your God, am a jealous God, visiting the iniquity of the fathers upon the children to the third and fourth generations of those who hate Me,

[10]And showing mercy *and* steadfast love to thousands *and* to a thousand generations of those who love Me and keep My commandments.

[11]You shall not take the name of the Lord your God in vain, for the Lord will not hold him guiltless who takes His name in falsehood *or* without purpose.

[12]Observe the Sabbath day to keep it holy, as the Lord your God commanded you.

[13]Six days you shall labor and do all your work,

[14]But the seventh day is a Sabbath to the Lord your God; in it you shall not do any work, you or your son or your daughter, or your manservant or your maidservant, or your ox or your donkey or any of your livestock, or the stranger *or* sojourner who is within your gates, that your manservant and your maidservant may rest as well as you.

[15]And [earnestly] remember that you were a servant in the land of Egypt and that the Lord your God brought you out from there with a mighty hand and an outstretched arm; therefore the Lord your God commanded you to observe *and* take heed to the Sabbath day.

[16]Honor your father and your mother, as the Lord your God commanded you, that your days may be prolonged and that it may go well with you in the land which the Lord your God gives you.

[17]You shall not murder.

[18]Neither shall you commit adultery.

---

[a] 48 Syriac (see also 3:9); Hebrew *Siyon*   [b] 49 Hebrew *the Sea of the Arabah*   [c] 3 Or *not only with our parents*   [d] 7 Or *besides*

## New International Version

19"You shall not steal.

20"You shall not give false testimony against your neighbor.

21"You shall not covet your neighbor's wife. You shall not set your desire on your neighbor's house or land, his male or female servant, his ox or donkey, or anything that belongs to your neighbor."

22These are the commandments the LORD proclaimed in a loud voice to your whole assembly there on the mountain from out of the fire, the cloud and the deep darkness; and he added nothing more. Then he wrote them on two stone tablets and gave them to me.

23When you heard the voice out of the darkness, while the mountain was ablaze with fire, all the leaders of your tribes and your elders came to me. 24And you said, "The LORD our God has shown us his glory and his majesty, and we have heard his voice from the fire. Today we have seen that a person can live even if God speaks with them. 25But now, why should we die? This great fire will consume us, and we will die if we hear the voice of the LORD our God any longer. 26For what mortal has ever heard the voice of the living God speaking out of fire, as we have, and survived? 27Go near and listen to all that the LORD our God says. Then tell us whatever the LORD our God tells you. We will listen and obey."

28The LORD heard you when you spoke to me, and the LORD said to me, "I have heard what this people said to you. Everything they said was good. 29Oh, that their hearts would be inclined to fear me and keep all my commands always, so that it might go well with them and their children forever!

30"Go, tell them to return to their tents. 31But you stay here with me so that I may give you all the commands, decrees and laws you are to teach them to follow in the land I am giving them to possess."

32So be careful to do what the LORD your God has commanded you; do not turn aside to the right or to the left. 33Walk in obedience to all that the LORD your God has commanded you, so that you may live and prosper and prolong your days in the land that you will possess.

### Love the LORD Your God

6 These are the commands, decrees and laws the LORD your God directed me to teach you to observe in the land that you are crossing the Jordan to possess, 2so that you, your children and their children after them may fear the LORD your God as long as you live by keeping all his decrees and commands that I give you, and so that you may enjoy long life. 3Hear, Israel, and be careful to obey so that it may go well with you and that you may increase greatly in a land flowing with milk and honey, just as the LORD, the God of your ancestors, promised you.

4Hear, O Israel: The LORD our God, the LORD is one.[a] 5Love the LORD your God with all your heart and with all your soul and with all your strength. 6These commandments that I give you today are to be on your hearts. 7Impress them on your children. Talk about them when you sit

## Amplified Bible

19Neither shall you act slyly or steal.

20Neither shall you witness falsely against your neighbor.

21Neither shall you covet your neighbor's wife, nor desire your neighbor's house, his field, his manservant or his maidservant, his ox or his donkey, or anything that is your neighbor's.

22These words the Lord spoke to all your assembly at the mountain out of the midst of the fire, the cloud, and the thick darkness, with a loud voice; and He spoke not again [added no more]. He wrote them on two tables of stone and gave them to me [Moses].

23And when you heard the voice out of the midst of the darkness, while the mountain was burning with fire, you came near me, all the heads of your tribes and your elders; 24And you said, Behold, the Lord our God has shown us His glory and His greatness, and we have heard His voice out of the midst of the fire; we have this day seen that God speaks with man and man still lives.

25Now therefore, why should we die? For this great fire will consume us; if we hear the voice of the Lord our God any longer, we shall die. 26For who is there of all flesh who has heard the voice of the living God speaking out of the midst of fire, as we have, and lived? 27Go near [Moses] and hear all that the Lord our God will say. And speak to us all that the Lord our God will speak to you; and we will hear and do it.

28And the Lord heard your words when you spoke to me and the Lord said to me, I have heard the words of this people which they have spoken to you. They have said well all that they have spoken.

29Oh, that they had such a [mind and] heart in them always [reverently] to fear Me and keep all My commandments, that it might go well with them and with their children forever!

30Go and say to them, Return to your tents.

31But you [Moses], stand here by Me, and I will tell you all the commandments and the statutes and the precepts which you shall teach them, that they may do them in the land which I give them to possess.

32Therefore you people shall be watchful to do as the Lord your God has commanded you; you shall not turn aside to the right hand or to the left.

33You shall walk in all the ways which the Lord your God has commanded you, that you may live and that it may go well with you and that you may live long in the land which you shall possess.

6 Now this is the instruction, the laws, and the precepts which the Lord your God commanded me to teach you, that you might do them in the land to which you go to possess it,

2That you may [reverently] fear the Lord your God, you and your son and your son's son, and keep all His statutes and His commandments which I command you all the days of your life, and that your days may be prolonged.

3Hear therefore, O Israel, and be watchful to do them, that it may be well with you and that you may increase exceedingly, as the Lord, the God of your fathers, has promised you, in a land flowing with milk and honey.

4Hear, O Israel: the Lord our God is one Lord [the only Lord].

5And you shall love the Lord your God with all your [mind and] heart and with your entire being and with all your might.

6And these words which I am commanding you this day shall be [first] in your [own] minds and hearts; [then]

7You shall whet and sharpen them so as to make them

---

a 4 Or The LORD our God is one LORD; or The LORD is our God, the LORD is one; or The LORD is our God, the LORD alone

## New International Version

at home and when you walk along the road, when you lie down and when you get up. [8]Tie them as symbols on your hands and bind them on your foreheads. [9]Write them on the doorframes of your houses and on your gates.

[10]When the LORD your God brings you into the land he swore to your fathers, to Abraham, Isaac and Jacob, to give you—a land with large, flourishing cities you did not build, [11]houses filled with all kinds of good things you did not provide, wells you did not dig, and vineyards and olive groves you did not plant—then when you eat and are satisfied, [12]be careful that you do not forget the LORD, who brought you out of Egypt, out of the land of slavery.

[13]Fear the LORD your God, serve him only and take your oaths in his name. [14]Do not follow other gods, the gods of the peoples around you; [15]for the LORD your God, who is among you, is a jealous God and his anger will burn against you, and he will destroy you from the face of the land. [16]Do not put the LORD your God to the test as you did at Massah. [17]Be sure to keep the commands of the LORD your God and the stipulations and decrees he has given you. [18]Do what is right and good in the LORD's sight, so that it may go well with you and you may go in and take over the good land the LORD promised on oath to your ancestors, [19]thrusting out all your enemies before you, as the LORD said.

[20]In the future, when your son asks you, "What is the meaning of the stipulations, decrees and laws the LORD our God has commanded you?" [21]tell him: "We were slaves of Pharaoh in Egypt, but the LORD brought us out of Egypt with a mighty hand. [22]Before our eyes the LORD sent signs and wonders—great and terrible—on Egypt and Pharaoh and his whole household. [23]But he brought us out from there to bring us in and give us the land he promised on oath to our ancestors. [24]The LORD commanded us to obey all these decrees and to fear the LORD our God, so that we might always prosper and be kept alive, as is the case today. [25]And if we are careful to obey all this law before the LORD our God, as he has commanded us, that will be our righteousness."

### Driving Out the Nations

**7** When the LORD your God brings you into the land you are entering to possess and drives out before you many nations—the Hittites, Girgashites, Amorites, Canaanites, Perizzites, Hivites and Jebusites, seven nations larger and stronger than you— [2]and when the LORD your God has delivered them over to you and you have defeated them, then you must destroy them totally.[a] Make no treaty with them, and show them no mercy. [3]Do not intermarry with them. Do not give your daughters to their sons or take their daughters for your sons, [4]for they will turn your children away from following me to serve other

## Amplified Bible

penetrate, *and* teach *and* impress them diligently upon the [minds and] hearts of your children, and shall talk of them when you sit in your house and when you walk by the way, and when you lie down and when you rise up.

[8]And you shall bind them as a sign upon your hand, and they shall be as frontlets (forehead bands) between your eyes.

[9]And you shall write them upon the doorposts of your house and on your gates.

[10]And when the Lord your God brings you into the land which He swore to your fathers, to Abraham, Isaac, and Jacob, to give you, with great and goodly cities which you did not build,

[11]And houses full of all good things which you did not fill, and cisterns hewn out which you did not hew, and vineyards and olive trees which you did not plant, and when you eat and are full,

[12]Then beware lest you forget the Lord, Who brought you out of the land of Egypt, out of the house of bondage.

[13]You shall [reverently] fear the Lord your God and serve Him and swear by His name [and presence].

[14]You shall not go after other gods, any of the gods of the peoples who are round about you;

[15]For the Lord your God in the midst of you is a jealous God; lest the anger of the Lord your God be kindled against you, and He destroy you from the face of the earth.

[16]You shall not tempt *and* try the Lord your God as you tempted *and* tried Him in Massah. [Exod. 17:7.]

[17]You shall diligently keep the commandments of the Lord your God and His exhortations and His statutes which He commanded you.

[18]And you shall do what is right and good in the sight of the Lord, that it may go well with you and that you may go in and possess the good land which the Lord swore to give to your fathers,

[19]To cast out all your enemies from before you, as the Lord has promised.

[20]When your son asks you in time to come, What is the meaning of the testimonies and statutes and precepts which the Lord our God has commanded you?

[21]Then you shall say to your son, We were Pharaoh's bondmen in Egypt, and the Lord brought us out of Egypt with a mighty hand.

[22]And the Lord showed signs and wonders, great and evil, against Egypt, against Pharaoh, and all his household, before our eyes;

[23]And He brought us out from there, that He might bring us in to give us the land which He swore to give our fathers.

[24]And the Lord commanded us to do all these statutes, to [reverently] fear the Lord our God for our good always, that He might preserve us alive, as it is this day.

[25]And it will be accounted as righteousness (conformity to God's will in word, thought, and action) for us if we are watchful to do all this commandment before the Lord our God, as He has commanded us.

**7** When the Lord your God brings you into the land which you are entering to possess and has plucked away many nations before you, the Hittites, the Girgashites, the Amorites, the Canaanites, the Perizzites, the Hivites, and the Jebusites, seven nations greater and mightier than you,

[2]And when the Lord your God gives them over to you and you smite them, then you must utterly destroy them. You shall make no covenant with them, or show mercy to them.

[3]You shall not make marriages with them; your daughter you shall not give to his son nor shall you take his daughter for your son,

[4]For they will turn away your sons from following Me,

---

[a] 2 The Hebrew term refers to the irrevocable giving over of things or persons to the LORD, often by totally destroying them; also in verse 26.

## New International Version

gods, and the LORD's anger will burn against you and will quickly destroy you. ⁵This is what you are to do to them: Break down their altars, smash their sacred stones, cut down their Asherah poles*a* and burn their idols in the fire. ⁶For you are a people holy to the LORD your God. The LORD your God has chosen you out of all the peoples on the face of the earth to be his people, his treasured possession.

⁷The LORD did not set his affection on you and choose you because you were more numerous than other peoples, for you were the fewest of all peoples. ⁸But it was because the LORD loved you and kept the oath he swore to your ancestors that he brought you out with a mighty hand and redeemed you from the land of slavery, from the power of Pharaoh king of Egypt. ⁹Know therefore that the LORD your God is God; he is the faithful God, keeping his covenant of love to a thousand generations of those who love him and keep his commandments. ¹⁰But

those who hate him he will repay to their face by destruction;
he will not be slow to repay to their face those who hate him.

¹¹Therefore, take care to follow the commands, decrees and laws I give you today.

¹²If you pay attention to these laws and are careful to follow them, then the LORD your God will keep his covenant of love with you, as he swore to your ancestors. ¹³He will love you and bless you and increase your numbers. He will bless the fruit of your womb, the crops of your land—your grain, new wine and olive oil—the calves of your herds and the lambs of your flocks in the land he swore to your ancestors to give you. ¹⁴You will be blessed more than any other people; none of your men or women will be childless, nor will any of your livestock be without young. ¹⁵The LORD will keep you free from every disease. He will not inflict on you the horrible diseases you knew in Egypt, but he will inflict them on all who hate you. ¹⁶You must destroy all the peoples the LORD your God gives over to you. Do not look on them with pity and do not serve their gods, for that will be a snare to you.

¹⁷You may say to yourselves, "These nations are stronger than we are. How can we drive them out?" ¹⁸But do not be afraid of them; remember well what the LORD your God did to Pharaoh and to all Egypt. ¹⁹You saw with your own eyes the great trials, the signs and wonders, the mighty hand and outstretched arm, with which the LORD your God brought you out. The LORD your God will do the same to all the peoples you now fear. ²⁰Moreover, the LORD your God will send the hornet among them until even the survivors who hide from you have perished. ²¹Do not be terrified by them, for the LORD your God, who is among you, is a great and awesome God. ²²The LORD your God will drive out those nations before you, little by little. You will not be allowed to eliminate them all at once, or the wild animals will multiply around you. ²³But the LORD your God will deliver them over to you, throwing them into great confusion until they are destroyed. ²⁴He will give their kings into

## Amplified Bible

that they may serve other gods; so will the anger of the Lord be kindled against you and He will destroy you quickly.

⁵But thus shall you deal with them: you shall break down their altars and dash in pieces their pillars and hew down their Asherim [symbols of the goddess Asherah] and burn their graven images with fire.

⁶For you are a holy *and* set-apart people to the Lord your God; the Lord your God has chosen you to be a special people to Himself out of all the peoples on the face of the earth.

⁷The Lord did not set His love upon you and choose you because you were more in number than any other people, for you were the fewest of all people.

⁸But because the Lord loves you and because He would keep the oath which He had sworn to your fathers, the Lord has brought you out with a mighty hand and redeemed you out of the house of bondage, from the hand of Pharaoh king of Egypt.

⁹Know, recognize, *and* understand therefore that the Lord your God, He is God, the faithful God, Who keeps covenant and steadfast love *and* mercy with those who love Him and keep His commandments, to a thousand generations,

¹⁰And repays those who hate Him to their face, by destroying them; He will not be slack to him who hates Him, but will requite him to his face.

¹¹You shall therefore keep and do the instruction, laws, and precepts which I command you this day.

¹²And if you hearken to these precepts and keep and do them, the Lord your God will keep with you the covenant and the steadfast love which He swore to your fathers.

¹³And He will love you, bless you, and multiply you; He will also bless the fruit of your body and the fruit of your land, your grain, your new wine, and your oil, the increase of your cattle and the young of your flock in the land which He swore to your fathers to give you.

¹⁴You shall be blessed above all peoples; there shall not be male or female barren among you, or among your cattle.

¹⁵And the Lord will take away from you all sickness, and none of the evil diseases of Egypt which you knew will He put upon you, but will lay them upon all who hate you.

¹⁶And you shall consume all the peoples whom the Lord your God will give over to you; your eye shall not pity them, neither shall you serve their gods, for that would be a snare to you.

¹⁷If you say in your [minds and] hearts, These nations are greater than we are; how can we dispossess them?

¹⁸You shall not be afraid of them, but remember [earnestly] what the Lord your God did to Pharaoh and to all Egypt,

¹⁹The great trials which your eyes saw, the signs, the wonders, the mighty hand and the outstretched arm by which the Lord your God brought you out. So shall the Lord your God do to all the people of whom you are afraid.

²⁰Moreover, the Lord your God will send the *a*hornet among them until those who are left and hide themselves from you are destroyed.

²¹You shall not dread them, for the Lord your God is among you, a mighty and terrible God.

²²And the Lord your God will clear out those nations before you, little by little; you may not consume them quickly, lest the beasts of the field increase among you.

²³But the Lord your God will give them over to you and will confuse them with a mighty panic until they are destroyed.

²⁴And He will give their kings into your hand, and you

---

*a* 5 That is, wooden symbols of the goddess Asherah; here and elsewhere in Deuteronomy

*a* " . . . the hornet" with the article, used in a collective sense as a species or kind, is thus evidently to be understood, as in Deut. 2:25, as the terrors of God which should go before Israel, with which also Josh. 24:12 and Ps. 44:2 fully agree (J. P. Lange, *A Commentary*).

## New International Version

your hand, and you will wipe out their names from under heaven. No one will be able to stand up against you; you will destroy them. 25The images of their gods you are to burn in the fire. Do not covet the silver and gold on them, and do not take it for yourselves, or you will be ensnared by it, for it is detestable to the LORD your God. 26Do not bring a detestable thing into your house or you, like it, will be set apart for destruction. Regard it as vile and utterly detest it, for it is set apart for destruction.

### Do Not Forget the LORD

**8** Be careful to follow every command I am giving you today, so that you may live and increase and may enter and possess the land the LORD promised on oath to your ancestors. 2Remember how the LORD your God led you all the way in the wilderness these forty years, to humble and test you in order to know what was in your heart, whether or not you would keep his commands. 3He humbled you, causing you to hunger and then feeding you with manna, which neither you nor your ancestors had known, to teach you that man does not live on bread alone but on every word that comes from the mouth of the LORD. 4Your clothes did not wear out and your feet did not swell during these forty years. 5Know then in your heart that as a man disciplines his son, so the LORD your God disciplines you.

6Observe the commands of the LORD your God, walking in obedience to him and revering him. 7For the LORD your God is bringing you into a good land—a land with brooks, streams, and deep springs gushing out into the valleys and hills; 8a land with wheat and barley, vines and fig trees, pomegranates, olive oil and honey; 9a land where bread will not be scarce and you will lack nothing; a land where the rocks are iron and you can dig copper out of the hills.

10When you have eaten and are satisfied, praise the LORD your God for the good land he has given you. 11Be careful that you do not forget the LORD your God, failing to observe his commands, his laws and his decrees that I am giving you this day. 12Otherwise, when you eat and are satisfied, when you build fine houses and settle down, 13and when your herds and flocks grow large and your silver and gold increase and all you have is multiplied, 14then your heart will become proud and you will forget the LORD your God, who brought you out of Egypt, out of the land of slavery. 15He led you through the vast and dreadful wilderness, that thirsty and waterless land, with its venomous snakes and scorpions. He brought you water out of hard rock. 16He gave you manna to eat in the wilderness, something your ancestors had never known, to humble and test you so that in the end it might go well with you. 17You may say to yourself, "My power and the strength of my hands have produced this wealth for me." 18But remember the LORD your God, for it is he who gives you the ability to produce wealth, and so confirms his covenant, which he swore to your ancestors, as it is today.

19If you ever forget the LORD your God and follow other gods and worship and bow down to them, I testify against you today that you will surely be destroyed. 20Like the na-

## Amplified Bible

shall make their name perish from under the heavens; there shall no man be able to stand before you, until you have destroyed them.

25The graven images of their gods you shall burn with fire. You shall not desire the silver or gold that is on them, nor take it for yourselves, lest you be ensnared by it, for it is an abomination to the Lord your God.

26Neither shall you bring an abomination (an idol) into your house, lest you become an accursed thing like it; but you shall utterly detest and abhor it, for it is an accursed thing.

**8** All the commandments which I command you this day you shall be watchful to do, that you may live and multiply and go in and possess the land which the Lord swore to give to your fathers.

2And you shall [earnestly] remember all the way which the Lord your God led you these forty years in the wilderness, to humble you and to prove you, to know what was in your [mind and] heart, whether you would keep His commandments or not.

3And He humbled you and allowed you to hunger and fed you with manna, which you did not know nor did your fathers know, that He might make you recognize *and* personally know that man does not live by bread only, but man lives by every word that proceeds out of the mouth of the Lord.

4Your clothing did not become old upon you nor did your feet swell these forty years.

5Know also in your [minds and] hearts that, as a man disciplines *and* instructs his son, so the Lord your God disciplines *and* instructs you.

6So you shall keep the commandments of the Lord your God, to walk in His ways and [reverently] fear Him. [Prov. 8:13.]

7For the Lord your God is bringing you into a good land, a land of brooks of water, of fountains and springs, flowing forth in valleys and hills;

8A land of wheat and barley, and vines and fig trees and pomegranates, a land of olive trees and honey;

9A land in which you shall eat food without shortage and lack nothing in it; a land whose stones are iron and out of whose hills you can dig copper.

10When you have eaten and are full, then you shall bless the Lord your God for all the good land which He has given you.

11Beware that you do not forget the Lord your God by not keeping His commandments, His precepts, and His statutes which I command you today,

12Lest when you have eaten and are full, and have built goodly houses and live in them,

13And when your herds and flocks multiply and your silver and gold is multiplied and all you have is multiplied,

14Then your [minds and] hearts be lifted up and you forget the Lord your God, Who brought you out of the land of Egypt, out of the house of bondage,

15Who led you through the great and terrible wilderness, with its fiery serpents and scorpions and thirsty ground where there was no water, but Who brought you forth water out of the flinty rock,

16Who fed you in the wilderness with manna, which your fathers did not know, that He might humble you and test you, to do you good in the end.

17And beware lest you say in your [mind and] heart, My power and the might of my hand have gotten me this wealth.

18But you shall [earnestly] remember the Lord your God, for it is He Who gives you power to get wealth, that He may establish His covenant which He swore to your fathers, as it is this day.

19And if you forget the Lord your God and walk after other gods and serve them and worship them, I testify against you this day that you shall surely perish.

## New International Version

tions the LORD destroyed before you, so you will be destroyed for not obeying the LORD your God.

### Not Because of Israel's Righteousness

**9** Hear, Israel: You are now about to cross the Jordan to go in and dispossess nations greater and stronger than you, with large cities that have walls up to the sky. [2]The people are strong and tall—Anakites! You know about them and have heard it said: "Who can stand up against the Anakites?" [3]But be assured today that the LORD your God is the one who goes across ahead of you like a devouring fire. He will destroy them; he will subdue them before you. And you will drive them out and annihilate them quickly, as the LORD has promised you.

[4]After the LORD your God has driven them out before you, do not say to yourself, "The LORD has brought me here to take possession of this land because of my righteousness." No, it is on account of the wickedness of these nations that the LORD is going to drive them out before you. [5]It is not because of your righteousness or your integrity that you are going in to take possession of their land; but on account of the wickedness of these nations, the LORD your God will drive them out before you, to accomplish what he swore to your fathers, to Abraham, Isaac and Jacob. [6]Understand, then, that it is not because of your righteousness that the LORD your God is giving you this good land to possess, for you are a stiff-necked people.

### The Golden Calf

[7]Remember this and never forget how you aroused the anger of the LORD your God in the wilderness. From the day you left Egypt until you arrived here, you have been rebellious against the LORD. [8]At Horeb you aroused the LORD's wrath so that he was angry enough to destroy you. [9]When I went up on the mountain to receive the tablets of stone, the tablets of the covenant that the LORD had made with you, I stayed on the mountain forty days and forty nights; I ate no bread and drank no water. [10]The LORD gave me two stone tablets inscribed by the finger of God. On them were all the commandments the LORD proclaimed to you on the mountain out of the fire, on the day of the assembly.

[11]At the end of the forty days and forty nights, the LORD gave me the two stone tablets, the tablets of the covenant. [12]Then the LORD told me, "Go down from here at once, because your people whom you brought out of Egypt have become corrupt. They have turned away quickly from what I commanded them and have made an idol for themselves."

[13]And the LORD said to me, "I have seen this people, and they are a stiff-necked people indeed! [14]Let me alone, so that I may destroy them and blot out their name from under heaven. And I will make you into a nation stronger and more numerous than they."

[15]So I turned and went down from the mountain while it was ablaze with fire. And the two tablets of the covenant were in my hands. [16]When I looked, I saw that you had sinned against the LORD your God; you had made for yourselves an idol cast in the shape of a calf. You had turned aside quickly from the way that the LORD had commanded you. [17]So I took the two tablets and threw them out of my hands, breaking them to pieces before your eyes.

[18]Then once again I fell prostrate before the LORD for forty days and forty nights; I ate no bread and drank no water, because of all the sin you had committed, doing what was evil in the LORD's sight and so arousing his anger. [19]I

## Amplified Bible

[20]Like the nations which the Lord makes to perish before you, so shall you perish, because you would not obey the voice of the Lord your God.

**9** Hear, O Israel. You are to cross the Jordan today to go in to dispossess nations greater and mightier than you are, cities great and fortified up to the heavens, [2]A people great and tall, the sons of the Anakim, whom you know and of whom you have heard it said, Who can stand before the sons of Anak? [3]Know therefore this day that the Lord your God is He Who goes over before you as a devouring fire. He will destroy them and bring them down before you; so you shall dispossess them and make them perish quickly, as the Lord has promised you.

[4]Do not say in your [mind and] heart, after the Lord your God has thrust them out from before you, It is because of my righteousness that the Lord has brought me in to possess this land—whereas it is because of the wickedness of these nations that the Lord is dispossessing them before you.

[5]Not for your righteousness or for the uprightness of your [minds and] hearts do you go to possess their land; but because of the wickedness of these nations the Lord your God is driving them out before you, and that He may fulfill the promise which the Lord swore to your fathers, Abraham, Isaac, and Jacob.

[6]Know therefore that the Lord your God does not give you this good land to possess because of your righteousness, for you are a hard *and* stubborn people.

[7][Earnestly] remember and forget not how you provoked the Lord your God to wrath in the wilderness; from the day you left the land of Egypt until you came to this place, you have been rebellious against the Lord.

[8]Even in Horeb you provoked the Lord to wrath, and the Lord was so angry with you that He would have destroyed you.

[9]When I went up the mountain to receive the tables of stone, the tables of the covenant which the Lord made with you, I remained on the mountain forty days and forty nights; I neither ate food nor drank water.

[10]And the Lord delivered to me the two tables of stone written with the finger of God; and on them were all the words which the Lord spoke with you on the mountain out of the midst of the fire in the day of the assembly.

[11]And at the end of forty days and forty nights the Lord gave me the two tables of stone, the tables of the covenant.

[12]And the Lord said to me, Arise, go down from here quickly, for your people whom you brought out of Egypt have corrupted themselves. They have quickly turned aside from the way which I commanded them; they have made for themselves a molten image.

[13]Furthermore the Lord said to me, I have seen this people, and behold, they are stubborn *and* hard.

[14]Let me alone, that I may destroy them and blot out their name from under the heavens; and I will make of you a nation mightier and greater than they.

[15]So I turned and came down from the mountain, and the mountain was burning with fire. And the two tables of the covenant were in my two hands.

[16]And I looked, and behold, you had sinned against the Lord your God; you had made for yourselves a molten calf. You had turned aside quickly from the way which the Lord had commanded you.

[17]I took the two tables, cast them out of my two hands, and broke them before your eyes.

[18]Then I fell down before the Lord as before, for forty days and forty nights; I neither ate food nor drank water, because of all the sin you had committed in doing wickedly in the sight of the Lord, to provoke Him to anger.

## New International Version

feared the anger and wrath of the LORD, for he was angry enough with you to destroy you. But again the LORD listened to me. [20]And the LORD was angry enough with Aaron to destroy him, but at that time I prayed for Aaron too. [21]Also I took that sinful thing of yours, the calf you had made, and burned it in the fire. Then I crushed it and ground it to powder as fine as dust and threw the dust into a stream that flowed down the mountain. [22]You also made the LORD angry at Taberah, at Massah and at Kibroth Hattaavah.

[23]And when the LORD sent you out from Kadesh Barnea, he said, "Go up and take possession of the land I have given you." But you rebelled against the command of the LORD your God. You did not trust him or obey him. [24]You have been rebellious against the LORD ever since I have known you.

[25]I lay prostrate before the LORD those forty days and forty nights because the LORD had said he would destroy you. [26]I prayed to the LORD and said, "Sovereign LORD, do not destroy your people, your own inheritance that you redeemed by your great power and brought out of Egypt with a mighty hand. [27]Remember your servants Abraham, Isaac and Jacob. Overlook the stubbornness of this people, their wickedness and their sin. [28]Otherwise, the country from which you brought us will say, 'Because the LORD was not able to take them into the land he had promised them, and because he hated them, he brought them out to put them to death in the wilderness.' [29]But they are your people, your inheritance that you brought out by your great power and your outstretched arm."

### Tablets Like the First Ones

**10** At that time the LORD said to me, "Chisel out two stone tablets like the first ones and come up to me on the mountain. Also make a wooden ark.[a] [2]I will write on the tablets the words that were on the first tablets, which you broke. Then you are to put them in the ark."

[3]So I made the ark out of acacia wood and chiseled out two stone tablets like the first ones, and I went up on the mountain with the two tablets in my hands. [4]The LORD wrote on these tablets what he had written before, the Ten Commandments he had proclaimed to you on the mountain, out of the fire, on the day of the assembly. And the LORD gave them to me. [5]Then I came back down the mountain and put the tablets in the ark I had made, as the LORD commanded me, and they are there now.

[6](The Israelites traveled from the wells of Bene Jaakan to Moserah. There Aaron died and was buried, and Eleazar his son succeeded him as priest. [7]From there they traveled to Gudgodah and on to Jotbathah, a land with streams of water. [8]At that time the LORD set apart the tribe of Levi to carry the ark of the covenant of the LORD, to stand before the LORD to minister and to pronounce blessings in his name, as they still do today. [9]That is why the

## Amplified Bible

[19]For I was afraid of the anger and hot displeasure which the Lord held against you, enough to destroy you. But the Lord listened to me that time also.

[20]And the Lord was very angry with Aaron, angry enough to have destroyed him, and I prayed for Aaron also at the same time.

[21]And I took your sin, the calf which you had made, and burned it with fire and crushed it, grinding it very small, until it was as fine as dust; and I cast the dust of it into the brook that came down out of the mountain.

[22]At Taberah also and at Massah and at Kibroth-hattaavah you provoked the Lord to wrath.

[23]Likewise when the Lord sent you from Kadesh-barnea, saying, Go up and possess the land which I have given you, then you rebelled against the commandment of the Lord your God, and you did not believe Him *or* trust *and* rely on Him or obey His voice.

[24]You have been rebellious against the Lord from the day that I knew you.

[25]So I fell down *and* lay prostrate before the Lord forty days and nights because the Lord had said He would destroy you.

[26]And I prayed to the Lord, O Lord God, do not destroy Your people and Your heritage, whom You have redeemed through Your greatness, whom You have brought out of Egypt with a mighty hand.

[27]Remember [earnestly] Your servants, Abraham, Isaac, and Jacob; look not at the stubbornness of this people or at their wickedness or at their sin,

[28]Lest the land from which You brought us out say, Because the Lord was not able to bring them into the land which He promised them, and because He hated them, He has brought them out to slay them in the wilderness.

[29]Yet they are Your people and Your inheritance, whom You brought out by Your mighty power and by Your outstretched arm.

**10** At that time the Lord said to me, Hew two tables of stone like the first and come up to Me on the mountain and make an ark of wood.

[2]And I will write on the tables the words that were on the first tables which you broke, and you shall put them in the ark.

[3]So I [Moses] made an ark of acacia wood and hewed two tables of stone like the first, and went up the mountain [a]with the two tables of stone in my [one] hand.

[4]And the Lord wrote on the tables as at the first writing, the Ten Commandments which the Lord had spoken to you on the mountain out of the midst of the fire on the day of the assembly; and the Lord gave them to me.

[5]And I turned and came down from the mountain and put the tables in the ark which I had made; and there they are, as the Lord commanded me.

[6](The Israelites journeyed from the wells of the sons of Jaakan to Moserah. There Aaron died, and there he was buried, and Eleazar his son ministered in the priest's office in his stead.

[7]From there they journeyed to Gudgodah, and then to Jotbathah, a land of brooks [dividing the valley].

[8]At that time the Lord set apart the tribe of Levi to bear the ark of the covenant of the Lord, to stand before the Lord to minister to Him and to bless in His name unto this day.

[a] One of the many misconceptions of articles and events mentioned in the Bible, innocently perpetuated by artists without adequate knowledge, is that of the size of the two tables of stone on which the Ten Commandments were written. They were not great tombstone-sized slabs, but probably small rectangular plates, two of which could easily be carried in one hand. Dr. George L. Robinson brought from the Sinai area a pair of "tables of stone" believed comparable to those mentioned here, which he put in his coat pocket. Moses says here, "I . . . went up the mountain with the two tables of stone in my [one] hand," and he confirms it in Exod. 34:4.

[a] 1 That is, a chest

## New International Version

Levites have no share or inheritance among their fellow Israelites; the LORD is their inheritance, as the LORD your God told them.)

10Now I had stayed on the mountain forty days and forty nights, as I did the first time, and the LORD listened to me at this time also. It was not his will to destroy you. 11"Go," the LORD said to me, "and lead the people on their way, so that they may enter and possess the land I swore to their ancestors to give them."

### Fear the LORD

12And now, Israel, what does the LORD your God ask of you but to fear the LORD your God, to walk in obedience to him, to love him, to serve the LORD your God with all your heart and with all your soul, 13and to observe the LORD's commands and decrees that I am giving you today for your own good?

14To the LORD your God belong the heavens, even the highest heavens, the earth and everything in it. 15Yet the LORD set his affection on your ancestors and loved them, and he chose you, their descendants, above all the nations—as it is today. 16Circumcise your hearts, therefore, and do not be stiff-necked any longer. 17For the LORD your God is God of gods and Lord of lords, the great God, mighty and awesome, who shows no partiality and accepts no bribes. 18He defends the cause of the fatherless and the widow, and loves the foreigner residing among you, giving them food and clothing. 19And you are to love those who are foreigners, for you yourselves were foreigners in Egypt. 20Fear the LORD your God and serve him. Hold fast to him and take your oaths in his name. 21He is the one you praise; he is your God, who performed for you those great and awesome wonders you saw with your own eyes. 22Your ancestors who went down into Egypt were seventy in all, and now the LORD your God has made you as numerous as the stars in the sky.

### Love and Obey the LORD

**11** Love the LORD your God and keep his requirements, his decrees, his laws and his commands always. 2Remember today that your children were not the ones who saw and experienced the discipline of the LORD your God: his majesty, his mighty hand, his outstretched arm; 3the signs he performed and the things he did in the heart of Egypt, both to Pharaoh king of Egypt and to his whole country; 4what he did to the Egyptian army, to its horses and chariots, how he overwhelmed them with the waters of the Red Sea[a] as they were pursuing you, and how the LORD brought lasting ruin on them. 5It was not your children who saw what he did for you in the wilderness until you arrived at this place, 6and what he did to Dathan and Abiram, sons of Eliab the Reubenite, when the earth opened its mouth right in the middle of all Israel and swallowed them up with their households, their tents and every living thing that belonged to them. 7But it was your own eyes that saw all these great things the LORD has done.

8Observe therefore all the commands I am giving you today, so that you may have the strength to go in and take over the land that you are crossing the Jordan to possess, 9and so that you may live long in the land the LORD swore to your ancestors to give to them and their descendants, a land flowing with milk and honey. 10The land you are

## Amplified Bible

9Therefore Levi has no part or inheritance with his brethren; the Lord is his inheritance, as the Lord your God promised him.)

10And I [Moses] stayed on the mountain, as the first time, forty days and nights, and the Lord listened to me at that time also; the Lord would not destroy you.

11And the Lord said to me, Arise, journey on before the people, that they may go in and possess the land which I swore to their fathers to give to them.

12And now, Israel, what does the Lord your God require of you but [reverently] to fear the Lord your God, [that is] to walk in all His ways, and to love Him, and to serve the Lord your God with all your [mind and] heart and with your entire being,

13To keep the commandments of the Lord and His statutes which I command you today for your good?

14Behold, the heavens and the heaven of heavens belong to the Lord your God, the earth also, with all that is in it *and* on it.

15Yet the Lord had a delight in loving your fathers, and He chose their descendants after them, you above all peoples, as it is this day.

16So circumcise the foreskin of your [minds and] hearts; be no longer stubborn *and* hardened.

17For the Lord your God is God of gods and Lord of lords, the great, the mighty, the terrible God, Who is not partial and takes no bribe.

18He executes justice for the fatherless and the widow, and loves the stranger *or* temporary resident and gives him food and clothing.

19Therefore love the stranger *and* sojourner, for you were strangers *and* sojourners in the land of Egypt.

20You shall [reverently] fear the Lord your God; you shall serve Him and cling to Him, and by His name *and* presence you shall swear.

21He is your praise; He is your God, Who has done for you these great and terrible things which your eyes have seen.

22Your fathers went down to Egypt seventy persons in all, and now the Lord your God has made you as the stars of the heavens for multitude.

**11** Therefore you shall love the Lord your God and keep His charge, His statutes, His precepts, and His commandments always.

2And know this day—for I am not speaking to your children who have not [personally] known and seen it—the instruction *and* discipline of the Lord your God: His greatness, His mighty hand, and His outstretched arm;

3His signs and His deeds which He did in Egypt to Pharaoh the king of Egypt and to all his land;

4And what He did to the army of Egypt, to their horses and chariots, how He made the waters of the Red Sea flow over them as they pursued you, and how the Lord has destroyed them to this day;

5And what He did to you in the wilderness until you came to this place;

6And what He did to Dathan and Abiram, sons of Eliab, the son of Reuben, how the earth opened its mouth and swallowed up them, their households, their tents, and every living thing that followed them, in the midst of all Israel. [Num. 26:9, 10.]

7For your eyes have seen all the great work of the Lord which He did.

8Therefore you shall keep all the commandments which I command you today, that you may be strong and go in and possess the land which you go across [the Jordan] to possess,

9And that you may live long in the land which the Lord swore to your fathers to give to them and to their descendants, a land flowing with milk and honey.

## New International Version

entering to take over is not like the land of Egypt, from which you have come, where you planted your seed and irrigated it by foot as in a vegetable garden. [11] But the land you are crossing the Jordan to take possession of is a land of mountains and valleys that drinks rain from heaven. [12] It is a land the LORD your God cares for; the eyes of the LORD your God are continually on it from the beginning of the year to its end.

[13] So if you faithfully obey the commands I am giving you today—to love the LORD your God and to serve him with all your heart and with all your soul— [14] then I will send rain on your land in its season, both autumn and spring rains, so that you may gather in your grain, new wine and olive oil. [15] I will provide grass in the fields for your cattle, and you will eat and be satisfied.

[16] Be careful, or you will be enticed to turn away and worship other gods and bow down to them. [17] Then the LORD's anger will burn against you, and he will shut up the heavens so that it will not rain and the ground will yield no produce, and you will soon perish from the good land the LORD is giving you. [18] Fix these words of mine in your hearts and minds; tie them as symbols on your hands and bind them on your foreheads. [19] Teach them to your children, talking about them when you sit at home and when you walk along the road, when you lie down and when you get up. [20] Write them on the doorframes of your houses and on your gates, [21] so that your days and the days of your children may be many in the land the LORD swore to give your ancestors, as many as the days that the heavens are above the earth.

[22] If you carefully observe all these commands I am giving you to follow—to love the LORD your God, to walk in obedience to him and to hold fast to him— [23] then the LORD will drive out all these nations before you, and you will dispossess nations larger and stronger than you. [24] Every place where you set your foot will be yours: Your territory will extend from the desert to Lebanon, and from the Euphrates River to the Mediterranean Sea. [25] No one will be able to stand against you. The LORD your God, as he promised you, will put the terror and fear of you on the whole land, wherever you go.

[26] See, I am setting before you today a blessing and a curse— [27] the blessing if you obey the commands of the LORD your God that I am giving you today; [28] the curse if you disobey the commands of the LORD your God and turn from the way that I command you today by following other gods, which you have not known. [29] When the LORD your God has brought you into the land you are entering to possess, you are to proclaim on Mount Gerizim the blessings, and on Mount Ebal the curses. [30] As you know, these mountains are across the Jordan, westward, toward the setting sun, near the great trees of Moreh, in the territory of those Canaanites living in the Arabah in the vicinity of Gilgal. [31] You are about to cross the Jordan to enter and take possession of the land the LORD your God is giving you. When you have taken it over and are living there, [32] be

## Amplified Bible

[10] For the land which you go in to possess is not like the land of Egypt, from which you came out, where you sowed your seed and watered it with your foot laboriously as in a garden of vegetables.

[11] But the land which you enter to possess is a land of hills and valleys which drinks water of the rain of the heavens,

[12] A land for which the Lord your God cares; the eyes of the Lord your God are always upon it from the beginning of the year to the end of the year.

[13] And if you will diligently heed My commandments which I command you this day—to love the Lord your God and to serve Him with all your [mind and] heart and with your entire being—

[14] I will give the rain for your land in its season, the early rain and the latter rain, that you may gather in your grain, your new wine, and your oil.

[15] And I will give grass in your fields for your cattle, that you may eat and be full.

[16] Take heed to yourselves, lest your [minds and] hearts be deceived and you turn aside and serve other gods and worship them,

[17] And the Lord's anger be kindled against you, and He shut up the heavens so that there will be no rain and the land will not yield its fruit, and you perish quickly off the good land which the Lord gives you.

[18] Therefore you shall lay up these My words in your [minds and] hearts and in your [entire] being, and bind them for a sign upon your hands and as forehead bands between your eyes.

[19] And you shall teach them to your children, speaking of them when you sit in your house and when you walk along the road, when you lie down and when you rise up.

[20] And you shall write them upon the doorposts of your house and on your gates,

[21] That your days and the days of your children may be multiplied in the land which the Lord swore to your fathers to give them, as long as the heavens are above the earth.

[22] For if you diligently keep all this commandment which I command you to do, to love the Lord your God, to walk in all His ways, and to cleave to Him—

[23] Then the Lord will drive out all these nations before you, and you shall dispossess nations greater and mightier than you.

[24] Every place upon which the sole of your foot shall tread shall be yours: from the wilderness to Lebanon, and from the River, the river Euphrates, to the western sea [the Mediterranean] your territory shall be.

[25] There shall no man be able to stand before you; the Lord your God shall lay the fear and the dread of you upon all the land that you shall tread, as He has said to you.

[26] Behold, I set before you this day a blessing and a curse—

[27] The blessing if you obey the commandments of the Lord your God which I command you this day;

[28] And the curse if you will not obey the commandments of the Lord your God, but turn aside from the way which I command you this day to go after other gods, which you have not known.

[29] And when the Lord your God has brought you into the land which you go to possess, you shall set the blessing on Mount Gerizim and the curse on Mount Ebal. [Josh. 8:33.]

[30] Are they not beyond the Jordan, west of the road, where the sun goes down, in the land of the Canaanites living in the Arabah opposite Gilgal, beside the oaks or terebinths of Moreh?

[31] For you are to cross over the Jordan to go in to possess the land which the Lord your God gives you, and you shall possess it and live in it.

## New International Version

sure that you obey all the decrees and laws I am setting before you today.

### The One Place of Worship

**12** These are the decrees and laws you must be careful to follow in the land that the LORD, the God of your ancestors, has given you to possess—as long as you live in the land. [2]Destroy completely all the places on the high mountains, on the hills and under every spreading tree, where the nations you are dispossessing worship their gods. [3]Break down their altars, smash their sacred stones and burn their Asherah poles in the fire; cut down the idols of their gods and wipe out their names from those places.

[4]You must not worship the LORD your God in their way. [5]But you are to seek the place the LORD your God will choose from among all your tribes to put his Name there for his dwelling. To that place you must go; [6]there bring your burnt offerings and sacrifices, your tithes and special gifts, what you have vowed to give and your freewill offerings, and the firstborn of your herds and flocks. [7]There, in the presence of the LORD your God, you and your families shall eat and shall rejoice in everything you have put your hand to, because the LORD your God has blessed you.

[8]You are not to do as we do here today, everyone doing as they see fit, [9]since you have not yet reached the resting place and the inheritance the LORD your God is giving you. [10]But you will cross the Jordan and settle in the land the LORD your God is giving you as an inheritance, and he will give you rest from all your enemies around you so that you will live in safety. [11]Then to the place the LORD your God will choose as a dwelling for his Name—there you are to bring everything I command you: your burnt offerings and sacrifices, your tithes and special gifts, and all the choice possessions you have vowed to the LORD. [12]And there rejoice before the LORD your God—you, your sons and daughters, your male and female servants, and the Levites from your towns who have no allotment or inheritance of their own. [13]Be careful not to sacrifice your burnt offerings anywhere you please. [14]Offer them only at the place the LORD will choose in one of your tribes, and there observe everything I command you.

[15]Nevertheless, you may slaughter your animals in any of your towns and eat as much of the meat as you want, as if it were gazelle or deer, according to the blessing the LORD your God gives you. Both the ceremonially unclean and the clean may eat it. [16]But you must not eat the blood; pour it out on the ground like water. [17]You must not eat in your own towns the tithe of your grain and new wine and

## Amplified Bible

[32]And you shall be watchful to do all the statutes and ordinances which I set before you this day.

**12** These are the statutes and ordinances which you shall be watchful to do in the land which the Lord, the God of your fathers, gives you to possess all the days you live on the earth. [2]You shall surely destroy all the places where the nations you dispossess served their gods, upon the high mountains and the hills and under every green tree. [3]You shall break down their altars and dash in pieces their pillars and burn their Asherim with fire; you shall hew down the graven images of their gods and destroy their name out of that place.

[4]You shall not behave so toward the Lord your God. [5]But you shall seek the place which the Lord your God shall choose out of all your tribes to put His [a]Name and make His dwelling place, and there shall you come; [6]And there you shall bring your burnt offerings and your sacrifices, your tithes and the offering of your hands, and your vows and your freewill offerings, and the firstlings of your herd and of your flock. [7]And there you shall eat before the Lord your God, and you shall rejoice in all to which you put your hand, you and your households, in which the Lord your God has blessed you.

[8]You [b]shall not do according to all we do here [in the camp] this day, every man doing whatever looks right in his own eyes. [9]For you have not yet come to the rest and to the inheritance which the Lord your God gives you. [10]But when you go over the Jordan and dwell in the land which the Lord your God causes you to inherit, and He gives you rest from all your enemies round about so that you dwell in safety, [11]Then there shall be a place which the Lord your God shall choose to cause His Name [and His Presence] to dwell there; to it you shall bring all that I command you: your burnt offerings, your sacrifices, your tithes and what the hand presents [as a first gift from the fruits of the ground], and all your choicest offerings which you vow to the Lord. [12]And you shall rejoice before the Lord your God, you and your sons and your daughters, and your menservants and your maidservants, and the Levite that is within your towns, since he has no part or inheritance with you. [13]Be watchful not to offer your burnt offerings in every place you see. [14]But in the place which the Lord shall choose in one of your tribes, there you shall offer your burnt offerings, and there you shall do all I command you. [15]However, you may kill and eat flesh in any of your towns whenever you desire, according to the provision for the support of life with which the Lord your God has blessed you; those [ceremonially] unclean and the clean may eat of it, as of the gazelle and the hart. [16]Only you shall not eat the blood; you shall pour it upon the ground as water. [17]You may not eat within your towns the tithe of your grain or of your new wine or of your oil, or the firstlings of

*a* The "Name" of God is equivalent to His gracious presence in passages such as this one. The place where God puts His Name is the place where the Lord Himself chooses to dwell. When it stands for God's presence at the sanctuary, "Name" is capitalized. *b* "It has been too often overlooked that the Law of Moses had a prophetic side. It was given to him and to Israel when they were not in a position to keep it [fully]. It was the law of the land which God would give them. In many ways its observance depended on the completion of the conquest of the land and upon the quietness of the times in which they lived. This prophetic aspect was certainly not unrecognized by the Jews, or they would not (for example) have neglected to dwell in booths at the Feast of Tabernacles from the time of Joshua to Nehemiah (Neh. 8:17)" (Charles J. Ellicott, *A Bible Commentary*).

## New International Version

olive oil, or the firstborn of your herds and flocks, or whatever you have vowed to give, or your freewill offerings or special gifts. 18Instead, you are to eat them in the presence of the Lord your God at the place the Lord your God will choose—you, your sons and daughters, your male and female servants, and the Levites from your towns—and you are to rejoice before the Lord your God in everything you put your hand to. 19Be careful not to neglect the Levites as long as you live in your land.

20When the Lord your God has enlarged your territory as he promised you, and you crave meat and say, "I would like some meat," then you may eat as much of it as you want. 21If the place where the Lord your God chooses to put his Name is too far away from you, you may slaughter animals from the herds and flocks the Lord has given you, as I have commanded you, and in your own towns you may eat as much of them as you want. 22Eat them as you would gazelle or deer. Both the ceremonially unclean and the clean may eat. 23But be sure you do not eat the blood, because the blood is the life, and you must not eat the life with the meat. 24You must not eat the blood; pour it out on the ground like water. 25Do not eat it, so that it may go well with you and your children after you, because you will be doing what is right in the eyes of the Lord.

26But take your consecrated things and whatever you have vowed to give, and go to the place the Lord will choose. 27Present your burnt offerings on the altar of the Lord your God, both the meat and the blood. The blood of your sacrifices must be poured beside the altar of the Lord your God, but you may eat the meat. 28Be careful to obey all these regulations I am giving you, so that it may always go well with you and your children after you, because you will be doing what is good and right in the eyes of the Lord your God.

29The Lord your God will cut off before you the nations you are about to invade and dispossess. But when you have driven them out and settled in their land, 30and after they have been destroyed before you, be careful not to be ensnared by inquiring about their gods, saying, "How do these nations serve their gods? We will do the same." 31You must not worship the Lord your God in their way, because in worshiping their gods, they do all kinds of detestable things the Lord hates. They even burn their sons and daughters in the fire as sacrifices to their gods.

32See that you do all I command you; do not add to it or take away from it.*a*

### Worshiping Other Gods

**13**b If a prophet, or one who foretells by dreams, appears among you and announces to you a sign or wonder, 2and if the sign or wonder spoken of takes place, and the prophet says, "Let us follow other gods" (gods you have not known) "and let us worship them," 3you must not listen to the words of that prophet or dreamer. The Lord your God is testing you to find out whether you love him with all your heart and with all your soul. 4It is the Lord your God you must follow, and him you must revere. Keep his commands and obey him; serve him and hold fast to him. 5That prophet or dreamer must be put to death for inciting rebellion against the Lord your God, who brought you out of Egypt and redeemed you from the land of slavery. That prophet or dreamer tried to turn you from the

## Amplified Bible

your herd or flock, or anything you have vowed, or your freewill offerings, or the offerings from your hand [of garden products].

18But you shall eat them before the Lord your God in the place which the Lord your God shall choose, you and your son and your daughter, your manservant and your maidservant, and the Levite that is within your towns; and you shall rejoice before the Lord your God in all that you undertake.

19Take heed not to forsake *or* neglect the Levite [God's minister] as long as you live in your land.

20When the Lord your God enlarges your territory, as He promised you, and you say, I will eat flesh, because you crave flesh, you may eat flesh whenever you desire.

21If the place where the Lord your God has chosen to put His Name [and Presence] is too far from you, then you shall kill from your herd or flock which the Lord has given you, as I [Moses] have commanded you; eat in your towns as much as you desire.

22Just as the roebuck and the hart is eaten, so you may eat of it [but not offer it]; the unclean and the clean alike may eat of it.

23Only be sure that you do not eat the blood, for the blood is the life, and you may not eat the life with the flesh.

24You shall not eat it; you shall pour it out on the earth like water.

25You shall not eat it, that all may go well with you and with your children after you, when you do what is right in the sight of the Lord.

26Only your holy things which you have [to offer] and what you have vowed you shall take, and go to the place [before the sanctuary] which the Lord shall choose.

27And offer your burnt offerings, the flesh and the blood, upon the altar of the Lord your God; and the blood of your sacrifices shall be poured out on the altar of the Lord your God, and you may eat the flesh.

28Be watchful and obey all these words which I command you, that it may go well with you and with your children after you forever, when you do what is good and right in the sight of the Lord your God.

29When the Lord your God cuts off before you the nations whom you go to dispossess, and you dispossess them and live in their land,

30Be watchful that you are not ensnared into following them after they have been destroyed before you and that you do not inquire after their gods, saying, How did these nations serve their gods? We will do likewise.

31You shall not do so to the Lord your God, for every abominable thing which the Lord hates they have done for their gods. For even their sons and their daughters they have burned in the fire to their gods.

32Whatever I command you, be watchful to do it; you shall not add to it or diminish it.

**13** If a prophet arises among you, or a dreamer of dreams, and gives you a sign or a wonder,

2And the sign or the wonder he foretells to you comes to pass, and if he says, Let us go after other gods—gods you have not known—and let us serve them,

3You shall not listen to the words of that prophet or to that dreamer of dreams. For the Lord your God is testing you to know whether you love the Lord your God with all your [mind and] heart and with your entire being.

4You shall walk after the Lord your God and [reverently] fear Him, and keep His commandments and obey His voice, and you shall serve Him and cling to Him.

5But that prophet or that dreamer of dreams shall be put to death, because he has talked rebellion *and* turning away from the Lord your God, Who brought you out of the land of Egypt and redeemed you out of the house of bondage; that man has tried to draw you aside from the way

---

*a 32 In Hebrew texts this verse (12:32) is numbered 13:1.   b In Hebrew texts 13:1-18 is numbered 13:2-19.

## New International Version

way the Lord your God commanded you to follow. You must purge the evil from among you.

6If your very own brother, or your son or daughter, or the wife you love, or your closest friend secretly entices you, saying, "Let us go and worship other gods" (gods that neither you nor your ancestors have known, 7gods of the peoples around you, whether near or far, from one end of the land to the other), 8do not yield to them or listen to them. Show them no pity. Do not spare them or shield them. 9You must certainly put them to death. Your hand must be the first in putting them to death, and then the hands of all the people. 10Stone them to death, because they tried to turn you away from the Lord your God, who brought you out of Egypt, out of the land of slavery. 11Then all Israel will hear and be afraid, and no one among you will do such an evil thing again.

12If you hear it said about one of the towns the Lord your God is giving you to live in 13that troublemakers have arisen among you and have led the people of their town astray, saying, "Let us go and worship other gods" (gods you have not known), 14then you must inquire, probe and investigate it thoroughly. And if it is true and it has been proved that this detestable thing has been done among you, 15you must certainly put to the sword all who live in that town. You must destroy it completely,*a* both its people and its livestock. 16You are to gather all the plunder of the town into the middle of the public square and completely burn the town and all its plunder as a whole burnt offering to the Lord your God. That town is to remain a ruin forever, never to be rebuilt, 17and none of the condemned things*a* are to be found in your hands. Then the Lord will turn from his fierce anger, will show you mercy, and will have compassion on you. He will increase your numbers, as he promised on oath to your ancestors— 18because you obey the Lord your God by keeping all his commands that I am giving you today and doing what is right in his eyes.

### Clean and Unclean Food

**14** You are the children of the Lord your God. Do not cut yourselves or shave the front of your heads for the dead, 2for you are a people holy to the Lord your God. Out of all the peoples on the face of the earth, the Lord has chosen you to be his treasured possession.

3Do not eat any detestable thing. 4These are the animals you may eat: the ox, the sheep, the goat, 5the deer, the gazelle, the roe deer, the wild goat, the ibex, the antelope and the mountain sheep.*b* 6You may eat any animal that has a divided hoof and that chews the cud. 7However, of those that chew the cud or that have a divided hoof you may not eat the camel, the rabbit or the hyrax. Although they chew the cud, they do not have a divided hoof; they are ceremonially unclean for you. 8The pig is also unclean; although it has a divided hoof, it does not chew the cud. You are not to eat their meat or touch their carcasses.

*a 15,17 The Hebrew term refers to the irrevocable giving over of things or persons to the Lord, often by totally destroying them.*
*b 5 The precise identification of some of the birds and animals in this chapter is uncertain.*

## Amplified Bible

in which the Lord your God commanded you to walk. So shall you put the evil away from your midst.

6If your brother, the son of your mother, or your son or daughter, or the wife of your bosom, or your friend who is as your own life entices you secretly, saying, Let us go and serve other gods—gods you have not known, you nor your fathers,

7Of the gods of the peoples who are round about you, near you or far away from you, from one end of the earth to the other—

8You shall not give consent to him or listen to him; nor shall your eye pity him, nor shall you spare him or conceal him.

9But you shall surely kill him; your hand shall be first upon him to put him to death, and afterwards the hands of all the people.

10And you shall stone him to death with stones, because he has tried to draw you away from the Lord your God, Who brought you out of the land of Egypt, from the house of bondage.

11And all Israel shall hear and [reverently] fear, and shall never again do any such wickedness as this among you.

12If you hear it said in one of your cities which the Lord your God has given you in which to dwell

13That certain base fellows have gone out from your midst and have enticed away the inhabitants of their city, saying, Let us go and serve other gods—gods you have not known—

14Then you shall inquire and make search and ask diligently. And behold, if it is true and certain that such an abominable thing has been done among you,

15You shall surely smite the inhabitants of that city with the edge of the sword, destroying it utterly and all who are in it and its beasts with the edge of the sword.

16And you shall collect all its spoil into the midst of its open square and shall burn the city with fire with every bit of its spoil [as a whole burnt offering] to the Lord your God. It shall be a heap [of ruins] forever; it shall not be built again.

17And nothing of the accursed thing shall cling to your hand, so that the Lord may turn from the fierceness of His anger, and show you mercy and have compassion on you and multiply you, as He swore to your fathers,

18If you obey the voice of the Lord your God, to keep all His commandments which I command you this day, to do what is right in the eyes of the Lord your God.

**14** You are the sons of the Lord your God; you shall not cut yourselves or make any baldness on your foreheads for the dead,

2For you are a holy people [set apart] to the Lord your God; and the Lord has chosen you to be a peculiar people to Himself, above all the nations on the earth.

3You shall not eat anything that is abominable [to the Lord and so forbidden by Him].

4These are the beasts which you may eat: the ox, the sheep, and the goat,

5The hart, the gazelle, the roebuck, the wild goat, the ibex, the antelope, and the mountain sheep.

6And every beast that parts the hoof and has it divided into two and brings up *and* chews the cud among the beasts you may eat.

7Yet these you shall not eat of those that chew the cud or have the hoof split in two: the camel, the hare, and the coney, because they chew the cud but divide not the hoof; they are unclean for you.

8And the swine, because it parts the hoof but does not chew the cud; it is unclean to you. You shall not eat of their flesh or touch their dead bodies.

## New International Version

⁹Of all the creatures living in the water, you may eat any that has fins and scales. ¹⁰But anything that does not have fins and scales you may not eat; for you it is unclean.

¹¹You may eat any clean bird. ¹²But these you may not eat: the eagle, the vulture, the black vulture, ¹³the red kite, the black kite, any kind of falcon, ¹⁴any kind of raven, ¹⁵the horned owl, the screech owl, the gull, any kind of hawk, ¹⁶the little owl, the great owl, the white owl, ¹⁷the desert owl, the osprey, the cormorant, ¹⁸the stork, any kind of heron, the hoopoe and the bat.

¹⁹All flying insects are unclean to you; do not eat them. ²⁰But any winged creature that is clean you may eat.

²¹Do not eat anything you find already dead. You may give it to the foreigner residing in any of your towns, and they may eat it, or you may sell it to any other foreigner. But you are a people holy to the Lord your God.

Do not cook a young goat in its mother's milk.

### Tithes

²²Be sure to set aside a tenth of all that your fields produce each year. ²³Eat the tithe of your grain, new wine and olive oil, and the firstborn of your herds and flocks in the presence of the Lord your God at the place he will choose as a dwelling for his Name, so that you may learn to revere the Lord your God always. ²⁴But if that place is too distant and you have been blessed by the Lord your God and cannot carry your tithe (because the place where the Lord will choose to put his Name is so far away), ²⁵then exchange your tithe for silver, and take the silver with you and go to the place the Lord your God will choose. ²⁶Use the silver to buy whatever you like: cattle, sheep, wine or other fermented drink, or anything you wish. Then you and your household shall eat there in the presence of the Lord your God and rejoice. ²⁷And do not neglect the Levites living in your towns, for they have no allotment or inheritance of their own.

²⁸At the end of every three years, bring all the tithes of that year's produce and store it in your towns, ²⁹so that the Levites (who have no allotment or inheritance of their own) and the foreigners, the fatherless and the widows who live in your towns may come and eat and be satisfied, and so that the Lord your God may bless you in all the work of your hands.

### The Year for Canceling Debts

**15** At the end of every seven years you must cancel debts. ²This is how it is to be done: Every creditor shall cancel any loan they have made to a fellow Israelite. They shall not require payment from anyone among their own people, because the Lord's time for canceling debts has been proclaimed. ³You may require payment from a foreigner, but you must cancel any debt your fellow Israelite owes you. ⁴However, there need be no poor people among you, for in the land the Lord your God is giving you to possess as your inheritance, he will richly bless you, ⁵if only you fully obey the Lord your God and are careful to follow all these commands I am giving you today. ⁶For the Lord your God will bless you as he has promised, and you

## Amplified Bible

⁹These you may eat of all that are in the waters: whatever has fins and scales you may eat,

¹⁰And whatever has not fins and scales you may not eat; it is unclean for you.

¹¹Of all clean birds you may eat.

¹²But these are the ones which you shall not eat: the eagle, the vulture, the ospray,

¹³The buzzard, the kite in its several species,

¹⁴The raven in all its species,

¹⁵The ostrich, the nighthawk, the sea gull, the hawk of any variety,

¹⁶The little owl, the great owl, the horned owl,

¹⁷The pelican, the carrion vulture, the cormorant,

¹⁸The stork, the heron of any variety, the hoopoe, and the bat.

¹⁹And all flying insects are unclean for you; they shall not be eaten.

²⁰But of all clean winged things you may eat.

²¹You shall not eat of anything that dies of itself. You may give it to the stranger *or* the foreigner who is within your towns, that he may eat it, or you may sell it to an alien. [They are not under God's law in this matter] but you are a people holy to the Lord your God. You shall not [even] boil a kid in its mother's milk.

²²You shall surely tithe all the yield of your seed produced by your field each year.

²³And you shall eat before the Lord your God in the place in which He will cause His Name [and Presence] to dwell the tithe (tenth) of your grain, your new wine, your oil, and the firstlings of your herd and your flock, that you may learn [reverently] to fear the Lord your God always.

²⁴And if the distance is too long for you to carry your tithe, or the place where the Lord your God chooses to set His Name [and Presence] is too far away for you, when the Lord your God has blessed you,

²⁵Then you shall turn it into money, and bind up the money in your hand, and shall go to the place [of worship] which the Lord your God has chosen.

²⁶And you may spend that money for whatever your appetite craves, for oxen, or sheep, or new wine or strong[er] drink, or whatever you desire; and you shall eat there before the Lord your God and you shall rejoice, you and your household.

²⁷And you shall not forsake *or* neglect the Levite [God's minister] in your towns, for he has been given no share or inheritance with you.

²⁸At the end of every three years you shall bring forth all the tithe of your increase the same year and lay it up within your towns.

²⁹And the Levite [because he has no part or inheritance with you] and the stranger *or* temporary resident, and the fatherless and the widow who are in your towns shall come and eat and be satisfied, so that the Lord your God may bless you in all the work of your hands that you do.

**15** At the end of every seven years you shall grant a release.

²And this is the manner of the release: every creditor shall release that which he has lent to his neighbor; he shall not exact it of his neighbor, his brother, for the Lord's release is proclaimed.

³Of a foreigner you may exact it, but whatever of yours is with your brother [Israelite] your hand shall release.

⁴But there will be no poor among you, for the Lord will surely bless you in the land which the Lord your God gives you for an inheritance to possess,

⁵If only you carefully listen to the voice of the Lord your God, to do watchfully all these commandments which I command you this day.

⁶When the Lord your God blesses you as He promised you, then you shall lend to many nations, but you shall not

## New International Version

will lend to many nations but will borrow from none. You will rule over many nations but none will rule over you.

[7]If anyone is poor among your fellow Israelites in any of the towns of the land the LORD your God is giving you, do not be hardhearted or tightfisted toward them. [8]Rather, be openhanded and freely lend them whatever they need. [9]Be careful not to harbor this wicked thought: "The seventh year, the year for canceling debts, is near," so that you do not show ill will toward the needy among your fellow Israelites and give them nothing. They may then appeal to the LORD against you, and you will be found guilty of sin. [10]Give generously to them and do so without a grudging heart; then because of this the LORD your God will bless you in all your work and in everything you put your hand to. [11]There will always be poor people in the land. Therefore I command you to be openhanded toward your fellow Israelites who are poor and needy in your land.

### Freeing Servants
[12]If any of your people—Hebrew men or women—sell themselves to you and serve you six years, in the seventh year you must let them go free. [13]And when you release them, do not send them away empty-handed. [14]Supply them liberally from your flock, your threshing floor and your winepress. Give to them as the LORD your God has blessed you. [15]Remember that you were slaves in Egypt and the LORD your God redeemed you. That is why I give you this command today.

[16]But if your servant says to you, "I do not want to leave you," because he loves you and your family and is well off with you, [17]then take an awl and push it through his earlobe into the door, and he will become your servant for life. Do the same for your female servant.

[18]Do not consider it a hardship to set your servant free, because their service to you these six years has been worth twice as much as that of a hired hand. And the LORD your God will bless you in everything you do.

### The Firstborn Animals
[19]Set apart for the LORD your God every firstborn male of your herds and flocks. Do not put the firstborn of your cows to work, and do not shear the firstborn of your sheep. [20]Each year you and your family are to eat them in the presence of the LORD your God at the place he will choose. [21]If an animal has a defect, is lame or blind, or has any serious flaw, you must not sacrifice it to the LORD your God. [22]You are to eat it in your own towns. Both the ceremonially unclean and the clean may eat it, as if it were gazelle or deer. [23]But you must not eat the blood; pour it out on the ground like water.

## Amplified Bible

borrow; and you shall rule over many nations, but they shall not rule over you.

[7]If there is among you a poor man, one of your kinsmen in any of the towns of your land which the Lord your God gives you, you shall not harden your [minds and] hearts or close your hands to your poor brother;

[8]But you shall open your hands wide to him and shall surely lend him sufficient for his need in whatever he lacks.

[9]Beware lest there be a base thought in your [minds and] hearts, and you say, The seventh year, the year of release, is at hand, and your eye be evil against your poor brother and you give him nothing, and he cry to the Lord against you, and it be sin in you.

[10]You shall give to him freely without begrudging it; because of this the Lord will bless you in all your work and in all you undertake.

[11]For the poor will never cease out of the land; therefore I command you, You shall open wide your hands to your brother, to your needy, and to your poor in your land.

[12]And if your brother, a Hebrew man or a Hebrew woman, is sold to you and serves you six years, then in the seventh year you shall let him go free from you.

[13]And when you send him out free from you, you shall not let him go away empty-handed.

[14]You shall furnish him liberally out of your flock, your threshing floor, and your winepress; of what the Lord your God has blessed you, you shall give to him.

[15]And you shall [earnestly] remember that you were a bondman in the land of Egypt and the Lord your God redeemed you; therefore I give you this command today.

[16]But if the servant says to you, I will not go away from you, because he loves you and your household, since he does well with you,

[17]Then take an awl and pierce his ear through to the door, and he shall be your servant always. And also to your bondwoman you shall do likewise.

[18]It shall not seem hard to you when you let him go free from you, for at half the cost of a hired servant he has served you six years; and the Lord your God will bless you in all you do.

[19]All the firstling males that are born of your herd and flock you shall set apart for the Lord your God; you shall do no work with the firstling of your herd, nor shear the firstling of your flock.

[20]You shall eat it before the Lord your God annually in the place [for worship] which the Lord shall choose, you and your household.

[21]But if it has any blemish, if it is lame, blind, or has any bad blemish whatsoever, you shall not sacrifice it to the Lord your God.

[22]You shall eat it within your towns; the [ceremonially] unclean and the clean alike may eat it, as if it were a gazelle or a hart.

[23]Only you shall not eat its blood; you shall pour it on the ground like water.

### The Passover
**16** Observe the month of Aviv and celebrate the Passover of the LORD your God, because in the month of Aviv he brought you out of Egypt by night. [2]Sacrifice as the Passover to the LORD your God an animal from your flock or herd at the place the LORD will choose as a dwelling for his Name. [3]Do not eat it with bread made with yeast, but for seven days eat unleavened bread, the bread of affliction, because you left Egypt in haste—so that all the days of your life you may remember the time of

**16** Observe the month of Abib and keep the Passover to the Lord your God, for in the month of Abib the Lord your God brought you out of Egypt by night.

[2]You shall offer the Passover sacrifice to the Lord your God from the flock or the herd in the place where the Lord will choose to make His Name [and His Presence] dwell.

[3]You shall eat no leavened bread with it; for seven days you shall eat it with unleavened bread, the bread of affliction—for you fled from the land of Egypt in haste—that all the days of your life you may [earnestly] remember the day when you came out of Egypt.

## New International Version

your departure from Egypt. [4]Let no yeast be found in your possession in all your land for seven days. Do not let any of the meat you sacrifice on the evening of the first day remain until morning.

[5]You must not sacrifice the Passover in any town the LORD your God gives you [6]except in the place he will choose as a dwelling for his Name. There you must sacrifice the Passover in the evening, when the sun goes down, on the anniversary[a] of your departure from Egypt. [7]Roast it and eat it at the place the LORD your God will choose. Then in the morning return to your tents. [8]For six days eat unleavened bread and on the seventh day hold an assembly to the LORD your God and do no work.

### The Festival of Weeks

[9]Count off seven weeks from the time you begin to put the sickle to the standing grain. [10]Then celebrate the Festival of Weeks to the LORD your God by giving a freewill offering in proportion to the blessings the LORD your God has given you. [11]And rejoice before the LORD your God at the place he will choose as a dwelling for his Name—you, your sons and daughters, your male and female servants, the Levites in your towns, and the foreigners, the fatherless and the widows living among you. [12]Remember that you were slaves in Egypt, and follow carefully these decrees.

### The Festival of Tabernacles

[13]Celebrate the Festival of Tabernacles for seven days after you have gathered the produce of your threshing floor and your winepress. [14]Be joyful at your festival—you, your sons and daughters, your male and female servants, and the Levites, the foreigners, the fatherless and the widows who live in your towns. [15]For seven days celebrate the festival to the LORD your God at the place the LORD will choose. For the LORD your God will bless you in all your harvest and in all the work of your hands, and your joy will be complete.

[16]Three times a year all your men must appear before the LORD your God at the place he will choose: at the Festival of Unleavened Bread, the Festival of Weeks and the Festival of Tabernacles. No one should appear before the LORD empty-handed: [17]Each of you must bring a gift in proportion to the way the LORD your God has blessed you.

### Judges

[18]Appoint judges and officials for each of your tribes in every town the LORD your God is giving you, and they shall judge the people fairly. [19]Do not pervert justice or show partiality. Do not accept a bribe, for a bribe blinds the eyes of the wise and twists the words of the innocent. [20]Follow justice and justice alone, so that you may live and possess the land the LORD your God is giving you.

### Worshiping Other Gods

[21]Do not set up any wooden Asherah pole beside the altar you build to the LORD your God, [22]and do not erect a sacred stone, for these the LORD your God hates.

**17** Do not sacrifice to the LORD your God an ox or a sheep that has any defect or flaw in it, for that would be detestable to him.

[2]If a man or woman living among you in one of the

## Amplified Bible

[4]No leaven shall be seen with you in all your territory for seven days; nor shall any of the flesh which you sacrificed the first day at evening be left all night until the morning.

[5]You may not offer the Passover sacrifice within any of your towns which the Lord your God gives you,

[6]But at the place which the Lord your God will choose in which to make His Name [and His Presence] dwell, there you shall offer the Passover sacrifice in the evening at sunset, at the season that you came out of Egypt.

[7]And you shall roast or boil and eat it in the place which the Lord your God will choose. And in the morning you shall turn and go to your tents.

[8]For six days you shall eat unleavened bread, and on the seventh day there shall be a solemn assembly to the Lord your God; you shall do no work on it.

[9]You shall count seven weeks; begin to number the seven weeks from the time you begin to put the sickle to the standing grain.

[10]Then you shall keep the Feast of Weeks to the Lord your God with a tribute of a freewill offering from your hand, which you shall give to the Lord your God, as the Lord your God blesses you.

[11]And you shall rejoice before the Lord your God, you and your son and daughter, your manservant and maidservant, and the Levite who is within your towns, the stranger or temporary resident, the fatherless, and the widow who are among you, at the place in which the Lord your God chooses to make His Name [and His Presence] dwell.

[12]And you shall [earnestly] remember that you were a slave in Egypt, and you shall be watchful and obey these statutes.

[13]You shall observe the Feast of Tabernacles or Booths for seven days after you have gathered in from your threshing floor and wine vat.

[14]You shall rejoice in your Feast, you, your son and daughter, your manservant and maidservant, the Levite, the transient and the stranger, the fatherless, and the widow who are within your towns.

[15]For seven days you shall keep a solemn Feast to the Lord your God in the place which the Lord chooses; because the Lord your God will bless you in all your produce and in all the works of your hands, so that you will be altogether joyful.

[16]Three times a year shall all your males appear before the Lord your God in the place which He chooses: at the Feast of Unleavened Bread, at the Feast of Weeks, and at the Feast of Tabernacles or Booths. They shall not appear before the Lord empty-handed:

[17]Every man shall give as he is able, according to the blessing of the Lord your God which He has given you.

[18]You shall appoint judges and officers in all your towns which the Lord your God gives you, according to your tribes, and they shall judge the people with righteous judgment.

[19]You shall not misinterpret or misapply judgment; you shall not be partial, or take a bribe, for a bribe blinds the eyes of the wise and perverts the words of the righteous.

[20]Follow what is altogether just (uncompromisingly righteous), that you may live and inherit the land which your God gives you.

[21]You shall not plant for yourselves any kind of tree dedicated to [the goddess] Asherah beside the altar of the Lord your God which you shall make.

[22]Neither shall you set up an idolatrous stone or image, which the Lord your God hates.

**17** You shall not sacrifice to the Lord your God an ox or sheep with a blemish or any defect whatsoever, for that is an abomination to the Lord your God.

[2]If there is found among you within any of your towns

## New International Version

towns the LORD gives you is found doing evil in the eyes of the LORD your God in violation of his covenant, ³and contrary to my command has worshiped other gods, bowing down to them or to the sun or the moon or the stars in the sky, ⁴and this has been brought to your attention, then you must investigate it thoroughly. If it is true and it has been proved that this detestable thing has been done in Israel, ⁵take the man or woman who has done this evil deed to your city gate and stone that person to death. ⁶On the testimony of two or three witnesses a person is to be put to death, but no one is to be put to death on the testimony of only one witness. ⁷The hands of the witnesses must be the first in putting that person to death, and then the hands of all the people. You must purge the evil from among you.

### Law Courts

⁸If cases come before your courts that are too difficult for you to judge—whether bloodshed, lawsuits or assaults—take them to the place the LORD your God will choose. ⁹Go to the Levitical priests and to the judge who is in office at that time. Inquire of them and they will give you the verdict. ¹⁰You must act according to the decisions they give you at the place the LORD will choose. Be careful to do everything they instruct you to do. ¹¹Act according to whatever they teach you and the decisions they give you. Do not turn aside from what they tell you, to the right or to the left. ¹²Anyone who shows contempt for the judge or for the priest who stands ministering there to the LORD your God is to be put to death. You must purge the evil from Israel. ¹³All the people will hear and be afraid, and will not be contemptuous again.

### The King

¹⁴When you enter the land the LORD your God is giving you and have taken possession of it and settled in it, and you say, "Let us set a king over us like all the nations around us," ¹⁵be sure to appoint over you a king the LORD your God chooses. He must be from among your fellow Israelites. Do not place a foreigner over you, one who is not an Israelite. ¹⁶The king, moreover, must not acquire great numbers of horses for himself or make the people return to Egypt to get more of them, for the LORD has told you, "You are not to go back that way again." ¹⁷He must not take many wives, or his heart will be led astray. He must not accumulate large amounts of silver and gold.

¹⁸When he takes the throne of his kingdom, he is to write for himself on a scroll a copy of this law, taken from that of the Levitical priests. ¹⁹It is to be with him, and he is to read it all the days of his life so that he may learn to revere the LORD his God and follow carefully all the words of this law and these decrees ²⁰and not consider himself better than his fellow Israelites and turn from the law to the right or to the left. Then he and his descendants will reign a long time over his kingdom in Israel.

## Amplified Bible

which the Lord your God gives you a man or woman who does what is wicked in the sight of the Lord your God by transgressing His covenant,

³Who has gone and served other gods and worshiped them, or the sun or moon or any of the host of the heavens, which I have forbidden,

⁴And it is told and you hear of it, then inquire diligently. And if it is certainly true that such an abomination has been committed in Israel,

⁵Then you shall bring forth to your town's gates that man or woman who has done that wicked thing and you shall stone that man or woman to death.

⁶On the evidence of two or three witnesses he who is worthy of death shall be put to death; he shall not be put to death on the evidence of one witness.

⁷The hands of the witnesses shall be the first against him to put him to death, and afterward the hands of all the people. So you shall purge the evil from among you.

⁸If there arises a matter too hard for you in judgment—between one kind of bloodshed and another, between one legality and another, between one kind of assault and another, matters of controversy within your towns—then arise and go to the place which the Lord your God chooses.

⁹And you shall come to the Levitical priests and to the judge who is in office in those days, and you shall consult them and they shall make clear to you the decision.

¹⁰And you shall do according to the decision which they declare to you from that place which the Lord chooses; and you shall be watchful to do according to all that they tell you;

¹¹According to the decision of the law which they shall teach you and the judgment which they shall announce to you, you shall do; you shall not turn aside from the verdict they give you, ᵃeither to the right hand or the left.

¹²The man who does presumptuously and will not listen to the priest who stands to minister there before the Lord your God or to the judge, that man shall die; so you shall purge the evil from Israel.

¹³And all the people shall hear and [reverently] fear, and not act presumptuously again.

¹⁴When you come to the land which the Lord your God gives you and you possess it and live there, and then say, We will set a king over us like all the nations that are about us,

¹⁵You shall surely set as king over you him whom the Lord your God will choose. One from among your brethren you shall set as king over you; you may not set a foreigner, who is not your brother, over you.

¹⁶But he shall not multiply horses to himself or cause the people to return to Egypt in order to multiply horses, since the Lord said to you, You shall never return that way.

¹⁷And he shall not multiply wives to himself, that his [mind and] heart turn not away; neither shall he greatly multiply to himself silver and gold.

¹⁸And when he sits on his royal throne, he shall write for himself a copy of this law in a book, out of what is before the Levitical priests.

¹⁹And he shall keep it with him, and he shall read in it all the days of his life, that he may learn [reverently] to fear the Lord his God, by keeping all the words of this law and these statutes and doing them,

²⁰That his [mind and] heart may not be lifted up above his brethren and that he may not turn aside from the commandment to the right hand or to the left; so that he may continue long, he and his sons, in his kingdom in Israel.

---

ᵃ The Hebrew is obscure.

## New International Version

### Offerings for Priests and Levites

**18** The Levitical priests—indeed, the whole tribe of Levi—are to have no allotment or inheritance with Israel. They shall live on the food offerings presented to the LORD, for that is their inheritance. ²They shall have no inheritance among their fellow Israelites; the LORD is their inheritance, as he promised them.

³This is the share due the priests from the people who sacrifice a bull or a sheep: the shoulder, the internal organs and the meat from the head. ⁴You are to give them the firstfruits of your grain, new wine and olive oil, and the first wool from the shearing of your sheep, ⁵for the LORD your God has chosen them and their descendants out of all your tribes to stand and minister in the LORD's name always.

⁶If a Levite moves from one of your towns anywhere in Israel where he is living, and comes in all earnestness to the place the LORD will choose, ⁷he may minister in the name of the LORD his God like all his fellow Levites who serve there in the presence of the LORD. ⁸He is to share equally in their benefits, even though he has received money from the sale of family possessions.

### Occult Practices

⁹When you enter the land the LORD your God is giving you, do not learn to imitate the detestable ways of the nations there. ¹⁰Let no one be found among you who sacrifices their son or daughter in the fire, who practices divination or sorcery, interprets omens, engages in witchcraft, ¹¹or casts spells, or who is a medium or spiritist or who consults the dead. ¹²Anyone who does these things is detestable to the LORD; because of these same detestable practices the LORD your God will drive out those nations before you. ¹³You must be blameless before the LORD your God.

### The Prophet

¹⁴The nations you will dispossess listen to those who practice sorcery or divination. But as for you, the LORD your God has not permitted you to do so. ¹⁵The LORD your God will raise up for you a prophet like me from among you, from your fellow Israelites. You must listen to him. ¹⁶For this is what you asked of the LORD your God at Horeb on the day of the assembly when you said, "Let us not hear the voice of the LORD our God nor see this great fire anymore, or we will die."

¹⁷The LORD said to me: "What they say is good. ¹⁸I will raise up for them a prophet like you from among their fellow Israelites, and I will put my words in his mouth. He will tell them everything I command him. ¹⁹I myself will call to account anyone who does not listen to my words that the prophet speaks in my name. ²⁰But a prophet who presumes to speak in my name anything I have not com-

## Amplified Bible

**18** The Levitical priests and all the tribe of Levi shall have no part or inheritance with Israel; they shall eat the offerings made by fire to the Lord, and His rightful dues.

²They shall have no inheritance among their brethren; the Lord is their inheritance, as He promised them.

³And this shall be the priest's due from the people, from those who offer a sacrifice, whether it be ox or sheep: they shall give to the priest the shoulder and the two cheeks and the stomach.

⁴The firstfruits of your grain, of your new wine, and of your oil, and the first *or* best of the fleece of your sheep you shall give the priest.

⁵For the Lord your God has chosen him out of all your tribes to stand to minister in the name [and presence] of the Lord, him and his sons forever.

⁶And if a Levite comes from any of your towns out of all Israel where he is a temporary resident, he may come whenever he desires to [the sanctuary] the place the Lord will choose;

⁷Then he may minister in the name [and presence of] the Lord his God like all his brethren the Levites who stand to minister there before the Lord.

⁸They shall have equal portions to eat, besides what may come of the sale of his patrimony. [Jer. 32:6-15.]

⁹When you come into the land which the Lord your God gives you, you shall not learn to follow the abominable practices of these nations.

¹⁰There shall not be found among you anyone who makes his son or daughter pass through the fire, or who uses divination, or is a soothsayer, or an augur, or a sorcerer,

¹¹Or a charmer, or a medium, or a wizard, or a necromancer.

¹²For all who do these things are an abomination to the Lord, and it is because of these abominable practices that the Lord your God is driving them out before you.

¹³You shall be blameless [and absolutely true] to the Lord your God.

¹⁴For these nations whom you shall dispossess listen to soothsayers and diviners. But as for you, the Lord your God has not allowed you to do so.

¹⁵The Lord your God will raise up for you ᵃa prophet (Prophet) from the midst of your brethren like me [Moses]; to him you shall listen. [Matt. 21:11; John 1:21.]

¹⁶This is what you desired [and asked] of the Lord your God at Horeb on the day of the assembly when you said, Let me not hear again the voice of the Lord my God or see this great fire any more, lest I die.

¹⁷And the Lord said to me, They have well said all that they have spoken.

¹⁸I will raise up for them a prophet (Prophet) from among their brethren like you, and will put My words in his mouth; and he shall speak to them all that I command him.

¹⁹And whoever will not hearken to My words which he shall speak in My name, I Myself will require it of him.

²⁰But the prophet who presumes to speak a word in My

ᵃ The insertion of this promise in connection with the preceding prohibition might warrant the application which some make of it to that order of true prophets whom God commissioned in unbroken succession to instruct, to direct, and warn His people; in this view the gist of it is, "there is no need to consult with diviners and soothsayers, for I shall afford you the benefit of divinely appointed prophets, for judging of whose identity a sure clue is given" (Deut. 18:20, 22). But the prophet here promised was preeminently the Messiah, for He alone was "like unto Moses in His mediatorial character; in the peculiar excellence of His ministry; in the number, variety, and magnitude of His miracles; in His close and familiar communion with God; and in His being the author of a new dispensation of religion." This prediction was fulfilled 1,500 years afterwards, and was expressly applied to Christ by Peter (Acts 3:22, 23) and by Stephen (Acts 7:37) (Robert Jamieson, A. R. Fausset and David Brown, *A Commentary*).

## New International Version

manded, or a prophet who speaks in the name of other gods, is to be put to death."
21You may say to yourselves, "How can we know when a message has not been spoken by the LORD?" 22If what a prophet proclaims in the name of the LORD does not take place or come true, that is a message the LORD has not spoken. That prophet has spoken presumptuously, so do not be alarmed.

### Cities of Refuge

**19** When the LORD your God has destroyed the nations whose land he is giving you, and when you have driven them out and settled in their towns and houses, 2then set aside for yourselves three cities in the land the LORD your God is giving you to possess. 3Determine the distances involved and divide into three parts the land the LORD your God is giving you as an inheritance, so that a person who kills someone may flee for refuge to one of these cities.

4This is the rule concerning anyone who kills a person and flees there for safety—anyone who kills a neighbor unintentionally, without malice aforethought. 5For instance, a man may go into the forest with his neighbor to cut wood, and as he swings his ax to fell a tree, the head may fly off and hit his neighbor and kill him. That man may flee to one of these cities and save his life. 6Otherwise, the avenger of blood might pursue him in a rage, overtake him if the distance is too great, and kill him even though he is not deserving of death, since he did it to his neighbor without malice aforethought. 7This is why I command you to set aside for yourselves three cities.

8If the LORD your God enlarges your territory, as he promised on oath to your ancestors, and gives you the whole land he promised them, 9because you carefully follow all these laws I command you today—to love the LORD your God and to walk always in obedience to him—then you are to set aside three more cities. 10Do this so that innocent blood will not be shed in your land, which the LORD your God is giving you as your inheritance, and so that you will not be guilty of bloodshed.

11But if out of hate someone lies in wait, assaults and kills a neighbor, and then flees to one of these cities, 12the killer shall be sent for by the town elders, be brought back from the city, and be handed over to the avenger of blood to die. 13Show no pity. You must purge from Israel the guilt of shedding innocent blood, so that it may go well with you.

14Do not move your neighbor's boundary stone set up by your predecessors in the inheritance you receive in the land the LORD your God is giving you to possess.

### Witnesses

15One witness is not enough to convict anyone accused of any crime or offense they may have committed. A matter must be established by the testimony of two or three witnesses.

16If a malicious witness takes the stand to accuse someone of a crime, 17the two people involved in the dispute must stand in the presence of the LORD before the priests and the judges who are in office at the time. 18The judges must make a thorough investigation, and if the witness proves to be a liar, giving false testimony against a fellow

## Amplified Bible

name which I have not commanded him to speak, or who speaks in the name of other gods, that same prophet shall die.

21And if you say in your [minds and] hearts, How shall we know which words the Lord has not spoken?
22When a prophet speaks in the name of the Lord, if the word does not come to pass or prove true, that is a word which the Lord has not spoken. The prophet has spoken it presumptuously; you shall not be afraid of him.

**19** When the Lord your God has cut off the nations whose land the Lord your God gives you, and you dispossess them and dwell in their cities and in their houses,

2You shall set apart three cities for yourselves in the land which the Lord your God gives you to possess.

3You shall prepare the road and divide into three parts the territory of your land which the Lord your God gives you to possess, so that any manslayer can flee to them.

4And this is the case of the slayer who shall flee there in order that he may live. Whoever kills his neighbor unintentionally, for whom he had no enmity in time past—

5As when a man goes into the wood with his neighbor to hew wood, and his hand strikes with the ax to cut down the tree, and the head slips off the handle and lights on his neighbor and kills him—he may flee to one of those cities and live;

6Lest the avenger of the blood pursue the slayer while his [mind and] heart are hot with anger and overtake him, because the way is long, and slay him even though the slayer was not worthy of death, since he had not been at enmity with him previously.

7Therefore I command you, You shall set apart three [refuge] cities.

8And if the Lord your God enlarges your territory, as He has sworn to your fathers to do, and gives you all the land which He promised to your fathers to give,

9If you keep all these commandments to do them, which I command you this day, to love the Lord your God and to walk always in His ways, then you shall add three other cities to these three,

10Lest innocent blood be shed in your land, which the Lord your God gives you as an inheritance, and so blood guilt be upon you.

11But if any man hates his neighbor and lies in wait for him, and attacks him and wounds him mortally so that he dies, and the assailant flees into one of these cities,

12Then the elders of his own city shall send for him and fetch him from there and give him over to the avenger of blood, so that he may die.

13Your eyes shall not pity him, but you shall clear Israel of the guilt of innocent blood, that it may go well with you.

14You shall not remove your neighbor's landmark in the land which the Lord your God gives you to possess, which the men of old [the first dividers of the land] set.

15One witness shall not prevail against a man for any crime or any wrong in connection with any sin he commits; only on the testimony of two or three witnesses shall a charge be established.

16If a false witness rises up against any man to accuse him of wrongdoing,

17Then both parties to the controversy shall stand before the Lord, before the priests and the judges who are in office in those days.

18The judges shall inquire diligently, and if the witness is a false witness and has accused his brother falsely,

## New International Version

Israelite, ¹⁹then do to the false witness as that witness intended to do to the other party. You must purge the evil from among you. ²⁰The rest of the people will hear of this and be afraid, and never again will such an evil thing be done among you. ²¹Show no pity: life for life, eye for eye, tooth for tooth, hand for hand, foot for foot.

### Going to War

**20** When you go to war against your enemies and see horses and chariots and an army greater than yours, do not be afraid of them, because the LORD your God, who brought you up out of Egypt, will be with you. ²When you are about to go into battle, the priest shall come forward and address the army. ³He shall say: "Hear, Israel: Today you are going into battle against your enemies. Do not be fainthearted or afraid; do not panic or be terrified by them. ⁴For the LORD your God is the one who goes with you to fight for you against your enemies to give you victory."

⁵The officers shall say to the army: "Has anyone built a new house and not yet begun to live in it? Let him go home, or he may die in battle and someone else may begin to live in it. ⁶Has anyone planted a vineyard and not begun to enjoy it? Let him go home, or he may die in battle and someone else enjoy it. ⁷Has anyone become pledged to a woman and not married her? Let him go home, or he may die in battle and someone else marry her." ⁸Then the officers shall add, "Is anyone afraid or fainthearted? Let him go home so that his fellow soldiers will not become disheartened too." ⁹When the officers have finished speaking to the army, they shall appoint commanders over it.

¹⁰When you march up to attack a city, make its people an offer of peace. ¹¹If they accept and open their gates, all the people in it shall be subject to forced labor and shall work for you. ¹²If they refuse to make peace and they engage you in battle, lay siege to that city. ¹³When the LORD your God delivers it into your hand, put to the sword all the men in it. ¹⁴As for the women, the children, the livestock and everything else in the city, you may take these as plunder for yourselves. And you may use the plunder the LORD your God gives you from your enemies. ¹⁵This is how you are to treat all the cities that are at a distance from you and do not belong to the nations nearby.

¹⁶However, in the cities of the nations the LORD your God is giving you as an inheritance, do not leave alive anything that breathes. ¹⁷Completely destroy[a] them—the Hittites, Amorites, Canaanites, Perizzites, Hivites and Jebusites—as the LORD your God has commanded you. ¹⁸Otherwise, they will teach you to follow all the detestable things they do in worshiping their gods, and you will sin against the LORD your God.

¹⁹When you lay siege to a city for a long time, fighting against it to capture it, do not destroy its trees by putting an ax to them, because you can eat their fruit. Do not cut them down. Are the trees people, that you should besiege

## Amplified Bible

¹⁹Then you shall do to him as he had intended to do to his brother. So you shall put away the evil from among you. ²⁰And those who remain shall hear and [reverently] fear, and shall henceforth commit no such evil among you. ²¹Your eyes shall not pity: it shall be life for life, eye for eye, tooth for tooth, hand for hand, foot for foot.

**20** When you go forth to battle against your enemies and see horses and chariots and an army greater than your own, do not be afraid of them, for the Lord your God, Who brought you out of the land of Egypt, is with you. ²And when you come near to the battle, the priest shall approach and speak to the men, ³And shall say to them, Hear, O Israel, you draw near this day to battle against your enemies. Let not your [minds and] hearts faint; fear not, and do not tremble or be terrified [and in dread] because of them. ⁴For the Lord your God is He Who goes with you to fight for you against your enemies to save you. [I Sam. 17:45.]

⁵And the officers shall speak to the people, saying, What man is there who has built a new house and has not dedicated it? Let him return to his house, lest he die in the battle and another man dedicate it. ⁶And what man has planted a vineyard and has not used the fruit of it? Let him also return to his house, lest he die in the battle and another man use the fruit of it. ⁷And what man has betrothed a wife and has not taken her? Let him return to his house, lest he die in the battle and another man take her. ⁸And the officers shall speak further to the people, and say, What man is fearful and fainthearted? Let him return to his house, lest [because of him] his brethren's [minds and] hearts faint as his own. ⁹And when the officers finish speaking to the people, they shall appoint commanders at the head of the people.

¹⁰When you draw near to a city to fight against it, then proclaim peace to it. ¹¹And if that city makes an answer of peace to you and opens to you, then all the people found in it shall be tributary to you and they shall serve you. ¹²But if it refuses to make peace with you and fights against you, then you shall besiege it. ¹³And when the Lord your God has given it into your hands, you shall smite every male there with the edge of the sword. ¹⁴But the women, the little ones, the beasts, and all that is in the city, all the spoil in it, you shall take for yourselves; and you shall use the spoil of your enemies which the Lord your God has given you. ¹⁵So shall you treat all the cities that are very far off from you, that do not belong to the cities of these nations. ¹⁶But in the cities of these people which the Lord your God gives you for an inheritance, you shall save alive nothing that breathes. ¹⁷But you shall utterly exterminate them, the Hittites, the Amorites, the Canaanites, the Perizzites, the Hivites, and the Jebusites, as the Lord your God has commanded you, ¹⁸So that they may not teach you all the abominable practices they have carried on for their gods, and so cause you to sin against the Lord your God.

¹⁹When you besiege a city for a long time, making war against it to take it, you shall not destroy its trees by using an ax on them, for you can eat their fruit; you must not cut them down, for is the tree of the field a man, that it should be besieged by you?

---

[a] 17 The Hebrew term refers to the irrevocable giving over of things or persons to the LORD, often by totally destroying them.

## New International Version

them?[a] 20However, you may cut down trees that you know are not fruit trees and use them to build siege works until the city at war with you falls.

### Atonement for an Unsolved Murder

**21** If someone is found slain, lying in a field in the land the LORD your God is giving you to possess, and it is not known who the killer was, 2your elders and judges shall go out and measure the distance from the body to the neighboring towns. 3Then the elders of the town nearest the body shall take a heifer that has never been worked and has never worn a yoke 4and lead it down to a valley that has not been plowed or planted and where there is a flowing stream. There in the valley they are to break the heifer's neck. 5The Levitical priests shall step forward, for the LORD your God has chosen them to minister and to pronounce blessings in the name of the LORD and to decide all cases of dispute and assault. 6Then all the elders of the town nearest the body shall wash their hands over the heifer whose neck was broken in the valley, 7and they shall declare: "Our hands did not shed this blood, nor did our eyes see it done. 8Accept this atonement for your people Israel, whom you have redeemed, LORD, and do not hold your people guilty of the blood of an innocent person." Then the bloodshed will be atoned for, 9and you will have purged from yourselves the guilt of shedding innocent blood, since you have done what is right in the eyes of the LORD.

### Marrying a Captive Woman

10When you go to war against your enemies and the LORD your God delivers them into your hands and you take captives, 11if you notice among the captives a beautiful woman and are attracted to her, you may take her as your wife. 12Bring her into your home and have her shave her head, trim her nails 13and put aside the clothes she was wearing when captured. After she has lived in your house and mourned her father and mother for a full month, then you may go to her and be her husband and she shall be your wife. 14If you are not pleased with her, let her go wherever she wishes. You must not sell her or treat her as a slave, since you have dishonored her.

### The Right of the Firstborn

15If a man has two wives, and he loves one but not the other, and both bear him sons but the firstborn is the son of the wife he does not love, 16when he wills his property to his sons, he must not give the rights of the firstborn to the son of the wife he loves in preference to his actual firstborn, the son of the wife he does not love. 17He must acknowledge the son of his unloved wife as the firstborn by giving him a double share of all he has. That son is the first sign of his father's strength. The right of the firstborn belongs to him.

### A Rebellious Son

18If someone has a stubborn and rebellious son who does not obey his father and mother and will not listen to them when they discipline him, 19his father and mother shall take hold of him and bring him to the elders at the gate of his town. 20They shall say to the elders, "This son

## Amplified Bible

20Only the trees which you know are not trees for food you may destroy and cut down, that you may build siege works against the city that makes war with you until it falls.

**21** If one is found slain in the land which the Lord your God gives you to possess, lying in the field, and it is not known who has killed him, 2Then your elders and judges shall come forth and measure the distance to the cities around him who is slain. 3And the city which is nearest to the slain man, the elders of that city shall take a heifer which has never been worked, never pulled in the yoke, 4And the elders of that city shall bring the heifer down to a valley with running water which is neither plowed nor sown, and shall break the heifer's neck there in the valley. 5And the priests, the sons of Levi, shall come near, for the Lord your God has chosen them to minister to Him and to bless in the name [and presence] of the Lord, and by their word shall every controversy and every assault be settled. 6And all the elders of that city nearest to the slain man shall wash their hands over the heifer whose neck was broken in the valley, 7And they shall testify, Our hands have not shed this blood, neither have our eyes seen it. 8Forgive, O Lord, Your people Israel, whom You have redeemed, and do not allow the shedding of innocent blood to be charged to Your people Israel. And the guilt of blood shall be forgiven them. 9So shall you purge the guilt of innocent blood from among you, when you do what is right in the sight of the Lord.

10When you go forth to battle against your enemies and the Lord your God has given them into your hands and you carry them away captive, 11And you see among the captives a beautiful woman and desire her, that you may have her as your wife, 12Then you shall bring her home to your house, and she shall shave her head and pare her nails [in purification from heathenism] 13And put off her prisoner's garb, and shall remain in your house and bewail her father and mother a full month. After that you may go in to her and be her husband and she shall be your wife. 14And if you have no delight in her, then you shall let her go absolutely free. You shall not sell her at all for money; you shall not deal with her as a slave or a servant, because you have humbled her.

15If a man has two wives, one loved and the other disliked, and they both have borne him children, and if the firstborn son is the son of the one who is disliked, 16Then on the day when he wills his possessions to his sons, he shall not put the firstborn of his loved wife in place of the [actual] firstborn of the disliked wife—her firstborn being older. 17But he shall acknowledge the son of the disliked as the firstborn by giving him a double portion of all that he has, for he was the first issue of his strength; the right of the firstborn is his. 18If a man has a stubborn and rebellious son who will not obey the voice of his father or his mother and though they chasten him will not listen to them, 19Then his father and mother shall take hold of him and bring him out to the elders of his city at the gate of the place where he lives, 20And they shall say to the elders of his city, This son of

---

[a] 19 Or *down to use in the siege, for the fruit trees are for the benefit of people.*

## New International Version

of ours is stubborn and rebellious. He will not obey us. He is a glutton and a drunkard." [21]Then all the men of his town are to stone him to death. You must purge the evil from among you. All Israel will hear of it and be afraid.

### Various Laws

[22]If someone guilty of a capital offense is put to death and their body is exposed on a pole, [23]you must not leave the body hanging on the pole overnight. Be sure to bury it that same day, because anyone who is hung on a pole is under God's curse. You must not desecrate the land the LORD your God is giving you as an inheritance.

**22** If you see your fellow Israelite's ox or sheep straying, do not ignore it but be sure to take it back to its owner. [2]If they do not live near you or if you do not know who owns it, take it home with you and keep it until they come looking for it. Then give it back. [3]Do the same if you find their donkey or cloak or anything else they have lost. Do not ignore it.

[4]If you see your fellow Israelite's donkey or ox fallen on the road, do not ignore it. Help the owner get it to its feet.

[5]A woman must not wear men's clothing, nor a man wear women's clothing, for the LORD your God detests anyone who does this.

[6]If you come across a bird's nest beside the road, either in a tree or on the ground, and the mother is sitting on the young or on the eggs, do not take the mother with the young. [7]You may take the young, but be sure to let the mother go, so that it may go well with you and you may have a long life.

[8]When you build a new house, make a parapet around your roof so that you may not bring the guilt of bloodshed on your house if someone falls from the roof.

[9]Do not plant two kinds of seed in your vineyard; if you do, not only the crops you plant but also the fruit of the vineyard will be defiled.[a]

[10]Do not plow with an ox and a donkey yoked together.

[11]Do not wear clothes of wool and linen woven together.

[12]Make tassels on the four corners of the cloak you wear.

### Marriage Violations

[13]If a man takes a wife and, after sleeping with her, dislikes her [14]and slanders her and gives her a bad name, saying, "I married this woman, but when I approached her, I did not find proof of her virginity," [15]then the young woman's father and mother shall bring to the town elders at the gate proof that she was a virgin. [16]Her father will say to the elders, "I gave my daughter in marriage to this man, but he dislikes her. [17]Now he has slandered her and said, 'I did not find your daughter to be a virgin.' But here is the proof of my daughter's virginity." Then her parents shall display the cloth before the elders of the town, [18]and the elders shall take the man and punish him. [19]They shall fine him a hundred shekels[b] of silver and give them to the young woman's father, because this man has given an Isra-

## Amplified Bible

ours is stubborn and rebellious. He will not obey our voice. He is a glutton and a drunkard. [Prov. 23:20-22.]

[21]Then all the men of his city shall stone him to death; so you shall cleanse out the evil from your midst, and all Israel shall hear and [reverently] fear.

[22]And if a man has committed a sin worthy of death and he is put to death and [afterward] you hang him on a tree, [Josh. 10:26, 27.]

[23]His body shall not remain all night upon the tree, but you shall surely bury him on the same day, for a hanged man is accursed by God. Thus you shall not defile your land which the Lord your God gives you for an inheritance. [Gal. 3:13.]

**22** You shall not see your brother's ox or his sheep being driven away or stolen, and hide yourself from [your duty to help] them; you shall surely take them back to your brother. [Prov. 24:12.]

[2]And if your brother [the owner] is not near you or if you do not know who he is, you shall bring the animal to your house and it shall be with you until your brother comes looking for it; then you shall restore it to him.

[3]And so shall you do with his donkey or his garment or with anything which your brother has lost and you have found. You shall not hide from [your duty concerning] them.

[4]You shall not see your brother's donkey or his ox fall down by the way, and hide from [your duty concerning] them; you shall surely help him to lift them up again.

[5]The woman shall not wear that which pertains to a man, neither shall a man put on a woman's garment, for all that do so are an abomination to the Lord your God.

[6]If a bird's nest should chance to be before you in the way, in any tree or on the ground, with young ones or eggs, and the mother bird is sitting on the young or on the eggs, you shall not take the mother bird with the young.

[7]You shall surely let the mother bird go, and take only the young, that it may be well with you and that you may prolong your days.

[8]When you build a new house, then you shall put a railing around your [flat] roof, so that no one may fall from there and bring guilt of blood upon your house.

[9]You shall not plant your vineyard with two kinds of seed, lest the whole crop be forfeited [under this ban], the seed which you have sown and the yield of the vineyard forfeited to the sanctuary.

[10]You shall not plow with an ox [a clean animal] and a donkey [unclean] together. [II Cor. 6:14-16.]

[11]You shall not wear a garment of mingled stuff, wool and linen together. [Ezek. 44:18; Rev. 19:8.]

[12]You shall make yourself tassels on the four corners of your cloak with which you cover yourself. [Num. 15:37-40.]

[13]If any man takes a wife and goes in to her, and then scorns her

[14]And charges her with shameful things and gives her an evil reputation, and says, I took this woman, but when I came to her, I did not find in her the tokens of a virgin,

[15]Then the father of the young woman, and her mother, shall get and bring out the tokens of her virginity to the elders of the city at the gate.

[16]And her father shall say to the elders, I gave my daughter to this man as wife, but he hates and spurns her;

[17]And behold, he has made shameful charges against her, saying, I found not in your daughter the evidences of her virginity. And yet these are the tokens of my daughter's virginity. And they shall spread the garment before the elders of the city,

[18]And the elders of that city shall take the man and rebuke and whip him.

[19]And they shall fine him 100 shekels of silver and give them to the father of the young woman, because he has

[a] 9 Or be forfeited to the sanctuary  [b] 19 That is, about 2 1/2 pounds or about 1.2 kilograms

## New International Version

elite virgin a bad name. She shall continue to be his wife; he must not divorce her as long as he lives.

[20]If, however, the charge is true and no proof of the young woman's virginity can be found, [21]she shall be brought to the door of her father's house and there the men of her town shall stone her to death. She has done an outrageous thing in Israel by being promiscuous while still in her father's house. You must purge the evil from among you.

[22]If a man is found sleeping with another man's wife, both the man who slept with her and the woman must die. You must purge the evil from Israel.

[23]If a man happens to meet in a town a virgin pledged to be married and he sleeps with her, [24]you shall take both of them to the gate of that town and stone them to death—the young woman because she was in a town and did not scream for help, and the man because he violated another man's wife. You must purge the evil from among you.

[25]But if out in the country a man happens to meet a young woman pledged to be married and rapes her, only the man who has done this shall die. [26]Do nothing to the woman; she has committed no sin deserving death. This case is like that of someone who attacks and murders a neighbor, [27]for the man found the young woman out in the country, and though the betrothed woman screamed, there was no one to rescue her.

[28]If a man happens to meet a virgin who is not pledged to be married and rapes her and they are discovered, [29]he shall pay her father fifty shekels[a] of silver. He must marry the young woman, for he has violated her. He can never divorce her as long as he lives.

[30]A man is not to marry his father's wife; he must not dishonor his father's bed.[b]

### Exclusion From the Assembly

**23**[c] No one who has been emasculated by crushing or cutting may enter the assembly of the LORD.

[2]No one born of a forbidden marriage[d] nor any of their descendants may enter the assembly of the LORD, not even in the tenth generation.

[3]No Ammonite or Moabite or any of their descendants may enter the assembly of the LORD, not even in the tenth generation. [4]For they did not come to meet you with bread and water on your way when you came out of Egypt, and they hired Balaam son of Beor from Pethor in Aram Naharaim[e] to pronounce a curse on you. [5]However, the LORD your God would not listen to Balaam but turned the curse into a blessing for you, because the LORD your God loves you. [6]Do not seek a treaty of friendship with them as long as you live.

[7]Do not despise an Edomite, for the Edomites are related to you. Do not despise an Egyptian, because you resided as foreigners in their country. [8]The third generation of children born to them may enter the assembly of the LORD.

### Uncleanness in the Camp

[9]When you are encamped against your enemies, keep away from everything impure. [10]If one of your men is un-

## Amplified Bible

brought an evil name upon a virgin of Israel. And she shall be his wife; he may not divorce her all his days.

[20]But if it is true that the evidences of virginity were not found in the young woman,

[21]Then they shall bring her to the door of her father's house and the men of her city shall stone her to death, because she has wrought [criminal] folly in Israel by playing the harlot in her father's house. So you shall put away the evil from among you.

[22]If a man is found lying with another man's wife, they shall both die, the man who lay with the woman and the woman. So you shall purge the evil from Israel.

[23]If a maiden who is a virgin is engaged to be married, and a man finds her in the city and lies with her,

[24]Then you shall bring them both out to the gate of that city and shall stone them to death—the young woman because she did not cry for help though she was in the city, and the man because he has violated his neighbor's [promised] wife. So shall you put away evil from among you.

[25]But if a man finds the betrothed maiden in the open country and the man seizes her and lies with her, then only the man who lay with her shall die.

[26]But you shall do nothing to the young woman; she has committed no sin punishable by death, for this is as when a man attacks and slays his neighbor,

[27]For he came upon her in the open country, and the betrothed girl cried out, but there was no one to save her.

[28]If a man finds a girl who is a virgin, who is not betrothed, and he seizes her and lies with her and they are found,

[29]Then the man who lay with her shall give to the girl's father fifty shekels of silver, and she shall be his wife, because he has violated her; he may not divorce her all his days.

[30]A man shall not take his father's former wife, nor shall he uncover her who belongs to his father.

**23** He who is wounded in the testicles, or has been made a eunuch, shall not enter into the congregation of the Lord.

[2]A person begotten out of wedlock shall not enter into the assembly of the Lord; even to his tenth generation shall his descendants not enter into the congregation of the Lord.

[3]An Ammonite or [a]Moabite shall not enter into the congregation of the Lord; even to their tenth generation their descendants shall not enter into the assembly of the Lord forever,

[4]Because they did not meet you with food and water on the way when you came forth out of Egypt, and because they hired Balaam son of Beor of Pethor of Mesopotamia against you to curse you.

[5]Nevertheless, the Lord your God would not listen to Balaam, but the Lord your God turned the curse into a blessing to you, because the Lord your God loves you.

[6]You shall not seek their peace or their prosperity all your days forever.

[7]You shall not abhor an Edomite, for he is your brother [Esau's descendant]. You shall not abhor an Egyptian, because you were a stranger *and* temporary resident in his land.

[8]Their children may enter into the congregation of the Lord in their third generation.

[9]When you go forth against your enemies and are in camp, you shall keep yourselves from every evil thing.

---

[a] It must be remembered that according to the Jewish law the children followed the father, not the mother. [Take the family of Boaz, for example. Although Boaz's wife Ruth was a Moabitess, his family was considered Israelite, including his wife]. The case of Ruth would not, therefore, be touched by this precept (Charles J. Ellicott, *A Bible Commentary*).

---

[a] 29 That is, about 1 1/4 pounds or about 575 grams    [b] 30 In Hebrew texts this verse (22:30) is numbered 23:1.    [c] In Hebrew texts 23:1-25 is numbered 23:2-26.    [d] 2 Or *one of illegitimate birth*    [e] 4 That is, Northwest Mesopotamia

## New International Version

clean because of a nocturnal emission, he is to go outside the camp and stay there. ¹¹But as evening approaches he is to wash himself, and at sunset he may return to the camp. ¹²Designate a place outside the camp where you can go to relieve yourself. ¹³As part of your equipment have something to dig with, and when you relieve yourself, dig a hole and cover up your excrement. ¹⁴For the Lord your God moves about in your camp to protect you and to deliver your enemies to you. Your camp must be holy, so that he will not see among you anything indecent and turn away from you.

### Miscellaneous Laws
¹⁵If a slave has taken refuge with you, do not hand them over to their master. ¹⁶Let them live among you wherever they like and in whatever town they choose. Do not oppress them.

¹⁷No Israelite man or woman is to become a shrine prostitute. ¹⁸You must not bring the earnings of a female prostitute or of a male prostitute[a] into the house of the Lord your God to pay any vow, because the Lord your God detests them both.

¹⁹Do not charge a fellow Israelite interest, whether on money or food or anything else that may earn interest. ²⁰You may charge a foreigner interest, but not a fellow Israelite, so that the Lord your God may bless you in everything you put your hand to in the land you are entering to possess.

²¹If you make a vow to the Lord your God, do not be slow to pay it, for the Lord your God will certainly demand it of you and you will be guilty of sin. ²²But if you refrain from making a vow, you will not be guilty. ²³Whatever your lips utter you must be sure to do, because you made your vow freely to the Lord your God with your own mouth.

²⁴If you enter your neighbor's vineyard, you may eat all the grapes you want, but do not put any in your basket. ²⁵If you enter your neighbor's grainfield, you may pick kernels with your hands, but you must not put a sickle to their standing grain.

**24** If a man marries a woman who becomes displeasing to him because he finds something indecent about her, and he writes her a certificate of divorce, gives it to her and sends her from his house, ²and if after she leaves his house she becomes the wife of another man, ³and her second husband dislikes her and writes her a certificate of divorce, gives it to her and sends her from his house, or if he dies, ⁴then her first husband, who divorced her, is not allowed to marry her again after she has been defiled. That would be detestable in the eyes of the Lord. Do not bring sin upon the land the Lord your God is giving you as an inheritance.

⁵If a man has recently married, he must not be sent to war or have any other duty laid on him. For one year he is

## Amplified Bible

¹⁰If there is among you any man who is not clean by reason of what happens to him at night, then he shall go outside the camp; he shall not come within the camp; ¹¹But when evening comes he shall bathe himself in water, and when the sun is down he may return to the camp.

¹²You shall have a place also outside the camp to which you shall go [as a comfort station];

¹³And you shall have a paddle or shovel among your weapons, and when you sit down outside [to relieve yourself], you shall dig a hole with it and turn back and cover up what has come from you.

¹⁴For the Lord your God walks in the midst of your camp to deliver you and to give up your enemies before you. Therefore shall your camp be holy, that He may see nothing indecent among you and turn away from you.

¹⁵You shall not give up to his master a servant who has escaped from his master to you.

¹⁶He shall dwell with you in your midst wherever he chooses in one of your towns where it pleases him best. You shall not defraud or oppress him.

¹⁷There shall be no cult prostitute among the daughters of Israel, neither shall there be a cult prostitute (a sodomite) among the sons of Israel.

¹⁸You shall not bring the hire of a harlot or the price of a dog (a sodomite) into the house of the Lord your God as payment of a vow, for both of these [the gift and the giver] are an abomination to the Lord your God.

¹⁹You shall not lend on interest to your brother—interest on money, on victuals, on anything that is lent for interest.

²⁰You may lend on interest to a foreigner, but to your brother you shall not lend on interest, that the Lord your God may bless you in all that you undertake in the land to which you go to possess it.

²¹When you make a vow to the Lord your God, you shall not be slack in paying it, for the Lord your God will surely require it of you, and slackness would be sin in you.

²²But if you refrain from vowing, it will not be sin in you.

²³The vow which has passed your lips you shall be watchful to perform, a voluntary offering which you have made to the Lord your God, which you have promised with your mouth.

²⁴When you come into your neighbor's vineyard, you may eat your fill of grapes, as many as you please, but you shall not put any in your vessel.

²⁵When you come into the standing grain of your neighbor, you may pluck the ears with your hand, but you shall not put a sickle to your neighbor's standing grain.

**24** When a man takes a wife and marries her, if then she finds no favor in his eyes because he has found some indecency in her, and he writes her a bill of divorce, puts it in her hand, and sends her out of his house,

²And when she departs out of his house she goes and marries another man,

³And if the latter husband dislikes her and writes her a bill of divorce and puts it in her hand and sends her out of his house, or if the latter husband dies, who took her as his wife,

⁴Then her former husband, who sent her away, may not take her again to be his wife after she is defiled. For that is an abomination before the Lord; and you shall not bring guilt upon the land which the Lord your God gives you as an inheritance.

⁵When a man is newly married, he shall not go out with the army or be charged with any business; he shall be free

---

ᵃ 18 Hebrew of a dog

## New International Version

to be free to stay at home and bring happiness to the wife he has married.

⁶Do not take a pair of millstones—not even the upper one—as security for a debt, because that would be taking a person's livelihood as security.

⁷If someone is caught kidnapping a fellow Israelite and treating or selling them as a slave, the kidnapper must die. You must purge the evil from among you.

⁸In cases of defiling skin diseases,ᵃ be very careful to do exactly as the Levitical priests instruct you. You must follow carefully what I have commanded them. ⁹Remember what the LORD your God did to Miriam along the way after you came out of Egypt.

¹⁰When you make a loan of any kind to your neighbor, do not go into their house to get what is offered to you as a pledge. ¹¹Stay outside and let the neighbor to whom you are making the loan bring the pledge out to you. ¹²If the neighbor is poor, do not go to sleep with their pledge in your possession. ¹³Return their cloak by sunset so that your neighbor may sleep in it. Then they will thank you, and it will be regarded as a righteous act in the sight of the LORD your God.

¹⁴Do not take advantage of a hired worker who is poor and needy, whether that worker is a fellow Israelite or a foreigner residing in one of your towns. ¹⁵Pay them their wages each day before sunset, because they are poor and are counting on it. Otherwise they may cry to the LORD against you, and you will be guilty of sin.

¹⁶Parents are not to be put to death for their children, nor children put to death for their parents; each will die for their own sin.

¹⁷Do not deprive the foreigner or the fatherless of justice, or take the cloak of the widow as a pledge. ¹⁸Remember that you were slaves in Egypt and the LORD your God redeemed you from there. That is why I command you to do this.

¹⁹When you are harvesting in your field and you overlook a sheaf, do not go back to get it. Leave it for the foreigner, the fatherless and the widow, so that the LORD your God may bless you in all the work of your hands. ²⁰When you beat the olives from your trees, do not go over the branches a second time. Leave what remains for the foreigner, the fatherless and the widow. ²¹When you harvest the grapes in your vineyard, do not go over the vines again. Leave what remains for the foreigner, the fatherless and the widow. ²²Remember that you were slaves in Egypt. That is why I command you to do this.

**25** When people have a dispute, they are to take it to court and the judges will decide the case, acquitting the innocent and condemning the guilty. ²If the guilty person deserves to be beaten, the judge shall make them lie down and have them flogged in his presence with the number of lashes the crime deserves, ³but the judge must not impose more than forty lashes. If the guilty party is flogged more than that, your fellow Israelite will be degraded in your eyes.

⁴Do not muzzle an ox while it is treading out the grain.

⁵If brothers are living together and one of them dies without a son, his widow must not marry outside the fami-

## Amplified Bible

at home one year and shall cheer his wife whom he has taken.

⁶No man shall take a mill or an upper millstone in pledge, for he would be taking a life in pledge.

⁷If a man is found kidnapping any of his brethren of the Israelites and treats him as a slave *or* a servant or sells him, then that thief shall die. So you shall put evil from among you.

⁸Take heed in the plague of leprosy, that you watch diligently and do according to all that the Levitical priests shall teach you. As I commanded them, so you shall be watchful and do. [Lev. 13:14, 15.]

⁹Remember [earnestly] what the Lord your God did to Miriam on the way after you had come out of Egypt. [Num. 12:10.]

¹⁰When you lend your brother anything, you shall not go into his house to get his pledge.

¹¹You shall stand outside and the man to whom you lend shall bring the pledge out to you.

¹²And if the man is poor, you shall not keep his pledge overnight.

¹³You shall surely restore to him the pledge at sunset, that he may sleep in his garment and bless you; and it shall be credited to you as righteousness (rightness and justice) before the Lord your God.

¹⁴You shall not oppress *or* extort from a hired servant who is poor and needy, whether he is of your brethren or of your strangers *and* sojourners who are in your land inside your towns.

¹⁵You shall give him his hire on the day he earns it before the sun goes down, for he is poor, and sets his heart upon it; lest he cry against you to the Lord, and it be sin to you.

¹⁶The fathers shall not be put to death for the children, neither shall the children be put to death for the fathers; only for his own sin shall anyone be put to death.

¹⁷You shall not pervert the justice due the stranger *or* the sojourner or the fatherless, or take a widow's garment in pledge.

¹⁸But you shall [earnestly] remember that you were a slave in Egypt and the Lord your God redeemed you from there; therefore I command you to do this.

¹⁹When you reap your harvest in your field and have forgotten a sheaf in the field, you shall not go back to get it; it shall be for the stranger *and* the sojourner, the fatherless, and the widow, that the Lord your God may bless you in all the work of your hands.

²⁰When you beat your olive tree, do not go over the boughs again; the leavings shall be for the stranger *and* the sojourner, the fatherless, and the widow.

²¹When you gather the grapes of your vineyard, you shall not glean it afterward; it shall be for the stranger *and* the sojourner, the fatherless, and the widow.

²²You shall [earnestly] remember that you were a slave in the land of Egypt; therefore I command you to do this.

**25** If there is a controversy between men, and they come into court and the judges decide between them, justifying the innocent and condemning the guilty,

²Then if the guilty man deserves to be beaten, the judge shall cause him to lie down and be beaten in his presence with a certain number of stripes according to his offense.

³Forty stripes may be given him but not more, lest, if he should be beaten with many stripes, your brother should [be treated like a beast and] seem low and worthless to you.

⁴You shall not muzzle the ox when he treads out the grain. [I Cor. 9:9, 10; I Tim. 5:17, 18.]

⁵If brothers live together and one of them dies and has no son, his wife shall not be married outside the family to a stranger [an excluded man]. Her husband's brother shall

---

## New International Version

ly. Her husband's brother shall take her and marry her and fulfill the duty of a brother-in-law to her. <sup>6</sup>The first son she bears shall carry on the name of the dead brother so that his name will not be blotted out from Israel.

<sup>7</sup>However, if a man does not want to marry his brother's wife, she shall go to the elders at the town gate and say, "My husband's brother refuses to carry on his brother's name in Israel. He will not fulfill the duty of a brother-in-law to me." <sup>8</sup>Then the elders of his town shall summon him and talk to him. If he persists in saying, "I do not want to marry her," <sup>9</sup>his brother's widow shall go up to him in the presence of the elders, take off one of his sandals, spit in his face and say, "This is what is done to the man who will not build up his brother's family line." <sup>10</sup>That man's line shall be known in Israel as The Family of the Unsandaled.

<sup>11</sup>If two men are fighting and the wife of one of them comes to rescue her husband from his assailant, and she reaches out and seizes him by his private parts, <sup>12</sup>you shall cut off her hand. Show her no pity.

<sup>13</sup>Do not have two differing weights in your bag—one heavy, one light. <sup>14</sup>Do not have two differing measures in your house—one large, one small. <sup>15</sup>You must have accurate and honest weights and measures, so that you may live long in the land the LORD your God is giving you. <sup>16</sup>For the LORD your God detests anyone who does these things, anyone who deals dishonestly.

<sup>17</sup>Remember what the Amalekites did to you along the way when you came out of Egypt. <sup>18</sup>When you were weary and worn out, they met you on your journey and attacked all who were lagging behind; they had no fear of God. <sup>19</sup>When the LORD your God gives you rest from all the enemies around you in the land he is giving you to possess as an inheritance, you shall blot out the name of Amalek from under heaven. Do not forget!

### Firstfruits and Tithes

**26** When you have entered the land the LORD your God is giving you as an inheritance and have taken possession of it and settled in it, <sup>2</sup>take some of the firstfruits of all that you produce from the soil of the land the LORD your God is giving you and put them in a basket. Then go to the place the LORD your God will choose as a dwelling for his Name <sup>3</sup>and say to the priest in office at the time, "I declare today to the LORD your God that I have come to the land the LORD swore to our ancestors to give us." <sup>4</sup>The priest shall take the basket from your hands and set it down in front of the altar of the LORD your God. <sup>5</sup>Then you shall declare before the LORD your God: "My father was a wandering Aramean, and he went down into Egypt with a few people and lived there and became a great nation, powerful and numerous. <sup>6</sup>But the Egyptians mistreated us and made us suffer, subjecting us to harsh labor. <sup>7</sup>Then we cried out to the LORD, the God of our ancestors, and the LORD heard our voice and saw our misery, toil and oppression. <sup>8</sup>So the LORD brought us out of Egypt

## Amplified Bible

go in to her and take her as his wife and perform the duty of a husband's brother to her.

<sup>6</sup>And the firstborn son shall succeed to the name of the dead brother, that his name may not be blotted out of Israel.

<sup>7</sup>And if the man does not want to take his brother's wife, then let his brother's wife go up to the gate to the elders, and say, My husband's brother refuses to continue his brother's name in Israel; he will not perform the duty of my husband's brother.

<sup>8</sup>Then the elders of his city shall call him and speak to him. And if he stands firm and says, I do not want to take her,

<sup>9</sup>Then shall his brother's wife come to him in the presence of the elders and pull his shoe off his foot and spit in his face and shall answer, So shall it be done to that man who does not build up his brother's house.

<sup>10</sup>And his family shall be called in Israel, The House of Him Whose Shoe Was Loosed.

<sup>11</sup>When men strive together one with another and the wife of the one draws near to rescue her husband out of the hand of him who is beating him, and puts out her hand and seizes the other man by the private parts,

<sup>12</sup>Then you shall cut off her hand; your eyes shall not pity her.

<sup>13</sup>You shall not have in your bag true and false weights, a large and a small.

<sup>14</sup>You shall not have in your house true and false measures, a large and a small.

<sup>15</sup>But you shall have a perfect and just weight and a perfect and just measure, that your days may be prolonged in the land which the Lord your God gives you.

<sup>16</sup>For all who do such things, all who do unrighteously, are an abomination to the Lord your God.

<sup>17</sup>Remember what Amalek did to you on the way when you had come forth from Egypt,

<sup>18</sup>How he did not fear God, but when you were faint and weary he attacked you along the way and cut off all the stragglers at your rear. [Exod. 17:14.]

<sup>19</sup>Therefore when the Lord your God has given you rest from all your enemies round about in the land which the Lord your God gives you to possess as an inheritance, you shall blot out the remembrance of Amalek from under the heavens; you must not forget.

**26** When you have come into the land which the Lord your God gives you as an inheritance and possess it and live in it,

<sup>2</sup>You shall take some of the first of all the produce of the soil which you harvest from the land the Lord your God gives you and put it in a basket, and go to the place [the sanctuary] which the Lord your God has chosen as the abiding place for His Name [and His Presence].

<sup>3</sup>And you shall go to the priest who is in office in those days, and say to him, I give thanks this day to the Lord your God that I have come to the land which the Lord swore to our fathers to give us.

<sup>4</sup>And the priest shall take the basket from your hand and set it down before the altar of the Lord your God.

<sup>5</sup>And you shall say before the Lord your God, A wandering *and* lost Aramean ready to perish was my father [Jacob], and he went down into Egypt and sojourned there, few in number, and he became there a nation, great, mighty, and numerous.

<sup>6</sup>And the Egyptians treated us very badly and afflicted us and laid upon us hard bondage.

<sup>7</sup>And when we cried to the Lord, the God of our fathers, the Lord heard our voice and looked on our affliction and our labor and our [cruel] oppression;

<sup>8</sup>And the Lord brought us forth out of Egypt with a

## New International Version

with a mighty hand and an outstretched arm, with great terror and with signs and wonders. ⁹He brought us to this place and gave us this land, a land flowing with milk and honey; ¹⁰and now I bring the firstfruits of the soil that you, LORD, have given me." Place the basket before the LORD your God and bow down before him. ¹¹Then you and the Levites and the foreigners residing among you shall rejoice in all the good things the LORD your God has given to you and your household.

¹²When you have finished setting aside a tenth of all your produce in the third year, the year of the tithe, you shall give it to the Levite, the foreigner, the fatherless and the widow, so that they may eat in your towns and be satisfied. ¹³Then say to the LORD your God: "I have removed from my house the sacred portion and have given it to the Levite, the foreigner, the fatherless and the widow, according to all you commanded. I have not turned aside from your commands nor have I forgotten any of them. ¹⁴I have not eaten any of the sacred portion while I was in mourning, nor have I removed any of it while I was unclean, nor have I offered any of it to the dead. I have obeyed the LORD my God; I have done everything you commanded me. ¹⁵Look down from heaven, your holy dwelling place, and bless your people Israel and the land you have given us as you promised on oath to our ancestors, a land flowing with milk and honey."

### Follow the LORD's Commands

¹⁶The LORD your God commands you this day to follow these decrees and laws; carefully observe them with all your heart and with all your soul. ¹⁷You have declared this day that the LORD is your God and that you will walk in obedience to him, that you will keep his decrees, commands and laws—that you will listen to him. ¹⁸And the LORD has declared this day that you are his people, his treasured possession as he promised, and that you are to keep all his commands. ¹⁹He has declared that he will set you in praise, fame and honor high above all the nations he has made and that you will be a people holy to the LORD your God, as he promised.

### The Altar on Mount Ebal

**27** Moses and the elders of Israel commanded the people: "Keep all these commands that I give you today. ²When you have crossed the Jordan into the land the LORD your God is giving you, set up some large stones and coat them with plaster. ³Write on them all the words of this law when you have crossed over to enter the land the LORD your God is giving you, a land flowing with milk and honey, just as the LORD, the God of your ancestors, promised you. ⁴And when you have crossed the Jordan, set up these stones on Mount Ebal, as I command you today, and coat them with plaster. ⁵Build there an altar to the LORD your God, an altar of stones. Do not use any iron tool on them. ⁶Build the altar of the LORD your God with fieldstones and offer burnt offerings on it to the LORD your God. ⁷Sacrifice fellowship offerings there, eating them and rejoicing in the presence of the LORD your God. ⁸And

## Amplified Bible

mighty hand and with an outstretched arm, and with great (awesome) power and with signs and with wonders; ⁹And He brought us into this place and gave us this land, a land flowing with milk and honey. ¹⁰And now, behold, I bring the firstfruits of the ground which You, O Lord, have given me. And you shall set it down before the Lord your God and worship before the Lord your God; ¹¹And you and the Levite and the stranger *and* the sojourner among you shall rejoice in all the good which the Lord your God has given you and your household.

¹²When you have finished paying all the tithe of your produce the third year, which is the year of tithing, and have given it to the Levite, the stranger *and* the sojourner, the fatherless, and to the widow, that they may eat within your towns and be filled,

¹³Then you shall say before the Lord your God, I have brought the hallowed things (the tithe) out of my house and moreover have given them to the Levite, to the stranger *and* the sojourner, to the fatherless, and to the widow, according to all Your commandments which You have commanded me; I have not transgressed any of Your commandments, neither have I forgotten them.

¹⁴I have not eaten of the tithe in my mourning [making the tithe unclean], nor have I handled any of it when I was unclean, nor given any of it to the dead. I have hearkened to the voice of the Lord my God; I have done according to all that You have commanded me.

¹⁵Look down from Your holy habitation, from heaven, and bless Your people Israel and the land which You have given us as You swore to our fathers, a land flowing with milk and honey.

¹⁶This day the Lord your God has commanded you to do these statutes and ordinances. Therefore you shall keep and do them with all your [mind and] heart and with all your being.

¹⁷You have [openly] declared the Lord this day to be your God, [pledging] to walk in His ways, to keep His statutes and His commandments and His precepts, and to hearken to His voice.

¹⁸And the Lord has declared this day that you are His peculiar people as He promised you, and you are to keep all His commandments;

¹⁹And He will make you high above all nations which He has made, in praise and in fame and in honor, and that you shall be a holy people to the Lord your God, as He has spoken.

**27** And Moses with the elders of Israel commanded the people, Keep all the commandments with which I charge you today.

²And on the day when you pass over the Jordan to the land which the Lord your God gives you, you shall set up great stones and cover them with plaster.

³And you shall write on them all the words of this law when you have passed over, that you may go into the land which the Lord your God is giving you, a land flowing with milk and honey, as the Lord, the God of your fathers, has promised you.

⁴And when you have gone over the Jordan, you shall set up these stones, as I command you this day, on Mount Ebal, and coat them with plaster.

⁵And there you shall build an altar to the Lord your God, an altar of stones; you shall not lift up any iron tool upon them.

⁶You shall build the altar of the Lord your God of whole stones and offer burnt offerings on it to Him;

⁷And you shall offer peace offerings, and eat there and rejoice before the Lord your God.

## New International Version

you shall write very clearly all the words of this law on these stones you have set up."

### Curses From Mount Ebal

⁹Then Moses and the Levitical priests said to all Israel, "Be silent, Israel, and listen! You have now become the people of the LORD your God. ¹⁰Obey the LORD your God and follow his commands and decrees that I give you today."

¹¹On the same day Moses commanded the people:

¹²When you have crossed the Jordan, these tribes shall stand on Mount Gerizim to bless the people: Simeon, Levi, Judah, Issachar, Joseph and Benjamin. ¹³And these tribes shall stand on Mount Ebal to pronounce curses: Reuben, Gad, Asher, Zebulun, Dan and Naphtali.

¹⁴The Levites shall recite to all the people of Israel in a loud voice:

¹⁵"Cursed is anyone who makes an idol—a thing detestable to the LORD, the work of skilled hands—and sets it up in secret."

Then all the people shall say, "Amen!"

¹⁶"Cursed is anyone who dishonors their father or mother."

Then all the people shall say, "Amen!"

¹⁷"Cursed is anyone who moves their neighbor's boundary stone."

Then all the people shall say, "Amen!"

¹⁸"Cursed is anyone who leads the blind astray on the road."

Then all the people shall say, "Amen!"

¹⁹"Cursed is anyone who withholds justice from the foreigner, the fatherless or the widow."

Then all the people shall say, "Amen!"

²⁰"Cursed is anyone who sleeps with his father's wife, for he dishonors his father's bed."

Then all the people shall say, "Amen!"

²¹"Cursed is anyone who has sexual relations with any animal."

Then all the people shall say, "Amen!"

²²"Cursed is anyone who sleeps with his sister, the daughter of his father or the daughter of his mother."

Then all the people shall say, "Amen!"

²³"Cursed is anyone who sleeps with his mother-in-law."

Then all the people shall say, "Amen!"

²⁴"Cursed is anyone who kills their neighbor secretly."

Then all the people shall say, "Amen!"

²⁵"Cursed is anyone who accepts a bribe to kill an innocent person."

Then all the people shall say, "Amen!"

²⁶"Cursed is anyone who does not uphold the words of this law by carrying them out."

Then all the people shall say, "Amen!"

### Blessings for Obedience

**28** If you fully obey the LORD your God and carefully follow all his commands I give you today, the LORD your God will set you high above all the nations on earth. ²All these blessings will come on you and accompany you if you obey the LORD your God:

³You will be blessed in the city and blessed in the country.

⁴The fruit of your womb will be blessed, and the crops of your land and the young of your livestock—the calves of your herds and the lambs of your flocks.

⁵Your basket and your kneading trough will be blessed.

⁶You will be blessed when you come in and blessed when you go out.

## Amplified Bible

⁸And you shall write upon the stones all the words of this law very plainly.

⁹And Moses and the Levitical priests said to all Israel, Keep silence and hear, O Israel! This day you have become the people of the Lord your God.

¹⁰So you shall obey the voice of the Lord your God and do His commandments and statutes which I command you today.

¹¹And Moses charged the people the same day, saying,

¹²These [tribes] shall stand on Mount Gerizim to bless the people, when you have passed over the Jordan: Simeon, Levi, Judah, Issachar, Joseph's [sons], and Benjamin.

¹³And these [tribes] shall stand on Mount Ebal to pronounce the curse [for disobedience]: Reuben, Gad, Asher, Zebulun, Dan, and Naphtali.

¹⁴And the Levites shall declare with a loud voice to all the men of Israel:

¹⁵Cursed is the man who makes a graven or molten image, an abomination to the Lord, the work of the hands of the craftsman, and sets it up in secret. All the people shall answer, Amen.

¹⁶Cursed is he who dishonors his father or his mother. All the people shall say, Amen.

¹⁷Cursed is he who moves [back] his neighbor's landmark. All the people shall say, Amen.

¹⁸Cursed is he who misleads a blind man on his way. All the people shall say, Amen.

¹⁹Cursed is he who perverts the justice due to the sojourner *or* the stranger, the fatherless, and the widow. All the people shall say, Amen.

²⁰Cursed is he who lies with his father's wife, because he uncovers what belongs to his father. All the people shall say, Amen.

²¹Cursed is he who lies with any beast. All the people shall say, Amen.

²²Cursed is he who lies with his half sister, whether his father's or his mother's daughter. All the people shall say, Amen.

²³Cursed is he who lies with his mother-in-law. All the people shall say, Amen.

²⁴Cursed is he who slays his neighbor secretly. All the people shall say, Amen.

²⁵Cursed is he who takes a bribe to slay an innocent person. All the people shall say, Amen.

²⁶Cursed is he who does not support *and* give assent to the words of this law to do them [as the rule of his life]. All the people shall say, Amen.

**28** If you will listen diligently to the voice of the Lord your God, being watchful to do all His commandments which I command you this day, the Lord your God will set you high above all the nations of the earth.

²And all these blessings shall come upon you and overtake you if you heed the voice of the Lord your God.

³Blessed shall you be in the city and blessed shall you be in the field.

⁴Blessed shall be the fruit of your body and the fruit of your ground and the fruit of your beasts, the increase of your cattle and the young of your flock.

⁵Blessed shall be your basket and your kneading trough.

⁶Blessed shall you be when you come in and blessed shall you be when you go out.

## New International Version

[7] The LORD will grant that the enemies who rise up against you will be defeated before you. They will come at you from one direction but flee from you in seven.

[8] The LORD will send a blessing on your barns and on everything you put your hand to. The LORD your God will bless you in the land he is giving you.

[9] The LORD will establish you as his holy people, as he promised you on oath, if you keep the commands of the LORD your God and walk in obedience to him. [10] Then all the peoples on earth will see that you are called by the name of the LORD, and they will fear you. [11] The LORD will grant you abundant prosperity—in the fruit of your womb, the young of your livestock and the crops of your ground—in the land he swore to your ancestors to give you.

[12] The LORD will open the heavens, the storehouse of his bounty, to send rain on your land in season and to bless all the work of your hands. You will lend to many nations but will borrow from none. [13] The LORD will make you the head, not the tail. If you pay attention to the commands of the LORD your God that I give you this day and carefully follow them, you will always be at the top, never at the bottom. [14] Do not turn aside from any of the commands I give you today, to the right or to the left, following other gods and serving them.

### Curses for Disobedience

[15] However, if you do not obey the LORD your God and do not carefully follow all his commands and decrees I am giving you today, all these curses will come on you and overtake you:

[16] You will be cursed in the city and cursed in the country.

[17] Your basket and your kneading trough will be cursed.

[18] The fruit of your womb will be cursed, and the crops of your land, and the calves of your herds and the lambs of your flocks.

[19] You will be cursed when you come in and cursed when you go out.

[20] The LORD will send on you curses, confusion and rebuke in everything you put your hand to, until you are destroyed and come to sudden ruin because of the evil you have done in forsaking him.[a] [21] The LORD will plague you with diseases until he has destroyed you from the land you are entering to possess. [22] The LORD will strike you with wasting disease, with fever and inflammation, with scorching heat and drought, with blight and mildew, which will plague you until you perish. [23] The sky over your head will be bronze, the ground beneath you iron. [24] The LORD will turn the rain of your country into dust and powder; it will come down from the skies until you are destroyed.

[25] The LORD will cause you to be defeated before your enemies. You will come at them from one direction but flee from them in seven, and you will become a thing of horror to all the kingdoms on earth. [26] Your carcasses will be food for all the birds and the wild animals, and there will be no one to frighten them away. [27] The LORD will afflict you with the boils of Egypt and with tumors, festering sores and the itch, from which you cannot be cured. [28] The LORD will afflict you with madness, blindness and confusion of

## Amplified Bible

[7] The Lord shall cause your enemies who rise up against you to be defeated before your face; they shall come out against you one way and flee before you seven ways.

[8] The Lord shall command the blessing upon you in your storehouse and in all that you undertake. And He will bless you in the land which the Lord your God gives you.

[9] The Lord will establish you as a people holy to Himself, as He has sworn to you, if you keep the commandments of the Lord your God and walk in His ways.

[10] And all people of the earth shall see that you are called by the name [and in the presence of] the Lord, and they shall be afraid of you.

[11] And the Lord shall make you have a surplus of prosperity, through the fruit of your body, of your livestock, and of your ground, in the land which the Lord swore to your fathers to give you.

[12] The Lord shall open to you His good treasury, the heavens, to give the rain of your land in its season and to bless all the work of your hands; and you shall lend to many nations, but you shall not borrow.

[13] And the Lord shall make you the head, and not the tail; and you shall be above only, and you shall not be beneath, if you heed the commandments of the Lord your God which I command you this day and are watchful to do them.

[14] And you shall not turn aside from any of the words which I command you this day, to the right hand or to the left, to go after other gods to serve them.

[15] But if you will not obey the voice of the Lord your God, being watchful to do all His commandments and His statutes which I command you this day, then all these curses shall come upon you and overtake you:

[16] Cursed shall you be in the city and cursed shall you be in the field.

[17] Cursed shall be your basket and your kneading trough.

[18] Cursed shall be the fruit of your body, of your land, of the increase of your cattle and the young of your sheep.

[19] Cursed shall you be when you come in and cursed shall you be when you go out.

[20] The Lord shall send you curses, confusion, and rebuke in every enterprise to which you set your hand, until you are destroyed, perishing quickly because of the evil of your doings by which you have forsaken me [Moses and God as one].

[21] The Lord will make the pestilence cling to you until He has consumed you from the land into which you go to possess.

[22] The Lord will smite you with consumption, with fever and inflammation, fiery heat, sword *and* drought, blasting and mildew; they shall pursue you until you perish.

[23] The heavens over your head shall be brass and the earth under you shall be iron.

[24] The Lord shall make the rain of your land powdered soil and dust; from the heavens it shall come down upon you until you are destroyed.

[25] The Lord shall cause you to be struck down before your enemies; you shall go out one way against them and flee seven ways before them, and you shall be tossed to and fro *and* be a terror among all the kingdoms of the earth. [Fulfilled in II Chron. 29:8.]

[26] And your dead body shall be food for all the birds of the air and the beasts of the earth, and there shall be no one to frighten them away.

[27] The Lord will smite you with the boils of Egypt and the tumors, the scurvy and the itch, from which you cannot be healed.

[28] The Lord will smite you with madness and blindness and dismay of [mind and] heart.

## New International Version

mind. 29 At midday you will grope about like a blind person in the dark. You will be unsuccessful in everything you do; day after day you will be oppressed and robbed, with no one to rescue you.

30 You will be pledged to be married to a woman, but another will take her and rape her. You will build a house, but you will not live in it. You will plant a vineyard, but you will not even begin to enjoy its fruit. 31 Your ox will be slaughtered before your eyes, but you will eat none of it. Your donkey will be forcibly taken from you and will not be returned. Your sheep will be given to your enemies, and no one will rescue them. 32 Your sons and daughters will be given to another nation, and you will wear out your eyes watching for them day after day, powerless to lift a hand. 33 A people that you do not know will eat what your land and labor produce, and you will have nothing but cruel oppression all your days. 34 The sights you see will drive you mad. 35 The LORD will afflict your knees and legs with painful boils that cannot be cured, spreading from the soles of your feet to the top of your head.

36 The LORD will drive you and the king you set over you to a nation unknown to you or your ancestors. There you will worship other gods, gods of wood and stone. 37 You will become a thing of horror, a byword and an object of ridicule among all the peoples where the LORD will drive you.

38 You will sow much seed in the field but you will harvest little, because locusts will devour it. 39 You will plant vineyards and cultivate them but you will not drink the wine or gather the grapes, because worms will eat them. 40 You will have olive trees throughout your country but you will not use the oil, because the olives will drop off. 41 You will have sons and daughters but you will not keep them, because they will go into captivity. 42 Swarms of locusts will take over all your trees and the crops of your land.

43 The foreigners who reside among you will rise above you higher and higher, but you will sink lower and lower. 44 They will lend to you, but you will not lend to them. They will be the head, but you will be the tail.

45 All these curses will come on you. They will pursue you and overtake you until you are destroyed, because you did not obey the LORD your God and observe the commands and decrees he gave you. 46 They will be a sign and a wonder to you and your descendants forever. 47 Because you did not serve the LORD your God joyfully and gladly in the time of prosperity, 48 therefore in hunger and thirst, in nakedness and dire poverty, you will serve the enemies the LORD sends against you. He will put an iron yoke on your neck until he has destroyed you.

49 The LORD will bring a nation against you from far away, from the ends of the earth, like an eagle swooping down, a nation whose language you will not understand, 50 a fierce-looking nation without respect for the old or pity

## Amplified Bible

29 And you shall grope at noonday as the blind grope in darkness. And you shall not prosper in your ways; and you shall be only oppressed and robbed continually, and there shall be no one to save you.

30 You shall betroth a wife, but another man shall lie with her; you shall build a house, but not live in it; you shall plant a vineyard, but not gather its grapes.

31 Your ox shall be slain before your eyes, but you shall not eat of it; your donkey shall be violently taken away before your face and not be restored to you; your sheep shall be given to your enemies, and you shall have no one to help you.

32 Your sons and daughters shall be given to another people, and your eyes shall look and fail with longing for them all the day; and there shall be no power in your hands to prevent it. [Fulfilled in II Chron. 29:9.]

33 A nation which you have not known shall eat up the fruit of your land and of all your labors, and you shall be only oppressed and crushed continually, [Fulfilled in Judg. 6:1-6; 13:1.]

34 So that you shall be driven mad by the sights which your eyes shall see.

35 The Lord will smite you on the knees and on the legs with a sore boil that cannot be healed, from the sole of your foot to the top of your head.

36 The Lord shall bring you and your king whom you have set over you to a nation which neither you nor your fathers have known, and there you shall [be forced to] serve other gods, of wood and stone. [Fulfilled in II Kings 17:4, 6; 24:12, 14; 25:7, 11; Dan. 6:11, 12.]

37 And you shall become an amazement, a proverb, and a byword among all the peoples to which the Lord will lead you.

38 You shall carry much seed out into the field and shall gather little in, for the locust shall consume it. [Fulfilled in Hag. 1:6.]

39 You shall plant vineyards and dress them but shall neither drink of the wine nor gather the grapes, for the worm shall eat them.

40 You shall have olive trees throughout all your territory but you shall not anoint yourselves with the oil, for your olive trees shall drop their fruit.

41 You shall beget sons and daughters but shall not enjoy them, for they shall go into captivity. [Fulfilled in Lam. 1:5.]

42 All your trees and the fruit of your ground shall the locust possess. [Fulfilled in Joel 1:4.]

43 The transient (stranger) among you shall mount up higher and higher above you, and you shall come down lower and lower.

44 He shall lend to you, but you shall not lend to him; he shall be the head, and you shall be the tail.

45 All these curses shall come upon you and shall pursue you and overtake you till you are destroyed, because you do not obey the voice of the Lord your God, to keep His commandments and His statutes which He commanded you.

46 They shall be upon you for a sign [of warning to other nations] and for a wonder, and upon your descendants forever.

47 Because you did not serve the Lord your God with joyfulness of [mind and] heart [in gratitude] for the abundance of all [with which He had blessed you],

48 Therefore you shall serve your enemies whom the Lord shall send against you, in hunger and thirst, in nakedness and in want of all things; and He will put a yoke of iron upon your neck until He has destroyed you.

49 The Lord will bring a nation against you from afar, from the end of the earth, as swift as the eagle flies, a nation whose language you shall not understand,

50 A nation of unyielding countenance who will not regard the person of the old or show favor to the young,

## New International Version

for the young. [51]They will devour the young of your livestock and the crops of your land until you are destroyed. They will leave you no grain, new wine or olive oil, nor any calves of your herds or lambs of your flocks until you are ruined. [52]They will lay siege to all the cities throughout your land until the high fortified walls in which you trust fall down. They will besiege all the cities throughout the land the LORD your God is giving you.

[53]Because of the suffering your enemy will inflict on you during the siege, you will eat the fruit of the womb, the flesh of the sons and daughters the LORD your God has given you. [54]Even the most gentle and sensitive man among you will have no compassion on his own brother or the wife he loves or his surviving children, [55]and he will not give to one of them any of the flesh of his children that he is eating. It will be all he has left because of the suffering your enemy will inflict on you during the siege of all your cities. [56]The most gentle and sensitive woman among you—so sensitive and gentle that she would not venture to touch the ground with the sole of her foot—will begrudge the husband she loves and her own son or daughter [57]the afterbirth from her womb and the children she bears. For in her dire need she intends to eat them secretly because of the suffering your enemy will inflict on you during the siege of your cities.

[58]If you do not carefully follow all the words of this law, which are written in this book, and do not revere this glorious and awesome name—the LORD your God— [59]the LORD will send fearful plagues on you and your descendants, harsh and prolonged disasters, and severe and lingering illnesses. [60]He will bring on you all the diseases of Egypt that you dreaded, and they will cling to you. [61]The LORD will also bring on you every kind of sickness and disaster not recorded in this Book of the Law, until you are destroyed. [62]You who were as numerous as the stars in the sky will be left but few in number, because you did not obey the LORD your God. [63]Just as it pleased the LORD to make you prosper and increase in number, so it will please him to ruin and destroy you. You will be uprooted from the land you are entering to possess.

[64]Then the LORD will scatter you among all nations, from one end of the earth to the other. There you will worship other gods—gods of wood and stone, which neither you nor your ancestors have known. [65]Among those nations you will find no repose, no resting place for the sole of your foot. There the LORD will give you an anxious mind, eyes weary with longing, and a despairing heart. [66]You will live in constant suspense, filled with dread both night and day, never sure of your life. [67]In the morning you

## Amplified Bible

[51]And shall eat the fruit of your cattle and the fruit of your ground until you are destroyed, who also shall not leave you grain, new wine, oil, the increase of your cattle or the young of your sheep until they have caused you to perish.

[52]They shall besiege you in all your towns until your high and fortified walls in which you trusted come down throughout all your land; and they shall besiege you in all your towns throughout all your land which the Lord your God has given you.

[53]And you shall eat the fruit of your own body, the flesh of your sons and daughters whom the Lord your God has given you, in the siege and in the [pressing] misery with which your enemies shall distress you. [Fulfilled in II Kings 6:24-29.]

[54]The man who is most tender among you and extremely particular *and* well-bred, his eye shall be cruel *and* grudging of food toward his brother and toward the wife of his bosom and toward those of his children still remaining,

[55]So that he will not give to any of them any of the flesh of his children which he is eating, because he has nothing left to him in the siege and in the distress with which your enemies shall distress you in all your towns.

[56]The most tender and daintily bred woman among you, who would not venture to set the sole of her foot upon the ground because she is so dainty and kind, will grudge to the husband of her bosom, to her son and to her daughter

[57]Her afterbirth that comes out from her body and the children whom she shall bear. For she will eat them secretly for want of anything else in the siege and distress with which your enemies shall distress you in your towns.

[58]If you will not be watchful to do all the words of this law that are written in this book, that you may [reverently] fear this glorious and fearful name [and presence]—THE LORD YOUR GOD--

[59]Then the Lord will bring upon you and your descendants extraordinary strokes and blows, great plagues of long continuance, and grievous sicknesses of long duration.

[60]Moreover, He will bring upon you all the diseases of Egypt of which you were afraid, and they shall cling to you.

[61]Also every sickness and every affliction which is not written in this Book of the Law the Lord will bring upon you until you are destroyed.

[62]And you shall be [a]left few in number, whereas you had been as the stars of the heavens for multitude, because you would not obey the voice of the Lord your God.

[63]And as the Lord rejoiced over you to do you good and to multiply you, so the Lord will rejoice to bring ruin upon you and to destroy you; and you shall be [b]plucked from the land into which you go to possess.

[64]And the Lord shall scatter you among all peoples from one end of the earth to the other; and there you shall [be forced to] serve other gods, of wood and stone, which neither you nor your fathers have known. [Fulfilled in Dan. 3:6.]

[65]And among these nations you shall find no ease and there shall be no rest for the sole of your foot; but the Lord will give you there a trembling heart, failing of eyes [from disappointment of hope], fainting of mind, *and* languishing of spirit.

[66]Your life shall hang in doubt before you; day and night you shall be worried, and have no assurance of your life.

---

[a] The informed reader scarcely needs to be reminded of how literally fulfilled have been many of these predictions of evil made against the chosen people because of their idolatry and rebellion against God. Such verses as Deut. 28:25, 32, 33, 36, 38, 41, 42, and 53 foretell historical facts now recorded in Jewish history, both sacred and secular. Here Deut. 28:62 foretells how the Jewish race has been "thinned and kept down," again and again. [b] The Roman emperor Hadrian issued a proclamation forbidding any Jews to reside in Judea, or even to approach its confines (James C. Gray and George M. Adams, *Bible Commentary*).

## New International Version

will say, "If only it were evening!" and in the evening, "If only it were morning!"—because of the terror that will fill your hearts and the sights that your eyes will see. [68]The Lord will send you back in ships to Egypt on a journey I said you should never make again. There you will offer yourselves for sale to your enemies as male and female slaves, but no one will buy you.

### Renewal of the Covenant

**29** [a] These are the terms of the covenant the Lord commanded Moses to make with the Israelites in Moab, in addition to the covenant he had made with them at Horeb.

[2]Moses summoned all the Israelites and said to them:

Your eyes have seen all that the Lord did in Egypt to Pharaoh, to all his officials and to all his land. [3]With your own eyes you saw those great trials, those signs and great wonders. [4]But to this day the Lord has not given you a mind that understands or eyes that see or ears that hear. [5]Yet the Lord says, "During the forty years that I led you through the wilderness, your clothes did not wear out, nor did the sandals on your feet. [6]You ate no bread and drank no wine or other fermented drink. I did this so that you might know that I am the Lord your God."

[7]When you reached this place, Sihon king of Heshbon and Og king of Bashan came out to fight against us, but we defeated them. [8]We took their land and gave it as an inheritance to the Reubenites, the Gadites and the half-tribe of Manasseh.

[9]Carefully follow the terms of this covenant, so that you may prosper in everything you do. [10]All of you are standing today in the presence of the Lord your God—your leaders and chief men, your elders and officials, and all the other men of Israel, [11]together with your children and your wives, and the foreigners living in your camps who chop your wood and carry your water. [12]You are standing here in order to enter into a covenant with the Lord your God, a covenant the Lord is making with you this day and sealing with an oath, [13]to confirm you this day as his people, that he may be your God as he promised you and as he swore to your fathers, Abraham, Isaac and Jacob. [14]I am making this covenant, with its oath, not only with you [15]who are standing here with us today in the presence of the Lord our God but also with those who are not here today.

[16]You yourselves know how we lived in Egypt and how we passed through the countries on the way here. [17]You saw among them their detestable images and idols of wood and stone, of silver and gold. [18]Make sure there is no man

## Amplified Bible

[67]In the morning you shall say, Would that it were evening! and at evening you shall say, Would that it were morning!—because of the anxiety *and* dread of your [minds and] hearts and the sights which you shall see with your [own] eyes.

[68]And the Lord shall [a]bring you into Egypt again with ships by the way about which I said to you, You shall never see it again. And there you shall be sold to your enemies as bondmen and bondwomen, but no man shall buy you. [Hos. 8:13.]

**29** These are the words of the covenant which the Lord commanded Moses to make with the Israelites in the land of Moab, besides the covenant which He made with them in Horeb.

[2]Moses called to all Israel and said to them, You have seen all that the Lord did before your eyes in the land of Egypt to Pharaoh, to all his servants, and to all his land;

[3]The great trials which your eyes saw, the signs, and those great wonders.

[4]Yet the Lord has not given you a [mind and] heart to understand and eyes to see and ears to hear, to this day.

[5]I have led you forty years in the wilderness; your clothes have not worn out upon you, and your sandals have not worn off your feet.

[6]You have not eaten [grain] bread, nor have you drunk wine or strong drink, that you might recognize *and* know [your dependence on Him Who is saying], I am the Lord your God.

[7]And when you came to this place, Sihon king of Heshbon and Og king of Bashan came out against us to battle, but we defeated them.

[8]We took their land and gave it as an inheritance to the Reubenites, the Gadites, and the half-tribe of the Manassites.

[9]Therefore keep the words of this covenant and do them, that you may deal wisely *and* prosper in all that you do.

[10]All of you stand today before the Lord your God—your heads, your tribes, your elders, and your officers, even all the men of Israel,

[11]Your little ones, your wives, and the stranger *and* sojourner in your camp, from the hewer of your wood to the drawer of your water—

[12]That you may enter into the covenant of the Lord your God, and into His oath which He makes with you today,

[13]That He may establish you this day as a people for Himself, and that He may be to you a God as He said to you and as He swore to your fathers, Abraham, Isaac, and Jacob.

[14]It is not with you only that I make this sworn covenant

[15]But with future Israelites who do not stand here with us today before the Lord our God, as well as with those who are here with us this day.

[16]You know how we lived in the land of Egypt and how we came through the midst of the nations you crossed.

[17]And you have seen their abominations and their idols of wood and stone, of silver and gold, which were among them.

[18]Beware lest there should be among you a man or

[a] "Observe the contrast: you came out from bondage by God's high hand, monuments of His grace and power; you shall be carried back into bondage in men's slave ships. This was literally fulfilled under [the Roman emperor] Titus, and also under Hadrian" (James C. Gray and George M. Adams, *Bible Commentary*). The curses . . . were also fulfilled in a terrible manner during the Middle Ages, and are still in a course of fulfillment, though frequently less sensibly felt (J. P. Lange, *A Commentary*). "Here, then, are prophecies delivered above 3,000 years ago and yet being fulfilled in the world at this very time . . . I must acknowledge that they not only convince but amaze and astonish me beyond expression; they are truly as Moses foretold (Deut. 28:45, 46) they would be, 'a sign and a wonder forever' " (Bishop Thomas Newton, cited by Robert Jamieson, A. R. Fausset and David Brown, *A Commentary*).

## New International Version

or woman, clan or tribe among you today whose heart turns away from the LORD our God to go and worship the gods of those nations; make sure there is no root among you that produces such bitter poison.

[19]When such a person hears the words of this oath and they invoke a blessing on themselves, thinking, "I will be safe, even though I persist in going my own way," they will bring disaster on the watered land as well as the dry. [20]The LORD will never be willing to forgive them; his wrath and zeal will burn against them. All the curses written in this book will fall on them, and the LORD will blot out their names from under heaven. [21]The LORD will single them out from all the tribes of Israel for disaster, according to all the curses of the covenant written in this Book of the Law.

[22]Your children who follow you in later generations and foreigners who come from distant lands will see the calamities that have fallen on the land and the diseases with which the LORD has afflicted it. [23]The whole land will be a burning waste of salt and sulfur—nothing planted, nothing sprouting, no vegetation growing on it. It will be like the destruction of Sodom and Gomorrah, Admah and Zeboyim, which the LORD overthrew in fierce anger. [24]All the nations will ask: "Why has the LORD done this to this land? Why this fierce, burning anger?"

[25]And the answer will be: "It is because this people abandoned the covenant of the LORD, the God of their ancestors, the covenant he made with them when he brought them out of Egypt. [26]They went off and worshiped other gods and bowed down to them, gods they did not know, gods he had not given them. [27]Therefore the LORD's anger burned against this land, so that he brought on it all the curses written in this book. [28]In furious anger and in great wrath the LORD uprooted them from their land and thrust them into another land, as it is now."

[29]The secret things belong to the LORD our God, but the things revealed belong to us and to our children forever, that we may follow all the words of this law.

### Prosperity After Turning to the LORD

**30** When all these blessings and curses I have set before you come on you and you take them to heart wherever the LORD your God disperses you among the nations, [2]and when you and your children return to the LORD your God and obey him with all your heart and with all your soul according to everything I command you today, [3]then the LORD your God will restore your fortunes[a] and have compassion on you and gather you again from all the nations where he scattered you. [4]Even if you have been banished to the most distant land under the heavens, from there the LORD your God will gather you and bring you back. [5]He will bring you to the land that belonged to your ancestors, and you will take possession of it. He will make you more prosperous and numerous than your ancestors.

## Amplified Bible

woman, or family or tribe, whose [mind and] heart turns away this day from the Lord our God to go and serve the gods of these nations; lest there should be among you a [poisonous] root that bears gall and wormwood,

[19]And lest, when he hears the words of this curse *and* oath, he flatters *and* congratulates himself in his [mind and] heart, saying, I shall have peace *and* safety, [a]though I walk in the stubbornness of my [mind and] heart [bringing down a hurricane of destruction] and sweep away the watered land with the dry.

[20]The Lord will not pardon him, but then the anger of the Lord and His jealousy will smoke against that man, and all the curses that are written in this book shall settle on him; the Lord will blot out his very name from under the heavens.

[21]And the Lord will single him out for ruin *and* destruction from all the tribes of Israel, according to all the curses of the covenant that are written in this Book of the Law,

[22]So that the next generation, your children who rise up after you, and the foreigner who shall come from a distant land, shall say, when they see the plagues of this land and the diseases with which the Lord has made it sick—

[23]The whole land is brimstone and salt and a burned waste, not sown or bearing anything, where no grass can take root, like the overthrow of Sodom and Gomorrah with Admah and Zeboiim, which the Lord overthrew in His anger and wrath—

[24]Even all the nations shall say, Why has the Lord done thus to this land? What does the heat of this great anger mean?

[25]Then men shall say, Because they forsook the covenant of the Lord, the God of their fathers, which He made with them when He brought them forth out of the land of Egypt.

[26]For they went and served other gods and worshiped them, gods they knew not and that He had not given to them.

[27]So the anger of the Lord was kindled against this land, bringing upon it all the curses that are written in this book.

[28]And the Lord rooted them out of their land in anger and in wrath and in great indignation and cast them into another land, as it is this day.

[29]The secret things belong unto the Lord our God, but the things which are revealed belong to us and to our children forever, that we may do all of the words of this law.

**30** And when all these things have come upon you, the blessings and the curses which I have set before you, and you shall call them to mind among all the nations where the Lord your God has driven you,

[2]And shall return to the Lord your God and obey His voice according to all that I command you today, you and your children, with all your [mind and] heart and with all your being,

[3]Then the Lord your God will restore your fortunes and have compassion upon you and will gather you again from all the nations where He has scattered you.

[4]Even if any of your dispersed are in the uttermost parts of the heavens, from there the Lord your God will gather you and from there will He bring you.

[5]And the Lord your God will bring you into the land which your fathers possessed, and you shall possess it; and He will do you good and multiply you above your fathers.

[a] It is on the strength of the Lord's oath to be Israel's God and so to protect them that this Israelite flatters himself into thinking he is secure, no matter how he may behave. In the history of religion such a delusion has been lamentably frequent, and persons depending upon the unlimited protection of election have presumed on this and recklessly indulged in evil (*The Cambridge Bible*). The Bible emphasizes the "security of the saints," but it is equally emphatic concerning the insecurity of those in conscious and continued indifference to God (Ezek. 3:20; 18:24, 26; Gal. 6:8; James 1:21; II Pet. 1:10, 11; Rev. 22:14).

[a] 3 Or *will bring you back from captivity*

## New International Version

6The LORD your God will circumcise your hearts and the hearts of your descendants, so that you may love him with all your heart and with all your soul, and live. 7The LORD your God will put all these curses on your enemies who hate and persecute you. 8You will again obey the LORD and follow all his commands I am giving you today. 9Then the LORD your God will make you most prosperous in all the work of your hands and in the fruit of your womb, the young of your livestock and the crops of your land. The LORD will again delight in you and make you prosperous, just as he delighted in your ancestors, 10if you obey the LORD your God and keep his commands and decrees that are written in this Book of the Law and turn to the LORD your God with all your heart and with all your soul.

### The Offer of Life or Death

11Now what I am commanding you today is not too difficult for you or beyond your reach. 12It is not up in heaven, so that you have to ask, "Who will ascend into heaven to get it and proclaim it to us so we may obey it?" 13Nor is it beyond the sea, so that you have to ask, "Who will cross the sea to get it and proclaim it to us so we may obey it?" 14No, the word is very near you; it is in your mouth and in your heart so you may obey it.

15See, I set before you today life and prosperity, death and destruction. 16For I command you today to love the LORD your God, to walk in obedience to him, and to keep his commands, decrees and laws; then you will live and increase, and the LORD your God will bless you in the land you are entering to possess.

17But if your heart turns away and you are not obedient, and if you are drawn away to bow down to other gods and worship them, 18I declare to you this day that you will certainly be destroyed. You will not live long in the land you are crossing the Jordan to enter and possess.

19This day I call the heavens and the earth as witnesses against you that I have set before you life and death, blessings and curses. Now choose life, so that you and your children may live 20and that you may love the LORD your God, listen to his voice, and hold fast to him. For the LORD is your life, and he will give you many years in the land he swore to give to your fathers, Abraham, Isaac and Jacob.

### Joshua to Succeed Moses

**31** Then Moses went out and spoke these words to all Israel: 2"I am now a hundred and twenty years old and I am no longer able to lead you. The LORD has said to me, 'You shall not cross the Jordan.' 3The LORD your God himself will cross over ahead of you. He will destroy these nations before you, and you will take possession of their land. Joshua also will cross over ahead of you, as the LORD said. 4And the LORD will do to them what he did to Sihon and Og, the kings of the Amorites, whom he destroyed along with their land. 5The LORD will deliver them to you, and you must do to them all that I have commanded you. 6Be strong and courageous. Do not be afraid or terrified because of them, for the LORD your God goes with you; he will never leave you nor forsake you."

## Amplified Bible

6And the Lord your God will circumcise your hearts and the hearts of your descendants, to love the Lord your God with all your [mind and] heart and with all your being, that you may live.

7And the Lord your God will put all these curses upon your enemies and on those who hate you, who persecute you.

8And you shall return and obey the voice of the Lord and do all His commandments which I command you to-day.

9And the Lord your God will make you abundantly prosperous in every work of your hand, in the fruit of your body, of your cattle, of your land, for good; for the Lord will again delight in prospering you, as He took delight in your fathers,

10If you obey the voice of the Lord your God, to keep His commandments and His statutes which are written in this Book of the Law, and if you turn to the Lord your God with all your [mind and] heart and with all your being.

11For this commandment which I command you this day is not too difficult for you, nor is it far off.

12It is not [a secret laid up] in heaven, that you should say, Who shall go up for us to heaven and bring it to us, that we may hear and do it?

13Neither is it beyond the sea, that you should say, Who shall go over the sea for us and bring it to us, that we may hear and do it?

14But the word is very near you, in your mouth and in your mind *and* in your heart, so that you can do it.

15See, I have set before you this day life and good, and death and evil.

16[If you obey the commandments of the Lord your God which] I command you today, to love the Lord your God, to walk in His ways, and to keep His commandments and His statutes and His ordinances, then you shall live and multiply, and the Lord your God will bless you in the land into which you go to possess.

17But if your [mind and] heart turn away and you will not hear, but are drawn away to worship other gods and serve them,

18I declare to you today that you shall surely perish, and you shall not live long in the land which you pass over the Jordan to enter and possess.

19I call heaven and earth to witness this day against you that I have set before you life and death, the blessings and the curses; therefore choose life, that you and your descendants may live

20And may love the Lord your God, obey His voice, and cling to Him. For He is your life and the length of your days, that you may dwell in the land which the Lord swore to give to your fathers, to Abraham, Isaac, and Jacob.

**31** And Moses went on speaking these words to all Israel:

2And he said to them, I am 120 years old this day; I can no more go out and come in. And the Lord has said to me, You shall not go over this Jordan.

3The Lord your God will Himself go over before you, and He will destroy these nations from before you, and you shall dispossess them. And Joshua shall go over before you, as the Lord has said.

4And the Lord will do to them as He did to Sihon and Og, the kings of the Amorites, and to their land, when He destroyed them.

5And the Lord will give them over to you, and you shall do to them according to all the commandments which I have commanded you.

6Be strong, courageous, *and* firm; fear not nor be in terror before them, for it is the Lord your God Who goes with you; He will not fail you or forsake you.

## New International Version

[7]Then Moses summoned Joshua and said to him in the presence of all Israel, "Be strong and courageous, for you must go with this people into the land that the LORD swore to their ancestors to give them, and you must divide it among them as their inheritance. [8]The LORD himself goes before you and will be with you; he will never leave you nor forsake you. Do not be afraid; do not be discouraged."

### Public Reading of the Law

[9]So Moses wrote down this law and gave it to the Levitical priests, who carried the ark of the covenant of the LORD, and to all the elders of Israel. [10]Then Moses commanded them: "At the end of every seven years, in the year for canceling debts, during the Festival of Tabernacles, [11]when all Israel comes to appear before the LORD your God at the place he will choose, you shall read this law before them in their hearing. [12]Assemble the people—men, women and children, and the foreigners residing in your towns—so they can listen and learn to fear the LORD your God and follow carefully all the words of this law. [13]Their children, who do not know this law, must hear it and learn to fear the LORD your God as long as you live in the land you are crossing the Jordan to possess."

### Israel's Rebellion Predicted

[14]The LORD said to Moses, "Now the day of your death is near. Call Joshua and present yourselves at the tent of meeting, where I will commission him." So Moses and Joshua came and presented themselves at the tent of meeting.

[15]Then the LORD appeared at the tent in a pillar of cloud, and the cloud stood over the entrance to the tent. [16]And the LORD said to Moses: "You are going to rest with your ancestors, and these people will soon prostitute themselves to the foreign gods of the land they are entering. They will forsake me and break the covenant I made with them. [17]And in that day I will become angry with them and forsake them; I will hide my face from them, and they will be destroyed. Many disasters and calamities will come on them, and in that day they will ask, 'Have not these disasters come on us because our God is not with us?' [18]And I will certainly hide my face in that day because of all their wickedness in turning to other gods.

[19]"Now write down this song and teach it to the Israelites and have them sing it, so that it may be a witness for me against them. [20]When I have brought them into the land flowing with milk and honey, the land I promised on oath to their ancestors, and when they eat their fill and thrive, they will turn to other gods and worship them, rejecting me and breaking my covenant. [21]And when many disasters and calamities come on them, this song will testify against them, because it will not be forgotten by their descendants. I know what they are disposed to do, even before I bring them into the land I promised them on oath." [22]So Moses wrote down this song that day and taught it to the Israelites.

[23]The LORD gave this command to Joshua son of Nun: "Be strong and courageous, for you will bring the Israelites into the land I promised them on oath, and I myself will be with you."

[24]After Moses finished writing in a book the words of this law from beginning to end, [25]he gave this command to the Levites who carried the ark of the covenant of the

## Amplified Bible

[7]And Moses called to Joshua and said to him in the sight of all Israel, Be strong, courageous, *and* firm, for you shall go with this people into the land which the Lord has sworn to their fathers to give them, and you shall cause them to possess it.

[8]It is the Lord Who goes before you; He will [march] with you; He will not fail you *or* let you go or forsake you; [let there be no cowardice or flinching, but] fear not, neither become broken [in spirit—depressed, dismayed, and unnerved with alarm].

[9]And Moses wrote this law and delivered it to the Levitical priests, who carried the ark of the covenant of the Lord, and to all the elders of Israel.

[10]And Moses commanded them, At the end of every seven years, at the set time of the year of release [of debtors from their debts], at the Feast of Booths,

[11]When all Israel comes to appear before the Lord your God in the place which He chooses [for His sanctuary], you shall read this law before all Israel in their hearing.

[12]Assemble the people—men, women, and children, and the stranger *and* the sojourner within your towns—that they may hear and learn [reverently] to fear the Lord your God and be watchful to do all the words of this law,

[13]And that their children, who have not known it, may hear and learn [reverently] to fear the Lord your God as long as you live in the land which you go over the Jordan to possess.

[14]And the Lord said to Moses, Behold, your days are nearing when you must die. Call Joshua and present yourselves at the Tent of Meeting, that I may give him his charge. And Moses and Joshua went and presented themselves at the Tent of Meeting.

[15]And the Lord appeared in the Tent in a pillar of cloud, and the pillar of cloud stood over the door of the Tent.

[16]And the Lord said to Moses, Behold, you shall sleep with your fathers, and this people will rise up and play the harlot after the strange gods of the land where they go to be among them; and they will forsake Me and break My covenant which I have made with them.

[17]Then My anger will be kindled against them in that day, and I will forsake them and hide My face from them. And they shall be devoured, and many evils and troubles shall befall them, so that they will say in that day, Have not these evils come upon us because our God is not among us?

[18]And I will surely hide My face in that day because of all the evil which they have done in turning to other gods.

[19]And now write this song for yourselves and teach it to the Israelites; put it in their mouths, that this song may be a witness for Me against the Israelites.

[20]For when I have brought them into the land which I swore to their fathers, a land flowing with milk and honey, and they have eaten and filled themselves and become fat, then they will turn to other gods and serve them, and despise *and* scorn Me and break My covenant.

[21]And when many evils and troubles have befallen them, this [sacred] song will confront them as a witness, for it will never be forgotten from the mouths of their descendants. For I know their strong desire *and* the purposes which they are forming even now, before I have brought them into the land which I swore to give them.

[22]Moses wrote this song the same day and taught it to the Israelites. [Deut. 32:1-43.]

[23]And [the Lord] charged Joshua son of Nun, Be strong and courageous *and* firm, for you shall bring the Israelites into the land which I swore to give them, and I will be with you.

[24]And when Moses had finished writing the words of this law in a book to the very end,

[25]He commanded the Levites who carried the ark of the covenant of the Lord,

## New International Version

Lord: 26"Take this Book of the Law and place it beside the ark of the covenant of the Lord your God. There it will remain as a witness against you. 27For I know how rebellious and stiff-necked you are. If you have been rebellious against the Lord while I am still alive and with you, how much more will you rebel after I die! 28Assemble before me all the elders of your tribes and all your officials, so that I can speak these words in their hearing and call the heavens and the earth to testify against them. 29For I know that after my death you are sure to become utterly corrupt and to turn from the way I have commanded you. In days to come, disaster will fall on you because you will do evil in the sight of the Lord and arouse his anger by what your hands have made."

### The Song of Moses

30And Moses recited the words of this song from beginning to end in the hearing of the whole assembly of Israel:

**32** Listen, you heavens, and I will speak;
hear, you earth, the words of my mouth.
2Let my teaching fall like rain
    and my words descend like dew,
like showers on new grass,
    like abundant rain on tender plants.

3I will proclaim the name of the Lord.
    Oh, praise the greatness of our God!
4He is the Rock, his works are perfect,
    and all his ways are just.
A faithful God who does no wrong,
    upright and just is he.

5They are corrupt and not his children;
    to their shame they are a warped and crooked
        generation.
6Is this the way you repay the Lord,
    you foolish and unwise people?
Is he not your Father, your Creator,*a*
    who made you and formed you?

7Remember the days of old;
    consider the generations long past.
Ask your father and he will tell you,
    your elders, and they will explain to you.
8When the Most High gave the nations their inheritance,
    when he divided all mankind,
he set up boundaries for the peoples
    according to the number of the sons of Israel.*b*
9For the Lord's portion is his people,
    Jacob his allotted inheritance.

10In a desert land he found him,
    in a barren and howling waste.
He shielded him and cared for him;
    he guarded him as the apple of his eye,
11like an eagle that stirs up its nest
    and hovers over its young,
that spreads its wings to catch them
    and carries them aloft.
12The Lord alone led him;
    no foreign god was with him.

13He made him ride on the heights of the land
    and fed him with the fruit of the fields.
He nourished him with honey from the rock,
    and with oil from the flinty crag,
14with curds and milk from herd and flock
    and with fattened lambs and goats,
with choice rams of Bashan
    and the finest kernels of wheat.
You drank the foaming blood of the grape.

*a 6 Or Father, who bought you    b 8 Masoretic Text; Dead Sea Scrolls (see also Septuagint) sons of God*

## Amplified Bible

26Take this Book of the Law and put it by the side of the ark of the covenant of the Lord your God, that it may be there for a witness against you.

27For I know your rebellion and stubbornness; behold, while I am yet alive with you today, you have been rebellious against the Lord; and how much more after my death!

28Gather to me all the elders of your tribes and your officers, that I may speak these words in their ears and call heaven and earth to witness against them.

29For I know that after my death you will utterly corrupt yourselves and turn aside from the way which I have commanded you; and evil will befall you in the latter days because you will do what is evil in the sight of the Lord, to provoke Him to anger through the work of your hands.

30And Moses spoke in the hearing of all the congregation of Israel the words of this song until they were ended:

**32** Give ear, O heavens, and I [Moses] will speak; and let the earth hear the words of my mouth.
2My message shall drop as the rain, my speech shall distil as the dew, as the light rain upon the tender grass, and as the showers upon the herb.
3For I will proclaim the name [and presence] of the Lord. Concede *and* ascribe greatness to our God.
4He is the Rock, His work is perfect, for all His ways are law *and* justice. A God of faithfulness without breach *or* deviation, just and right is He.
5They [Israel] have spoiled themselves. They are not sons to Him, and that is their blemish—a perverse and crooked generation!
6Do you thus repay the Lord, you foolish and senseless people? Is not He your Father Who acquired you for His own, Who made and established you [as a nation]?
7Remember the days of old; consider the years of many generations. Ask your father and he will show you, your elders, and they will tell you.
8When the Most High gave to the nations their inheritance, when He separated the children of men, He set the bounds of the peoples according to the number of the Israelites.
9For the Lord's portion is His people; Jacob (Israel) is the lot of His inheritance.
10He found him in a desert land, in the howling void of the wilderness; He kept circling around him, He scanned him [penetratingly], He kept him as the pupil of His eye.
11As an eagle that stirs up her nest, that flutters over her young, He spread abroad His wings and He took them, He bore them on His pinions. [Luke 13:34.]
12So the Lord alone led him; there was no foreign god with Him.
13He made Israel ride on the high places of the earth, and he ate the increase of the field; and He made him suck honey out of the rock and oil out of the flinty rock,
14Butter *and* curds of the herd and milk of the flock, with fat of lambs, and rams of the breed of Bashan, and he-goats, with the finest of the wheat; and you drank wine of the blood of the grape.

## New International Version

15 Jeshurun[a] grew fat and kicked;
    filled with food, they became heavy and sleek.
They abandoned the God who made them
    and rejected the Rock their Savior.
16 They made him jealous with their foreign gods
    and angered him with their detestable idols.
17 They sacrificed to false gods, which are not God—
    gods they had not known,
    gods that recently appeared,
    gods your ancestors did not fear.
18 You deserted the Rock, who fathered you;
    you forgot the God who gave you birth.

19 The LORD saw this and rejected them
    because he was angered by his sons and daughters.
20 "I will hide my face from them," he said,
    "and see what their end will be;
for they are a perverse generation,
    children who are unfaithful.
21 They made me jealous by what is no god
    and angered me with their worthless idols.
I will make them envious by those who are not a
    people;
    I will make them angry by a nation that has no
    understanding.
22 For a fire will be kindled by my wrath,
    one that burns down to the realm of the dead below.
It will devour the earth and its harvests
    and set afire the foundations of the mountains.

23 "I will heap calamities on them
    and spend my arrows against them.
24 I will send wasting famine against them,
    consuming pestilence and deadly plague;
I will send against them the fangs of wild beasts,
    the venom of vipers that glide in the dust.
25 In the street the sword will make them childless;
    in their homes terror will reign.
The young men and young women will perish,
    the infants and those with gray hair.
26 I said I would scatter them
    and erase their name from human memory,
27 but I dreaded the taunt of the enemy,
    lest the adversary misunderstand
and say, 'Our hand has triumphed;
    the LORD has not done all this.'"

28 They are a nation without sense,
    there is no discernment in them.
29 If only they were wise and would understand this
    and discern what their end will be!
30 How could one man chase a thousand,
    or two put ten thousand to flight,
unless their Rock had sold them,
    unless the LORD had given them up?
31 For their rock is not like our Rock,
    as even our enemies concede.
32 Their vine comes from the vine of Sodom
    and from the fields of Gomorrah.
Their grapes are filled with poison,
    and their clusters with bitterness.
33 Their wine is the venom of serpents,
    the deadly poison of cobras.

34 "Have I not kept this in reserve
    and sealed it in my vaults?
35 It is mine to avenge; I will repay.
    In due time their foot will slip;
their day of disaster is near
    and their doom rushes upon them."

## Amplified Bible

15 But Jeshurun (Israel) grew fat and kicked. You became fat, you grew thick, you were gorged *and* sleek! Then he forsook God Who made him and forsook *and* despised the Rock of his salvation.
16 They provoked Him to jealousy with strange gods, with abominations they provoked Him to anger.
17 They sacrificed to demons, not to God—to gods whom they knew not, to new gods lately come up, whom your fathers never knew or feared.
18 Of the Rock Who bore you you were unmindful; you forgot the God Who travailed in your birth.
19 And the Lord saw it and He spurned *and* rejected them, out of indignation with His sons and His daughters.
20 And He said, I will hide My face from them, I will see what their end will be; for they are a perverse generation, children in whom is no faithfulness.
21 They have moved Me to jealousy with what is not God; they have angered Me with their idols. So I will move them to jealousy with those who are not a people; I will anger them with a foolish nation.
22 For a fire is kindled by My anger, and it burns to the depths of Sheol, devours the earth with its increase, and sets on fire the foundations of the mountains.
23 And I will heap evils upon them; I will spend My arrows upon them.
24 They shall be wasted with hunger and devoured with burning heat and poisonous pestilence; and the teeth of beasts will I send against them, with the poison of crawling things of the dust.
25 From without the sword shall bereave, and in the chambers shall be terror, destroying both young man and virgin, the sucking child with the man of gray hairs.
26 I said, I would scatter them afar and I would have made the remembrance of them to cease from among men,
27 Had I not feared the provocation of the foe, lest their enemies misconstrue it and lest they should say, Our own hand has prevailed; all this was not the work of the Lord.
28 For they are a nation void of counsel, and there is no understanding in them.
29 O that they were wise and would see through this [present triumph] to their ultimate fate!
30 How could one have chased a thousand, and two put ten thousand to flight, except their Rock had sold them, and the Lord had delivered them up?
31 For their rock is not like our Rock, even our enemies themselves judge this.
32 For their vine comes from the vine of Sodom and from the fields of Gomorrah; their grapes are grapes of [poisonous] gall, their clusters are bitter.
33 Their wine is the [furious] venom of serpents, and the pitiless poison of vipers.
34 Is not this laid up in store with Me, sealed up in My treasuries?
35 Vengeance is Mine, and recompense, in the time when their foot shall slide; for the day of their disaster is at hand and their doom comes speedily.

a 15 *Jeshurun* means *the upright one*, that is, Israel.

## New International Version

36 The LORD will vindicate his people
   and relent concerning his servants
when he sees their strength is gone
   and no one is left, slave or free.[a]
37 He will say: "Now where are their gods,
   the rock they took refuge in,
38 the gods who ate the fat of their sacrifices
   and drank the wine of their drink offerings?
Let them rise up to help you!
   Let them give you shelter!

39 "See now that I myself am he!
   There is no god besides me.
I put to death and I bring to life,
   I have wounded and I will heal,
   and no one can deliver out of my hand.
40 I lift my hand to heaven and solemnly swear:
   As surely as I live forever,
41 when I sharpen my flashing sword
   and my hand grasps it in judgment,
I will take vengeance on my adversaries
   and repay those who hate me.
42 I will make my arrows drunk with blood,
   while my sword devours flesh:
the blood of the slain and the captives,
   the heads of the enemy leaders."

43 Rejoice, you nations, with his people,[b,c]
   for he will avenge the blood of his servants;
he will take vengeance on his enemies
   and make atonement for his land and people.

44 Moses came with Joshua[d] son of Nun and spoke all the words of this song in the hearing of the people. 45 When Moses finished reciting all these words to all Israel, 46 he said to them, "Take to heart all the words I have solemnly declared to you this day, so that you may command your children to obey carefully all the words of this law. 47 They are not just idle words for you—they are your life. By them you will live long in the land you are crossing the Jordan to possess."

### Moses to Die on Mount Nebo

48 On that same day the LORD told Moses, 49 "Go up into the Abarim Range to Mount Nebo in Moab, across from Jericho, and view Canaan, the land I am giving the Israelites as their own possession. 50 There on the mountain that you have climbed you will die and be gathered to your people, just as your brother Aaron died on Mount Hor and was gathered to his people. 51 This is because both of you broke faith with me in the presence of the Israelites at the waters of Meribah Kadesh in the Desert of Zin and because you did not uphold my holiness among the Israelites. 52 Therefore, you will see the land only from a distance; you will not enter the land I am giving to the people of Israel."

### Moses Blesses the Tribes

**33** This is the blessing that Moses the man of God pronounced on the Israelites before his death. 2 He said:

"The LORD came from Sinai
   and dawned over them from Seir;
   he shone forth from Mount Paran.
He came with[e] myriads of holy ones
   from the south, from his mountain slopes.[f]

## Amplified Bible

36 For the Lord will revoke sentence for His people and relent for His servants' sake when He sees that their power is gone and none remains, whether bond or free.
37 And He will say, Where are their gods, the rock in which they took refuge,
38 Who ate the fat of their sacrifices and drank the wine of their drink offering? Let them rise up and help you, let them be your protection!
39 See now that I, I am He, and there is no god beside Me; I kill and I make alive, I wound and I heal, and there is none who can deliver out of My hand.
40 For I lift up My hand to heaven and swear, As I live forever,
41 If I whet My lightning sword and My hand takes hold on judgment, I will wreak vengeance on My foes and recompense those who hate Me.
42 I will make My arrows drunk with blood, and My sword shall devour flesh, with the blood of the slain and the captives, from the long-haired heads of the foe.
43 Rejoice [with] His people, O you nations, for He avenges the blood of His servants, and vengeance He inflicts on His foes and clears guilt from the land of His people.
44 And Moses came and spoke all the words of this song in the ears of the people, he and Hoshea (Joshua) son of Nun.
45 And when Moses had finished speaking all these words to all Israel,
46 He said to them, Set your [minds and] hearts on all the words which I command you this day, that you may command them to your children, that they may be watchful to do all the words of this law.
47 For it is not an empty *and* worthless trifle for you; it is your [very] life. By it you shall live long in the land which you are going over the Jordan to possess.
48 And the Lord said to Moses that same day,
49 Get up into this mountain of the Abarim, Mount Nebo, which is in the land of Moab, opposite Jericho, and look at the land of Canaan which I give to the Israelites for a possession.
50 And die on the mountain which you ascend and be gathered to your people, as Aaron your brother died on Mount Hor and was gathered to his people,
51 Because you broke faith with Me in the midst of the Israelites at the waters of Meribah-kadesh in the Wilderness of Zin and because you did not set Me apart as holy in the midst of the Israelites.
52 For you shall see the land opposite you at a distance, but you shall not go there, into the land which I give the Israelites.

**33** This is the blessing with which Moses the man of God blessed the Israelites before his death.
2 He said, The Lord came from Sinai and beamed upon us from Seir; He flashed forth from Mount Paran, from among ten thousands of holy ones, a flaming fire, a law, at His right hand.

---

*a 36 Or and they are without a ruler or leader    b 43 Or Make his people rejoice, you nations    c 43 Masoretic Text; Dead Sea Scrolls (see also Septuagint) people, / and let all the angels worship him, /    d 44 Hebrew Hoshea, a variant of Joshua    e 2 Or from    f 2 The meaning of the Hebrew for this phrase is uncertain.*

## New International Version

3 Surely it is you who love the people;
  all the holy ones are in your hand.
At your feet they all bow down,
  and from you receive instruction,
4 the law that Moses gave us,
  the possession of the assembly of Jacob.
5 He was king over Jeshurun[a]
  when the leaders of the people assembled,
  along with the tribes of Israel.

6 "Let Reuben live and not die,
  nor[b] his people be few."

7 And this he said about Judah:

"Hear, Lord, the cry of Judah;
  bring him to his people.
With his own hands he defends his cause.
  Oh, be his help against his foes!"

8 About Levi he said:

"Your Thummim and Urim belong
  to your faithful servant.
You tested him at Massah;
  you contended with him at the waters of Meribah.
9 He said of his father and mother,
  'I have no regard for them.'
He did not recognize his brothers
  or acknowledge his own children,
but he watched over your word
  and guarded your covenant.
10 He teaches your precepts to Jacob
  and your law to Israel.
He offers incense before you
  and whole burnt offerings on your altar.
11 Bless all his skills, Lord,
  and be pleased with the work of his hands.
Strike down those who rise against him,
  his foes till they rise no more."

12 About Benjamin he said:

"Let the beloved of the Lord rest secure in him,
  for he shields him all day long,
  and the one the Lord loves rests between his
    shoulders."

13 About Joseph he said:

"May the Lord bless his land
  with the precious dew from heaven above
  and with the deep waters that lie below;
14 with the best the sun brings forth
  and the finest the moon can yield;
15 with the choicest gifts of the ancient mountains
  and the fruitfulness of the everlasting hills;
16 with the best gifts of the earth and its fullness
  and the favor of him who dwelt in the burning bush.
Let all these rest on the head of Joseph,
  on the brow of the prince among[c] his brothers.
17 In majesty he is like a firstborn bull;
  his horns are the horns of a wild ox.
With them he will gore the nations,
  even those at the ends of the earth.
Such are the ten thousands of Ephraim;
  such are the thousands of Manasseh."

18 About Zebulun he said:

"Rejoice, Zebulun, in your going out,
  and you, Issachar, in your tents.

---

a 5 *Jeshurun* means *the upright one*, that is, Israel; also in verse 26.
b 6 Or *but let*    c 16 Or *of the one separated from*

## Amplified Bible

3 Yes, He loves [the tribes] His people; all those conse-crated to Him are in Your hand. They followed in Your steps; they [accepted Your word and] received direction from You,
4 When Moses commanded us a law, as a possession for the assembly of Jacob.
5 [The Lord] was King in Jeshurun (Israel) when the heads of the people were gathered, all the tribes of Israel together.
6 Let [the tribe of] Reuben live and not die out, but a let his men be few.
7 And this he [Moses] said of Judah: Hear, O Lord, the voice of Judah, and bring him to his people! With his hands he contended for himself; but may You be a help against his enemies.
8 And of Levi he said: Your Thummim and Your Urim [by which the priest sought God's will for the nation] are for Your pious one [Aaron on behalf of the tribe], whom You tried *and* proved at Massah, with whom You contend-ed at the waters of Meribah; [Num. 20:1-13.]
9 [Aaron] who b said of his father and mother, I do not re-gard them; nor did he acknowledge his brothers or openly recognize his own children. For the priests observed Your word and kept Your covenant [as to their limitations].
10 [The priests] shall teach Jacob Your ordinances and Israel Your law. They shall put incense before You and whole burnt offerings upon Your altar.
11 Bless, O Lord, [Levi's] substance, and accept the work of his hands; crush the loins of his adversaries, and of those who hate him, that they arise no more.
12 Of Benjamin he said: The beloved of the Lord shall c dwell in safety by Him; He covers him all the day long, and makes His dwelling between his shoulders.
13 And of Joseph he said: Blessed by the Lord be his land, with the precious gifts of heaven from the dew and from the deep that couches beneath,
14 With the precious things of the fruits of the sun and with the precious yield of the months,
15 With the chief products of the ancient mountains and with the precious things of the everlasting hills,
16 With the precious things of the earth and its fullness and the favor *and* goodwill of Him Who dwelt in the bush. Let these blessings come upon the head of Joseph, upon the crown of the head of him who was separate *and* prince among his brothers. [Exod. 3:4.]
17 Like a firstling young bull his majesty is, and his horns like the horns of the wild ox; with them he shall push the peoples, all of them, to the ends of the earth. And they are the ten thousands of Ephraim, and they are the thousands of Manasseh.
18 And of Zebulun he said: d Rejoice, Zebulun, in your in-terests abroad, and you, Issachar, in your tents [at home].

---

a The earlier Bible translators could not believe that Moses meant to say of Reuben, "let his men be few," so they put "not" in italics: "let *not* his men be few." But Reuben had committed a grave offense (Gen. 49:3, 4) which cancelled his birthright, and God meant exactly what He directed Moses to say, as continuous fulfillment of the prophecy proves. "In Judg. 5:16 the tribe [of Reuben] is scorned for its failure to join the others against the Canaanites, and except for I Chron. 5:3-20 it does not again appear in Israel's history. Nor does Misha of Moab, ninth century, B.C., name it" *(The Cambridge Bible).* Furthermore, by A.D. 1951 no Jew was permitted to enter the territory once allotted to the tribe of Reuben. "The whole territory, which is . . . quite capable of cultivation, is now deserted by its settled inhabitants" (John D. Davis, *A Dictionary of the Bible).* It was then being restored not by Israelites but by Arabs. b The law required that the high priest act just as impartially when one of his immediate family died, as if the departed were no kin to him (Lev. 21:10-12). This throws light on Christ's attitude toward His mother and brothers in Matt. 12:46-50 (see also Heb. 3:1-3; 8:1-6). c The temple in Jerusalem was located almost between the ridges of the territory of Benjamin, suggesting "between his shoulders" (see also Josh. 15:8). Moses sees it as a symbol of the Lord's presence covering Benjamin continually. d Not until 1934 was this prophecy notably in process of fulfillment, when Haifa's bay became one of the great harbors of the Mediterranean Sea, with commerce affecting the whole world.

## New International Version

19 They will summon peoples to the mountain
     and there offer the sacrifices of the righteous;
they will feast on the abundance of the seas,
     on the treasures hidden in the sand."

20 About Gad he said:

"Blessed is he who enlarges Gad's domain!
     Gad lives there like a lion,
     tearing at arm or head.
21 He chose the best land for himself;
     the leader's portion was kept for him.
When the heads of the people assembled,
     he carried out the LORD's righteous will,
     and his judgments concerning Israel."

22 About Dan he said:

"Dan is a lion's cub,
     springing out of Bashan."

23 About Naphtali he said:

"Naphtali is abounding with the favor of the LORD
     and is full of his blessing;
he will inherit southward to the lake."

24 About Asher he said:

"Most blessed of sons is Asher;
     let him be favored by his brothers,
     and let him bathe his feet in oil.
25 The bolts of your gates will be iron and bronze,
     and your strength will equal your days.

26 "There is no one like the God of Jeshurun,
     who rides across the heavens to help you
     and on the clouds in his majesty.
27 The eternal God is your refuge,
     and underneath are the everlasting arms.
He will drive out your enemies before you,
     saying, 'Destroy them!'
28 So Israel will live in safety;
     Jacob will dwell[a] secure
in a land of grain and new wine,
     where the heavens drop dew.
29 Blessed are you, Israel!
     Who is like you,
     a people saved by the LORD?
He is your shield and helper
     and your glorious sword.
Your enemies will cower before you,
     and you will tread on their heights."

### The Death of Moses

**34** Then Moses climbed Mount Nebo from the plains of Moab to the top of Pisgah, across from Jericho. There the LORD showed him the whole land—from Gilead

## Amplified Bible

19 They shall call the people unto Mount [Carmel]; there they shall offer sacrifices of righteousness, for ᵃ they shall suck the abundance of the seas and the treasures hid in the sand.
20 And of Gad he said: Blessed is He Who enlarges Gad! Gad lurks like a lioness, and tears the arm, yes, the crown of the head.
21 He selected the best land for himself, for there was the leader's portion reserved; yet he came with the chiefs of the nation, and the righteous will of the Lord he performed, and His ordinances with Israel. [Num. 32:29-33.]
22 Of Dan he said: Dan is a lion's whelp that leaps forth from Bashan.
23 Of Naphtali he said: O Naphtali, ᵇ satisfied with favor and full of the blessing of the Lord, possess the Sea [of Galilee] and [its warm, sunny climate like] the south.
24 Of Asher he said: Blessed above sons is Asher; let him be acceptable to his brothers, and ᶜ let him dip his foot in oil.
25 Your castles and strongholds shall have bars of iron and bronze, and as your day, so shall your strength, your rest *and* security, be.
26 There is none like God, O Jeshurun [Israel], Who rides through the heavens to your help and in His majestic glory through the skies.
27 The eternal God is your refuge *and* dwelling place, and underneath are the everlasting arms; He drove the enemy before you *and* thrust them out, saying, Destroy!
28 And Israel dwells in safety, the fountain of Jacob alone in a land of grain and new wine; yes, His heavens drop dew.
29 Happy are you, O Israel, *and* blessing is yours! Who is like you, a people saved by the Lord, the Shield of your help, the Sword that exalts you! Your enemies shall come fawning *and* cringing, *and* submit feigned obedience to you, and you shall march on their high places.

**34** And Moses went up from the plains of Moab to Mount Nebo, to the top of Pisgah, that is opposite Jericho. And the Lord showed him all the land—from Gilead to Dan,

---

ᵃ The great oil pipeline path across Palestine was first opened in 1935. Until then this prophecy fell far short of fulfillment. But 3,400 years before, Moses sent out the inspired headlines, "Zebulun . . . Issachar . . . shall suck the abundance of the seas, and the treasures hid in the sand." Our omnipotent God was "declaring the end *and* the result from the beginning, and from ancient times the things that are not yet done, saying, My counsel shall stand" (Isa. 46:10). ᵇ For many centuries much of the territory of upper Naphtali was little more than a miasmic swamp, unfit for man or beast. But when the Jews returned to Palestine, they drained and redeemed the area, and by 1940 it was dotted over with thriving colonies, as Moses had foretold, "satisfied with favor and full of the blessing of the Lord." ᶜ The maps of the territory of Asher sometimes suggest the shape of the sole of a foot, sometimes that of a leg and foot; but in either case the Great International Iraq-Petroleum Enterprise, opened in 1935, crossed the area just at the toe of Asher's "foot." Oil brought nearly 1,000 miles across the sands from Mesopotamia began pouring through pipes into the Haifa harbor, a million gallons of oil a day. Jacob had prophesied about Asher, " . . . his bread *shall be* fat" (Gen. 49:20 KJV), and here Moses says of Asher, "Let him dip his foot in oil"!

---

ᵃ 28 Septuagint; Hebrew *Jacob's spring is*

## New International Version

to Dan, [2]all of Naphtali, the territory of Ephraim and Manasseh, all the land of Judah as far as the Mediterranean Sea, [3]the Negev and the whole region from the Valley of Jericho, the City of Palms, as far as Zoar. [4]Then the LORD said to him, "This is the land I promised on oath to Abraham, Isaac and Jacob when I said, 'I will give it to your descendants.' I have let you see it with your eyes, but you will not cross over into it."

[5]And Moses the servant of the LORD died there in Moab, as the LORD had said. [6]He buried him[a] in Moab, in the valley opposite Beth Peor, but to this day no one knows where his grave is. [7]Moses was a hundred and twenty years old when he died, yet his eyes were not weak nor his strength gone. [8]The Israelites grieved for Moses in the plains of Moab thirty days, until the time of weeping and mourning was over.

[9]Now Joshua son of Nun was filled with the spirit[b] of wisdom because Moses had laid his hands on him. So the Israelites listened to him and did what the LORD had commanded Moses.

[10]Since then, no prophet has risen in Israel like Moses, whom the LORD knew face to face, [11]who did all those signs and wonders the LORD sent him to do in Egypt—to Pharaoh and to all his officials and to his whole land. [12]For no one has ever shown the mighty power or performed the awesome deeds that Moses did in the sight of all Israel.

## Amplified Bible

[2]And all Naphtali, and the land of Ephraim and Manasseh, and all the land of Judah to the western [Mediterranean] sea,

[3]And the South (the Negeb) and the plain, that is, the Valley of Jericho, the City of Palm Trees, as far as Zoar.

[4]And the Lord said to him, This is the land which I swore to Abraham, Isaac, and Jacob, saying, I will give it to your descendants. I have let you see it with your eyes, but you shall not go over there.

[5]So Moses the servant of the Lord died there in the land of Moab, according to the word of the Lord,

[6]And He buried him in the valley of the land of Moab opposite Beth-peor, but no man knows where his tomb is to this day.

[7]Moses was 120 years old when he died; his eye was not dim nor his natural force abated. [Deut. 31:2.]

[8]And the Israelites wept for Moses in the plains of Moab thirty days; then the days of weeping and mourning for Moses were ended.

[9]And Joshua son of Nun was full of the spirit of wisdom, for Moses had laid his hands upon him; so the Israelites listened to him and did as the Lord commanded Moses.

[10]And there arose not a prophet since in Israel like Moses, whom the Lord knew face to face,

[11][None equal to him] in all the signs and wonders which the Lord sent him to do in the land of Egypt—to Pharaoh and to all his servants and to all his land,

[12]And in all the mighty power and all the great and terrible deeds which Moses wrought in the sight of all Israel.

[a] 6 Or *He was buried*   [b] 9 Or *Spirit*

# Joshua

## Joshua Installed as Leader

**1** After the death of Moses the servant of the LORD, the LORD said to Joshua son of Nun, Moses' aide: ²"Moses my servant is dead. Now then, you and all these people, get ready to cross the Jordan River into the land I am about to give to them—to the Israelites. ³I will give you every place where you set your foot, as I promised Moses. ⁴Your territory will extend from the desert to Lebanon, and from the great river, the Euphrates—all the Hittite country—to the Mediterranean Sea in the west. ⁵No one will be able to stand against you all the days of your life. As I was with Moses, so I will be with you; I will never leave you nor forsake you. ⁶Be strong and courageous, because you will lead these people to inherit the land I swore to their ancestors to give them.

⁷"Be strong and very courageous. Be careful to obey all the law my servant Moses gave you; do not turn from it to the right or to the left, that you may be successful wherever you go. ⁸Keep this Book of the Law always on your lips; meditate on it day and night, so that you may be careful to do everything written in it. Then you will be prosperous and successful. ⁹Have I not commanded you? Be strong and courageous. Do not be afraid; do not be discouraged, for the LORD your God will be with you wherever you go."

¹⁰So Joshua ordered the officers of the people: ¹¹"Go through the camp and tell the people, 'Get your provisions ready. Three days from now you will cross the Jordan here to go in and take possession of the land the LORD your God is giving you for your own.'"

¹²But to the Reubenites, the Gadites and the half-tribe of Manasseh, Joshua said, ¹³"Remember the command that Moses the servant of the LORD gave you after he said, 'The LORD your God will give you rest by giving you this land.' ¹⁴Your wives, your children and your livestock may stay in the land that Moses gave you east of the Jordan, but all your fighting men, ready for battle, must cross over ahead of your fellow Israelites. You are to help them ¹⁵until the LORD gives them rest, as he has done for you, and until they too have taken possession of the land the LORD your God is giving them. After that, you may go back and occupy your own land, which Moses the servant of the LORD gave you east of the Jordan toward the sunrise."

¹⁶Then they answered Joshua, "Whatever you have commanded us we will do, and wherever you send us we will go. ¹⁷Just as we fully obeyed Moses, so we will obey

# Joshua

**1** After the death of Moses the servant of the Lord, the Lord said to Joshua son of Nun, Moses' minister, [Deut. 34:4-8.]

²Moses My servant is dead. So now arise [take his place], go over this Jordan, you and all this people, into the land which I am giving to them, the Israelites.

³Every place upon which the sole of your foot shall tread, that have I given to you, as I promised Moses.

⁴From the wilderness and this Lebanon to the great river Euphrates—all the land of the *a*Hittites [Canaan]—and to the Great [Mediterranean] Sea on the west shall be your territory.

⁵No man shall be able to stand before you all the days of your life. As I was with Moses, so I will be with you; I will not fail you or forsake you.

⁶Be strong (confident) and of good courage, for you shall cause this people to inherit the land which I swore to their fathers to give them.

⁷Only you be strong and very courageous, that you may do according to all the law which Moses My servant commanded you. Turn not from it to the right hand or to the left, that you may prosper wherever you go.

⁸This Book of the Law shall not depart out of your mouth, but you shall meditate on it day and night, that you may observe *and* do according to all that is written in it. For then you shall make your way prosperous, and then you shall deal wisely *and* have good *b*success.

⁹Have not I commanded you? Be strong, vigorous, and very courageous. Be not afraid, neither be dismayed, for the Lord your God is with you wherever you go.

¹⁰Then Joshua commanded the officers of the people, saying,

¹¹Pass through the camp and command the people, Prepare your provisions, for within three days you shall pass over this Jordan to go in to take possession of the land which the Lord your God is giving you to possess.

¹²And to the Reubenites, the Gadites, and the half-tribe of Manasseh, Joshua said,

¹³Remember what Moses the servant of the Lord commanded you, saying, The Lord your God is giving you [of these two and a half tribes a place of] rest and will give you this land [east of the Jordan].

¹⁴Your wives, your little ones, and your cattle shall dwell in the land which Moses gave you on this side of the Jordan, but all your mighty men of valor shall pass on before your brethren [of the other tribes] armed, and help them [possess their land]

¹⁵Until the Lord gives your brethren rest, as He has given you, and they also possess the land the Lord your God is giving them. Then you shall return to the land of your possession and possess it, the land Moses the Lord's servant gave you on the sunrise side of the Jordan.

¹⁶They answered Joshua, All you command us we will do, and wherever you send us we will go.

¹⁷As we hearkened to Moses in all things, so will we

---

*a* Although the Hittites are mentioned forty-eight times in the Bible, some critics long refused to accept the possibility, or at least the probability, of the importance of such an ancient people. But archaeological discoveries of the twentieth century have confirmed the importance of the Hittites beyond all question. For instance, G. A. Barton in *Archaeology and the Bible* records the existence of an archive of clay tablets containing among other things a military treaty made by the Egyptians and the Hittites nearly thirteen centuries before the birth of Christ. *b* This is the only place in the early English versions where the word "success" is found. The secret of success is given in verses 5 through 9. Joshua accepted Moses' place of leadership without misgivings. God's will for him was his will, and he did not hesitate. To go "all out" for God was already habitual with him; it is the unfailing prerequisite of eternal success (Deut. 6:3-5; Ps. 1:1-3; Luke 10:25-28).

## New International Version

you. Only may the LORD your God be with you as he was with Moses. [18]Whoever rebels against your word and does not obey it, whatever you may command them, will be put to death. Only be strong and courageous!"

### Rahab and the Spies

**2** Then Joshua son of Nun secretly sent two spies from Shittim. "Go, look over the land," he said, "especially Jericho." So they went and entered the house of a prostitute named Rahab and stayed there.

[2]The king of Jericho was told, "Look, some of the Israelites have come here tonight to spy out the land." [3]So the king of Jericho sent this message to Rahab: "Bring out the men who came to you and entered your house, because they have come to spy out the whole land."

[4]But the woman had taken the two men and hidden them. She said, "Yes, the men came to me, but I did not know where they had come from. [5]At dusk, when it was time to close the city gate, they left. I don't know which way they went. Go after them quickly. You may catch up with them." [6](But she had taken them up to the roof and hidden them under the stalks of flax she had laid out on the roof.) [7]So the men set out in pursuit of the spies on the road that leads to the fords of the Jordan, and as soon as the pursuers had gone out, the gate was shut.

[8]Before the spies lay down for the night, she went up on the roof [9]and said to them, "I know that the LORD has given you this land and that a great fear of you has fallen on us, so that all who live in this country are melting in fear because of you. [10]We have heard how the LORD dried up the water of the Red Sea[a] for you when you came out of Egypt, and what you did to Sihon and Og, the two kings of the Amorites east of the Jordan, whom you completely destroyed.[b] [11]When we heard of it, our hearts melted in fear and everyone's courage failed because of you, for the LORD your God is God in heaven above and on the earth below.

[12]"Now then, please swear to me by the LORD that you will show kindness to my family, because I have shown kindness to you. Give me a sure sign [13]that you will spare the lives of my father and mother, my brothers and sisters, and all who belong to them—and that you will save us from death."

[14]"Our lives for your lives!" the men assured her. "If you don't tell what we are doing, we will treat you kindly and faithfully when the LORD gives us the land."

[15]So she let them down by a rope through the window, for the house she lived in was part of the city wall. [16]She said to them, "Go to the hills so the pursuers will not find you. Hide yourselves there three days until they return, and then go on your way."

[17]Now the men had said to her, "This oath you made us swear will not be binding on us [18]unless, when we enter the land, you have tied this scarlet cord in the window through which you let us down, and unless you have brought your father and mother, your brothers and all your family into

## Amplified Bible

hearken to you; only may the Lord your God be with you as He was with Moses. [18]Whoever rebels against your commandment and will not hearken to all you command him shall be put to death. Only be strong, vigorous, *and* of good courage.

**2** Joshua son of Nun sent two men secretly from Shittim as scouts, saying, Go, view the land, especially Jericho. And they went and came to the house of a harlot named Rahab and lodged there.

[2]It was told the king of Jericho, Behold, there came men in here tonight of the Israelites to search out the country.

[3]And the king of Jericho sent to Rahab, saying, Bring forth the men who have come to you, who entered your house, for they have come to search out the land.

[4]But the woman had taken the two men and hidden them. So she said, Yes, two men came to me, but I did not know from where they had come.

[5]And at gate closing time, after dark, the men went out. Where they went I do not know. Pursue them quickly, for you will overtake them.

[6]But she had brought them up to the roof and hidden them under the stalks of flax which she had laid in order there.

[7]So the men pursued them to the Jordan as far as the fords. As soon as the pursuers had gone, the city's gate was shut.

[8]Before the two men had lain down, Rahab came up to them on the roof,

[9]And she said to the men, I know that the Lord has given you the land and that your terror is fallen upon us and that all the inhabitants of the land faint because of you.

[10]For we have heard how the Lord dried up the water of the Red Sea for you when you came out of Egypt, and what you did to the two kings of the Amorites who were on the [east] side of the Jordan, Sihon and Og, whom you utterly destroyed.

[11]When we heard it, our hearts melted, neither did spirit *or* courage remain any more in any man because of you, for the Lord your God, He is God in heaven above and on earth beneath. [Heb. 11:31.]

[12]Now then, I pray you, swear to me by the Lord, since I have shown you kindness, that you also will show kindness to my father's house, and give me a sure sign,

[13]And save alive my father and mother, my brothers and sisters, and all they have, and deliver us from death.

[14]And the men said to her, Our lives for yours! If you do not tell this business of ours, then when the Lord gives us the land we will deal kindly and faithfully with you.

[15]Then she let them down by a rope through the window, for her house was built into the [town] wall so that she dwelt in the wall.

[16]And she said to them, Get to the mountain, lest the pursuers meet you; hide yourselves there three days until the pursuers have returned; and afterward you may go your way.

[17]The men said to her, We will be blameless of this oath you have made us swear. [The responsibility is now yours.]

[18]Behold, when we come into the land, you shall bind this scarlet cord in the window through which you let us down, and you shall bring your father and mother, your brothers, and all your father's household into your house.

---

[a] 10 Or *the Sea of Reeds*    [b] 10 The Hebrew term refers to the irrevocable giving over of things or persons to the LORD, often by totally destroying them.

## New International Version

your house. <sup>19</sup>If any of them go outside your house into the street, their blood will be on their own heads; we will not be responsible. As for those who are in the house with you, their blood will be on our head if a hand is laid on them. <sup>20</sup>But if you tell what we are doing, we will be released from the oath you made us swear."

<sup>21</sup>"Agreed," she replied. "Let it be as you say."

So she sent them away, and they departed. And she tied the scarlet cord in the window.

<sup>22</sup>When they left, they went into the hills and stayed there three days, until the pursuers had searched all along the road and returned without finding them. <sup>23</sup>Then the two men started back. They went down out of the hills, forded the river and came to Joshua son of Nun and told him everything that had happened to them. <sup>24</sup>They said to Joshua, "The LORD has surely given the whole land into our hands; all the people are melting in fear because of us."

### Crossing the Jordan

**3** Early in the morning Joshua and all the Israelites set out from Shittim and went to the Jordan, where they camped before crossing over. <sup>2</sup>After three days the officers went throughout the camp, <sup>3</sup>giving orders to the people: "When you see the ark of the covenant of the LORD your God, and the Levitical priests carrying it, you are to move out from your positions and follow it. <sup>4</sup>Then you will know which way to go, since you have never been this way before. But keep a distance of about two thousand cubits[a] between you and the ark; do not go near it."

<sup>5</sup>Joshua told the people, "Consecrate yourselves, for tomorrow the LORD will do amazing things among you."

<sup>6</sup>Joshua said to the priests, "Take up the ark of the covenant and pass on ahead of the people." So they took it up and went ahead of them.

<sup>7</sup>And the LORD said to Joshua, "Today I will begin to exalt you in the eyes of all Israel, so they may know that I am with you as I was with Moses. <sup>8</sup>Tell the priests who carry the ark of the covenant: 'When you reach the edge of the Jordan's waters, go and stand in the river.'"

<sup>9</sup>Joshua said to the Israelites, "Come here and listen to the words of the LORD your God. <sup>10</sup>This is how you will know that the living God is among you and that he will certainly drive out before you the Canaanites, Hittites, Hivites, Perizzites, Girgashites, Amorites and Jebusites. <sup>11</sup>See, the ark of the covenant of the Lord of all the earth will go into the Jordan ahead of you. <sup>12</sup>Now then, choose twelve men from the tribes of Israel, one from each tribe. <sup>13</sup>And as soon as the priests who carry the ark of the LORD—the Lord of all the earth—set foot in the Jordan, its waters flowing downstream will be cut off and stand up in a heap."

<sup>14</sup>So when the people broke camp to cross the Jordan, the priests carrying the ark of the covenant went ahead of them. <sup>15</sup>Now the Jordan is at flood stage all during harvest. Yet as soon as the priests who carried the ark reached the Jordan and their feet touched the water's edge, <sup>16</sup>the wa-

## Amplified Bible

<sup>19</sup>And if anyone goes out of the doors of your house into the street, his blood shall be upon his head, and we will be guiltless; but if a hand is laid upon anyone who is with you in the house, his blood shall be on our head.

<sup>20</sup>But if you tell this business of ours, we shall be guiltless of your oath which you made us swear.

<sup>21</sup>And she said, According to your words, so it is. Then she sent them away and they departed; and she bound the <sup>a</sup>scarlet cord in the window.

<sup>22</sup>They left and went to the mountain and stayed there three days, until the pursuers returned, who had searched all along the way without finding them.

<sup>23</sup>So the two men descended from the mountain, passed over [the Jordan], and came to Joshua son of Nun, and told him all that had befallen them.

<sup>24</sup>They said to Joshua, Truly the Lord has given all the land into our hands; for all the inhabitants of the country are faint because of us.

**3** Joshua rose early in the morning and they removed from Shittim and came to the Jordan, he and all the Israelites, and lodged there before passing over.

<sup>2</sup>After three days the officers went through the camp,

<sup>3</sup>Commanding the people: When you see the ark of the covenant of the Lord your God being borne by the Levitical priests, set out from where you are and follow it.

<sup>4</sup>Yet a space must be kept between you and it, about 2,000 cubits by measure; come not near it, that you may [be able to see the ark and] know the way you must go, for you have not passed this way before.

<sup>5</sup>And Joshua said to the people, Sanctify yourselves [that is, separate yourselves for a special holy purpose], for tomorrow the Lord will do wonders among you.

<sup>6</sup>Joshua said to the priests, Take up the ark of the covenant and pass over before the people. And they took it up and went on before the people.

<sup>7</sup>The Lord said to Joshua, This day I will begin to magnify you in the sight of all Israel, so they may know that as I was with Moses, so I will be with you.

<sup>8</sup>You shall command the priests who bear the ark of the covenant, When you come to the brink of the waters of the Jordan, you shall stand still in the Jordan.

<sup>9</sup>Joshua said to the Israelites, Come near, hear the words of the Lord your God.

<sup>10</sup>Joshua said, Hereby you shall know that the living God is among you and that He will surely drive out from before you the Canaanites, Hittites, Hivites, Perizzites, Girgashites, Amorites, and Jebusites.

<sup>11</sup>Behold, the ark of the covenant of the Lord of all the earth is passing over before you into the Jordan!

<sup>12</sup>So now take twelve men from the tribes of Israel, one from each tribe.

<sup>13</sup>When the soles of the feet of the priests who bear the ark of the Lord of all the earth shall rest in the Jordan, the waters of the Jordan coming down from above shall be cut off and they shall stand in one heap.

<sup>14</sup>So when the people set out from their tents to pass over the Jordan, with the priests bearing the ark of the covenant before the people,

<sup>15</sup>And when those who bore the ark had come to the Jordan and the feet of the priests bearing the ark were in the brink of the water—for the Jordan overflows all its banks throughout the time of harvest—

---

<sup>a</sup> What the blood on the doorposts on the first Passover night in Egypt was to the houses of Israel (Exod. 12:13), the scarlet cord in the window was to the house of Rahab. Her sinful years of ignorance God ignored (Acts 17:30, 31); she became an ancestress, as did Ruth, of David and of Jesus Christ (Matt. 1:1, 5, 6).

---

<sup>a</sup> 4 That is, about 3,000 feet or about 900 meters

## New International Version

ter from upstream stopped flowing. It piled up in a heap a great distance away, at a town called Adam in the vicinity of Zarethan, while the water flowing down to the Sea of the Arabah (that is, the Dead Sea) was completely cut off. So the people crossed over opposite Jericho. ¹⁷The priests who carried the ark of the covenant of the LORD stopped in the middle of the Jordan and stood on dry ground, while all Israel passed by until the whole nation had completed the crossing on dry ground.

**4** When the whole nation had finished crossing the Jordan, the LORD said to Joshua, ²"Choose twelve men from among the people, one from each tribe, ³and tell them to take up twelve stones from the middle of the Jordan, from right where the priests are standing, and carry them over with you and put them down at the place where you stay tonight."

⁴So Joshua called together the twelve men he had appointed from the Israelites, one from each tribe, ⁵and said to them, "Go over before the ark of the LORD your God into the middle of the Jordan. Each of you is to take up a stone on his shoulder, according to the number of the tribes of the Israelites, ⁶to serve as a sign among you. In the future, when your children ask you, 'What do these stones mean?' ⁷tell them that the flow of the Jordan was cut off before the ark of the covenant of the LORD. When it crossed the Jordan, the waters of the Jordan were cut off. These stones are to be a memorial to the people of Israel forever."

⁸So the Israelites did as Joshua commanded them. They took twelve stones from the middle of the Jordan, according to the number of the tribes of the Israelites, as the LORD had told Joshua; and they carried them over with them to their camp, where they put them down. ⁹Joshua set up the twelve stones that had been*ᵃ* in the middle of the Jordan at the spot where the priests who carried the ark of the covenant had stood. And they are there to this day.

¹⁰Now the priests who carried the ark remained standing in the middle of the Jordan until everything the LORD had commanded Joshua was done by the people, just as Moses had directed Joshua. The people hurried over, ¹¹and as soon as all of them had crossed, the ark of the LORD and the priests came to the other side while the people watched. ¹²The men of Reuben, Gad and the half-tribe of Manasseh crossed over, ready for battle, in front of the Israelites, as Moses had directed them. ¹³About forty thousand armed for battle crossed over before the LORD to the plains of Jericho for war.

¹⁴That day the LORD exalted Joshua in the sight of all Israel; and they stood in awe of him all the days of his life, just as they had stood in awe of Moses.

¹⁵Then the LORD said to Joshua, ¹⁶"Command the priests carrying the ark of the covenant law to come up out of the Jordan."

*ᵃ 9 Or Joshua also set up twelve stones*

## Amplified Bible

¹⁶Then the ᵃwaters which came down from above stood and rose up in a heap far off, at Adam, the city that is beside Zarethan; and those flowing down toward the Sea of the Arabah, the Salt [Dead] Sea, were wholly cut off. And the people passed over opposite Jericho. [Ps. 114.]

¹⁷And while all Israel passed over on dry ground, the priests who bore the ark of the covenant of the Lord stood firm on dry ground in the midst of the Jordan, until all the nation finished passing over the Jordan.

**4** When all the nation had fully passed over the Jordan, the Lord said to Joshua,

²Take twelve men from among the people, one man out of every tribe,

³And command them, Take twelve stones out of the midst of the Jordan from the place where the priests' feet stood firm; carry them over with you and leave them at the place where you lodge tonight.

⁴Then Joshua called the twelve men of the Israelites whom he had appointed, a man from each tribe.

⁵And Joshua said to them, Pass over before the ark of the Lord your God in the midst of the Jordan, and take up every man of you a stone on his shoulder, as is the number of the tribes of the Israelites,

⁶That this may be a sign among you when your children ask in time to come, What do these stones mean to you?

⁷Then you shall tell them that the waters of the Jordan were cut off before the ark of the covenant of the Lord; when it passed over the Jordan, the waters of Jordan were cut off. So these stones shall be to the Israelites a memorial forever.

⁸And the Israelites did as Joshua commanded, and took up twelve stones out of the midst of the Jordan, according to the number of the tribes of the Israelites, as the Lord told Joshua, and carried them over with them to the place where they lodged and laid them down there.

⁹And Joshua set up twelve stones in the midst of the Jordan in the place where the feet of the priests bearing the ark of the covenant had stood. And they are there to this day.

¹⁰For the priests who bore the ark stood in the midst of the Jordan until everything was finished that the Lord commanded Joshua to tell the people, according to all that Moses had commanded Joshua. The people passed over in haste.

¹¹When all the people had passed over, the ark of the Lord and the priests went over in the presence of the people.

¹²And the sons of Reuben, Gad, and half the tribe of Manasseh passed over armed before the [other] Israelites, as Moses had bidden them;

¹³About 40,000 [of these] prepared for war passed over before the Lord to the plains of Jericho for battle.

¹⁴On that day the Lord magnified Joshua in the sight of all Israel; and they stood in awe of him, as they stood in awe of Moses, all the days of his life.

¹⁵And the Lord said to Joshua,

¹⁶Order the priests bearing the ark of the Testimony to come up out of the Jordan.

ᵃ The city of Adam has been placed 16 miles up the river from Jericho, and it seems probable that a stretch of 20 or 30 miles of the riverbed was left dry. An interesting parallel of the event here recorded has been found in the pages of an Arabic historian telling how in A.D. 1266, near a place many experts have identified with Adam, the bed of the [Jordan] river was left dry for ten hours as the result of a landslide. John Garstang (*The Story of Jericho*) cites other parallels. But to accept this "natural" explanation of what happened centuries earlier does not detract in any way from the supernatural intervention which opened the way to Israel just at the moment when they needed to cross. The sight of the priests standing in the dry bed of the river as the whole nation passed over was the sign (Josh. 3:10) that this was the doing of the Lord (F. Davidson, ed., *The New Bible Commentary*).

## New International Version

¹⁷So Joshua commanded the priests, "Come up out of the Jordan."

¹⁸And the priests came up out of the river carrying the ark of the covenant of the LORD. No sooner had they set their feet on the dry ground than the waters of the Jordan returned to their place and ran at flood stage as before.

¹⁹On the tenth day of the first month the people went up from the Jordan and camped at Gilgal on the eastern border of Jericho. ²⁰And Joshua set up at Gilgal the twelve stones they had taken out of the Jordan. ²¹He said to the Israelites, "In the future when your descendants ask their parents, 'What do these stones mean?' ²²tell them, 'Israel crossed the Jordan on dry ground.' ²³For the LORD your God dried up the Jordan before you until you had crossed over. The LORD your God did to the Jordan what he had done to the Red Sea<sup>a</sup> when he dried it up before us until we had crossed over. ²⁴He did this so that all the peoples of the earth might know that the hand of the LORD is powerful and so that you might always fear the LORD your God."

**5** Now when all the Amorite kings west of the Jordan and all the Canaanite kings along the coast heard how the LORD had dried up the Jordan before the Israelites until they<sup>b</sup> had crossed over, their hearts melted in fear and they no longer had the courage to face the Israelites.

### Circumcision and Passover at Gilgal

²At that time the LORD said to Joshua, "Make flint knives and circumcise the Israelites again." ³So Joshua made flint knives and circumcised the Israelites at Gibeath Haaraloth.<sup>c</sup>

⁴Now this is why he did so: All those who came out of Egypt—all the men of military age—died in the wilderness on the way after leaving Egypt. ⁵All the people that came out had been circumcised, but all the people born in the wilderness during the journey from Egypt had not. ⁶The Israelites had moved about in the wilderness forty years until all the men who were of military age when they left Egypt had died, since they had not obeyed the LORD. For the LORD had sworn to them that they would not see the land he had solemnly promised their ancestors to give us, a land flowing with milk and honey. ⁷So he raised up their sons in their place, and these were the ones Joshua circumcised. They were still uncircumcised because they had not been circumcised on the way. ⁸And after the whole nation had been circumcised, they remained where they were in camp until they were healed.

⁹Then the LORD said to Joshua, "Today I have rolled away the reproach of Egypt from you." So the place has been called Gilgal<sup>d</sup> to this day.

¹⁰On the evening of the fourteenth day of the month, while camped at Gilgal on the plains of Jericho, the Israelites celebrated the Passover. ¹¹The day after the Passover, that very day, they ate some of the produce of the land: unleavened bread and roasted grain. ¹²The manna stopped the day after<sup>e</sup> they ate this food from the land; there was no longer any manna for the Israelites, but that year they ate the produce of Canaan.

## Amplified Bible

¹⁷So Joshua commanded the priests, Come up out of the Jordan.

¹⁸And when the priests who bore the ark of the covenant of the Lord had come up out of the midst of the Jordan, and the soles of their feet were lifted up to the dry land, the waters of the Jordan returned to their place and flowed over all its banks as they had before.

¹⁹And the people came up out of the Jordan on the tenth day of the first month and encamped in Gilgal on the east border of Jericho.

²⁰And those twelve stones which they took out of the Jordan Joshua set up in Gilgal.

²¹And he said to the Israelites, When your children ask their fathers in time to come, What do these stones mean?

²²You shall let your children know, Israel came over this Jordan on dry ground.

²³For the Lord your God dried up the waters of the Jordan for you until you passed over, as the Lord your God did to the Red Sea, which He dried up for us until we passed over,

²⁴That all the peoples of the earth may know that the hand of the Lord is mighty and that you may reverence *and* fear the Lord your God forever.

**5** When all the kings of the Amorites who were beyond the Jordan to the west and all the kings of the Canaanites who were by the sea heard that the Lord had dried up the waters of the Jordan before the Israelites until we had crossed over, their hearts melted and there was no spirit in them any more because of the Israelites.

²At that time the Lord said to Joshua, Make knives of flint and circumcise the [new generation of] Israelites as before.

³So Joshua made knives of flint and circumcised the sons of Israel at Gibeath-haaraloth.

⁴And this is the reason Joshua circumcised them: all the males of the people who came out of Egypt, all the men of war, had died in the wilderness on the way after they came out of Egypt.

⁵Though all the people who came out were circumcised, yet all the people who were born in the wilderness on the way after Israel came out of Egypt had not been circumcised.

⁶For the Israelites walked forty years in the wilderness till all who were men of war who came out of Egypt perished, because they did not hearken to the voice of the Lord; to them the Lord swore that He would not let them see the land which the Lord swore to their fathers to give us, a land flowing with milk and honey.

⁷So it was their uncircumcised children whom He raised up in their stead whom Joshua circumcised, because the rite had not been performed on the way.

⁸When they finished circumcising all the males of the nation, they remained in their places in the camp till they were healed.

⁹And the Lord said to Joshua, This day have I rolled away the reproach of Egypt from you. So the name of the place is called Gilgal [rolling] to this day.

¹⁰And the Israelites encamped in Gilgal; and they kept the Passover on the fourteenth day of the month at evening in the plains of Jericho.

¹¹And on that same day they ate the produce of the land: unleavened cakes and parched grain.

¹²And the manna ceased on the day after they ate of the produce of the land; and the Israelites had manna no more, but they ate of the fruit of the land of Canaan that year.

---

<sup>a</sup> 23 Or *the Sea of Reeds*    <sup>b</sup> 1 Another textual tradition *we*
<sup>c</sup> 3 *Gibeath Haaraloth* means *the hill of foreskins.*    <sup>d</sup> 9 *Gilgal* sounds like the Hebrew for *roll.*    <sup>e</sup> 12 Or *the day*

# New International Version

## The Fall of Jericho

¹³Now when Joshua was near Jericho, he looked up and saw a man standing in front of him with a drawn sword in his hand. Joshua went up to him and asked, "Are you for us or for our enemies?"

¹⁴"Neither," he replied, "but as commander of the army of the LORD I have now come." Then Joshua fell facedown to the ground in reverence, and asked him, "What message does my Lord*a* have for his servant?"

¹⁵The commander of the LORD's army replied, "Take off your sandals, for the place where you are standing is holy." And Joshua did so.

**6** Now the gates of Jericho were securely barred because of the Israelites. No one went out and no one came in.

²Then the LORD said to Joshua, "See, I have delivered Jericho into your hands, along with its king and its fighting men. ³March around the city once with all the armed men. Do this for six days. ⁴Have seven priests carry trumpets of rams' horns in front of the ark. On the seventh day, march around the city seven times, with the priests blowing the trumpets. ⁵When you hear them sound a long blast on the trumpets, have the whole army give a loud shout; then the wall of the city will collapse and the army will go up, everyone straight in."

⁶So Joshua son of Nun called the priests and said to them, "Take up the ark of the covenant of the LORD and have seven priests carry trumpets in front of it." ⁷And he ordered the army, "Advance! March around the city, with an armed guard going ahead of the ark of the LORD."

⁸When Joshua had spoken to the people, the seven priests carrying the seven trumpets before the LORD went forward, blowing their trumpets, and the ark of the LORD's covenant followed them. ⁹The armed guard marched ahead of the priests who blew the trumpets, and the rear guard followed the ark. All this time the trumpets were sounding. ¹⁰But Joshua had commanded the army, "Do not give a war cry, do not raise your voices, do not say a word until the day I tell you to shout. Then shout!" ¹¹So he had the ark of the LORD carried around the city, circling it once. Then the army returned to camp and spent the night there.

¹²Joshua got up early the next morning and the priests took up the ark of the LORD. ¹³The seven priests carrying the seven trumpets went forward, marching before the ark of the LORD and blowing the trumpets. The armed men went ahead of them and the rear guard followed the ark of the LORD, while the trumpets kept sounding. ¹⁴So on the second day they marched around the city once and returned to the camp. They did this for six days.

¹⁵On the seventh day, they got up at daybreak and

# Amplified Bible

¹³When Joshua was by Jericho, he looked up, and behold, a Man stood near him with His drawn sword in His hand. And Joshua went to Him and said to Him, Are you for us or for our adversaries?

¹⁴And He said, No [neither], but as Prince of the Lord's host have I now come. And Joshua fell on his face to the earth and worshiped, and said to Him, What says my Lord to His servant?

¹⁵And the Prince of the Lord's host said to Joshua, *a*Loose your shoes from off your feet, for the place where you stand is holy. And Joshua did so. [Exod. 3:5.]

**6** Now Jericho [a fenced town with high walls] was tightly closed because of the Israelites; no one went out or came in.

²And the Lord said to Joshua, See, I have given Jericho, its king and mighty men of valor, into your hands.

³You shall march around the enclosure, all the men of war going around the city once. This you shall do for six days.

⁴And seven priests shall bear before the ark seven trumpets of rams' horns; and on the seventh day you shall march around the enclosure seven times, and the priests shall blow the trumpets.

⁵When they make a long blast with the ram's horn and you hear the sound of the trumpet, all the people shall shout with a great shout; and the wall of the enclosure shall fall down in its place and the people shall go up [over it], every man straight before him.

⁶So Joshua son of Nun called the priests and said to them, Take up the ark of the covenant and let seven priests bear seven trumpets of rams' horns before the ark of the Lord.

⁷He said to the people, Go on! March around the enclosure, and let the armed men pass on before the ark of the Lord.

⁸When Joshua had spoken to the people, the seven priests bearing the seven trumpets of rams' horns passed on before the Lord and blew the trumpets, and the ark of the covenant of the Lord followed them.

⁹The armed men went before the priests who blew the trumpets, and the rear guard came after the ark, the priests blowing the trumpets as they went.

¹⁰But Joshua commanded the people, You shall not shout or let your voice be heard, nor shall any word proceed out of your mouth until the day I tell you to shout. Then you shall shout!

¹¹So he caused the ark of the Lord to go around the city once; and they came into the camp and lodged in the camp.

¹²Joshua rose early in the morning and the priests took up the ark of the Lord.

¹³And the seven priests bearing the seven trumpets of rams' horns before the ark of the Lord passed on, blowing the trumpets continually; and the armed men went before them and the rear guard came after the ark of the Lord, the priests blowing the trumpets as they went.

¹⁴On the second day they compassed the city enclosure once and returned to the camp. So they did for six days.

¹⁵On the seventh day they rose early at daybreak and

---

*a* "The real character of this personage was disclosed by His accepting the homage of worship (cf. Acts 10:25, 26; Rev. 19:10), and still further in the command, 'Loose thy shoe from off thy foot' " (KJV) (Robert Jamieson, A. R. Fausset and David Brown, *A Commentary*). *The New Bible Commentary* supports this position (as do J. P. Lange, *The Cambridge Bible,* Charles Ellicott, and many others) when it says, "We believe that this was the Son of God Himself."

*a* 14 Or *lord*

## New International Version

marched around the city seven times in the same manner, except that on that day they circled the city seven times. ¹⁶The seventh time around, when the priests sounded the trumpet blast, Joshua commanded the army, "Shout! For the LORD has given you the city! ¹⁷The city and all that is in it are to be devoted[a] to the LORD. Only Rahab the prostitute and all who are with her in her house shall be spared, because she hid the spies we sent. ¹⁸But keep away from the devoted things, so that you will not bring about your own destruction by taking any of them. Otherwise you will make the camp of Israel liable to destruction and bring trouble on it. ¹⁹All the silver and gold and the articles of bronze and iron are sacred to the LORD and must go into his treasury."

²⁰When the trumpets sounded, the army shouted, and at the sound of the trumpet, when the men gave a loud shout, the wall collapsed; so everyone charged straight in, and they took the city. ²¹They devoted the city to the LORD and destroyed with the sword every living thing in it—men and women, young and old, cattle, sheep and donkeys.

²²Joshua said to the two men who had spied out the land, "Go into the prostitute's house and bring her out and all who belong to her, in accordance with your oath to her." ²³So the young men who had done the spying went in and brought out Rahab, her father and mother, her brothers and sisters and all who belonged to her. They brought out her entire family and put them in a place outside the camp of Israel.

²⁴Then they burned the whole city and everything in it, but they put the silver and gold and the articles of bronze and iron into the treasury of the LORD's house. ²⁵But Joshua spared Rahab the prostitute, with her family and all who belonged to her, because she hid the men Joshua had sent as spies to Jericho—and she lives among the Israelites to this day.

²⁶At that time Joshua pronounced this solemn oath: "Cursed before the LORD is the one who undertakes to rebuild this city, Jericho:

"At the cost of his firstborn son
  he will lay its foundations;
at the cost of his youngest
  he will set up its gates."

²⁷So the LORD was with Joshua, and his fame spread throughout the land.

## Amplified Bible

marched around the city as usual, only on that day they compassed the city [a] seven times.

¹⁶And the seventh time, when the priests had blown the trumpets, Joshua said to the people, Shout! For the Lord has given you the city.

¹⁷And the city and all that is in it shall be devoted to the Lord [for destruction]; only Rahab the harlot and all who are with her in her house shall live, because she hid the messengers whom we sent.

¹⁸But you, keep yourselves from the accursed *and* devoted things, lest when you have devoted it [to destruction], you take of the accursed thing, and so make the camp of Israel accursed and trouble it.

¹⁹But all the silver and gold and vessels of bronze and iron are consecrated to the Lord; they shall come into the treasury of the Lord.

²⁰So the people shouted, and the trumpets were blown. When the people heard the sound of the trumpet, they raised a great shout, and [Jericho's] wall fell down in its place, so that the [Israelites] went up into the city, every man straight before him, and they took the city.

²¹Then they utterly destroyed all that was in the city, both man and woman, young and old, ox, sheep, and donkey, with the edge of the sword.

²²But Joshua said to the two men who had spied out the land, Go into the harlot's house and bring out the woman and all she has, as you swore to her.

²³So the young men, the spies, went in and brought out Rahab, her father and mother, her brethren, and all that she had; and they brought out all her kindred and set them outside the camp of Israel.

²⁴And they [b] burned the city with fire and all that was in it; only the silver, the gold, and the vessels of bronze and of iron they put into the treasury of the house of the Lord.

²⁵So Joshua saved Rahab the harlot, with her father's household and all that she had; and she lives in Israel even to this day, because she hid the messengers whom Joshua sent to spy out Jericho.

²⁶Then Joshua laid this oath on them, Cursed is the man before the Lord who rises up and rebuilds this city, Jericho. With the loss of his firstborn shall he lay its foundation, and with the loss of his youngest son shall he set up its gates. [I Kings 16:34.]

²⁷So the Lord was with Joshua, and his fame was in all the land.

*a* Any walled town was called a "city" and its headman was called "a king" in ancient times, but the fact that Joshua's army could march around the whole of Jericho seven times in one day shows that it was a very small place. Sir Charles Marston (*New Bible Evidence*) echoes the reports of other archaeologists when he says that the excavations of ancient Jericho do not confirm the conceptions of our youth. Though the walls were so formidable, the area they enclosed only measures seven acres. The whole circumference of the city was about 650 yards. Our disappointment is somewhat modified by the fact that Jebusite Jerusalem, which David captured, was about the same size. Schliemann experienced a similar disillusionment in 1873 when he excavated the city of Troy, which Homer tells us so long withstood the Grecian hosts. Indeed it would almost seem that these ancient cities were more in the nature of places of refuge resorted to when an enemy approached. Under peaceful conditions a large proportion of the inhabitants would dwell outside the city's walls (Sir Charles Marston, *New Bible Evidence*). *b* Important details of this story are fully substantiated by the findings of Dr. J. B. Garstang in his several excavations of Jericho: 1. The city was thoroughly burned by fire. 2. It had not been thoroughly plundered. Stored grain, for example, was found burned but undisturbed. 3. The "silver, the gold, and the vessels of bronze and of iron" were missing. 4. The walls had fallen, but the one gate had a tower left standing. 5. Well-supported houses had been built on the walls. 6. The gate tower was "an imposing edifice," 54 ft. by 24 ft., remarkably well built of gray brick. Its ruins still stand 16 ft. high. 7. Only on one side of Jericho is there a mountain, and that is a mountain ridge beginning a mile west of the city (John Garstang, *The Story of Jericho*, Joseph P. Free, *Archaeology and Bible History*, and other sources).

*a 17* The Hebrew term refers to the irrevocable giving over of things or persons to the LORD, often by totally destroying them; also in verses 18 and 21.

## New International Version

### Achan's Sin

**7** But the Israelites were unfaithful in regard to the devoted things[a]; Achan son of Karmi, the son of Zimri,[b] the son of Zerah, of the tribe of Judah, took some of them. So the LORD's anger burned against Israel.

[2] Now Joshua sent men from Jericho to Ai, which is near Beth Aven to the east of Bethel, and told them, "Go up and spy out the region." So the men went up and spied out Ai. [3] When they returned to Joshua, they said, "Not all the army will have to go up against Ai. Send two or three thousand men to take it and do not weary the whole army, for only a few people live there." [4] So about three thousand went up; but they were routed by the men of Ai, [5] who killed about thirty-six of them. They chased the Israelites from the city gate as far as the stone quarries and struck them down on the slopes. At this the hearts of the people melted in fear and became like water.

[6] Then Joshua tore his clothes and fell facedown to the ground before the ark of the LORD, remaining there till evening. The elders of Israel did the same, and sprinkled dust on their heads. [7] And Joshua said, "Alas, Sovereign LORD, why did you ever bring this people across the Jordan to deliver us into the hands of the Amorites to destroy us? If only we had been content to stay on the other side of the Jordan! [8] Pardon your servant, Lord. What can I say, now that Israel has been routed by its enemies? [9] The Canaanites and the other people of the country will hear about this and they will surround us and wipe out our name from the earth. What then will you do for your own great name?"

[10] The LORD said to Joshua, "Stand up! What are you doing down on your face? [11] Israel has sinned; they have violated my covenant, which I commanded them to keep. They have taken some of the devoted things; they have stolen, they have lied, they have put them with their own possessions. [12] That is why the Israelites cannot stand against their enemies; they turn their backs and run because they have been made liable to destruction. I will not be with you anymore unless you destroy whatever among you is devoted to destruction.

[13] "Go, consecrate the people. Tell them, 'Consecrate yourselves in preparation for tomorrow; for this is what the LORD, the God of Israel, says: There are devoted things among you, Israel. You cannot stand against your enemies until you remove them.

[14] "'In the morning, present yourselves tribe by tribe. The tribe the LORD chooses shall come forward clan by clan; the clan the LORD chooses shall come forward family by family; and the family the LORD chooses shall come forward man by man. [15] Whoever is caught with the devoted things shall be destroyed by fire, along with all that belongs to him. He has violated the covenant of the LORD and has done an outrageous thing in Israel!'"

[16] Early the next morning Joshua had Israel come forward by tribes, and Judah was chosen. [17] The clans of Judah came forward, and the Zerahites were chosen. He had the clan of the Zerahites come forward by families, and Zimri was chosen. [18] Joshua had his family come forward man by man, and Achan son of Karmi, the son of Zimri, the son of Zerah, of the tribe of Judah, was chosen.

## Amplified Bible

**7** But the Israelites committed a trespass in regard to the devoted things; for Achan son of Carmi, the son of Zabdi, the son of Zerah, of the tribe of Judah, took some of the things devoted [for destruction]. And the anger of the Lord burned against Israel.

[2] Joshua sent men from Jericho to Ai, which is near Beth-aven, east of Bethel, and said to them, Go up and spy out the land. So the men went up and spied out Ai. [3] And they returned to Joshua and said to him, Let not all the men go up; but let about two thousand or three thousand go up and attack Ai; do not make the whole army toil up there, for they of Ai are few.

[4] So about three thousand Israelites went up there, but they fled before the men of Ai.

[5] And the men of Ai killed about thirty-six of them, for they chased them from before the gate as far as Shebarim, and slew them at the descent. And the hearts of the people melted and became as water.

[6] Then Joshua rent his clothes and lay on the earth upon his face before the ark of the Lord until evening, he and the elders of Israel; and they put dust on their heads. [7] Joshua said, Alas, O Lord God, why have You brought this people over the Jordan at all only to give us into the hands of the Amorites to destroy us? Would that we had been content to dwell beyond the Jordan!

[8] O Lord, what can I say, now that Israel has turned to flee before their enemies! [9] For the Canaanites and all the inhabitants of the land will hear of it and will surround us and cut off our name from the earth. And what will You do for Your great name? [10] The Lord said to Joshua, Get up! Why do you lie thus upon your face?

[11] Israel has sinned; they have transgressed My covenant which I commanded them. They have taken some of the things devoted [for destruction]; they have stolen, and lied, and put them among their own baggage.

[12] That is why the Israelites could not stand before their enemies, but fled before them; they are accursed *and* have become devoted [for destruction]. I will cease to be with you unless you destroy the accursed [devoted] things among you.

[13] Up, sanctify (set apart for a holy purpose) the people, and say, Sanctify yourselves for tomorrow; for thus says the Lord, the God of Israel: There are accursed things in the midst of you, O Israel. You can not stand before your enemies until you take away from among you the things devoted [to destruction].

[14] In the morning therefore, you shall present your tribes. And the tribe which the Lord takes shall come by families; and the family which the Lord takes shall come by households; and the household which the Lord takes shall come by persons.

[15] And he who is taken with the devoted things shall be [killed and his body] burned with fire, he and all he has, because he has transgressed the covenant of the Lord and because he has done a shameful *and* wicked thing in Israel. [Josh. 7:25.]

[16] So Joshua rose up early in the morning and brought Israel near by their tribes, and the tribe of Judah was taken.

[17] He brought near the family of Judah, and the family of the Zerahites was taken; and he brought near the family of the Zerahites man by man, and Zabdi was taken.

[18] He brought near his household man by man, and Achan son of Carmi, the son of Zabdi, the son of Zerah, of the tribe of Judah, was taken.

---

[a] 1 The Hebrew term refers to the irrevocable giving over of things or persons to the LORD, often by totally destroying them; also in verses 11, 12, 13 and 15.   [b] 1 See Septuagint and 1 Chron. 2:6; Hebrew *Zabdi*; also in verses 17 and 18.

## New International Version

19Then Joshua said to Achan, "My son, give glory to the LORD, the God of Israel, and honor him. Tell me what you have done; do not hide it from me."

20Achan replied, "It is true! I have sinned against the LORD, the God of Israel. This is what I have done: 21When I saw in the plunder a beautiful robe from Babylonia,*a* two hundred shekels*b* of silver and a bar of gold weighing fifty shekels,*c* I coveted them and took them. They are hidden in the ground inside my tent, with the silver underneath."

22So Joshua sent messengers, and they ran to the tent, and there it was, hidden in his tent, with the silver underneath. 23They took the things from the tent, brought them to Joshua and all the Israelites and spread them out before the LORD.

24Then Joshua, together with all Israel, took Achan son of Zerah, the silver, the robe, the gold bar, his sons and daughters, his cattle, donkeys and sheep, his tent and all that he had, to the Valley of Achor. 25Joshua said, "Why have you brought this trouble on us? The LORD will bring trouble on you today."

Then all Israel stoned him, and after they had stoned the rest, they burned them. 26Over Achan they heaped up a large pile of rocks, which remains to this day. Then the LORD turned from his fierce anger. Therefore that place has been called the Valley of Achor*d* ever since.

### Ai Destroyed

**8** Then the LORD said to Joshua, "Do not be afraid; do not be discouraged. Take the whole army with you, and go up and attack Ai. For I have delivered into your hands the king of Ai, his people, his city and his land. 2You shall do to Ai and its king as you did to Jericho and its king, except that you may carry off their plunder and livestock for yourselves. Set an ambush behind the city."

3So Joshua and the whole army moved out to attack Ai. He chose thirty thousand of his best fighting men and sent them out at night 4with these orders: "Listen carefully. You are to set an ambush behind the city. Don't go very far from it. All of you be on the alert. 5I and all those with me will advance on the city, and when the men come out against us, as they did before, we will flee from them. 6They will pursue us until we have lured them away from the city, for they will say, 'They are running away from us as they did before.' So when we flee from them, 7you are to rise up from ambush and take the city. The LORD your God will give it into your hand. 8When you have taken the city, set it on fire. Do what the LORD has commanded. See to it; you have my orders."

9Then Joshua sent them off, and they went to the place of ambush and lay in wait between Bethel and Ai, to the west of Ai—but Joshua spent that night with the people.

10Early the next morning Joshua mustered his army, and he and the leaders of Israel marched before them to Ai. 11The entire force that was with him marched up and approached the city and arrived in front of it. They set up camp north of Ai, with the valley between them and the

## Amplified Bible

19And Joshua said to Achan, My son, give glory to the Lord, the God of Israel, and make confession to Him. And tell me now what you have done; do not hide it from me.

20And Achan answered Joshua, In truth, I have sinned against the Lord, the God of Israel, and this have I done:

21When I saw among the spoils an attractive mantle from Shinar and two hundred shekels of silver and a bar of gold weighing fifty shekels, I coveted them and took them. Behold, they are hidden in the earth inside my tent, with the silver underneath.

22So Joshua sent messengers, who ran to the tent, and behold, the spoil was hidden in his tent, with the silver underneath.

23And they took them from the tent and brought them to Joshua and all the Israelites and laid them out before the Lord.

24And Joshua and all Israel with him took Achan son of Zerah, and the silver, the garment, the wedge of gold, his sons, his daughters, his oxen, his donkeys, his sheep, his tent, and all that he had; and they brought them to the Valley of Achor.

25And Joshua said, Why have you brought trouble on us? The Lord will trouble you this day. And all Israel stoned him and those with him with stones, and afterward burned their bodies with fire.

26And they raised over him a great heap of stones that remains to this day. Then the Lord turned from the fierceness of His anger. Therefore the name of that place has been called the Valley of Achor *or* Troubling to this day.

**8** And the Lord said to Joshua, Fear not nor be dismayed. Take all the men of war with you, and arise, go up to Ai; see, I have given into your hand the king of Ai, his people, his city, and his land.

2And you shall do to Ai and its king as you did to Jericho and its king, except that its spoil and its cattle [this time] you shall take as booty for yourselves. Lay an ambush against the city behind it.

3So Joshua arose, and all the people of war, to go up against Ai; [he] chose thirty thousand mighty men of strength and sent them forth by night.

4And he commanded them, Behold, you shall lie in wait against the city behind it. Do not go very far from the city, but all of you be ready.

5And I and all the people who are with me will approach the city. And when they come out against us, as the first time, we will flee before them

6Till we have drawn them from the city, for they will say, They are fleeing from us as before. So we will flee before them.

7Then you shall rise up from the ambush and seize the city, for the Lord your God will deliver it into your hand.

8When you have taken the city, you shall set it afire; as the Lord commanded, you shall do. See, I have commanded you.

9So Joshua sent them forth, and they went to the place of ambush and remained between Bethel and Ai, on the west side of Ai; but Joshua lodged that night among the people.

10Joshua rose up early in the morning and mustered the men, and went up with the elders of Israel before the warriors to Ai.

11And all the fighting men who were with him went up and drew near before the city and encamped on the north side of [it], with a ravine between them and Ai.

---

*a 21* Hebrew *Shinar*   *b 21* That is, about 5 pounds or about 2.3 kilograms   *c 21* That is, about 1 1/4 pounds or about 575 grams   *d 26 Achor* means *trouble.*

## New International Version

city. [12]Joshua had taken about five thousand men and set them in ambush between Bethel and Ai, to the west of the city. [13]So the soldiers took up their positions—with the main camp to the north of the city and the ambush to the west of it. That night Joshua went into the valley.

[14]When the king of Ai saw this, he and all the men of the city hurried out early in the morning to meet Israel in battle at a certain place overlooking the Arabah. But he did not know that an ambush had been set against him behind the city. [15]Joshua and all Israel let themselves be driven back before them, and they fled toward the wilderness. [16]All the men of Ai were called to pursue them, and they pursued Joshua and were lured away from the city. [17]Not a man remained in Ai or Bethel who did not go after Israel. They left the city open and went in pursuit of Israel.

[18]Then the LORD said to Joshua, "Hold out toward Ai the javelin that is in your hand, for into your hand I will deliver the city." So Joshua held out toward the city the javelin that was in his hand. [19]As soon as he did this, the men in the ambush rose quickly from their position and rushed forward. They entered the city and captured it and quickly set it on fire.

[20]The men of Ai looked back and saw the smoke of the city rising up into the sky, but they had no chance to escape in any direction; the Israelites who had been fleeing toward the wilderness had turned back against their pursuers. [21]For when Joshua and all Israel saw that the ambush had taken the city and that smoke was going up from it, they turned around and attacked the men of Ai. [22]Those in the ambush also came out of the city against them, so that they were caught in the middle, with Israelites on both sides. Israel cut them down, leaving them neither survivors nor fugitives. [23]But they took the king of Ai alive and brought him to Joshua.

[24]When Israel had finished killing all the men of Ai in the fields and in the wilderness where they had chased them, and when every one of them had been put to the sword, all the Israelites returned to Ai and killed those who were in it. [25]Twelve thousand men and women fell that day—all the people of Ai. [26]For Joshua did not draw back the hand that held out his javelin until he had destroyed[a] all who lived in Ai. [27]But Israel did carry off for themselves the livestock and plunder of this city, as the LORD had instructed Joshua.

[28]So Joshua burned Ai[b] and made it a permanent heap of ruins, a desolate place to this day. [29]He impaled the body of the king of Ai on a pole and left it there until evening. At sunset, Joshua ordered them to take the body from the pole and throw it down at the entrance of the city gate. And they raised a large pile of rocks over it, which remains to this day.

### The Covenant Renewed at Mount Ebal

[30]Then Joshua built on Mount Ebal an altar to the LORD, the God of Israel, [31]as Moses the servant of the LORD had commanded the Israelites. He built it according to what is written in the Book of the Law of Moses—an altar of uncut stones, on which no iron tool had been used. On it they offered to the LORD burnt offerings and sacrificed fellow-

## Amplified Bible

[12]And he took about five thousand men and set them in ambush between Bethel and Ai, west of the city. [13]So they stationed all the army—the main encampment that was north of the city and their men in ambush behind *and* on the west of the city—and Joshua went that night into the midst of the ravine.

[14]When the king [and people] of Ai saw it, they hastily rose early, and the men of the city went out against Israel to battle [at a time and place appointed] before the Arabah [plain]. But he did not know of the ambush against him behind the city.

[15]And Joshua and all Israel pretended to be beaten by them, and fled toward the wilderness.

[16]So all the people in Ai were called together to pursue them, and they pursued Joshua and were drawn away from the city.

[17]Not a man was left in Ai or Bethel who did not go out after Israel. Leaving the city open, they pursued Israel.

[18]Then the Lord said to Joshua, Stretch out the javelin that is in your hand toward Ai, for I will give it into your hand. So Joshua stretched out the javelin in his hand toward the city.

[19]The men in the ambush arose quickly out of their place and ran when he stretched out his hand; and they entered the city and took it, and then hastened and set it afire.

[20]When the men of Ai looked back, behold, the smoke of the city went up to the heavens, and they had no power to flee this way or that way. Then the Israelites who fled to the wilderness turned back upon the pursuers.

[21]When Joshua and all Israel saw that the ambush had taken the city and that the smoke of the city went up, they turned again and slew the men of Ai.

[22]And the others came forth out of the city against them [of Ai], so that they were in the midst of Israel, some on this side and some on that side. And [the Israelites] smote them, so that they let none of them remain or escape.

[23]But they took the king of Ai alive and brought him to Joshua.

[24]When Israel had finished slaying all the inhabitants of Ai in the field and in the wilderness into which they pursued them, and they were all fallen by the sword until they were consumed, then all the Israelites returned to Ai and smote it with the sword.

[25]And all that fell that day, both men and women, were twelve thousand, including all the men of Ai.

[26]For Joshua drew not back his hand with which he stretched out the javelin until he had utterly destroyed all the inhabitants of Ai.

[27]Only the livestock and the spoil of that city Israel took as booty for themselves, according to the word of the Lord which He commanded Joshua.

[28]So Joshua burned Ai and made it a heap of ruins for ever, even a desolation to this day.

[29]And he hanged the king of Ai on a tree until evening; and at sunset, Joshua commanded and they took the body down from the tree and cast it at the entrance of the city gate and raised a great heap of stones over it that is there to this day.

[30]Then Joshua built an altar to the Lord, the God of Israel, on Mount Ebal,

[31]As Moses the servant of the Lord commanded the Israelites, as it is written in the Book of the Law of Moses, an altar of unhewn stones, upon which no man has lifted up an iron tool; and they offered on it burnt offerings to the Lord and sacrificed peace offerings.

---

[a] 26 The Hebrew term refers to the irrevocable giving over of things or persons to the LORD, often by totally destroying them. [b] 28 *Ai* means *the ruin.*

## New International Version

ship offerings. [32]There, in the presence of the Israelites, Joshua wrote on stones a copy of the law of Moses. [33]All the Israelites, with their elders, officials and judges, were standing on both sides of the ark of the covenant of the LORD, facing the Levitical priests who carried it. Both the foreigners living among them and the native-born were there. Half of the people stood in front of Mount Gerizim and half of them in front of Mount Ebal, as Moses the servant of the LORD had formerly commanded when he gave instructions to bless the people of Israel.

[34]Afterward, Joshua read all the words of the law—the blessings and the curses—just as it is written in the Book of the Law. [35]There was not a word of all that Moses had commanded that Joshua did not read to the whole assembly of Israel, including the women and children, and the foreigners who lived among them.

### The Gibeonite Deception

**9** Now when all the kings west of the Jordan heard about these things—the kings in the hill country, in the western foothills, and along the entire coast of the Mediterranean Sea as far as Lebanon (the kings of the Hittites, Amorites, Canaanites, Perizzites, Hivites and Jebusites) — [2]they came together to wage war against Joshua and Israel.

[3]However, when the people of Gibeon heard what Joshua had done to Jericho and Ai, [4]they resorted to a ruse: They went as a delegation whose donkeys were loaded[a] with worn-out sacks and old wineskins, cracked and mended. [5]They put worn and patched sandals on their feet and wore old clothes. All the bread of their food supply was dry and moldy. [6]Then they went to Joshua in the camp at Gilgal and said to him and the Israelites, "We have come from a distant country; make a treaty with us."

[7]The Israelites said to the Hivites, "But perhaps you live near us, so how can we make a treaty with you?"

[8]"We are your servants," they said to Joshua.

But Joshua asked, "Who are you and where do you come from?"

[9]They answered: "Your servants have come from a very distant country because of the fame of the LORD your God. For we have heard reports of him: all that he did in Egypt, [10]and all that he did to the two kings of the Amorites east of the Jordan—Sihon king of Heshbon, and Og king of Bashan, who reigned in Ashtaroth. [11]And our elders and all those living in our country said to us, 'Take provisions for your journey; go and meet them and say to them, "We are your servants; make a treaty with us."' [12]This bread of ours was warm when we packed it at home on the day we left to come to you. But now see how dry and moldy it is. [13]And these wineskins that we filled were new, but see how cracked they are. And our clothes and sandals are worn out by the very long journey."

[14]The Israelites sampled their provisions but did not inquire of the LORD. [15]Then Joshua made a treaty of peace with them to let them live, and the leaders of the assembly ratified it by oath.

[16]Three days after they made the treaty with the Gibeonites, the Israelites heard that they were neighbors, living near them. [17]So the Israelites set out and on the third day came to their cities: Gibeon, Kephirah, Beeroth and

## Amplified Bible

[32]And there, in the presence of the Israelites, [Joshua] wrote on the stones a copy of the law of Moses.

[33]And all Israel, sojourner as well as he who was born among them, with their elders, officers, and judges, stood on either side of the ark before the Levitical priests who carried the ark of the covenant of the Lord, half of them in front of Mount Gerizim and half of them in front of Mount Ebal, as Moses the servant of the Lord had commanded before that they should bless the Israelites.

[34]Afterward, Joshua read all the words of the law, the blessings and cursings, all that is written in the Book of the Law.

[35]There was not a word of all that Moses commanded which Joshua did not read before all the assembly of Israel, and the women, and little ones, and the foreigners who were living among them.

**9** When all the kings beyond the Jordan in the hill country and in the lowland and all along the coast of the Great [Mediterranean] Sea toward Lebanon, the Hittites, Amorites, Canaanites, Perizzites, Hivites, and Jebusites heard this,

[2]They gathered together with one accord to fight Joshua and Israel.

[3]But when the people of Gibeon heard what Joshua had done to Jericho and Ai,

[4]They worked cunningly, and went pretending to be ambassadors and took [provisions and] old sacks on their donkeys and wineskins, old, torn, and mended,

[5]And old and patched shoes on their feet and wearing old garments; and all their supply of food was dry and moldy.

[6]And they went to Joshua in the camp at Gilgal and said to him and the men of Israel, We have come from a far country; so now, make a covenant with us.

[7]But the men of Israel said to the Hivites, Perhaps you live among us; how then can we make a covenant with you?

[8]They said to Joshua, We are your servants. And Joshua said to them, Who are you? From where have you come?

[9]They said to him, From a very far country your servants have come because of the name of the Lord your God. For we have heard the fame of Him, and all that He did in Egypt,

[10]And all that He did to the two kings of the Amorites who were beyond the Jordan, to Sihon king of Heshbon, and to Og king of Bashan, who lived in Ashtaroth.

[11]So our elders and all the residents of our country said to us, Take provisions for the journey and go to meet [the Israelites] and say to them, We are your servants; and now make a covenant with us.

[12]This our bread we took hot for our provision out of our houses on the day we set out to go to you; but now behold, it is dry and has become moldy.

[13]These wineskins (bottles) which we filled were new, and behold, they are torn; and our garments and our shoes have become old because of the very long journey.

[14]So the [Israelite] men partook of their food and did not consult the Lord.

[15]Joshua made peace with them, covenanting with them to let them live, and the assembly's leaders swore to them.

[16]Then three days after they had made a covenant with [the strangers, the Israelites] heard that they were their neighbors and that they dwelt among them.

[17]And the Israelites set out and came to their cities on the third day. Now their cities were Gibeon, Chephirah, Beeroth, and Kiriath-jearim.

---

[a] 4 Most Hebrew manuscripts; some Hebrew manuscripts, Vulgate and Syriac (see also Septuagint) *They prepared provisions and loaded their donkeys*

## New International Version

Kiriath Jearim. [18]But the Israelites did not attack them, because the leaders of the assembly had sworn an oath to them by the LORD, the God of Israel.

The whole assembly grumbled against the leaders, [19]but all the leaders answered, "We have given them our oath by the LORD, the God of Israel, and we cannot touch them now. [20]This is what we will do to them: We will let them live, so that God's wrath will not fall on us for breaking the oath we swore to them." [21]They continued, "Let them live, but let them be woodcutters and water carriers in the service of the whole assembly." So the leaders' promise to them was kept.

[22]Then Joshua summoned the Gibeonites and said, "Why did you deceive us by saying, 'We live a long way from you,' while actually you live near us? [23]You are now under a curse: You will never be released from service as woodcutters and water carriers for the house of my God."

[24]They answered Joshua, "Your servants were clearly told how the LORD your God had commanded his servant Moses to give you the whole land and to wipe out all its inhabitants from before you. So we feared for our lives because of you, and that is why we did this. [25]We are now in your hands. Do to us whatever seems good and right to you."

[26]So Joshua saved them from the Israelites, and they did not kill them. [27]That day he made the Gibeonites woodcutters and water carriers for the assembly, to provide for the needs of the altar of the LORD at the place the LORD would choose. And that is what they are to this day.

### The Sun Stands Still

**10** Now Adoni-Zedek king of Jerusalem heard that Joshua had taken Ai and totally destroyed[a] it, doing to Ai and its king as he had done to Jericho and its king, and that the people of Gibeon had made a treaty of peace with Israel and had become their allies. [2]He and his people were very much alarmed at this, because Gibeon was an important city, like one of the royal cities; it was larger than Ai, and all its men were good fighters. [3]So Adoni-Zedek king of Jerusalem appealed to Hoham king of Hebron, Piram king of Jarmuth, Japhia king of Lachish and Debir king of Eglon. [4]"Come up and help me attack Gibeon," he said, "because it has made peace with Joshua and the Israelites."

[5]Then the five kings of the Amorites—the kings of Jerusalem, Hebron, Jarmuth, Lachish and Eglon—joined forces. They moved up with all their troops and took up positions against Gibeon and attacked it.

[6]The Gibeonites then sent word to Joshua in the camp at Gilgal: "Do not abandon your servants. Come up to us quickly and save us! Help us, because all the Amorite kings from the hill country have joined forces against us."

[7]So Joshua marched up from Gilgal with his entire army, including all the best fighting men. [8]The LORD said to Joshua, "Do not be afraid of them; I have given them into your hand. Not one of them will be able to withstand you."

[9]After an all-night march from Gilgal, Joshua took them by surprise. [10]The LORD threw them into confusion before Israel, so Joshua and the Israelites defeated them completely at Gibeon. Israel pursued them along the road going up to Beth Horon and cut them down all the way to Azekah and Makkedah. [11]As they fled before Israel on the

## Amplified Bible

[18]But the Israelites did not slay them, because the leaders of the assembly had sworn to them by the Lord, the God of Israel, [to spare them]. And all the assembly murmured against the leaders.

[19]But all the leaders said to all the assembly, We have sworn to them by the Lord, the God of Israel, so now we may not touch them.

[20]This we will do to them: we will let them live, lest wrath be upon us because of the oath which we swore to them.

[21]And the leaders said to them, Let them live [and be our slaves]. So they became hewers of wood and drawers of water for all the assembly, just as the leaders had said of them.

[22]Joshua called the men and said, Why did you deceive us, saying, We live very far from you, when you dwell among us?

[23]Now therefore you are cursed, and of you there shall always be slaves, hewers of wood and drawers of water for the house of my God.

[24]They answered Joshua, Because it was surely told your servants that the Lord your God commanded His servant Moses to give you all the land and to destroy all the land's inhabitants from before us. So we feared greatly for our lives because of you, and have done this thing.

[25]And now, behold, we are in your hand; do as it seems good and right in your sight to do to us.

[26]So he did to them, and delivered them out of the hand of the Israelites, so that they did not kill them.

[27]But Joshua then made them hewers of wood and drawers of water for the congregation and for the altar of the Lord, to this day, in the place which He should choose.

**10** When Adoni-zedek king of Jerusalem heard how Joshua had taken Ai and had utterly destroyed it, doing to Jericho and its king as he had done to Ai and its king, and how the residents of Gibeon had made peace with Israel and were among them,

[2]He feared greatly, because Gibeon was a great city, like one of the royal cities, and because it was greater than Ai, and all its men were mighty.

[3]So Adoni-zedek king of Jerusalem sent to Hoham king of Hebron, to Piram king of Jarmuth, to Japhia king of Lachish, and to Debir king of Eglon, saying,

[4]Come up to me and help me, and let us smite Gibeon, for it has made peace with Joshua and with the Israelites.

[5]Then the five kings of the Amorites—the kings of Jerusalem, Hebron, Jarmuth, Lachish, and Eglon—gathered their forces and went up with all their armies and encamped before Gibeon to fight against it.

[6]And the men of Gibeon sent to Joshua at the camp in Gilgal, saying, Do not relax your hand from your servants; come up to us quickly and save us and help us, for all the kings of the Amorites who dwell in the hill country are gathered against us.

[7]So Joshua went up from Gilgal, he and all the warriors with him and all the mighty men of valor.

[8]And the Lord said to Joshua, Do not fear them, for I have given them into your hand; there shall not a man of them stand before you.

[9]So Joshua came upon them suddenly, having gone up from Gilgal all night.

[10]And the Lord caused [the enemies] to panic before Israel, who slew them with a great slaughter at Gibeon and chased them along the way that goes up to Beth-horon and smote them as far as Azekah and Makkedah.

[11]As they fled before Israel, while they were descend-

---

[a] 1 The Hebrew term refers to the irrevocable giving over of things or persons to the LORD, often by totally destroying them; also in verses 28, 35, 37, 39 and 40.

## New International Version

road down from Beth Horon to Azekah, the LORD hurled large hailstones down on them, and more of them died from the hail than were killed by the swords of the Israelites.

¹²On the day the LORD gave the Amorites over to Israel, Joshua said to the LORD in the presence of Israel:

"Sun, stand still over Gibeon,
    and you, moon, over the Valley of Aijalon."
¹³So the sun stood still,
    and the moon stopped,
    till the nation avenged itself on*a* its enemies,

as it is written in the Book of Jashar.

The sun stopped in the middle of the sky and delayed going down about a full day. ¹⁴There has never been a day like it before or since, a day when the LORD listened to a human being. Surely the LORD was fighting for Israel! ¹⁵Then Joshua returned with all Israel to the camp at Gilgal.

### Five Amorite Kings Killed

¹⁶Now the five kings had fled and hidden in the cave at Makkedah. ¹⁷When Joshua was told that the five kings had been found hiding in the cave at Makkedah, ¹⁸he said, "Roll large rocks up to the mouth of the cave, and post some men there to guard it. ¹⁹But don't stop; pursue your enemies! Attack them from the rear and don't let them reach their cities, for the LORD your God has given them into your hand."

²⁰So Joshua and the Israelites defeated them completely, but a few survivors managed to reach their fortified cities. ²¹The whole army then returned safely to Joshua in the camp at Makkedah, and no one uttered a word against the Israelites.

²²Joshua said, "Open the mouth of the cave and bring those five kings out to me." ²³So they brought the five kings out of the cave—the kings of Jerusalem, Hebron, Jarmuth, Lachish and Eglon. ²⁴When they had brought these kings to Joshua, he summoned all the men of Israel and said to the army commanders who had come with him, "Come here and put your feet on the necks of these kings." So they came forward and placed their feet on their necks.

²⁵Joshua said to them, "Do not be afraid; do not be discouraged. Be strong and courageous. This is what the LORD will do to all the enemies you are going to fight." ²⁶Then Joshua put the kings to death and exposed their bodies on five poles, and they were left hanging on the poles until evening.

²⁷At sunset Joshua gave the order and they took them down from the poles and threw them into the cave where they had been hiding. At the mouth of the cave they placed large rocks, which are there to this day.

### Southern Cities Conquered

²⁸That day Joshua took Makkedah. He put the city and its king to the sword and totally destroyed everyone in it. He left no survivors. And he did to the king of Makkedah as he had done to the king of Jericho.

²⁹Then Joshua and all Israel with him moved on from Makkedah to Libnah and attacked it. ³⁰The LORD also gave that city and its king into Israel's hand. The city and everyone in it Joshua put to the sword. He left no survi-

## Amplified Bible

ing [the pass] to Beth-horon, the Lord cast great stones from the heavens on them as far as Azekah, killing them. More died because of the hailstones than the Israelites slew with the sword.

¹²Then Joshua spoke to the Lord on the day when the Lord gave the Amorites over to the Israelites, and he said in the sight of Israel, Sun, be silent *and* stand still at Gibeon, and you, moon, in the Valley of Ajalon!

¹³And the sun stood still, and the moon stayed, until the nation took vengeance upon their enemies. Is not this written in the Book of Jasher? So the sun stood still in the midst of the heavens and did not hasten to go down for about a whole day.

¹⁴There was no day like it before or since, when the Lord heeded the voice of a man. For the Lord fought for Israel.

¹⁵Then Joshua returned, and all Israel with him, to the camp at Gilgal.

¹⁶Those five kings fled and hid themselves in the cave of Makkedah.

¹⁷And it was told Joshua, The five kings are hidden in the cave at Makkedah.

¹⁸Joshua said, Roll great stones to the cave's mouth, and set men to guard them.

¹⁹But do not stay. Pursue your enemies and fall upon their rear; do not allow them to enter their cities, for the Lord your God has given them into your hand.

²⁰When Joshua and the Israelites had ended slaying them until they were wiped out and the remnant remaining of them had entered into fortified cities,

²¹All the people returned to the camp to Joshua at Makkedah in peace; none moved his tongue against any of the Israelites.

²²Then said Joshua, Open the mouth of the cave and bring out those five kings to me from the cave.

²³They brought the five kings out of the cave to him—the kings of Jerusalem, Hebron, Jarmuth, Lachish, and Eglon.

²⁴When they brought out those kings to Joshua, [he] called for all the Israelites and told the commanders of the men of war who went with him, Come, put your feet on necks of these kings. And they came and put their feet on the [kings'] necks.

²⁵Joshua said to them, Fear not nor be dismayed; be strong and of good courage. For thus shall the Lord do to all your enemies against whom you fight.

²⁶Afterward Joshua smote and slew them and hanged their bodies on five trees, and they hung on the trees until evening.

²⁷At sunset Joshua ordered and they took the bodies down from the trees and cast them into the cave where the kings had hidden and laid great stones on the cave's mouth, which remain to this very day.

²⁸Joshua took Makkedah that day and smote it and its king with the sword and utterly destroyed everyone in it. He left none remaining. And he did to the king of Makkedah as he had done to the king of Jericho. [Josh. 6:21.]

²⁹Then Joshua and all Israel went from Makkedah to Libnah and attacked Libnah.

³⁰And the Lord gave it also and its king into Israel's hands, and Joshua smote it with the sword, and all the

---

*a* 13 Or *nation triumphed over*

## New International Version

vors there. And he did to its king as he had done to the king of Jericho.

³¹Then Joshua and all Israel with him moved on from Libnah to Lachish; he took up positions against it and attacked it. ³²The LORD gave Lachish into Israel's hands, and Joshua took it on the second day. The city and everyone in it he put to the sword, just as he had done to Libnah. ³³Meanwhile, Horam king of Gezer had come up to help Lachish, but Joshua defeated him and his army—until no survivors were left.

³⁴Then Joshua and all Israel with him moved on from Lachish to Eglon; they took up positions against it and attacked it. ³⁵They captured it that same day and put it to the sword and totally destroyed everyone in it, just as they had done to Lachish.

³⁶Then Joshua and all Israel with him went up from Eglon to Hebron and attacked it. ³⁷They took the city and put it to the sword, together with its king, its villages and everyone in it. They left no survivors. Just as at Eglon, they totally destroyed it and everyone in it.

³⁸Then Joshua and all Israel with him turned around and attacked Debir. ³⁹They took the city, its king and its villages, and put them to the sword. Everyone in it they totally destroyed. They left no survivors. They did to Debir and its king as they had done to Libnah and its king and to Hebron.

⁴⁰So Joshua subdued the whole region, including the hill country, the Negev, the western foothills and the mountain slopes, together with all their kings. He left no survivors. He totally destroyed all who breathed, just as the LORD, the God of Israel, had commanded. ⁴¹Joshua subdued them from Kadesh Barnea to Gaza and from the whole region of Goshen to Gibeon. ⁴²All these kings and their lands Joshua conquered in one campaign, because the LORD, the God of Israel, fought for Israel.

⁴³Then Joshua returned with all Israel to the camp at Gilgal.

### Northern Kings Defeated

**11** When Jabin king of Hazor heard of this, he sent word to Jobab king of Madon, to the kings of Shimron and Akshaph, ²and to the northern kings who were in the mountains, in the Arabah south of Kinnereth, in the western foothills and in Naphoth Dor on the west; ³to the Canaanites in the east and west; to the Amorites, Hittites, Perizzites and Jebusites in the hill country; and to the Hivites below Hermon in the region of Mizpah. ⁴They came out with all their troops and a large number of horses and chariots—a huge army, as numerous as the sand on the

## Amplified Bible

people in it. He left none remaining in it. And he did to its king as he had done to the king of Jericho.

³¹And Joshua passed from Libnah, and all Israel with him, to Lachish and encamped against it and attacked it.

³²And the Lord delivered Lachish into the hands of Israel, and Joshua took it on the second day and smote it with the sword, and all the people in it, as he had done to Libnah.

³³Then Horam king of Gezer came up to help Lachish, and Joshua smote him and his people—until he had left none remaining.

³⁴From Lachish Joshua and all Israel went on to Eglon, laid siege to it, and attacked it.

³⁵And they took it that day and smote it with the sword and utterly destroyed all who were in it that day, as he had done to Lachish.

³⁶Then Joshua with all Israel went up from Eglon to Hebron, and they attacked it

³⁷And took it and smote it with the sword, and its king and all its towns and everyone in it. He left none remaining, as he had done to Eglon, and utterly destroyed it and all its people.

³⁸And Joshua and all Israel with him returned to Debir and attacked it.

³⁹And he took it, with its king and all its towns, and they smote them with the sword and utterly destroyed everyone in it. He left none remaining. As he had done to Hebron and to Libnah and its king, so he did to Debir and its king.

⁴⁰So Joshua smote all the land, the hill country, the South, the lowland, and the slopes, and all their kings. He left none remaining, but utterly destroyed all that breathed, as the ᵃLord, the God of Israel, commanded. [Deut. 20:16.]

⁴¹And Joshua smote them from Kadesh-barnea even to Gaza, and all the country of Goshen even to Gibeon.

⁴²Joshua took all these kings and their land at one time, because the Lord, the God of Israel, fought for Israel.

⁴³And Joshua returned, and all Israel with him, to the camp at Gilgal.

**11** When Jabin king of Hazor heard of this, he sent to Jobab king of Madon, and to the kings of Shimron and Achshaph,

²And to the kings who were in the north in the hill country and in the Arabah south of Chinneroth and in the lowland and in the heights of Dor on the west;

³To the Canaanites in the east and west; to the Amorites, the Hittites, the Perizzites, the Jebusites in the hill country; and to the Hivites below [Mount] Hermon in the land of Mizpah.

⁴And they went out with all their hosts, much people, like the sand on the seashore in number, with very many horses and chariots.

ᵃ As the presence of "the Prince of the Lord's host" (Josh. 5:13-15) indicates, the Lord will take part in this conflict not as an ally or an adversary but as Commander In Chief. It is not Israel's quarrel, in which they are to ask divine assistance. It is the Lord's own quarrel, and Israel and Joshua are but a division in His host. The wars of Israel in Canaan are always presented by the Old Testament as "the wars of the Lord." The conquest of Canaan is too often treated as an enterprise of the Israelites, carried out with great cruelties, for which they claimed divine sanction. The Old Testament presents the matter in an entirely different light. The Lord fights for His own right hand, and Israel is but a fragment of His army. "The sun stood still"(Josh. 10:13), the stars in their courses fought against His foes (Judg. 5:20) (Charles Ellicott, *A Bible Commentary*).

## New International Version

seashore. ⁵All these kings joined forces and made camp together at the Waters of Merom to fight against Israel.

⁶The LORD said to Joshua, "Do not be afraid of them, because by this time tomorrow I will hand all of them, slain, over to Israel. You are to hamstring their horses and burn their chariots."

⁷So Joshua and his whole army came against them suddenly at the Waters of Merom and attacked them, ⁸and the LORD gave them into the hand of Israel. They defeated them and pursued them all the way to Greater Sidon, to Misrephoth Maim, and to the Valley of Mizpah on the east, until no survivors were left. ⁹Joshua did to them as the LORD had directed: He hamstrung their horses and burned their chariots.

¹⁰At that time Joshua turned back and captured Hazor and put its king to the sword. (Hazor had been the head of all these kingdoms.) ¹¹Everyone in it they put to the sword. They totally destroyed*a* them, not sparing anyone that breathed, and he burned Hazor itself.

¹²Joshua took all these royal cities and their kings and put them to the sword. He totally destroyed them, as Moses the servant of the LORD had commanded. ¹³Yet Israel did not burn any of the cities built on their mounds—except Hazor, which Joshua burned. ¹⁴The Israelites carried off for themselves all the plunder and livestock of these cities, but all the people they put to the sword until they completely destroyed them, not sparing anyone that breathed. ¹⁵As the LORD commanded his servant Moses, so Moses commanded Joshua, and Joshua did it; he left nothing undone of all that the LORD commanded Moses.

¹⁶So Joshua took this entire land: the hill country, all the Negev, the whole region of Goshen, the western foothills, the Arabah and the mountains of Israel with their foothills, ¹⁷from Mount Halak, which rises toward Seir, to Baal Gad in the Valley of Lebanon below Mount Hermon. He captured all their kings and put them to death. ¹⁸Joshua waged war against all these kings for a long time. ¹⁹Except for the Hivites living in Gibeon, not one city made a treaty of peace with the Israelites, who took them all in battle. ²⁰For it was the LORD himself who hardened their hearts to wage war against Israel, so that he might destroy them totally, exterminating them without mercy, as the LORD had commanded Moses.

²¹At that time Joshua went and destroyed the Anakites from the hill country: from Hebron, Debir and Anab, from all the hill country of Judah, and from all the hill country of Israel. Joshua totally destroyed them and their towns. ²²No Anakites were left in Israelite territory; only in Gaza, Gath and Ashdod did any survive.

²³So Joshua took the entire land, just as the LORD had

## Amplified Bible

⁵And all these kings met and came and encamped together at the Waters of Merom, to fight against Israel.

⁶But the Lord said to Joshua, Do not be afraid because of them, for tomorrow by this time I will give them up all slain to Israel; you shall hamstring their horses and burn their chariots with fire.

⁷So Joshua and all the people of war with him came against them suddenly by the Waters of Merom and fell upon them.

⁸And the Lord gave them into the hand of Israel, who smote them and chased them [toward] populous Sidon and Misrephoth-maim, and eastward as far as the Valley of Mizpah; they smote them until none remained.

⁹And Joshua did to them as the Lord had commanded him: he hamstrung their horses and burned their chariots with fire.

¹⁰And Joshua at that time turned back and took Hazor and smote its king with the sword; for Hazor previously was the head of all those kingdoms.

¹¹They smote all the people in it with the sword, utterly destroying them; none were left alive, and he burned Hazor with fire.

¹²And Joshua took all the cities of those kings and all the kings and smote them with the sword, utterly destroying them, as Moses the servant of the Lord commanded. [Deut. 20:16.]

¹³But Israel burned none of the cities that stood [fortified] on their mounds—except Hazor only, which Joshua burned.

¹⁴And all the spoil of these cities and the livestock the Israelites took for their booty; but every man they smote with the sword until they had destroyed them, and they left none who breathed.

¹⁵As the Lord had commanded Moses His servant, so Moses commanded Joshua, and so Joshua did; he left nothing undone of all that the Lord commanded Moses.

¹⁶So Joshua took all that land: the hill country, all the South, all the land of Goshen, the lowland, the Arabah [plain], the hill country of Israel and its lowland,

¹⁷From Mount Halak, which rises toward Seir, as far as Baal-gad in the Valley of Lebanon below Mount Hermon. He captured all their kings and slew them.

¹⁸Joshua had waged war a long time [at least five years] with all those kings.

¹⁹Not a city made peace with the Israelites except the Hivites, the people of Gibeon; all the others they took in battle.

²⁰For it was of the Lord to harden their hearts that they should come against Israel in battle, that [Israel] might *a*destroy them utterly, and that without favor *and* mercy, as the Lord commanded Moses.

²¹Joshua came at that time and cut off the Anakim [large in stature] from the hill country: from Hebron, from Debir, from Anab, and from all the hill country of Judah and the hill country of Israel. Joshua destroyed them utterly with their cities.

²²None of the Anakim were left in the land of the Israelites; only in Gaza, Gath, and Ashdod [of Philistia] did some remain.

²³So Joshua took the whole land, according to all that

*a* "Infidels say that it seems wholly inconsistent with what we should suppose to be the merciful character of God that He should thus command whole nations to be destroyed by the sword . . . [But] when we see juries in our own country bringing in a verdict of guilty, the judge pronouncing the sentence of death, and that sentence executed, we do not complain that there is anything unjust in the act. These Canaanites are proved to have polluted and stained the land with [intolerable] crimes; it was merely the holy Judge [the Lord] pronouncing the sentence on flagrant criminals and [Joshua] the righteous governor executing that sentence to the letter. It was not an act of arbitrary or private revenge, but the execution of the sentence of retributive justice, and as such had perhaps as great mercy to the innocent as justice to the guilty" (John Cumming, cited by James C. Gray and George M. Adams, *Bible Commentary*).

*a* 11 The Hebrew term refers to the irrevocable giving over of things or persons to the LORD, often by totally destroying them; also in verses 12, 20 and 21.

## New International Version

directed Moses, and he gave it as an inheritance to Israel according to their tribal divisions. Then the land had rest from war.

### List of Defeated Kings

**12** These are the kings of the land whom the Israelites had defeated and whose territory they took over east of the Jordan, from the Arnon Gorge to Mount Hermon, including all the eastern side of the Arabah:

²Sihon king of the Amorites, who reigned in Heshbon.

He ruled from Aroer on the rim of the Arnon Gorge—from the middle of the gorge—to the Jabbok River, which is the border of the Ammonites. This included half of Gilead. ³He also ruled over the eastern Arabah from the Sea of Galilee*a* to the Sea of the Arabah (that is, the Dead Sea), to Beth Jeshimoth, and then southward below the slopes of Pisgah.

⁴And the territory of Og king of Bashan, one of the last of the Rephaites, who reigned in Ashtaroth and Edrei.

⁵He ruled over Mount Hermon, Salekah, all of Bashan to the border of the people of Geshur and Maakah, and half of Gilead to the border of Sihon king of Heshbon.

⁶Moses, the servant of the Lord, and the Israelites conquered them. And Moses the servant of the Lord gave their land to the Reubenites, the Gadites and the half-tribe of Manasseh to be their possession.

⁷Here is a list of the kings of the land that Joshua and the Israelites conquered on the west side of the Jordan, from Baal Gad in the Valley of Lebanon to Mount Halak, which rises toward Seir. Joshua gave their lands as an inheritance to the tribes of Israel according to their tribal divisions. ⁸The lands included the hill country, the western foothills, the Arabah, the mountain slopes, the wilderness and the Negev. These were the lands of the Hittites, Amorites, Canaanites, Perizzites, Hivites and Jebusites. These were the kings:

| | |
|---|---|
| ⁹the king of Jericho | one |
| the king of Ai (near Bethel) | one |
| ¹⁰the king of Jerusalem | one |
| the king of Hebron | one |
| ¹¹the king of Jarmuth | one |
| the king of Lachish | one |
| ¹²the king of Eglon | one |
| the king of Gezer | one |
| ¹³the king of Debir | one |
| the king of Geder | one |
| ¹⁴the king of Hormah | one |
| the king of Arad | one |
| ¹⁵the king of Libnah | one |
| the king of Adullam | one |
| ¹⁶the king of Makkedah | one |
| the king of Bethel | one |
| ¹⁷the king of Tappuah | one |
| the king of Hepher | one |
| ¹⁸the king of Aphek | one |
| the king of Lasharon | one |
| ¹⁹the king of Madon | one |
| the king of Hazor | one |
| ²⁰the king of Shimron Meron | one |
| the king of Akshaph | one |
| ²¹the king of Taanach | one |
| the king of Megiddo | one |
| ²²the king of Kedesh | one |
| the king of Jokneam in Carmel | one |

*a 3* Hebrew *Kinnereth*

## Amplified Bible

the Lord had spoken to Moses, and Joshua gave it for an inheritance to Israel according to their allotments by tribes. And the land had rest from war.

**12** Now these are the kings of the land whom the Israelites defeated and whose land they took possession of east of the Jordan, from the river Arnon to Mount Hermon, and all the Arabah eastward:

²Sihon king of the Amorites, who dwelt in Heshbon, and ruled from Aroer on the edge of the Valley of the [river] Arnon, and from the middle of the valley as far as the river Jabbok, the boundary of the Ammonites, including half of Gilead;

³And the Arabah to the Sea of Chinneroth eastward, and in the direction of Beth-jeshimoth, to the Sea of the Arabah, the Salt [or Dead] Sea, southward to the foot of the slopes of Pisgah.

⁴And Og king of Bashan, one of the remnant of the Rephaim, who lived at Ashtaroth and at Edrei,

⁵And ruled over Mount Hermon and Salecah and all of Bashan to the boundary of the Geshurites and the Maacathites, and over half of Gilead to the boundary of Sihon king of Heshbon.

⁶These Moses the servant of the Lord and the Israelites defeated; and Moses the servant of the Lord gave their land for a possession to the Reubenites, the Gadites, and the half-tribe of Manasseh. [Num. 21; 32:33; Deut. 2; 3.]

⁷These are the kings of the land whom Joshua and the Israelites defeated on the west side of the Jordan, from Baal-gad in the Valley of Lebanon to Mount Halak, which rises toward Seir. Joshua gave their land to the tribes of Israel for a possession according to their allotments,

⁸In the hill country, in the lowland, in the Arabah, on the slopes, in the wilderness, and in the Negeb—the lands of the Hittites, Amorites, Canaanites, Perizzites, Hivites, and Jebusites:

⁹The king of Jericho, one; the king of Ai, which is beside Bethel, one;

¹⁰The king of Jerusalem, one; the king of Hebron, one;

¹¹The king of Jarmuth, one; the king of Lachish, one;

¹²The king of Eglon, one; the king of Gezer, one;

¹³The king of Debir, one; the king of Geder, one;

¹⁴The king of Hormah, one; the king of Arad, one;

¹⁵The king of Libnah, one; the king of Adullam, one;

¹⁶The king of Makkedah, one; the king of Bethel, one;

¹⁷The king of Tappuah, one; the king of Hepher, one;

¹⁸The king of Aphek, one; the king of Lasharon, one;

¹⁹The king of Madon, one; the king of Hazor, one;

²⁰The king of Shimron-meron, one; the king of Achshaph, one;

²¹The king of Taanach, one; the king of Megiddo, one;

²²The king of Kedesh, one; the king of Jokneam in Carmel, one;

## New International Version

<table>
<tr><td>23the king of Dor (in Naphoth Dor)</td><td>one</td></tr>
<tr><td>the king of Goyim in Gilgal</td><td>one</td></tr>
<tr><td>24the king of Tirzah</td><td>one</td></tr>
<tr><td></td><td>thirty-one kings in all.</td></tr>
</table>

### Land Still to Be Taken

**13** When Joshua had grown old, the LORD said to him, "You are now very old, and there are still very large areas of land to be taken over.

2"This is the land that remains: all the regions of the Philistines and Geshurites, 3from the Shihor River on the east of Egypt to the territory of Ekron on the north, all of it counted as Canaanite though held by the five Philistine rulers in Gaza, Ashdod, Ashkelon, Gath and Ekron; the territory of the Avvites 4on the south; all the land of the Canaanites, from Arah of the Sidonians as far as Aphek and the border of the Amorites; 5the area of Byblos; and all Lebanon to the east, from Baal Gad below Mount Hermon to Lebo Hamath.

6"As for all the inhabitants of the mountain regions from Lebanon to Misrephoth Maim, that is, all the Sidonians, I myself will drive them out before the Israelites. Be sure to allocate this land to Israel for an inheritance, as I have instructed you, 7and divide it as an inheritance among the nine tribes and half of the tribe of Manasseh."

### Division of the Land East of the Jordan

8The other half of Manasseh,ᵃ the Reubenites and the Gadites had received the inheritance that Moses had given them east of the Jordan, as he, the servant of the LORD, had assigned it to them.

9It extended from Aroer on the rim of the Arnon Gorge, and from the town in the middle of the gorge, and included the whole plateau of Medeba as far as Dibon, 10and all the towns of Sihon king of the Amorites, who ruled in Heshbon, out to the border of the Ammonites. 11It also included Gilead, the territory of the people of Geshur and Maakah, all of Mount Hermon and all Bashan as far as Salekah— 12that is, the whole kingdom of Og in Bashan, who had reigned in Ashtaroth and Edrei. (He was the last of the Rephaites.) Moses had defeated them and taken over their land. 13But the Israelites did not drive out the people of Geshur and Maakah, so they continue to live among the Israelites to this day.

14But to the tribe of Levi he gave no inheritance, since the food offerings presented to the LORD, the God of Israel, are their inheritance, as he promised them.

15This is what Moses had given to the tribe of Reuben, according to its clans:

16The territory from Aroer on the rim of the Arnon Gorge, and from the town in the middle of the gorge, and the whole plateau past Medeba 17to Heshbon and all its towns on the plateau, including Dibon, Bamoth Baal, Beth Baal Meon, 18Jahaz, Kedemoth, Mephaath, 19Kiriathaim, Sibmah, Zereth Shahar on the hill in the valley, 20Beth Peor, the slopes of Pisgah, and Beth Jeshimoth— 21all the towns on the plateau and the entire realm of Sihon king of the Amorites, who ruled at Heshbon. Moses had defeated him and the Midianite chiefs, Evi, Rekem, Zur, Hur and Reba— princes allied with Sihon—who lived in that country. 22In addition to those slain in battle, the Israelites had put to the sword Balaam son of Beor, who prac-

### Amplified Bible

23The king of Dor in the heights of Dor, one; the king of Goiim in Gilgal, one;
24The king of Tirzah, one. In all, thirty-one kings.

**13** Now Joshua was old and gone far in years [over 100], and the Lord said to him, You have grown old and are gone far in years, and very much of the land still remains to be possessed.

2This is the land that remains: all the regions of the Philistines and all those of the Geshurites:

3From the Shihor [River] which is east of Egypt, northward to the boundary of Ekron, all of it counted as Canaanite; there are five rulers of the Philistines, those of Gaza, Ashdod, Ashkelon, Gath, and Ekron, and those of the Avvites;

4In the south, all the land of the Canaanites, and Mearah, which belongs to the Sidonians, to Aphek, to the boundary of the Amorites,

5And the land of the Gebalites; and all Lebanon toward the east, from Baal-gad below Mount Hermon to the gate of Hamath.

6As for all the inhabitants of the hill country from Lebanon to Misrephoth-maim, even all the Sidonians, I will Myself drive them out from before the Israelites; only allot the land to Israel for an inheritance, as I have commanded you.

7So now divide this land for an inheritance to the nine tribes and the half-tribe of Manasseh.

8With the other half-tribe of Manasseh, the Reubenites and the Gadites received their inheritance beyond the Jordan eastward, as Moses the servant of the Lord gave them:

9From Aroer on the edge of the Valley of the [river] Arnon, and the city in the midst of the valley, and all the tableland of Medeba as far as Dibon;

10And all the cities of Sihon king of the Amorites, who ruled in Heshbon, as far as the boundary of the Ammonites;

11And Gilead, and the region of the Geshurites and Maacathites, and all Mount Hermon, and all Bashan to Salecah—

12All the kingdom of Og in Bashan, who reigned in Ashtaroth and Edrei and alone was left of the Rephaim [giants]; for these Moses had defeated and driven out.

13Yet the Israelites did not drive out the Geshurites or the Maacathites, but Geshur and Maacath dwell among [them] still.

14Only to the tribe of Levi Moses gave no inheritance; the sacrifices made by fire to the Lord, the God of Israel, are their inheritance, as He said to him.

15And Moses gave an inheritance to the tribe of the Reubenites according to their families:

16Their territory was from Aroer on the edge of the Valley of the [river] Arnon, and the city in the midst of the valley, and all the tableland by Medeba:

17With Heshbon and all its cities which are on the plain; Dibon, Bamoth-baal, and Beth-baal-meon,

18Jahaz, Kedemoth, Mephaath,

19Kiriathaim, Sibmah, and Zereth-shahar on the hill of the valley,

20Beth-peor, Pisgah's slopes, and Beth-jeshimoth,

21All the cities of the plain and all the kingdom of Sihon king of the Amorites, who ruled in Heshbon, whom Moses defeated along with the leaders of Midian, Evi, Rekem, Zur, Hur, and Reba, the princes of Sihon who lived in the land.

22Balaam son of Beor, the soothsayer, the Israelites also killed with the sword among the rest of their slain. [Num. 31:16.]

---

ᵃ 8 Hebrew *With it* (that is, with the other half of Manasseh)

## New International Version

ticed divination. <sup>23</sup>The boundary of the Reubenites was the bank of the Jordan. These towns and their villages were the inheritance of the Reubenites, according to their clans.

<sup>24</sup>This is what Moses had given to the tribe of Gad, according to its clans:

<sup>25</sup>The territory of Jazer, all the towns of Gilead and half the Ammonite country as far as Aroer, near Rabbah; <sup>26</sup>and from Heshbon to Ramath Mizpah and Betonim, and from Mahanaim to the territory of Debir; <sup>27</sup>and in the valley, Beth Haram, Beth Nimrah, Sukkoth and Zaphon with the rest of the realm of Sihon king of Heshbon (the east side of the Jordan, the territory up to the end of the Sea of Galilee<sup>a</sup>). <sup>28</sup>These towns and their villages were the inheritance of the Gadites, according to their clans.

<sup>29</sup>This is what Moses had given to the half-tribe of Manasseh, that is, to half the family of the descendants of Manasseh, according to its clans:

<sup>30</sup>The territory extending from Mahanaim and including all of Bashan, the entire realm of Og king of Bashan—all the settlements of Jair in Bashan, sixty towns, <sup>31</sup>half of Gilead, and Ashtaroth and Edrei (the royal cities of Og in Bashan). This was for the descendants of Makir son of Manasseh—for half of the sons of Makir, according to their clans.

<sup>32</sup>This is the inheritance Moses had given when he was in the plains of Moab across the Jordan east of Jericho. <sup>33</sup>But to the tribe of Levi, Moses had given no inheritance; the LORD, the God of Israel, is their inheritance, as he promised them.

### Division of the Land West of the Jordan

**14** Now these are the areas the Israelites received as an inheritance in the land of Canaan, which Eleazar the priest, Joshua son of Nun and the heads of the tribal clans of Israel allotted to them. <sup>2</sup>Their inheritances were assigned by lot to the nine and a half tribes, as the LORD had commanded through Moses. <sup>3</sup>Moses had granted the two and a half tribes their inheritance east of the Jordan but had not granted the Levites an inheritance among the rest, <sup>4</sup>for Joseph's descendants had become two tribes—Manasseh and Ephraim. The Levites received no share of the land but only towns to live in, with pasturelands for their flocks and herds. <sup>5</sup>So the Israelites divided the land, just as the LORD had commanded Moses.

### Allotment for Caleb

<sup>6</sup>Now the people of Judah approached Joshua at Gilgal, and Caleb son of Jephunneh the Kenizzite said to him, "You know what the LORD said to Moses the man of God at Kadesh Barnea about you and me. <sup>7</sup>I was forty years old when Moses the servant of the LORD sent me from Kadesh Barnea to explore the land. And I brought him back a report according to my convictions, <sup>8</sup>but my fellow Israelites who went up with me made the hearts of the people melt in fear. I, however, followed the LORD my God wholeheartedly. <sup>9</sup>So on that day Moses swore to me, 'The land on which your feet have walked will be your inheritance and that of your children forever, because you have followed the LORD my God wholeheartedly.'<sup>b</sup>

<sup>10</sup>"Now then, just as the LORD promised, he has kept me alive for forty-five years since the time he said this to Moses, while Israel moved about in the wilderness. So here I am today, eighty-five years old! <sup>11</sup>I am still as strong

## Amplified Bible

<sup>23</sup>And the border of the Reubenites was the Jordan. This was the inheritance of the Reubenites according to their families, with their cities and villages.

<sup>24</sup>Moses gave an inheritance also to the tribe of the Gadites according to their families.

<sup>25</sup>Their territory was Jazer, and all the cities of Gilead, and half the land of the Ammonites as far as Aroer east of Rabbah;

<sup>26</sup>And from Heshbon to Ramath-mizpeh and Betonim, and from Mahanaim to the territory of Debir;

<sup>27</sup>And in the valley, Beth-haram, Beth-nimrah, Succoth, and Zaphon, the rest of the realm of Sihon king of Heshbon, with the Jordan as a boundary, to the lower end of the Sea of Chinnereth east of the Jordan.

<sup>28</sup>This is the inheritance of the Gadites according to their families, with their cities and villages.

<sup>29</sup>And Moses gave an inheritance to the half-tribe of Manasseh; it was allotted to them according to their families.

<sup>30</sup>Their region extended from Mahanaim through all Bashan, the entire kingdom of Og king of Bashan, and all the towns of Jair, which are in Bashan, sixty cities,

<sup>31</sup>And half of Gilead, and Ashtaroth and Edrei, cities of the kingdom of Og in Bashan; these were allotted to the people of Machir son of Manasseh for half of the Machirites according to their families.

<sup>32</sup>These are the inheritances which Moses distributed in the plains of Moab beyond the Jordan east of Jericho.

<sup>33</sup>But to the tribe of Levi, Moses gave no inheritance; the Lord, the God of Israel, is their inheritance, as He told them.

**14** These are the inheritances in the land of Canaan distributed to the Israelites by Eleazar the priest, Joshua son of Nun, and the heads of the fathers' houses of their tribes.

<sup>2</sup>Their inheritance was by lot, as the Lord commanded Moses, for the nine and one-half tribes.

<sup>3</sup>For Moses had given an inheritance to the two and one-half tribes beyond the Jordan, but to the Levites he gave no inheritance among them,

<sup>4</sup>For the people of Joseph were two tribes, Manasseh and Ephraim. And no part was given in the land to the Levites except cities in which to live, with their pasturelands for their livestock and for their possessions.

<sup>5</sup>As the Lord commanded Moses, so the Israelites did, and they divided the land.

<sup>6</sup>Then the people of Judah came to Joshua in Gilgal, and Caleb son of Jephunneh the Kenizzite said to him, You know what the Lord said to Moses the man of God concerning me and you in Kadesh-barnea.

<sup>7</sup>Forty years old was I when Moses the servant of the Lord sent me from Kadesh-barnea to scout out the land. And I brought him a report as it was in my heart.

<sup>8</sup>But my brethren who went up with me made the hearts of the people melt; yet I wholly followed the Lord my God.

<sup>9</sup>And Moses swore on that day, Surely the land on which your feet have walked shall be an inheritance to you and your children always, because you have wholly followed the Lord my God. [Deut. 1:35, 36.]

<sup>10</sup>And now, behold, the Lord has kept me alive, as He said, these forty-five years since the Lord spoke this word to Moses, while the Israelites wandered in the wilderness; and now, behold, I am this day eighty-five years old.

---

<sup>a</sup> 27 Hebrew *Kinnereth*   <sup>b</sup> 9 Deut. 1:36

## New International Version

today as the day Moses sent me out; I'm just as vigorous to go out to battle now as I was then. [12]Now give me this hill country that the LORD promised me that day. You yourself heard that the Anakites were there and their cities were large and fortified, but, the LORD helping me, I will drive them out just as he said."

[13]Then Joshua blessed Caleb son of Jephunneh and gave him Hebron as his inheritance. [14]So Hebron has belonged to Caleb son of Jephunneh the Kenizzite ever since, because he followed the LORD, the God of Israel, wholeheartedly. [15](Hebron used to be called Kiriath Arba after Arba, who was the greatest man among the Anakites.)

Then the land had rest from war.

### Allotment for Judah

**15** The allotment for the tribe of Judah, according to its clans, extended down to the territory of Edom, to the Desert of Zin in the extreme south. [2]Their southern boundary started from the bay at the southern end of the Dead Sea, [3]crossed south of Scorpion Pass, continued on to Zin and went over to the south of Kadesh Barnea. Then it ran past Hezron up to Addar and curved around to Karka. [4]It then passed along to Azmon and joined the Wadi of Egypt, ending at the Mediterranean Sea. This is their[a] southern boundary.

[5]The eastern boundary is the Dead Sea as far as the mouth of the Jordan.

The northern boundary started from the bay of the sea at the mouth of the Jordan, [6]went up to Beth Hoglah and continued north of Beth Arabah to the Stone of Bohan son of Reuben. [7]The boundary then went up to Debir from the Valley of Achor and turned north to Gilgal, which faces the Pass of Adummim south of the gorge. It continued along to the waters of En Shemesh and came out at En Rogel. [8]Then it ran up the Valley of Ben Hinnom along the southern slope of the Jebusite city (that is, Jerusalem). From there it climbed to the top of the hill west of the Hinnom Valley at the northern end of the Valley of Rephaim. [9]From the hilltop the boundary headed toward the spring of the waters of Nephtoah, came out at the towns of Mount Ephron and went down toward Baalah (that is, Kiriath Jearim). [10]Then it curved westward from Baalah to Mount Seir, ran along the northern slope of Mount Jearim (that is, Kesalon), continued down to Beth Shemesh and crossed to Timnah. [11]It went to the northern slope of Ekron, turned toward Shikkeron, passed along to Mount Baalah and reached Jabneel. The boundary ended at the sea.

[12]The western boundary is the coastline of the Mediterranean Sea.

These are the boundaries around the people of Judah by their clans.

[13]In accordance with the LORD's command to him, Joshua gave to Caleb son of Jephunneh a portion in Judah— Kiriath Arba, that is, Hebron. (Arba was the forefather of Anak.) [14]From Hebron Caleb drove out the three Anakites—Sheshai, Ahiman and Talmai, the sons of Anak. [15]From there he marched against the people living in Debir (formerly called Kiriath Sepher). [16]And Caleb said, "I

## Amplified Bible

[11]Yet I am as strong today as I was the day Moses sent me; as my strength was then, so is my strength now for war and to go out and to come in.

[12]So now give me this hill country of which the Lord spoke that day. For you heard then how the [giantlike] Anakim were there and that the cities were great and fortified; if the Lord will be with me, I shall drive them out just as the Lord said.

[13]Then Joshua blessed him and gave Hebron to Caleb son of Jephunneh for an inheritance.

[14]So Hebron became the inheritance of Caleb son of Jephunneh the Kenizzite to this day, because he wholly followed the Lord, the God of Israel.

[15]The name of Hebron before was Kiriath-arba [city of Arba]. This Arba was the greatest of the Anakim. And the land had rest from war.

**15** The lot for the tribe of Judah according to its families reached southward to the boundary of Edom, to the Wilderness of Zin at its most southern part. [2]And their south boundary was from the end of the Salt [Dead] Sea, from the bay that faces southward; [3]It went out south of the ascent of Akrabbim, passed along to Zin, and went up south of Kadesh-barnea, along by Hezron, up to Addar, and turned about to Karka, [4]Passed along to Azmon, went out by the Brook of Egypt, and ended at the sea. This was their southern frontier.

[5]The eastern boundary was the Salt [Dead] Sea as far as the mouth of the Jordan. The northern boundary was from the bay of the sea at the mouth of the Jordan; [6]And the boundary went up to Beth-hogla and passed along north of Beth-arabah and [it] went up to the [landmark] Stone of Bohan son of Reuben. [7]And the boundary went up to Debir from the Valley of Achor, and so northward, turning toward Gilgal, which is opposite the ascent to Adummim on the south side of the valley; and it passed on to the waters of En-shemesh and ended at En-rogel. [8]Then the boundary went up by the Valley of Ben-hinnom [son of Hinnom] at the southern shoulder of the Jebusite [city]—that is, Jerusalem; and the boundary went up to the top of the mountain that lies before the Valley of Hinnom on the west, at the northern end of the Valley of Rephaim. [9]Then the boundary extended from the top of the mountain to the spring of the waters of Nephtoah and went on to the cities of Mount Ephron; then it bent round to Baalah, that is, Kiriath-jearim; [10]And the boundary went around west of Baalah to Mount Seir, passed along to the northern side of Mount Jearim, which is Chesalon, went down to Beth-shemesh, and then passed on by Timnah. [11]And the boundary went out to the shoulder of the hill north of Ekron, then bent round to Shikkeron, and passed along to Mount Baalah, and went out to Jabneel. Then the boundary ended at the sea. [12]And the west boundary was the Great Sea with its coastline. This is the boundary round about the people of Judah according to their families. [13]And to Caleb son of Jephunneh, [Joshua] gave a part among the people of Judah, as the Lord commanded [him]; it was Kiriath-arba, which is Hebron, [named for] Arba the father of Anak. [14]And Caleb drove from there the three sons of Anak— Sheshai and Ahiman and Talmai—the descendants of Anak. [15]He went up from there against the people of Debir. Debir was formerly named Kiriath-sepher.

## New International Version

will give my daughter Aksah in marriage to the man who attacks and captures Kiriath Sepher." ¹⁷Othniel son of Kenaz, Caleb's brother, took it; so Caleb gave his daughter Aksah to him in marriage.

¹⁸One day when she came to Othniel, she urged him[a] to ask her father for a field. When she got off her donkey, Caleb asked her, "What can I do for you?"

¹⁹She replied, "Do me a special favor. Since you have given me land in the Negev, give me also springs of water." So Caleb gave her the upper and lower springs.

²⁰This is the inheritance of the tribe of Judah, according to its clans:

²¹The southernmost towns of the tribe of Judah in the Negev toward the boundary of Edom were:

Kabzeel, Eder, Jagur, ²²Kinah, Dimonah, Adadah, ²³Kedesh, Hazor, Ithnan, ²⁴Ziph, Telem, Bealoth, ²⁵Hazor Hadattah, Kerioth Hezron (that is, Hazor), ²⁶Amam, Shema, Moladah, ²⁷Hazar Gaddah, Heshmon, Beth Pelet, ²⁸Hazar Shual, Beersheba, Biziothiah, ²⁹Baalah, Iyim, Ezem, ³⁰Eltolad, Kesil, Hormah, ³¹Ziklag, Madmannah, Sansannah, ³²Lebaoth, Shilhim, Ain and Rimmon—a total of twenty-nine towns and their villages.

³³In the western foothills:

Eshtaol, Zorah, Ashnah, ³⁴Zanoah, En Gannim, Tappuah, Enam, ³⁵Jarmuth, Adullam, Sokoh, Azekah, ³⁶Shaaraim, Adithaim and Gederah (or Gederothaim)[b]—fourteen towns and their villages.

³⁷Zenan, Hadashah, Migdal Gad, ³⁸Dilean, Mizpah, Joktheel, ³⁹Lachish, Bozkath, Eglon, ⁴⁰Kabbon, Lahmas, Kitlish, ⁴¹Gederoth, Beth Dagon, Naamah and Makkedah—sixteen towns and their villages.

⁴²Libnah, Ether, Ashan, ⁴³Iphtah, Ashnah, Nezib, ⁴⁴Keilah, Akzib and Mareshah—nine towns and their villages.

⁴⁵Ekron, with its surrounding settlements and villages; ⁴⁶west of Ekron, all that were in the vicinity of Ashdod, together with their villages; ⁴⁷Ashdod, its surrounding settlements and villages; and Gaza, its settlements and villages, as far as the Wadi of Egypt and the coastline of the Mediterranean Sea.

⁴⁸In the hill country:

Shamir, Jattir, Sokoh, ⁴⁹Dannah, Kiriath Sannah (that is, Debir), ⁵⁰Anab, Eshtemoh, Anim, ⁵¹Goshen, Holon and Giloh—eleven towns and their villages.

⁵²Arab, Dumah, Eshan, ⁵³Janim, Beth Tappuah, Aphekah, ⁵⁴Humtah, Kiriath Arba (that is, Hebron) and Zior—nine towns and their villages.

⁵⁵Maon, Carmel, Ziph, Juttah, ⁵⁶Jezreel, Jokdeam, Zanoah, ⁵⁷Kain, Gibeah and Timnah—ten towns and their villages.

⁵⁸Halhul, Beth Zur, Gedor, ⁵⁹Maarath, Beth Anoth and Eltekon—six towns and their villages.[c]

⁶⁰Kiriath Baal (that is, Kiriath Jearim) and Rabbah—two towns and their villages.

⁶¹In the wilderness:

Beth Arabah, Middin, Sekakah, ⁶²Nibshan, the

## Amplified Bible

¹⁶Caleb said, He who smites Kiriath-sepher and takes it, to him will I give Achsah my daughter as wife.

¹⁷And Othniel son of Kenaz, Caleb's brother, took it; and he gave him Achsah his daughter as wife.

¹⁸When Achsah came to Othniel, she got his consent to ask her father for a field. Then she returned to Caleb and when she lighted off her donkey, Caleb said, What do you wish?

¹⁹Achsah answered, Give me a present. Since you have set me in the [dry] Negeb, give me also springs of water. And he gave her the [sloping field with] upper and lower springs.

²⁰This is the inheritance of the tribe of Judah according to their families.

²¹The cities of the tribe of Judah in the extreme south toward the boundary of Edom were: Kabzeel, Eder, Jagur, ²²Kinah, Dimonah, Adadah, ²³Kedesh, Hazor, Ithnan, ²⁴Ziph, Telem, Bealoth, ²⁵Hazor-hadattah, Kerioth-hezron (Hazor), ²⁶Amam, Shema, Moladah, ²⁷Hazar-gaddah, Heshmon, Beth-pelet, ²⁸Hazar-shual, Beersheba, Biziothiah, ²⁹Baalah, Iim, Ezem, ³⁰Eltolad, Chesil, Hormah, ³¹Ziklag, Madmannah, Sansannah, ³²Lebaoth, Shilhim, Ain, and Rimmon. All the cities were twenty-nine [later thirty-six] with their villages.

³³In the lowland: Eshtaol, Zorah, Ashnah, ³⁴Zanoah, En-gannim, Tappuah, Enam, ³⁵Jarmuth, Adullam, Socoh, Azekah, ³⁶Shaaraim, Adithaim, and Gederah and Gederothaim; fourteen cities with their villages.

³⁷Zenan, Hadashah, Migdal-gad, ³⁸Dilean, Mizpah, Joktheel, ³⁹Lachish, Bozkath, Eglon, ⁴⁰Cabbon, Lahmas, Chitlish, ⁴¹Gederoth, Beth-dagon, Naamah, and Makkedah; sixteen cities with their villages.

⁴²Libnah, Ether, Ashan, ⁴³Iphtah, Ashnah, Nezib, ⁴⁴Keilah, Achzib, and Mareshah; nine cities with their villages.

⁴⁵Ekron, with its towns and villages.

⁴⁶From Ekron to the sea, all that lay beside Ashdod, with their villages;

⁴⁷Ashdod, with its towns and its villages; Gaza, with its towns and its villages, as far as the Brook of Egypt, and the Great [Mediterranean] Sea with its coastline.

⁴⁸In the hill country: Shamir, Jattir, Socoh, ⁴⁹Dannah, Kiriath-sannah (that is, Debir), ⁵⁰Anab, Eshtemoh, Anim, ⁵¹Goshen, Holon, and Giloh; eleven cities with their villages.

⁵²Arab, Dumah, Eshan, ⁵³Janim, Beth-tappuah, Aphekah, ⁵⁴Humtah, Kiriath-arba (that is, Hebron), and Zior; nine cities with their villages.

⁵⁵Maon, Carmel, Ziph, Juttah, ⁵⁶Jezreel, Jokdeam, Zanoah, ⁵⁷Kain, Gibeah, and Timnah; ten cities with their villages.

⁵⁸Halhul, Beth-zur, Gedor, ⁵⁹Maarath, Beth-anoth, and Eltekon; six cities with their villages.

⁶⁰Kiriath-baal (that is, Kiriath-jearim) and Rabbah; two cities with their villages.

⁶¹In the wilderness: Beth-arabah, Middin, Secacah,

---

[a] 18 Hebrew and some Septuagint manuscripts; other Septuagint manuscripts (see also note at Judges 1:14) *Othniel, he urged her*
[b] 36 Or *Gederah and Gederothaim*  [c] 59 The Septuagint adds another district of eleven towns, including Tekoa and Ephrathah (Bethlehem).

| New International Version | Amplified Bible |
|---|---|

**New International Version**

City of Salt and En Gedi—six towns and their villages.
⁶³Judah could not dislodge the Jebusites, who were living in Jerusalem; to this day the Jebusites live there with the people of Judah.

### Allotment for Ephraim and Manasseh

**16** The allotment for Joseph began at the Jordan, east of the springs of Jericho, and went up from there through the desert into the hill country of Bethel. ²It went on from Bethel (that is, Luz),ᵃ crossed over to the territory of the Arkites in Ataroth, ³descended westward to the territory of the Japhletites as far as the region of Lower Beth Horon and on to Gezer, ending at the Mediterranean Sea.
⁴So Manasseh and Ephraim, the descendants of Joseph, received their inheritance.

⁵This was the territory of Ephraim, according to its clans:

The boundary of their inheritance went from Ataroth Addar in the east to Upper Beth Horon ⁶and continued to the Mediterranean Sea. From Mikmethath on the north it curved eastward to Taanath Shiloh, passing by it to Janoah on the east. ⁷Then it went down from Janoah to Ataroth and Naarah, touched Jericho and came out at the Jordan. ⁸From Tappuah the border went west to the Kanah Ravine and ended at the Mediterranean Sea. This was the inheritance of the tribe of the Ephraimites, according to its clans. ⁹It also included all the towns and their villages that were set aside for the Ephraimites within the inheritance of the Manassites.
¹⁰They did not dislodge the Canaanites living in Gezer; to this day the Canaanites live among the people of Ephraim but are required to do forced labor.

**17** This was the allotment for the tribe of Manasseh as Joseph's firstborn, that is, for Makir, Manasseh's firstborn. Makir was the ancestor of the Gileadites, who had received Gilead and Bashan because the Makirites were great soldiers. ²So this allotment was for the rest of the people of Manasseh—the clans of Abiezer, Helek, Asriel, Shechem, Hepher and Shemida. These are the other male descendants of Manasseh son of Joseph by their clans.
³Now Zelophehad son of Hepher, the son of Gilead, the son of Makir, the son of Manasseh, had no sons but only daughters, whose names were Mahlah, Noah, Hoglah, Milkah and Tirzah. ⁴They went to Eleazar the priest, Joshua son of Nun, and the leaders and said, "The Lᴏʀᴅ commanded Moses to give us an inheritance among our relatives." So Joshua gave them an inheritance along with the brothers of their father, according to the Lᴏʀᴅ's command. ⁵Manasseh's share consisted of ten tracts of land besides Gilead and Bashan east of the Jordan, ⁶because the daughters of the tribe of Manasseh received an inheritance among the sons. The land of Gilead belonged to the rest of the descendants of Manasseh.
⁷The territory of Manasseh extended from Asher to Mikmethath east of Shechem. The boundary ran southward from there to include the people living at En Tappuah. ⁸(Manasseh had the land of Tappuah,

**Amplified Bible**

⁶²Nibshan, the City of Salt, and En-gedi; six cities with their villages.
⁶³But the Jebusites, the inhabitants of Jerusalem, the people of Judah could not drive out; so the Jebusites dwell with the people of Judah at Jerusalem to this day.

**16** The allotment for the people of Joseph went from the Jordan by Jericho, east of the waters of Jericho, into the wilderness, going up from Jericho into the hill country to Bethel;
²Then it went from Bethel to Luz and passed on to Ataroth, the border of the Archites.
³And it went down westward to the territory of the Japhletites as far as the outskirts of Lower Beth-horon, then to Gezer, and ended at the sea.
⁴The descendants of Joseph, Manasseh and Ephraim, received their inheritance.
⁵The boundary of the Ephraimites according to their families was thus: on the east side their border was Ataroth-addar as far as Upper Beth-horon.
⁶Then the boundary went from there to the sea; on the north was Michmethath; then on the east the boundary went out to Taanath-shiloh, and eastward to Janoah,
⁷Then it went down from Janoah to Ataroth and to Naarah, touched Jericho, and ended at the Jordan [River].
⁸The border went out from Tappuah westward to the brook Kanah and ended at the [Mediterranean] Sea. This is the inheritance of the Ephraimites by their families,
⁹With the towns set apart for the Ephraimites within the inheritance of the Manassites, all those towns with their villages.
¹⁰But they did not drive out the Canaanites who dwelt in Gezer; but the Canaanites dwell among the Ephraimites to this day, and they became slaves required to do forced labor.

**17** Allotment was made for the tribe of Manasseh, for he was the firstborn of Joseph. To Machir the firstborn of Manasseh, the father of Gilead, were allotted Gilead and Bashan because he was a man of war.
²Allotment was also made for the other Manassites by their families—for the sons of Abiezer, of Helek, Asriel, Shechem, Hepher, and Shemida, the male offspring of Manasseh son of Joseph by their families.
³But Zelophehad son of Hepher, the son of Gilead, the son of Machir, the son of Manasseh, had no sons but only daughters; their names were Mahlah, Noah, Hoglah, Milcah, and Tirzah.
⁴They came before Eleazar the priest and Joshua son of Nun and the leaders and said, The Lord commanded Moses to give us an inheritance with our brethren. So according to the Lord's command, Joshua gave them an inheritance among their father's brethren.
⁵So there fell ten portions to Manasseh besides the land of Gilead and Bashan, which is on the other side of the Jordan,
⁶Because the [five] daughters of Manasseh received an inheritance among his [five] sons. The land of Gilead belonged to the other [half] of the Manassites.
⁷The territory of Manasseh reached from Asher to Michmethah east of Shechem; and the border went along southward to the inhabitants of En-tappuah.
⁸The land of Tappuah belonged to Manasseh, but the

---

ᵃ 2 Septuagint; Hebrew *Bethel to Luz*

## New International Version

but Tappuah itself, on the boundary of Manasseh, belonged to the Ephraimites.) 9Then the boundary continued south to the Kanah Ravine. There were towns belonging to Ephraim lying among the towns of Manasseh, but the boundary of Manasseh was the northern side of the ravine and ended at the Mediterranean Sea. 10On the south the land belonged to Ephraim, on the north to Manasseh. The territory of Manasseh reached the Mediterranean Sea and bordered Asher on the north and Issachar on the east.
11Within Issachar and Asher, Manasseh also had Beth Shan, Ibleam and the people of Dor, Endor, Taanach and Megiddo, together with their surrounding settlements (the third in the list is Naphoth*a*).
12Yet the Manassites were not able to occupy these towns, for the Canaanites were determined to live in that region. 13However, when the Israelites grew stronger, they subjected the Canaanites to forced labor but did not drive them out completely.
14The people of Joseph said to Joshua, "Why have you given us only one allotment and one portion for an inheritance? We are a numerous people, and the LORD has blessed us abundantly."
15"If you are so numerous," Joshua answered, "and if the hill country of Ephraim is too small for you, go up into the forest and clear land for yourselves there in the land of the Perizzites and Rephaites."
16The people of Joseph replied, "The hill country is not enough for us, and all the Canaanites who live in the plain have chariots fitted with iron, both those in Beth Shan and its settlements and those in the Valley of Jezreel."
17But Joshua said to the tribes of Joseph—to Ephraim and Manasseh—"You are numerous and very powerful. You will have not only one allotment 18but the forested hill country as well. Clear it, and its farthest limits will be yours; though the Canaanites have chariots fitted with iron and though they are strong, you can drive them out."

### Division of the Rest of the Land

**18** The whole assembly of the Israelites gathered at Shiloh and set up the tent of meeting there. The country was brought under their control, 2but there were still seven Israelite tribes who had not yet received their inheritance.
3So Joshua said to the Israelites: "How long will you wait before you begin to take possession of the land that the LORD, the God of your ancestors, has given you? 4Appoint three men from each tribe. I will send them out to make a survey of the land and to write a description of it, according to the inheritance of each. Then they will return to me. 5You are to divide the land into seven parts. Judah is to remain in its territory on the south and the tribes of Joseph in their territory on the north. 6After you have written descriptions of the seven parts of the land, bring them here to me and I will cast lots for you in the presence of the LORD our God. 7The Levites, however, do not get a portion among you, because the priestly service of the LORD is their inheritance. And Gad, Reuben and the half-tribe of Manasseh have already received their inheritance on the east side of the Jordan. Moses the servant of the LORD gave it to them."
8As the men started on their way to map out the land, Joshua instructed them, "Go and make a survey of the land and write a description of it. Then return to me, and

## Amplified Bible

town of Tappuah on the border of Manasseh belonged to the Ephraimites.
9Then the boundary went down to the brook Kanah. The cities south of the brook lying among the cities of Manasseh belonged to Ephraim. But Manasseh's boundary went on north of the brook and ended at the sea.
10The land to the south was Ephraim's and that to the north was Manasseh's, and the sea was the boundary; on the north Asher was reached, and on the east Issachar.
11Also Manasseh had in Issachar and in Asher [these six towns], their inhabitants and their villages: Beth-shean, Ibleam, Dor, Endor, Taanach, and Megiddo.
12Yet the sons of Manasseh could not drive out the inhabitants of those cities, but the Canaanites persisted in dwelling in that land.
13When the Israelites became strong, they put the Canaanites to forced labor but did not utterly drive them out.
14The tribe of Joseph spoke to Joshua, saying, Why have you given [us] but one lot and one portion as an inheritance when [we] are a great [abundant] people, for until now the Lord has blessed [us]?
15Joshua replied, If you are a great people, get up to the forest and clear ground for yourselves in the land of the Perizzites and the Rephaim, since the Ephraim hill country is too narrow for you.
16The Josephites said, The hill country is not enough for us, and all the Canaanites who dwell in the valley have iron chariots, both those in Beth-shean and its villages and in the Valley of Jezreel.
17And Joshua said to the house of Joseph, to Ephraim and to Manasseh, You are a great *and* numerous people and have great power; you shall not have only one lot
18But the hill country shall be yours; though it is a forest, you shall clear and possess it to its farthest borders; for you shall drive out the Canaanites, though they have iron chariots and are strong.

**18** And the whole congregation of the Israelites assembled at Shiloh and set up the Tent of Meeting there; and the land was subdued before them.
2And there remained among the Israelites seven tribes who had not yet divided their inheritance.
3Joshua asked the Israelites, How long will you be slack to go in and possess the land which the Lord, the God of your fathers, has given you?
4Provide three men from each tribe, and I will send them to go through the land and write a description of it according to their [tribal] inheritances; then they shall return to me.
5And they shall divide it into seven parts. Judah shall remain in its territory on the south and the house of Joseph shall remain in its territory on the north.
6You shall describe the land in seven divisions, and bring the description here to me, that I may cast lots for you here before the Lord our God.
7But the Levites have no portion among you, for the priesthood of the Lord is their inheritance. Gad and Reuben and half the tribe of Manasseh have received their inheritance east of the Jordan, which Moses the servant of the Lord gave them.
8So the men arose and went, and Joshua charged them saying, Go and walk through the land and describe it and

*a 11* That is, Naphoth Dor

## New International Version

I will cast lots for you here at Shiloh in the presence of the LORD." ⁹So the men left and went through the land. They wrote its description on a scroll, town by town, in seven parts, and returned to Joshua in the camp at Shiloh. ¹⁰Joshua then cast lots for them in Shiloh in the presence of the LORD, and there he distributed the land to the Israelites according to their tribal divisions.

### Allotment for Benjamin

¹¹The first lot came up for the tribe of Benjamin according to its clans. Their allotted territory lay between the tribes of Judah and Joseph:

¹²On the north side their boundary began at the Jordan, passed the northern slope of Jericho and headed west into the hill country, coming out at the wilderness of Beth Aven. ¹³From there it crossed to the south slope of Luz (that is, Bethel) and went down to Ataroth Addar on the hill south of Lower Beth Horon.

¹⁴From the hill facing Beth Horon on the south the boundary turned south along the western side and came out at Kiriath Baal (that is, Kiriath Jearim), a town of the people of Judah. This was the western side.

¹⁵The southern side began at the outskirts of Kiriath Jearim on the west, and the boundary came out at the spring of the waters of Nephtoah. ¹⁶The boundary went down to the foot of the hill facing the Valley of Ben Hinnom, north of the Valley of Rephaim. It continued down the Hinnom Valley along the southern slope of the Jebusite city and so to En Rogel. ¹⁷It then curved north, went to En Shemesh, continued to Geliloth, which faces the Pass of Adummim, and ran down to the Stone of Bohan son of Reuben. ¹⁸It continued to the northern slope of Beth Arabah[a] and on down into the Arabah. ¹⁹It then went to the northern slope of Beth Hoglah and came out at the northern bay of the Dead Sea, at the mouth of the Jordan in the south. This was the southern boundary. ²⁰The Jordan formed the boundary on the eastern side.

These were the boundaries that marked out the inheritance of the clans of Benjamin on all sides.

²¹The tribe of Benjamin, according to its clans, had the following towns:

Jericho, Beth Hoglah, Emek Keziz, ²²Beth Arabah, Zemaraim, Bethel, ²³Avvim, Parah, Ophrah, ²⁴Kephar Ammoni, Ophni and Geba—twelve towns and their villages.

²⁵Gibeon, Ramah, Beeroth, ²⁶Mizpah, Kephirah, Mozah, ²⁷Rekem, Irpeel, Taralah, ²⁸Zelah, Haeleph, the Jebusite city (that is, Jerusalem), Gibeah and Kiriath—fourteen towns and their villages.

This was the inheritance of Benjamin for its clans.

### Allotment for Simeon

**19** The second lot came out for the tribe of Simeon according to its clans. Their inheritance lay within the territory of Judah. ²It included:

## Amplified Bible

come again to me, and I will cast lots for you here before the Lord in Shiloh.

⁹And the men went and passed through the land and described it by cities in seven portions in a book; and they came again to Joshua to the camp at Shiloh.

¹⁰Joshua cast lots for them in Shiloh before the Lord, and there [he] divided the land to the Israelites, to each [tribe] his portion.

¹¹And the lot of the Benjamites came up according to their families; and the territory of their lot fell between the tribes of Judah and Joseph.

¹²On the north side their boundary began at the Jordan; then it went up to the shoulder of Jericho on the north and up through the hill country westward and ended at the Beth-aven wilderness.

¹³Then the boundary passed over southward toward Luz, to the shoulder of Luz (that is, Bethel); then it went down to Ataroth-addar by the mountain that lies south of Lower Beth-horon.

¹⁴The boundary extended from there, and turning about on the western side southward from the mountain that lies to the south opposite Beth-horon, it ended at Kiriath-baal (that is, Kiriath-jearim), a city of the tribe of Judah. This formed the western side [of Benjamin's territory].

¹⁵The southern side began at the edge of Kiriath-jearim, and the boundary went on westward to the spring of the waters of Nephtoah.

¹⁶Then the boundary went down to the edge of the mountain overlooking the Valley of Ben-hinnom [son of Hinnom], which is at the north end of the Valley of Rephaim; and it descended to the Valley of Hinnom, south of the shoulder of the Jebusites, and went on down to En-rogel.

¹⁷Then it bent toward the north and went on to En-shemesh and on to Geliloth, which was opposite the ascent of Adummim, and went down to the Stone of Bohan son of Reuben.

¹⁸And it went on to the north of the shoulder [of Beth]-Arabah and down to the Arabah.

¹⁹Then the boundary passed along to the north of the shoulder of Beth-hoglah and ended at the northern bay of the Salt [Dead] Sea, at the south end of the Jordan. This was the southern border.

²⁰And the Jordan was its boundary on the east side. This was the inheritance of the sons of Benjamin by their boundaries round about, according to their families.

²¹Now the cities of the tribe of Benjamin according to [their] families were: Jericho, Beth-hoglah, Emek-keziz, ²²Beth-arabah, Zemaraim, Bethel, ²³Avvim, Parah, Ophrah, ²⁴Chephar-ammoni, Ophni, and Geba; twelve cities with their villages; ²⁵Gibeon, Ramah, Beeroth, ²⁶Mizpah, Chephirah, Mozah, ²⁷Rekem, Irpeel, Taralah, ²⁸Zelah, Haeleph, the Jebusite [city]—that is, Jerusalem—Gibeah, and Kiriath-[jearim]; fourteen cities with their villages. This is the inheritance of the tribe of Benjamin according to their families.

**19** The second lot fell to Simeon, to the tribe of the Simeonites according to their families; and their inheritance lay within that of the people of Judah.

---

a 18 Septuagint; Hebrew *slope facing the Arabah*

## New International Version

Beersheba (or Sheba),*a* Moladah, ³Hazar Shual, Balah, Ezem, ⁴Eltolad, Bethul, Hormah, ⁵Ziklag, Beth Markaboth, Hazar Susah, ⁶Beth Lebaoth and Sharuhen—thirteen towns and their villages;

⁷Ain, Rimmon, Ether and Ashan—four towns and their villages— ⁸and all the villages around these towns as far as Baalath Beer (Ramah in the Negev). This was the inheritance of the tribe of the Simeonites, according to its clans. ⁹The inheritance of the Simeonites was taken from the share of Judah, because Judah's portion was more than they needed. So the Simeonites received their inheritance within the territory of Judah.

### Allotment for Zebulun

¹⁰The third lot came up for Zebulun according to its clans:

The boundary of their inheritance went as far as Sarid. ¹¹Going west it ran to Maralah, touched Dabbesheth, and extended to the ravine near Jokneam. ¹²It turned east from Sarid toward the sunrise to the territory of Kisloth Tabor and went on to Daberath and up to Japhia. ¹³Then it continued eastward to Gath Hepher and Eth Kazin; it came out at Rimmon and turned toward Neah. ¹⁴There the boundary went around on the north to Hannathon and ended at the Valley of Iphtah El. ¹⁵Included were Kattath, Nahalal, Shimron, Idalah and Bethlehem. There were twelve towns and their villages.

¹⁶These towns and their villages were the inheritance of Zebulun, according to its clans.

### Allotment for Issachar

¹⁷The fourth lot came out for Issachar according to its clans. ¹⁸Their territory included:

Jezreel, Kesulloth, Shunem, ¹⁹Hapharaim, Shion, Anaharath, ²⁰Rabbith, Kishion, Ebez, ²¹Remeth, En Gannim, En Haddah and Beth Pazzez. ²²The boundary touched Tabor, Shahazumah and Beth Shemesh, and ended at the Jordan. There were sixteen towns and their villages.

²³These towns and their villages were the inheritance of the tribe of Issachar, according to its clans.

### Allotment for Asher

²⁴The fifth lot came out for the tribe of Asher according to its clans. ²⁵Their territory included:

Helkath, Hali, Beten, Akshaph, ²⁶Allammelek, Amad and Mishal. On the west the boundary touched Carmel and Shihor Libnath. ²⁷It then turned east toward Beth Dagon, touched Zebulun and the Valley of Iphtah El, and went north to Beth Emek and Neiel, passing Kabul on the left. ²⁸It went to Abdon,*b* Rehob, Hammon and Kanah, as far as Greater Sidon. ²⁹The boundary then turned back toward Ramah and went to the fortified city of Tyre, turned toward Hosah and came out at the Mediterranean Sea in the region of Akzib, ³⁰Ummah, Aphek and Rehob. There were twenty-two towns and their villages.

## Amplified Bible

²And they had for their inheritance: Beersheba or Sheba, Moladah,

³Hazarshual, Balah, Ezem,

⁴Eltolad, Bethul, Hormah,

⁵Ziklag, Beth-marcaboth, Hazar-susah,

⁶Beth-lebaoth, and Sharuhen; [making] thirteen cities and their villages;

⁷Ain [with] Rimmon, Ether, and Ashan; [making] four cities and their villages;

⁸And all the villages around these cities as far as Baalath-beer, or Ramah of the Negeb. This was the possession of the Simeonites according to their families.

⁹Out of the part assigned to the Judahites was the inheritance of the tribe of Simeon, for the portion of the tribe of Judah was too large for them. Therefore the tribe of Simeon had its inheritance in the midst of Judah's inheritance.

¹⁰The third lot came up for the tribe of Zebulun according to their families. The border of its inheritance extended to Sarid.

¹¹Then its boundary went up westward and on to Maralah and reached to Dabbesheth and to the brook east of Jokneam.

¹²And it turned from Sarid eastward to the border of Chisloth-tabor and it went out to Daberath and on up to Japhia,

¹³Then passed eastward to Gath-hepher [Jonah's birthplace] and to Eth-kazin, and went on to Rimmon bending toward Neah.

¹⁴The boundary circled on the north to Hannathon, ending at the Valley of Iphtah-el.

¹⁵Included were Kattath, Nahalal, Shimron, Idalah, and Bethlehem; twelve cities with their villages.

¹⁶This is the inheritance of the people of Zebulun according to their families, these cities with their villages.

¹⁷The fourth lot fell to Issachar, to its people according to their families.

¹⁸Their territory included: Jezreel, Chesulloth, Shunem,

¹⁹Hapharaim, Shion, Anaharath,

²⁰Rabbith, Kishion, Ebez,

²¹Remeth, En-gannim, En-haddah, and Beth-pazzez.

²²The boundary reached to Tabor, Shahazumah, and Beth-shemesh, and ended at the Jordan; sixteen cities with their villages.

²³This is the inheritance of the tribe of Issachar according to their families, the cities and their villages.

²⁴The fifth lot fell to the tribe of Asher according to their families.

²⁵Their territory included: Helkath, Hali, Beten, Achshaph,

²⁶Allammelech, Amad, and Mishal; and on the west it touched Carmel and Shihor-libnath.

²⁷Then it turned eastward to Beth-dagon, touching Zebulun and the Valley of Iphtah-el northward to Beth-emek and Neiel, and continued in the north to Cabul,

²⁸Ebron, Rehob, Hammon, and Kanah, even to populous Sidon.

²⁹Then the boundary turned to Ramah, reaching to the fortified city of Tyre; and it turned to Hosah, and ended at the sea—Mahalab, Achzib,

³⁰Ummah, Aphek, and Rehob; twenty-two cities with their villages.

---

*a* 2 Or *Beersheba, Sheba*; 1 Chron. 4:28 does not have *Sheba*.
*b* 28 Some Hebrew manuscripts (see also 21:30); most Hebrew manuscripts *Ebron*

## New International Version

³¹These towns and their villages were the inheritance of the tribe of Asher, according to its clans.

### Allotment for Naphtali

³²The sixth lot came out for Naphtali according to its clans:

³³Their boundary went from Heleph and the large tree in Zaanannim, passing Adami Nekeb and Jabneel to Lakkum and ending at the Jordan. ³⁴The boundary ran west through Aznoth Tabor and came out at Hukkok. It touched Zebulun on the south, Asher on the west and the Jordan*a* on the east. ³⁵The fortified towns were Ziddim, Zer, Hammath, Rakkath, Kinnereth, ³⁶Adamah, Ramah, Hazor, ³⁷Kedesh, Edrei, En Hazor, ³⁸Iron, Migdal El, Horem, Beth Anath and Beth Shemesh. There were nineteen towns and their villages.

³⁹These towns and their villages were the inheritance of the tribe of Naphtali, according to its clans.

### Allotment for Dan

⁴⁰The seventh lot came out for the tribe of Dan according to its clans. ⁴¹The territory of their inheritance included:

Zorah, Eshtaol, Ir Shemesh, ⁴²Shaalabbin, Aijalon, Ithlah, ⁴³Elon, Timnah, Ekron, ⁴⁴Eltekeh, Gibbethon, Baalath, ⁴⁵Jehud, Bene Berak, Gath Rimmon, ⁴⁶Me Jarkon and Rakkon, with the area facing Joppa.

⁴⁷(When the territory of the Danites was lost to them, they went up and attacked Leshem, took it, put it to the sword and occupied it. They settled in Leshem and named it Dan after their ancestor.)

⁴⁸These towns and their villages were the inheritance of the tribe of Dan, according to its clans.

### Allotment for Joshua

⁴⁹When they had finished dividing the land into its allotted portions, the Israelites gave Joshua son of Nun an inheritance among them, ⁵⁰as the LORD had commanded. They gave him the town he asked for—Timnath Serah*b* in the hill country of Ephraim. And he built up the town and settled there.

⁵¹These are the territories that Eleazar the priest, Joshua son of Nun and the heads of the tribal clans of Israel assigned by lot at Shiloh in the presence of the LORD at the entrance to the tent of meeting. And so they finished dividing the land.

### Cities of Refuge

**20** Then the LORD said to Joshua: ²"Tell the Israelites to designate the cities of refuge, as I instructed you through Moses, ³so that anyone who kills a person accidentally and unintentionally may flee there and find protection from the avenger of blood. ⁴When they flee to one of these cities, they are to stand in the entrance of the city gate and state their case before the elders of that city. Then the elders are to admit the fugitive into their city and provide a place to live among them. ⁵If the avenger of blood comes in pursuit, the elders must not surrender

## Amplified Bible

³¹This is the inheritance of the tribe of Asher according to their families, these cities with their villages.

³²The sixth lot fell to the tribe of Naphtali according to their families.

³³Their boundary ran from Heleph, from the oak in Zaanannim and Adami-nekeb and Jabneel as far as Lakkum; and it ended at the Jordan.

³⁴Then the boundary turned westward to Aznoth-tabor and went from there to Hukkok, touching Zebulun on the south, Asher on the west, and Judah on the east at the Jordan.

³⁵The fortified cities included Ziddim, Zer, Hammath, Rakkath, Chinnereth,

³⁶Adamah, Ramah, Hazor,

³⁷Kedesh, Edrei, En-hazor,

³⁸Yiron, Migdal-el, Horem, Beth-anath, and Beth-shemesh; nineteen cities and their villages.

³⁹This is the inheritance of the tribe of Naphtali according to their families, the cities and their villages.

⁴⁰And the seventh lot fell to the tribe of Dan according to their families.

⁴¹The territory of their inheritance included: Zorah, Eshtaol, Ir-shemesh,

⁴²Shaalabbin, Aijalon, Ithlah,

⁴³Elon, Timnah, Ekron,

⁴⁴Eltekeh, Gibbethon, Baalath,

⁴⁵Jehud, Bene-berak, Gath-rimmon,

⁴⁶Me-jarkon, and Rakkon, with the territory before Joppa.

⁴⁷The territory of the tribe of Dan had to be extended [because of the crowding in of the Amorites and Philistines]; so the sons of Dan went up to fight against Leshem (Laish) and took it and smote it with the sword and possessed it and dwelt there, and they called Leshem (Laish) Dan after Dan their [forefather]. [Judg. 1:34; 18:7-10, 27.]

⁴⁸This is the inheritance of the tribe of Dan according to their families, these cities with their villages.

⁴⁹When they had finished dividing the land for inheritance by their boundaries, the Israelites gave an inheritance among them to Joshua son of Nun.

⁵⁰According to the word of the Lord they gave him the city for which he asked—Timnath-serah in the hills of Ephraim. And he built the city and dwelt in it.

⁵¹These are the inheritances which Eleazar the priest, Joshua son of Nun, and the heads of the tribes' houses of the tribes of Israel distributed by lot in Shiloh before the Lord at the door of the Tent of Meeting. So they finished dividing the land.

**20** The Lord said also to Joshua,
²Say to the Israelites, Appoint among you cities of refuge, of which I spoke to you through Moses,

³That the slayer who kills anyone accidentally and unintentionally may flee there; and they shall be your refuge from the avenger of blood. [Num. 35:10ff.]

⁴He who flees to one of those cities shall stand at the entrance of the gate of the city and explain his case to the elders of that city; they shall receive him to [the protection of] that city and give him a place to dwell among them.

⁵If the avenger of blood pursues him, they shall not deliver the slayer into his hand, because he killed his

---

*a 34* Septuagint; Hebrew *west, and Judah, the Jordan,*   *b 50* Also known as *Timnath Heres* (see Judges 2:9)

## New International Version

the fugitive, because the fugitive killed their neighbor unintentionally and without malice aforethought. ⁶They are to stay in that city until they have stood trial before the assembly and until the death of the high priest who is serving at that time. Then they may go back to their own home in the town from which they fled."

⁷So they set apart Kedesh in Galilee in the hill country of Naphtali, Shechem in the hill country of Ephraim, and Kiriath Arba (that is, Hebron) in the hill country of Judah. ⁸East of the Jordan (on the other side from Jericho) they designated Bezer in the wilderness on the plateau in the tribe of Reuben, Ramoth in Gilead in the tribe of Gad, and Golan in Bashan in the tribe of Manasseh. ⁹Any of the Israelites or any foreigner residing among them who killed someone accidentally could flee to these designated cities and not be killed by the avenger of blood prior to standing trial before the assembly.

### Towns for the Levites

**21** Now the family heads of the Levites approached Eleazar the priest, Joshua son of Nun, and the heads of the other tribal families of Israel ²at Shiloh in Canaan and said to them, "The Lᴏʀᴅ commanded through Moses that you give us towns to live in, with pasturelands for our livestock." ³So, as the Lᴏʀᴅ had commanded, the Israelites gave the Levites the following towns and pasturelands out of their own inheritance:

⁴The first lot came out for the Kohathites, according to their clans. The Levites who were descendants of Aaron the priest were allotted thirteen towns from the tribes of Judah, Simeon and Benjamin. ⁵The rest of Kohath's descendants were allotted ten towns from the clans of the tribes of Ephraim, Dan and half of Manasseh.

⁶The descendants of Gershon were allotted thirteen towns from the clans of the tribes of Issachar, Asher, Naphtali and the half-tribe of Manasseh in Bashan.

⁷The descendants of Merari, according to their clans, received twelve towns from the tribes of Reuben, Gad and Zebulun.

⁸So the Israelites allotted to the Levites these towns and their pasturelands, as the Lᴏʀᴅ had commanded through Moses.

⁹From the tribes of Judah and Simeon they allotted the following towns by name ¹⁰(these towns were assigned to the descendants of Aaron who were from the Kohathite clans of the Levites, because the first lot fell to them):

¹¹They gave them Kiriath Arba (that is, Hebron), with its surrounding pastureland, in the hill country of Judah. (Arba was the forefather of Anak.) ¹²But the fields and villages around the city they had given to Caleb son of Jephunneh as his possession.

¹³So to the descendants of Aaron the priest they gave Hebron (a city of refuge for one accused of murder), Libnah, ¹⁴Jattir, Eshtemoa, ¹⁵Holon, Debir, ¹⁶Ain, Juttah and Beth Shemesh, together with their pasturelands—nine towns from these two tribes.

## Amplified Bible

neighbor unintentionally, having had no hatred for him previously.

⁶And he shall dwell in that city until he has been tried before the congregation and until the death of him who is the high priest in those days. Then the slayer shall return to his own city from which he fled and to his own house.

⁷And they set apart *and* consecrated Kedesh in Galilee in the hill country of Naphtali and Shechem in the hill country of Ephraim and Kiriath-arba (that is, Hebron) in the hill country of Judah.

⁸Beyond the Jordan east of Jericho they appointed Bezer in the wilderness tableland from the tribe of Reuben, and Ramoth in Gilead from the tribe of Gad, and Golan in Bashan from the tribe of Manasseh.

⁹These cities were for all the Israelites and the stranger sojourning among them, that whoever killed a person unintentionally might flee there and not be slain by the avenger of blood until he had been tried before the congregation.

**21** Then the heads of the fathers' houses of the Levites came to Eleazar the priest and Joshua son of Nun and the heads of the fathers' houses of the Israelite tribes.

²They said to them at Shiloh in Canaan, The Lord commanded through Moses that we should be given cities to dwell in, with their pasturelands (suburbs) for our cattle.

³So the Israelites gave to the Levites out of their own inheritance, at the command of the Lord, these cities and their suburbs.

⁴The [first] lot came out for the families of the Kohathites. So those ᵃLevites who were descendants of Aaron the priest received by lot from the tribes of Judah, Simeon, and Benjamin thirteen cities.

⁵And the rest of the Kohathites received by lot from the families of the tribes of Ephraim, Dan, and the half-tribe of Manasseh ten cities.

⁶The Gershonites received by lot from the families of the tribes of Issachar, Asher, Naphtali, and the half-tribe of Manasseh in Bashan thirteen cities.

⁷The Merarites received according to their families from the tribes of Reuben, Gad, and Zebulun twelve cities.

⁸The Israelites gave by lot to the Levites these cities with their pasturelands (suburbs), as the Lord commanded through Moses.

⁹They gave from the tribes of Judah and Simeon the cities here mentioned by name,

¹⁰Which went to the families of the descendants of Aaron, of the Kohathite branch of the Levites, for the lot fell to them first.

¹¹They gave them [the city of] Kiriath-arba, Arba being the father of Anak, which city is Hebron, in the hill country of Judah, with its pasturelands round about it.

¹²But the city's fields and villages they gave to Caleb son of Jephunneh as his own.

¹³Thus to the descendants of Aaron the priest they gave Hebron, the city of refuge for the slayer, with its pasturelands (suburbs), and together with their suburbs, Libnah,

¹⁴Jattir, Eshtemoa,

¹⁵Holon, Debir,

¹⁶Ain, Juttah, and Beth-shemesh; nine cities, each with its suburbs, out of those two tribes.

---

ᵃ The Levites were divided into three groups, the descendants of Levi's three sons, Gershon, Kohath, and Merari. But only those Israelites who were descendants of Levi through Kohath's grandson Aaron could be priests. The priesthood was made hereditary in the family of Aaron and restricted to it; however, even some of these were debarred by legal disabilities (Lev. 21:16ff.). The other families of Levi's descendants, the Gershonites and Merarites and those Kohathites who were not descended from Aaron, were charged with the care of the sanctuary. The priests ministered at the altar.

## New International Version

[17] And from the tribe of Benjamin they gave them Gibeon, Geba, [18] Anathoth and Almon, together with their pasturelands—four towns.

[19] The total number of towns for the priests, the descendants of Aaron, came to thirteen, together with their pasturelands.

[20] The rest of the Kohathite clans of the Levites were allotted towns from the tribe of Ephraim:

[21] In the hill country of Ephraim they were given Shechem (a city of refuge for one accused of murder) and Gezer, [22] Kibzaim and Beth Horon, together with their pasturelands—four towns.

[23] Also from the tribe of Dan they received Eltekeh, Gibbethon, [24] Aijalon and Gath Rimmon, together with their pasturelands—four towns.

[25] From half the tribe of Manasseh they received Taanach and Gath Rimmon, together with their pasturelands—two towns.

[26] All these ten towns and their pasturelands were given to the rest of the Kohathite clans.

[27] The Levite clans of the Gershonites were given:
from the half-tribe of Manasseh,
Golan in Bashan (a city of refuge for one accused of murder) and Be Eshterah, together with their pasturelands—two towns;
[28] from the tribe of Issachar,
Kishion, Daberath, [29] Jarmuth and En Gannim, together with their pasturelands—four towns;
[30] from the tribe of Asher,
Mishal, Abdon, [31] Helkath and Rehob, together with their pasturelands—four towns;
[32] from the tribe of Naphtali,
Kedesh in Galilee (a city of refuge for one accused of murder), Hammoth Dor and Kartan, together with their pasturelands—three towns.
[33] The total number of towns of the Gershonite clans came to thirteen, together with their pasturelands.

[34] The Merarite clans (the rest of the Levites) were given:
from the tribe of Zebulun,
Jokneam, Kartah, [35] Dimnah and Nahalal, together with their pasturelands—four towns;
[36] from the tribe of Reuben,
Bezer, Jahaz, [37] Kedemoth and Mephaath, together with their pasturelands—four towns;
[38] from the tribe of Gad,
Ramoth in Gilead (a city of refuge for one accused of murder), Mahanaim, [39] Heshbon and Jazer, together with their pasturelands—four towns in all.
[40] The total number of towns allotted to the Merarite clans, who were the rest of the Levites, came to twelve.

[41] The towns of the Levites in the territory held by the Israelites were forty-eight in all, together with their pasturelands. [42] Each of these towns had pasturelands surrounding it; this was true for all these towns.

[43] So the LORD gave Israel all the land he had sworn to give their ancestors, and they took possession of it and settled there. [44] The LORD gave them rest on every side, just as he had sworn to their ancestors. Not one of their enemies withstood them; the LORD gave all their enemies into their hands. [45] Not one of all the LORD's good promises to Israel failed; every one was fulfilled.

## Amplified Bible

[17] Out of the tribe of Benjamin, Gibeon, Geba,
[18] Anathoth, and Almon; four cities, each with its suburbs.
[19] The cities of the sons of Aaron, the priests, were thirteen, with their suburbs.
[20] The rest of the Kohathites belonging to the Levitical families were allotted cities out of the tribe of Ephraim.
[21] To them were given, each with its pasturelands (suburbs), Shechem in the hill country of Ephraim, as the city of refuge for the slayer, and Gezer,
[22] And Kibzaim, and Beth-horon; four cities, each with its pasturelands (suburbs).
[23] And out of the tribe of Dan, each with its pasturelands (suburbs), Eltekeh, Gibbethon,
[24] Aijalon, and Gath-rimmon; four cities, each with its pasturelands (suburbs).
[25] And out of the half-tribe of Manasseh, Taanach, and [another] Gath-rimmon; two cities, each with its pasturelands (suburbs).
[26] All the cities for the families of the remaining Kohathites were ten, with their pasturelands (suburbs).
[27] And to the Gershonites of the families of the Levites they gave out of the other half-tribe of Manasseh the city of Golan in Bashan, as the city of refuge for the slayer, and Be-eshterah; two cities, each with its pasturelands.
[28] Out of the tribe of Issachar, Kishion, Daberath,
[29] Jarmuth, and En-gannim; four cities, each with its suburbs.
[30] Out of the tribe of Asher, Mishal, Abdon,
[31] Helkath, and Rehob; four cities, each with its pasturelands.
[32] And out of the tribe of Naphtali, Kedesh in Galilee, city of refuge for the slayer, and Hammoth-dor, and Kartan; three cities, each with its suburbs.
[33] All the cities of the Gershonite families were thirteen, with their pasturelands (suburbs).
[34] And to the families of the Merarites, the rest of the Levites, out of the tribe of Zebulun were given Jokneam, Kartah,
[35] Dimnah, and Nahalal; four cities, each with its pasturelands (suburbs).
[36] And out of the tribe of Reuben, Bezer, Jahaz,
[37] Kedemoth, and Mephaath; four cities, each with its pasturelands (suburbs).
[38] And out of the tribe of Gad, Ramoth in Gilead, as the city of refuge for the slayer, and Mahanaim,
[39] Heshbon, and Jazer; four cities in all, each with its pasturelands (suburbs).
[40] So all the cities allotted to the Merarite families, that is, the remainder of the Levite families, were twelve cities.
[41] The cities of the Levites in the midst of the possession of the Israelites were forty-eight cities in all, with their pasturelands (suburbs).
[42] These cities all had their pasturelands (suburbs) around them.
[43] And the Lord gave to Israel all the land which He had sworn to give to their fathers, and they possessed it and dwelt in it.
[44] The Lord gave them rest round about, just as He had sworn to their fathers. Not one of all their enemies withstood them; the Lord delivered all their enemies into their hands.
[45] There failed no part of any good thing which the Lord had promised to the house of Israel; all came to pass.

## New International Version

### Eastern Tribes Return Home

**22** Then Joshua summoned the Reubenites, the Gadites and the half-tribe of Manasseh ²and said to them, "You have done all that Moses the servant of the LORD commanded, and you have obeyed me in everything I commanded. ³For a long time now—to this very day—you have not deserted your fellow Israelites but have carried out the mission the LORD your God gave you. ⁴Now that the LORD your God has given them rest as he promised, return to your homes in the land that Moses the servant of the LORD gave you on the other side of the Jordan. ⁵But be very careful to keep the commandment and the law that Moses the servant of the LORD gave you: to love the LORD your God, to walk in obedience to him, to keep his commands, to hold fast to him and to serve him with all your heart and with all your soul."

⁶Then Joshua blessed them and sent them away, and they went to their homes. ⁷(To the half-tribe of Manasseh Moses had given land in Bashan, and to the other half of the tribe Joshua gave land on the west side of the Jordan along with their fellow Israelites.) When Joshua sent them home, he blessed them, ⁸saying, "Return to your homes with your great wealth—with large herds of livestock, with silver, gold, bronze and iron, and a great quantity of clothing—and divide the plunder from your enemies with your fellow Israelites."

⁹So the Reubenites, the Gadites and the half-tribe of Manasseh left the Israelites at Shiloh in Canaan to return to Gilead, their own land, which they had acquired in accordance with the command of the LORD through Moses.

¹⁰When they came to Geliloth near the Jordan in the land of Canaan, the Reubenites, the Gadites and the half-tribe of Manasseh built an imposing altar there by the Jordan. ¹¹And when the Israelites heard that they had built the altar on the border of Canaan at Geliloth near the Jordan on the Israelite side, ¹²the whole assembly of Israel gathered at Shiloh to go to war against them.

¹³So the Israelites sent Phinehas son of Eleazar, the priest, to the land of Gilead—to Reuben, Gad and the half-tribe of Manasseh. ¹⁴With him they sent ten of the chief men, one from each of the tribes of Israel, each the head of a family division among the Israelite clans.

¹⁵When they went to Gilead—to Reuben, Gad and the half-tribe of Manasseh—they said to them: ¹⁶"The whole assembly of the LORD says: 'How could you break faith with the God of Israel like this? How could you turn away from the LORD and build yourselves an altar in rebellion against him now? ¹⁷Was not the sin of Peor enough for us? Up to this very day we have not cleansed ourselves from that sin, even though a plague fell on the community of the LORD! ¹⁸And are you now turning away from the LORD?

"'If you rebel against the LORD today, tomorrow he will be angry with the whole community of Israel. ¹⁹If the

## Amplified Bible

**22** Then Joshua called the Reubenites, the Gadites, and the half-tribe of Manasseh, ²And said to them, You have kept all that Moses the servant of the Lord commanded you, and have obeyed my voice in all that I commanded you.

³You have not deserted your brethren [the other tribes] these many days to this day but have carefully kept the charge of the Lord your God.

⁴But now the Lord your God has given rest to your brethren, as He promised them; so now go, return to your homes in the land of your possession, which Moses the servant of the Lord gave you on the [east] side of the Jordan.

⁵But take diligent heed to do the commandment and the law which Moses the servant of the Lord charged you: to love the Lord your God and to walk in all His ways and to keep His commandments and to cling to *and* unite with Him and to serve Him with all your heart and soul [your very life].

⁶So Joshua blessed them and sent them away, and they went to their homes.

⁷Now to one-half of the tribe of Manasseh Moses had given a possession in Bashan, but to the other half Joshua gave a possession on the west side of the Jordan among their brethren. So when Joshua sent them away to their homes, he blessed them,

⁸And he said to them, Return with much riches to your tents and with very much livestock, with silver, gold, bronze, iron, and very much clothing. Divide the spoil of your enemies with your brethren.

⁹So the Reubenites, Gadites, and the half-tribe of Manasseh returned home, parting from the [other] Israelites at Shiloh in the land of Canaan to go to the land of Gilead, their own land of which they had been given possession by the command of the Lord through Moses.

¹⁰And when they came to the region of the Jordan in the land of Canaan, the Reubenites, Gadites, and the half-tribe of Manasseh built there an altar by the Jordan, an altar great to behold.

¹¹And the [other] Israelites heard it said, Behold, the Reubenites, Gadites, and the half-tribe of Manasseh have built an altar at the edge of the land of Canaan in the region [west] of the Jordan in the passage [belonging to us], the Israelites.

¹²When the Israelites heard of it, the whole congregation of the sons of Israel gathered at Shiloh to make war on them.

¹³And the [other] Israelites sent to the Reubenites, Gadites, and the half-tribe of Manasseh, in the land of Gilead, Phinehas son of Eleazar, the priest,

¹⁴And with him ten chiefs, one from each of the tribal families of Israel; and each one was a head of a father's house among the clans of Israel.

¹⁵And they came to the Reubenites, Gadites, and the half-tribe of Manasseh, in the land of Gilead, and they said to them,

¹⁶The whole congregation of the Lord says, What trespass is this that you have committed against the God of Israel, to turn away this day from following the Lord, in that you have built yourselves an altar to rebel this day against the Lord?

¹⁷Is the iniquity of Peor too little for us, from which we are not cleansed even now, although there came a plague [in which 24,000 died] in the congregation of the Lord, [Num. 25:1-9.]

¹⁸That you must turn away this day from following the Lord? The result will be, since you rebel today against the Lord, that tomorrow He will be angry with the whole congregation of Israel.

## New International Version

land you possess is defiled, come over to the LORD's land, where the LORD's tabernacle stands, and share the land with us. But do not rebel against the LORD or against us by building an altar for yourselves, other than the altar of the LORD our God. [20]When Achan son of Zerah was unfaithful in regard to the devoted things,[a] did not wrath come on the whole community of Israel? He was not the only one who died for his sin.'"

[21]Then Reuben, Gad and the half-tribe of Manasseh replied to the heads of the clans of Israel: [22]"The Mighty One, God, the LORD! The Mighty One, God, the LORD! He knows! And let Israel know! If this has been in rebellion or disobedience to the LORD, do not spare us this day. [23]If we have built our own altar to turn away from the LORD and to offer burnt offerings and grain offerings, or to sacrifice fellowship offerings on it, may the LORD himself call us to account.

[24]"No! We did it for fear that some day your descendants might say to ours, 'What do you have to do with the LORD, the God of Israel? [25]The LORD has made the Jordan a boundary between us and you—you Reubenites and Gadites! You have no share in the LORD.' So your descendants might cause ours to stop fearing the LORD.

[26]"That is why we said, 'Let us get ready and build an altar—but not for burnt offerings or sacrifices.' [27]On the contrary, it is to be a witness between us and you and the generations that follow, that we will worship the LORD at his sanctuary with our burnt offerings, sacrifices and fellowship offerings. Then in the future your descendants will not be able to say to ours, 'You have no share in the LORD.'

[28]"And we said, 'If they ever say this to us, or to our descendants, we will answer: Look at the replica of the LORD's altar, which our ancestors built, not for burnt offerings and sacrifices, but as a witness between us and you.'

[29]"Far be it from us to rebel against the LORD and turn away from him today by building an altar for burnt offerings, grain offerings and sacrifices, other than the altar of the LORD our God that stands before his tabernacle."

[30]When Phinehas the priest and the leaders of the community—the heads of the clans of the Israelites—heard what Reuben, Gad and Manasseh had to say, they were pleased. [31]And Phinehas son of Eleazar, the priest, said to Reuben, Gad and Manasseh, "Today we know that the LORD is with us, because you have not been unfaithful to the LORD in this matter. Now you have rescued the Israelites from the LORD's hand."

[32]Then Phinehas son of Eleazar, the priest, and the leaders returned to Canaan from their meeting with the Reubenites and Gadites in Gilead and reported to the Israelites. [33]They were glad to hear the report and praised God. And they talked no more about going to war against them to devastate the country where the Reubenites and the Gadites lived.

[34]And the Reubenites and the Gadites gave the altar this name: A Witness Between Us—that the LORD is God.

## Amplified Bible

[19]But now, if your land is unclean, pass over into the Lord's land, where the Lord's tabernacle resides, and take for yourselves a possession among us. But do not rebel against the Lord or rebel against us by building for yourselves an altar other than the altar of the Lord our God.

[20]Did not Achan son of Zerah commit a trespass in the matter of taking accursed things [devoted to destruction] and wrath fall on all the congregation of Israel? And he did not perish alone in his perversity and iniquity. [Josh. 7.]

[21]Then the Reubenites, Gadites, and the half-tribe of Manasseh said to the heads of the clans of Israel,

[22]The Mighty One, God, the Lord! The Mighty One, God, the Lord! He knows, and let Israel itself know! If it was in rebellion or in transgression against the Lord, spare us not today.

[23]If we have built us an altar to turn away from following the Lord, or if we did so to offer on it burnt offerings or cereal offerings or peace offerings, may the Lord Himself take vengeance.

[24]No! But we did it for fear that in time to come your children might say to our children, What have you to do with the Lord, the God of Israel?

[25]For the Lord has made the Jordan a boundary between us and you, you Reubenites and Gadites; you have no part in the Lord. So your children might make our children cease from fearing the Lord.

[26]So we said, Let us now prepare to build us an altar, not for burnt offering nor for sacrifice,

[27]But to be a witness between us and you and between the generations after us, that we will perform the service of the Lord before Him with our burnt offerings and sacrifices and peace offerings; lest your children say to our children in time to come, You have no portion in the Lord.

[28]So we thought, if that should be said to us or to our descendants in time to come, we can reply, Behold the copy of the altar of the Lord, which our fathers made, not for burnt offerings nor for sacrifices, but to be a witness between us and you.

[29]Far be it from us that we should rebel against the Lord and turn away this day from following the Lord to build an altar for burnt offerings, for cereal offerings, or for sacrifices, besides the altar of the Lord our God that is before His tabernacle.

[30]And when Phinehas the priest and the chiefs of the congregation and heads of the clans of Israel who were with him heard the words that the Reubenites, Gadites, and Manassites spoke, it pleased them.

[31]Phinehas son of Eleazar, the priest, said to the Reubenites, Gadites, and Manassites, Today we know that the Lord is among us, because you have not committed this trespass and treachery against the Lord; now you have saved the Israelites from the Lord's hand.

[32]Then Phinehas son of Eleazar, the priest, and the chiefs returned from the Reubenites and Gadites in the land of Gilead to the land of Canaan, to the [other] Israelites, and brought back word to them.

[33]The report pleased the Israelites and they blessed God; and they spoke no more of going to war against them to destroy the land in which the Reubenites and Gadites dwelt.

[34]The Reubenites and Gadites called the altar Ed [witness], saying, It shall be: A Witness Between Us that the Lord is God.

---

[a] 20 The Hebrew term refers to the irrevocable giving over of things or persons to the LORD, often by totally destroying them.

## New International Version

### Joshua's Farewell to the Leaders

**23** After a long time had passed and the LORD had given Israel rest from all their enemies around them, Joshua, by then a very old man, ²summoned all Israel—their elders, leaders, judges and officials—and said to them: "I am very old. ³You yourselves have seen everything the LORD your God has done to all these nations for your sake; it was the LORD your God who fought for you. ⁴Remember how I have allotted as an inheritance for your tribes all the land of the nations that remain—the nations I conquered—between the Jordan and the Mediterranean Sea in the west. ⁵The LORD your God himself will push them out for your sake. He will drive them out before you, and you will take possession of their land, as the LORD your God promised you.

⁶"Be very strong; be careful to obey all that is written in the Book of the Law of Moses, without turning aside to the right or to the left. ⁷Do not associate with these nations that remain among you; do not invoke the names of their gods or swear by them. You must not serve them or bow down to them. ⁸But you are to hold fast to the LORD your God, as you have until now.

⁹"The LORD has driven out before you great and powerful nations; to this day no one has been able to withstand you. ¹⁰One of you routs a thousand, because the LORD your God fights for you, just as he promised. ¹¹So be very careful to love the LORD your God.

¹²"But if you turn away and ally yourselves with the survivors of these nations that remain among you and if you intermarry with them and associate with them, ¹³then you may be sure that the LORD your God will no longer drive out these nations before you. Instead, they will become snares and traps for you, whips on your backs and thorns in your eyes, until you perish from this good land, which the LORD your God has given you.

¹⁴"Now I am about to go the way of all the earth. You know with all your heart and soul that not one of all the good promises the LORD your God gave you has failed. Every promise has been fulfilled; not one has failed. ¹⁵But just as all the good things the LORD your God has promised you have come to you, so he will bring on you all the evil things he has threatened, until the LORD your God has destroyed you from this good land he has given you. ¹⁶If you violate the covenant of the LORD your God, which he commanded you, and go and serve other gods and bow down to them, the LORD's anger will burn against you, and you will quickly perish from the good land he has given you."

## Amplified Bible

**23** A long time after that, when the Lord had given Israel rest from all their enemies round about, and Joshua had grown old and advanced in years, ²Joshua summoned all Israel, their elders, heads, judges, and officers, and said to them, I am old and advanced in years.

³And you have seen all that the Lord your God has done to all these nations for your sake; for it is the Lord your God Who has fought for you. [Exod. 14:14.]

⁴Behold, I have allotted to you as an inheritance for your tribes those nations that remain, with all the nations I have cut off, from the Jordan to the Great Sea on the west.

⁵The Lord your God will thrust them out from before you and drive them out of your sight, and you shall possess their land, as the Lord your God ᵃpromised you.

⁶So be very courageous *and* steadfast to keep and do all that is written in the Book of the Law of Moses, turning not aside from it to the right hand or the left,

⁷That you may not mix with these nations that remain among you, or make mention of the names of their gods or swear by them or serve them or bow down to them.

⁸But cling to the Lord your God as you have done to this day.

⁹For the Lord has driven out from before you great and strong nations; and as for you, no man has been able to withstand you to this day.

¹⁰One man of you shall put to flight a thousand, for it is the Lord your God Who fights for you, as He promised you.

¹¹Be very watchful of yourselves, therefore, to ᵇlove the Lord your God.

¹²For if you turn back and adhere to the remnant of these nations left among you and make marriages with them, you marrying their women and they yours,

¹³Know with certainty that the Lord your God will not continue to drive these nations from before you; but they shall be a snare and trap to you, and a scourge in your sides and thorns in your eyes, until you perish from off this good land which the Lord your God has given you.

¹⁴And behold, this day I am going the way of all the earth. Know in all your hearts and in all your souls that not one thing has failed of all the good things which the Lord your God promised concerning you. All have come to pass for you; not one thing of them has failed.

¹⁵But just as all good things which the Lord promised you have come to you, so will the Lord carry out [His] every [warning of] evil upon you, until He has destroyed you from off this good land which the Lord your God has given you.

¹⁶If you transgress the covenant of the Lord your God, which He commanded you, if you serve other gods and bow down to them, then the anger of the Lord will be kindled against you, and you shall perish quickly from off the good land He has given you.

---

ᵃ All through the time of Joshua's leadership he kept giving as his warrant of faith the fact that the Lord had spoken, the Lord had promised. The word of God is the guaranty of faith. Genuine faith always advances on the authority expressed in Heb. 13:5, 6, "**He** [God] Himself has said, . . . So **we** take comfort *and* are encouraged *and* confidently *and* boldly say . . ." (emphasis added). ᵇ Everything depended on whether or not Israel would continue to be faithful to the covenant. Joshua's words do not conceal his apprehension. Seven times he refers to the idolatrous nations still left in Canaan. He knew the snare they would be to Israel, and he therefore prescribed three safeguards. First, there must be brave **adherence to God's word** (Josh. 23:6). Second, there must be a vigilantly continued **separation** from the Canaanite nations (Josh. 23:7). Finally, there must be a cleaving to the Lord with real and fervent **love** (Josh. 23:8-11) (J. Sidlow Baxter, *Explore the Book*).

## New International Version

### The Covenant Renewed at Shechem

**24** Then Joshua assembled all the tribes of Israel at Shechem. He summoned the elders, leaders, judges and officials of Israel, and they presented themselves before God.

[2] Joshua said to all the people, "This is what the LORD, the God of Israel, says: 'Long ago your ancestors, including Terah the father of Abraham and Nahor, lived beyond the Euphrates River and worshiped other gods. [3] But I took your father Abraham from the land beyond the Euphrates and led him throughout Canaan and gave him many descendants. I gave him Isaac, [4] and to Isaac I gave Jacob and Esau. I assigned the hill country of Seir to Esau, but Jacob and his family went down to Egypt.

[5] "'Then I sent Moses and Aaron, and I afflicted the Egyptians by what I did there, and I brought you out. [6] When I brought your people out of Egypt, you came to the sea, and the Egyptians pursued them with chariots and horsemen[a] as far as the Red Sea.[b] [7] But they cried to the LORD for help, and he put darkness between you and the Egyptians; he brought the sea over them and covered them. You saw with your own eyes what I did to the Egyptians. Then you lived in the wilderness for a long time.

[8] "'I brought you to the land of the Amorites who lived east of the Jordan. They fought against you, but I gave them into your hands. I destroyed them from before you, and you took possession of their land. [9] When Balak son of Zippor, the king of Moab, prepared to fight against Israel, he sent for Balaam son of Beor to put a curse on you. [10] But I would not listen to Balaam, so he blessed you again and again, and I delivered you out of his hand.

[11] "'Then you crossed the Jordan and came to Jericho. The citizens of Jericho fought against you, as did also the Amorites, Perizzites, Canaanites, Hittites, Girgashites, Hivites and Jebusites, but I gave them into your hands. [12] I sent the hornet ahead of you, which drove them out before you—also the two Amorite kings. You did not do it with your own sword and bow. [13] So I gave you a land on which you did not toil and cities you did not build; and you live in them and eat from vineyards and olive groves that you did not plant.'

[14] "Now fear the LORD and serve him with all faithfulness. Throw away the gods your ancestors worshiped beyond the Euphrates River and in Egypt, and serve the LORD. [15] But if serving the LORD seems undesirable to you, then choose for yourselves this day whom you will serve, whether the gods your ancestors served beyond the Euphrates, or the gods of the Amorites, in whose land you are living. But as for me and my household, we will serve the LORD."

[16] Then the people answered, "Far be it from us to forsake the LORD to serve other gods! [17] It was the LORD our God himself who brought us and our parents up out of Egypt, from that land of slavery, and performed those great signs before our eyes. He protected us on our entire journey and among all the nations through which we traveled. [18] And the LORD drove out before us all the nations, including the Amorites, who lived in the land. We too will serve the LORD, because he is our God."

[19] Joshua said to the people, "You are not able to serve the LORD. He is a holy God; he is a jealous God. He will not forgive your rebellion and your sins. [20] If you forsake

## Amplified Bible

**24** Then Joshua gathered all the tribes of Israel to Shechem, and summoned the elders of Israel and their heads, their judges, and their officers; they presented themselves before God.

[2] Joshua said to all the people, Thus says the Lord, the God of Israel, Your fathers dwelt in olden times beyond the Euphrates River, including Terah the father of Abraham and Nahor, and they served other gods.

[3] And I took your father Abraham from beyond the Euphrates River and led him through all the land of Canaan and multiplied his offspring. I gave him Isaac,

[4] And I gave to Isaac Jacob and Esau. And I gave to Esau the hill country of Seir to possess, but Jacob and his children went down to Egypt.

[5] I sent Moses and Aaron, and I plagued Egypt with what I did in the midst of it; and afterward I brought you out.

[6] I brought your fathers out of Egypt, and you came to the sea; and the Egyptians pursued your fathers with chariots and horsemen to the Red Sea.

[7] When they cried to the Lord, He put darkness between you and the Egyptians, and brought the sea upon them and covered them; and your eyes saw what I did in Egypt. And you lived in the wilderness a long time [forty years]. [Josh. 5:6.]

[8] I brought you into the land of the Amorites who lived on the other side of the Jordan; they fought with you, and I gave them into your hand, and you possessed their land, and I destroyed them before you.

[9] Then Balak son of Zippor, king of Moab, arose and warred against Israel, and sent and called Balaam son of Beor to curse you.

[10] But I would not listen to Balaam; therefore he blessed you; so I delivered you out of Balak's hand. [Deut. 23:5.]

[11] You went over the Jordan and came to Jericho; and the men of Jericho fought against you, as did the Amorites, Perizzites, Canaanites, Hittites, Girgashites, Hivites, and Jebusites, and I gave them into your hands.

[12] I sent the [a]hornet [that is, the terror of you] before you, which drove the two kings of the Amorites out before you; but it was not by your sword or by your bow. [Exod. 23:27, 28; Deut. 2:25; 7:20.]

[13] I have given you a land for which you did not labor and cities you did not build, and you dwell in them; you eat from vineyards and olive yards you did not plant.

[14] Now therefore, [reverently] fear the Lord and serve Him in sincerity and in truth; put away the gods which your fathers served on the other side of the [Euphrates] River and in Egypt, and serve the Lord.

[15] And if it seems evil to you to serve the Lord, choose for yourselves this day whom you will serve, whether the gods which your fathers served on the other side of the River, or the gods of the Amorites, in whose land you dwell; but as for me and my house, we will serve the Lord.

[16] The people answered, Far be it from us to forsake the Lord to serve other gods;

[17] For it is the Lord our God Who brought us and our fathers up out of the land of Egypt, from the house of bondage, Who did those great signs in our sight and preserved us in all the way that we went and among all the peoples through whom we passed.

[18] And the Lord drove out before us all the people, the Amorites who dwelt in the land. Therefore we also will serve the Lord, for He is our God.

[19] And Joshua said to the people, You cannot serve the Lord, for He is a holy God; He is a jealous God. He will not forgive your transgressions or your sins.

---

[a] 6 Or *charioteers*    [b] 6 Or *the Sea of Reeds*

[a] See footnote on Deut. 7:20.

## New International Version

the LORD and serve foreign gods, he will turn and bring disaster on you and make an end of you, after he has been good to you."

²¹But the people said to Joshua, "No! We will serve the LORD."

²²Then Joshua said, "You are witnesses against yourselves that you have chosen to serve the LORD."

"Yes, we are witnesses," they replied.

²³"Now then," said Joshua, "throw away the foreign gods that are among you and yield your hearts to the LORD, the God of Israel."

²⁴And the people said to Joshua, "We will serve the LORD our God and obey him."

²⁵On that day Joshua made a covenant for the people, and there at Shechem he reaffirmed for them decrees and laws. ²⁶And Joshua recorded these things in the Book of the Law of God. Then he took a large stone and set it up there under the oak near the holy place of the LORD.

²⁷"See!" he said to all the people. "This stone will be a witness against us. It has heard all the words the LORD has said to us. It will be a witness against you if you are untrue to your God."

²⁸Then Joshua dismissed the people, each to their own inheritance.

### Buried in the Promised Land

²⁹After these things, Joshua son of Nun, the servant of the LORD, died at the age of a hundred and ten. ³⁰And they buried him in the land of his inheritance, at Timnath Serah*a* in the hill country of Ephraim, north of Mount Gaash.

³¹Israel served the LORD throughout the lifetime of Joshua and of the elders who outlived him and who had experienced everything the LORD had done for Israel.

³²And Joseph's bones, which the Israelites had brought up from Egypt, were buried at Shechem in the tract of land that Jacob bought for a hundred pieces of silver*b* from the sons of Hamor, the father of Shechem. This became the inheritance of Joseph's descendants.

³³And Eleazar son of Aaron died and was buried at Gibeah, which had been allotted to his son Phinehas in the hill country of Ephraim.

## Amplified Bible

²⁰If you forsake the Lord and *a*serve strange gods, then He will turn and do you harm and consume you, after having done you good.

²¹And the people said to Joshua, No; but we will serve the Lord.

²²Then Joshua said to the people, You are witnesses against yourselves that you have chosen the Lord, to serve Him. And they said, We are witnesses.

²³Then put away, said he, the foreign gods that are among you and incline your hearts to the Lord, the God of Israel.

²⁴The people said to Joshua, The Lord our God we will serve; His voice we will obey.

²⁵So Joshua made a covenant with the people that day, and made statutes and ordinances for them at Shechem.

²⁶And Joshua wrote these words in the Book of the Law of God; and he took a great stone and set it up there under an oak that was in [the court of] the sanctuary of the Lord.

²⁷And Joshua said to all the people, See, this stone shall be a witness against us, for it has heard all the words the Lord spoke to us; so it shall be a witness against you, lest [afterward] you lie (pretend) *and* deny your God.

²⁸So Joshua sent the people away, every man to his inheritance.

²⁹After this, Joshua son of Nun, the servant of the Lord, died, being 110 years old.

³⁰They buried him at the edge of his inheritance in Timnath-serah in the hill country of Ephraim, on the north side of the hill of Gaash.

³¹Israel served the Lord all the days of Joshua and of the elders who outlived Joshua and had known all the works the Lord had done for Israel.

³²And the bones of Joseph, which the Israelites brought up out of Egypt, they buried in Shechem in the portion of ground Jacob bought from the sons of Hamor, the father of Shechem, for 100 pieces of money; and it became the inheritance of the Josephites.

³³And Eleazar son of Aaron died; and they buried him at Gibeah [on the hill] of Phinehas his son, which was given him in the hill country of Ephraim.

---

*a* Anything which we keep in our hearts in the place which God ought to have is an idol, whether it be an image of wood or stone or gold, or whether it be money, or desire for fame, or love of pleasure, or some secret sin which we will not give up. If God does not really occupy the highest place in our hearts, controlling all, something else does, and that something else is an idol (J. R. Miller, *Devotional Hours with the Bible*).

---

*a 30* Also known as *Timnath Heres* (see Judges 2:9)    *b 32* Hebrew *hundred kesitahs*; a kesitah was a unit of money of unknown weight and value.

# Judges

## Israel Fights the Remaining Canaanites

**1** After the death of Joshua, the Israelites asked the LORD, "Who of us is to go up first to fight against the Canaanites?"

[2] The LORD answered, "Judah shall go up; I have given the land into their hands."

[3] The men of Judah then said to the Simeonites their fellow Israelites, "Come up with us into the territory allotted to us, to fight against the Canaanites. We in turn will go with you into yours." So the Simeonites went with them.

[4] When Judah attacked, the LORD gave the Canaanites and Perizzites into their hands, and they struck down ten thousand men at Bezek. [5] It was there that they found Adoni-Bezek and fought against him, putting to rout the Canaanites and Perizzites. [6] Adoni-Bezek fled, but they chased him and caught him, and cut off his thumbs and big toes.

[7] Then Adoni-Bezek said, "Seventy kings with their thumbs and big toes cut off have picked up scraps under my table. Now God has paid me back for what I did to them." They brought him to Jerusalem, and he died there.

[8] The men of Judah attacked Jerusalem also and took it. They put the city to the sword and set it on fire.

[9] After that, Judah went down to fight against the Canaanites living in the hill country, the Negev and the western foothills. [10] They advanced against the Canaanites living in Hebron (formerly called Kiriath Arba) and defeated Sheshai, Ahiman and Talmai. [11] From there they advanced against the people living in Debir (formerly called Kiriath Sepher).

[12] And Caleb said, "I will give my daughter Aksah in marriage to the man who attacks and captures Kiriath Sepher." [13] Othniel son of Kenaz, Caleb's younger brother, took it; so Caleb gave his daughter Aksah to him in marriage.

[14] One day when she came to Othniel, she urged him[a] to ask her father for a field. When she got off her donkey, Caleb asked her, "What can I do for you?"

[15] She replied, "Do me a special favor. Since you have given me land in the Negev, give me also springs of water." So Caleb gave her the upper and lower springs.

[16] The descendants of Moses' father-in-law, the Kenite, went up from the City of Palms[b] with the people of Judah to live among the inhabitants of the Desert of Judah in the Negev near Arad.

[17] Then the men of Judah went with the Simeonites their fellow Israelites and attacked the Canaanites living in Zephath, and they totally destroyed[c] the city. Therefore it was called Hormah.[d] [18] Judah also took[e] Gaza, Ashkelon and Ekron—each city with its territory.

[19] The LORD was with the men of Judah. They took possession of the hill country, but they were unable to drive the people from the plains, because they had chariots fitted with iron. [20] As Moses had promised, Hebron was given to Caleb, who drove from it the three sons of Anak. [21] The Benjamites, however, did not drive out the Jebusites, who were living in Jerusalem; to this day the Jebusites live there with the Benjamites.

---

*a 14* Hebrew; Septuagint and Vulgate *Othniel, he urged her*    *b 16* That is, Jericho    *c 17* The Hebrew term refers to the irrevocable giving over of things or persons to the LORD, often by totally destroying them.    *d 17 Hormah* means *destruction.*    *e 18* Hebrew; Septuagint *Judah did not take*

# Judges

**1** After the death of Joshua, the Israelites asked the Lord, Who shall go up first for us against the Canaanites to fight against them?

[2] And the Lord said, Judah shall go up; behold, I have delivered the land into his hand.

[3] And Judah [the tribe] said to [the tribe of] Simeon his brother, Come up with me into my allotted territory, so that we may fight against the Canaanites; and I likewise will go with you into your territory. So Simeon went with him.

[4] Then Judah went up and the Lord delivered the Canaanites and the Perizzites into their hand, and they smote 10,000 of them in Bezek.

[5] And they found Adoni-bezek in Bezek and fought against him, and they smote the Canaanites and the Perizzites.

[6] Adoni-bezek fled, but they pursued him and caught him and cut off his thumbs and his big toes.

[7] Adoni-bezek said, Seventy kings with their thumbs and big toes cut off had to gather their food under my table. As I have done, so God has repaid me. And they brought him to Jerusalem, and there he died.

[8] And the men of Judah fought against [Jebusite] Jerusalem and took it, and smote it with the edge of the sword and set the city on fire.

[9] Afterward the men of Judah went down to fight against the Canaanites who dwelt in the hill country, in the South (the Negeb), and in the lowland.

[10] And Judah went against the Canaanites who dwelt in Hebron. The name of Hebron before was Kiriath-arba. And they defeated Sheshai and Ahiman and Talmai.

[11] From there [Judah] went against the inhabitants of Debir. The name of Debir before was Kiriath-sepher [city of books and scribes].

[12] And Caleb said, Whoever attacks Kiriath-sepher and takes it, to him will I give Achsah, my daughter, as wife.

[13] And Othniel son of Kenaz, Caleb's younger brother, took it; and he gave him Achsah, his daughter, as wife.

[14] And when she came to [Othniel], she got his consent to ask her father for a [sloping] field. And she alighted off her donkey, and Caleb said to her, What do you want?

[15] And she said to him, Give me a present; since you have set me in the land of the South (the Negeb), give me also springs of water. And Caleb gave her the upper and lower springs.

[16] And the descendants of the Kenite, Moses' father-in-law, went up with the Judahites from the City of Palms (Jericho) into the Wilderness of Judah, which lies in the South (the Negeb) near Arad; and they went and dwelt with the people.

[17] And [the tribe of] Judah went with Simeon his brother, and they slew the Canaanites who inhabited Zephath and utterly destroyed it. So the city was called Hormah [destruction].

[18] Also Judah took Gaza, Askelon, and Ekron—each with its territory.

[19] The Lord was with Judah, and [Judah] drove out the inhabitants of the hill country, but he could not drive out those inhabiting the [difficult] valley basin because they had chariots of iron.

[20] Hebron was given to Caleb as Moses said, and he expelled from there the three sons of Anak. [Josh. 14:6, 9.]

[21] But the Benjamites did not drive out the Jebusites who inhabited Jerusalem; the Jebusites dwell with the Benjamites in Jerusalem to this day.

## New International Version

²²Now the tribes of Joseph attacked Bethel, and the LORD was with them. ²³When they sent men to spy out Bethel (formerly called Luz), ²⁴the spies saw a man coming out of the city and they said to him, "Show us how to get into the city and we will see that you are treated well." ²⁵So he showed them, and they put the city to the sword but spared the man and his whole family. ²⁶He then went to the land of the Hittites, where he built a city and called it Luz, which is its name to this day.

²⁷But Manasseh did not drive out the people of Beth Shan or Taanach or Dor or Ibleam or Megiddo and their surrounding settlements, for the Canaanites were determined to live in that land. ²⁸When Israel became strong, they pressed the Canaanites into forced labor but never drove them out completely. ²⁹Nor did Ephraim drive out the Canaanites living in Gezer, but the Canaanites continued to live there among them. ³⁰Neither did Zebulun drive out the Canaanites living in Kitron or Nahalol, so these Canaanites lived among them, but Zebulun did subject them to forced labor. ³¹Nor did Asher drive out those living in Akko or Sidon or Ahlab or Akzib or Helbah or Aphek or Rehob. ³²The Asherites lived among the Canaanite inhabitants of the land because they did not drive them out. ³³Neither did Naphtali drive out those living in Beth Shemesh or Beth Anath; but the Naphtalites too lived among the Canaanite inhabitants of the land, and those living in Beth Shemesh and Beth Anath became forced laborers for them. ³⁴The Amorites confined the Danites to the hill country, not allowing them to come down into the plain. ³⁵And the Amorites were determined also to hold out in Mount Heres, Aijalon and Shaalbim, but when the power of the tribes of Joseph increased, they too were pressed into forced labor. ³⁶The boundary of the Amorites was from Scorpion Pass to Sela and beyond.

### The Angel of the LORD at Bokim

**2** The angel of the LORD went up from Gilgal to Bokim and said, "I brought you up out of Egypt and led you into the land I swore to give to your ancestors. I said, 'I will never break my covenant with you, ²and you shall not make a covenant with the people of this land, but you shall break down their altars.' Yet you have disobeyed me. Why have you done this? ³And I have also said, 'I will not drive them out before you; they will become traps for you, and their gods will become snares to you.'"

⁴When the angel of the LORD had spoken these things to all the Israelites, the people wept aloud, ⁵and they called that place Bokim.ᵃ There they offered sacrifices to the LORD.

### Disobedience and Defeat

⁶After Joshua had dismissed the Israelites, they went to take possession of the land, each to their own inheritance. ⁷The people served the LORD throughout the lifetime of

## Amplified Bible

²²The house of Joseph also went up against Bethel, and the Lord was with them.

²³And the house of Joseph was sent to spy out Bethel. The name of the city formerly had been Luz.

²⁴And the spies saw a man coming out of the city and they said to him, Show us, we pray you, the way into the city and we will show you mercy.

²⁵When he showed them the entrance to the city, they smote the city with the sword, but they let the man and all his family go.

²⁶And the man went into the land of the Hittites and built a city and called it Luz, which is its name to this day.

²⁷Neither did Manasseh drive out the inhabitants of Beth-shean and its villages, or of Taanach or Dor or Ibleam or Megiddo and their villages, but the Canaanites remained in that land.

²⁸When Israel became strong, they put the Canaanites to forced labor but did not utterly drive them out.

²⁹Neither did Ephraim drive out the Canaanites who dwelt in Gezer, but the Canaanites dwelt in Gezer among them.

³⁰Neither did Zebulun drive out the inhabitants of Kitron or of Nahalol, but the Canaanites dwelt among them and were put to forced labor.

³¹Neither did Asher drive out the inhabitants of Acco or of Sidon or of Ahlab or of Achzib or of Helbah or of Aphik or of Rehob;

³²But the Asherites dwelt among the Canaanites, the inhabitants of the land, for they did not drive them out.

³³Neither did Naphtali drive out the inhabitants of Beth-shemesh or of Beth-anath, but dwelt among the Canaanites, the inhabitants of the land; but the inhabitants of Beth-shemesh and of Beth-anath became subject to forced labor for them.

³⁴The Amorites forced the Danites back into the hill country, for they would not allow them to come down into the plain;

³⁵The Amorites remained fixed in Mount Heres [mountain of the sun], in Aijalon, and in Shaalbim; yet the hand of the house of Joseph prevailed, so that they became subject to forced labor.

³⁶And the border of the Amorites was from the ascent of Akrabbim, from the rock Sela and onward.

**2** Now the ᵃAngel of the Lord went up from Gilgal to Bochim. And He said, I brought you up from Egypt and have brought you to the land which I swore to give to your fathers, and I said, I will never break My covenant with you; [Exod. 20:2.]

²And you shall make no covenant with the inhabitants of this land; but you shall break down their altars. But you have not obeyed My voice. Why have you done this?

³So now I say, I will not drive them out from before you; but they shall be as thorns in your sides, and their gods shall be a snare to you.

⁴When the Angel of the Lord spoke these words to all the Israelites, the people lifted up their voice and wept.

⁵They named that place Bochim [weepers], and they sacrificed there to the Lord.

⁶And when Joshua had let the people go, the Israelites went every man to his inheritance to possess the land.

⁷And the people served the Lord all the days of Joshua and all the days of the elders who outlived Joshua, who

---

ᵃ 5 *Bokim* means *weepers*.

ᵃ See footnote on Gen. 16:7.

## New International Version

Joshua and of the elders who outlived him and who had seen all the great things the LORD had done for Israel. ⁸Joshua son of Nun, the servant of the LORD, died at the age of a hundred and ten. ⁹And they buried him in the land of his inheritance, at Timnath Heres*ᵃ* in the hill country of Ephraim, north of Mount Gaash.

¹⁰After that whole generation had been gathered to their ancestors, another generation grew up who knew neither the LORD nor what he had done for Israel. ¹¹Then the Israelites did evil in the eyes of the LORD and served the Baals. ¹²They forsook the LORD, the God of their ancestors, who had brought them out of Egypt. They followed and worshiped various gods of the peoples around them. They aroused the LORD's anger ¹³because they forsook him and served Baal and the Ashtoreths. ¹⁴In his anger against Israel the LORD gave them into the hands of raiders who plundered them. He sold them into the hands of their enemies all around, whom they were no longer able to resist. ¹⁵Whenever Israel went out to fight, the hand of the LORD was against them to defeat them, just as he had sworn to them. They were in great distress.

¹⁶Then the LORD raised up judges,*ᵇ* who saved them out of the hands of these raiders. ¹⁷Yet they would not listen to their judges but prostituted themselves to other gods and worshiped them. They quickly turned from the ways of their ancestors, who had been obedient to the LORD's commands. ¹⁸Whenever the LORD raised up a judge for them, he was with the judge and saved them out of the hands of their enemies as long as the judge lived; for the LORD relented because of their groaning under those who oppressed and afflicted them. ¹⁹But when the judge died, the people returned to ways even more corrupt than those of their ancestors, following other gods and serving and worshiping them. They refused to give up their evil practices and stubborn ways.

²⁰Therefore the LORD was very angry with Israel and said, "Because this nation has violated the covenant I ordained for their ancestors and has not listened to me, ²¹I will no longer drive out before them any of the nations Joshua left when he died. ²²I will use them to test Israel and see whether they will keep the way of the LORD and walk in it as their ancestors did." ²³The LORD had allowed those nations to remain; he did not drive them out at once by giving them into the hands of Joshua.

**3** These are the nations the LORD left to test all those Israelites who had not experienced any of the wars in Canaan ²(he did this only to teach warfare to the descendants of the Israelites who had not had previous battle experience): ³the five rulers of the Philistines, all the Canaanites, the Sidonians, and the Hivites living in the Lebanon mountains from Mount Baal Hermon to Lebo Ha-

## Amplified Bible

had seen all the great works of the Lord which He did for Israel.

⁸And Joshua son of Nun, the servant of the Lord, died, being 110 years old.

⁹And they buried him within the boundary of his inheritance in Timnath-heres in the hill country of Ephraim, north of Mount Gaash.

¹⁰And also all that generation were gathered to their fathers, and there arose another generation after them who did not know (recognize, understand) the Lord, or even the work which He had done for Israel.

¹¹And the people of Israel did evil in the sight of the Lord and served the Baals.

¹²And they forsook the Lord, the God of their fathers, Who brought them out of the land of Egypt. They went after other gods of the peoples round about them and bowed down to them, and provoked the Lord to anger.

¹³And they forsook the Lord and served Baal [the god worshiped by the Canaanites] and the Ashtaroth [female deities such as Ashtoreth and Asherah].

¹⁴So the anger of the Lord was kindled against Israel, and He gave them into the power of plunderers who robbed them; and He sold them into the hands of their enemies round about, so that they could no longer stand before their foes.

¹⁵Whenever they went out, the hand of the Lord was against them for evil as the Lord had said, and as the Lord had sworn to them; and they were bitterly distressed. [Lev. 26:14-46.]

¹⁶But the Lord raised up judges, who delivered them out of the hands of those who robbed them.

¹⁷And yet they did not listen to their judges, for they played the harlot after other gods and bowed down to them. They turned quickly out of the way in which their fathers had walked, who had obeyed the commandments of the Lord, and they did not so.

¹⁸When the Lord raised them up judges, then He was with the judge and delivered them out of the hands of their enemies all the days of the judge; for the Lord was moved to relent because of their groanings by reason of those who oppressed and vexed them.

¹⁹But when the judge was dead, they turned back and corrupted themselves more than their fathers, following and serving other gods, and bowing down to them. They did not cease from their practices or their stubborn way.

²⁰So the anger of the Lord was kindled against Israel; and He said, Because this people have transgressed My covenant which I commanded their fathers and have not listened to My voice,

²¹I from now on will also not drive out from before them any of the nations which Joshua left when he died,

²²That through them I may prove Israel, whether they will keep the way of the Lord to walk in it, as their fathers kept it, or not.

²³So the Lord left those nations, without driving them out at once, nor had He delivered them into Joshua's power.

**3** Now these are the nations which the Lord left to prove Israel by them, that is, all in Israel who had not previously experienced war in Canaan;

²It was only that the generations of the Israelites might know and be taught war, at least those who previously knew nothing of it.

³The remaining nations are: the five lords of the Philistines, all the Canaanites, the Sidonians, and the Hivites who dwelt on Mount Lebanon from Mount Baal-hermon to the entrance of Hamath.

---

ᵃ 9 Also known as *Timnath Serah* (see Joshua 19:50 and 24:30)
ᵇ 16 Or *leaders*; similarly in verses 17-19

## New International Version

math. [4]They were left to test the Israelites to see whether they would obey the LORD's commands, which he had given their ancestors through Moses.

[5]The Israelites lived among the Canaanites, Hittites, Amorites, Perizzites, Hivites and Jebusites. [6]They took their daughters in marriage and gave their own daughters to their sons, and served their gods.

### Othniel

[7]The Israelites did evil in the eyes of the LORD; they forgot the LORD their God and served the Baals and the Asherahs. [8]The anger of the LORD burned against Israel so that he sold them into the hands of Cushan-Rishathaim king of Aram Naharaim,[a] to whom the Israelites were subject for eight years. [9]But when they cried out to the LORD, he raised up for them a deliverer, Othniel son of Kenaz, Caleb's younger brother, who saved them. [10]The Spirit of the LORD came on him, so that he became Israel's judge[b] and went to war. The LORD gave Cushan-Rishathaim king of Aram into the hands of Othniel, who overpowered him. [11]So the land had peace for forty years, until Othniel son of Kenaz died.

### Ehud

[12]Again the Israelites did evil in the eyes of the LORD, and because they did this evil the LORD gave Eglon king of Moab power over Israel. [13]Getting the Ammonites and Amalekites to join him, Eglon came and attacked Israel, and they took possession of the City of Palms.[c] [14]The Israelites were subject to Eglon king of Moab for eighteen years.

[15]Again the Israelites cried out to the LORD, and he gave them a deliverer—Ehud, a left-handed man, the son of Gera the Benjamite. The Israelites sent him with tribute to Eglon king of Moab. [16]Now Ehud had made a double-edged sword about a cubit[d] long, which he strapped to his right thigh under his clothing. [17]He presented the tribute to Eglon king of Moab, who was a very fat man. [18]After Ehud had presented the tribute, he sent on their way those who had carried it. [19]But on reaching the stone images near Gilgal he himself went back to Eglon and said, "Your Majesty, I have a secret message for you."

The king said to his attendants, "Leave us!" And they all left.

[20]Ehud then approached him while he was sitting alone in the upper room of his palace[e] and said, "I have a message from God for you." As the king rose from his seat, [21]Ehud reached with his left hand, drew the sword from his right thigh and plunged it into the king's belly. [22]Even the handle sank in after the blade, and his bowels discharged. Ehud did not pull the sword out, and the fat closed in over it. [23]Then Ehud went out to the porch[f]; he shut the doors of the upper room behind him and locked them.

[24]After he had gone, the servants came and found the doors of the upper room locked. They said, "He must be relieving himself in the inner room of the palace." [25]They waited to the point of embarrassment, but when he did not

## Amplified Bible

[4]They were for the testing *and* proving of Israel to know whether Israel would listen *and* obey the commandments of the Lord, which He commanded their fathers by Moses.

[5]And the Israelites dwelt among the Canaanites, Hittites, Amorites, Perizzites, Hivites, and Jebusites;

[6]And they married their daughters and gave their own daughters to their sons, and served their gods. [Exod. 34:12-16.]

[7]And the Israelites did evil in the sight of the Lord and forgot the Lord their God and served the Baals and the Ashtaroth. [Judg. 2:13.]

[8]So the anger of the Lord was kindled against Israel, and He sold them into the hand of Chushan-rishathaim king of Mesopotamia; and the Israelites served Chushan-rishathaim eight years.

[9]But when the Israelites cried to the Lord, the Lord raised up a deliverer for the people of Israel to deliver them, Othniel son of Kenaz, Caleb's younger brother.

[10]The Spirit of the Lord came upon him, and he judged Israel. He went out to war, and the Lord delivered Chushan-rishathaim king of Mesopotamia into his hand and his hand prevailed over Chushan-rishathaim.

[11]And the land had rest forty years. Then Othniel son of Kenaz died.

[12]And the Israelites again did evil in the sight of the Lord, and the Lord strengthened Eglon king of Moab against Israel because they had done what was evil in the sight of the Lord.

[13]And [Eglon] gathered to him the men of Ammon and Amalek, and went and smote Israel, and they possessed the City of Palm Trees (Jericho).

[14]And the Israelites served Eglon king of Moab eighteen years.

[15]But when the Israelites cried to the Lord, the Lord raised them up a deliverer, Ehud son of Gera, a Benjamite, a left-handed man; and by him the Israelites sent tribute to Eglon king of Moab.

[16]Ehud made for himself a sword, a cubit long, which had two edges, and he girded it on his right thigh under his clothing.

[17]And he brought the tribute to Eglon king of Moab. Now Eglon was a very fat man.

[18]And when Ehud had finished presenting the tribute, he sent away the people who had carried it.

[19]He himself went [with them] as far as the sculptured [boundary] stones near Gilgal, and then turned back and came to Eglon and said, I have a secret errand to you, O king. Eglon commanded silence, and all who stood by him went out from him.

[20]When Ehud had come [near] to him as he was sitting alone in his cool upper apartment, Ehud said, I have a commission from God to execute to you. And the king arose from his seat.

[21]Then Ehud put forth his left hand and took the sword from his right thigh and thrust it into Eglon's belly.

[22]And the hilt also went in after the blade, and the fat closed upon the blade, for [Ehud] did not draw the sword out of his belly, and the dirt came out.

[23]Then Ehud went out into the vestibule and shut the doors of the upper room upon [Eglon] and locked them.

[24]When [Ehud] had gone out, [Eglon's] servants came. And when they saw the doors of the upper room were locked, they thought, Surely he [is seeking privacy while he] relieves himself in the closet of the cool chamber.

[25]They waited a long time until they became embarrassed *and* uneasy, but when he still did not open the doors

---

[a] 8 That is, Northwest Mesopotamia   [b] 10 Or *leader*   [c] 13 That is, Jericho   [d] 16 That is, about 18 inches or about 45 centimeters   [e] 20 The meaning of the Hebrew for this word is uncertain; also in verse 24.   [f] 23 The meaning of the Hebrew for this word is uncertain.

## New International Version

open the doors of the room, they took a key and unlocked them. There they saw their lord fallen to the floor, dead. <sup>26</sup>While they waited, Ehud got away. He passed by the stone images and escaped to Seirah. <sup>27</sup>When he arrived there, he blew a trumpet in the hill country of Ephraim, and the Israelites went down with him from the hills, with him leading them. <sup>28</sup>"Follow me," he ordered, "for the LORD has given Moab, your enemy, into your hands." So they followed him down and took possession of the fords of the Jordan that led to Moab; they allowed no one to cross over. <sup>29</sup>At that time they struck down about ten thousand Moabites, all vigorous and strong; not one escaped. <sup>30</sup>That day Moab was made subject to Israel, and the land had peace for eighty years.

### Shamgar

<sup>31</sup>After Ehud came Shamgar son of Anath, who struck down six hundred Philistines with an oxgoad. He too saved Israel.

### Deborah

**4** Again the Israelites did evil in the eyes of the LORD, now that Ehud was dead. <sup>2</sup>So the LORD sold them into the hands of Jabin king of Canaan, who reigned in Hazor. Sisera, the commander of his army, was based in Harosheth Haggoyim. <sup>3</sup>Because he had nine hundred chariots fitted with iron and had cruelly oppressed the Israelites for twenty years, they cried to the LORD for help.

<sup>4</sup>Now Deborah, a prophet, the wife of Lappidoth, was leading<sup>a</sup> Israel at that time. <sup>5</sup>She held court under the Palm of Deborah between Ramah and Bethel in the hill country of Ephraim, and the Israelites went up to her to have their disputes decided. <sup>6</sup>She sent for Barak son of Abinoam from Kedesh in Naphtali and said to him, "The LORD, the God of Israel, commands you: 'Go, take with you ten thousand men of Naphtali and Zebulun and lead them up to Mount Tabor. <sup>7</sup>I will lead Sisera, the commander of Jabin's army, with his chariots and his troops to the Kishon River and give him into your hands.'"

<sup>8</sup>Barak said to her, "If you go with me, I will go; but if you don't go with me, I won't go."

<sup>9</sup>"Certainly I will go with you," said Deborah. "But because of the course you are taking, the honor will not be yours, for the LORD will deliver Sisera into the hands of a woman." So Deborah went with Barak to Kedesh. <sup>10</sup>There Barak summoned Zebulun and Naphtali, and ten thousand men went up under his command. Deborah also went up with him.

<sup>11</sup>Now Heber the Kenite had left the other Kenites, the descendants of Hobab, Moses' brother-in-law,<sup>b</sup> and

## Amplified Bible

of the upper room, they took the key and opened them, and there lay their master fallen to the floor, dead! <sup>26</sup>Ehud escaped while they delayed and passed beyond the sculptured [boundary] stones (images) and escaped to Seirah.

<sup>27</sup>When he arrived, he blew a trumpet in the hill country of Ephraim, and the Israelites went down from the hill country, with him at their head.

<sup>28</sup>And he said to them, Follow me, for the Lord has delivered your enemies the Moabites into your hand. So they went down after him and seized the fords of the Jordan against the Moabites and permitted not a man to pass over.

<sup>29</sup>They slew at that time about 10,000 Moabites, all strong, courageous men; not a man escaped.

<sup>30</sup>So Moab was subdued that day under the hand of Israel, and the land had peace *and* rest for eighty years.

<sup>31</sup>After [Ehud] was Shamgar son of Anath, who slew 600 Philistine men with an oxgoad. He also delivered Israel.

**4** But after Ehud died the Israelites again did evil in the sight of the Lord.

<sup>2</sup>So the Lord sold them into the hand of Jabin king of Canaan, who reigned in Hazor. The commander of his army was Sisera, who dwelt in Harosheth-hagoiim [fortress or city of the nations].

<sup>3</sup>Then the Israelites cried to the Lord, for [Jabin] had 900 chariots of iron and had severely oppressed the Israelites for twenty years.

<sup>4</sup>Now Deborah, a <sup>a</sup>prophetess, the wife of Lappidoth, judged Israel at that time.

<sup>5</sup>She sat under the palm tree of Deborah between Ramah and Bethel in the hill country of Ephraim, and the Israelites came up to her for judgment.

<sup>6</sup>And she sent and called Barak son of Abinoam from Kedesh in Naphtali and said to him, Has not the Lord, the God of Israel, commanded [you], Go, gather your men at Mount Tabor, taking 10,000 men from the tribes of Naphtali and Zebulun?

<sup>7</sup>And I will draw out Sisera, the general of Jabin's army, to meet you at the river Kishon with his chariots and his multitude, and I will deliver him into your hand?

<sup>8</sup>And Barak said to her, If you will go with me, then I will go; but if you will not go with me, I will not go.

<sup>9</sup>And she said, I will surely go with you; nevertheless, the trip you take will not be for your glory, for the Lord will sell Sisera into the hand of a woman. And Deborah arose and went with Barak to Kedesh. [Fulfilled in Judg. 4:22.]

<sup>10</sup>And Barak called Zebulun and Naphtali to Kedesh, and he went up with 10,000 men at his heels, and Deborah went up with him.

<sup>11</sup>Now Heber the Kenite, of the descendants of Hobab, the father-in-law of Moses, had separated from the

<sup>a</sup> According to Num. 11:25, the prophetic gift has its source in the "Spirit of the Lord." The prophet is a spokesman of God and for God. Miriam was the first prophetess who praised God before all the people (Exod. 15:20). Deborah was not like Miriam, the sister of such men as Moses and Aaron. The objective Spirit of her God elevates her above her people, above heroes before and after her. Not only the ecstasy of enthusiasm, but also the calm wisdom of that Spirit Who informs the law dwells in her. Of no judge until Samuel [the last of the major judges] is it expressly said that he was a "prophet." Of none until him can it be said that he was possessed of the popular authority necessary for the office of judge. The position of Deborah in Israel is therefore a twofold testimony: it proves the relaxation of spiritual and manly energy, and, secondly, the undying might of divine truth, as delivered by Moses, comes brilliantly to view. History shows many instances where in times of distress, when men despaired, women arose and saved their nation; but in all such cases there must be an unextinguished spark of the old fire in the people themselves. Israel, formerly encouraged by the great exploit of a left-handed man—Ehud (Judg. 3:15), is now quickened by the glowing word of a noble woman (J. P. Lange, *A Commentary*).

<sup>a</sup> 4 Traditionally *judging*    <sup>b</sup> 11 Or *father-in-law*

## New International Version

pitched his tent by the great tree in Zaanannim near Kedesh.

¹²When they told Sisera that Barak son of Abinoam had gone up to Mount Tabor, ¹³Sisera summoned from Harosheth Haggoyim to the Kishon River all his men and his nine hundred chariots fitted with iron.

¹⁴Then Deborah said to Barak, "Go! This is the day the LORD has given Sisera into your hands. Has not the LORD gone ahead of you?" So Barak went down Mount Tabor, with ten thousand men following him. ¹⁵At Barak's advance, the LORD routed Sisera and all his chariots and army by the sword, and Sisera got down from his chariot and fled on foot.

¹⁶Barak pursued the chariots and army as far as Harosheth Haggoyim, and all Sisera's troops fell by the sword; not a man was left. ¹⁷Sisera, meanwhile, fled on foot to the tent of Jael, the wife of Heber the Kenite, because there was an alliance between Jabin king of Hazor and the family of Heber the Kenite.

¹⁸Jael went out to meet Sisera and said to him, "Come, my lord, come right in. Don't be afraid." So he entered her tent, and she covered him with a blanket.

¹⁹"I'm thirsty," he said. "Please give me some water." She opened a skin of milk, gave him a drink, and covered him up.

²⁰"Stand in the doorway of the tent," he told her. "If someone comes by and asks you, 'Is anyone in there?' say 'No.'"

²¹But Jael, Heber's wife, picked up a tent peg and a hammer and went quietly to him while he lay fast asleep, exhausted. She drove the peg through his temple into the ground, and he died.

²²Just then Barak came by in pursuit of Sisera, and Jael went out to meet him. "Come," she said, "I will show you the man you're looking for." So he went in with her, and there lay Sisera with the tent peg through his temple—dead.

²³On that day God subdued Jabin king of Canaan before the Israelites. ²⁴And the hand of the Israelites pressed harder and harder against Jabin king of Canaan until they destroyed him.

### The Song of Deborah

**5** On that day Deborah and Barak son of Abinoam sang this song:

²"When the princes in Israel take the lead,
   when the people willingly offer themselves—
   praise the LORD!

³"Hear this, you kings! Listen, you rulers!
   I, even I, will sing to*ᵃ* the LORD;
   I will praise the LORD, the God of Israel, in song.

⁴"When you, LORD, went out from Seir,
   when you marched from the land of Edom,
   the earth shook, the heavens poured,
   the clouds poured down water.

⁵The mountains quaked before the LORD, the One of Sinai,
   before the LORD, the God of Israel.

⁶"In the days of Shamgar son of Anath,
   in the days of Jael, the highways were abandoned;
   travelers took to winding paths.

⁷Villagers in Israel would not fight;
   they held back until I, Deborah, arose,
   until I arose, a mother in Israel.

*ᵃ 3 Or of*

## Amplified Bible

Kenites and encamped as far away as the oak in Zaanannim, which is near Kedesh.

¹²When it was told Sisera that Barak son of Abinoam had gone up to Mount Tabor,

¹³Sisera gathered together all his chariots, even 900 chariots of iron, and all the men who were with him from Harosheth-hagoiim to the river Kishon.

¹⁴And Deborah said to Barak, Up! For this is the day when the Lord has given Sisera into your hand. Is not the Lord gone out before you? So Barak went down from Mount Tabor with 10,000 men following him.

¹⁵And the Lord confused *and* terrified Sisera and all his chariot drivers and all his army before Barak with the sword. And Sisera alighted from his chariot and fled on foot.

¹⁶But Barak pursued after the chariots and the army to Harosheth-hagoiim, and all the army of Sisera fell by the sword; not a man was left.

¹⁷But Sisera fled on foot to the tent of Jael, the wife of Heber the Kenite, for there was peace between Jabin the king of Hazor and the house of Heber the Kenite.

¹⁸And Jael went out to meet Sisera and said to him, Turn aside, my lord, turn aside to me; have no fear. So he turned aside to her into the tent, and she covered him with a rug.

¹⁹And he said to her, Give me, I pray you, a little water to drink for I am thirsty. And she opened a skin of milk and gave him a drink and covered him.

²⁰And he said to her, Stand at the door of the tent, and if any man comes and asks you, Is there any man here? Tell him, No.

²¹But Jael, Heber's wife, took a tent pin and a hammer in her hand and went softly to him and drove the pin through his temple and into the ground; for he was in a deep sleep from weariness. So he died.

²²And behold, as Barak pursued Sisera, Jael came out to meet him and said to him, Come, and I will show you the man you seek. And when he came into her tent, behold, Sisera lay dead, and the tent pin was in his temples.

²³So God subdued on that day Jabin king of Canaan before the Israelites.

²⁴And the hand of the Israelites bore more and more upon Jabin king of Canaan until they had destroyed [him].

**5** Then sang Deborah and Barak son of Abinoam on that day, saying,

²For the leaders who took the lead in Israel, for the people who offered themselves willingly, bless the Lord!

³Hear, O kings; give ear, O princes; I will sing to the Lord. I will sing praise to the Lord, the God of Israel.

⁴Lord, when You went forth out of Seir, when You marched out of the field of Edom, the earth trembled and the heavens also dropped, yes, the clouds dropped water.

⁵The mountains quaked at the presence of the Lord, yes, yonder Sinai at the presence of the Lord, the God of Israel.

⁶After the days of Shamgar son of Anath, after the days of Jael [meaning here Ehud] the caravans ceased, travelers walked through byways.

⁷The villages were unoccupied *and* rulers ceased in Israel until *ᵃ*you arose—you, Deborah, arose—a mother in Israel.

*ᵃ F. F. Bruce in The New Bible Dictionary calls attention to the fact that the repeated Hebrew verb here "may be understood not as the normal first person singular ('I arose') but as an archaic second person singular ('thou didst arise')."*

## New International Version

8 God chose new leaders
    when war came to the city gates,
but not a shield or spear was seen
    among forty thousand in Israel.
9 My heart is with Israel's princes,
    with the willing volunteers among the people.
    Praise the LORD!

10 "You who ride on white donkeys,
    sitting on your saddle blankets,
    and you who walk along the road,
consider 11 the voice of the singers*a* at the watering
    places.
    They recite the victories of the LORD,
    the victories of his villagers in Israel.

"Then the people of the LORD
    went down to the city gates.
12 'Wake up, wake up, Deborah!
    Wake up, wake up, break out in song!
    Arise, Barak!
    Take captive your captives, son of Abinoam.'

13 "The remnant of the nobles came down;
    the people of the LORD came down to me against the
      mighty.
14 Some came from Ephraim, whose roots were in
    Amalek;
    Benjamin was with the people who followed you.
From Makir captains came down,
    from Zebulun those who bear a commander's*a* staff.
15 The princes of Issachar were with Deborah;
    yes, Issachar was with Barak,
    sent under his command into the valley.
In the districts of Reuben
    there was much searching of heart.
16 Why did you stay among the sheep pens*b*
    to hear the whistling for the flocks?
In the districts of Reuben
    there was much searching of heart.
17 Gilead stayed beyond the Jordan.
    And Dan, why did he linger by the ships?
Asher remained on the coast
    and stayed in his coves.
18 The people of Zebulun risked their very lives;
    so did Naphtali on the terraced fields.

19 "Kings came, they fought,
    the kings of Canaan fought.
At Taanach, by the waters of Megiddo,
    they took no plunder of silver.
20 From the heavens the stars fought,
    from their courses they fought against Sisera.
21 The river Kishon swept them away,
    the age-old river, the river Kishon.
    March on, my soul; be strong!
22 Then thundered the horses' hooves—
    galloping, galloping go his mighty steeds.
23 'Curse Meroz,' said the angel of the LORD.
    'Curse its people bitterly,
because they did not come to help the LORD,
    to help the LORD against the mighty.'

24 "Most blessed of women be Jael,
    the wife of Heber the Kenite,
    most blessed of tent-dwelling women.
25 He asked for water, and she gave him milk;
    in a bowl fit for nobles she brought him curdled milk.
26 Her hand reached for the tent peg,
    her right hand for the workman's hammer.
She struck Sisera, she crushed his head,
    she shattered and pierced his temple.

*a* 11,14 The meaning of the Hebrew for this word is uncertain.
*b* 16 Or the *campfires*; or the *saddlebags*

## Amplified Bible

8 [Formerly] they chose new gods; then war was in the gates. Was there a shield or spear seen among 40,000 in Israel?
9 My heart goes out to the commanders of Israel who offered themselves willingly among the people. Bless the Lord!
10 Tell of it—you who ride on white donkeys, you who sit on rich carpets, and you who walk by the way.
11 Far from the noise of archers in the places of drawing water, there shall they rehearse the righteous acts of the Lord, even the righteous acts toward His villagers in Israel. Then the people of the Lord went down to the gates.
12 Awake, awake, Deborah! Awake, awake, utter a song! Arise, Barak, and lead away your captives, you son of Abinoam.
13 Then down marched the remnant of the nobles, the people of the Lord marched down for Me against the mighty.
14 Out of Ephraim they came down whose root is in Amalek, after you, Benjamin, with your kinsmen. Out of Machir came down commanders *and* lawgivers, and out of Zebulun those who *a* handle the pen *or* stylus of the writer.
15 And the princes of Issachar came with Deborah, and Issachar was faithful to Barak; into the valley they rushed forth at his heels. [But] among the clans of Reuben were great searchings of heart.
16 Why [Reuben] did you linger among the sheepfolds listening to the piping for the flocks? Among the clans of Reuben there were great searchings of heart.
17 Gilead remained beyond the Jordan, and why did Dan stay with the ships? Asher sat still on the seacoast and remained by his creeks. [These came not forth to battle for God's people.]
18 But Zebulun was a people who endangered their lives to the death; Naphtali did also on the heights of the field.
19 The kings came and fought, then fought the kings of Canaan at Taanach by the waters of Megiddo. Gain of booty they did not obtain.
20 From the heavens the stars fought, from their courses they fought against Sisera.
21 The torrent Kishon swept [the foe] away, the onrushing torrent, the torrent Kishon. O my soul, march on with strength!
22 Then the horses' hoofs beat loudly because of the galloping of [fleeing] valiant riders.
23 Curse Meroz, said the messenger of the Lord. Curse bitterly its inhabitants, because they came not to the help of the Lord, to the help of the Lord against the mighty!
24 Blessed above women shall Jael, the wife of Heber the Kenite, be; blessed shall she be above women in the tent.
25 [Sisera] asked for water, and she gave [him] milk; she brought him curds in a lordly dish.
26 She put her [left] hand to the tent pin, and her right hand to the workmen's hammer. And with the wooden hammer she smote Sisera, she smote his head, yes, she struck and pierced his temple.

*a* Reference at this date (about 1150 B.C.) to a writer is no more surprising than the mention of "the city of books" in Judg. 1:11. Writing, and alphabetical writing at that, had been practiced for some centuries along the Syrian Coast . . . Quantities of papyrus [the pith of papyrus was used for writing] were exported from Egypt to Phoenicia at around 1100 B.C. (Judg. 8:14) (F. Davidson, ed., *The New Bible Commentary*). "Zebulun, formerly known only for [its] experts with the ciphering-pencil, had now become a people courageous unto death" (J. P. Lange, *A Commentary*).

## New International Version

27 At her feet he sank,
he fell; there he lay.
At her feet he sank, he fell;
where he sank, there he fell—dead.

28 "Through the window peered Sisera's mother;
behind the lattice she cried out,
'Why is his chariot so long in coming?
Why is the clatter of his chariots delayed?'
29 The wisest of her ladies answer her;
indeed, she keeps saying to herself,
30 'Are they not finding and dividing the spoils:
a woman or two for each man,
colorful garments as plunder for Sisera,
colorful garments embroidered,
highly embroidered garments for my neck—
all this as plunder?'

31 "So may all your enemies perish, LORD!
But may all who love you be like the sun
when it rises in its strength."

Then the land had peace forty years.

### Gideon

**6** The Israelites did evil in the eyes of the LORD, and for seven years he gave them into the hands of the Midianites. ²Because the power of Midian was so oppressive, the Israelites prepared shelters for themselves in mountain clefts, caves and strongholds. ³Whenever the Israelites planted their crops, the Midianites, Amalekites and other eastern peoples invaded the country. ⁴They camped on the land and ruined the crops all the way to Gaza and did not spare a living thing for Israel, neither sheep nor cattle nor donkeys. ⁵They came up with their livestock and their tents like swarms of locusts. It was impossible to count them or their camels; they invaded the land to ravage it. ⁶Midian so impoverished the Israelites that they cried out to the LORD for help.

⁷When the Israelites cried out to the LORD because of Midian, ⁸he sent them a prophet, who said, "This is what the LORD, the God of Israel, says: I brought you up out of Egypt, out of the land of slavery. ⁹I rescued you from the hand of the Egyptians. And I delivered you from the hand of all your oppressors; I drove them out before you and gave you their land. ¹⁰I said to you, 'I am the LORD your God; do not worship the gods of the Amorites, in whose land you live.' But you have not listened to me."

¹¹The angel of the LORD came and sat down under the oak in Ophrah that belonged to Joash the Abiezrite, where his son Gideon was threshing wheat in a winepress to keep it from the Midianites. ¹²When the angel of the LORD appeared to Gideon, he said, "The LORD is with you, mighty warrior."

¹³"Pardon me, my lord," Gideon replied, "but if the LORD is with us, why has all this happened to us? Where are all his wonders that our ancestors told us about when they said, 'Did not the LORD bring us up out of Egypt?' But now the LORD has abandoned us and given us into the hand of Midian."

¹⁴The LORD turned to him and said, "Go in the strength

## Amplified Bible

27 He sank, he fell, he lay still at her feet. At her feet he sank, he fell; where he sank, there he fell—dead!

28 The ᵃmother of Sisera looked out at a window and wailed through the lattice, Why is his chariot so long in coming? Why do the hoofbeats of his chariots tarry?

29 Her wise ladies answered her, yet she repeated her words to herself,

30 Have they not found and been dividing the spoil? A maiden or two for every man, a spoil of dyed garments for Sisera, a spoil of dyed stuffs embroidered, two pieces of dyed work embroidered for my neck as spoil?

31 So let all Your enemies perish, O Lord! But let those who love Him be like the sun when it rises in its might. And the land had peace *and* rest for forty years.

**6** But the Israelites did evil in the sight of the Lord, and the Lord gave them into the hand of Midian for seven years.

²And the hand of Midian prevailed against Israel. Because of Midian the Israelites made themselves the dens which are in the mountains and the caves and the strongholds.

³For whenever Israel had sown their seed, the Midianites and the Amalekites and the people of the east came up against them.

⁴They would encamp against them and destroy the crops as far as Gaza and leave no nourishment for Israel, and no ox or sheep or donkey.

⁵For they came up with their cattle and their tents, and they came like locusts for multitude; both they and their camels could not be counted. So they wasted the land as they entered it.

⁶And Israel was greatly impoverished because of the Midianites, and the Israelites cried to the Lord.

⁷And when they cried to the Lord because of Midian,

⁸The Lord sent a prophet to the Israelites, who said to them, Thus says the Lord, the God of Israel, I brought you up from Egypt and brought you forth out of the house of bondage.

⁹And I delivered you out of the hand of the Egyptians and out of the hand of all who oppressed you, and drove them out from before you and gave you their land.

¹⁰And I said to you, I am the Lord your God; fear not the gods of the Amorites, in whose land you dwell. But you have not obeyed My voice.

¹¹Now the ᵇAngel of the Lord came and sat under the oak (terebinth) at Ophrah, which belonged to Joash the Abiezrite, and his son Gideon was beating wheat in the winepress to hide it from the Midianites.

¹²And the Angel of the Lord appeared to him and said to him, The Lord is with you, you mighty man of [fearless] courage.

¹³And Gideon said to him, O sir, if the Lord is with us, why is all this befallen us? And where are all His wondrous works of which our fathers told us, saying, Did not the Lord bring us up from Egypt? But now the Lord has forsaken us and given us into the hand of Midian.

¹⁴The Lord turned to him and said, Go in this your

---

ᵃ "Who should first suffer anxiety [in the palace of the women] if not the mother? Of a wife, nothing is said; such love thrives not in the harem of a prince. He is his mother's pride, the great hero, who had hitherto been invincible. What she has in him, and what she loses, concerns no other woman" (J. P. Lange, *A Commentary*). ᵇ See footnote on Gen. 16:7.

## New International Version

you have and save Israel out of Midian's hand. Am I not sending you?"

15"Pardon me, my lord," Gideon replied, "but how can I save Israel? My clan is the weakest in Manasseh, and I am the least in my family."

16The LORD answered, "I will be with you, and you will strike down all the Midianites, leaving none alive."

17Gideon replied, "If now I have found favor in your eyes, give me a sign that it is really you talking to me. 18Please do not go away until I come back and bring my offering and set it before you."

And the LORD said, "I will wait until you return."

19Gideon went inside, prepared a young goat, and from an ephahᵃ of flour he made bread without yeast. Putting the meat in a basket and its broth in a pot, he brought them out and offered them to him under the oak.

20The angel of God said to him, "Take the meat and the unleavened bread, place them on this rock, and pour out the broth." And Gideon did so. 21Then the angel of the LORD touched the meat and the unleavened bread with the tip of the staff that was in his hand. Fire flared from the rock, consuming the meat and the bread. And the angel of the LORD disappeared. 22When Gideon realized that it was the angel of the LORD, he exclaimed, "Alas, Sovereign LORD! I have seen the angel of the LORD face to face!"

23But the LORD said to him, "Peace! Do not be afraid. You are not going to die."

24So Gideon built an altar to the LORD there and called it The LORD Is Peace. To this day it stands in Ophrah of the Abiezrites.

25That same night the LORD said to him, "Take the second bull from your father's herd, the one seven years old.ᵇ Tear down your father's altar to Baal and cut down the Asherah poleᶜ beside it. 26Then build a proper kind ofᵈ altar to the LORD your God on the top of this height. Using the wood of the Asherah pole that you cut down, offer the secondᵉ bull as a burnt offering."

27So Gideon took ten of his servants and did as the LORD told him. But because he was afraid of his family and the townspeople, he did it at night rather than in the daytime.

28In the morning when the people of the town got up, there was Baal's altar, demolished, with the Asherah pole beside it cut down and the second bull sacrificed on the newly built altar!

29They asked each other, "Who did this?"

When they carefully investigated, they were told, "Gideon son of Joash did it."

30The people of the town demanded of Joash, "Bring out your son. He must die, because he has broken down Baal's altar and cut down the Asherah pole beside it."

31But Joash replied to the hostile crowd around him, "Are you going to plead Baal's cause? Are you trying to save him? Whoever fights for him shall be put to death by morning! If Baal really is a god, he can defend himself when someone breaks down his altar." 32So because Gideon broke down Baal's altar, they gave him the name Jerub-Baalᶠ that day, saying, "Let Baal contend with him."

33Now all the Midianites, Amalekites and other eastern peoples joined forces and crossed over the Jordan and

## Amplified Bible

might, and you shall save Israel from the hand of Midian. Have I not sent you?

15Gideon said to Him, Oh Lord, how can I deliver Israel? Behold, my clan is the poorest in Manasseh, and I am the least in my father's house.

16The Lord said to him, Surely I will be with you, and you shall smite the Midianites as one man.

17Gideon said to Him, If now I have found favor in Your sight, then show me a sign that it is You Who talks with me.

18Do not leave here, I pray You, until I return to You and bring my offering and set it before You. And He said, I will wait until you return.

19Then Gideon went in and prepared a kid and unleavened cakes of an ephah of flour. The meat he put in a basket and the broth in a pot, and brought them to Him under the oak and presented them.

20And the Angel of God said to him, Take the meat and unleavened cakes and lay them on this rock and pour the broth over them. And he did so.

21Then the Angel of the Lord reached out the tip of the staff that was in His hand, and touched the meat and the unleavened cakes, and there flared up fire from the rock and consumed the meat and the unleavened cakes. Then the Angel of the Lord vanished from his sight.

22And when Gideon perceived that He was the Angel of the Lord, Gideon said, Alas, O Lord God! For now I have seen the Angel of the Lord face to face!

23The Lord said to him, Peace be to you, do not fear; you shall not die.

24Then Gideon built an altar there to the Lord and called it, The Lord is Peace. To this day it still stands in Ophrah, which belongs to the Abiezrites.

25That night the Lord said to Gideon, Take your father's bull, the second bull seven years old, and pull down the altar of Baal that your father has and cut down the Asherah [symbol of the goddess Asherah] that is beside it;

26And build an altar to the Lord your God on top of this stronghold with stones laid in proper order. Then take the second bull and offer a burnt sacrifice with the wood of the Asherah which you shall cut down.

27Then Gideon took ten men of his servants and did as the Lord had told him, but because he was too afraid of his father's household and the men of the city to do it by day, he did it by night.

28And when the men of the city arose early in the morning, behold, the altar of Baal was cast down, and the Asherah was cut down that was beside it, and the second bull was offered on the altar which had been built.

29And they said to one another, Who has done this thing? And when they searched and asked, they were told, Gideon son of Joash has done this thing.

30Then the men of the city commanded Joash, Bring out your son, that he may die, for he has pulled down the altar of Baal and cut down the Asherah beside it.

31But Joash said to all who stood against him, Will you contend for Baal? Or will you save him? He who will contend for Baal, let him be put to death while it is still morning. If Baal is a god, let him contend for himself because one has pulled down his altar.

32Therefore on that day he called Gideon Jerubbaal, meaning, Let Baal contend against him, because he had pulled down his altar.

33Then all the Midianites and the Amalekites and the people of the east came together and, crossing the Jordan, encamped in the Valley of Jezreel.

---

ᵃ 19 That is, probably about 36 pounds or about 16 kilograms
ᵇ 25 Or Take a full-grown, mature bull from your father's herd    ᶜ 25 That is, a wooden symbol of the goddess Asherah; also in verses 26, 28 and 30
ᵈ 26 Or build with layers of stone an    ᵉ 26 Or full-grown; also in verse 28
ᶠ 32 Jerub-Baal probably means let Baal contend.

## New International Version

camped in the Valley of Jezreel. ³⁴Then the Spirit of the LORD came on Gideon, and he blew a trumpet, summoning the Abiezrites to follow him. ³⁵He sent messengers throughout Manasseh, calling them to arms, and also into Asher, Zebulun and Naphtali, so that they too went up to meet them.

³⁶Gideon said to God, "If you will save Israel by my hand as you have promised— ³⁷look, I will place a wool fleece on the threshing floor. If there is dew only on the fleece and all the ground is dry, then I will know that you will save Israel by my hand, as you said." ³⁸And that is what happened. Gideon rose early the next day; he squeezed the fleece and wrung out the dew—a bowlful of water.

³⁹Then Gideon said to God, "Do not be angry with me. Let me make just one more request. Allow me one more test with the fleece, but this time make the fleece dry and let the ground be covered with dew." ⁴⁰That night God did so. Only the fleece was dry; all the ground was covered with dew.

### Gideon Defeats the Midianites

**7** Early in the morning, Jerub-Baal (that is, Gideon) and all his men camped at the spring of Harod. The camp of Midian was north of them in the valley near the hill of Moreh. ²The LORD said to Gideon, "You have too many men. I cannot deliver Midian into their hands, or Israel would boast against me, 'My own strength has saved me.' ³Now announce to the army, 'Anyone who trembles with fear may turn back and leave Mount Gilead.'" So twenty-two thousand men left, while ten thousand remained.

⁴But the LORD said to Gideon, "There are still too many men. Take them down to the water, and I will thin them out for you there. If I say, 'This one shall go with you,' he shall go; but if I say, 'This one shall not go with you,' he shall not go." ⁵So Gideon took the men down to the water. There the LORD told him, "Separate those who lap the water with their tongues as a dog laps from those who kneel down to drink." ⁶Three hundred of them drank from cupped hands, lapping like dogs. All the rest got down on their knees to drink.

⁷The LORD said to Gideon, "With the three hundred men that lapped I will save you and give the Midianites into your hands. Let all the others go home." ⁸So Gideon sent the rest of the Israelites home but kept the three hundred, who took over the provisions and trumpets of the others.

Now the camp of Midian lay below him in the valley. ⁹During that night the LORD said to Gideon, "Get up, go down against the camp, because I am going to give it into your hands. ¹⁰If you are afraid to attack, go down to the camp with your servant Purah ¹¹and listen to what they are saying. Afterward, you will be encouraged to attack the camp." So he and Purah his servant went down to the outposts of the camp. ¹²The Midianites, the Amalekites

## Amplified Bible

³⁴But the Spirit of the Lord clothed Gideon with Himself *and* took possession of him, and he blew a trumpet, and [the clan of] Abiezer was gathered to him.

³⁵And he sent messengers throughout all Manasseh, and the Manassites were called to follow him; and he sent messengers to Asher, to Zebulun, and to Naphtali, and they came up to meet them.

³⁶And Gideon said to God, If You will deliver Israel by my hand as You have said,

³⁷Behold, I will put a fleece of wool on the threshing floor. If there is dew on the fleece only and it is dry on all the ground, then I shall know that You will deliver Israel by my hand, as You have said.

³⁸And it was so. When he rose early next morning and squeezed the dew out of the fleece, he wrung from it a bowlful of water.

³⁹And Gideon said to God, Let not your anger be kindled against me, and I will speak but this once. Let me make trial only this once with the fleece, I pray you; let it now be dry only upon the fleece and upon all the ground let there be dew.

⁴⁰And God did so that night, for it was dry on the fleece only, and there was dew on all the ground.

**7** Then Jerubbaal, that is, Gideon, and all the people who were with him rose early and encamped beside the spring of Harod; and the camp of Midian was north of them by the hill of Moreh in the valley.

²The Lord said to Gideon, The people who are with you are too many for Me to give the Midianites into their hands, lest Israel boast about themselves against Me, saying, My own hand has delivered me.

³So now proclaim in the ears of the men, saying, Whoever is fearful and trembling, let him turn back and depart from Mount Gilead. And 22,000 of the men returned, but 10,000 remained.

⁴And the Lord said to Gideon, The men are still too many; bring them down to the water, and I will test them for you there. And he of whom I say to you, This man shall go with you, shall go with you; and he of whom I say to you, This man shall not go with you, shall not go.

⁵So he brought the men down to the water, and the Lord said to Gideon, Everyone who laps up the water with his tongue as a dog laps it, you shall set by himself, likewise everyone who bows down on his knees to drink.

⁶And the number of those who lapped, putting their hand to their mouth, was 300 men, but all the rest of the people bowed down upon their knees to drink water.

⁷And the Lord said to Gideon, With the 300 men who lapped I will deliver you, and give the Midianites into your hand. Let all the others return every man to his home.

⁸So the people took provisions and their trumpets in their hands, and he sent all the rest of Israel every man to his home and retained those 300 men. And the host of Midian was below him in the valley.

⁹That same night the Lord said to Gideon, Arise, go down against their camp, for I have given it into your hand.

¹⁰But if you fear to go down, go with Purah your servant down to the camp

¹¹And you shall hear what they say, and afterward your hands shall be strengthened to go down against the camp. Then he went down with Purah his servant to the outposts of the camp of the armed men.

¹²And the Midianites and the Amalekites and all the

## New International Version

and all the other eastern peoples had settled in the valley, thick as locusts. Their camels could no more be counted than the sand on the seashore.

[13] Gideon arrived just as a man was telling a friend his dream. "I had a dream," he was saying. "A round loaf of barley bread came tumbling into the Midianite camp. It struck the tent with such force that the tent overturned and collapsed."

[14] His friend responded, "This can be nothing other than the sword of Gideon son of Joash, the Israelite. God has given the Midianites and the whole camp into his hands."

[15] When Gideon heard the dream and its interpretation, he bowed down and worshiped. He returned to the camp of Israel and called out, "Get up! The LORD has given the Midianite camp into your hands." [16] Dividing the three hundred men into three companies, he placed trumpets and empty jars in the hands of all of them, with torches inside.

[17] "Watch me," he told them. "Follow my lead. When I get to the edge of the camp, do exactly as I do. [18] When I and all who are with me blow our trumpets, then from all around the camp blow yours and shout, 'For the LORD and for Gideon.'"

[19] Gideon and the hundred men with him reached the edge of the camp at the beginning of the middle watch, just after they had changed the guard. They blew their trumpets and broke the jars that were in their hands. [20] The three companies blew the trumpets and smashed the jars. Grasping the torches in their left hands and holding in their right hands the trumpets they were to blow, they shouted, "A sword for the LORD and for Gideon!" [21] While each man held his position around the camp, all the Midianites ran, crying out as they fled.

[22] When the three hundred trumpets sounded, the LORD caused the men throughout the camp to turn on each other with their swords. The army fled to Beth Shittah toward Zererah as far as the border of Abel Meholah near Tabbath. [23] Israelites from Naphtali, Asher and all Manasseh were called out, and they pursued the Midianites. [24] Gideon sent messengers throughout the hill country of Ephraim, saying, "Come down against the Midianites and seize the waters of the Jordan ahead of them as far as Beth Barah."

So all the men of Ephraim were called out and they seized the waters of the Jordan as far as Beth Barah. [25] They also captured two of the Midianite leaders, Oreb and Zeeb. They killed Oreb at the rock of Oreb, and Zeeb at the winepress of Zeeb. They pursued the Midianites and brought the heads of Oreb and Zeeb to Gideon, who was by the Jordan.

### Zebah and Zalmunna

**8** Now the Ephraimites asked Gideon, "Why have you treated us like this? Why didn't you call us when you went to fight Midian?" And they challenged him vigorously.

[2] But he answered them, "What have I accomplished compared to you? Aren't the gleanings of Ephraim's grapes better than the full grape harvest of Abiezer? [3] God

## Amplified Bible

sons of the east lay along the valley like locusts for multitude; and their camels were without number, as the sand on the seashore for multitude.

[13] When Gideon arrived, behold, a man was telling a dream to his comrade. And he said, Behold, I dreamed a dream, and behold, a cake of [a] barley bread tumbled into the camp of Midian and came to the tent and struck it so that it fell, and turned it upside down so that the tent lay flat.

[14] And his comrade replied, This is nothing else but the sword of Gideon son of Joash, a man of Israel. Into his hand God has given Midian and all the host.

[15] When Gideon heard the telling of the dream and its interpretation, he worshiped and returned to the camp of Israel and said, Arise, for the Lord has given into your hand the host of Midian.

[16] And he divided the 300 men into three companies, and he put into the hands of all of them trumpets and empty pitchers, with torches inside the pitchers.

[17] And he said to them, Look at me, then do likewise. When I come to the edge of their camp, do as I do.

[18] When I blow the trumpet, I and all who are with me, then you blow the trumpets also on every side of all the camp and shout, For the Lord and for Gideon!

[19] So Gideon and the 100 men who were with him came to the outskirts of the camp at the beginning of the middle watch, when the guards had just been changed, and they blew the trumpets and smashed the pitchers that were in their hands.

[20] And the three companies blew the trumpets and shattered the pitchers, holding the torches in their left hands, and in their right hands the trumpets to blow [leaving no chance to use swords], and they cried, The sword for the Lord and Gideon!

[21] They stood every man in his place round about the camp, and all the [Midianite] army ran—they cried out and fled.

[22] When [Gideon's men] blew the 300 trumpets, the Lord set every [Midianite's] sword against his comrade and against all the army, and the army fled as far as Beth-shittah toward Zererah, as far as the border of Abel-meholah by Tabbath.

[23] And the men of Israel were called together out of Naphtali and Asher and all Manasseh, and they pursued Midian.

[24] And Gideon sent messengers throughout all the hill country of Ephraim, saying, Come down against the Midianites and take all the intervening fords as far as Beth-barah and also the Jordan. So all the men of Ephraim were gathered together and took all the fords as far as Beth-barah and also the Jordan.

[25] And [the men of Ephraim] took the two princes of Midian, Oreb and Zeeb, and they slew Oreb at the rock of Oreb, and Zeeb they slew at the winepress of Zeeb, and pursued Midian; and they brought the heads of Oreb and Zeeb to Gideon beyond the Jordan.

**8** And the men of Ephraim said to Gideon, Why have you treated us like this, not calling us when you went to fight with Midian? And they quarreled with him furiously.

[2] And he said to them, What have I done now in comparison with you? Is not the gleaning of the grapes of [your big tribe of] Ephraim better than the vintage of [my little clan of] Abiezer?

---

[a] Alluding to the insignificance of Gideon and his family, or perhaps his whole troop. Barley then, as it is still, was distinguished from "fine flour." "To heare himselfe but a Barly-cake, troubled him not. It matters not how base wee be thought, so wee be victorious" (Bishop Joseph Hall, cited by *The Cambridge Bible*).

## New International Version

gave Oreb and Zeeb, the Midianite leaders, into your hands. What was I able to do compared to you?" At this, their resentment against him subsided.

⁴Gideon and his three hundred men, exhausted yet keeping up the pursuit, came to the Jordan and crossed it. ⁵He said to the men of Sukkoth, "Give my troops some bread; they are worn out, and I am still pursuing Zebah and Zalmunna, the kings of Midian."

⁶But the officials of Sukkoth said, "Do you already have the hands of Zebah and Zalmunna in your possession? Why should we give bread to your troops?"

⁷Then Gideon replied, "Just for that, when the LORD has given Zebah and Zalmunna into my hand, I will tear your flesh with desert thorns and briers."

⁸From there he went up to Peniel*a* and made the same request of them, but they answered as the men of Sukkoth had. ⁹So he said to the men of Peniel, "When I return in triumph, I will tear down this tower."

¹⁰Now Zebah and Zalmunna were in Karkor with a force of about fifteen thousand men, all that were left of the armies of the eastern peoples; a hundred and twenty thousand swordsmen had fallen. ¹¹Gideon went up by the route of the nomads east of Nobah and Jogbehah and attacked the unsuspecting army. ¹²Zebah and Zalmunna, the two kings of Midian, fled, but he pursued them and captured them, routing their entire army.

¹³Gideon son of Joash then returned from the battle by the Pass of Heres. ¹⁴He caught a young man of Sukkoth and questioned him, and the young man wrote down for him the names of the seventy-seven officials of Sukkoth, the elders of the town. ¹⁵Then Gideon came and said to the men of Sukkoth, "Here are Zebah and Zalmunna, about whom you taunted me by saying, 'Do you already have the hands of Zebah and Zalmunna in your possession? Why should we give bread to your exhausted men?'" ¹⁶He took the elders of the town and taught the men of Sukkoth a lesson by punishing them with desert thorns and briers. ¹⁷He also pulled down the tower of Peniel and killed the men of the town.

¹⁸Then he asked Zebah and Zalmunna, "What kind of men did you kill at Tabor?"

"Men like you," they answered, "each one with the bearing of a prince."

¹⁹Gideon replied, "Those were my brothers, the sons of my own mother. As surely as the LORD lives, if you had spared their lives, I would not kill you." ²⁰Turning to Jether, his oldest son, he said, "Kill them!" But Jether did not draw his sword, because he was only a boy and was afraid.

²¹Zebah and Zalmunna said, "Come, do it yourself. 'As is the man, so is his strength.'" So Gideon stepped forward and killed them, and took the ornaments off their camels' necks.

### Gideon's Ephod

²²The Israelites said to Gideon, "Rule over us—you, your son and your grandson—because you have saved us from the hand of Midian."

²³But Gideon told them, "I will not rule over you, nor will my son rule over you. The LORD will rule over you."

## Amplified Bible

³*a*God has given into your hands the princes of Midian, Oreb and Zeeb, and what was I able to do in comparison with you? Then their anger toward him was abated when he had said that.

⁴And Gideon came to the Jordan and passed over, he and the 300 men with him, faint yet pursuing.

⁵And he said to the men of Succoth, Give, I pray you, loaves of bread to the people who follow me, for they are faint, and I am pursuing Zebah and Zalmunna, kings of Midian.

⁶And the princes of Succoth said, Are Zebah and Zalmunna already in your hand, that we should give bread to your army?

⁷And Gideon said, For that, when the Lord has delivered Zebah and Zalmunna into my hand, I will thresh your flesh with the thorns and briers of the wilderness!

⁸And he went from there up to Penuel and made the same request, and the men of Penuel answered him as the men of Succoth had done.

⁹And [Gideon] said to the men of Penuel, When I come again in peace, I will break down this tower.

¹⁰Now Zebah and Zalmunna were in Karkor with their army—about 15,000 men, all who were left of all the army of the sons of the east, for there had fallen 120,000 men who drew the sword.

¹¹And Gideon went up by the route of those who dwelt in tents east of Nobah and Jogbehah and smote their camp [unexpectedly], for the army thought itself secure.

¹²And Zebah and Zalmunna fled, and he pursued them and took the two kings of Midian, Zebah and Zalmunna, and terrified all the army.

¹³Then Gideon son of Joash returned from the battle by the ascent of Heres.

¹⁴And he caught a young man of Succoth and inquired of him, and [the youth] wrote down for him [the names of] the officials of Succoth and its elders, seventy-seven men.

¹⁵And he came to the men of Succoth and said, Behold Zebah and Zalmunna, about whom you scoffed at me, saying, Are Zebah and Zalmunna now in your hand, that we should give bread to your men who are faint?

¹⁶And he took the elders of the city and thorns of the wilderness and briers, and with them he taught the men of Succoth [a lesson].

¹⁷And he broke down the tower of Penuel and slew the men of the city.

¹⁸Then [Gideon] said to Zebah and Zalmunna, What kind of men were they whom you slew at Tabor? And they replied, They were like you, each of them resembled the son of a king.

¹⁹And he said, They were my brothers, the sons of my mother. As the Lord lives, if you had saved them alive, I would not slay you.

²⁰And [Gideon] said to Jether his firstborn [to embarrass them], Up, and slay them. But the youth drew not his sword, for he feared because he was yet a lad.

²¹Then Zebah and Zalmunna said, Rise yourself and fall on us; for as the man is, so is his strength. And Gideon arose and slew Zebah and Zalmunna and took the [crescent-shaped] ornaments that were on their camels' necks.

²²Then the men of Israel said to Gideon, Rule over us—you and your son and your son's son also—for you have delivered us from the hand of Midian.

²³And Gideon said to them, I will not rule over you, and my son will not rule over you; the Lord will rule over you.

---

*a* "Gideon's good words were as victorious as his sword" (Bishop Joseph Hall, cited by Charles Ellicott, *A Bible Commentary*). "He might have said that he could place but little dependence upon his brethren when, through faintheartedness, 22,000 left him at one time (Judg. 7:3), but he passed this by and took a more excellent way" (Adam Clarke, *The Holy Bible with A Commentary*). "The improving of a victory is often more honorable and of greater consequence than the winning of it . . . Humility of deportment is the . . . surest method of ending strife" (Matthew Henry, *Commentary on the Holy Bible*).

*a* 8 Hebrew *Penuel*, a variant of *Peniel*; also in verses 9 and 17

## New International Version

²⁴And he said, "I do have one request, that each of you give me an earring from your share of the plunder." (It was the custom of the Ishmaelites to wear gold earrings.) ²⁵They answered, "We'll be glad to give them." So they spread out a garment, and each of them threw a ring from his plunder onto it. ²⁶The weight of the gold rings he asked for came to seventeen hundred shekels,ᵃ not counting the ornaments, the pendants and the purple garments worn by the kings of Midian or the chains that were on their camels' necks. ²⁷Gideon made the gold into an ephod, which he placed in Ophrah, his town. All Israel prostituted themselves by worshiping it there, and it became a snare to Gideon and his family.

### Gideon's Death

²⁸Thus Midian was subdued before the Israelites and did not raise its head again. During Gideon's lifetime, the land had peace forty years.

²⁹Jerub-Baal son of Joash went back home to live. ³⁰He had seventy sons of his own, for he had many wives. ³¹His concubine, who lived in Shechem, also bore him a son, whom he named Abimelek. ³²Gideon son of Joash died at a good old age and was buried in the tomb of his father Joash in Ophrah of the Abiezrites.

³³No sooner had Gideon died than the Israelites again prostituted themselves to the Baals. They set up Baal-Berith as their god ³⁴and did not remember the Lᴏʀᴅ their God, who had rescued them from the hands of all their enemies on every side. ³⁵They also failed to show any loyalty to the family of Jerub-Baal (that is, Gideon) in spite of all the good things he had done for them.

### Abimelek

**9** Abimelek son of Jerub-Baal went to his mother's brothers in Shechem and said to them and to all his mother's clan, ²"Ask all the citizens of Shechem, 'Which is better for you: to have all seventy of Jerub-Baal's sons rule over you, or just one man?' Remember, I am your flesh and blood."

³When the brothers repeated all this to the citizens of Shechem, they were inclined to follow Abimelek, for they said, "He is related to us." ⁴They gave him seventy shekelsᵇ of silver from the temple of Baal-Berith, and Abimelek used it to hire reckless scoundrels, who became his followers. ⁵He went to his father's home in Ophrah and on one stone murdered his seventy brothers, the sons of Jerub-Baal. But Jotham, the youngest son of Jerub-Baal, escaped by hiding. ⁶Then all the citizens of Shechem and Beth Millo gathered beside the great tree at the pillar in Shechem to crown Abimelek king.

⁷When Jotham was told about this, he climbed up on the top of Mount Gerizim and shouted to them, "Listen to me, citizens of Shechem, so that God may listen to you. ⁸One day the trees went out to anoint a king for themselves. They said to the olive tree, 'Be our king.'

## Amplified Bible

²⁴And Gideon said to them, Let me make a request of you—every man of you give me the earrings of his spoil. For [the Midianites] had gold earrings because they were Ishmaelites [general term for all descendants of Keturah].

²⁵And they answered, We will willingly give them. And they spread a garment, and every man cast on it the earrings of his spoil.

²⁶And the weight of the golden earrings that he requested was 1,700 shekels of gold, besides the crescents and pendants and the purple garments worn by the kings of Midian, and the chains that were about their camels' necks.

²⁷And Gideon made an ephod [a sacred, high priest's garment] of it, and put it in his city of Ophrah, and all Israel paid homage to it there, and ᵃit became a snare to Gideon and to his family.

²⁸Thus was Midian subdued before the Israelites so that they lifted up their heads no more. And the land had peace *and* rest for forty years in the days of Gideon.

²⁹Jerubbaal (Gideon) son of Joash went and dwelt in his own house.

³⁰Now Gideon had seventy sons born to him, for he had many wives.

³¹And his concubine, who was in Shechem, also bore him a son, whom he named Abimelech.

³²Gideon son of Joash died at a good old age and was buried in the tomb of Joash his father in Ophrah of the Abiezrites.

³³As soon as Gideon was dead, the Israelites turned again and played the harlot after the Baals and made Baal-berith their god.

³⁴And the Israelites did not remember the Lord their God, Who had delivered them out of the hand of all their enemies on every side;

³⁵Neither did they show kindness to the family of Jerubbaal, that is, Gideon, in return for all the good which he had done for Israel.

**9** Now Abimelech son of Jerubbaal (Gideon) went to Shechem to his mother's kinsmen and said to them and to the whole clan of his mother's family,

²Say, I pray you, in the hearing of all the men of Shechem, Which is better for you: that all seventy of the sons of Jerubbaal reign over you, or that one man rule over you? Remember also that I am your bone and your flesh.

³And his mother's kinsmen spoke all these words concerning him in the hearing of all the men of Shechem, and their hearts inclined to follow Abimelech, for they said, He is our brother.

⁴And they gave him seventy pieces of silver out of the house of Baal-berith, with which Abimelech hired worthless and foolhardy men who followed him.

⁵And he went to his father's house at Ophrah and slew his brothers the sons of Jerubbaal, seventy men, on one stone. But Jotham, the youngest son of Jerubbaal, was left, for he hid himself.

⁶And all the men of Shechem gathered together and all of Beth-millo, and they went and made Abimelech king by the oak (terebinth) of the pillar at Shechem.

⁷When it was told to Jotham, he went and stood at the top of Mount Gerizim and shouted to them, Hear me, men of Shechem, that God may hear you.

⁸One time the trees went forth to anoint a king over them, and they said to the olive tree, Reign over us.

---

ᵃ The gold and purple of the spoil enabled Gideon to make an ephod, presumably on the pattern of that described in Exod. 28. It was not exactly an idol but a kind of fetish, and it diverted the thoughts of the people from Shiloh and the spiritual worship of the unseen and eternal God. So apt is the human heart to cling to some outward emblem—it may be a crucifix, a wafer, or a church—and miss that worship in spirit and in truth which the Father seeks (John 4:23) (F. B. Meyer, *Devotional Commentary on Joshua—II Kings*).

---

ᵃ 26 That is, about 43 pounds or about 20 kilograms      ᵇ 4 That is, about 1 3/4 pounds or about 800 grams

## New International Version

⁹"But the olive tree answered, 'Should I give up my oil, by which both gods and humans are honored, to hold sway over the trees?'

¹⁰"Next, the trees said to the fig tree, 'Come and be our king.'

¹¹"But the fig tree replied, 'Should I give up my fruit, so good and sweet, to hold sway over the trees?'

¹²"Then the trees said to the vine, 'Come and be our king.'

¹³"But the vine answered, 'Should I give up my wine, which cheers both gods and humans, to hold sway over the trees?'

¹⁴"Finally all the trees said to the thornbush, 'Come and be our king.'

¹⁵"The thornbush said to the trees, 'If you really want to anoint me king over you, come and take refuge in my shade; but if not, then let fire come out of the thornbush and consume the cedars of Lebanon!'

¹⁶"Have you acted honorably and in good faith by making Abimelek king? Have you been fair to Jerub-Baal and his family? Have you treated him as he deserves? ¹⁷Remember that my father fought for you and risked his life to rescue you from the hand of Midian. ¹⁸But today you have revolted against my father's family. You have murdered his seventy sons on a single stone and have made Abimelek, the son of his female slave, king over the citizens of Shechem because he is related to you. ¹⁹So have you acted honorably and in good faith toward Jerub-Baal and his family today? If you have, may Abimelek be your joy, and may you be his, too! ²⁰But if you have not, let fire come out from Abimelek and consume you, the citizens of Shechem and Beth Millo, and let fire come out from you, the citizens of Shechem and Beth Millo, and consume Abimelek!"

²¹Then Jotham fled, escaping to Beer, and he lived there because he was afraid of his brother Abimelek.

²²After Abimelek had governed Israel three years, ²³God stirred up animosity between Abimelek and the citizens of Shechem so that they acted treacherously against Abimelek. ²⁴God did this in order that the crime against Jerub-Baal's seventy sons, the shedding of their blood, might be avenged on their brother Abimelek and on the citizens of Shechem, who had helped him murder his brothers. ²⁵In opposition to him these citizens of Shechem set men on the hilltops to ambush and rob everyone who passed by, and this was reported to Abimelek.

²⁶Now Gaal son of Ebed moved with his clan into Shechem, and its citizens put their confidence in him. ²⁷After they had gone out into the fields and gathered the grapes and trodden them, they held a festival in the temple of their god. While they were eating and drinking, they cursed Abimelek. ²⁸Then Gaal son of Ebed said, "Who is Abimelek, and why should we Shechemites be subject to him? Isn't he Jerub-Baal's son, and isn't Zebul his deputy? Serve the family of Hamor, Shechem's father! Why should we serve Abimelek? ²⁹If only this people were under my command! Then I would get rid of him. I would say to Abimelek, 'Call out your whole army!'"ᵃ

³⁰When Zebul the governor of the city heard what Gaal son of Ebed said, he was very angry. ³¹Under cover he sent messengers to Abimelek, saying, "Gaal son of Ebed and his clan have come to Shechem and are stirring up the

ᵃ 29 Septuagint; Hebrew him." Then he said to Abimelek, "Call out your whole army!"

## Amplified Bible

⁹But the olive tree said to them, Should I leave my fatness, by which God and man are honored, and go to wave over the trees?

¹⁰Then the trees said to the fig tree, You come and reign over us.

¹¹But the fig tree said to them, Should I leave my sweetness and my good fruit and go to wave over the trees?

¹²Then the trees said to the vine (grapevine), You come and reign over us.

¹³And the vine (grapevine) replied, Should I leave my new wine, which rejoices God and man, and go to wave over the trees?

¹⁴Then all the trees said to the bramble, You come and reign over us.

¹⁵And the bramble said to the trees, If in good faith you are anointing me king over you, then come and take refuge in my shade; but if not, let fire come out of the bramble and devour the cedars of Lebanon.

¹⁶Now therefore, if you acted sincerely and honorably when you made Abimelech king, and if you have dealt well with Jerubbaal and his house and have done to him as his deeds deserved—

¹⁷For my father fought for you, jeopardized his life, and rescued you from the hand of Midian;

¹⁸And you have risen up against my father's house this day and have slain his sons, seventy men, on one stone and have made Abimelech, son of his maidservant, king over the people of Shechem because he is your kinsman—

¹⁹If you then have acted sincerely and honorably with Jerubbaal and his house this day, then rejoice in Abimelech, and let him also rejoice in you;

²⁰But if not, let fire come out from Abimelech and devour the people of Shechem and Beth-millo, and let fire come out from the people of Shechem and Beth-millo and devour Abimelech.

²¹And Jotham ran away and fled, and went to Beer and dwelt there for fear of Abimelech his brother.

²²Abimelech reigned three years over Israel.

²³And God sent an evil spirit between Abimelech and the men of Shechem, and the men of Shechem dealt treacherously with Abimelech,

²⁴That the violence done to the seventy sons of Jerubbaal might come, and that their blood might be laid upon Abimelech their brother, who slew them, and upon the men of Shechem, who strengthened his hands to slay his brothers.

²⁵And the men of Shechem set men in ambush against [Abimelech] on the mountaintops, and they robbed all who passed by them along that way; and it was told to Abimelech.

²⁶And Gaal son of Ebed came with his kinsmen and moved into Shechem, and the men of Shechem put confidence in him.

²⁷And they went out into the field, gathered their vineyard fruits and trod them, and held a festival; and going into the house of their god, they ate and drank and cursed Abimelech.

²⁸Gaal son of Ebed said, Who is Abimelech, and who are we of Shechem, that we should serve him? Were not the son of Jerubbaal and Zebul, his officer, servants of the men of Hamor the father and founder of Shechem? Then why should we serve him?

²⁹Would that this people were under my hand! Then would I remove Abimelech and say to him, Increase your army and come out.

³⁰When Zebul the city's mayor heard the words of Gaal son of Ebed, his anger was kindled.

³¹And he sent messengers to Abimelech slyly, saying, Behold, Gaal son of Ebed and his kinsmen have come to Shechem; and behold, they stir up the city to rise against you.

## New International Version

city against you. 32Now then, during the night you and your men should come and lie in wait in the fields. 33In the morning at sunrise, advance against the city. When Gaal and his men come out against you, seize the opportunity to attack them."

34So Abimelek and all his troops set out by night and took up concealed positions near Shechem in four companies. 35Now Gaal son of Ebed had gone out and was standing at the entrance of the city gate just as Abimelek and his troops came out from their hiding place.

36When Gaal saw them, he said to Zebul, "Look, people are coming down from the tops of the mountains!"

Zebul replied, "You mistake the shadows of the mountains for men."

37But Gaal spoke up again: "Look, people are coming down from the central hill,a and a company is coming from the direction of the diviners' tree."

38Then Zebul said to him, "Where is your big talk now, you who said, 'Who is Abimelek that we should be subject to him?' Aren't these the men you ridiculed? Go out and fight them!"

39So Gaal led outb the citizens of Shechem and fought Abimelek. 40Abimelek chased him all the way to the entrance of the gate, and many were killed as they fled. 41Then Abimelek stayed in Arumah, and Zebul drove Gaal and his clan out of Shechem.

42The next day the people of Shechem went out to the fields, and this was reported to Abimelek. 43So he took his men, divided them into three companies and set an ambush in the fields. When he saw the people coming out of the city, he rose to attack them. 44Abimelek and the companies with him rushed forward to a position at the entrance of the city gate. Then two companies attacked those in the fields and struck them down. 45All that day Abimelek pressed his attack against the city until he had captured it and killed its people. Then he destroyed the city and scattered salt over it.

46On hearing this, the citizens in the tower of Shechem went into the stronghold of the temple of El-Berith. 47When Abimelek heard that they had assembled there, 48he and all his men went up Mount Zalmon. He took an ax and cut off some branches, which he lifted to his shoulders. He ordered the men with him, "Quick! Do what you have seen me do!" 49So all the men cut branches and followed Abimelek. They piled them against the stronghold and set it on fire with the people still inside. So all the people in the tower of Shechem, about a thousand men and women, also died.

50Next Abimelek went to Thebez and besieged it and

## Amplified Bible

32Now therefore, rise up by night, you and the men with you, and lie in wait in the field.

33Then in the morning, as soon as the sun is up, rise early and set upon the city; and when Gaal and the men with him come out against you, do to them as opportunity permits.

34And Abimelech rose up by night, and all the men with him, and they laid in wait against Shechem in four companies.

35And Gaal son of Ebed came out and stood in the entrance of the city's gate. Then Abimelech and the men with him rose up from ambush.

36When Gaal saw the men, he said to Zebul, Look, men are coming down from the mountaintops! Zebul said to him, The shadow of the mountains looks to you like men.

37And Gaal spoke again and said, See, men are coming down from the center of the land, and one company is coming from the direction of the oak of Meonenim [the sorcerers].

38Then said Zebul to Gaal, Where is your [big] mouth now, you who said, Who is Abimelech, that we should serve him? Are not these the men whom you have despised? Go out now and fight with them.

39And Gaal went out ahead of the men of Shechem and fought with Abimelech.

40And Abimelech chased him, and he fled before him; and many fell wounded—even to the entrance of the gate.

41And Abimelech lodged at Arumah, and Zebul thrust out Gaal and his kinsmen so that they could not live in Shechem.

42The next day the men went out into the fields, and Abimelech was told.

43He took his men and divided them into three companies and laid in wait in the field; and he looked and behold, the people were coming out of the city. And he rose up against them and smote them.

44And Abimelech and the company with him rushed forward and stood in the entrance of the city's gate, while the two other companies rushed upon all who were in the field and slew them.

45And Abimelech fought against the city all that day. He took the city and slew the people who were in it. He demolished the city and a sowed it with salt.

46And when all the men of the Tower of Shechem heard of it, they entered the stronghold of the house of El-berith [the god of Berith].

47Abimelech was told that all the people of the Tower of Shechem were gathered together.

48And Abimelech went up to Mount Zalmon, he and all the men with him; and Abimelech took an ax in his hand and cut down a bundle of brush, picked it up, and laid it on his shoulder. And he said to the men with him, What you have seen me do, make haste to do also.

49So each of the men cut down his bundle and following Abimelech put it against the stronghold and set [the stronghold] on fire over the people in it, so that all the people of the Tower of Shechem also died, about 1,000 men and women.

50Then Abimelech went to Thebez and encamped against Thebez and took it.

---

a This strewing of salt over Shechem was not intended (even if Abimelech had been able to supply enough salt) actually to make the ground unfruitful; but it was a symbol of perpetual desolation, and a sign that Shechem never would be rebuilt. However, such a forecast of a city's fate made by a true prophet of God, or by the Lord Himself, was one thing. This forecast, symbolized by the wicked usurper Abimelech, was quite another thing. For Shechem was later rebuilt (I Kings 12:25), and so was denounced Jericho (I Kings 16:34; see also Josh. 6). But this is not true of Samaria (Mic. 1:6), or Nineveh (Nah. 1:9-12), or Ashkelon (Zeph. 2:4), or the cities of Edom (Ezek. 35:9), or Tyre (Ezek. 26:3, 14), or Chorazin, or Bethsaida, or Capernaum (Matt. 11:20, 21, 23). That these cities, as such, would never be rebuilt permanently was foretold on the authority and by order of God Himself. "Sky and earth will pass away, but My words will not pass away" (Matt. 24:35).

---

a 37 The Hebrew for this phrase means *the navel of the earth.*
b 39 Or *Gaal went out in the sight of*

## New International Version

captured it. ⁵¹Inside the city, however, was a strong tower, to which all the men and women—all the people of the city—had fled. They had locked themselves in and climbed up on the tower roof. ⁵²Abimelek went to the tower and attacked it. But as he approached the entrance to the tower to set it on fire, ⁵³a woman dropped an upper millstone on his head and cracked his skull.

⁵⁴Hurriedly he called to his armor-bearer, "Draw your sword and kill me, so that they can't say, 'A woman killed him.'" So his servant ran him through, and he died. ⁵⁵When the Israelites saw that Abimelek was dead, they went home.

⁵⁶Thus God repaid the wickedness that Abimelek had done to his father by murdering his seventy brothers. ⁵⁷God also made the people of Shechem pay for all their wickedness. The curse of Jotham son of Jerub-Baal came on them.

### Tola

**10** After the time of Abimelek, a man of Issachar named Tola son of Puah, the son of Dodo, rose to save Israel. He lived in Shamir, in the hill country of Ephraim. ²He led*ᵃ* Israel twenty-three years; then he died, and was buried in Shamir.

### Jair

³He was followed by Jair of Gilead, who led Israel twenty-two years. ⁴He had thirty sons, who rode thirty donkeys. They controlled thirty towns in Gilead, which to this day are called Havvoth Jair.*ᵇ* ⁵When Jair died, he was buried in Kamon.

### Jephthah

⁶Again the Israelites did evil in the eyes of the Lord. They served the Baals and the Ashtoreths, and the gods of Aram, the gods of Sidon, the gods of Moab, the gods of the Ammonites and the gods of the Philistines. And because the Israelites forsook the Lord and no longer served him, ⁷he became angry with them. He sold them into the hands of the Philistines and the Ammonites, ⁸who that year shattered and crushed them. For eighteen years they oppressed all the Israelites on the east side of the Jordan in Gilead, the land of the Amorites. ⁹The Ammonites also crossed the Jordan to fight against Judah, Benjamin and Ephraim; Israel was in great distress. ¹⁰Then the Israelites cried out to the Lord, "We have sinned against you, forsaking our God and serving the Baals."

¹¹The Lord replied, "When the Egyptians, the Amorites, the Ammonites, the Philistines, ¹²the Sidonians, the Amalekites and the Maonites*ᶜ* oppressed you and you cried to me for help, did I not save you from their hands? ¹³But you have forsaken me and served other gods, so I will no longer save you. ¹⁴Go and cry out to the gods you have chosen. Let them save you when you are in trouble!"

¹⁵But the Israelites said to the Lord, "We have sinned. Do with us whatever you think best, but please rescue us now." ¹⁶Then they got rid of the foreign gods among them and served the Lord. And he could bear Israel's misery no longer.

¹⁷When the Ammonites were called to arms and camped in Gilead, the Israelites assembled and camped

## Amplified Bible

⁵¹But there was a strong tower in the city, and all the people of the city—men and women—fled to it, shut themselves in, and went to the roof of the tower.

⁵²And Abimelech came to the tower and fought against it and drew near the door of the tower to burn it with fire. ⁵³But a certain woman cast an upper millstone [down] upon Abimelech's head and broke his skull.

⁵⁴Then he called hastily to the young man, his armorbearer, and said to him, Draw your sword and slay me, so that men may not say of me, A woman slew him. And his young man thrust him through, and he died.

⁵⁵And when the men of Israel saw that Abimelech was dead, they departed each man to his home.

⁵⁶Thus God repaid the wickedness of Abimelech which he had done to his father [Gideon] by slaying his seventy brothers;

⁵⁷And all the wickedness of the men of Shechem God repaid upon their heads and caused to come upon them the curse of Jotham son of Jerubbaal. [Judg. 9:19, 20.]

**10** After Abimelech there arose to rescue Israel, Tola son of Puah, the son of Dodo, a man of Issachar; and he lived at Shamir in the hill country of Ephraim.

²He judged Israel twenty-three years; then he died and was buried in Shamir.

³After him arose Jair the Gileadite, and he judged Israel twenty-two years.

⁴And he had thirty sons who rode on thirty donkey colts, and they had thirty towns called Havvoth-jair [towns of Jair] which to this day are in the land of Gilead.

⁵And Jair died and was buried in Kamon.

⁶And the Israelites again did what was evil in the sight of the Lord, served the Baals, the Ashtaroth [female deities], the gods of Syria, the gods of Sidon, the gods of Moab, the gods of the Ammonites, and the gods of the Philistines. They forsook the Lord and did not serve Him.

⁷And the anger of the Lord was kindled against Israel, and He sold them into the hands of the Philistines and the Ammonites,

⁸And they oppressed and crushed *and* broke the Israelites that year. For eighteen years they oppressed all the Israelites beyond the Jordan in the land of the Amorites, which is in Gilead.

⁹And the Ammonites passed over the Jordan to fight against Judah, Benjamin, and the house of Ephraim, so that Israel was sorely distressed.

¹⁰And the Israelites cried to the Lord, saying, We have sinned against You, because we have forsaken our God and have served the Baals.

¹¹And the Lord said to the Israelites, Did I not deliver you from the Egyptians, the Amorites, the Ammonites, and the Philistines?

¹²Also when the Sidonians, the Amalekites, and the Maonites oppressed *and* crushed you, you cried to Me, and I delivered you out of their hands.

¹³Yet you have forsaken Me and served other gods; therefore I will deliver you no more.

¹⁴Go, cry to the gods you have chosen; let them deliver you in your time of distress.

¹⁵And the Israelites said to the Lord, We have sinned, do to us whatever seems good to You; only deliver us, we pray You, this day.

¹⁶So they put away the foreign gods from among them and served the Lord, and His heart became impatient over the misery of Israel.

¹⁷Then the Ammonites were gathered together and they encamped in Gilead. And the Israelites assembled and encamped at Mizpah.

---

*ᵃ* 2 Traditionally *judged*; also in verse 3    *ᵇ* 4 Or *called the settlements of Jair*    *ᶜ* 12 Hebrew; some Septuagint manuscripts *Midianites*

## New International Version

at Mizpah. [18]The leaders of the people of Gilead said to each other, "Whoever will take the lead in attacking the Ammonites will be head over all who live in Gilead."

**11** Jephthah the Gileadite was a mighty warrior. His father was Gilead; his mother was a prostitute. [2]Gilead's wife also bore him sons, and when they were grown up, they drove Jephthah away. "You are not going to get any inheritance in our family," they said, "because you are the son of another woman." [3]So Jephthah fled from his brothers and settled in the land of Tob, where a gang of scoundrels gathered around him and followed him.

[4]Some time later, when the Ammonites were fighting against Israel, [5]the elders of Gilead went to get Jephthah from the land of Tob. [6]"Come," they said, "be our commander, so we can fight the Ammonites."

[7]Jephthah said to them, "Didn't you hate me and drive me from my father's house? Why do you come to me now, when you're in trouble?"

[8]The elders of Gilead said to him, "Nevertheless, we are turning to you now; come with us to fight the Ammonites, and you will be head over all of us who live in Gilead."

[9]Jephthah answered, "Suppose you take me back to fight the Ammonites and the LORD gives them to me—will I really be your head?"

[10]The elders of Gilead replied, "The LORD is our witness; we will certainly do as you say." [11]So Jephthah went with the elders of Gilead, and the people made him head and commander over them. And he repeated all his words before the LORD in Mizpah.

[12]Then Jephthah sent messengers to the Ammonite king with the question: "What do you have against me that you have attacked my country?"

[13]The king of the Ammonites answered Jephthah's messengers, "When Israel came up out of Egypt, they took away my land from the Arnon to the Jabbok, all the way to the Jordan. Now give it back peaceably."

[14]Jephthah sent back messengers to the Ammonite king, [15]saying:

"This is what Jephthah says: Israel did not take the land of Moab or the land of the Ammonites. [16]But when they came up out of Egypt, Israel went through the wilderness to the Red Sea[a] and on to Kadesh. [17]Then Israel sent messengers to the king of Edom, saying, 'Give us permission to go through your country,' but the king of Edom would not listen. They sent also to the king of Moab, and he refused. So Israel stayed at Kadesh.

[18]"Next they traveled through the wilderness, skirted the lands of Edom and Moab, passed along the eastern side of the country of Moab, and camped on the other side of the Arnon. They did not enter the territory of Moab, for the Arnon was its border.

[19]"Then Israel sent messengers to Sihon king of the Amorites, who ruled in Heshbon, and said to him, 'Let us pass through your country to our own place.' [20]Sihon, however, did not trust Israel[b] to pass

## Amplified Bible

[18]And the leaders of Gilead [the Israelites] said one to another, Who is the man who will begin to fight against the Ammonites? He shall be head over all the inhabitants of Gilead.

**11** Now Jephthah the Gileadite was a mighty warrior, but he was the son of a harlot. Gilead was Jephthah's father.

[2]And Gilead's wife also bore him sons, and when his wife's sons grew up, they thrust Jephthah out and said to him, You shall not have an inheritance in our father's house, for you are the son of another woman.

[3]Then Jephthah fled from his brothers and dwelt in the land of Tob; and worthless men gathered around Jephthah and went on raids with him.

[4]And after a time, the Ammonites made war against Israel.

[5]And when the Ammonites made war against Israel, the elders of Gilead went to bring Jephthah out of the land of Tob;

[6]And they said to Jephthah, Come and be our leader, that we may fight with the Ammonites.

[7]But Jephthah said to the elders of Gilead, Did you not hate me and drive me out of my father's house? Why have you come to me now when you are in trouble?

[8]And the elders of Gilead said to Jephthah, This is why we have turned to you now, that you may go with us and fight the Ammonites and be our head over all the citizens of Gilead.

[9]Jephthah said to the elders of Gilead, If you bring me home again to fight against the Ammonites and the Lord gives them over to me, [understand that] I will be your head.

[10]And the elders of Gilead said to Jephthah, The Lord is witness between us, if we do not do as you have said.

[11]So Jephthah went with the elders of Gilead, and the people made him head and leader over them. And Jephthah repeated all he had promised before the Lord at Mizpah.

[12]And Jephthah sent messengers to the king of the Ammonites, saying, What have you to do with me, that you have come against me to fight in my land?

[13]The Ammonites' king replied to the messengers of Jephthah, Because Israel took away my land [which was not true] when they came up out of Egypt [300 years before], from the Arnon even to Jabbok and to the Jordan; now therefore, restore those lands peaceably.

[14]And Jephthah sent messengers again to the king of the Ammonites

[15]And said to him, Thus says Jephthah, Israel did not take the land of Moab or the land of the Ammonites.

[16]But when [Israel] came up from Egypt, [they] walked through the wilderness to the Red Sea and came to Kadesh.

[17]Then Israel sent messengers to the king of Edom, saying, Let us, we pray, pass through your land, but the king of Edom would not listen. Also they sent to the king of Moab, but he would not consent. So Israel remained at Kadesh.

[18]Then they went through the wilderness and went around the land of Edom and the land of Moab, and came by the east side of the land of Moab and camped on the other side of the Arnon; but they came not within the territory of Moab, for the Arnon was the boundary of Moab.

[19]Then Israel sent messengers to Sihon king of the Amorites, king of Heshbon, and Israel said to him, Let us pass, we pray you, through your land to our country.

[20]But Sihon did not trust Israel to pass through his ter-

---

[a] 16 Or the Sea of Reeds    [b] 20 Or however, would not make an agreement for Israel

## New International Version

through his territory. He mustered all his troops and encamped at Jahaz and fought with Israel.

²¹"Then the LORD, the God of Israel, gave Sihon and his whole army into Israel's hands, and they defeated them. Israel took over all the land of the Amorites who lived in that country, ²²capturing all of it from the Arnon to the Jabbok and from the desert to the Jordan.

²³"Now since the LORD, the God of Israel, has driven the Amorites out before his people Israel, what right have you to take it over? ²⁴Will you not take what your god Chemosh gives you? Likewise, whatever the LORD our God has given us, we will possess. ²⁵Are you any better than Balak son of Zippor, king of Moab? Did he ever quarrel with Israel or fight with them? ²⁶For three hundred years Israel occupied Heshbon, Aroer, the surrounding settlements and all the towns along the Arnon. Why didn't you retake them during that time? ²⁷I have not wronged you, but you are doing me wrong by waging war against me. Let the LORD, the Judge, decide the dispute this day between the Israelites and the Ammonites."

²⁸The king of Ammon, however, paid no attention to the message Jephthah sent him.

²⁹Then the Spirit of the LORD came on Jephthah. He crossed Gilead and Manasseh, passed through Mizpah of Gilead, and from there he advanced against the Ammonites. ³⁰And Jephthah made a vow to the LORD: "If you give the Ammonites into my hands, ³¹whatever comes out of the door of my house to meet me when I return in triumph from the Ammonites will be the LORD's, and I will sacrifice it as a burnt offering."

³²Then Jephthah went over to fight the Ammonites, and the LORD gave them into his hands. ³³He devastated twenty towns from Aroer to the vicinity of Minnith, as far as Abel Keramim. Thus Israel subdued Ammon.

³⁴When Jephthah returned to his home in Mizpah, who should come out to meet him but his daughter, dancing to the sound of timbrels! She was an only child. Except for her he had neither son nor daughter. ³⁵When he saw her, he tore his clothes and cried, "Oh no, my daughter! You have brought me down and I am devastated. I have made a vow to the LORD that I cannot break."

³⁶"My father," she replied, "you have given your word to the LORD. Do to me just as you promised, now that the LORD has avenged you of your enemies, the Ammonites. ³⁷But grant me this one request," she said. "Give me two months to roam the hills and weep with my friends, because I will never marry."

³⁸"You may go," he said. And he let her go for two months. She and her friends went into the hills and wept because she would never marry. ³⁹After the two months,

## Amplified Bible

ritory; so Sihon gathered all his people together and encamped at Jahaz and fought with Israel.

²¹And the Lord, the God of Israel, gave Sihon and all his people into the hand of Israel, and they defeated them; so Israel took possession of all the land of the Amorites, the inhabitants of that country.

²²They possessed all the territory of the Amorites, from the Arnon even to the Jabbok, and from the wilderness even to the Jordan.

²³So now the Lord God of Israel has dispossessed the Amorites from before His people Israel, and should you possess them?

²⁴Will you not possess what Chemosh your god gives you to possess? And all the Lord our God dispossessed before us, we will possess.

²⁵Now are you any better than Balak son of Zippor, king of Moab? Did he ever strive against Israel or did he ever go to war with them?

²⁶While Israel dwelt in Heshbon and its villages, and in Aroer and its villages, and in all the cities along the banks of the Arnon for 300 years, why did you not recover [your lost lands] during that time?

²⁷So I have not sinned against you, but you are doing me wrong to war against me. The Lord, the [righteous] Judge, judge this day between the Israelites and the Ammonites.

²⁸But the king of the Ammonites did not listen to the message Jephthah sent him.

²⁹Then the Spirit of the Lord came upon Jephthah, and he passed through Gilead and Manasseh, and Mizpah of Gilead, and from Mizpah of Gilead he passed on to the Ammonites.

³⁰And Jephthah made a vow to the Lord and said, If You will indeed give the Ammonites into my hand,

³¹Then whatever or whoever comes forth from the doors of my house to meet me when I return in peace from the Ammonites, it shall be the Lord's, and I will offer it or him up as a burnt offering.

³²Then Jephthah crossed over to the Ammonites to fight with them, and the Lord gave them into his hand.

³³And from Aroer to Minnith he smote them, twenty cities, and as far as Abel-cheramim [the meadow of vineyards], with a very great slaughter. So the Ammonites were subdued before the Israelites.

³⁴Then Jephthah came to Mizpah to his home, and behold, his daughter came out to meet him with timbrels and with dances! And she was his only child; beside her he had neither son nor daughter.

³⁵And when he saw her, he rent his clothes and said, Alas, my daughter! You have brought me very low, and you are the cause of great trouble to me; for I have opened my mouth [in a vow] to the Lord, and I cannot take it back.

³⁶And she said to him, My father, if you have opened your mouth to the Lord, do to me according to what you have vowed, since the Lord has taken vengeance for you on your enemies, the Ammonites.

³⁷And she said to her father, Let this thing be done for me; let me alone two months, that I may go and wander upon the mountains and bewail my virginity, I and my companions.

³⁸And he said, Go. And he sent her away for two months, and she went with her companions and bewailed her virginity upon the mountains.

³⁹At the end of two months she returned to her father,

## New International Version

she returned to her father, and he did to her as he had vowed. And she was a virgin.

From this comes the Israelite tradition [40]that each year the young women of Israel go out for four days to commemorate the daughter of Jephthah the Gileadite.

### Jephthah and Ephraim

**12** The Ephraimite forces were called out, and they crossed over to Zaphon. They said to Jephthah, "Why did you go to fight the Ammonites without calling us to go with you? We're going to burn down your house over your head."

[2]Jephthah answered, "I and my people were engaged in a great struggle with the Ammonites, and although I called, you didn't save me out of their hands. [3]When I saw that you wouldn't help, I took my life in my hands and crossed over to fight the Ammonites, and the LORD gave me the victory over them. Now why have you come up today to fight me?"

[4]Jephthah then called together the men of Gilead and fought against Ephraim. The Gileadites struck them down because the Ephraimites had said, "You Gileadites are renegades from Ephraim and Manasseh." [5]The Gileadites captured the fords of the Jordan leading to Ephraim, and whenever a survivor of Ephraim said, "Let me cross over," the men of Gilead asked him, "Are you an Ephraimite?" If he replied, "No," [6]they said, "All right, say 'Shibboleth.'" If he said, "Sibboleth," because he could not pronounce the word correctly, they seized him and killed him at the fords of the Jordan. Forty-two thousand Ephraimites were killed at that time.

[7]Jephthah led[a] Israel six years. Then Jephthah the Gileadite died and was buried in a town in Gilead.

### Ibzan, Elon and Abdon

[8]After him, Ibzan of Bethlehem led Israel. [9]He had thirty sons and thirty daughters. He gave his daughters away in marriage to those outside his clan, and for his sons he brought in thirty young women as wives from outside his clan. Ibzan led Israel seven years. [10]Then Ibzan died and was buried in Bethlehem.

[11]After him, Elon the Zebulunite led Israel ten years. [12]Then Elon died and was buried in Aijalon in the land of Zebulun.

[13]After him, Abdon son of Hillel, from Pirathon, led Israel. [14]He had forty sons and thirty grandsons, who rode on seventy donkeys. He led Israel eight years. [15]Then Abdon son of Hillel died and was buried at Pirathon in Ephraim, in the hill country of the Amalekites.

## Amplified Bible

who [a]did with her according to his vow which he had vowed. She never mated with a man. This became a custom in Israel—

[40]That the daughters of Israel went yearly to mourn the daughter of Jephthah the Gileadite four days in a year.

**12** The men of Ephraim were summoned together and they crossed to Zaphon and said to Jephthah, Why did you cross over to fight with the Ammonites and did not summon us to go with you? We will burn your house over you with fire.

[2]And Jephthah said to them, I and my people were in a severe conflict with the Ammonites, and I when I called you, you did not rescue me from their hands.

[3]And when I saw that you would not rescue me, I put my life in my hands and crossed over against the Ammonites, and the Lord delivered them into my hand. Why then have you come up to me this day to fight against me?

[4]Then Jephthah gathered all the men of Gilead and fought with Ephraim; and the men of Gilead smote Ephraim because they had said, You Gileadites are fugitives of Ephraim in the midst of Ephraim and Manasseh.

[5]And the Gileadites took the fords of the Jordan before the Ephraimites; and when any of those Ephraimites who had escaped said, Let me go over, the men of Gilead said to him, Are you an Ephraimite? If he said, No,

[6]They said to him, Then say Shibboleth; and he said, Sibboleth, for he could not pronounce it right. Then they seized him and slew him at the fords of the Jordan. And there fell at that time 42,000 of the Ephraimites.

[7]Jephthah judged Israel six years. Then Jephthah the Gileadite died and was buried in one of the cities of Gilead.

[8]And after him Ibzan of Bethlehem judged Israel.

[9]And he had thirty sons and thirty daughters whom he gave [to husbands] outside his tribe, and thirty daughters [daughters-in-law] whom he brought in from outside his tribe for his sons. And he judged Israel seven years.

[10]Then Ibzan died and was buried at Bethlehem.

[11]After him Elon the Zebulunite judged Israel, and he judged Israel ten years.

[12]Then Elon the Zebulunite died and was buried at Aijalon in the land of Zebulun.

[13]And after him Abdon son of Hillel the Pirathonite judged Israel.

[14]And he had forty sons and thirty grandsons who rode on seventy donkey colts; and he judged Israel eight years.

[15]Then Abdon son of Hillel the Pirathonite died, and was buried at Pirathon in the land of Ephraim, in the hill country of the Amalekites.

---

[a] Scholars fail to agree as to what Jephthah really did. For example, "This plain and restrained statement that 'he did with her according to his vow' is best taken as implying her actual sacrifice. Although human sacrifice was strictly forbidden to Israelites, we need not be surprised at a man of Jephthah's half-Canaanite antecedents following Canaanite usage in this matter" (F. Davidson, ed., *The New Bible Commentary*). And, "Although the lapse of two months might be supposed to have afforded time for reflection and a better sense of his duty, there is but too much reason to conclude that he was impelled to the fulfillment by the dictates of a pious but unenlightened conscience" (Robert Jamieson, A. R. Fausset and David Brown, *A Commentary*). And, "The religious system of Israel had fallen into suspension. From the days of Phinehas (Judg. 20:28) to the time of Samuel, we hear nothing of the high priest, the ark or the tabernacle" (*The Cambridge Bible*). On the other hand, J. P. Lange (*A Commentary*) articulates the position of many scholars when he calls attention to stories in Greek mythology in which the virginity of a goddess was celebrated by Greek maidens with song and dance. Summing up, Lange says, "At all events, it does not 'stand there in the text,' as Luther wrote, that she was offered in sacrifice." And the fact that the maidens mourned her virginity and not her death seems to prove that she did not die.

---

[a] 7 Traditionally *judged*; also in verses 8-14

## New International Version

### The Birth of Samson

**13** Again the Israelites did evil in the eyes of the LORD, so the LORD delivered them into the hands of the Philistines for forty years.

²A certain man of Zorah, named Manoah, from the clan of the Danites, had a wife who was childless, unable to give birth. ³The angel of the LORD appeared to her and said, "You are barren and childless, but you are going to become pregnant and give birth to a son. ⁴Now see to it that you drink no wine or other fermented drink and that you do not eat anything unclean. ⁵You will become pregnant and have a son whose head is never to be touched by a razor because the boy is to be a Nazirite, dedicated to God from the womb. He will take the lead in delivering Israel from the hands of the Philistines."

⁶Then the woman went to her husband and told him, "A man of God came to me. He looked like an angel of God, very awesome. I didn't ask him where he came from, and he didn't tell me his name. ⁷But he said to me, 'You will become pregnant and have a son. Now then, drink no wine or other fermented drink and do not eat anything unclean, because the boy will be a Nazirite of God from the womb until the day of his death.'"

⁸Then Manoah prayed to the LORD: "Pardon your servant, Lord. I beg you to let the man of God you sent to us come again to teach us how to bring up the boy who is to be born."

⁹God heard Manoah, and the angel of God came again to the woman while she was out in the field; but her husband Manoah was not with her. ¹⁰The woman hurried to tell her husband, "He's here! The man who appeared to me the other day!"

¹¹Manoah got up and followed his wife. When he came to the man, he said, "Are you the man who talked to my wife?"

"I am," he said.

¹²So Manoah asked him, "When your words are fulfilled, what is to be the rule that governs the boy's life and work?"

¹³The angel of the LORD answered, "Your wife must do all that I have told her. ¹⁴She must not eat anything that comes from the grapevine, nor drink any wine or other fermented drink nor eat anything unclean. She must do everything I have commanded her."

¹⁵Manoah said to the angel of the LORD, "We would like you to stay until we prepare a young goat for you."

¹⁶The angel of the LORD replied, "Even though you detain me, I will not eat any of your food. But if you prepare a burnt offering, offer it to the LORD." (Manoah did not realize that it was the angel of the LORD.)

¹⁷Then Manoah inquired of the angel of the LORD, "What is your name, so that we may honor you when your word comes true?"

¹⁸He replied, "Why do you ask my name? It is beyond understanding.ᵃ" ¹⁹Then Manoah took a young goat, together with the grain offering, and sacrificed it on a rock to the LORD. And the LORD did an amazing thing while Manoah and his wife watched: ²⁰As the flame blazed up from the altar toward heaven, the angel of the LORD ascended in the flame. Seeing this, Manoah and his wife fell with their faces to the ground. ²¹When the angel of the LORD did not show himself again to Manoah and his wife, Manoah realized that it was the angel of the LORD.

²²"We are doomed to die!" he said to his wife. "We have seen God!"

## Amplified Bible

**13** And the Israelites again did what was evil in the sight of the Lord, and the Lord gave them into the hands of the Philistines for forty years.

²And there was a certain man of Zorah, of the tribe of the Danites, whose name was Manoah; and his wife was barren and had no children.

³And the ᵃAngel of the Lord appeared to the woman and said to her, Behold, you are barren and have no children, but you shall become pregnant and bear a son.

⁴Therefore beware and drink no wine or strong drink and eat nothing unclean.

⁵For behold, you shall become pregnant and bear a son. No razor shall come upon his head, for the child shall be a Nazirite to God from birth, and he shall begin to deliver Israel out of the hands of the Philistines.

⁶Then the woman went and told her husband, saying, A ᵇMan of God came to me and his face was like the face of the Angel of God, to be greatly and reverently feared. I did not ask him from where he came, and he did not tell me his name.

⁷But he said to me, Behold, you shall become pregnant and bear a son, and now drink no wine or strong drink and eat nothing unclean, for the child shall be a Nazirite to God from birth to the day of his death.

⁸Then Manoah entreated the Lord and said, O Lord, let the Man of God whom You sent come again to us and teach us what we shall do with the child that shall be born.

⁹And God listened to the voice of Manoah, and the Angel of God came again to the woman as she sat in the field; but Manoah her husband was not with her.

¹⁰And the woman ran in haste and told her husband and said to him, Behold, the Man who came to me the other day has appeared to me.

¹¹And Manoah arose and went after his wife and came to the Man and said to him, Are you the Man who spoke to this woman? And he said, I am.

¹²And Manoah said, Now when your words come true, how shall we manage the child, and what is he to do?

¹³And the Angel of the Lord said to Manoah, Let the mother beware of all that I told her.

¹⁴She may not eat of anything that comes from the grapevine, nor drink wine or strong drink nor eat any unclean thing. All that I commanded her let her observe.

¹⁵And Manoah said to the Angel of the Lord, Pray, let us detain you that we may prepare a kid for you.

¹⁶And the Angel of the Lord said to Manoah, Though you detain me, I will not eat of your food, but if you make ready a burnt offering, offer it to the Lord. For Manoah did not know that he was the Angel of the Lord.

¹⁷And Manoah said to the Angel of the Lord, What is your name, so that when your words come true, we may do you honor?

¹⁸And the Angel of the Lord said to him, Why do you ask my name, seeing it is wonderful? [Isa. 9:6.]

¹⁹So Manoah took the kid with the cereal offering and offered it upon a rock to the Lord, the Angel working wonders, while Manoah and his wife looked on.

²⁰For when the flame went up toward the heavens from the altar, the Angel of the Lord ascended in the altar flame. And Manoah and his wife looked on, and they fell on their faces to the ground.

²¹The Angel of the Lord did not appear again to Manoah or to his wife. Then Manoah knew that he was the Angel of the Lord.

²²And Manoah said to his wife, We shall surely die, because we have seen God.

---

ᵃ 18 Or *is wonderful*

ᵃ See footnote on Gen. 16:7. Note that in Judg. 13:22 the Angel of the Lord is identified with God. ᵇ It is clear from Judg. 13:3, 21 that this messenger was the Angel of the Lord.

## New International Version

²³But his wife answered, "If the LORD had meant to kill us, he would not have accepted a burnt offering and grain offering from our hands, nor shown us all these things or now told us this."

²⁴The woman gave birth to a boy and named him Samson. He grew and the LORD blessed him, ²⁵and the Spirit of the LORD began to stir him while he was in Mahaneh Dan, between Zorah and Eshtaol.

### Samson's Marriage

**14** Samson went down to Timnah and saw there a young Philistine woman. ²When he returned, he said to his father and mother, "I have seen a Philistine woman in Timnah; now get her for me as my wife."

³His father and mother replied, "Isn't there an acceptable woman among your relatives or among all our people? Must you go to the uncircumcised Philistines to get a wife?"

But Samson said to his father, "Get her for me. She's the right one for me." ⁴(His parents did not know that this was from the LORD, who was seeking an occasion to confront the Philistines; for at that time they were ruling over Israel.)

⁵Samson went down to Timnah together with his father and mother. As they approached the vineyards of Timnah, suddenly a young lion came roaring toward him. ⁶The Spirit of the LORD came powerfully upon him so that he tore the lion apart with his bare hands as he might have torn a young goat. But he told neither his father nor his mother what he had done. ⁷Then he went down and talked with the woman, and he liked her.

⁸Some time later, when he went back to marry her, he turned aside to look at the lion's carcass, and in it he saw a swarm of bees and some honey. ⁹He scooped out the honey with his hands and ate as he went along. When he rejoined his parents, he gave them some, and they too ate it. But he did not tell them that he had taken the honey from the lion's carcass.

¹⁰Now his father went down to see the woman. And there Samson held a feast, as was customary for young men. ¹¹When the people saw him, they chose thirty men to be his companions.

¹²"Let me tell you a riddle," Samson said to them. "If you can give me the answer within the seven days of the feast, I will give you thirty linen garments and thirty sets of clothes. ¹³If you can't tell me the answer, you must give me thirty linen garments and thirty sets of clothes."

"Tell us your riddle," they said. "Let's hear it."

¹⁴He replied,

"Out of the eater, something to eat;
    out of the strong, something sweet."

For three days they could not give the answer.

¹⁵On the fourth[a] day, they said to Samson's wife, "Coax your husband into explaining the riddle for us, or we will burn you and your father's household to death. Did you invite us here to steal our property?"

¹⁶Then Samson's wife threw herself on him, sobbing, "You hate me! You don't really love me. You've given my people a riddle, but you haven't told me the answer."

"I haven't even explained it to my father or mother," he replied, "so why should I explain it to you?" ¹⁷She cried the

## Amplified Bible

²³But his [sensible] wife said to him, If the Lord were pleased to kill us, He would not have received a burnt offering and a cereal offering from our hands, nor have shown us all these things or now have announced such things as these.

²⁴And the woman [in due time] bore a son and called his name Samson; and the child grew and the Lord blessed him.

²⁵And the Spirit of the Lord began to move him at times in Mahaneh-dan [the camp of Dan] between Zorah and Eshtaol.

**14** Samson went down to Timnah and at Timnah saw one of the daughters of the Philistines.

²And he came up and told his father and mother, I saw one of the daughters of the Philistines at Timnah; now get her for me as my wife.

³But his father and mother said to him, Is there not a woman among the daughters of your kinsmen or among all our people, that you must go to take a wife from the uncircumcised Philistines? And Samson said to his father, Get her for me, for she is all right in my eyes.

⁴His father and mother did not know that it was of the Lord, and that He sought an occasion for assailing the Philistines. At that time the Philistines had dominion over Israel.

⁵Then Samson and his father and mother went down to Timnah and came to the vineyards of Timnah. And behold, a young lion roared against him.

⁶And the Spirit of the Lord came mightily upon him, and he tore the lion as he would have torn a kid, and he had nothing in his hand; but he did not tell his father or mother what he had done.

⁷And he went down and talked with the woman, and she pleased Samson well.

⁸And after a while he returned to take her, and he turned aside to see the body of the lion, and behold, a swarm of bees and honey were in the body of the lion.

⁹And he scraped some of the honey out into his hands and went along eating. And he came to his father and mother and gave them some, and they ate it; but he did not tell them he had taken the honey from the body of the lion.

¹⁰His father went down to the woman, and Samson made a feast there, for that was the customary thing for young men to do.

¹¹And when the people saw him, they brought thirty companions to be with him.

¹²And Samson said to them, I will now put forth a riddle to you; if you can tell me what it is within the seven days of the feast, and find it out, then I will give you thirty linen undergarments and thirty changes of raiment.

¹³But if you cannot declare it to me, then shall you give me thirty linen undergarments and thirty changes of festive [costly] raiment. And they said to him, Put forth your riddle, that we may hear it.

¹⁴And he said to them, Out of the eater came forth food, and out of the strong came forth sweetness. And they could not solve the riddle in three days.

¹⁵And on the seventh day they said to Samson's wife, Entice your husband to declare to us the riddle, lest we burn you and your father's household with fire. Have you invited us to make us poor? Is this not true?

¹⁶And Samson's wife wept before him and said, You only hate me, you do not love me; you have put forth a riddle to my countrymen and have not told the answer to me. And he said to her, Behold, I have not told my father or my mother, and shall I tell you?

---

ᵃ 15 Some Septuagint manuscripts and Syriac; Hebrew *seventh*

## New International Version

whole seven days of the feast. So on the seventh day he finally told her, because she continued to press him. She in turn explained the riddle to her people.

[18]Before sunset on the seventh day the men of the town said to him,

"What is sweeter than honey?
  What is stronger than a lion?"

Samson said to them,

"If you had not plowed with my heifer,
  you would not have solved my riddle."

[19]Then the Spirit of the LORD came powerfully upon him. He went down to Ashkelon, struck down thirty of their men, stripped them of everything and gave their clothes to those who had explained the riddle. Burning with anger, he returned to his father's home. [20]And Samson's wife was given to one of his companions who had attended him at the feast.

### Samson's Vengeance on the Philistines

**15** Later on, at the time of wheat harvest, Samson took a young goat and went to visit his wife. He said, "I'm going to my wife's room." But her father would not let him go in.

[2]"I was so sure you hated her," he said, "that I gave her to your companion. Isn't her younger sister more attractive? Take her instead."

[3]Samson said to them, "This time I have a right to get even with the Philistines; I will really harm them." [4]So he went out and caught three hundred foxes and tied them tail to tail in pairs. He then fastened a torch to every pair of tails, [5]lit the torches and let the foxes loose in the standing grain of the Philistines. He burned up the shocks and standing grain, together with the vineyards and olive groves.

[6]When the Philistines asked, "Who did this?" they were told, "Samson, the Timnite's son-in-law, because his wife was given to his companion."

So the Philistines went up and burned her and her father to death. [7]Samson said to them, "Since you've acted like this, I swear that I won't stop until I get my revenge on you." [8]He attacked them viciously and slaughtered many of them. Then he went down and stayed in a cave in the rock of Etam.

[9]The Philistines went up and camped in Judah, spreading out near Lehi. [10]The people of Judah asked, "Why have you come to fight us?"

"We have come to take Samson prisoner," they answered, "to do to him as he did to us."

[11]Then three thousand men from Judah went down to the cave in the rock of Etam and said to Samson, "Don't you realize that the Philistines are rulers over us? What have you done to us?"

He answered, "I merely did to them what they did to me."

[12]They said to him, "We've come to tie you up and hand you over to the Philistines."

Samson said, "Swear to me that you won't kill me yourselves."

[13]"Agreed," they answered. "We will only tie you up and hand you over to them. We will not kill you." So they bound him with two new ropes and led him up from the rock. [14]As he approached Lehi, the Philistines came toward him shouting. The Spirit of the LORD came powerfully upon him. The ropes on his arms became like charred flax, and the bindings dropped from his hands. [15]Finding a fresh

## Amplified Bible

[17]And Samson's wife wept before him the seven days their feast lasted, and on the seventh day he told her because she pressed him with entreaties. Then she told the riddle to her countrymen.

[18]And the men of the city said to [Samson] on the seventh day before sundown, What is sweeter than honey? What is stronger than a lion? And he said to them, If you had not plowed with my heifer, you would not have solved my riddle.

[19]And the Spirit of the Lord came upon him, and he went down to Ashkelon and slew thirty men of them and took their apparel [as spoil], and gave the changes of garments to those who explained the riddle. And his anger was kindled, and he went up to his father's house.

[20]But Samson's wife was [given] to his companion who was his [best] friend.

**15** But some days later, in the time of wheat harvest, Samson went to visit his wife, taking along a kid [as a token of reconciliation]; and he said, I will go unto my wife in the inner chamber. But her father would not allow him to go in.

[2]And her father said, I truly thought you utterly hated her, so I gave her to your companion. Is her younger sister not fairer than she? Take her, I pray you, instead.

[3]And Samson said of them, This time shall I be blameless as regards the Philistines, though I do them evil.

[4]So Samson went and caught 300 foxes or jackals and took torches and turning the foxes tail to tail, he put a torch between each pair of tails.

[5]And when he had set the torches ablaze, he let the foxes go into the standing grain of the Philistines, and he burned up the shocks and the standing grain, along with the olive orchards.

[6]Then the Philistines said, Who has done this? And they were told, Samson, the son-in-law of the Timnite, because he [the Timnite] has taken his [Samson's] wife and has given her to his companion. And the Philistines came up and burned her and her father with fire.

[7]And Samson said to them, If this is the way you act, surely I will take revenge on you, and after that I will quit.

[8]And he smote them hip and thigh [unsparingly], a great slaughter; and he went down and dwelt in the cleft of the rock of Etam.

[9]Then the Philistines came up and encamped in Judah and spread themselves in Lehi.

[10]And the men of Judah said, Why have you come up against us? And they answered, We have come up to bind Samson, to do to him as he has done to us.

[11]Then 3,000 men of Judah went down to the cleft of the rock Etam and said to Samson, Have you not known that the Philistines are rulers over us? What is this that you have done to us? He said to them, As they did to me, so have I done to them.

[12]And they said to him, We have come down to bind you, that we may deliver you into the hands of the Philistines. And Samson said to them, Swear to me that you will not fall upon me yourselves.

[13]And they said to him, No, we will bind you fast and give you into their hand; but surely we will not kill you. So they bound him with two new ropes and brought him up from the rock.

[14]And when he came to Lehi, the Philistines came shouting to meet him. And the Spirit of the Lord came mightily upon [Samson], and the ropes on his arms became as flax that had caught fire, and his bonds melted off his hands.

## New International Version

jawbone of a donkey, he grabbed it and struck down a thousand men.

16Then Samson said,

"With a donkey's jawbone
  I have made donkeys of them.*
With a donkey's jawbone
  I have killed a thousand men."

17When he finished speaking, he threw away the jawbone; and the place was called Ramath Lehi.b

18Because he was very thirsty, he cried out to the LORD, "You have given your servant this great victory. Must I now die of thirst and fall into the hands of the uncircumcised?" 19Then God opened up the hollow place in Lehi, and water came out of it. When Samson drank, his strength returned and he revived. So the spring was called En Hakkore,c and it is still there in Lehi.

20Samson ledd Israel for twenty years in the days of the Philistines.

### Samson and Delilah

**16** One day Samson went to Gaza, where he saw a prostitute. He went in to spend the night with her. 2The people of Gaza were told, "Samson is here!" So they surrounded the place and lay in wait for him all night at the city gate. They made no move during the night, saying, "At dawn we'll kill him."

3But Samson lay there only until the middle of the night. Then he got up and took hold of the doors of the city gate, together with the two posts, and tore them loose, bar and all. He lifted them to his shoulders and carried them to the top of the hill that faces Hebron.

4Some time later, he fell in love with a woman in the Valley of Sorek whose name was Delilah. 5The rulers of the Philistines went to her and said, "See if you can lure him into showing you the secret of his great strength and how we can overpower him so we may tie him up and subdue him. Each one of us will give you eleven hundred shekelse of silver."

6So Delilah said to Samson, "Tell me the secret of your great strength and how you can be tied up and subdued."

7Samson answered her, "If anyone ties me with seven fresh bowstrings that have not been dried, I'll become as weak as any other man."

8Then the rulers of the Philistines brought her seven fresh bowstrings that had not been dried, and she tied him with them. 9With men hidden in the room, she called to him, "Samson, the Philistines are upon you!" But he snapped the bowstrings as easily as a piece of string snaps when it comes close to a flame. So the secret of his strength was not discovered.

10Then Delilah said to Samson, "You have made a fool of me; you lied to me. Come now, tell me how you can be tied."

11He said, "If anyone ties me securely with new ropes that have never been used, I'll become as weak as any other man."

12So Delilah took new ropes and tied him with them. Then, with men hidden in the room, she called to him, "Samson, the Philistines are upon you!" But he snapped the ropes off his arms as if they were threads.

13Delilah then said to Samson, "All this time you have been making a fool of me and lying to me. Tell me how you can be tied."

He replied, "If you weave the seven braids of my head into the fabric on the loom and tighten it with the pin, I'll become as weak as any other man." So while he was sleep-

## Amplified Bible

15And he found a still moist jawbone of a donkey and reached out and took it and slew 1,000 men with it.

16And Samson said, With the jawbone of a donkey, heaps upon heaps, with the jawbone of a donkey I have slain 1,000 men!

17And when he stopped speaking, he cast the jawbone from his hand; and that place was called Ramath-lehi [the hill of the jawbone].

18Samson was very thirsty, and he prayed to the Lord and said, You have given this great deliverance by the hand of Your servant, and now shall I die of thirst and fall into the hands of the uncircumcised?

19And God split open the hollow place that was at Lehi, and water came out of it. And when he drank, his spirit returned and he revived. Therefore the name of it was called En-hakkore [the spring of him who prayed], which is at Lehi to this day.

20And [Samson] judged (defended) Israel in the days of the Philistines twenty years. [Judg. 17:6.]

**16** Then Samson went to Gaza and saw a harlot there, and went in to her. 2The Gazites were told, Samson has come here. So they surrounded the place and lay in wait for him all night at the gate of the city. They were quiet all night, saying, In the morning, when it is light, we will kill him.

3But Samson lay until midnight, and [then] he arose and took hold of the doors of the city's gate and the two posts, and pulling them up, bar and all, he put them on his shoulders and carried them to the top of the hill that is before Hebron.

4After this he loved a woman in the Valley of Sorek whose name was Delilah.

5And the lords of the Philistines came to her and said to her, Entice him and see in what his great strength lies, and by what means we may overpower him that we may bind him to subdue him. And we will each give you 1,100 pieces of silver.

6And Delilah said to Samson, Tell me, I pray you, wherein your great strength lies, and with what you might be bound to subdue you.

7And Samson said to her, If they bind me with seven fresh, strong gutstrings, still moist, then shall I be weak and be like any other man.

8Then the Philistine lords brought to her seven fresh, strong bowstrings, still moist, and she bound him with them.

9Now she had men lying in wait in an inner room. And she said to him, The Philistines are upon you, Samson! And he broke the bowstrings as a string of tow breaks when it touches the fire. So the secret of his strength was not known.

10And Delilah said to Samson, Behold, you have mocked me and told me lies; now tell me, I pray you, how you might be bound.

11And he said to her, If they bind me fast with new ropes that have not been used, then I shall become weak and be like any other man.

12So Delilah took new ropes and bound him with them and said to him, The Philistines are upon you, Samson! And the men lay in wait were in the inner room. But he snapped the ropes off his arms like [sewing] thread.

13And Delilah said to Samson, Until now you have mocked me and told me lies; tell me with what you might be bound. And he said to her, If you weave the seven braids of [the hair of] my head with the web.

---

*a 16 Or made a heap or two*; the Hebrew for *donkey* sounds like the Hebrew for *heap*.   *b 17 Ramath Lehi* means *jawbone hill*.   *c 19 En Hakkore* means *caller's spring*.   *d 20 Traditionally judged*   *e 5 That* is, about 28 pounds or about 13 kilograms

## New International Version

ing, Delilah took the seven braids of his head, wove them into the fabric [14]and[a] tightened it with the pin.

Again she called to him, "Samson, the Philistines are upon you!" He awoke from his sleep and pulled up the pin and the loom, with the fabric.

[15]Then she said to him, "How can you say, 'I love you,' when you won't confide in me? This is the third time you have made a fool of me and haven't told me the secret of your great strength." [16]With such nagging she prodded him day after day until he was sick to death of it.

[17]So he told her everything. "No razor has ever been used on my head," he said, "because I have been a Nazirite dedicated to God from my mother's womb. If my head were shaved, my strength would leave me, and I would become as weak as any other man."

[18]When Delilah saw that he had told her everything, she sent word to the rulers of the Philistines, "Come back once more; he has told me everything." So the rulers of the Philistines returned with the silver in their hands. [19]After putting him to sleep on her lap, she called for someone to shave off the seven braids of his hair, and so began to subdue him.[b] And his strength left him.

[20]Then she called, "Samson, the Philistines are upon you!"

He awoke from his sleep and thought, "I'll go out as before and shake myself free." But he did not know that the LORD had left him.

[21]Then the Philistines seized him, gouged out his eyes and took him down to Gaza. Binding him with bronze shackles, they set him to grinding grain in the prison. [22]But the hair on his head began to grow again after it had been shaved.

### The Death of Samson

[23]Now the rulers of the Philistines assembled to offer a great sacrifice to Dagon their god and to celebrate, saying, "Our god has delivered Samson, our enemy, into our hands."

[24]When the people saw him, they praised their god, saying,

"Our god has delivered our enemy
    into our hands,
the one who laid waste our land
    and multiplied our slain."

[25]While they were in high spirits, they shouted, "Bring out Samson to entertain us." So they called Samson out of the prison, and he performed for them.

When they stood him among the pillars, [26]Samson said to the servant who held his hand, "Put me where I can feel the pillars that support the temple, so that I may lean against them." [27]Now the temple was crowded with men and women; all the rulers of the Philistines were there, and on the roof were about three thousand men and women watching Samson perform. [28]Then Samson prayed to the LORD, "Sovereign LORD, remember me. Please, God, strengthen me just once more, and let me with one blow get revenge on the Philistines for my two eyes." [29]Then Samson reached toward the two central pillars on which the temple stood. Bracing himself against them, his right hand on the one and his left hand on the other, [30]Samson said, "Let me die with the Philistines!" Then he pushed with all his might, and down came the temple on the rulers and all the people in it. Thus he killed many more when he died than while he lived.

[31]Then his brothers and his father's whole family went

## Amplified Bible

[14]And she did so and fastened it with the pin and said to him, The Philistines are upon you, Samson! And he awoke out of his sleep and went away with the pin of the [weaver's] beam and with the web.

[15]And she said to him, How can you say, I love you, when your heart is not with me? You have mocked me these three times and have not told me in what your great strength lies.

[16]And when she pressed him day after day with her words and urged him, he was vexed to death.

[17]Then he told her all his mind and said to her, A razor has never come upon my head, for I have been a Nazirite to God from my birth. If I am shaved, then my strength will go from me, and I shall become weak and be like any other man.

[18]And when Delilah saw that he had told her all his mind, she went and called for the Philistine lords, saying, Come up this once, for he has told me all he knows. Then the Philistine lords came up to her and brought the money in their hands.

[19]And she made Samson sleep upon her knees, and she called a man and caused him to shave off the seven braids of his head. Then she began to torment [Samson], and his strength went from him.

[20]She said, The Philistines are upon you, Samson! And he awoke out of his sleep and said, I will go out as I have time after time and shake myself free. For Samson did not know that the Lord had departed from him.

[21]But the Philistines laid hold of him, bored out his eyes, and brought him down to Gaza and bound him with [two] bronze fetters; and he ground at the mill in the prison.

[22]But the hair of his head began to grow again after it had been shaved.

[23]Then the Philistine lords gathered together to offer a great sacrifice to Dagon their god and to rejoice, for they said, Our god has given Samson our enemy into our hands.

[24]And when the people saw Samson, they praised their god, for they said, Our god has delivered into our hands our enemy, the ravager of our country, who has slain many of us.

[25]And when their hearts were merry, they said, Call for Samson, that he may make sport for us. So they called [blind] Samson out of the prison, and he made sport before them. They made him stand between the pillars.

[26]And Samson said to the lad who held him by the hand, Allow me to feel the pillars upon which the house rests, that I may lean against them.

[27]Now the house was full of men and women; all the Philistine princes were there, and on the roof were about 3,000 men and women who looked on while Samson made sport.

[28]Then Samson called to the Lord and said, O Lord God, [earnestly] remember me, I pray You, and strengthen me, I pray You, only this once, O God, and let me have one vengeance upon the Philistines for both my eyes.

[29]And Samson laid hold of the two middle pillars by which the house was borne up, one with his right hand and the other with his left.

[30]And Samson cried, Let me die with the Philistines! And he bowed himself mightily, and the house fell upon the princes and upon all the people that were in it. So the dead whom he slew at his death were more than they whom he slew in his life.

[31]Then his kinsmen and all the tribal family of his fa-

---

[a] 13,14 Some Septuagint manuscripts; Hebrew *replied, "I can if you weave the seven braids of my head into the fabric on the loom."* [14]*So she*
[b] 19 Hebrew; some Septuagint manuscripts *and he began to weaken*

## New International Version

down to get him. They brought him back and buried him between Zorah and Eshtaol in the tomb of Manoah his father. He had led[a] Israel twenty years.

### Micah's Idols

**17** Now a man named Micah from the hill country of Ephraim [2] said to his mother, "The eleven hundred shekels[b] of silver that were taken from you and about which I heard you utter a curse—I have that silver with me; I took it."

Then his mother said, "The LORD bless you, my son!"

[3] When he returned the eleven hundred shekels of silver to his mother, she said, "I solemnly consecrate my silver to the LORD for my son to make an image overlaid with silver. I will give it back to you."

[4] So after he returned the silver to his mother, she took two hundred shekels[c] of silver and gave them to a silversmith, who used them to make the idol. And it was put in Micah's house.

[5] Now this man Micah had a shrine, and he made an ephod and some household gods and installed one of his sons as his priest. [6] In those days Israel had no king; everyone did as they saw fit.

[7] A young Levite from Bethlehem in Judah, who had been living within the clan of Judah, [8] left that town in search of some other place to stay. On his way[d] he came to Micah's house in the hill country of Ephraim.

[9] Micah asked him, "Where are you from?"

"I'm a Levite from Bethlehem in Judah," he said, "and I'm looking for a place to stay."

[10] Then Micah said to him, "Live with me and be my father and priest, and I'll give you ten shekels[e] of silver a year, your clothes and your food." [11] So the Levite agreed to live with him, and the young man became like one of his sons to him. [12] Then Micah installed the Levite, and the young man became his priest and lived in his house. [13] And Micah said, "Now I know that the LORD will be good to me, since this Levite has become my priest."

### The Danites Settle in Laish

**18** In those days Israel had no king.

And in those days the tribe of the Danites was seeking a place of their own where they might settle, because they had not yet come into an inheritance among the tribes of Israel. [2] So the Danites sent five of their leading men from Zorah and Eshtaol to spy out the land and explore it. These men represented all the Danites. They told them, "Go, explore the land."

So they entered the hill country of Ephraim and came to the house of Micah, where they spent the night. [3] When they were near Micah's house, they recognized the voice of the young Levite; so they turned in there and asked him, "Who brought you here? What are you doing in this place? Why are you here?"

[4] He told them what Micah had done for him, and said, "He has hired me and I am his priest."

[5] Then they said to him, "Please inquire of God to learn whether our journey will be successful."

[6] The priest answered them, "Go in peace. Your journey has the LORD's approval."

## Amplified Bible

ther came down, took his body, and brought it up; and they buried him between Zorah and Eshtaol in the burial place of Manoah his father. He had judged Israel [that is, had defended the Israelites] twenty years. [Judg. 17:6; Heb. 11:32.]

**17** There was a man of the hill country of Ephraim whose name was Micah.

[2] And he said to his mother, The 1,100 shekels of silver that were taken from you, about which you cursed and also spoke about in my hearing, behold, I have the silver with me; I took it. And his mother said, Blessed be you by the Lord, my son!

[3] He restored the 1,100 shekels of silver to his mother, and she said, I had truly dedicated the silver to the Lord from my hand for my son to make a graven image and a molten image; now therefore, I will restore it to you.

[4] So when he restored the money to his mother, she took 200 pieces of silver and gave them to the silversmith, who made of it a graven image and a molten image; and they were in the house of Micah.

[5] And the man Micah had a house of gods, and he made an ephod and teraphim and dedicated one of his sons, who became his priest.

[6] In those days there was no king in Israel; every man did what was right in his own eyes.

[7] And there was a young man in Bethlehem of Judah, of the family of Judah, who was a Levite; and he sojourned there.

[8] And the man departed from the town of Bethlehem in Judah to sojourn where he could find a place, and as he journeyed he came to the hill country of Ephraim to the house of Micah.

[9] And Micah said to him, From where do you come? And he said to him, I am a Levite of Bethlehem in Judah, and I go to sojourn where I may find a place.

[10] And Micah said to him, Dwell with me and be to me a father and a priest, and I will give you ten pieces of silver each year, a suit of clothes, and your living. So the Levite went in.

[11] And the Levite was content to dwell with the man, and the young man was to Micah as one of his sons.

[12] And Micah consecrated the Levite, and the young man became his priest and was in the house of Micah.

[13] Then said Micah, Now I know that the Lord will favor me, since I have a Levite to be my priest.

**18** In those days there was no king in Israel. And in those days the tribe of the Danites sought for itself an inheritance to dwell in, for until then no [sufficient] inheritance had been acquired by them among the tribes of Israel.

[2] So the Danites sent from the whole number of their tribe five brave men from Zorah and Eshtaol to spy out the land and to explore it, and they said to them, Go, explore the land. They came to the hill country of Ephraim, to the house of Micah, and lodged there.

[3] When they went by the house of Micah, they recognized the voice of the young Levite, and they turned aside there and said to him, Who brought you here? And what do you do in this place? And what have you here?

[4] And he said to them, Thus and thus Micah deals with me and has hired me, and I am his priest.

[5] And they said to him, Ask counsel, we pray you, of God that we may know whether our journey will be successful.

[6] And the priest said to them, Go in peace. The way in which you go is before (under the eye of) the Lord.

---

*a 31 Traditionally *judged*   *b 2* That is, about 28 pounds or about 13 kilograms   *c 4* That is, about 5 pounds or about 2.3 kilograms   *d 8* Or *To carry on his profession*   *e 10* That is, about 4 ounces or about 115 grams

## New International Version

[7] So the five men left and came to Laish, where they saw that the people were living in safety, like the Sidonians, at peace and secure. And since their land lacked nothing, they were prosperous.[a] Also, they lived a long way from the Sidonians and had no relationship with anyone else.[b]

[8] When they returned to Zorah and Eshtaol, their fellow Danites asked them, "How did you find things?"

[9] They answered, "Come on, let's attack them! We have seen the land, and it is very good. Aren't you going to do something? Don't hesitate to go there and take it over. [10] When you get there, you will find an unsuspecting people and a spacious land that God has put into your hands, a land that lacks nothing whatever."

[11] Then six hundred men of the Danites, armed for battle, set out from Zorah and Eshtaol. [12] On their way they set up camp near Kiriath Jearim in Judah. This is why the place west of Kiriath Jearim is called Mahaneh Dan[c] to this day. [13] From there they went on to the hill country of Ephraim and came to Micah's house.

[14] Then the five men who had spied out the land of Laish said to their fellow Danites, "Do you know that one of these houses has an ephod, some household gods and an image overlaid with silver? Now you know what to do." [15] So they turned in there and went to the house of the young Levite at Micah's place and greeted him. [16] The six hundred Danites, armed for battle, stood at the entrance of the gate. [17] The five men who had spied out the land went inside and took the idol, the ephod and the household gods while the priest and the six hundred armed men stood at the entrance of the gate.

[18] When the five men went into Micah's house and took the idol, the ephod and the household gods, the priest said to them, "What are you doing?"

[19] They answered him, "Be quiet! Don't say a word. Come with us, and be our father and priest. Isn't it better that you serve a tribe and clan in Israel as priest rather than just one man's household?" [20] The priest was very pleased. He took the ephod, the household gods and the idol and went along with the people. [21] Putting their little children, their livestock and their possessions in front of them, they turned away and left.

[22] When they had gone some distance from Micah's house, the men who lived near Micah were called together and overtook the Danites. [23] As they shouted after them, the Danites turned and said to Micah, "What's the matter with you that you called out your men to fight?"

[24] He replied, "You took the gods I made, and my priest, and went away. What else do I have? How can you ask, 'What's the matter with you?'"

[25] The Danites answered, "Don't argue with us, or some of the men may get angry and attack you, and you and your family will lose your lives." [26] So the Danites went their way, and Micah, seeing that they were too strong for him, turned around and went back home.

## Amplified Bible

[7] Then the five men departed and came to Laish and saw the people who were there, how they dwelt securely after the manner of the Sidonians, quiet and feeling safe; and there was no magistrate in the land, who might put them to shame in anything or injure them; and they were far from the Sidonians and had no dealings with anyone.

[8] The five men came back to their brethren at Zorah and Eshtaol, and their brethren said to them, What do you say?

[9] They said, Arise, let us go up against them, for we have seen the land, and behold, it is very fertile. And will you do nothing? Do not be slow to go and enter in and possess the land.

[10] When you go, you will come to people [feeling] safe and secure. The land is broad [widely extended on all sides]; and God has given it into your hands—a place where there is no want of anything that is in the earth.

[11] And there went from there of the tribe of the Danites, out of Zorah and Eshtaol, 600 men armed with weapons of war.

[12] And they went up and encamped at Kiriath-jearim in Judah. Therefore they called that place Mahaneh-dan [camp of Dan] to this day; it is west of Kiriath-jearim.

[13] And they passed from there to the hill country of Ephraim and came to Micah's house.

[14] Then the five men who had gone to spy out the country of Laish said to their brethren, Do you know that there are in these houses an ephod, teraphim, a graven image, and a molten image? Now therefore, consider what you have to do.

[15] And they turned in that direction and came to the house of the young Levite, at the home of Micah, and saluted him.

[16] Now the 600 Danites with their weapons of war stood at Micah's gate.

[17] And the five men who had gone to spy out the land went up and entered the house and took the graven image, the ephod, the teraphim, and the molten image, while the priest stood by the entrance of the gate with the 600 men armed with weapons of war.

[18] And when these went into Micah's house and took the carved image, the ephod, the teraphim, and the molten image, the priest said to them, What are you doing?

[19] And they said to him, Be still, put your hand over your mouth, and come with us, and be to us a father and a priest. Is it better for you to be a priest to the house of one man, or that you be a priest to a tribe and family in Israel?

[20] And the priest's heart was glad, and he took the ephod, the teraphim, and the graven image, and went in the midst of the people.

[21] So they turned and departed and put the little ones, the cattle, and the baggage in front of them.

[22] When they were a good way from the house of Micah, the men who were Micah's near neighbors were called out and overtook the Danites.

[23] They shouted to the Danites, who turned and said to Micah, What ails you, that you come with such a company?

[24] And he said, You take away my gods which I made and the priest, and go away; and what have I left? How can you say to me, What ails you?

[25] And the men of Dan said to him, Let not your voice be heard among us, lest angry fellows fall upon you and you lose your life with the lives of your household.

[26] And the Danites went their way; and when Micah saw that they were too strong for him, he turned and went back to his house.

---

[a] 7 The meaning of the Hebrew for this clause is uncertain.
[b] 7 Hebrew; some Septuagint manuscripts *with the Arameans*
[c] 12 *Mahaneh Dan* means *Dan's camp.*

## New International Version

27Then they took what Micah had made, and his priest, and went on to Laish, against a people at peace and secure. They attacked them with the sword and burned down their city. 28There was no one to rescue them because they lived a long way from Sidon and had no relationship with anyone else. The city was in a valley near Beth Rehob.

The Danites rebuilt the city and settled there. 29They named it Dan after their ancestor Dan, who was born to Israel—though the city used to be called Laish. 30There the Danites set up for themselves the idol, and Jonathan son of Gershom, the son of Moses,a and his sons were priests for the tribe of Dan until the time of the captivity of the land. 31They continued to use the idol Micah had made, all the time the house of God was in Shiloh.

### A Levite and His Concubine

**19** In those days Israel had no king.

Now a Levite who lived in a remote area in the hill country of Ephraim took a concubine from Bethlehem in Judah. 2But she was unfaithful to him. She left him and went back to her parents' home in Bethlehem, Judah. After she had been there four months, 3her husband went to her to persuade her to return. He had with him his servant and two donkeys. She took him into her parents' home, and when her father saw him, he gladly welcomed him. 4His father-in-law, the woman's father, prevailed on him to stay; so he remained with him three days, eating and drinking, and sleeping there.

5On the fourth day they got up early and he prepared to leave, but the woman's father said to his son-in-law, "Refresh yourself with something to eat; then you can go." 6So the two of them sat down to eat and drink together. Afterward the woman's father said, "Please stay tonight and enjoy yourself." 7And when the man got up to go, his father-in-law persuaded him, so he stayed there that night. 8On the morning of the fifth day, when he rose to go, the woman's father said, "Refresh yourself. Wait till afternoon!" So the two of them ate together.

9Then when the man, with his concubine and his servant, got up to leave, his father-in-law, the woman's father, said, "Now look, it's almost evening. Spend the night here; the day is nearly over. Stay and enjoy yourself. Early tomorrow morning you can get up and be on your way home." 10But, unwilling to stay another night, the man left and went toward Jebus (that is, Jerusalem), with his two saddled donkeys and his concubine.

11When they were near Jebus and the day was almost gone, the servant said to his master, "Come, let's stop at this city of the Jebusites and spend the night."

12His master replied, "No. We won't go into any city whose people are not Israelites. We will go on to Gibeah." 13He added, "Come, let's try to reach Gibeah or Ramah and spend the night in one of those places." 14So they went on, and the sun set as they neared Gibeah in Benjamin.

## Amplified Bible

27And they took the things which Micah had made, and his priest, and came to Laish, to a people quiet and feeling secure, and they smote them with the sword and burned the city.

28And there was no deliverer because it was far from Sidon, and they had no business with anyone. It was in the valley which belongs to Beth-rehob. And they rebuilt the city and dwelt in it.

29They named the city Dan, after Dan their forefather who was born to Israel; however, the name of the city was Laish at first.

30And the Danites set up the graven image for themselves; and Jonathan son of Gershom, the son of Moses, and his sons were priests to the tribe of Dan until the day of the captivity of the land.

31So they set them up Micah's graven image which he made, as long as the house of God was at Shiloh.

**19** In those days, when there was no king in Israel, a certain Levite was living temporarily in the most remote part of the hill district of Ephraim, who took to himself a concubine [of inferior status than a wife] from Bethlehem in Judah.

2And his concubine was untrue to him and went away from him to her father's house at Bethlehem of Judah and stayed there the space of four months.

3Then her husband arose and went after her to speak kindly to her [to her heart] and to bring her back, having with him his servant and a couple of donkeys. And she brought him into her father's house, and when her father saw him, he rejoiced to meet him.

4And his father-in-law, the girl's father, [insistently] detained him, and he remained with him three days. So they ate and drank, and he lodged there.

5On the fourth day they arose early in the morning, and the [Levite] prepared to leave, but the girl's father said to his son-in-law, Strengthen your heart with a morsel of bread and afterward go your way.

6So both men sat down and ate and drank together, and the girl's father said to the man, Consent to stay all night and let your heart be merry.

7And when the man rose up to depart, his father-in-law urged him; so he lodged there again.

8And he arose early in the morning on the fifth day to depart, but the girl's father said, Strengthen your heart and tarry until toward evening. So they ate, both of them.

9And when the man and his concubine and his servant rose up to leave, his father-in-law, the girl's father, said to him, Behold, now the day draws toward evening, I pray you stay all night. Behold, now the day grows to an end, lodge here and let your heart be merry, and tomorrow get early on your way and go home.

10But the man would not stay that night; so he rose up and departed and came opposite to Jebus, which is Jerusalem. With him were two saddled donkeys [and his servant] and his concubine.

11When they were near Jebus, it was late, and the servant said to his master, Come I pray, and let us turn into this Jebusite city and lodge in it.

12His master said to him, We will not turn aside into the city of foreigners where there are no Israelites. We will go on to Gibeah.

13And he said to his servant, Come and let us go to one of these places and spend the night in Gibeah or in Ramah.

14So they passed on and went their way, and the sun went down on them near Gibeah, which belongs to Benjamin,

a 30 Many Hebrew manuscripts, some Septuagint manuscripts and Vulgate; many other Hebrew manuscripts and some other Septuagint manuscripts *Manasseh*

## New International Version

¹⁵There they stopped to spend the night. They went and sat in the city square, but no one took them in for the night. ¹⁶That evening an old man from the hill country of Ephraim, who was living in Gibeah (the inhabitants of the place were Benjamites), came in from his work in the fields. ¹⁷When he looked and saw the traveler in the city square, the old man asked, "Where are you going? Where did you come from?"

¹⁸He answered, "We are on our way from Bethlehem in Judah to a remote area in the hill country of Ephraim where I live. I have been to Bethlehem in Judah and now I am going to the house of the LORD.ᵃ No one has taken me in for the night. ¹⁹We have both straw and fodder for our donkeys and bread and wine for ourselves your servants—me, the woman and the young man with us. We don't need anything."

²⁰"You are welcome at my house," the old man said. "Let me supply whatever you need. Only don't spend the night in the square." ²¹So he took him into his house and fed his donkeys. After they had washed their feet, they had something to eat and drink.

²²While they were enjoying themselves, some of the wicked men of the city surrounded the house. Pounding on the door, they shouted to the old man who owned the house, "Bring out the man who came to your house so we can have sex with him."

²³The owner of the house went outside and said to them, "No, my friends, don't be so vile. Since this man is my guest, don't do this outrageous thing. ²⁴Look, here is my virgin daughter, and his concubine. I will bring them out to you now, and you can use them and do to them whatever you wish. But as for this man, don't do such an outrageous thing."

²⁵But the men would not listen to him. So the man took his concubine and sent her outside to them, and they raped her and abused her throughout the night, and at dawn they let her go. ²⁶At daybreak the woman went back to the house where her master was staying, fell down at the door and lay there until daylight.

²⁷When her master got up in the morning and opened the door of the house and stepped out to continue on his way, there lay his concubine, fallen in the doorway of the house, with her hands on the threshold. ²⁸He said to her, "Get up; let's go." But there was no answer. Then the man put her on his donkey and set out for home.

²⁹When he reached home, he took a knife and cut up his concubine, limb by limb, into twelve parts and sent them into all the areas of Israel. ³⁰Everyone who saw it was saying to one another, "Such a thing has never been seen or done, not since the day the Israelites came up out of Egypt. Just imagine! We must do something! So speak up!"

### The Israelites Punish the Benjamites

**20** Then all Israel from Dan to Beersheba and from the land of Gilead came together as one and assembled before the LORD in Mizpah. ²The leaders of all the people of the tribes of Israel took their places in the assembly of God's people, four hundred thousand men armed with swords. ³(The Benjamites heard that the Israelites had gone up to Mizpah.) Then the Israelites said, "Tell us how this awful thing happened."

---

ᵃ 18 Hebrew, Vulgate, Syriac and Targum; Septuagint *going home*

## Amplified Bible

¹⁵And they turned aside there to go in and lodge at Gibeah. And the Levite went in and sat down in the open square of the city, for no man took them into his house to spend the night.

¹⁶And behold, an old man was coming from his work in the field at evening. He was from the hill country of Ephraim but was living temporarily in Gibeah, but the men of the place were Benjamites.

¹⁷And when he looked up, he saw the wayfarer in the city square, and the old man said, Where are you going? And from where did you come?

¹⁸The Levite replied, We are passing from Bethlehem of Judah to the rear side of the hill country of Ephraim; I am from there. I went to Bethlehem of Judah, but I am [now] going [home] to the house of the Lord [where I serve], and there is no man who receives me into his house.

¹⁹Yet we have both straw and provender for our donkeys and bread and wine also for me, your handmaid, and the young man who is with your servants; there is no lack of anything.

²⁰And the old man said, Peace be to you, but leave all your wants to me; only do not lodge in the street.

²¹So he brought him into his house and gave provender to the donkeys. And the guests washed their feet and ate and drank.

²²Now as they were making their hearts merry, behold, the men of the city, certain worthless fellows, beset the house round about, beat on the door, and said to the master of the house, the old man, Bring forth the man who came to your house, that we may have intercourse with him.

²³And the man, the master of the house, went out and said to them, No, my kinsmen, I pray you, do not act so wickedly; seeing that this man is my guest, do not do this [wicked] folly.

²⁴Behold, here are my virgin daughter and this man's concubine; them I will bring out now; debase them and do with them what seems good to you, but to this man do not so vile a thing.

²⁵But the men would not listen to him. So the man took his concubine and forced her forth to them, and they had intercourse with her and abused her all the night until morning. And when the dawn began to break, they let her go.

²⁶At daybreak the woman came and fell down and lay at the door of the man's house where her master was, till it was light.

²⁷And her master rose up in the morning and opened the doors of the house and went out to go his way; and behold, his concubine had fallen down at the door of the house, and her hands were upon the threshold.

²⁸And he said to her, Up, and let us be going. But there was no answer [for she was dead]. Then he put her [body] upon the donkey, and the man rose up and went home.

²⁹And when he came into his house, he took a knife, and took hold of his dead concubine and divided her [body] limb by limb into twelve pieces and sent her [body] throughout all the territory of Israel.

³⁰And all who saw it said, There was no such deed done or seen from the day that the Israelites came up out of Egypt to this day; consider it, take counsel, and speak [your minds].

**20** Then all the Israelites came out, and the congregation assembled as one man to the Lord at Mizpah, from Dan even to Beersheba, including the land of Gilead.

²And the chiefs of all the people, of all the tribes of Israel, presented themselves in the assembly of the people of God, 400,000 men on foot who drew the sword.

³(Now the Benjamites [among whom the vile tragedy occurred] heard that the [other] Israelites had gone up to Mizpah.) There the Israelites asked, How did this wickedness happen?

## New International Version

[4]So the Levite, the husband of the murdered woman, said, "I and my concubine came to Gibeah in Benjamin to spend the night. [5]During the night the men of Gibeah came after me and surrounded the house, intending to kill me. They raped my concubine, and she died. [6]I took my concubine, cut her into pieces and sent one piece to each region of Israel's inheritance, because they committed this lewd and outrageous act in Israel. [7]Now, all you Israelites, speak up and tell me what you have decided to do."

[8]All the men rose up together as one, saying, "None of us will go home. No, not one of us will return to his house. [9]But now this is what we'll do to Gibeah: We'll go up against it in the order decided by casting lots. [10]We'll take ten men out of every hundred from all the tribes of Israel, and a hundred from a thousand, and a thousand from ten thousand, to get provisions for the army. Then, when the army arrives at Gibeah[a] in Benjamin, it can give them what they deserve for this outrageous act done in Israel." [11]So all the Israelites got together and united as one against the city.

[12]The tribes of Israel sent messengers throughout the tribe of Benjamin, saying, "What about this awful crime that was committed among you? [13]Now turn those wicked men of Gibeah over to us so that we may put them to death and purge the evil from Israel."

But the Benjamites would not listen to their fellow Israelites. [14]From their towns they came together at Gibeah to fight against the Israelites. [15]At once the Benjamites mobilized twenty-six thousand swordsmen from their towns, in addition to seven hundred able young men from those living in Gibeah. [16]Among all these soldiers there were seven hundred select troops who were left-handed, each of whom could sling a stone at a hair and not miss.

[17]Israel, apart from Benjamin, mustered four hundred thousand swordsmen, all of them fit for battle.

[18]The Israelites went up to Bethel[b] and inquired of God. They said, "Who of us is to go up first to fight against the Benjamites?"

The LORD replied, "Judah shall go first."

[19]The next morning the Israelites got up and pitched camp near Gibeah. [20]The Israelites went out to fight the Benjamites and took up battle positions against them at Gibeah. [21]The Benjamites came out of Gibeah and cut down twenty-two thousand Israelites on the battlefield that day. [22]But the Israelites encouraged one another and again took up their positions where they had stationed themselves the first day. [23]The Israelites went up and wept before the LORD until evening, and they inquired of the LORD. They said, "Shall we go up again to fight against the Benjamites, our fellow Israelites?"

The LORD answered, "Go up against them."

[24]Then the Israelites drew near to Benjamin the second day. [25]This time, when the Benjamites came out from Gibeah to oppose them, they cut down another eighteen thousand Israelites, all of them armed with swords.

## Amplified Bible

[4]And the Levite, the husband of the woman who was murdered, replied, I came to Gibeah which belongs to Benjamin, I and my concubine, to spend the night. [5]And the men of Gibeah rose against me and beset the house round about me by night; they meant to kill me and they raped my concubine, and she is dead. [6]And I took my concubine and cut her in pieces and sent her throughout all the country of the inheritance of Israel, for they have committed abomination and [wicked] folly in Israel. [7]Behold, you Israelites, all of you, give here your advice and counsel.

[8]And all the people arose as one man, saying, Not any of us will go to his tent, and none of us will return to his home. [9]But now this we will do to Gibeah: we will go up by lot against it, [10]And we will take ten men of 100 throughout all the tribes of Israel, and 100 of 1,000, and 1,000 out of 10,000, to bring provisions for the men, that when they come to Gibeah of Benjamin they may do to them according to all the [wicked] folly which they have committed in Israel. [11]So all the men of Israel gathered against the city, united as one man.

[12]And the tribes of Israel sent men through all the tribe of Benjamin, saying, What wickedness is this that has been done among you? [13]Now therefore, give up the men [involved], the base fellows in Gibeah, that we may put them to death and put away evil from Israel. But the Benjamites would not listen to the voice of their kinsmen the Israelites. [14]But the Benjamites out of the cities assembled at Gibeah to go out to battle against the other Israelites. [15]And the Benjamites mustered out of their cities at that time 26,000 men who drew the sword, besides the inhabitants of Gibeah, who mustered 700 chosen men. [16]Among all these were 700 chosen left-handed men; every one could sling stones at a hair and not miss.

[17]And the men of Israel, other than Benjamin, mustered 400,000 men who drew the sword; all these were men of war.

[18]The Israelites arose and went up to the house of God [Bethel] and asked counsel of God and said, Which of us shall take the lead to battle against the Benjamites? And the Lord said, Judah shall go up first.

[19]Then the Israelites rose in the morning and encamped against Gibeah.

[20]And the men of Israel went out to battle against Benjamin and set the battle in array against them at Gibeah. [21]The Benjamites came forth out of Gibeah and felled to the ground that day 22,000 men of the Israelites. [22]But the people, the men of Israel, took courage and strengthened themselves and again set their battle line in the same place where they formed it the first day. [23]And the Israelites went up and wept before the Lord until evening and asked of the Lord, Shall we go up again to battle against our brethren the Benjamites? And the Lord said, Go up against them.

[24]So the Israelites came near against the Benjamites the second day. [25]And Benjamin went forth out of Gibeah against them the second day and felled to the ground the Israelites again, 18,000 men, all of whom were swordsmen.

---

[a] 10 One Hebrew manuscript; most Hebrew manuscripts Geba, a variant of Gibeah   [b] 18 Or to the house of God; also in verse 26

## New International Version

²⁶Then all the Israelites, the whole army, went up to Bethel, and there they sat weeping before the LORD. They fasted that day until evening and presented burnt offerings and fellowship offerings to the LORD. ²⁷And the Israelites inquired of the LORD. (In those days the ark of the covenant of God was there, ²⁸with Phinehas son of Eleazar, the son of Aaron, ministering before it.) They asked, "Shall we go up again to fight against the Benjamites, our fellow Israelites, or not?"

The LORD responded, "Go, for tomorrow I will give them into your hands."

²⁹Then Israel set an ambush around Gibeah. ³⁰They went up against the Benjamites on the third day and took up positions against Gibeah as they had done before. ³¹The Benjamites came out to meet them and were drawn away from the city. They began to inflict casualties on the Israelites as before, so that about thirty men fell in the open field and on the roads—the one leading to Bethel and the other to Gibeah. ³²While the Benjamites were saying, "We are defeating them as before," the Israelites were saying, "Let's retreat and draw them away from the city to the roads."

³³All the men of Israel moved from their places and took up positions at Baal Tamar, and the Israelite ambush charged out of its place on the west[a] of Gibeah.[b] ³⁴Then ten thousand of Israel's able young men made a frontal attack on Gibeah. The fighting was so heavy that the Benjamites did not realize how near disaster was. ³⁵The LORD defeated Benjamin before Israel, and on that day the Israelites struck down 25,100 Benjamites, all armed with swords. ³⁶Then the Benjamites saw that they were beaten.

Now the men of Israel had given way before Benjamin, because they relied on the ambush they had set near Gibeah. ³⁷Those who had been in ambush made a sudden dash into Gibeah, spread out and put the whole city to the sword. ³⁸The Israelites had arranged with the ambush that they should send up a great cloud of smoke from the city, ³⁹and then the Israelites would counterattack.

The Benjamites had begun to inflict casualties on the Israelites (about thirty), and they said, "We are defeating them as in the first battle." ⁴⁰But when the column of smoke began to rise from the city, the Benjamites turned and saw the whole city going up in smoke. ⁴¹Then the Israelites counterattacked, and the Benjamites were terrified, because they realized that disaster had come on them. ⁴²So they fled before the Israelites in the direction of the wilderness, but they could not escape the battle. And the Israelites who came out of the towns cut them down there. ⁴³They surrounded the Benjamites, chased them and easily[c] overran them in the vicinity of Gibeah on the east. ⁴⁴Eighteen thousand Benjamites fell, all of them valiant fighters. ⁴⁵As they turned and fled toward the wilderness to the rock of Rimmon, the Israelites cut down five thousand men along the roads. They kept pressing after the Benjamites as far as Gidom and struck down two thousand more.

⁴⁶On that day twenty-five thousand Benjamite swordsmen fell, all of them valiant fighters. ⁴⁷But six hundred

## Amplified Bible

²⁶Then all the Israelites, the whole army, went up and came to the house of God [Bethel] and wept; and they sat there before the Lord and fasted that day until evening and offered burnt offerings and peace offerings before the Lord.

²⁷And the Israelites inquired of the Lord—for the ark of the covenant of God was there [at Bethel] in those days,

²⁸And Phinehas son of Eleazar, the son of Aaron, ministered before it in those days—saying, Shall we yet again go out to battle against our brethren the Benjamites or shall we quit? And the Lord said, Go up, for tomorrow I will deliver them into your hand.

²⁹So Israel set men in ambush round about Gibeah.

³⁰And the Israelites went up against the Benjamites on the third day and set themselves in array against Gibeah as at other times.

³¹And the Benjamites went out against their army and were drawn away from the city; and they began to smite and kill some of the people as at other times, in the highways, one of which goes up to Bethel and the other to Gibeah, and in the open country—about thirty men of Israel.

³²And the Benjamites said, They are routed before us as at first. But the Israelites said, Let us flee and draw them from the city to the highways.

³³And all the men of Israel rose out of their places and set themselves in array at Baal-tamar, and the men of Israel in ambush rushed out of their place in the meadow of Geba.

³⁴And there came against Gibeah 10,000 chosen men out of all Israel, and the battle was hard; but the Benjamites did not know disaster was close upon them.

³⁵And the Lord overcame Benjamin before Israel, and the Israelites destroyed of the Benjamites that day 25,100 men, all of whom were swordsmen.

³⁶So the Benjamites saw that they were defeated. The men of Israel gave ground to the Benjamites, because they trusted in the men in ambush whom they had set against Gibeah.

³⁷And the men in ambush quickly rushed upon Gibeah, and the liers-in-wait moved out and smote all the city with the sword.

³⁸Now the appointed signal between the men of Israel and the men in ambush was that when they made a great cloud of smoke arise from the city,

³⁹The men of Israel should all turn back in battle. Now Benjamin had begun to smite and kill some of the men of Israel, about thirty persons. They said, Surely they are falling before us as in the first battle.

⁴⁰But when the [signal] cloud began to rise out of the city in a pillar of smoke, the Benjamites looked behind them, and behold, the whole of the city went up in smoke to the heavens.

⁴¹When the men of Israel turned back again, the men of Benjamin were dismayed, for they saw that disaster had come upon them.

⁴²Therefore they turned their backs before the men of Israel and fled toward the wilderness, but the battle followed close behind *and* overtook them; and the inhabitants of the cities destroyed those [Benjamites] who came through them in their midst.

⁴³They surrounded the Benjamites, pursued them, and overtook *and* trod them down at their resting-place as far as opposite Gibeah toward the east.

⁴⁴And there fell 18,000 men of Benjamin, all of them men of valor.

⁴⁵And [the Benjamites] turned and fled toward the wilderness to the rock of Rimmon, and Israel picked off on the highways 5,000 men of them; they pursued hard after them to Gidom and slew 2,000 more of them.

⁴⁶So that all of Benjamin who fell that day were 25,000 men who drew the sword, all of them men of valor.

---

[a] 33 Some Septuagint manuscripts and Vulgate; the meaning of the Hebrew for this word is uncertain.   [b] 33 Hebrew *Geba*, a variant of *Gibeah*   [c] 43 The meaning of the Hebrew for this word is uncertain.

## New International Version

of them turned and fled into the wilderness to the rock of Rimmon, where they stayed four months. 48The men of Israel went back to Benjamin and put all the towns to the sword, including the animals and everything else they found. All the towns they came across they set on fire.

### Wives for the Benjamites

**21** The men of Israel had taken an oath at Mizpah: "Not one of us will give his daughter in marriage to a Benjamite."

2The people went to Bethel,*a* where they sat before God until evening, raising their voices and weeping bitterly. 3"LORD, God of Israel," they cried, "why has this happened to Israel? Why should one tribe be missing from Israel today?"

4Early the next day the people built an altar and presented burnt offerings and fellowship offerings.

5Then the Israelites asked, "Who from all the tribes of Israel has failed to assemble before the LORD?" For they had taken a solemn oath that anyone who failed to assemble before the LORD at Mizpah was to be put to death.

6Now the Israelites grieved for the tribe of Benjamin, their fellow Israelites. "Today one tribe is cut off from Israel," they said. "How can we provide wives for those who are left, since we have taken an oath by the LORD not to give them any of our daughters in marriage?" 8Then they asked, "Which one of the tribes of Israel failed to assemble before the LORD at Mizpah?" They discovered that no one from Jabesh Gilead had come to the camp for the assembly. 9For when they counted the people, they found that none of the people of Jabesh Gilead were there.

10So the assembly sent twelve thousand fighting men with instructions to go to Jabesh Gilead and put to the sword those living there, including the women and children. 11"This is what you are to do," they said. "Kill every male and every woman who is not a virgin." 12They found among the people living in Jabesh Gilead four hundred young women who had never slept with a man, and they took them to the camp at Shiloh in Canaan.

13Then the whole assembly sent an offer of peace to the Benjamites at the rock of Rimmon. 14So the Benjamites returned at that time and were given the women of Jabesh Gilead who had been spared. But there were not enough for all of them.

15The people grieved for Benjamin, because the LORD had made a gap in the tribes of Israel. 16And the elders of the assembly said, "With the women of Benjamin destroyed, how shall we provide wives for the men who are left? 17The Benjamite survivors must have heirs," they said, "so that a tribe of Israel will not be wiped out. 18We can't give them our daughters as wives, since we Israelites have taken this oath: 'Cursed be anyone who gives a wife to a Benjamite.' 19But look, there is the annual festival of the LORD in Shiloh, which lies north of Bethel, east of the road that goes from Bethel to Shechem, and south of Lebonah."

## Amplified Bible

47But 600 men turned and fled to the wilderness to the rock Rimmon and remained at the rock Rimmon four months.

48And the men of Israel turned back against the Benjamites and smote them with the sword, men and beasts and all that they found. Also they set on fire all the towns to which they came.

**21** Now the men of Israel had sworn at Mizpah, None of us shall give his daughter in marriage to Benjamin.

2And the Israelites came to the house of God [Bethel] and sat there until evening before God and lifted up their voices and wept bitterly. [Judg. 20:27.]

3And they said, O Lord, the God of Israel, why has this come to pass in Israel, that there should be today one tribe lacking in Israel?

4And next morning the people rose early, and built there an altar, and offered burnt offerings and peace offerings.

5And the Israelites said, Which among all the tribes of Israel did not come up with the assembly to the Lord? For they had taken a great oath concerning him who did not come up to the Lord to Mizpah, saying, He shall surely die.

6And the Israelites changed their purpose [and had compassion] for the Benjamites their kinsmen and said, There is one tribe cut off from Israel today.

7What shall we do for wives for those who are left, seeing we have sworn by the Lord that we will not give them our daughters as wives?

8And they said, Which one is there of the tribes of Israel that did not come up to Mizpah to the Lord? And behold, no one had come to the camp from Jabesh-gilead, to the assembly.

9For when the people were mustered, behold, not one of the citizens of Jabesh-gilead was there.

10And the congregation sent there 12,000 of the bravest men, saying, Go and smite the inhabitants of Jabesh-gilead with the sword, also the women and the little ones.

11And this is what you shall do; utterly destroy every male and every woman who is not a virgin.

12And they found among the inhabitants of Jabesh-gilead 400 young virgins, who had known no man by lying with him; and they brought them to the camp at Shiloh, which is in the land of Canaan.

13And the whole congregation sent word to the Benjamites who were at the rock of Rimmon and invited them to be friendly with them.

14And Benjamin returned at that time, and they gave them the women whom they had saved alive of the women of Jabesh-gilead; and yet there were not enough for them.

15And the people had compassion on Benjamin, because the Lord had made a breach in the tribes of Israel.

16Then the elders of the congregation said, What shall we do for wives for those who are left, since the women of Benjamin are destroyed?

17And they said, There must be an inheritance for the survivors of Benjamin, so that a tribe shall not be wiped out of Israel.

18But we cannot give them wives of our daughters, for the Israelites have sworn, Cursed be he who gives a wife to Benjamin.

19So they said, Behold, there is the yearly feast of the Lord at Shiloh, which is north of Bethel, on the east of the highway that goes up from Bethel to Shechem and south of Lebonah.

---

*a 2 Or to the house of God*

## New International Version

[20]So they instructed the Benjamites, saying, "Go and hide in the vineyards [21]and watch. When the young women of Shiloh come out to join in the dancing, rush from the vineyards and each of you seize one of them to be your wife. Then return to the land of Benjamin. [22]When their fathers or brothers complain to us, we will say to them, 'Do us the favor of helping them, because we did not get wives for them during the war. You will not be guilty of breaking your oath because you did not give your daughters to them.'"

[23]So that is what the Benjamites did. While the young women were dancing, each man caught one and carried her off to be his wife. Then they returned to their inheritance and rebuilt the towns and settled in them.

[24]At that time the Israelites left that place and went home to their tribes and clans, each to his own inheritance.

[25]In those days Israel had no king; everyone did as they saw fit.

## Amplified Bible

[20]So they commanded the Benjamites, Go and lie in wait in the vineyards,

[21]And watch; if the daughters of Shiloh come out to dance in the dances, then come out of the vineyards and catch every man his wife from the daughters of Shiloh and go to the land of Benjamin.

[22]And when their fathers or their brothers come to us to complain, we will say to them, Grant them graciously unto us, because we did not reserve a wife for each of them in battle, neither did you give wives to them, for that would have made you guilty [of breaking your oath].

[23]And the Benjamites did so and took wives, according to their number, from the dancers whom they carried off; then they went and returned to their inheritance and repaired the towns and dwelt in them.

[24]And the Israelites left there then, every man to his tribe and family, and they went out from there every man to his inheritance.

[25]In those days [a]there was no king in Israel; every man did what was right in his own eyes.

[a] This statement is made three times in these latter chapters. All was well while Joshua and those who assisted him lived; then gradually came disorder. "What is the meaning of this? . . . There was no king [or counselor] in Israel because in Israel there was no God. The Lord is King. You cannot have a [true] king if you have not a God. There was no nominal renunciation of God, no public and blatant atheism, no boastful impiety; there was a deadlier heresy—namely, keeping God as a sign but paying no tribute to Him as a King, worshiping Him possibly in outward form but knowing nothing of the subduing and directing power of godliness. That is more to be dreaded than any intellectual difficulty of a theological kind . . . Dead consciences, prayerless prayers, mechanical formalities—these are the impediments which overturn . . . the chariots of progress. This was the case in Israel. Where God is, the king is not [merely] a man with a crown on, but a king in the sense of kingliness, sovereignty, authority, rule—the spirit of obligation and responsibility . . . You find the right monarch where you find the right God" (Joseph Parker, cited by James C. Gray and George M. Adams, *Bible Commentary*).

# Ruth

### Naomi Loses Her Husband and Sons

**1** In the days when the judges ruled,[a] there was a famine in the land. So a man from Bethlehem in Judah, together with his wife and two sons, went to live for a while in the country of Moab. [2] The man's name was Elimelek, his wife's name was Naomi, and the names of his two sons were Mahlon and Kilion. They were Ephrathites from Bethlehem, Judah. And they went to Moab and lived there.

[3] Now Elimelek, Naomi's husband, died, and she was left with her two sons. [4] They married Moabite women, one named Orpah and the other Ruth. After they had lived there about ten years, [5] both Mahlon and Kilion also died, and Naomi was left without her two sons and her husband.

### Naomi and Ruth Return to Bethlehem

[6] When Naomi heard in Moab that the LORD had come to the aid of his people by providing food for them, she and her daughters-in-law prepared to return home from there. [7] With her two daughters-in-law she left the place where she had been living and set out on the road that would take them back to the land of Judah.

[8] Then Naomi said to her two daughters-in-law, "Go back, each of you, to your mother's home. May the LORD show you kindness, as you have shown kindness to your dead husbands and to me. [9] May the LORD grant that each of you will find rest in the home of another husband."

Then she kissed them goodbye and they wept aloud [10] and said to her, "We will go back with you to your people."

[11] But Naomi said, "Return home, my daughters. Why would you come with me? Am I going to have any more sons, who could become your husbands? [12] Return home, my daughters; I am too old to have another husband. Even if I thought there was still hope for me—even if I had a husband tonight and then gave birth to sons— [13] would you wait until they grew up? Would you remain unmarried for them? No, my daughters. It is more bitter for me than for you, because the LORD's hand has turned against me!"

[14] At this they wept aloud again. Then Orpah kissed her mother-in-law goodbye, but Ruth clung to her.

[15] "Look," said Naomi, "your sister-in-law is going back to her people and her gods. Go back with her."

[16] But Ruth replied, "Don't urge me to leave you or to turn back from you. Where you go I will go, and where you stay I will stay. Your people will be my people and your God my God. [17] Where you die I will die, and there I will be buried. May the LORD deal with me, be it ever so severely, if even death separates you and me." [18] When Naomi real-

# Ruth

**1** In the days when the judges ruled, there was a famine in the land. And a certain man of Bethlehem of Judah went to sojourn in the country of Moab, he, his wife, and his two sons.

[2] The man's name was Elimelech and his wife's name was Naomi and his two sons were named Mahlon [invalid] and Chilion [pining]; they were Ephrathites from Bethlehem of Judah. They went to the country of Moab and continued there.

[3] But Elimelech, who Naomi's husband, died, and she was left with her two sons.

[4] And they took wives of the women of Moab; the name of the one was Orpah and the name of the other Ruth. They dwelt there about ten years;

[5] And Mahlon and Chilion died also, both of them, so the woman was bereft of her two sons and her husband.

[6] Then she arose with her daughters-in-law to return from the country of Moab, for she had heard in Moab how the Lord had visited His people in giving them food.

[7] So she left the place where she was, her two daughters-in-law with her, and they started on the way back to Judah.

[8] And Naomi said to her two daughters-in-law, Go, return each of you to her mother's house. May the Lord deal kindly with you, as you have dealt with the dead and with me.

[9] The Lord grant that you may find a home *and* rest, each in the house of her husband! Then she kissed them and they wept aloud.

[10] And they said to her, No, we will return with you to your people.

[11] But Naomi said, Turn back, my daughters, why will you go with me? Have I yet sons in my womb that may become your husbands?

[12] Turn back, my daughters, go; for I am too old to have a husband. If I should say I have hope, even if I should have a husband tonight and should bear sons,

[13] Would you therefore wait till they were grown? Would you therefore refrain from marrying? No, my daughters; it is far more bitter for me than for you that the hand of the Lord is gone out against me.

[14] Then they wept aloud again; and Orpah [a] kissed her mother-in-law [good-bye], but Ruth clung to her.

[15] And Naomi said, See, your sister-in-law has gone back to her people and to her gods; return after your sister-in-law.

[16] And Ruth said, Urge me not to leave you or to turn back from following you; for where you go I will go, and where you lodge I will lodge. [b] Your people shall be my people and your God my God.

[17] Where you die I will die, and there will I be buried. The Lord do so to me, and more also, if anything but death parts me from you.

---

[a] "How many part with Christ at this crossway! Like Orpah they go a furlong or two with Christ, till He goes to take them off from their worldly hopes and bids them prepare for hardship, and then they fairly kiss and leave Him" (William Gurnall, cited by James C. Gray and George M. Adams, *Bible Commentary*). [b] "Ruth is a prophecy, than which none could be more beautiful and engaging, of the entrance of the heathen world into the kingdom of God. She comes forth out of Moab, an idolatrous people full of wantonness and sin, and is herself so tender and pure. In a land where dissolute sensuality formed one of the elements of idol worship, a woman appears, as wife and daughter, chaste as the rose of spring and unsurpassed in these relations by any other [human] character in Holy Writ. . . . Ruth's confession of God and His people originated in the home of her married life. It sprang from the love with which she was permitted to embrace Israelites . . . . The conduct of one Israelitish woman [Naomi] in a foreign land was able to call forth a love and a confession of God like that of Ruth . . . . Ruth loves a woman, and is thereby led to the God Whom that woman confesses" (J. P. Lange, *A Commentary*).

## New International Version

ized that Ruth was determined to go with her, she stopped urging her.

[19]So the two women went on until they came to Bethlehem. When they arrived in Bethlehem, the whole town was stirred because of them, and the women exclaimed, "Can this be Naomi?"

[20]"Don't call me Naomi,[a]" she told them. "Call me Mara,[b] because the Almighty[c] has made my life very bitter. [21]I went away full, but the LORD has brought me back empty. Why call me Naomi? The LORD has afflicted[d] me; the Almighty has brought misfortune upon me."

[22]So Naomi returned from Moab accompanied by Ruth the Moabite, her daughter-in-law, arriving in Bethlehem as the barley harvest was beginning.

### Ruth Meets Boaz in the Grain Field

**2** Now Naomi had a relative on her husband's side, a man of standing from the clan of Elimelek, whose name was Boaz.

[2]And Ruth the Moabite said to Naomi, "Let me go to the fields and pick up the leftover grain behind anyone in whose eyes I find favor."

Naomi said to her, "Go ahead, my daughter." [3]So she went out, entered a field and began to glean behind the harvesters. As it turned out, she was working in a field belonging to Boaz, who was from the clan of Elimelek.

[4]Just then Boaz arrived from Bethlehem and greeted the harvesters, "The LORD be with you!"

"The LORD bless you!" they answered.

[5]Boaz asked the overseer of his harvesters, "Who does that young woman belong to?"

[6]The overseer replied, "She is the Moabite who came back from Moab with Naomi. [7]She said, 'Please let me glean and gather among the sheaves behind the harvesters.' She came into the field and has remained here from morning till now, except for a short rest in the shelter."

[8]So Boaz said to Ruth, "My daughter, listen to me. Don't go and glean in another field and don't go away from here. Stay here with the women who work for me. [9]Watch the field where the men are harvesting, and follow along after the women. I have told the men not to lay a hand on you. And whenever you are thirsty, go and get a drink from the water jars the men have filled."

[10]At this, she bowed down with her face to the ground. She asked him, "Why have I found such favor in your eyes that you notice me—a foreigner?"

[11]Boaz replied, "I've been told all about what you have done for your mother-in-law since the death of your husband—how you left your father and mother and your homeland and came to live with a people you did not know before. [12]May the LORD repay you for what you have done. May you be richly rewarded by the LORD, the God of Israel, under whose wings you have come to take refuge."

[13]"May I continue to find favor in your eyes, my lord," she said. "You have put me at ease by speaking kindly to your servant—though I do not have the standing of one of your servants."

[14]At mealtime Boaz said to her, "Come over here. Have some bread and dip it in the wine vinegar."

When she sat down with the harvesters, he offered her some roasted grain. She ate all she wanted and had some left over. [15]As she got up to glean, Boaz gave orders to his men, "Let her gather among the sheaves and don't

## Amplified Bible

[18]When Naomi saw that Ruth was determined to go with her, she said no more.

[19]So they both went on until they came to Bethlehem. And when they arrived in Bethlehem, the whole town was stirred about them, and said, Is this Naomi?

[20]And she said to them, Call me not Naomi [pleasant]; call me Mara [bitter], for the Almighty has dealt very bitterly with me.

[21]I went out full, but the Lord has brought me home again empty. Why call me Naomi, since the Lord has testified against me, and the Almighty has afflicted me?

[22]So Naomi returned, and Ruth the Moabitess, her daughter-in-law, with her, who returned from the country of Moab. And they came to Bethlehem at the beginning of barley harvest.

**2** Now Naomi had a kinsman of her husband's, a man of wealth, of the family of Elimelech, whose name was Boaz.

[2]And Ruth the Moabitess said to Naomi, Let me go to the field and glean among the ears of grain after him in whose sight I shall find favor. Naomi said to her, Go, my daughter.

[3]And [Ruth] went and gleaned in a field after the reapers; and she happened to stop at the part of the field belonging to Boaz, who was of the family of Elimelech.

[4]And behold, Boaz came from Bethlehem and said to the reapers, The Lord be with you! And they answered him, The Lord bless you!

[5]Then Boaz said to his servant who was set over the reapers, Whose maiden is this?

[6]And the servant set over the reapers answered, She is the Moabitish girl who came back with Naomi from the country of Moab.

[7]And she said, I pray you, let me glean and gather after the reapers among the sheaves. So she came and has continued from early morning until now, except when she rested a little in the house.

[8]Then Boaz said to Ruth, Listen, my daughter, do not go to glean in another field or leave this one, but stay here close by my maidens.

[9]Watch which field they reap, and follow them. Have I not charged the young men not to molest you? And when you are thirsty, go to the vessels and drink what the young men have drawn.

[10]Then she fell on her face, bowing to the ground, and said to him, Why have I found favor in your eyes that you should notice me, when I am a foreigner?

[11]And Boaz said to her, I have been made fully aware of all you have done for your mother-in-law since the death of your husband, and how you have left your father and mother and the land of your birth and have come to a people unknown to you before.

[12]The Lord recompense you for what you have done, and a full reward be given you by the Lord, the God of Israel, under Whose wings you have come to take refuge!

[13]Then she said, Let me find favor in your sight, my lord. For you have comforted me and have spoken to the heart of your maidservant, though I am not as one of your maidservants.

[14]And at mealtime Boaz said to her, Come here and eat of the bread and dip your morsel in the sour wine [mixed with oil]. And she sat beside the reapers; and he passed her some parched grain, and she ate until she was satisfied and she had some left [for Naomi].

[15]And when she got up to glean, Boaz ordered his young men, Let her glean even among the sheaves, and do not reproach her.

---

[a] 20 *Naomi* means *pleasant*.   [b] 20 *Mara* means *bitter*.   [c] 20 Hebrew *Shaddai*; also in verse 21   [d] 21 Or *has testified against*

## New International Version

reprimand her. [16]Even pull out some stalks for her from the bundles and leave them for her to pick up, and don't rebuke her."

[17]So Ruth gleaned in the field until evening. Then she threshed the barley she had gathered, and it amounted to about an ephah.[a] [18]She carried it back to town, and her mother-in-law saw how much she had gathered. Ruth also brought out and gave her what she had left over after she had eaten enough.

[19]Her mother-in-law asked her, "Where did you glean today? Where did you work? Blessed be the man who took notice of you!"

Then Ruth told her mother-in-law about the one at whose place she had been working. "The name of the man I worked with today is Boaz," she said.

[20]"The LORD bless him!" Naomi said to her daughter-in-law. "He has not stopped showing his kindness to the living and the dead." She added, "That man is our close relative; he is one of our guardian-redeemers.[b]"

[21]Then Ruth the Moabite said, "He even said to me, 'Stay with my workers until they finish harvesting all my grain.'"

[22]Naomi said to Ruth her daughter-in-law, "It will be good for you, my daughter, to go with the women who work for him, because in someone else's field you might be harmed."

[23]So Ruth stayed close to the women of Boaz to glean until the barley and wheat harvests were finished. And she lived with her mother-in-law.

### Ruth and Boaz at the Threshing Floor

**3** One day Ruth's mother-in-law Naomi said to her, "My daughter, I must find a home[c] for you, where you will be well provided for. [2]Now Boaz, with whose women you have worked, is a relative of ours. Tonight he will be winnowing barley on the threshing floor. [3]Wash, put on perfume, and get dressed in your best clothes. Then go down to the threshing floor, but don't let him know you are there until he has finished eating and drinking. [4]When he lies down, note the place where he is lying. Then go and uncover his feet and lie down. He will tell you what to do."

[5]"I will do whatever you say," Ruth answered. [6]So she went down to the threshing floor and did everything her mother-in-law told her to do.

[7]When Boaz had finished eating and drinking and was in good spirits, he went over to lie down at the far end of the grain pile. Ruth approached quietly, uncovered his feet and lay down. [8]In the middle of the night something startled the man; he turned—and there was a woman lying at his feet!

[9]"Who are you?" he asked.

"I am your servant Ruth," she said. "Spread the corner of your garment over me, since you are a guardian-redeemer[d] of our family."

[10]"The LORD bless you, my daughter," he replied. "This kindness is greater than that which you showed earlier: You have not run after the younger men, whether rich or poor. [11]And now, my daughter, don't be afraid. I will do for you all you ask. All the people of my town know that you are a woman of noble character. [12]Although it is true that I am a guardian-redeemer of our family, there is another who is more closely related than I. [13]Stay here for the night, and in the morning if he wants to do his duty as your guardian-redeemer, good; let him redeem you. But if he is not willing, as surely as the LORD lives I will do it. Lie here until morning."

## Amplified Bible

[16]And let fall some handfuls for her on purpose and let them lie there for her to glean, and do not rebuke her.

[17]So she gleaned in the field until evening. Then she beat out what she had gleaned. It was about an ephah of barley.

[18]And she took it up and went into the town; she showed her mother-in-law what she had gleaned, and she also brought forth and gave her the food she had reserved after she was satisfied.

[19]And her mother-in-law said to her, Where have you gleaned today? Where did you work? Blessed be the man who noticed you. So [Ruth] told [her], The name of him with whom I worked today is Boaz.

[20]And Naomi said to her daughter-in-law, Blessed be he of the Lord who has not ceased his kindness to the living and to the dead. And Naomi said to her, The man is a near relative of ours, one who has the right to redeem us. [Lev. 25:25.]

[21]And Ruth the Moabitess said, He said to me also, Stay close to my young men until they have harvested my entire crop.

[22]And Naomi said to Ruth, It is good, my daughter, for you to go out with his maidens, lest in any other field you be molested.

[23]So she kept close to the maidens of Boaz, gleaning until the end of the barley and wheat harvests. And she lived with her mother-in-law.

**3** Then Naomi her mother-in-law said to Ruth, My daughter, shall I not seek rest or a home for you, that you may prosper?

[2]And now is not Boaz, with whose maidens you were, our relative? See, he is winnowing barley tonight at the threshing floor.

[3]Wash and anoint yourself therefore, and put on your best clothes and go down to the threshing floor, but do not make yourself known to the man until he has finished eating and drinking.

[4]But when he lies down, notice the place where he lies; then go and uncover his feet and lie down. And he will tell you what to do.

[5]And Ruth said to her, All that you say to me I will do.

[6]So she went down to the threshing floor and did just as her mother-in-law had told her.

[7]And when Boaz had eaten and drunk and his heart was merry, he went to lie down at the end of the heap of grain. Then [Ruth] came softly and uncovered his feet and lay down.

[8]At midnight the man was startled, and he turned over, and behold, a woman lay at his feet!

[9]And he said, Who are you? And she answered, I am Ruth your maidservant. Spread your wing [of protection] over your maidservant, for you are a next of kin.

[10]And he said, Blessed be you of the Lord, my daughter. For you have made this last loving-kindness greater than the former, for you have not gone after young men, whether poor or rich.

[11]And now, my daughter, fear not. I will do for you all you require, for all my people in the city know that you are a woman of strength (worth, bravery, capability).

[12]It is true that I am your near kinsman; however, there is a kinsman nearer than I.

[13]Remain tonight, and in the morning if he will perform for you the part of a kinsman, good; let him do it. But if he will not do the part of a kinsman for you, then, as the Lord lives, I will do the part of a kinsman for you. Lie down until the morning.

---

[a] 17 That is, probably about 30 pounds or about 13 kilograms
[b] 20 The Hebrew word for *guardian-redeemer* is a legal term for one who has the obligation to redeem a relative in serious difficulty (see Lev. 25:25-55).   [c] 1 Hebrew *find rest* (see 1:9)   [d] 9 The Hebrew word for *guardian-redeemer* is a legal term for one who has the obligation to redeem a relative in serious difficulty (see Lev. 25:25-55); also in verses 12 and 13.

## New International Version

¹⁴So she lay at his feet until morning, but got up before anyone could be recognized; and he said, "No one must know that a woman came to the threshing floor."

¹⁵He also said, "Bring me the shawl you are wearing and hold it out." When she did so, he poured into it six measures of barley and placed the bundle on her. Then he*ᵃ* went back to town.

¹⁶When Ruth came to her mother-in-law, Naomi asked, "How did it go, my daughter?"

Then she told her everything Boaz had done for her ¹⁷and added, "He gave me these six measures of barley, saying, 'Don't go back to your mother-in-law empty-handed.'"

¹⁸Then Naomi said, "Wait, my daughter, until you find out what happens. For the man will not rest until the matter is settled today."

### Boaz Marries Ruth

**4** Meanwhile Boaz went up to the town gate and sat down there just as the guardian-redeemer*ᵇ* he had mentioned came along. Boaz said, "Come over here, my friend, and sit down." So he went over and sat down.

²Boaz took ten of the elders of the town and said, "Sit here," and they did so. ³Then he said to the guardian-redeemer, "Naomi, who has come back from Moab, is selling the piece of land that belonged to our relative Elimelek. ⁴I thought I should bring the matter to your attention and suggest that you buy it in the presence of these seated here and in the presence of the elders of my people. If you will redeem it, do so. But if you*ᶜ* will not, tell me, so I will know. For no one has the right to do it except you, and I am next in line."

"I will redeem it," he said.

⁵Then Boaz said, "On the day you buy the land from Naomi, you also acquire Ruth the Moabite, the*ᵈ* dead man's widow, in order to maintain the name of the dead with his property."

⁶At this, the guardian-redeemer said, "Then I cannot redeem it because I might endanger my own estate. You redeem it yourself. I cannot do it."

⁷(Now in earlier times in Israel, for the redemption and transfer of property to become final, one party took off his sandal and gave it to the other. This was the method of legalizing transactions in Israel.)

⁸So the guardian-redeemer said to Boaz, "Buy it yourself." And he removed his sandal.

⁹Then Boaz announced to the elders and all the people, "Today you are witnesses that I have bought from Naomi all the property of Elimelek, Kilion and Mahlon. ¹⁰I have also acquired Ruth the Moabite, Mahlon's widow, as my wife, in order to maintain the name of the dead with his property, so that his name will not disappear from among his family or from his hometown. Today you are witnesses!"

¹¹Then the elders and all the people at the gate said, "We are witnesses. May the LORD make the woman who is coming into your home like Rachel and Leah, who together built up the family of Israel. May you have standing in Ephrathah and be famous in Bethlehem. ¹²Through the offspring the LORD gives you by this young woman, may your family be like that of Perez, whom Tamar bore to Judah."

### Naomi Gains a Son

¹³So Boaz took Ruth and she became his wife. When he made love to her, the LORD enabled her to conceive,

## Amplified Bible

¹⁴And she lay at his feet until the morning, but arose before one could recognize another; for he said, Let it not be known that the woman came to the threshing floor.

¹⁵Also he said, Bring the mantle you are wearing and hold it. So [Ruth] held it, and he measured out six measures of barley and laid it on her. And she went into the town.

¹⁶And when she came home, her mother-in-law said, How have you fared, my daughter? And Ruth told her all that the man had done for her.

¹⁷And she said, He gave me these six measures of barley, for he said to me, Do not go empty-handed to your mother-in-law.

¹⁸Then said she, Sit still, my daughter, until you learn how the matter turns out; for the man will not rest until he finishes the matter today.

**4** Then Boaz went up to the city's gate and sat down there, and behold, the kinsman of whom Boaz had spoken came by. He said to him, Ho! Turn aside and sit down here. So he turned aside and sat down.

²And Boaz took ten men of the elders of the city and said, Sit down here. And they sat down.

³And he said to the kinsman, Naomi, who has returned from the country of Moab, has sold the parcel of land which belonged to our brother Elimelech.

⁴And I thought to let you hear of it, saying, Buy it in the presence of those sitting here and before the elders of my people. If you will redeem it, redeem it; but if you will not redeem it, then say so, that I may know; for there is no one besides you to redeem it, and I am [next of kin] after you. And he said, I will redeem it.

⁵Then Boaz said, The day you buy the field of Naomi, you must buy also Ruth the Moabitess, the widow of the dead man, to restore the name of the dead to his inheritance.

⁶And the kinsman said, I cannot redeem it for myself, lest [by marrying a Moabitess] I endanger my own inheritance. Take my right of redemption yourself, for I cannot redeem it. [Deut. 23:3, 4.]

⁷Now formerly in Israel this was the custom concerning redeeming and exchanging. To confirm a transaction, a man pulled off his sandal and gave it to the other. This was the way of attesting in Israel.

⁸Therefore, when the kinsman said to Boaz, Buy it for yourself, he pulled off his sandal.

⁹And Boaz said to the elders and to all the people, You are witnesses this day that I have bought all that was Elimelech's and all that was Chilion's and Mahlon's from the hand of Naomi.

¹⁰Also Ruth the Moabitess, the widow of Mahlon, I have bought to be my wife to restore the name of the dead to his inheritance, that the name of the dead may not be cut off from among his brethren and from the gate of his birthplace. You are witnesses this day.

¹¹And all the people at the gate and the elders said, We are witnesses. May the Lord make the woman who is coming into your house like Rachel and Leah, the two who built the household of Israel. May you do worthily *and* get wealth (power) in Ephratah and be famous in Bethlehem.

¹²And let your house be like the house of Perez, whom Tamar bore to Judah, because of the offspring which the Lord will give you by this young woman.

¹³So Boaz took Ruth and she became his wife. And he went in to her, and the Lord caused her to conceive, and she bore a son.

---

*ᵃ 15* Most Hebrew manuscripts; many Hebrew manuscripts, Vulgate and Syriac *she*   *ᵇ 1* The Hebrew word for *guardian-redeemer* is a legal term for one who has the obligation to redeem a relative in serious difficulty (see Lev. 25:25-55); also in verses 3, 6, 8 and 14.   *ᶜ 4* Many Hebrew manuscripts, Septuagint, Vulgate and Syriac; most Hebrew manuscripts *he*   *ᵈ 5* Vulgate and Syriac; Hebrew (see also Septuagint) *Naomi and from Ruth the Moabite, you acquire the*

## New International Version

and she gave birth to a son. [14]The women said to Naomi: "Praise be to the LORD, who this day has not left you without a guardian-redeemer. May he become famous throughout Israel! [15]He will renew your life and sustain you in your old age. For your daughter-in-law, who loves you and who is better to you than seven sons, has given him birth."

[16]Then Naomi took the child in her arms and cared for him. [17]The women living there said, "Naomi has a son!" And they named him Obed. He was the father of Jesse, the father of David.

### The Genealogy of David

[18]This, then, is the family line of Perez:

Perez was the father of Hezron,
[19]Hezron the father of Ram,
Ram the father of Amminadab,
[20]Amminadab the father of Nahshon,
Nahshon the father of Salmon,[a]
[21]Salmon the father of Boaz,
Boaz the father of Obed,
[22]Obed the father of Jesse,
and Jesse the father of David.

## Amplified Bible

[14]And the women said to Naomi, Blessed be the Lord, Who has not left you this day without a close kinsman, and may his name be famous in Israel.

[15]And may he be to you a restorer of life and a nourisher *and* supporter in your old age, for your daughter-in-law who loves you, who is better to you than seven sons, has borne him.

[16]Then Naomi took the child and laid him in her bosom and became his nurse.

[17]And her neighbor women gave him a name, saying, A son is born to Naomi. They named him Obed. He was the father of Jesse, the father of David [the ancestor of Jesus Christ].

[18]Now these are the descendants of Perez: Perez was the father of Hezron,

[19]Hezron of Ram, Ram of Amminadab,
[20]Amminadab of Nahshon, Nahshon of Salmon,
[21]Salmon of Boaz, Boaz of Obed,
[22]Obed of Jesse, and Jesse of David [the ancestor of Jesus Christ].

---

[a] 20 A few Hebrew manuscripts, some Septuagint manuscripts and Vulgate (see also verse 21 and Septuagint of 1 Chron. 2:11); most Hebrew manuscripts *Salma*

# 1 Samuel

### The Birth of Samuel

**1** There was a certain man from Ramathaim, a Zuphite[a] from the hill country of Ephraim, whose name was Elkanah son of Jeroham, the son of Elihu, the son of Tohu, the son of Zuph, an Ephraimite. [2] He had two wives; one was called Hannah and the other Peninnah. Peninnah had children, but Hannah had none.

[3] Year after year this man went up from his town to worship and sacrifice to the LORD Almighty at Shiloh, where Hophni and Phinehas, the two sons of Eli, were priests of the LORD. [4] Whenever the day came for Elkanah to sacrifice, he would give portions of the meat to his wife Peninnah and to all her sons and daughters. [5] But to Hannah he gave a double portion because he loved her, and the LORD had closed her womb. [6] Because the LORD had closed Hannah's womb, her rival kept provoking her in order to irritate her. [7] This went on year after year. Whenever Hannah went up to the house of the LORD, her rival provoked her till she wept and would not eat. [8] Her husband Elkanah would say to her, "Hannah, why are you weeping? Why don't you eat? Why are you downhearted? Don't I mean more to you than ten sons?"

[9] Once when they had finished eating and drinking in Shiloh, Hannah stood up. Now Eli the priest was sitting on his chair by the doorpost of the LORD's house. [10] In her deep anguish Hannah prayed to the LORD, weeping bitterly. [11] And she made a vow, saying, "LORD Almighty, if you will only look on your servant's misery and remember me, and not forget your servant but give her a son, then I will give him to the LORD for all the days of his life, and no razor will ever be used on his head."

[12] As she kept on praying to the LORD, Eli observed her mouth. [13] Hannah was praying in her heart, and her lips were moving but her voice was not heard. Eli thought she was drunk [14] and said to her, "How long are you going to stay drunk? Put away your wine."

[15] "Not so, my lord," Hannah replied, "I am a woman who is deeply troubled. I have not been drinking wine or beer; I was pouring out my soul to the LORD. [16] Do not take your servant for a wicked woman; I have been praying here out of my great anguish and grief."

[17] Eli answered, "Go in peace, and may the God of Israel grant you what you have asked of him."

[18] She said, "May your servant find favor in your eyes." Then she went her way and ate something, and her face was no longer downcast.

[19] Early the next morning they arose and worshiped before the LORD and then went back to their home at Ramah. Elkanah made love to his wife Hannah, and the LORD remembered her. [20] So in the course of time Hannah became pregnant and gave birth to a son. She named him Samuel,[b] saying, "Because I asked the LORD for him."

### Hannah Dedicates Samuel

[21] When her husband Elkanah went up with all his family to offer the annual sacrifice to the LORD and to fulfill his

# Samuel

**1** There was a certain man of Ramathaim-zophim, of the hill country of Ephraim, named Elkanah son of Jeroham, the son of Elihu, the son of Tohu, the son of Zuph, an Ephraimite. [2] He had two wives, one named Hannah and the other named Peninnah. Peninnah had children, but Hannah had none.

[3] This man went from his city year by year to worship and sacrifice to the Lord of hosts at Shiloh, where Hophni and Phinehas, the two sons of Eli, were the Lord's priests. [4] When the day came that Elkanah sacrificed, he would give to Peninnah his wife and all her sons and daughters portions [of the sacrificial meat]. [5] But to Hannah he gave a double portion, for he loved Hannah, but the Lord had given her no children.

[6] [This embarrassed and grieved Hannah] and her rival provoked her greatly to vex her, because the Lord had left her childless. [7] So it was year after year; whenever Hannah went up to the Lord's house, Peninnah provoked her, so she wept and did not eat. [8] Then Elkanah her husband said to her, Hannah, why do you cry? And why do you not eat? And why are you grieving? Am I not more to you than ten sons?

[9] So Hannah rose after they had eaten and drunk in Shiloh. Now Eli the priest was sitting on his seat beside a post of the temple (tent) of the Lord. [10] And [Hannah] was in distress of soul, praying to the Lord and weeping bitterly. [11] She vowed, saying, O Lord of hosts, if You will indeed look on the affliction of Your handmaid and [earnestly] remember, and not forget Your handmaid but will give me a son, I will give him to the Lord all his life; no razor shall touch his head.

[12] And as she continued praying before the Lord, Eli noticed her mouth. [13] Hannah was speaking in her heart; only her lips moved but her voice was not heard. So Eli thought she was drunk. [14] Eli said to her, How long will you be intoxicated? Put wine away from you.

[15] But Hannah answered, No, my lord, I am a woman of a sorrowful spirit. I have drunk neither wine nor strong drink, but I was pouring out my soul before the Lord. [Gen. 19:34.]

[16] Regard not your handmaid as a wicked woman; for out of my great complaint and bitter provocation I have been speaking.

[17] Then Eli said, Go in peace, and may the God of Israel grant your petition which you have asked of Him.

[18] Hannah said, Let your handmaid find grace in your sight. So [she] went her way and ate, her countenance no longer sad.

[19] The family rose early the next morning, worshiped before the Lord, and returned to their home in Ramah. Elkanah knew Hannah his wife, and the Lord remembered her.

[20] Hannah became pregnant and in due time bore a son and named him Samuel [heard of God], Because, she said, I have asked him of the Lord.

[21] And Elkanah and all his house went up to offer to the Lord the yearly sacrifice and pay his vow.

---

[a] 1 See Septuagint and 1 Chron. 6:26-27,33-35; or *from Ramathaim Zuphim.*   [b] 20 *Samuel* sounds like the Hebrew for *heard by God.*

## New International Version

vow, [22]Hannah did not go. She said to her husband, "After the boy is weaned, I will take him and present him before the LORD, and he will live there always."[a]

[23]"Do what seems best to you," her husband Elkanah told her. "Stay here until you have weaned him; only may the LORD make good his[b] word." So the woman stayed at home and nursed her son until she had weaned him.

[24]After he was weaned, she took the boy with her, young as he was, along with a three-year-old bull,[c] an ephah[d] of flour and a skin of wine, and brought him to the house of the LORD at Shiloh. [25]When the bull had been sacrificed, they brought the boy to Eli, [26]and she said to him, "Pardon me, my lord. As surely as you live, I am the woman who stood here beside you praying to the LORD. [27]I prayed for this child, and the LORD has granted me what I asked of him. [28]So now I give him to the LORD. For his whole life he will be given over to the LORD." And he worshiped the LORD there.

### Hannah's Prayer

**2** Then Hannah prayed and said:

"My heart rejoices in the LORD;
  in the LORD my horn[e] is lifted high.
My mouth boasts over my enemies,
  for I delight in your deliverance.

[2]"There is no one holy like the LORD;
  there is no one besides you;
  there is no Rock like our God.

[3]"Do not keep talking so proudly
  or let your mouth speak such arrogance,
for the LORD is a God who knows,
  and by him deeds are weighed.

[4]"The bows of the warriors are broken,
  but those who stumbled are armed with strength.
[5]Those who were full hire themselves out for food,
  but those who were hungry are hungry no more.
She who was barren has borne seven children,
  but she who has had many sons pines away.

[6]"The LORD brings death and makes alive;
  he brings down to the grave and raises up.
[7]The LORD sends poverty and wealth;
  he humbles and he exalts.
[8]He raises the poor from the dust
  and lifts the needy from the ash heap;
he seats them with princes
  and has them inherit a throne of honor.

"For the foundations of the earth are the LORD's;
  on them he has set the world.
[9]He will guard the feet of his faithful servants,
  but the wicked will be silenced in the place of darkness.

"It is not by strength that one prevails;
[10]  those who oppose the LORD will be broken.
The Most High will thunder from heaven;
  the LORD will judge the ends of the earth.

"He will give strength to his king
  and exalt the horn of his anointed."

[11]Then Elkanah went home to Ramah, but the boy ministered before the LORD under Eli the priest.

---

## Amplified Bible

[22]But Hannah did not go, for she said to her husband, I will not go until the child is weaned, and then I will bring him, that he may appear before the Lord and remain there as long as he lives.

[23]Elkanah her husband said to her, Do what seems best to you. Wait until you have weaned him; only may the Lord establish His word. So Hannah remained and nursed her son until she weaned him.

[24]When she had [a]weaned him, she took him with her, with a three-year-old bull, an ephah of flour, and a skin bottle of wine [to pour over the burnt offering for a sweet odor], and brought Samuel to the Lord's house in Shiloh. The child was growing.

[25]Then they slew the bull, and brought the child to Eli.

[26]Hannah said, Oh, my lord! As your soul lives, my lord, I am the woman who stood by you here praying to the Lord.

[27]For this child I prayed, and the Lord has granted my petition made to Him.

[28]Therefore I have given him to the Lord; as long as he lives he is given to the Lord. And they worshiped the Lord there.

**2** Hannah prayed, and said, My heart exults and triumphs in the Lord; my horn (my strength) is lifted up in the Lord. My mouth is no longer silent, for it is opened wide over my enemies, because I rejoice in Your salvation.

[2]There is none holy like the Lord, there is none besides You; there is no Rock like our God.

[3]Talk no more so very proudly; let not arrogance go forth from your mouth, for the Lord is a God of knowledge, and by Him actions are weighed.

[4]The bows of the mighty are broken, and those who stumbled are girded with strength.

[5]Those who were full have hired themselves out for bread, but those who were hungry have ceased to hunger. The barren has borne seven, but she who has many children languishes and is forlorn.

[6]The Lord slays and makes alive; He brings down to Sheol and raises up.

[7]The Lord makes poor and makes rich; He brings low and He lifts up.

[8]He raises up the poor out of the dust and lifts up the needy from the ash heap, to make them sit with nobles and inherit the throne of glory. For the pillars of the earth are the Lord's, and He has set the world upon them.

[9]He will guard the feet of His godly ones, but the wicked shall be silenced and perish in darkness; for by strength shall no man prevail.

[10]The adversaries of the Lord shall be broken to pieces; against them will He thunder in heaven. The Lord will judge [all peoples] to the ends of the earth; and He will give strength to [b]His king (King) and exalt the power of His anointed (Anointed [c]His Christ). [Luke 1:46.]

[11]Elkanah and his wife Hannah returned to Ramah to his house. But the child ministered to the Lord before Eli the priest.

---

[a] 22 Masoretic Text; Dead Sea Scrolls *always. I have dedicated him as a Nazirite—all the days of his life.*   [b] 23 Masoretic Text; Dead Sea Scrolls, Septuagint and Syriac *your*   [c] 24 Dead Sea Scrolls, Septuagint and Syriac; Masoretic Text *with three bulls*   [d] 24 That is, probably about 36 pounds or about 16 kilograms   [e] 1 *Horn* here symbolizes strength; also in verse 10.

[a] He would then be two or three years old. There were women engaged in tabernacle service to whose care he might have been committed. It was important that he should be dedicated as soon as possible. The earliest impressions of his boyhood were to be those of the house of God (*The Cambridge Bible*).   [b] Hannah's prophetic prayer was but partially fulfilled in the king soon to be anointed by her son as the deliverer of Israel; it reaches forward to . . . the King Messiah, in Whom alone the lofty anticipations of the prophetess are to be completely realized (*The Cambridge Bible*).   [c] Both *The Septuagint* (Greek translation of the Old Testament) and *The Latin Vulgate* read "His Christ" (Luke 2:26).

## New International Version

### Eli's Wicked Sons

[12]Eli's sons were scoundrels; they had no regard for the LORD. [13]Now it was the practice of the priests that, whenever any of the people offered a sacrifice, the priest's servant would come with a three-pronged fork in his hand while the meat was being boiled [14]and would plunge the fork into the pan or kettle or caldron or pot. Whatever the fork brought up the priest would take for himself. This is how they treated all the Israelites who came to Shiloh. [15]But even before the fat was burned, the priest's servant would come and say to the person who was sacrificing, "Give the priest some meat to roast; he won't accept boiled meat from you, but only raw."

[16]If the person said to him, "Let the fat be burned first, and then take whatever you want," the servant would answer, "No, hand it over now; if you don't, I'll take it by force."

[17]This sin of the young men was very great in the LORD's sight, for they[a] were treating the LORD's offering with contempt.

[18]But Samuel was ministering before the LORD—a boy wearing a linen ephod. [19]Each year his mother made him a little robe and took it to him when she went up with her husband to offer the annual sacrifice. [20]Eli would bless Elkanah and his wife, saying, "May the LORD give you children by this woman to take the place of the one she prayed for and gave to[b] the LORD." Then they would go home. [21]And the LORD was gracious to Hannah; she gave birth to three sons and two daughters. Meanwhile, the boy Samuel grew up in the presence of the LORD.

[22]Now Eli, who was very old, heard about everything his sons were doing to all Israel and how they slept with the women who served at the entrance to the tent of meeting. [23]So he said to them, "Why do you do such things? I hear from all the people about these wicked deeds of yours. [24]No, my sons; the report I hear spreading among the LORD's people is not good. [25]If one person sins against another, God[c] may mediate for the offender; but if anyone sins against the LORD, who will intercede for them?" His sons, however, did not listen to their father's rebuke, for it was the LORD's will to put them to death.

[26]And the boy Samuel continued to grow in stature and in favor with the LORD and with people.

### Prophecy Against the House of Eli

[27]Now a man of God came to Eli and said to him, "This is what the LORD says: 'Did I not clearly reveal myself to your ancestor's family when they were in Egypt under Pharaoh? [28]I chose your ancestor out of all the tribes of Israel to be my priest, to go up to my altar, to burn incense, and to wear an ephod in my presence. I also gave your ancestor's family all the food offerings presented by the Israelites. [29]Why do you[d] scorn my sacrifice and offering that I prescribed for my dwelling? Why do you honor your sons more than me by fattening yourselves on the choice parts of every offering made by my people Israel?'

[30]"Therefore the LORD, the God of Israel, declares: 'I promised that members of your family would minister before me forever.' But now the LORD declares: 'Far be it from me! Those who honor me I will honor, but those who despise me will be disdained. [31]The time is coming when I will cut short your strength and the strength of your priestly house, so that no one in it will reach old age, [32]and you will see distress in my dwelling. Although good

## Amplified Bible

[12]The sons of Eli were base *and* worthless; they did not know *or* regard the Lord.

[13]And the custom of the priests with the people was this: when any man offered sacrifice, the priest's servant came while the flesh was boiling with a fleshhook of three prongs in his hand;

[14]And he thrust it into the pan or kettle or caldron or pot; all that the fleshhook brought up the priest took for himself. So they did in Shiloh with all the Israelites who came there.

[15]Also, before they burned the fat, the priest's servant came and said to the man who sacrificed, Give the priest meat to roast, for he will not accept boiled meat from you, but raw.

[16]And if the man said to him, Let them burn the fat first, and then you may take as much as you want, the priest's servant would say, No! Give it to me now or I will take it by force.

[17]So the sin of the [two] young men was very great before the Lord, for they despised the offering of the Lord.

[18]But Samuel ministered before the Lord, a child girded with a linen ephod.

[19]Moreover, his mother made him a little robe and brought it to him from year to year when she came up with her husband to offer the yearly sacrifice.

[20]And Eli would bless Elkanah and his wife and say, May the Lord give you children by this woman for the gift she asked for *and* gave to the Lord. Then they would go to their own home.

[21]And the Lord visited Hannah, so that she bore three sons and two daughters. And the child Samuel grew before the Lord.

[22]Now Eli was very old, and he heard all that his sons did to all Israel and how they lay with the women who served at the door of the Tent of Meeting.

[23]And he said to them, Why do you do such things? For I hear of your evil dealings from all the people.

[24]No, my sons; it is no good report which I hear the Lord's people spreading abroad.

[25]If one man wrongs another, God will mediate for him; but if a man wrongs the Lord, who shall intercede for him? Yet they did not listen to their father, for it was the Lord's will to slay them.

[26]Now the boy Samuel grew and was in favor both with the Lord and with men.

[27]A man of God came to Eli and said to him, Thus has the Lord said: I plainly revealed Myself to the house of your father [forefather Aaron] when they were in Egypt in bondage to Pharaoh's house.

[28]Moreover, I selected him out of all the tribes of Israel to be My priest, to offer on My altar, to burn incense, to wear an ephod before Me. And I gave [from then on] to the house of your father [forefather] all the offerings of the Israelites made by fire.

[29]Why then do you kick [trample upon, treat with contempt] My sacrifice and My offering which I commanded, and honor your sons above Me by fattening yourselves upon the choicest part of every offering of My people Israel?

[30]Therefore the Lord, the God of Israel, says, I did promise that your house and that of your father [forefather Aaron] should go in and out before Me forever. But now the Lord says, Be it far from Me. For those who honor Me I will honor, and those who despise Me shall be lightly esteemed.

[31]Behold, the time is coming when I will cut off your strength and the strength of your own father's house, that there shall not be an old man in your house.

[32]And you shall behold the distress of My house, even

---

[a] 17 Dead Sea Scrolls and Septuagint; Masoretic Text *people*
[b] 20 Dead Sea Scrolls; Masoretic Text *and asked from*   [c] 25 Or *the judges*   [d] 29 The Hebrew is plural.

## New International Version

will be done to Israel, no one in your family line will ever reach old age. ³³Every one of you that I do not cut off from serving at my altar I will spare only to destroy your sight and sap your strength, and all your descendants will die in the prime of life.

³⁴"'And what happens to your two sons, Hophni and Phinehas, will be a sign to you—they will both die on the same day. ³⁵I will raise up for myself a faithful priest, who will do according to what is in my heart and mind. I will firmly establish his priestly house, and they will minister before my anointed one always. ³⁶Then everyone left in your family line will come and bow down before him for a piece of silver and a loaf of bread and plead, "Appoint me to some priestly office so I can have food to eat."'"

### The Lord Calls Samuel

3 The boy Samuel ministered before the Lord under Eli. In those days the word of the Lord was rare; there were not many visions.

²One night Eli, whose eyes were becoming so weak that he could barely see, was lying down in his usual place. ³The lamp of God had not yet gone out, and Samuel was lying down in the house of the Lord, where the ark of God was. ⁴Then the Lord called Samuel.

Samuel answered, "Here I am." ⁵And he ran to Eli and said, "Here I am; you called me."

But Eli said, "I did not call; go back and lie down." So he went and lay down.

⁶Again the Lord called, "Samuel!" And Samuel got up and went to Eli and said, "Here I am; you called me."

"My son," Eli said, "I did not call; go back and lie down."

⁷Now Samuel did not yet know the Lord: The word of the Lord had not yet been revealed to him.

⁸A third time the Lord called, "Samuel!" And Samuel got up and went to Eli and said, "Here I am; you called me."

Then Eli realized that the Lord was calling the boy. ⁹So Eli told Samuel, "Go and lie down, and if he calls you, say, 'Speak, Lord, for your servant is listening.'" So Samuel went and lay down in his place.

¹⁰The Lord came and stood there, calling as at the other times, "Samuel! Samuel!"

Then Samuel said, "Speak, for your servant is listening."

¹¹And the Lord said to Samuel: "See, I am about to do something in Israel that will make the ears of everyone who hears it tingle. ¹²At that time I will carry out against Eli everything I spoke against his family—from beginning to end. ¹³For I told him that I would judge his family forever because of the sin he knew about; his sons blasphemed God,ᵃ and he failed to restrain them. ¹⁴Therefore I swore to the house of Eli, 'The guilt of Eli's house will never be atoned for by sacrifice or offering.'"

¹⁵Samuel lay down until morning and then opened the doors of the house of the Lord. He was afraid to tell Eli the vision, ¹⁶but Eli called him and said, "Samuel, my son."

Samuel answered, "Here I am."

¹⁷"What was it he said to you?" Eli asked. "Do not hide it from me. May God deal with you, be it ever so severely, if you hide from me anything he told you." ¹⁸So Samuel

## Amplified Bible

in all the prosperity which God will give Israel, and there shall not be an old man in your house forever.

³³Yet I will not cut off from My altar every man of yours; some shall survive to weep and mourn [over the family's ruin], but all the increase of your house shall die in their best years. [I Sam. 22:17-20.]

³⁴And what befalls your two sons, Hophni and Phinehas, shall be a sign to you—in one day they both shall die. [Fulfilled in I Sam. 4:17, 18.]

³⁵And I will raise up for Myself a ᵃfaithful priest (Priest), who shall do according to what is in My heart and mind. And I will build him a sure house, and he shall walk before My anointed (Anointed) forever. [I Sam. 2:10.]

³⁶Everyone who is left in your house shall come crouching to him for a piece of silver and a bit of bread and say, Put me, I pray you, into a priest's office so I may have a piece of bread.

3 Now the boy Samuel ministered to the Lord before Eli. The word of the Lord was rare *and* precious in those days; there was no frequent *or* widely spread vision.

²At that time Eli, whose eyesight had dimmed so that he could not see, was lying down in his own place. ³The lamp of God had not yet gone out in the temple of the Lord, where the ark of God was, and Samuel was lying down

⁴When the Lord called, Samuel! And he answered, Here I am.

⁵He ran to Eli and said, Here I am, for you called me. Eli said, I did not call you; lie down again. So he went and lay down.

⁶And the Lord called again, Samuel! And Samuel arose and went to Eli and said, Here am I; you did call me. Eli answered, I did not call, my son; lie down again.

⁷Now Samuel did not yet know the Lord, and the word of the Lord was not yet revealed to him.

⁸And the Lord called Samuel the third time. And he went to Eli and said, Here I am, for you did call me. Then Eli perceived that the Lord was calling the boy.

⁹So Eli said to Samuel, Go, lie down. And if He calls you, you shall say, Speak, Lord, for Your servant is listening. So Samuel went and lay down in his place.

¹⁰And the Lord came and stood and called as at other times, Samuel! Samuel! Then Samuel answered, Speak, Lord, for Your servant is listening.

¹¹The Lord told Samuel, Behold, I am about to do a thing in Israel at which both ears of all who hear it shall tingle.

¹²On that day I will perform against Eli all that I have spoken concerning his house, from beginning to end.

¹³And I [now] announce to him that I will judge *and* punish his house forever for the iniquity of which he knew, for his sons were bringing a curse upon themselves [blaspheming God], and he did not restrain them.

¹⁴Therefore I have sworn to the house of Eli that the iniquity of Eli's house shall not be atoned for *or* purged with sacrifice or offering forever.

¹⁵Samuel lay until morning; then he opened the doors of the Lord's house. And [he] was afraid to tell the vision to Eli.

¹⁶But Eli called Samuel and said, Samuel, my son. And he answered, Here I am.

¹⁷Eli said, What is it He told you? Pray do not hide it from me. May God do so to you, and more also, if you hide anything from me of all that He said to you.

---

ᵃ This person is not identified, but this prophecy found its fulfillment from the standpoint of historical exposition in Samuel (J. P. Lange, *A Commentary*). Christian writers usually adopt also the Messianic interpretation. The text does not allow an exclusive reference to Christ, since it does look plainly to the then existing order of things; however, it also points to Christ as the consummation of the blessedness which it promises.

---

ᵃ 13 An ancient Hebrew scribal tradition (see also Septuagint); Masoretic Text *sons made themselves contemptible*

## New International Version

told him everything, hiding nothing from him. Then Eli said, "He is the LORD; let him do what is good in his eyes." ¹⁹The LORD was with Samuel as he grew up, and he let none of Samuel's words fall to the ground. ²⁰And all Israel from Dan to Beersheba recognized that Samuel was attested as a prophet of the LORD. ²¹The LORD continued to appear at Shiloh, and there he revealed himself to Samuel through his word.

4 And Samuel's word came to all Israel.

### The Philistines Capture the Ark

Now the Israelites went out to fight against the Philistines. The Israelites camped at Ebenezer, and the Philistines at Aphek. ²The Philistines deployed their forces to meet Israel, and as the battle spread, Israel was defeated by the Philistines, who killed about four thousand of them on the battlefield. ³When the soldiers returned to camp, the elders of Israel asked, "Why did the LORD bring defeat on us today before the Philistines? Let us bring the ark of the LORD's covenant from Shiloh, so that he may go with us and save us from the hand of our enemies."

⁴So the people sent men to Shiloh, and they brought back the ark of the covenant of the LORD Almighty, who is enthroned between the cherubim. And Eli's two sons, Hophni and Phinehas, were there with the ark of the covenant of God.

⁵When the ark of the LORD's covenant came into the camp, all Israel raised such a great shout that the ground shook. ⁶Hearing the uproar, the Philistines asked, "What's all this shouting in the Hebrew camp?"

When they learned that the ark of the LORD had come into the camp, ⁷the Philistines were afraid. "A god has[a] come into the camp," they said. "Oh no! Nothing like this has happened before. ⁸We're doomed! Who will deliver us from the hand of these mighty gods? They are the gods who struck the Egyptians with all kinds of plagues in the wilderness. ⁹Be strong, Philistines! Be men, or you will be subject to the Hebrews, as they have been to you. Be men, and fight!"

¹⁰So the Philistines fought, and the Israelites were defeated and every man fled to his tent. The slaughter was very great; Israel lost thirty thousand foot soldiers. ¹¹The ark of God was captured, and Eli's two sons, Hophni and Phinehas, died.

### Death of Eli

¹²That same day a Benjamite ran from the battle line and went to Shiloh with his clothes torn and dust on his head. ¹³When he arrived, there was Eli sitting on his chair by the side of the road, watching, because his heart feared for the ark of God. When the man entered the town and told what had happened, the whole town sent up a cry.

¹⁴Eli heard the outcry and asked, "What is the meaning of this uproar?"

The man hurried over to Eli, ¹⁵who was ninety-eight years old and whose eyes had failed so that he could not see. ¹⁶He told Eli, "I have just come from the battle line; I fled from it this very day."

Eli asked, "What happened, my son?"

¹⁷The man who brought the news replied, "Israel fled before the Philistines, and the army has suffered heavy losses. Also your two sons, Hophni and Phinehas, are dead, and the ark of God has been captured."

## Amplified Bible

¹⁸And Samuel told him everything, hiding nothing. And Eli said, It is the Lord; let Him do what seems good to Him. ¹⁹Samuel grew; the Lord was with him and let none of his words fall to the ground. [Josh. 23:14.] ²⁰And all Israel from Dan to Beersheba knew that Samuel was established to be a prophet of the Lord. ²¹And the Lord continued to appear in Shiloh, for the Lord revealed Himself to Samuel in Shiloh through the word of the Lord.

4 And the word of [the Lord through] Samuel came to all Israel. Now Israel went out to battle against the Philistines and encamped beside Ebenezer; the Philistines encamped at Aphek. ²The Philistines drew up against Israel, and when the battle spread, Israel was smitten by the Philistines, who slew about 4,000 men on the battlefield. ³When the troops had come into the camp, the elders of Israel said, Why has the Lord smitten us today before the Philistines? Let us bring the ark of the covenant of the Lord here from Shiloh, that He may come among us and save us from the power of our enemies. ⁴So the people sent to Shiloh and brought from there the ark of the covenant of the Lord of hosts, Who dwells above the cherubim. And the two sons of Eli, Hophni and Phinehas, were with the ark of the covenant of God. ⁵And when the ark of the covenant of the Lord came into the camp, all Israel shouted with a great shout, so that the earth resounded. ⁶And when the Philistines heard the noise of the shout, they said, What does this great shout in the camp of the Hebrews mean? When they understood that the ark of the Lord had come into the camp, ⁷The Philistines were afraid, for they said, God has come into the camp. And they said, Woe to us! For such a thing has not happened before. ⁸Woe to us! Who shall deliver us out of the hand of these mighty gods? These are the gods that smote the Egyptians with every kind of plague in the wilderness. ⁹Be strong, and acquit yourselves like men, O you Philistines, that you may not become servants to the Hebrews, as they have been to you; behave yourselves like men, and fight!

¹⁰And the Philistines fought; Israel was smitten and they fled every man to his own home. There was a very great slaughter; for 30,000 foot soldiers of Israel fell. ¹¹And the ark of God was taken, and the two sons of Eli, Hophni and Phinehas, were slain. [Foretold in I Sam. 2:34.]

¹²Now a man of Benjamin ran from the battle line and came to Shiloh that day, with his clothes torn and earth on his head. ¹³When he arrived, Eli was sitting by the road watching, for his heart trembled for the ark of God. When the man told the news in the city, all the city [people] cried out. ¹⁴When Eli heard the noise of the crying, he said, What is this uproar? And the man came hastily and told Eli. ¹⁵Now Eli was 98 years old; his eyes were dim so that he could not see. ¹⁶The man said to Eli, I have come from the battle; I fled from the battle today. Eli said, How did it go, my son? ¹⁷The messenger replied, Israel fled before the Philistines, and there has been a great slaughter among the people. Also your two sons, Hophni and Phinehas, are dead, and the ark of God is captured.

---

[a] 7 Or "Gods have" (see Septuagint)

## New International Version

[18]When he mentioned the ark of God, Eli fell backward off his chair by the side of the gate. His neck was broken and he died, for he was an old man, and he was heavy. He had led[a] Israel forty years.

[19]His daughter-in-law, the wife of Phinehas, was pregnant and near the time of delivery. When she heard the news that the ark of God had been captured and that her father-in-law and her husband were dead, she went into labor and gave birth, but was overcome by her labor pains. [20]As she was dying, the women attending her said, "Don't despair; you have given birth to a son." But she did not respond or pay any attention.

[21]She named the boy Ichabod,[b] saying, "The Glory has departed from Israel"—because of the capture of the ark of God and the deaths of her father-in-law and her husband. [22]She said, "The Glory has departed from Israel, for the ark of God has been captured."

### The Ark in Ashdod and Ekron

**5** After the Philistines had captured the ark of God, they took it from Ebenezer to Ashdod. [2]Then they carried the ark into Dagon's temple and set it beside Dagon. [3]When the people of Ashdod rose early the next day, there was Dagon, fallen on his face on the ground before the ark of the LORD! They took Dagon and put him back in his place. [4]But the following morning when they rose, there was Dagon, fallen on his face on the ground before the ark of the LORD! His head and hands had been broken off and were lying on the threshold; only his body remained. [5]That is why to this day neither the priests of Dagon nor any others who enter Dagon's temple at Ashdod step on the threshold.

[6]The LORD's hand was heavy on the people of Ashdod and its vicinity; he brought devastation on them and afflicted them with tumors.[c] [7]When the people of Ashdod saw what was happening, they said, "The ark of the god of Israel must not stay here with us, because his hand is heavy on us and on Dagon our god." [8]So they called together all the rulers of the Philistines and asked them, "What shall we do with the ark of the god of Israel?"

They answered, "Have the ark of the god of Israel moved to Gath." So they moved the ark of the God of Israel.

[9]But after they had moved it, the LORD's hand was against that city, throwing it into a great panic. He afflicted the people of the city, both young and old, with an outbreak of tumors.[d] [10]So they sent the ark of God to Ekron.

As the ark of God was entering Ekron, the people of Ekron cried out, "They have brought the ark of the god of Israel around to us to kill us and our people." [11]So they called together all the rulers of the Philistines and said, "Send the ark of the god of Israel away; let it go back to its own place, or it[e] will kill us and our people." For death had filled the city with panic; God's hand was very heavy on it. [12]Those who did not die were afflicted with tumors, and the outcry of the city went up to heaven.

### The Ark Returned to Israel

**6** When the ark of the LORD had been in Philistine territory seven months, [2]the Philistines called for the priests and the diviners and said, "What shall we do with

## Amplified Bible

[18]And when he mentioned the ark of God, Eli fell off the seat backward by the side of the gate. His neck was broken and he died, for he was an old man and heavy. He had judged Israel forty years.

[19]Now his daughter-in-law, Phinehas' wife, was with child, about to be delivered. And when she heard that the ark of God was captured and that her father-in-law and her husband were dead, she bowed herself and gave birth, for her pains came upon her.

[20]And about the time of her death the women attending her said to her, Fear not, for you have borne a son. But she did not answer or notice.

[21]And she named the child Ichabod, saying, The glory is departed from Israel!—because the ark of God had been captured and because of her father-in-law and her husband.

[22]She said, The glory is gone from Israel, for the ark of God has been taken.

**5** The Philistines brought the ark of God from Ebenezer to Ashdod.

[2]They took the ark of God into the house of Dagon and set it beside Dagon [their idol].

[3]When they of Ashdod arose early on the morrow, behold, Dagon had fallen upon his face on the ground before the ark of the Lord. So they took Dagon and set him in his place again.

[4]But when they arose early the next morning, behold, Dagon had again fallen on his face on the ground before the ark of the Lord, and [his] head and both the palms of his hands were lying cut off on the threshold; only the trunk of Dagon was left him.

[5]This is the reason neither the priests of Dagon nor any who come into Dagon's house tread on the threshold of Dagon in Ashdod to this day.

[6]But the hand of the Lord was heavy upon the people of Ashdod, and He caused [mice to spring up and there was] very deadly destruction and He smote the people with [very painful] tumors or boils, both Ashdod and its territory.

[7]When the men of Ashdod saw that it was so, they said, The ark of the God of Israel must not remain with us, for His hand is heavy on us and on Dagon our god.

[8]So they sent and gathered all the lords of the Philistines to them and said, What shall we do with the ark of the God of Israel? They answered, Let [it] be carried around to Gath. So they carried the ark of the God of Israel there.

[9]But after they had carried it to Gath, the hand of the Lord was against the city, causing an exceedingly great panic [at the deaths from the plague], for He afflicted the people of the city, both small and great, and tumors or boils broke out on them.

[10]So they sent the ark of God to Ekron. And as [it] came, the people of Ekron cried out, They have brought the ark of the God of Israel to us to slay us and our people!

[11]So they sent and assembled all the lords of the Philistines and said, Send away the ark of the God of Israel; let it return to its own place, that it may not slay us and our people. For there was a deadly panic throughout all the city; the hand of God was very heavy there.

[12]The men who had not died were stricken with very painful tumors or boils, and the cry of the city went up to heaven.

**6** The ark of the Lord was in the country of the Philistines seven months.

[2]And the Philistines called for the priests and the divin-

---

[a] 18 Traditionally *judged*   [b] 21 *Ichabod* means *no glory.*   [c] 6 Hebrew; Septuagint and Vulgate *tumors. And rats appeared in their land, and there was death and destruction throughout the city*   [d] 9 Or *with tumors in the groin* (see Septuagint)   [e] 11 Or *he*

## New International Version

the ark of the Lord? Tell us how we should send it back to its place."

³They answered, "If you return the ark of the god of Israel, do not send it back to him without a gift; by all means send a guilt offering to him. Then you will be healed, and you will know why his hand has not been lifted from you." ⁴The Philistines asked, "What guilt offering should we send to him?"

They replied, "Five gold tumors and five gold rats, according to the number of the Philistine rulers, because the same plague has struck both you and your rulers. ⁵Make models of the tumors and of the rats that are destroying the country, and give glory to Israel's god. Perhaps he will lift his hand from you and your gods and your land. ⁶Why do you harden your hearts as the Egyptians and Pharaoh did? When Israel's god dealt harshly with them, did they not send the Israelites out so they could go on their way?

⁷"Now then, get a new cart ready, with two cows that have calved and have never been yoked. Hitch the cows to the cart, but take their calves away and pen them up. ⁸Take the ark of the Lord and put it on the cart, and in a chest beside it put the gold objects you are sending back to him as a guilt offering. Send it on its way, ⁹but keep watching it. If it goes up to its own territory, toward Beth Shemesh, then the Lord has brought this great disaster on us. But if it does not, then we will know that it was not his hand that struck us but that it happened to us by chance."

¹⁰So they did this. They took two such cows and hitched them to the cart and penned up their calves. ¹¹They placed the ark of the Lord on the cart and along with it the chest containing the gold rats and the models of the tumors. ¹²Then the cows went straight up toward Beth Shemesh, keeping on the road and lowing all the way; they did not turn to the right or to the left. The rulers of the Philistines followed them as far as the border of Beth Shemesh.

¹³Now the people of Beth Shemesh were harvesting their wheat in the valley, and when they looked up and saw the ark, they rejoiced at the sight. ¹⁴The cart came to the field of Joshua of Beth Shemesh, and there it stopped beside a large rock. The people chopped up the wood of the cart and sacrificed the cows as a burnt offering to the Lord. ¹⁵The Levites took down the ark of the Lord, together with the chest containing the gold objects, and placed them on the large rock. On that day the people of Beth Shemesh offered burnt offerings and made sacrifices to the Lord. ¹⁶The five rulers of the Philistines saw all this and then returned that same day to Ekron.

¹⁷These are the gold tumors the Philistines sent as a guilt offering to the Lord—one each for Ashdod, Gaza, Ashkelon, Gath and Ekron. ¹⁸And the number of the gold rats was according to the number of Philistine towns belonging to the five rulers—the fortified towns with their country villages. The large rock on which the Levites set the ark of the Lord is a witness to this day in the field of Joshua of Beth Shemesh.

¹⁹But God struck down some of the inhabitants of Beth Shemesh, putting seventy[a] of them to death because they looked into the ark of the Lord. The people mourned because of the heavy blow the Lord had dealt them. ²⁰And the people of Beth Shemesh asked, "Who can stand in the presence of the Lord, this holy God? To whom will the ark go up from here?"

## Amplified Bible

ers, saying, What shall we do to the ark of the Lord? Tell us with what we shall send it to its place.

³And they said, If you send away the ark of the God of Israel, do not send it empty, but at least return to Him a guilt offering. Then you will be healed, and it will be known to you why His hand is not removed [and healing granted you].

⁴Then they said, What shall be the guilt offering which we shall return to Him? They answered, Five golden tumors and five golden mice, according to the number of the Philistine lords, for one plague was on you all, even on your lords.

⁵Therefore you must make images of your tumors and of your mice that destroy the land, and give glory to the God of Israel. Perhaps He will lighten His hand from off you and your gods and your land.

⁶Why then do you harden your hearts as the Egyptians and Pharaoh hardened their hearts? When He had done wonders *and* made a mock of them, did they not let the people go, and they departed?

⁷Now then, make and prepare a new cart and two milch cows on which no yoke has ever come; and yoke the cows to the cart, but take their calves home, away from them.

⁸And take the ark of the Lord and place it upon the cart, and put in a box at its side the figures of gold which you are returning to Him as a guilt offering. Then send it away and let it be gone.

⁹And watch. If it goes up by the way of its own land to Beth-shemesh, then He has done us this great evil. But if not, then we shall know that it was not His hand that struck us; it happened to us by chance.

¹⁰And the men did so, and took two milch cows and yoked them to the cart and shut up their calves at home.

¹¹And they put the ark of the Lord on the cart and along with it the box with the mice of gold and the images of their tumors.

¹²And the cows went straight toward Beth-shemesh along the highway, lowing as they went, and turned not aside to the right or the left. And the Philistine lords followed them as far as the border of Beth-shemesh.

¹³Now the men of Beth-shemesh were reaping their wheat harvest in the valley, and they lifted up their eyes and saw the ark, and rejoiced to see it.

¹⁴The cart came into the field of Joshua of Beth-shemesh and stopped there. A great stone was there; and the men split up the wood of the cart and offered the cows as a burnt offering to the Lord.

¹⁵The Levites took down the ark of the Lord and the box beside it in which were the figures of gold and put them upon the great stone. And the men of Beth-shemesh offered burnt offerings and made sacrifices that day to the Lord.

¹⁶When the five lords of the Philistines saw it, they returned that day to Ekron.

¹⁷And these are the tumors of gold which the Philistines returned for a guilt offering to the Lord: one each for Ashdod, Gaza, Ashkelon, Gath and Ekron;

¹⁸Also the mice of gold was according to the number of all the cities of the Philistines belonging to the five lords, both fortified cities and country villages. The great stone, on which they set the ark of the Lord, remains as a witness to this day in the field of Joshua of Beth-shemesh.

¹⁹And the Lord slew some of the men of Beth-shemesh because they had looked into the ark of the Lord; He slew ᵃseventy men of them, and the people mourned because the Lord had made a great slaughter among them.

²⁰And the men of Beth-shemesh said, Who is able to stand before the Lord, this holy God? And to whom shall He go away from us?

ᵃ 19 A few Hebrew manuscripts; most Hebrew manuscripts and Septuagint *50,070*

ᵃ Most Hebrew manuscripts read 50,070.

# New International Version

21Then they sent messengers to the people of Kiriath Jearim, saying, "The Philistines have returned the ark of the LORD. Come down and take it up to your town."

**7** 1So the men of Kiriath Jearim came and took up the ark of the LORD. They brought it to Abinadab's house on the hill and consecrated Eleazar his son to guard the ark of the LORD. 2The ark remained at Kiriath Jearim a long time—twenty years in all.

### Samuel Subdues the Philistines at Mizpah

Then all the people of Israel turned back to the LORD. 3So Samuel said to all the Israelites, "If you are returning to the LORD with all your hearts, then rid yourselves of the foreign gods and the Ashtoreths and commit yourselves to the LORD and serve him only, and he will deliver you out of the hand of the Philistines." 4So the Israelites put away their Baals and Ashtoreths, and served the LORD only.

5Then Samuel said, "Assemble all Israel at Mizpah, and I will intercede with the LORD for you." 6When they had assembled at Mizpah, they drew water and poured it out before the LORD. On that day they fasted and there they confessed, "We have sinned against the LORD." Now Samuel was serving as leader*a* of Israel at Mizpah.

7When the Philistines heard that Israel had assembled at Mizpah, the rulers of the Philistines came up to attack them. When the Israelites heard of it, they were afraid because of the Philistines. 8They said to Samuel, "Do not stop crying out to the LORD our God for us, that he may rescue us from the hand of the Philistines." 9Then Samuel took a suckling lamb and sacrificed it as a whole burnt offering to the LORD. He cried out to the LORD on Israel's behalf, and the LORD answered him.

10While Samuel was sacrificing the burnt offering, the Philistines drew near to engage Israel in battle. But that day the LORD thundered with loud thunder against the Philistines and threw them into such a panic that they were routed before the Israelites. 11The men of Israel rushed out of Mizpah and pursued the Philistines, slaughtering them along the way to a point below Beth Kar.

12Then Samuel took a stone and set it up between Mizpah and Shen. He named it Ebenezer,*b* saying, "Thus far the LORD has helped us."

13So the Philistines were subdued and they stopped invading Israel's territory. Throughout Samuel's lifetime, the hand of the LORD was against the Philistines. 14The towns from Ekron to Gath that the Philistines had captured from Israel were restored to Israel, and Israel delivered the neighboring territory from the hands of the Philistines. And there was peace between Israel and the Amorites.

15Samuel continued as Israel's leader all the days of his life. 16From year to year he went on a circuit from Bethel to Gilgal to Mizpah, judging Israel in all those places. 17But he always went back to Ramah, where his home was, and there he also held court for Israel. And he built an altar there to the LORD.

### Israel Asks for a King

**8** When Samuel grew old, he appointed his sons as Israel's leaders.*c* 2The name of his firstborn was Joel and the name of his second was Abijah, and they served at Beersheba. 3But his sons did not follow his ways. They turned aside after dishonest gain and accepted bribes and perverted justice.

# Amplified Bible

21And they sent messengers to the inhabitants of Kiriath-jearim, saying, The Philistines have returned the ark of the Lord. Come down and take it up to you.

**7** So the men of Kiriath-jearim came and took the ark of the Lord and brought it into the house of Abinadab on the hill and consecrated Eleazar his son to have charge of the ark of the Lord.

2And the ark remained in Kiriath-jearim a very long time [nearly 100 years, through Samuel's entire judgeship, Saul's reign, and well into David's, when it was brought to Jerusalem]. For it was twenty years before all the house of Israel lamented after the Lord. [I Chron. 13:5-7.]

3Then Samuel said to all the house of Israel, If you are returning to the Lord with all your hearts, then put away the foreign gods and the Ashtaroth [female deities] from among you and direct your hearts to the Lord and serve Him only, and He will deliver you out of the hand of the Philistines.

4So the Israelites put away the Baals and the Ashtaroth, and served the Lord only.

5Samuel said, Gather all Israel to Mizpah and I will pray to the Lord for you.

6So they gathered at Mizpah and drew water and poured it out before the Lord and fasted on that day and said there, We have sinned against the Lord. And Samuel judged the Israelites at Mizpah.

7Now when the Philistines heard that the Israelites had gathered at Mizpah, the lords of the Philistines went up against Israel. And when the Israelites heard of it, they were afraid of the Philistines.

8And the Israelites said to Samuel, Do not cease to cry to the Lord our God for us, that He may save us from the hand of the Philistines.

9So Samuel took a sucking lamb and offered it as a whole burnt offering to the Lord; and Samuel cried to the Lord for Israel, and the Lord answered him.

10As Samuel was offering up the burnt offering, the Philistines drew near to attack Israel. But the Lord thundered with a great voice that day against the Philistines and threw them into confusion, and they were defeated before Israel.

11And the men of Israel went out of Mizpah and pursued the Philistines and smote them as far as below Beth-car.

12Then Samuel took a stone and set it between Mizpah and Shen, and he called the name of it Ebenezer [stone of help], saying, Heretofore the Lord has helped us.

13So the Philistines were subdued and came no more into Israelite territory. And the hand of the Lord was against the Philistines all the days of Samuel.

14The cities the Philistines had taken from Israel were restored to Israel, from Ekron to Gath, and Israel rescued [the cities'] territory from the Philistines. There was peace also between Israel and the Amorites.

15And Samuel judged Israel all his days.

16And he went from year to year on a circuit to Bethel, Gilgal, and Mizpah, and was judge for Israel in all those places.

17Then he would return to Ramah, for his home was there; there he judged Israel, and there he built an altar to the Lord.

**8** When Samuel was old, he made his sons judges over Israel.

2Now the name of his firstborn was Joel and the name of his second, Abijah. They were judges in Beersheba.

3His sons did not walk in his ways, but turned aside after gain, took bribes, and perverted justice.

---

*a* 6 Traditionally *judge*; also in verse 15    *b* 12 *Ebenezer* means *stone of help*.    *c* 1 Traditionally *judges*

## New International Version

[4] So all the elders of Israel gathered together and came to Samuel at Ramah. [5] They said to him, "You are old, and your sons do not follow your ways; now appoint a king to lead[a] us, such as all the other nations have."

[6] But when they said, "Give us a king to lead us," this displeased Samuel; so he prayed to the LORD. [7] And the LORD told him: "Listen to all that the people are saying to you; it is not you they have rejected, but they have rejected me as their king. [8] As they have done from the day I brought them up out of Egypt until this day, forsaking me and serving other gods, so they are doing to you. [9] Now listen to them; but warn them solemnly and let them know what the king who will reign over them will claim as his rights."

[10] Samuel told all the words of the LORD to the people who were asking him for a king. [11] He said, "This is what the king who will reign over you will claim as his rights: He will take your sons and make them serve with his chariots and horses, and they will run in front of his chariots. [12] Some he will assign to be commanders of thousands and commanders of fifties, and others to plow his ground and reap his harvest, and still others to make weapons of war and equipment for his chariots. [13] He will take your daughters to be perfumers and cooks and bakers. [14] He will take the best of your fields and vineyards and olive groves and give them to his attendants. [15] He will take a tenth of your grain and of your vintage and give it to his officials and attendants. [16] Your male and female servants and the best of your cattle[b] and donkeys he will take for his own use. [17] He will take a tenth of your flocks, and you yourselves will become his slaves. [18] When that day comes, you will cry out for relief from the king you have chosen, but the LORD will not answer you in that day."

[19] But the people refused to listen to Samuel. "No!" they said. "We want a king over us. [20] Then we will be like all the other nations, with a king to lead us and to go out before us and fight our battles."

[21] When Samuel heard all that the people said, he repeated it before the LORD. [22] The LORD answered, "Listen to them and give them a king."

Then Samuel said to the Israelites, "Everyone go back to your own town."

## Amplified Bible

[4] All the elders of Israel assembled and came to Samuel at Ramah

[5] And said to him, Behold, you are old, and your sons do not walk in your ways; now appoint us a king to rule over us like all the other nations.

[6] But it displeased Samuel when they said, Give us a king to govern us. And Samuel prayed to the Lord.

[7] And the Lord said to Samuel, Hearken to the voice of the people in all they say to you; for they have not rejected you, but they have rejected Me, that I should not be King over them.

[8] According to all the works which they have done since I brought them up out of Egypt even to this day, forsaking Me and serving other gods, so they also do to you.

[9] So listen now to their voice; only solemnly warn them and show them the ways of the king who shall reign over them.

[10] So Samuel told all the words of the Lord to the people who asked of him a king.

[11] And he said, These will be the ways of the king who shall reign over you: he will take your sons and appoint them to his chariots and to be his horsemen and to run before his chariots.

[12] He will appoint them for himself to be commanders over thousands and over fifties, and some to plow his ground and to reap his harvest and to make his implements of war and equipment for his chariots.

[13] He will take your daughters to be perfumers, cooks, and bakers.

[14] He will take your fields, your vineyards, and your olive orchards, even the best of them, and give them to his servants.

[15] He will take a tenth of your grain and of your vineyards and give it to his officers and to his servants.

[16] He will take your men and women servants and the best of your cattle and your donkeys and put them to his work.

[17] He will take a tenth of your flocks, and you yourselves shall be his slaves.

[18] In that day you will cry out because of your king you have chosen for yourselves, but the Lord will not hear you then.

[19] Nevertheless, the people refused to listen to the voice of Samuel, and they said, No! We will have a king over us,

[20] That we also may be like all the nations, and that our king may govern us and go out before us and fight our battles.

[21] Samuel heard all the people's words and repeated them in the Lord's ears.

[22] And the Lord said to Samuel, Hearken to their voice and appoint them a king. And Samuel said to the men of Israel, Go every man to his city.

### Samuel Anoints Saul

**9** There was a Benjamite, a man of standing, whose name was Kish son of Abiel, the son of Zeror, the son of Bekorath, the son of Aphiah of Benjamin. [2] Kish had a son named Saul, as handsome a young man as could be found anywhere in Israel, and he was a head taller than anyone else.

[3] Now the donkeys belonging to Saul's father Kish were lost, and Kish said to his son Saul, "Take one of the servants with you and go and look for the donkeys." [4] So he passed through the hill country of Ephraim and through the area around Shalisha, but they did not find them. They went on into the district of Shaalim, but the donkeys were

**9** There was a man of Benjamin whose name was Kish son of Abiel, the son of Zeror, the son of Becorath, the son of Aphiah, a Benjamite, a mighty man of wealth *and* valor.

[2] Kish had a son named Saul, a choice young man and handsome; among all the Israelites there was not a man more handsome than he. He was a head taller than any of the people.

[3] The donkeys of Kish, Saul's father, were lost. Kish said to Saul, Take a servant with you and go, look for the donkeys.

[4] And they passed through the hill country of Ephraim and the land of Shalishah, but did not find them. Then they

---

[a] 5 Traditionally *judge*; also in verses 6 and 20    [b] 16 Septuagint; Hebrew *young men*

## New International Version

not there. Then he passed through the territory of Benjamin, but they did not find them.

⁵When they reached the district of Zuph, Saul said to the servant who was with him, "Come, let's go back, or my father will stop thinking about the donkeys and start worrying about us."

⁶But the servant replied, "Look, in this town there is a man of God; he is highly respected, and everything he says comes true. Let's go there now. Perhaps he will tell us what way to take."

⁷Saul said to his servant, "If we go, what can we give the man? The food in our sacks is gone. We have no gift to take to the man of God. What do we have?"

⁸The servant answered him again. "Look," he said, "I have a quarter of a shekel[a] of silver. I will give it to the man of God so that he will tell us what way to take." ⁹(Formerly in Israel, if someone went to inquire of God, they would say, "Come, let us go to the seer," because the prophet of today used to be called a seer.)

¹⁰"Good," Saul said to his servant. "Come, let's go." So they set out for the town where the man of God was.

¹¹As they were going up the hill to the town, they met some young women coming out to draw water, and they asked them, "Is the seer here?"

¹²"He is," they answered. "He's ahead of you. Hurry now; he has just come to our town today, for the people have a sacrifice at the high place. ¹³As soon as you enter the town, you will find him before he goes up to the high place to eat. The people will not begin eating until he comes, because he must bless the sacrifice; afterward, those who are invited will eat. Go up now; you should find him about this time."

¹⁴They went up to the town, and as they were entering it, there was Samuel, coming toward them on his way up to the high place.

¹⁵Now the day before Saul came, the Lᴏʀᴅ had revealed this to Samuel: ¹⁶"About this time tomorrow I will send you a man from the land of Benjamin. Anoint him ruler over my people Israel; he will deliver them from the hand of the Philistines. I have looked on my people, for their cry has reached me."

¹⁷When Samuel caught sight of Saul, the Lᴏʀᴅ said to him, "This is the man I spoke to you about; he will govern my people."

¹⁸Saul approached Samuel in the gateway and asked, "Would you please tell me where the seer's house is?"

¹⁹"I am the seer," Samuel replied. "Go up ahead of me to the high place, for today you are to eat with me, and in the morning I will send you on your way and will tell you all that is in your heart. ²⁰As for the donkeys you lost three days ago, do not worry about them; they have been found. And to whom is all the desire of Israel turned, if not to you and your whole family line?"

²¹Saul answered, "But am I not a Benjamite, from the smallest tribe of Israel, and is not my clan the least of all the clans of the tribe of Benjamin? Why do you say such a thing to me?"

²²Then Samuel brought Saul and his servant into the hall and seated them at the head of those who were invited—about thirty in number. ²³Samuel said to the cook, "Bring the piece of meat I gave you, the one I told you to lay aside."

²⁴So the cook took up the thigh with what was on it and set it in front of Saul. Samuel said, "Here is what has been kept for you. Eat, because it was set aside for you for this occasion from the time I said, 'I have invited guests.'" And Saul dined with Samuel that day.

## Amplified Bible

went through the land of Shaalim and the land of Benjamin, but did not find them.

⁵And when they came to the land of Zuph, Saul said to his servant, Come, let us return, lest my father stop worrying about the donkeys and become concerned about us.

⁶The servant said to him, Behold now, there is in this city a man of God, a man held in honor; all that he says surely comes true. Now let us go there. Perhaps he can show us where we should go.

⁷Then Saul said to his servant, But if we go, what shall we bring the man? The bread in our sacks is gone, and there is no gift for the man of God. What have we?

⁸The servant replied, I have here a quarter of a shekel of silver. I will give that to the man of God to tell us our way—

⁹(Formerly in Israel, when a man went to inquire of God, he said, Come, let us go to the seer, for he that is now called a prophet was formerly called a seer.)

¹⁰Saul said to his servant, Well said; come, let us go. So they went to the city where the man of God was.

¹¹As they went up the hill to the city, they met young maidens going out to draw water, and said to them, Is the seer here?

¹²They answered, He is; behold, he is just beyond you. Hurry, for he came today to the city because the people have a sacrifice today on the high place.

¹³As you enter the city, you will find him before he goes up to the high place to eat. The people will not eat until he comes to ask the blessing on the sacrifice. Afterward, those who are invited eat. So go on up, for about now you will find him.

¹⁴So they went up to the city, and as they were entering, behold, Samuel came toward them, going up to the high place.

¹⁵Now a day before Saul came, the Lord had revealed to Samuel in his ear,

¹⁶Tomorrow about this time I will send you a man from the land of Benjamin, and you shall anoint him to be leader over My people Israel; and he shall save them out of the hand of the Philistines. For I have looked upon the distress of My people, because their cry has come to Me.

¹⁷When Samuel saw Saul, the Lord told him, There is the man of whom I told you. He shall have authority over My people.

¹⁸Then Saul came near to Samuel in the gate and said, Tell me where is the seer's house?

¹⁹Samuel answered Saul, I am the seer. Go up before me to the high place, for you shall eat with me today, and tomorrow I will let you go and will tell you all that is on your mind.

²⁰As for your donkeys that were lost three days ago, do not be thinking about them, for they are found. And for whom are all the desirable things of Israel? Are they not for you and for all your father's house?

²¹And Saul said, Am I not a Benjamite, of the smallest of the tribes of Israel? And is not my family the least of all the families of the clans of Benjamin? Why then do you speak this way to me?

²²Then Samuel took Saul and his servant and brought them into the guest room [at the high place] and had them sit in the chief place among the persons—about thirty of them—who were invited. [The other people feasted outside.]

²³And Samuel said to the cook, Bring the portion which I gave you, of which I said to you, Set it aside.

²⁴And the cook lifted high the shoulder and what was on it [indicating that it was the priest's honored portion] and set it before Saul. [Samuel] said, See what was reserved for you. Eat, for until the hour appointed it was kept for you, ever since I invited the people. So Saul ate that day with Samuel.

---

ᵃ 8 That is, about 1/10 ounce or about 3 grams

## New International Version

25After they came down from the high place to the town, Samuel talked with Saul on the roof of his house. 26They rose about daybreak, and Samuel called to Saul on the roof, "Get ready, and I will send you on your way." When Saul got ready, he and Samuel went outside together. 27As they were going down to the edge of the town, Samuel said to Saul, "Tell the servant to go on ahead of us"—and the servant did so—"but you stay here for a while, so that I may give you a message from God."

**10** Then Samuel took a flask of olive oil and poured it on Saul's head and kissed him, saying, "Has not the LORD anointed you ruler over his inheritance?*a* 2When you leave me today, you will meet two men near Rachel's tomb, at Zelzah on the border of Benjamin. They will say to you, 'The donkeys you set out to look for have been found. And now your father has stopped thinking about them and is worried about you. He is asking, "What shall I do about my son?"'

3"Then you will go on from there until you reach the great tree of Tabor. Three men going up to worship God at Bethel will meet you there. One will be carrying three young goats, another three loaves of bread, and another a skin of wine. 4They will greet you and offer you two loaves of bread, which you will accept from them.

5"After that you will go to Gibeah of God, where there is a Philistine outpost. As you approach the town, you will meet a procession of prophets coming down from the high place with lyres, timbrels, pipes and harps being played before them, and they will be prophesying. 6The Spirit of the LORD will come powerfully upon you, and you will prophesy with them; and you will be changed into a different person. 7Once these signs are fulfilled, do whatever your hand finds to do, for God is with you.

8"Go down ahead of me to Gilgal. I will surely come down to you to sacrifice burnt offerings and fellowship offerings, but you must wait seven days until I come to you and tell you what you are to do."

### Saul Made King

9As Saul turned to leave Samuel, God changed Saul's heart, and all these signs were fulfilled that day. 10When he and his servant arrived at Gibeah, a procession of prophets met him; the Spirit of God came powerfully upon him, and he joined in their prophesying. 11When all those who had formerly known him saw him prophesying with the prophets, they asked each other, "What is this that has happened to the son of Kish? Is Saul also among the prophets?"

12A man who lived there answered, "And who is their father?" So it became a saying: "Is Saul also among the prophets?" 13After Saul stopped prophesying, he went to the high place.

14Now Saul's uncle asked him and his servant, "Where have you been?"

"Looking for the donkeys," he said. "But when we saw they were not to be found, we went to Samuel."

15Saul's uncle said, "Tell me what Samuel said to you."

16Saul replied, "He assured us that the donkeys had been found." But he did not tell his uncle what Samuel had said about the kingship.

17Samuel summoned the people of Israel to the LORD

## Amplified Bible

25When they had come down from the high place into the city, Samuel conversed with Saul on the top of the house.

26They arose early and about dawn Samuel called Saul [who was sleeping] on the top of the house, saying, Get up, that I may send you on your way. Saul arose, and both he and Samuel went out on the street.

27And as they were going down to the outskirts of the city, Samuel said to Saul, Bid the servant pass on before us—and he passed on—but you stand still, first, that I may cause you to hear the word of God.

**10** Then Samuel took the vial of oil and poured it on Saul's head and kissed him and said, Has not the Lord anointed you to be prince over His heritage Israel?

2When you have left me today, you will meet two men by Rachel's tomb in the territory of Benjamin at Zelzah, and they will say to you, The donkeys you sought are found. And your father has quit caring about them and is anxious for you, asking, What shall I do about my son?

3Then you will go on from there and you will come to the oak of Tabor, and three men going up to God at Bethel will meet you there, one carrying three kids, another carrying three loaves of bread, and another carrying a skin bottle of wine.

4They will greet you and give you two loaves of bread, which you shall accept from their hand.

5After that you will come to the hill of God, where the garrison of the Philistines is; and when you come to the city, you will meet a company of prophets coming down from the high place with harp, tambourine, flute, and lyre before them, prophesying.

6Then the Spirit of the Lord will come upon you mightily, and you will show yourself to be a prophet with them; and you will be turned into another man.

7When these signs meet you, do whatever you find to be done, for God is with you.

8You shall go down before me to Gilgal; and behold, I will come down to you to offer burnt offerings and to sacrifice peace offerings. You shall wait seven days until I come to you and show you what you shall do.

9And when [Saul] had turned his back to leave Samuel, God gave him another heart, and all these signs came to pass that day.

10When they came to the hill [Gibeah], behold, a band of prophets met him; and the Spirit of God came mightily upon him, and he spoke under divine inspiration among them.

11And when all who knew Saul before saw that he spoke by inspiration among the [schooled] prophets, the people said one to another, What has come over [him, who is nobody but] the son of Kish? Is Saul also among the prophets?

12One from that same place answered, But who is the father of the others? So it became a proverb, Is Saul also among the prophets?

13When [Saul] had ended his inspired speaking, he went to the high place.

14Saul's uncle said to him and to his servant, Where did you go? And Saul said, To look for the donkeys, and when we found them nowhere, we went to Samuel.

15Saul's uncle said, Tell me, what did Samuel say to you?

16And Saul said to his uncle, He told us plainly that the donkeys were found. But of the matter of the kingdom of which Samuel spoke he told him nothing.

17And Samuel called the people together to the Lord at Mizpah

---

*a 1 Hebrew; Septuagint and Vulgate over his people Israel? You will reign over the LORD's people and save them from the power of their enemies round about. And this will be a sign to you that the LORD has anointed you ruler over his inheritance:*

## New International Version

at Mizpah [18]and said to them, "This is what the Lord, the God of Israel, says: 'I brought Israel up out of Egypt, and I delivered you from the power of Egypt and all the kingdoms that oppressed you.' [19]But you have now rejected your God, who saves you out of all your disasters and calamities. And you have said, 'No, appoint a king over us.' So now present yourselves before the Lord by your tribes and clans."

[20]When Samuel had all Israel come forward by tribes, the tribe of Benjamin was taken by lot. [21]Then he brought forward the tribe of Benjamin, clan by clan, and Matri's clan was taken. Finally Saul son of Kish was taken. But when they looked for him, he was not to be found. [22]So they inquired further of the Lord, "Has the man come here yet?"

And the Lord said, "Yes, he has hidden himself among the supplies."

[23]They ran and brought him out, and as he stood among the people he was a head taller than any of the others. [24]Samuel said to all the people, "Do you see the man the Lord has chosen? There is no one like him among all the people."

Then the people shouted, "Long live the king!"

[25]Samuel explained to the people the rights and duties of kingship. He wrote them down on a scroll and deposited it before the Lord. Then Samuel dismissed the people to go to their own homes.

[26]Saul also went to his home in Gibeah, accompanied by valiant men whose hearts God had touched. [27]But some scoundrels said, "How can this fellow save us?" They despised him and brought him no gifts. But Saul kept silent.

### Saul Rescues the City of Jabesh

**11** Nahash[a] the Ammonite went up and besieged Jabesh Gilead. And all the men of Jabesh said to him, "Make a treaty with us, and we will be subject to you."

[2]But Nahash the Ammonite replied, "I will make a treaty with you only on the condition that I gouge out the right eye of every one of you and so bring disgrace on all Israel."

[3]The elders of Jabesh said to him, "Give us seven days so we can send messengers throughout Israel; if no one comes to rescue us, we will surrender to you."

[4]When the messengers came to Gibeah of Saul and reported these terms to the people, they all wept aloud. [5]Just then Saul was returning from the fields, behind his oxen, and he asked, "What is wrong with everyone? Why are they weeping?" Then they repeated to him what the men of Jabesh had said.

[6]When Saul heard their words, the Spirit of God came powerfully upon him, and he burned with anger. [7]He took a pair of oxen, cut them into pieces, and sent the pieces by messengers throughout Israel, proclaiming, "This is what will be done to the oxen of anyone who does not follow Saul and Samuel." Then the terror of the Lord fell on the people, and they came out together as one. [8]When Saul mustered them at Bezek, the men of Israel numbered three hundred thousand and those of Judah thirty thousand.

[9]They told the messengers who had come, "Say to the men of Jabesh Gilead, 'By the time the sun is hot tomorrow, you will be rescued.'" When the messengers went and reported this to the men of Jabesh, they were elated.

<hr/>

[a] 1 Masoretic Text; Dead Sea Scrolls gifts. Now Nahash king of the Ammonites oppressed the Gadites and Reubenites severely. He gouged out all their right eyes and struck terror and dread in Israel. Not a man remained among the Israelites beyond the Jordan whose right eye was not gouged out by Nahash king of the Ammonites, except that seven thousand men fled from the Ammonites and entered Jabesh Gilead. About a month later, [1]Nahash

## Amplified Bible

[18]And said to the Israelites, Thus says the Lord, the God of Israel: It was I Who brought up Israel out of Egypt and delivered you out of the hands of the Egyptians and of all the kingdoms that oppressed you.

[19]But you have this day rejected your God, Who Himself saves you from all your calamities and distresses; and you have said to Him, No! Set a king over us. So now present yourselves before the Lord by your tribes and by your thousands.

[20]And when Samuel had caused all the tribes of Israel to come near, the tribe of Benjamin was taken [probably by lot].

[21]When he had caused the tribe of Benjamin to come near by their families, the family of Matri was taken. And Saul son of Kish was taken. But when they looked for him, he could not be found.

[22]Therefore they inquired of the Lord further, if the man would yet come back. And the Lord answered, Behold, he has hidden himself among the baggage. [Exod. 28:30.]

[23]They ran and brought him from there. And when he stood among the people, he was a head taller than any of them.

[24]And Samuel said to all the people, Do you see him whom the Lord has chosen, that none like him is among all the people? And all the people shouted and said, Long live the king!

[25]Then Samuel told the people the manner of the kingdom [defining the position of the king in relation to God and to the people], and wrote it in a book and laid it before the Lord. And Samuel sent all the people away, each one to his home.

[26]Saul also went home to Gibeah; and there went with him a band of valiant men whose hearts God had touched.

[27]But some worthless fellows said, How can this man save us? And they despised him and brought him no gift. But he held his peace and was as if deaf.

**11** And Nahash the Ammonite went up and besieged Jabesh-gilead; and all the men of Jabesh said to Nahash, Make a treaty with us, and we will serve you.

[2]But Nahash the Ammonite told them, On this condition I will make a treaty with you, that I thrust out all your right eyes and thus lay disgrace on all Israel.

[3]The elders of Jabesh said to Nahash, Give us seven days' time, that we may send messengers through all the territory of Israel. Then, if there is no man to save us, we will come out to you.

[4]Then messengers came to Gibeah of Saul and told the news in the ears of the people; and all the people wept aloud.

[5]Now Saul came out of the field after the oxen, and [he] said, What ails the people that they are weeping? And they told him the words of the men of Jabesh.

[6]The Spirit of God came mightily upon Saul when he heard those tidings, and his anger was greatly kindled.

[7]And he took a yoke of oxen and cut them in pieces and sent them throughout all the territory of Israel by the hands of messengers, saying, Whoever does not come forth after Saul and Samuel, so shall it be done to his oxen! And terror from the Lord fell on the people, and they came out with one consent.

[8]And he numbered them at Bezek, and the Israelites were 300,000 and the men of Judah 30,000.

[9]The messengers who came were told, Say to the men of Jabesh-gilead, Tomorrow, by the time the sun is hot, you shall have help. The messengers came and reported to the men of Jabesh, and they were glad.

## New International Version

[10]They said to the Ammonites, "Tomorrow we will surrender to you, and you can do to us whatever you like."

[11]The next day Saul separated his men into three divisions; during the last watch of the night they broke into the camp of the Ammonites and slaughtered them until the heat of the day. Those who survived were scattered, so that no two of them were left together.

### Saul Confirmed as King

[12]The people then said to Samuel, "Who was it that asked, 'Shall Saul reign over us?' Turn these men over to us so that we may put them to death."

[13]But Saul said, "No one will be put to death today, for this day the LORD has rescued Israel."

[14]Then Samuel said to the people, "Come, let us go to Gilgal and there renew the kingship." [15]So all the people went to Gilgal and made Saul king in the presence of the LORD. There they sacrificed fellowship offerings before the LORD, and Saul and all the Israelites held a great celebration.

### Samuel's Farewell Speech

**12** Samuel said to all Israel, "I have listened to everything you said to me and have set a king over you. [2]Now you have a king as your leader. As for me, I am old and gray, and my sons are here with you. I have been your leader from my youth until this day. [3]Here I stand. Testify against me in the presence of the LORD and his anointed. Whose ox have I taken? Whose donkey have I taken? Whom have I cheated? Whom have I oppressed? From whose hand have I accepted a bribe to make me shut my eyes? If I have done any of these things, I will make it right."

[4]"You have not cheated or oppressed us," they replied. "You have not taken anything from anyone's hand."

[5]Samuel said to them, "The LORD is witness against you, and also his anointed is witness this day, that you have not found anything in my hand."

"He is witness," they said.

[6]Then Samuel said to the people, "It is the LORD who appointed Moses and Aaron and brought your ancestors up out of Egypt. [7]Now then, stand here, because I am going to confront you with evidence before the LORD as to all the righteous acts performed by the LORD for you and your ancestors.

[8]"After Jacob entered Egypt, they cried to the LORD for help, and the LORD sent Moses and Aaron, who brought your ancestors out of Egypt and settled them in this place.

[9]"But they forgot the LORD their God; so he sold them into the hand of Sisera, the commander of the army of Hazor, and into the hands of the Philistines and the king of Moab, who fought against them. [10]They cried out to the LORD and said, 'We have sinned; we have forsaken the LORD and served the Baals and the Ashtoreths. But now deliver us from the hands of our enemies, and we will serve you.' [11]Then the LORD sent Jerub-Baal,[a] Barak,[b] Jephthah and Samuel,[c] and he delivered you from the hands of your enemies all around you, so that you lived in safety.

[12]"But when you saw that Nahash king of the Ammonites was moving against you, you said to me, 'No, we want a king to rule over us'—even though the LORD your God was your king. [13]Now here is the king you have chosen, the one you asked for; see, the LORD has set a king over you. [14]If you fear the LORD and serve and obey him and do not rebel against his commands, and if both you and the king who reigns over you follow the LORD your God—

## Amplified Bible

[10]So the men of Jabesh said to Nahash, Tomorrow we will come out to you, and you may do to us all that seems good to you.

[11]The next day Saul put the men in three companies; and they came into the midst of the enemy's camp in the [darkness of the] morning watch and slew the Ammonites until midday; and the survivors were scattered, so that no two of them remained together.

[12]The people said to Samuel, Who is he who said, Shall Saul reign over us? Bring the men, that we may put them to death.

[13]But Saul said, There shall not a man be put to death this day, for today the Lord has brought deliverance to Israel.

[14]Samuel said to the people, Come, let us go to Gilgal and there renew the kingdom.

[15]All the people went to Gilgal and there they made Saul king before the Lord. And there they sacrificed peace offerings before the Lord, and there Saul and all the men of Israel rejoiced greatly.

**12** And Samuel said to all Israel, I have listened to you in all that you have said to me and have made a king over you.

[2]And now, behold, the king walks before you. And I am old and gray, and behold, my sons are with you. And I have walked before you from my childhood to this day.

[3]Here I am; testify against me before the Lord and Saul His anointed. Whose ox or donkey have I taken? Or whom have I defrauded or oppressed? Or from whose hand have I received any bribe to blind my eyes? Tell me and I will restore it to you.

[4]And they said, You have not defrauded us or oppressed us or taken anything from any man's hand.

[5]And Samuel said to them, The Lord is witness against you, and His anointed is witness this day, that you have not found anything in my hand. And they answered, He is witness.

[6]And Samuel said to the people, It is the Lord Who appointed Moses and Aaron and brought your fathers up out of Egypt.

[7]Now present yourselves, that I may plead with you before the Lord concerning all the righteous acts of the Lord which He did for you and for your fathers.

[8]When Jacob and his sons had come into Egypt [and the Egyptians oppressed them], and your fathers cried to the Lord, then the Lord sent Moses and Aaron, who brought forth your fathers out of Egypt and made them dwell in this place.

[9]But when they forgot the Lord their God, He sold them into the hand of Sisera, commander of Hazor's army, and into the hands of the Philistines and of the king of Moab, and they fought those foes.

[10]And they cried to the Lord, saying, We have sinned because we have forsaken the Lord and have served the Baals and the Ashtaroth; but now deliver us from the hands of our enemies, and we will serve You.

[11]And the Lord sent Jerubbaal and Barak and Jephthah and Samuel, and He delivered you out of the hands of your enemies on every side, and you dwelt safely.

[12]But when you saw that Nahash king of the Ammonites came against you, you said to me, No! A king shall reign over us—when the Lord your God was your King!

[13]Now see the king whom you have chosen and for whom you have asked; behold, the Lord has set a king over you.

[14]If you will revere *and* fear the Lord and serve Him and hearken to His voice and not rebel against His commandment, and if both you and your king will follow the Lord your God, it will be good!

---

[a] 11 Also called *Gideon*   [b] 11 Some Septuagint manuscripts and Syriac; Hebrew *Bedan*   [c] 11 Hebrew; some Septuagint manuscripts and Syriac *Samson*

# New International Version

good! [15]But if you do not obey the LORD, and if you rebel against his commands, his hand will be against you, as it was against your ancestors.

[16]"Now then, stand still and see this great thing the LORD is about to do before your eyes! [17]Is it not wheat harvest now? I will call on the LORD to send thunder and rain. And you will realize what an evil thing you did in the eyes of the LORD when you asked for a king."

[18]Then Samuel called on the LORD, and that same day the LORD sent thunder and rain. So all the people stood in awe of the LORD and of Samuel.

[19]The people all said to Samuel, "Pray to the LORD your God for your servants so that we will not die, for we have added to all our other sins the evil of asking for a king."

[20]"Do not be afraid," Samuel replied. "You have done all this evil; yet do not turn away from the LORD, but serve the LORD with all your heart. [21]Do not turn away after useless idols. They can do you no good, nor can they rescue you, because they are useless. [22]For the sake of his great name the LORD will not reject his people, because the LORD was pleased to make you his own. [23]As for me, far be it from me that I should sin against the LORD by failing to pray for you. And I will teach you the way that is good and right. [24]But be sure to fear the LORD and serve him faithfully with all your heart; consider what great things he has done for you. [25]Yet if you persist in doing evil, both you and your king will perish."

## Samuel Rebukes Saul

**13** Saul was thirty[a] years old when he became king, and he reigned over Israel forty-[b] two years.

[2]Saul chose three thousand men from Israel; two thousand were with him at Mikmash and in the hill country of Bethel, and a thousand were with Jonathan at Gibeah in Benjamin. The rest of the men he sent back to their homes.

[3]Jonathan attacked the Philistine outpost at Geba, and the Philistines heard about it. Then Saul had the trumpet blown throughout the land and said, "Let the Hebrews hear!" [4]So all Israel heard the news: "Saul has attacked the Philistine outpost, and now Israel has become obnoxious to the Philistines." And the people were summoned to join Saul at Gilgal.

[5]The Philistines assembled to fight Israel, with three thousand[c] chariots, six thousand charioteers, and soldiers as numerous as the sand on the seashore. They went up and camped at Mikmash, east of Beth Aven. [6]When the Israelites saw that their situation was critical and that their army was hard pressed, they hid in caves and thickets, among the rocks, and in pits and cisterns. [7]Some Hebrews even crossed the Jordan to the land of Gad and Gilead.

Saul remained at Gilgal, and all the troops with him were quaking with fear. [8]He waited seven days, the time set by Samuel; but Samuel did not come to Gilgal, and Saul's men began to scatter. [9]So he said, "Bring me the burnt offering and the fellowship offerings." And Saul offered up the burnt offering. [10]Just as he finished making the offering, Samuel arrived, and Saul went out to greet him.

# Amplified Bible

[15]But if you will not hearken to the Lord's voice, but rebel against His commandment, then the hand of the Lord will be against you, as it was against your fathers.

[16]So stand still and see this great thing the Lord will do before your eyes now.

[17]Is it not wheat harvest today? I will call to the Lord and He will send thunder and rain; then you shall know and see that your wickedness is great which you have done in the sight of the Lord in asking for a king for yourselves.

[18]So Samuel called to the Lord, and He sent thunder and rain that day; and all the people greatly feared the Lord and Samuel.

[19]And [they] all said to Samuel, Pray for your servants to the Lord your God, that we may not die, for we have added to all our sins this evil—to ask for a king.

[20]And Samuel said to the people, Fear not. You have indeed done all this evil; yet turn not aside from following the Lord, but serve Him with all your heart.

[21]And turn not aside after vain *and* worthless things which cannot profit or deliver you, for they are empty *and* futile.

[22]The Lord will not forsake His people for His great name's sake, for it has pleased Him to make you a people for Himself.

[23]Moreover, as for me, far be it from me that I should sin against the Lord by ceasing to pray for you; but I will instruct you in the good and right way.

[24]Only fear the Lord and serve Him faithfully with all your heart; for consider how great are the things He has done for you.

[25]But if you still do wickedly, both you and your king shall be swept away.

**13** Saul was [a] [forty] years old when he began to reign; and when he had reigned two years over Israel,

[2]Saul chose 3,000 men of Israel; 2,000 were with [him] in Michmash and the hill country of Bethel, and 1,000 with Jonathan in Gibeah of Benjamin. The rest of the men he sent away, each one to his home.

[3]Jonathan smote the Philistine garrison at Geba, and the Philistines heard of it. And Saul blew the trumpet throughout all the land, saying, Let the Hebrews hear!

[4]All Israel heard that Saul had defeated the Philistine garrison and also that Israel had become an abomination to the Philistines. And the people were called out to join Saul at Gilgal.

[5]And the Philistines gathered to fight with Israel, 30,000 chariots and 6,000 horsemen and troops like sand on the seashore. They came up and encamped at Michmash, east of Beth-aven.

[6]When the men of Israel saw that they were in a tight situation—for their troops were hard pressed—they hid in caves, holes, rocks, tombs, and pits *or* cisterns.

[7]Some Hebrews had gone over the Jordan to the land of Gad and Gilead. As for Saul, he was still in Gilgal, and all the people followed him trembling.

[8]Saul waited seven days, according to the set time Samuel had appointed. But Samuel had not come to Gilgal, and the people were scattering from Saul.

[9]So Saul said, Bring me the burnt offering and the peace offerings. And he offered the burnt offering [which he was forbidden to do].

[10]And just as he finished offering the burnt offering, behold, Samuel came! Saul went out to meet and greet him.

---

[a] 1 A few late manuscripts of the Septuagint; Hebrew does not have *thirty*.  [b] 1 Probable reading of the original Hebrew text (see Acts 13:21); Masoretic Text does not have *forty-*.  [c] 5 Some Septuagint manuscripts and Syriac; Hebrew *thirty thousand*

[a] The complete numbers in this verse are missing in the Hebrew. The word "forty" is supplied by the best available estimate.

## New International Version

[11]"What have you done?" asked Samuel.

Saul replied, "When I saw that the men were scattering, and that you did not come at the set time, and that the Philistines were assembling at Mikmash, [12]I thought, 'Now the Philistines will come down against me at Gilgal, and I have not sought the LORD's favor.' So I felt compelled to offer the burnt offering."

[13]"You have done a foolish thing," Samuel said. "You have not kept the command the LORD your God gave you; if you had, he would have established your kingdom over Israel for all time. [14]But now your kingdom will not endure; the LORD has sought out a man after his own heart and appointed him ruler of his people, because you have not kept the LORD's command."

[15]Then Samuel left Gilgal[a] and went up to Gibeah in Benjamin, and Saul counted the men who were with him. They numbered about six hundred.

### Israel Without Weapons

[16]Saul and his son Jonathan and the men with them were staying in Gibeah[b] in Benjamin, while the Philistines camped at Mikmash. [17]Raiding parties went out from the Philistine camp in three detachments. One turned toward Ophrah in the vicinity of Shual, [18]another toward Beth Horon, and the third toward the borderland overlooking the Valley of Zeboyim facing the wilderness.

[19]Not a blacksmith could be found in the whole land of Israel, because the Philistines had said, "Otherwise the Hebrews will make swords or spears!" [20]So all Israel went down to the Philistines to have their plow points, mattocks, axes and sickles[c] sharpened. [21]The price was two-thirds of a shekel[d] for sharpening plow points and mattocks, and a third of a shekel[e] for sharpening forks and axes and for repointing goads.

[22]So on the day of the battle not a soldier with Saul and Jonathan had a sword or spear in his hand; only Saul and his son Jonathan had them.

### Jonathan Attacks the Philistines

[23]Now a detachment of Philistines had gone out to the pass at Mikmash. **14** [1]One day Jonathan son of Saul said to his young armor-bearer, "Come, let's go over to the Philistine outpost on the other side." But he did not tell his father.

[2]Saul was staying on the outskirts of Gibeah under a pomegranate tree in Migron. With him were about six hundred men, [3]among whom was Ahijah, who was wearing an ephod. He was a son of Ichabod's brother Ahitub son of Phinehas, the son of Eli, the LORD's priest in Shiloh. No one was aware that Jonathan had left.

[4]On each side of the pass that Jonathan intended to cross to reach the Philistine outpost was a cliff; one was called Bozez and the other Seneh. [5]One cliff stood to the north toward Mikmash, the other to the south toward Geba.

[6]Jonathan said to his young armor-bearer, "Come, let's go over to the outpost of those uncircumcised men. Perhaps the LORD will act in our behalf. Nothing can hinder the LORD from saving, whether by many or by few."

[7]"Do all that you have in mind," his armor-bearer said. "Go ahead; I am with you heart and soul."

## Amplified Bible

[11]Samuel said, What have you done? Saul said, Because I saw that the people were scattering from me, and that you did not come within the days appointed, and that the Philistines were assembled at Michmash,

[12]I thought, The Philistines will come down now upon me to Gilgal, and I have not made supplication to the Lord. So I forced myself to offer a burnt offering.

[13]And Samuel said to Saul, You have done foolishly! You have not kept the commandment of the Lord your God which He commanded you; for the Lord would have established your kingdom over Israel forever;

[14]But now your kingdom shall not continue; the Lord has sought out [David] a man after His own [a]heart, and the Lord has commanded him to be prince *and* ruler over His people, because you have not kept what the Lord commanded you.

[15]And Samuel went up from Gilgal to Gibeah of Benjamin. And Saul numbered the people that were left with him, [only] about 600.

[16]Saul and Jonathan his son and the people with them remained in Gibeah of Benjamin, but the Philistines encamped at Michmash.

[17]And raiders came out of the Philistine camp in three companies; one company turned toward Ophrah, to the land of Shual,

[18]Another turned toward Beth-horon, and another toward the border overlooking the Valley of Zeboim toward the wilderness.

[19]Now there was no metal worker to be found throughout all the land of Israel, for the Philistines said, Lest the Hebrews make swords or spears.

[20]But each of the Israelites had to go down to the Philistines to get his plowshare, mattock, axe, or sickle sharpened.

[21]And the price for plowshares and mattocks was a pim, and a third of a shekel for axes and for setting goads [with resulting blunt edges on the sickles, mattocks, forks, axes, and goads.]

[22]So on the day of battle neither sword nor spear was found in the hand of any of the men who were with Saul and Jonathan; but Saul and Jonathan his son had them.

[23]And the garrison of the Philistines went out to the pass of Michmash.

**14** One day Jonathan son of Saul said to his armor-bearer, Come, let us go over to the Philistine garrison on the other side. But he did not tell his father.

[2]Saul was remaining in the outskirts of Gibeah under a pomegranate tree in Migron; and with him were about 600 men,

[3]And Ahijah son of Ahitub, Ichabod's brother, the son of Phinehas, the son of Eli, the Lord's priest in Shiloh, was wearing the ephod. And the people did not know that Jonathan was gone.

[4]Between the passes by which Jonathan sought to go over to the Philistine garrison there was a rocky crag on the one side and a rocky crag on the other side; one was named Bozez, and the other Seneh.

[5]The one crag rose on the north in front of Michmash, and the other on the south in front of Geba.

[6]And Jonathan said to his young armor-bearer, Come, and let us go over to the garrison of these uncircumcised; it may be that the Lord will work for us. For there is nothing to prevent the Lord from saving by many or by few.

[7]And his armor-bearer said to him, Do all that is in your mind; I am with you in whatever you think [best].

---

[a] 15 Hebrew; Septuagint *Gilgal and went his way; the rest of the people went after Saul to meet the army, and they went out of Gilgal*
[b] 16 Two Hebrew manuscripts; most Hebrew manuscripts *Geba,* a variant of *Gibeah*  [c] 20 Septuagint; Hebrew *plow points*  [d] 21 That is, about 1/4 ounce or about 8 grams  [e] 21 That is, about 1/8 ounce or about 4 grams

[a] See footnote on I Sam. 27:10.

## New International Version

[8]Jonathan said, "Come on, then; we will cross over toward them and let them see us. [9]If they say to us, 'Wait there until we come to you,' we will stay where we are and not go up to them. [10]But if they say, 'Come up to us,' we will climb up, because that will be our sign that the LORD has given them into our hands."

[11]So both of them showed themselves to the Philistine outpost. "Look!" said the Philistines. "The Hebrews are crawling out of the holes they were hiding in." [12]The men of the outpost shouted to Jonathan and his armor-bearer, "Come up to us and we'll teach you a lesson."

So Jonathan said to his armor-bearer, "Climb up after me; the LORD has given them into the hand of Israel."

[13]Jonathan climbed up, using his hands and feet, with his armor-bearer right behind him. The Philistines fell before Jonathan, and his armor-bearer followed and killed behind him. [14]In that first attack Jonathan and his armor-bearer killed some twenty men in an area of about half an acre.

### Israel Routs the Philistines

[15]Then panic struck the whole army—those in the camp and field, and those in the outposts and raiding parties—and the ground shook. It was a panic sent by God.[a]

[16]Saul's lookouts at Gibeah in Benjamin saw the army melting away in all directions. [17]Then Saul said to the men who were with him, "Muster the forces and see who has left us." When they did, it was Jonathan and his armor-bearer who were not there.

[18]Saul said to Ahijah, "Bring the ark of God." (At that time it was with the Israelites.)[b] [19]While Saul was talking to the priest, the tumult in the Philistine camp increased more and more. So Saul said to the priest, "Withdraw your hand."

[20]Then Saul and all his men assembled and went to the battle. They found the Philistines in total confusion, striking each other with their swords. [21]Those Hebrews who had previously been with the Philistines and had gone up with them to their camp went over to the Israelites who were with Saul and Jonathan. [22]When all the Israelites who had hidden in the hill country of Ephraim heard that the Philistines were on the run, they joined the battle in hot pursuit. [23]So on that day the LORD saved Israel, and the battle moved on beyond Beth Aven.

### Jonathan Eats Honey

[24]Now the Israelites were in distress that day, because Saul had bound the people under an oath, saying, "Cursed be anyone who eats food before evening comes, before I have avenged myself on my enemies!" So none of the troops tasted food.

[25]The entire army entered the woods, and there was honey on the ground. [26]When they went into the woods, they saw the honey oozing out; yet no one put his hand to his mouth, because they feared the oath. [27]But Jonathan had not heard that his father had bound the people with the oath, so he reached out the end of the staff that was in his hand and dipped it into the honeycomb. He raised his hand to his mouth, and his eyes brightened.[c] [28]Then one of the soldiers told him, "Your father bound the army under a strict oath, saying, 'Cursed be anyone who eats food today!' That is why the men are faint."

## Amplified Bible

[8]Jonathan said, We will pass over to these men and we will let them see us.

[9]If they say to us, Wait until we come to you, then we will stand still in our place and will not go up to them.

[10]But if they say, Come up to us, we will go up, for the Lord has delivered them into our hand, and this will be our sign.

[11]So both of them let the Philistine garrison see them. And the Philistines said, Behold, the Hebrews are coming out of the holes where they have hidden themselves.

[12]The garrison men said to Jonathan and his armor-bearer, Come up to us and we will show you a thing. Jonathan said to his armor-bearer, Come up after me, for the Lord has given them into Israel's hand.

[13]Then Jonathan climbed up on his hands and feet, his armor-bearer after him; and the enemy fell before Jonathan, and his armor-bearer killed them after him.

[14]And that first slaughter which Jonathan and his armor-bearer made was about twenty men within about a half acre of land [which a yoke of oxen might plow].

[15]And there was trembling and panic in the [Philistine] camp, in the field, and among all the men; the garrison, and even the raiders trembled; the earth quaked, and it became a terror from God.

[16]Saul's watchmen in Gibeah of Benjamin looked, and behold, the multitude melted away and went hither and thither.

[17]Then Saul said to the men with him, Number and see who is gone from us. When they numbered, behold, Jonathan and his armor-bearer were missing.

[18]Saul said to Ahijah, Bring here the ark of God—for at that time the ark of God was with the children of Israel.

[19]While Saul talked to the priest, the tumult in the Philistine camp kept increasing. Then Saul said to the priest, Withdraw your hand.

[20]Then Saul and all the people with him rallied and went into the battle, and behold, every [Philistine's] sword was against his fellow in wild confusion.

[21]Moreover, the Hebrews who were with the Philistines before that time, who went up with them into the camp from the country round about, even they also turned to be with the Israelites who were with Saul and Jonathan.

[22]Likewise, all the men of Israel who had hid themselves in the hill country of Ephraim, when they heard that the Philistines fled, they also went after them in hot pursuit in the battle.

[23]So the Lord delivered Israel that day, and the battle passed beyond Beth-aven.

[24]But the men of Israel were distressed that day, for Saul had caused them to take an oath, saying, Cursed be the man who eats any food before evening and until I have taken vengeance on my enemies. So none of the men tasted any food.

[25]And all the people of the land came to a wood, and there was honey on the ground.

[26]When the men entered the wood, behold, the honey was dripping, but no man tasted it, for the men feared the oath.

[27]But Jonathan had not heard when his father charged the people with the oath. So he dipped the end of the rod in his hand into a honeycomb and put it to his mouth, and his [weary] eyes brightened.

[28]Then one of the men told him, Your father strictly charged the men with an oath, saying, Cursed be the man who eats any food today. And the people were exhausted and faint.

---

[a] 15 Or a terrible panic    [b] 18 Hebrew; Septuagint "Bring the ephod."
(At that time he wore the ephod before the Israelites.)    [c] 27 Or his
strength was renewed; similarly in verse 29

## New International Version

29Jonathan said, "My father has made trouble for the country. See how my eyes brightened when I tasted a little of this honey. 30How much better it would have been if the men had eaten today some of the plunder they took from their enemies. Would not the slaughter of the Philistines have been even greater?"

31That day, after the Israelites had struck down the Philistines from Mikmash to Aijalon, they were exhausted. 32They pounced on the plunder and, taking sheep, cattle and calves, they butchered them on the ground and ate them, together with the blood. 33Then someone said to Saul, "Look, the men are sinning against the Lord by eating meat that has blood in it."

"You have broken faith," he said. "Roll a large stone over here at once." 34Then he said, "Go out among the men and tell them, 'Each of you bring me your cattle and sheep, and slaughter them here and eat them. Do not sin against the Lord by eating meat with blood still in it.'"

So everyone brought his ox that night and slaughtered it there. 35Then Saul built an altar to the Lord; it was the first time he had done this.

36Saul said, "Let us go down and pursue the Philistines by night and plunder them till dawn, and let us not leave one of them alive."

"Do whatever seems best to you," they replied.

But the priest said, "Let us inquire of God here."

37So Saul asked God, "Shall I go down and pursue the Philistines? Will you give them into Israel's hand?" But God did not answer him that day.

38Saul therefore said, "Come here, all you who are leaders of the army, and let us find out what sin has been committed today. 39As surely as the Lord who rescues Israel lives, even if the guilt lies with my son Jonathan, he must die." But not one of them said a word.

40Saul then said to all the Israelites, "You stand over there; I and Jonathan my son will stand over here."

"Do what seems best to you," they replied.

41Then Saul prayed to the Lord, the God of Israel, "Why have you not answered your servant today? If the fault is in me or my son Jonathan, respond with Urim, but if the men of Israel are at fault,*a* respond with Thummim." Jonathan and Saul were taken by lot, and the men were cleared.

42Saul said, "Cast the lot between me and Jonathan my son." And Jonathan was taken.

43Then Saul said to Jonathan, "Tell me what you have done."

So Jonathan told him, "I tasted a little honey with the end of my staff. And now I must die!"

44Saul said, "May God deal with me, be it ever so severely, if you do not die, Jonathan."

45But the men said to Saul, "Should Jonathan die—he who has brought about this great deliverance in Israel? Never! As surely as the Lord lives, not a hair of his head will fall to the ground, for he did this today with God's help." So the men rescued Jonathan, and he was not put to death.

46Then Saul stopped pursuing the Philistines, and they withdrew to their own land.

47After Saul had assumed rule over Israel, he fought against their enemies on every side: Moab, the Ammonites, Edom, the kings*b* of Zobah, and the Philistines. Wherever he turned, he inflicted punishment on them.*c* 48He fought valiantly and defeated the Amalekites, delivering Israel from the hands of those who had plundered them.

### Saul's Family

49Saul's sons were Jonathan, Ishvi and Malki-Shua. The name of his older daughter was Merab, and that of

## Amplified Bible

29Then Jonathan said, My father has troubled the land. See how my eyes have brightened because I tasted a little of this honey.

30How much better if the men had eaten freely today of the spoil of their enemies which they found! For now the slaughter of the Philistines has not been great.

31They smote the Philistines that day from Michmash to Aijalon. And the people were very faint.

32[When night came and the oath expired] the men flew upon the spoil. They took sheep, oxen, and calves, slew them on the ground, and ate them [raw] with the blood.

33Then Saul was told, Behold, the men are sinning against the Lord by eating with the blood. And he said, You have transgressed; roll a great stone to me here.

34Saul said, Disperse yourselves among the people and tell them, Bring me every man his ox or his sheep, and butcher them here and eat; and sin not against the Lord by eating the blood. So all the men brought each one his ox that night and butchered it there.

35And Saul built an altar to the Lord; it was the first altar he built to the Lord.

36Then Saul said, Let us go down after the Philistines by night and seize and plunder them until daylight, and let us not leave a man of them. They said, Do whatever seems good to you. Then the priest said, Let us draw near here to God.

37And Saul asked counsel of God, Shall I go down after the Philistines? Will You deliver them into the hand of Israel? But He did not answer him that day.

38Then Saul said, Draw near, all the chiefs of the people, and let us see how this sin [causing God's silence] arose today.

39For as the Lord lives, Who delivers Israel, though it be in Jonathan my son, he shall surely die. But not a man among all the people answered him.

40Then he said to all Israel, You be on one side; and I and Jonathan my son will be on the other side. The people said to Saul, Do what seems good to you.

41Therefore Saul said to the Lord, the God of Israel, Give a perfect lot *and* show the right. And Saul and Jonathan were taken [by lot], but the other men went free.

42Saul said, Cast lots between me and Jonathan my son. And Jonathan was taken.

43Saul said to Jonathan, Tell me what you have done. And Jonathan said, I tasted a little honey with the end of the rod that was in my hand. And behold, I must die.

44Saul answered, May God do so, and more also, for you shall surely die, Jonathan.

45But the people said to Saul, Shall Jonathan, who has wrought this great deliverance to Israel, die? God forbid! As the Lord lives, there shall not one hair of his head perish, for he has wrought this great deliverance with God this day. So the people rescued Jonathan, and he did not die.

46Then Saul ceased pursuing the Philistines, and they went to their own place.

47When Saul took over the kingdom of Israel, he fought against all his enemies on every side: Moab, the Ammonites, Edom, the kings of Zobah, and the Philistines. Wherever he turned, he made it worse for them.

48He did valiantly and smote the Amalekites, and delivered Israel out of the hands of those who plundered them.

49Now Saul's sons were Jonathan, Ishvi, and Malchishua; and the names of his two daughters were, of the firstborn, Merab; and of the younger, Michal.

---

*a* 41 Septuagint; Hebrew does not have *"Why . . . at fault.*
*b* 47 Masoretic Text; Dead Sea Scrolls and Septuagint *king*
*c* 47 Hebrew; Septuagint *he was victorious*

## New International Version

the younger was Michal. [50]His wife's name was Ahinoam daughter of Ahimaaz. The name of the commander of Saul's army was Abner son of Ner, and Ner was Saul's uncle. [51]Saul's father Kish and Abner's father Ner were sons of Abiel.

[52]All the days of Saul there was bitter war with the Philistines, and whenever Saul saw a mighty or brave man, he took him into his service.

### The Lord Rejects Saul as King

**15** Samuel said to Saul, "I am the one the Lord sent to anoint you king over his people Israel; so listen now to the message from the Lord. [2]This is what the Lord Almighty says: 'I will punish the Amalekites for what they did to Israel when they waylaid them as they came up from Egypt. [3]Now go, attack the Amalekites and totally destroy[a] all that belongs to them. Do not spare them; put to death men and women, children and infants, cattle and sheep, camels and donkeys.'"

[4]So Saul summoned the men and mustered them at Telaim—two hundred thousand foot soldiers and ten thousand from Judah. [5]Saul went to the city of Amalek and set an ambush in the ravine. [6]Then he said to the Kenites, "Go away, leave the Amalekites so that I do not destroy you along with them; for you showed kindness to all the Israelites when they came up out of Egypt." So the Kenites moved away from the Amalekites.

[7]Then Saul attacked the Amalekites all the way from Havilah to Shur, near the eastern border of Egypt. [8]He took Agag king of the Amalekites alive, and all his people he totally destroyed with the sword. [9]But Saul and the army spared Agag and the best of the sheep and cattle, the fat calves[b] and lambs—everything that was good. These they were unwilling to destroy completely, but everything that was despised and weak they totally destroyed.

[10]Then the word of the Lord came to Samuel: [11]"I regret that I have made Saul king, because he has turned away from me and has not carried out my instructions." Samuel was angry, and he cried out to the Lord all that night.

[12]Early in the morning Samuel got up and went to meet Saul, but he was told, "Saul has gone to Carmel. There he has set up a monument in his own honor and has turned and gone on down to Gilgal."

[13]When Samuel reached him, Saul said, "The Lord bless you! I have carried out the Lord's instructions."

[14]But Samuel said, "What then is this bleating of sheep in my ears? What is this lowing of cattle that I hear?"

[15]Saul answered, "The soldiers brought them from the Amalekites; they spared the best of the sheep and cattle to sacrifice to the Lord your God, but we totally destroyed the rest."

[16]"Enough!" Samuel said to Saul. "Let me tell you what the Lord said to me last night."

"Tell me," Saul replied.

[17]Samuel said, "Although you were once small in your own eyes, did you not become the head of the tribes of Israel? The Lord anointed you king over Israel. [18]And he sent you on a mission, saying, 'Go and completely destroy those wicked people, the Amalekites; wage war against them until you have wiped them out.' [19]Why did you not obey the Lord? Why did you pounce on the plunder and do evil in the eyes of the Lord?"

## Amplified Bible

[50]The name of Saul's wife was Ahinoam daughter of Ahimaaz. The commander of his army was Abner son of Ner, Saul's uncle.

[51]Kish the father of Saul and Ner the father of Abner were sons of Abiel.

[52]There was severe war against the Philistines all the days of Saul, and whenever Saul saw any mighty or [outstandingly] courageous man, he attached him to himself.

**15** Samuel told Saul, The Lord sent me to anoint you king over His people Israel. Now listen and heed the words of the Lord.

[2]Thus says the Lord of hosts, I have considered *and* will punish what Amalek did to Israel, how he set himself against him in the way when [Israel] came out of Egypt.

[3]Now go and smite Amalek and utterly destroy all they have; do not spare them, but kill both man and woman, infant and suckling, ox and sheep, camel and donkey.

[4]So Saul assembled the men and numbered them at Telaim—200,000 men on foot and 10,000 men of Judah.

[5]And Saul came to the city of Amalek and laid wait in the valley.

[6]Saul warned the Kenites, Go, depart, get down from among the Amalekites, lest I destroy you with them; for you showed kindness to all the Israelites when they came up out of Egypt. So the Kenites departed from among the Amalekites.

[7]Saul smote the Amalekites from Havilah as far as Shur, which is east of Egypt.

[8]And he took Agag king of the Amalekites alive, though he utterly destroyed all the rest of the people with the sword.

[9]Saul and the people spared Agag and the best of the sheep, oxen, fatlings, lambs, and all that was good, and would not utterly destroy them; but all that was undesirable or worthless they destroyed utterly.

[10]Then the word of the Lord came to Samuel, saying,

[11]I regret making Saul king, for he has turned back from following Me and has not performed My commands. And Samuel was grieved *and* angry [with Saul], and he cried to the Lord all night.

[12]When Samuel rose early to meet Saul in the morning, he was told, Saul came to Carmel, and behold, he set up for himself a monument or trophy [of his victory] and passed on and went down to Gilgal.

[13]And Samuel came to Saul, and Saul said to him, Blessed are you of the Lord. I have performed what the Lord ordered.

[14]And Samuel said, What then means this bleating of the sheep in my ears, and the lowing of the oxen which I hear?

[15]Saul said, They have brought them from the Amalekites; for the people spared the best of the sheep and oxen to sacrifice to the Lord your God, but the rest we have utterly destroyed.

[16]Then Samuel said to Saul, Stop! I will tell you what the Lord said to me tonight. Saul said to him, Say on.

[17]Samuel said, When you were small in your own sight, were you not made the head of the tribes of Israel, and the Lord anointed you king over Israel?

[18]And the Lord sent you on a mission and said, Go, utterly destroy the sinners, the Amalekites; and fight against them until they are consumed.

[19]Why then did you not obey the voice of the Lord, but swooped down upon the plunder and did evil in the Lord's sight?

---

[a] 3 The Hebrew term refers to the irrevocable giving over of things or persons to the Lord, often by totally destroying them; also in verses 8, 9, 15, 18, 20 and 21.  [b] 9 Or *the grown bulls*; the meaning of the Hebrew for this phrase is uncertain.

## New International Version

20 "But I did obey the Lord," Saul said. "I went on the mission the Lord assigned me. I completely destroyed the Amalekites and brought back Agag their king. 21 The soldiers took sheep and cattle from the plunder, the best of what was devoted to God, in order to sacrifice them to the Lord your God at Gilgal."
22 But Samuel replied:

"Does the Lord delight in burnt offerings and sacrifices
    as much as in obeying the Lord?
To obey is better than sacrifice,
    and to heed is better than the fat of rams.
23 For rebellion is like the sin of divination,
    and arrogance like the evil of idolatry.
Because you have rejected the word of the Lord,
    he has rejected you as king."

24 Then Saul said to Samuel, "I have sinned. I violated the Lord's command and your instructions. I was afraid of the men and so I gave in to them. 25 Now I beg you, forgive my sin and come back with me, so that I may worship the Lord."
26 But Samuel said to him, "I will not go back with you. You have rejected the word of the Lord, and the Lord has rejected you as king over Israel!"
27 As Samuel turned to leave, Saul caught hold of the hem of his robe, and it tore. 28 Samuel said to him, "The Lord has torn the kingdom of Israel from you today and has given it to one of your neighbors—to one better than you. 29 He who is the Glory of Israel does not lie or change his mind; for he is not a human being, that he should change his mind."
30 Saul replied, "I have sinned. But please honor me before the elders of my people and before Israel; come back with me, so that I may worship the Lord your God." 31 So Samuel went back with Saul, and Saul worshiped the Lord.
32 Then Samuel said, "Bring me Agag king of the Amalekites."

Agag came to him in chains.[a] And he thought, "Surely the bitterness of death is past."
33 But Samuel said,

"As your sword has made women childless,
    so will your mother be childless among women."

And Samuel put Agag to death before the Lord at Gilgal.
34 Then Samuel left for Ramah, but Saul went up to his home in Gibeah of Saul. 35 Until the day Samuel died, he did not go to see Saul again, though Samuel mourned for him. And the Lord regretted that he had made Saul king over Israel.

### Samuel Anoints David

**16** The Lord said to Samuel, "How long will you mourn for Saul, since I have rejected him as king over Israel? Fill your horn with oil and be on your way; I am sending you to Jesse of Bethlehem. I have chosen one of his sons to be king."
2 But Samuel said, "How can I go? If Saul hears about it, he will kill me."

The Lord said, "Take a heifer with you and say, 'I have come to sacrifice to the Lord.' 3 Invite Jesse to the sacrifice, and I will show you what to do. You are to anoint for me the one I indicate."
4 Samuel did what the Lord said. When he arrived at Bethlehem, the elders of the town trembled when they met him. They asked, "Do you come in peace?"
5 Samuel replied, "Yes, in peace; I have come to sacrifice to the Lord. Consecrate yourselves and come to the sacrifice with me." Then he consecrated Jesse and his sons and invited them to the sacrifice.

## Amplified Bible

20 Saul said to Samuel, Yes, I have obeyed the voice of the Lord and have gone the way which the Lord sent me, and have brought Agag king of Amalek and have utterly destroyed the Amalekites.
21 But the people took from the spoil sheep and oxen, the chief of the things to be utterly destroyed, to sacrifice to the Lord your God in Gilgal.
22 Samuel said, Has the Lord as great a delight in burnt offerings and sacrifices as in obeying the voice of the Lord? Behold, to obey is better than sacrifice, and to hearken than the fat of rams.
23 For rebellion is as the sin of witchcraft, and stubbornness is as idolatry and teraphim (household good luck images). Because you have rejected the word of the Lord, He also has rejected you from being king.
24 And Saul said to Samuel, I have sinned; for I have transgressed the commandment of the Lord and your words, because I feared the people and obeyed their voice.
25 Now, I pray you, pardon my sin and go back with me, that I may worship the Lord.
26 And Samuel said to Saul, I will not return with you; for you have rejected the word of the Lord, and the Lord has rejected you from being king over Israel.
27 And as Samuel turned to go away, Saul seized the skirt of Samuel's mantle, and it tore.
28 And Samuel said to him, The Lord has torn the kingdom of Israel from you this day and has given it to a neighbor of yours who is better than you.
29 And also the Strength of Israel will not lie or repent; for He is not a man, that He should repent.
30 Saul said, I have sinned; yet honor me now, I pray you, before the elders of my people and before Israel, and return with me, that I may worship the Lord your God.
31 So Samuel turned back after Saul, and Saul worshiped the Lord.
32 Then Samuel said, Bring here to me Agag king of the Amalekites. And Agag came to him cheerfully. And Agag said, Surely the bitterness of death is past.
33 Samuel said, As your sword has made women childless, so shall your mother be childless among women. And Samuel hewed Agag in pieces before the Lord in Gilgal.
34 Then Samuel went to Ramah, but Saul went up to his house in Gibeah of Saul.
35 And Samuel came no more to see Saul until the day of his death, though Samuel grieved over Saul. And the Lord repented that He had made Saul king over Israel.

**16** The Lord said to Samuel, How long will you mourn for Saul, seeing I have rejected him from reigning over Israel? Fill your horn with oil; I will send you to Jesse the Bethlehemite. For I have provided for Myself a king among his sons.
2 Samuel said, How can I go? If Saul hears it, he will kill me. And the Lord said, Take a heifer with you and say, I have come to sacrifice to the Lord.
3 And invite Jesse to the sacrifice, and I will show you what you shall do; and you shall anoint for Me the one I name to you.
4 And Samuel did what the Lord said, and came to Bethlehem. And the elders of the town trembled at his coming and said, Have you come peaceably?
5 And he said, Peaceably; I have come to sacrifice to the Lord. Consecrate yourselves and come with me to the sacrifice. And he consecrated Jesse and his sons and called them to the sacrifice.

---

*a 32 The meaning of the Hebrew for this phrase is uncertain.

## New International Version

6When they arrived, Samuel saw Eliab and thought, "Surely the LORD's anointed stands here before the LORD." 7But the LORD said to Samuel, "Do not consider his appearance or his height, for I have rejected him. The LORD does not look at the things people look at. People look at the outward appearance, but the LORD looks at the heart." 8Then Jesse called Abinadab and had him pass in front of Samuel. But Samuel said, "The LORD has not chosen this one either." 9Jesse then had Shammah pass by, but Samuel said, "Nor has the LORD chosen this one." 10Jesse had seven of his sons pass before Samuel, but Samuel said to him, "The LORD has not chosen these." 11So he asked Jesse, "Are these all the sons you have?"

"There is still the youngest," Jesse answered. "He is tending the sheep."

Samuel said, "Send for him; we will not sit down until he arrives."

12So he sent for him and had him brought in. He was glowing with health and had a fine appearance and handsome features.

Then the LORD said, "Rise and anoint him; this is the one."

13So Samuel took the horn of oil and anointed him in the presence of his brothers, and from that day on the Spirit of the LORD came powerfully upon David. Samuel then went to Ramah.

### David in Saul's Service

14Now the Spirit of the LORD had departed from Saul, and an evil[a] spirit from the LORD tormented him. 15Saul's attendants said to him, "See, an evil spirit from God is tormenting you. 16Let our lord command his servants here to search for someone who can play the lyre. He will play when the evil spirit from God comes on you, and you will feel better."

17So Saul said to his attendants, "Find someone who plays well and bring him to me."

18One of the servants answered, "I have seen a son of Jesse of Bethlehem who knows how to play the lyre. He is a brave man and a warrior. He speaks well and is a fine-looking man. And the LORD is with him."

19Then Saul sent messengers to Jesse and said, "Send me your son David, who is with the sheep." 20So Jesse took a donkey loaded with bread, a skin of wine and a young goat and sent them with his son David to Saul.

21David came to Saul and entered his service. Saul liked him very much, and David became one of his armor-bearers. 22Then Saul sent word to Jesse, saying, "Allow David to remain in my service, for I am pleased with him."

23Whenever the spirit from God came on Saul, David would take up his lyre and play. Then relief would come to Saul; he would feel better, and the evil spirit would leave him.

### David and Goliath

**17** Now the Philistines gathered their forces for war and assembled at Sokoh in Judah. They pitched camp at Ephes Dammim, between Sokoh and Azekah. 2Saul and the Israelites assembled and camped in the Valley of Elah and drew up their battle line to meet the Philistines. 3The Philistines occupied one hill and the Israelites another, with the valley between them.

4A champion named Goliath, who was from Gath, came out of the Philistine camp. His height was six cubits and

## Amplified Bible

6When they had come, he looked on Eliab [the eldest son] and said, Surely the Lord's anointed is before Him. 7But the Lord said to Samuel, Look not on his appearance or at the height of his stature, for I have rejected him. For the Lord sees not as man sees; for man looks on the outward appearance, but the Lord looks on the heart. 8Then Jesse called Abinadab and made him pass before Samuel. But Samuel said, Neither has the Lord chosen this one. 9Then Jesse made Shammah pass by. Samuel said, Nor has the Lord chosen him. 10Jesse made seven of his sons pass before Samuel. And Samuel said to Jesse, The Lord has not chosen any of these. 11Then [he] said to Jesse, Are all your sons here? [Jesse] said, There is yet the youngest; he is tending the sheep. Samuel said to Jesse, Send for him; for we will not sit down until he is here.

12Jesse sent and brought him. David had a healthy reddish complexion and beautiful eyes, and was fine-looking. The Lord said [to Samuel], Arise, anoint him; this is he. 13Then Samuel took the horn of oil and anointed David in the midst of his brothers; and the Spirit of the Lord came mightily upon David from that day forward. And Samuel arose and went to Ramah.

14But the Spirit of the Lord departed from Saul, and an evil spirit from the Lord tormented and troubled him. 15Saul's servants said to him, Behold, an evil spirit from God torments you. 16Let our lord now command your servants here before you to find a man who plays skillfully on the lyre; and when the evil spirit from God is upon you, he will play it, and you will be well. 17Saul told his servants, Find me a man who plays well and bring him to me. 18One of the young men said, I have seen a son of Jesse the Bethlehemite who plays skillfully, a valiant man, a man of war, prudent in speech and eloquent, an attractive person; and the Lord is with him. 19So Saul sent messengers to Jesse and said, Send me David your son, who is with the sheep. 20And Jesse took a donkey loaded with bread, a skin of wine, and a kid and sent them by David his son to Saul. 21And David came to Saul and served him. Saul became very fond of him, and he became his armor-bearer. 22Saul sent to Jesse, saying, Let David remain in my service, for he pleases me. 23And when the evil spirit from God was upon Saul, David took a lyre and played it; so Saul was refreshed and became well, and the evil spirit left him.

**17** Now the Philistines gathered their armies for battle and were assembled at Socoh, which belongs to Judah, and encamped between Socoh and Azekah in Ephes-dammim. 2Saul and the men of Israel were encamped in the Valley of Elah and drew up in battle array against the Philistines. 3And the Philistines stood on a mountain on one side and Israel stood on a mountain on the other side, with the valley between them. 4And a champion went out of the camp of the Philistines named Goliath of Gath, whose height was six cubits and a span [almost ten feet].

---

[a] 14 Or *and a harmful*; similarly in verses 15, 16 and 23

## New International Version

a span.*a* 5He had a bronze helmet on his head and wore a coat of scale armor of bronze weighing five thousand shekels*b*; 6on his legs he wore bronze greaves, and a bronze javelin was slung on his back. 7His spear shaft was like a weaver's rod, and its iron point weighed six hundred shekels.*c* His shield bearer went ahead of him.

8Goliath stood and shouted to the ranks of Israel, "Why do you come out and line up for battle? Am I not a Philistine, and are you not the servants of Saul? Choose a man and have him come down to me. 9If he is able to fight and kill me, we will become your subjects; but if I overcome him and kill him, you will become our subjects and serve us." 10Then the Philistine said, "This day I defy the armies of Israel! Give me a man and let us fight each other." 11On hearing the Philistine's words, Saul and all the Israelites were dismayed and terrified.

12Now David was the son of an Ephrathite named Jesse, who was from Bethlehem in Judah. Jesse had eight sons, and in Saul's time he was very old. 13Jesse's three oldest sons had followed Saul to the war: The firstborn was Eliab; the second, Abinadab; and the third, Shammah. 14David was the youngest. The three oldest followed Saul, 15but David went back and forth from Saul to tend his father's sheep at Bethlehem.

16For forty days the Philistine came forward every morning and evening and took his stand.

17Now Jesse said to his son David, "Take this ephah*d* of roasted grain and these ten loaves of bread for your brothers and hurry to their camp. 18Take along these ten cheeses to the commander of their unit. See how your brothers are and bring back some assurance*e* from them. 19They are with Saul and all the men of Israel in the Valley of Elah, fighting against the Philistines."

20Early in the morning David left the flock in the care of a shepherd, loaded up and set out, as Jesse had directed. He reached the camp as the army was going out to its battle positions, shouting the war cry. 21Israel and the Philistines were drawing up their lines facing each other. 22David left his things with the keeper of supplies, ran to the battle lines and asked his brothers how they were. 23As he was talking with them, Goliath, the Philistine champion from Gath, stepped out from his lines and shouted his usual defiance, and David heard it. 24Whenever the Israelites saw the man, they all fled from him in great fear.

25Now the Israelites had been saying, "Do you see how this man keeps coming out? He comes out to defy Israel. The king will give great wealth to the man who kills him. He will also give him his daughter in marriage and will exempt his family from taxes in Israel."

26David asked the men standing near him, "What will be done for the man who kills this Philistine and removes this disgrace from Israel? Who is this uncircumcised Philistine that he should defy the armies of the living God?" 27They repeated to him what they had been saying and told him, "This is what will be done for the man who kills him."

## Amplified Bible

5And he had a bronze helmet on his head and wore a coat of mail, and the coat weighed 5,000 shekels of bronze.

6He had bronze shin armor on his legs and a bronze javelin across his shoulders.

7And the shaft of his spear was like a weaver's beam; his spear's head weighed 600 shekels of iron. And a shield bearer went before him.

8Goliath stood and shouted to the ranks of Israel, Why have you come out to draw up for battle? Am I not a Philistine, and are you not servants of Saul? Choose a man for yourselves and let him come down to me.

9If he is able to fight with me and kill me, then we will be your servants; but if I prevail against him and kill him, then you shall be our servants and serve us.

10And the Philistine said, I defy the ranks of Israel this day; give me a man, that we may fight together.

11When Saul and all Israel heard those words of the Philistine, they were dismayed and greatly afraid.

12David was the son of an Ephrathite of Bethlehem in Judah named Jesse, who had eight sons. [Jesse] in the days of Saul was old, advanced in years.

13[His] three eldest sons had followed Saul into battle. Their names were Eliab the firstborn; next, Abinadab; and third, Shammah.

14David was the youngest. The three eldest followed Saul,

15But David went back and forth from Saul to feed his father's sheep at Bethlehem.

16The Philistine came out morning and evening, presenting himself for forty days.

17And Jesse said to David his son, Take for your brothers an ephah of this parched grain and these ten loaves and carry them quickly to your brothers at the camp.

18Also take these ten cheeses to the commander of their thousand. See how your brothers fare and bring some token from them.

19Now Saul and the brothers and all the men of Israel were in the Valley of Elah, fighting with the Philistines.

20So David rose up early next morning, left the sheep with a keeper, took the provisions, and went, as Jesse had commanded him. And he came to the encampment as the host going forth to the battleground shouted the battle cry.

21And Israel and the Philistines put the battle in array, army against army.

22David left his packages in the care of the baggage keeper and ran into the ranks and came and greeted his brothers.

23As they talked, behold, Goliath, the champion, the Philistine of Gath, came forth from the Philistine ranks and spoke the same words as before, and David heard him.

24And all the men of Israel, when they saw the man, fled from him, terrified.

25And the Israelites said, Have you seen this man who has come out? Surely he has come out to defy Israel; and the man who kills him the king will enrich with great riches, and will give him his daughter and make his father's house free [from taxes and service] in Israel.

26And David said to the men standing by him, What shall be done for the man who kills this Philistine and takes away the reproach from Israel? For who is this uncircumcised Philistine that he should defy the armies of the living God?

27And the [men] told him, Thus shall it be done for the man who kills him.

---

*a 4* That is, about 9 feet 9 inches or about 3 meters  *b 5* That is, about 125 pounds or about 58 kilograms  *c 7* That is, about 15 pounds or about 6.9 kilograms  *d 17* That is, probably about 36 pounds or about 16 kilograms  *e 18* Or *some token; or some pledge of spoils*

## New International Version

28When Eliab, David's oldest brother, heard him speaking with the men, he burned with anger at him and asked, "Why have you come down here? And with whom did you leave those few sheep in the wilderness? I know how conceited you are and how wicked your heart is; you came down only to watch the battle."

29"Now what have I done?" said David. "Can't I even speak?" 30He then turned away to someone else and brought up the same matter, and the men answered him as before. 31What David said was overheard and reported to Saul, and Saul sent for him.

32David said to Saul, "Let no one lose heart on account of this Philistine; your servant will go and fight him."

33Saul replied, "You are not able to go out against this Philistine and fight him; you are only a young man, and he has been a warrior from his youth."

34But David said to Saul, "Your servant has been keeping his father's sheep. When a lion or a bear came and carried off a sheep from the flock, 35I went after it, struck it and rescued the sheep from its mouth. When it turned on me, I seized it by its hair, struck it and killed it. 36Your servant has killed both the lion and the bear; this uncircumcised Philistine will be like one of them, because he has defied the armies of the living God. 37The LORD who rescued me from the paw of the lion and the paw of the bear will rescue me from the hand of this Philistine."

Saul said to David, "Go, and the LORD be with you."

38Then Saul dressed David in his own tunic. He put a coat of armor on him and a bronze helmet on his head. 39David fastened on his sword over the tunic and tried walking around, because he was not used to them.

"I cannot go in these," he said to Saul, "because I am not used to them." So he took them off. 40Then he took his staff in his hand, chose five smooth stones from the stream, put them in the pouch of his shepherd's bag and, with his sling in his hand, approached the Philistine.

41Meanwhile, the Philistine, with his shield bearer in front of him, kept coming closer to David. 42He looked David over and saw that he was little more than a boy, glowing with health and handsome, and he despised him. 43He said to David, "Am I a dog, that you come at me with sticks?" And the Philistine cursed David by his gods. 44"Come here," he said, "and I'll give your flesh to the birds and the wild animals!"

45David said to the Philistine, "You come against me with sword and spear and javelin, but I come against you in the name of the LORD Almighty, the God of the armies of Israel, whom you have defied. 46This day the LORD will deliver you into my hands, and I'll strike you down and cut off your head. This very day I will give the carcasses of the Philistine army to the birds and the wild animals, and the whole world will know that there is a God in Israel. 47All those gathered here will know that it is not by sword or spear that the LORD saves; for the battle is the LORD's, and he will give all of you into our hands."

48As the Philistine moved closer to attack him, David ran quickly toward the battle line to meet him. 49Reaching into his bag and taking out a stone, he slung it and

## Amplified Bible

28Now Eliab his eldest brother heard what he said to the men; and Eliab's anger was kindled against David and he said, Why did you come here? With whom have you left those few sheep in the wilderness? I know your presumption and evilness of heart; for you came down that you might see the battle.

29And David said, What have I done now? Was it not a harmless question?

30And David turned away from Eliab to another and he asked the same question, and again the men gave him the same answer.

31When David's words were heard, they were repeated to Saul, and he sent for him.

32David said to Saul, Let no man's heart fail because of this Philistine; your servant will go out and fight with him.

33And Saul said to David, You are not able to go to fight against this Philistine. You are only an adolescent, and he has been a warrior from his youth.

34And David said to Saul, Your servant kept his father's sheep. And when there came a lion or again a bear and took a lamb out of the flock,

35I went out after it and smote it and delivered the lamb out of its mouth; and when it arose against me, I caught it by its beard and smote it and killed it.

36Your servant killed both the lion and the bear; and this uncircumcised Philistine shall be like one of them, for he has defied the armies of the living God!

37David said, The Lord Who delivered me out of the paw of the lion and out of the paw of the bear, He will deliver me out of the hand of this Philistine. And Saul said to David, Go, and the Lord be with you!

38Then Saul clothed David with his armor; he put a bronze helmet on his head and clothed him with a coat of mail.

39And David girded his sword over his armor. Then he tried to go, but could not, for he was not used to it. And David said to Saul, I cannot go with these, for I am not used to them. And David took them off.

40Then he took his staff in his hand and chose five smooth stones out of the brook and put them in his shepherd's bag [a whole kid's skin slung from his shoulder], in his pouch, and his sling was in his hand, and he drew near the Philistine.

41The Philistine came on and drew near to David, the man who bore the shield going before him.

42And when the Philistine looked around and saw David, he scorned *and* despised him, for he was but an adolescent, with a healthy reddish color and a fair face.

43And the Philistine said to David, Am I a dog, that you should come to me with sticks? And the Philistine cursed David by his gods.

44The Philistine said to David, Come to me, and I will give your flesh to the birds of the air and the beasts of the field.

45Then said David to the Philistine, You come to me with a sword, a spear, and a javelin, but I come to you in the name of the Lord of hosts, the God of the ranks of Israel, Whom you have defied.

46This day the Lord will deliver you into my hand, and I will smite you and cut off your head. And I will give the corpses of the army of the Philistines this day to the birds of the air and the wild beasts of the earth, that all the earth may know that there is a God in Israel.

47And all this assembly shall know that the Lord saves not with sword and spear; for the battle is the Lord's, and He will give you into our hands.

48When the Philistine came forward to meet David, David ran quickly toward the battle line to meet the Philistine.

49David put his hand into his bag and took out a stone

## New International Version

struck the Philistine on the forehead. The stone sank into his forehead, and he fell facedown on the ground.

⁵⁰So David triumphed over the Philistine with a sling and a stone; without a sword in his hand he struck down the Philistine and killed him.

⁵¹David ran and stood over him. He took hold of the Philistine's sword and drew it from the sheath. After he killed him, he cut off his head with the sword.

When the Philistines saw that their hero was dead, they turned and ran. ⁵²Then the men of Israel and Judah surged forward with a shout and pursued the Philistines to the entrance of Gath*ᵃ* and to the gates of Ekron. Their dead were strewn along the Shaaraim road to Gath and Ekron. ⁵³When the Israelites returned from chasing the Philistines, they plundered their camp.

⁵⁴David took the Philistine's head and brought it to Jerusalem; he put the Philistine's weapons in his own tent.

⁵⁵As Saul watched David going out to meet the Philistine, he said to Abner, commander of the army, "Abner, whose son is that young man?"

Abner replied, "As surely as you live, Your Majesty, I don't know."

⁵⁶The king said, "Find out whose son this young man is."

⁵⁷As soon as David returned from killing the Philistine, Abner took him and brought him before Saul, with David still holding the Philistine's head.

⁵⁸"Whose son are you, young man?" Saul asked him.

David said, "I am the son of your servant Jesse of Bethlehem."

### Saul's Growing Fear of David

**18** After David had finished talking with Saul, Jonathan became one in spirit with David, and he loved him as himself. ²From that day Saul kept David with him and did not let him return home to his family. ³And Jonathan made a covenant with David because he loved him as himself. ⁴Jonathan took off the robe he was wearing and gave it to David, along with his tunic, and even his sword, his bow and his belt.

⁵Whatever mission Saul sent him on, David was so successful that Saul gave him a high rank in the army. This pleased all the troops, and Saul's officers as well.

⁶When the men were returning home after David had killed the Philistine, the women came out from all the towns of Israel to meet King Saul with singing and dancing, with joyful songs and with timbrels and lyres. ⁷As they danced, they sang:

"Saul has slain his thousands,
    and David his tens of thousands."

⁸Saul was very angry; this refrain displeased him greatly. "They have credited David with tens of thousands," he thought, "but me with only thousands. What more can he get but the kingdom?" ⁹And from that time on Saul kept a close eye on David.

¹⁰The next day an evil*ᵇ* spirit from God came forcefully on Saul. He was prophesying in his house, while David was playing the lyre, as he usually did. Saul had a spear in his hand ¹¹and he hurled it, saying to himself, "I'll pin David to the wall." But David eluded him twice.

¹²Saul was afraid of David, because the LORD was with David but had departed from Saul. ¹³So he sent David

## Amplified Bible

and slung it, and it struck the Philistine, sinking into his forehead, and he fell on his face to the earth.

⁵⁰So David prevailed over the Philistine with a sling and with a stone, and struck down the Philistine and slew him. But no sword was in David's hand.

⁵¹So he ran and stood over the Philistine, took his sword and drew it out of its sheath, and killed him, and cut off his head with it. When the Philistines saw that their mighty champion was dead, they fled.

⁵²And the men of Israel and Judah rose with a shout and pursued the Philistines as far as Gath and the gates of Ekron. So the wounded Philistines fell along the way from Shaaraim as far as Gath and Ekron.

⁵³The Israelites returned from their pursuit of the Philistines and plundered their tents.

⁵⁴David took the head of the Philistine and brought it to Jerusalem, but he put his armor in his tent.

⁵⁵When Saul saw David go out against the Philistine, he said to Abner, the captain of the host, Abner, whose son is this youth? And Abner said, As your soul lives, O king, I cannot tell.

⁵⁶And the king said, Inquire whose son the stripling is.

⁵⁷When David returned from killing Goliath the Philistine, Abner brought him before Saul with the head of the Philistine in his hand.

⁵⁸And Saul said to him, Whose son are you, young man? And David answered, I am the son of your servant Jesse of Bethlehem.

**18** When David had finished speaking to Saul, the soul of Jonathan was knit with the soul of David, and Jonathan loved him as his own life.

²Saul took David that day and would not let him return to his father's house.

³Then Jonathan made a covenant with David, because he loved him as his own life.

⁴And Jonathan stripped himself of the robe that was on him and gave it to David, and his armor, even his sword, his bow, and his girdle.

⁵And David went out wherever Saul sent him, and he prospered *and* behaved himself wisely; and Saul set him over the men of war. And it was satisfactory both to the people and to Saul's servants.

⁶As they were coming home, when David returned from killing the Philistine, the women came out of all the Israelite towns, singing and dancing, to meet King Saul with timbrels, songs of joy, and instruments of music.

⁷And the women responded as they laughed *and* frolicked, saying, Saul has slain his thousands, and David his ten thousands.

⁸And Saul was very angry, for the saying displeased him; and he said, They have ascribed to David ten thousands, but to me they have ascribed only thousands. What more can he have but the kingdom?

⁹And Saul [jealously] eyed David from that day forward.

¹⁰The next day an evil spirit from God came mightily upon Saul, and he raved [madly] in his house, while David played [the lyre] with his hand, as at other times; and there was a javelin in Saul's hand.

¹¹And Saul cast the javelin, for he thought, I will pin David to the wall. And David evaded him twice.

¹²Saul was afraid of David, because the Lord was with him but had departed from Saul.

¹³So Saul removed David from him and made him his

---

*ᵃ 52* Some Septuagint manuscripts; Hebrew *of a valley*    *ᵇ 10* Or *a harmful*

## New International Version

away from him and gave him command over a thousand men, and David led the troops in their campaigns. ¹⁴In everything he did he had great success, because the LORD was with him. ¹⁵When Saul saw how successful he was, he was afraid of him. ¹⁶But all Israel and Judah loved David, because he led them in their campaigns.

¹⁷Saul said to David, "Here is my older daughter Merab. I will give her to you in marriage; only serve me bravely and fight the battles of the LORD." For Saul said to himself, "I will not raise a hand against him. Let the Philistines do that!"

¹⁸But David said to Saul, "Who am I, and what is my family or my clan in Israel, that I should become the king's son-in-law?" ¹⁹So[a] when the time came for Merab, Saul's daughter, to be given to David, she was given in marriage to Adriel of Meholah.

²⁰Now Saul's daughter Michal was in love with David, and when they told Saul about it, he was pleased. ²¹"I will give her to him," he thought, "so that she may be a snare to him and so that the hand of the Philistines may be against him." So Saul said to David, "Now you have a second opportunity to become my son-in-law."

²²Then Saul ordered his attendants: "Speak to David privately and say, 'Look, the king likes you, and his attendants all love you; now become his son-in-law.'"

²³They repeated these words to David. But David said, "Do you think it is a small matter to become the king's son-in-law? I'm only a poor man and little known."

²⁴When Saul's servants told him what David had said, ²⁵Saul replied, "Say to David, 'The king wants no other price for the bride than a hundred Philistine foreskins, to take revenge on his enemies.'" Saul's plan was to have David fall by the hands of the Philistines.

²⁶When the attendants told David these things, he was pleased to become the king's son-in-law. So before the allotted time elapsed, ²⁷David took his men with him and went out and killed two hundred Philistines and brought back their foreskins. They counted out the full number to the king so that David might become the king's son-in-law. Then Saul gave him his daughter Michal in marriage.

²⁸When Saul realized that the LORD was with David and that his daughter Michal loved David, ²⁹Saul became still more afraid of him, and he remained his enemy the rest of his days.

³⁰The Philistine commanders continued to go out to battle, and as often as they did, David met with more success than the rest of Saul's officers, and his name became well known.

### Saul Tries to Kill David

**19** Saul told his son Jonathan and all the attendants to kill David. But Jonathan had taken a great liking to David ²and warned him, "My father Saul is looking for a chance to kill you. Be on your guard tomorrow morning; go into hiding and stay there. ³I'll go out and stand with my father in the field where you are. I'll speak to him about you and will tell you what I find out."

⁴Jonathan spoke well of David to Saul his father and said to him, "Let not the king do wrong to his servant David;

## Amplified Bible

commander over a thousand; and he went out and came in before the people.

¹⁴David acted wisely in all his ways *and* succeeded, and the Lord was with him.

¹⁵When Saul saw how capable *and* successful David was, he stood in awe of him.

¹⁶But all Israel and Judah loved David, for he went out and came in before them.

¹⁷Saul said to David, My elder daughter Merab I will give you as wife; only serve me courageously and fight the Lord's battles. For Saul thought, Let not my hand, but the Philistines' hand, be upon him.

¹⁸David said to Saul, Who am I, and what is my life or my father's family in Israel, that I should be the king's son-in-law?

¹⁹But at the time when Merab, Saul's daughter, should have been given to David, she was given to Adriel the Meholathite as wife.

²⁰Now Michal, Saul's daughter, loved David; and they told Saul, and it pleased him.

²¹Saul thought, I will give her to him that she may be a snare to him and that the hand of the Philistines may be against him. So Saul said to David a second time, You shall now be my son-in-law.

²²And Saul commanded his servants to speak to David privately and say, The king delights in you, and all his servants love you; now then, become [his] son-in-law.

²³Saul's servants told those words to David. David said, Does it seem to you a light thing to be a king's son-in-law, seeing I am a poor man and lightly esteemed?

²⁴And the servants of Saul told him what David said.

²⁵Saul said, Say this to David, The king wants no dowry but a hundred foreskins of the Philistines, to avenge himself of the king's enemies. But Saul thought to make David fall by the Philistines' hands.

²⁶When his servants told David these words, it pleased [him] well to become the king's son-in-law. Before the days expired,

²⁷David went, he and his men, and slew two hundred Philistine men, and brought their foreskins and gave them in full number to the king, that he might become the king's son-in-law. And Saul gave him Michal his daughter as wife.

²⁸When Saul saw and knew that the Lord was with David and that Michal [his] daughter loved him,

²⁹Saul was still more afraid of David; and Saul became David's constant enemy.

³⁰Then the Philistine princes came out to battle, and when they did so, David had more success *and* behaved himself more wisely than all Saul's servants, so that his name was very dear *and* highly esteemed.

**19** Now Saul told Jonathan his son and all his servants that they must kill David.

²But Jonathan, Saul's son, delighted much in David, and he told David, Saul my father is seeking to kill you. Now therefore, take heed to yourself in the morning, and stay in a secret place and hide yourself.

³And I will go out and stand beside my father in the field where you are; and I will converse with my father about you and if I learn anything, I will tell you.

⁴And Jonathan spoke well of David to Saul his father and said to him, Let not the king sin against his servant

---

## New International Version

he has not wronged you, and what he has done has benefited you greatly. ⁵He took his life in his hands when he killed the Philistine. The LORD won a great victory for all Israel, and you saw it and were glad. Why then would you do wrong to an innocent man like David by killing him for no reason?"

⁶Saul listened to Jonathan and took this oath: "As surely as the LORD lives, David will not be put to death."

⁷So Jonathan called David and told him the whole conversation. He brought him to Saul, and David was with Saul as before.

⁸Once more war broke out, and David went out and fought the Philistines. He struck them with such force that they fled before him.

⁹But an evil[a] spirit from the LORD came on Saul as he was sitting in his house with his spear in his hand. While David was playing the lyre, ¹⁰Saul tried to pin him to the wall with his spear, but David eluded him as Saul drove the spear into the wall. That night David made good his escape.

¹¹Saul sent men to David's house to watch it and to kill him in the morning. But Michal, David's wife, warned him, "If you don't run for your life tonight, tomorrow you'll be killed." ¹²So Michal let David down through a window, and he fled and escaped. ¹³Then Michal took an idol and laid it on the bed, covering it with a garment and putting some goats' hair at the head.

¹⁴When Saul sent the men to capture David, Michal said, "He is ill."

¹⁵Then Saul sent the men back to see David and told them, "Bring him up to me in his bed so that I may kill him." ¹⁶But when the men entered, there was the idol in the bed, and at the head was some goats' hair.

¹⁷Saul said to Michal, "Why did you deceive me like this and send my enemy away so that he escaped?"

Michal told him, "He said to me, 'Let me get away. Why should I kill you?'"

¹⁸When David had fled and made his escape, he went to Samuel at Ramah and told him all that Saul had done to him. Then he and Samuel went to Naioth and stayed there. ¹⁹Word came to Saul: "David is in Naioth at Ramah"; ²⁰so he sent men to capture him. But when they saw a group of prophets prophesying, with Samuel standing there as their leader, the Spirit of God came on Saul's men, and they also prophesied. ²¹Saul was told about it, and he sent more men, and they prophesied too. Saul sent men a third time, and they also prophesied. ²²Finally, he himself left for Ramah and went to the great cistern at Seku. And he asked, "Where are Samuel and David?"

"Over in Naioth at Ramah," they said.

²³So Saul went to Naioth at Ramah. But the Spirit of God came even on him, and he walked along prophesying until he came to Naioth. ²⁴He stripped off his garments, and he too prophesied in Samuel's presence. He lay naked all that day and all that night. This is why people say, "Is Saul also among the prophets?"

## Amplified Bible

David, for he has not sinned against you, and his deeds have been of good service to you.

⁵For he took his life in his hands and slew the Philistine, and the Lord wrought a great deliverance for all Israel; you saw it and rejoiced. Why then will you sin against innocent blood and kill David without a cause?

⁶Saul heeded Jonathan and swore, As the Lord lives, David shall not be slain.

⁷So Jonathan called David and told him all these things. And Jonathan brought David to Saul, and he was in his presence as in times past.

⁸Then there was war again, and David went out and fought with the Philistines, and made a great slaughter among them and they fled before him.

⁹Then an evil spirit from the Lord came upon Saul as he sat in his house with his spear in his hand; and David was playing [the lyre] with his hand.

¹⁰Saul sought to pin David to the wall with the spear, but he slipped away, so that Saul struck the spear into the wall. Then David fled and escaped that night.

¹¹Saul sent messengers that night to David's house to watch him, that he might kill him in the morning. But Michal, David's wife, told him, If you do not save your life tonight, tomorrow you will be killed.

¹²So Michal let David down through the window, and he fled and escaped.

¹³And Michal took the teraph (household good luck image) and laid it in the bed, put a pillow of goats' hair at its head, and covered it with a bedspread.

¹⁴And when Saul sent messengers to take David, she said, He is sick.

¹⁵Then Saul sent the messengers again to see David, saying, Bring him up to me in the bed, that I may slay him.

¹⁶And when the messengers came in, behold, there was an image in the bed, with a pillow of goats' hair at its head.

¹⁷Saul said to Michal, Why have you deceived me so and sent away my enemy so that he has escaped? Michal answered Saul, He said to me, Let me go. Why should I kill you?

¹⁸So David fled and escaped and came to Samuel at Ramah and told him all that Saul had done to him. And he and Samuel went and dwelt in Naioth.

¹⁹And it was told Saul, Behold, David is at Naioth in Ramah.

²⁰And Saul sent messengers to take David; and when they saw the company of the prophets prophesying, and Samuel standing as appointed head over them, the Spirit of God came upon the messengers of Saul and they also prophesied.

²¹When it was told Saul, he sent other messengers, and they also prophesied. And Saul sent messengers again the third time, and they also prophesied.

²²Then Saul himself went to Ramah and came to a great well that is in Secu; and he asked, Where are Samuel and David? And he was told, They are at Naioth in Ramah.

²³So he went on to Naioth in Ramah; and the Spirit of God came upon him also, and as he went on he prophesied until he came to Naioth in Ramah.

²⁴He took off his royal robes and prophesied before Samuel and lay down stripped thus all that day and night. So they say, Is Saul also among the prophets? [I Sam. 10:10.]

### David and Jonathan

**20** Then David fled from Naioth at Ramah and went to Jonathan and asked, "What have I done? What is my crime? How have I wronged your father, that he is trying to kill me?"

**20** David fled from Naioth in Ramah and came and said to Jonathan, What have I done? Of what am I guilty? What is my sin before your father, that he seeks my life?

[a] 9 Or *But a harmful*

## New International Version

2"Never!" Jonathan replied. "You are not going to die! Look, my father doesn't do anything, great or small, without letting me know. Why would he hide this from me? It isn't so!"

3But David took an oath and said, "Your father knows very well that I have found favor in your eyes, and he has said to himself, 'Jonathan must not know this or he will be grieved.' Yet as surely as the LORD lives and as you live, there is only a step between me and death."

4Jonathan said to David, "Whatever you want me to do, I'll do for you."

5So David said, "Look, tomorrow is the New Moon feast, and I am supposed to dine with the king; but let me go and hide in the field until the evening of the day after tomorrow. 6If your father misses me at all, tell him, 'David earnestly asked my permission to hurry to Bethlehem, his hometown, because an annual sacrifice is being made there for his whole clan.' 7If he says, 'Very well,' then your servant is safe. But if he loses his temper, you can be sure that he is determined to harm me. 8As for you, show kindness to your servant, for you have brought him into a covenant with you before the LORD. If I am guilty, then kill me yourself! Why hand me over to your father?"

9"Never!" Jonathan said. "If I had the least inkling that my father was determined to harm you, wouldn't I tell you?"

10David asked, "Who will tell me if your father answers you harshly?"

11"Come," Jonathan said, "let's go out into the field." So they went there together.

12Then Jonathan said to David, "I swear by the LORD, the God of Israel, that I will surely sound out my father by this time the day after tomorrow! If he is favorably disposed toward you, will I not send you word and let you know? 13But if my father intends to harm you, may the LORD deal with Jonathan, be it ever so severely, if I do not let you know and send you away in peace. May the LORD be with you as he has been with my father. 14But show me unfailing kindness like the LORD's kindness as long as I live, so that I may not be killed, 15and do not ever cut off your kindness from my family—not even when the LORD has cut off every one of David's enemies from the face of the earth."

16So Jonathan made a covenant with the house of David, saying, "May the LORD call David's enemies to account." 17And Jonathan had David reaffirm his oath out of love for him, because he loved him as he loved himself.

18Then Jonathan said to David, "Tomorrow is the New Moon feast. You will be missed, because your seat will be empty. 19The day after tomorrow, toward evening, go to the place where you hid when this trouble began, and wait by the stone Ezel. 20I will shoot three arrows to the side of it, as though I were shooting at a target. 21Then I will send a boy and say, 'Go, find the arrows.' If I say to him, 'Look, the arrows are on this side of you; bring them here,' then come, because, as surely as the LORD lives, you are safe; there is no danger. 22But if I say to the boy, 'Look, the arrows are beyond you,' then you must go, because the LORD has sent you away. 23And about the matter you and I discussed—remember, the LORD is witness between you and me forever."

24So David hid in the field, and when the New Moon feast came, the king sat down to eat. 25He sat in his cus-

## Amplified Bible

2Jonathan said, God forbid! You shall not die. My father does nothing great or small but what he tells me. And why should [he] hide this thing from me? It is not so.

3But David replied, Your father certainly knows that I have found favor in your eyes, and he thinks, Let not Jonathan know this, lest he be grieved. But truly as the Lord lives and as your soul lives, there is but a step between me and death.

4Then Jonathan said to David, Whatever you desire, I will do for you.

5David said to Jonathan, Tomorrow is the New Moon [festival], and I should not fail to sit at the table with the king; but let me go, that I may hide myself in the field till the third day at evening.

6If your father misses me at all, then say, David earnestly asked leave of me that he might run to Bethlehem, his city, for there is a yearly sacrifice there for all the family.

7If he says, All right, then it will be well with your servant; but if he is angry, then be sure that evil is determined by him.

8Therefore deal kindly with your servant, for you have brought [me] into a covenant of the Lord with you. But if there is guilt in me, kill me yourself; for why should you bring me to your father?

9And Jonathan said, Far be it from you! If I knew that evil was determined for you by my father, would I not tell you?

10Then said David to Jonathan, Who will tell me if your father answers you roughly?

11Jonathan said, Come, let us go into the field. So they went into the field.

12Jonathan said to David, The Lord, the God of Israel, be witness. When I have sounded out my father about this time tomorrow, or the third day, behold, if he is well inclined toward David, and I do not send and let you know it, 13The Lord do so, and much more, to Jonathan. But if it please my father to do you harm, then I will disclose it to you and send you away, that you may go in safety. And may the Lord be with you as He has been with my father.

14While I am still alive you shall not only show me the loving-kindness of the Lord, so that I die not, 15But also you shall not cut off your kindness from my house forever—no, not even when the Lord has cut off every enemy of David from the face of the earth.

16So Jonathan made a covenant with the house of David, saying, And the Lord will require that this covenant be kept at the hands of David's enemies.

17And Jonathan caused David to swear again by his love for him, for Jonathan loved him as he loved his own life.

18Then Jonathan said to David, Tomorrow is the New Moon festival; and you will be missed, for your seat will be empty.

19On the third day you will go quickly and come to the place where you hid yourself when the matter was in hand, and remain by the stone Ezel.

20And I will shoot three arrows on the side of it, as though I shot at a mark.

21And I will send a lad, saying, Go, find the arrows. If I expressly say to the lad, Look, the arrows are on this side of you, take them—then you are to come, for it is safe for you and there is no danger, as the Lord lives.

22But if I say to the youth, Look, the arrows are beyond you—then go, for the Lord has sent you away.

23And as touching the matter of which you and I have spoken, behold, the Lord is between you and me forever.

24So David hid himself in the field, and when the New Moon [festival] came, the king sat down to eat food.

25The king sat, as at other times, on his seat by the wall,

## New International Version

tomary place by the wall, opposite Jonathan,[a] and Abner sat next to Saul, but David's place was empty. 26Saul said nothing that day, for he thought, "Something must have happened to David to make him ceremonially unclean—surely he is unclean." 27But the next day, the second day of the month, David's place was empty again. Then Saul said to his son Jonathan, "Why hasn't the son of Jesse come to the meal, either yesterday or today?"

28Jonathan answered, "David earnestly asked me for permission to go to Bethlehem. 29He said, 'Let me go, because our family is observing a sacrifice in the town and my brother has ordered me to be there. If I have found favor in your eyes, let me get away to see my brothers.' That is why he has not come to the king's table."

30Saul's anger flared up at Jonathan and he said to him, "You son of a perverse and rebellious woman! Don't I know that you have sided with the son of Jesse to your own shame and to the shame of the mother who bore you? 31As long as the son of Jesse lives on this earth, neither you nor your kingdom will be established. Now send someone to bring him to me, for he must die!"

32"Why should he be put to death? What has he done?" Jonathan asked his father. 33But Saul hurled his spear at him to kill him. Then Jonathan knew that his father intended to kill David.

34Jonathan got up from the table in fierce anger; on that second day of the feast he did not eat, because he was grieved at his father's shameful treatment of David.

35In the morning Jonathan went out to the field for his meeting with David. He had a small boy with him, 36and he said to the boy, "Run and find the arrows I shoot." As the boy ran, he shot an arrow beyond him. 37When the boy came to the place where Jonathan's arrow had fallen, Jonathan called out after him, "Isn't the arrow beyond you?" 38Then he shouted, "Hurry! Go quickly! Don't stop!" The boy picked up the arrow and returned to his master. 39(The boy knew nothing about all this; only Jonathan and David knew.) 40Then Jonathan gave his weapons to the boy and said, "Go, carry them back to town."

41After the boy had gone, David got up from the south side of the stone and bowed down before Jonathan three times, with his face to the ground. Then they kissed each other and wept together—but David wept the most.

42Jonathan said to David, "Go in peace, for we have sworn friendship with each other in the name of the LORD, saying, 'The LORD is witness between you and me, and between your descendants and my descendants forever.'" Then David left, and Jonathan went back to the town.[b]

### David at Nob

**21** [c] David went to Nob, to Ahimelek the priest. Ahimelek trembled when he met him, and asked, "Why are you alone? Why is no one with you?"

2David answered Ahimelek the priest, "The king sent me on a mission and said to me, 'No one is to know anything about the mission I am sending you on.' As for my men, I have told them to meet me at a certain place. 3Now

## Amplified Bible

and Jonathan sat opposite, and Abner sat by Saul's side, but David's place was empty.

26Yet Saul said nothing that day, for he thought, Something has befallen him and he is not clean—surely he is not clean.

27But on the morrow, the second day after the new moon, David's place was empty; and Saul said to Jonathan his son, Why has not the son of Jesse come to the meal, either yesterday or today?

28And Jonathan answered, David earnestly asked leave of me to go to Bethlehem.

29He said, Let me go, I pray, for our family holds a sacrifice in the city and my brother commanded me to be there. Now, if I have found favor in your eyes, let me get away and see my brothers. That is why he has not come to the king's table.

30Then Saul's anger was kindled against Jonathan and he said to him, You son of a perverse, rebellious woman, do not I know that you have chosen the son of Jesse to your own shame and to the shame of your mother who bore you?

31For as long as the son of Jesse lives upon the earth, you shall not be established nor shall your kingdom. So now send and bring him to me, for he shall surely die.

32Jonathan answered Saul his father, Why should he be killed? What has he done?

33But Saul cast his spear at him to smite him, by which Jonathan knew that his father had determined to kill David.

34So Jonathan arose from the table in fierce anger, and ate no food that second day of the month, for he grieved for David because his father had disgraced him.

35In the morning Jonathan went out into the field at the time appointed with David, and a little lad was with him.

36And he said to his lad, Run, find the arrows which I shoot. And as the lad ran, he shot an arrow beyond him.

37When the lad came to the place where Jonathan had shot the arrow, Jonathan called to [him], Is not the arrow beyond you?

38And Jonathan cried after the lad, Make speed, haste, stay not! The lad gathered up the arrow and came to his master.

39But the lad knew nothing; only Jonathan and David knew the matter.

40Jonathan gave his weapons to his lad and told him, Go, carry them to the city.

41And as soon as the lad was gone, David arose from beside the heap of stones and fell on his face to the ground and bowed himself three times. And they kissed one another and wept with one another until David got control of himself.

42And Jonathan told David, Go in peace, forasmuch as we have sworn to each other in the name of the Lord, saying, The Lord shall be between me and you, and between my descendants and yours forever. And Jonathan arose and departed into the city.

**21** Then David went to Nob, to Ahimelech the priest; and Ahimelech was afraid at meeting David, and said to him, Why are you alone and no man with you?

2David said to Ahimelech the priest, The king has charged me with a matter and has told me, Let no man know anything of the mission on which I send you and with what I have charged you. I have appointed the young men to a certain place.

---

[a] 25 Septuagint; Hebrew *wall. Jonathan arose*   [b] 42 In Hebrew texts this sentence (20:42b) is numbered 21:1.   [c] In Hebrew texts 21:1-15 is numbered 21:2-16.

## New International Version

then, what do you have on hand? Give me five loaves of bread, or whatever you can find."

⁴But the priest answered David, "I don't have any ordinary bread on hand; however, there is some consecrated bread here—provided the men have kept themselves from women."

⁵David replied, "Indeed women have been kept from us, as usual whenever*ᵃ* I set out. The men's bodies are holy even on missions that are not holy. How much more so today!" ⁶So the priest gave him the consecrated bread, since there was no bread there except the bread of the Presence that had been removed from before the LORD and replaced by hot bread on the day it was taken away.

⁷Now one of Saul's servants was there that day, detained before the LORD; he was Doeg the Edomite, Saul's chief shepherd.

⁸David asked Ahimelek, "Don't you have a spear or a sword here? I haven't brought my sword or any other weapon, because the king's mission was urgent."

⁹The priest replied, "The sword of Goliath the Philistine, whom you killed in the Valley of Elah, is here; it is wrapped in a cloth behind the ephod. If you want it, take it; there is no sword here but that one."

David said, "There is none like it; give it to me."

### David at Gath

¹⁰That day David fled from Saul and went to Achish king of Gath. ¹¹But the servants of Achish said to him, "Isn't this David, the king of the land? Isn't he the one they sing about in their dances:

"'Saul has slain his thousands,
    and David his tens of thousands'?"

¹²David took these words to heart and was very much afraid of Achish king of Gath. ¹³So he pretended to be insane in their presence; and while he was in their hands he acted like a madman, making marks on the doors of the gate and letting saliva run down his beard.

¹⁴Achish said to his servants, "Look at the man! He is insane! Why bring him to me? ¹⁵Am I so short of madmen that you have to bring this fellow here to carry on like this in front of me? Must this man come into my house?"

### David at Adullam and Mizpah

**22** David left Gath and escaped to the cave of Adullam. When his brothers and his father's household heard about it, they went down to him there. ²All those who were in distress or in debt or discontented gathered around him, and he became their commander. About four hundred men were with him.

³From there David went to Mizpah in Moab and said to the king of Moab, "Would you let my father and mother come and stay with you until I learn what God will do for me?" ⁴So he left them with the king of Moab, and they stayed with him as long as David was in the stronghold.

⁵But the prophet Gad said to David, "Do not stay in the stronghold. Go into the land of Judah." So David left and went to the forest of Hereth.

### Saul Kills the Priests of Nob

⁶Now Saul heard that David and his men had been discovered. And Saul was seated, spear in hand, under the tamarisk tree on the hill at Gibeah, with all his officials standing at his side. ⁷He said to them, "Listen, men of Benjamin! Will the son of Jesse give all of you fields and vineyards? Will he make all of you commanders of thousands and commanders of hundreds? ⁸Is that why you

## Amplified Bible

³Now what do you have on hand? Give me five loaves of bread, or whatever you may have.

⁴And the priest answered David, There is no common bread on hand, but there is hallowed bread—if the young men have kept themselves at least from women.

⁵And David told the priest, Truly women have been kept from us in these three days since I came out, and the food bags *and* utensils of the young men are clean, and although the bread will be used in a secular way, it will be set apart in the clean bags.

⁶So the priest gave him holy bread, for there was no bread there but the showbread which was taken from before the Lord to put hot bread in its place the day when it was taken away.

⁷Now a certain man of Saul's servants was there that day, detained before the Lord; his name was Doeg the Edomite, the chief of Saul's herdsmen.

⁸David said to Ahimelech, Do you have at hand a sword or spear? The king's business required haste, and I brought neither my sword nor my weapons with me.

⁹The priest said, The sword of Goliath the Philistine, whom you slew in the Valley of Elah, see, it is here wrapped in a cloth behind the ephod; if you will take it, do so, for there is no other here. And David said, There is none like that; give it to me.

¹⁰David arose and fled that day from Saul and went to Achish king of Gath.

¹¹The servants of Achish said to him, Is not this David, the king of the land? Did they not sing one to another of him in their dances: Saul has slain his thousands, and David his ten thousands?

¹²David took these words to heart and was much afraid of Achish king of Gath.

¹³And he changed his behavior before them, and pretended to be insane in their [Philistine] hands, and scribbled on the gate doors, and drooled on his beard.

¹⁴Then said Achish to his servants, You see the man is mad. Why then have you brought him to me?

¹⁵Have I need of madmen, that you bring this fellow to play the madman in my presence? Shall this fellow come into my house?

**22** So David departed and escaped to the cave of Adullam: and when his brothers and all his father's house heard it, they went down there to him.

²And everyone in distress or in debt or discontented gathered to him, and he became a commander over them. And there were with him about 400 men.

³And David went from there to Mizpah of Moab; and he said to the king of Moab, Let my father [of Moabite descent] and my mother, I pray you, come out [of Judah] and be with you till I know what God will do for me. [Ruth 4:13, 17.]

⁴And he brought them before the king of Moab, and they dwelt with him all the while that David was in the stronghold [in Moab].

⁵Then the prophet Gad said to David, Do not remain in the stronghold; leave, and get into the land of Judah. So David left and went into the forest of Hareth.

⁶Saul heard that David was discovered, and the men that were with him. Saul was sitting in Gibeah under the tamarisk tree on the height, his spear in his hand and all his servants standing about him.

⁷Saul said to his servants who stood about him, Hear now, you Benjamites! Will the son of Jesse give every one of you fields and vineyards and make you all commanders of thousands and hundreds,

---

*ᵃ 5 Or from us in the past few days since*

## New International Version

have all conspired against me? No one tells me when my son makes a covenant with the son of Jesse. None of you is concerned about me or tells me that my son has incited my servant to lie in wait for me, as he does today."

⁹But Doeg the Edomite, who was standing with Saul's officials, said, "I saw the son of Jesse come to Ahimelek son of Ahitub at Nob. ¹⁰Ahimelek inquired of the LORD for him; he also gave him provisions and the sword of Goliath the Philistine."

¹¹Then the king sent for the priest Ahimelek son of Ahitub and all the men of his family, who were the priests at Nob, and they all came to the king. ¹²Saul said, "Listen now, son of Ahitub."

"Yes, my lord," he answered.

¹³Saul said to him, "Why have you conspired against me, you and the son of Jesse, giving him bread and a sword and inquiring of God for him, so that he has rebelled against me and lies in wait for me, as he does today?"

¹⁴Ahimelek answered the king, "Who of all your servants is as loyal as David, the king's son-in-law, captain of your bodyguard and highly respected in your household? ¹⁵Was that day the first time I inquired of God for him? Of course not! Let not the king accuse your servant or any of his father's family, for your servant knows nothing at all about this whole affair."

¹⁶But the king said, "You will surely die, Ahimelek, you and your whole family."

¹⁷Then the king ordered the guards at his side: "Turn and kill the priests of the LORD, because they too have sided with David. They knew he was fleeing, yet they did not tell me."

But the king's officials were unwilling to raise a hand to strike the priests of the LORD.

¹⁸The king then ordered Doeg, "You turn and strike down the priests." So Doeg the Edomite turned and struck them down. That day he killed eighty-five men who wore the linen ephod. ¹⁹He also put to the sword Nob, the town of the priests, with its men and women, its children and infants, and its cattle, donkeys and sheep.

²⁰But one son of Ahimelek son of Ahitub, named Abiathar, escaped and fled to join David. ²¹He told David that Saul had killed the priests of the LORD. ²²Then David said to Abiathar, "That day, when Doeg the Edomite was there, I knew he would be sure to tell Saul. I am responsible for the death of your whole family. ²³Stay with me; don't be afraid. The man who wants to kill you is trying to kill me too. You will be safe with me."

### David Saves Keilah

**23** When David was told, "Look, the Philistines are fighting against Keilah and are looting the threshing floors," ²he inquired of the LORD, saying, "Shall I go and attack these Philistines?"

The LORD answered him, "Go, attack the Philistines and save Keilah."

³But David's men said to him, "Here in Judah we are afraid. How much more, then, if we go to Keilah against the Philistine forces!"

⁴Once again David inquired of the LORD, and the LORD answered him, "Go down to Keilah, for I am going to give the Philistines into your hand." ⁵So David and his men went to Keilah, fought the Philistines and carried off their

## Amplified Bible

⁸That all of you have conspired against me? No one discloses to me when my son makes a league with the son of Jesse. None of you is sorry for me or discloses that my son has stirred up my servant against me to lie in wait, as he does this day?

⁹Then Doeg the Edomite, who stood with Saul's servants, said, I saw the son of Jesse come to Nob, to Ahimelech son of Ahitub.

¹⁰And [Ahimelech] inquired of the Lord for him, and gave him provisions and the sword of Goliath the Philistine.

¹¹Then the king sent to call Ahimelech the priest, the son of Ahitub, and all his father's house, the priests who were at Nob, and they all came to the king.

¹²Saul said, Hear now, you son of Ahitub. He replied, Here I am, my lord.

¹³Saul said to him, Why have you conspired against me, you and the son of Jesse, giving him bread and a sword and inquiring of God for him, so he could rise against me to lie in wait, as he does this day?

¹⁴Then Ahimelech answered the king, And who is so faithful among all your servants as David, who is the king's son-in-law, and is taken into your council and honored in your house?

¹⁵Have I only today begun inquiring of God for him? No! Let not the king impute any wrong to his servant or to all the house of my father, for your servant has known nothing of all this, little or much.

¹⁶[Saul] said, You shall surely die, Ahimelech, you and all your father's house.

¹⁷And the king said to the guard that stood about him, Turn and slay the Lord's priests, because their hand also is with David and because they knew that he fled and did not disclose it to me. But the servants of the king would not put forth their hands against the Lord's priests.

¹⁸The king said to Doeg, You turn and fall upon the priests. And Doeg the Edomite turned and attacked the priests and slew that day eighty-five persons who wore the priest's linen ephod.

¹⁹And Nob, the city of the priests, he smote with the sword; both men and women, children and sucklings, oxen and donkeys and sheep, he put to the sword.

²⁰And one of the sons of Ahimelech son of Ahitub named Abiathar escaped and fled after David.

²¹And Abiathar told David that Saul had slain the Lord's priests.

²²David said to Abiathar, I knew that day, when Doeg the Edomite was there, that he would surely tell Saul. I have occasioned the death of all your father's house.

²³Stay with me, fear not; for he who seeks my life seeks your life. But with me you shall be safeguarded.

**23** Then they told David, Behold, the Philistines are fighting against Keilah and are robbing the threshing floors.

²So David inquired of the Lord, Shall I go and attack these Philistines? And the Lord said to David, Go, smite the Philistines and save Keilah.

³David's men said to him, Behold, we are afraid here in Judah. How much more, then, if we come to Keilah against the armies of the Philistines?

⁴Then David inquired of the Lord again. And the Lord answered him, Arise, go down to Keilah, for I will deliver the Philistines into your hand.

⁵So David and his men went to Keilah and fought the

## New International Version

livestock. He inflicted heavy losses on the Philistines and saved the people of Keilah. <sup>6</sup>(Now Abiathar son of Ahimelek had brought the ephod down with him when he fled to David at Keilah.)

### Saul Pursues David

<sup>7</sup>Saul was told that David had gone to Keilah, and he said, "God has delivered him into my hands, for David has imprisoned himself by entering a town with gates and bars." <sup>8</sup>And Saul called up all his forces for battle, to go down to Keilah to besiege David and his men.

<sup>9</sup>When David learned that Saul was plotting against him, he said to Abiathar the priest, "Bring the ephod." <sup>10</sup>David said, "Lord, God of Israel, your servant has heard definitely that Saul plans to come to Keilah and destroy the town on account of me. <sup>11</sup>Will the citizens of Keilah surrender me to him? Will Saul come down, as your servant has heard? Lord, God of Israel, tell your servant."

And the Lord said, "He will."

<sup>12</sup>Again David asked, "Will the citizens of Keilah surrender me and my men to Saul?"

And the Lord said, "They will."

<sup>13</sup>So David and his men, about six hundred in number, left Keilah and kept moving from place to place. When Saul was told that David had escaped from Keilah, he did not go there.

<sup>14</sup>David stayed in the wilderness strongholds and in the hills of the Desert of Ziph. Day after day Saul searched for him, but God did not give David into his hands.

<sup>15</sup>While David was at Horesh in the Desert of Ziph, he learned that<sup>a</sup> Saul had come out to take his life. <sup>16</sup>And Saul's son Jonathan went to David at Horesh and helped him find strength in God. <sup>17</sup>"Don't be afraid," he said. "My father Saul will not lay a hand on you. You will be king over Israel, and I will be second to you. Even my father Saul knows this." <sup>18</sup>The two of them made a covenant before the Lord. Then Jonathan went home, but David remained at Horesh.

<sup>19</sup>The Ziphites went up to Saul at Gibeah and said, "Is not David hiding among us in the strongholds at Horesh, on the hill of Hakilah, south of Jeshimon? <sup>20</sup>Now, Your Majesty, come down whenever it pleases you to do so, and we will be responsible for giving him into your hands."

<sup>21</sup>Saul replied, "The Lord bless you for your concern for me. <sup>22</sup>Go and get more information. Find out where David usually goes and who has seen him there. They tell me he is very crafty. <sup>23</sup>Find out about all the hiding places he uses and come back to me with definite information. Then I will go with you; if he is in the area, I will track him down among all the clans of Judah."

<sup>24</sup>So they set out and went to Ziph ahead of Saul. Now David and his men were in the Desert of Maon, in the Arabah south of Jeshimon. <sup>25</sup>Saul and his men began the search, and when David was told about it, he went down to the rock and stayed in the Desert of Maon. When Saul heard this, he went into the Desert of Maon in pursuit of David.

<sup>26</sup>Saul was going along one side of the mountain, and David and his men were on the other side, hurrying to get

## Amplified Bible

Philistines with a great slaughter and brought away their cattle. So David delivered the people of Keilah.

<sup>6</sup>When Abiathar son of Ahimelech fled to David at Keilah, he came with an ephod in his hand.

<sup>7</sup>Now it was told Saul that David had come to Keilah. Saul said, God has delivered him into my hand, for he is shut in by going into a town that has gates and bars.

<sup>8</sup>Saul summoned all the men for war, to go to Keilah to besiege David and his men.

<sup>9</sup>David knew that Saul was plotting evil against him; and he said to Abiathar the priest, Bring the ephod here.

<sup>10</sup>Then David said, O Lord, the God of Israel, Your servant has surely heard that Saul intends to come and destroy the city of Keilah on my account.

<sup>11</sup>Will the men of Keilah deliver me into his hand? Will Saul come down, as Your servant has heard? O Lord, God of Israel, I beseech You, tell Your servant. And the Lord said, He will come down.

<sup>12</sup>Then David asked, Will the men of Keilah deliver me and my men into Saul's hand? The Lord said, They will deliver you up.

<sup>13</sup>Then David and his men, about 600, arose and left Keilah, going wherever they could go. When Saul was told that David had escaped from Keilah, he gave up going there.

<sup>14</sup>David remained in the wilderness strongholds in the hill country of the Wilderness of Ziph. Saul sought him every day, but God did not give him into his hands.

<sup>15</sup>David saw that Saul had come out to seek his life. David was in the Wilderness of Ziph in the wood [at Horesh].

<sup>16</sup>And Jonathan, Saul's son, rose and went into the wood to David [at Horesh] and strengthened his hand in God.

<sup>17</sup>He said to him, Fear not; the hand of Saul my father shall not find you. You shall be king over Israel, and I shall be next to you. Saul my father knows that too.

<sup>18</sup>And the two of them made a covenant before the Lord. And David remained in the wood [at Horesh], and Jonathan went to his house.

<sup>19</sup>Then the Ziphites came to Saul at Gibeah, saying, Does not David hide himself with us in strongholds in the wood [at Horesh], on the hill of Hachilah, which is south of Jeshimon?

<sup>20</sup>Now come down, O king, according to all your heart's desire to come down, and our part shall be to deliver him into the king's hands.

<sup>21</sup>And Saul said, The Lord bless you, for you have compassion on me.

<sup>22</sup>Go, make yet more sure; and know and see where his haunt is and who has seen him there; for I am told he deals very craftily.

<sup>23</sup>See and take note of all his hiding places and come back to me with the certain facts, and I will go with you. If he is in the land, I will search him out among all the thousands of Judah.

<sup>24</sup>So they arose and went to Ziph ahead of Saul. Now David and his men were in the Wilderness of Maon, in the Arabah south of Jeshimon.

<sup>25</sup>Saul and his men went to seek him. And David was told; so he went down to the rock in the Wilderness of Maon and stayed. When Saul heard that, he pursued David in the Wilderness of Maon.

<sup>26</sup>And Saul went on one side of the mountain, and David and his men on the other side of the mountain. And

---

<sup>a</sup> 15 Or *he was afraid because*

## New International Version

away from Saul. As Saul and his forces were closing in on David and his men to capture them, [27]a messenger came to Saul, saying, "Come quickly! The Philistines are raiding the land." [28]Then Saul broke off his pursuit of David and went to meet the Philistines. That is why they call this place Sela Hammahlekoth.[a] [29]And David went up from there and lived in the strongholds of En Gedi.[b]

### David Spares Saul's Life

**24**[c] After Saul returned from pursuing the Philistines, he was told, "David is in the Desert of En Gedi." [2]So Saul took three thousand able young men from all Israel and set out to look for David and his men near the Crags of the Wild Goats.

[3]He came to the sheep pens along the way; a cave was there, and Saul went in to relieve himself. David and his men were far back in the cave. [4]The men said, "This is the day the LORD spoke of when he said[d] to you, 'I will give your enemy into your hands for you to deal with as you wish.'" Then David crept up unnoticed and cut off a corner of Saul's robe.

[5]Afterward, David was conscience-stricken for having cut off a corner of his robe. [6]He said to his men, "The LORD forbid that I should do such a thing to my master, the LORD's anointed, or lay my hand on him; for he is the anointed of the LORD." [7]With these words David sharply rebuked his men and did not allow them to attack Saul. And Saul left the cave and went his way.

[8]Then David went out of the cave and called out to Saul, "My lord the king!" When Saul looked behind him, David bowed down and prostrated himself with his face to the ground. [9]He said to Saul, "Why do you listen when men say, 'David is bent on harming you'? [10]This day you have seen with your own eyes how the LORD delivered you into my hands in the cave. Some urged me to kill you, but I spared you; I said, 'I will not lay my hand on my lord, because he is the LORD's anointed.' [11]See, my father, look at this piece of your robe in my hand! I cut off the corner of your robe but did not kill you. See that there is nothing in my hand to indicate that I am guilty of wrongdoing or rebellion. I have not wronged you, but you are hunting me down to take my life. [12]May the LORD judge between you and me. And may the LORD avenge the wrongs you have done to me, but my hand will not touch you. [13]As the old saying goes, 'From evildoers come evil deeds,' so my hand will not touch you.

[14]"Against whom has the king of Israel come out? Who are you pursuing? A dead dog? A flea? [15]May the LORD be our judge and decide between us. May he consider my cause and uphold it; may he vindicate me by delivering me from your hand."

[16]When David finished saying this, Saul asked, "Is that your voice, David my son?" And he wept aloud. [17]"You are more righteous than I," he said. "You have treated me well, but I have treated you badly. [18]You have just now told me about the good you did to me; the LORD delivered me into your hands, but you did not kill me. [19]When a man finds

## Amplified Bible

David made haste to get away for fear of Saul, for Saul and his men were surrounding [him] and his men to capture them.

[27]But a messenger came to Saul, saying, Make haste and come, for the Philistines have made a raid on the land.

[28]So Saul returned from pursuing David and went against the Philistines. So they called that place the Rock of Escape.

[29]David went up from there and dwelt in the strongholds of En-gedi.

**24** When Saul returned from following the Philistines, he was told, Behold, David is in the Wilderness of En-gedi.

[2]Then Saul took 3,000 chosen men out of all Israel and went to seek David and his men among the Rocks of the Wild Goats.

[3]He came to the sheepfolds on the way, where there was a cave, and Saul went in to relieve himself. Now David and his men were sitting in the cave's innermost recesses.

[4]David's men said to him, Behold the day of which the Lord said to you, Behold, I will deliver your enemy into your hands and you shall do to him as seems good to you. Then David arose [in the darkness] and stealthily cut off the skirt of Saul's robe.

[5]Afterward, David's heart smote him because he had cut off Saul's skirt.

[6]He said to his men, The Lord forbid that I should do this to my master, the Lord's anointed, to put my hand out against him, when he is the anointed of the Lord.

[7]So David checked his men with these words and did not let them rise against Saul. But Saul rose up and left the cave and went on his way.

[8]David also arose afterward and went out of the cave and called after Saul, saying, My lord the king! And when Saul looked behind him, David bowed with his face to the earth and did obeisance.

[9]And David said to Saul, Why do you listen to the words of men who say, David seeks to do you harm?

[10]Behold, your eyes have seen how the Lord gave you today into my hands in the cave. Some told me to kill you, but I spared you; I said, I will not put forth my hand against my lord, for he is the Lord's anointed.

[11]See, my father, see the skirt of your robe in my hand! Since I cut off the skirt of your robe and did not kill you, you know and see that there is no evil or treason in my hands. I have not sinned against you, yet you hunt my life to take it.

[12]May the Lord judge between me and you, and may the Lord avenge me upon you, but my hand shall not be upon you.

[13]As the proverb of the ancients says, Out of the wicked comes forth wickedness; but my hand shall not be against you.

[14]After whom has the king of Israel come out? After whom do you pursue? After a dead dog? After a flea?

[15]May the Lord be judge and judge between me and you, and see and plead my cause, and deliver me out of your hands. [Ps. 142.]

[16]When David had said this to Saul, Saul said, Is this your voice, my son David? And Saul lifted up his voice and wept.

[17]He said to David, You are more upright in God's eyes than I, for you have repaid me good, but I have rewarded you evil.

[18]You have declared today how you have dealt well with me; for when the Lord gave me into your hand, you did not kill me.

---

[a] 28 *Sela Hammahlekoth* means *rock of parting.*    [b] 29 In Hebrew texts this verse (23:29) is numbered 24:1.    [c] In Hebrew texts 24:1-22 is numbered 24:2-23.    [d] 4 Or *"Today the LORD is saying*

## New International Version

his enemy, does he let him get away unharmed? May the LORD reward you well for the way you treated me today. [20]I know that you will surely be king and that the kingdom of Israel will be established in your hands. [21]Now swear to me by the LORD that you will not kill off my descendants or wipe out my name from my father's family."

[22]So David gave his oath to Saul. Then Saul returned home, but David and his men went up to the stronghold.

### David, Nabal and Abigail

**25** Now Samuel died, and all Israel assembled and mourned for him; and they buried him at his home in Ramah. Then David moved down into the Desert of Paran.[a]

[2]A certain man in Maon, who had property there at Carmel, was very wealthy. He had a thousand goats and three thousand sheep, which he was shearing in Carmel. [3]His name was Nabal and his wife's name was Abigail. She was an intelligent and beautiful woman, but her husband was surly and mean in his dealings—he was a Calebite.

[4]While David was in the wilderness, he heard that Nabal was shearing sheep. [5]So he sent ten young men and said to them, "Go up to Nabal at Carmel and greet him in my name. [6]Say to him: 'Long life to you! Good health to you and your household! And good health to all that is yours!

[7]"'Now I hear that it is sheep-shearing time. When your shepherds were with us, we did not mistreat them, and the whole time they were at Carmel nothing of theirs was missing. [8]Ask your own servants and they will tell you. Therefore be favorable toward my men, since we come at a festive time. Please give your servants and your son David whatever you can find for them.'"

[9]When David's men arrived, they gave Nabal this message in David's name. Then they waited.

[10]Nabal answered David's servants, "Who is this David? Who is this son of Jesse? Many servants are breaking away from their masters these days. [11]Why should I take my bread and water, and the meat I have slaughtered for my shearers, and give it to men coming from who knows where?"

[12]David's men turned around and went back. When they arrived, they reported every word. [13]David said to his men, "Each of you strap on your sword!" So they did, and David strapped his on as well. About four hundred men went up with David, while two hundred stayed with the supplies.

[14]One of the servants told Abigail, Nabal's wife, "David sent messengers from the wilderness to give our master his greetings, but he hurled insults at them. [15]Yet these men were very good to us. They did not mistreat us, and the whole time we were out in the fields near them nothing was missing. [16]Night and day they were a wall around us the whole time we were herding our sheep near them. [17]Now think it over and see what you can do, because disaster is hanging over our master and his whole household. He is such a wicked man that no one can talk to him."

## Amplified Bible

[19]For if a man finds his enemy, will he let him go away unharmed? Therefore may the Lord reward you with good for what you have done for me this day.

[20]And now, behold, I well know that you shall surely be king and that the kingdom of Israel shall be established in your hands.

[21]Swear now therefore to me by the Lord that you will not cut off my descendants after me and that you will not destroy my name out of my father's house.

[22]David gave Saul his oath; and Saul went home, but David and his men went up to the stronghold.

**25** Now Samuel died, and all the Israelites assembled and mourned for him, and buried him at his house in Ramah. David arose and went to the Wilderness of Paran.

[2]A very rich man was in Maon, whose possessions *and* business were in Carmel. He had 3,000 sheep and 1,000 goats, and he was shearing his sheep in Carmel.

[3]The man's name was Nabal and his wife's name was Abigail; she was a woman of good understanding, and beautiful. But the man was rough and evil in his doings; he was a Calebite.

[4]David heard in the wilderness that Nabal was shearing his sheep.

[5]And David sent out ten young men and said to [them], Go up to Carmel to Nabal and greet him in my name;

[6]And salute him thus: Peace be to you and to your house and to all that you have.

[7]I have heard that you have shearers. Now your shepherds have been with us and we did them no harm, and they missed nothing all the time they were in Carmel.

[8]Ask your young men and they will tell you. Therefore let my young men find favor in your sight, for we come at an opportune time. I pray you, give whatever you have at hand to your servants and to your son David.

[9]And when David's young men came, they said all this to Nabal in the name of David, and then paused.

[10]And Nabal answered David's servants and said, Who is this David? Who is the son of Jesse? There are many servants nowadays who are each breaking away from his master.

[11]Shall I then take my bread and my water, and my meat that I have killed for my shearers, and give it to men when I do not know where they belong?

[12]So David's young men turned away, and came and told him all that was said.

[13]And David said to his men, Every man gird on his sword. And they did so, and David also girded on his sword; and there went up after David about 400 men, and 200 remained with the baggage.

[14]But one of Nabal's young men told Abigail, Nabal's wife, Behold, David sent messengers out of the wilderness to salute our master, and he railed at them.

[15]But David's men were very good to us, and we were not harmed, nor did we miss anything as long as we went with them, when we were in the fields.

[16]They were a wall to us night and day, all the time we were with them keeping the sheep.

[17]So know this and consider what you will do, for evil is determined against our master and all his house. For he is such a wicked man that one cannot speak to him.

---

[a] 1 Hebrew and some Septuagint manuscripts; other Septuagint manuscripts *Maon*

## New International Version

18Abigail acted quickly. She took two hundred loaves of bread, two skins of wine, five dressed sheep, five seahs*a* of roasted grain, a hundred cakes of raisins and two hundred cakes of pressed figs, and loaded them on donkeys. 19Then she told her servants, "Go on ahead; I'll follow you." But she did not tell her husband Nabal.

20As she came riding her donkey into a mountain ravine, there were David and his men descending toward her, and she met them. 21David had just said, "It's been useless—all my watching over this fellow's property in the wilderness so that nothing of his was missing. He has paid me back evil for good. 22May God deal with David,*b* be it ever so severely, if by morning I leave alive one male of all who belong to him!"

23When Abigail saw David, she quickly got off her donkey and bowed down before David with her face to the ground. 24She fell at his feet and said: "Pardon your servant, my lord, and let me speak to you; hear what your servant has to say. 25Please pay no attention, my lord, to that wicked man Nabal. He is just like his name—his name means Fool, and folly goes with him. And as for me, your servant, I did not see the men my lord sent. 26And now, my lord, as surely as the LORD your God lives and as you live, since the LORD has kept you from bloodshed and from avenging yourself with your own hands, may your enemies and all who are intent on harming my lord be like Nabal. 27And let this gift, which your servant has brought to my lord, be given to the men who follow you.

28"Please forgive your servant's presumption. The LORD your God will certainly make a lasting dynasty for my lord, because you fight the LORD's battles, and no wrongdoing will be found in you as long as you live. 29Even though someone is pursuing you to take your life, the life of my lord will be bound securely in the bundle of the living by the LORD your God, but the lives of your enemies he will hurl away as from the pocket of a sling. 30When the LORD has fulfilled for my lord every good thing he promised concerning him and has appointed him ruler over Israel, 31my lord will not have on his conscience the staggering burden of needless bloodshed or of having avenged himself. And when the LORD your God has brought my lord success, remember your servant."

32David said to Abigail, "Praise be to the LORD, the God of Israel, who has sent you today to meet me. 33May you be blessed for your good judgment and for keeping me from bloodshed this day and from avenging myself with my own

## Amplified Bible

18Then Abigail made haste and took 200 loaves, two skins of wine, five sheep already dressed, five measures of parched grain, 100 clusters of raisins, and 200 cakes of figs, and laid them on donkeys.

19And she said to her servants, Go on before me; behold, I come after you. But she did not tell her husband Nabal.

20As she rode on her donkey, she came down hidden by the mountain, and behold, David and his men came down opposite her, and she met them.

21Now David had said, Surely in vain have I protected all that this fellow has in the wilderness, so that nothing was missed of all that belonged to him; and he has repaid me evil for good.

22May God do so, and more also, to David *a*if I leave of all who belong to him one male alive by morning.

23When Abigail saw David, she hastened and lighted off the donkey, and fell before David on her face and did obeisance.

24Kneeling at his feet she said, Upon me alone let this guilt be, my lord. And let your handmaid, I pray you, speak in your presence, and hear the words of your handmaid.

25Let not my lord, I pray you, regard this foolish *and* wicked fellow Nabal, for as his name is, so is he—Nabal [foolish, wicked] is his name, and folly is with him. But I, your handmaid, did not see my lord's young men whom you sent.

26So now, my lord, as the Lord lives and as your soul lives, seeing that the Lord has prevented you from bloodguiltiness and from avenging yourself with your own hand, now let your enemies and those who seek to do evil to my lord be as Nabal.

27And now this gift, which your handmaid has brought my lord, let it be given to the young men who follow my lord.

28Forgive, I pray you, the trespass of your handmaid, for the Lord will certainly make my lord a sure house, because my lord is fighting the Lord's battles, and evil has not been found in you all your days.

29Though man is risen up to pursue you and to seek your life, yet the life of my lord shall be bound in the living bundle with the Lord your God. And the lives of your enemies—them shall He sling out as out of the center of a sling.

30And when the Lord has done to my lord according to all the good that He has promised concerning you and has made you ruler over Israel,

31This shall be no staggering grief to you or cause for pangs of conscience to my lord, either that you have shed blood without cause or that my lord has avenged himself. And when the Lord has dealt well with my lord, then [*b*earnestly] remember your handmaid.

32And David said to Abigail, Blessed be the Lord, the God of Israel, Who sent you this day to meet me.

33And blessed be your discretion *and* advice, and blessed be you who have kept me today from bloodguiltiness and from avenging myself with my own hand.

---

*a The Septuagint* (Greek translation of the Old Testament) so reads. The Hebrew reads "David's enemies." *b* Whenever God's inspired Word says "[earnestly] remember," one is certain to miss something if he does not stop, look, and really listen to what the Holy Spirit is wanting to tell him—or her. "[Earnestly] remember" Abigail, the woman whom God has specifically held up as a pattern of right behavior in an unfortunate marriage. Here a dozen vital questions are answered through Abigail's example. She could not have known that thousands of years later people in similar circumstances would become "more than conquerors" because of her, but God knew. Study her until you know her God-given secrets of success; then pass them on to the people who are letting an unfortunate marriage wreck them rather than sanctify them for service. F. B. Meyer (*Through the Bible Day by Day*) said, "Never let the evil disposition of one mate hinder the devotion and grace of the other. Never let the difficulties of your home lead you to abdicate your throne. Do not step down to the level of your circumstances, but lift them to your own high calling in Christ. 'Be not conformed . . . but be ye transformed' (Rom. 12:1, 2 KJV)."

---

## New International Version

hands. 34Otherwise, as surely as the LORD, the God of Israel, lives, who has kept me from harming you, if you had not come quickly to meet me, not one male belonging to Nabal would have been left alive by daybreak."

35Then David accepted from her hand what she had brought him and said, "Go home in peace. I have heard your words and granted your request."

36When Abigail went to Nabal, he was in the house holding a banquet like that of a king. He was in high spirits and very drunk. So she told him nothing at all until daybreak. 37Then in the morning, when Nabal was sober, his wife told him all these things, and his heart failed him and he became like a stone. 38About ten days later, the LORD struck Nabal and he died.

39When David heard that Nabal was dead, he said, "Praise be to the LORD, who has upheld my cause against Nabal for treating me with contempt. He has kept his servant from doing wrong and has brought Nabal's wrongdoing down on his own head."

Then David sent word to Abigail, asking her to become his wife. 40His servants went to Carmel and said to Abigail, "David has sent us to you to take you to become his wife."

41She bowed down with her face to the ground and said, "I am your servant and am ready to serve you and wash the feet of my lord's servants." 42Abigail quickly got on a donkey and, attended by her five female servants, went with David's messengers and became his wife. 43David had also married Ahinoam of Jezreel, and they both were his wives. 44But Saul had given his daughter Michal, David's wife, to Paltiel[a] son of Laish, who was from Gallim.

### David Again Spares Saul's Life

**26** The Ziphites went to Saul at Gibeah and said, "Is not David hiding on the hill of Hakilah, which faces Jeshimon?"

2So Saul went down to the Desert of Ziph, with his three thousand select Israelite troops, to search there for David. 3Saul made his camp beside the road on the hill of Hakilah facing Jeshimon, but David stayed in the wilderness. When he saw that Saul had followed him there, 4he sent out scouts and learned that Saul had definitely arrived.

5Then David set out and went to the place where Saul had camped. He saw where Saul and Abner son of Ner, the commander of the army, had lain down. Saul was lying inside the camp, with the army encamped around him.

6David then asked Ahimelek the Hittite and Abishai son of Zeruiah, Joab's brother, "Who will go down into the camp with me to Saul?"

"I'll go with you," said Abishai.

7So David and Abishai went to the army by night, and there was Saul, lying asleep inside the camp with his spear stuck in the ground near his head. Abner and the soldiers were lying around him.

8Abishai said to David, "Today God has delivered your enemy into your hands. Now let me pin him to the ground with one thrust of the spear; I won't strike him twice."

## Amplified Bible

34For as the Lord, the God of Israel, lives, Who has prevented me from hurting you, if you had not hurried and come to meet me, surely by morning there would not have been left so much as one male to Nabal.

35So David accepted what she had brought him and said to her, Go up in peace to your house. See, I have hearkened to your voice and have granted your petition.

36And Abigail came to Nabal, and behold, he was holding a feast in his house like the feast of a king. And [his] heart was merry, for he was very drunk; so she told him nothing at all until the morning light.

37But in the morning, when the wine was gone out of Nabal, and his wife told him these things, his heart died within him and he became [paralyzed, helpless as] a stone.

38And about ten days after that, the Lord smote Nabal and he died.

39When David heard that Nabal was dead, he said, Blessed be the Lord, Who has pleaded the cause of my reproach at the hand of Nabal, and kept His servant from evil. For the Lord has returned the wickedness of Nabal upon his own head. And David sent and communed with Abigail, to take her to him as his wife.

40And when the servants of David had come to Abigail at Carmel, they said to her, David sent us to you to take you to him to be his wife.

41And she arose and bowed herself to the earth and said, Behold, let your handmaid be a servant to wash the feet of the servants of my lord.

42And Abigail hastened and arose and rode on a donkey, with five of her maids who followed her, and she went after the messengers of David and became his wife.

43David also took Ahinoam of Jezreel, and they both became his wives.

44Saul had given Michal his daughter, David's wife, to Phalti son of Laish, who was of Gallim.

**26** The Ziphites came to Saul at Gibeah, saying, Does not David hide himself on the hill of Hachilah, east of Jeshimon?

2So Saul arose and went down to the Wilderness of Ziph, with 3,000 chosen men of Israel, to seek David [there].

3Saul encamped on the hill of Hachilah, which is beside the road east of Jeshimon. But David remained in the wilderness. And when he saw that Saul came after him into the wilderness,

4David sent out spies and learned that Saul had actually come.

5David arose and came to the place where Saul had encamped, and saw where Saul lay with Abner son of Ner, commander of his army; and Saul was lying in the encampment, with the army encamped around him.

6Then David said to Ahimelech the Hittite and to Abishai son of Zeruiah, brother of Joab, Who will go down with me into the camp of Saul? And Abishai said, I will go down with you.

7So David and Abishai went to the army by night, and there Saul lay sleeping within the encampment with his spear stuck in the ground at his head; and Abner and the army lay round about him.

8Then said Abishai to David, God has given your enemy into your hands this day. Now therefore let me smite him to the earth at once with one stroke of the spear, and I will not strike him twice.

## New International Version

⁹But David said to Abishai, "Don't destroy him! Who can lay a hand on the Lord's anointed and be guiltless? ¹⁰As surely as the Lord lives," he said, "the Lord himself will strike him, or his time will come and he will die, or he will go into battle and perish. ¹¹But the Lord forbid that I should lay a hand on the Lord's anointed. Now get the spear and water jug that are near his head, and let's go."

¹²So David took the spear and water jug near Saul's head, and they left. No one saw or knew about it, nor did anyone wake up. They were all sleeping, because the Lord had put them into a deep sleep.

¹³Then David crossed over to the other side and stood on top of the hill some distance away; there was a wide space between them. ¹⁴He called out to the army and to Abner son of Ner, "Aren't you going to answer me, Abner?"

Abner replied, "Who are you who calls to the king?"

¹⁵David said, "You're a man, aren't you? And who is like you in Israel? Why didn't you guard your lord the king? Someone came to destroy your lord the king. ¹⁶What you have done is not good. As surely as the Lord lives, you and your men must die, because you did not guard your master, the Lord's anointed. Look around you. Where are the king's spear and water jug that were near his head?"

¹⁷Saul recognized David's voice and said, "Is that your voice, David my son?"

David replied, "Yes it is, my lord the king." ¹⁸And he added, "Why is my lord pursuing his servant? What have I done, and what wrong am I guilty of? ¹⁹Now let my lord the king listen to his servant's words. If the Lord has incited you against me, then may he accept an offering. If, however, people have done it, may they be cursed before the Lord! They have driven me today from my share in the Lord's inheritance and have said, 'Go, serve other gods.' ²⁰Now do not let my blood fall to the ground far from the presence of the Lord. The king of Israel has come out to look for a flea—as one hunts a partridge in the mountains."

²¹Then Saul said, "I have sinned. Come back, David my son. Because you considered my life precious today, I will not try to harm you again. Surely I have acted like a fool and have been terribly wrong."

²²"Here is the king's spear," David answered. "Let one of your young men come over and get it. ²³The Lord rewards everyone for their righteousness and faithfulness. The Lord delivered you into my hands today, but I would not lay a hand on the Lord's anointed. ²⁴As surely as I valued your life today, so may the Lord value my life and deliver me from all trouble."

²⁵Then Saul said to David, "May you be blessed, David my son; you will do great things and surely triumph."

So David went on his way, and Saul returned home.

## Amplified Bible

⁹David said to Abishai, Do not destroy him; for who can raise his hand against the Lord's anointed and be guiltless?

¹⁰David said, As the Lord lives, [He] will smite him; or his day will come to die or he will go down in battle and perish.

¹¹The Lord forbid that I should raise my hand against the Lord's anointed; but take now the spear that is at his head and the bottle of water, and let us go.

¹²So David took the spear and the bottle of water from Saul's head, and they got away. And no man saw or knew or wakened, for they were all asleep, because a deep sleep from the Lord had fallen upon them.

¹³Then David went over to the other side and stood on the top of the mountain afar off, a great space being between them.

¹⁴David called to the army and Abner son of Ner, Will you answer, Abner? Abner replied, Who are you, calling [and disturbing] the king?

¹⁵David said to Abner, Are you not a valiant man? Who is like you in Israel? Why then have you not guarded your lord the king? For one of the people came in [to your camp] to destroy the king your lord.

¹⁶This thing is not good that you have done. As the Lord lives, you deserve to die, because you have not guarded your master, the Lord's anointed. And now see where the king's spear is and the bottle of water that was at his head.

¹⁷And Saul knew David's voice and said, Is this your voice, my son David? And David said, My voice, my lord O king!

¹⁸And David said, Why does my lord thus pursue his servant? What have I done? Or what evil is in my hand [tonight]?

¹⁹Now therefore, I pray you, let my lord the king hear the words of his servant. If the Lord has stirred you up against me, let Him accept an offering; but if it is men, may they be cursed before the Lord, for they have driven me out this day that I should have no share in the inheritance of the Lord, saying, Go, serve other gods.

²⁰Now therefore, let not my blood fall to the earth away from the presence of the Lord; for the king of Israel is come out to seek one flea, as when one hunts a partridge in the mountains.

²¹Then said Saul, I have sinned. Return, my son David, for I will no more do you harm, because my life was precious in your eyes this day. Behold, I have ᵃplayed the fool and have erred exceedingly.

²²David answered, See the king's spear! Let one of the young men come and get it.

²³The Lord rewards every man for his righteousness and his faithfulness; for the Lord delivered you into my hands today, but I would not stretch forth my hand against the Lord's anointed.

²⁴And behold, as your life was precious today in my sight, so let my life be precious in the sight of the Lord, and let Him deliver me out of all tribulation.

²⁵Then Saul said to David, May you be blessed, my son David; you will both do mightily and surely prevail. So David went on his way, and Saul returned to his place.

ᵃ "When for a moment a man is off guard, in all probability you will know more truth about him than in all his attempts either to reveal himself or to hide himself. The ever-present consciousness, habitually hidden, flashes forth. Later he may apologize and say he did not mean what he said. The fact is that he was surprised into saying what he was constantly thinking. In all probability Saul had never said that before and would never say it again, but he had been thinking it for a long time—'I played the fool.' There is no escape for any man, as long as reason continues, from the naked truth about himself. He may practice deceit so skillfully as not only to hide himself from his fellowmen, but in his unutterable folly to imagine he has hidden himself from God; but he can never hide himself from **himself**. In some moment of stress and strain he says what he has been thinking all the time . . . . Ere Saul knew it, he had said, 'Behold, I have played the fool.' That is the whole story of the man" (G. Campbell Morgan, cited by J. Sidlow Baxter, *Explore the Book*).

## New International Version

### David Among the Philistines

**27** But David thought to himself, "One of these days I will be destroyed by the hand of Saul. The best thing I can do is to escape to the land of the Philistines. Then Saul will give up searching for me anywhere in Israel, and I will slip out of his hand."

²So David and the six hundred men with him left and went over to Achish son of Maok king of Gath. ³David and his men settled in Gath with Achish. Each man had his family with him, and David had his two wives: Ahinoam of Jezreel and Abigail of Carmel, the widow of Nabal. ⁴When Saul was told that David had fled to Gath, he no longer searched for him.

⁵Then David said to Achish, "If I have found favor in your eyes, let a place be assigned to me in one of the country towns, that I may live there. Why should your servant live in the royal city with you?"

⁶So on that day Achish gave him Ziklag, and it has belonged to the kings of Judah ever since. ⁷David lived in Philistine territory a year and four months.

⁸Now David and his men went up and raided the Geshurites, the Girzites and the Amalekites. (From ancient times these peoples had lived in the land extending to Shur and Egypt.) ⁹Whenever David attacked an area, he did not leave a man or woman alive, but took sheep and cattle, donkeys and camels, and clothes. Then he returned to Achish.

¹⁰When Achish asked, "Where did you go raiding today?" David would say, "Against the Negev of Judah" or "Against the Negev of Jerahmeel" or "Against the Negev of the Kenites." ¹¹He did not leave a man or woman alive to be brought to Gath, for he thought, "They might inform on us and say, 'This is what David did.'" And such was his practice as long as he lived in Philistine territory. ¹²Achish trusted David and said to himself, "He has become so obnoxious to his people, the Israelites, that he will be my servant for life."

**28** In those days the Philistines gathered their forces to fight against Israel. Achish said to David, "You must understand that you and your men will accompany me in the army."

²David said, "Then you will see for yourself what your servant can do."

Achish replied, "Very well, I will make you my bodyguard for life."

### Saul and the Medium at Endor

³Now Samuel was dead, and all Israel had mourned for him and buried him in his own town of Ramah. Saul had expelled the mediums and spiritists from the land.

⁴The Philistines assembled and came and set up camp at Shunem, while Saul gathered all Israel and set up camp at Gilboa. ⁵When Saul saw the Philistine army, he was

## Amplified Bible

**27** But David said in his heart, I shall now perish one day by the hand of Saul. There is nothing better for me than that I should escape into the land of the Philistines. Then Saul will despair of seeking me any more within the borders of Israel, and I shall escape out of his hand.

²So David arose and went over with the 600 men who were with him to Achish son of Maoch, king of Gath.

³And David dwelt with Achish at Gath, he and his men, every man with his household, and David with his two wives, Ahinoam the Jezreelitess and Abigail the Carmelitess, Nabal's widow.

⁴When it was told Saul that David had fled to Gath, he sought for him no more.

⁵And David said to Achish, If I have now found favor in your eyes, let me be given a place to dwell in some country town; for why should your servant live in the royal city with you?

⁶Then Achish gave David the town of Ziklag that day. Therefore Ziklag belongs to the kings of Judah to this day.

⁷The time David dwelt in the Philistines' country was a year and four months.

⁸Now David and his men went up and made attacks on the Geshurites, Girzites, and Amalekites [enemies of Israel Joshua had failed to exterminate]. For from of old those nations inhabited the land, as one goes to Shur even to the land of Egypt. [Deut. 25:19; Josh. 13:1, 2, 13.]

⁹And David smote the land and left neither man nor woman alive, and took away the sheep, oxen, donkeys, camels, and the apparel, and returned to Achish.

¹⁰Achish would ask, Against whom have you made a raid today? And David would reply, ᵃAgainst the South (Negeb) of Judah, or of the Jerahmeelites, or of the Kenites.

¹¹And David saved neither man nor woman alive to bring tidings to Gath, thinking, Lest they should say about us, So did David, and so will he do as long as he dwells in the Philistines' country.

¹²And Achish believed David, saying, He has made his people Israel utterly abhor him; so he shall be my servant always.

**28** In those days the Philistines gathered their forces for war against Israel. Achish said to David, Understand that you and your men shall go with me to battle.

²David said to Achish, All right, you shall know what your servant can do. Achish said to David, Therefore I will make you my bodyguard always.

³Now Samuel was dead, and all Israel had mourned for him and buried him in Ramah, his own city. And Saul had put the mediums and the wizards out of the land.

⁴And the Philistines assembled and came and encamped at Shunem; and Saul gathered all Israel and they encamped at Gilboa.

⁵When Saul saw the Philistine host, he was afraid; his heart trembled greatly.

---

ᵃ How could David be "a man after His [God's] own heart" (I Sam. 13:14) and lie and deceive like that? God hates lying (Prov. 12:22), and those who deal in falsehood and deception are to be excluded from heaven (Rev. 22:15). The truth is that David had gone through such a long period of persecution and threatening circumstances that he had fallen into a bit of mistrust of God Himself. God had sworn to make him king, to rid him of his enemies, to give him a sure house; yet here he was in a panic, concluding that God had forsaken him and that if he was to remain alive he must manage it himself. It was very dishonoring to God. But God was standing by His stricken child, waiting for the moment when he would realize his own utter helplessness and turn in blessed surrender to the almighty arms of Him who had been watching over him all along. That time came at Ziklag, when, in the bitterest hour of his life, we are told, "But David encouraged *and* strengthened himself in the Lord his God" (I Sam. 30:6), truly "a man after God's own heart."

## New International Version

afraid; terror filled his heart. [6]He inquired of the LORD, but the LORD did not answer him by dreams or Urim or prophets. [7]Saul then said to his attendants, "Find me a woman who is a medium, so I may go and inquire of her."

"There is one in Endor," they said.

[8]So Saul disguised himself, putting on other clothes, and at night he and two men went to the woman. "Consult a spirit for me," he said, "and bring up for me the one I name."

[9]But the woman said to him, "Surely you know what Saul has done. He has cut off the mediums and spiritists from the land. Why have you set a trap for my life to bring about my death?"

[10]Saul swore to her by the LORD, "As surely as the LORD lives, you will not be punished for this."

[11]Then the woman asked, "Whom shall I bring up for you?"

"Bring up Samuel," he said.

[12]When the woman saw Samuel, she cried out at the top of her voice and said to Saul, "Why have you deceived me? You are Saul!"

[13]The king said to her, "Don't be afraid. What do you see?"

The woman said, "I see a ghostly figure[a] coming up out of the earth."

[14]"What does he look like?" he asked.

"An old man wearing a robe is coming up," she said.

Then Saul knew it was Samuel, and he bowed down and prostrated himself with his face to the ground.

[15]Samuel said to Saul, "Why have you disturbed me by bringing me up?"

"I am in great distress," Saul said. "The Philistines are fighting against me, and God has departed from me. He no longer answers me, either by prophets or by dreams. So I have called on you to tell me what to do."

[16]Samuel said, "Why do you consult me, now that the LORD has departed from you and become your enemy? [17]The LORD has done what he predicted through me. The LORD has torn the kingdom out of your hands and given it to one of your neighbors—to David. [18]Because you did not obey the LORD or carry out his fierce wrath against the Amalekites, the LORD has done this to you today. [19]The LORD will deliver both Israel and you into the hands of the Philistines, and tomorrow you and your sons will be with me. The LORD will also give the army of Israel into the hands of the Philistines."

[20]Immediately Saul fell full length on the ground, filled with fear because of Samuel's words. His strength was gone, for he had eaten nothing all that day and all that night.

[21]When the woman came to Saul and saw that he was greatly shaken, she said, "Look, your servant has obeyed you. I took my life in my hands and did what you told me to do. [22]Now please listen to your servant and let me give you some food so you may eat and have the strength to go on your way."

[23]He refused and said, "I will not eat."

But his men joined the woman in urging him, and he listened to them. He got up from the ground and sat on the couch.

[24]The woman had a fattened calf at the house, which she butchered at once. She took some flour, kneaded it and baked bread without yeast. [25]Then she set it before Saul and his men, and they ate. That same night they got up and left.

## Amplified Bible

[6]When Saul inquired of the Lord, He refused to answer him, either by dreams or by Urim [a symbol worn by the priest when seeking the will of God for Israel] or by the prophets. [Prov. 1:24-30.]

[7]Then Saul said to his servants, Find me a woman who is a medium [between the living and the dead], that I may go and inquire of her. His servants said, Behold, there is a woman who is a medium at Endor.

[8]So Saul disguised himself, put on other raiment, and he and two men with him went and came to the woman at night. He said to her, Perceive for me by the familiar spirit and bring up for me the dead person whom I shall name to you.

[9]The woman said, See here, you know what Saul has done, how he has cut off those who are mediums and wizards out of the land. Why then do you lay a trap for my life to cause my death?

[10]And Saul swore to her by the Lord, saying, As the Lord lives, there shall no punishment come to you for this.

[11]The woman said, Whom shall I bring up for you? He said, Bring up Samuel for me.

[12]And when the woman saw Samuel, she screamed and she said to Saul, Why have you deceived me? For you are Saul!

[13]The king said to her, Be not afraid; what do you see? The woman said to Saul, I see a god [terrifying superhuman being] coming up out of the earth!

[14]He said to her, In what form is he? And she said, An old man comes up, covered with a mantle. And Saul perceived that it was Samuel, and he stooped with his face to the ground and made obeisance.

[15]And Samuel said to Saul, Why have you disturbed me to bring me up? Saul answered, I am bitterly distressed; for the Philistines make war against me, and God has departed from me and answers me no more, either by prophets or by dreams. Therefore I have called you, that you may make known to me what I should do.

[16]Samuel said, Why then do you ask me, seeing that the Lord has turned from you and has become your enemy?

[17]The Lord has done to you as He said through me He would do; for [He] has torn the kingdom out of your hands and given it to your neighbor David. [I Sam. 15:22-28.]

[18]Because you did not obey the voice of the Lord or execute His fierce wrath upon Amalek, therefore the Lord has done this thing to you this day.

[19]Moreover, the Lord will also give Israel with you into the hands of the Philistines, and tomorrow you and your sons shall be with me [among the dead]. The Lord also will give the army of Israel into the hands of the Philistines.

[20]Then immediately Saul fell full length upon the earth floor [of the medium's house], and was exceedingly afraid because of Samuel's words. There was no strength in him, for he had eaten nothing all day and all night.

[21]The woman came to Saul, and seeing that he was greatly troubled, she said to him, Behold, your handmaid has obeyed you, and I have put my life in my hands and have listened to what you said to me.

[22]So now, I pray you, listen also to the voice of your handmaid and let me set a morsel of food before you, and eat, so you may have strength when you go on your way.

[23]But he said, I will not eat. But his servants, together with the woman, urged him, and he heeded their words. So he arose from the ground and sat upon the bed.

[24]The woman had a fat calf in the house; she hurried and killed it, and took flour, kneaded it, and baked unleavened bread.

[25]Then she brought it before Saul and his servants, and they ate. Then they rose up and went away that night.

---

[a] 13 Or see spirits; or see gods

## New International Version

### Achish Sends David Back to Ziklag

**29** The Philistines gathered all their forces at Aphek, and Israel camped by the spring in Jezreel. ²As the Philistine rulers marched with their units of hundreds and thousands, David and his men were marching at the rear with Achish. ³The commanders of the Philistines asked, "What about these Hebrews?"

Achish replied, "Is this not David, who was an officer of Saul king of Israel? He has already been with me for over a year, and from the day he left Saul until now, I have found no fault in him."

⁴But the Philistine commanders were angry with Achish and said, "Send the man back, that he may return to the place you assigned him. He must not go with us into battle, or he will turn against us during the fighting. How better could he regain his master's favor than by taking the heads of our own men? ⁵Isn't this the David they sang about in their dances:

"'Saul has slain his thousands,
and David his tens of thousands'?"

⁶So Achish called David and said to him, "As surely as the LORD lives, you have been reliable, and I would be pleased to have you serve with me in the army. From the day you came to me until today, I have found no fault in you, but the rulers don't approve of you. ⁷Now turn back and go in peace; do nothing to displease the Philistine rulers."

⁸"But what have I done?" asked David. "What have you found against your servant from the day I came to you until now? Why can't I go and fight against the enemies of my lord the king?"

⁹Achish answered, "I know that you have been as pleasing in my eyes as an angel of God; nevertheless, the Philistine commanders have said, 'He must not go up with us into battle.' ¹⁰Now get up early, along with your master's servants who have come with you, and leave in the morning as soon as it is light."

¹¹So David and his men got up early in the morning to go back to the land of the Philistines, and the Philistines went up to Jezreel.

### David Destroys the Amalekites

**30** David and his men reached Ziklag on the third day. Now the Amalekites had raided the Negev and Ziklag. They had attacked Ziklag and burned it, ²and had taken captive the women and everyone else in it, both young and old. They killed none of them, but carried them off as they went on their way.

³When David and his men reached Ziklag, they found it destroyed by fire and their wives and sons and daughters taken captive. ⁴So David and his men wept aloud until they had no strength left to weep. ⁵David's two wives had been captured—Ahinoam of Jezreel and Abigail, the widow of Nabal of Carmel. ⁶David was greatly distressed because the men were talking of stoning him; each one was bitter in spirit because of his sons and daughters. But David found strength in the LORD his God.

⁷Then David said to Abiathar the priest, the son of

## Amplified Bible

**29** Now the Philistines gathered all their forces at Aphek, and the Israelites encamped by the fountain in Jezreel.

²As the Philistine lords were passing on by hundreds and by thousands, and David and his men were in the rear with Achish,

³The Philistine princes said, What are these Hebrews doing here? Achish said to the Philistine princes, Is not this David, the servant of Saul king of Israel, who has been with me these days and years, and I have found no fault in him since he deserted to me to this day?

⁴And the Philistine princes were angry with Achish and they said to him, Make this fellow return, that he may go again to his place where you have assigned him, and let him not go down with us to battle, lest in the battle he become an adversary to us. For how could David reconcile himself to his master? Would it not be with the heads of the men here?

⁵Is not this David, of whom they sang to one another in dances, Saul slew his thousands, and David his ten thousands?

⁶Then Achish called David and said to him, As surely as the Lord lives, you have been honest *and* upright, and for you to go out and come in with me in the army is good in my sight; for I have found no evil in you from the day of your coming to me to this day. Yet the lords do not approve of you.

⁷So return now and go peaceably, so as not to displease the Philistine lords.

⁸David said to Achish, But what have I done? And what have you found in your servant as long as I have been with you to this day, that I may not go and fight against the enemies of my lord the king?

⁹And Achish said to David, I know that you are as blameless in my sight as an angel of God; nevertheless the princes of the Philistines have said, He shall not go up with us to the battle.

¹⁰So now rise up early in the morning, with your master's servants who have come with you, and as soon as you are and have light, depart.

¹¹So David and his men rose up early in the morning to return to the land of the Philistines. But the Philistines went up to Jezreel [to fight against Israel].

**30** Now when David and his men came home to Ziklag on the third day, they found that the Amalekites had made a raid on the South (the Negeb) and on Ziklag, and had struck Ziklag and burned it with fire,

²And had taken the women and all who were there, both great and small, captive. They killed no one, but carried them off and went on their way.

³So David and his men came to the town, and behold, it was burned, and their wives and sons and daughters were taken captive.

⁴Then David and the men with him lifted up their voices and wept until they had no more strength to weep.

⁵David's two wives also had been taken captive, Ahinoam the Jezreelitess and Abigail, the widow of Nabal the Carmelite.

⁶David was greatly distressed, for the men spoke of stoning him because the souls of them all were bitterly grieved, each man for his sons and daughters. But David encouraged *and* strengthened himself in the Lord his God.

⁷David said to Abiathar the priest, Ahimelech's son, I

## New International Version

Ahimelek, "Bring me the ephod." Abiathar brought it to him, [8]and David inquired of the LORD, "Shall I pursue this raiding party? Will I overtake them?"

"Pursue them," he answered. "You will certainly overtake them and succeed in the rescue."

[9]David and the six hundred men with him came to the Besor Valley, where some stayed behind. [10]Two hundred of them were too exhausted to cross the valley, but David and the other four hundred continued the pursuit.

[11]They found an Egyptian in a field and brought him to David. They gave him water to drink and food to eat— [12]part of a cake of pressed figs and two cakes of raisins. He ate and was revived, for he had not eaten any food or drunk any water for three days and three nights.

[13]David asked him, "Who do you belong to? Where do you come from?"

He said, "I am an Egyptian, the slave of an Amalekite. My master abandoned me when I became ill three days ago. [14]We raided the Negev of the Kerethites, some territory belonging to Judah and the Negev of Caleb. And we burned Ziklag."

[15]David asked him, "Can you lead me down to this raiding party?"

He answered, "Swear to me before God that you will not kill me or hand me over to my master, and I will take you down to them."

[16]He led David down, and there they were, scattered over the countryside, eating, drinking and reveling because of the great amount of plunder they had taken from the land of the Philistines and from Judah. [17]David fought them from dusk until the evening of the next day, and none of them got away, except four hundred young men who rode off on camels and fled. [18]David recovered everything the Amalekites had taken, including his two wives. [19]Nothing was missing: young or old, boy or girl, plunder or anything else they had taken. David brought everything back. [20]He took all the flocks and herds, and his men drove them ahead of the other livestock, saying, "This is David's plunder."

[21]Then David came to the two hundred men who had been too exhausted to follow him and who were left behind at the Besor Valley. They came out to meet David and the men with him. As David and his men approached, he asked them how they were. [22]But all the evil men and troublemakers among David's followers said, "Because they did not go out with us, we will not share with them the plunder we recovered. However, each man may take his wife and children and go."

[23]David replied, "No, my brothers, you must not do that with what the LORD has given us. He has protected us and delivered into our hands the raiding party that came against us. [24]Who will listen to what you say? The share of the man who stayed with the supplies is to be the same as that of him who went down to the battle. All will share alike." [25]David made this a statute and ordinance for Israel from that day to this.

[26]When David reached Ziklag, he sent some of the plunder to the elders of Judah, who were his friends, saying, "Here is a gift for you from the plunder of the LORD's enemies."

## Amplified Bible

pray you, bring me the ephod. And Abiathar brought him the ephod.

[8]And David inquired of the Lord, saying, Shall I pursue this troop? Shall I overtake them? The Lord answered him, Pursue, for you shall surely overtake them and without fail recover all.

[9]So David went, he and the 600 men with him, and came to the brook Besor; there those remained who were left behind.

[10]But David pursued, he and 400 men, for 200 stayed behind who were too exhausted *and* faint to cross the brook Besor.

[11]They found an Egyptian in the field and brought him to David, and gave him bread and he ate, and water to drink,

[12]And a piece of a cake of figs and two clusters of raisins; and when he had eaten, his spirit returned to him, for he had eaten no food or drunk any water for three days and three nights.

[13]And David said to him, To whom do you belong? And from where have you come? He said, I am a young man of Egypt, servant to an Amalekite; and my master left me because three days ago I fell sick.

[14]We had made a raid on the South (Negeb) of the Cherethites and upon that which belongs to Judah and upon the South (Negeb) of Caleb. And we burned Ziklag with fire.

[15]And David said to him, Can you take me down to this band? And he said, Swear to me by God that you will neither kill me nor deliver me into the hands of my master, and I will bring you down to this band.

[16]And when he had brought David down, behold, the raiders were spread abroad over all the land, eating and drinking and dancing because of all the great spoil they had taken from the land of the Philistines and from the land of Judah.

[17]And David smote them from twilight even to the evening of the next day, and not a man of them escaped, except 400 youths who rode camels and fled.

[18]David recovered all that the Amalekites had taken and rescued his two wives.

[19]Nothing was missing, small or great, sons or daughters, spoil or anything that had been taken; David recovered all.

[20]Also David captured all the flocks and herds [which the enemy had], and the people drove those animals before him and said, This is David's spoil.

[21]And David came to the 200 men who were so exhausted *and* faint that they could not follow [him] and had been left at the brook Besor [with the baggage]. They came to meet David and those with him, and when he came near to the men, he saluted them.

[22]Then all the wicked and base men who went with David said, Because they did not go with us, we will give them nothing of the spoil we have recovered, except that every man may lead away his wife and children and depart.

[23]David said, You shall not do so, my brethren, with what the Lord has given us. He has preserved us and has delivered into our hands the troop that came against us.

[24]Who would listen to you in this matter? For as is the share of him who goes into the battle, so shall his share be who stays by the baggage. They shall share alike.

[25]And from that day to this he made it a statute and ordinance for Israel.

[26]When David came to Ziklag, he sent part of the spoil to the elders of Judah, his friends, saying, Here is a gift for you of the spoil of the enemies of the Lord:

## New International Version

27 David sent it to those who were in Bethel, Ramoth Negev and Jattir; 28 to those in Aroer, Siphmoth, Eshtemoa 29 and Rakal; to those in the towns of the Jerahmeelites and the Kenites; 30 to those in Hormah, Bor Ashan, Athak 31 and Hebron; and to those in all the other places where he and his men had roamed.

### Saul Takes His Life

**31** Now the Philistines fought against Israel; the Israelites fled before them, and many fell dead on Mount Gilboa. 2 The Philistines were in hot pursuit of Saul and his sons, and they killed his sons Jonathan, Abinadab and Malki-Shua. 3 The fighting grew fierce around Saul, and when the archers overtook him, they wounded him critically.

4 Saul said to his armor-bearer, "Draw your sword and run me through, or these uncircumcised fellows will come and run me through and abuse me."

But his armor-bearer was terrified and would not do it; so Saul took his own sword and fell on it. 5 When the armor-bearer saw that Saul was dead, he too fell on his sword and died with him. 6 So Saul and his three sons and his armor-bearer and all his men died together that same day.

7 When the Israelites along the valley and those across the Jordan saw that the Israelite army had fled and that Saul and his sons had died, they abandoned their towns and fled. And the Philistines came and occupied them.

8 The next day, when the Philistines came to strip the dead, they found Saul and his three sons fallen on Mount Gilboa. 9 They cut off his head and stripped off his armor, and they sent messengers throughout the land of the Philistines to proclaim the news in the temple of their idols and among their people. 10 They put his armor in the temple of the Ashtoreths and fastened his body to the wall of Beth Shan.

11 When the people of Jabesh Gilead heard what the Philistines had done to Saul, 12 all their valiant men marched through the night to Beth Shan. They took down the bodies of Saul and his sons from the wall of Beth Shan and went to Jabesh, where they burned them. 13 Then they took their bones and buried them under a tamarisk tree at Jabesh, and they fasted seven days.

## Amplified Bible

27 For those in Bethel, Ramoth of the Negeb, Jattir, 28 Aroer, Siphmoth, Eshtemoa, 29 Racal, the cities of the Jerahmeelites, the cities of the Kenites; 30 Hormah, Bor-ashan, Athach, 31 Hebron, and for those in all the places David and his men had habitually haunted.

**31** Now the Philistines fought against Israel; and the men of Israel fled before [them] and fell slain on Mount Gilboa. 2 And the Philistines pursued Saul and his sons, and slew Jonathan and Abinadab and Malchi-shua, Saul's sons. 3 The battle went heavily against Saul, and the archers severely wounded him.

4 Saul said to his armor-bearer, Draw your sword and thrust me through, lest these uncircumcised come and thrust me through and abuse *and* mock me. But his armor-bearer would not, for he was terrified. So *a* Saul took a sword and fell upon it.

5 When his armor-bearer saw that Saul was dead, he likewise fell upon his sword and died with him. 6 So Saul, his three sons, his armor-bearer, and all his men died that day together.

7 And when the men of Israel on the other side of the valley and beyond the Jordan saw that the Israelites had fled and that Saul and his sons were dead, they forsook the cities and fled; and the Philistines came and dwelt in them.

8 The next day, when the Philistines came to strip the slain, they found Saul and his three sons fallen on Mount Gilboa.

9 They cut off Saul's head and stripped off his armor and sent it round about the land of the Philistines to publish it in the house of their idols and among the people.

10 And they put Saul's armor in the house of the Ashtaroth [the idols representing the female deities Ashtoreth and Asherah], and they fastened his body to the wall of Beth-shan.

11 When the people of Jabesh-gilead heard what the Philistines had done to Saul,

12 All the valiant men arose and went all night, and they took the bodies of Saul and his sons from the wall of Beth-shan and came to Jabesh and cremated them there.

13 And they took their bones and buried them under a tree at Jabesh, and fasted seven days.

*a* This account of Saul's death obviously contradicts that given by the Amalekite who came to David with Saul's spear and crown, claiming to have killed him (II Sam. 1:9ff). His story was probably a fabrication. He found the king's body on the battlefield, stripped it, and brought the spoil to David hoping for a reward, as *The Cambridge Bible* comments. However, it is possible that Saul was not entirely dead when the Amalekite found him, though his armor-bearer had thought him dead and had killed himself, in which case the Amalekite's story may have been true.

# 2 Samuel

# Samuel

## David Hears of Saul's Death

**1** After the death of Saul, David returned from striking down the Amalekites and stayed in Ziklag two days. ²On the third day a man arrived from Saul's camp with his clothes torn and dust on his head. When he came to David, he fell to the ground to pay him honor.

³"Where have you come from?" David asked him.

He answered, "I have escaped from the Israelite camp."

⁴"What happened?" David asked. "Tell me."

"The men fled from the battle," he replied. "Many of them fell and died. And Saul and his son Jonathan are dead."

⁵Then David said to the young man who brought him the report, "How do you know that Saul and his son Jonathan are dead?"

⁶"I happened to be on Mount Gilboa," the young man said, "and there was Saul, leaning on his spear, with the chariots and their drivers in hot pursuit. ⁷When he turned around and saw me, he called out to me, and I said, 'What can I do?'

⁸"He asked me, 'Who are you?'

"'An Amalekite,' I answered.

⁹"Then he said to me, 'Stand here by me and kill me! I'm in the throes of death, but I'm still alive.'

¹⁰"So I stood beside him and killed him, because I knew that after he had fallen he could not survive. And I took the crown that was on his head and the band on his arm and have brought them here to my lord."

¹¹Then David and all the men with him took hold of their clothes and tore them. ¹²They mourned and wept and fasted till evening for Saul and his son Jonathan, and for the army of the LORD and for the nation of Israel, because they had fallen by the sword.

¹³David said to the young man who brought him the report, "Where are you from?"

"I am the son of a foreigner, an Amalekite," he answered.

¹⁴David asked him, "Why weren't you afraid to lift your hand to destroy the LORD's anointed?"

¹⁵Then David called one of his men and said, "Go, strike him down!" So he struck him down, and he died. ¹⁶For David had said to him, "Your blood be on your own head. Your own mouth testified against you when you said, 'I killed the LORD's anointed.'"

## David's Lament for Saul and Jonathan

¹⁷David took up this lament concerning Saul and his son Jonathan, ¹⁸and he ordered that the people of Judah be taught this lament of the bow (it is written in the Book of Jashar):

¹⁹"A gazelle*a* lies slain on your heights, Israel.
　　How the mighty have fallen!

²⁰"Tell it not in Gath,
　　proclaim it not in the streets of Ashkelon,
　lest the daughters of the Philistines be glad,
　　lest the daughters of the uncircumcised rejoice.

²¹"Mountains of Gilboa,
　　may you have neither dew nor rain,
　　may no showers fall on your terraced fields.*b*
　For there the shield of the mighty was despised,
　　the shield of Saul—no longer rubbed with oil.

²²"From the blood of the slain,
　　from the flesh of the mighty,
　the bow of Jonathan did not turn back,
　　the sword of Saul did not return unsatisfied.

---

*a 19 Gazelle* here symbolizes a human dignitary.　*b 21* Or / *nor fields that yield grain for offerings*

**1** Now after the death of Saul, when David returned from the slaughter of the Amalekites, he had stayed two days in Ziklag,

²When on the third day a man came from Saul's camp with his clothes torn and dust on his head. When he came to David, he fell to the ground and did obeisance.

³David said to him, Where have you come from? He said, I have escaped from the camp of Israel.

⁴David said to him, How did it go? Tell me. He answered, The men have fled from the battle. Many have fallen and are dead; Saul and Jonathan his son are dead also.

⁵David said to the young man, How do you know Saul and Jonathan his son are dead?

⁶The young man said, By chance I happened to be on Mount Gilboa and I saw Saul leaning on his spear, and behold, the chariots and horsemen were close behind him.

⁷When he looked behind him, he saw me and called to me. I answered, Here I am.

⁸He asked me, Who are you? I answered, An Amalekite.

⁹He said to me, Rise up against me and slay me; for terrible dizziness has come upon me, yet my life is still in me [and I will be taken alive].

¹⁰So I stood up against him and slew him, because I was sure he could not live after he had fallen. So I took the crown on his head and the bracelet on his arm and have brought them here to my lord. [I Sam. 31:4.]

¹¹Then David grasped his own clothes and tore them; so did all the men with him.

¹²They mourned and wept for Saul and Jonathan his son, and fasted until evening for the Lord's people and the house of Israel, because of their defeat in battle.

¹³David said to the young man who told him, Where are you from? He answered, I am the son of a foreigner, an Amalekite.

¹⁴David said to him, Why were you not afraid to stretch forth your hand to destroy the Lord's anointed?

¹⁵David called one of the young men and said, Go near and fall upon him. And he smote him so that he died.

¹⁶David said to [the fallen man], Your blood be upon your own head; for you have testified against yourself, saying, I have slain the Lord's anointed.

¹⁷David lamented with this lamentation over Saul and Jonathan his son,

¹⁸And he commanded to teach it, [the lament of] the bow, to the Israelites. Behold, it is written in the Book of Jashar:

¹⁹Your glory, O Israel, is slain upon your high places. How have the mighty fallen!

²⁰Tell it not in Gath, announce it not in the streets of Ashkelon, lest the daughters of the Philistines rejoice, lest the daughters of the uncircumcised exult.

²¹O mountains of Gilboa, let there be no dew or rain upon you, or fields with offerings. For there the shield of the mighty was defiled, the shield of Saul, as though he were not anointed with oil.

²²From the blood of the slain, from the fat of the mighty, the bow of Jonathan turned not back, and the sword of Saul returned not empty.

## New International Version

23 Saul and Jonathan—
  in life they were loved and admired,
  and in death they were not parted.
They were swifter than eagles,
  they were stronger than lions.

24 "Daughters of Israel,
  weep for Saul,
who clothed you in scarlet and finery,
  who adorned your garments with ornaments of gold.

25 "How the mighty have fallen in battle!
  Jonathan lies slain on your heights.
26 I grieve for you, Jonathan my brother;
  you were very dear to me.
Your love for me was wonderful,
  more wonderful than that of women.

27 "How the mighty have fallen!
  The weapons of war have perished!"

### David Anointed King Over Judah

2 In the course of time, David inquired of the LORD. "Shall I go up to one of the towns of Judah?" he asked.
The LORD said, "Go up."
David asked, "Where shall I go?"
"To Hebron," the LORD answered.
2 So David went up there with his two wives, Ahinoam of Jezreel and Abigail, the widow of Nabal of Carmel. 3 David also took the men who were with him, each with his family, and they settled in Hebron and its towns. 4 Then the men of Judah came to Hebron, and there they anointed David king over the tribe of Judah.
  When David was told that it was the men from Jabesh Gilead who had buried Saul, 5 he sent messengers to them to say to them, "The LORD bless you for showing this kindness to Saul your master by burying him. 6 May the LORD now show you kindness and faithfulness, and I too will show you the same favor because you have done this. 7 Now then, be strong and brave, for Saul your master is dead, and the people of Judah have anointed me king over them."

### War Between the Houses of David and Saul

8 Meanwhile, Abner son of Ner, the commander of Saul's army, had taken Ish-Bosheth son of Saul and brought him over to Mahanaim. 9 He made him king over Gilead, Ashuri and Jezreel, and also over Ephraim, Benjamin and all Israel.
10 Ish-Bosheth son of Saul was forty years old when he became king over Israel, and he reigned two years. The tribe of Judah, however, remained loyal to David. 11 The length of time David was king in Hebron over Judah was seven years and six months.
12 Abner son of Ner, together with the men of Ish-Bosheth son of Saul, left Mahanaim and went to Gibeon. 13 Joab son of Zeruiah and David's men went out and met them at the pool of Gibeon. One group sat down on one side of the pool and one group on the other side. 14 Then Abner said to Joab, "Let's have some of the young men get up and fight hand to hand in front of us."
"All right, let them do it," Joab said.
15 So they stood up and were counted off—twelve men

## Amplified Bible

23 Saul and Jonathan, beloved and lovely! In their lives and in their deaths they were not divided. They were swifter than eagles, they were stronger than lions.
24 You daughters of Israel, weep over Saul, who clothed you in scarlet with [other] delights, who put ornaments of gold upon your apparel.
25 How have the mighty fallen in the midst of the battle! Jonathan lies slain upon your high places.
26 I am distressed for you, my brother Jonathan; very pleasant have you been to me. Your love to me was wonderful, passing the love of women.
27 How have the mighty fallen, and the weapons of war perished!

2 After this, David inquired of the Lord, saying, Shall I go up into any of the cities of Judah? And the Lord said to him, Go up. David said, To which shall I go up? And He said, To Hebron.
2 So David went up there with his two wives, Ahinoam the Jezreelitess and Abigail, the widow of Nabal of Carmel.
3 And David brought up his men who were with him, each one with his household, and they dwelt in the towns of Hebron.
4 And the men of Judah came and there they anointed David king over the house of Judah. They told David, The men of Jabesh-gilead buried Saul. [I Sam. 31:11-13.]
5 And David sent messengers to the men of Jabesh-gilead, saying, May the Lord bless you because you showed kindness and loyalty to Saul your king and buried him.
6 And now may the Lord show loving-kindness and faithfulness to you. I also will do well by you because you have done this.
7 So now, let your hands be strengthened and be valiant, for your master Saul is dead, and the house of Judah has anointed me king over them.
8 Now Abner son of Ner, commander of Saul's army, took Ish-bosheth son of Saul and brought him over to Mahanaim.
9 And he made him king over Gilead, the Ashurites, Jezreel, Ephraim, Benjamin, and all Israel.
10 Ish-bosheth, Saul's son, was forty years old when he began his two-year reign over Israel. But the house of Judah followed David.
11 And David was king in Hebron over the house of Judah for seven years and six months.
12 And Abner son of Ner and the servants of Ish-bosheth son of Saul went out from Mahanaim to Gibeon.
13 Joab son of Zeruiah and the servants of David went out also; and the two groups met by the pool of Gibeon, seating themselves with one group on either side of the pool.
14 And Abner said to Joab, Let the young men now arise and have a contest before us. And Joab said, Let them arise.
15 Then there arose and went over by number—twelve

## New International Version

for Benjamin and Ish-Bosheth son of Saul, and twelve for David. [16]Then each man grabbed his opponent by the head and thrust his dagger into his opponent's side, and they fell down together. So that place in Gibeon was called Helkath Hazzurim.[a]
[17]The battle that day was very fierce, and Abner and the Israelites were defeated by David's men.
[18]The three sons of Zeruiah were there: Joab, Abishai and Asahel. Now Asahel was as fleet-footed as a wild gazelle. [19]He chased Abner, turning neither to the right nor to the left as he pursued him. [20]Abner looked behind him and asked, "Is that you, Asahel?"
"It is," he answered.
[21]Then Abner said to him, "Turn aside to the right or to the left; take on one of the young men and strip him of his weapons." But Asahel would not stop chasing him.
[22]Again Abner warned Asahel, "Stop chasing me! Why should I strike you down? How could I look your brother Joab in the face?"
[23]But Asahel refused to give up the pursuit; so Abner thrust the butt of his spear into Asahel's stomach, and the spear came out through his back. He fell there and died on the spot. And every man stopped when he came to the place where Asahel had fallen and died.
[24]But Joab and Abishai pursued Abner, and as the sun was setting, they came to the hill of Ammah, near Giah on the way to the wasteland of Gibeon. [25]Then the men of Benjamin rallied behind Abner. They formed themselves into a group and took their stand on top of a hill.
[26]Abner called out to Joab, "Must the sword devour forever? Don't you realize that this will end in bitterness? How long before you order your men to stop pursuing their fellow Israelites?"
[27]Joab answered, "As surely as God lives, if you had not spoken, the men would have continued pursuing them until morning."
[28]So Joab blew the trumpet, and all the troops came to a halt; they no longer pursued Israel, nor did they fight anymore.
[29]All that night Abner and his men marched through the Arabah. They crossed the Jordan, continued through the morning hours[b] and came to Mahanaim.
[30]Then Joab stopped pursuing Abner and assembled the whole army. Besides Asahel, nineteen of David's men were found missing. [31]But David's men had killed three hundred and sixty Benjamites who were with Abner. [32]They took Asahel and buried him in his father's tomb at Bethlehem. Then Joab and his men marched all night and arrived at Hebron by daybreak.

**3** The war between the house of Saul and the house of David lasted a long time. David grew stronger and stronger, while the house of Saul grew weaker and weaker.
[2]Sons were born to David in Hebron:
His firstborn was Amnon the son of Ahinoam of Jezreel;

## Amplified Bible

of Benjamin who were with Ish-bosheth son of Saul, and twelve of the servants of David.
[16]And each caught his opponent by the head and thrust his sword into his side; so they all fell together. Therefore that place was called the Field of Sharp Knives, which is at Gibeon.
[17]A very fierce battle followed, and Abner and the men of Israel were beaten before the servants of David.
[18]Three sons of Zeruiah [the half sister of David] were there: Joab, Abishai, and Asahel. Now Asahel was as light of foot as a wild roe or antelope.
[19]Asahel pursued Abner, and as he ran he turned not to the right hand or to the left from following Abner.
[20]Then Abner looked behind him and said, Are you Asahel? He answered, I am.
[21]Abner said to him, Turn aside to your right or left, and seize one of the young men and take his armor. But Asahel would not turn aside from following him.
[22]And Abner said again to Asahel, Turn aside from following me. Why should I strike you to the ground? How then should I be able to face Joab your brother?
[23]Asahel refused to turn aside; so Abner with the rear end of his spear smote him through the abdomen, and he fell and died where he fell. And all who came to the place where Asahel fell and died stood still.
[24]But Joab and Abishai [his brothers] pursued Abner; the sun was going down as they came to the hill of Ammah, before Giah on the way to the wilderness of Gibeon.
[25]And the Benjamites gathered together behind Abner and became one troop and took their stand on the top of a hill.
[26]Then Abner called to Joab, Shall the sword devour forever? Do you not know that bitterness will be the result? How long will it be then before you bid the people to stop pursuing their brethren?
[27]Joab said, As God lives, if you had not spoken, surely the men would have stopped pursuing their brethren in the morning.
[28]So Joab blew a trumpet, and all the people stood still and pursued Israel no more, nor did they fight any more.
[29]Abner and his men went all night through the Arabah [plain], crossed the Jordan, and went through the whole Bithron [district of ravines] and came to Mahanaim.
[30]Joab returned from pursuing Abner, and when he had gathered all the people together, there were missing of David's servants nineteen men besides Asahel.
[31]But the servants of David had slain of Benjamin 360 of Abner's men.
[32]And they took up Asahel and buried him in the tomb of his father at Bethlehem. And Joab and his men walked all night and came to Hebron at daybreak.

**3** There was a long war between the house of Saul and the house of David. But David grew stronger and stronger, and the house of Saul grew weaker and weaker.
[2]Sons were born to David in Hebron: his firstborn was Amnon, by Ahinoam the Jezreelitess;

---

[a] 16 *Helkath Hazzurim* means *field of daggers* or *field of hostilities.*
[b] 29 See Septuagint; the meaning of the Hebrew for this phrase is uncertain.

## New International Version

3his second, Kileab the son of Abigail the widow of Nabal of Carmel;
the third, Absalom the son of Maakah daughter of Talmai king of Geshur;
4the fourth, Adonijah the son of Haggith;
the fifth, Shephatiah the son of Abital;
5and the sixth, Ithream the son of David's wife Eglah.
These were born to David in Hebron.

### Abner Goes Over to David

6During the war between the house of Saul and the house of David, Abner had been strengthening his own position in the house of Saul. 7Now Saul had had a concubine named Rizpah daughter of Aiah. And Ish-Bosheth said to Abner, "Why did you sleep with my father's concubine?"

8Abner was very angry because of what Ish-Bosheth said. So he answered, "Am I a dog's head—on Judah's side? This very day I am loyal to the house of your father Saul and to his family and friends. I haven't handed you over to David. Yet now you accuse me of an offense involving this woman! 9May God deal with Abner, be it ever so severely, if I do not do for David what the LORD promised him on oath 10and transfer the kingdom from the house of Saul and establish David's throne over Israel and Judah from Dan to Beersheba." 11Ish-Bosheth did not dare to say another word to Abner, because he was afraid of him.

12Then Abner sent messengers on his behalf to say to David, "Whose land is it? Make an agreement with me, and I will help you bring all Israel over to you."

13"Good," said David. "I will make an agreement with you. But I demand one thing of you: Do not come into my presence unless you bring Michal daughter of Saul when you come to see me." 14Then David sent messengers to Ish-Bosheth son of Saul, demanding, "Give me my wife Michal, whom I betrothed to myself for the price of a hundred Philistine foreskins."

15So Ish-Bosheth gave orders and had her taken away from her husband Paltiel son of Laish. 16Her husband, however, went with her, weeping behind her all the way to Bahurim. Then Abner said to him, "Go back home!" So he went back.

17Abner conferred with the elders of Israel and said, "For some time you have wanted to make David your king. 18Now do it! For the LORD promised David, 'By my servant David I will rescue my people Israel from the hand of the Philistines and from the hand of all their enemies.'"

19Abner also spoke to the Benjamites in person. Then he went to Hebron to tell David everything that Israel and the whole tribe of Benjamin wanted to do. 20When Abner, who had twenty men with him, came to David at Hebron, David prepared a feast for him and his men. 21Then Abner said to David, "Let me go at once and assemble all Israel for my lord the king, so that they may make a covenant with you, and that you may rule over all that your heart desires." So David sent Abner away, and he went in peace.

### Joab Murders Abner

22Just then David's men and Joab returned from a raid and brought with them a great deal of plunder. But Abner was no longer with David in Hebron, because David had sent him away, and he had gone in peace. 23When Joab and all the soldiers with him arrived, he was told that Abner son of Ner had come to the king and that the king had sent him away and that he had gone in peace.

24So Joab went to the king and said, "What have you

## Amplified Bible

3His second, Chileab, by Abigail widow of Nabal of Carmel; the third, Absalom the son of Maacah daughter of Talmai king of Geshur;
4The fourth, Adonijah the son of Haggith; the fifth, Shephatiah the son of Abital;
5And the sixth, Ithream, by Eglah, David's wife. These were born to David in Hebron.

6While there was war between the houses of Saul and David, Abner was making himself strong in the house of Saul.

7Now Saul had a concubine whose name was Rizpah daughter of Aiah. And Ish-bosheth said to Abner, Why have you gone in to my father's concubine?

8Then Abner was very angry at the words of Ish-bosheth and said, Am I a dog's head [despicable and hostile] against Judah? This day I keep showing kindness and loyalty to the house of Saul your father, to his brothers, and his friends, and have not delivered you into the hands of David; and yet you charge me today with a fault concerning this woman!

9May God do so to Abner, and more also, if I do not do for David what the Lord has sworn to him,

10To transfer the kingdom from the house of Saul and set the throne of David over Israel and Judah from Dan to Beersheba.

11And Ish-bosheth could not answer Abner a word, because he feared him.

12And Abner sent messengers to David where he was [at Hebron], saying, Whose is the land? Make your league with me, and my hand shall be with you to bring all Israel over to you.

13And David said, Good. I will make a league with you. But I require one thing of you: that is, you shall not see my face unless you first bring Michal, Saul's daughter, when you come to see me.

14And David sent messengers to Ish-bosheth, Saul's son, saying, Give me my wife Michal, whom I betrothed for a hundred foreskins of the Philistines.

15And Ish-bosheth sent and took her from her [second] husband, from Paltiel son of Laish [to whom Saul had given her].

16But her husband went with her, weeping behind her all the way to Bahurim. Then Abner said to him, Go back. And he did so.

17Abner talked with the seniors of Israel, saying, In times past you sought to make David king over you.

18Now then, do it! For the Lord has spoken of David, saying, By the hand of My servant David I will save My people Israel from the hands of the Philistines and of all their enemies. [I Sam. 9:16.]

19Abner also spoke to [the men of] Benjamin. Then [he] went to Hebron to tell David all that seemed good to Israel and the whole house of Benjamin to do.

20So Abner came to David at Hebron, and twenty men along with him. And David made Abner and the men with him a feast.

21Abner said to David, I will go and gather all Israel to my lord the king, that they may make a league with you, and that you may reign over all that your heart desires. So David sent Abner away in peace.

22Then the servants of David came with Joab from pursuing a troop and brought much spoil with them. But Abner was not with David in Hebron, for he had sent him away, and he had gone in peace.

23When Joab and all the army with him had come, it was told to Joab, Abner son of Ner came to the king, and he has sent him away, and he is gone in peace.

24Then Joab came to the king and said, What have you

## New International Version

done? Look, Abner came to you. Why did you let him go? Now he is gone! 25You know Abner son of Ner; he came to deceive you and observe your movements and find out everything you are doing."

26Joab then left David and sent messengers after Abner, and they brought him back from the cistern at Sirah. But David did not know it. 27Now when Abner returned to Hebron, Joab took him aside into an inner chamber, as if to speak with him privately. And there, to avenge the blood of his brother Asahel, Joab stabbed him in the stomach, and he died.

28Later, when David heard about this, he said, "I and my kingdom are forever innocent before the LORD concerning the blood of Abner son of Ner. 29May his blood fall on the head of Joab and on his whole family! May Joab's family never be without someone who has a running sore or leprosy[a] or who leans on a crutch or who falls by the sword or who lacks food."

30(Joab and his brother Abishai murdered Abner because he had killed their brother Asahel in the battle at Gibeon.)

31Then David said to Joab and all the people with him, "Tear your clothes and put on sackcloth and walk in mourning in front of Abner." King David himself walked behind the bier. 32They buried Abner in Hebron, and the king wept aloud at Abner's tomb. All the people wept also.

33The king sang this lament for Abner:

"Should Abner have died as the lawless die?
34    Your hands were not bound,
       your feet were not fettered.
You fell as one falls before the wicked."

And all the people wept over him again.

35Then they all came and urged David to eat something while it was still day; but David took an oath, saying, "May God deal with me, be it ever so severely, if I taste bread or anything else before the sun sets!"

36All the people took note and were pleased; indeed, everything the king did pleased them. 37So on that day all the people there and all Israel knew that the king had no part in the murder of Abner son of Ner.

38Then the king said to his men, "Do you not realize that a commander and a great man has fallen in Israel this day? 39And today, though I am the anointed king, I am weak, and these sons of Zeruiah are too strong for me. May the LORD repay the evildoer according to his evil deeds!"

## Amplified Bible

done? Behold, Abner came to you. Why is it you have sent him away and he is quite gone?

25You know that Abner son of Ner came to deceive you and to know your going out and coming in and all you are doing.

26When Joab came from seeing David, he sent messengers after Abner, and they brought him back from the well of Sirah; but David did not know it.

27And when Abner returned to Hebron, Joab took him aside to the center of the gate to speak to him privately, and there he smote Abner in the abdomen, so that he died to avenge the blood of Asahel, Joab's brother.

28When David heard of it, he said, I and my kingdom are guiltless before the Lord forever of the blood of Abner son of Ner.

29Let it fall on the head of Joab and on all his father's house; and let the house of Joab never be without one who has a discharge or is a leper or walks with a crutch or is a distaff holder [unfit for war] or who falls by the sword or lacks food!

30So Joab and Abishai his brother slew Abner because he had slain their brother Asahel at Gibeon in the battle.

31And David said to Joab and to all the people with him, Rend your clothes, gird yourselves with sackcloth, and mourn before Abner. And King David followed the bier.

32They buried Abner in Hebron. And the king lifted up his voice and wept at the grave of Abner, and all the people wept.

33And the king lamented over Abner and said, Should Abner die as a fool dies?

34Your hands were not bound or your feet put into fetters; as a man falls before wicked men, so you fell. And all the people wept again over him.

35All the people came to urge David to eat food while it was yet day; but David took an oath, saying, May God do so to me, and more also, if I taste bread or anything else, till the sun is down.

36And all the people took notice of it, and it pleased them, as whatever the king did pleased all the people.

37For all the people and all Israel understood that day that it was not the king's will to slay Abner son of Ner.

38King David said to his servants, Do you not know that a prince and a great man has fallen this day in Israel?

39And I am this day weak, though anointed [but not crowned] king; these sons of Zeruiah are too hard for me. May the Lord repay the evildoer according to his wickedness!

### Ish-Bosheth Murdered

**4** When Ish-Bosheth son of Saul heard that Abner had died in Hebron, he lost courage, and all Israel became alarmed. 2Now Saul's son had two men who were leaders of raiding bands. One was named Baanah and the other Rekab; they were sons of Rimmon the Beerothite from the tribe of Benjamin—Beeroth is considered part of Benjamin, 3because the people of Beeroth fled to Gittaim and have resided there as foreigners to this day.

4(Jonathan son of Saul had a son who was lame in both feet. He was five years old when the news about Saul and Jonathan came from Jezreel. His nurse picked him up and fled, but as she hurried to leave, he fell and became disabled. His name was Mephibosheth.)

5Now Rekab and Baanah, the sons of Rimmon the Be-

**4** When Ish-bosheth, Saul's son [king over Israel], heard that Abner was dead in Hebron, his courage failed, and all the Israelites were troubled and dismayed.

2Saul's son had two men who were captains of raiding bands. One was named Baanah and the other Rechab, sons of Rimmon the Beerothite of Benjamin—for Beeroth also was reckoned to Benjamin,

3And the Beerothites fled to Gittaim and have been sojourners there to this day.

4Jonathan, Saul's son, had a son who was a cripple in his feet. He was five years old when the news came out of Jezreel [of the deaths] of Saul and Jonathan. And the boy's nurse took him up and fled; and in her haste, he fell and became lame. His name was Mephibosheth.

5Now the sons of Rimmon the Beerothite, Rechab and

---

[a] 29 The Hebrew for *leprosy* was used for various diseases affecting the skin.

## New International Version

erothite, set out for the house of Ish-Bosheth, and they arrived there in the heat of the day while he was taking his noonday rest. 6They went into the inner part of the house as if to get some wheat, and they stabbed him in the stomach. Then Rekab and his brother Baanah slipped away.

7They had gone into the house while he was lying on the bed in his bedroom. After they stabbed and killed him, they cut off his head. Taking it with them, they traveled all night by way of the Arabah. 8They brought the head of Ish-Bosheth to David at Hebron and said to the king, "Here is the head of Ish-Bosheth son of Saul, your enemy, who tried to kill you. This day the LORD has avenged my lord the king against Saul and his offspring."

9David answered Rekab and his brother Baanah, the sons of Rimmon the Beerothite, "As surely as the LORD lives, who has delivered me out of every trouble, 10when someone told me, 'Saul is dead,' and thought he was bringing good news, I seized him and put him to death in Ziklag. That was the reward I gave him for his news! 11How much more—when wicked men have killed an innocent man in his own house and on his own bed—should I not now demand his blood from your hand and rid the earth of you!"

12So David gave an order to his men, and they killed them. They cut off their hands and feet and hung the bodies by the pool in Hebron. But they took the head of Ish-Bosheth and buried it in Abner's tomb at Hebron.

### David Becomes King Over Israel

**5** All the tribes of Israel came to David at Hebron and said, "We are your own flesh and blood. 2In the past, while Saul was king over us, you were the one who led Israel on their military campaigns. And the LORD said to you, 'You will shepherd my people Israel, and you will become their ruler.'"

3When all the elders of Israel had come to King David at Hebron, the king made a covenant with them at Hebron before the LORD, and they anointed David king over Israel.

4David was thirty years old when he became king, and he reigned forty years. 5In Hebron he reigned over Judah seven years and six months, and in Jerusalem he reigned over all Israel and Judah thirty-three years.

### David Conquers Jerusalem

6The king and his men marched to Jerusalem to attack the Jebusites, who lived there. The Jebusites said to David, "You will not get in here; even the blind and the lame can ward you off." They thought, "David cannot get in here." 7Nevertheless, David captured the fortress of Zion—which is the City of David.

8On that day David had said, "Anyone who conquers the Jebusites will have to use the water shaft to reach those 'lame and blind' who are David's enemies.a" That is why they say, "The 'blind and lame' will not enter the palace."

9David then took up residence in the fortress and called it the City of David. He built up the area around it, from the terracesb inward. 10And he became more and more powerful, because the LORD God Almighty was with him.

11Now Hiram king of Tyre sent envoys to David, along with cedar logs and carpenters and stonemasons, and they built a palace for David. 12Then David knew that the LORD had established him as king over Israel and had exalted his kingdom for the sake of his people Israel.

## Amplified Bible

Baanah, went about in the heat of the day to the house of Ish-bosheth, who lay resting on his bed at noon.

6And they came into the interior of the house as though they were delivering wheat, and they smote him in the body; and Rechab and Baanah his brother escaped.

7Now when they had come into the house and he lay on his bed in his bedroom, they [not only] smote and slew him, [but] beheaded him and took his head and went by the way of the plain all night.

8And they brought the head of Ish-bosheth to David at Hebron and said to the king, Behold, the head of Ish-bosheth son of Saul, your enemy, who sought your life; and the Lord has avenged my lord the king this day on Saul and on his offspring.

9And David answered Rechab and Baanah his brother, sons of Rimmon the Beerothite, As the Lord lives, Who redeemed my life out of all adversity,

10When one told me, Behold, Saul is dead, thinking he was bringing good news, I seized and slew him in Ziklag who expected me to give him a reward for his news.

11How much more—when wicked men have slain a just man in his own house on his bed—shall I not now require his blood of your hand and remove you from the earth!

12David commanded his young men, and they slew them and cut off their hands and feet and hanged them over the pool in Hebron. But they took Ish-bosheth's head and buried it in Hebron in the tomb of Abner [his relative and once chief supporter].

**5** Then all the tribes of Israel came to David at Hebron and said, Behold, we are your bone and your flesh.

2In times past, when Saul was king over us, it was you who led out and brought in Israel. And the Lord told you, You shall feed My people Israel and be prince over [them]. [I Sam. 15:27-29; 16:1.]

3So all the elders of Israel came to the king at Hebron, and King David made a covenant with them [there] before the Lord, and they anointed [him] king over Israel.

4David was thirty years old when he began his forty-year reign.

5In Hebron he reigned over Judah seven years and six months, and in Jerusalem he reigned thirty-three years over all Israel and Judah.

6And the king and his men went to Jerusalem against the Jebusites, the inhabitants of the land, who said to David, You shall not enter here, for the blind and the lame will prevent you; they thought, David cannot come in here.

7Nevertheless, David took the stronghold of Zion, that is, the City of David.

8David said on that day, Whoever smites the Jebusites, let him get up through the water shaft and smite the lame and the blind who are detested by David's soul. So they say, The blind and the lame shall not come into the house.

9So David dwelt in the stronghold and called it the City of David. And he built round about from the Millo and inward.

10David became greater and greater, for the Lord God of hosts was with him.

11Hiram king of Tyre sent messengers to David, and cedar trees, carpenters, and masons; and they built David a house.

12And David perceived that the Lord had established him king over Israel and that He had exalted his kingdom for His people Israel's sake.

---

a 8 Or are hated by David    b 9 Or the Millo

## New International Version

13After he left Hebron, David took more concubines and wives in Jerusalem, and more sons and daughters were born to him. 14These are the names of the children born to him there: Shammua, Shobab, Nathan, Solomon, 15Ibhar, Elishua, Nepheg, Japhia, 16Elishama, Eliada and Eliphelet.

### David Defeats the Philistines

17When the Philistines heard that David had been anointed king over Israel, they went up in full force to search for him, but David heard about it and went down to the stronghold. 18Now the Philistines had come and spread out in the Valley of Rephaim; 19so David inquired of the LORD, "Shall I go and attack the Philistines? Will you deliver them into my hands?"

The LORD answered him, "Go, for I will surely deliver the Philistines into your hands."

20So David went to Baal Perazim, and there he defeated them. He said, "As waters break out, the LORD has broken out against my enemies before me." So that place was called Baal Perazim.a 21The Philistines abandoned their idols there, and David and his men carried them off.

22Once more the Philistines came up and spread out in the Valley of Rephaim; 23so David inquired of the LORD, and he answered, "Do not go straight up, but circle around behind them and attack them in front of the poplar trees. 24As soon as you hear the sound of marching in the tops of the poplar trees, move quickly, because that will mean the LORD has gone out in front of you to strike the Philistine army." 25So David did as the LORD commanded him, and he struck down the Philistines all the way from Gibeonb to Gezer.

### The Ark Brought to Jerusalem

**6** David again brought together all the able young men of Israel—thirty thousand. 2He and all his men went to Baalahc in Judah to bring up from there the ark of God, which is called by the Name,d the name of the LORD Almighty, who is enthroned between the cherubim on the ark. 3They set the ark of God on a new cart and brought it from the house of Abinadab, which was on the hill. Uzzah and Ahio, sons of Abinadab, were guiding the new cart 4with the ark of God on it,e and Ahio was walking in front of it. 5David and all Israel were celebrating with all their might before the LORD, with castanets,f harps, lyres, timbrels, sistrums and cymbals.

6When they came to the threshing floor of Nakon, Uzzah reached out and took hold of the ark of God, because the oxen stumbled. 7The LORD's anger burned against Uzzah because of his irreverent act; therefore God struck him down, and he died there beside the ark of God.

8Then David was angry because the LORD's wrath had broken out against Uzzah, and to this day that place is called Perez Uzzah.g

9David was afraid of the LORD that day and said, "How can the ark of the LORD ever come to me?" 10He was not

## Amplified Bible

13And David took more concubines and wives out of Jerusalem, after he came from Hebron, and other sons and daughters were born to [him].

14And these are the names of those who were born to him in Jerusalem: Shammua, Shobab, Nathan, Solomon, 15Ibhar, Elishua, Nepheg, Japhia, 16Elishama, Eliada, and Eliphelet.

17When the Philistines heard that David had been anointed king over Israel, they all went up to find [him], but [he] heard of it and went down to the stronghold. 18The Philistines also came and spread themselves in the Valley of Rephaim.

19David inquired of the Lord, saying, Shall I go up against the Philistines? Will You deliver them into my hand? And the Lord said to David, Go up, for I will surely deliver [them] into your hand.

20And David came to Baal-perazim, and he smote them there, and said, The Lord has broken through my enemies before me, like the bursting out of great waters. So he called the name of that place Baal-perazim [Lord of breaking through].

21There the Philistines left their aimages, and David and his men took them away.

22The Philistines came up again and spread themselves out in the Valley of Rephaim.

23When David inquired of the Lord, He said, You shall not go up, but go around behind them and come upon them over opposite the mulberry (or balsam) trees.

24And when you hear the sound of marching in the tops of the mulberry trees, then bestir yourselves, for then has the Lord gone out before you to smite the army of the Philistines.

25And David did as the Lord had commanded him, and smote the Philistines from Geba to Gezer.

**6** Again David gathered together all the chosen men of Israel, 30,000.

2And [he] arose and went with all the people who were with him to Baale-judah [Kiriath-jearim] to bring up from there the ark of God, which is called by the name of the Lord of hosts, Who sits enthroned above the cherubim.

3And they set the ark of God upon a new cart and brought it bout of the house of Abinadab, which was on the hill; and Uzzah and Ahio, sons of Abinadab, drove the new cart.

4And they brought it out of the house of Abinadab, which was on the hill, with the ark of God; and Ahio went before the ark.

5And David and all The house of Israel played before the Lord with all their might, with songs, lyres, harps, tambourines, castanets, and cymbals.

6And when they came to Nacon's threshing floor, Uzzah put out his hand to the ark of God and took hold of it, for the oxen stumbled *and* shook it.

7And the anger of the Lord was kindled against Uzzah; and God smote him there for touching the ark, and he died there by the ark of God.

8David was grieved *and* offended because the Lord had broken forth upon Uzzah, and that place is called Perezuzzah [the breaking forth upon Uzzah] to this day.

9David was afraid of the Lord that day and said, How can the ark of the Lord come to me?

---

a 20 *Baal Perazim* means *the lord who breaks out.*    b 25 Septuagint (see also 1 Chron. 14:16); Hebrew *Geba*    c 2 That is, Kiriath Jearim (see 1 Chron. 13:6)    d 2 Hebrew; Septuagint and Vulgate do not have *the Name.*    e 3,4 Dead Sea Scrolls and some Septuagint manuscripts; Masoretic Text *cart* 4*and they brought it with the ark of God from the house of Abinadab, which was on the hill*    f 5 Masoretic Text; Dead Sea Scrolls and Septuagint (see also 1 Chron. 13:8) *songs*    g 8 *Perez Uzzah* means *outbreak against Uzzah.*

---

a The Israelites took as spoil the images of the Philistines, perhaps to display in triumphal procession, though they were afterward burned (I Chron. 14:12) in compliance with the law of Deut. 7:5, 25. Thus the old disgrace of the capture of the ark by the Philistines was avenged (I Sam. 4:4, 10, 11) (*The Cambridge Bible*).    b How long had the ark been in the house of Abinadab (see I Sam. 7:2)?

## New International Version

willing to take the ark of the Lord to be with him in the City of David. Instead, he took it to the house of Obed-Edom the Gittite. ¹¹The ark of the Lord remained in the house of Obed-Edom the Gittite for three months, and the Lord blessed him and his entire household.

¹²Now King David was told, "The Lord has blessed the household of Obed-Edom and everything he has, because of the ark of God." So David went to bring up the ark of God from the house of Obed-Edom to the City of David with rejoicing. ¹³When those who were carrying the ark of the Lord had taken six steps, he sacrificed a bull and a fattened calf. ¹⁴Wearing a linen ephod, David was dancing before the Lord with all his might, ¹⁵while he and all Israel were bringing up the ark of the Lord with shouts and the sound of trumpets.

¹⁶As the ark of the Lord was entering the City of David, Michal daughter of Saul watched from a window. And when she saw King David leaping and dancing before the Lord, she despised him in her heart.

¹⁷They brought the ark of the Lord and set it in its place inside the tent that David had pitched for it, and David sacrificed burnt offerings and fellowship offerings before the Lord. ¹⁸After he had finished sacrificing the burnt offerings and fellowship offerings, he blessed the people in the name of the Lord Almighty. ¹⁹Then he gave a loaf of bread, a cake of dates and a cake of raisins to each person in the whole crowd of Israelites, both men and women. And all the people went to their homes.

²⁰When David returned home to bless his household, Michal daughter of Saul came out to meet him and said, "How the king of Israel has distinguished himself today, going around half-naked in full view of the slave girls of his servants as any vulgar fellow would!"

²¹David said to Michal, "It was before the Lord, who chose me rather than your father or anyone from his house when he appointed me ruler over the Lord's people Israel—I will celebrate before the Lord. ²²I will become even more undignified than this, and I will be humiliated in my own eyes. But by these slave girls you spoke of, I will be held in honor."

²³And Michal daughter of Saul had no children to the day of her death.

### God's Promise to David

**7** After the king was settled in his palace and the Lord had given him rest from all his enemies around him, ²he said to Nathan the prophet, "Here I am, living in a house of cedar, while the ark of God remains in a tent."

³Nathan replied to the king, "Whatever you have in mind, go ahead and do it, for the Lord is with you."

⁴But that night the word of the Lord came to Nathan, saying:

⁵"Go and tell my servant David, 'This is what the Lord says: Are you the one to build me a house to dwell in? ⁶I have not dwelt in a house from the day I brought the Israelites up out of Egypt to this day. I have been moving from place to place with a tent as my dwelling. ⁷Wherever I have moved with all the Israelites, did I ever say to any of their rulers whom I commanded to shepherd my people Israel, "Why have you not built me a house of cedar?"'

## Amplified Bible

¹⁰So David was not willing to take the ark of the Lord to him into the City of David; but he took it aside into the house of Obed-edom the Gittite.

¹¹And the ark of the Lord remained in the house of Obed-edom the Gittite for three months, and the Lord blessed Obed-edom and all his household.

¹²And it was told King David, The Lord has blessed the house of Obed-edom and all that belongs to him, because of the ark of God. So David went and brought up the ark of God from the house of Obed-edom into the City of David with rejoicing;

¹³And when those who bore the ark of the Lord had gone six paces, he sacrificed an ox and a fatling.

¹⁴And David danced before the Lord with all his might, clad in a linen ephod [a priest's upper garment].

¹⁵So David and all the house of Israel brought up the ark of the Lord with shouting and with the sound of the trumpet.

¹⁶As the ark of the Lord came into the City of David, Michal, Saul's daughter [David's wife], looked out of the window and saw King David leaping and dancing before the Lord, and she despised him in her heart.

¹⁷They brought in the ark of the Lord and set it in its place inside the tent which David had pitched for it, and David offered burnt offerings and peace offerings before the Lord.

¹⁸When David had finished offering the burnt offerings and peace offerings, he blessed the people in the name [and presence] of the Lord of hosts,

¹⁹And distributed among all the people, the whole multitude of Israel, both to men and women, to each a cake of bread, a portion of meat, and a cake of raisins. So all the people departed, each to his house.

²⁰Then David returned to bless his household. And [his wife] Michal daughter of Saul came out to meet David and said, How glorious was the king of Israel today, who stripped himself of his kingly robes *and* uncovered himself in the eyes of his servants' maids as one of the worthless fellows shamelessly uncovers himself!

²¹David said to Michal, It was before the Lord, Who chose me above your father and all his house to appoint me as prince over Israel, the people of the Lord. Therefore will I make merry [in pure enjoyment] before the Lord.

²²I will be still more lightly esteemed than this, and will humble *and* lower myself in my own sight [and yours]. But by the maids you mentioned, I will be held in honor.

²³And Michal the daughter of Saul had no child to the day of her death.

**7** When King David dwelt in his house and the Lord had given him rest from all his surrounding enemies,

²The king said to Nathan the prophet, See now, I dwell in a house of cedar, but the ark of God dwells within curtains.

³And Nathan said to the king, Go, do all that is in your heart, for the Lord is with you.

⁴That night the word of the Lord came to Nathan, saying,

⁵Go and tell My servant David, Thus says the Lord: Shall you build Me a house in which to dwell?

⁶For I have not dwelt in a house since I brought the Israelites out of Egypt to this day, but have moved about with a tent for My dwelling.

⁷In all the places where I have moved with all the Israelites, did I speak a word to any from the tribes of Israel whom I commanded to be shepherd of My people Israel, asking, Why do you not build Me a house of cedar?

## New International Version

8"Now then, tell my servant David, 'This is what the LORD Almighty says: I took you from the pasture, from tending the flock, and appointed you ruler over my people Israel. 9I have been with you wherever you have gone, and I have cut off all your enemies from before you. Now I will make your name great, like the names of the greatest men on earth. 10And I will provide a place for my people Israel and will plant them so that they can have a home of their own and no longer be disturbed. Wicked people will not oppress them anymore, as they did at the beginning 11and have done ever since the time I appointed leaders*a* over my people Israel. I will also give you rest from all your enemies.

"'The LORD declares to you that the LORD himself will establish a house for you: 12When your days are over and you rest with your ancestors, I will raise up your offspring to succeed you, your own flesh and blood, and I will establish his kingdom. 13He is the one who will build a house for my Name, and I will establish the throne of his kingdom forever. 14I will be his father, and he will be my son. When he does wrong, I will punish him with a rod wielded by men, with floggings inflicted by human hands. 15But my love will never be taken away from him, as I took it away from Saul, whom I removed from before you. 16Your house and your kingdom will endure forever before me*b*; your throne will be established forever.'"

17Nathan reported to David all the words of this entire revelation.

### David's Prayer

18Then King David went in and sat before the LORD, and he said:

"Who am I, Sovereign LORD, and what is my family, that you have brought me this far? 19And as if this were not enough in your sight, Sovereign LORD, you have also spoken about the future of the house of your servant—and this decree, Sovereign LORD, is for a mere human!*c*

20"What more can David say to you? For you know your servant, Sovereign LORD. 21For the sake of your word and according to your will, you have done this great thing and made it known to your servant.

22"How great you are, Sovereign LORD! There is no one like you, and there is no God but you, as we have heard with our own ears. 23And who is like your people Israel—the one nation on earth that God went out to redeem as a people for himself, and to make a name for himself, and to perform great and awesome wonders by driving out nations and their gods from before your people, whom you redeemed from Egypt?*d* 24You have established your people Israel as your very own forever, and you, LORD, have become their God.

25"And now, LORD God, keep forever the promise you have made concerning your servant and his house. Do as you promised, 26so that your name will be great forever. Then people will say, 'The LORD Almighty is God over Israel!' And the house of your servant David will be established in your sight.

27"LORD Almighty, God of Israel, you have revealed this to your servant, saying, 'I will build a house for you.' So your servant has found courage to pray this prayer to you. 28Sovereign LORD, you are God! Your

## Amplified Bible

8So now say this to My servant David, Thus says the Lord of hosts: I took you from the pasture, from following the sheep, to be prince over My people Israel.

9And I was with you wherever you went, and have cut off all your enemies from before you; and I will make you a great name, like [that] of the great men of the earth.

10And I will appoint a place for My people Israel and will plant them, that they may dwell in a place of their own and be moved no more. And wicked men shall afflict them no more, as formerly

11And as from the time that I appointed judges over My people Israel; and I will cause you to rest from all your enemies. Also the Lord declares to you that He will make for you a house:

12And when your days are fulfilled and you sleep with your fathers, I will set up after you your offspring who shall be born to you, and I will establish his kingdom.

13He shall build a house for My *a*Name [and My Presence], and I will establish the throne of his kingdom forever.

14I will be his Father, and he shall be My son. When he commits iniquity, I will chasten him with the rod of men and with the stripes of the sons of men.

15But My mercy *and* loving-kindness shall not depart from him, as I took [them] from Saul, whom I took away from before you.

16And your house and your kingdom shall be made sure forever before you; your throne shall be established forever.

17In accordance with all these words and all this vision Nathan spoke to David.

18Then King David went in and sat before the Lord, and said, Who am I, O Lord God, and what is my house, that You have brought me this far?

19Then as if this were a little thing in Your eyes, O Lord God, You have spoken also of Your servant's house in the far distant future. And this is the law for man, O Lord God!

20What more can David say to You? For You know Your servant, O Lord God.

21Because of Your promise and as Your own heart dictates, You have done all these astounding things to make Your servant know *and* understand.

22Therefore You are great, O Lord God; for none is like You, nor is there any God besides You, according to all [You have made] our ears to hear.

23What [other] one nation on earth is like Your people Israel, whom God went to redeem to be a people for Himself and to make for Himself a name? You have done great and terrible things for Yourself *and* for Your land, before Your people, whom You redeemed *and* delivered for Yourself from Egypt, from the nations and their gods.

24And You have established for Yourself Your people Israel to be Your people forever, and You, Lord, became their God.

25Now, O Lord God, confirm forever the word You have given as to Your servant and his house; and do as You have said,

26And Your name [and presence] shall be magnified forever, saying, The Lord of hosts is God over Israel; and the house of Your servant David will be made firm before You.

27For You, O Lord of hosts, God of Israel, have revealed this to Your servant: I will build you a house. So Your servant has found courage to pray this prayer to You.

28And now, O Lord God, You are God, and Your words

---

*a 11* Traditionally *judges*   *b 16* Some Hebrew manuscripts and Septuagint; most Hebrew manuscripts *you*   *c 19* Or *for the human race*   *d 23* See Septuagint and 1 Chron. 17:21; Hebrew *wonders for your land and before your people, whom you redeemed from Egypt, from the nations and their gods.*

*a* "Name" is equivalent to "Me" in II Sam. 7:5. See also footnote on Deut. 12:5.

## New International Version

covenant is trustworthy, and you have promised these good things to your servant. ²⁹Now be pleased to bless the house of your servant, that it may continue forever in your sight; for you, Sovereign LORD, have spoken, and with your blessing the house of your servant will be blessed forever."

### David's Victories

**8** In the course of time, David defeated the Philistines and subdued them, and he took Metheg Ammah from the control of the Philistines.

²David also defeated the Moabites. He made them lie down on the ground and measured them off with a length of cord. Every two lengths of them were put to death, and the third length was allowed to live. So the Moabites became subject to David and brought him tribute.

³Moreover, David defeated Hadadezer son of Rehob, king of Zobah, when he went to restore his monument at*a* the Euphrates River. ⁴David captured a thousand of his chariots, seven thousand charioteers*b* and twenty thousand foot soldiers. He hamstrung all but a hundred of the chariot horses.

⁵When the Arameans of Damascus came to help Hadadezer king of Zobah, David struck down twenty-two thousand of them. ⁶He put garrisons in the Aramean kingdom of Damascus, and the Arameans became subject to him and brought tribute. The LORD gave David victory wherever he went.

⁷David took the gold shields that belonged to the officers of Hadadezer and brought them to Jerusalem. ⁸From Tebah*c* and Berothai, towns that belonged to Hadadezer, King David took a great quantity of bronze.

⁹When Tou*d* king of Hamath heard that David had defeated the entire army of Hadadezer, ¹⁰he sent his son Joram*e* to King David to greet him and congratulate him on his victory in battle over Hadadezer, who had been at war with Tou. Joram brought with him articles of silver, of gold and of bronze.

¹¹King David dedicated these articles to the LORD, as he had done with the silver and gold from all the nations he had subdued: ¹²Edom*f* and Moab, the Ammonites and the Philistines, and Amalek. He also dedicated the plunder taken from Hadadezer son of Rehob, king of Zobah.

¹³And David became famous after he returned from striking down eighteen thousand Edomites*g* in the Valley of Salt.

¹⁴He put garrisons throughout Edom, and all the Edomites became subject to David. The LORD gave David victory wherever he went.

### David's Officials

¹⁵David reigned over all Israel, doing what was just and right for all his people. ¹⁶Joab son of Zeruiah was over the army; Jehoshaphat son of Ahilud was recorder; ¹⁷Zadok son of Ahitub and Ahimelek son of Abiathar were priests; Seraiah was secretary; ¹⁸Benaiah son of Jehoiada was over the Kerethites and Pelethites; and David's sons were priests.*h*

## Amplified Bible

are truth, and You have promised this good thing to Your servant.

²⁹Therefore now let it please You to bless the house of Your servant, that it may continue forever before You; for You, O Lord God, have spoken it, and with Your blessing let [his] house be blessed forever.

**8** After this David smote the Philistines and subdued them, and he took Metheg-ammah out of the hands of the Philistines.

²He defeated Moab, and measured them with a line, making them lie down on the ground; two lines he measured to be put to death, and one full line to keep alive. And the Moabites became servants to David, bringing tribute.

³David also defeated Hadadezer son of Rehob, king of Zobah, as he went to restore his power at the river [Euphrates].

⁴David took from him 1,700 horsemen and 20,000 foot soldiers; and David hamstrung all the chariot horses, except he reserved enough of them for 100 chariots.

⁵And when the Syrians of Damascus came to help Hadadezer king of Zobah, David slew 22,000 of them.

⁶David put garrisons in Syrian Damascus, and the Syrians became [his] servants and brought tribute. The Lord preserved *and* gave victory to David wherever he went.

⁷And David took the shields of gold that were on the servants of Hadadezer and brought them to Jerusalem.

⁸And from Betah and Berothai, cities of Hadadezer, King David exacted an immense amount of bronze.

⁹When Toi king of Hamath heard about David's defeat of all the forces of Hadadezer,

¹⁰[He] sent Joram his son to King David to salute *and* congratulate him about his battle and defeat of Hadadezer. For Hadadezer had had wars with Toi. Joram brought vessels of silver, gold, and bronze.

¹¹These King David dedicated to the Lord, with the silver and gold that he had dedicated from all the nations he subdued:

¹²From Syria, Moab, the Ammonites, the Philistines, Amalek, and from the spoil of Hadadezer son of Rehob, king of Zobah.

¹³David won renown. When he returned he slew 18,000 Edomites in the Valley of Salt.

¹⁴He put garrisons throughout all Edom, and all the Edomites became his servants. And the Lord preserved *and* gave victory to [him] wherever he went.

¹⁵So David reigned over all Israel, and executed justice and righteousness for all his people.

¹⁶Joab son of Zeruiah was over the army; Jehoshaphat son of Ahilud was recorder;

¹⁷Zadok son of Ahitub and Ahimelech son of Abiathar were the [chief] priests, and Seraiah was the scribe;

¹⁸Benaiah son of Jehoiada was over both the Cherethites and Pelethites [the king's bodyguards]; and David's sons were chief [confidential] assistants to the king.

---

*a 3* Or *his control along*    *b 4* Septuagint (see also Dead Sea Scrolls and 1 Chron. 18:4); Masoretic Text *captured seventeen hundred of his charioteers*    *c 8* See some Septuagint manuscripts (see also 1 Chron. 18:8); Hebrew *Betah*.    *d 9* Hebrew *Toi,* a variant of *Tou*; also in verse 10    *e 10* A variant of *Hadoram*    *f 12* Some Hebrew manuscripts, Septuagint and Syriac (see also 1 Chron. 18:11); most Hebrew manuscripts *Aram*    *g 13* A few Hebrew manuscripts, Septuagint and Syriac (see also 1 Chron. 18:12); most Hebrew manuscripts *Aram* (that is, Arameans)    *h 18* Or *were chief officials* (see Septuagint and Targum; also 1 Chron. 18:17)

| New International Version | Amplified Bible |
|---|---|

## New International Version

### David and Mephibosheth

**9** David asked, "Is there anyone still left of the house of Saul to whom I can show kindness for Jonathan's sake?"

²Now there was a servant of Saul's household named Ziba. They summoned him to appear before David, and the king said to him, "Are you Ziba?"

"At your service," he replied.

³The king asked, "Is there no one still alive from the house of Saul to whom I can show God's kindness?"

Ziba answered the king, "There is still a son of Jonathan; he is lame in both feet."

⁴"Where is he?" the king asked.

Ziba answered, "He is at the house of Makir son of Ammiel in Lo Debar."

⁵So King David had him brought from Lo Debar, from the house of Makir son of Ammiel.

⁶When Mephibosheth son of Jonathan, the son of Saul, came to David, he bowed down to pay him honor.

David said, "Mephibosheth!"

"At your service," he replied.

⁷"Don't be afraid," David said to him, "for I will surely show you kindness for the sake of your father Jonathan. I will restore to you all the land that belonged to your grandfather Saul, and you will always eat at my table."

⁸Mephibosheth bowed down and said, "What is your servant, that you should notice a dead dog like me?"

⁹Then the king summoned Ziba, Saul's steward, and said to him, "I have given your master's grandson everything that belonged to Saul and his family. ¹⁰You and your sons and your servants are to farm the land for him and bring in the crops, so that your master's grandson may be provided for. And Mephibosheth, grandson of your master, will always eat at my table." (Now Ziba had fifteen sons and twenty servants.)

¹¹Then Ziba said to the king, "Your servant will do whatever my lord the king commands his servant to do." So Mephibosheth ate at David's*ᵃ* table like one of the king's sons.

¹²Mephibosheth had a young son named Mika, and all the members of Ziba's household were servants of Mephibosheth. ¹³And Mephibosheth lived in Jerusalem, because he always ate at the king's table; he was lame in both feet.

### David Defeats the Ammonites

**10** In the course of time, the king of the Ammonites died, and his son Hanun succeeded him as king. ²David thought, "I will show kindness to Hanun son of Nahash, just as his father showed kindness to me." So David sent a delegation to express his sympathy to Hanun concerning his father.

When David's men came to the land of the Ammonites, ³the Ammonite commanders said to Hanun their lord, "Do you think David is honoring your father by sending envoys to you to express sympathy? Hasn't David sent them to you only to explore the city and spy it out and overthrow it?" ⁴So Hanun seized David's envoys, shaved off half of each man's beard, cut off their garments at the buttocks, and sent them away.

⁵When David was told about this, he sent messengers to meet the men, for they were greatly humiliated. The king said, "Stay at Jericho till your beards have grown, and then come back."

⁶When the Ammonites realized that they had become obnoxious to David, they hired twenty thousand Aramean foot soldiers from Beth Rehob and Zobah, as well as the king of Maakah with a thousand men, and also twelve thousand men from Tob.

## Amplified Bible

**9** And David said, Is there still anyone left of the house of Saul to whom I may show kindness for Jonathan's sake?

²And of the house of Saul there was a servant whose name was Ziba. When they had called him to David, he said to him, Are you Ziba? He said, I, your servant, am he.

³The king said, Is there not still someone of the house of Saul to whom I may show the [unfailing, unsought, unlimited] mercy *and* kindness of God? Ziba replied, Jonathan has yet a son who is lame in his feet. [I Sam. 20:14-17.]

⁴And the king said, Where is he? Ziba replied, He is in the house of Machir son of Ammiel in Lo-debar.

⁵Then King David sent and brought him from the house of Machir son of Ammiel at Lo-debar.

⁶And Mephibosheth son of Jonathan, the son of Saul, came to David and fell on his face and did obeisance. David said, Mephibosheth! And he answered, Behold your servant!

⁷David said to him, Fear not, for I will surely show you kindness for Jonathan your father's sake, and will restore to you all the land of Saul your father [grandfather], and you shall eat at my table always.

⁸And [the cripple] bowed himself and said, What is your servant, that you should look upon such a dead dog as I am?

⁹Then the king called to Ziba, Saul's servant, and said to him, I have given your master's son [grandson] all that belonged to Saul and to all his house.

¹⁰And you shall till the land for him, you, your sons, and your servants, and you shall bring in the produce, that your master's heir may have food to eat; but Mephibosheth, your master's son [grandson], shall eat always at my table. Now Ziba had fifteen sons and twenty servants.

¹¹Then Ziba said to the king, Your servant will do according to all my lord the king commands. So Mephibosheth ate at David's table as one of the king's sons.

¹²Mephibosheth had a young son whose name was Micha. And all who dwelt in Ziba's house were servants to Mephibosheth.

¹³So Mephibosheth dwelt in Jerusalem, for he ate continually at the king's table, [even though] he was lame in both feet.

**10** Later, the king of the Ammonites died, and Hanun his son reigned in his stead.

²David said, I will show kindness to Hanun son of Nahash, as his father did to me. So David sent his servants to console him for his father's death; and they came into the land of the Ammonites.

³But the princes of the Ammonites said to Hanun their lord, Do you think that it is because David honors your father that he has sent comforters to you? Has he not rather sent his servants to you to search the city, spy it out, and overthrow it?

⁴So Hanun took David's servants and shaved off half their beards and cut off their garments in the middle at their hips and sent them away.

⁵When it was told David, he sent to meet them, for the men were greatly ashamed. And the king said, Tarry at Jericho until your beards are grown, and then return.

⁶And when the Ammonites saw that they had made themselves obnoxious *and* disgusting to David, they sent and hired the Syrians of Beth-rehob and of Zobah, 20,000 foot soldiers, and of the king of Maacah 1,000 men, and of Tob 12,000 men.

---

*ᵃ 11* Septuagint; Hebrew *my*

## New International Version

[7]On hearing this, David sent Joab out with the entire army of fighting men. [8]The Ammonites came out and drew up in battle formation at the entrance of their city gate, while the Arameans of Zobah and Rehob and the men of Tob and Maakah were by themselves in the open country. [9]Joab saw that there were battle lines in front of him and behind him; so he selected some of the best troops in Israel and deployed them against the Arameans. [10]He put the rest of the men under the command of Abishai his brother and deployed them against the Ammonites. [11]Joab said, "If the Arameans are too strong for me, then you are to come to my rescue; but if the Ammonites are too strong for you, then I will come to rescue you. [12]Be strong, and let us fight bravely for our people and the cities of our God. The LORD will do what is good in his sight."

[13]Then Joab and the troops with him advanced to fight the Arameans, and they fled before him. [14]When the Ammonites realized that the Arameans were fleeing, they fled before Abishai and went inside the city. So Joab returned from fighting the Ammonites and came to Jerusalem.

[15]After the Arameans saw that they had been routed by Israel, they regrouped. [16]Hadadezer had Arameans brought from beyond the Euphrates River; they went to Helam, with Shobak the commander of Hadadezer's army leading them.

[17]When David was told of this, he gathered all Israel, crossed the Jordan and went to Helam. The Arameans formed their battle lines to meet David and fought against him. [18]But they fled before Israel, and David killed seven hundred of their charioteers and forty thousand of their foot soldiers.[a] He also struck down Shobak the commander of their army, and he died there. [19]When all the kings who were vassals of Hadadezer saw that they had been routed by Israel, they made peace with the Israelites and became subject to them.

So the Arameans were afraid to help the Ammonites anymore.

## Amplified Bible

[7]When David heard of it, he sent Joab and all the army of the mighty men.

[8]And the Ammonites came out and put the battle in array at the entrance of the gate, but the Syrians of Zobah and of Rehob and the men of Tob and Maacah were stationed by themselves in the open country.

[9]When Joab saw that the battlefront was against him before and behind, he picked some of all the choice men of Israel and put them in array against the Syrians.

[10]The rest of the men Joab gave over to Abishai his brother, that he might put them in array against the Ammonites.

[11]Joab said, If the Syrians are too strong for me, then you shall help me; but if the Ammonites are too strong for you, I will come and help you.

[12]Be of good courage; let us play the man for our people and the cities of our God. And may the Lord do what seems good to Him.

[13]And Joab and the people who were with him drew near to battle against the Syrians, and they fled before him.

[14]And when the Ammonites saw that the Syrians had fled, they also fled before Abishai and entered the city. So Joab returned from battling against the Ammonites and came to Jerusalem.

[15]When the Syrians saw that they were defeated by Israel, they gathered together.

[16]Hadadezer sent and brought the Syrians who were beyond the river [Euphrates]; and they came to Helam, with Shobach commander of the army of Hadadezer leading them.

[17]When David was told, he gathered all Israel, crossed the Jordan, and came to Helam. Then the Syrians set themselves in array against David and fought with him.

[18]The Syrians fled before Israel, and David slew of [them] the men of 700 chariots and 40,000 horsemen and smote Shobach captain of their army, who died there.

[19]And when all the kings serving Hadadezer saw that they were defeated by Israel, they made peace with Israel and served them. So the Syrians were afraid to help the Ammonites any more.

### David and Bathsheba

**11** In the spring, at the time when kings go off to war, David sent Joab out with the king's men and the whole Israelite army. They destroyed the Ammonites and besieged Rabbah. But David remained in Jerusalem.

[2]One evening David got up from his bed and walked around on the roof of the palace. From the roof he saw a woman bathing. The woman was very beautiful, [3]and David sent someone to find out about her. The man said, "She is Bathsheba, the daughter of Eliam and the wife of Uriah the Hittite." [4]Then David sent messengers to get her. She came to him, and he slept with her. (Now she was purifying herself from her monthly uncleanness.) Then she went back home. [5]The woman conceived and sent word to David, saying, "I am pregnant."

[6]So David sent this word to Joab: "Send me Uriah the Hittite." And Joab sent him to David. [7]When Uriah came to him, David asked him how Joab was, how the soldiers were and how the war was going. [8]Then David said to Uriah, "Go down to your house and wash your feet." So Uriah left the palace, and a gift from the king was sent after him. [9]But Uriah slept at the entrance to the palace with all his master's servants and did not go down to his house.

**11** In the spring, when kings go forth to battle, David sent Joab with his servants and all Israel, and they ravaged the Ammonites [country] and besieged Rabbah. But David remained in Jerusalem.

[2]One evening David arose from his couch and was walking on the roof of the king's house, when from there he saw a woman bathing; and she was very lovely to behold.

[3]David sent and inquired about the woman. One said, Is not this Bathsheba, the daughter of Eliam and the wife of Uriah the Hittite?

[4]And David sent messengers and took her. And she came in to him, and he lay with her—for she was purified from her uncleanness. Then she returned to her house.

[5]And the woman became pregnant and sent and told David, I am with child.

[6]David sent to Joab, saying, Send me Uriah the Hittite. So Joab sent [him] Uriah.

[7]When Uriah had come to him, David asked him how Joab was, how the people fared, and how the war progressed.

[8]David said to Uriah, Go down to your house and wash your feet. Uriah went out of the king's house, and there followed him a mess of food [a gift] from the king.

[9]But Uriah slept at the door of the king's house with all the servants of his lord and did not go down to his house.

---

[a] 18 Some Septuagint manuscripts (see also 1 Chron. 19:18); Hebrew *horsemen*

## New International Version

[10] David was told, "Uriah did not go home." So he asked Uriah, "Haven't you just come from a military campaign? Why didn't you go home?"

[11] Uriah said to David, "The ark and Israel and Judah are staying in tents,[a] and my commander Joab and my lord's men are camped in the open country. How could I go to my house to eat and drink and make love to my wife? As surely as you live, I will not do such a thing!"

[12] Then David said to him, "Stay here one more day, and tomorrow I will send you back." So Uriah remained in Jerusalem that day and the next. [13] At David's invitation, he ate and drank with him, and David made him drunk. But in the evening Uriah went out to sleep on his mat among his master's servants; he did not go home.

[14] In the morning David wrote a letter to Joab and sent it with Uriah. [15] In it he wrote, "Put Uriah out in front where the fighting is fiercest. Then withdraw from him so he will be struck down and die."

[16] So while Joab had the city under siege, he put Uriah at a place where he knew the strongest defenders were. [17] When the men of the city came out and fought against Joab, some of the men in David's army fell; moreover, Uriah the Hittite died.

[18] Joab sent David a full account of the battle. [19] He instructed the messenger: "When you have finished giving the king this account of the battle, [20] the king's anger may flare up, and he may ask you, 'Why did you get so close to the city to fight? Didn't you know they would shoot arrows from the wall? [21] Who killed Abimelek son of Jerub-Besheth[b]? Didn't a woman drop an upper millstone on him from the wall, so that he died in Thebez? Why did you get so close to the wall?' If he asks you this, then say to him, 'Moreover, your servant Uriah the Hittite is dead.'"

[22] The messenger set out, and when he arrived he told David everything Joab had sent him to say. [23] The messenger said to David, "The men overpowered us and came out against us in the open, but we drove them back to the entrance of the city gate. [24] Then the archers shot arrows at your servants from the wall, and some of the king's men died. Moreover, your servant Uriah the Hittite is dead."

[25] David told the messenger, "Say this to Joab: 'Don't let this upset you; the sword devours one as well as another. Press the attack against the city and destroy it.' Say this to encourage Joab."

[26] When Uriah's wife heard that her husband was dead, she mourned for him. [27] After the time of mourning was over, David had her brought to his house, and she became his wife and bore him a son. But the thing David had done displeased the LORD.

### Nathan Rebukes David

**12** The LORD sent Nathan to David. When he came to him, he said, "There were two men in a certain town, one rich and the other poor. [2] The rich man had a very large number of sheep and cattle, [3] but the poor man had nothing except one little ewe lamb he had bought. He raised it, and it grew up with him and his children. It shared his food, drank from his cup and even slept in his arms. It was like a daughter to him.

## Amplified Bible

[10] When they told David, Uriah did not go down to his house, David said to Uriah, Have you not come from a journey? Why did you not go down to your house?

[11] Uriah said to David, The ark and Israel and Judah live in tents, and my lord Joab and the servants of my lord are camping in the open field. Shall I then go to my house to eat and drink and lie with my wife? As you live and as my soul lives, I will not do this thing.

[12] And David said to Uriah, Remain here today also, and tomorrow I will let you depart. So Uriah remained in Jerusalem that day and the next.

[13] David invited him, and he ate with him and drank, so that he made him drunk; but that night he went out to lie on his bed with the servants of his lord and did not go down to his house.

[14] In the morning David wrote a letter to Joab and sent it with Uriah.

[15] And he wrote in the letter, Put Uriah in the front line of the heaviest fighting and withdraw from him, that he may be struck down and die.

[16] So when Joab was besieging the city, he assigned Uriah opposite where he knew the enemy's most valiant men were.

[17] And the men of the city came out and fought with Joab, and some of the servants of David fell. Uriah the Hittite died also.

[18] Then Joab sent and told David all the things concerning the war.

[19] And he charged the messenger, When you have finished reporting matters of the war to the king,

[20] Then if the king's anger rises and he says to you, Why did you go so near to the city to fight? Did you not know they would shoot from the wall?

[21] Who killed Abimelech son of Jerubbesheth (Gideon)? Did not a woman cast an upper millstone upon him from the wall, so that he died in Thebez? Why did you go near the wall? Then say, Your servant Uriah the Hittite is dead also. [Judg. 9:35, 53.]

[22] So the messenger went and told David all for which Joab had sent him.

[23] The messenger said to David, Surely the men prevailed against us and came out to us in to the field, but we were upon them even to the entrance of the gate.

[24] Then the archers shot at your servants from the wall. Some of the king's servants are dead, and your servant Uriah the Hittite is dead also.

[25] Then David said to the messenger, Say to Joab, Let not this thing disturb you, for the sword devours one as well as another. Strengthen your attack upon the city and overthrow it. And encourage Joab.

[26] When Uriah's wife heard that her husband was dead, she mourned for Uriah.

[27] And when the mourning was past, David sent and brought her to his house, and she became his wife and bore him a son. But the thing that David had done was evil in the sight of the Lord.

**12** And the Lord sent Nathan to David. He came and said to him, There were two men in a city, one rich and the other poor.

[2] The rich man had very many flocks and herds,

[3] But the poor man had nothing but one little ewe lamb which he had bought and brought up, and it grew up with him and his children. It ate of his own morsel, drank from his own cup, lay in his bosom, and was like a daughter to him.

---

[a] 11 Or *staying at Sukkoth*    [b] 21 Also known as *Jerub-Baal* (that is, Gideon)

## New International Version

⁴"Now a traveler came to the rich man, but the rich man refrained from taking one of his own sheep or cattle to prepare a meal for the traveler who had come to him. Instead, he took the ewe lamb that belonged to the poor man and prepared it for the one who had come to him."

⁵David burned with anger against the man and said to Nathan, "As surely as the LORD lives, the man who did this must die! ⁶He must pay for that lamb four times over, because he did such a thing and had no pity."

⁷Then Nathan said to David, "You are the man! This is what the LORD, the God of Israel, says: 'I anointed you king over Israel, and I delivered you from the hand of Saul. ⁸I gave your master's house to you, and your master's wives into your arms. I gave you all Israel and Judah. And if all this had been too little, I would have given you even more. ⁹Why did you despise the word of the LORD by doing what is evil in his eyes? You struck down Uriah the Hittite with the sword and took his wife to be your own. You killed him with the sword of the Ammonites. ¹⁰Now, therefore, the sword will never depart from your house, because you despised me and took the wife of Uriah the Hittite to be your own.'

¹¹"This is what the LORD says: 'Out of your own household I am going to bring calamity on you. Before your very eyes I will take your wives and give them to one who is close to you, and he will sleep with your wives in broad daylight. ¹²You did it in secret, but I will do this thing in broad daylight before all Israel.'"

¹³Then David said to Nathan, "I have sinned against the LORD."

Nathan replied, "The LORD has taken away your sin. You are not going to die. ¹⁴But because by doing this you have shown utter contempt for[a] the LORD, the son born to you will die."

¹⁵After Nathan had gone home, the LORD struck the child that Uriah's wife had borne to David, and he became ill. ¹⁶David pleaded with God for the child. He fasted and spent the nights lying in sackcloth[b] on the ground. ¹⁷The elders of his household stood beside him to get him up from the ground, but he refused, and he would not eat any food with them.

¹⁸On the seventh day the child died. David's attendants were afraid to tell him that the child was dead, for they thought, "While the child was still living, he wouldn't listen to us when we spoke to him. How can we now tell him the child is dead? He may do something desperate."

¹⁹David noticed that his attendants were whispering among themselves, and he realized the child was dead. "Is the child dead?" he asked.

"Yes," they replied, "he is dead."

²⁰Then David got up from the ground. After he had washed, put on lotions and changed his clothes, he went into the house of the LORD and worshiped. Then he went to his own house, and at his request they served him food, and he ate.

## Amplified Bible

⁴Now a traveler came to the rich man, and to avoid taking one of his own flock or herd to prepare for the wayfaring man who had come to him, he took the poor man's lamb and prepared it for his guest.

⁵Then David's anger was greatly kindled against the man, and he said to Nathan, As the Lord lives, the man who has done this is a son [worthy] of death.

⁶He shall restore the lamb fourfold, because he did this thing and had no pity.

⁷Then Nathan said to David, You are the man! Thus says the Lord, the God of Israel: I anointed you king over Israel, and I delivered you out of the hand of Saul.

⁸And I gave you your master's house, and your master's wives into your bosom, and gave you the house of Israel and of Judah; and if that had been too little, I would have added that much again.

⁹Why have you despised the commandment of the Lord, doing evil in His sight? You have slain Uriah the Hittite with the sword and have taken his wife to be your wife. You have murdered him with the sword of the Ammonites. [Lev. 20:10; 24:17.]

¹⁰Now, therefore, the sword shall never depart from your house, because [you have not only despised My command, but] you have despised Me and have taken the wife of Uriah the Hittite to be your wife.

¹¹Thus says the Lord, Behold, I will raise up evil against you out of your ᵃown house; and I will take your wives before your eyes and give them to your neighbor, and he shall lie with your wives in the sight of this sun.

¹²For you did it secretly, but I will do this thing before all Israel and before the sun. [Fulfilled in II Sam. 16:21, 22.]

¹³And David said to Nathan, I have sinned against the Lord. And Nathan said to David, The Lord also has put away your sin; you shall not die. [Ps. 51.]

¹⁴Nevertheless, because by this deed you have utterly scorned the Lord and given great occasion to the enemies of the Lord to blaspheme, the child that is born to you shall surely die.

¹⁵Then Nathan departed to his house. And the Lord struck the child that Uriah's widow bore to David, and he was very sick.

¹⁶David therefore besought God for the child; and David fasted and went in and lay all night [repeatedly] on the floor.

¹⁷His older house servants arose [in the night] and went to him to raise him up from the floor, but he would not, nor did he eat food with them.

¹⁸And on the seventh day the child died. David's servants feared to tell him that the child was dead, for they said, While the child was yet alive, we spoke to him and he would not listen to our voices; will he then harm himself if we tell him the child is dead?

¹⁹But when David saw that his servants whispered, he perceived that the child was dead. So he said to them, Is the child dead? And they said, He is.

²⁰Then David arose from the floor, washed, anointed himself, changed his apparel, and went into the house of the Lord and worshiped. Then he came to his own house, and when he asked, they set food before him, and he ate.

---

ᵃ This sentence was fulfilled in the agony brought on David by his lawless children: Amnon's scandalous behavior with his half sister Tamar (13:14) and his consequent murder by his brother Absalom (13:28, 29); Absalom's escape to a foreign land (13:38) and his return after three years; Absalom without recognition by David for two more years (14:28); Absalom's deliberate, rebellious attempt to win the hearts of the people and supplant his father (15:6); David's flight from Jerusalem, with the mass of the people against him (15:14), the terrible battle in the forest of Ephraim, won by David's forces, with Absalom killed in flight (18:6ff.). David's agony of heart is echoed repeatedly in the history of these tragedies [II Sam. 13:1–19:8] and in some of his psalms. Even when the great king was dying, his son Adonijah was attempting to usurp the throne, and was later executed as a traitor (II Kings 1:5; 2:25).

---

ᵃ 14 An ancient Hebrew scribal tradition; Masoretic Text *for the enemies of*   ᵇ 16 Dead Sea Scrolls and Septuagint; Masoretic Text does not have *in sackcloth*.

## New International Version

²¹His attendants asked him, "Why are you acting this way? While the child was alive, you fasted and wept, but now that the child is dead, you get up and eat!"

²²He answered, "While the child was still alive, I fasted and wept. I thought, 'Who knows? The Lᴏʀᴅ may be gracious to me and let the child live.' ²³But now that he is dead, why should I go on fasting? Can I bring him back again? I will go to him, but he will not return to me."

²⁴Then David comforted his wife Bathsheba, and he went to her and made love to her. She gave birth to a son, and they named him Solomon. The Lᴏʀᴅ loved him; ²⁵and because the Lᴏʀᴅ loved him, he sent word through Nathan the prophet to name him Jedidiah.ᵃ

²⁶Meanwhile Joab fought against Rabbah of the Ammonites and captured the royal citadel. ²⁷Joab then sent messengers to David, saying, "I have fought against Rabbah and taken its water supply. ²⁸Now muster the rest of the troops and besiege the city and capture it. Otherwise I will take the city, and it will be named after me."

²⁹So David mustered the entire army and went to Rabbah, and attacked and captured it. ³⁰David took the crown from their king'sᵇ head, and it was placed on his own head. It weighed a talentᶜ of gold, and it was set with precious stones. David took a great quantity of plunder from the city ³¹and brought out the people who were there, consigning them to labor with saws and with iron picks and axes, and he made them work at brickmaking.ᵈ David did this to all the Ammonite towns. Then he and his entire army returned to Jerusalem.

## Amplified Bible

²¹Then his servants said to him, What is this that you have done? You fasted and wept while the child was alive, but when the child was dead, you arose and ate food.

²²David said, While the child was still alive, I fasted and wept; for I said, Who knows whether the Lord will be gracious to me and let the child live?

²³But now he is dead; why should I fast? Can I bring him back again? I shall go to him, but he will not return to me.

²⁴David comforted Bathsheba his wife, and went to her and lay with her; and she bore a son, and she called his name Solomon. And the Lord loved [the child];

²⁵He sent [a message] by the hand of Nathan the prophet, and [Nathan] called the boy's [special] name Jedidiah [beloved of the Lord], because the Lord [loved the child].

²⁶Now Joab fought against Rabbah of the Ammonites and took the royal city.

²⁷And Joab sent messengers to David and said, I have fought against Rabbah, and have taken the city of waters.

²⁸Now therefore assemble the rest of the men, encamp against the city, and take it, lest I take the city, and it be called after my name.

²⁹So David gathered all the men, went to Rabbah, fought against it, and took it.

³⁰And he took the crown of their king [of Malcham] from his head; the weight of it was a talent of gold, and in it were precious stones; and it was set on David's head. And he brought forth exceedingly much spoil from the city.

³¹And he brought forth the people who were there, and put them to [work with] saws and iron threshing sledges and axes, and made them labor at the brickkiln. And he did this to all the Ammonite cities. Then [he] and all the men returned to Jerusalem.

### Amnon and Tamar

**13** In the course of time, Amnon son of David fell in love with Tamar, the beautiful sister of Absalom son of David.

²Amnon became so obsessed with his sister Tamar that he made himself ill. She was a virgin, and it seemed impossible for him to do anything to her.

³Now Amnon had an adviser named Jonadab son of Shimeah, David's brother. Jonadab was a very shrewd man. ⁴He asked Amnon, "Why do you, the king's son, look so haggard morning after morning? Won't you tell me?"

Amnon said to him, "I'm in love with Tamar, my brother Absalom's sister."

⁵"Go to bed and pretend to be ill," Jonadab said. "When your father comes to see you, say to him, 'I would like my sister Tamar to come and give me something to eat. Let her prepare the food in my sight so I may watch her and then eat it from her hand.'"

⁶So Amnon lay down and pretended to be ill. When the king came to see him, Amnon said to him, "I would like my sister Tamar to come and make some special bread in my sight, so I may eat from her hand."

⁷David sent word to Tamar at the palace: "Go to the house of your brother Amnon and prepare some food for him." ⁸So Tamar went to the house of her brother Amnon, who was lying down. She took some dough, kneaded it, made the bread in his sight and baked it. ⁹Then she took the pan and served him the bread, but he refused to eat.

"Send everyone out of here," Amnon said. So everyone left him. ¹⁰Then Amnon said to Tamar, "Bring the food

**13** Absalom son of David had a fair sister whose name was Tamar, and Amnon [her half brother] son of David loved her.

²And Amnon was so troubled that he fell sick for his [half] sister Tamar, for she was a virgin, and Amnon thought it impossible for him to do anything to her.

³But Amnon had a friend whose name was Jonadab son of Shimeah, David's brother; and Jonadab was a very crafty man.

⁴He said to Amnon, Why are you, the king's son, so lean and weak-looking from day to day? Will you not tell me? And Amnon said to him, I love Tamar, my [half] brother Absalom's sister.

⁵Jonadab said to him, Go to bed and pretend you are sick; and when your father David comes to see you, say to him, Let my sister Tamar come and give me food and prepare it in my sight, that I may see it and eat it from her hand.

⁶So Amnon lay down and pretended to be sick; and when the king came to see him, Amnon said to the king, I pray you, let my sister Tamar come and make me a couple of cakes in my sight, that I may eat from her hand.

⁷Then David sent home and told Tamar, Go now to your brother Amnon's house and prepare food for him.

⁸So Tamar went to her brother Amnon's house, and he was in bed. And she took dough and kneaded it and made cakes in his sight and baked them.

⁹She took the pan and emptied it out before him, but he refused to eat. And Amnon said, Send everyone out from me. So everyone went out from him.

¹⁰Then Amnon said to Tamar, Bring the food here into

---

ᵃ 25 *Jedidiah* means *loved by the* Lᴏʀᴅ.    ᵇ 30 Or *from Milkom's* (that is, Molek's)    ᶜ 30 That is, about 75 pounds or about 34 kilograms    ᵈ 31 The meaning of the Hebrew for this clause is uncertain.

## New International Version

here into my bedroom so I may eat from your hand." And Tamar took the bread she had prepared and brought it to her brother Amnon in his bedroom. [11]But when she took it to him to eat, he grabbed her and said, "Come to bed with me, my sister."

[12]"No, my brother!" she said to him. "Don't force me! Such a thing should not be done in Israel! Don't do this wicked thing. [13]What about me? Where could I get rid of my disgrace? And what about you? You would be like one of the wicked fools in Israel. Please speak to the king; he will not keep me from being married to you." [14]But he refused to listen to her, and since he was stronger than she, he raped her.

[15]Then Amnon hated her with intense hatred. In fact, he hated her more than he had loved her. Amnon said to her, "Get up and get out!"

[16]"No!" she said to him. "Sending me away would be a greater wrong than what you have already done to me."

But he refused to listen to her. [17]He called his personal servant and said, "Get this woman out of my sight and bolt the door after her." [18]So his servant put her out and bolted the door after her. She was wearing an ornate[a] robe, for this was the kind of garment the virgin daughters of the king wore. [19]Tamar put ashes on her head and tore the ornate robe she was wearing. She put her hands on her head and went away, weeping aloud as she went.

[20]Her brother Absalom said to her, "Has that Amnon, your brother, been with you? Be quiet for now, my sister; he is your brother. Don't take this thing to heart." And Tamar lived in her brother Absalom's house, a desolate woman.

[21]When King David heard all this, he was furious. [22]And Absalom never said a word to Amnon, either good or bad; he hated Amnon because he had disgraced his sister Tamar.

### Absalom Kills Amnon

[23]Two years later, when Absalom's sheepshearers were at Baal Hazor near the border of Ephraim, he invited all the king's sons to come there. [24]Absalom went to the king and said, "Your servant has had shearers come. Will the king and his attendants please join me?"

[25]"No, my son," the king replied. "All of us should not go; we would only be a burden to you." Although Absalom urged him, he still refused to go but gave him his blessing.

[26]Then Absalom said, "If not, please let my brother Amnon come with us."

The king asked him, "Why should he go with you?" [27]But Absalom urged him, so he sent with him Amnon and the rest of the king's sons.

[28]Absalom ordered his men, "Listen! When Amnon is in high spirits from drinking wine and I say to you, 'Strike Amnon down,' then kill him. Don't be afraid. Haven't I given you this order? Be strong and brave." [29]So Absalom's men did to Amnon what Absalom had ordered. Then all the king's sons got up, mounted their mules and fled.

[30]While they were on their way, the report came to David: "Absalom has struck down all the king's sons; not one of them is left." [31]The king stood up, tore his clothes and lay down on the ground; and all his attendants stood by with their clothes torn.

[32]But Jonadab son of Shimeah, David's brother, said,

## Amplified Bible

the bedroom, so I may eat from your hand. So Tamar took the cakes she had made and brought them into the room to Amnon her brother.

[11]And when she brought them to him, he took hold of her and said, Come lie with me, my sister.

[12]She replied, No, my brother! Do not force and humble me, for no such thing should be done in Israel! Do not do this foolhardy, scandalous thing! [Gen. 34:7.]

[13]And I, how could I rid myself of my shame? And you, you will be [considered] one of the stupid fools in Israel. Now therefore, I pray you, speak to the king, for he will not withhold me from you.

[14]But he would not listen to her, and being stronger than she, he forced her and lay with her.

[15]Then Amnon hated her exceedingly, so that his hatred for her was greater than the love with which he had loved her. And Amnon said to her, Get up and get out!

[16]But she said, No! This great evil of sending me away is worse than what you did to me. But he would not listen to her.

[17]He called the servant who served him and said, Put this woman out of my presence now, and bolt the door after her!

[18]Now [Tamar] was wearing a long robe with sleeves and of various colors, for in such robes were the king's virgin daughters clad of old. Then Amnon's servant brought her out and bolted the door after her.

[19]And [she] put ashes on her head and tore the long, sleeved robe which she wore, and she laid her hand on her head and went away shrieking and wailing.

[20]And Absalom her brother said to her, Has your brother Amnon been with you? Be quiet now, my sister. He is your brother; take not this matter to heart. So Tamar dwelt in her brother Absalom's house, a desolate woman.

[21]But when King David heard of all these things, he was very angry.

[22]And Absalom spoke to Amnon neither good nor bad; for Absalom hated Amnon because he had humbled his sister Tamar.

[23]After two full years Absalom had sheepshearers at Baal-hazor near Ephraim, and Absalom invited all the king's sons.

[24]Absalom came to the king and said, Behold, your servant has sheepshearers; I pray you, let the king and his servants go with your servant.

[25]And the king said to Absalom, No, my son, let us not all go, lest we be burdensome to you. Absalom urged David; still he would not go, but he blessed him.

[26]Then said Absalom, If not, I pray you, let my brother Amnon go with us. And the king said to him, Why should he go with you?

[27]But Absalom urged him, and he let Amnon and all the king's sons go with him.

[28]Now Absalom commanded his servants, Notice now, when Amnon's heart is merry with wine and when I say to you, Strike Amnon, then kill him. Fear not; have I not commanded you? Be courageous and brave.

[29]And the servants of Absalom did to Amnon as Absalom had commanded. Then all the king's sons arose and every man mounted his mule and fled.

[30]While they were on the way, the word came to David, Absalom has killed all the king's sons, and not one of them is left.

[31]Then the king arose and tore his garments and lay on the floor; and all his servants standing by tore their clothes.

[32]But Jonadab son of Shimeah, David's brother, said,

---

[a] 18 The meaning of the Hebrew for this word is uncertain; also in verse 19.

## New International Version

"My lord should not think that they killed all the princes; only Amnon is dead. This has been Absalom's express intention ever since the day Amnon raped his sister Tamar. [33]My lord the king should not be concerned about the report that all the king's sons are dead. Only Amnon is dead."

[34]Meanwhile, Absalom had fled.

Now the man standing watch looked up and saw many people on the road west of him, coming down the side of the hill. The watchman went and told the king, "I see men in the direction of Horonaim, on the side of the hill."[a]

[35]Jonadab said to the king, "See, the king's sons have come; it has happened just as your servant said."

[36]As he finished speaking, the king's sons came in, wailing loudly. The king, too, and all his attendants wept very bitterly.

[37]Absalom fled and went to Talmai son of Ammihud, the king of Geshur. But King David mourned many days for his son.

[38]After Absalom fled and went to Geshur, he stayed there three years. [39]And King David longed to go to Absalom, for he was consoled concerning Amnon's death.

### Absalom Returns to Jerusalem

**14** Joab son of Zeruiah knew that the king's heart longed for Absalom. [2]So Joab sent someone to Tekoa and had a wise woman brought from there. He said to her, "Pretend you are in mourning. Dress in mourning clothes, and don't use any cosmetic lotions. Act like a woman who has spent many days grieving for the dead. [3]Then go to the king and speak these words to him." And Joab put the words in her mouth.

[4]When the woman from Tekoa went[b] to the king, she fell with her face to the ground to pay him honor, and she said, "Help me, Your Majesty!"

[5]The king asked her, "What is troubling you?"

She said, "I am a widow; my husband is dead. [6]I your servant had two sons. They got into a fight with each other in the field, and no one was there to separate them. One struck the other and killed him. [7]Now the whole clan has risen up against your servant; they say, 'Hand over the one who struck his brother down, so that we may put him to death for the life of his brother whom he killed; then we will get rid of the heir as well.' They would put out the only burning coal I have left, leaving my husband neither name nor descendant on the face of the earth."

[8]The king said to the woman, "Go home, and I will issue an order in your behalf."

[9]But the woman from Tekoa said to him, "Let my lord the king pardon me and my family, and let the king and his throne be without guilt."

[10]The king replied, "If anyone says anything to you, bring them to me, and they will not bother you again."

[11]She said, "Then let the king invoke the LORD his God to prevent the avenger of blood from adding to the destruction, so that my son will not be destroyed."

"As surely as the LORD lives," he said, "not one hair of your son's head will fall to the ground."

[12]Then the woman said, "Let your servant speak a word to my lord the king."

"Speak," he replied.

[13]The woman said, "Why then have you devised a thing like this against the people of God? When the king says this, does he not convict himself, for the king has not brought back his banished son? [14]Like water spilled on

## Amplified Bible

Let not my lord suppose they have killed all the king's sons; for Amnon only is dead. This purpose has shown itself on Absalom's determined mouth ever since the day Amnon humiliated his sister Tamar. [33]So let not my lord the king take the thing to heart and think all the king's sons are dead; for Amnon only is dead.

[34]But Absalom fled. And the young man who kept the watch looked up, and behold, many people were coming by the way of the hillside behind him.

[35]And Jonadab said to the king, See, the king's sons are coming. It is as your servant said.

[36]And as he finished speaking, the king's sons came and lifted up their voices and wept; and the king also and all his servants wept very bitterly.

[37]But Absalom fled and went to [his mother's father] Talmai son of Ammihud, king of Geshur. And David mourned for his son [Amnon] every day.

[38]So Absalom fled to Geshur and was there three years.

[39]And the spirit of King David longed to go forth to Absalom, for he was comforted about Amnon, seeing that he was dead.

**14** Now Joab son of Zeruiah knew that the king's heart was toward Absalom.

[2]And Joab sent to Tekoah and brought from there a wise woman and said to her, Pretend to be a mourner; put on mourning apparel, do not anoint yourself with oil, but act like a woman who has long been mourning for the dead.

[3]And go to the king and speak thus to him. And Joab told her what to say.

[4]When the woman of Tekoah spoke to the king, she fell on her face to the ground and did obeisance, and said, Help, O king!

[5]The king asked her, What troubles you? She said, I am a widow; my husband is dead.

[6]And your handmaid had two sons, and they quarreled with one another in the field. There was no one to separate them, and one struck the other and killed him.

[7]And behold, our whole family has risen against your handmaid, and they say, Deliver him who slew his brother, that we may kill him for the life of his brother whom he slew; and so they would destroy the heir also. And so quenching my coal which is left, they would leave to my husband neither name nor remnant upon the earth.

[8]David said to the woman, Go home, and I will give orders concerning you.

[9]And the woman of Tekoah said to the king, My lord, O king, let the guilt be on me and on my father's house; let the king and his throne be guiltless.

[10]The king said, If anyone says anything to you, bring him to me, and he shall not touch you again.

[11]Then she said, I pray you, let the king remember the Lord your God, that the avenger of blood destroy not any more, lest they destroy my son. And David said, As the Lord lives, there shall not one hair of your son fall to the earth.

[12]Then the woman said, Let your handmaid, I pray you, speak one word to my lord the king. He said, Say on.

[13][She] said, Why then have you planned such a thing against God's people? For in speaking this word the king is like one who is guilty, in that [he] does not bring home his banished one.

---

[a] 34 Septuagint; Hebrew does not have this sentence.  [b] 4 Many Hebrew manuscripts, Septuagint, Vulgate and Syriac; most Hebrew manuscripts *spoke*

## New International Version

the ground, which cannot be recovered, so we must die. But that is not what God desires; rather, he devises ways so that a banished person does not remain banished from him.

¹⁵"And now I have come to say this to my lord the king because the people have made me afraid. Your servant thought, 'I will speak to the king; perhaps he will grant his servant's request. ¹⁶Perhaps the king will agree to deliver his servant from the hand of the man who is trying to cut off both me and my son from God's inheritance.'

¹⁷"And now your servant says, 'May the word of my lord the king secure my inheritance, for my lord the king is like an angel of God in discerning good and evil. May the LORD your God be with you.'"

¹⁸Then the king said to the woman, "Don't keep from me the answer to what I am going to ask you."

"Let my lord the king speak," the woman said.

¹⁹The king asked, "Isn't the hand of Joab with you in all this?"

The woman answered, "As surely as you live, my lord the king, no one can turn to the right or to the left from anything my lord the king says. Yes, it was your servant Joab who instructed me to do this and who put all these words into the mouth of your servant. ²⁰Your servant Joab did this to change the present situation. My lord has wisdom like that of an angel of God—he knows everything that happens in the land."

²¹The king said to Joab, "Very well, I will do it. Go, bring back the young man Absalom."

²²Joab fell with his face to the ground to pay him honor, and he blessed the king. Joab said, "Today your servant knows that he has found favor in your eyes, my lord the king, because the king has granted his servant's request."

²³Then Joab went to Geshur and brought Absalom back to Jerusalem. ²⁴But the king said, "He must go to his own house; he must not see my face." So Absalom went to his own house and did not see the face of the king.

²⁵In all Israel there was not a man so highly praised for his handsome appearance as Absalom. From the top of his head to the sole of his foot there was no blemish in him. ²⁶Whenever he cut the hair of his head—he used to cut his hair once a year because it became too heavy for him—he would weigh it, and its weight was two hundred shekels[a] by the royal standard.

²⁷Three sons and a daughter were born to Absalom. His daughter's name was Tamar, and she became a beautiful woman.

²⁸Absalom lived two years in Jerusalem without seeing the king's face. ²⁹Then Absalom sent for Joab in order to send him to the king, but Joab refused to come to him. So he sent a second time, but he refused to come. ³⁰Then he said to his servants, "Look, Joab's field is next to mine, and he has barley there. Go and set it on fire." So Absalom's servants set the field on fire.

³¹Then Joab did go to Absalom's house, and he said to him, "Why have your servants set my field on fire?"

³²Absalom said to Joab, "Look, I sent word to you and said, 'Come here so I can send you to the king to ask, "Why have I come from Geshur? It would be better for me if I were still there!"' Now then, I want to see the king's face, and if I am guilty of anything, let him put me to death."

## Amplified Bible

¹⁴We must all die; we are like water spilled on the ground, which cannot be gathered up again. And God does not take away life, but devises means so that he who is banished may not be an utter outcast from Him.

¹⁵And now I have come to speak of this thing to my lord the king because the people have made me afraid. And I thought, I will speak to the king; it may be that he will perform the request of his servant.

¹⁶For the king will hear to deliver his handmaid from the hand of the man who would destroy me and my son together from [Israel] the inheritance of God.

¹⁷And the woman said, The word of my lord the king will now give me rest *and* security, for as an angel of God is my lord the king to hear *and* discern good and evil. May the Lord your God be with you!

¹⁸Then the king said to the woman, Hide not from me anything I ask you. And the woman said, Let my lord the king speak.

¹⁹The king said, Is the hand of Joab with you in all this? And the woman answered, As your soul lives, my lord king, none can turn to the right hand or to the left from anything my lord the king has said. It was your servant Joab who directed me; he put all these words in my mouth.

²⁰In order to change the course of matters [between Absalom and his father] your servant Joab did this. But my lord has wisdom like the wisdom of the angel of God—to know all things that are on the earth.

²¹Then the king said to Joab, Behold now, I grant this; go, bring back the young man Absalom.

²²And Joab fell to the ground on his face and did obeisance and thanked the king. And Joab said, Today your servant knows that I have found favor in your sight, my lord, O king, in that the king has performed the request of his servant.

²³So Joab arose, went to Geshur, and brought Absalom to Jerusalem.

²⁴And the king said, Let him go to his own house, and let him not see my face. So Absalom went to his own house and did not see the king's face.

²⁵But in all Israel there was none so much to be praised for his beauty as Absalom; from the sole of his foot to the crown of his head there was no blemish in him.

²⁶And when he cut the hair of his head, he weighed it—for at each year's end he cut it, because its weight was a burden to him—and it weighed 200 shekels by the king's weight.

²⁷There were born to Absalom three sons and one daughter whose name was Tamar; she was a beautiful woman.

²⁸Absalom dwelt two full years in Jerusalem and did not see the king's face.

²⁹So Absalom sent for Joab to send him to the king, but he would not come to him; even when he sent again the second time, he would not come.

³⁰Therefore Absalom said to his servants, See, Joab's field is near mine, and he has barley there; go and set it on fire. So Absalom's servants set the field afire.

³¹Then Joab arose and went to Absalom at his house and said to him, Why have your servants set my field on fire?

³²Absalom answered Joab, I sent to you, saying, Come here, that I may send you to the king to ask, Why have I come from Geshur? It would be better for me to be there still. Now therefore [Joab], let me see the king, and if there is iniquity *and* guilt in me, let him kill me.

---

*a 26 That is, about 5 pounds or about 2.3 kilograms

## New International Version

[33]So Joab went to the king and told him this. Then the king summoned Absalom, and he came in and bowed down with his face to the ground before the king. And the king kissed Absalom.

### Absalom's Conspiracy

**15** In the course of time, Absalom provided himself with a chariot and horses and with fifty men to run ahead of him. [2]He would get up early and stand by the side of the road leading to the city gate. Whenever anyone came with a complaint to be placed before the king for a decision, Absalom would call out to him, "What town are you from?" He would answer, "Your servant is from one of the tribes of Israel." [3]Then Absalom would say to him, "Look, your claims are valid and proper, but there is no representative of the king to hear you." [4]And Absalom would add, "If only I were appointed judge in the land! Then everyone who has a complaint or case could come to me and I would see that they receive justice." [5]Also, whenever anyone approached him to bow down before him, Absalom would reach out his hand, take hold of him and kiss him. [6]Absalom behaved in this way toward all the Israelites who came to the king asking for justice, and so he stole the hearts of the people of Israel.

[7]At the end of four[a] years, Absalom said to the king, "Let me go to Hebron and fulfill a vow I made to the LORD. [8]While your servant was living at Geshur in Aram, I made this vow: 'If the LORD takes me back to Jerusalem, I will worship the LORD in Hebron.[b]'"

[9]The king said to him, "Go in peace." So he went to Hebron.

[10]Then Absalom sent secret messengers throughout the tribes of Israel to say, "As soon as you hear the sound of the trumpets, then say, 'Absalom is king in Hebron.'" [11]Two hundred men from Jerusalem had accompanied Absalom. They had been invited as guests and went quite innocently, knowing nothing about the matter. [12]While Absalom was offering sacrifices, he also sent for Ahithophel the Gilonite, David's counselor, to come from Giloh, his hometown. And so the conspiracy gained strength, and Absalom's following kept on increasing.

### David Flees

[13]A messenger came and told David, "The hearts of the people of Israel are with Absalom."

[14]Then David said to all his officials who were with him in Jerusalem, "Come! We must flee, or none of us will escape from Absalom. We must leave immediately, or he will move quickly to overtake us and bring ruin on us and put the city to the sword."

[15]The king's officials answered him, "Your servants are ready to do whatever our lord the king chooses."

[16]The king set out, with his entire household following him; but he left ten concubines to take care of the palace. [17]So the king set out, with all the people following him, and they halted at the edge of the city. [18]All his men marched past him, along with all the Kerethites and Pelethites; and all the six hundred Gittites who had accompanied him from Gath marched before the king.

[19]The king said to Ittai the Gittite, "Why should you come along with us? Go back and stay with King Absalom. You are a foreigner, an exile from your homeland. [20]You came only yesterday. And today shall I make you wander about with us, when I do not know where I am going? Go back, and take your people with you. May the LORD show you kindness and faithfulness."[c]

## Amplified Bible

[33]So Joab came to the king and told him. And when David had called for Absalom, he came to him and bowed himself on his face to the ground before the king; and [David] kissed Absalom.

**15** After this, Absalom got a chariot and horses, and fifty men to run before him. [2]And [he] rose up early and stood beside the gateway; and when any man who had a controversy came to the king for judgment, Absalom called to him, Of what city are you? And he would say, Your servant is of such and such a tribe of Israel.

[3]Absalom would say to him, Your claims are good and right, but there is no man appointed as the king's agent to hear you.

[4]Absalom added, Oh, that I were judge in the land! Then every man with any suit or cause might come to me and I would do him justice!

[5]And whenever a man came near to do obeisance to him, he would put out his hand, take hold of him, and kiss him.

[6]Thus Absalom did to all Israel who came to the king for judgment. So Absalom stole the hearts of the men of Israel.

[7]And after [four] years, Absalom said to the king, I pray you, let me go to Hebron [his birthplace] and pay my vow to the Lord.

[8]For your servant vowed while I dwelt at Geshur in Syria, If the Lord will bring me again to Jerusalem, then I will serve the Lord [by offering a sacrifice].

[9]And the king said to him, Go in peace. So he arose and went to Hebron.

[10]But Absalom sent secret messengers throughout all the tribes of Israel, saying, As soon as you hear the sound of the trumpet, then say, Absalom is king at Hebron.

[11]With Absalom went 200 men from Jerusalem, who were invited [as guests to his sacrificial feast]; and they went in their simplicity, and they knew not a thing.

[12]And while Absalom was offering the sacrifices, he sent for Ahithophel the Gilonite, David's counselor, from his city Giloh. And the conspiracy was strong; the people with Absalom increased continually.

[13]And there came a messenger to David, saying, The hearts of the men of Israel have gone after Absalom.

[14]David said to all his servants who were with him at Jerusalem, Arise and let us flee, or else none of us will escape from Absalom. Make haste to depart, lest he overtake us suddenly and bring evil upon us and smite the city with the sword.

[15]And the king's servants said to the king, Behold, your servants are ready to do whatever my lord the king says.

[16]So the king and all his household after him went forth. But he left ten women who were concubines to keep the house. [II Sam. 12:11; 20:3.]

[17]The king went forth with all the people after him, and halted at the last house.

[18]All David's servants passed on beside him, along with [his bodyguards] all the Cherethites, Pelethites; also all the Gittites, 600 men who came after him from Gath, passed on before the king.

[19]The king said to Ittai the Gittite, Why do you go with us also? Return to your place and remain with the king [Absalom], for you are a foreigner and an exile.

[20]Since you came only yesterday, should I make you go up and down with us? Since I must go where I may, you return, and take back your brethren with you. May lovingkindness and faithfulness be with you.

---

[a] 7 Some Septuagint manuscripts, Syriac and Josephus; Hebrew *forty*
[b] 8 Some Septuagint manuscripts; Hebrew does not have *in Hebron.*
[c] 20 Septuagint; Hebrew *May kindness and faithfulness be with you*

## New International Version

²¹But Ittai replied to the king, "As surely as the LORD lives, and as my lord the king lives, wherever my lord the king may be, whether it means life or death, there will your servant be."

²²David said to Ittai, "Go ahead, march on." So Ittai the Gittite marched on with all his men and the families that were with him.

²³The whole countryside wept aloud as all the people passed by. The king also crossed the Kidron Valley, and all the people moved on toward the wilderness.

²⁴Zadok was there, too, and all the Levites who were with him were carrying the ark of the covenant of God. They set down the ark of God, and Abiathar offered sacrifices until all the people had finished leaving the city.

²⁵Then the king said to Zadok, "Take the ark of God back into the city. If I find favor in the LORD's eyes, he will bring me back and let me see it and his dwelling place again. ²⁶But if he says, 'I am not pleased with you,' then I am ready; let him do to me whatever seems good to him."

²⁷The king also said to Zadok the priest, "Do you understand? Go back to the city with my blessing. Take your son Ahimaaz with you, and also Abiathar's son Jonathan. You and Abiathar return with your two sons. ²⁸I will wait at the fords in the wilderness until word comes from you to inform me." ²⁹So Zadok and Abiathar took the ark of God back to Jerusalem and stayed there.

³⁰But David continued up the Mount of Olives, weeping as he went; his head was covered and he was barefoot. All the people with him covered their heads too and were weeping as they went up. ³¹Now David had been told, "Ahithophel is among the conspirators with Absalom." So David prayed, "LORD, turn Ahithophel's counsel into foolishness."

³²When David arrived at the summit, where people used to worship God, Hushai the Arkite was there to meet him, his robe torn and dust on his head. ³³David said to him, "If you go with me, you will be a burden to me. ³⁴But if you return to the city and say to Absalom, 'Your Majesty, I will be your servant; I was your father's servant in the past, but now I will be your servant,' then you can help me by frustrating Ahithophel's advice. ³⁵Won't the priests Zadok and Abiathar be there with you? Tell them anything you hear in the king's palace. ³⁶Their two sons, Ahimaaz son of Zadok and Jonathan son of Abiathar, are there with them. Send them to me with anything you hear."

³⁷So Hushai, David's confidant, arrived at Jerusalem as Absalom was entering the city.

### David and Ziba

**16** When David had gone a short distance beyond the summit, there was Ziba, the steward of Mephibosheth, waiting to meet him. He had a string of donkeys saddled and loaded with two hundred loaves of bread, a hundred cakes of raisins, a hundred cakes of figs and a skin of wine.

²The king asked Ziba, "Why have you brought these?"

Ziba answered, "The donkeys are for the king's household to ride on, the bread and fruit are for the men to eat, and the wine is to refresh those who become exhausted in the wilderness."

³The king then asked, "Where is your master's grandson?"

Ziba said to him, "He is staying in Jerusalem, because he thinks, 'Today the Israelites will restore to me my grandfather's kingdom.'"

## Amplified Bible

²¹But Ittai answered the king, As the Lord lives, and as my lord the king lives, wherever my lord the king shall be, whether for death or life, even there also will your servant be.

²²So David said to Ittai, Go on and pass over [the Kidron]. And Ittai the Gittite passed over and all his men and all the little ones who were with him.

²³All the country wept with a loud voice as all the people passed over. The king crossed the brook Kidron, and all the people went on toward the wilderness.

²⁴Abiathar [the priest] and behold, Zadok came also, and all the Levites with him, bearing the ark of the covenant of God. And they set down the ark of God until all the people had gone from the city.

²⁵Then the king told Zadok, Take back the ark of God to the city. If I find favor in the Lord's eyes, He will bring me back and let me see both it and His house.

²⁶But if He says, I have no delight in you, then here I am; let Him do to me what seems good to Him.

²⁷The king also said to Zadok the priest, Are you not a seer? [You and Abiathar] return to the city in peace, and your two sons with you, Ahimaaz your son and Jonathan son of Abiathar.

²⁸See, I will wait at the fords [at the Jordan] of the wilderness until word comes from you to inform me.

²⁹Zadok, therefore, and Abiathar carried the ark of God back to Jerusalem and they stayed there.

³⁰And David went up over the Mount of Olives and wept as he went, barefoot and his head covered. And all the people who were with him covered their heads, weeping as they went.

³¹David was told, Ahithophel [your counselor] is among the conspirators with Absalom. David said, O Lord, I pray You, turn Ahithophel's counsel into foolishness.

³²When David came to the summit [of Olivet], where he worshiped God, behold, Hushai the Archite came to meet him with his coat rent and earth upon his head.

³³David said to him, If you go with me, you will be a burden to me.

³⁴But if you return to the city and say to Absalom, I will be your servant, O king; as I have been your father's servant in the past, so will I be your servant now, then you may defeat for me the counsel of Ahithophel.

³⁵Will not Zadok and Abiathar the priests be with you? So whatever you hear from the king's house, just tell it to [them].

³⁶Behold, their two sons are there with them, Ahimaaz, Zadok's son and Jonathan, Abiathar's son; and by them send to me everything you hear.

³⁷So Hushai, David's friend, returned, and Absalom also came into Jerusalem.

**16** When David was a little past the top [of Olivet], behold, Ziba, the servant of Mephibosheth, met him with a couple of donkeys saddled, and upon them 200 loaves of bread, 100 bunches of raisins, 100 summer fruits, and a skin of wine.

²The king said to Ziba, What do you mean by these? Ziba said, The donkeys are for the king's household to ride on, the bread and summer fruit for the young men to eat, and the wine is for those to drink who become faint in the wilderness.

³The king said, And where is your master's son [grandson Mephibosheth]? Ziba said to the king, Behold, he remains in Jerusalem, for he said, Today the house of Israel will give me back the kingdom of my father [grandfather Saul].

## New International Version

<sup>4</sup>Then the king said to Ziba, "All that belonged to Mephibosheth is now yours."

"I humbly bow," Ziba said. "May I find favor in your eyes, my lord the king."

### Shimei Curses David

<sup>5</sup>As King David approached Bahurim, a man from the same clan as Saul's family came out from there. His name was Shimei son of Gera, and he cursed as he came out. <sup>6</sup>He pelted David and all the king's officials with stones, though all the troops and the special guard were on David's right and left. <sup>7</sup>As he cursed, Shimei said, "Get out, get out, you murderer, you scoundrel! <sup>8</sup>The LORD has repaid you for all the blood you shed in the household of Saul, in whose place you have reigned. The LORD has given the kingdom into the hands of your son Absalom. You have come to ruin because you are a murderer!"

<sup>9</sup>Then Abishai son of Zeruiah said to the king, "Why should this dead dog curse my lord the king? Let me go over and cut off his head."

<sup>10</sup>But the king said, "What does this have to do with you, you sons of Zeruiah? If he is cursing because the LORD said to him, 'Curse David,' who can ask, 'Why do you do this?'"

<sup>11</sup>David then said to Abishai and all his officials, "My son, my own flesh and blood, is trying to kill me. How much more, then, this Benjamite! Leave him alone; let him curse, for the LORD has told him to. <sup>12</sup>It may be that the LORD will look upon my misery and restore to me his covenant blessing instead of his curse today."

<sup>13</sup>So David and his men continued along the road while Shimei was going along the hillside opposite him, cursing as he went and throwing stones at him and showering him with dirt. <sup>14</sup>The king and all the people with him arrived at their destination exhausted. And there he refreshed himself.

### The Advice of Ahithophel and Hushai

<sup>15</sup>Meanwhile, Absalom and all the men of Israel came to Jerusalem, and Ahithophel was with him. <sup>16</sup>Then Hushai the Arkite, David's confidant, went to Absalom and said to him, "Long live the king! Long live the king!"

<sup>17</sup>Absalom said to Hushai, "So this is the love you show your friend? If he's your friend, why didn't you go with him?"

<sup>18</sup>Hushai said to Absalom, "No, the one chosen by the LORD, by these people, and by all the men of Israel—his I will be, and I will remain with him. <sup>19</sup>Furthermore, whom should I serve? Should I not serve the son? Just as I served your father, so I will serve you."

<sup>20</sup>Absalom said to Ahithophel, "Give us your advice. What should we do?"

<sup>21</sup>Ahithophel answered, "Sleep with your father's concubines whom he left to take care of the palace. Then all Israel will hear that you have made yourself obnoxious to your father, and the hands of everyone with you will be more resolute." <sup>22</sup>So they pitched a tent for Absalom on the roof, and he slept with his father's concubines in the sight of all Israel.

<sup>23</sup>Now in those days the advice Ahithophel gave was like that of one who inquires of God. That was how both David and Absalom regarded all of Ahithophel's advice.

## Amplified Bible

<sup>4</sup>Then the king said to Ziba, Behold, all that belonged to Mephibosheth is now yours. Ziba said, I do obeisance; let me ever find favor in your sight, my lord O king.

<sup>5</sup>When King David came to Bahurim, a man of the family of the house of Saul, Shimei son of Gera, came out and cursed continually as he came.

<sup>6</sup>And he cast stones at David and at all the servants of King David; and all the people and all the mighty men were on his right hand and on his left.

<sup>7</sup>Shimei said as he cursed, Get out, get out, you man of blood, you base fellow!

<sup>8</sup>The Lord has avenged upon you all the blood of the house of Saul, in whose stead you have reigned; and the Lord has delivered the kingdom into the hands of Absalom your son. Behold, the calamity is upon you because you are a bloody man!

<sup>9</sup>Then said [David's nephew] Abishai son of Zeruiah to the king, Why should this dead dog curse my lord the king? Let me go over and take off his head.

<sup>10</sup>The king said, What have I to do with you, you sons of Zeruiah? If he is cursing because the Lord said to him, Curse David, who then shall ask, Why have you done so?

<sup>11</sup>And David said to Abishai and to all his servants, Behold, my son, who was born to me, seeks my life. With how much more reason now may this Benjamite do it? Let him alone; and let him curse, for the Lord has bidden him to do it.

<sup>12</sup>It may be that the Lord will look on the iniquity done me and will recompense me with good for his cursing this day.

<sup>13</sup>So David and his men went by the road, and Shimei went along on the hillside opposite David and cursed as he went and threw stones at him and dust at him.

<sup>14</sup>And the king and all the people who were with him came [to the Jordan] weary, and he refreshed himself there.

<sup>15</sup>And Absalom and all the people, the men of Israel, came to Jerusalem, and Ahithophel with him.

<sup>16</sup>And when Hushai the Archite, David's friend, came to Absalom, Hushai said to [him], Long live the king! Long live the king!

<sup>17</sup>Absalom said to Hushai, Is this your kindness *and* loyalty to your friend? Why did you not go with your friend?

<sup>18</sup>Hushai said to Absalom, No, for whom the Lord and this people and all the men of Israel choose, his will I be, and with him I will remain.

<sup>19</sup>And again, whom should I serve? Should it not be his son? As I have served your father, so will I serve you.

<sup>20</sup>Then Absalom said to Ahithophel, Give your counsel. What shall we do?

<sup>21</sup>And Ahithophel said to Absalom, Go in to your father's concubines whom he has left to keep the house; and all Israel will hear that you are abhorred by your father. Then the hands of all who are with you will be made strong.

<sup>22</sup>So they spread for Absalom a tent on the top of the [king's] house, and Absalom went in to his father's harem in the sight of all Israel.

<sup>23</sup>And the counsel of Ahithophel in those days was as if a man had consulted the word of God; so was all Ahithophel's counsel considered both by David and by Absalom.

## New International Version

**17** Ahithophel said to Absalom, "I would[a] choose twelve thousand men and set out tonight in pursuit of David. [2] I would attack him while he is weary and weak. I would strike him with terror, and then all the people with him will flee. I would strike down only the king [3] and bring all the people back to you. The death of the man you seek will mean the return of all; all the people will be unharmed." [4] This plan seemed good to Absalom and to all the elders of Israel.

[5] But Absalom said, "Summon also Hushai the Arkite, so we can hear what he has to say as well." [6] When Hushai came to him, Absalom said, "Ahithophel has given this advice. Should we do what he says? If not, give us your opinion."

[7] Hushai replied to Absalom, "The advice Ahithophel has given is not good this time. [8] You know your father and his men; they are fighters, and as fierce as a wild bear robbed of her cubs. Besides, your father is an experienced fighter; he will not spend the night with the troops. [9] Even now, he is hidden in a cave or some other place. If he should attack your troops first,[b] whoever hears about it will say, 'There has been a slaughter among the troops who follow Absalom.' [10] Then even the bravest soldier, whose heart is like the heart of a lion, will melt with fear, for all Israel knows that your father is a fighter and that those with him are brave.

[11] "So I advise you: Let all Israel, from Dan to Beersheba—as numerous as the sand on the seashore—be gathered to you, with you yourself leading them into battle. [12] Then we will attack him wherever he may be found, and we will fall on him as dew settles on the ground. Neither he nor any of his men will be left alive. [13] If he withdraws into a city, then all Israel will bring ropes to that city, and we will drag it down to the valley until not so much as a pebble is left."

[14] Absalom and all the men of Israel said, "The advice of Hushai the Arkite is better than that of Ahithophel." For the LORD had determined to frustrate the good advice of Ahithophel in order to bring disaster on Absalom.

[15] Hushai told Zadok and Abiathar, the priests, "Ahithophel has advised Absalom and the elders of Israel to do such and such, but I have advised them to do so and so. [16] Now send a message at once and tell David, 'Do not spend the night at the fords in the wilderness; cross over without fail, or the king and all the people with him will be swallowed up.'"

[17] Jonathan and Ahimaaz were staying at En Rogel. A female servant was to go and inform them, and they were to go and tell King David, for they could not risk being seen entering the city. [18] But a young man saw them and told Absalom. So the two of them left at once and went to the house of a man in Bahurim. He had a well in his courtyard, and they climbed down into it. [19] His wife took a covering and spread it out over the opening of the well and scattered grain over it. No one knew anything about it.

[20] When Absalom's men came to the woman at the house, they asked, "Where are Ahimaaz and Jonathan?"

The woman answered them, "They crossed over the brook."[c] The men searched but found no one, so they returned to Jerusalem.

## Amplified Bible

**17** Moreover, Ahithophel said to Absalom, Let me choose 12,000 men and I will set out and pursue David this night.

[2] I will come upon him while he is exhausted and weak, and cause him to panic; all the people with him will flee. Then I will strike down the king alone.

[3] I will bring back all the people to you. [The removal of] the man whom you seek is the assurance that all will return; and all the people will be at peace.

[4] And what he said pleased Absalom well and all the elders of Israel.

[5] Absalom said, Now call Hushai the Archite also, and let us hear what he says.

[6] When Hushai came, Absalom said to him, Ahithophel has counseled thus. Shall we do what he says? If not, speak up.

[7] And Hushai said to Absalom, The counsel that Ahithophel has given is not good at this time.

[8] For, said Hushai, you know your father and his men, that they are mighty men, and they are embittered *and* enraged like a bear robbed of her whelps in the field. And your father is a man of war, and will not lodge with the people.

[9] Behold, he is hidden even now in some pit or other place; and when some of them are overthrown at the first, whoever hears it will say, There is a slaughter among the followers of Absalom.

[10] And even he who is brave, whose heart is as the heart of a lion, will utterly melt, for all Israel knows that your father is a mighty man and that those who are with him are brave men.

[11] Therefore I counsel that all [the men of] Israel be gathered to you, from Dan even to Beersheba, as the sand that is by the sea for multitude, and that you go to battle in your own person.

[12] So shall we come upon [David] some place where he shall be found, and we will light upon him as the dew settles [unseen and unheard] on the ground; and of him and of all the men with him there shall not be left so much as one.

[13] If he withdraws into a city, then shall all Israel bring ropes to that city, and we will drag it into the ravine until not one pebble is left there.

[14] Absalom and all the men of Israel said, The counsel of Hushai the Archite is better than that of Ahithophel. For the Lord had ordained to defeat the good counsel of Ahithophel, so that the Lord might bring evil upon Absalom.

[15] Then said Hushai to Zadok and Abiathar the priests, Thus and thus did Ahithophel counsel Absalom and the elders of Israel, and thus and thus have I counseled.

[16] Now send quickly and tell David, Lodge not this night at the fords [at the Jordan] of the wilderness, but by all means pass over, lest the king be swallowed up and all the people with him.

[17] Now [the youths] Jonathan and Ahimaaz stayed at En-rogel, for they must not be seen coming into the city. But a maidservant went and told them, and they went and told King David.

[18] But a lad saw them and told Absalom; but they left quickly and came to the house of a man in Bahurim, who had a well in his court, and they went down into it.

[19] And the woman spread a covering over the well's mouth and spread ground corn on it; and the thing was not discovered.

[20] For when Absalom's servants came to the woman at the house, they said, Where are Ahimaaz and Jonathan? And the woman said to them, They went over the brook of water. When they had sought and could not find them, they returned to Jerusalem.

---

[a] 1 Or *Let me*     [b] 9 Or *When some of the men fall at the first attack*
[c] 20 Or *"They passed by the sheep pen toward the water."*

## New International Version

²¹After they had gone, the two climbed out of the well and went to inform King David. They said to him, "Set out and cross the river at once; Ahithophel has advised such and such against you." ²²So David and all the people with him set out and crossed the Jordan. By daybreak, no one was left who had not crossed the Jordan.

²³When Ahithophel saw that his advice had not been followed, he saddled his donkey and set out for his house in his hometown. He put his house in order and then hanged himself. So he died and was buried in his father's tomb.

### Absalom's Death

²⁴David went to Mahanaim, and Absalom crossed the Jordan with all the men of Israel. ²⁵Absalom had appointed Amasa over the army in place of Joab. Amasa was the son of Jether,ᵃ an Ishmaeliteᵇ who had married Abigail,ᶜ the daughter of Nahash and sister of Zeruiah the mother of Joab. ²⁶The Israelites and Absalom camped in the land of Gilead.

²⁷When David came to Mahanaim, Shobi son of Nahash from Rabbah of the Ammonites, and Makir son of Ammiel from Lo Debar, and Barzillai the Gileadite from Rogelim ²⁸brought bedding and bowls and articles of pottery. They also brought wheat and barley, flour and roasted grain, beans and lentils,ᵈ ²⁹honey and curds, sheep, and cheese from cows' milk for David and his people to eat. For they said, "The people have become exhausted and hungry and thirsty in the wilderness."

**18** David mustered the men who were with him and appointed over them commanders of thousands and commanders of hundreds. ²David sent out his troops, a third under the command of Joab, a third under Joab's brother Abishai son of Zeruiah, and a third under Ittai the Gittite. The king told the troops, "I myself will surely march out with you."

³But the men said, "You must not go out; if we are forced to flee, they won't care about us. Even if half of us die, they won't care; but you are worth ten thousand of us.ᵉ It would be better now for you to give us support from the city."

⁴The king answered, "I will do whatever seems best to you."

So the king stood beside the gate while all his men marched out in units of hundreds and of thousands. ⁵The king commanded Joab, Abishai and Ittai, "Be gentle with the young man Absalom for my sake." And all the troops heard the king giving orders concerning Absalom to each of the commanders.

⁶David's army marched out of the city to fight Israel, and the battle took place in the forest of Ephraim. ⁷There Israel's troops were routed by David's men, and the casualties that day were great—twenty thousand men. ⁸The battle spread out over the whole countryside, and the forest swallowed up more men that day than the sword.

⁹Now Absalom happened to meet David's men. He was riding his mule, and as the mule went under the thick branches of a large oak, Absalom's hair got caught in the tree. He was left hanging in midair, while the mule he was riding kept on going.

¹⁰When one of the men saw what had happened, he told Joab, "I just saw Absalom hanging in an oak tree."

¹¹Joab said to the man who had told him this, "What! You saw him? Why didn't you strike him to the ground

## Amplified Bible

²¹After they had departed, the boys came up out of the well and went and told King David, and said, Arise and pass quickly over the river Jordan; for thus and so has Ahithophel counseled against you.

²²David arose and all the people with him and passed over the Jordan. By daybreak, not one was left who had not crossed.

²³But when Ahithophel saw that his counsel was not followed, he saddled his donkey, went home to his city, put his household in order, and hanged himself and died, and was buried in the tomb of his father.

²⁴Then David came to Mahanaim. And Absalom passed over the Jordan, he and all the men of Israel with him.

²⁵Absalom made Amasa captain of the army instead of Joab. Amasa was the son of an [Ishmaelite] named Ithra, who married Abigail daughter of Nahash, [half sister of David and] sister of Zeruiah, Joab's mother.

²⁶So Israel and Absalom encamped in the land of Gilead.

²⁷When David came to Mahanaim, Shobi son of Nahash of Rabbah of the Ammonites, and Machir son of Ammiel of Lo-debar, and Barzillai the Gileadite of Rogelim ²⁸Brought beds, basins, earthen vessels, wheat, barley, meal, parched grain, beans, lentils, parched [pulse—seeds of peas and beans],

²⁹Honey, curds, sheep, and cheese of cows for David and the people with him to eat; for they said, The people are hungry, weary, and thirsty in the wilderness.

**18** David numbered the men who were with him and set over them commanders of thousands and of hundreds.

²David sent forth the army, a third under command of Joab, a third under Abishai son of Zeruiah, Joab's brother, and a third under Ittai the Gittite. [He] told the men, I myself will go out with you also.

³But the men said, You shall not go out. For if we flee, they will not care about us; if half of us die, they will not care about us. But you are worth 10,000 such as we are. So now it is better that you be able to help us from the city.

⁴The king said to them, Whatever seems best to you I will do. So he stood beside the gate, and all the army came out by hundreds and by thousands.

⁵The king commanded Joab, Abishai, and Ittai, saying, Deal gently for my sake with the young man Absalom. And all the people heard when the king gave orders to all the commanders about Absalom.

⁶So the army went out into the field against Israel, and the battle was fought in the forest of Ephraim.

⁷[Absalom's] men of Israel were defeated by the servants of David, and there was a great slaughter that day of 20,000 men.

⁸For the battle spread over the face of all the country, and the forest devoured more men that day than did the sword.

⁹Then Absalom [unavoidably] met the servants of David. Absalom rode on a mule, and the mule went under the thick boughs of a great oak, and Absalom's head caught fast [in a fork] of the oak; and the mule under him ran away, leaving him hanging between the heavens and the earth.

¹⁰A certain man saw it and told Joab, Behold, I saw Absalom hanging in an oak.

¹¹Joab said to the man, You saw him! Why did you not

---

ᵃ 25 Hebrew *Ithra*, a variant of *Jether*    ᵇ 25 Some Septuagint manuscripts (see also 1 Chron. 2:17); Hebrew and other Septuagint manuscripts *Israelite*    ᶜ 25 Hebrew *Abigal*, a variant of *Abigail*    ᵈ 28 Most Septuagint manuscripts and Syriac; Hebrew *lentils, and roasted grain*    ᵉ 3 Two Hebrew manuscripts, some Septuagint manuscripts and Vulgate; most Hebrew manuscripts *care; for now there are ten thousand like us*

## New International Version

right there? Then I would have had to give you ten shek-els[a] of silver and a warrior's belt."

¹²But the man replied, "Even if a thousand shekels[b] were weighed out into my hands, I would not lay a hand on the king's son. In our hearing the king commanded you and Abishai and Ittai, 'Protect the young man Absalom for my sake.[c]' ¹³And if I had put my life in jeopardy[d]—and nothing is hidden from the king—you would have kept your distance from me."

¹⁴Joab said, "I'm not going to wait like this for you." So he took three javelins in his hand and plunged them into Absalom's heart while Absalom was still alive in the oak tree. ¹⁵And ten of Joab's armor-bearers surrounded Absalom, struck him and killed him.

¹⁶Then Joab sounded the trumpet, and the troops stopped pursuing Israel, for Joab halted them. ¹⁷They took Absalom, threw him into a big pit in the forest and piled up a large heap of rocks over him. Meanwhile, all the Israelites fled to their homes.

¹⁸During his lifetime Absalom had taken a pillar and erected it in the King's Valley as a monument to himself, for he thought, "I have no son to carry on the memory of my name." He named the pillar after himself, and it is called Absalom's Monument to this day.

### David Mourns

¹⁹Now Ahimaaz son of Zadok said, "Let me run and take the news to the king that the LORD has vindicated him by delivering him from the hand of his enemies."

²⁰"You are not the one to take the news today," Joab told him. "You may take the news another time, but you must not do so today, because the king's son is dead."

²¹Then Joab said to a Cushite, "Go, tell the king what you have seen." The Cushite bowed down before Joab and ran off.

²²Ahimaaz son of Zadok again said to Joab, "Come what may, please let me run behind the Cushite."

But Joab replied, "My son, why do you want to go? You don't have any news that will bring you a reward."

²³He said, "Come what may, I want to run."

So Joab said, "Run!" Then Ahimaaz ran by way of the plain[e] and outran the Cushite.

²⁴While David was sitting between the inner and outer gates, the watchman went up to the roof of the gateway by the wall. As he looked out, he saw a man running alone. ²⁵The watchman called out to the king and reported it.

The king said, "If he is alone, he must have good news." And the runner came closer and closer.

²⁶Then the watchman saw another runner, and he called down to the gatekeeper, "Look, another man running alone!"

The king said, "He must be bringing good news, too."

²⁷The watchman said, "It seems to me that the first one runs like Ahimaaz son of Zadok."

"He's a good man," the king said. "He comes with good news."

²⁸Then Ahimaaz called out to the king, "All is well!" He bowed down before the king with his face to the ground and said, "Praise be to the LORD your God! He has delivered up those who lifted their hands against my lord the king."

²⁹The king asked, "Is the young man Absalom safe?"

Ahimaaz answered, "I saw great confusion just as Joab was about to send the king's servant and me, your servant, but I don't know what it was."

³⁰The king said, "Stand aside and wait here." So he stepped aside and stood there.

## Amplified Bible

strike him down to the ground? I would have given you ten shekels of silver and a girdle.

¹²The man told Joab, Though I should receive 1,000 pieces of silver, yet I would not put forth my hand against the king's son. For in our hearing the king charged you, Abishai, and Ittai, Have a care, whoever you be, for the young man Absalom.

¹³Otherwise, if I had dealt falsely against his life—for nothing is hidden from the king—you yourself would have taken sides against me.

¹⁴Joab said, I will not tarry thus with you. He took three darts in his hand and thrust them into the body of Absalom while he was yet alive in the midst of the oak.

¹⁵And ten young men, Joab's armor-bearers, surrounded and struck Absalom and killed him.

¹⁶Then Joab blew the trumpet, and the troops returned from pursuing Israel, for Joab restrained *and* spared them.

¹⁷They took Absalom and cast him into a great pit in the forest and raised a very great heap of stones upon him. And all Israel fled, everyone to his own home.

¹⁸Now Absalom in his lifetime had reared up for himself a pillar which is in the King's Valley, for he said, I have no son to keep my name in remembrance. He called the pillar after his own name, and to this day it is called Absalom's Monument.

¹⁹Then said Ahimaaz son of Zadok, Let me now run and bear the king tidings of how the Lord has avenged David of his enemies.

²⁰Joab told him, You shall not carry news today, but another time. Today you shall bear no news, for the king's son is dead.

²¹Then said Joab to the Cushite [an Ethiopian], Go tell the king what you have seen. And the Cushite bowed to Joab and ran.

²²Then said Ahimaaz son of Zadok again to Joab, But anyhow, let me, I pray you, also run after the Cushite. Joab said, Why should you run, my son, seeing you will have no reward, for you have not sufficient tidings?

²³But he said, Let me run anyhow. So Joab said to him, Run. Then Ahimaaz ran by the way of the plain and outran the Cushite.

²⁴Now David was sitting between the two gates; and the watchman went up to the roof over the gate by the wall, and when he looked, he saw a man running alone.

²⁵The watchman called out and told the king. The king said, If he is alone, he has news to tell. And he came on and drew near.

²⁶Then the watchman saw another man running, and the watchman called to the gatekeeper, Behold, another man running alone. The king said, He also brings news.

²⁷The watchman said, I think the man in front runs like Ahimaaz son of Zadok. The king said, He is a good man and comes with good tidings.

²⁸And Ahimaaz called and said to the king, All is well! And he fell down to the ground on his face before the king and said, Blessed be the Lord your God, Who has shut up the men who lifted up their hands against my lord the king.

²⁹The king said, Is the young man Absalom safe? Ahimaaz answered, When Joab sent the king's servant and me, your servant, I saw a great tumult, but I do not know what it was.

³⁰The king told him, Turn aside; stand here. And he turned aside and stood still.

---

*a 11 That is, about 4 ounces or about 115 grams     b 12 That is, about 25 pounds or about 12 kilograms     c 12 A few Hebrew manuscripts, Septuagint, Vulgate and Syriac; most Hebrew manuscripts may be translated Absalom, whoever you may be.     d 13 Or Otherwise, if I had acted treacherously toward him     e 23 That is, the plain of the Jordan*

## New International Version

³¹Then the Cushite arrived and said, "My lord the king, hear the good news! The Lord has vindicated you today by delivering you from the hand of all who rose up against you."

³²The king asked the Cushite, "Is the young man Absalom safe?"

The Cushite replied, "May the enemies of my lord the king and all who rise up to harm you be like that young man."

³³The king was shaken. He went up to the room over the gateway and wept. As he went, he said: "O my son Absalom! My son, my son Absalom! If only I had died instead of you—O Absalom, my son, my son!"ᵃ

**19**ᵇ Joab was told, "The king is weeping and mourning for Absalom." ²And for the whole army the victory that day was turned into mourning, because on that day the troops heard it said, "The king is grieving for his son." ³The men stole into the city that day as men steal in who are ashamed when they flee from battle. ⁴The king covered his face and cried aloud, "O my son Absalom! O Absalom, my son, my son!"

⁵Then Joab went into the house to the king and said, "Today you have humiliated all your men, who have just saved your life and the lives of your sons and daughters and the lives of your wives and concubines. ⁶You love those who hate you and hate those who love you. You have made it clear today that the commanders and their men mean nothing to you. I see that you would be pleased if Absalom were alive today and all of us were dead. ⁷Now go out and encourage your men. I swear by the Lord that if you don't go out, not a man will be left with you by nightfall. This will be worse for you than all the calamities that have come on you from your youth till now."

⁸So the king got up and took his seat in the gateway. When the men were told, "The king is sitting in the gateway," they all came before him.

Meanwhile, the Israelites had fled to their homes.

### David Returns to Jerusalem

⁹Throughout the tribes of Israel, all the people were arguing among themselves, saying, "The king delivered us from the hand of our enemies; he is the one who rescued us from the hand of the Philistines. But now he has fled the country to escape from Absalom; ¹⁰and Absalom, whom we anointed to rule over us, has died in battle. So why do you say nothing about bringing the king back?"

¹¹King David sent this message to Zadok and Abiathar, the priests: "Ask the elders of Judah, 'Why should you be the last to bring the king back to his palace, since what is being said throughout Israel has reached the king at his quarters? ¹²You are my relatives, my own flesh and blood. So why should you be the last to bring back the king?' ¹³And say to Amasa, 'Are you not my own flesh and blood? May God deal with me, be it ever so severely, if you are not the commander of my army for life in place of Joab.'"

¹⁴He won over the hearts of the men of Judah so that they were all of one mind. They sent word to the king, "Return, you and all your men." ¹⁵Then the king returned and went as far as the Jordan.

Now the men of Judah had come to Gilgal to go out and meet the king and bring him across the Jordan. ¹⁶Shimei

## Amplified Bible

³¹And behold, the Cushite (Ethiopian) came, and he said, News, my lord the king! For the Lord has delivered you this day from all who rose up against you.

³²The king said to the Cushite, Is the young man Absalom safe? The Cushite replied, May the enemies of my lord the king and all who rise against you to do evil be like that young man is.

³³And the king was deeply moved and went up to the chamber over the gate and wept. And as he went, he said, O my son Absalom, my son, my son Absalom! Would to God I had died for you, O Absalom, my son, my son!

**19** It was told Joab, Behold, the king is weeping and mourning for Absalom.

²So the victory that day was turned into mourning for all the people, for they heard it said, The king grieves for his son.

³The people slipped into the city stealthily that day as humiliated people steal away when they flee in battle.

⁴But the king covered his face and cried with a loud voice, O my son Absalom, O Absalom, my son, my son!

⁵And Joab came into the house to the king and said, You have today covered the faces of all your servants with shame, who this day have saved your life and the lives of your sons and your daughters and the lives of your wives and concubines.

⁶For you love those who hate you and hate those who love you. You have declared today that princes and servants are nothing to you; for today I see that if Absalom had lived and all the rest of us had died, you would be well pleased.

⁷So now arise, go out and speak kindly and encouragingly to your servants; for I swear by the Lord that if you do not go, not a man will remain with you this night. And this will be worse for you than all the evil that has befallen you from your youth until now.

⁸Then the king arose and sat in the gate. And all [his followers] were told, The king is sitting in the gate, and they all came before the king. Now Israel [Absalom's troops] had fled, every man to his home.

⁹And all the people were at strife throughout all the tribes of Israel, saying, The king delivered us from the hands of our enemies, and he saved us from the hands of the Philistines. And now he has fled out of the land from Absalom.

¹⁰And Absalom, whom we anointed over us, is dead in battle. So now, why do you say nothing about bringing back the king?

¹¹And King David sent to Zadok and to Abiathar the priests, saying, Say to the elders of Judah, Why are you the last to bring the king back to his house, when the word of all Israel has come to the king, to bring him to his house?

¹²You are my kinsmen; you are my bone and my flesh. Why then are you the last to bring back the king?

¹³And say to Amasa, Are you not of my bone and of my flesh? May God do so to me, and more also, if you are not commander of my army hereafter in place of Joab.

¹⁴He inclined the hearts of all the men of Judah as one man, so they sent word to [him], Return, you and all your servants.

¹⁵So [David] returned and came to the Jordan. And Judah came to Gilgal to meet the king, to conduct him over the Jordan.

ᵃ 33 In Hebrew texts this verse (18:33) is numbered 19:1.   ᵇ In Hebrew texts 19:1-43 is numbered 19:2-44.

## New International Version

son of Gera, the Benjamite from Bahurim, hurried down with the men of Judah to meet King David. [17]With him were a thousand Benjamites, along with Ziba, the steward of Saul's household, and his fifteen sons and twenty servants. They rushed to the Jordan, where the king was. [18]They crossed at the ford to take the king's household over and to do whatever he wished.

When Shimei son of Gera crossed the Jordan, he fell prostrate before the king [19]and said to him, "May my lord not hold me guilty. Do not remember how your servant did wrong on the day my lord the king left Jerusalem. May the king put it out of his mind. [20]For I your servant know that I have sinned, but today I have come here as the first from the tribes of Joseph to come down and meet my lord the king."

[21]Then Abishai son of Zeruiah said, "Shouldn't Shimei be put to death for this? He cursed the LORD's anointed."

[22]David replied, "What does this have to do with you, you sons of Zeruiah? What right do you have to interfere? Should anyone be put to death in Israel today? Don't I know that today I am king over Israel?" [23]So the king said to Shimei, "You shall not die." And the king promised him on oath.

[24]Mephibosheth, Saul's grandson, also went down to meet the king. He had not taken care of his feet or trimmed his mustache or washed his clothes from the day the king left until the day he returned safely. [25]When he came from Jerusalem to meet the king, the king asked him, "Why didn't you go with me, Mephibosheth?"

[26]He said, "My lord the king, since I your servant am lame, I said, 'I will have my donkey saddled and will ride on it, so I can go with the king.' But Ziba my servant betrayed me. [27]And he has slandered your servant to my lord the king. My lord the king is like an angel of God; so do whatever you wish. [28]All my grandfather's descendants deserved nothing but death from my lord the king, but you gave your servant a place among those who eat at your table. So what right do I have to make any more appeals to the king?"

[29]The king said to him, "Why say more? I order you and Ziba to divide the land."

[30]Mephibosheth said to the king, "Let him take everything, now that my lord the king has returned home safely."

[31]Barzillai the Gileadite also came down from Rogelim to cross the Jordan with the king and to send him on his way from there. [32]Now Barzillai was very old, eighty years of age. He had provided for the king during his stay in Mahanaim, for he was a very wealthy man. [33]The king said to Barzillai, "Cross over with me and stay with me in Jerusalem, and I will provide for you."

[34]But Barzillai answered the king, "How many more years will I live, that I should go up to Jerusalem with the king? [35]I am now eighty years old. Can I tell the difference between what is enjoyable and what is not? Can your servant taste what he eats and drinks? Can I still hear the voices of male and female singers? Why should your servant be an added burden to my lord the king? [36]Your servant will cross over the Jordan with the king for a short distance, but why should the king reward me in this way? [37]Let your servant return, that I may die in my own town

## Amplified Bible

[16]And Shimei son of Gera, a Benjamite of Bahurim, hastily came down with the men of Judah to meet King David,

[17]And 1,000 men of Benjamin with him. And Ziba, the servant of the house of Saul, and his fifteen sons and twenty servants with him, rushed to the Jordan *and* pressed quickly into the king's presence.

[18]And there went over a ferryboat to bring over the king's household and to do what he thought good. And Shimei son of Gera fell down before the king as David came to the Jordan,

[19]And said to the king, Let not my lord impute iniquity to me *and* hold me guilty, nor remember what your servant did the day my lord went out of Jerusalem [when Shimei grossly insulted David]; may the king not take it to heart.

[20]For your servant knows that I have sinned; therefore, behold, I am today the first of all the house of Joseph to come down to meet my lord the king.

[21]But Abishai son of Zeruiah said, Shall not Shimei be put to death for this, because he cursed the Lord's anointed?

[22]David said, What have I to do with you, you sons of Zeruiah, that you should be an adversary to me today? Shall anyone be put to death today in Israel? For do not I know that I am this day king over Israel?

[23]Therefore the king said to Shimei, You shall not die [at my hand]. And the king gave him his oath. [I Kings 2:44-46.]

[24]Mephibosheth the son [grandson] of Saul came down to meet the king, and had not dressed his feet, trimmed his beard, or washed his clothes from the day the king left until he returned in peace *and* safety.

[25]And when he came to Jerusalem to meet the king, David said to him, Why did you not go with me, Mephibosheth?

[26]He said, My lord O king, my servant [Ziba] deceived me; for I said, Saddle me the donkey that I may ride on it and go to the king, for your servant is lame [but he took the donkey and left without me].

[27]He has slandered your servant to my lord the king. But the king is as an angel of God; so do what is good in your eyes.

[28]For all of my father's house were but doomed to death before my lord the king; yet you set your servant among those who ate at your own table. What right therefore have I to cry any more to the king?

[29]The king said to him, Why speak any more of your affairs? I say, You and Ziba divide the land.

[30]Mephibosheth said to the king, Oh, let him take it all, since my lord the king has returned home in safety *and* peace.

[31]Now Barzillai the Gileadite came down from Rogelim and went on to the Jordan with the king to conduct him over the Jordan.

[32]Now Barzillai was a very aged man, even eighty years old; and he had provided the king with food while he remained at Mahanaim, for he was a very great man.

[33]And the king said to Barzillai, Come over with me, and I will provide for you with me in Jerusalem.

[34]And Barzillai said to the king, How much longer have I to live, that it would be worthwhile for me to go up with the king to Jerusalem?

[35]I am this day eighty years old. Could I now [be useful as a counselor to] discern between good and evil? Can your servant appreciate what I eat or drink? Can I any longer enjoy the voices of singing men and women? Why then should your servant be still a burden to my lord the king?

[36]Your servant will only go over the Jordan with the king. Why should the king repay me with such a reward?

[37]Let your servant turn back again, that I may die in

## New International Version

near the tomb of my father and mother. But here is your servant Kimham. Let him cross over with my lord the king. Do for him whatever you wish."

38The king said, "Kimham shall cross over with me, and I will do for him whatever you wish. And anything you desire from me I will do for you."

39So all the people crossed the Jordan, and then the king crossed over. The king kissed Barzillai and bid him farewell, and Barzillai returned to his home.

40When the king crossed over to Gilgal, Kimham crossed with him. All the troops of Judah and half the troops of Israel had taken the king over.

41Soon all the men of Israel were coming to the king and saying to him, "Why did our brothers, the men of Judah, steal the king away and bring him and his household across the Jordan, together with all his men?"

42All the men of Judah answered the men of Israel, "We did this because the king is closely related to us. Why are you angry about it? Have we eaten any of the king's provisions? Have we taken anything for ourselves?"

43Then the men of Israel answered the men of Judah, "We have ten shares in the king; so we have a greater claim on David than you have. Why then do you treat us with contempt? Weren't we the first to speak of bringing back our king?"

But the men of Judah pressed their claims even more forcefully than the men of Israel.

### Sheba Rebels Against David

**20** Now a troublemaker named Sheba son of Bikri, a Benjamite, happened to be there. He sounded the trumpet and shouted,

"We have no share in David,
    no part in Jesse's son!
Every man to his tent, Israel!"

2So all the men of Israel deserted David to follow Sheba son of Bikri. But the men of Judah stayed by their king all the way from the Jordan to Jerusalem.

3When David returned to his palace in Jerusalem, he took the ten concubines he had left to take care of the palace and put them in a house under guard. He provided for them but had no sexual relations with them. They were kept in confinement till the day of their death, living as widows.

4Then the king said to Amasa, "Summon the men of Judah to come to me within three days, and be here yourself." 5But when Amasa went to summon Judah, he took longer than the time the king had set for him.

6David said to Abishai, "Now Sheba son of Bikri will do us more harm than Absalom did. Take your master's men and pursue him, or he will find fortified cities and escape from us."*a* 7So Joab's men and the Kerethites and Pelethites and all the mighty warriors went out under the command of Abishai. They marched out from Jerusalem to pursue Sheba son of Bikri.

8While they were at the great rock in Gibeon, Amasa came to meet them. Joab was wearing his military tunic, and strapped over it at his waist was a belt with a dagger in its sheath. As he stepped forward, it dropped out of its sheath.

9Joab said to Amasa, "How are you, my brother?" Then Joab took Amasa by the beard with his right hand to kiss him. 10Amasa was not on his guard against the dagger in Joab's hand, and Joab plunged it into his belly, and his intestines spilled out on the ground. Without being stabbed

## Amplified Bible

my own city and be buried by the grave of my father and mother. But here is your servant Chimham; let him go over with my lord the king. And do to him what shall seem good to you.

38The king answered, Chimham shall go over with me, and I will do to him what seems good to you; and whatever you ask of me I will do for you.

39So all the people went over the Jordan. When the king had crossed over, he kissed Barzillai and blessed him, and [the great man] returned to his own place.

40Then the king went on to Gilgal, and Chimham went with him; and all the people of Judah and also half the people of Israel escorted the king.

41And all the men of Israel came to the king and said to him, Why have our kinsmen, the men of Judah, stolen you away and have brought the king and his household over the Jordan, and all David's men with him?

42But all the men of Judah answered the men of Israel, Because the king is near of kin to us. Why then be angry about it? Have we eaten at all at the king's expense? Or has he given us any gift?

43Then the men of Israel answered the men of Judah, We have ten [tribes'] shares in the king; and we have more right to David than you have. Why then did you despise *and* ignore us? Were we not the first to speak of our bringing back our king? But the words of the men of Judah were more violent than the charges of the men of Israel.

**20** There happened to be there a base *and* contemptible fellow named Sheba son of Bichri, a Benjamite. He blew a trumpet and said, We have no portion in David and no inheritance in the son of Jesse! Every man to his tents, O Israel!

2So all the men of Israel withdrew from David and followed Sheba son of Bichri; but the men of Judah stayed faithfully with their king, from the Jordan to Jerusalem.

3So David came to his house at Jerusalem. And the king took the ten women, his concubines, whom he had left to keep the house, and put them away under guard and provided for them, but did not go in to them. So they were shut up to the day of their death, living in widowhood.

4Then said the king to Amasa, Assemble the men of Judah to me within three days, and you be present here.

5So Amasa went to assemble the men of Judah, but he tarried longer than the set time which had been appointed him.

6And David said to Abishai, Now will Sheba son of Bichri do us more harm than Absalom did. Take your lord's servants and pursue him, lest he get for himself fenced cities and snatch away our very eyes.

7And there went after him Joab's men and [David's bodyguards] the Cherethites and Pelethites and all the mighty men; they went out from Jerusalem to pursue Sheba son of Bichri.

8When they were at the great stone in Gibeon, Amasa came to meet them. Joab was wearing a soldier's garment, and over it was a sheathed sword fastened around his hips; and as he went forward, it fell out.

9Joab said to Amasa, Are you well, my brother? And Joab took Amasa by the beard with the right hand [as if] to kiss him.

10But Amasa did not notice the sword in Joab's hand. So [Joab] struck him [who was to have been his successor] with it in the body, shedding his bowels to the ground

*a* 6 Or *and do us serious injury*

## New International Version

again, Amasa died. Then Joab and his brother Abishai pursued Sheba son of Bikri.

[11]One of Joab's men stood beside Amasa and said, "Whoever favors Joab, and whoever is for David, let him follow Joab!" [12]Amasa lay wallowing in his blood in the middle of the road, and the man saw that all the troops came to a halt there. When he realized that everyone who came up to Amasa stopped, he dragged him from the road into a field and threw a garment over him. [13]After Amasa had been removed from the road, everyone went on with Joab to pursue Sheba son of Bikri.

[14]Sheba passed through all the tribes of Israel to Abel Beth Maakah and through the entire region of the Bikrites,[a] who gathered together and followed him. [15]All the troops with Joab came and besieged Sheba in Abel Beth Maakah. They built a siege ramp up to the city, and it stood against the outer fortifications. While they were battering the wall to bring it down, [16]a wise woman called from the city, "Listen! Listen! Tell Joab to come here so I can speak to him." [17]He went toward her, and she asked, "Are you Joab?"

"I am," he answered.

She said, "Listen to what your servant has to say."

"I'm listening," he said.

[18]She continued, "Long ago they used to say, 'Get your answer at Abel,' and that settled it. [19]We are the peaceful and faithful in Israel. You are trying to destroy a city that is a mother in Israel. Why do you want to swallow up the Lord's inheritance?"

[20]"Far be it from me!" Joab replied, "Far be it from me to swallow up or destroy! [21]That is not the case. A man named Sheba son of Bikri, from the hill country of Ephraim, has lifted up his hand against the king, against David. Hand over this one man, and I'll withdraw from the city."

The woman said to Joab, "His head will be thrown to you from the wall."

[22]Then the woman went to all the people with her wise advice, and they cut off the head of Sheba son of Bikri and threw it to Joab. So he sounded the trumpet, and his men dispersed from the city, each returning to his home. And Joab went back to the king in Jerusalem.

### David's Officials

[23]Joab was over Israel's entire army; Benaiah son of Jehoiada was over the Kerethites and Pelethites; [24]Adoniram[b] was in charge of forced labor; Jehoshaphat son of Ahilud was recorder; [25]Sheva was secretary; Zadok and Abiathar were priests; [26]and Ira the Jairite[c] was David's priest.

## Amplified Bible

without another blow; and [soon] he died. So Joab and Abishai his brother pursued Sheba son of Bichri.

[11]And one of Joab's men stood by him and said, Whoever favors Joab and is for David, follow Joab!

[12]And Amasa wallowed in his blood in the highway. And when the man saw that all the people who came by stood still, he removed Amasa out of the highway into the field and spread a cloth over him.

[13]When Amasa was removed from the highway, all the people went on after Joab to pursue Sheba son of Bichri.

[14]Joab went through all the tribes of Israel to Abel of Beth-maacah, and all the Berites assembled and also went after [Sheba] ardently.

[15]And they came and besieged Sheba in Abel of Beth-maacah, and they cast up a siege mound against the city, and it stood against the rampart; and all the men with Joab battered *and* undermined the wall to make it fall.

[16]Then a wise woman of the city cried, Hear, hear! Say to Joab, Come here so I can speak to you.

[17]And when he came near her, the woman said, Are you Joab? He answered, I am. Then she said to him, Hear the words of your handmaid. He answered, I am listening.

[18]Then she said, People used to say, Let them but ask counsel at Abel, and so they settled the matter.

[19]I am one of the peaceable and faithful in Israel. You seek to destroy a city which is a mother in Israel. Why will you swallow up the inheritance of the Lord?

[20]Joab answered, Far be it, far be it from me that I should swallow up or destroy!

[21]That is not true. But a man of the hill country of Ephraim, Sheba son of Bichri, has lifted up his hand against King David. Deliver him only, and I will depart from the city. And the woman said, Behold, his head shall be thrown to you over the wall.

[22]Then the woman in her wisdom went to all the people. And they cut off the head of Sheba of Bichri and cast it down to Joab. So he blew the trumpet, and they retired from the city, every man to his own home. And Joab returned to Jerusalem to the king. [Eccl. 9:13-16.]

[23]Joab was over the host of Israel; Benaiah son of Jehoiada was over [the king's bodyguards] the Cherethites and Pelethites;

[24]Adoram was over the tribute; Jehoshaphat son of Ahilud was recorder;

[25]Sheva was scribe; and Zadok and Abiathar were priests;

[26]Also Ira the Jairite was chief minister to David.

### The Gibeonites Avenged

**21** During the reign of David, there was a famine for three successive years; so David sought the face of the Lord. The Lord said, "It is on account of Saul and his blood-stained house; it is because he put the Gibeonites to death."

[2]The king summoned the Gibeonites and spoke to them. (Now the Gibeonites were not a part of Israel but were survivors of the Amorites; the Israelites had sworn to spare them, but Saul in his zeal for Israel and Judah had tried to annihilate them.) [3]David asked the Gibeonites, "What shall I do for you? How shall I make atonement so that you will bless the Lord's inheritance?"

**21** There was a three-year famine in the days of David, year after year; and David inquired of the Lord. The Lord replied, It is on account of Saul and his bloody house, for he put to death the Gibeonites.

[2]So the king called the Gibeonites—now the Gibeonites were not Israelites but of the remnant of the Amorites. The Israelites had sworn to spare them, but Saul in his zeal for the people of Israel and Judah had sought to slay the Gibeonites—

[3]So David said to the Gibeonites, What shall I do for you? How can I make atonement that you may bless the Lord's inheritance?

[a] 14 See Septuagint and Vulgate; Hebrew *Berites*.   [b] 24 Some Septuagint manuscripts (see also 1 Kings 4:6 and 5:14); Hebrew *Adoram*   [c] 26 Hebrew; some Septuagint manuscripts and Syriac (see also 23:38) *Ithrite*

## New International Version

[4]The Gibeonites answered him, "We have no right to demand silver or gold from Saul or his family, nor do we have the right to put anyone in Israel to death."

"What do you want me to do for you?" David asked.

[5]They answered the king, "As for the man who destroyed us and plotted against us so that we have been decimated and have no place anywhere in Israel, [6]let seven of his male descendants be given to us to be killed and their bodies exposed before the Lord at Gibeah of Saul—the Lord's chosen one."

So the king said, "I will give them to you."

[7]The king spared Mephibosheth son of Jonathan, the son of Saul, because of the oath before the Lord between David and Jonathan son of Saul. [8]But the king took Armoni and Mephibosheth, the two sons of Aiah's daughter Rizpah, whom she had borne to Saul, together with the five sons of Saul's daughter Merab,[a] whom she had borne to Adriel son of Barzillai the Meholathite. [9]He handed them over to the Gibeonites, who killed them and exposed their bodies on a hill before the Lord. All seven of them fell together; they were put to death during the first days of the harvest, just as the barley harvest was beginning.

[10]Rizpah daughter of Aiah took sackcloth and spread it out for herself on a rock. From the beginning of the harvest till the rain poured down from the heavens on the bodies, she did not let the birds touch them by day or the wild animals by night. [11]When David was told what Aiah's daughter Rizpah, Saul's concubine, had done, [12]he went and took the bones of Saul and his son Jonathan from the citizens of Jabesh Gilead. (They had stolen their bodies from the public square at Beth Shan, where the Philistines had hung them after they struck Saul down on Gilboa.) [13]David brought the bones of Saul and his son Jonathan from there, and the bones of those who had been killed and exposed were gathered up.

[14]They buried the bones of Saul and his son Jonathan in the tomb of Saul's father Kish, at Zela in Benjamin, and did everything the king commanded. After that, God answered prayer in behalf of the land.

### Wars Against the Philistines

[15]Once again there was a battle between the Philistines and Israel. David went down with his men to fight against the Philistines, and he became exhausted. [16]And Ishbi-Benob, one of the descendants of Rapha, whose bronze spearhead weighed three hundred shekels[b] and who was armed with a new sword, said he would kill David. [17]But Abishai son of Zeruiah came to David's rescue; he struck the Philistine down and killed him. Then David's men swore to him, saying, "Never again will you go out with us to battle, so that the lamp of Israel will not be extinguished."

[18]In the course of time, there was another battle with the Philistines, at Gob. At that time Sibbekai the Hushathite killed Saph, one of the descendants of Rapha.

[19]In another battle with the Philistines at Gob, Elhanan son of Jair[c] the Bethlehemite killed the brother of[d] Goliath the Gittite, who had a spear with a shaft like a weaver's rod.

[20]In still another battle, which took place at Gath, there was a huge man with six fingers on each hand and six toes on each foot—twenty-four in all. He also was descended from Rapha. [21]When he taunted Israel, Jonathan son of Shimeah, David's brother, killed him.

[22]These four were descendants of Rapha in Gath, and they fell at the hands of David and his men.

## Amplified Bible

[4]The Gibeonites said to him, We will accept no silver or gold of Saul or of his house; neither for us shall you kill any man in Israel. David said, I will do for you what you say.

[5]They said to the king, The man who consumed us and planned to prevent us from remaining in any territory of Israel,

[6]Let seven men of his sons be delivered to us and we will hang them up before the Lord at Gibeah of Saul, [on the mountain] of the Lord. And the king said, I will give them.

[7]But the king spared Mephibosheth son of Jonathan, the son of Saul, because of the Lord's oath that was between David and Jonathan son of Saul.

[8]But the king took the two sons of Rizpah daughter of Aiah, whom she bore to Saul, Armoni and Mephibosheth, and the five sons of [Merab] daughter of Saul, whom she bore to Adriel son of Barzillai the Meholathite.

[9]He delivered them into the hands of the Gibeonites, and they hung them up on the hill before the Lord, and all seven perished together. They were put to death in the first days of barley harvest.

[10]Rizpah daughter of Aiah took sackcloth and spread it for herself on the rock, from the beginning of harvest until rain fell on them, and she did not allow either the birds of the air to come upon them by day or the beasts of the field by night.

[11]It was told David what Rizpah daughter of Aiah, the concubine of Saul, had done.

[12]And David went and took the bones of Saul and Jonathan his son from the men of Jabesh-gilead, who had stolen them from the street of Beth-shan, where the Philistines had hung them up when the Philistines had slain Saul in Gilboa.

[13]He brought from there the bones of Saul and of Jonathan his son, and they gathered the bones of those who were hung up.

[14]And the bones of Saul and Jonathan his son they buried in the country of Benjamin in Zelah in the tomb of Kish, [Saul's] father, and they did all that the king commanded. And after that, God heard *and* answered when His people prayed for the land.

[15]The Philistines had war again with Israel. And David went down and his servants with him and fought against the Philistines, and David became faint.

[16]Ishbi-benob, who was of the sons of the giants, the weight of whose spear was 300 shekels of bronze, was girded with a new sword, and thought to kill David.

[17]But Abishai son of Zeruiah came to David's aid, and smote and killed the Philistine. Then David's men charged him, You shall no more go out with us to battle, lest you quench the lamp of Israel.

[18]After this, there was again war with the Philistines at Gob (Gezer). Then Sibbecai the Hushathite slew Saph (Sippai), who was a descendant of the giant.

[19]There was again war at Gob with the Philistines, and Elhanan son of Jaare-oregim, a Bethlehemite, slew Goliath the Gittite, whose spear shaft was like a weaver's beam.

[20]And there was again war at Gath, where there was a man of great stature who had six fingers on each hand and six toes on each foot, twenty-four in number; he also was a descendant of the giants.

[21]And when he defied Israel, Jonathan son of Shimei, brother of David, slew him.

[22]These four were descended from the giant in Gath, and they fell by the hands of David and his servants.

---

*a* 8 Two Hebrew manuscripts, some Septuagint manuscripts and Syriac (see also 1 Samuel 18:19); most Hebrew and Septuagint manuscripts *Michal*    *b* 16 That is, about 7 1/2 pounds or about 3.5 kilograms
*c* 19 See 1 Chron. 20:5; Hebrew *Jaare-Oregim.*    *d* 19 See 1 Chron. 20:5; Hebrew does not have *the brother of.*

## New International Version

### David's Song of Praise

**22** David sang to the LORD the words of this song when the LORD delivered him from the hand of all his enemies and from the hand of Saul. ²He said:

"The LORD is my rock, my fortress and my deliverer;
3  my God is my rock, in whom I take refuge,
  my shield*ᵃ* and the horn*ᵇ* of my salvation.
He is my stronghold, my refuge and my savior—
  from violent people you save me.

⁴"I called to the LORD, who is worthy of praise,
  and have been saved from my enemies.
⁵The waves of death swirled about me;
  the torrents of destruction overwhelmed me.
⁶The cords of the grave coiled around me;
  the snares of death confronted me.

⁷"In my distress I called to the LORD;
  I called out to my God.
From his temple he heard my voice;
  my cry came to his ears.
⁸The earth trembled and quaked,
  the foundations of the heavens*ᶜ* shook;
  they trembled because he was angry.
⁹Smoke rose from his nostrils;
  consuming fire came from his mouth,
  burning coals blazed out of it.
¹⁰He parted the heavens and came down;
  dark clouds were under his feet.
¹¹He mounted the cherubim and flew;
  he soared*ᵈ* on the wings of the wind.
¹²He made darkness his canopy around him—
  the dark*ᵉ* rain clouds of the sky.
¹³Out of the brightness of his presence
  bolts of lightning blazed forth.
¹⁴The LORD thundered from heaven;
  the voice of the Most High resounded.
¹⁵He shot his arrows and scattered the enemy,
  with great bolts of lightning he routed them.
¹⁶The valleys of the sea were exposed
  and the foundations of the earth laid bare
at the rebuke of the LORD,
  at the blast of breath from his nostrils.

¹⁷"He reached down from on high and took hold of me;
  he drew me out of deep waters.
¹⁸He rescued me from my powerful enemy,
  from my foes, who were too strong for me.
¹⁹They confronted me in the day of my disaster,
  but the LORD was my support.
²⁰He brought me out into a spacious place;
  he rescued me because he delighted in me.

²¹"The LORD has dealt with me according to my righteousness;
  according to the cleanness of my hands he has
  rewarded me.
²²For I have kept the ways of the LORD;
  I am not guilty of turning from my God.
²³All his laws are before me;
  I have not turned away from his decrees.
²⁴I have been blameless before him
  and have kept myself from sin.
²⁵The LORD has rewarded me according to my
  righteousness,
  according to my cleanness*ᶠ* in his sight.

²⁶"To the faithful you show yourself faithful,
  to the blameless you show yourself blameless,

## Amplified Bible

**22** David spoke to the Lord the words of this song on the day when the Lord delivered him from the hands of all his enemies and from the hand of Saul.

²He said: The Lord is my Rock [of escape from Saul] and my Fortress [in the wilderness] and my Deliverer; [I Sam. 23:14, 25, 28.]

³My God, my Rock, in Him will I take refuge; my Shield and the Horn of my salvation; my Stronghold and my Refuge, my Savior—You save me from violence. [Gen. 15:1.]

⁴I call on the Lord, Who is worthy to be praised, and I am saved from my enemies.

⁵For the waves of death enveloped me; the torrents of destruction made me afraid.

⁶The cords of Sheol were entangling me; I encountered the snares of death.

⁷In my distress I called upon the Lord; I cried to my God, and He heard my voice from His temple; my cry came into His ears.

⁸Then the earth reeled and quaked, the foundations of the heavens trembled and shook because He was angry.

⁹Smoke went up from His nostrils, and devouring fire from His mouth; coals were kindled by it.

¹⁰He bowed the heavens and came down; thick darkness was under His feet.

¹¹He rode on a cherub and flew; He was seen upon the wings of the wind.

¹²He made darkness His canopy around Him, gathering of waters, thick clouds of the skies.

¹³Out of the brightness before Him coals of fire flamed forth.

¹⁴The Lord thundered from heaven, and the Most High uttered His voice.

¹⁵He sent out arrows and scattered them; lightning confused *and* troubled them.

¹⁶The channels of the sea were visible, the foundations of the world were uncovered at the rebuke of the Lord, at the blast of the breath of His nostrils.

¹⁷He sent from above, He took me; He drew me out of great waters.

¹⁸He delivered me from my strong enemy, from those who hated me, for they were too mighty for me.

¹⁹They came upon me in the day of my calamity, but the Lord was my stay.

²⁰He brought me forth into a large place; He delivered me because He delighted in me.

²¹The Lord rewarded me according to my uprightness with Him; He compensated *and* benefited me according to the cleanness of my hands.

²²For I have kept the ways of the Lord, and have not wickedly departed from my God.

²³For all His ordinances were before me; and from His statutes I did not turn aside.

²⁴I was also blameless before Him and kept myself from guilt *and* iniquity.

²⁵Therefore the Lord has recompensed me according to my righteousness, according to my cleanness in His [holy] sight.

²⁶Toward the loving *and* loyal You will show Yourself loving *and* loyal, and with the upright *and* blameless You will show Yourself upright *and* blameless.

---

*ᵃ 3* Or *sovereign*  *ᵇ 3 Horn* here symbolizes strength.  *ᶜ 8* Hebrew; Vulgate and Syriac (see also Psalm 18:7) *mountains*  *ᵈ 11* Many Hebrew manuscripts (see also Psalm 18:10); most Hebrew manuscripts *appeared*  *ᵉ 12* Septuagint (see also Psalm 18:11); Hebrew *massed*  *ᶠ 25* Hebrew; Septuagint and Vulgate (see also Psalm 18:24) *to the cleanness of my hands*

## New International Version

27 to the pure you show yourself pure,
  but to the devious you show yourself shrewd.
28 You save the humble,
  but your eyes are on the haughty to bring them low.
29 You, LORD, are my lamp;
  the LORD turns my darkness into light.
30 With your help I can advance against a troop[a];
  with my God I can scale a wall.

31 "As for God, his way is perfect:
  The LORD's word is flawless;
  he shields all who take refuge in him.
32 For who is God besides the LORD?
  And who is the Rock except our God?
33 It is God who arms me with strength[b]
  and keeps my way secure.
34 He makes my feet like the feet of a deer;
  he causes me to stand on the heights.
35 He trains my hands for battle;
  my arms can bend a bow of bronze.
36 You make your saving help my shield;
  your help has made[c] me great.
37 You provide a broad path for my feet,
  so that my ankles do not give way.

38 "I pursued my enemies and crushed them;
  I did not turn back till they were destroyed.
39 I crushed them completely, and they could not rise;
  they fell beneath my feet.
40 You armed me with strength for battle;
  you humbled my adversaries before me.
41 You made my enemies turn their backs in flight,
  and I destroyed my foes.
42 They cried for help, but there was no one to save them—
  to the LORD, but he did not answer.
43 I beat them as fine as the dust of the earth;
  I pounded and trampled them like mud in the streets.

44 "You have delivered me from the attacks of the peoples;
  you have preserved me as the head of nations.
People I did not know now serve me,
45   foreigners cower before me;
  as soon as they hear of me, they obey me.
46 They all lose heart;
  they come trembling[d] from their strongholds.

47 "The LORD lives! Praise be to my Rock!
  Exalted be my God, the Rock, my Savior!
48 He is the God who avenges me,
  who puts the nations under me,
49   who sets me free from my enemies.
You exalted me above my foes;
  from a violent man you rescued me.
50 Therefore I will praise you, LORD, among the nations;
  I will sing the praises of your name.

51 "He gives his king great victories;
  he shows unfailing kindness to his anointed,
  to David and his descendants forever."

### David's Last Words

23 These are the last words of David:

"The inspired utterance of David son of Jesse,
  the utterance of the man exalted by the Most High,

## Amplified Bible

27 To the pure You will show Yourself pure, and to the willful You will show Yourself willful.
28 And the afflicted people You will deliver, but Your eyes are upon the haughty, whom You will bring down.
29 For You, O Lord, are my Lamp; the Lord lightens my darkness.
30 For by You I run through a troop; by my God I leap over a wall.
31 As for God, His way is perfect; the word of the Lord is tried. He is a Shield to all those who trust and take refuge in Him.
32 For who is God but the Lord? And who is a Rock except our God?
33 God is my strong Fortress; He guides the blameless in His way and sets him free.
34 He makes my feet like the hinds' [firm and able]; He sets me secure and confident upon the heights.
35 He trains my hands for war, so that my arms can bend a bow of bronze.
36 You have also given me the shield of Your salvation; and Your condescension and gentleness have made me great.
37 You have enlarged my steps under me, so that my feet have not slipped.
38 I have pursued my enemies and destroyed them; and I did not turn back until they were consumed.
39 I consumed them and thrust them through, so that they did not arise; they fell at my feet.
40 For You girded me with strength for the battle; those who rose up against me You subdued under me.
41 You have made my enemies turn their backs to me, that I might cut off those who hate me.
42 They looked, but there was none to save—even to the Lord, but He did not answer them.
43 Then I beat them small as the dust of the earth; I crushed them as the mire of the street and scattered them abroad.
44 You also have delivered me from strife with my people; You kept me as the head of the nations. People whom I had not known served me.
45 Foreigners yielded feigned obedience to me; as soon as they heard of me, they became obedient to me.
46 Foreigners faded away; they came limping and trembling from their strongholds.
47 The Lord lives; blessed be my Rock, and exalted be God, the Rock of my salvation.
48 It is God Who executes vengeance for me and Who brought down [and disciplined] the peoples under me,
49 Who brought me out from my enemies. You also lifted me up above those who rose up against me; You delivered me from the violent man.
50 For this I will give thanks and extol You, O Lord, among the nations; I will sing praises to Your name.
51 He is a Tower of salvation and great deliverance to His king, and shows loving-kindness to His anointed, to David and his offspring forever.

23 Now these are the last words of David: David son of Jesse says, and the man who was raised on high,

---

a 30 Or *can run through a barricade*   b 33 Dead Sea Scrolls, some Septuagint manuscripts, Vulgate and Syriac (see also Psalm 18:32); Masoretic Text *who is my strong refuge*   c 36 Dead Sea Scrolls; Masoretic Text *shield; / you stoop down to make*   d 46 Some Septuagint manuscripts and Vulgate (see also Psalm 18:45); Masoretic Text *they arm themselves*

## New International Version

the man anointed by the God of Jacob,
  the hero of Israel's songs:

2"The Spirit of the LORD spoke through me;
  his word was on my tongue.
3The God of Israel spoke,
  the Rock of Israel said to me:
'When one rules over people in righteousness,
  when he rules in the fear of God,
4he is like the light of morning at sunrise
  on a cloudless morning,
like the brightness after rain
  that brings grass from the earth.'

5"If my house were not right with God,
  surely he would not have made with me an
    everlasting covenant,
  arranged and secured in every part;
surely he would not bring to fruition my salvation
  and grant me my every desire.
6But evil men are all to be cast aside like thorns,
  which are not gathered with the hand.
7Whoever touches thorns
  uses a tool of iron or the shaft of a spear;
  they are burned up where they lie."

### David's Mighty Warriors
8These are the names of David's mighty warriors:
Josheb-Basshebeth,*a* a Tahkemonite,*b* was chief of the
Three; he raised his spear against eight hundred men,
whom he killed*c* in one encounter.
9Next to him was Eleazar son of Dodai the Ahohite. As
one of the three mighty warriors, he was with David when
they taunted the Philistines gathered at Pas Dammim*d* for
battle. Then the Israelites retreated, 10but Eleazar stood
his ground and struck down the Philistines till his hand
grew tired and froze to the sword. The LORD brought about
a great victory that day. The troops returned to Eleazar,
but only to strip the dead.
11Next to him was Shammah son of Agee the Hararite.
When the Philistines banded together at a place where
there was a field full of lentils, Israel's troops fled from
them. 12But Shammah took his stand in the middle of the
field. He defended it and struck the Philistines down, and
the LORD brought about a great victory.
13During harvest time, three of the thirty chief warriors
came down to David at the cave of Adullam, while a band
of Philistines was encamped in the Valley of Rephaim. 14At
that time David was in the stronghold, and the Philistine
garrison was at Bethlehem. 15David longed for water and
said, "Oh, that someone would get me a drink of water
from the well near the gate of Bethlehem!" 16So the three
mighty warriors broke through the Philistine lines, drew
water from the well near the gate of Bethlehem and carried it back to David. But he refused to drink it; instead, he
poured it out before the LORD. 17"Far be it from me, LORD,
to do this!" he said. "Is it not the blood of men who went
at the risk of their lives?" And David would not drink it.
  Such were the exploits of the three mighty warriors.
18Abishai the brother of Joab son of Zeruiah was chief
of the Three.*e* He raised his spear against three hundred
men, whom he killed, and so he became as famous as the
Three. 19Was he not held in greater honor than the Three?
He became their commander, even though he was not included among them.
20Benaiah son of Jehoiada, a valiant fighter from Kab-

## Amplified Bible

the anointed of the God of Jacob, and the sweet psalmist
of Israel, says,
2The Spirit of the Lord spoke in *and* by me, and His
word was upon my tongue.
3The God of Israel spoke, the Rock of Israel said to me,
When one rules over men righteously, ruling in the fear
of God,
4He dawns on them like the morning light when the
sun rises on a cloudless morning, when the tender grass
springs out of the earth through clear shining after rain.
5Truly does not my house stand so with God? For He
has made with me an everlasting covenant, ordered in all
things, and sure. For will He not cause to prosper all my
help and my desire?
6But wicked, godless, *and* worthless lives are all like
thorns to be thrust away, because they cannot be taken
with the hand.
7But the man who touches them arms himself with iron
and the shaft of a spear, and they are utterly consumed
with fire on the spot.
8These are the names of the mighty men whom David
had: Josheb-basshebeth, a Tahchemonite, chief of the
Three [heroes], known also as Adino the Eznite; he wielded his spear and went against 800 men, who were slain at
one time. [I Chron. 11:11.]
9Next to him among the three mighty men was Eleazar
son of Dodo, son of Ahohi. He was with David when they
defied the Philistines assembled there for battle, and the
men of Israel had departed.
10[Eleazar] arose and struck down the Philistines until his hand was weary and clung to the sword. The Lord
wrought a great deliverance *and* victory that day; the men
returned after him only to take the spoil.
11Next to [Eleazar] was Shammah son of Agee the Hararite. The Philistines were gathered at Lehi on a piece
of ground full of lentils; and the [Israelites] fled from the
Philistines.
12But he stood in the midst of the ground and defended
it and slew the Philistines; and the Lord wrought a great
victory.
13And three of the thirty chief men went down at harvest time to David in the cave of Adullam, and a troop of
Philistines was encamped in the Valley of Rephaim.
14And David was then in the stronghold, and the garrison of the Philistines was then in Bethlehem.
15And David said longingly, Oh, that someone would
give me a drink of water from the well of Bethlehem by
the gate!
16And the three mighty men broke through the army
of the Philistines and drew water out of the well of Bethlehem by the gate and brought it to David. But he would not
drink it, but poured it out to the Lord.
17And he said, Be it far from me, O Lord, to drink this.
Is it not [the same as] the blood of the men who went at the
risk of their lives? So he would not drink it. These things
did the three mighty men.
18Now Abishai the brother of Joab son of Zeruiah was
chief of the Three. He wielded his spear against 300 men
and slew them, and won a name beside the Three.
19Was he not most renowned of the Three? So he was
their captain; however, he did not attain to the Three.
20And Benaiah son of Jehoiada, a valiant man of

*a* 8 Hebrew; some Septuagint manuscripts suggest *Ish-Bosheth,* that
is, *Esh-Baal* (see also 1 Chron. 11:11 *Jashobeam*).   *b* 8 Probably a
variant of *Hakmonite* (see 1 Chron. 11:11)   *c* 8 Some Septuagint
manuscripts (see also 1 Chron. 11:11); Hebrew and other Septuagint
manuscripts *Three; it was Adino the Eznite who killed eight hundred men*
*d* 9 See 1 Chron. 11:13; Hebrew *gathered there.*   *e* 18 Most Hebrew
manuscripts (see also 1 Chron. 11:20); two Hebrew manuscripts and
Syriac *Thirty*

## New International Version

zeel, performed great exploits. He struck down Moab's two mightiest warriors. He also went down into a pit on a snowy day and killed a lion. [21]And he struck down a huge Egyptian. Although the Egyptian had a spear in his hand, Benaiah went against him with a club. He snatched the spear from the Egyptian's hand and killed him with his own spear. [22]Such were the exploits of Benaiah son of Jehoiada; he too was as famous as the three mighty warriors. [23]He was held in greater honor than any of the Thirty, but he was not included among the Three. And David put him in charge of his bodyguard.

[24]Among the Thirty were:
Asahel the brother of Joab,
Elhanan son of Dodo from Bethlehem,
[25]Shammah the Harodite,
Elika the Harodite,
[26]Helez the Paltite,
Ira son of Ikkesh from Tekoa,
[27]Abiezer from Anathoth,
Sibbekai[a] the Hushathite,
[28]Zalmon the Ahohite,
Maharai the Netophathite,
[29]Heled[b] son of Baanah the Netophathite,
Ithai son of Ribai from Gibeah in Benjamin,
[30]Benaiah the Pirathonite,
Hiddai[c] from the ravines of Gaash,
[31]Abi-Albon the Arbathite,
Azmaveth the Barhumite,
[32]Eliahba the Shaalbonite,
the sons of Jashen,
Jonathan [33]son of[d] Shammah the Hararite,
Ahiam son of Sharar[e] the Hararite,
[34]Eliphelet son of Ahasbai the Maakathite,
Eliam son of Ahithophel the Gilonite,
[35]Hezro the Carmelite,
Paarai the Arbite,
[36]Igal son of Nathan from Zobah,
the son of Hagri,[f]
[37]Zelek the Ammonite,
Naharai the Beerothite, the armor-bearer of Joab
son of Zeruiah,
[38]Ira the Ithrite,
Gareb the Ithrite
[39]and Uriah the Hittite.
There were thirty-seven in all.

### David Enrolls the Fighting Men

**24** Again the anger of the Lord burned against Israel, and he incited David against them, saying, "Go and take a census of Israel and Judah."

[2]So the king said to Joab and the army commanders[g] with him, "Go throughout the tribes of Israel from Dan to Beersheba and enroll the fighting men, so that I may know how many there are."

[3]But Joab replied to the king, "May the Lord your God multiply the troops a hundred times over, and may the eyes of my lord the king see it. But why does my lord the king want to do such a thing?"

[4]The king's word, however, overruled Joab and the army commanders; so they left the presence of the king to enroll the fighting men of Israel.

[5]After crossing the Jordan, they camped near Aroer, south of the town in the gorge, and then went through Gad and on to Jazer. [6]They went to Gilead and the region

a 27 Some Septuagint manuscripts (see also 21:18; 1 Chron. 11:29); Hebrew *Mebunnai*    b 29 Some Hebrew manuscripts and Vulgate (see also 1 Chron. 11:30); most Hebrew manuscripts *Heleb*    c 30 Hebrew; some Septuagint manuscripts (see also 1 Chron. 11:32) *Hurai*    d 33 Some Septuagint manuscripts (see also 1 Chron. 11:34); Hebrew does not have *son of*.    e 33 Hebrew; some Septuagint manuscripts (see also 1 Chron. 11:35) *Sakar*    f 36 Some Septuagint manuscripts (see also 1 Chron. 11:38); Hebrew *Haggadi*    g 2 Septuagint (see also verse 4 and 1 Chron. 21:2); Hebrew *Joab the army commander*

## Amplified Bible

Kabzeel, who had done many notable acts, slew two lion-like men of Moab. He went down also and slew a lion in a pit on a snowy day.

[21]And he slew an Egyptian, a handsome man. The Egyptian had a spear in his hand, but Benaiah went down to him with a staff, snatched the spear out of the Egyptian's hand, and slew the man with his own spear.

[22]These things Benaiah son of Jehoiada did, and won a name beside the three mighty men.

[23]He was more renowned than the Thirty, but he attained not to the [first] Three. David set him over his guard *or* council.

[24]Asahel brother of Joab was one of the Thirty; then Elhanan son of Dodo of Bethlehem,
[25]Shammah of Harod, Elika of Harod,
[26]Helez the Paltite, Ira son of Ikkesh of Tekoa,
[27]Abiezer of Anathoth, Mebunnai the Hushathite,
[28]Zalmon the Ahohite, Maharai of Netophah,
[29]Heleb son of Baanah of Netophah, Ittai son of Ribai of Gibeah of the Benjamites.
[30]Benaiah of Pirathon, Hiddai of the brooks of Gaash,
[31]Abi-albon the Arbathite, Azmaveth the Barhumite,
[32]Eliahba of Shaalbon, the sons of Jashen, Jonathan,
[33]Shammah the Hararite, Ahiam son of Sharar the Hararite,
[34]Eliphelet son of Ahasbai, son of Maacah, Eliam son of Ahithophel of Giloh,
[35]Hezro (Hezrai) of Carmel, Paarai the Arbite,
[36]Igal son of Nathan of Zobah, Bani the Gadite,
[37]Zelek the Ammonite, Naharai of Beeroth, armor-bearer of Joab son of Zeruiah,
[38]Ira the Ithrite, Gareb the Ithrite,
[39]Uriah the Hittite—thirty-seven in all.

**24** Again the anger of the Lord was kindled against Israel, and He moved David against them, saying, Go, number Israel and Judah.

[2]For the king said to Joab the captain of the host who was with him, Go now through all the tribes of Israel, from Dan even to Beersheba, and count the people, that I may know their number.

[3]And Joab said to the king, May the Lord your God add a hundred times as many people as there are, and let the eyes of my lord the king see it; but why does my lord the king delight in this thing?

[4]But the king's word prevailed against Joab and the commanders of the army. So they went from the king's presence to number the Israelites.

[5]They passed over the Jordan and encamped in Aroer, on the south side of the city lying in the midst of the ravine [of the Arnon] toward Gad, and on to Jazer.

[6]Then they came to Gilead, and to the land of Tahtim-hodshi, and they came to Dan-jaan [Dan in the forest] and around to Sidon,

## New International Version

of Tahtim Hodshi, and on to Dan Jaan and around toward Sidon. 7Then they went toward the fortress of Tyre and all the towns of the Hivites and Canaanites. Finally, they went on to Beersheba in the Negev of Judah.

8After they had gone through the entire land, they came back to Jerusalem at the end of nine months and twenty days.

9Joab reported the number of the fighting men to the king: In Israel there were eight hundred thousand able-bodied men who could handle a sword, and in Judah five hundred thousand.

10David was conscience-stricken after he had counted the fighting men, and he said to the LORD, "I have sinned greatly in what I have done. Now, LORD, I beg you, take away the guilt of your servant. I have done a very foolish thing."

11Before David got up the next morning, the word of the LORD had come to Gad the prophet, David's seer: 12"Go and tell David, 'This is what the LORD says: I am giving you three options. Choose one of them for me to carry out against you.'"

13So Gad went to David and said to him, "Shall there come on you threeᵃ years of famine in your land? Or three months of fleeing from your enemies while they pursue you? Or three days of plague in your land? Now then, think it over and decide how I should answer the one who sent me."

14David said to Gad, "I am in deep distress. Let us fall into the hands of the LORD, for his mercy is great; but do not let me fall into human hands."

15So the LORD sent a plague on Israel from that morning until the end of the time designated, and seventy thousand of the people from Dan to Beersheba died. 16When the angel stretched out his hand to destroy Jerusalem, the LORD relented concerning the disaster and said to the angel who was afflicting the people, "Enough! Withdraw your hand." The angel of the LORD was then at the threshing floor of Araunah the Jebusite.

17When David saw the angel who was striking down the people, he said to the LORD, "I have sinned; I, the shepherd,ᵇ have done wrong. These are but sheep. What have they done? Let your hand fall on me and my family."

### David Builds an Altar

18On that day Gad went to David and said to him, "Go up and build an altar to the LORD on the threshing floor of Araunah the Jebusite." 19So David went up, as the LORD had commanded through Gad. 20When Araunah looked and saw the king and his officials coming toward him, he went out and bowed down before the king with his face to the ground.

21Araunah said, "Why has my lord the king come to his servant?"

"To buy your threshing floor," David answered, "so I can build an altar to the LORD, that the plague on the people may be stopped."

22Araunah said to David, "Let my lord the king take whatever he wishes and offer it up. Here are oxen for the burnt offering, and here are threshing sledges and ox yokes for the wood. 23Your Majesty, Araunahᶜ gives all this to the king." Araunah also said to him, "May the LORD your God accept you."

24But the king replied to Araunah, "No, I insist on paying you for it. I will not sacrifice to the LORD my God burnt offerings that cost me nothing."

So David bought the threshing floor and the oxen and paid fifty shekelsᵈ of silver for them. 25David built an altar to the LORD there and sacrificed burnt offerings and fellowship offerings. Then the LORD answered his prayer in behalf of the land, and the plague on Israel was stopped.

ᵃ 13 Septuagint (see also 1 Chron. 21:12); Hebrew seven    ᵇ 17 Dead Sea Scrolls and Septuagint; Masoretic Text does not have the shepherd.
ᶜ 23 Some Hebrew manuscripts and Septuagint; most Hebrew manuscripts King Araunah    ᵈ 24 That is, about 1 1/4 pounds or about 575 grams

## Amplified Bible

7And came to the stronghold of Tyre and to all the cities of the Hivites and Canaanites; and they went out to the South (the Negeb) of Judah at Beersheba.

8So when they had gone through all the land [taking the census], they came to Jerusalem at the end of nine months and twenty days.

9And Joab gave the sum of the numbering of the people to the king. There were in Israel 800,000 valiant men who drew the sword, and the men of Judah were 500,000.

10But David's heart smote him after he had numbered the people. David said to the Lord, I have sinned greatly in what I have done. I beseech You, O Lord, take away the iniquity of Your servant, for I have done very foolishly.

11When David arose in the morning, the word of the Lord came to the prophet Gad, David's seer, saying,

12Go and say to David, Thus says the Lord, I hold over you three choices; select one of them, so I may bring it upon you.

13So Gad came to David and told him and said, Shall seven years of famine come to your land? Or will you flee three months before your pursuing enemies? Or do you prefer three days of pestilence in your land? Consider and see what answer I shall return to Him Who sent me.

14And David said to Gad, I am in great distress. Let us fall into the hands of the Lord, for His mercies are many and great; but let me not fall into the hands of man.

15So the Lord sent a pestilence upon Israel from the morning even to the time appointed; and there died of the people from Dan even to Beersheba 70,000 men.

16And when the angel stretched out his hand upon Jerusalem to destroy it, the Lord relented of the evil and reversed His judgment and said to the destroying angel, It is enough; now stay your hand. And the angel of the Lord was by the threshing floor of Araunah the Jebusite.

17When David saw the angel who was smiting the people, he spoke to the Lord and said, Behold, I have sinned and I have done wickedly; but these sheep, what have they done? Let Your hand, I pray You, be [only] against me and against my father's house.

18Then Gad came to David and said, Go up, rear an altar to the Lord on the threshing floor of Araunah the Jebusite.

19So David went up according to Gad's word, as the Lord commanded.

20Araunah looked and saw the king and his servants coming toward him; and [he] went out and bowed himself before the king with his face to the ground.

21Araunah said, Why has my lord the king come to his servant? And David said, To buy the threshing floor from you, to build there an altar to the Lord, that the plague may be stayed from the people.

22And Araunah said to David, Let my lord the king take and offer up what seems good to him. Behold, here are oxen for burnt sacrifice, and threshing instruments and the yokes of the oxen for wood.

23All this, O king, Araunah gives to the king. And Araunah said to the king, The Lord your God accept you.

24But King David said to Araunah, No, but I will buy it of you for a price. I will not offer burnt offerings to the Lord my God of that which costs me nothing. So David bought the threshing floor and the oxen for fifty shekels of silver.

25David built there an altar to the Lord and offered burnt offerings and peace offerings. So the Lord heeded the prayers for the land, and Israel's plague was stayed.

# 1 Kings

# Kings

## Adonijah Sets Himself Up as King

**1** When King David was very old, he could not keep warm even when they put covers over him. ²So his attendants said to him, "Let us look for a young virgin to serve the king and take care of him. She can lie beside him so that our lord the king may keep warm."

³Then they searched throughout Israel for a beautiful young woman and found Abishag, a Shunammite, and brought her to the king. ⁴The woman was very beautiful; she took care of the king and waited on him, but the king had no sexual relations with her.

⁵Now Adonijah, whose mother was Haggith, put himself forward and said, "I will be king." So he got chariots and horses[a] ready, with fifty men to run ahead of him. ⁶(His father had never rebuked him by asking, "Why do you behave as you do?" He was also very handsome and was born next after Absalom.)

⁷Adonijah conferred with Joab son of Zeruiah and with Abiathar the priest, and they gave him their support. ⁸But Zadok the priest, Benaiah son of Jehoiada, Nathan the prophet, Shimei and Rei and David's special guard did not join Adonijah.

⁹Adonijah then sacrificed sheep, cattle and fattened calves at the Stone of Zoheleth near En Rogel. He invited all his brothers, the king's sons, and all the royal officials of Judah, ¹⁰but he did not invite Nathan the prophet or Benaiah or the special guard or his brother Solomon.

¹¹Then Nathan asked Bathsheba, Solomon's mother, "Have you not heard that Adonijah, the son of Haggith, has become king, and our lord David knows nothing about it? ¹²Now then, let me advise you how you can save your own life and the life of your son Solomon. ¹³Go in to King David and say to him, 'My lord the king, did you not swear to me your servant: "Surely Solomon your son shall be king after me, and he will sit on my throne"? Why then has Adonijah become king?' ¹⁴While you are still there talking to the king, I will come in and add my word to what you have said."

¹⁵So Bathsheba went to see the aged king in his room, where Abishag the Shunammite was attending him. ¹⁶Bathsheba bowed down, prostrating herself before the king.

"What is it you want?" the king asked.

¹⁷She said to him, "My lord, you yourself swore to me your servant by the LORD your God: 'Solomon your son shall be king after me, and he will sit on my throne.' ¹⁸But now Adonijah has become king, and you, my lord the king, do not know about it. ¹⁹He has sacrificed great numbers of cattle, fattened calves, and sheep, and has invited all the king's sons, Abiathar the priest and Joab the commander of the army, but he has not invited Solomon your servant. ²⁰My lord the king, the eyes of all Israel are on you, to learn from you who will sit on the throne of my lord the king after him. ²¹Otherwise, as soon as my lord the king is laid to rest with his ancestors, I and my son Solomon will be treated as criminals."

**1** And King David was old and advanced in years; they covered him with [bed]clothes, but he could not get warm.

²So his servants [the ᵃphysicians] said to him, Let there be sought for my lord the king a young virgin, and let her wait on and be useful to the king; let her lie in your bosom, that my lord the king may get warm.

³So they sought a fair maiden through all the territory of Israel and found Abishag the Shunammite, and brought her to the king.

⁴The maiden was beautiful; and she waited on and nursed him. But the king had no intercourse with her.

⁵Then Adonijah son of [David's wife] Haggith exalted himself, saying, I [the eldest living son] will be king. And he prepared for himself chariots and horsemen, with fifty men to run before him.

⁶David his father had never in his life displeased him by asking, Why have you done so? He was also a very attractive man and was born after Absalom.

⁷He conferred with ᵇJoab son of Zeruiah [David's half sister] and with Abiathar the priest, and they followed Adonijah and helped him.

⁸But Zadok the priest, Benaiah son of Jehoiada, Nathan the prophet, Shimei, Rei, and David's mighty men did not side with Adonijah.

⁹Adonijah sacrificed sheep, oxen, and fatlings by the Stone of Zoheleth, which is beside [the well] En-rogel; and he invited all his brothers, the king's sons, and all the royal officials of Judah.

¹⁰But Nathan the prophet, Benaiah, the mighty men, and Solomon his brother he did not invite.

¹¹Then Nathan said to Bathsheba the mother of Solomon, Have you not heard that Adonijah, the son of Haggith, reigns and David our lord does not know it?

¹²Come now, let me advise you how to save your own life and your son Solomon's.

¹³Go to King David and say, Did you not, my lord, O king, swear to your handmaid, saying, Assuredly Solomon your son shall reign after me, and he shall sit upon my throne? Why then does Adonijah reign?

¹⁴Behold, while you are still talking there with the king, I also will come in after you and confirm your words.

¹⁵So Bathsheba went in to the king in his chamber. Now the king was very old *and* feeble, and Abishag the Shunammite was ministering to [him].

¹⁶Bathsheba bowed and did obeisance to the king. The king said, What do you wish?

¹⁷And she said to him, My lord, you swore by the Lord your God to your handmaid, saying, Assuredly Solomon your son shall reign after me and sit upon my throne.

¹⁸And now, behold, Adonijah is reigning, and, my lord the king, you do not know it.

¹⁹He has sacrificed oxen and fatlings and sheep in abundance, and has invited all the king's sons and Abiathar the priest and Joab the commander of the army. But he did not invite Solomon your servant.

²⁰Now, my lord O king, the eyes of all Israel are on you, to tell who shall sit on the throne of my lord the king after you.

²¹Otherwise, when my lord the king shall sleep with his fathers, I and my son Solomon shall be counted as offenders.

---

ᵃ 5 Or *charioteers*

ᵃ Josephus, *Antiquities of the Jews* 14, 3.   ᵇ The commander of Israel's army.

## New International Version

22While she was still speaking with the king, Nathan the prophet arrived. 23And the king was told, "Nathan the prophet is here." So he went before the king and bowed with his face to the ground.

24Nathan said, "Have you, my lord the king, declared that Adonijah shall be king after you, and that he will sit on your throne? 25Today he has gone down and sacrificed great numbers of cattle, fattened calves, and sheep. He has invited all the king's sons, the commanders of the army and Abiathar the priest. Right now they are eating and drinking with him and saying, 'Long live King Adonijah!' 26But me your servant, and Zadok the priest, and Benaiah son of Jehoiada, and your servant Solomon he did not invite. 27Is this something my lord the king has done without letting his servants know who should sit on the throne of my lord the king after him?"

### David Makes Solomon King

28Then King David said, "Call in Bathsheba." So she came into the king's presence and stood before him. 29The king then took an oath: "As surely as the LORD lives, who has delivered me out of every trouble, 30I will surely carry out this very day what I swore to you by the LORD, the God of Israel: Solomon your son shall be king after me, and he will sit on my throne in my place."

31Then Bathsheba bowed down with her face to the ground, prostrating herself before the king, and said, "May my lord King David live forever!"

32King David said, "Call in Zadok the priest, Nathan the prophet and Benaiah son of Jehoiada." When they came before the king, 33he said to them: "Take your lord's servants with you and have Solomon my son mount my own mule and take him down to Gihon. 34There have Zadok the priest and Nathan the prophet anoint him king over Israel. Blow the trumpet and shout, 'Long live King Solomon!' 35Then you are to go up with him, and he is to come and sit on my throne and reign in my place. I have appointed him ruler over Israel and Judah."

36Benaiah son of Jehoiada answered the king, "Amen! May the LORD, the God of my lord the king, so declare it. 37As the LORD was with my lord the king, so may he be with Solomon to make his throne even greater than the throne of my lord King David!"

38So Zadok the priest, Nathan the prophet, Benaiah son of Jehoiada, the Kerethites and the Pelethites went down and had Solomon mount King David's mule, and they escorted him to Gihon. 39Zadok the priest took the horn of oil from the sacred tent and anointed Solomon. Then they sounded the trumpet and all the people shouted, "Long live King Solomon!" 40And all the people went up after him, playing pipes and rejoicing greatly, so that the ground shook with the sound.

41Adonijah and all the guests who were with him heard it as they were finishing their feast. On hearing the sound of the trumpet, Joab asked, "What's the meaning of all the noise in the city?"

42Even as he was speaking, Jonathan son of Abiathar the priest arrived. Adonijah said, "Come in. A worthy man like you must be bringing good news."

43"Not at all!" Jonathan answered. "Our lord King David has made Solomon king. 44The king has sent with him Zadok the priest, Nathan the prophet, Benaiah son of Jehoi-

## Amplified Bible

22While she was still talking with the king, Nathan the prophet also came in.

23The king was told, Here is Nathan the prophet. And when he came before the king, he bowed himself before him with his face to the ground.

24And Nathan said, My lord the king, have you said, Adonijah shall reign after me, and he shall sit on my throne?

25He has gone this day and sacrificed oxen, fatlings, and sheep in abundance, and has invited all the king's sons, the captains of the host, and Abiathar the priest; and they eat and drink before him and say, Long live King Adonijah!

26But me your servant, and Zadok the priest, and Benaiah son of Jehoiada, and your servant Solomon he has not invited.

27Is this done by my lord the king and you have not shown your servants who shall succeed my lord the king?

28Then King David answered, Call Bathsheba. And she came into the king's presence and stood before him.

29And the king took an oath and said, As the Lord lives, Who has redeemed my soul out of all distress,

30Even as I swore to you by the Lord, the God of Israel, saying, Assuredly Solomon your son shall reign after me, and he shall sit upon my throne in my stead—even so will I certainly do this day.

31Bathsheba bowed with her face to the ground and did obeisance to the king and said, Let my lord King David live forever!

32King David said, Call Zadok the priest, Nathan the prophet, and Benaiah son of Jehoiada. And they came before the king.

33The king told them, Take the servants of your lord and cause Solomon my son to ride on my own mule and bring him down to Gihon [in the Kidron Valley].

34And let Zadok the priest and Nathan the prophet anoint him there king over Israel. Then blow the trumpet and say, Long live King Solomon!

35Then you shall come up after him, and he shall come and sit on my throne, for he shall be king in my stead; I have appointed him ruler over Israel and Judah.

36And Benaiah son of Jehoiada answered the king and said, Amen! May the Lord, the God of my lord the king, say so too.

37As the Lord has been with my lord the king, even so may He be with Solomon and make his throne greater than the throne of my lord King David.

38So Zadok the priest, Nathan the prophet, Benaiah son of Jehoiada, the Cherethites, and the Pelethites [the king's bodyguards] went down and caused Solomon to ride upon King David's mule and brought him to Gihon.

39Zadok the priest took a horn of oil out of the tent and anointed Solomon. They blew the trumpet and all the people said, Long live King Solomon!

40All the people followed him; they played on pipes and rejoiced greatly, so that the earth [resounded] with the joyful sound.

41And Adonijah and all the guests with him heard it as they finished feasting. When Joab heard the trumpet sound, he said, What does this uproar in the city mean?

42While he was still speaking, behold, Jonathan son of Abiathar the priest came. And Adonijah said, Come in, for you are a trustworthy man and bring good news.

43Jonathan replied, Adonijah, truly our lord King David has made Solomon king!

44The king has sent him with Zadok the priest, Nathan the prophet, Benaiah son of Jehoiada, the Cherethites and

## New International Version

ada, the Kerethites and the Pelethites, and they have put him on the king's mule, [45]and Zadok the priest and Nathan the prophet have anointed him king at Gihon. From there they have gone up cheering, and the city resounds with it. That's the noise you hear. [46]Moreover, Solomon has taken his seat on the royal throne. [47]Also, the royal officials have come to congratulate our lord King David, saying, 'May your God make Solomon's name more famous than yours and his throne greater than yours!' And the king bowed in worship on his bed [48]and said, 'Praise be to the LORD, the God of Israel, who has allowed my eyes to see a successor on my throne today.'"

[49]At this, all Adonijah's guests rose in alarm and dispersed. [50]But Adonijah, in fear of Solomon, went and took hold of the horns of the altar. [51]Then Solomon was told, "Adonijah is afraid of King Solomon and is clinging to the horns of the altar. He says, 'Let King Solomon swear to me today that he will not put his servant to death with the sword.'"

[52]Solomon replied, "If he shows himself to be worthy, not a hair of his head will fall to the ground; but if evil is found in him, he will die." [53]Then King Solomon sent men, and they brought him down from the altar. And Adonijah came and bowed down to King Solomon, and Solomon said, "Go to your home."

### David's Charge to Solomon

**2** When the time drew near for David to die, he gave a charge to Solomon his son.

[2]"I am about to go the way of all the earth," he said. "So be strong, act like a man, [3]and observe what the LORD your God requires: Walk in obedience to him, and keep his decrees and commands, his laws and regulations, as written in the Law of Moses. Do this so that you may prosper in all you do and wherever you go [4]and that the LORD may keep his promise to me: 'If your descendants watch how they live, and if they walk faithfully before me with all their heart and soul, you will never fail to have a successor on the throne of Israel.'

[5]"Now you yourself know what Joab son of Zeruiah did to me—what he did to the two commanders of Israel's armies, Abner son of Ner and Amasa son of Jether. He killed them, shedding their blood in peacetime as if in battle, and with that blood he stained the belt around his waist and the sandals on his feet. [6]Deal with him according to your wisdom, but do not let his gray head go down to the grave in peace.

[7]"But show kindness to the sons of Barzillai of Gilead and let them be among those who eat at your table. They stood by me when I fled from your brother Absalom.

[8]"And remember, you have with you Shimei son of Gera, the Benjamite from Bahurim, who called down bitter curses on me the day I went to Mahanaim. When he came down to meet me at the Jordan, I swore to him by the LORD: 'I will not put you to death by the sword.' [9]But now, do not consider him innocent. You are a man of wisdom; you will know what to do to him. Bring his gray head down to the grave in blood."

[10]Then David rested with his ancestors and was buried

## Amplified Bible

the Pelethites, and they have caused him to ride upon the king's mule.

[45]Zadok the priest and Nathan the prophet have anointed him king in Gihon; they have come up from there rejoicing, so the city resounds. This is the noise you heard.

[46]Solomon sits on the royal throne.

[47]Moreover, the king's servants came to congratulate our lord King David, saying, May God make the name of Solomon better than your name and make his throne greater than your throne. And the king bowed himself upon the bed

[48]And said, Blessed be the Lord, the God of Israel, Who has granted me to see one of my offspring sitting on my throne this day.

[49]And all the guests that were with Adonijah were afraid and rose up and went every man his way.

[50]And Adonijah feared because of Solomon, and arose and went [to the tabernacle tent on Mt. Zion] and caught hold of the horns of the altar [as a fugitive's refuge].

[51]And it was told Solomon, Behold, Adonijah fears King Solomon, for behold, he has caught hold of the horns of the altar, saying, Let King Solomon swear to me first that he will not slay his servant with the sword.

[52]Solomon said, If he will show himself to be a worthy man, not a hair of him shall fall to the ground; but if wickedness is found in him, he shall die.

[53]So King Solomon sent, and they brought Adonijah down from the altar [in front of the tabernacle]. He came and bowed himself to King Solomon, and Solomon said to him, Go to your house.

**2** When David's time to die was near, he charged Solomon his son, saying,

[2]I go the way of all the earth. Be strong and show yourself a man;

[3]Keep the charge of the Lord your God, walk in His ways, keep His statutes, His commandments, His precepts, and His testimonies, as it is written in the Law of Moses, that you may do wisely and prosper in all that you do and wherever you turn;

[4]That the Lord may fulfill His promise to me, saying, If your sons take heed to their way, to walk before Me in truth with all their heart and mind and with all their soul, there shall not fail you [to have] a man on the throne of Israel.

[5]You know also what Joab son of Zeruiah did to me, and what he did to the two captains of the hosts of Israel, Abner son of Ner and Amasa son of Jether, whom he murdered, avenging in time of peace blood shed in war, and putting innocent blood of war on the girdle on his loins and on the sandals of his feet.

[6]Do therefore according to your wisdom, but let not his hoary head go down to Sheol (the place of the dead) in peace.

[7]But show kindness to the sons of Barzillai the Gileadite and let them be among those who eat at your table; for with such kindness they met me when I fled because of Absalom your brother. [II Sam. 17:27-29.]

[8]And you have with you Shimei son of Gera, the Benjamite of Bahurim, who cursed me with a grievous curse in the day when I went to Mahanaim. But he came down to meet me at the Jordan [on my return], and I swore to him by the Lord, saying, I will not put you to death with the sword.

[9]So do not hold him guiltless; for you are a wise man and know what you should do to him. His hoary head bring down to the grave with blood.

[10]So David slept with his fathers and was buried in the City of David.

## New International Version

in the City of David. [11]He had reigned forty years over Israel—seven years in Hebron and thirty-three in Jerusalem. [12]So Solomon sat on the throne of his father David, and his rule was firmly established.

### Solomon's Throne Established

[13]Now Adonijah, the son of Haggith, went to Bathsheba, Solomon's mother. Bathsheba asked him, "Do you come peacefully?"

He answered, "Yes, peacefully." [14]Then he added, "I have something to say to you."

"You may say it," she replied.

[15]"As you know," he said, "the kingdom was mine. All Israel looked to me as their king. But things changed, and the kingdom has gone to my brother; for it has come to him from the LORD. [16]Now I have one request to make of you. Do not refuse me."

"You may make it," she said.

[17]So he continued, "Please ask King Solomon—he will not refuse you—to give me Abishag the Shunammite as my wife."

[18]"Very well," Bathsheba replied, "I will speak to the king for you."

[19]When Bathsheba went to King Solomon to speak to him for Adonijah, the king stood up to meet her, bowed down to her and sat down on his throne. He had a throne brought for the king's mother, and she sat down at his right hand.

[20]"I have one small request to make of you," she said. "Do not refuse me."

The king replied, "Make it, my mother; I will not refuse you."

[21]So she said, "Let Abishag the Shunammite be given in marriage to your brother Adonijah."

[22]King Solomon answered his mother, "Why do you request Abishag the Shunammite for Adonijah? You might as well request the kingdom for him—after all, he is my older brother—yes, for him and for Abiathar the priest and Joab son of Zeruiah!"

[23]Then King Solomon swore by the LORD: "May God deal with me, be it ever so severely, if Adonijah does not pay with his life for this request! [24]And now, as surely as the LORD lives—he who has established me securely on the throne of my father David and has founded a dynasty for me as he promised—Adonijah shall be put to death today!" [25]So King Solomon gave orders to Benaiah son of Jehoiada, and he struck down Adonijah and he died.

[26]To Abiathar the priest the king said, "Go back to your fields in Anathoth. You deserve to die, but I will not put you to death now, because you carried the ark of the Sovereign LORD before my father David and shared all my father's hardships." [27]So Solomon removed Abiathar from the priesthood of the LORD, fulfilling the word the LORD had spoken at Shiloh about the house of Eli.

[28]When the news reached Joab, who had conspired with Adonijah though not with Absalom, he fled to the tent of the LORD and took hold of the horns of the altar. [29]King Solomon was told that Joab had fled to the tent of the LORD and was beside the altar. Then Solomon ordered Benaiah son of Jehoiada, "Go, strike him down!"

[30]So Benaiah entered the tent of the LORD and said to Joab, "The king says, 'Come out!'"

But he answered, "No, I will die here."

Benaiah reported to the king, "This is how Joab answered me."

[31]Then the king commanded Benaiah, "Do as he says.

## Amplified Bible

[11]David reigned over Israel forty years—seven years in Hebron and thirty-three years in Jerusalem.

[12]Then Solomon sat on the throne of David his father, and his kingdom was firmly established.

[13]Adonijah, the son of [David and] Haggith, came to Bathsheba, the mother of Solomon. She said, Do you come peaceably? And he said, Peaceably.

[14]He said, I have something to say to you. And she said, Say on.

[15]He said, You know that the kingdom belonged to me [as the eldest living son], and all Israel looked to me to reign. However, the kingdom has passed from me to my brother; for it was his from the Lord.

[16]Now I make one request of you; do not deny me. And she said, Say on.

[17]He said, I pray you, ask King Solomon, for he will not refuse you, to give me Abishag the Shunammite to be my wife. [I Kings 1:1-4.]

[18]And Bathsheba said, Very well; I will speak for you to the king.

[19]So Bathsheba went to King Solomon to speak to him for Adonijah. The king rose to meet her, bowed to her, sat down on his throne, and caused a seat to be set at his right hand for her, the king's mother.

[20]Then she said, I have one small request to make of you; do not refuse me. The king said to her, Ask on, my mother, for I will not refuse you.

[21]She said, Give Abishag the Shunammite to Adonijah your brother to be his wife.

[22]King Solomon answered his mother, And why do you ask Abishag the Shunammite for Adonijah? Ask for him the kingdom also—for he is my elder brother—[ask it] even for him and for [his supporters] Abiathar the priest and Joab son of Zeruiah.

[23]Then King Solomon swore by the Lord, saying, May God do so to me, and more also, if Adonijah has not requested this against his own life.

[24]Therefore, as the Lord lives, Who has established me and set me on the throne of David my father and Who has made me a house as He promised, Adonijah shall be put to death this day.

[25]So King Solomon sent Benaiah son of Jehoiada, who attacked [Adonijah] and he died.

[26]And to Abiathar the priest the king said, Get to Anathoth to your own estate; for you deserve death, but I will not put you to death now, because you bore the ark of the Lord God before my father David and were afflicted in all my father endured.

[27]So Solomon expelled Abiathar [descendant of Eli] from being priest to the Lord, fulfilling the word of the Lord which He spoke concerning the house of Eli in Shiloh. [I Sam. 2:27-36.]

[28]When the news came to Joab, for Joab had followed Adonijah though he had not followed Absalom, [he] fled to the tent (tabernacle) of the Lord and caught hold of the horns of the altar [before it].

[29]King Solomon was told that Joab had fled to the tent of the Lord and was at the altar. Then Solomon sent Benaiah son of Jehoiada, saying, Go, strike him down.

[30]So Benaiah came to the tent of the Lord and told Joab, The king commands, Come forth. But Joab said, No, I will die here. Then Benaiah brought the king word again, Thus said Joab, and thus he answered me.

[31]The king said to him, Do as he has said. Strike him

## New International Version

Strike him down and bury him, and so clear me and my whole family of the guilt of the innocent blood that Joab shed. ³²The LORD will repay him for the blood he shed, because without my father David knowing it he attacked two men and killed them with the sword. Both of them—Abner son of Ner, commander of Israel's army, and Amasa son of Jether, commander of Judah's army—were better men and more upright than he. ³³May the guilt of their blood rest on the head of Joab and his descendants forever. But on David and his descendants, his house and his throne, may there be the LORD's peace forever."

³⁴So Benaiah son of Jehoiada went up and struck down Joab and killed him, and he was buried at his home out in the country. ³⁵The king put Benaiah son of Jehoiada over the army in Joab's position and replaced Abiathar with Zadok the priest.

³⁶Then the king sent for Shimei and said to him, "Build yourself a house in Jerusalem and live there, but do not go anywhere else. ³⁷The day you leave and cross the Kidron Valley, you can be sure you will die; your blood will be on your own head."

³⁸Shimei answered the king, "What you say is good. Your servant will do as my lord the king has said." And Shimei stayed in Jerusalem for a long time.

³⁹But three years later, two of Shimei's slaves ran off to Achish son of Maakah, king of Gath, and Shimei was told, "Your slaves are in Gath." ⁴⁰At this, he saddled his donkey and went to Achish at Gath in search of his slaves. So Shimei went away and brought the slaves back from Gath.

⁴¹When Solomon was told that Shimei had gone from Jerusalem to Gath and had returned, ⁴²the king summoned Shimei and said to him, "Did I not make you swear by the LORD and warn you, 'On the day you leave to go anywhere else, you can be sure you will die'? At that time you said to me, 'What you say is good. I will obey.' ⁴³Why then did you not keep your oath to the LORD and obey the command I gave you?"

⁴⁴The king also said to Shimei, "You know in your heart all the wrong you did to my father David. Now the LORD will repay you for your wrongdoing. ⁴⁵But King Solomon will be blessed, and David's throne will remain secure before the LORD forever."

⁴⁶Then the king gave the order to Benaiah son of Jehoiada, and he went out and struck Shimei down and he died.

The kingdom was now established in Solomon's hands.

### Solomon Asks for Wisdom

**3** Solomon made an alliance with Pharaoh king of Egypt and married his daughter. He brought her to the City of David until he finished building his palace and the temple of the LORD, and the wall around Jerusalem. ²The people, however, were still sacrificing at the high places, because a temple had not yet been built for the Name of the LORD. ³Solomon showed his love for the LORD by walking according to the instructions given him by his father David, except that he offered sacrifices and burned incense on the high places.

⁴The king went to Gibeon to offer sacrifices, for that

## Amplified Bible

down and bury him, that you may take away from [me and from] my father's house the innocent blood which Joab shed.

³²The Lord shall return his bloody deeds upon his own head, for he fell upon two men more [uncompromisingly] righteous and honorable than he and slew them with the sword, without my father knowing of it: Abner son of Ner, captain of the host of Israel, and Amasa son of Jether, captain of the host of Judah.

³³So shall their blood return upon the head of Joab and of his descendants forever. But upon David, his descendants, his house, and his throne, there shall be peace from the Lord forever.

³⁴So Benaiah son of Jehoiada went up and struck and killed Joab, and he was buried at his own house in the wilderness.

³⁵The king put Benaiah son of Jehoiada in Joab's place over the army and put Zadok the priest in place of Abiathar.

³⁶The king sent for Shimei and said to him, Build yourself a house in Jerusalem and dwell there, and do not leave there.

³⁷For on the day you go out and pass over the brook Kidron, know with certainty that you shall die; your blood shall be upon your own head.

³⁸And Shimei said to the king, The saying is good. As my lord the king has said, so your servant will do. And Shimei dwelt in Jerusalem many days.

³⁹But after three years, two of Shimei's servants ran away to Achish son of Maacah, king of Gath. And Shimei was told, Behold, your [runaway] servants are in Gath.

⁴⁰So Shimei arose, saddled his donkey, and went to Gath to King Achish to seek his servants, and brought them from Gath.

⁴¹It was told Solomon that Shimei went from Jerusalem to Gath and had returned.

⁴²And the king sent for Shimei and said to him, Did I not make you swear by the Lord and warn you, saying, Know with certainty, on the day you go out and walk abroad anywhere, you shall surely die? And you said to me, I have heard your word. It is accepted.

⁴³Why then have you not kept the oath of the Lord and the command with which I have charged you?

⁴⁴The king also said to Shimei, You are aware in your own heart of all the evil you did to my father David; so the Lord will return your evil upon your own head.

⁴⁵But King Solomon shall be blessed, and the throne of David shall be established before the Lord forever.

⁴⁶So the king commanded Benaiah son of Jehoiada, who went out and struck down Shimei, and he died. And the kingdom was established in the hands of Solomon.

**3** And Solomon made an alliance with Pharaoh king of Egypt and took Pharaoh's daughter and brought her into the City of David until he had finished building his own house and the house of the Lord, and the wall around Jerusalem.

²But the people sacrificed [to God] in the high places [as the heathen did to their idols], for there was no house yet built to the ᵃName of the Lord.

³Solomon loved the Lord, walking [at first] in the statutes *and* practices of David his father, only he sacrificed and burned incense in the high places.

⁴The king went to Gibeon [near Jerusalem, where stood the tabernacle and the bronze altar] to sacrifice there, for

ᵃ See footnote on Deut. 12:5.

## New International Version

was the most important high place, and Solomon offered a thousand burnt offerings on that altar. ⁵At Gibeon the LORD appeared to Solomon during the night in a dream, and God said, "Ask for whatever you want me to give you."

⁶Solomon answered, "You have shown great kindness to your servant, my father David, because he was faithful to you and righteous and upright in heart. You have continued this great kindness to him and have given him a son to sit on his throne this very day.

⁷"Now, LORD my God, you have made your servant king in place of my father David. But I am only a little child and do not know how to carry out my duties. ⁸Your servant is here among the people you have chosen, a great people, too numerous to count or number. ⁹So give your servant a discerning heart to govern your people and to distinguish between right and wrong. For who is able to govern this great people of yours?"

¹⁰The Lord was pleased that Solomon had asked for this. ¹¹So God said to him, "Since you have asked for this and not for long life or wealth for yourself, nor have asked for the death of your enemies but for discernment in administering justice, ¹²I will do what you have asked. I will give you a wise and discerning heart, so that there will never have been anyone like you, nor will there ever be. ¹³Moreover, I will give you what you have not asked for—both wealth and honor—so that in your lifetime you will have no equal among kings. ¹⁴And if you walk in obedience to me and keep my decrees and commands as David your father did, I will give you a long life." ¹⁵Then Solomon awoke—and he realized it had been a dream.

He returned to Jerusalem, stood before the ark of the Lord's covenant and sacrificed burnt offerings and fellowship offerings. Then he gave a feast for all his court.

### A Wise Ruling

¹⁶Now two prostitutes came to the king and stood before him. ¹⁷One of them said, "Pardon me, my lord. This woman and I live in the same house, and I had a baby while she was there with me. ¹⁸The third day after my child was born, this woman also had a baby. We were alone; there was no one in the house but the two of us.

¹⁹"During the night this woman's son died because she lay on him. ²⁰So she got up in the middle of the night and took my son from my side while I your servant was asleep. She put him by her breast and put her dead son by my breast. ²¹The next morning, I got up to nurse my son—and he was dead! But when I looked at him closely in the morning light, I saw that it wasn't the son I had borne."

²²The other woman said, "No! The living one is my son; the dead one is yours."

But the first one insisted, "No! The dead one is yours; the living one is mine." And so they argued before the king.

²³The king said, "This one says, 'My son is alive and your son is dead,' while that one says, 'No! Your son is dead and mine is alive.'"

## Amplified Bible

that was the great high place. One thousand burnt offerings Solomon offered on that altar.

⁵In Gibeon the Lord appeared to Solomon in a dream by night. And God said, ᵃAsk what I shall give you.

⁶Solomon said, You have shown to Your servant David my father great mercy and loving-kindness, according as he walked before You in faithfulness, righteousness, and uprightness of heart with You; and You have kept for him this great kindness and steadfast love, that You have given him a son to sit on his throne this day.

⁷Now, O Lord my God, You have made Your servant king instead of David my father, and I am ᵇbut a lad [in wisdom and experience]; I know not how to go out (begin) or come in (finish).

⁸Your servant is in the midst of Your people whom You have chosen, a great people who cannot be counted for multitude.

⁹So give Your servant an understanding mind and a hearing heart to judge Your people, that I may discern between good and bad. For who is able to judge and rule this Your great people? [James 1:5.]

¹⁰It pleased the Lord that Solomon had asked this.

¹¹God said to him, Because you have asked this and have not asked for long life or for riches, nor for the lives of your enemies, but have asked for yourself understanding to recognize what is just and right,

¹²Behold, I have done as you asked. I have given you a wise, discerning mind, so that no one before you was your equal, nor shall any arise after you equal to you.

¹³I have also given you what you have not asked, both riches and honor, so that there shall not be any among the kings equal to you all your days.

¹⁴And if you will go My way, keep My statutes and My commandments as your father David did, then I will lengthen your days.

¹⁵Solomon awoke, and behold, it was a dream. He came to Jerusalem, stood before the ark of the covenant of the Lord, and offered burnt offerings and peace offerings, and made a feast for all his servants.

¹⁶Then two women who had become mothers out of wedlock came and stood before the king.

¹⁷And one woman said, O my lord, I and this woman dwell in one house; and I was delivered of a child with her in the house.

¹⁸And the third day after I was delivered, this woman also was delivered. And we were together; no stranger was with us, just we two in the house.

¹⁹And this woman's child died in the night because she lay on him.

²⁰And she arose at midnight and took my son from beside me while your handmaid slept and laid him in her bosom and laid her dead child in my bosom.

²¹And when I rose to nurse my child, behold, he was dead. But when I had considered him in the morning, behold, it was not the son I had borne.

²²But the other woman said, No! But the living one is my son, and the dead one is your son! And this one said, No! But the dead son is your son, and the living is my son. Thus they spoke before the king.

²³The king said, One says, This is my son that is alive and yours is the dead one. The other woman says, No! But your son is the dead one and mine is the living one.

---

ᵃ This is the high privilege of the child of God. Each one's life tells what he has asked for—"in heaven above or in the earth beneath." Which shall it be, God's will and glory, or our own?   ᵇ Solomon was already a father (see I Kings 11:42; 14:21).

## New International Version

24Then the king said, "Bring me a sword." So they brought a sword for the king. 25He then gave an order: "Cut the living child in two and give half to one and half to the other."

26The woman whose son was alive was deeply moved out of love for her son and said to the king, "Please, my lord, give her the living baby! Don't kill him!"

But the other said, "Neither I nor you shall have him. Cut him in two!"

27Then the king gave his ruling: "Give the living baby to the first woman. Do not kill him; she is his mother."

28When all Israel heard the verdict the king had given, they held the king in awe, because they saw that he had wisdom from God to administer justice.

### Solomon's Officials and Governors

4 So King Solomon ruled over all Israel. 2And these were his chief officials:

Azariah son of Zadok—the priest;
3Elihoreph and Ahijah, sons of Shisha—secretaries;
Jehoshaphat son of Ahilud—recorder;
4Benaiah son of Jehoiada—commander in chief;
Zadok and Abiathar—priests;
5Azariah son of Nathan—in charge of the district governors;
Zabud son of Nathan—a priest and adviser to the king;
6Ahishar—palace administrator;
Adoniram son of Abda—in charge of forced labor.

7Solomon had twelve district governors over all Israel, who supplied provisions for the king and the royal household. Each one had to provide supplies for one month in the year. 8These are their names:

Ben-Hur—in the hill country of Ephraim;
9Ben-Deker—in Makaz, Shaalbim, Beth Shemesh and Elon Bethhanan;
10Ben-Hesed—in Arubboth (Sokoh and all the land of Hepher were his);
11Ben-Abinadab—in Naphoth Dor (he was married to Taphath daughter of Solomon);
12Baana son of Ahilud—in Taanach and Megiddo, and in all of Beth Shan next to Zarethan below Jezreel, from Beth Shan to Abel Meholah across to Jokmeam;
13Ben-Geber—in Ramoth Gilead (the settlements of Jair son of Manasseh in Gilead were his, as well as the region of Argob in Bashan and its sixty large walled cities with bronze gate bars);
14Ahinadab son of Iddo—in Mahanaim;
15Ahimaaz—in Naphtali (he had married Basemath daughter of Solomon);
16Baana son of Hushai—in Asher and in Aloth;
17Jehoshaphat son of Paruah—in Issachar;
18Shimei son of Ela—in Benjamin;
19Geber son of Uri—in Gilead (the country of Sihon king of the Amorites and the country of Og king of Bashan). He was the only governor over the district.

### Solomon's Daily Provisions

20The people of Judah and Israel were as numerous as the sand on the seashore; they ate, they drank and they were happy. 21And Solomon ruled over all the kingdoms from the Euphrates River to the land of the Philistines, as far as the border of Egypt. These countries brought tribute and were Solomon's subjects all his life.

22Solomon's daily provisions were thirty cors*a* of the finest flour and sixty cors*b* of meal, 23ten head of stall-fed cat-

*a* 22 That is, probably about 5 1/2 tons or about 5 metric tons
*b* 22 That is, probably about 11 tons or about 10 metric tons

## Amplified Bible

24And the king said, Bring me a sword. And they brought a sword to the king.

25And the king said, Divide the living child in two and give half to the one and half to the other.

26Then the mother of the living child said to the king, for she yearned over her son, O my lord, give her the living baby, and by no means slay him. But the other said, Let him not be mine or yours, but divide him.

27Then the king said, Give her [who pleads for his life] the living baby, and by no means slay him. She is the child's mother.

28And all Israel heard of the judgment which the king had made, and they stood in awe of him, for they saw that the wisdom of God was in him to do justice.

4 King Solomon was king over all Israel.
2These were his chief officials: Azariah son of Zadok was the [high] priest;
3Elihoreph and Ahijah, sons of Shisha, were secretaries; Jehoshaphat son of Ahilud was recorder;
4Benaiah son of Jehoiada commanded the army; Zadok and Abiathar were priests;
5Azariah son of Nathan was over the officers; Zabud son of Nathan was priest and the king's friend *and* private advisor;
6Ahishar was in charge of the palace; and Adoniram son of Abda was in charge of the forced labor.
7Solomon had twelve officers over all Israel, who secured provisions for the king and his household; each man had to provide for a month in a year.
8These were their names: Ben-hur, in the hill country of Ephraim;
9Ben-deker, in Makaz, Shaalbim, Beth-shemesh, and Elon-beth-hanan;
10Ben-hesed, in Arubboth (to him belonged Socoh and all the land of Hepher);
11Ben-abinadab, in Naphoth-dor (he had Taphath, Solomon's daughter, as wife);
12Baana son of Ahilud, in Taanach, Megiddo, and all Beth-shean which is beside Zarethan below Jezreel, from Beth-shean to Abel-meholah as far as beyond Jokmeam;
13Ben-geber, in Ramoth-gilead (to him belonged the villages of Jair son of Manasseh which are in Gilead, also the region of Argob which is in Bashan, sixty great cities with walls and bronze bars);
14Ahinadab son of Iddo, in Mahanaim;
15Ahimaaz, in Naphtali (he had taken Basemath, Solomon's daughter, as his wife);
16Baana son of Hushai, in Asher and Bealoth;
17Jehoshaphat son of Paruah, in Issachar;
18Shimei son of Ela, in Benjamin;
19Geber son of Uri, in Gilead, the country of Sihon king of the Amorites and of Og king of Bashan; only one officer was over all the country [at one time, each serving for one month].
20Judah and Israel were many, like the sand which is by the sea in multitude; they ate, drank, and rejoiced.
21Solomon reigned *a* over all the kingdoms from the [Euphrates] River to the land of the Philistines and to the border of Egypt; they brought tribute and served Solomon all the days of his life.
22Solomon's provision for one day was thirty measures of fine flour, sixty measures of meal,

*a* That King Solomon's empire was as great as is definitely indicated here and in II Chron. 9:26 has frequently been questioned because of the great empires of Assyria on the Euphrates and Egypt on the Nile. But archaeological discoveries prove that "precisely during the period 1100-900 B.C., when the kingdom of Israel was being built up, 'the weak and inglorious twenty-first dynasty' was ruling in Egypt and at the same time Assyria went into a period of decline" (J. P. Free, *Archaeology and Bible History*, citing A. T. Olmstead, *History of Assyria*).

## New International Version

tle, twenty of pasture-fed cattle and a hundred sheep and goats, as well as deer, gazelles, roebucks and choice fowl. [24] For he ruled over all the kingdoms west of the Euphrates River, from Tiphsah to Gaza, and had peace on all sides. [25] During Solomon's lifetime Judah and Israel, from Dan to Beersheba, lived in safety, everyone under their own vine and under their own fig tree. [26] Solomon had four[a] thousand stalls for chariot horses, and twelve thousand horses.[b]

[27] The district governors, each in his month, supplied provisions for King Solomon and all who came to the king's table. They saw to it that nothing was lacking. [28] They also brought to the proper place their quotas of barley and straw for the chariot horses and the other horses.

### Solomon's Wisdom

[29] God gave Solomon wisdom and very great insight, and a breadth of understanding as measureless as the sand on the seashore. [30] Solomon's wisdom was greater than the wisdom of all the people of the East, and greater than all the wisdom of Egypt. [31] He was wiser than anyone else, including Ethan the Ezrahite—wiser than Heman, Kalkol and Darda, the sons of Mahol. And his fame spread to all the surrounding nations. [32] He spoke three thousand proverbs and his songs numbered a thousand and five. [33] He spoke about plant life, from the cedar of Lebanon to the hyssop that grows out of walls. He also spoke about animals and birds, reptiles and fish. [34] From all nations people came to listen to Solomon's wisdom, sent by all the kings of the world, who had heard of his wisdom.[c]

### Preparations for Building the Temple

**5**[d] When Hiram king of Tyre heard that Solomon had been anointed king to succeed his father David, he sent his envoys to Solomon, because he had always been on friendly terms with David. [2] Solomon sent back this message to Hiram:

[3] "You know that because of the wars waged against my father David from all sides, he could not build a temple for the Name of the LORD his God until the LORD put his enemies under his feet. [4] But now the LORD my God has given me rest on every side, and there is no adversary or disaster. [5] I intend, therefore, to build a temple for the Name of the LORD my God, as the LORD told my father David, when he said, 'Your son whom I will put on the throne in your place will build the temple for my Name.'

[6] "So give orders that cedars of Lebanon be cut for me. My men will work with yours, and I will pay you for your men whatever wages you set. You know that we have no one so skilled in felling timber as the Sidonians."

[7] When Hiram heard Solomon's message, he was greatly pleased and said, "Praise be to the LORD today, for he has given David a wise son to rule over this great nation." [8] So Hiram sent word to Solomon:

"I have received the message you sent me and will do all you want in providing the cedar and juniper logs. [9] My men will haul them down from Lebanon to the Mediterranean Sea, and I will float them as rafts by sea to the place you specify. There I will separate them and you can take them away. And you are to grant my wish by providing food for my royal household."

## Amplified Bible

[23] Ten fat oxen, twenty pasture-fed cattle, a hundred sheep, besides harts, gazelles, roebucks, and fatted fowl of choice kinds.

[24] For he had dominion over all the region west of the [Euphrates] River, from Tiphsah to Gaza, over all the kings west of the River, and he had peace on all sides around him.

[25] Judah and Israel dwelt safely, every man under his vine and fig tree, from Dan to Beersheba, all of Solomon's days.

[26] Solomon also had 40,000 stalls of horses for his chariots, and 12,000 horsemen.

[27] And those officers provided food for King Solomon and for all who came to his table, every man in his month; they let nothing be lacking.

[28] Barley also and straw for the horses and swift steeds they brought to the place where it was needed, each according to his assignment.

[29] And God gave Solomon exceptionally much wisdom and understanding, and breadth of mind like the sand of the seashore.

[30] Solomon's wisdom excelled the wisdom of all the people of the East and all the wisdom of Egypt.

[31] For he was wiser [a] than all other men—than Ethan the Ezrahite, and Heman, Calcol, and Darda, the sons of Mahol. His fame was in all the nations round about.

[32] He also originated 3,000 proverbs, and his songs were 1,005.

[33] He spoke of trees, from the cedar that is in Lebanon to the hyssop that grows out of the wall; he spoke also of beasts, of birds, of creeping things, and of fish.

[34] Men came from all peoples to hear the wisdom of Solomon, and from all kings of the earth who had heard of his wisdom.

**5** Hiram king of Tyre sent his servants to Solomon, when he heard that he was anointed king in place of his father, for Hiram always loved David.

[2] And Solomon sent to Hiram, saying,

[3] You know how David my father could not build a house to the Name of the Lord his God because wars were about him on every side, until the Lord put his foes under his feet. [II Sam. 7:4ff.; I Chron. 22:8.]

[4] But now the Lord my God has given me rest on every side, so that there is neither adversary nor evil confronting me.

[5] And I purpose to build a house to the Name of the Lord my God, as the Lord said to David my father, Your son whom I will set on your throne in your place shall build the house to My Name *and* Presence.

[6] So, Hiram, command them to hew me cedar trees out of Lebanon; my servants shall join yours, and I will give you whatever wages you set for your servants. For you know that no one among us can equal the skill of the Sidon men in cutting timber.

[7] When Hiram heard the words of Solomon, he rejoiced greatly and said, Blessed be the Lord this day, Who has given David a wise son to be over this great people.

[8] And Hiram sent to Solomon, saying, I have considered the things for which you sent to me; I will do all you wish concerning the cedar and cypress timber.

[9] My servants shall bring the logs down from Lebanon to the sea, make them into rafts, and float them by sea to the place that you direct. I will have them released there, and you shall take them away. And you shall fulfill my desire by providing food for my household.

---

[a] 26 Some Septuagint manuscripts (see also 2 Chron. 9:25); Hebrew *forty*
[b] 26 Or *charioteers*   [c] 34 In Hebrew texts 4:21-34 is numbered 5:1-14.
[d] In Hebrew texts 5:1-18 is numbered 5:15-32.

[a] "Wiser than all other men," until Christ came. Jesus said, "Someone more *and* greater than Solomon is here" (Matt. 12:42).

## New International Version

[10]In this way Hiram kept Solomon supplied with all the cedar and juniper logs he wanted, [11]and Solomon gave Hiram twenty thousand cors*a* of wheat as food for his household, in addition to twenty thousand baths*b,c* of pressed olive oil. Solomon continued to do this for Hiram year after year. [12]The LORD gave Solomon wisdom, just as he had promised him. There were peaceful relations between Hiram and Solomon, and the two of them made a treaty.

[13]King Solomon conscripted laborers from all Israel—thirty thousand men. [14]He sent them off to Lebanon in shifts of ten thousand a month, so that they spent one month in Lebanon and two months at home. Adoniram was in charge of the forced labor. [15]Solomon had seventy thousand carriers and eighty thousand stonecutters in the hills, [16]as well as thirty-three hundred*d* foremen who supervised the project and directed the workers. [17]At the king's command they removed from the quarry large blocks of high-grade stone to provide a foundation of dressed stone for the temple. [18]The craftsmen of Solomon and Hiram and workers from Byblos cut and prepared the timber and stone for the building of the temple.

### Solomon Builds the Temple

**6** In the four hundred and eightieth*e* year after the Israelites came out of Egypt, in the fourth year of Solomon's reign over Israel, in the month of Ziv, the second month, he began to build the temple of the LORD.

[2]The temple that King Solomon built for the LORD was sixty cubits long, twenty wide and thirty high.*f* [3]The portico at the front of the main hall of the temple extended the width of the temple, that is twenty cubits,*g* and projected ten cubits*h* from the front of the temple. [4]He made narrow windows high up in the temple walls. [5]Against the walls of the main hall and inner sanctuary he built a structure around the building, in which there were side rooms. [6]The lowest floor was five cubits*i* wide, the middle floor six cubits*j* and the third floor seven.*k* He made offset ledges around the outside of the temple so that nothing would be inserted into the temple walls.

[7]In building the temple, only blocks dressed at the quarry were used, and no hammer, chisel or any other iron tool was heard at the temple site while it was being built.

[8]The entrance to the lowest*l* floor was on the south side of the temple; a stairway led up to the middle level and from there to the third. [9]So he built the temple and completed it, roofing it with beams and cedar planks. [10]And he built the side rooms all along the temple. The height of each was five cubits, and they were attached to the temple by beams of cedar.

[11]The word of the LORD came to Solomon: [12]"As for this temple you are building, if you follow my decrees, observe my laws and keep all my commands and obey them, I will fulfill through you the promise I gave to David your father. [13]And I will live among the Israelites and will not abandon my people Israel."

*a 11* That is, probably about 3,600 tons or about 3,250 metric tons      *b 11* Septuagint (see also 2 Chron. 2:10); Hebrew *twenty cors*      *c 11* That is, about 120,000 gallons or about 440,000 liters      *d 16* Hebrew; some Septuagint manuscripts (see also 2 Chron. 2:2,18) *thirty-six hundred*      *e 1* Hebrew; Septuagint *four hundred and fortieth*      *f 2* That is, about 90 feet long, 30 feet wide and 45 feet high or about 27 meters long, 9 meters wide and 14 meters high      *g 3* That is, about 30 feet or about 9 meters; also in verses 16 and 20      *h 3* That is, about 15 feet or about 4.5 meters; also in verses 23-26      *i 6* That is, about 7 1/2 feet or about 2.3 meters; also in verses 10 and 24      *j 6* That is, about 9 feet or about 2.7 meters      *k 6* That is, about 11 feet or about 3.2 meters      *l 8* Septuagint; Hebrew *middle*

## Amplified Bible

[10]So Hiram gave Solomon all the cedar and cypress trees he desired,

[11]And Solomon gave Hiram 20,000 measures of wheat for food for his household, and 20 measures of pure, beaten oil. He gave these to Hiram yearly.

[12]The Lord gave Solomon wisdom, as He promised him; and there was peace between Hiram and Solomon, and they made a treaty.

[13]King Solomon raised a levy [of forced labor] out of all Israel; and the levy was 30,000 men.

[14]He sent them to Lebanon, 10,000 a month by divisions; one month they were in Lebanon and two months at home. Adoniram was over the levy.

[15]And Solomon had 70,000 burden bearers and 80,000 hewers [of stone] in the hill country of Judah,

[16]Besides Solomon's 3,300 overseers in charge of the people doing the work.

[17]The king commanded, and they hewed *and* brought out *a*great, costly stones in order to lay the foundation of the house with dressed stone.

[18]Solomon's builders and Hiram's builders and the men of Gebal did the hewing and prepared the timber and stones to build the house.

**6** And 480 years after the Israelites came out of the land of Egypt, in the fourth year of Solomon's reign over Israel, in the second month, Ziv, he began to build the Lord's house.

[2]The length of the house Solomon built for the Lord was sixty cubits, its breadth twenty, and its height thirty cubits.

[3]The length of the vestibule in front of the temple was twenty cubits, equal to the width of the house, and its depth in front of the house was ten cubits.

[4]For the house he made narrow [latticed] windows.

[5]Against the wall of the house he built chambers running round the walls of the house both of the Holy Place and of the Holy of Holies; and he made side chambers all around.

[6]The first story's side chambers were five cubits wide, those of the middle story six cubits wide, and of the third story seven cubits wide; for around the outside of the wall of the house he made offsets in order that the supporting beams should not be thrust into the walls of the house.

[7]When the house was being built, its stone was made ready at the quarry, and no hammer, ax, or tool of iron was heard in the house while it was in building.

[8]The entrance to the lowest side chamber was on the right [or south] side of the house; and one went up winding stairs into the middle chamber and from the middle into the third.

[9]So Solomon built the temple building and finished it, and roofed the house with beams and boards of cedar.

[10]Then he built the stories of chambers [the lean-to] against all the house, each [story] five cubits high; and it was joined to the house with timbers of cedar.

[11]Now the word of the Lord came to Solomon, saying,

[12]Concerning this house which you are building, if you will walk in My statutes, execute My precepts, and keep all My commandments to walk in them, then I will fulfill to you My promises which I made to David your father.

[13]And I will dwell among the Israelites and will not forsake My people Israel.

*a* These great foundation stones remain to this day. One of them is almost thirty-nine feet long, one of the most interesting stones of the world. It is the chief cornerstone of the Mosque of Omar's massive wall, placed in its present position 3,000 years ago. Markings on the stones represent the culture of Phoenicia, the region around Tyre from which Solomon received building materials for the temple.

## New International Version

[14] So Solomon built the temple and completed it. [15] He lined its interior walls with cedar boards, paneling them from the floor of the temple to the ceiling, and covered the floor of the temple with planks of juniper. [16] He partitioned off twenty cubits at the rear of the temple with cedar boards from floor to ceiling to form within the temple an inner sanctuary, the Most Holy Place. [17] The main hall in front of this room was forty cubits[a] long. [18] The inside of the temple was cedar, carved with gourds and open flowers. Everything was cedar; no stone was to be seen.

[19] He prepared the inner sanctuary within the temple to set the ark of the covenant of the LORD there. [20] The inner sanctuary was twenty cubits long, twenty wide and twenty high. He overlaid the inside with pure gold, and he also overlaid the altar of cedar. [21] Solomon covered the inside of the temple with pure gold, and he extended gold chains across the front of the inner sanctuary, which was overlaid with gold. [22] So he overlaid the whole interior with gold. He also overlaid with gold the altar that belonged to the inner sanctuary.

[23] For the inner sanctuary he made a pair of cherubim out of olive wood, each ten cubits high. [24] One wing of the first cherub was five cubits long, and the other wing five cubits—ten cubits from wing tip to wing tip. [25] The second cherub also measured ten cubits, for the two cherubim were identical in size and shape. [26] The height of each cherub was ten cubits. [27] He placed the cherubim inside the innermost room of the temple, with their wings spread out. The wing of one cherub touched one wall, while the wing of the other touched the other wall, and their wings touched each other in the middle of the room. [28] He overlaid the cherubim with gold.

[29] On the walls all around the temple, in both the inner and outer rooms, he carved cherubim, palm trees and open flowers. [30] He also covered the floors of both the inner and outer rooms of the temple with gold. [31] For the entrance to the inner sanctuary he made doors out of olive wood that were one fifth of the width of the sanctuary. [32] And on the two olive-wood doors he carved cherubim, palm trees and open flowers, and overlaid the cherubim and palm trees with hammered gold. [33] In the same way, for the entrance to the main hall he made doorframes out of olive wood that were one fourth of the width of the hall. [34] He also made two doors out of juniper wood, each having two leaves that turned in sockets. [35] He carved cherubim, palm trees and open flowers on them and overlaid them with gold hammered evenly over the carvings.

[36] And he built the inner courtyard of three courses of dressed stone and one course of trimmed cedar beams.

[37] The foundation of the temple of the LORD was laid in the fourth year, in the month of Bul, [38] In the eleventh year in the month of Bul, the eighth month, the temple was finished in all its details according to its specifications. He had spent seven years building it.

## Amplified Bible

[14] So Solomon built the house and finished it.

[15] He built the walls of the house (the Holy Place and the Holy of Holies) within with boards of cedar, from the floor of the house to the rafters of the ceiling. He covered the inside with wood, and the floor of the house with boards of cypress.

[16] He built twenty cubits of the rear of the house with boards of cedar from the floor to the rafters; he built it within for the sanctuary, the Holy of Holies.

[17] The [rest of the] house, that is, the temple in front of the Holy of Holies, was forty cubits long.

[18] The cedar on the house within was carved with gourds and open flowers. All was cedar; no stone was visible.

[19] And he prepared the Holy of Holies in the inner room in which to set the ark of the covenant of the Lord.

[20] The Holy of Holies was twenty cubits in length, in breadth, and in height. He overlaid it with pure gold. He also overlaid the cedar altar.

[21] Solomon overlaid the house within with pure gold, and he drew chains of gold across in front of the Holy of Holies and overlaid it with gold.

[22] And the whole house he overlaid with gold, until all the house was finished. Also the whole [incense] altar that [stood outside the door but] belonged to the Holy of Holies he overlaid with gold.

[23] Within the Holy of Holies he made two cherubim of olive wood, each ten cubits high.

[24] Five cubits was the length of one wing of the cherub and five cubits its other wing; from the tip of one wing to the tip of the other was ten cubits.

[25] The wings of the other cherub were also ten cubits. Both cherubim were the same,

[26] The height of one cherub ten cubits, as was the other.

[27] He put the cherubim within the inner sanctuary. Their wings were stretched out, so that the wing of one touched one wall, and the wing of the other cherub touched the other wall, and their inner wings touched in the midst of the room.

[28] Solomon overlaid the cherubim with gold.

[29] He carved all the walls of the house (these two holy rooms) round about with figures of cherubim, palm trees, and open flowers, within and without.

[30] The floor of the house he overlaid with gold, inside and out.

[31] For the Holy of Holies he made [folding] doors of olive wood; their entire width was one-fifth that of the wall.

[32] On the two doors of olive wood he carved cherubim, palm trees, and open flowers; he overlaid them with gold, and spread gold on the cherubim and palm trees.

[33] Also he made for the door of the Holy Place four-sided posts of olive wood.

[34] The two doors were of cypress wood; the two leaves of each door were folding.

[35] He carved on them cherubim, palm trees, and open flowers, covered with gold evenly applied on the carved work.

[36] He built the inner court with three rows of hewn stone and a row of cedar beams.

[37] In the fourth year the foundation of the Lord's house was laid, in the [second] month, Ziv.

[38] In the eleventh year, in Bul, the eighth month, the house was finished throughout according to all its specifications. So he was seven years in building it.

---

[a] 17 That is, about 60 feet or about 18 meters

## New International Version

### Solomon Builds His Palace

**7** It took Solomon thirteen years, however, to complete the construction of his palace. [2]He built the Palace of the Forest of Lebanon a hundred cubits long, fifty wide and thirty high,[a] with four rows of cedar columns supporting trimmed cedar beams. [3]It was roofed with cedar above the beams that rested on the columns—forty-five beams, fifteen to a row. [4]Its windows were placed high in sets of three, facing each other. [5]All the doorways had rectangular frames; they were in the front part in sets of three, facing each other.[b]

[6]He made a colonnade fifty cubits long and thirty wide.[c] In front of it was a portico, and in front of that were pillars and an overhanging roof.

[7]He built the throne hall, the Hall of Justice, where he was to judge, and he covered it with cedar from floor to ceiling.[d] [8]And the palace in which he was to live, set farther back, was similar in design. Solomon also made a palace like this hall for Pharaoh's daughter, whom he had married.

[9]All these structures, from the outside to the great courtyard and from foundation to eaves, were made of blocks of high-grade stone cut to size and smoothed on their inner and outer faces. [10]The foundations were laid with large stones of good quality, some measuring ten cubits[e] and some eight.[f] [11]Above were high-grade stones, cut to size, and cedar beams. [12]The great courtyard was surrounded by a wall of three courses of dressed stone and one course of trimmed cedar beams, as was the inner courtyard of the temple of the LORD with its portico.

### The Temple's Furnishings

[13]King Solomon sent to Tyre and brought Huram,[g] [14]whose mother was a widow from the tribe of Naphtali and whose father was from Tyre and a skilled craftsman in bronze. Huram was filled with wisdom, with understanding and with knowledge to do all kinds of bronze work. He came to King Solomon and did all the work assigned to him.

[15]He cast two bronze pillars, each eighteen cubits high and twelve cubits in circumference.[h] [16]He also made two capitals of cast bronze to set on the tops of the pillars; each capital was five cubits[i] high. [17]A network of interwoven chains adorned the capitals on top of the pillars, seven for each capital. [18]He made pomegranates in two rows[j] encircling each network to decorate the capitals on top of the pillars.[k] He did the same for each capital. [19]The capitals on top of the pillars in the portico were in the shape of lilies, four cubits[l] high. [20]On the capitals of both pillars, above the bowl-shaped part next to the network, were the two hundred pomegranates in rows all around. [21]He erected the pillars at the portico of the temple. The pillar to the south he named Jakin[m] and the one to the north Boaz.[n] [22]The capitals on top were in the shape of lilies. And so the work on the pillars was completed.

[23]He made the Sea of cast metal, circular in shape, measuring ten cubits from rim to rim and five cubits high. It took a line of thirty cubits[o] to measure around it. [24]Below

---

[a] 2 That is, about 150 feet long, 75 feet wide and 45 feet high or about 45 meters long, 23 meters wide and 14 meters high   [b] 5 The meaning of the Hebrew for this verse is uncertain.   [c] 6 That is, about 75 feet long and 45 feet wide or about 23 meters long and 14 meters wide   [d] 7 Vulgate and Syriac; Hebrew *floor*   [e] 10 That is, about 15 feet or about 4.5 meters; also in verse 23   [f] 10 That is, about 12 feet or about 3.6 meters   [g] 13 Hebrew *Hiram*, a variant of *Huram*; also in verses 40 and 45   [h] 15 That is, about 27 feet high and 18 feet in circumference or about 8.1 meters high and 5.4 meters in circumference   [i] 16 That is, about 7 1/2 feet or about 2.3 meters; also in verse 23   [j] 18 Two Hebrew manuscripts and Septuagint; most Hebrew manuscripts *made the pillars, and there were two rows*   [k] 18 Many Hebrew manuscripts and Syriac; most Hebrew manuscripts *pomegranates*   [l] 19 That is, about 6 feet or about 1.8 meters; also in verse 38   [m] 21 *Jakin* probably means *he establishes*.   [n] 21 *Boaz* probably means *in him is strength*.   [o] 23 That is, about 45 feet or about 14 meters

## Amplified Bible

**7** Solomon was building his own house [a]thirteen years, and he finished all of it.

[2]He built also the Forest of Lebanon House; its length was a hundred cubits, its breadth fifty, and its height thirty cubits, upon four rows of cedar pillars, with cedar beams upon the pillars.

[3]And it was covered with cedar above the side chambers that were upon the forty-five pillars, fifteen in a row.

[4]There were window frames in three rows, and window opposite window in three tiers.

[5]All the doorways and windows were square cut, and window was opposite window in three tiers.

[6]He also made the Hall of Pillars; its length was fifty cubits and its breadth thirty cubits. There was a porch in front, and pillars and a cornice before them.

[7]He made the porch for the throne where he was to judge, the Porch of Judgment; it was covered with cedar from floor to ceiling.

[8]His house where he was to dwell had another court behind the Porch of Judgment of similar work. Solomon also made a house like this porch for Pharaoh's daughter, whom he had married.

[9]All were of costly stones hewn according to measure, sawed with saws back and front, even from foundation to coping, and from the outside to the great court.

[10]The foundation was of costly stones, even great stones of eight and ten cubits.

[11]And above were costly stones hewn according to measure, and cedar timbers.

[12]Also the great encircling court had three courses of hewn stone and a course of cedar beams, like was around the inner court of the house of the Lord and the porch of the house.

[13]King Solomon brought Hiram from Tyre.

[14]He was the son of a widow of the tribe of Naphtali, and his father was a man of Tyre, a worker in bronze. He was full of wisdom, understanding, and skill to do any kind of work in bronze. So he came to King Solomon and did all his [bronze] work.

[15]He fashioned the two pillars of bronze, each eighteen cubits high, and a line of twelve cubits measured its circumference.

[16]He made two capitals of molten bronze to set upon the tops of the pillars; the height of each capital was five cubits.

[17]Nets of checkerwork and wreaths of chainwork for the capitals were on the tops of the pillars, seven for each capital.

[18]So Hiram made the pillars. There were two rows of pomegranates encircling each network to cover the capitals that were upon the top.

[19]The capitals that were upon the top of the pillars in the porch were of lily work [design], four cubits.

[20]The capitals were upon the two pillars and also above the rounded projection beside the network. There were 200 pomegranates in two rows round about, and so with the other capital.

[21]Hiram set up the pillars of the porch of the temple; he set up the right pillar and called its name Jachin [he will establish], and he set up the left pillar and called its name Boaz [in strength].

[22]On the tops of the pillars was lily work [design]. So the work of the pillars was finished.

[23]He made a round molten Sea, ten cubits from brim to brim, five cubits high and thirty cubits in circumference. [Exod. 30:17-21; II Chron. 4:6.]

---

[a] Solomon built God's house first, then his own. That his took much longer is no reflection on Solomon, for David had made every possible preparation for building the temple, greatly reducing the time needed to finish it (I Chron. 22:2-5). David even left for Solomon plans and patterns for the temple and loyal friends eager to help (I Kings 5:1; I Chron. 28:14-19).

## New International Version

the rim, gourds encircled it—ten to a cubit. The gourds were cast in two rows in one piece with the Sea. [25]The Sea stood on twelve bulls, three facing north, three facing west, three facing south and three facing east. The Sea rested on top of them, and their hindquarters were toward the center. [26]It was a handbreadth[a] in thickness, and its rim was like the rim of a cup, like a lily blossom. It held two thousand baths.[b] [27]He also made ten movable stands of bronze; each was four cubits long, four wide and three high.[c] [28]This is how the stands were made: They had side panels attached to uprights. [29]On the panels between the uprights were lions, bulls and cherubim—and on the uprights as well. Above and below the lions and bulls were wreaths of hammered work. [30]Each stand had four bronze wheels with bronze axles, and each had a basin resting on four supports, cast with wreaths on each side. [31]On the inside of the stand there was an opening that had a circular frame one cubit[d] deep. This opening was round, and with its basework it measured a cubit and a half.[e] Around its opening there was engraving. The panels of the stands were square, not round. [32]The four wheels were under the panels, and the axles of the wheels were attached to the stand. The diameter of each wheel was a cubit and a half. [33]The wheels were made like chariot wheels; the axles, rims, spokes and hubs were all of cast metal.

[34]Each stand had four handles, one on each corner, projecting from the stand. [35]At the top of the stand there was a circular band half a cubit[f] deep. The supports and panels were attached to the top of the stand. [36]He engraved cherubim, lions and palm trees on the surfaces of the supports and on the panels, in every available space, with wreaths all around. [37]This is the way he made the ten stands. They were all cast in the same molds and were identical in size and shape.

[38]He then made ten bronze basins, each holding forty baths[g] and measuring four cubits across, one basin to go on each of the ten stands. [39]He placed five of the stands on the south side of the temple and five on the north. He placed the Sea on the south side, at the southeast corner of the temple. [40]He also made the pots[h] and shovels and sprinkling bowls.

So Huram finished all the work he had undertaken for King Solomon in the temple of the LORD:

[41]the two pillars;
the two bowl-shaped capitals on top of the pillars;
the two sets of network decorating the two bowl-shaped capitals on top of the pillars;
[42]the four hundred pomegranates for the two sets of network (two rows of pomegranates for each network decorating the bowl-shaped capitals on top of the pillars);
[43]the ten stands with their ten basins;
[44]the Sea and the twelve bulls under it;
[45]the pots, shovels and sprinkling bowls.

All these objects that Huram made for King Solomon for the temple of the LORD were of burnished bronze. [46]The king had them cast in clay molds in the plain of the Jordan between Sukkoth and Zarethan. [47]Solomon left all these things unweighed, because there were so many; the weight of the bronze was not determined.

## Amplified Bible

[24]Under its brim were gourds encircling the Sea, ten to a cubit; the gourds were in two rows, cast in one piece with it. [25]It stood upon twelve oxen, three facing north, three west, three south, and three east; the Sea was set upon them, and all their rears pointed inward. [26]It was a handbreadth thick, and its brim was made like the brim of a cup, like a lily blossom. It held 2,000 baths [Hebrew liquid measurement]. [27]Hiram made ten bronze bases [for the lavers]; their length and breadth were four cubits, and the height three cubits. [28]This is the way the bases were made: they had panels between the ledges. [29]On the panels between the ledges were lions, oxen, and cherubim; and upon the ledges there was a pedestal above. Beneath the lions and oxen were wreaths of hanging work. [30]And every base had four bronze wheels and axles of bronze, and at the four corners were supports for a laver. Beneath the laver the supports were cast, with wreaths at the side of each. [31]Its mouth within the capital projected upward a cubit, and its mouth was round like the work of a pedestal, a cubit and a half. Also upon its mouth were carvings, and their borders were square, not round. [32]Under the borders were four wheels, and the axles of the wheels were one piece with the base. And the height of a wheel was a cubit and a half. [33]The wheels were made like a chariot wheel: their axles, their rims, their spokes, and their hubs were all cast. [34]There were four supports to the four corners of each base; the supports were part of the base itself. [35]On the top of the base there was a circular elevation half a cubit high, and on the top of the base its stays and panels were of one piece with it. [36]And on the surface of its stays and its panels Hiram carved cherubim, lions, and palm trees, according to the space of each, with wreaths round about. [37]Thus he made the ten bases. They all had one casting, one measure, and one form. [38]Then he made ten lavers of bronze; each laver held forty baths and measured four cubits, and there was one laver on each of the ten bases. [39]He put the bases five on the south side of the house and five on the north side; and he set the Sea at the southeast corner of the house. [40]Hiram made the lavers, the shovels, and the basins. So Hiram finished all the work that he did for King Solomon on the house of the Lord: [41]The two pillars; and the two bowls of the capitals that were on the tops of the two pillars; and the two networks to cover the two bowls; [42]And the 400 pomegranates for the two networks, two rows of pomegranates for each network, to cover the two bowls of the capitals that were upon the pillars; [43]The ten bases and the ten lavers on the bases; [44]One Sea, and the twelve oxen under it; [45]The pots, the shovels, and the basins. All these vessels which Hiram made for King Solomon in the house of the Lord were of burnished bronze. [46]In the Jordan plain the king cast them, in clay ground between Succoth and Zarethan. [47]Solomon left all the vessels unweighed, because they were so many; the weight of the bronze was not found out.

---

[a] 26 That is, about 3 inches or about 7.5 centimeters     [b] 26 That is, about 12,000 gallons or about 44,000 liters; the Septuagint does not have this sentence.     [c] 27 That is, about 6 feet long and wide and about 4 1/2 feet high or about 1.8 meters long and wide and 1.4 meters high     [d] 31 That is, about 18 inches or about 45 centimeters     [e] 31 That is, about 2 1/4 feet or about 68 centimeters; also in verse 32     [f] 35 That is, about 9 inches or about 23 centimeters     [g] 38 That is, about 240 gallons or about 880 liters     [h] 40 Many Hebrew manuscripts, Septuagint, Syriac and Vulgate (see also verse 45 and 2 Chron. 4:11); many other Hebrew manuscripts basins

## New International Version

<sup>48</sup>Solomon also made all the furnishings that were in the LORD's temple:

the golden altar;
the golden table on which was the bread of the Presence;
<sup>49</sup>the lampstands of pure gold (five on the right and five on the left, in front of the inner sanctuary);
the gold floral work and lamps and tongs;
<sup>50</sup>the pure gold basins, wick trimmers, sprinkling bowls, dishes and censers;
and the gold sockets for the doors of the innermost room, the Most Holy Place, and also for the doors of the main hall of the temple.

<sup>51</sup>When all the work King Solomon had done for the temple of the LORD was finished, he brought in the things his father David had dedicated—the silver and gold and the furnishings—and he placed them in the treasuries of the LORD's temple.

### The Ark Brought to the Temple

**8** Then King Solomon summoned into his presence at Jerusalem the elders of Israel, all the heads of the tribes and the chiefs of the Israelite families, to bring up the ark of the LORD's covenant from Zion, the City of David. <sup>2</sup>All the Israelites came together to King Solomon at the time of the festival in the month of Ethanim, the seventh month.

<sup>3</sup>When all the elders of Israel had arrived, the priests took up the ark, <sup>4</sup>and they brought up the ark of the LORD and the tent of meeting and all the sacred furnishings in it. The priests and Levites carried them up, <sup>5</sup>and King Solomon and the entire assembly of Israel that had gathered about him were before the ark, sacrificing so many sheep and cattle that they could not be recorded or counted.

<sup>6</sup>The priests then brought the ark of the LORD's covenant to its place in the inner sanctuary of the temple, the Most Holy Place, and put it beneath the wings of the cherubim. <sup>7</sup>The cherubim spread their wings over the place of the ark and overshadowed the ark and its carrying poles. <sup>8</sup>These poles were so long that their ends could be seen from the Holy Place in front of the inner sanctuary, but not from outside the Holy Place; and they are still there today. <sup>9</sup>There was nothing in the ark except the two stone tablets that Moses had placed in it at Horeb, where the LORD made a covenant with the Israelites after they came out of Egypt.

<sup>10</sup>When the priests withdrew from the Holy Place, the cloud filled the temple of the LORD. <sup>11</sup>And the priests could not perform their service because of the cloud, for the glory of the LORD filled his temple.

<sup>12</sup>Then Solomon said, "The LORD has said that he would dwell in a dark cloud; <sup>13</sup>I have indeed built a magnificent temple for you, a place for you to dwell forever."

<sup>14</sup>While the whole assembly of Israel was standing there, the king turned around and blessed them. <sup>15</sup>Then he said:

"Praise be to the LORD, the God of Israel, who with his own hand has fulfilled what he promised with his own mouth to my father David. For he said, <sup>16</sup>'Since the day I brought my people Israel out of Egypt, I

## Amplified Bible

<sup>48</sup>Solomon made all the other vessels of the Lord's house: the [incense] altar of gold; the table of gold for the showbread;

<sup>49</sup>The lampstands of pure gold, five on the right side and five on the left, in front of the Holy of Holies; with the flowers, the lamps, and the tongs of gold;

<sup>50</sup>The cups, snuffers, basins, spoons, firepans—of pure gold; and the hinges of gold for the doors of the innermost room, the Holy of Holies, and for the doors of the Holy Place.

<sup>51</sup>So all the work that King Solomon did on the house of the Lord was completed. Solomon brought in the things which David his father had dedicated—the silver, the gold, and the vessels—and put them in the treasuries of the Lord's house.

**8** Then Solomon assembled the elders of Israel and all the heads of the tribes, the chiefs of the fathers' houses of the Israelites, before the king in Jerusalem, to bring up the ark of the covenant of the Lord out of Zion, the City of David.

<sup>2</sup>All the men of Israel assembled themselves before King Solomon at the feast in the seventh month, Ethanim.

<sup>3</sup>All the elders of Israel came, and the priests took up the ark.

<sup>4</sup>And they brought up the ark of the Lord, the Tent of Meeting, and all the holy vessels that were in the tent; the priests and the Levites brought them up.

<sup>5</sup>King Solomon and all the congregation of Israel who had assembled before him were with him before the ark, sacrificing sheep and oxen, so many that they could not be reported or counted.

<sup>6</sup>And the priests brought the ark of the covenant of the Lord to its place in the Holy of Holies of the house, under the wings of the cherubim.

<sup>7</sup>For the cherubim spread forth their two wings over the place of the ark, and the cherubim covered the ark and its poles.

<sup>8</sup>The poles were so long that the ends of them were seen from the Holy Place before the Holy of Holies, but they were not seen outside; they are there to this day.

<sup>9</sup>There was nothing in the ark except the two tables of stone which Moses put there at Horeb, where the Lord made a covenant with the Israelites when they came out of the land of Egypt. [Deut. 10:2-5.]

<sup>10</sup>When the priests had come out of the Holy Place, the cloud filled the Lord's house,

<sup>11</sup>So the priests could not stand to minister because of the cloud, for the glory of the Lord had filled the Lord's house.

<sup>12</sup>Then Solomon said, The Lord said that He would dwell in the thick darkness.

<sup>13</sup>I have surely built You a house of habitation, a settled place for You to dwell in forever.

<sup>14</sup>And the king turned his face about and blessed all the assembly of Israel, and all the assembly of Israel stood.

<sup>15</sup>He said, Blessed be the Lord, the God of Israel, Who spoke with His mouth to David my father and has with His hand fulfilled it, saying,

<sup>16</sup>Since the day that I brought forth My people Israel

## New International Version

have not chosen a city in any tribe of Israel to have a temple built so that my Name might be there, but I have chosen David to rule my people Israel.'

[17]"My father David had it in his heart to build a temple for the Name of the LORD, the God of Israel. [18]But the LORD said to my father David, 'You did well to have it in your heart to build a temple for my Name. [19]Nevertheless, you are not the one to build the temple, but your son, your own flesh and blood—he is the one who will build the temple for my Name.'

[20]"The LORD has kept the promise he made: I have succeeded David my father and now I sit on the throne of Israel, just as the LORD promised, and I have built the temple for the Name of the LORD, the God of Israel. [21]I have provided a place there for the ark, in which is the covenant of the LORD that he made with our ancestors when he brought them out of Egypt."

### Solomon's Prayer of Dedication

[22]Then Solomon stood before the altar of the LORD in front of the whole assembly of Israel, spread out his hands toward heaven [23]and said:

"LORD, the God of Israel, there is no God like you in heaven above or on earth below—you who keep your covenant of love with your servants who continue wholeheartedly in your way. [24]You have kept your promise to your servant David my father; with your mouth you have promised and with your hand you have fulfilled it—as it is today. [25]"Now LORD, the God of Israel, keep for your servant David my father the promises you made to him when you said, 'You shall never fail to have a successor to sit before me on the throne of Israel, if only your descendants are careful in all they do to walk before me faithfully as you have done.' [26]And now, God of Israel, let your word that you promised your servant David my father come true.

[27]"But will God really dwell on earth? The heavens, even the highest heaven, cannot contain you. How much less this temple I have built! [28]Yet give attention to your servant's prayer and his plea for mercy, LORD my God. Hear the cry and the prayer that your servant is praying in your presence this day. [29]May your eyes be open toward this temple night and day, this place of which you said, 'My Name shall be there,' so that you will hear the prayer your servant prays toward this place. [30]Hear the supplication of your servant and of your people Israel when they pray toward this place. Hear from heaven, your dwelling place, and when you hear, forgive.

[31]"When anyone wrongs their neighbor and is required to take an oath and they come and swear the oath before your altar in this temple, [32]then hear from heaven and act. Judge between your servants, condemning the guilty by bringing down on their heads what they have done, and vindicating the innocent by treating them in accordance with their innocence.

[33]"When your people Israel have been defeated by an enemy because they have sinned against you, and when they turn back to you and give praise to your name, praying and making supplication to you in this

## Amplified Bible

out of Egypt, I chose no city out of all the tribes of Israel in which to build a house that My Name [and My Presence] might be in it, but I chose David to be over My people Israel.

[17]Now it was in the heart of David my father to build a house for the Name [the Presence] of the Lord, the God of Israel.

[18]And the Lord said to David my father, Whereas it was in your heart to build a house for My Name, you did well that it was in your heart.

[19]Yet you shall not build the house, but your son, who shall be born to you, shall build it to My Name [and My actively present Person].

[20]And the Lord has fulfilled His promise which He made: I have risen up in the place of David my father, and sit on the throne of Israel, as the Lord promised, and have built a house for the Name (renown) of the Lord, the God of Israel.

[21]And I have made there a place for the ark [the token of [a] His presence], in which is the covenant [the Ten Commandments] of the Lord which He made with our fathers when He brought them out of the land of Egypt. [Exod. 34:28.]

[22]Then Solomon stood [in the court] before the Lord's burnt offering altar in the presence of all the assembly of Israel, and spread forth his hands toward heaven

[23]And he said, O Lord, the God of Israel, there is no God like You in heaven above or on earth beneath, keeping covenant and showing mercy and loving-kindness to Your servants who walk before You with all their heart.

[24]You have kept what You promised Your servant David my father. You also spoke with Your mouth and have fulfilled it with Your hand, as it is this day.

[25]Therefore now, O Lord, the God of Israel, keep with Your servant David my father what You promised him when You said, There shall not fail you a man before Me to sit on the throne of Israel, if only your children take heed to their way, that they walk before Me as you have done.

[26]Now, O God of Israel, let Your word which You spoke to Your servant David my father be confirmed [by experience].

[27]But will God indeed dwell with men on the earth? Behold, the heavens and heaven of heavens [in its most extended compass] cannot contain You; how much less this house that I have built?

[28]Yet graciously consider the prayer and supplication of Your servant, O Lord my God, to hearken to the [loud] cry and prayer which he prays before You today,

[29]That Your eyes may be open toward this house night and day, toward the place of which You have said, My Name [and the token of My presence] shall be there, that You may hearken to the prayer which Your servant shall make in [or facing toward] this place.

[30]Hearken to the prayer of Your servant and of Your people Israel when they pray in or toward this place. Hear in heaven, Your dwelling place, and when You hear, forgive.

[31]Whenever a man sins against his neighbor and is made to take an oath and comes and swears the oath before Your altar in this house,

[32]Then hear in heaven and do and judge Your servants, condemning the wicked by bringing his guilt upon his own head and justifying the [uncompromisingly] righteous by rewarding him according to his righteousness (his uprightness, right standing with God).

[33]When Your people Israel are struck down before the enemy because they have sinned against You, and they turn again to You, confess Your [b]name (Your revelation of Yourself), and pray, beseeching You in this house,

---

[a] God acknowledged the ark as a token of His presence (Matthew Henry, *Commentary on the Holy Bible*). The ark of the covenant is the pledge of the divine gracious presence, and the cloud that filled the house (I Kings 8:10) is the sign that Yahweh will dwell here (J. P. Lange, *A Commentary*). [b] See footnote on Exod. 3:15.

## New International Version

temple, 34then hear from heaven and forgive the sin of your people Israel and bring them back to the land you gave to their ancestors.

35"When the heavens are shut up and there is no rain because your people have sinned against you, and when they pray toward this place and give praise to your name and turn from their sin because you have afflicted them, 36then hear from heaven and forgive the sin of your servants, your people Israel. Teach them the right way to live, and send rain on the land you gave your people for an inheritance.

37"When famine or plague comes to the land, or blight or mildew, locusts or grasshoppers, or when an enemy besieges them in any of their cities, whatever disaster or disease may come, 38and when a prayer or plea is made by anyone among your people Israel—being aware of the afflictions of their own hearts, and spreading out their hands toward this temple—39then hear from heaven, your dwelling place. Forgive and act; deal with everyone according to all they do, since you know their hearts (for you alone know every human heart), 40so that they will fear you all the time they live in the land you gave our ancestors.

41"As for the foreigner who does not belong to your people Israel but has come from a distant land because of your name— 42for they will hear of your great name and your mighty hand and your outstretched arm—when they come and pray toward this temple, 43then hear from heaven, your dwelling place. Do whatever the foreigner asks of you, so that all the peoples of the earth may know your name and fear you, as do your own people Israel, and may know that this house I have built bears your Name.

44"When your people go to war against their enemies, wherever you send them, and when they pray to the LORD toward the city you have chosen and the temple I have built for your Name, 45then hear from heaven their prayer and their plea, and uphold their cause.

46"When they sin against you—for there is no one who does not sin—and you become angry with them and give them over to their enemies, who take them captive to their own lands, far away or near; 47and if they have a change of heart in the land where they are held captive, and repent and plead with you in the land of their captors and say, 'We have sinned, we have done wrong, we have acted wickedly'; 48and if they turn back to you with all their heart and soul in the land of their enemies who took them captive, and pray to you toward the land you gave their ancestors, toward the city you have chosen and the temple I have built for your Name; 49then from heaven, your dwelling place, hear their prayer and their plea, and uphold their cause. 50And forgive your people, who have sinned against you; forgive all the offenses they have committed against you, and cause their captors to show them mercy; 51for they are your people and your inheritance, whom you brought out of Egypt, out of that iron-smelting furnace.

52"May your eyes be open to your servant's plea and to the plea of your people Israel, and may you listen to them whenever they cry out to you. 53For

## Amplified Bible

34Then hear in heaven and forgive the sin of Your people Israel and return them to the land You gave to their fathers.

35When heaven is shut up and no rain falls because they have sinned against You, if they pray in [or toward] this place and confess Your name (Your revelation of Yourself) and turn from their sin when You afflict them,

36Then hear in heaven and forgive the sin of Your servants, Your people Israel, when You teach them the good way in which they should walk. And give rain upon Your land which You have given to Your people as an inheritance.

37If there is famine in the land or pestilence, blight, mildew, locust, or caterpillar, if their enemy besieges them in the land of their cities, whatever plague, whatever sickness there is,

38Whatever prayer or supplication is made by any or all of Your people Israel—each man knowing the affliction of his own heart, and spreading forth his hands toward this house [and its pledge of Your presence]—

39Then hear in heaven, Your dwelling place, and forgive and act and give to every man according to his ways, whose heart You know, for You and You only know the hearts of all the children of men,

40That they may fear and revere You all the days that they live in the land which You gave to our fathers.

41Moreover, concerning a stranger who is not of Your people Israel but comes from a far country for the sake of Your name [and Your active Presence]—

42For they will hear of Your great name (Your revelation of Yourself), Your strong hand, and outstretched arm—when he shall pray in [or toward] this house,

43Hear in heaven, Your dwelling place, and do according to all that the stranger asks of You, so that all peoples of the earth may know Your name [and [a] Your revelation of Your presence] and fear and revere You, as do Your people Israel, and may know and comprehend that this house which I have built is called by Your Name [and contains the token of Your presence].

44If Your people go out to battle against their enemy, wherever You shall send them, and shall pray to the Lord toward the city which You have chosen and the house that I have built for Your Name [and Your revelation of Yourself],

45Then hear in heaven their prayer and supplication, and defend their cause and maintain their right.

46If they sin against You—for there is no man who does not sin—and You are angry with them and deliver them to the enemy, so that they are carried away captive to the enemy's land, far or near;

47Yet if they think and consider in the land where they were carried captive, and repent and make supplication to You there, saying, We have sinned and have done perversely and wickedly;

48If they repent and turn to You with all their mind and with all their heart in the land of their enemies who took them captive, and pray to You toward their land which You gave to their fathers, the city which You have chosen, and the house which I have built for Your Name;

49Then hear their prayer and their supplication in heaven, Your dwelling place, and defend their cause and maintain their right.

50And forgive Your people, who have sinned against You, and all their transgressions against You, and grant them compassion before those who took them captive, that they may have pity and be merciful to them;

51For they are Your people and Your heritage, which You brought out of Egypt, from the midst of the iron furnace.

52Let Your eyes be open to the supplication of Your servant and of Your people Israel, to hearken to them in all for which they call to You.

[a] See footnote on Exod. 3:15.

## New International Version

you singled them out from all the nations of the world to be your own inheritance, just as you declared through your servant Moses when you, Sovereign LORD, brought our ancestors out of Egypt."

54 When Solomon had finished all these prayers and supplications to the LORD, he rose from before the altar of the LORD, where he had been kneeling with his hands spread out toward heaven. 55 He stood and blessed the whole assembly of Israel in a loud voice, saying:

56 "Praise be to the LORD, who has given rest to his people Israel just as he promised. Not one word has failed of all the good promises he gave through his servant Moses. 57 May the LORD our God be with us as he was with our ancestors; may he never leave us nor forsake us. 58 May he turn our hearts to him, to walk in obedience to him and keep the commands, decrees and laws he gave our ancestors. 59 And may these words of mine, which I have prayed before the LORD, be near to the LORD our God day and night, that he may uphold the cause of his servant and the cause of his people Israel according to each day's need, 60 so that all the peoples of the earth may know that the LORD is God and that there is no other. 61 And may your hearts be fully committed to the LORD our God, to live by his decrees and obey his commands, as at this time."

### The Dedication of the Temple

62 Then the king and all Israel with him offered sacrifices before the LORD. 63 Solomon offered a sacrifice of fellowship offerings to the LORD: twenty-two thousand cattle and a hundred and twenty thousand sheep and goats. So the king and all the Israelites dedicated the temple of the LORD.

64 On that same day the king consecrated the middle part of the courtyard in front of the temple of the LORD, and there he offered burnt offerings, grain offerings and the fat of the fellowship offerings, because the bronze altar that stood before the LORD was too small to hold the burnt offerings, the grain offerings and the fat of the fellowship offerings.

65 So Solomon observed the festival at that time, and all Israel with him—a vast assembly, people from Lebo Hamath to the Wadi of Egypt. They celebrated it before the LORD our God for seven days and seven days more, fourteen days in all. 66 On the following day he sent the people away. They blessed the king and then went home, joyful and glad in heart for all the good things the LORD had done for his servant David and his people Israel.

### The LORD Appears to Solomon

**9** When Solomon had finished building the temple of the LORD and the royal palace, and had achieved all he had desired to do, 2 the LORD appeared to him a second time, as he had appeared to him at Gibeon. 3 The LORD said to him:

"I have heard the prayer and plea you have made before me; I have consecrated this temple, which you have built, by putting my Name there forever. My eyes and my heart will always be there.

4 "As for you, if you walk before me faithfully with integrity of heart and uprightness, as David your father did, and do all I command and observe my de-

## Amplified Bible

53 For You separated them from among all the peoples of the earth to be Your heritage, as You declared through Moses Your servant when You brought our fathers out of Egypt, O Lord God.

54 When Solomon finished offering all this prayer and supplication to the Lord, he arose from before the Lord's altar, where he had knelt with hands stretched toward heaven.

55 And he stood and blessed all the assembly of Israel with a loud voice, saying,

56 Blessed be the Lord, Who has given rest to His people Israel, according to all that He promised. Not one word has failed of all His good promise which He promised through Moses His servant.

57 May the Lord our God be with us as He was with our fathers; may He not leave us or forsake us,

58 That He may incline our hearts to Him, to walk in all His ways and to keep His commandments, His statutes, and His precepts which He commanded our fathers.

59 Let these my words, with which I have made supplication before the Lord, be near to the Lord our God day and night, that He may maintain the cause *and* right of His servant and of His people Israel as each day requires,

60 That all the earth's people may know that the Lord is God and that there is no other.

61 Let your hearts therefore be blameless *and* wholly true to the Lord our God, to walk in His statutes and to keep His commandments, as today.

62 And the king and all Israel with him offered sacrifice before the Lord.

63 Solomon offered as peace offerings to the Lord: 22,000 oxen and 120,000 sheep. So the king and all the Israelites dedicated the house of the Lord.

64 On that same day the king consecrated the middle of the court that was before the Lord's house; there he offered burnt offerings, cereal offerings, and the fat of the peace offerings, because the bronze altar that was before the Lord was too small to receive [all] the offerings.

65 So at that time Solomon held the feast, and all Israel with him, a great assembly, from the entrance of Hamath to the Brook of Egypt, before the Lord our God, for seven days [for the dedication] and seven days [for the Feast of Tabernacles], fourteen days in all.

66 On the eighth day he sent the people away; they blessed the king and went to their tents with greatest joy and gratitude for all the goodness the Lord had shown to David His servant and Israel His people.

**9** When Solomon finished the building of the Lord's house and the king's house, and all he desired and was pleased to do,

2 The Lord appeared to Solomon the second time, as He had appeared to him at Gibeon.

3 The Lord told him, I have heard your prayer and supplication which you have made before Me; I have hallowed this house which you have built, and I have put My Name [and My Presence] there forever. My eyes and My heart shall be there perpetually.

4 And if you will walk before Me, as David your father walked, in integrity of heart and uprightness, doing according to all that I have commanded you, keeping My statutes and My precepts,

## New International Version

crees and laws, [5]I will establish your royal throne over Israel forever, as I promised David your father when I said, 'You shall never fail to have a successor on the throne of Israel.'

[6]"But if you[a] or your descendants turn away from me and do not observe the commands and decrees I have given you[a] and go off to serve other gods and worship them, [7]then I will cut off Israel from the land I have given them and will reject this temple I have consecrated for my Name. Israel will then become a byword and an object of ridicule among all peoples. [8]This temple will become a heap of rubble. All[b] who pass by will be appalled and will scoff and say, 'Why has the LORD done such a thing to this land and to this temple?' [9]People will answer, 'Because they have forsaken the LORD their God, who brought their ancestors out of Egypt, and have embraced other gods, worshiping and serving them—that is why the LORD brought all this disaster on them.'"

### Solomon's Other Activities

[10]At the end of twenty years, during which Solomon built these two buildings—the temple of the LORD and the royal palace— [11]King Solomon gave twenty towns in Galilee to Hiram king of Tyre, because Hiram had supplied him with all the cedar and juniper and gold he wanted. [12]But when Hiram went from Tyre to see the towns that Solomon had given him, he was not pleased with them. [13]"What kind of towns are these you have given me, my brother?" he asked. And he called them the Land of Kabul,[c] a name they have to this day. [14]Now Hiram had sent to the king 120 talents[d] of gold.

[15]Here is the account of the forced labor King Solomon conscripted to build the LORD's temple, his own palace, the terraces,[e] the wall of Jerusalem, and Hazor, Megiddo and Gezer. [16](Pharaoh king of Egypt had attacked and captured Gezer. He had set it on fire. He killed its Canaanite inhabitants and then gave it as a wedding gift to his daughter, Solomon's wife. [17]And Solomon rebuilt Gezer.) He built up Lower Beth Horon, [18]Baalath, and Tadmor[f] in the desert, within his land, [19]as well as all his store cities and the towns for his chariots and for his horses[g]—whatever he desired to build in Jerusalem, in Lebanon and throughout all the territory he ruled.

[20]There were still people left from the Amorites, Hittites, Perizzites, Hivites and Jebusites (these peoples were not Israelites). [21]Solomon conscripted the descendants of all these peoples remaining in the land—whom the Israelites could not exterminate[h]—to serve as slave labor, as it is to this day. [22]But Solomon did not make slaves of any of the Israelites; they were his fighting men, his government officials, his officers, his captains, and the commanders of his chariots and charioteers. [23]They were also the chief officials in charge of Solomon's projects—550 officials supervising those who did the work.

## Amplified Bible

[5]Then I will establish your royal throne over Israel forever, as I promised David your father, saying, There shall not fail you [to have] a man upon the throne of Israel.

[6]But if you turn away from following Me, you or your children, and will not keep My commandments and My statutes which I have set before you but go and serve other gods and worship them,

[7]Then I will cut off Israel from the land I have given them, and this house I have hallowed for My Name (renown) I will cast from My sight. And Israel shall be a proverb and a byword among all the peoples.

[8]This house shall become a heap of ruins; every passerby shall be astonished and shall hiss [with surprise] and say, Why has the Lord done thus to this land and to this house?

[9]Then they will answer, Because they forsook the Lord their God, Who brought their fathers out of the land of Egypt, and have laid hold of other gods and have worshiped and served them; therefore the Lord has brought on them all this evil.

[10]At the end of twenty years, in which Solomon had built the two houses, the Lord's house and the king's house,

[11]For which Hiram king of Tyre had furnished Solomon with as much cedar and cypress timber and gold as he desired, King Solomon gave Hiram twenty cities in the land of Galilee.

[12]And Hiram came from Tyre to see the cities which Solomon had given him, and they did not please him.

[13]He said, What are these cities worth which you have given me, my brother? So they are called the Cabul [unproductive] Land to this day.

[14]And Hiram sent to the king 120 talents of gold.

[15]This is the account of the levy [of forced labor] which King Solomon raised to build the house of the Lord, his own house, the Millo, the wall of Jerusalem, Hazor, Megiddo, and Gezer.

[16]For Pharaoh king of Egypt had gone up and taken Gezer, burned it with fire, slew the Canaanites who dwelt in the city, and had given it as dowry to his daughter, Solomon's wife.

[17]So Solomon rebuilt Gezer and Lower Beth-horon,

[18]Baalath and Tamar (Tadmor) in the wilderness, in the land of Judah,

[19]And all the store cities which Solomon had and cities for his chariots and cities for his horsemen, and whatever Solomon desired to build [a]for his pleasure in Jerusalem, in Lebanon, and in all the land of his dominion.

[20]As for all the people who were left of the Amorites, Hittites, Perizzites, Hivites, and Jebusites, who were not Israelites,

[21]Their children who were left after them in the land, whom the Israelites were not able utterly to destroy, of them Solomon made a forced levy of slaves to this day.

[22]But Solomon made no slaves of the Israelites; they were the soldiers, his officials, attendants, commanders, captains, chariot officers, and horsemen.

[23]These were the chief officers over Solomon's work, 550 who had charge of the people who did the work.

---

[a] Once on the throne Solomon became a thoroughgoing despot. All political power was taken out of the hands of the tribal sheiks . . . and placed in the hands of officers who were simply puppets of Solomon. The resources of the nation were expended not on works of public utility but on the personal aggrandizement of the monarch. In the means he took to gratify his passions he showed himself to be little better than a savage (James Orr et al., eds., *The International Standard Bible Encyclopedia*). The division of the nation at Solomon's death with all the weakness and misery that it caused [idolatry, ignoring God, captivity, exile, the loss of the ten tribes] through the coming centuries was the direct outgrowth of Solomon's unholy self-indulgence (Amos R. Wells, *Bible Miniatures*). Because of his extensive building program and his extravagant expenditures in the maintenance of his luxurious court, he resorted to forced labor and heavy taxation. Bitter opposition to his rule thus engendered the division of the united kingdom after his death (*The New Jewish Encyclopedia*).

---

[a] 6 The Hebrew is plural.     [b] 8 See some Septuagint manuscripts, Old Latin, Syriac, Arabic and Targum; Hebrew *And though this temple is now imposing, all*     [c] 13 *Kabul* sounds like the Hebrew for *good-for-nothing*.     [d] 14 That is, about 4 1/2 tons or about 4 metric tons     [e] 15 Or *the Millo*; also in verse 24     [f] 18 The Hebrew may also be read *Tamar*.     [g] 19 Or *charioteers*     [h] 21 The Hebrew term refers to the irrevocable giving over of things or persons to the LORD, often by totally destroying them.

## New International Version

24After Pharaoh's daughter had come up from the City of David to the palace Solomon had built for her, he constructed the terraces.

25Three times a year Solomon sacrificed burnt offerings and fellowship offerings on the altar he had built for the LORD, burning incense before the LORD along with them, and so fulfilled the temple obligations.

26King Solomon also built ships at Ezion Geber, which is near Elath in Edom, on the shore of the Red Sea.[a] 27And Hiram sent his men—sailors who knew the sea—to serve in the fleet with Solomon's men. 28They sailed to Ophir and brought back 420 talents[b] of gold, which they delivered to King Solomon.

### The Queen of Sheba Visits Solomon

**10** When the queen of Sheba heard about the fame of Solomon and his relationship to the LORD, she came to test Solomon with hard questions. 2Arriving at Jerusalem with a very great caravan—with camels carrying spices, large quantities of gold, and precious stones—she came to Solomon and talked with him about all that she had on her mind. 3Solomon answered all her questions; nothing was too hard for the king to explain to her. 4When the queen of Sheba saw all the wisdom of Solomon and the palace he had built, 5the food on his table, the seating of his officials, the attending servants in their robes, his cupbearers, and the burnt offerings he made at[c] the temple of the LORD, she was overwhelmed.

6She said to the king, "The report I heard in my own country about your achievements and your wisdom is true. 7But I did not believe these things until I came and saw with my own eyes. Indeed, not even half was told me; in wisdom and wealth you have far exceeded the report I heard. 8How happy your people must be! How happy your officials, who continually stand before you and hear your wisdom! 9Praise be to the LORD your God, who has delighted in you and placed you on the throne of Israel. Because of the LORD's eternal love for Israel, he has made you king to maintain justice and righteousness."

10And she gave the king 120 talents[d] of gold, large quantities of spices, and precious stones. Never again were so many spices brought in as those the queen of Sheba gave to King Solomon.

11(Hiram's ships brought gold from Ophir; and from there they brought great cargoes of almugwood[e] and precious stones. 12The king used the almugwood to make supports[f] for the temple of the LORD and for the royal palace, and to make harps and lyres for the musicians. So much almugwood has never been imported or seen since that day.)

13King Solomon gave the queen of Sheba all she desired and asked for, besides what he had given her out of his royal bounty. Then she left and returned with her retinue to her own country.

### Solomon's Splendor

14The weight of the gold that Solomon received yearly was 666 talents,[g] 15not including the revenues from merchants and traders and from all the Arabian kings and the governors of the territories.

16King Solomon made two hundred large shields of hammered gold; six hundred shekels[h] of gold went into each shield. 17He also made three hundred small shields of hammered gold, with three minas[i] of gold in each shield. The king put them in the Palace of the Forest of Lebanon.

## Amplified Bible

24But Pharaoh's daughter came up out of the City of David to her house which Solomon had built for her; then he built the Millo.

25Three times a year Solomon offered burnt offerings and peace offerings on the altar he built to the Lord, and he burned incense with them before the Lord. So he finished the house.

26And King Solomon made a fleet of ships in Eziongeber, which is beside Eloth, on the shore of the Red Sea, in Edom.

27And Hiram sent with the fleet his servants, shipmen who had knowledge of the sea, with the servants of Solomon.

28They came to Ophir and got 420 talents of gold and brought it to King Solomon.

**10** When the queen of Sheba heard of [the constant connection of] the fame of Solomon with the name of the Lord, she came to prove him with hard questions (problems and riddles).

2She came to Jerusalem with a very great train, with camels bearing spices, very much gold, and precious stones. When she had come to Solomon, she communed with him about all that was in her mind.

3Solomon answered all her questions; there was nothing hidden from the king which he failed to explain to her.

4When the queen of Sheba had seen all Solomon's wisdom *and* skill, the house he had built,

5The food of his table, the seating of his officials, the standing at attention of his servants, their apparel, his cupbearers, his ascent by which he went up to the house of the Lord [or the burnt offerings he sacrificed], she was breathless *and* overcome.

6She said to the king, It was a true report I heard in my own land of your acts *and* sayings and wisdom.

7I did not believe it until I came and my eyes had seen. Behold, the half was not told me. You have added wisdom and goodness exceeding the fame I heard.

8Happy are your men! Happy are these your servants who stand continually before you, hearing your wisdom!

9Blessed be the Lord your God, Who delighted in you and set you on the throne of Israel! Because the Lord loved Israel forever, He made you king to execute justice and righteousness.

10And she gave the king 120 talents of gold and of spices a very great store and precious stones. Never again came such abundance of spices as these the queen of Sheba gave King Solomon.

11The navy also of Hiram brought from Ophir gold and a great plenty of almug (algum) wood and precious stones.

12Of the almug wood the king made pillars for the house of the Lord and for the king's house, and lyres also and harps for the singers. No such almug wood came again or has been seen to this day.

13King Solomon gave to the queen of Sheba all she wanted, whatever she asked, besides his gifts to her from his royal bounty. So she returned to her own country, she and her servants.

14Now the weight of gold that came to Solomon in one [particular] year was 666 talents of gold,

15Besides what the traders brought and the traffic of the merchants and from all the [tributary] kings and governors of the land of Arabia.

16King Solomon made 200 large shields of beaten gold; 600 shekels of gold went into each shield.

17And he made 300 shields of beaten gold; three minas of gold went into each shield. The king put them in the House of the Forest of Lebanon.

---

*a 26* Or *the Sea of Reeds*    *b 28* That is, about 16 tons or about 14 metric tons    *c 5* Or *the ascent by which he went up to*    *d 10* That is, about 4 1/2 tons or about 4 metric tons    *e 11* Probably a variant of *algumwood*; also in verse 12    *f 12* The meaning of the Hebrew for this word is uncertain.    *g 14* That is, about 25 tons or about 23 metric tons    *h 16* That is, about 15 pounds or about 6.9 kilograms; also in verse 29    *i 17* That is, about 3 3/4 pounds or about 1.7 kilograms; or perhaps reference is to double minas, that is, about 7 1/2 pounds or about 3.5 kilograms.

## New International Version

18Then the king made a great throne covered with ivory and overlaid with fine gold. 19The throne had six steps, and its back had a rounded top. On both sides of the seat were armrests, with a lion standing beside each of them. 20Twelve lions stood on the six steps, one at either end of each step. Nothing like it had ever been made for any other kingdom. 21All King Solomon's goblets were gold, and all the household articles in the Palace of the Forest of Lebanon were pure gold. Nothing was made of silver, because silver was considered of little value in Solomon's days. 22The king had a fleet of trading ships[a] at sea along with the ships of Hiram. Once every three years it returned, carrying gold, silver and ivory, and apes and baboons.

23King Solomon was greater in riches and wisdom than all the other kings of the earth. 24The whole world sought audience with Solomon to hear the wisdom God had put in his heart. 25Year after year, everyone who came brought a gift—articles of silver and gold, robes, weapons and spices, and horses and mules.

26Solomon accumulated chariots and horses; he had fourteen hundred chariots and twelve thousand horses,[b] which he kept in the chariot cities and also with him in Jerusalem. 27The king made silver as common in Jerusalem as stones, and cedar as plentiful as sycamore-fig trees in the foothills. 28Solomon's horses were imported from Egypt and from Kue[c]—the royal merchants purchased them from Kue at the current price. 29They imported a chariot from Egypt for six hundred shekels of silver, and a horse for a hundred and fifty.[d] They also exported them to all the kings of the Hittites and of the Arameans.

### Solomon's Wives

**11** King Solomon, however, loved many foreign women besides Pharaoh's daughter—Moabites, Ammonites, Edomites, Sidonians and Hittites. 2They were from nations about which the LORD had told the Israelites, "You must not intermarry with them, because they will surely turn your hearts after their gods." Nevertheless, Solomon held fast to them in love. 3He had seven hundred wives of royal birth and three hundred concubines, and his wives led him astray. 4As Solomon grew old, his wives turned his heart after other gods, and his heart was not fully devoted to the LORD his God, as the heart of David his father had been. 5He followed Ashtoreth the goddess of the Sidonians, and Molek the detestable god of the Ammonites. 6So Solomon did evil in the eyes of the LORD; he did not follow the LORD completely, as David his father had done.

7On a hill east of Jerusalem, Solomon built a high place for Chemosh the detestable god of Moab, and for Molek the detestable god of the Ammonites. 8He did the same

## Amplified Bible

18Also the king made a great throne of ivory and overlaid it with the finest gold.

19The throne had six steps, and attached at the rear of the top of the throne was a round covering or canopy. On either side of the seat were armrests, and two lions stood beside the armrests.

20Twelve lions stood there, one on either end of each of the six steps; there was nothing like it ever made in any kingdom.

21All King Solomon's drinking vessels were of gold, and all vessels of the House of the Forest of Lebanon were of pure gold. None were of silver; it was accounted as nothing in the days of Solomon.

22For the king had a fleet of ships of Tarshish at sea with the fleet of Hiram. Once every three years the fleet of ships of Tarshish came bringing gold, silver, ivory, apes, and peacocks.

23So King Solomon exceeded all the kings of the earth in riches and in wisdom (skill).

24And all the earth sought the presence of Solomon to hear his wisdom which God had put in his mind.

25Every man brought tribute: vessels of silver and gold, garments, equipment, spices, horses, and mules, so much year by year.

26Solomon collected chariots and horsemen; he had 1,400 chariots and 12,000 horsemen, which he stationed in the chariot cities and with the king in Jerusalem.

27The king made silver as common in Jerusalem as stones, and cedars as plentiful as the sycamore trees in the lowlands.

28Solomon's horses were brought out of Egypt, and the king's merchants received them in droves, each at a price. [Deut. 17:15, 16.]

29A chariot could be brought out of Egypt for 600 shekels of silver, and a horse for 150. And so to all the kings of the Hittites and of Syria they were exported by the king's merchants.

**11** But King Solomon [defiantly] loved many foreign women—the [a]daughter of Pharaoh, women of the Moabites, Ammonites, Edomites, Sidonians, and Hittites.

2They were of the very nations of whom the Lord said to the Israelites, You shall not mingle with them, neither shall they mingle with you, for surely they will turn away your hearts after their gods. Yet Solomon clung to these in love. [Deut. 17:17.]

3He had 700 wives, princesses, and 300 concubines, and his wives turned away his heart from God.

4For when Solomon was old, his wives turned away his heart after other gods, and his heart was not perfect (complete and whole) with the Lord his God, as was the heart of David his father.

5For Solomon went after Ashtoreth the goddess of the Sidonians, and after Milcom the abominable idol of the Ammonites! [I Kings 9:6-9.]

6Solomon did evil in the sight of the Lord, and went not fully after the Lord, as David his father did.

7Then Solomon built a high place for Chemosh the abominable idol of Moab, on the hill opposite Jerusalem, and for Molech the abominable idol of the Ammonites.

---

[a] "Solomon brought the daughter of Pharaoh out of the City of David into the house he had built for her, for he said, My wife shall not dwell in the house of David king of Israel, because the places are holy to which the ark of the Lord has come" (II Chron. 8:11). God had given Solomon the name "Jedidiah [beloved of the Lord]" (II Sam. 12:25), yet he chose to be the beloved of heathen women instead, in defiance of God's covenant with him.

[a] 22 Hebrew of ships of Tarshish    [b] 26 Or charioteers    [c] 28 Probably Cilicia    [d] 29 That is, about 3 3/4 pounds or about 1.7 kilograms

## New International Version

for all his foreign wives, who burned incense and offered sacrifices to their gods.

⁹The LORD became angry with Solomon because his heart had turned away from the LORD, the God of Israel, who had appeared to him twice. ¹⁰Although he had forbidden Solomon to follow other gods, Solomon did not keep the LORD's command. ¹¹So the LORD said to Solomon, "Since this is your attitude and you have not kept my covenant and my decrees, which I commanded you, I will most certainly tear the kingdom away from you and give it to one of your subordinates. ¹²Nevertheless, for the sake of David your father, I will not do it during your lifetime. I will tear it out of the hand of your son. ¹³Yet I will not tear the whole kingdom from him, but will give him one tribe for the sake of David my servant and for the sake of Jerusalem, which I have chosen."

### Solomon's Adversaries

¹⁴Then the LORD raised up against Solomon an adversary, Hadad the Edomite, from the royal line of Edom. ¹⁵Earlier when David was fighting with Edom, Joab the commander of the army, who had gone up to bury the dead, had struck down all the men in Edom. ¹⁶Joab and all the Israelites stayed there for six months, until they had destroyed all the men in Edom. ¹⁷But Hadad, still only a boy, fled to Egypt with some Edomite officials who had served his father. ¹⁸They set out from Midian and went to Paran. Then taking people from Paran with them, they went to Egypt, to Pharaoh king of Egypt, who gave Hadad a house and land and provided him with food.

¹⁹Pharaoh was so pleased with Hadad that he gave him a sister of his own wife, Queen Tahpenes, in marriage. ²⁰The sister of Tahpenes bore him a son named Genubath, whom Tahpenes brought up in the royal palace. There Genubath lived with Pharaoh's own children.

²¹While he was in Egypt, Hadad heard that David rested with his ancestors and that Joab the commander of the army was also dead. Then Hadad said to Pharaoh, "Let me go, that I may return to my own country."

²²"What have you lacked here that you want to go back to your own country?" Pharaoh asked.

"Nothing," Hadad replied, "but do let me go!"

²³And God raised up against Solomon another adversary, Rezon son of Eliada, who had fled from his master, Hadadezer king of Zobah. ²⁴When David destroyed Zobah's army, Rezon gathered a band of men around him and became their leader; they went to Damascus, where they settled and took control. ²⁵Rezon was Israel's adversary as long as Solomon lived, adding to the trouble caused by Hadad. So Rezon ruled in Aram and was hostile toward Israel.

### Jeroboam Rebels Against Solomon

²⁶Also, Jeroboam son of Nebat rebelled against the king. He was one of Solomon's officials, an Ephraimite from Zeredah, and his mother was a widow named Zeruah.

²⁷Here is the account of how he rebelled against the king: Solomon had built the terraces[a] and had filled in the gap in the wall of the city of David his father. ²⁸Now Jeroboam was a man of standing, and when Solomon saw how well the young man did his work, he put him in charge of the whole labor force of the tribes of Joseph.

## Amplified Bible

⁸And he did so [a] for all of his foreign wives, who burned incense and sacrificed to their gods.

⁹And the Lord was angry with Solomon because his heart was turned from the Lord, the God of Israel, Who had appeared to him twice,

¹⁰And had commanded him concerning this thing, that he should not go after other gods, but he did not do what the Lord commanded.

¹¹Therefore the Lord said to Solomon, Because you are doing this and have not kept My covenant and My statutes, which I have commanded you, I will surely rend the kingdom from you and will give it to your servant!

¹²However, in your days I will not do it, for David your father's sake. But I will rend it out of the hand of your son!

¹³However, I will not tear away all the kingdom, but will give one tribe to your son for David My servant's sake and for the sake of Jerusalem, which I have chosen.

¹⁴The Lord stirred up an adversary against Solomon, Hadad the Edomite; he was of royal descent in Edom.

¹⁵For when David was in Edom, and Joab the commander of Israel's army went up to bury the slain, he slew every male in Edom.

¹⁶For Joab and all Israel remained there for six months, until he had cut off every male in Edom.

¹⁷But Hadad fled, he and certain Edomites of his father's servants, to Egypt, Hadad being yet a little child.

¹⁸They set out from Midian and came to Paran, and took men with them out of Paran and came to Egypt, to Pharaoh king of Egypt, who gave [young] Hadad a house and land and ordered provisions for him.

¹⁹Hadad found great favor with Pharaoh, so that he gave him in marriage the sister of his own wife Tahpenes the queen.

²⁰The sister of Tahpenes bore Hadad Genubath his son, whom Tahpenes weaned in Pharaoh's house; and Genubath was in Pharaoh's household among the sons of Pharaoh.

²¹But when Hadad heard in Egypt that David slept with his fathers and that Joab the commander of Israel's army was dead, Hadad said to Pharaoh, Let me depart, that I may go to my own country.

²²Then Pharaoh said to him, But what have you lacked with me that now you want to go to your own country? He replied, Nothing. However, let me go anyhow.

²³God raised up for [Hadad] another adversary, Rezon son of Eliada, who had fled from his master, Hadadezer king of Zobah.

²⁴Rezon gathered men about him and became leader of a marauding band after the slaughter by David. They went to Damascus and dwelt and made [Rezon] king in Damascus.

²⁵And Rezon was an adversary to Israel all the days of Solomon, besides the mischief that Hadad did. Rezon abhorred Israel and reigned over Syria.

²⁶Jeroboam son of Nebat, an Ephrathite of Zereda, Solomon's servant, whose mother's name was Zeruah, a widow woman, rebelled against the king—

²⁷And for this reason: Solomon built the Millo and repaired the breaches of the city of David his father.

²⁸The man Jeroboam was a mighty man of courage. Solomon, seeing that the young man was industrious, put him in charge over all the [forced] labor of the house of Joseph.

---

[a] What all this did to Solomon's sweet fellowship with God is to be seen in Ecclesiastes. Take the sun out of the sky, and all earth's beauty and fruitfulness will go also. Take God out of your sky, and life's joys will be turned to dregs, bitterness, and futility. Solomon had deliberately chosen to live "under the sun" instead of under God. In the awareness of his own unquestionable greatness, he had become indifferent to the fact that "here is more than Solomon" (Luke 11:31) and to scorn or ignore God is fatal. With all his wisdom he failed to recognize that "God will not allow Himself to be sneered at (scorned, disdained, or mocked by mere pretensions or professions or by His precepts being set aside) . . . For whatever a man sows, that *and* that only is what he will reap" (Gal. 6:7).

## New International Version

²⁹About that time Jeroboam was going out of Jerusalem, and Ahijah the prophet of Shiloh met him on the way, wearing a new cloak. The two of them were alone out in the country, ³⁰and Ahijah took hold of the new cloak he was wearing and tore it into twelve pieces. ³¹Then he said to Jeroboam, "Take ten pieces for yourself, for this is what the Lord, the God of Israel, says: 'See, I am going to tear the kingdom out of Solomon's hand and give you ten tribes. ³²But for the sake of my servant David and the city of Jerusalem, which I have chosen out of all the tribes of Israel, he will have one tribe. ³³I will do this because they have*ᵃ* forsaken me and worshiped Ashtoreth the goddess of the Sidonians, Chemosh the god of the Moabites, and Molek the god of the Ammonites, and have not walked in obedience to me, nor done what is right in my eyes, nor kept my decrees and laws as David, Solomon's father, did. ³⁴"'But I will not take the whole kingdom out of Solomon's hand; I have made him ruler all the days of his life for the sake of David my servant, whom I chose and who obeyed my commands and decrees. ³⁵I will take the kingdom from his son's hands and give you ten tribes. ³⁶I will give one tribe to his son so that David my servant may always have a lamp before me in Jerusalem, the city where I chose to put my Name. ³⁷However, as for you, I will take you, and you will rule over all that your heart desires; you will be king over Israel. ³⁸If you do whatever I command you and walk in obedience to me and do what is right in my eyes by obeying my decrees and commands, as David my servant did, I will be with you. I will build you a dynasty as enduring as the one I built for David and will give Israel to you. ³⁹I will humble David's descendants because of this, but not forever.'"

⁴⁰Solomon tried to kill Jeroboam, but Jeroboam fled to Egypt, to Shishak the king, and stayed there until Solomon's death.

### Solomon's Death

⁴¹As for the other events of Solomon's reign—all he did and the wisdom he displayed—are they not written in the book of the annals of Solomon? ⁴²Solomon reigned in Jerusalem over all Israel forty years. ⁴³Then he rested with his ancestors and was buried in the city of David his father. And Rehoboam his son succeeded him as king.

### Israel Rebels Against Rehoboam

**12** Rehoboam went to Shechem, for all Israel had gone there to make him king. ²When Jeroboam son of Nebat heard this (he was still in Egypt, where he had fled from King Solomon), he returned from*ᵇ* Egypt. ³So they sent for Jeroboam, and he and the whole assembly of Israel went to Rehoboam and said to him: ⁴"Your father put a heavy yoke on us, but now lighten the harsh labor and the heavy yoke he put on us, and we will serve you."

⁵Rehoboam answered, "Go away for three days and then come back to me." So the people went away.

⁶Then King Rehoboam consulted the elders who had served his father Solomon during his lifetime. "How would you advise me to answer these people?" he asked.

⁷They replied, "If today you will be a servant to these

## Amplified Bible

²⁹At that time, when Jeroboam went out of Jerusalem, the prophet Ahijah the Shilonite met him on the way. Ahijah had clad himself with a new garment; and they were alone in the field.

³⁰Ahijah caught the new garment he wore and tore it into twelve pieces.

³¹He said to Jeroboam, You take ten pieces, for thus says the Lord, the God of Israel, Behold, I will tear the kingdom from the hand of Solomon and will give you ten tribes.

³²But he shall have one tribe, for My servant David's sake and for Jerusalem's sake, the city which I have chosen out of all the tribes of Israel,

³³Because they have forsaken Me and have worshiped Ashtoreth the goddess of the Sidonians, Chemosh the god of the Moabites, and Milcom the god of the Ammonites, and have not walked in My ways, to do what is right in My sight, keeping My statutes and My ordinances as did David his father.

³⁴However, I will not take the whole kingdom out of his hand; but I will make him ruler all the days of his life for David My servant's sake, whom I chose because he kept My commandments and My statutes.

³⁵But I will take the kingdom out of his son's hand and give it to you, ten tribes.

³⁶Yet to his son I will give one tribe, that David My servant may always have a light before Me in Jerusalem, the city where I have chosen to put My Name.

³⁷And I will take you, and you shall reign according to all that your soul desires; and you shall be king over Israel.

³⁸And if you will hearken to all I command you and will walk in My ways and do right in My sight, keeping My statutes and My commandments, as David My servant did, I will be with you and build you a sure house, as I built for David, and will give Israel to you.

³⁹And I will for this afflict the descendants of David, but not forever.

⁴⁰Solomon sought therefore to kill Jeroboam. But Jeroboam arose and fled into Egypt, to Shishak king of Egypt, and was in Egypt until Solomon died.

⁴¹The rest of the acts of Solomon—and all that he did, and his wisdom (skill)—are they not written in the book of the acts of Solomon?

⁴²The time Solomon reigned in Jerusalem over all Israel was forty years.

⁴³And Solomon slept with his fathers and was buried in the city of David his father. Rehoboam his son reigned in his stead.

**12** Rehoboam went to Shechem, for all Israel had come to Shechem to make him king.

²And when Jeroboam son of Nebat heard of it—for he still dwelt in Egypt, where he had fled from King Solomon—[he] returned from Egypt.

³And they sent and called him, and Jeroboam and all the assembly of Israel came and said to Rehoboam,

⁴Your father made our yoke heavy; now therefore lighten the hard service and the heavy yoke your father put upon us, and we will serve you.

⁵He replied, Go away for three days and then return to me. So the people departed.

⁶And King Rehoboam consulted with the old men who stood before Solomon his father while he yet lived and said, How do you advise me to answer this people?

⁷And they said to him, If you will be a servant to this

---

*ᵃ 33 Hebrew; Septuagint, Vulgate and Syriac because he has    ᵇ 2 Or he remained in*

## New International Version

people and serve them and give them a favorable answer, they will always be your servants."

8 But Rehoboam rejected the advice the elders gave him and consulted the young men who had grown up with him and were serving him. 9 He asked them, "What is your advice? How should we answer these people who say to me, 'Lighten the yoke your father put on us'?"

10 The young men who had grown up with him replied, "These people have said to you, 'Your father put a heavy yoke on us, but make our yoke lighter.' Now tell them, 'My little finger is thicker than my father's waist. 11 My father laid on you a heavy yoke; I will make it even heavier. My father scourged you with whips; I will scourge you with scorpions.'"

12 Three days later Jeroboam and all the people returned to Rehoboam, as the king had said, "Come back to me in three days." 13 The king answered the people harshly. Rejecting the advice given him by the elders, 14 he followed the advice of the young men and said, "My father made your yoke heavy; I will make it even heavier. My father scourged you with whips; I will scourge you with scorpions." 15 So the king did not listen to the people, for this turn of events was from the LORD, to fulfill the word the LORD had spoken to Jeroboam son of Nebat through Ahijah the Shilonite.

16 When all Israel saw that the king refused to listen to them, they answered the king:

"What share do we have in David,
    what part in Jesse's son?
To your tents, Israel!
    Look after your own house, David!"

So the Israelites went home. 17 But as for the Israelites who were living in the towns of Judah, Rehoboam still ruled over them.

18 King Rehoboam sent out Adoniram,[a] who was in charge of forced labor, but all Israel stoned him to death. King Rehoboam, however, managed to get into his chariot and escape to Jerusalem. 19 So Israel has been in rebellion against the house of David to this day.

20 When all the Israelites heard that Jeroboam had returned, they sent and called him to the assembly and made him king over all Israel. Only the tribe of Judah remained loyal to the house of David.

21 When Rehoboam arrived in Jerusalem, he mustered all Judah and the tribe of Benjamin—a hundred and eighty thousand able young men—to go to war against Israel and to regain the kingdom for Rehoboam son of Solomon.

22 But this word of God came to Shemaiah the man of God: 23 "Say to Rehoboam son of Solomon king of Judah, to all Judah and Benjamin, and to the rest of the people, 24 'This is what the LORD says: Do not go up to fight against your brothers, the Israelites. Go home, every one of you, for this is my doing.'" So they obeyed the word of the LORD and went home again, as the LORD had ordered.

### Golden Calves at Bethel and Dan

25 Then Jeroboam fortified Shechem in the hill country of Ephraim and lived there. From there he went out and built up Peniel.[b]

26 Jeroboam thought to himself, "The kingdom will now likely revert to the house of David. 27 If these people go up

## Amplified Bible

people today and serve them and answer them with good words, they will be your servants forever.

8 But he forsook the counsel the old men gave him and consulted the young men who grew up with him and stood before him.

9 He said to them, What do you advise that we answer this people who have said, Make the yoke your father put on us lighter?

10 The young men who grew up with him answered, To the people who told you, Your father made our yoke heavy, but you make it lighter for us—say this, My little finger shall be thicker than my father's loins.

11 And now whereas my father loaded you with a heavy yoke, I will add to your yoke. My father chastised you with whips, but I will chastise you with scorpions.

12 So Jeroboam and all the people came to Rehoboam on the third day, as the king had appointed.

13 And the king answered the people roughly and forsook the counsel the old men had given him,

14 And spoke to them after the counsel of the young men, saying, My father made your yoke heavy, but I will add to your yoke; he chastised you with whips, but I will chastise you with scorpions.

15 So the king did not hearken to the people, for the situation was from the Lord, that He might fulfill His word which He spoke by Ahijah the Shilonite to Jeroboam son of Nebat. [I Kings 11:29-33.]

16 So when all Israel saw that the king did not heed them, they answered the king, What portion have we in David? We have no inheritance in the son of Jesse. To your tents, O Israel! Look now to your own house, David! So Israel went to their tents.

17 But Rehoboam reigned over the Israelites who dwelt in the cities of Judah.

18 Then King Rehoboam sent Adoram, who was over the tribute [taskmaster over the forced labor], and all Israel stoned him to death with stones. So King Rehoboam hastened to get into his chariot to flee to Jerusalem.

19 So Israel has rebelled against the house of David to this day.

20 When all Israel heard that Jeroboam had returned, they sent and called him to the assembly and made him king over all Israel. None followed the house of David except the tribe of Judah only.

21 And when Rehoboam had come to Jerusalem, he assembled all the house of Judah, with the tribe of Benjamin, 180,000 chosen warriors, to fight against the house of Israel to bring the kingdom back to Rehoboam son of Solomon.

22 But the word of God came to Shemaiah the man of God, saying,

23 Tell Rehoboam son of Solomon king of Judah and all the house of Judah and Benjamin and the remnant of the people,

24 Thus says the Lord, You shall not go up or fight against your brethren, the Israelites. Return every man to his house, for this thing is from Me. So they hearkened to the Lord's word and returned home, according to the Lord's word.

25 Then Jeroboam built Shechem in the hill country of Ephraim and lived there. He went out from there and built Penuel.

26 Jeroboam said in his heart, Now the kingdom will return to the house of David.

---

a 18 Some Septuagint manuscripts and Syriac (see also 4:6 and 5:14); Hebrew *Adoram*   b 25 Hebrew *Penuel*, a variant of *Peniel*

## New International Version

to offer sacrifices at the temple of the LORD in Jerusalem, they will again give their allegiance to their lord, Rehoboam king of Judah. They will kill me and return to King Rehoboam."

²⁸After seeking advice, the king made two golden calves. He said to the people, "It is too much for you to go up to Jerusalem. Here are your gods, Israel, who brought you up out of Egypt." ²⁹One he set up in Bethel, and the other in Dan. ³⁰And this thing became a sin; the people came to worship the one at Bethel and went as far as Dan to worship the other.ᵃ

³¹Jeroboam built shrines on high places and appointed priests from all sorts of people, even though they were not Levites. ³²He instituted a festival on the fifteenth day of the eighth month, like the festival held in Judah, and offered sacrifices on the altar. This he did in Bethel, sacrificing to the calves he had made. And at Bethel he also installed priests at the high places he had made. ³³On the fifteenth day of the eighth month, a month of his own choosing, he offered sacrifices on the altar he had built at Bethel. So he instituted the festival for the Israelites and went up to the altar to make offerings.

### The Man of God From Judah

**13** By the word of the LORD a man of God came from Judah to Bethel, as Jeroboam was standing by the altar to make an offering. ²By the word of the LORD he cried out against the altar: "Altar, altar! This is what the LORD says: 'A son named Josiah will be born to the house of David. On you he will sacrifice the priests of the high places who make offerings here, and human bones will be burned on you.'" ³That same day the man of God gave a sign: "This is the sign the LORD has declared: The altar will be split apart and the ashes on it will be poured out."

⁴When King Jeroboam heard what the man of God cried out against the altar at Bethel, he stretched out his hand from the altar and said, "Seize him!" But the hand he stretched out toward the man shriveled up, so that he could not pull it back. ⁵Also, the altar was split apart and its ashes poured out according to the sign given by the man of God by the word of the LORD.

⁶Then the king said to the man of God, "Intercede with the LORD your God and pray for me that my hand may be restored." So the man of God interceded with the LORD, and the king's hand was restored and became as it was before.

⁷The king said to the man of God, "Come home with me for a meal, and I will give you a gift."

⁸But the man of God answered the king, "Even if you were to give me half your possessions, I would not go with you, nor would I eat bread or drink water here. ⁹For I was commanded by the word of the LORD: 'You must not eat bread or drink water or return by the way you came.'" ¹⁰So he took another road and did not return by the way he had come to Bethel.

¹¹Now there was a certain old prophet living in Bethel, whose sons came and told him all that the man of God had done there that day. They also told their father what he had said to the king. ¹²Their father asked them, "Which

## Amplified Bible

²⁷If this people goes up to the house of the Lord at Jerusalem to sacrifice, then the heart of this people will turn again to their lord, to Rehoboam king of Judah; and they will kill me and go back to Rehoboam king of Judah.

²⁸So the king took counsel and made two calves of gold. And he said to the people, It is too much for you to go [all the way] up to Jerusalem. Behold your gods, O Israel, who brought you up out of the land of Egypt.

²⁹And he set the one golden calf in Bethel, and the other he put in Dan.

³⁰And this thing became a sin; for the people went to worship each of them even as far as Dan.

³¹Jeroboam also made houses on high places and made priests of people who were not Levites.

³²And Jeroboam appointed a feast on the fifteenth day of the eighth month, like the feast kept in Judah, and he offered sacrifices upon the altar. So he did in Bethel, sacrificing to the calves he had made. And he placed in Bethel the priests of the high places he had made.

³³So he offered upon the altar he had made in Bethel on the fifteenth day of the eighth month, a date which he chose individually; and he appointed a feast for the Israelites and he went up to the altar to burn incense [in defiance of God's law.]

**13** And behold, there came a man of God out of Judah by the word of the Lord to Bethel. Jeroboam stood by the altar to burn incense.

²The man cried against the altar by the word of the Lord, O altar, altar, thus says the Lord: Behold, a son shall be born to the house of David, Josiah by name; and on you shall he offer the priests of the high places who burn incense on you, and men's bones shall be burned on you.

³And he gave a sign the same day, saying, This is the sign which the Lord has spoken: Behold, the altar shall be split and the ashes that are upon it shall be poured out. [Fulfilled in II Kings 23:15, 16.]

⁴When King Jeroboam heard the words the man of God cried against the altar in Bethel, he thrust out his hand, saying, Lay hold on him! And his hand which he put forth against him dried up, so that he could not draw it to him again.

⁵The altar also was split and the ashes poured out from the altar according to the sign which the man of God had given by the word of the Lord.

⁶And the king said to the man of God, Entreat now the favor of the Lord your God and pray for me, that my hand may be restored to me. And the man of God entreated the Lord, and the king's hand was restored and became as it was before.

⁷And the king said to the man of God, Come home with me and refresh yourself, and I will give you a reward.

⁸And the man of God said to the king, If you give me half your house, I will not go in with you, and I will not eat bread or drink water in this place.

⁹For I was commanded by the word of the Lord, You shall eat no bread or drink water or return by the way you came.

¹⁰So he went another way and did not return by the way that he came to Bethel.

¹¹Now there dwelt an old prophet in Bethel; and his sons came and told him all that the man of God had done that day in Bethel; the words which he had spoken to the king they told also to their father.

¹²Their father asked them, Which way did he go? For

---

ᵃ 30 Probable reading of the original Hebrew text; Masoretic Text *people went to the one as far as Dan*

## New International Version

way did he go?" And his sons showed him which road the man of God from Judah had taken. ¹³So he said to his sons, "Saddle the donkey for me." And when they had saddled the donkey for him, he mounted it ¹⁴and rode after the man of God. He found him sitting under an oak tree and asked, "Are you the man of God who came from Judah?"

"I am," he replied.

¹⁵So the prophet said to him, "Come home with me and eat."

¹⁶The man of God said, "I cannot turn back and go with you, nor can I eat bread or drink water with you in this place. ¹⁷I have been told by the word of the Lord: 'You must not eat bread or drink water there or return by the way you came.'"

¹⁸The old prophet answered, "I too am a prophet, as you are. And an angel said to me by the word of the Lord: 'Bring him back with you to your house so that he may eat bread and drink water.'" (But he was lying to him.) ¹⁹So the man of God returned with him and ate and drank in his house.

²⁰While they were sitting at the table, the word of the Lord came to the old prophet who had brought him back. ²¹He cried out to the man of God who had come from Judah, "This is what the Lord says: 'You have defied the word of the Lord and have not kept the command the Lord your God gave you. ²²You came back and ate bread and drank water in the place where he told you not to eat or drink. Therefore your body will not be buried in the tomb of your ancestors.'"

²³When the man of God had finished eating and drinking, the prophet who had brought him back saddled his donkey for him. ²⁴As he went on his way, a lion met him on the road and killed him, and his body was left lying on the road, with both the donkey and the lion standing beside it. ²⁵Some people who passed by saw the body lying there, with the lion standing beside the body, and they went and reported it in the city where the old prophet lived.

²⁶When the prophet who had brought him back from his journey heard of it, he said, "It is the man of God who defied the word of the Lord. The Lord has given him over to the lion, which has mauled him and killed him, as the word of the Lord had warned him."

²⁷The prophet said to his sons, "Saddle the donkey for me," and they did so. ²⁸Then he went out and found the body lying on the road, with the donkey and the lion standing beside it. The lion had neither eaten the body nor mauled the donkey. ²⁹So the prophet picked up the body of the man of God, laid it on the donkey, and brought it back to his own city to mourn for him and bury him. ³⁰Then he laid the body in his own tomb, and they mourned over him and said, "Alas, my brother!"

³¹After burying him, he said to his sons, "When I die, bury me in the grave where the man of God is buried; lay my bones beside his bones. ³²For the message he declared by the word of the Lord against the altar in Bethel and against all the shrines on the high places in the towns of Samaria will certainly come true."

³³Even after this, Jeroboam did not change his evil ways, but once more appointed priests for the high places from all sorts of people. Anyone who wanted to become a priest he consecrated for the high places. ³⁴This was the sin of the house of Jeroboam that led to its downfall and to its destruction from the face of the earth.

## Amplified Bible

his sons had seen which way the man of God who came from Judah had gone. ¹³He said to his sons, Saddle the donkey for me. So they saddled the donkey and he rode on it

¹⁴And went after the man of God. And he found him sitting under an oak, and he said to him, Are you the man of God who came from Judah? And he said, I am.

¹⁵Then he said to him, Come home with me and eat bread.

¹⁶He said, I may not return with you or go in with you, neither will I eat bread or drink water with you in this place.

¹⁷For I was told by the word of the Lord, You shall not eat bread or drink water there or return by the way that you came.

¹⁸He answered, I am a prophet also, as you are. And an angel spoke to me by the word of the Lord, saying, Bring him back with you to your house, that he may eat bread and drink water. But he lied to him.

¹⁹So the man from Judah went back with him and ate and drank water in his house.

²⁰And as they sat at the table, the word of the Lord came to the prophet who brought him back.

²¹And he cried to the man of God who came from Judah, Thus says the Lord: Because you have disobeyed the word of the Lord and have not kept the command which the Lord your God commanded you,

²²But have come back and have eaten bread and drunk water in the place of which the Lord said to you, Eat no bread and drink no water—your corpse shall not come to the tomb of your fathers.

²³And after the prophet of the house had eaten bread and drunk, he saddled the donkey for the man he had brought back.

²⁴And when he had gone, a lion met him by the road and slew him, and his corpse was cast in the way, and the donkey stood by it; the lion also stood by the corpse.

²⁵And behold, men passed by and saw the corpse thrown in the road, and the lion standing by the corpse, and they came and told it in the city where the old prophet dwelt.

²⁶When the prophet who brought him back from the way heard of it, he said, It is the man of God who was disobedient to the word of the Lord; therefore the Lord has given him to the lion, which has torn him and slain him, according to the word of the Lord which He spoke to him.

²⁷And he said to his sons, Saddle the donkey for me. And they saddled it.

²⁸And he went and found the corpse thrown in the road, and the donkey and the lion stood by the body; the lion had not eaten the corpse or torn the donkey.

²⁹The prophet took up the corpse of the man of God and laid it upon the donkey and brought it back, and the old prophet came into the city to mourn and to bury him.

³⁰And he laid the body in his own grave, and they mourned over him, saying, Alas, my brother!

³¹After he had buried him, he said to his sons, When I am dead, bury me in the grave in which the man of God is buried; lay my bones beside his bones.

³²For the saying which he cried by the word of the Lord against the altar in Bethel and against all the houses of the high places which are in the cities of Samaria shall surely come to pass.

³³After this thing, Jeroboam turned not from his evil way, but made priests for the high places again from among all the people. Whoever would, he consecrated, that there might be priests for the high places.

³⁴And this thing became the sin of the dynasty of Jeroboam that caused it to be abolished and destroyed from the face of the earth.

## New International Version

### Ahijah's Prophecy Against Jeroboam

**14** At that time Abijah son of Jeroboam became ill, ²and Jeroboam said to his wife, "Go, disguise yourself, so you won't be recognized as the wife of Jeroboam. Then go to Shiloh. Ahijah the prophet is there—the one who told me I would be king over this people. ³Take ten loaves of bread with you, some cakes and a jar of honey, and go to him. He will tell you what will happen to the boy." ⁴So Jeroboam's wife did what he said and went to Ahijah's house in Shiloh.

Now Ahijah could not see; his sight was gone because of his age. ⁵But the Lᴏʀᴅ had told Ahijah, "Jeroboam's wife is coming to ask you about her son, for he is ill, and you are to give her such and such an answer. When she arrives, she will pretend to be someone else."

⁶So when Ahijah heard the sound of her footsteps at the door, he said, "Come in, wife of Jeroboam. Why this pretense? I have been sent to you with bad news. ⁷Go, tell Jeroboam that this is what the Lᴏʀᴅ, the God of Israel, says: 'I raised you up from among the people and appointed you ruler over my people Israel. ⁸I tore the kingdom away from the house of David and gave it to you, but you have not been like my servant David, who kept my commands and followed me with all his heart, doing only what was right in my eyes. ⁹You have done more evil than all who lived before you. You have made for yourself other gods, idols made of metal; you have aroused my anger and turned your back on me.

¹⁰"'Because of this, I am going to bring disaster on the house of Jeroboam. I will cut off from Jeroboam every last male in Israel—slave or free.ᵃ I will burn up the house of Jeroboam as one burns dung, until it is all gone. ¹¹Dogs will eat those belonging to Jeroboam who die in the city, and the birds will feed on those who die in the country. The Lᴏʀᴅ has spoken!'

¹²"As for you, go back home. When you set foot in your city, the boy will die. ¹³All Israel will mourn for him and bury him. He is the only one belonging to Jeroboam who will be buried, because he is the only one in the house of Jeroboam in whom the Lᴏʀᴅ, the God of Israel, has found anything good.

¹⁴"The Lᴏʀᴅ will raise up for himself a king over Israel who will cut off the family of Jeroboam. Even now this is beginning to happen.ᵇ ¹⁵And the Lᴏʀᴅ will strike Israel, so that it will be like a reed swaying in the water. He will uproot Israel from this good land that he gave to their ancestors and scatter them beyond the Euphrates River, because they aroused the Lᴏʀᴅ's anger by making Asherah poles.ᶜ ¹⁶And he will give Israel up because of the sins Jeroboam has committed and has caused Israel to commit."

¹⁷Then Jeroboam's wife got up and left and went to Tirzah. As soon as she stepped over the threshold of the

## Amplified Bible

**14** Then Abijah [the little] son of Jeroboam became sick.

²And Jeroboam said to his wife, Arise, I pray you, and disguise yourself, that you may not be recognized as Jeroboam's wife, and go to Shiloh. Behold, Ahijah the prophet is there, who told me that I should be king over this people.

³Take ten loaves, some cakes, and a bottle of honey, and go to him. He will tell you what shall happen to the child.

⁴Jeroboam's wife did so. She arose and went [twenty miles] to Shiloh and came to the house of Ahijah. Ahijah could not see, for his eyes were dim because of his age.

⁵And the Lord said to Ahijah, Behold, the ᵃwife of Jeroboam is coming to ask you concerning her son, for he is sick. Thus and thus shall you say to her. When she came, she pretended to be another woman.

⁶But when Ahijah heard the sound of her feet as she came in at the door, he said, Come in, wife of Jeroboam. Why do you pretend to be another? For I am charged with heavy news for you.

⁷Go, tell Jeroboam, Thus says the Lord, the God of Israel: Because I exalted you from among the people and made you leader over My people Israel

⁸And rent the kingdom away from the house of David and gave it to you—and yet you have not been as My servant David, who kept My commandments and followed Me with all his heart, to do only what was right in My eyes,

⁹But have done evil above all who were before you; for you have made yourself other gods, molten images, to provoke Me to anger and have cast Me behind your back—

¹⁰Therefore behold, I will bring evil upon the house of Jeroboam and will cut off from [him] every male, both bond and free, in Israel, and will utterly sweep away the house of Jeroboam as a man sweeps away dung, till it is all gone.

¹¹Anyone belonging to Jeroboam who dies in the city the dogs shall eat, and any who dies in the field the birds of the heavens shall eat. For the Lord has spoken it.

¹²Arise therefore [Ano, Jeroboam's wife], get to your own house. When your feet enter the city, the child shall die.

¹³And all Israel shall mourn for him and bury him; for he only of Jeroboam's family shall come to the grave, because in him there is found something good *and* pleasing to the Lord, the God of Israel, in the house of Jeroboam.

¹⁴Moreover, the Lord will raise up for Himself a king over Israel who shall cut off the house of Jeroboam this day. From now on

¹⁵The Lord will smite Israel, as a reed is shaken in the water; and He will root up Israel out of this good land which He gave to their fathers and will scatter them beyond the [Euphrates] River, because they have made their Asherim [idolatrous symbols of the goddess Asherah], provoking the Lord to anger.

¹⁶He will give Israel up because of the sins of Jeroboam which he has sinned and made Israel to sin.

¹⁷So Jeroboam's wife departed and came to Tirzah. When she came to the threshold of the house, the child died.

---

ᵃ The Hebrew text gives no particulars about the background of Jeroboam's wife, but there is an insertion in *The Septuagint* (Greek translation of the Old Testament), found in the Vatican manuscript after I Kings 12:24, in which we find further information about her. When Jeroboam, then taskmaster over the forced labor of the house of Joseph, fled to Egypt to escape death at the hands of King Solomon, he went to King Shishak of Egypt and was with him until the death of Solomon. Jeroboam asked permission of King Shishak to return to his own land, and the king told him, "Ask of me a request, and I will give it to you." And he gave to Jeroboam Ano, the elder sister of his own wife Thekemina (Tahpenes), to be his wife. She was great among the daughters of the king, and bore to Jeroboam Abias (Abijah) his son [who in this chapter lies dying in the palace of Jeroboam while Queen Ano, his mother, is about to hear what the old prophet was required by God to tell her] (Charles Ellicott, *A Bible Commentary*).

---

ᵃ 10 Or *Israel—every ruler or leader*   ᵇ 14 The meaning of the Hebrew for this sentence is uncertain.   ᶜ 15 That is, wooden symbols of the goddess Asherah; here and elsewhere in 1 Kings

## New International Version

house, the boy died. [18]They buried him, and all Israel mourned for him, as the LORD had said through his servant the prophet Ahijah.

[19]The other events of Jeroboam's reign, his wars and how he ruled, are written in the book of the annals of the kings of Israel. [20]He reigned for twenty-two years and then rested with his ancestors. And Nadab his son succeeded him as king.

### Rehoboam King of Judah

[21]Rehoboam son of Solomon was king in Judah. He was forty-one years old when he became king, and he reigned seventeen years in Jerusalem, the city the LORD had chosen out of all the tribes of Israel in which to put his Name. His mother's name was Naamah; she was an Ammonite. [22]Judah did evil in the eyes of the LORD. By the sins they committed they stirred up his jealous anger more than those who were before them had done. [23]They also set up for themselves high places, sacred stones and Asherah poles on every high hill and under every spreading tree. [24]There were even male shrine prostitutes in the land; the people engaged in all the detestable practices of the nations the LORD had driven out before the Israelites.

[25]In the fifth year of King Rehoboam, Shishak king of Egypt attacked Jerusalem. [26]He carried off the treasures of the temple of the LORD and the treasures of the royal palace. He took everything, including all the gold shields Solomon had made. [27]So King Rehoboam made bronze shields to replace them and assigned these to the commanders of the guard on duty at the entrance to the royal palace. [28]Whenever the king went to the LORD's temple, the guards bore the shields, and afterward they returned them to the guardroom.

[29]As for the other events of Rehoboam's reign, and all he did, are they not written in the book of the annals of the kings of Judah? [30]There was continual warfare between Rehoboam and Jeroboam. [31]And Rehoboam rested with his ancestors and was buried with them in the City of David. His mother's name was Naamah; she was an Ammonite. And Abijah[a] his son succeeded him as king.

### Abijah King of Judah

**15** In the eighteenth year of the reign of Jeroboam son of Nebat, Abijah[b] became king of Judah, [2]and he reigned in Jerusalem three years. His mother's name was Maakah daughter of Abishalom.[c]

[3]He committed all the sins his father had done before him; his heart was not fully devoted to the LORD his God, as the heart of David his forefather had been. [4]Nevertheless, for David's sake the LORD his God gave him a lamp in Jerusalem by raising up a son to succeed him and by making Jerusalem strong. [5]For David had done what was right in the eyes of the LORD and had not failed to keep any of the LORD's commands all the days of his life—except in the case of Uriah the Hittite.

[6]There was war between Abijah[d] and Jeroboam throughout Abijah's lifetime. [7]As for the other events of Abijah's reign, and all he did, are they not written in the

[a] 31 Some Hebrew manuscripts and Septuagint (see also 2 Chron. 12:16); most Hebrew manuscripts *Abijam*  [b] 1 Some Hebrew manuscripts and Septuagint (see also 2 Chron. 12:16); most Hebrew manuscripts *Abijam*; also in verses 7 and 8  [c] 2 A variant of *Absalom*; also in verse 10  [d] 6 Some Hebrew manuscripts and Syriac *Abijam* (that is, Abijah); most Hebrew manuscripts *Rehoboam*

## Amplified Bible

[18]And all Israel buried him and mourned for him, according to the word of the Lord spoken by His servant Ahijah the prophet.

[19]The rest of the acts of Jeroboam, how he warred and how he reigned, behold, they are written in the Book of the Chronicles of the Kings of Israel. [20]Jeroboam reigned for twenty-two years, and he slept with his fathers; and Nadab his son reigned in his stead.

[21]And Rehoboam son of Solomon reigned in Judah. Rehoboam was forty-one years old when he began to reign, and he reigned seventeen years in Jerusalem, the city the Lord chose out of all the tribes of Israel to put His Name [and the pledge of His presence] there. His mother's name was Naamah the Ammonitess.

[22]And Judah did evil in the sight of the Lord, Whom they provoked to jealousy with the sins they committed, above all that their fathers had done.

[23]For they also built themselves [idolatrous] high places, pillars, and Asherim [idolatrous symbols of the goddess Asherah] on every high hill and under every green tree.

[24]There were also sodomites (male cult prostitutes) in the land. They did all the abominations of the nations whom the Lord cast out before the Israelites.

[25]In the fifth year of King Rehoboam, Shishak king of Egypt [Jeroboam's brother-in-law] came up against Jerusalem.

[26]He took away the treasures of the house of the Lord and of the king's house; he took away all, including all the shields of gold which Solomon had made.

[27]King Rehoboam made in their stead bronze shields and committed them to the hands of the captains of the guard who kept the door of the king's house.

[28]And as often as the king went into the house of the Lord, the guards bore them and brought them back into the guardroom.

[29]The rest of the acts of Rehoboam, and all that he did, are they not written in the Book of the Chronicles of the Kings of Judah?

[30]There was war between Rehoboam and Jeroboam continually.

[31]Rehoboam slept with his fathers and was buried with them in the City of David. His mother's name was Naamah the Ammonitess. Abijam (Abijah) his son reigned in his stead.

**15** In the eighteenth year of King Jeroboam son of Nebat, Abijam began to reign over Judah.

[2]He reigned three years in Jerusalem. His mother was Maacah (Micaiah) daughter [granddaughter] of Abishalom (Absalom).

[3]He walked in all the sins of his father [Rehoboam] before him; and his heart was not blameless with the Lord his God, as the heart of David his father [forefather].

[4]Nevertheless, for David's sake the Lord his God gave him a lamp in Jerusalem, setting up his son after him and establishing Jerusalem,

[5]Because David did what was right in the eyes of the Lord and turned not aside from anything that He commanded him all the days of his life, except in the matter of Uriah the Hittite.

[6]There was war between [Abijam's father] Rehoboam and Jeroboam all the days of [Rehoboam's] life.

[7]The rest of the acts of Abijam, and all that he did, are they not written in the Book of the Chronicles of the

## New International Version

book of the annals of the kings of Judah? There was war between Abijah and Jeroboam. [8]And Abijah rested with his ancestors and was buried in the City of David. And Asa his son succeeded him as king.

### Asa King of Judah

[9]In the twentieth year of Jeroboam king of Israel, Asa became king of Judah, [10]and he reigned in Jerusalem forty-one years. His grandmother's name was Maakah daughter of Abishalom.

[11]Asa did what was right in the eyes of the LORD, as his father David had done. [12]He expelled the male shrine prostitutes from the land and got rid of all the idols his ancestors had made. [13]He even deposed his grandmother Maakah from her position as queen mother, because she had made a repulsive image for the worship of Asherah. Asa cut it down and burned it in the Kidron Valley. [14]Although he did not remove the high places, Asa's heart was fully committed to the LORD all his life. [15]He brought into the temple of the LORD the silver and gold and the articles that he and his father had dedicated.

[16]There was war between Asa and Baasha king of Israel throughout their reigns. [17]Baasha king of Israel went up against Judah and fortified Ramah to prevent anyone from leaving or entering the territory of Asa king of Judah.

[18]Asa then took all the silver and gold that was left in the treasuries of the LORD's temple and of his own palace. He entrusted it to his officials and sent them to Ben-Hadad son of Tabrimmon, the son of Hezion, the king of Aram, who was ruling in Damascus. [19]"Let there be a treaty between me and you," he said, "as there was between my father and your father. See, I am sending you a gift of silver and gold. Now break your treaty with Baasha king of Israel so he will withdraw from me."

[20]Ben-Hadad agreed with King Asa and sent the commanders of his forces against the towns of Israel. He conquered Ijon, Dan, Abel Beth Maakah and all Kinnereth in addition to Naphtali. [21]When Baasha heard this, he stopped building Ramah and withdrew to Tirzah. [22]Then King Asa issued an order to all Judah—no one was exempt—and they carried away from Ramah the stones and timber Baasha had been using there. With them King Asa built up Geba in Benjamin, and also Mizpah.

[23]As for all the other events of Asa's reign, all his achievements, all he did and the cities he built, are they not written in the book of the annals of the kings of Judah? In his old age, however, his feet became diseased. [24]Then Asa rested with his ancestors and was buried with them in the city of his father David. And Jehoshaphat his son succeeded him as king.

### Nadab King of Israel

[25]Nadab son of Jeroboam became king of Israel in the second year of Asa king of Judah, and he reigned over Israel two years. [26]He did evil in the eyes of the LORD, following the ways of his father and committing the same sin his father had caused Israel to commit.

[27]Baasha son of Ahijah from the tribe of Issachar plotted against him, and he struck him down at Gibbethon, a Philistine town, while Nadab and all Israel were besieging

## Amplified Bible

Kings of Judah? And there was war between Abijam and Jeroboam.

[8]Abijam slept with his fathers and they buried him in the City of David. Asa his son reigned in his stead.

[9]In the twentieth year of Jeroboam king of Israel, Asa began to reign over Judah.

[10]Forty-one years he reigned in Jerusalem. His mother was [also named] Maacah (Micaiah) daughter of Abishalom (Absalom). [I Kings 15:2.]

[11]And Asa did right in the eyes of the Lord, as did David his father [forefather].

[12]He put away the sodomites (male cult prostitutes) out of the land and removed all the idols that his fathers [Solomon, Rehoboam, and Abijam] had made or promoted. [I Kings 11:5-11; 14:22.]

[13]Also Maacah his mother he removed from being queen mother, because she had an image made for [the goddess] Asherah. Asa destroyed her image, burning it by the brook Kidron.

[14]But the high places were not removed. Yet Asa's heart was blameless with the Lord all his days.

[15]He brought the things which his father had dedicated and the things which he himself had dedicated into the house of the Lord—silver, gold, and vessels.

[16]There was war between Asa and Baasha king of Israel all their days.

[17]Baasha king of Israel went up against Judah and built up Ramah, that he might allow no one to go out or come in to Asa king of Judah.

[18]Then Asa took all the silver and gold left in the treasuries of the house of the Lord and of the king's house and delivered them into the hands of his servants. And King Asa sent them to Ben-hadad son of Tabrimmon, the son of Hezion, king of Syria, who dwelt at Damascus, saying,

[19]Let there be a league between me and you, as was between my father and your father. Behold, I am sending you a present of silver and gold; go, break your league with Baasha king of Israel, that he may withdraw from me.

[20]So Ben-hadad hearkened to king Asa and sent the commanders of his armies against the cities of Israel, and smote Ijon, Dan, Abel-beth-maacah, and all Chinneroth, with all the land of Naphtali.

[21]When Baasha heard of it, he quit building up Ramah and dwelt in Tirzah.

[22]Then King Asa made a proclamation to all Judah—none was exempted. They carried away the stones of Ramah and its timber with which Baasha had been building. And King Asa built up with them Geba of Benjamin, and also Mizpah.

[23]The rest of all the acts of Asa, all his might, all that he did, and the cities which he built, are they not written in the Book of the Chronicles of the Kings of Judah? But in the time of his old age he was diseased in his feet.

[24]Asa slept with his fathers and was buried with them in the city of David his father. Jehoshaphat his son reigned in his stead.

[25]Nadab son of Jeroboam began to reign over Israel in the second year of Asa king of Judah, and reigned two years.

[26]He did evil in the sight of the Lord and walked in the way of his father and in his sin, with which he made Israel sin.

[27]Baasha son of Ahijah of the house of Issachar conspired against Nadab, and Baasha smote him at Gibbethon, which belonged to the Philistines, for Nadab and all Israel were laying siege to Gibbethon.

## New International Version

it. ²⁸Baasha killed Nadab in the third year of Asa king of Judah and succeeded him as king.

²⁹As soon as he began to reign, he killed Jeroboam's whole family. He did not leave Jeroboam anyone that breathed, but destroyed them all, according to the word of the LORD given through his servant Ahijah the Shilonite. ³⁰This happened because of the sins Jeroboam had committed and had caused Israel to commit, and because he aroused the anger of the LORD, the God of Israel.

³¹As for the other events of Nadab's reign, and all he did, are they not written in the book of the annals of the kings of Israel? ³²There was war between Asa and Baasha king of Israel throughout their reigns.

### Baasha King of Israel

³³In the third year of Asa king of Judah, Baasha son of Ahijah became king of all Israel in Tirzah, and he reigned twenty-four years. ³⁴He did evil in the eyes of the LORD, following the ways of Jeroboam and committing the same sin Jeroboam had caused Israel to commit.

**16** Then the word of the LORD came to Jehu son of Hanani concerning Baasha: ²"I lifted you up from the dust and appointed you ruler over my people Israel, but you followed the ways of Jeroboam and caused my people Israel to sin and to arouse my anger by their sins. ³So I am about to wipe out Baasha and his house, and I will make your house like that of Jeroboam son of Nebat. ⁴Dogs will eat those belonging to Baasha who die in the city, and birds will feed on those who die in the country."

⁵As for the other events of Baasha's reign, what he did and his achievements, are they not written in the book of the annals of the kings of Israel? ⁶Baasha rested with his ancestors and was buried in Tirzah. And Elah his son succeeded him as king.

⁷Moreover, the word of the LORD came through the prophet Jehu son of Hanani to Baasha and his house, because of all the evil he had done in the eyes of the LORD, arousing his anger by the things he did, becoming like the house of Jeroboam—and also because he destroyed it.

### Elah King of Israel

⁸In the twenty-sixth year of Asa king of Judah, Elah son of Baasha became king of Israel, and he reigned in Tirzah two years.

⁹Zimri, one of his officials, who had command of half his chariots, plotted against him. Elah was in Tirzah at the time, getting drunk in the home of Arza, the palace administrator at Tirzah. ¹⁰Zimri came in, struck him down and killed him in the twenty-seventh year of Asa king of Judah. Then he succeeded him as king.

¹¹As soon as he began to reign and was seated on the throne, he killed off Baasha's whole family. He did not spare a single male, whether relative or friend. ¹²So Zimri destroyed the whole family of Baasha, in accordance with the word of the LORD spoken against Baasha through the prophet Jehu— ¹³because of all the sins Baasha and his son Elah had committed and had caused Israel to commit, so that they aroused the anger of the LORD, the God of Israel, by their worthless idols.

¹⁴As for the other events of Elah's reign, and all he did, are they not written in the book of the annals of the kings of Israel?

## Amplified Bible

²⁸In the third year of Asa king of Judah Baasha slew Nadab and reigned in his stead.

²⁹As soon as he was king, Baasha killed all the household of Jeroboam. He left to [it] not one who breathed, until he had destroyed it, according to the word of the Lord which He spoke by His servant Ahijah the Shilonite— [I Kings 14:9-16.]

³⁰Because of the sins of Jeroboam which he sinned and by which he made Israel to sin, and because of his provocation of the Lord, the God of Israel, to anger.

³¹The rest of Nadab's acts, and all that he did, are they not written in the Book of the Chronicles of the Kings of Israel?

³²There was war between Asa and Baasha king of Israel all their days.

³³In the third year of Asa king of Judah, Baasha son of Ahijah began his reign of twenty-four years over all Israel in Tirzah.

³⁴He did evil in the sight of the Lord and walked in the way of Jeroboam and in his sin, with which he made Israel sin.

**16** And the word of the Lord came to Jehu son of Hanani against Baasha, saying,

²Because I exalted you [Baasha] out of the dust and made you leader over My people Israel, and you have walked in the way of Jeroboam and have made My people Israel sin, to provoke Me to anger with their sins,

³Behold, I will utterly sweep away Baasha and his house, and will make your house like [that] of Jeroboam son of Nebat.

⁴Any of Baasha's family who dies in the city the dogs shall eat, and any who dies in the field the birds of the heavens shall eat.

⁵Now the rest of the acts of Baasha, what he did and his might, are they not written in the Book of the Chronicles of the Kings of Israel?

⁶Baasha slept with his fathers and was buried in Tirzah. Elah his son reigned in his stead.

⁷Also the word of the Lord against Baasha and his house came through the prophet Jehu son of Hanani for all the evil that Baasha did in the sight of the Lord in provoking Him to anger with the work of his hands [idols], in being like the house of Jeroboam, and also because he destroyed it [the family of Jeroboam, of his own accord].

⁸In the twenty-sixth year of Asa king of Judah, Elah son of Baasha began his reign of two years over Israel in Tirzah.

⁹Elah's servant Zimri, captain of half his chariots, conspired against Elah. He was in Tirzah, drinking himself drunk in the house of Arza, who was over the household in Tirzah.

¹⁰Zimri came in and smote and killed him in the twenty-seventh year of Asa king of Judah, and reigned in his stead.

¹¹When he began to reign, as soon as he sat on his throne, he killed all the household of Baasha; he left not one male of his kinsmen or his friends.

¹²Thus Zimri destroyed all the house of Baasha, according to the word of the Lord which He spoke against Baasha through Jehu the prophet, [I Kings 16:3.]

¹³For all the sins of Baasha and of Elah his son by which they sinned and made Israel sin, in provoking the Lord, the God of Israel, to anger with their idols.

¹⁴The rest of the acts of Elah, and all he did, are they not written in the Book of the Chronicles of the Kings of Israel?

## New International Version

### Zimri King of Israel

[15] In the twenty-seventh year of Asa king of Judah, Zimri reigned in Tirzah seven days. The army was encamped near Gibbethon, a Philistine town. [16] When the Israelites in the camp heard that Zimri had plotted against the king and murdered him, they proclaimed Omri, the commander of the army, king over Israel that very day there in the camp. [17] Then Omri and all the Israelites with him withdrew from Gibbethon and laid siege to Tirzah. [18] When Zimri saw that the city was taken, he went into the citadel of the royal palace and set the palace on fire around him. So he died, [19] because of the sins he had committed, doing evil in the eyes of the LORD and following the ways of Jeroboam and committing the same sin Jeroboam had caused Israel to commit.

[20] As for the other events of Zimri's reign, and the rebellion he carried out, are they not written in the book of the annals of the kings of Israel?

### Omri King of Israel

[21] Then the people of Israel were split into two factions; half supported Tibni son of Ginath for king, and the other half supported Omri. [22] But Omri's followers proved stronger than those of Tibni son of Ginath. So Tibni died and Omri became king.

[23] In the thirty-first year of Asa king of Judah, Omri became king of Israel, and he reigned twelve years, six of them in Tirzah. [24] He bought the hill of Samaria from Shemer for two talents[a] of silver and built a city on the hill, calling it Samaria, after Shemer, the name of the former owner of the hill.

[25] But Omri did evil in the eyes of the LORD and sinned more than all those before him. [26] He followed completely the ways of Jeroboam son of Nebat, committing the same sin Jeroboam had caused Israel to commit, so that they aroused the anger of the LORD, the God of Israel, by their worthless idols.

[27] As for the other events of Omri's reign, what he did and the things he achieved, are they not written in the book of the annals of the kings of Israel? [28] Omri rested with his ancestors and was buried in Samaria. And Ahab his son succeeded him as king.

### Ahab Becomes King of Israel

[29] In the thirty-eighth year of Asa king of Judah, Ahab son of Omri became king of Israel, and he reigned in Samaria over Israel twenty-two years. [30] Ahab son of Omri did more evil in the eyes of the LORD than any of those before him. [31] He not only considered it trivial to commit the sins of Jeroboam son of Nebat, but he also married Jezebel daughter of Ethbaal king of the Sidonians, and began to serve Baal and worship him. [32] He set up an altar for Baal in the temple of Baal that he built in Samaria. [33] Ahab also made an Asherah pole and did more to arouse the anger of the LORD, the God of Israel, than did all the kings of Israel before him.

[34] In Ahab's time, Hiel of Bethel rebuilt Jericho. He laid its foundations at the cost of his firstborn son Abiram, and he set up its gates at the cost of his youngest son Segub, in accordance with the word of the LORD spoken by Joshua son of Nun.

### Elijah Announces a Great Drought

**17** Now Elijah the Tishbite, from Tishbe[b] in Gilead, said to Ahab, "As the LORD, the God of Israel, lives, whom I serve, there will be neither dew nor rain in the next few years except at my word."

## Amplified Bible

[15] In the twenty-seventh year of Asa king of Judah, Zimri reigned for seven days in Tirzah. The troops were encamped against Gibbethon, which belonged to the Philistines, [16] And they heard the rumor, Zimri has conspired and slain the king! So all Israel made Omri, the commander of the army, king over Israel that day in the camp. [17] So Omri went up from Gibbethon, and all Israel with him, and they besieged Tirzah. [18] And when Zimri saw that the city was taken, he went into the stronghold of the king's house and burned the king's house over him with fire and died, [19] Because of his sins committed in doing evil in the sight of the Lord, in walking in the way of Jeroboam, and his sin in causing Israel to sin.

[20] The rest of the acts of Zimri, and his deeds of treason, are they not written in the Book of the Chronicles of the Kings of Israel?

[21] Then the people of Israel were divided into two factions. Half of the people followed Tibni son of Ginath, to make him king, and half followed Omri.

[22] But the people who followed Omri prevailed against those who followed Tibni son of Ginath. So Tibni died and Omri reigned.

[23] In the thirty-first year of Asa king of Judah, Omri began his reign of twelve years over Israel. He reigned six years in Tirzah.

[24] Omri bought the hill Samaria from Shemer for two talents of silver. He built a city on the hill *and* fortified it, and called it Samaria (Shomeron), after the owner of the hill, Shemer.

[25] But Omri did evil in the eyes of the Lord, even worse than all who were before him.

[26] He walked in all the ways of Jeroboam son of Nebat and in his sin, by which he made Israel sin, to provoke the Lord, the God of Israel, to anger with their idols.

[27] The rest of the acts of Omri, and his might that he showed, are they not written in the Book of the Chronicles of the Kings of Israel?

[28] So Omri slept with his fathers and was buried in Samaria. Ahab his son reigned in his stead.

[29] In the thirty-eighth year of Asa king of Judah, Ahab son of Omri began his reign of twenty-two years over Israel in Samaria.

[30] And Ahab son of Omri did evil in the sight of the Lord above all before him.

[31] As if it had been a light thing for Ahab to walk in the sins of Jeroboam son of Nebat, he took for a wife Jezebel daughter of Ethbaal king of the Sidonians, and served Baal and worshiped him.

[32] He erected an altar for Baal in the house of Baal which he built in Samaria.

[33] And Ahab made an Asherah [idolatrous symbol of the goddess Asherah]. Ahab did more to provoke the Lord, the God of Israel, to anger than all the kings of Israel before him.

[34] In his days, Hiel the Bethelite built Jericho. He laid its foundations at the cost of the life of Abiram his firstborn, and set up its gates with the loss of his youngest son Segub, according to the word of the Lord which He spoke through Joshua son of Nun. [Josh. 6:26.]

**17** Elijah the Tishbite, of the temporary residents of Gilead, said to Ahab, As the Lord, the God of Israel, lives, before Whom I stand, there shall be not be dew or rain these years but according to My word.

---

[a] *24* That is, about 150 pounds or about 68 kilograms    [b] *1* Or *Tishbite, of the settlers*

## New International Version

## Amplified Bible

### Elijah Fed by Ravens

[2]Then the word of the LORD came to Elijah: [3]"Leave here, turn eastward and hide in the Kerith Ravine, east of the Jordan. [4]You will drink from the brook, and I have directed the ravens to supply you with food there."

[5]So he did what the LORD had told him. He went to the Kerith Ravine, east of the Jordan, and stayed there. [6]The ravens brought him bread and meat in the morning and bread and meat in the evening, and he drank from the brook.

### Elijah and the Widow at Zarephath

[7]Some time later the brook dried up because there had been no rain in the land. [8]Then the word of the LORD came to him: [9]"Go at once to Zarephath in the region of Sidon and stay there. I have directed a widow there to supply you with food." [10]So he went to Zarephath. When he came to the town gate, a widow was there gathering sticks. He called to her and asked, "Would you bring me a little water in a jar so I may have a drink?" [11]As she was going to get it, he called, "And bring me, please, a piece of bread."

[12]"As surely as the LORD your God lives," she replied, "I don't have any bread—only a handful of flour in a jar and a little olive oil in a jug. I am gathering a few sticks to take home and make a meal for myself and my son, that we may eat it—and die."

[13]Elijah said to her, "Don't be afraid. Go home and do as you have said. But first make a small loaf of bread for me from what you have and bring it to me, and then make something for yourself and your son. [14]For this is what the LORD, the God of Israel, says: 'The jar of flour will not be used up and the jug of oil will not run dry until the day the LORD sends rain on the land.'"

[15]She went away and did as Elijah had told her. So there was food every day for Elijah and for the woman and her family. [16]For the jar of flour was not used up and the jug of oil did not run dry, in keeping with the word of the LORD spoken by Elijah.

[17]Some time later the son of the woman who owned the house became ill. He grew worse and worse, and finally stopped breathing. [18]She said to Elijah, "What do you have against me, man of God? Did you come to remind me of my sin and kill my son?"

[19]"Give me your son," Elijah replied. He took him from her arms, carried him to the upper room where he was staying, and laid him on his bed. [20]Then he cried out to the LORD, "LORD my God, have you brought tragedy even on this widow I am staying with, by causing her son to die?" [21]Then he stretched himself out on the boy three times and cried out to the LORD, "LORD my God, let this boy's life return to him!"

[22]The LORD heard Elijah's cry, and the boy's life returned to him, and he lived. [23]Elijah picked up the child and carried him down from the room into the house. He gave him to his mother and said, "Look, your son is alive!"

[24]Then the woman said to Elijah, "Now I know that you are a man of God and that the word of the LORD from your mouth is the truth."

[2]And the word of the Lord came to him, saying,

[3]Go from here and turn east and hide yourself by the brook Cherith, east of the Jordan.

[4]You shall drink of the brook, and I have commanded the ravens to feed you there.

[5]So he did according to the word of the Lord; he went and dwelt by the brook Cherith, east of the Jordan.

[6]And the ravens brought him bread and flesh in the morning and bread and flesh in the evening, and he drank of the brook.

[7]After a while the brook dried up because there was no rain in the land.

[8]And the word of the Lord came to him:

[9]Arise, go to Zarephath, which belongs to Sidon, and dwell there. Behold, I have commanded a widow there to provide for you.

[10]So he arose and went to Zarephath. When he came to the gate of the city, behold, a widow was there gathering sticks. He called to her, Bring me a little water in a vessel, that I may drink.

[11]As she was going to get it, he called to her and said, Bring me a morsel of bread in your hand.

[12]And she said, As the Lord your God lives, I have not a loaf baked but only a handful of meal in the jar and a little oil in the bottle. See, I am gathering two sticks, that I may go in and bake it for me and my son, that we may eat it—and die.

[13]Elijah said to her, Fear not; go and do as you have said. But make me a little cake of [it] first and bring it to me, and afterward prepare some for yourself and your son.

[14]For thus says the Lord, the God of Israel: The jar of meal shall not waste away or the bottle of oil fail until the day that the Lord sends rain on the earth.

[15]She did as Elijah said. And she and he and her household ate for many days.

[16]The jar of meal was not spent nor did the bottle of oil fail, according to the word which the Lord spoke through Elijah.

[17]After these things, the son of the woman, the mistress of the house, became sick; and his sickness was so severe that there was no breath left in him.

[18]And she said to Elijah, What have you against me, O man of God? Have you come to me to call my sin to remembrance and to slay my son?

[19]He said to her, Give me your son. And he took him from her bosom and carried him up into the chamber where he stayed and laid him upon his own bed.

[20]And Elijah cried to the Lord and said, O Lord my God, have You brought further calamity upon the widow with whom I sojourn, by slaying her son?

[21]And he stretched himself upon the child three times and cried to the Lord and said, O Lord my God, I pray You, let this child's soul come back into him.

[22]And the Lord heard the voice of Elijah, and the soul of the child came into him again, and he revived.

[23]And Elijah took the child, and brought him down out of the chamber into the [lower part of the] house and gave him to his mother; and Elijah said, See, your son is alive!

[24]And the woman said to Elijah, By this I know that you are a man of God and that the word of the Lord in your mouth is truth.

### Elijah and Obadiah

**18** After a long time, in the third year, the word of the LORD came to Elijah: "Go and present yourself to Ahab, and I will send rain on the land." [2]So Elijah went to present himself to Ahab.

**18** After many days, the word of the Lord came to Elijah in the third year, saying, Go, show yourself to Ahab, and I will send rain upon the earth.

## New International Version

Now the famine was severe in Samaria, ³and Ahab had summoned Obadiah, his palace administrator. (Obadiah was a devout believer in the LORD. ⁴While Jezebel was killing off the LORD's prophets, Obadiah had taken a hundred prophets and hidden them in two caves, fifty in each, and had supplied them with food and water.) ⁵Ahab had said to Obadiah, "Go through the land to all the springs and valleys. Maybe we can find some grass to keep the horses and mules alive so we will not have to kill any of our animals." ⁶So they divided the land they were to cover, Ahab going in one direction and Obadiah in another.

⁷As Obadiah was walking along, Elijah met him. Obadiah recognized him, bowed down to the ground, and said, "Is it really you, my lord Elijah?"

⁸"Yes," he replied. "Go tell your master, 'Elijah is here.'"

⁹"What have I done wrong," asked Obadiah, "that you are handing your servant over to Ahab to be put to death? ¹⁰As surely as the LORD your God lives, there is not a nation or kingdom where my master has not sent someone to look for you. And whenever a nation or kingdom claimed you were not there, he made them swear they could not find you. ¹¹But now you tell me to go to my master and say, 'Elijah is here.' ¹²I don't know where the Spirit of the LORD may carry you when I leave you. If I go and tell Ahab and he doesn't find you, he will kill me. Yet I your servant have worshiped the LORD since my youth. ¹³Haven't you heard, my lord, what I did while Jezebel was killing the prophets of the LORD? I hid a hundred of the LORD's prophets in two caves, fifty in each, and supplied them with food and water. ¹⁴And now you tell me to go to my master and say, 'Elijah is here.' He will kill me!"

¹⁵Elijah said, "As the LORD Almighty lives, whom I serve, I will surely present myself to Ahab today."

### Elijah on Mount Carmel

¹⁶So Obadiah went to meet Ahab and told him, and Ahab went to meet Elijah. ¹⁷When he saw Elijah, he said to him, "Is that you, you troubler of Israel?"

¹⁸"I have not made trouble for Israel," Elijah replied. "But you and your father's family have. You have abandoned the LORD's commands and have followed the Baals. ¹⁹Now summon the people from all over Israel to meet me on Mount Carmel. And bring the four hundred and fifty prophets of Baal and the four hundred prophets of Asherah, who eat at Jezebel's table."

²⁰So Ahab sent word throughout all Israel and assembled the prophets on Mount Carmel. ²¹Elijah went before the people and said, "How long will you waver between two opinions? If the LORD is God, follow him; but if Baal is God, follow him."

But the people said nothing.

²²Then Elijah said to them, "I am the only one of the LORD's prophets left, but Baal has four hundred and fifty prophets. ²³Get two bulls for us. Let Baal's prophets choose one for themselves, and let them cut it into pieces and put it on the wood but not set fire to it. I will prepare the other bull and put it on the wood but not set fire to it. ²⁴Then you call on the name of your god, and I will call on the name of the LORD. The god who answers by fire—he is God."

Then all the people said, "What you say is good."

²⁵Elijah said to the prophets of Baal, "Choose one of the bulls and prepare it first, since there are so many of you. Call on the name of your god, but do not light the fire." ²⁶So they took the bull given them and prepared it.

## Amplified Bible

²So Elijah went to show himself to Ahab. Now the famine was severe in Samaria.

³And Ahab called Obadiah, who was the governor of his house. (Now Obadiah feared the Lord greatly;

⁴For when Jezebel cut off the prophets of the Lord, Obadiah took a hundred prophets and hid them by fifties in a cave and fed them with bread and water.)

⁵And Ahab said to Obadiah, Go into the land to all the fountains of water and to all the brooks; perhaps we may find grass to keep the horses and mules alive, that we lose none of the beasts.

⁶So they divided the land between them to pass through it. Ahab went one way and Obadiah went another way, each by himself.

⁷As Obadiah was on the way, behold, Elijah met him. He recognized him and fell on his face and said, Are you my lord Elijah?

⁸He answered him, It is I. Go tell your lord, Behold, Elijah is here.

⁹And he said, What sin have I committed, that you would deliver your servant into the hands of Ahab to be slain?

¹⁰As the Lord your God lives, there is no nation or kingdom where my lord has not sent to seek you. And when they said, He is not here, he took an oath from the kingdom or nation that they had not found you.

¹¹And now you say, Go tell your lord, Behold, Elijah is here.

¹²And as soon as I have gone out from you, the Spirit of the Lord will carry you I know not where; so when I come and tell Ahab and he cannot find you, he will kill me. But I your servant have feared *and* revered the Lord from my youth.

¹³Was it not told my lord what I did when Jezebel slew the prophets of the Lord, how I hid a hundred men of the Lord's prophets by fifties in a cave and fed them with bread and water?

¹⁴And now you say, Go tell your lord, Behold, Elijah is here; and he will kill me.

¹⁵Elijah said, As the Lord of hosts lives, before Whom I stand, I will surely show myself to Ahab today.

¹⁶So Obadiah went to meet Ahab and told him, and Ahab went to meet Elijah.

¹⁷When Ahab saw Elijah, Ahab said to him, Are you he who troubles Israel?

¹⁸Elijah replied, I have not troubled Israel, but you have, and your father's house, by forsaking the commandments of the Lord and by following the Baals.

¹⁹Therefore send and gather to me all Israel at Mount Carmel, and the 450 prophets of Baal and the 400 prophets of [the goddess] Asherah, who eat at [Queen] Jezebel's table.

²⁰So Ahab sent to all the Israelites and assembled the prophets at Mount Carmel.

²¹Elijah came near to all the people and said, How long will you halt *and* limp between two opinions? If the Lord is God, follow Him! But if Baal, then follow him. And the people did not answer him a word.

²²Then Elijah said to the people, I, I only, remain a prophet of the Lord, but Baal's prophets are 450 men.

²³Let two bulls be given us; let them choose one bull for themselves and cut it in pieces and lay it on the wood but put no fire to it. I will dress the other bull, lay it on the wood, and put no fire to it.

²⁴Then you call on the name of your god, and I will call on the name of the Lord; and the One Who answers by fire, let Him be God. And all the people answered, It is well spoken.

²⁵Elijah said to the prophets of Baal, Choose one bull for yourselves and dress it first, for you are many; and call on the name of your god, but put no fire under it.

²⁶So they took the bull given them, dressed it, and

## New International Version

Then they called on the name of Baal from morning till noon. "Baal, answer us!" they shouted. But there was no response; no one answered. And they danced around the altar they had made.

27At noon Elijah began to taunt them. "Shout louder!" he said. "Surely he is a god! Perhaps he is deep in thought, or busy, or traveling. Maybe he is sleeping and must be awakened." 28So they shouted louder and slashed themselves with swords and spears, as was their custom, until their blood flowed. 29Midday passed, and they continued their frantic prophesying until the time for the evening sacrifice. But there was no response, no one answered, no one paid attention.

30Then Elijah said to all the people, "Come here to me." They came to him, and he repaired the altar of the LORD, which had been torn down. 31Elijah took twelve stones, one for each of the tribes descended from Jacob, to whom the word of the LORD had come, saying, "Your name shall be Israel." 32With the stones he built an altar in the name of the LORD, and he dug a trench around it large enough to hold two seahs*a* of seed. 33He arranged the wood, cut the bull into pieces and laid it on the wood. Then he said to them, "Fill four large jars with water and pour it on the offering and on the wood."

34"Do it again," he said, and they did it again.

"Do it a third time," he ordered, and they did it the third time. 35The water ran down around the altar and even filled the trench.

36At the time of sacrifice, the prophet Elijah stepped forward and prayed: "LORD, the God of Abraham, Isaac and Israel, let it be known today that you are God in Israel and that I am your servant and have done all these things at your command. 37Answer me, LORD, answer me, so these people will know that you, LORD, are God, and that you are turning their hearts back again."

38Then the fire of the LORD fell and burned up the sacrifice, the wood, the stones and the soil, and also licked up the water in the trench.

39When all the people saw this, they fell prostrate and cried, "The LORD—he is God! The LORD—he is God!"

40Then Elijah commanded them, "Seize the prophets of Baal. Don't let anyone get away!" They seized them, and Elijah had them brought down to the Kishon Valley and slaughtered there.

41And Elijah said to Ahab, "Go, eat and drink, for there is the sound of a heavy rain." 42So Ahab went off to eat and drink, but Elijah climbed to the top of Carmel, bent down to the ground and put his face between his knees.

43"Go and look toward the sea," he told his servant. And he went up and looked.

"There is nothing there," he said.

Seven times Elijah said, "Go back."

44The seventh time the servant reported, "A cloud as small as a man's hand is rising from the sea."

So Elijah said, "Go and tell Ahab, 'Hitch up your chariot and go down before the rain stops you.'"

45Meanwhile, the sky grew black with clouds, the wind rose, a heavy rain started falling and Ahab rode off to Jezreel. 46The power of the LORD came on Elijah and, tucking his cloak into his belt, he ran ahead of Ahab all the way to Jezreel.

## Amplified Bible

called on the name of Baal from morning until noon, saying, O Baal, hear *and* answer us! But there was no voice; no one answered. And they leaped upon *or* limped about the altar they had made.

27At noon Elijah mocked them, saying, Cry aloud, for he is a god; either he is musing, or he has gone aside, or he is on a journey, or perhaps he is asleep and must be awakened.

28And they cried aloud and cut themselves after their custom with knives and lances until the blood gushed out upon them.

29Midday passed, and they played the part of prophets until the time for offering the evening sacrifice, but there was no voice, no answer, no one who paid attention.

30Then Elijah said to all the people, Come near to me. And all the people came near him. And he repaired the [old] altar of the Lord that had been broken down [by Jezebel]. [I Kings 18:13; 19:10.]

31Then Elijah took twelve stones, according to the number of the tribes of the sons of Jacob, to whom the word of the Lord came, saying, Israel shall be your name. [Gen. 32:28.]

32And with the stones Elijah built an altar in the name [and self-revelation] of the Lord. He made a trench about the altar as great as would contain two measures of seed.

33He put the wood in order and cut the bull in pieces and laid it on the wood and said, Fill four jars with water and pour it on the burnt offering and the wood.

34And he said, Do it the second time. And they did it the second time. And he said, Do it the third time. And they did it the third time.

35The water ran round about the altar, and he filled the trench also with water.

36At the time of the offering of the evening sacrifice, Elijah the prophet came near and said, O Lord, the God of Abraham, Isaac, and Israel, let it be known this day that You are God in Israel and that I am Your servant and that I have done all these things at Your word.

37Hear me, O Lord, hear me, that this people may know that You, the Lord, are God, and have turned their hearts back [to You].

38Then the fire of the Lord fell and consumed the burnt sacrifice and the wood and the stones and the dust, and also licked up the water that was in the trench.

39When all the people saw it, they fell on their faces and they said, The Lord, He is God! The Lord, He is God!

40And Elijah said, Seize the prophets of Baal; let not one escape. They seized them, and Elijah brought them down to the brook Kishon, and [as God's law required] slew them there. [Deut. 13:5; 18:20.]

41And Elijah said to Ahab, Go up, eat and drink, for there is the sound of abundance of rain.

42So Ahab went up to eat and to drink. And Elijah went up to the top of Carmel; and he bowed himself down upon the earth and put his face between his knees

43And said to his servant, Go up now, look toward the sea. And he went up and looked and said, There is nothing. Elijah said, Go again seven times.

44And at the seventh time the servant said, A cloud as small as a man's hand is arising out of the sea. And Elijah said, Go up, say to Ahab, Hitch your chariot and go down, lest the rain stop you.

45In a little while, the heavens were black with windswept clouds, and there was a great rain. And Ahab went to Jezreel.

46The hand of the Lord was on Elijah. He girded up his loins and ran before Ahab to the entrance of Jezreel [nearly twenty miles].

---

*a 32* That is, probably about 24 pounds or about 11 kilograms

## New International Version

### Elijah Flees to Horeb

**19** Now Ahab told Jezebel everything Elijah had done and how he had killed all the prophets with the sword. ²So Jezebel sent a messenger to Elijah to say, "May the gods deal with me, be it ever so severely, if by this time tomorrow I do not make your life like that of one of them."

³Elijah was afraid*a* and ran for his life. When he came to Beersheba in Judah, he left his servant there, ⁴while he himself went a day's journey into the wilderness. He came to a broom bush, sat down under it and prayed that he might die. "I have had enough, LORD," he said. "Take my life; I am no better than my ancestors." ⁵Then he lay down under the bush and fell asleep.

All at once an angel touched him and said, "Get up and eat." ⁶He looked around, and there by his head was some bread baked over hot coals, and a jar of water. He ate and drank and then lay down again.

⁷The angel of the LORD came back a second time and touched him and said, "Get up and eat, for the journey is too much for you." ⁸So he got up and ate and drank. Strengthened by that food, he traveled forty days and forty nights until he reached Horeb, the mountain of God. ⁹There he went into a cave and spent the night.

### The LORD Appears to Elijah

And the word of the LORD came to him: "What are you doing here, Elijah?"

¹⁰He replied, "I have been very zealous for the LORD God Almighty. The Israelites have rejected your covenant, torn down your altars, and put your prophets to death with the sword. I am the only one left, and now they are trying to kill me too."

¹¹The LORD said, "Go out and stand on the mountain in the presence of the LORD, for the LORD is about to pass by."

Then a great and powerful wind tore the mountains apart and shattered the rocks before the LORD, but the LORD was not in the wind. After the wind there was an earthquake, but the LORD was not in the earthquake. ¹²After the earthquake came a fire, but the LORD was not in the fire. And after the fire came a gentle whisper. ¹³When Elijah heard it, he pulled his cloak over his face and went out and stood at the mouth of the cave.

Then a voice said to him, "What are you doing here, Elijah?"

¹⁴He replied, "I have been very zealous for the LORD God Almighty. The Israelites have rejected your covenant, torn down your altars, and put your prophets to death with the sword. I am the only one left, and now they are trying to kill me too."

¹⁵The LORD said to him, "Go back the way you came, and go to the Desert of Damascus. When you get there, anoint Hazael*a* king over Aram. ¹⁶Also, anoint Jehu son of Nimshi king over Israel, and anoint Elisha son of Shaphat from Abel Meholah to succeed you as prophet. ¹⁷Jehu will put to death any who escape the sword of Hazael, and Elisha will put to death any who escape the sword of Jehu. ¹⁸Yet I reserve seven thousand in Israel—all whose knees have not bowed down to Baal and whose mouths have not kissed him."

## Amplified Bible

**19** Ahab told Jezebel all that Elijah had done and how he had slain all the prophets [of Baal] with the sword.

²Then Jezebel sent a messenger to Elijah, saying, So let the gods do to me, and more also, if I make not your life as the life of one of them by this time tomorrow.

³Then he was afraid and arose and went for his life and came to Beersheba of Judah [over eighty miles, and out of Jezebel's realm] and left his servant there.

⁴But he himself went a day's journey into the wilderness and came and sat down under a lone broom *or* juniper tree and asked that he might die. He said, It is enough; now, O Lord, take away my life; for I am no better than my fathers.

⁵As he lay asleep under the broom *or* juniper tree, behold, an angel touched him and said to him, Arise and eat.

⁶He looked, and behold, there was a cake baked on the coals, and a bottle of water at his head. And he ate and drank and lay down again.

⁷The angel of the Lord came the second time and touched him and said, Arise and eat, for the journey is too great for you.

⁸So he arose and ate and drank, and went in the strength of that food forty days and nights to Horeb, the mount of God.

⁹There he came to a cave and lodged in it; and behold, the word of the Lord came to him, and He said to him, What are you doing here, Elijah?

¹⁰He replied, I have been very jealous for the Lord God of hosts; for the Israelites have forsaken Your covenant, thrown down Your altars, and killed Your prophets with the sword. And I, I only, am left; and they seek my life, to take it away.

¹¹And He said, Go out and stand on the mount before the Lord. And behold, the Lord passed by, and a great and strong wind rent the mountains and broke in pieces the rocks before the Lord, but the Lord was not in the wind; and after the wind an earthquake, but the Lord was not in the earthquake;

¹²And after the earthquake a fire, but the Lord was not in the fire; and after the fire [a sound of gentle stillness and] a still, small voice.

¹³When Elijah heard the voice, he wrapped his face in his mantle and went out and stood in the entrance of the cave. And behold, there came a voice to him and said, What are you doing here, Elijah?

¹⁴He said, I have been very jealous for the Lord God of hosts, because the Israelites have forsaken Your covenant, thrown down Your altars, and slain Your prophets with the sword. And I, I only, am left, and they seek my life, to destroy it.

¹⁵And the Lord said to him, Go, return on your way to the Wilderness of Damascus; and when you arrive, anoint Hazael to be king over Syria.

¹⁶And anoint Jehu son of Nimshi to be king over Israel, and anoint Elisha son of Shaphat of Abel-meholah to be prophet in your place.

¹⁷And him who escapes from the sword of *a*Hazael Jehu shall slay, and him who escapes the sword of Jehu Elisha shall slay.

¹⁸Yet I will leave Myself 7,000 in Israel, all the knees that have not bowed to Baal and every mouth that has not kissed him.

*a* Ahab had again fallen under the sway of Jezebel. Therefore, Baal worship would recover from the blow dealt it by Elijah. Elijah is accordingly instructed to take the necessary steps for the destruction of Baal worship. They were three. First, Ahab was to be attacked from without by the Syrians, and for that purpose warlike Hazael was to take the Syrian throne. Second, when Ahab was thus weakened, Jehu was to seize his throne, since Jehu was a known opponent of Baal worship, and also a ruthless soldier. Third, Elijah was to appoint as his own successor the vigorous and wholehearted Elisha, who might be trusted under Jehu to complete the destruction of the adherents of Baal (*The Cambridge Bible*).

*a 3 Or Elijah saw*

## New International Version

### The Call of Elisha

19So Elijah went from there and found Elisha son of Shaphat. He was plowing with twelve yoke of oxen, and he himself was driving the twelfth pair. Elijah went up to him and threw his cloak around him. 20Elisha then left his oxen and ran after Elijah. "Let me kiss my father and mother goodbye," he said, "and then I will come with you."

"Go back," Elijah replied. "What have I done to you?"

21So Elisha left him and went back. He took his yoke of oxen and slaughtered them. He burned the plowing equipment to cook the meat and gave it to the people, and they ate. Then he set out to follow Elijah and became his servant.

### Ben-Hadad Attacks Samaria

**20** Now Ben-Hadad king of Aram mustered his entire army. Accompanied by thirty-two kings with their horses and chariots, he went up and besieged Samaria and attacked it. 2He sent messengers into the city to Ahab king of Israel, saying, "This is what Ben-Hadad says: 3'Your silver and gold are mine, and the best of your wives and children are mine.'"

4The king of Israel answered, "Just as you say, my lord the king. I and all I have are yours."

5The messengers came again and said, "This is what Ben-Hadad says: 'I sent to demand your silver and gold, your wives and your children. 6But about this time tomorrow I am going to send my officials to search your palace and the houses of your officials. They will seize everything you value and carry it away.'"

7The king of Israel summoned all the elders of the land and said to them, "See how this man is looking for trouble! When he sent for my wives and my children, my silver and my gold, I did not refuse him."

8The elders and the people all answered, "Don't listen to him or agree to his demands."

9So he replied to Ben-Hadad's messengers, "Tell my lord the king, 'Your servant will do all you demanded the first time, but this demand I cannot meet.'" They left and took the answer back to Ben-Hadad.

10Then Ben-Hadad sent another message to Ahab: "May the gods deal with me, be it ever so severely, if enough dust remains in Samaria to give each of my men a handful."

11The king of Israel answered, "Tell him: 'One who puts on his armor should not boast like one who takes it off.'"

12Ben-Hadad heard this message while he and the kings were drinking in their tents,ᵃ and he ordered his men: "Prepare to attack." So they prepared to attack the city.

### Ahab Defeats Ben-Hadad

13Meanwhile a prophet came to Ahab king of Israel and announced, "This is what the LORD says: 'Do you see this vast army? I will give it into your hand today, and then you will know that I am the LORD.'"

14"But who will do this?" asked Ahab.

The prophet replied, "This is what the LORD says: 'The junior officers under the provincial commanders will do it.'"

"And who will start the battle?" he asked.

The prophet answered, "You will."

15So Ahab summoned the 232 junior officers under the provincial commanders. Then he assembled the rest of the Israelites, 7,000 in all. 16They set out at noon while Ben-Hadad and the 32 kings allied with him were in their

## Amplified Bible

19So Elijah left there and found Elisha son of Shaphat, whose plowing was being done with twelve yoke of oxen, and he drove the twelfth. Elijah crossed over to him and cast his mantle upon him.

20He left the oxen and ran after Elijah and said, Let me kiss my father and mother, and then I will follow you. And he [testing Elisha] said, Go on back. What have I done to you? [Settle it for yourself.]

21So Elisha went back from him. Then he took a yoke of oxen, slew them, boiled their flesh with the oxen's yoke [as fuel], and gave to the people, and they ate. Then he arose, followed Elijah, and served him. [II Kings 3:11.]

**20** Ben-hadad king of Syria gathered all his army together; thirty-two kings were with him, and horses and chariots. And he went up and besieged Samaria, warring against it.

2He sent messengers into Samaria to Ahab king of Israel and said to him, Thus says Ben-hadad:

3Your silver and your gold are mine; your wives and your children, even the fairest, also are mine.

4And the king of Israel answered and said, My lord, O king, according to what you say, I am yours, and all that I have.

5The messengers came again and said, Thus says Ben-hadad: Although I have sent to you, saying, You shall deliver to me your silver, your gold, your wives, and your children—

6Yet I will send my servants to you tomorrow about this time, and they shall search your house and the houses of your servants; and all the desire of your eyes they shall lay hands upon and take it away.

7Then the king of Israel called all the elders of the land and said, Notice now and see how this man is seeking our destruction. He sent to me for my wives, my children, my silver, and my gold, and I did not refuse him.

8And all the elders and all the people said to him, Do not heed him or consent.

9So he said to Ben-hadad's messengers, Tell my lord the king, All you first sent for to your servant I will do, but this thing I cannot do. And the messengers left; then they brought him word again.

10Ben-hadad sent to him and said, May the gods do so to me, and more also, if the rubbish of Samaria shall be enough for each one of all the people who are at my feet *and* follow me to get a handful.

11The king of Israel answered, Tell him: Let not him who girds on his harness boast as he who puts it off.

12When Ben-hadad heard this message as he and the kings were drinking in the booths, he said to his servants, Set the army in array. And they set themselves in array against [Samaria].

13Then a prophet came to Ahab king of Israel and said, Thus says the Lord: Have you seen all this great multitude? Behold, I will deliver it into your hand today, and you shall know *and* realize that I am the Lord.

14Ahab said, By whom? And he said, Thus says the Lord: By the young men [the attendants or bodyguards] of the governors of the districts. Then Ahab said, Who shall order the battle? And he answered, You.

15Ahab numbered the attendants of the governors of the districts, and they were 232. After them he numbered all the people of [the army of] Israel, 7,000. [I Kings 19:18.]

16And they went out at noon. But Ben-hadad was drinking himself drunk in the booths, he and the thirty-two kings who helped him.

---

ᵃ 12 Or *in Sukkoth*; also in verse 16

## New International Version

tents getting drunk. ¹⁷The junior officers under the provincial commanders went out first.

Now Ben-Hadad had dispatched scouts, who reported, "Men are advancing from Samaria."

¹⁸He said, "If they have come out for peace, take them alive; if they have come out for war, take them alive."

¹⁹The junior officers under the provincial commanders marched out of the city with the army behind them ²⁰and each one struck down his opponent. At that, the Arameans fled, with the Israelites in pursuit. But Ben-Hadad king of Aram escaped on horseback with some of his horsemen. ²¹The king of Israel advanced and overpowered the horses and chariots and inflicted heavy losses on the Arameans.

²²Afterward, the prophet came to the king of Israel and said, "Strengthen your position and see what must be done, because next spring the king of Aram will attack you again."

²³Meanwhile, the officials of the king of Aram advised him, "Their gods are gods of the hills. That is why they were too strong for us. But if we fight them on the plains, surely we will be stronger than they. ²⁴Do this: Remove all the kings from their commands and replace them with other officers. ²⁵You must also raise an army like the one you lost—horse for horse and chariot for chariot—so we can fight Israel on the plains. Then surely we will be stronger than they." He agreed with them and acted accordingly.

²⁶The next spring Ben-Hadad mustered the Arameans and went up to Aphek to fight against Israel. ²⁷When the Israelites were also mustered and given provisions, they marched out to meet them. The Israelites camped opposite them like two small flocks of goats, while the Arameans covered the countryside.

²⁸The man of God came up and told the king of Israel, "This is what the LORD says: 'Because the Arameans think the LORD is a god of the hills and not a god of the valleys, I will deliver this vast army into your hands, and you will know that I am the LORD.'"

²⁹For seven days they camped opposite each other, and on the seventh day the battle was joined. The Israelites inflicted a hundred thousand casualties on the Aramean foot soldiers in one day. ³⁰The rest of them escaped to the city of Aphek, where the wall collapsed on twenty-seven thousand of them. And Ben-Hadad fled to the city and hid in an inner room.

³¹His officials said to him, "Look, we have heard that the kings of Israel are merciful. Let us go to the king of Israel with sackcloth around our waists and ropes around our heads. Perhaps he will spare your life."

³²Wearing sackcloth around their waists and ropes around their heads, they went to the king of Israel and said, "Your servant Ben-Hadad says: 'Please let me live.'"

The king answered, "Is he still alive? He is my brother."

³³The men took this as a good sign and were quick to pick up his word. "Yes, your brother Ben-Hadad!" they said.

"Go and get him," the king said. When Ben-Hadad came out, Ahab had him come up into his chariot.

³⁴"I will return the cities my father took from your father," Ben-Hadad offered. "You may set up your own market areas in Damascus, as my father did in Samaria."

Ahab said, "On the basis of a treaty I will set you free." So he made a treaty with him, and let him go.

### A Prophet Condemns Ahab

³⁵By the word of the LORD one of the company of the prophets said to his companion, "Strike me with your weapon," but he refused.

## Amplified Bible

¹⁷The servants of the governors of the districts went out first; and Ben-hadad sent out, and they told him, saying, There are men come out of Samaria.

¹⁸And he said, Whether they have come out for peace or for war, take them alive.

¹⁹So these [strong young guards] of the governors of the districts went out of [Samaria], and the army followed them.

²⁰And each one killed his man; the Syrians fled, and Israel pursued them. Ben-hadad king of Syria escaped on a horse with the horsemen.

²¹The king of Israel went out and smote [the riders of] the horses and chariots and slew the Syrians with a great slaughter.

²²The prophet came to the king of Israel and said to him, Go, fortify yourself and become strong and give attention to what you must do, for at the first of next year the king of Syria will return against you.

²³And the servants of the king of Syria said to him, Israel's gods are gods of the hills; therefore they were stronger than we. But let us fight against them in the plain, and surely we shall be stronger than they.

²⁴And do this thing: Remove the kings, each from his place, and put governors in their stead.

²⁵And muster yourself an army like the army you have lost, horse for horse and chariot for chariot. And we will fight against them in the plain, and surely we shall be stronger than they. And he heeded their speech and did so.

²⁶And at the return of the year, Ben-hadad mustered the Syrians and went up to Aphek to fight against Israel.

²⁷The Israelites were counted and, all present, went against them. The Israelites encamped before the enemy like two little flocks of lost kids [absolutely everything against them but Almighty God], but the Syrians filled the country.

²⁸A man of God came and said to the king of Israel, Thus says the Lord: Because the Syrians have said, The Lord is God of the hills but He is not God of the valleys, therefore I will deliver all this great multitude into your hands, and you shall know and recognize by experience that I am the Lord. [Phil. 4:13.]

²⁹They encamped opposite each other seven days. Then the battle was joined; and the Israelites slew of the Syrians 100,000 foot soldiers in one day.

³⁰But the rest fled to the city of Aphek, and the wall fell upon 27,000 men who were left. Ben-hadad fled into the city and from chamber to chamber.

³¹His servants said to him, We have heard that the kings of the house of Israel are merciful kings. Let us put sackcloth on our loins and ropes about our necks, and go out to the king of Israel; perhaps he will spare your life.

³²So they girded sackcloth on their loins and put ropes on their necks, and came to the king of Israel and said, Your servant Ben-hadad says, I pray you, let me live. And King [Ahab] said, Is he yet alive? He is my brother.

³³Now the men took it as an omen and they hastily took it up and said, Yes, your brother Ben-hadad. Then the king said, Go, bring him. Then Ben-hadad came forth to him, and the victorious king caused him to come up into the chariot.

³⁴Ben-hadad [tempting him] said, The cities which my father took from your father I will restore; and you may maintain bazaars of your own in Damascus, as my father did in Samaria. Then, said Ahab, I will send you away on these terms. So he made a covenant with him and sent him away.

³⁵And a certain man of the sons of the prophets said to his neighbor, At the command of the Lord, strike me, I pray you. And the man refused to strike him.

## New International Version

36So the prophet said, "Because you have not obeyed the LORD, as soon as you leave me a lion will kill you." And after the man went away, a lion found him and killed him.

37The prophet found another man and said, "Strike me, please." So the man struck him and wounded him. 38Then the prophet went and stood by the road waiting for the king. He disguised himself with his headband down over his eyes. 39As the king passed by, the prophet called out to him, "Your servant went into the thick of the battle, and someone came to me with a captive and said, 'Guard this man. If he is missing, it will be your life for his life, or you must pay a talent*a* of silver.' 40While your servant was busy here and there, the man disappeared."

"That is your sentence," the king of Israel said. "You have pronounced it yourself."

41Then the prophet quickly removed the headband from his eyes, and the king of Israel recognized him as one of the prophets. 42He said to the king, "This is what the LORD says: 'You have set free a man I had determined should die.*b* Therefore it is your life for his life, your people for his people.'" 43Sullen and angry, the king of Israel went to his palace in Samaria.

### Naboth's Vineyard

**21** Some time later there was an incident involving a vineyard belonging to Naboth the Jezreelite. The vineyard was in Jezreel, close to the palace of Ahab king of Samaria. 2Ahab said to Naboth, "Let me have your vineyard to use for a vegetable garden, since it is close to my palace. In exchange I will give you a better vineyard or, if you prefer, I will pay you whatever it is worth."

3But Naboth replied, "The LORD forbid that I should give you the inheritance of my ancestors."

4So Ahab went home, sullen and angry because Naboth the Jezreelite had said, "I will not give you the inheritance of my ancestors." He lay on his bed sulking and refused to eat.

5His wife Jezebel came in and asked him, "Why are you so sullen? Why won't you eat?"

6He answered her, "Because I said to Naboth the Jezreelite, 'Sell me your vineyard; or if you prefer, I will give you another vineyard in its place.' But he said, 'I will not give you my vineyard.'"

7Jezebel his wife said, "Is this how you act as king over Israel? Get up and eat! Cheer up. I'll get you the vineyard of Naboth the Jezreelite."

8So she wrote letters in Ahab's name, placed his seal on them, and sent them to the elders and nobles who lived in Naboth's city with him. 9In those letters she wrote:

"Proclaim a day of fasting and seat Naboth in a prominent place among the people. 10But seat two scoundrels opposite him and have them bring charges that he has cursed both God and the king. Then take him out and stone him to death."

11So the elders and nobles who lived in Naboth's city did as Jezebel directed in the letters she had written to them. 12They proclaimed a fast and seated Naboth in a prominent place among the people. 13Then two scoundrels came and sat opposite him and brought charges against Naboth

## Amplified Bible

36Then said he to him, Because you have not obeyed the voice of the Lord, behold, as soon as you have left me a lion will slay you. And as soon as he departed from him, a lion found him and killed him.

37Then [the prophet] found another man and said, Strike me, I pray you. And the man struck him, so that in striking, he wounded him.

38So the prophet departed and waited for King Ahab by the way, and disguised himself with ashes upon his face.

39And as the king passed by, the [prophet] cried out to him, Your servant went out into the midst of the battle, and behold, a man turned aside and brought a man to me and said, Keep this man. If for any reason he is missing, then your life shall be required for his life, or else you shall pay a talent of silver.

40But while your servant was busy here and there, he was gone. And the king of Israel said to him, Such is your own verdict; you yourself have decided it.

41The man hastily removed the ashes from his face, and Ahab king of Israel recognized him as one of the prophets.

42And he said to the king, Thus says the Lord: Because you have let go out of your hand the man I had devoted to destruction, therefore your life shall go for his life, and your people for his people.

43And King [Ahab] of Israel went to his house resentful and sullen, and came to Samaria. [I Kings 22:34-36.]

**21** Now Naboth the Jezreelite had a vineyard in Jezreel, close beside the palace of Ahab king of Samaria; and after these things,

2Ahab said to Naboth, Give me your vineyard, that I may have it for a garden of herbs, because it is near my house. I will give you a better vineyard for it or, if you prefer, I will give you its worth in money.

3Naboth said to Ahab, The Lord forbid that I should give the inheritance of my fathers to you.

4And Ahab [already depressed by the Lord's message to him] came into his house [more] resentful and sullen because of what Naboth the Jezreelite had said to him; for he had said, I will not give you the inheritance of my fathers. And he lay down on his bed, turned away his face, and would eat no food.

5But Jezebel his wife came and said to him, Why is your spirit so troubled that you eat no food?

6And he said to her, Because I spoke to Naboth the Jezreelite and said to him, Give me your vineyard for money; or if you prefer, I will give you another vineyard for it. And he answered, I will not give you my vineyard.

7Jezebel his wife said to him, Do you not govern Israel? Arise, eat food, and let your heart be happy. I will give you the vineyard of Naboth the Jezreelite.

8So she wrote letters in Ahab's name and sealed them with his seal and sent them to the elders and nobles who dwelt with Naboth in his city.

9And in the letters she said, Proclaim a fast and set Naboth up high among the people.

10And set two men, base fellows, before him, and let them bear witness against him, saying, You cursed *and* renounced God and the king. Then carry him out and stone him to death.

11And the men of his city, the elders and the nobles who dwelt there, did as Jezebel had directed in the letters sent them.

12They proclaimed a fast and set Naboth on high among the people.

13Two base fellows came in and sat opposite him and they charged Naboth before the people, saying, Naboth

---

*a 39 That is, about 75 pounds or about 34 kilograms    b 42 The Hebrew term refers to the irrevocable giving over of things or persons to the LORD, often by totally destroying them.

## New International Version

before the people, saying, "Naboth has cursed both God and the king." So they took him outside the city and stoned him to death. [14]Then they sent word to Jezebel: "Naboth has been stoned to death."

[15]As soon as Jezebel heard that Naboth had been stoned to death, she said to Ahab, "Get up and take possession of the vineyard of Naboth the Jezreelite that he refused to sell you. He is no longer alive, but dead." [16]When Ahab heard that Naboth was dead, he got up and went down to take possession of Naboth's vineyard.

[17]Then the word of the LORD came to Elijah the Tishbite: [18]"Go down to meet Ahab king of Israel, who rules in Samaria. He is now in Naboth's vineyard, where he has gone to take possession of it. [19]Say to him, 'This is what the LORD says: Have you not murdered a man and seized his property?' Then say to him, 'This is what the LORD says: In the place where dogs licked up Naboth's blood, dogs will lick up your blood—yes, yours!'"

[20]Ahab said to Elijah, "So you have found me, my enemy!"

"I have found you," he answered, "because you have sold yourself to do evil in the eyes of the LORD. [21]He says, 'I am going to bring disaster on you. I will wipe out your descendants and cut off from Ahab every last male in Israel—slave or free.[a] [22]I will make your house like that of Jeroboam son of Nebat and that of Baasha son of Ahijah, because you have aroused my anger and have caused Israel to sin.'

[23]"And also concerning Jezebel the LORD says: 'Dogs will devour Jezebel by the wall of[b] Jezreel.'

[24]"Dogs will eat those belonging to Ahab who die in the city, and the birds will feed on those who die in the country."

[25] (There was never anyone like Ahab, who sold himself to do evil in the eyes of the LORD, urged on by Jezebel his wife. [26]He behaved in the vilest manner by going after idols, like the Amorites the LORD drove out before Israel.)

[27]When Ahab heard these words, he tore his clothes, put on sackcloth and fasted. He lay in sackcloth and went around meekly.

[28]Then the word of the LORD came to Elijah the Tishbite: [29]"Have you noticed how Ahab has humbled himself before me? Because he has humbled himself, I will not bring this disaster in his day, but I will bring it on his house in the days of his son."

## Amplified Bible

cursed *and* renounced God and the king. Then he was carried out of the city and stoned to death.

[14]Then they sent to Jezebel, saying, Naboth has been stoned and is dead.

[15]Then Jezebel said to Ahab, Arise, take possession of the vineyard of Naboth the Jezreelite which he refused to sell you, for Naboth is not alive, but dead.

[16]When Ahab heard that, he arose to go down to the vineyard of Naboth the Jezreelite to take possession of it.

[17]Then the word of the Lord came to Elijah the Tishbite, saying,

[18]Arise, go down to meet Ahab king of Israel in Samaria. He is in the vineyard of Naboth, where he has gone to possess it.

[19]Say to him, Thus says the Lord: Have you killed and also taken possession? Thus says the Lord: In the place where dogs licked the blood of Naboth shall dogs lick your blood, even yours.

[20]And Ahab said to Elijah, Have you found me, O my enemy? And he answered, I have found you, because you have sold yourself to do evil in the sight of the Lord.

[21]See [says the Lord], I will bring evil on you and utterly sweep away and cut off from Ahab every male, bond and free,

[22]And will make your household like that of Jeroboam son of Nebat and like the household of Baasha son of Ahijah, for the provocation with which you have provoked Me to anger and made Israel to sin.

[23]Also the Lord said of Jezebel: The dogs shall eat Jezebel by the wall of Jezreel.

[24]Any belonging to Ahab who dies in the city the dogs shall eat, and any who dies in the field the birds of the air shall eat. [I Kings 14:11; 16:4.]

[25]For there was no one who sold himself to do evil in the sight of the Lord as did Ahab, incited by his wife Jezebel.

[26]He did very abominably in going after idols, as had the Amorites, whom the Lord cast out before the Israelites.

[27]When Ahab heard those words of Elijah, he tore his clothes, put sackcloth on his flesh, fasted, lay in sackcloth, and went quietly.

[28]And the word of the Lord came to Elijah the Tishbite, saying,

[29]Do you see how Ahab humbles himself before Me? Because he humbles himself before Me, I will not bring the evil in his lifetime, but in his son's day I will bring the evil upon his house.

### Micaiah Prophesies Against Ahab

**22** For three years there was no war between Aram and Israel. [2]But in the third year Jehoshaphat king of Judah went down to see the king of Israel. [3]The king of Israel had said to his officials, "Don't you know that Ramoth Gilead belongs to us and yet we are doing nothing to retake it from the king of Aram?"

[4]So he asked Jehoshaphat, "Will you go with me to fight against Ramoth Gilead?"

Jehoshaphat replied to the king of Israel, "I am as you are, my people as your people, my horses as your horses." [5]But Jehoshaphat also said to the king of Israel, "First seek the counsel of the LORD."

[6]So the king of Israel brought together the prophets—

**22** Syria and Israel continued without war for three years.

[2]In the third year Jehoshaphat king of Judah came down to the king of Israel.

[3]And [Ahab] king of Israel said to his servants, Do you know that Ramoth in Gilead is ours, and we keep silence and do not take it from the king of Syria?

[4]And [Ahab] said to Jehoshaphat, Will you go with me to Ramoth-gilead to battle? Jehoshaphat said to the king of Israel, I am as you are, my people as your people, my horses as your horses.

[5]But Jehoshaphat said to the king of Israel, Inquire first, I pray you, for the word of the Lord today.

[6]Then [Ahab] king of Israel gathered the prophets to-

[a] 21 Or *Israel—every ruler or leader*   [b] 23 Most Hebrew manuscripts; a few Hebrew manuscripts, Vulgate and Syriac (see also 2 Kings 9:26) *the plot of ground at*

## New International Version

about four hundred men—and asked them, "Shall I go to war against Ramoth Gilead, or shall I refrain?"

"Go," they answered, "for the Lord will give it into the king's hand."

⁷But Jehoshaphat asked, "Is there no longer a prophet of the LORD here whom we can inquire of?"

⁸The king of Israel answered Jehoshaphat, "There is still one prophet through whom we can inquire of the LORD, but I hate him because he never prophesies anything good about me, but always bad. He is Micaiah son of Imlah."

"The king should not say such a thing," Jehoshaphat replied.

⁹So the king of Israel called one of his officials and said, "Bring Micaiah son of Imlah at once."

¹⁰Dressed in their royal robes, the king of Israel and Jehoshaphat king of Judah were sitting on their thrones at the threshing floor by the entrance of the gate of Samaria, with all the prophets prophesying before them. ¹¹Now Zedekiah son of Kenaanah had made iron horns and he declared, "This is what the LORD says: 'With these you will gore the Arameans until they are destroyed.'"

¹²All the other prophets were prophesying the same thing. "Attack Ramoth Gilead and be victorious," they said, "for the LORD will give it into the king's hand."

¹³The messenger who had gone to summon Micaiah said to him, "Look, the other prophets without exception are predicting success for the king. Let your word agree with theirs, and speak favorably."

¹⁴But Micaiah said, "As surely as the LORD lives, I can tell him only what the LORD tells me."

¹⁵When he arrived, the king asked him, "Micaiah, shall we go to war against Ramoth Gilead, or not?"

"Attack and be victorious," he answered, "for the LORD will give it into the king's hand."

¹⁶The king said to him, "How many times must I make you swear to tell me nothing but the truth in the name of the LORD?"

¹⁷Then Micaiah answered, "I saw all Israel scattered on the hills like sheep without a shepherd, and the LORD said, 'These people have no master. Let each one go home in peace.'"

¹⁸The king of Israel said to Jehoshaphat, "Didn't I tell you that he never prophesies anything good about me, but only bad?"

¹⁹Micaiah continued, "Therefore hear the word of the LORD: I saw the LORD sitting on his throne with all the multitudes of heaven standing around him on his right and on his left. ²⁰And the LORD said, 'Who will entice Ahab into attacking Ramoth Gilead and going to his death there?'

"One suggested this, and another that. ²¹Finally, a spirit came forward, stood before the LORD and said, 'I will entice him.'

²²"'By what means?' the LORD asked.

"'I will go out and be a deceiving spirit in the mouths of all his prophets,' he said.

"'You will succeed in enticing him,' said the LORD. 'Go and do it.'

²³"So now the LORD has put a deceiving spirit in the mouths of all these prophets of yours. The LORD has decreed disaster for you."

²⁴Then Zedekiah son of Kenaanah went up and slapped Micaiah in the face. "Which way did the spirit from*ᵃ* the LORD go when he went from me to speak to you?" he asked.

²⁵Micaiah replied, "You will find out on the day you go to hide in an inner room."

²⁶The king of Israel then ordered, "Take Micaiah and send him back to Amon the ruler of the city and to Joash the king's son ²⁷and say, 'This is what the king says: Put

## Amplified Bible

gether, about 400 men, and said to them, Shall I go against Ramoth-gilead to battle, or shall I hold back? And they said, Go up, for the Lord will deliver it into the hand of the king.

⁷Jehoshaphat said, Is there not another prophet of the Lord here whom we may ask?

⁸[Ahab] king of Israel said to Jehoshaphat, There is yet one man, Micaiah son of Imlah, by whom we may inquire of the Lord, but I hate him, for he never prophesies good for me, but evil. Jehoshaphat said, Let not the king say that.

⁹Then [Ahab] king of Israel told an officer, Bring quickly Micaiah son of Imlah.

¹⁰Now the king of Israel and Jehoshaphat king of Judah were sitting in [royal] robes [or armor], each on his throne in an open place [on a threshing floor] at the entrance of the gate of Samaria; and all the prophets prophesied before them.

¹¹And Zedekiah son of Chenaanah made him horns of iron and said, Thus says the Lord: With these you shall push the Syrians until they are destroyed.

¹²And all the prophets agreed, saying, Go up to Ramoth-gilead and prosper, for the Lord will deliver it into the king's hand.

¹³The messenger who went to call Micaiah said to him, Behold now, the prophets unanimously declare good to the king. Let your answer, I pray you, be like theirs, and say what is good.

¹⁴But Micaiah said, As the Lord lives, I will speak what the Lord says to me.

¹⁵So he came to the king. King [Ahab] said, Micaiah, shall we go against Ramoth-gilead to battle, or shall we hold back? And he answered, Go and prosper, for the Lord will deliver it into the king's hand.

¹⁶And the king said to him, How many times must I charge you to tell me nothing but the truth in the name of the Lord?

¹⁷And he said, I saw all Israel scattered upon the hills as sheep that have no shepherd, and the Lord said, These have no master. Let them return every man to his house in peace.

¹⁸Then the king of Israel said to Jehoshaphat, Did I not tell you that he would prophesy no good concerning me, but evil?

¹⁹And Micaiah said, Hear the word of the Lord: I saw the Lord sitting on His throne, and all the host of heaven standing by Him on His right hand and on His left.

²⁰And the Lord said, Who will entice Ahab to go up and fall at Ramoth-gilead? One said this way, another said that way.

²¹Then there came forth a spirit [of whom I am about to tell] and stood before the Lord and said, I will entice him.

²²The Lord said to him, By what means? And he said, I will go forth and be a lying spirit in the mouths of all his prophets. [The Lord] said, You shall entice him and succeed also. Go forth and do it.

²³So the Lord has put a lying spirit in the mouths of all these prophets; and the Lord has spoken evil concerning you.

²⁴But Zedekiah son of Chenaanah went near and struck Micaiah on the cheek and said, Which way went the Spirit of the Lord from me to speak to you?

²⁵Micaiah said, Behold, you shall see on that day when you go into an inner chamber to hide yourself.

²⁶[Ahab] king of Israel said, Take Micaiah, carry him back to Amon the governor of the city and to Joash the king's son,

²⁷And say, The king says, Put this fellow in prison and

---

*ᵃ 24 Or Spirit of*

## New International Version

this fellow in prison and give him nothing but bread and water until I return safely.'"

28Micaiah declared, "If you ever return safely, the LORD has not spoken through me." Then he added, "Mark my words, all you people!"

### Ahab Killed at Ramoth Gilead

29So the king of Israel and Jehoshaphat king of Judah went up to Ramoth Gilead. 30The king of Israel said to Jehoshaphat, "I will enter the battle in disguise, but you wear your royal robes." So the king of Israel disguised himself and went into battle.

31Now the king of Aram had ordered his thirty-two chariot commanders, "Do not fight with anyone, small or great, except the king of Israel." 32When the chariot commanders saw Jehoshaphat, they thought, "Surely this is the king of Israel." So they turned to attack him, but when Jehoshaphat cried out, 33the chariot commanders saw that he was not the king of Israel and stopped pursuing him.

34But someone drew his bow at random and hit the king of Israel between the sections of his armor. The king told his chariot driver, "Wheel around and get me out of the fighting. I've been wounded." 35All day long the battle raged, and the king was propped up in his chariot facing the Arameans. The blood from his wound ran onto the floor of the chariot, and that evening he died. 36As the sun was setting, a cry spread through the army: "Every man to his town. Every man to his land!"

37So the king died and was brought to Samaria, and they buried him there. 38They washed the chariot at a pool in Samaria (where the prostitutes bathed),*a* and the dogs licked up his blood, as the word of the LORD had declared.

39As for the other events of Ahab's reign, including all he did, the palace he built and adorned with ivory, and the cities he fortified, are they not written in the book of the annals of the kings of Israel? 40Ahab rested with his ancestors. And Ahaziah his son succeeded him as king.

### Jehoshaphat King of Judah

41Jehoshaphat son of Asa became king of Judah in the fourth year of Ahab king of Israel. 42Jehoshaphat was thirty-five years old when he became king, and he reigned in Jerusalem twenty-five years. His mother's name was Azubah daughter of Shilhi. 43In everything he followed the ways of his father Asa and did not stray from them; he did what was right in the eyes of the LORD. The high places, however, were not removed, and the people continued to offer sacrifices and burn incense there.*b* 44Jehoshaphat was also at peace with the king of Israel.

45As for the other events of Jehoshaphat's reign, the things he achieved and his military exploits, are they not written in the book of the annals of the kings of Judah? 46He rid the land of the rest of the male shrine prostitutes who remained there even after the reign of his father Asa. 47There was then no king in Edom; a provincial governor ruled.

48Now Jehoshaphat built a fleet of trading ships*c* to go to Ophir for gold, but they never set sail—they were wrecked at Ezion Geber. 49At that time Ahaziah son of Ahab said to Jehoshaphat, "Let my men sail with yours," but Jehoshaphat refused.

50Then Jehoshaphat rested with his ancestors and was buried with them in the city of David his father. And Jehoram his son succeeded him as king.

## Amplified Bible

feed him with bread and water of affliction until I come in peace.

28Micaiah said, If you return at all in peace, the Lord has not spoken by me. He [added], Hear, O people, every one of you!

29So [Ahab] king of Israel and Jehoshaphat the king of Judah went up to Ramoth-gilead.

30And the king of Israel said to Jehoshaphat, I will disguise myself and enter the battle, but you put on your [royal] clothing. And the king of Israel disguised himself and went into the battle.

31But the king of Syria had commanded the thirty-two captains of his chariots, Fight neither with small nor great, but only with [Ahab] king of Israel.

32And when the captains of the chariots saw Jehoshaphat, they said, Surely it is the king of Israel. They turned to fight against him, but Jehoshaphat cried out.

33And when the captains of the chariots saw that it was not the king of Israel, they turned back from pursuing him.

34But a certain man drew a bow at a venture and smote [Ahab] the king of Israel between the joints of the armor. So he said to the driver of his chariot, Turn around and carry me out of the army, for I am wounded.

35The battle increased that day, and [Ahab] the king was propped up in his chariot facing the Syrians, and at nightfall he died. And the blood of his wound flowed onto the floor of the chariot.

36And there went a cry throughout the army about sundown, saying, Every man to his city and his own country,

37For the king is dead! And [Ahab] was brought to Samaria, where they buried him.

38And they washed [his] chariot by the pool of Samaria, where the harlots bathed, and the dogs licked up his blood, as the Lord had predicted. [I Kings 21:19.]

39The rest of Ahab's acts, all he did, the ivory palace and all the cities he built, are they not written in the Book of the Chronicles of the Kings of Israel?

40So Ahab slept with his fathers. Ahaziah his son reigned in his stead.

41Jehoshaphat son of Asa began to reign over Judah in the fourth year of Ahab king of Israel.

42Jehoshaphat was thirty-five years old when he began to reign, and he reigned twenty-five years in Jerusalem. His mother was Azubah daughter of Shilhi.

43He walked in all the ways or customs of Asa his father, never swerving from it, doing right in the sight of the Lord. However, the [idolatrous] high places were not taken away; for the people still sacrificed and burned incense in the high places.

44And Jehoshaphat made peace with Israel's king.

45The rest of the acts of Jehoshaphat, his might that he showed and how he warred, are they not written in the Book of the Chronicles of the Kings of Judah?

46And the remnant of the sodomites (the male cult prostitutes) who remained in the days of his father Asa, [Jehoshaphat] expelled from the country.

47There was no king in Edom; a deputy was acting king.

48Jehoshaphat ordered ships of Tarshish to go to Ophir for gold, but they did not go, for the ships were wrecked at Ezion-geber.

49When Ahaziah son of Ahab said to Jehoshaphat, Let my servants go with your servants in the ships, Jehoshaphat refused.

50Jehoshaphat slept with his fathers and was buried with them in the city of David his father [forefather]. And Jehoram his son reigned in his stead.

---

*a* 38 Or *Samaria and cleaned the weapons*   *b* 43 In Hebrew texts this sentence (22:43b) is numbered 22:44, and 22:44-53 is numbered 22:45-54.   *c* 48 Hebrew *of ships of Tarshish*

## New International Version

### Ahaziah King of Israel

51 Ahaziah son of Ahab became king of Israel in Samaria in the seventeenth year of Jehoshaphat king of Judah, and he reigned over Israel two years. 52 He did evil in the eyes of the LORD, because he followed the ways of his father and mother and of Jeroboam son of Nebat, who caused Israel to sin. 53 He served and worshiped Baal and aroused the anger of the LORD, the God of Israel, just as his father had done.

## Amplified Bible

51 Ahaziah son of Ahab began his two-year reign over Israel in Samaria in the seventeenth year of Jehoshaphat king of Judah.

52 He did evil in the sight of the Lord and walked in the ways of his father [Ahab] and of his mother [Jezebel] and of Jeroboam son of Nebat, who made Israel sin.

53 He served Baal and worshiped him and provoked the Lord, the God of Israel, to anger in all the ways his father had done.

# 2 Kings

## The LORD's Judgment on Ahaziah

**1** After Ahab's death, Moab rebelled against Israel. ²Now Ahaziah had fallen through the lattice of his upper room in Samaria and injured himself. So he sent messengers, saying to them, "Go and consult Baal-Zebub, the god of Ekron, to see if I will recover from this injury."

³But the angel of the LORD said to Elijah the Tishbite, "Go up and meet the messengers of the king of Samaria and ask them, 'Is it because there is no God in Israel that you are going off to consult Baal-Zebub, the god of Ekron?' ⁴Therefore this is what the LORD says: 'You will not leave the bed you are lying on. You will certainly die!'" So Elijah went.

⁵When the messengers returned to the king, he asked them, "Why have you come back?"

⁶"A man came to meet us," they replied. "And he said to us, 'Go back to the king who sent you and tell him, "This is what the LORD says: Is it because there is no God in Israel that you are sending messengers to consult Baal-Zebub, the god of Ekron? Therefore you will not leave the bed you are lying on. You will certainly die!"'"

⁷The king asked them, "What kind of man was it who came to meet you and told you this?"

⁸They replied, "He had a garment of hair[a] and had a leather belt around his waist."

The king said, "That was Elijah the Tishbite."

⁹Then he sent to Elijah a captain with his company of fifty men. The captain went up to Elijah, who was sitting on the top of a hill, and said to him, "Man of God, the king says, 'Come down!'"

¹⁰Elijah answered the captain, "If I am a man of God, may fire come down from heaven and consume you and your fifty men!" Then fire fell from heaven and consumed the captain and his men.

¹¹At this the king sent to Elijah another captain with his fifty men. The captain said to him, "Man of God, this is what the king says, 'Come down at once!'"

¹²"If I am a man of God," Elijah replied, "may fire come down from heaven and consume you and your fifty men!" Then the fire of God fell from heaven and consumed him and his fifty men.

¹³So the king sent a third captain with his fifty men. This third captain went up and fell on his knees before Elijah. "Man of God," he begged, "please have respect for my life and the lives of these fifty men, your servants! ¹⁴See, fire has fallen from heaven and consumed the first two captains and all their men. But now have respect for my life!"

¹⁵The angel of the LORD said to Elijah, "Go down with him; do not be afraid of him." So Elijah got up and went down with him to the king.

¹⁶He told the king, "This is what the LORD says: Is it because there is no God in Israel for you to consult that you have sent messengers to consult Baal-Zebub, the god of Ekron? Because you have done this, you will never leave the bed you are lying on. You will certainly die!" ¹⁷So he died, according to the word of the LORD that Elijah had spoken.

Because Ahaziah had no son, Joram[b] succeeded him as king in the second year of Jehoram son of Jehoshaphat

# Kings

**1** Moab rebelled against Israel after the death of Ahab. ²[King] Ahaziah fell down through a lattice in his upper chamber in Samaria and lay sick. He sent messengers, saying, Go, ask Baal-zebub, the god of [Philistine] Ekron, if I shall recover from this illness.

³But the angel of the Lord said to Elijah the Tishbite, Arise, go up to meet the messengers of the king in Samaria and say to them, Is it because there is no God in Israel that you are going to inquire of Baal-zebub, the god of Ekron?

⁴Therefore the Lord says: You [Ahaziah] shall not leave the bed on which you lie, but shall surely die. And Elijah departed.

⁵When the messengers returned to Ahaziah, he said, Why have you turned back?

⁶They replied, A man came up to meet us who said, Go back to the king who sent you and tell him, Thus says the Lord: Is there no God in Israel that you send to inquire of Baal-zebub, the god of Ekron? Therefore you shall not leave the bed on which you lie, but shall surely die.

⁷The king asked, What was the man like who came to meet you saying these things?

⁸They answered, He was a hairy man with a girdle of leather about his loins. And he said, It is Elijah the Tishbite.

⁹Then the king sent to Elijah a captain of fifty men with his fifty [to seize him]. He found Elijah sitting on a hilltop and said, Man of God, the king says, Come down.

¹⁰Elijah said to the captain of fifty, If I am a man of God, then let fire come down from heaven and consume you and your fifty. And fire fell from heaven and consumed him and his fifty.

¹¹Again King [Ahaziah] sent to him another captain of fifty with his fifty. And he said to Elijah, Man of God, the king says, Come down quickly!

¹²And Elijah answered, If I am a man of God, let fire come down from heaven and consume you and your fifty. And the fire of God came down from heaven and consumed him and his fifty.

¹³Ahaziah sent again a captain of a third fifty with his fifty. And the third captain of fifty went up and fell on his knees before Elijah and besought him and said to him, O man of God, I pray you, let my life and the lives of these fifty, your servants, be precious in your sight.

¹⁴Behold, fire came down from heaven and burned up the two captains of the former fifties with their fifties. Therefore let my life now be precious in your sight.

¹⁵The angel of the Lord said to Elijah, Go down with him; do not be afraid of him. So he arose and went with him to the king.

¹⁶Elijah said to [King] Ahaziah, Thus says the Lord: Since you have sent messengers to inquire of Baal-zebub, god of Ekron, is it because there is no God in Israel of Whom to inquire His word? Therefore you shall not leave the bed on which you lie, but shall surely die.

¹⁷So Ahaziah died according to the word of the Lord which Elijah had spoken. [a]Joram [also a son of Ahab] reigned in Israel in his stead in the second year of Jehoram son of Jehoshaphat king of Judah, because Ahaziah had no son [but his brother].

---

a 8 Or *He was a hairy man*   b 17 Hebrew *Jehoram*, a variant of *Joram*     a Hebrew *Jehoram*, a variant of *Joram*.

## New International Version

king of Judah. ¹⁸As for all the other events of Ahaziah's reign, and what he did, are they not written in the book of the annals of the kings of Israel?

### Elijah Taken Up to Heaven

**2** When the LORD was about to take Elijah up to heaven in a whirlwind, Elijah and Elisha were on their way from Gilgal. ²Elijah said to Elisha, "Stay here; the LORD has sent me to Bethel."

But Elisha said, "As surely as the LORD lives and as you live, I will not leave you." So they went down to Bethel.

³The company of the prophets at Bethel came out to Elisha and asked, "Do you know that the LORD is going to take your master from you today?"

"Yes, I know," Elisha replied, "so be quiet."

⁴Then Elijah said to him, "Stay here, Elisha; the LORD has sent me to Jericho."

And he replied, "As surely as the LORD lives and as you live, I will not leave you." So they went to Jericho.

⁵The company of the prophets at Jericho went up to Elisha and asked him, "Do you know that the LORD is going to take your master from you today?"

"Yes, I know," he replied, "so be quiet."

⁶Then Elijah said to him, "Stay here; the LORD has sent me to the Jordan."

And he replied, "As surely as the LORD lives and as you live, I will not leave you." So the two of them walked on.

⁷Fifty men from the company of the prophets went and stood at a distance, facing the place where Elijah and Elisha had stopped at the Jordan. ⁸Elijah took his cloak, rolled it up and struck the water with it. The water divided to the right and to the left, and the two of them crossed over on dry ground.

⁹When they had crossed, Elijah said to Elisha, "Tell me, what can I do for you before I am taken from you?"

"Let me inherit a double portion of your spirit," Elisha replied.

¹⁰"You have asked a difficult thing," Elijah said, "yet if you see me when I am taken from you, it will be yours— otherwise, it will not."

¹¹As they were walking along and talking together, suddenly a chariot of fire and horses of fire appeared and separated the two of them, and Elijah went up to heaven in a whirlwind. ¹²Elisha saw this and cried out, "My father! My father! The chariots and horsemen of Israel!" And Elisha saw him no more. Then he took hold of his garment and tore it in two.

¹³Elisha then picked up Elijah's cloak that had fallen from him and went back and stood on the bank of the Jordan. ¹⁴He took the cloak that had fallen from Elijah and struck the water with it. "Where now is the LORD, the God of Elijah?" he asked. When he struck the water, it divided to the right and to the left, and he crossed over.

¹⁵The company of the prophets from Jericho, who were watching, said, "The spirit of Elijah is resting on Elisha." And they went to meet him and bowed to the ground before him. ¹⁶"Look," they said, "we your servants have fifty able men. Let them go and look for your master. Perhaps the Spirit of the LORD has picked him up and set him down on some mountain or in some valley."

"No," Elisha replied, "do not send them."

¹⁷But they persisted until he was too embarrassed to refuse. So he said, "Send them." And they sent fifty men, who searched for three days but did not find him. ¹⁸When they returned to Elisha, who was staying in Jericho, he said to them, "Didn't I tell you not to go?"

## Amplified Bible

¹⁸Now the rest of the acts of Ahaziah, are they not written in the Book of the Chronicles of the Kings of Israel?

**2** When the Lord was about to take Elijah up to heaven by a whirlwind, Elijah and Elisha were going from Gilgal.

²And Elijah said to Elisha, Tarry here, I pray you, for the Lord has sent me to Bethel. But Elisha replied, As the Lord lives and as your soul lives, I will not leave you. So they went down to Bethel.

³The prophets' sons who were at Bethel came to Elisha and said, Do you know that the Lord will take your master away from you today? He said, Yes, I know it; hold your peace.

⁴Elijah said to him, Elisha, tarry here, I pray you, for the Lord has sent me to Jericho. But he said, As the Lord lives and as your soul lives, I will not leave you. So they came to Jericho.

⁵The sons of the prophets who were at Jericho came to Elisha and said, Do you know that the Lord will take your master away from you today? And he answered, Yes, I know it; hold your peace.

⁶Elijah said to him, Tarry here, I pray you, for the Lord has sent me to the Jordan. But he said, As the Lord lives and as your soul lives, I will not leave you. And the two of them went on.

⁷Fifty men of the sons of the prophets also went and stood [to watch] afar off; and the two of them stood by the Jordan.

⁸And Elijah took his mantle and rolled it up and struck the waters, and they divided this way and that, so that the two of them went over on dry ground.

⁹And when they had gone over, Elijah said to Elisha, Ask what I shall do for you before I am taken from you. And Elisha said, I pray you, let a double portion of your spirit be upon me.

¹⁰He said, You have asked a hard thing. However, if you see me when I am taken from you, it shall be so for you— but if not, it shall not be so.

¹¹As they still went on and talked, behold, a chariot of fire and horses of fire parted the two of them, and Elijah went up by a whirlwind into heaven.

¹²And Elisha saw it and he cried, My father, my father! The chariot of Israel and its horsemen! And he saw him no more. And he took hold of his own clothes and tore them in two pieces.

¹³He took up also the mantle of Elijah that fell from him and went back and stood by the bank of the Jordan.

¹⁴And he took the mantle that fell from Elijah and struck the waters and said, Where is the Lord, the God of Elijah? And when he had struck the waters, they parted this way and that, and Elisha went over.

¹⁵When the sons of the prophets who were [watching] at Jericho saw him, they said, The spirit of Elijah rests on Elisha. And they came to meet him and bowed themselves to the ground before him.

¹⁶And they said to him, Behold now, there are among your servants fifty strong men; let them go, we pray you, and seek your master. It may be that the Spirit of the Lord has taken him up and cast him on some mountain or into some valley. And he said, You shall not send.

¹⁷But when they urged him till he was embarrassed, he said, Send. So they sent fifty men, who sought for three days but did not find him.

¹⁸When they returned to Elisha, who had waited at Jericho, he said to them, Did I not tell you, Do not go?

## New International Version

### Healing of the Water

[19]The people of the city said to Elisha, "Look, our lord, this town is well situated, as you can see, but the water is bad and the land is unproductive."

[20]"Bring me a new bowl," he said, "and put salt in it." So they brought it to him.

[21]Then he went out to the spring and threw the salt into it, saying, "This is what the LORD says: 'I have healed this water. Never again will it cause death or make the land unproductive.'" [22]And the water has remained pure to this day, according to the word Elisha had spoken.

### Elisha Is Jeered

[23]From there Elisha went up to Bethel. As he was walking along the road, some boys came out of the town and jeered at him. "Get out of here, baldy!" they said. "Get out of here, baldy!" [24]He turned around, looked at them and called down a curse on them in the name of the LORD. Then two bears came out of the woods and mauled forty-two of the boys. [25]And he went on to Mount Carmel and from there returned to Samaria.

### Moab Revolts

**3** Joram[a] son of Ahab became king of Israel in Samaria in the eighteenth year of Jehoshaphat king of Judah, and he reigned twelve years. [2]He did evil in the eyes of the LORD, but not as his father and mother had done. He got rid of the sacred stone of Baal that his father had made. [3]Nevertheless he clung to the sins of Jeroboam son of Nebat, which he had caused Israel to commit; he did not turn away from them.

[4]Now Mesha king of Moab raised sheep, and he had to pay the king of Israel a tribute of a hundred thousand lambs and the wool of a hundred thousand rams. [5]But after Ahab died, the king of Moab rebelled against the king of Israel. [6]So at that time King Joram set out from Samaria and mobilized all Israel. [7]He also sent this message to Jehoshaphat king of Judah: "The king of Moab has rebelled against me. Will you go with me to fight against Moab?"

"I will go with you," he replied. "I am as you are, my people as your people, my horses as your horses."

[8]"By what route shall we attack?" he asked.

"Through the Desert of Edom," he answered.

[9]So the king of Israel set out with the king of Judah and the king of Edom. After a roundabout march of seven days, the army had no more water for themselves or for the animals with them.

[10]"What!" exclaimed the king of Israel. "Has the LORD called us three kings together only to deliver us into the hands of Moab?"

[11]But Jehoshaphat asked, "Is there no prophet of the LORD here, through whom we may inquire of the LORD?"

An officer of the king of Israel answered, "Elisha son of Shaphat is here. He used to pour water on the hands of Elijah.[b]"

[12]Jehoshaphat said, "The word of the LORD is with him." So the king of Israel and Jehoshaphat and the king of Edom went down to him.

[13]Elisha said to the king of Israel, "Why do you want to involve me? Go to the prophets of your father and the prophets of your mother."

"No," the king of Israel answered, "because it was the

## Amplified Bible

[19]And the men of the city said to Elisha, Behold, inhabiting of this city is pleasant, as my lord sees, but the water is bad and the locality causes miscarriage *and* barrenness [in all animals].

[20]He said, Bring me a new bowl and put salt [the symbol of God's purifying power] in it. And they brought it to him.

[21]Then Elisha went to the spring of the waters and cast the salt in it and said, Thus says the Lord: I [not the salt] have healed these waters; there shall not be any more death, miscarriage *or* barrenness [and bereavement] because of it.

[22]So the waters were healed to this day, as Elisha had said.

[23]He went up from Jericho to Bethel. On the way, [a]young [maturing and accountable] boys came out of the city and mocked him and said to him, Go up [in a whirlwind], you baldhead! Go up, you baldhead!

[24]And he turned around and looked at them and called a curse down on them in the name of the Lord. And two she-bears came out of the woods and ripped up forty-two of the boys.

[25]Elisha went from there to Mount Carmel, and from there he returned to Samaria.

**3** Joram son of Ahab began to reign over Israel in Samaria in the eighteenth year of Jehoshaphat king of Judah, and reigned twelve years.

[2]He did evil in the sight of the Lord, but not like his father and mother; for he put away the pillar of Baal that his father had made.

[3]Yet he clung to the sins of Jeroboam son of Nebat, which made Israel to sin; he departed not from them.

[4][b]Mesha king of Moab was a sheepmaster, and paid in tribute to the king of Israel [annually] 100,000 lambs and 100,000 rams, with the wool.

[5]But when Ahab died, the king of Moab rebelled against the king of Israel.

[6]So King Joram went out of Samaria at that time and mustered all Israel.

[7]And he sent to Jehoshaphat king of Judah, saying, The king of Moab has rebelled against me. Will you go with me to war against Moab? And he said, I will go; I am as you are, my people as your people, my horses as your horses.

[8]Joram said, Which way shall we go up? Jehoshaphat answered, The way through the Wilderness of Edom.

[9]So the king of Israel went with the king of Judah and the king of Edom. They made a circuit of seven days' journey, but there was no water for the army or for the animals following them.

[10]Then the king of Israel said, Alas! The Lord has called [us] three kings together to be delivered into Moab's hand!

[11]But Jehoshaphat said, Is there no prophet of the Lord here by whom we may inquire of the Lord? One of the king of Israel's servants answered, Elisha son of Shaphat, who served Elijah, is here.

[12]Jehoshaphat said, The word of the Lord is with him. So Joram king of Israel and Jehoshaphat and the king of Edom went down to Elisha.

[13]And Elisha said to the king of Israel, What have I to do with you? Go to the prophets of your [wicked] father Ahab and your [wicked] mother Jezebel. But the king of Israel

[a] This incident has long been misunderstood because the Hebrew word "naar" was translated "little boys." That these characteristic juvenile delinquents were old enough to be fully accountable is obvious from the use of the word elsewhere. For example, it was used by David of his son Solomon and translated "young and inexperienced," when Solomon was a father (I Chron. 22:5; cf. I Kings 14:21 and II Chron. 9:30). It was used of Joseph when he was seventeen (Gen. 37:2). In fact, not less than seventy times in the *King James Version* this word "naar" is translated "young man" or "young men." [b] This name of the king of Moab occurs in the first line of the Moabite Stone. In that inscription the Moabite king mentions his successes against Omri and Omri's successor (I Kings 16:23).

---

[a] 1 Hebrew *Jehoram*, a variant of *Joram*; also in verse 6  [b] 11 That is, he was Elijah's personal servant.

## New International Version

Lord who called us three kings together to deliver us into the hands of Moab."

14 Elisha said, "As surely as the Lord Almighty lives, whom I serve, if I did not have respect for the presence of Jehoshaphat king of Judah, I would not pay any attention to you. 15 But now bring me a harpist."

While the harpist was playing, the hand of the Lord came on Elisha 16 and he said, "This is what the Lord says: I will fill this valley with pools of water. 17 For this is what the Lord says: You will see neither wind nor rain, yet this valley will be filled with water, and you, your cattle and your other animals will drink. 18 This is an easy thing in the eyes of the Lord; he will also deliver Moab into your hands. 19 You will overthrow every fortified city and every major town. You will cut down every good tree, stop up all the springs, and ruin every good field with stones."

20 The next morning, about the time for offering the sacrifice, there it was—water flowing from the direction of Edom! And the land was filled with water.

21 Now all the Moabites had heard that the kings had come to fight against them; so every man, young and old, who could bear arms was called up and stationed on the border. 22 When they got up early in the morning, the sun was shining on the water. To the Moabites across the way, the water looked red—like blood. 23 "That's blood!" they said. "Those kings must have fought and slaughtered each other. Now to the plunder, Moab!"

24 But when the Moabites came to the camp of Israel, the Israelites rose up and fought them until they fled. And the Israelites invaded the land and slaughtered the Moabites. 25 They destroyed the towns, and each man threw a stone on every good field until it was covered. They stopped up all the springs and cut down every good tree. Only Kir Hareseth was left with its stones in place, but men armed with slings surrounded it and attacked it.

26 When the king of Moab saw that the battle had gone against him, he took with him seven hundred swordsmen to break through to the king of Edom, but they failed. 27 Then he took his firstborn son, who was to succeed him as king, and offered him as a sacrifice on the city wall. The fury against Israel was great; they withdrew and returned to their own land.

### The Widow's Olive Oil

4 The wife of a man from the company of the prophets cried out to Elisha, "Your servant my husband is dead, and you know that he revered the Lord. But now his creditor is coming to take my two boys as his slaves."

2 Elisha replied to her, "How can I help you? Tell me, what do you have in your house?"

"Your servant has nothing there at all," she said, "except a small jar of olive oil."

3 Elisha said, "Go around and ask all your neighbors for empty jars. Don't ask for just a few. 4 Then go inside and shut the door behind you and your sons. Pour oil into all the jars, and as each is filled, put it to one side."

5 She left him and shut the door behind her and her sons. They brought the jars to her and she kept pouring. 6 When all the jars were full, she said to her son, "Bring me another one."

But he replied, "There is not a jar left." Then the oil stopped flowing.

## Amplified Bible

said to him, No, for the Lord has called [us] three kings together to be delivered into the hand of Moab.

14 And Elisha said, As the Lord of hosts lives, before Whom I stand, surely, were it not that I respect the presence of Jehoshaphat king of Judah, I would neither look at you nor see you [King Joram].

15 But now bring me a minstrel. And while the minstrel played, the hand *and* power of the Lord came upon [Elisha].

16 And he said, Thus says the Lord: Make this [dry] brook bed full of trenches.

17 For thus says the Lord: You shall not see wind or rain, yet that ravine shall be filled with water, so you, your cattle, and your beasts [of burden] may drink.

18 This is but a light thing in the sight of the Lord. He will deliver the Moabites also into your hands.

19 You shall smite every fenced city and every choice city, and shall fell every good tree and stop all wells of water and mar every good piece of land with stones.

20 In the morning, when the sacrifice was offered, behold, there came water by the way of Edom, and the country was filled with water.

21 When all the Moabites heard that the kings had come up to fight against them, all who were able to put on armor, young and old, gathered and drew up at the border.

22 When they rose up early next morning, and the sun shone upon the water, the Moabites saw the water across from them as red as blood.

23 And they said, This is blood; the kings have surely been fighting and have slain one another. Now then, Moab, to the spoil!

24 But when they came to the camp of Israel, the Israelites rose up and smote the Moabites, so that they fled before them. And they went forward, slaying the Moabites as they went.

25 They beat down the cities [walls], and on every good piece of land every man cast a stone, covering it [with stones]. And they stopped all the springs of water and felled all the good trees, until only the stones [of the walls of Moab's capital city] of Kir-hareseth were left standing, and the slingers surrounded and took it.

26 And when the king of Moab saw that the battle was against him, he took with him 700 swordsmen to break through to the king of Edom, but they could not.

27 Then he [Moab's king] took his eldest son, who was to reign in his stead, and offered him for a burnt offering on the wall [in full view of the horrified enemy kings]. And there was great indignation, wrath, *and* bitterness against Israel; and they [his allies Judah and Edom] withdrew from [Joram] and returned to their own land.

4 Now the wife of a son of the prophets cried to Elisha, Your servant my husband is dead, and you know that your servant feared the Lord. But the creditor has come to take my two sons to be his slaves.

2 Elisha said to her, What shall I do for you? Tell me, what have you [of sale value] in the house? She said, Your handmaid has nothing in the house except a jar of oil.

3 Then he said, Go around and borrow vessels from all your neighbors, empty vessels—and not a few.

4 And when you come in, shut the door upon you and your sons. Then pour out [the oil you have] into all those vessels, setting aside each one when it is full.

5 So she went from him and shut the door upon herself and her sons, who brought to her the vessels as she poured the oil.

6 When the vessels were all full, she said to her son, Bring me another vessel. And he said to her, There is not a one left. Then the oil stopped multiplying.

## New International Version

[7] She went and told the man of God, and he said, "Go, sell the oil and pay your debts. You and your sons can live on what is left."

### The Shunammite's Son Restored to Life

[8] One day Elisha went to Shunem. And a well-to-do woman was there, who urged him to stay for a meal. So whenever he came by, he stopped there to eat. [9] She said to her husband, "I know that this man who often comes our way is a holy man of God. [10] Let's make a small room on the roof and put in it a bed and a table, a chair and a lamp for him. Then he can stay there whenever he comes to us."

[11] One day when Elisha came, he went up to his room and lay down there. [12] He said to his servant Gehazi, "Call the Shunammite." So he called her, and she stood before him. [13] Elisha said to him, "Tell her, 'You have gone to all this trouble for us. Now what can be done for you? Can we speak on your behalf to the king or the commander of the army?'"

She replied, "I have a home among my own people."

[14] "What can be done for her?" Elisha asked.

Gehazi said, "She has no son, and her husband is old."

[15] Then Elisha said, "Call her." So he called her, and she stood in the doorway. [16] "About this time next year," Elisha said, "you will hold a son in your arms."

"No, my lord!" she objected. "Please, man of God, don't mislead your servant!"

[17] But the woman became pregnant, and the next year about that same time she gave birth to a son, just as Elisha had told her.

[18] The child grew, and one day he went out to his father, who was with the reapers. [19] He said to his father, "My head! My head!"

His father told a servant, "Carry him to his mother." [20] After the servant had lifted him up and carried him to his mother, the boy sat on her lap until noon, and then he died. [21] She went up and laid him on the bed of the man of God, then shut the door and went out.

[22] She called her husband and said, "Please send me one of the servants and a donkey so I can go to the man of God quickly and return."

[23] "Why go to him today?" he asked. "It's not the New Moon or the Sabbath."

"That's all right," she said.

[24] She saddled the donkey and said to her servant, "Lead on; don't slow down for me unless I tell you." [25] So she set out and came to the man of God at Mount Carmel.

When he saw her in the distance, the man of God said to his servant Gehazi, "Look! There's the Shunammite! [26] Run to meet her and ask her, 'Are you all right? Is your husband all right? Is your child all right?'"

"Everything is all right," she said.

[27] When she reached the man of God at the mountain, she took hold of his feet. Gehazi came over to push her away, but the man of God said, "Leave her alone! She is in bitter distress, but the LORD has hidden it from me and has not told me why."

[28] "Did I ask you for a son, my lord?" she said. "Didn't I tell you, 'Don't raise my hopes'?"

[29] Elisha said to Gehazi, "Tuck your cloak into your belt, take my staff in your hand and run. Don't greet anyone you meet, and if anyone greets you, do not answer. Lay my staff on the boy's face."

[30] But the child's mother said, "As surely as the LORD lives and as you live, I will not leave you." So he got up and followed her.

## Amplified Bible

[7] Then she came and told the man of God. He said, Go, sell the oil and pay your debt, and you and your sons live on the rest.

[8] One day Elisha went on to Shunem, where a rich and influential woman lived, who insisted on his eating a meal. Afterward, whenever he passed by, he stopped there for a meal.

[9] And she said to her husband, Behold now, I perceive that this is a holy man of God who passes by continually.

[10] Let us make a small chamber on the [housetop] and put there for him a bed, a table, a chair, and a lamp. Then whenever he comes to us, he can go [up the outside stairs and rest] here.

[11] One day he came and turned into the chamber and lay there.

[12] And he said to Gehazi his servant, Call this Shunammite. When he had called her, she stood before him.

[13] And he said to Gehazi, Say now to her, You have been most painstakingly *and* reverently concerned for us; what is to be done for you? Would you like to be spoken for to the king or to the commander of the army? She answered, I dwell among my own people [they are sufficient].

[14] Later Elisha said, What then is to be done for her? Gehazi answered, She has no child and her husband is old.

[15] He said, Call her. [Gehazi] called her, and she stood in the doorway.

[16] Elisha said, At this season when the time comes round, you shall embrace a son. She said, No, my lord, you man of God, do not lie to your handmaid.

[17] But the woman conceived and bore a son at that season the following year, as Elisha had said to her.

[18] When the child had grown, he went out one day to his father with the reapers.

[19] But he said to his father, My head, my head! The man said to his servant, Carry him to his mother.

[20] And when he was brought to his mother, he sat on her knees till noon, and then died.

[21] And she went up and laid him on the bed of the man of God, and shut the door upon him and went out.

[22] And she called to her husband and said, Send me one of the servants and one of the donkeys, that I may go quickly to the man of God and come back again.

[23] And he said, Why go to him today? It is neither the New Moon nor the Sabbath. And she said, It will be all right.

[24] Then she saddled the donkey and said to her servant, Ride fast; do not slacken your pace for me unless I tell you.

[25] So she set out and came to the man of God at Mount Carmel. When the man of God saw her afar off, he said to Gehazi his servant, Behold, yonder is that Shunammite.

[26] Run to meet her and say, Is it well with you? Well with your husband? Well with the child? And she answered, It is well.

[27] When she came to the mountain to the man of God, she clung to his feet. Gehazi came to thrust her away, but the man of God said, Let her alone, for her soul is bitter *and* vexed within her, and the Lord has hid it from me and has not told me.

[28] Then she said, Did I desire a son of my lord? Did I not say, Do not deceive me?

[29] Then he said to Gehazi, Gird up your loins and take my staff in your hand and go lay my staff on the face of the child. If you meet any man, do not salute him. If he salutes you, do not answer him.

[30] The mother of the child said, As the Lord lives and as my soul lives, I will not leave you. And he arose and followed her.

## New International Version

31Gehazi went on ahead and laid the staff on the boy's face, but there was no sound or response. So Gehazi went back to meet Elisha and told him, "The boy has not awakened."

32When Elisha reached the house, there was the boy lying dead on his couch. 33He went in, shut the door on the two of them and prayed to the Lord. 34Then he got on the bed and lay on the boy, mouth to mouth, eyes to eyes, hands to hands. As he stretched himself out on him, the boy's body grew warm. 35Elisha turned away and walked back and forth in the room and then got on the bed and stretched out on him once more. The boy sneezed seven times and opened his eyes.

36Elisha summoned Gehazi and said, "Call the Shunammite." And he did. When she came, he said, "Take your son." 37She came in, fell at his feet and bowed to the ground. Then she took her son and went out.

### Death in the Pot

38Elisha returned to Gilgal and there was a famine in that region. While the company of the prophets was meeting with him, he said to his servant, "Put on the large pot and cook some stew for these prophets."

39One of them went out into the fields to gather herbs and found a wild vine and picked as many of its gourds as his garment could hold. When he returned, he cut them up into the pot of stew, though no one knew what they were. 40The stew was poured out for the men, but as they began to eat it, they cried out, "Man of God, there is death in the pot!" And they could not eat it.

41Elisha said, "Get some flour." He put it into the pot and said, "Serve it to the people to eat." And there was nothing harmful in the pot.

### Feeding of a Hundred

42A man came from Baal Shalishah, bringing the man of God twenty loaves of barley bread baked from the first ripe grain, along with some heads of new grain. "Give it to the people to eat," Elisha said.

43"How can I set this before a hundred men?" his servant asked.

But Elisha answered, "Give it to the people to eat. For this is what the Lord says: 'They will eat and have some left over.'" 44Then he set it before them, and they ate and had some left over, according to the word of the Lord.

### Naaman Healed of Leprosy

**5** Now Naaman was commander of the army of the king of Aram. He was a great man in the sight of his master and highly regarded, because through him the Lord had given victory to Aram. He was a valiant soldier, but he had leprosy.[a]

2Now bands of raiders from Aram had gone out and had taken captive a young girl from Israel, and she served Naaman's wife. 3She said to her mistress, "If only my master would see the prophet who is in Samaria! He would cure him of his leprosy."

4Naaman went to his master and told him what the girl from Israel had said. 5"By all means, go," the king of Aram replied. "I will send a letter to the king of Israel." So Naaman left, taking with him ten talents[b] of silver, six thousand shekels[c] of gold and ten sets of clothing. 6The letter that he took to the king of Israel read: "With this letter I am sending my servant Naaman to you so that you may cure him of his leprosy."

7As soon as the king of Israel read the letter, he tore

a 1 The Hebrew for leprosy was used for various diseases affecting the skin; also in verses 3, 6, 7, 11 and 27.   b 5 That is, about 750 pounds or about 340 kilograms   c 5 That is, about 150 pounds or about 69 kilograms

## Amplified Bible

31Gehazi passed on before them and laid the staff on the child's face, but the boy neither spoke nor heard. So he went back to meet Elisha and said to him, The child has not awakened.

32When Elisha arrived in the house, the child was dead and laid upon his bed.

33So he went in, shut the door on the two of them, and prayed to the Lord.

34He went up and lay on the child, put his mouth on his mouth, his eyes on his eyes, and his hands on his hands. And as he stretched himself on him and embraced him, the child's flesh became warm.

35Then he returned and walked in the house to and fro and went up again and stretched himself upon him. And the child sneezed seven times, and then opened his eyes.

36Then [Elisha] called Gehazi and said, Call this Shunammite. So he called her. And when she came, he said, Take up your son.

37She came and fell at his feet, bowing herself to the ground. Then she took up her son and went out.

38Elisha came back to Gilgal during a famine in the land. The sons of the prophets were sitting before him, and he said to his servant, Set on the big pot and cook pottage for the sons of the prophets.

39Then one went into the field to gather herbs and gathered from a wild vine his lap full of wild gourds, and returned and cut them up into the pot of pottage, for they were unknown to them.

40So they poured it out for the men to eat. But as they ate of the pottage, they cried out, O man of God, there is death in the pot! And they could not eat it.

41But he said, Bring meal [as a symbol of God's healing power]. And he cast it into the pot and said, Pour it out for the people that they may eat. Then there was no harm in the pot.

42[At another time] a man from Baal-shalisha came and brought the man of God bread of the firstfruits, twenty loaves of barley, and fresh ears of grain [in the husk] in his sack. And Elisha said, Give to the men that they may eat.

43His servant said, How am I to set [only] this before a hundred [hungry] men? He said, Give to the men that they may eat. For thus says the Lord: They shall be fed and have some left.

44So he set it before them, and they ate and left some, as the Lord had said.

**5** Naaman, commander of the army of the king of Syria, was a great man with his master, accepted [and acceptable], because by him the Lord had given victory to Syria. He was also a mighty man of valor, but he was a leper.

2The Syrians had gone out in bands and had brought away captive out of the land of Israel a little maid, and she waited on Naaman's wife.

3She said to her mistress, Would that my lord were with the prophet who is in Samaria! For he would heal him of his leprosy.

4[Naaman] went in and told his king, Thus and thus said the maid from Israel.

5And the king of Syria said, Go now, and I will send a letter to the king of Israel. And he departed and took with him ten talents of silver, 6,000 shekels of gold, and ten changes of raiment.

6And he brought the letter to the king of Israel. It said, When this letter comes to you, I will with it have sent to you my servant Naaman, that you may cure him of leprosy.

7When the king of Israel read the letter, he rent his

## New International Version

his robes and said, "Am I God? Can I kill and bring back to life? Why does this fellow send someone to me to be cured of his leprosy? See how he is trying to pick a quarrel with me!"

[8]When Elisha the man of God heard that the king of Israel had torn his robes, he sent him this message: "Why have you torn your robes? Have the man come to me and he will know that there is a prophet in Israel." [9]So Naaman went with his horses and chariots and stopped at the door of Elisha's house. [10]Elisha sent a messenger to say to him, "Go, wash yourself seven times in the Jordan, and your flesh will be restored and you will be cleansed."

[11]But Naaman went away angry and said, "I thought that he would surely come out to me and stand and call on the name of the LORD his God, wave his hand over the spot and cure me of my leprosy. [12]Are not Abana and Pharpar, the rivers of Damascus, better than all the waters of Israel? Couldn't I wash in them and be cleansed?" So he turned and went off in a rage.

[13]Naaman's servants went to him and said, "My father, if the prophet had told you to do some great thing, would you not have done it? How much more, then, when he tells you, 'Wash and be cleansed'!" [14]So he went down and dipped himself in the Jordan seven times, as the man of God had told him, and his flesh was restored and became clean like that of a young boy.

[15]Then Naaman and all his attendants went back to the man of God. He stood before him and said, "Now I know that there is no God in all the world except in Israel. So please accept a gift from your servant."

[16]The prophet answered, "As surely as the LORD lives, whom I serve, I will not accept a thing." And even though Naaman urged him, he refused.

[17]"If you will not," said Naaman, "please let me, your servant, be given as much earth as a pair of mules can carry, for your servant will never again make burnt offerings and sacrifices to any other god but the LORD. [18]But may the LORD forgive your servant for this one thing: When my master enters the temple of Rimmon to bow down and he is leaning on my arm and I have to bow there also—when I bow down in the temple of Rimmon, may the LORD forgive your servant for this."

[19]"Go in peace," Elisha said.

After Naaman had traveled some distance, [20]Gehazi, the servant of Elisha the man of God, said to himself, "My master was too easy on Naaman, this Aramean, by not accepting from him what he brought. As surely as the LORD lives, I will run after him and get something from him."

[21]So Gehazi hurried after Naaman. When Naaman saw him running toward him, he got down from the chariot to meet him. "Is everything all right?" he asked.

[22]"Everything is all right," Gehazi answered. "My master sent me to say, 'Two young men from the company of the prophets have just come to me from the hill country of Ephraim. Please give them a talent[a] of silver and two sets of clothing.'"

[23]"By all means, take two talents," said Naaman. He urged Gehazi to accept them, and then tied up the two talents of silver in two bags, with two sets of clothing. He gave them to two of his servants, and they carried them ahead of Gehazi. [24]When Gehazi came to the hill, he took the things from the servants and put them away in the house. He sent the men away and they left.

[25]When he went in and stood before his master, Elisha asked him, "Where have you been, Gehazi?"

"Your servant didn't go anywhere," Gehazi answered.

## Amplified Bible

clothes and said, Am I God, to kill and to make alive, that this man sends to me to heal a man of his leprosy? Just consider and see how he is seeking a quarrel with me.

[8]When Elisha the man of God heard that the king of Israel had rent his clothes, he sent to the king, asking, Why have you rent your clothes? Let Naaman come now to me and he shall know that there is a prophet in Israel.

[9]So Naaman came with his horses and chariots and stopped at Elisha's door.

[10]Elisha sent a messenger to him, saying, Go and wash in the Jordan seven times, and your flesh shall be restored and you shall be clean.

[11]But Naaman was angry and went away and said, Behold, I thought he would surely come out to me and stand and call on the name of the Lord his God, and wave his hand over the place and heal the leper.

[12]Are not Abana and Pharpar, the rivers of Damascus, better than all the waters of Israel? May I not wash in them and be clean? So he turned and went away in a rage.

[13]And his servants came near and said to him, My father, if the prophet had bid you to do some great thing, would you not have done it? How much rather, then, when he says to you, Wash and be clean?

[14]Then he went down and dipped himself seven times in the Jordan, as the man of God had said, and his flesh was restored like that of a little child, and he was clean.

[15]Then Naaman returned to the man of God, he and all his company, and stood before him. He said, Behold, now I know that there is no God in all the earth but in Israel. So now accept a gift from your servant.

[16]Elisha said, As the Lord lives, before Whom I stand, I will accept none. He urged him to take it, but Elisha refused.

[17]Naaman said, Then, I pray you, let there be given to me, your servant, two mules' burden of earth. For your servant will henceforth offer neither burnt offering nor sacrifice to other gods, but only to the Lord.

[18]In this thing may the Lord pardon your servant: when my master [the king] goes into the house of [his god] Rimmon to worship there, and he leans on my hand and I bow myself in the house of Rimmon, when I bow down myself in the house of Rimmon, may the Lord pardon your servant in this thing.

[19]Elisha said to him, Go in peace. So Naaman departed from him a little way.

[20]But Gehazi, the servant of Elisha the man of God, said, Behold, my master spared this Naaman the Syrian, in not receiving from his hands what he brought. But as the Lord lives, I will run after him and get something from him.

[21]So Gehazi followed after Naaman. When Naaman saw one running after him, he lighted down from the chariot to meet him and said, Is all well?

[22]And he said, All is well. My master has sent me to say, There have just come to me from the hill country of Ephraim two young men of the sons of the prophets. I pray you, give them a talent of silver and two changes of garments.

[23]And Naaman said, Be pleased to take two talents. And he urged him, and bound two talents of silver in two bags with two changes of garments and laid them upon two of his servants, and they bore them before Gehazi.

[24]When he came to the hill, he took them from their hands and put them in the house; and he sent the men away, and they left.

[25]He went in and stood before his master. Elisha said, Where have you been, Gehazi? He said, Your servant went nowhere.

---

[a] 22 That is, about 75 pounds or about 34 kilograms

## New International Version

26But Elisha said to him, "Was not my spirit with you when the man got down from his chariot to meet you? Is this the time to take money or to accept clothes—or olive groves and vineyards, or flocks and herds, or male and female slaves? 27Naaman's leprosy will cling to you and to your descendants forever." Then Gehazi went from Elisha's presence and his skin was leprous—it had become as white as snow.

### An Axhead Floats

**6** The company of the prophets said to Elisha, "Look, the place where we meet with you is too small for us. 2Let us go to the Jordan, where each of us can get a pole; and let us build a place there for us to meet."

And he said, "Go."

3Then one of them said, "Won't you please come with your servants?"

"I will," Elisha replied. 4And he went with them.

They went to the Jordan and began to cut down trees. 5As one of them was cutting down a tree, the iron axhead fell into the water. "Oh no, my lord!" he cried out. "It was borrowed!"

6The man of God asked, "Where did it fall?" When he showed him the place, Elisha cut a stick and threw it there, and made the iron float. 7"Lift it out," he said. Then the man reached out his hand and took it.

### Elisha Traps Blinded Arameans

8Now the king of Aram was at war with Israel. After conferring with his officers, he said, "I will set up my camp in such and such a place."

9The man of God sent word to the king of Israel: "Beware of passing that place, because the Arameans are going down there." 10So the king of Israel checked on the place indicated by the man of God. Time and again Elisha warned the king, so that he was on his guard in such places.

11This enraged the king of Aram. He summoned his officers and demanded of them, "Tell me! Which of us is on the side of the king of Israel?"

12"None of us, my lord the king," said one of his officers, "but Elisha, the prophet who is in Israel, tells the king of Israel the very words you speak in your bedroom."

13"Go, find out where he is," the king ordered, "so I can send men and capture him." The report came back: "He is in Dothan." 14Then he sent horses and chariots and a strong force there. They went by night and surrounded the city.

15When the servant of the man of God got up and went out early the next morning, an army with horses and chariots had surrounded the city. "Oh no, my lord! What shall we do?" the servant asked.

16"Don't be afraid," the prophet answered. "Those who are with us are more than those who are with them."

17And Elisha prayed, "Open his eyes, Lord, so that he may see." Then the Lord opened the servant's eyes, and he looked and saw the hills full of horses and chariots of fire all around Elisha.

18As the enemy came down toward him, Elisha prayed to the Lord, "Strike this army with blindness." So he struck them with blindness, as Elisha had asked.

19Elisha told them, "This is not the road and this is not the city. Follow me, and I will lead you to the man you are looking for." And he led them to Samaria.

20After they entered the city, Elisha said, "Lord, open the eyes of these men so they can see." Then the Lord opened their eyes and they looked, and there they were, inside Samaria.

## Amplified Bible

26Elisha said to him, Did not my spirit go with you when the man turned from his chariot to meet you? Was it a time to accept money, garments, olive orchards, vineyards, sheep, oxen, menservants, and maidservants?

27Therefore the leprosy of Naaman shall cleave to you and to your offspring forever. And Gehazi went from his presence a leper as white as snow.

**6** The sons of the prophets said to Elisha, Look now, the place where we live before you is too small for us. 2Let us go to the Jordan, and each man get there a [house] beam; and let us make us a place there where we may dwell. And he answered, Go.

3One said, Be pleased to go with your servants. He answered, I will go.

4So he went with them. And when they came to the Jordan, they cut down trees.

5But as one was felling his beam, the axhead fell into the water; and he cried, Alas, my master, for it was borrowed!

6The man of God said, Where did it fall? When shown the place, Elisha cut off a stick and threw it in there, and the iron floated.

7He said, Pick it up. And he put out his hand and took it.

8When the king of Syria was warring against Israel, after counseling with his servants, he said, In such and such a place shall be my camp.

9Then the man of God sent to the king of Israel, saying, Beware that you pass not such a place, for the Syrians are coming down there.

10Then the king of Israel sent to the place of which [Elisha] told and warned him; and thus he protected and saved himself there repeatedly.

11Therefore the mind of the king of Syria was greatly troubled by this thing. He called his servants and said, Will you show me who of us is for the king of Israel?

12One of his servants said, None, my lord O king; but Elisha, the prophet who is in Israel, tells the king of Israel the words that you speak in your bedchamber.

13He said, Go and see where he is, that I may send and seize him. And it was told him, He is in Dothan.

14So [the Syrian king] sent there horses, chariots, and a great army. They came by night and surrounded the city.

15When the servant of the man of God rose early and went out, behold, an army with horses and chariots was around the city. Elisha's servant said to him, Alas, my master! What shall we do?

16[Elisha] answered, Fear not; for those with us are more than those with them.

17Then Elisha prayed, Lord, I pray You, open his eyes that he may see. And the Lord opened the young man's eyes, and he saw, and behold, the mountain was full of horses and chariots of fire round about Elisha.

18And when the Syrians came down to him, Elisha prayed to the Lord, Smite this people with blindness, I pray You. And God smote them with blindness, as Elisha asked.

19Elisha said to the Syrians, This is not the way or the city. Follow me, and I will bring you to the man whom you seek. And he led them to Samaria.

20And when they had come into Samaria, Elisha said, Lord, open the eyes of these men that they may see. And the Lord opened their eyes, and they saw. Behold, they were in the midst of Samaria!

## New International Version

21When the king of Israel saw them, he asked Elisha, "Shall I kill them, my father? Shall I kill them?"
22"Do not kill them," he answered. "Would you kill those you have captured with your own sword or bow? Set food and water before them so that they may eat and drink and then go back to their master." 23So he prepared a great feast for them, and after they had finished eating and drinking, he sent them away, and they returned to their master. So the bands from Aram stopped raiding Israel's territory.

### Famine in Besieged Samaria

24Some time later, Ben-Hadad king of Aram mobilized his entire army and marched up and laid siege to Samaria. 25There was a great famine in the city; the siege lasted so long that a donkey's head sold for eighty shekels*a* of silver, and a quarter of a cab*b* of seed pods*c* for five shekels.*d*
26As the king of Israel was passing by on the wall, a woman cried to him, "Help me, my lord the king!"
27The king replied, "If the LORD does not help you, where can I get help for you? From the threshing floor? From the winepress?" 28Then he asked her, "What's the matter?"
She answered, "This woman said to me, 'Give up your son so we may eat him today, and tomorrow we'll eat my son.' 29So we cooked my son and ate him. The next day I said to her, 'Give up your son so we may eat him,' but she had hidden him."
30When the king heard the woman's words, he tore his robes. As he went along the wall, the people looked, and they saw that, under his robes, he had sackcloth on his body. 31He said, "May God deal with me, be it ever so severely, if the head of Elisha son of Shaphat remains on his shoulders today!"
32Now Elisha was sitting in his house, and the elders were sitting with him. The king sent a messenger ahead, but before he arrived, Elisha said to the elders, "Don't you see how this murderer is sending someone to cut off my head? Look, when the messenger comes, shut the door and hold it shut against him. Is not the sound of his master's footsteps behind him?" 33While he was still talking to them, the messenger came down to him.
The king said, "This disaster is from the LORD. Why should I wait for the LORD any longer?"

**7** Elisha replied, "Hear the word of the LORD. This is what the LORD says: About this time tomorrow, a seah*e* of the finest flour will sell for a shekel*f* and two seahs*g* of barley for a shekel at the gate of Samaria."
2The officer on whose arm the king was leaning said to the man of God, "Look, even if the LORD should open the floodgates of the heavens, could this happen?"
"You will see it with your own eyes," answered Elisha, "but you will not eat any of it!"

### The Siege Lifted

3Now there were four men with leprosy*h* at the entrance of the city gate. They said to each other, "Why stay here until we die? 4If we say, 'We'll go into the city'—the famine

## Amplified Bible

21When the king of Israel saw them, he said to Elisha, My father, shall I slay them? Shall I slay them?
22[Elisha] answered, You shall not slay them. Would you slay those you have taken captive with your sword and bow? Set bread and water before them, that they may eat and drink and return to their master.
23So [the king] prepared great provision for them, and when they had eaten and drunk, he sent them away, and they went to their master. And the bands of Syria came no more into the land of Israel.
24Afterward, Ben-hadad king of Syria gathered his whole army and went up and besieged Samaria,
25And a great famine came to Samaria. They besieged it until a donkey's head was sold for eighty shekels of silver, and a fourth of a kab of dove's dung [a wild vegetable] for five shekels of silver.
26As the king of Israel was passing by upon the wall, a woman cried to him, Help, my lord, O king!
27He said, [For] if he does not help you [No, let the Lord help you!], from where can I get you help? Out of the threshing floor, or out of the winepress?
28And the king said to her, What ails you? She answered, This woman said to me, Give me your son so we may eat him today, and we will eat my son tomorrow.
29So we boiled my son and ate him. The next day I said to her, Give your son so we may eat him, but she had hidden her son.
30When the king heard the woman's words, he rent his clothes. As he went on upon the wall, the people looked, and behold, he wore sackcloth inside on his flesh.
31Then he said, May God do so to me, and more also, if the head of Elisha son of Shaphat shall stand on him this day!
32Now Elisha sat in his house, and the elders sat with him. And the king sent a man from before him [to behead Elisha]. But before the messenger arrived, Elisha said to the elders, See how this son of [Jezebel] a murderer is sending to remove my head? Look, when the messenger comes, shut the door and hold it fast against him. Is not the sound of his master's feet [just] behind him?
33And while Elisha was talking with them, behold, [the messenger] came to him [and then the king came also]. And [the relenting king] said, This evil is from the Lord! Why should I any longer wait [expecting Him to withdraw His punishment? What, Elisha, can be done now]?

**7** Then Elisha said, Hear the word of the Lord. Thus says the Lord: Tomorrow about this time a measure of fine flour will sell for a shekel and two measures of barley for a shekel in the gate of Samaria!
2Then the captain on whose hand the king leaned answered the man of God and said, If the Lord should make windows in heaven, could this thing be? But Elisha said, You shall see it with your own eyes, but you shall not eat of it.
3Now four men who were lepers were at the entrance of the city's gate; and they said to one another, Why do we sit here until we die?
4If we say, We will enter the city—then the famine is in

---

*a 25* That is, about 2 pounds or about 920 grams    *b 25* That is, probably about 1/4 pound or about 100 grams    *c 25* Or *of doves' dung*    *d 25* That is, about 2 ounces or about 58 grams    *e 1* That is, probably about 12 pounds or about 5.5 kilograms of flour; also in verses 16 and 18    *f 1* That is, about 2/5 ounce or about 12 grams; also in verses 16 and 18    *g 1* That is, probably about 20 pounds or about 9 kilograms of barley; also in verses 16 and 18    *h 3* The Hebrew for *leprosy* was used for various diseases affecting the skin; also in verse 8.

## New International Version

is there, and we will die. And if we stay here, we will die. So let's go over to the camp of the Arameans and surrender. If they spare us, we live; if they kill us, then we die."

⁵At dusk they got up and went to the camp of the Arameans. When they reached the edge of the camp, no one was there, ⁶for the Lord had caused the Arameans to hear the sound of chariots and horses and a great army, so that they said to one another, "Look, the king of Israel has hired the Hittite and Egyptian kings to attack us!" ⁷So they got up and fled in the dusk and abandoned their tents and their horses and donkeys. They left the camp as it was and ran for their lives.

⁸The men who had leprosy reached the edge of the camp, entered one of the tents and ate and drank. Then they took silver, gold and clothes, and went off and hid them. They returned and entered another tent and took some things from it and hid them also.

⁹Then they said to each other, "What we're doing is not right. This is a day of good news and we are keeping it to ourselves. If we wait until daylight, punishment will overtake us. Let's go at once and report this to the royal palace."

¹⁰So they went and called out to the city gatekeepers and told them, "We went into the Aramean camp and no one was there—not a sound of anyone—only tethered horses and donkeys, and the tents left just as they were." ¹¹The gatekeepers shouted the news, and it was reported within the palace.

¹²The king got up in the night and said to his officers, "I will tell you what the Arameans have done to us. They know we are starving; so they have left the camp to hide in the countryside, thinking, 'They will surely come out, and then we will take them alive and get into the city.'" ¹³One of his officers answered, "Have some men take five of the horses that are left in the city. Their plight will be like that of all the Israelites left here—yes, they will only be like all these Israelites who are doomed. So let us send them to find out what happened."

¹⁴So they selected two chariots with their horses, and the king sent them after the Aramean army. He commanded the drivers, "Go and find out what has happened." ¹⁵They followed them as far as the Jordan, and they found the whole road strewn with the clothing and equipment the Arameans had thrown away in their headlong flight. So the messengers returned and reported to the king. ¹⁶Then the people went out and plundered the camp of the Arameans. So a seah of the finest flour sold for a shekel, and two seahs of barley sold for a shekel, as the Lᴏʀᴅ had said.

¹⁷Now the king had put the officer on whose arm he leaned in charge of the gate, and the people trampled him in the gateway, and he died, just as the man of God had foretold when the king came down to his house. ¹⁸It happened as the man of God had said to the king: "About this time tomorrow, a seah of the finest flour will sell for a shekel and two seahs of barley for a shekel at the gate of Samaria."

¹⁹The officer had said to the man of God, "Look, even if the Lᴏʀᴅ should open the floodgates of the heavens, could this happen?" The man of God had replied, "You will see it with your own eyes, but you will not eat any of it!" ²⁰And that is exactly what happened to him, for the people trampled him in the gateway, and he died.

## Amplified Bible

the city, and we shall die there; and if we sit still here, we die also. So now come, let us go over to the army of the Syrians. If they spare us alive, we shall live; and if they kill us, we shall but die.

⁵So they arose in the twilight and went to the Syrian camp. But when they came to the edge of the camp, no man was there.

⁶For the Lord had made the Syrian army hear a noise of chariots and horses, the noise of a great army. They had said to one another, The king of Israel has hired the Hittite and Egyptian kings to come upon us.

⁷So the Syrians arose and fled in the twilight and left their tents, horses, donkeys, even the camp as it was, and fled for their lives.

⁸And when these lepers came to the edge of the camp, they went into one tent and ate and drank, and carried away silver, gold, and clothing, and went and hid them [in the darkness]. Then they entered another tent and carried from there also and went and hid it.

⁹Then they said one to another, We are not doing right. This is a day of [glad] good news and we are silent *and* do not speak up! If we wait until daylight, some punishment will come upon us [for not reporting at once]. So now come, let us go and tell the king's household.

¹⁰So they came and called to the gatekeepers of the city. They told them, We came to the camp of the Syrians, and behold, there was neither sight nor sound of man there— only the horses and donkeys tied, and the tents as they were.

¹¹Then the gatekeepers called out, and it was told to the king's household within.

¹²And the king rose in the night and said to his servants, I will tell you what the Syrians have done to us. They know that we are hungry; therefore they have gone out of the camp to hide themselves in the open country, thinking, When they come out of the city, we shall take them alive and get into the city.

¹³One of his servants said, Let some men take five of the remaining horses; [if they are caught and killed] they will be no worse off than all the multitude of Israel left in the city to be consumed. Let us send and see.

¹⁴So they took two chariot horses, and the king sent them after the Syrian army, saying, Go and see.

¹⁵They went after them to the Jordan. All the way was strewn with clothing and equipment which the Syrians had cast away in their flight. And the messengers returned and told the king.

¹⁶Then the people went out and plundered the tents of the Syrians. So a measure of fine flour was sold for a shekel, and two measures of barley for a shekel, as the Lord had spoken [through Elisha]. [II Kings 7:1.]

¹⁷The king had appointed the captain on whose hand he leaned to have charge of the gate, and the [starving] people trampled him in the gate [as they struggled to get through for food], and he died, as the man of God had foretold when the king came down to him.

¹⁸When the man of God had told the king, Two measures of barley shall sell for a shekel and a measure of fine flour for a shekel tomorrow about this time in the gate of Samaria,

¹⁹The captain had told the man of God, If the Lord should make windows in heaven, could such a thing be? And he said, You shall see it with your own eyes, but you shall not eat of it. [II Kings 7:2.]

²⁰And so it was fulfilled to him, for the people trampled on him in the gate, and he died.

<table>
<tr><td>

## New International Version

### The Shunammite's Land Restored

**8** Now Elisha had said to the woman whose son he had restored to life, "Go away with your family and stay for a while wherever you can, because the LORD has decreed a famine in the land that will last seven years." ²The woman proceeded to do as the man of God said. She and her family went away and stayed in the land of the Philistines seven years.

³At the end of the seven years she came back from the land of the Philistines and went to appeal to the king for her house and land. ⁴The king was talking to Gehazi, the servant of the man of God, and had said, "Tell me about all the great things Elisha has done." ⁵Just as Gehazi was telling the king how Elisha had restored the dead to life, the woman whose son Elisha had brought back to life came to appeal to the king for her house and land.

Gehazi said, "This is the woman, my lord the king, and this is her son whom Elisha restored to life." ⁶The king asked the woman about it, and she told him.

Then he assigned an official to her case and said to him, "Give back everything that belonged to her, including all the income from her land from the day she left the country until now."

### Hazael Murders Ben-Hadad

⁷Elisha went to Damascus, and Ben-Hadad king of Aram was ill. When the king was told, "The man of God has come all the way up here," ⁸he said to Hazael, "Take a gift with you and go to meet the man of God. Consult the LORD through him; ask him, 'Will I recover from this illness?'"

⁹Hazael went to meet Elisha, taking with him as a gift forty camel-loads of all the finest wares of Damascus. He went in and stood before him, and said, "Your son Ben-Hadad king of Aram has sent me to ask, 'Will I recover from this illness?'"

¹⁰Elisha answered, "Go and say to him, 'You will certainly recover.' Nevertheless,[a] the LORD has revealed to me that he will in fact die." ¹¹He stared at him with a fixed gaze until Hazael was embarrassed. Then the man of God began to weep.

¹²"Why is my lord weeping?" asked Hazael.

"Because I know the harm you will do to the Israelites," he answered. "You will set fire to their fortified places, kill their young men with the sword, dash their little children to the ground, and rip open their pregnant women." ¹³Hazael said, "How could your servant, a mere dog, accomplish such a feat?"

"The LORD has shown me that you will become king of Aram," answered Elisha.

¹⁴Then Hazael left Elisha and returned to his master. When Ben-Hadad asked, "What did Elisha say to you?" Hazael replied, "He told me that you would certainly recover." ¹⁵But the next day he took a thick cloth, soaked it in water and spread it over the king's face, so that he died. Then Hazael succeeded him as king.

### Jehoram King of Judah

¹⁶In the fifth year of Joram son of Ahab king of Israel, when Jehoshaphat was king of Judah, Jehoram son of Jehoshaphat began his reign as king of Judah. ¹⁷He was thirty-two years old when he became king, and he reigned in Jerusalem eight years. ¹⁸He followed the ways of the kings of Israel, as the house of Ahab had done, for he married a daughter of Ahab. He did evil in the eyes of the LORD. ¹⁹Nevertheless, for the sake of his servant David, the LORD was not willing to destroy Judah. He had promised to maintain a lamp for David and his descendants forever.

</td><td>

## Amplified Bible

**8** Now Elisha had said to the woman whose son he had restored to life, Arise and go with your household and sojourn wherever you can, for the Lord has called for a famine, and moreover, it will come upon the land for seven years.

²So the woman arose and did as the man of God had said. She went with her household and sojourned in the land of the Philistines seven years.

³At the end of the seven years the woman returned from the land of the Philistines, and she went to appeal to the king for her house and land.

⁴The king talked with Gehazi, the servant of the man of God, saying, Tell me all the great things Elisha has done. ⁵And as Gehazi was telling the king how [Elisha] had restored the dead to life, behold, the woman whose son he had restored to life appealed to the king for her house and land. And Gehazi said, My lord O king, this is the woman, and this is her son whom Elisha brought back to life.

⁶When the king asked the woman, she told him. So the king appointed to her a certain officer, saying, Restore all that was hers, and all the fruits of the field since the day that she left the land even until now.

⁷Elisha came to Damascus, and Ben-hadad king of Syria was sick; and he was told, The man of God has come here.

⁸And the king said to Hazael, Take a present in your hand and go meet the man of God, and inquire of the Lord by him, saying, Shall I recover from this disease?

⁹So Hazael went to meet Elisha and took a present with him of every good thing of Damascus, forty camel loads, and came and stood before him and said, Your son Ben-hadad king of Syria has sent me to you, asking, Shall I recover from this disease?

¹⁰And Elisha said, Go, say to him, You shall certainly recover; but the Lord has shown me that he shall certainly die.

¹¹Elisha stared steadily at him until Hazael was embarrassed. And the man of God wept.

¹²And Hazael said, Why do you weep, my lord? He answered, Because I know the evil that you will do to the Israelites. You will burn their strongholds, slay their young men with the sword, dash their infants in pieces, and rip up their pregnant women.

¹³And Hazael said, What is your servant, only a dog, that he should do this monstrous thing? And Elisha answered, The Lord has shown me that you will be king over Syria.

¹⁴Then [Hazael] departed from Elisha and came to his master, who said to him, What did Elisha say to you? And he answered, He told me you would surely recover.

¹⁵But the next day Hazael took the bedspread and dipped it in water and spread it on [the Syrian king's] face, so that he died. And Hazael reigned in his stead.

¹⁶In the fifth year of Joram son of Ahab king of Israel, Jehoshaphat being then king of Judah, Jehoram son of Jehoshaphat king of Judah began to reign.

¹⁷He was thirty-two years old when he began to reign, and he reigned eight years in Jerusalem.

¹⁸He walked in the ways of the kings of Israel, as did the house of Ahab, for [Athaliah] the daughter of Ahab was his wife. He did evil in the sight of the Lord.

¹⁹Yet, for David His servant's sake, the Lord would not destroy Judah, for He promised to give him and his sons a lamp forever.

</td></tr>
</table>

---

[a] 10 The Hebrew may also be read *Go and say, 'You will certainly not recover,' for.*

## New International Version

20In the time of Jehoram, Edom rebelled against Judah and set up its own king. 21So Jehoram*a* went to Zair with all his chariots. The Edomites surrounded him and his chariot commanders, but he rose up and broke through by night; his army, however, fled back home. 22To this day Edom has been in rebellion against Judah. Libnah revolted at the same time.

23As for the other events of Jehoram's reign, and all he did, are they not written in the book of the annals of the kings of Judah? 24Jehoram rested with his ancestors and was buried with them in the City of David. And Ahaziah his son succeeded him as king.

### Ahaziah King of Judah

25In the twelfth year of Joram son of Ahab king of Israel, Ahaziah son of Jehoram king of Judah began to reign. 26Ahaziah was twenty-two years old when he became king, and he reigned in Jerusalem one year. His mother's name was Athaliah, a granddaughter of Omri king of Israel. 27He followed the ways of the house of Ahab and did evil in the eyes of the LORD, as the house of Ahab had done, for he was related by marriage to Ahab's family.

28Ahaziah went with Joram son of Ahab to war against Hazael king of Aram at Ramoth Gilead. The Arameans wounded Joram; 29so King Joram returned to Jezreel to recover from the wounds the Arameans had inflicted on him at Ramoth*b* in his battle with Hazael king of Aram.

Then Ahaziah son of Jehoram king of Judah went down to Jezreel to see Joram son of Ahab, because he had been wounded.

### Jehu Anointed King of Israel

**9** The prophet Elisha summoned a man from the company of the prophets and said to him, "Tuck your cloak into your belt, take this flask of olive oil with you and go to Ramoth Gilead. 2When you get there, look for Jehu son of Jehoshaphat, the son of Nimshi. Go to him, get him away from his companions and take him into an inner room. 3Then take the flask and pour the oil on his head and declare, 'This is what the LORD says: I anoint you king over Israel.' Then open the door and run; don't delay!"

4So the young prophet went to Ramoth Gilead. 5When he arrived, he found the army officers sitting together. "I have a message for you, commander," he said.

"For which of us?" asked Jehu.

"For you, commander," he replied.

6Jehu got up and went into the house. Then the prophet poured the oil on Jehu's head and declared, "This is what the LORD, the God of Israel, says: 'I anoint you king over the LORD's people Israel. 7You are to destroy the house of Ahab your master, and I will avenge the blood of my servants the prophets and the blood of all the LORD's servants shed by Jezebel. 8The whole house of Ahab will perish. I will cut off from Ahab every last male in Israel—slave or free.*c* 9I will make the house of Ahab like the house of Jeroboam son of Nebat and like the house of Baasha son of Ahijah. 10As for Jezebel, dogs will devour her on the plot of ground at Jezreel, and no one will bury her.'" Then he opened the door and ran.

11When Jehu went out to his fellow officers, one of them asked him, "Is everything all right? Why did this maniac come to you?"

## Amplified Bible

20In his days, Edom revolted from the rule of Judah and set up a king over themselves.

21So Jehoram [of Judah] went over to Zair with all his chariots. He and his chariot commanders rose up by night and slew the Edomites who had surrounded them; and [escaping] his army fled home.

22So Edom revolted from the rule of Judah to this day. Then Libnah revolted at the same time.

23The rest of the acts of Jehoram, and all that he did, are they not written in the Book of the Chronicles of the Kings of Judah?

24Jehoram slept with his fathers and was buried with [them] in the City of David. Ahaziah his son reigned in his stead.

25In the twelfth year of Joram son of Ahab king of Israel, Ahaziah son of Jehoram king of Judah began to reign. 26Ahaziah was twenty-two years old when he began to reign, and he reigned one year in Jerusalem. His mother's name was Athaliah, the granddaughter of Omri king of Israel.

27He walked in the ways of the house of Ahab and did evil in the sight of the Lord, as did the house of Ahab, for his father was son-in-law of Ahab.

28Ahaziah went with Joram son of Ahab to war against Hazael king of Syria in Ramoth-gilead; and the Syrians wounded Joram.

29King Joram returned to Jezreel to be healed of the wounds which the Syrians had given him at Ramah when he fought against Hazael king of Syria. And Ahaziah son of Jehoram king of Judah went down to see Joram son of Ahab in Jezreel, because he was sick.

**9** And Elisha the prophet called one of the sons of the prophets and said to him, Gird up your loins, take this flask of oil in your hand, and go to Ramoth-gilead.

2When you arrive, look there for Jehu son of Jehoshaphat son of Nimshi; and go in and have him arise from among his brethren and lead him to an inner chamber.

3Then take the cruse of oil and pour it on his head and say, Thus says the Lord: I have anointed you king over Israel. Then open the door and flee; do not tarry.

4So the young man, the young prophet, went to Ramoth-gilead.

5And when he came, the captains of the army were sitting outside; and he said, I have a message for you, O captain. Jehu said, To which of us? And he said, To you, O captain.

6And Jehu arose, and they went into the house. And the prophet poured the oil on Jehu's head and said to him, Thus says the Lord, the God of Israel: I have anointed you king over the people of the Lord, even over Israel.

7You shall strike down the house of Ahab your master, that I may avenge the blood of My servants the prophets and of all the servants of the Lord [who have died] at the hands of Jezebel.

8For the whole house of Ahab shall perish, and I will cut off from Ahab every male, bond or free, in Israel.

9I will make the house of Ahab like the house of Jeroboam son of Nebat and like the house of Baasha son of Ahijah. [I Kings 21:22.]

10And the dogs shall eat Jezebel in the portion of Jezreel, and none shall bury her. And he opened the door and fled. [Fulfilled in II Kings 9:33-37.]

11When Jehu came out to the servants of his master, one said to him, Is all well? Why did this mad fellow come to

---

*a* 21 Hebrew *Joram*, a variant of *Jehoram*; also in verses 23 and 24
*b* 29 Hebrew *Ramah*, a variant of *Ramoth*    *c* 8 Or *Israel—every ruler or leader*

## New International Version

"You know the man and the sort of things he says," Jehu replied.

¹²"That's not true!" they said. "Tell us."

Jehu said, "Here is what he told me: 'This is what the Lord says: I anoint you king over Israel.'"

¹³They quickly took their cloaks and spread them under him on the bare steps. Then they blew the trumpet and shouted, "Jehu is king!"

### Jehu Kills Joram and Ahaziah

¹⁴So Jehu son of Jehoshaphat, the son of Nimshi, conspired against Joram. (Now Joram and all Israel had been defending Ramoth Gilead against Hazael king of Aram, ¹⁵but King Joram*ᵃ* had returned to Jezreel to recover from the wounds the Arameans had inflicted on him in the battle with Hazael king of Aram.) Jehu said, "If you desire to make me king, don't let anyone slip out of the city to go and tell the news in Jezreel." ¹⁶Then he got into his chariot and rode to Jezreel, because Joram was resting there and Ahaziah king of Judah had gone down to see him.

¹⁷When the lookout standing on the tower in Jezreel saw Jehu's troops approaching, he called out, "I see some troops coming."

"Get a horseman," Joram ordered. "Send him to meet them and ask, 'Do you come in peace?'"

¹⁸The horseman rode off to meet Jehu and said, "This is what the king says: 'Do you come in peace?'"

"What do you have to do with peace?" Jehu replied. "Fall in behind me."

The lookout reported, "The messenger has reached them, but he isn't coming back."

¹⁹So the king sent out a second horseman. When he came to them he said, "This is what the king says: 'Do you come in peace?'"

Jehu replied, "What do you have to do with peace? Fall in behind me."

²⁰The lookout reported, "He has reached them, but he isn't coming back either. The driving is like that of Jehu son of Nimshi—he drives like a maniac."

²¹"Hitch up my chariot," Joram ordered. And when it was hitched up, Joram king of Israel and Ahaziah king of Judah rode out, each in his own chariot, to meet Jehu. They met him at the plot of ground that had belonged to Naboth the Jezreelite. ²²When Joram saw Jehu he asked, "Have you come in peace, Jehu?"

"How can there be peace," Jehu replied, "as long as all the idolatry and witchcraft of your mother Jezebel abound?"

²³Joram turned about and fled, calling out to Ahaziah, "Treachery, Ahaziah!"

²⁴Then Jehu drew his bow and shot Joram between the shoulders. The arrow pierced his heart and he slumped down in his chariot. ²⁵Jehu said to Bidkar, his chariot officer, "Pick him up and throw him on the field that belonged to Naboth the Jezreelite. Remember how you and I were riding together in chariots behind Ahab his father when the Lord spoke this prophecy against him: ²⁶'Yesterday I saw the blood of Naboth and the blood of his sons, declares the Lord, and I will surely make you pay for it on this plot of ground, declares the Lord.'*ᵇ* Now then, pick him up and throw him on that plot, in accordance with the word of the Lord."

²⁷When Ahaziah king of Judah saw what had happened, he fled up the road to Beth Haggan.*ᶜ* Jehu chased him, shouting, "Kill him too!" They wounded him in his chariot on the way up to Gur near Ibleam, but he escaped to Megiddo and died there. ²⁸His servants took him by chariot to Jerusalem and buried him with his ancestors in his tomb

## Amplified Bible

you? And he said to them, You know that class of man and what he would say.

¹²And they said, That is false; tell us now. And he said, Thus and thus he spoke to me, saying, Thus says the Lord: I have anointed you king over Israel.

¹³Then they hastily took every man his garment and put it [for a cushion] under Jehu on the top of the [outside] stairs, and blew with trumpets, saying, Jehu is king!

¹⁴So Jehu son of Jehoshaphat, the son of Nimshi, conspired against Joram [to dethrone and slay him]. Now Joram was holding Ramoth-gilead, he and all Israel, against Hazael king of Syria,

¹⁵But King Joram had returned to be healed in Jezreel of the wounds which the Syrians had given him when he fought with Hazael king of Syria. And Jehu said, If this is your mind, let no one make his escape from the city [Ramoth-gilead] to go and tell it in Jezreel [the capital].

¹⁶So Jehu rode in a chariot and went to Jezreel, for Joram lay there. And Ahaziah king of Judah had come down to see Joram.

¹⁷A watchman on the tower in Jezreel spied the company of Jehu as he came, and said, I see a company. And Joram said, Send a horseman to meet them and have him ask, Do you come in peace?

¹⁸So one on horseback went to meet him and said, Thus says the king: Is it peace? And Jehu said, What have you to do with peace? Rein in behind me. And the watchman reported, The messenger came to them, but he does not return.

¹⁹Then Joram sent out a second man on horseback, who came to them and said, Thus says the king: Is it peace? Jehu replied, What have you to do with peace? Ride behind me.

²⁰And the watchman reported, He came to them, but does not return; also the driving is like the driving of Jehu son of Nimshi, for he drives furiously.

²¹Joram said, Make ready. When his chariot was made ready, Joram king of Israel and Ahaziah king of Judah went out, each in his chariot. Thus they went out to meet Jehu and met him in the field of Naboth the Jezreelite.

²²When Joram saw Jehu, he said, Is it peace, Jehu? And he answered, How can peace exist as long as the fornications of your mother Jezebel and her witchcrafts are so many?

²³Then Joram reined about and fled, and he said to Ahaziah, Treachery, Ahaziah!

²⁴But Jehu drew his bow with his full strength and shot Joram between his shoulders; and the arrow went out through his heart, and he sank down in his chariot.

²⁵Then said Jehu to Bidkar his captain, Take [Joram] up and cast him in the plot of Naboth the Jezreelite's field; for remember how, when I and you rode together after Ahab his father, the Lord uttered this prophecy against him:

²⁶As surely as I saw yesterday the blood of Naboth and the blood of his sons, says the Lord, I will repay you on this plot of ground, says the Lord. Now therefore, take and cast Joram into the plot of ground [of Naboth], as the word of the Lord said. [I Kings 21:15-29.]

²⁷When Ahaziah king of Judah saw this, he fled by the way of the garden house. Jehu followed him and said, Smite him also in the chariot. And they did so at the ascent to Gur, which is by Ibleam. And [Ahaziah] fled to Megiddo and died there.

²⁸His servants took him in a chariot to Jerusalem, and buried him in his sepulcher with his fathers in the City of David.

---

*ᵃ 15* Hebrew *Jehoram*, a variant of *Joram*; also in verses 17 and 21-24
*ᵇ 26* See 1 Kings 21:19.    *ᶜ 27* Or *fled by way of the garden house*

## New International Version

in the City of David. ²⁹(In the eleventh year of Joram son of Ahab, Ahaziah had become king of Judah.)

### Jezebel Killed

³⁰Then Jehu went to Jezreel. When Jezebel heard about it, she put on eye makeup, arranged her hair and looked out of a window. ³¹As Jehu entered the gate, she asked, "Have you come in peace, you Zimri, you murderer of your master?"ᵃ

³²He looked up at the window and called out, "Who is on my side? Who?" Two or three eunuchs looked down at him. ³³"Throw her down!" Jehu said. So they threw her down, and some of her blood spattered the wall and the horses as they trampled her underfoot.

³⁴Jehu went in and ate and drank. "Take care of that cursed woman," he said, "and bury her, for she was a king's daughter." ³⁵But when they went out to bury her, they found nothing except her skull, her feet and her hands. ³⁶They went back and told Jehu, who said, "This is the word of the LORD that he spoke through his servant Elijah the Tishbite: On the plot of ground at Jezreel dogs will devour Jezebel's flesh.ᵇ ³⁷Jezebel's body will be like dung on the ground in the plot at Jezreel, so that no one will be able to say, 'This is Jezebel.'"

### Ahab's Family Killed

**10** Now there were in Samaria seventy sons of the house of Ahab. So Jehu wrote letters and sent them to Samaria: to the officials of Jezreel,ᶜ to the elders and to the guardians of Ahab's children. He said, ²"You have your master's sons with you and you have chariots and horses, a fortified city and weapons. Now as soon as this letter reaches you, ³choose the best and most worthy of your master's sons and set him on his father's throne. Then fight for your master's house."

⁴But they were terrified and said, "If two kings could not resist him, how can we?"

⁵So the palace administrator, the city governor, the elders and the guardians sent this message to Jehu: "We are your servants and we will do anything you say. We will not appoint anyone as king; you do whatever you think best."

⁶Then Jehu wrote them a second letter, saying, "If you are on my side and will obey me, take the heads of your master's sons and come to me in Jezreel by this time tomorrow."

Now the royal princes, seventy of them, were with the leading men of the city, who were rearing them. ⁷When the letter arrived, these men took the princes and slaughtered all seventy of them. They put their heads in baskets and sent them to Jehu in Jezreel. ⁸When the messenger arrived, he told Jehu, "They have brought the heads of the princes."

Then Jehu ordered, "Put them in two piles at the entrance of the city gate until morning."

⁹The next morning Jehu went out. He stood before all the people and said, "You are innocent. It was I who conspired against my master and killed him, but who killed all these? ¹⁰Know, then, that not a word the LORD has spoken against the house of Ahab will fail. The LORD has done what he announced through his servant Elijah." ¹¹So Jehu killed everyone in Jezreel who remained of the house of Ahab, as well as all his chief men, his close friends and his priests, leaving him no survivor.

## Amplified Bible

²⁹In the eleventh year of Joram son of Ahab, Ahaziah's reign over Judah began.

³⁰Now when Jehu came to Jezreel, Jezebel heard of it, and she painted her eyes and beautified her head and looked out of [an upper] window. ³¹And as Jehu entered in at the gate, she said, [Have you come in] peace, you Zimri, who slew his master? [I Kings 16:9, 10.]

³²Jehu lifted up his face to the window and said, Who is on my side? Who? And two or three eunuchs looked out at him.

³³And he said, Throw her down! So they threw her down, and some of her blood splattered on the wall and on the horses, and he drove over her.

³⁴When he came in, he ate and drank, and said, See now to this cursed woman and bury her, for she is a king's daughter.

³⁵They went to bury her, but they found nothing left of her except the skull, feet, and palms of her hands.

³⁶They came again and told Jehu. He said, This is the word of the Lord which He spoke by His servant Elijah the Tishbite, In the portion of Jezreel shall dogs eat the flesh of Jezebel. [I Kings 21:23.]

³⁷The corpse of Jezebel shall be like dung upon the face of the field in the portion of Jezreel, so that they shall not say, This is Jezebel.

**10** Ahab had seventy [grandsons] in Samaria. So Jehu wrote letters and sent them from Jezreel to the rulers of Samaria, to the elders, and to those who brought up Ahab's [grandsons], saying,

²Now as soon as this letter comes to you, seeing your master [Joram's] sons are with you and also chariots and horses, a fortified city, and weapons,

³Select the best and most fit of your master's sons and set him on his father's throne; and fight for your master's house.

⁴But they were exceedingly afraid and reasoned, The two kings could not stand before [Jehu]; how then can we stand?

⁵And he who was over the household, he who was over the city, the elders also, and the guardians *and* tutors sent to Jehu, saying, We are your servants and will do all that you bid us; [but] we will not make any man king; do what is good in your eyes.

⁶Then [Jehu] wrote a second letter to them, saying, If you are with me and will obey me, take the heads of your master [Joram's] sons and come to me at Jezreel by tomorrow this time. Now the [dead] king's sons, seventy persons, were with the great men of the city, who were bringing them up.

⁷When the letter came to these men, they took the king's sons and slew them, seventy persons, and put their heads in baskets and sent them to Jehu at Jezreel.

⁸When a messenger came and told him, They have brought the heads of the king's sons, he said, Lay them in two heaps at the entrance of the city gate until morning.

⁹The next morning he went out and stood and said to all the people, You are just *and* innocent. Behold, I conspired against my master and slew him, but who smote all these?

¹⁰Know now that nothing which the Lord spoke concerning the house of Ahab shall be unfulfilled *or* ineffective; for the Lord has done what He said through His servant Elijah.

¹¹So Jehu slew all that remained of the house of Ahab in Jezreel, and all his great men, his familiar friends, and his priests, until he left him none remaining.

---

ᵃ 31 Or *"Was there peace for Zimri, who murdered his master?"*
ᵇ 36 See 1 Kings 21:23.   ᶜ 1 Hebrew; some Septuagint manuscripts and Vulgate *of the city*

## New International Version

¹²Jehu then set out and went toward Samaria. At Beth Eked of the Shepherds, ¹³he met some relatives of Ahaziah king of Judah and asked, "Who are you?"

They said, "We are relatives of Ahaziah, and we have come down to greet the families of the king and of the queen mother."

¹⁴"Take them alive!" he ordered. So they took them alive and slaughtered them by the well of Beth Eked—forty-two of them. He left no survivor.

¹⁵After he left there, he came upon Jehonadab son of Rekab, who was on his way to meet him. Jehu greeted him and said, "Are you in accord with me, as I am with you?"

"I am," Jehonadab answered.

"If so," said Jehu, "give me your hand." So he did, and Jehu helped him up into the chariot. ¹⁶Jehu said, "Come with me and see my zeal for the LORD." Then he had him ride along in his chariot.

¹⁷When Jehu came to Samaria, he killed all who were left there of Ahab's family; he destroyed them, according to the word of the LORD spoken to Elijah.

### Servants of Baal Killed

¹⁸Then Jehu brought all the people together and said to them, "Ahab served Baal a little; Jehu will serve him much. ¹⁹Now summon all the prophets of Baal, all his servants and all his priests. See that no one is missing, because I am going to hold a great sacrifice for Baal. Anyone who fails to come will no longer live." But Jehu was acting deceptively in order to destroy the servants of Baal.

²⁰Jehu said, "Call an assembly in honor of Baal." So they proclaimed it. ²¹Then he sent word throughout Israel, and all the servants of Baal came; not one stayed away. They crowded into the temple of Baal until it was full from one end to the other. ²²And Jehu said to the keeper of the wardrobe, "Bring robes for all the servants of Baal." So he brought out robes for them.

²³Then Jehu and Jehonadab son of Rekab went into the temple of Baal. Jehu said to the servants of Baal, "Look around and see that no one who serves the LORD is here with you—only servants of Baal." ²⁴Now Jehu had posted eighty men outside with this warning: "If one of you lets any of the men I am placing in your hands escape, it will be your life for his life."

²⁵As soon as Jehu had finished making the burnt offering, he ordered the guards and officers: "Go in and kill them; let no one escape." So they cut them down with the sword. The guards and officers threw the bodies out and then entered the inner shrine of the temple of Baal. ²⁶They brought the sacred stone out of the temple of Baal and burned it. ²⁷They demolished the sacred stone of Baal and tore down the temple of Baal, and people have used it for a latrine to this day.

²⁸So Jehu destroyed Baal worship in Israel. ²⁹However, he did not turn away from the sins of Jeroboam son of Nebat, which he had caused Israel to commit—the worship of the golden calves at Bethel and Dan.

³⁰The LORD said to Jehu, "Because you have done well in accomplishing what is right in my eyes and have done to the house of Ahab all I had in mind to do, your descendants will sit on the throne of Israel to the fourth generation." ³¹Yet Jehu was not careful to keep the law of the LORD, the God of Israel, with all his heart. He did not turn away from the sins of Jeroboam, which he had caused Israel to commit.

## Amplified Bible

¹²And he arose and went to Samaria. And as he was at the shearing house of the shepherds on the way,

¹³Jehu met the kinsmen of Ahaziah king of Judah and said, Who are you? They answered, We are the kinsmen of Ahaziah, and we came down to visit the royal princes and the sons of [Jezebel] the queen mother.

¹⁴He said, Take them alive. And they did so and slew them at the cistern of the shearing house, forty-two men; he left none of them.

¹⁵When Jehu left there, he met Jehonadab son of Rechab coming to meet him. He saluted him and said to him, Is your heart right, as my heart is with yours? Jehonadab answered, It is. [Jehu said] If it is, give me your hand. He gave him his hand, and Jehu took him up into the chariot.

¹⁶And he said, Come with me and see my zeal for the Lord. So they made [the Rechabite] ride in Jehu's chariot.

¹⁷When Jehu came to Samaria, he slew all who remained of Ahab's family in Samaria, till he had destroyed them all, according to what the Lord said to Elijah.

¹⁸Jehu assembled all the people and said to them, Ahab served Baal a little; but Jehu will serve him much.

¹⁹So call to me all the prophets of Baal, all his worshipers, and all his priests. Let none be missing, for I have a great sacrifice to make to Baal; whoever is missing shall not live. But Jehu did it with trickery, intending to destroy the Baal worshipers.

²⁰Jehu said, Sanctify a solemn assembly for Baal. And they proclaimed it.

²¹Jehu sent through all Israel, and all the worshipers of Baal came; not a man failed to come. They went to the house or temple of Baal, filling it from one end to the other.

²²And he said to the man over the vestry, Bring vestments for all the worshipers of Baal. And he brought them vestments.

²³Then Jehu with Jehonadab son of Rechab went into the house of Baal and said to the worshipers of Baal, Search and see that there are here with you none of the servants of the Lord—but Baal worshipers only.

²⁴And when they went in to offer sacrifices and burnt offerings, Jehu appointed eighty men outside and said, If any of the men whom I have brought into your hands escape, he who lets him go shall forfeit his own life for his life.

²⁵As soon as he had finished offering the burnt offering, Jehu said to the guards and to the officers, Go in and slay them; let none escape. And they smote them with the sword; and the guards or runners [before the king] and the officers threw their bodies out and went into the inner dwelling of the house of Baal.

²⁶They brought out the pillars or obelisks of the house of Baal and burned them.

²⁷They broke down the pillars of Baal and the house of Baal, and made it [forever unclean] a privy to this day.

²⁸Thus Jehu rooted Baal out of Israel.

²⁹But Jehu did not give up the sins of Jeroboam son of Nebat, by which he made Israel to sin, that is, the golden calves at Bethel and Dan. [I Kings 12:28ff.]

³⁰And the Lord said to Jehu, Because you have executed well what is right in My eyes and have done to the house of Ahab as I willed, your sons to the fourth generation shall sit on Israel's throne. [Fulfilled in II Kings 15:12.]

³¹But Jehu paid no attention to walking in the law of the Lord, the God of Israel, with all his heart. He did not quit the sins with which Jeroboam made Israel to sin.

## New International Version

[32]In those days the LORD began to reduce the size of Israel. Hazael overpowered the Israelites throughout their territory [33]east of the Jordan in all the land of Gilead (the region of Gad, Reuben and Manasseh), from Aroer by the Arnon Gorge through Gilead to Bashan.

[34]As for the other events of Jehu's reign, all he did, and all his achievements, are they not written in the book of the annals of the kings of Israel?

[35]Jehu rested with his ancestors and was buried in Samaria. And Jehoahaz his son succeeded him as king. [36]The time that Jehu reigned over Israel in Samaria was twenty-eight years.

### Athaliah and Joash

**11** When Athaliah the mother of Ahaziah saw that her son was dead, she proceeded to destroy the whole royal family. [2]But Jehosheba, the daughter of King Jehoram[a] and sister of Ahaziah, took Joash son of Ahaziah and stole him away from among the royal princes, who were about to be murdered. She put him and his nurse in a bedroom to hide him from Athaliah; so he was not killed. [3]He remained hidden with his nurse at the temple of the LORD for six years while Athaliah ruled the land.

[4]In the seventh year Jehoiada sent for the commanders of units of a hundred, the Carites and the guards and had them brought to him at the temple of the LORD. He made a covenant with them and put them under oath at the temple of the LORD. Then he showed them the king's son. [5]He commanded them, saying, "This is what you are to do: You who are in the three companies that are going on duty on the Sabbath—a third of you guarding the royal palace, [6]a third at the Sur Gate, and a third at the gate behind the guard, who take turns guarding the temple— [7]and you who are in the other two companies that normally go off Sabbath duty are all to guard the temple for the king. [8]Station yourselves around the king, each of you with weapon in hand. Anyone who approaches your ranks[b] is to be put to death. Stay close to the king wherever he goes."

[9]The commanders of units of a hundred did just as Jehoiada the priest ordered. Each one took his men—those who were going on duty on the Sabbath and those who were going off duty—and came to Jehoiada the priest. [10]Then he gave the commanders the spears and shields that had belonged to King David and that were in the temple of the LORD. [11]The guards, each with weapon in hand, stationed themselves around the king—near the altar and the temple, from the south side to the north side of the temple.

[12]Jehoiada brought out the king's son and put the crown on him; he presented him with a copy of the covenant and proclaimed him king. They anointed him, and the people clapped their hands and shouted, "Long live the king!"

[13]When Athaliah heard the noise made by the guards and the people, she went to the people at the temple of the LORD. [14]She looked and there was the king, standing by the pillar, as the custom was. The officers and the trumpeters were beside the king, and all the people of the land were rejoicing and blowing trumpets. Then Athaliah tore her robes and called out, "Treason! Treason!"

## Amplified Bible

[32][So] in those days the Lord began to cut off parts of Israel. Hazael [of Syria] defeated them in all the [across the Jordan] territory of Israel

[33]From the Jordan east, all the land of Gilead, the Gadites, Reubenites, and Manassites, from Aroer which is by the Valley of the Arnon, even Gilead and Bashan.

[34]The rest of the acts of Jehu, and all that he did, and all his might, are they not written in the Book of the Chronicles of the Kings of Israel?

[35]Jehu slept with his fathers. They buried him in Samaria. Jehoahaz his son reigned in his stead. [36]The time that Jehu reigned over Israel in Samaria was twenty-eight years.

**11** When Athaliah the mother of [King] Ahaziah [of Judah] saw that her son was dead, she arose and destroyed all the royal descendants.

[2]But Jehosheba, the daughter of King Jehoram, [half] sister of Ahaziah, stole Joash son of Ahaziah from among the king's sons, who were to be slain, even him and his nurse, and hid them from Athaliah in an inner storeroom for beds; so he was not slain.

[3]Joash was with his nurse hidden in the house of the Lord for six years. And Athaliah reigned over the land.

[4]In the seventh year Jehoiada [the priest, Jehosheba's husband] sent for the captains over hundreds of the Carites and of the guards or runners and brought them to him to the house of the Lord and made a covenant with them and took an oath from them in the house of the Lord and showed them the king's [hidden] son.

[5]And he commanded them, saying, This is the thing you shall do: a third of you who come in on the Sabbath shall keep watch of the king's house,

[6]A third shall be at the gate Sur, and a third at the gate behind the guard. So you shall keep watch of the palace [from three places] and be a barrier.

[7]And two divisions of all you who should go off duty on the Sabbath shall keep the watch of the house of the Lord to [protect] the king.

[8]You shall surround the [little] king, every man with his weapons in his hand. And let anyone who breaks through the ranks be put to death. You be with the king when he goes out and when he comes in.

[9]The captains over the hundreds did all that Jehoiada the priest commanded; and they took every man his men who were to come on duty on the Sabbath with those who should go off duty on the Sabbath, and came to Jehoiada the priest.

[10]To the captains over hundreds the priest gave the spears and shields that had been King David's, which were in the house of the Lord.

[11]And the guards stood, every man with his weapons in his hand, from the right corner to the left corner of the temple area, along by the altar [in the court] and the temple proper.

[12]And Jehoiada brought out the king's son and put the crown on him and gave him the Testimony [the Mosaic Law]; and they proclaimed him king and anointed him, and they clapped their hands and said, Long live the king!

[13]When Athaliah heard the noise of the guards and the people, she went into the house of the Lord to the people.

[14]When she looked, there stood the king [on the platform] by the pillar, as was customary [on such occasions], and the captains and the trumpeters beside the king, with all the people of the land rejoicing and blowing trumpets. And Athaliah rent her clothes and cried, Treason! Treason!

---

[a] 2 Hebrew *Joram*, a variant of *Jehoram*    [b] 8 Or *approaches the precincts*

## New International Version

[15]Jehoiada the priest ordered the commanders of units of a hundred, who were in charge of the troops: "Bring her out between the ranks[a] and put to the sword anyone who follows her." For the priest had said, "She must not be put to death in the temple of the LORD." [16]So they seized her as she reached the place where the horses enter the palace grounds, and there she was put to death.

[17]Jehoiada then made a covenant between the LORD and the king and people that they would be the LORD's people. He also made a covenant between the king and the people. [18]All the people of the land went to the temple of Baal and tore it down. They smashed the altars and idols to pieces and killed Mattan the priest of Baal in front of the altars.

Then Jehoiada the priest posted guards at the temple of the LORD. [19]He took with him the commanders of hundreds, the Carites, the guards and all the people of the land, and together they brought the king down from the temple of the LORD and went into the palace, entering by way of the gate of the guards. The king then took his place on the royal throne. [20]All the people of the land rejoiced, and the city was calm, because Athaliah had been slain with the sword at the palace.

[21]Joash[b] was seven years old when he began to reign.[c]

### Joash Repairs the Temple

**12**[d] In the seventh year of Jehu, Joash[e] became king, and he reigned in Jerusalem forty years. His mother's name was Zibiah; she was from Beersheba. [2]Joash did what was right in the eyes of the LORD all the years Jehoiada the priest instructed him. [3]The high places, however, were not removed; the people continued to offer sacrifices and burn incense there.

[4]Joash said to the priests, "Collect all the money that is brought as sacred offerings to the temple of the LORD—the money collected in the census, the money received from personal vows and the money brought voluntarily to the temple. [5]Let every priest receive the money from one of the treasurers, then use it to repair whatever damage is found in the temple."

[6]But by the twenty-third year of King Joash the priests still had not repaired the temple. [7]Therefore King Joash summoned Jehoiada the priest and the other priests and asked them, "Why aren't you repairing the damage done to the temple? Take no more money from your treasurers, but hand it over for repairing the temple." [8]The priests agreed that they would not collect any more money from the people and that they would not repair the temple themselves.

[9]Jehoiada the priest took a chest and bored a hole in its lid. He placed it beside the altar, on the right side as one enters the temple of the LORD. The priests who guarded the entrance put into the chest all the money that was brought to the temple of the LORD. [10]Whenever they saw that there was a large amount of money in the chest, the royal secretary and the high priest came, counted the money that had been brought into the temple of the LORD and put it into bags. [11]When the amount had been determined, they gave the money to the men appointed to supervise the work on the temple. With it they paid those who worked on the temple of the LORD—the carpenters

## Amplified Bible

[15]Then Jehoiada the priest commanded the captains of hundreds set over the army and said to them, Take her forth outside the ranks, and him who follows her kill with the sword. For the priest had said, Let her not be slain in the house of the Lord.

[16]They seized her, and she went through the horses' entrance to the king's house, and there she was slain.

[17]And Jehoiada made a covenant between the Lord, the king, and the people that they would be the Lord's people—and also between the king and the people.

[18]Then all the people of the land went to the house of Baal and destroyed it. His altar and his images they broke completely in pieces, and Mattan the priest of Baal they slew before the altars. And [Jehoiada] the priest appointed watchmen to guard the house of the Lord.

[19]Then he took the rulers over hundreds, the captains, the guard, and all the people of the land, and they brought the king down from the house of the Lord and came by way of the guards' gate to the king's house. And [little] Joash was seated on the throne of the kings.

[20]So all the people of the land rejoiced, and the city was quiet after Athaliah had been slain with the sword beside the king's house.

[21]Joash was seven years old when he began to reign.

**12** In the seventh year of Jehu, [a]Joash began to reign, and he reigned forty years in Jerusalem. His mother was Zibiah of Beersheba.

[2]Joash did right in the sight of the Lord all his days in which Jehoiada the priest instructed him.

[3]Yet the high places were not taken away; the people still sacrificed and burned incense in the high places.

[4]And Joash said to the priests, All the current money brought into the house of the Lord to provide the dedicated things, also the money [which the priests by command have] assessed on all those bound by vows, also all the money that it comes into any man's heart voluntarily to bring into the house of the Lord,

[5]Let the priests solicit *and* receive such contributions, every man from his acquaintance, and let them repair the Lord's house wherever any such need may be found.

[6]But in the twenty-third year of King Joash's reign the priests had not made the needed repairs on the Lord's house.

[7]Then King Joash called for Jehoiada the priest and the other priests and said to them, Why are you not repairing the [Lord's] house? Do not take any more money from your acquaintances, but turn it all over for the repair of the house. [You are no longer responsible for this work. I will take it into my own hands.]

[8]And the priests consented to receive no more money from the people, nor to repair the breaches of the house.

[9]Then Jehoiada the priest took a chest and bored a hole in the lid of it and set it beside the altar on the right side as one entered the house of the Lord; and the priests who guarded the door put in the chest all the money that was brought into the house of the Lord.

[10]And whenever they saw that there was much money in the chest, the king's scribe and the high priest came up and counted the money that was found in the house of the Lord and tied it up in bags.

[11]Then they gave the money, when it was weighed, into the hands of those who were doing the work, who had the oversight of the house of the Lord; and they paid it out to the carpenters and builders who worked on the house of the Lord

---

[a] Judah and Israel each had a king named Joash or Jehoash, and the Hebrew uses the two forms of the name interchangeably. Since the time of their reigns overlapped, it became difficult not to confuse them. So this version will call the first one Joash, referring to the king of Judah who began his reign at seven years of age, and the other one Jehoash (as the Hebrew does in II Kings 13:10 and 14:17), referring to the king of Israel who began his reign thirty-seven years later.

---

[a] 15 Or *out from the precincts*   [b] 21 Hebrew *Jehoash*, a variant of *Joash*   [c] 21 In Hebrew texts this verse (11:21) is numbered 12:1.   [d] In Hebrew texts 12:1-21 is numbered 12:2-22.   [e] 1 Hebrew *Jehoash*, a variant of *Joash*; also in verses 2, 4, 6, 7 and 18

## New International Version

and builders, [12]the masons and stonecutters. They purchased timber and blocks of dressed stone for the repair of the temple of the LORD, and met all the other expenses of restoring the temple.

[13]The money brought into the temple was not spent for making silver basins, wick trimmers, sprinkling bowls, trumpets or any other articles of gold or silver for the temple of the LORD; [14]it was paid to the workers, who used it to repair the temple. [15]They did not require an accounting from those to whom they gave the money to pay the workers, because they acted with complete honesty. [16]The money from the guilt offerings and sin offerings[a] was not brought into the temple of the LORD; it belonged to the priests.

[17]About this time Hazael king of Aram went up and attacked Gath and captured it. Then he turned to attack Jerusalem. [18]But Joash king of Judah took all the sacred objects dedicated by his predecessors—Jehoshaphat, Jehoram and Ahaziah, the kings of Judah—and the gifts he himself had dedicated and all the gold found in the treasuries of the temple of the LORD and of the royal palace, and he sent them to Hazael king of Aram, who then withdrew from Jerusalem.

[19]As for the other events of the reign of Joash, and all he did, are they not written in the book of the annals of the kings of Judah? [20]His officials conspired against him and assassinated him at Beth Millo, on the road down to Silla. [21]The officials who murdered him were Jozabad son of Shimeath and Jehozabad son of Shomer. He died and was buried with his ancestors in the City of David. And Amaziah his son succeeded him as king.

### Jehoahaz King of Israel

**13** In the twenty-third year of Joash son of Ahaziah king of Judah, Jehoahaz son of Jehu became king of Israel in Samaria, and he reigned seventeen years. [2]He did evil in the eyes of the LORD by following the sins of Jeroboam son of Nebat, which he had caused Israel to commit, and he did not turn away from them. [3]So the LORD's anger burned against Israel, and for a long time he kept them under the power of Hazael king of Aram and Ben-Hadad his son.

[4]Then Jehoahaz sought the LORD's favor, and the LORD listened to him, for he saw how severely the king of Aram was oppressing Israel. [5]The LORD provided a deliverer for Israel, and they escaped from the power of Aram. So the Israelites lived in their own homes as they had before. [6]But they did not turn away from the sins of the house of Jeroboam, which he had caused Israel to commit; they continued in them. Also, the Asherah pole[b] remained standing in Samaria.

[7]Nothing had been left of the army of Jehoahaz except fifty horsemen, ten chariots and ten thousand foot soldiers, for the king of Aram had destroyed the rest and made them like the dust at threshing time.

[8]As for the other events of the reign of Jehoahaz, all he did and his achievements, are they not written in the book of the annals of the kings of Israel? [9]Jehoahaz rested with his ancestors and was buried in Samaria. And Jehoash[c] his son succeeded him as king.

## Amplified Bible

[12]And to the masons and stonecutters, and to buy timber and hewn stone for making the repairs on the house of the Lord, and for all that was outlay for repairing the house.

[13]However, there were not made for the house of the Lord basins of silver, snuffers, bowls, trumpets, any vessels of gold or of silver, from the money that was brought into the house of the Lord.

[14]But they gave that to the workmen, and repaired with it the house of the Lord.

[15]Moreover, they did not require an accounting from the men into whose hands they delivered the money to be paid to the workmen, for they dealt faithfully.

[16]The money from the guilt offerings and sin offerings was not brought into the house of the Lord; it was the priests'.

[17]Then Hazael king of Syria went up, fought against Gath [in Philistia], and took it. And Hazael set his face to go up to Jerusalem.

[18]And Joash king of Judah took all the hallowed things that Jehoshaphat, Jehoram, and Ahaziah, his [forefathers], kings of Judah, had dedicated and his own hallowed things and all the gold that was found in the treasuries of the house of the Lord and in the king's house, and sent them to Hazael king of Syria; and Hazael went away from Jerusalem.

[19]The rest of the acts of Joash, and all that he did, are they not written in the Book of the Chronicles of the Kings of Judah?

[20]His servants arose and made a conspiracy and slew Joash [in revenge] in the house of Millo, on the way that goes down to Silla. [II Chron. 24:22-25.]

[21]It was Jozachar son of Shimeath and Jehozabad son of Shomer, his servants, who smote him so that he died. They buried [Joash] with his fathers in the City of David. Amaziah his son reigned in his stead.

**13** In the twenty-third year of Joash son of Ahaziah king of Judah, Jehoahaz son of Jehu began to reign over Israel in Samaria, and reigned seventeen years.

[2]He did evil in the sight of the Lord and followed the sins of Jeroboam son of Nebat, which made Israel to sin, and did not depart from them.

[3]The anger of the Lord was kindled against Israel, and He delivered them into the hand of Hazael king of Syria and of Ben-hadad son of Hazael continually.

[4]But Jehoahaz besought the Lord, and the Lord hearkened to him, for He saw the oppression of Israel, how the king of Syria burdened them.

[5]Then the Lord gave Israel a savior [one to rescue and give them peace], so that they escaped from under the hand of the Syrians; and the Israelites dwelt in their tents *or* homes as before.

[6]Yet they did not depart from the sins of the house of Jeroboam, who made Israel sin; but the nation walked in them. And the Asherah [symbol of the goddess Asherah] remained in Samaria.

[7][Ben-hadad] of Syria did not leave to Jehoahaz of [Israel] an army of more than fifty horsemen, ten chariots, and 10,000 footmen, for the Syrian king had destroyed them and made them like dust to be trampled.

[8]The rest of the acts of Jehoahaz, all that he did and his might, are they not written in the Book of the Chronicles of the Kings of Israel?

[9]Jehoahaz slept with his fathers, and they buried him in Samaria. [a]Jehoash his son reigned in his stead.

---

[a] 16 Or *purification offerings*   [b] 6 That is, a wooden symbol of the goddess Asherah; here and elsewhere in 2 Kings   [c] 9 Hebrew *Joash*, a variant of *Jehoash*; also in verses 12-14 and 25

[a] See footnote on II Kings 12:1.

| New International Version | Amplified Bible |
|---|---|

## Jehoash King of Israel

[10] In the thirty-seventh year of Joash king of Judah, Jehoash son of Jehoahaz became king of Israel in Samaria, and he reigned sixteen years. [11] He did evil in the eyes of the LORD and did not turn away from any of the sins of Jeroboam son of Nebat, which he had caused Israel to commit; he continued in them.

[12] As for the other events of the reign of Jehoash, all he did and his achievements, including his war against Amaziah king of Judah, are they not written in the book of the annals of the kings of Israel? [13] Jehoash rested with his ancestors, and Jeroboam succeeded him on the throne. Jehoash was buried in Samaria with the kings of Israel.

[14] Now Elisha had been suffering from the illness from which he died. Jehoash king of Israel went down to see him and wept over him. "My father! My father!" he cried. "The chariots and horsemen of Israel!" [15] Elisha said, "Get a bow and some arrows," and he did so. [16] "Take the bow in your hands," he said to the king of Israel. When he had taken it, Elisha put his hands on the king's hands.

[17] "Open the east window," he said, and he opened it. "Shoot!" Elisha said, and he shot. "The LORD's arrow of victory, the arrow of victory over Aram!" Elisha declared. "You will completely destroy the Arameans at Aphek." [18] Then he said, "Take the arrows," and the king took them. Elisha told him, "Strike the ground." He struck it three times and stopped. [19] The man of God was angry with him and said, "You should have struck the ground five or six times; then you would have defeated Aram and completely destroyed it. But now you will defeat it only three times."

[20] Elisha died and was buried.

Now Moabite raiders used to enter the country every spring. [21] Once while some Israelites were burying a man, suddenly they saw a band of raiders; so they threw the man's body into Elisha's tomb. When the body touched Elisha's bones, the man came to life and stood up on his feet.

[22] Hazael king of Aram oppressed Israel throughout the reign of Jehoahaz. [23] But the LORD was gracious to them and had compassion and showed concern for them because of his covenant with Abraham, Isaac and Jacob. To this day he has been unwilling to destroy them or banish them from his presence.

[24] Hazael king of Aram died, and Ben-Hadad his son succeeded him as king. [25] Then Jehoash son of Jehoahaz recaptured from Ben-Hadad son of Hazael the towns he had taken in battle from his father Jehoahaz. Three times Jehoash defeated him, and so he recovered the Israelite towns.

[10] In the thirty-seventh year of Joash king of Judah, Jehoash son of Jehoahaz began to reign over Israel in Samaria, and reigned sixteen years. [11] He did evil in the sight of the Lord; he departed not from all the sins of Jeroboam son of Nebat, who made Israel sin; he walked in them.

[12] The rest of the acts of Jehoash, all that he did, and his might with which he fought against Amaziah king of Judah, are they not written in the Book of the Chronicles of the Kings of Israel?

[13] Jehoash slept with his fathers, and Jeroboam [II] sat on his throne. Jehoash was buried in Samaria with the kings of Israel.

[14] Now Elisha [previously] had become ill of the illness of which he died. And Jehoash king of Israel came down to him and wept over him and said, O my father, my father, the chariot of Israel and the horsemen of it! [II Kings 2:12.]

[15] And Elisha said to him, Take bow and arrows. And he took bow and arrows.

[16] And he said to the king of Israel, Put your hand upon the bow. And he put his hand upon it, and Elisha put his hands upon the king's hands.

[17] And he said, Open the window to the east. And he opened it. Then Elisha said, Shoot. And he shot. And he said, The Lord's arrow of victory, the arrow of victory over Syria. For you shall smite the Syrians in Aphek till you have destroyed them.

[18] Then he said, Take the arrows. And he took them. And he said to the king of Israel, Strike on the ground. And he struck three times and stopped.

[19] And the man of God was angry with him and said, You should have struck five or six times; then you would have struck down Syria until you had destroyed it. But now you shall strike Syria down only three times.

[20] Elisha died, and they buried him. Bands of the Moabites invaded the land in the spring of the next year.

[21] As a man was being buried [on an open bier], such a band was seen coming; and the man was cast into Elisha's grave. And when the man being let down touched the bones of Elisha, he revived and stood on his feet.

[22] Hazael king of Syria oppressed Israel all the days of Jehoahaz.

[23] But the Lord was gracious to them and had compassion on them and turned toward them because of [a] His covenant with Abraham, Isaac, and Jacob, and would not destroy them or cast them from His presence yet. [Mal. 3:6.]

[24] Hazael king of Syria died; Ben-hadad his son reigned in his stead.

[25] Jehoash son of Jehoahaz recovered from Ben-hadad son of Hazael the cities which he had taken from Jehoahaz his father by war. Three times Jehoash defeated him, and recovered the cities of Israel. [II Kings 13:19.]

## Amaziah King of Judah

**14** In the second year of Jehoash[a] son of Jehoahaz king of Israel, Amaziah son of Joash king of Judah began to reign. [2] He was twenty-five years old when he became king, and he reigned in Jerusalem twenty-nine years. His mother's name was Jehoaddan; she was from Jerusalem. [3] He did what was right in the eyes of the LORD, but not as his father David had done. In everything he followed the example of his father Joash. [4] The high places, however, were not removed; the people continued to offer sacrifices and burn incense there.

**14** In the second year of Jehoash son of Jehoahaz king of Israel, Amaziah son of Joash king of Judah reigned. [2] He was twenty-five years old when he began his twenty-nine-year reign in Jerusalem. His mother was Jehoaddin of Jerusalem. [3] He did right in the sight of the Lord, yet not like David his [forefather]. He did all things as Joash his father did. [4] But the high places were not removed; the people still sacrificed and burned incense on the high places.

---

[a] 1 Hebrew *Joash*, a variant of *Jehoash*; also in verses 13, 23 and 27

[a] Abraham, Isaac, and Jacob had been dead a thousand years, yet God's covenant with them was undiminishingly effective.

## New International Version

[5]After the kingdom was firmly in his grasp, he executed the officials who had murdered his father the king. [6]Yet he did not put the children of the assassins to death, in accordance with what is written in the Book of the Law of Moses where the LORD commanded: "Parents are not to be put to death for their children, nor children put to death for their parents; each will die for their own sin."[a]

[7]He was the one who defeated ten thousand Edomites in the Valley of Salt and captured Sela in battle, calling it Joktheel, the name it has to this day.

[8]Then Amaziah sent messengers to Jehoash son of Jehoahaz, the son of Jehu, king of Israel, with the challenge: "Come, let us face each other in battle."

[9]But Jehoash king of Israel replied to Amaziah king of Judah: "A thistle in Lebanon sent a message to a cedar in Lebanon, 'Give your daughter to my son in marriage.' Then a wild beast in Lebanon came along and trampled the thistle underfoot. [10]You have indeed defeated Edom and now you are arrogant. Glory in your victory, but stay at home! Why ask for trouble and cause your own downfall and that of Judah also?"

[11]Amaziah, however, would not listen, so Jehoash king of Israel attacked. He and Amaziah king of Judah faced each other at Beth Shemesh in Judah. [12]Judah was routed by Israel, and every man fled to his home. [13]Jehoash king of Israel captured Amaziah king of Judah, the son of Joash, the son of Ahaziah, at Beth Shemesh. Then Jehoash went to Jerusalem and broke down the wall of Jerusalem from the Ephraim Gate to the Corner Gate—a section about four hundred cubits long.[b] [14]He took all the gold and silver and all the articles found in the temple of the LORD and in the treasuries of the royal palace. He also took hostages and returned to Samaria.

[15]As for the other events of the reign of Jehoash, what he did and his achievements, including his war against Amaziah king of Judah, are they not written in the book of the annals of the kings of Israel? [16]Jehoash rested with his ancestors and was buried in Samaria with the kings of Israel. And Jeroboam his son succeeded him as king.

[17]Amaziah son of Joash king of Judah lived for fifteen years after the death of Jehoash son of Jehoahaz king of Israel. [18]As for the other events of Amaziah's reign, are they not written in the book of the annals of the kings of Judah?

[19]They conspired against him in Jerusalem, and he fled to Lachish, but they sent men after him to Lachish and killed him there. [20]He was brought back by horse and was buried in Jerusalem with his ancestors, in the City of David.

[21]Then all the people of Judah took Azariah,[c] who was sixteen years old, and made him king in place of his father Amaziah. [22]He was the one who rebuilt Elath and restored it to Judah after Amaziah rested with his ancestors.

### Jeroboam II King of Israel

[23]In the fifteenth year of Amaziah son of Joash king of Judah, Jeroboam son of Jehoash king of Israel became king in Samaria, and he reigned forty-one years. [24]He did evil in the eyes of the LORD and did not turn away from any of the sins of Jeroboam son of Nebat, which he had caused Israel to commit. [25]He was the one who restored the boundaries of Israel from Lebo Hamath to the Dead Sea,[d] in accordance with the word of the LORD, the God of Israel, spoken through his servant Jonah son of Amittai, the prophet from Gath Hepher.

## Amplified Bible

[5]As soon as the kingdom was established in Amaziah's hand, he slew his servants who had slain the king his father. [II Kings 12:20.]

[6]But he did not slay the children of the murderers, in compliance with what is written in the Book of the Law of Moses, in which the Lord commanded, The fathers shall not be put to death for the children, nor the children for the fathers; but every man shall die for his own sin only.

[7]Amaziah slew of Edom in the Valley of Salt 10,000, and took Sela (Greek *petra* [rock]) by war, and called it Joktheel, which is the name of it to this day.

[8]Then Amaziah sent messengers to Jehoash son of Jehoahaz, the son of Jehu, king of Israel, saying, Come, let us look one another in the face *and* test each other.

[9]Jehoash king of Israel replied to Amaziah king of Judah, The thistle in Lebanon sent to the cedar in Lebanon, saying, Give your daughter to my son as wife. And a wild beast of Lebanon passed by and trampled the thistle [leaving the cedar unharmed].

[10]You have indeed smitten Edom, and your heart has lifted you up. Glory in that, and stay at home; for why should you meddle to your hurt *and* provoke calamity, causing you to fall, you and Judah with you?

[11]But Amaziah would not hear. So Jehoash king of Israel went up; and he and Amaziah king of Judah measured swords at Beth-shemesh, which belongs to Judah.

[12]But Judah was defeated by Israel, and every man fled home.

[13]And Jehoash king of Israel captured Amaziah king of Judah, son of Joash, the son of Ahaziah, at Beth-shemesh, and came to Jerusalem and broke down the wall of Jerusalem from the Ephraim Gate to the Corner Gate, 400 cubits.

[14]He seized all the gold and silver and all the vessels found in the Lord's house and in the treasuries of the king's house, also hostages, and returned to Samaria.

[15]The rest of the acts of Jehoash, his might, and how he fought with Amaziah king of Judah, are they not written in the Book of the Chronicles of Israel's Kings?

[16]Jehoash slept with his fathers, and was buried in Samaria with Israel's kings. Jeroboam [II] reigned in his stead.

[17]Amaziah son of Joash king of Judah lived after the death of Jehoash son of Jehoahaz king of Israel fifteen years.

[18]The rest of the acts of Amaziah, are they not written in the Book of the Chronicles of the Kings of Judah?

[19]Now a conspiracy was made against him in Jerusalem, and Amaziah fled to Lachish, but they sent after him to Lachish and slew him there.

[20]They brought him on horses and he was buried at Jerusalem with his fathers in the City of David.

[21]And all the people of Judah took Azariah, sixteen years old, and made him king instead of his father Amaziah.

[22]He built Elath and restored it to Judah after the king [his father] died.

[23]In the fifteenth year of Amaziah son of Joash king of Judah Jeroboam [II] son of Jehoash king of Israel began to reign in Samaria, and reigned forty-one years.

[24]He did evil in the sight of the Lord; he did not depart from all the sins of Jeroboam [I] son of Nebat, with which he made Israel to sin.

[25]Jeroboam restored Israel's border from the entrance of Hamath to the [Dead] Sea of the Arabah, according to the word of the Lord, the God of Israel, which He spoke through His servant Jonah son of Amittai, the prophet from Gath-hepher.

---

[a] 6 Deut. 24:16    [b] 13 That is, about 600 feet or about 180 meters
[c] 21 Also called *Uzziah*    [d] 25 Hebrew *the Sea of the Arabah*

# New International Version

<sup>26</sup>The LORD had seen how bitterly everyone in Israel, whether slave or free, was suffering;<sup>a</sup> there was no one to help them. <sup>27</sup>And since the LORD had not said he would blot out the name of Israel from under heaven, he saved them by the hand of Jeroboam son of Jehoash.

<sup>28</sup>As for the other events of Jeroboam's reign, all he did, and his military achievements, including how he recovered for Israel both Damascus and Hamath, which had belonged to Judah, are they not written in the book of the annals of the kings of Israel? <sup>29</sup>Jeroboam rested with his ancestors, the kings of Israel. And Zechariah his son succeeded him as king.

## Azariah King of Judah

**15** In the twenty-seventh year of Jeroboam king of Israel, Azariah<sup>b</sup> son of Amaziah king of Judah began to reign. <sup>2</sup>He was sixteen years old when he became king, and he reigned in Jerusalem fifty-two years. His mother's name was Jekoliah; she was from Jerusalem. <sup>3</sup>He did what was right in the eyes of the LORD, just as his father Amaziah had done. <sup>4</sup>The high places, however, were not removed; the people continued to offer sacrifices and burn incense there.

<sup>5</sup>The LORD afflicted the king with leprosy<sup>c</sup> until the day he died, and he lived in a separate house.<sup>d</sup> Jotham the king's son had charge of the palace and governed the people of the land.

<sup>6</sup>As for the other events of Azariah's reign, and all he did, are they not written in the book of the annals of the kings of Judah? <sup>7</sup>Azariah rested with his ancestors and was buried near them in the City of David. And Jotham his son succeeded him as king.

## Zechariah King of Israel

<sup>8</sup>In the thirty-eighth year of Azariah king of Judah, Zechariah son of Jeroboam became king of Israel in Samaria, and he reigned six months. <sup>9</sup>He did evil in the eyes of the LORD, as his predecessors had done. He did not turn away from the sins of Jeroboam son of Nebat, which he had caused Israel to commit.

<sup>10</sup>Shallum son of Jabesh conspired against Zechariah. He attacked him in front of the people,<sup>e</sup> assassinated him and succeeded him as king. <sup>11</sup>The other events of Zechariah's reign are written in the book of the annals of the kings of Israel. <sup>12</sup>So the word of the LORD spoken to Jehu was fulfilled: "Your descendants will sit on the throne of Israel to the fourth generation."<sup>f</sup>

## Shallum King of Israel

<sup>13</sup>Shallum son of Jabesh became king in the thirty-ninth year of Uzziah king of Judah, and he reigned in Samaria one month. <sup>14</sup>Then Menahem son of Gadi went from Tirzah up to Samaria. He attacked Shallum son of Jabesh in Samaria, assassinated him and succeeded him as king.

<sup>15</sup>The other events of Shallum's reign, and the conspiracy he led, are written in the book of the annals of the kings of Israel.

<sup>16</sup>At that time Menahem, starting out from Tirzah, attacked Tiphsah and everyone in the city and its vicinity, because they refused to open their gates. He sacked Tiphsah and ripped open all the pregnant women.

# Amplified Bible

<sup>26</sup>For the Lord saw as very bitter the affliction of Israel; there was no one left, bond or free, nor any helper for Israel.

<sup>27</sup>But the Lord had not said that He would blot out the name of Israel from under the heavens, so He saved them by the hand of Jeroboam [II] son of Jehoash.

<sup>28</sup>The rest of the acts of Jeroboam [II], all that he did, his might, how he warred, and how he recovered for Israel Damascus and Hamath, which had belonged to Judah, are they not written in the Book of the Chronicles of the Kings of Israel?

<sup>29</sup>Jeroboam [II] slept with his fathers, the kings of Israel. Zechariah his son reigned in his stead.

**15** In the twenty-seventh year of Jeroboam [II] king of Israel, Azariah (Uzziah) son of Amaziah king of Judah began to reign. <sup>2</sup>He was sixteen years old when he began his fifty-two-year reign in Jerusalem. His mother was Jecoliah of Jerusalem. <sup>3</sup>He did right in the Lord's sight, in keeping with all his father Amaziah had done— <sup>4</sup>Except the high places were not removed; the people sacrificed and burned incense still on the high places. <sup>5</sup>And the Lord smote the king, so that he was a leper to his dying day, and dwelt in a separate house. Jotham the king's son was over the household, judging the people of the land. [II Chron. 26:16-21.]

<sup>6</sup>The rest of Azariah's acts, all that he did, are they not written in the Book of the Chronicles of the Kings of Judah? <sup>7</sup>Azariah slept with his fathers, and they buried him with them in the City of David. Jotham his son reigned in his stead.

<sup>8</sup>In the thirty-eighth year of Azariah king of Judah Zechariah son of Jeroboam [II] reigned over Israel in Samaria six months. <sup>9</sup>He did evil in the sight of the Lord, as his fathers had done; he departed not from the sins of Jeroboam [I] son of Nebat, with which he made Israel to sin.

<sup>10</sup>Shallum son of Jabesh conspired against Zechariah and struck and killed him before the people and reigned in his stead. <sup>11</sup>The rest of the acts of Zechariah, see, they are written in the Book of the Chronicles of the Kings of Israel. <sup>12</sup>This was the fulfillment of the promise to Jehu from the Lord: Your sons shall sit on the throne of Israel to the fourth generation. And so it came to pass. [II Kings 10:30.]

<sup>13</sup>Shallum son of Jabesh, in the thirty-ninth year of Uzziah king of Judah, began his reign of a full month in Samaria.

<sup>14</sup>For Menahem son of Gadi went up from Tirzah and came to Samaria, and smote and killed Shallum son of Jabesh in Samaria and reigned in his stead.

<sup>15</sup>The rest of Shallum's acts, his conspiracy, see, they are written in the Book of the Chronicles of the Kings of Israel.

<sup>16</sup>Then Menahem smote Tiphsah and all who were in it and its territory from Tirzah on; he attacked it because they did not open to him. And all <sup>a</sup>the women there who were with child he ripped up.

---

<sup>a</sup> 26 Or *Israel was suffering. They were without a ruler or leader,*
*and*   <sup>b</sup> 1 Also called *Uzziah*; also in verses 6, 7, 8, 17, 23 and 27
<sup>c</sup> 5 The Hebrew for *leprosy* was used for various diseases affecting
the skin.   <sup>d</sup> 5 Or *in a house where he was relieved of responsibilities*
<sup>e</sup> 10 Hebrew; some Septuagint manuscripts *in Ibleam*   <sup>f</sup> 12 2 Kings
10:30

<sup>a</sup> This savage conduct was among the enormities that a heathen ruler might perpetrate, but only here do we find such cruelty employed by an Israelite. It shows the great degradation and barbarity of the times (*The Cambridge Bible*).

## New International Version

### Menahem King of Israel

¹⁷In the thirty-ninth year of Azariah king of Judah, Menahem son of Gadi became king of Israel, and he reigned in Samaria ten years. ¹⁸He did evil in the eyes of the LORD. During his entire reign he did not turn away from the sins of Jeroboam son of Nebat, which he had caused Israel to commit.

¹⁹Then Pul[a] king of Assyria invaded the land, and Menahem gave him a thousand talents[b] of silver to gain his support and strengthen his own hold on the kingdom. ²⁰Menahem exacted this money from Israel. Every wealthy person had to contribute fifty shekels[c] of silver to be given to the king of Assyria. So the king of Assyria withdrew and stayed in the land no longer.

²¹As for the other events of Menahem's reign, and all he did, are they not written in the book of the annals of the kings of Israel? ²²Menahem rested with his ancestors. And Pekahiah his son succeeded him as king.

### Pekahiah King of Israel

²³In the fiftieth year of Azariah king of Judah, Pekahiah son of Menahem became king of Israel in Samaria, and he reigned two years. ²⁴Pekahiah did evil in the eyes of the LORD. He did not turn away from the sins of Jeroboam son of Nebat, which he had caused Israel to commit. ²⁵One of his chief officers, Pekah son of Remaliah, conspired against him. Taking fifty men of Gilead with him, he assassinated Pekahiah, along with Argob and Arieh, in the citadel of the royal palace at Samaria. So Pekah killed Pekahiah and succeeded him as king.

²⁶The other events of Pekahiah's reign, and all he did, are written in the book of the annals of the kings of Israel.

### Pekah King of Israel

²⁷In the fifty-second year of Azariah king of Judah, Pekah son of Remaliah became king of Israel in Samaria, and he reigned twenty years. ²⁸He did evil in the eyes of the LORD. He did not turn away from the sins of Jeroboam son of Nebat, which he had caused Israel to commit.

²⁹In the time of Pekah king of Israel, Tiglath-Pileser king of Assyria came and took Ijon, Abel Beth Maakah, Janoah, Kedesh and Hazor. He took Gilead and Galilee, including all the land of Naphtali, and deported the people to Assyria. ³⁰Then Hoshea son of Elah conspired against Pekah son of Remaliah. He attacked and assassinated him, and then succeeded him as king in the twentieth year of Jotham son of Uzziah.

³¹As for the other events of Pekah's reign, and all he did, are they not written in the book of the annals of the kings of Israel?

### Jotham King of Judah

³²In the second year of Pekah son of Remaliah king of Israel, Jotham son of Uzziah king of Judah began to reign. ³³He was twenty-five years old when he became king, and he reigned in Jerusalem sixteen years. His mother's name was Jerusha daughter of Zadok. ³⁴He did what was right in the eyes of the LORD, just as his father Uzziah had done. ³⁵The high places, however, were not removed; the people continued to offer sacrifices and burn incense there. Jotham rebuilt the Upper Gate of the temple of the LORD.

³⁶As for the other events of Jotham's reign, and what he did, are they not written in the book of the annals of the

## Amplified Bible

¹⁷In the thirty-ninth year of Azariah king of Judah, Menahem son of Gadi began his ten-year reign over Israel in Samaria.

¹⁸He did evil in the sight of the Lord; he did not depart all his days from the sins of Jeroboam son of Nebat, which he caused Israel to sin.

¹⁹There came against the land Pul king of Assyria, and Menahem gave Pul 1,000 talents of silver, that he might help him to confirm his kingship.

²⁰Menahem exacted the money from Israel, from all the men of wealth, from each man fifty shekels of silver to give to the king of Assyria. So the king of Assyria turned back and did not stay in the land.

²¹The rest of Menahem's acts, all that he did, are they not written in the Book of the Chronicles of the Kings of Israel?

²²Menahem slept with his fathers; Pekahiah his son reigned in his stead.

²³In the fiftieth year of Azariah king of Judah, Pekahiah son of Menahem began his two-year reign over Israel in Samaria.

²⁴He did evil in the sight of the Lord; he did not depart from the sins of Jeroboam [I] son of Nebat, which he made Israel sin.

²⁵But Pekah son of Remaliah, his captain, conspired against [Pekahiah] and attacked him in Samaria, in the citadel of the king's house, with Argob and Arieh; [for] with [Pekah] were fifty Gileadites. And he killed him and reigned in his stead.

²⁶The rest of the acts of Pekahiah, all he did, see, they are written in the Book of the Chronicles of the Kings of Israel.

²⁷In the fifty-second year of Azariah king of Judah, Pekah son of Remaliah began his twenty-year reign over Israel in Samaria.

²⁸He did evil in the Lord's sight; he did not depart from the sins of Jeroboam [I] son of Nebat, which he made Israel sin.

²⁹In the days of Pekah king of Israel, Tiglath-pileser king of Assyria came and took Ijon, Abel-beth-maacah, Janoah, Kedesh, Hazor, Gilead, and Galilee, all the land of Naphtali, and carried the people captive to Assyria.

³⁰Hoshea son of Elah conspired against Pekah son of Remaliah [of Israel]; he smote and killed him, and reigned in his stead in the twentieth year of Jotham son of Uzziah king of Judah.

³¹The rest of Pekah's acts, all that he did, behold, they are written in the Book of the Chronicles of Israel's Kings.

³²In the second year of Pekah son of Remaliah king of Israel, Jotham son of Uzziah king of Judah became king.

³³When he was twenty-five years old, he began his reign of sixteen years in Jerusalem. His mother was Jerusha daughter of Zadok.

³⁴He did right in the Lord's sight, according to all his father Uzziah had done.

³⁵Yet the high places were not removed; the people sacrificed and burned incense still on the high places. He built the Upper Gate of the house of the Lord.

³⁶The rest of the acts of Jotham, all he did, are they not written in the Book of the Chronicles of Judah's Kings?

---

a 19 Also called *Tiglath-Pileser*   b 19 That is, about 38 tons or about 34 metric tons   c 20 That is, about 1 1/4 pounds or about 575 grams

## New International Version

kings of Judah? [37] (In those days the LORD began to send Rezin king of Aram and Pekah son of Remaliah against Judah.) [38] Jotham rested with his ancestors and was buried with them in the City of David, the city of his father. And Ahaz his son succeeded him as king.

### Ahaz King of Judah

**16** In the seventeenth year of Pekah son of Remaliah, Ahaz son of Jotham king of Judah began to reign. [2] Ahaz was twenty years old when he became king, and he reigned in Jerusalem sixteen years. Unlike David his father, he did not do what was right in the eyes of the LORD his God. [3] He followed the ways of the kings of Israel and even sacrificed his son in the fire, engaging in the detestable practices of the nations the LORD had driven out before the Israelites. [4] He offered sacrifices and burned incense at the high places, on the hilltops and under every spreading tree.

[5] Then Rezin king of Aram and Pekah son of Remaliah king of Israel marched up to fight against Jerusalem and besieged Ahaz, but they could not overpower him. [6] At that time, Rezin king of Aram recovered Elath for Aram by driving out the people of Judah. Edomites then moved into Elath and have lived there to this day. [7] Ahaz sent messengers to say to Tiglath-Pileser king of Assyria, "I am your servant and vassal. Come up and save me out of the hand of the king of Aram and of the king of Israel, who are attacking me." [8] And Ahaz took the silver and gold found in the temple of the LORD and in the treasuries of the royal palace and sent it as a gift to the king of Assyria. [9] The king of Assyria complied by attacking Damascus and capturing it. He deported its inhabitants to Kir and put Rezin to death.

[10] Then King Ahaz went to Damascus to meet Tiglath-Pileser king of Assyria. He saw an altar in Damascus and sent to Uriah the priest a sketch of the altar, with detailed plans for its construction. [11] So Uriah the priest built an altar in accordance with all the plans that King Ahaz had sent from Damascus and finished it before King Ahaz returned. [12] When the king came back from Damascus and saw the altar, he approached it and presented offerings[a] on it. [13] He offered up his burnt offering and grain offering, poured out his drink offering, and splashed the blood of his fellowship offerings against the altar. [14] As for the bronze altar that stood before the LORD, he brought it from the front of the temple—from between the new altar and the temple of the LORD—and put it on the north side of the new altar.

[15] King Ahaz then gave these orders to Uriah the priest: "On the large new altar, offer the morning burnt offering and the evening grain offering, the king's burnt offering and his grain offering, and the burnt offering of all the people of the land, and their grain offering and their drink offering. Splash against this altar the blood of all the burnt offerings and sacrifices. But I will use the bronze altar for seeking guidance." [16] And Uriah the priest did just as King Ahaz had ordered.

## Amplified Bible

[37] In those days the Lord began sending Rezin king of Syria and Pekah son of Remaliah against Judah. [38] Jotham slept with his fathers and was buried [with them] in the city of David his [forefather]. Ahaz his son succeeded him.

**16** In the seventeenth year of Pekah son of Remaliah, Ahaz son of Jotham king of Judah became king. [2] Ahaz was twenty years old when he began his sixteen-year reign in Jerusalem. He did not do right in the sight of the Lord his God, like David his [forefather]. [3] But he walked in the ways of Israel's kings, yes, and made his son pass through the fire [and offered him as a sacrifice], in accord with the abominable [idolatrous] practices of the [heathen] nations whom the Lord drove out before the Israelites. [4] He sacrificed and burned incense in the high places, on the hills, and under every green tree.

[5] Then Rezin king of Syria and Pekah son of Remaliah king of Israel came up to Jerusalem to wage war; they besieged Ahaz, but could not conquer him. [6] At that time, Rezin king of Syria got back Elath [in Edom] for Syria and drove the Jews from [it]. The Syrians came to Elath and dwell there to this day. [7] So Ahaz sent messengers to Tiglath-pileser king of Assyria, saying, I am your servant and son. Come up and save me out of the hands of the kings of Syria and of Israel, who are attacking me. [8] And Ahaz took the silver and gold in the house of the Lord and in the treasuries of the king's house and sent a present to the king of Assyria. [9] Assyria's king hearkened to him; he went up against Damascus, took it, carried its people captive to Kir, and slew Rezin.

[10] King Ahaz went to Damascus to meet Tiglath-pileser king of Assyria, and saw there their [heathen] altar. King Ahaz sent to Urijah the priest a model of the altar and an exact pattern for its construction. [11] So Urijah the priest built an altar according to all that King Ahaz had sent from Damascus, finishing it before King Ahaz returned. [12] When the king came from Damascus, he looked at the altar and offered on it. [13] King Ahaz burned his burnt offering and his cereal offering, poured his drink offering, and dashed the blood of his peace offerings upon that altar. [14] The bronze altar which was before the Lord he removed from the front of the house, from between his [new] altar and the house of the Lord, and put it on the north side of his altar. [15] And King Ahaz commanded Urijah the priest: Upon the principal (the new) altar, burn the morning burnt offering, the evening cereal offering, the king's burnt sacrifice and his cereal offering, with the burnt offering and cereal offering and drink offering of all the people of the land; and dash upon the [new] altar all the blood of the burnt offerings and the sacrifices. But the [old] bronze altar shall be kept for me to use to inquire by [of the Lord]. [16] Urijah the priest did all this as King Ahaz commanded.

---

[a] 12 Or *and went up*

## New International Version

[17]King Ahaz cut off the side panels and removed the basins from the movable stands. He removed the Sea from the bronze bulls that supported it and set it on a stone base. [18]He took away the Sabbath canopy[a] that had been built at the temple and removed the royal entryway outside the temple of the LORD, in deference to the king of Assyria. [19]As for the other events of the reign of Ahaz, and what he did, are they not written in the book of the annals of the kings of Judah? [20]Ahaz rested with his ancestors and was buried with them in the City of David. And Hezekiah his son succeeded him as king.

### Hoshea Last King of Israel

**17** In the twelfth year of Ahaz king of Judah, Hoshea son of Elah became king of Israel in Samaria, and he reigned nine years. [2]He did evil in the eyes of the LORD, but not like the kings of Israel who preceded him. [3]Shalmaneser king of Assyria came up to attack Hoshea, who had been Shalmaneser's vassal and had paid him tribute. [4]But the king of Assyria discovered that Hoshea was a traitor, for he had sent envoys to So[b] king of Egypt, and he no longer paid tribute to the king of Assyria, as he had done year by year. Therefore Shalmaneser seized him and put him in prison. [5]The king of Assyria invaded the entire land, marched against Samaria and laid siege to it for three years. [6]In the ninth year of Hoshea, the king of Assyria captured Samaria and deported the Israelites to Assyria. He settled them in Halah, in Gozan on the Habor River and in the towns of the Medes.

### Israel Exiled Because of Sin

[7]All this took place because the Israelites had sinned against the LORD their God, who had brought them up out of Egypt from under the power of Pharaoh king of Egypt. They worshiped other gods [8]and followed the practices of the nations the LORD had driven out before them, as well as the practices that the kings of Israel had introduced. [9]The Israelites secretly did things against the LORD their God that were not right. From watchtower to fortified city they built themselves high places in all their towns. [10]They set up sacred stones and Asherah poles on every high hill and under every spreading tree. [11]At every high place they burned incense, as the nations whom the LORD had driven out before them had done. They did wicked things that aroused the LORD's anger. [12]They worshiped idols, though the LORD had said, "You shall not do this."[c] [13]The LORD warned Israel and Judah through all his prophets and seers: "Turn from your evil ways. Observe my commands and decrees, in accordance with the entire Law that I commanded your ancestors to obey and that I delivered to you through my servants the prophets."

[14]But they would not listen and were as stiff-necked as their ancestors, who did not trust in the LORD their God. [15]They rejected his decrees and the covenant he had made with their ancestors and the statutes he had warned them to keep. They followed worthless idols and themselves became worthless. They imitated the nations around them although the LORD had ordered them, "Do not do as they do."

## Amplified Bible

[17][To keep Assyria's king from getting them] King Ahaz cut off the panels of the bases [of the ten lavers] and removed the laver from each of them; and he took down the Sea from off the bronze oxen that were under it and put it upon stone supports. [18]And the covered way for the Sabbath that they had built in the temple court, and the king's outer entrance, he removed from the house of the Lord, because of the king of Assyria [who if he heard of them might seize them]. [19]The rest of the acts of Ahaz, are they not written in the Book of the Chronicles of the Kings of Judah? [20]Ahaz slept with his fathers and was buried [with them] in the City of David. Hezekiah his son reigned in his stead.

**17** In the twelfth year of Ahaz king of Judah, Hoshea son of Elah began his nine-year reign in Samaria over Israel.

[2]He did evil in the sight of the Lord, but not as Israel's kings before him did.

[3]Against him came up Shalmaneser king of Assyria, and Hoshea became his servant and brought him tribute.

[4]But the king of Assyria found treachery in Hoshea, for he had sent messengers to So king of Egypt and offered no tribute to the king of Assyria, as he had done year by year; therefore the king of Assyria shut him up and bound him in prison.

[5]Then the king of Assyria invaded all the land and went up to Samaria and besieged it for three years.

[6]In the ninth year of Hoshea, the king of Assyria took Samaria and carried the Israelites away into Assyria, and placed them in Halah and in Habor by the river of Gozan and in the cities of the Medes.

[7]This was so because the Israelites had sinned against the Lord their God, Who had brought them out of the land of Egypt, from under the hand of Pharaoh king of Egypt; and they had feared other gods

[8]And walked in the customs of the [heathen] nations whom the Lord drove out before the Israelites, customs the kings of Israel had introduced.

[9]The Israelites did secretly against the Lord their God things not right. They built for themselves high places in all their towns, from [lonely] watchtower to [populous] fortified city.

[10]They set up for themselves pillars and Asherim [symbols of the goddess Asherah] on every high hill and under every green tree.

[11]There they burned incense on all the high places, as did the nations whom the Lord carried away before them; and they did wicked things provoking the Lord to anger.

[12]And they served idols, of which the Lord had said to them, You shall not do this thing.

[13]Yet the Lord warned Israel and Judah through all the prophets and all the seers, saying, Turn from your evil ways and keep My commandments and My statutes, according to all the Law which I commanded your fathers and which I sent to you by My servants the prophets.

[14]Yet they would not hear, but hardened their necks as did their fathers who did not believe (trust in, rely on, and remain steadfast to) the Lord their God.

[15]They despised *and* rejected His statutes and His covenant which He made with their fathers and His warnings to them, and they followed vanity (false gods—falsehood, emptiness, and futility) and [they themselves and their prayers] became false (empty and futile). They went after the heathen round about them, of whom the Lord had charged them that they should not do as they did.

---

*a 18* Or *the dais of his throne* (see Septuagint)    *b 4 So* is probably an abbreviation for *Osorkon.*    *c 12* Exodus 20:4,5

## New International Version

[16]They forsook all the commands of the LORD their God and made for themselves two idols cast in the shape of calves, and an Asherah pole. They bowed down to all the starry hosts, and they worshiped Baal. [17]They sacrificed their sons and daughters in the fire. They practiced divination and sought omens and sold themselves to do evil in the eyes of the LORD, arousing his anger.

[18]So the LORD was very angry with Israel and removed them from his presence. Only the tribe of Judah was left, [19]and even Judah did not keep the commands of the LORD their God. They followed the practices Israel had introduced. [20]Therefore the LORD rejected all the people of Israel; he afflicted them and gave them into the hands of plunderers, until he thrust them from his presence.

[21]When he tore Israel away from the house of David, they made Jeroboam son of Nebat their king. Jeroboam enticed Israel away from following the LORD and caused them to commit a great sin. [22]The Israelites persisted in all the sins of Jeroboam and did not turn away from them [23]until the LORD removed them from his presence, as he had warned through all his servants the prophets. So the people of Israel were taken from their homeland into exile in Assyria, and they are still there.

### Samaria Resettled

[24]The king of Assyria brought people from Babylon, Kuthah, Avva, Hamath and Sepharvaim and settled them in the towns of Samaria to replace the Israelites. They took over Samaria and lived in its towns. [25]When they first lived there, they did not worship the LORD; so he sent lions among them and they killed some of the people. [26]It was reported to the king of Assyria: "The people you deported and resettled in the towns of Samaria do not know what the god of that country requires. He has sent lions among them, which are killing them off, because the people do not know what he requires."

[27]Then the king of Assyria gave this order: "Have one of the priests you took captive from Samaria go back to live there and teach the people what the god of the land requires." [28]So one of the priests who had been exiled from Samaria came to live in Bethel and taught them how to worship the LORD.

[29]Nevertheless, each national group made its own gods in the several towns where they settled, and set them up in the shrines the people of Samaria had made at the high places. [30]The people from Babylon made Sukkoth Benoth, those from Kuthah made Nergal, and those from Hamath made Ashima; [31]the Avvites made Nibhaz and Tartak, and the Sepharvites burned their children in the fire as sacrifices to Adrammelek and Anammelek, the gods of Sepharvaim. [32]They worshiped the LORD, but they also appointed all sorts of their own people to officiate for them as priests in the shrines at the high places. [33]They worshiped the LORD, but they also served their own gods in accordance with the customs of the nations from which they had been brought.

[34]To this day they persist in their former practices. They neither worship the LORD nor adhere to the decrees and regulations, the laws and commands that the LORD gave the descendants of Jacob, whom he named Israel. [35]When the LORD made a covenant with the Israelites, he commanded them: "Do not worship any other gods or bow down to them, serve them or sacrifice to them. [36]But the

## Amplified Bible

[16]And they forsook all the commandments of the Lord their God and made for themselves molten images, even two calves, and made an Asherah and worshiped all the [starry] hosts of the heavens and served Baal.

[17]They caused their sons and their daughters to pass through the fire and used divination and enchantments and sold themselves to do evil in the sight of the Lord, provoking Him to anger.

[18]Therefore the Lord was very angry with Israel and removed them out of His sight. None was left but the tribe of Judah.

[19]Judah also did not keep the commandments of the Lord their God, but walked in the customs which Israel introduced.

[20]The Lord rejected all the descendants of Israel and afflicted them and delivered them into the hands of spoilers, until He had cast them out of His sight.

[21]For He tore Israel from the house of David; and they made Jeroboam son of Nebat king. And Jeroboam drew *and* drove Israel away from following the Lord and made them sin a great sin.

[22]For the Israelites walked in all the sins Jeroboam committed; they departed not from them

[23]Until the Lord removed Israel from His sight, as He had foretold by all His servants the prophets. So Israel was carried away from their own land to Assyria to this day.

[24]The king of Assyria brought men from Babylon, Cuthah, Avva, Hamath, and Sepharvaim and placed them in the cities of Samaria instead of the Israelites. They possessed Samaria and dwelt in its cities.

[25]At the beginning of their dwelling there, they did not fear *and* revere the Lord. Therefore the Lord sent lions among them, which killed some of them.

[26]So the king of Assyria was told: The nations you removed and placed in the cities of Samaria do not know the manner in which the God of the land requires their worship. Therefore He has sent lions among them, and behold, they are killing them, because they do not know the manner of [worship demanded by] the God of the land.

[27]Then the king of Assyria commanded, Take to Samaria one of the priests you brought from there, and let him [and his helpers] go and live there and let him teach the people the law of the God of the land.

[28]So one of the priests whom they had carried away from Samaria came and dwelt in Bethel and taught them how they should fear *and* revere the Lord.

[29]But every nationality still made gods of their own and put them in the shrines of the high places which the Samaritans had made, every nationality in the city in which they dwelt.

[30]The men of Babylon made [and worshiped their deity] Succoth-benoth, the men of Cuth made Nergal, the men of Hamath made Ashima;

[31]The Avvites made Nibhaz and Tartak, and the Sepharvites burned their children in the fire to Adrammelech and Anammelech, the gods of Sepharvaim.

[32]So they feared the Lord, yet appointed from among themselves, whether high or low, priests of the high places, who sacrificed for them in the shrines of the high places.

[33]They feared the Lord, yet served their own gods, as did the nations from among whom they had been carried away.

[34]Unto this day they do after their former custom: they do not fear the Lord [as God sees it], neither do they obey the statutes or the ordinances or the law and commandment which the Lord commanded the children of Jacob, whom He named Israel,

[35]With whom the Lord had made a covenant and commanded them, You shall not fear other gods or bow yourselves to them or serve them or sacrifice to them.

## New International Version

LORD, who brought you up out of Egypt with mighty power and outstretched arm, is the one you must worship. To him you shall bow down and to him offer sacrifices. [37] You must always be careful to keep the decrees and regulations, the laws and commands he wrote for you. Do not worship other gods. [38] Do not forget the covenant I have made with you, and do not worship other gods. [39] Rather, worship the LORD your God; it is he who will deliver you from the hand of all your enemies."

[40] They would not listen, however, but persisted in their former practices. [41] Even while these people were worshiping the LORD, they were serving their idols. To this day their children and grandchildren continue to do as their ancestors did.

### Hezekiah King of Judah

**18** In the third year of Hoshea son of Elah king of Israel, Hezekiah son of Ahaz king of Judah began to reign. [2] He was twenty-five years old when he became king, and he reigned in Jerusalem twenty-nine years. His mother's name was Abijah[a] daughter of Zechariah. [3] He did what was right in the eyes of the LORD, just as his father David had done. [4] He removed the high places, smashed the sacred stones and cut down the Asherah poles. He broke into pieces the bronze snake Moses had made, for up to that time the Israelites had been burning incense to it. (It was called Nehushtan.[b])

[5] Hezekiah trusted in the LORD, the God of Israel. There was no one like him among all the kings of Judah, either before him or after him. [6] He held fast to the LORD and did not stop following him; he kept the commands the LORD had given Moses. [7] And the LORD was with him; he was successful in whatever he undertook. He rebelled against the king of Assyria and did not serve him. [8] From watchtower to fortified city, he defeated the Philistines, as far as Gaza and its territory.

[9] In King Hezekiah's fourth year, which was the seventh year of Hoshea son of Elah king of Israel, Shalmaneser king of Assyria marched against Samaria and laid siege to it. [10] At the end of three years the Assyrians took it. So Samaria was captured in Hezekiah's sixth year, which was the ninth year of Hoshea king of Israel. [11] The king of Assyria deported Israel to Assyria and settled them in Halah, in Gozan on the Habor River and in towns of the Medes. [12] This happened because they had not obeyed the LORD their God, but had violated his covenant—all that Moses the servant of the LORD commanded. They neither listened to the commands nor carried them out.

[13] In the fourteenth year of King Hezekiah's reign, Sennacherib king of Assyria attacked all the fortified cities of Judah and captured them. [14] So Hezekiah king of Judah sent this message to the king of Assyria at Lachish: "I have done wrong. Withdraw from me, and I will pay whatever you demand of me." The king of Assyria exacted from Hezekiah king of Judah three hundred talents[c] of silver and thirty talents[d] of gold. [15] So Hezekiah gave him all the silver that was found in the temple of the LORD and in the treasuries of the royal palace.

## Amplified Bible

[36] But you shall [reverently] fear, bow yourselves to, and sacrifice to the Lord, Who brought you out of the land of Egypt with great power and an outstretched arm. [37] And the statutes, ordinances, law, and commandment which He wrote for you you shall observe and do forevermore; you shall not fear other gods. [38] And the covenant that I have made with you you shall not forget; you shall not fear other gods. [39] But the Lord your God you shall [reverently] fear; then He will deliver you out of the hands of all your enemies.

[40] However, they did not listen, but they did as they had done formerly. [41] So these nations [vainly] feared the Lord and also served their graven images, as did their children and their children's children. As their fathers did, so do they to this day.

**18** In the third year of Hoshea son of Elah king of Israel, Hezekiah son of Ahaz king of Judah began to reign. [2] He was twenty-five years old when he began his twenty-nine-year reign in Jerusalem. His mother was Abi daughter of Zechariah. [3] Hezekiah did right in the sight of the Lord, according to all that David his [forefather] had done. [4] He removed the high places, broke the images, cut down the Asherim, and broke in pieces the bronze serpent that Moses had made, for until then the Israelites had burned incense to it; but he called it Nehushtan [a bronze trifle]. [5] Hezekiah trusted in, leaned on, and was confident in the Lord, the God of Israel; so that neither after him nor before him was any one of all the kings of Judah like him. [6] For he clung and held fast to the Lord and ceased not to follow Him, but kept His commandments, as the Lord commanded Moses.

[7] And the Lord was with Hezekiah; he prospered wherever he went. And he rebelled against the king of Assyria and refused to serve him. [8] He smote the Philistines, even to Gaza [the most distant city] and its borders, from the [isolated] watchtower to the [populous] fortified city. [9] In the fourth year of King Hezekiah, which was the seventh of Hoshea son of Elah king of Israel, Shalmaneser king of Assyria came up against Samaria and besieged it. [10] After three years it was taken; in the sixth year of Hezekiah, which was the ninth year of Hoshea king of Israel, Samaria was taken. [11] The king of Assyria carried Israel away to Assyria, and put them in Halah, and on the Habor, the river of Gozan, and in the cities of the Medes, [12] Because they did not obey the voice of the Lord their God, but transgressed His covenant, even all that Moses the servant of the Lord commanded, and would not hear it or do it. [13] In the fourteenth year of Hezekiah, Sennacherib king of Assyria came up against all the fortified cities of Judah and took them. [14] Then Hezekiah king of Judah sent to the king of Assyria at Lachish, saying, I have done wrong. Depart from me; what you put on me I will bear. And the king of Assyria exacted of Hezekiah king of Judah 300 talents of silver and thirty talents of gold. [15] And Hezekiah gave him all the silver that was found in the house of the Lord and in the treasuries of the king's house.

---

[a] 2 Hebrew *Abi*, a variant of *Abijah*.    [b] 4 *Nehushtan* sounds like the Hebrew for both *bronze* and *snake*.    [c] 14 That is, about 11 tons or about 10 metric tons    [d] 14 That is, about 1 ton or about 1 metric ton

## New International Version

16At this time Hezekiah king of Judah stripped off the gold with which he had covered the doors and doorposts of the temple of the LORD, and gave it to the king of Assyria.

### Sennacherib Threatens Jerusalem

17The king of Assyria sent his supreme commander, his chief officer and his field commander with a large army, from Lachish to King Hezekiah at Jerusalem. They came up to Jerusalem and stopped at the aqueduct of the Upper Pool, on the road to the Washerman's Field. 18They called for the king; and Eliakim son of Hilkiah the palace administrator, Shebna the secretary, and Joah son of Asaph the recorder went out to them.

19The field commander said to them, "Tell Hezekiah:

"'This is what the great king, the king of Assyria, says: On what are you basing this confidence of yours? 20You say you have the counsel and the might for war—but you speak only empty words. On whom are you depending, that you rebel against me? 21Look, I know you are depending on Egypt, that splintered reed of a staff, which pierces the hand of anyone who leans on it! Such is Pharaoh king of Egypt to all who depend on him. 22But if you say to me, "We are depending on the LORD our God"—isn't he the one whose high places and altars Hezekiah removed, saying to Judah and Jerusalem, "You must worship before this altar in Jerusalem"?

23"'Come now, make a bargain with my master, the king of Assyria: I will give you two thousand horses—if you can put riders on them! 24How can you repulse one officer of the least of my master's officials, even though you are depending on Egypt for chariots and horsemen*a*? 25Furthermore, have I come to attack and destroy this place without word from the LORD? The LORD himself told me to march against this country and destroy it.'"

26Then Eliakim son of Hilkiah, and Shebna and Joah said to the field commander, "Please speak to your servants in Aramaic, since we understand it. Don't speak to us in Hebrew in the hearing of the people on the wall."

27But the commander replied, "Was it only to your master and you that my master sent me to say these things, and not to the people sitting on the wall—who, like you, will have to eat their own excrement and drink their own urine?"

28Then the commander stood and called out in Hebrew, "Hear the word of the great king, the king of Assyria! 29This is what the king says: Do not let Hezekiah deceive you. He cannot deliver you from my hand. 30Do not let Hezekiah persuade you to trust in the LORD when he says, 'The LORD will surely deliver us; this city will not be given into the hand of the king of Assyria.'

31"Do not listen to Hezekiah. This is what the king of Assyria says: Make peace with me and come out to me. Then each of you will eat fruit from your own vine and fig tree and drink water from your own cistern, 32until I come and take you to a land like your own—a land of grain and new wine, a land of bread and vineyards, a land of olive trees and honey. Choose life and not death!

"Do not listen to Hezekiah, for he is misleading you when he says, 'The LORD will deliver us.' 33Has the god of any nation ever delivered his land from the hand of the king of Assyria? 34Where are the gods of Hamath and Arpad? Where are the gods of Sepharvaim, Hena and Ivvah? Have they rescued Samaria from my hand? 35Who of all the gods of these countries has been able to save his land from me? How then can the LORD deliver Jerusalem from my hand?"

*a 24 Or charioteers*

## Amplified Bible

16Then Hezekiah stripped off the gold from the doors of the temple of the Lord and from the doorposts which he as king of Judah had overlaid, and gave it to the king of Assyria.

17And the king of Assyria sent the Tartan, the Rabsaris, and the Rabshakeh [the high officials] from Lachish to King Hezekiah at Jerusalem with a great army. They went up to Jerusalem, and when they arrived, they came and stood by the canal of the Upper Pool, which is on the highway to the Fuller's Field. [II Chron. 32:9-19; Isa. 36:1-22.]

18When they called for the king, there came out to them Eliakim son of Hilkiah, who was over the king's household, and Shebna the scribe, and Joah son of Asaph the recorder.

19The Rabshakeh told them, Say to Hezekiah, Thus says the great king of Assyria: What justifies this confidence of yours?

20You say—but they are empty words—There is counsel and strength for war. Now on whom do you rely, that you rebel against me?

21Behold, you are relying on Egypt, that broken reed of a staff; if a man leans on it, it will pierce his hand. So is Pharaoh king of Egypt to all who trust *and* rely on him.

22But if you tell me, We trust in *and* rely on the Lord our God, is it not He Whose high places and altars Hezekiah has removed, saying to Judah and Jerusalem, You shall worship before this altar in Jerusalem?

23So now, make a wager *and* give pledges to my lord the king of Assyria: I will deliver you 2,000 horses—if you can on your part put riders on them.

24How then can you beat back one captain among the least of my master's servants, when your trust is put in Egypt for chariots and horsemen?

25Have I come up without the Lord against this place to destroy it? The Lord said to me, Go up against this land and destroy it.

26Then Eliakim son of Hilkiah and Shebna and Joah said to the Rabshakeh, We pray you, speak to your servants in the Aramaic (Syrian) language, for we understand it; and do not speak to us in the Jews' language in the hearing of the people on the wall.

27But the Rabshakeh said to them, Has my master sent me to your master and you to say these things? Has he not sent me to the men who sit on the wall [whom Hezekiah has doomed to be forced] to eat their own dung and drink their own urine along with you?

28Then the Rabshakeh stood and cried with a loud voice in the Jews' language, Hear the word of the great king of Assyria!

29Thus says the king: Let not Hezekiah deceive you. For he will not be able to deliver you out of my hand.

30Nor let Hezekiah make you trust in *and* rely on the Lord, saying, The Lord will surely deliver us, and this city will not be given into the hand of Assyria's king.

31Hearken not to Hezekiah, for thus says the king of Assyria: Make your peace with me and come out to me, and eat every man from his own vine and fig tree and drink every man the waters of his own cistern,

32Until I come and take you away to a land like your own, a land of grain and vintage fruit, of bread and vineyards, of olive trees and honey, that you may live and not die. Do not listen to Hezekiah when he urges you, saying, The Lord will deliver us.

33Has any one of the gods of the nations ever delivered his land out of the hand of the king of Assyria?

34Where are the gods of Hamath and Arpad [in Syria]? Where are the gods of Sepharvaim, Hena, and Ivvah [in the Euphrates Valley]? Have they delivered Samaria [Israel's capital] out of my hand?

35Who of all the gods of the countries has delivered his country out of my hand, that the Lord should deliver Jerusalem out of my hand?

## New International Version

³⁶But the people remained silent and said nothing in reply, because the king had commanded, "Do not answer him."

³⁷Then Eliakim son of Hilkiah the palace administrator, Shebna the secretary, and Joah son of Asaph the recorder went to Hezekiah, with their clothes torn, and told him what the field commander had said.

### Jerusalem's Deliverance Foretold

**19** When King Hezekiah heard this, he tore his clothes and put on sackcloth and went into the temple of the LORD. ²He sent Eliakim the palace administrator, Shebna the secretary, and the leading priests, all wearing sackcloth, to the prophet Isaiah son of Amoz. ³They told him, "This is what Hezekiah says: This day is a day of distress and rebuke and disgrace, as when children come to the moment of birth and there is no strength to deliver them. ⁴It may be that the LORD your God will hear all the words of the field commander, whom his master, the king of Assyria, has sent to ridicule the living God, and that he will rebuke him for the words the LORD your God has heard. Therefore pray for the remnant that still survives."

⁵When King Hezekiah's officials came to Isaiah, ⁶Isaiah said to them, "Tell your master, 'This is what the LORD says: Do not be afraid of what you have heard—those words with which the underlings of the king of Assyria have blasphemed me. ⁷Listen! When he hears a certain report, I will make him want to return to his own country, and there I will have him cut down with the sword.'"

⁸When the field commander heard that the king of Assyria had left Lachish, he withdrew and found the king fighting against Libnah.

⁹Now Sennacherib received a report that Tirhakah, the king of Cush,ᵃ was marching out to fight against him. So he again sent messengers to Hezekiah with this word: ¹⁰"Say to Hezekiah king of Judah: Do not let the god you depend on deceive you when he says, 'Jerusalem will not be given into the hands of the king of Assyria.' ¹¹Surely you have heard what the kings of Assyria have done to all the countries, destroying them completely. And will you be delivered? ¹²Did the gods of the nations that were destroyed by my predecessors deliver them—the gods of Gozan, Harran, Rezeph and the people of Eden who were in Tel Assar? ¹³Where is the king of Hamath or the king of Arpad? Where are the kings of Lair, Sepharvaim, Hena and Ivvah?"

### Hezekiah's Prayer

¹⁴Hezekiah received the letter from the messengers and read it. Then he went up to the temple of the LORD and spread it out before the LORD. ¹⁵And Hezekiah prayed to the LORD: "LORD, the God of Israel, enthroned between the cherubim, you alone are God over all the kingdoms of the earth. You have made heaven and earth. ¹⁶Give ear, LORD, and hear; open your eyes, LORD, and see; listen to the words Sennacherib has sent to ridicule the living God.

¹⁷"It is true, LORD, that the Assyrian kings have laid waste these nations and their lands. ¹⁸They have thrown their gods into the fire and destroyed them, for they were not gods but only wood and stone, fashioned by human hands. ¹⁹Now, LORD our God, deliver us from his hand, so that all the kingdoms of the earth may know that you alone, LORD, are God."

## Amplified Bible

³⁶But the people were silent and answered him not a word, for Hezekiah had commanded, Do not answer him.

³⁷Then Eliakim son of Hilkiah, who was over the royal household, and Shebna the scribe, and Joah son of Asaph the recorder came to Hezekiah with their clothes rent, and told him what the Rabshakeh had said.

**19** When King Hezekiah heard it, he rent his clothes and covered himself with sackcloth and went into the house of the Lord. [Isa. 37:1-13.]

²And he sent Eliakim, who was over his household, Shebna the scribe, and the older priests, covered with sackcloth, to Isaiah the prophet the son of Amoz.

³They said to him, Hezekiah says: This is a day of [extreme danger and] distress, of rebuke *and* chastisement, and blasphemous *and* insolent insult; for children have come to the birth, and there is no strength to bring them forth.

⁴It may be that the Lord your God will hear all the words of the Rabshakeh, whom the king of Assyria has sent to mock, reproach, insult, *and* defy the living God, and will rebuke the words which the Lord your God has heard. So raise your prayer for the remnant [of His people] that is left.

⁵So the servants of King Hezekiah came to Isaiah.

⁶Isaiah said to them, Say to your master, Thus says the Lord: Do not be afraid because of the words you have heard, with which the servants of the king of Assyria have reviled *and* blasphemed Me.

⁷Behold, I will put a spirit in him so that he will hear a rumor and return to his own land, and I will cause him to fall by the sword in his own country.

⁸So the Rabshakeh returned and found the king of Assyria fighting against Libnah [a fortified city of Judah]; for he had heard that the king had left Lachish.

⁹And Sennacherib king of Assyria heard concerning Tirhakah king of Ethiopia, He has come to make war against you. And when he heard it, he sent messengers again to Hezekiah, saying,

¹⁰Say this to Hezekiah king of Judah: Let not your God on Whom you rely deceive you by saying, Jerusalem shall not be delivered into the hand of the king of Assyria.

¹¹Behold, you have heard what the Assyrian kings have done to all lands, destroying them utterly. And shall you be delivered?

¹²Have the gods of the nations delivered those whom my ancestors have destroyed, as Gozan, Haran [of Mesopotamia], Rezeph, and the people of Eden who were in Telassar?

¹³Where are the kings of Hamath, of Arpad [of northern Syria], of the city of Sepharvaim, of Hena, and Ivvah?

¹⁴Hezekiah received the letter from the hand of the messengers and read it. And he went up into the house of the Lord and spread it before the Lord. [Isa. 37:14-20.]

¹⁵And Hezekiah prayed: O Lord, the God of Israel, Who [in symbol] is enthroned above the cherubim [of the ark in the temple], You are the God, You alone, of all the kingdoms of the earth. You have made the heavens and the earth.

¹⁶Lord, bow down Your ear and hear; Lord, open Your eyes and see; hear the words of Sennacherib which he has sent to mock, reproach, insult, *and* defy the living God.

¹⁷It is true, Lord, that the Assyrian kings have laid waste the nations and their lands

¹⁸And have cast the gods of those peoples into the fire, for they were not gods but the work of men's hands, wood and stone. So they [could destroy and] have destroyed them.

¹⁹Now therefore, O Lord our God, I beseech You, save us out of his hand, that all the kingdoms of the earth may know *and* understand that You, O Lord, are God alone.

ᵃ 9 That is, the upper Nile region

## New International Version

### Isaiah Prophesies Sennacherib's Fall

²⁰Then Isaiah son of Amoz sent a message to Hezekiah: "This is what the LORD, the God of Israel, says: I have heard your prayer concerning Sennacherib king of Assyria. ²¹This is the word that the LORD has spoken against him:

"'Virgin Daughter Zion
  despises you and mocks you.
Daughter Jerusalem
  tosses her head as you flee.
²²Who is it you have ridiculed and blasphemed?
  Against whom have you raised your voice
and lifted your eyes in pride?
  Against the Holy One of Israel!
²³By your messengers
  you have ridiculed the Lord.
And you have said,
  "With my many chariots
I have ascended the heights of the mountains,
  the utmost heights of Lebanon.
I have cut down its tallest cedars,
  the choicest of its junipers.
I have reached its remotest parts,
  the finest of its forests.
²⁴I have dug wells in foreign lands
  and drunk the water there.
With the soles of my feet
  I have dried up all the streams of Egypt."

²⁵"'Have you not heard?
  Long ago I ordained it.
In days of old I planned it;
  now I have brought it to pass,
that you have turned fortified cities
  into piles of stone.
²⁶Their people, drained of power,
  are dismayed and put to shame.
They are like plants in the field,
  like tender green shoots,
like grass sprouting on the roof,
  scorched before it grows up.

²⁷"'But I know where you are
  and when you come and go
  and how you rage against me.
²⁸Because you rage against me
  and because your insolence has reached my ears,
I will put my hook in your nose
  and my bit in your mouth,
and I will make you return
  by the way you came.'

²⁹"This will be the sign for you, Hezekiah:

"This year you will eat what grows by itself,
  and the second year what springs from that.
But in the third year sow and reap,
  plant vineyards and eat their fruit.
³⁰Once more a remnant of the kingdom of Judah
  will take root below and bear fruit above.
³¹For out of Jerusalem will come a remnant,
  and out of Mount Zion a band of survivors.

"The zeal of the LORD Almighty will accomplish this.

³²"Therefore this is what the LORD says concerning the king of Assyria:

"'He will not enter this city
  or shoot an arrow here.
He will not come before it with shield
  or build a siege ramp against it.
³³By the way that he came he will return;
  he will not enter this city,

declares the LORD.

## Amplified Bible

²⁰Then Isaiah son of Amoz sent to Hezekiah, saying, Thus says the Lord, the God of Israel: Your prayer to Me about Sennacherib king of Assyria I have heard. [Isa. 37:21-38.]
²¹This is the word that the Lord has spoken concerning him: The Virgin Daughter of Zion has despised you and laughed you to scorn; the Daughter of Jerusalem has wagged her head behind you.
²²Whom have you mocked *and* reviled and insulted *and* blasphemed? Against Whom have you raised your voice and haughtily lifted your eyes? Against the Holy One of Israel!
²³By your messengers you have mocked, reproached, insulted, *and* defied the Lord, and have said, With my many chariots I have gone up to the heights of the mountains, to the far recesses of Lebanon. I cut down its tall cedar trees and its choicest cypress trees. I entered its most distant retreat, its densest forest.
²⁴I dug wells and drank foreign waters, and with the sole of my feet have I dried up all [the defense and] the streams of Egypt.
²⁵[But, says the God of Israel] Have you not heard how I ordained long ago what now I have brought to pass? I planned it in olden times, that you [king of Assyria] should [be My instrument to] lay waste fortified cities, making them ruinous heaps.
²⁶That is why their inhabitants had little power, they were dismayed and confounded; they were like plants of the field, the green herb, the grass on the housetops, blasted before it is grown up.
²⁷But [O Sennacherib] I [the Lord] know your sitting down, your going out, your coming in, and your raging against Me.
²⁸Because your raging against Me and your arrogance *and* careless ease have come to My ears, therefore I will put My hook in your nose and My bridle in your lips, and I will turn you back by the way you came, O king of Assyria.
²⁹And [Hezekiah, says the Lord] this shall be the sign [of these things] to you: you shall eat this year what grows of itself, also in the second year what springs up voluntarily. But in the third year sow and reap, plant vineyards and eat their fruit.
³⁰And the remnant that has survived of the house of Judah shall again take root downward and bear fruit upward.
³¹For out of Jerusalem shall go forth a remnant, and a band of survivors out of Mount Zion. The zeal of the Lord of hosts shall perform this.
³²Therefore thus says the Lord concerning the king of Assyria: He shall not come into this city or shoot an arrow here or come before it with shield or cast up a siege mound against it.
³³By the way that he came, by that way shall he return, and he shall not come into this city, says the Lord.

## New International Version

³⁴I will defend this city and save it,
    for my sake and for the sake of David my servant.'"

³⁵That night the angel of the LORD went out and put to death a hundred and eighty-five thousand in the Assyrian camp. When the people got up the next morning—there were all the dead bodies! ³⁶So Sennacherib king of Assyria broke camp and withdrew. He returned to Nineveh and stayed there.

³⁷One day, while he was worshiping in the temple of his god Nisrok, his sons Adrammelek and Sharezer killed him with the sword, and they escaped to the land of Ararat. And Esarhaddon his son succeeded him as king.

### Hezekiah's Illness

**20** In those days Hezekiah became ill and was at the point of death. The prophet Isaiah son of Amoz went to him and said, "This is what the LORD says: Put your house in order, because you are going to die; you will not recover."

²Hezekiah turned his face to the wall and prayed to the LORD, ³"Remember, LORD, how I have walked before you faithfully and with wholehearted devotion and have done what is good in your eyes." And Hezekiah wept bitterly.

⁴Before Isaiah had left the middle court, the word of the LORD came to him: ⁵"Go back and tell Hezekiah, the ruler of my people, 'This is what the LORD, the God of your father David, says: I have heard your prayer and seen your tears; I will heal you. On the third day from now you will go up to the temple of the LORD. ⁶I will add fifteen years to your life. And I will deliver you and this city from the hand of the king of Assyria. I will defend this city for my sake and for the sake of my servant David.'"

⁷Then Isaiah said, "Prepare a poultice of figs." They did so and applied it to the boil, and he recovered.

⁸Hezekiah had asked Isaiah, "What will be the sign that the LORD will heal me and that I will go up to the temple of the LORD on the third day from now?"

⁹Isaiah answered, "This is the LORD's sign to you that the LORD will do what he has promised: Shall the shadow go forward ten steps, or shall it go back ten steps?"

¹⁰"It is a simple matter for the shadow to go forward ten steps," said Hezekiah. "Rather, have it go back ten steps."

¹¹Then the prophet Isaiah called on the LORD, and the LORD made the shadow go back the ten steps it had gone down on the stairway of Ahaz.

### Envoys From Babylon

¹²At that time Marduk-Baladan son of Baladan king of Babylon sent Hezekiah letters and a gift, because he had heard of Hezekiah's illness. ¹³Hezekiah received the en-

## Amplified Bible

³⁴For I will defend this city to save it, for My own sake and for My servant David's sake.

³⁵And it all came to pass, for that night the ᵃAngel of the Lord went forth and slew 185,000 in the camp of the Assyrians; and when [the living] arose early in the morning, behold, all these were dead bodies.

³⁶So Sennacherib king of Assyria departed and returned and dwelt at Nineveh.

³⁷And as he was worshiping in the house of Nisroch his god, Adrammelech and Sharezer his sons killed him with the sword, and they escaped to the land of Armenia or Ararat. Esarhaddon his son reigned in his stead.

**20** In those days Hezekiah became deadly ill. The prophet Isaiah son of Amoz came and said to him, Thus says the Lord: Set your house in order, for you shall die; you shall not recover. [II Chron. 32:24-26; Isa. 38:1-8.]

²Then Hezekiah turned his face to the wall and prayed to the Lord, saying,

³I beseech You, O Lord, [earnestly] remember now how I have walked before You in faithfulness *and* truth and with a whole heart [entirely devoted to You] and have done what is good in Your sight. And Hezekiah wept bitterly.

⁴Before Isaiah had gone out of the middle court, the word of the Lord came to him:

⁵Turn back and tell Hezekiah, the leader of My people, Thus says the Lord, the God of David your [forefather]: I have heard your prayer, I have seen your tears; behold, I will heal you. On the third day you shall go up to the house of the Lord.

⁶I will ᵇadd to your life fifteen years and deliver you and this city [Jerusalem] out of the hand of the king of Assyria; and I will defend this city for My own sake and for My servant David's sake.

⁷And Isaiah said, Bring a cake of figs. Let them lay it on the burning inflammation, that he may recover.

⁸Hezekiah said to Isaiah, What shall be the sign that the Lord will heal me and that I shall go up into the house of the Lord on the third day?

⁹And Isaiah said, This is the sign to you from the Lord that He will do the thing He has promised: shall the shadow [denoting the time of day] go forward ten steps, or go back ten steps?

¹⁰Hezekiah answered, It is an easy matter for the shadow to go forward ten steps; so let the shadow go back ten steps.

¹¹So Isaiah the prophet cried to the Lord, and He brought the shadow the ten steps backward by which it had gone down on the sundial of Ahaz.

¹²At that time Merodach-baladan son of Baladan king of Babylon sent letters and a present to Hezekiah, for he had heard of Hezekiah's illness. [Isa. 39:1-8.]

¹³And Hezekiah rejoiced *and* welcomed the embassy

---

ᵃ See footnote on Gen. 16:7. ᵇ Good King Hezekiah's prayer life holds a mighty challenge and a clear and terrible warning for every believer. In his nation's darkest hour (18:13-17), he prayed (19:15), and God performed a miracle, one He had foretold (19:20, 32-37). It is a wonderful thing to have such power as that with God! But in this chapter (20) and the next, that power has become a terrible thing; for Hezekiah had put himself on God's "ways and means committee," as chairman in fact. God virtually said, "Your time has come to die" (20:1). But Hezekiah's words and tears implied, "No! I want to live and have sons who will do mighty things, and I myself have my best years ahead of me!" Read this chapter and the next, and note at least ten terrible things (see also footnote on II Kings 20:17) that resulted which only God could foresee and that only Hezekiah's death executed at the time God intended it would have prevented. But Hezekiah interfered. The only safe prayer policy is "God's will; nothing more; nothing less; nothing else; at any cost" (see Luke 22:42, Acts 21:14). It pays triumphantly! Martin Luther is quoted as saying, "Blessed is he who submits to the will of God; he can never be unhappy. Men may deal with him as they will . . . ; he is without care; he knows that 'all things work together for good' for him" (Rom. 8:28) (Martin Luther, cited by J. P. Lange, *A Commentary*).

## New International Version

voys and showed them all that was in his storehouses—the silver, the gold, the spices and the fine olive oil—his armory and everything found among his treasures. There was nothing in his palace or in all his kingdom that Hezekiah did not show them.

14Then Isaiah the prophet went to King Hezekiah and asked, "What did those men say, and where did they come from?"

"From a distant land," Hezekiah replied. "They came from Babylon."

15The prophet asked, "What did they see in your palace?"

"They saw everything in my palace," Hezekiah said. "There is nothing among my treasures that I did not show them."

16Then Isaiah said to Hezekiah, "Hear the word of the LORD: 17The time will surely come when everything in your palace, and all that your predecessors have stored up until this day, will be carried off to Babylon. Nothing will be left, says the LORD. 18And some of your descendants, your own flesh and blood who will be born to you, will be taken away, and they will become eunuchs in the palace of the king of Babylon."

19"The word of the LORD you have spoken is good," Hezekiah replied. For he thought, "Will there not be peace and security in my lifetime?"

20As for the other events of Hezekiah's reign, all his achievements and how he made the pool and the tunnel by which he brought water into the city, are they not written in the book of the annals of the kings of Judah? 21Hezekiah rested with his ancestors. And Manasseh his son succeeded him as king.

### Manasseh King of Judah

**21** Manasseh was twelve years old when he became king, and he reigned in Jerusalem fifty-five years. His mother's name was Hephzibah. 2He did evil in the eyes of the LORD, following the detestable practices of the nations the LORD had driven out before the Israelites. 3He rebuilt the high places his father Hezekiah had destroyed; he also erected altars to Baal and made an Asherah pole, as Ahab king of Israel had done. He bowed down to all the starry hosts and worshiped them. 4He built altars in the temple of the LORD, of which the LORD had said, "In Jerusalem I will put my Name." 5In the two courts of the temple of the LORD, he built altars to all the starry hosts. 6He sacrificed his own son in the fire, practiced divination, sought omens, and consulted mediums and spiritists. He did much evil in the eyes of the LORD, arousing his anger.

7He took the carved Asherah pole he had made and put it in the temple, of which the LORD had said to David and to his son Solomon, "In this temple and in Jerusalem, which I have chosen out of all the tribes of Israel, I will put my Name forever. 8I will not again make the feet of the Israelites wander from the land I gave their ancestors, if only they will be careful to do everything I commanded them and will keep the whole Law that my servant Moses gave them." 9But the people did not listen. Manasseh led them astray, so that they did more evil than the nations the LORD had destroyed before the Israelites.

## Amplified Bible

and showed them all his treasure-house—the silver, gold, spices, precious ointment, his armory, and all that was found in his treasuries. There was nothing in his house or in all his realm that Hezekiah did not show them.

14Then Isaiah the prophet came to King Hezekiah and said, What did these men say? From where did they come to you? Hezekiah said, They are from a far country, from Babylon.

15Isaiah said, What have they seen in your house? Hezekiah answered, They have seen all that is in my house. There is no treasure of mine that I have not shown them.

16Then Isaiah said to Hezekiah, Hear the word of the Lord!

17Behold, the time is coming when a all that is in your house, and that which your forefathers have stored up till this day, shall be carried to Babylon; nothing shall be left, says the Lord.

18And some of your sons who shall be born to you shall be taken away, and they shall be eunuchs in the palace of Babylon's king.

19Then said Hezekiah to Isaiah, The word of the Lord you have spoken is good. For he thought, Is it not good, if [all this evil is meant for the future and] peace and security shall be in my days?

20The rest of the acts of Hezekiah, and all his might, and how he made the pool and the canal and brought water into the city, are they not written in the Book of the Chronicles of the Kings of Judah?

21Hezekiah slept with his fathers. Manasseh his son reigned in his stead.

**21** Manasseh was twelve years old when he began his fifty-five-year [wicked] reign in Jerusalem. His mother's name was Hephzibah.

2He [Hezekiah's son] did evil in the sight of the Lord, after the [idolatrous] practices of the [heathen] nations whom the Lord cast out before the Israelites.

3For he built up again the high places which Hezekiah his father had destroyed; and he reared up altars for Baal and made an Asherah, as did Ahab king of Israel, and worshiped all the [starry] hosts of the heavens and served them!

4And he built [heathen] altars in the house of the Lord, of which the Lord said, In Jerusalem will I put My b Name [and the pledge of My presence].

5And he [good Hezekiah's son] built altars for all the hosts of the heavens in the two courts of the house of the Lord!

6And he made his son pass through the fire *and* burned him as an offering [to Molech]; he practiced soothsaying and augury, and dealt with mediums and wizards! He did much wickedness in the sight of the Lord, provoking Him to anger.

7He made a graven image of [the goddess] Asherah and set it in the house, of which the Lord said to David and to Solomon his son, In this house and in Jerusalem, which I have chosen out of all the tribes of Israel, will I put My Name [and the pledge of My presence] forever;

8And I will not cause the feet of Israel to wander any more out of the land which I gave their fathers, if only they will observe to do according to all that I have commanded them and according to all the law that My servant Moses commanded them.

9But they would not listen; and Manasseh seduced them to do more evil than the nations did whom the Lord destroyed before the Israelites!

a This is the first of ten tragic results of Hezekiah's self-willed prayer, which God's plan for Hezekiah's death would have prevented (see the footnote on 20:6). For a listing of these results see II Kings 20:18; 21:1, 3, 4, 6, 9, 14, 16, 20.  b See footnote on Deut. 12:5.

## New International Version

[10]The LORD said through his servants the prophets: [11]"Manasseh king of Judah has committed these detestable sins. He has done more evil than the Amorites who preceded him and has led Judah into sin with his idols. [12]Therefore this is what the LORD, the God of Israel, says: I am going to bring such disaster on Jerusalem and Judah that the ears of everyone who hears of it will tingle. [13]I will stretch out over Jerusalem the measuring line used against Samaria and the plumb line used against the house of Ahab. I will wipe out Jerusalem as one wipes a dish, wiping it and turning it upside down. [14]I will forsake the remnant of my inheritance and give them into the hands of enemies. They will be looted and plundered by all their enemies; [15]they have done evil in my eyes and have aroused my anger from the day their ancestors came out of Egypt until this day."

[16]Moreover, Manasseh also shed so much innocent blood that he filled Jerusalem from end to end—besides the sin that he had caused Judah to commit, so that they did evil in the eyes of the LORD.

[17]As for the other events of Manasseh's reign, and all he did, including the sin he committed, are they not written in the book of the annals of the kings of Judah? [18]Manasseh rested with his ancestors and was buried in his palace garden, the garden of Uzza. And Amon his son succeeded him as king.

### Amon King of Judah

[19]Amon was twenty-two years old when he became king, and he reigned in Jerusalem two years. His mother's name was Meshullemeth daughter of Haruz; she was from Jotbah. [20]He did evil in the eyes of the LORD, as his father Manasseh had done. [21]He followed completely the ways of his father, worshiping the idols his father had worshiped, and bowing down to them. [22]He forsook the LORD, the God of his ancestors, and did not walk in obedience to him.

[23]Amon's officials conspired against him and assassinated the king in his palace. [24]Then the people of the land killed all who had plotted against King Amon, and they made Josiah his son king in his place.

[25]As for the other events of Amon's reign, and what he did, are they not written in the book of the annals of the kings of Judah? [26]He was buried in his tomb in the garden of Uzza. And Josiah his son succeeded him as king.

### The Book of the Law Found

**22** Josiah was eight years old when he became king, and he reigned in Jerusalem thirty-one years. His mother's name was Jedidah daughter of Adaiah; she was from Bozkath. [2]He did what was right in the eyes of the LORD and followed completely the ways of his father David, not turning aside to the right or to the left.

[3]In the eighteenth year of his reign, King Josiah sent the secretary, Shaphan son of Azaliah, the son of Meshullam, to the temple of the LORD. He said: [4]"Go up to Hilkiah the high priest and have him get ready the money that has been brought into the temple of the LORD, which the doorkeepers have collected from the people. [5]Have them entrust it to the men appointed to supervise the work on

## Amplified Bible

[10]And the Lord said through His servants the prophets: [11]Because Manasseh king of Judah has committed these abominations, and has done wickedly above all that the Amorites did who were before him, and has made Judah also to sin with his idols,

[12]Therefore thus says the Lord, the God of Israel: Behold, I am bringing such evil upon Jerusalem and Judah, that whoever hears of it, both his ears shall tingle!

[13]And I will stretch over Jerusalem the measuring line of Samaria and the plummet of the house of Ahab; and I will wipe out Jerusalem as one wipes a dish, wiping it and turning it upside down.

[14]And I will cast off the rest of My inheritance and deliver them into the hands of their enemies; and they shall become a prey and a spoil to all their enemies,

[15]For they have done evil in My sight and have provoked Me to anger since their fathers came out of Egypt to this day.

[16]Moreover, Manasseh shed very much innocent blood, filling Jerusalem from one end to another—besides his sin in making Judah sin, by doing evil in the sight of the Lord! [II Chron. 33:1-10.]

[17]The rest of the acts of Manasseh, all that he did, and his sin that he committed, are they not written in the Book of the Chronicles of the Kings of Judah?

[18]Manasseh slept with his fathers and was buried in the garden of his own house, in the garden of Uzza. Amon his son reigned in his stead.

[19]Amon was twenty-two years old when he began his two-year reign in Jerusalem. His mother was Meshullemeth daughter of Haruz of Jotbah.

[20][But] he also did evil in the sight of the Lord, as his father Manasseh had done. [II Kings 23:26, 27; 24:3, 4.]

[21]He walked in all the ways of his father; and he served the idols that his father served, and worshiped them;

[22]He forsook the Lord, the God of his [forefathers], and did not walk in the way of the Lord.

[23]The servants of Amon conspired against him and killed the king in his own house.

[24]But the people of the land killed all those who had conspired against King Amon, and made Josiah his son king in his stead.

[25]The rest of the acts of Amon, are they not written in the Book of the Chronicles of the Kings of Judah?

[26]He was buried in his tomb in the garden of Uzza. Josiah his son succeeded him.

**22** Josiah was eight years old when he began his thirty-one-year reign in Jerusalem. His mother was Jedidah daughter of Adaiah of Bozkath.

[2]He did right in the sight of the Lord and walked in all the ways of David his [forefather], and turned not aside to the right hand or to the left.

[3]In the eighteenth year of King Josiah, he sent Shaphan son of Azaliah, the son of Meshullam, the scribe, to the Lord's house, saying,

[4]Go up to Hilkiah the high priest, that he may count the money brought into the house of the Lord, which the keepers of the door have gathered from the people. [II Kings 12:4ff.]

[5]And let them deliver it into the hands of the workmen

## New International Version

the temple. And have these men pay the workers who repair the temple of the LORD— ⁶the carpenters, the builders and the masons. Also have them purchase timber and dressed stone to repair the temple. ⁷But they need not account for the money entrusted to them, because they are honest in their dealings."

⁸Hilkiah the high priest said to Shaphan the secretary, "I have found the Book of the Law in the temple of the LORD." He gave it to Shaphan, who read it. ⁹Then Shaphan the secretary went to the king and reported to him: "Your officials have paid out the money that was in the temple of the LORD and have entrusted it to the workers and supervisors at the temple." ¹⁰Then Shaphan the secretary informed the king, "Hilkiah the priest has given me a book." And Shaphan read from it in the presence of the king.

¹¹When the king heard the words of the Book of the Law, he tore his robes. ¹²He gave these orders to Hilkiah the priest, Ahikam son of Shaphan, Akbor son of Micaiah, Shaphan the secretary and Asaiah the king's attendant: ¹³"Go and inquire of the LORD for me and for the people and for all Judah about what is written in this book that has been found. Great is the LORD's anger that burns against us because those who have gone before us have not obeyed the words of this book; they have not acted in accordance with all that is written there concerning us."

¹⁴Hilkiah the priest, Ahikam, Akbor, Shaphan and Asaiah went to speak to the prophet Huldah, who was the wife of Shallum son of Tikvah, the son of Harhas, keeper of the wardrobe. She lived in Jerusalem, in the New Quarter.

¹⁵She said to them, "This is what the LORD, the God of Israel, says: Tell the man who sent you to me, ¹⁶'This is what the LORD says: I am going to bring disaster on this place and its people, according to everything written in the book the king of Judah has read. ¹⁷Because they have forsaken me and burned incense to other gods and aroused my anger by all the idols their hands have made,ᵃ my anger will burn against this place and will not be quenched.' ¹⁸Tell the king of Judah, who sent you to inquire of the LORD, 'This is what the LORD, the God of Israel, says concerning the words you heard: ¹⁹Because your heart was responsive and you humbled yourself before the LORD when you heard what I have spoken against this place and its people—that they would become a curseᵇ and be laid waste—and because you tore your robes and wept in my presence, I also have heard you, declares the LORD. ²⁰Therefore I will gather you to your ancestors, and you will be buried in peace. Your eyes will not see all the disaster I am going to bring on this place.'"

So they took her answer back to the king.

### Josiah Renews the Covenant

**23** Then the king called together all the elders of Judah and Jerusalem. ²He went up to the temple of the LORD with the people of Judah, the inhabitants of Jerusalem, the priests and the prophets—all the people from the least to the greatest. He read in their hearing all the words of the Book of the Covenant, which had been found in the temple of the LORD. ³The king stood by the pillar and renewed the covenant in the presence of the LORD—to

ᵃ 17 Or by everything they have done    ᵇ 19 That is, their names would be used in cursing (see Jer. 29:22); or, others would see that they are cursed.

## Amplified Bible

who have oversight of the Lord's house, to give to the laborers engaged in the repairing of the Lord's house— ⁶That is, to the carpenters, builders, and masons—and to buy timber and hewn stone to repair the house.

⁷However, there was no accounting required of them for the money delivered into their hands, because they dealt faithfully.

⁸Hilkiah the high priest said to Shaphan the scribe, I have found the Book of the Law in the house of the Lord! Hilkiah gave the book to Shaphan, and he read it.

⁹And Shaphan the scribe came to the king and reported to him: Your servants have gathered the money that was found in the house and have delivered it into the hands of the workmen who have oversight of the house of the Lord.

¹⁰Then Shaphan the scribe told the king, Hilkiah the priest has given me a book. And Shaphan read it before the king.

¹¹And when the king heard the words of the Book of the Law, he rent his clothes.

¹²And the king commanded Hilkiah the priest, Ahikam son of Shaphan, Achbor son of Micaiah, Shaphan the scribe, and Asaiah servant of the king,

¹³Go, inquire of the Lord for me and for the people and for all Judah concerning the words of this book that has been found. For great is the wrath of the Lord that is kindled against us because our fathers have not listened and obeyed the words of this book, to do according to all that is written concerning us.

¹⁴So Hilkiah the priest, Ahikam, Achbor, Shaphan, and Asaiah went to Huldah the prophetess, the wife of Shallum son of Tikvah, the son of Harhas, keeper of the wardrobe—now she dwelt in Jerusalem, in the Second Quarter—and they talked with her.

¹⁵She said to them, Thus says the Lord, the God of Israel: Tell the man who sent you to me,

¹⁶Thus says the Lord: Behold, I will bring evil upon this place and upon its inhabitants, according to all the words of the book which the king of Judah has read.

¹⁷Because they have forsaken Me and have burned incense to other gods, provoking Me to anger with all the work of their hands, therefore My wrath will be kindled against this place and will not be quenched.

¹⁸But to the king of Judah, who sent you to inquire of the Lord, say this, Thus says the Lord, the God of Israel, regarding the words you heard:

¹⁹Because your heart was [tender and] penitent and you humbled yourself before the Lord when you heard what I said against this place and against its inhabitants, that they should become a desolation, [an astonishment and] a curse, and you have rent your clothes and wept before Me, I also have heard you, says the Lord.

²⁰Behold, therefore [King Josiah], I will gather you to your fathers, taken to your grave in peace, and your eyes shall not see all the evil which I will bring on this place. And they brought the king word.

**23** King Josiah sent and gathered to him all the elders of Judah and of Jerusalem.

²The king went up to the house of the Lord, and with him all the men of Judah, all the inhabitants of Jerusalem, the priests, the prophets, and all the people, both small and great. And he read in their ears all the words of the Book of the Covenant, which was found in the Lord's house.

³The king stood [on the platform] by the pillar and made a covenant before the Lord—to walk after the Lord

## New International Version

follow the LORD and keep his commands, statutes and decrees with all his heart and all his soul, thus confirming the words of the covenant written in this book. Then all the people pledged themselves to the covenant.

⁴The king ordered Hilkiah the high priest, the priests next in rank and the doorkeepers to remove from the temple of the LORD all the articles made for Baal and Asherah and all the starry hosts. He burned them outside Jerusalem in the fields of the Kidron Valley and took the ashes to Bethel. ⁵He did away with the idolatrous priests appointed by the kings of Judah to burn incense on the high places of the towns of Judah and on those around Jerusalem—those who burned incense to Baal, to the sun and moon, to the constellations and to all the starry hosts. ⁶He took the Asherah pole from the temple of the LORD to the Kidron Valley outside Jerusalem and burned it there. He ground it to powder and scattered the dust over the graves of the common people. ⁷He also tore down the quarters of the male shrine prostitutes that were in the temple of the LORD, the quarters where women did weaving for Asherah.

⁸Josiah brought all the priests from the towns of Judah and desecrated the high places, from Geba to Beersheba, where the priests had burned incense. He broke down the gateway at the entrance of the Gate of Joshua, the city governor, which was on the left of the city gate. ⁹Although the priests of the high places did not serve at the altar of the LORD in Jerusalem, they ate unleavened bread with their fellow priests.

¹⁰He desecrated Topheth, which was in the Valley of Ben Hinnom, so no one could use it to sacrifice their son or daughter in the fire to Molek. ¹¹He removed from the entrance to the temple of the LORD the horses that the kings of Judah had dedicated to the sun. They were in the courtᵃ near the room of an official named Nathan-Melek. Josiah then burned the chariots dedicated to the sun.

¹²He pulled down the altars the kings of Judah had erected on the roof near the upper room of Ahaz, and the altars Manasseh had built in the two courts of the temple of the LORD. He removed them from there, smashed them to pieces and threw the rubble into the Kidron Valley. ¹³The king also desecrated the high places that were east of Jerusalem on the south of the Hill of Corruption—the ones Solomon king of Israel had built for Ashtoreth the vile goddess of the Sidonians, for Chemosh the vile god of Moab, and for Molek the detestable god of the people of Ammon. ¹⁴Josiah smashed the sacred stones and cut down the Asherah poles and covered the sites with human bones.

¹⁵Even the altar at Bethel, the high place made by Jeroboam son of Nebat, who had caused Israel to sin—even that altar and high place he demolished. He burned the high place and ground it to powder, and burned the Asherah pole also. ¹⁶Then Josiah looked around, and when he saw the tombs that were there on the hillside, he had the bones removed from them and burned on the altar to defile it, in accordance with the word of the LORD proclaimed by the man of God who foretold these things.

¹⁷The king asked, "What is that tombstone I see?"

The people of the city said, "It marks the tomb of the man of God who came from Judah and pronounced against the altar of Bethel the very things you have done to it."

¹⁸"Leave it alone," he said. "Don't let anyone disturb his

## Amplified Bible

and to keep His commandments, His testimonies, and His statutes with all his heart and soul, to confirm the words of this covenant that were written in this book. And all the people stood to join in the covenant.

⁴And the king commanded Hilkiah the high priest and the priests of the second rank and the keepers of the threshold to bring out of the temple of the Lord all the vessels made for Baal, for [the goddess] Asherah, and for all the hosts of the heavens; and he burned them outside Jerusalem in the fields of the Kidron, and carried their ashes to Bethel [where Israel's idolatry began]. [I Kings 12:28, 29.]

⁵He put away the idolatrous priests whom the kings of Judah had ordained to burn incense in the high places in Judah's cities and round about Jerusalem—also those who burned incense to Baal, to the sun, to the moon, to the constellations [or twelve signs of the zodiac], and to all the hosts of the heavens.

⁶And Josiah brought the Asherah from the house of the Lord to outside Jerusalem to the brook Kidron and burned it there, and beat it to dust and cast its dust upon the graves of the common people [who had sacrificed to it].

⁷And he broke down the houses of the male cult prostitutes, which were by the house of the Lord, where the women wove [tent] hangings for the Asherah [shrines].

⁸And [Josiah] brought all the [idolatrous] priests out of the city of Judah and defiled the high places, where the priests had burned incense, from Geba to Beersheba [north to south], and broke down the high places both at the entrance of the Gate of Joshua the governor of the city and that which was on one's left at the city's gate.

⁹However, the priests of the high places were not allowed to sacrifice upon the Lord's altar in Jerusalem, but they ate unleavened bread among their brethren.

¹⁰And Josiah defiled Topheth, which is in the Valley of Ben-hinnom [son of Hinnom], that no man might ever burn there his son or his daughter as an offering to Molech. [Ezek. 16:21.]

¹¹And he removed the horses that the kings of Judah had devoted to the sun from the entrance of the house of the Lord, by the chamber of Nathan-melech the chamberlain, which was in the area, and he burned the chariots of the sun with fire.

¹²And the altars on the roof of the upper chamber of Ahaz, which the kings of Judah had made, and the altars which Manasseh had made in the two courts of the house of the Lord, [Josiah] pulled down and beat them in pieces, and he [ran and] cast their dust into the brook Kidron.

¹³And the king defiled the high places east of Jerusalem, south of the Mount of Corruption, which Solomon the king of Israel had built for Ashtoreth the abominable [goddess] of the Sidonians, for Chemosh the abominable god of the Moabites, and for Milcom the abominable [god] of the Ammonites.

¹⁴He broke in pieces the pillars (images) and cut down the Asherim and replaced them with the bones of men [to defile the places forever].

¹⁵Moreover, the altar at Bethel, the high place made by Jeroboam son of Nebat, who made Israel to sin, that altar with the high place Josiah tore down *and* broke in pieces its stones, beating them to dust, and burned the Asherah.

¹⁶And as Josiah turned, he saw the tombs across on the mount, and he sent and brought the bones out of the tombs and burned them upon the altar and defiled it, in fulfillment of the word of the Lord which the man of God prophesied, who predicted these things [about this altar, naming Josiah before he was born]. [I Kings 13:2-5.]

¹⁷Josiah said, What is that monument I see? The men of the city told him, It is the tomb of the man of God who came from Judah and foretold these things that you have just done against the altar of Bethel.

¹⁸He said, Let him alone; let no man move his bones. So

---

ᵃ 11 The meaning of the Hebrew for this word is uncertain.

## New International Version

bones." So they spared his bones and those of the prophet who had come from Samaria.

[19]Just as he had done at Bethel, Josiah removed all the shrines at the high places that the kings of Israel had built in the towns of Samaria and that had aroused the LORD's anger. [20]Josiah slaughtered all the priests of those high places on the altars and burned human bones on them. Then he went back to Jerusalem.

[21]The king gave this order to all the people: "Celebrate the Passover to the LORD your God, as it is written in this Book of the Covenant." [22]Neither in the days of the judges who led Israel nor in the days of the kings of Israel and the kings of Judah had any such Passover been observed. [23]But in the eighteenth year of King Josiah, this Passover was celebrated to the LORD in Jerusalem.

[24]Furthermore, Josiah got rid of the mediums and spiritists, the household gods, the idols and all the other detestable things seen in Judah and Jerusalem. This he did to fulfill the requirements of the law written in the book that Hilkiah the priest had discovered in the temple of the LORD. [25]Neither before nor after Josiah was there a king like him who turned to the LORD as he did—with all his heart and with all his soul and with all his strength, in accordance with all the Law of Moses.

[26]Nevertheless, the LORD did not turn away from the heat of his fierce anger, which burned against Judah because of all that Manasseh had done to arouse his anger. [27]So the LORD said, "I will remove Judah also from my presence as I removed Israel, and I will reject Jerusalem, the city I chose, and this temple, about which I said, 'My Name shall be there.'[a]"

[28]As for the other events of Josiah's reign, and all he did, are they not written in the book of the annals of the kings of Judah?

[29]While Josiah was king, Pharaoh Necho king of Egypt went up to the Euphrates River to help the king of Assyria. King Josiah marched out to meet him in battle, but Necho faced him and killed him at Megiddo. [30]Josiah's servants brought his body in a chariot from Megiddo to Jerusalem and buried him in his own tomb. And the people of the land took Jehoahaz son of Josiah and anointed him and made him king in place of his father.

### Jehoahaz King of Judah

[31]Jehoahaz was twenty-three years old when he became king, and he reigned in Jerusalem three months. His mother's name was Hamutal daughter of Jeremiah; she was from Libnah. [32]He did evil in the eyes of the LORD, just as his predecessors had done. [33]Pharaoh Necho put him in chains at Riblah in the land of Hamath so that he might not reign in Jerusalem, and he imposed on Judah a levy of a hundred talents[b] of silver and a talent[c] of gold. [34]Pharaoh Necho made Eliakim son of Josiah king in place of his father Josiah and changed Eliakim's name to Jehoiakim. But he took Jehoahaz and carried him off to Egypt, and there he died. [35]Jehoiakim paid Pharaoh Necho the silver and gold he demanded. In order to do so, he taxed the land and exacted the silver and gold from the people of the land according to their assessments.

## Amplified Bible

they let his bones alone, with the bones of the prophet that came out of Samaria. [I Kings 13:31, 32.]

[19]Also Josiah took away all the houses of the high places in the cities of Samaria which the kings of Israel had made, provoking the Lord to anger, and he did to them all that he had done in Bethel.

[20]He slew all the priests of the high places that were there upon the altars and burned men's bones upon them [to defile the places forever]. Then he returned to Jerusalem.

[21]The king commanded all the people, Keep the Passover to the Lord your God, as it is written in this Book of the Covenant.

[22]Surely such a Passover was not held from the days of Israel's judges, even in all the days of the kings of Israel or Judah.

[23]But in the eighteenth year of King Josiah, this Passover was kept to the Lord in Jerusalem.

[24]Moreover, Josiah put away the mediums, the wizards, the teraphim (household gods), the idols, and all the abominations that were seen in Judah and in Jerusalem, that he might establish the words of the law written in the book found by Hilkiah the priest in the house of the Lord.

[25]There was no king like him before or after [Josiah] who turned to the Lord with all his heart and all his soul and all his might, according to all the Law of Moses.

[26]Still the Lord did not turn from the fierceness of His great wrath, kindled against Judah because of all the provocations with which Manasseh had provoked Him.

[27]And the Lord said, I will remove Judah also out of My sight as I have removed Israel, and will cast off this city, Jerusalem, which I have chosen, and the house, of which I said, My Name [and the pledge of My presence] shall be there.

[28]The rest of the acts of Josiah, all that he did, are they not written in the Book of the Chronicles of Judah's Kings?

[29]In his days Pharaoh Necho king of Egypt went up against the king of Assyria to the river Euphrates. King Josiah went out against him, but he slew Josiah at Megiddo when he saw him.

[30]Josiah's servants carried him dead in a chariot from Megiddo, brought him to Jerusalem, and buried him in his own tomb. The people of the land anointed Jehoahaz son of Josiah king in his stead.

[31]Jehoahaz was twenty-three years old when he began his three-month reign in Jerusalem. His mother was Hamutal daughter of Jeremiah of Libnah.

[32]He did evil in the sight of the Lord, according to all [the evil] his forefathers had done.

[33]And Pharaoh Necho put him in bonds at Riblah in the land of Hamath, that he might not reign in Jerusalem, and laid a tribute of a hundred talents of silver and a talent of gold upon the land.

[34]Pharaoh Necho made Eliakim son of Josiah king in place of Josiah and changed his name to Jehoiakim. But he took Jehoahaz away to Egypt, where he died.

[35]Jehoiakim gave the silver and the gold to Pharaoh, but he taxed the land to give the money as Pharaoh commanded. He exacted the silver and gold of the people of the land, from everyone according to his assessment, to give it to Pharaoh Necho.

---

[a] 27 1 Kings 8:29   [b] 33 That is, about 3 3/4 tons or about 3.4 metric tons   [c] 33 That is, about 75 pounds or about 34 kilograms

## New International Version

### Jehoiakim King of Judah

[36]Jehoiakim was twenty-five years old when he became king, and he reigned in Jerusalem eleven years. His mother's name was Zebidah daughter of Pedaiah; she was from Rumah. [37]And he did evil in the eyes of the LORD, just as his predecessors had done.

**24** During Jehoiakim's reign, Nebuchadnezzar king of Babylon invaded the land, and Jehoiakim became his vassal for three years. But then he turned against Nebuchadnezzar and rebelled. [2]The LORD sent Babylonian,[a] Aramean, Moabite and Ammonite raiders against him to destroy Judah, in accordance with the word of the LORD proclaimed by his servants the prophets. [3]Surely these things happened to Judah according to the LORD's command, in order to remove them from his presence because of the sins of Manasseh and all he had done, [4]including the shedding of innocent blood. For he had filled Jerusalem with innocent blood, and the LORD was not willing to forgive.

[5]As for the other events of Jehoiakim's reign, and all he did, are they not written in the book of the annals of the kings of Judah? [6]Jehoiakim rested with his ancestors. And Jehoiachin his son succeeded him as king.

[7]The king of Egypt did not march out from his own country again, because the king of Babylon had taken all his territory, from the Wadi of Egypt to the Euphrates River.

### Jehoiachin King of Judah

[8]Jehoiachin was eighteen years old when he became king, and he reigned in Jerusalem three months. His mother's name was Nehushta daughter of Elnathan; she was from Jerusalem. [9]He did evil in the eyes of the LORD, just as his father had done.

[10]At that time the officers of Nebuchadnezzar king of Babylon advanced on Jerusalem and laid siege to it, [11]and Nebuchadnezzar himself came up to the city while his officers were besieging it. [12]Jehoiachin king of Judah, his mother, his attendants, his nobles and his officials all surrendered to him.

In the eighth year of the reign of the king of Babylon, he took Jehoiachin prisoner. [13]As the LORD had declared, Nebuchadnezzar removed the treasures from the temple of the LORD and from the royal palace, and cut up the gold articles that Solomon king of Israel had made for the temple of the LORD. [14]He carried all Jerusalem into exile: all the officers and fighting men, and all the skilled workers and artisans—a total of ten thousand. Only the poorest people of the land were left.

[15]Nebuchadnezzar took Jehoiachin captive to Babylon. He also took from Jerusalem to Babylon the king's mother, his wives, his officials and the prominent people of the land. [16]The king of Babylon also deported to Babylon the entire force of seven thousand fighting men, strong and fit for war, and a thousand skilled workers and artisans. [17]He made Mattaniah, Jehoiachin's uncle, king in his place and changed his name to Zedekiah.

## Amplified Bible

[36]Jehoiakim was twenty-five years old when he began his eleven-year reign in Jerusalem. His mother was Zebidah daughter of Pedaiah of Rumah. [37]He did evil in the sight of the Lord, like all his [forefathers] had done.

**24** In his days, Nebuchadnezzar king of Babylon came up, and Jehoiakim became his servant for three years; then he turned and rebelled against him. [2]The Lord sent against Jehoiakim bands of Chaldeans, of Syrians, of Moabites, and of Ammonites. And He sent them against Judah to destroy it, according to the word of the Lord which He spoke by His servants the prophets. [3]Surely this came upon Judah at the command of the Lord, to remove them out of His sight because of the sins of Manasseh according to all he had done, [4]And also for the innocent blood that he shed. For he filled Jerusalem with innocent blood, and the Lord would not pardon.

[5]The rest of the acts of Jehoiakim, all that he did, are they not written in the Book of the Chronicles of Judah's Kings?

[6]So Jehoiakim slept with his fathers. Jehoiachin his son reigned in his stead.

[7]The king of Egypt came no more out of his land, for the king of Babylon had taken all that belonged to Egypt's king, from the River of Egypt to the river Euphrates.

[8]Jehoiachin was eighteen years old when he began his three-month reign in Jerusalem. His mother was Nehushta daughter of Elnathan of Jerusalem. [9]And he did evil in the sight of the Lord, in keeping with all his father had done.

[10]At that time the servants of Nebuchadnezzar king of Babylon came up to Jerusalem, and the city was besieged.

[11]Nebuchadnezzar king of Babylon came to the city while his servants were besieging it. [12]Jehoiachin king of Judah surrendered to the king of Babylon, he, his mother, his servants, princes, and palace officials. The king of Babylon took him prisoner in the eighth year of Nebuchadnezzar's reign.

[13]He carried off all the treasures of the Lord's house and the king's house, and cut in pieces all the vessels of gold in the temple of the Lord, which Solomon king of Israel had made, as the Lord had said.

[14]He carried away all Jerusalem, all the princes, all the mighty men of valor, 10,000 captives, and all the craftsmen and smiths. None remained except the poorest of the land.

[15]Nebuchadnezzar took captive to Babylon King Jehoiachin; his mother, his wives, his officials, and the chief *and* mighty men of the land [the prophet Ezekiel included] he took from Jerusalem to Babylon into exile. [Ezek. 1:1.]

[16]And the king of Babylon brought captive to Babylon all the men of valor, 7,000, and craftsmen and smiths, 1,000, all strong and fit for war.

[17]And the king of Babylon made Mattaniah, Jehoiachin's uncle, king in his stead and changed his name to Zedekiah.

## New International Version

### Zedekiah King of Judah

¹⁸Zedekiah was twenty-one years old when he became king, and he reigned in Jerusalem eleven years. His mother's name was Hamutal daughter of Jeremiah; she was from Libnah. ¹⁹He did evil in the eyes of the LORD, just as Jehoiakim had done. ²⁰It was because of the LORD's anger that all this happened to Jerusalem and Judah, and in the end he thrust them from his presence.

### The Fall of Jerusalem

Now Zedekiah rebelled against the king of Babylon.

**25** So in the ninth year of Zedekiah's reign, on the tenth day of the tenth month, Nebuchadnezzar king of Babylon marched against Jerusalem with his whole army. He encamped outside the city and built siege works all around it. ²The city was kept under siege until the eleventh year of King Zedekiah.

³By the ninth day of the fourthᵃ month the famine in the city had become so severe that there was no food for the people to eat. ⁴Then the city wall was broken through, and the whole army fled at night through the gate between the two walls near the king's garden, though the Babyloniansᵇ were surrounding the city. They fled toward the Arabah,ᶜ ⁵but the Babylonianᵈ army pursued the king and overtook him in the plains of Jericho. All his soldiers were separated from him and scattered, ⁶and he was captured.

He was taken to the king of Babylon at Riblah, where sentence was pronounced on him. ⁷They killed the sons of Zedekiah before his eyes. Then they put out his eyes, bound him with bronze shackles and took him to Babylon.

⁸On the seventh day of the fifth month, in the nineteenth year of Nebuchadnezzar king of Babylon, Nebuzaradan commander of the imperial guard, an official of the king of Babylon, came to Jerusalem. ⁹He set fire to the temple of the LORD, the royal palace and all the houses of Jerusalem. Every important building he burned down. ¹⁰The whole Babylonian army under the commander of the imperial guard broke down the walls around Jerusalem. ¹¹Nebuzaradan the commander of the guard carried into exile the people who remained in the city, along with the rest of the populace and those who had deserted to the king of Babylon. ¹²But the commander left behind some of the poorest people of the land to work the vineyards and fields.

¹³The Babylonians broke up the bronze pillars, the movable stands and the bronze Sea that were at the temple of the LORD and they carried the bronze to Babylon. ¹⁴They also took away the pots, shovels, wick trimmers, dishes and all the bronze articles used in the temple service. ¹⁵The commander of the imperial guard took away the censers and sprinkling bowls—all that were made of pure gold or silver.

¹⁶The bronze from the two pillars, the Sea and the movable stands, which Solomon had made for the temple of the LORD, was more than could be weighed. ¹⁷Each pillar was eighteen cubitsᵉ high. The bronze capital on top of one pillar was three cubitsᶠ high and was decorated with a network and pomegranates of bronze all around. The other pillar, with its network, was similar.

¹⁸The commander of the guard took as prisoners Sera-

## Amplified Bible

¹⁸Zedekiah was twenty-one years old when he began his eleven-year reign in Jerusalem. His mother was Hamutal daughter of Jeremiah of Libnah. ¹⁹He did evil in the sight of the Lord, in keeping with all Jehoiakim had done. ²⁰For because of the anger of the Lord it came to the point in Jerusalem and Judah that He cast them out of His presence. And Zedekiah rebelled against the king of Babylon.

**25** In the ninth year of Zedekiah's reign, on the tenth day of the tenth month, Nebuchadnezzar king of Babylon came with all his army against Jerusalem and laid siege to it, and they built siege works against it round about. ²The city was besieged [nearly two years] until the eleventh year of King Zedekiah.

³On the ninth day of the fourth month the famine was complete in the city; there was no food for the people of the land. ⁴Then the city was broken through; the king and all the warriors fled by night by way of the gate between the two walls by the king's garden, though the Chaldeans were round about the city. [The king] went by the way toward the Arabah (the plain). ⁵The Chaldean army pursued the king and overtook him in the plains of Jericho. All his army was scattered from him. ⁶So they captured Zedekiah and brought him to the king of Babylon at Riblah, and sentence was passed on him.

⁷And they slew the sons of Zedekiah before his eyes and put out the eyes of Zedekiah and bound him in double fetters [hands and feet] and carried him to Babylon. [Foretold in Jer. 34:3; Ezek. 12:13.]

⁸On the seventh day of the fifth month of the nineteenth year of King Nebuchadnezzar of Babylon, Nebuzaradan, captain of the Babylonian king's guard, came to Jerusalem.

⁹He burned the house of the Lord, the king's house, and all the houses of Jerusalem; every great house he burned down.

¹⁰All the army of the Chaldeans who were with the captain of the [Babylonian] guard broke down the walls around Jerusalem.

¹¹Now the rest of the people left in the city and the deserters who fell away to the king of Babylon, along with the rest of the multitude, Nebuzaradan the captain of the guard carried into exile.

¹²But the captain of the guard left some of the poorest of the land to be vinedressers and soil tillers.

¹³The bronze pillars in the Lord's house and [its] bases and the bronze Sea the Chaldeans smashed and carried the bronze to Babylon.

¹⁴And they took away the pots, shovels, snuffers, dishes for incense, all the bronze vessels used in the temple service,

¹⁵The firepans, and bowls. Such things as were of gold the captain of the guard took away as gold, and what was of silver [he took away] as silver.

¹⁶The two pillars, the one Sea, and the bases, which Solomon had made for the house of the Lord, the bronze of all these articles was incalculable.

¹⁷The height of the one pillar was eighteen cubits, and upon it was a capital of bronze. The height of the capital was three cubits; a network and pomegranates round about the capital were all of bronze. And the second pillar had the same as these, with a network.

¹⁸The captain of the guard took Seraiah the chief priest,

---

ᵃ 3 Probable reading of the original Hebrew text (see Jer. 52:6); Masoretic Text does not have *fourth*.   ᵇ Or *Chaldeans*; also in verses 13, 25 and 26   ᶜ 4 Or *the Jordan Valley*   ᵈ 5 Or *Chaldean*; also in verses 10 and 24   ᵉ 17 That is, about 27 feet or about 8.1 meters   ᶠ 17 That is, about 4 1/2 feet or about 1.4 meters

## New International Version

iah the chief priest, Zephaniah the priest next in rank and the three doorkeepers. [19]Of those still in the city, he took the officer in charge of the fighting men, and five royal advisers. He also took the secretary who was chief officer in charge of conscripting the people of the land and sixty of the conscripts who were found in the city. [20]Nebuzaradan the commander took them all and brought them to the king of Babylon at Riblah. [21]There at Riblah, in the land of Hamath, the king had them executed.

So Judah went into captivity, away from her land.

[22]Nebuchadnezzar king of Babylon appointed Gedaliah son of Ahikam, the son of Shaphan, to be over the people he had left behind in Judah. [23]When all the army officers and their men heard that the king of Babylon had appointed Gedaliah as governor, they came to Gedaliah at Mizpah—Ishmael son of Nethaniah, Johanan son of Kareah, Seraiah son of Tanhumeth the Netophathite, Jaazaniah the son of the Maakathite, and their men. [24]Gedaliah took an oath to reassure them and their men. "Do not be afraid of the Babylonian officials," he said. "Settle down in the land and serve the king of Babylon, and it will go well with you."

[25]In the seventh month, however, Ishmael son of Nethaniah, the son of Elishama, who was of royal blood, came with ten men and assassinated Gedaliah and also the men of Judah and the Babylonians who were with him at Mizpah. [26]At this, all the people from the least to the greatest, together with the army officers, fled to Egypt for fear of the Babylonians.

### Jehoiachin Released

[27]In the thirty-seventh year of the exile of Jehoiachin king of Judah, in the year Awel-Marduk became king of Babylon, he released Jehoiachin king of Judah from prison. He did this on the twenty-seventh day of the twelfth month. [28]He spoke kindly to him and gave him a seat of honor higher than those of the other kings who were with him in Babylon. [29]So Jehoiachin put aside his prison clothes and for the rest of his life ate regularly at the king's table. [30]Day by day the king gave Jehoiachin a regular allowance as long as he lived.

## Amplified Bible

Zephaniah the second priest, and the three keepers of the threshold.

[19]And out of the city he took an officer who was in command of the men of war and five men of the king's personal advisors, who were found in the city, and the scribe of the captain of the army who mustered the people of the land and sixty men of the people who were found in the city.

[20]Nebuzaradan the captain of the guard took these and brought them to the king of Babylon at Riblah.

[21]The king of Babylon smote and killed them at Riblah in the land of Hamath [north of Damascus]. So Judah was taken into exile.

[22]Over the people whom Nebuchadnezzar king of Babylon had left in the land of Judah he appointed as governor Gedaliah son of Ahikam, the son of Shaphan.

[23]And when all the captains of the forces and their men heard that the king of Babylon had made Gedaliah governor, they came with their men to Gedaliah at Mizpah, namely, Ishmael son of Nethaniah, Johanan son of Kareah, Seraiah son of Tanhumeth the Netophathite, and Jaazaniah son of the Maacathite.

[24]And Gedaliah swore to them and their men, saying, Do not be afraid of the Chaldean officials. Dwell in the land and serve the king of Babylon, and it shall be well with you.

[25]But in the seventh month Ishmael son of Nethaniah, the son of Elishama, of the royal family [so having a claim to be governor], came with ten men and smote and killed Gedaliah and the Jews and the Chaldeans who were with him at Mizpah.

[26]Then all the people, both small and great, and the captains of the forces arose and went to Egypt, for they were afraid of the Chaldeans.

[27]And in the thirty-seventh year of the captivity of Jehoiachin king of Judah, on the twenty-seventh day of the twelfth month, Evil-merodach king of Babylon, in the year that he began to reign, showed favor to Jehoiachin king of Judah *and* released him from prison;

[28]He spoke kindly to him and ranked him above the kings with him in Babylon.

[29]Jehoiachin put off his prison garments, and he dined regularly at the king's table the remainder of his life.

[30]And his allowance, a continual one, was given him by the king, every day a portion, for the rest of his life.

# 1 Chronicles

## Historical Records From Adam to Abraham

*To Noah's Sons*

**1** Adam, Seth, Enosh, ²Kenan, Mahalalel, Jared, ³Enoch, Methuselah, Lamech, Noah.

⁴The sons of Noah:[a]
Shem, Ham and Japheth.

*The Japhethites*

⁵The sons[b] of Japheth:
Gomer, Magog, Madai, Javan, Tubal, Meshek and Tiras.
⁶The sons of Gomer:
Ashkenaz, Riphath[c] and Togarmah.
⁷The sons of Javan:
Elishah, Tarshish, the Kittites and the Rodanites.

*The Hamites*

⁸The sons of Ham:
Cush, Egypt, Put and Canaan.
⁹The sons of Cush:
Seba, Havilah, Sabta, Raamah and Sabteka.
The sons of Raamah:
Sheba and Dedan.
¹⁰Cush was the father[d] of
Nimrod, who became a mighty warrior on earth.
¹¹Egypt was the father of
the Ludites, Anamites, Lehabites, Naphtuhites, ¹²Pathrusites, Kasluhites (from whom the Philistines came) and Caphtorites.
¹³Canaan was the father of
Sidon his firstborn,[e] and of the Hittites, ¹⁴Jebusites, Amorites, Girgashites, ¹⁵Hivites, Arkites, Sinites, ¹⁶Arvadites, Zemarites and Hamathites.

*The Semites*

¹⁷The sons of Shem:
Elam, Ashur, Arphaxad, Lud and Aram.
The sons of Aram:[f]
Uz, Hul, Gether and Meshek.
¹⁸Arphaxad was the father of Shelah,
and Shelah the father of Eber.
¹⁹Two sons were born to Eber:
One was named Peleg,[g] because in his time the earth was divided; his brother was named Joktan.
²⁰Joktan was the father of
Almodad, Sheleph, Hazarmaveth, Jerah, ²¹Hadoram, Uzal, Diklah, ²²Obal,[h] Abimael, Sheba, ²³Ophir, Havilah and Jobab. All these were sons of Joktan.

²⁴Shem, Arphaxad,[i] Shelah,
²⁵Eber, Peleg, Reu,
²⁶Serug, Nahor, Terah
²⁷and Abram (that is, Abraham).

## The Family of Abraham

²⁸The sons of Abraham:
Isaac and Ishmael.

# Chronicles

**1** Adam [his genealogical line], Seth, Enosh, ²Kenan, Mahalalel, Jared, ³Enoch, Methuselah, Lamech, ⁴Noah, Shem, Ham, and Japheth.
⁵The sons of Japheth: Gomer, Magog, Madai, Javan, Tubal, Meshech, and Tiras.
⁶The sons of Gomer: Ashkenaz, Diphath, and Togarmah.
⁷The sons of Javan: Elishah, Tarshish, Kittim, and Rodanim.
⁸The sons of Ham: Cush, Mizraim (Egypt), Put, and Canaan.
⁹The sons of Cush: Seba, Havilah, Sabta, Raamah, and Sabteca. The sons of Raamah: Sheba and Dedan.
¹⁰Cush was the father of Nimrod; he began to be a mighty one upon the earth.
¹¹Mizraim (Egypt) was the father of the Ludim, Anamim, Lehabim, Naphtuhim,
¹²Pathrusim, Casluhim, from whom came the Philistines, and the Caphtorim.
¹³Canaan was the father of Sidon his firstborn, and Heth,
¹⁴The Jebusites, Amorites, Girgashites,
¹⁵Hivites, Arkites, Sinites,
¹⁶Arvadites, Zemarites, and Hamathites.
¹⁷The sons of Shem: Elam, Asshur, Arpachshad, Lud, Aram, Uz, Hul, Gether, and Meshech.
¹⁸Arpachshad was the father of Shelah, Shelah of Eber.
¹⁹To Eber were born two sons: the name of the one was Peleg, because in his days [the population of] the earth was divided [according to its languages], and his brother's name was Joktan.
²⁰Joktan was the father of Almodad, Sheleph, Hazarmaveth, Jerah,
²¹Hadoram, Uzal, Diklah,
²²Ebal, Abimael, Sheba,
²³Ophir, Havilah, and Jobab. All these were the sons of Joktan.
²⁴Shem, Arpachshad, Shelah,
²⁵Eber, Peleg, Reu,
²⁶Serug, Nahor, Terah,
²⁷Abram, the same as Abraham.
²⁸The sons of Abraham: Isaac and Ishmael.

---

*a* 4 Septuagint; Hebrew does not have this line.   *b* 5 *Sons* may mean *descendants* or *successors* or *nations*; also in verses 6-9, 17 and 23.   *c* 6 Many Hebrew manuscripts and Vulgate (see also Septuagint and Gen. 10:3); most Hebrew manuscripts *Diphath*   *d* 10 *Father* may mean *ancestor* or *predecessor*; also in verses 11, 13, 18 and 20.   *e* 13 Or *of the Sidonians, the foremost*   *f* 17 One Hebrew manuscript and some Septuagint manuscripts (see also 10:23); most Hebrew manuscripts do not have this line.   *g* 19 *Peleg* means *division.*   *h* 22 Some Hebrew manuscripts and Syriac (see also Gen. 10:28); most Hebrew manuscripts *Ebal*   *i* 24 Hebrew; some Septuagint manuscripts *Arphaxad, Cainan* (see also note at Gen. 11:10)

## New International Version

*Descendants of Hagar*
29 These were their descendants:
Nebaioth the firstborn of Ishmael, Kedar, Adbeel, Mibsam, 30 Mishma, Dumah, Massa, Hadad, Tema, 31 Jetur, Naphish and Kedemah. These were the sons of Ishmael.

*Descendants of Keturah*
32 The sons born to Keturah, Abraham's concubine:
Zimran, Jokshan, Medan, Midian, Ishbak and Shuah.
The sons of Jokshan:
Sheba and Dedan.
33 The sons of Midian:
Ephah, Epher, Hanok, Abida and Eldaah.
All these were descendants of Keturah.

*Descendants of Sarah*
34 Abraham was the father of Isaac.
The sons of Isaac:
Esau and Israel.

### Esau's Sons
35 The sons of Esau:
Eliphaz, Reuel, Jeush, Jalam and Korah.
36 The sons of Eliphaz:
Teman, Omar, Zepho,*a* Gatam and Kenaz;
by Timna: Amalek.*b*
37 The sons of Reuel:
Nahath, Zerah, Shammah and Mizzah.

*The People of Seir in Edom*
38 The sons of Seir:
Lotan, Shobal, Zibeon, Anah, Dishon, Ezer and Dishan.
39 The sons of Lotan:
Hori and Homam. Timna was Lotan's sister.
40 The sons of Shobal:
Alvan,*c* Manahath, Ebal, Shepho and Onam.
The sons of Zibeon:
Aiah and Anah.
41 The son of Anah:
Dishon.
The sons of Dishon:
Hemdan,*d* Eshban, Ithran and Keran.
42 The sons of Ezer:
Bilhan, Zaavan and Akan.*e*
The sons of Dishan*f*:
Uz and Aran.

*The Rulers of Edom*
43 These were the kings who reigned in Edom before any Israelite king reigned:
Bela son of Beor, whose city was named Dinhabah.
44 When Bela died, Jobab son of Zerah from Bozrah succeeded him as king.
45 When Jobab died, Husham from the land of the Temanites succeeded him as king.
46 When Husham died, Hadad son of Bedad, who defeated Midian in the country of Moab, succeeded him as king. His city was named Avith.
47 When Hadad died, Samlah from Masrekah succeeded him as king.

*a 36* Many Hebrew manuscripts, some Septuagint manuscripts and Syriac (see also Gen. 36:11); most Hebrew manuscripts *Zephi*    *b 36* Some Septuagint manuscripts (see also Gen. 36:12); Hebrew *Gatam, Kenaz, Timna and Amalek*    *c 40* Many Hebrew manuscripts and some Septuagint manuscripts (see also Gen. 36:23); most Hebrew manuscripts *Alian*    *d 41* Many Hebrew manuscripts and some Septuagint manuscripts (see also Gen. 36:26); most Hebrew manuscripts *Hamran*    *e 42* Many Hebrew and Septuagint manuscripts (see also Gen. 36:27); most Hebrew manuscripts *Zaavan, Jaakan*    *f 42* See Gen. 36:28; Hebrew *Dishon*, a variant of *Dishan*

## Amplified Bible

29 These are their descendants: The firstborn of Ishmael, Nebaioth; Kedar, Adbeel, Mibsam,
30 Mishma, Dumah, Massa, Hadad, Tema,
31 Jetur, Naphish, and Kedemah. These are the sons of Ishmael.
32 Now the sons of Keturah, Abraham's concubine: she bore Zimran, Jokshan, Medan, Midian, Ishbak, and Shuah. The sons of Jokshan: Sheba and Dedan.
33 The sons of Midian: Ephah, Epher, Hanoch, Abida, and Eldaah. All these are the sons [and grandsons] of Keturah.
34 Abraham was the father of Isaac. The sons of Isaac: Esau and Israel.
35 The sons of Esau: Eliphaz, Reuel, Jeush, Jalam, and Korah.
36 The sons of Eliphaz: Teman, Omar, Zephi, Gatam, Kenaz, Timna, and Amalek.
37 The sons of Reuel: Nahath, Zerah, Shammah, and Mizzah.
38 The sons of Seir: Lotan, Shobal, Zibeon, Anah, Dishon, Ezer, and Dishan.
39 The sons of Lotan: Hori and Homam; and Timna was Lotan's sister.
40 The sons of Shobal: Alian, Manahath, Ebal, Shephi, and Onam. The sons of Zibeon: Aiah and Anah.
41 The son of Anah: Dishon. The sons of Dishon: Hamran, Eshban, Ithran, and Cheran.
42 The sons of Ezer: Bilhan, Zaavan, [and] Jaakan. The sons of Dishan: Uz and Aran.
43 These are the kings who reigned in the land of Edom before any king reigned over the Israelites: Bela son of Beor; the name of his city was Dinhabah.
44 When Bela died, Jobab son of Zerah of Bozrah reigned in his stead.
45 When Jobab died, Husham of the land of the Temanites reigned in his stead.
46 When Husham died, Hadad [I of Edom] son of Bedad, who defeated Midian in the field of Moab, reigned in his stead; his city was Avith.
47 When Hadad [I] died, Samlah of Masrekah reigned in his stead.

## New International Version

⁴⁸When Samlah died, Shaul from Rehoboth on the river[a] succeeded him as king. ⁴⁹When Shaul died, Baal-Hanan son of Akbor succeeded him as king. ⁵⁰When Baal-Hanan died, Hadad succeeded him as king. His city was named Pau,[b] and his wife's name was Mehetabel daughter of Matred, the daughter of Me-Zahab. ⁵¹Hadad also died.

The chiefs of Edom were:

Timna, Alvah, Jetheth, ⁵²Oholibamah, Elah, Pinon, ⁵³Kenaz, Teman, Mibzar, ⁵⁴Magdiel and Iram. These were the chiefs of Edom.

### Israel's Sons

**2** These were the sons of Israel:
Reuben, Simeon, Levi, Judah, Issachar, Zebulun, ²Dan, Joseph, Benjamin, Naphtali, Gad and Asher.

### Judah

*To Hezron's Sons*

³The sons of Judah:
Er, Onan and Shelah. These three were born to him by a Canaanite woman, the daughter of Shua. Er, Judah's firstborn, was wicked in the LORD's sight; so the LORD put him to death. ⁴Judah's daughter-in-law Tamar bore Perez and Zerah to Judah. He had five sons in all.

⁵The sons of Perez:
Hezron and Hamul.

⁶The sons of Zerah:
Zimri, Ethan, Heman, Kalkol and Darda[c]—five in all.

⁷The sons of Karmi:
Achar,[d] who brought trouble on Israel by violating the ban on taking devoted things.[e]

⁸The son of Ethan:
Azariah.

⁹The sons born to Hezron were:
Jerahmeel, Ram and Caleb.[f]

*From Ram Son of Hezron*

¹⁰Ram was the father of
Amminadab, and Amminadab the father of Nahshon, the leader of the people of Judah. ¹¹Nahshon was the father of Salmon,[g] Salmon the father of Boaz, ¹²Boaz the father of Obed and Obed the father of Jesse.

¹³Jesse was the father of
Eliab his firstborn; the second son was Abinadab, the third Shimea, ¹⁴the fourth Nethanel, the fifth Raddai, ¹⁵the sixth Ozem and the seventh David. ¹⁶Their sisters were Zeruiah and Abigail. Zeruiah's three sons were Abishai, Joab and Asahel. ¹⁷Abigail was the mother of Amasa, whose father was Jether the Ishmaelite.

*Caleb Son of Hezron*

¹⁸Caleb son of Hezron had children by his wife Azubah (and by Jerioth). These were her sons: Jesher, Shobab and Ardon. ¹⁹When Azubah died, Caleb married Ephrath, who bore him Hur. ²⁰Hur was the father of Uri, and Uri the father of Bezalel.

---

*a 48* Possibly the Euphrates    *b 50* Many Hebrew manuscripts, some Septuagint manuscripts, Vulgate and Syriac (see also Gen. 36:39); most Hebrew manuscripts *Pai*    *c 6* Many Hebrew manuscripts, some Septuagint manuscripts and Syriac (see also 1 Kings 4:31); most Hebrew manuscripts *Dara*    *d 7 Achar* means *trouble*; *Achar* is called *Achan* in Joshua.    *e 7* The Hebrew term refers to the irrevocable giving over of things or persons to the LORD, often by totally destroying them. *f 9* Hebrew *Kelubai*, a variant of *Caleb*    *g 11* Septuagint (see also Ruth 4:21); Hebrew *Salma*

## Amplified Bible

⁴⁸When Samlah died, Shaul of Rehoboth on the River [Euphrates] reigned in his stead. ⁴⁹When Shaul died, Baal-hanan son of Achbor reigned in his stead. ⁵⁰When Baal-hanan died, Hadad [II] reigned in his stead; his city was Pai; his wife was Mehetabel daughter of Matred, the daughter of Mezahab. ⁵¹Hadad died also. The chiefs of Edom were: chiefs Timna, Aliah, Jetheth, ⁵²Oholibamah, Elah, Pinon, ⁵³Kenaz, Teman, Mibzar, ⁵⁴Magdiel, and Iram. These are the chiefs of Edom.

**2** These are the sons of Israel: Reuben, Simeon, Levi, Judah, Issachar, Zebulun, ²Dan, Joseph, Benjamin, Naphtali, Gad, and Asher.

³The sons of Judah: Er, Onan, and Shelah, whom Shua's daughter the Canaanitess bore him. Er, Judah's eldest, was evil in the Lord's sight, and He slew him. ⁴Tamar, Judah's daughter-in-law, bore him Pharez and Zerah. All Judah's sons were five. ⁵The sons of Pharez: Hezron and Hamul. ⁶The sons of Zerah: Zimri, Ethan, Heman, Calcol, and Dara—five in all. [I Kings 4:31.] ⁷The son of Carmi: Achar, the troubler of Israel, who transgressed in the matter of the devoted things. [Josh. 7:1.] ⁸The son of Ethan: Azariah. ⁹The sons of Hezron who were born to him: Jerahmeel, Ram, and Chelubai (that is, Caleb). ¹⁰Ram was the father of Amminadab, and Amminadab of Nahshon, prince of the sons of Judah. ¹¹Nahshon was the father of Salma, Salma of Boaz, ¹²Boaz of Obed, and Obed of Jesse. ¹³Jesse was the father of Eliab his firstborn, Abinadab second, Shimea third, ¹⁴Nethanel fourth, Raddai fifth, ¹⁵Ozem sixth, David seventh. ¹⁶Their sisters were Zeruiah and Abigail. The sons of Zeruiah: Abishai, Joab, and Asahel, three. ¹⁷Abigail bore Amasa, and the father of Amasa was Jether the Ishmaelite. ¹⁸And Caleb son of Hezron had sons by his wife Azubah and by Jerioth. [Azubah's] sons were: Jesher, Shobab, and Ardon. ¹⁹Azubah died, and Caleb married Ephrath, who bore him Hur. ²⁰Hur was the father of Uri, and Uri of Bezalel [the skillful craftsman who made the furnishings of the tabernacle]. [Exod. 31:2-5.]

## New International Version

21 Later, Hezron, when he was sixty years old, married the daughter of Makir the father of Gilead. He made love to her, and she bore him Segub. 22 Segub was the father of Jair, who controlled twenty-three towns in Gilead. 23 (But Geshur and Aram captured Havvoth Jair,*a* as well as Kenath with its surrounding settlements—sixty towns.) All these were descendants of Makir the father of Gilead.

24 After Hezron died in Caleb Ephrathah, Abijah the wife of Hezron bore him Ashhur the father*b* of Tekoa.

### Jerahmeel Son of Hezron

25 The sons of Jerahmeel the firstborn of Hezron:
Ram his firstborn, Bunah, Oren, Ozem and*c* Ahijah. 26 Jerahmeel had another wife, whose name was Atarah; she was the mother of Onam.
27 The sons of Ram the firstborn of Jerahmeel:
Maaz, Jamin and Eker.
28 The sons of Onam:
Shammai and Jada.
The sons of Shammai:
Nadab and Abishur.
29 Abishur's wife was named Abihail, who bore him Ahban and Molid.
30 The sons of Nadab:
Seled and Appaim. Seled died without children.
31 The son of Appaim:
Ishi, who was the father of Sheshan.
Sheshan was the father of Ahlai.
32 The sons of Jada, Shammai's brother:
Jether and Jonathan. Jether died without children.
33 The sons of Jonathan:
Peleth and Zaza.
These were the descendants of Jerahmeel.
34 Sheshan had no sons—only daughters.
He had an Egyptian servant named Jarha. 35 Sheshan gave his daughter in marriage to his servant Jarha, and she bore him Attai.
36 Attai was the father of Nathan,
Nathan the father of Zabad,
37 Zabad the father of Ephlal,
Ephlal the father of Obed,
38 Obed the father of Jehu,
Jehu the father of Azariah,
39 Azariah the father of Helez,
Helez the father of Eleasah,
40 Eleasah the father of Sismai,
Sismai the father of Shallum,
41 Shallum the father of Jekamiah,
and Jekamiah the father of Elishama.

### The Clans of Caleb

42 The sons of Caleb the brother of Jerahmeel:
Mesha his firstborn, who was the father of Ziph, and his son Mareshah,*d* who was the father of Hebron.
43 The sons of Hebron:
Korah, Tappuah, Rekem and Shema. 44 Shema was the father of Raham, and Raham the father of Jorkeam. Rekem was the father of Shammai. 45 The son of Shammai was Maon, and Maon was the father of Beth Zur.
46 Caleb's concubine Ephah was the mother of Haran, Moza and Gazez. Haran was the father of Gazez.
47 The sons of Jahdai:
Regem, Jotham, Geshan, Pelet, Ephah and Shaaph.

## Amplified Bible

21 Later, when Hezron was sixty years old, he married the daughter of Machir the father of Gilead, and she bore him Segub.
22 Segub was the father of Jair, who had twenty-three cities in the land of Gilead.
23 But Geshur and Aram took from them Havvoth-jair, with Kenath and its villages, sixty towns. All these were the descendants of Machir the father of Gilead.
24 After Hezron died in Caleb-ephrathah, Abiah, Hezron's wife, bore to him Ashhur the father of Tekoa.
25 The sons of Jerahmeel the firstborn of Hezron: Ram the firstborn, Bunah, Oren, Ozem, and Ahijah.
26 Jerahmeel had another wife, named Atarah; she was the mother of Onam.
27 The sons of Ram the firstborn of Jerahmeel were: Maaz, Jamin, and Eker.
28 The sons of Onam: Shammai and Jada. The sons of Shammai: Nadab and Abishur.
29 Abishur's wife was Abihail; she bore him Ahban and Molid.
30 The sons of Nadab: Seled and Appaim. Seled died childless.
31 The son of Appaim: Ishi. The son of Ishi: Sheshan. The son of Sheshan: Ahlai.
32 The sons of Jada the brother of Shammai: Jether and Jonathan. Jether died childless.
33 The sons of Jonathan: Peleth and Zaza. These were the descendants of Jerahmeel.
34 Sheshan had no sons—only daughters. But Sheshan had a servant, an Egyptian, whose name was Jarha.
35 Sheshan gave his daughter to Jarha his servant as wife; she bore him Attai.
36 Attai was the father of Nathan, and Nathan of Zabad.
37 Zabad was the father of Ephlal, and Ephlal of Obed.
38 Obed was the father of Jehu, and Jehu of Azariah.
39 Azariah was the father of Helez, and Helez of Eleasah.
40 Eleasah was the father of Sismai, and Sismai of Shallum.
41 Shallum was the father of Jekamiah, and Jekamiah of Elishama.
42 The sons of Caleb the brother of Jerahmeel: Mesha his firstborn was the father of Ziph; and his son Mareshah [he was] the father of Hebron.
43 The sons of Hebron: Korah, Tappuah, Rekem, and Shema.
44 Shema was the father of Raham, the father of Jorkeam. And Rekem was the father of Shammai.
45 The son of Shammai was Maon; Maon's son was Beth-zur.
46 Ephah, Caleb's concubine, bore Haran, Moza, and Gazez; Haran was the father of Gazez.
47 The sons of Jahdai: Regem, Jotham, Geshan, Pelet, Ephah, and Shaaph.

---

*a 23* Or *captured the settlements of Jair*   *b 24 Father* may mean *civic leader* or *military leader*; also in verses 42, 45, 49-52 and possibly elsewhere.   *c 25* Or *Oren and Ozem, by*   *d 42* The meaning of the Hebrew for this phrase is uncertain.

| New International Version | Amplified Bible |
|---|---|

## New International Version

⁴⁸Caleb's concubine Maakah was the mother of Sheber and Tirhanah. ⁴⁹She also gave birth to Shaaph the father of Madmannah and to Sheva the father of Makbenah and Gibea. Caleb's daughter was Aksah. ⁵⁰These were the descendants of Caleb.

The sons of Hur the firstborn of Ephrathah:
Shobal the father of Kiriath Jearim, ⁵¹Salma the father of Bethlehem, and Hareph the father of Beth Gader.
⁵²The descendants of Shobal the father of Kiriath Jearim were:
Haroeh, half the Manahathites, ⁵³and the clans of Kiriath Jearim: the Ithrites, Puthites, Shumathites and Mishraites. From these descended the Zorathites and Eshtaolites.
⁵⁴The descendants of Salma:
Bethlehem, the Netophathites, Atroth Beth Joab, half the Manahathites, the Zorites, ⁵⁵and the clans of scribes*ᵃ* who lived at Jabez: the Tirathites, Shimeathites and Sucathites. These are the Kenites who came from Hammath, the father of the Rekabites.*ᵇ*

### The Sons of David

**3** These were the sons of David born to him in Hebron:
The firstborn was Amnon the son of Ahinoam of Jezreel;
the second, Daniel the son of Abigail of Carmel;
²the third, Absalom the son of Maakah daughter of Talmai king of Geshur;
the fourth, Adonijah the son of Haggith;
³the fifth, Shephatiah the son of Abital;
and the sixth, Ithream, by his wife Eglah.
⁴These six were born to David in Hebron, where he reigned seven years and six months.
David reigned in Jerusalem thirty-three years, ⁵and these were the children born to him there:
Shammua,*ᶜ* Shobab, Nathan and Solomon. These four were by Bathsheba*ᵈ* daughter of Ammiel. ⁶There were also Ibhar, Elishua,*ᵉ* Eliphelet, ⁷Nogah, Nepheg, Japhia, ⁸Elishama, Eliada and Eliphelet—nine in all. ⁹All these were the sons of David, besides his sons by his concubines. And Tamar was their sister.

### The Kings of Judah

¹⁰Solomon's son was Rehoboam,
Abijah his son,
Asa his son,
Jehoshaphat his son,
¹¹Jehoram*ᶠ* his son,
Ahaziah his son,
Joash his son,
¹²Amaziah his son,
Azariah his son,
Jotham his son,
¹³Ahaz his son,
Hezekiah his son,
Manasseh his son,
¹⁴Amon his son,
Josiah his son.
¹⁵The sons of Josiah:
Johanan the firstborn,
Jehoiakim the second son,
Zedekiah the third,
Shallum the fourth.

## Amplified Bible

⁴⁸Maacah, Caleb's concubine, bore Sheber and Tirhanah, and also ⁴⁹Shaaph the father of Madmannah and Sheva the father of Machbenah and of Gibea; and the daughter of Caleb was Achsah.
⁵⁰These were the descendants of Caleb. The sons of Hur the firstborn of Ephrathah: Shobal the father of Kiriath-jearim, ⁵¹Salma the father of Bethlehem, and Hareph the father of Beth-gader.
⁵²Shobal the father of Kiriath-jearim had [other] descendants: Haroeh, half [of the inhabitants] of Menuhoth [in Judah],
⁵³And the families of Kiriath-jearim: the Ithrites, Puthites, Shumathites, and Mishraites. From these came the Zorathites and the Eshtaolites.
⁵⁴The descendants of Salma: Bethlehem, the Netophathites, Atroth-beth-joab, and half of the Manahathites, [and] the Zorites,
⁵⁵And the families of scribes who dwelt at Jabez: the Tirathites, Shimeathites, and Sucathites. These are the Kenites who came from Hammath, the father of the house of Rechab.

**3** These sons of David were born to him in Hebron: the firstborn was Amnon, of Ahinoam the Jezreelitess; second, Daniel (Chileab), of Abigail the Carmelitess;
²Third, Absalom the son of Maacah daughter of Talmai king of Geshur; fourth, Adonijah, of Haggith;
³Fifth, Shephatiah, of Abital; sixth, Ithream, of his wife Eglah.
⁴These six were born to David in Hebron; there he reigned seven years and six months, and in Jerusalem he reigned thirty-three years.
⁵These were born to [David] in Jerusalem: Shimea, Shobab, Nathan, Solomon—four of Bathshua (Bathsheba) daughter of Ammiel (Eliam);
⁶Then Ibhar, Elishama, Eliphelet,
⁷Nogah, Nepheg, Japhia,
⁸Elishama, Eliada, and Eliphelet—nine in all.
⁹These were all the sons of David, besides the sons of the concubines. And Tamar was their sister.
¹⁰Solomon's descendants [omitting nonreigning offspring] were: his son Rehoboam. Abijah was his son, Asa his son, Jehoshaphat his son,
¹¹Jehoram (Joram) his son, Ahaziah his son, Joash his son,
¹²Amaziah his son, Azariah his son, Jotham his son,
¹³Ahaz his son, Hezekiah his son, Manasseh his son,
¹⁴Amon his son, Josiah his son.
¹⁵The descendants of Josiah: firstborn, Johanan; second, Jehoiakim; third, Zedekiah; fourth, Shallum.

---

*ᵃ 55* Or *of the Sopherites*   *ᵇ 55* Or *father of Beth Rekab*   *ᶜ 5* Hebrew *Shimea,* a variant of *Shammua*   *ᵈ 5* One Hebrew manuscript and Vulgate (see also Septuagint and 2 Samuel 11:3); most Hebrew manuscripts *Bathshua*   *ᵉ 6* Two Hebrew manuscripts (see also 2 Samuel 5:15 and 1 Chron. 14:5); most Hebrew manuscripts *Elishama*   *ᶠ 11* Hebrew *Joram,* a variant of *Jehoram*

## New International Version

16 The successors of Jehoiakim:
Jehoiachin[a] his son,
and Zedekiah.

### The Royal Line After the Exile
17 The descendants of Jehoiachin the captive:
Shealtiel his son, 18 Malkiram, Pedaiah, Shenazzar,
Jekamiah, Hoshama and Nedabiah.
19 The sons of Pedaiah:
Zerubbabel and Shimei.
The sons of Zerubbabel:
Meshullam and Hananiah.
Shelomith was their sister.
20 There were also five others:
Hashubah, Ohel, Berekiah, Hasadiah and Jushab-
Hesed.
21 The descendants of Hananiah:
Pelatiah and Jeshaiah, and the sons of Rephaiah, of
Arnan, of Obadiah and of Shekaniah.
22 The descendants of Shekaniah:
Shemaiah and his sons:
Hattush, Igal, Bariah, Neariah and Shaphat—six
in all.
23 The sons of Neariah:
Elioenai, Hizkiah and Azrikam—three in all.
24 The sons of Elioenai:
Hodaviah, Eliashib, Pelaiah, Akkub, Johanan, De-
laiah and Anani—seven in all.

### Other Clans of Judah
4 The descendants of Judah:
Perez, Hezron, Karmi, Hur and Shobal.
2 Reaiah son of Shobal was the father of Jahath, and Jahath the father of Ahumai and Lahad. These were
the clans of the Zorathites.
3 These were the sons[b] of Etam:
Jezreel, Ishma and Idbash. Their sister was named
Hazzelelponi. 4 Penuel was the father of Gedor, and
Ezer the father of Hushah.
These were the descendants of Hur, the firstborn of
Ephrathah and father[c] of Bethlehem.
5 Ashhur the father of Tekoa had two wives, Helah and
Naarah.
6 Naarah bore him Ahuzzam, Hepher, Temeni and Ha-
ahashtari. These were the descendants of Naarah.
7 The sons of Helah:
Zereth, Zohar, Ethnan, 8 and Koz, who was the fa-
ther of Anub and Hazzobebah and of the clans of
Aharhel son of Harum.

9 Jabez was more honorable than his brothers. His mother had named him Jabez,[d] saying, "I gave birth to him in
pain." 10 Jabez cried out to the God of Israel, "Oh, that you
would bless me and enlarge my territory! Let your hand
be with me, and keep me from harm so that I will be free
from pain." And God granted his request.

11 Kelub, Shuhah's brother, was the father of Mehir,
who was the father of Eshton. 12 Eshton was the
father of Beth Rapha, Paseah and Tehinnah the father of Ir Nahash.[e] These were the men of Rekah.

13 The sons of Kenaz:
Othniel and Seraiah.
The sons of Othniel:
Hathath and Meonothai.[f] 14 Meonothai was the fa-
ther of Ophrah.
Seraiah was the father of Joab,

## Amplified Bible

16 The descendants of Jehoiakim: Jehoiachin (Jeconiah)
his son, Zedekiah his son.
17 The descendants of Jehoiachin the captive: Shealtiel
his son,
18 Malchiram, Pedaiah, Shenazzar, Jekamiah, Hoshama,
and Nedabiah.
19 The sons of Pedaiah: Zerubbabel and Shimei. The
sons of Zerubbabel: Meshullam, Hananiah. And Shelomith was their sister;
20 And Hashubah, Ohel, Berechiah, Hasadiah, [and]
Jushab-hesed—five [the sons of Meshullam?].
21 The sons of Hananiah: Pelatiah and Jeshaiah, whose
son was Rephaiah, his son Arnan, his son Obadiah, his
son Shecaniah.
22 The son of Shecaniah: Shemaiah. The sons of Shemaiah: Hattush, Igal, Bariah, Neariah, and Shaphat—six
in all.
23 The sons of Neariah: Elioenai, Hizkiah, and Azrikam—three in all.
24 The sons of Elioenai: Hodaviah, Eliashib, Pelaiah, Akkub, Johanan, Delaiah, and Anani—seven in all.

4 The sons of Judah: Perez, Hezron, Carmi, Hur, and
Shobal.
2 Reaiah son of Shobal was the father of Jahath, and Jahath of Ahumai and Lahad. These were the families of the
Zorathites.
3 These were the sons of [Hur] the father of Etam: Jezreel, Ishma, and Idbash. And their sister was Hazzelelponi.
4 And Penuel was the father of Gedor, and Ezer the father of Hushah. These were the sons of Hur, the eldest of
Ephrathah (Ephrath), the father of Bethlehem.
5 Ashur the father of Tekoa had two wives, Helah and
Naarah.
6 Naarah bore him Ahuzzam, Hepher, Temeni, and Haa-
hashtari. These were Naarah's sons.
7 The sons of Helah: Zereth, Izhar, and Ethnan.
8 Koz was the father of Anub, Zobebah, and the families
of Aharhel son of Harum.
9 Jabez was honorable above his brothers; but his mother named him Jabez [sorrow maker], saying, Because I
bore him in pain.
10 Jabez cried to the God of Israel, saying, Oh, that You
would bless me and enlarge my border, and that Your hand
might be with me, and You would keep me from evil so it
might not hurt me! And God granted his request.
11 Chelub the brother of Shuhah was the father of Mehir,
the father of Eshton.
12 Eshton was the father of Beth-rapha, Paseah, and
Tehinnah the father of Ir-nahash. These are the men of
Recah.
13 The sons of Kenaz: Othniel and Seraiah. The sons of
Othniel: Hathath [and Meonothai].
14 Meonothai was father of Ophrah, and Seraiah of Joab

---

a 16 Hebrew Jeconiah, a variant of Jehoiachin; also in verse 17
b 3 Some Septuagint manuscripts (see also Vulgate); Hebrew father
c 4 Father may mean civic leader or military leader; also in verses 12,
14, 17, 18 and possibly elsewhere.   d 9 Jabez sounds like the Hebrew
for pain.   e 12 Or of the city of Nahash   f 13 Some Septuagint
manuscripts and Vulgate; Hebrew does not have and Meonothai.

## New International Version

the father of Ge Harashim.*ª* It was called this because its people were skilled workers.
<sup></sup>¹⁵The sons of Caleb son of Jephunneh:
Iru, Elah and Naam.
The son of Elah:
Kenaz.
¹⁶The sons of Jehallelel:
Ziph, Ziphah, Tiria and Asarel.
¹⁷The sons of Ezrah:
Jether, Mered, Epher and Jalon. One of Mered's wives gave birth to Miriam, Shammai and Ishbah the father of Eshtemoa. ¹⁸(His wife from the tribe of Judah gave birth to Jered the father of Gedor, Heber the father of Soko, and Jekuthiel the father of Zanoah.) These were the children of Pharaoh's daughter Bithiah, whom Mered had married.
¹⁹The sons of Hodiah's wife, the sister of Naham:
the father of Keilah the Garmite, and Eshtemoa the Maakathite.
²⁰The sons of Shimon:
Amnon, Rinnah, Ben-Hanan and Tilon.
The descendants of Ishi:
Zoheth and Ben-Zoheth.
²¹The sons of Shelah son of Judah:
Er the father of Lekah, Laadah the father of Mareshah and the clans of the linen workers at Beth Ashbea, ²²Jokim, the men of Kozeba, and Joash and Saraph, who ruled in Moab and Jashubi Lehem. (These records are from ancient times.) ²³They were the potters who lived at Netaim and Gederah; they stayed there and worked for the king.

### Simeon

²⁴The descendants of Simeon:
Nemuel, Jamin, Jarib, Zerah and Shaul;
²⁵Shallum was Shaul's son, Mibsam his son and Mishma his son.
²⁶The descendants of Mishma:
Hammuel his son, Zakkur his son and Shimei his son.
²⁷Shimei had sixteen sons and six daughters, but his brothers did not have many children; so their entire clan did not become as numerous as the people of Judah. ²⁸They lived in Beersheba, Moladah, Hazar Shual, ²⁹Bilhah, Ezem, Tolad, ³⁰Bethuel, Hormah, Ziklag, ³¹Beth Markaboth, Hazar Susim, Beth Biri and Shaaraim. These were their towns until the reign of David. ³²Their surrounding villages were Etam, Ain, Rimmon, Token and Ashan—five towns— ³³and all the villages around these towns as far as Baalath.*ᵇ* These were their settlements. And they kept a genealogical record.

³⁴Meshobab, Jamlech, Joshah son of Amaziah, ³⁵Joel, Jehu son of Joshibiah, the son of Seraiah, the son of Asiel, ³⁶also Elioenai, Jaakobah, Jeshohaiah, Asaiah, Adiel, Jesimiel, Benaiah, ³⁷and Ziza son of Shiphi, the son of Allon, the son of Jedaiah, the son of Shimri, the son of Shemaiah.

³⁸The men listed above by name were leaders of their clans. Their families increased greatly, ³⁹and they went to the outskirts of Gedor to the east of the valley in search of pasture for their flocks. ⁴⁰They found rich, good pasture, and the land was spacious, peaceful and quiet. Some Hamites had lived there formerly.
⁴¹The men whose names were listed came in the days of Hezekiah king of Judah. They attacked the Hamites in their dwellings and also the Meunites who were there and completely destroyed*ᶜ* them, as is evident to this day. Then they settled in their place, because there was pasture for

## Amplified Bible

the father of Ge-harashim [the Valley of Craftsmen], so named because they were craftsmen.
¹⁵The sons of Caleb [Joshua's companion] son of Jephunneh: Iru, Elah, and Naam. The son of Elah: Kenaz.
¹⁶The sons of Jehallelel: Ziph, Ziphah, Tiria, and Asarel.
¹⁷The sons of Ezrah: Jether, Mered, Epher, and Jalon. *ª*These are the sons of Bithiah daughter of Pharaoh, whom Mered married: she bore Miriam, Shammai, and Ishbah the father of Eshtemoa.
¹⁸And Mered's Jewish wife bore Jered the father of Gedor, Heber the father of Soco, and Jekuthiel the father of Zanoah.
¹⁹The sons of the wife of Hodiah, the sister of Naham, were: the father of Keilah the Garmite, and Eshtemoa the Maacathite.
²⁰The sons of Shimon: Amnon, Rinnah, Ben-hanan, and Tilon. The sons of Ishi: Zoheth and Ben-zoheth.
²¹The sons of Shelah son of Judah: Er the father of Lecah, and Laadah the father of Mareshah, and the families of the house of the linen workers at Beth-ashbea,
²²And Jokim, the men of Cozeba, Joash, and Saraph, who ruled in Moab, and returned to [Bethlehem]. These are ancient matters.
²³These were the potters and those who dwelt among plantations and hedges at Netaim and Gederah; there they dwelt with the king for his work.
²⁴The sons of Simeon: Nemuel, Jamin, Jarib, Zerah, and Shaul;
²⁵Shallum was his [Shaul's] son, Mibsam his son, Mishma his son.
²⁶The sons of Mishma: Hammuel his son, Zaccur his son, Shimei his son.
²⁷Shimei had sixteen sons and six daughters, but his brothers did not have many children; neither did all their family multiply like the children of Judah.
²⁸They dwelt at Beersheba, Moladah, Hazar-shual,
²⁹Bilhah, Ezem, Tolad,
³⁰Bethuel, Hormah, Ziklag,
³¹Beth-marcaboth, Hazar-susim, Beth-biri, and at Shaaraim. These were their towns [and villages] until the reign of David.
³²There were also Etam, Ain, Rimmon, Tochen, and Ashan—five towns—
³³And all their villages that were round about these towns, as far as Baal[-ath-beer]. These were their settlements, and they had their genealogical record.
³⁴Meshobab, Jamlech, Joshah son of Amaziah,
³⁵Joel, Jehu son of Joshibiah, the son of Seraiah, the son of Asiel,
³⁶Also Elioenai, Jaakobah, Jeshohaiah, Asaiah, Adiel, Jesimiel, Benaiah,
³⁷Ziza son of Shiphi, the son of Allon, the son of Jedaiah, the son of Shimri, the son of Shemaiah.
³⁸These mentioned by name were princes in their families; and their fathers' houses increased greatly [so they needed more room].
³⁹And they journeyed to the entrance of Gedor to the east side of the valley to seek pasture for their flocks.
⁴⁰And they found rich, good pasture, and the [cleared] land was wide, quiet, and peaceful, because people of Ham had dwelt there of old [and had left it a better place for those who came after them].
⁴¹And these registered by name came in the days of Hezekiah king of Judah and destroyed their tents and the Meunim [foreigners] who were found there and exterminated them to this day, and they settled in their stead, because there was pasture for their flocks.

---

*ª 14 Ge Harashim* means *valley of skilled workers.* *ᵇ 33* Some Septuagint manuscripts (see also Joshua 19:8); Hebrew *Baal* *ᶜ 41* The Hebrew term refers to the irrevocable giving over of things or persons to the Lᴏʀᴅ, often by totally destroying them.

*ª* This clause, "These are the sons of Bithiah daughter of Pharaoh, whom Mered married," has been transposed from I Chron. 4:18 to I Chron. 4:17.

## New International Version

their flocks. ⁴²And five hundred of these Simeonites, led by Pelatiah, Neariah, Rephaiah and Uzziel, the sons of Ishi, invaded the hill country of Seir. ⁴³They killed the remaining Amalekites who had escaped, and they have lived there to this day.

### Reuben

**5** The sons of Reuben the firstborn of Israel (he was the firstborn, but when he defiled his father's marriage bed, his rights as firstborn were given to the sons of Joseph son of Israel; so he could not be listed in the genealogical record in accordance with his birthright, ²and though Judah was the strongest of his brothers and a ruler came from him, the rights of the firstborn belonged to Joseph) — ³the sons of Reuben the firstborn of Israel:

Hanok, Pallu, Hezron and Karmi.

⁴The descendants of Joel:
Shemaiah his son, Gog his son,
Shimei his son, ⁵Micah his son,
Reaiah his son, Baal his son,
⁶and Beerah his son, whom Tiglath-Pileserᵃ king of Assyria took into exile. Beerah was a leader of the Reubenites.

⁷Their relatives by clans, listed according to their genealogical records:
Jeiel the chief, Zechariah, ⁸and Bela son of Azaz, the son of Shema, the son of Joel. They settled in the area from Aroer to Nebo and Baal Meon. ⁹To the east they occupied the land up to the edge of the desert that extends to the Euphrates River, because their livestock had increased in Gilead. ¹⁰During Saul's reign they waged war against the Hagrites, who were defeated at their hands; they occupied the dwellings of the Hagrites throughout the entire region east of Gilead.

### Gad

¹¹The Gadites lived next to them in Bashan, as far as Salekah:
¹²Joel was the chief, Shapham the second, then Janai and Shaphat, in Bashan.

¹³Their relatives, by families, were:
Michael, Meshullam, Sheba, Jorai, Jakan, Zia and Eber — seven in all.

¹⁴These were the sons of Abihail son of Huri, the son of Jaroah, the son of Gilead, the son of Michael, the son of Jeshishai, the son of Jahdo, the son of Buz.

¹⁵Ahi son of Abdiel, the son of Guni, was head of their family.

¹⁶The Gadites lived in Gilead, in Bashan and its outlying villages, and on all the pasturelands of Sharon as far as they extended.

¹⁷All these were entered in the genealogical records during the reigns of Jotham king of Judah and Jeroboam king of Israel.

¹⁸The Reubenites, the Gadites and the half-tribe of Manasseh had 44,760 men ready for military service — able-bodied men who could handle shield and sword, who could use a bow, and who were trained for battle. ¹⁹They waged war against the Hagrites, Jetur, Naphish and Nodab. ²⁰They were helped in fighting them, and God delivered the Hagrites and all their allies into their hands, because they cried out to him during the battle. He answered their prayers, because they trusted in him. ²¹They seized the livestock of the Hagrites — fifty thousand camels, two hundred fifty thousand sheep and two thousand donkeys. They also took one hundred thousand people captive, ²²and many others fell slain, because the battle was God's. And they occupied the land until the exile.

## Amplified Bible

⁴²And some of them from the sons of Simeon, 500 men, went to Mount Seir, having for their leaders Pelatiah, and Neariah, Rephaiah, and Uzziel, the sons of Ishi. ⁴³They destroyed the remnant of the Amalekites who had escaped, and they have dwelt there to this day.

**5** Now [we come to] the sons of Reuben the firstborn of Israel. For [Reuben] was the eldest, but because he polluted his father's couch [with Bilhah his father's concubine] his birthright was given to the sons of Joseph [favorite] son of Israel; so the genealogy is not to be reckoned according to the birthright. [Gen. 35:22; 48:15-22; 49:3, 4.]

²Judah prevailed above his brethren, and from him came the prince *and* leader [and eventually the Messiah]; yet the birthright was Joseph's. [Gen. 49:10; Mic. 5:2.]

³The sons of Reuben the firstborn of Israel: Hanoch, Pallu, Hezron, and Carmi.

⁴The sons of Joel: Shemaiah his son, Gog his son, Shimei his son,

⁵Micah his son, Reaiah his son, Baal his son,

⁶Beerah his son, whom Tilgath-pilneser king of Assyria carried away captive; he was a prince of the Reubenites.

⁷And his brethren by their families, when the genealogy of their generations was reckoned: the chief Jeiel, and Zechariah,

⁸Bela son of Azaz, the son of Shema, the son of Joel, who dwelt in Aroer as far as Nebo and Baal-meon.

⁹Eastward [Bela] inhabited the land as far as the entrance into the desert this [west] side of the river Euphrates, because their cattle had multiplied in the land of Gilead.

¹⁰In the days of [King] Saul they made war with the Hagrites *or* Ishmaelites, who fell by their hands; they dwelt in their tents in all the land east of Gilead.

¹¹The children of Gad who dwelt opposite them in the land of Bashan, as far as Salecah:

¹²Joel the chief, Shapham the next, Janai, and Shaphat in Bashan.

¹³Their kinsmen of the houses of their fathers: Michael, Meshullam, Sheba, Jorai, Jacan, Zia, and Eber — seven in all.

¹⁴These were the sons of Abihail son of Huri, the son of Jaroah, the son of Gilead, the son of Michael, the son of Jeshishai, the son of Jahdo, the son of Buz.

¹⁵Ahi son of Abdiel, the son of Guni, was chief in their fathers' houses.

¹⁶They dwelt in Gilead, in Bashan and in its towns, and in all the suburbs *and* pasturelands of Sharon to their limits.

¹⁷All these were enrolled by genealogies in the days of Jotham king of Judah and in the days of Jeroboam [II] king of Israel.

¹⁸The sons of Reuben, the Gadites, and the half-tribe of Manasseh — valiant men able to bear buckler and sword and to shoot with bow and skillful in war — were 44,760 able *and* ready to go forth to war.

¹⁹And [these Israelites, on the east side of the Jordan River] made war with the Hagrites [a tribe of northern Arabia], Jetur, Naphish, and Nodab.

²⁰They were given help against them, and the Hagrites *or* Ishmaelites were delivered into their hands, and all who were allied with them, for they cried to God in the battle; and He granted their entreaty, because they relied on, clung to, *and* trusted in Him.

²¹And [these Israelites] took away their adversaries' herds: of their camels 50,000, and of sheep 250,000, and of donkeys 2,000, and of the lives of men 100,000.

²²For a great number fell mortally wounded, because the battle was God's. And [these Israelites] dwelt in their territory until the captivity [by Assyria more than five centuries later]. [II Kings 15:29.]

ᵃ 6 Hebrew *Tilgath-Pilneser,* a variant of *Tiglath-Pileser*; also in verse 26

## New International Version

### The Half-Tribe of Manasseh

23The people of the half-tribe of Manasseh were numerous; they settled in the land from Bashan to Baal Hermon, that is, to Senir (Mount Hermon).

24These were the heads of their families: Epher, Ishi, Eliel, Azriel, Jeremiah, Hodaviah and Jahdiel. They were brave warriors, famous men, and heads of their families. 25But they were unfaithful to the God of their ancestors and prostituted themselves to the gods of the peoples of the land, whom God had destroyed before them. 26So the God of Israel stirred up the spirit of Pul king of Assyria (that is, Tiglath-Pileser king of Assyria), who took the Reubenites, the Gadites and the half-tribe of Manasseh into exile. He took them to Halah, Habor, Hara and the river of Gozan, where they are to this day.

### Levi

**6**a The sons of Levi:
  Gershon, Kohath and Merari.
2The sons of Kohath:
  Amram, Izhar, Hebron and Uzziel.
3The children of Amram:
  Aaron, Moses and Miriam.
The sons of Aaron:
  Nadab, Abihu, Eleazar and Ithamar.
4Eleazar was the father of Phinehas,
  Phinehas the father of Abishua,
5Abishua the father of Bukki,
  Bukki the father of Uzzi,
6Uzzi the father of Zerahiah,
  Zerahiah the father of Meraioth,
7Meraioth the father of Amariah,
  Amariah the father of Ahitub,
8Ahitub the father of Zadok,
  Zadok the father of Ahimaaz,
9Ahimaaz the father of Azariah,
  Azariah the father of Johanan,
10Johanan the father of Azariah (it was he who served as priest in the temple Solomon built in Jerusalem),
11Azariah the father of Amariah,
  Amariah the father of Ahitub,
12Ahitub the father of Zadok,
  Zadok the father of Shallum,
13Shallum the father of Hilkiah,
  Hilkiah the father of Azariah,
14Azariah the father of Seraiah,
  and Seraiah the father of Jozadak.b

15Jozadak was deported when the LORD sent Judah and Jerusalem into exile by the hand of Nebuchadnezzar.

16The sons of Levi:
  Gershon,c Kohath and Merari.
17These are the names of the sons of Gershon:
  Libni and Shimei.
18The sons of Kohath:
  Amram, Izhar, Hebron and Uzziel.
19The sons of Merari:
  Mahli and Mushi.
These are the clans of the Levites listed according to their fathers:
20Of Gershon:
  Libni his son, Jahath his son,
  Zimmah his son, 21Joah his son,
  Iddo his son, Zerah his son
  and Jeatherai his son.

## Amplified Bible

23And the people of the half-tribe of Manasseh dwelt in the land; their settlements spread from Bashan to Baalhermon, Senir, and Mount Hermon.

24And these were the heads of their fathers' houses: Epher, Ishi, Eliel, Azriel, Jeremiah, Hodaviah, and Jahdiel, mighty men of strength of mind *and* spirit [enabling them to encounter danger with firmness and personal bravery], famous men, and heads of the houses of their fathers.

25They transgressed against the God of their fathers and played the harlot [by unfaithfulness to their own God and running] after the gods of the native peoples, whom God had destroyed before them.

26So the God of Israel stirred up the spirit of Pul king of Assyria, [that is,] the spirit of Tilgath-pilneser king of Assyria, and he carried them away, the Reubenites, Gadites, and half-tribe of Manasseh and brought them to Halah, Habor, Hara, and the river Gozan, to this day.

**6** The sons of Levi: Gershom, Kohath, and Merari.
2The sons of Kohath: Amram, Izhar, Hebron, and Uzziel.

3The children of Amram: Aaron, Moses, and Miriam. The sons also of Aaron: Nadab, Abihu, Eleazar, and Ithamar.

4Eleazar was the father of Phinehas, Phinehas of Abishua.

5Abishua was the father of Bukki, and Bukki of Uzzi,

6Uzzi of Zerahiah, and Zerahiah of Meraioth,

7Meraioth of Amariah, and Amariah of Ahitub,

8Ahitub of Zadok, and Zadok of Ahimaaz,

9Ahimaaz of Azariah, and Azariah of Johanan,

10Johanan of Azariah, who was priest in the temple Solomon built in Jerusalem,

11Azariah of Amariah, and Amariah of Ahitub,

12Ahitub of Zadok, and Zadok of Shallum,

13Shallum of Hilkiah, and Hilkiah of Azariah,

14Azariah of Seraiah, and Seraiah of Jehozadak;

15Jehozadak went into captivity when the Lord sent Judah and Jerusalem into exile by the hand of Nebuchadnezzar.

16The sons of Levi: Gershom, Kohath, and Merari.

17These are the names of the sons of Gershom: Libni and Shimei.

18The sons of Kohath: Amram, Izhar, Hebron, and Uzziel.

19The sons of Merari: Mahli and Mushi. These are the families of the Levites according to their fathers:

20Of Gershom: Libni his son, Jahath his son, Zimmah his son,

21Joah his son, Iddo his son, Zerah his son, Jeatherai his son.

---

a In Hebrew texts 6:1-15 is numbered 5:27-41, and 6:16-81 is numbered 6:1-66.   b 14 Hebrew *Jehozadak*, a variant of *Jozadak*; also in verse 15   c 16 Hebrew *Gershom*, a variant of *Gershon*; also in verses 17, 20, 43, 62 and 71

## New International Version

22The descendants of Kohath:
    Amminadab his son, Korah his son,
    Assir his son, 23Elkanah his son,
    Ebiasaph his son, Assir his son,
24Tahath his son, Uriel his son,
    Uzziah his son and Shaul his son.
25The descendants of Elkanah:
    Amasai, Ahimoth,
26Elkanah his son,*a* Zophai his son,
    Nahath his son, 27Eliab his son,
    Jeroham his son, Elkanah his son
    and Samuel his son.*b*
28The sons of Samuel:
    Joel*c* the firstborn
    and Abijah the second son.
29The descendants of Merari:
    Mahli, Libni his son,
    Shimei his son, Uzzah his son,
30Shimea his son, Haggiah his son
    and Asaiah his son.

*The Temple Musicians*
31These are the men David put in charge of the music in the house of the LORD after the ark came to rest there. 32They ministered with music before the tabernacle, the tent of meeting, until Solomon built the temple of the LORD in Jerusalem. They performed their duties according to the regulations laid down for them.
33Here are the men who served, together with their sons:
From the Kohathites:
    Heman, the musician,
    the son of Joel, the son of Samuel,
34the son of Elkanah, the son of Jeroham,
    the son of Eliel, the son of Toah,
35the son of Zuph, the son of Elkanah,
    the son of Mahath, the son of Amasai,
36the son of Elkanah, the son of Joel,
    the son of Azariah, the son of Zephaniah,
37the son of Tahath, the son of Assir,
    the son of Ebiasaph, the son of Korah,
38the son of Izhar, the son of Kohath,
    the son of Levi, the son of Israel;
39and Heman's associate Asaph, who served at his right hand:
    Asaph son of Berekiah, the son of Shimea,
40the son of Michael, the son of Baaseiah,*d*
    the son of Malkijah, 41the son of Ethni,
    the son of Zerah, the son of Adaiah,
42the son of Ethan, the son of Zimmah,
    the son of Shimei, 43the son of Jahath,
    the son of Gershon, the son of Levi;
44and from their associates, the Merarites, at his left hand:
    Ethan son of Kishi, the son of Abdi,
    the son of Malluk, 45the son of Hashabiah,
    the son of Amaziah, the son of Hilkiah,
46the son of Amzi, the son of Bani,
    the son of Shemer, 47the son of Mahli,
    the son of Mushi, the son of Merari,
    the son of Levi.

48Their fellow Levites were assigned to all the other duties of the tabernacle, the house of God. 49But Aaron and his descendants were the ones who presented offerings on the altar of burnt offering and on the altar of incense in

---

*a 26* Some Hebrew manuscripts, Septuagint and Syriac; most Hebrew manuscripts *Ahimoth 26and Elkanah. The sons of Elkanah:*   *b 27* Some Septuagint manuscripts (see also 1 Samuel 1:19,20 and 1 Chron. 6:33,34); Hebrew does not have *and Samuel his son.*   *c 28* Some Septuagint manuscripts and Syriac (see also 1 Samuel 8:2 and 1 Chron. 6:33); Hebrew does not have *Joel.*   *d 40* Most Hebrew manuscripts; some Hebrew manuscripts, one Septuagint manuscript and Syriac *Maaseiah*

## Amplified Bible

22The sons of Kohath: Amminadab his son, Korah his son, Assir his son,
23Elkanah his son, Ebiasaph his son, Assir his son,
24Tahath his son, Uriel his son, Uzziah his son, and Shaul his son.
25And the sons of Elkanah: Amasai, Ahimoth,
26Elkanah his son, Zophai his son, Nahath his son,
27Eliab his son, Jeroham his son, Elkanah [Samuel's father] his son.
28The sons of Samuel: the firstborn [Joel] and Abijah.
29The sons of Merari: Mahli, Libni his son, Shimei his son, Uzza his son,
30Shimea his son, Haggiah his son, Asaiah his son.
31These David put over the service of song in the house of the Lord after the ark of the covenant rested there [after being taken by the Philistines and later placed in the house of Abinadab, where it remained for nearly 100 years during the rest of Samuel's judgeship and Saul's entire reign and into David's reign].
32They ministered before the tabernacle of the Tent of Meeting with singing until Solomon had built the Lord's house in Jerusalem, performing their service in due order.
33These and their sons served of the Kohathites: Heman, the singer, the son of Joel, the son of Samuel [the great prophet and judge],
34The son of Elkanah [III], the son of Jeroham, the son of Eliel, the son of Toah,
35The son of Zuph, the son of Elkanah [II], the son of Mahath, the son of Amasai,
36The son of Elkanah [I], the son of Joel, the son of Azariah, the son of Zephaniah,
37The son of Tahath, the son of Assir, the son of Ebiasaph, the son of Korah,
38The son of Izhar, the son of Kohath, the son of Levi, the son of Israel (Jacob).
39Heman's [tribal] brother Asaph stood at his right hand: Asaph son of Berechiah, the son of Shimea,
40The son of Michael, the son of Baaseiah, the son of Malchijah,
41The son of Ethni, the son of Zerah, the son of Adaiah,
42The son of Ethan, the son of Zimmah, the son of Shimei,
43The son of Jahath, the son of Gershom, the son of Levi.
44Their kinsmen the sons of Merari stood at the left hand: Ethan son of Kishi, the son of Abdi, the son of Malluch,
45The son of Hashabiah, the son of Amaziah, the son of Hilkiah,
46The son of Amzi, the son of Bani, the son of Shemer,
47The son of Mahli, the son of Mushi, the son of Merari, the son of Levi.
48And their brethren the Levites [who were not descended from Aaron] were appointed for all other kinds of service of the tabernacle of the house of God.
49But [the line of] Aaron and his sons offered upon the altar of burnt offering and the altar of incense, ministering

## New International Version

connection with all that was done in the Most Holy Place, making atonement for Israel, in accordance with all that Moses the servant of God had commanded.

50 These were the descendants of Aaron:
Eleazar his son, Phinehas his son,
Abishua his son, 51 Bukki his son,
Uzzi his son, Zerahiah his son,
52 Meraioth his son, Amariah his son,
Ahitub his son, 53 Zadok his son
and Ahimaaz his son.

54 These were the locations of their settlements allotted as their territory (they were assigned to the descendants of Aaron who were from the Kohathite clan, because the first lot was for them):
55 They were given Hebron in Judah with its surrounding pasturelands. 56 But the fields and villages around the city were given to Caleb son of Jephunneh.
57 So the descendants of Aaron were given Hebron (a city of refuge), and Libnah,*a* Jattir, Eshtemoa, 58 Hilen, Debir, 59 Ashan, Juttah*b* and Beth Shemesh, together with their pasturelands. 60 And from the tribe of Benjamin they were given Gibeon,*c* Geba, Alemeth and Anathoth, together with their pasturelands.
The total number of towns distributed among the Kohathite clans came to thirteen.
61 The rest of Kohath's descendants were allotted ten towns from the clans of half the tribe of Manasseh.
62 The descendants of Gershon, clan by clan, were allotted thirteen towns from the tribes of Issachar, Asher and Naphtali, and from the part of the tribe of Manasseh that is in Bashan.
63 The descendants of Merari, clan by clan, were allotted twelve towns from the tribes of Reuben, Gad and Zebulun.
64 So the Israelites gave the Levites these towns and their pasturelands. 65 From the tribes of Judah, Simeon and Benjamin they allotted the previously named towns.
66 Some of the Kohathite clans were given as their territory towns from the tribe of Ephraim.
67 In the hill country of Ephraim they were given Shechem (a city of refuge), and Gezer,*d* 68 Jokmeam, Beth Horon, 69 Aijalon and Gath Rimmon, together with their pasturelands.
70 And from half the tribe of Manasseh the Israelites gave Aner and Bileam, together with their pasturelands, to the rest of the Kohathite clans.

71 The Gershonites received the following:
From the clan of the half-tribe of Manasseh
they received Golan in Bashan and also Ashtaroth, together with their pasturelands;
72 from the tribe of Issachar
they received Kedesh, Daberath, 73 Ramoth and Anem, together with their pasturelands;
74 from the tribe of Asher
they received Mashal, Abdon, 75 Hukok and Rehob, together with their pasturelands;
76 and from the tribe of Naphtali
they received Kedesh in Galilee, Hammon and Kiriathaim, together with their pasturelands.

77 The Merarites (the rest of the Levites) received the following:
From the tribe of Zebulun
they received Jokneam, Kartah,*e* Rimmono and Tabor, together with their pasturelands;

## Amplified Bible

for all the work of the Holy of Holies, and to make atonement for Israel, according to all that Moses, God's servant, had commanded.

50 The sons of Aaron: Eleazar his son, Phinehas his son, Abishua his son,
51 Bukki his son, Uzzi his son, Zerahiah his son,
52 Meraioth his son, Amariah his son, Ahitub his son,
53 Zadok his son, Ahimaaz his son.
54 Their dwelling places are according to their settlements within their borders: to the sons of Aaron of the families of the Kohathites, for theirs was the [first] lot— [Josh. 21:10.]
55 To them they gave Hebron in the land of Judah and its surrounding suburbs.
56 But the fields of the city and its villages they gave to Caleb son of Jephunneh.
57 To the sons of Aaron they gave the city of refuge, Hebron; also Libnah with its pasturelands, Jattir, Eshtemoa with its pasturelands, [Josh. 21:13.]
58 Hilen with its pasturelands, Debir with its pasturelands,
59 Ashan with its pasturelands, and Beth-shemesh with its pasturelands.
60 And out of the tribe of Benjamin: Geba, Alemeth, and Anathoth, with their pasturelands. All their cities according to their families were thirteen.
61 And to the rest of the Kohathites ten cities were given by lot out of the family of the tribe [of Ephraim and of Dan and], of the half-tribe, the half of Manasseh. [Josh. 21:5.]
62 To the Gershomites, according to their families, [were allotted] thirteen cities out of the tribes of Issachar, Asher, Naphtali, and Manasseh in Bashan.
63 To the Merarites were given by lot, according to their families, twelve cities out of the tribes of Reuben, Gad, and Zebulun.
64 And the Israelites gave to the Levites these cities with their pasturelands.
65 They gave by lot out of the tribes of Judah, Simeon, and Benjamin these cities whose names are mentioned.
66 Some of the families of the Kohathites had cities in the allotted territory out of the tribe of Ephraim.
67 And [the Ephraimites] gave to [the Levites] the city of refuge, Shechem in the hill country of Ephraim; also Gezer, [both] with their suburbs *and* pasturelands;
68 Jokmeam, Beth-horon,
69 Aijalon, and Gath-rimmon, with their suburbs *and* pasturelands;
70 And out of the half-tribe of Manasseh [these cities], with their suburbs *and* pasturelands: Aner and Bileam, for the rest of the families of the sons of Kohath.
71 To the Gershomites were given out of the half-tribe of Manasseh: Golan in Bashan and Ashtaroth, with their suburbs *and* pasturelands;
72 Out of the tribe of Issachar, with their suburbs *and* pasturelands: Kedesh, Daberath,
73 Ramoth, and Anem;
74 Out of the tribe of Asher, with their suburbs *and* pasturelands: Mashal, Abdon,
75 Hukok, and Rehob;
76 And out of the tribe of Naphtali, with their suburbs *and* pasturelands: Kedesh in Galilee, Hammon, and Kiriathaim.
77 To the rest of the Merarites were given from the tribe of Zebulun: Rimmono and Tabor, with their suburbs *and* pasturelands;

---

*a 57 See Joshua 21:13; Hebrew given the cities of refuge: Hebron, Libnah.*
*b 59 Syriac (see also Septuagint and Joshua 21:16); Hebrew does not have Juttah.  c 60 See Joshua 21:17; Hebrew does not have Gibeon.*
*d 67 See Joshua 21:21; Hebrew given the cities of refuge: Shechem, Gezer.*
*e 77 See Septuagint and Joshua 21:34; Hebrew does not have Jokneam, Kartah.*

## New International Version

78 from the tribe of Reuben across the Jordan east of Jericho

they received Bezer in the wilderness, Jahzah, 79 Kedemoth and Mephaath, together with their pasturelands;

80 and from the tribe of Gad

they received Ramoth in Gilead, Mahanaim, 81 Heshbon and Jazer, together with their pasturelands.

### Issachar

**7** The sons of Issachar:
Tola, Puah, Jashub and Shimron—four in all.
2 The sons of Tola:
Uzzi, Rephaiah, Jeriel, Jahmai, Ibsam and Samuel—heads of their families. During the reign of David, the descendants of Tola listed as fighting men in their genealogy numbered 22,600.
3 The son of Uzzi:
Izrahiah.
The sons of Izrahiah:
Michael, Obadiah, Joel and Ishiah. All five of them were chiefs. 4 According to their family genealogy, they had 36,000 men ready for battle, for they had many wives and children.
5 The relatives who were fighting men belonging to all the clans of Issachar, as listed in their genealogy, were 87,000 in all.

### Benjamin

6 Three sons of Benjamin:
Bela, Beker and Jediael.
7 The sons of Bela:
Ezbon, Uzzi, Uzziel, Jerimoth and Iri, heads of families—five in all. Their genealogical record listed 22,034 fighting men.
8 The sons of Beker:
Zemirah, Joash, Eliezer, Elioenai, Omri, Jeremoth, Abijah, Anathoth and Alemeth. All these were the sons of Beker. 9 Their genealogical record listed the heads of families and 20,200 fighting men.
10 The son of Jediael:
Bilhan.
The sons of Bilhan:
Jeush, Benjamin, Ehud, Kenaanah, Zethan, Tarshish and Ahishahar. 11 All these sons of Jediael were heads of families. There were 17,200 fighting men ready to go out to war.
12 The Shuppites and Huppites were the descendants of Ir, and the Hushites*a* the descendants of Aher.

### Naphtali

13 The sons of Naphtali:
Jahziel, Guni, Jezer and Shillem*b*—the descendants of Bilhah.

### Manasseh

14 The descendants of Manasseh:
Asriel was his descendant through his Aramean concubine. She gave birth to Makir the father of Gilead. 15 Makir took a wife from among the Huppites and Shuppites. His sister's name was Maakah.
Another descendant was named Zelophehad, who had only daughters.
16 Makir's wife Maakah gave birth to a son and named him Peresh. His brother was named Sheresh, and his sons were Ulam and Rakem.

## Amplified Bible

78 On the other side of the Jordan, on the east side by Jericho, the Levites were given out of the tribe of Reuben [these cities], with their suburbs *and* pasturelands: Bezer in the wilderness, Jahzah, 79 Kedemoth, and Mephaath; 80 Out of the tribe of Gad [these cities], with their suburbs *and* pasturelands: Ramoth in Gilead, Mahanaim, 81 Heshbon, and Jazer.

**7** The sons of Issachar were: Tola, Puah, Jashub, and Shimron—four in all.
2 The sons of Tola: Uzzi, Rephaiah, Jeriel, Jahmai, Ibsam, Shemuel (Samuel)—heads of their fathers' houses, descendants of Tola. They were mighty men of valor in their generations; their number in David's days was 22,600.
3 The son of Uzzi: Izrahiah. The sons of Izrahiah: Michael, Obadiah, Joel, Isshiah—five, all of them chief men.
4 And with them by their generations according to their fathers' houses were units of the army for war, 36,000, for they had many wives and children [with them].
5 Their kinsmen from all the families of Issachar, mighty men of valor, registered by genealogies, were in all 87,000.
6 The sons of Benjamin: Bela, Becher, and Jediael—three in all.
7 The sons of Bela: Ezbon, Uzzi, Uzziel, Jerimoth, and Iri—five, heads of the houses of their fathers, mighty men of valor. By their genealogies they numbered 22,034.
8 The sons of Becher: Zemirah, Joash, Eliezer, Elioenai, Omri, Jeremoth, Abijah, Anathoth, and Alemeth, all sons of Becher.
9 The number of them by their genealogies by generations, as heads of their fathers' houses, mighty warriors, was 20,200.
10 The son of Jediael: Bilhan. The sons of Bilhan: Jeush, Benjamin, Ehud, Chenaanah, Zethan, Tarshish, and Ahishahar.
11 All these were the sons of Jediael, according to the heads of their fathers' houses, mighty men of valor, 17,200, able *and* fit for service in war.
12 Shuppim and Huppim were the sons of Ir, and Hushim the son of Aher.
13 The sons of Naphtali: Jahziel, Guni, Jezer, and Shallum, whose [grandmother] was Bilhah.
14 The sons of Manasseh: Ashriel, whom his concubine the Aramitess bore; she bore Machir the father of Gilead.
15 And Machir took as wife the sister of Huppim and Shuppim; her name was Maacah. The name of a second [and later descendant, the first being Gilead], was Zelophehad; and Zelophehad had daughters [only]. [Num. 27:1-7.]
16 Maacah the wife of Machir bore a son; she called his name Peresh. The name of his brother was Sheresh; his sons were Ulam and Rakem.

---

*a* 12 Or *Ir. The sons of Dan: Hushim,* (see Gen. 46:23); Hebrew does not have *The sons of Dan.* *b* 13 Some Hebrew and Septuagint manuscripts (see also Gen. 46:24 and Num. 26:49); most Hebrew manuscripts *Shallum*

## New International Version

[17] The son of Ulam:

Bedan.

These were the sons of Gilead son of Makir, the son of Manasseh. [18] His sister Hammoleketh gave birth to Ishhod, Abiezer and Mahlah.

[19] The sons of Shemida were:

Ahian, Shechem, Likhi and Aniam.

### Ephraim

[20] The descendants of Ephraim:

Shuthelah, Bered his son,

Tahath his son, Eleadah his son,

Tahath his son, [21] Zabad his son

and Shuthelah his son.

Ezer and Elead were killed by the native-born men of Gath, when they went down to seize their livestock. [22] Their father Ephraim mourned for them many days, and his relatives came to comfort him. [23] Then he made love to his wife again, and she became pregnant and gave birth to a son. He named him Beriah,[a] because there had been misfortune in his family. [24] His daughter was Sheerah, who built Lower and Upper Beth Horon as well as Uzzen Sheerah.

[25] Rephah was his son, Resheph his son,[b]

Telah his son, Tahan his son,

[26] Ladan his son, Ammihud his son,

Elishama his son, [27] Nun his son

and Joshua his son.

[28] Their lands and settlements included Bethel and its surrounding villages, Naaran to the east, Gezer and its villages to the west, and Shechem and its villages all the way to Ayyah and its villages. [29] Along the borders of Manasseh were Beth Shan, Taanach, Megiddo and Dor, together with their villages. The descendants of Joseph son of Israel lived in these towns.

### Asher

[30] The sons of Asher:

Imnah, Ishvah, Ishvi and Beriah. Their sister was Serah.

[31] The sons of Beriah:

Heber and Malkiel, who was the father of Birzaith.

[32] Heber was the father of Japhlet, Shomer and Hotham and of their sister Shua.

[33] The sons of Japhlet:

Pasak, Bimhal and Ashvath.

These were Japhlet's sons.

[34] The sons of Shomer:

Ahi, Rohgah,[c] Hubbah and Aram.

[35] The sons of his brother Helem:

Zophah, Imna, Shelesh and Amal.

[36] The sons of Zophah:

Suah, Harnepher, Shual, Beri, Imrah, [37] Bezer, Hod, Shamma, Shilshah, Ithran[d] and Beera.

[38] The sons of Jether:

Jephunneh, Pispah and Ara.

[39] The sons of Ulla:

Arah, Hanniel and Rizia.

[40] All these were descendants of Asher—heads of families, choice men, brave warriors and outstanding leaders. The number of men ready for battle, as listed in their genealogy, was 26,000.

### The Genealogy of Saul the Benjamite

**8** Benjamin was the father of Bela his firstborn,
Ashbel the second son, Aharah the third,
[2] Nohah the fourth and Rapha the fifth.
[3] The sons of Bela were:

## Amplified Bible

[17] The son of Ulam: Bedan. These were the sons of Gilead son of Machir, the son of Manasseh.

[18] His sister Hammolecheth bore Ishbod, Abiezer, and Mahlah.

[19] The sons of Shemida were: Ahian, Shechem, Likhi, and Aniam.

[20] The sons of Ephraim: Shuthelah, Bered his son, Tahath [I] his son, Eleadah his son, Tahath [II] his son,

[21] Zabad his son, and Shuthelah his son. [During Ephraim's lifetime, his sons] Ezer and Elead were slain by men of Gath born in the land, who had come down to steal the cattle [of the Ephraimites, probably before the Israelites left Egypt].

[22] And Ephraim their father mourned many days, and his brethren came to comfort him.

[23] Then his wife conceived and bore a son, and he called his name Beriah [in evil], because calamity had befallen his house.

[24] [Beriah's] daughter was Sheerah, who built both Lower and Upper Beth-horon, and also Uzzen-sheerah.

[25] Rephah was his son, and Resheph [his son]; Resheph's son was Telah, Tahan his son,

[26] Ladan his son, Ammihud his son, Elishama his son,

[27] Nun his son, Joshua [Moses' successor] his son.

[28] And their possessions and settlements were Bethel and its towns, and eastward Naaran, and westward Gezer, and Shechem, and as far as Azzah (Gaza) with all their towns,

[29] And along the borders of the Manassites, Beth-shean, Taanach, Megiddo, Dor, with all their towns. In these dwelt the sons of Joseph son of Israel.

[30] The sons of Asher: Imnah, Ishvah, Ishvi, Beriah; and Serah their sister.

[31] The sons of Beriah: Heber and Malchiel, who was the father of Birzaith.

[32] Heber was the father of Japhlet, Shomer, Hotham, and Shua their sister.

[33] The sons of Japhlet: Pasach, Bimhal, and Ashvath. These were the sons of Japhlet.

[34] The sons of Shemer (Shomer) his brother: Rohgah, Jehubbah, and Aram.

[35] The sons of his brother Helem (Hotham): Zophah, Imna, Shelesh, and Amal.

[36] The sons of Zophah: Suah, Harnepher, Shual, Beri, Imrah,

[37] Bezer, Hod, Shamma, Shilshah, Ithran, and Beera.

[38] The sons of Jether: Jephunneh, Pispa, and Ara.

[39] The sons of Ulla: Arah, Hanniel, and Rizia.

[40] All these were offspring of Asher, heads of their fathers' houses, approved men, mighty warriors, chief of the princes. Their number enrolled by genealogies for service in war, was 26,000 men.

**8** Benjamin was the father of Bela his firstborn, Ashbel the second, Aharah the third,
[2] Nohah the fourth, and Rapha the fifth.
[3] Bela's sons were: Addar, Gera, Abihud,

---

[a] 23 *Beriah* sounds like the Hebrew for *misfortune.* [b] 25 Some Septuagint manuscripts; Hebrew does not have *his son.* [c] 34 Or *of his brother Shomer: Rohgah* [d] 37 Possibly a variant of *Jether*

## New International Version

Addar, Gera, Abihud,[a] 4Abishua, Naaman, Ahoah,
5Gera, Shephuphan and Huram.

6These were the descendants of Ehud, who were heads of families of those living in Geba and were deported to Manahath:

7Naaman, Ahijah, and Gera, who deported them and who was the father of Uzza and Ahihud.

8Sons were born to Shaharaim in Moab after he had divorced his wives Hushim and Baara. 9By his wife Hodesh he had Jobab, Zibia, Mesha, Malkam, 10Jeuz, Sakia and Mirmah. These were his sons, heads of families. 11By Hushim he had Abitub and Elpaal.

12The sons of Elpaal:

Eber, Misham, Shemed (who built Ono and Lod with its surrounding villages), 13and Beriah and Shema, who were heads of families of those living in Aijalon and who drove out the inhabitants of Gath.

14Ahio, Shashak, Jeremoth, 15Zebadiah, Arad, Eder, 16Michael, Ishpah and Joha were the sons of Beriah.

17Zebadiah, Meshullam, Hizki, Heber, 18Ishmerai, Izliah and Jobab were the sons of Elpaal.

19Jakim, Zikri, Zabdi, 20Elienai, Zillethai, Eliel, 21Adaiah, Beraiah and Shimrath were the sons of Shimei.

22Ishpan, Eber, Eliel, 23Abdon, Zikri, Hanan, 24Hananiah, Elam, Anthothijah, 25Iphdeiah and Penuel were the sons of Shashak.

26Shamsherai, Sheariah, Athaliah, 27Jareshiah, Elijah and Zikri were the sons of Jeroham.

28All these were heads of families, chiefs as listed in their genealogy, and they lived in Jerusalem.

29Jeiel[b] the father[c] of Gibeon lived in Gibeon. His wife's name was Maakah, 30and his firstborn son was Abdon, followed by Zur, Kish, Baal, Ner,[d] Nadab, 31Gedor, Ahio, Zeker 32and Mikloth, who was the father of Shimeah. They too lived near their relatives in Jerusalem.

33Ner was the father of Kish, Kish the father of Saul, and Saul the father of Jonathan, Malki-Shua, Abinadab and Esh-Baal.[e]

34The son of Jonathan:

Merib-Baal,[f] who was the father of Micah.

35The sons of Micah:

Pithon, Melek, Tarea and Ahaz.

36Ahaz was the father of Jehoaddah, Jehoaddah was the father of Alemeth, Azmaveth and Zimri, and Zimri was the father of Moza. 37Moza was the father of Binea; Raphah was his son, Eleasah his son and Azel his son.

38Azel had six sons, and these were their names: Azrikam, Bokeru, Ishmael, Sheariah, Obadiah and Hanan. All these were the sons of Azel.

39The sons of his brother Eshek:

Ulam his firstborn, Jeush the second son and Eliphelet the third. 40The sons of Ulam were brave warriors who could handle the bow. They had many sons and grandsons—150 in all.

All these were the descendants of Benjamin.

## Amplified Bible

4Abishua, Naaman, Ahoah,
5Gera, Shephuphan, and Huram.

6The sons of Ehud: These are the heads of the fathers' houses of the inhabitants of Geba; they were exiled to Manahath:

7Naaman, Ahijah, and Gera, that is, Heglam, who was the father of Uzza and Ahihud.

8Shaharaim had sons in the country of Moab after he had [divorced and] sent away Hushim and Baara his wives.

9And by Hodesh his [Moabitish] wife he was the father of Jobab, Zibia, Mesha, Malcam,

10Jeuz, Sachia, and Mirmah. These were his sons, heads of fathers' houses.

11By Hushim [divorced] he had had sons: Abitub and Elpaal.

12The sons of Elpaal: Eber, Misham, and Shemed, who built Ono and Lod with its towns,

13And Beriah and Shema, who were heads of fathers' houses of the inhabitants of Aijalon, who put to flight the inhabitants of Gath.

14And Ahio, Shashak, and Jeremoth.

15The sons of Beriah: Zebadiah, Arad, Eder,

16Michael, Ishpah, and Joha.

17Zebadiah, Meshullam, Hizki, Heber,

18Ishmerai, Izliah, and Jobab were the sons of Elpaal.

19Jakim, Zichri, Zabdi,

20Elienai, Zillethai, Eliel,

21Adaiah, Beraiah, and Shimrath were the sons of Shimei.

22Ishpan, Eber, Eliel,

23Abdon, Zichri, Hanan,

24Hananiah, Elam, Anthothijah,

25Iphdeiah, and Penuel were the sons of Shashak.

26Shamsherai, Sheariah, Athaliah,

27Jaareshiah, Elijah, and Zichri were the sons of Jeroham.

28These were heads of the fathers' houses, according to their generations, chief men. These dwelt in Jerusalem.

29At Gibeon dwelt [Jeiel] the father of Gibeon, whose wife's name was Maacah.

30His firstborn son was Abdon, then Zur, Kish, Baal, Nadab,

31Gedor, Ahio, Zecher,

32And Mikloth the father of Shimeah. These dwelt together opposite their kinsmen in Jerusalem.

33Ner was the father of Kish, and Kish of [King] Saul the father of Jonathan, Malchi-shua, Abinadab, and Esh-baal (Ish-bosheth).

34The son of Jonathan was Merib-baal (Mephibosheth) the father of Micah.

35The sons of Micah: Pithon, Melech, Tarea, and Ahaz.

36Ahaz was the father of Jehoaddah, and Jehoaddah of Alemeth, Azmaveth, and Zimri; Zimri was the father of Moza.

37Moza was the father of Binea; Raphah was his son, Eleasah his son, Azel his son.

38Azel had six sons: Azrikam, Bocheru, Ishmael, Sheariah, Obadiah, and Hanan. All these were the sons of Azel.

39The sons of Eshek his brother: Ulam his firstborn, Jehush the second, Eliphelet the third.

40The sons of Ulam were mighty warriors, archers, with many sons and grandsons—150 in all. All these were Benjamites.

a 3 Or Gera the father of Ehud    b 29 Some Septuagint manuscripts (see also 9:35); Hebrew does not have Jeiel.    c 29 Father may mean civic leader or military leader.    d 30 Some Septuagint manuscripts (see also 9:36); Hebrew does not have Ner.    e 33 Also known as Ish-Bosheth
f 34 Also known as Mephibosheth

| New International Version | Amplified Bible |
|---|---|

**New International Version**

**9** All Israel was listed in the genealogies recorded in the book of the kings of Israel and Judah. They were taken captive to Babylon because of their unfaithfulness.

### The People in Jerusalem
2 Now the first to resettle on their own property in their own towns were some Israelites, priests, Levites and temple servants.
3 Those from Judah, from Benjamin, and from Ephraim and Manasseh who lived in Jerusalem were:
4 Uthai son of Ammihud, the son of Omri, the son of Imri, the son of Bani, a descendant of Perez son of Judah.
5 Of the Shelanites<sup>a</sup>:
Asaiah the firstborn and his sons.
6 Of the Zerahites:
Jeuel.
The people from Judah numbered 690.
7 Of the Benjamites:
Sallu son of Meshullam, the son of Hodaviah, the son of Hassenuah;
8 Ibneiah son of Jeroham; Elah son of Uzzi, the son of Mikri; and Meshullam son of Shephatiah, the son of Reuel, the son of Ibnijah.
9 The people from Benjamin, as listed in their genealogy, numbered 956. All these men were heads of their families.
10 Of the priests:
Jedaiah; Jehoiarib; Jakin;
11 Azariah son of Hilkiah, the son of Meshullam, the son of Zadok, the son of Meraioth, the son of Ahitub, the official in charge of the house of God;
12 Adaiah son of Jeroham, the son of Pashhur, the son of Malkijah; and Maasai son of Adiel, the son of Jahzerah, the son of Meshullam, the son of Meshillemith, the son of Immer.
13 The priests, who were heads of families, numbered 1,760. They were able men, responsible for ministering in the house of God.
14 Of the Levites:
Shemaiah son of Hasshub, the son of Azrikam, the son of Hashabiah, a Merarite; 15 Bakbakkar, Heresh, Galal and Mattaniah son of Mika, the son of Zikri, the son of Asaph; 16 Obadiah son of Shemaiah, the son of Galal, the son of Jeduthun; and Berekiah son of Asa, the son of Elkanah, who lived in the villages of the Netophathites.
17 The gatekeepers:
Shallum, Akkub, Talmon, Ahiman and their fellow Levites, Shallum their chief 18 being stationed at the King's Gate on the east, up to the present time. These were the gatekeepers belonging to the camp of the Levites. 19 Shallum son of Kore, the son of Ebiasaph, the son of Korah, and his fellow gatekeepers from his family (the Korahites) were responsible for guarding the thresholds of the tent just as their ancestors had been responsible for guarding the entrance to the dwelling of the LORD. 20 In earlier times Phinehas son of Eleazar was the official in charge of the gatekeepers, and the LORD was with him. 21 Zechariah son of Meshelemiah was the gatekeeper at the entrance to the tent of meeting.
22 Altogether, those chosen to be gatekeepers at the thresholds numbered 212. They were registered by genealogy in their villages. The gatekeepers had been assigned to their positions of trust by David and Samuel the seer.
23 They and their descendants were in charge of guarding the gates of the house of the LORD—the house called

**Amplified Bible**

**9** So all Israel was enrolled by genealogies; and they are written in the Book of the Kings of Israel. And Judah was carried away captive to Babylon for their unfaithfulness to God.
2 Now the first [of the returned exiles] to dwell again in their possessions in the cities of Israel were the priests, Levites, and the Nethinim [the temple servants].
3 In Jerusalem dwelt some of the people of Judah, Benjamin, Ephraim, and Manasseh:
4 Uthai son of Ammihud, the son of Omri, the son of Imri, the son of Bani, of the sons of Pharez son of Judah.
5 Of the Shilonites: Asaiah the firstborn and his sons.
6 Of the sons of Zerah: Jeuel and their kinsmen, 690.
7 Of the Benjamites: Sallu son of Meshullam, the son of Hodaviah, the son of Hassenuah;
8 Ibneiah son of Jeroham; Elah son of Uzzi, the son of Michri; and Meshullam son of Shephatiah, the son of Reuel, the son of Ibnijah;
9 And their kinsmen, according to their generations, 956. All these were heads of fathers' houses according to their fathers' houses.
10 Of the priests: Jedaiah; Jehoiarib; Jachin;
11 Azariah son of Hilkiah, the son of Meshullam, the son of Zadok, the son of Meraioth, the son of Ahitub, the chief officer of God's house;
12 And Adaiah son of Jeroham, the son of Pashhur, the son of Malchijah; Massai son of Adiel, the son of Jahzerah, the son of Meshullam, the son of Meshillemith, the son of Immer;
13 And their kinsmen, heads of their fathers' houses, 1,760—very able men for the work of the service of the house of God.
14 Of the Levites: Shemaiah son of Hasshub, the son of Azrikam, the son of Hashabiah, of the sons of Merari;
15 And Bakbakkar, Heresh, Galal, and Mattaniah son of Mica, the son of Zichri, the son of Asaph;
16 Obadiah son of Shemaiah, the son of Galal, the son of Jeduthun; and Berechiah son of Asa, the son of Elkanah, who dwelt in the villages of the Netophathites [near Jerusalem].
17 The gatekeepers were: Shallum, Akkub, Talmon, Ahiman, and their kinsmen, Shallum being the chief
18 Who hitherto was assigned to the king's east side gate. They were the gatekeepers of the camp of the Levites.
19 Shallum son of Kore, the son of Ebiasaph, the son of Korah, and his kinsmen of his father's house, the Korahites, were in charge of the work of the service, keepers of the thresholds of the Tent, as their fathers had been in charge of the camp of the Lord, keepers of the entrance.
20 Phinehas son of Eleazar was ruler over them in times past, and the Lord was with him.
21 Zechariah son of Meshelemiah was gatekeeper at the entrance of the Tent of Meeting.
22 All these chosen to be keepers at the thresholds were 212. These were enrolled by their genealogies in their villages [around Jerusalem], these men [whose grandfathers] David and Samuel the seer had established to their office of trust.
23 So they and their sons had oversight of the gates of the Lord's house, that is, the house of the tabernacle, by wards.

---

<sup>a</sup> 5 See Num. 26:20; Hebrew *Shilonites*.

## New International Version

the tent of meeting. 24The gatekeepers were on the four sides: east, west, north and south. 25Their fellow Levites in their villages had to come from time to time and share their duties for seven-day periods. 26But the four principal gatekeepers, who were Levites, were entrusted with the responsibility for the rooms and treasuries in the house of God. 27They would spend the night stationed around the house of God, because they had to guard it; and they had charge of the key for opening it each morning.

28Some of them were in charge of the articles used in the temple service; they counted them when they were brought in and when they were taken out. 29Others were assigned to take care of the furnishings and all the other articles of the sanctuary, as well as the special flour and wine, and the olive oil, incense and spices. 30But some of the priests took care of mixing the spices. 31A Levite named Mattithiah, the firstborn son of Shallum the Korahite, was entrusted with the responsibility for baking the offering bread. 32Some of the Kohathites, their fellow Levites, were in charge of preparing for every Sabbath the bread set out on the table.

33Those who were musicians, heads of Levite families, stayed in the rooms of the temple and were exempt from other duties because they were responsible for the work day and night.

34All these were heads of Levite families, chiefs as listed in their genealogy, and they lived in Jerusalem.

### The Genealogy of Saul

35Jeiel the father[a] of Gibeon lived in Gibeon.

His wife's name was Maakah, 36and his firstborn son was Abdon, followed by Zur, Kish, Baal, Ner, Nadab, 37Gedor, Ahio, Zechariah and Mikloth. 38Mikloth was the father of Shimeam. They too lived near their relatives in Jerusalem.

39Ner was the father of Kish, Kish the father of Saul, and Saul the father of Jonathan, Malki-Shua, Abinadab and Esh-Baal.[b]

40The son of Jonathan:

Merib-Baal,[c] who was the father of Micah.

41The sons of Micah:

Pithon, Melek, Tahrea and Ahaz.[d]

42Ahaz was the father of Jadah, Jadah[e] was the father of Alemeth, Azmaveth and Zimri, and Zimri was the father of Moza. 43Moza was the father of Binea; Rephaiah was his son, Eleasah his son and Azel his son.

44Azel had six sons, and these were their names:

Azrikam, Bokeru, Ishmael, Sheariah, Obadiah and Hanan. These were the sons of Azel.

### Saul Takes His Life

**10** Now the Philistines fought against Israel; the Israelites fled before them, and many fell dead on Mount Gilboa. 2The Philistines were in hot pursuit of Saul and his sons, and they killed his sons Jonathan, Abinadab and Malki-Shua. 3The fighting grew fierce around Saul, and when the archers overtook him, they wounded him.

4Saul said to his armor-bearer, "Draw your sword and run me through, or these uncircumcised fellows will come and abuse me."

But his armor-bearer was terrified and would not do

a 35 *Father* may mean *civic leader* or *military leader.*   b 39 Also known as *Ish-Bosheth*   c 40 Also known as *Mephibosheth*   d 41 Vulgate and Syriac (see also Septuagint and 8:35); Hebrew does not have *and Ahaz.*   e 42 Some Hebrew manuscripts and Septuagint (see also 8:36); most Hebrew manuscripts *Jarah, Jarah*

## Amplified Bible

24The gatekeepers were stationed on the four sides [of the house of the Lord]—on the east, west, north, and south.

25Their brethren in their villages were to come in every seven days to be with them.

26But these Levites, the four chief gatekeepers, were in charge of the chambers and treasuries of the house of God.

27They lodged round about God's house, for the duty [of watching] was theirs, as well as the opening of the house every morning.

28Some of them had charge of the serving utensils, being required to count them when they brought them in or took them out.

29Some of them also were appointed over the furniture and over all the sacred utensils, as well as over the fine flour, wine, oil, frankincense, and spices.

30Other sons of the priests prepared the ointment of spices.

31Mattithiah, one of the Levites, the firstborn of Shallum the Korahite, was responsible for the things baked in pans.

32Of their Kohathite kinsmen, some were to prepare the showbread every Sabbath.

33These are the singers, heads of the fathers' houses of the Levites, dwelling in the temple chambers, free from other service because they were on duty day and night.

34These were heads of fathers' houses of the Levites, according to their generations, chief men, who lived in Jerusalem.

35In Gibeon dwelt the father of Gibeon, Jeiel, whose wife's name was Maacah,

36His firstborn son Abdon, then Zur, Kish, Baal, Ner, Nadab,

37Gedor, Ahio, Zechariah, and Mikloth.

38Mikloth was the father of Shimeam. They also dwelt beside their brethren, opposite their kinsmen in Jerusalem.

39Ner was the father of Kish, Kish of [King] Saul, Saul of Jonathan, Malchi-shua, Abinadab, and Esh-baal.

40The son of Jonathan was Merib-baal (Mephibosheth); Merib-baal was the father of Micah.

41The sons of Micah: Pithon, Melech, Tahrea, and Ahaz.

42Ahaz was the father of Jarah, and Jarah of Alemeth, Azmaveth, and Zimri; Zimri was the father of Moza,

43Moza of Binea; Rephaiah was his son, Eleasah his son, Azel his son.

44Azel had six sons: Azrikam, Bocheru, Ishmael, Sheariah, Obadiah, and Hanan. These were the sons of Azel.

**10** Now the Philistines fought against Israel; and the men of Israel fled from before them and fell slain on Mount Gilboa.

2And the Philistines followed close after Saul and his sons *and* overtook them, and the Philistines slew Jonathan, Abinadab, and Malchi-shua, the sons of Saul.

3And the battle raged about Saul, and the archers found and wounded him.

4Then Saul said to his armor-bearer, Draw your sword and thrust me through with it, lest these uncircumcised come and abuse *and* make sport of me. But his armor-bearer would not, for he was terrified. So Saul took his own sword and fell on it.

## New International Version

it; so Saul took his own sword and fell on it. [5]When the armor-bearer saw that Saul was dead, he too fell on his sword and died. [6]So Saul and his three sons died, and all his house died together.

[7]When all the Israelites in the valley saw that the army had fled and that Saul and his sons had died, they abandoned their towns and fled. And the Philistines came and occupied them.

[8]The next day, when the Philistines came to strip the dead, they found Saul and his sons fallen on Mount Gilboa. [9]They stripped him and took his head and his armor, and sent messengers throughout the land of the Philistines to proclaim the news among their idols and their people. [10]They put his armor in the temple of their gods and hung up his head in the temple of Dagon.

[11]When all the inhabitants of Jabesh Gilead heard what the Philistines had done to Saul, [12]all their valiant men went and took the bodies of Saul and his sons and brought them to Jabesh. Then they buried their bones under the great tree in Jabesh, and they fasted seven days.

[13]Saul died because he was unfaithful to the LORD; he did not keep the word of the LORD and even consulted a medium for guidance, [14]and did not inquire of the LORD. So the LORD put him to death and turned the kingdom over to David son of Jesse.

### David Becomes King Over Israel

**11** All Israel came together to David at Hebron and said, "We are your own flesh and blood. [2]In the past, even while Saul was king, you were the one who led Israel on their military campaigns. And the LORD your God said to you, 'You will shepherd my people Israel, and you will become their ruler.'"

[3]When all the elders of Israel had come to King David at Hebron, he made a covenant with them at Hebron before the LORD, and they anointed David king over Israel, as the LORD had promised through Samuel.

### David Conquers Jerusalem

[4]David and all the Israelites marched to Jerusalem (that is, Jebus). The Jebusites who lived there [5]said to David, "You will not get in here." Nevertheless, David captured the fortress of Zion—which is the City of David.

[6]David had said, "Whoever leads the attack on the Jebusites will become commander-in-chief." Joab son of Zeruiah went up first, and so he received the command.

[7]David then took up residence in the fortress, and so it was called the City of David. [8]He built up the city around it, from the terraces[a] to the surrounding wall, while Joab restored the rest of the city. [9]And David became more and more powerful, because the LORD Almighty was with him.

### David's Mighty Warriors

[10]These were the chiefs of David's mighty warriors—they, together with all Israel, gave his kingship strong support to extend it over the whole land, as the LORD had promised— [11]this is the list of David's mighty warriors:

Jashobeam,[b] a Hakmonite, was chief of the officers[c]; he raised his spear against three hundred men, whom he killed in one encounter.

## Amplified Bible

[5]When his armor-bearer saw that Saul was dead, he also fell on his sword and died.

[6]So Saul died; he and his three sons and all his house died together.

[7]And when all the men of Israel who were in the valley saw that the army had fled and that Saul and his sons were dead, they forsook their cities and fled; and the Philistines came and dwelt in them.

[8]The next day, when the Philistines came to strip the slain, they found Saul and his sons fallen on Mount Gilboa. [9]They stripped [Saul] and took his head and his armor, and sent [them] round about in Philistia to carry the news to their idols and to the people.

[10]And they put [Saul's] armor in the house of their gods and fastened his head in the temple of Dagon.

[11]When all Jabesh-gilead heard all that the Philistines had done to Saul, [12]All the brave men arose, took away the bodies of Saul and his sons, brought them to Jabesh, and buried their bones under the oak in Jabesh; then they fasted seven days. [I Sam. 31:12.]

[13]So Saul died for his trespass against the Lord [in sparing Amalek], for his unfaithfulness in not keeping God's word, and also for consulting [a medium with] a spirit of the dead to inquire pleadingly of it, [14]And inquired not so of the Lord [in earnest penitence]. Therefore the Lord slew him and turned the kingdom over to David son of Jesse. [I Sam. 28:6.]

**11** Then [after the death of Ish-bosheth, Saul's son, who ruled over eleven tribes of Israel for two troubled years after Saul's death] all Israel gathered at Hebron and said to David, Behold, we are your bone and your flesh. [II Sam. 2:8-10.]

[2]In times past, even when Saul was king, it was you who led out and brought in Israel; and the Lord your God said to you, You shall be shepherd of My people Israel, and you shall be prince *and* leader over [them].

[3]So all the elders of Israel came to the king at Hebron, and David made a covenant with them there before the Lord, and they anointed [him] king over Israel, according to the word of the Lord through Samuel. [I Sam. 16:1, 12, 13.]

[4]And David and all Israel went to Jerusalem, that is Jebus, where the Jebusites, the inhabitants of the land, were.

[5]Then the Jebusites said to David, You shall not come in here! But David took the stronghold of Zion, that is, the City of David.

[6]And David said, Whoever smites the Jebusites first shall be chief and commander. Joab son of Zeruiah [David's half sister] went up first, and so he was made chief.

[7]David dwelt in the stronghold; so it was called the City of David.

[8]He built the city from the Millo [a fortification] on around; and Joab repaired *and* revived the rest of the [old Jebusite] city.

[9]And David became greater and greater, for the Lord of hosts was with him.

[10]Now these are the chiefs of David's mighty men, who strongly supported him in his kingdom, together with all Israel, to make him king, according to the word of the Lord concerning Israel.

[11]And this is the number [thirty, and list] of David's mighty men: Jashobeam, a Hachmonite, the chief of the Thirty [captains]. He lifted up his spear against 300, whom he slew at one time.

---

[a] 8 Or *the Millo*  [b] 11 Possibly a variant of *Jashob-Baal*  
[c] 11 Or *Thirty*; some Septuagint manuscripts *Three* (see also 2 Samuel 23:8)

## New International Version

¹²Next to him was Eleazar son of Dodai the Ahohite, one of the three mighty warriors. ¹³He was with David at Pas Dammim when the Philistines gathered there for battle. At a place where there was a field full of barley, the troops fled from the Philistines. ¹⁴But they took their stand in the middle of the field. They defended it and struck the Philistines down, and the LORD brought about a great victory.

¹⁵Three of the thirty chiefs came down to David to the rock at the cave of Adullam, while a band of Philistines was encamped in the Valley of Rephaim. ¹⁶At that time David was in the stronghold, and the Philistine garrison was at Bethlehem. ¹⁷David longed for water and said, "Oh, that someone would get me a drink of water from the well near the gate of Bethlehem!" ¹⁸So the Three broke through the Philistine lines, drew water from the well near the gate of Bethlehem and carried it back to David. But he refused to drink it; instead, he poured it out to the LORD. ¹⁹"God forbid that I should do this!" he said. "Should I drink the blood of these men who went at the risk of their lives?" Because they risked their lives to bring it back, David would not drink it.

Such were the exploits of the three mighty warriors.

²⁰Abishai the brother of Joab was chief of the Three. He raised his spear against three hundred men, whom he killed, and so he became as famous as the Three. ²¹He was doubly honored above the Three and became their commander, even though he was not included among them.

²²Benaiah son of Jehoiada, a valiant fighter from Kabzeel, performed great exploits. He struck down Moab's two mightiest warriors. He also went down into a pit on a snowy day and killed a lion. ²³And he struck down an Egyptian who was five cubits*a* tall. Although the Egyptian had a spear like a weaver's rod in his hand, Benaiah went against him with a club. He snatched the spear from the Egyptian's hand and killed him with his own spear. ²⁴Such were the exploits of Benaiah son of Jehoiada; he too was as famous as the three mighty warriors. ²⁵He was held in greater honor than any of the Thirty, but he was not included among the Three. And David put him in charge of his bodyguard.

²⁶The mighty warriors were:
    Asahel the brother of Joab,
    Elhanan son of Dodo from Bethlehem,
²⁷Shammoth the Harorite,
    Helez the Pelonite,
²⁸Ira son of Ikkesh from Tekoa,
    Abiezer from Anathoth,
²⁹Sibbekai the Hushathite,
    Ilai the Ahohite,
³⁰Maharai the Netophathite,
    Heled son of Baanah the Netophathite,
³¹Ithai son of Ribai from Gibeah in Benjamin,
    Benaiah the Pirathonite,
³²Hurai from the ravines of Gaash,
    Abiel the Arbathite,
³³Azmaveth the Baharumite,
    Eliahba the Shaalbonite,
³⁴the sons of Hashem the Gizonite,
    Jonathan son of Shagee the Hararite,
³⁵Ahiam son of Sakar the Hararite,
    Eliphal son of Ur,
³⁶Hepher the Mekerathite,
    Ahijah the Pelonite,
³⁷Hezro the Carmelite,
    Naarai son of Ezbai,
³⁸Joel the brother of Nathan,
    Mibhar son of Hagri,
³⁹Zelek the Ammonite,
    Naharai the Berothite, the armor-bearer of Joab son of Zeruiah,

## Amplified Bible

¹²Next to him in rank was Eleazar son of Dodo the Ahohite, one of the three mighty men. ¹³He was with David at Pas-dammim [where David had long before slain Goliath], and there the Philistines were gathered for battle, where there was a plot of ground full of barley *or* lentils; and the men [of Israel] fled before the Philistines. ¹⁴And Eleazar [one of the Three] stood in the midst of that plot and defended it and slew the Philistines [until his hand was weary, and his hand cleaved to the sword], and the Lord saved by a great victory *and* deliverance. [II Sam. 23:9, 10.]

¹⁵Three of the thirty chief men went down to the rock to David, into the cave of Adullam, and the army of the Philistines was encamped in the Valley of Rephaim.

¹⁶David was then in the stronghold, and the Philistines' garrison was in Bethlehem.

¹⁷And David longingly said, Oh, that someone would give me water to drink from the well of Bethlehem which is by the gate!

¹⁸Then the Three [mighty men] broke through the camp of the Philistines and drew water out of the well of Bethlehem which was by the gate and brought it to David. But David would not drink it; he poured it out to the Lord,

¹⁹And said, My God forbid that I should do this thing. Shall I drink the blood of these men who have put their lives in jeopardy? For at the risk of their lives they brought it. So he would not drink it. These things did these three mighty men.

²⁰Abishai the brother of Joab was chief of the Three. For he lifted up his spear against 300 and slew them, and was named among the Three.

²¹Of the Three [in the second rank] he was more renowned than the two, and became their captain; however, he attained not to the first three.

²²Benaiah son of Jehoiada, whose father was a valiant man of Kabzeel, had done mighty deeds. He slew the two sons of Ariel of Moab. Also he went down and slew a lion in a pit in time of snow.

²³He slew an Egyptian also, a man of great stature, five cubits tall. The Egyptian held a spear like a weaver's beam, and [Benaiah] went to him with a staff and plucked the spear out of the Egyptian's hand and slew him with the man's own spear.

²⁴These things did Benaiah son of Jehoiada, and won a name beside the three mighty men.

²⁵He was renowned among the Thirty, but he did not attain to the rank of the first three. David put him over his guard *and* council.

²⁶Also the mighty men of the armies were: Asahel the brother of Joab, Elhanan son of Dodo of Bethlehem,
²⁷Shammoth of Harod, Helez the Pelonite,
²⁸Ira son of Ikkesh of Tekoa, Abiezer of Anathoth,
²⁹Sibbecai the Hushathite, Ilai the Ahohite,
³⁰Maharai of Netophah, Heled son of Baanah of Netophah,
³¹Ithai son of Ribai of Gibeah of the Benjamites, Benaiah of Pirathon,
³²Hurai of the brooks of Gaash, Abiel the Arbathite,
³³Azmaveth of Baharum, Eliahba of Shaalbon,
³⁴The sons of Hashem the Gizonite, Jonathan son of Shagee the Hararite,
³⁵Ahiam son of Sacar the Hararite, Eliphal son of Ur,
³⁶Hepher the Mecherathite, Ahijah the Pelonite,
³⁷Hezro of Carmel, Naarai son of Ezbai,
³⁸Joel the brother of Nathan, Mibhar son of Hagri,
³⁹Zelek the Ammonite, Naharai the Berothite, the armor-bearer of Joab son of Zeruiah [David's half sister],

---

*a 23* That is, about 7 feet 6 inches or about 2.3 meters

## New International Version

40 Ira the Ithrite,
Gareb the Ithrite,
41 Uriah the Hittite,
Zabad son of Ahlai,
42 Adina son of Shiza the Reubenite, who was chief of the Reubenites, and the thirty with him,
43 Hanan son of Maakah,
Joshaphat the Mithnite,
44 Uzzia the Ashterathite,
Shama and Jeiel the sons of Hotham the Aroerite,
45 Jediael son of Shimri,
his brother Joha the Tizite,
46 Eliel the Mahavite,
Jeribai and Joshaviah the sons of Elnaam,
Ithmah the Moabite,
47 Eliel, Obed and Jaasiel the Mezobaite.

### Warriors Join David

**12** These were the men who came to David at Ziklag, while he was banished from the presence of Saul son of Kish (they were among the warriors who helped him in battle; 2 they were armed with bows and were able to shoot arrows or to sling stones right-handed or left-handed; they were relatives of Saul from the tribe of Benjamin):

3 Ahiezer their chief and Joash the sons of Shemaah the Gibeathite; Jeziel and Pelet the sons of Azmaveth; Berakah, Jehu the Anathothite, 4 and Ishmaiah the Gibeonite, a mighty warrior among the Thirty, who was a leader of the Thirty; Jeremiah, Jahaziel, Johanan, Jozabad the Gederathite,ᵃ 5 Eluzai, Jerimoth, Bealiah, Shemariah and Shephatiah the Haruphite; 6 Elkanah, Ishiah, Azarel, Joezer and Jashobeam the Korahites; 7 and Joelah and Zebadiah the sons of Jeroham from Gedor.

8 Some Gadites defected to David at his stronghold in the wilderness. They were brave warriors, ready for battle and able to handle the shield and spear. Their faces were the faces of lions, and they were as swift as gazelles in the mountains.

9 Ezer was the chief,
Obadiah the second in command, Eliab the third,
10 Mishmannah the fourth, Jeremiah the fifth,
11 Attai the sixth, Eliel the seventh,
12 Johanan the eighth, Elzabad the ninth,
13 Jeremiah the tenth and Makbannai the eleventh.

14 These Gadites were army commanders; the least was a match for a hundred, and the greatest for a thousand. 15 It was they who crossed the Jordan in the first month when it was overflowing all its banks, and they put to flight everyone living in the valleys, to the east and to the west.

16 Other Benjamites and some men from Judah also came to David in his stronghold. 17 David went out to meet them and said to them, "If you have come to me in peace to help me, I am ready for you to join me. But if you have come to betray me to my enemies when my hands are free from violence, may the God of our ancestors see it and judge you."

18 Then the Spirit came on Amasai, chief of the Thirty, and he said:

"We are yours, David!
We are with you, son of Jesse!
Success, success to you,
and success to those who help you,
for your God will help you."

So David received them and made them leaders of his raiding bands.

## Amplified Bible

40 Ira the Ithrite, Gareb the Ithrite,
41 Uriah the Hittite [Bathsheba's husband], Zabad son of Ahlai,
42 Adina son of Shiza, a leader of the Reubenites, and thirty heroes with him,
43 Hanan son of Maacah, and Joshaphat the Mithnite,
44 Uzzia the Ashterathite, Shama and Jeiel the sons of Hotham the Aroerite,
45 Jediael son of Shimri, and Joha his brother, the Tizite,
46 Eliel the Mahavite, Jeribai and Joshaviah sons of Elnaam, Ithmah the Moabite,
47 Eliel, Obed, and Jaasiel the Mezobaite.

**12** These are the ones who came to David at Ziklag, while he yet concealed himself because of Saul son of Kish; they were among the mighty men, his helpers in war.

2 They were bowmen and could use the right hand or the left to sling stones or shoot arrows from the bow; they were of Saul's kinsmen of Benjamin.

3 The chief was Ahiezer and then Joash the sons of Shemaah of Gibeah; Jeziel and Pelet the sons of Azmaveth; Beracah, and Jehu of Anathoth,
4 Ishmaiah of Gibeon, a mighty man among the Thirty and a [leader] over them; Jeremiah, Jahaziel, Johanan, Jozabad of Gederah,
5 Eluzai, Jerimoth, Bealiah, Shemariah, Shephatiah the Haruphite;
6 Elkanah, Isshiah, Azarel, Joezer, and Jashobeam, the Korahites;
7 Joelah and Zebadiah the sons of Jeroham of Gedor.

8 Of the Gadites there went over to David to the stronghold in the wilderness men of might, men trained for war who could handle shield and spear, whose faces were like the faces of lions, and who were swift as gazelles on the mountains:

9 Ezer the chief, Obadiah the second, Eliab the third,
10 Mishmannah the fourth, Jeremiah the fifth,
11 Attai the sixth, Eliel the seventh,
12 Johanan the eighth, Elzabad the ninth,
13 Jeremiah the tenth, Machbannai the eleventh.

14 These Gadites were officers of the army. The lesser was equal to *and* over a hundred, and the greater equal to *and* over a thousand.

15 These are the men who went over the Jordan in the first month when it had overflowed all its banks, and put to flight all those in the valleys, east and west.

16 There came some of the men of Benjamin and Judah to the stronghold to David.

17 David went out to meet them and said to them, If you have come peaceably to me to help me, my heart shall be knit to you; but if you have come to betray me to my adversaries, although there is no violence *or* wrong in my hands, may the God of our fathers look upon and rebuke you.

18 Then the Spirit came upon Amasai, who was chief of the captains, and he said, Yours we are, David, and on your side, you son of Jesse! Peace, peace be to you, and peace be to your helpers, for your God helps you. Then David received them and made them officers of his troops.

---

ᵃ 4 In Hebrew texts the second half of this verse (*Jeremiah . . . Gederathite*) is numbered 12:5, and 12:5-40 is numbered 12:6-41.

## New International Version

19Some of the tribe of Manasseh defected to David when he went with the Philistines to fight against Saul. (He and his men did not help the Philistines because, after consultation, their rulers sent him away. They said, "It will cost us our heads if he deserts to his master Saul.") 20When David went to Ziklag, these were the men of Manasseh who defected to him: Adnah, Jozabad, Jediael, Michael, Jozabad, Elihu and Zillethai, leaders of units of a thousand in Manasseh. 21They helped David against raiding bands, for all of them were brave warriors, and they were commanders in his army. 22Day after day men came to help David, until he had a great army, like the army of God.a

### Others Join David at Hebron

23These are the numbers of the men armed for battle who came to David at Hebron to turn Saul's kingdom over to him, as the LORD had said:
24from Judah, carrying shield and spear—6,800 armed for battle;
25from Simeon, warriors ready for battle—7,100;
26from Levi—4,600, 27including Jehoiada, leader of the family of Aaron, with 3,700 men, 28and Zadok, a brave young warrior, with 22 officers from his family;
29from Benjamin, Saul's tribe—3,000, most of whom had remained loyal to Saul's house until then;
30from Ephraim, brave warriors, famous in their own clans—20,800;
31from half the tribe of Manasseh, designated by name to come and make David king—18,000;
32from Issachar, men who understood the times and knew what Israel should do—200 chiefs, with all their relatives under their command;
33from Zebulun, experienced soldiers prepared for battle with every type of weapon, to help David with undivided loyalty—50,000;
34from Naphtali—1,000 officers, together with 37,000 men carrying shields and spears;
35from Dan, ready for battle—28,600;
36from Asher, experienced soldiers prepared for battle—40,000;
37and from east of the Jordan, from Reuben, Gad and the half-tribe of Manasseh, armed with every type of weapon—120,000.
38All these were fighting men who volunteered to serve in the ranks. They came to Hebron fully determined to make David king over all Israel. All the rest of the Israelites were also of one mind to make David king. 39The men spent three days there with David, eating and drinking, for their families had supplied provisions for them. 40Also, their neighbors from as far away as Issachar, Zebulun and Naphtali came bringing food on donkeys, camels, mules and oxen. There were plentiful supplies of flour, fig cakes, raisin cakes, wine, olive oil, cattle and sheep, for there was joy in Israel.

### Bringing Back the Ark

**13** David conferred with each of his officers, the commanders of thousands and commanders of hundreds. 2He then said to the whole assembly of Israel, "If it seems good to you and if it is the will of the LORD our

## Amplified Bible

19Some of the men of Manasseh deserted to David when he came with the Philistines for the battle against Saul. But [David's] men did not actually fight with them, for the lords of the Philistines, upon advisement, sent him away, saying, He will desert to his master Saul at the risk of our heads. [I Sam. 29:2-9.]
20As David went to Ziklag, there deserted to him of Manasseh: Adnah, Jozabad, Jediael, Michael, Jozabad, Elihu, and Zillethai, chiefs of thousands in Manasseh.
21They helped David against the band of raiders, for they were all mighty men of courage, and [all seven] became commanders in [his] army.
22For at that time day by day men kept coming to David to help him, until there was a great army, like the army of God.
23These are the numbers of the armed divisions who came to David at Hebron to turn the kingdom of Saul to him, according to the word of the Lord:
24Those of Judah, who bore shield and spear, were 6,800 armed for war;
25Those of Simeon, mighty and brave warriors, 7,100;
26Those of Levi, 4,600—
27Jehoiada was the leader of the Aaronite [priests], and with him were 3,700,
28And Zadok, a young man mighty in valor, and twenty-two captains from his own father's house;
29Of the Benjamites, the kindred of [King] Saul, 3,000—hitherto the majority of them had kept their allegiance [to Saul] and the charge of the house of Saul;
30Of the Ephraimites, 20,800, mighty in valor, famous in their fathers' houses;
31Of the half-tribe of Manasseh, 18,000, who were mentioned by name to come and make David king;
32And of Issachar, men who had understanding of the times to know what Israel ought to do, 200 chiefs; and all their kinsmen were under their command;
33Of Zebulun, 50,000 experienced troops, fitted out with all kinds of weapons and instruments of war that could order and set the battle in array, men not of double purpose but stable and trustworthy.
34Of Naphtali, 1,000 captains, and with them 37,000 [of the rank and file armed] with shield and spear;
35Of Dan, 28,600, men who could set the battle in array;
36Of Asher, men able to go forth to battle, fit for active service, 40,000;
37On the other [the east] side of the Jordan River, of Reuben and Gad and the half-tribe of Manasseh, 120,000 men, armed with all the weapons and instruments of war.
38All these, being men of war arrayed in battle order, came with a perfect and sincere heart to Hebron to make David king over all Israel; and all the rest also of Israel were of one mind to make David king.
39And they were there with David for three days, eating and drinking, for their brethren had prepared for them.
40Also those who were near them from as far as Issachar, Zebulun, and Naphtali brought food on donkeys, camels, mules, and oxen, abundant supplies of meal, cakes of figs, bunches of raisins, wine, oil, oxen, and sheep, for there was joy in Israel.

**13** David consulted the captains of thousands and hundreds, even with every leader.
2And David said to all the assembly of Israel, If it seems good to you and if it is of the Lord our God, let us send

a 22 Or a great and mighty army

## New International Version

God, let us send word far and wide to the rest of our people throughout the territories of Israel, and also to the priests and Levites who are with them in their towns and pasturelands, to come and join us. ³Let us bring the ark of our God back to us, for we did not inquire of[a] it[b] during the reign of Saul." ⁴The whole assembly agreed to do this, because it seemed right to all the people.

⁵So David assembled all Israel, from the Shihor River in Egypt to Lebo Hamath, to bring the ark of God from Kiriath Jearim. ⁶David and all Israel went to Baalah of Judah (Kiriath Jearim) to bring up from there the ark of God the LORD, who is enthroned between the cherubim—the ark that is called by the Name.

⁷They moved the ark of God from Abinadab's house on a new cart, with Uzzah and Ahio guiding it. ⁸David and all the Israelites were celebrating with all their might before God, with songs and with harps, lyres, timbrels, cymbals and trumpets.

⁹When they came to the threshing floor of Kidon, Uzzah reached out his hand to steady the ark, because the oxen stumbled. ¹⁰The LORD's anger burned against Uzzah, and he struck him down because he had put his hand on the ark. So he died there before God.

¹¹Then David was angry because the LORD's wrath had broken out against Uzzah, and to this day that place is called Perez Uzzah.[c]

¹²David was afraid of God that day and asked, "How can I ever bring the ark of God to me?" ¹³He did not take the ark to be with him in the City of David. Instead, he took it to the house of Obed-Edom the Gittite. ¹⁴The ark of God remained with the family of Obed-Edom in his house for three months, and the LORD blessed his household and everything he had.

### David's House and Family

**14** Now Hiram king of Tyre sent messengers to David, along with cedar logs, stonemasons and carpenters to build a palace for him. ²And David knew that the LORD had established him as king over Israel and that his kingdom had been highly exalted for the sake of his people Israel.

³In Jerusalem David took more wives and became the father of more sons and daughters. ⁴These are the names of the children born to him there: Shammua, Shobab, Nathan, Solomon, ⁵Ibhar, Elishua, Elpelet, ⁶Nogah, Nepheg, Japhia, ⁷Elishama, Beeliada[d] and Eliphelet.

### David Defeats the Philistines

⁸When the Philistines heard that David had been anointed king over all Israel, they went up in full force to search for him, but David heard about it and went out to meet them. ⁹Now the Philistines had come and raided the Valley of Rephaim; ¹⁰so David inquired of God: "Shall I go and attack the Philistines? Will you deliver them into my hands?"

The LORD answered him, "Go, I will deliver them into your hands."

¹¹So David and his men went up to Baal Perazim, and there he defeated them. He said, "As waters break out, God has broken out against my enemies by my hand." So that place was called Baal Perazim.[e] ¹²The Philistines had

## Amplified Bible

abroad everywhere to our brethren who are left in all the land of Israel, and with them to the priests and Levites in their cities that have suburbs *and* pasturelands, that they may gather together with us.

³And let us bring again the ark of our God to us, for we did not seek it during the days of Saul.

⁴And all the assembly agreed to do so, for the thing seemed right in the eyes of all the people.

⁵So David gathered all Israel together, from the Shihor, the brook of Egypt [that marked the southeast border of Palestine], to the entrance of Hemath, to bring the ark of God from Kiriath-jearim.

⁶And David and all Israel went up to Baalah, that is, to Kiriath-jearim which belonged to Judah, to bring up from there the ark of God the Lord, which is called by the name of Him Who sits [enthroned] above the cherubim.

⁷And they carried the ark of God on a new cart and brought it out of the house of Abinadab, and Uzza and Ahio [his brother] drove the cart.

⁸And David and all Israel merrily celebrated before God with all their might, with songs and lyres and harps and tambourines and cymbals and trumpets.

⁹And when they came to the threshing floor of Chidon, Uzza put out his hand to steady the ark, for the oxen [that were drawing the cart] stumbled *and* were restive.

¹⁰And the anger of the Lord was kindled against Uzza, and He smote him because he touched the ark; and there he died before God. [Num. 4:15.]

¹¹And David was offended because the Lord had broken forth upon Uzza; that place to this day is called Perez-uzza [the breaking forth upon Uzza].

¹²And David was afraid of God that day, and he said, How can I bring the ark of God home to me?

¹³So David did not bring the ark home to the City of David, but carried it aside into the house of Obed-edom the Gittite [a Levitical porter born in Gath-rimmon]. [Josh. 21:20, 24; I Chron. 15:24.]

¹⁴And the ark of God remained with the family of Obed-edom in his house three months. And the Lord blessed the house of Obed-edom and all that he had.

**14** And Hiram king of Tyre sent messengers to David, and cedar timbers, with masons and carpenters, to build him a house.

²And David perceived that the Lord had established *and* confirmed him as king over Israel, for his kingdom was exalted highly for His people Israel's sake.

³And David took more wives to Jerusalem, and [he] became the father of more sons and daughters.

⁴Now these are the names of the children whom he had in Jerusalem: Shammua, Shobab, Nathan, Solomon,

⁵Ibhar, Elishua, Elpelet,

⁶Nogah, Nepheg, Japhia,

⁷Elishama, Beeliada, and Eliphelet.

⁸And when the Philistines heard that David was anointed king over all Israel, [they] all went up to seek David. And [he] heard of it and went out before them.

⁹Now the Philistines had come and made a raid in the Valley of Rephaim.

¹⁰David asked God, Shall I go up against the Philistines? And will You deliver them into my hand? And the Lord said, Go up, and I will deliver them into your hand.

¹¹So [Israel] came up to Baal-perazim, and David smote [the Philistines] there. Then David said, God has broken my enemies by my hand, like the bursting forth of waters. Therefore they called the name of that place Baal-perazim [Lord of breaking through].

---

[a] 3 Or *we neglected*    [b] 3 Or *him*    [c] 11 *Perez Uzzah* means *outbreak against Uzzah.*    [d] 7 A variant of *Eliada*    [e] 11 *Baal Perazim* means *the lord who breaks out.*

## New International Version

abandoned their gods there, and David gave orders to burn them in the fire.

[13]Once more the Philistines raided the valley; [14]so David inquired of God again, and God answered him, "Do not go directly after them, but circle around them and attack them in front of the poplar trees. [15]As soon as you hear the sound of marching in the tops of the poplar trees, move out to battle, because that will mean God has gone out in front of you to strike the Philistine army." [16]So David did as God commanded him, and they struck down the Philistine army, all the way from Gibeon to Gezer.

[17]So David's fame spread throughout every land, and the LORD made all the nations fear him.

### The Ark Brought to Jerusalem

**15** After David had constructed buildings for himself in the City of David, he prepared a place for the ark of God and pitched a tent for it. [2]Then David said, "No one but the Levites may carry the ark of God, because the LORD chose them to carry the ark of the LORD and to minister before him forever."

[3]David assembled all Israel in Jerusalem to bring up the ark of the LORD to the place he had prepared for it. [4]He called together the descendants of Aaron and the Levites:

[5]From the descendants of Kohath,
    Uriel the leader and 120 relatives;
[6]from the descendants of Merari,
    Asaiah the leader and 220 relatives;
[7]from the descendants of Gershon,[a]
    Joel the leader and 130 relatives;
[8]from the descendants of Elizaphan,
    Shemaiah the leader and 200 relatives;
[9]from the descendants of Hebron,
    Eliel the leader and 80 relatives;
[10]from the descendants of Uzziel,
    Amminadab the leader and 112 relatives.

[11]Then David summoned Zadok and Abiathar the priests, and Uriel, Asaiah, Joel, Shemaiah, Eliel and Amminadab the Levites. [12]He said to them, "You are the heads of the Levitical families; you and your fellow Levites are to consecrate yourselves and bring up the ark of the LORD, the God of Israel, to the place I have prepared for it. [13]It was because you, the Levites, did not bring it up the first time that the LORD our God broke out in anger against us. We did not inquire of him about how to do it in the prescribed way." [14]So the priests and Levites consecrated themselves in order to bring up the ark of the LORD, the God of Israel. [15]And the Levites carried the ark of God with the poles on their shoulders, as Moses had commanded in accordance with the word of the LORD.

[16]David told the leaders of the Levites to appoint their fellow Levites as musicians to make a joyful sound with musical instruments: lyres, harps and cymbals.

[17]So the Levites appointed Heman son of Joel; from his relatives, Asaph son of Berekiah; and from their relatives the Merarites, Ethan son of Kushaiah; [18]and with them their relatives next in rank: Zechariah,[b] Jaaziel, Shemiramoth, Jehiel, Unni, Eliab, Benaiah, Maaseiah, Mattithiah, Eliphelehu, Mikneiah, Obed-Edom and Jeiel,[c] the gatekeepers.

[19]The musicians Heman, Asaph and Ethan were to sound the bronze cymbals; [20]Zechariah, Jaaziel,[d] Shemiramoth, Jehiel, Unni, Eliab, Maaseiah and Benaiah were to play the lyres according to *alamoth*,[e] [21]and Mattithiah,

## Amplified Bible

[12][The Philistines] left their gods there; David commanded and they were burned.

[13]And the Philistines again made a raid in the valley.

[14]And David inquired again of God, and God said to him, Do not go up after them; turn away from them and come [around] upon them over opposite the mulberry trees.

[15]And when you hear a sound of marching in the tops of the mulberry *or* balsam trees, then go out to battle, for God has gone out before you to smite the Philistine host.

[16]So David did as God commanded him, and they smote the army of the Philistines from Gibeon even to Gezer.

[17]And the fame of David went out into all lands, and the Lord brought the fear of him upon all nations.

**15** David made for himself houses in the City of David, and he prepared a place for the ark of God and pitched a tent for it.

[2]Then David said, None should carry the ark of God but the Levites, for the Lord chose them to carry the ark of God and to minister to Him forever.

[3]And David assembled all Israel at Jerusalem to bring up the ark of the Lord to its place, which he had prepared for it.

[4]And David gathered together the sons of Aaron and the Levites:

[5]Of the sons of Kohath, Uriel the chief, with 120 kinsmen;
[6]Of the sons of Merari, Asaiah the chief, with 220 kinsmen;
[7]Of the sons of Gershom, Joel the chief, with 130 kinsmen;
[8]Of the sons of Elizaphan, Shemaiah the chief, with 200 kinsmen;
[9]Of the sons of Hebron, Eliel the chief, with 80 kinsmen;
[10]Of the sons of Uzziel, Amminadab the chief, with 112 kinsmen.

[11]And David called for Zadok and Abiathar the priests, and for the Levites—Uriel, Asaiah, Joel, Shemaiah, Eliel, and Amminadab,

[12]And said to them, You are the heads of the fathers' houses of the Levites; sanctify yourselves, both you and your brethren, that you may bring up the ark of the Lord, the God of Israel, to the place that I have prepared for it.

[13]For because you bore it not [as God directed] at the first, the Lord our God broke forth upon us—because we did not seek Him in the way He ordained. [Num. 1:50; I Chron. 13:7-10.]

[14]So the priests and the Levites sanctified themselves to bring up the ark of the Lord, the God of Israel.

[15]The Levites carried the ark of God on their shoulders with the poles, as Moses commanded by the word of the Lord.

[16]David told the chief Levites to appoint their brethren the singers with instruments of music—harps, lyres, and cymbals—to play loudly and lift up their voices with joy.

[17]So the Levites appointed Heman son of Joel; and of his brethren, Asaph son of Berechiah; and of the sons of Merari their brethren, Ethan son of Kushaiah;

[18]And with them their brethren of the second class: Zechariah, Ben, Jaaziel, Shemiramoth, Jehiel, Unni, Eliab, Benaiah, Maaseiah, Mattithiah, Eliphelehu, and Mikneiah, and also the gatekeepers, Obed-edom and Jeiel.

[19]So the singers Heman, Asaph, and Ethan, were appointed to sound bronze cymbals;

[20]Zechariah, Aziel, Shemiramoth, Jehiel, Unni, Eliab, Maaseiah, and Benaiah were to play harps [resembling guitars] set to Alamoth [probably the treble voice];

---

[a] 7 Hebrew *Gershom*, a variant of *Gershon*     [b] 18 Three Hebrew manuscripts and most Septuagint manuscripts (see also verse 20 and 16:5); most Hebrew manuscripts *Zechariah son and* or *Zechariah, Ben and*     [c] 18 Hebrew; Septuagint (see also verse 21) *Jeiel and Azaziah*     [d] 20 See verse 18; Hebrew *Aziel*, a variant of *Jaaziel*.     [e] 20 Probably a musical term

## New International Version

Eliphelehu, Mikneiah, Obed-Edom, Jeiel and Azaziah were to play the harps, directing according to *sheminith.*[a] [22]Kenaniah the head Levite was in charge of the singing; that was his responsibility because he was skillful at it. [23]Berekiah and Elkanah were to be doorkeepers for the ark. [24]Shebaniah, Joshaphat, Nethanel, Amasai, Zechariah, Benaiah and Eliezer the priests were to blow trumpets before the ark of God. Obed-Edom and Jehiah were also to be doorkeepers for the ark.

[25]So David and the elders of Israel and the commanders of units of a thousand went to bring up the ark of the covenant of the LORD from the house of Obed-Edom, with rejoicing. [26]Because God had helped the Levites who were carrying the ark of the covenant of the LORD, seven bulls and seven rams were sacrificed. [27]Now David was clothed in a robe of fine linen, as were all the Levites who were carrying the ark, and as were the musicians, and Kenaniah, who was in charge of the singing of the choirs. David also wore a linen ephod. [28]So all Israel brought up the ark of the covenant of the LORD with shouts, with the sounding of rams' horns and trumpets, and of cymbals, and the playing of lyres and harps.

[29]As the ark of the covenant of the LORD was entering the City of David, Michal daughter of Saul watched from a window. And when she saw King David dancing and celebrating, she despised him in her heart.

### Ministering Before the Ark

**16** They brought the ark of God and set it inside the tent that David had pitched for it, and they presented burnt offerings and fellowship offerings before God. [2]After David had finished sacrificing the burnt offerings and fellowship offerings, he blessed the people in the name of the LORD. [3]Then he gave a loaf of bread, a cake of dates and a cake of raisins to each Israelite man and woman.

[4]He appointed some of the Levites to minister before the ark of the LORD, to extol,[b] thank, and praise the LORD, the God of Israel: [5]Asaph was the chief, and next to him in rank were Zechariah, then Jaaziel,[c] Shemiramoth, Jehiel, Mattithiah, Eliab, Benaiah, Obed-Edom and Jeiel. They were to play the lyres and harps, Asaph was to sound the cymbals, [6]and Benaiah and Jahaziel the priests were to blow the trumpets regularly before the ark of the covenant of God.

[7]That day David first appointed Asaph and his associates to give praise to the LORD in this manner:

[8]Give praise to the LORD, proclaim his name;
    make known among the nations what he has done.
[9]Sing to him, sing praise to him;
    tell of all his wonderful acts.
[10]Glory in his holy name;
    let the hearts of those who seek the LORD rejoice.
[11]Look to the LORD and his strength;
    seek his face always.
[12]Remember the wonders he has done,
    his miracles, and the judgments he pronounced,
[13]you his servants, the descendants of Israel,
    his chosen ones, the children of Jacob.
[14]He is the LORD our God;
    his judgments are in all the earth.

## Amplified Bible

[21]Mattithiah, Eliphelehu, Mikneiah, Obed-edom, Jeiel, and Azaziah were to lead with lyres set to Sheminith [the bass voice].

[22]Chenaniah, leader of the Levites in singing, was put in charge of carrying the ark *and* lifting up song. He instructed about these matters because he was skilled *and* able.

[23]Berechiah and Elkanah were gatekeepers for the ark. [24]Shebaniah, Joshaphat, Nethanel, Amasai, Zechariah, Benaiah, and Eliezer the priests were to blow the trumpets before the ark of God. And Obed-edom and Jehiah (Jeiel) were also gatekeepers for the ark.

[25]So David, the elders of Israel, and the captains over thousands went to bring up the ark of the covenant of the Lord out of the house of Obed-edom with joy.

[26]And when God helped the Levites who carried the ark of the covenant of the Lord [with a safe start], they offered seven bulls and seven rams.

[27]David was clothed with a robe of fine linen, as were the Levites who bore the ark, and the singers, and Chenaniah, director of the music of the singers. David also wore an ephod [a priestly upper garment] of linen.

[28]Thus all Israel brought up the ark of the covenant of the Lord with shouting, sound of the cornet, trumpets, and cymbals, sounding aloud with harps and lyres.

[29]As the ark of the covenant of the Lord came to the City of David, Michal [David's wife] daughter of Saul, looking from a window, saw King David leaping as in sport, and she despised him in her heart.

**16** So they brought the ark of God and set it in the midst of the tent which David had pitched for it, and they offered burnt offerings and peace offerings before God. [2]And when David had finished offering the burnt offerings and the peace offerings, he blessed the people in the name of the Lord. [3]And he distributed to everyone of Israel, both man and woman, to everyone a loaf of bread, a portion of meat, and a cake of raisins.

[4]He appointed Levites to minister before the ark of the Lord and to celebrate [by calling to mind], thanking and praising the Lord, the God of Israel: [5]Asaph was the chief, next to him Zechariah, Jeiel (Jaaziel), Shemiramoth, Jehiel, Mattithiah, Eliab, and Benaiah, Obed-edom, and Jeiel, who were to play harps and lyres; Asaph was to sound the cymbals; [6]Benaiah and Jahaziel the priests were to blow trumpets continually before the ark of the covenant of God.

[7]Then on that day David first entrusted to Asaph and his brethren the singing of thanks to the Lord [as their chief task]:

[8]O give thanks to the Lord, call on His name; make known His doings among the peoples!
[9]Sing to Him, sing praises to Him; meditate on *and* talk of all His wondrous works *and* devoutly praise them!
[10]Glory in His holy name; let the hearts of those rejoice who seek the Lord!
[11]Seek the Lord and His strength; yearn for *and* seek His face *and* to be in His presence continually!
[12][Earnestly] remember the marvelous deeds which He has done, His miracles, and the judgments He uttered [as in Egypt],
[13]O you offspring of [Abraham and] of Israel His servants, you children of Jacob, His chosen ones!
[14]He is the Lord our God; His judgments are in all the earth.

---

[a] 21 Probably a musical term    [b] 4 Or *petition*; or *invoke*
[c] 5 See 15:18,20; Hebrew *Jeiel*, possibly another name for *Jaaziel*.

## New International Version

15 He remembers[a] his covenant forever,
　　the promise he made, for a thousand generations,
16 the covenant he made with Abraham,
　　the oath he swore to Isaac.
17 He confirmed it to Jacob as a decree,
　　to Israel as an everlasting covenant:
18 "To you I will give the land of Canaan
　　as the portion you will inherit."

19 When they were but few in number,
　　few indeed, and strangers in it,
20 they[b] wandered from nation to nation,
　　from one kingdom to another.
21 He allowed no one to oppress them;
　　for their sake he rebuked kings:
22 "Do not touch my anointed ones;
　　do my prophets no harm."

23 Sing to the LORD, all the earth;
　　proclaim his salvation day after day.
24 Declare his glory among the nations,
　　his marvelous deeds among all peoples.

25 For great is the LORD and most worthy of praise;
　　he is to be feared above all gods.
26 For all the gods of the nations are idols,
　　but the LORD made the heavens.
27 Splendor and majesty are before him;
　　strength and joy are in his dwelling place.

28 Ascribe to the LORD, all you families of nations,
　　ascribe to the LORD glory and strength.
29 Ascribe to the LORD the glory due his name;
　　bring an offering and come before him.
　Worship the LORD in the splendor of his[c] holiness.
30 　Tremble before him, all the earth!
　　The world is firmly established; it cannot be moved.

31 Let the heavens rejoice, let the earth be glad;
　　let them say among the nations, "The LORD reigns!"
32 Let the sea resound, and all that is in it;
　　let the fields be jubilant, and everything in them!
33 Let the trees of the forest sing,
　　let them sing for joy before the LORD,
　　for he comes to judge the earth.

34 Give thanks to the LORD, for he is good;
　　his love endures forever.
35 Cry out, "Save us, God our Savior;
　　gather us and deliver us from the nations,
　that we may give thanks to your holy name,
　　and glory in your praise."
36 Praise be to the LORD, the God of Israel,
　　from everlasting to everlasting.

Then all the people said "Amen" and "Praise the LORD."

37 David left Asaph and his associates before the ark of the covenant of the LORD to minister there regularly, according to each day's requirements. 38 He also left Obed-Edom and his sixty-eight associates to minister with them. Obed-Edom son of Jeduthun, and also Hosah, were gatekeepers.
39 David left Zadok the priest and his fellow priests before the tabernacle of the LORD at the high place in Gibeon 40 to present burnt offerings to the LORD on the altar of burnt offering regularly, morning and evening, in accordance with everything written in the Law of the LORD, which he had given Israel. 41 With them were Heman and Jeduthun and the rest of those chosen and designated by name to give thanks to the LORD, "for his love endures forever." 42 Heman and Jeduthun were responsible for the

## Amplified Bible

15 Be mindful of His covenant forever, the promise which He commanded and established to a thousand generations,
16 The covenant which He made with Abraham, and His sworn promise to Isaac.
17 He confirmed it as a statute to Jacob, and to Israel for an everlasting covenant, [Gen. 35:11, 12.]
18 Saying, To you I will give the land of Canaan, the measured portion of your possession and inheritance.
19 When they were but few, even a very few, and only temporary residents and strangers in it,
20 When they went from nation to nation, and from one kingdom to another people,
21 He allowed no man to do them wrong; yes, He reproved kings for their sakes, [Gen. 12:17; 20:3; Exod. 7:15-18.]
22 Saying, Touch not My anointed, and do My prophets no harm. [Gen. 20:7.]
23 Sing to the Lord, all the earth; show forth from day to day His salvation.
24 Declare His glory among the nations, His marvelous works among all peoples.
25 For great is the Lord and greatly to be praised; He also is to be [reverently] feared above all so-called gods.
26 For all the gods of the people are [lifeless] idols, but the Lord made the heavens.
27 Honor and majesty are [found] in His presence; strength and joy are [found] in His sanctuary.
28 Ascribe to the Lord, you families of the peoples, ascribe to the Lord glory and strength.
29 Ascribe to the Lord the glory due His name. Bring an offering and come before Him; worship the Lord in the beauty of holiness and in holy array.
30 Tremble and reverently fear before Him, all the earth's peoples; the world also shall be established, so it cannot be moved.
31 Let the heavens be glad and let the earth rejoice; and let men say among the nations, The Lord reigns!
32 Let the sea roar, and all the things that fill it; let the fields rejoice, and all that is in them.
33 Then shall the trees of the wood sing out for joy before the Lord, for He comes to judge and govern the earth.
34 O give thanks to the Lord, for He is good; for His mercy and loving-kindness endure forever!
35 And say, Save us, O God of our salvation; gather us together and deliver us from the nations, that we may give thanks to Your holy name and glory in Your praise.
36 Blessed be the Lord, the God of Israel, forever and ever! And all the people said Amen! and praised the Lord.
37 So David left Asaph and his brethren before the ark of the covenant of the Lord to minister before the ark continually, as each day's work required,
38 And Obed-edom with [his] sixty-eight kinsmen. Also Obed-edom son of Jeduthun, and Hosah, were to be gatekeepers.
39 And David left Zadok the priest and his brethren the priests before the tabernacle of the Lord in the high place that was at Gibeon
40 To offer burnt offerings to the Lord upon the altar of burnt offering continually, morning and evening, and to do all that is written in the Law of the Lord which He commanded Israel.
41 With them were Heman and Jeduthun and the rest who were chosen and expressly named to give thanks to the Lord, for His mercy and loving-kindness endure forever.
42 With them were Heman and Jeduthun with trumpets

---

a 15 Some Septuagint manuscripts (see also Psalm 105:8); Hebrew *Remember*　b 18-20 One Hebrew manuscript, Septuagint and Vulgate (see also Psalm 105:12); most Hebrew manuscripts *inherit, / 19though you are but few in number, / few indeed, and strangers in it." / 20They*　c 29 Or LORD *with the splendor of*

## New International Version

sounding of the trumpets and cymbals and for the playing of the other instruments for sacred song. The sons of Jeduthun were stationed at the gate.

⁴³Then all the people left, each for their own home, and David returned home to bless his family.

### God's Promise to David

**17** After David was settled in his palace, he said to Nathan the prophet, "Here I am, living in a house of cedar, while the ark of the covenant of the LORD is under a tent."

²Nathan replied to David, "Whatever you have in mind, do it, for God is with you."

³But that night the word of God came to Nathan, saying:

⁴"Go and tell my servant David, 'This is what the LORD says: You are not the one to build me a house to dwell in. ⁵I have not dwelt in a house from the day I brought Israel up out of Egypt to this day. I have moved from one tent site to another, from one dwelling place to another. ⁶Wherever I have moved with all the Israelites, did I ever say to any of their leaders*ᵃ* whom I commanded to shepherd my people, "Why have you not built me a house of cedar?"'

⁷"Now then, tell my servant David, 'This is what the LORD Almighty says: I took you from the pasture, from tending the flock, and appointed you ruler over my people Israel. ⁸I have been with you wherever you have gone, and I have cut off all your enemies from before you. Now I will make your name like the names of the greatest men on earth. ⁹And I will provide a place for my people Israel and will plant them so that they can have a home of their own and no longer be disturbed. Wicked people will not oppress them anymore, as they did at the beginning ¹⁰and have done ever since the time I appointed leaders over my people Israel. I will also subdue all your enemies.

"'I declare to you that the LORD will build a house for you: ¹¹When your days are over and you go to be with your ancestors, I will raise up your offspring to succeed you, one of your own sons, and I will establish his kingdom. ¹²He is the one who will build a house for me, and I will establish his throne forever. ¹³I will be his father, and he will be my son. I will never take my love away from him, as I took it away from your predecessor. ¹⁴I will set him over my house and my kingdom forever; his throne will be established forever.'"

¹⁵Nathan reported to David all the words of this entire revelation.

### David's Prayer

¹⁶Then King David went in and sat before the LORD, and he said:

"Who am I, LORD God, and what is my family, that you have brought me this far? ¹⁷And as if this were not enough in your sight, my God, you have spoken about the future of the house of your servant. You, LORD God, have looked on me as though I were the most exalted of men.

## Amplified Bible

and cymbals for those who should sound aloud, and instruments for accompanying the songs of God. And the sons of Jeduthun were to be at the gate.

⁴³Then all the people departed, each man to his house, and David returned home to bless his household.

**17** As David sat in his house, he said to Nathan the prophet, Behold, I dwell in a house of cedars, but the ark of the covenant of the Lord remains under tent curtains.

²Then Nathan said to David, Do all that is in your heart, for God is with you.

³And that same night the word of God came to Nathan, saying,

⁴Go and tell David My servant, Thus says the Lord: You shall not build Me a house to dwell in,

⁵For I have not dwelt in a house since the day that I brought up Israel from Egypt until this day; but I have gone from tent to tent, and from one tabernacle to another.

⁶Wherever I have walked with all Israel, did I say a word to any of the judges of Israel whom I commanded to feed My people, saying, Why have you not built Me a house of cedar?

⁷Now therefore, thus shall you say to My servant David, Thus says the Lord of hosts: I took you from the sheepfold, from following the sheep, that you should be prince over My people Israel.

⁸And I have been with you wherever you have gone, and I have cut off all your enemies from before you, and I will make your name like the name of the great ones of the earth.

⁹Also I will appoint a place for My people Israel and will plant them, that they may dwell in their own place and be moved no more; neither shall the children of wickedness waste them any more, as at the first,

¹⁰Since the time that I commanded judges to be over My people Israel. Moreover, I will subdue all your enemies. Furthermore, I foretell to you that the Lord will build you a house (a blessed posterity).

¹¹And it shall come to pass that when your days are fulfilled to go to be with your fathers, I will raise up your offspring after you, one of your own sons, and I will establish his kingdom.

¹²He shall build Me a house, and I will establish his throne forever. [I Chron. 28:7.]

¹³I will be his father, and he shall be My son; and I will not take My mercy *and* steadfast love away from him, as I took it from him [King Saul] who was before you. [Heb. 1:5, 6.]

¹⁴But I will settle *ᵃ*him (Him) in My house and in My kingdom forever; and his (His) throne shall be established forevermore. [Isa. 9:7.]

¹⁵According to all these words and according to all this vision, so Nathan spoke to David.

¹⁶And David the king went in and sat before the Lord and said, Who am I, O Lord God, and what is my house *and* family, that You have brought me up to this?

¹⁷And yet this was a small thing in Your eyes, O God; for You have spoken of Your servant's house for a great while to come, and have regarded me according to the estate of a man of high degree, O Lord God!

---

ᵃ The "house" or "kingdom of God," in which this preservation or confirming of the seed of David is to take place, has two points of reference: first, the Old Testament theocracy [government of a state by the immediate direction of God], and second, the Messianic kingdom of the new covenant. The text of II Sam. 7:16 (KJV) differs: "And thine house and thy kingdom shall be established forever before thee, and thy throne shall be established forever." The sense of both is Messianic [though the writer in earlier verses definitely referred not to Christ but to Solomon (I Chron. 17:11-13 and II Sam. 7:13, 14)] (J. P. Lange, *A Commentary*). "The reference in this prophecy looks beyond Solomon to Him of Whom the greatest princes of the house of David were but imperfect types" (Charles Ellicott, *A Bible Commentary*).

---

ᵃ 6 Traditionally *judges*; also in verse 10

## New International Version

18"What more can David say to you for honoring your servant? For you know your servant, 19LORD. For the sake of your servant and according to your will, you have done this great thing and made known all these great promises.

20"There is no one like you, LORD, and there is no God but you, as we have heard with our own ears. 21And who is like your people Israel—the one nation on earth whose God went out to redeem a people for himself, and to make a name for yourself, and to perform great and awesome wonders by driving out nations from before your people, whom you redeemed from Egypt? 22You made your people Israel your very own forever, and you, LORD, have become their God.

23"And now, LORD, let the promise you have made concerning your servant and his house be established forever. Do as you promised, 24so that it will be established and that your name will be great forever. Then people will say, 'The LORD Almighty, the God over Israel, is Israel's God!' And the house of your servant David will be established before you.

25"You, my God, have revealed to your servant that you will build a house for him. So your servant has found courage to pray to you. 26You, LORD, are God! You have promised these good things to your servant. 27Now you have been pleased to bless the house of your servant, that it may continue forever in your sight; for you, LORD, have blessed it, and it will be blessed forever."

### David's Victories

**18** In the course of time, David defeated the Philistines and subdued them, and he took Gath and its surrounding villages from the control of the Philistines.

2David also defeated the Moabites, and they became subject to him and brought him tribute.

3Moreover, David defeated Hadadezer king of Zobah, in the vicinity of Hamath, when he went to set up his monument at*a* the Euphrates River. 4David captured a thousand of his chariots, seven thousand charioteers and twenty thousand foot soldiers. He hamstrung all but a hundred of the chariot horses.

5When the Arameans of Damascus came to help Hadadezer king of Zobah, David struck down twenty-two thousand of them. 6He put garrisons in the Aramean kingdom of Damascus, and the Arameans became subject to him and brought him tribute. The LORD gave David victory wherever he went.

7David took the gold shields carried by the officers of Hadadezer and brought them to Jerusalem. 8From Tebah*b* and Kun, towns that belonged to Hadadezer, David took a great quantity of bronze, which Solomon used to make the bronze Sea, the pillars and various bronze articles.

9When Tou king of Hamath heard that David had defeated the entire army of Hadadezer king of Zobah, 10he sent his son Hadoram to King David to greet him and congratulate him on his victory in battle over Hadadezer, who had been at war with Tou. Hadoram brought all kinds of articles of gold, of silver and of bronze.

11King David dedicated these articles to the LORD, as he had done with the silver and gold he had taken from all these nations: Edom and Moab, the Ammonites and the Philistines, and Amalek.

12Abishai son of Zeruiah struck down eighteen thousand Edomites in the Valley of Salt. 13He put garrisons in

## Amplified Bible

18What more can David say to You for thus honoring Your servant? For You know Your servant.

19O Lord, for Your servant's sake and in accord with Your own heart, You have wrought all this greatness, to make known all these great things.

20O Lord, there is none like You, nor is there any God beside You, according to all that our ears have heard.

21And what nation on the earth is like Your people Israel, whom God went to redeem to Himself as a people, making Yourself a name by great and terrible things, by driving out nations from before Your people, whom You redeemed out of Egypt?

22You made Your people Israel Your own forever, and You, Lord, became their God.

23Therefore now, Lord, let the word which You have spoken concerning Your servant and his house be established forever, and do as You have said.

24Let it be established and let Your name [and the character that name denotes] be magnified forever, saying, The Lord of hosts, the God of Israel, is Israel's God; and the house of David Your servant will be established before You.

25For You, O my God, have told Your servant that You will build for him a house (a blessed posterity); therefore Your servant has found courage *and* confidence to pray before You.

26And now, Lord, You are God, and have promised this good thing to Your servant.

27Therefore may it please You to bless the house (posterity) of Your servant, that it may continue before You forever; for what You bless, O Lord, is blessed forever.

**18** After this, David smote and subdued the Philistines, and took Gath and its villages out of the hand of the Philistines.

2He smote Moab, and the Moabites became David's servants and brought tribute.

3Also David defeated Hadadezer king of Zobah toward Hamath, as he went to establish his dominion by the river Euphrates.

4David took from him 1,000 chariots, 7,000 horsemen, and 20,000 foot soldiers. David also hamstrung all the chariot horses, but reserved enough for 100 chariots.

5When the Syrians of Damascus came to help Hadadezer king of Zobah, David slew of the Syrians 22,000 men.

6Then David put garrisons in Syria, [whose capital was] Damascus; the Syrians became David's servants and brought tribute. Thus the Lord preserved *and* gave victory to David wherever he went.

7David took the shields of gold that were carried by the servants of Hadadezer and brought them to Jerusalem.

8Likewise from Tibhath and from Cun, cities of Hadadezer, David brought very much bronze, with which Solomon later made the bronze laver, the pillars, and the vessels of bronze.

9When Tou king of Hamath heard how David had defeated all the hosts of Hadadezer king of Zobah,

10He sent Hadoram his son to King David to salute him and to congratulate him because he had fought and defeated Hadadezer, for Hadadezer had had wars with Tou. And Hadoram brought with him all manner of vessels of gold, silver, and bronze.

11King David dedicated them also to the Lord, with the silver and the gold he brought from all these nations: Edom, Moab, the Ammonites, the Philistines, and the Amalekites.

12Also Abishai son of Zeruiah slew 18,000 of the Edomites in the Valley of Salt.

---

*a* 3 Or *to restore his control over*    *b* 8 Hebrew *Tibhath,* a variant of *Tebah*

## New International Version

Edom, and all the Edomites became subject to David. The LORD gave David victory wherever he went.

### David's Officials

[14]David reigned over all Israel, doing what was just and right for all his people. [15]Joab son of Zeruiah was over the army; Jehoshaphat son of Ahilud was recorder; [16]Zadok son of Ahitub and Ahimelek[a] son of Abiathar were priests; Shavsha was secretary; [17]Benaiah son of Jehoiada was over the Kerethites and Pelethites; and David's sons were chief officials at the king's side.

### David Defeats the Ammonites

**19** In the course of time, Nahash king of the Ammonites died, and his son succeeded him as king. [2]David thought, "I will show kindness to Hanun son of Nahash, because his father showed kindness to me." So David sent a delegation to express his sympathy to Hanun concerning his father.

When David's envoys came to Hanun in the land of the Ammonites to express sympathy to him, [3]the Ammonite commanders said to Hanun, "Do you think David is honoring your father by sending envoys to you to express sympathy? Haven't his envoys come to you only to explore and spy out the country and overthrow it?" [4]So Hanun seized David's envoys, shaved them, cut off their garments at the buttocks, and sent them away.

[5]When someone came and told David about the men, he sent messengers to meet them, for they were greatly humiliated. The king said, "Stay at Jericho till your beards have grown, and then come back."

[6]When the Ammonites realized that they had become obnoxious to David, Hanun and the Ammonites sent a thousand talents[b] of silver to hire chariots and charioteers from Aram Naharaim,[c] Aram Maakah and Zobah. [7]They hired thirty-two thousand chariots and charioteers, as well as the king of Maakah with his troops, who came and camped near Medeba, while the Ammonites were mustered from their towns and moved out for battle.

[8]On hearing this, David sent Joab out with the entire army of fighting men. [9]The Ammonites came out and drew up in battle formation at the entrance to their city, while the kings who had come were by themselves in the open country.

[10]Joab saw that there were battle lines in front of him and behind him; so he selected some of the best troops in Israel and deployed them against the Arameans. [11]He put the rest of the men under the command of Abishai his brother, and they were deployed against the Ammonites. [12]Joab said, "If the Arameans are too strong for me, then you are to rescue me; but if the Ammonites are too strong for you, then I will rescue you. [13]Be strong, and let us fight bravely for our people and the cities of our God. The LORD will do what is good in his sight."

[14]Then Joab and the troops with him advanced to fight the Arameans, and they fled before him. [15]When the Ammonites realized that the Arameans were fleeing, they too fled before his brother Abishai and went inside the city. So Joab went back to Jerusalem.

[16]After the Arameans saw that they had been routed by Israel, they sent messengers and had Arameans brought from beyond the Euphrates River, with Shophak the commander of Hadadezer's army leading them.

## Amplified Bible

[13]He put garrisons in Edom, and all the Edomites became David's servants. Thus the Lord preserved *and* gave victory to David wherever he went.

[14]So David reigned over all Israel and executed judgment and justice among all his people.

[15]Joab son of Zeruiah [David's half sister] was over the army; and Jehoshaphat son of Ahilud was the recorder; [16]Zadok son of Ahitub and Abimelech son of Abiathar were the priests; and Shavsha was secretary [of state]; [17]Benaiah son of Jehoiada was over [David's bodyguards] the Cherethites and the Pelethites; and David's sons were chiefs next to the king.

**19** After this, Nahash king of the Ammonites died, and his son reigned in his stead. [2]David said, I will show kindness to Hanun son of Nahash, because his father showed kindness to me. And David sent messengers to comfort him concerning his father's death. So the servants of David came into the land of the Ammonites to comfort Hanun.

[3]But the princes of the Ammonites said to Hanun, Do you think that David has sent comforters to you because he honors your father? Have his servants not come to you to search, to overthrow, and to spy out the land? [4]Therefore Hanun took David's servants, shaved them, cut off their garments in the middle near their buttocks, and sent them away.

[5]When David was told how the men were served, he sent to meet them, for [they] were greatly shamed *and* embarrassed. The king said, Stay in Jericho until your beards are grown, and then return.

[6]When the Ammonites saw that they had made themselves hateful to David, Hanun and [his people] sent 1,000 talents of silver to hire chariots and horsemen from Mesopotamia and Aram-maacah and Zobah. [7]So they hired 32,000 chariots, and the king of Maacah and his troops, who came and pitched before Medeba. And the Ammonites gathered from their cities and came to battle.

[8]When David heard of it, he sent Joab and all the army of mighty men.

[9]And the Ammonites came out and lined up in battle array before the entrance of the city [Medeba], and the kings who had come were by themselves in the open country.

[10]When Joab saw that the battle was set against him before and behind, he chose from all the choice men of Israel and put them in array against the Syrians. [11]The rest of the soldiers he delivered to Abishai his brother, and they were arrayed against the Ammonites. [12]And he said, If the Syrians are too strong for me, you help me; but if the Ammonites are too strong for you, I will help you. [13]Be of good courage and let us behave ourselves courageously for our people and for the cities of our God; and may the Lord do what is good in His sight.

[14]So Joab and the people who were with him drew near before the Syrians for battle, and they fled before him. [15]And when the Ammonites saw that the Syrians fled, they likewise fled before Abishai, Joab's brother, and entered into the city [Medeba]. Then Joab came to Jerusalem.

[16]When the Syrians saw that they were defeated by Israel, they sent messengers and drew forth the Syrians who were beyond the Euphrates River, with Shophach the commander of the army of Hadadezer at their head.

---

[a] 16 Some Hebrew manuscripts, Vulgate and Syriac (see also 2 Samuel 8:17); most Hebrew manuscripts *Abimelek*   [b] 6 That is, about 38 tons or about 34 metric tons   [c] 6 That is, Northwest Mesopotamia

## New International Version

17When David was told of this, he gathered all Israel and crossed the Jordan; he advanced against them and formed his battle lines opposite them. David formed his lines to meet the Arameans in battle, and they fought against him. 18But they fled before Israel, and David killed seven thousand of their charioteers and forty thousand of their foot soldiers. He also killed Shophak the commander of their army.
19When the vassals of Hadadezer saw that they had been routed by Israel, they made peace with David and became subject to him.

So the Arameans were not willing to help the Ammonites anymore.

### The Capture of Rabbah

**20** In the spring, at the time when kings go off to war, Joab led out the armed forces. He laid waste the land of the Ammonites and went to Rabbah and besieged it, but David remained in Jerusalem. Joab attacked Rabbah and left it in ruins. 2David took the crown from the head of their king*a*—its weight was found to be a talent*b* of gold, and it was set with precious stones—and it was placed on David's head. He took a great quantity of plunder from the city 3and brought out the people who were there, consigning them to labor with saws and with iron picks and axes. David did this to all the Ammonite towns. Then David and his entire army returned to Jerusalem.

### War With the Philistines

4In the course of time, war broke out with the Philistines, at Gezer. At that time Sibbekai the Hushathite killed Sippai, one of the descendants of the Rephaites, and the Philistines were subjugated.
5In another battle with the Philistines, Elhanan son of Jair killed Lahmi the brother of Goliath the Gittite, who had a spear with a shaft like a weaver's rod.
6In still another battle, which took place at Gath, there was a huge man with six fingers on each hand and six toes on each foot—twenty-four in all. He also was descended from Rapha. 7When he taunted Israel, Jonathan son of Shimea, David's brother, killed him.
8These were descendants of Rapha in Gath, and they fell at the hands of David and his men.

### David Counts the Fighting Men

**21** Satan rose up against Israel and incited David to take a census of Israel. 2So David said to Joab and the commanders of the troops, "Go and count the Israelites from Beersheba to Dan. Then report back to me so that I may know how many there are."
3But Joab replied, "May the LORD multiply his troops a hundred times over. My lord the king, are they not all my lord's subjects? Why does my lord want to do this? Why should he bring guilt on Israel?"
4The king's word, however, overruled Joab; so Joab left and went throughout Israel and then came back to Jerusalem. 5Joab reported the number of the fighting men to David: In all Israel there were one million one hundred thousand men who could handle a sword, including four hundred and seventy thousand in Judah.
6But Joab did not include Levi and Benjamin in the numbering, because the king's command was repulsive to him. 7This command was also evil in the sight of God; so he punished Israel.
8Then David said to God, "I have sinned greatly by doing this. Now, I beg you, take away the guilt of your servant. I have done a very foolish thing."

## Amplified Bible

17It was told to David, and he gathered all Israel and crossed the Jordan and drew up his army against them. So when David set the battle in array against the Syrians, they fought with him. 18But the Syrians fled before Israel, and David slew of the Syrians 7,000 men in chariots and 40,000 foot soldiers, and killed Shophach the commander of the army.
19When the servants of Hadadezer saw that they were defeated before Israel, they made peace with David and became subject to him; nor would the Syrians any longer help the Ammonites.

**20** After the end of the year, when kings go out to battle, Joab led forth the army and devastated the land of the Ammonites, and came and besieged Rabbah. But David tarried at Jerusalem. Joab smote Rabbah and overthrew it.
2David took their king's crown from off his head and found that it weighed a talent of gold and that precious stones were in it. It was set upon David's head. He brought also very much spoil out of the city of Rabbah.
3He brought out the people who were in it and set them at cutting with saws, iron wedges, and axes. So David dealt with all the Ammonite cities. And David and all the army returned to Jerusalem.
4After this, there arose war at Gezer with the Philistines; then Sibbecai the Hushathite slew Sippai, of the sons of the giant, and they were subdued.
5There was war again with the Philistines, and Elhanan son of Jair slew Lahmi the brother of Goliath the Gittite, the staff of whose spear was like a weaver's beam.
6And again there was war at Gath, where was a man of great stature who had twenty-four fingers and toes, six on each hand and each foot. He also was born to the giant.
7And when he reproached *and* defied Israel, Jonathan son of Shimea, David's brother, slew him.
8These were born to the giant [clan] in Gath, and they fell by the hands of David and his servants.

**21** Satan [an adversary] stood up against Israel and stirred up David to number Israel.
2David said to Joab and the rulers of the people, Go, number Israel from Beersheba to Dan, and bring me the total, that I may know it.
3And Joab answered, May the Lord multiply His people a hundred times! But, my lord the king, are they not all my lord's servants? Why then does my lord require this? Why will he bring guilt upon Israel?
4But the king's word prevailed against Joab. So Joab departed and went throughout all Israel and came to Jerusalem.
5Joab gave the total number of the people to David. And all of Israel were 1,100,000 who drew the sword, and of Judah 470,000 who drew the sword.
6But Levi and Benjamin he did not include among them, for the king's order was detestable to Joab.
7And God was displeased with this [reliance on human resources], and He smote Israel.
8And David said to God, I have sinned greatly because I have done this thing. But now, I beseech You, take away the hateful wickedness of Your servant; for I have done very foolishly.

---

*a 2 Or of Milkom, that is, Molek* *b 2 That is, about 75 pounds or about 34 kilograms*

## New International Version

[9] The LORD said to Gad, David's seer, [10] "Go and tell David, 'This is what the LORD says: I am giving you three options. Choose one of them for me to carry out against you.'"

[11] So Gad went to David and said to him, "This is what the LORD says: 'Take your choice: [12] three years of famine, three months of being swept away[a] before your enemies, with their swords overtaking you, or three days of the sword of the LORD — days of plague in the land, with the angel of the LORD ravaging every part of Israel.' Now then, decide how I should answer the one who sent me."

[13] David said to Gad, "I am in deep distress. Let me fall into the hands of the LORD, for his mercy is very great; but do not let me fall into human hands."

[14] So the LORD sent a plague on Israel, and seventy thousand men of Israel fell dead. [15] And God sent an angel to destroy Jerusalem. But as the angel was doing so, the LORD saw it and relented concerning the disaster and said to the angel who was destroying the people, "Enough! Withdraw your hand." The angel of the LORD was then standing at the threshing floor of Araunah[b] the Jebusite.

[16] David looked up and saw the angel of the LORD standing between heaven and earth, with a drawn sword in his hand extended over Jerusalem. Then David and the elders, clothed in sackcloth, fell facedown.

[17] David said to God, "Was it not I who ordered the fighting men to be counted? I, the shepherd,[c] have sinned and done wrong. These are but sheep. What have they done? LORD my God, let your hand fall on me and my family, but do not let this plague remain on your people."

### David Builds an Altar

[18] Then the angel of the LORD ordered Gad to tell David to go up and build an altar to the LORD on the threshing floor of Araunah the Jebusite. [19] So David went up in obedience to the word that Gad had spoken in the name of the LORD.

[20] While Araunah was threshing wheat, he turned and saw the angel; his four sons who were with him hid themselves. [21] Then David approached, and when Araunah looked and saw him, he left the threshing floor and bowed down before David with his face to the ground.

[22] David said to him, "Let me have the site of your threshing floor so I can build an altar to the LORD, that the plague on the people may be stopped. Sell it to me at the full price."

[23] Araunah said to David, "Take it! Let my lord the king do whatever pleases him. Look, I will give the oxen for the burnt offerings, the threshing sledges for the wood, and the wheat for the grain offering. I will give all this."

[24] But King David replied to Araunah, "No, I insist on paying the full price. I will not take for the LORD what is yours, or sacrifice a burnt offering that costs me nothing."

[25] So David paid Araunah six hundred shekels[d] of gold for the site. [26] David built an altar to the LORD there and sacrificed burnt offerings and fellowship offerings. He called on the LORD, and the LORD answered him with fire from heaven on the altar of burnt offering.

[27] Then the LORD spoke to the angel, and he put his sword back into its sheath. [28] At that time, when David saw that the LORD had answered him on the threshing floor of Araunah the Jebusite, he offered sacrifices there. [29] The tabernacle of the LORD, which Moses had made in the wilderness, and the altar of burnt offering were at that time on the high place at Gibeon. [30] But David could not go

## Amplified Bible

[9] And the Lord said to Gad, David's seer,

[10] Go and tell David, Thus says the Lord: I offer you three things; choose one of them, that I may do it to you.

[11] So Gad came to David and said to him, Thus says the Lord: Take which one you will:

[12] Either three years of famine, or three months of devastation before your foes, while the sword of your enemies overtakes you, or else three days of the sword of the Lord and pestilence in the land, and the angel of the Lord destroying throughout all the borders of Israel. Now therefore, consider what answer I shall return to Him Who sent me.

[13] And David said to Gad, I am in great *and* distressing perplexity; let me fall, I pray you, into the hands of the Lord, for very great *and* many are His mercies; but let me not fall into the hands of man.

[14] So the Lord sent a pestilence upon Israel, and there fell of Israel 70,000 men.

[15] God sent an angel to Jerusalem to destroy it, and as he was destroying, the Lord beheld, and He regretted *and* relented of the evil and said to the destroying angel, It is enough; now stay your hand. And the angel of the Lord stood by the threshing floor of Ornan the Jebusite.

[16] David lifted up his eyes and saw the angel of the Lord standing between earth and the heavens, having a drawn sword in his hand stretched out over Jerusalem. Then David and the elders, clothed in sackcloth, fell upon their faces.

[17] And David said to God, Is it not I who commanded the people to be numbered? It is I who has sinned and done evil indeed; but as for these sheep, what have they done? Let Your hand, I pray You, O Lord my God, be on me and on my father's house, but not on Your people, that they should be plagued.

[18] Then the angel of the Lord commanded Gad to say to David that David should go up and set up an altar to the Lord in the threshing floor of Ornan the Jebusite.

[19] So David went up at Gad's word, which he spoke in the name of the Lord.

[20] Now Ornan was threshing wheat, and he turned back and saw the angel; and his four sons hid themselves.

[21] And as David came to Ornan, Ornan looked and saw him, and went out from the threshing floor and bowed himself to David with his face to the ground.

[22] Then David said to Ornan, Grant me the site of this threshing floor, that I may build an altar on it to the Lord. You shall charge me the full price for it, that the plague may be averted from the people.

[23] Ornan said to David, Take it; and let my lord the king do what is good in his eyes. I give you the oxen also for burnt offerings and the threshing sledges for wood and the wheat for the meal offering. I give it all.

[24] And King David said to Ornan, No, but I will pay the full price. I will not take what is yours for the Lord, nor offer burnt offerings which cost me nothing.

[25] So David gave to Ornan for the site 600 shekels of gold by weight.

[26] And David built there an altar to the Lord and offered burnt offerings and peace offerings and called upon the Lord; and He answered him by fire from heaven upon the altar of burnt offering.

[27] Then the Lord commanded the [avenging] angel, and he put his sword back into its sheath.

[28] When David saw that the Lord had answered him at the threshing floor of Ornan the Jebusite, he sacrificed there.

[29] For the tabernacle of the Lord, which Moses made in the wilderness, and the altar of burnt offering were at that time in the high place at Gibeon.

---

[a] 12 Hebrew; Septuagint and Vulgate (see also 2 Samuel 24:13) *of fleeing*    [b] 15 Hebrew *Ornan,* a variant of *Araunah;* also in verses 18-28    [c] 17 Probable reading of the original Hebrew text (see 2 Samuel 24:17 and note); Masoretic Text does not have *the shepherd.*    [d] 25 That is, about 15 pounds or about 6.9 kilograms

## New International Version

before it to inquire of God, because he was afraid of the sword of the angel of the LORD.

**22** Then David said, "The house of the LORD God is to be here, and also the altar of burnt offering for Israel."

### Preparations for the Temple

²So David gave orders to assemble the foreigners residing in Israel, and from among them he appointed stonecutters to prepare dressed stone for building the house of God. ³He provided a large amount of iron to make nails for the doors of the gateways and for the fittings, and more bronze than could be weighed. ⁴He also provided more cedar logs than could be counted, for the Sidonians and Tyrians had brought large numbers of them to David.

⁵David said, "My son Solomon is young and inexperienced, and the house to be built for the LORD should be of great magnificence and fame and splendor in the sight of all the nations. Therefore I will make preparations for it." So David made extensive preparations before his death.

⁶Then he called for his son Solomon and charged him to build a house for the LORD, the God of Israel. ⁷David said to Solomon: "My son, I had it in my heart to build a house for the Name of the LORD my God. ⁸But this word of the LORD came to me: 'You have shed much blood and have fought many wars. You are not to build a house for my Name, because you have shed much blood on the earth in my sight. ⁹But you will have a son who will be a man of peace and rest, and I will give him rest from all his enemies on every side. His name will be Solomon,ᵃ and I will grant Israel peace and quiet during his reign. ¹⁰He is the one who will build a house for my Name. He will be my son, and I will be his father. And I will establish the throne of his kingdom over Israel forever.'

¹¹"Now, my son, the LORD be with you, and may you have success and build the house of the LORD your God, as he said you would. ¹²May the LORD give you discretion and understanding when he puts you in command over Israel, so that you may keep the law of the LORD your God. ¹³Then you will have success if you are careful to observe the decrees and laws that the LORD gave Moses for Israel. Be strong and courageous. Do not be afraid or discouraged.

¹⁴"I have taken great pains to provide for the temple of the LORD a hundred thousand talentsᵇ of gold, a million talentsᶜ of silver, quantities of bronze and iron too great to be weighed, and wood and stone. And you may add to them. ¹⁵You have many workers: stonecutters, masons and carpenters, as well as those skilled in every kind of work ¹⁶in gold and silver, bronze and iron—craftsmen beyond number. Now begin the work, and the LORD be with you."

¹⁷Then David ordered all the leaders of Israel to help his son Solomon. ¹⁸He said to them, "Is not the LORD your God with you? And has he not granted you rest on every side? For he has given the inhabitants of the land into my hands, and the land is subject to the LORD and to his people. ¹⁹Now devote your heart and soul to seeking the LORD your God. Begin to build the sanctuary of the LORD God, so that you may bring the ark of the covenant of the LORD and the sacred articles belonging to God into the temple that will be built for the Name of the LORD."

## Amplified Bible

³⁰But David could not go before it to inquire of God, for he was afraid of the sword of the angel of the Lord.

**22** Then David said, Here shall be the house of the Lord God, and here the altar of the burnt offering for Israel.

²David commanded to gather together the strangers who were in the land of Israel, and he set stonecutters to hew out stones to build the house of God.

³David prepared iron in abundance for nails for the doors of the gates and for the couplings, and bronze in abundance without weighing,

⁴Also cedar trees without number, for the Sidonians and they of Tyre brought much cedar timber to David.

⁵David said, Solomon my son is young and inexperienced, and the house that is to be built for the Lord must be exceedingly magnificent, of fame and glory throughout all lands. I will therefore make preparation for it. So David prepared abundantly before his death.

⁶Then he called for Solomon his son and charged him to build a house for the Lord, the God of Israel.

⁷David said to Solomon, My son, it was in my heart to build a house to the ᵃName *and* [for the symbol of] the Presence of the Lord my God.

⁸But the word of the Lord came to me, saying, You have shed much blood and have waged great wars; you shall not build a house to My Name, because you have shed much blood on the earth in My sight.

⁹Behold, a son shall be born to you who shall be a man of peace. I will give him rest from all his enemies round about; for his name shall be Solomon [peaceable], and I will give peace and quiet to Israel in his days. [II Sam. 12:24, 25.]

¹⁰He shall build a house for My Name *and* [the symbol of My] Presence. He shall be My son, and I will be his father; and I will establish his royal throne over Israel forever.

¹¹Now, my son, the Lord be with and prosper you in building the house of the Lord your God, as He has spoken concerning you.

¹²Only may the Lord give you wisdom and understanding as you are put in charge of Israel, that you may keep the law of the Lord your God.

¹³Then you will prosper if you are careful to keep *and* fulfill the statutes and ordinances with which the Lord charged Moses concerning Israel. Be strong and of good courage. Dread not *and* fear not; be not dismayed.

¹⁴In my affliction *and* trouble I have provided for the house of the Lord 100,000 talents of gold, 1,000,000 talents of silver, and bronze and iron without weighing. I have also provided timber and stone; you must add to them.

¹⁵You have workmen in abundance: hewers, workers of stone and timber, and all kinds of craftsmen without number, skillful in doing every kind of work

¹⁶With gold, silver, bronze, and iron. So arise and be doing, and the Lord be with you!

¹⁷David also commanded all the princes of Israel to help Solomon his son, saying,

¹⁸Is not the Lord your God with you? And has He not given you peace on every side? For He has given the inhabitants of the land into my hand, and the land is subdued before the Lord and His people.

¹⁹Now set your mind and heart to seek (inquire of and require as your vital necessity) the Lord your God. Arise and build the sanctuary of the Lord God, so that the ark of the covenant of the Lord and the holy vessels of God may be brought into the house built to the Name *and* renown of the Lord.

---

ᵃ 9 *Solomon* sounds like and may be derived from the Hebrew for *peace.*
ᵇ 14 That is, about 3,750 tons or about 3,400 metric tons    ᶜ 14 That is, about 37,500 tons or about 34,000 metric tons

ᵃ See footnote on Deut. 12:5.

## New International Version

### The Levites

**23** When David was old and full of years, he made his son Solomon king over Israel.

[2] He also gathered together all the leaders of Israel, as well as the priests and Levites. [3] The Levites thirty years old or more were counted, and the total number of men was thirty-eight thousand. [4] David said, "Of these, twenty-four thousand are to be in charge of the work of the temple of the LORD and six thousand are to be officials and judges. [5] Four thousand are to be gatekeepers and four thousand are to praise the LORD with the musical instruments I have provided for that purpose."

[6] David separated the Levites into divisions corresponding to the sons of Levi: Gershon, Kohath and Merari.

### Gershonites

[7] Belonging to the Gershonites:
Ladan and Shimei.
[8] The sons of Ladan:
Jehiel the first, Zetham and Joel—three in all.
[9] The sons of Shimei:
Shelomoth, Haziel and Haran—three in all.
These were the heads of the families of Ladan.
[10] And the sons of Shimei:
Jahath, Ziza,[a] Jeush and Beriah.
These were the sons of Shimei—four in all.
[11] Jahath was the first and Ziza the second, but Jeush and Beriah did not have many sons; so they were counted as one family with one assignment.

### Kohathites

[12] The sons of Kohath:
Amram, Izhar, Hebron and Uzziel—four in all.
[13] The sons of Amram:
Aaron and Moses.
Aaron was set apart, he and his descendants forever, to consecrate the most holy things, to offer sacrifices before the LORD, to minister before him and to pronounce blessings in his name forever. [14] The sons of Moses the man of God were counted as part of the tribe of Levi.
[15] The sons of Moses:
Gershom and Eliezer.
[16] The descendants of Gershom:
Shubael was the first.
[17] The descendants of Eliezer:
Rehabiah was the first.
Eliezer had no other sons, but the sons of Rehabiah were very numerous.
[18] The sons of Izhar:
Shelomith was the first.
[19] The sons of Hebron:
Jeriah the first, Amariah the second, Jahaziel the third and Jekameam the fourth.
[20] The sons of Uzziel:
Micah the first and Ishiah the second.

### Merarites

[21] The sons of Merari:
Mahli and Mushi.
The sons of Mahli:
Eleazar and Kish.
[22] Eleazar died without having sons: he had only daughters. Their cousins, the sons of Kish, married them.
[23] The sons of Mushi:
Mahli, Eder and Jerimoth—three in all.

[24] These were the descendants of Levi by their families—the heads of families as they were registered under

[a] 10 One Hebrew manuscript, Septuagint and Vulgate (see also verse 11); most Hebrew manuscripts *Zina*

## Amplified Bible

**23** When David was old and full of days, he made Solomon his son king over Israel.

[2] David assembled all the leaders of Israel, with the priests and Levites.
[3] The Levites thirty years old and upward numbered, man by man, 38,000,
[4] Of whom [a] 24,000 were to oversee the work of the house of the Lord and 6,000 were to be officers and judges.
[5] And, said David, 4,000 shall be gatekeepers and 4,000 are to praise the Lord with the instruments which I made for praise.
[6] And David organized them in sections according to the sons of Levi: Gershon, Kohath, and Merari.
[7] Of the Gershonites: Ladan (Libni) and Shimei.
[8] The sons of Ladan: Jehiel the chief, Zetham, and Joel—three in all.
[9] The sons of Shimei: Shelomoth, Haziel, and Haran—three in all. These were the heads of the fathers' houses of Ladan.
[10] And the sons of Shimei: Jahath, Zina (Zizah), Jeush, and Beriah. Of these four sons of Shimei,
[11] Jahath was chief and Zizah the second, but Jeush and Beriah had not many sons [not enough for a father's house or clan]; so they were counted together as one father's house.
[12] The sons of Kohath: Amram, Izhar, Hebron, and Uzziel—four in all.
[13] The sons of Amram: Aaron and Moses. Aaron was set apart to sanctify him as most holy *and* to consecrate the most holy things, that he and his sons forever might burn incense before the Lord, minister to Him, and bless in His name [and the character which that name denotes] forever.
[14] But the sons of Moses the man of God were named among the tribe of Levi.
[15] The sons of Moses: Gershom and Eliezer.
[16] The son of Gershom: Shebuel the chief.
[17] The son of Eliezer: Rehabiah the chief. Eliezer had no other sons, but Rehabiah's sons were very many.
[18] The sons of Izhar: Shelomith was the chief.
[19] The sons of Hebron: Jeriah the first, Amariah the second, Jahaziel the third, and Jekameam the fourth.
[20] The sons of Uzziel: Micah the first and Isshiah the second.
[21] The sons of Merari: Mahli and Mushi. The sons of Mahli: Eleazar and Kish.
[22] Eleazar died and had no sons, but daughters only, and their kinsmen, sons of Kish, took them as wives.
[23] The sons of Mushi: Mahli, Eder, and Jeremoth—three in all.
[24] These were the Levites by their fathers' houses, the heads of the fathers' houses of those registered, accord-

[a] The reader may be tempted to consider these figures absurdly high if he does not get the whole picture. Note these features of it: 1. The Levites were divided into twenty-four rotating divisions (I Chron. 24:6-19). 2. One thousand Levites on duty at one time for Solomon's temple, considering the many purposes and cost of the building, its ornate ritual, and the scale of the work, is not unreasonable according to authorities. 3. In the primitive simplicity of the wilderness, the worshiper killed the animal he brought for an offering, skinned it, cut it in pieces, and washed the entrails and legs. But now all these services were the duty of the Levites or Nethinim (servants of the temple); in addition, the number of worshipers had greatly increased (hence the need for a large number of Levites).

## New International Version

their names and counted individually, that is, the workers twenty years old or more who served in the temple of the LORD. 25 For David had said, "Since the LORD, the God of Israel, has granted rest to his people and has come to dwell in Jerusalem forever, 26 the Levites no longer need to carry the tabernacle or any of the articles used in its service." 27 According to the last instructions of David, the Levites were counted from those twenty years old or more.

28 The duty of the Levites was to help Aaron's descendants in the service of the temple of the LORD: to be in charge of the courtyards, the side rooms, the purification of all sacred things and the performance of other duties at the house of God. 29 They were in charge of the bread set out on the table, the special flour for the grain offerings, the thin loaves made without yeast, the baking and the mixing, and all measurements of quantity and size. 30 They were also to stand every morning to thank and praise the LORD. They were to do the same in the evening 31 and whenever burnt offerings were presented to the LORD on the Sabbaths, at the New Moon feasts and at the appointed festivals. They were to serve before the LORD regularly in the proper number and in the way prescribed for them.

32 And so the Levites carried out their responsibilities for the tent of meeting, for the Holy Place and, under their relatives the descendants of Aaron, for the service of the temple of the LORD.

### The Divisions of Priests

**24** These were the divisions of the descendants of Aaron:

The sons of Aaron were Nadab, Abihu, Eleazar and Ithamar. 2 But Nadab and Abihu died before their father did, and they had no sons; so Eleazar and Ithamar served as the priests. 3 With the help of Zadok a descendant of Eleazar and Ahimelek a descendant of Ithamar, David separated them into divisions for their appointed order of ministering. 4 A larger number of leaders were found among Eleazar's descendants than among Ithamar's, and they were divided accordingly: sixteen heads of families from Eleazar's descendants and eight heads of families from Ithamar's descendants. 5 They divided them impartially by casting lots, for there were officials of the sanctuary and officials of God among the descendants of both Eleazar and Ithamar.

6 The scribe Shemaiah son of Nethanel, a Levite, recorded their names in the presence of the king and of the officials: Zadok the priest, Ahimelek son of Abiathar and the heads of families of the priests and of the Levites—one family being taken from Eleazar and then one from Ithamar.

7 The first lot fell to Jehoiarib,
  the second to Jedaiah,
8 the third to Harim,
  the fourth to Seorim,
9 the fifth to Malkijah,
  the sixth to Mijamin,
10 the seventh to Hakkoz,
  the eighth to Abijah,
11 the ninth to Jeshua,
  the tenth to Shekaniah,
12 the eleventh to Eliashib,
  the twelfth to Jakim,
13 the thirteenth to Huppah,
  the fourteenth to Jeshebeab,
14 the fifteenth to Bilgah,
  the sixteenth to Immer,
15 the seventeenth to Hezir,
  the eighteenth to Happizzez,
16 the nineteenth to Pethahiah,
  the twentieth to Jehezkel,

## Amplified Bible

ing to the number of names of the individuals who were the servants of the house of the Lord, from twenty years old and upward.

25 For David said, The Lord, the God of Israel has given peace *and* rest to His people, and He dwells in Jerusalem forever.

26 So the Levites no more have need to carry the tabernacle and all its vessels for its service.

27 For by the last words *and* acts of David, these were the number of the Levites from twenty years old and above.

28 But their duty should be to wait on [the priests] the sons of Aaron in the service of the house of the Lord, caring for the courts, the chambers, the cleansing of all holy things, and any work of the service of God's house,

29 For the showbread also, and for the fine flour for a cereal offering, whether of unleavened wafers or of what is baked on the griddle or soaked [in oil], and for all measuring of amount and size [as the Law of Moses required].

30 They are also to stand every morning to thank and praise the Lord, and likewise at evening,

31 And to assist in offering all burnt sacrifices to the Lord on Sabbaths, New Moon festivals, and set feast days by number according to the ordinance concerning them, continually before the Lord.

32 So they shall keep charge of the Tent of Meeting and the Holy Place and shall attend to the sons of Aaron their kinsmen, for the service of the house of the Lord.

**24** The courses *or* divisions of the priests, the sons of Aaron, were these: The sons of Aaron: Nadab, and Abihu, Eleazar, and Ithamar.

2 But Nadab and Abihu died before their father and had no children; therefore Eleazar and Ithamar executed the priest's office.

3 And David, with Zadok of the sons of Eleazar and Ahimelech of the sons of Ithamar, divided *and* distributed them according to their assigned duties.

4 Since there were more chief men found among the sons of Eleazar [because of the misfortunes of Eli, and Saul's slaughter of the priests at Nob] than among the sons of Ithamar, they were divided thus: sixteen heads of fathers' houses of the sons of Eleazar and eight of the sons of Ithamar according to their fathers' houses.

5 Thus were they divided by lot, one group with the other, for there were chiefs of the sanctuary and chiefs of God [high priests] drawn both from the sons of Eleazar and from the sons of Ithamar.

6 Shemaiah the scribe, son of Nethanel, a Levite, recorded them in the presence of the king, the princes, Zadok the priest, Ahimelech son of Abiathar [the priest who escaped being killed at Nob by Saul and fled to David], and the heads of the fathers' houses of the priests and Levites—one father's house being taken alternately for Eleazar and one for Ithamar.

7 The lots fell, the first one to Jehoiarib, the second to Jedaiah,
8 The third to Harim, the fourth to Se-orim,
9 The fifth to Malchijah, the sixth to Mijamin,
10 The seventh to Hakkoz, the eighth to Abijah,
11 The ninth to Jeshua, the tenth to Shecaniah,
12 The eleventh to Eliashib, the twelfth to Jakim,
13 The thirteenth to Huppah, the fourteenth to Jeshebeab,
14 The fifteenth to Bilgah, the sixteenth to Immer,
15 The seventeenth to Hezir, the eighteenth to Happizzez,
16 The nineteenth to Pethahiah, the twentieth to Jehezkel,

## New International Version

<sup>17</sup>the twenty-first to Jakin,
  the twenty-second to Gamul,
<sup>18</sup>the twenty-third to Delaiah
  and the twenty-fourth to Maaziah.

<sup>19</sup>This was their appointed order of ministering when they entered the temple of the LORD, according to the regulations prescribed for them by their ancestor Aaron, as the LORD, the God of Israel, had commanded him.

### The Rest of the Levites

<sup>20</sup>As for the rest of the descendants of Levi:
  from the sons of Amram: Shubael;
    from the sons of Shubael: Jehdeiah.
<sup>21</sup>As for Rehabiah, from his sons:
  Ishiah was the first.
<sup>22</sup>From the Izharites: Shelomoth;
  from the sons of Shelomoth: Jahath.
<sup>23</sup>The sons of Hebron: Jeriah the first,<sup>a</sup> Amariah the second, Jahaziel the third and Jekameam the fourth.
<sup>24</sup>The son of Uzziel: Micah;
  from the sons of Micah: Shamir.
<sup>25</sup>The brother of Micah: Ishiah;
  from the sons of Ishiah: Zechariah.
<sup>26</sup>The sons of Merari: Mahli and Mushi.
  The son of Jaaziah: Beno.
<sup>27</sup>The sons of Merari:
  from Jaaziah: Beno, Shoham, Zakkur and Ibri.
<sup>28</sup>From Mahli: Eleazar, who had no sons.
<sup>29</sup>From Kish: the son of Kish:
  Jerahmeel.
<sup>30</sup>And the sons of Mushi: Mahli, Eder and Jerimoth.

These were the Levites, according to their families. <sup>31</sup>They also cast lots, just as their relatives the descendants of Aaron did, in the presence of King David and of Zadok, Ahimelek, and the heads of families of the priests and of the Levites. The families of the oldest brother were treated the same as those of the youngest.

### The Musicians

**25** David, together with the commanders of the army, set apart some of the sons of Asaph, Heman and Jeduthun for the ministry of prophesying, accompanied by harps, lyres and cymbals. Here is the list of the men who performed this service:

<sup>2</sup>From the sons of Asaph:
  Zakkur, Joseph, Nethaniah and Asarelah. The sons of Asaph were under the supervision of Asaph, who prophesied under the king's supervision.
<sup>3</sup>As for Jeduthun, from his sons:
  Gedaliah, Zeri, Jeshaiah, Shimei,<sup>b</sup> Hashabiah and Mattithiah, six in all, under the supervision of their father Jeduthun, who prophesied, using the harp in thanking and praising the LORD.
<sup>4</sup>As for Heman, from his sons:
  Bukkiah, Mattaniah, Uzziel, Shubael and Jerimoth; Hananiah, Hanani, Eliathah, Giddalti and Romamti-Ezer; Joshbekashah, Mallothi, Hothir and Mahazioth. <sup>5</sup>(All these were sons of Heman the king's seer. They were given him through the promises of God to exalt him. God gave Heman fourteen sons and three daughters.

<sup>6</sup>All these men were under the supervision of their father for the music of the temple of the LORD, with cymbals, lyres and harps, for the ministry at the house of God. Asaph, Jeduthun and Heman were under the supervi-

## Amplified Bible

<sup>17</sup>The twenty-first to Jachin, the twenty-second to Gamul,
<sup>18</sup>The twenty-third to Delaiah, the twenty-fourth to Maaziah.

<sup>19</sup>This was their order for coming on duty to serve in the house of the Lord, according to the procedure ordered for them by their [forefather] Aaron, as the Lord, the God of Israel, had commanded him.

<sup>20</sup>As for the rest of the sons of Levi: of the sons of Amram: Shubael; of the sons of Shubael: Jehdeiah.
<sup>21</sup>Of Rehabiah: of the sons of Rehabiah: Isshiah the chief.
<sup>22</sup>Of the Izharites: Shelomoth; of the sons of Shelomoth: Jahath.
<sup>23</sup>The sons of Hebron: Jeriah the first, Amariah the second, Jahaziel the third, Jekameam the fourth.
<sup>24</sup>The son of Uzziel: Micah; of the sons of Micah: Shamir.
<sup>25</sup>The brother of Micah: Isshiah; of the sons of Isshiah: Zechariah.
<sup>26</sup>The sons of Merari: Mahli and Mushi. The son of Jaaziah: Beno.
<sup>27</sup>The sons of Merari: by Jaaziah: Beno, Shoham, Zaccur, and Ibri.
<sup>28</sup>Of Mahli: Eleazar, who had no sons.
<sup>29</sup>Of Kish: the son of Kish: Jerahmeel.
<sup>30</sup>The sons of Mushi: Mahli, Eder, and Jerimoth. These were the sons of the Levites, according to their fathers' houses.
<sup>31</sup>These likewise cast lots, as did their kinsmen the sons of Aaron, in the presence of David the king, Zadok, Ahimelech, and the heads of the fathers' houses of the priests and Levites—the head of each father's house and his younger brother alike.

**25** Also David and the chiefs of the host [of the Lord] separated to the [temple] service some of the sons of Asaph, Heman, and Jeduthun, who should prophesy [being inspired] with lyres, harps, and cymbals. The list of the musicians according to their service was:

<sup>2</sup>Of the sons of Asaph: Zaccur, Joseph, Nethaniah, and Asharelah, the sons of Asaph under the direction of Asaph, who prophesied (witnessed and testified under divine inspiration) in keeping with the king's order.

<sup>3</sup>Of the sons of Jeduthun: Gedaliah, Zeri, Jeshaiah, Shimei, Hashabiah, and Mattithiah, six in all, under the direction of their father Jeduthun, who witnessed and prophesied under divine inspiration with the lyre in thanksgiving and praise to the Lord.

<sup>4</sup>Of Heman: the sons of Heman: Bukkiah, Mattaniah, Uzziel, Shebuel, Jerimoth, Hananiah, Hanani, Eliathah, Giddalti, Romamti-ezer, Joshbekashah, Mallothi, Hothir, and Mahazioth.

<sup>5</sup>All these were the sons of Heman the king's seer [his mediator] in the words *and* things of God to exalt Him; for God gave to Heman fourteen sons and three daughters. [Ps. 68:25.]

<sup>6</sup>All of whom were [in the choir] under the direction of their father for song in the house of the Lord, with cymbals, harps, and lyres, for the service of the house of God. Asaph, Jeduthun, and Heman were under the order of the king.

---

<sup>a</sup> 23 Two Hebrew manuscripts and some Septuagint manuscripts (see also 23:19); most Hebrew manuscripts *The sons of Jeriah:*
<sup>b</sup> 3 One Hebrew manuscript and some Septuagint manuscripts (see also verse 17); most Hebrew manuscripts do not have *Shimei.*

## New International Version

sion of the king. ⁷Along with their relatives—all of them trained and skilled in music for the LORD—they numbered 288. ⁸Young and old alike, teacher as well as student, cast lots for their duties.

⁹The first lot, which was for Asaph, fell to Joseph,
his sons and relatives*a*     12*b*
the second to Gedaliah,
him and his relatives and sons     12
¹⁰the third to Zakkur,
his sons and relatives     12
¹¹the fourth to Izri,*c*
his sons and relatives     12
¹²the fifth to Nethaniah,
his sons and relatives     12
¹³the sixth to Bukkiah,
his sons and relatives     12
¹⁴the seventh to Jesarelah,*d*
his sons and relatives     12
¹⁵the eighth to Jeshaiah,
his sons and relatives     12
¹⁶the ninth to Mattaniah,
his sons and relatives     12
¹⁷the tenth to Shimei,
his sons and relatives     12
¹⁸the eleventh to Azarel,*e*
his sons and relatives     12
¹⁹the twelfth to Hashabiah,
his sons and relatives     12
²⁰the thirteenth to Shubael,
his sons and relatives     12
²¹the fourteenth to Mattithiah,
his sons and relatives     12
²²the fifteenth to Jerimoth,
his sons and relatives     12
²³the sixteenth to Hananiah,
his sons and relatives     12
²⁴the seventeenth to Joshbekashah,
his sons and relatives     12
²⁵the eighteenth to Hanani,
his sons and relatives     12
²⁶the nineteenth to Mallothi,
his sons and relatives     12
²⁷the twentieth to Eliathah,
his sons and relatives     12
²⁸the twenty-first to Hothir,
his sons and relatives     12
²⁹the twenty-second to Giddalti,
his sons and relatives     12
³⁰the twenty-third to Mahazioth,
his sons and relatives     12
³¹the twenty-fourth to Romamti-Ezer,
his sons and relatives     12.

### The Gatekeepers

**26** The divisions of the gatekeepers:

From the Korahites: Meshelemiah son of Kore, one of the sons of Asaph.
²Meshelemiah had sons:
Zechariah the firstborn,
Jediael the second,
Zebadiah the third,
Jathniel the fourth,
³Elam the fifth,
Jehohanan the sixth
and Eliehoenai the seventh.
⁴Obed-Edom also had sons:
Shemaiah the firstborn,

*a 9* See Septuagint; Hebrew does not have *his sons and relatives.*
*b 9* See the total in verse 7; Hebrew does not have *twelve.*
*c 11* A variant of *Zeri*     *d 14* A variant of *Asarelah*     *e 18* A variant of *Uzziel*

## Amplified Bible

⁷So the number of them [who led the remainder of the 4,000], with their kinsmen who were specially trained in songs for the Lord, all who were talented singers, was 288. [I Chron. 23:5.]

⁸[The musicians] cast lots for their duties, small and great, teacher and scholar alike.

⁹The first lot fell for Asaph to Joseph; the second to Gedaliah, to him, his brethren and his sons, twelve;

¹⁰The third to Zaccur, his sons and his brethren, twelve;

¹¹The fourth to Izri, his sons and his brethren, twelve;

¹²The fifth to Nethaniah, his sons and his brethren, twelve;

¹³The sixth to Bukkiah, his sons and his brethren, twelve;

¹⁴The seventh to Jesharelah, his sons and his brethren, twelve;

¹⁵The eighth to Jeshaiah, his sons and his brethren, twelve;

¹⁶The ninth to Mattaniah, his sons and his brethren, twelve;

¹⁷The tenth to Shimei, his sons and his brethren, twelve;

¹⁸The eleventh to Azarel, his sons and his brethren, twelve;

¹⁹The twelfth to Hashabiah, his sons and his brethren, twelve;

²⁰The thirteenth to Shubael, his sons and his brethren, twelve;

²¹The fourteenth to Mattithiah, his sons and his brethren, twelve;

²²The fifteenth to Jeremoth, his sons and his brethren, twelve;

²³The sixteenth to Hananiah, his sons and his brethren, twelve;

²⁴The seventeenth of Joshbekashah, his sons and his brethren, twelve;

²⁵The eighteenth to Hanani, his sons and his brethren, twelve;

²⁶The nineteenth to Mallothi, his sons and his brethren, twelve;

²⁷The twentieth to Eliathah, his sons and his brethren, twelve;

²⁸The twenty-first to Hothir, his sons and his brethren, twelve;

²⁹The twenty-second to Giddalti, his sons and his brethren, twelve;

³⁰The twenty-third to Mahazioth, his sons and his brethren, twelve;

³¹The twenty-fourth to Romamti-ezer, his sons and his brethren, twelve.

**26** For the divisions of the gatekeepers: Of the Korahites was: Meshelemiah son of Kore, of the sons of Asaph.

²And Meshelemiah had sons: Zechariah the firstborn, Jediael the second, Zebadiah the third, Jathniel the fourth,

³Elam the fifth, Jehohanan the sixth, Eliehoenai the seventh.

⁴Obed-edom had sons: Shemaiah the firstborn, Jehoz-

## New International Version

Jehozabad the second,
Joah the third,
Sakar the fourth,
Nethanel the fifth,
[5] Ammiel the sixth,
Issachar the seventh
and Peullethai the eighth.
(For God had blessed Obed-Edom.)

[6] Obed-Edom's son Shemaiah also had sons, who were leaders in their father's family because they were very capable men. [7] The sons of Shemaiah: Othni, Rephael, Obed and Elzabad; his relatives Elihu and Semakiah were also able men. [8] All these were descendants of Obed-Edom; they and their sons and their relatives were capable men with the strength to do the work—descendants of Obed-Edom, 62 in all.

[9] Meshelemiah had sons and relatives, who were able men—18 in all.

[10] Hosah the Merarite had sons: Shimri the first (although he was not the firstborn, his father had appointed him the first), [11] Hilkiah the second, Tabaliah the third and Zechariah the fourth. The sons and relatives of Hosah were 13 in all.

[12] These divisions of the gatekeepers, through their leaders, had duties for ministering in the temple of the LORD, just as their relatives had. [13] Lots were cast for each gate, according to their families, young and old alike. [14] The lot for the East Gate fell to Shelemiah.[a] Then lots were cast for his son Zechariah, a wise counselor, and the lot for the North Gate fell to him. [15] The lot for the South Gate fell to Obed-Edom, and the lot for the storehouse fell to his sons. [16] The lots for the West Gate and the Shalleketh Gate on the upper road fell to Shuppim and Hosah.

Guard was alongside of guard: [17] There were six Levites a day on the east, four a day on the north, four a day on the south and two at a time at the storehouse. [18] As for the court[b] to the west, there were four at the road and two at the court[b] itself.

[19] These were the divisions of the gatekeepers who were descendants of Korah and Merari.

### The Treasurers and Other Officials

[20] Their fellow Levites were[c] in charge of the treasuries of the house of God and the treasuries for the dedicated things.

[21] The descendants of Ladan, who were Gershonites through Ladan and who were heads of families belonging to Ladan the Gershonite, were Jehieli, [22] the sons of Jehieli, Zetham and his brother Joel. They were in charge of the treasuries of the temple of the LORD.

[23] From the Amramites, the Izharites, the Hebronites and the Uzzielites:

[24] Shubael, a descendant of Gershom son of Moses, was the official in charge of the treasuries. [25] His relatives through Eliezer: Rehabiah his son, Jeshaiah his son, Joram his son, Zikri his son and Shelomith his son. [26] Shelomith and his relatives were in charge of all the treasuries for the things dedicated by King David, by the heads of families who were the commanders of thousands and commanders of hundreds, and by the other army commanders. [27] Some of the plunder taken in battle they dedicated for the repair of the temple of the LORD. [28] And everything dedicated by Samuel the seer and by Saul son of Kish, Abner son of Ner and Joab son of Zeruiah, and all the other dedicated things were in the care of Shelomith and his relatives.

*a 14* A variant of *Meshelemiah*   *b 18* The meaning of the Hebrew for this word is uncertain.   *c 20* Septuagint; Hebrew *As for the Levites, Ahijah was*

## Amplified Bible

abad the second, Joah the third, Sacar the fourth, Nethanel the fifth,
[5] Ammiel the sixth, Issachar the seventh, Peullethai the eighth; for God blessed him.

[6] Also to Shemaiah his son were sons born, who were rulers in their fathers' houses, for they were mighty men of ability *and* courage.

[7] The sons of Shemaiah: Othni, Rephael, Obed, and Elzabad, whose brethren were strong *and* able men, Elihu and Semachiah.

[8] All these were sons of Obed-edom [in whose house the ark was kept], with their sons and brethren, strong *and* able men for the service—sixty-two in all. [I Chron. 13:13, 14.]

[9] Meshelemiah had sons and brethren, strong *and* able men—eighteen in all.

[10] Also Hosah, of the sons of Merari, had sons: Shimri the chief (he was not the firstborn, yet his father made him chief),

[11] Hilkiah the second, Tebaliah the third, Zechariah the fourth; all the sons and brethren of Hosah were thirteen in all.

[12] Of these were the divisions of the gatekeepers, even of the chief men, having duties, as did their brethren, to minister in the house of the Lord.

[13] And they cast lots by fathers' houses, small and great alike, for every gate.

[14] The lot for the east fell to Shelemiah. They cast lots also for Zechariah his son, a wise counselor, and his lot came out for the north.

[15] To Obed-edom it came out for the south, and to his sons the storehouse was allotted.

[16] To Shuppim and Hosah the lot fell for the west, by the refuse gate that goes into the ascending highway, post opposite post.

[17] On the east were six Levites, on the north four a day, on the south four a day, and two by two at the storehouse.

[18] At the [a]colonnade on the west side [of the outer court of the temple], there were four at the road and two at the colonnade.

[19] These were the divisions of the gatekeepers among the Korahites and the sons of Merari.

[20] Of the Levites, Ahijah was over the treasuries of the house of God and the treasuries of the dedicated gifts.

[21] The sons of Ladan, the descendants of Gershon through Ladan, the heads of families of Ladan the Gershonite: Jehieli,

[22] The sons of Jehieli, Zetham and Joel his brother, who were over the treasuries of the house of the Lord.

[23] Of the Amramites, Izharites, Hebronites, and Uzzielites:

[24] Shebuel son of Gershom, the son of Moses, was ruler over the treasuries.

[25] His brethren from Eliezer were his son Rehabiah, his son Jeshaiah, his son Joram, his son Zichri, and his son Shelomoth.

[26] This Shelomoth and his brethren were over all the treasuries of the dedicated gifts, which King David, the heads of the fathers' houses, the officers over thousands and hundreds, and the commanders of the army had dedicated.

[27] From spoil won in battles they dedicated gifts to maintain the house of the Lord.

[28] Also all that Samuel the seer, Saul son of Kish, Abner son of Ner, and Joab son of Zeruiah had dedicated, and whatever anyone had dedicated, it was in the charge of Shelomoth and his brethren.

*a* Hebrew *Parbar*, possibly court or colonnade.

## New International Version

29 From the Izharites: Kenaniah and his sons were assigned duties away from the temple, as officials and judges over Israel.
30 From the Hebronites: Hashabiah and his relatives—seventeen hundred able men—were responsible in Israel west of the Jordan for all the work of the LORD and for the king's service. 31 As for the Hebronites, Jeriah was their chief according to the genealogical records of their families. In the fortieth year of David's reign a search was made in the records, and capable men among the Hebronites were found at Jazer in Gilead. 32 Jeriah had twenty-seven hundred relatives, who were able men and heads of families, and King David put them in charge of the Reubenites, the Gadites and the half-tribe of Manasseh for every matter pertaining to God and for the affairs of the king.

### Army Divisions

**27** This is the list of the Israelites—heads of families, commanders of thousands and commanders of hundreds, and their officers, who served the king in all that concerned the army divisions that were on duty month by month throughout the year. Each division consisted of 24,000 men.

2 In charge of the first division, for the first month, was Jashobeam son of Zabdiel. There were 24,000 men in his division. 3 He was a descendant of Perez and chief of all the army officers for the first month.
4 In charge of the division for the second month was Dodai the Ahohite; Mikloth was the leader of his division. There were 24,000 men in his division.
5 The third army commander, for the third month, was Benaiah son of Jehoiada the priest. He was chief and there were 24,000 men in his division. 6 This was the Benaiah who was a mighty warrior among the Thirty and was over the Thirty. His son Ammizabad was in charge of his division.
7 The fourth, for the fourth month, was Asahel the brother of Joab; his son Zebadiah was his successor. There were 24,000 men in his division.
8 The fifth, for the fifth month, was the commander Shamhuth the Izrahite. There were 24,000 men in his division.
9 The sixth, for the sixth month, was Ira the son of Ikkesh the Tekoite. There were 24,000 men in his division.
10 The seventh, for the seventh month, was Helez the Pelonite, an Ephraimite. There were 24,000 men in his division.
11 The eighth, for the eighth month, was Sibbekai the Hushathite, a Zerahite. There were 24,000 men in his division.
12 The ninth, for the ninth month, was Abiezer the Anathothite, a Benjamite. There were 24,000 men in his division.
13 The tenth, for the tenth month, was Maharai the Netophathite, a Zerahite. There were 24,000 men in his division.
14 The eleventh, for the eleventh month, was Benaiah the Pirathonite, an Ephraimite. There were 24,000 men in his division.
15 The twelfth, for the twelfth month, was Heldai the Netophathite, from the family of Othniel. There were 24,000 men in his division.

### Leaders of the Tribes

16 The leaders of the tribes of Israel:

over the Reubenites: Eliezer son of Zikri;
over the Simeonites: Shephatiah son of Maakah;

## Amplified Bible

29 Of the Izharites: Chenaniah and his sons were appointed to outside duties for Israel, as officers and judges.
30 Of the Hebronites: Hashabiah and his brethren, men of courage *and* ability, 1,700 in all, were officers over Israel on the west side of the Jordan in all the Lord's business and the king's service.
31 Of the Hebronites: Jerijah was the chief, according to their generations by fathers' houses. In the fortieth year of David's reign a search was made, and men of great courage *and* ability were found among them at Jazer in Gilead.
32 Jerijah's kinsmen, men of courage *and* ability, were 2,700 heads of fathers' houses; King David made them overseers of the Reubenites, the Gadites, and the half-tribe of Manasseh, for everything pertaining to God and for the affairs of the king.

**27** This is the list of the Israelites, the heads of fathers' houses, the commanders of thousands and hundreds, and their officers who served the king in all matters of the divisions that came and went, month by month throughout the year, each division numbering 24,000.

2 Over the first division for the first month was Jashobeam son of Zabdiel. In his division were 24,000.
3 He was descended from Perez and was chief of all the commanders of the army for the first month.
4 Over the division for the second month was Dodai the Ahohite; and of his division Mikloth was the chief officer. In his division were 24,000.
5 The third commander of the army for the third month was Benaiah son of Jehoiada the priest, as chief. In his division were 24,000.
6 This is the Benaiah who was a mighty man of the Thirty and over the Thirty; and in his division was Ammizabad his son.
7 The fourth, for the fourth month, Asahel brother of Joab, and Zebadiah his son after him. In his division were 24,000.
8 The fifth, for the fifth month, Shamhuth the Izrahite. In his division were 24,000.
9 The sixth, for the sixth month, Ira son of Ikkesh the Tekoite. In his division were 24,000.
10 The seventh, for the seventh month, Helez the Pelonite, of the Ephraimites. In his division were 24,000.
11 The eighth, for the eighth month, Sibbecai the Hushathite, of the Zarahites. In his division were 24,000.
12 The ninth, for the ninth month, Abiezer of Anathoth, a Benjamite. In his division were 24,000.
13 The tenth, for the tenth month, Maharai from Netophah, of the Zerahites. In his division were 24,000.
14 The eleventh, for the eleventh month, Benaiah the Pirathonite, of the sons of Ephraim. In his division were 24,000.
15 The twelfth, for the twelfth month, Heldai the Netophathite, of Othniel. In his division were 24,000.
16 Also over the tribes of Israel: of the Reubenites: Eliezer son of Zichri was chief officer; of the Simeonites: Shephatiah son of Maachah;

## New International Version

17 over Levi: Hashabiah son of Kemuel;
over Aaron: Zadok;
18 over Judah: Elihu, a brother of David;
over Issachar: Omri son of Michael;
19 over Zebulun: Ishmaiah son of Obadiah;
over Naphtali: Jerimoth son of Azriel;
20 over the Ephraimites: Hoshea son of Azaziah;
over half the tribe of Manasseh: Joel son of Pedaiah;
21 over the half-tribe of Manasseh in Gilead: Iddo son of
Zechariah;
over Benjamin: Jaasiel son of Abner;
22 over Dan: Azarel son of Jeroham.
These were the leaders of the tribes of Israel.

23 David did not take the number of the men twenty
years old or less, because the LORD had promised to make
Israel as numerous as the stars in the sky. 24 Joab son of
Zeruiah began to count the men but did not finish. God's
wrath came on Israel on account of this numbering, and
the number was not entered in the book*a* of the annals of
King David.

### The King's Overseers

25 Azmaveth son of Adiel was in charge of the royal
storehouses.
Jonathan son of Uzziah was in charge of the storehouses in the outlying districts, in the towns, the villages and
the watchtowers.
26 Ezri son of Kelub was in charge of the workers who
farmed the land.
27 Shimei the Ramathite was in charge of the vineyards.
Zabdi the Shiphmite was in charge of the produce of the
vineyards for the wine vats.
28 Baal-Hanan the Gederite was in charge of the olive
and sycamore-fig trees in the western foothills.
Joash was in charge of the supplies of olive oil.
29 Shitrai the Sharonite was in charge of the herds grazing in Sharon.
Shaphat son of Adlai was in charge of the herds in the
valleys.
30 Obil the Ishmaelite was in charge of the camels.
Jehdeiah the Meronothite was in charge of the donkeys.
31 Jaziz the Hagrite was in charge of the flocks.
All these were the officials in charge of King David's
property.

32 Jonathan, David's uncle, was a counselor, a man of insight and a scribe. Jehiel son of Hakmoni took care of the
king's sons.
33 Ahithophel was the king's counselor.
Hushai the Arkite was the king's confidant. 34 Ahithophel was succeeded by Jehoiada son of Benaiah and by
Abiathar.
Joab was the commander of the royal army.

### David's Plans for the Temple

**28** David summoned all the officials of Israel to assemble at Jerusalem: the officers over the tribes,
the commanders of the divisions in the service of the king,
the commanders of thousands and commanders of hundreds, and the officials in charge of all the property and
livestock belonging to the king and his sons, together with
the palace officials, the warriors and all the brave fighting
men.
2 King David rose to his feet and said: "Listen to me, my
fellow Israelites, my people. I had it in my heart to build
a house as a place of rest for the ark of the covenant of
the LORD, for the footstool of our God, and I made plans
to build it. 3 But God said to me, 'You are not to build a
house for my Name, because you are a warrior and have
shed blood.'
4 "Yet the LORD, the God of Israel, chose me from my

## Amplified Bible

17 Of Levi: Hashabiah son of Kemuel; of Aaron: Zadok;
18 Of Judah: Elihu, one of David's brothers; of Issachar:
Omri son of Michael;
19 Of Zebulun: Ishmaiah son of Obadiah; of Naphtali:
Jerimoth son of Azriel;
20 Of the Ephraimites: Hoshea son of Azaziah; of the
half-tribe of Manasseh: Joel son of Pedaiah;
21 Of the half-tribe of Manasseh in Gilead: Iddo son of
Zechariah; of Benjamin: Jaasiel son of Abner;
22 Of Dan: Azarel son of Jeroham. These were the leaders of the tribes of Israel.
23 But David did not number those under twenty years
of age, for the Lord had promised to make Israel as the
stars of the heavens.
24 Joab son of Zeruiah began a census but did not finish,
because the census brought wrath upon Israel, and the
number was not recorded in the chronicles of King David.
25 Over the king's treasuries was Azmaveth son of Adiel;
and over the treasuries in the country, cities, villages, and
towers *or* forts was Jonathan son of Uzziah;
26 Over those who did the work of the field of tilling the
soil was Ezri son of Chelub;
27 Over the vineyards was Shimei the Ramathite; over
the produce of the vineyards for the wine cellars, Zabdi
the Shiphmite;
28 Over the olive and sycamore trees in the low plains,
Baal-hanan the Gederite; over the stores of oil, Joash;
29 Over the herds pasturing in Sharon, Shitrai the Sharonite; over the herds in the valleys, Shaphat son of Adlai;
30 Over the camels, Obil the Ishmaelite; over the she-
donkeys, Jehdeiah the Meronothite;
31 And over the flocks, Jaziz the Hagrite. All these were
stewards of King David's property.
32 Also Jonathan, David's uncle, was a counselor, a wise
man and a scribe; he and Jehiel son of Hachmoni attended
the king's sons [as tutors]. [II Kings 10:6.]
33 Ahithophel was the king's counselor; Hushai the Archite was the king's companion *and* friend.
34 Ahithophel was succeeded by Jehoiada son of Benaiah and by Abiathar. Joab was the commander of the king's
army.

**28** David assembled at Jerusalem all the leaders of Israel and of the tribes, the officers of the divisions
that served the king in courses, and those over thousands
and hundreds, and the stewards over all the property and
livestock of the king and his sons, with the palace officers,
the mighty men, and all the mighty warriors.
2 Then David the king rose to his feet and said, Hear me,
my brethren and my people. I myself intended to build a
house of rest for the ark of the covenant of the Lord, as
a footstool for our God, and I prepared materials for the
building.
3 But God said to me, You shall not build a house for My
Name [and Presence], because you have been a man of
war and have shed blood.
4 However, the Lord, the God of Israel, chose me before

*a 24 Septuagint; Hebrew number*

## New International Version

whole family to be king over Israel forever. He chose Judah as leader, and from the tribe of Judah he chose my family, and from my father's sons he was pleased to make me king over all Israel. ⁵Of all my sons—and the LORD has given me many—he has chosen my son Solomon to sit on the throne of the kingdom of the LORD over Israel. ⁶He said to me: 'Solomon your son is the one who will build my house and my courts, for I have chosen him to be my son, and I will be his father. ⁷I will establish his kingdom forever if he is unswerving in carrying out my commands and laws, as is being done at this time.'

⁸"So now I charge you in the sight of all Israel and of the assembly of the LORD, and in the hearing of our God: Be careful to follow all the commands of the LORD your God, that you may possess this good land and pass it on as an inheritance to your descendants forever.

⁹"And you, my son Solomon, acknowledge the God of your father, and serve him with wholehearted devotion and with a willing mind, for the LORD searches every heart and understands every desire and every thought. If you seek him, he will be found by you; but if you forsake him, he will reject you forever. ¹⁰Consider now, for the LORD has chosen you to build a house as the sanctuary. Be strong and do the work."

¹¹Then David gave his son Solomon the plans for the portico of the temple, its buildings, its storerooms, its upper parts, its inner rooms and the place of atonement. ¹²He gave him the plans of all that the Spirit had put in his mind for the courts of the temple of the LORD and all the surrounding rooms, for the treasuries of the temple of God and for the treasuries for the dedicated things. ¹³He gave him instructions for the divisions of the priests and Levites, and for all the work of serving in the temple of the LORD, as well as for all the articles to be used in its service. ¹⁴He designated the weight of gold for all the gold articles to be used in various kinds of service, and the weight of silver for all the silver articles to be used in various kinds of service: ¹⁵the weight of gold for the gold lampstands and their lamps, with the weight for each lampstand and its lamps; and the weight of silver for each silver lampstand and its lamps, according to the use of each lampstand; ¹⁶the weight of gold for each table for consecrated bread; the weight of silver for the silver tables; ¹⁷the weight of pure gold for the forks, sprinkling bowls and pitchers; the weight of gold for each gold dish; the weight of silver for each silver dish; ¹⁸and the weight of the refined gold for the altar of incense. He also gave him the plan for the chariot, that is, the cherubim of gold that spread their wings and overshadow the ark of the covenant of the LORD.

## Amplified Bible

all my father's house to be king over Israel forever. For He chose Judah to be the ruler; and of the house of Judah he chose the house of my father; and among the sons of my father He was pleased to make me king over all Israel;

⁵And of all my sons, for the Lord has given me many sons, He has chosen Solomon my son to sit upon the throne of the kingdom of the Lord over Israel.

⁶And He said to me, Solomon your son shall build My house and My courts, for I have chosen him to be My son, and I will be his father.

⁷I will establish his kingdom forever if he loyally *and* continuously obeys My commandments and My ordinances, as he does today.

⁸Now therefore, in the sight of all Israel, the assembly of the Lord, and in the hearing of our God, keep and seek [to be familiar with] all the commandments of the Lord your God, that you may possess this good land and leave it as an inheritance for your children after you forever.

⁹And you, Solomon my son, know the God of your father [have personal knowledge of Him, be acquainted with, and understand Him; appreciate, heed, and cherish Him] and serve Him with a blameless heart and a willing mind. For the Lord searches all hearts *and* minds and understands all the wanderings of the thoughts. If you seek Him [inquiring for and of Him and requiring Him as your first and vital necessity] you will find Him; but ᵃif you forsake Him, He will cast you off forever!

¹⁰Take heed now, for the Lord has chosen you to build a house for the sanctuary. Be strong and do it!

¹¹Then David gave Solomon his son the plan of the vestibule of the temple, its houses, its treasuries, its upper chambers, its inner rooms, and of the place for the [ark and its] mercy seat;

¹²And the plan of all that he had in mind [by the Spirit] for the courts of the house of the Lord, all the surrounding chambers, the treasuries of the house of God, and the treasuries for the dedicated gifts;

¹³The plan for the divisions of the priests and the Levites, for all the work of the service in the house of the Lord; for all the vessels for service in the house of the Lord:

¹⁴The weight of gold and silver for all the gold and silver articles of every kind of service—

¹⁵The weight of the golden lampstands and their lamps, the weight of gold or silver for each lampstand and its lamps, according to the use of each lampstand;

¹⁶The gold by weight for each table of showbread, and the silver for the tables of silver;

¹⁷Also pure gold for the forks, basins, and cups; for the golden bowls by weight of each; for the silver bowls by weight of each;

¹⁸For the incense altar refined gold by weight, and gold for the plan of the chariot of the cherubim that spread their wings and covered the ark of the Lord's covenant.

---

ᵃ God's promises to men and women invariably are dependent upon the other party to the covenant meeting His conditions, whether He says so at the time or not. In I Chron. 28:7 we find Him promising to establish Solomon's kingdom forever. Yet in I Kings 11:9-11 we find that God became angry with Solomon for all his degenerate and abominable conduct and his treachery of heart toward Him; and without mercy, except for David's sake, God declared that the kingdom would be torn from him. Was God breaking His covenant with Solomon? No, Solomon had broken and nullified that covenant long before; it no longer existed. There was now no promise for God to keep. Christians are prone to think that God will keep His part of a bargain whether they do or not, but the wisest man who ever lived died knowing that God is not mocked; "[He inevitably deludes himself who attempts to delude God.] For whatever a man sows, that *and* that only is what he will reap" (Gal. 6:7). "If you seek Him [inquiring for and of Him and requiring Him as your first and vital necessity], you will find Him; but if you forsake Him, He will cast you off forever!" David was telling Solomon all this, but as the new king grew in power, popularity, and personal aggrandizement, step by step he set himself up as privileged to ignore God. In all his wisdom he failed to comprehend that "Something greater *and* more exalted *and* more majestic than the temple is here! . . . Someone more *and* greater than Solomon is here" (Matt. 12:6, 42).

## New International Version

[19]"All this," David said, "I have in writing as a result of the LORD's hand on me, and he enabled me to understand all the details of the plan." [20]David also said to Solomon his son, "Be strong and courageous, and do the work. Do not be afraid or discouraged, for the LORD God, my God, is with you. He will not fail you or forsake you until all the work for the service of the temple of the LORD is finished. [21]The divisions of the priests and Levites are ready for all the work on the temple of God, and every willing person skilled in any craft will help you in all the work. The officials and all the people will obey your every command."

### Gifts for Building the Temple

**29** Then King David said to the whole assembly: "My son Solomon, the one whom God has chosen, is young and inexperienced. The task is great, because this palatial structure is not for man but for the LORD God. [2]With all my resources I have provided for the temple of my God—gold for the gold work, silver for the silver, bronze for the bronze, iron for the iron and wood for the wood, as well as onyx for the settings, turquoise,[a] stones of various colors, and all kinds of fine stone and marble—all of these in large quantities. [3]Besides, in my devotion to the temple of my God I now give my personal treasures of gold and silver for the temple of my God, over and above everything I have provided for this holy temple: [4]three thousand talents[b] of gold (gold of Ophir) and seven thousand talents[c] of refined silver, for the overlaying of the walls of the buildings, [5]for the gold work and the silver work, and for all the work to be done by the craftsmen. Now, who is willing to consecrate themselves to the LORD today?"

[6]Then the leaders of families, the officers of the tribes of Israel, the commanders of thousands and commanders of hundreds, and the officials in charge of the king's work gave willingly. [7]They gave toward the work on the temple of God five thousand talents[d] and ten thousand darics[e] of gold, ten thousand talents[f] of silver, eighteen thousand talents[g] of bronze and a hundred thousand talents[h] of iron. [8]Anyone who had precious stones gave them to the treasury of the temple of the LORD in the custody of Jehiel the Gershonite. [9]The people rejoiced at the willing response of their leaders, for they had given freely and wholeheartedly to the LORD. David the king also rejoiced greatly.

### David's Prayer

[10]David praised the LORD in the presence of the whole assembly, saying,

"Praise be to you, LORD,
  the God of our father Israel,
  from everlasting to everlasting.
[11]Yours, LORD, is the greatness and the power
  and the glory and the majesty and the splendor,
  for everything in heaven and earth is yours.
Yours, LORD, is the kingdom;
  you are exalted as head over all.
[12]Wealth and honor come from you;
  you are the ruler of all things.
In your hands are strength and power
  to exalt and give strength to all.
[13]Now, our God, we give you thanks,
  and praise your glorious name.

[14]"But who am I, and who are my people, that we should be able to give as generously as this? Everything comes

## Amplified Bible

[19]All this the Lord made me understand by the writing by His hand upon me, all the work to be done according to the plan. [20]Also David told Solomon his son, Be strong and courageous, and do it. Fear not, be not dismayed, for the Lord God, my God, is with you. He will not fail or forsake you until you have finished all the work for the service of the house of the Lord. [21]And see, [you have] the divisions of the priests and Levites for all the service of God's house, and with you in all the kinds of work will be every willing, skillful man for any kind of service. Also the officers and all the people will be wholly at your command.

**29** And King David said to all the assembly, Solomon my son, whom alone God has chosen, is yet young, tender, *and* inexperienced; and the work is great, for the palace is not to be for man but for the Lord God. [2]So I have provided with all my might for the house of my God the gold for things to be of gold, silver for things of silver, bronze for things of bronze, iron for things of iron, and wood for things of wood, as well as onyx *or* beryl stones, stones to be set, stones of antimony, stones of various colors, and all sorts of precious stones, and marble stones in abundance. [3]Moreover, because I have set my affection on the house of my God, in addition to all I have prepared for the holy house, I have a private treasure of gold and silver which I give for the house of my God: [4]It is 3,000 talents of gold, gold of Ophir, 7,000 talents of refined silver for overlaying the walls of the house, [5]Gold for the uses of gold, silver for the uses of silver, and for every work to be done by craftsmen. Now who will offer willingly to fill his hand [and consecrate it] today to the Lord [like one consecrating himself to the priesthood]? [6]Then the chiefs of the fathers and princes of the tribes of Israel and the captains of thousands and of hundreds, with the rulers of the king's work, offered willingly [7]And gave for the service of the house of God—of gold 5,000 talents and 10,000 darics, of silver 10,000 talents, of bronze 18,000 talents, and 100,000 talents of iron. [8]And whoever had precious stones gave them to the treasury of the house of the Lord in the care of Jehiel the Gershonite. [9]Then the people rejoiced because these had given willingly, for with a whole *and* blameless heart they had offered freely to the Lord. King David also rejoiced greatly. [10]Therefore David blessed the Lord before all the assembly and said, Be praised, adored, *and* thanked, O Lord, the God of Israel our [forefather], forever and ever. [11]Yours, O Lord, is the greatness and the power and the glory and the victory and the majesty, for all that is in the heavens and the earth is Yours; Yours is the kingdom, O Lord, and Yours it is to be exalted as Head over all. [12]Both riches and honor come from You, and You reign over all. In Your hands are power and might; in Your hands it is to make great and to give strength to all. [13]Now therefore, our God, we thank You and praise Your glorious name *and* those attributes which that name denotes. [14]But who am I, and what are my people, that we should retain strength *and* be able to offer thus so willingly? For

---

*a* 2 The meaning of the Hebrew for this word is uncertain.  *b* 4 That is, about 110 tons or about 100 metric tons  *c* 4 That is, about 260 tons or about 235 metric tons  *d* 7 That is, about 190 tons or about 170 metric tons  *e* 7 That is, about 185 pounds or about 84 kilograms  *f* 7 That is, about 380 tons or about 340 metric tons  *g* 7 That is, about 675 tons or about 610 metric tons  *h* 7 That is, about 3,800 tons or about 3,400 metric tons

## New International Version

from you, and we have given you only what comes from your hand. [15]We are foreigners and strangers in your sight, as were all our ancestors. Our days on earth are like a shadow, without hope. [16]LORD our God, all this abundance that we have provided for building you a temple for your Holy Name comes from your hand, and all of it belongs to you. [17]I know, my God, that you test the heart and are pleased with integrity. All these things I have given willingly and with honest intent. And now I have seen with joy how willingly your people who are here have given to you. [18]LORD, the God of our fathers Abraham, Isaac and Israel, keep these desires and thoughts in the hearts of your people forever, and keep their hearts loyal to you. [19]And give my son Solomon the wholehearted devotion to keep your commands, statutes and decrees and to do everything to build the palatial structure for which I have provided."

[20]Then David said to the whole assembly, "Praise the LORD your God." So they all praised the LORD, the God of their fathers; they bowed down, prostrating themselves before the LORD and the king.

### Solomon Acknowledged as King

[21]The next day they made sacrifices to the LORD and presented burnt offerings to him: a thousand bulls, a thousand rams and a thousand male lambs, together with their drink offerings, and other sacrifices in abundance for all Israel. [22]They ate and drank with great joy in the presence of the LORD that day.

Then they acknowledged Solomon son of David as king a second time, anointing him before the LORD to be ruler and Zadok to be priest. [23]So Solomon sat on the throne of the LORD as king in place of his father David. He prospered and all Israel obeyed him. [24]All the officers and warriors, as well as all of King David's sons, pledged their submission to King Solomon.

[25]The LORD highly exalted Solomon in the sight of all Israel and bestowed on him royal splendor such as no king over Israel ever had before.

### The Death of David

[26]David son of Jesse was king over all Israel. [27]He ruled over Israel forty years—seven in Hebron and thirty-three in Jerusalem. [28]He died at a good old age, having enjoyed long life, wealth and honor. His son Solomon succeeded him as king.

[29]As for the events of King David's reign, from beginning to end, they are written in the records of Samuel the seer, the records of Nathan the prophet and the records of Gad the seer, [30]together with the details of his reign and power, and the circumstances that surrounded him and Israel and the kingdoms of all the other lands.

## Amplified Bible

all things come from You, and out of Your own [hand] we have given You.

[15]For we are strangers before You, and sojourners, as all our fathers were; our days on the earth are like a shadow, and there is no hope or expectation of remaining.

[16]O Lord our God, all this store that we have prepared to build You a house for Your holy Name and the token of Your presence comes from Your hand, and is all Your own.

[17]I know also, my God, that You try the heart and delight in uprightness. In the uprightness of my heart I have freely offered all these things. And now I have seen with joy Your people who are present here offer voluntarily and freely to You.

[18]O Lord, God of Abraham, Isaac, and Israel, our fathers, keep forever such purposes and thoughts in the minds of Your people, and direct and establish their hearts toward You.

[19]And give to Solomon my son a blameless heart to keep Your commandments, testimonies, and statutes, and to do all that is necessary to build the palace [for You] for which I have made provision.

[20]And David said to all the assembly, Now adore (praise and thank) the Lord your God! And all the assembly blessed the Lord, the God of their fathers, and bowed down and did obeisance to the Lord and to the king [as His earthly representative].

[21]The next day they offered sacrifices and burnt offerings to the Lord: 1,000 bulls, 1,000 rams, and 1,000 lambs, with their drink offerings, and sacrifices in abundance for all Israel.

[22]They ate and drank before the Lord on that day with great rejoicing. They made Solomon son of David king a second time, and anointed him as prince for the Lord and Zadok to be high priest.

[23]Then Solomon sat on the throne of the Lord as king instead of David his father; and he prospered, and all Israel obeyed him.

[24]All the leaders and mighty men, and also all the sons of King David, pledged allegiance to King Solomon.

[25]And the Lord magnified Solomon exceedingly in the sight of all Israel and bestowed upon him such royal majesty as had not been on any king before him in Israel.

[26]Thus David son of Jesse reigned over all Israel.

[27]The time he reigned over Israel was forty years—he reigned seven years in Hebron and thirty-three years in Jerusalem.

[28]He died in a good old age [his seventy-first year], full and satisfied with days, riches, and honor. Solomon his son reigned in his stead.

[29]Now the acts of King David, from first to last, are written in the recorded words of Samuel the seer, Nathan the prophet, and Gad the seer,

[30]With accounts of all his reign and his might, and the times through which he and Israel passed, as did all the kingdoms of the countries.

# 2 Chronicles

# Chronicles

## Solomon Asks for Wisdom

**1** Solomon son of David established himself firmly over his kingdom, for the LORD his God was with him and made him exceedingly great.

²Then Solomon spoke to all Israel—to the commanders of thousands and commanders of hundreds, to the judges and to all the leaders in Israel, the heads of families— ³and Solomon and the whole assembly went to the high place at Gibeon, for God's tent of meeting was there, which Moses the LORD's servant had made in the wilderness. ⁴Now David had brought up the ark of God from Kiriath Jearim to the place he had prepared for it, because he had pitched a tent for it in Jerusalem. ⁵But the bronze altar that Bezalel son of Uri, the son of Hur, had made was in Gibeon in front of the tabernacle of the LORD; so Solomon and the assembly inquired of him there. ⁶Solomon went up to the bronze altar before the LORD in the tent of meeting and offered a thousand burnt offerings on it.

⁷That night God appeared to Solomon and said to him, "Ask for whatever you want me to give you."

⁸Solomon answered God, "You have shown great kindness to David my father and have made me king in his place. ⁹Now, LORD God, let your promise to my father David be confirmed, for you have made me king over a people who are as numerous as the dust of the earth. ¹⁰Give me wisdom and knowledge, that I may lead this people, for who is able to govern this great people of yours?"

¹¹God said to Solomon, "Since this is your heart's desire and you have not asked for wealth, possessions or honor, nor for the death of your enemies, and since you have not asked for a long life but for wisdom and knowledge to govern my people over whom I have made you king, ¹²therefore wisdom and knowledge will be given you. And I will also give you wealth, possessions and honor, such as no king who was before you ever had and none after you will have."

¹³Then Solomon went to Jerusalem from the high place at Gibeon, from before the tent of meeting. And he reigned over Israel.

¹⁴Solomon accumulated chariots and horses; he had fourteen hundred chariots and twelve thousand horses,[a] which he kept in the chariot cities and also with him in Jerusalem. ¹⁵The king made silver and gold as common in Jerusalem as stones, and cedar as plentiful as sycamore-fig trees in the foothills. ¹⁶Solomon's horses were imported from Egypt and from Kue[b]—the royal merchants purchased them from Kue at the current price. ¹⁷They imported a chariot from Egypt for six hundred shekels[c] of silver, and a horse for a hundred and fifty.[d] They also exported them to all the kings of the Hittites and of the Arameans.

**1** Solomon son of David was strengthened in his kingdom, and the Lord his God was with him and made him exceedingly great.

²Solomon spoke to all Israel, to the captains of thousands and of hundreds, and to the judges, and to every prince in all Israel, the heads of the fathers' houses.

³And Solomon and all the assembly [a united nation] with him went to the high place that was at Gibeon, for the Tent of Meeting of God, which Moses the servant of the Lord had made in the wilderness, was there [where the Canaanites had habitually worshiped].

⁴But David had brought up the ark of God from Kiriath-jearim to the place which David had prepared for it, for he had pitched a tent for it at Jerusalem.

⁵Moreover, the bronze altar that Bezalel son of Uri, the son of Hur, had made was there before the tabernacle of the Lord, and Solomon and the assembly sought [the Lord].

⁶Solomon went up there to the bronze altar before the Lord at the Tent of Meeting and offered 1,000 burnt offerings on it.

⁷That night God appeared to Solomon and said to him, Ask what I shall give you.

⁸And Solomon said to God, You have shown great mercy and loving-kindness to David my father and have made me king in his place.

⁹Now, O Lord God, let Your promise to David my father be fulfilled, for you have made me king over a people like the dust of the earth in multitude.

¹⁰Give me now wisdom and knowledge to go out and come in before this people, for who can rule this Your people who are so great?

¹¹God replied to Solomon, Because this was in your heart and you have not asked for riches, possessions, honor, *and* glory, or the life of your foes, or even for long life, but have asked wisdom and knowledge for yourself, that you may rule *and* judge My people over whom I have made you king,

¹²Wisdom and knowledge are granted you. And I will give you riches, possessions, honor, *and* glory, such as none of the kings had before you, and none after you shall have their equal.

¹³Then Solomon came from the high place at Gibeon, from before the Tent of Meeting, to Jerusalem. And he reigned over Israel.

¹⁴Solomon gathered chariots and horsemen; he had 1,400 chariots and 12,000 horsemen, which he placed in the cities [suited for the use] of chariots and with the king at Jerusalem.

¹⁵And the king made silver and gold in Jerusalem as common as stones, and he made cedar as plentiful as the sycamores of the lowland.

¹⁶Solomon's horses were brought out of Egypt; the king's merchants received them in droves, ªeach drove at a price.

¹⁷They imported from Egypt a chariot for 600 shekels of silver, and a horse for 150; so they brought out horses for all the Hittite and Syrian kings as export agents.

---

ª 14 Or *charioteers*   ᵇ 16 Probably Cilicia   ᶜ 17 That is, about 15 pounds or about 6.9 kilograms     ᵈ 17 That is, about 3 3/4 pounds or about 1.7 kilograms

ª Solomon's actions were in violation of the commands given through Moses in Deut. 17:16, 17 (see also I Kings 4:26; I Kings 10:26-11:1-4).

## New International Version

### Preparations for Building the Temple

**2** [a] Solomon gave orders to build a temple for the Name of the LORD and a royal palace for himself. [2] He conscripted 70,000 men as carriers and 80,000 as stonecutters in the hills and 3,600 as foremen over them.

[3] Solomon sent this message to Hiram[b] king of Tyre:

"Send me cedar logs as you did for my father David when you sent him cedar to build a palace to live in. [4] Now I am about to build a temple for the Name of the LORD my God and to dedicate it to him for burning fragrant incense before him, for setting out the consecrated bread regularly, and for making burnt offerings every morning and evening and on the Sabbaths, at the New Moons and at the appointed festivals of the LORD our God. This is a lasting ordinance for Israel.

[5] "The temple I am going to build will be great, because our God is greater than all other gods. [6] But who is able to build a temple for him, since the heavens, even the highest heavens, cannot contain him? Who then am I to build a temple for him, except as a place to burn sacrifices before him?

[7] "Send me, therefore, a man skilled to work in gold and silver, bronze and iron, and in purple, crimson and blue yarn, and experienced in the art of engraving, to work in Judah and Jerusalem with my skilled workers, whom my father David provided.

[8] "Send me also cedar, juniper and algum[c] logs from Lebanon, for I know that your servants are skilled in cutting timber there. My servants will work with yours [9] to provide me with plenty of lumber, because the temple I build must be large and magnificent. [10] I will give your servants, the woodsmen who cut the timber, twenty thousand cors[d] of ground wheat, twenty thousand cors[e] of barley, twenty thousand baths[f] of wine and twenty thousand baths of olive oil."

[11] Hiram king of Tyre replied by letter to Solomon:

"Because the LORD loves his people, he has made you their king."

[12] And Hiram added:

"Praise be to the LORD, the God of Israel, who made heaven and earth! He has given King David a wise son, endowed with intelligence and discernment, who will build a temple for the LORD and a palace for himself.

[13] "I am sending you Huram-Abi, a man of great skill, [14] whose mother was from Dan and whose father was from Tyre. He is trained to work in gold and silver, bronze and iron, stone and wood, and with purple and blue and crimson yarn and fine linen. He is experienced in all kinds of engraving and can execute any design given to him. He will work with your skilled workers and with those of my lord, David your father.

[15] "Now let my lord send his servants the wheat and barley and the olive oil and wine he promised, [16] and we will cut all the logs from Lebanon that you need and will float them as rafts by sea down to Joppa. You can then take them up to Jerusalem."

[17] Solomon took a census of all the foreigners residing in Israel, after the census his father David had taken; and they were found to be 153,600. [18] He assigned 70,000 of them to be carriers and 80,000 to be stonecutters in the hills, with 3,600 foremen over them to keep the people working.

---

[a] In Hebrew texts 2:1 is numbered 1:18, and 2:2-18 is numbered 2:1-17.
[b] 3 Hebrew *Huram*, a variant of *Hiram*; also in verses 11 and 12
[c] 8 Probably a variant of *almug*    [d] 10 That is, probably about 3,600 tons or about 3,200 metric tons of wheat    [e] 10 That is, probably about 3,000 tons or about 2,700 metric tons of barley    [f] 10 That is, about 120,000 gallons or about 440,000 liters

## Amplified Bible

**2** Solomon determined to build a temple for the [a] Name of the Lord and a royal capitol. [2] And Solomon counted out 70,000 men to bear burdens, 80,000 to be stonecutters in the hill country, and 3,600 overseers.

[3] And Solomon sent to Hiram king of Tyre, saying, As you dealt with David my father and sent him cedars to build himself a house in which to dwell, even so deal with me.

[4] Behold, I am about to build a house for the Name of the Lord my God, dedicated to Him for the burning of incense of sweet spices before Him, for the continual showbread, and for the burnt offerings morning and evening, on the Sabbaths, New Moons, and on the solemn feasts of the Lord our God, as ordained forever for Israel.

[5] The house which I am to build is great, for our God is greater than all gods.

[6] But who is able to build Him a house, since heaven, even highest heaven, cannot contain Him? Who am I to build Him a house, except as a place to burn incense in worship before Him?

[7] Now therefore, send a man skilled to work in gold, silver, bronze, and iron, and in purple, crimson, and blue colors, who is a trained engraver, to work with the skilled men who are with me in Judah and Jerusalem, whom David my father provided.

[8] Send me also from Lebanon cedar, cypress, and algum timber, for I know your servants can skillfully cut timber in Lebanon; and my servants will be with your servants,

[9] To prepare for me timber in abundance, for the house I am about to build shall be great and wonderful.

[10] And I will give to your servants who cut timber 20,000 measures of crushed wheat and also of barley, and 20,000 baths of wine and also of oil.

[11] Then Hiram king of Tyre replied in writing sent to Solomon, Because the Lord loves His people, He has made you king over them.

[12] Hiram said also, Blessed be the Lord, the God of Israel, Who made heaven and earth, Who has given to David the king a wise son, endued with prudence and understanding, who should build a house for the Lord and a royal palace as his capitol.

[13] Now I have sent a skilled man, endued with understanding, even Huram-abi, my trusted counselor,

[14] The son of a woman of the daughters of [b] Dan; his father was a man of Tyre. He is a trained worker in gold, silver, bronze, iron, stone, and wood; in purple, blue, and crimson colors, and in fine linen; and also to engrave any type of engraving and to carry out any design given him, with your skilled men and those of my lord, David your father.

[15] Now therefore, the wheat, barley, oil, and wine of which my lord has spoken, let him send them to his servants,

[16] And we will cut whatever timber you need from Lebanon and bring it to you in rafts by sea to Joppa, so you may take it up to Jerusalem.

[17] Then Solomon took a census of all the aliens in the land of Israel, like the census of them which his father David had taken. They were found to be 153,600.

[18] And he assigned 70,000 of them to be burden bearers, 80,000 to work in the mountain quarries, and 3,600 as overseers to direct the people's work.

---

[a] See footnote on Deut. 12:5.   [b] I Kings 7:14 says that this woman was of the tribe of Naphtali. Doubtless her mother's marriage identified her with a tribe of which she was not a native.

## New International Version

### Solomon Builds the Temple

**3** Then Solomon began to build the temple of the LORD in Jerusalem on Mount Moriah, where the LORD had appeared to his father David. It was on the threshing floor of Araunah*ᵃ* the Jebusite, the place provided by David. ²He began building on the second day of the second month in the fourth year of his reign.

³The foundation Solomon laid for building the temple of God was sixty cubits long and twenty cubits wide*ᵇ* (using the cubit of the old standard). ⁴The portico at the front of the temple was twenty cubits*ᶜ* long across the width of the building and twenty*ᵈ* cubits high.

He overlaid the inside with pure gold. ⁵He paneled the main hall with juniper and covered it with fine gold and decorated it with palm tree and chain designs. ⁶He adorned the temple with precious stones. And the gold he used was gold of Parvaim. ⁷He overlaid the ceiling beams, doorframes, walls and doors of the temple with gold, and he carved cherubim on the walls.

⁸He built the Most Holy Place, its length corresponding to the width of the temple—twenty cubits long and twenty cubits wide. He overlaid the inside with six hundred talents*ᵉ* of fine gold. ⁹The gold nails weighed fifty shekels.*ᶠ* He also overlaid the upper parts with gold.

¹⁰For the Most Holy Place he made a pair of sculptured cherubim and overlaid them with gold. ¹¹The total wingspan of the cherubim was twenty cubits. One wing of the first cherub was five cubits*ᵍ* long and touched the temple wall, while its other wing, also five cubits long, touched the wing of the other cherub. ¹²Similarly one wing of the second cherub was five cubits long and touched the other temple wall, and its other wing, also five cubits long, touched the wing of the first cherub. ¹³The wings of these cherubim extended twenty cubits. They stood on their feet, facing the main hall.*ʰ*

¹⁴He made the curtain of blue, purple and crimson yarn and fine linen, with cherubim worked into it.

¹⁵For the front of the temple he made two pillars, which together were thirty-five cubits*ⁱ* long, each with a capital five cubits high. ¹⁶He made interwoven chains*ʲ* and put them on top of the pillars. He also made a hundred pomegranates and attached them to the chains. ¹⁷He erected the pillars in the front of the temple, one to the south and one to the north. The one to the south he named Jakin*ᵏ* and the one to the north Boaz.*ˡ*

### The Temple's Furnishings

**4** He made a bronze altar twenty cubits long, twenty cubits wide and ten cubits high.*ᵐ* ²He made the Sea of cast metal, circular in shape, measuring ten cubits from rim to rim and five cubits*ⁿ* high. It took a line of thirty cubits*ᵒ* to measure around it. ³Below the rim, figures of

---

*ᵃ 1* Hebrew *Ornan*, a variant of *Araunah*   *ᵇ 3* That is, about 90 feet long and 30 feet wide or about 27 meters long and 9 meters wide   *ᶜ 4* That is, about 30 feet or about 9 meters; also in verses 8, 11 and 13   *ᵈ 4* Some Septuagint and Syriac manuscripts; Hebrew *and a hundred and twenty*   *ᵉ 8* That is, about 23 tons or about 21 metric tons   *ᶠ 9* That is, about 1 1/4 pounds or about 575 grams   *ᵍ 11* That is, about 7 1/2 feet or about 2.3 meters; also in verse 15   *ʰ 13* Or *facing inward*   *ⁱ 15* That is, about 53 feet or about 16 meters   *ʲ 16* Or possibly *made chains in the inner sanctuary*; the meaning of the Hebrew for this phrase is uncertain.   *ᵏ 17* *Jakin* probably means *he establishes.*   *ˡ 17* *Boaz* probably means *in him is strength.*   *ᵐ 1* That is, about 30 feet long and wide and 15 feet high or about 9 meters long and wide and 4.5 meters high   *ⁿ 2* That is, about 7 1/2 feet or about 2.3 meters   *ᵒ 2* That is, about 45 feet or about 14 meters

## Amplified Bible

**3** Then Solomon began to build the house of the Lord at Jerusalem on Mount Moriah, where the Lord appeared to David his father, in the place that David had appointed, on the threshing floor of Ornan the Jebusite. [I Chron. 21:20-22.]

²And Solomon began to build on the second day of the second month in the fourth year of his reign.

³Now these are the measurements for the foundations which Solomon laid for the house of God. The length in cubits by the former measure was sixty cubits, and the breadth twenty cubits.

⁴The porch *or* vestibule across the front of the house was the same length as the house's breadth, twenty cubits, and the *ᵃ*height 120 cubits. He overlaid it inside with pure gold.

⁵And the greater house (the Holy Place) he lined with cypress and overlaid it with fine gold and made palm trees and chains on it.

⁶And he adorned the house with precious stones for beauty; and the gold was gold of Parvaim.

⁷He lined the house (the Holy Place), its beams, thresholds, walls, and doors with gold, and engraved cherubim on the walls.

⁸He made the Most Holy Place, its length equaling the breadth of the house, twenty cubits, and its breadth twenty cubits; he overlaid it with 600 talents of fine gold.

⁹The weight of the nails was fifty shekels of gold. And he lined the upper chambers with gold.

¹⁰And in the Most Holy Place he made two cherubim of image work, and they were overlaid with gold.

¹¹And the wings of the cherubim [combined] extended twenty cubits: one wing of one cherub was five cubits, reaching to the wall of the house, and its other wing of five cubits touched the other cherub's wing.

¹²And of the other cherub one wing of five cubits touched the wall of the house, and the other wing, also five cubits, joined the wing of the first cherub.

¹³The wings of these cherubim extended twenty cubits; the cherubim stood on their feet, their faces toward the Holy Place.

¹⁴And he made the veil [between the Holy Place and the Most Holy Place] of blue, purple, and crimson colors, and fine linen, and embroidered cherubim on it.

¹⁵Before the house he made two pillars, 35 cubits high, with a capital on the top of each which was five cubits.

¹⁶He made chains like a necklace and put them on the heads of the pillars, and he made 100 pomegranates and put them on the chains.

¹⁷He erected the pillars before the temple, one on the right, the other on the left, and called the one on the right Jachin [he shall establish] and the one on the left Boaz [in it is strength].

**4** Also Solomon made an altar of bronze, its top twenty by twenty cubits and its height ten cubits.

²Also he made a round Sea of molten metal, ten cubits from brim to brim and five cubits high, and a line of thirty cubits measured around it.

---

*ᵃ* This extreme height is believed by most scholars to be a copyist's error, but II Chron. 7:21 seems to confirm it. It reads, ". . . this house, which was so high . . ."

## New International Version

bulls encircled it—ten to a cubit.[a] The bulls were cast in two rows in one piece with the Sea.

⁴The Sea stood on twelve bulls, three facing north, three facing west, three facing south and three facing east. The Sea rested on top of them, and their hindquarters were toward the center. ⁵It was a handbreadth[b] in thickness, and its rim was like the rim of a cup, like a lily blossom. It held three thousand baths.[c]

⁶He then made ten basins for washing and placed five on the south side and five on the north. In them the things to be used for the burnt offerings were rinsed, but the Sea was to be used by the priests for washing.

⁷He made ten gold lampstands according to the specifications for them and placed them in the temple, five on the south side and five on the north.

⁸He made ten tables and placed them in the temple, five on the south side and five on the north. He also made a hundred gold sprinkling bowls.

⁹He made the courtyard of the priests, and the large court and the doors for the court, and overlaid the doors with bronze. ¹⁰He placed the Sea on the south side, at the southeast corner.

¹¹And Huram also made the pots and shovels and sprinkling bowls.

So Huram finished the work he had undertaken for King Solomon in the temple of God:

¹²the two pillars;

the two bowl-shaped capitals on top of the pillars;

the two sets of network decorating the two bowl-shaped capitals on top of the pillars;

¹³the four hundred pomegranates for the two sets of network (two rows of pomegranates for each network, decorating the bowl-shaped capitals on top of the pillars);

¹⁴the stands with their basins;

¹⁵the Sea and the twelve bulls under it;

¹⁶the pots, shovels, meat forks and all related articles.

All the objects that Huram-Abi made for King Solomon for the temple of the LORD were of polished bronze. ¹⁷The king had them cast in clay molds in the plain of the Jordan between Sukkoth and Zarethan.[d] ¹⁸All these things that Solomon made amounted to so much that the weight of the bronze could not be calculated.

¹⁹Solomon also made all the furnishings that were in God's temple:

the golden altar;

the tables on which was the bread of the Presence;

²⁰the lampstands of pure gold with their lamps, to burn in front of the inner sanctuary as prescribed;

²¹the gold floral work and lamps and tongs (they were solid gold);

²²the pure gold wick trimmers, sprinkling bowls, dishes and censers; and the gold doors of the temple: the inner doors to the Most Holy Place and the doors of the main hall.

**5** When all the work Solomon had done for the temple of the LORD was finished, he brought in the things his father David had dedicated—the silver and gold and all the furnishings—and he placed them in the treasuries of God's temple.

### The Ark Brought to the Temple

²Then Solomon summoned to Jerusalem the elders of Israel, all the heads of the tribes and the chiefs of the Israelite families, to bring up the ark of the LORD's covenant

## Amplified Bible

³Under it were figures of oxen encircling it, ten to a cubit. The oxen were in two rows, cast in one piece with it.

⁴It stood upon twelve oxen, three looking north, three west, three south, three east; and the Sea rested upon them, and all their hind parts were inward.

⁵Its thickness was a handbreadth; its brim was like the brim of a cup, like the flower of a lily; it held 3,000 baths (measures).

⁶He made also ten lavers in which to wash and put five on the right (south) side and five on the left (north). Such things as they offered for the burnt offering they washed in them, but the Sea was for the priests to wash in.

⁷And he made ten golden lampstands as directed and set them in the temple, five on the right side and five on the left.

⁸He made also ten tables and placed them in the temple, five each on the right and left sides, and 100 basins of gold.

⁹Moreover, he made the priests' court, and the great court and doors for the court, and overlaid their doors with bronze.

¹⁰And he set the Sea at the southeast corner of the house.

¹¹And Huram made the pots, shovels, and basins. So Huram finished the work of God's house that he did for King Solomon:

¹²The two pillars; the bowls; the capitals on top of the two pillars; and the two networks to cover the two bowls of the capitals on top of the pillars;

¹³And 400 pomegranates for the two networks, two rows of pomegranates for each network, to cover the two bowls of the capitals upon the pillars;

¹⁴He made also bases *or* stands and lavers upon the bases;

¹⁵One Sea and the twelve oxen under it;

¹⁶The pots, shovels, and fleshhooks, and all their equipment Huram his trusted counselor made of burnished bronze for King Solomon for the house of the Lord.

¹⁷In the plain of the Jordan the king cast them, in the clay ground between Succoth and Zeredah.

¹⁸Solomon made all these things in such great numbers that the weight of the bronze was not computed.

¹⁹And Solomon made all the vessels for the house of God: the golden altar also; and the tables for the showbread (the bread of the Presence);

²⁰And the lampstands with their lamps of pure gold, to burn before the inner sanctuary (the Holy of Holies) as directed;

²¹The flowers, lamps, and tongs, of purest gold;

²²The snuffers, basins, dishes for incense, and firepans, of pure gold; and for the temple entry, the inner doors for the Most Holy Place and the doors of the Holy Place were of gold.

**5** Thus all the work that Solomon did for the house of the Lord was finished. He brought in all the things that David his father had dedicated, and the silver, the gold, and all the vessels he put in the treasuries of the house of God.

²Then Solomon assembled the elders of Israel and all the heads of the tribes, the chiefs of the fathers' houses of the Israelites, to Jerusalem to bring up the ark of the covenant of the Lord out of the City of David, which is Zion.

---

a 3 That is, about 18 inches or about 45 centimeters    b 5 That is, about 3 inches or about 7.5 centimeters    c 5 That is, about 18,000 gallons or about 66,000 liters    d 17 Hebrew Zeredatha, a variant of Zarethan

## New International Version

from Zion, the City of David. ³And all the Israelites came together to the king at the time of the festival in the seventh month.

⁴When all the elders of Israel had arrived, the Levites took up the ark, ⁵and they brought up the ark and the tent of meeting and all the sacred furnishings in it. The Levitical priests carried them up; ⁶and King Solomon and the entire assembly of Israel that had gathered about him were before the ark, sacrificing so many sheep and cattle that they could not be recorded or counted.

⁷The priests then brought the ark of the LORD's covenant to its place in the inner sanctuary of the temple, the Most Holy Place, and put it beneath the wings of the cherubim. ⁸The cherubim spread their wings over the place of the ark and covered the ark and its carrying poles. ⁹These poles were so long that their ends, extending from the ark, could be seen from in front of the inner sanctuary, but not from outside the Holy Place; and they are still there today. ¹⁰There was nothing in the ark except the two tablets that Moses had placed in it at Horeb, where the LORD made a covenant with the Israelites after they came out of Egypt.

¹¹The priests then withdrew from the Holy Place. All the priests who were there had consecrated themselves, regardless of their divisions. ¹²All the Levites who were musicians—Asaph, Heman, Jeduthun and their sons and relatives—stood on the east side of the altar, dressed in fine linen and playing cymbals, harps and lyres. They were accompanied by 120 priests sounding trumpets. ¹³The trumpeters and musicians joined in unison to give praise and thanks to the LORD. Accompanied by trumpets, cymbals and other instruments, the singers raised their voices in praise to the LORD and sang:

"He is good;
his love endures forever."

Then the temple of the LORD was filled with the cloud, ¹⁴and the priests could not perform their service because of the cloud, for the glory of the LORD filled the temple of God.

**6** Then Solomon said, "The LORD has said that he would dwell in a dark cloud; ²I have built a magnificent temple for you, a place for you to dwell forever."

³While the whole assembly of Israel was standing there, the king turned around and blessed them. ⁴Then he said:

"Praise be to the LORD, the God of Israel, who with his hands has fulfilled what he promised with his mouth to my father David. For he said, ⁵'Since the day I brought my people out of Egypt, I have not chosen a city in any tribe of Israel to have a temple built so that my Name might be there, nor have I chosen anyone to be ruler over my people Israel. ⁶But now I have chosen Jerusalem for my Name to be there, and I have chosen David to rule my people Israel.'

## Amplified Bible

³All the men of Israel gathered to the king at the feast in the seventh month.

⁴And all the elders of Israel came, and the Levites took up the ark.

⁵And the priests and Levites brought up the ark, the Tent of Meeting, and all the holy vessels that were in the Tent.

⁶Also King Solomon and all the assembly of Israel who were gathered to him before the ark sacrificed sheep and oxen so numerous that they could not be counted or reported.

⁷And the priests brought the ark of the covenant of the Lord to its place, to the sanctuary of the house, into the Holy of Holies, under the wings of the cherubim.

⁸For the cherubim spread out their wings over the place of the ark, making a covering above the ark and its poles.

⁹And they drew out the poles of the ark, so that the ends of the poles protruding from the ark were visible from the front of the Holy of Holies, but were not visible from without. It is there to this day.

¹⁰There was nothing in the ark except the two tables [the Ten Commandments] which Moses put in it at Mount Horeb, when the Lord made a covenant with the Israelites when they came out of Egypt.

¹¹And when the priests had come out of the Holy Place—for all the priests present had sanctified themselves, separating themselves from everything that defiles, without regard to their divisions;

¹²And all the Levites who were singers—all of those of Asaph, Heman, and Jeduthun, with their sons and kinsmen, arrayed in fine linen, having cymbals, harps, and lyres—stood at the east end of the altar, and with them 120 priests blowing trumpets;

¹³And when the trumpeters and singers were joined in unison, making one sound to be heard in praising and thanking the Lord, and when they lifted up their voice with the trumpets and cymbals and other instruments for song and praised the Lord, saying, For He is good, for His mercy *and* loving-kindness endure forever, then the house of the Lord was filled with a cloud,

¹⁴So that the priests could not stand to minister because of the cloud, for the glory of the Lord filled the house of God.

**6** Then Solomon said, The Lord has said that He would dwell in the thick darkness;

²I have built You a house, [in which the dark Holy of Holies seems] a [fitting] abode for You, a place for You to dwell in forever.

³And the king turned his face and blessed all the assembly of Israel, and they all stood.

⁴And he said, Blessed be the Lord, the God of Israel, Who has fulfilled with His hands what He promised with His mouth to David my father, saying,

⁵Since the day that I brought My people out of the land of Egypt, I chose no city among all the tribes of Israel to build a house in, that My Name might be there, ᵃneither chose I any man to be a ruler over My people Israel;

⁶But I have chosen Jerusalem, that My Name [and the symbol of My presence] might be there, and I have chosen David to be over My people Israel.

ᵃ God is plainly saying here that it was not His desire for Israel to have a king. To be sure, when to Samuel's attempt to dissuade them they replied, "No! We will have a king over us, that we also may be like all the nations" (I Sam. 8:19-20), God said to Samuel, "They have rejected Me, that I should not be King over them . . . appoint them a king" (I Sam. 8:7, 22). But Saul was originally the people's choice, not God's choice. The Bible nowhere teaches that "the voice of the people is the voice of God." But it does teach that when people make demands of God that are not in harmony with His will, He may grant them to their sorrow, and send "leanness into their souls" (Ps. 106:15).

## New International Version

[7]"My father David had it in his heart to build a temple for the Name of the LORD, the God of Israel. [8]But the LORD said to my father David, 'You did well to have it in your heart to build a temple for my Name. [9]Nevertheless, you are not the one to build the temple, but your son, your own flesh and blood—he is the one who will build the temple for my Name.'

[10]"The LORD has kept the promise he made. I have succeeded David my father and now I sit on the throne of Israel, just as the LORD promised, and I have built the temple for the Name of the LORD, the God of Israel. [11]There I have placed the ark, in which is the covenant of the LORD that he made with the people of Israel."

### Solomon's Prayer of Dedication

[12]Then Solomon stood before the altar of the LORD in front of the whole assembly of Israel and spread out his hands. [13]Now he had made a bronze platform, five cubits long, five cubits wide and three cubits high,[a] and had placed it in the center of the outer court. He stood on the platform and then knelt down before the whole assembly of Israel and spread out his hands toward heaven. [14]He said:

"LORD, the God of Israel, there is no God like you in heaven or on earth—you who keep your covenant of love with your servants who continue wholeheartedly in your way. [15]You have kept your promise to your servant David my father; with your mouth you have promised and with your hand you have fulfilled it—as it is today.

[16]"Now, LORD, the God of Israel, keep for your servant David the promises you made to him when you said, 'You shall never fail to have a successor to sit before me on the throne of Israel, if only your descendants are careful in all they do to walk before me according to my law, as you have done.' [17]And now, LORD, the God of Israel, let your word that you promised your servant David come true.

[18]"But will God really dwell on earth with humans? The heavens, even the highest heavens, cannot contain you. How much less this temple I have built! [19]Yet, LORD my God, give attention to your servant's prayer and his plea for mercy. Hear the cry and the prayer that your servant is praying in your presence. [20]May your eyes be open toward this temple day and night, this place of which you said you would put your Name there. May you hear the prayer your servant prays toward this place. [21]Hear the supplications of your servant and of your people Israel when they pray toward this place. Hear from heaven, your dwelling place; and when you hear, forgive.

[22]"When anyone wrongs their neighbor and is required to take an oath and they come and swear the oath before your altar in this temple, [23]then hear from heaven and act. Judge between your servants, condemning the guilty and bringing down on their heads what they have done, and vindicating the innocent by treating them in accordance with their innocence.

[24]"When your people Israel have been defeated by an enemy because they have sinned against you and when they turn back and give praise to your name, praying and making supplication before you in this temple, [25]then hear from heaven and forgive the sin of your people Israel and bring them back to the land you gave to them and their ancestors.

## Amplified Bible

[7]Now it was in the heart of David my father to build a house for the Name and renown of the Lord, the God of Israel. [8]But the Lord said to David my father, Since it was in your heart to build a house for My Name and renown, you did well that it was in your heart. [9]Yet you shall not build the house, but your son, who shall be born to you—he shall build the house for My Name.

[10]The Lord therefore has performed His word that He has spoken, for I have risen up in the place of David my father and sit on the throne of Israel, as the Lord promised, and have built the house for the Name of the Lord, the God of Israel.

[11]In it have I put the ark [the symbol of His presence], in which is the covenant of the Lord [the Ten Commandments] which He made with the people of Israel.

[12]And Solomon stood before the altar of the Lord in the presence of all the assembly of Israel and spread forth his hands.

[13]For he had made a bronze scaffold, five cubits square and three cubits high, and had set it in the midst of the court; upon it he stood, and he knelt upon his knees before all the assembly of Israel and spread forth his hands toward heaven,

[14]And said, O Lord, God of Israel, there is no God like You in the heavens or in the earth, keeping covenant and showing mercy and loving-kindness to Your servants who walk before You with all their hearts,

[15]You Who have kept Your promises to my father David and fulfilled with Your hand what You spoke with Your mouth, as it is today.

[16]Now therefore, O Lord, God of Israel, keep with Your servant David my father that which You promised him, saying, There shall not fail a man in My sight to sit on the throne of Israel, provided your children are careful to walk in My law as you, David, have walked before Me.

[17]Now then, O Lord, God of Israel, let Your word to Your servant David be verified.

[18]But will God actually dwell with men on the earth? Behold, heaven and the heaven of heavens cannot contain You; how much less this house which I have built!

[19]Yet have respect for the prayer of Your servant and for his supplication, O Lord my God, to listen to the cry and the prayer which Your servant prays before You,

[20]That Your eyes may be open upon this house day and night, toward the place in which You have said You would put Your Name [and the symbol of your presence], to listen to and heed the prayer which Your servant prays facing this place.

[21]So listen to and heed the requests of Your servant and Your people Israel which they shall make facing this place. Hear from Your dwelling place, heaven; and when You hear, forgive.

[22]If a man sins against his neighbor, and he is required to take an oath, and the oath comes before Your altar in this house,

[23]Then hear from heaven and do; and judge Your servants, requiting the wicked by bringing his conduct upon his own head, and justifying the [uncompromisingly] righteous by giving him according to his righteousness (his uprightness and right standing with God).

[24]If Your people Israel have been defeated before the enemy because they have sinned against You, and shall return, confess Your name [and You Yourself], and pray and make supplication before You in this house,

[25]Then hear from heaven and forgive the sin of Your people Israel and bring them again to the land which You gave to them and their fathers.

---

[a] 13 That is, about 7 1/2 feet long and wide and 4 1/2 feet high or about 2.3 meters long and wide and 1.4 meters high

## New International Version

[26]"When the heavens are shut up and there is no rain because your people have sinned against you, and when they pray toward this place and give praise to your name and turn from their sin because you have afflicted them, [27]then hear from heaven and forgive the sin of your servants, your people Israel. Teach them the right way to live, and send rain on the land you gave your people for an inheritance.

[28]"When famine or plague comes to the land, or blight or mildew, locusts or grasshoppers, or when enemies besiege them in any of their cities, whatever disaster or disease may come, [29]and when a prayer or plea is made by anyone among your people Israel—being aware of their afflictions and pains, and spreading out their hands toward this temple—[30]then hear from heaven, your dwelling place. Forgive, and deal with everyone according to all they do, since you know their hearts (for you alone know the human heart), [31]so that they will fear you and walk in obedience to you all the time they live in the land you gave our ancestors.

[32]"As for the foreigner who does not belong to your people Israel but has come from a distant land because of your great name and your mighty hand and your outstretched arm—when they come and pray toward this temple, [33]then hear from heaven, your dwelling place. Do whatever the foreigner asks of you, so that all the peoples of the earth may know your name and fear you, as do your own people Israel, and may know that this house I have built bears your Name.

[34]"When your people go to war against their enemies, wherever you send them, and when they pray to you toward this city you have chosen and the temple I have built for your Name, [35]then hear from heaven their prayer and their plea, and uphold their cause.

[36]"When they sin against you—for there is no one who does not sin—and you become angry with them and give them over to the enemy, who takes them captive to a land far away or near; [37]and if they have a change of heart in the land where they are held captive, and repent and plead with you in the land of their captivity and say, 'We have sinned, we have done wrong and acted wickedly'; [38]and if they turn back to you with all their heart and soul in the land of their captivity where they were taken, and pray toward the land you gave their ancestors, toward the city you have chosen and toward the temple I have built for your Name; [39]then from heaven, your dwelling place, hear their prayer and their pleas, and uphold their cause. And forgive your people, who have sinned against you.

[40]"Now, my God, may your eyes be open and your ears attentive to the prayers offered in this place.

[41]"Now arise, LORD God, and come to your resting place,
    you and the ark of your might.
May your priests, LORD God, be clothed with
    salvation,
    may your faithful people rejoice in your
    goodness.

## Amplified Bible

[26]When the heavens are shut up and there is no rain because Your people have sinned against You, yet if they pray toward this place, confess your name [and You Yourself], and turn from their sin when You afflict them,

[27]Then hear from heaven and forgive the sin of Your servants, [all of] Your people Israel, when You have taught them the good way in which they should walk. And send rain upon Your land which You have given to Your people for an inheritance.

[28]If there is famine in the land, if there is pestilence, blight, mildew, locusts, or caterpillars, if their enemies besiege them in any of their cities, whatever plague or sickness there may be,

[29]Then whatever prayer or supplication any man or all of Your people Israel shall make—each knowing his own affliction and his own sorrow and stretching out his hands toward this house—

[30]Then hear from heaven, Your dwelling place, and forgive, and render to every man according to all his ways, whose heart You know; for You, You only, know men's hearts,

[31]That they may fear You and walk in Your ways as long as they live in the land which You gave to our fathers.

[32]Also concerning the stranger who is not of Your people Israel but has come from a far country for Your great name's sake and Your mighty power and Your outstretched arm—if he comes and prays toward this house,

[33]Hear from heaven, from Your dwelling place, and do all for which the stranger calls to You, that all peoples of the earth may know Your name and fear You [reverently and worshipfully], as do Your people Israel, and may know that this house which I have built is called by Your Name.

[34]If Your people go out to war against their enemies by the way that You send them, and they pray to You facing this city [Jerusalem] which You have chosen and the house which I have built for Your Name,

[35]Then hear from heaven their prayer and supplication, and maintain their cause.

[36]If they sin against You—for there is no man who does not sin—and You are angry with them and give them to enemies who take them captive to a land far or near;

[37]Yet if they repent in the land to which they have been carried captive, and turn and pray there, saying, We have sinned, we have done wrong, and have dealt wickedly;

[38]If they return to You with all their heart and soul in the land of their captivity, and pray facing their land which You gave to their fathers and toward the city which You have chosen and the house which I have built for Your Name;

[39]Then hear from heaven, Your dwelling place, their prayer and supplications, and maintain their cause; and forgive Your people, who have sinned against You.

[40]Now, O my God, I beseech You, let Your eyes be open and Your ears attentive to the prayer offered in this temple.

[41]So now arise, O Lord God, and come into Your resting place, You and the ark of Your strength *and* power. Let Your priests, O Lord God, be clothed with salvation, and let Your saints (Your zealous ones) rejoice in good *and* in Your goodness.

## New International Version

42 LORD God, do not reject your anointed one.
    Remember the great love promised to David
        your servant."

### The Dedication of the Temple

**7** When Solomon finished praying, fire came down from
    heaven and consumed the burnt offering and the sac-
rifices, and the glory of the LORD filled the temple. ²The
priests could not enter the temple of the LORD because
the glory of the LORD filled it. ³When all the Israelites saw
the fire coming down and the glory of the LORD above the
temple, they knelt on the pavement with their faces to the
ground, and they worshiped and gave thanks to the LORD,
saying,

"He is good;
    his love endures forever."

⁴Then the king and all the people offered sacrifices before
the LORD. ⁵And King Solomon offered a sacrifice of twenty-two thousand head of cattle and a hundred and twenty
thousand sheep and goats. So the king and all the people
dedicated the temple of God. ⁶The priests took their positions, as did the Levites with the LORD's musical instruments, which King David had made for praising the LORD
and which were used when he gave thanks, saying, "His
love endures forever." Opposite the Levites, the priests
blew their trumpets, and all the Israelites were standing.
    ⁷Solomon consecrated the middle part of the courtyard
in front of the temple of the LORD, and there he offered
burnt offerings and the fat of the fellowship offerings, because the bronze altar he had made could not hold the
burnt offerings, the grain offerings and the fat portions.
    ⁸So Solomon observed the festival at that time for sev-
en days, and all Israel with him—a vast assembly, people
from Lebo Hamath to the Wadi of Egypt. ⁹On the eighth
day they held an assembly, for they had celebrated the
dedication of the altar for seven days and the festival for
seven days more. ¹⁰On the twenty-third day of the seventh
month he sent the people to their homes, joyful and glad
in heart for the good things the LORD had done for David
and Solomon and for his people Israel.

### The LORD Appears to Solomon

¹¹When Solomon had finished the temple of the LORD
and the royal palace, and had succeeded in carrying out all
he had in mind to do in the temple of the LORD and in his
own palace, ¹²the LORD appeared to him at night and said:

"I have heard your prayer and have chosen this
place for myself as a temple for sacrifices.
¹³"When I shut up the heavens so that there is no
rain, or command locusts to devour the land or send
a plague among my people, ¹⁴if my people, who are

## Amplified Bible

42 O Lord God, ªturn not away the face of [me] Your
anointed one; [earnestly] remember Your good deeds,
mercy, *and* steadfast love for David Your servant.

**7** When Solomon had finished praying, the fire came
    down from heaven and consumed the burnt offering
and the sacrifices, and the glory of the Lord filled the
house.
    ²The priests could not enter the house of the Lord, be-
cause the glory of the Lord had filled the Lord's house.
    ³And when all the people of Israel saw how the fire
came down and the glory of the Lord upon the house, they
bowed with their faces upon the pavement and worshiped
and praised the Lord, saying, For He is good, for His mercy *and* loving-kindness endure forever.
    ⁴Then the king and all the people offered sacrifices be-
fore the Lord.
    ⁵King Solomon offered a sacrifice of 22,000 oxen and
120,000 sheep. So the king and all the people dedicated
God's house.
    ⁶The priests stood at their posts, and the Levites also,
with instruments of music to the Lord, which King David
had made to praise *and* give thanks to the Lord—for His
mercy *and* loving-kindness endure forever—whenever
David praised through their ministry; the priests blew
trumpets before them, and all Israel stood.
    ⁷Moreover, Solomon consecrated the middle of the
court that was before the house of the Lord, for there he
offered burnt offerings and the fat of the peace offerings,
because the bronze altar which [he] had made was not
sufficient to receive the burnt offerings, the cereal offerings, and the fat.
    ⁸At that time Solomon held the feast for seven days,
and all Israel with him, a very great assembly, from the
entrance of Hamath to the Brook of Egypt.
    ⁹The eighth day they made a solemn assembly, for they
had kept the dedication of the altar and the feast, each for
seven days.
    ¹⁰And on the twenty-third day of the seventh month he
sent the people away to their homes, glad and merry in
heart for the goodness that the Lord had shown to David,
to Solomon, and to Israel His people.
    ¹¹Thus Solomon finished the Lord's house and the
king's house; all that [he] had planned to do in the Lord's
house and his own house he accomplished successfully.
    ¹²And the Lord appeared to Solomon by night and said
to him: I have heard your prayer and have chosen this
place for Myself as a house of sacrifice.
    ¹³If I shut up heaven so no rain falls, or if I command
locusts to devour the land, or if I send pestilence among
My people,

---

ª Young Solomon seems, and doubtless is, utterly sincere as he offers
this prayer of which God shows His approval by the miraculous
demonstration of His presence in the next verse. It raises the ever-
present question, How could Solomon have begun his career like
this, and have written his unquestionably divinely inspired books,
and yet have fallen eventually into utter defiance of God's will? Not as
the result of one false step, as with David, but as the habit of his life
for the remainder of his days! Not broken with unspeakable sorrow
for his awful sin, as was his penitent father (Ps. 51), but without ever
apparently repenting or confessing his awful defiance of God and His
explicit commands and warnings, given specifically to Solomon himself
(II Chron. 7:17-22). Possibly in this closing sentence of Solomon's prayer
we detect the fallacy in the young king's thinking. He seems to be saying
in substance, "O Lord God, I am **Your responsibility** now; it will be
for **You** to see that my face does not turn away from You; and not for my
sake, but [since my name is identified with this temple as well as Yours,
You must keep my face turned toward You] for Your own sake!" God lost
no unnecessary time in attempting to set the young man straight as to
whose is the responsibility for sin—in his case specifically (II Chron.
7:12, 17-22). But there is no evidence that Solomon applied it to himself;
though he preached a bit to others, he seems to have considered himself
exempt from obeying God's commands—an attitude which has brought
disaster upon every person who has ever taken it, however great, or
wise, or rich, or otherwise sufficient.

## New International Version

called by my name, will humble themselves and pray and seek my face and turn from their wicked ways, then I will hear from heaven, and I will forgive their sin and will heal their land. [15]Now my eyes will be open and my ears attentive to the prayers offered in this place. [16]I have chosen and consecrated this temple so that my Name may be there forever. My eyes and my heart will always be there.

[17]"As for you, if you walk before me faithfully as David your father did, and do all I command, and observe my decrees and laws, [18]I will establish your royal throne, as I covenanted with David your father when I said, 'You shall never fail to have a successor to rule over Israel.'

[19]"But if you[a] turn away and forsake the decrees and commands I have given you[a] and go off to serve other gods and worship them, [20]then I will uproot Israel from my land, which I have given them, and will reject this temple I have consecrated for my Name. I will make it a byword and an object of ridicule among all peoples. [21]This temple will become a heap of rubble. All[b] who pass by will be appalled and say, 'Why has the LORD done such a thing to this land and to this temple?' [22]People will answer, 'Because they have forsaken the LORD, the God of their ancestors, who brought them out of Egypt, and have embraced other gods, worshiping and serving them—that is why he brought all this disaster on them.'"

### Solomon's Other Activities

**8** At the end of twenty years, during which Solomon built the temple of the LORD and his own palace, [2]Solomon rebuilt the villages that Hiram[c] had given him, and settled Israelites in them. [3]Solomon then went to Hamath Zobah and captured it. [4]He also built up Tadmor in the desert and all the store cities he had built in Hamath. [5]He rebuilt Upper Beth Horon and Lower Beth Horon as fortified cities, with walls and with gates and bars, [6]as well as Baalath and all his store cities, and all the cities for his chariots and for his horses[d]—whatever he desired to build in Jerusalem, in Lebanon and throughout all the territory he ruled.

[7]There were still people left from the Hittites, Amorites, Perizzites, Hivites and Jebusites (these people were not Israelites). [8]Solomon conscripted the descendants of all these people remaining in the land—whom the Israelites had not destroyed—to serve as slave labor, as it is to this day. [9]But Solomon did not make slaves of the Israelites for his work; they were his fighting men, commanders of his captains, and commanders of his chariots and charioteers. [10]They were also King Solomon's chief officials—two hundred and fifty officials supervising the men.

[11]Solomon brought Pharaoh's daughter up from the City of David to the palace he had built for her, for he said, "My wife must not live in the palace of David king of Israel, because the places the ark of the LORD has entered are holy."

[12]On the altar of the LORD that he had built in front of the portico, Solomon sacrificed burnt offerings to the LORD, [13]according to the daily requirement for offerings commanded by Moses for the Sabbaths, the New Moons and the three annual festivals—the Festival of Unleavened Bread, the Festival of Weeks and the Festival of

## Amplified Bible

[14]If My people, who are called by My name, shall humble themselves, pray, seek, crave, *and* require of necessity My face and turn from their wicked ways, then will I hear from heaven, forgive their sin, and heal their land.

[15]Now My eyes will be open and My ears attentive to prayer offered in this place.

[16]For I have chosen and sanctified (set apart for holy use) this house, that My Name may be here forever, and My eyes and My heart will be here perpetually.

[17]As for you [Solomon], if you will walk before me as David your father walked, and do all I have commanded you, and observe My statutes and My ordinances, [I Kings 11:1-11.]

[18]Then I will establish the throne of your kingdom, as I covenanted with David your father, saying, There shall not fail you a man to be ruler in Israel.

[19]But if you [people] turn away and forsake My statutes and My commandments which I have set before you and go and serve other gods and worship them,

[20]Then will I pluck [Israel] up by the roots out of My land which I have given them; and this house which I have hallowed for My Name will I cast out of My sight, and will make it to be a proverb and a byword among all nations. [Jer. 24:9, 10.]

[21]And this house, which was so high, shall be an astonishment to everyone passing it, and they will say, Why has the Lord done thus to this land and to this house?

[22]Then men will say, Because they forsook the Lord, the God of their fathers, Who brought them out of Egypt, and they laid hold of other gods and worshiped and served them; therefore has He brought all this evil upon them.

**8** At the end of twenty years, in which Solomon had built the house of the Lord and his own house,

[2]The cities which Huram had given to [him] Solomon rebuilt *and* fortified, and caused the Israelites to dwell there.

[3]And Solomon took Hamath-zobah.

[4]He built Tadmor in the wilderness and all his store cities in Hamath.

[5]Also he built Upper Beth-horon and Lower Beth-horon, fortified cities with walls, gates, and bars,

[6]And Baalath and all the store cities [he] had, and all the cities for his chariots and the cities for his horsemen, and all that Solomon desired to build in Jerusalem, in Lebanon, and in all his dominion.

[7]All the people who were left of the Hittites, Amorites, Perizzites, Hivites, and Jebusites, who were not of Israel,

[8]But descendants of those who were left in the land, whom the Israelites had not destroyed—of them Solomon made a levy for forced labor to this day.

[9]But of the Israelites Solomon made no slaves for his work; but they were men of war, chiefs of his captains, and captains of his chariots and horsemen.

[10]These were the chiefs of King Solomon's officers, 250 in authority over the people.

[11]Solomon brought the daughter of Pharaoh out of the City of David into the house he had built for her, for he said, My wife shall not dwell in the house of David king of Israel, because the places are holy to which the ark of the Lord has come.

[12]Then Solomon offered burnt offerings to the Lord on the Lord's altar which he had built before the [temple] porch *or* vestibule,

[13]A certain number every day, offering as Moses commanded for the Sabbaths, the New Moons, and the solemn feast days three times in the year—the Feasts of Unleavened Bread, of Weeks, and of Tabernacles.

---

[a] *19* The Hebrew is plural.   [b] *21* See some Septuagint manuscripts, Old Latin, Syriac, Arabic and Targum; Hebrew *And though this temple is now so imposing, all*   [c] *2* Hebrew *Huram,* a variant of *Hiram;* also in verse 18   [d] *6* Or *charioteers*

## New International Version

Tabernacles. ¹⁴In keeping with the ordinance of his father David, he appointed the divisions of the priests for their duties, and the Levites to lead the praise and to assist the priests according to each day's requirement. He also appointed the gatekeepers by divisions for the various gates, because this was what David the man of God had ordered. ¹⁵They did not deviate from the king's commands to the priests or to the Levites in any matter, including that of the treasuries.

¹⁶All Solomon's work was carried out, from the day the foundation of the temple of the Lord was laid until its completion. So the temple of the Lord was finished.

¹⁷Then Solomon went to Ezion Geber and Elath on the coast of Edom. ¹⁸And Hiram sent him ships commanded by his own men, sailors who knew the sea. These, with Solomon's men, sailed to Ophir and brought back four hundred and fifty talents*a* of gold, which they delivered to King Solomon.

### The Queen of Sheba Visits Solomon

**9** When the queen of Sheba heard of Solomon's fame, she came to Jerusalem to test him with hard questions. Arriving with a very great caravan—with camels carrying spices, large quantities of gold, and precious stones—she came to Solomon and talked with him about all she had on her mind. ²Solomon answered all her questions; nothing was too hard for him to explain to her. ³When the queen of Sheba saw the wisdom of Solomon, as well as the palace he had built, ⁴the food on his table, the seating of his officials, the attending servants in their robes, the cupbearers in their robes and the burnt offerings he made at*b* the temple of the Lord, she was overwhelmed.

⁵She said to the king, "The report I heard in my own country about your achievements and your wisdom is true. ⁶But I did not believe what they said until I came and saw with my own eyes. Indeed, not even half the greatness of your wisdom was told me; you have far exceeded the report I heard. ⁷How happy your people must be! How happy your officials, who continually stand before you and hear your wisdom! ⁸Praise be to the Lord your God, who has delighted in you and placed you on his throne as king to rule for the Lord your God. Because of the love of your God for Israel and his desire to uphold them forever, he has made you king over them, to maintain justice and righteousness."

⁹Then she gave the king 120 talents*c* of gold, large quantities of spices, and precious stones. There had never been such spices as those the queen of Sheba gave to King Solomon.

¹⁰(The servants of Hiram and the servants of Solomon brought gold from Ophir; they also brought algumwood*d* and precious stones. ¹¹The king used the algumwood to make steps for the temple of the Lord and for the royal palace, and to make harps and lyres for the musicians. Nothing like them had ever been seen in Judah.)

¹²King Solomon gave the queen of Sheba all she desired and asked for; he gave her more than she had brought to him. Then she left and returned with her retinue to her own country.

### Solomon's Splendor

¹³The weight of the gold that Solomon received yearly was 666 talents,*e* ¹⁴not including the revenues brought in by merchants and traders. Also all the kings of Arabia and the governors of the territories brought gold and silver to Solomon.

---

*a 18 That is, about 17 tons or about 15 metric tons    b 4 Or and the ascent by which he went up to    c 9 That is, about 4 1/2 tons or about 4 metric tons    d 10 Probably a variant of almugwood    e 13 That is, about 25 tons or about 23 metric tons*

## Amplified Bible

¹⁴And he appointed, as ordered by David his father, the divisions of the priests for their service, and the Levites to their offices to praise and to serve before the priests as the duty of every day required, and the gatekeepers also by their divisions at every gate; for so had David the man of God commanded.

¹⁵And they did not turn from the command of the king to the priests and Levites in any respect or concerning the treasuries.

¹⁶Thus all the work of Solomon was prepared from the day the foundation of the Lord's house was laid until it was finished. So the house of the Lord was completed.

¹⁷Then Solomon went to Ezion-geber and to Eloth on the shore of the [Red] Sea in the land of Edom. ¹⁸And Huram sent him by his servants ships and servants familiar with the sea; and they went with the servants of Solomon to Ophir and took from there 450 talents of gold and brought them to King Solomon.

**9** When the queen of Sheba heard of the fame of Solomon, she came to test him with hard questions, accompanied by very many attendants and camels bearing spices, much gold, and precious stones. And when she came to Solomon, she talked with him of all that was on her mind.

²And Solomon answered all her questions; there was nothing hidden from [him] which he was unable to make clear to her.

³And when the queen of Sheba had seen Solomon's wisdom, the house he had built,

⁴The food of his table, the seating of his officials, the [standing at] attention of his servants, their apparel, his cupbearers also and their apparel, and his burnt offerings which he offered at the house of the Lord, there was no more spirit in her.

⁵She said to the king, The report which I heard in my own land of your acts *and* sayings and of your wisdom was true,

⁶But I did not believe their words until I came and my eyes had seen it. Behold, the half of the greatness of your wisdom was not told me; you surpass the fame that I heard of you.

⁷Happy are your wives *and* men, and happy are these your servants who stand continually before you and hear your wisdom!

⁸Blessed be the Lord your God, Who delighted in you and set you on His throne to be king for the Lord your God! Because your God loved Israel and would establish them forever, He made you king over them, to do justice and righteousness.

⁹She gave the king 120 talents of gold, a very large quantity of spices, and precious stones; such spice was not anywhere as that which the queen of Sheba gave King Solomon.

¹⁰The servants of Huram and [those] of Solomon, who brought gold from Ophir, also brought algum trees and precious stones.

¹¹The king made of the algum trees terraces *or* walks to the house of the Lord and to the king's palace, and lyres and harps for the singers; none such had ever been seen before in the land of Judah.

¹²And King Solomon gave to the queen of Sheba all her desire, whatever she asked, besides what she had brought to the king. So she with her servants returned to her own land.

¹³Now the weight of gold that came to Solomon in one year was 666 talents,

¹⁴Besides what traders and merchants brought; and all the kings of Arabia and governors of the country brought gold and silver to Solomon.

## New International Version

[15]King Solomon made two hundred large shields of hammered gold; six hundred shekels[a] of hammered gold went into each shield. [16]He also made three hundred small shields of hammered gold, with three hundred shekels[b] of gold in each shield. The king put them in the Palace of the Forest of Lebanon.

[17]Then the king made a great throne covered with ivory and overlaid with pure gold. [18]The throne had six steps, and a footstool of gold was attached to it. On both sides of the seat were armrests, with a lion standing beside each of them. [19]Twelve lions stood on the six steps, one at either end of each step. Nothing like it had ever been made for any other kingdom. [20]All King Solomon's goblets were gold, and all the household articles in the Palace of the Forest of Lebanon were pure gold. Nothing was made of silver, because silver was considered of little value in Solomon's day. [21]The king had a fleet of trading ships[c] manned by Hiram's[d] servants. Once every three years it returned, carrying gold, silver and ivory, and apes and baboons.

[22]King Solomon was greater in riches and wisdom than all the other kings of the earth. [23]All the kings of the earth sought audience with Solomon to hear the wisdom God had put in his heart. [24]Year after year, everyone who came brought a gift—articles of silver and gold, and robes, weapons and spices, and horses and mules.

[25]Solomon had four thousand stalls for horses and chariots, and twelve thousand horses,[e] which he kept in the chariot cities and also with him in Jerusalem. [26]He ruled over all the kings from the Euphrates River to the land of the Philistines, as far as the border of Egypt. [27]The king made silver as common in Jerusalem as stones, and cedar as plentiful as sycamore-fig trees in the foothills. [28]Solomon's horses were imported from Egypt and from all other countries.

### Solomon's Death

[29]As for the other events of Solomon's reign, from beginning to end, are they not written in the records of Nathan the prophet, in the prophecy of Ahijah the Shilonite and in the visions of Iddo the seer concerning Jeroboam son of Nebat? [30]Solomon reigned in Jerusalem over all Israel forty years. [31]Then he rested with his ancestors and was buried in the city of David his father. And Rehoboam his son succeeded him as king.

### Israel Rebels Against Rehoboam

**10** Rehoboam went to Shechem, for all Israel had gone there to make him king. [2]When Jeroboam son of Nebat heard this (he was in Egypt, where he had fled from King Solomon), he returned from Egypt. [3]So they sent for Jeroboam, and he and all Israel went to Rehoboam and said to him: [4]"Your father put a heavy yoke on us, but now lighten the harsh labor and the heavy yoke he put on us, and we will serve you."

[5]Rehoboam answered, "Come back to me in three days." So the people went away.

[6]Then King Rehoboam consulted the elders who had served his father Solomon during his lifetime. "How would you advise me to answer these people?" he asked.

[7]They replied, "If you will be kind to these people and

## Amplified Bible

[15]And King Solomon made 200 large shields or bucklers of beaten gold; 600 shekels of beaten gold went into each shield. [16]And he made 300 shields of beaten gold, with 300 shekels of gold spread on each shield. And the king put them in the House of the Forest of Lebanon.

[17]Moreover, [he] made a great throne of ivory and overlaid it with pure gold. [18]There were six steps to the throne and a gold footstool attached to the throne, and arms on each side of the seat, with two lions standing beside the arms. [19]And twelve lions stood there one on either end of each of the six steps. The like of it was never made in any kingdom before. [20]King Solomon's drinking vessels were all of gold, and all the vessels of the House of the Forest of Lebanon were of pure gold; silver was not counted as anything in the days of Solomon. [21]For the king's ships went to Tarshish with Huram's servants; once every three years the ships of Tarshish came bringing gold, silver, ivory, apes, and peacocks.

[22]King Solomon surpassed all the kings of the earth in riches and wisdom. [23]And all the kings of the earth sought the presence of Solomon to hear his wisdom which God had put into his mind. [24]And every man brought his tribute: silver and gold articles, robes, armor, spices, horses, and mules, so much year by year. [25]Solomon had 4,000 stalls for horses and chariots, and 12,000 horsemen, stationed in chariot cities or at Jerusalem with the king. [Deut. 17:16, 17.]

[26]And he ruled over [a]all the kings from the [Euphrates] River to the land of Philistia and to the frontier of Egypt. [27]The king made silver in Jerusalem as common as stones, and cedar wood as plentiful as sycamore trees in the lowlands. [28]And they imported horses for Solomon from Egypt and from all lands.

[29]Now the rest of the acts of Solomon, from first to last, are they not written in the history of Nathan the prophet and in the prophecy of Ahijah the Shilonite and in the visions of Iddo the seer concerning Jeroboam the son of Nebat?

[30]Solomon reigned in Jerusalem over all Israel forty years.

[31]Then Solomon slept with his fathers; he was buried in the city of David his father. Rehoboam his son reigned in his stead.

**10** Rehoboam went to Shechem, for all Israel had gone to Shechem to make him king.

[2]Jeroboam the son of Nebat was in Egypt, where he had fled from the presence of King Solomon, when he heard about the new king; so Jeroboam returned from Egypt.

[3]And the people sent for him. So Jeroboam and all Israel came to Rehoboam, saying,

[4]Your father [King Solomon] made our yoke grievous. So now make lighter the grievous service of your father and his heavy yoke that he put upon us, and we will serve you.

[5]Rehoboam replied, Come again to me after three days. And the people departed.

[6]King Rehoboam took counsel with the old men who stood before Solomon his father while he was alive, saying, What counsel do you give me in reply to the people?

[7]And they answered him, If you are kind to [these]

## New International Version

please them and give them a favorable answer, they will always be your servants."

[8]But Rehoboam rejected the advice the elders gave him and consulted the young men who had grown up with him and were serving him. [9]He asked them, "What is your advice? How should we answer these people who say to me, 'Lighten the yoke your father put on us'?"

[10]The young men who had grown up with him replied, "The people have said to you, 'Your father put a heavy yoke on us, but make our yoke lighter.' Now tell them, 'My little finger is thicker than my father's waist. [11]My father laid on you a heavy yoke; I will make it even heavier. My father scourged you with whips; I will scourge you with scorpions.'"

[12]Three days later Jeroboam and all the people returned to Rehoboam, as the king had said, "Come back to me in three days." [13]The king answered them harshly. Rejecting the advice of the elders, [14]he followed the advice of the young men and said, "My father made your yoke heavy; I will make it even heavier. My father scourged you with whips; I will scourge you with scorpions." [15]So the king did not listen to the people, for this turn of events was from God, to fulfill the word the LORD had spoken to Jeroboam son of Nebat through Ahijah the Shilonite.

[16]When all Israel saw that the king refused to listen to them, they answered the king:

"What share do we have in David,
　　what part in Jesse's son?
To your tents, Israel!
　　Look after your own house, David!"

So all the Israelites went home. [17]But as for the Israelites who were living in the towns of Judah, Rehoboam still ruled over them.

[18]King Rehoboam sent out Adoniram,[a] who was in charge of forced labor, but the Israelites stoned him to death. King Rehoboam, however, managed to get into his chariot and escape to Jerusalem. [19]So Israel has been in rebellion against the house of David to this day.

**11** When Rehoboam arrived in Jerusalem, he mustered Judah and Benjamin—a hundred and eighty thousand able young men—to go to war against Israel and to regain the kingdom for Rehoboam.

[2]But this word of the LORD came to Shemaiah the man of God: [3]"Say to Rehoboam son of Solomon king of Judah and to all Israel in Judah and Benjamin, [4]'This is what the LORD says: Do not go up to fight against your fellow Israelites. Go home, every one of you, for this is my doing.'" So they obeyed the words of the LORD and turned back from marching against Jeroboam.

### Rehoboam Fortifies Judah

[5]Rehoboam lived in Jerusalem and built up towns for defense in Judah: [6]Bethlehem, Etam, Tekoa, [7]Beth Zur, Soko, Adullam, [8]Gath, Mareshah, Ziph, [9]Adoraim, Lachish, Azekah, [10]Zorah, Aijalon and Hebron. These were fortified cities in Judah and Benjamin. [11]He strengthened

## Amplified Bible

people and please them and speak good words to them, they will be your servants forever.

[8]But the king forsook the counsel which the old men gave him and took counsel with the young men who were brought up with him and stood before him.

[9]And he said to them, What answer do you advise that we give to the demand of [these] people, Make the yoke your father put upon us lighter?

[10]The young men who were brought up with him said to him, Tell the people who said to you, Your father made our yoke heavy, but you make it lighter: My little finger is thicker than my father's loins.

[11]For whereas my father put a heavy yoke upon you, I will add to your yoke. My father chastised you with whips, but I will chastise you with scorpions.

[12]The third day Jeroboam and all the people returned to Rehoboam as he had said.

[13]And the king answered them harshly, forsaking the counsel of the old men,

[14]And answered them after the advice of the young men, saying, My father made your yoke heavy, but I will add to it; my father chastised you with whips, but I will chastise you with scorpions.

[15]So the king did not heed the people, for it was [a]brought about of God, that the Lord might perform His word which He spoke by Ahijah the Shilonite to Jeroboam son of Nebat. [I Kings 11:29-39.]

[16]And when all Israel saw that the king would not listen to *and* heed them, they answered [him], What portion have we in David? We have no inheritance in the son of Jesse. Every man to your tents, O Israel! Now, David [tribe of Judah], see to your own house [under your tyrant King Rehoboam]! So all Israel went to their homes.

[17]But as for the Israelites who dwelt in Judah's cities, Rehoboam ruled over them.

[18]Then King Rehoboam sent Hadoram, who was over the forced labor, and the Israelites stoned him and he died. But King Rehoboam hastened to get up to his royal chariot to flee to Jerusalem.

[19]And Israel has rebelled against the house of David to this day.

**11** And when Rehoboam came to Jerusalem, he assembled of the house of Judah and Benjamin 180,000 chosen warriors to fight against [the ten rebellious tribes of] Israel to bring the kingdom again to Rehoboam.

[2]But the word of the Lord came to Shemaiah the man of God, saying,

[3]Say to Rehoboam son of Solomon king of Judah and to all Israel in Judah and Benjamin,

[4]Thus says the Lord: You shall not go up or fight against your brethren. Return every man to his house, for this thing is from Me. And they obeyed the Lord and returned from going against Jeroboam.

[5]Rehoboam dwelt in Jerusalem and built cities for defense in Judah.

[6]He built Bethlehem, Etam, Tekoa,

[7]Beth-zur, Soco, Adullam,

[8]Gath, Mareshah, Ziph,

[9]Adoraim, Lachish, Azekah,

[10]Zorah, Aijalon, and Hebron, which are fortified cities in Judah and Benjamin.

---

[a] God permitted the revolt of the northern tribes, intending it as a punishment of the house of David for Solomon's apostasy (Robert Jamieson, A. R. Fausset and David Brown, *A Commentary*).

[a] 18 Hebrew *Hadoram*, a variant of *Adoniram*

## New International Version

their defenses and put commanders in them, with supplies of food, olive oil and wine. [12]He put shields and spears in all the cities, and made them very strong. So Judah and Benjamin were his.

[13]The priests and Levites from all their districts throughout Israel sided with him. [14]The Levites even abandoned their pasturelands and property and came to Judah and Jerusalem, because Jeroboam and his sons had rejected them as priests of the LORD [15]when he appointed his own priests for the high places and for the goat and calf idols he had made. [16]Those from every tribe of Israel who set their hearts on seeking the LORD, the God of Israel, followed the Levites to Jerusalem to offer sacrifices to the LORD, the God of their ancestors. [17]They strengthened the kingdom of Judah and supported Rehoboam son of Solomon three years, following the ways of David and Solomon during this time.

### Rehoboam's Family

[18]Rehoboam married Mahalath, who was the daughter of David's son Jerimoth and of Abihail, the daughter of Jesse's son Eliab. [19]She bore him sons: Jeush, Shemariah and Zaham. [20]Then he married Maakah daughter of Absalom, who bore him Abijah, Attai, Ziza and Shelomith. [21]Rehoboam loved Maakah daughter of Absalom more than any of his other wives and concubines. In all, he had eighteen wives and sixty concubines, twenty-eight sons and sixty daughters.

[22]Rehoboam appointed Abijah son of Maakah as crown prince among his brothers, in order to make him king. [23]He acted wisely, dispersing some of his sons throughout the districts of Judah and Benjamin, and to all the fortified cities. He gave them abundant provisions and took many wives for them.

### Shishak Attacks Jerusalem

**12** After Rehoboam's position as king was established and he had become strong, he and all Israel[a] with him abandoned the law of the LORD. [2]Because they had been unfaithful to the LORD, Shishak king of Egypt attacked Jerusalem in the fifth year of King Rehoboam. [3]With twelve hundred chariots and sixty thousand horsemen and the innumerable troops of Libyans, Sukkites and Cushites[b] that came with him from Egypt, [4]he captured the fortified cities of Judah and came as far as Jerusalem.

[5]Then the prophet Shemaiah came to Rehoboam and to the leaders of Judah who had assembled in Jerusalem for fear of Shishak, and he said to them, "This is what the LORD says, 'You have abandoned me; therefore, I now abandon you to Shishak.'"

[6]The leaders of Israel and the king humbled themselves and said, "The LORD is just."

[7]When the LORD saw that they humbled themselves, this word of the LORD came to Shemaiah: "Since they have humbled themselves, I will not destroy them but will soon give them deliverance. My wrath will not be poured out on Jerusalem through Shishak. [8]They will, however, become subject to him, so that they may learn the difference between serving me and serving the kings of other lands."

## Amplified Bible

[11]He fortified the strongholds and put captains in them, with stores of food, oil, and vintage fruits.

[12]And in each city he put shields and spears, and made them very strong. So he held Judah and Benjamin.

[13]And the priests and the Levites who were in all Israel came over to Rehoboam from wherever they lived.

[14]For the Levites left their suburbs and their possessions and came to Judah and Jerusalem, for Jeroboam and his sons had cast them out from executing the priest's office to the Lord.

[15]And he appointed his own priests for the high places and for the [idols of demon] he-goats, and calves he had made. [I Kings 12:28.]

[16]And after them out of all the tribes of Israel there came to Jerusalem those who set their hearts to seek *and* inquire of the Lord, the God of Israel, to sacrifice to the Lord, the God of their fathers.

[17]So they strengthened the kingdom of Judah and upheld Rehoboam son of Solomon for three years; for they walked in the ways of David and Solomon for three years.

[18]Rehoboam took as wife Mahalath, whose father was Jerimoth son of David; her mother was Abihail daughter of Eliab son of Jesse.

[19]She bore him sons: Jeush, Shamariah, and Zaham.

[20]And after her he took Maacah daughter [grand-daughter] of Absalom, who bore him Abijah, Attai, Ziza, and Shelomith.

[21]And Rehoboam loved Maacah daughter [granddaughter] of Absalom more than all his wives and concubines— for he took eighteen wives and sixty concubines, and he had twenty-eight sons and sixty daughters.

[22]And Rehoboam made Abijah son of Maacah the chief prince among his brethren, for he intended to make him king.

[23]And he dealt understandingly and dispersed his children throughout all Judah and Benjamin to every fortified city. He gave them abundant supplies, and he sought many wives for them.

**12** When Rehoboam had established the kingdom and had strengthened himself, he forsook the law of the Lord, and all Israel with him.

[2]And in the fifth year of King Rehoboam, because they had transgressed *and* been unfaithful to the Lord, Shishak king of Egypt came up against Jerusalem

[3]With 1,200 chariots and 60,000 horsemen, and the people were without number who came with him from Egypt—the Libyans, Sukkiim, and Ethiopians.

[4]And he took the fortified cities of Judah and came on to Jerusalem.

[5]Then Shemaiah the prophet came to Rehoboam and the princes of Judah who had gathered at Jerusalem because of Shishak, and said to them, Thus says the Lord: You have forsaken Me, so I have abandoned you into the hands of Shishak.

[6]Then the princes of Israel and the king humbled themselves and said, The Lord is righteous.

[7]And when the Lord saw that they humbled themselves, the word of the Lord came to Shemaiah, saying, They have humbled themselves, so I will not destroy them; but I will grant them some deliverance; and My wrath shall not be poured out upon Jerusalem by the hand of Shishak.

[8]Nevertheless, they shall be his servants, that they may know [the difference between] My service and the service of the kingdoms of the countries.

---

[a] *1* That is, Judah, as frequently in 2 Chronicles    [b] *3* That is, people from the upper Nile region

## New International Version

⁹When Shishak king of Egypt attacked Jerusalem, he carried off the treasures of the temple of the LORD and the treasures of the royal palace. He took everything, including the gold shields Solomon had made. ¹⁰So King Rehoboam made bronze shields to replace them and assigned these to the commanders of the guard on duty at the entrance to the royal palace. ¹¹Whenever the king went to the LORD's temple, the guards went with him, bearing the shields, and afterward they returned them to the guardroom.

¹²Because Rehoboam humbled himself, the LORD's anger turned from him, and he was not totally destroyed. Indeed, there was some good in Judah.

¹³King Rehoboam established himself firmly in Jerusalem and continued as king. He was forty-one years old when he became king, and he reigned seventeen years in Jerusalem, the city the LORD had chosen out of all the tribes of Israel in which to put his Name. His mother's name was Naamah; she was an Ammonite. ¹⁴He did evil because he had not set his heart on seeking the LORD.

¹⁵As for the events of Rehoboam's reign, from beginning to end, are they not written in the records of Shemaiah the prophet and of Iddo the seer that deal with genealogies? There was continual warfare between Rehoboam and Jeroboam. ¹⁶Rehoboam rested with his ancestors and was buried in the City of David. And Abijah his son succeeded him as king.

### Abijah King of Judah

**13** In the eighteenth year of the reign of Jeroboam, Abijah became king of Judah, ²and he reigned in Jerusalem three years. His mother's name was Maakah,ᵃ a daughterᵇ of Uriel of Gibeah.

There was war between Abijah and Jeroboam. ³Abijah went into battle with an army of four hundred thousand able fighting men, and Jeroboam drew up a battle line against him with eight hundred thousand able troops.

⁴Abijah stood on Mount Zemaraim, in the hill country of Ephraim, and said, "Jeroboam and all Israel, listen to me! ⁵Don't you know that the LORD, the God of Israel, has given the kingship of Israel to David and his descendants forever by a covenant of salt? ⁶Yet Jeroboam son of Nebat, an official of Solomon son of David, rebelled against his master. ⁷Some worthless scoundrels gathered around him and opposed Rehoboam son of Solomon when he was young and indecisive and not strong enough to resist them.

⁸"And now you plan to resist the kingdom of the LORD, which is in the hands of David's descendants. You are indeed a vast army and have with you the golden calves Jeroboam made to be your gods. ⁹But didn't you drive out the priests of the LORD, the sons of Aaron, and the Levites, and make priests of your own as the peoples of other lands do? Whoever comes to consecrate himself with a young bull and seven rams may become a priest of what are not gods.

¹⁰"As for us, the LORD is our God, and we have not forsaken him. The priests who serve the LORD are sons of Aaron, and the Levites assist them. ¹¹Every morning and evening they present burnt offerings and fragrant incense to the LORD. They set out the bread on the ceremonially

## Amplified Bible

⁹So Shishak king of Egypt came up against Jerusalem; he took away the treasures of the house of the Lord and of the king's house. He took everything. He took away also the shields of gold Solomon had made.

¹⁰Instead of them King Rehoboam made shields of bronze and committed them to the hands of the officers of the guard who kept the door of the king's house.

¹¹And whenever the king entered the Lord's house, the guards came and got the shields of bronze and brought them again into the guard chamber.

¹²When Rehoboam humbled himself, the wrath of the Lord turned from him, so as not to destroy him entirely; also in Judah conditions were good.

¹³So King Rehoboam established *and* strengthened himself in Jerusalem and reigned. Rehoboam was forty-one years old when he began to reign, and he reigned seventeen years in Jerusalem, the city in which the Lord had chosen out of all the tribes of Israel to put His Name [and the symbol of His presence]. His mother was Naamah an Ammonitess.

¹⁴And he did evil because he did not set his heart to seek (inquire of, yearn for) the Lord with all his desire.

¹⁵Now the acts of Rehoboam, from first to last, are they not written in the histories of Shemaiah the prophet and of Iddo the seer regarding genealogies? There were wars between Rehoboam of Judah and Jeroboam of Israel continually.

¹⁶And Rehoboam slept with his fathers and was buried in the City of David; and Abijah his son reigned in his stead.

**13** In the eighteenth year of King Jeroboam, Abijah began to reign over Judah.

²He reigned three years in Jerusalem. His mother was Micaiah daughter of Uriel of Gibeah. And there was war between Abijah and Jeroboam of Israel.

³And Abijah prepared for battle with an army of valiant men of war, 400,000 chosen men. Jeroboam set the battle in array against him with 800,000 chosen men, mighty men of valor.

⁴And Abijah stood on Mount Zemaraim, in the hill country of Ephraim, and said, Hear me, O Jeroboam and all Israel!

⁵Ought you not to know that the Lord, the God of Israel, gave the kingship over Israel to David forever, even to him and to his sons by a covenant of salt?

⁶Yet Jeroboam son of Nebat, a servant of Solomon son of David, rose up and rebelled against his lord [the king].

⁷And there gathered to him worthless men, base fellows, who strengthened themselves against Rehoboam son of Solomon when Rehoboam was young [as king], irresolute, *and* inexperienced and did not withstand them with firmness and strength.

⁸And now you think to withstand the kingdom of the Lord which is in the hands of the sons of David, because you are a great multitude and you have with you the golden calves which Jeroboam made for you for gods.

⁹Have you not driven out the priests of the Lord, the sons of Aaron, and the Levites, and made priests for yourselves like the peoples of other lands? So whoever comes to consecrate himself with a young bull and seven rams may be a priest of idols that are not gods.

¹⁰But as for us, the Lord is our God, and we have not forsaken Him. We have priests ministering to the Lord who are sons of Aaron, and Levites for their service.

¹¹They offer to the Lord every morning and every evening burnt sacrifices and incense of sweet spices; they set in order the showbread on the table of pure gold and

---

ᵃ 2 Most Septuagint manuscripts and Syriac (see also 11:20 and 1 Kings 15:2); Hebrew *Micaiah*   ᵇ 2 Or *granddaughter*

# New International Version

clean table and light the lamps on the gold lampstand every evening. We are observing the requirements of the LORD our God. But you have forsaken him. [12]God is with us; he is our leader. His priests with their trumpets will sound the battle cry against you. People of Israel, do not fight against the LORD, the God of your ancestors, for you will not succeed."

[13]Now Jeroboam had sent troops around to the rear, so that while he was in front of Judah the ambush was behind them. [14]Judah turned and saw that they were being attacked at both front and rear. Then they cried out to the LORD. The priests blew their trumpets [15]and the men of Judah raised the battle cry. At the sound of their battle cry, God routed Jeroboam and all Israel before Abijah and Judah. [16]The Israelites fled before Judah, and God delivered them into their hands. [17]Abijah and his troops inflicted heavy losses on them, so that there were five hundred thousand casualties among Israel's able men. [18]The Israelites were subdued on that occasion, and the people of Judah were victorious because they relied on the LORD, the God of their ancestors.

[19]Abijah pursued Jeroboam and took from him the towns of Bethel, Jeshanah and Ephron, with their surrounding villages. [20]Jeroboam did not regain power during the time of Abijah. And the LORD struck him down and he died.

[21]But Abijah grew in strength. He married fourteen wives and had twenty-two sons and sixteen daughters.

[22]The other events of Abijah's reign, what he did and what he said, are written in the annotations of the prophet Iddo.

**14** [a] And Abijah rested with his ancestors and was buried in the City of David. Asa his son succeeded him as king, and in his days the country was at peace for ten years.

### Asa King of Judah

[2]Asa did what was good and right in the eyes of the LORD his God. [3]He removed the foreign altars and the high places, smashed the sacred stones and cut down the Asherah poles.[b] [4]He commanded Judah to seek the LORD, the God of their ancestors, and to obey his laws and commands. [5]He removed the high places and incense altars in every town in Judah, and the kingdom was at peace under him. [6]He built up the fortified cities of Judah, since the land was at peace. No one was at war with him during those years, for the LORD gave him rest.

[7]"Let us build up these towns," he said to Judah, "and put walls around them, with towers, gates and bars. The land is still ours, because we have sought the LORD our God; we sought him and he has given us rest on every side." So they built and prospered.

[8]Asa had an army of three hundred thousand men from Judah, equipped with large shields and with spears, and two hundred and eighty thousand from Benjamin, armed with small shields and with bows. All these were brave fighting men.

[9]Zerah the Cushite marched out against them with an army of thousands upon thousands and three hundred chariots, and came as far as Mareshah. [10]Asa went out to meet him, and they took up battle positions in the Valley of Zephathah near Mareshah.

[11]Then Asa called to the LORD his God and said, "LORD,

*a In Hebrew texts 14:1 is numbered 13:23, and 14:2-15 is numbered 14:1-14. b 3 That is, wooden symbols of the goddess Asherah; here and elsewhere in 2 Chronicles*

# Amplified Bible

attend to the golden lampstand, that its lamps may be lighted every evening. For we keep the charge of the Lord our God, but you have forsaken Him.

[12]Behold, God Himself is with us at our head, and His priests with their battle trumpets to sound an alarm against you. O Israelites, fight not against the Lord, the God of your fathers, for you cannot prosper.

[13]But Jeroboam caused an ambushment to come around them from behind, so his troops were before Judah and the ambush behind.

[14]When Judah looked, behold, the battle was before and behind; and they cried to the Lord, and the priests blew the trumpets.

[15]Then the men of Judah gave a shout; and as they shouted, God smote Jeroboam and all Israel before Abijah and Judah.

[16]And the Israelites fled before Judah, and God delivered them into their hands.

[17]And Abijah and his people slew them with a great slaughter, so there fell of Israel 500,000 chosen men.

[18]Thus the Israelites were brought low at that time, and the people of Judah prevailed because they relied upon the Lord, the God of their fathers.

[19]And Abijah pursued Jeroboam and took some cities from him, Bethel, Jeshanah, and Ephraim (Ephron), with their towns.

[20]Jeroboam did not recover strength again in the days of Abijah. And the Lord smote him and he died.

[21]But Abijah became mighty. He married fourteen wives and had twenty-two sons and sixteen daughters.

[22]And the rest of the acts of Abijah, his ways and his sayings, are written in the story of the prophet Iddo.

**14** So Abijah slept with his fathers, and they buried him in the City of David; and Asa his son reigned in his stead. In his days the land was at rest for ten years.

[2]And Asa did what was good and right in the eyes of the Lord his God.

[3]He took away the foreign altars and high places and broke down the idol pillars or obelisks and cut down the Asherim [symbols of the goddess Asherah]

[4]And commanded Judah to seek the Lord, the God of their fathers [to inquire of and for Him and crave Him as a vital necessity], and to obey the law and the commandment.

[5]Also Asa took out of all the cities of Judah the idolatrous high places and the incense altars. And the kingdom had rest under his reign.

[6]And he built fortified cities in Judah, for the land had rest. He had no war in those years, for the Lord gave him peace.

[7]Therefore he said to Judah, Let us build these cities and surround them with walls, towers, gates, and bars. The land is still ours, because we have sought the Lord our God; we sought Him [yearning for Him with all our desire] and He has given us rest *and* peace on every side. So they built and prospered.

[8]Asa had an army of 300,000 men out of Judah, who bore bucklers and spears, and 280,000 out of Benjamin, who bore shields and drew bows, all mighty men of courage.

[9]There came out against Judah Zerah the Ethiopian with a host of a million [that is, too many to be numbered] and 300 chariots, and came as far as Mareshah.

[10]Then Asa went out against him, and they set up their lines of battle in the Valley of Zephathah at Mareshah.

[11]Asa cried to the Lord his God, O Lord, there is none

## New International Version

there is no one like you to help the powerless against the mighty. Help us, Lord our God, for we rely on you, and in your name we have come against this vast army. Lord, you are our God; do not let mere mortals prevail against you."

[12]The Lord struck down the Cushites before Asa and Judah. The Cushites fled, [13]and Asa and his army pursued them as far as Gerar. Such a great number of Cushites fell that they could not recover; they were crushed before the Lord and his forces. The men of Judah carried off a large amount of plunder. [14]They destroyed all the villages around Gerar, for the terror of the Lord had fallen on them. They looted all these villages, since there was much plunder there. [15]They also attacked the camps of the herders and carried off droves of sheep and goats and camels. Then they returned to Jerusalem.

### Asa's Reform

**15** The Spirit of God came on Azariah son of Oded. [2]He went out to meet Asa and said to him, "Listen to me, Asa and all Judah and Benjamin. The Lord is with you when you are with him. If you seek him, he will be found by you, but if you forsake him, he will forsake you. [3]For a long time Israel was without the true God, without a priest to teach and without the law. [4]But in their distress they turned to the Lord, the God of Israel, and sought him, and he was found by them. [5]In those days it was not safe to travel about, for all the inhabitants of the lands were in great turmoil. [6]One nation was being crushed by another and one city by another, because God was troubling them with every kind of distress. [7]But as for you, be strong and do not give up, for your work will be rewarded."

[8]When Asa heard these words and the prophecy of Azariah son of[a] Oded the prophet, he took courage. He removed the detestable idols from the whole land of Judah and Benjamin and from the towns he had captured in the hills of Ephraim. He repaired the altar of the Lord that was in front of the portico of the Lord's temple.

[9]Then he assembled all Judah and Benjamin and the people from Ephraim, Manasseh and Simeon who had settled among them, for large numbers had come over to him from Israel when they saw that the Lord his God was with him.

[10]They assembled at Jerusalem in the third month of the fifteenth year of Asa's reign. [11]At that time they sacrificed to the Lord seven hundred head of cattle and seven thousand sheep and goats from the plunder they had brought back. [12]They entered into a covenant to seek the Lord, the God of their ancestors, with all their heart and soul. [13]All who would not seek the Lord, the God of Israel, were to be put to death, whether small or great, man or woman. [14]They took an oath to the Lord with loud acclamation, with shouting and with trumpets and horns. [15]All Judah rejoiced about the oath because they had sworn it wholeheartedly. They sought God eagerly, and he was found by them. So the Lord gave them rest on every side.

[16]King Asa also deposed his grandmother Maakah from her position as queen mother, because she had made a repulsive image for the worship of Asherah. Asa cut it down, broke it up and burned it in the Kidron Valley. [17]Although

---

*[a] 8 Vulgate and Syriac (see also Septuagint and verse 1); Hebrew does not have Azariah son of.*

## Amplified Bible

besides You to help, and it makes no difference to You whether the one You help is mighty or powerless. Help us, O Lord our God! For we rely on You, and we go against this multitude in Your name. O Lord, You are our God; let no man prevail against You!

[12]So the Lord smote the Ethiopians before Asa and Judah, and the Ethiopians fled.

[13]Asa and the people with him pursued them to Gerar; and the Ethiopians were overthrown, so that none remained alive; for they were destroyed before the Lord and His host, who carried away very much booty.

[14]And they smote all the cities round about Gerar, for the fear of the Lord came upon them. They plundered all the cities, for there was much plunder in them.

[15]They smote also the cattle encampments and carried away sheep in abundance and camels; and they returned to Jerusalem.

**15** The Spirit of God came upon Azariah son of Oded. [2]And he went out to meet Asa and said to him, Hear me, Asa, and all Judah and Benjamin: the Lord is with you while you are with Him. If you seek Him [inquiring for and of Him, craving Him as your soul's first necessity], He will be found by you; but if you [become indifferent and] forsake Him, He will forsake you.

[3]Now for a long time Israel was without the true God, without a teaching priest, and without law.

[4]But when they in their trouble turned to the Lord, the God of Israel, and [in desperation earnestly] sought Him, He was found by them.

[5]And in those times there was no peace to him who went out nor to him who came in, but great *and* vexing afflictions *and* disturbances were upon all the inhabitants of the countries.

[6]Nation was broke in pieces against nation, and city against city, for God vexed *and* troubled them with all sorts of adversity.

[7]Be strong, therefore, and let not your hands be weak *and* slack, for your work shall be rewarded.

[8]And when Asa heard these words, the prophecy of Oded the prophet, he took courage and put away the abominable idols from all the land of Judah and Benjamin and from the cities which he had taken in the hill country of Ephraim; and he repaired the altar [of burnt offering] of the Lord which was in front of the porch *or* vestibule [of the house] of the Lord.

[9]And he gathered all Judah and Benjamin and the strangers with them out of Ephraim, Manasseh, and Simeon, for they came over to Asa out of Israel in large numbers when they saw that the Lord his God was with him.

[10]So they gathered at Jerusalem in the third month of the fifteenth year of the reign of Asa.

[11]And they sacrificed to the Lord on that day from the spoil which they had brought—700 oxen and 7,000 sheep.

[12]And they entered into a covenant to seek the Lord, the God of their fathers, *and* to yearn for Him with all their heart's desire and with all their soul;

[13]And that whoever would not seek the Lord, the God of Israel, should be put to death, whether young or old, man or woman.

[14]They took an oath to the Lord with a loud voice, with shouting, with trumpets, and with cornets.

[15]And all Judah rejoiced at the oath, for they had sworn with all their heart and sought Him [yearning for Him] with their whole desire, and He was found by them. And the Lord gave them rest *and* peace round about.

[16]Also Maacah, King Asa's mother, he removed from being queen mother, because she had made an abominable image for [the goddess] Asherah. Asa cut down her idol, crushed it, and burned it at the brook Kidron.

## New International Version

he did not remove the high places from Israel, Asa's heart was fully committed to the LORD all his life. [18]He brought into the temple of God the silver and gold and the articles that he and his father had dedicated.

[19]There was no more war until the thirty-fifth year of Asa's reign.

### Asa's Last Years

**16** In the thirty-sixth year of Asa's reign Baasha king of Israel went up against Judah and fortified Ramah to prevent anyone from leaving or entering the territory of Asa king of Judah.

[2]Asa then took the silver and gold out of the treasuries of the LORD's temple and of his own palace and sent it to Ben-Hadad king of Aram, who was ruling in Damascus. [3]"Let there be a treaty between me and you," he said, "as there was between my father and your father. See, I am sending you silver and gold. Now break your treaty with Baasha king of Israel so he will withdraw from me."

[4]Ben-Hadad agreed with King Asa and sent the commanders of his forces against the towns of Israel. They conquered Ijon, Dan, Abel Maim[a] and all the store cities of Naphtali. [5]When Baasha heard this, he stopped building Ramah and abandoned his work. [6]Then King Asa brought all the men of Judah, and they carried away from Ramah the stones and timber Baasha had been using. With them he built up Geba and Mizpah.

[7]At that time Hanani the seer came to Asa king of Judah and said to him: "Because you relied on the king of Aram and not on the LORD your God, the army of the king of Aram has escaped from your hand. [8]Were not the Cushites[b] and Libyans a mighty army with great numbers of chariots and horsemen[c]? Yet when you relied on the LORD, he delivered them into your hand. [9]For the eyes of the LORD range throughout the earth to strengthen those whose hearts are fully committed to him. You have done a foolish thing, and from now on you will be at war."

[10]Asa was angry with the seer because of this; he was so enraged that he put him in prison. At the same time Asa brutally oppressed some of the people.

[11]The events of Asa's reign, from beginning to end, are written in the book of the kings of Judah and Israel. [12]In the thirty-ninth year of his reign Asa was afflicted with a disease in his feet. Though his disease was severe, even in his illness he did not seek help from the LORD, but only from the physicians. [13]Then in the forty-first year of his reign Asa died and rested with his ancestors. [14]They buried him in the tomb that he had cut out for himself in the City of David. They laid him on a bier covered with spices and various blended perfumes, and they made a huge fire in his honor.

### Jehoshaphat King of Judah

**17** Jehoshaphat his son succeeded him as king and strengthened himself against Israel. [2]He stationed troops in all the fortified cities of Judah and put garrisons in Judah and in the towns of Ephraim that his father Asa had captured.

[3]The LORD was with Jehoshaphat because he followed the ways of his father David before him. He did not consult

## Amplified Bible

[17]But the high places were not taken out of Israel. Nevertheless, the heart of Asa was blameless all his days. [18]And he brought into the house of God the things that his father [Abijah] had dedicated and those he himself had dedicated—silver and gold and vessels.

[19]And there was no more war until the thirty-fifth year of the reign of Asa.

**16** In the thirty-sixth year of Asa's reign, Baasha king of Israel came up against Judah, and built (fortified) Ramah intending to intercept anyone going out or coming in to Asa king of Judah.

[2]Then Asa brought silver and gold out of the treasuries of the house of the Lord and of the king's house and sent them to Ben-hadad king of Syria, who dwelt at Damascus, saying,

[3]Let there be a league between me and you, as was between my father and your father. Behold, I am sending you silver and gold; go, break your league with Baasha king of Israel, that he may withdraw from me.

[4]And Ben-hadad hearkened to King Asa and sent the captains of his armies against the cities of Israel; and they smote Ijon, Dan, Abel-maim, and all the store cities of Naphtali.

[5]And when Baasha heard it, he stopped building Ramah and let his work cease.

[6]Then King Asa took all Judah, and they carried away the stones of Ramah and its timber with which Baasha had been building, and with them he built Geba and Mizpah.

[7]At that time Hanani the seer came to Asa king of Judah and said to him, Because you relied on the king of Syria and not on the Lord your God, the army of the king of Syria has escaped you.

[8]Were not the Ethiopians and Libyans a huge host with very many chariots and horsemen? Yet because you relied then on the Lord, He gave them into your hand.

[9]For the eyes of the Lord run to and fro throughout the whole earth to show Himself strong in behalf of those whose hearts are blameless toward Him. You have done foolishly in this; therefore, from now on you shall have wars.

[10]Then Asa was angry with the seer and put him in prison [in the stocks], for he was enraged with him because of this. Asa oppressed some of the people at the same time.

[11]The acts of Asa, from first to last, are written in the Book of the Kings of Judah and Israel.

[12]In the thirty-ninth year of his reign Asa was diseased in his feet—until his disease became very severe; yet in his disease he did not seek the Lord, but relied on the physicians.

[13]And Asa slept with his fathers, dying in the forty-first year of his reign.

[14]And they buried him in his own tomb which he had hewn out for himself in the City of David, and they laid him on a bier which was filled with sweet odors and various kinds [of spices] prepared by the perfumers' art; and they made a very great burning [of spices] in his honor.

**17** Jehoshaphat his son reigned in Asa's stead and strengthened himself against Israel.

[2]And he placed forces in all the fortified cities of Judah and set garrisons in the land of Judah and in the cities of Ephraim which Asa his father had taken.

[3]The Lord was with Jehoshaphat because he walked in the first ways of his father [David]. He did not seek the Baals

---

[a] 4 Also known as *Abel Beth Maakah*   [b] 8 That is, people from the upper Nile region   [c] 8 Or *charioteers*

## New International Version

the Baals ⁴but sought the God of his father and followed his commands rather than the practices of Israel. ⁵The LORD established the kingdom under his control; and all Judah brought gifts to Jehoshaphat, so that he had great wealth and honor. ⁶His heart was devoted to the ways of the LORD; furthermore, he removed the high places and the Asherah poles from Judah.

⁷In the third year of his reign he sent his officials Ben-Hail, Obadiah, Zechariah, Nethanel and Micaiah to teach in the towns of Judah. ⁸With them were certain Levites—Shemaiah, Nethaniah, Zebadiah, Asahel, Shemiramoth, Jehonathan, Adonijah, Tobijah and Tob-Adonijah—and the priests Elishama and Jehoram. ⁹They taught throughout Judah, taking with them the Book of the Law of the LORD; they went around to all the towns of Judah and taught the people.

¹⁰The fear of the LORD fell on all the kingdoms of the lands surrounding Judah, so that they did not go to war against Jehoshaphat. ¹¹Some Philistines brought Jehoshaphat gifts and silver as tribute, and the Arabs brought him flocks: seven thousand seven hundred rams and seven thousand seven hundred goats.

¹²Jehoshaphat became more and more powerful; he built forts and store cities in Judah ¹³and had large supplies in the towns of Judah. He also kept experienced fighting men in Jerusalem. ¹⁴Their enrollment by families was as follows:

From Judah, commanders of units of 1,000:
Adnah the commander, with 300,000 fighting men;
¹⁵next, Jehohanan the commander, with 280,000;
¹⁶next, Amasiah son of Zikri, who volunteered himself for the service of the LORD, with 200,000.
¹⁷From Benjamin:
Eliada, a valiant soldier, with 200,000 men armed with bows and shields;
¹⁸next, Jehozabad, with 180,000 men armed for battle.

¹⁹These were the men who served the king, besides those he stationed in the fortified cities throughout Judah.

### Micaiah Prophesies Against Ahab

**18** Now Jehoshaphat had great wealth and honor, and he allied himself with Ahab by marriage. ²Some years later he went down to see Ahab in Samaria. Ahab slaughtered many sheep and cattle for him and the people with him and urged him to attack Ramoth Gilead. ³Ahab king of Israel asked Jehoshaphat king of Judah, "Will you go with me against Ramoth Gilead?"

Jehoshaphat replied, "I am as you are, and my people as your people; we will join you in the war." ⁴But Jehoshaphat also said to the king of Israel, "First seek the counsel of the LORD."

⁵So the king of Israel brought together the prophets—four hundred men—and asked them, "Shall we go to war against Ramoth Gilead, or shall I not?"

"Go," they answered, "for God will give it into the king's hand."

⁶But Jehoshaphat asked, "Is there no longer a prophet of the LORD here whom we can inquire of?"

⁷The king of Israel answered Jehoshaphat, "There is still one prophet through whom we can inquire of the LORD, but I hate him because he never prophesies anything good about me, but always bad. He is Micaiah son of Imlah."

"The king should not say such a thing," Jehoshaphat replied.

## Amplified Bible

⁴But sought *and* yearned with all his desire for the Lord, the God of his father, and walked in His commandments and not after the ways of Israel.

⁵Therefore the Lord established the kingdom in his hand; and all Judah brought tribute to Jehoshaphat, and he had great riches and honor.

⁶His heart was cheered *and* his courage was high in the ways of the Lord; moreover, he took away the high places and the Asherim out of Judah.

⁷Also in the third year of his reign he sent his princes Ben-hail, Obadiah, Zechariah, Nethanel, and Micaiah to teach in the cities of Judah;

⁸And with them were the Levites—Shemaiah, Nethaniah, Zebadiah, Asahel, Shemiramoth, Jehonathan, Adonijah, Tobijah, and Tob-adonijah; and with these Levites were the priests Elishama and Jehoram.

⁹And they taught in Judah, and had the Book of the Law of the Lord with them; they went about throughout all the cities of Judah and taught among the people.

¹⁰And a terror from the Lord fell upon all the kingdoms of the lands that were round about Judah, so that they made no war against Jehoshaphat.

¹¹And some of the Philistines brought Jehoshaphat gifts and tribute silver, and the Arabs brought him flocks: 7,700 each of rams and of he-goats.

¹²And Jehoshaphat became very great. He built in Judah fortresses and store cities,

¹³And he had many works in the cities of Judah, and soldiers, mighty men of courage, in Jerusalem.

¹⁴This was the number of them by their fathers' houses: Of Judah, the captains of thousands: Adnah the chief, with 300,000 mighty men of valor;

¹⁵Next to him was Jehohanan the captain, with 280,000;

¹⁶And next to him Amasiah son of Zichri, who willingly offered himself to the Lord, with 200,000 mighty men of valor.

¹⁷Of Benjamin: Eliada, a mighty man of valor, with 200,000 men armed with bow and shield;

¹⁸Next to him was Jehozabad with 180,000 armed for war.

¹⁹These were in the king's service, besides those [he] had placed in fortified cities throughout all Judah.

**18** Now Jehoshaphat had great riches and honor, but was allied [by marriage] with Ahab.

²After some years he went down to Ahab in Samaria. And Ahab killed sheep and oxen for him in abundance and for the people with him and persuaded him to go up with him against Ramoth-gilead.

³Ahab king of Israel said to Jehoshaphat king of Judah, Will you go with me to Ramoth-gilead? He answered, I am as you are, and my people as your people; we will be with you in the war.

⁴And Jehoshaphat said to the king of Israel, Inquire first, I pray you, for the word of the Lord today.

⁵So King [Ahab] of Israel gathered together the prophets, 400 men, and said to them, Shall we go to Ramoth-gilead to battle, or shall I forbear? And they said, Go up, for God will deliver it into the king's hand.

⁶But Jehoshaphat said, Is there not another prophet of the Lord here by whom we may inquire?

⁷King [Ahab] of Israel said to Jehoshaphat, There is another man, Micaiah son of Imla, by whom we may inquire of the Lord, but I hate him, for he never has prophesied good for me, but always evil. And Jehoshaphat said, Let not the king say so.

## New International Version

⁸So the king of Israel called one of his officials and said, "Bring Micaiah son of Imlah at once."

⁹Dressed in their royal robes, the king of Israel and Jehoshaphat king of Judah were sitting on their thrones at the threshing floor by the entrance of the gate of Samaria, with all the prophets prophesying before them. ¹⁰Now Zedekiah son of Kenaanah had made iron horns, and he declared, "This is what the LORD says: 'With these you will gore the Arameans until they are destroyed.'"

¹¹All the other prophets were prophesying the same thing. "Attack Ramoth Gilead and be victorious," they said, "for the LORD will give it into the king's hand."

¹²The messenger who had gone to summon Micaiah said to him, "Look, the other prophets without exception are predicting success for the king. Let your word agree with theirs, and speak favorably."

¹³But Micaiah said, "As surely as the LORD lives, I can tell him only what my God says."

¹⁴When he arrived, the king asked him, "Micaiah, shall we go to war against Ramoth Gilead, or shall I not?"

"Attack and be victorious," he answered, "for they will be given into your hand."

¹⁵The king said to him, "How many times must I make you swear to tell me nothing but the truth in the name of the LORD?"

¹⁶Then Micaiah answered, "I saw all Israel scattered on the hills like sheep without a shepherd, and the LORD said, 'These people have no master. Let each one go home in peace.'"

¹⁷The king of Israel said to Jehoshaphat, "Didn't I tell you that he never prophesies anything good about me, but only bad?"

¹⁸Micaiah continued, "Therefore hear the word of the LORD: I saw the LORD sitting on his throne with all the multitudes of heaven standing on his right and on his left. ¹⁹And the LORD said, 'Who will entice Ahab king of Israel into attacking Ramoth Gilead and going to his death there?'

"One suggested this, and another that. ²⁰Finally, a spirit came forward, stood before the LORD and said, 'I will entice him.'

"'By what means?' the LORD asked.

²¹"'I will go and be a deceiving spirit in the mouths of all his prophets,' he said.

"'You will succeed in enticing him,' said the LORD. 'Go and do it.'

²²"So now the LORD has put a deceiving spirit in the mouths of these prophets of yours. The LORD has decreed disaster for you."

²³Then Zedekiah son of Kenaanah went up and slapped Micaiah in the face. "Which way did the spirit from[a] the LORD go when he went from me to speak to you?" he asked.

²⁴Micaiah replied, "You will find out on the day you go to hide in an inner room."

²⁵The king of Israel then ordered, "Take Micaiah and send him back to Amon the ruler of the city and to Joash the king's son, ²⁶and say, 'This is what the king says: Put this fellow in prison and give him nothing but bread and water until I return safely.'"

²⁷Micaiah declared, "If you ever return safely, the LORD has not spoken through me." Then he added, "Mark my words, all you people!"

### Ahab Killed at Ramoth Gilead

²⁸So the king of Israel and Jehoshaphat king of Judah went up to Ramoth Gilead. ²⁹The king of Israel said to

## Amplified Bible

⁸And King [Ahab] of Israel called for one of his officers and said, Bring quickly Micaiah son of Imla.

⁹The king of Israel and Jehoshaphat king of Judah sat each on his throne, arrayed in their robes; they were sitting in an open place [at the threshing floor] at the entrance of the gate of Samaria; all the prophets were prophesying before them.

¹⁰And Zedekiah son of Chenaanah had made himself horns of iron, and said, Thus says the Lord: With these you shall push the Syrians until they are destroyed.

¹¹All the prophets prophesied so, saying, Go up to Ramoth-gilead and prosper; the Lord will deliver it into the king's hand.

¹²The messenger who went to call Micaiah said to him, Behold, the words of the prophets foretell good to the king with one accord. So let your word be like one of them, and speak favorably.

¹³But Micaiah said, As the Lord lives, what my God says, that will I speak.

¹⁴And when he had come to the king, King [Ahab] said to him, Micaiah, shall we go to Ramoth-gilead to battle, or shall I forbear? And he said, Go up and prosper, and they shall be delivered into your hand.

¹⁵And the king said to him, How many times shall I warn you to tell nothing but the truth to me in the name of the Lord?

¹⁶Then Micaiah said, I did see all Israel scattered upon the mountains as sheep that have no shepherd, and the Lord said, These have no master. Let each return to his house in peace.

¹⁷And King [Ahab] of Israel said to Jehoshaphat, Did I not tell you that he would not prophesy good to me, but evil?

¹⁸[Micaiah] said, Therefore hear the word of the Lord: I saw the Lord sitting on His throne, and all the host of heaven standing at His right hand and His left.

¹⁹And the Lord said, Who shall entice Ahab king of Israel, that he may go up and fall at Ramoth-gilead? And one said this thing, and another that.

²⁰Then there came a spirit and stood before the Lord and said, I will entice him. The Lord said to him, By what means?

²¹And he said, I will go out and be a lying spirit in the mouths of all his prophets. And the Lord said, You shall entice him and also succeed. Go forth and do so.

²²Now, you see, the Lord put a lying spirit in the mouths of your prophets; and the Lord has spoken evil concerning you.

²³Then Zedekiah the son of Chenaanah came near and smote Micaiah upon the cheek and said, Which way went the Spirit of the Lord from me to speak to you?

²⁴And Micaiah said, Behold, you shall see on that day when you shall go into an inner chamber to hide yourself.

²⁵Then King [Ahab] of Israel said, Take Micaiah back to Amon the governor of the city and to Joash the king's son,

²⁶And say, Thus says the king: Put this fellow in prison and feed him with bread and water of affliction until I return in peace.

²⁷Micaiah said, If you return at all in peace, the Lord has not spoken by me. And he [added], Hear it, you people, all of you!

²⁸So Ahab king of Israel and Jehoshaphat king of Judah went up to Ramoth-gilead.

---

a 23 Or *Spirit of*

## New International Version

Jehoshaphat, "I will enter the battle in disguise, but you wear your royal robes." So the king of Israel disguised himself and went into battle.

³⁰Now the king of Aram had ordered his chariot commanders, "Do not fight with anyone, small or great, except the king of Israel." ³¹When the chariot commanders saw Jehoshaphat, they thought, "This is the king of Israel." So they turned to attack him, but Jehoshaphat cried out, and the LORD helped him. God drew them away from him, ³²for when the chariot commanders saw that he was not the king of Israel, they stopped pursuing him.

³³But someone drew his bow at random and hit the king of Israel between the breastplate and the scale armor. The king told the chariot driver, "Wheel around and get me out of the fighting. I've been wounded." ³⁴All day long the battle raged, and the king of Israel propped himself up in his chariot facing the Arameans until evening. Then at sunset he died.

**19** When Jehoshaphat king of Judah returned safely to his palace in Jerusalem, ²Jehu the seer, the son of Hanani, went out to meet him and said to the king, "Should you help the wicked and love[a] those who hate the LORD? Because of this, the wrath of the LORD is on you. ³There is, however, some good in you, for you have rid the land of the Asherah poles and have set your heart on seeking God."

### Jehoshaphat Appoints Judges

⁴Jehoshaphat lived in Jerusalem, and he went out again among the people from Beersheba to the hill country of Ephraim and turned them back to the LORD, the God of their ancestors. ⁵He appointed judges in the land, in each of the fortified cities of Judah. ⁶He told them, "Consider carefully what you do, because you are not judging for mere mortals but for the LORD, who is with you whenever you give a verdict. ⁷Now let the fear of the LORD be on you. Judge carefully, for with the LORD our God there is no injustice or partiality or bribery."

⁸In Jerusalem also, Jehoshaphat appointed some of the Levites, priests and heads of Israelite families to administer the law of the LORD and to settle disputes. And they lived in Jerusalem. ⁹He gave them these orders: "You must serve faithfully and wholeheartedly in the fear of the LORD. ¹⁰In every case that comes before you from your people who live in the cities—whether bloodshed or other concerns of the law, commands, decrees or regulations—you are to warn them not to sin against the LORD; otherwise his wrath will come on you and your people. Do this, and you will not sin.

¹¹"Amariah the chief priest will be over you in any matter concerning the LORD, and Zebadiah son of Ishmael, the leader of the tribe of Judah, will be over you in any matter concerning the king, and the Levites will serve as officials before you. Act with courage, and may the LORD be with those who do well."

### Jehoshaphat Defeats Moab and Ammon

**20** After this, the Moabites and Ammonites with some of the Meunites[b] came to wage war against Jehoshaphat.

## Amplified Bible

²⁹And [Ahab] king of Israel said to Jehoshaphat, I will disguise myself and will go to the battle, but you put on your royal robes. So King Ahab of Israel disguised himself, and they went into the battle.

³⁰Now Syria's king had commanded his chariot captains, Fight not with small or great, but only with the king of Israel.

³¹And when the captains of the chariots saw Jehoshaphat [of Judah], they said, It is the king of Israel. So they turned to fight against him, but Jehoshaphat cried out, and the Lord helped him; and God moved them to depart from him.

³²For when the captains of the chariots saw that it was not the king of Israel, they turned back from pursuing him.

³³A certain man drew his bow at a venture and smote King [Ahab] of Israel between the lower armor and the breastplate. So Ahab said to his chariot driver, Turn, carry me out of the battle, for I am wounded.

³⁴And the battle increased that day; however, King [Ahab] of Israel propped himself up in his chariot opposite the Syrians until evening, and about sunset he died.

**19** Jehoshaphat the king of Judah returned safely to his house in Jerusalem.

²Jehu son of Hanani, the seer, went out to meet him and said to Jehoshaphat, Should you help the ungodly and love those who hate the Lord? Because of this, wrath has gone out against you from the Lord.

³But there are good things found in you, for you have destroyed the Asherim out of the land and have set your heart to seek God [with all your soul's desire].

⁴Jehoshaphat dwelt at Jerusalem, and he went out again among the people from Beersheba to the hill country of Ephraim and brought them back to the Lord, the God of their fathers.

⁵He appointed judges throughout all the fortified cities of Judah, city by city,

⁶And said to the judges, Be careful what you do, for you judge not for man but for the Lord, and He is with you in the matter of judgment.

⁷So now let the reverence *and* fear of the Lord be upon you; take heed what you do, for there is no injustice with the Lord our God, or partiality or taking of bribes.

⁸Also in Jerusalem, Jehoshaphat set certain Levites, priests, and heads of families of Israel to give judgment for the Lord and decide controversies. When they [of the commission] returned to Jerusalem,

⁹The king charged them, Do this in the fear of the Lord, faithfully, with integrity *and* a blameless heart.

¹⁰Whenever any controversy shall come to you from your brethren who dwell in their cities, between blood and blood, between law and commandment, statutes and judgments, you shall warn *and* instruct them that they may not be guilty before the Lord; otherwise wrath will come upon you and your brethren. Do this and you will not be guilty.

¹¹And behold, Amariah the chief priest is over you in all matters of the Lord, and Zebadiah son of Ishmael, the governor of the house of Judah, in all the king's matters; also the Levites will serve you as officers. Deal courageously [be strong and do], and may the Lord be with the good!

**20** After this, the Moabites, the Ammonites, and with them the Meunites came against Jehoshaphat to battle.

---

*a* 2 Or *and make alliances with*    *b* 1 Some Septuagint manuscripts; Hebrew *Ammonites*

## New International Version

[2] Some people came and told Jehoshaphat, "A vast army is coming against you from Edom,[a] from the other side of the Dead Sea. It is already in Hazezon Tamar" (that is, En Gedi). [3] Alarmed, Jehoshaphat resolved to inquire of the LORD, and he proclaimed a fast for all Judah. [4] The people of Judah came together to seek help from the LORD; indeed, they came from every town in Judah to seek him.

[5] Then Jehoshaphat stood up in the assembly of Judah and Jerusalem at the temple of the LORD in the front of the new courtyard [6] and said:

"LORD, the God of our ancestors, are you not the God who is in heaven? You rule over all the kingdoms of the nations. Power and might are in your hand, and no one can withstand you. [7] Our God, did you not drive out the inhabitants of this land before your people Israel and give it forever to the descendants of Abraham your friend? [8] They have lived in it and have built in it a sanctuary for your Name, saying, [9] 'If calamity comes upon us, whether the sword of judgment, or plague or famine, we will stand in your presence before this temple that bears your Name and will cry out to you in our distress, and you will hear us and save us.'

[10] "But now here are men from Ammon, Moab and Mount Seir, whose territory you would not allow Israel to invade when they came from Egypt; so they turned away from them and did not destroy them. [11] See how they are repaying us by coming to drive us out of the possession you gave us as an inheritance. [12] Our God, will you not judge them? For we have no power to face this vast army that is attacking us. We do not know what to do, but our eyes are on you."

[13] All the men of Judah, with their wives and children and little ones, stood there before the LORD.

[14] Then the Spirit of the LORD came on Jahaziel son of Zechariah, the son of Benaiah, the son of Jeiel, the son of Mattaniah, a Levite and descendant of Asaph, as he stood in the assembly.

[15] He said: "Listen, King Jehoshaphat and all who live in Judah and Jerusalem! This is what the LORD says to you: 'Do not be afraid or discouraged because of this vast army. For the battle is not yours, but God's. [16] Tomorrow march down against them. They will be climbing up by the Pass of Ziz, and you will find them at the end of the gorge in the Desert of Jeruel. [17] You will not have to fight this battle. Take up your positions; stand firm and see the deliverance the LORD will give you, Judah and Jerusalem. Do not be afraid; do not be discouraged. Go out to face them tomorrow, and the LORD will be with you.'"

[18] Jehoshaphat bowed down with his face to the ground, and all the people of Judah and Jerusalem fell down in worship before the LORD. [19] Then some Levites from the Kohathites and Korahites stood up and praised the LORD, the God of Israel, with a very loud voice.

[20] Early in the morning they left for the Desert of Tekoa. As they set out, Jehoshaphat stood and said, "Listen to me, Judah and people of Jerusalem! Have faith in the LORD your God and you will be upheld; have faith in his prophets and you will be successful." [21] After consulting the people, Jehoshaphat appointed men to sing to the LORD and to

## Amplified Bible

[2] It was told Jehoshaphat, A great multitude has come against you from beyond the [Dead] Sea, from Edom; and behold they are in Hazazon-tamar, which is En-gedi.

[3] Then Jehoshaphat feared, and set himself [determinedly, as his vital need] to seek the Lord; he proclaimed a fast in all Judah.

[4] And Judah gathered together to ask help from the Lord; even out of all the cities of Judah they came to seek the Lord [yearning for Him with all their desire].

[5] And Jehoshaphat stood in the assembly of Judah and Jerusalem in the house of the Lord before the new court

[6] And said, O Lord, God of our fathers, are You not God in heaven? And do You not rule over all the kingdoms of the nations? In Your hand are power and might, so that none is able to withstand You.

[7] Did not You, O our God, drive out the inhabitants of this land before Your people Israel and give it forever to the descendants of Abraham Your friend?

[8] They dwelt in it and have built You a sanctuary in it for Your Name, saying,

[9] If evil comes upon us, the sword of judgment, or pestilence, or famine, we will stand before this house and before You—for Your Name [and the symbol of Your presence] is in this house—and cry to You in our affliction, and You will hear and save.

[10] And now behold, the men of Ammon, Moab, and Mount Seir, whom You would not let Israel invade when they came from the land of Egypt, and whom they turned from and did not destroy—[Deut. 2:9.]

[11] Behold, they reward us by coming to drive us out of Your possession which You have given us to inherit.

[12] O our God, will You not exercise judgment upon them? For we have no might to stand against this great company that is coming against us. We do not know what to do, but our eyes are upon You.

[13] And all Judah stood before the Lord, with their children and their wives.

[14] Then the Spirit of the Lord came upon Jahaziel son of Zechariah, the son of Benaiah, the son of Jeiel, the son of Mattaniah, a Levite of the sons of Asaph, in the midst of the assembly.

[15] He said, Hearken, all Judah, you inhabitants of Jerusalem, and you King Jehoshaphat. The Lord says this to you: Be not afraid or dismayed at this great multitude; for the battle is not yours, but God's.

[16] Tomorrow go down to them. Behold, they will come up by the Ascent of Ziz, and you will find them at the end of the ravine before the Wilderness of Jeruel.

[17] You shall not need to fight in this battle; take your positions, stand still, and see the deliverance of the Lord [Who is] with you, O Judah and Jerusalem. Fear not nor be dismayed. Tomorrow go out against them, for the Lord is with you.

[18] And Jehoshaphat bowed his head with his face to the ground, and all Judah and the inhabitants of Jerusalem fell down before the Lord, worshiping Him.

[19] And some Levites of the Kohathites and Korahites stood up to praise the Lord, the God of Israel, with a very loud voice.

[20] And they rose early in the morning and went out into the Wilderness of Tekoa; and as they went out, Jehoshaphat stood and said, Hear me, O Judah, and you inhabitants of Jerusalem! Believe in the Lord your God and you shall be established; believe *and* remain steadfast to His prophets and you shall prosper.

[21] When he had consulted with the people, he appointed singers to sing to the Lord and praise Him in their holy

---

[a] 2 One Hebrew manuscript; most Hebrew manuscripts, Septuagint and Vulgate *Aram*

## New International Version

praise him for the splendor of his[a] holiness as they went out at the head of the army, saying:

"Give thanks to the LORD,
   for his love endures forever."

22As they began to sing and praise, the LORD set ambushes against the men of Ammon and Moab and Mount Seir who were invading Judah, and they were defeated. 23The Ammonites and Moabites rose up against the men from Mount Seir to destroy and annihilate them. After they finished slaughtering the men from Seir, they helped to destroy one another.

24When the men of Judah came to the place that overlooks the desert and looked toward the vast army, they saw only dead bodies lying on the ground; no one had escaped. 25So Jehoshaphat and his men went to carry off their plunder, and they found among them a great amount of equipment and clothing[b] and also articles of value—more than they could take away. There was so much plunder that it took three days to collect it. 26On the fourth day they assembled in the Valley of Berakah, where they praised the LORD. This is why it is called the Valley of Berakah[c] to this day.

27Then, led by Jehoshaphat, all the men of Judah and Jerusalem returned joyfully to Jerusalem, for the LORD had given them cause to rejoice over their enemies. 28They entered Jerusalem and went to the temple of the LORD with harps and lyres and trumpets.

29The fear of God came on all the surrounding kingdoms when they heard how the LORD had fought against the enemies of Israel. 30And the kingdom of Jehoshaphat was at peace, for his God had given him rest on every side.

### The End of Jehoshaphat's Reign

31So Jehoshaphat reigned over Judah. He was thirty-five years old when he became king of Judah, and he reigned in Jerusalem twenty-five years. His mother's name was Azubah daughter of Shilhi. 32He followed the ways of his father Asa and did not stray from them; he did what was right in the eyes of the LORD. 33The high places, however, were not removed, and the people still had not set their hearts on the God of their ancestors.

34The other events of Jehoshaphat's reign, from beginning to end, are written in the annals of Jehu son of Hanani, which are recorded in the book of the kings of Israel.

35Later, Jehoshaphat king of Judah made an alliance with Ahaziah king of Israel, whose ways were wicked. 36He agreed with him to construct a fleet of trading ships.[d] After these were built at Ezion Geber, 37Eliezer son of Dodavahu of Mareshah prophesied against Jehoshaphat, saying, "Because you have made an alliance with Ahaziah, the LORD will destroy what you have made." The ships were wrecked and were not able to set sail to trade.[e]

**21** Then Jehoshaphat rested with his ancestors and was buried with them in the City of David. And Jehoram his son succeeded him as king. 2Jehoram's brothers, the sons of Jehoshaphat, were Azariah, Jehiel, Zechariah, Azariahu, Michael and Shephatiah. All these were sons of Jehoshaphat king of Israel.[f] 3Their father had given them many gifts of silver and gold and articles of value, as well as fortified cities in Judah, but he had given the kingdom to Jehoram because he was his firstborn son.

## Amplified Bible

[priestly] garments as they went out before the army, saying, Give thanks to the Lord, for His mercy *and* lovingkindness endure forever!

22And when they began to sing and to praise, the Lord set ambushments against the men of Ammon, Moab, and Mount Seir who had come against Judah, and they were [self-] slaughtered;

23For [suspecting betrayal] the men of Ammon and Moab rose against those of Mount Seir, utterly destroying them. And when they had made an end of the men of Seir, they all helped to destroy one another.

24And when Judah came to the watchtower of the wilderness, they looked at the multitude, and behold, they were dead bodies fallen to the earth, and none had escaped!

25When Jehoshaphat and his people came to take the spoil, they found among them much cattle, goods, garments, and precious things which they took for themselves, more than they could carry away, so much they were three days in gathering the spoil.

26On the fourth day they assembled in the Valley of Beracah. There they blessed the Lord. So the name of the place is still called the Valley of Beracah [blessing].

27Then they returned, every man of Judah and Jerusalem, Jehoshaphat leading them, to Jerusalem with joy, for the Lord had made them to rejoice over their enemies.

28They came to Jerusalem with harps, lyres, and trumpets to the house of the Lord.

29And the fear of God came upon all the kingdoms of those countries when they heard that the Lord had fought against the enemies of Israel.

30So the realm of Jehoshaphat was quiet, for his God gave him rest round about.

31Thus Jehoshaphat reigned over Judah. He was thirty-five years old when he began his twenty-five-year reign in Jerusalem. His mother was Azubah daughter of Shilhi.

32And he walked in the ways of Asa his father and departed not from it, doing what was right in the sight of the Lord.

33But the high places [of idolatry] were not taken away, for the people had not yet set their hearts on their fathers' God.

34Now the rest of the acts of Jehoshaphat, from first to last, they are written in the records of Jehu son of Hanani, which are in the Book of the Kings of Israel.

35After this, Jehoshaphat king of Judah joined with Ahaziah king of Israel, who did very wickedly.

36He joined him in building ships to go to Tarshish, building them in Ezion-geber.

37Then Eliezer son of Dodavahu of Mareshah prophesied against Jehoshaphat, saying, Because you have joined Ahaziah, the Lord will destroy your works. So the ships were wrecked and unable to go to Tarshish.

**21** Jehoshaphat slept with his fathers and was buried with [them] in the City of David. Jehoram his son reigned in his stead.

2He had brothers: Azariah, Jehiel, Zechariah, Azariah, Michael, and Shephatiah, all the sons of Jehoshaphat king of Israel.

3Their father gave them great gifts of silver, gold, and precious things, together with fortified cities in Judah, but the kingdom he gave to Jehoram, the firstborn.

---

*a 21* Or *him with the splendor of*   *b 25* Some Hebrew manuscripts and Vulgate; most Hebrew manuscripts *corpses*   *c 26 Berakah* means *praise.*   *d 36* Hebrew *of ships that could go to Tarshish*   *e 37* Hebrew *sail for Tarshish*   *f 2* That is, Judah, as frequently in 2 Chronicles

# New International Version

## Jehoram King of Judah

[4]When Jehoram established himself firmly over his father's kingdom, he put all his brothers to the sword along with some of the officials of Israel. [5]Jehoram was thirty-two years old when he became king, and he reigned in Jerusalem eight years. [6]He followed the ways of the kings of Israel, as the house of Ahab had done, for he married a daughter of Ahab. He did evil in the eyes of the LORD. [7]Nevertheless, because of the covenant the LORD had made with David, the LORD was not willing to destroy the house of David. He had promised to maintain a lamp for him and his descendants forever.

[8]In the time of Jehoram, Edom rebelled against Judah and set up its own king. [9]So Jehoram went there with his officers and all his chariots. The Edomites surrounded him and his chariot commanders, but he rose up and broke through by night. [10]To this day Edom has been in rebellion against Judah.

Libnah revolted at the same time, because Jehoram had forsaken the LORD, the God of his ancestors. [11]He had also built high places on the hills of Judah and had caused the people of Jerusalem to prostitute themselves and had led Judah astray.

[12]Jehoram received a letter from Elijah the prophet, which said:

"This is what the LORD, the God of your father David, says: 'You have not followed the ways of your father Jehoshaphat or of Asa king of Judah. [13]But you have followed the ways of the kings of Israel, and you have led Judah and the people of Jerusalem to prostitute themselves, just as the house of Ahab did. You have also murdered your own brothers, members of your own family, men who were better than you. [14]So now the LORD is about to strike your people, your sons, your wives and everything that is yours, with a heavy blow. [15]You yourself will be very ill with a lingering disease of the bowels, until the disease causes your bowels to come out.'"

[16]The LORD aroused against Jehoram the hostility of the Philistines and of the Arabs who lived near the Cushites. [17]They attacked Judah, invaded it and carried off all the goods found in the king's palace, together with his sons and wives. Not a son was left to him except Ahaziah,[a] the youngest.

[18]After all this, the LORD afflicted Jehoram with an incurable disease of the bowels. [19]In the course of time, at the end of the second year, his bowels came out because of the disease, and he died in great pain. His people made no funeral fire in his honor, as they had for his predecessors.

[20]Jehoram was thirty-two years old when he became king, and he reigned in Jerusalem eight years. He passed away, to no one's regret, and was buried in the City of David, but not in the tombs of the kings.

## Ahaziah King of Judah

**22** The people of Jerusalem made Ahaziah, Jehoram's youngest son, king in his place, since the raiders, who came with the Arabs into the camp, had killed all the older sons. So Ahaziah son of Jehoram king of Judah began to reign. [2]Ahaziah was twenty-two[b] years old when he became king, and he reigned in Jerusalem one year. His mother's name was Athaliah, a granddaughter of Omri. [3]He too followed the ways of the house of Ahab, for his

# Amplified Bible

[4]When Jehoram had ascended to the kingship of his father, he strengthened himself and slew all his brethren with the sword and also some of Israel's princes.

[5]Jehoram at thirty-two years of age began his eight-year reign in Jerusalem.

[6]He walked in the ways of the kings of Israel, as did the house of Ahab, for he married the daughter of Ahab and did what was evil in the eyes of the Lord.

[7]But the Lord would not destroy the house of David, because He had made a covenant with David and promised to give a light to him and to his sons forever.

[8]In Jehoram's days, the Edomites revolted from the rule of Judah and set up for themselves a king.

[9]Then Jehoram passed over [the Jordan] with his captains and all his chariots, and rose up by night and smote the Edomites who had surrounded him and his chariot captains.

[10]So Edom revolted from the rule of Judah to this day. Then Libnah also revolted from Jehoram's rule, because he had forsaken the Lord, the God of his fathers.

[11]Moreover, he made idolatrous high places in the hill country of Judah and debauched spiritually the inhabitants of Jerusalem and led Judah astray [compelling the people's cooperation].

[12]And there came a letter to Jehoram from Elijah the prophet, saying, Thus says the Lord, the God of David your father [forefather]: Because you have not walked in the ways of Jehoshaphat your father nor in the ways of Asa king of Judah,

[13]But have walked in the ways of Israel's kings, and made Judah and the inhabitants of Jerusalem play the harlot like the [spiritual] harlotry of Ahab's house, and also have slain your brothers of your father's house, who were better than you,

[14]Behold, the Lord will smite your people, and your children, your wives, and all your possessions with a great plague.

[15]And you yourself shall have a severe illness because of an intestinal disease, until your bowels fall out because of the sickness, day after day.

[16]And the Lord stirred up against Jehoram the anger of the Philistines and of the Arabs who were near the Ethiopians.

[17]They came against Judah, invaded it, and carried away all the possessions found in *and* around the king's house, together with his sons and his wives; so there was not a son left to him except Jehoahaz, the youngest.

[18]And after all this, the Lord smote [Jehoram] with an incurable intestinal disease.

[19]In process of time, after two years, his bowels fell out because of his disease. So he died in severe distress. And his people made no funeral fire to honor him, like the fires for his fathers.

[20]Thirty-two years old was Jehoram when he began to reign, and he reigned in Jerusalem eight years, and departed without being wanted. Yet they buried him in the City of David, but not in the tombs of the kings.

**22** The people of Jerusalem made Ahaziah, his youngest son, king in his stead, for the troop that came with the Arabs to the camp had slain all the older sons. So Ahaziah son of Jehoram king of Judah reigned. [2]Forty-two years old was Ahaziah when he began his one-year reign in Jerusalem. His mother was Athaliah, a granddaughter of Omri. [II Kings 8:26.]

[3]He also walked in the ways of the house of Ahab, for his mother was his counselor to do wickedly.

---

[a] 17 Hebrew *Jehoahaz*, a variant of *Ahaziah*   [b] 2 Some Septuagint manuscripts and Syriac (see also 2 Kings 8:26); Hebrew *forty-two*

## New International Version

mother encouraged him to act wickedly. [4]He did evil in the eyes of the LORD, as the house of Ahab had done, for after his father's death they became his advisers, to his undoing. [5]He also followed their counsel when he went with Joram[a] son of Ahab king of Israel to wage war against Hazael king of Aram at Ramoth Gilead. The Arameans wounded Joram; [6]so he returned to Jezreel to recover from the wounds they had inflicted on him at Ramoth[b] in his battle with Hazael king of Aram.

Then Ahaziah[c] son of Jehoram king of Judah went down to Jezreel to see Joram son of Ahab because he had been wounded.

[7]Through Ahaziah's visit to Joram, God brought about Ahaziah's downfall. When Ahaziah arrived, he went out with Joram to meet Jehu son of Nimshi, whom the LORD had anointed to destroy the house of Ahab. [8]While Jehu was executing judgment on the house of Ahab, he found the officials of Judah and the sons of Ahaziah's relatives, who had been attending Ahaziah, and he killed them. [9]He then went in search of Ahaziah, and his men captured him while he was hiding in Samaria. He was brought to Jehu and put to death. They buried him, for they said, "He was a son of Jehoshaphat, who sought the LORD with all his heart." So there was no one in the house of Ahaziah powerful enough to retain the kingdom.

### Athaliah and Joash

[10]When Athaliah the mother of Ahaziah saw that her son was dead, she proceeded to destroy the whole royal family of the house of Judah. [11]But Jehosheba,[d] the daughter of King Jehoram, took Joash son of Ahaziah and stole him away from among the royal princes who were about to be murdered and put him and his nurse in a bedroom. Because Jehosheba,[d] the daughter of King Jehoram and wife of the priest Jehoiada, was Ahaziah's sister, she hid the child from Athaliah so she could not kill him. [12]He remained hidden with them at the temple of God for six years while Athaliah ruled the land.

**23** In the seventh year Jehoiada showed his strength. He made a covenant with the commanders of units of a hundred: Azariah son of Jeroham, Ishmael son of Jehohanan, Azariah son of Obed, Maaseiah son of Adaiah, and Elishaphat son of Zikri. [2]They went throughout Judah and gathered the Levites and the heads of Israelite families from all the towns. When they came to Jerusalem, [3]the whole assembly made a covenant with the king at the temple of God.

Jehoiada said to them, "The king's son shall reign, as the LORD promised concerning the descendants of David. [4]Now this is what you are to do: A third of you priests and Levites who are going on duty on the Sabbath are to keep watch at the doors, [5]a third of you at the royal palace and a third at the Foundation Gate, and all the others are to be in the courtyards of the temple of the LORD. [6]No one is to enter the temple of the LORD except the priests and Levites on duty; they may enter because they are consecrated, but all the others are to observe the LORD's command not to enter.[e] [7]The Levites are to station themselves around the king, each with weapon in hand. Anyone who enters the

## Amplified Bible

[4]So he did evil in the sight of the Lord like the house of Ahab, for they were his counselors after his father's death, to his destruction.

[5]He followed their counsel and even went with [a]Joram son of Ahab king of Israel to war against Hazael king of Syria at Ramoth-gilead. And the Syrians wounded Joram; [II Kings 8:28ff.]

[6]And he returned to be healed in Jezreel of the wounds given him at Ramah when he fought against Hazael king of Syria. Azariah son of Jehoram king of Judah went down to see Joram son of Ahab because he was sick.

[7]But the destruction of Ahaziah was ordained of God in his coming to visit Joram. For when he got there he went out with Joram against Jehu son of Nimshi, whom the Lord had anointed to destroy the house of Ahab.

[8]And when Jehu was executing judgment upon the house of Ahab, he met the princes of Judah and the sons of Ahaziah's slain brothers, who attended Ahaziah, and he slew them.

[9]And [Jehu] sought Ahaziah, who was hiding in Samaria; he was captured, brought to Jehu, and slain. They buried him, for they said, After all, he is the grandson of Jehoshaphat, who sought the Lord with all his heart. So the house of Ahaziah had no one left able to rule the kingdom.

[10]But when Athaliah mother of Ahaziah saw that her son was dead, she arose and destroyed all the royal family of Judah.

[11]But Jehosheba, the daughter of the king, took Joash [infant] son of Ahaziah and stole him away from among the king's sons who were to be slain, and she put him and his nurse in a bedchamber. So Jehosheba daughter of King Jehoram, sister of Ahaziah, and wife of Jehoiada the priest, hid [Joash] from [his grandmother] Athaliah, so that she did not slay him.

[12]And Joash was with them hidden in the house of God six years, and Athaliah reigned over the land.

**23** In the seventh year Jehoiada [the priest] took strength *and* courage and made a covenant with the captains of hundreds: Azariah son of Jeroham, Ishmael son of Jehohanan, Azariah son of Obed, Maaseiah son of Adaiah, and Elishaphat son of Zichri.

[2]And they went about in Judah and gathered the Levites out of all the cities, and the chiefs of the fathers' houses of Israel, and they came to Jerusalem.

[3]And all the assembly made a covenant in the house of God with the king [little Joash, to suddenly proclaim his sovereignty and overthrow Athaliah's tyranny]. And Jehoiada the priest said to them, Behold, the king's son shall reign, as the Lord has said of the offspring of David.

[4]This is what you shall do: a third of you priests and Levites who are resuming service on the Sabbath shall be doorkeepers,

[5]A [second] third shall be at the king's house, and [the final] third at the Foundation Gate; and all the people shall be in the courts [only] of the house of the Lord.

[6]But let none come into the [main] house of the Lord except the priests and those of the Levites who minister; they may go in, for they are holy, but let all the rest of the people carefully observe the law against entering the holy place of the Lord.

[7]And the Levites shall surround the young king, every man with his weapons in his hand; and whoever comes into the house [breaking through the ranks of the guard

## New International Version

temple is to be put to death. Stay close to the king wherever he goes."

[8]The Levites and all the men of Judah did just as Jehoiada the priest ordered. Each one took his men—those who were going on duty on the Sabbath and those who were going off duty—for Jehoiada the priest had not released any of the divisions. [9]Then he gave the commanders of units of a hundred the spears and the large and small shields that had belonged to King David and that were in the temple of God. [10]He stationed all the men, each with his weapon in his hand, around the king—near the altar and the temple, from the south side to the north side of the temple.

[11]Jehoiada and his sons brought out the king's son and put the crown on him; they presented him with a copy of the covenant and proclaimed him king. They anointed him and shouted, "Long live the king!"

[12]When Athaliah heard the noise of the people running and cheering the king, she went to them at the temple of the LORD. [13]She looked, and there was the king, standing by his pillar at the entrance. The officers and the trumpeters were beside the king, and all the people of the land were rejoicing and blowing trumpets, and musicians with their instruments were leading the praises. Then Athaliah tore her robes and shouted, "Treason! Treason!"

[14]Jehoiada the priest sent out the commanders of units of a hundred, who were in charge of the troops, and said to them: "Bring her out between the ranks[a] and put to the sword anyone who follows her." For the priest had said, "Do not put her to death at the temple of the LORD." [15]So they seized her as she reached the entrance of the Horse Gate on the palace grounds, and there they put her to death.

[16]Jehoiada then made a covenant that he, the people and the king[b] would be the LORD's people. [17]All the people went to the temple of Baal and tore it down. They smashed the altars and idols and killed Mattan the priest of Baal in front of the altars.

[18]Then Jehoiada placed the oversight of the temple of the LORD in the hands of the Levitical priests, to whom David had made assignments in the temple, to present the burnt offerings of the LORD as written in the Law of Moses, with rejoicing and singing, as David had ordered. [19]He also stationed gatekeepers at the gates of the LORD's temple so that no one who was in any way unclean might enter.

[20]He took with him the commanders of hundreds, the nobles, the rulers of the people and all the people of the land and brought the king down from the temple of the LORD. They went into the palace through the Upper Gate and seated the king on the royal throne. [21]All the people of the land rejoiced, and the city was calm, because Athaliah had been slain with the sword.

### Joash Repairs the Temple

**24** Joash was seven years old when he became king, and he reigned in Jerusalem forty years. His mother's name was Zibiah; she was from Beersheba. [2]Joash did what was right in the eyes of the LORD all the years of Jehoiada the priest. [3]Jehoiada chose two wives for him, and he had sons and daughters.

## Amplified Bible

to get near Joash] shall be put to death. But you be with the king when he comes in [from the temple chamber where he is hiding] and when he goes out.

[8]So the Levites and all Judah did according to all that Jehoiada the priest had commanded; and took every man his men who were to resume duty on the Sabbath, with those who were to go out on the Sabbath, for Jehoiada the priest did not dismiss the divisions [of priests and Levites].

[9]Also Jehoiada the priest gave the captains of hundreds spears, bucklers, and shields that had been King David's, which were in the house of God.

[10]And he set all the people as a guard for the king, every man having his weapon (missile) in his hand, from the right side to the left side of the temple, around the altar and the temple.

[11]Then they brought out the king's son and put the crown on him and gave him the testimony *or* law and made him king. And Jehoiada and his sons anointed him and said, Long live the king!

[12]When Athaliah heard the noise of the people running and praising the king, she went into the Lord's house to the people.

[13]And behold, there the king stood by his pillar at the entrance, the captains and the trumpeters beside him; and all the people of the land rejoicing and blowing trumpets, and the singers with musical instruments led in singing of praise. Athaliah rent her clothes and cried, Treason! Treason!

[14]Then Jehoiada the priest commanded the captains of hundreds who were over the army, Bring her out between the ranks, and whoever follows her, let him be slain with the sword. For the priest said, Do not slay her in the Lord's house.

[15]So they made way for Athaliah, and she went into the entrance of the Horse Gate of the king's house; there they slew her.

[16]Then Jehoiada made a covenant between himself, all the people, and the king, that they should be the Lord's people.

[17]Then all the people went to the house of Baal, tore it down, and broke its altars and its images in pieces, and slew Mattan the priest of Baal before the altars.

[18]Also Jehoiada appointed the offices *and* officers [for the care] of the house of the Lord under the direction of the Levitical priests, whom David had distributed [in his day] in the house of the Lord, to offer the burnt offerings of the Lord as written in the Law of Moses, with rejoicing and singing, as ordered by David.

[19]Jehoiada set the gatekeepers at the gates of the house of the Lord so that no one should enter who was in any way unclean.

[20]And he took the captains of hundreds and the nobles and governors of the people and all the people of the land and brought down the king from the house of the Lord; and they came through the Upper Gate to the king's house and set the king upon the throne of the kingdom.

[21]So all the people of the land rejoiced, and the city was quiet after Athaliah had been slain with the sword.

**24** Joash was seven years old when he began his forty-year reign in Jerusalem. His mother was Zibiah of Beersheba.

[2]And Joash did what was right in the sight of the Lord all the days of Jehoiada the priest [his uncle].

[3]And Jehoiada took for him two wives, and he had sons and daughters.

---

[a] 14 Or *out from the precincts*    [b] 16 Or *covenant between the LORD and the people and the king that they* (see 2 Kings 11:17)

## New International Version

⁴Some time later Joash decided to restore the temple of the LORD. ⁵He called together the priests and Levites and said to them, "Go to the towns of Judah and collect the money due annually from all Israel, to repair the temple of your God. Do it now." But the Levites did not act at once.
⁶Therefore the king summoned Jehoiada the chief priest and said to him, "Why haven't you required the Levites to bring in from Judah and Jerusalem the tax imposed by Moses the servant of the LORD and by the assembly of Israel for the tent of the covenant law?"
⁷Now the sons of that wicked woman Athaliah had broken into the temple of God and had used even its sacred objects for the Baals.
⁸At the king's command, a chest was made and placed outside, at the gate of the temple of the LORD. ⁹A proclamation was then issued in Judah and Jerusalem that they should bring to the LORD the tax that Moses the servant of God had required of Israel in the wilderness. ¹⁰All the officials and all the people brought their contributions gladly, dropping them into the chest until it was full. ¹¹Whenever the chest was brought in by the Levites to the king's officials and they saw that there was a large amount of money, the royal secretary and the officer of the chief priest would come and empty the chest and carry it back to its place. They did this regularly and collected a great amount of money. ¹²The king and Jehoiada gave it to those who carried out the work required for the temple of the LORD. They hired masons and carpenters to restore the LORD's temple, and also workers in iron and bronze to repair the temple.
¹³The men in charge of the work were diligent, and the repairs progressed under them. They rebuilt the temple of God according to its original design and reinforced it. ¹⁴When they had finished, they brought the rest of the money to the king and Jehoiada, and with it were made articles for the LORD's temple: articles for the service and for the burnt offerings, and also dishes and other objects of gold and silver. As long as Jehoiada lived, burnt offerings were presented continually in the temple of the LORD.
¹⁵Now Jehoiada was old and full of years, and he died at the age of a hundred and thirty. ¹⁶He was buried with the kings in the City of David, because of the good he had done in Israel for God and his temple.

### The Wickedness of Joash
¹⁷After the death of Jehoiada, the officials of Judah came and paid homage to the king, and he listened to them. ¹⁸They abandoned the temple of the LORD, the God of their ancestors, and worshiped Asherah poles and idols. Because of their guilt, God's anger came on Judah and Jerusalem. ¹⁹Although the LORD sent prophets to the people to bring them back to him, and though they testified against them, they would not listen.
²⁰Then the Spirit of God came on Zechariah son of Jehoiada the priest. He stood before the people and said, "This is what God says: 'Why do you disobey the LORD's commands? You will not prosper. Because you have forsaken the LORD, he has forsaken you.'"
²¹But they plotted against him, and by order of the king they stoned him to death in the courtyard of the LORD's

## Amplified Bible

⁴After this, Joash decided to repair the Lord's house.
⁵He gathered the priests and the Levites and said to them, Go out to the cities of Judah, and gather from all Israel money to repair the house of your God from year to year; and see that you hasten the matter. But the Levites did not hasten it.
⁶So the king called for Jehoiada the high priest and said to him, Why have you not required the Levites to bring in from Judah and Jerusalem the tax authorized by Moses the servant of the Lord and of the assembly of Israel for the Tent of the Testimony?
⁷For the sons of Athaliah, that wicked woman, had broken into the house of God and also had used for the Baals all the dedicated things of the house of the Lord.
⁸And at the king's command they made a chest and set it outside the gate of the house of the Lord.
⁹And they made a proclamation through Judah and Jerusalem to bring in for the Lord the tax that Moses the servant of God laid upon Israel in the wilderness.
¹⁰And all the princes and people rejoiced and brought their tax and dropped it into the chest until they had finished.
¹¹When the Levites brought the chest to the king's office, and whenever they saw that there was much money, the king's secretary and the high priest's officer came and emptied the chest and carried it to its place again. Thus they did day by day and collected money in abundance.
¹²And the king and Jehoiada gave it to those who did the work of the temple service; and they hired masons and carpenters and also those who worked in iron and bronze to repair the house of the Lord.
¹³So the workmen labored, and the work of repairing went forward in their hands; and they set up the house of God according to its design and strengthened it.
¹⁴When they had finished it, they brought the rest of the money before the king and Jehoiada; from it were made utensils for the Lord's house, vessels for ministering and for offerings, and cups and vessels of gold and silver. And they offered burnt offerings in the house of the Lord continually all the days of Jehoiada.
¹⁵But Jehoiada became old and full of [the handicaps of great] age, and he died. He was 130 years old at his death.
¹⁶They buried him in the City of David among the kings, because he had done good in Israel and toward God and His house.
¹⁷Now after the death of Jehoiada [the priest, who had hidden Joash], the princes of Judah came and made obeisance to King Joash; then the king hearkened to them.
¹⁸They forsook the house of the Lord, the God of their fathers, and served the Asherim and idols; and wrath came upon Judah and Jerusalem for their sin (guilt).
¹⁹Yet [God] sent prophets to them to bring them again to the Lord; these testified against them, but they would not listen.
²⁰Then the Spirit of God came upon Zechariah son of Jehoiada the priest, who stood over the people, and he said to them, Thus says God: Why do you transgress the commandments of the Lord so that you cannot prosper? Because you have forsaken the Lord, He also has forsaken you.
²¹They conspired against Zechariah the priest and stoned him at the command of the king in the court of the Lord's house!

## New International Version

temple. <sup>22</sup>King Joash did not remember the kindness Zechariah's father Jehoiada had shown him but killed his son, who said as he lay dying, "May the LORD see this and call you to account."

<sup>23</sup>At the turn of the year,<sup>a</sup> the army of Aram marched against Joash; it invaded Judah and Jerusalem and killed all the leaders of the people. They sent all the plunder to their king in Damascus. <sup>24</sup>Although the Aramean army had come with only a few men, the LORD delivered into their hands a much larger army. Because Judah had forsaken the LORD, the God of their ancestors, judgment was executed on Joash. <sup>25</sup>When the Arameans withdrew, they left Joash severely wounded. His officials conspired against him for murdering the son of Jehoiada the priest, and they killed him in his bed. So he died and was buried in the City of David, but not in the tombs of the kings.

<sup>26</sup>Those who conspired against him were Zabad,<sup>b</sup> son of Shimeath an Ammonite woman, and Jehozabad, son of Shimrith<sup>c</sup> a Moabite woman. <sup>27</sup>The account of his sons, the many prophecies about him, and the record of the restoration of the temple of God are written in the annotations on the book of the kings. And Amaziah his son succeeded him as king.

### Amaziah King of Judah

**25** Amaziah was twenty-five years old when he became king, and he reigned in Jerusalem twenty-nine years. His mother's name was Jehoaddin; she was from Jerusalem. <sup>2</sup>He did what was right in the eyes of the LORD, but not wholeheartedly. <sup>3</sup>After the kingdom was firmly in his control, he executed the officials who had murdered his father the king. <sup>4</sup>Yet he did not put their children to death, but acted in accordance with what is written in the Law, in the Book of Moses, where the LORD commanded: "Parents shall not be put to death for their children, nor children be put to death for their parents; each will die for their own sin."<sup>d</sup>

<sup>5</sup>Amaziah called the people of Judah together and assigned them according to their families to commanders of thousands and commanders of hundreds for all Judah and Benjamin. He then mustered those twenty years old or more and found that there were three hundred thousand men fit for military service, able to handle the spear and shield. <sup>6</sup>He also hired a hundred thousand fighting men from Israel for a hundred talents<sup>e</sup> of silver.

<sup>7</sup>But a man of God came to him and said, "Your Majesty, these troops from Israel must not march with you, for the LORD is not with Israel—not with any of the people of Ephraim. <sup>8</sup>Even if you go and fight courageously in battle, God will overthrow you before the enemy, for God has the power to help or to overthrow."

<sup>9</sup>Amaziah asked the man of God, "But what about the hundred talents I paid for these Israelite troops?"

The man of God replied, "The LORD can give you much more than that."

<sup>10</sup>So Amaziah dismissed the troops who had come to him from Ephraim and sent them home. They were furious with Judah and left for home in a great rage.

<sup>11</sup>Amaziah then marshaled his strength and led his army to the Valley of Salt, where he killed ten thousand

## Amplified Bible

<sup>22</sup>Thus Joash the king did not remember the kindness which Jehoiada, Zechariah's father, had done him, but slew his son. And when [Zechariah the priest] was dying, he said, May the Lord see and avenge!

<sup>23</sup>At the end of the year, the army of Syria came up against Joash. They came to Judah and Jerusalem and destroyed all the princes from among the people and sent all their spoil to the king of Damascus.

<sup>24</sup>Though the army of the Syrians came with a small company of men, the Lord delivered a very great host into their hands, because Joash and Judah had forsaken the Lord, the God of their fathers. So the Syrians executed judgment against Joash.

<sup>25</sup>And when they had departed from Joash, leaving him very ill, his own servants conspired against him for the blood of the sons of Jehoiada the priest, and they slew him on his bed. So he died and they buried him in the City of David, but not in the tombs of the kings.

<sup>26</sup>The conspirators against Joash were Zabad son of Shimeath the Ammonitess, and Jehozabad son of Shimrith the Moabitess.

<sup>27</sup>Now concerning his sons and the greatness of the prophecies uttered against him and the rebuilding of the house of God, they are written in the commentary on the Book of Kings. And Amaziah his [Joash's] son reigned in his stead.

**25** Amaziah was twenty-five years old when he began to reign, and he reigned twenty-nine years in Jerusalem. His mother was Jehoaddan of Jerusalem.

<sup>2</sup>He did right in the Lord's sight, but not with a perfect or blameless heart.

<sup>3</sup>When his kingdom was firmly established, he slew his servants who had killed the king his father.

<sup>4</sup>But he did not slay their children; he did as it is written in the Law, in the Book of Moses, where the Lord commanded, The fathers shall not die for the children, or the children die for the fathers; but every man shall die for his own sin.

<sup>5</sup>Amaziah assembled the men of Judah and set them by fathers' houses under commanders of thousands and of hundreds for all Judah and Benjamin. He numbered them from twenty years old and over and found them to be 300,000 choice men fit for war and able to handle spear and shield.

<sup>6</sup>He hired also 100,000 mighty men of valor from Israel for 100 talents of silver.

<sup>7</sup>But a man of God came to him, saying, O king, do not let all this army of Ephraimites of Israel go with you [of Judah], for the Lord is not with you,

<sup>8</sup>For if you go [in spite of warning], no matter how strong you are for battle, God will cast you down before the enemy, for God has power to help and to cast down.

<sup>9</sup>And Amaziah said to the man of God, But what shall we do about the 100 talents which I have given to the army of Israel? The man of God answered, The Lord is able to give you much more than this.

<sup>10</sup>So Amaziah discharged the army that came to him from Ephraim to go home. So their anger was greatly kindled against Judah; they returned home in fierce wrath.

<sup>11</sup>And Amaziah took courage and led forth his people to the Valley of Salt and smote 10,000 of the men of Seir [Edom].

---

<sup>a</sup> 23 Probably in the spring   <sup>b</sup> 26 A variant of *Jozabad*   <sup>c</sup> 26 A variant of *Shomer*   <sup>d</sup> 4 Deut. 24:16   <sup>e</sup> 6 That is, about 3 3/4 tons or about 3.4 metric tons; also in verse 9

## New International Version

men of Seir. [12]The army of Judah also captured ten thousand men alive, took them to the top of a cliff and threw them down so that all were dashed to pieces.

[13]Meanwhile the troops that Amaziah had sent back and had not allowed to take part in the war raided towns belonging to Judah from Samaria to Beth Horon. They killed three thousand people and carried off great quantities of plunder.

[14]When Amaziah returned from slaughtering the Edomites, he brought back the gods of the people of Seir. He set them up as his own gods, bowed down to them and burned sacrifices to them. [15]The anger of the LORD burned against Amaziah, and he sent a prophet to him, who said, "Why do you consult this people's gods, which could not save their own people from your hand?"

[16]While he was still speaking, the king said to him, "Have we appointed you an adviser to the king? Stop! Why be struck down?"

So the prophet stopped but said, "I know that God has determined to destroy you, because you have done this and have not listened to my counsel."

[17]After Amaziah king of Judah consulted his advisers, he sent this challenge to Jehoash[a] son of Jehoahaz, the son of Jehu, king of Israel: "Come, let us face each other in battle."

[18]But Jehoash king of Israel replied to Amaziah king of Judah: "A thistle in Lebanon sent a message to a cedar in Lebanon, 'Give your daughter to my son in marriage.' Then a wild beast in Lebanon came along and trampled the thistle underfoot. [19]You say to yourself that you have defeated Edom, and now you are arrogant and proud. But stay at home! Why ask for trouble and cause your own downfall and that of Judah also?"

[20]Amaziah, however, would not listen, for God so worked that he might deliver them into the hands of Jehoash, because they sought the gods of Edom. [21]So Jehoash king of Israel attacked. He and Amaziah king of Judah faced each other at Beth Shemesh in Judah. [22]Judah was routed by Israel, and every man fled to his home. [23]Jehoash king of Israel captured Amaziah king of Judah, the son of Joash, the son of Ahaziah,[b] at Beth Shemesh. Then Jehoash brought him to Jerusalem and broke down the wall of Jerusalem from the Ephraim Gate to the Corner Gate—a section about four hundred cubits[c] long. [24]He took all the gold and silver and all the articles found in the temple of God that had been in the care of Obed-Edom, together with the palace treasures and the hostages, and returned to Samaria.

[25]Amaziah son of Joash king of Judah lived for fifteen years after the death of Jehoash son of Jehoahaz king of Israel. [26]As for the other events of Amaziah's reign, from beginning to end, are they not written in the book of the kings of Judah and Israel? [27]From the time that Amaziah turned away from following the LORD, they conspired against him in Jerusalem and he fled to Lachish, but they sent men after him to Lachish and killed him there. [28]He was brought back by horse and was buried with his ancestors in the City of Judah.[d]

## Amplified Bible

[12]Another 10,000 the men of Judah captured alive and brought them to the top of a crag and cast them down from it, and they were all dashed to pieces.

[13]But the soldiers of the band which Amaziah sent back, not allowing them to go with him to battle, fell upon the cities of Judah, from Samaria even to Beth-horon, and smote 3,000 [men] and took much spoil.

[14]After Amaziah came back from the slaughter of the Edomites, he brought their gods and set them up to be his gods and bowed before them and burned incense to them.

[15]So the anger of the Lord was kindled against Amaziah, and He sent to him a prophet, who said, Why have you sought after the gods of the people, which could not deliver their own people out of your hand?

[16]As he was talking, the king said to him, Have we made you the king's counselor? Stop it! Why should you be put to death? The prophet stopped but said, I know that God has determined to destroy you, because you have done this and ignored my counsel.

[17]Then Amaziah king of Judah took counsel and sent to [a]Jehoash son of Jehoahaz, the son of Jehu, king of Israel, saying, Come [to battle], let us look one another in the face. [II Kings 14:8-20.]

[18]Jehoash king of Israel sent to Amaziah king of Judah, saying, A little thistle in Lebanon sent to a great cedar in Lebanon, saying, Give your daughter to my son as wife. And a wild beast of Lebanon passed by and trampled down the thistle.

[19]You say, See, [I] have smitten Edom! Your heart lifts you up to boast. Stay at home; why should you meddle [and court disaster], so you will fall and Judah with you?

[20]But Amaziah would not hear, for it came from God, that He might deliver Judah into the hands of their enemies, because they sought after the gods of Edom.

[21]So Jehoash king of Israel went up; and he and Amaziah king of Judah faced one another at Beth-shemesh of Judah.

[22]And Judah was defeated before Israel, and they fled every man to his tent.

[23]And Jehoash king of Israel took Amaziah king of Judah, the son of Joash, the son of Jehoahaz, at Beth-shemesh and brought him to Jerusalem and broke down the wall of Jerusalem from the Ephraim Gate to the Corner Gate, 400 cubits.

[24]And he took all the gold, the silver, and all the vessels found in God's house with [the doorkeeper] Obed-edom, and the treasures of the king's house and hostages also, and returned to Samaria.

[25]And Amaziah son of Joash king of Judah lived after the death of Jehoash son of Jehoahaz king of Israel fifteen years.

[26]The rest of the acts of Amaziah, from first to last, are they not written in the Book of the Kings of Judah and Israel?

[27]Now after Amaziah turned away from the Lord, they made a conspiracy against him in Jerusalem, and he fled to Lachish. But they sent to Lachish and slew him there.

[28]And they brought him upon horses and buried him with his fathers in the City of [David in] Judah.

---

[a] 17 Hebrew *Joash,* a variant of *Jehoash*; also in verses 18, 21, 23 and 25   [b] 23 Hebrew *Jehoahaz,* a variant of *Ahaziah*   [c] 23 That is, about 600 feet or about 180 meters   [d] 28 Most Hebrew manuscripts; some Hebrew manuscripts, Septuagint, Vulgate and Syriac (see also 2 Kings 14:20) *David*

[a] Hebrew *Joash,* a variant of *Jehoash*.

## New International Version

### Uzziah King of Judah

**26** Then all the people of Judah took Uzziah,[a] who was sixteen years old, and made him king in place of his father Amaziah. [2] He was the one who rebuilt Elath and restored it to Judah after Amaziah rested with his ancestors.

[3] Uzziah was sixteen years old when he became king, and he reigned in Jerusalem fifty-two years. His mother's name was Jekoliah; she was from Jerusalem. [4] He did what was right in the eyes of the LORD, just as his father Amaziah had done. [5] He sought God during the days of Zechariah, who instructed him in the fear[b] of God. As long as he sought the LORD, God gave him success.

[6] He went to war against the Philistines and broke down the walls of Gath, Jabneh and Ashdod. He then rebuilt towns near Ashdod and elsewhere among the Philistines. [7] God helped him against the Philistines and against the Arabs who lived in Gur Baal and against the Meunites. [8] The Ammonites brought tribute to Uzziah, and his fame spread as far as the border of Egypt, because he had become very powerful.

[9] Uzziah built towers in Jerusalem at the Corner Gate, at the Valley Gate and at the angle of the wall, and he fortified them. [10] He also built towers in the wilderness and dug many cisterns, because he had much livestock in the foothills and in the plain. He had people working his fields and vineyards in the hills and in the fertile lands, for he loved the soil.

[11] Uzziah had a well-trained army, ready to go out by divisions according to their numbers as mustered by Jeiel the secretary and Maaseiah the officer under the direction of Hananiah, one of the royal officials. [12] The total number of family leaders over the fighting men was 2,600. [13] Under their command was an army of 307,500 men trained for war, a powerful force to support the king against his enemies. [14] Uzziah provided shields, spears, helmets, coats of armor, bows and slingstones for the entire army. [15] In Jerusalem he made devices invented for use on the towers and on the corner defenses so that soldiers could shoot arrows and hurl large stones from the walls. His fame spread far and wide, for he was greatly helped until he became powerful.

[16] But after Uzziah became powerful, his pride led to his downfall. He was unfaithful to the LORD his God, and entered the temple of the LORD to burn incense on the altar of incense. [17] Azariah the priest with eighty other courageous priests of the LORD followed him in. [18] They confronted King Uzziah and said, "It is not right for you, Uzziah, to burn incense to the LORD. That is for the priests, the descendants of Aaron, who have been consecrated to burn incense. Leave the sanctuary, for you have been unfaithful; and you will not be honored by the LORD God."

[19] Uzziah, who had a censer in his hand ready to burn incense, became angry. While he was raging at the priests in their presence before the incense altar in the LORD's temple, leprosy[c] broke out on his forehead. [20] When Azariah the chief priest and all the other priests looked at him, they saw that he had leprosy on his forehead, so they hurried him out. Indeed, he himself was eager to leave, because the LORD had afflicted him.

## Amplified Bible

**26** Then all the people of Judah took Uzziah, who was sixteen years old, and made him king in place of his father Amaziah. [2] He built Eloth and restored it to Judah after Amaziah slept with his fathers.

[3] Uzziah was sixteen years old when he began his fifty-two-year reign in Jerusalem. His mother was Jecoliah of Jerusalem. [4] He did right in the Lord's sight, to the extent of all that his father Amaziah had done.

[5] He set himself to seek God in the days of Zechariah, who instructed him in the things of God; and as long as he sought (inquired of, yearned for) the Lord, God made him prosper.

[6] He went out against the Philistines and broke down the walls of Gath, of Jabneh, and of Ashdod, and built cities near Ashdod and elsewhere among the Philistines. [7] And God helped him against the Philistines, and the Arabs who dwelt in Gur-baal and the Meunim. [8] The Ammonites paid tribute to Uzziah, and his fame spread abroad even to the border of Egypt, for he became very strong.

[9] Also Uzziah built towers in Jerusalem at the Corner Gate, the Valley Gate, and at the angle of the wall, and fortified them. [10] Also he built towers in the wilderness and hewed out many cisterns, for he had much livestock, both in the lowlands and in the tableland. And he had farmers and vinedressers in the hills and in the fertile fields [of Carmel], for he loved farming.

[11] And Uzziah had a combat army for waging war by regiments according to the number as recorded by Jeiel the secretary and Maaseiah the officer under the direction of Hananiah, one of the king's commanders. [12] The whole number of the heads of fathers' houses of mighty men of valor was 2,600. [13] Under their command was an army of 307,500 who could fight with mighty power to help the king against the enemy. [14] Uzziah prepared for all the army shields, spears, helmets, coats of mail, bows, and stones to sling. [15] In Jerusalem he made machines invented by skillful men to be on the towers and the [corner] bulwarks, with which to shoot arrows and great stones. And his fame spread far, for he was marvelously helped till he was strong.

[16] But when [King Uzziah] was strong, he became proud to his destruction; and he trespassed against the Lord his God, for he went [a]into the temple of the Lord to burn incense on the altar of incense.

[17] And Azariah the priest went in after him and with him eighty priests of the Lord, men of courage. [18] They opposed King Uzziah and said to him, It is not for you, Uzziah, to burn incense to the Lord, but for the priests, the sons of Aaron, who are set apart to burn incense. Withdraw from the sanctuary; you have trespassed, and that will not be to your credit *and* honor before the Lord God.

[19] Then Uzziah was enraged, and he had a censer in his hand to burn incense. And while he was enraged with the priests, leprosy broke out on his forehead before the priests in the house of the Lord, beside the incense altar. [20] And as Azariah the chief priest and all the priests looked upon him, behold, he was leprous on his forehead! So they forced him out of there; and he also made haste to get out, because the Lord had smitten him.

---

[a] 1 Also called *Azariah*   [b] 5 Many Hebrew manuscripts, Septuagint and Syriac; other Hebrew manuscripts *vision*   [c] 19 The Hebrew for *leprosy* was used for various diseases affecting the skin; also in verses 20, 21 and 23.

[a] No one but an ordained priest was permitted by law to enter the tabernacle or later the temple proper, even in Jesus' time. See footnote on Num. 3:38.

## New International Version

[21] King Uzziah had leprosy until the day he died. He lived in a separate house[a]—leprous, and banned from the temple of the LORD. Jotham his son had charge of the palace and governed the people of the land.

[22] The other events of Uzziah's reign, from beginning to end, are recorded by the prophet Isaiah son of Amoz. [23] Uzziah rested with his ancestors and was buried near them in a cemetery that belonged to the kings, for people said, "He had leprosy." And Jotham his son succeeded him as king.

### Jotham King of Judah

**27** Jotham was twenty-five years old when he became king, and he reigned in Jerusalem sixteen years. His mother's name was Jerusha daughter of Zadok. [2] He did what was right in the eyes of the LORD, just as his father Uzziah had done, but unlike him he did not enter the temple of the LORD. The people, however, continued their corrupt practices. [3] Jotham rebuilt the Upper Gate of the temple of the LORD and did extensive work on the wall at the hill of Ophel. [4] He built towns in the hill country of Judah and forts and towers in the wooded areas.

[5] Jotham waged war against the king of the Ammonites and conquered them. That year the Ammonites paid him a hundred talents[b] of silver, ten thousand cors[c] of wheat and ten thousand cors[d] of barley. The Ammonites brought him the same amount also in the second and third years.

[6] Jotham grew powerful because he walked steadfastly before the LORD his God.

[7] The other events in Jotham's reign, including all his wars and the other things he did, are written in the book of the kings of Israel and Judah. [8] He was twenty-five years old when he became king, and he reigned in Jerusalem sixteen years. [9] Jotham rested with his ancestors and was buried in the City of David. And Ahaz his son succeeded him as king.

### Ahaz King of Judah

**28** Ahaz was twenty years old when he became king, and he reigned in Jerusalem sixteen years. Unlike David his father, he did not do what was right in the eyes of the LORD. [2] He followed the ways of the kings of Israel and also made idols for worshiping the Baals. [3] He burned sacrifices in the Valley of Ben Hinnom and sacrificed his children in the fire, engaging in the detestable practices of the nations the LORD had driven out before the Israelites. [4] He offered sacrifices and burned incense at the high places, on the hilltops and under every spreading tree.

[5] Therefore the LORD his God delivered him into the hands of the king of Aram. The Arameans defeated him and took many of his people as prisoners and brought them to Damascus.

He was also given into the hands of the king of Israel, who inflicted heavy casualties on him. [6] In one day Pekah son of Remaliah killed a hundred and twenty thousand soldiers in Judah—because Judah had forsaken the LORD, the God of their ancestors. [7] Zikri, an Ephraimite warrior, killed Maaseiah the king's son, Azrikam the officer in charge of the palace, and Elkanah, second to the king. [8] The men of Israel took captive from their fellow Israelites who were from Judah two hundred thousand wives, sons and daughters. They also took a great deal of plunder, which they carried back to Samaria.

## Amplified Bible

[21] And King Uzziah was a leper to the day of his death, and, being a leper, he dwelt in a separate house, for he was excluded from the Lord's house. And Jotham his son took charge of the king's household, ruling the people of the land.

[22] Now the rest of the acts of Uzziah, from first to last, Isaiah the prophet, the son of Amoz, wrote. [Isa. 1:1.]

[23] So Uzziah slept with his fathers, and they buried him in the burial field of the kings [outside the royal tombs], for they said, He is a leper. Jotham his son reigned in his stead.

**27** Jotham was twenty-five years old when he began to reign, and he reigned sixteen years in Jerusalem. His mother was Jerushah daughter of Zadok. [2] He did right in the sight of the Lord, to the extent of all that his father Uzziah had done. However, he did not invade the temple of the Lord. But the people still did corruptly.

[3] He built the Upper Gate of the Lord's house and did much building on the wall of Ophel.

[4] Moreover, he built cities in the hill country of Judah, and in the forests he built forts and towers.

[5] He fought with the king of the Ammonites and prevailed against them. The Ammonites gave him that year 100 talents of silver and 10,000 measures each of wheat and of barley. That much the Ammonites paid to him also the second year and third year.

[6] So Jotham grew mighty, for he ordered his ways in the sight of the Lord his God.

[7] Now the rest of Jotham's acts, and all his wars and his ways, behold, they are written in the Book of the Kings of Israel and Judah.

[8] He was twenty-five years old when he began to reign, and he reigned sixteen years in Jerusalem.

[9] And Jotham slept with his fathers, and they buried him in the City of David. Ahaz his son reigned in his stead.

**28** Ahaz was twenty years old when he began his sixteen-year reign in Jerusalem. He did not do right in the sight of the Lord, like David his father [forefather].

[2] But he walked in the ways of the kings of Israel and even made molten images for the Baals.

[3] And he burned incense in the Valley of Ben-hinnom [son of Hinnom] and burned his sons as an offering, after the abominable customs of the [heathen] nations whom the Lord drove out before the Israelites.

[4] He sacrificed also and burnt incense in the high places, on the hills, and under every green tree.

[5] Therefore the Lord his God gave Ahaz into the power of the king of Syria, who defeated him and carried away a great multitude of the Jews as captives, taking them to Damascus. And he was also delivered into the hands of the king of Israel, who smote Judah with a great slaughter.

[6] For Pekah son of Remaliah slew in Judah 120,000 in one day, all courageous men, because they had forsaken the Lord, the God of their fathers.

[7] And Zichri, a mighty man of Ephraim, slew Maaseiah, King Ahaz' son, and Azrikam the governor of the house, and Elkanah, who was second to the king.

[8] And the Israelites carried away captive 200,000 of their kinsmen [of Judah]—women, sons, and daughters— and also took much plunder from them and brought it to Samaria.

---

[a] 21 Or *in a house where he was relieved of responsibilities*   [b] 5 That is, about 3 3/4 tons or about 3.4 metric tons   [c] 5 That is, probably about 1,800 tons or about 1,600 metric tons of wheat   [d] 5 That is, probably about 1,500 tons or about 1,350 metric tons of barley

## New International Version

⁹But a prophet of the LORD named Oded was there, and he went out to meet the army when it returned to Samaria. He said to them, "Because the LORD, the God of your ancestors, was angry with Judah, he gave them into your hand. But you have slaughtered them in a rage that reaches to heaven. ¹⁰And now you intend to make the men and women of Judah and Jerusalem your slaves. But aren't you also guilty of sins against the LORD your God? ¹¹Now listen to me! Send back your fellow Israelites you have taken as prisoners, for the LORD's fierce anger rests on you."

¹²Then some of the leaders in Ephraim—Azariah son of Jehohanan, Berekiah son of Meshillemoth, Jehizkiah son of Shallum, and Amasa son of Hadlai—confronted those who were arriving from the war. ¹³"You must not bring those prisoners here," they said, "or we will be guilty before the LORD. Do you intend to add to our sin and guilt? For our guilt is already great, and his fierce anger rests on Israel."

¹⁴So the soldiers gave up the prisoners and plunder in the presence of the officials and all the assembly. ¹⁵The men designated by name took the prisoners, and from the plunder they clothed all who were naked. They provided them with clothes and sandals, food and drink, and healing balm. All those who were weak they put on donkeys. So they took them back to their fellow Israelites at Jericho, the City of Palms, and returned to Samaria.

¹⁶At that time King Ahaz sent to the kings[a] of Assyria for help. ¹⁷The Edomites had again come and attacked Judah and carried away prisoners, ¹⁸while the Philistines had raided towns in the foothills and in the Negev of Judah. They captured and occupied Beth Shemesh, Aijalon and Gederoth, as well as Soko, Timnah and Gimzo, with their surrounding villages. ¹⁹The LORD had humbled Judah because of Ahaz king of Israel,[b] for he had promoted wickedness in Judah and had been most unfaithful to the LORD. ²⁰Tiglath-Pileser[c] king of Assyria came to him, but he gave him trouble instead of help. ²¹Ahaz took some of the things from the temple of the LORD and from the royal palace and from the officials and presented them to the king of Assyria, but that did not help him.

²²In his time of trouble King Ahaz became even more unfaithful to the LORD. ²³He offered sacrifices to the gods of Damascus, who had defeated him; for he thought, "Since the gods of the kings of Aram have helped them, I will sacrifice to them so they will help me." But they were his downfall and the downfall of all Israel.

²⁴Ahaz gathered together the furnishings from the temple of God and cut them in pieces. He shut the doors of the LORD's temple and set up altars at every street corner in Jerusalem. ²⁵In every town in Judah he built high places to burn sacrifices to other gods and aroused the anger of the LORD, the God of his ancestors.

²⁶The other events of his reign and all his ways, from beginning to end, are written in the book of the kings of Judah and Israel. ²⁷Ahaz rested with his ancestors and was buried in the city of Jerusalem, but he was not placed in the tombs of the kings of Israel. And Hezekiah his son succeeded him as king.

## Amplified Bible

⁹But a prophet of the Lord was there whose name was Oded, and he went out to meet the army that was returning to Samaria and said to them, Behold, because the Lord, the God of your fathers, was angry with Judah, He delivered them into your hand; but you have slain them in a fury that reaches up to heaven.

¹⁰And now you intend to suppress the people of Judah and Jerusalem, both men and women, as your slaves. But are not you yourselves guilty of crimes against the Lord your God?

¹¹Now hear me therefore, and set the prisoners free again whom you have taken captive of your kinsmen, for the fierce wrath of the Lord is upon you.

¹²Then certain of the heads of the Ephraimites [Israel]—Azariah son of Johanan, Berechiah son of Meshillemoth, Jehizkiah son of Shallum, and Amasa son of Hadlai—stood up against those returning from the war

¹³And said, You shall not bring the captives in here; we are guilty before the Lord already, and what you intend will add more to our sins and our guilt. For our trespass (guilt) is great, and there is fierce anger against Israel.

¹⁴So the armed men [of Israel] left the captives and the spoil [of Judah] before the princes and all the assembly.

¹⁵And the men who have been mentioned by name rose up and took the captives, and with the spoil they clothed all who were naked among them; and having clothed them, shod them, given them food and drink, anointed them [as was a host's duty], and carried all the feeble of them upon donkeys, they brought them to Jericho, the City of Palm Trees, to their brethren. Then they returned to Samaria. [Luke 10:25-37.]

¹⁶At that time King Ahaz sent to the king of Assyria to help him.

¹⁷For again the Edomites had come and smitten Judah and carried away captives.

¹⁸The Philistines had invaded the cities of the low country and of the South (the Negeb) of Judah, and had taken Beth-shemesh, Aijalon, Gederoth, and Soco, and also Timnah and Gimzo, with their villages, and they settled there.

¹⁹For the Lord brought Judah low because of Ahaz king of Israel, for Ahaz had dealt with reckless cruelty against Judah and had been faithless [had transgressed sorely] against the Lord.

²⁰So Tilgath-pilneser king of Assyria came to him and distressed him without strengthening him.

²¹For Ahaz took [treasure] from the house of the Lord and out of the house of the king and from the princes and gave it as tribute to the king of Assyria, but it did not help Ahaz.

²²In the time of his distress he became still more unfaithful to the Lord—this same King Ahaz.

²³For he sacrificed to the gods of Damascus, which had defeated him, for he said, Since the gods of the kings of Syria helped them, I will sacrifice to them that they may help me. But they were the ruin of him and of all Israel.

²⁴And Ahaz collected the utensils of the house of God and cut them in pieces; and he shut up the doors of the Lord's temple [the Holy Place and the Holy of Holies] and made himself altars in every corner of Jerusalem.

²⁵In each city of Judah he made high places to burn incense to other gods, provoking to anger the Lord, the God of his fathers.

²⁶Now the rest of his acts and of all his ways, from first to last, behold, they are written in the Book of the Kings of Judah and Israel.

²⁷And Ahaz slept with his fathers, and they buried him in the city, in Jerusalem, but they did not bring him into the tombs of the kings of Israel. And Hezekiah his son reigned in his stead.

---

ᵃ 16 Most Hebrew manuscripts; one Hebrew manuscript, Septuagint and Vulgate (see also 2 Kings 16:7) *king*    ᵇ 19 That is, Judah, as frequently in 2 Chronicles    ᶜ 20 Hebrew *Tilgath-Pilneser,* a variant of *Tiglath-Pileser*

## New International Version

### Hezekiah Purifies the Temple

**29** Hezekiah was twenty-five years old when he became king, and he reigned in Jerusalem twenty-nine years. His mother's name was Abijah daughter of Zechariah. [2] He did what was right in the eyes of the LORD, just as his father David had done.

[3] In the first month of the first year of his reign, he opened the doors of the temple of the LORD and repaired them. [4] He brought in the priests and the Levites, assembled them in the square on the east side [5] and said: "Listen to me, Levites! Consecrate yourselves now and consecrate the temple of the LORD, the God of your ancestors. Remove all defilement from the sanctuary. [6] Our parents were unfaithful; they did evil in the eyes of the LORD our God and forsook him. They turned their faces away from the LORD's dwelling place and turned their backs on him. [7] They also shut the doors of the portico and put out the lamps. They did not burn incense or present any burnt offerings at the sanctuary to the God of Israel. [8] Therefore, the anger of the LORD has fallen on Judah and Jerusalem; he has made them an object of dread and horror and scorn, as you can see with your own eyes. [9] This is why our fathers have fallen by the sword and why our sons and daughters and our wives are in captivity. [10] Now I intend to make a covenant with the LORD, the God of Israel, so that his fierce anger will turn away from us. [11] My sons, do not be negligent now, for the LORD has chosen you to stand before him and serve him, to minister before him and to burn incense."

[12] Then these Levites set to work:
from the Kohathites,
Mahath son of Amasai and Joel son of Azariah;
from the Merarites,
Kish son of Abdi and Azariah son of Jehallelel;
from the Gershonites,
Joah son of Zimmah and Eden son of Joah;
[13] from the descendants of Elizaphan,
Shimri and Jeiel;
from the descendants of Asaph,
Zechariah and Mattaniah;
[14] from the descendants of Heman,
Jehiel and Shimei;
from the descendants of Jeduthun,
Shemaiah and Uzziel.

[15] When they had assembled their fellow Levites and consecrated themselves, they went in to purify the temple of the LORD, as the king had ordered, following the word of the LORD. [16] The priests went into the sanctuary of the LORD to purify it. They brought out to the courtyard of the LORD's temple everything unclean that they found in the temple of the LORD. The Levites took it and carried it out to the Kidron Valley. [17] They began the consecration on the first day of the first month, and by the eighth day of the month they reached the portico of the LORD. For eight more days they consecrated the temple of the LORD itself, finishing on the sixteenth day of the first month.

[18] Then they went in to King Hezekiah and reported: "We have purified the entire temple of the LORD, the altar of burnt offering with all its utensils, and the table for setting out the consecrated bread, with all its articles. [19] We have prepared and consecrated all the articles that King Ahaz removed in his unfaithfulness while he was king. They are now in front of the LORD's altar."

[20] Early the next morning King Hezekiah gathered the city officials together and went up to the temple of the

## Amplified Bible

**29** Hezekiah began to reign when he was twenty-five years old, and he reigned twenty-nine years in Jerusalem. His mother was Abijah daughter of Zechariah. [2] And he did right in the sight of the Lord, according to all that David his father [forefather] had done.

[3] In the first year of his reign, in the first month, he opened the doors of the house of the Lord [which his father had closed] and repaired them. [4] He brought together the priests and Levites in the square on the east [5] And said to them, Levites, hear me! Now sanctify (purify and make free from sin) yourselves and the house of the Lord, the God of your fathers, and carry out the filth from the Holy Place. [6] For our fathers have trespassed and have done what was evil in the sight of the Lord our God, and they have forsaken Him and have turned away their faces from the dwelling place of the Lord and have turned their backs. [7] Also they have closed the doors of the porch and put out the lamps, and they have not burned incense or offered burnt offerings in the place holy to the God of Israel. [II Kings 16:10-16.] [8] Therefore the wrath of the Lord was upon Judah and Jerusalem, and He has delivered them to be a terror *and* a cause of trembling, to be an astonishment, and a hissing, as you see with your own eyes. [9] For, behold, our fathers have fallen by the sword, and our sons, our daughters, and our wives are in captivity for this. [10] Now it is in my heart to make a covenant with the Lord, the God of Israel, that His fierce anger may turn away from us. [11] My sons, do not now be negligent, for the Lord has chosen you to stand in His presence, to serve Him, to be His ministers, and to burn incense to Him.

[12] Then the Levites arose: Mahath son of Amasai, Joel son of Azariah, of the sons of the Kohathites; of the sons of Merari: Kish son of Abdi, Azariah son of Jehallelel; of the Gershonites: Joah son of Zimmah and Eden son of Joah; [13] Of the sons of Elizaphan: Shimri and Jeiel; of the sons of Asaph: Zechariah, and Mattaniah; [14] Of the sons of Heman: Jehiel and Shimei; and of the sons of Jeduthun: Shemaiah and Uzziel.

[15] They gathered their brethren and sanctified themselves and went in, as the king had commanded by the words of the Lord, to cleanse the house of the Lord. [16] The priests went into the inner part of the house of the Lord to cleanse it, and brought out all the uncleanness they found in the temple of the Lord into the court of the Lord's house. And the Levites carried it out to the brook Kidron.

[17] They began on the first day of the first month, and on the eighth day they came to the porch of the Lord. Then for eight days they sanctified the house of the Lord, and on the sixteenth day they finished. [18] Then they went to King Hezekiah and said, We have cleansed all the house of the Lord and the altar of burnt offering with all its utensils and the showbread table with all its utensils. [19] Moreover, all the utensils which King Ahaz in his reign cast away when he was transgressing [faithless] we have made ready and sanctified; and behold, they are before the altar of the Lord.

[20] Then King Hezekiah rose early and gathered the officials of the city and went up to the house of the Lord.

## New International Version

LORD. [21]They brought seven bulls, seven rams, seven male lambs and seven male goats as a sin offering[a] for the kingdom, for the sanctuary and for Judah. The king commanded the priests, the descendants of Aaron, to offer these on the altar of the LORD. [22]So they slaughtered the bulls, and the priests took the blood and splashed it against the altar; next they slaughtered the rams and splashed their blood against the altar; then they slaughtered the lambs and splashed their blood against the altar. [23]The goats for the sin offering were brought before the king and the assembly, and they laid their hands on them. [24]The priests then slaughtered the goats and presented their blood on the altar for a sin offering to atone for all Israel, because the king had ordered the burnt offering and the sin offering for all Israel.

[25]He stationed the Levites in the temple of the LORD with cymbals, harps and lyres in the way prescribed by David and Gad the king's seer and Nathan the prophet; this was commanded by the LORD through his prophets. [26]So the Levites stood ready with David's instruments, and the priests with their trumpets.

[27]Hezekiah gave the order to sacrifice the burnt offering on the altar. As the offering began, singing to the LORD began also, accompanied by trumpets and the instruments of David king of Israel. [28]The whole assembly bowed in worship, while the musicians played and the trumpets sounded. All this continued until the sacrifice of the burnt offering was completed.

[29]When the offerings were finished, the king and everyone present with him knelt down and worshiped. [30]King Hezekiah and his officials ordered the Levites to praise the LORD with the words of David and of Asaph the seer. So they sang praises with gladness and bowed down and worshiped.

[31]Then Hezekiah said, "You have now dedicated yourselves to the LORD. Come and bring sacrifices and thank offerings to the temple of the LORD." So the assembly brought sacrifices and thank offerings, and all whose hearts were willing brought burnt offerings.

[32]The number of burnt offerings the assembly brought was seventy bulls, a hundred rams and two hundred male lambs—all of them for burnt offerings to the LORD. [33]The animals consecrated as sacrifices amounted to six hundred bulls and three thousand sheep and goats. [34]The priests, however, were too few to skin all the burnt offerings; so their relatives the Levites helped them until the task was finished and until other priests had been consecrated, for the Levites had been more conscientious in consecrating themselves than the priests had been. [35]There were burnt offerings in abundance, together with the fat of the fellowship offerings and the drink offerings that accompanied the burnt offerings.

So the service of the temple of the LORD was reestablished. [36]Hezekiah and all the people rejoiced at what God had brought about for his people, because it was done so quickly.

### Hezekiah Celebrates the Passover

**30** Hezekiah sent word to all Israel and Judah and also wrote letters to Ephraim and Manasseh, inviting them to come to the temple of the LORD in Jerusalem and celebrate the Passover to the LORD, the God of Israel. [2]The king and his officials and the whole assem-

## Amplified Bible

[21]They brought seven each of bulls, rams, lambs, and he-goats for a sin offering for the kingdom, the sanctuary, and Judah. He commanded the priests, the sons of Aaron, to offer them on the Lord's altar. [22]So they killed the bulls, and the priests received the blood and dashed it against the altar. Likewise, when they had killed the rams and then the lambs, they dashed the blood against the altar. [23]Then the he-goats for the sin offering were brought before the king and the assembly, and they laid their hands on them. [24]The priests killed them and made a sin offering with their blood upon the altar to make atonement for all Israel, for the king commanded that the burnt offering and sin offering be made for all Israel.

[25]Hezekiah stationed the Levites in the Lord's house with cymbals, harps, and lyres, as David [his forefather] and Gad the king's seer and Nathan the prophet had commanded; for the commandment was from the Lord through His prophets. [26]The Levites stood with the instruments of David, and the priests with the trumpets. [27]Hezekiah commanded to offer the burnt offering upon the altar. And when the burnt offering began, the song of the Lord began also with the trumpets and with the instruments ordained by King David of Israel. [28]And all the congregation worshiped, the singers sang, and the trumpeters sounded; all this continued until the burnt offering was finished. [29]When they had stopped offering, the king and all present with him bowed themselves and worshiped.

[30]Also King Hezekiah and the princes ordered the Levites to sing praises to the Lord with the words of David and of Asaph the seer. And they sang praises with gladness and bowed themselves and worshiped.

[31]Then Hezekiah said, Now you have consecrated yourselves to the Lord; come near and bring sacrifices and thank offerings into the house of the Lord. And the assembly brought in sacrifices and thank offerings, and as many as were of a willing heart brought burnt offerings. [32]And the number of the burnt offerings which the assembly brought was 70 bulls, 100 rams, and 200 lambs. All these were for a burnt offering to the Lord. [33]And the consecrated things were 600 oxen and 3,000 sheep. [34]But the priests were too few and could not skin all the burnt offerings. So until the other priests had sanctified themselves, their Levite kinsmen helped them until the work was done, for the Levites were more upright in heart than the priests in sanctifying themselves. [35]Also the burnt offerings were in abundance, with the fat of the peace offerings, and the drink offerings for every burnt offering. So the service of the Lord's house was set in order.

[36]Thus Hezekiah rejoiced, and all the people, because of what God had prepared for the people, for it was done suddenly.

**30** Hezekiah sent to all Israel [as well as] Judah and wrote letters also to Ephraim and Manasseh to come to the Lord's house at Jerusalem to keep the Passover to the Lord, the God of Israel. [2]For the king and his princes and all the assembly in Je-

---

[a] 21 Or *purification offering*; also in verses 23 and 24

## New International Version

bly in Jerusalem decided to celebrate the Passover in the second month. ³They had not been able to celebrate it at the regular time because not enough priests had consecrated themselves and the people had not assembled in Jerusalem. ⁴The plan seemed right both to the king and to the whole assembly. ⁵They decided to send a proclamation throughout Israel, from Beersheba to Dan, calling the people to come to Jerusalem and celebrate the Passover to the LORD, the God of Israel. It had not been celebrated in large numbers according to what was written.

⁶At the king's command, couriers went throughout Israel and Judah with letters from the king and from his officials, which read:

"People of Israel, return to the LORD, the God of Abraham, Isaac and Israel, that he may return to you who are left, who have escaped from the hand of the kings of Assyria. ⁷Do not be like your parents and your fellow Israelites, who were unfaithful to the LORD, the God of their ancestors, so that he made them an object of horror, as you see. ⁸Do not be stiff-necked, as your ancestors were; submit to the LORD. Come to his sanctuary, which he has consecrated forever. Serve the LORD your God, so that his fierce anger will turn away from you. ⁹If you return to the LORD, then your fellow Israelites and your children will be shown compassion by their captors and will return to this land, for the LORD your God is gracious and compassionate. He will not turn his face from you if you return to him."

¹⁰The couriers went from town to town in Ephraim and Manasseh, as far as Zebulun, but people scorned and ridiculed them. ¹¹Nevertheless, some from Asher, Manasseh and Zebulun humbled themselves and went to Jerusalem. ¹²Also in Judah the hand of God was on the people to give them unity of mind to carry out what the king and his officials had ordered, following the word of the LORD.

¹³A very large crowd of people assembled in Jerusalem to celebrate the Festival of Unleavened Bread in the second month. ¹⁴They removed the altars in Jerusalem and cleared away the incense altars and threw them into the Kidron Valley.

¹⁵They slaughtered the Passover lamb on the fourteenth day of the second month. The priests and the Levites were ashamed and consecrated themselves and brought burnt offerings to the temple of the LORD. ¹⁶Then they took up their regular positions as prescribed in the Law of Moses the man of God. The priests splashed against the altar the blood handed to them by the Levites. ¹⁷Since many in the crowd had not consecrated themselves, the Levites had to kill the Passover lambs for all those who were not ceremonially clean and could not consecrate their lambs[a] to the LORD. ¹⁸Although most of the many people who came from Ephraim, Manasseh, Issachar and Zebulun had not purified themselves, yet they ate the Passover, contrary to what was written. But Hezekiah prayed for them, saying, "May the LORD, who is good, pardon everyone ¹⁹who sets their heart on seeking God—the LORD, the God of their ancestors—even if they are not clean according to the rules of the sanctuary." ²⁰And the LORD heard Hezekiah and healed the people.

²¹The Israelites who were present in Jerusalem celebrated the Festival of Unleavened Bread for seven days

a 17 Or consecrate themselves

## Amplified Bible

rusalem took counsel to keep the Passover in the [a]second month. [Num. 9:10, 11.]

³For they could not keep it at the set time because not enough priests had sanctified themselves, neither had the people assembled in Jerusalem.

⁴The new time pleased the king and all the assembly.

⁵So they decreed to make a proclamation throughout all Israel, from Beersheba to Dan, that the people should come to keep the Passover to the Lord, the God of Israel, at Jerusalem. For they had not kept it collectively as prescribed for a long time.

⁶So the posts went with the letters from the king and his princes throughout all Israel and Judah, as the king commanded, saying, O Israelites, return to the Lord, the God of Abraham, Isaac, and Israel, that He may return to those left of you who escaped out of the hands of the kings of Assyria.

⁷Do not be like your fathers and brethren, who were unfaithful to the Lord, the God of their fathers, so that He gave them up to desolation [to be an astonishment], as you see.

⁸Now be not stiff-necked, as your fathers were, but yield yourselves to the Lord and come to His sanctuary, which He has sanctified forever, and serve the Lord your God, that His fierce anger may turn away from you.

⁹For if you return to the Lord, your brethren and your children shall find compassion with their captors and return to this land. For the Lord your God is gracious and merciful, and He will not turn away His face from you if you return to Him.

¹⁰So the posts passed from city to city through the country of Ephraim and Manasseh, even to Zebulun, but the people laughed them to scorn and mocked them.

¹¹Yet, a few of Asher, Manasseh, and Zebulun humbled themselves and came to Jerusalem.

¹²Also the hand of God came upon Judah to give them one heart to do the commandment of the king and of the princes, by the word of the Lord.

¹³And many people came to Jerusalem to keep the Feast of Unleavened Bread in the second month, a very great assembly.

¹⁴They rose up and took away the altars [to idols] that were in Jerusalem, and all the altars and utensils for incense [to the gods] they took away and threw into the Kidron Valley [dumping place for the ashes of such abominations].

¹⁵Then they killed the Passover lamb on the fourteenth day of the second month. And the priests and the Levites were ashamed and sanctified themselves and brought burnt offerings to the Lord's house.

¹⁶They stood in their accustomed places, as directed in the Law of Moses the man of God. The priests threw [against the altar] the blood they received from the hand of the Levites.

¹⁷For many were in the assembly who had not sanctified themselves [become clean and free from all sin]. So the Levites had to kill the Passover lambs for all who were not clean, in order to make them holy to the Lord.

¹⁸For a multitude of the people, many from Ephraim, Manasseh, Issachar, and Zebulun, had not cleansed themselves, yet they ate the Passover otherwise than Moses directed. For Hezekiah had prayed for them, saying, May the good Lord pardon everyone

¹⁹Who sets his heart to seek and yearn for God—the Lord, the God of his fathers—even though not complying with the purification regulations of the sanctuary.

²⁰And the Lord hearkened to Hezekiah and healed the people.

²¹And the Israelites who were in Jerusalem kept the Feast of Unleavened Bread for seven days with great joy.

a Postponement from the first month is graciously permitted by God (see Num. 9:10-11).

## New International Version

with great rejoicing, while the Levites and priests praised the LORD every day with resounding instruments dedicated to the LORD.[a]

[22]Hezekiah spoke encouragingly to all the Levites, who showed good understanding of the service of the LORD. For the seven days they ate their assigned portion and offered fellowship offerings and praised[b] the LORD, the God of their ancestors.

[23]The whole assembly then agreed to celebrate the festival seven more days; so for another seven days they celebrated joyfully. [24]Hezekiah king of Judah provided a thousand bulls and seven thousand sheep and goats for the assembly, and the officials provided them with a thousand bulls and ten thousand sheep and goats. A great number of priests consecrated themselves. [25]The entire assembly of Judah rejoiced, along with the priests and Levites and all who had assembled from Israel, including the foreigners who had come from Israel and also those who resided in Judah. [26]There was great joy in Jerusalem, for since the days of Solomon son of David king of Israel there had been nothing like this in Jerusalem. [27]The priests and the Levites stood to bless the people, and God heard them, for their prayer reached heaven, his holy dwelling place.

**31** When all this had ended, the Israelites who were there went out to the towns of Judah, smashed the sacred stones and cut down the Asherah poles. They destroyed the high places and the altars throughout Judah and Benjamin and in Ephraim and Manasseh. After they had destroyed all of them, the Israelites returned to their own towns and to their own property.

### Contributions for Worship

[2]Hezekiah assigned the priests and Levites to divisions—each of them according to their duties as priests or Levites—to offer burnt offerings and fellowship offerings, to minister, to give thanks and to sing praises at the gates of the LORD's dwelling. [3]The king contributed from his own possessions for the morning and evening burnt offerings and for the burnt offerings on the Sabbaths, at the New Moons and at the appointed festivals as written in the Law of the LORD. [4]He ordered the people living in Jerusalem to give the portion due the priests and Levites so they could devote themselves to the Law of the LORD. [5]As soon as the order went out, the Israelites generously gave the firstfruits of their grain, new wine, olive oil and honey and all that the fields produced. They brought a great amount, a tithe of everything. [6]The people of Israel and Judah who lived in the towns of Judah also brought a tithe of their herds and flocks and a tithe of the holy things dedicated to the LORD their God, and they piled them in heaps. [7]They began doing this in the third month and finished in the seventh month. [8]When Hezekiah and his officials came and saw the heaps, they praised the LORD and blessed his people Israel.

[9]Hezekiah asked the priests and Levites about the heaps; [10]and Azariah the chief priest, from the family of Zadok, answered, "Since the people began to bring their contributions to the temple of the LORD, we have had enough to eat and plenty to spare, because the LORD has blessed his people, and this great amount is left over."

[11]Hezekiah gave orders to prepare storerooms in the temple of the LORD, and this was done. [12]Then they faithfully brought in the contributions, tithes and dedicated

## Amplified Bible

The Levites and priests praised the Lord day by day, singing with instruments of much volume to the Lord.

[22]Hezekiah spoke encouragingly to all the Levites who had good understanding in the Lord's work. So the people ate the seven-day appointed feast, offering peace offerings, making confession [and giving thanks] to the Lord, the God of their fathers.

[23]And the whole assembly took counsel to prolong the feast another seven days; and they kept it another seven days with joy.

[24]For Hezekiah king of Judah gave to the assembly 1,000 young bulls and 7,000 sheep, and the princes gave 1,000 young bulls and 10,000 sheep. And a great number of priests sanctified themselves [for service].

[25]All the assembly of Judah, with the priests, the Levites, and all the assembly who with the sojourners came from the land of Israel to dwell in Judah, rejoiced.

[26]So there was great joy in Jerusalem, for since the time of Solomon son of David king of Israel there was nothing like this in Jerusalem.

[27]Then the priests and Levites arose and blessed the people; and their voice was heard and their prayer came up to [God's] holy habitation in heaven.

**31** Now when all this was finished, all Israel present there went out to the cities of Judah and broke in pieces the pillars or obelisks, cut down the Asherim, and threw down the high places [of idolatry] and the altars in all Judah and Benjamin, in Ephraim and Manasseh, until they had utterly destroyed them all. Then all the Israelites returned to their own cities, every man to his possession.

[2]And Hezekiah appointed the priests and the Levites after their divisions, each man according to his service, the priests and Levites for burnt offerings and for peace offerings, to minister, to give thanks, and to praise in the gates of the camp of the Lord.

[3]King Hezekiah's personal contribution was for the burnt offerings: [those] of morning and evening, for the Sabbaths, for the New Moons, and for the appointed feasts, as written in the Law of the Lord.

[4]He commanded the people living in Jerusalem to give the portion due the priests and Levites, that they might [be free to] give themselves to the Law of the Lord.

[5]As soon as the command went abroad, the Israelites gave in abundance the firstfruits of grain, vintage fruit, oil, honey, and of all the produce of the field; and they brought in abundantly the tithe of everything.

[6]The people of Israel and Judah who lived in Judah's cities also brought the tithe of cattle and sheep and of the dedicated things which were consecrated to the Lord their God, and they laid them in heaps.

[7]In the third month [at the end of wheat harvest] they began to lay the foundation or beginning of the heaps and finished them in the seventh month.

[8]When Hezekiah and the princes came and saw the heaps, they blessed the Lord and His people Israel.

[9]Then Hezekiah questioned the priests and Levites about the heaps.

[10]Azariah the high priest, of the house of Zadok, answered him, Since the people began to bring the offerings into the Lord's house, we have eaten and have plenty left, for the Lord has blessed His people, and what is left is this great store.

[11]Then Hezekiah commanded them to prepare chambers [for storage] in the house of the Lord, and they prepared them

[12]And brought in the offerings, tithes, and dedicated

---

[a] 21 Or priests sang to the LORD every day, accompanied by the LORD's instruments of praise    [b] 22 Or and confessed their sins to

## New International Version

gifts. Konaniah, a Levite, was the overseer in charge of these things, and his brother Shimei was next in rank. [13]Jehiel, Azaziah, Nahath, Asahel, Jerimoth, Jozabad, Eliel, Ismakiah, Mahath and Benaiah were assistants of Konaniah and Shimei his brother. All these served by appointment of King Hezekiah and Azariah the official in charge of the temple of God.

[14]Kore son of Imnah the Levite, keeper of the East Gate, was in charge of the freewill offerings given to God, distributing the contributions made to the LORD and also the consecrated gifts. [15]Eden, Miniamin, Jeshua, Shemaiah, Amariah and Shekaniah assisted him faithfully in the towns of the priests, distributing to their fellow priests according to their divisions, old and young alike.

[16]In addition, they distributed to the males three years old or more whose names were in the genealogical records—all who would enter the temple of the LORD to perform the daily duties of their various tasks, according to their responsibilities and their divisions. [17]And they distributed to the priests enrolled by their families in the genealogical records and likewise to the Levites twenty years old or more, according to their responsibilities and their divisions. [18]They included all the little ones, the wives, and the sons and daughters of the whole community listed in these genealogical records. For they were faithful in consecrating themselves.

[19]As for the priests, the descendants of Aaron, who lived on the farmlands around their towns or in any other towns, men were designated by name to distribute portions to every male among them and to all who were recorded in the genealogies of the Levites.

[20]This is what Hezekiah did throughout Judah, doing what was good and right and faithful before the LORD his God. [21]In everything that he undertook in the service of God's temple and in obedience to the law and the commands, he sought his God and worked wholeheartedly. And so he prospered.

### Sennacherib Threatens Jerusalem

**32** After all that Hezekiah had so faithfully done, Sennacherib king of Assyria came and invaded Judah. He laid siege to the fortified cities, thinking to conquer them for himself. [2]When Hezekiah saw that Sennacherib had come and that he intended to wage war against Jerusalem, [3]he consulted with his officials and military staff about blocking off the water from the springs outside the city, and they helped him. [4]They gathered a large group of people who blocked all the springs and the stream that flowed through the land. "Why should the kings of Assyria come and find plenty of water?" they said. [5]Then he worked hard repairing all the broken sections of the wall and building towers on it. He built another wall outside that one and reinforced the terraces[b] of the City of David. He also made large numbers of weapons and shields.

[6]He appointed military officers over the people and assembled them before him in the square at the city gate and encouraged them with these words: [7]"Be strong and courageous. Do not be afraid or discouraged because of the king of Assyria and the vast army with him, for there is a greater power with us than with him. [8]With him is only the arm of flesh, but with us is the LORD our God to help us and to fight our battles." And the people gained confidence from what Hezekiah the king of Judah said.

[9]Later, when Sennacherib king of Assyria and all his forces were laying siege to Lachish, he sent his officers to Jerusalem with this message for Hezekiah king of Judah and for all the people of Judah who were there:

## Amplified Bible

things faithfully. Conaniah the Levite was in charge of them, and Shimei his brother came next.

[13]And Jehiel, Azaziah, Nahath, Asahel, Jerimoth, Jozabad, Eliel, Ismachiah, Mahath, and Benaiah were overseers directed by Conaniah and Shimei his brother, at the appointment of King Hezekiah and Azariah the chief officer of the house of God.

[14]Kore son of Imnah the Levite, keeper of the East Gate, was over the freewill offerings to God, to apportion the contributions of the Lord and the most holy things.

[15]Under him were Eden, Miniamin, Jeshua, Shemaiah, Amariah, and Shecaniah, in the priests' cities, in their office of trust faithfully to give to their brethren by divisions, to great and small alike,

[16]Except those [Levites] registered as males from three years old and upward—who were consecrated to the temple service [in Jerusalem, for their daily portion] as the duty of every day required, for their service according to their offices by their divisions.

[17]The registration of the priests was according to their fathers' houses; that of the Levites from twenty years old and upward was according to their offices by their divisions;

[18]Also there was the registration of all their little ones, their wives, and their older sons and daughters through all the congregation. For in their office of trust they cleansed themselves *and* set themselves apart in holiness.

[19]Also for the sons of Aaron the priests, who were in the fields of the suburbs of their cities or in every city, there were men who were mentioned by name to give portions to all the males among the priests and to all who were registered among the Levites.

[20]Hezekiah did this throughout all Judah, and he did what was good, right, and faithful before the Lord his God.

[21]And every work that he began in the service of the house of God, in keeping with the law and the commandments to seek his God [inquiring of and yearning for Him], he did with all his heart, and he prospered.

**32** After these things and this loyalty, Sennacherib king of Assyria came, invaded Judah, and encamped against the fortified cities, thinking to take them.

[2]When Hezekiah saw that Sennacherib had come and intended to fight against Jerusalem,

[3]He decided with his officers and his mighty men to stop up the waters of the fountains which were outside the city [by enclosing them with masonry and concealing them], and they helped him.

[4]So many people gathered, and they stopped up all the springs and the brook which flowed through the land, saying, Why should the kings of Assyria come and find much water?

[5]Also Hezekiah took courage and built up all the wall that was broken, and raised towers upon it, and he built another wall outside and strengthened the Millo in the City of David and made weapons and shields in abundance.

[6]And he set captains of war over the people and gathered them together to him in the street of the gate of the city and spoke encouragingly to them, saying,

[7]Be strong and courageous. Be not afraid or dismayed before the king of Assyria and all the horde that is with him, for there is Another with us greater than [all those] with him.

[8]With him is an arm of flesh, but with us is the Lord our God to help us and to fight our battles. And the people relied on the words of Hezekiah king of Judah.

[9]And this Sennacherib king of Assyria, while he himself with all his forces was before Lachish, sent his servants to Jerusalem, to Hezekiah king of Judah, and to all Judah who were at Jerusalem, saying,

---

[a] 4 Hebrew; Septuagint and Syriac *king*    [b] 5 Or *the Millo*

## New International Version

[10]"This is what Sennacherib king of Assyria says: On what are you basing your confidence, that you remain in Jerusalem under siege? [11]When Hezekiah says, 'The LORD our God will save us from the hand of the king of Assyria,' he is misleading you, to let you die of hunger and thirst. [12]Did not Hezekiah himself remove this god's high places and altars, saying to Judah and Jerusalem, 'You must worship before one altar and burn sacrifices on it'?

[13]"Do you not know what I and my predecessors have done to all the peoples of the other lands? Were the gods of those nations ever able to deliver their land from my hand? [14]Who of all the gods of these nations that my predecessors destroyed has been able to save his people from me? How then can your god deliver you from my hand? [15]Now do not let Hezekiah deceive you and mislead you like this. Do not believe him, for no god of any nation or kingdom has been able to deliver his people from my hand or the hand of my predecessors. How much less will your god deliver you from my hand!"

[16]Sennacherib's officers spoke further against the LORD God and against his servant Hezekiah. [17]The king also wrote letters ridiculing the LORD, the God of Israel, and saying this against him: "Just as the gods of the peoples of the other lands did not rescue their people from my hand, so the god of Hezekiah will not rescue his people from my hand." [18]Then they called out in Hebrew to the people of Jerusalem who were on the wall, to terrify them and make them afraid in order to capture the city. [19]They spoke about the God of Jerusalem as they did about the gods of the other peoples of the world—the work of human hands.

[20]King Hezekiah and the prophet Isaiah son of Amoz cried out in prayer to heaven about this. [21]And the LORD sent an angel, who annihilated all the fighting men and the commanders and officers in the camp of the Assyrian king. So he withdrew to his own land in disgrace. And when he went into the temple of his god, some of his sons, his own flesh and blood, cut him down with the sword.

[22]So the LORD saved Hezekiah and the people of Jerusalem from the hand of Sennacherib king of Assyria and from the hand of all others. He took care of them[a] on every side. [23]Many brought offerings to Jerusalem for the LORD and valuable gifts for Hezekiah king of Judah. From then on he was highly regarded by all the nations.

### Hezekiah's Pride, Success and Death

[24]In those days Hezekiah became ill and was at the point of death. He prayed to the LORD, who answered him and gave him a miraculous sign. [25]But Hezekiah's heart was proud and he did not respond to the kindness shown him; therefore the LORD's wrath was on him and on Judah and Jerusalem. [26]Then Hezekiah repented of the pride of his heart, as did the people of Jerusalem; therefore the LORD's wrath did not come on them during the days of Hezekiah.

[27]Hezekiah had very great wealth and honor, and he made treasuries for his silver and gold and for his precious stones, spices, shields and all kinds of valuables. [28]He also made buildings to store the harvest of grain, new wine and olive oil; and he made stalls for various kinds of cattle, and pens for the flocks. [29]He built villages and acquired great numbers of flocks and herds, for God had given him very great riches.

## Amplified Bible

[10]Thus says Sennacherib king of Assyria: On what do you trust, that you remain in the strongholds in Jerusalem?

[11]Is not Hezekiah leading you on in order to let you die by famine and thirst, saying, The Lord our God will deliver us out of the hand of the king of Assyria?

[12]Has not the same Hezekiah taken away his high places and his altars, and commanded Judah and Jerusalem, You shall worship before one altar and burn incense upon it?

[13]Do you not know what I and my fathers have done to all the peoples of other lands? Were the gods of the nations of those lands in any way able to deliver their lands out of my hand?

[14]Who among all the gods of those nations that my fathers utterly destroyed was able to deliver his people out of my hand, that your God should be able to deliver you out of my hand?

[15]So now, do not let Hezekiah deceive or mislead you in this way, and do not believe him, for no god of any nation or kingdom was able to deliver his people out of my hand or the hand of my fathers. How much less will your God deliver you out of my hand!

[16]And his servants said still more against the Lord God and against His servant Hezekiah.

[17]The Assyrian king also wrote letters insulting the Lord, the God of Israel, and speaking against Him, saying, As the gods of the nations of other lands have not delivered their people out of my hand, so shall not the God of Hezekiah deliver His people out of my hand.

[18]And they shouted it loudly in the Jewish language to the people of Jerusalem who were on the wall, to frighten and terrify them, that they might take the city.

[19]And they spoke of the God of Jerusalem as they spoke of the gods of the peoples of the earth, which are the work of the hands of men.

[20]For this cause Hezekiah the king and the prophet Isaiah son of Amoz prayed and cried to heaven.

[21]And the Lord sent an angel, who cut off all the mighty warriors and commanders and officers in the camp of the king of Assyria. So the Assyrian king returned with shamed face to his own land. And when he came into the house of his god, they who were his own offspring slew him there with the sword. [II Kings 19:35-37.]

[22]Thus the Lord saved Hezekiah and the inhabitants of Jerusalem from the hand of Sennacherib the king of Assyria and from the hand of all his enemies, and He guided them on every side.

[23]And many brought gifts to Jerusalem to the Lord and presents to Hezekiah king of Judah; so from then on he was magnified in the sight of all nations.

[24]In those days Hezekiah was sick to the point of death; and he prayed to the Lord and He answered him and gave him a sign.

[25]But Hezekiah did not make return [to the Lord] according to the benefit done to him, for his heart became proud [at such a spectacular response to his prayer]; therefore there was wrath upon him and upon Judah and Jerusalem.

[26]But Hezekiah humbled himself for the pride of his heart, both he and the inhabitants of Jerusalem, so that the wrath of the Lord came not upon them in the days of Hezekiah.

[27]And Hezekiah had very great wealth and honor, and he made for himself treasuries for silver, gold, precious stones, spices, shields, and all kinds of attractive vessels,

[28]Storehouses also for the increase of grain, vintage fruits, and oil, and stalls for all kinds of cattle, and sheepfolds.

[29]Moreover, he provided for himself cities and flocks and herds in abundance, for God had given him very great possessions.

[a] 22 Hebrew; Septuagint and Vulgate *He gave them rest*

## New International Version

30It was Hezekiah who blocked the upper outlet of the Gihon spring and channeled the water down to the west side of the City of David. He succeeded in everything he undertook. 31But when envoys were sent by the rulers of Babylon to ask him about the miraculous sign that had occurred in the land, God left him to test him and to know everything that was in his heart.

32The other events of Hezekiah's reign and his acts of devotion are written in the vision of the prophet Isaiah son of Amoz in the book of the kings of Judah and Israel. 33Hezekiah rested with his ancestors and was buried on the hill where the tombs of David's descendants are. All Judah and the people of Jerusalem honored him when he died. And Manasseh his son succeeded him as king.

### Manasseh King of Judah

**33** Manasseh was twelve years old when he became king, and he reigned in Jerusalem fifty-five years. 2He did evil in the eyes of the LORD, following the detestable practices of the nations the LORD had driven out before the Israelites. 3He rebuilt the high places his father Hezekiah had demolished; he also erected altars to the Baals and made Asherah poles. He bowed down to all the starry hosts and worshiped them. 4He built altars in the temple of the LORD, of which the LORD had said, "My Name will remain in Jerusalem forever." 5In both courts of the temple of the LORD, he built altars to all the starry hosts. 6He sacrificed his children in the fire in the Valley of Ben Hinnom, practiced divination and witchcraft, sought omens, and consulted mediums and spiritists. He did much evil in the eyes of the LORD, arousing his anger.

7He took the image he had made and put it in God's temple, of which God had said to David and to his son Solomon, "In this temple and in Jerusalem, which I have chosen out of all the tribes of Israel, I will put my Name forever. 8I will not again make the feet of the Israelites leave the land I assigned to your ancestors, if only they will be careful to do everything I commanded them concerning all the laws, decrees and regulations given through Moses." 9But Manasseh led Judah and the people of Jerusalem astray, so that they did more evil than the nations the LORD had destroyed before the Israelites.

10The LORD spoke to Manasseh and his people, but they paid no attention. 11So the LORD brought against them the army commanders of the king of Assyria, who took Manasseh prisoner, put a hook in his nose, bound him with bronze shackles and took him to Babylon. 12In his distress he sought the favor of the LORD his God and humbled himself greatly before the God of his ancestors. 13And when he prayed to him, the LORD was moved by his entreaty and listened to his plea; so he brought him back to Jerusalem and to his kingdom. Then Manasseh knew that the LORD is God.

14Afterward he rebuilt the outer wall of the City of David, west of the Gihon spring in the valley, as far as the entrance of the Fish Gate and encircling the hill of Ophel; he also made it much higher. He stationed military commanders in all the fortified cities in Judah.

## Amplified Bible

30This same Hezekiah also closed the upper springs of Gihon and directed the waters down to the west side of the City of David. And Hezekiah prospered in all his works.

31And so in the matter of the ambassadors of the princes of Babylon who were sent to him to inquire about the wonder that was done in the land, God left him to himself to try him, that He might know all that was in his heart. [Isa. 39:1-7.]

32Now the rest of the acts of Hezekiah and his good deeds, behold, they are written in the vision of Isaiah the prophet, the son of Amoz, and in the Book of the Kings of Judah and Israel.

33And Hezekiah slept with his fathers and was buried in the ascent of the tombs of the descendants of David; and all Judah and the inhabitants of Jerusalem did him honor at his death. Manasseh his son reigned in his stead.

**33** Manasseh was twelve years old when he began to reign, and he reigned fifty-five years in Jerusalem. 2But he did evil in the Lord's sight, like the abominations of the heathen whom the Lord drove out before the Israelites.

3For he built again the [idolatrous] high places which Hezekiah his father had broken down, and he reared altars for the Baals and made the Asherim and worshiped all the hosts of the heavens and served them.

4Also he built [heathen] altars in the Lord's house, of which the Lord had said, In Jerusalem shall My Name be forever.

5He built altars for all the hosts of the heavens in the two courts of the Lord's house.

6And he burned his children as an offering [to his god] in the Valley of Ben-hinnom [son of Hinnom], and practiced soothsaying, augury, and sorcery, and dealt with mediums and wizards. He did much evil in the sight of the Lord, provoking Him to anger.

7And he set a carved image, the idol which he had made, in the house of God, of which God had said to David and to Solomon his son, In this house and in Jerusalem, which I have chosen before all the tribes of Israel, will I put My Name [and Presence] forever;

8And I will no more remove Israel from the land which I appointed for your fathers, if they will only take heed to do all that I have commanded them, the whole law, the statutes, and the ordinances given through Moses.

9So Manasseh led Judah and the inhabitants of Jerusalem to do more evil than the heathen whom the Lord had destroyed before the Israelites.

10The Lord spoke to Manasseh and to his people, but they would not hearken.

11So the Lord brought against them the commanders of the host of the king of Assyria, who took Manasseh with hooks and in fetters and brought him to Babylon.

12When he was in affliction, he besought the Lord his God and humbled himself greatly before the God of his fathers.

13He prayed to Him, and God, entreated by him, heard his supplication and brought him again to Jerusalem to his kingdom. Then Manasseh knew that the Lord is God.

14And he built an outer wall to the City of David west of Gihon in the valley, to the entrance of the Fish Gate, and ran it around Ophel, raising it to a very great height; and he put commanders of the army in all the fortified cities of Judah.

## New International Version

[15]He got rid of the foreign gods and removed the image from the temple of the LORD, as well as all the altars he had built on the temple hill and in Jerusalem; and he threw them out of the city. [16]Then he restored the altar of the LORD and sacrificed fellowship offerings and thank offerings on it, and told Judah to serve the LORD, the God of Israel. [17]The people, however, continued to sacrifice at the high places, but only to the LORD their God.

[18]The other events of Manasseh's reign, including his prayer to his God and the words the seers spoke to him in the name of the LORD, the God of Israel, are written in the annals of the kings of Israel.[a] [19]His prayer and how God was moved by his entreaty, as well as all his sins and unfaithfulness, and the sites where he built high places and set up Asherah poles and idols before he humbled himself—all these are written in the records of the seers.[b] [20]Manasseh rested with his ancestors and was buried in his palace. And Amon his son succeeded him as king.

### Amon King of Judah

[21]Amon was twenty-two years old when he became king, and he reigned in Jerusalem two years. [22]He did evil in the eyes of the LORD, as his father Manasseh had done. Amon worshiped and offered sacrifices to all the idols Manasseh had made. [23]But unlike his father Manasseh, he did not humble himself before the LORD; Amon increased his guilt.

[24]Amon's officials conspired against him and assassinated him in his palace. [25]Then the people of the land killed all who had plotted against King Amon, and they made Josiah his son king in his place.

### Josiah's Reforms

**34** Josiah was eight years old when he became king, and he reigned in Jerusalem thirty-one years. [2]He did what was right in the eyes of the LORD and followed the ways of his father David, not turning aside to the right or to the left.

[3]In the eighth year of his reign, while he was still young, he began to seek the God of his father David. In his twelfth year he began to purge Judah and Jerusalem of high places, Asherah poles and idols. [4]Under his direction the altars of the Baals were torn down; he cut to pieces the incense altars that were above them, and smashed the Asherah poles and the idols. These he broke to pieces and scattered over the graves of those who had sacrificed to them. [5]He burned the bones of the priests on their altars, and so he purged Judah and Jerusalem. [6]In the towns of Manasseh, Ephraim and Simeon, as far as Naphtali, and in the ruins around them, [7]he tore down the altars and the Asherah poles and crushed the idols to powder and cut to pieces all the incense altars throughout Israel. Then he went back to Jerusalem.

[8]In the eighteenth year of Josiah's reign, to purify the land and the temple, he sent Shaphan son of Azaliah and Maaseiah the ruler of the city, with Joah son of Joahaz, the recorder, to repair the temple of the LORD his God. [9]They went to Hilkiah the high priest and gave him the money that had been brought into the temple of God,

## Amplified Bible

[15]And he took away the foreign gods and the idol out of the house of the Lord and all the altars that he had built on the mount of the house of the Lord and in Jerusalem; and he cast them out of the city. [16]And he restored the Lord's altar and sacrificed on it offerings of peace and of thanksgiving; and he commanded Judah to serve the Lord, the God of Israel. [17]Yet the people still sacrificed in the high places, but only to the Lord their God.

[18]Now the rest of the acts of Manasseh, and his prayer to his God, and the words of the seers who spoke to him in the name of the Lord, the God of Israel, behold, they are written in the Book of the Kings of Israel. [19]His prayer and how God heard him, and all his sins and unfaithfulness, and the sites on which he built high places and set up the Asherim and graven images before he humbled himself, behold, they are written in the Chronicles of the Seers.

[20]So Manasseh slept with his fathers, and they buried him in his own house [garden]. And Amon his son reigned in his stead.

[21]Amon was twenty-two years old when he began his two-year reign in Jerusalem. [22]But he did evil in the sight of the Lord, as did Manasseh his father; for Amon sacrificed to all the images which Manasseh his father had made, and served them, [23]And he did not humble himself before the Lord, as Manasseh his father [finally] did; but Amon trespassed and became more and more guilty.

[24]And his servants conspired against him and killed him in his own house. [25]But the people of the land slew all those who had conspired against King Amon, and they made Josiah his son king in his stead.

**34** Josiah was eight years old when he began his thirty-one-year reign in Jerusalem. [2]He did right in the sight of the Lord and walked in the ways of David his father [forefather] and turned aside neither to the right hand nor to the left.

[3]For in the eighth year of his reign, while he was yet young [sixteen], he began to seek after and yearn for the God of David his father [forefather]; and in the twelfth year he began to purge Judah and Jerusalem of the high places, the Asherim, and the carved and molten images. [4]They broke down the altars of the Baals in his presence; the sun-images that were high above them he hewed down; the Asherim and the graven images and the molten images he broke in pieces and made dust of them and strewed it upon the graves of those who sacrificed to them. [5]Josiah burned the bones of the [idolatrous] priests upon their altars, and so cleansed Judah and Jerusalem. [6]So he did in the cities of Manasseh, Ephraim, and Simeon, even to Naphtali, in their ruins round about [with their axes], [7]He broke down the altars and the Asherim and beat the graven images into powder and hewed down all the sun-images throughout all the land of Israel. Then he returned to Jerusalem.

[8]In the eighteenth year of Josiah's reign, when he had purged the land and the [Lord's] house, he sent Shaphan son of Azaliah, and Maaseiah governor of the city, and Joah son of Joahaz, the recorder, to repair the house of the Lord his God. [9]When they came to Hilkiah the high priest, they delivered the money that had been brought into the house of

---

[a] 18 That is, Judah, as frequently in 2 Chronicles   [b] 19 One Hebrew manuscript and Septuagint; most Hebrew manuscripts *of Hozai*

## New International Version

which the Levites who were the gatekeepers had collected from the people of Manasseh, Ephraim and the entire remnant of Israel and from all the people of Judah and Benjamin and the inhabitants of Jerusalem. [10]Then they entrusted it to the men appointed to supervise the work on the LORD's temple. These men paid the workers who repaired and restored the temple. [11]They also gave money to the carpenters and builders to purchase dressed stone, and timber for joists and beams for the buildings that the kings of Judah had allowed to fall into ruin.

[12]The workers labored faithfully. Over them to direct them were Jahath and Obadiah, Levites descended from Merari, and Zechariah and Meshullam, descended from Kohath. The Levites—all who were skilled in playing musical instruments— [13]had charge of the laborers and supervised all the workers from job to job. Some of the Levites were secretaries, scribes and gatekeepers.

### The Book of the Law Found

[14]While they were bringing out the money that had been taken into the temple of the LORD, Hilkiah the priest found the Book of the Law of the LORD that had been given through Moses. [15]Hilkiah said to Shaphan the secretary, "I have found the Book of the Law in the temple of the LORD." He gave it to Shaphan.

[16]Then Shaphan took the book to the king and reported to him: "Your officials are doing everything that has been committed to them. [17]They have paid out the money that was in the temple of the LORD and have entrusted it to the supervisors and workers." [18]Then Shaphan the secretary informed the king, "Hilkiah the priest has given me a book." And Shaphan read from it in the presence of the king.

[19]When the king heard the words of the Law, he tore his robes. [20]He gave these orders to Hilkiah, Ahikam son of Shaphan, Abdon son of Micah,[a] Shaphan the secretary and Asaiah the king's attendant: [21]"Go and inquire of the LORD for me and for the remnant in Israel and Judah about what is written in this book that has been found. Great is the LORD's anger that is poured out on us because those who have gone before us have not kept the word of the LORD; they have not acted in accordance with all that is written in this book."

[22]Hilkiah and those the king had sent with him[b] went to speak to the prophet Huldah, who was the wife of Shallum son of Tokhath,[c] the son of Hasrah,[d] keeper of the wardrobe. She lived in Jerusalem, in the New Quarter.

[23]She said to them, "This is what the LORD, the God of Israel, says: Tell the man who sent you to me, [24]'This is what the LORD says: I am going to bring disaster on this place and its people—all the curses written in the book that has been read in the presence of the king of Judah. [25]Because they have forsaken me and burned incense to other gods and aroused my anger by all that their hands have made,[e] my anger will be poured out on this place and will not be quenched.' [26]Tell the king of Judah, who sent you to inquire of the LORD, 'This is what the LORD, the God of Israel, says concerning the words you heard: [27]Because your heart was responsive and you humbled yourself before God when you heard what he spoke against this place and its people, and because you humbled yourself before

## Amplified Bible

God, which the Levites who kept the doors had collected from Manasseh, Ephraim, all the remnant of Israel, and from all Judah, Benjamin, and Jerusalem.

[10]They delivered it to the workmen who had oversight of the Lord's house, who gave it to repair and restore the temple:

[11]To the carpenters and builders to buy hewn stone, and timber for couplings and beams for the houses which the kings of Judah had destroyed [by neglect].

[12]The men did the work faithfully. Their overseers were Jahath and Obadiah, Levites of the sons of Merari, and Zechariah and Meshullam, of the sons of the Kohathites. The Levites—all who were skillful with instruments of music—

[13]Also had oversight of the burden bearers and all who did work in any kind of service; and some of the Levites were scribes, officials, and gatekeepers.

[14]When they were bringing out the money that was brought into the house of the Lord, Hilkiah the priest found the Book of the Law of the Lord given by Moses.

[15]Hilkiah told Shaphan the scribe, I have found the Book of the Law in the Lord's house. And [he] gave the book to Shaphan.

[16]Shaphan took the book to King Josiah, but [first] reported to him, All that was committed to your servants they are doing.

[17]They have emptied out the money that was found in the house of the Lord and have delivered it into the hand of the overseers and the workmen.

[18]Then Shaphan the scribe said to the king, Hilkiah the priest has given me a book. And Shaphan read it before the king.

[19]When King Josiah had heard the words of the Law, he rent his clothes.

[20]And the king commanded Hilkiah, Ahikam son of Shaphan, Abdon son of Micah, Shaphan the scribe, and Asaiah a servant of the king, saying,

[21]Go, inquire of the Lord for me and for those who are left in Israel and in Judah about the words of the book that is found. For great is the Lord's wrath that is poured out on us because our fathers have not kept the word of the Lord, to do according to all that is written in this book.

[22]And Hilkiah and they whom the king had appointed went to Huldah the prophetess, the wife of Shallum son of Tokhath, the son of Hasrah, keeper of the wardrobe. She dwelt in Jerusalem, in the Second Quarter. They spoke to her to that effect.

[23]And she answered them, Thus says the Lord, the God of Israel: Tell the man who sent you to me,

[24]Thus says the Lord: Behold, I will bring evil upon this place and upon its inhabitants, even all the curses that are written in the book which they have read before the king of Judah.

[25]Because they have forsaken Me and have burned incense to other gods, that they might provoke Me to anger with all the works of their hands, therefore My wrath shall be poured out upon this place and shall not be quenched.

[26]But say to King Josiah of Judah, who sent you to inquire of the Lord, Thus says the Lord, the God of Israel, concerning the words which you have heard:

[27]Because your heart was tender *and* penitent and you humbled yourself before God when you heard His words against this place and its inhabitants, and humbled your-

---

[a] 20 Also called *Akbor son of Micaiah*   [b] 22 One Hebrew manuscript, Vulgate and Syriac; most Hebrew manuscripts do not have *had sent with him*.   [c] 22 Also called *Tikvah*   [d] 22 Also called *Harhas*   [e] 25 Or *by everything they have done*

## New International Version

me and tore your robes and wept in my presence, I have heard you, declares the LORD. [28]Now I will gather you to your ancestors, and you will be buried in peace. Your eyes will not see all the disaster I am going to bring on this place and on those who live here.'"

So they took her answer back to the king.

[29]Then the king called together all the elders of Judah and Jerusalem. [30]He went up to the temple of the LORD with the people of Judah, the inhabitants of Jerusalem, the priests and the Levites—all the people from the least to the greatest. He read in their hearing all the words of the Book of the Covenant, which had been found in the temple of the LORD. [31]The king stood by his pillar and renewed the covenant in the presence of the LORD—to follow the LORD and keep his commands, statutes and decrees with all his heart and all his soul, and to obey the words of the covenant written in this book.

[32]Then he had everyone in Jerusalem and Benjamin pledge themselves to it; the people of Jerusalem did this in accordance with the covenant of God, the God of their ancestors.

[33]Josiah removed all the detestable idols from all the territory belonging to the Israelites, and he had all who were present in Israel serve the LORD their God. As long as he lived, they did not fail to follow the LORD, the God of their ancestors.

### Josiah Celebrates the Passover

**35** Josiah celebrated the Passover to the LORD in Jerusalem, and the Passover lamb was slaughtered on the fourteenth day of the first month. [2]He appointed the priests to their duties and encouraged them in the service of the LORD's temple. [3]He said to the Levites, who instructed all Israel and who had been consecrated to the LORD: "Put the sacred ark in the temple that Solomon son of David king of Israel built. It is not to be carried about on your shoulders. Now serve the LORD your God and his people Israel. [4]Prepare yourselves by families in your divisions, according to the instructions written by David king of Israel and by his son Solomon.

[5]"Stand in the holy place with a group of Levites for each subdivision of the families of your fellow Israelites, the lay people. [6]Slaughter the Passover lambs, consecrate yourselves and prepare the lambs for your fellow Israelites, doing what the LORD commanded through Moses."

[7]Josiah provided for all the lay people who were there a total of thirty thousand lambs and goats for the Passover offerings, and also three thousand cattle—all from the king's own possessions.

[8]His officials also contributed voluntarily to the people and the priests and Levites. Hilkiah, Zechariah and Jehiel, the officials in charge of God's temple, gave the priests twenty-six hundred Passover offerings and three hundred cattle. [9]Also Konaniah along with Shemaiah and Nethanel, his brothers, and Hashabiah, Jeiel and Jozabad, the leaders of the Levites, provided five thousand Passover offerings and five hundred head of cattle for the Levites.

[10]The service was arranged and the priests stood in their places with the Levites in their divisions as the king had ordered. [11]The Passover lambs were slaughtered, and the priests splashed against the altar the blood handed to them, while the Levites skinned the animals. [12]They set aside the burnt offerings to give them to the subdivi-

## Amplified Bible

self before Me and rent your clothes and wept before Me, I have heard you, says the Lord.

[28]Behold, I will gather you to your fathers, and you shall be gathered to your grave in peace, and your eyes shall not see all the evil that I will bring upon this place and its inhabitants. So they brought the king word again.

[29]Then King Josiah sent and gathered all the elders of Judah and Jerusalem.

[30]And [he] went up into the house of the Lord, as did all the men of Judah, the inhabitants of Jerusalem, the priests, the Levites, and all the people, great and small; and he [the king] read in their hearing all the words of the Book of the Covenant that was found in the Lord's house.

[31]Then the king stood in his place and made a covenant before the Lord—to walk after the Lord and to keep His commandments, His testimonies, and His statutes with all his heart and with all his soul, to perform the words of the covenant that are written in this book.

[32]And he caused all who were present in Jerusalem and Benjamin to stand in confirmation of it. And the inhabitants of Jerusalem did according to the covenant of God, the God of their fathers.

[33]Josiah removed all the [idolatrous] abominations from all the territory that belonged to the Israelites, and made all who were in Israel serve the Lord their God. All his days they did not turn from following the Lord, the God of their fathers.

**35** Josiah kept the Passover to the Lord in Jerusalem; they killed the Passover lamb on the fourteenth day of the first month.

[2]He appointed the priests to their positions and encouraged them in the service of the house of the Lord.

[3]To the Levites who taught all Israel and were holy to the Lord he said: Put the holy ark in the house which Solomon son of David king of Israel, built; it shall no longer be a burden carried on your shoulders. Now serve the Lord your God and His people Israel.

[4]Prepare yourselves according to your fathers' houses by your divisions, after the directions of David king of Israel and of Solomon his son.

[5]And stand in the holy court of the priests according to the sections of the fathers' families of your kinsmen, the common people, and let there be a section of the Levites [to attend] to each division of the families of the people.

[6]Kill the Passover lambs and sanctify yourselves and prepare for your brethren to do according to the word of the Lord by Moses.

[7]Then Josiah contributed to the lay people lambs and kids of the flock as Passover offerings for all who were present, to the number of 30,000, and 3,000 young bulls—all from the king's possessions.

[8]And his princes gave for a freewill offering to the people, to the priests, and the Levites. Hilkiah, Zechariah, and Jehiel, chief officers of God's house, gave the priests for the Passover offerings 2,600 [lambs and kids] and 300 bulls.

[9]Conaniah also, and Shemaiah and Nethanel his brothers, and Hashabiah, Jeiel, and Jozabad, chiefs of the Levites, gave to the Levites for Passover offerings 5,000 [lambs and kids] and 500 bulls.

[10]When the service was ready, the priests stood in their place and the Levites in their divisions as the king commanded.

[11]They killed the Passover lambs, and the priests sprinkled the blood they received from the Levites who skinned the animals.

[12]Then they removed the burnt offerings, that they might distribute them according to the divisions of the lay

## New International Version

sions of the families of the people to offer to the LORD, as it is written in the Book of Moses. They did the same with the cattle. [13]They roasted the Passover animals over the fire as prescribed, and boiled the holy offerings in pots, caldrons and pans and served them quickly to all the people. [14]After this, they made preparations for themselves and for the priests, because the priests, the descendants of Aaron, were sacrificing the burnt offerings and the fat portions until nightfall. So the Levites made preparations for themselves and for the Aaronic priests.

[15]The musicians, the descendants of Asaph, were in the places prescribed by David, Asaph, Heman and Jeduthun the king's seer. The gatekeepers at each gate did not need to leave their posts, because their fellow Levites made the preparations for them.

[16]So at that time the entire service of the LORD was carried out for the celebration of the Passover and the offering of burnt offerings on the altar of the LORD, as King Josiah had ordered. [17]The Israelites who were present celebrated the Passover at that time and observed the Festival of Unleavened Bread for seven days. [18]The Passover had not been observed like this in Israel since the days of the prophet Samuel; and none of the kings of Israel had ever celebrated such a Passover as did Josiah, with the priests, the Levites and all Judah and Israel who were there with the people of Jerusalem. [19]This Passover was celebrated in the eighteenth year of Josiah's reign.

### The Death of Josiah

[20]After all this, when Josiah had set the temple in order, Necho king of Egypt went up to fight at Carchemish on the Euphrates, and Josiah marched out to meet him in battle. [21]But Necho sent messengers to him, saying, "What quarrel is there, king of Judah, between you and me? It is not you I am attacking at this time, but the house with which I am at war. God has told me to hurry; so stop opposing God, who is with me, or he will destroy you."

[22]Josiah, however, would not turn away from him, but disguised himself to engage him in battle. He would not listen to what Necho had said at God's command but went to fight him on the plain of Megiddo.

[23]Archers shot King Josiah, and he told his officers, "Take me away; I am badly wounded." [24]So they took him out of his chariot, put him in his other chariot and brought him to Jerusalem, where he died. He was buried in the tombs of his ancestors, and all Judah and Jerusalem mourned for him.

[25]Jeremiah composed laments for Josiah, and to this day all the male and female singers commemorate Josiah in the laments. These became a tradition in Israel and are written in the Laments.

[26]The other events of Josiah's reign and his acts of devotion in accordance with what is written in the Law of the LORD— [27]all the events, from beginning to end, are written

**36** in the book of the kings of Israel and Judah. [1]And the people of the land took Jehoahaz son of Josiah and made him king in Jerusalem in place of his father.

### Jehoahaz King of Judah

[2]Jehoahaz[a] was twenty-three years old when he became king, and he reigned in Jerusalem three months. [3]The king of Egypt dethroned him in Jerusalem and imposed

---

a 2 Hebrew *Joahaz*, a variant of *Jehoahaz*; also in verse 4

## Amplified Bible

families to offer to the Lord, as directed in the Book of Moses. And so they did with the bulls.

[13]And they roasted the Passover lambs with fire according to the ordinance; and they cooked the holy offerings in pots, in caldrons, and in pans and carried them quickly to all the people.

[14]Afterward [the Levites] prepared for themselves and the priests, because the priests, the sons of Aaron, were busy in offering the burnt offerings and the fat until night; so the Levites prepared for themselves and also for the priests, the sons of Aaron.

[15]The singers, the sons of Asaph, were in their places according to the command of David, Asaph, Heman, and Jeduthun the king's seer. And the gatekeepers were at every gate; they did not need to leave their service, for their brethren the Levites prepared for them.

[16]So all the Lord's service was prepared the same day to keep the Passover and to offer burnt offerings upon the Lord's altar, as King Josiah commanded.

[17]And the Israelites who were present kept the Passover at that time, and the Feast of Unleavened Bread for seven days.

[18]No Passover like it had been kept in Israel since the days of Samuel the prophet, even by any of the kings of Israel, as was kept by Josiah and the priests, the Levites, and all Judah and Israel who were present, and the inhabitants of Jerusalem.

[19]In the eighteenth year of the reign of Josiah this Passover was kept.

[20]After all this, when Josiah had prepared the temple, Neco king of Egypt went out to fight against Carchemish on the Euphrates, and Josiah went out against him.

[21]But [Neco] sent ambassadors to [Josiah], saying, What have I to do with you, you king of Judah? I come not against you this day, but against the house with which I am at war; and God has commanded me to make haste. Refrain from opposing God, Who is with me, lest He destroy you.

[22]Yet Josiah would not turn away from him, but disguised himself in order to fight with him. He did not heed the words of Neco from the mouth of God, but came to fight with him in the valley of Megiddo.

[23]And the archers shot King Josiah, and the king said to his servants, Take me away, for I am severely wounded.

[24]So his servants took him out of the chariot and put him in his second chariot and brought him to Jerusalem. And he died and was buried in the tombs of his fathers. All Judah and Jerusalem mourned for Josiah.

[25]Jeremiah gave a lament for Josiah, and all the singing men and women have spoken of Josiah in their laments to this day. They made them an ordinance in Israel; behold, they are written in the Laments. [Lam. 4:20.]

[26]Now the rest of the acts of Josiah and his deeds, according to what is written in the Law of the Lord,

[27]And his acts, from first to last, behold, they are written in the Book of the Kings of Israel and Judah.

**36** Then the people of the land took Jehoahaz son of Josiah and made him king in his father's stead in Jerusalem.

[2]Jehoahaz was [then] twenty-three years old; he reigned three months in Jerusalem.

[3]Then the king of Egypt deposed him at Jerusalem and

## New International Version

on Judah a levy of a hundred talents[a] of silver and a talent[b] of gold. [4]The king of Egypt made Eliakim, a brother of Jehoahaz, king over Judah and Jerusalem and changed Eliakim's name to Jehoiakim. But Necho took Eliakim's brother Jehoahaz and carried him off to Egypt.

### Jehoiakim King of Judah

[5]Jehoiakim was twenty-five years old when he became king, and he reigned in Jerusalem eleven years. He did evil in the eyes of the LORD his God. [6]Nebuchadnezzar king of Babylon attacked him and bound him with bronze shackles to take him to Babylon. [7]Nebuchadnezzar also took to Babylon articles from the temple of the LORD and put them in his temple[c] there.

[8]The other events of Jehoiakim's reign, the detestable things he did and all that was found against him, are written in the book of the kings of Israel and Judah. And Jehoiachin his son succeeded him as king.

### Jehoiachin King of Judah

[9]Jehoiachin was eighteen[d] years old when he became king, and he reigned in Jerusalem three months and ten days. He did evil in the eyes of the LORD. [10]In the spring, King Nebuchadnezzar sent for him and brought him to Babylon, together with articles of value from the temple of the LORD, and he made Jehoiachin's uncle,[e] Zedekiah, king over Judah and Jerusalem.

### Zedekiah King of Judah

[11]Zedekiah was twenty-one years old when he became king, and he reigned in Jerusalem eleven years. [12]He did evil in the eyes of the LORD his God and did not humble himself before Jeremiah the prophet, who spoke the word of the LORD. [13]He also rebelled against King Nebuchadnezzar, who had made him take an oath in God's name. He became stiff-necked and hardened his heart and would not turn to the LORD, the God of Israel. [14]Furthermore, all the leaders of the priests and the people became more and more unfaithful, following all the detestable practices of the nations and defiling the temple of the LORD, which he had consecrated in Jerusalem.

### The Fall of Jerusalem

[15]The LORD, the God of their ancestors, sent word to them through his messengers again and again, because he had pity on his people and on his dwelling place. [16]But they mocked God's messengers, despised his words and scoffed at his prophets until the wrath of the LORD was aroused against his people and there was no remedy. [17]He brought up against them the king of the Babylonians,[f] who killed their young men with the sword in the sanctuary, and did not spare young men or young women, the elderly or the infirm. God gave them all into the hands of Nebuchadnezzar. [18]He carried to Babylon all the articles from the temple of God, both large and small, and the treasures of the LORD's temple and the treasures of the king and his officials. [19]They set fire to God's temple and broke down the wall of Jerusalem; they burned all the palaces and destroyed everything of value there.

[20]He carried into exile to Babylon the remnant, who escaped from the sword, and they became servants to him and his successors until the kingdom of Persia came to power. [21]The land enjoyed its sabbath rests; all the time of its desolation it rested, until the seventy years were completed in fulfillment of the word of the LORD spoken by Jeremiah.

## Amplified Bible

fined the land a hundred talents of silver and a talent of gold.

[4]And the king of Egypt made Eliakim, Jehoahaz' brother, king over Judah and Jerusalem and changed his name to Jehoiakim. But Neco took Jehoahaz his brother and carried him to Egypt.

[5]Jehoiakim was twenty-five years old when he began to reign, and he reigned eleven years in Jerusalem. He did evil in the sight of the Lord his God.

[6]Against him came up Nebuchadnezzar king of Babylon and bound him in fetters to take him to Babylon.

[7]Nebuchadnezzar also took some of the vessels of the house of the Lord to Babylon and put them in his temple or palace there.

[8]Now the rest of the acts of Jehoiakim, and the abominations which he did, and what was found against him, behold, they are written in the Book of the Kings of Israel and Judah. And Jehoiachin his son reigned in his stead.

[9]Jehoiachin was eight[een] years old then; he reigned three months and ten days in Jerusalem. He did evil in the Lord's sight. [II Kings 24:8.]

[10]In the spring, King Nebuchadnezzar sent and brought him to Babylon, with the precious vessels of the house of the Lord, and made Zedekiah the [boy's] brother king over Judah and Jerusalem.

[11]Zedekiah was twenty-one years old when he became king, and he reigned eleven years in Jerusalem.

[12]He did evil in the sight of the Lord his God and did not humble himself before Jeremiah the prophet, who spoke at the dictation of the Lord.

[13]He also rebelled against King Nebuchadnezzar, who made him swear by God. He stiffened his neck and hardened his heart against turning to the Lord, the God of Israel.

[14]Also all the chiefs of the priests and the people trespassed greatly in accord with all the abominations of the heathen, and they polluted the house of the Lord which He had hallowed in Jerusalem.

[15]And the Lord, the God of their fathers, sent to them persistently by His messengers, because He had compassion on His people and on His dwelling place.

[16]But they kept mocking the messengers of God and despising His words and scoffing at His prophets till the wrath of the Lord rose against His people, till there was no remedy or healing.

[17]Therefore He brought against them the king of the Chaldeans, who slew their young men with the sword in the house of their sanctuary, and had no compassion on young man or virgin, old man or hoary-headed; He gave them all into his hand.

[18]And all the vessels of the house of God, great and small, and the treasures of the Lord's house, of the king, and of his princes, all these he brought to Babylon.

[19]And they burned God's house and broke down Jerusalem's wall and burned all its palaces with fire and destroyed all its choice vessels.

[20]Those who had escaped from the sword he took away to Babylon, where they were servants to him and his sons until the kingdom of Persia was established there,

[21]To fulfill the Lord's word by Jeremiah, till the land had enjoyed its sabbaths; for as long as it lay desolate it kept sabbath to fulfill seventy years. [Lev. 25:4; 26:43; Jer. 25:11; 29:10.]

---

[a] 3 That is, about 3 3/4 tons or about 3.4 metric tons    [b] 3 That is, about 75 pounds or about 34 kilograms    [c] 7 Or *palace*    [d] 9 One Hebrew manuscript, some Septuagint manuscripts and Syriac (see also 2 Kings 24:8); most Hebrew manuscripts *eight*    [e] 10 Hebrew *brother*, that is, relative (see 2 Kings 24:17)    [f] 17 Or *Chaldeans*

## New International Version

<sup>22</sup>In the first year of Cyrus king of Persia, in order to fulfill the word of the LORD spoken by Jeremiah, the LORD moved the heart of Cyrus king of Persia to make a proclamation throughout his realm and also to put it in writing:

<sup>23</sup>"This is what Cyrus king of Persia says:

"'The LORD, the God of heaven, has given me all the kingdoms of the earth and he has appointed me to build a temple for him at Jerusalem in Judah. Any of his people among you may go up, and may the LORD their God be with them.'"

## Amplified Bible

<sup>22</sup>Now in the first year of Cyrus king of Persia, that the word of the Lord by the mouth of Jeremiah might be accomplished, the Lord stirred up the spirit of Cyrus king of Persia so that he made a proclamation throughout all his kingdom and also put it in writing:

<sup>23</sup>Thus says Cyrus king of Persia: All the kingdoms of the earth has the Lord, the God of heaven, has given me, and He has charged me to build Him a house in Jerusalem, which is in Judah. Whoever there is among you of all His people, may the Lord his God be with him, and let him go up [to Jerusalem].

## New International Version

# Ezra

### Cyrus Helps the Exiles to Return

**1** In the first year of Cyrus king of Persia, in order to fulfill the word of the LORD spoken by Jeremiah, the LORD moved the heart of Cyrus king of Persia to make a proclamation throughout his realm and also to put it in writing:

² "This is what Cyrus king of Persia says:

"'The LORD, the God of heaven, has given me all the kingdoms of the earth and he has appointed me to build a temple for him at Jerusalem in Judah. ³Any of his people among you may go up to Jerusalem in Judah and build the temple of the LORD, the God of Israel, the God who is in Jerusalem, and may their God be with them. ⁴And in any locality where survivors may now be living, the people are to provide them with silver and gold, with goods and livestock, and with freewill offerings for the temple of God in Jerusalem.'"

⁵Then the family heads of Judah and Benjamin, and the priests and Levites—everyone whose heart God had moved—prepared to go up and build the house of the LORD in Jerusalem. ⁶All their neighbors assisted them with articles of silver and gold, with goods and livestock, and with valuable gifts, in addition to all the freewill offerings.

⁷Moreover, King Cyrus brought out the articles belonging to the temple of the LORD, which Nebuchadnezzar had carried away from Jerusalem and had placed in the temple of his god.ᵃ ⁸Cyrus king of Persia had them brought by Mithredath the treasurer, who counted them out to Sheshbazzar the prince of Judah.

⁹This was the inventory:

| | |
|---|---:|
| gold dishes | 30 |
| silver dishes | 1,000 |
| silver pansᵇ | 29 |
| ¹⁰gold bowls | 30 |
| matching silver bowls | 410 |
| other articles | 1,000 |

¹¹In all, there were 5,400 articles of gold and of silver. Sheshbazzar brought all these along with the exiles when they came up from Babylon to Jerusalem.

### The List of the Exiles Who Returned

**2** Now these are the people of the province who came up from the captivity of the exiles, whom Nebuchadnezzar king of Babylon had taken captive to Babylon (they returned to Jerusalem and Judah, each to their own town, ²in company with Zerubbabel, Joshua, Nehemiah, Seraiah, Reelaiah, Mordecai, Bilshan, Mispar, Bigvai, Rehum and Baanah):

The list of the men of the people of Israel:

| | |
|---|---:|
| ³the descendants of Parosh | 2,172 |
| ⁴of Shephatiah | 372 |

ᵃ 7 Or *gods*    ᵇ 9 The meaning of the Hebrew for this word is uncertain.

## Amplified Bible

THE BOOK OF

# Ezra

**1** Now in the first year of ᵃCyrus king of Persia [almost seventy years after the first Jewish captives were taken to Babylon], that the word of the Lord by the mouth of Jeremiah might begin to be accomplished, the Lord stirred up the spirit of Cyrus king of Persia so that he made a proclamation throughout all his kingdom and put it also in writing: [Jer. 29:10-14.]

²Thus says Cyrus king of Persia: The Lord, the God of heaven, has given me all the kingdoms of the earth, and He has charged me to build Him a house at Jerusalem in Judah.

³Whoever is among you of all His people, may his God be with him, and let him go up to Jerusalem in Judah and rebuild the house of the Lord, the God of Israel, in Jerusalem; He is God.

⁴And in any place where a survivor [of the Babylonian captivity of the Jews] sojourns, let the men of that place assist him with silver and gold, with goods and beasts, besides freewill offerings for the house of God in Jerusalem.

⁵Then rose up the heads of the fathers' houses of Judah and Benjamin, and the priests and Levites, with all those whose spirits God had stirred up, to go up to rebuild the house of the Lord in Jerusalem.

⁶And all those who were around them aided them with vessels of silver, with gold, goods, beasts, and precious things, besides all that was willingly *and* freely offered.

⁷Also Cyrus the king brought out the vessels of the house of the Lord, which Nebuchadnezzar had brought from Jerusalem [when he took that city] and had put in the house of his gods.

⁸These Cyrus king of Persia directed Mithredath the treasurer to bring forth and count out to Sheshbazzar [who is Zerubbabel, recognized as the legitimate heir to the throne of David] the prince of Judah.

⁹And they numbered: 30 basins of gold; 1,000 basins of silver; 29 sacrificial dishes;

¹⁰Of gold bowls, 30; another sort of silver bowl, 410; and other vessels, 1,000.

¹¹All the vessels of gold and of silver were 5,400. All these Sheshbazzar [the governor] brought with the people of the captivity from Babylon to Jerusalem.

**2** Now these are the people of the province [of Judah] who went up out of the captivity of those exiles whom Nebuchadnezzar the king of Babylon had carried away to Babylon, but who came again to Jerusalem and Judah, everyone to his own city.

²These came with Zerubbabel: Jeshua, Nehemiah [not the author], Seraiah, Reelaiah, Mordecai [not Esther's relative], Bilshan, Mispar, Bigvai, Rehum, Baanah. The number of the men of Israel:

³The sons [meaning male descendants] of Parosh, 2,172.

⁴The sons of Shephatiah, 372.

ᵃ Cyrus, a heathen ruler of a heathen empire (Persia), was "twice named [before his birth] in the book of Isaiah as anointed of God and predestined to conquer kings and fortified places and to set the Jews free from captivity (Isa. 44:28; 45:1-14). Daniel . . . records that during the night that followed a great feast, Belshazzar, the king of the Chaldeans, was slain, and Darius the Mede received the kingdom (Dan. 5:30, 31). Darius was the predecessor of Cyrus, or his regent, in Babylonia (Dan. 6:28)" (John D. Davis, *A Dictionary of the Bible*). God gave Cyrus the resolution and the desire to execute His intention. That the Lord at this time chose a heathen as His instrument was in accordance with the new position that the empires of the world were henceforth to assume toward the kingdom of God (J. P. Lange, *A Commentary*).

## New International Version

5 of Arah   775
6 of Pahath-Moab (through the line of
  Jeshua and Joab)   2,812
7 of Elam   1,254
8 of Zattu   945
9 of Zakkai   760
10 of Bani   642
11 of Bebai   623
12 of Azgad   1,222
13 of Adonikam   666
14 of Bigvai   2,056
15 of Adin   454
16 of Ater (through Hezekiah)   98
17 of Bezai   323
18 of Jorah   112
19 of Hashum   223
20 of Gibbar   95

21 the men of Bethlehem   123
22 of Netophah   56
23 of Anathoth   128
24 of Azmaveth   42
25 of Kiriath Jearim,a Kephirah and Beeroth   743
26 of Ramah and Geba   621
27 of Mikmash   122
28 of Bethel and Ai   223
29 of Nebo   52
30 of Magbish   156
31 of the other Elam   1,254
32 of Harim   320
33 of Lod, Hadid and Ono   725
34 of Jericho   345
35 of Senaah   3,630

36 The priests:

the descendants of Jedaiah (through the
  family of Jeshua)   973
37 of Immer   1,052
38 of Pashhur   1,247
39 of Harim   1,017

40 The Levites:

the descendants of Jeshua and Kadmiel
  (of the line of Hodaviah)   74

41 The musicians:

the descendants of Asaph   128

42 The gatekeepers of the temple:

the descendants of
  Shallum, Ater, Talmon,
  Akkub, Hatita and Shobai   139

43 The temple servants:

the descendants of
  Ziha, Hasupha, Tabbaoth,
44 Keros, Siaha, Padon,
45 Lebanah, Hagabah, Akkub,
46 Hagab, Shalmai, Hanan,
47 Giddel, Gahar, Reaiah,
48 Rezin, Nekoda, Gazzam,
49 Uzza, Paseah, Besai,

## Amplified Bible

5 The sons of Arah, 775.
6 The sons of Pahath-moab, namely of the sons of Jeshua and Joab, 2,812.
7 The sons of Elam, 1,254.
8 The sons of Zattu, 945.
9 The sons of Zaccai, 760.
10 The sons of Bani, 642.
11 The sons of Bebai, 623.
12 The sons of Azgad, 1,222.
13 The sons of Adonikam, 666.
14 The sons of Bigvai, 2,056.
15 The sons of Adin, 454.
16 The sons of Ater, namely of Hezekiah, 98.
17 The sons of Bezai, 323.
18 The sons of Jorah, 112.
19 The sons of Hashum, 223.
20 The sons of Gibbar, 95.
21 The sons of Bethlehem, 123.
22 The men of Netophah, 56.
23 The men of Anathoth, 128.
24 The sons of Azmaveth, 42.
25 The sons of Kiriath-arim, Chephirah, and Beeroth, 743.
26 The sons of Ramah and Geba, 621.
27 The men of Michmas, 122.
28 The men of Bethel and Ai, 223.
29 The sons of Nebo, 52.
30 The sons of Magbish, 156.
31 The sons of the other Elam, 1,254.
32 The sons of Harim, 320.
33 The sons of Lod, Hadid, and Ono, 725.
34 The sons of Jericho, 345.
35 The sons of Senaah, 3,630.
36 The priests: the sons of Jedaiah, of the house of Jeshua, 973.
37 The sons of Immer, 1,052.
38 The sons of Pashhur, 1,247.
39 The sons of Harim, 1,017.
40 The Levites: the sons of Jeshua and Kadmiel, of the house of Hodaviah, 74.
41 The singers: the sons of Asaph, 128.
42 The sons of the gatekeepers: of Shallum, Ater, Talmon, Akkub, Hatita, and Shobai, in all 139.
43 The Nethinim [the temple servants]: the sons of Ziba, Hasupha, Tabbaoth,
44 The sons of Keros, Siaha, Padon,
45 The sons of Lebanah, Hagabah, Akkub,
46 The sons of Hagab, Shalmai, Hanan,
47 The sons of Giddel, Gahar, Reaiah,
48 The sons of Rezin, Nekoda, Gazzam,
49 The sons of Uzza, Paseah, Besai,

---

a 25 See Septuagint (see also Neh. 7:29); Hebrew *Kiriath Arim.*

## New International Version

50 Asnah, Meunim, Nephusim,
51 Bakbuk, Hakupha, Harhur,
52 Bazluth, Mehida, Harsha,
53 Barkos, Sisera, Temah,
54 Neziah and Hatipha

55 The descendants of the servants of Solomon:

the descendants of
Sotai, Hassophereth, Peruda,
56 Jaala, Darkon, Giddel,
57 Shephatiah, Hattil,
Pokereth-Hazzebaim and Ami

58 The temple servants and the descendants
of the servants of Solomon      392

59 The following came up from the towns of Tel Me-lah, Tel Harsha, Kerub, Addon and Immer, but they could not show that their families were descended from Israel:

60 The descendants of
Delaiah, Tobiah and Nekoda      652

61 And from among the priests:

The descendants of
Hobaiah, Hakkoz and Barzillai (a man who had married a daughter of Barzillai the Gileadite and was called by that name).

62 These searched for their family records, but they could not find them and so were excluded from the priesthood as unclean. 63 The governor ordered them not to eat any of the most sacred food until there was a priest ministering with the Urim and Thummim.

64 The whole company numbered 42,360, 65 besides their 7,337 male and female slaves; and they also had 200 male and female singers. 66 They had 736 horses, 245 mules, 67 435 camels and 6,720 donkeys.

68 When they arrived at the house of the Lord in Jerusalem, some of the heads of the families gave freewill offerings toward the rebuilding of the house of God on its site. 69 According to their ability they gave to the treasury for this work 61,000 darics[a] of gold, 5,000 minas[b] of silver and 100 priestly garments. 70 The priests, the Levites, the musicians, the gatekeepers and the temple servants settled in their own towns, along with some of the other people, and the rest of the Israelites settled in their towns.

### Rebuilding the Altar

**3** When the seventh month came and the Israelites had settled in their towns, the people assembled together as one in Jerusalem. 2 Then Joshua son of Jozadak and his fellow priests and Zerubbabel son of Shealtiel and his associates began to build the altar of the God of Israel to sacri-

## Amplified Bible

50 The sons of Asnah, Meunim, Nephisim,
51 The sons of Bakbuk, Hakupha, Harhur,
52 The sons of Bazluth, Mehida, Harsha,
53 The sons of Barkos, Sisera, Temah,
54 The sons of Neziah [and] of Hatipha.

55 The sons of [King] Solomon's servants: the sons of Sotai, Sophereth (Hassophereth), Peruda,
56 The sons of Jaalah, Darkon, Giddel,
57 The sons of Shephatiah, Hattil, Pochereth-hazzebaim, Ami.

58 All the Nethinim [the temple servants] and the sons of Solomon's servants were 392.

59 And these were they who came up from Tel-melah, Tel-harsha, Cherub, Addan, and Immer, but they could not show a record of their fathers' houses or prove their descent, whether they were of Israel:

60 The sons of Delaiah, Tobiah, and Nekoda, 652.

61 And of the sons of the priests: the sons of Habaiah, of Hakkoz, and of Barzillai, who had taken a wife from the daughters of Barzillai the [noted] Gileadite and had assumed their name. [II Sam. 17:27, 28; 19:31-39.]

62 These sought their names among those enrolled in the genealogies, but they were not found; so they were excluded from the priesthood as [ceremonially] unclean.

63 [Zerubbabel] the governor told them they should not eat of the most holy things [the priests' food] until there should be a priest with Urim and Thummim [who by consulting these articles in his breastplate could [a]know God's will in the matter].

64 The whole congregation numbered 42,360,
65 Besides their menservants and maidservants, 7,337; and among them they had 200 men and women singers.
66 Their horses were 736; their mules, 245;
67 Their camels were 435; their donkeys, 6,720.
68 Some of the heads of families, when they came to the house of the Lord in Jerusalem, made freewill offerings for the house of God to [re]build it on its site.
69 They gave as they were able to the treasury for the work 61,000 darics of gold, 5,000 minas of silver, and 100 priests' garments.
70 So the priests, the Levites, some of the people, the singers, the gatekeepers, and the temple servants lived in their own towns, and all Israel [gradually settled] into their towns.

**3** When the seventh month came and the Israelites were in the towns, the people gathered together as one man to Jerusalem.
2 Then stood up Jeshua son of Jozadak, and his brethren the priests, and Zerubbabel son of Shealtiel, and his brethren, and they built the altar of the God of Israel to offer

---

a But the effort doubtless would have been in vain. Long-standing disobedience had apparently caused Israel's priests to forfeit the divine gift of guidance through Urim and Thummim, and it was never recovered. Except for a similar incident in Neh. 7:65, Urim and Thummim are not again mentioned in the Scriptures. The higher revelation by the prophets superseded them as interpreters of the will of God (see also Exod. 28:30; Amos 3:7).

---

a 69 That is, about 1,100 pounds or about 500 kilograms    b 69 That is, about 3 tons or about 2.8 metric tons

## New International Version

fice burnt offerings on it, in accordance with what is written in the Law of Moses the man of God. [3]Despite their fear of the peoples around them, they built the altar on its foundation and sacrificed burnt offerings on it to the LORD, both the morning and evening sacrifices. [4]Then in accordance with what is written, they celebrated the Festival of Tabernacles with the required number of burnt offerings prescribed for each day. [5]After that, they presented the regular burnt offerings, the New Moon sacrifices and the sacrifices for all the appointed sacred festivals of the LORD, as well as those brought as freewill offerings to the LORD. [6]On the first day of the seventh month they began to offer burnt offerings to the LORD, though the foundation of the LORD's temple had not yet been laid.

### Rebuilding the Temple

[7]Then they gave money to the masons and carpenters, and gave food and drink and olive oil to the people of Sidon and Tyre, so that they would bring cedar logs by sea from Lebanon to Joppa, as authorized by Cyrus king of Persia. [8]In the second month of the second year after their arrival at the house of God in Jerusalem, Zerubbabel son of Shealtiel, Joshua son of Jozadak and the rest of the people (the priests and the Levites and all who had returned from the captivity to Jerusalem) began the work. They appointed Levites twenty years old and older to supervise the building of the house of the LORD. [9]Joshua and his sons and brothers and Kadmiel and his sons (descendants of Hodaviah[a]) and the sons of Henadad and their sons and brothers—all Levites—joined together in supervising those working on the house of God.

[10]When the builders laid the foundation of the temple of the LORD, the priests in their vestments and with trumpets, and the Levites (the sons of Asaph) with cymbals, took their places to praise the LORD, as prescribed by David king of Israel. [11]With praise and thanksgiving they sang to the LORD:

"He is good;
his love toward Israel endures forever."

And all the people gave a great shout of praise to the LORD, because the foundation of the house of the LORD was laid. [12]But many of the older priests and Levites and family heads, who had seen the former temple, wept aloud when they saw the foundation of this temple being laid, while many others shouted for joy. [13]No one could distinguish the sound of the shouts of joy from the sound of weeping, because the people made so much noise. And the sound was heard far away.

### Opposition to the Rebuilding

**4** When the enemies of Judah and Benjamin heard that the exiles were building a temple for the LORD, the God of Israel, [2]they came to Zerubbabel and to the heads of the families and said, "Let us help you build because,

## Amplified Bible

burnt offerings upon it, as it is written in the [a]instructions of Moses the man of God.

[3]And they set the altar [in its place] upon its base, for fear was upon them because of the peoples of the countries; and they offered burnt offerings on it to the Lord morning and evening.

[4]They kept also the Feast of Tabernacles, as it is written, and offered the daily burnt offerings by number according to the ordinances, as each day's duty required,

[5]And after that, the continual burnt offering, the offering at the New Moon, and at all the appointed feasts of the Lord, and the offerings of everyone who made a freewill offering to the Lord.

[6]From the first day of the seventh month they began to offer burnt offerings to the Lord, but the foundation of the temple of the Lord was not yet laid.

[7]They gave money also to the masons and to the carpenters, and gave food, drink, and oil to the Sidonians and the Tyrians, to bring cedar trees from Lebanon to the seaport of Joppa, according to the grant they had from Cyrus king of Persia.

[8]In the second year of their coming to God's house at Jerusalem, in the second month, Zerubbabel son of Shealtiel and Jeshua son of Jozadak made a beginning, with the rest of their brethren—the priests and Levites and all who had come to Jerusalem out of the captivity. They appointed the Levites from twenty years old and upward to oversee the work of the Lord's house.

[9]Then Jeshua with his sons and his kinsmen, Kadmiel and his sons, sons of Judah, together took the oversight of the workmen in the house of God—the sons of Henadad, with their sons and Levite kinsmen.

[10]And when the builders laid the foundation of the temple of the Lord, the priests stood in their vestments with trumpets, and the Levite sons of Asaph with their cymbals, to praise the Lord, after the order of David king of Israel.

[11]They sang responsively, praising and giving thanks to the Lord, saying, For He is good, for His mercy *and* lovingkindness endure forever toward Israel. And all the people shouted with a great shout when they praised the Lord, because the foundation of the house of the Lord was laid!

[12]But many of the priests and Levites and heads of fathers' houses, old men who had seen the first house [Solomon's temple], when the foundation of this house was laid before their eyes, wept with a loud voice, though many shouted aloud for joy.

[13]So the people could not distinguish the shout of joy from the sound of the weeping of the people, for the people shouted with a loud shout, and the sound was heard far off.

**4** Now when [the Samaritans] the adversaries of Judah and Benjamin heard that the exiles from the captivity were building a temple to the Lord, the God of Israel,

[2]They came to Zerubbabel [now governor] and to the heads of the fathers' houses and said, Let us build with

[a] The Hebrew word here is *torah*, and although usually translated "law," that is only one phase of its meaning, and so to use it, to the exclusion of its fuller sense, may defeat its intended purpose at times. The word *torah* is used more than 200 times in the Old Testament. When capitalized, *Torah* means the whole of the Pentateuch, the five books of Moses. Says *Baker's Dictionary of Theology* (E. F. Harrison et al., eds.), "The Hebrew *torah* originally signified authoritative instruction (Prov. 1:8); hence it most commonly means an 'oracle' or 'word' of the Lord, whether delivered through an accredited spokesman such as Moses, or a prophet or priest. Thus *torah* comes to have the wider sense of 'instruction' (as in RV margin) from God. . . . It is therefore a synonym for the whole of the revealed will of God—the word, commandments, ways, judgments, precepts, etc., of the Lord, as in Gen. 26:5, and especially throughout Ps. 119."

[a] 9 Hebrew *Yehudah*, a variant of *Hodaviah*

## New International Version

like you, we seek your God and have been sacrificing to him since the time of Esarhaddon king of Assyria, who brought us here."

³But Zerubbabel, Joshua and the rest of the heads of the families of Israel answered, "You have no part with us in building a temple to our God. We alone will build it for the LORD, the God of Israel, as King Cyrus, the king of Persia, commanded us."

⁴Then the peoples around them set out to discourage the people of Judah and make them afraid to go on building.[a] ⁵They bribed officials to work against them and frustrate their plans during the entire reign of Cyrus king of Persia and down to the reign of Darius king of Persia.

### Later Opposition Under Xerxes and Artaxerxes

⁶At the beginning of the reign of Xerxes,[b] they lodged an accusation against the people of Judah and Jerusalem.

⁷And in the days of Artaxerxes king of Persia, Bishlam, Mithredath, Tabeel and the rest of his associates wrote a letter to Artaxerxes. The letter was written in Aramaic script and in the Aramaic language.[c,d]

⁸Rehum the commanding officer and Shimshai the secretary wrote a letter against Jerusalem to Artaxerxes the king as follows:

⁹Rehum the commanding officer and Shimshai the secretary, together with the rest of their associates— the judges, officials and administrators over the people from Persia, Uruk and Babylon, the Elamites of Susa, ¹⁰and the other people whom the great and honorable Ashurbanipal deported and settled in the city of Samaria and elsewhere in Trans-Euphrates.

¹¹(This is a copy of the letter they sent him.)

To King Artaxerxes,

From your servants in Trans-Euphrates:

¹²The king should know that the people who came up to us from you have gone to Jerusalem and are rebuilding that rebellious and wicked city. They are restoring the walls and repairing the foundations.

¹³Furthermore, the king should know that if this city is built and its walls are restored, no more taxes, tribute or duty will be paid, and eventually the royal revenues will suffer.[e] ¹⁴Now since we are under obligation to the palace and it is not proper for us to see the king dishonored, we are sending this message to inform the king, ¹⁵so that a search may be made in the archives of your predecessors. In these records you will find that this city is a rebellious city, troublesome to kings and provinces, a place with a long history of sedition. That is why this city was destroyed. ¹⁶We inform the king that if this city is built and its walls are restored, you will be left with nothing in Trans-Euphrates.

¹⁷The king sent this reply:

To Rehum the commanding officer, Shimshai the secretary and the rest of their associates living in Samaria and elsewhere in Trans-Euphrates:

Greetings:

¹⁸The letter you sent us has been read and translated in my presence. ¹⁹I issued an order and a search was made, and it was found that this city has a long history of revolt against kings and has been a place of rebellion and sedition. ²⁰Jerusalem has had powerful kings ruling over the whole of Trans-Euphrates, and taxes, tribute and duty were paid to them. ²¹Now

## Amplified Bible

you, for we seek *and* worship your God as you do, and we have sacrificed to Him since the days of Esarhaddon king of Assyria, who brought us here. [II Kings 17:24-29.]

³But Zerubbabel and Jeshua and the rest of the heads of fathers' houses of Israel said to them, You have nothing to do with us in building a house to our God; but we ourselves will together build to the Lord, the God of Israel, as King Cyrus, the king of Persia, has commanded us.

⁴Then [the Samaritans] the people of the land [continually] weakened the hands of the people of Judah and troubled *and* terrified them in building

⁵And hired counselors against them to frustrate their purpose *and* plans all the days of Cyrus king of Persia, even until the reign of Darius [II] king of Persia.

⁶And in the reign of Ahasuerus [or Xerxes], in the beginning of his reign, [the Samaritans] wrote to him an accusation against the [returned] inhabitants of Judah and Jerusalem.

⁷Later, in the days of King Artaxerxes, Bishlam, Mithredath, Tabeel, and the rest of their associates wrote to Artaxerxes king of Persia; and the letter was written in the Syrian *or* Aramaic script and interpreted in that language.

⁸Rehum the [Persian] commander [of the Samaritans] and Shimshai the scribe wrote a letter against Jerusalem to Artaxerxes the king of this sort—

⁹Then wrote Rehum the [Persian] commander, Shimshai the scribe, and the rest of their associates—the Dinaites, the Apharsathchites, the Tarpelites, the Apharsites, the Archevites, the Babylonians, the Susanchites, the Dehaites, the Elamites,

¹⁰And the rest of the nations whom the great and noble Osnappar deported and settled in the city of Samaria and the rest of the country beyond [west of] the Euphrates River, and so forth.

¹¹This is a copy of the letter which they sent to King Artaxerxes: Your servants, the men beyond [that is, west of] the River [Euphrates], and so forth.

¹²Be it known to the king that the Jews who came up from you to us have come to Jerusalem. This rebellious and bad city they are rebuilding, and have restored its walls and repaired the foundations.

¹³Be it known now to the king that if this city is rebuilt and the walls finished, then they will not pay tribute, custom, or toll, and the royal revenue will be diminished.

¹⁴Now because we eat the salt of the king's palace and it is not proper for us to witness the king's discredit, therefore we send to inform the king,

¹⁵In order that a search may be made in the book of the records of your fathers, in which you will learn that this is a rebellious city, hurtful to kings and provinces, and that sedition was stirred up in it of old. That is why [it] was laid waste.

¹⁶We declare to the king that if this city is rebuilt and its walls finished, it will mean that you will have no portion on this side of the [Euphrates] River.

¹⁷Then the king sent an answer: To Rehum the [Persian] official, to Shimshai the scribe, to the rest of their companions who dwell in Samaria and in the rest of the country beyond the River: Greetings.

¹⁸The letter which you sent to us has been plainly read before me.

¹⁹I commanded and search has been made, and it is found that this city [Jerusalem] of old time has made insurrection against kings and that rebellion and sedition have been made in it.

²⁰There have been mighty kings also over Jerusalem who have ruled over all countries beyond [west of] the [Euphrates] River, and tribute, custom, and toll were paid to them.

---

[a] 4 Or *and troubled them as they built*   [b] 6 Hebrew *Ahasuerus*
[c] 7 Or *written in Aramaic and translated*   [d] 7 The text of 4:8–6:18 is in Aramaic.   [e] 13 The meaning of the Aramaic for this clause is uncertain.

## New International Version

issue an order to these men to stop work, so that this city will not be rebuilt until I so order. [22]Be careful not to neglect this matter. Why let this threat grow, to the detriment of the royal interests?

[23]As soon as the copy of the letter of King Artaxerxes was read to Rehum and Shimshai the secretary and their associates, they went immediately to the Jews in Jerusalem and compelled them by force to stop.

[24]Thus the work on the house of God in Jerusalem came to a standstill until the second year of the reign of Darius king of Persia.

### Tattenai's Letter to Darius

**5** Now Haggai the prophet and Zechariah the prophet, a descendant of Iddo, prophesied to the Jews in Judah and Jerusalem in the name of the God of Israel, who was over them. [2]Then Zerubbabel son of Shealtiel and Joshua son of Jozadak set to work to rebuild the house of God in Jerusalem. And the prophets of God were with them, supporting them. [3]At that time Tattenai, governor of Trans-Euphrates, and Shethar-Bozenai and their associates went to them and asked, "Who authorized you to rebuild this temple and to finish it?"[a] [4]They[a] also asked, "What are the names of those who are constructing this building?" [5]But the eye of their God was watching over the elders of the Jews, and they were not stopped until a report could go to Darius and his written reply be received.

[6]This is a copy of the letter that Tattenai, governor of Trans-Euphrates, and Shethar-Bozenai and their associates, the officials of Trans-Euphrates, sent to King Darius. [7]The report they sent him read as follows:

To King Darius:

Cordial greetings.

[8]The king should know that we went to the district of Judah, to the temple of the great God. The people are building it with large stones and placing the timbers in the walls. The work is being carried on with diligence and is making rapid progress under their direction.

[9]We questioned the elders and asked them, "Who authorized you to rebuild this temple and to finish it?" [10]We also asked them their names, so that we could write down the names of their leaders for your information.

[11]This is the answer they gave us:

"We are the servants of the God of heaven and earth, and we are rebuilding the temple that was built many years ago, one that a great king of Israel built and finished. [12]But because our ancestors angered the God of heaven, he gave them into the hands of Nebuchadnezzar the Chaldean, king of Babylon, who destroyed this temple and deported the people to Babylon.

[13]"However, in the first year of Cyrus king of Babylon, King Cyrus issued a decree to rebuild this house of God. [14]He even removed from the temple[b] of Babylon the gold and silver articles of the house of God, which Nebuchadnezzar had taken from the temple in Jerusalem and brought to the temple[b] in Babylon. Then King Cyrus gave them to a man named Sheshbazzar, whom he had appointed governor,

## Amplified Bible

[21]Therefore give a decree to make these men stop, that this city not be rebuilt, until a command is given by me. [22]Be sure that you do this. Why should damage grow, to the hurt of the kings?

[23]When the copy of King Artaxerxes' letter was read before Rehum, Shimshai the scribe, and their companions, they went up in haste to Jerusalem to the Jews and by force and power made them cease.

[24]Then the [a]work on the house of God in Jerusalem stopped. It stopped until the second year of Darius [I] king of Persia.

**5** Now the prophets, Haggai and Zechariah son [grandson] of Iddo, prophesied to the Jews in Judah and Jerusalem in the name of the God of Israel, Whose [Spirit] was upon them.

[2]Then rose up Zerubbabel son of Shealtiel [heir to the throne of Judah] and Jeshua son of Jozadak and began to build the house of God in Jerusalem; and with them were the prophets of God [Haggai and Zechariah], helping them. [Hag. 1:12-14; Matt. 1:12, 13.]

[3]Then Tattenai, governor on the west side of the [Euphrates] River, and Shethar-bozenai and their companions came to them and said, Who [b]authorized you to build this house and to restore this wall?

[4]Then we told them [in reply] the names of the men who were building this building.

[5]But the eye of their God was upon the elders of the Jews, so the enemy could not make them stop until the matter came before Darius [I] and an answer was returned by letter concerning it.

[6]This is a copy of the letter that Tattenai, governor on this side of the River, and Shethar-bozenai and his associates, the Apharsachites who were on this [west] side of the River, sent to Darius [I] the king.

[7]They wrote: To Darius the king: All peace.

[8]Be it known to the king that we went to the province of Judah, to the house of the great God. It is being built with huge stones, with timber laid in the walls; this work goes on with diligence *and* care and prospers in their hands.

[9]Then we asked those elders, Who authorized you to build this house and restore these walls?

[10]We asked their names also, that we might record the names of the men at their head and notify you.

[11]They replied, We are servants of the God of heaven and earth, rebuilding the house which was erected and finished many years ago by a great king of Israel.

[12]But after our fathers had provoked the God of heaven to wrath, He gave them into the hand of Nebuchadnezzar king of Babylon, the Chaldean, who destroyed this house and carried the people away into Babylon.

[13]But in the first year of Cyrus king of Babylon, the same King Cyrus made a decree to rebuild this house of God.

[14]And the vessels also of gold and silver of the house of God, which Nebuchadnezzar took from the temple in Jerusalem and brought into the temple of Babylon, King Cyrus took from the temple of Babylon and delivered to a man named Sheshbazzar, whom he had made governor.

---

[a] The long digression in Ezra 4:6-23 describes later opposition to Jewish efforts to restore the walls and rebuild the city during the reigns of Xerxes (486-465 B.C.) and Artaxerxes I (465-424). Here in Ezra 4:24 Ezra reverts back to the time of Darius I (522-486) and the rebuilding of the temple, which ceased because of the discouragement described in Ezra 4:4-5, resumed again (Ezra 5:2), and was completed in the sixth year of the reign of Darius I (Ezra 6:15). [b] Seventeen or eighteen years had elapsed since Cyrus issued his decree. One other king had succeeded him. The second, Darius [I], was just assuring his position upon the throne after two years of incessant warring, and it was entirely possible that during this interval the affairs of a comparatively unimportant city . . . may well have been almost forgotten (*The Cambridge Bible*).

---

[a] 4 See Septuagint; Aramaic *We*.    [b] 14 Or *palace*

## New International Version

15and he told him, 'Take these articles and go and deposit them in the temple in Jerusalem. And rebuild the house of God on its site.'

16"So this Sheshbazzar came and laid the foundations of the house of God in Jerusalem. From that day to the present it has been under construction but is not yet finished."

17Now if it pleases the king, let a search be made in the royal archives of Babylon to see if King Cyrus did in fact issue a decree to rebuild this house of God in Jerusalem. Then let the king send us his decision in this matter.

### The Decree of Darius

**6** King Darius then issued an order, and they searched in the archives stored in the treasury at Babylon. 2A scroll was found in the citadel of Ecbatana in the province of Media, and this was written on it:

Memorandum:

3In the first year of King Cyrus, the king issued a decree concerning the temple of God in Jerusalem:

Let the temple be rebuilt as a place to present sacrifices, and let its foundations be laid. It is to be sixty cubits*a* high and sixty cubits wide, 4with three courses of large stones and one of timbers. The costs are to be paid by the royal treasury. 5Also, the gold and silver articles of the house of God, which Nebuchadnezzar took from the temple in Jerusalem and brought to Babylon, are to be returned to their places in the temple in Jerusalem; they are to be deposited in the house of God.

6Now then, Tattenai, governor of Trans-Euphrates, and Shethar-Bozenai and you other officials of that province, stay away from there. 7Do not interfere with the work on this temple of God. Let the governor of the Jews and the Jewish elders rebuild this house of God on its site.

8Moreover, I hereby decree what you are to do for these elders of the Jews in the construction of this house of God:

Their expenses are to be fully paid out of the royal treasury, from the revenues of Trans-Euphrates, so that the work will not stop. 9Whatever is needed—young bulls, rams, male lambs for burnt offerings to the God of heaven, and wheat, salt, wine and olive oil, as requested by the priests in Jerusalem—must be given them daily without fail, 10so that they may offer sacrifices pleasing to the God of heaven and pray for the well-being of the king and his sons.

11Furthermore, I decree that if anyone defies this edict, a beam is to be pulled from their house and they are to be impaled on it. And for this crime their house is to be made a pile of rubble. 12May God, who has caused his Name to dwell there, overthrow any king or people who lifts a hand to change this decree or to destroy this temple in Jerusalem.

I Darius have decreed it. Let it be carried out with diligence.

### Completion and Dedication of the Temple

13Then, because of the decree King Darius had sent, Tattenai, governor of Trans-Euphrates, and Shethar-Bozenai and their associates carried it out with diligence. 14So the elders of the Jews continued to build and prosper under the preaching of Haggai the prophet and Zechariah, a descendant of Iddo. They finished building the temple according to the command of the God of Israel and the decrees of Cyrus, Darius and Artaxerxes, kings of Persia.

*a 3 That is, about 90 feet or about 27 meters*

## Amplified Bible

15And King Cyrus said to him, Go, take these vessels to Jerusalem and carry them into the temple, and let the house of God be built upon its site.

16Then came this Sheshbazzar and laid the foundation of the house of God in Jerusalem; and since that time until now it has been in the process of being rebuilt and is not completed yet.

17So now, if it seems good to the king, let a search be made in the royal archives there in Babylon to see if it is true that King Cyrus issued a decree to build this house of God at Jerusalem; and let the king send us his pleasure in this matter.

**6** Then King Darius [I] decreed, and a search was made in Babylonia in the house where the treasured records were stored.

2And at Ecbatana in the capital in the province of Media, a scroll was found on which this was recorded:

3In the first year of King Cyrus, [he] made a decree: Concerning the house of God in Jerusalem, let the house, the place where they offer sacrifices, be built, and let its foundations be strongly laid, its height and its breadth each 60 cubits,

4With three courses of great stones and one course of new timber. Let the cost be paid from the royal treasury.

5Also let the gold and silver vessels of the house of God, which Nebuchadnezzar took from the temple in Jerusalem and brought to Babylon, be restored and brought back to the temple in Jerusalem, each put in its place in the house of God.

6Now therefore, Tattenai, governor of the province [west of] the River, Shethar-bozenai, and your associates, the Apharsachites who are [west of] the River, keep far away from there.

7Leave the work on this house of God alone; let the governor and the elders of the Jews build this house of God on its site.

8Moreover, I make a decree as to what you shall do for these elders of the Jews for the rebuilding of this house of God: the cost is to be paid in full to these men at once from the king's revenue, the tribute of the province [west of] the River, that they may not be hindered.

9And all they need, including young bulls, rams, and lambs for the burnt offerings to the God of heaven, and wheat, salt, wine, and oil, according to the word of the priests at Jerusalem, let it be given them each day without fail,

10That they may offer pleasing sacrifices to the God of heaven and pray for the life of the king and his sons.

11Also I make a decree that whoever shall change or infringe on this order, let a beam be pulled from his house and erected; then let him be fastened to it, and let his house be made a dunghill for this.

12May the God Who has caused His *a*Name to dwell there overthrow all kings and peoples who put forth their hands to alter this or to destroy this house of God in Jerusalem. I Darius make a decree; let it be executed speedily *and* exactly.

13Then Tattenai, governor of the province this side of the River, with Shethar-bozenai and their associates, diligently did what King Darius had decreed.

14And the elders of the Jews built and prospered through the prophesying of Haggai the prophet and Zechariah son of Iddo. They finished their building as commanded by the God of Israel and by decree of Cyrus and Darius and Artaxerxes king of Persia.

*a See footnote on Deut. 12:5.*

## New International Version

¹⁵The temple was completed on the third day of the month Adar, in the sixth year of the reign of King Darius.

¹⁶Then the people of Israel—the priests, the Levites and the rest of the exiles—celebrated the dedication of the house of God with joy. ¹⁷For the dedication of this house of God they offered a hundred bulls, two hundred rams, four hundred male lambs and, as a sin offering*a* for all Israel, twelve male goats, one for each of the tribes of Israel. ¹⁸And they installed the priests in their divisions and the Levites in their groups for the service of God at Jerusalem, according to what is written in the Book of Moses.

### The Passover

¹⁹On the fourteenth day of the first month, the exiles celebrated the Passover. ²⁰The priests and Levites had purified themselves and were all ceremonially clean. The Levites slaughtered the Passover lamb for all the exiles, for their relatives the priests and for themselves. ²¹So the Israelites who had returned from the exile ate it, together with all who had separated themselves from the unclean practices of their Gentile neighbors in order to seek the LORD, the God of Israel. ²²For seven days they celebrated with joy the Festival of Unleavened Bread, because the LORD had filled them with joy by changing the attitude of the king of Assyria so that he assisted them in the work on the house of God, the God of Israel.

### Ezra Comes to Jerusalem

**7** After these things, during the reign of Artaxerxes king of Persia, Ezra son of Seraiah, the son of Azariah, the son of Hilkiah, ²the son of Shallum, the son of Zadok, the son of Ahitub, ³the son of Amariah, the son of Azariah, the son of Meraioth, ⁴the son of Zerahiah, the son of Uzzi, the son of Bukki, ⁵the son of Abishua, the son of Phinehas, the son of Eleazar, the son of Aaron the chief priest— ⁶this Ezra came up from Babylon. He was a teacher well versed in the Law of Moses, which the LORD, the God of Israel, had given. The king had granted him everything he asked, for the hand of the LORD his God was on him. ⁷Some of the Israelites, including priests, Levites, musicians, gatekeepers and temple servants, also came up to Jerusalem in the seventh year of King Artaxerxes.

⁸Ezra arrived in Jerusalem in the fifth month of the seventh year of the king. ⁹He had begun his journey from Babylon on the first day of the first month, and he arrived in Jerusalem on the first day of the fifth month, for the gracious hand of his God was on him. ¹⁰For Ezra had devoted himself to the study and observance of the Law of the LORD, and to teaching its decrees and laws in Israel.

## Amplified Bible

¹⁵And this house was finished on the third day of the month of Adar, in the sixth year of the reign of King Darius.

¹⁶And the Israelites—the priests, the Levites, and the rest of the returned exiles—celebrated the dedication of this house of God with joy.

¹⁷They offered at the dedication of this house of God 100 young bulls, 200 rams, 400 lambs, and, for a sin offering for all Israel, 12 he-goats, according to the number of Israel's tribes.

¹⁸And they set the priests in their divisions and the Levites in their courses for the service of God at Jerusalem, as it is written in the Book of Moses.

¹⁹The returned exiles kept the Passover on the fourteenth day of the first month.

²⁰For the priests and the Levites had purified themselves together; all of them were clean. So they killed the Passover lamb for all the returned exiles, for their brother priests, and for themselves.

²¹It was eaten by the Israelites who had returned from exile and by all who had joined them and separated themselves from the pollutions of the peoples of the land to seek the Lord, the God of Israel.

²²They kept the Feast of Unleavened Bread for seven days with joy, for the Lord had made them joyful and had turned the heart of the king of Assyria [referring to Darius king of Persia] to them, so that he strengthened their hands in the work of the house of God, the God of Israel.

**7** Now *a*after this, in the reign of Artaxerxes [son of Xerxes, or Ahasuerus] king of Persia, Ezra son of Seraiah, the son of Azariah, the son of Hilkiah,

²The son of Shallum, the son of Zadok, the son of Ahitub,

³The son of Amariah, the son of Azariah, the son of Meraioth,

⁴The son of Zerahiah, the son of Uzzi, the son of Bukki,

⁵The son of Abishua, the son of Phinehas, the son of Eleazar, the son of Aaron the chief priest—

⁶This Ezra went up from Babylon. He was a skilled scribe in the five books of Moses, which the Lord, the God of Israel, had given. And the king granted him all he asked, for the hand of the Lord his God was upon him.

⁷And also some of the Israelites, with some of the priests and Levites, the singers and gatekeepers, and the temple servants, went up [from Babylon] to Jerusalem in the seventh year of King Artaxerxes.

⁸Ezra came to Jerusalem in the fifth month of the seventh year of the king.

⁹On the first of the first month he started out from Babylon, and on the first of the fifth month he arrived in Jerusalem, for upon him was the good hand of his God.

¹⁰For Ezra had *b*prepared *and* set his heart to seek the Law of the Lord [to inquire for it and of it, to require and yearn for it], and to do and teach in Israel its statutes and its ordinances.

---

*a* There is about a sixty-year silence in the book of Ezra between chapters six and seven, including the years 516-458 B.C. It is during this time that events of the book of Esther took place. The Ahasuerus of the book of Esther is identified with the Xerxes who invaded Greece, was stopped at Thermopylae, defeated at the naval battle at Salamis, and nearly annihilated at Plataea (479 B.C.). The French excavations at Susa in 1880-1890 disclosed the great palace of Xerxes (Ahasuerus), where Esther would have lived. The building covered two and one-half acres. The finds at Susa from this period were so astonishing that the Louvre in Paris devoted two large rooms to the exhibition of the treasures (J. P. Free, *Archaeology and Bible History*). *b* God can use mightily one whose whole heart craves a knowledge of Him and His Word like that. Watch Ezra throughout the remainder of his story, as he turns the homes of his nation back from heathendom to God—in the pouring rain! He was not merely righteous, he was "[uncompromisingly] righteous" (I Kings 8:32); he worshiped God, Who is not merely just and righteous, but "rigidly just *and* righteous" (Ezra 9:15.)

---

# New International Version

## King Artaxerxes' Letter to Ezra

[11]This is a copy of the letter King Artaxerxes had given to Ezra the priest, a teacher of the Law, a man learned in matters concerning the commands and decrees of the LORD for Israel:

[12]Artaxerxes, king of kings,

To Ezra the priest, teacher of the Law of the God of heaven:

Greetings.

[13]Now I decree that any of the Israelites in my kingdom, including priests and Levites, who volunteer to go to Jerusalem with you, may go. [14]You are sent by the king and his seven advisers to inquire about Judah and Jerusalem with regard to the Law of your God, which is in your hand. [15]Moreover, you are to take with you the silver and gold that the king and his advisers have freely given to the God of Israel, whose dwelling is in Jerusalem, [16]together with all the silver and gold you may obtain from the province of Babylon, as well as the freewill offerings of the people and priests for the temple of their God in Jerusalem. [17]With this money be sure to buy bulls, rams and male lambs, together with their grain offerings and drink offerings, and sacrifice them on the altar of the temple of your God in Jerusalem.

[18]You and your fellow Israelites may then do whatever seems best with the rest of the silver and gold, in accordance with the will of your God. [19]Deliver to the God of Jerusalem all the articles entrusted to you for worship in the temple of your God. [20]And anything else needed for the temple of your God that you are responsible to supply, you may provide from the royal treasury.

[21]Now I, King Artaxerxes, decree that all the treasurers of Trans-Euphrates are to provide with diligence whatever Ezra the priest, the teacher of the Law of the God of heaven, may ask of you— [22]up to a hundred talents[a] of silver, a hundred cors[b] of wheat, a hundred baths[c] of wine, a hundred baths[c] of olive oil, and salt without limit. [23]Whatever the God of heaven has prescribed, let it be done with diligence for the temple of the God of heaven. Why should his wrath fall on the realm of the king and of his sons? [24]You are also to know that you have no authority to impose taxes, tribute or duty on any of the priests, Levites, musicians, gatekeepers, temple servants or other workers at this house of God. [25]And you, Ezra, in accordance with the wisdom of your God, which you possess, appoint magistrates and judges to administer justice to all the people of Trans-Euphrates—all who know the laws of your God. And you are to teach any who do not know them. [26]Whoever does not obey the law of your God and the law of the king must surely be punished by death, banishment, confiscation of property, or imprisonment.[d]

[27]Praise be to the LORD, the God of our ancestors, who has put it into the king's heart to bring honor to the house of the LORD in Jerusalem in this way [28]and who has extended his good favor to me before the king and his advisers and all the king's powerful officials. Because the hand of the LORD my God was on me, I took courage and gathered leaders from Israel to go up with me.

# Amplified Bible

[11]Now this is the copy of the letter that King Artaxerxes gave to Ezra the priest, the scribe, even a scribe [occupied with] the words of the commands of the Lord and of His statutes to Israel:

[12]Artaxerxes, king of kings, to Ezra the priest, scribe of the instructions of the God of heaven: Greetings.

[13]I make a decree that all of the people of Israel and of their priests and Levites in my realm, who offer freely to go up to Jerusalem, may go with you.

[14]For you are sent by the king and his seven counselors to inquire about Judah and Jerusalem according to the instruction of your God, which is in your hand,

[15]And to carry the silver and gold which the king and his counselors have freely offered to the God of Israel, Whose dwelling is in Jerusalem,

[16]And all the silver and gold that you may find in all the province of Babylonia, with the freewill offerings of the people and of the priests, offered willingly for the house of their God in Jerusalem.

[17]Therefore you shall with all speed *and* exactness buy with this money young bulls, rams, lambs, with their cereal offerings and drink offerings, and offer them on the altar of the house of your God in Jerusalem.

[18]And whatever shall seem good to you and to your brethren to do with the rest of the silver and the gold, that do after the will of your God.

[19]The vessels also that are given to you for the service of the house of your God, those deliver before the God of Jerusalem.

[20]And whatever more shall be needful for the house of your God which you shall have occasion to provide, provide it out of the king's treasury.

[21]And I, Artaxerxes the king, make a decree to all the treasurers in the province beyond the [Euphrates] River that whatever Ezra the priest, the scribe of the instructions of the God of heaven, shall require of you, it shall be done exactly *and* at once—

[22]Up to 100 talents of silver, 100 measures of wheat, 100 baths of wine, 100 baths of oil, and salt not specified.

[23]Whatever is commanded by the God of heaven, let it be done diligently *and* honorably for the house of the God of heaven, lest His wrath be against the realm of the king and his sons.

[24]Also we notify you that as to any of the priests and Levites, singers, gatekeepers, temple servants, or other servants of this house of God, it shall not be lawful to impose tribute, custom, or toll on them.

[25]You, Ezra, after the wisdom of your God, which is [in His instructions] in your hand, set magistrates and judges who may judge all the people [west] of the River; choose those who know the instructions of your God, and teach him who does not know them.

[26]And whoever will not do the law of your God and the law of the king, let judgment be executed upon him exactly *and* speedily, whether it be unto death or banishment or confiscation of goods or imprisonment.

[27]Blessed be the Lord, the God of our fathers [said Ezra], Who put such a thing as this into the king's heart, to beautify the house of the Lord in Jerusalem,

[28]And Who has extended His mercy *and* steadfast love to me before the king, his counselors, and all the king's mighty officers. I was strengthened and encouraged, for the hand of the Lord my God was upon me, and I gathered together outstanding men of Israel to go with me to Jerusalem.

---

[a] 22 That is, about 3 3/4 tons or about 3.4 metric tons    [b] 22 That is, probably about 18 tons or about 16 metric tons    [c] 22 That is, about 600 gallons or about 2,200 liters    [d] 26 The text of 7:12-26 is in Aramaic.

## New International Version

### List of the Family Heads Returning With Ezra

**8** These are the family heads and those registered with them who came up with me from Babylon during the reign of King Artaxerxes:

[2] of the descendants of Phinehas, Gershom;

of the descendants of Ithamar, Daniel;

of the descendants of David, Hattush [3] of the descendants of Shekaniah;

of the descendants of Parosh, Zechariah, and with him were registered 150 men;

[4] of the descendants of Pahath-Moab, Eliehoenai son of Zerahiah, and with him 200 men;

[5] of the descendants of Zattu,[a] Shekaniah son of Jahaziel, and with him 300 men;

[6] of the descendants of Adin, Ebed son of Jonathan, and with him 50 men;

[7] of the descendants of Elam, Jeshaiah son of Athaliah, and with him 70 men;

[8] of the descendants of Shephatiah, Zebadiah son of Michael, and with him 80 men;

[9] of the descendants of Joab, Obadiah son of Jehiel, and with him 218 men;

[10] of the descendants of Bani,[b] Shelomith son of Josiphiah, and with him 160 men;

[11] of the descendants of Bebai, Zechariah son of Bebai, and with him 28 men;

[12] of the descendants of Azgad, Johanan son of Hakkatan, and with him 110 men;

[13] of the descendants of Adonikam, the last ones, whose names were Eliphelet, Jeuel and Shemaiah, and with them 60 men;

[14] of the descendants of Bigvai, Uthai and Zakkur, and with him 70 men.

### The Return to Jerusalem

[15] I assembled them at the canal that flows toward Ahava, and we camped there three days. When I checked among the people and the priests, I found no Levites there. [16] So I summoned Eliezer, Ariel, Shemaiah, Elnathan, Jarib, Elnathan, Nathan, Zechariah and Meshullam, who were leaders, and Joiarib and Elnathan, who were men of learning, [17] and I ordered them to go to Iddo, the leader in Kasiphia. I told them what to say to Iddo and his fellow Levites, the temple servants in Kasiphia, so that they might bring attendants to us for the house of our God. [18] Because the gracious hand of our God was on us, they brought us Sherebiah, a capable man, from the descendants of Mahli son of Levi, the son of Israel, and Sherebiah's sons and brothers, 18 in all; [19] and Hashabiah, together with Jeshaiah from the descendants of Merari, and his brothers and nephews, 20 in all. [20] They also brought 220 of the temple servants—a body that David and the officials had established to assist the Levites. All were registered by name.

[21] There, by the Ahava Canal, I proclaimed a fast, so that we might humble ourselves before our God and ask him for a safe journey for us and our children, with all our possessions. [22] I was ashamed to ask the king for soldiers and horsemen to protect us from enemies on the road, because we had told the king, "The gracious hand of our God is on everyone who looks to him, but his great anger is against all who forsake him." [23] So we fasted and petitioned our God about this, and he answered our prayer.

[24] Then I set apart twelve of the leading priests, namely, Sherebiah, Hashabiah and ten of their brothers, [25] and I weighed out to them the offering of silver and gold and the articles that the king, his advisers, his officials and

## Amplified Bible

**8** These are the heads of their fathers' houses and this is the genealogy of those who went up with me from Babylonia in the reign of King Artaxerxes:

[2] Of the sons of Phinehas, Gershom; of Ithamar, Daniel; of David, Hattush

[3] Of the sons of Shecaniah; of the sons of Parosh, Zechariah, and with him were registered 150 men by genealogy;

[4] Of the sons of Pahath-moab, Eliehoenai son of Zerahiah, with 200 men;

[5] Of the sons of Zattu, Shecaniah son of Jahaziel, with 300 men;

[6] Of the sons of Adin, Ebed son of Jonathan, with 50 men;

[7] Of the sons of Elam, Jeshaiah son of Athaliah, with 70 men;

[8] Of the sons of Shephatiah, Zebadiah son of Michael, with 80 men;

[9] Of the sons of Joab, Obadiah son of Jehiel, with 218 men;

[10] Of the sons of [Bani], Shelomith son of Josiphiah, with 160 men;

[11] Of the sons of Bebai, Zechariah son of Bebai, with 28 men;

[12] Of the sons of Azgad, Johanan son of Hakkatan, with 110 men;

[13] Of the sons of Adonikam, the last to come, their names are Eliphelet, Jeuel, and Shemaiah, with 60 men;

[14] Of the sons of Bigvai, Uthai and Zabbud [Zaccur], with 70 men.

[15] I [Ezra] gathered them together at the river that runs to Ahava, and there we encamped three days. I reviewed the people and the priests, and found no Levites. [16] Then I sent for Eliezer, Ariel, Shemaiah, Elnathan, Jarib, Elnathan, Nathan, Zechariah, Meshullam, who were chief men, and also for Joiarib and Elnathan, who were teachers. [17] And I sent them to Iddo, the leading man at the place Casiphia, telling them to say to Iddo and his brethren the Nethinim [temple servants] at the place Casiphia, Bring to us servants for the house of our God. [18] And by the good hand of our God upon us, they brought us a man of understanding, of the sons of Mahli son of Levi, the son of Israel, named Sherebiah, with his sons and his kinsmen, 18; [19] And Hashabiah, and with him Jeshaiah of the sons of Merari, with his kinsmen and their sons, 20; [20] Also 220 of the Nethinim, whose forefathers David and the officials had set apart [with their descendants] to attend the Levites. They were all mentioned by name. [21] Then I proclaimed a fast there, at the river Ahava, that we might humble ourselves before our God to seek from Him a straight *and* right way for us, our little ones, and all our possessions. [22] For I was ashamed to request of the king a band of soldiers and horsemen to protect us against the enemy along the way, because we had told the king, The hand of our God is upon all them for good who seek Him, but His power and His wrath are against all those who forsake Him. [23] So we fasted and besought our God for this, and He heard our entreaty. [24] Then I set apart twelve leading priests, Sherebiah, Hashabiah, and ten of their kinsmen, [25] And weighed out to them the silver, the gold, and the vessels, the offering for the house of our God which the

---

a 5 Some Septuagint manuscripts (also 1 Esdras 8:32); Hebrew does not have *Zattu*.    b 10 Some Septuagint manuscripts (also 1 Esdras 8:36); Hebrew does not have *Bani*.

## New International Version

all Israel present there had donated for the house of our God. ²⁶I weighed out to them 650 talents*ᵃ* of silver, silver articles weighing 100 talents,*ᵇ* 100 talents*ᵇ* of gold, ²⁷20 bowls of gold valued at 1,000 darics,*ᶜ* and two fine articles of polished bronze, as precious as gold.

²⁸I said to them, "You as well as these articles are consecrated to the LORD. The silver and gold are a freewill offering to the LORD, the God of your ancestors. ²⁹Guard them carefully until you weigh them out in the chambers of the house of the LORD in Jerusalem before the leading priests and the Levites and the family heads of Israel." ³⁰Then the priests and Levites received the silver and gold and sacred articles that had been weighed out to be taken to the house of our God in Jerusalem.

³¹On the twelfth day of the first month we set out from the Ahava Canal to go to Jerusalem. The hand of our God was on us, and he protected us from enemies and bandits along the way. ³²So we arrived in Jerusalem, where we rested three days.

³³On the fourth day, in the house of our God, we weighed out the silver and gold and the sacred articles into the hands of Meremoth son of Uriah, the priest. Eleazar son of Phinehas was with him, and so were the Levites Jozabad son of Jeshua and Noadiah son of Binnui. ³⁴Everything was accounted for by number and weight, and the entire weight was recorded at that time.

³⁵Then the exiles who had returned from captivity sacrificed burnt offerings to the God of Israel: twelve bulls for all Israel, ninety-six rams, seventy-seven male lambs, as a sin offering,*ᵈ* twelve male goats. All this was a burnt offering to the LORD. ³⁶They also delivered the king's orders to the royal satraps and to the governors of Trans-Euphrates, who then gave assistance to the people and to the house of God.

### Ezra's Prayer About Intermarriage

**9** After these things had been done, the leaders came to me and said, "The people of Israel, including the priests and the Levites, have not kept themselves separate from the neighboring peoples with their detestable practices, like those of the Canaanites, Hittites, Perizzites, Jebusites, Ammonites, Moabites, Egyptians and Amorites. ²They have taken some of their daughters as wives for themselves and their sons, and have mingled the holy race with the peoples around them. And the leaders and officials have led the way in this unfaithfulness."

³When I heard this, I tore my tunic and cloak, pulled hair from my head and beard and sat down appalled. ⁴Then everyone who trembled at the words of the God of Israel gathered around me because of this unfaithfulness of the exiles. And I sat there appalled until the evening sacrifice.

⁵Then, at the evening sacrifice, I rose from my self-abasement, with my tunic and cloak torn, and fell on my knees with my hands spread out to the LORD my God ⁶and prayed:

"I am too ashamed and disgraced, my God, to lift up my face to you, because our sins are higher than our heads and our guilt has reached to the heavens. ⁷From the days of our ancestors until now, our guilt

## Amplified Bible

king, his counselors, his lords, and all Israel there present had offered.

²⁶I weighed into their hands 650 talents of silver, and silver vessels valued at 100 talents, and 100 talents of gold; ²⁷Also 20 basins of gold worth 1,000 darics, and two vessels of fine bright bronze, precious as gold.

²⁸And I said to them, You are holy to the Lord, the vessels are holy also, and the silver and the gold are a freewill offering to the Lord, the God of your fathers. ²⁹Guard and keep them until you weigh them before the chief priests and Levites and heads of the fathers' houses of Israel in Jerusalem in the chambers of the house of the Lord.

³⁰So the priests and the Levites received the weight of the silver, the gold, and the vessels to bring them to Jerusalem into the house of our God.

³¹We left the river Ahava on the twelfth day of the first month to go to Jerusalem; and the hand of our God was upon us, and He delivered us from the enemy and those who lay in wait by the way.

³²And we came to Jerusalem, and [had been] there three days.

³³On the fourth day, the silver, the gold, and the vessels were weighed in the house of our God into the hands of Meremoth the priest, son of Uriah, and with him was Eleazar son of Phinehas, and with them were Jozabad son of Jeshua and Noadiah son of Binnui—the Levites.

³⁴Every piece was counted and weighed, and all the weight was recorded at once.

³⁵Also those returned exiles whose parents had been carried into captivity offered burnt offerings to the God of Israel: twelve young bulls for all Israel, ninety-six rams, seventy-seven lambs, and twelve he-goats for a sin offering. All this was a burnt offering to the Lord.

³⁶And they delivered the king's commissions to the king's lieutenants and to the governors west of the River, and they aided the people and God's house.

**9** Afterward, the officials came to me and said, The Israelites and the priests and Levites have not separated themselves from the peoples of the lands, but have committed the abominations of the Canaanites, Hittites, Perizzites, Jebusites, Ammonites, Moabites, Egyptians, and Amorites.

²For they have taken as wives some of their daughters for themselves and for their sons, so that the holy offspring have mixed themselves with the peoples of the lands. Indeed, the officials and chief men have been foremost in this wicked act *and* direct violation [of God's will]. [Deut. 7:3, 4.]

³When I heard this, I rent my undergarment and my mantle, I pulled hair from my head and beard and sat down appalled.

⁴Then all those who trembled at the words of the God of Israel because of the offensive violation of His will by the returned exiles gathered around me as I sat astounded until the evening sacrifice.

⁵At the evening sacrifice I arose from my depression, and, having rent my undergarment and my mantle, I fell on my knees and spread out my hands to the Lord my God,

⁶Saying, O my God, I am ashamed and blush to lift my face to You, my God, for our iniquities have risen higher than our heads and our guilt has mounted to the heavens.

⁷Since the days of our fathers we have been exceed-

---

*ᵃ 26* That is, about 24 tons or about 22 metric tons   *ᵇ 26* That is, about 3 3/4 tons or about 3.4 metric tons   *ᶜ 27* That is, about 19 pounds or about 8.4 kilograms   *ᵈ 35* Or *purification offering*

## New International Version

has been great. Because of our sins, we and our kings and our priests have been subjected to the sword and captivity, to pillage and humiliation at the hand of foreign kings, as it is today.

8"But now, for a brief moment, the LORD our God has been gracious in leaving us a remnant and giving us a firm place[a] in his sanctuary, and so our God gives light to our eyes and a little relief in our bondage. 9Though we are slaves, our God has not forsaken us in our bondage. He has shown us kindness in the sight of the kings of Persia: He has granted us new life to rebuild the house of our God and repair its ruins, and he has given us a wall of protection in Judah and Jerusalem.

10"But now, our God, what can we say after this? For we have forsaken the commands 11you gave through your servants the prophets when you said: 'The land you are entering to possess is a land polluted by the corruption of its peoples. By their detestable practices they have filled it with their impurity from one end to the other. 12Therefore, do not give your daughters in marriage to their sons or take their daughters for your sons. Do not seek a treaty of friendship with them at any time, that you may be strong and eat the good things of the land and leave it to your children as an everlasting inheritance.'

13"What has happened to us is a result of our evil deeds and our great guilt, and yet, our God, you have punished us less than our sins deserved and have given us a remnant like this. 14Shall we then break your commands again and intermarry with the peoples who commit such detestable practices? Would you not be angry enough with us to destroy us, leaving us no remnant or survivor? 15LORD, the God of Israel, you are righteous! We are left this day as a remnant. Here we are before you in our guilt, though because of it not one of us can stand in your presence."

### The People's Confession of Sin

**10** While Ezra was praying and confessing, weeping and throwing himself down before the house of God, a large crowd of Israelites—men, women and children—gathered around him. They too wept bitterly. 2Then Shekaniah son of Jehiel, one of the descendants of Elam, said to Ezra, "We have been unfaithful to our God by marrying foreign women from the peoples around us. But in spite of this, there is still hope for Israel. 3Now let us make a covenant before our God to send away all these women and their children, in accordance with the counsel of my lord and of those who fear the commands of our God. Let it be done according to the Law. 4Rise up; this matter is in your hands. We will support you, so take courage and do it."

5So Ezra rose up and put the leading priests and Levites and all Israel under oath to do what had been suggested. And they took the oath. 6Then Ezra withdrew from before the house of God and went to the room of Jehohanan son of Eliashib. While he was there, he ate no food and drank no water, because he continued to mourn over the unfaithfulness of the exiles.

7A proclamation was then issued throughout Judah and Jerusalem for all the exiles to assemble in Jerusalem. 8Anyone who failed to appear within three days would forfeit all his property, in accordance with the decision of the officials and elders, and would himself be expelled from the assembly of the exiles.

## Amplified Bible

ingly guilty; and for our willfulness we, our kings, and our priests have been delivered into the hand of the kings of the lands, to the sword, captivity, plundering, and utter shame, as it is today.

8And now, for a brief moment, grace has been shown us by the Lord our God, Who has left us a remnant to escape and has given us a secure hold in His holy place, that our God may brighten our eyes and give us a little reviving in our bondage.

9For we are bondmen; yet our God has not forsaken us in our bondage, but has extended mercy and steadfast love to us before the kings of Persia, to give us some reviving to set up the house of our God, to repair its ruins, and to give us a wall [of protection] in Judah and Jerusalem.

10Now, O our God, what can we say after this? For we have forsaken Your commands

11Which You have commanded by Your servants the prophets, saying, The land which you are entering to possess is an unclean land with the pollutions of the peoples of the lands, through their abominations which have filled it from one end to the other with their filthiness.

12Therefore, do not give your daughters to their sons or take their daughters for your sons; and never seek their peace or prosperity, that you may be strong and eat the good of the land and leave it as an inheritance to your children always.

13And after all that has come upon us for our evil deeds and for our great guilt, seeing that You, our God, have punished us less than our iniquities deserved and have given us such a remnant,

14Shall we break Your commandments again and intermarry with the peoples who practice these abominations? Would You not be angry with us till You had consumed us, so that there would be no remnant nor any to escape? [Deut. 7:2-4.]

15O Lord, the God of Israel, You are rigidly just and righteous, for we are left a remnant that is escaped, as it is this day. Behold, we are before You in our guilt, for none can stand before You because of this.

**10** Now while Ezra prayed and made confession, weeping and casting himself down before the house of God, there gathered to him out of Israel a very great assembly of men, women, and children; for the people wept bitterly.

2And Shecaniah [II] son of Jehiel [one of the congregation], of the sons of Elam, said to Ezra: We have broken faith and dealt treacherously against our God and have married foreign women of the peoples of the land; yet now there is still hope for Israel in spite of this thing.

3Therefore let us make a covenant with our God to put away all the foreign wives and their children, according to the counsel of my lord and of those who tremble at the command of our God; and let it be done according to the Law.

4Arise, for it is your duty, and we are with you. Be strong and brave and do it.

5Then Ezra arose and made the chiefs of the priests, the Levites, and all Israel swear that they would do as had been said. So they took the oath.

6Then Ezra came from before the house of God and went into the lodging place of Jehohanan son of Eliashib [for the night]. There he ate no bread and drank no water, for he mourned over the returned exiles' faithlessness [and violation of God's law].

7And proclamation was made throughout Judah and Jerusalem to all the returned exiles, that they should assemble in Jerusalem,

8And that whoever did not come within three days, by order of the officials and the elders, all his property should be forfeited and he himself banned from the assembly of the exiles.

## New International Version

⁹Within the three days, all the men of Judah and Benjamin had gathered in Jerusalem. And on the twentieth day of the ninth month, all the people were sitting in the square before the house of God, greatly distressed by the occasion and because of the rain. ¹⁰Then Ezra the priest stood up and said to them, "You have been unfaithful; you have married foreign women, adding to Israel's guilt. ¹¹Now honor*a* the LORD, the God of your ancestors, and do his will. Separate yourselves from the peoples around you and from your foreign wives."

¹²The whole assembly responded with a loud voice: "You are right! We must do as you say. ¹³But there are many people here and it is the rainy season; so we cannot stand outside. Besides, this matter cannot be taken care of in a day or two, because we have sinned greatly in this thing. ¹⁴Let our officials act for the whole assembly. Then let everyone in our towns who has married a foreign woman come at a set time, along with the elders and judges of each town, until the fierce anger of our God in this matter is turned away from us." ¹⁵Only Jonathan son of Asahel and Jahzeiah son of Tikvah, supported by Meshullam and Shabbethai the Levite, opposed this.

¹⁶So the exiles did as was proposed. Ezra the priest selected men who were family heads, one from each family division, and all of them designated by name. On the first day of the tenth month they sat down to investigate the cases, ¹⁷and by the first day of the first month they finished dealing with all the men who had married foreign women.

### Those Guilty of Intermarriage

¹⁸Among the descendants of the priests, the following had married foreign women:

From the descendants of Joshua son of Jozadak, and his brothers: Maaseiah, Eliezer, Jarib and Gedaliah. ¹⁹(They all gave their hands in pledge to put away their wives, and for their guilt they each presented a ram from the flock as a guilt offering.)
²⁰From the descendants of Immer:
Hanani and Zebadiah.
²¹From the descendants of Harim:
Maaseiah, Elijah, Shemaiah, Jehiel and Uzziah.
²²From the descendants of Pashhur:
Elioenai, Maaseiah, Ishmael, Nethanel, Jozabad and Elasah.

²³Among the Levites:

Jozabad, Shimei, Kelaiah (that is, Kelita), Pethahiah, Judah and Eliezer.
²⁴From the musicians:
Eliashib.
From the gatekeepers:
Shallum, Telem and Uri.

²⁵And among the other Israelites:

From the descendants of Parosh:
Ramiah, Izziah, Malkijah, Mijamin, Eleazar, Malkijah and Benaiah.

## Amplified Bible

⁹Then all the men of Judah and Benjamin gathered at Jerusalem within three days. It was the twentieth day of the ninth month, and all the people sat in the open space before the house of God, trembling because of this matter and because of the heavy rain.

¹⁰And Ezra the priest stood up and said to them, You have acted wickedly *and* broken faith [with God] and have married foreign (heathen) women, increasing the guilt of Israel.

¹¹So now make confession *and* give thanks to the Lord, the God of your fathers [for not consuming you], and do His will. *a*Separate yourselves from the peoples of the land and from [your] foreign (heathen) wives.

¹²Then all the assembly answered with a loud voice, As you have said, so must we do.

¹³But the people are many and it is a time of heavy rain; we cannot stand outside. Nor can this work be done in a day or two, for we have greatly transgressed in this matter.

¹⁴Let our officials stand for the whole assembly; let all in our cities who have foreign wives come by appointment, and with each group the elders of that city and its judges, until the fierce wrath of our God over this matter is turned away from us.

¹⁵Only Jonathan son of Asahel and Jahzeiah son of Tikvah opposed this, and Meshullam and Shabbethai the Levite supported them.

¹⁶Then the returned exiles did so. Ezra the priest and certain heads of fathers' houses were selected, according to their fathers' houses, each of them by name; and they sat down on the first day of the tenth month to investigate the matter.

¹⁷And by the first day of the first month they had come to the end of the cases of the men married to foreign wives.

¹⁸Of the sons of the priests who had married non-Jewish women were found: of the sons of Jeshua [the high priest] son of Jozadak, and his brethren: Maaseiah, Eliezer, Jarib, and Gedaliah.

¹⁹They solemnly vowed to put away their [heathen] wives, and, being guilty, [each] offered a ram of the flock for [his] guilt.

²⁰Of the sons of Immer: Hanani and Zebadiah.

²¹Of the sons of Harim: Maaseiah, Elijah, Shemaiah, Jehiel, and Uzziah.

²²Of the sons of Pashhur: Elioenai, Maaseiah, Ishmael, Nethanel, Jozabad, and Elasah.

²³Of the Levites: Jozabad, Shimei, Kelaiah (Kelita), Pethahiah, Judah, and Eliezer.

²⁴Of the singers: Eliashib. Of the gatekeepers: Shallum, Telem, and Uri.

²⁵And of Israel: of the sons of Parosh: Ramiah, Izziah, Malchijah, Mijamin, Eleazar, Malchijah (Hashabiah), and Benaiah.

*a* The apparently great severity which characterized Ezra's divorce policy, as shown in chapters 9 and 10, becomes thoroughly justified when Israel's tragic experiences because of marriages with heathen women are considered. The consequent idolatry, first of King Solomon, for example, and then of the whole nation, was fatal. God's wrath had been so great that He not only took the kingship from Solomon, but eventually turned the Israelites over to their enemies and left the promised land desolate, while the people bewailed their fate as captives in a heathen country. Ezra, to whom the keeping of God's law was of constant concern, had been born in captivity among exiles who hung their harps on the willow trees and grieved for the country, for the peace and prosperity which their now justly offended God had once given them. Nothing could have been more abhorrent to Ezra than that the Jews should again fall into the snare of idolatry. His action in leading the exiles to give up their foreign wives and their children was the only way out if God's consuming wrath was not again to be incurred. That those still living of the 42,360 men who over eighty years before had made up the congregation (Ezra 2:64) also saw complete separation from the foreign women as the unavoidable solution is obvious from the fact that only four (Ezra 10:15) spoke against it. However, those who were now actually married to native heathen women were only 17 priests, 10 Levites, and 86 laymen—113 in all, according to the records, though the list may be incomplete.

*a* 11 Or *Now make confession to*

## New International Version

26 From the descendants of Elam:

Mattaniah, Zechariah, Jehiel, Abdi, Jeremoth and Elijah.

27 From the descendants of Zattu:

Elioenai, Eliashib, Mattaniah, Jeremoth, Zabad and Aziza.

28 From the descendants of Bebai:

Jehohanan, Hananiah, Zabbai and Athlai.

29 From the descendants of Bani:

Meshullam, Malluk, Adaiah, Jashub, Sheal and Jeremoth.

30 From the descendants of Pahath-Moab:

Adna, Kelal, Benaiah, Maaseiah, Mattaniah, Bezalel, Binnui and Manasseh.

31 From the descendants of Harim:

Eliezer, Ishijah, Malkijah, Shemaiah, Shimeon, 32 Benjamin, Malluk and Shemariah.

33 From the descendants of Hashum:

Mattenai, Mattattah, Zabad, Eliphelet, Jeremai, Manasseh and Shimei.

34 From the descendants of Bani:

Maadai, Amram, Uel, 35 Benaiah, Bedeiah, Keluhi, 36 Vaniah, Meremoth, Eliashib, 37 Mattaniah, Mattenai and Jaasu.

38 From the descendants of Binnui:ᵃ

Shimei, 39 Shelemiah, Nathan, Adaiah, 40 Maknadebai, Shashai, Sharai, 41 Azarel, Shelemiah, Shemariah, 42 Shallum, Amariah and Joseph.

43 From the descendants of Nebo:

Jeiel, Mattithiah, Zabad, Zebina, Jaddai, Joel and Benaiah.

44 All these had married foreign women, and some of them had children by these wives.ᵇ

## Amplified Bible

26 Of the sons of Elam: Mattaniah, Zechariah, Jehiel, Abdi, Jeremoth, and Elijah.

27 Of the sons of Zattu: Elioenai, Eliashib, Mattaniah, Jeremoth, Zabad, and Aziza.

28 Of the sons also of Bebai: Jehohanan, Hananiah, Zabbai, and Athlai.

29 Of the sons of Bani: Meshullam, Malluch, Adaiah, Jashub, Sheal, and Jeremoth.

30 Of the sons of Pahath-moab: Adna, Chelal, Benaiah, Maaseiah, Mattaniah, Bezalel, Binnui, and Manasseh.

31 Of the sons of Harim: Eliezer, Isshijah, Malchijah, Shemaiah, Shimeon,

32 Benjamin, Malluch, and Shemariah.

33 Of the sons of Hashum: Mattenai, Mattattah, Zabad, Eliphelet, Jeremai, Manasseh, and Shimei.

34 Of the sons of Bani: Maadai, Amram, Uel,

35 Benaiah, Bedeiah, Cheluhi (Cheluhu),

36 Vaniah, Meremoth, Eliashib,

37 Mattaniah, Mattenai, Jaasu [Jaasai],

38 Bani, Binnui, Shimei,

39 Shelemiah, Nathan, Adaiah,

40 Machnadebai, Shashai, Sharai,

41 Azarel, Shelemiah, Shemariah,

42 Shallum, Amariah, and Joseph.

43 Of the sons of Nebo: Jeiel, Mattithiah, Zabad, Zebina, Iddo (Jaddai), Joel, and Benaiah.

44 All these had married foreign women, and some of the wives had borne children.

---

ᵃ 37,38 See Septuagint (also 1 Esdras 9:34); Hebrew Jaasu ³⁸and Bani and Binnui,   ᵇ 44 Or and they sent them away with their children

# Nehemiah

# Nehemiah

## Nehemiah's Prayer

**1** The words of Nehemiah son of Hakaliah:

In the month of Kislev in the twentieth year, while I was in the citadel of Susa, ²Hanani, one of my brothers, came from Judah with some other men, and I questioned them about the Jewish remnant that had survived the exile, and also about Jerusalem.

³They said to me, "Those who survived the exile and are back in the province are in great trouble and disgrace. The wall of Jerusalem is broken down, and its gates have been burned with fire."

⁴When I heard these things, I sat down and wept. For some days I mourned and fasted and prayed before the God of heaven. ⁵Then I said:

"LORD, the God of heaven, the great and awesome God, who keeps his covenant of love with those who love him and keep his commandments, ⁶let your ear be attentive and your eyes open to hear the prayer your servant is praying before you day and night for your servants, the people of Israel. I confess the sins we Israelites, including myself and my father's family, have committed against you. ⁷We have acted very wickedly toward you. We have not obeyed the commands, decrees and laws you gave your servant Moses.

⁸"Remember the instruction you gave your servant Moses, saying, 'If you are unfaithful, I will scatter you among the nations, ⁹but if you return to me and obey my commands, then even if your exiled people are at the farthest horizon, I will gather them from there and bring them to the place I have chosen as a dwelling for my Name.'

¹⁰"They are your servants and your people, whom you redeemed by your great strength and your mighty hand. ¹¹Lord, let your ear be attentive to the prayer of this your servant and to the prayer of your servants who delight in revering your name. Give your servant success today by granting him favor in the presence of this man."

I was cupbearer to the king.

## Artaxerxes Sends Nehemiah to Jerusalem

**2** In the month of Nisan in the twentieth year of King Artaxerxes, when wine was brought for him, I took the wine and gave it to the king. I had not been sad in his presence before, ²so the king asked me, "Why does your face look so sad when you are not ill? This can be nothing but sadness of heart."

I was very much afraid, ³but I said to the king, "May the king live forever! Why should my face not look sad when the city where my ancestors are buried lies in ruins, and its gates have been destroyed by fire?"

⁴The king said to me, "What is it you want?"

Then I prayed to the God of heaven, ⁵and I answered the king, "If it pleases the king and if your servant has found favor in his sight, let him send me to the city in Judah where my ancestors are buried so that I can rebuild it."

⁶Then the king, with the queen sitting beside him, asked me, "How long will your journey take, and when will you get back?" It pleased the king to send me; so I set a time.

**1** The words or story of Nehemiah son of Hacaliah: Now in the month of Chislev in the twentieth year [of the Persian king], as I was in the castle of Shushan, ²Hanani, one of my kinsmen, came with certain men from Judah, and I asked them about the surviving Jews who had escaped exile, and about Jerusalem.

³And they said to me, The remnant there in the province who escaped exile are in great trouble and reproach; the wall of Jerusalem is broken down, and its [fortified] gates are destroyed by fire.

⁴When I heard this, I sat down and wept and mourned for days and fasted and prayed [constantly] before the God of heaven,

⁵And I said, O Lord God of heaven, the great and terrible God, Who keeps covenant, loving-kindness, *and* mercy for those who love Him and keep His commandments,

⁶Let Your ear now be attentive and Your eyes open to listen to the prayer of Your servant which I pray before You day and night for the Israelites, Your servants, confessing the sins of the Israelites which we have sinned against You. Yes, I and my father's house have sinned.

⁷We have acted very corruptly against You and have not kept the commandments, statutes, and ordinances which You commanded Your servant Moses. [Deut. 6:1-9.]

⁸Remember [earnestly] what You commanded Your servant Moses: If you transgress *and* are unfaithful, I will scatter you abroad among the nations; [Lev. 26:33.]

⁹But if you return to Me and keep My commandments and do them, though your outcasts were in the farthest part of the heavens [the expanse of outer space], yet will I gather them from there and will bring them to the place in which I have chosen to set My *a*Name. [Deut. 30:1-5.]

¹⁰Now these are Your servants and Your people, whom You have redeemed by Your great power and by Your strong hand.

¹¹O Lord, let Your ear be attentive to the prayer of Your servant and the prayer of Your servants who delight to revere *and* fear Your name (Your nature and attributes); and prosper, I pray You, Your servant this day and grant him mercy in the sight of this man. For I was cupbearer to the king.

**2** In the month of Nisan in the twentieth year of King Artaxerxes, when wine was before him, I took up the wine and gave it to the king. Now I had not been sad before in his presence.

²So the king said to me, Why do you look sad, since you are not sick? This is nothing but sorrow of heart. Then I was very much afraid

³And said to the king, Let the king live forever! Why should I not be sad faced when the city, the place of my fathers' sepulchers, lies waste, and its [fortified] gates are consumed by fire?

⁴The king said to me, For what do you ask? So I prayed to the God of heaven.

⁵And I said to [him], If it pleases the king and if your servant has found favor in your sight, I ask that you will send me to Judah, to the city of my fathers' sepulchers, that I may rebuild it.

⁶The king, beside whom the queen was sitting, asked me, How long will your journey take, and when will you return? So it pleased [him] to send me; and I set him a time.

*a* See footnote on Deut. 12:5.

## New International Version

[7] I also said to him, "If it pleases the king, may I have letters to the governors of Trans-Euphrates, so that they will provide me safe-conduct until I arrive in Judah? [8] And may I have a letter to Asaph, keeper of the royal park, so he will give me timber to make beams for the gates of the citadel by the temple and for the city wall and for the residence I will occupy?" And because the gracious hand of my God was on me, the king granted my requests. [9] So I went to the governors of Trans-Euphrates and gave them the king's letters. The king had also sent army officers and cavalry with me.

[10] When Sanballat the Horonite and Tobiah the Ammonite official heard about this, they were very much disturbed that someone had come to promote the welfare of the Israelites.

### Nehemiah Inspects Jerusalem's Walls

[11] I went to Jerusalem, and after staying there three days [12] I set out during the night with a few others. I had not told anyone what my God had put in my heart to do for Jerusalem. There were no mounts with me except the one I was riding on. [13] By night I went out through the Valley Gate toward the Jackal[a] Well and the Dung Gate, examining the walls of Jerusalem, which had been broken down, and its gates, which had been destroyed by fire. [14] Then I moved on toward the Fountain Gate and the King's Pool, but there was not enough room for my mount to get through; [15] so I went up the valley by night, examining the wall. Finally, I turned back and reentered through the Valley Gate. [16] The officials did not know where I had gone or what I was doing, because as yet I had said nothing to the Jews or the priests or nobles or officials or any others who would be doing the work. [17] Then I said to them, "You see the trouble we are in: Jerusalem lies in ruins, and its gates have been burned with fire. Come, let us rebuild the wall of Jerusalem, and we will no longer be in disgrace." [18] I also told them about the gracious hand of my God on me and what the king had said to me.

They replied, "Let us start rebuilding." So they began this good work.

[19] But when Sanballat the Horonite, Tobiah the Ammonite official and Geshem the Arab heard about it, they mocked and ridiculed us. "What is this you are doing?" they asked. "Are you rebelling against the king?"

[20] I answered them by saying, "The God of heaven will give us success. We his servants will start rebuilding, but as for you, you have no share in Jerusalem or any claim or historic right to it."

### Builders of the Wall

**3** Eliashib the high priest and his fellow priests went to work and rebuilt the Sheep Gate. They dedicated it and set its doors in place, building as far as the Tower of the Hundred, which they dedicated, and as far as the Tower of Hananel. [2] The men of Jericho built the adjoining section, and Zakkur son of Imri built next to them.

[3] The Fish Gate was rebuilt by the sons of Hassenaah. They laid its beams and put its doors and bolts and bars in place. [4] Meremoth son of Uriah, the son of Hakkoz, repaired the next section. Next to him Meshullam son of Berekiah, the son of Meshezabel, made repairs, and next to him Zadok son of Baana also made repairs. [5] The next section was repaired by the men of Tekoa, but their nobles did not put their shoulders to the work under their supervisors.[b]

[6] The Jeshanah[c] Gate was repaired by Joiada son of Paseah and Meshullam son of Besodeiah. They laid its beams and put its doors with their bolts and bars in place. [7] Next

## Amplified Bible

[7] Also I said to the king, If it pleases the king, let letters be given me for the governors beyond the [Euphrates] River, that they may let me pass through to Judah;

[8] And a letter to Asaph, keeper of the king's forest or park, that he may give me timber to make beams for the gates of the fortress of the temple and for the city wall and for the house that I shall occupy. And the king granted what I asked, for the good hand of my God was upon me.

[9] Then I came to the governors beyond the River and gave them the king's letters. Now the king had sent captains of the army and horsemen with me.

[10] When Sanballat the Horonite and Tobiah the servant, the Ammonite, heard this, it distressed them exceedingly that a man had come to inquire for and require the good and prosperity of the Israelites.

[11] So I came to Jerusalem and had been there three days.

[12] Then I arose in the night, I and a few men with me. And I told no one what my God had put in my heart to do for Jerusalem. No beast was with me except the one I rode.

[13] I went out by night by the Valley Gate toward the Dragon's Well and to the Dung Gate and inspected the walls of Jerusalem, which were broken down, and its gates, which had been destroyed by fire.

[14] I passed over to the Fountain Gate and to the King's Pool, but there was no place for the beast that was under me to pass.

[15] So [gradually] I went up by the brook [Kidron] in the night and inspected the wall; then I turned back and entered [the city] by the Valley Gate, and so returned.

[16] And the magistrates knew not where I went or what I did; nor had I yet told the Jews, the priests, the nobles, the officials, or the rest who did the work.

[17] Then I said to them, You see the bad situation we are in—how Jerusalem lies in ruins, and its gates are burned with fire. Come, let us build up the wall of Jerusalem, that we may no longer be a disgrace.

[18] Then I told them of the hand of my God which was upon me for good, and also the words that the king had spoken to me. And they said, Let us rise up and build! So they strengthened their hands for the good work.

[19] But when Sanballat the Horonite and Tobiah the servant, the Ammonite, and Geshem the Arab heard of it, they laughed us to scorn and despised us and said, What is this thing you are doing? Will you rebel against the king?

[20] I answered them, The God of heaven will prosper us; therefore we His servants will arise and build, but you have no portion or right or memorial in Jerusalem.

**3** Then Eliashib the high priest rose up with his brethren the priests and built the Sheep Gate. They consecrated it and set up its doors; they consecrated it even to the Tower of Hammeah or the Hundred, as far as the Tower of Hananel.

[2] And next to him [Eliashib] the men of Jericho built. Next to [them] Zaccur son of Imri built.

[3] And the Fish Gate the sons of Hassenaah built; they laid its beams and set up its doors, its bolts, and its bars.

[4] And next to them Meremoth son of Uriah, the son of Hakkoz, repaired. Next to them Meshullam son of Berechiah, the son of Meshezabel, repaired. Next to them Zadok son of Baana repaired.

[5] Next to them the Tekoites repaired, but their nobles or lords did not put their necks to the work of their Lord.

[6] Moreover, the Old Gate Joiada son of Paseah and Meshullam son of Besodeiah repaired. They laid its beams and set up its doors, its bolts, and its bars.

---

[a] 13 Or *Serpent* or *Fig*  [b] 5 Or *their Lord* or *the governor*  [c] 6 Or *Old*

## New International Version

to them, repairs were made by men from Gibeon and Mizpah—Melatiah of Gibeon and Jadon of Meronoth—places under the authority of the governor of Trans-Euphrates. [8]Uzziel son of Harhaiah, one of the goldsmiths, repaired the next section; and Hananiah, one of the perfume-makers, made repairs next to that. They restored Jerusalem as far as the Broad Wall. [9]Rephaiah son of Hur, ruler of a half-district of Jerusalem, repaired the next section. [10]Adjoining this, Jedaiah son of Harumaph made repairs opposite his house, and Hattush son of Hashabneiah made repairs next to him. [11]Malkijah son of Harim and Hasshub son of Pahath-Moab repaired another section and the Tower of the Ovens. [12]Shallum son of Hallohesh, ruler of a half-district of Jerusalem, repaired the next section with the help of his daughters.

[13]The Valley Gate was repaired by Hanun and the residents of Zanoah. They rebuilt it and put its doors with their bolts and bars in place. They also repaired a thousand cubits[a] of the wall as far as the Dung Gate.

[14]The Dung Gate was repaired by Malkijah son of Rekab, ruler of the district of Beth Hakkerem. He rebuilt it and put its doors with their bolts and bars in place.

[15]The Fountain Gate was repaired by Shallun son of Kol-Hozeh, ruler of the district of Mizpah. He rebuilt it, roofing it over and putting its doors and bolts and bars in place. He also repaired the wall of the Pool of Siloam,[b] by the King's Garden, as far as the steps going down from the City of David. [16]Beyond him, Nehemiah son of Azbuk, ruler of a half-district of Beth Zur, made repairs up to a point opposite the tombs[c] of David, as far as the artificial pool and the House of the Heroes.

[17]Next to him, the repairs were made by the Levites under Rehum son of Bani. Beside him, Hashabiah, ruler of half the district of Keilah, carried out repairs for his district. [18]Next to him, the repairs were made by their fellow Levites under Binnui[d] son of Henadad, ruler of the other half-district of Keilah. [19]Next to him, Ezer son of Jeshua, ruler of Mizpah, repaired another section, from a point facing the ascent to the armory as far as the angle of the wall. [20]Next to him, Baruch son of Zabbai zealously repaired another section, from the angle to the entrance of the house of Eliashib the high priest. [21]Next to him, Meremoth son of Uriah, the son of Hakkoz, repaired another section, from the entrance of Eliashib's house to the end of it.

[22]The repairs next to him were made by the priests from the surrounding region. [23]Beyond them, Benjamin and Hasshub made repairs in front of their house; and next to them, Azariah son of Maaseiah, the son of Ananiah, made repairs beside his house. [24]Next to him, Binnui son of Henadad repaired another section, from Azariah's house to the angle and the corner, [25]and Palal son of Uzai worked opposite the angle and the tower projecting from the upper palace near the court of the guard. Next to him, Pedaiah son of Parosh [26]and the temple servants living on the hill of Ophel made repairs up to a point opposite the Water Gate toward the east and the projecting tower. [27]Next to them, the men of Tekoa repaired another section, from the great projecting tower to the wall of Ophel.

## Amplified Bible

[7]Next to them repaired Melatiah the Gibeonite and Jadon the Meronothite, the men of Gibeon and of Mizpah, [up] to the seat or residence of the governor [west of] the River [Euphrates, there in Jerusalem].

[8]Next to them repaired Uzziel son of Harhaiah, one of the goldsmiths. Next to him repaired Hananiah, one of the perfumers, and they abandoned [fortification of] Jerusalem as far as the Broad Wall [omitting that part of the ancient city and reducing the area].

[9]Next to them repaired Rephaiah son of Hur, ruler of half the district of Jerusalem.

[10]Next to them repaired Jedaiah son of Harumaph, opposite his own house. And next to him repaired Hattush son of Hashabneiah.

[11]Malchijah son of Harim and Hasshub son of Pahath-moab repaired another portion and the Tower of the Furnaces.

[12]Next to [them] repaired Shallum son of Hallohesh, the ruler of half the district of Jerusalem, he and his daughters.

[13]The Valley Gate [the main entrance in the west wall, the Jaffa Gate] was repaired by Hanun and the inhabitants of Zanoah. They built it and set up its doors, its bolts, and its bars and repaired a thousand cubits of the wall, as far as the Dung Gate.

[14]The Dung Gate was repaired by Malchijah son of Rechab, the ruler of the district of Beth-haccherem. He rebuilt it and set its doors, its bolts, and its bars.

[15]The Fountain Gate was repaired by Shallum son of Col-hozeh, ruler of the district of Mizpah. He rebuilt and covered it and set up its doors, its bolts, and its bars, and the wall of the Pool of Shelah (Siloam), by the King's Garden, as far as the stairs that go down [the eastern slope] from the [portion of Jerusalem known as] the City of David.

[16]After him Nehemiah [III] son of Azbuk, ruler of half the district of Beth-zur, repaired [the wall] to a point opposite the sepulchers of David, and to the artificial pool and the house of the guards.

[17]After him the Levites: Rehum son of Bani. Next to him repaired Hashabiah, ruler of half the district of Keilah.

[18]After him repaired their brethren under Bavvai son of Henadad, ruler of [the other] half of the district of Keilah.

[19]Next to him repaired Ezer son of Jeshua, ruler of Mizpah, another district over opposite the ascent to the armory at the angle [in the wall].

[20]After him Baruch son of Zabbai (Zaccai) earnestly repaired another portion [toward the hill] from the angular turning of the wall to the door of the house of Eliashib the high priest.

[21]After him Meremoth son of Uriah, the son of Hakkoz, repaired from the door of Eliashib's house to the end of his house.

[22]After him the priests, men of the plain, repaired.

[23]After them Benjamin and Hasshub repaired opposite their house. After them repaired Azariah son of Maaseiah, the son of Ananiah beside his own house.

[24]After him Binnui son of Henadad repaired another section [of the wall], from the house of Azariah to the angular turn of the wall and to the corner.

[25]Palal son of Uzai repaired opposite the angular turn of the wall and the tower which stands out from the upper house of the king by the court of the guard. After him Pedaiah son of Parosh

[26]And the servants of the priests dwelling on Ophel [the hill south of the temple] repaired to opposite the Water Gate on the east and the projecting tower.

[27]After them the Tekoites repaired another portion opposite the great projecting tower to the wall of Ophel.

---

[a] 13 That is, about 1,500 feet or about 450 meters   [b] 15 Hebrew *Shelah*, a variant of *Shiloah*, that is, Siloam   [c] 16 Hebrew; Septuagint, some Vulgate manuscripts and Syriac *tomb*   [d] 18 Two Hebrew Hebrew manuscripts (see also Septuagint and verse 24); most Hebrew manuscripts *Bavvai*

## New International Version

28Above the Horse Gate, the priests made repairs, each in front of his own house. 29Next to them, Zadok son of Immer made repairs opposite his house. Next to him, Shemaiah son of Shekaniah, the guard at the East Gate, made repairs. 30Next to him, Hananiah son of Shelemiah, and Hanun, the sixth son of Zalaph, repaired another section. Next to them, Meshullam son of Berekiah made repairs opposite his living quarters. 31Next to him, Malkijah, one of the goldsmiths, made repairs as far as the house of the temple servants and the merchants, opposite the Inspection Gate, and as far as the room above the corner; 32and between the room above the corner and the Sheep Gate the goldsmiths and merchants made repairs.

### Opposition to the Rebuilding

4a When Sanballat heard that we were rebuilding the wall, he became angry and was greatly incensed. He ridiculed the Jews, 2and in the presence of his associates and the army of Samaria, he said, "What are those feeble Jews doing? Will they restore their wall? Will they offer sacrifices? Will they finish in a day? Can they bring the stones back to life from those heaps of rubble—burned as they are?"

3Tobiah the Ammonite, who was at his side, said, "What they are building—even a fox climbing up on it would break down their wall of stones!"

4Hear us, our God, for we are despised. Turn their insults back on their own heads. Give them over as plunder in a land of captivity. 5Do not cover up their guilt or blot out their sins from your sight, for they have thrown insults in the face ofb the builders.

6So we rebuilt the wall till all of it reached half its height, for the people worked with all their heart.

7But when Sanballat, Tobiah, the Arabs, the Ammonites and the people of Ashdod heard that the repairs to Jerusalem's walls had gone ahead and that the gaps were being closed, they were very angry. 8They all plotted together to come and fight against Jerusalem and stir up trouble against it. 9But we prayed to our God and posted a guard day and night to meet this threat.

10Meanwhile, the people in Judah said, "The strength of the laborers is giving out, and there is so much rubble that we cannot rebuild the wall."

11Also our enemies said, "Before they know it or see us, we will be right there among them and will kill them and put an end to the work."

12Then the Jews who lived near them came and told us ten times over, "Wherever you turn, they will attack us."

13Therefore I stationed some of the people behind the lowest points of the wall at the exposed places, posting them by families, with their swords, spears and bows. 14After I looked things over, I stood up and said to the nobles, the officials and the rest of the people, "Don't be afraid of them. Remember the Lord, who is great and awesome, and fight for your families, your sons and your daughters, your wives and your homes."

15When our enemies heard that we were aware of their plot and that God had frustrated it, we all returned to the wall, each to our own work.

## Amplified Bible

28Above the Horse Gate the priests repaired, everyone opposite his own house.

29After them repaired Zadok son of Immer opposite his house. Then Shemaiah son of Shecaniah, keeper of the East Gate, repaired.

30After him Hananiah son of Shelemiah, and Hanun, the sixth son of Zalaph, repaired another section. After him Meshullam son of Berechiah repaired opposite his chamber.

31After him Malchijah, one of the goldsmiths, repaired as far as the house of the temple servants and of the merchants, opposite the Muster Gate, and to the ascent *and* upper room of the corner.

32And from the ascent *and* upper room of the corner to the Sheep Gate the goldsmiths and merchants repaired.

4But when Sanballat heard that we were building the wall, he was angry and in a great rage, and he ridiculed the Jews.

2And he said before his brethren and the army of Samaria, What are these feeble Jews doing? Will they restore things [at will and by themselves]? Will they [try to bribe their God] with sacrifices? Will they finish up in a day? Will they revive the stones out of the heaps of rubbish, seeing they are burned?

3Now Tobiah the Ammonite was near him, and he said, What they build—if a fox climbs upon it, he will break down their stone wall.

4[And Nehemiah prayed] Hear, O our God, for we are despised. Turn their taunts upon their own heads, and give them for a prey in a land of their captivity.

5Cover not their iniquity and let not their sin be blotted out before You, for they have vexed [with alarm] the builders *and* provoked You.

6So we built the wall, and all [of it] was joined together to half its height, for the people had a heart *and* mind to work.

7But when Sanballat, Tobiah, the Arabians, Ammonites, and Ashdodites heard that the walls of Jerusalem were going up and that the breaches were being closed, they were very angry.

8And they all plotted together to come and fight against Jerusalem, to injure *and* cause confusion *and* failure in it.

9But because of them we made our prayer to our God and set a watch against them day and night.

10And [the leaders of] Judah said, The strength of the burden bearers is weakening, and there is much rubbish; we are not able to work on the wall.

11And our enemies said, They will not know or see till we come into their midst and kill them and stop the work.

12And when the Jews who lived near them came, they said to us ten times, You must return [to guard our little villages]; from all places where they dwell they will be upon us.

13So I set [armed men] behind the wall in places where it was least protected; I even thus used the people as families with their swords, spears, and bows.

14I looked [them over] and rose up and said to the nobles and officials and the other people, Do not be afraid of the enemy; [earnestly] remember the Lord *and* imprint Him [on your minds], great and terrible, and [take from Him courage to] fight for your brethren, your sons, your daughters, your wives, and your homes.

15And when our enemies heard that their plot was known to us and that God had frustrated their purpose, we all returned to the wall, everyone to his work.

---

a In Hebrew texts 4:1-6 is numbered 3:33-38, and 4:7-23 is numbered 4:1-17.    b 5 Or *have aroused your anger before*

## New International Version

16From that day on, half of my men did the work, while the other half were equipped with spears, shields, bows and armor. The officers posted themselves behind all the people of Judah 17who were building the wall. Those who carried materials did their work with one hand and held a weapon in the other, 18and each of the builders wore his sword at his side as he worked. But the man who sounded the trumpet stayed with me.

19Then I said to the nobles, the officials and the rest of the people, "The work is extensive and spread out, and we are widely separated from each other along the wall. 20Wherever you hear the sound of the trumpet, join us there. Our God will fight for us!"

21So we continued the work with half the men holding spears, from the first light of dawn till the stars came out. 22At that time I also said to the people, "Have every man and his helper stay inside Jerusalem at night, so they can serve us as guards by night and as workers by day." 23Neither I nor my brothers nor my men nor the guards with me took off our clothes; each had his weapon, even when he went for water.[a]

### Nehemiah Helps the Poor

5 Now the men and their wives raised a great outcry against their fellow Jews. 2Some were saying, "We and our sons and daughters are numerous; in order for us to eat and stay alive, we must get grain."

3Others were saying, "We are mortgaging our fields, our vineyards and our homes to get grain during the famine."

4Still others were saying, "We have had to borrow money to pay the king's tax on our fields and vineyards. 5Although we are of the same flesh and blood as our fellow Jews and though our children are as good as theirs, yet we have to subject our sons and daughters to slavery. Some of our daughters have already been enslaved, but we are powerless, because our fields and our vineyards belong to others."

6When I heard their outcry and these charges, I was very angry. 7I pondered them in my mind and then accused the nobles and officials. I told them, "You are charging your own people interest!" So I called together a large meeting to deal with them 8and said: "As far as possible, we have bought back our fellow Jews who were sold to the Gentiles. Now you are selling your own people, only for them to be sold back to us!" They kept quiet, because they could find nothing to say.

9So I continued, "What you are doing is not right. Shouldn't you walk in the fear of our God to avoid the reproach of our Gentile enemies? 10I and my brothers and my men are also lending the people money and grain. But let us stop charging interest! 11Give back to them immediately their fields, vineyards, olive groves and houses, and also the interest you are charging them—one percent of the money, grain, new wine and olive oil."

12"We will give it back," they said. "And we will not demand anything more from them. We will do as you say."

Then I summoned the priests and made the nobles and officials take an oath to do what they had promised. 13I also shook out the folds of my robe and said, "In this way may God shake out of their house and possessions anyone

## Amplified Bible

16And from that time forth, half of my servants worked at the task, and the other half held the spears, shields, bows, and coats of mail; and the leaders stood behind all the house of Judah.

17Those who built the wall and those who bore burdens loaded themselves so that everyone worked with one hand and held a weapon with the other hand,

18And every builder had his sword girded by his side, and so worked. And he who sounded the trumpet was at my side.

19And I said to the nobles and officials and the rest of the people, The work is great and scattered, and we are separated on the wall, one far from another.

20In whatever place you hear the sound of the trumpet, rally to us there. Our God will fight for us.

21So we labored at the work while half of them held the spears from dawn until the stars came out.

22At that time also I said to the people, Let everyone with his servant lodge within Jerusalem, that at night they may be a guard to us and a laborer during the day.

23So none of us—I, my kinsmen, my servants, nor the men of the guard who followed me—took off our clothes; each kept his weapon [in his hand for days].

5 Now there arose a great cry of the [poor] people and of their wives [driven to borrowing] against their Jewish brethren [the few who could afford to lend].

2For some said, We, our sons and daughters, are many; therefore allow us to take grain, that we may eat and live! If we are not given grain, let us take it!

3Also some said, We are mortgaging our lands, vineyards, and houses to buy grain because of the scarcity.

4Others said, We have borrowed money on our fields and vineyards to pay the [Persian] king's heavy tax.

5Although our flesh is the same as that of our brethren and our children are as theirs, yet we are forced to sell our children as slaves; some of our daughters have already been thus sold, and we are powerless to redeem them, for others have our lands and vineyards.

6I [Nehemiah] was very angry when I heard their cry and these words.

7I thought it over and then rebuked the nobles and officials. I told them, You are exacting interest from your own kinsmen. And I held a great assembly against them.

8I said to them, We, according to our ability, have bought back our Jewish brethren who were sold to the nations; but will you even sell your brethren, that they may be sold to us? Then they were silent and found not a word to say.

9Also I said, What you are doing is not good. Should you not walk in the fear of our God to prevent the taunts and reproach of the nations, our enemies?

10I, my brethren, and my servants are lending them money and grain. Let us stop this forbidden interest! [Exod. 22:25.]

11Return this very day to them their fields, vineyards, olive groves, and houses, and also a hundredth of all the money, grain, new wine, and oil that you have exacted from them.

12Then they said, We will restore these and require nothing from them. We will do as you say. Then I called the priests and took an oath of the lenders that they would do according to this promise.

13I shook out my lap and said, So may God shake out every man from his house and from [the exercise and fruits

---

[a] 23 The meaning of the Hebrew for this clause is uncertain.

## New International Version

who does not keep this promise. So may such a person be shaken out and emptied!"

At this the whole assembly said, "Amen," and praised the LORD. And the people did as they had promised.

[14]Moreover, from the twentieth year of King Artaxerxes, when I was appointed to be their governor in the land of Judah, until his thirty-second year—twelve years—neither I nor my brothers ate the food allotted to the governor. [15]But the earlier governors—those preceding me—placed a heavy burden on the people and took forty shekels[a] of silver from them in addition to food and wine. Their assistants also lorded it over the people. But out of reverence for God I did not act like that. [16]Instead, I devoted myself to the work on this wall. All my men were assembled there for the work; we[b] did not acquire any land.

[17]Furthermore, a hundred and fifty Jews and officials ate at my table, as well as those who came to us from the surrounding nations. [18]Each day one ox, six choice sheep and some poultry were prepared for me, and every ten days an abundant supply of wine of all kinds. In spite of all this, I never demanded the food allotted to the governor, because the demands were heavy on these people.

[19]Remember me with favor, my God, for all I have done for these people.

### Further Opposition to the Rebuilding

**6** When word came to Sanballat, Tobiah, Geshem the Arab and the rest of our enemies that I had rebuilt the wall and not a gap was left in it—though up to that time I had not set the doors in the gates— [2]Sanballat and Geshem sent me this message: "Come, let us meet together in one of the villages[c] on the plain of Ono."

But they were scheming to harm me; [3]so I sent messengers to them with this reply: "I am carrying on a great project and cannot go down. Why should the work stop while I leave it and go down to you?" [4]Four times they sent me the same message, and each time I gave them the same answer.

[5]Then, the fifth time, Sanballat sent his aide to me with the same message, and in his hand was an unsealed letter [6]in which was written:

"It is reported among the nations—and Geshem[d] says it is true—that you and the Jews are plotting to revolt, and therefore you are building the wall. Moreover, according to these reports you are about to become their king [7]and have even appointed prophets to make this proclamation about you in Jerusalem: 'There is a king in Judah!' Now this report will get back to the king; so come, let us meet together."

[8]I sent him this reply: "Nothing like what you are saying is happening; you are just making it up out of your head."

[9]They were all trying to frighten us, thinking, "Their hands will get too weak for the work, and it will not be completed."

But I prayed, "Now strengthen my hands."

[10]One day I went to the house of Shemaiah son of Delaiah, the son of Mehetabel, who was shut in at his home. He said, "Let us meet in the house of God, inside the temple, and let us close the temple doors, because men are coming to kill you—by night they are coming to kill you."

[11]But I said, "Should a man like me run away? Or should someone like me go into the temple to save his life? I will

## Amplified Bible

of] his labor who does not keep this promise! So may he be shaken out and emptied. And all the assembly said, Amen, and praised the Lord. And the people did according to this promise.

[14]Also, in the twelve years after I was appointed to be their governor in Judah, from the twentieth to the thirty-second year of King Artaxerxes, neither I nor my kin ate the food allowed to [me] the governor.

[15]But the former governors lived at the expense of the people and took from them food and wine, besides forty shekels of silver [a large monthly official salary]; yes, even their servants assumed authority over the people. But I did not so because of my [reverent] fear of God.

[16]I also held fast to the work on this wall; and we bought no land. And all my servants were gathered there for the work.

[17]And there were at my table 150 Jews and officials, besides those who came to us from the nations about us.

[18]Now these were prepared for each day: one ox and six choice sheep; also fowls were prepared for me, and once in ten days a store of all sorts of wine. Yet for all this, I did not demand [my rights] the food allowed me as governor, for the [tribute] bondage was heavy upon this people.

[19]O my God, [earnestly] remember me for good for all I have done for this people. [Heb. 6:10.]

**6** Now when Sanballat, Tobiah, Geshem the Arab, and the rest of our enemies heard that I had built the wall and that there was no breach left in it, although at that time I had not set up the doors in the gates,

[2]Sanballat and Geshem sent to me, saying, Come, let us meet together in one of the villages in the plain of Ono. But they intended to do me harm.

[3]And I sent messengers to them, saying, I am doing a great work and cannot come down. Why should the work stop while I leave to come down to you?

[4]They sent to me four times this way, and I answered them as before.

[5]Then Sanballat sent his servant to me again the fifth time with an open letter.

[6]In it was written: It is reported among the neighboring nations, and Gashmu says it, that you and the Jews plan to rebel; therefore you are building the wall, that you may be their king, according to the report.

[7]Also you have set up prophets to announce concerning you in Jerusalem, There is a king in Judah. And now this will be reported to the [Persian] king. So, come now and let us take counsel together.

[8]I replied to him, No such things as you say have been done; you are inventing them out of your own heart *and* mind.

[9]For they all wanted to frighten us, thinking, Their hands will be so weak that the work will not be done. But now strengthen my hands!

[10]I went into the house of Shemaiah son of Delaiah, the son of Mehetabel, who was shut up. He said, Let us meet together in the house of God, within the temple, and let us shut the doors of the temple, for they are coming to kill you—at night they are coming to kill you.

[11]But I said, Should such a man as I flee? And what man such as I could go into the temple [where only the priests are allowed to go] and yet live? I will not go in.

---

[a] 15 That is, about 1 pound or about 460 grams   [b] 16 Most Hebrew manuscripts; some Hebrew manuscripts, Septuagint, Vulgate and Syriac *I*   [c] 2 Or *in Kephirim*   [d] 6 Hebrew *Gashmu*, a variant of *Geshem*

## New International Version

not go!" ¹²I realized that God had not sent him, but that he had prophesied against me because Tobiah and Sanballat had hired him. ¹³He had been hired to intimidate me so that I would commit a sin by doing this, and then they would give me a bad name to discredit me.

¹⁴Remember Tobiah and Sanballat, my God, because of what they have done; remember also the prophet Noadiah and how she and the rest of the prophets have been trying to intimidate me. ¹⁵So the wall was completed on the twenty-fifth of Elul, in fifty-two days.

### Opposition to the Completed Wall

¹⁶When all our enemies heard about this, all the surrounding nations were afraid and lost their self-confidence, because they realized that this work had been done with the help of our God.

¹⁷Also, in those days the nobles of Judah were sending many letters to Tobiah, and replies from Tobiah kept coming to them. ¹⁸For many in Judah were under oath to him, since he was son-in-law to Shekaniah son of Arah, and his son Jehohanan had married the daughter of Meshullam son of Berekiah. ¹⁹Moreover, they kept reporting to me his good deeds and then telling him what I said. And Tobiah sent letters to intimidate me.

**7** After the wall had been rebuilt and I had set the doors in place, the gatekeepers, the musicians and the Levites were appointed. ²I put in charge of Jerusalem my brother Hanani, along with Hananiah the commander of the citadel, because he was a man of integrity and feared God more than most people do. ³I said to them, "The gates of Jerusalem are not to be opened until the sun is hot. While the gatekeepers are still on duty, have them shut the doors and bar them. Also appoint residents of Jerusalem as guards, some at their posts and some near their own houses."

### The List of the Exiles Who Returned

⁴Now the city was large and spacious, but there were few people in it, and the houses had not yet been rebuilt. ⁵So my God put it into my heart to assemble the nobles, the officials and the common people for registration by families. I found the genealogical record of those who had been the first to return. This is what I found written there:

⁶These are the people of the province who came up from the captivity of the exiles whom Nebuchadnezzar king of Babylon had taken captive (they returned to Jerusalem and Judah, each to his own town, ⁷in company with Zerubbabel, Joshua, Nehemiah, Azariah, Raamiah, Nahamani, Mordecai, Bilshan, Mispereth, Bigvai, Nehum and Baanah):

The list of the men of Israel:

| | |
|---|---|
| ⁸the descendants of Parosh | 2,172 |
| ⁹of Shephatiah | 372 |
| ¹⁰of Arah | 652 |
| ¹¹of Pahath-Moab (through the line of Jeshua and Joab) | 2,818 |
| ¹²of Elam | 1,254 |
| ¹³of Zattu | 845 |
| ¹⁴of Zakkai | 760 |
| ¹⁵of Binnui | 648 |
| ¹⁶of Bebai | 628 |
| ¹⁷of Azgad | 2,322 |

## Amplified Bible

¹²And behold, I saw that God had not sent him, but he made this prophecy against me because Tobiah and Sanballat had hired him. ¹³He was hired that I should be made afraid and do as he said and sin, that they might have matter for an evil report with which to taunt *and* reproach me. ¹⁴My God, think on Tobiah and Sanballat according to these their works, and on the prophetess Noadiah and the rest of the prophets who would have put me in fear. ¹⁵So the wall was finished on the twenty-fifth day of the month Elul, in fifty-two days.

¹⁶When all our enemies heard of it, all the nations around us feared and fell far in their own esteem, for they saw that this work was done by our God. ¹⁷Moreover, in those days the nobles of Judah sent many letters to Tobiah, and Tobiah's letters came to them. ¹⁸For many in Judah were bound by oath to him, because he was the son-in-law of Shecaniah son of Arah, and his son Jehohanan had married the daughter of Meshullam son of Berechiah. ¹⁹Also they spoke of [Tobiah's] good deeds before me and told him what I said. And Tobiah sent letters to frighten me.

**7** Now when the wall was built and I had set up the doors, and the gatekeepers, singers, and Levites had been appointed,

²I gave my brother Hanani, with Hananiah the ruler of the castle, charge over Jerusalem, for Hananiah was a more faithful and God-fearing man than many.

³I said to them, Let not the gates of Jerusalem be opened until the sun is hot; and while the watchmen are still on guard, let them shut and bar the doors. Appoint guards from the people of Jerusalem, each to his watch [on the wall] and each opposite his own house.

⁴Now the city was wide and large, but the people in it were few, and their houses were not yet built.

⁵And my God put it into my mind *and* heart to assemble the nobles, the officers, and the people, that they might be counted by genealogy. And I found a register of the genealogy of those who came [from Babylon] at the first, and found written in it:

⁶These are the people of the province who came up out of the captivity of those exiles whom Nebuchadnezzar the king of Babylon had carried away; they returned to Jerusalem and to Judah, each to his town,

⁷Who came with Zerubbabel, Jeshua, Nehemiah [not the author], Azariah, Raamiah, Nahamani, Mordecai, Bilshan, Mispereth, Bigvai, Nehum, Baanah. The men of Israel numbered:

⁸The sons of Parosh, 2,172.

⁹The sons of Shephatiah, 372.

¹⁰The sons of Arah, 652.

¹¹The sons of Pahath-moab, namely the sons of Jeshua and Joab, 2,818.

¹²The sons of Elam, 1,254.

¹³The sons of Zattu, 845.

¹⁴The sons of Zaccai, 760.

¹⁵The sons of Binnui, 648.

¹⁶The sons of Bebai, 628.

¹⁷The sons of Azgad, 2,322.

## New International Version

18 of Adonikam     667
19 of Bigvai     2,067
20 of Adin     655
21 of Ater (through Hezekiah)     98
22 of Hashum     328
23 of Bezai     324
24 of Hariph     112
25 of Gibeon     95
26 the men of Bethlehem and Netophah     188
27 of Anathoth     128
28 of Beth Azmaveth     42
29 of Kiriath Jearim, Kephirah and Beeroth     743
30 of Ramah and Geba     621
31 of Mikmash     122
32 of Bethel and Ai     123
33 of the other Nebo     52
34 of the other Elam     1,254
35 of Harim     320
36 of Jericho     345
37 of Lod, Hadid and Ono     721
38 of Senaah     3,930

39 The priests:

the descendants of Jedaiah (through the
family of Jeshua)     973
40 of Immer     1,052
41 of Pashhur     1,247
42 of Harim     1,017

43 The Levites:

the descendants of Jeshua (through Kadmiel
through the line of Hodaviah)     74

44 The musicians:

the descendants of Asaph     148

45 The gatekeepers:

the descendants of
Shallum, Ater, Talmon, Akkub, Hatita and
Shobai     138

46 The temple servants:

the descendants of
Ziha, Hasupha, Tabbaoth,
47 Keros, Sia, Padon,
48 Lebana, Hagaba, Shalmai,
49 Hanan, Giddel, Gahar,
50 Reaiah, Rezin, Nekoda,
51 Gazzam, Uzza, Paseah,
52 Besai, Meunim, Nephusim,
53 Bakbuk, Hakupha, Harhur,
54 Bazluth, Mehida, Harsha,
55 Barkos, Sisera, Temah,
56 Neziah and Hatipha

57 The descendants of the servants of Solomon:

the descendants of
Sotai, Sophereth, Perida,
58 Jaala, Darkon, Giddel,
59 Shephatiah, Hattil,
Pokereth-Hazzebaim and Amon

## Amplified Bible

18 The sons of Adonikam, 667.
19 The sons of Bigvai, 2,067.
20 The sons of Adin, 655.
21 The sons of Ater, namely of Hezekiah, 98.
22 The sons of Hashum, 328.
23 The sons of Bezai, 324.
24 The sons of Hariph, 112.
25 The sons of Gibeon, 95.
26 The men of Bethlehem and Netophah, 188.
27 The men of Anathoth, 128.
28 The men of Beth-azmaveth, 42.
29 The men of Kiriath-jearim, Chephirah, and Beeroth, 743.
30 The men of Ramah and Geba, 621.
31 The men of Michmas, 122.
32 The men of Bethel and Ai, 123.
33 The men of the other Nebo, 52.
34 The sons of the other Elam, 1,254.
35 The sons of Harim, 320.
36 The sons of Jericho, 345.
37 The sons of Lod, Hadid, and Ono, 721.
38 The sons of Senaah, 3,930.
39 The priests: the sons of Jedaiah, namely the house of Jeshua, 973.
40 The sons of Immer, 1,052.
41 The sons of Pashhur, 1,247.
42 The sons of Harim, 1,017.
43 The Levites: the sons of Jeshua, namely of Kadmiel of the sons of Hodevah, 74.
44 The singers: the sons of Asaph, 148.
45 The gatekeepers: the sons of Shallum, of Ater, of Talmon, of Akkub, of Hatita, and of Shobai, 138.
46 The Nethinim [temple servants]: the sons of Ziha, of Hasupha, of Tabbaoth,
47 Of Keros, of Sia, of Padon,
48 Of Lebana, of Hagaba, of Shalmai,
49 Of Hanan, of Giddel, of Gahar,
50 Of Reaiah, of Rezin, of Nekoda,
51 Of Gazzam, of Uzza, of Paseah,
52 Of Besai, of Meunim, of Nephushesim,
53 Of Bakbuk, of Hakupha, of Harhur,
54 Of Bazlith, of Mehida, of Harsha,
55 Of Barkos, of Sisera, of Temah,
56 Of Neziah, of Hatipha.
57 The sons of Solomon's servants: the sons of Sotai, of Sophereth, of Perida,
58 Of Jaala, of Darkon, of Giddel,
59 Of Shephatiah, of Hattil, of Pochereth-hazzebaim, of Amon.

## New International Version

[60] The temple servants and the descendants
of the servants of Solomon          392

[61] The following came up from the towns of Tel Melah, Tel Harsha, Kerub, Addon and Immer, but they could not show that their families were descended from Israel:

[62] the descendants of
Delaiah, Tobiah and Nekoda          642

[63] And from among the priests:

the descendants of
Hobaiah, Hakkoz and Barzillai (a man who had married a daughter of Barzillai the Gileadite and was called by that name).
[64] These searched for their family records, but they could not find them and so were excluded from the priesthood as unclean. [65] The governor, therefore, ordered them not to eat any of the most sacred food until there should be a priest ministering with the Urim and Thummim.

[66] The whole company numbered 42,360, [67] besides their 7,337 male and female slaves; and they also had 245 male and female singers. [68] There were 736 horses, 245 mules,[a] [69] 435 camels and 6,720 donkeys.

[70] Some of the heads of the families contributed to the work. The governor gave to the treasury 1,000 darics[b] of gold, 50 bowls and 530 garments for priests. [71] Some of the heads of the families gave to the treasury for the work 20,000 darics[c] of gold and 2,200 minas[d] of silver. [72] The total given by the rest of the people was 20,000 darics of gold, 2,000 minas[e] of silver and 67 garments for priests. [73] The priests, the Levites, the gatekeepers, the musicians and the temple servants, along with certain of the people and the rest of the Israelites, settled in their own towns.

### Ezra Reads the Law

When the seventh month came and the Israelites had settled in their towns, [1] all the people came together as one in the square before the Water Gate. They told Ezra the teacher of the Law to bring out the Book of the Law of Moses, which the LORD had commanded for Israel. [2] So on the first day of the seventh month Ezra the priest brought the Law before the assembly, which was made up of men and women and all who were able to understand. [3] He read it aloud from daybreak till noon as he faced the square before the Water Gate in the presence of the men, women and others who could understand. And all the people listened attentively to the Book of the Law. [4] Ezra the teacher of the Law stood on a high wooden platform built for the occasion. Beside him on his right stood Mattithiah, Shema, Anaiah, Uriah, Hilkiah and Maaseiah; and on his left were Pedaiah, Mishael, Malkijah, Hashum, Hashbaddanah, Zechariah and Meshullam. [5] Ezra opened the book. All the people could see him because he was standing above them; and as he opened it, the people all stood up. [6] Ezra praised the LORD, the great God; and all the people lifted their hands and responded, "Amen! Amen!" Then they bowed down and worshiped the LORD with their faces to the ground. [7] The Levites—Jeshua, Bani, Sherebiah, Jamin, Akkub, Shabbethai, Hodiah, Maaseiah, Kelita, Azariah, Jozabad,

## Amplified Bible

[60] All the Nethinim [temple servants] and the sons of Solomon's servants, 392.

[61] And these were they who went up also from Tel-melah, Tel-harsha, Cherub, Addon, and Immer, but they [had no birth records and] could not prove their father's house nor their descent, whether they were of Israel:

[62] The sons of Delaiah, of Tobiah, of Nekoda, 642.

[63] Of the priests: the sons of Hobaiah, of Hakkoz, and of Barzillai, who [was so named because he] married one of the daughters of the [noted] Gileadite Barzillai and was called by their name.

[64] These sought their registration among those recorded in the genealogies, but it was not found; so they were excluded from the priesthood as [ceremonially] unclean.

[65] The governor told them that they should refrain from eating any of the most holy food until a priest with Urim and Thummim should arise [to determine the will of God in the matter].

[66] The congregation all together was 42,360,

[67] Besides their manservants and their maidservants, of whom there were 7,337; and they had 245 singers, men and women.

[68] Their horses were 736; their mules, 245;

[69] Their camels, 435; their donkeys, 6,720.

[70] And some of the heads of fathers' houses gave to the work. The Tirshatha or governor gave to the treasury 1,000 darics of gold, 50 basins, 530 priests' garments.

[71] Some of the heads of fathers' houses gave to the treasury for the work 20,000 darics of gold and 2,200 minas of silver.

[72] What the rest of the people gave was 20,000 darics of gold, 2,000 minas of silver, and 67 priests' garments.

[73] So the priests, the Levites, the gatekeepers, the singers, some of the people, the Nethinim [the temple servants], along with all Israel, dwelt in their towns, and were in them when the seventh month came.

Then all the people gathered together as one man in the broad place before the Water Gate; and they asked Ezra the scribe to bring the Book of the Law of Moses, which the Lord had given to Israel. [2] And Ezra the priest brought the Law before the assembly of both men and women and all who could hear with understanding, on the first of the seventh month. [3] He read from it, facing the broad place before the Water Gate, from early morning until noon, in the presence of the men and women and those who could understand; and all the people were attentive to the Book of the Law. [4] Ezra the scribe stood on a wooden pulpit which they had made for the purpose. And beside him stood Mattithiah, Shema, Anaiah, Uriah, Hilkiah, and Maaseiah on his right hand; and on his left hand, Pedaiah, Mishael, Malchijah, Hashum, Hashbaddana, Zechariah, and Meshullam. [5] Ezra opened the book in sight of all the people, for he was standing above them; and when he opened it, all the people stood up. [6] And Ezra blessed the Lord, the great God. And all the people answered, Amen, Amen, lifting up their hands; and they bowed their heads and worshiped the Lord with faces to the ground. [7] Also Jeshua, Bani, Sherebiah, Jamin, Akkub, Shabbethai, Hodiah, Maaseiah, Kelita, Azariah, Jozabad, Han-

---

[a] 68 Some Hebrew manuscripts (see also Ezra 2:66); most Hebrew manuscripts do not have this verse.    [b] 70 That is, about 19 pounds or about 8.4 kilograms    [c] 71 That is, about 375 pounds or about 170 kilograms; also in verse 72    [d] 71 That is, about 1 1/3 tons or about 1.2 metric tons    [e] 72 That is, about 1 1/4 tons or about 1.1 metric tons

## New International Version

Hanan and Pelaiah—instructed the people in the Law while the people were standing there. [8]They read from the Book of the Law of God, making it clear[a] and giving the meaning so that the people understood what was being read.

[9]Then Nehemiah the governor, Ezra the priest and teacher of the Law, and the Levites who were instructing the people said to them all, "This day is holy to the LORD your God. Do not mourn or weep." For all the people had been weeping as they listened to the words of the Law.

[10]Nehemiah said, "Go and enjoy choice food and sweet drinks, and send some to those who have nothing prepared. This day is holy to our Lord. Do not grieve, for the joy of the LORD is your strength."

[11]The Levites calmed all the people, saying, "Be still, for this is a holy day. Do not grieve."

[12]Then all the people went away to eat and drink, to send portions of food and to celebrate with great joy, because they now understood the words that had been made known to them.

[13]On the second day of the month, the heads of all the families, along with the priests and the Levites, gathered around Ezra the teacher to give attention to the words of the Law. [14]They found written in the Law, which the LORD had commanded through Moses, that the Israelites were to live in temporary shelters during the festival of the seventh month [15]and that they should proclaim this word and spread it throughout their towns and in Jerusalem: "Go out into the hill country and bring back branches from olive and wild olive trees, and from myrtles, palms and shade trees, to make temporary shelters"—as it is written.[b]

[16]So the people went out and brought back branches and built themselves temporary shelters on their own roofs, in their courtyards, in the courts of the house of God and in the square by the Water Gate and the one by the Gate of Ephraim. [17]The whole company that had returned from exile built temporary shelters and lived in them. From the days of Joshua son of Nun until that day, the Israelites had not celebrated it like this. And their joy was very great.

[18]Day after day, from the first day to the last, Ezra read from the Book of the Law of God. They celebrated the festival for seven days, and on the eighth day, in accordance with the regulation, there was an assembly.

### The Israelites Confess Their Sins

**9** On the twenty-fourth day of the same month, the Israelites gathered together, fasting and wearing sackcloth and putting dust on their heads. [2]Those of Israelite descent had separated themselves from all foreigners. They stood in their places and confessed their sins and the sins of their ancestors. [3]They stood where they were and read from the Book of the Law of the LORD their God for a quarter of the day, and spent another quarter in confession and in worshiping the LORD their God. [4]Standing on the stairs of the Levites were Jeshua, Bani, Kadmiel, Shebaniah, Bunni, Sherebiah, Bani and Kenani. They cried out with loud voices to the LORD their God. [5]And the Levites— Jeshua, Kadmiel, Bani, Hashabneiah, Sherebiah, Hodiah, Shebaniah and Pethahiah—said: "Stand up and praise the LORD your God, who is from everlasting to everlasting.[c]"

"Blessed be your glorious name, and may it be exalted above all blessing and praise. [6]You alone are the LORD. You made the heavens, even the highest heavens, and all their starry host, the earth and all that is on it, the seas and all that is in them. You give

## Amplified Bible

an, Pelaiah—the Levites—helped the people to understand the Law, and the people [remained] in their place.

[8]So they read from the Book of the Law of God distinctly, faithfully amplifying *and* giving the sense so that [the people] understood the reading.

[9]And Nehemiah, who was the governor, and Ezra the priest and scribe, and the Levites who taught the people said to all of them, This day is holy to the Lord your God; mourn not nor weep. For all the people wept when they heard the words of the Law.

[10]Then [Ezra] told them, Go your way, eat the fat, drink the sweet drink, and send portions to him for whom nothing is prepared; for this day is holy to our Lord. And be not grieved *and* depressed, for the joy of the Lord is your strength *and* stronghold.

[11]So the Levites quieted all the people, saying, Be still, for the day is holy. And do not be grieved *and* sad.

[12]And all the people went their way to eat, drink, send portions, and make great rejoicing, for they had understood the words that were declared to them.

[13]On the second day, all the heads of fathers' houses, with the priests and Levites, gathered to Ezra the scribe to study *and* understand the words of [a]divine instruction.

[14]And they found written in the law, which the Lord had commanded through Moses, that the Israelites should dwell in booths during the feast of the seventh month

[15]And that they should publish and proclaim in all their towns and in Jerusalem, saying, Go out to the hills and bring branches of olive, wild olive, myrtle, palm, and other leafy trees to make booths, as it is written. [Lev. 23:39, 40.]

[16]So the people went out and brought them and made themselves booths, each on the roof of his house and in their courts and the courts of God's house and in the squares of the Water Gate and the Gate of Ephraim.

[17]All the assembly of returned exiles made booths and dwelt in them; for since the days of Jeshua (Joshua) son of Nun up to that day, the Israelites had not done so. And there was very great rejoicing.

[18]Also day by day, from the first day to the last, Ezra read from the Book of the Law of God. They kept the feast for seven days; the eighth day was a [closing] solemn assembly, according to the ordinance.

**9** Now on the twenty-fourth day of this month, the Israelites were assembled with fasting and in sackcloth and with earth upon their heads.

[2]And the Israelites separated themselves from all foreigners and stood and confessed their sins and the iniquities of their fathers.

[3]And they stood in their place and read from the Book of the Law of the Lord their God for a fourth of the day, and for another fourth of it they confessed and worshiped the Lord their God.

[4]On the stairs of the Levites stood Jeshua, Bani, Kadmiel, Shebaniah, Bunni, Sherebiah, Bani, and Chenani, and they cried with a loud voice to the Lord their God.

[5]Then the Levites—Jeshua, Kadmiel, Bani, Hashabneiah, Sherebiah, Hodiah, Shebaniah, and Pethahiah—said, Stand up and bless the Lord your God from everlasting to everlasting. Blessed be Your glorious name which is exalted above all blessing and praise.

[6][And Ezra said], You are the Lord, You alone; You have made heaven, the heaven of heavens, with all their host, the earth, and all that is on it, the seas and all that is in

---

[a] 8 Or *God, translating it ever and ever*   [b] 15 See Lev. 23:37-40.   [c] 5 Or *God for*

[a] See footnote on Ezra 3:2.

## New International Version

life to everything, and the multitudes of heaven worship you.

7"You are the LORD God, who chose Abram and brought him out of Ur of the Chaldeans and named him Abraham. 8You found his heart faithful to you, and you made a covenant with him to give to his descendants the land of the Canaanites, Hittites, Amorites, Perizzites, Jebusites and Girgashites. You have kept your promise because you are righteous.

9"You saw the suffering of our ancestors in Egypt; you heard their cry at the Red Sea.ᵃ 10You sent signs and wonders against Pharaoh, against all his officials and all the people of his land, for you knew how arrogantly the Egyptians treated them. You made a name for yourself, which remains to this day. 11You divided the sea before them, so that they passed through it on dry ground, but you hurled their pursuers into the depths, like a stone into mighty waters. 12By day you led them with a pillar of cloud, and by night with a pillar of fire to give them light on the way they were to take.

13"You came down on Mount Sinai; you spoke to them from heaven. You gave them regulations and laws that are just and right, and decrees and commands that are good. 14You made known to them your holy Sabbath and gave them commands, decrees and laws through your servant Moses. 15In their hunger you gave them bread from heaven and in their thirst you brought them water from the rock; you told them to go in and take possession of the land you had sworn with uplifted hand to give them.

16"But they, our ancestors, became arrogant and stiff-necked, and they did not obey your commands. 17They refused to listen and failed to remember the miracles you performed among them. They became stiff-necked and in their rebellion appointed a leader in order to return to their slavery. But you are a forgiving God, gracious and compassionate, slow to anger and abounding in love. Therefore you did not desert them, 18even when they cast for themselves an image of a calf and said, 'This is your god, who brought you up out of Egypt,' or when they committed awful blasphemies.

19"Because of your great compassion you did not abandon them in the wilderness. By day the pillar of cloud did not fail to guide them on their path, nor the pillar of fire by night to shine on the way they were

## Amplified Bible

them; and You preserve them all, and the hosts of heaven worship You.

7You are the Lord, the God Who chose Abram and brought him out of Ur of the Chaldees and gave him the name Abraham.

8You found his heart faithful before You, and You made the covenant with him to give his descendants the land of the Canaanite, Hittite, Amorite, Perizzite, Jebusite, and Girgashite. And You have fulfilled Your promise, for You are just *and* righteous.

9You saw our fathers' affliction in Egypt, and You heard their cry at the Red Sea.

10You performed signs and wonders against Pharaoh and all his servants and all the people of his land, for You knew that they dealt insolently against the Israelites. And You got for Yourself a name, as it is today.

11You divided the sea before them, so that they went through its midst on dry land; their persecutors You threw into the depths, as a stone into mighty waters.

12Moreover, by a pillar of cloud You led them by day, and by a pillar of fire by night to light the way they should go.

13You came down also upon Mount Sinai and spoke with them from Heaven and gave them right ordinances and true laws, good statutes and commandments.

14And You made known to them Your holy Sabbath and gave them commandments, statutes, and a law through Moses Your servant.

15You gave them bread from heaven for their hunger and brought water for them out of the rock for their thirst; and You told them to go in and possess the land You had sworn to give them. [John 6:31-34.]

16But they and our fathers acted presumptuously and stiffened their necks, and did not heed Your commandments.

17They refused to obey, nor were they mindful of Your wonders *and* miracles which You did among them; but they stiffened their necks and in their rebellion appointed a captain, that they might return to their bondage [in Egypt]. But You are a God ready to pardon, gracious and merciful, slow to anger, and of great steadfast love; and You did not forsake them.

18Even when they had made for themselves a molten calf and said, This is your god, who brought you out of Egypt, and had committed great *and* contemptible blasphemies,

19You in Your great mercy forsook them not in the wilderness; the pillar of the cloud departed not from them by day to lead them in the way, nor the pillar of fire by night to light the way they should go.

---

ᵃ 9 Or *the Sea of Reeds*

## New International Version

to take. [20]You gave your good Spirit to instruct them. You did not withhold your manna from their mouths, and you gave them water for their thirst. [21]For forty years you sustained them in the wilderness; they lacked nothing, their clothes did not wear out nor did their feet become swollen.

[22]"You gave them kingdoms and nations, allotting to them even the remotest frontiers. They took over the country of Sihon[a] king of Heshbon and the country of Og king of Bashan. [23]You made their children as numerous as the stars in the sky, and you brought them into the land that you told their parents to enter and possess. [24]Their children went in and took possession of the land. You subdued before them the Canaanites, who lived in the land; you gave the Canaanites into their hands, along with their kings and the peoples of the land, to deal with them as they pleased. [25]They captured fortified cities and fertile land; they took possession of houses filled with all kinds of good things, wells already dug, vineyards, olive groves and fruit trees in abundance. They ate to the full and were well-nourished; they reveled in your great goodness.

[26]"But they were disobedient and rebelled against you; they turned their backs on your law. They killed your prophets, who had warned them in order to turn them back to you; they committed awful blasphemies. [27]So you delivered them into the hands of their enemies, who oppressed them. But when they were oppressed they cried out to you. From heaven you heard them, and in your great compassion you gave them deliverers, who rescued them from the hand of their enemies.

[28]"But as soon as they were at rest, they again did what was evil in your sight. Then you abandoned them to the hand of their enemies so that they ruled over them. And when they cried out to you again, you heard from heaven, and in your compassion you delivered them time after time.

[29]"You warned them in order to turn them back to your law, but they became arrogant and disobeyed your commands. They sinned against your ordinances, of which you said, 'The person who obeys them will live by them.' Stubbornly they turned their backs on you, became stiff-necked and refused to listen. [30]For many years you were patient with them. By your Spirit you warned them through your prophets. Yet they paid no attention, so you gave them into the hands of the neighboring peoples. [31]But in your great mercy you did not put an end to them or abandon them, for you are a gracious and merciful God.

## Amplified Bible

[20]You also gave Your good Spirit to instruct them, and withheld not Your manna from them, and gave water for their thirst.

[21]Forty years You sustained them in the wilderness; they lacked nothing, their clothes did not wear out, and their feet did not swell.

[22]Also You gave them kingdoms and peoples and allotted to them every corner. So they possessed the land of Sihon king of Heshbon and the land of Og king of Bashan.

[23]Their children You also multiplied as the stars of heaven and brought them into the land which You told their fathers they should go in and possess.

[24]So the descendants went in and possessed the land; and You subdued before them the inhabitants of the land, the Canaanites, and gave them into their hands, with their kings and the peoples of the land, that they might do with them as they would.

[25]And they captured fortified cities and a rich land and took possession of houses full of all good things, cisterns hewn out, vineyards, olive orchards, and fruit trees in abundance. So they ate and were filled and became fat and delighted themselves in Your great goodness.

[26]Yet they were disobedient and rebelled against You and cast Your law behind their back and killed Your prophets who accused *and* warned them to turn to You again; and they committed great *and* contemptible blasphemies.

[27]Therefore You delivered them into the hand of their enemies, who distressed them. In the time of their suffering when they cried to You, You heard them from heaven, and according to Your abundant mercy You gave them deliverers, who saved them from their enemies.

[28]But after they had rest, they did evil again before You; therefore You left them in the hand of their enemies, so that they had dominion over them. Yet when they turned and cried to You, You heard them from heaven, and many times You delivered them according to Your mercies,

[29]And reproved *and* warned them, that You might bring them again to Your law. Yet they acted presumptuously and did not heed Your commandments, but sinned against Your ordinances, which by keeping, a man shall live. And they turned a stubborn shoulder, stiffened their neck, and would not listen.

[30]Yet You bore with them many years more and reproved *and* warned them by Your Spirit through Your prophets; still they would not listen. Therefore You gave them into the power of the peoples of the lands.

[31]Yet in Your great mercies You did not utterly consume them or forsake them, for You are a gracious and merciful God.

---

[a] 22 One Hebrew manuscript and Septuagint; most Hebrew manuscripts *Sihon, that is, the country of the*

## New International Version

[32] "Now therefore, our God, the great God, mighty and awesome, who keeps his covenant of love, do not let all this hardship seem trifling in your eyes—the hardship that has come on us, on our kings and leaders, on our priests and prophets, on our ancestors and all your people, from the days of the kings of Assyria until today. [33] In all that has happened to us, you have remained righteous; you have acted faithfully, while we acted wickedly. [34] Our kings, our leaders, our priests and our ancestors did not follow your law; they did not pay attention to your commands or the statutes you warned them to keep. [35] Even while they were in their kingdom, enjoying your great goodness to them in the spacious and fertile land you gave them, they did not serve you or turn from their evil ways.

[36] "But see, we are slaves today, slaves in the land you gave our ancestors so they could eat its fruit and the other good things it produces. [37] Because of our sins, its abundant harvest goes to the kings you have placed over us. They rule over our bodies and our cattle as they please. We are in great distress.

### The Agreement of the People

[38] "In view of all this, we are making a binding agreement, putting it in writing, and our leaders, our Levites and our priests are affixing their seals to it."[a]

# 10[b] Those who sealed it were:

Nehemiah the governor, the son of Hakaliah.

Zedekiah, [2] Seraiah, Azariah, Jeremiah,
[3] Pashhur, Amariah, Malkijah,
[4] Hattush, Shebaniah, Malluk,
[5] Harim, Meremoth, Obadiah,
[6] Daniel, Ginnethon, Baruch,
[7] Meshullam, Abijah, Mijamin,
[8] Maaziah, Bilgai and Shemaiah.
These were the priests.

[9] The Levites:

Jeshua son of Azaniah, Binnui of the sons of Henadad, Kadmiel,
[10] and their associates: Shebaniah,
Hodiah, Kelita, Pelaiah, Hanan,
[11] Mika, Rehob, Hashabiah,
[12] Zakkur, Sherebiah, Shebaniah,
[13] Hodiah, Bani and Beninu.

[14] The leaders of the people:

Parosh, Pahath-Moab, Elam, Zattu, Bani,
[15] Bunni, Azgad, Bebai,
[16] Adonijah, Bigvai, Adin,
[17] Ater, Hezekiah, Azzur,
[18] Hodiah, Hashum, Bezai,
[19] Hariph, Anathoth, Nebai,
[20] Magpiash, Meshullam, Hezir,
[21] Meshezabel, Zadok, Jaddua,

## Amplified Bible

[32] Now therefore, our God, the great, mighty, and terrible God, Who keeps covenant and mercy *and* lovingkindness, let not all the trouble *and* hardship seem little to You—the hardship that has come upon us, our kings, our princes, our priests, our prophets, our fathers, and on all Your people, since the time of the kings of Assyria to this day.

[33] However, You are just in all that has come upon us; for You have dealt faithfully, but we have done wickedly;

[34] Our kings, our princes, our priests, and our fathers have not kept Your law or hearkened to Your commandments and Your warnings *and* reproofs which You gave them.

[35] They did not serve You in their kingdom, and in Your great goodness that You gave them and in the large and rich land You set before them, nor did they turn from their wicked works.

[36] Behold, we are slaves this day, and as for the land that You gave to our fathers to eat the fruit and the good of it, behold, we are slaves in it.

[37] And its rich yield goes to the kings whom You have set over us because of our sins; they have power also over our bodies and over our livestock at their pleasure. And we are in great distress.

[38] Because of all this, we make a firm *and* sure written covenant, and our princes, Levites, and priests set their seal to it.

# 10 These set their seal: Nehemiah the governor, the son of Hacaliah. And Zedekiah,

[2] Seraiah, Azariah, Jeremiah,
[3] Pashhur, Amariah, Malchijah,
[4] Hattush, Shebaniah, Malluch,
[5] Harim, Meremoth, Obadiah,
[6] Daniel, Ginnethon, Baruch,
[7] Meshullam, Abijah, Mijamin,
[8] Maaziah, Bilgai, Shemaiah—these were the priests.
[9] And the Levites: Jeshua son of Azaniah, Binnui of the sons of Henadad, Kadmiel,
[10] And their brethren: Shebaniah, Hodiah, Kelita, Pelaiah, Hanan,
[11] Mica, Rehob, Hashabiah,
[12] Zaccur, Sherebiah, Shebaniah,
[13] Hodiah, Bani, Beninu.
[14] The chiefs of the people: Parosh, Pahath-moab, Elam, Zattu, Bani,
[15] Bunni, Azgad, Bebai,
[16] Adonijah, Bigvai, Adin,
[17] Ater, Hezekiah, Azzur,
[18] Hodiah, Hashum, Bezai,
[19] Hariph, Anathoth, Nebai,
[20] Magpiash, Meshullam, Hezir,
[21] Meshezabel, Zadok, Jaddua,

---

[a] 38 In Hebrew texts this verse (9:38) is numbered 10:1.    [b] In Hebrew texts 10:1-39 is numbered 10:2-40.

## New International Version

22 Pelatiah, Hanan, Anaiah,
23 Hoshea, Hananiah, Hasshub,
24 Hallohesh, Pilha, Shobek,
25 Rehum, Hashabnah, Maaseiah,
26 Ahiah, Hanan, Anan,
27 Malluk, Harim and Baanah.

28 "The rest of the people—priests, Levites, gatekeepers, musicians, temple servants and all who separated themselves from the neighboring peoples for the sake of the Law of God, together with their wives and all their sons and daughters who are able to understand— 29 all these now join their fellow Israelites the nobles, and bind themselves with a curse and an oath to follow the Law of God given through Moses the servant of God and to obey carefully all the commands, regulations and decrees of the LORD our Lord.

30 "We promise not to give our daughters in marriage to the peoples around us or take their daughters for our sons.

31 "When the neighboring peoples bring merchandise or grain to sell on the Sabbath, we will not buy from them on the Sabbath or on any holy day. Every seventh year we will forgo working the land and will cancel all debts.

32 "We assume the responsibility for carrying out the commands to give a third of a shekel[a] each year for the service of the house of our God: 33 for the bread set out on the table; for the regular grain offerings and burnt offerings; for the offerings on the Sabbaths, at the New Moon feasts and at the appointed festivals; for the holy offerings; for sin offerings[b] to make atonement for Israel; and for all the duties of the house of our God.

34 "We—the priests, the Levites and the people—have cast lots to determine when each of our families is to bring to the house of our God at set times each year a contribution of wood to burn on the altar of the LORD our God, as it is written in the Law.

35 "We also assume responsibility for bringing to the house of the LORD each year the firstfruits of our crops and of every fruit tree.

36 "As it is also written in the Law, we will bring the firstborn of our sons and of our cattle, of our herds and of our flocks to the house of our God, to the priests ministering there.

37 "Moreover, we will bring to the storerooms of the house of our God, to the priests, the first of our ground meal, of our grain offerings, of the fruit of all our trees and of our new wine and olive oil. And we will bring a tithe of our crops to the Levites, for it is the Levites who collect the tithes in all the towns where we work. 38 A priest descended from Aaron is to accompany the Levites when they receive the tithes, and the Levites are to bring a tenth of the tithes up to the house of our God, to the storerooms of the treasury. 39 The people of Israel, including the Levites, are to bring their contributions of grain, new wine and olive oil to the storerooms, where the articles for the sanctuary and for the ministering priests, the gatekeepers and the musicians are also kept.

"We will not neglect the house of our God."

### The New Residents of Jerusalem

**11** Now the leaders of the people settled in Jerusalem. The rest of the people cast lots to bring one out of every ten of them to live in Jerusalem, the holy city, while the remaining nine were to stay in their own towns.

## Amplified Bible

22 Pelatiah, Hanan, Anaiah,
23 Hoshea, Hananiah, Hasshub,
24 Hallohesh, Pilha, Shobek,
25 Rehum, Hashabnah, Maaseiah,
26 Ahiah, Hanan, Anan,
27 Malluch, Harim, Baanah.

28 And the rest of the people—the priests, Levites, gatekeepers, singers, Nethinim [temple servants], and all they who had separated themselves from the peoples of the lands to the Law of God, their wives, their sons, their daughters, all who had knowledge and understanding—

29 Join now, with their brethren, their nobles, and enter into a curse and an oath to walk in God's Law which was given to Moses the servant of God and to observe and do all the commandments of the Lord our Lord, and His ordinances and His statutes:

30 We shall not give our daughters to the peoples of the land or take their daughters for our sons.

31 And if the peoples of the land bring wares or any grain on the Sabbath day to sell, we shall not buy it on the Sabbath or on a holy day; and we shall forego raising crops the seventh year [letting the land lie fallow] and the compulsory payment of every debt. [Exod. 23:10, 11; Deut. 15:1, 2.]

32 Also we pledge ourselves to pay yearly a third of a shekel for the service expenses of the house of our God [which are]:

33 For the showbread; for the continual cereal offerings and burnt offerings; [for the offerings on] the Sabbaths, the New Moons, the set feasts; for the holy things, for the sin offerings to make atonement for Israel; and for all the work of the house of our God.

34 We also cast lots—the priests, the Levites, and the people—for the wood offering, to bring it into the house of our God, according to our fathers' houses, at appointed times year by year, to burn upon the altar of the Lord our God, as it is written in the Law.

35 And [we obligate ourselves] to bring the firstfruits of our ground and the first of all the fruit of all trees year by year to the house of the Lord,

36 As well as the firstborn of our sons and of our cattle, as is written in the Law, and the firstlings of our herds and flocks, to bring to the house of our God, to the priests who minister in [His] house.

37 And we shall bring the first *and* best of our coarse meal, our contributions, the fruit of all kinds of trees, of new wine, and of oil to the priests, to the chambers of the house of our God. And we shall bring the tithes from our ground to the Levites, for they, the Levites, collect the tithes in all our rural towns.

38 And the priest, the son of Aaron, shall be with the Levites when [they] receive tithes, and [they] shall bring one-tenth of the tithes to the house of our God, to the chambers, into the storehouse.

39 For the Israelites and the sons of Levi shall bring the offering of grain, new wine, and oil to the chambers where the vessels of the sanctuary are, along with the priests who minister and the gatekeepers and singers. We will not forsake *or* neglect the house of our God.

**11** Now the leaders of the people dwelt at Jerusalem; the rest of the people also cast lots to bring one of ten to dwell in Jerusalem, the holy city, while nine-tenths dwelt in other towns *and* villages.

---

*a 32* That is, about 1/8 ounce or about 4 grams   *b 33* Or *purification offerings*

## New International Version

2The people commended all who volunteered to live in Jerusalem.

3These are the provincial leaders who settled in Jerusalem (now some Israelites, priests, Levites, temple servants and descendants of Solomon's servants lived in the towns of Judah, each on their own property in the various towns, 4while other people from both Judah and Benjamin lived in Jerusalem):

From the descendants of Judah:

Athaiah son of Uzziah, the son of Zechariah, the son of Amariah, the son of Shephatiah, the son of Mahalalel, a descendant of Perez; 5and Maaseiah son of Baruch, the son of Kol-Hozeh, the son of Hazaiah, the son of Adaiah, the son of Joiarib, the son of Zechariah, a descendant of Shelah. 6The descendants of Perez who lived in Jerusalem totaled 468 men of standing.

7From the descendants of Benjamin:

Sallu son of Meshullam, the son of Joed, the son of Pedaiah, the son of Kolaiah, the son of Maaseiah, the son of Ithiel, the son of Jeshaiah, 8and his followers, Gabbai and Sallai—928 men. 9Joel son of Zikri was their chief officer, and Judah son of Hassenuah was over the New Quarter of the city.

10From the priests:

Jedaiah; the son of Joiarib; Jakin; 11Seraiah son of Hilkiah, the son of Meshullam, the son of Zadok, the son of Meraioth, the son of Ahitub, the official in charge of the house of God, 12and their associates, who carried on work for the temple—822 men; Adaiah son of Jeroham, the son of Pelaliah, the son of Amzi, the son of Zechariah, the son of Pashhur, the son of Malkijah, 13and his associates, who were heads of families—242 men; Amashsai son of Azarel, the son of Ahzai, the son of Meshillemoth, the son of Immer, 14and his[a] associates, who were men of standing—128. Their chief officer was Zabdiel son of Haggedolim.

15From the Levites:

Shemaiah son of Hasshub, the son of Azrikam, the son of Hashabiah, the son of Bunni; 16Shabbethai and Jozabad, two of the heads of the Levites, who had charge of the outside work of the house of God; 17Mattaniah son of Mika, the son of Zabdi, the son of Asaph, the director who led in thanksgiving and prayer; Bakbukiah, second among his associates; and Abda son of Shammua, the son of Galal, the son of Jeduthun. 18The Levites in the holy city totaled 284.

19The gatekeepers:

Akkub, Talmon and their associates, who kept watch at the gates—172 men.

20The rest of the Israelites, with the priests and Levites, were in all the towns of Judah, each on their ancestral property.

21The temple servants lived on the hill of Ophel, and Ziha and Gishpa were in charge of them.

22The chief officer of the Levites in Jerusalem was Uzzi son of Bani, the son of Hashabiah, the son of Mattaniah, the son of Mika. Uzzi was one of Asaph's descendants, who were the musicians responsible for the service of the house of God. 23The musicians were under the king's orders, which regulated their daily activity.

24Pethahiah son of Meshezabel, one of the descendants of Zerah son of Judah, was the king's agent in all affairs relating to the people.

## Amplified Bible

2And the people blessed all the men who willingly offered to live in Jerusalem.

3These are the province chiefs who dwelt in Jerusalem, but in the towns of Judah everyone lived on his property there—Israelites, the priests, the Levites, the temple servants, and the descendants of Solomon's servants.

4And at Jerusalem dwelt certain of the sons of Judah and Benjamin. Of Judah: Athaiah son of Uzziah, the son of Zechariah, the son of Amariah, the son of Shephatiah, the son of Mahalalel, of the sons of Perez;

5Maaseiah son of Baruch, the son of Col-hozeh, the son of Hazaiah, the son of Adaiah, the son of Joiarib, the son of Zechariah, the son of the Shilonite.

6All the sons of Perez who dwelt at Jerusalem were 468 valiant men.

7These are the sons of Benjamin: Sallu son of Meshullam, the son of Joed, the son of Pedaiah, the son of Kolaiah, the son of Maaseiah, the son of Ithiel, son of Jeshaiah,

8And after him Gabbai and Sallai, 928.

9Joel son of Zichri was overseer, and Judah son of Hassenuah was second over the city.

10Of the priests: Jedaiah son of Joiarib; Jachin;

11Seraiah son of Hilkiah, the son of Meshullam, the son of Zadok, the son of Meraioth, the son of Ahitub, ruler of the house of God,

12And their brethren, who did the work of the house, 822; and Adaiah son of Jeroham, the son of Pelaliah, the son of Amzi, the son of Zechariah, the son of Pashhur, the son of Malchijah,

13And his brethren, chiefs of fathers' houses, 242; and Amashsai son of Azarel, the son of Ahzai, the son of Meshillemoth, the son of Immer,

14And their brethren, mighty men of valor, 128. Their overseer was Zabdiel son of Haggedolim [one of the great men].

15And of the Levites: Shemaiah son of Hasshub, the son of Azrikam, the son of Hashabiah, the son of Bunni;

16And Shabbethai and Jozabad, of the chiefs of the Levites, who had charge of the outside work of the house of God;

17Mattaniah son of Mica, the son of Zabdi, the son of Asaph, the leader to begin the thanksgiving in prayer; and Bakbukiah, second among his brethren; and Abda son of Shammua, the son of Galal, the son of Jeduthun.

18The Levites in the holy city were 284.

19The gatekeepers: Akkub, Talmon, and their brethren, who kept watch, were 172.

20And the rest of Israel, with the priests and the Levites, were in all the cities of Judah, each in his inheritance.

21But the temple servants dwelt on [the hill] Ophel; Ziha and Gishpa were over [them].

22Overseer of the Levites in Jerusalem and the work of God's house was Uzzi son of Bani, the son of Hashabiah, the son of Mattaniah, the son of Mica, of Asaph's sons, the singers.

23For the [Persian] king had ordered concerning them that a certain provision be made for the singers, as each day required.

24Pethahiah son of Meshezabel, of the sons of Zerah son of Judah, was at the king's hand in all matters concerning the people.

---

a 14 Most Septuagint manuscripts; Hebrew *their*

## New International Version

25As for the villages with their fields, some of the people of Judah lived in Kiriath Arba and its surrounding settlements, in Dibon and its settlements, in Jekabzeel and its villages, 26in Jeshua, in Moladah, in Beth Pelet, 27in Hazar Shual, in Beersheba and its settlements, 28in Ziklag, in Mekonah and its settlements, 29in En Rimmon, in Zorah, in Jarmuth, 30Zanoah, Adullam and their villages, in Lachish and its fields, and in Azekah and its settlements. So they were living all the way from Beersheba to the Valley of Hinnom.

31The descendants of the Benjamites from Geba lived in Mikmash, Aija, Bethel and its settlements, 32in Anathoth, Nob and Ananiah, 33in Hazor, Ramah and Gittaim, 34in Hadid, Zeboim and Neballat, 35in Lod and Ono, and in Ge Harashim.

36Some of the divisions of the Levites of Judah settled in Benjamin.

### Priests and Levites

**12** These were the priests and Levites who returned with Zerubbabel son of Shealtiel and with Joshua:
Seraiah, Jeremiah, Ezra,
2Amariah, Malluk, Hattush,
3Shekaniah, Rehum, Meremoth,
4Iddo, Ginnethon,a Abijah,
5Mijamin,b Moadiah, Bilgah,
6Shemaiah, Joiarib, Jedaiah,
7Sallu, Amok, Hilkiah and Jedaiah.
These were the leaders of the priests and their associates in the days of Joshua.

8The Levites were Jeshua, Binnui, Kadmiel, Sherebiah, Judah, and also Mattaniah, who, together with his associates, was in charge of the songs of thanksgiving. 9Bakbukiah and Unni, their associates, stood opposite them in the services.

10Joshua was the father of Joiakim, Joiakim the father of Eliashib, Eliashib the father of Joiada, 11Joiada the father of Jonathan, and Jonathan the father of Jaddua.

12In the days of Joiakim, these were the heads of the priestly families:
of Seraiah's family, Meraiah;
of Jeremiah's, Hananiah;
13of Ezra's, Meshullam;
of Amariah's, Jehohanan;
14of Malluk's, Jonathan;
of Shekaniah's,c Joseph;
15of Harim's, Adna;
of Meremoth's,d Helkai;
16of Iddo's, Zechariah;
of Ginnethon's, Meshullam;
17of Abijah's, Zikri;
of Miniamin's and of Moadiah's, Piltai;
18of Bilgah's, Shammua;
of Shemaiah's, Jehonathan;
19of Joiarib's, Mattenai;
of Jedaiah's, Uzzi;
20of Sallu's, Kallai;
of Amok's, Eber;
21of Hilkiah's, Hashabiah;
of Jedaiah's, Nethanel.

22The family heads of the Levites in the days of Eliashib, Joiada, Johanan and Jaddua, as well as those of the priests, were recorded in the reign of Darius the Persian. 23The family heads among the descendants of Levi up to

## Amplified Bible

25As for the villages with their fields, some people of Judah dwelt in Kiriath-arba, Dibon, and Jekabzeel, and their villages,
26In Jeshua, Moladah, Beth-pelet,
27Hazar-shual, Beersheba and its villages,
28Ziklag, Meconah and its villages,
29En-rimmon, Zorah, Jarmuth,
30Zanoah, Adullam, and their villages, Lachish and its fields, Azekah and its villages. So they encamped from Beersheba to the Hinnom Valley.

31The people of Benjamin also dwelt from Geba onward, at Michmash, Aija, Bethel and its villages,
32At Anathoth, Nob, Ananiah,
33Hazor, Ramah, Gittaim,
34Hadid, Zeboim, Neballat,
35Lod, and Ono, the Valley of the Craftsmen.
36And certain divisions of the Levites in Judah were joined to Benjamin.

**12** Now these are the priests and Levites who went up with Zerubbabel son of Shealtiel and with Jeshua:
Seraiah, Jeremiah, Ezra,
2Amariah, Malluch, Hattush,
3Shecaniah, Rehum, Meremoth,
4Iddo, Ginnethoi, Abijah,
5Mijamin, Maadiah, Bilgah,
6Shemaiah, Joiarib, Jedaiah,
7Sallu, Amok, Hilkiah, and Jedaiah. These were the chiefs of the priests and their brethren in the days of Jeshua.

8And the Levites were Jeshua, Binnui, Kadmiel, Sherebiah, Judah, and Mattaniah, who, with his brethren, was over the thanksgiving [choirs].
9Bakbukiah and Unni, their brethren, stood opposite them according to their offices.

10And Jeshua was the father of Joiakim, Joiakim of Eliashib, Eliashib of Joiada,
11Joiada was the father of Jonathan, and Jonathan of Jaddua.

12And in the days of Joiakim were priests, heads of fathers' houses: of Seraiah, Meraiah; of Jeremiah, Hananiah;
13Of Ezra, Meshullam; of Amariah, Jehohanan;
14Of Malluchi, Jonathan; of Shebaniah, Joseph;
15Of Harim, Adna; of Meraioth, Helkai;
16Of Iddo, Zechariah; of Ginnethon, Meshullam;
17Of Abijah, Zichri; of Miniamin and of Moadiah, Piltai;
18Of Bilgah, Shammua; of Shemaiah, Jehonathan;
19Of Joiarib, Mattenai; of Jedaiah, Uzzi;
20Of Sallai, Kallai; of Amok, Eber;
21Of Hilkiah, Hashabiah; of Jedaiah, Nethanel.

22As for the Levites in the days of Eliashib, Joiada, Johanan, and Jaddua, the heads of fathers' houses were recorded, as well as the priests, until the reign of Darius the Persian.

23The sons of Levi, heads of fathers' houses, were re-

---

a 4 Many Hebrew manuscripts and Vulgate (see also verse 16); most Hebrew manuscripts *Ginnethoi*    b 5 A variant of *Miniamin*
c 14 Very many Hebrew manuscripts, some Septuagint manuscripts and Syriac (see also verse 3); most Hebrew manuscripts *Shebaniah's*
d 15 Some Septuagint manuscripts (see also verse 3); Hebrew *Meraioth's*

## New International Version

the time of Johanan son of Eliashib were recorded in the book of the annals. [24]And the leaders of the Levites were Hashabiah, Sherebiah, Jeshua son of Kadmiel, and their associates, who stood opposite them to give praise and thanksgiving, one section responding to the other, as prescribed by David the man of God.

[25]Mattaniah, Bakbukiah, Obadiah, Meshullam, Talmon and Akkub were gatekeepers who guarded the storerooms at the gates. [26]They served in the days of Joiakim son of Joshua, the son of Jozadak, and in the days of Nehemiah the governor and of Ezra the priest, the teacher of the Law.

### Dedication of the Wall of Jerusalem

[27]At the dedication of the wall of Jerusalem, the Levites were sought out from where they lived and were brought to Jerusalem to celebrate joyfully the dedication with songs of thanksgiving and with the music of cymbals, harps and lyres. [28]The musicians also were brought together from the region around Jerusalem—from the villages of the Netophathites, [29]from Beth Gilgal, and from the area of Geba and Azmaveth, for the musicians had built villages for themselves around Jerusalem. [30]When the priests and Levites had purified themselves ceremonially, they purified the people, the gates and the wall.

[31]I had the leaders of Judah go up on top of[a] the wall. I also assigned two large choirs to give thanks. One was to proceed on top of[b] the wall to the right, toward the Dung Gate. [32]Hoshaiah and half the leaders of Judah followed them, [33]along with Azariah, Ezra, Meshullam, [34]Judah, Benjamin, Shemaiah, Jeremiah, [35]as well as some priests with trumpets, and also Zechariah son of Jonathan, the son of Shemaiah, the son of Mattaniah, the son of Micaiah, the son of Zakkur, the son of Asaph, [36]and his associates—Shemaiah, Azarel, Milalai, Gilalai, Maai, Nethanel, Judah and Hanani—with musical instruments prescribed by David the man of God. Ezra the teacher of the Law led the procession. [37]At the Fountain Gate they continued directly up the steps of the City of David on the ascent to the wall and passed above the site of David's palace to the Water Gate on the east.

[38]The second choir proceeded in the opposite direction. I followed them on top of[c] the wall, together with half the people—past the Tower of the Ovens to the Broad Wall, [39]over the Gate of Ephraim, the Jeshanah[d] Gate, the Fish Gate, the Tower of Hananel and the Tower of the Hundred, as far as the Sheep Gate. At the Gate of the Guard they stopped.

[40]The two choirs that gave thanks then took their places in the house of God; so did I, together with half the officials, [41]as well as the priests—Eliakim, Maaseiah, Miniamin, Micaiah, Elioenai, Zechariah and Hananiah with their trumpets— [42]and also Maaseiah, Shemaiah, Eleazar, Uzzi, Jehohanan, Malkijah, Elam and Ezer. The choirs sang under the direction of Jezrahiah. [43]And on that day they offered great sacrifices, rejoicing because God had given them great joy. The women and children also rejoiced. The sound of rejoicing in Jerusalem could be heard far away.

[44]At that time men were appointed to be in charge of the storerooms for the contributions, firstfruits and tithes. From the fields around the towns they were to bring into the storerooms the portions required by the Law for the priests and the Levites, for Judah was pleased with the ministering priests and Levites. [45]They performed the

## Amplified Bible

corded in the Book of the Chronicles until the days of Johanan son of Eliashib.

[24]And the chiefs of the Levites were Hashabiah, Sherebiah, and Jeshua son of Kadmiel, with their brethren opposite them, to praise and to give thanks, as David, God's man, commanded, [one] watch [singing] in response to [the men in the opposite] watch.

[25]Mattaniah, Bakbukiah, Obadiah, Meshullam, Talmon, and Akkub were gatekeepers guarding at the storehouses of the gates.

[26]These were in the days of Joiakim son of Jeshua, the son of Jozadak, and in the days of Nehemiah the governor and of Ezra the priest and scribe.

[27]And for the dedication of the wall of Jerusalem, they sought the Levites in all their places to bring them to Jerusalem to celebrate the dedication with gladness, with thanksgivings, and with singing, cymbals, harps, and lyres.

[28]And the sons of the singers gathered together from the plain *and* circuit around Jerusalem and from the villages of the Netophathites,

[29]And also from Beth-gilgal and the fields of Geba and Azmaveth, for the singers had built for themselves villages around Jerusalem.

[30]And the priests and the Levites purified themselves, the people, the gates, and the wall.

[31]Then I brought the princes of Judah up on the wall, and I appointed two great companies of them who gave thanks and went in procession. One went to the right upon the wall toward the Dung Gate.

[32]And after them went Hoshaiah and half of the princes of Judah,

[33]And Azariah, Ezra, Meshullam,

[34]Judah, Benjamin, Shemaiah, and Jeremiah,

[35]And certain of the priests' sons with trumpets, and Zechariah son of Jonathan, the son of Shemaiah, the son of Mattaniah, the son of Micaiah, the son of Zaccur, the son of Asaph,

[36]And his kinsmen—Shemaiah, Azarel, Milalai, Gilalai, Maai, Nethanel, Judah, Hanani—with the musical instruments of David, God's man. And Ezra the scribe went before them.

[37]At the Fountain Gate they went up straight ahead by the stairs of the City of David at the wall's ascent above David's house to the Water Gate on the east.

[38]The other company of those who gave thanks went to the left; I followed with half of the people upon the wall, above the Tower of the Furnaces to the Broad Wall,

[39]And above the Gate of Ephraim, and by the Old Gate and by the Fish Gate and by the Tower of Hananel and the Tower of Hammeah, even to the Sheep Gate; and they stopped at the Gate of the Guard.

[40]So the two companies of those who gave thanks stood in the house of God, and I, and the half of the officials with me;

[41]And the priests Eliakim, Maaseiah, Miniamin, Micaiah, Elioenai, Zechariah, and Hananiah, with trumpets;

[42]And Maaseiah, Shemaiah, Eleazar, Uzzi, Jehohanan, Malchijah, Elam, and Ezer. And the singers sang *and* made themselves heard, with Jezrahiah as leader.

[43]Also that day they offered great sacrifices and rejoiced, for God had made them rejoice with great joy; the women also and the children rejoiced. The joy of Jerusalem was heard even afar off.

[44]On that day men were appointed over the chambers for the stores, the contributions, the firstfruits, and the tithes, to gather into them the portions required by law for the priests and the Levites according to the fields of the towns, for Judah rejoiced over the priests and Levites who served [faithfully].

---

[a] 31 Or *go alongside*    [b] 31 Or *proceed alongside*    [c] 38 Or *them alongside*    [d] 39 Or *Old*

## New International Version

service of their God and the service of purification, as did also the musicians and gatekeepers, according to the commands of David and his son Solomon. 46For long ago, in the days of David and Asaph, there had been directors for the musicians and for the songs of praise and thanksgiving to God. 47So in the days of Zerubbabel and of Nehemiah, all Israel contributed the daily portions for the musicians and the gatekeepers. They also set aside the portion for the other Levites, and the Levites set aside the portion for the descendants of Aaron.

### Nehemiah's Final Reforms

**13** On that day the Book of Moses was read aloud in the hearing of the people and there it was found written that no Ammonite or Moabite should ever be admitted into the assembly of God, 2because they had not met the Israelites with food and water but had hired Balaam to call a curse down on them. (Our God, however, turned the curse into a blessing.) 3When the people heard this law, they excluded from Israel all who were of foreign descent.

4Before this, Eliashib the priest had been put in charge of the storerooms of the house of our God. He was closely associated with Tobiah, 5and he had provided him with a large room formerly used to store the grain offerings and incense and temple articles, and also the tithes of grain, new wine and olive oil prescribed for the Levites, musicians and gatekeepers, as well as the contributions for the priests.

6But while all this was going on, I was not in Jerusalem, for in the thirty-second year of Artaxerxes king of Babylon I had returned to the king. Some time later I asked his permission 7and came back to Jerusalem. Here I learned about the evil thing Eliashib had done in providing Tobiah a room in the courts of the house of God. 8I was greatly displeased and threw all Tobiah's household goods out of the room. 9I gave orders to purify the rooms, and then I put back into them the equipment of the house of God, with the grain offerings and the incense.

10I also learned that the portions assigned to the Levites had not been given to them, and that all the Levites and musicians responsible for the service had gone back to their own fields. 11So I rebuked the officials and asked them, "Why is the house of God neglected?" Then I called them together and stationed them at their posts.

12All Judah brought the tithes of grain, new wine and olive oil into the storerooms. 13I put Shelemiah the priest, Zadok the scribe, and a Levite named Pedaiah in charge of the storerooms and made Hanan son of Zakkur, the son of Mattaniah, their assistant, because they were considered trustworthy. They were made responsible for distributing the supplies to their fellow Levites.

14Remember me for this, my God, and do not blot out what I have so faithfully done for the house of my God and its services.

15In those days I saw people in Judah treading winepresses on the Sabbath and bringing in grain and loading it on donkeys, together with wine, grapes, figs and all other kinds of loads. And they were bringing all this into Jerusalem on the Sabbath. Therefore I warned them against

## Amplified Bible

45And they performed the due service of their God and of the purification; so did the singers and gatekeepers, as David and his son Solomon had commanded.

46For in the days of David and Asaph of old, there was a chief of singers and songs of praise and thanksgiving to God.

47And all Israel in the days of Zerubbabel and [later] of Nehemiah gave the daily portions for the singers and the gatekeepers; and they set apart what was for the Levites, and the Levites set apart what was for the sons of Aaron [the priests].

**13** On that day they read in the Book of Moses in the audience of the people, and in it was found written that no Ammonite or Moabite should ever come into the assembly of God,

2For they met not the Israelites with food and drink but hired Balaam to curse them; yet our God turned the curse into a blessing. [Num. 22:3-11; Deut. 23:5, 6.]

3When [the Jews] heard the law, they separated from Israel all who were of foreign descent.

4Now before this, Eliashib the priest, who was appointed over the chambers of the house of our God, and was related [by marriage] to Tobiah [our adversary],

5Prepared for Tobiah a large chamber where previously they had put the cereal offerings, the frankincense, the vessels, and the tithes of grain, new wine, and oil which were given by commandment to the Levites, the singers, and gatekeepers, and the contributions for the priests.

6But in all this time I was not at Jerusalem, for in the thirty-second year of Artaxerxes [Persian] king of Babylon I went to the king. Then later I asked leave of him

7And came to Jerusalem. Then I discovered the evil that Eliashib had done for Tobiah in preparing him [an adversary] a chamber in the courts of the house of God!

8And it grieved me exceedingly, and I threw all the house furnishings of Tobiah out of the chamber.

9Then I commanded, and they cleansed the chambers; and I brought back there the vessels of the house of God, with the cereal offerings and the frankincense.

10And I perceived that the portions of the Levites had not been given them, so that the Levites and the singers who did the work [forced by necessity] had each fled to his field.

11Then I contended with the officials and said, Why is the house of God neglected *and* forsaken? I gathered the Levites and singers and set them in their stations.

12Then all Judah brought the tithe of the grain, the new wine, and the oil to the storerooms.

13I set treasurers over the storerooms: Shelemiah the priest, Zadok the scribe, and Pedaiah of the Levites; assisting them was Hanan son of Zaccur, the son of Mattaniah, for they were counted faithful, and their task was to distribute to their brethren.

14O my God, [earnestly] remember me concerning this and wipe not out my good deeds *and* kindnesses done for the house of my God and for His service.

15In those days I saw in Judah men treading winepresses on the Sabbath, bringing in sheaves *or* heaps of grain with which they loaded donkeys, as well as wine, grapes, figs, and all sorts of burdens, which they brought into Jerusalem on the Sabbath day. And I protested *and* warned them on the day they sold the produce.

## New International Version

selling food on that day. [16]People from Tyre who lived in Jerusalem were bringing in fish and all kinds of merchandise and selling them in Jerusalem on the Sabbath to the people of Judah. [17]I rebuked the nobles of Judah and said to them, "What is this wicked thing you are doing—desecrating the Sabbath day? [18]Didn't your ancestors do the same things, so that our God brought all this calamity on us and on this city? Now you are stirring up more wrath against Israel by desecrating the Sabbath."

[19]When evening shadows fell on the gates of Jerusalem before the Sabbath, I ordered the doors to be shut and not opened until the Sabbath was over. I stationed some of my own men at the gates so that no load could be brought in on the Sabbath day. [20]Once or twice the merchants and sellers of all kinds of goods spent the night outside Jerusalem. [21]But I warned them and said, "Why do you spend the night by the wall? If you do this again, I will arrest you." From that time on they no longer came on the Sabbath. [22]Then I commanded the Levites to purify themselves and go and guard the gates in order to keep the Sabbath day holy.

Remember me for this also, my God, and show mercy to me according to your great love.

[23]Moreover, in those days I saw men of Judah who had married women from Ashdod, Ammon and Moab. [24]Half of their children spoke the language of Ashdod or the language of one of the other peoples, and did not know how to speak the language of Judah. [25]I rebuked them and called curses down on them. I beat some of the men and pulled out their hair. I made them take an oath in God's name and said: "You are not to give your daughters in marriage to their sons, nor are you to take their daughters in marriage for your sons or for yourselves. [26]Was it not because of marriages like these that Solomon king of Israel sinned? Among the many nations there was no king like him. He was loved by his God, and God made him king over all Israel, but even he was led into sin by foreign women. [27]Must we hear now that you too are doing all this terrible wickedness and are being unfaithful to our God by marrying foreign women?"

[28]One of the sons of Joiada son of Eliashib the high priest was son-in-law to Sanballat the Horonite. And I drove him away from me.

[29]Remember them, my God, because they defiled the priestly office and the covenant of the priesthood and of the Levites.

[30]So I purified the priests and the Levites of everything foreign, and assigned them duties, each to his own task. [31]I also made provision for contributions of wood at designated times, and for the firstfruits.

Remember me with favor, my God.

## Amplified Bible

[16]There dwelt men of Tyre there also who brought fish and all kinds of wares and sold on the Sabbath to the people of Judah and in Jerusalem.

[17]Then I reproved the nobles of Judah and said, What evil thing is this that you do—profaning the Sabbath day?

[18]Did not your fathers do thus, and did not our God bring all this evil upon us and upon this city? Yet you bring more wrath upon Israel by profaning the Sabbath.

[19]And when it began to get dark at the gates of Jerusalem before the Sabbath [day began], I commanded that the gates should be shut and not be opened till after the Sabbath. And I set some of my servants at the gates to prevent any burden being brought in on the Sabbath day.

[20]So the merchants and sellers of all kinds of wares lodged outside Jerusalem once or twice.

[21]But I reproved *and* warned them, saying, Why do you lodge by the wall? If you do so again, I will lay hands on you. Then they stopped coming on the Sabbath.

[22]And I commanded the Levites to cleanse themselves and come and guard the gates to keep the Sabbath day holy. O my God, [earnestly] remember me concerning this also and spare me according to the greatness of Your mercy *and* loving-kindness.

[23]In those days also I saw Jews who had married wives from Ashdod, Ammon, and Moab.

[24]And their children spoke half in the speech of Ashdod, and could not speak the Hebrew, but in the language of each people.

[25]And I contended with them and reviled them and beat some of them and pulled out their hair and made them swear by God, saying, You shall not give your daughters to their sons, nor take their daughters for your sons or for yourselves.

[26]Did not Solomon king of Israel act treacherously against God *and* miss the mark on account of such women? Among many nations there was no king like him. He was loved by his God, and God made him king over all Israel; yet strange women even caused him to sin [when he was old he turned treacherously away from the Lord to other gods, and God rent his kingdom from him]. [I Kings 11:1-11.]

[27]Shall we then listen to you to do all this great evil and act treacherously against our God by marrying strange (heathen) women?

[28]One of the sons of Joiada son of Eliashib the high priest was son-in-law to Sanballat the Horonite; therefore I chased him from me.

[29]O my God, [earnestly] remember them, because they have defiled the priesthood and the covenant of the priests and Levites.

[30]Thus I cleansed them from everything foreign (heathen), and I defined the duties of the priests and Levites, everyone in his work;

[31]And I provided for the wood offering at appointed times, and for the firstfruits. O my God, [earnestly] remember me for good *and* imprint me [on Your heart]!

# New International Version

## Esther

### Queen Vashti Deposed

**1** This is what happened during the time of Xerxes,[a] the Xerxes who ruled over 127 provinces stretching from India to Cush[b]: [2] At that time King Xerxes reigned from his royal throne in the citadel of Susa, [3] and in the third year of his reign he gave a banquet for all his nobles and officials. The military leaders of Persia and Media, the princes, and the nobles of the provinces were present.

[4] For a full 180 days he displayed the vast wealth of his kingdom and the splendor and glory of his majesty. [5] When these days were over, the king gave a banquet, lasting seven days, in the enclosed garden of the king's palace, for all the people from the least to the greatest who were in the citadel of Susa. [6] The garden had hangings of white and blue linen, fastened with cords of white linen and purple material to silver rings on marble pillars. There were couches of gold and silver on a mosaic pavement of porphyry, marble, mother-of-pearl and other costly stones. [7] Wine was served in goblets of gold, each one different from the other, and the royal wine was abundant, in keeping with the king's liberality. [8] By the king's command each guest was allowed to drink with no restrictions, for the king instructed all the wine stewards to serve each man what he wished.

[9] Queen Vashti also gave a banquet for the women in the royal palace of King Xerxes.

[10] On the seventh day, when King Xerxes was in high spirits from wine, he commanded the seven eunuchs who served him—Mehuman, Biztha, Harbona, Bigtha, Abagtha, Zethar and Karkas— [11] to bring before him Queen Vashti, wearing her royal crown, in order to display her beauty to the people and nobles, for she was lovely to look at. [12] But when the attendants delivered the king's command, Queen Vashti refused to come. Then the king became furious and burned with anger.

[13] Since it was customary for the king to consult experts in matters of law and justice, he spoke with the wise men who understood the times [14] and were closest to the king—Karshena, Shethar, Admatha, Tarshish, Meres, Marsena and Memukan, the seven nobles of Persia and Media who had special access to the king and were highest in the kingdom.

[15] "According to law, what must be done to Queen Vashti?" he asked. "She has not obeyed the command of King Xerxes that the eunuchs have taken to her."

[16] Then Memukan replied in the presence of the king and the nobles, "Queen Vashti has done wrong, not only against the king but also against all the nobles and the peoples of all the provinces of King Xerxes. [17] For the queen's conduct will become known to all the women, and so they will despise their husbands and say, 'King Xerxes commanded Queen Vashti to be brought before him, but she would not come.' [18] This very day the Persian and Median women of the nobility who have heard about the queen's conduct will respond to all the king's nobles in the same way. There will be no end of disrespect and discord.

[19] "Therefore, if it pleases the king, let him issue a royal decree and let it be written in the laws of Persia and Me-

# Amplified Bible

## THE BOOK OF

## Esther

**1** It was in the days of Ahasuerus [Xerxes], the Ahasuerus who reigned from India to Ethiopia over 127 provinces.

[2] In those days when King Ahasuerus sat on his royal throne which was in Shushan *or* Susa [the capital of the Persian Empire] in the palace *or* castle,

[3] In the third year of his reign he made a feast for all his princes and his courtiers. The chief officers of the Persian and Median army and the nobles and governors of the provinces were there before him

[4] While he showed the riches of his glorious kingdom and the splendor and excellence of his majesty for many days, even 180 days.

[5] And when these days were completed, the king made a feast for all the people present in Shushan the capital, both great and small, a seven-day feast in the court of the garden of the king's palace.

[6] There were hangings of fine white cloth, of green and of blue [cotton], fastened with cords of fine linen and purple to silver rings *or* rods and marble pillars. The couches of gold and silver rested on a [mosaic] pavement of porphyry, white marble, mother-of-pearl, and [precious] colored stones.

[7] Drinks were served in different kinds of golden goblets, and there was royal wine in abundance, according to the liberality of the king.

[8] And drinking was according to the law; no one was compelled to drink, for the king had directed all the officials of his palace to serve wine only as each guest desired.

[9] Also Queen Vashti gave a banquet for the women in the royal house which belonged to King Ahasuerus.

[10] On the seventh day, when the king's heart was merry with wine, he commanded Mehuman, Biztha, Harbona, Bigtha, Abagtha, Zethar, and Carkas, the seven eunuchs who ministered to King Ahasuerus as attendants,

[11] To bring Queen Vashti before the king, with her royal crown, to show the peoples and the princes her beauty, for she was fair to behold.

[12] But Queen Vashti refused to come at the king's command conveyed by the eunuchs. Therefore the king was enraged, and his anger burned within him.

[13] Then the king spoke to the wise men who knew the times—for this was the king's procedure toward all who were familiar with law and judgment—

[14] Those next to him being Carshena, Shethar, Admatha, Tarshish, Meres, Marsena, and Memucan, the seven princes of Persia and Media who were in the king's presence and held first place in the kingdom.

[15] [He said] According to the law, what is to be done to Queen Vashti because she has not done the bidding of King Ahasuerus conveyed by the eunuchs?

[16] And Memucan answered before the king and the princes, Vashti the queen has not only done wrong to the king but also to all the princes and to all the peoples who are in all the provinces of King Ahasuerus.

[17] For this deed of the queen will become known to all women, making their husbands contemptible in their eyes, since they will say, King Ahasuerus commanded Queen Vashti to be brought before him, but she did not come.

[18] This very day the ladies of Persia and Media who have heard of the queen's behavior will be telling it to all the king's princes. So contempt and wrath in plenty will arise.

[19] If it pleases the king, let a royal command go forth from him and let it be written among the laws of the Persians and Medes, so that it may not be changed, that

---

[a] 1 Hebrew *Ahasuerus*; here and throughout Esther    [b] 1 That is, the upper Nile region

## New International Version

dia, which cannot be repealed, that Vashti is never again to enter the presence of King Xerxes. Also let the king give her royal position to someone else who is better than she. [20]Then when the king's edict is proclaimed throughout all his vast realm, all the women will respect their husbands, from the least to the greatest."

[21]The king and his nobles were pleased with this advice, so the king did as Memukan proposed. [22]He sent dispatches to all parts of the kingdom, to each province in its own script and to each people in their own language, proclaiming that every man should be ruler over his own household, using his native tongue.

### Esther Made Queen

**2** Later when King Xerxes' fury had subsided, he remembered Vashti and what she had done and what he had decreed about her. [2]Then the king's personal attendants proposed, "Let a search be made for beautiful young virgins for the king. [3]Let the king appoint commissioners in every province of his realm to bring all these beautiful young women into the harem at the citadel of Susa. Let them be placed under the care of Hegai, the king's eunuch, who is in charge of the women; and let beauty treatments be given to them. [4]Then let the young woman who pleases the king be queen instead of Vashti." This advice appealed to the king, and he followed it.

[5]Now there was in the citadel of Susa a Jew of the tribe of Benjamin, named Mordecai son of Jair, the son of Shimei, the son of Kish, [6]who had been carried into exile from Jerusalem by Nebuchadnezzar king of Babylon, among those taken captive with Jehoiachin[a] king of Judah. [7]Mordecai had a cousin named Hadassah, whom he had brought up because she had neither father nor mother. This young woman, who was also known as Esther, had a lovely figure and was beautiful. Mordecai had taken her as his own daughter when her father and mother died.

[8]When the king's order and edict had been proclaimed, many young women were brought to the citadel of Susa and put under the care of Hegai. Esther also was taken to the king's palace and entrusted to Hegai, who had charge of the harem. [9]She pleased him and won his favor. Immediately he provided her with her beauty treatments and special food. He assigned to her seven female attendants selected from the king's palace and moved her and her attendants into the best place in the harem.

[10]Esther had not revealed her nationality and family background, because Mordecai had forbidden her to do so. [11]Every day he walked back and forth near the courtyard of the harem to find out how Esther was and what was happening to her.

[12]Before a young woman's turn came to go in to King Xerxes, she had to complete twelve months of beauty treatments prescribed for the women, six months with oil of myrrh and six with perfumes and cosmetics. [13]And this is how she would go to the king: Anything she wanted was given her to take with her from the harem to the king's palace. [14]In the evening she would go there and in the morning return to another part of the harem to the care of Shaashgaz, the king's eunuch who was in charge of the concubines. She would not return to the king unless he was pleased with her and summoned her by name.

## Amplified Bible

Vashti is to [be divorced and] come no more before King Ahasuerus; and let the king give her royal position to another who is better than she.

[20]So when the king's decree is made and proclaimed throughout all his kingdom, extensive as it is, all wives will give honor to their husbands, high and low.

[21]This advice pleased the king and the princes, and the king did what Memucan proposed.

[22]He sent letters to all the royal provinces, to each in its own script and to every people in their own language, saying that every man should rule in his own house and speak there in the language of his own people. [If he had foreign wives, let them learn his language.]

**2** After these things, when the wrath of King Ahasuerus was pacified, he [earnestly] remembered Vashti and what she had done and what was decreed against her.

[2]Then the king's servants who ministered to him said, Let beautiful young virgins be sought for the king.

[3]And let the king appoint officers in all the provinces of his kingdom to gather all the beautiful young virgins to the capital in Shushan, to the harem under the custody of Hegai, the king's eunuch, who is in charge of the women; and let their things for purification be given them.

[4]And let the maiden who pleases the king be queen instead of Vashti. This pleased the king, and he did so.

[5]There was a certain Jew in the capital in Shushan whose name was Mordecai son of Jair, the son of Shimei, the son of Kish, a Benjamite,

[6]Who had been carried away from Jerusalem with the captives taken away with Jeconiah king of Judah, whom Nebuchadnezzar the king of Babylon had carried into exile.

[7]He had brought up Hadassah, that is Esther, his uncle's daughter, for she had neither father nor mother. The maiden was beautiful and lovely, and when her father and mother died, Mordecai took her as his own daughter.

[8]So when the king's command and his decree were proclaimed and when many maidens were gathered in Shushan the capital under the custody of Hegai, Esther also was taken to the king's house into the custody of Hegai, keeper of the women.

[9]And the maiden pleased [Hegai] and obtained his favor. And he speedily gave her the things for her purification and her portion of food and the seven chosen maids to be given her from the king's palace; and he removed her and her maids to the best [apartment] in the harem.

[10]Esther had not made known her nationality or her kindred, for Mordecai had charged her not to do so.

[11]And Mordecai [who was an [a]attendant in the king's court] walked every day before the court of the harem to learn how Esther was and what would become of her.

[12]Now when the turn of each maiden came to go in to King Ahasuerus, after the regulations for the women had been carried out for twelve months—since this was the regular period for their beauty treatments, six months with oil of myrrh and six months with sweet spices *and* perfumes and the things for the purifying of the women—

[13]Then in this way the maiden came to the king: whatever she desired was given her to take with her from the harem into the king's palace.

[14]In the evening she went and next day she returned into the second harem in the custody of Shaashgaz, the king's eunuch who was in charge of the concubines. She came to the king no more unless the king delighted in her and she was called for by name.

---

[a] 6 Hebrew *Jeconiah*, a variant of *Jehoiachin*

[a] So says *The Septuagint* (Greek translation of the Old Testament).

## New International Version

<sup>15</sup>When the turn came for Esther (the young woman Mordecai had adopted, the daughter of his uncle Abihail) to go to the king, she asked for nothing other than what Hegai, the king's eunuch who was in charge of the harem, suggested. And Esther won the favor of everyone who saw her. <sup>16</sup>She was taken to King Xerxes in the royal residence in the tenth month, the month of Tebeth, in the seventh year of his reign.

<sup>17</sup>Now the king was attracted to Esther more than to any of the other women, and she won his favor and approval more than any of the other virgins. So he set a royal crown on her head and made her queen instead of Vashti. <sup>18</sup>And the king gave a great banquet, Esther's banquet, for all his nobles and officials. He proclaimed a holiday throughout the provinces and distributed gifts with royal liberality.

### Mordecai Uncovers a Conspiracy

<sup>19</sup>When the virgins were assembled a second time, Mordecai was sitting at the king's gate. <sup>20</sup>But Esther had kept secret her family background and nationality just as Mordecai had told her to do, for she continued to follow Mordecai's instructions as she had done when he was bringing her up.

<sup>21</sup>During the time Mordecai was sitting at the king's gate, Bigthana<sup>a</sup> and Teresh, two of the king's officers who guarded the doorway, became angry and conspired to assassinate King Xerxes. <sup>22</sup>But Mordecai found out about the plot and told Queen Esther, who in turn reported it to the king, giving credit to Mordecai. <sup>23</sup>And when the report was investigated and found to be true, the two officials were impaled on poles. All this was recorded in the book of the annals in the presence of the king.

### Haman's Plot to Destroy the Jews

**3** After these events, King Xerxes honored Haman son of Hammedatha, the Agagite, elevating him and giving him a seat of honor higher than that of all the other nobles. <sup>2</sup>All the royal officials at the king's gate knelt down and paid honor to Haman, for the king had commanded this concerning him. But Mordecai would not kneel down or pay him honor.

<sup>3</sup>Then the royal officials at the king's gate asked Mordecai, "Why do you disobey the king's command?" <sup>4</sup>Day after day they spoke to him but he refused to comply. Therefore they told Haman about it to see whether Mordecai's behavior would be tolerated, for he had told them he was a Jew.

<sup>5</sup>When Haman saw that Mordecai would not kneel down or pay him honor, he was enraged. <sup>6</sup>Yet having learned who Mordecai's people were, he scorned the idea of killing only Mordecai. Instead Haman looked for a way to destroy all Mordecai's people, the Jews, throughout the whole kingdom of Xerxes.

<sup>7</sup>In the twelfth year of King Xerxes, in the first month, the month of Nisan, the *pur* (that is, the lot) was cast in the presence of Haman to select a day and month. And the lot fell on<sup>b</sup> the twelfth month, the month of Adar.

## Amplified Bible

<sup>15</sup>Now when the turn for Esther the daughter of Abihail, the uncle of Mordecai who had taken her as his own daughter, had come to go in to the king, she required nothing but what Hegai the king's attendant, the keeper of the women, suggested. And Esther won favor in the sight of all who saw her.

<sup>16</sup>So Esther was taken to King Ahasuerus into his royal palace in the tenth month, the month of Tebeth, in the seventh year of his reign.

<sup>17</sup>And the king loved Esther more than all the women, and she obtained grace and favor in his sight more than all the maidens, so that he set the royal crown on her head and made her queen instead of Vashti.

<sup>18</sup>Then the king gave a great feast for all his princes and his servants, Esther's feast; and he gave a holiday [or a lessening of taxes] to the provinces and gave gifts in keeping with the generosity of the king.

<sup>19</sup>And when the maidens were gathered together the second time, Mordecai was sitting at the king's gate.

<sup>20</sup>Now Esther had not yet revealed her nationality or her people, for she obeyed Mordecai's command to her [<sup>a</sup>to fear God and execute His commands] just as when she was being brought up by him.

<sup>21</sup>In those days, while Mordecai sat at the king's gate, two of the king's eunuchs, Bigthan and Teresh, of those who guarded the door, were angry and sought to lay hands on King Ahasuerus.

<sup>22</sup>And this was known to Mordecai, who told it to Queen Esther, and Esther told the king in Mordecai's name.

<sup>23</sup>When it was investigated and found to be true, both men were hanged on the gallows. And it was recorded in the Book of the Chronicles in the king's presence.

**3** After these things, King <sup>b</sup>Ahasuerus promoted Haman the son of Hammedatha the Agagite and advanced him and set his seat above all the princes who were with him.

<sup>2</sup>And all the king's servants who were at the king's gate bowed down and did reverence to Haman, for the king had so commanded concerning him. But Mordecai did not bow down or do him reverence.

<sup>3</sup>Then the king's servants who were at the king's gate said to Mordecai, Why do you transgress the king's command?

<sup>4</sup>Now when they spoke to him day after day and he paid no attention to them, they told Haman to see whether Mordecai's conduct would stand, for he had told them that he was a Jew.

<sup>5</sup>And when Haman saw that Mordecai did not bow down or do him reverence, he was very angry.

<sup>6</sup>But he scorned laying hands only on Mordecai. So since they had told him Mordecai's nationality, Haman sought to destroy all the Jews, the people of Mordecai, throughout the whole kingdom of Ahasuerus.

<sup>7</sup>In the first month, the month of Nisan, in the twelfth year of King Ahasuerus, Haman caused Pur, that is, lots, to be cast before him day after day [to find a lucky day for his venture], month after month, until the twelfth, the month of Adar.

---

<sup>a</sup> So *The Septuagint* (Greek translation of the Old Testament) reads. The name of God is nowhere mentioned directly in the Hebrew text. <sup>b</sup> There seems to be little doubt that King Ahasuerus is to be identified with the well-known Xerxes, who reigned from 486 to 465 B.C. *The Zondervan Pictorial Bible Dictionary* (Merrill C. Tenney, ed.) gives four close similarities between them which support this identification. Also, "the Ahasuerus of Ezra 4:6, to whom were written accusations against the Jews of Jerusalem, is in all probability the same Xerxes, although sometimes identified with Cambyses son of Cyrus."

---

<sup>a</sup> 21 Hebrew *Bigthan*, a variant of *Bigthana* does not have *And the lot fell on*.　　<sup>b</sup> 7 Septuagint; Hebrew does not have *And the lot fell on*.

## New International Version

[8]Then Haman said to King Xerxes, "There is a certain people dispersed among the peoples in all the provinces of your kingdom who keep themselves separate. Their customs are different from those of all other people, and they do not obey the king's laws; it is not in the king's best interest to tolerate them. [9]If it pleases the king, let a decree be issued to destroy them, and I will give ten thousand talents[a] of silver to the king's administrators for the royal treasury."

[10]So the king took his signet ring from his finger and gave it to Haman son of Hammedatha, the Agagite, the enemy of the Jews. [11]"Keep the money," the king said to Haman, "and do with the people as you please."

[12]Then on the thirteenth day of the first month the royal secretaries were summoned. They wrote out in the script of each province and in the language of each people all Haman's orders to the king's satraps, the governors of the various provinces and the nobles of the various peoples. These were written in the name of King Xerxes himself and sealed with his own ring. [13]Dispatches were sent by couriers to all the king's provinces with the order to destroy, kill and annihilate all the Jews—young and old, women and children—on a single day, the thirteenth day of the twelfth month, the month of Adar, and to plunder their goods. [14]A copy of the text of the edict was to be issued as law in every province and made known to the people of every nationality so they would be ready for that day.

[15]The couriers went out, spurred on by the king's command, and the edict was issued in the citadel of Susa. The king and Haman sat down to drink, but the city of Susa was bewildered.

### Mordecai Persuades Esther to Help

**4** When Mordecai learned of all that had been done, he tore his clothes, put on sackcloth and ashes, and went out into the city, wailing loudly and bitterly. [2]But he went only as far as the king's gate, because no one clothed in sackcloth was allowed to enter it. [3]In every province to which the edict and order of the king came, there was great mourning among the Jews, with fasting, weeping and wailing. Many lay in sackcloth and ashes.

[4]When Esther's eunuchs and female attendants came and told her about Mordecai, she was in great distress. She sent clothes for him to put on instead of his sackcloth, but he would not accept them. [5]Then Esther summoned Hathak, one of the king's eunuchs assigned to attend her, and ordered him to find out what was troubling Mordecai and why.

[6]So Hathak went out to Mordecai in the open square of the city in front of the king's gate. [7]Mordecai told him everything that had happened to him, including the exact amount of money Haman had promised to pay into the royal treasury for the destruction of the Jews. [8]He also gave him a copy of the text of the edict for their annihilation, which had been published in Susa, to show to Esther and explain it to her, and he told him to instruct her to go into the king's presence to beg for mercy and plead with him for her people.

[9]Hathak went back and reported to Esther what Mordecai had said. [10]Then she instructed him to say to Mor-

## Amplified Bible

[8]Then Haman said to King Ahasuerus, There is a certain people scattered abroad and dispersed among the peoples in all the provinces of your kingdom; their laws are different from every other people, neither do they keep the king's laws. Therefore it is not for the king's profit to tolerate them.

[9]If it pleases the king, let it be decreed that they be destroyed, and I will pay 10,000 talents of silver into the hands of those who have charge of the king's business, that it may be brought into the king's treasuries.

[10]And the king took his signet ring from his hand [with which to seal his letters by the king's authority] and gave it to Haman son of Hammedatha the Agagite, the Jews' enemy.

[11]And the king said to Haman, The silver is given to you, the people also, to do with them as it seems good to you.

[12]Then the king's secretaries were called in on the thirteenth day of the first month, and all that Haman had commanded was written to the king's chief rulers and to the governors who were over all the provinces and to the princes of each people, to every province in its own script and to each people in their own language; it was written in the name of King Ahasuerus and it was sealed with the king's [signet] ring.

[13]And letters were sent by special messengers to all the king's provinces—to destroy, to slay, and to do away with all Jews, both young and old, little children and women, in one day, the thirteenth day of the twelfth month, the month of Adar, and to seize their belongings as spoil.

[14]A copy of the writing was to be published *and* given out as a decree in every province to all the peoples to be ready for that day.

[15]The special messengers went out in haste by order of the king, and the decree was given out in Shushan, the capital. And the king and Haman sat down to drink, but the city of Shushan was perplexed [at the strange and alarming decree].

**4** Now when Mordecai learned all that was done, [he] rent his clothes and put on sackcloth with ashes and went out into the midst of the city and cried with a loud and bitter cry.

[2]He came *and* stood before the king's gate, for no one might enter the king's gate clothed with sackcloth.

[3]And in every province, wherever the king's commandment and his decree came, there was great mourning among the Jews, with fasting, weeping, and wailing, and many lay in sackcloth and ashes.

[4]When Esther's maids and her attendants came and told it to her, the queen was exceedingly grieved *and* distressed. She sent garments to clothe Mordecai, with orders to take his sackcloth from off him, but he would not receive them.

[5]Then Esther called for Hathach, one of the king's attendants whom he had appointed to attend her, and ordered him to go to Mordecai to learn what this was and why it was.

[6]So Hathach went out to Mordecai in the open square of the city, which was in front of the king's gate.

[7]And Mordecai told him of all that had happened to him, and the exact sum of money that Haman had promised to pay to the king's treasuries for the Jews to be destroyed.

[8][Mordecai] also gave him a copy of the decree to destroy them, that was given out in Shushan, that he might show it to Esther, explain it to her, and charge her to go to the king, make supplication to him, and plead with him for the lives of her people.

[9]And Hathach came and told Esther the words of Mordecai.

[10]Then Esther spoke to Hathach and gave him a message for Mordecai, saying,

---

[a] 9 That is, about 375 tons or about 340 metric tons

## New International Version

decai, [11]"All the king's officials and the people of the royal provinces know that for any man or woman who approaches the king in the inner court without being summoned the king has but one law: that they be put to death unless the king extends the gold scepter to them and spares their lives. But thirty days have passed since I was called to go to the king."

[12]When Esther's words were reported to Mordecai, [13]he sent back this answer: "Do not think that because you are in the king's house you alone of all the Jews will escape. [14]For if you remain silent at this time, relief and deliverance for the Jews will arise from another place, but you and your father's family will perish. And who knows but that you have come to your royal position for such a time as this?"

[15]Then Esther sent this reply to Mordecai: [16]"Go, gather together all the Jews who are in Susa, and fast for me. Do not eat or drink for three days, night or day. I and my attendants will fast as you do. When this is done, I will go to the king, even though it is against the law. And if I perish, I perish."

[17]So Mordecai went away and carried out all of Esther's instructions.

### Esther's Request to the King

5 On the third day Esther put on her royal robes and stood in the inner court of the palace, in front of the king's hall. The king was sitting on his royal throne in the hall, facing the entrance. [2]When he saw Queen Esther standing in the court, he was pleased with her and held out to her the gold scepter that was in his hand. So Esther approached and touched the tip of the scepter.

[3]Then the king asked, "What is it, Queen Esther? What is your request? Even up to half the kingdom, it will be given you."

[4]"If it pleases the king," replied Esther, "let the king, together with Haman, come today to a banquet I have prepared for him."

[5]"Bring Haman at once," the king said, "so that we may do what Esther asks."

So the king and Haman went to the banquet Esther had prepared. [6]As they were drinking wine, the king again asked Esther, "Now what is your petition? It will be given you. And what is your request? Even up to half the kingdom, it will be granted."

[7]Esther replied, "My petition and my request is this: [8]If the king regards me with favor and if it pleases the king to grant my petition and fulfill my request, let the king and Haman come tomorrow to the banquet I will prepare for them. Then I will answer the king's question."

### Haman's Rage Against Mordecai

[9]Haman went out that day happy and in high spirits. But when he saw Mordecai at the king's gate and observed that he neither rose nor showed fear in his presence, he was filled with rage against Mordecai. [10]Nevertheless, Haman restrained himself and went home.

Calling together his friends and Zeresh, his wife, [11]Haman boasted to them about his vast wealth, his many sons, and all the ways the king had honored him and how he had elevated him above the other nobles and officials. [12]"And that's not all," Haman added. "I'm the only person Queen Esther invited to accompany the king to the banquet she gave. And she has invited me along with the king tomor-

## Amplified Bible

[11]All the king's servants and the people of the king's provinces know that any person, be it man or woman, who shall go into the inner court to the king without being called shall be put to death; there is but one law for him, except [him] to whom the king shall hold out the golden scepter, that he may live. But I have not been called to come to the king for these thirty days.

[12]And they told Mordecai what Esther said.

[13]Then Mordecai told them to return this answer to Esther, Do not flatter yourself that you shall escape in the king's palace any more than all the other Jews.

[14]For if you keep silent at this time, relief and deliverance shall arise for the Jews from elsewhere, but you and your father's house will perish. And who knows but that you have come to the kingdom for such a time as this *and* for this very occasion?

[15]Then Esther told them to give this answer to Mordecai,

[16]Go, gather together all the Jews that are present in Shushan, and fast for me; and neither eat nor drink for three days, night or day. I also and my maids will fast as you do. Then I will go to the king, though it is against the law; and if I perish, I perish.

[17]So Mordecai went away and did all that Esther had commanded him.

5 On the third day [of the fast] Esther put on her royal robes and stood in the royal *or* inner court of the king's palace opposite his [throne room]. The king was sitting on his throne, facing the main entrance of the palace.

[2]And when the king saw Esther the queen standing in the court, she obtained favor in his sight, and he held out to [her] the golden scepter that was in his hand. So Esther drew near and touched the tip of the scepter.

[3]Then the king said to her, What will you have, Queen Esther? What is your request? It shall be given you, even to the half of the kingdom.

[4]And Esther said, If it seems good to the king, let the king and Haman come this day to the dinner that I have prepared for the king.

[5]Then the king said, Cause Haman to come quickly, that what Esther has said may be done.

[6]So the king and Haman came to the dinner that Esther had prepared.

[7]And during the serving of wine, the king said to Esther, What is your petition? It shall be granted you. And what is your request? Even to the half of the kingdom, it shall be performed.

[8]Then Esther said, My petition and my request is: If I have found favor in the sight of the king and if it pleases the king to grant my petition and to perform my request, let the king and Haman come tomorrow to the dinner that I shall prepare for them; and I will do tomorrow as the king has said.

[9]Haman went away that day joyful and elated in heart. But when he saw Mordecai at the king's gate refusing to stand up or show fear before him, he was filled with wrath against Mordecai.

[10]Nevertheless, Haman restrained himself and went home. There he sent and called for his friends and Zeresh his wife.

[11]And Haman recounted to them the glory of his riches, the abundance of his [ten] sons, all the things in which the king had promoted him, and how he had advanced him above the princes and servants of the king.

[12]Haman added, Yes, and today Queen Esther did not let any man come with the king to the dinner she had prepared but myself; and tomorrow also I am invited by her together with the king.

## New International Version

row. ¹³But all this gives me no satisfaction as long as I see that Jew Mordecai sitting at the king's gate."

¹⁴His wife Zeresh and all his friends said to him, "Have a pole set up, reaching to a height of fifty cubits,ᵃ and ask the king in the morning to have Mordecai impaled on it. Then go with the king to the banquet and enjoy yourself." This suggestion delighted Haman, and he had the pole set up.

### Mordecai Honored

**6** That night the king could not sleep; so he ordered the book of the chronicles, the record of his reign, to be brought in and read to him. ²It was found recorded there that Mordecai had exposed Bigthana and Teresh, two of the king's officers who guarded the doorway, who had conspired to assassinate King Xerxes.

³"What honor and recognition has Mordecai received for this?" the king asked.

"Nothing has been done for him," his attendants answered.

⁴The king said, "Who is in the court?" Now Haman had just entered the outer court of the palace to speak to the king about impaling Mordecai on the pole he had set up for him.

⁵His attendants answered, "Haman is standing in the court."

"Bring him in," the king ordered.

⁶When Haman entered, the king asked him, "What should be done for the man the king delights to honor?"

Now Haman thought to himself, "Who is there that the king would rather honor than me?" ⁷So he answered the king, "For the man the king delights to honor, ⁸have them bring a royal robe the king has worn and a horse the king has ridden, one with a royal crest placed on its head. ⁹Then let the robe and horse be entrusted to one of the king's most noble princes. Let them robe the man the king delights to honor, and lead him on the horse through the city streets, proclaiming before him, 'This is what is done for the man the king delights to honor!'"

¹⁰"Go at once," the king commanded Haman. "Get the robe and the horse and do just as you have suggested for Mordecai the Jew, who sits at the king's gate. Do not neglect anything you have recommended."

¹¹So Haman got the robe and the horse. He robed Mordecai, and led him on horseback through the city streets, proclaiming before him, "This is what is done for the man the king delights to honor!"

¹²Afterward Mordecai returned to the king's gate. But Haman rushed home, with his head covered in grief, ¹³and told Zeresh his wife and all his friends everything that had happened to him.

His advisers and his wife Zeresh said to him, "Since Mordecai, before whom your downfall has started, is of Jewish origin, you cannot stand against him—you will surely come to ruin!" ¹⁴While they were still talking with him, the king's eunuchs arrived and hurried Haman away to the banquet Esther had prepared.

### Haman Impaled

**7** So the king and Haman went to Queen Esther's banquet, ²and as they were drinking wine on the second day, the king again asked, "Queen Esther, what is your petition? It will be given you. What is your request? Even up to half the kingdom, it will be granted."

³Then Queen Esther answered, "If I have found favor with you, Your Majesty, and if it pleases you, grant me my

## Amplified Bible

¹³Yet all this benefits me nothing as long as I see Mordecai the Jew sitting at the king's gate.

¹⁴Then Zeresh his wife and all his friends said to him, Let a gallows be made, fifty cubits [seventy-five feet] high, and in the morning speak to the king, that Mordecai may be hanged on it; then you go in merrily with the king to the dinner. And the thing pleased Haman, and he caused the gallows to be made.

**6** On that night the king could not sleep; and he ordered that the book of memorable deeds, the chronicles, be brought, and they were read before the king.

²And it was found written there how Mordecai had told of Bigthana and Teresh, two of the king's attendants who guarded the door, who had sought to lay hands on King Ahasuerus.

³And the king said, What honor or distinction has been given Mordecai for this? Then the king's servants who ministered to him said, Nothing has been done for him.

⁴The king said, Who is in the court? Now Haman had just come into the outer court of the king's palace to ask the king to hang Mordecai on the gallows he had prepared for him.

⁵And the king's servants said to him, Behold, Haman is standing in the court. And the king said, Let him come in.

⁶So Haman came in. And the king said to him, What shall be done to the man whom the king delights to honor? Now Haman said to himself, To whom would the king delight to do honor more than to me?

⁷And Haman said to the king, For the man whom the king delights to honor,

⁸Let royal apparel be brought which the king has worn and the horse which the king has ridden, and a royal crown be set on his head.

⁹And let the apparel and the horse be delivered to the hand of one of the king's most noble princes. Let him array the man whom the king delights to honor, and conduct him on horseback through the open square of the city, and proclaim before him, Thus shall it be done to the man whom the king delights to honor.

¹⁰Then the king said to Haman, Make haste and take the apparel and the horse, as you have said, and do so to Mordecai the Jew, who sits at the king's gate. Leave out nothing that you have spoken.

¹¹Then Haman took the apparel and the horse and conducted Mordecai on horseback through the open square of the city, proclaiming before him, Thus shall it be done to the man whom the king delights to honor.

¹²Then Mordecai came again to the king's gate. But Haman hastened to his house, mourning and having his head covered.

¹³And Haman recounted to Zeresh his wife and all his friends everything that had happened to him. Then his wise men and Zeresh his wife said to him, If Mordecai, before whom you have begun to fall, is of the offspring of the Jews, you cannot prevail against him, but shall surely fall before him.

¹⁴While they were yet talking with him, the king's attendants came and hastily brought Haman to the dinner that Esther had prepared.

**7** So the king and Haman came to dine with Esther the queen.

²And the king said again to Esther on the second day when wine was being served, What is your petition, Queen Esther? It shall be granted. And what is your request? Even to the half of the kingdom, it shall be performed.

³Then Queen Esther said, If I have found favor in your

---

ᵃ *14* That is, about 75 feet or about 23 meters

## New International Version

life—this is my petition. And spare my people—this is my request. [4]For I and my people have been sold to be destroyed, killed and annihilated. If we had merely been sold as male and female slaves, I would have kept quiet, because no such distress would justify disturbing the king.[a]"

[5]King Xerxes asked Queen Esther, "Who is he? Where is he—the man who has dared to do such a thing?"

[6]Esther said, "An adversary and enemy! This vile Haman!"

Then Haman was terrified before the king and queen. [7]The king got up in a rage, left his wine and went out into the palace garden. But Haman, realizing that the king had already decided his fate, stayed behind to beg Queen Esther for his life.

[8]Just as the king returned from the palace garden to the banquet hall, Haman was falling on the couch where Esther was reclining.

The king exclaimed, "Will he even molest the queen while she is with me in the house?"

As soon as the word left the king's mouth, they covered Haman's face. [9]Then Harbona, one of the eunuchs attending the king, said, "A pole reaching to a height of fifty cubits[b] stands by Haman's house. He had it set up for Mordecai, who spoke up to help the king."

The king said, "Impale him on it!" [10]So they impaled Haman on the pole he had set up for Mordecai. Then the king's fury subsided.

### The King's Edict in Behalf of the Jews

**8** That same day King Xerxes gave Queen Esther the estate of Haman, the enemy of the Jews. And Mordecai came into the presence of the king, for Esther had told how he was related to her. [2]The king took off his signet ring, which he had reclaimed from Haman, and presented it to Mordecai. And Esther appointed him over Haman's estate.

[3]Esther again pleaded with the king, falling at his feet and weeping. She begged him to put an end to the evil plan of Haman the Agagite, which he had devised against the Jews. [4]Then the king extended the gold scepter to Esther and she arose and stood before him.

[5]"If it pleases the king," she said, "and if he regards me with favor and thinks it the right thing to do, and if he is pleased with me, let an order be written overruling the dispatches that Haman son of Hammedatha, the Agagite, devised and wrote to destroy the Jews in all the king's provinces. [6]For how can I bear to see disaster fall on my people? How can I bear to see the destruction of my family?"

[7]King Xerxes replied to Queen Esther and to Mordecai the Jew, "Because Haman attacked the Jews, I have given his estate to Esther, and they have impaled him on the pole he set up. [8]Now write another decree in the king's name in behalf of the Jews as seems best to you, and seal it with the king's signet ring—for no document written in the king's name and sealed with his ring can be revoked."

[9]At once the royal secretaries were summoned—on the twenty-third day of the third month, the month of Sivan. They wrote out all Mordecai's orders to the Jews, and to the satraps, governors and nobles of the 127 provinces stretching from India to Cush.[c] These orders were written in the script of each province and the language of

## Amplified Bible

sight, O king and if it pleases the king, let my life be given me at my petition and my people at my request.

[4]For we are sold, I and my people, to be destroyed, slain, and wiped out of existence! But if we had been sold for bondmen and bondwomen, I would have held my tongue, for our affliction is not to be compared with the damage this will do to the king.

[5]Then King Ahasuerus said to Queen Esther, Who is he, and where is he who dares presume in his heart to do that?

[6]And Esther said, An adversary and an enemy, even this wicked Haman. Then Haman was afraid before the king and queen.

[7]And the king arose from the feast in his wrath and went into the palace garden; and Haman stood up to make request for his life to Queen Esther, for he saw that there was evil determined against him by the king.

[8]When the king returned out of the palace garden into the place of the drinking of wine, Haman was falling upon the couch where Esther was. Then said the king, Will he even forcibly assault the queen in my presence, in my own palace? As the king spoke the words, [the servants] covered Haman's face.

[9]Then said Harbonah, one of the attendants serving the king, Behold, the gallows fifty cubits high, which Haman has made for Mordecai, whose warning saved the king, stands at the house of Haman. And the king said, Hang him on it!

[10]So they hanged Haman on the gallows that he had prepared for Mordecai. Then the king's wrath was pacified.

**8** On that day King Ahasuerus gave the house of Haman, the Jews' enemy, to Queen Esther. And Mordecai came before the king, for Esther had told what he was to her.

[2]And the king took off his [signet] ring, which he had taken from Haman, and gave it to Mordecai. And Esther set Mordecai over the house of Haman.

[3]And Esther spoke yet again to the king and fell down at his feet and besought him with tears to avert the evil plot of Haman the Agagite and his scheme that he had devised against the Jews.

[4]Then the king held out to Esther the golden scepter. So Esther arose and stood before the king.

[5]And she said, If it pleases the king and if I have found favor in his sight and the thing seems right before the king and I am pleasing in his eyes, let it be written to reverse the letters devised by Haman son of Hammedatha, the Agagite, which he wrote to destroy the Jews who are in all the king's provinces.

[6]For how can I endure to see the evil that shall come upon my people? Or how can I endure to see the destruction of my kindred?

[7]Then the King Ahasuerus said to Queen Esther and to Mordecai the Jew, Behold, I have given Esther the house of Haman, and him they have hanged upon the gallows because he laid his hand upon the Jews.

[8]Write also concerning the Jews as it pleases you in the king's name, and seal it with the king's [signet] ring—for writing which is in the king's name and sealed with the king's ring no man can reverse.

[9]Then the king's scribes were called, in the third month, the month of Sivan, on the twenty-third day, and it was written according to all that Mordecai commanded to the Jews, to the chief rulers, and the governors and princes of the provinces from India to Ethiopia, 127 provinces, to every province in its own script and to every people in

---

[a] 4 Or *quiet, but the compensation our adversary offers cannot be compared with the loss the king would suffer*   [b] 9 That is, about 75 feet or about 23 meters   [c] 9 That is, the upper Nile region

## New International Version

each people and also to the Jews in their own script and language. ¹⁰Mordecai wrote in the name of King Xerxes, sealed the dispatches with the king's signet ring, and sent them by mounted couriers, who rode fast horses especially bred for the king.

¹¹The king's edict granted the Jews in every city the right to assemble and protect themselves; to destroy, kill and annihilate the armed men of any nationality or province who might attack them and their women and children,ᵃ and to plunder the property of their enemies. ¹²The day appointed for the Jews to do this in all the provinces of King Xerxes was the thirteenth day of the twelfth month, the month of Adar. ¹³A copy of the text of the edict was to be issued as law in every province and made known to the people of every nationality so that the Jews would be ready on that day to avenge themselves on their enemies.

¹⁴The couriers, riding the royal horses, went out, spurred on by the king's command, and the edict was issued in the citadel of Susa.

### The Triumph of the Jews

¹⁵When Mordecai left the king's presence, he was wearing royal garments of blue and white, a large crown of gold and a purple robe of fine linen. And the city of Susa held a joyous celebration. ¹⁶For the Jews it was a time of happiness and joy, gladness and honor. ¹⁷In every province and in every city to which the edict of the king came, there was joy and gladness among the Jews, with feasting and celebrating. And many people of other nationalities became Jews because fear of the Jews had seized them.

**9** On the thirteenth day of the twelfth month, the month of Adar, the edict commanded by the king was to be carried out. On this day the enemies of the Jews had hoped to overpower them, but now the tables were turned and the Jews got the upper hand over those who hated them. ²The Jews assembled in their cities in all the provinces of King Xerxes to attack those determined to destroy them. No one could stand against them, because the people of all the other nationalities were afraid of them. ³And all the nobles of the provinces, the satraps, the governors and the king's administrators helped the Jews, because fear of Mordecai had seized them. ⁴Mordecai was prominent in the palace; his reputation spread throughout the provinces, and he became more and more powerful.

⁵The Jews struck down all their enemies with the sword, killing and destroying them, and they did what they pleased to those who hated them. ⁶In the citadel of Susa, the Jews killed and destroyed five hundred men. ⁷They also killed Parshandatha, Dalphon, Aspatha, ⁸Poratha, Adalia, Aridatha, ⁹Parmashta, Arisai, Aridai and Vaizatha, ¹⁰the ten sons of Haman son of Hammedatha, the enemy of the Jews. But they did not lay their hands on the plunder.

¹¹The number of those killed in the citadel of Susa was reported to the king that same day. ¹²The king said to Queen Esther, "The Jews have killed and destroyed five hundred men and the ten sons of Haman in the citadel of Susa. What have they done in the rest of the king's provinces? Now what is your petition? It will be given you. What is your request? It will also be granted."

## Amplified Bible

their own language and to the Jews according to their writing and according to their language.

¹⁰He wrote in the name of King Ahasuerus and sealed it with the king's ring and sent letters by messengers on horseback, riding on swift steeds, mules, and young dromedaries used in the king's service, bred from the [royal] stud.

¹¹In it the king granted the Jews who were in every city to gather and defend their lives; to destroy, to slay, and to wipe out any armed force that might attack them, their little ones, and women; and to take the enemies' goods for spoil.

¹²On one day in all the provinces of King Ahasuerus, the thirteenth day of the twelfth month, the month of Adar,

¹³A copy of the writing was to be issued as a decree in every province and as a proclamation to all peoples, and the Jews should be ready on that day to avenge themselves upon their enemies.

¹⁴So the couriers, who were mounted on swift beasts that were used in the king's service, went out, being hurried and urged on by the king's command; and the decree was released in Shushan, the capital.

¹⁵And Mordecai went forth from the presence of the king in royal apparel of blue and white, with a great crown of gold and with a robe of fine linen and purple; and the city of Shushan shouted and rejoiced.

¹⁶The Jews had light [a dawn of new hope] and gladness and joy and honor.

¹⁷And in every province and in every city, wherever the king's command and his decree came, the Jews had gladness and joy, a feast and a holiday. And many from among the peoples of the land [submitted themselves to Jewish rite and] became Jews, for the fear of the Jews had fallen upon them.

**9** Now in the twelfth month, the month of Adar, on the thirteenth day of Adar when the king's command and his edict were about to be executed, on the [very] day that the enemies of the Jews had planned for a massacre of them, it was turned to the contrary and the Jews had rule over those who hated them.

²The Jews gathered together in their cities throughout all the provinces of King Ahasuerus to lay hands on such as sought their hurt; and no man could withstand them, for the fear of them had fallen upon all the peoples.

³And all the princes of the provinces and the chief rulers and the governors and they who attended to the king's business helped the Jews, because the fear of Mordecai had fallen upon them.

⁴For Mordecai was great in the king's palace; and his fame went forth throughout all the provinces, for the man Mordecai became more and more powerful.

⁵So the Jews smote all their enemies with the sword, slaughtering and destroying them, and did as they chose with those who hated them.

⁶In Shushan, the capital itself, the Jews slew and destroyed 500 men.

⁷And they killed Parshandatha,

⁸Dalphon, Aspatha, Poratha, Adalia,

⁹Aridatha, Parmashta, Arisai, Aridai,

¹⁰And Vaizatha, the ten sons of Haman son of Hammedatha, the Jews' enemy; but on the spoil they laid not their hands.

¹¹On that day the number of those who were slain in Shushan, the capital, was brought before the king.

¹²And the king said to Esther the queen, The Jews have slain and destroyed 500 men in Shushan, the capital, and the ten sons of Haman. What then have they done in the rest of the king's provinces! What then is your petition? It shall be granted to you. Or what is your request further? It shall be done.

---

ᵃ 11 Or *province, together with their women and children, who might attack them;*

## New International Version

[13]"If it pleases the king," Esther answered, "give the Jews in Susa permission to carry out this day's edict tomorrow also, and let Haman's ten sons be impaled on poles."

[14]So the king commanded that this be done. An edict was issued in Susa, and they impaled the ten sons of Haman. [15]The Jews in Susa came together on the fourteenth day of the month of Adar, and they put to death in Susa three hundred men, but they did not lay their hands on the plunder.

[16]Meanwhile, the remainder of the Jews who were in the king's provinces also assembled to protect themselves and get relief from their enemies. They killed seventy-five thousand of them but did not lay their hands on the plunder. [17]This happened on the thirteenth day of the month of Adar, and on the fourteenth they rested and made it a day of feasting and joy.

[18]The Jews in Susa, however, had assembled on the thirteenth and fourteenth, and then on the fifteenth they rested and made it a day of feasting and joy.

[19]That is why rural Jews—those living in villages—observe the fourteenth of the month of Adar as a day of joy and feasting, a day for giving presents to each other.

### Purim Established

[20]Mordecai recorded these events, and he sent letters to all the Jews throughout the provinces of King Xerxes, near and far, [21]to have them celebrate annually the fourteenth and fifteenth days of the month of Adar [22]as the time when the Jews got relief from their enemies, and as the month when their sorrow was turned into joy and their mourning into a day of celebration. He wrote them to observe the days as days of feasting and joy and giving presents of food to one another and gifts to the poor.

[23]So the Jews agreed to continue the celebration they had begun, doing what Mordecai had written to them. [24]For Haman son of Hammedatha, the Agagite, the enemy of all the Jews, had plotted against the Jews to destroy them and had cast the *pur* (that is, the lot) for their ruin and destruction. [25]But when the plot came to the king's attention,[a] he issued written orders that the evil scheme Haman had devised against the Jews should come back onto his own head, and that he and his sons should be impaled on poles. [26](Therefore these days were called Purim, from the word *pur*.) Because of everything written in this letter and because of what they had seen and what had happened to them, [27]the Jews took it on themselves to establish the custom that they and their descendants and all who join them should without fail observe these two days every year, in the way prescribed and at the time appointed. [28]These days should be remembered and observed in every generation by every family, and in every province and in every city. And these days of Purim should never fail to be celebrated by the Jews—nor should the memory of these days die out among their descendants.

[29]So Queen Esther, daughter of Abihail, along with Mordecai the Jew, wrote with full authority to confirm this second letter concerning Purim. [30]And Mordecai sent letters to all the Jews in the 127 provinces of Xerxes' kingdom—words of goodwill and assurance— [31]to establish these days of Purim at their designated times, as Morde-

## Amplified Bible

[13]Then said Esther, If it pleases the king, let it be granted to the Jews which are in Shushan to do tomorrow also according to this day's decree, and let [the dead bodies of] Haman's ten sons be hanged on the gallows. [Esth. 9:10.]

[14]And the king commanded it to be done; the decree was given in Shushan, and they hanged [the bodies of] Haman's ten sons.

[15]And the Jews that were in Shushan gathered together on the fourteenth day also of the month of Adar and slew 300 men in Shushan, but on the spoil they laid not their hands.

[16]And the other Jews who were in the king's provinces gathered to defend their lives and had relief *and* rest from their enemies and slew of them that hated them 75,000; but on the spoil they laid not their hands.

[17]This was done on the thirteenth day of the month of Adar, and on the fourteenth day they rested and made it a day of feasting and gladness.

[18]But the Jews who were in Shushan [Susa] assembled on the thirteenth day and on the fourteenth, and on the fifteenth day they rested and made it a day of feasting and gladness.

[19]Therefore the Jews of the villages, who dwell in the unwalled towns, make the fourteenth day of the month of Adar a day of gladness and feasting, a holiday, and a day for sending choice portions to one another.

[20]And Mordecai recorded these things, and he sent letters to all the Jews who were in all the provinces of the King Ahasuerus, both near and far,

[21]To command them to keep the fourteenth day of the month of Adar and also the fifteenth, yearly,

[22]As the days on which the Jews got rest from their enemies, and as the month which was turned for them from sorrow to gladness and from mourning into a holiday—that they should make them days of feasting and gladness, days of sending choice portions to one another and gifts to the poor.

[23]So the Jews undertook to do as they had begun and as Mordecai had written to them—

[24]Because Haman son of Hammedatha, the Agagite, the enemy of all the Jews, had plotted against the Jews to destroy them and had cast Pur, that is, the lot, [to find a lucky day] to crush *and* consume and destroy them.

[25]But when Esther brought the matter before the king, he commanded in writing that Haman's wicked scheme which he had devised against the Jews should return upon his own head, and that he and his sons should be hanged on the gallows.

[26]Therefore they called these days Purim, after the name Pur [lot]. Therefore, because of all that was in this letter and what they had faced in this matter and what had happened to them,

[27]The Jews ordained and took it upon themselves and their descendants and all who joined them that without fail every year they would keep these two days at the appointed time and as it was written,

[28]That these days should be remembered (imprinted on their minds) and kept throughout every generation in every family, province, and city, and that these days of Purim should never cease from among the Jews, nor the commemoration of them cease among their descendants.

[29]Then Queen Esther, the daughter of Abihail, with Mordecai the Jew, gave full power [written authority], confirming this second letter about Purim.

[30]And letters were sent to all the Jews, to the 127 provinces of the kingdom of Ahasuerus, in words of peace and truth,

[31]To confirm that these days of Purim should be observed at their appointed times, as Mordecai the Jew and

---

[a] 25 Or *when Esther came before the king*

## New International Version

cai the Jew and Queen Esther had decreed for them, and as they had established for themselves and their descendants in regard to their times of fasting and lamentation. [32]Esther's decree confirmed these regulations about Purim, and it was written down in the records.

### The Greatness of Mordecai

**10** King Xerxes imposed tribute throughout the empire, to its distant shores. [2]And all his acts of power and might, together with a full account of the greatness of Mordecai, whom the king had promoted, are they not written in the book of the annals of the kings of Media and Persia? [3]Mordecai the Jew was second in rank to King Xerxes, preeminent among the Jews, and held in high esteem by his many fellow Jews, because he worked for the good of his people and spoke up for the welfare of all the Jews.

## Amplified Bible

Queen Esther had commanded [the Jews], and as they had ordained for themselves and for their descendants in the matter of their fasts and their lamenting. [32]And the command of Esther confirmed these observances of Purim, and it was written in the book.

**10** King Ahasuerus laid a tribute (tax) on the land and on the coastlands of the sea. [2]And all the acts of his power and of his might, and the full account of the greatness of Mordecai to which the king advanced him, are they not written in the Book of the Chronicles of the Kings of Media and Persia? [3]For Mordecai the Jew was next to King Ahasuerus and great among the Jews, and was a favorite with the multitude of his brethren, for he sought the welfare of his people and spoke peace to his whole race.

THE BOOK OF

# Job

## Prologue

**1** In the land of Uz there lived a man whose name was Job. This man was blameless and upright; he feared God and shunned evil. [2]He had seven sons and three daughters, [3]and he owned seven thousand sheep, three thousand camels, five hundred yoke of oxen and five hundred donkeys, and had a large number of servants. He was the greatest man among all the people of the East.

[4]His sons used to hold feasts in their homes on their birthdays, and they would invite their three sisters to eat and drink with them. [5]When a period of feasting had run its course, Job would make arrangements for them to be purified. Early in the morning he would sacrifice a burnt offering for each of them, thinking, "Perhaps my children have sinned and cursed God in their hearts." This was Job's regular custom.

[6]One day the angels[a] came to present themselves before the LORD, and Satan[b] also came with them. [7]The LORD said to Satan, "Where have you come from?"

Satan answered the LORD, "From roaming throughout the earth, going back and forth on it."

[8]Then the LORD said to Satan, "Have you considered my servant Job? There is no one on earth like him; he is blameless and upright, a man who fears God and shuns evil."

[9]"Does Job fear God for nothing?" Satan replied. [10]"Have you not put a hedge around him and his household and everything he has? You have blessed the work of his hands, so that his flocks and herds are spread throughout the land. [11]But now stretch out your hand and strike everything he has, and he will surely curse you to your face."

[12]The LORD said to Satan, "Very well, then, everything he has is in your power, but on the man himself do not lay a finger."

Then Satan went out from the presence of the LORD.

[13]One day when Job's sons and daughters were feasting and drinking wine at the oldest brother's house, [14]a messenger came to Job and said, "The oxen were plowing and the donkeys were grazing nearby, [15]and the Sabeans attacked and made off with them. They put the servants to the sword, and I am the only one who has escaped to tell you!"

[16]While he was still speaking, another messenger came and said, "The fire of God fell from the heavens and burned up the sheep and the servants, and I am the only one who has escaped to tell you!"

[17]While he was still speaking, another messenger came and said, "The Chaldeans formed three raiding parties and swept down on your camels and made off with them. They put the servants to the sword, and I am the only one who has escaped to tell you!"

[18]While he was still speaking, yet another messenger came and said, "Your sons and daughters were feasting and drinking wine at the oldest brother's house, [19]when suddenly a mighty wind swept in from the desert and struck the four corners of the house. It collapsed on them and they are dead, and I am the only one who has escaped to tell you!"

**1** There was a man in the land of Uz whose name was Job; and that man was blameless and upright, and one who [reverently] feared God and abstained from *and* shunned evil [because it was wrong].

[2]And there were born to him seven sons and three daughters.

[3]He possessed 7,000 sheep, 3,000 camels, 500 yoke of oxen, 500 female donkeys, and a very great body of servants, so that this man was the greatest of all the men of the East.

[4]His sons used to go and feast in the house of each on his day (birthday) in turn, and they invited their three sisters to eat and drink with them. [Gen. 21:8; 40:20.]

[5]And when the days of their feasting were over, Job sent for them to purify *and* hallow them, and rose up early in the morning and offered burnt offerings according to the number of them all. For Job said, It may be that my sons have sinned and cursed *or* disowned God in their hearts. Thus did Job at all [such] times.

[6]Now there was a day when the sons (the angels) of God came to present themselves before the Lord, and Satan (the adversary and accuser) also came among them. [Rev. 12:10.]

[7]And the Lord said to Satan, From where did you come? Then Satan answered the Lord, From going to and fro on the earth and from walking up and down on it.

[8]And the Lord said to Satan, Have you considered My servant Job, that there is none like him on the earth, a blameless and upright man, one who [reverently] fears God and abstains from *and* shuns evil [because it is wrong]?

[9]Then Satan answered the Lord, Does Job [reverently] fear God for nothing?

[10]Have You not put a hedge about him and his house and all that he has, on every side? You have conferred prosperity *and* happiness upon him in the work of his hands, and his possessions have increased in the land.

[11]But put forth Your hand now and touch all that he has, and he will curse You to Your face.

[12]And the Lord said to Satan (the adversary and the accuser), Behold, all that he has is in your power, only upon the man himself put not forth your hand. So Satan went forth from the presence of the Lord.

[13]And there was a day when [Job's] sons and his daughters were eating and drinking wine in their eldest brother's house [on his birthday],

[14]And there came a messenger to Job and said, The oxen were plowing and the donkeys feeding beside them,

[15]And the Sabeans swooped down upon them and took away [the animals]. Indeed, they have slain the servants with the edge of the sword, and I alone have escaped to tell you.

[16]While he was yet speaking, there came also another and said, The fire of God (lightning) has fallen from the heavens and has burned up the sheep and the servants and consumed them, and I alone have escaped to tell you.

[17]While he was yet speaking, there came also another and said, The Chaldeans divided into three bands and made a raid upon the camels and have taken them away, yes, and have slain the servants with the edge of the sword, and I alone have escaped to tell you.

[18]While he was yet speaking, there came also another and said, Your sons and your daughters were eating and drinking wine in their eldest brother's house,

[19]And behold, there came a great [whirlwind] from the desert, and smote the four corners of the house, and it fell upon the young people and they are dead, and I alone have escaped to tell you.

---

[a] 6 Hebrew *the sons of God*    [b] 6 Hebrew *satan* means *adversary*.

# New International Version

<sup>20</sup>At this, Job got up and tore his robe and shaved his head. Then he fell to the ground in worship <sup>21</sup>and said:

"Naked I came from my mother's womb,
and naked I will depart.<sup>a</sup>
The LORD gave and the LORD has taken away;
may the name of the LORD be praised."

<sup>22</sup>In all this, Job did not sin by charging God with wrongdoing.

**2** On another day the angels<sup>b</sup> came to present themselves before the LORD, and Satan also came with them to present himself before him. <sup>2</sup>And the LORD said to Satan, "Where have you come from?"

Satan answered the LORD, "From roaming throughout the earth, going back and forth on it."

<sup>3</sup>Then the LORD said to Satan, "Have you considered my servant Job? There is no one on earth like him; he is blameless and upright, a man who fears God and shuns evil. And he still maintains his integrity, though you incited me against him to ruin him without any reason."

<sup>4</sup>"Skin for skin!" Satan replied. "A man will give all he has for his own life. <sup>5</sup>But now stretch out your hand and strike his flesh and bones, and he will surely curse you to your face."

<sup>6</sup>The LORD said to Satan, "Very well, then, he is in your hands; but you must spare his life."

<sup>7</sup>So Satan went out from the presence of the LORD and afflicted Job with painful sores from the soles of his feet to the crown of his head. <sup>8</sup>Then Job took a piece of broken pottery and scraped himself with it as he sat among the ashes.

<sup>9</sup>His wife said to him, "Are you still maintaining your integrity? Curse God and die!"

<sup>10</sup>He replied, "You are talking like a foolish<sup>c</sup> woman. Shall we accept good from God, and not trouble?"

In all this, Job did not sin in what he said.

<sup>11</sup>When Job's three friends, Eliphaz the Temanite, Bildad the Shuhite and Zophar the Naamathite, heard about all the troubles that had come upon him, they set out from their homes and met together by agreement to go and sympathize with him and comfort him. <sup>12</sup>When they saw him from a distance, they could hardly recognize him; they began to weep aloud, and they tore their robes and sprinkled dust on their heads. <sup>13</sup>Then they sat on the ground with him for seven days and seven nights. No one said a word to him, because they saw how great his suffering was.

## Job Speaks

**3** After this, Job opened his mouth and cursed the day of his birth. <sup>2</sup>He said:

<sup>3</sup>"May the day of my birth perish,
and the night that said, 'A boy is conceived!'
<sup>4</sup>That day—may it turn to darkness;
may God above not care about it;
may no light shine on it.
<sup>5</sup>May gloom and utter darkness claim it once more;
may a cloud settle over it;
may blackness overwhelm it.
<sup>6</sup>That night—may thick darkness seize it;
may it not be included among the days of the year
nor be entered in any of the months.

# Amplified Bible

<sup>20</sup>Then Job arose and rent his robe and shaved his head and fell down upon the ground and worshiped

<sup>21</sup>And said, Naked (without possessions) came I [into this world] from my mother's womb, and naked (without possessions) shall I depart. The Lord gave and the Lord has taken away; blessed (praised and magnified in worship) be the name of the Lord!

<sup>22</sup>In all this Job sinned not nor charged God foolishly.

**2** Again there was a day when the sons of God [the angels] came to present themselves before the Lord, and Satan (the adversary and the accuser) came also among them to present himself before the Lord.

<sup>2</sup>And the Lord said to Satan, From where do you come? And Satan (the adversary and the accuser) answered the Lord, From going to and fro on the earth and from walking up and down on it.

<sup>3</sup>And the Lord said to Satan, Have you considered My servant Job, that there is none like him on the earth, a blameless and upright man, one who [reverently] fears God and abstains from *and* shuns all evil [because it is wrong]? And still he holds fast his integrity, although you moved Me against him to destroy him without cause.

<sup>4</sup>Then Satan answered the Lord, Skin for skin! Yes, all that a man has will he give for his life.

<sup>5</sup>But put forth Your hand now, and touch his bone and his flesh, and he will curse *and* renounce You to Your face.

<sup>6</sup>And the Lord said to Satan, Behold, he is in your hand; only spare his life.

<sup>7</sup>So Satan went forth from the presence of the Lord and smote Job with loathsome *and* painful sores from the sole of his foot to the crown of his head.

<sup>8</sup>And he took a piece of broken pottery with which to scrape himself, and he sat [down] among the ashes.

<sup>9</sup>Then his wife said to him, Do you still hold fast your blameless uprightness? Renounce God and die!

<sup>10</sup>But he said to her, You speak as one of the impious *and* foolish women would speak. What? Shall we accept [only] good at the hand of God and shall we not accept [also] misfortune *and* what is of a bad nature? In [spite of] all this, Job did not sin with his lips.

<sup>11</sup>Now when Job's three friends heard of all this evil that was come upon him, they came each one from his own place, Eliphaz the Temanite and Bildad the Shuhite and Zophar the Naamathite, for they had made an appointment together to come to condole with him and to comfort him.

<sup>12</sup>And when they looked from afar off and saw him [disfigured] beyond recognition, they lifted up their voices and wept; and each one tore his robe, and they cast dust over their heads toward the heavens.

<sup>13</sup>So they sat down with [Job] on the ground for seven days and seven nights, and none spoke a word to him, for they saw that his grief *and* pain were very great.

**3** After this, Job opened his mouth and cursed his day (birthday).

<sup>2</sup>And Job said,

<sup>3</sup>Let the day perish wherein I was born, and the night which announced, There is a man-child conceived.

<sup>4</sup>Let that day be darkness! May not God above regard it, nor light shine upon it.

<sup>5</sup>Let gloom and deep darkness claim it for their own; let a cloud dwell upon it; let all that blackens the day terrify it (the day that I was born).

<sup>6</sup>As for that night, let thick darkness seize it; let it not rejoice among the days of the year; let it not come into the number of the months.

---

<sup>a</sup> 21 Or *will return there*  <sup>b</sup> 1 Hebrew *the sons of God*
<sup>c</sup> 10 The Hebrew word rendered *foolish* denotes moral deficiency.

## New International Version

7 May that night be barren;
    may no shout of joy be heard in it.
8 May those who curse days[a] curse that day,
    those who are ready to rouse Leviathan.
9 May its morning stars become dark;
    may it wait for daylight in vain
    and not see the first rays of dawn,
10 for it did not shut the doors of the womb on me
    to hide trouble from my eyes.

11 "Why did I not perish at birth,
    and die as I came from the womb?
12 Why were there knees to receive me
    and breasts that I might be nursed?
13 For now I would be lying down in peace;
    I would be asleep and at rest
14 with kings and rulers of the earth,
    who built for themselves places now lying in ruins,
15 with princes who had gold,
    who filled their houses with silver.
16 Or why was I not hidden away in the ground like a
        stillborn child,
    like an infant who never saw the light of day?
17 There the wicked cease from turmoil,
    and there the weary are at rest.
18 Captives also enjoy their ease;
    they no longer hear the slave driver's shout.
19 The small and the great are there,
    and the slaves are freed from their owners.

20 "Why is light given to those in misery,
    and life to the bitter of soul,
21 to those who long for death that does not come,
    who search for it more than for hidden treasure,
22 who are filled with gladness
    and rejoice when they reach the grave?
23 Why is life given to a man
    whose way is hidden,
    whom God has hedged in?
24 For sighing has become my daily food;
    my groans pour out like water.
25 What I feared has come upon me;
    what I dreaded has happened to me.
26 I have no peace, no quietness;
    I have no rest, but only turmoil."

### Eliphaz

**4** Then Eliphaz the Temanite replied:

2 "If someone ventures a word with you, will you be
        impatient?
    But who can keep from speaking?
3 Think how you have instructed many,
    how you have strengthened feeble hands.
4 Your words have supported those who stumbled;
    you have strengthened faltering knees.
5 But now trouble comes to you, and you are
        discouraged;
    it strikes you, and you are dismayed.
6 Should not your piety be your confidence
    and your blameless ways your hope?

7 "Consider now: Who, being innocent, has ever
        perished?
    Where were the upright ever destroyed?
8 As I have observed, those who plow evil
    and those who sow trouble reap it.
9 At the breath of God they perish;
    at the blast of his anger they are no more.
10 The lions may roar and growl,
    yet the teeth of the great lions are broken.

## Amplified Bible

7 Yes, let that night be solitary *and* barren; let no joyful
voice come into it.
8 Let those curse it who curse the day, who are skilled in
rousing up Leviathan.
9 Let the stars of the early dawn of that day be dark; let
[the morning] look in vain for the light, nor let it behold
the day's dawning,
10 Because it shut not the doors of my mother's womb
nor hid sorrow *and* trouble from my eyes.
11 Why was I not stillborn? Why did I not give up the
ghost when my mother bore me?
12 Why did the knees receive me? Or why the breasts,
that I should suck?
13 For then would I have lain down and been quiet; I
would have slept; then would I have been at rest [in death]
14 With kings and counselors of the earth, who built up
[now] desolate ruins for themselves,
15 Or with princes who had gold, who filled their houses
with silver.
16 Or [why] was I not a miscarriage, hidden *and* put
away, as infants who never saw light?
17 There [in death] the wicked cease from troubling, and
there the weary are at rest.
18 There the [captive] prisoners rest together; they hear
not the taskmaster's voice.
19 The small and the great are there, and the servant is
free from his master. [Jer. 20:14-18.]
20 Why is light [of life] given to him who is in misery, and
life to the bitter in soul,
21 Who long *and* wait for death, but it comes not, and dig
for it more than for hidden treasures,
22 Who rejoice exceedingly and are elated when they
find the grave?
23 [Why is the light of day given] to a man whose way is
hidden, and whom God has hedged in?
24 For my sighing comes before my food, and my groanings are poured out like water.
25 For the thing which I greatly fear comes upon me, and
that of which I am afraid befalls me.
26 I was not *or* am not at ease, nor had I *or* have I rest,
nor was I *or* am I quiet, yet trouble came *and* still comes
[upon me].

**4** Then Eliphaz the Temanite answered and said,
2 If we venture to converse with you, will you be offended? Yet who can restrain himself from speaking?
3 Behold, you have instructed many, and you have
strengthened the weak hands.
4 Your words have held firm him who was falling, and
you have strengthened the feeble knees.
5 But now it is come upon you, and you faint *and* are
grieved; it touches you, and you are troubled *and* dismayed.
6 Is not your [reverent] fear of God your confidence and
the integrity *and* uprightness of your ways your hope?
7 Think [earnestly], I beg of you: who, being innocent,
ever perished? Or where were those upright *and* in right
standing with God cut off?
8 As I myself have seen, those who plow iniquity and sow
trouble *and* mischief reap the same.
9 By the breath of God they perish, and by the blast of
His anger they are consumed.
10 The roaring of the lion and the voice of the fierce lion,
and the teeth of the young lions are broken.

---

a 8 Or *curse the sea*

## New International Version

[11] The lion perishes for lack of prey,
and the cubs of the lioness are scattered.

[12] "A word was secretly brought to me,
my ears caught a whisper of it.
[13] Amid disquieting dreams in the night,
when deep sleep falls on people,
[14] fear and trembling seized me
and made all my bones shake.
[15] A spirit glided past my face,
and the hair on my body stood on end.
[16] It stopped,
but I could not tell what it was.
A form stood before my eyes,
and I heard a hushed voice:
[17] 'Can a mortal be more righteous than God?
Can even a strong man be more pure than his
Maker?
[18] If God places no trust in his servants,
if he charges his angels with error,
[19] how much more those who live in houses of clay,
whose foundations are in the dust,
who are crushed more readily than a moth!
[20] Between dawn and dusk they are broken to pieces;
unnoticed, they perish forever.
[21] Are not the cords of their tent pulled up,
so that they die without wisdom?'

**5** "Call if you will, but who will answer you?
To which of the holy ones will you turn?
[2] Resentment kills a fool,
and envy slays the simple.
[3] I myself have seen a fool taking root,
but suddenly his house was cursed.
[4] His children are far from safety,
crushed in court without a defender.
[5] The hungry consume his harvest,
taking it even from among thorns,
and the thirsty pant after his wealth.
[6] For hardship does not spring from the soil,
nor does trouble sprout from the ground.
[7] Yet man is born to trouble
as surely as sparks fly upward.

[8] "But if I were you, I would appeal to God;
I would lay my cause before him.
[9] He performs wonders that cannot be fathomed,
miracles that cannot be counted.
[10] He provides rain for the earth;
he sends water on the countryside.
[11] The lowly he sets on high,
and those who mourn are lifted to safety.
[12] He thwarts the plans of the crafty,
so that their hands achieve no success.
[13] He catches the wise in their craftiness,
and the schemes of the wily are swept away.
[14] Darkness comes upon them in the daytime;
at noon they grope as in the night.
[15] He saves the needy from the sword in their mouth;
he saves them from the clutches of the powerful.
[16] So the poor have hope,
and injustice shuts its mouth.

[17] "Blessed is the one whom God corrects;
so do not despise the discipline of the Almighty.[a]

## Amplified Bible

[11] The old and strong lion perishes for lack of prey, and the whelps of the lioness are scattered abroad.
[12] Now a thing was secretly brought to me, and my ear received a whisper of it.
[13] In thoughts from the visions of the night, when deep sleep falls on men,
[14] Fear came upon me and trembling, which made all my bones shake.
[15] Then a spirit passed before my face; the hair of my flesh stood up!
[16] [The spirit] stood still, but I could not discern the appearance of it. A form was before my eyes; there was silence, and then I heard a voice, saying,
[17] Can mortal man be just before God, or be more right than He is? Can a man be pure before his Maker, or be more cleansed than He is? [I John 1:7; Rev. 1:5.]
[18] Even in His [heavenly] servants He puts no trust or confidence, and His angels He charges with folly and error—
[19] How much more those who dwell in houses (bodies) of clay, whose foundations are in the dust, who are crushed like the moth.
[20] Between morning and evening they are destroyed; without anyone noticing it they perish forever.
[21] Is not their tent cord plucked up within them [so that the tent falls]? Do they not die, and that without [acquiring] wisdom?

**5** Call now—is there any who will answer you? And to which of the holy [angels] will you turn?
[2] For [a] vexation and rage kill the foolish man; jealousy and indignation slay the simple.
[3] I have seen the foolish taking root [and outwardly prospering], but suddenly I saw that his dwelling was cursed [for his doom was certain].
[4] His children are far from safety; [involved in their father's ruin] they are crushed in the [court of justice in the city's] gate, and there is no one to deliver them.
[5] His harvest the hungry eat and take it even [when it grows] among the thorns; the snare opens for [his] wealth.
[6] For affliction comes not forth from the dust, neither does trouble spring forth out of the ground.
[7] But man is born to trouble as the sparks and the flames fly upward.
[8] As for me, I would seek God and inquire of and require Him, and to God would I commit my cause—
[9] Who does great things and unsearchable, marvelous things without number,
[10] Who gives rain upon the earth and sends waters upon the fields,
[11] So that He sets on high those who are lowly, and those who mourn He lifts to safety.
[12] He frustrates the devices of the crafty, so that their hands cannot perform their enterprise or anything of [lasting] worth.
[13] He catches the [so-called] wise in their own trickiness, and the counsel of the schemers is brought to a quick end. [I Cor. 3:19, 20.]
[14] In the daytime they meet in darkness, and at noon they grope as in the night.
[15] But [God] saves [the fatherless] from the sword of their mouth, and the needy from the hand of the mighty.
[16] So the poor have hope, and iniquity shuts her mouth.
[17] Happy and fortunate is the man whom God reproves; so do not despise or reject the correction of the Almighty [subjecting you to trial and suffering].

---

[a] This was written many centuries ago, but physicians and psychiatrists today are continually emphasizing the importance of recognizing the principle it lays down if one would avoid being among the constantly increasing number of the mentally ill and those killed by avoidable illnesses.

---

[a] 17 Hebrew *Shaddai*; here and throughout Job

## New International Version

18 For he wounds, but he also binds up;
    he injures, but his hands also heal.
19 From six calamities he will rescue you;
    in seven no harm will touch you.
20 In famine he will deliver you from death,
    and in battle from the stroke of the sword.
21 You will be protected from the lash of the tongue,
    and need not fear when destruction comes.
22 You will laugh at destruction and famine,
    and need not fear the wild animals.
23 For you will have a covenant with the stones of the
    field,
    and the wild animals will be at peace with you.
24 You will know that your tent is secure;
    you will take stock of your property and find
        nothing missing.
25 You will know that your children will be many,
    and your descendants like the grass of the earth.
26 You will come to the grave in full vigor,
    like sheaves gathered in season.

27 "We have examined this, and it is true.
    So hear it and apply it to yourself."

## Job

**6** Then Job replied:

2 "If only my anguish could be weighed
    and all my misery be placed on the scales!
3 It would surely outweigh the sand of the seas—
    no wonder my words have been impetuous.
4 The arrows of the Almighty are in me,
    my spirit drinks in their poison;
    God's terrors are marshaled against me.
5 Does a wild donkey bray when it has grass,
    or an ox bellow when it has fodder?
6 Is tasteless food eaten without salt,
    or is there flavor in the sap of the mallow*a*?
7 I refuse to touch it;
    such food makes me ill.

8 "Oh, that I might have my request,
    that God would grant what I hope for,
9 that God would be willing to crush me,
    to let loose his hand and cut off my life!
10 Then I would still have this consolation—
    my joy in unrelenting pain—
    that I had not denied the words of the Holy One.

11 "What strength do I have, that I should still hope?
    What prospects, that I should be patient?
12 Do I have the strength of stone?
    Is my flesh bronze?
13 Do I have any power to help myself,
    now that success has been driven from me?

14 "Anyone who withholds kindness from a friend
    forsakes the fear of the Almighty.
15 But my brothers are as undependable as intermittent
    streams,
    as the streams that overflow
16 when darkened by thawing ice
    and swollen with melting snow,
17 but that stop flowing in the dry season,
    and in the heat vanish from their channels.
18 Caravans turn aside from their routes;
    they go off into the wasteland and perish.
19 The caravans of Tema look for water,
    the traveling merchants of Sheba look in hope.
20 They are distressed, because they had been confident;
    they arrive there, only to be disappointed.

*a 6 The meaning of the Hebrew for this phrase is uncertain.*

## Amplified Bible

18 For He wounds, but He binds up; He smites, but His
hands heal.
19 He will rescue you in six troubles; in seven nothing
that is evil [for you] will touch you.
20 In famine He will redeem you from death, and in war
from the power of the sword.
21 You shall be hidden from the scourge of the tongue,
neither shall you be afraid of destruction when it comes.
22 At destruction and famine you shall laugh, neither
shall you be afraid of the living creatures of the earth.
23 For you shall be in league with the stones of the field,
and the beasts of the field shall be at peace with you.
24 And you shall know that your tent shall be in peace,
and you shall visit your fold *and* your dwelling and miss
nothing [from them].
25 You shall know also that your children shall be many,
and your offspring as the grass of the earth.
26 You shall come to your grave in ripe old age, and as a
shock of grain goes up [to the threshing floor] in its season.
27 This is what we have searched out; it is true. Hear *and*
heed it and know for yourself [for your good].

**6** Then Job answered,
2 Oh, that my impatience *and* vexation might be
[thoroughly] weighed and all my calamity be laid up over
against them in the balances, one against the other [to see
if my grief is unmanly]!
3 For now it would be heavier than the sand of the sea;
therefore my words have been rash *and* wild,
4 [But it is] because the arrows of the Almighty are within me, the poison which my spirit drinks up; the terrors of
God set themselves in array against me.
5 Does the wild ass bray when it has grass? Or does the
ox low over its fodder?
6 Can that which has no taste to it be eaten without salt?
Or is there any flavor in the white of an egg?
7 [These afflictions] my soul refuses to touch! Such
things are like diseased food to me [sickening and repug-
nant]!
8 Oh, that I might have my request, and that God would
grant me the thing that I long for!
9 I even wish that it would please God to crush me, that
He would let loose His hand and cut me off!
10 Then would I still have consolation—yes, I would
leap [for joy] amid unsparing pain [though I shrink from
it]—that I have not concealed *or* denied the words of the
Holy One!
11 What strength have I left, that I should wait *and* hope?
And what is ahead of me, that I should be patient?
12 Is my strength *and* endurance that of stones? Or is my
flesh made of bronze?
13 Is it not that I have no help in myself, and that wisdom
is quite driven from me?
14 To him who is about to faint *and* despair, kindness
is due from his friend, lest he forsake the fear of the Almighty.
15 [You] my brethren have dealt deceitfully as a brook,
as the channel of brooks that pass away,
16 Which are black *and* turbid by reason of the ice, *and*
in which the snows hides itself;
17 When they get warm, they shrink *and* disappear;
when it is hot, they vanish out of their place.
18 The caravans which travel by way of them turn aside;
they go into the waste places and perish. [Such is my disappointment in you, the friends I fully trusted.]
19 The caravans of Tema looked [for water], the companies of Sheba waited for them [in vain].
20 They were confounded because they had hoped [to
find water]; they came there and were bitterly disappointed.

## New International Version

21 Now you too have proved to be of no help;
    you see something dreadful and are afraid.
22 Have I ever said, 'Give something on my behalf,
    pay a ransom for me from your wealth,
23 deliver me from the hand of the enemy,
    rescue me from the clutches of the ruthless'?

24 "Teach me, and I will be quiet;
    show me where I have been wrong.
25 How painful are honest words!
    But what do your arguments prove?
26 Do you mean to correct what I say,
    and treat my desperate words as wind?
27 You would even cast lots for the fatherless
    and barter away your friend.

28 "But now be so kind as to look at me.
    Would I lie to your face?
29 Relent, do not be unjust;
    reconsider, for my integrity is at stake.*a*
30 Is there any wickedness on my lips?
    Can my mouth not discern malice?

**7** "Do not mortals have hard service on earth?
    Are not their days like those of hired laborers?
2 Like a slave longing for the evening shadows,
    or a hired laborer waiting to be paid,
3 so I have been allotted months of futility,
    and nights of misery have been assigned to me.
4 When I lie down I think, 'How long before I get up?'
    The night drags on, and I toss and turn until dawn.
5 My body is clothed with worms and scabs,
    my skin is broken and festering.

6 "My days are swifter than a weaver's shuttle,
    and they come to an end without hope.
7 Remember, O God, that my life is but a breath;
    my eyes will never see happiness again.
8 The eye that now sees me will see me no longer;
    you will look for me, but I will be no more.
9 As a cloud vanishes and is gone,
    so one who goes down to the grave does not return.
10 He will never come to his house again;
    his place will know him no more.

11 "Therefore I will not keep silent;
    I will speak out in the anguish of my spirit,
    I will complain in the bitterness of my soul.
12 Am I the sea, or the monster of the deep,
    that you put me under guard?
13 When I think my bed will comfort me
    and my couch will ease my complaint,
14 even then you frighten me with dreams
    and terrify me with visions,
15 so that I prefer strangling and death,
    rather than this body of mine.
16 I despise my life; I would not live forever.
    Let me alone; my days have no meaning.

17 "What is mankind that you make so much of them,
    that you give them so much attention,
18 that you examine them every morning
    and test them every moment?
19 Will you never look away from me,
    or let me alone even for an instant?
20 If I have sinned, what have I done to you,
    you who see everything we do?
    Why have you made me your target?
    Have I become a burden to you?*b*

*a 29* Or *my righteousness still stands*   *b 20* A few manuscripts of the
Masoretic Text, an ancient Hebrew scribal tradition and Septuagint;
most manuscripts of the Masoretic Text *I have become a burden to myself.*

## Amplified Bible

21 Now to me you are [like a dried-up brook]; you see
my dismay *and* terror, and [believing me to be a victim
of God's anger] you are afraid [to sympathize with me].
22 Did I ever say, Bring me a gift, or Pay a bribe on my
account from your wealth
23 To deliver me from the adversary's hand, or Redeem
me from the hand of the oppressors?
24 Teach me, and I will hold my peace; and cause me to
understand wherein I have erred.
25 How forcible are words of straightforward speech!
But what does your arguing argue *and* prove *or* your reproof reprove?
26 Do you imagine your words to be an argument, but
the speeches of one who is desperate to be as wind?
27 Yes, you would cast lots over the fatherless and bargain away your friend.
28 Now be pleased to look upon me, that it may be evident to you if I lie [for surely I would not lie to your face].
29 Return [from your suspicion], I pray you, let there be
no injustice; yes, return again [to confidence in me], my
vindication is in it.
30 Is there wrong on my tongue? Cannot my taste discern what is destructive?

**7** Is there not an [appointed] warfare *and* hard labor to
man upon earth? And are not his days like the days
of a hireling?
2 As a servant earnestly longs for the shade *and* the evening shadows, and as a hireling who looks for the reward
of his work,
3 So am I allotted months of futile [suffering], and [long]
nights of misery are appointed to me.
4 When I lie down I say, When shall I arise and the night
be gone? And I am full of tossing to and fro till the dawning of the day.
5 My flesh is clothed with worms and clods of dust; my
skin is broken and has become loathsome, *and* it closes up
and breaks out afresh.
6 My days are swifter than a weaver's shuttle, and are
spent without hope.
7 Oh, remember that my life is but wind (a puff, a breath,
a sob); my eye shall see good no more.
8 The eye of him who sees me shall see me no more;
while your eyes are upon me, I shall be gone.
9 As the cloud is consumed and vanishes away, so he
who goes down to Sheol (the place of the dead) shall come
up no more.
10 He shall return no more to his house, neither shall his
place know him any more.
11 Therefore I will not restrain my mouth; I will speak in
the anguish of my spirit, I will complain in the bitterness
of my soul [O Lord]!
12 Am I the sea, or the sea monster, that You set a watch
over me?
13 When I say, My bed shall comfort me, my couch shall
ease my complaint,
14 Then You scare me with dreams and terrify me
through visions,
15 So that I would choose strangling *and* death rather
than these my bones.
16 I loathe my life; I would not live forever. Let me alone,
for my days are a breath (futility).
17 What is man that You should magnify him *and* think
him important? And that You should set Your mind upon
him? [Ps. 8:4.]
18 And that You should visit him every morning and try
him every moment?
19 How long will Your [plaguing] glance not look away
from me, nor You let me alone till I swallow my spittle?
20 If I have sinned, what [harm] have I done You, O You
Watcher *and* Keeper of men? Why have You set me as a
mark for You, so that I am a burden to myself [and You]?

## New International Version

21 Why do you not pardon my offenses
  and forgive my sins?
For I will soon lie down in the dust;
  you will search for me, but I will be no more."

### Bildad

**8** Then Bildad the Shuhite replied:

2 "How long will you say such things?
  Your words are a blustering wind.
3 Does God pervert justice?
  Does the Almighty pervert what is right?
4 When your children sinned against him,
  he gave them over to the penalty of their sin.
5 But if you will seek God earnestly
  and plead with the Almighty,
6 if you are pure and upright,
  even now he will rouse himself on your behalf
  and restore you to your prosperous state.
7 Your beginnings will seem humble,
  so prosperous will your future be.

8 "Ask the former generation
  and find out what their ancestors learned,
9 for we were born only yesterday and know nothing,
  and our days on earth are but a shadow.
10 Will they not instruct you and tell you?
  Will they not bring forth words from their
    understanding?
11 Can papyrus grow tall where there is no marsh?
  Can reeds thrive without water?
12 While still growing and uncut,
  they wither more quickly than grass.
13 Such is the destiny of all who forget God;
  so perishes the hope of the godless.
14 What they trust in is fragile*a*;
  what they rely on is a spider's web.
15 They lean on the web, but it gives way;
  they cling to it, but it does not hold.
16 They are like a well-watered plant in the sunshine,
  spreading its shoots over the garden;
17 it entwines its roots around a pile of rocks
  and looks for a place among the stones.
18 But when it is torn from its spot,
  that place disowns it and says, 'I never saw you.'
19 Surely its life withers away,
  and*b* from the soil other plants grow.

20 "Surely God does not reject one who is blameless
  or strengthen the hands of evildoers.
21 He will yet fill your mouth with laughter
  and your lips with shouts of joy.
22 Your enemies will be clothed in shame,
  and the tents of the wicked will be no more."

### Job

**9** Then Job replied:

2 "Indeed, I know that this is true.
  But how can mere mortals prove their innocence
    before God?
3 Though they wished to dispute with him,
  they could not answer him one time out of a
    thousand.
4 His wisdom is profound, his power is vast.
  Who has resisted him and come out unscathed?
5 He moves mountains without their knowing it
  and overturns them in his anger.
6 He shakes the earth from its place
  and makes its pillars tremble.

## Amplified Bible

21 And why do You not pardon my transgression and
take away my iniquity? For now shall I lie down in the dust;
and [even if] You will seek me diligently, [it will be too
late, for] I shall not be.

**8** Then answered Bildad the Shuhite,
2 How long will you say these things [Job]? And how
long shall the words of your mouth be as a mighty wind?
3 Does God pervert justice? Or does the Almighty pervert righteousness?
4 If your children have sinned against Him, then He has
delivered them into the power of their transgression.
5 If you will seek God diligently and make your supplication to the Almighty,
6 Then, if you are pure and upright, surely He will bestir
Himself for you and make your righteous dwelling prosperous again.
7 And though your beginning was small, yet your latter
end would greatly increase.
8 For inquire, I pray you, of the former age and apply
yourself to that which their fathers have searched out,
9 For we are but of yesterday and know nothing, because
our days upon earth are a shadow.
10 Shall not [the forefathers] teach you and tell you and
utter words out of their hearts (the deepest part of their
nature)?
11 Can the rush *or* papyrus grow up without marsh? Can
the flag *or* reed grass grow without water?
12 While it is yet green, in flower, and not cut down, it
withers before any other herb [when without water].
13 So are the ways of all who forget God; and the hope of
the godless shall perish.
14 For his confidence breaks, and [the object of] his trust
is a spider's web.
15 He shall lean upon his house, but it shall not stand; he
shall hold fast to it, but it shall not last.
16 He is green before the sun, and his shoots go forth
over his garden.
17 [Godless] his roots are wrapped about the [stone]
heap, and see their way [promisingly] among the rocks.
18 But if [God] snatches him from his property, [then
having passed into the hands of others] it [his property]
will forget *and* deny him, [saying,] I have never seen you
[before, as if ashamed of him—like his former friends].
19 See, this is the joy of going the way [of the ungodly]!
And from the dust others will spring up [to take his place].
20 Behold, as surely as God will never uphold wrongdoers, He will never cast away a blameless man.
21 He will yet fill your mouth with laughter [Job] and
your lips with joyful shouting.
22 Those who hate you will be clothed with shame, and
the tents of the wicked shall be no more.

**9** Then Job answered and said,
2 Yes, I know it is true. But how can mortal man be
right before God?
3 If one should want to contend with Him, he cannot answer one [of His questions] in a thousand.
4 [God] is wise in heart and mighty in strength; who
has [ever] hardened himself against Him and prospered
*or* even been safe?
5 [God] Who removes the mountains, and they know it
not when He overturns them in His anger;
6 Who shakes the earth out of its place, and the pillars
of it tremble;

---

*a* 14 The meaning of the Hebrew for this word is uncertain.
*b* 19 Or *Surely all the joy it has / is that*

## New International Version

⁷He speaks to the sun and it does not shine;
  he seals off the light of the stars.
⁸He alone stretches out the heavens
  and treads on the waves of the sea.
⁹He is the Maker of the Bear*ᵃ* and Orion,
  the Pleiades and the constellations of the south.
¹⁰He performs wonders that cannot be fathomed,
  miracles that cannot be counted.
¹¹When he passes me, I cannot see him;
  when he goes by, I cannot perceive him.
¹²If he snatches away, who can stop him?
  Who can say to him, 'What are you doing?'
¹³God does not restrain his anger;
  even the cohorts of Rahab cowered at his feet.

¹⁴"How then can I dispute with him?
  How can I find words to argue with him?
¹⁵Though I were innocent, I could not answer him;
  I could only plead with my Judge for mercy.
¹⁶Even if I summoned him and he responded,
  I do not believe he would give me a hearing.
¹⁷He would crush me with a storm
  and multiply my wounds for no reason.
¹⁸He would not let me catch my breath
  but would overwhelm me with misery.
¹⁹If it is a matter of strength, he is mighty!
  And if it is a matter of justice, who can challenge
  him*ᵇ*?
²⁰Even if I were innocent, my mouth would condemn me;
  if I were blameless, it would pronounce me guilty.

²¹"Although I am blameless,
  I have no concern for myself;
  I despise my own life.
²²It is all the same; that is why I say,
  'He destroys both the blameless and the wicked.'
²³When a scourge brings sudden death,
  he mocks the despair of the innocent.
²⁴When a land falls into the hands of the wicked,
  he blindfolds its judges.
  If it is not he, then who is it?

²⁵"My days are swifter than a runner;
  they fly away without a glimpse of joy.
²⁶They skim past like boats of papyrus,
  like eagles swooping down on their prey.
²⁷If I say, 'I will forget my complaint,
  I will change my expression, and smile,'
²⁸I still dread all my sufferings,
  for I know you will not hold me innocent.
²⁹Since I am already found guilty,
  why should I struggle in vain?
³⁰Even if I washed myself with soap
  and my hands with cleansing powder,
³¹you would plunge me into a slime pit
  so that even my clothes would detest me.

³²"He is not a mere mortal like me that I might answer
  him,
  that we might confront each other in court.
³³If only there were someone to mediate between us,
  someone to bring us together,
³⁴someone to remove God's rod from me,
  so that his terror would frighten me no more.
³⁵Then I would speak up without fear of him,
  but as it now stands with me, I cannot.

**10** "I loathe my very life;
  therefore I will give free rein to my complaint
  and speak out in the bitterness of my soul.
²I say to God: Do not declare me guilty,
  but tell me what charges you have against me.

## Amplified Bible

⁷Who commands the sun, and it rises not; Who seals up
the stars [from view];
⁸Who alone stretches out the heavens and treads upon
the waves *and* high places of the sea;
⁹Who made [the constellations] the Bear, Orion, and
the [loose cluster] Pleiades, and the [vast starry] spaces
of the south;
¹⁰Who does great things past finding out, yes, marvelous things without number.
¹¹Behold, He goes by me, and I see Him not; He passes
on also, but I perceive Him not.
¹²Behold, He snatches away; who can hinder *or* turn
Him back? Who will say to Him, What are You doing?
¹³God will not withdraw His anger; the [proud] helpers
of Rahab [arrogant monster of the sea] bow under Him.

¹⁴How much less shall I answer Him, choosing out my
words to reason with Him
¹⁵Whom, though I were righteous (upright and innocent) yet I could not answer? I must appeal for mercy to
my Opponent *and* Judge [for my right].
¹⁶If I called and He answered me, yet would I not believe
that He listened to my voice.
¹⁷For He overwhelms *and* breaks me with a tempest and
multiplies my wounds without cause.
¹⁸He will not allow me to catch my breath, but fills me
with bitterness.
¹⁹If I speak of strength, behold, He is mighty! And if of
justice, Who, says He, will summon Me?
²⁰Though I am innocent *and* in the right, my own mouth
would condemn me; though I am blameless, He would
prove me perverse.
²¹Though I am blameless, I regard not myself; I despise
my life.
²²It is all one; therefore I say, God [does not discriminate, but] destroys the blameless and the wicked.
²³When [His] scourge slays suddenly, He mocks at the
calamity *and* trial of the innocent.
²⁴The earth is given into the hands of the wicked; He
covers the faces of its judges [so that they are blinded to
justice]. If it is not [God], who then is it [responsible for all
this inequality]?
²⁵Now my days are swifter than a runner; they flee
away, they see no good.
²⁶They are passed away like the swift rowboats made
of reeds, or like the eagle that swoops down on the prey.
²⁷If I say, I will forget my complaint, I will put off my
sad countenance, and be of good cheer *and* brighten up,
²⁸I become afraid of all my pains *and* sorrows [yet to
come], for I know You will not pronounce me innocent [by
removing them].
²⁹I shall be held guilty *and* be condemned; why then
should I labor in vain [to appear innocent]?
³⁰If I wash myself with snow and cleanse my hands with
lye,
³¹Yet You will plunge me into the ditch, and my own
clothes will abhor me [and refuse to cover so foul a body].
³²For [God] is not a [mere] man, as I am, that I should
answer Him, that we should come together in court.
³³There is no umpire between us, who might lay his
hand upon us both, [would that there were!] [I Tim. 2:5.]
³⁴That He might take His rod away from [threatening]
me, and that the fear of Him might not terrify me.
³⁵[Then] would I speak and not fear Him, but I am not
so in myself [to make me afraid, were only a fair trial given
me].

**10** I am weary of my life *and* loathe it! I will give free
  expression to my complaint; I will speak in the bitterness of my soul.
²I will say to God, Do not condemn me [do not make me
guilty]! Show me why You contend with me.

---

*ᵃ 9 Or of Leo*   *ᵇ 19 See Septuagint; Hebrew me.*

# New International Version

³ Does it please you to oppress me,
    to spurn the work of your hands,
        while you smile on the plans of the wicked?
⁴ Do you have eyes of flesh?
    Do you see as a mortal sees?
⁵ Are your days like those of a mortal
    or your years like those of a strong man,
⁶ that you must search out my faults
    and probe after my sin—
⁷ though you know that I am not guilty
    and that no one can rescue me from your hand?

⁸ "Your hands shaped me and made me.
    Will you now turn and destroy me?
⁹ Remember that you molded me like clay.
    Will you now turn me to dust again?
¹⁰ Did you not pour me out like milk
    and curdle me like cheese,
¹¹ clothe me with skin and flesh
    and knit me together with bones and sinews?
¹² You gave me life and showed me kindness,
    and in your providence watched over my spirit.

¹³ "But this is what you concealed in your heart,
    and I know that this was in your mind:
¹⁴ If I sinned, you would be watching me
    and would not let my offense go unpunished.
¹⁵ If I am guilty—woe to me!
    Even if I am innocent, I cannot lift my head,
for I am full of shame
    and drowned in^a my affliction.
¹⁶ If I hold my head high, you stalk me like a lion
    and again display your awesome power against me.
¹⁷ You bring new witnesses against me
    and increase your anger toward me;
    your forces come against me wave upon wave.

¹⁸ "Why then did you bring me out of the womb?
    I wish I had died before any eye saw me.
¹⁹ If only I had never come into being,
    or had been carried straight from the womb to the grave!
²⁰ Are not my few days almost over?
    Turn away from me so I can have a moment's joy
²¹ before I go to the place of no return,
    to the land of gloom and utter darkness,
²² to the land of deepest night,
    of utter darkness and disorder,
    where even the light is like darkness."

## Zophar

**11** Then Zophar the Naamathite replied:

² "Are all these words to go unanswered?
    Is this talker to be vindicated?
³ Will your idle talk reduce others to silence?
    Will no one rebuke you when you mock?
⁴ You say to God, 'My beliefs are flawless
    and I am pure in your sight.'
⁵ Oh, how I wish that God would speak,
    that he would open his lips against you
⁶ and disclose to you the secrets of wisdom,
    for true wisdom has two sides.
    Know this: God has even forgotten some of your sin.

⁷ "Can you fathom the mysteries of God?
    Can you probe the limits of the Almighty?
⁸ They are higher than the heavens above—what can you do?
    They are deeper than the depths below—what can you know?

^a 15 Or and aware of

# Amplified Bible

³ Does it seem good to You that You should oppress, that You should despise and reject the work of Your hands, and favor the schemes of the wicked?
⁴ Have You eyes of flesh? Do You see as man sees?
⁵ Are Your days as the days of man, are Your years as man's [years],
⁶ That You inquire after my iniquity and search for my sin—
⁷ Although You know that I am not wicked or guilty and that there is none who can deliver me out of Your hand?
⁸ Your hands have formed me and made me. Would You turn around and destroy me?
⁹ Remember [earnestly], I beseech You, that You have fashioned me as clay [out of the same earth material, exquisitely and elaborately]. And will You bring me into dust again?
¹⁰ Have You not poured me out like milk and curdled me like cheese?
¹¹ You have clothed me with skin and flesh and have knit me together with bones and sinews.
¹² You have granted me life and favor, and Your providence has preserved my spirit.
¹³ Yet these [the present evils] have You hid in Your heart [for me since my creation]; I know that this was with You [in Your purpose and thought].
¹⁴ If I sin, then You observe me, and You will not acquit me from my iniquity and guilt.
¹⁵ If I am wicked, woe unto me! And if I am righteous, yet must I not lift up my head, for I am filled with disgrace and the sight of my affliction.
¹⁶ If I lift myself up, You hunt me like a lion and again show Yourself [inflicting] marvelous [trials] upon me.
¹⁷ You renew Your witnesses against me and increase Your indignation toward me; I am as if attacked by a troop time after time.
¹⁸ Why then did You bring me forth out of the womb? Would that I had perished and no eye had seen me!
¹⁹ I should have been as though I had not existed; I should have been carried from the womb to the grave.
²⁰ Are not my days few? Cease then and let me alone, that I may take a little comfort and cheer up
²¹ Before I go whence I shall not return, even to the land of darkness and the shadow of death,
²² The land of sunless gloom as intense darkness, [the land] of the shadow of death, without any order, and where the light is as thick darkness.

**11** Then Zophar the Naamathite replied,
² Should not the multitude of words be answered? And should a man full of talk [and making such great professions] be pronounced free from guilt or blame?
³ Should your boastings and babble make men keep silent? And when you mock and scoff, shall no man make you ashamed?
⁴ For you have said, My doctrine [that God afflicts the righteous knowingly] is pure, and I am clean in [God's] eyes. [Job 10:7.]
⁵ But oh, that God would speak, and open His lips against you,
⁶ And that He would show you the secrets of wisdom! For He is manifold in understanding! Know therefore that God exacts of you less than your guilt and iniquity [deserve].
⁷ Can you find out the deep things of God, or can you by searching find out the limits of the Almighty [explore His depths, ascend to His heights, extend to His breadths, and comprehend His infinite perfection]?
⁸ His wisdom is as high as the heights of heaven! What can you do? It is deeper than Sheol (the place of the dead)! What can you know?

# New International Version

⁹Their measure is longer than the earth
and wider than the sea.

¹⁰"If he comes along and confines you in prison
and convenes a court, who can oppose him?
¹¹Surely he recognizes deceivers;
and when he sees evil, does he not take note?
¹²But the witless can no more become wise
than a wild donkey's colt can be born human.ᵃ

¹³"Yet if you devote your heart to him
and stretch out your hands to him,
¹⁴if you put away the sin that is in your hand
and allow no evil to dwell in your tent,
¹⁵then, free of fault, you will lift up your face;
you will stand firm and without fear.
¹⁶You will surely forget your trouble,
recalling it only as waters gone by.
¹⁷Life will be brighter than noonday,
and darkness will become like morning.
¹⁸You will be secure, because there is hope;
you will look about you and take your rest in safety.
¹⁹You will lie down, with no one to make you afraid,
and many will court your favor.
²⁰But the eyes of the wicked will fail,
and escape will elude them;
their hope will become a dying gasp."

## Job

**12** Then Job replied:

²"Doubtless you are the only people who matter,
and wisdom will die with you!
³But I have a mind as well as you;
I am not inferior to you.
Who does not know all these things?

⁴"I have become a laughingstock to my friends,
though I called on God and he answered—
a mere laughingstock, though righteous and
blameless!
⁵Those who are at ease have contempt for misfortune
as the fate of those whose feet are slipping.
⁶The tents of marauders are undisturbed,
and those who provoke God are secure—
those God has in his hand.ᵇ

⁷"But ask the animals, and they will teach you,
or the birds in the sky, and they will tell you;
⁸or speak to the earth, and it will teach you,
or let the fish in the sea inform you.
⁹Which of all these does not know
that the hand of the LORD has done this?
¹⁰In his hand is the life of every creature
and the breath of all mankind.
¹¹Does not the ear test words
as the tongue tastes food?
¹²Is not wisdom found among the aged?
Does not long life bring understanding?

¹³"To God belong wisdom and power;
counsel and understanding are his.
¹⁴What he tears down cannot be rebuilt;
those he imprisons cannot be released.
¹⁵If he holds back the waters, there is drought;
if he lets them loose, they devastate the land.
¹⁶To him belong strength and insight;
both deceived and deceiver are his.

# Amplified Bible

⁹Longer in measure [and scope] is it than the earth, and
broader than the sea.

¹⁰If [God] sweeps in and arrests and calls into judgment, who can hinder Him? [If He is against a man, who
shall call Him to account for it?]
¹¹For He recognizes and knows hollow, wicked, and
useless men (men of falsehood); when He sees iniquity,
will He not consider it?
¹²But a stupid man will get wisdom [only] when a wild
donkey's colt is born a man [as when he thinks himself
free because he is lifted up in pride].
¹³If you set your heart aright and stretch out your hands
to [God],
¹⁴If you put sin out of your hand and far away from you
and let not evil dwell in your tents;
¹⁵Then can you lift up your face to Him without stain
[of sin, and unashamed]; yes, you shall be steadfast and
secure; you shall not fear.
¹⁶For you shall forget your misery; you shall remember
it as waters that pass away.
¹⁷And [your] life shall be clearer than the noonday and
rise above it; though there be darkness, it shall be as the
morning.
¹⁸And you shall be secure and feel confident because
there is hope; yes, you shall search about you, and you
shall take your rest in safety.
¹⁹You shall lie down, and none shall make you afraid;
yes, many shall sue for your favor.
²⁰But the eyes of the wicked shall look [for relief] in
vain, and they shall not escape [the justice of God]; and
their hope shall be to give up the ghost.

**12** Then Job answered,
²No doubt you are the [only wise] people [in the
world], and wisdom will die with you!
³But I have understanding as well as you; I am not inferior to you. Who does not know such things as these [of
God's wisdom and might]?
⁴I am become one who is a laughingstock to his friend;
I, one whom God answered when he called upon Him—a
just, upright (blameless) man—laughed to scorn!
⁵In the thought of him who is at ease there is contempt
for misfortune—but it is ready for those whose feet slip.
⁶The dwellings of robbers prosper; those who provoke
God are [apparently] secure; God supplies them abundantly [who have no god but their own hands and power].
⁷For ask now the animals, and they will teach you [that
God does not deal with His creatures according to their
character]; ask the birds of the air, and they will tell you;
⁸Or speak to the earth [with its other forms of life], and
it will teach you; and the fish of the sea will declare [this
truth] to you.
⁹Who [is so blind as] not to recognize in all these [that
good and evil are promiscuously scattered throughout
nature and human life] that it is God's hand which does
it [and God's way]?
¹⁰In His hand is the life of every living thing and the
breath of all mankind.
¹¹Is it not the task of the ear to discriminate between
[wise and unwise] words, just as the mouth distinguishes
[between desirable and undesirable] food?
¹²With the aged [you say] is wisdom, and with length of
days comes understanding.
¹³But [only] with [God] are [perfect] wisdom and
might; He [alone] has [true] counsel and understanding.
¹⁴Behold, He tears down, and it cannot be built again;
He shuts a man in, and none can open.
¹⁵He withholds the waters, and the land dries up; again,
He sends forth [rains], and they overwhelm the land or
transform it.
¹⁶With Him are might and wisdom; the deceived and
the deceiver are His [and in His power].

---

ᵃ 12 Or wild donkey can be born tame ᵇ 6 Or those whose god is in their
own hand

## New International Version

17 He leads rulers away stripped
   and makes fools of judges.
18 He takes off the shackles put on by kings
   and ties a loincloth*a* around their waist.
19 He leads priests away stripped
   and overthrows officials long established.
20 He silences the lips of trusted advisers
   and takes away the discernment of elders.
21 He pours contempt on nobles
   and disarms the mighty.
22 He reveals the deep things of darkness
   and brings utter darkness into the light.
23 He makes nations great, and destroys them;
   he enlarges nations, and disperses them.
24 He deprives the leaders of the earth of their reason;
   he makes them wander in a trackless waste.
25 They grope in darkness with no light;
   he makes them stagger like drunkards.

**13** "My eyes have seen all this,
   my ears have heard and understood it.
2 What you know, I also know;
   I am not inferior to you.
3 But I desire to speak to the Almighty
   and to argue my case with God.
4 You, however, smear me with lies;
   you are worthless physicians, all of you!
5 If only you would be altogether silent!
   For you, that would be wisdom.
6 Hear now my argument;
   listen to the pleas of my lips.
7 Will you speak wickedly on God's behalf?
   Will you speak deceitfully for him?
8 Will you show him partiality?
   Will you argue the case for God?
9 Would it turn out well if he examined you?
   Could you deceive him as you might deceive a mortal?
10 He would surely call you to account
   if you secretly showed partiality.
11 Would not his splendor terrify you?
   Would not the dread of him fall on you?
12 Your maxims are proverbs of ashes;
   your defenses are defenses of clay.

13 "Keep silent and let me speak;
   then let come to me what may.
14 Why do I put myself in jeopardy
   and take my life in my hands?
15 Though he slay me, yet will I hope in him;
   I will surely*b* defend my ways to his face.
16 Indeed, this will turn out for my deliverance,
   for no godless person would dare come before him!
17 Listen carefully to what I say;
   let my words ring in your ears.
18 Now that I have prepared my case,
   I know I will be vindicated.
19 Can anyone bring charges against me?
   If so, I will be silent and die.

20 "Only grant me these two things, God,
   and then I will not hide from you:
21 Withdraw your hand far from me,
   and stop frightening me with your terrors.

## Amplified Bible

17 He leads [great and scheming] counselors away stripped *and* barefoot and makes the judges fools [in human estimation, by overthrowing their plans].
18 He looses the fetters [ordered] by kings and has [the] waistcloth [of a slave] bound about their [own] loins.
19 He leads away priests as spoil, and men firmly seated He overturns.
20 He deprives of speech those who are trusted and takes away the discernment *and* discretion of the aged.
21 He pours contempt on princes and loosens the belt of the strong [disabling them, bringing low the pride of the learned].
22 He uncovers deep things out of darkness and brings into light black gloom *and* the shadow of death.
23 He makes nations great, and He destroys them; He enlarges nations [and then straitens and shrinks them again], and leads them [away captive].
24 He takes away understanding from the leaders of the people of the land *and* of the earth, and causes them to wander in a wilderness where there is no path.
25 They grope in the dark without light, and He makes them to stagger *and* wander like a drunken man.

**13** [Job continued:] Behold, my eye has seen all this, my ear has heard and understood it.
2 What you know, I also know; I am not inferior to you.
3 Surely I wish to speak to the Almighty, and I desire to argue *and* reason my case with God [that He may explain the conflict between what I believe of Him and what I see of Him].
4 But you are forgers of lies [you defame my character most untruthfully]; you are all physicians of no value *and* have no remedy to offer.
5 Oh, that you would altogether hold your peace! Then you would evidence your wisdom *and* you might pass for wise men.
6 Hear now my reasoning, and listen to the pleadings of my lips.
7 Will you speak unrighteously for God and talk deceitfully for Him?
8 Will you show partiality to Him [be unjust to me in order to gain favor with Him]? Will you act as special pleaders for God?
9 Would it be profitable for you if He should investigate your tactics [with me]? Or as one deceives *and* mocks a man, do you deceive *and* mock Him?
10 He will surely reprove you if you do secretly show partiality.
11 Shall not His majesty make you afraid, and should not your awe for Him restrain you?
12 Your memorable sayings are proverbs of ashes [valueless]; your defenses are defenses of clay [and will crumble].
13 Hold your peace! Let me alone, so I may speak; and let come on me what may.
14 Why should I take my flesh in my teeth and put my life in my hands [incurring the danger of God's wrath]?
15 [I do it because, though He slay me, yet will I wait for and trust Him and] behold, He will slay me; I have no hope—nevertheless, I will maintain *and* argue my ways before Him *and* even to His face.
16 This will be my salvation, that a polluted *and* godless man shall not come before Him.
17 Listen diligently to my speech, and let my declaration be in your ears.
18 Behold now, I have prepared my case; I know that I shall be justified *and* vindicated.
19 Who is he who will argue against *and* refute me? For then I would hold my peace and expire.
20 Only [O Lord] grant two conditions to me, and then will I not hide myself from You:
21 Withdraw Your hand and take this bodily suffering far from me; and let not my [reverent] dread of You terrify me.

---

*a* 18 Or *shackles of kings / and ties a belt*     *b* 15 Or *He will surely slay me;*
*I have no hope — / yet I will*

# New International Version

## Amplified Bible

### New International Version

22Then summon me and I will answer,
 or let me speak, and you reply to me.
23How many wrongs and sins have I committed?
 Show me my offense and my sin.
24Why do you hide your face
 and consider me your enemy?
25Will you torment a windblown leaf?
 Will you chase after dry chaff?
26For you write down bitter things against me
 and make me reap the sins of my youth.
27You fasten my feet in shackles;
 you keep close watch on all my paths
 by putting marks on the soles of my feet.

28"So man wastes away like something rotten,
 like a garment eaten by moths.

**14** "Mortals, born of woman,
 are of few days and full of trouble.
2They spring up like flowers and wither away;
 like fleeting shadows, they do not endure.
3Do you fix your eye on them?
 Will you bring them*a* before you for judgment?
4Who can bring what is pure from the impure?
 No one!
5A person's days are determined;
 you have decreed the number of his months
 and have set limits he cannot exceed.
6So look away from him and let him alone,
 till he has put in his time like a hired laborer.

7"At least there is hope for a tree:
 If it is cut down, it will sprout again,
 and its new shoots will not fail.
8Its roots may grow old in the ground
 and its stump die in the soil,
9yet at the scent of water it will bud
 and put forth shoots like a plant.
10But a man dies and is laid low;
 he breathes his last and is no more.
11As the water of a lake dries up
 or a riverbed becomes parched and dry,
12so he lies down and does not rise;
 till the heavens are no more, people will not awake
 or be roused from their sleep.

13"If only you would hide me in the grave
 and conceal me till your anger has passed!
 If only you would set me a time
 and then remember me!
14If someone dies, will they live again?
 All the days of my hard service
 I will wait for my renewal*b* to come.
15You will call and I will answer you;
 you will long for the creature your hands have made.
16Surely then you will count my steps
 but not keep track of my sin.
17My offenses will be sealed up in a bag;
 you will cover over my sin.

18"But as a mountain erodes and crumbles
 and as a rock is moved from its place,
19as water wears away stones
 and torrents wash away the soil,
 so you destroy a person's hope.
20You overpower them once for all, and they are gone;
 you change their countenance and send them away.
21If their children are honored, they do not know it;
 if their offspring are brought low, they do not see it.

*a 3* Septuagint, Vulgate and Syriac; Hebrew *me*    *b 14* Or *release*

### Amplified Bible

22Then [Lord] call and I will answer, or let me speak, and You answer me.
23How many are my iniquities and sins [that so much sorrow should come to me]? Make me recognize *and* know my transgression and my sin. [Rom. 8:1.]
24Why do You hide Your face [as if offended] and alienate me as if I were Your enemy?
25Will You harass *and* frighten a [poor, helpless] leaf driven to and fro, and will You pursue the chaff of the dry stubble?
26For You write bitter things against me [in Your bill of indictment] and make me inherit *and* be accountable now for the iniquities of my youth.
27You put my feet also in the stocks and observe critically all my paths; You set a circle *and* limit around the soles of my feet [which I must not overstep].
28And he wastes away as a rotten thing, like a garment that is moth-eaten.

**14** Man who is born of a woman is of few days and full of trouble.
2He comes forth like a flower and withers; he flees also like a shadow and continues not.
3And [Lord] do You open Your eyes upon such a one, and bring me into judgment with You?
4Who can bring a clean thing out of an unclean? No one! [Isa. 1:18; I John 1:7.]
5Since a man's days are already determined, and the number of his months is wholly in Your control, and he cannot pass the bounds of his allotted time—
6[O God] turn from him [and cease to watch him so pitilessly]; let him rest until he has accomplished as does a hireling the appointed time for his day.
7For there is hope for a tree if it is cut down, that it will sprout again and that the tender shoots of it will not cease. [But there is no such hope for man.]
8Though its roots grow old in the earth and its stock dies in the ground,
9Yet through the scent [and breathing] of water [the stump of the tree] will bud and bring forth boughs like a young plant.
10But [the brave, strong] man must die and lie prostrate; yes, man breathes his last, and where is he?
11As waters evaporate from the lake, and the river drains and dries up,
12So man lies down and does not rise [to his former state]. Till the heavens are no more, men will not awake nor be raised [physically] out of their sleep.
13Oh, that You would hide me in Sheol (the unseen state), that You would conceal me until Your wrath is past, that You would set a definite time and then remember me earnestly [and imprint me on your heart]!
14If a man dies, shall he live again? All the days of my warfare *and* service I will wait, till my change *and* release shall come. [John 5:25; 6:40; I Thess. 4:16.]
15[Then] You would call and I would answer You; You would yearn for [me] the work of Your hands.
16But now You number each of my steps and take note of my every sin.
17My transgression is sealed up in a bag, and You glue up my iniquity [to preserve it in full for the day of reckoning].
18But as a mountain, if it falls, crumbles to nothing, and as the rock is removed out of its place,
19As waters wear away the stones and as floods wash away the soil of the earth, so You [O Lord] destroy the hope of man.
20You prevail forever against him, and he passes on; You change his appearance [in death] and send him away [from the presence of the living].
21His sons come to honor, and he knows it not; they are brought low, and he perceives it not.

## New International Version

22They feel but the pain of their own bodies
and mourn only for themselves."

### Eliphaz

**15** Then Eliphaz the Temanite replied:

2"Would a wise person answer with empty notions
or fill their belly with the hot east wind?
3Would they argue with useless words,
with speeches that have no value?
4But you even undermine piety
and hinder devotion to God.
5Your sin prompts your mouth;
you adopt the tongue of the crafty.
6Your own mouth condemns you, not mine;
your own lips testify against you.

7"Are you the first man ever born?
Were you brought forth before the hills?
8Do you listen in on God's council?
Do you have a monopoly on wisdom?
9What do you know that we do not know?
What insights do you have that we do not have?
10The gray-haired and the aged are on our side,
men even older than your father.
11Are God's consolations not enough for you,
words spoken gently to you?
12Why has your heart carried you away,
and why do your eyes flash,
13so that you vent your rage against God
and pour out such words from your mouth?

14"What are mortals, that they could be pure,
or those born of woman, that they could be
righteous?
15If God places no trust in his holy ones,
if even the heavens are not pure in his eyes,
16how much less mortals, who are vile and corrupt,
who drink up evil like water!

17"Listen to me and I will explain to you;
let me tell you what I have seen,
18what the wise have declared,
hiding nothing received from their ancestors
19(to whom alone the land was given
when no foreigners moved among them):
20All his days the wicked man suffers torment,
the ruthless man through all the years stored up for
him.
21Terrifying sounds fill his ears;
when all seems well, marauders attack him.
22He despairs of escaping the realm of darkness;
he is marked for the sword.
23He wanders about for food like a vulture;
he knows the day of darkness is at hand.
24Distress and anguish fill him with terror;
troubles overwhelm him, like a king poised to
attack,
25because he shakes his fist at God
and vaunts himself against the Almighty,
26defiantly charging against him
with a thick, strong shield.

27"Though his face is covered with fat
and his waist bulges with flesh,
28he will inhabit ruined towns
and houses where no one lives,
houses crumbling to rubble.

## Amplified Bible

22But his body [lamenting its decay in the grave] shall
grieve over him, and his soul shall mourn [over the body
of clay which it once enlivened].

**15** Then Eliphaz the Temanite answered [Job],
2Should a wise man utter such windy knowledge
[as we have just heard] and fill himself with the east wind
[of withering, parching, and violent accusations]?
3Should he reason with unprofitable talk? Or with
speeches with which he can do no good?
4Indeed, you are doing away with [reverential] fear, and
you are hindering and diminishing meditation and devotion before God.
5For your iniquity teaches your mouth, and you choose
the tongue of the crafty.
6Your own mouth condemns you, and not I; yes, your
own lips testify against you.
7Are you the first man that was born [the original wise
man]? Or were you created before the hills?
8Were you present to hear the secret counsel of God?
And do you limit [the possession of] wisdom to yourself?
9What do you know that we know not? What do you understand that is not equally clear to us?
10Among us are both the gray-haired and the aged,
older than your father by far.
11Are God's consolations [as we have interpreted them
to you] too trivial for you? Is there any secret thing (any
bosom sin) which you have not given up? [Or] were we
too gentle [in our first speech] toward you to be effective?
12Why does your heart carry you away [why allow yourself to be controlled by feeling]? And why do your eyes
flash [in anger or contempt],
13That you turn your spirit against God and let [such]
words [as you have spoken] go out of your mouth?
14What is man, that he could be pure and clean? And he
who is born of a woman, that he could be right and just?
15Behold, [God] puts no trust in His holy ones [the
angels]; indeed, the heavens are not clean in His sight—
16How much less that which is abominable and corrupt,
a man who drinks iniquity like water?
17I will show you, hear me; and that which I have seen
I will relate,
18What wise men have not hid but have freely communicated; it was told to them by their fathers,
19Unto whom alone the land was given, and no stranger
intruded or passed among them [corrupting the truth].
20The wicked man suffers with [self-inflicted] torment
all his days, through all the years that are numbered and
laid up for him, the oppressor.
21A [dreadful] sound of terrors is in his ears; in prosperity the destroyer shall come upon him [the dwellings of
robbers are not at peace].
22He believes that he will not return out of darkness,
and [because of his guilt] he is waited for by the sword [of
God's vengeance].
23He wanders abroad for food, saying, Where is it? He
knows that the day of darkness and destruction is already
close upon him.
24Distress and anguish terrify him; [he knows] they
shall prevail against him, like a king ready for battle.
25Because he has stretched out his hand against God
and bids defiance and behaves himself proudly against the
Almighty,
26Running stubbornly against Him with a thickly ornamented shield;
27Because he has covered his face with his fat, adding
layers of fat on his loins [giving himself up to animal plea-
sures],
28And has lived in desolate [God-forsaken] cities and in
houses which no man should inhabit, which were destined
to become heaps [of ruins];

## New International Version

29 He will no longer be rich and his wealth will not
endure,
   nor will his possessions spread over the land.
30 He will not escape the darkness;
   a flame will wither his shoots,
   and the breath of God's mouth will carry him away.
31 Let him not deceive himself by trusting what is
worthless,
   for he will get nothing in return.
32 Before his time he will wither,
   and his branches will not flourish.
33 He will be like a vine stripped of its unripe grapes,
   like an olive tree shedding its blossoms.
34 For the company of the godless will be barren,
   and fire will consume the tents of those who love
bribes.
35 They conceive trouble and give birth to evil;
   their womb fashions deceit."

### Job

# 16 Then Job replied:

2 "I have heard many things like these;
   you are miserable comforters, all of you!
3 Will your long-winded speeches never end?
   What ails you that you keep on arguing?
4 I also could speak like you,
   if you were in my place;
 I could make fine speeches against you
   and shake my head at you.
5 But my mouth would encourage you;
   comfort from my lips would bring you relief.

6 "Yet if I speak, my pain is not relieved;
   and if I refrain, it does not go away.
7 Surely, God, you have worn me out;
   you have devastated my entire household.
8 You have shriveled me up—and it has become a
witness;
   my gauntness rises up and testifies against me.
9 God assails me and tears me in his anger
   and gnashes his teeth at me;
   my opponent fastens on me his piercing eyes.
10 People open their mouths to jeer at me;
   they strike my cheek in scorn
   and unite together against me.
11 God has turned me over to the ungodly
   and thrown me into the clutches of the wicked.
12 All was well with me, but he shattered me;
   he seized me by the neck and crushed me.
 He has made me his target;
13  his archers surround me.
 Without pity, he pierces my kidneys
   and spills my gall on the ground.
14 Again and again he bursts upon me;
   he rushes at me like a warrior.

## Amplified Bible

29 He shall not be rich, neither shall his wealth last, neither shall his produce bend to the earth nor his possessions be extended on the earth.
30 He shall not depart out of darkness [and escape from
calamity; the wrath of God] shall consume him as flame
consumes a dry tree, and by the blast of His mouth he
shall be swept away.
31 Let him not deceive himself and trust in vanity (emptiness, falseness, and futility), for these shall be his recompense [for such living].
32 It shall be accomplished and paid in full while he still
lives, and his branch shall not be green [but shall wither
away].
33 He shall fail to bring his grapes to maturity [leaving
them to wither unnourished] on the vine and shall cast off
blossoms [and fail to bring forth fruit] like the olive tree.
34 For the company of the godless shall be barren, and
fire shall consume the tents of bribery (wrong and injustice).
35 They conceive mischief and bring forth iniquity, and
their inmost soul hatches deceit.

# 16 Then Job answered,
2 I have heard many such things; wearisome and
miserable comforters are you all!
3 Will your futile words of wind have no end? Or what
makes you so bold to answer [me like this]?
4 I also could speak as you do, if you were in my stead; I
could join words together against you and shake my head
at you.
5 [But] I would strengthen and encourage you with [the
words of] my mouth, and the consolation of my lips would
soothe your suffering.
6 If I speak [to you miserable comforters], my sorrow is
not soothed or lessened; and if I refrain [from speaking],
in what way am I eased? [I hardly know whether to answer
you or be silent.]
7 But now [God] has taken away my strength. You
[O Lord] have made desolate all my family and associates.
8 You have laid firm hold on me and have shriveled me
up, which is a witness against me; and my leanness [and
wretched state of body] are further evidence [against me];
[they] testify to my face.
9 [a My adversary Satan] has torn [me] in his wrath and
hated and persecuted me; he has gnashed upon me with
his teeth; my adversary sharpens his eyes against me.
10 [The forces of evil] have gaped at me with their
mouths; they have struck me upon the cheek insolently;
they massed themselves together and conspired unanimously against me. [Ps. 22:13; 35:21.]
11 God has delivered me to the ungodly (to the evil one)
and cast me [headlong] into the hands of the wicked (Satan's host).
12 I was living at ease, but [Satan] crushed me and broke
me apart; yes, he seized me by the neck and dashed me in
pieces; then he set me up for his target.
13 [Satan's] arrows whiz around me. He slashes open
my vitals and does not spare; he pours out my gall on the
ground.
14 [Satan] stabs me, making breach after breach and attacking again and again; he runs at me like a giant and
irresistible warrior.

---

a The next six verses leave the casual reader at a loss to know of whom
Job is speaking—of God, of Eliphaz, or of Satan, each of whom has been
the choice of various translators and commentators. But careful study
of the text itself, particularly the eleventh verse, seems to leave no
question that while Job is blaming God for abandoning him to Satanic
forces, nevertheless the monstrous, appalling, and disgusting behavior
which Job describes is by him being attributed to Satan himself. Verse
eleven in any translation seems to reveal what the reader has known all
along but which Job only now sees. He still does not understand God's
motive, but he is facing the facts as they are: he is at the mercy of Satan!
But God's thrilling and rewarding motive is still unknown to him.

## New International Version

15 "I have sewed sackcloth over my skin
  and buried my brow in the dust.
16 My face is red with weeping,
  dark shadows ring my eyes;
17 yet my hands have been free of violence
  and my prayer is pure.

18 "Earth, do not cover my blood;
  may my cry never be laid to rest!
19 Even now my witness is in heaven;
  my advocate is on high.
20 My intercessor is my friend[a]
  as my eyes pour out tears to God;
21 on behalf of a man he pleads with God
  as one pleads for a friend.

22 "Only a few years will pass
  before I take the path of no return.

**17** 1 My spirit is broken,
  my days are cut short,
  the grave awaits me.
2 Surely mockers surround me;
  my eyes must dwell on their hostility.

3 "Give me, O God, the pledge you demand.
  Who else will put up security for me?
4 You have closed their minds to understanding;
  therefore you will not let them triumph.
5 If anyone denounces their friends for reward,
  the eyes of their children will fail.

6 "God has made me a byword to everyone,
  a man in whose face people spit.
7 My eyes have grown dim with grief;
  my whole frame is but a shadow.
8 The upright are appalled at this;
  the innocent are aroused against the ungodly.
9 Nevertheless, the righteous will hold to their ways,
  and those with clean hands will grow stronger.

10 "But come on, all of you, try again!
  I will not find a wise man among you.
11 My days have passed, my plans are shattered.
  Yet the desires of my heart
12 turn night into day;
  in the face of the darkness light is near.
13 If the only home I hope for is the grave,
  if I spread out my bed in the realm of darkness,
14 if I say to corruption, 'You are my father,'
  and to the worm, 'My mother' or 'My sister,'
15 where then is my hope—
  who can see any hope for me?
16 Will it go down to the gates of death?
  Will we descend together into the dust?"

### Bildad

**18** Then Bildad the Shuhite replied:

2 "When will you end these speeches?
  Be sensible, and then we can talk.
3 Why are we regarded as cattle
  and considered stupid in your sight?
4 You who tear yourself to pieces in your anger,
  is the earth to be abandoned for your sake?
  Or must the rocks be moved from their place?

## Amplified Bible

15 I have sewed sackcloth over my skin [as a sign of mourning] and have defiled my horn (my insignia of strength) in the dust.
16 My face is red *and* swollen with weeping, and on my eyelids is the shadow of death [my eyes are dimmed],
17 Although there is no guilt *or* violence in my hands and my prayer is pure.
18 O earth, cover not my blood, and let my cry have no resting-place [where it will cease being heard].
19 Even now, behold, my Witness is in heaven, and He who vouches for me is on high. [Rom. 1:9.]
20 My friends scorn me, but my eye pours out tears to God.
21 Oh, that there might be one who would plead for a man with God *and* that he would maintain his right with Him, as a son of man pleads with *or* for his neighbor! [I Tim. 2:5.]
22 For when a few years are come, I shall go the way from which I shall not return.

**17** 1 My spirit is broken, my days are spent (snuffed out); the grave is ready for me.
2 Surely there are mockers *and* mockery around me, and my eye dwells on their obstinacy, insults, *and* resistance.
3 Give me a pledge with Yourself [acknowledge my innocence before my death]; who is there that will give security for me?
4 But their hearts [Lord] You have closed to understanding; therefore You will not let them triumph [by giving them a verdict against me].
5 He who denounces his friends [in order to make them] a prey *and* get a share, the eyes of his children shall fail [to find food].
6 But He has made me a byword among the people, and they spit before my face.
7 My eye has grown dim because of grief, and all my members are [wasted away] like a shadow.
8 Upright men shall be astonished *and* appalled at this, and the innocent shall stir himself up against the godless *and* polluted.
9 Yet shall the righteous (those upright and in right standing with God) hold to their ways, and he who has clean hands shall grow stronger and stronger. [Ps. 24:4.]
10 But as for you, come on again, all of you, though I find not a wise man among you.
11 My days are past, my purposes *and* plans are frustrated; even the thoughts (desires and possessions) of my heart [are broken off].
12 These [thoughts] extend from the night into the day, [so that] the light is short because of darkness.
13 But if I look to Sheol (the unseen state) as my abode, if I spread my couch in the darkness,
14 If I say to the grave *and* corruption, You are my father, and to the worm [that feeds on decay], You are my mother and my sister [because I will soon be closest to you],
15 Where then is my hope? And if I have hope, who will see [its fulfillment]?
16 [My hope] shall go down to the bars of Sheol (the unseen state) when once there is rest in the dust.

**18** Then Bildad the Shuhite answered,
2 How long will you lay snares for words *and* have to hunt for your argument? Do some clear thinking, and then we will reply.
3 Why are we counted as beasts [as if we had no sense]? Why are we unclean in your sight?
4 You who tear yourself in your anger, shall the earth be forsaken for you, or the rock be removed out of its place?

---

[a] 20 Or *My friends treat me with scorn*

## New International Version

5 "The lamp of a wicked man is snuffed out;
   the flame of his fire stops burning.
6 The light in his tent becomes dark;
   the lamp beside him goes out.
7 The vigor of his step is weakened;
   his own schemes throw him down.
8 His feet thrust him into a net;
   he wanders into its mesh.
9 A trap seizes him by the heel;
   a snare holds him fast.
10 A noose is hidden for him on the ground;
   a trap lies in his path.
11 Terrors startle him on every side
   and dog his every step.
12 Calamity is hungry for him;
   disaster is ready for him when he falls.
13 It eats away parts of his skin;
   death's firstborn devours his limbs.
14 He is torn from the security of his tent
   and marched off to the king of terrors.
15 Fire resides*a* in his tent;
   burning sulfur is scattered over his dwelling.
16 His roots dry up below
   and his branches wither above.
17 The memory of him perishes from the earth;
   he has no name in the land.
18 He is driven from light into the realm of darkness
   and is banished from the world.
19 He has no offspring or descendants among his people,
   no survivor where once he lived.
20 People of the west are appalled at his fate;
   those of the east are seized with horror.
21 Surely such is the dwelling of an evil man;
   such is the place of one who does not know God."

**Job**

# 19
Then Job replied:

2 "How long will you torment me
   and crush me with words?
3 Ten times now you have reproached me;
   shamelessly you attack me.
4 If it is true that I have gone astray,
   my error remains my concern alone.
5 If indeed you would exalt yourselves above me
   and use my humiliation against me,
6 then know that God has wronged me
   and drawn his net around me.

7 "Though I cry, 'Violence!' I get no response;
   though I call for help, there is no justice.
8 He has blocked my way so I cannot pass;
   he has shrouded my paths in darkness.
9 He has stripped me of my honor
   and removed the crown from my head.
10 He tears me down on every side till I am gone;
   he uproots my hope like a tree.
11 His anger burns against me;
   he counts me among his enemies.
12 His troops advance in force;
   they build a siege ramp against me
   and encamp around my tent.

13 "He has alienated my family from me;
   my acquaintances are completely estranged from
   me.

## Amplified Bible

5 Yes, the light of the wicked shall be put out, and the flame of his fire shall not shine. [Prov. 13:9; 24:20.]
6 The light shall be dark in his dwelling, and his lamp beside him shall be put out. [Ps. 18:28.]
7 The steps of his strength shall be shortened, and his own counsel *and* the plans in which he trusted shall bring about his downfall.
8 For the wicked is cast into a net by his own feet, and he walks upon a lattice-covered pit.
9 A trap will catch him by the heel, and a snare will lay hold on him.
10 A noose is hidden for him on the ground and a trap for him in the way.
11 Terrors shall make him afraid on every side and shall chase him at his heels.
12 The strength [of the wicked] shall be hunger-bitten, and calamity is ready at his side [if he halts].
13 By disease his strength *and* his skin shall be devoured; the firstborn of death [the worst of diseases] shall consume his limbs.
14 He shall be rooted out of his dwelling place in which he trusted, and he shall be brought to the king of terrors [death].
15 There shall dwell in his tent that which is none of his [family]; sulphur shall be scattered over his dwelling [to purify it after his going].
16 The roots [of the wicked] shall be dried up beneath, and above shall his branch be cut off *and* wither.
17 His remembrance shall perish from the earth, and he shall have no name in the street.
18 He shall be thrust from light into darkness and driven out of the world.
19 He shall neither have son nor grandson among his people, nor any remaining where he sojourned.
20 They [of the west] that come after [the wicked man] shall be astonished *and* appalled at his day, as they [of the east] that went before were seized with horror.
21 Surely such are the dwellings of the ungodly, and such is the place of him who knows not (recognizes not and honors not) God.

# 19
Then Job answered:

2 How long will you vex *and* torment me and break me in pieces with words?
3 These ten times you have reproached me; you are not ashamed that you make yourselves strange [harden yourselves against me and deal severely with me].
4 And if it were true that I have erred, my error would remain with me [I would be conscious of it].
5 If indeed you magnify yourselves against me and plead against me my reproach *and* humiliation,
6 Know that God has overthrown *and* put me in the wrong and has closed His net about me.
7 Behold, I cry out, Violence! but I am not heard; I cry aloud for help, but there is no justice.
8 He has walled up my way so that I cannot pass, and He has set darkness upon my paths.
9 He has stripped me of my glory and taken the crown from my head.
10 He has broken me down on every side, and I am gone; my hope has He pulled up like a tree.
11 He has also kindled His wrath against me, and He counts me as one of His adversaries.
12 His troops come together and cast up their way *and* siege works against me and encamp round about my tent.
13 He has put my brethren far from me, and my acquaintances are wholly estranged from me.

---

*a* 15 Or *Nothing he had remains*

## New International Version

<sup>14</sup>My relatives have gone away;
  my closest friends have forgotten me.
<sup>15</sup>My guests and my female servants count me a
    foreigner;
  they look on me as on a stranger.
<sup>16</sup>I summon my servant, but he does not answer,
  though I beg him with my own mouth.
<sup>17</sup>My breath is offensive to my wife;
  I am loathsome to my own family.
<sup>18</sup>Even the little boys scorn me;
  when I appear, they ridicule me.
<sup>19</sup>All my intimate friends detest me;
  those I love have turned against me.
<sup>20</sup>I am nothing but skin and bones;
  I have escaped only by the skin of my teeth.<sup>a</sup>

<sup>21</sup>"Have pity on me, my friends, have pity,
  for the hand of God has struck me.
<sup>22</sup>Why do you pursue me as God does?
  Will you never get enough of my flesh?

<sup>23</sup>"Oh, that my words were recorded,
  that they were written on a scroll,
<sup>24</sup>that they were inscribed with an iron tool on<sup>b</sup> lead,
  or engraved in rock forever!
<sup>25</sup>I know that my redeemer<sup>c</sup> lives,
  and that in the end he will stand on the earth.<sup>d</sup>
<sup>26</sup>And after my skin has been destroyed,
  yet<sup>e</sup> in<sup>f</sup> my flesh I will see God;
<sup>27</sup>I myself will see him
  with my own eyes—I, and not another.
  How my heart yearns within me!

<sup>28</sup>"If you say, 'How we will hound him,
  since the root of the trouble lies in him,<sup>g</sup>'
<sup>29</sup>you should fear the sword yourselves;
  for wrath will bring punishment by the sword,
  and then you will know that there is judgment.<sup>h</sup>"

### Zophar

**20** Then Zophar the Naamathite replied:

<sup>2</sup>"My troubled thoughts prompt me to answer
  because I am greatly disturbed.
<sup>3</sup>I hear a rebuke that dishonors me,
  and my understanding inspires me to reply.

<sup>4</sup>"Surely you know how it has been from of old,
  ever since mankind<sup>i</sup> was placed on the earth,
<sup>5</sup>that the mirth of the wicked is brief,
  the joy of the godless lasts but a moment.
<sup>6</sup>Though the pride of the godless person reaches to the
    heavens
  and his head touches the clouds,
<sup>7</sup>he will perish forever, like his own dung;
  those who have seen him will say, 'Where is he?'
<sup>8</sup>Like a dream he flies away, no more to be found,
  banished like a vision of the night.
<sup>9</sup>The eye that saw him will not see him again;
  his place will look on him no more.
<sup>10</sup>His children must make amends to the poor;
  his own hands must give back his wealth.
<sup>11</sup>The youthful vigor that fills his bones
  will lie with him in the dust.

<sup>12</sup>"Though evil is sweet in his mouth
  and he hides it under his tongue,
<sup>13</sup>though he cannot bear to let it go
  and lets it linger in his mouth,

## Amplified Bible

<sup>14</sup>My kinsfolk have failed me, and my familiar friends have forgotten me.
<sup>15</sup>Those who live temporarily in my house and my maids count me as a stranger; I am an alien in their sight.
<sup>16</sup>I call to my servant, but he gives me no answer, though I beseech him with words.
<sup>17</sup>I am repulsive to my wife and loathsome to the children of my own mother.
<sup>18</sup>Even young children despise me; when I get up, they speak against me.
<sup>19</sup>All the men of my council *and* my familiar friends abhor me; those whom I loved are turned against me.
<sup>20</sup>My bone clings to my skin and to my flesh, and I have escaped with the skin *or* gums of my teeth.
<sup>21</sup>Have pity on me! Have pity on me, O you my friends, for the hand of God has touched me!
<sup>22</sup>Why do you, as if you were God, pursue *and* persecute me? [Acting like wild beasts] why are you not satisfied with my flesh?
<sup>23</sup>Oh, that the words I now speak were written! Oh, that they were inscribed in a book [carved on a tablet of stone]!
<sup>24</sup>That with an iron pen and [molten] lead they were graven in the rock forever!
<sup>25</sup>For I know that my Redeemer *and* Vindicator lives, and at last He [the Last One] will stand upon the earth. [Isa. 44:6; 48:12.]
<sup>26</sup>And after my skin, even this body, has been destroyed, then from my flesh *or* without it I shall see God,
<sup>27</sup>Whom I, even I, shall see for myself *and* on my side! And my eyes shall behold Him, and not as a stranger! My heart pines away *and* is consumed within me.
<sup>28</sup>If you say, How we will pursue him! [and continue to persecute me with the claim] that the root [cause] of all these [afflictions] is found in me,
<sup>29</sup>Then beware *and* be afraid of the sword [of divine vengeance], for wrathful are the punishments of that sword, that you may know there is a judgment.

**20** Then Zophar the Naamathite answered,
<sup>2</sup>Therefore do my thoughts give me an answer, and I make haste [to offer it] for this reason.
<sup>3</sup>I have heard the reproof which puts me to shame, but out of my understanding my spirit answers me.
<sup>4</sup>Do you not know from of old, since the time that man was placed on the earth,
<sup>5</sup>That the triumphing of the wicked is short, and the joy of the godless *and* defiled is but for a moment? [Ps. 37:35, 36.]
<sup>6</sup>Though his [proud] height mounts up to the heavens and his head reaches to the clouds,
<sup>7</sup>Yet he will perish forever like his own dung; those who have seen him will say, Where is he?
<sup>8</sup>He will fly away like a dream and will not be found; yes, he will be chased away as a vision of the night.
<sup>9</sup>The eye which saw him will see him no more, neither will his [accustomed] place any more behold him.
<sup>10</sup>The poor will oppress his children, and his hands will give back his [ill-gotten] wealth.
<sup>11</sup>His bones are full of youthful energy, but it will lie down with him in the dust.
<sup>12</sup>Though wickedness is sweet in his mouth, though he hides it under his tongue,
<sup>13</sup>Though he is loath to let it go but keeps it still within his mouth,

---

<sup>a</sup> 20 Or *only by my gums*  <sup>b</sup> 24 Or *and*  <sup>c</sup> 25 Or *vindicator*
<sup>d</sup> 25 Or *on my grave*  <sup>e</sup> 26 Or *And after I awake, / though this body has been destroyed, / then*  <sup>f</sup> 26 Or *destroyed, / apart from*  <sup>g</sup> 28 Many Hebrew manuscripts, Septuagint and Vulgate; most Hebrew manuscripts *me*  <sup>h</sup> 29 Or *sword, / that you may come to know the Almighty*  <sup>i</sup> 4 Or *Adam*

## New International Version

¹⁴yet his food will turn sour in his stomach;
 it will become the venom of serpents within him.
¹⁵He will spit out the riches he swallowed;
 God will make his stomach vomit them up.
¹⁶He will suck the poison of serpents;
 the fangs of an adder will kill him.
¹⁷He will not enjoy the streams,
 the rivers flowing with honey and cream.
¹⁸What he toiled for he must give back uneaten;
 he will not enjoy the profit from his trading.
¹⁹For he has oppressed the poor and left them destitute;
 he has seized houses he did not build.

²⁰"Surely he will have no respite from his craving;
 he cannot save himself by his treasure.
²¹Nothing is left for him to devour;
 his prosperity will not endure.
²²In the midst of his plenty, distress will overtake him;
 the full force of misery will come upon him.
²³When he has filled his belly,
 God will vent his burning anger against him
 and rain down his blows on him.
²⁴Though he flees from an iron weapon,
 a bronze-tipped arrow pierces him.
²⁵He pulls it out of his back,
 the gleaming point out of his liver.
 Terrors will come over him;
²⁶ total darkness lies in wait for his treasures.
 A fire unfanned will consume him
 and devour what is left in his tent.
²⁷The heavens will expose his guilt;
 the earth will rise up against him.
²⁸A flood will carry off his house,
 rushing waters*a* on the day of God's wrath.
²⁹Such is the fate God allots the wicked,
 the heritage appointed for them by God."

**Job**

# 21

Then Job replied:

²"Listen carefully to my words;
 let this be the consolation you give me.
³Bear with me while I speak,
 and after I have spoken, mock on.

⁴"Is my complaint directed to a human being?
 Why should I not be impatient?
⁵Look at me and be appalled;
 clap your hand over your mouth.
⁶When I think about this, I am terrified;
 trembling seizes my body.
⁷Why do the wicked live on,
 growing old and increasing in power?
⁸They see their children established around them,
 their offspring before their eyes.
⁹Their homes are safe and free from fear;
 the rod of God is not on them.
¹⁰Their bulls never fail to breed;
 their cows calve and do not miscarry.
¹¹They send forth their children as a flock;
 their little ones dance about.
¹²They sing to the music of timbrel and lyre;
 they make merry to the sound of the pipe.
¹³They spend their years in prosperity
 and go down to the grave in peace.*b*

---

*a 28* Or *The possessions in his house will be carried off, / washed away*
*b 13* Or *in an instant*

## Amplified Bible

¹⁴Yet his food turns [to poison] in his stomach; it is the venom of asps within him.
¹⁵He has swallowed down [his ill-gotten] riches, and he shall vomit them up again; God will cast them out of his belly.
¹⁶He shall suck the poison of asps [which ill-gotten wealth contains]; the viper's tongue shall slay him.
¹⁷He shall not look upon the rivers, the flowing streams of honey and butter [to enjoy his wealth].
¹⁸That which he labored for shall he give back and shall not swallow it down [to enjoy it]; according to his wealth shall the restitution be, and he shall not rejoice in it.
¹⁹For he has oppressed and forsaken the poor; he has violently taken away a house which he did not build.
²⁰Because his desire *and* greed knew no quietness within him, he will not save anything of that in which he delights.
²¹There was nothing left that he did not devour; therefore his prosperity will not endure.
²²In the fullness of his sufficiency [in the time of his great abundance] he shall be poor and in straits; every hand of everyone who is in misery shall come upon him [he is but a wretch on every side].
²³When he is about to fill his belly [as in the wilderness when God sent the quails], God will cast the fierceness of His wrath upon him and will rain it upon him while he is eating. [Num. 11:33; Ps. 78:26-31.]
²⁴He will flee from the iron weapon, but the bow of bronze shall strike him through.
²⁵[The arrow] is drawn forth and it comes out after passing through his body; yes, the glittering point comes out of his gall. Terrors march in upon him;
²⁶Every misfortune is laid up for his treasures. A fire not blown by man shall devour him; it shall consume what is left in his tent [and it shall go ill with him who remains there].
²⁷The heavens shall reveal his iniquity, and the earth shall rise up against him.
²⁸The produce *and* increase of his house will go into exile [with the victors], dragged away in the day of [God's] wrath.
²⁹This is the wicked man's portion from God, and the heritage appointed to him by God.

# 21

Then Job answered,
²Hear diligently my speech, and let this [your attention] be your consolation [given me].
³Allow me, and I also will speak; and after I have spoken, mock on.
⁴As for me, is my complaint to man *or* of him? And why should I not be impatient *and* my spirit be troubled?
⁵Look at me and be astonished (appalled); and lay your hand upon your mouth.
⁶Even when I remember, I am troubled *and* afraid; horror *and* trembling take hold of my flesh.
⁷Why do the wicked live, become old, and become mighty in power?
⁸Their children are established with them in their sight, and their offspring before their eyes.
⁹Their houses are safe *and* in peace, without fear; neither is the rod of God upon them.
¹⁰Their bull breeds and fails not; their cows calve and do not miscarry.
¹¹They send forth their little ones like a flock, and their children skip about.
¹²They themselves lift up their voices *and* sing to the tambourine and the lyre and rejoice to the sound of the pipe.
¹³They spend their days in prosperity and go down to Sheol (the unseen state) in a moment *and* peacefully.

## New International Version

14 Yet they say to God, 'Leave us alone!
　We have no desire to know your ways.
15 Who is the Almighty, that we should serve him?
　What would we gain by praying to him?'
16 But their prosperity is not in their own hands,
　so I stand aloof from the plans of the wicked.

17 "Yet how often is the lamp of the wicked snuffed out?
　How often does calamity come upon them,
　　the fate God allots in his anger?
18 How often are they like straw before the wind,
　like chaff swept away by a gale?
19 It is said, 'God stores up the punishment of the wicked
　for their children.'
　Let him repay the wicked, so that they themselves
　　will experience it!
20 Let their own eyes see their destruction;
　let them drink the cup of the wrath of the Almighty.
21 For what do they care about the families they leave
　behind
　when their allotted months come to an end?

22 "Can anyone teach knowledge to God,
　since he judges even the highest?
23 One person dies in full vigor,
　completely secure and at ease,
24 well nourished in body,*a*
　bones rich with marrow.
25 Another dies in bitterness of soul,
　never having enjoyed anything good.
26 Side by side they lie in the dust,
　and worms cover them both.

27 "I know full well what you are thinking,
　the schemes by which you would wrong me.
28 You say, 'Where now is the house of the great,
　the tents where the wicked lived?'
29 Have you never questioned those who travel?
　Have you paid no regard to their accounts—
30 that the wicked are spared from the day of calamity,
　that they are delivered from*b* the day of wrath?
31 Who denounces their conduct to their face?
　Who repays them for what they have done?
32 They are carried to the grave,
　and watch is kept over their tombs.
33 The soil in the valley is sweet to them;
　everyone follows after them,
　and a countless throng goes*c* before them.

34 "So how can you console me with your nonsense?
　Nothing is left of your answers but falsehood!"

### Eliphaz
**22** Then Eliphaz the Temanite replied:

2 "Can a man be of benefit to God?
　Can even a wise person benefit him?
3 What pleasure would it give the Almighty if you were
　righteous?
　What would he gain if your ways were blameless?
4 "Is it for your piety that he rebukes you
　and brings charges against you?
5 Is not your wickedness great?
　Are not your sins endless?
6 You demanded security from your relatives for no
　reason;
　you stripped people of their clothing, leaving them
　　naked.
7 You gave no water to the weary
　and you withheld food from the hungry,

## Amplified Bible

14 Yet they say to God, Depart from us, for we do not
desire the knowledge of Your ways.
15 Who is the Almighty, that we should serve Him? And
what profit do we have if we pray to Him? [Exod. 5:2.]
16 But notice, [you say] the prosperity of the wicked is
not in their power; the mystery [of God's dealings] with
the ungodly is far from my comprehension.
17 How often [then] is it that the lamp of the wicked is
put out? That their calamity comes upon them? That God
distributes pains *and* sorrows to them in His anger? [Luke
12:46.]
18 That they are like stubble before the wind and like
chaff that the storm steals *and* carries away?
19 You say, God lays up [the punishment of the wicked
man's] iniquity for his children. Let Him recompense it to
the man himself, that he may know *and* feel it.
20 Let his own eyes see his destruction, and let him
drink of the wrath of the Almighty.
21 For what pleasure *or* interest has a man in his house
*and* family after he is dead, when the number of his
months is cut off?
22 Shall any teach God knowledge, seeing that He judges
those who are on high? [Rom. 11:34; I Cor. 2:16.]
23 One dies in his full strength, being wholly at ease and
quiet;
24 His pails are full of milk [his veins are filled with nour-
ishment], and the marrow of his bones is fresh *and* moist,
25 Whereas another man dies in bitterness of soul and
never tastes of pleasure *or* good fortune.
26 They lie down alike in the dust, and the worm spreads
a covering over them.
27 Behold, I know your thoughts *and* plans and the devices with which you would wrong me.
28 For you say, Where is the house of the rich *and* liberal
prince [meaning me]? And where is the tent in which the
wicked [Job] dwelt?
29 Have you not asked those who travel this way, and do
you not accept their testimony *and* evidences—
30 That the evil man is [now] spared in the day of calamity *and* destruction, and they are led forth *and* away on the
day of [God's] wrath?
31 But who declares [a man's] way [and rebukes] him to
his face? And who pays him back for what he has done?
32 When he is borne to the grave, watch is kept over his
tomb.
33 The clods of the valley are sweet to him, and every
man shall follow him to a grave, as innumerable people
[have gone] before him.
34 How then can you comfort me with empty *and* futile
words, since in your replies there lurks falsehood?

**22** Then Eliphaz the Temanite answered [Job],
　2 Can a man be profitable to God? Surely he that is
wise is profitable to himself. [Ps. 16:2; Luke 17:10.]
3 Is it any pleasure *or* advantage to the Almighty that you
are righteous (upright and in right standing with Him)?
Or is it gain to Him that you make your ways perfect? [Isa.
62:3; Zech. 2:8; Mal. 3:17; Acts 20:28.]
4 Is it for your [reverential] fear of Him that He [thus]
reproves you, that He enters with you into judgment?
5 Is not your wickedness great? There is no end to your
iniquities.
6 For you have taken pledges of your brother for nothing,
and stripped the naked of their clothing.
7 You have not given water to the weary to drink, and
you have withheld bread from the hungry. [Matt. 25:42.]

---

*a 24 The meaning of the Hebrew for this word is uncertain.*
*b 30 Or wicked are reserved for the day of calamity, / that they are brought*
*forth to　c 33 Or them, / as a countless throng went*

## New International Version

⁸though you were a powerful man, owning land—
   an honored man, living on it.
⁹And you sent widows away empty-handed
   and broke the strength of the fatherless.
¹⁰That is why snares are all around you,
   why sudden peril terrifies you,
¹¹why it is so dark you cannot see,
   and why a flood of water covers you.

¹²"Is not God in the heights of heaven?
   And see how lofty are the highest stars!
¹³Yet you say, 'What does God know?
   Does he judge through such darkness?
¹⁴Thick clouds veil him, so he does not see us
   as he goes about in the vaulted heavens.'
¹⁵Will you keep to the old path
   that the wicked have trod?
¹⁶They were carried off before their time,
   their foundations washed away by a flood.
¹⁷They said to God, 'Leave us alone!
   What can the Almighty do to us?'
¹⁸Yet it was he who filled their houses with good things,
   so I stand aloof from the plans of the wicked.
¹⁹The righteous see their ruin and rejoice;
   the innocent mock them, saying,
²⁰'Surely our foes are destroyed,
   and fire devours their wealth.'

²¹"Submit to God and be at peace with him;
   in this way prosperity will come to you.
²²Accept instruction from his mouth
   and lay up his words in your heart.
²³If you return to the Almighty, you will be restored:
   If you remove wickedness far from your tent
²⁴and assign your nuggets to the dust,
   your gold of Ophir to the rocks in the ravines,
²⁵then the Almighty will be your gold,
   the choicest silver for you.
²⁶Surely then you will find delight in the Almighty
   and will lift up your face to God.
²⁷You will pray to him, and he will hear you,
   and you will fulfill your vows.
²⁸What you decide on will be done,
   and light will shine on your ways.
²⁹When people are brought low and you say, 'Lift them up!'
   then he will save the downcast.
³⁰He will deliver even one who is not innocent,
   who will be delivered through the cleanness of your hands."

## Job

**23** Then Job replied:

²"Even today my complaint is bitter;
   his hand*ᵃ* is heavy in spite of*ᵇ* my groaning.
³If only I knew where to find him;
   if only I could go to his dwelling!
⁴I would state my case before him
   and fill my mouth with arguments.
⁵I would find out what he would answer me,
   and consider what he would say to me.
⁶Would he vigorously oppose me?
   No, he would not press charges against me.
⁷There the upright can establish their innocence before him,
   and there I would be delivered forever from my judge.

ᵃ 2 Septuagint and Syriac; Hebrew / *the hand on me*   ᵇ 2 Or *heavy on me in*

## Amplified Bible

⁸But [you, Job] the man with power possessed the land, and the favored *and* accepted man dwelt in it.
⁹You have sent widows away empty-handed, and the arms of the fatherless have been broken.
¹⁰Therefore snares are round about you, and sudden fear troubles *and* overwhelms you;
¹¹Your light is darkened, so that you cannot see, and a flood of water covers you.
¹²Is not God in the height of heaven? And behold the height of the stars, how high they are!
¹³Therefore you say, How *and* what does God know [about me]? Can He judge through the thick darkness?
¹⁴Thick clouds are a covering to Him, so that He does not see, and He walks on the vault of the heavens.
¹⁵Will you pay attention *and* keep to the old way that wicked men trod [in Noah's time], [II Pet. 2:5.]
¹⁶Men who were snatched away before their time, whose foundations were poured out like a stream [during the flood]?
¹⁷They said to God, Depart from us, and, What can the Almighty do for *or* to us?
¹⁸Yet He filled their houses with good [things]. But the counsel of the ungodly is far from me.
¹⁹The righteous see it and are glad; and the innocent laugh them to scorn [saying],
²⁰Surely those who rose up against us are cut off, and that which remained to them the fire has consumed.
²¹Acquaint now yourself with Him [agree with God and show yourself to be conformed to His will] and be at peace; by that [you shall prosper and great] good shall come to you.
²²Receive, I pray you, the law *and* instruction from His mouth and lay up His words in your heart. [Ps. 119:11.]
²³If you return to the Almighty [and submit and humble yourself before Him], you will be built up; if you put away unrighteousness far from your tents,
²⁴If you lay gold in the dust, and the gold of Ophir among the stones of the brook [considering them of little worth],
²⁵And make the Almighty your gold and [the Lord] your precious silver treasure,
²⁶Then you will have delight in the Almighty, and you will lift up your face to God.
²⁷You will make your prayer to Him, and He will hear you, and you will pay your vows.
²⁸You shall also decide *and* decree a thing, and it shall be established for you; and the light [of God's favor] shall shine upon your ways.
²⁹When they make [you] low, you will say, [There is] a lifting up; and the humble person He lifts up *and* saves.
³⁰He will even deliver the one [for whom you intercede] who is not innocent; yes, he will be delivered through the cleanness of your hands. [Job 42:7, 8.]

**23** Then Job answered,

²Even today my complaint is rebellious *and* bitter; my stroke is heavier than my groaning.
³Oh, that I knew where I might find Him, that I might come even to His seat!
⁴I would lay my cause before Him and fill my mouth with arguments.
⁵I would learn what He would answer me, and understand what He would say to me.
⁶Would He plead against me with His great power? No, He would give heed to me. [Isa. 27:4, 5; 57:16.]
⁷There the righteous [one who is upright and in right standing with God] could reason with Him; so I should be acquitted by my Judge forever.

## New International Version

8 "But if I go to the east, he is not there;
   if I go to the west, I do not find him.
9 When he is at work in the north, I do not see him;
   when he turns to the south, I catch no glimpse of
   him.
10 But he knows the way that I take;
   when he has tested me, I will come forth as gold.
11 My feet have closely followed his steps;
   I have kept to his way without turning aside.
12 I have not departed from the commands of his lips;
   I have treasured the words of his mouth more than
   my daily bread.

13 "But he stands alone, and who can oppose him?
   He does whatever he pleases.
14 He carries out his decree against me,
   and many such plans he still has in store.
15 That is why I am terrified before him;
   when I think of all this, I fear him.
16 God has made my heart faint;
   the Almighty has terrified me.
17 Yet I am not silenced by the darkness,
   by the thick darkness that covers my face.

**24** "Why does the Almighty not set times for
   judgment?
   Why must those who know him look in vain for such
   days?
2 There are those who move boundary stones;
   they pasture flocks they have stolen.
3 They drive away the orphan's donkey
   and take the widow's ox in pledge.
4 They thrust the needy from the path
   and force all the poor of the land into hiding.
5 Like wild donkeys in the desert,
   the poor go about their labor of foraging food;
   the wasteland provides food for their children.
6 They gather fodder in the fields
   and glean in the vineyards of the wicked.
7 Lacking clothes, they spend the night naked;
   they have nothing to cover themselves in the cold.
8 They are drenched by mountain rains
   and hug the rocks for lack of shelter.
9 The fatherless child is snatched from the breast;
   the infant of the poor is seized for a debt.
10 Lacking clothes, they go about naked;
   they carry the sheaves, but still go hungry.
11 They crush olives among the terraces[a];
   they tread the winepresses, yet suffer thirst.
12 The groans of the dying rise from the city,
   and the souls of the wounded cry out for help.
   But God charges no one with wrongdoing.

13 "There are those who rebel against the light,
   who do not know its ways
   or stay in its paths.
14 When daylight is gone, the murderer rises up,
   kills the poor and needy,
   and in the night steals forth like a thief.
15 The eye of the adulterer watches for dusk;
   he thinks, 'No eye will see me,'
   and he keeps his face concealed.
16 In the dark, thieves break into houses,
   but by day they shut themselves in;
   they want nothing to do with the light.

## Amplified Bible

8 Behold, I go forward [and to the east], but He is not
there; I go backward [and to the west], but I cannot perceive Him.
9 On the left hand [and to the north] where He works [I
seek Him], but I cannot behold Him; He turns Himself to
the right hand [and to the south], but I cannot see Him.
10 But He knows the way that I take [He has concern for
it, appreciates, and pays attention to it]. When He has tried
me, I shall come forth as refined gold [pure and luminous].
[Ps. 17:3; 66:10; James 1:12.]
11 My foot has held fast to His steps; His ways have I kept
and not turned aside.
12 I have not gone back from the commandment of His
lips; I have esteemed *and* treasured the words of His
mouth more than my necessary food.
13 But He is unchangeable, and who can turn Him? And
what He wants to do, that He does.
14 For He performs [that which He has] planned for me,
and of many such matters He is mindful.
15 Therefore am I troubled *and* terrified at His presence;
when I consider, I am in dread and afraid of Him.
16 For God has made my heart faint, timid, *and* broken,
and the Almighty has terrified me,
17 Because I was not cut off before the darkness [of these
woes befell me], neither has He covered the thick darkness from my face.

**24** Why [seeing times are not hidden from the Al-
   mighty] does He not set seasons for judgment?
Why do those who know Him see not His days [for punishment of the wicked]? [Acts 1:7.]
2 Some remove the landmarks; they violently take away
flocks and pasture them [appropriating land and flocks
openly].
3 They drive away the donkey of the fatherless; they take
the widow's ox for a pledge.
4 They crowd the poor *and* needy off the road; the poor
*and* meek of the earth all hide themselves.
5 Behold, as wild asses in the desert, [the poor] go forth
to their work, seeking diligently for prey *and* food; the
wilderness yields them bread for their children [in roots
and herbage].
6 They reap each one his fodder in a field [that is not his
own], and they glean the vintage of the wicked man.
7 They lie all night naked, without clothing, and have no
covering in the cold.
8 They are wet with the showers of the mountains and
cling to the rock for want of shelter.
9 [The violent men whose wickedness seems unno-
ticed] pluck the fatherless infants from the breast [to sell
or make them slaves], and take [the clothing on] the poor
for a pledge,
10 So that the needy go about naked for lack of clothing,
and though hungry, they must carry [but not eat from]
the sheaves.
11 Among the olive rows [of the wicked, the poor] make
oil; they tread [the fresh juice of the grape from] the presses, but suffer thirst.
12 From out of the populous city men groan, and the very
life of the wounded cries for help; yet God [seemingly] regards not the wrong done them.
13 These wrongdoers are of those who rebel against the
light; they know not its ways nor stay in its paths.
14 The murderer rises with the light; he kills the poor
and the needy, and in the night he becomes as a thief.
15 The eye also of the adulterer waits for the twilight,
saying, No eye shall see me, and he puts a disguise upon
his face.
16 In the dark, they dig through [the penetrable walls
of] houses; by day they shut themselves up; they do not
know the sunlight.

---

*a* 11 The meaning of the Hebrew for this word is uncertain.

## New International Version

¹⁷For all of them, midnight is their morning;
they make friends with the terrors of darkness.

¹⁸"Yet they are foam on the surface of the water;
their portion of the land is cursed,
so that no one goes to the vineyards.
¹⁹As heat and drought snatch away the melted snow,
so the grave snatches away those who have sinned.
²⁰The womb forgets them,
the worm feasts on them;
the wicked are no longer remembered
but are broken like a tree.
²¹They prey on the barren and childless woman,
and to the widow they show no kindness.
²²But God drags away the mighty by his power;
though they become established, they have no
assurance of life.
²³He may let them rest in a feeling of security,
but his eyes are on their ways.
²⁴For a little while they are exalted, and then they are
gone;
they are brought low and gathered up like all others;
they are cut off like heads of grain.

²⁵"If this is not so, who can prove me false
and reduce my words to nothing?"

### Bildad

**25** Then Bildad the Shuhite replied:

²"Dominion and awe belong to God;
he establishes order in the heights of heaven.
³Can his forces be numbered?
On whom does his light not rise?
⁴How then can a mortal be righteous before God?
How can one born of woman be pure?
⁵If even the moon is not bright
and the stars are not pure in his eyes,
⁶how much less a mortal, who is but a maggot—
a human being, who is only a worm!"

### Job

**26** Then Job replied:

²"How you have helped the powerless!
How you have saved the arm that is feeble!
³What advice you have offered to one without wisdom!
And what great insight you have displayed!
⁴Who has helped you utter these words?
And whose spirit spoke from your mouth?

⁵"The dead are in deep anguish,
those beneath the waters and all that live in them.
⁶The realm of the dead is naked before God;
Destructionᵃ lies uncovered.
⁷He spreads out the northern skies over empty space;
he suspends the earth over nothing.
⁸He wraps up the waters in his clouds,
yet the clouds do not burst under their weight.
⁹He covers the face of the full moon,
spreading his clouds over it.
¹⁰He marks out the horizon on the face of the waters
for a boundary between light and darkness.
¹¹The pillars of the heavens quake,
aghast at his rebuke.
¹²By his power he churned up the sea;
by his wisdom he cut Rahab to pieces.

## Amplified Bible

¹⁷For midnight is morning to all of them; for they are
familiar with the terrors of deep darkness.
¹⁸[You say] Swiftly such men pass away on the face of
the waters; their portion is cursed in the earth; [no tread-
er] turns into their vineyards.
¹⁹Drought and heat consume the snow waters; so does
Sheol (the place of the dead) those who have sinned.
²⁰The womb shall forget him, the worm shall feed
sweetly on him; he shall be no more remembered, and unrighteousness shall be broken like a tree [which cannot be
healed]. [Prov. 10:7.]
²¹[The evil man] preys upon the barren, childless woman and does no good to the widow.
²²Yet [God] prolongs the life of the [wicked] mighty by
His power; they rise up when they had despaired of life.
²³God gives them security, and they rest on it; and His
eyes are upon their ways.
²⁴They are exalted for a little while, and then are gone
and brought low; they are taken out of the way as all others
are and are cut off as the tops of the ears of grain.
²⁵And if this is not so, who will prove me a liar and make
my speech worthless?

**25** Then Bildad the Shuhite answered,
²Dominion and fear are with [God]; He makes
peace in His high places.
³Is there any number to His armies? And upon whom
does not His light arise?
⁴How then can man be justified *and* righteous before
God? Or how can he who is born of a woman be pure *and*
clean? [Ps. 130:3; 143:2.]
⁵Behold, even the moon has no brightness [compared
to God's glory] and the stars are not pure in His sight—
⁶How much less man, who is a maggot! And a son of
man, who is a worm!

**26** But Job answered,
²How you have helped him who is without power!
How you have sustained the arm that is without strength!
³How you have counseled him who has no wisdom! And
how plentifully you have declared to him sound knowledge!
⁴With whose assistance have you uttered these words?
And whose spirit [inspired what] came forth from you?
⁵The shades of the dead tremble underneath the waters
and their inhabitants.
⁶Sheol (the place of the dead) is naked before God, and
Abaddon (the place of destruction) has no covering [from
His eyes].
⁷He it is Who spreads out the northern skies over emptiness and ᵃhangs the earth upon *or* over nothing.
⁸He holds the waters bound in His clouds [which otherwise would spill on earth all at once], and the cloud is not
rent under them.
⁹He covers the face of His throne and spreads over it
His cloud.
¹⁰He has placed an enclosing limit [the horizon] upon
the waters at the boundary between light and darkness.
¹¹The pillars of the heavens tremble and are astonished
at His rebuke.
¹²He stills *or* stirs up the sea by His power, and by His
understanding He smites proud Rahab.

---

ᵃ For millenniums, various theories of what supports the earth—
elephants, giants, and other fantastic means—were accepted by
mankind as truth. The Bible made no such absurd error. How could Job,
more than 3,000 years ago, possibly have known that God "hangs the
earth upon *or* over nothing," except by divine inspiration?

---

ᵃ 6 Hebrew *Abaddon*

## New International Version

13 By his breath the skies became fair;
  his hand pierced the gliding serpent.
14 And these are but the outer fringe of his works;
  how faint the whisper we hear of him!
  Who then can understand the thunder of his
    power?"

### Job's Final Word to His Friends

**27** And Job continued his discourse:

2 "As surely as God lives, who has denied me justice,
  the Almighty, who has made my life bitter,
3 as long as I have life within me,
  the breath of God in my nostrils,
4 my lips will not say anything wicked,
  and my tongue will not utter lies.
5 I will never admit you are in the right;
  till I die, I will not deny my integrity.
6 I will maintain my innocence and never let go of it;
  my conscience will not reproach me as long as I live.

7 "May my enemy be like the wicked,
  my adversary like the unjust!
8 For what hope have the godless when they are cut off,
  when God takes away their life?
9 Does God listen to their cry
  when distress comes upon them?
10 Will they find delight in the Almighty?
  Will they call on God at all times?

11 "I will teach you about the power of God;
  the ways of the Almighty I will not conceal.
12 You have all seen this yourselves.
  Why then this meaningless talk?

13 "Here is the fate God allots to the wicked,
  the heritage a ruthless man receives from the
    Almighty:
14 However many his children, their fate is the sword;
  his offspring will never have enough to eat.
15 The plague will bury those who survive him,
  and their widows will not weep for them.
16 Though he heaps up silver like dust
  and clothes like piles of clay,
17 what he lays up the righteous will wear,
  and the innocent will divide his silver.
18 The house he builds is like a moth's cocoon,
  like a hut made by a watchman.
19 He lies down wealthy, but will do so no more;
  when he opens his eyes, all is gone.
20 Terrors overtake him like a flood;
  a tempest snatches him away in the night.
21 The east wind carries him off, and he is gone;
  it sweeps him out of his place.
22 It hurls itself against him without mercy
  as he flees headlong from its power.
23 It claps its hands in derision
  and hisses him out of his place."

### Interlude: Where Wisdom Is Found

**28** There is a mine for silver
  and a place where gold is refined.
2 Iron is taken from the earth,
  and copper is smelted from ore.
3 Mortals put an end to the darkness;
  they search out the farthest recesses
  for ore in the blackest darkness.
4 Far from human dwellings they cut a shaft,
  in places untouched by human feet;
  far from other people they dangle and sway.

## Amplified Bible

13 By His breath the heavens are garnished; His hand
pierced the [swiftly] fleeing serpent. [Ps. 33:6.]
14 Yet these are but [a small part of His doings] the outskirts of His ways *or* the mere fringes of His force, the
faintest whisper of His voice! Who dares contemplate *or*
who can understand the thunders of His full, magnificent
power?

**27** Job again took up his discourse and said,
2 As God lives, Who has taken away my right *and*
denied me justice, and the Almighty, Who has vexed *and*
embittered my life,
3 As long as my life is still whole within me, and the
breath of God is [yet] in my nostrils,
4 My lips shall not speak untruth, nor shall my tongue
utter deceit.
5 God forbid that I should justify you—saying you are
right [in your accusations against me]; till I die, I will not
put away my integrity from me.
6 My uprightness *and* my right standing with God I hold
fast and will not let them go; my heart does not reproach
me for any of my days *and* it shall not reproach me as long
as I live.
7 Let my enemy be as the wicked, and let him who rises
up against me be as the unrighteous.
8 For what is the hope of the godless *and* polluted, even
though he has gained [in this world], when God cuts him
off *and* takes away his life?
9 Will God hear his cry when trouble comes upon him?
10 Will he take delight in the Almighty? Will he call upon
God at all times?
11 I will teach you regarding the hand *and* handiwork of
God; that which is with the Almighty [God's actual treatment of the wicked man] will I not conceal.
12 Behold, all of you have seen it yourselves; why then have
you become altogether vain [cherishing foolish notions]?
13 This [which I am about to tell] is the portion of a wicked man with God, and the heritage which oppressors shall
receive from the Almighty:
14 If his children are multiplied, it is for the sword; and
his offspring will not have sufficient bread.
15 Those who survive him, [the pestilence] will bury,
and [their] widows will make no lamentation.
16 Though he heaps up silver like dust and piles up clothing like clay,
17 He may prepare it, but the just will wear it, and the
innocent will divide the silver.
18 He builds his house like a moth *or* a spider, like a
booth which a watchman makes [to last for a season].
19 [The wicked] will lie down rich, but does it not again;
he opens his eyes, and [his wealth] is gone.
20 Terrors overtake him like a [suddenly loosened]
flood; a windstorm steals him away in the night.
21 The east wind lifts him up, and he is gone; it sweeps
him out of his place.
22 For [God and the storm] hurl at him without pity *and*
unsparingly [their thunderbolts of wrath]; he flees in
haste before His power.
23 [God causes] men to clap their hands at him [in malignant joy] and hiss him out of his place.

**28** Surely there is a mine for silver, and a place for
gold where they refine it.
2 Iron is taken out of the earth, and copper is smelted
from the stone ore.
3 Man sets an end to darkness, and he searches out the
farthest bounds for the ore buried in gloom and deep darkness.
4 Men break open shafts away from where people sojourn, in places forgotten by [human] foot; and [descend
into them], hanging afar from men, they swing *or* flit to
and fro.

## New International Version

⁵The earth, from which food comes,
  is transformed below as by fire;
⁶lapis lazuli comes from its rocks,
  and its dust contains nuggets of gold.
⁷No bird of prey knows that hidden path,
  no falcon's eye has seen it.
⁸Proud beasts do not set foot on it,
  and no lion prowls there.
⁹People assault the flinty rock with their hands
  and lay bare the roots of the mountains.
¹⁰They tunnel through the rock;
  their eyes see all its treasures.
¹¹They search[a] the sources of the rivers
  and bring hidden things to light.

¹²But where can wisdom be found?
  Where does understanding dwell?
¹³No mortal comprehends its worth;
  it cannot be found in the land of the living.
¹⁴The deep says, "It is not in me";
  the sea says, "It is not with me."
¹⁵It cannot be bought with the finest gold,
  nor can its price be weighed out in silver.
¹⁶It cannot be bought with the gold of Ophir,
  with precious onyx or lapis lazuli.
¹⁷Neither gold nor crystal can compare with it,
  nor can it be had for jewels of gold.
¹⁸Coral and jasper are not worthy of mention;
  the price of wisdom is beyond rubies.
¹⁹The topaz of Cush cannot compare with it;
  it cannot be bought with pure gold.

²⁰Where then does wisdom come from?
  Where does understanding dwell?
²¹It is hidden from the eyes of every living thing,
  concealed even from the birds in the sky.
²²Destruction[b] and Death say,
  "Only a rumor of it has reached our ears."
²³God understands the way to it
  and he alone knows where it dwells,
²⁴for he views the ends of the earth
  and sees everything under the heavens.
²⁵When he established the force of the wind
  and measured out the waters,
²⁶when he made a decree for the rain
  and a path for the thunderstorm,
²⁷then he looked at wisdom and appraised it;
  he confirmed it and tested it.
²⁸And he said to the human race,
  "The fear of the Lord—that is wisdom,
  and to shun evil is understanding."

### Job's Final Defense

**29** Job continued his discourse:

²"How I long for the months gone by,
  for the days when God watched over me,
³when his lamp shone on my head
  and by his light I walked through darkness!
⁴Oh, for the days when I was in my prime,
  when God's intimate friendship blessed my house,
⁵when the Almighty was still with me
  and my children were around me,
⁶when my path was drenched with cream
  and the rock poured out for me streams of olive oil.

⁷"When I went to the gate of the city
  and took my seat in the public square,

---

ᵃ 11 Septuagint, Aquila and Vulgate; Hebrew *They dam up*
ᵇ 22 Hebrew *Abaddon*

## Amplified Bible

⁵As for the earth, out of it comes bread, but underneath [its surface, down deep in the mine] there is ᵃblasting, turning it up as by fire.
⁶Its stones are the bed of sapphires; it holds dust of gold [which he wins].
⁷That path no bird of prey knows, and the falcon's eye has not seen it.
⁸The proud beasts [and their young] have not trodden it, nor has the fierce lion passed over it.
⁹Man puts forth his hand upon the flinty rock; he overturns the mountains by the roots.
¹⁰He cuts out channels *and* passages among the rocks; and his eye sees every precious thing.
¹¹[Man] binds the streams so that they do not trickle [into the mine], and the thing that is hidden he brings forth to light.

¹²But where shall ᵇWisdom be found? And where is the place of understanding?
¹³Man knows not the price of it; neither is it found in the land of the living.
¹⁴The deep says, [Wisdom] is not in me; and the sea says, It is not with me.
¹⁵It cannot be gotten for gold, neither shall silver be weighed for the price of it.
¹⁶It cannot be valued in [terms of] the gold of Ophir, in the precious onyx *or* beryl, or the sapphire.
¹⁷Gold and glass cannot equal [Wisdom], nor can it be exchanged for jewels *or* vessels of fine gold.
¹⁸No mention shall be made of coral or of crystal; for the possession of Wisdom is even above rubies *or* pearls.
¹⁹The topaz of Ethiopia cannot compare with it, nor can it be valued in pure gold.

²⁰From where then does Wisdom come? And where is the place of understanding?
²¹It is hidden from the eyes of all living, and knowledge of it is withheld from the birds of the heavens.
²²Abaddon (the place of destruction) and Death say, We have [only] heard the report of it with our ears.
²³God understands the way [to Wisdom] and He knows the place of it [Wisdom is with God alone].
²⁴For He looks to the ends of the earth and sees everything under the heavens.
²⁵When He gave to the wind weight *or* pressure and allotted the waters by measure,
²⁶When He made a decree for the rain and a way for the lightning of the thunder,
²⁷Then He saw [Wisdom] and declared it; He established it, yes, and searched it out [for His own use, and He alone possesses it].
²⁸But to man He said, Behold, the reverential *and* worshipful fear of the Lord—that is Wisdom; and to depart from evil is understanding.

**29** And Job again took up his discussion and said,
²Oh, that I were as in the months of old, as in the days when God watched over me, [Eccl. 7:10.]
³When His lamp shone above *and* upon my head and by His light I walked through darkness;
⁴As I was in the [prime] ripeness of my days, when the friendship *and* counsel of God were over my tent,
⁵When the Almighty was yet with me and my children were about me,
⁶When my steps [through rich pasturage] were washed with butter and the rock poured out for me streams of oil!
⁷When I went out to the gate of the city, when I prepared my seat in the street [the broad place for the council at the city's gate],

---

ᵃ Blasting of rocks is said to have been practiced on a large scale by the ancients (*Speaker's Commentary*).   ᵇ Wisdom is capitalized as a reminder of its divine implications. Note that the pronouns referring to wisdom are not capitalized. See footnote on Prov. 1:23.

## New International Version

8the young men saw me and stepped aside
  and the old men rose to their feet;
9the chief men refrained from speaking
  and covered their mouths with their hands;
10the voices of the nobles were hushed,
  and their tongues stuck to the roof of their mouths.
11Whoever heard me spoke well of me,
  and those who saw me commended me,
12because I rescued the poor who cried for help,
  and the fatherless who had none to assist them.
13The one who was dying blessed me;
  I made the widow's heart sing.
14I put on righteousness as my clothing;
  justice was my robe and my turban.
15I was eyes to the blind
  and feet to the lame.
16I was a father to the needy;
  I took up the case of the stranger.
17I broke the fangs of the wicked
  and snatched the victims from their teeth.

18"I thought, 'I will die in my own house,
  my days as numerous as the grains of sand.
19My roots will reach to the water,
  and the dew will lie all night on my branches.
20My glory will not fade;
  the bow will be ever new in my hand.'

21"People listened to me expectantly,
  waiting in silence for my counsel.
22After I had spoken, they spoke no more;
  my words fell gently on their ears.
23They waited for me as for showers
  and drank in my words as the spring rain.
24When I smiled at them, they scarcely believed it;
  the light of my face was precious to them.a
25I chose the way for them and sat as their chief;
  I dwelt as a king among his troops;
  I was like one who comforts mourners.

**30** "But now they mock me,
  men younger than I,
  whose fathers I would have disdained
  to put with my sheep dogs.
2Of what use was the strength of their hands to me,
  since their vigor had gone from them?
3Haggard from want and hunger,
  they roamedb the parched land
  in desolate wastelands at night.
4In the brush they gathered salt herbs,
  and their foodc was the root of the broom bush.
5They were banished from human society,
  shouted at as if they were thieves.
6They were forced to live in the dry stream beds,
  among the rocks and in holes in the ground.
7They brayed among the bushes
  and huddled in the undergrowth.
8A base and nameless brood,
  they were driven out of the land.

9"And now those young men mock me in song;
  I have become a byword among them.
10They detest me and keep their distance;
  they do not hesitate to spit in my face.

## Amplified Bible

8The young men saw me and hid themselves; the aged rose up *and* stood;
9The princes refrained from talking and laid their hands on their mouths;
10The voices of the nobles were hushed, and their tongues cleaved to the roof of their mouths.
11For when the ear heard, it called me happy *and* blessed me; and when the eye saw, it testified for me [approvingly],
12Because I delivered the poor who cried, the fatherless and him who had none to help him.
13The blessing of him who was about to perish came upon me, and I caused the widow's heart to sing for joy.
14I put on *a*righteousness, and it clothed me *or* clothed itself with me; my justice was like a robe and a turban *or* a diadem *or* a crown!
15I was eyes to the blind, and feet was I to the lame.
16I was a father to the poor *and* needy; the cause of him I did not know I searched out.
17And I broke the jaws *or* the big teeth of the unrighteous and plucked the prey out of his teeth.
18Then I said, I shall die in *or* beside my nest, and I shall multiply my days as the sand.
19My root is spread out *and* open to the waters, and the dew lies all night upon my branch.
20My glory *and* honor are fresh in me [being constantly renewed], and my bow gains [ever] new strength in my hand.
21Men listened to me and waited and kept silence for my counsel.
22After I spoke, they did not speak again, and my speech dropped upon them [like a refreshing shower].
23And they waited for me as for the rain, and they opened their mouths wide as for the spring rain.
24I smiled on them when they had no confidence, and their depression did not cast down the light of my countenance.
25I chose their way [for them] and sat as [their] chief, and dwelt like a king among his soldiers, like one who comforts mourners.

**30** But now they who are younger than I have me in derision, whose fathers I disdained to set with the dogs of my flock.
2Yes, how could the strength of their hands profit me? They were men whose ripe age *and* vigor had perished.
3They are gaunt with want and famine; they gnaw the dry *and* barren ground *or* flee into the wilderness, into the gloom of wasteness and desolation.
4They pluck saltwort *or* mallows among the bushes, and roots of the broom for their food *or* to warm them.
5They are driven from among men, who shout after them as after a thief.
6They must dwell in the clefts of frightful valleys (gullies made by torrents) and in holes of the earth and of the rocks.
7Among the bushes they bray *and* howl [like wild animals]; beneath the prickly scrub they fling themselves *and* huddle together.
8Sons of the worthless and nameless, they have been scourged *and* crushed out of the land.
9And now I have become their song; yes, I am a byword to them.
10They abhor me, they stand aloof from me, and do not refrain from spitting in my face *or* at the sight of me.

*a* Blameless and upright as Job had been—and God had so pronounced him—his misunderstood afflictions had caused him to get dangerously off-center. Instead of keeping his mind stayed on God and justifying Him, he is giving his whole thought to justifying himself. Instead of humility there is only self-righteousness. In this chapter he uses pronouns referring to himself fifty times. But when he was able to see himself as God saw him, he loathed himself and repented "in dust and ashes" (Job 42:6).

---

a 24 The meaning of the Hebrew for this clause is uncertain.
b 3 Or *gnawed*   c 4 Or *fuel*

## New International Version

[11] Now that God has unstrung my bow and afflicted me,
    they throw off restraint in my presence.
[12] On my right the tribe[a] attacks;
    they lay snares for my feet,
    they build their siege ramps against me.
[13] They break up my road;
    they succeed in destroying me.
    'No one can help him,' they say.
[14] They advance as through a gaping breach;
    amid the ruins they come rolling in.
[15] Terrors overwhelm me;
    my dignity is driven away as by the wind,
    my safety vanishes like a cloud.

[16] "And now my life ebbs away;
    days of suffering grip me.
[17] Night pierces my bones;
    my gnawing pains never rest.
[18] In his great power God becomes like clothing to me[b];
    he binds me like the neck of my garment.
[19] He throws me into the mud,
    and I am reduced to dust and ashes.

[20] "I cry out to you, God, but you do not answer;
    I stand up, but you merely look at me.
[21] You turn on me ruthlessly;
    with the might of your hand you attack me.
[22] You snatch me up and drive me before the wind;
    you toss me about in the storm.
[23] I know you will bring me down to death,
    to the place appointed for all the living.

[24] "Surely no one lays a hand on a broken man
    when he cries for help in his distress.
[25] Have I not wept for those in trouble?
    Has not my soul grieved for the poor?
[26] Yet when I hoped for good, evil came;
    when I looked for light, then came darkness.
[27] The churning inside me never stops;
    days of suffering confront me.
[28] I go about blackened, but not by the sun;
    I stand up in the assembly and cry for help.
[29] I have become a brother of jackals,
    a companion of owls.
[30] My skin grows black and peels;
    my body burns with fever.
[31] My lyre is tuned to mourning,
    and my pipe to the sound of wailing.

**31** "I made a covenant with my eyes
    not to look lustfully at a young woman.
[2] For what is our lot from God above,
    our heritage from the Almighty on high?
[3] Is it not ruin for the wicked,
    disaster for those who do wrong?
[4] Does he not see my ways
    and count my every step?

[5] "If I have walked with falsehood
    or my foot has hurried after deceit—
[6] let God weigh me in honest scales
    and he will know that I am blameless—
[7] if my steps have turned from the path,
    if my heart has been led by my eyes,
    or if my hands have been defiled,
[8] then may others eat what I have sown,
    and may my crops be uprooted.

[9] "If my heart has been enticed by a woman,
    or if I have lurked at my neighbor's door,

## Amplified Bible

[11] For God has loosed my bowstring and afflicted *and* humbled me; they have cast off the bridle [of restraint] before me.
[12] On my right hand rises the rabble brood; they jostle me *and* push away my feet, and they cast up against me their ways of destruction [like an advancing army].
[13] They break up *and* clutter my path [embarrassing my plans]; they urge on my calamity, even though they have no helper [and are themselves helpless].
[14] As through a wide breach they come in; amid the crash [of falling walls] they roll themselves upon me.
[15] Terrors are turned upon me; my honor *and* reputation they chase away like the wind, and my welfare has passed away as a cloud.
[16] And now my life is poured out within me; the days of affliction have gripped me.
[17] My bones are pierced [with aching] in the night season, and the pains that gnaw me take no rest.
[18] By the great force [of my disease] my garment is disguised *and* disfigured; it binds me about like the collar of my coat.
[19] [God] has cast me into the mire, and I have become like dust and ashes.
[20] I cry to You, [Lord,] and You do not answer me; I stand up, but You [only] gaze [indifferently] at me.
[21] You have become harsh *and* cruel to me; with the might of Your hand You [keep me alive only to] persecute me.
[22] You lift me up on the wind; You cause me to ride upon it, and You toss me about in the tempest.
[23] For I know that You will bring me to death and to the house [of meeting] appointed for all the living.
[24] However, does not one falling in a heap of ruins stretch out his hand? Or in his calamity will he not therefore cry for help?
[25] Did not I weep for him who was in trouble? Was not my heart grieved for the poor *and* needy?
[26] But when I looked for good, then evil came to me; and when I waited for light, there came darkness.
[27] My heart is troubled and does not rest; days of affliction come to meet me.
[28] I go about blackened, but not by the sun; I stand up in the congregation and cry for help.
[29] I am a brother to jackals [which howl], and a companion to ostriches [which scream dismally].
[30] My skin falls from me in blackened flakes, and my bones are burned with heat.
[31] Therefore my lyre is turned to mourning, and my pipe into the voice of those who weep.

**31** I dictated a covenant (an agreement) to my eyes; how then could I have [lustfully] upon a girl?
[2] For what portion should I have from God above [if I were lewd], and what heritage from the Almighty on high?
[3] Does not calamity [justly] befall the unrighteous, and disaster the workers of iniquity?
[4] Does not [God] see my ways and count all my steps?
[5] If I have walked with falsehood *or* vanity, or if my foot has hastened to deceit—
[6] Oh, let me be weighed in a just balance *and* let Him weigh me, that God may know my integrity!
[7] If my step has turned out of [God's] way, and my heart has gone the way my eyes [covetously] invited, and if any spot has stained my hands with guilt,
[8] Then let me sow and let another eat; yes, let the produce of my field *or* my offspring be rooted out.
[9] If my heart has been deceived *and* I made a fool by a woman, or if I have [covetously] laid wait at my neighbor's door [until his departure],

---

*a 12* The meaning of the Hebrew for this word is uncertain.
*b 18* Hebrew; Septuagint *power he grasps my clothing*

## New International Version

10 then may my wife grind another man's grain,
  and may other men sleep with her.
11 For that would have been wicked,
  a sin to be judged.
12 It is a fire that burns to Destruction<sup>a</sup>;
  it would have uprooted my harvest.

13 "If I have denied justice to any of my servants,
  whether male or female,
  when they had a grievance against me,
14 what will I do when God confronts me?
  What will I answer when called to account?
15 Did not he who made me in the womb make them?
  Did not the same one form us both within our
  mothers?

16 "If I have denied the desires of the poor
  or let the eyes of the widow grow weary,
17 if I have kept my bread to myself,
  not sharing it with the fatherless—
18 but from my youth I reared them as a father would,
  and from my birth I guided the widow—
19 if I have seen anyone perishing for lack of clothing,
  or the needy without garments,
20 and their hearts did not bless me
  for warming them with the fleece from my sheep,
21 if I have raised my hand against the fatherless,
  knowing that I had influence in court,
22 then let my arm fall from the shoulder,
  let it be broken off at the joint.
23 For I dreaded destruction from God,
  and for fear of his splendor I could not do such
  things.

24 "If I have put my trust in gold
  or said to pure gold, 'You are my security,'
25 if I have rejoiced over my great wealth,
  the fortune my hands had gained,
26 if I have regarded the sun in its radiance
  or the moon moving in splendor,
27 so that my heart was secretly enticed
  and my hand offered them a kiss of homage,
28 then these also would be sins to be judged,
  for I would have been unfaithful to God on high.

29 "If I have rejoiced at my enemy's misfortune
  or gloated over the trouble that came to him—
30 I have not allowed my mouth to sin
  by invoking a curse against their life—
31 if those of my household have never said,
  'Who has not been filled with Job's meat?'—
32 but no stranger had to spend the night in the street,
  for my door was always open to the traveler—
33 if I have concealed my sin as people do,<sup>b</sup>
  by hiding my guilt in my heart
34 because I so feared the crowd
  and so dreaded the contempt of the clans
  that I kept silent and would not go outside—

35 ("Oh, that I had someone to hear me!
  I sign now my defense—let the Almighty answer
  me;
  let my accuser put his indictment in writing.
36 Surely I would wear it on my shoulder,
  I would put it on like a crown.

## Amplified Bible

10 Then let my wife grind [meal, like a bondslave] for
another, and let others bow down upon her.
11 For [adultery] is a heinous *and* chief crime, an iniquity
[to demand action by] the judges *and* punishment. [Deut.
22:22; John 8:5.]
12 For [uncontrolled passion] is a fire which consumes to
Abaddon (to destruction, ruin, and the place of final torment); [that fire once lighted would rage until all is con-
sumed] and would burn to the root all my [life's] increase.
13 If I have despised *and* rejected the cause of my
manservant or my maidservant when they contended *or*
brought a complaint against me,
14 What then shall I do when God rises up [to judge]?
When He visits [to inquire of me], what shall I answer
Him? [Ps. 44:21.]
15 Did not He Who made me in the womb make [my
servant]? And did not One fashion us both in the womb?
[Prov. 14:31; 22:2; Mal. 2:10.]
16 If I have withheld from the poor *and* needy what they
desired, or have caused the eyes of the widow to look in
vain [for relief],
17 Or have eaten my morsel alone and have not shared it
with the fatherless—
18 No, but from my youth [the fatherless] grew up with
me as a father, and I have been [the widow's] guide from
my mother's womb—
19 If I have seen anyone perish for want of clothing, or
any poor person without covering,
20 If his loins have not blessed me [for clothing them],
and if he was not warmed with the fleece of my sheep,
21 If I have lifted my hand against the fatherless when I
saw [that the judges would be favorable and be] my help
at the [council] gate,
22 Then let my shoulder fall away from my shoulder
blade, and my arm be broken from its socket.
23 For calamity from God was a terror to me, and because of His majesty I could not endure [to face Him] *and*
could do nothing. [Isa. 13:6; Joel 1:15.]
24 If I have made gold my trust *and* hope or have said to
fine gold, You are my confidence,
25 If I rejoiced because my wealth was great and because
my [powerful] hand [alone] had gotten much,
26 If I beheld [as an object of worship] the sunlight when
it shone or the moon walking in its brightness,
27 And my heart has been secretly enticed by them or
my mouth has kissed my hand [in homage to them],
28 This also would have been [a heinous and principal]
iniquity to demand the judges' action *and* punishment,
for I would have denied *and* been false to the God Who is
above. [Deut. 4:19; 17:2-7.]
29 If I rejoiced at the destruction of him who hated me or
lifted myself up [in malicious triumph] when evil overtook
him—
30 No, I have let my mouth sin neither by cursing my
enemy nor by praying that he might die—
31 [Just ask] if the men of my tent will not say, Who can
find one in need who has not been satisfied with food he
gave them?—
32 The temporary resident has not lodged in the street,
but I have opened my door to the wayfaring man—
33 If like Adam *or* like [other] men I have concealed my
transgressions, by hiding my iniquity in my bosom
34 Because I feared the great multitude and the contempt of families terrified me so that I kept silence and
did not go out of the door—
35 Oh, for a hearing! Oh, for an answer from the Almighty! Let my adversary write out His indictment [and
put His vague accusations in tangible form] in a book!
36 Surely I would [proudly] bear it on my shoulder and
wind the scroll about my head as a diadem.

---

<sup>a</sup> 12 Hebrew *Abaddon*   <sup>b</sup> 33 Or *as Adam did*

## New International Version

37 I would give him an account of my every step;
   I would present it to him as to a ruler.) —

38 "if my land cries out against me
   and all its furrows are wet with tears,
39 if I have devoured its yield without payment
   or broken the spirit of its tenants,
40 then let briers come up instead of wheat
   and stinkweed instead of barley."

The words of Job are ended.

### Elihu

**32** So these three men stopped answering Job, because he was righteous in his own eyes. 2 But Elihu son of Barakel the Buzite, of the family of Ram, became very angry with Job for justifying himself rather than God. 3 He was also angry with the three friends, because they had found no way to refute Job, and yet had condemned him.*a* 4 Now Elihu had waited before speaking to Job because they were older than he. 5 But when he saw that the three men had nothing more to say, his anger was aroused.

6 So Elihu son of Barakel the Buzite said:

"I am young in years,
   and you are old;
that is why I was fearful,
   not daring to tell you what I know.
7 I thought, 'Age should speak;
   advanced years should teach wisdom.'
8 But it is the spirit*b* in a person,
   the breath of the Almighty, that gives them
      understanding.
9 It is not only the old*c* who are wise,
   not only the aged who understand what is right.

10 "Therefore I say: Listen to me;
   I too will tell you what I know.
11 I waited while you spoke,
   I listened to your reasoning;
while you were searching for words,
12   I gave you my full attention.
But not one of you has proved Job wrong;
   none of you has answered his arguments.
13 Do not say, 'We have found wisdom;
   let God, not a man, refute him.'
14 But Job has not marshaled his words against me,
   and I will not answer him with your arguments.

15 "They are dismayed and have no more to say;
   words have failed them.
16 Must I wait, now that they are silent,
   now that they stand there with no reply?
17 I too will have my say;
   I too will tell what I know.
18 For I am full of words,
   and the spirit within me compels me;
19 inside I am like bottled-up wine,
   like new wineskins ready to burst.
20 I must speak and find relief;
   I must open my lips and reply.
21 I will show no partiality,
   nor will I flatter anyone;
22 for if I were skilled in flattery,
   my Maker would soon take me away.

## Amplified Bible

37 I would count out to Him the number of my steps [with every detail of my life], approaching His presence as a prince—
38 For if my land has cried out against me and its furrows have complained together with tears [that I have no right to them],
39 If I have eaten its fruits without paying for them or have caused its [rightful] owners to breathe their last,
40 Let thistles grow instead of wheat and cockleburs instead of barley. The [controversial] words of Job [with his friends] are ended.

**32** So these three men ceased to answer Job, because he was [rigidly] righteous (upright and in right standing with God) in his own eyes. [But there was a fifth man there also.]
2 Elihu son of Barachel the Buzite, of the family of Ram, became indignant. His indignation was kindled against Job because he justified himself rather than God [even made himself out to be better than God].
3 Also against [Job's] three friends was [Elihu's] anger kindled, because they had found no answer [were unable to show his real error], and yet they had declared him to be in the wrong [and responsible for his own afflictions].
4 Now Elihu had waited to speak to Job because the others were older than he.
5 But when Elihu saw that there was no answer in the mouths of these three men, he became angry.
6 Then Elihu son of Barachel the Buzite said, I am young, and you are aged; for that reason I was timid *and* restrained and dared not declare my opinion to you.
7 I said, Age should speak, and a multitude of years should teach wisdom [so let it be heard].
8 But there is [a vital force] a spirit [of intelligence] in man, and the breath of the Almighty gives men understanding. [Prov. 2:6.]
9 It is not the great [necessarily] who are wise, nor [always] the aged who understand justice.
10 So I say, Listen to me; I also will give you my opinion [about Job's situation] *and* my knowledge.
11 You see, I waited for your words, I listened to your wise reasons, while you searched out what to say.
12 Yes, I paid attention to what you said, and behold, not one of you convinced Job or made [satisfactory] replies to his words [you could not refute him].
13 Beware lest you say, We have found wisdom; God thrusts [Job] down [justly], not man [God alone is dealing with him].
14 Now [Job] has not directed his words against me [therefore I have no cause for irritation], neither will I answer him with speeches like yours. [I speak for truth, not for revenge].
15 [Job's friends] are amazed *and* embarrassed, they answer no more; they have not a thing to say [reports Elihu].
16 And shall I wait, because they say nothing but stand still and answer no more?
17 I also will answer my [God-assigned] part; I also will declare my opinion *and* my knowledge.
18 For I am full of words; the spirit within me constrains me.
19 My breast is as wine that has no vent; like new wineskins, it is ready to burst.
20 I must speak, that I may get relief *and* be refreshed; I will open my lips and answer.
21 I will not [I warn you] be influenced by respect for any man's person *and* show partiality, neither will I flatter any man.
22 For I know not how to flatter, [wasting my time in mere formalities, for then] my Maker would soon take me away.

---

*a* 3 Masoretic Text; an ancient Hebrew scribal tradition *Job, and so had condemned God*   *b* 8 Or *Spirit*; also in verse 18   *c* 9 Or *many*; or *great*

## New International Version

**33** "But now, Job, listen to my words;
pay attention to everything I say.
[2] I am about to open my mouth;
my words are on the tip of my tongue.
[3] My words come from an upright heart;
my lips sincerely speak what I know.
[4] The Spirit of God has made me;
the breath of the Almighty gives me life.
[5] Answer me then, if you can;
stand up and argue your case before me.
[6] I am the same as you in God's sight;
I too am a piece of clay.
[7] No fear of me should alarm you,
nor should my hand be heavy on you.

[8] "But you have said in my hearing—
I heard the very words—
[9] 'I am pure, I have done no wrong;
I am clean and free from sin.
[10] Yet God has found fault with me;
he considers me his enemy.
[11] He fastens my feet in shackles;
he keeps close watch on all my paths.'

[12] "But I tell you, in this you are not right,
for God is greater than any mortal.
[13] Why do you complain to him
that he responds to no one's words[a]?
[14] For God does speak—now one way, now another—
though no one perceives it.
[15] In a dream, in a vision of the night,
when deep sleep falls on people
as they slumber in their beds,
[16] he may speak in their ears
and terrify them with warnings,
[17] to turn them from wrongdoing
and keep them from pride,
[18] to preserve them from the pit,
their lives from perishing by the sword.[b]

[19] "Or someone may be chastened on a bed of pain
with constant distress in their bones,
[20] so that their body finds food repulsive
and their soul loathes the choicest meal.
[21] Their flesh wastes away to nothing,
and their bones, once hidden, now stick out.
[22] They draw near to the pit,
and their life to the messengers of death.[c]
[23] Yet if there is an angel at their side,
a messenger, one out of a thousand,
sent to tell them how to be upright,
[24] and he is gracious to that person and says to God,
'Spare them from going down to the pit;
I have found a ransom for them—
[25] let their flesh be renewed like a child's;
let them be restored as in the days of their youth'—
[26] then that person can pray to God and find favor with him,
they will see God's face and shout for joy;
he will restore them to full well-being.
[27] And they will go to others and say,
'I have sinned, I have perverted what is right,
but I did not get what I deserved.

## Amplified Bible

**33** Be that as it may, Job, I beg of you to hear what I have to say and give heed to all my words.
[2] Behold, here I am with open mouth; here is my tongue talking.
[3] My words shall express the uprightness of my heart, and my lips shall speak what they know with utter sincerity.
[4] [It is] the Spirit of God that made me [which has stirred me up], and the breath of the Almighty that gives me life [which inspires me].
[5] Answer me now, if you can; set your words in order before me; take your stand.
[6] Behold, I am toward God *and* before Him even as you are; I also am formed out of the clay [though I speak with abnormal wisdom because of a divine illumination].
[7] See my terror [for I am only a fellow mortal, not God]; I shall not make you afraid, neither shall my pressure be heavy upon you.
[8] Surely you have spoken in my hearing, and I have heard the voice of your words, saying,
[9] I am clean, without transgression; I am innocent, neither is there iniquity in me.
[10] But behold, God finds occasions against me *and* causes of alienation *and* indifference; He counts me as His enemy.
[11] He puts my feet in the stocks; He [untrustingly] watches all my paths [you say].
[12] I reply to you, Behold, in this you are not just; God is superior to man.
[13] Why do you contend against Him? For He does not give account of any of His actions. [Sufficient for us it should be to know that it is He Who does them.]
[14] For God [does reveal His will; He] speaks not only once, but more than once, even though men do not regard it [including you, Job].
[15] [One may hear God's voice] in a dream, in a vision of the night, when deep sleep falls on men while slumbering upon the bed,
[16] Then He opens the ears of men and seals their instruction [terrifying them with warnings],
[17] That He may withdraw man from his purpose and cut off pride from him [disgusting him with his own disappointing self-sufficiency].
[18] He holds him back from the pit [of destruction], and his life from perishing by the sword [of God's destructive judgments].
[19] [God's voice may be heard by man when] he is chastened with pain upon his bed and with continual strife in his bones *or* while all his bones are firmly set,
[20] So that his desire makes him loathe food, and even dainty dishes [nauseate him].
[21] His flesh is so wasted away that it cannot be seen, and his bones that were not seen stick out.
[22] Yes, his soul draws near to corruption, and his life to the inflicters of death (the destroyers).
[23] [God's voice may be heard] if there is for the hearer a messenger *or* an angel, an interpreter, one among a thousand, to show to man what is right for him [how to be upright and in right standing with God],
[24] Then [God] is gracious to him and says, Deliver him from going down into the pit [of destruction]; I have found a ransom (a price of redemption, an atonement)!
[25] [Then the man's] flesh shall be restored; it becomes fresher *and* more tender than a child's; he returns to the days of his youth.
[26] He prays to God, and He is favorable to him, so that he sees His face with joy; for [God] restores to him his righteousness (his uprightness and right standing with God—with its joys).
[27] He looks upon other men *or* sings out to them, I have sinned and perverted that which was right, and it did not profit me, *or* He did not requite me [according to my iniquity]!

---

[a] 13 Or *that he does not answer for any of his actions*   [b] 18 Or *from crossing the river*   [c] 22 Or *to the place of the dead*

## New International Version

28 God has delivered me from going down to the pit,
    and I shall live to enjoy the light of life.'
29 "God does all these things to a person—
    twice, even three times—
30 to turn them back from the pit,
    that the light of life may shine on them.
31 "Pay attention, Job, and listen to me;
    be silent, and I will speak.
32 If you have anything to say, answer me;
    speak up, for I want to vindicate you.
33 But if not, then listen to me;
    be silent, and I will teach you wisdom."

# 34

Then Elihu said:

2 "Hear my words, you wise men;
    listen to me, you men of learning.
3 For the ear tests words
    as the tongue tastes food.
4 Let us discern for ourselves what is right;
    let us learn together what is good.

5 "Job says, 'I am innocent,
    but God denies me justice.
6 Although I am right,
    I am considered a liar;
although I am guiltless,
    his arrow inflicts an incurable wound.'
7 Is there anyone like Job,
    who drinks scorn like water?
8 He keeps company with evildoers;
    he associates with the wicked.
9 For he says, 'There is no profit
    in trying to please God.'

10 "So listen to me, you men of understanding.
    Far be it from God to do evil,
    from the Almighty to do wrong.
11 He repays everyone for what they have done;
    he brings on them what their conduct deserves.
12 It is unthinkable that God would do wrong,
    that the Almighty would pervert justice.
13 Who appointed him over the earth?
    Who put him in charge of the whole world?
14 If it were his intention
    and he withdrew his spirit[a] and breath,
15 all humanity would perish together
    and mankind would return to the dust.

16 "If you have understanding, hear this;
    listen to what I say.
17 Can someone who hates justice govern?
    Will you condemn the just and mighty One?
18 Is he not the One who says to kings, 'You are
      worthless,'
    and to nobles, 'You are wicked,'
19 who shows no partiality to princes
    and does not favor the rich over the poor,
    for they are all the work of his hands?
20 They die in an instant, in the middle of the night;
    the people are shaken and they pass away;
    the mighty are removed without human hand.

21 "His eyes are on the ways of mortals;
    he sees their every step.
22 There is no deep shadow, no utter darkness,
    where evildoers can hide.
23 God has no need to examine people further,
    that they should come before him for judgment.
24 Without inquiry he shatters the mighty
    and sets up others in their place.

## Amplified Bible

28 [God] has redeemed my life from going down to the
pit [of destruction], and my life shall see the light!
29 [Elihu comments] Behold, God does all these things
twice, yes, three times, with a man,
30 To bring back his life from the pit [of destruction],
that he may be enlightened with the light of the living.
31 Give heed, O Job, listen to me; hold your peace, and
I will speak.
32 If you have anything to say, answer me; speak, for I
desire to justify you.
33 If [you do] not [have anything to say], listen to me;
hold your peace, and I will teach you wisdom.

# 34

Elihu answered (continued his discourse) and
said,

2 Hear my words, you wise men, and give ear to me, you
who have [so much] knowledge.
3 For the ear tries words as the palate tastes food.
4 Let us choose for ourselves that which is right; let us
know among ourselves what is good.
5 For Job has said, I am [innocent and uncompromising-
ly] righteous, but God has taken away my right; [Job 33:9.]
6 Would I lie against my right? Yet, notwithstanding my
right, I am counted a liar. My wound is incurable, though
I am without transgression.
7 What man is like Job, who drinks up scoffing and
scorning like water,
8 Who goes in company with the workers of iniquity and
walks with wicked men?
9 For he has said, It profits a man nothing that he should
delight himself with God and consent to Him.
10 Therefore hear me, you men of understanding. Far be
it from God that He should do wickedness, and from the
Almighty that He should commit iniquity.
11 For according to the deeds of a man God will [exactly]
proportion his pay, and He will cause every man to find
[recompense] according to his ways.
12 Truly God will not do wickedly, neither will the Almighty pervert justice.
13 Who put [God] in charge over the earth? Or who laid
on Him the whole world?
14 If [God] should set His heart upon him [man] and
withdraw His [life-giving] spirit and His breath [from
man] to Himself,
15 All flesh would perish together, and man would turn
again to dust. [Ps. 104:29; Eccl. 12:7.]
16 If now you have understanding, hear this; listen to my
words.
17 Is it possible that an enemy of right should govern?
And will you condemn Him Who is just and mighty?
18 [God] Who says to a king, You are worthless and vile,
or to princes and nobles, You are ungodly and evil?
19 [God] is not partial to princes, nor does He regard
the rich more than the poor, for they all are the work of
His hands.
20 In a moment they die; even at midnight the people are
shaken and pass away, and the mighty are taken away by
no [human] hand.
21 For [God's] eyes are upon the ways of a man, and He
sees all his steps. [Ps. 34:15; Prov. 5:21; Jer. 16:17.]
22 There is no darkness nor thick gloom where the evildoers may hide themselves.
23 [God] sets before man no appointed time, that he
should appear before [Him] in judgment.
24 He breaks in pieces mighty men without inquiry [be-
fore a jury] and in ways past finding out and sets others in
their stead. [Dan. 2:21.]

---

a 14 Or *Spirit*

## New International Version

25 Because he takes note of their deeds,
　　he overthrows them in the night and they are
　　　crushed.
26 He punishes them for their wickedness
　　where everyone can see them,
27 because they turned from following him
　　and had no regard for any of his ways.
28 They caused the cry of the poor to come before him,
　　so that he heard the cry of the needy.
29 But if he remains silent, who can condemn him?
　　If he hides his face, who can see him?
　　Yet he is over individual and nation alike,
30 　to keep the godless from ruling,
　　from laying snares for the people.

31 "Suppose someone says to God,
　　'I am guilty but will offend no more.
32 Teach me what I cannot see;
　　if I have done wrong, I will not do so again.'
33 Should God then reward you on your terms,
　　when you refuse to repent?
　You must decide, not I;
　　so tell me what you know.

34 "Men of understanding declare,
　　wise men who hear me say to me,
35 'Job speaks without knowledge;
　　his words lack insight.'
36 Oh, that Job might be tested to the utmost
　　for answering like a wicked man!
37 To his sin he adds rebellion;
　　scornfully he claps his hands among us
　　and multiplies his words against God."

## 35 Then Elihu said:

2 "Do you think this is just?
　　You say, 'I am in the right, not God.'
3 Yet you ask him, 'What profit is it to me,[a]
　　and what do I gain by not sinning?'

4 "I would like to reply to you
　　and to your friends with you.
5 Look up at the heavens and see;
　　gaze at the clouds so high above you.
6 If you sin, how does that affect him?
　　If your sins are many, what does that do to him?
7 If you are righteous, what do you give to him,
　　or what does he receive from your hand?
8 Your wickedness only affects humans like yourself,
　　and your righteousness only other people.

9 "People cry out under a load of oppression;
　　they plead for relief from the arm of the powerful.
10 But no one says, 'Where is God my Maker,
　　who gives songs in the night,
11 who teaches us more than he teaches[b] the beasts of
　　　the earth
　　and makes us wiser than[c] the birds in the sky?'
12 He does not answer when people cry out
　　because of the arrogance of the wicked.
13 Indeed, God does not listen to their empty plea;
　　the Almighty pays no attention to it.
14 How much less, then, will he listen
　　when you say that you do not see him,
　that your case is before him
　　and you must wait for him,

## Amplified Bible

25 Therefore He takes knowledge of their works, and He
overturns them in the night, so that they are crushed *and*
destroyed.
26 God strikes them down as wicked men in the open
sight of beholders,
27 Because they turned aside from Him and would not
consider *or* show regard for any of His ways, [I Sam.
15:11.]
28 So that they caused the cry of the poor to come to
Him, and He heard the cry of the afflicted. [Exod. 22:23;
James 5:4.]
29 When He gives quietness (peace and security from
oppression), who then can condemn? When He hides His
face [withdrawing His favor and help], who then can behold Him [and make Him gracious], whether it be a nation
or a man by himself?—
30 That the godless man may not reign, that there be no
one to ensnare the people.
31 For has anyone said to God, I have borne my chastisement; I will not offend any more;
32 Teach me what I do not see [in regard to how I have
sinned]; if I have done iniquity, I will do it no more?
33 Should [God's] recompense [for your sins] be as you
will it, when you refuse to accept it? For you must do the
choosing, and not I; therefore say what is your truthful
conclusion.
34 Men of understanding will tell me, indeed, every wise
man who hears me [will agree],
35 That Job speaks without knowledge, and his words
are without wisdom *and* insight.
36 [Would that Job's afflictions be continued and] he be
tried to the end because of his answering like wicked men!
37 For he adds rebellion [in his unsubmissive, defiant attitude toward God] to his unacknowledged sin; he claps
his hands [in open mockery and contempt of God] among
us, and he multiplies his words of accusation against God.

## 35 Elihu spoke further [to Job] and said,

2 Do you think this is your right, *or* are you saying,
My righteousness is more than God's,
3 That you ask, What advantage have you? How am I
profited more than if I had sinned?
4 I will answer you and your companions with you.
5 Look to the heavens and see; and behold the skies
which are higher than you.
6 If you have sinned, how does that affect God? And if
your transgressions are multiplied, what have you done
to Him?
7 If you are righteous, what do you [by that] give God?
Or what does He receive from your hand?
8 Your wickedness touches and affects a man such as
you are, and your righteousness is for yourself, one of the
human race [but it cannot touch God, Who is above such
influence.]
9 Because of the multitudes of oppressions the people
cry out; they cry for help because of the violence of the
mighty.
10 But no one says, Where is God my Maker, Who gives
songs of rejoicing in the night, [Acts 16:25.]
11 Who teaches us more than the beasts of the earth and
makes us wiser than the birds of the heavens?
12 [The people] cry out because of the pride of evil men,
but He does not answer.
13 Surely God will refuse to answer [the cry which is]
vanity (vain and empty—instead of abiding trust); neither
will the Almighty regard it—
14 How much less when [missing His righteous judgment on earth] you say that you do not see Him, that your
cause is before Him, and you are waiting for Him!

---

*a* 3 Or *you*　*b* 10,11 Or *night, / 11who teaches us by*　*c* 11 Or *us wise by*

## New International Version

15 and further, that his anger never punishes
and he does not take the least notice of wickedness.*
16 So Job opens his mouth with empty talk;
without knowledge he multiplies words."

**36** Elihu continued:

2 "Bear with me a little longer and I will show you
that there is more to be said in God's behalf.
3 I get my knowledge from afar;
I will ascribe justice to my Maker.
4 Be assured that my words are not false;
one who has perfect knowledge is with you.

5 "God is mighty, but despises no one;
he is mighty, and firm in his purpose.
6 He does not keep the wicked alive
but gives the afflicted their rights.
7 He does not take his eyes off the righteous;
he enthrones them with kings
and exalts them forever.
8 But if people are bound in chains,
held fast by cords of affliction,
9 he tells them what they have done—
that they have sinned arrogantly.
10 He makes them listen to correction
and commands them to repent of their evil.
11 If they obey and serve him,
they will spend the rest of their days in prosperity
and their years in contentment.
12 But if they do not listen,
they will perish by the sword*
and die without knowledge.

13 "The godless in heart harbor resentment;
even when he fetters them, they do not cry for help.
14 They die in their youth,
among male prostitutes of the shrines.
15 But those who suffer he delivers in their suffering;
he speaks to them in their affliction.

16 "He is wooing you from the jaws of distress
to a spacious place free from restriction,
to the comfort of your table laden with choice food.
17 But now you are laden with the judgment due the wicked;
judgment and justice have taken hold of you.
18 Be careful that no one entices you by riches;
do not let a large bribe turn you aside.
19 Would your wealth or even all your mighty efforts
sustain you so you would not be in distress?
20 Do not long for the night,
to drag people away from their homes.*
21 Beware of turning to evil,
which you seem to prefer to affliction.

22 "God is exalted in his power.
Who is a teacher like him?
23 Who has prescribed his ways for him,
or said to him, 'You have done wrong'?
24 Remember to extol his work,
which people have praised in song.
25 All humanity has seen it;
mortals gaze on it from afar.
26 How great is God—beyond our understanding!
The number of his years is past finding out.

27 "He draws up the drops of water,
which distill as rain to the streams*;

*a 15* Symmachus, Theodotion and Vulgate; the meaning of the
Hebrew for this word is uncertain.    *b 12* Or *will cross the river*
*c 20* The meaning of the Hebrew for verses 18-20 is uncertain.
*d 27* Or *distill from the mist as rain*

## Amplified Bible

15 But now because God has not [speedily] punished in
His anger and seems to be unaware of the wrong *and* oppression [of which a person is guilty],
16 Job uselessly opens his mouth and multiplies words
without knowledge [drawing the worthless conclusion that
the righteous have no more advantage than the wicked].

**36** Elihu proceeded and said,

2 Bear with me *and* wait a little longer, and I will
show you, for I have something still to say on God's behalf.
3 I will bring my knowledge from afar and will ascribe
righteousness to my Maker.
4 For truly my words shall not be false; He Who is perfect in knowledge is with you.
5 Behold! God is mighty, and yet despises no one nor
regards anything as trivial; He is mighty in power of understanding *and* heart.
6 He does not prolong the life of the wicked, but gives
the needy *and* afflicted their right.
7 He withdraws not His eyes from the righteous (the upright in right standing with God); but He sets them forever
with kings upon the throne, and they are exalted.
8 And if they are bound in fetters [of adversity] and held
by cords of affliction, [Ps. 107:10, 11.]
9 Then He shows to them [the true character of] their
deeds and their transgressions, that they have acted arrogantly [with presumption and self-sufficiency].
10 He also opens their ears to instruction *and* discipline,
and commands that they return from iniquity.
11 If they obey and serve Him, they shall spend their
days in prosperity and their years in pleasantness *and* joy.
12 But if they obey not, they shall perish by the sword [of
God's destructive judgments], and they shall die in ignorance of true knowledge.
13 But the godless *and* profane in heart heap up anger
[at the divine discipline]; they do not cry to Him when He
binds them [with cords of affliction]. [Rom. 2:5.]
14 They die in youth, and their life perishes among the
unclean (those who are sodomites).
15 He delivers the afflicted in their affliction and opens
their ears [to His voice] in adversity.
16 Indeed, God would have allured you out of the mouth
of distress into a broad place where there is no situation
of perplexity *or* privation; and that which would be set on
your table would be full of fatness.
17 But if you [Job] are filled with the judgment of the
wicked, judgment and justice will keep hold on you.
18 For let not wrath entice you into scorning chastisements; and let not the greatness of the ransom [the suffering, if rightly endured] turn you aside.
19 Will your cry be sufficient to keep you from distress,
or will all the force of your strength do it?
20 Desire not the night, when peoples are cut off from
their places;
21 Take heed, turn not to iniquity, for this [the iniquity
of complaining against God] you have chosen rather than
[submission in] affliction.
22 Behold, God exalts *and* does loftily in His power; who
is a ruler *or* a teacher like Him?
23 Who has appointed God His way? Or who can say, You
have done unrighteousness?
24 Remember that [by submission] you magnify God's
work, of which men have sung.
25 All men have looked upon God's work; man may behold it afar off.
26 Behold, God is great, and we know Him not! The number of His years is unsearchable. [I Cor. 13:12.]
27 For He draws up the drops of water, which distil as
rain from His vapor,

## New International Version

28 the clouds pour down their moisture
and abundant showers fall on mankind.
29 Who can understand how he spreads out the clouds,
how he thunders from his pavilion?
30 See how he scatters his lightning about him,
bathing the depths of the sea.
31 This is the way he governs<sup>a</sup> the nations
and provides food in abundance.
32 He fills his hands with lightning
and commands it to strike its mark.
33 His thunder announces the coming storm;
even the cattle make known its approach.<sup>b</sup>

**37** "At this my heart pounds
and leaps from its place.
2 Listen! Listen to the roar of his voice,
to the rumbling that comes from his mouth.
3 He unleashes his lightning beneath the whole heaven
and sends it to the ends of the earth.
4 After that comes the sound of his roar;
he thunders with his majestic voice.
When his voice resounds,
he holds nothing back.
5 God's voice thunders in marvelous ways;
he does great things beyond our understanding.
6 He says to the snow, 'Fall on the earth,'
and to the rain shower, 'Be a mighty downpour.'
7 So that everyone he has made may know his work,
he stops all people from their labor.<sup>c</sup>
8 The animals take cover;
they remain in their dens.
9 The tempest comes out from its chamber,
the cold from the driving winds.
10 The breath of God produces ice,
and the broad waters become frozen.
11 He loads the clouds with moisture;
he scatters his lightning through them.
12 At his direction they swirl around
over the face of the whole earth
to do whatever he commands them.
13 He brings the clouds to punish people,
or to water his earth and show his love.

14 "Listen to this, Job;
stop and consider God's wonders.
15 Do you know how God controls the clouds
and makes his lightning flash?
16 Do you know how the clouds hang poised,
those wonders of him who has perfect knowledge?
17 You who swelter in your clothes
when the land lies hushed under the south wind,
18 can you join him in spreading out the skies,
hard as a mirror of cast bronze?

19 "Tell us what we should say to him;
we cannot draw up our case because of our darkness.
20 Should he be told that I want to speak?
Would anyone ask to be swallowed up?
21 Now no one can look at the sun,
bright as it is in the skies
after the wind has swept them clean.
22 Out of the north he comes in golden splendor;
God comes in awesome majesty.
23 The Almighty is beyond our reach and exalted in power;
in his justice and great righteousness, he does not oppress.

## Amplified Bible

28 Which the skies pour down and drop abundantly upon [the multitudes of] mankind.
29 Not only that, but can anyone understand the spreadings of the clouds or the thunderings of His pavilion? [Ps. 18:11; Isa. 40:22.]
30 Behold, He spreads His lightning against the dark clouds and covers the roots of the sea.
31 For by [His clouds] God executes judgment upon the peoples; He gives food in abundance.
32 He covers His hands with the lightning and commands it to strike the mark.
33 His thunderings speak [awesomely] concerning Him; the cattle are told of His coming storm.

**37** Indeed, [at His thunderings] my heart also trembles and leaps out of its place.
2 Hear, oh, hear the roar of His voice and the sound of rumbling that goes out of His mouth!
3 Under the whole heaven He lets it loose, and His lightning to the ends of the earth.
4 After it His voice roars; He thunders with the voice of His majesty, and He restrains not [His lightnings against His adversaries] when His voice is heard.
5 God thunders marvelously with His voice; He does great things which we cannot comprehend.
6 For He says to the snow, Fall on the earth; likewise He speaks to the showers and to the downpour of His mighty rains.
7 God seals up (stops, brings to a standstill by severe weather) the hand of every man [and now under His seal their hands are forced to inactivity], that all men whom He has made may know His doings (His sovereign power and their subjection to it).
8 Then the beasts go into dens and remain in their lairs.
9 Out of its chamber comes the whirlwind, and cold from the scattering winds.
10 By the breath of God ice is given, and the breadth of the waters is frozen over. [Ps. 147:17, 18.]
11 He loads the thick cloud with moisture; He scatters the cloud of His lightning.
12 And it is turned round about by His guidance, that they may do whatever He commands them upon the face of the habitable earth.
13 Whether it be for correction or for His earth [generally] or for His mercy and loving-kindness, He causes it to come. [Exod. 9:18, 23; I Sam. 12:18, 19.]
14 Hear this, O Job; stand still and consider the wondrous works of God.
15 Do you know how God lays His command upon them and causes the lightning of His [storm] cloud to shine?
16 Do you know how the clouds are balanced [and poised in the heavens], the wonderful works of Him Who is perfect in knowledge?
17 [Or] why your garments are hot when He quiets the earth [in sultry summer] with the [oppressive] south wind?
18 Can you along with Him spread out the sky, [which is] strong as a molten mirror?
19 Tell us [Job] with what words of man we may address such a Being; we cannot state our case because we are in the dark [in the presence of the unsearchable God].
20 So shall it be told Him that I wish to speak? If a man speaks, shall he be swallowed up?
21 And now men cannot look upon the light when it is bright in the skies, when the wind has passed and cleared them.
22 Golden brightness and splendor come out of the north; [if men can scarcely look upon it, how much less upon the] terrible splendor and majesty God has upon Himself!
23 Touching the Almighty, we cannot find Him out; He is excellent in power; and to justice and plenteous righteousness He does no violence [He will disregard no right]. [I Tim. 6:16.]

---

<sup>a</sup> 31 Or nourishes   <sup>b</sup> 33 Or announces his coming— / the One zealous against evil   <sup>c</sup> 7 Or work, / he fills all people with fear by his power

## New International Version

24 Therefore, people revere him,
for does he not have regard for all the wise in heart?[a]"

### The LORD Speaks

**38** Then the LORD spoke to Job out of the storm. He said:

2 "Who is this that obscures my plans
with words without knowledge?
3 Brace yourself like a man;
I will question you,
and you shall answer me.

4 "Where were you when I laid the earth's foundation?
Tell me, if you understand.
5 Who marked off its dimensions? Surely you know!
Who stretched a measuring line across it?
6 On what were its footings set,
or who laid its cornerstone—
7 while the morning stars sang together
and all the angels[b] shouted for joy?

8 "Who shut up the sea behind doors
when it burst forth from the womb,
9 when I made the clouds its garment
and wrapped it in thick darkness,
10 when I fixed limits for it
and set its doors and bars in place,
11 when I said, 'This far you may come and no farther;
here is where your proud waves halt'?

12 "Have you ever given orders to the morning,
or shown the dawn its place,
13 that it might take the earth by the edges
and shake the wicked out of it?
14 The earth takes shape like clay under a seal;
its features stand out like those of a garment.
15 The wicked are denied their light,
and their upraised arm is broken.

16 "Have you journeyed to the springs of the sea
or walked in the recesses of the deep?
17 Have the gates of death been shown to you?
Have you seen the gates of the deepest darkness?
18 Have you comprehended the vast expanses of the earth?
Tell me, if you know all this.

19 "What is the way to the abode of light?
And where does darkness reside?
20 Can you take them to their places?
Do you know the paths to their dwellings?
21 Surely you know, for you were already born!
You have lived so many years!

22 "Have you entered the storehouses of the snow
or seen the storehouses of the hail,
23 which I reserve for times of trouble,
for days of war and battle?
24 What is the way to the place where the lightning is dispersed,
or the place where the east winds are scattered over the earth?
25 Who cuts a channel for the torrents of rain,
and a path for the thunderstorm,
26 to water a land where no one lives,
an uninhabited desert,
27 to satisfy a desolate wasteland
and make it sprout with grass?
28 Does the rain have a father?
Who fathers the drops of dew?
29 From whose womb comes the ice?
Who gives birth to the frost from the heavens
30 when the waters become hard as stone,
when the surface of the deep is frozen?

a 24 Or for he does not have regard for any who think they are wise.
b 7 Hebrew the sons of God

## Amplified Bible

24 Men therefore [reverently] fear Him; He regards and respects not any who are wise in heart [in their own understanding and conceit]. [Matt. 10:28.]

**38** Then the Lord answered Job out of the whirlwind and said,

2 Who is this that darkens counsel by words without knowledge? [Job 35:16.]
3 Gird up now your loins like a man, and I will demand of you, and you declare to Me.
4 Where were you when I laid the foundation of the earth? Declare to Me, if you have and know understanding.
5 Who determined the measures of the earth, if you know? Or who stretched the measuring line upon it?
6 Upon what were the foundations of it fastened, or who laid its cornerstone,
7 When the morning stars sang together and all the sons of God shouted for joy?
8 Or who shut up the sea with doors when it broke forth and issued out of the womb?—
9 When I made the clouds the garment of it, and thick darkness a swaddling band for it,
10 And marked for it My appointed boundary and set bars and doors, [Jer. 5:22.]
11 And said, Thus far shall you come and no farther; and here shall your proud waves be stayed? [Ps. 89:9; 93:4.]
12 Have you commanded the morning since your days began and caused the dawn to know its place,
13 So that [light] may get hold of the corners of the earth and shake the wickedness [of night] out of it?
14 It is changed like clay into which a seal is pressed; and things stand out like a many-colored garment.
15 From the wicked their light is withheld, and their uplifted arm is broken.
16 Have you explored the springs of the sea? Or have you walked in the recesses of the deep?
17 Have the gates of death been revealed to you? Or have you seen the doors of deep darkness?
18 Have you comprehended the breadth of the earth? Tell Me, if you know it all.
19 Where is the [a]way where light dwells? And as for darkness, where is its abode,
20 That you may conduct it to its home, and may know the paths to its house?
21 You must know, since you were born then! Or because you are so extremely old!
22 Have you entered the treasuries of the snow, or have you seen the treasuries of the hail,
23 Which I have reserved for the time of trouble, for the day of battle and war? [Exod. 9:18; Josh. 10:11; Isa. 30:30; Rev. 16:21.]
24 By what way is the light distributed, or the east wind spread over the earth?
25 Who has prepared a channel for the torrents of rain, or a path for the thunderbolt,
26 To cause it to rain on the uninhabited land [and] on the desert where no man lives,
27 To satisfy the waste and desolate ground and to cause the tender grass to spring forth?
28 Has the rain a father? Or who has begotten the drops of dew?
29 Out of whose womb came the ice? And the hoary frost of heaven, who has given it birth?
30 The waters are congealed like stone, and the face of the deep is frozen.

a How, except by divine inspiration, could Job have known that light does not dwell in a **place**, but a **way**? For light, as modern man has discovered, involves motion (wave motion). Traveling 186,000 miles a second, it can only dwell in a way.

## New International Version

31 "Can you bind the chains[a] of the Pleiades?
  Can you loosen Orion's belt?
32 Can you bring forth the constellations in their seasons[b]
  or lead out the Bear[c] with its cubs?
33 Do you know the laws of the heavens?
  Can you set up God's[d] dominion over the earth?

34 "Can you raise your voice to the clouds
  and cover yourself with a flood of water?
35 Do you send the lightning bolts on their way?
  Do they report to you, 'Here we are'?
36 Who gives the ibis wisdom[e]
  or gives the rooster understanding?[f]
37 Who has the wisdom to count the clouds?
  Who can tip over the water jars of the heavens
38 when the dust becomes hard
  and the clods of earth stick together?

39 "Do you hunt the prey for the lioness
  and satisfy the hunger of the lions
40 when they crouch in their dens
  or lie in wait in a thicket?
41 Who provides food for the raven
  when its young cry out to God
  and wander about for lack of food?

**39** "Do you know when the mountain goats give birth?
  Do you watch when the doe bears her fawn?
2 Do you count the months till they bear?
  Do you know the time they give birth?
3 They crouch down and bring forth their young;
  their labor pains are ended.
4 Their young thrive and grow strong in the wilds;
  they leave and do not return.

5 "Who let the wild donkey go free?
  Who untied its ropes?
6 I gave it the wasteland as its home,
  the salt flats as its habitat.
7 It laughs at the commotion in the town;
  it does not hear a driver's shout.
8 It ranges the hills for its pasture
  and searches for any green thing.

9 "Will the wild ox consent to serve you?
  Will it stay by your manger at night?
10 Can you hold it to the furrow with a harness?
  Will it till the valleys behind you?
11 Will you rely on it for its great strength?
  Will you leave your heavy work to it?
12 Can you trust it to haul in your grain
  and bring it to your threshing floor?

13 "The wings of the ostrich flap joyfully,
  though they cannot compare
  with the wings and feathers of the stork.
14 She lays her eggs on the ground
  and lets them warm in the sand,
15 unmindful that a foot may crush them,
  that some wild animal may trample them.
16 She treats her young harshly, as if they were not hers;
  she cares not that her labor was in vain,
17 for God did not endow her with wisdom
  or give her a share of good sense.
18 Yet when she spreads her feathers to run,
  she laughs at horse and rider.

19 "Do you give the horse its strength
  or clothe its neck with a flowing mane?

---

a 31 Septuagint; Hebrew *beauty*    b 32 Or *the morning star in its season*    c 32 Or *out Leo*    d 33 Or *their*    e 36 That is, wisdom about the flooding of the Nile    f 36 That is, understanding of when to crow; the meaning of the Hebrew for this verse is uncertain.

## Amplified Bible

31 Can you bind the chains of [the cluster of stars called] Pleiades, or loose the cords of [the constellation] Orion?
32 Can you lead forth the signs of the zodiac in their season? Or can you guide [the stars of] the Bear with her young?
33 Do you know the ordinances of the heavens? Can you establish their rule upon the earth?
34 Can you lift up your voice to the clouds, so that an abundance of waters may cover you?
35 Can you send lightnings, that they may go and say to you, Here we are?
36 Who has put wisdom in the inward parts [or in the dark clouds]? Or who has given understanding to the mind [or to the meteor]?
37 Who can number the clouds by wisdom? Or who can pour out the [water] bottles of the heavens
38 When [heat has caused] the dust to run into a mass and the clods to cleave fast together?
39 Can you [Job] hunt the prey for the lion? Or satisfy the appetite of the young lions
40 When they couch in their dens or lie in wait in their hiding place?
41 Who provides for the raven its prey when its young ones cry to God and wander about for lack of food?

**39** Do you know the time when the wild goats of the rock bring forth [their young]? [Or] do you observe when the hinds are giving birth? [Do you attend to all this, Job?]
2 Can you number the months that they carry their offspring? Or do you know the time when they are delivered,
3 When they bow themselves, bring forth their young ones, [and] cast out their pains?
4 Their young ones become strong, they grow up in the open field; they go forth and return not to them.
5 Who has sent out the wild donkey, giving him his freedom? Or who has loosed the bands of the swift donkey [by which his tame brother is bound—he, the shy, the swift-footed, and the untamable],
6 Whose home I have made the wilderness, and the salt land his dwelling place?
7 He scorns the tumult of the city and hears not the shoutings of the taskmaster.
8 The range of the mountains is his pasture, and he searches after every green thing.
9 Will the wild ox be willing to serve you, or remain beside your manger?
10 Can you bind the wild ox with a harness to the plow in the furrow? Or will he harrow the furrows for you?
11 Will you trust him because his strength is great, or to him will you leave your labor?
12 Will you depend upon him to bring home your seed and gather the grain of your threshing floor? [Who, Job, was the author of this strange variance in the disposition of animals so alike in appearance? Was it you?]
13 The wings of the ostrich wave proudly, [but] are they the pinions and plumage of love?
14 The ostrich leaves her eggs on the ground and warms them in the dust,
15 Forgetting that a foot may crush them or that the wild beast may trample them.
16 She is hardened against her young ones, as though they were not hers; her labor is in vain because she has no sense of danger [for her unborn brood],
17 For God has deprived her of wisdom, neither has He imparted to her understanding.
18 Yet when she lifts herself up in flight, [so swift is she that] she can laugh to scorn the horse and his rider.
19 Have you given the horse his might? Have you clothed his neck with quivering *and* a shaking mane?

# New International Version

20 Do you make it leap like a locust,
 striking terror with its proud snorting?
21 It paws fiercely, rejoicing in its strength,
 and charges into the fray.
22 It laughs at fear, afraid of nothing;
 it does not shy away from the sword.
23 The quiver rattles against its side,
 along with the flashing spear and lance.
24 In frenzied excitement it eats up the ground;
 it cannot stand still when the trumpet sounds.
25 At the blast of the trumpet it snorts, 'Aha!'
 It catches the scent of battle from afar,
 the shout of commanders and the battle cry.

26 "Does the hawk take flight by your wisdom
 and spread its wings toward the south?
27 Does the eagle soar at your command
 and build its nest on high?
28 It dwells on a cliff and stays there at night;
 a rocky crag is its stronghold.
29 From there it looks for food;
 its eyes detect it from afar.
30 Its young ones feast on blood,
 and where the slain are, there it is."

# 40

The LORD said to Job:

2 "Will the one who contends with the Almighty correct
 him?
 Let him who accuses God answer him!"

3 Then Job answered the LORD:

4 "I am unworthy—how can I reply to you?
 I put my hand over my mouth.
5 I spoke once, but I have no answer—
 twice, but I will say no more."

6 Then the LORD spoke to Job out of the storm:

7 "Brace yourself like a man;
 I will question you,
 and you shall answer me.

8 "Would you discredit my justice?
 Would you condemn me to justify yourself?
9 Do you have an arm like God's,
 and can your voice thunder like his?
10 Then adorn yourself with glory and splendor,
 and clothe yourself in honor and majesty.
11 Unleash the fury of your wrath,
 look at all who are proud and bring them low,
12 look at all who are proud and humble them,
 crush the wicked where they stand.
13 Bury them all in the dust together;
 shroud their faces in the grave.
14 Then I myself will admit to you
 that your own right hand can save you.

15 "Look at Behemoth,
 which I made along with you
 and which feeds on grass like an ox.
16 What strength it has in its loins,
 what power in the muscles of its belly!
17 Its tail sways like a cedar;
 the sinews of its thighs are close-knit.
18 Its bones are tubes of bronze,
 its limbs like rods of iron.

# Amplified Bible

20 Was it you [Job] who made him to leap like a locust?
The majesty of his [snorting] nostrils is terrible.
21 He paws in the valley and exults in his strength; he
goes out to meet the weapons [of armed men].
22 He mocks at fear and is not dismayed or terrified; neither does he turn back [in battle] from the sword.
23 The quiver rattles upon him, as do the glittering spear
and the lance [of his rider].
24 [He seems in running to] devour the ground with
fierceness and rage; neither can he stand still at the sound
of the [war] trumpet.
25 As often as the trumpet sounds he says, Ha, ha! And
he smells the battle from afar, the thunder of the captains,
and the shouting.
26 Is it by your wisdom [Job] that the hawk soars and
stretches her wings toward the south [as winter approach-
es]?
27 Does the eagle mount up at your command and make
his nest on [a] high [inaccessible place]?
28 On the cliff he dwells and remains securely, upon the
point of the rock and the stronghold.
29 From there he spies out the prey; and his eyes see it
afar off.
30 His young ones suck up blood, and where the slain
are, there is he.

# 40

Moreover, the Lord said to Job,
2 Shall he who would find fault with the Almighty
contend with Him? He who disputes with God, let him answer it.

3 Then Job replied to the Lord:

4 Behold, I am of small account and vile! What shall I
answer You? I lay my hand upon my mouth. [Ezra 9:6; Ps.
51:4.]
5 I have spoken once, but I will not reply again—indeed,
twice [have I answered], but I will proceed no further.

6 Then the Lord answered Job out of the whirlwind, saying,
7 Gird up your loins now like a man; I will demand of you,
and you answer Me.
8 Will you also annul (set aside and render void) My
judgment? Will you condemn Me [your God], that you may
[appear] righteous and justified?
9 Have you an arm like God? Or can you thunder with a
voice like His?
10 [Since you question the manner of the Almighty's
rule] deck yourself now with the excellency and dignity
[of the Supreme Ruler, and yourself undertake the government of the world if you are so wise], and array yourself
with honor and majesty.
11 Pour forth the overflowings of your anger, and look on
everyone who is proud and abase him;
12 Look on everyone who is proud and bring him low,
and tread down the wicked where they stand [if you are
so able, Job].
13 [Bury and] hide them all in the dust together; [and]
shut them up [in the prison house of death].
14 [If you can do all this, Job, proving yourself of divine
might] then will I [God] praise you also [and acknowledge
that] your own right hand can save you.
15 Behold now the behemoth (the hippopotamus), which
I created as I did you; he eats grass like an ox.
16 See now, his strength is in his loins, and his power is
in the sinews of his belly.
17 He moves his tail like a cedar tree; the tendons of his
thighs are twisted together [like a rope].
18 His bones are like tubes of bronze; his limbs [or ribs]
are like bars of iron.

## New International Version

19 It ranks first among the works of God,
yet its Maker can approach it with his sword.
20 The hills bring it their produce,
and all the wild animals play nearby.
21 Under the lotus plants it lies,
hidden among the reeds in the marsh.
22 The lotuses conceal it in their shadow;
the poplars by the stream surround it.
23 A raging river does not alarm it;
it is secure, though the Jordan should surge against
its mouth.
24 Can anyone capture it by the eyes,
or trap it and pierce its nose?

**41** [a] "Can you pull in Leviathan with a fishhook
or tie down its tongue with a rope?
2 Can you put a cord through its nose
or pierce its jaw with a hook?
3 Will it keep begging you for mercy?
Will it speak to you with gentle words?
4 Will it make an agreement with you
for you to take it as your slave for life?
5 Can you make a pet of it like a bird
or put it on a leash for the young women in your
house?
6 Will traders barter for it?
Will they divide it up among the merchants?
7 Can you fill its hide with harpoons
or its head with fishing spears?
8 If you lay a hand on it,
you will remember the struggle and never do it
again!
9 Any hope of subduing it is false;
the mere sight of it is overpowering.
10 No one is fierce enough to rouse it.
Who then is able to stand against me?
11 Who has a claim against me that I must pay?
Everything under heaven belongs to me.
12 "I will not fail to speak of Leviathan's limbs,
its strength and its graceful form.
13 Who can strip off its outer coat?
Who can penetrate its double coat of armor[b]?
14 Who dares open the doors of its mouth,
ringed about with fearsome teeth?
15 Its back has[c] rows of shields
tightly sealed together;
16 each is so close to the next
that no air can pass between.
17 They are joined fast to one another;
they cling together and cannot be parted.
18 Its snorting throws out flashes of light;
its eyes are like the rays of dawn.
19 Flames stream from its mouth;
sparks of fire shoot out.
20 Smoke pours from its nostrils
as from a boiling pot over burning reeds.
21 Its breath sets coals ablaze,
and flames dart from its mouth.
22 Strength resides in its neck;
dismay goes before it.
23 The folds of its flesh are tightly joined;
they are firm and immovable.
24 Its chest is hard as rock,
hard as a lower millstone.

## Amplified Bible

19 [The hippopotamus] is the first [in magnitude and
power] of the works of God [in animal life]; [only] He Who
made him provides him with his [swordlike tusks, or only
God Who made him can bring near His sword to master
him].
20 Surely the mountains bring him food, where all the
wild animals play.
21 He lies under the lotus trees, in the covert of the reeds
in the marsh.
22 The lotus trees cover him with their shade; the willows of the brook compass him about.
23 Behold, if a river is violent *and* overflows, he does not
tremble; he is confident, though the Jordan [River] swells
and rushes against his mouth.
24 Can any take him when he is on the watch, or pierce
through his nose with a snare?

**41** Can you draw out the leviathan (the crocodile)
with a fishhook? Or press down his tongue with
a cord?
2 Can you put a rope into his nose? Or pierce his jaw
through with a hook *or* a spike?
3 Will he make many supplications to you [begging to
be spared]? Will he speak soft words to you [to coax you
to treat him kindly]?
4 Will he make a covenant with you to take him for your
servant forever?
5 Will you play with [the crocodile] as with a bird? Or
will you put him on a leash for your maidens?
6 Will traders bargain over him? Will they divide him up
among the merchants?
7 Can you fill his skin with harpoons? Or his head with
fishing spears?
8 Lay your hand upon him! Remember your battle with
him; you will not do [such an ill-advised thing] again!
9 Behold, the hope of [his assailant] is disappointed; one
is cast down even at the sight of him!
10 No one is so fierce [and foolhardy] that he dares to stir
up [the crocodile]; who then is he who can stand before
Me [the beast's Creator, or dares to contend with Me]?
11 Who has first given to Me, that I should repay him?
Whatever is under the whole heavens is Mine. [Therefore,
who can have a claim against Me, God Who made the
unmastered crocodile?] [Rom. 11:35.]
12 I will not keep silence concerning his limbs, nor his
mighty strength, nor his goodly frame.
13 Who can strip off [the crocodile's] outer garment?
[Who can penetrate his double coat of mail?] Who shall
come within his jaws?
14 Who can open the doors of his [lipless] mouth? His
[extended jaws and bare] teeth are terrible round about.
15 His scales are [the crocodile's] pride, [for his back is
made of rows of shields] shut up together [as with] a tight
seal;
16 One is so near to another that no air can come between them.
17 They are joined one to another; they stick together so
that they cannot be separated.
18 His sneezings flash forth light, and his eyes are like
the [reddish] eyelids of the dawn.
19 Out of his mouth go burning torches, [and] sparks of
fire leap out.
20 Out of his nostrils goes forth smoke, as out of a seeth-
ing pot over a fire of rushes.
21 His breath kindles coals, and a flame goes forth from
his mouth.
22 In [the crocodile's] neck abides strength, and terror
dances before him.
23 The folds of his flesh cleave together; they are firm
upon him, and they cannot shake [when he moves].
24 His heart is as firm as a stone, indeed, as solid as a
nether millstone.

---

[a] In Hebrew texts 41:1-8 is numbered 40:25-32, and 41:9-34 is numbered
41:1-26.   [b] 13 Septuagint; Hebrew *double bridle*   [c] 15 Or *Its pride
is its*

## New International Version

25 When it rises up, the mighty are terrified;
  they retreat before its thrashing.
26 The sword that reaches it has no effect,
  nor does the spear or the dart or the javelin.
27 Iron it treats like straw
  and bronze like rotten wood.
28 Arrows do not make it flee;
  slingstones are like chaff to it.
29 A club seems to it but a piece of straw;
  it laughs at the rattling of the lance.
30 Its undersides are jagged potsherds,
  leaving a trail in the mud like a threshing sledge.
31 It makes the depths churn like a boiling caldron
  and stirs up the sea like a pot of ointment.
32 It leaves a glistening wake behind it;
  one would think the deep had white hair.
33 Nothing on earth is its equal—
  a creature without fear.
34 It looks down on all that are haughty;
  it is king over all that are proud."

### Job

**42** Then Job replied to the LORD:

2 "I know that you can do all things;
  no purpose of yours can be thwarted.
3 You asked, 'Who is this that obscures my plans
    without knowledge?'
  Surely I spoke of things I did not understand,
  things too wonderful for me to know.

4 "You said, 'Listen now, and I will speak;
  I will question you,
  and you shall answer me.'
5 My ears had heard of you
  but now my eyes have seen you.
6 Therefore I despise myself
  and repent in dust and ashes."

### Epilogue

7 After the LORD had said these things to Job, he said to Eliphaz the Temanite, "I am angry with you and your two friends, because you have not spoken the truth about me, as my servant Job has. 8 So now take seven bulls and seven rams and go to my servant Job and sacrifice a burnt offering for yourselves. My servant Job will pray for you, and I will accept his prayer and not deal with you according to your folly. You have not spoken the truth about me, as my servant Job has." 9 So Eliphaz the Temanite, Bildad the Shuhite and Zophar the Naamathite did what the LORD told them; and the LORD accepted Job's prayer.

10 After Job had prayed for his friends, the LORD restored his fortunes and gave him twice as much as he had before. 11 All his brothers and sisters and everyone who had known him before came and ate with him in his house. They comforted and consoled him over all the trouble the LORD had brought on him, and each one gave him a piece of silver[a] and a gold ring. 12 The LORD blessed the latter part of Job's life more than the former part. He had fourteen thousand sheep, six thousand camels, a thousand yoke of oxen and a thousand

## Amplified Bible

25 When [the crocodile] raises himself up, the mighty are afraid; because of terror and the crashing they are beside themselves.
26 Even if one strikes at him with the sword, it cannot get any hold, nor does the spear, the dart, or the javelin.
27 He counts iron as straw and bronze as rotten wood.
28 The arrow cannot make [the crocodile] flee; slingstones are treated by him as stubble.
29 Clubs [also] are counted as stubble; he laughs at the rushing and the rattling of the javelin.
30 His underparts are like sharp pieces of broken pottery; he spreads [grooves like] a threshing sledge upon the mire.
31 He makes the deep boil like a pot; he makes the sea like a [foaming] pot of ointment.
32 [His swift darting] makes a shining track behind him; one would think the deep to be hoary [with foam].
33 Upon earth there is not [the crocodile's] equal, a creature made without fear and he behaves fearlessly.
34 He looks all mighty [beasts of prey] in the face [without terror]; he is monarch over all the sons of pride. [And now, Job, a who are you who dares not arouse the unmastered crocodile, yet who dares resist Me, the beast's Creator, to My face? Everything under the heavens is Mine; therefore, who can have a claim against God?]

**42** Then Job said to the Lord,
2 I know that You can do all things, and that no thought or purpose of Yours can be restrained or thwarted.
3 [You said to me] Who is this that darkens and obscures counsel [by words] without knowledge? Therefore [I now see] I have [rashly] uttered what I did not understand, things too wonderful for me, which I did not know. [Job 38:2.]
4 [I had virtually said to You what You have said to me:] Hear, I beseech You, and I will speak; I will demand of You, and You declare to me.
5 I had heard of You [only] by the hearing of the ear, but now my [spiritual] eye sees You.
6 Therefore I loathe [my words] and abhor myself and repent in dust and ashes.
7 After the Lord had spoken the previous words to Job, the Lord said to Eliphaz the Temanite, My wrath is kindled against you and against your two friends, for you have not spoken of Me the thing that is right, as My servant Job has.
8 Now therefore take seven bullocks and seven rams and go to My servant Job and offer up for yourselves a burnt offering; and My servant Job shall pray for you, for I will accept [his prayer] that I deal not with you after your folly, in that you have not spoken of Me the thing that is right, as My servant Job has.
9 So Eliphaz the Temanite and Bildad the Shuhite and Zophar the Naamathite went and did as the Lord commanded them; and the Lord accepted [Job's prayer].
10 And the Lord turned the captivity of Job and restored his fortunes, when he prayed for his friends; also the Lord gave Job twice as much as he had before. [Deut. 30:1-3; Ps. 126:1, 2.]
11 Then there came to him all his brothers and sisters and all who had known him before, and they ate bread with him in his house; and they sympathized with him and comforted him over all the [distressing] calamities that the Lord had brought upon him. Every man also gave him a piece of money, and every man an earring of gold.
12 And the Lord blessed the latter days of Job more than his beginning; for he had 14,000 sheep, 6,000 camels, 1,000 yoke of oxen, and 1,000 female donkeys. [Job 1:3.]

---

a 11 Hebrew him a kesitah; a kesitah was a unit of money of unknown weight and value.

a This repeats the thought of verses ten and eleven of this chapter, which is the key and climax to God's argument with Job.

## New International Version

donkeys. [13]And he also had seven sons and three daughters. [14]The first daughter he named Jemimah, the second Keziah and the third Keren-Happuch. [15]Nowhere in all the land were there found women as beautiful as Job's daughters, and their father granted them an inheritance along with their brothers.

[16]After this, Job lived a hundred and forty years; he saw his children and their children to the fourth generation. [17]And so Job died, an old man and full of years.

## Amplified Bible

[13]He had also seven sons and three daughters.

[14]And he called the name of the first Jemimah, and the name of the second Keziah, and the name of the third Keren-happuch.

[15]And in all the land there were no women so fair as the daughters of Job, and their father gave them inheritance among their brothers.

[16]After this, Job lived 140 years, and saw his sons and his sons' sons, even to four generations.

[17]So Job died, an old man and full of days. [James 5:11.]

# Psalms

# Psalms

## BOOK I

*Psalms 1–41*

### Psalm 1

¹Blessed is the one
  who does not walk in step with the wicked
or stand in the way that sinners take
  or sit in the company of mockers,
²but whose delight is in the law of the LORD,
  and who meditates on his law day and night.
³That person is like a tree planted by streams of water,
  which yields its fruit in season
and whose leaf does not wither—
  whatever they do prospers.

⁴Not so the wicked!
  They are like chaff
  that the wind blows away.
⁵Therefore the wicked will not stand in the judgment,
  nor sinners in the assembly of the righteous.

⁶For the LORD watches over the way of the righteous,
  but the way of the wicked leads to destruction.

### Psalm 2

¹Why do the nations conspire*a*
  and the peoples plot in vain?
²The kings of the earth rise up
  and the rulers band together
  against the LORD and against his anointed, saying,
³"Let us break their chains
  and throw off their shackles."

⁴The One enthroned in heaven laughs;
  the Lord scoffs at them.
⁵He rebukes them in his anger
  and terrifies them in his wrath, saying,
⁶"I have installed my king
  on Zion, my holy mountain."

## BOOK ONE

### Psalm 1 *a*

¹Blessed (happy, fortunate, prosperous, and enviable) is the man who walks *and* lives not in the counsel of the ungodly [following their advice, their plans and purposes], nor stands [submissive and inactive] in the path where sinners walk, nor sits down [to relax and rest] where the scornful [and the mockers] gather.

²But his delight *and* desire are in the law of the Lord, and on His law (the precepts, the instructions, the teachings of God) he habitually meditates (ponders and studies) by day and by night. [Rom. 13:8-10; Gal. 3:1-29; II Tim. 3:16.]

³And he shall be like a tree firmly planted [and tended] by the streams of water, ready to bring forth its fruit in its season; its leaf also shall not fade *or* wither; and everything he does shall prosper [and come to maturity]. [Jer. 17:7, 8.]

⁴Not so the wicked [those disobedient and living without God are not so]. But they are like the chaff [worthless, dead, without substance] which the wind drives away.

⁵Therefore the wicked [those disobedient and living without God] shall not stand [justified] in the judgment, nor *b*sinners in the congregation of the righteous [those who are upright and in right standing with God].

⁶For the Lord knows *and* is fully acquainted with the way of the righteous, but the way of the ungodly [those living outside God's will] shall perish (end in ruin and come to nought).

### Psalm 2

¹Why do the nations assemble with commotion [uproar and confusion of voices], and why do the people imagine (meditate upon and devise) an empty scheme?

²The kings of the earth take their places; the rulers take counsel together against the Lord and His Anointed One (the Messiah, the Christ). *They say,* [Acts 4:25-27.]

³Let us break Their bands [of restraint] asunder and cast Their cords [of control] from us.

⁴He Who sits in the heavens laughs; the Lord has them in derision [and in supreme contempt He mocks them].

⁵He speaks to them in His deep anger and troubles (terrifies and confounds) them in His displeasure *and* fury, *saying,*

⁶Yet have I anointed (installed and placed) My King [firmly] on My holy hill of Zion.

---

*a 1* Hebrew; Septuagint *rage*

*a* This has been called "The Preface Psalm" because in some respects it may be considered "the text upon which the whole of the Psalms make up a divine sermon." It opens with a benediction, "Blessed," as does our Lord's Sermon on the Mount (Matt. 5:3).  *b* Charles Haddon Spurgeon (*The Treasury of David*) said, "Sinners cannot live in heaven. They would be out of their element. Sooner could a fish live upon a tree than the wicked in paradise." The only way they will ever be able to endure heaven is to be born again and become new creatures with pure hearts able fully to enjoy the presence of God, His holy angels, and the redeemed.

# New International Version

7 I will proclaim the LORD's decree:

He said to me, "You are my son;
  today I have become your father.
8 Ask me,
  and I will make the nations your inheritance,
  the ends of the earth your possession.
9 You will break them with a rod of iron[a];
  you will dash them to pieces like pottery."

10 Therefore, you kings, be wise;
  be warned, you rulers of the earth.
11 Serve the LORD with fear
  and celebrate his rule with trembling.
12 Kiss his son, or he will be angry
  and your way will lead to your destruction,
for his wrath can flare up in a moment.
  Blessed are all who take refuge in him.

## Psalm 3[b]

*A psalm of David. When he fled from his son Absalom.*

1 LORD, how many are my foes!
  How many rise up against me!
2 Many are saying of me,
  "God will not deliver him."[c]

3 But you, LORD, are a shield around me,
  my glory, the One who lifts my head high.
4 I call out to the LORD,
  and he answers me from his holy mountain.

5 I lie down and sleep;
  I wake again, because the LORD sustains me.
6 I will not fear though tens of thousands
  assail me on every side.

7 Arise, LORD!
  Deliver me, my God!
Strike all my enemies on the jaw;
  break the teeth of the wicked.

8 From the LORD comes deliverance.
  May your blessing be on your people.

## Psalm 4[d]

*For the director of music. With stringed instruments.*
*A psalm of David.*

1 Answer me when I call to you,
  my righteous God.
Give me relief from my distress;
  have mercy on me and hear my prayer.

2 How long will you people turn my glory into shame?
  How long will you love delusions and seek false
  gods[e]?[f]
3 Know that the LORD has set apart his faithful servant
  for himself;
  the LORD hears when I call to him.

4 Tremble and[g] do not sin;
  when you are on your beds,
  search your hearts and be silent.
5 Offer the sacrifices of the righteous
  and trust in the LORD.

6 Many, LORD, are asking, "Who will bring us
  prosperity?"
  Let the light of your face shine on us.

# Amplified Bible

7 I will declare the decree of the Lord: He said to Me,
You are My Son; this day [I declare] I have begotten You.
[Heb. 1:5; 3:5, 6; II Pet. 1:17, 18.]
8 Ask of Me, and I will give You the nations as Your inheritance, and the uttermost parts of the earth as Your
possession.
9 You shall break them with a rod of iron; You shall dash
them in pieces like potters' ware. [Rev. 12:5; 19:15.]
10 Now therefore, O you kings, act wisely; be instructed
*and* warned, O you rulers of the earth.
11 Serve the Lord with reverent awe *and* worshipful fear;
rejoice *and* be in high spirits with trembling [lest you displease Him].
12 Kiss the Son [pay homage to Him in purity], lest He be
angry and you perish in the way, for soon shall His wrath
be kindled. O blessed (happy, fortunate, and to be envied)
are all those who seek refuge *and* put their trust in Him!

## Psalm 3

A Psalm of David. When he fled from Absalom his son.

1 Lord, how they are increased who trouble me! Many
are they who rise up against me.
2 Many are saying of me, There is no help for him in
God. Selah [pause, and calmly think of that]!
3 But You, O Lord, are a shield for me, my glory, and the
lifter of my head.
4 With my voice I cry to the Lord, and He hears and answers me out of His holy hill. Selah [pause, and calmly
think of that]!
5 I lay down and slept; I wakened again, for the Lord
sustains me.
6 I will not be afraid of ten thousands of people who have
set themselves against me round about.
7 Arise, O Lord; save me, O my God! For You have struck
all my enemies on the cheek; You have broken the teeth
of the ungodly.
8 Salvation belongs to the Lord; May Your blessing be
upon Your people. Selah [pause, and calmly think of that]!

## Psalm 4

To the Chief Musician; on stringed instruments.
A Psalm of David.

1 Answer me when I call, O God of my righteousness
(uprightness, justice, and right standing with You)! You
have freed me when I was hemmed in *and* enlarged me
when I was in distress; have mercy upon me and hear my
prayer.
2 O you sons of men, how long will you turn my honor
*and* glory into shame? How long will you love vanity *and*
futility *and* seek after lies? Selah [pause, and calmly think
of that]!
3 But know that the Lord has set apart for Himself [and
given distinction to] him who is godly [the man of loving-
kindness]. The Lord listens *and* heeds when I call to Him.
4 Be angry [or stand in awe] and sin not; commune with
your own hearts upon your beds and be silent (sorry for
the things you say in your hearts). Selah [pause, and calmly think of that]! [Eph. 4:26.]
5 Offer just *and* right sacrifices; trust (lean on and be
confident) in the Lord.
6 Many say, Oh, that we might see some good! Lift up
the light of Your countenance upon us, O Lord.

---

*a* 9 Or *will rule them with an iron scepter* (see Septuagint and Syriac)
*b* In Hebrew texts 3:1-8 is numbered 3:2-9.   *c* 2 The Hebrew has *Selah*
(a word of uncertain meaning) here and at the end of verses 4 and 8.
*d* In Hebrew texts 4:1-8 is numbered 4:2-9.   *e* 2 Or *seek lies*   *f* 2 The
Hebrew has *Selah* (a word of uncertain meaning) here and at the end of
verse 4.   *g* 4 Or *In your anger* (see Septuagint)

## New International Version

⁷Fill my heart with joy
  when their grain and new wine abound.
⁸In peace I will lie down and sleep,
  for you alone, LORD,
  make me dwell in safety.

### Psalm 5ᵃ

*For the director of music. For pipes. A psalm of David.*

¹Listen to my words, LORD,
  consider my lament.
²Hear my cry for help,
  my King and my God,
  for to you I pray.

³In the morning, LORD, you hear my voice;
  in the morning I lay my requests before you
  and wait expectantly.
⁴For you are not a God who is pleased with wickedness;
  with you, evil people are not welcome.
⁵The arrogant cannot stand
  in your presence.
You hate all who do wrong;
⁶  you destroy those who tell lies.
The bloodthirsty and deceitful
  you, LORD, detest.
⁷But I, by your great love,
  can come into your house;
in reverence I bow down
  toward your holy temple.

⁸Lead me, LORD, in your righteousness
  because of my enemies—
  make your way straight before me.
⁹Not a word from their mouth can be trusted;
  their heart is filled with malice.
Their throat is an open grave;
  with their tongues they tell lies.
¹⁰Declare them guilty, O God!
  Let their intrigues be their downfall.
Banish them for their many sins,
  for they have rebelled against you.
¹¹But let all who take refuge in you be glad;
  let them ever sing for joy.
Spread your protection over them,
  that those who love your name may rejoice in you.

¹²Surely, LORD, you bless the righteous;
  you surround them with your favor as with a shield.

### Psalm 6ᵇ

*For the director of music. With stringed instruments.
According to* sheminith.ᶜ *A psalm of David.*

¹LORD, do not rebuke me in your anger
  or discipline me in your wrath.
²Have mercy on me, LORD, for I am faint;
  heal me, LORD, for my bones are in agony.
³My soul is in deep anguish.
  How long, LORD, how long?

⁴Turn, LORD, and deliver me;
  save me because of your unfailing love.
⁵Among the dead no one proclaims your name.
  Who praises you from the grave?

⁶I am worn out from my groaning.

All night long I flood my bed with weeping
  and drench my couch with tears.
⁷My eyes grow weak with sorrow;
  they fail because of all my foes.

## Amplified Bible

⁷You have put more joy *and* rejoicing in my heart than
[they know] when their wheat and new wine have yielded
abundantly.
⁸In peace I will both lie down and sleep, for You, Lord,
alone make me dwell in safety *and* confident trust.

### Psalm 5

To the Chief Musician; on wind instruments. A Psalm of David.

¹Listen to my words, O Lord, give heed to my sighing
*and* groaning.
²Hear the sound of my cry, my King and my God, for
to You do I pray.
³In the morning You hear my voice, O Lord; in the
morning I prepare [a prayer, a sacrifice] for You and watch
*and* wait [for You to speak to my heart].
⁴For You are not a God Who takes pleasure in wickedness; neither will the evil [man] so much as dwell [tempo-
rarily] with You.
⁵Boasters can have no standing in Your sight; You abhor
all evildoers.
⁶You will destroy those who speak lies; the Lord abhors
[and rejects] the bloodthirsty and deceitful man.
⁷But as for me, I will enter Your house through the
abundance of Your steadfast love *and* mercy; I will worship toward *and* at Your holy temple in reverent fear *and*
awe of You.
⁸Lead me, O Lord, in Your righteousness because of my
enemies; make Your way level (straight and right) before
my face.
⁹For there is nothing trustworthy *or* steadfast *or* truthful in their talk; their heart is destruction [or a destructive
chasm, a yawning gulf]; their throat is an open sepulcher;
they flatter and make smooth with their tongue. [Rom.
3:13.]
¹⁰Hold them guilty, O God; let them fall by their own designs *and* counsels; cast them out because of the multitude
of their transgressions, for they have rebelled against You.
¹¹But let all those who take refuge *and* put their trust in
You rejoice; let them ever sing *and* shout for joy, because
You make a covering over them *and* defend them; let those
also who love Your name be joyful in You *and* be in high
spirits.
¹²For You, Lord, will bless the [uncompromisingly]
righteous [him who is upright and in right standing with
You]; as with a shield You will surround him with goodwill
(pleasure and favor).

### Psalm 6

To the Chief Musician; on stringed instruments, set [possibly]
an octave below. A Psalm of David.

¹O Lord, rebuke me not in Your anger nor discipline *and*
chasten me in Your hot displeasure.
²Have mercy on me *and* be gracious to me, O Lord, for
I am weak (faint and withered away); O Lord, heal me, for
my bones are troubled.
³My [inner] self [as well as my body] is also exceedingly
disturbed *and* troubled. But You, O Lord, how long [until
You return and speak peace to me]?
⁴Return [to my relief], O Lord, deliver my life; save me
for the sake of Your steadfast love *and* mercy.
⁵For in death there is no remembrance of You; in Sheol
(the place of the dead) who will give You thanks?
⁶I am weary with my groaning; all night I soak my pillow with tears, I drench my couch with my weeping.
⁷My eye grows dim because of grief; it grows old because of all my enemies.

---

ᵃ In Hebrew texts 5:1-12 is numbered 5:2-13.  ᵇ In Hebrew texts 6:1-10
is numbered 6:2-11.  ᶜ Title: Probably a musical term

## New International Version

8 Away from me, all you who do evil,
for the LORD has heard my weeping.
9 The LORD has heard my cry for mercy;
the LORD accepts my prayer.
10 All my enemies will be overwhelmed with shame and
anguish;
they will turn back and suddenly be put to shame.

### Psalm 7[a]

*A shiggaion[b] of David, which he sang to the LORD
concerning Cush, a Benjamite.*

1 LORD my God, I take refuge in you;
save and deliver me from all who pursue me,
2 or they will tear me apart like a lion
and rip me to pieces with no one to rescue me.

3 LORD my God, if I have done this
and there is guilt on my hands—
4 if I have repaid my ally with evil
or without cause have robbed my foe—
5 then let my enemy pursue and overtake me;
let him trample my life to the ground
and make me sleep in the dust.[c]

6 Arise, LORD, in your anger;
rise up against the rage of my enemies.
Awake, my God; decree justice.
7 Let the assembled peoples gather around you,
while you sit enthroned over them on high.
8     Let the LORD judge the peoples.
Vindicate me, LORD, according to my righteousness,
according to my integrity, O Most High.
9 Bring to an end the violence of the wicked
and make the righteous secure—
you, the righteous God
who probes minds and hearts.

10 My shield[d] is God Most High,
who saves the upright in heart.
11 God is a righteous judge,
a God who displays his wrath every day.
12 If he does not relent,
he[e] will sharpen his sword;
he will bend and string his bow.
13 He has prepared his deadly weapons;
he makes ready his flaming arrows.

14 Whoever is pregnant with evil
conceives trouble and gives birth to disillusionment.
15 Whoever digs a hole and scoops it out
falls into the pit they have made.
16 The trouble they cause recoils on them;
their violence comes down on their own heads.

17 I will give thanks to the LORD because of his
righteousness;
I will sing the praises of the name of the LORD Most
High.

### Psalm 8[f]

*For the director of music. According to* gittith.[g]
*A psalm of David.*

1 LORD, our Lord,
how majestic is your name in all the earth!

You have set your glory
in the heavens.

## Amplified Bible

8 Depart from me, all you workers of iniquity, for the
Lord has heard the voice of my weeping. [Matt. 7:23; Luke
13:27.]
9 The Lord has heard my supplication; the Lord receives
my prayer.
10 Let all my enemies be ashamed and sorely troubled;
let them turn back *and* be put to shame suddenly.

### Psalm 7

An Ode of David, [probably] in a wild, irregular, enthusiastic
strain, which he sang to the Lord concerning the words
of Cush, a Benjamite.

1 O Lord my God, in You I take refuge *and* put my trust;
save me from all those who pursue *and* persecute me, and
deliver me,
2 Lest my foe tear my life [from my body] like a lion,
dragging *me* away while there is none to deliver.
3 O Lord my God, if I have done this, if there is wrong
in my hands,
4 If I have paid back with evil him who was at peace with
me or without cause have robbed him who was my enemy,
5 Let the enemy pursue my life and take it; yes, let him
trample my life to the ground and lay my honor in the dust.
Selah [pause, and calmly think of that]!
6 Arise, O Lord, in Your anger; lift up Yourself against
the rage of my enemies; and awake [and stir up] for me
the justice *and* vindication [that] You have commanded.
7 Let the assembly of the peoples be gathered about You,
and return on high over them.
8 The Lord judges the people; judge me, O Lord, *and* do
me justice according to my righteousness [my rightness,
justice, and right standing with You] and according to the
integrity that is in me.
9 Oh, let the wickedness of the wicked come to an end,
but establish the [uncompromisingly] righteous [those
upright and in harmony with You]; for You, Who try the
hearts and emotions *and* thinking powers, are a righteous
God. [Rev. 2:23.]
10 My defense *and* shield depend on God, Who saves the
upright in heart.
11 God is a righteous Judge, yes, a God Who is indignant
every day.
12 If a man does not turn *and* repent, [God] will whet His
sword; He has strung *and* bent His [huge] bow and made
it ready [by treading it with His foot].
13 He has also prepared for him deadly weapons; He
makes His arrows fiery shafts.
14 Behold, [the wicked man] conceives iniquity and is
pregnant with mischief and gives birth to lies.
15 He made a pit and hollowed it out and has fallen into
the hole which he made [before the trap was completed].
16 His mischief shall fall back in return upon his own
head, and his violence come down [with the loose dirt]
upon his own scalp.
17 I will give to the Lord the thanks due to His rightness
*and* justice, and I will sing praise to the name of the Lord
Most High.

### Psalm 8

To the Chief Musician; set to a Philistine lute, or [possibly]
to a particular Hittite tune. A Psalm of David.

1 O Lord, our Lord, how excellent (majestic and glorious) is Your name in all the earth! You have set Your glory
on [or above] the heavens.

---

*a* In Hebrew texts 7:1-17 is numbered 7:2-18.     *b* Title: Probably a
literary or musical term     *c* 5 The Hebrew has *Selah* (a word of
uncertain meaning) here.     *d* 10 Or *sovereign*     *e* 12 Or *If anyone
does not repent, / God*     *f* In Hebrew texts 8:1-9 is numbered 8:2-10.
*g* Title: Probably a musical term

# New International Version

[2]Through the praise of children and infants
    you have established a stronghold against your
        enemies,
    to silence the foe and the avenger.
[3]When I consider your heavens,
    the work of your fingers,
  the moon and the stars,
    which you have set in place,
[4]what is mankind that you are mindful of them,
    human beings that you care for them?[a]

[5]You have made them[b] a little lower than the angels[c]
    and crowned them[b] with glory and honor.
[6]You made them rulers over the works of your hands;
    you put everything under their[d] feet:
[7]all flocks and herds,
    and the animals of the wild,
[8]the birds in the sky,
    and the fish in the sea,
    all that swim the paths of the seas.

[9]Lord, our Lord,
    how majestic is your name in all the earth!

## Psalm 9[e,f]

*For the director of music. To the tune of "The Death of the Son."
A psalm of David.*

[1]I will give thanks to you, Lord, with all my heart;
    I will tell of all your wonderful deeds.
[2]I will be glad and rejoice in you;
    I will sing the praises of your name, O Most High.

[3]My enemies turn back;
    they stumble and perish before you.
[4]For you have upheld my right and my cause,
    sitting enthroned as the righteous judge.
[5]You have rebuked the nations and destroyed the wicked;
    you have blotted out their name for ever and ever.
[6]Endless ruin has overtaken my enemies,
    you have uprooted their cities;
    even the memory of them has perished.

[7]The Lord reigns forever;
    he has established his throne for judgment.
[8]He rules the world in righteousness
    and judges the peoples with equity.
[9]The Lord is a refuge for the oppressed,
    a stronghold in times of trouble.
[10]Those who know your name trust in you,
    for you, Lord, have never forsaken those who seek
        you.

[11]Sing the praises of the Lord, enthroned in Zion;
    proclaim among the nations what he has done.
[12]For he who avenges blood remembers;
    he does not ignore the cries of the afflicted.

[13]Lord, see how my enemies persecute me!
    Have mercy and lift me up from the gates of death,
[14]that I may declare your praises
    in the gates of Daughter Zion,
    and there rejoice in your salvation.

[15]The nations have fallen into the pit they have dug;
    their feet are caught in the net they have hidden.
[16]The Lord is known by his acts of justice;
    the wicked are ensnared by the work of their hands.[g]

---

[a] 4 Or *what is a human being that you are mindful of him, / a son of man
that you care for him?*   [b] 5 Or *him*   [c] 5 Or *than God*   [d] 6 Or *made
him ruler . . . ; / . . . his*   [e] Psalms 9 and 10 may originally have
been a single acrostic poem in which alternating lines began with
the successive letters of the Hebrew alphabet. In the Septuagint they
constitute one psalm.   [f] In Hebrew texts 9:1-20 is numbered 9:2-21.
[g] 16 The Hebrew has *Higgaion* and *Selah* (words of uncertain meaning)
here; *Selah* occurs also at the end of verse 20.

# Amplified Bible

[2]Out of the mouths of babes and unweaned infants You
have established strength because of Your foes, that You
might silence the enemy and the avenger. [Matt. 21:15,
16.]
[3]When I view *and* consider Your heavens, the work of
Your fingers, the moon and the stars, which You have ordained *and* established,
[4]What is man that You are mindful of him, and the son
of [earthborn] man that You care for him?
[5]Yet You have made him but a little lower than God [or
heavenly beings], and You have crowned him with glory
and honor.
[6]You made him to have dominion over the works of Your
hands; You have put all things under his feet: [I Cor. 15:27;
Eph. 1:22, 23; Heb. 2:6-8.]
[7]All sheep and oxen, yes, and the beasts of the field,
[8]The birds of the air, and the fish of the sea, *and* whatever passes along the paths of the seas.
[9]O Lord, our Lord, how excellent (majestic and glorious) is Your name in all the earth!

## Psalm 9

To the Chief Musician; set for [possibly] soprano voices.
A Psalm of David.

[1]I Will praise You, O Lord, with my whole heart; I will
show forth (recount and tell aloud) all Your marvelous
works *and* wonderful deeds!
[2]I will rejoice in You and be in high spirits; I will sing
praise to Your name, O Most High!
[3]When my enemies turned back, they stumbled and
perished before You.
[4]For You have maintained my right and my cause; You
sat on the throne judging righteously.
[5]You have rebuked the nations, You have destroyed the
wicked; You have blotted out their name forever and ever.
[6]The enemy have been cut off *and* have vanished in everlasting ruins, You have plucked up *and* overthrown their
cities; the very memory of them has perished *and* vanished.
[7]But the Lord shall remain *and* continue forever; He has
prepared *and* established His throne for judgment. [Heb.
1:11.]
[8]And He will judge the world in righteousness (rightness and equity); He will minister justice to the peoples in
uprightness. [Acts 17:31.]
[9]The Lord also will be a refuge *and* a high tower for the
oppressed, a refuge *and* a stronghold in times of trouble
(high cost, destitution, and desperation).
[10]And they who know Your name [who have experience
and acquaintance with Your mercy] will lean on *and* confidently put their trust in You, for You, Lord, have not forsak-
en those who seek (inquire of and for) You [on the authority
of God's Word and the right of their necessity]. [Ps. 42:1.]
[11]Sing praises to the Lord, Who dwells in Zion! Declare
among the peoples His doings!
[12]For He Who avenges the blood [of His people shed
unjustly] remembers them; He does not forget the cry of
the afflicted (the poor and the humble).
[13]Have mercy upon me *and* be gracious *to me,* O Lord;
consider how I am afflicted by those who hate me, You
Who lift me up from the gates of death,
[14]That I may show forth (recount and tell aloud) all Your
praises! In the gates of the Daughter of Zion I will rejoice
in Your salvation *and* Your saving help.
[15]The nations have sunk down in the pit that they made;
in the net which they hid is their own foot caught.
[16]The Lord has made Himself known; He executes
judgment; the wicked are snared in the work of their own
hands. Higgaion [meditation]. Selah [pause, and calmly
think of that]!

## New International Version

17 The wicked go down to the realm of the dead,
　　all the nations that forget God.
18 But God will never forget the needy;
　　the hope of the afflicted will never perish.

19 Arise, LORD, do not let mortals triumph;
　　let the nations be judged in your presence.
20 Strike them with terror, LORD;
　　let the nations know they are only mortal.

### Psalm 10 *a*

1 Why, LORD, do you stand far off?
　　Why do you hide yourself in times of trouble?

2 In his arrogance the wicked man hunts down the
　　　weak,
　　who are caught in the schemes he devises.
3 He boasts about the cravings of his heart;
　　he blesses the greedy and reviles the LORD.
4 In his pride the wicked man does not seek him;
　　in all his thoughts there is no room for God.
5 His ways are always prosperous;
　　your laws are rejected by *b* him;
　　he sneers at all his enemies.
6 He says to himself, "Nothing will ever shake me."
　　He swears, "No one will ever do me harm."

7 His mouth is full of lies and threats;
　　trouble and evil are under his tongue.
8 He lies in wait near the villages;
　　from ambush he murders the innocent.
　　His eyes watch in secret for his victims;
9 　like a lion in cover he lies in wait.
　　He lies in wait to catch the helpless;
　　he catches the helpless and drags them off in his
　　　net.
10 His victims are crushed, they collapse;
　　they fall under his strength.
11 He says to himself, "God will never notice;
　　he covers his face and never sees."

12 Arise, LORD! Lift up your hand, O God.
　　Do not forget the helpless.
13 Why does the wicked man revile God?
　　Why does he say to himself,
　　"He won't call me to account"?
14 But you, God, see the trouble of the afflicted;
　　you consider their grief and take it in hand.
　　The victims commit themselves to you;
　　you are the helper of the fatherless.
15 Break the arm of the wicked man;
　　call the evildoer to account for his wickedness
　　that would not otherwise be found out.

16 The LORD is King for ever and ever;
　　the nations will perish from his land.
17 You, LORD, hear the desire of the afflicted;
　　you encourage them, and you listen to their cry,
18 defending the fatherless and the oppressed,
　　so that mere earthly mortals
　　will never again strike terror.

## Amplified Bible

17 The wicked shall be turned back [headlong into premature death] into Sheol (the place of the departed spirits
of the wicked), even all the nations that forget *or* are for-
getful of God.
18 For the needy shall not always be forgotten, and the
expectation *and* hope of the meek *and* the poor shall not
perish forever.
19 Arise, O Lord! Let not man prevail; let the nations be
judged before You.
20 Put them in fear [make them realize their frail na-
ture], O Lord, that the nations may know themselves to be
but men. Selah [pause, and calmly think of that]!

### Psalm 10

1 Why do you stand afar off, O Lord? Why do You hide
Yourself, [veiling Your eyes] in times of trouble (distress
and desperation)?
2 The wicked in pride *and* arrogance hotly pursue *and*
persecute the poor; let them be taken in the schemes
which they have devised.
3 For the wicked *man* boasts (sings the praises) of his
own heart's desire, and the one greedy for gain curses *and*
spurns, yes, renounces *and* despises the Lord.
4 The wicked one in the pride of his countenance will not
seek, inquire for, *and* yearn for God; all his thoughts are
that there is no God [so He never punishes].
5 His ways are grievous [or persist] at all times; Your
judgments [Lord] are far above *and* on high out of his
sight [so he never thinks about them]; as for all his foes,
he sniffs *and* sneers at them.
6 He thinks in his heart, I shall not be moved; for
throughout all generations I shall not come to want *or* be
in adversity.
7 His mouth is full of cursing, deceit, oppression (fraud);
under his tongue are trouble and sin (mischief and iniquity).
8 He sits in ambush in the villages; in hiding places he
slays the innocent; he watches stealthily for the poor (the
helpless and unfortunate).
9 He lurks in secret places like a lion in his thicket; he
lies in wait that he may seize the poor (the helpless and
the unfortunate); he seizes the poor when he draws him
into his net.
10 [The prey] is crushed, sinks down; and the helpless
falls by his mighty [claws].
11 [The foe] thinks in his heart, God has quite forgotten;
He has hidden His face; He will never see [my deed].
12 Arise, O Lord! O God, lift up Your hand; forget not the
humble [patient and crushed].
13 Why does the wicked [man] condemn (spurn and renounce) God? Why has he thought in his heart, You will
not call to account?
14 You have seen it; yes, You note trouble and grief
(vexation) to requite it with Your hand. The unfortunate
commits himself to You; You are the helper of the fatherless.
15 Break the arm of the wicked man; and as for the evil
man, search out his wickedness until You find no more.
16 The Lord is King forever and ever; the nations will
perish out of His land.
17 O Lord, You have heard the desire *and* the longing of the humble *and* oppressed; You will prepare *and*
strengthen *and* direct their hearts, You will cause Your
ear to hear,
18 To do justice to the fatherless and the oppressed, so
that man, who is of the earth, may not terrify them any
more.

---

*a* Psalms 9 and 10 may originally have been a single acrostic poem in
which alternating lines began with the successive letters of the Hebrew
alphabet. In the Septuagint they constitute one psalm.　*b* 5 See
Septuagint; Hebrew / *they are haughty, and your laws are far from*

# New International Version

## Psalm 11

*For the director of music. Of David.*

¹ In the LORD I take refuge.
　How then can you say to me:
　"Flee like a bird to your mountain.
² For look, the wicked bend their bows;
　they set their arrows against the strings
to shoot from the shadows
　at the upright in heart.
³ When the foundations are being destroyed,
　what can the righteous do?"

⁴ The LORD is in his holy temple;
　the LORD is on his heavenly throne.
He observes everyone on earth;
　his eyes examine them.
⁵ The LORD examines the righteous,
　but the wicked, those who love violence,
　he hates with a passion.
⁶ On the wicked he will rain
　fiery coals and burning sulfur;
　a scorching wind will be their lot.

⁷ For the LORD is righteous,
　he loves justice;
　the upright will see his face.

## Psalm 12ᵃ

*For the director of music. According to* sheminith.ᵇ
*A psalm of David.*

¹ Help, LORD, for no one is faithful anymore;
　those who are loyal have vanished from the human
　　race.
² Everyone lies to their neighbor;
　they flatter with their lips
　but harbor deception in their hearts.

³ May the LORD silence all flattering lips
　and every boastful tongue—
⁴ those who say,
　"By our tongues we will prevail;
　our own lips will defend us—who is lord over us?"

⁵ "Because the poor are plundered and the needy groan,
　I will now arise," says the LORD.
　"I will protect them from those who malign them."
⁶ And the words of the LORD are flawless,
　like silver purified in a crucible,
　like goldᶜ refined seven times.

⁷ You, LORD, will keep the needy safe
　and will protect us forever from the wicked,
⁸ who freely strut about
　when what is vile is honored by the human race.

## Psalm 13ᵈ

*For the director of music. A psalm of David.*

¹ How long, LORD? Will you forget me forever?
　How long will you hide your face from me?
² How long must I wrestle with my thoughts
　and day after day have sorrow in my heart?
　How long will my enemy triumph over me?

³ Look on me and answer, LORD my God.
　Give light to my eyes, or I will sleep in death,
⁴ and my enemy will say, "I have overcome him,"
　and my foes will rejoice when I fall.

⁵ But I trust in your unfailing love;
　my heart rejoices in your salvation.

---

ᵃ In Hebrew texts 12:1-8 is numbered 12:2-9.　ᵇ Title: Probably a
musical term　ᶜ 6 Probable reading of the original Hebrew text;
Masoretic Text *earth*　ᵈ In Hebrew texts 13:1-6 is numbered 13:2-6.

# Amplified Bible

## Psalm 11

To the Chief Musician *or* Choir Leader. [A Psalm] of David.

¹ In the Lord I take refuge [and put my trust]; how can
you say to me, Flee like a bird to your mountain?
² For see, the wicked are bending the bow; they make
ready their arrow upon the string, that they [furtively] in
darkness may shoot at the upright in heart.
³ If the foundations are destroyed, what can the [un-
yieldingly] righteous do, *or* what has He [the Righteous
One] wrought *or* accomplished?
⁴ The Lord is in His holy temple; the Lord's throne is in
heaven. His eyes behold; His eyelids test *and* prove the
children of men. [Acts 7:49; Rev. 4:2.]
⁵ The Lord tests *and* proves the [unyieldingly] righteous, but His soul abhors the wicked and him who loves
violence. [James 1:12.]
⁶ Upon the wicked He will rain quick burning coals *or*
snares; fire, brimstone, and a [dreadful] scorching wind
shall be the portion of their cup.
⁷ For the Lord is [rigidly] righteous, He loves righteous
deeds; the upright shall behold His face, *or* He beholds
the upright.

## Psalm 12

To the Chief Musician; set [possibly] an octave below.
A Psalm of David.

¹ Help, Lord! For principled *and* godly people are here
no more; faithfulness *and* the faithful vanish from among
the sons of men.
² To his neighbor each one speaks words without use *or*
worth *or* truth; with flattering lips and double heart [de-
ceitfully] they speak.
³ May the Lord cut off all flattering lips *and* the tongues
that speak proud boasting,
⁴ Those who say, With our tongues we will prevail; our lips
are our own [to command at our will]—who is lord *and*
master over us?
⁵ Now will I arise, says the Lord, because the poor are
oppressed, because of the groans of the needy; I will set
him in safety *and* in the salvation for which he pants.
⁶ The words *and* promises of the Lord are pure words,
like silver refined in an earthen furnace, purified seven
times over.
⁷ You will keep them and preserve them, O Lord; You
will guard *and* keep us from this [evil] generation forever.
⁸ The wicked walk *or* prowl about on every side, as vile-
ness is exalted [and baseness is rated high] among the
sons of men.

## Psalm 13

To the Chief Musician. A Psalm of David.

¹ How long will You forget me, O Lord? Forever? How
long will You hide Your face from me?
² How long must I lay up cares within me and have sorrow in my heart day after day? How long shall my enemy
exalt himself over me?
³ Consider and answer me, O Lord my God; lighten the
eyes [of my faith to behold Your face in the pitchlike dark-
ness], lest I sleep the sleep of death,
⁴ Lest my enemy say, I have prevailed over him, *and*
those that trouble me rejoice when I am shaken.
⁵ But I have trusted, leaned on, *and* been confident in
Your mercy *and* loving-kindness; my heart shall rejoice
*and* be in high spirits in Your salvation.

## New International Version

6 I will sing the LORD's praise,
    for he has been good to me.

### Psalm 14

*For the director of music. Of David.*

1 The fool[a] says in his heart,
    "There is no God."
They are corrupt, their deeds are vile;
    there is no one who does good.

2 The LORD looks down from heaven
    on all mankind
to see if there are any who understand,
    any who seek God.
3 All have turned away, all have become corrupt;
    there is no one who does good,
    not even one.

4 Do all these evildoers know nothing?

They devour my people as though eating bread;
    they never call on the LORD.
5 But there they are, overwhelmed with dread,
    for God is present in the company of the righteous.
6 You evildoers frustrate the plans of the poor,
    but the LORD is their refuge.

7 Oh, that salvation for Israel would come out of Zion!
    When the LORD restores his people,
    let Jacob rejoice and Israel be glad!

### Psalm 15

*A psalm of David.*

1 LORD, who may dwell in your sacred tent?
    Who may live on your holy mountain?

2 The one whose walk is blameless,
    who does what is righteous,
    who speaks the truth from their heart;
3 whose tongue utters no slander,
    who does no wrong to a neighbor,
    and casts no slur on others;
4 who despises a vile person
    but honors those who fear the LORD;
who keeps an oath even when it hurts,
    and does not change their mind;
5 who lends money to the poor without interest;
    who does not accept a bribe against the innocent.

Whoever does these things
    will never be shaken.

### Psalm 16

*A miktam[b] of David.*

1 Keep me safe, my God,
    for in you I take refuge.

2 I say to the LORD, "You are my Lord;
    apart from you I have no good thing."
3 I say of the holy people who are in the land,
    "They are the noble ones in whom is all my delight."
4 Those who run after other gods will suffer more and
    more.

## Amplified Bible

6 I will sing to the Lord, because He has dealt bountifully with me.

### Psalm 14

To the Chief Musician. [A Psalm] of David.

1 The [empty-headed] fool has said in his heart, There is no God. They are corrupt, they have done abominable deeds; there is none that does good *or* right. [Rom. 3:10.]
2 The Lord looked down from heaven upon the children of men to see if there were any who understood, dealt wisely, *and* sought after God, inquiring for *and* of Him *and* requiring Him [of vital necessity].
3 They are all gone aside, they have *all* together become filthy; there is none that does good *or* right, no, not one. [Rom. 3:11, 12.]
4 Have all the workers of iniquity no knowledge, who eat up my people as they eat bread and who do not call on the Lord?
5 There they shall be in great fear [literally—dreading a dread], for God is with the generation of the [uncompromisingly] righteous (those upright and in right standing with Him).
6 You [evildoers] would put to shame *and* confound the plans of the poor *and* patient, but the Lord is his safe refuge.
7 Oh, that the salvation of Israel would come out of Zion! When the Lord shall restore the fortunes of His people, then Jacob shall rejoice *and* Israel shall be glad. [Rom. 11:25-27.]

### Psalm 15

A Psalm of David.

1 Lord, who shall dwell [temporarily] in Your tabernacle? Who shall dwell [permanently] on Your holy hill?
2 He who walks *and* lives uprightly *and* blamelessly, who works rightness *and* justice and speaks *and* thinks the truth in his heart,
3 He who does not slander with his tongue, nor does evil to his friend, nor takes up a reproach against his neighbor;
4 In whose eyes a vile person is despised, but he who honors those who fear the Lord (who revere and worship Him); who swears to his own hurt and does not change;
5 [He who] does not put out his money for *a*interest [to one of his own people] and who will not take a bribe against the innocent. He who does these things shall never be moved. [Exod. 22:25, 26.]

### Psalm 16

A Poem of David; [probably] intended to record memorable thoughts.

1 Keep *and* protect me, O God, for in You I have found refuge, *and* in You do I put my trust *and* hide myself.
2 I say to the Lord, You are my Lord; I have no good beside *or* beyond You.
3 As for the godly (the saints) who are in the land, they are the excellent, the noble, *and* the glorious, in whom is all my delight.
4 Their sorrows shall be multiplied who choose another

---

*a* "Israel was originally not a mercantile people, and the law aimed at an equal diffusion of wealth, not at enriching some while others were poor. The spirit of the law still is obligatory—not to take advantage of a brother's distress to lend at interest ruinous to him—but the letter of the law is abrogated, and a loan at moderate interest is often of great service to the poor. Hence, it is referred to by our Lord in parables, apparently as a lawful as well as recognized usage. (Matt. 25:27; Luke 19:23)" (A. R. Fausset, *Bible Encyclopedia and Dictionary*).

---

*a* 1 The Hebrew words rendered *fool* in Psalms denote one who is morally deficient.   *b* Title: Probably a literary or musical term

## New International Version

I will not pour out libations of blood to such gods
 or take up their names on my lips.
⁵ LORD, you alone are my portion and my cup;
 you make my lot secure.
⁶ The boundary lines have fallen for me in pleasant
 places;
 surely I have a delightful inheritance.
⁷ I will praise the LORD, who counsels me;
 even at night my heart instructs me.
⁸ I keep my eyes always on the LORD.
 With him at my right hand, I will not be shaken.

⁹ Therefore my heart is glad and my tongue rejoices;
 my body also will rest secure,
¹⁰ because you will not abandon me to the realm of the
 dead,
 nor will you let your faithful*a* one see decay.
¹¹ You make known to me the path of life;
 you will fill me with joy in your presence,
 with eternal pleasures at your right hand.

### Psalm 17

*A prayer of David.*

¹ Hear me, LORD, my plea is just;
 listen to my cry.
 Hear my prayer—
 it does not rise from deceitful lips.
² Let my vindication come from you;
 may your eyes see what is right.

³ Though you probe my heart,
 though you examine me at night and test me,
 you will find that I have planned no evil;
 my mouth has not transgressed.
⁴ Though people tried to bribe me,
 I have kept myself from the ways of the violent
 through what your lips have commanded.
⁵ My steps have held to your paths;
 my feet have not stumbled.

⁶ I call on you, my God, for you will answer me;
 turn your ear to me and hear my prayer.
⁷ Show me the wonders of your great love,
 you who save by your right hand
 those who take refuge in you from their foes.
⁸ Keep me as the apple of your eye;
 hide me in the shadow of your wings
⁹ from the wicked who are out to destroy me,
 from my mortal enemies who surround me.

¹⁰ They close up their callous hearts,
 and their mouths speak with arrogance.
¹¹ They have tracked me down, they now surround me,
 with eyes alert, to throw me to the ground.
¹² They are like a lion hungry for prey,
 like a fierce lion crouching in cover.

¹³ Rise up, LORD, confront them, bring them down;
 with your sword rescue me from the wicked.
¹⁴ By your hand save me from such people, LORD,
 from those of this world whose reward is in this life.
 May what you have stored up for the wicked fill their
 bellies;
 may their children gorge themselves on it,
 and may there be leftovers for their little ones.

¹⁵ As for me, I will be vindicated and will see your face;
 when I awake, I will be satisfied with seeing your
 likeness.

## Amplified Bible

god; their drink offerings of blood will I not offer or take
their names upon my lips.
⁵ The Lord is my chosen *and* assigned portion, my cup;
You hold *and* maintain my lot.
⁶ The lines have fallen for me in pleasant places; yes, I
have a good heritage.
⁷ I will bless the Lord, Who has given me counsel; yes,
my heart instructs me in the night seasons.
⁸ I have set the Lord continually before me; because He
is at my right hand, I shall not be moved.
⁹ Therefore my heart is glad and my glory [my inner
self] rejoices; my body too shall rest *and* confidently dwell
in safety,
¹⁰ For You will not abandon me to Sheol (the place of the
dead), neither will You suffer Your holy one [Holy One] to
see corruption. [Acts 13:35.]
¹¹ You will show me the path of life; in Your presence
is fullness of joy, at Your right hand there are pleasures
forevermore. [Acts 2:25-28, 31.]

### Psalm 17

A Prayer of David.

¹ Hear the right (my righteous cause), O Lord; listen to
my shrill, piercing cry! Give ear to my prayer, that comes
from unfeigned *and* guileless lips.
² Let my sentence of vindication come from You! May
Your eyes behold the things that are just *and* upright.
³ You have proved my heart; You have visited *me* in the
night; You have tried me and find nothing [no evil purpose
in me]; I have purposed that my mouth shall not transgress.
⁴ Concerning the works of men, by the word of Your lips
I have avoided the ways of the violent (the paths of the
destroyer).
⁵ My steps have held closely to Your paths [to the tracks
of the One Who has gone on before]; my feet have not
slipped.
⁶ I have called upon You, O God, for You will hear me;
incline Your ear to me *and* hear my speech.
⁷ Show Your marvelous loving-kindness, O You Who
save by Your right hand those who trust *and* take refuge
in You from those who rise up against them.
⁸ Keep *and* guard me as the pupil of Your eye; hide me in
the shadow of Your wings
⁹ From the wicked who despoil *and* oppress me, my
deadly adversaries who surround me.
¹⁰ They are enclosed in their own prosperity *and* have
shut up their hearts to pity; with their mouths they make
exorbitant claims *and* proudly *and* arrogantly speak.
¹¹ They track us down in each step we take; now they
surround us; they set their eyes to cast us to the ground,
¹² Like a lion greedy *and* eager to tear his prey, and as a
young lion lurking in hidden places.
¹³ Arise, O Lord! Confront *and* forestall them, cast them
down! Deliver my life from the wicked by Your sword,
¹⁴ From men by Your hand, O Lord, from men of *this*
world [these poor moths of the night] whose portion in
life is idle *and* vain. Their bellies are filled with Your hidden treasure [what You have stored up]; their children are
satiated, and they leave the rest [of their] wealth to their
babes.
¹⁵ As for me, I will continue beholding Your face in righteousness (rightness, justice, and right standing with
You); I shall be fully satisfied, when I awake [to find my-
self] beholding Your form [and having sweet communion
with You].

---

*a 10 Or holy*

## New International Version

### Psalm 18[a]

*For the director of music. Of David the servant of the LORD.*
*He sang to the LORD the words of this song when the LORD*
*delivered him from the hand of all his enemies*
*and from the hand of Saul. He said:*

[1] I love you, LORD, my strength.

[2] The LORD is my rock, my fortress and my deliverer;
  my God is my rock, in whom I take refuge,
  my shield[b] and the horn[c] of my salvation, my
    stronghold.

[3] I called to the LORD, who is worthy of praise,
  and I have been saved from my enemies.

[4] The cords of death entangled me;
  the torrents of destruction overwhelmed me.

[5] The cords of the grave coiled around me;
  the snares of death confronted me.

[6] In my distress I called to the LORD;
  I cried to my God for help.
  From his temple he heard my voice;
    my cry came before him, into his ears.

[7] The earth trembled and quaked,
  and the foundations of the mountains shook;
  they trembled because he was angry.

[8] Smoke rose from his nostrils;
  consuming fire came from his mouth,
  burning coals blazed out of it.

[9] He parted the heavens and came down;
  dark clouds were under his feet.

[10] He mounted the cherubim and flew;
  he soared on the wings of the wind.

[11] He made darkness his covering, his canopy around
    him—
  the dark rain clouds of the sky.

[12] Out of the brightness of his presence clouds advanced,
  with hailstones and bolts of lightning.

[13] The LORD thundered from heaven;
  the voice of the Most High resounded.[d]

[14] He shot his arrows and scattered the enemy,
  with great bolts of lightning he routed them.

[15] The valleys of the sea were exposed
  and the foundations of the earth laid bare
  at your rebuke, LORD,
  at the blast of breath from your nostrils.

[16] He reached down from on high and took hold of me;
  he drew me out of deep waters.

[17] He rescued me from my powerful enemy,
  from my foes, who were too strong for me.

[18] They confronted me in the day of my disaster,
  but the LORD was my support.

[19] He brought me out into a spacious place;
  he rescued me because he delighted in me.

[20] The LORD has dealt with me according to my
    righteousness;
  according to the cleanness of my hands he has
    rewarded me.

[21] For I have kept the ways of the LORD;
  I am not guilty of turning from my God.

[22] All his laws are before me;
  I have not turned away from his decrees.

[23] I have been blameless before him
  and have kept myself from sin.

## Amplified Bible

### Psalm 18

To the Chief Musician. [A Psalm] of David the servant of the
Lord, who spoke the words of this song to the Lord on the day
when the Lord delivered him from the hand of all his enemies
and from the hand of Saul. And he said:

[1] I love you fervently *and* devotedly, O Lord, my
Strength.

[2] The Lord is my Rock, my Fortress, and my Deliverer;
my God, my keen *and* firm Strength in Whom I will trust
*and* take refuge, my Shield, and the Horn of my salvation,
my High Tower. [Heb. 2:13.]

[3] I will call upon the Lord, Who is to be praised; so shall
I be saved from my enemies. [Rev. 5:12.]

[4] The cords *or* bands of death surrounded me, and the
streams of ungodliness *and* the torrents of ruin terrified
me.

[5] The cords of Sheol (the place of the dead) surrounded
me; the snares of death confronted *and* came upon me.

[6] In my distress [when seemingly closed in] I called
upon the Lord and cried to my God; He heard my voice
out of His temple (heavenly dwelling place), and my cry
came before Him, into His [very] ears.

[7] Then the earth quaked and rocked, the foundations
also of the mountains trembled; they moved *and* were
shaken because He was indignant *and* angry.

[8] There went up smoke from His nostrils; and lightning
out of His mouth devoured; coals were kindled by it.

[9] He bowed the heavens also and came down; and thick
darkness was under His feet.

[10] And He rode upon a cherub [a storm] and flew [swift-
ly]; yes, He sped on with the wings of the wind.

[11] He made darkness His secret hiding place; as His pavilion (His canopy) round about Him were dark waters *and*
thick clouds of the skies.

[12] Out of the brightness before Him there broke forth
through His thick clouds hailstones and coals of fire.

[13] The Lord also thundered from the heavens, and the
Most High uttered His voice, amid hailstones and coals
of fire.

[14] And He sent out His arrows and scattered them; and
He flashed forth lightnings and put them to rout.

[15] Then the beds of the sea appeared and the foundations of the world were laid bare at Your rebuke, O Lord,
at the blast of the breath of Your nostrils.

[16] He reached from on high, He took me; He drew me
out of many waters.

[17] He delivered me from my strong enemy and from
those who hated *and* abhorred me, for they were too
strong for me.

[18] They confronted *and* came upon me in the day of my
calamity, but the Lord was my stay and support.

[19] He brought me forth also into a large place; He was
delivering me because He was pleased with me *and* delighted in me.

[20] The Lord rewarded me according to my righteousness (my conscious integrity and sincerity with Him); according to the cleanness of my hands has He recompensed
me.

[21] For I have kept the ways of the Lord and have not wickedly departed from my God.

[22] For all His ordinances were before me, and I put not
away His statutes from me.

[23] I was upright before Him *and* blameless with Him,
ever [on guard] to keep myself free from my sin *and* guilt.

---

*a* In Hebrew texts 18:1-50 is numbered 18:2-51.     *b* 2 Or *sovereign*
*c* 2 *Horn* here symbolizes strength.     *d* 13 Some Hebrew manuscripts
and Septuagint (see also 2 Samuel 22:14); most Hebrew manuscripts
*resounded, / amid hailstones and bolts of lightning*

## New International Version

24The LORD has rewarded me according to my
righteousness,
according to the cleanness of my hands in his sight.

25To the faithful you show yourself faithful,
to the blameless you show yourself blameless,
26to the pure you show yourself pure,
but to the devious you show yourself shrewd.
27You save the humble
but bring low those whose eyes are haughty.
28You, LORD, keep my lamp burning;
my God turns my darkness into light.
29With your help I can advance against a troop*a*;
with my God I can scale a wall.

30As for God, his way is perfect:
The LORD's word is flawless;
he shields all who take refuge in him.
31For who is God besides the LORD?
And who is the Rock except our God?
32It is God who arms me with strength
and keeps my way secure.
33He makes my feet like the feet of a deer;
he causes me to stand on the heights.
34He trains my hands for battle;
my arms can bend a bow of bronze.
35You make your saving help my shield,
and your right hand sustains me;
your help has made me great.
36You provide a broad path for my feet,
so that my ankles do not give way.

37I pursued my enemies and overtook them;
I did not turn back till they were destroyed.
38I crushed them so that they could not rise;
they fell beneath my feet.
39You armed me with strength for battle;
you humbled my adversaries before me.
40You made my enemies turn their backs in flight,
and I destroyed my foes.
41They cried for help, but there was no one to save
them—
to the LORD, but he did not answer.
42I beat them as fine as windblown dust;
I trampled them*b* like mud in the streets.
43You have delivered me from the attacks of the people;
you have made me the head of nations.
People I did not know now serve me,
44    foreigners cower before me;
as soon as they hear of me, they obey me.
45They all lose heart;
they come trembling from their strongholds.

46The LORD lives! Praise be to my Rock!
Exalted be God my Savior!
47He is the God who avenges me,
who subdues nations under me,
48    who saves me from my enemies.
You exalted me above my foes;
from a violent man you rescued me.
49Therefore I will praise you, LORD, among the nations;
I will sing the praises of your name.

50He gives his king great victories;
he shows unfailing love to his anointed,
to David and to his descendants forever.

## Amplified Bible

24Therefore has the Lord recompensed me according
to my righteousness (my uprightness and right standing
with Him), according to the cleanness of my hands in His
sight.
25With the kind *and* merciful You will show Yourself
kind *and* merciful, with an upright man You will show
Yourself upright,
26With the pure You will show Yourself pure, and with
the perverse You will show Yourself contrary.
27For You deliver an afflicted *and* humble people but
will bring down those with haughty looks.
28For You cause my lamp to be lighted *and* to shine; the
Lord my God illumines my darkness.
29For by You I can run through a troop, and by my God
I can leap over a wall.
30As for God, His way is perfect! The word of the Lord is
tested *and* tried; He is a shield to all those who take refuge
*and* put their trust in Him.
31For who is God except the Lord? Or who is the Rock
save our God,
32The God who girds me with strength and makes my
way perfect?
33He makes my feet like hinds' feet [able to stand firmly
or make progress on the dangerous heights of testing and
trouble]; He sets me securely upon my high places.
34He teaches my hands to war, so that my arms can
bend a bow of bronze.
35You have also given me the shield of Your salvation,
and Your right hand has held me up; Your gentleness *and*
condescension have made me great.
36You have given plenty of room for my steps under me,
that my feet would not slip.
37I pursued my enemies and overtook them; neither did
I turn again till they were consumed.
38I smote them so that they were not able to rise; they
fell wounded under my feet.
39For You have girded me with strength for the battle;
You have subdued under me and caused to bow down
those who rose up against me.
40You have also made my enemies turn their backs to
me, that I might cut off those who hate me.
41They cried [for help], but there was none to deliver—
even unto the Lord, but He answered them not.
42Then I beat them small as the dust before the wind; I
emptied them out as the dirt *and* mire of the streets.
43You have delivered me from the strivings of the people; You made me the head of the nations; a people I had
not known served me.
44As soon as they heard of me, they obeyed me; foreigners submitted themselves cringingly *and* yielded feigned
obedience to me.
45Foreigners lost heart and came trembling out of their
caves *or* strongholds.
46The Lord lives! Blessed be my Rock; and let the God
of my salvation be exalted,
47The God Who avenges me and subdues peoples under
me,
48Who delivers me from my enemies; yes, You lift me up
above those who rise up against me; You deliver me from
the man of violence.
49Therefore will I give thanks *and* extol You, O Lord,
among the nations, and sing praises to Your name. [Rom.
15:9.]
50Great deliverances *and* triumphs gives He to His king;
and He shows mercy *and* steadfast love to His anointed, to
David and his offspring forever. [II Sam. 22:2-51.]

---

*a* 29 Or *can run through a barricade*    *b* 42 Many Hebrew manuscripts,
Septuagint, Syriac and Targum (see also 2 Samuel 22:43); Masoretic
Text *I poured them out*

# New International Version

## Psalm 19[a]

*For the director of music. A psalm of David.*

[1] The heavens declare the glory of God;
  the skies proclaim the work of his hands.
[2] Day after day they pour forth speech;
  night after night they reveal knowledge.
[3] They have no speech, they use no words;
  no sound is heard from them.
[4] Yet their voice[b] goes out into all the earth,
  their words to the ends of the world.
In the heavens God has pitched a tent for the sun.
[5]   It is like a bridegroom coming out of his chamber,
  like a champion rejoicing to run his course.
[6] It rises at one end of the heavens
  and makes its circuit to the other;
  nothing is deprived of its warmth.

[7] The law of the LORD is perfect,
  refreshing the soul.
The statutes of the LORD are trustworthy,
  making wise the simple.
[8] The precepts of the LORD are right,
  giving joy to the heart.
The commands of the LORD are radiant,
  giving light to the eyes.
[9] The fear of the LORD is pure,
  enduring forever.
The decrees of the LORD are firm,
  and all of them are righteous.

[10] They are more precious than gold,
  than much pure gold;
they are sweeter than honey,
  than honey from the honeycomb.
[11] By them your servant is warned;
  in keeping them there is great reward.
[12] But who can discern their own errors?
  Forgive my hidden faults.
[13] Keep your servant also from willful sins;
  may they not rule over me.
Then I will be blameless,
  innocent of great transgression.

[14] May these words of my mouth and this meditation of
    my heart
  be pleasing in your sight,
LORD, my Rock and my Redeemer.

## Psalm 20[c]

*For the director of music. A psalm of David.*

[1] May the LORD answer you when you are in distress;
  may the name of the God of Jacob protect you.
[2] May he send you help from the sanctuary
  and grant you support from Zion.
[3] May he remember all your sacrifices
  and accept your burnt offerings.[d]
[4] May he give you the desire of your heart
  and make all your plans succeed.
[5] May we shout for joy over your victory
  and lift up our banners in the name of our God.

May the LORD grant all your requests.

[6] Now this I know:
  The LORD gives victory to his anointed.
He answers him from his heavenly sanctuary
  with the victorious power of his right hand.
[7] Some trust in chariots and some in horses,
  but we trust in the name of the LORD our God.

# Amplified Bible

## Psalm 19

To the Chief Musician. A Psalm of David.

[1] The heavens declare the glory of God; and the firmament shows *and* proclaims His handiwork. [Rom. 1:20, 21.]
[2] Day after day pours forth speech, and night after night shows forth knowledge.
[3] There is no speech nor spoken word [from the stars]; their voice is not heard.
[4] Yet their voice [in evidence] goes out through all the earth, their sayings to the end of the world. Of the heavens has God made a tent for the sun, [Rom. 10:18.]
[5] Which is as a bridegroom coming out of his chamber; and it rejoices as a strong man to run his course.
[6] Its going forth is from the end of the heavens, and its circuit to the ends of it; and nothing [yes, no one] is hidden from the heat of it.
[7] The law of the Lord is perfect, restoring the [whole] person; the testimony of the Lord is sure, making wise the simple.
[8] The precepts of the Lord are right, rejoicing the heart; the commandment of the Lord is pure *and* bright, enlightening the eyes.
[9] The [reverent] fear of the Lord is clean, enduring forever; the ordinances of the Lord are true and righteous altogether.
[10] More to be desired are they than gold, even than much fine gold; they are sweeter also than honey and drippings from the honeycomb.
[11] Moreover, by them is Your servant warned (reminded, illuminated, and instructed); and in keeping them there is great reward.
[12] Who can discern his lapses *and* errors? Clear me from hidden [and unconscious] faults.
[13] Keep back Your servant also from presumptuous sins; let them not have dominion over me! Then shall I be blameless, and I shall be innocent *and* clear of great transgression.
[14] Let the words of my mouth and the meditation of my heart be acceptable in Your sight, O Lord, my [firm, impenetrable] Rock and my Redeemer.

## Psalm 20

To the Chief Musician. A Psalm of David.

[1] May the Lord answer you in the day of trouble! May the name of the God of Jacob set you up on high [and defend you];
[2] Send you help from the sanctuary and support, refresh, *and* strengthen you from Zion;
[3] Remember all your offerings and accept your burnt sacrifice. Selah [pause, and think of that]!
[4] May He grant you according to your heart's desire and fulfill all your plans.
[5] We will [shout in] triumph at your salvation *and* victory, and in the name of our God we will set up our banners. May the Lord fulfill all your petitions.
[6] Now I know that the Lord saves His anointed; He will answer him from His holy heaven with the saving strength of His right hand.
[7] Some trust in *and* boast of chariots and some of horses, but we will trust in *and* boast of the name of the Lord our God.

---

[a] In Hebrew texts 19:1-14 is numbered 19:2-15.    [b] 4 Septuagint, Jerome and Syriac; Hebrew *measuring line*    [c] In Hebrew texts 20:1-9 is numbered 20:2-10.    [d] 3 The Hebrew has *Selah* (a word of uncertain meaning) here.

## New International Version

8They are brought to their knees and fall,
  but we rise up and stand firm.
9LORD, give victory to the king!
  Answer us when we call!

### Psalm 21ᵃ

*For the director of music. A psalm of David.*

1The king rejoices in your strength, LORD.
  How great is his joy in the victories you give!

2You have granted him his heart's desire
  and have not withheld the request of his lips.ᵇ
3You came to greet him with rich blessings
  and placed a crown of pure gold on his head.
4He asked you for life, and you gave it to him—
  length of days, for ever and ever.
5Through the victories you gave, his glory is great;
  you have bestowed on him splendor and majesty.
6Surely you have granted him unending blessings
  and made him glad with the joy of your presence.
7For the king trusts in the LORD;
  through the unfailing love of the Most High
  he will not be shaken.

8Your hand will lay hold on all your enemies;
  your right hand will seize your foes.
9When you appear for battle,
  you will burn them up as in a blazing furnace.
The LORD will swallow them up in his wrath,
  and his fire will consume them.
10You will destroy their descendants from the earth,
  their posterity from mankind.
11Though they plot evil against you
  and devise wicked schemes, they cannot succeed.
12You will make them turn their backs
  when you aim at them with drawn bow.

13Be exalted in your strength, LORD;
  we will sing and praise your might.

### Psalm 22ᶜ

*For the director of music. To the tune of "The Doe of the
Morning." A psalm of David.*

1My God, my God, why have you forsaken me?
  Why are you so far from saving me,
  so far from my cries of anguish?
2My God, I cry out by day, but you do not answer,
  by night, but I find no rest.ᵈ

3Yet you are enthroned as the Holy One;
  you are the one Israel praises.ᵉ
4In you our ancestors put their trust;
  they trusted and you delivered them.
5To you they cried out and were saved;
  in you they trusted and were not put to shame.

6But I am a worm and not a man,
  scorned by everyone, despised by the people.
7All who see me mock me;
  they hurl insults, shaking their heads.

## Amplified Bible

8They are bowed down and fallen, but we are risen and
stand upright.
9O Lord, give victory; let the King answer us when we
call.

### Psalm 21

To the Chief Musician. A Psalm of David.

1The king [David] shall joy in Your strength, O Lord;
and in Your salvation how greatly shall he rejoice!
2You have given him his heart's desire and have not
withheld the request of his lips. Selah [pause, and think
of that]!
3For You send blessings of good things to meet him;
You set a crown of pure gold on his head.
4He asked life of You, *and* You gave it to him—long life
forever and evermore.
5His glory is great because of Your aid; splendor and
majesty You bestow upon him.
6For You make him to be blessed *and* a blessing forever;
You make him exceedingly glad with the joy of Your presence. [Gen. 12:2.]
7For the king trusts, relies on, *and* is confident in the
Lord, and through the mercy *and* steadfast love of the
Most High he will never be moved.

8Your hand shall find all Your enemies; Your right hand
shall find all those who hate You.
9You will make them as if in a blazing oven in the time
of Your anger; the Lord will swallow them up in His wrath,
and the fire will utterly consume them.
10Their offspring You will destroy from the earth, and
their sons from among the children of men.
11For they planned evil against You; they conceived a
mischievous plot which they are not able to perform.
12For You will make them turn their backs; You will aim
Your bow [of divine justice] at their faces.

13Be exalted, Lord, in Your strength; we will sing and
praise Your power.

### Psalm 22ᵃ

To the Chief Musician; set to [the tune of] Aijeleth
Hashshahar [the hind of the morning dawn].
A Psalm of David.

1My God, my God, why have You forsaken me? Why
are You so far from helping me, and from the words of my
groaning? [Matt. 27:46.]
2O my God, I cry in the daytime, but You answer not;
and by night I am not silent *or* find no rest.

3But You are holy, O You Who dwell in [the holy place
where] the praises of Israel [are offered].
4Our fathers trusted in You; they trusted (leaned on, relied on You, and were confident) and You delivered them.
5They cried to You and were delivered; they trusted
in, leaned on, *and* confidently relied on You, and were not
ashamed *or* confounded *or* disappointed.

6But I am a worm, and no man; I am the scorn of men,
and despised by the people. [Matt. 27:39-44.]
7All who see me laugh at me *and* mock me; they shoot
out the lip, they shake the head, saying, [Matt. 27:43.]

ᵃ "This is beyond all others 'The Psalm of the Cross.' It may have been
actually repeated by our Lord when hanging on the tree; it would be too
bold to say so, but even a casual reader may see that it might have been.
It begins with, 'My God, my God, why hast thou forsaken me?' and ends
[with the thought], 'It is finished.' For plaintive expressions uprising from
unutterable depths of woe, we may say of this psalm, 'There is none like
it' " (Charles Haddon Spurgeon, *The Treasury of David*). Quoted in the
Gospels (Matt. 27:46; Mark 15:34; and alluded to in Matt. 27:35, 39, 43
and John 19:23-24, 28) as being fulfilled at Christ's crucifixion.

---

ᵃ In Hebrew texts 21:1-13 is numbered 21:2-14.    ᵇ 2 The Hebrew has
*Selah* (a word of uncertain meaning) here.    ᶜ In Hebrew texts 22:1-31
is numbered 22:2-32.    ᵈ 2 Or *night, and am not silent*    ᵉ 3 Or *Yet you
are holy, / enthroned on the praises of Israel*

## New International Version

8 "He trusts in the Lord," they say,
  "let the Lord rescue him.
  Let him deliver him,
  since he delights in him."
9 Yet you brought me out of the womb;
  you made me trust in you, even at my mother's breast.
10 From birth I was cast on you;
  from my mother's womb you have been my God.
11 Do not be far from me,
  for trouble is near
  and there is no one to help.

12 Many bulls surround me;
  strong bulls of Bashan encircle me.
13 Roaring lions that tear their prey
  open their mouths wide against me.
14 I am poured out like water,
  and all my bones are out of joint.
  My heart has turned to wax;
  it has melted within me.
15 My mouth*a* is dried up like a potsherd,
  and my tongue sticks to the roof of my mouth;
  you lay me in the dust of death.

16 Dogs surround me,
  a pack of villains encircles me;
  they pierce*b* my hands and my feet.
17 All my bones are on display;
  people stare and gloat over me.
18 They divide my clothes among them
  and cast lots for my garment.

19 But you, Lord, do not be far from me.
  You are my strength; come quickly to help me.
20 Deliver me from the sword,
  my precious life from the power of the dogs.
21 Rescue me from the mouth of the lions;
  save me from the horns of the wild oxen.

22 I will declare your name to my people;
  in the assembly I will praise you.
23 You who fear the Lord, praise him!
  All you descendants of Jacob, honor him!
  Revere him, all you descendants of Israel!
24 For he has not despised or scorned
  the suffering of the afflicted one;
  he has not hidden his face from him
  but has listened to his cry for help.

25 From you comes the theme of my praise in the great assembly;
  before those who fear you*c* I will fulfill my vows.
26 The poor will eat and be satisfied;
  those who seek the Lord will praise him—
  may your hearts live forever!

27 All the ends of the earth
  will remember and turn to the Lord,
  and all the families of the nations
  will bow down before him,
28 for dominion belongs to the Lord
  and he rules over the nations.

29 All the rich of the earth will feast and worship;
  all who go down to the dust will kneel before him—
  those who cannot keep themselves alive.
30 Posterity will serve him;
  future generations will be told about the Lord.
31 They will proclaim his righteousness,
  declaring to a people yet unborn:
  He has done it!

*a 15* Probable reading of the original Hebrew text; Masoretic Text *strength*   *b 16* Dead Sea Scrolls and some manuscripts of the Masoretic Text, Septuagint and Syriac; most manuscripts of the Masoretic Text *me, / like a lion*   *c 25* Hebrew *him*

## Amplified Bible

8 He trusted *and* rolled himself on the Lord, that He would deliver him. Let Him deliver him, seeing that He delights in him! [Matt. 27:39, 43; Mark 15:29, 30; Luke 23:35.]
9 Yet You are He Who took me out of the womb; You made me hope *and* trust when I was on my mother's breasts.
10 I was cast upon You from my very birth; from my mother's womb You have been my God.
11 Be not far from me, for trouble is near and there is none to help.
12 Many [foes like] bulls have surrounded me; strong bulls of Bashan have hedged me in. [Ezek. 39:18.]
13 Against me they opened their mouths wide, like a ravening and roaring lion.
14 I am poured out like water, and all my bones are out of joint. My heart is like wax; it is softened [with anguish] *and* melted down within me.
15 My strength is dried up like a fragment of clay pottery; [with thirst] my tongue cleaves to my jaws; and You have brought me into the dust of death. [John 19:28.]
16 For [like a pack of] dogs they have encompassed me; a company of evildoers has encircled me, they pierced my hands and my feet. [Isa. 53:7; John 19:37.]
17 I can count all my bones; [the evildoers] gaze at me. [Luke 23:27, 35.]
18 They part my clothing among them and cast lots for my raiment (a long, shirtlike garment, a seamless under-tunic). [John 19:23, 24.])
19 But be not far from me, O Lord; O my Help, hasten to aid me!
20 Deliver my life from the sword, my dear life [my only one] from the power of the dog [the agent of execution].
21 Save me from the lion's mouth; for You have answered me [kindly] from the horns of the wild oxen.
22 I will declare Your name to my brethren; in the midst of the congregation will I praise You. [John 20:17; Rom. 8:29; Heb. 2:12.]
23 You who fear (revere and worship) the Lord, praise Him! All you offspring of Jacob, glorify Him. Fear (revere and worship) Him, all you offspring of Israel.
24 For He has not despised or abhorred the affliction of the afflicted; neither has He hidden His face from him, but when he cried to Him, He heard.
25 My praise shall be of You in the great congregation. I will pay to Him my vows [made in the time of trouble] before them who fear (revere and worship) Him.
26 The poor *and* afflicted shall eat and be satisfied; they shall praise the Lord—they who [diligently] seek for, inquire of *and* for Him, *and* require Him [as their greatest need]. May your hearts be quickened now *and* forever!
27 All the ends of the earth shall remember and turn to the Lord, and all the families of the nations shall bow down *and* worship before You,
28 For the kingship *and* the kingdom are the Lord's, and He is the ruler over the nations.
29 All the mighty ones upon earth shall eat [in thanksgiving] and worship; all they that go down to the dust shall bow before Him, even he who cannot keep himself alive.
30 Posterity shall serve Him; they shall tell of the Lord to the next generation.
31 They shall come and shall declare His righteousness to a people yet to be born—that He has done it [that it is finished]! [John 19:30.]

## New International Version

### Psalm 23

*A psalm of David.*

¹The LORD is my shepherd, I lack nothing.
² He makes me lie down in green pastures,
he leads me beside quiet waters,
³ he refreshes my soul.
He guides me along the right paths
for his name's sake.
⁴Even though I walk
through the darkest valley,ᵃ
I will fear no evil,
for you are with me;
your rod and your staff,
they comfort me.

⁵You prepare a table before me
in the presence of my enemies.
You anoint my head with oil;
my cup overflows.
⁶Surely your goodness and love will follow me
all the days of my life,
and I will dwell in the house of the LORD
forever.

### Psalm 24

*Of David. A psalm.*

¹The earth is the LORD's, and everything in it,
the world, and all who live in it;
²for he founded it on the seas
and established it on the waters.

³Who may ascend the mountain of the LORD?
Who may stand in his holy place?
⁴The one who has clean hands and a pure heart,
who does not trust in an idol
or swear by a false god.ᵇ

⁵They will receive blessing from the LORD
and vindication from God their Savior.
⁶Such is the generation of those who seek him,
who seek your face, God of Jacob.ᶜ,ᵈ

⁷Lift up your heads, you gates;
be lifted up, you ancient doors,
that the King of glory may come in.
⁸Who is this King of glory?
The LORD strong and mighty,
the LORD mighty in battle.
⁹Lift up your heads, you gates;
lift them up, you ancient doors,
that the King of glory may come in.
¹⁰Who is he, this King of glory?
The LORD Almighty—
he is the King of glory.

### Psalm 25ᵉ

*Of David.*

¹In you, LORD my God,
I put my trust.

²I trust in you;
do not let me be put to shame,
nor let my enemies triumph over me.
³No one who hopes in you
will ever be put to shame,

---

ᵃ 4 Or *the valley of the shadow of death*    ᵇ 4 Or *swear falsely*
ᶜ 6 Two Hebrew manuscripts and Syriac (see also Septuagint); most
Hebrew manuscripts *face, Jacob*    ᵈ 6 The Hebrew has *Selah* (a word of
uncertain meaning) here and at the end of verse 10.    ᵉ This psalm is
an acrostic poem, the verses of which begin with the successive letters
of the Hebrew alphabet.

## Amplified Bible

### Psalm 23

A Psalm of David.

¹The Lord is my Shepherd [to feed, guide, and shield
me], I shall not lack.
²He makes me lie down in [fresh, tender] green pastures; He leads me beside the still *and* restful waters. [Rev.
7:17.]
³He refreshes *and* restores my life (my self); He leads
me in the paths of righteousness [uprightness and right
standing with Him—not for my earning it, but] for His
name's sake.
⁴Yes, though I walk through the [deep, sunless] valley of the shadow of death, I will fear *or* dread no evil, for
You are with me; Your rod [to protect] and Your staff [to
guide], they comfort me.
⁵You prepare a table before me in the presence of my
enemies. You anoint my head with ᵃoil; my [brimming]
cup runs over.
⁶Surely *or* only goodness, mercy, *and* unfailing love
shall follow me all the days of my life, and through the
length of my days the house of the Lord [and His pres-
ence] shall be my dwelling place.

### Psalm 24

A Psalm of David.

¹The Earth is the Lord's, and the fullness of it, the world
and they who dwell in it. [I Cor. 10:26.]
²For He has founded it upon the seas and established it
upon the currents *and* the rivers.
³Who shall go up into the mountain of the Lord? Or who
shall stand in His Holy Place?
⁴He who has clean hands and a pure heart, who has not
lifted himself up to falsehood *or* to what is false, nor sworn
deceitfully. [Matt. 5:8.]
⁵He shall receive blessing from the Lord and righteousness from the God of his salvation.
⁶This is the generation [description] of those who seek
Him [who inquire of and for Him and of necessity require
Him], who seek Your face, [O God of] Jacob. Selah [pause,
and think of that]! [Ps. 42:1.]
⁷Lift up your heads, O you gates; and be lifted up, you
age-abiding doors, that the King of glory may come in.
⁸Who is the King of glory? The Lord strong and mighty,
the Lord mighty in battle.
⁹Lift up your heads, O you gates; yes, lift them up, you
age-abiding doors, that the King of glory may come in.
¹⁰Who is [He then] this King of glory? The Lord of
hosts, He is the King of glory. Selah [pause, and think of
that]!

### Psalm 25

[A Psalm] of David.

¹Unto you, O lord, do I bring my life.
²O my God, I trust, lean on, rely on, *and* am confident
in You. Let me not be put to shame *or* [my hope in You] be
disappointed; let not my enemies triumph over me.
³Yes, let none who trust *and* wait hopefully *and* look
for You be put to shame *or* be disappointed; let them be

---

ᵃ It is difficult for those living in a temperate climate to appreciate, but
it was customary in hot climates to anoint the body with oil to protect
it from excessive perspiration. When mixed with perfume, the oil
imparted a delightfully refreshing and invigorating sensation. Athletes
anointed their bodies as a matter of course before running a race. As the
body, therefore, anointed with oil was refreshed, invigorated, and better
fitted for action, so the Lord would anoint His "sheep" with the Holy
Spirit, Whom oil symbolizes, to fit them to engage more freely in His
service and run in the way He directs—in heavenly fellowship with Him.

## New International Version

but shame will come on those
who are treacherous without cause.

4 Show me your ways, LORD,
teach me your paths.
5 Guide me in your truth and teach me,
for you are God my Savior,
and my hope is in you all day long.
6 Remember, LORD, your great mercy and love,
for they are from of old.
7 Do not remember the sins of my youth
and my rebellious ways;
according to your love remember me,
for you, LORD, are good.

8 Good and upright is the LORD;
therefore he instructs sinners in his ways.
9 He guides the humble in what is right
and teaches them his way.
10 All the ways of the LORD are loving and faithful
toward those who keep the demands of his
covenant.
11 For the sake of your name, LORD,
forgive my iniquity, though it is great.

12 Who, then, are those who fear the LORD?
He will instruct them in the ways they should
choose.*a*
13 They will spend their days in prosperity,
and their descendants will inherit the land.
14 The LORD confides in those who fear him;
he makes his covenant known to them.
15 My eyes are ever on the LORD,
for only he will release my feet from the snare.

16 Turn to me and be gracious to me,
for I am lonely and afflicted.
17 Relieve the troubles of my heart
and free me from my anguish.
18 Look on my affliction and my distress
and take away all my sins.
19 See how numerous are my enemies
and how fiercely they hate me!
20 Guard my life and rescue me;
do not let me be put to shame,
for I take refuge in you.
21 May integrity and uprightness protect me,
because my hope, LORD,*b* is in you.

22 Deliver Israel, O God,
from all their troubles!

### Psalm 26

*Of David.*

1 Vindicate me, LORD,
for I have led a blameless life;
I have trusted in the LORD
and have not faltered.
2 Test me, LORD, and try me,
examine my heart and my mind;
3 for I have always been mindful of your unfailing love
and have lived in reliance on your faithfulness.

4 I do not sit with the deceitful,
nor do I associate with hypocrites.
5 I abhor the assembly of evildoers
and refuse to sit with the wicked.
6 I wash my hands in innocence,
and go about your altar, LORD,
7 proclaiming aloud your praise
and telling of all your wonderful deeds.

## Amplified Bible

ashamed who forsake the right *or* deal treacherously without cause.
4 Show me Your ways, O Lord; teach me Your paths.
5 Guide me in Your truth *and* faithfulness and teach me,
for You are the God of my salvation; for You [You only and
altogether] do I wait [expectantly] all the day long.
6 Remember, O Lord, Your tender mercy and loving-
kindness; for they have been ever from of old.
7 Remember not the sins (the lapses and frailties) of my
youth or my transgressions; according to Your mercy *and*
steadfast love remember me, for Your goodness' sake,
O Lord.
8 Good and upright is the Lord; therefore will He instruct sinners in [His] way.
9 He leads the humble in what is right, and the humble
He teaches His way.
10 All the paths of the Lord are mercy *and* steadfast love,
even truth *and* faithfulness are they for those who keep
His covenant and His testimonies.
11 For Your name's sake, O Lord, pardon my iniquity *and*
my guilt, for [they are] great.
12 Who is the man who reverently fears *and* worships
the Lord? Him shall He teach in the way that he should
choose.
13 He himself shall dwell at ease, and his offspring shall
inherit the land.
14 The secret [of the sweet, satisfying companionship]
of the Lord have they who fear (revere and worship) Him,
and He will show them His covenant *and* reveal to them its
[deep, inner] meaning. [John 7:17; 15:15.]
15 My eyes are ever toward the Lord, for He will pluck
my feet out of the net.
16 [Lord] turn to me and be gracious to me, for I am
lonely and afflicted.
17 The troubles of my heart are multiplied; bring me out
of my distresses.
18 Behold my affliction and my pain and forgive all my
sins [of thinking and doing].
19 Consider my enemies, for they abound; they hate me
with cruel hatred.
20 O keep me, Lord, and deliver me; let me not be
ashamed *or* disappointed, for my trust *and* my refuge are
in You.
21 Let integrity and uprightness preserve me, for I wait
for *and* expect You.
22 Redeem Israel, O God, out of all their troubles.

### Psalm 26

[A Psalm] of David.

1 Vindicate me, O Lord, for I have walked in my integrity; I have [expectantly] trusted in, leaned on, *and* relied
on the Lord without wavering *and* I shall not slide.
2 Examine me, O Lord, and prove me; test my heart and
my mind.
3 For Your loving-kindness is before my eyes, and I have
walked in Your truth [faithfully].
4 I do not sit with false persons, nor fellowship with pretenders;
5 I hate the company of evildoers and will not sit with
the wicked.
6 I will wash my hands in innocence, and go about Your
altar, O Lord,
7 That I may make the voice of thanksgiving heard and
may tell of all Your wondrous works.

---

*a 12 Or ways he chooses*    *b 21 Septuagint; Hebrew does not have LORD.*

## New International Version

[8] LORD, I love the house where you live,
the place where your glory dwells.
[9] Do not take away my soul along with sinners,
my life with those who are bloodthirsty,
[10] in whose hands are wicked schemes,
whose right hands are full of bribes.
[11] I lead a blameless life;
deliver me and be merciful to me.
[12] My feet stand on level ground;
in the great congregation I will praise the LORD.

### Psalm 27

*Of David.*

[1] The LORD is my light and my salvation—
whom shall I fear?
The LORD is the stronghold of my life—
of whom shall I be afraid?
[2] When the wicked advance against me
to devour[a] me,
it is my enemies and my foes
who will stumble and fall.
[3] Though an army besiege me,
my heart will not fear;
though war break out against me,
even then I will be confident.

[4] One thing I ask from the LORD,
this only do I seek:
that I may dwell in the house of the LORD
all the days of my life,
to gaze on the beauty of the LORD
and to seek him in his temple.
[5] For in the day of trouble
he will keep me safe in his dwelling;
he will hide me in the shelter of his sacred tent
and set me high upon a rock.

[6] Then my head will be exalted
above the enemies who surround me;
at his sacred tent I will sacrifice with shouts of joy;
I will sing and make music to the LORD.

[7] Hear my voice when I call, LORD;
be merciful to me and answer me.
[8] My heart says of you, "Seek his face!"
Your face, LORD, I will seek.
[9] Do not hide your face from me,
do not turn your servant away in anger;
you have been my helper.
Do not reject me or forsake me,
God my Savior.
[10] Though my father and mother forsake me,
the LORD will receive me.
[11] Teach me your way, LORD;
lead me in a straight path
because of my oppressors.
[12] Do not turn me over to the desire of my foes,
for false witnesses rise up against me,
spouting malicious accusations.

[13] I remain confident of this:
I will see the goodness of the LORD
in the land of the living.
[14] Wait for the LORD;
be strong and take heart
and wait for the LORD.

## Amplified Bible

[8] Lord, I love the habitation of Your house, and the place where Your glory dwells.
[9] Gather me not with sinners *and* sweep me not away [with them], nor my life with bloodthirsty men,
[10] In whose hands is wickedness, and their right hands are full of bribes.
[11] But as for me, I will walk in my integrity; redeem me and be merciful *and* gracious to me.
[12] My foot stands on an even place; in the congregations will I bless the Lord.

### Psalm 27

[A Psalm] of David.

[1] The Lord is my Light and my Salvation—whom shall I fear *or* dread? The Lord is the Refuge *and* Stronghold of my life—of whom shall I be afraid?
[2] When the wicked, even my enemies and my foes, came upon me to eat up my flesh, they stumbled and fell.
[3] Though a host encamp against me, my heart shall not fear; though war arise against me, [even then] in this will I be confident.
[4] One thing have I asked of the Lord, that will I seek, inquire for, *and* [insistently] require: that I may dwell in the house of the Lord [in His presence] all the days of my life, to behold *and* gaze upon the beauty [the sweet attractiveness and the delightful loveliness] of the Lord and to meditate, consider, *and* inquire in His temple. [Ps. 16:11; 18:6; 65:4; Luke 2:37.]
[5] For in the day of trouble He will hide me in His shelter; in the secret place of His tent will He hide me; He will set me high upon a rock.
[6] And now shall my head be lifted up above my enemies round about me; in His tent I will offer sacrifices *and* shouting of joy; I will sing, yes, I will sing praises to the Lord.
[7] Hear, O Lord, when I cry aloud; have mercy *and* be gracious to me and answer me!
[8] You have said, Seek My face [inquire for and require My presence as your vital need]. My heart says to You, Your face (Your presence), Lord, will I seek, inquire for, *and* require [of necessity and on the authority of Your Word].
[9] Hide not Your face from me; turn not Your servant away in anger, You Who have been my help! Cast me not off, neither forsake me, O God of my salvation!
[10] Although my father and my mother have forsaken me, yet the Lord will take me up [adopt me as His child]. [Ps. 22:10.]
[11] Teach me Your way, O Lord, and lead me in a plain *and* even path because of my enemies [those who lie in wait for me].
[12] Give me not up to the will of my adversaries, for false witnesses have risen up against me; they breathe out cruelty *and* violence.
[13] [What, what would have become of me] had I not believed that I would see the Lord's goodness in the land of the living!
[14] Wait *and* hope for *and* expect the Lord; be brave *and* of good courage and let your heart be stout *and* enduring. Yes, wait for *and* hope for *and* expect the Lord.

---

[a] 2 Or *slander*

# New International Version

## Psalm 28

*Of David.*

¹To you, Lord, I call;
    you are my Rock,
    do not turn a deaf ear to me.
For if you remain silent,
    I will be like those who go down to the pit.
²Hear my cry for mercy
    as I call to you for help,
as I lift up my hands
    toward your Most Holy Place.

³Do not drag me away with the wicked,
    with those who do evil,
who speak cordially with their neighbors
    but harbor malice in their hearts.
⁴Repay them for their deeds
    and for their evil work;
repay them for what their hands have done
    and bring back on them what they deserve.
⁵Because they have no regard for the deeds of the Lord
    and what his hands have done,
he will tear them down
    and never build them up again.

⁶Praise be to the Lord,
    for he has heard my cry for mercy.
⁷The Lord is my strength and my shield;
    my heart trusts in him, and he helps me.
My heart leaps for joy,
    and with my song I praise him.

⁸The Lord is the strength of his people,
    a fortress of salvation for his anointed one.
⁹Save your people and bless your inheritance;
    be their shepherd and carry them forever.

## Psalm 29

*A psalm of David.*

¹Ascribe to the Lord, you heavenly beings,
    ascribe to the Lord glory and strength.
²Ascribe to the Lord the glory due his name;
    worship the Lord in the splendor of his*a* holiness.

³The voice of the Lord is over the waters;
    the God of glory thunders,
    the Lord thunders over the mighty waters.
⁴The voice of the Lord is powerful;
    the voice of the Lord is majestic.
⁵The voice of the Lord breaks the cedars;
    the Lord breaks in pieces the cedars of Lebanon.
⁶He makes Lebanon leap like a calf,
    Sirion*b* like a young wild ox.
⁷The voice of the Lord strikes
    with flashes of lightning.
⁸The voice of the Lord shakes the desert;
    the Lord shakes the Desert of Kadesh.
⁹The voice of the Lord twists the oaks*c*
    and strips the forests bare.
    And in his temple all cry, "Glory!"

¹⁰The Lord sits enthroned over the flood;
    the Lord is enthroned as King forever.
¹¹The Lord gives strength to his people;
    the Lord blesses his people with peace.

# Amplified Bible

## Psalm 28

[A Psalm] of David.

¹Unto you do I cry, O Lord my Rock, be not deaf *and* silent to me, lest, if You be silent to me, I become like those going down to the pit [the grave].
²Hear the voice of my supplication as I cry to You for help, as I lift up my hands toward Your innermost sanctuary (the Holy of Holies).
³Drag me not away with the wicked, with the workers of iniquity, who speak peace with their neighbors, but malice *and* mischief are in their hearts.
⁴Repay them according to their work and according to the wickedness of their doings; repay them according to the work of their hands; render to them what they deserve. [II Tim. 4:14; Rev. 18:6.]
⁵Because they regard not the works of the Lord nor the operations of His hands, He will break them down and not rebuild them.
⁶Blessed be the Lord, because He has heard the voice of my supplications.
⁷The Lord is my Strength and my [impenetrable] Shield; my heart trusts in, relies on, *and* confidently leans on Him, and I am helped; therefore my heart greatly rejoices, and with my song will I praise Him.
⁸The Lord is their [unyielding] Strength, and He is the Stronghold of salvation to [me] His anointed.
⁹Save Your people and bless Your heritage; nourish *and* shepherd them and carry them forever.

## Psalm 29*a*

A Psalm of David.

¹Ascribe to the Lord, O sons of the mighty, ascribe to the Lord glory and strength.
²Give to the Lord the glory due to His name; worship the Lord in the beauty of holiness *or* in holy array.
³The voice of the Lord is upon the waters; the God of glory thunders; the Lord is upon many (great) waters.
⁴The voice of the Lord is powerful; the voice of the Lord is full of majesty.
⁵The voice of the Lord breaks the cedars; yes, the Lord breaks in pieces the cedars of Lebanon.
⁶He makes them also to skip like a calf; Lebanon and Sirion (Mount Hermon) like a young, wild ox.
⁷The voice of the Lord splits *and* flashes forth forked lightning.
⁸The voice of the Lord makes the wilderness tremble; the Lord shakes the Wilderness of Kadesh.
⁹The voice of the Lord makes the hinds bring forth their young, and His voice strips bare the forests, while in His temple everyone is saying, Glory!
¹⁰The Lord sat as King over the deluge; the Lord [still] sits as King [and] forever!
¹¹The Lord will give [unyielding and impenetrable] strength to His people; the Lord will bless His people with peace.

---

*a 2* Or *Lord with the splendor of*    *b 6* That is, Mount Hermon
*c 9* Or *Lord makes the deer give birth*

*a* This psalm has been called "The Song of the Thunderstorm," a glorious psalm of praise sung during an earthshaking tempest which reminds the psalmist of the time of Noah and the deluge (see Ps. 29:10).

## New International Version

### Psalm 30[a]

*A psalm. A song. For the dedication of the temple.[b] Of David.*

[1] I will exalt you, LORD,
  for you lifted me out of the depths
  and did not let my enemies gloat over me.
[2] LORD my God, I called to you for help,
  and you healed me.
[3] You, LORD, brought me up from the realm of the dead;
  you spared me from going down to the pit.

[4] Sing the praises of the LORD, you his faithful people;
  praise his holy name.
[5] For his anger lasts only a moment,
  but his favor lasts a lifetime;
  weeping may stay for the night,
  but rejoicing comes in the morning.

[6] When I felt secure, I said,
  "I will never be shaken."
[7] LORD, when you favored me,
  you made my royal mountain[c] stand firm;
  but when you hid your face,
  I was dismayed.

[8] To you, LORD, I called;
  to the Lord I cried for mercy:
[9] "What is gained if I am silenced,
  if I go down to the pit?
  Will the dust praise you?
  Will it proclaim your faithfulness?
[10] Hear, LORD, and be merciful to me;
  LORD, be my help."

[11] You turned my wailing into dancing;
  you removed my sackcloth and clothed me with joy,
[12] that my heart may sing your praises and not be silent.
  LORD my God, I will praise you forever.

### Psalm 31[d]

*For the director of music. A psalm of David.*

[1] In you, LORD, I have taken refuge;
  let me never be put to shame;
  deliver me in your righteousness.
[2] Turn your ear to me,
  come quickly to my rescue;
  be my rock of refuge,
  a strong fortress to save me.
[3] Since you are my rock and my fortress,
  for the sake of your name lead and guide me.
[4] Keep me free from the trap that is set for me,
  for you are my refuge.
[5] Into your hands I commit my spirit;
  deliver me, LORD, my faithful God.

[6] I hate those who cling to worthless idols;
  as for me, I trust in the LORD.
[7] I will be glad and rejoice in your love,
  for you saw my affliction
  and knew the anguish of my soul.
[8] You have not given me into the hands of the enemy
  but have set my feet in a spacious place.

[9] Be merciful to me, LORD, for I am in distress;
  my eyes grow weak with sorrow,
  my soul and body with grief.
[10] My life is consumed by anguish
  and my years by groaning;
  my strength fails because of my affliction,[e]
  and my bones grow weak.

## Amplified Bible

### Psalm 30

A Psalm; a Song at the Dedication of the Temple.
[A Psalm] of David.

[1] I will extol You, O Lord, for You have lifted me up and have not let my foes rejoice over me.
[2] O Lord my God, I cried to You and You have healed me.
[3] O Lord, You have brought my life up from Sheol (the place of the dead); You have kept me alive, that I should not go down to the pit (the grave).
[4] Sing to the Lord, O you saints of His, and give thanks at the remembrance of His holy name.
[5] For His anger is but for a moment, but His favor is for a lifetime *or* in His favor is life. Weeping may endure for a night, but joy comes in the morning. [II Cor. 4:17.]
[6] As for me, in my prosperity I said, I shall never be moved.
[7] By Your favor, O Lord, You have established me as a strong mountain; You hid Your face, and I was troubled.
[8] I cried to You, O Lord, and to the Lord I made supplication.
[9] What profit is there in my blood, when I go down to the pit (the grave)? Will the dust praise You? Will it declare Your truth *and* faithfulness to men?
[10] Hear, O Lord, have mercy *and* be gracious to me! O Lord, be my helper!
[11] You have turned my mourning into dancing for me; You have put off my sackcloth and girded me with gladness,
[12] To the end that my tongue *and* my heart *and* everything glorious within me may sing praise to You and not be silent. O Lord my God, I will give thanks to You forever.

### Psalm 31

To the Chief Musician. A Psalm of David.

[1] In you, O Lord, do I put my trust *and* seek refuge; let me never be put to shame *or* [have my hope in You] disappointed; deliver me in Your righteousness!
[2] Bow down Your ear to me, deliver me speedily! Be my Rock of refuge, a strong Fortress to save me!
[3] Yes, You are my Rock and my Fortress; therefore for Your name's sake lead me and guide me.
[4] Draw me out of the net that they have laid secretly for me, for You are my Strength *and* my Stronghold.
[5] Into Your hands I commit my spirit; You have redeemed me, O Lord, the God of truth *and* faithfulness. [Luke 23:46; Acts 7:59.]
[6] [You and] I abhor those who pay regard to vain idols; but I trust in, rely on, *and* confidently lean on the Lord.
[7] I will be glad and rejoice in Your mercy *and* steadfast love, because You have seen my affliction, You have taken note of my life's distresses,
[8] And You have not given me into the hand of the enemy; You have set my feet in a broad place.
[9] Have mercy *and* be gracious unto me, O Lord, for I am in trouble; with grief my eye is weakened, also my inner self and my body.
[10] For my life is spent with sorrow and my years with sighing; my strength has failed because of my iniquity, and even my bones have wasted away.

---

[a] In Hebrew texts 30:1-12 is numbered 30:2-13.   [b] Title: Or *palace*
[c] 7 That is, Mount Zion   [d] In Hebrew texts 31:1-24 is numbered 31:2-25.   [e] 10 Or *guilt*

## New International Version

11 Because of all my enemies,
    I am the utter contempt of my neighbors
and an object of dread to my closest friends—
    those who see me on the street flee from me.
12 I am forgotten as though I were dead;
    I have become like broken pottery.
13 For I hear many whispering,
    "Terror on every side!"
They conspire against me
    and plot to take my life.
14 But I trust in you, LORD;
    I say, "You are my God."
15 My times are in your hands;
    deliver me from the hands of my enemies,
    from those who pursue me.
16 Let your face shine on your servant;
    save me in your unfailing love.
17 Let me not be put to shame, LORD,
    for I have cried out to you;
but let the wicked be put to shame
    and be silent in the realm of the dead.
18 Let their lying lips be silenced,
    for with pride and contempt
    they speak arrogantly against the righteous.

19 How abundant are the good things
    that you have stored up for those who fear you,
    that you bestow in the sight of all,
    on those who take refuge in you.
20 In the shelter of your presence you hide them
    from all human intrigues;
    you keep them safe in your dwelling
    from accusing tongues.
21 Praise be to the LORD,
    for he showed me the wonders of his love
    when I was in a city under siege.
22 In my alarm I said,
    "I am cut off from your sight!"
Yet you heard my cry for mercy
    when I called to you for help.

23 Love the LORD, all his faithful people!
    The LORD preserves those who are true to him,
    but the proud he pays back in full.
24 Be strong and take heart,
    all you who hope in the LORD.

### Psalm 32

*Of David. A maskil.*[a]

1 Blessed is the one
    whose transgressions are forgiven,
    whose sins are covered.
2 Blessed is the one
    whose sin the LORD does not count against them
    and in whose spirit is no deceit.

3 When I kept silent,
    my bones wasted away
    through my groaning all day long.
4 For day and night
    your hand was heavy on me;
my strength was sapped
    as in the heat of summer.[b]

5 Then I acknowledged my sin to you
    and did not cover up my iniquity.

## Amplified Bible

11 To all my enemies I have become a reproach, but especially to my neighbors, and a dread to my acquaintances, who flee from me on the street.
12 I am forgotten like a dead man, and out of mind; like a broken vessel am I.
13 For I have heard the slander of many; terror is on every side! While they schemed together against me, they plotted to take my life.
14 But I trusted in, relied on, *and* was confident in You, O Lord; I said, You are my God.
15 My times are in Your hands; deliver me from the hands of my foes and those who pursue me *and* persecute me.
16 Let Your face shine on Your servant; save me for Your mercy's sake *and* in Your loving-kindness.
17 Let me not be put to shame, O Lord, *or* disappointed, for I am calling upon You; let the wicked be put to shame, let them be silent in Sheol (the place of the dead).
18 Let the lying lips be silenced, which speak insolently against the [consistently] righteous with pride and contempt.
19 Oh, how great is Your goodness, which You have laid up for those who fear, revere, *and* worship You, goodness which You have wrought for those who trust *and* take refuge in You before the sons of men!
20 In the secret place of Your presence You hide them from the plots of men; You keep them secretly in Your pavilion from the strife of tongues.
21 Blessed be the Lord! For He has shown me His marvelous loving favor when I was beset as in a besieged city.
22 As for me, I said in my haste *and* alarm, I am cut off from before Your eyes. But You heard the voice of my supplications when I cried to You for aid.
23 O love the Lord, all you His saints! The Lord preserves the faithful, and plentifully pays back him who deals haughtily.
24 Be strong and let your heart take courage, all you who wait for *and* hope for *and* expect the Lord!

### Psalm 32

[A Psalm of David.] A skillful song, *or* a didactic *or* reflective poem.

1 Blessed (happy, fortunate, to be envied) is he who has forgiveness of his transgression continually exercised upon him, whose sin is covered.
2 Blessed (happy, fortunate, to be envied) is the man to whom the Lord imputes no iniquity and in whose spirit there is no deceit. [Rom. 4:7, 8.]
3 When I kept silence [before I confessed], my bones wasted away through my groaning all the day long.
4 For day and night Your hand [of displeasure] was heavy upon me; my moisture was turned into the drought of summer. Selah [pause, and calmly think of that]!
5 I acknowledged my sin to You, and my iniquity I did

---

*a* Title: Probably a literary or musical term     *b* 4 The Hebrew has *Selah* (a word of uncertain meaning) here and at the end of verses 5 and 7.

## New International Version

I said, "I will confess
my transgressions to the LORD."
And you forgave
the guilt of my sin.

[6] Therefore let all the faithful pray to you
while you may be found;
surely the rising of the mighty waters
will not reach them.
[7] You are my hiding place;
you will protect me from trouble
and surround me with songs of deliverance.

[8] I will instruct you and teach you in the way you should
go;
I will counsel you with my loving eye on you.
[9] Do not be like the horse or the mule,
which have no understanding
but must be controlled by bit and bridle
or they will not come to you.
[10] Many are the woes of the wicked,
but the LORD's unfailing love
surrounds the one who trusts in him.

[11] Rejoice in the LORD and be glad, you righteous;
sing, all you who are upright in heart!

### Psalm 33

[1] Sing joyfully to the LORD, you righteous;
it is fitting for the upright to praise him.
[2] Praise the LORD with the harp;
make music to him on the ten-stringed lyre.
[3] Sing to him a new song;
play skillfully, and shout for joy.

[4] For the word of the LORD is right and true;
he is faithful in all he does.
[5] The LORD loves righteousness and justice;
the earth is full of his unfailing love.

[6] By the word of the LORD the heavens were made,
their starry host by the breath of his mouth.
[7] He gathers the waters of the sea into jars[a];
he puts the deep into storehouses.
[8] Let all the earth fear the LORD;
let all the people of the world revere him.
[9] For he spoke, and it came to be;
he commanded, and it stood firm.

[10] The LORD foils the plans of the nations;
he thwarts the purposes of the peoples.
[11] But the plans of the LORD stand firm forever,
the purposes of his heart through all generations.

[12] Blessed is the nation whose God is the LORD,
the people he chose for his inheritance.
[13] From heaven the LORD looks down
and sees all mankind;
[14] from his dwelling place he watches
all who live on earth—
[15] he who forms the hearts of all,
who considers everything they do.

[16] No king is saved by the size of his army;
no warrior escapes by his great strength.
[17] A horse is a vain hope for deliverance;
despite all its great strength it cannot save.
[18] But the eyes of the LORD are on those who fear him,
on those whose hope is in his unfailing love,

[a] 7 Or *sea as into a heap*

## Amplified Bible

not hide. I said, I will confess my transgressions to the
Lord [continually unfolding the past till all is told]—then
You [instantly] forgave me the guilt *and* iniquity of my sin.
Selah [pause, and calmly think of that]!
[6] For this [forgiveness] let everyone who is godly pray—
pray to You in a time when You may be found; surely when
the great waters [of trial] overflow, they shall not reach
[the spirit in] him.
[7] You are a hiding place for me; You, Lord, preserve me
from trouble, You surround me with songs *and* shouts of
deliverance. Selah [pause, and calmly think of that]!
[8] I [the Lord] will instruct you and teach you in the way
you should go; I will counsel you with My eye upon you.
[9] Be not like the horse or the mule, which lack understanding, which must have their mouths held firm with bit
and bridle, or else they will not come with you.
[10] Many are the sorrows of the wicked, but he who trusts
in, relies on, *and* confidently leans on the Lord shall be
compassed about with mercy *and* with loving-kindness.
[11] Be glad in the Lord and rejoice, you [uncompromis-
ingly] righteous [you who are upright and in right standing with Him]; shout for joy, all you upright in heart!

### Psalm 33

[1] Rejoice in the Lord, O you [uncompromisingly] righteous [you upright in right standing with God]; for praise
is becoming *and* appropriate for those who are upright [in
heart].
[2] Give thanks to the Lord with the lyre; sing praises to
Him with the harp of ten strings.
[3] Sing to Him a new song; play skillfully [on the strings]
with a loud *and* joyful sound.
[4] For the word of the Lord is right; and all His work is
done in faithfulness.
[5] He loves righteousness and justice; the earth is full of
the loving-kindness of the Lord.
[6] By the word of the Lord were the heavens made, and
all their host by the breath of His mouth. [Heb. 11:3; II Pet.
3:5.]
[7] He gathers the waters of the sea as in a bottle; He puts
the deeps in storage places.
[8] Let all the earth fear the Lord [revere and worship
Him]; let all the inhabitants of the world stand in awe of
Him.
[9] For He spoke, and it was done; He commanded, and
it stood fast.
[10] The Lord brings the counsel of the nations to nought;
He makes the thoughts *and* plans of the peoples of no effect.
[11] The counsel of the Lord stands forever, the thoughts
of His heart through all generations.
[12] Blessed (happy, fortunate, to be envied) is the nation
whose God is the Lord, the people He has chosen as His
heritage.
[13] The Lord looks from heaven, He beholds all the sons
of men;
[14] From His dwelling place He looks [intently] upon all
the inhabitants of the earth—
[15] He Who fashions the hearts of them all, Who considers all their doings.
[16] No king is saved by the great size *and* power of
his army; a mighty man is not delivered by [his] much
strength.
[17] A horse is devoid of value for victory; neither does he
deliver any by his great power.
[18] Behold, the Lord's eye is upon those who fear Him
[who revere and worship Him with awe], who wait for Him
*and* hope in His mercy *and* loving-kindness,

## New International Version

19 to deliver them from death
and keep them alive in famine.

20 We wait in hope for the LORD;
he is our help and our shield.
21 In him our hearts rejoice,
for we trust in his holy name.
22 May your unfailing love be with us, LORD,
even as we put our hope in you.

### Psalm 34[a,b]

*Of David. When he pretended to be insane before Abimelek, who
drove him away, and he left.*

1 I will extol the LORD at all times;
his praise will always be on my lips.
2 I will glory in the LORD;
let the afflicted hear and rejoice.
3 Glorify the LORD with me;
let us exalt his name together.

4 I sought the LORD, and he answered me;
he delivered me from all my fears.
5 Those who look to him are radiant;
their faces are never covered with shame.
6 This poor man called, and the LORD heard him;
he saved him out of all his troubles.
7 The angel of the LORD encamps around those who fear
him,
and he delivers them.

8 Taste and see that the LORD is good;
blessed is the one who takes refuge in him.
9 Fear the LORD, you his holy people,
for those who fear him lack nothing.
10 The lions may grow weak and hungry,
but those who seek the LORD lack no good thing.
11 Come, my children, listen to me;
I will teach you the fear of the LORD.
12 Whoever of you loves life
and desires to see many good days,
13 keep your tongue from evil
and your lips from telling lies.
14 Turn from evil and do good;
seek peace and pursue it.

15 The eyes of the LORD are on the righteous,
and his ears are attentive to their cry;
16 but the face of the LORD is against those who do evil,
to blot out their name from the earth.

17 The righteous cry out, and the LORD hears them;
he delivers them from all their troubles.
18 The LORD is close to the brokenhearted
and saves those who are crushed in spirit.

19 The righteous person may have many troubles,
but the LORD delivers him from them all;
20 he protects all his bones,
not one of them will be broken.

21 Evil will slay the wicked;
the foes of the righteous will be condemned.
22 The LORD will rescue his servants;
no one who takes refuge in him will be condemned.

## Amplified Bible

19 To deliver them from death and keep them alive in
famine.
20 Our inner selves wait [earnestly] for the Lord; He is
our Help and our Shield.
21 For in Him does our heart rejoice, because we have
trusted (relied on and been confident) in His holy name.
22 Let Your mercy *and* loving-kindness, O Lord, be upon
us, in proportion to our waiting *and* hoping for You.

### Psalm 34

[A Psalm] of David; when he pretended to be insane
before Abimelech, who drove him out, and he went away.

1 I will bless the Lord at all times; His praise shall continually be in my mouth.
2 My life makes its boast in the Lord; let the humble *and*
afflicted hear and be glad.
3 O magnify the Lord with me, and let us exalt His name
together.
4 I sought (inquired of) the Lord *and* required Him [of
necessity and on the authority of His Word], and He heard
me, and delivered me from all my fears. [Ps. 73:25; Matt.
7:7.]
5 They looked to Him and were radiant; their faces shall
never blush for shame *or* be confused.
6 This poor man cried, and the Lord heard him, and
saved him out of all his troubles.
7a The Angel of the Lord encamps around those who
fear Him [who revere and worship Him with awe] and each
of them He delivers. [Ps. 18:1; 145:20.]
8 O taste and see that the Lord [our God] is good!
Blessed (happy, fortunate, to be envied) is the man who
trusts *and* takes refuge in Him. [I Pet. 2:2, 3.]
9 O fear the Lord, you His saints [revere and worship
Him]! For there is no want to those who truly revere *and*
worship Him *with* godly fear.
10 The young lions lack food and suffer hunger, but they
who seek (inquire of and require) the Lord [by right of
their need and on the authority of His Word], none of them
shall lack any beneficial thing.
11 Come, you children, listen to me; I will teach you to
revere *and* worshipfully fear the Lord.
12 What man is he who desires life *and* longs for many
days, that he may see good?
13 Keep your tongue from evil and your lips from speaking deceit.
14 Depart from evil and do good; seek, inquire for, *and*
crave peace and pursue (go after) it!
15 The eyes of the Lord are toward the [uncompromis-
ingly] righteous and His ears are open to their cry.
16 The face of the Lord is against those who do evil, to
cut off the remembrance of them from the earth. [I Pet.
3:10-12.]
17 When the *righteous* cry for help, the Lord hears, and
delivers them out of all their distress *and* troubles.
18 The Lord is close to those who are of a broken heart
and saves such as are crushed with sorrow for sin *and* are
humbly *and* thoroughly penitent.
19 Many evils confront the [consistently] righteous, but
the Lord delivers him out of them all.
20 He keeps all his bones; not one of them is broken.
21 Evil shall cause the death of the wicked; and they who
hate the just *and* righteous shall be held guilty *and* shall
be condemned.
22 The Lord redeems the lives of His servants, and none
of those who take refuge *and* trust in Him shall be condemned *or* held guilty.

---

*a* This psalm is an acrostic poem, the verses of which begin with the
successive letters of the Hebrew alphabet.    *b* In Hebrew texts 34:1-22
is numbered 34:2-23.

*a* See footnote on Gen. 16:7.

## New International Version

### Psalm 35

#### Of David.

[1] Contend, LORD, with those who contend with me;
  fight against those who fight against me.
[2] Take up shield and armor;
  arise and come to my aid.
[3] Brandish spear and javelin[a]
  against those who pursue me.
Say to me,
  "I am your salvation."

[4] May those who seek my life
  be disgraced and put to shame;
may those who plot my ruin
  be turned back in dismay.
[5] May they be like chaff before the wind,
  with the angel of the LORD driving them away;
[6] may their path be dark and slippery,
  with the angel of the LORD pursuing them.

[7] Since they hid their net for me without cause
  and without cause dug a pit for me,
[8] may ruin overtake them by surprise—
  may the net they hid entangle them,
  may they fall into the pit, to their ruin.
[9] Then my soul will rejoice in the LORD
  and delight in his salvation.
[10] My whole being will exclaim,
  "Who is like you, LORD?
You rescue the poor from those too strong for them,
  the poor and needy from those who rob them."

[11] Ruthless witnesses come forward;
  they question me on things I know nothing about.
[12] They repay me evil for good
  and leave me like one bereaved.
[13] Yet when they were ill, I put on sackcloth
  and humbled myself with fasting.
When my prayers returned to me unanswered,
[14]   I went about mourning
  as though for my friend or brother.
I bowed my head in grief
  as though weeping for my mother.
[15] But when I stumbled, they gathered in glee;
  assailants gathered against me without my
    knowledge.
  They slandered me without ceasing.
[16] Like the ungodly they maliciously mocked;[b]
  they gnashed their teeth at me.

[17] How long, Lord, will you look on?
  Rescue me from their ravages,
  my precious life from these lions.
[18] I will give you thanks in the great assembly;
  among the throngs I will praise you.
[19] Do not let those gloat over me
  who are my enemies without cause;
do not let those who hate me without reason
  maliciously wink the eye.
[20] They do not speak peaceably,
  but devise false accusations
  against those who live quietly in the land.
[21] They sneer at me and say, "Aha! Aha!
  With our own eyes we have seen it."

[22] LORD, you have seen this; do not be silent.
  Do not be far from me, Lord.
[23] Awake, and rise to my defense!
  Contend for me, my God and Lord.
[24] Vindicate me in your righteousness, LORD my God;
  do not let them gloat over me.

## Amplified Bible

### Psalm 35

#### [A Psalm] of David.

[1] Contend, O lord, with those who contend with me;
fight against those who fight against me!
[2] Take hold of shield and buckler, and stand up for my
help!
[3] Draw out also the spear and javelin *and* close up the
way of those who pursue *and* persecute me. Say to me, I
am your deliverance!
[4] Let them be put to shame and dishonor who seek *and*
require my life; let them be turned back and confounded
who plan my hurt!
[5] Let them be as chaff before the wind, with the [a]Angel
of the Lord driving them on!
[6] Let their way be through dark and slippery places,
with the Angel of the Lord pursuing *and* afflicting them.
[7] For without cause they hid for me their net; a pit of
destruction without cause they dug for my life.
[8] Let destruction befall [my foe] unawares; let the net
he hid for me catch him; let him fall into that very destruction.
[9] Then I shall be joyful in the Lord; I shall rejoice in His
deliverance.
[10] All my bones shall say, Lord, who is like You, You
Who deliver the poor *and* the afflicted from him who is
too strong for him, yes, the poor and the needy from him
who snatches away his goods?
[11] Malicious *and* unrighteous witnesses rise up; they ask
me of things that I know not.
[12] They reward me evil for good to my personal bereavement.
[13] But as for me, when they were sick, my clothing was
sackcloth; I afflicted myself with fasting, and I prayed with
head bowed on my breast.
[14] I behaved as if grieving for my friend *or* my brother;
I bowed down in sorrow, as one who bewails his mother.
[15] But in my stumbling *and* limping they rejoiced and
gathered together [against me]; the smiters (slanderers
and revilers) gathered against me, and I knew them not;
they ceased not to slander *and* revile me.
[16] Like profane mockers at feasts [making sport for the
price of a cake] they gnashed at me with their teeth.
[17] Lord, how long will You look on [without action]? Rescue my life from their destructions, my dear *and* only life
from the lions!
[18] I will give You thanks in the great assembly; I will
praise You among a mighty throng.
[19] Let not those who are wrongfully my foes rejoice over
me; neither let them wink with the eye who hate me without cause. [John 15:24, 25.]
[20] For they do not speak peace, but they devise deceitful
matters against those who are quiet in the land.
[21] Yes, they open their mouths wide against me; they
say, Aha! Aha! Our eyes have seen it!
[22] You have seen this, O Lord; keep not silence! O Lord,
be not far from me!
[23] Arouse Yourself, awake to the justice due me, even to
my cause, my God and my Lord!
[24] Judge *and* vindicate me, O Lord my God, according
to Your righteousness (Your rightness and justice); and
let [my foes] not rejoice over me!

---

*a* 3 Or *and block the way*    *b* 16 Septuagint; Hebrew may mean *Like an*
*ungodly circle of mockers,*

*a* See footnote on Gen. 16:7.

## New International Version

25 Do not let them think, "Aha, just what we wanted!"
or say, "We have swallowed him up."

26 May all who gloat over my distress
be put to shame and confusion;
may all who exalt themselves over me
be clothed with shame and disgrace.

27 May those who delight in my vindication
shout for joy and gladness;
may they always say, "The LORD be exalted,
who delights in the well-being of his servant."

28 My tongue will proclaim your righteousness,
your praises all day long.

### Psalm 36[a]

*For the director of music. Of David the servant of the LORD.*

1 I have a message from God in my heart
concerning the sinfulness of the wicked:[b]
There is no fear of God
before their eyes.

2 In their own eyes they flatter themselves
too much to detect or hate their sin.

3 The words of their mouths are wicked and deceitful;
they fail to act wisely or do good.

4 Even on their beds they plot evil;
they commit themselves to a sinful course
and do not reject what is wrong.

5 Your love, LORD, reaches to the heavens,
your faithfulness to the skies.

6 Your righteousness is like the highest mountains,
your justice like the great deep.
You, LORD, preserve both people and animals.

7 How priceless is your unfailing love, O God!
People take refuge in the shadow of your wings.

8 They feast on the abundance of your house;
you give them drink from your river of delights.

9 For with you is the fountain of life;
in your light we see light.

10 Continue your love to those who know you,
your righteousness to the upright in heart.

11 May the foot of the proud not come against me,
nor the hand of the wicked drive me away.

12 See how the evildoers lie fallen—
thrown down, not able to rise!

### Psalm 37[c]

*Of David.*

1 Do not fret because of those who are evil
or be envious of those who do wrong;

2 for like the grass they will soon wither,
like green plants they will soon die away.

3 Trust in the LORD and do good;
dwell in the land and enjoy safe pasture.

4 Take delight in the LORD,
and he will give you the desires of your heart.

5 Commit your way to the LORD;
trust in him and he will do this:

## Amplified Bible

25 Let them not say in their hearts, Aha, that is what we wanted! Let them not say, We have swallowed him up *and* utterly destroyed him.

26 Let them be put to shame and confusion together who rejoice at my calamity! Let them be clothed with shame and dishonor who magnify *and* exalt themselves over me!

27 Let those who favor my righteous cause *and* have pleasure in my uprightness shout for joy and be glad and say continually, Let the Lord be magnified, Who takes pleasure in the prosperity of His servant.

28 And my tongue shall talk of Your righteousness, rightness, *and* justice, and of [my reasons for] Your praise all the day long.

### Psalm 36

To the Chief Musician. [A Psalm] of David the servant
of the Lord.

1 Transgression [like an oracle] speaks to the wicked deep in his heart. There is no fear *or* dread of God before his eyes. [Rom. 3:18.]

2 For he flatters *and* deceives himself in his own eyes that his iniquity will not be found out and be hated.

3 The words of his mouth are wrong and deceitful; he has ceased to be wise *and* to do good.

4 He plans wrongdoing on his bed; he sets himself in a way that is not good; he does not reject *or* despise evil.

5 Your mercy *and* loving-kindness, O Lord, extend to the skies, *and* Your faithfulness to the clouds.

6 Your righteousness is like the mountains of God, Your judgments are like the great deep. O Lord, You preserve man and beast.

7 How precious is Your steadfast love, O God! The children of men take refuge *and* put their trust under the shadow of Your wings.

8 They relish *and* feast on the abundance of Your house; and You cause them to drink of the stream of Your pleasures.

9 For with You is the fountain of life; in Your light do we see light. [John 4:10, 14.]

10 O continue Your loving-kindness to those who know You, Your righteousness (salvation) to the upright in heart.

11 Let not the foot of pride overtake me, and let not the hand of the wicked drive me away.

12 There the workers of iniquity fall *and* lie prostrate; they are thrust down and shall not be able to rise.

### Psalm 37

[A Psalm] of David.

1 Fret not yourself because of evildoers, neither be envious against those who work unrighteousness (that which is not upright or in right standing with God).

2 For they shall soon be cut down like the grass, and wither as the green herb.

3 Trust (lean on, rely on, and be confident) in the Lord and do good; so shall you dwell in the land and feed surely on His faithfulness, *and* truly you shall be fed.

4 Delight yourself also in the Lord, and He will give you the desires *and* secret petitions of your heart.

5 Commit your way to the Lord [roll and repose each care of your load on Him]; trust (lean on, rely on, and be confident) also in Him and He will bring it to pass.

---

[a] In Hebrew texts 36:1-12 is numbered 36:2-13.    [b] 1 Or *A message from God: The transgression of the wicked / resides in their hearts.*    [c] This psalm is an acrostic poem, the stanzas of which begin with the successive letters of the Hebrew alphabet.

## New International Version

6 He will make your righteous reward shine like the
        dawn,
    your vindication like the noonday sun.

7 Be still before the Lord
    and wait patiently for him;
  do not fret when people succeed in their ways,
    when they carry out their wicked schemes.

8 Refrain from anger and turn from wrath;
    do not fret—it leads only to evil.
9 For those who are evil will be destroyed,
    but those who hope in the Lord will inherit the land.

10 A little while, and the wicked will be no more;
    though you look for them, they will not be found.
11 But the meek will inherit the land
    and enjoy peace and prosperity.

12 The wicked plot against the righteous
    and gnash their teeth at them;
13 but the Lord laughs at the wicked,
    for he knows their day is coming.

14 The wicked draw the sword
    and bend the bow
  to bring down the poor and needy,
    to slay those whose ways are upright.
15 But their swords will pierce their own hearts,
    and their bows will be broken.

16 Better the little that the righteous have
    than the wealth of many wicked;
17 for the power of the wicked will be broken,
    but the Lord upholds the righteous.

18 The blameless spend their days under the Lord's care,
    and their inheritance will endure forever.
19 In times of disaster they will not wither;
    in days of famine they will enjoy plenty.

20 But the wicked will perish:
    Though the Lord's enemies are like the flowers of
        the field,
    they will be consumed, they will go up in smoke.

21 The wicked borrow and do not repay,
    but the righteous give generously;
22 those the Lord blesses will inherit the land,
    but those he curses will be destroyed.

23 The Lord makes firm the steps
    of the one who delights in him;
24 though he may stumble, he will not fall,
    for the Lord upholds him with his hand.

25 I was young and now I am old,
    yet I have never seen the righteous forsaken
    or their children begging bread.
26 They are always generous and lend freely;
    their children will be a blessing.[a]

27 Turn from evil and do good;
    then you will dwell in the land forever.
28 For the Lord loves the just
    and will not forsake his faithful ones.

  Wrongdoers will be completely destroyed[b];
    the offspring of the wicked will perish.
29 The righteous will inherit the land
    and dwell in it forever.

30 The mouths of the righteous utter wisdom,
    and their tongues speak what is just.
31 The law of their God is in their hearts;
    their feet do not slip.

## Amplified Bible

6 And He will make your uprightness and right standing with God go forth as the light, and your justice and right as [the shining sun of] the noonday.
7 Be still and rest in the Lord; wait for Him and patiently lean yourself upon Him; fret not yourself because of him who prospers in his way, because of the man who brings wicked devices to pass.
8 Cease from anger and forsake wrath; fret not yourself—it tends only to evildoing.
9 For evildoers shall be cut off, but those who wait and hope for the Lord [in the end] shall inherit the earth. [Isa. 57:13c.]
10 For yet a little while, and the evildoers will be no more; though you look with care where they used to be, they will not be found. [Heb. 10:36, 37; Rev. 21:7, 8.]
11 But the meek [in the end] shall inherit the earth and shall delight themselves in the abundance of peace. [Ps. 37:29; Matt. 5:5.]
12 The wicked plot against the [uncompromisingly] righteous (the upright in right standing with God); they gnash at them with their teeth.
13 The Lord laughs at [the wicked], for He sees that their own day [of defeat] is coming.
14 The wicked draw the sword and bend their bows to cast down the poor and needy, to slay those who walk uprightly (blameless in conduct and in conversation).
15 The swords [of the wicked] shall enter their own hearts, and their bows shall be broken.
16 Better is the little that the [uncompromisingly] righteous have than the abundance [of possessions] of many who are wrong and wicked. [I Tim. 6:6, 7.]
17 For the arms of the wicked shall be broken, but the Lord upholds the [consistently] righteous.
18 The Lord knows the days of the upright and blameless, and their heritage will abide forever.
19 They shall not be put to shame in the time of evil; and in the days of famine they shall be satisfied.
20 But the wicked shall perish, and the enemies of the Lord shall be as the fat of lambs [that is consumed in smoke] and as the glory of the pastures. They shall vanish; like smoke shall they consume away.
21 The wicked borrow and pay not again [for they may be unable], but the [uncompromisingly] righteous deal kindly and give [for they are able].
22 For such as are blessed of God shall [in the end] inherit the earth, but they that are cursed of Him shall be cut off. [Isa. 57:13c.]
23 The steps of a [good] man are directed and established by the Lord when He delights in his way [and He busies Himself with his every step].
24 Though he falls, he shall not be utterly cast down, for the Lord grasps his hand in support and upholds him.
25 I have been young and now am old, yet have I not seen the [uncompromisingly] righteous forsaken or their seed begging bread.
26 All day long they are merciful and deal graciously; they lend, and their offspring are blessed.
27 Depart from evil and do good; and you will dwell forever [securely].
28 For the Lord delights in justice and forsakes not His saints; they are preserved forever, but the offspring of the wicked [in time] shall be cut off.
29 [Then] the [consistently] righteous shall inherit the land and dwell upon it forever.
30 The mouth of the [uncompromisingly] righteous utters wisdom, and his tongue speaks with justice.
31 The law of his God is in his heart; none of his steps shall slide.

---

a 26 Or freely; / the names of their children will be used in blessings (see Gen. 48:20); or freely; / others will see that their children are blessed
b 28 See Septuagint; Hebrew They will be protected forever

## New International Version

32 The wicked lie in wait for the righteous,
   intent on putting them to death;
33 but the LORD will not leave them in the power of the
   wicked
   or let them be condemned when brought to trial.

34 Hope in the LORD
   and keep his way.
He will exalt you to inherit the land;
   when the wicked are destroyed, you will see it.

35 I have seen a wicked and ruthless man
   flourishing like a luxuriant native tree,
36 but he soon passed away and was no more;
   though I looked for him, he could not be found.

37 Consider the blameless, observe the upright;
   a future awaits those who seek peace.[a]
38 But all sinners will be destroyed;
   there will be no future[b] for the wicked.

39 The salvation of the righteous comes from the LORD;
   he is their stronghold in time of trouble.
40 The LORD helps them and delivers them;
   he delivers them from the wicked and saves them,
   because they take refuge in him.

### Psalm 38[c]

*A psalm of David. A petition.*

1 LORD, do not rebuke me in your anger
   or discipline me in your wrath.
2 Your arrows have pierced me,
   and your hand has come down on me.
3 Because of your wrath there is no health in my body;
   there is no soundness in my bones because of my
   sin.
4 My guilt has overwhelmed me
   like a burden too heavy to bear.

5 My wounds fester and are loathsome
   because of my sinful folly.
6 I am bowed down and brought very low;
   all day long I go about mourning.
7 My back is filled with searing pain;
   there is no health in my body.
8 I am feeble and utterly crushed;
   I groan in anguish of heart.

9 All my longings lie open before you, Lord;
   my sighing is not hidden from you.
10 My heart pounds, my strength fails me;
   even the light has gone from my eyes.
11 My friends and companions avoid me because of my
   wounds;
   my neighbors stay far away.
12 Those who want to kill me set their traps,
   those who would harm me talk of my ruin;
   all day long they scheme and lie.

13 I am like the deaf, who cannot hear,
   like the mute, who cannot speak;
14 I have become like one who does not hear,
   whose mouth can offer no reply.
15 LORD, I wait for you;
   you will answer, Lord my God.
16 For I said, "Do not let them gloat
   or exalt themselves over me when my feet slip."

17 For I am about to fall,
   and my pain is ever with me.
18 I confess my iniquity;
   I am troubled by my sin.

## Amplified Bible

32 The wicked lie in wait for the [uncompromisingly]
righteous and seek to put them to death.
33 The Lord will not leave them in their hands, or [suffer
them to] condemn them when they are judged.
34 Wait for *and* expect the Lord and keep *and* heed His
way, and He will exalt you to inherit the land; [in the end]
when the wicked are cut off, you shall see it.
35 I have seen a wicked man in great power and spreading himself like a green tree in its native soil,
36 Yet he passed away, and behold, he was not; yes, I
sought *and* inquired for him, but he could not be found.
37 Mark the blameless man and behold the upright, for
there is a happy end for the man of peace.
38 As for transgressors, they shall be destroyed together; in the end the wicked shall be cut off.
39 But the salvation of the [consistently] righteous is of
the Lord; He is their Refuge *and* secure Stronghold in the
time of trouble.
40 And the Lord helps them and delivers them; He delivers them from the wicked and saves them, because they
trust *and* take refuge in Him.

### Psalm 38

A Psalm of David; to bring to remembrance
*and* make memorial.

1 O Lord, rebuke me not in Your wrath, neither chasten
me in Your hot displeasure.
2 For Your arrows have sunk into me *and* stick fast, and
Your hand has come down upon me *and* pressed me sorely.
3 There is no soundness in my flesh because of Your indignation; neither is there any health *or* rest in my bones
because of my sin.
4 For my iniquities have gone over my head [like waves
of a flood]; as a heavy burden they weigh too much for me.
5 My wounds are loathsome and corrupt because of my
foolishness.
6 I am bent and bowed down greatly; I go about mourning all the day long.
7 For my loins are filled with burning; and there is no
soundness in my flesh.
8 I am faint and sorely bruised [deadly cold and quite
worn out]; I groan by reason of the disquiet *and* moaning
of my heart.
9 Lord, all my desire is before You; and my sighing is not
hidden from You.
10 My heart throbs, my strength fails me; as for the light
of my eyes, it also is gone from me.
11 My lovers and my friends stand aloof from my plague;
and my neighbors *and* my near ones stand afar off. [Luke
23:49.]
12 They also that seek *and* demand my life lay snares for
me, and they that seek *and* require my hurt speak crafty
*and* mischievous things; they meditate treachery *and* deceit all the day long.
13 But I, like a deaf man, hear not; and I am like a dumb
man who opens not his mouth.
14 Yes, I have become like a man who hears not, in whose
mouth are no arguments *or* replies.
15 For in You, O Lord, do I hope; You will answer, O Lord
my God.
16 For I pray, Let them not rejoice over me, who when my
foot slips boast against me.
17 For I am ready to halt *and* fall; my pain *and* sorrow are
continually before me.
18 For I do confess my guilt *and* iniquity; I am filled with
sorrow for my sin. [II Cor. 7:9, 10.]

---

[a] 37 Or *upright; / those who seek peace will have posterity*
[b] 38 Or *posterity*    [c] In Hebrew texts 38:1-22 is numbered 38:2-23.

## New International Version

¹⁹Many have become my enemies without cause*ᵃ*;
 those who hate me without reason are numerous.
²⁰Those who repay my good with evil
 lodge accusations against me,
 though I seek only to do what is good.
²¹Lᴏʀᴅ, do not forsake me;
 do not be far from me, my God.
²²Come quickly to help me,
 my Lord and my Savior.

### Psalm 39ᵇ

*For the director of music. For Jeduthun. A psalm of David.*

¹I said, "I will watch my ways
 and keep my tongue from sin;
I will put a muzzle on my mouth
 while in the presence of the wicked."
²So I remained utterly silent,
 not even saying anything good.
But my anguish increased;
³ my heart grew hot within me.
While I meditated, the fire burned;
 then I spoke with my tongue:

⁴"Show me, Lᴏʀᴅ, my life's end
 and the number of my days;
 let me know how fleeting my life is.
⁵You have made my days a mere handbreadth;
 the span of my years is as nothing before you.
Everyone is but a breath,
 even those who seem secure.*ᶜ*

⁶"Surely everyone goes around like a mere phantom;
 in vain they rush about, heaping up wealth
 without knowing whose it will finally be.

⁷"But now, Lord, what do I look for?
 My hope is in you.
⁸Save me from all my transgressions;
 do not make me the scorn of fools.
⁹I was silent; I would not open my mouth,
 for you are the one who has done this.
¹⁰Remove your scourge from me;
 I am overcome by the blow of your hand.
¹¹When you rebuke and discipline anyone for their sin,
 you consume their wealth like a moth—
 surely everyone is but a breath.

¹²"Hear my prayer, Lᴏʀᴅ,
 listen to my cry for help;
 do not be deaf to my weeping.
I dwell with you as a foreigner,
 a stranger, as all my ancestors were.
¹³Look away from me, that I may enjoy life again
 before I depart and am no more."

### Psalm 40ᵈ

*For the director of music. Of David. A psalm.*

¹I waited patiently for the Lᴏʀᴅ;
 he turned to me and heard my cry.
²He lifted me out of the slimy pit,
 out of the mud and mire;
he set my feet on a rock
 and gave me a firm place to stand.
³He put a new song in my mouth,
 a hymn of praise to our God.
Many will see and fear the Lᴏʀᴅ
 and put their trust in him.

## Amplified Bible

¹⁹But my enemies are vigorous *and* strong, and those
who hate me wrongfully are multiplied.
²⁰They also that render evil for good are adversaries to
me, because I follow the thing that is good.
²¹Forsake me not, O Lord; O my God, be not far from
me.
²²Make haste to help me, O Lord, my Salvation.

### Psalm 39

To the Chief Musician; for Jeduthun [founder of an official
musical family]. A Psalm of David.

¹I said, I will take heed *and* guard my ways, that I may
sin not with my tongue; I will muzzle my mouth as with a
bridle while the wicked are before me.
²I was dumb with silence, I held my peace without profit
and had no comfort away from good, while my distress
was renewed.
³My heart was hot within me. While I was musing, the
fire burned; then I spoke with my tongue:
⁴Lord, make me to know my end and [to appreciate] the
measure of my days—what it is; let me know *and* realize
how frail I am [how transient is my stay here].
⁵Behold, You have made my days as [short as] hand-
breadths, and my lifetime as nothing in Your sight. Truly every man at his best is merely a breath! Selah [pause,
and think calmly of that]!
⁶Surely every man walks to and fro—like a shadow in
a pantomime; surely for futility *and* emptiness he is in
turmoil; each one heaps up riches, not knowing who will
gather them. [I Cor. 7:31; James 4:14.]
⁷And now, Lord, what do I wait for *and* expect? My hope
*and* expectation are in You.
⁸Deliver me from all my transgressions; make me not
the scorn *and* reproach of the [self-confident] fool!
⁹I am dumb, I open not my mouth, for it is You Who
has done it.
¹⁰Remove Your stroke away from me; I am consumed by
the conflict *and* the blow of Your hand.
¹¹When with rebukes You correct *and* chasten man for
sin, You waste his beauty like a moth *and* what is dear to
him consumes away; surely every man is a mere breath.
Selah [pause, and think calmly of that]!
¹²Hear my prayer, O Lord, and give ear to my cry; hold
not Your peace at my tears! For I am Your passing guest, a
temporary resident, as all my fathers were.
¹³O look away from me *and* spare me, that I may recover
cheerfulness *and* encouraging strength *and* know gladness before I go and am no more!

### Psalm 40

To the Chief Musician. A Psalm of David.

¹I waited patiently *and* expectantly for the Lord; and He
inclined to me and heard my cry.
²He drew me up out of a horrible pit [a pit of tumult and
of destruction], out of the miry clay (froth and slime), and
set my feet upon a rock, steadying my steps *and* establishing my goings.
³And He has put a new song in my mouth, a song of
praise to our God. Many shall see and fear (revere and
worship) and put their trust *and* confident reliance in the
Lord. [Ps. 5:11.]

---

*ᵃ 19* One Dead Sea Scrolls manuscript; Masoretic Text *my vigorous*
*enemies*    *ᵇ* In Hebrew texts 39:1-13 is numbered 39:2-14.    *ᶜ 5* The
Hebrew has *Selah* (a word of uncertain meaning) here and at the end of
verse 11.    *ᵈ* In Hebrew texts 40:1-17 is numbered 40:2-18.

## New International Version

[4] Blessed is the one
    who trusts in the LORD,
who does not look to the proud,
    to those who turn aside to false gods.[a]
[5] Many, LORD my God,
    are the wonders you have done,
    the things you planned for us.
None can compare with you;
    were I to speak and tell of your deeds,
    they would be too many to declare.

[6] Sacrifice and offering you did not desire—
    but my ears you have opened[b]—
    burnt offerings and sin offerings[c] you did not
      require.
[7] Then I said, "Here I am, I have come—
    it is written about me in the scroll.[d]
[8] I desire to do your will, my God;
    your law is within my heart."

[9] I proclaim your saving acts in the great assembly;
    I do not seal my lips, LORD,
    as you know.
[10] I do not hide your righteousness in my heart;
    I speak of your faithfulness and your saving help.
I do not conceal your love and your faithfulness
    from the great assembly.

[11] Do not withhold your mercy from me, LORD;
    may your love and faithfulness always protect me.
[12] For troubles without number surround me;
    my sins have overtaken me, and I cannot see.
They are more than the hairs of my head,
    and my heart fails within me.
[13] Be pleased to save me, LORD;
    come quickly, LORD, to help me.

[14] May all who want to take my life
    be put to shame and confusion;
may all who desire my ruin
    be turned back in disgrace.
[15] May those who say to me, "Aha! Aha!"
    be appalled at their own shame.
[16] But may all who seek you
    rejoice and be glad in you;
may those who long for your saving help always say,
    "The LORD is great!"

[17] But as for me, I am poor and needy;
    may the Lord think of me.
You are my help and my deliverer;
    you are my God, do not delay.

## Amplified Bible

[4] Blessed (happy, fortunate, to be envied) is the man who makes the Lord his refuge *and* trust, and turns not to the proud or to followers of false gods.
[5] Many, O Lord my God, are the wonderful works which You have done, and Your thoughts toward us; no one can compare with You! If I should declare and speak of them, they are too many to be numbered.
[6] Sacrifice and offering You do not desire, *nor* have You delight in them; You have given me the capacity to hear *and* obey [Your law, a more valuable service than] burnt offerings and sin offerings [which] You do not require.
[7] Then said I, Behold, I come; in the volume of the book it is written of me;
[8] I delight to do Your will, O my God; yes, Your law is within my heart. [Heb. 10:5-9.]
[9] I have proclaimed glad tidings of righteousness in the great assembly [tidings of uprightness and right standing with God]. Behold, I have not restrained my lips, as You know, O Lord.
[10] I have not concealed Your righteousness within my heart; I have proclaimed Your faithfulness and Your salvation. I have not hid away Your steadfast love and Your truth from the great assembly. [Acts 20:20, 27.]
[11] Withhold not Your tender mercy from me, O Lord; let Your loving-kindness and Your truth continually preserve me!
[12] For innumerable evils have compassed me about; my iniquities have taken such hold on me that I am not able to look up. They are more than the hairs of my head, and my heart has failed me *and* forsaken me.
[13] Be pleased, O Lord, to deliver me; O Lord, make haste to help me!
[14] Let them be put to shame and confounded together who seek *and* require my life to destroy it; let them be driven backward and brought to dishonor who wish me evil *and* delight in my hurt!
[15] Let them be desolate by reason of their shame who say to me, Aha, aha!
[16] Let all those that seek *and* require You rejoice and be glad in You; let such as love Your salvation say continually, The Lord be magnified!
[17] [As for me] I am poor and needy, yet the Lord takes thought *and* plans for me. You are my Help and my Deliverer. O my God, do not tarry! [Ps. 70:1-5; I Pet. 5:7.]

---

### Psalm 41[e]

*For the director of music. A psalm of David.*

[1] Blessed are those who have regard for the weak;
    the LORD delivers them in times of trouble.
[2] The LORD protects and preserves them—
    they are counted among the blessed in the land—
    he does not give them over to the desire of their
      foes.
[3] The LORD sustains them on their sickbed
    and restores them from their bed of illness.

[4] I said, "Have mercy on me, LORD;
    heal me, for I have sinned against you."

### Psalm 41

To the Chief Musician. A Psalm of David.

[1] Blessed (happy, fortunate, to be envied) is he who considers the weak *and* the poor; the Lord will deliver him in the time of evil *and* trouble.
[2] The Lord will protect him and keep him alive; he shall be called blessed in the land; and You will not deliver him to the will of his enemies.
[3] The Lord will sustain, refresh, *and* strengthen him on his bed of languishing; all his bed You [O Lord] will turn, change, *and* transform in his illness.
[4] I said, Lord, be merciful *and* gracious to me; heal my inner self, for I have sinned against You.

---

[a] 4 Or *to lies*   [b] 6 Hebrew; some Septuagint manuscripts *but a body you have prepared for me*   [c] 6 Or *purification offerings*   [d] 7 Or *come / with the scroll written for me*   [e] In Hebrew texts 41:1-13 is numbered 41:2-14.

## New International Version

5 My enemies say of me in malice,
  "When will he die and his name perish?"
6 When one of them comes to see me,
  he speaks falsely, while his heart gathers slander;
  then he goes out and spreads it around.

7 All my enemies whisper together against me;
  they imagine the worst for me, saying,
8 "A vile disease has afflicted him;
  he will never get up from the place where he lies."
9 Even my close friend,
  someone I trusted,
  one who shared my bread,
  has turned[a] against me.

10 But may you have mercy on me, LORD;
  raise me up, that I may repay them.
11 I know that you are pleased with me,
  for my enemy does not triumph over me.
12 Because of my integrity you uphold me
  and set me in your presence forever.

13 Praise be to the LORD, the God of Israel,
  from everlasting to everlasting.
    Amen and Amen.

### BOOK II

*Psalms 42–72*

### Psalm 42[b,c]

*For the director of music. A* maskil[d] *of the Sons of Korah.*

1 As the deer pants for streams of water,
  so my soul pants for you, my God.
2 My soul thirsts for God, for the living God.
  When can I go and meet with God?
3 My tears have been my food
  day and night,
  while people say to me all day long,
  "Where is your God?"
4 These things I remember
  as I pour out my soul:
  how I used to go to the house of God
  under the protection of the Mighty One[e]
  with shouts of joy and praise
  among the festive throng.

5 Why, my soul, are you downcast?
  Why so disturbed within me?
  Put your hope in God,
  for I will yet praise him,
  my Savior and my God.

6 My soul is downcast within me;
  therefore I will remember you
  from the land of the Jordan,
  the heights of Hermon—from Mount Mizar.
7 Deep calls to deep
  in the roar of your waterfalls;
  all your waves and breakers
  have swept over me.

8 By day the LORD directs his love,
  at night his song is with me—
  a prayer to the God of my life.

9 I say to God my Rock,
  "Why have you forgotten me?
  Why must I go about mourning,
  oppressed by the enemy?"

## Amplified Bible

5 My enemies speak evil of me, [saying], When will he
die and his name perish?
6 And when one comes to see me, he speaks falsehood
*and* empty words, while his heart gathers mischievous
gossip [against me]; when he goes away, he tells it abroad.
7 All who hate me whisper together about me; against
me do they devise my hurt [imagining the worst for me].
8 An evil disease, say they, is poured out upon him *and*
cleaves fast to him; and now that he is bedfast, he will not
rise up again.
9 Even my own familiar friend, in whom I trusted (relied
on and was confident), who ate of my bread, has lifted up
his heel against me. [John 13:18.]
10 But You, O Lord, be merciful *and* gracious to me, and
raise me up, that I may requite them.
11 By this I know that You favor *and* delight in me, because my enemy does not triumph over me.
12 And as for me, You have upheld me in my integrity and
set me in Your presence forever.
13 Blessed be the Lord, the God of Israel, from everlasting and to everlasting [from this age to the next, and for-
ever]! Amen and Amen (so be it).

### BOOK TWO

### Psalm 42

To the Chief Musician. A skillful song, *or* a didactic *or*
reflective poem, of the sons of Korah.

1 As the hart pants *and* longs for the water brooks, so I
pant *and* long for You, O God.
2 My inner self thirsts for God, for the living God. When
shall I come and behold the face of God? [John 7:37;
I Thess. 1:9, 10.]
3 My tears have been my food day and night, while men
say to me all day long, Where is your God?
4 These things I [earnestly] remember and pour myself
out within me: how I went slowly before the throng and
led them in procession to the house of God [like a band-
master before his band, timing the steps to the sound of
music and the chant of song], with the voice of shouting
and praise, a throng keeping festival.
5 Why are you cast down, O my inner self? And why
should you moan over me *and* be disquieted within me?
Hope in God *and* wait expectantly for Him, for I shall yet
praise Him, my Help and my God.
6 O my God, my life is cast down upon me [and I find the
burden more than I can bear]; therefore will I [earnestly]
remember You from the land of the Jordan [River] and the
[summits of Mount] Hermon, from the little mountain
Mizar.
7 [Roaring] deep calls to [roaring] deep at the thunder
of Your waterspouts; all Your breakers and Your rolling
waves have gone over me.
8 Yet the Lord will command His loving-kindness in the
daytime, and in the night His song shall be with me, a
prayer to the God of my life.
9 I will say to God my Rock, Why have You forgotten
me? Why go I mourning because of the oppression of the
enemy?

---

*a* 9 Hebrew *has lifted up his heel*    *b* In many Hebrew manuscripts Psalms
42 and 43 constitute one psalm.    *c* In Hebrew texts 42:1-11 is numbered
42:2-12.    *d* Title: Probably a literary or musical term    *e* 4 See
Septuagint and Syriac; the meaning of the Hebrew for this line is uncertain.

## New International Version

10 My bones suffer mortal agony
    as my foes taunt me,
saying to me all day long,
    "Where is your God?"
11 Why, my soul, are you downcast?
    Why so disturbed within me?
Put your hope in God,
    for I will yet praise him,
    my Savior and my God.

### Psalm 43[a]

1 Vindicate me, my God,
    and plead my cause
    against an unfaithful nation.
Rescue me from those who are
    deceitful and wicked.
2 You are God my stronghold.
    Why have you rejected me?
Why must I go about mourning,
    oppressed by the enemy?
3 Send me your light and your faithful care,
    let them lead me;
let them bring me to your holy mountain,
    to the place where you dwell.
4 Then I will go to the altar of God,
    to God, my joy and my delight.
I will praise you with the lyre,
    O God, my God.

5 Why, my soul, are you downcast?
    Why so disturbed within me?
Put your hope in God,
    for I will yet praise him,
    my Savior and my God.

### Psalm 44[b]

*For the director of music. Of the Sons of Korah. A maskil.[c]*

1 We have heard it with our ears, O God;
    our ancestors have told us
what you did in their days,
    in days long ago.
2 With your hand you drove out the nations
    and planted our ancestors;
you crushed the peoples
    and made our ancestors flourish.
3 It was not by their sword that they won the land,
    nor did their arm bring them victory;
it was your right hand, your arm,
    and the light of your face, for you loved them.

4 You are my King and my God,
    who decrees[d] victories for Jacob.
5 Through you we push back our enemies;
    through your name we trample our foes.
6 I put no trust in my bow,
    my sword does not bring me victory;
7 but you give us victory over our enemies,
    you put our adversaries to shame.
8 In God we make our boast all day long,
    and we will praise your name forever.[e]

9 But now you have rejected and humbled us;
    you no longer go out with our armies.
10 You made us retreat before the enemy,
    and our adversaries have plundered us.

## Amplified Bible

10 As with a sword [crushing] in my bones, my enemies taunt *and* reproach me, while they say continually to me, Where is your God?
11 Why are you cast down, O my inner self? And why should you moan over me *and* be disquieted within me? Hope in God *and* wait expectantly for Him, for I shall yet praise Him, Who is the help of my countenance, and my God.

### Psalm 43

1 Judge *and* vindicate me, O God; plead and defend my cause against an ungodly nation. O deliver me from the deceitful and unjust man!
2 For You are the God of my strength [my Stronghold—in Whom I take refuge]; why have You cast me off? Why go I mourning because of the oppression of the enemy?
3 O send out Your light and Your truth, let them lead me; let them bring me to Your holy hill and to Your dwelling.
4 Then will I go to the altar of God, to God, my exceeding joy; yes, with the lyre will I praise You, O God, my God!
5 Why are you cast down, O my inner self? And why should you moan over me *and* be disquieted within me? Hope in God *and* wait expectantly for Him, for I shall yet praise Him, Who is the help of my [sad] countenance, and my God.

### Psalm 44

To the Chief Musician. [A Psalm] of the sons of Korah. A skillful song, *or* a didactic *or* reflective poem.

1 We have heard with our ears, O God; our fathers have told us [what] work You did in their days, in the days of old.
2 You drove out the nations with Your hand *and* it was Your power that gave [Israel] a home by rooting out the [heathen] peoples, but [Israel] You spread out.
3 For they got not the land [of Canaan] in possession by their own sword, neither did their own arm save them; but Your right hand and Your arm and the light of Your countenance [did it], because You were favorable toward *and* did delight in them.
4 You are my King, O God; command victories *and* deliverance for Jacob (Israel).
5 Through You shall we push down our enemies; through Your name shall we tread them under who rise up against us.
6 For I will not trust in *and* lean on my bow, neither shall my sword save me.
7 But You have saved us from our foes and have put them to shame who hate us.
8 In God we have made our boast all the day long, and we will give thanks to Your name forever. Selah [pause, and calmly think of that]!
9 But now You have cast us off and brought us to dishonor, and You go not out with our armies.
10 You make us to turn back from the enemy, and they who hate us take spoil for themselves.

---

*a* In many Hebrew manuscripts Psalms 42 and 43 constitute one psalm.   *b* In Hebrew texts 44:1-26 is numbered 44:2-27.   *c* Title: Probably a literary or musical term   *d 4* Septuagint, Aquila and Syriac; Hebrew *King, O God; / command*   *e 8* The Hebrew has *Selah* (a word of uncertain meaning) here.

# New International Version

[11] You gave us up to be devoured like sheep
and have scattered us among the nations.
[12] You sold your people for a pittance,
gaining nothing from their sale.

[13] You have made us a reproach to our neighbors,
the scorn and derision of those around us.
[14] You have made us a byword among the nations;
the peoples shake their heads at us.
[15] I live in disgrace all day long,
and my face is covered with shame
[16] at the taunts of those who reproach and revile me,
because of the enemy, who is bent on revenge.

[17] All this came upon us,
though we had not forgotten you;
we had not been false to your covenant.
[18] Our hearts had not turned back;
our feet had not strayed from your path.
[19] But you crushed us and made us a haunt for jackals;
you covered us over with deep darkness.

[20] If we had forgotten the name of our God
or spread out our hands to a foreign god,
[21] would not God have discovered it,
since he knows the secrets of the heart?
[22] Yet for your sake we face death all day long;
we are considered as sheep to be slaughtered.

[23] Awake, Lord! Why do you sleep?
Rouse yourself! Do not reject us forever.
[24] Why do you hide your face
and forget our misery and oppression?

[25] We are brought down to the dust;
our bodies cling to the ground.
[26] Rise up and help us;
rescue us because of your unfailing love.

## Psalm 45[a]

*For the director of music. To the tune of "Lilies." Of the Sons
of Korah. A maskil.[b] A wedding song.*

[1] My heart is stirred by a noble theme
as I recite my verses for the king;
my tongue is the pen of a skillful writer.

[2] You are the most excellent of men
and your lips have been anointed with grace,
since God has blessed you forever.

[3] Gird your sword on your side, you mighty one;
clothe yourself with splendor and majesty.
[4] In your majesty ride forth victoriously
in the cause of truth, humility and justice;
let your right hand achieve awesome deeds.
[5] Let your sharp arrows pierce the hearts of the king's
enemies;
let the nations fall beneath your feet.
[6] Your throne, O God,[c] will last for ever and ever;
a scepter of justice will be the scepter of your
kingdom.
[7] You love righteousness and hate wickedness;
therefore God, your God, has set you above your
companions
by anointing you with the oil of joy.
[8] All your robes are fragrant with myrrh and aloes and
cassia;
from palaces adorned with ivory
the music of the strings makes you glad.
[9] Daughters of kings are among your honored women;
at your right hand is the royal bride in gold of Ophir.

---

[a] In Hebrew texts 45:1-17 is numbered 45:2-18.    [b] Title: Probably a
literary or musical term    [c] 6 Here the king is addressed as God's
representative.

# Amplified Bible

[11] You have made us like sheep intended for mutton and
have scattered us in exile among the nations.
[12] You sell Your people for nothing, and have not increased Your wealth by their price.

[13] You have made us the taunt of our neighbors, a scoffing and a derision to those who are round about us.
[14] You make us a byword among the nations, a shaking
of the heads among the people.
[15] My dishonor is before me all day long, and shame has
covered my face
[16] At the words of the taunter and reviler, by reason of
the enemy and the revengeful.

[17] All this is come upon us, yet have we not forgotten
You, neither have we been false to Your covenant [which
You made with our fathers].
[18] Our hearts are not turned back, neither have our
steps declined from Your path,
[19] Though You have distressingly broken us in the place
of jackals and covered us with deep darkness, even with
the shadow of death.

[20] If we had forgotten the name of our God or stretched
out our hands to a strange god,
[21] Would not God discover this? For He knows the secrets of the heart.
[22] No, but for Your sake we are killed all the day long; we
are accounted as sheep for the slaughter. [Rom. 8:35-39.]
[23] Awake! Why do You sleep, O Lord? Arouse Yourself,
cast us not off forever!
[24] Why do You hide Your face *and* forget our affliction
and our oppression?
[25] For our lives are bowed down to the dust; our bodies
cleave to the ground.
[26] Rise up! Come to our help, and deliver us for Your
mercy's sake *and* because of Your steadfast love!

## Psalm 45

To the Chief Musician; [set to the tune of] "Lilies" [probably a
popular air. A Psalm] of the sons of Korah. A skillful song, *or* a
didactic *or* reflective poem. A song of love.

[1] My heart overflows with a [a]goodly theme; I address
my psalm to a King. My tongue is like the pen of a ready
writer.
[2] You are fairer than the children of men; graciousness
is poured upon Your lips; therefore God has blessed You
forever.
[3] Gird Your sword upon Your thigh, O mighty One, in
Your glory and Your majesty!
[4] And in Your majesty ride on triumphantly for the cause
of truth, humility, *and* righteousness (uprightness and
right standing with God); and let Your right hand guide
You to tremendous things.
[5] Your arrows are sharp; the peoples fall under You;
Your darts pierce the hearts of the King's enemies.
[6] Your throne, O God, is forever and ever; the scepter of
righteousness is the scepter of Your kingdom.
[7] You love righteousness, uprightness, *and* right standing with God and hate wickedness; therefore God, Your
God, has anointed You with the oil of gladness above Your
fellows. [Heb. 1:8, 9.]
[8] Your garments are all fragrant with myrrh, aloes, *and*
cassia; stringed instruments make You glad.
[9] Kings' daughters are among Your honorable women; at
Your right hand stands the queen in gold of Ophir.

---

[a] Jesus spoke of what was written of Him "in the Psalms" (see Luke
24:44). This is one such Messianic psalm. However, the capitalization
indicating the deity is offered provisionally. The chapter is written
against the background of a secular royal wedding. But the New
Testament reference to this psalm in Heb. 1:8, 9, where verses 6 and
7 of Psalm 45 are quoted and applied to Christ, makes any other
interpretation seem incidental in importance.

## New International Version

10 Listen, daughter, and pay careful attention:
    Forget your people and your father's house.
11 Let the king be enthralled by your beauty;
    honor him, for he is your lord.
12 The city of Tyre will come with a gift,[a]
    people of wealth will seek your favor.
13 All glorious is the princess within her chamber;
    her gown is interwoven with gold.
14 In embroidered garments she is led to the king;
    her virgin companions follow her—
    those brought to be with her.
15 Led in with joy and gladness,
    they enter the palace of the king.

16 Your sons will take the place of your fathers;
    you will make them princes throughout the land.

17 I will perpetuate your memory through all
    generations;
    therefore the nations will praise you for ever and
    ever.

### Psalm 46[b]

*For the director of music. Of the Sons of Korah.*
*According to* alamoth.[c] *A song.*

1 God is our refuge and strength,
    an ever-present help in trouble.
2 Therefore we will not fear, though the earth give way
    and the mountains fall into the heart of the sea,
3 though its waters roar and foam
    and the mountains quake with their surging.[d]

4 There is a river whose streams make glad the city of
    God,
    the holy place where the Most High dwells.
5 God is within her, she will not fall;
    God will help her at break of day.
6 Nations are in uproar, kingdoms fall;
    he lifts his voice, the earth melts.

7 The LORD Almighty is with us;
    the God of Jacob is our fortress.

8 Come and see what the LORD has done,
    the desolations he has brought on the earth.
9 He makes wars cease
    to the ends of the earth.
He breaks the bow and shatters the spear;
    he burns the shields[e] with fire.
10 He says, "Be still, and know that I am God;
    I will be exalted among the nations,
    I will be exalted in the earth."

11 The LORD Almighty is with us;
    the God of Jacob is our fortress.

### Psalm 47[f]

*For the director of music. Of the Sons of Korah. A psalm.*

1 Clap your hands, all you nations;
    shout to God with cries of joy.

2 For the LORD Most High is awesome,
    the great King over all the earth.
3 He subdued nations under us,
    peoples under our feet.

## Amplified Bible

10 Hear, O daughter, consider, submit, *and* consent to my instruction: forget also your own people and your father's house;
11 So will the King desire your beauty; because He is your Lord, be submissive *and* reverence *and* honor Him.
12 And, O daughter of Tyre, the richest of the people shall entreat your favor with a gift.
13 The King's daughter in the inner part [of the palace] is all glorious; her clothing is inwrought with gold. [Rev. 19:7, 8.]
14 She shall be brought to the King in raiment of needlework; with the virgins, her companions that follow her, she shall be brought to You.
15 With gladness and rejoicing will they be brought; they will enter into the King's palace.
16 Instead of Your fathers shall be Your sons, whom You will make princes in all the land.
17 I will make Your name to be remembered in all generations; therefore shall the people praise and give You thanks forever and ever.

### Psalm 46

To the Chief Musician. [A Psalm] of the sons of Korah, set
to treble voices. A song.

1 God is our Refuge and Strength [mighty *and* impenetrable to temptation], a very present *and* well-proved help in trouble.
2 Therefore we will not fear, though the earth should change and though the mountains be shaken into the midst of the seas,
3 Though its waters roar and foam, though the mountains tremble at its swelling *and* tumult. Selah [pause, and calmly think of that]!
4 There is a river whose streams shall make glad the city of God, the holy place of the tabernacles of the Most High.
5 God is in the midst of her, she shall not be moved; God will help her right early [at the dawn of the morning].
6 The nations raged, the kingdoms tottered *and* were moved; He uttered His voice, the earth melted.
7 The Lord of hosts is with us; the God of Jacob is our Refuge (our Fortress and High Tower). Selah [pause, and calmly think of that]!
8 Come, behold the works of the Lord, Who has wrought desolations *and* wonders in the earth.
9 He makes wars to cease to the end of the earth; He breaks the bow into pieces and snaps the spear in two; He burns the chariots in the fire.
10 Let be *and* be still, and know (recognize and understand) that I am God. I will be exalted among the nations! I will be exalted in the earth!
11 The Lord of hosts is with us; the God of Jacob is our Refuge (our High Tower and Stronghold). Selah [pause, and calmly think of that]!

### Psalm 47

To the Chief Musician. A Psalm of the sons of Korah.

1 O clap your hands, all you peoples! Shout to God with the voice of triumph *and* songs of joy!
2 For the Lord Most High excites terror, awe, *and* dread; He is a great King over all the earth.
3 He subdued peoples under us, and nations under our feet.

---

[a] 12 Or *A Tyrian robe is among the gifts*   [b] In Hebrew texts 46:1-11 is numbered 46:2-12.   [c] Title: Probably a musical term   [d] 3 The Hebrew has *Selah* (a word of uncertain meaning) here and at the end of verses 7 and 11.   [e] 9 Or *chariots*   [f] In Hebrew texts 47:1-9 is numbered 47:2-10.

## New International Version

[4] He chose our inheritance for us,
the pride of Jacob, whom he loved.[a]

[5] God has ascended amid shouts of joy,
the LORD amid the sounding of trumpets.
[6] Sing praises to God, sing praises;
sing praises to our King, sing praises.
[7] For God is the King of all the earth;
sing to him a psalm of praise.

[8] God reigns over the nations;
God is seated on his holy throne.
[9] The nobles of the nations assemble
as the people of the God of Abraham,
for the kings[b] of the earth belong to God;
he is greatly exalted.

### Psalm 48[c]

*A song. A psalm of the Sons of Korah.*

[1] Great is the LORD, and most worthy of praise,
in the city of our God, his holy mountain.

[2] Beautiful in its loftiness,
the joy of the whole earth,
like the heights of Zaphon[d] is Mount Zion,
the city of the Great King.
[3] God is in her citadels;
he has shown himself to be her fortress.

[4] When the kings joined forces,
when they advanced together,
[5] they saw her and were astounded;
they fled in terror.
[6] Trembling seized them there,
pain like that of a woman in labor.
[7] You destroyed them like ships of Tarshish
shattered by an east wind.

[8] As we have heard,
so we have seen
in the city of the LORD Almighty,
in the city of our God:
God makes her secure
forever.[a]

[9] Within your temple, O God,
we meditate on your unfailing love.
[10] Like your name, O God,
your praise reaches to the ends of the earth;
your right hand is filled with righteousness.
[11] Mount Zion rejoices,
the villages of Judah are glad
because of your judgments.

[12] Walk about Zion, go around her,
count her towers,
[13] consider well her ramparts,
view her citadels,
that you may tell of them
to the next generation.

[14] For this God is our God for ever and ever;
he will be our guide even to the end.

### Psalm 49[e]

*For the director of music. Of the Sons of Korah. A psalm.*

[1] Hear this, all you peoples;
listen, all who live in this world,
[2] both low and high,
rich and poor alike:

## Amplified Bible

[4] He chose our inheritance for us, the glory *and* pride of Jacob, whom He loves. Selah [pause, and calmly think of that]! [I Pet. 1:4, 5.]
[5] God has ascended amid shouting, the Lord with the sound of a trumpet.
[6] Sing praises to God, sing praises! Sing praises to our King, sing praises!
[7] For God is the King of all the earth; sing praises in a skillful psalm *and* with understanding.
[8] God reigns over the nations; God sits upon His holy throne.
[9] The princes *and* nobles of the peoples are gathered together, a [united] people for the God of Abraham, for the shields of the earth belong to God; He is highly exalted.

### Psalm 48

A song; a Psalm of the sons of Korah.

[1] Great is the Lord, and highly to be praised in the city of our God! His holy mountain,
[2] Fair *and* beautiful in elevation, is the joy of all the earth—[a] Mount Zion [the City of David], to the northern side [Mount Moriah and the temple], the [whole] city of the Great King! [Matt. 5:35.]
[3] God has made Himself known in her palaces as a Refuge (a High Tower and a Stronghold).
[4] For, behold, the kings assembled, they came onward *and* they passed away together.
[5] They looked, they were amazed; they were stricken with terror *and* took to flight [affrighted and dismayed].
[6] Trembling took hold of them there, and pain as of a woman in childbirth.
[7] With the east wind You shattered the ships of Tarshish.
[8] As we have heard, so have we seen in the city of the Lord of hosts, in the city of our God: God will establish it forever. Selah [pause, and calmly think of that]!
[9] We have thought of Your steadfast love, O God, in the midst of Your temple.
[10] As is Your name, O God, so is Your praise to the ends of the earth; Your right hand is full of righteousness (rightness and justice).
[11] Let Mount Zion be glad! Let the daughters of Judah rejoice because of Your [righteous] judgments!
[12] Walk about Zion, and go round about her, number her towers (her lofty and noble deeds of past days),
[13] Consider well her ramparts, go through her palaces *and* citadels, that you may tell the next generation [and cease recalling disappointments].
[14] For this God is our God forever and ever; He will be our guide [even] until death.

### Psalm 49

To the Chief Musician. A Psalm of the sons of Korah.

[1] Hear this, all you peoples; give ear, all you inhabitants of the world,
[2] Both low and high, rich and poor together:

---

[a] 4,8 The Hebrew has *Selah* (a word of uncertain meaning) here.
[b] 9 Or *shields*   [c] In Hebrew texts 48:1-14 is numbered 48:2-15.
[d] 2 *Zaphon* was the most sacred mountain of the Canaanites.
[e] In Hebrew texts 49:1-20 is numbered 49:2-21.

[a] Psalm 48 is a celebration of the security of Zion. See the beauty of Zion as God's unconquerable fortress.

## New International Version

³My mouth will speak words of wisdom;
  the meditation of my heart will give you
    understanding.
⁴I will turn my ear to a proverb;
  with the harp I will expound my riddle:

⁵Why should I fear when evil days come,
  when wicked deceivers surround me—
⁶those who trust in their wealth
  and boast of their great riches?
⁷No one can redeem the life of another
  or give to God a ransom for them—
⁸the ransom for a life is costly,
  no payment is ever enough—
⁹so that they should live on forever
  and not see decay.
¹⁰For all can see that the wise die,
  that the foolish and the senseless also perish,
    leaving their wealth to others.
¹¹Their tombs will remain their housesᵃ forever,
  their dwellings for endless generations,
    though they hadᵇ named lands after themselves.

¹²People, despite their wealth, do not endure;
  they are like the beasts that perish.

¹³This is the fate of those who trust in themselves,
  and of their followers, who approve their sayings.ᶜ
¹⁴They are like sheep and are destined to die;
  death will be their shepherd
    (but the upright will prevail over them in the
      morning).
Their forms will decay in the grave,
  far from their princely mansions.
¹⁵But God will redeem me from the realm of the dead;
  he will surely take me to himself.
¹⁶Do not be overawed when others grow rich,
  when the splendor of their houses increases;
¹⁷for they will take nothing with them when they die,
  their splendor will not descend with them.
¹⁸Though while they live they count themselves
    blessed—
  and people praise you when you prosper—
¹⁹they will join those who have gone before them,
  who will never again see the light of life.

²⁰People who have wealth but lack understanding
  are like the beasts that perish.

### Psalm 50

*A psalm of Asaph.*

¹The Mighty One, God, the Lᴏʀᴅ,
  speaks and summons the earth
    from the rising of the sun to where it sets.
²From Zion, perfect in beauty,
  God shines forth.
³Our God comes
  and will not be silent;
a fire devours before him,
  and around him a tempest rages.
⁴He summons the heavens above,
  and the earth, that he may judge his people:
⁵"Gather to me this consecrated people,
  who made a covenant with me by sacrifice."
⁶And the heavens proclaim his righteousness,
  for he is a God of justice.ᵈ,ᵉ

---

ᵃ 11 Septuagint and Syriac; Hebrew *In their thoughts their houses will
remain*  ᵇ 11 Or *generations, / for they have*  ᶜ 13 The Hebrew has
*Selah* (a word of uncertain meaning) here and at the end of verse 15.
ᵈ 6 With a different word division of the Hebrew; Masoretic Text *for
God himself is judge*  ᵉ 6 The Hebrew has *Selah* (a word of uncertain
meaning) here.

## Amplified Bible

³My mouth shall speak wisdom; and the meditation of
my heart shall be understanding.
⁴I will submit *and* consent to a parable *or* proverb; to
the music of a lyre I will unfold my riddle (my problem).
⁵Why should I fear in the days of evil, when the iniquity
of those who would supplant me surrounds me on every
side,
⁶Even of those who trust in *and* lean on their wealth and
boast of the abundance of their riches?
⁷None of them can by any means redeem [either himself or] his brother, nor give to God a ransom for him—
⁸For the ransom of a life is too costly, and [the price one
can pay] can never suffice—
⁹So that he should live on forever *and* never see the pit
(the grave) *and* corruption.
¹⁰For he sees that even wise men die; the [self-con-
fident] fool and the stupid alike perish and leave their
wealth to others.
¹¹Their inward thought is that their houses will continue forever, *and* their dwelling places to all generations;
they call their lands their own [apart from God] *and* after
their own names.
¹²But man, with all his honor *and* pomp, does not remain; he is like the beasts that perish.
¹³This is the fate of those who are foolishly confident,
yet after them men approve their sayings. Selah [pause,
and calmly think of that]!
¹⁴Like sheep they are appointed for Sheol (the place of
the dead); death shall be their shepherd. And the upright
shall have dominion over them in the morning; and their
form *and* beauty shall be consumed, for Sheol shall be
their dwelling.
¹⁵But God will redeem me from the power of Sheol (the
place of the dead); for He will receive me. Selah [pause,
and calmly think of that]!
¹⁶Be not afraid when [an ungodly] one is made rich,
when the wealth *and* glory of his house are increased;
¹⁷For when he dies he will carry nothing away; his glory
will not descend after him.
¹⁸Though while he lives he counts himself happy *and*
prosperous, and though a man gets praise when he does
well [for himself],
¹⁹He will go to the generation of his fathers, who will
nevermore see the light.
²⁰A man who is held in honor and understands not is
like the beasts that perish.

### Psalm 50

A Psalm of ᵃAsaph

¹The mighty One, God, the Lord, speaks and calls the
earth from the rising of the sun to its setting.
²Out of Zion, the perfection of beauty, God shines forth.
³Our God comes and does not keep silence; a fire devours before Him, and round about Him a mighty tempest
rages.
⁴He calls to the heavens above and to the earth, that He
may judge His people:
⁵Gather together to Me My saints [those who have
found grace in My sight], those who have made a covenant
with Me by sacrifice.
⁶And the heavens declare His righteousness (rightness
and justice), for God, He is judge. Selah [pause, and calmly
think of that]!

---

ᵃ Asaph was a Levite and one of the leaders of David's choir. He was the
head of one of the three families permanently charged with the temple
music. His family formed a guild which bore his name and is frequently
mentioned (II Chron. 20:14; 29:13; 29:30). Twelve psalms (50; 73-83)
are attributed in the titles to the family of Asaph. 128 of Asaph's family
members, all singers, came back from Babylon and took part when the
foundations of Zerubbabel's temple were laid (Ezra 2:41; 3:10).

## New International Version

7 "Listen, my people, and I will speak;
  I will testify against you, Israel:
  I am God, your God.
8 I bring no charges against you concerning your
    sacrifices
  or concerning your burnt offerings, which are ever
    before me.
9 I have no need of a bull from your stall
  or of goats from your pens,
10 for every animal of the forest is mine,
  and the cattle on a thousand hills.
11 I know every bird in the mountains,
  and the insects in the fields are mine.
12 If I were hungry I would not tell you,
  for the world is mine, and all that is in it.
13 Do I eat the flesh of bulls
  or drink the blood of goats?

14 "Sacrifice thank offerings to God,
  fulfill your vows to the Most High,
15 and call on me in the day of trouble;
  I will deliver you, and you will honor me."

16 But to the wicked person, God says:

"What right have you to recite my laws
  or take my covenant on your lips?
17 You hate my instruction
  and cast my words behind you.
18 When you see a thief, you join with him;
  you throw in your lot with adulterers.
19 You use your mouth for evil
  and harness your tongue to deceit.
20 You sit and testify against your brother
  and slander your own mother's son.
21 When you did these things and I kept silent,
  you thought I was exactly[a] like you.
But I now arraign you
  and set my accusations before you.

22 "Consider this, you who forget God,
  or I will tear you to pieces, with no one to rescue you:
23 Those who sacrifice thank offerings honor me,
  and to the blameless[b] I will show my salvation."

### Psalm 51[c]

*For the director of music. A psalm of David. When the prophet
Nathan came to him after David had committed adultery
with Bathsheba.*

1 Have mercy on me, O God,
    according to your unfailing love;
  according to your great compassion
    blot out my transgressions.
2 Wash away all my iniquity
  and cleanse me from my sin.

3 For I know my transgressions,
  and my sin is always before me.
4 Against you, you only, have I sinned
  and done what is evil in your sight;
  so you are right in your verdict
    and justified when you judge.
5 Surely I was sinful at birth,
  sinful from the time my mother conceived me.
6 Yet you desired faithfulness even in the womb;
  you taught me wisdom in that secret place.

7 Cleanse me with hyssop, and I will be clean;
  wash me, and I will be whiter than snow.
8 Let me hear joy and gladness;
  let the bones you have crushed rejoice.

## Amplified Bible

7 Hear, O My people, and I will speak; O Israel, I will testify to you *and* against you: I am God, your God.
8 I do not reprove you for your sacrifices; your burnt offerings are continually before Me.
9 I will accept no bull from your house nor he-goat out of your folds.
10 For every beast of the forest is Mine, *and* the cattle upon a thousand hills *or* upon the mountains where thousands are.
11 I know *and* am acquainted with all the birds of the mountains, and the wild animals of the field are Mine *and* are with Me, in My mind.
12 If I were hungry, I would not tell you, for the world and its fullness are Mine. [I Cor. 10:26.]
13 Shall I eat the flesh of bulls or drink the blood of goats?
14 Offer to God the sacrifice of thanksgiving, and pay your vows to the Most High,
15 And call on Me in the day of trouble; I will deliver you, and you shall honor *and* glorify Me.
16 But to the wicked, God says: What right have you to recite My statutes or take My covenant *or* pledge on your lips,
17 Seeing that you hate instruction *and* correction and cast My words behind you [discarding them]?
18 When you see a thief, you associate with him, and you have taken part with adulterers.
19 You give your mouth to evil, and your tongue frames deceit.
20 You sit and speak against your brother; you slander your own mother's son.
21 These things you have done and I kept silent; you thought I was once entirely like you. But [now] I will reprove you and put [the charge] in order before your eyes.
22 Now consider this, you who forget God, lest I tear you in pieces, and there be none to deliver.
23 He who brings an offering of praise *and* thanksgiving honors *and* glorifies Me; and he who orders his way aright [who prepares the way that I may show him], to him I will demonstrate the salvation of God.

### Psalm 51

To the Chief Musician. A Psalm of David; when Nathan the prophet came to him after he had sinned with Bathsheba.

1 Have mercy upon me, O God, according to Your steadfast love; according to the multitude of Your tender mercy *and* loving-kindness blot out my transgressions.
2 Wash me thoroughly [and repeatedly] from my iniquity *and* guilt and cleanse me *and* make me wholly pure from my sin!
3 For I am conscious of my transgressions *and* I acknowledge them; my sin is ever before me.
4 Against You, You only, have I sinned and done that which is evil in Your sight, so that You are justified in Your sentence and faultless in Your judgment. [Rom. 3:4.]
5 Behold, I was brought forth in [a state of] iniquity; my mother was sinful who conceived me [and I too am sinful]. [John 3:6; Rom. 5:12; Eph. 2:3.]
6 Behold, You desire truth in the inner being; make me therefore to know wisdom in my inmost heart.
7 Purify me with hyssop, and I shall be clean [ceremonially]; wash me, and I shall [in reality] be whiter than snow.
8 Make me to hear joy and gladness *and* be satisfied; let the bones which You have broken rejoice.

---

[a] 21 Or *thought the 'I AM' was*   [b] 23 Probable reading of the original Hebrew text; the meaning of the Masoretic Text for this phrase is uncertain.   [c] In Hebrew texts 51:1-19 is numbered 51:3-21.

## New International Version

⁹Hide your face from my sins
    and blot out all my iniquity.

¹⁰Create in me a pure heart, O God,
    and renew a steadfast spirit within me.
¹¹Do not cast me from your presence
    or take your Holy Spirit from me.
¹²Restore to me the joy of your salvation
    and grant me a willing spirit, to sustain me.

¹³Then I will teach transgressors your ways,
    so that sinners will turn back to you.
¹⁴Deliver me from the guilt of bloodshed, O God,
    you who are God my Savior,
    and my tongue will sing of your righteousness.
¹⁵Open my lips, Lord,
    and my mouth will declare your praise.
¹⁶You do not delight in sacrifice, or I would bring it;
    you do not take pleasure in burnt offerings.
¹⁷My sacrifice, O God, isᵃ a broken spirit;
    a broken and contrite heart
    you, God, will not despise.

¹⁸May it please you to prosper Zion,
    to build up the walls of Jerusalem.
¹⁹Then you will delight in the sacrifices of the righteous,
    in burnt offerings offered whole;
    then bulls will be offered on your altar.

### Psalm 52ᵇ

*For the director of music. A maskilᶜ of David. When Doeg the
Edomite had gone to Saul and told him: "David has gone to the
house of Ahimelek."*

¹Why do you boast of evil, you mighty hero?
    Why do you boast all day long,
    you who are a disgrace in the eyes of God?
²You who practice deceit,
    your tongue plots destruction;
    it is like a sharpened razor.
³You love evil rather than good,
    falsehood rather than speaking the truth.ᵈ
⁴You love every harmful word,
    you deceitful tongue!

⁵Surely God will bring you down to everlasting ruin:
    He will snatch you up and pluck you from your tent;
    he will uproot you from the land of the living.
⁶The righteous will see and fear;
    they will laugh at you, saying,
⁷"Here now is the man
    who did not make God his stronghold
    but trusted in his great wealth
    and grew strong by destroying others!"

⁸But I am like an olive tree
    flourishing in the house of God;
I trust in God's unfailing love
    for ever and ever.
⁹For what you have done I will always praise you
    in the presence of your faithful people.
And I will hope in your name,
    for your name is good.

## Amplified Bible

⁹Hide Your face from my sins and blot out all my guilt
*and* iniquities.

¹⁰Create in me a clean heart, O God, and renew a right,
persevering, *and* steadfast spirit within me.
¹¹Cast me not away from Your presence and take not
Your Holy Spirit from me.
¹²Restore to me the joy of Your salvation and uphold me
with a willing spirit.
¹³Then will I teach transgressors Your ways, and sinners shall be converted *and* return to You.
¹⁴Deliver me from bloodguiltiness *and* death, O God,
the God of my salvation, *and* my tongue shall sing aloud
of Your righteousness (Your rightness and Your justice).
¹⁵O Lord, open my lips, and my mouth shall show forth
Your praise.
¹⁶For You delight not in sacrifice, or else would I give
it; You find no pleasure in burnt offering. [I Sam. 15:22.]
¹⁷My sacrifice [the sacrifice acceptable] to God is a
broken spirit; a broken and a contrite heart [broken down
with sorrow for sin and humbly and thoroughly penitent],
such, O God, You will not despise.
¹⁸Do good in Your good pleasure to Zion; rebuild the
walls of Jerusalem.
¹⁹Then will You delight in the sacrifices of righteousness, justice, *and* right, with burnt offering and whole
burnt offering; then bullocks will be offered upon Your
altar.

### Psalm 52

To the Chief Musician. A skillful song, *or* a didactic *or*
reflective poem. [A Psalm] of David, when Doeg the
Edomite came and told Saul, David has come to the house
of Ahimelech.

¹Why boast you of mischief done against the loving-
kindness of God [and the godly], O mighty [sinful] man,
day after day?
²Your tongue devises wickedness; it is like a sharp razor, working deceitfully.
³You love evil more than good, and lying rather than to
speak righteousness, justice, *and* right. Selah [pause, and
calmly think of that]!
⁴You love all destroying *and* devouring words, O deceitful tongue.
⁵God will likewise break you down *and* destroy you forever; He will lay hold of you and pluck you out of your tent
and uproot you from the land of the living. Selah [pause,
and calmly think of that]!
⁶The [uncompromisingly] righteous also shall see [it]
and be in reverent fear *and* awe, but about you they will
[scoffingly] laugh, saying,
⁷See, this is the man who made not God his strength
(his stronghold and high tower) but trusted in *and* confidently relied on the abundance of his riches, seeking
refuge *and* security for himself through his wickedness.
⁸But I am like a green olive tree in the house of God; I
trust in *and* confidently rely on the loving-kindness *and*
the mercy of God forever and ever.
⁹I will thank You *and* confide in You forever, because
You have done it [delivered me and kept me safe]. I will
wait on, hope in *and* expect in Your name, for it is good, in
the presence of Your saints (Your kind and pious ones).

---

ᵃ 17 Or *The sacrifices of God are*    ᵇ In Hebrew texts 52:1-9 is numbered
52:3-11.    ᶜ Title: Probably a literary or musical term    ᵈ 3 The
Hebrew has *Selah* (a word of uncertain meaning) here and at the end of
verse 5.

# New International Version

## Psalm 53[a]

*For the director of music. According to* mahalath.[b]
*A maskil[c] of David.*

[1] The fool says in his heart,
    "There is no God."
They are corrupt, and their ways are vile;
    there is no one who does good.

[2] God looks down from heaven
    on all mankind
to see if there are any who understand,
    any who seek God.
[3] Everyone has turned away, all have become corrupt;
    there is no one who does good,
    not even one.

[4] Do all these evildoers know nothing?

They devour my people as though eating bread;
    they never call on God.
[5] But there they are, overwhelmed with dread,
    where there was nothing to dread.
God scattered the bones of those who attacked you;
    you put them to shame, for God despised them.

[6] Oh, that salvation for Israel would come out of Zion!
    When God restores his people,
    let Jacob rejoice and Israel be glad!

## Psalm 54[d]

*For the director of music. With stringed instruments. A maskil[c]
of David. When the Ziphites had gone to Saul and said, "Is not
David hiding among us?"*

[1] Save me, O God, by your name;
    vindicate me by your might.
[2] Hear my prayer, O God;
    listen to the words of my mouth.

[3] Arrogant foes are attacking me;
    ruthless people are trying to kill me—
    people without regard for God.[e]

[4] Surely God is my help;
    the Lord is the one who sustains me.

[5] Let evil recoil on those who slander me;
    in your faithfulness destroy them.

[6] I will sacrifice a freewill offering to you;
    I will praise your name, LORD, for it is good.
[7] You have delivered me from all my troubles,
    and my eyes have looked in triumph on my foes.

## Psalm 55[f]

*For the director of music. With stringed instruments.
A maskil[c] of David.*

[1] Listen to my prayer, O God,
    do not ignore my plea;
[2]     hear me and answer me.
My thoughts trouble me and I am distraught
[3]     because of what my enemy is saying,
    because of the threats of the wicked;
for they bring down suffering on me
    and assail me in their anger.

[4] My heart is in anguish within me;
    the terrors of death have fallen on me.

# Amplified Bible

## Psalm 53

To the Chief Musician; in a mournful strain. A skillful song,
*or* didactic *or* reflective poem of David.

[1] The [empty-headed] fool has said in his heart, There is
no God. Corrupt *and* evil are they, and doing abominable
iniquity; there is none who does good.
[2] God looked down from heaven upon the children of
men to see if there were any who understood, who sought
(inquired after and desperately required) God.
[3] Every one of them has gone back [backslidden and fall-
en away]; they have altogether become filthy *and* corrupt;
there is none who does good, no, not one. [Rom. 3:10-12.]
[4] Have those who work evil no knowledge (no understanding)? They eat up My people as they eat bread; they
do not call upon God.
[5] There they are, in terror *and* dread, where there was
[and had been] no terror *and* dread! For God has scattered
the bones of him who encamps against you; you have put
them to shame, because God has rejected them.
[6] Oh, that the salvation *and* deliverance of Israel would
come out of Zion! When God restores the fortunes of His
people, then will Jacob rejoice and Israel be glad.

## Psalm 54

To the Chief Musician; with stringed instruments. A skillful
song, *or* a didactic *or* reflective poem, of David, when the
Ziphites went and told Saul, David is hiding among us.

[1] Save me, O God, by Your name; judge *and* vindicate me
by Your mighty strength *and* power.
[2] Hear my pleading *and* my prayer, O God; give ear to
the words of my mouth.
[3] For strangers *and* insolent men are rising up against
me, and violent men *and* ruthless ones seek *and* demand
my life; they do not set God before them. Selah [pause, and
calmly think of that]!
[4] Behold, God is my helper *and* ally; the Lord is my up-
holder *and* is with them who uphold my life.
[5] He will pay back evil to my enemies; in Your faithfulness [Lord] put an end to them.
[6] With a freewill offering I will sacrifice to You; I will
give thanks *and* praise Your name, O Lord, for it is good.
[7] For He has delivered me out of every trouble, and my
eye has looked [in triumph] on my enemies.

## Psalm 55

To the Chief Musician; with stringed instruments. A skillful
song, *or* a didactic *or* reflective poem, of David.

[1] Listen to my prayer, O God, and hide not Yourself from
my supplication!
[2] Attend to me and answer me; I am restless *and* distraught in my complaint and must moan
[3] [And I am distracted] at the noise of the enemy, because of the oppression *and* threats of the wicked; for they
would cast trouble upon me, and in wrath they persecute
me.
[4] My heart is grievously pained within me, and the terrors of death have fallen upon me.

---

[a] In Hebrew texts 53:1-6 is numbered 53:2-7.   [b] Title: Probably a
musical term   [c] Title: Probably a literary or musical term   [d] In
Hebrew texts 54:1-7 is numbered 54:3-9.   [e] 3 The Hebrew has *Selah*
(a word of uncertain meaning) here.   [f] In Hebrew texts 55:1-23 is
numbered 55:2-24.

## New International Version

[5] Fear and trembling have beset me;
  horror has overwhelmed me.
[6] I said, "Oh, that I had the wings of a dove!
  I would fly away and be at rest.
[7] I would flee far away
  and stay in the desert;[a]
[8] I would hurry to my place of shelter,
  far from the tempest and storm."

[9] Lord, confuse the wicked, confound their words,
  for I see violence and strife in the city.
[10] Day and night they prowl about on its walls;
  malice and abuse are within it.
[11] Destructive forces are at work in the city;
  threats and lies never leave its streets.

[12] If an enemy were insulting me,
  I could endure it;
if a foe were rising against me,
  I could hide.
[13] But it is you, a man like myself,
  my companion, my close friend,
[14] with whom I once enjoyed sweet fellowship
  at the house of God,
as we walked about
  among the worshipers.

[15] Let death take my enemies by surprise;
  let them go down alive to the realm of the dead,
  for evil finds lodging among them.

[16] As for me, I call to God,
  and the LORD saves me.
[17] Evening, morning and noon
  I cry out in distress,
  and he hears my voice.
[18] He rescues me unharmed
  from the battle waged against me,
  even though many oppose me.
[19] God, who is enthroned from of old,
  who does not change—
he will hear them and humble them,
  because they have no fear of God.

[20] My companion attacks his friends;
  he violates his covenant.
[21] His talk is smooth as butter,
  yet war is in his heart;
his words are more soothing than oil,
  yet they are drawn swords.

[22] Cast your cares on the LORD
  and he will sustain you;
he will never let
  the righteous be shaken.
[23] But you, God, will bring down the wicked
  into the pit of decay;
the bloodthirsty and deceitful
  will not live out half their days.

But as for me, I trust in you.

### Psalm 56[b]

*For the director of music. To the tune of "A Dove on Distant
Oaks." Of David. A miktam.[c] When the Philistines
had seized him in Gath.*

[1] Be merciful to me, my God,
  for my enemies are in hot pursuit;
  all day long they press their attack.
[2] My adversaries pursue me all day long;
  in their pride many are attacking me.

## Amplified Bible

[5] Fear and trembling have come upon me; horror *and*
fright have overwhelmed me.
[6] And I say, Oh, that I had wings like a dove! I would fly
away and be at rest.
[7] Yes, I would wander far away, I would lodge in the wilderness. Selah [pause, and calmly think of that]!
[8] I would hasten to escape *and* to find a shelter from the
stormy wind and tempest.
[9] Destroy [their schemes], O Lord, confuse their
tongues, for I have seen violence and strife in the city.
[10] Day and night they go about on its walls; iniquity and
mischief are in its midst.
[11] Violence *and* ruin are within it; fraud and guile do not
depart from its streets *and* marketplaces.
[12] For it is not an enemy who reproaches *and* taunts
me—then I might bear it; nor is it one who has hated me
who insolently vaunts himself against me—then I might
hide from him.
[13] But it was you, a man my equal, my companion and
my familiar friend.
[14] We had sweet fellowship together and used to walk to
the house of God in company.
[15] Let desolations *and* death come suddenly upon them;
let them go down alive to Sheol (the place of the dead),
for evils are in their habitations, in their hearts, *and* their
inmost part.
[16] As for me, I will call upon God, and the Lord will save
me.
[17] Evening and morning and at noon will I utter my complaint and moan *and* sigh, and He will hear my voice.
[18] He has redeemed my life in peace from the battle that
was against me [so that none came near me], for they were
many who strove with me.
[19] God will hear and humble them, even He Who abides
of old—Selah [pause, and calmly think of that]!—because
in them there has been no change [of heart], and they do
not fear, revere, *and* worship God.
[20] [My companion] has put forth his hands against those
who were at peace with him; he has broken *and* profaned
his agreement [of friendship and loyalty].
[21] The words of his mouth were smoother than cream *or*
butter, but war was in his heart; his words were softer than
oil, yet they were drawn swords.
[22] Cast your burden on the Lord [releasing the weight of
it] and He will sustain you; He will never allow the [consis-
tently] righteous to be moved (made to slip, fall, or fail).
[I Pet. 5:7.]
[23] But You, O God, will bring down the wicked into the
pit of destruction; men of blood and treachery shall not
live out half their days. But I will trust in, lean on, *and*
confidently rely on You.

### Psalm 56

To the Chief Musician; [set to the tune of] "Silent Dove Among
Those Far Away." Of David. A record of memorable thoughts
when the Philistines seized him in Gath.

[1] Be merciful *and* gracious to me, O God, for man would
trample me *or* devour me; all the day long the adversary
oppresses me.
[2] They that lie in wait for me would swallow me up *or*
trample me all day long, for they are many who fight
against me, O Most High!

---

[a] 7 The Hebrew has *Selah* (a word of uncertain meaning) here and in the
middle of verse 19.  [b] In Hebrew texts 56:1-13 is numbered 56:2-14.
[c] Title: Probably a literary or musical term

## New International Version

[3]When I am afraid, I put my trust in you.
[4]   In God, whose word I praise—
in God I trust and am not afraid.
      What can mere mortals do to me?

[5]All day long they twist my words;
   all their schemes are for my ruin.
[6]They conspire, they lurk,
   they watch my steps,
   hoping to take my life.
[7]Because of their wickedness do not[a] let them escape;
   in your anger, God, bring the nations down.

[8]Record my misery;
   list my tears on your scroll[b]—
   are they not in your record?
[9]Then my enemies will turn back
   when I call for help.
   By this I will know that God is for me.

[10]In God, whose word I praise,
   in the LORD, whose word I praise—
[11]in God I trust and am not afraid.
   What can man do to me?

[12]I am under vows to you, my God;
   I will present my thank offerings to you.
[13]For you have delivered me from death
   and my feet from stumbling,
   that I may walk before God
   in the light of life.

### Psalm 57[c]

*For the director of music. To the tune of "Do Not Destroy."*
*Of David. A miktam.[d] When he had fled from Saul into the cave.*

[1]Have mercy on me, my God, have mercy on me,
   for in you I take refuge.
I will take refuge in the shadow of your wings
   until the disaster has passed.

[2]I cry out to God Most High,
   to God, who vindicates me.
[3]He sends from heaven and saves me,
   rebuking those who hotly pursue me—[e]
   God sends forth his love and his faithfulness.

[4]I am in the midst of lions;
   I am forced to dwell among ravenous beasts—
men whose teeth are spears and arrows,
   whose tongues are sharp swords.

[5]Be exalted, O God, above the heavens;
   let your glory be over all the earth.

[6]They spread a net for my feet—
   I was bowed down in distress.
They dug a pit in my path—
   but they have fallen into it themselves.

[7]My heart, O God, is steadfast,
   my heart is steadfast;
   I will sing and make music.
[8]Awake, my soul!
   Awake, harp and lyre!
   I will awaken the dawn.

[9]I will praise you, Lord, among the nations;
   I will sing of you among the peoples.
[10]For great is your love, reaching to the heavens;
   your faithfulness reaches to the skies.

## Amplified Bible

[3]What time I am afraid, I will have confidence in *and* put my trust *and* reliance in You.
[4]By [the help of] God I will praise His word; on God I lean, rely, *and* confidently put my trust; I will not fear. What can man, who is flesh, do to me?
[5]All day long they twist my words *and* trouble my affairs; all their thoughts are against me for evil *and* my hurt.
[6]They gather themselves together, they hide themselves, they watch my steps, even as they have [expectantly] waited for my life.
[7]They think to escape with iniquity, *and* shall they? In Your indignation bring down the peoples, O God.
[8]You number *and* record my wanderings; put my tears into Your bottle—are they not in Your book?
[9]Then shall my enemies turn back in the day that I cry out; this I know, for God is for me. [Rom. 8:31.]
[10]In God, Whose word I praise, in the Lord, Whose word I praise,
[11]In God have I put my trust *and* confident reliance; I will not be afraid. What can man do to me?
[12]Your vows are upon me, O God; I will render praise to You *and* give You thank offerings.
[13]For You have delivered my life from death, yes, and my feet from falling, that I may walk before God in the light of life *and* of the living.

### Psalm 57

To the Chief Musician; [set to the tune of] "Do Not Destroy."
A record of memorable thoughts of David when he fled
from Saul in the cave.

[1]Be merciful *and* gracious to me, O God, be merciful *and* gracious to me, for my soul takes refuge *and* finds shelter *and* confidence in You; yes, in the shadow of Your wings will I take refuge *and* be confident until calamities *and* destructive storms are passed.
[2]I will cry to God Most High, Who performs on my behalf *and* rewards me [Who brings to pass His purposes for me and surely completes them]!
[3]He will send from heaven and save me from the slanders *and* reproaches of him who would trample me down *or* swallow me up, *and* He will put him to shame. Selah [pause, and calmly think of that]! God will send forth His mercy *and* loving-kindness *and* His truth *and* faithfulness.
[4]My life is among lions; I must lie among those who are aflame—the sons of men whose teeth are spears and arrows, their tongues sharp swords.
[5]Be exalted, O God, above the heavens! Let Your glory be over all the earth!
[6]They set a net for my steps; my very life was bowed down. They dug a pit in my way; into the midst of it they themselves have fallen. Selah [pause, and calmly think of that]!
[7]My heart is fixed, O God, my heart is steadfast *and* confident! I will sing and make melody.
[8]Awake, my glory (my inner self); awake, harp and lyre! I will awake right early [I will awaken the dawn]!
[9]I will praise *and* give thanks to You, O Lord, among the peoples; I will sing praises to You among the nations.
[10]For Your mercy *and* loving-kindness are great, reaching to the heavens, and Your truth *and* faithfulness to the clouds.

---

[a] 7 Probable reading of the original Hebrew text; Masoretic Text does not have *do not*.   [b] 8 Or *misery; / put my tears in your wineskin*   [c] In Hebrew texts 57:1-11 is numbered 57:2-12.   [d] Title: Probably a literary or musical term   [e] 3 The Hebrew has *Selah* (a word of uncertain meaning) here and at the end of verse 6.

# New International Version

11 Be exalted, O God, above the heavens;
    let your glory be over all the earth.

## Psalm 58[a]

*For the director of music. To the tune of "Do Not Destroy."*
*Of David. A miktam.[b]*

1 Do you rulers indeed speak justly?
    Do you judge people with equity?
2 No, in your heart you devise injustice,
    and your hands mete out violence on the earth.

3 Even from birth the wicked go astray;
    from the womb they are wayward, spreading lies.
4 Their venom is like the venom of a snake,
    like that of a cobra that has stopped its ears,
5 that will not heed the tune of the charmer,
    however skillful the enchanter may be.

6 Break the teeth in their mouths, O God;
    LORD, tear out the fangs of those lions!
7 Let them vanish like water that flows away;
    when they draw the bow, let their arrows fall short.
8 May they be like a slug that melts away as it moves
        along,
    like a stillborn child that never sees the sun.

9 Before your pots can feel the heat of the thorns—
    whether they be green or dry—the wicked will be
        swept away.[c]
10 The righteous will be glad when they are avenged,
    when they dip their feet in the blood of the wicked.
11 Then people will say,
    "Surely the righteous still are rewarded;
    surely there is a God who judges the earth."

## Psalm 59[d]

*For the director of music. To the tune of "Do Not Destroy."*
*Of David. A miktam.[b] When Saul had sent men to watch David's*
*house in order to kill him.*

1 Deliver me from my enemies, O God;
    be my fortress against those who are attacking me.
2 Deliver me from evildoers
    and save me from those who are after my blood.

3 See how they lie in wait for me!
    Fierce men conspire against me
    for no offense or sin of mine, LORD.
4 I have done no wrong, yet they are ready to attack me.
    Arise to help me; look on my plight!
5 You, LORD God Almighty,
    you who are the God of Israel,
    rouse yourself to punish all the nations;
    show no mercy to wicked traitors.[e]

6 They return at evening,
    snarling like dogs,
    and prowl the city.
7 See what they spew from their mouths—
    the words from their lips are sharp as swords,
    and they think, "Who can hear us?"
8 But you laugh at them, LORD;
    you scoff at all those nations.

9 You are my strength, I watch for you;
    you, God, are my fortress,

# Amplified Bible

11 Be exalted, O God, above the heavens; let Your glory
be over all the earth.

## Psalm 58

*To the Chief Musician; [set to the tune of] "Do Not Destroy." A*
*record of memorable thoughts of David.*

1 Do you indeed in silence speak righteousness, O you
mighty ones? [Or is the righteousness, rightness, and justice you should speak quite dumb?] Do you judge fairly
*and* uprightly, O you sons of men?
2 No, in your heart you devise wickedness; you deal out
in the land the violence of your hands.
3 The ungodly are perverse *and* estranged from the womb;
they go astray as soon as they are born, speaking lies.
4 Their poison is like the venom of a serpent; they are
like the deaf adder *or* asp that stops its ear,
5 Which listens not to the voice of charmers *or* of the
enchanter never casting spells so cunningly.
6 Break their teeth, O God, in their mouths; break out
the fangs of the young lions, O Lord.
7 Let them melt away as water which runs on apace;
when he aims his arrows, let them be as if they were head-
less *or* split apart.
8 Let them be as a snail dissolving slime as it passes on
*or* as a festering sore which wastes away, like [the child
to which] a woman gives untimely birth that has not seen
the sun.
9 Before your pots can feel the thorns [that are placed
under them for fuel], He will take them away as with a
whirlwind, the green and the burning ones alike.
10 The [unyieldingly] righteous shall rejoice when he
sees the vengeance; he will bathe his feet in the blood of
the wicked.
11 Men will say, Surely there is a reward for the [uncom-
promisingly] righteous; surely there is a God Who judges
on the earth.

## Psalm 59

*To the Chief Musician; [set to the tune of] "Do Not Destroy."*
*Of David, a record of memorable thoughts when Saul sent men*
*to watch his house in order to kill him.*

1 Deliver me from my enemies, O my God; defend *and*
protect me from those who rise up against me.
2 Deliver me from *and* lift me above those who work evil
and save me from bloodthirsty men.
3 For, behold, they lie in wait for my life; fierce *and*
mighty men are banding together against me, not for my
transgression nor for any sin of mine, O Lord.
4 They run and prepare themselves, though there is no
fault in me; rouse Yourself [O Lord] to meet *and* help me,
and see!
5 You, O Lord God of hosts, the God of Israel, arise to
visit all the nations; spare none *and* be not merciful to
any who treacherously plot evil. Selah [pause, and calmly
think of that]!
6 They return at evening, they howl *and* snarl like dogs,
and go [prowling] about the city.
7 Behold, they belch out [insults] with their mouths;
swords [of sarcasm, ridicule, slander, and lies] are in their
lips, for who, they think, hears us?
8 But You, O Lord, will laugh at them [in scorn]; You will
hold all the nations in derision.
9 O my Strength, I will watch *and* give heed to You *and*
sing praises; for God is my Defense (my Protector and
High Tower).

---

[a] In Hebrew texts 58:1-11 is numbered 58:2-12.    [b] Title: Probably a
literary or musical term    [c] 9 The meaning of the Hebrew for this
verse is uncertain.    [d] In Hebrew texts 59:1-17 is numbered 59:2-18.
[e] 5 The Hebrew has *Selah* (a word of uncertain meaning) here and at the
end of verse 13.

# New International Version

<sup>10</sup> my God on whom I can rely.

God will go before me
  and will let me gloat over those who slander me.
<sup>11</sup> But do not kill them, Lord our shield,<sup>a</sup>
  or my people will forget.
In your might uproot them
  and bring them down.
<sup>12</sup> For the sins of their mouths,
  for the words of their lips,
    let them be caught in their pride.
For the curses and lies they utter,
<sup>13</sup>   consume them in your wrath,
    consume them till they are no more.
Then it will be known to the ends of the earth
  that God rules over Jacob.

<sup>14</sup> They return at evening,
  snarling like dogs,
  and prowl about the city.
<sup>15</sup> They wander about for food
  and howl if not satisfied.
<sup>16</sup> But I will sing of your strength,
  in the morning I will sing of your love;
for you are my fortress,
  my refuge in times of trouble.

<sup>17</sup> You are my strength, I sing praise to you;
  you, God, are my fortress,
  my God on whom I can rely.

## Psalm 60<sup>b</sup>

*For the director of music. To the tune of "The Lily of the Covenant." A miktam<sup>c</sup> of David. For teaching. When he fought Aram Naharaim<sup>d</sup> and Aram Zobah,<sup>e</sup> and when Joab returned and struck down twelve thousand Edomites in the Valley of Salt.*

<sup>1</sup> You have rejected us, God, and burst upon us;
  you have been angry—now restore us!
<sup>2</sup> You have shaken the land and torn it open;
  mend its fractures, for it is quaking.
<sup>3</sup> You have shown your people desperate times;
  you have given us wine that makes us stagger.
<sup>4</sup> But for those who fear you, you have raised a banner
  to be unfurled against the bow.<sup>f</sup>

<sup>5</sup> Save us and help us with your right hand,
  that those you love may be delivered.
<sup>6</sup> God has spoken from his sanctuary:
  "In triumph I will parcel out Shechem
    and measure off the Valley of Sukkoth.
<sup>7</sup> Gilead is mine, and Manasseh is mine;
  Ephraim is my helmet,
  Judah is my scepter.
<sup>8</sup> Moab is my washbasin,
  on Edom I toss my sandal;
  over Philistia I shout in triumph."

<sup>9</sup> Who will bring me to the fortified city?
  Who will lead me to Edom?
<sup>10</sup> Is it not you, God, you who have now rejected us
  and no longer go out with our armies?
<sup>11</sup> Give us aid against the enemy,
  for human help is worthless.
<sup>12</sup> With God we will gain the victory,
  and he will trample down our enemies.

# Amplified Bible

<sup>10</sup> My God in His mercy *and* steadfast love will meet me; God will let me look [triumphantly] on my enemies (those who lie in wait for me).
<sup>11</sup> Slay them not, lest my people forget; scatter them by Your power *and* make them wander to and fro, and bring them down, O Lord our Shield!
<sup>12</sup> For the sin of their mouths and the words of their lips, let them even be trapped *and* taken in their pride, and for the cursing and lying which they utter.
<sup>13</sup> Consume them in wrath, consume them so that they shall be no more; and let them know unto the ends of the earth that God rules over Jacob (Israel). Selah [pause, and calmly think of that]!
<sup>14</sup> And at evening let them return; let them howl *and* snarl like dogs, and go prowling about the city.
<sup>15</sup> Let them wander up and down for food and tarry all night if they are not satisfied (not getting their fill).
<sup>16</sup> But I will sing of Your mighty strength *and* power; yes, I will sing aloud of Your mercy *and* loving-kindness in the morning; for You have been to me a defense (a fortress and a high tower) and a refuge in the day of my distress.
<sup>17</sup> Unto You, O my Strength, I will sing praises; for God is my Defense, my Fortress, *and* High Tower, the God Who shows me mercy *and* steadfast love.

## Psalm 60

To the Chief Musician; [set to the tune of] "The Lily of the Testimony." A poem of David intended to record memorable thoughts and to teach; when he had striven with the Arameans of Mesopotamia and the Arameans of Zobah, and when Joab returned and smote twelve thousand Edomites in the Valley of Salt.

<sup>1</sup> O God, you have rejected us *and* cast us off, broken down [our defenses], *and* scattered us; You have been angry—O restore us *and* turn Yourself to us again!
<sup>2</sup> You have made the land to quake *and* tremble, You have rent it [open]; repair its breaches, for it shakes *and* totters.
<sup>3</sup> You have made Your people suffer hard things; You have given us to drink wine that makes us reel *and* be dazed.
<sup>4</sup> [But now] You have set up a banner for those who fear *and* worshipfully revere You [to which they may flee from the bow], a standard displayed because of the truth. Selah [pause, and calmly think of that]!
<sup>5</sup> That Your beloved ones may be delivered, save with Your right hand and answer us [or me].
<sup>6</sup> God has spoken in His holiness [in His promises]: I will rejoice, I will divide and portion out [the land] Shechem and the Valley of Succoth [west to east].
<sup>7</sup> Gilead is Mine, and Manasseh is Mine; Ephraim also is My helmet (the defense of My head); Judah is My scepter *and* My lawgiver.
<sup>8</sup> Moab is My washpot [reduced to vilest servitude]; upon Edom I cast My shoe in triumph; over Philistia I raise the shout of victory.
<sup>9</sup> Who will bring me [David] into the strong city [of Petra]? Who will lead me into Edom?
<sup>10</sup> Have You not rejected us, O God? And will You not go forth, O God, with our armies?
<sup>11</sup> O give us help against the adversary, for vain (ineffectual and to no purpose) is the help or salvation of man.
<sup>12</sup> Through God we shall do valiantly, for He it is Who shall tread down our adversaries.

---

<sup>a</sup> 11 Or *sovereign*    <sup>b</sup> In Hebrew texts 60:1-12 is numbered 60:3-14.
<sup>c</sup> Title: Probably a literary or musical term    <sup>d</sup> Title: That is, Arameans of Northwest Mesopotamia    <sup>e</sup> Title: That is, Arameans of central Syria
<sup>f</sup> 4 The Hebrew has *Selah* (a word of uncertain meaning) here.

## New International Version

### Psalm 61[a]

*For the director of music. With stringed instruments. Of David.*

[1] Hear my cry, O God;
  listen to my prayer.
[2] From the ends of the earth I call to you,
  I call as my heart grows faint;
  lead me to the rock that is higher than I.
[3] For you have been my refuge,
  a strong tower against the foe.

[4] I long to dwell in your tent forever
  and take refuge in the shelter of your wings.[b]
[5] For you, God, have heard my vows;
  you have given me the heritage of those who fear
    your name.

[6] Increase the days of the king's life,
  his years for many generations.
[7] May he be enthroned in God's presence forever;
  appoint your love and faithfulness to protect him.

[8] Then I will ever sing in praise of your name
  and fulfill my vows day after day.

### Psalm 62[c]

*For the director of music. For Jeduthun. A psalm of David.*

[1] Truly my soul finds rest in God;
  my salvation comes from him.
[2] Truly he is my rock and my salvation;
  he is my fortress, I will never be shaken.

[3] How long will you assault me?
  Would all of you throw me down—
  this leaning wall, this tottering fence?
[4] Surely they intend to topple me
  from my lofty place;
  they take delight in lies.
  With their mouths they bless,
  but in their hearts they curse.[d]

[5] Yes, my soul, find rest in God;
  my hope comes from him.
[6] Truly he is my rock and my salvation;
  he is my fortress, I will not be shaken.
[7] My salvation and my honor depend on God[e];
  he is my mighty rock, my refuge.
[8] Trust in him at all times, you people;
  pour out your hearts to him,
  for God is our refuge.

[9] Surely the lowborn are but a breath,
  the highborn are but a lie.
  If weighed on a balance, they are nothing;
  together they are only a breath.
[10] Do not trust in extortion
  or put vain hope in stolen goods;
  though your riches increase,
  do not set your heart on them.

[11] One thing God has spoken,
  two things I have heard:
  "Power belongs to you, God,
[12]   and with you, Lord, is unfailing love";
  and, "You reward everyone
    according to what they have done."

## Amplified Bible

### Psalm 61

To the Chief Musician; on stringed instruments.
[A Psalm] of David.

[1] Hear my cry, O God; listen to my prayer.
[2] From the end of the earth will I cry to You, when my heart is overwhelmed *and* fainting; lead me to the rock that is higher than I [yes, a rock that is too high for me].
[3] For You have been a shelter *and* a refuge for me, a strong tower against the adversary.
[4] I will dwell in Your tabernacle forever; let me find refuge *and* trust in the shelter of Your wings. Selah [pause, and calmly think of that]!
[5] For You, O God, have heard my vows; You have given me the heritage of those who fear, revere, *and* honor Your name.
[6] May You prolong the [true] [a]King's life [adding days upon days], and may His years be to the last generation [of this world and the generations of the world to come].
[7] May He sit enthroned forever before [the face of] God; O ordain that loving-kindness and faithfulness may watch over Him!
[8] So will I sing praise to Your name forever, paying my vows day by day.

### Psalm 62

To the Chief Musician; according to Jeduthun [Ethan, the noted musician, founder of an official musical family].
A Psalm of David.

[1] For God alone my soul waits in silence; from Him comes my salvation.
[2] He only is my Rock and my Salvation, my Defense *and* my Fortress, I shall not be greatly moved.
[3] How long will you set upon a man that you may slay him, all of you, like a leaning wall, like a tottering fence?
[4] They only consult to cast him down from his height [to dishonor him]; they delight in lies. They bless with their mouths, but they curse inwardly. Selah [pause, and calmly think of that]!
[5] My soul, wait only upon God *and* silently submit to Him; for my hope *and* expectation are from Him.
[6] He only is my Rock and my Salvation; He is my Defense *and* my Fortress, I shall not be moved.
[7] With God rests my salvation and my glory; He is my Rock of unyielding strength *and* impenetrable hardness, and my refuge is in God!
[8] Trust in, lean on, rely on, *and* have confidence in Him at all times, you people; pour out your hearts before Him. God is a refuge for us (a fortress and a high tower). Selah [pause, and calmly think of that]!
[9] Men of low degree [in the social scale] are emptiness (futility, a breath) *and* men of high degree [in the same scale] are a lie *and* a delusion. In the balances they go up; they are together lighter than a breath.
[10] Trust not in *and* rely confidently not on extortion *and* oppression, and do not vainly hope in robbery; if riches increase, set not your heart on them.
[11] God has spoken once, twice have I heard this: that power belongs to God.
[12] Also to You, O Lord, belong mercy *and* loving-kindness, for You render to every man according to his work. [Jer. 17:10; Rev. 22:12.]

---

[a] In Hebrew texts 61:1-8 is numbered 61:2-9.   [b] 4 The Hebrew has *Selah* (a word of uncertain meaning) here.   [c] In Hebrew texts 62:1-12 is numbered 62:2-13.   [d] 4 The Hebrew has *Selah* (a word of uncertain meaning) here and at the end of verse 8.   [e] 7 Or / *God Most High is my salvation and my honor*

[a] The thoughts of these verses (6-7) are fulfilled in Christ, David's great Son.

## New International Version

### Psalm 63[a]

*A psalm of David. When he was in the Desert of Judah.*

[1] You, God, are my God,
 earnestly I seek you;
I thirst for you,
 my whole being longs for you,
in a dry and parched land
 where there is no water.

[2] I have seen you in the sanctuary
 and beheld your power and your glory.
[3] Because your love is better than life,
 my lips will glorify you.
[4] I will praise you as long as I live,
 and in your name I will lift up my hands.
[5] I will be fully satisfied as with the richest of foods;
 with singing lips my mouth will praise you.

[6] On my bed I remember you;
 I think of you through the watches of the night.
[7] Because you are my help,
 I sing in the shadow of your wings.
[8] I cling to you;
 your right hand upholds me.

[9] Those who want to kill me will be destroyed;
 they will go down to the depths of the earth.
[10] They will be given over to the sword
 and become food for jackals.

[11] But the king will rejoice in God;
 all who swear by God will glory in him,
 while the mouths of liars will be silenced.

### Psalm 64[b]

*For the director of music. A psalm of David.*

[1] Hear me, my God, as I voice my complaint;
 protect my life from the threat of the enemy.

[2] Hide me from the conspiracy of the wicked,
 from the plots of evildoers.
[3] They sharpen their tongues like swords
 and aim cruel words like deadly arrows.
[4] They shoot from ambush at the innocent;
 they shoot suddenly, without fear.

[5] They encourage each other in evil plans,
 they talk about hiding their snares;
 they say, "Who will see it[c]?"
[6] They plot injustice and say,
 "We have devised a perfect plan!"
 Surely the human mind and heart are cunning.

[7] But God will shoot them with his arrows;
 they will suddenly be struck down.
[8] He will turn their own tongues against them
 and bring them to ruin;
 all who see them will shake their heads in scorn.
[9] All people will fear;
 they will proclaim the works of God
 and ponder what he has done.

[10] The righteous will rejoice in the LORD
 and take refuge in him;
 all the upright in heart will glory in him!

### Psalm 65[d]

*For the director of music. A psalm of David. A song.*

[1] Praise awaits[e] you, our God, in Zion;
 to you our vows will be fulfilled.

## Amplified Bible

### Psalm 63

A Psalm of David; when he was in the Wilderness of Judah.

[1] O God, you are my God, earnestly will I seek You; my inner self thirsts for You, my flesh longs *and* is faint for You, in a dry and weary land where no water is.
[2] So I have looked upon You in the sanctuary to see Your power and Your glory.
[3] Because Your loving-kindness is better than life, my lips shall praise You.
[4] So will I bless You while I live; I will lift up my hands in Your name.
[5] My whole being shall be satisfied as with marrow and fatness; and my mouth shall praise You with joyful lips
[6] When I remember You upon my bed and meditate on You in the night watches.
[7] For You have been my help, and in the shadow of Your wings will I rejoice.
[8] My whole being follows hard after You *and* clings closely to You; Your right hand upholds me.
[9] But those who seek *and* demand my life to ruin *and* destroy it shall [themselves be destroyed and] go into the lower parts of the earth [into the underworld of the dead].
[10] They shall be given over to the power of the sword; they shall be a prey for foxes *and* jackals.
[11] But the king shall rejoice in God; everyone who swears by Him [that is, who binds himself by God's authority, acknowledging His supremacy, and devoting himself to His glory and service alone; every such one] shall glory, for the mouths of those who speak lies shall be stopped.

### Psalm 64

To the Chief Musician. A Psalm of David.

[1] Hear my voice, O God, in my complaint; guard *and* preserve my life from the terror of the enemy.
[2] Hide me from the secret counsel *and* conspiracy of the ungodly, from the scheming of evildoers,
[3] Who whet their tongues like a sword, who aim venomous words like arrows,
[4] Who shoot from ambush at the blameless man; suddenly do they shoot at him, without self-reproach *or* fear.
[5] They encourage themselves in an evil purpose, they talk of laying snares secretly; they say, Who will discover *us*?
[6] They think out acts of injustice and say, We have accomplished a well-devised thing! For the inward thought of each one [is unsearchable] and his heart is deep.
[7] But God will shoot an unexpected arrow at them; and suddenly shall they be wounded.
[8] And they will be made to stumble, their own tongues turning against them; all who gaze upon them will shake their heads *and* flee away.
[9] And all men shall [reverently] fear *and* be in awe; and they will declare the work of God, for they will wisely consider *and* acknowledge that it is His doing.
[10] The [uncompromisingly] righteous shall be glad in the Lord and shall trust *and* take refuge in Him; and all the upright in heart shall glory *and* offer praise.

### Psalm 65

To the Chief Musician. A Psalm of David. A song.

[1] To you belongs silence (the submissive wonder of reverence which bursts forth into praise) *and* praise is due *and* fitting to You, O God, in Zion; and to You shall the vow be performed.

---

[a] In Hebrew texts 63:1-11 is numbered 63:2-12.   [b] In Hebrew texts 64:1-10 is numbered 64:2-11.   [c] 5 Or *us*   [d] In Hebrew texts 65:1-13 is numbered 65:2-14.   [e] 1 Or *befits*; the meaning of the Hebrew for this word is uncertain.

## New International Version

2You who answer prayer,
  to you all people will come.
3When we were overwhelmed by sins,
  you forgave*a* our transgressions.
4Blessed are those you choose
  and bring near to live in your courts!
We are filled with the good things of your house,
  of your holy temple.

5You answer us with awesome and righteous deeds,
  God our Savior,
the hope of all the ends of the earth
  and of the farthest seas,
6who formed the mountains by your power,
  having armed yourself with strength,
7who stilled the roaring of the seas,
  the roaring of their waves,
  and the turmoil of the nations.
8The whole earth is filled with awe at your wonders;
  where morning dawns, where evening fades,
  you call forth songs of joy.

9You care for the land and water it;
  you enrich it abundantly.
The streams of God are filled with water
  to provide the people with grain,
  for so you have ordained it.*b*
10You drench its furrows and level its ridges;
  you soften it with showers and bless its crops.
11You crown the year with your bounty,
  and your carts overflow with abundance.
12The grasslands of the wilderness overflow;
  the hills are clothed with gladness.
13The meadows are covered with flocks
  and the valleys are mantled with grain;
  they shout for joy and sing.

### Psalm 66

*For the director of music. A song. A psalm.*

1Shout for joy to God, all the earth!
2   Sing the glory of his name;
  make his praise glorious!
3Say to God, "How awesome are your deeds!
  So great is your power
  that your enemies cringe before you.
4All the earth bows down to you;
  they sing praise to you,
  they sing the praises of your name."*c*

5Come and see what God has done,
  his awesome deeds for mankind!
6He turned the sea into dry land,
  they passed through the waters on foot—
  come, let us rejoice in him.
7He rules forever by his power,
  his eyes watch the nations—
  let not the rebellious rise up against him.

8Praise our God, all peoples,
  let the sound of his praise be heard;
9he has preserved our lives
  and kept our feet from slipping.
10For you, God, tested us;
  you refined us like silver.
11You brought us into prison
  and laid burdens on our backs.

## Amplified Bible

2O You Who hear prayer, to You shall all flesh come.
3Iniquities *and* much varied guilt prevail against me;
[yet] as for our transgressions, You forgive *and* purge
them away [make atonement for them and cover them out
of Your sight]!
4Blessed (happy, fortunate, to be envied) is the man
whom You choose and cause to come near, that he may
dwell in Your courts! We shall be satisfied with the goodness of Your house, Your holy temple.

5By fearful *and* glorious things [that terrify the wicked
but make the godly sing praises] do You answer us in righteousness (rightness and justice), O God of our salvation,
You Who are the confidence and hope of all the ends of the
earth and of those far off on the seas;
6Who by [Your] might have founded the mountains, being girded with power,
7Who still the roaring of the seas, the roaring of their
waves, and the tumult of the peoples,
8So that those who dwell in earth's farthest parts are
afraid of [nature's] signs of Your presence. You make the
places where morning and evening have birth to shout for
joy.
9You visit the earth and saturate it with water; You
greatly enrich it; the river of God is full of water; You
provide them with grain when You have so prepared the
earth.
10You water the field's furrows abundantly, You settle
the ridges of it; You make the soil soft with showers, blessing the sprouting of its vegetation.
11You crown the year with Your bounty *and* goodness,
and the tracks of Your [chariot wheels] drip with fatness.
12The [luxuriant] pastures in the uncultivated country
drip [with moisture], and the hills gird themselves with
joy.
13The meadows are clothed with flocks, the valleys
also are covered with grain; they shout for joy and sing
together.

### Psalm 66

To the Chief Musician. A song. A Psalm.

1Make a joyful noise unto God, all the earth;
2Sing forth the honor *and* glory of His name; make His
praise glorious!
3Say to God, How awesome *and* fearfully glorious are
Your works! Through the greatness of Your power shall
Your enemies submit themselves to You [with feigned and
reluctant obedience].
4All the earth shall bow down to You and sing [praises]
to You; they shall praise Your name in song. Selah [pause,
and calmly think of that]!

5Come and see the works of God; see how [to save His
people He smites their foes; He is] terrible in His doings
toward the children of men.
6He turned the sea into dry land, they crossed through
the river on foot; there did we rejoice in Him.
7He rules by His might forever, His eyes observe *and*
keep watch *over* the nations; let not the rebellious exalt
themselves. Selah [pause, and calmly think of that]!

8Bless our God, O peoples, give Him grateful thanks
*and* make the voice of His praise be heard,
9Who put *and* kept us among the living, and has not
allowed our feet to slip.
10For You, O God, have proved us; You have tried us as
silver is tried, refined, *and* purified.
11You brought us into the net (the prison fortress, the
dungeon); You laid a heavy burden upon our loins.

---

*a 3* Or *made atonement for*    *b 9* Or *for that is how you prepare the land*
*c 4* The Hebrew has *Selah* (a word of uncertain meaning) here and at the
end of verses 7 and 15.

## New International Version

¹²You let people ride over our heads;
    we went through fire and water,
    but you brought us to a place of abundance.

¹³I will come to your temple with burnt offerings
    and fulfill my vows to you —
¹⁴vows my lips promised and my mouth spoke
    when I was in trouble.
¹⁵I will sacrifice fat animals to you
    and an offering of rams;
    I will offer bulls and goats.

¹⁶Come and hear, all you who fear God;
    let me tell you what he has done for me.
¹⁷I cried out to him with my mouth;
    his praise was on my tongue.
¹⁸If I had cherished sin in my heart,
    the Lord would not have listened;
¹⁹but God has surely listened
    and has heard my prayer.
²⁰Praise be to God,
    who has not rejected my prayer
    or withheld his love from me!

### Psalm 67ᵃ

*For the director of music. With stringed instruments.
A psalm. A song.*

¹May God be gracious to us and bless us
    and make his face shine on us—ᵇ
²so that your ways may be known on earth,
    your salvation among all nations.

³May the peoples praise you, God;
    may all the peoples praise you.
⁴May the nations be glad and sing for joy,
    for you rule the peoples with equity
    and guide the nations of the earth.
⁵May the peoples praise you, God;
    may all the peoples praise you.

⁶The land yields its harvest;
    God, our God, blesses us.
⁷May God bless us still,
    so that all the ends of the earth will fear him.

### Psalm 68ᶜ

*For the director of music. Of David. A psalm. A song.*

¹May God arise, may his enemies be scattered;
    may his foes flee before him.
²May you blow them away like smoke—
    as wax melts before the fire,
    may the wicked perish before God.
³But may the righteous be glad
    and rejoice before God;
    may they be happy and joyful.

⁴Sing to God, sing in praise of his name,
    extol him who rides on the cloudsᵈ;
    rejoice before him—his name is the LORD.
⁵A father to the fatherless, a defender of widows,
    is God in his holy dwelling.
⁶God sets the lonely in families,ᵉ
    he leads out the prisoners with singing;
    but the rebellious live in a sun-scorched land.

## Amplified Bible

¹²You caused men to ride over our heads [when we were prostrate]; we went through fire and through water, but You brought us out into a broad, moist place [to abundance and refreshment and the open air].
¹³I will come into Your house with burnt offerings [of entire consecration]; I will pay You my vows,
¹⁴Which my lips uttered and my mouth promised when I was in distress.
¹⁵I will offer to You burnt offerings of fat lambs, with rams consumed in sweet-smelling smoke; I will offer bullocks and he-goats. Selah [pause, and calmly think of that]!
¹⁶Come and hear, all you who reverently *and* worshipfully fear God, and I will declare what He has done for me!
¹⁷I cried aloud to Him; He was extolled *and* high praise was under my tongue.
¹⁸If I regard iniquity in my heart, the Lord will not hear me; [Prov. 15:29; 28:9; Isa. 1:15; John 9:31; James 4:3.]
¹⁹But certainly God has heard me; He has given heed to the voice of my prayer.
²⁰Blessed be God, Who has not rejected my prayer nor removed His mercy *and* loving-kindness from being [as it always is] with me.

### Psalm 67

To the Chief Musician; on stringed instruments.
A Psalm. A song.

¹God be merciful *and* gracious to us and bless us and cause His face to shine upon us *and* among us—Selah [pause, and calmly think of that]!—
²That Your way may be known upon earth, Your saving power (Your deliverances and Your salvation) among all nations.
³Let the peoples praise You [turn away from their idols] *and* give thanks to You, O God; let all the peoples praise *and* give thanks to You.
⁴O let the nations be glad and sing for joy, for You will judge the peoples fairly and guide, lead, *or* drive the nations upon earth. Selah [pause, and calmly think of that]!
⁵Let the peoples praise You [turn away from their idols] *and* give thanks to You, O God; let all the peoples praise *and* give thanks to You!
⁶The earth has yielded its harvest [in evidence of God's approval]; God, even our own God, will bless us.
⁷God will bless us, and all the ends of the earth shall reverently fear Him.

### Psalm 68

To the Chief Musician. A Psalm of David. A song.

¹God is [already] beginning to arise, and His enemies to scatter; let them also who hate Him flee before Him!
²As smoke is driven away, so drive them away; as wax melts before the fire, so let the wicked perish before the presence of God.
³But let the [uncompromisingly] righteous be glad; let them be in high spirits *and* glory before God, yes, let them [jubilantly] rejoice!
⁴Sing to God, sing praises to His name, cast up a highway for Him Who rides through the deserts—His name is the Lord—be in high spirits *and* glory before Him!
⁵A father of the fatherless and a judge *and* protector of the widows *is* God in His holy habitation.
⁶God places the solitary in families *and* gives the desolate a home in which to dwell; He leads the prisoners out to prosperity; but the rebellious dwell in a parched land.

---

ᵃ In Hebrew texts 67:1-7 is numbered 67:2-8.    ᵇ 1 The Hebrew has *Selah* (a word of uncertain meaning) here and at the end of verse 4.
ᶜ In Hebrew texts 68:1-35 is numbered 68:2-36.    ᵈ 4 Or *name, / prepare the way for him who rides through the deserts*    ᵉ 6 Or *the desolate in a homeland*

## New International Version

7 When you, God, went out before your people,
  when you marched through the wilderness,[a]
8 the earth shook, the heavens poured down rain,
  before God, the One of Sinai,
  before God, the God of Israel.
9 You gave abundant showers, O God;
  you refreshed your weary inheritance.
10 Your people settled in it,
  and from your bounty, God, you provided for the
    poor.
11 The Lord announces the word,
  and the women who proclaim it are a mighty throng:
12 "Kings and armies flee in haste;
  the women at home divide the plunder.
13 Even while you sleep among the sheep pens,[b]
  the wings of my dove are sheathed with silver,
  its feathers with shining gold."
14 When the Almighty[c] scattered the kings in the land,
  it was like snow fallen on Mount Zalmon.
15 Mount Bashan, majestic mountain,
  Mount Bashan, rugged mountain,
16 why gaze in envy, you rugged mountain,
  at the mountain where God chooses to reign,
  where the LORD himself will dwell forever?
17 The chariots of God are tens of thousands
  and thousands of thousands;
  the Lord has come from Sinai into his sanctuary.[d]
18 When you ascended on high,
  you took many captives;
  you received gifts from people,
even from[e] the rebellious—
  that you,[f] LORD God, might dwell there.

19 Praise be to the Lord, to God our Savior,
  who daily bears our burdens.
20 Our God is a God who saves;
  from the Sovereign LORD comes escape from death.
21 Surely God will crush the heads of his enemies,
  the hairy crowns of those who go on in their sins.
22 The Lord says, "I will bring them from Bashan;
  I will bring them from the depths of the sea,
23 that your feet may wade in the blood of your foes,
  while the tongues of your dogs have their share."
24 Your procession, God, has come into view,
  the procession of my God and King into the
    sanctuary.
25 In front are the singers, after them the musicians;
  with them are the young women playing the
    timbrels.
26 Praise God in the great congregation;
  praise the LORD in the assembly of Israel.
27 There is the little tribe of Benjamin, leading them,
  there the great throng of Judah's princes,
  and there the princes of Zebulun and of Naphtali.

## Amplified Bible

7 O God, when You went forth before Your people, when You marched through the wilderness—Selah [pause, and calmly think of that]!—
8 The earth trembled, the heavens also poured down [rain] at the presence of God; yonder Sinai quaked at the presence of God, the God of Israel.
9 You, O God, did send a plentiful rain; You did restore and confirm Your heritage when it languished and was weary.
10 Your flock found a dwelling place in it; You, O God, in Your goodness did provide for the poor and needy.
11 The Lord gives the word [of power]; the women who bear and publish [the news] are a great host.
12 The kings of the enemies' armies, they flee, they flee! She who tarries at home divides the spoil [left behind].
13 Though you [the slackers] may lie among the sheepfolds [in slothful ease, yet for Israel] the wings of a dove are covered with silver, its pinions excessively green with gold [are trophies taken from the enemy].
14 When the Almighty scattered kings in [the land], it was as when it snows on Zalmon [a wooded hill near Shechem].
15 Is Mount Bashan the high mountain of summits, Mount Bashan [east of the Jordan] the mount of God?
16 Why do you look with grudging and envy, you many-peaked mountains, at the mountain [of the city called Zion] which God has desired for His dwelling place? Yes, the Lord will dwell in it forever.
17 The chariots of God are twenty thousand, even thousands upon thousands. The Lord is among them as He was in Sinai, [so also] in the Holy Place (the sanctuary in Jerusalem).
18 aYou have ascended on high. You have led away captive a train of vanquished foes; You have received gifts of men, yes, of the rebellious also, that the Lord God might dwell there with them. [Eph. 4:8.]
19 Blessed be the Lord, Who bears our burdens and carries us day by day, even the God Who is our salvation! Selah [pause, and calmly think of that]!
20 God is to us a God of deliverances and salvation; and to God the Lord belongs escape from death [setting us free].
21 But God will shatter the heads of His enemies, the hairy scalp of such a one as goes on still in his trespasses and guilty ways.
22 The Lord said, I will bring back [your enemies] from Bashan; I will bring them back from the depths of the [Red] Sea,
23 That you may crush them, dipping your foot in blood, that the tongues of your dogs may have their share from the foe.
24 They see Your goings, O God, even the [solemn processions] of my God, my King, into the sanctuary [in holiness].
25 The singers go in front, the players on instruments last; between them the maidens are playing on tambourines.
26 Bless, give thanks, and gratefully praise God in full congregations, even the Lord, O you who are from [Jacob] the fountain of Israel.
27 There is little Benjamin in the lead [in the procession], the princes of Judah and their company, the princes of Zebulun, and the princes of Naphtali.

a David sang of the ark of the covenant, which after a great victory was transferred or brought back to Zion. In this fact he sees the principle of the history of the kingdom of God appearing in ever-widening circles and nobler manner. The earthly celebration of victory in battle, with the processional bearing of the ark into the temple, is to him a type of the method and course of the Messiah's kingdom, i.e., the certain triumph of God's kingdom and Christ's ascension to His place of enthronement. So the apostle Paul (in Eph. 4:8) is perfectly justified in finding the psalmist's eye directed toward Christ, and so interpreting it. The "on high" in the psalm is first of all Mount Zion, but this is a type of heaven, as Paul makes clear (J. P. Lange, A Commentary).

a 7 The Hebrew has Selah (a word of uncertain meaning) here and at the end of verses 19 and 32.    b 13 Or the campfires; or the saddlebags
c 14 Hebrew Shaddai    d 17 Probable reading of the original Hebrew text; Masoretic Text Lord is among them at Sinai in holiness
e 18 Or gifts for people, / even    f 18 Or they

## New International Version

28 Summon your power, God<sup>a</sup>;
  show us your strength, our God, as you have done before.
29 Because of your temple at Jerusalem
  kings will bring you gifts.
30 Rebuke the beast among the reeds,
  the herd of bulls among the calves of the nations.
  Humbled, may the beast bring bars of silver.
  Scatter the nations who delight in war.
31 Envoys will come from Egypt;
  Cush<sup>b</sup> will submit herself to God.

32 Sing to God, you kingdoms of the earth,
  sing praise to the Lord,
33 to him who rides across the highest heavens, the ancient heavens,
  who thunders with mighty voice.
34 Proclaim the power of God,
  whose majesty is over Israel,
  whose power is in the heavens.
35 You, God, are awesome in your sanctuary;
  the God of Israel gives power and strength to his people.

Praise be to God!

### Psalm 69<sup>c</sup>

*For the director of music. To the tune of "Lilies." Of David.*

1 Save me, O God,
  for the waters have come up to my neck.
2 I sink in the miry depths,
  where there is no foothold.
I have come into the deep waters;
  the floods engulf me.
3 I am worn out calling for help;
  my throat is parched.
My eyes fail,
  looking for my God.
4 Those who hate me without reason
  outnumber the hairs of my head;
many are my enemies without cause,
  those who seek to destroy me.
I am forced to restore
  what I did not steal.

5 You, God, know my folly;
  my guilt is not hidden from you.

6 Lord, the LORD Almighty,
  may those who hope in you
  not be disgraced because of me;
God of Israel,
  may those who seek you
  not be put to shame because of me.
7 For I endure scorn for your sake,
  and shame covers my face.
8 I am a foreigner to my own family,
  a stranger to my own mother's children;
9 for zeal for your house consumes me,
  and the insults of those who insult you fall on me.
10 When I weep and fast,
  I must endure scorn;
11 when I put on sackcloth,
  people make sport of me.
12 Those who sit at the gate mock me,
  and I am the song of the drunkards.

13 But I pray to you, LORD,
  in the time of your favor;

## Amplified Bible

28 Your God has commanded your strength [your might in His service and impenetrable hardness to temptation];
O God, display Your might *and* strengthen what You have wrought for us!
29 [Out of respect] for Your temple at Jerusalem kings shall bring gifts to You.
30 Rebuke the wild beasts dwelling among the reeds [in Egypt], the herd of bulls (the leaders) with the calves of the peoples; trample underfoot those who lust for tribute money; scatter the peoples who delight in war.
31 Princes shall come out of Egypt; Ethiopia shall hasten to stretch out her hands [with the offerings of submission] to God.
32 Sing to God, O kingdoms of the earth, sing praises to the Lord! Selah [pause, and calmly think of that]!
33 [Sing praises] to Him Who rides upon the heavens, the ancient heavens; behold, He sends forth His voice, His mighty voice.
34 Ascribe power *and* strength to God; His majesty is over Israel, and His strength *and* might are in the skies.
35 O God, awe-inspiring, profoundly impressive, *and* terrible are You out of Your holy places; the God of Israel Himself gives strength and fullness of might to His people. Blessed be God!

### Psalm 69

To the Chief Musician; [set to the tune of] "Lilies."
[A Psalm] of David.

1 Save me, O God, for the waters have come up to my neck [they threaten my life].
2 I sink in deep mire, where there is no foothold; I have come into deep waters, where the floods overwhelm me.
3 I am weary with my crying; my throat is parched; my eyes fail with waiting [hopefully] for my God.
4 Those who hate me without cause are more than the hairs of my head; those who would cut me off *and* destroy me, being my enemies wrongfully, are many *and* mighty. I am [forced] to restore what I did not steal. [John 15:25.]
5 O God, You know my folly *and* blundering; my sins *and* my guilt are not hidden from You.
6 Let not those who wait *and* hope *and* look for You, O Lord of hosts, be put to shame through me; let not those who seek *and* inquire for *and* require You [as their vital necessity] be brought to confusion *and* dishonor through me, O God of Israel.
7 Because for Your sake I have borne taunt *and* reproach; confusion *and* shame have covered my face.
8 I have become a stranger to my brethren, and an alien to my mother's children. [John 7:3-5.]
9 For zeal for Your house has eaten me up, and the reproaches *and* insults of those who reproach *and* insult You have fallen upon me. [John 2:17; Rom. 15:3.]
10 When I wept *and* humbled myself with fasting, I was jeered at *and* humiliated;
11 When I made sackcloth my clothing, I became a byword (an object of scorn) to them.
12 They who sit in [the city's] gate talk about me, and I am the song of the drunkards.
13 But as for me, my prayer is to You, O Lord. At an acceptable *and* opportune time, O God, in the multitude of

---

<sup>a</sup> 28 Many Hebrew manuscripts, Septuagint and Syriac; most Hebrew manuscripts *Your God has summoned power for you*   <sup>b</sup> 31 That is, the upper Nile region   <sup>c</sup> In Hebrew texts 69:1-36 is numbered 69:2-37.

## New International Version

in your great love, O God,
 answer me with your sure salvation.
14 Rescue me from the mire,
 do not let me sink;
deliver me from those who hate me,
 from the deep waters.
15 Do not let the floodwaters engulf me
 or the depths swallow me up
 or the pit close its mouth over me.

16 Answer me, LORD, out of the goodness of your love;
 in your great mercy turn to me.
17 Do not hide your face from your servant;
 answer me quickly, for I am in trouble.
18 Come near and rescue me;
 deliver me because of my foes.

19 You know how I am scorned, disgraced and shamed;
 all my enemies are before you.
20 Scorn has broken my heart
 and has left me helpless;
I looked for sympathy, but there was none,
 for comforters, but I found none.
21 They put gall in my food
 and gave me vinegar for my thirst.

22 May the table set before them become a snare;
 may it become retribution and[a] a trap.
23 May their eyes be darkened so they cannot see,
 and their backs be bent forever.
24 Pour out your wrath on them;
 let your fierce anger overtake them.
25 May their place be deserted;
 let there be no one to dwell in their tents.
26 For they persecute those you wound
 and talk about the pain of those you hurt.
27 Charge them with crime upon crime;
 do not let them share in your salvation.
28 May they be blotted out of the book of life
 and not be listed with the righteous.

29 But as for me, afflicted and in pain—
 may your salvation, God, protect me.

30 I will praise God's name in song
 and glorify him with thanksgiving.
31 This will please the LORD more than an ox,
 more than a bull with its horns and hooves.
32 The poor will see and be glad—
 you who seek God, may your hearts live!
33 The LORD hears the needy
 and does not despise his captive people.

34 Let heaven and earth praise him,
 the seas and all that move in them,
35 for God will save Zion
 and rebuild the cities of Judah.
 Then people will settle there and possess it;
36   the children of his servants will inherit it,
 and those who love his name will dwell there.

## Amplified Bible

Your mercy *and* the abundance of Your loving-kindness hear me, *and* in the truth *and* faithfulness of Your salvation answer me.
14 Rescue me out of the mire, and let me not sink; let me be delivered from those who hate me and from out of the deep waters.
15 Let not the floodwaters overflow *and* overwhelm me, neither let the deep swallow me up nor the [dug] pit [with water perhaps in the bottom] close its mouth over me.
16 Hear *and* answer me, O Lord, for Your loving-kindness is sweet *and* comforting; according to Your plenteous tender mercy *and* steadfast love turn to me.
17 Hide not Your face from Your servant, for I am in distress; O answer me speedily!
18 Draw close to me and redeem me; ransom *and* set me free because of my enemies [lest they glory in my prolonged distress]!
19 You know my reproach and my shame and my dishonor; my adversaries are all before You [fully known to You].
20 Insults *and* reproach have broken my heart; I am full of heaviness *and* I am distressingly sick. I looked for pity, but there was none, and for comforters, but I found none.
21 They gave me also gall [poisonous and bitter] for my food, and in my thirst they gave me vinegar (a soured wine) to drink. [Matt. 27:34, 48.]
22 Let their own table [with all its abundance and luxury] become a snare to them; and when they are secure in peace [or at their sacrificial feasts, let it become] a trap to them.
23 Let their eyes be darkened so that they cannot see, and make their loins tremble continually [from terror, dismay, and feebleness].
24 Pour out Your indignation upon them, and let the fierceness of Your burning anger catch up with them.
25 Let their habitation *and* their encampment be a desolation; let no one dwell in their tents. [Matt. 23:38; Acts 1:20.]
26 For they pursue *and* persecute him whom You have smitten, and they gossip about those whom You have wounded, [adding] to their grief *and* pain.
27 Let one [unforgiven] perverseness *and* iniquity accumulate upon another for them [in Your book], and let them not come into Your righteousness *or* be justified and acquitted by You.
28 Let them be blotted out of the book of the living *and* the book of life and not be enrolled among the [uncompromisingly] righteous (those upright and in right standing with God). [Rev. 3:4, 5; 20:12, 15; 21:27.]
29 But I am poor, sorrowful, and in pain; let Your salvation, O God, set me up on high.
30 I will praise the name of God with a song and will magnify Him with thanksgiving,
31 And it will please the Lord better than an ox or a bullock that has horns and hoofs.
32 The humble shall see it and be glad; you who seek God, inquiring for *and* requiring Him [as your first need], let your hearts revive *and* live! [Ps. 22:26; 42:1.]
33 For the Lord hears the poor *and* needy and despises not His prisoners (His miserable and wounded ones).
34 Let heaven and earth praise Him, the seas and everything that moves in them.
35 For God will save Zion and rebuild the cities of Judah; and [His servants] shall remain *and* dwell there and have it in their possession;
36 The children of His servants shall inherit it, and those who love His Name shall dwell in it.

---

*a* 22 Or snare / and their fellowship become

## New International Version

### Psalm 70[a]

*For the director of music. Of David. A petition.*

[1] Hasten, O God, to save me;
  come quickly, Lord, to help me.

[2] May those who want to take my life
  be put to shame and confusion;
may all who desire my ruin
  be turned back in disgrace.
[3] May those who say to me, "Aha! Aha!"
  turn back because of their shame.
[4] But may all who seek you
  rejoice and be glad in you;
may those who long for your saving help always say,
  "The Lord is great!"

[5] But as for me, I am poor and needy;
  come quickly to me, O God.
You are my help and my deliverer;
  Lord, do not delay.

### Psalm 71

[1] In you, Lord, I have taken refuge;
  let me never be put to shame.
[2] In your righteousness, rescue me and deliver me;
  turn your ear to me and save me.
[3] Be my rock of refuge,
  to which I can always go;
give the command to save me,
  for you are my rock and my fortress.
[4] Deliver me, my God, from the hand of the wicked,
  from the grasp of those who are evil and cruel.

[5] For you have been my hope, Sovereign Lord,
  my confidence since my youth.
[6] From birth I have relied on you;
  you brought me forth from my mother's womb.
  I will ever praise you.
[7] I have become a sign to many;
  you are my strong refuge.
[8] My mouth is filled with your praise,
  declaring your splendor all day long.

[9] Do not cast me away when I am old;
  do not forsake me when my strength is gone.
[10] For my enemies speak against me;
  those who wait to kill me conspire together.
[11] They say, "God has forsaken him;
  pursue him and seize him,
  for no one will rescue him."
[12] Do not be far from me, my God;
  come quickly, God, to help me.
[13] May my accusers perish in shame;
  may those who want to harm me
  be covered with scorn and disgrace.

[14] As for me, I will always have hope;
  I will praise you more and more.

[15] My mouth will tell of your righteous deeds,
  of your saving acts all day long—
  though I know not how to relate them all.
[16] I will come and proclaim your mighty acts, Sovereign Lord;
  I will proclaim your righteous deeds, yours alone.
[17] Since my youth, God, you have taught me,
  and to this day I declare your marvelous deeds.
[18] Even when I am old and gray,
  do not forsake me, my God,
till I declare your power to the next generation,
  your mighty acts to all who are to come.

## Amplified Bible

### Psalm 70

To the Chief Musician. [A Psalm] of David, to bring
to remembrance *or* make memorial.

[1] Make haste, O God, to deliver me; make haste to help
me, O Lord!
[2] Let them be put to shame *and* confounded that seek
*and* demand my life; let them be turned backward and
brought to confusion *and* dishonor who desire *and* delight
in my hurt.
[3] Let them be turned back *and* appalled because of their
shame *and* disgrace who say, Aha, aha!
[4] May all those who seek, inquire of *and* for You, *and*
require You [as their vital need] rejoice and be glad in You;
and may those who love Your salvation say continually, Let
God be magnified!
[5] But I am poor and needy; hasten to me, O God! You are
my Help and my Deliverer; O Lord, do not tarry!

### Psalm 71

[1] In you, O Lord, do I put my trust *and* confidently take
refuge; let me never be put to shame *or* confusion!
[2] Deliver me in Your righteousness and cause me to escape; bow down Your ear to me and save me!
[3] Be to me a rock of refuge in which to dwell, *and* a shel-
tering stronghold to which I may continually resort, which
You have appointed to save me, for You are my Rock and
my Fortress.
[4] Rescue me, O my God, out of the hand of the wicked,
out of the grasp of the unrighteous and ruthless man.
[5] For You are my hope; O Lord God, You are my trust
from my youth *and* the source of my confidence.
[6] Upon You have I leaned *and* relied from birth; You are
He Who took me from my mother's womb *and* You have
been my benefactor from that day. My praise is continually of You.
[7] I am as a wonder *and* surprise to many, but You are my
strong refuge.
[8] My mouth shall be filled with Your praise and with
Your honor all the day.
[9] Cast me not off *nor* send me away in the time of old
age; forsake me not when my strength is spent *and* my
powers fail.
[10] For my enemies talk against me; those who watch for
my life consult together,
[11] Saying, God has forsaken him; pursue *and* persecute
and take him, for there is none to deliver him.
[12] O God, be not far from me! O my God, make haste
to help me!
[13] Let them be put to shame and consumed who are adversaries to my life; let them be covered with reproach,
scorn, *and* dishonor who seek *and* require my hurt.
[14] But I will hope continually, and will praise You yet
more and more.
[15] My mouth shall tell of Your righteous acts *and* of Your
deeds of salvation all the day, for their number is more
than I know.
[16] I will come in the strength *and* with the mighty acts
of the Lord God; I will mention *and* praise Your righteousness, even Yours alone.
[17] O God, You have taught me from my youth, and hitherto have I declared Your wondrous works.
[18] Yes, even when I am old and gray-headed, O God, forsake me not, [but keep me alive] until I have declared Your
mighty strength to [this] generation, and Your might *and*
power to all that are to come.

---

[a] In Hebrew texts 70:1-5 is numbered 70:2-6.

## New International Version

19 Your righteousness, God, reaches to the heavens,
   you who have done great things.
   Who is like you, God?
20 Though you have made me see troubles,
   many and bitter,
   you will restore my life again;
from the depths of the earth
   you will again bring me up.
21 You will increase my honor
   and comfort me once more.

22 I will praise you with the harp
   for your faithfulness, my God;
I will sing praise to you with the lyre,
   Holy One of Israel.
23 My lips will shout for joy
   when I sing praise to you—
   I whom you have delivered.
24 My tongue will tell of your righteous acts
   all day long,
for those who wanted to harm me
   have been put to shame and confusion.

### Psalm 72

*Of Solomon.*

1 Endow the king with your justice, O God,
   the royal son with your righteousness.
2 May he judge your people in righteousness,
   your afflicted ones with justice.

3 May the mountains bring prosperity to the people,
   the hills the fruit of righteousness.
4 May he defend the afflicted among the people
   and save the children of the needy;
   may he crush the oppressor.
5 May he endure*a* as long as the sun,
   as long as the moon, through all generations.
6 May he be like rain falling on a mown field,
   like showers watering the earth.
7 In his days may the righteous flourish
   and prosperity abound till the moon is no more.

8 May he rule from sea to sea
   and from the River*b* to the ends of the earth.
9 May the desert tribes bow before him
   and his enemies lick the dust.
10 May the kings of Tarshish and of distant shores
   bring tribute to him.
   May the kings of Sheba and Seba
   present him gifts.
11 May all kings bow down to him
   and all nations serve him.

12 For he will deliver the needy who cry out,
   the afflicted who have no one to help.
13 He will take pity on the weak and the needy
   and save the needy from death.
14 He will rescue them from oppression and violence,
   for precious is their blood in his sight.

## Amplified Bible

19 Your righteousness also, O God, is very high [reaching to the heavens], You Who have done great things; O God, who is like You, *or* who is Your equal?
20 You Who have shown us [all] troubles great and sore will quicken us again and will bring us up again from the depths of the earth.
21 Increase my greatness (my honor) and turn and comfort me.
22 I will also praise You with the harp, even Your truth and faithfulness, O my God; unto You will I sing praises with the lyre, O Holy One of Israel.
23 My lips shall shout for joy when I sing praises to You, and my inner being, which You have redeemed.
24 My tongue also shall talk of Your righteousness all the day long; for they are put to shame, for they are confounded, who seek *and* demand my hurt.

### Psalm 72*a*

[A Psalm] for Solomon.

1 Give the king [knowledge of] Your [way of] judging, O God, and [the spirit of] Your righteousness to the king's son [to control all his actions].
2 Let him judge *and* govern Your people with righteousness, and Your poor *and* afflicted ones with judgment *and* justice.
3 The mountains shall bring peace to the people, and the hills, through [the general establishment of] righteousness.
4 May he judge *and* defend the poor of the people, deliver the children of the needy, and crush the oppressor,
5 So that they may revere *and* fear You while the sun and moon endure, throughout all generations.
6 May he [Solomon as a type of King David's greater Son] be like rain that comes down upon the mown grass, like showers that water the earth.
7 In *b* His [Christ's] days shall the [uncompromisingly] righteous flourish and peace abound till there is a moon no longer. [Isa. 11:3-9.]
8 He [Christ] shall have dominion also from sea to sea and from the River [Euphrates] to the ends of the earth. [Zech. 14:9.]
9 Those who dwell in the wilderness shall bow before Him and His enemies shall lick the dust.
10 The kings of Tarshish and of the coasts shall bring offerings; the kings of Sheba and Seba shall offer gifts.
11 Yes, all kings shall fall down before Him, all nations shall serve Him. [Ps. 138:4.]
12 For He delivers the needy when he calls out, the poor also and him who has no helper.
13 He will have pity on the poor *and* weak and needy and will save the lives of the needy.
14 He will redeem their lives from oppression *and* fraud and violence, and precious *and* costly shall their blood be in His sight.

---

*a* "This psalm, in highly wrought figurative style, describes the reign of a king as 'righteous, universal, beneficent, and perpetual.' By the older Jewish and most of the modern Christian interpreters it has been applied to Christ, Whose reign present and prospective alone corresponds with its statements. As the imagery of the Second Psalm was drawn from the martial character of David's reign, that of this is from the peaceful and prosperous state of Solomon's" (Robert Jamieson, A. R. Fausset and David Brown, *A Commentary*). "Jesus is here, beyond all doubt, in the glory of His reign, both as He now is and as He shall be revealed in the latter-day glory" (Charles Haddon Spurgeon, *The Treasury of David*). *b* See footnote on Ps. 72:1. The ideal concept of the king and the glorious effects of his reign are described, the fulfillment of which is experienced in Christ.

---

*a* 5 Septuagint; Hebrew *You will be feared*   *b* 8 That is, the Euphrates

# New International Version

15 Long may he live!
    May gold from Sheba be given him.
May people ever pray for him
    and bless him all day long.
16 May grain abound throughout the land;
    on the tops of the hills may it sway.
May the crops flourish like Lebanon
    and thrive[a] like the grass of the field.
17 May his name endure forever;
    may it continue as long as the sun.

Then all nations will be blessed through him,[b]
    and they will call him blessed.

18 Praise be to the LORD God, the God of Israel,
    who alone does marvelous deeds.
19 Praise be to his glorious name forever;
    may the whole earth be filled with his glory.
        Amen and Amen.

20 This concludes the prayers of David son of Jesse.

## BOOK III

*Psalms 73–89*

### Psalm 73

*A psalm of Asaph.*

1 Surely God is good to Israel,
    to those who are pure in heart.

2 But as for me, my feet had almost slipped;
    I had nearly lost my foothold.
3 For I envied the arrogant
    when I saw the prosperity of the wicked.

4 They have no struggles;
    their bodies are healthy and strong.[c]
5 They are free from common human burdens;
    they are not plagued by human ills.
6 Therefore pride is their necklace;
    they clothe themselves with violence.
7 From their callous hearts comes iniquity[d];
    their evil imaginations have no limits.
8 They scoff, and speak with malice;
    with arrogance they threaten oppression.
9 Their mouths lay claim to heaven,
    and their tongues take possession of the earth.
10 Therefore their people turn to them
    and drink up waters in abundance.[e]
11 They say, "How would God know?
    Does the Most High know anything?"

12 This is what the wicked are like—
    always free of care, they go on amassing wealth.

13 Surely in vain I have kept my heart pure
    and have washed my hands in innocence.
14 All day long I have been afflicted,
    and every morning brings new punishments.

15 If I had spoken out like that,
    I would have betrayed your children.
16 When I tried to understand all this,
    it troubled me deeply
17 till I entered the sanctuary of God;
    then I understood their final destiny.

# Amplified Bible

15 And He shall live; and to Him shall be given gold of Sheba; prayer also shall be made for Him *and* through Him continually, *and* they shall bless *and* praise Him all the day long.
16 There shall be abundance of grain in the soil upon the top of the mountains [the least fruitful places in the land]; the fruit of it shall wave like [the forests of] Lebanon, and [the inhabitants of] the city shall flourish like grass of the earth.
17 His name shall endure forever; His name shall continue as long as the sun [indeed, His name continues before the sun]. And men shall be blessed *and* bless themselves by Him; all nations shall call Him blessed!
18 Blessed be the Lord God, the God of Israel, Who alone does wondrous things!
19 Blessed be His glorious name forever; let the whole earth be filled with His glory! Amen and Amen!
20 The prayers of David son of Jesse are ended.

## BOOK THREE

### Psalm 73

A Psalm of Asaph.

1 Truly God is [only] good to Israel, even to those who are upright *and* pure in heart.
2 But as for me, my feet were almost gone, my steps had well-nigh slipped.
3 For I was envious of the foolish *and* arrogant when I saw the prosperity of the wicked.
4 For they suffer no violent pangs in their death, but their strength is firm.
5 They are not in trouble as other men; neither are they smitten *and* plagued like other men.
6 Therefore pride is about their necks like a chain; violence covers them like a garment [like a long, luxurious robe].
7 Their eyes stand out with fatness, they have more than heart could wish; *and* the imaginations of their minds overflow [with follies].
8 They scoff, and wickedly utter oppression; they speak loftily [from on high, maliciously and blasphemously].
9 They set their mouths against *and* speak down from heaven, and their tongues swagger through the earth [invading even heaven with blasphemy and smearing earth with slanders]. [Rev. 13:6.]
10 Therefore His people return here, and waters of a full cup [offered by the wicked] are [blindly] drained by them.
11 And they say, How does God know? Is there knowledge in the Most High?
12 Behold, these are the ungodly, who always prosper *and* are at ease in the world; they increase in riches.
13 Surely then in vain have I cleansed my heart and washed my hands in innocency.
14 For all the day long have I been smitten *and* plagued, and chastened every morning.
15 Had I spoken thus [and given expression to my feelings], I would have been untrue *and* have dealt treacherously against the generation of Your children.
16 But when I considered how to understand this, it was too great an effort for me *and* too painful
17 Until I went into the sanctuary of God; then I understood [for I considered] their end.

---

*a* 16 Probable reading of the original Hebrew text; Masoretic Text *Lebanon, / from the city*  *b* 17 Or *will use his name in blessings* (see Gen. 48:20)  *c* 4 With a different word division of the Hebrew; Masoretic Text *struggles at their death; / their bodies are healthy*
*d* 7 Syriac (see also Septuagint); Hebrew *Their eyes bulge with fat*
*e* 10 The meaning of the Hebrew for this verse is uncertain.

## New International Version

18 Surely you place them on slippery ground;
 you cast them down to ruin.
19 How suddenly are they destroyed,
 completely swept away by terrors!
20 They are like a dream when one awakes;
 when you arise, Lord,
 you will despise them as fantasies.

21 When my heart was grieved
 and my spirit embittered,
22 I was senseless and ignorant;
 I was a brute beast before you.

23 Yet I am always with you;
 you hold me by my right hand.
24 You guide me with your counsel,
 and afterward you will take me into glory.
25 Whom have I in heaven but you?
 And earth has nothing I desire besides you.
26 My flesh and my heart may fail,
 but God is the strength of my heart
 and my portion forever.

27 Those who are far from you will perish;
 you destroy all who are unfaithful to you.
28 But as for me, it is good to be near God.
 I have made the Sovereign Lord my refuge;
 I will tell of all your deeds.

### Psalm 74

*A maskil*[a] *of Asaph.*

1 O God, why have you rejected us forever?
 Why does your anger smolder against the sheep of
 your pasture?
2 Remember the nation you purchased long ago,
 the people of your inheritance, whom you
 redeemed—
 Mount Zion, where you dwelt.
3 Turn your steps toward these everlasting ruins,
 all this destruction the enemy has brought on the
 sanctuary.

4 Your foes roared in the place where you met with us;
 they set up their standards as signs.
5 They behaved like men wielding axes
 to cut through a thicket of trees.
6 They smashed all the carved paneling
 with their axes and hatchets.
7 They burned your sanctuary to the ground;
 they defiled the dwelling place of your Name.
8 They said in their hearts, "We will crush them
 completely!"
 They burned every place where God was worshiped
 in the land.

9 We are given no signs from God;
 no prophets are left,
 and none of us knows how long this will be.
10 How long will the enemy mock you, God?
 Will the foe revile your name forever?
11 Why do you hold back your hand, your right hand?
 Take it from the folds of your garment and destroy
 them!

12 But God is my King from long ago;
 he brings salvation on the earth.

13 It was you who split open the sea by your power;
 you broke the heads of the monster in the waters.
14 It was you who crushed the heads of Leviathan
 and gave it as food to the creatures of the desert.

## Amplified Bible

18 [After all] You do set the [wicked] in slippery places;
You cast them down to ruin *and* destruction.
19 How they become a desolation in a moment! They are
utterly consumed with terrors!
20 As a dream [which seems real] until one awakens,
so, O Lord, when You arouse Yourself [to take note of the
wicked], You will despise their outward show.

21 For my heart was grieved, embittered, *and* in a state of
ferment, and I was pricked in my heart [as with the sharp
fang of an adder].
22 So foolish, stupid, *and* brutish was I, and ignorant; I
was like a beast before You.
23 Nevertheless I am continually with You; You do hold
my right hand.
24 You will guide me with Your counsel, and afterward
receive me to honor *and* glory.
25 Whom have I in heaven but You? And I have no delight
*or* desire on earth besides You.
26 My flesh and my heart may fail, but God is the Rock
*and* firm Strength of my heart and my Portion forever.

27 For behold, those who are far from You shall perish;
You will destroy all who are false to You *and* like [spiritual]
harlots depart from You.
28 But it is good for me to draw near to God; I have put
my trust in the Lord God *and* made Him my refuge, that I
may tell of all Your works.

### Psalm 74

A skillful song, or a didactic or reflective poem, of Asaph.

1 O God, why do You cast us off forever? Why does Your
anger burn *and* smoke against the sheep of Your pasture?
2 [Earnestly] remember Your congregation which You
have acquired of old, which You have redeemed to be the
tribe of Your heritage; remember Mount Zion, where You
have dwelt.
3 Direct Your feet [quickly] to the perpetual ruins *and*
desolations; the foe has devastated *and* desecrated everything in the sanctuary.
4 In the midst of Your Holy Place Your enemies have
roared [with their battle cry]; they set up their own [idol]
emblems for signs [of victory].
5 They seemed like men who lifted up axes upon a thicket of trees to make themselves a record.
6 And then all the carved wood of the Holy Place they
broke down with hatchets and hammers.
7 They have set Your sanctuary on fire; they have profaned the dwelling place of Your [a] Name by casting it to
the ground.
8 They said in their hearts, Let us make havoc [of such
places] altogether. They have burned up all God's meet-
inghouses in the land.
9 We do not see our symbols; there is no longer any
prophet, neither does any among us know for how long.
10 O God, how long is the adversary to scoff *and* reproach? Is the enemy to blaspheme *and* revile Your name
forever?
11 Why do You hold back Your hand, even Your right
hand? Draw it out of Your bosom *and* consume them
[make an end of them]!
12 Yet God is my King of old, working salvation in the
midst of the earth.
13 You did divide the [Red] Sea by Your might; You broke
the heads of the [Egyptian] dragons in the waters. [Exod.
14:21.]
14 You crushed the heads of Leviathan (Egypt); You did
give him as food for the creatures inhabiting the wilderness.

---

## New International Version

¹⁵ It was you who opened up springs and streams;
  you dried up the ever-flowing rivers.
¹⁶ The day is yours, and yours also the night;
  you established the sun and moon.
¹⁷ It was you who set all the boundaries of the earth;
  you made both summer and winter.

¹⁸ Remember how the enemy has mocked you, LORD,
  how foolish people have reviled your name.
¹⁹ Do not hand over the life of your dove to wild beasts;
  do not forget the lives of your afflicted people
    forever.
²⁰ Have regard for your covenant,
  because haunts of violence fill the dark places of the
    land.
²¹ Do not let the oppressed retreat in disgrace;
  may the poor and needy praise your name.
²² Rise up, O God, and defend your cause;
  remember how fools mock you all day long.
²³ Do not ignore the clamor of your adversaries,
  the uproar of your enemies, which rises continually.

### Psalm 75ª

*For the director of music. To the tune of "Do Not Destroy."*
*A psalm of Asaph. A song.*

¹ We praise you, God,
  we praise you, for your Name is near;
  people tell of your wonderful deeds.

² You say, "I choose the appointed time;
  it is I who judge with equity.
³ When the earth and all its people quake,
  it is I who hold its pillars firm.ᵇ
⁴ To the arrogant I say, 'Boast no more,'
  and to the wicked, 'Do not lift up your horns.ᶜ
⁵ Do not lift your horns against heaven;
  do not speak so defiantly.'"

⁶ No one from the east or the west
  or from the desert can exalt themselves.
⁷ It is God who judges:
  He brings one down, he exalts another.
⁸ In the hand of the LORD is a cup
  full of foaming wine mixed with spices;
he pours it out, and all the wicked of the earth
  drink it down to its very dregs.

⁹ As for me, I will declare this forever;
  I will sing praise to the God of Jacob,
¹⁰ who says, "I will cut off the horns of all the wicked,
  but the horns of the righteous will be lifted up."

### Psalm 76ᵈ

*For the director of music. With stringed instruments.*
*A psalm of Asaph. A song.*

¹ God is renowned in Judah;
  in Israel his name is great.
² His tent is in Salem,
  his dwelling place in Zion.

## Amplified Bible

¹⁵ You did cleave open [the rock bringing forth] fountains and streams; You dried up mighty, ever-flowing rivers (the Jordan). [Exod. 17:6; Num. 20:11; Josh. 3:13.]
¹⁶ The day is Yours, the night also is Yours; You have established the [starry] light and the sun.
¹⁷ You have fixed all the borders of the earth [the divisions of land and sea and of the nations]; You have made summer and winter. [Acts 17:26.]
¹⁸ [Earnestly] remember how the enemy has scoffed, O Lord, *and* reproached You, and how a foolish *and* impious people has blasphemed Your name.
¹⁹ Oh, do not deliver the life of Your turtledove to the wild beast (to the greedy multitude); forget not the life [of the multitude] of Your poor forever.
²⁰ Have regard for the covenant [You made with Abraham], for the dark places of the land are full of the habitations of violence.
²¹ Oh, let not the downtrodden return in shame; let the oppressed and needy praise Your name.
²² Arise, O God, plead Your own cause; remember [earnestly] how the foolish *and* impious man scoffs *and* reproaches You day after day *and* all day long.
²³ Do not forget the [clamoring] voices of Your adversaries, the tumult of those who rise up against You, which ascends continually.

### Psalm 75

To the Chief Musician; [set to the tune of] "Do Not Destroy."
A Psalm of Asaph. A song.

¹ We give praise *and* thanks to You, O God, we praise *and* give thanks; Your wondrous works declare that Your ᵃName is near *and* they who invoke Your Name rehearse Your wonders.
² When the proper time has come [for executing My judgments], I will judge uprightly [says the Lord].
³ When the earth totters, and all the inhabitants of it, it is I Who will poise *and* keep steady its pillars. Selah [pause, and calmly think of that]!
⁴ I said to the arrogant *and* boastful, Deal not arrogantly [do not boast]; and to the wicked, Lift not up the horn [of personal aggrandizement].
⁵ Lift not up your [aggressive] horn on high, speak not with a stiff neck *and* insolent arrogance.
⁶ For not from the east nor from the west nor from the south come promotion *and* lifting up. [Isa. 14:13.]
⁷ But God is the Judge! He puts down one and lifts up another.
⁸ For in the hand of the Lord there is a cup [of His wrath], and the wine foams *and* is red, well mixed; and He pours out from it, and all the wicked of the earth must drain it and drink its dregs. [Ps. 60:3; Jer. 25:15; Rev. 14:9, 10; 16:19.]
⁹ But I will declare *and* rejoice forever; I will sing praises to the God of Jacob.
¹⁰ All the horns of the ungodly also will I cut off [says the Lord], but the horns of the [uncompromisingly] righteous shall be exalted.

### Psalm 76

To the Chief Musician; on stringed instruments.
A Psalm of Asaph. A song.

¹ In Judah God is known *and* renowned; His name is highly praised *and* is great in Israel.
² In [Jeru]Salem also is His tabernacle, and His dwelling place is in Zion.

---

ª In Hebrew texts 75:1-10 is numbered 75:2-11.  ᵇ 3 The Hebrew has *Selah* (a word of uncertain meaning) here.  ᶜ 4 *Horns* here symbolize strength; also in verses 5 and 10.  ᵈ In Hebrew texts 76:1-12 is numbered 76:2-13.

ᵃ See footnote on Deut. 12:5.

## New International Version

3 There he broke the flashing arrows,
  the shields and the swords, the weapons of war.[a]

4 You are radiant with light,
  more majestic than mountains rich with game.
5 The valiant lie plundered,
  they sleep their last sleep;
 not one of the warriors
  can lift his hands.
6 At your rebuke, God of Jacob,
  both horse and chariot lie still.

7 It is you alone who are to be feared.
  Who can stand before you when you are angry?
8 From heaven you pronounced judgment,
  and the land feared and was quiet—
9 when you, God, rose up to judge,
  to save all the afflicted of the land.
10 Surely your wrath against mankind brings you praise,
  and the survivors of your wrath are restrained.[b]

11 Make vows to the LORD your God and fulfill them;
  let all the neighboring lands
  bring gifts to the One to be feared.
12 He breaks the spirit of rulers;
  he is feared by the kings of the earth.

### Psalm 77[c]

*For the director of music. For Jeduthun. Of Asaph. A psalm.*

1 I cried out to God for help;
  I cried out to God to hear me.
2 When I was in distress, I sought the Lord;
  at night I stretched out untiring hands,
  and I would not be comforted.

3 I remembered you, God, and I groaned;
  I meditated, and my spirit grew faint.[d]
4 You kept my eyes from closing;
  I was too troubled to speak.
5 I thought about the former days,
  the years of long ago;
6 I remembered my songs in the night.
  My heart meditated and my spirit asked:

7 "Will the Lord reject forever?
  Will he never show his favor again?
8 Has his unfailing love vanished forever?
  Has his promise failed for all time?
9 Has God forgotten to be merciful?
  Has he in anger withheld his compassion?"

10 Then I thought, "To this I will appeal:
  the years when the Most High stretched out his
  right hand.
11 I will remember the deeds of the LORD;
  yes, I will remember your miracles of long ago.
12 I will consider all your works
  and meditate on all your mighty deeds."

13 Your ways, God, are holy.
  What god is as great as our God?
14 You are the God who performs miracles;
  you display your power among the peoples.
15 With your mighty arm you redeemed your people,
  the descendants of Jacob and Joseph.

---

[a] 3 The Hebrew has *Selah* (a word of uncertain meaning) here and at the end of verse 9.   [b] 10 Or *Surely the wrath of mankind brings you praise,* / *and with the remainder of wrath you arm yourself*   [c] In Hebrew texts 77:1-20 is numbered 77:2-21.   [d] 3 The Hebrew has *Selah* (a word of uncertain meaning) here and at the end of verses 9 and 15.

## Amplified Bible

3 There He broke the bow's flashing arrows, the shield, the sword, and the weapons of war. Selah [pause, and calmly think of that]!
4 Glorious *and* excellent are You from the mountains of prey [splendid and majestic, more than the everlasting mountains].
5 The stouthearted are stripped of their spoil, they have slept the sleep [of death]; and none of the men of might could raise their hands.
6 At Your rebuke, O God of Jacob, both chariot [rider] and horse are cast into a dead sleep [of death]. [Exod. 15:1, 21; Nah. 2:13; Zech. 12:4.]
7 You, even You, are to be feared [with awe and reverence]! Who may stand in Your presence when once Your anger is roused?
8 You caused sentence to be heard from heaven; the earth feared and was still—
9 When God arose to [establish] judgment, to save all the meek *and* oppressed of the earth. Selah [pause, and calmly think of that]!
10 Surely the wrath of man shall praise You; the remainder of wrath shall You restrain *and* gird *and* arm Yourself with it.
11 Vow and pay to the Lord your God; let all who are round about Him bring presents to Him Who ought to be [reverently] feared.
12 He will cut off the spirit [of pride and fury] of princes; He is terrible to the [ungodly] kings of the earth.

### Psalm 77

To the Chief Musician; after the manner of Jeduthun [one of David's three chief musicians, founder of an official musical family]. A Psalm of Asaph.

1 I will cry to God with my voice, even to God with my voice, and He will give ear *and* hearken to me.
2 In the day of my trouble I seek (inquire of and desperately require) the Lord; in the night my hand is stretched out [in prayer] without slacking up; I refuse to be comforted.
3 I [earnestly] remember God; I am disquieted *and* I groan; I muse in prayer, and my spirit faints [overwhelmed]. Selah [pause, and calmly think of that]!
4 You hold my eyes from closing; I am so troubled that I cannot speak.
5 I consider the days of old, the years of bygone times [of prosperity].
6 I call to remembrance my song in the night; with my heart I meditate and my spirit searches diligently:
7 Will the Lord cast off forever? And will He be favorable no more?
8 Have His mercy *and* loving-kindness ceased forever? Have His promises ended for all time?
9 Has God [deliberately] abandoned *or* forgotten His graciousness? Has He in anger shut up His compassion? Selah [pause, and calmly think of that]!
10 And I say, This [apparent desertion of Israel by God] is my appointed lot *and* trial, but I will recall the years of the right hand of the Most High [in loving-kindness extended toward us], for this is my grief, that the right hand of the Most High changes.
11 I will [earnestly] recall the deeds of the Lord; yes, I will [earnestly] remember the wonders [You performed for our fathers] of old.
12 I will meditate also upon all Your works and consider all Your [mighty] deeds.
13 Your way, O God, is in the sanctuary [in holiness, away from sin and guilt]. Who is a great God like our God?
14 You are the God Who does wonders; You have demonstrated Your power among the peoples.
15 You have with Your [mighty] arm redeemed Your people, the sons of Jacob and Joseph. Selah [pause, and calmly think of that]!

## New International Version

16The waters saw you, God,
  the waters saw you and writhed;
  the very depths were convulsed.
17The clouds poured down water,
  the heavens resounded with thunder;
  your arrows flashed back and forth.
18Your thunder was heard in the whirlwind,
  your lightning lit up the world;
  the earth trembled and quaked.
19Your path led through the sea,
  your way through the mighty waters,
  though your footprints were not seen.

20You led your people like a flock
  by the hand of Moses and Aaron.

### Psalm 78

*A maskil*a *of Asaph.*

1My people, hear my teaching;
  listen to the words of my mouth.
2I will open my mouth with a parable;
  I will utter hidden things, things from of old—
3things we have heard and known,
  things our ancestors have told us.
4We will not hide them from their descendants;
  we will tell the next generation
the praiseworthy deeds of the LORD,
  his power, and the wonders he has done.
5He decreed statutes for Jacob
  and established the law in Israel,
which he commanded our ancestors
  to teach their children,
6so the next generation would know them,
  even the children yet to be born,
  and they in turn would tell their children.
7Then they would put their trust in God
  and would not forget his deeds
  but would keep his commands.
8They would not be like their ancestors—
  a stubborn and rebellious generation,
whose hearts were not loyal to God,
  whose spirits were not faithful to him.

9The men of Ephraim, though armed with bows,
  turned back on the day of battle;
10they did not keep God's covenant
  and refused to live by his law.
11They forgot what he had done,
  the wonders he had shown them.
12He did miracles in the sight of their ancestors
  in the land of Egypt, in the region of Zoan.
13He divided the sea and led them through;
  he made the water stand up like a wall.
14He guided them with the cloud by day
  and with light from the fire all night.
15He split the rocks in the wilderness
  and gave them water as abundant as the seas;
16he brought streams out of a rocky crag
  and made water flow down like rivers.

17But they continued to sin against him,
  rebelling in the wilderness against the Most High.
18They willfully put God to the test
  by demanding the food they craved.
19They spoke against God;
  they said, "Can God really
  spread a table in the wilderness?

## Amplified Bible

16When the waters [at the Red Sea and the Jordan] saw You, O God, they were afraid; the deep shuddered also, for [all] the waters saw You.
17The clouds poured down water, the skies sent out a sound [of rumbling thunder]; Your arrows went forth [in forked lightning].
18The voice of Your thunder was in the whirlwind, the lightnings illumined the world; the earth trembled and shook.
19Your way [in delivering Your people] was through the sea, and Your paths through the great waters, yet Your footsteps were not traceable, *but* were obliterated.
20You led Your people like a flock by the hand of Moses and Aaron.

### Psalm 78

*A skillful song, or* a didactic *or* reflective poem, of Asaph.

1Give ear, O my people, to my teaching; incline your ears to the words of my mouth.
2I will open my mouth in a parable (in instruction by numerous examples); I will utter dark sayings of old [that hide important truth]—[Matt. 13:34, 35.]
3Which we have heard and known, and our fathers have told us.
4We will not hide them from their children, but we will tell to the generation to come the praiseworthy deeds of the Lord, and His might, and the wonderful works that He has performed.
5For He established a testimony (an express precept) in Jacob and appointed a law in Israel, commanding our fathers that they should make [the great facts of God's dealings with Israel] known to their children,
6That the generation to come might know them, that the children still to be born might arise and recount them to their children,
7That they might set their hope in God and not forget the works of God, but might keep His commandments
8And might not be as their fathers—a stubborn and rebellious generation, a generation that set not their hearts aright *nor* prepared their hearts to know God, and whose spirits were not steadfast *and* faithful to God.
9The children of Ephraim were armed and carrying bows, yet they turned back in the day of battle.
10They kept not the covenant of God and refused to walk according to His law
11And forgot His works and His wonders that He had shown them.
12Marvelous things did He in the sight of their fathers in the land of Egypt, in the field of Zoan [where Pharaoh resided].
13He divided the [Red] Sea and caused them to pass through it, and He made the waters stand like a heap. [Exod. 14:22.]
14In the daytime also He led them with a [pillar of] cloud and all the night with a light of fire. [Exod. 13:21; 14:24.]
15He split rocks in the wilderness and gave them drink abundantly as out of the deep.
16He brought streams also out of the rock [at Rephidim and Kadesh] and caused waters to run down like rivers. [Exod. 17:6; Num. 20:11.]
17Yet they still went on to sin against Him by provoking *and* rebelling against the Most High in the wilderness (in the land of drought).
18And they tempted God in their hearts by asking for food according to their [selfish] desire *and* appetite.
19Yes, they spoke against God; they said, Can God furnish [the food for] a table in the wilderness?

---

a Title: Probably a literary or musical term

## New International Version

20 True, he struck the rock,
  and water gushed out,
  streams flowed abundantly,
  but can he also give us bread?
  Can he supply meat for his people?"
21 When the LORD heard them, he was furious;
  his fire broke out against Jacob,
  and his wrath rose against Israel,
22 for they did not believe in God
  or trust in his deliverance.
23 Yet he gave a command to the skies above
  and opened the doors of the heavens;
24 he rained down manna for the people to eat,
  he gave them the grain of heaven.
25 Human beings ate the bread of angels;
  he sent them all the food they could eat.
26 He let loose the east wind from the heavens
  and by his power made the south wind blow.
27 He rained meat down on them like dust,
  birds like sand on the seashore.
28 He made them come down inside their camp,
  all around their tents.
29 They ate till they were gorged—
  he had given them what they craved.
30 But before they turned from what they craved,
  even while the food was still in their mouths,
31 God's anger rose against them;
  he put to death the sturdiest among them,
  cutting down the young men of Israel.

32 In spite of all this, they kept on sinning;
  in spite of his wonders, they did not believe.
33 So he ended their days in futility
  and their years in terror.
34 Whenever God slew them, they would seek him;
  they eagerly turned to him again.
35 They remembered that God was their Rock,
  that God Most High was their Redeemer.
36 But then they would flatter him with their mouths,
  lying to him with their tongues;
37 their hearts were not loyal to him,
  they were not faithful to his covenant.
38 Yet he was merciful;
  he forgave their iniquities
  and did not destroy them.
  Time after time he restrained his anger
  and did not stir up his full wrath.
39 He remembered that they were but flesh,
  a passing breeze that does not return.
40 How often they rebelled against him in the wilderness
  and grieved him in the wasteland!
41 Again and again they put God to the test;
  they vexed the Holy One of Israel.
42 They did not remember his power—
  the day he redeemed them from the oppressor,
43 the day he displayed his signs in Egypt,
  his wonders in the region of Zoan.
44 He turned their river into blood;
  they could not drink from their streams.
45 He sent swarms of flies that devoured them,
  and frogs that devastated them.
46 He gave their crops to the grasshopper,
  their produce to the locust.
47 He destroyed their vines with hail
  and their sycamore-figs with sleet.
48 He gave over their cattle to the hail,
  their livestock to bolts of lightning.

## Amplified Bible

20 Behold, He did smite the rock so that waters gushed out and the streams overflowed; but can He give bread also? Can He provide flesh for His people?
21 Therefore, when the Lord heard, He was [full of] wrath; a fire was kindled against Jacob, His anger mounted up against Israel,
22 Because in God they believed not [they relied not on Him, they adhered not to Him], and they trusted not in His salvation (His power to save).
23 Yet He commanded the clouds above and opened the doors of heaven;
24 And He rained down upon them manna to eat and gave them heaven's grain. [Exod. 16:14; John 6:31.]
25 Everyone ate the bread of the mighty [man ate angels' food]; God sent them meat in abundance.
26 He let forth the east wind to blow in the heavens, and by His power He guided the south wind.
27 He rained flesh also upon them like the dust, and winged birds [quails] like the sand of the seas. [Num. 11:31.]
28 And He let [the birds] fall in the midst of their camp, round about their tents.
29 So they ate and were well filled; He gave them what they craved and lusted after.
30 But scarce had they stilled their craving, and while their meat was yet in their mouths, [Num. 11:33.]
31 The wrath of God came upon them and slew the strongest and sturdiest of them and smote down Israel's chosen youth.
32 In spite of all this, they sinned still more, for they believed not in (relied not on and adhered not to Him for) His wondrous works.
33 Therefore their days He consumed like a breath [in emptiness, falsity, and futility] and their years in terror and sudden haste.
34 When He slew [some of] them, [the remainder] inquired after Him diligently, and they repented and sincerely sought God [for a time].
35 And they [earnestly] remembered that God was their Rock, and the Most High God their Redeemer.
36 Nevertheless they flattered Him with their mouths and lied to Him with their tongues.
37 For their hearts were not right or sincere with Him, neither were they faithful and steadfast to His covenant. [Acts 8:21.]
38 But He, full of [merciful] compassion, forgave their iniquity and destroyed them not; yes, many a time He turned His anger away and did not stir up all His wrath and indignation.
39 For He [earnestly] remembered that they were but flesh, a wind that goes and does not return.
40 How often they defied and rebelled against Him in the wilderness and grieved Him in the desert!
41 And time and again they turned back and tempted God, provoking and incensing the Holy One of Israel.
42 They remembered not [seriously the miracles of the working of] His hand, nor the day when He delivered them from the enemy,
43 How He wrought His miracles in Egypt and His wonders in the field of Zoan [where Pharaoh resided]
44 And turned their rivers into blood, and their streams, so that they could not drink from them.
45 He sent swarms of [venomous] flies among them which devoured them, and frogs which destroyed them.
46 He gave also their crops to the caterpillar and [the fruit of] their labor to the locust.
47 He destroyed their vines with hail and their sycamore trees with frost and [great chunks of] ice.
48 He [caused them to shut up their cattle or] gave them up also to the hail and their flocks to hot thunderbolts. [Exod. 9:18-21.]

## New International Version

49 He unleashed against them his hot anger,
his wrath, indignation and hostility —
a band of destroying angels.
50 He prepared a path for his anger;
he did not spare them from death
but gave them over to the plague.
51 He struck down all the firstborn of Egypt,
the firstfruits of manhood in the tents of Ham.
52 But he brought his people out like a flock;
he led them like sheep through the wilderness.
53 He guided them safely, so they were unafraid;
but the sea engulfed their enemies.
54 And so he brought them to the border of his holy land,
to the hill country his right hand had taken.
55 He drove out nations before them
and allotted their lands to them as an inheritance;
he settled the tribes of Israel in their homes.

56 But they put God to the test
and rebelled against the Most High;
they did not keep his statutes.
57 Like their ancestors they were disloyal and faithless,
as unreliable as a faulty bow.
58 They angered him with their high places;
they aroused his jealousy with their idols.
59 When God heard them, he was furious;
he rejected Israel completely.
60 He abandoned the tabernacle of Shiloh,
the tent he had set up among humans.
61 He sent the ark of his might into captivity,
his splendor into the hands of the enemy.
62 He gave his people over to the sword;
he was furious with his inheritance.
63 Fire consumed their young men,
and their young women had no wedding songs;
64 their priests were put to the sword,
and their widows could not weep.

65 Then the Lord awoke as from sleep,
as a warrior wakes from the stupor of wine.
66 He beat back his enemies;
he put them to everlasting shame.
67 Then he rejected the tents of Joseph,
he did not choose the tribe of Ephraim;
68 but he chose the tribe of Judah,
Mount Zion, which he loved.
69 He built his sanctuary like the heights,
like the earth that he established forever.
70 He chose David his servant
and took him from the sheep pens;
71 from tending the sheep he brought him
to be the shepherd of his people Jacob,
of Israel his inheritance.
72 And David shepherded them with integrity of heart;
with skillful hands he led them.

## Amplified Bible

49 He let loose upon them the fierceness of His anger,
His wrath and indignation and distress, by sending [a mission of] angels of calamity *and* woe among them.
50 He leveled *and* made a straight path for His anger [to give it free course]; He did not spare [the Egyptian families] from death but gave their beasts over to the pestilence *and* the life [of their eldest] over to the plague.
51 He smote all the firstborn in Egypt, the chief of their strength in the tents [of the land of the sons] of Ham.
52 But [God] led His own people forth like sheep and guided them [with a shepherd's care] like a flock in the wilderness.
53 And He led them on safely *and* in confident trust, so that they feared not; but the sea overwhelmed their enemies. [Exod. 14:27, 28.]
54 And He brought them to His holy border, the border of [Canaan] His sanctuary, even to this mountain [Zion] which His right hand had acquired.
55 He drove out the nations also before [Israel] and allotted their land as a heritage, measured out *and* partitioned; and He made the tribes of Israel to dwell in the tents of those dispossessed.
56 Yet they tempted and provoked *and* rebelled against the Most High God and kept not His testimonies.
57 But they turned back and dealt unfaithfully *and* treacherously like their fathers; they were twisted like a warped *and* deceitful bow [that will not respond to the archer's aim].
58 For they provoked Him to [righteous] anger with their high places [for idol worship] and moved Him to jealousy with their graven images.
59 When God heard this, He was full of [holy] wrath; and He utterly rejected Israel, greatly abhorring *and* loathing [her ways],
60 So that He forsook the tabernacle at Shiloh, the tent in which He had dwelt among men [and never returned to it again],
61 And delivered His strength *and* power (the ark of the covenant) into captivity, and His glory into the hands of the foe (the Philistines). [I Sam. 4:21.]
62 He gave His people over also to the sword and was wroth with His heritage [Israel]. [I Sam. 4:10.]
63 The fire [of war] devoured their young men, and their bereaved virgins were not praised in a wedding song.
64 Their priests [Hophni and Phinehas] fell by the sword, and their widows made no lamentation [for the bodies came not back from the scene of battle, and the widow of Phinehas also died that day]. [I Sam. 4:11, 19, 20.]
65 Then the Lord awakened as from sleep, as a strong man whose consciousness of power is heightened by wine.
66 And He smote His adversaries in the back [as they fled]; He put them to lasting shame *and* reproach.
67 Moreover, He rejected the tent of Joseph and chose not the tribe of Ephraim [in which the tabernacle had been accustomed to stand].
68 But He chose the tribe of Judah [as Israel's leader], Mount Zion, which He loved [to replace Shiloh as His capital].
69 And He built His sanctuary [exalted] like the heights [of the heavens] and like the earth which He established forever.
70 He chose David His servant and took him from the sheepfolds; [I Sam. 16:11, 12.]
71 From tending the ewes that had their young He brought him to be the shepherd of Jacob His people, of Israel His inheritance. [II Sam. 7:7, 8.]
72 So [David] was their shepherd with an upright heart; he guided them by the discernment *and* skillfulness [which controlled] his hands.

## New International Version

### Psalm 79

*A psalm of Asaph.*

1 O God, the nations have invaded your inheritance;
    they have defiled your holy temple,
    they have reduced Jerusalem to rubble.
2 They have left the dead bodies of your servants
    as food for the birds of the sky,
    the flesh of your own people for the animals of the
        wild.
3 They have poured out blood like water
    all around Jerusalem,
    and there is no one to bury the dead.
4 We are objects of contempt to our neighbors,
    of scorn and derision to those around us.

5 How long, LORD? Will you be angry forever?
    How long will your jealousy burn like fire?
6 Pour out your wrath on the nations
    that do not acknowledge you,
  on the kingdoms
    that do not call on your name;
7 for they have devoured Jacob
    and devastated his homeland.

8 Do not hold against us the sins of past generations;
    may your mercy come quickly to meet us,
    for we are in desperate need.
9 Help us, God our Savior,
    for the glory of your name;
  deliver us and forgive our sins
    for your name's sake.
10 Why should the nations say,
    "Where is their God?"

Before our eyes, make known among the nations
    that you avenge the outpoured blood of your
        servants.
11 May the groans of the prisoners come before you;
    with your strong arm preserve those condemned to
        die.
12 Pay back into the laps of our neighbors seven times
    the contempt they have hurled at you, Lord.
13 Then we your people, the sheep of your pasture,
    will praise you forever;
  from generation to generation
    we will proclaim your praise.

### Psalm 80[a]

*For the director of music. To the tune of "The Lilies of the
Covenant." Of Asaph. A psalm.*

1 Hear us, Shepherd of Israel,
    you who lead Joseph like a flock.
  You who sit enthroned between the cherubim,
    shine forth 2 before Ephraim, Benjamin and
        Manasseh.
  Awaken your might;
    come and save us.

3 Restore us, O God;
    make your face shine on us,
    that we may be saved.

4 How long, LORD God Almighty,
    will your anger smolder
    against the prayers of your people?
5 You have fed them with the bread of tears;
    you have made them drink tears by the bowlful.
6 You have made us an object of derision[b] to our
        neighbors,
    and our enemies mock us.

---

a In Hebrew texts 80:1-19 is numbered 80:2-20.    b 6 Probable reading
of the original Hebrew text; Masoretic Text *contention*

## Amplified Bible

### Psalm 79

A Psalm of Asaph.

1 O God, the nations have come into [the land of Your
people] Your inheritance; Your sacred temple have they
defiled; they have made Jerusalem heaps of ruins.
2 The dead bodies of Your servants they have given as
food to the birds of the heavens, the flesh of Your saints to
the beasts of the earth.
3 Their blood they have poured out like water round
about Jerusalem, and there was none to bury them.
4 [Because of such humiliation] we have become a taunt
*and* reproach to our neighbors, a mocking and derision to
those who are round about us.
5 How long, O Lord? Will You be angry forever? Shall
Your jealousy [which cannot endure a divided allegiance]
burn like fire?
6 Pour out Your wrath on the Gentile nations who do not
acknowledge You, and upon the kingdoms that do not call
on Your name. [II Thess. 1:8.]
7 For they have devoured Jacob and laid waste his dwelling *and* his pasture.
8 O do not [earnestly] remember against us the iniquities *and* guilt of our forefathers! Let Your compassion *and*
tender mercy speedily come to meet us, for we are brought
very low.
9 Help us, O God of our salvation, for the glory of Your
name! Deliver us, forgive us, *and* purge away our sins for
Your name's sake.
10 Why should the Gentile nations say, Where is their
God? Let vengeance for the blood of Your servants which
is poured out be known among the nations in our sight [not
delaying until some future generation].
11 Let the groaning *and* sighing of the prisoner come
before You; according to the greatness of Your power *and*
Your arm spare those who are appointed to die!
12 And return into the bosom of our neighbors sevenfold
the taunts with which they have taunted *and* scoffed at
You, O Lord!
13 Then we Your people, the sheep of Your pasture, will
give You thanks forever; we will show forth *and* publish
Your praise from generation to generation.

### Psalm 80

To the Chief Musician; [set to the tune of] "Lilies, a
Testimony." A Psalm of Asaph.

1 Give ear, O Shepherd of Israel, You Who lead Joseph
like a flock; You Who sit enthroned upon the cherubim [of
the ark of the covenant], shine forth
2 Before *a* Ephraim and Benjamin and Manasseh! Stir up
Your might, and come to save us!
3 Restore us again, O God; and cause Your face to shine
[in pleasure and approval on us], and we shall be saved!
4 O Lord God of hosts, how long will You be angry with
Your people's prayers?
5 You have fed them with the bread of tears, and You
have given them tears to drink in large measure.
6 You make us a strife *and* scorn to our neighbors, and
our enemies laugh among themselves.

---

a It is supposed that these three tribes represented the whole twelve
tribes of Israel, Benjamin being incorporated with Judah, Manasseh
embracing the country beyond the Jordan, and Ephraim the remainder.
It was natural for the Israelites to think of the three in one group, for
they had camped together on the west side of the tabernacle during
the years in the wilderness, and also they were the only descendants of
Jacob's wife Rachel.

## New International Version

7 Restore us, God Almighty;
　　make your face shine on us,
　　that we may be saved.

8 You transplanted a vine from Egypt;
　　you drove out the nations and planted it.
9 You cleared the ground for it,
　　and it took root and filled the land.
10 The mountains were covered with its shade,
　　the mighty cedars with its branches.
11 Its branches reached as far as the Sea,[a]
　　its shoots as far as the River.[b]

12 Why have you broken down its walls
　　so that all who pass by pick its grapes?
13 Boars from the forest ravage it,
　　and insects from the fields feed on it.
14 Return to us, God Almighty!
　　Look down from heaven and see!
　　Watch over this vine,
15　　the root your right hand has planted,
　　the son[c] you have raised up for yourself.

16 Your vine is cut down, it is burned with fire;
　　at your rebuke your people perish.
17 Let your hand rest on the man at your right hand,
　　the son of man you have raised up for yourself.
18 Then we will not turn away from you;
　　revive us, and we will call on your name.

19 Restore us, Lord God Almighty;
　　make your face shine on us,
　　that we may be saved.

### Psalm 81[d]

*For the director of music. According to* gittith.[e] *Of Asaph.*

1 Sing for joy to God our strength;
　　shout aloud to the God of Jacob!
2 Begin the music, strike the timbrel,
　　play the melodious harp and lyre.

3 Sound the ram's horn at the New Moon,
　　and when the moon is full, on the day of our festival;
4 this is a decree for Israel,
　　an ordinance of the God of Jacob.
5 When God went out against Egypt,
　　he established it as a statute for Joseph.

I heard an unknown voice say:

6 "I removed the burden from their shoulders;
　　their hands were set free from the basket.
7 In your distress you called and I rescued you,
　　I answered you out of a thundercloud;
　　I tested you at the waters of Meribah.[f]
8 Hear me, my people, and I will warn you—
　　if you would only listen to me, Israel!
9 You shall have no foreign god among you;
　　you shall not worship any god other than me.
10 I am the Lord your God,
　　who brought you up out of Egypt.
　　Open wide your mouth and I will fill it.

11 "But my people would not listen to me;
　　Israel would not submit to me.
12 So I gave them over to their stubborn hearts
　　to follow their own devices.

## Amplified Bible

7 Restore us again, O God of hosts; and cause Your face to shine [upon us with favor as of old], and we shall be saved!

8 You brought a vine [Israel] out of Egypt; You drove out the [heathen] nations and planted it [in Canaan].
9 You prepared room before it, and it took deep root and it filled the land.
10 The mountains were covered with the shadow of it, and the boughs of it were like the great cedars [cedars of God].
11 [Israel] sent out its boughs to the [Mediterranean] Sea and its branches to the [Euphrates] River. [I Kings 4:21.]

12 Why have You broken down its hedges *and* walls so that all who pass by pluck from its fruit?
13 The boar out of the wood wastes it and the wild beast of the field feeds on it.
14 Turn again, we beseech You, O God of hosts! Look down from heaven and see, visit, *and* have regard for this vine!
15 [Protect and maintain] the stock which Your right hand planted, and the branch (the son) that You have reared *and* made strong for Yourself.

16 They have burned it with fire, it is cut down; may they perish at the rebuke of Your countenance.
17 Let Your hand be upon the man of Your right hand, upon the son of man whom You have made strong for Yourself.
18 Then will we not depart from You; revive us (give us life) and we will call upon Your name.

19 Restore us, O Lord God of hosts; cause Your face to shine [in pleasure, approval, and favor on us], and we shall be saved!

### Psalm 81

To the Chief Musician; set to Philistine lute, or [possibly] a particular Gittite tune. [A Psalm] of Asaph.

1 Sing aloud to God our Strength! Shout for joy to the God of Jacob!
2 Raise a song, sound the timbrel, the sweet lyre with the harp.
3 Blow the trumpet at the New Moon, at the full moon, on our feast day.
4 For this is a statute for Israel, an ordinance of the God of Jacob.
5 This He ordained in Joseph [the [a]savior] for a testimony when He went out over the land of Egypt. The speech of One Whom I knew not did I hear [saying],
6 I removed his shoulder from the burden; his hands were freed from the basket.
7 You called in distress and I delivered you; I answered you in the secret place of thunder; I tested you at the waters of Meribah. Selah [pause, and calmly think of that]! [Num. 20:3, 13, 24.]
8 Hear, O My people, and I will admonish you—O Israel, if you would listen to Me!
9 There shall no strange god be among you, neither shall you worship any alien god.
10 I am the Lord your God, Who brought you up out of the land of Egypt. Open your mouth wide and I will fill it.
11 But My people would not hearken to My voice, and Israel would have none of Me.
12 So I gave them up to their own hearts' lust *and* let them go after their own stubborn will, that they might follow their own counsels. [Acts 7:42, 43; 14:16; Rom. 1:24, 26.]

a Joseph had once gone out over Egypt with the title "Zaphenath-paneah," meaning, according to some, "Savior of the Age," to bring deliverance from famine to the Egyptians (Gen. 41:45). Later they forgot their benefactor and severely oppressed his family and descendants. "Then Joseph's God arose and went forth over the land [of Egypt] in righteous judgment, yet still as Savior of that people [Israel], in whom dwelt the germ of blessing for all nations." (David M. Kay, cited by James C. Gray and George M. Adams, *Bible Commentary*).

---

a 11 Probably the Mediterranean　　b 11 That is, the Euphrates
c 15 Or *branch*　　d In Hebrew texts 81:1-16 is numbered 81:2-17.
e Title: Probably a musical term　　f 7 The Hebrew has *Selah* (a word of uncertain meaning) here.

## New International Version

13 "If my people would only listen to me,
   if Israel would only follow my ways,
14 how quickly I would subdue their enemies
   and turn my hand against their foes!
15 Those who hate the LORD would cringe before him,
   and their punishment would last forever.
16 But you would be fed with the finest of wheat;
   with honey from the rock I would satisfy you."

### Psalm 82

*A psalm of Asaph.*

1 God presides in the great assembly;
   he renders judgment among the "gods":

2 "How long will you[a] defend the unjust
   and show partiality to the wicked?[b]
3 Defend the weak and the fatherless;
   uphold the cause of the poor and the oppressed.
4 Rescue the weak and the needy;
   deliver them from the hand of the wicked.

5 "The 'gods' know nothing, they understand nothing.
   They walk about in darkness;
   all the foundations of the earth are shaken.

6 "I said, 'You are "gods";
   you are all sons of the Most High.'
7 But you will die like mere mortals;
   you will fall like every other ruler."

8 Rise up, O God, judge the earth,
   for all the nations are your inheritance.

### Psalm 83[c]

*A song. A psalm of Asaph.*

1 O God, do not remain silent;
   do not turn a deaf ear,
   do not stand aloof, O God.
2 See how your enemies growl,
   how your foes rear their heads.
3 With cunning they conspire against your people;
   they plot against those you cherish.
4 "Come," they say, "let us destroy them as a nation,
   so that Israel's name is remembered no more."

5 With one mind they plot together;
   they form an alliance against you—
6 the tents of Edom and the Ishmaelites,
   of Moab and the Hagrites,
7 Byblos, Ammon and Amalek,
   Philistia, with the people of Tyre.
8 Even Assyria has joined them
   to reinforce Lot's descendants.[b]

9 Do to them as you did to Midian,
   as you did to Sisera and Jabin at the river Kishon,
10 who perished at Endor
   and became like dung on the ground.
11 Make their nobles like Oreb and Zeeb,
   all their princes like Zebah and Zalmunna,
12 who said, "Let us take possession
   of the pasturelands of God."

13 Make them like tumbleweed, my God,
   like chaff before the wind.
14 As fire consumes the forest
   or a flame sets the mountains ablaze,

## Amplified Bible

13 Oh, that My people would listen to Me, that Israel would walk in My ways!
14 Speedily then I would subdue their enemies and turn My hand against their adversaries.
15 [Had Israel listened to Me in Egypt, then] those who hated the Lord would have come cringing before Him, and their defeat would have lasted forever.
16 [God] would feed [Israel now] also with the finest of the wheat; and with honey out of the rock would I satisfy you.

### Psalm 82

A Psalm of Asaph.

1 God stands in the assembly [of the representatives] of God; in the midst of the magistrates *or* judges He gives judgment [as] among the gods.
2 How long will you [magistrates or judges] judge unjustly and show partiality to the wicked? Selah [pause, and calmly think of that]!
3 Do justice to the weak (poor) and fatherless; maintain the rights of the afflicted and needy.
4 Deliver the poor and needy; rescue them out of the hand of the wicked.
5 [The magistrates and judges] know not, neither will they understand; they walk on in the darkness [of complacent satisfaction]; all the foundations of the earth [the fundamental principles upon which rests the administration of justice] are shaking.
6 I said, You are gods [since you judge on My behalf, as My representatives]; indeed, all of you are children of the Most High. [John 10:34-36; Rom. 13:1, 2.]
7 But you shall die like men and fall as one of the princes.
8 Arise, O God, judge the earth! For to You belong all the nations. [Rev. 11:15.]

### Psalm 83

A song. A Psalm of Asaph.

1 Keep not silence, O God; hold not Your peace or be still, O God.
2 For, behold, Your enemies are in tumult, and those who hate You have raised their heads. [Acts 4:25, 26.]
3 They lay crafty schemes against Your people and consult together against Your hidden *and* precious ones.
4 They have said, Come, and let us wipe them out as a nation; let the name of Israel be in remembrance no more.
5 For they have consulted together with one accord *and* one heart; against You they make a covenant—
6 The tents of Edom and the Ishmaelites, of Moab and the Hagrites,
7 Gebal and Ammon and Amalek, the Philistines, with the inhabitants of Tyre.
8 Assyria also has joined with them; they have helped the children of Lot [the Ammonites and the Moabites] *and* have been an arm to them. Selah [pause, and calmly think of that]!
9 Do to them as [You did to] the Midianites, as to Sisera and Jabin at the brook of Kishon, [Judg. 4:12-24.]
10 Who perished at Endor, who became like manure for the earth.
11 Make their nobles like Oreb and Zeeb, yes, all their princes as Zebah and Zalmunna, [Judg. 7:23-25; 8:10-21.]
12 Who say, Let us take possession for ourselves of the pastures of God.
13 O my God, make them like whirling dust, like stubble *or* chaff before the wind!
14 As fire consumes the forest, and as the flame sets the mountains ablaze,

---

*a 2* The Hebrew is plural.  *b 2,8* The Hebrew has *Selah* (a word of uncertain meaning) here.  *c* In Hebrew texts 83:1-18 is numbered 83:2-19.

## New International Version

[15] so pursue them with your tempest
and terrify them with your storm.
[16] Cover their faces with shame, LORD,
so that they will seek your name.

[17] May they ever be ashamed and dismayed;
may they perish in disgrace.
[18] Let them know that you, whose name is the LORD—
that you alone are the Most High over all the earth.

### Psalm 84[a]

*For the director of music. According to* gittith.[b] *Of the Sons of Korah. A psalm.*

[1] How lovely is your dwelling place,
LORD Almighty!
[2] My soul yearns, even faints,
for the courts of the LORD;
my heart and my flesh cry out
for the living God.
[3] Even the sparrow has found a home,
and the swallow a nest for herself,
where she may have her young—
a place near your altar,
LORD Almighty, my King and my God.
[4] Blessed are those who dwell in your house;
they are ever praising you.[c]

[5] Blessed are those whose strength is in you,
whose hearts are set on pilgrimage.
[6] As they pass through the Valley of Baka,
they make it a place of springs;
the autumn rains also cover it with pools.[d]
[7] They go from strength to strength,
till each appears before God in Zion.

[8] Hear my prayer, LORD God Almighty;
listen to me, God of Jacob.
[9] Look on our shield,[e] O God;
look with favor on your anointed one.

[10] Better is one day in your courts
than a thousand elsewhere;
I would rather be a doorkeeper in the house of my God
than dwell in the tents of the wicked.
[11] For the LORD God is a sun and shield;
the LORD bestows favor and honor;
no good thing does he withhold
from those whose walk is blameless.

[12] LORD Almighty,
blessed is the one who trusts in you.

### Psalm 85[f]

*For the director of music. Of the Sons of Korah. A psalm.*

[1] You, LORD, showed favor to your land;
you restored the fortunes of Jacob.
[2] You forgave the iniquity of your people
and covered all their sins.[g]
[3] You set aside all your wrath
and turned from your fierce anger.

[4] Restore us again, God our Savior,
and put away your displeasure toward us.
[5] Will you be angry with us forever?
Will you prolong your anger through all
generations?
[6] Will you not revive us again,
that your people may rejoice in you?

---

[a] In Hebrew texts 84:1-12 is numbered 84:2-13.   [b] Title: Probably a musical term   [c] 4 The Hebrew has *Selah* (a word of uncertain meaning) here and at the end of verse 8.   [d] 6 Or *blessings*
[e] 9 Or *sovereign*   [f] In Hebrew texts 85:1-13 is numbered 85:2-14.
[g] 2 The Hebrew has *Selah* (a word of uncertain meaning) here.

## Amplified Bible

[15] So pursue *and* afflict them with Your tempest and terrify them with Your tornado *or* hurricane.
[16] Fill their faces with shame, that they may seek, inquire for, *and* insistently require Your name, O Lord.
[17] Let them be put to shame and dismayed forever; yes, let them be put to shame and perish,
[18] That they may know that You, Whose name alone is the Lord, are the Most High over all the earth.

### Psalm 84

To the Chief Musician; set to a Philistine lute, or [possibly] a particular Gittite tune. A Psalm of the sons of Korah.

[1] How lovely are Your tabernacles, O Lord of hosts!
[2] My soul yearns, yes, even pines *and* is homesick for the courts of the Lord; my heart and my flesh cry out *and* sing for joy to the living God.
[3] Yes, the sparrow has found a house, and the swallow a nest for herself, where she may lay her young—even Your altars, O Lord of hosts, my King and my God.
[4] Blessed (happy, fortunate, to be envied) are those who dwell in Your house *and* Your presence; they will be singing Your praises all the day long. Selah [pause, and calmly think of that]!
[5] Blessed (happy, fortunate, to be envied) is the man whose strength is in You, in whose heart are the highways to Zion.
[6] Passing through the Valley of Weeping (Baca), they make it a place of springs; the early rain also fills [the pools] with blessings.
[7] They go from strength to strength [increasing in victorious power]; each of them appears before God in Zion.
[8] O Lord God of hosts, hear my prayer; give ear, O God of Jacob! Selah [pause, and calmly think of that]!
[9] Behold our shield [the king as Your agent], O God, and look upon the face of Your anointed!
[10] For a day in Your courts is better than a thousand [anywhere else]; I would rather be a doorkeeper *and* stand at the threshold in the house of my God than to dwell [at ease] in the tents of wickedness.
[11] For the Lord God is a Sun and Shield; the Lord bestows [present] grace *and* favor and [future] glory (honor, splendor, and heavenly bliss)! No good thing will He withhold from those who walk uprightly.
[12] O Lord of hosts, blessed (happy, fortunate, to be envied) is the man who trusts in You [leaning and believing on You, committing all and confidently looking to You, and that without fear or misgiving]!

### Psalm 85

To the Chief Musician. A Psalm of the sons of Korah.

[1] Lord, you have [at last] been favorable *and* have dealt graciously with Your land [of Canaan]; You have brought back [from Babylon] the captives of Jacob.
[2] You have forgiven *and* taken away the iniquity of Your people, You have covered all their sin. Selah [pause, and calmly realize what that means]!
[3] You have withdrawn all Your wrath *and* indignation, You have turned away from the blazing anger [which You had let loose].
[4] Restore us, O God of our salvation, and cause Your anger toward us to cease [forever].
[5] Will You be angry with us forever? Will You prolong Your anger [and disfavor] *and* spread it out to all generations?
[6] Will You not revive us again, that Your people may rejoice in You?

## New International Version

⁷Show us your unfailing love, Lᴏʀᴅ,
  and grant us your salvation.

⁸I will listen to what God the Lᴏʀᴅ says;
  he promises peace to his people, his faithful
    servants—
  but let them not turn to folly.
⁹Surely his salvation is near those who fear him,
  that his glory may dwell in our land.

¹⁰Love and faithfulness meet together;
  righteousness and peace kiss each other.
¹¹Faithfulness springs forth from the earth,
  and righteousness looks down from heaven.
¹²The Lᴏʀᴅ will indeed give what is good,
  and our land will yield its harvest.
¹³Righteousness goes before him
  and prepares the way for his steps.

### Psalm 86

*A prayer of David.*

¹Hear me, Lᴏʀᴅ, and answer me,
  for I am poor and needy.
²Guard my life, for I am faithful to you;
  save your servant who trusts in you.
  You are my God; ³have mercy on me, Lord,
  for I call to you all day long.
⁴Bring joy to your servant, Lord,
  for I put my trust in you.

⁵You, Lord, are forgiving and good,
  abounding in love to all who call to you.
⁶Hear my prayer, Lᴏʀᴅ;
  listen to my cry for mercy.
⁷When I am in distress, I call to you,
  because you answer me.

⁸Among the gods there is none like you, Lord;
  no deeds can compare with yours.
⁹All the nations you have made
  will come and worship before you, Lord;
  they will bring glory to your name.
¹⁰For you are great and do marvelous deeds;
  you alone are God.

¹¹Teach me your way, Lᴏʀᴅ,
  that I may rely on your faithfulness;
give me an undivided heart,
  that I may fear your name.
¹²I will praise you, Lord my God, with all my heart;
  I will glorify your name forever.
¹³For great is your love toward me;
  you have delivered me from the depths,
  from the realm of the dead.

¹⁴Arrogant foes are attacking me, O God;
  ruthless people are trying to kill me—
  they have no regard for you.
¹⁵But you, Lord, are a compassionate and gracious God,
  slow to anger, abounding in love and faithfulness.
¹⁶Turn to me and have mercy on me;
  show your strength in behalf of your servant;
  save me, because I serve you
    just as my mother did.
¹⁷Give me a sign of your goodness,
  that my enemies may see it and be put to shame,
  for you, Lᴏʀᴅ, have helped me and comforted me.

## Amplified Bible

⁷Show us Your mercy *and* loving-kindness, O Lord, and grant us Your salvation.

⁸I will listen [with expectancy] to what God the Lord will say, for He will speak peace to His people, to His saints (those who are in right standing with Him)—but let them not turn again to [self-confident] folly.

⁹Surely His salvation is near to those who reverently *and* worshipfully fear Him, [and is ready to be appropriated] that [the manifest presence of God, His] glory may tabernacle *and* abide in our land.

¹⁰Mercy *and* loving-kindness and truth have met together; righteousness and peace have kissed each other.

¹¹Truth shall spring up from the earth, and righteousness shall look down from heaven.

¹²Yes, the Lord will give what is good, and our land will yield its increase.

¹³Righteousness shall go before Him and shall make His footsteps a way in which to walk.

### Psalm 86

A Prayer of David.

¹Incline your ear, O Lord, and answer me, for I am poor *and* distressed, needy *and* desiring.

²Preserve my life, for I am godly *and* dedicated; O my God, save Your servant, for I trust in You [leaning and believing on You, committing all and confidently looking to You, without fear or doubt].

³Be merciful *and* gracious to me, O Lord, for to You do I cry all the day.

⁴Make me, Your servant, to rejoice, O Lord, for to You do I lift myself up.

⁵For You, O Lord, are good, and ready to forgive [our trespasses, sending them away, letting them go completely and forever]; and You are abundant in mercy *and* loving-kindness to all those who call upon You.

⁶Give ear, O Lord, to my prayer; and listen to the cry of my supplications.

⁷In the day of my trouble I will call on You, for You will answer me.

⁸There is none like unto You among the gods, O Lord, neither are their works like unto Yours.

⁹All nations whom You have made shall come and fall down before You, O Lord; and they shall glorify Your name.

¹⁰For You are great and work wonders! You alone are God.

¹¹Teach me Your way, O Lord, that I may walk *and* live in Your truth; direct *and* unite my heart [solely, reverently] to fear *and* honor Your name. [Ps. 5:11; 69:36.]

¹²I will confess *and* praise You, O Lord my God, with my whole (united) heart; and I will glorify Your name forevermore.

¹³For great is Your mercy *and* loving-kindness toward me; and You have delivered me from the depths of Sheol [from the exceeding depths of affliction].

¹⁴O God, the proud *and* insolent are risen against me; a rabble of violent *and* ruthless men has sought *and* demanded my life, and they have not set You before them.

¹⁵But You, O Lord, are a God merciful and gracious, slow to anger and abounding in mercy *and* loving-kindness and truth.

¹⁶O turn to me and have mercy *and* be gracious to me; grant strength (might and inflexibility to temptation) to Your servant and save the son of Your handmaiden.

¹⁷Show me a sign of [Your evident] goodwill *and* favor, that those who hate me may see it and be put to shame, because You, Lord, [will show Your approval of me when You] help and comfort me.

# New International Version

## Psalm 87

*Of the Sons of Korah. A psalm. A song.*

[1] He has founded his city on the holy mountain.
[2] The LORD loves the gates of Zion
  more than all the other dwellings of Jacob.

[3] Glorious things are said of you,
  city of God:[a]
[4] "I will record Rahab[b] and Babylon
  among those who acknowledge me—
Philistia too, and Tyre, along with Cush[c]—
  and will say, 'This one was born in Zion.'"[d]
[5] Indeed, of Zion it will be said,
  "This one and that one were born in her,
  and the Most High himself will establish her."
[6] The LORD will write in the register of the peoples:
  "This one was born in Zion."

[7] As they make music they will sing,
  "All my fountains are in you."

## Psalm 88[e]

*A song. A psalm of the Sons of Korah. For the director
of music. According to* mahalath leannoth.[f] *A* maskil[g]
*of Heman the Ezrahite.*

[1] LORD, you are the God who saves me;
  day and night I cry out to you.
[2] May my prayer come before you;
  turn your ear to my cry.

[3] I am overwhelmed with troubles
  and my life draws near to death.
[4] I am counted among those who go down to the pit;
  I am like one without strength.
[5] I am set apart with the dead,
  like the slain who lie in the grave,
  whom you remember no more,
  who are cut off from your care.

[6] You have put me in the lowest pit,
  in the darkest depths.
[7] Your wrath lies heavily on me;
  you have overwhelmed me with all your waves.[h]
[8] You have taken from me my closest friends
  and have made me repulsive to them.
  I am confined and cannot escape;
[9]  my eyes are dim with grief.

  I call to you, LORD, every day;
  I spread out my hands to you.
[10] Do you show your wonders to the dead?
  Do their spirits rise up and praise you?
[11] Is your love declared in the grave,
  your faithfulness in Destruction[i]?
[12] Are your wonders known in the place of darkness,
  or your righteous deeds in the land of oblivion?

[13] But I cry to you for help, LORD;
  in the morning my prayer comes before you.
[14] Why, LORD, do you reject me
  and hide your face from me?

# Amplified Bible

## Psalm 87

*A Psalm of the sons of Korah. A song.*

[1] On the holy hills stands the city [of Jerusalem and the
temple] God founded.
[2] The Lord loves the gates of Zion [through which the
crowds of pilgrims enter from all nations] more than all
the dwellings of Jacob (Israel).
[3] Glorious things are spoken of you, O city of God. Selah
[pause, and calmly realize what that means]!
[4] I will make mention of Rahab [the poetic name for
Egypt] and Babylon as among those who know [the city of
God]—behold, Philistia and Tyre, with Ethiopia (Cush)—
[saying], This man was born there.
[5] Yes, of Zion it shall be said, This man and that man
were born in her, for the Most High Himself will establish
her.
[6] The Lord shall count, when He registers the peoples,
that this man was born there. Selah [pause, and calmly
think of that]!
[7] The singers as well as the players on instruments shall
say, All my springs (my sources of life and joy) are in you
[city of our God].

## Psalm 88

*A song. A Psalm of the sons of Korah. To the Chief Musician;
set to chant mournfully. A didactic or reflective poem
of Heman the Ezrahite.*

[1] O Lord, the God of my salvation, I have cried to You for
help by day; at night I am in Your presence. [Luke 18:7.]
[2] Let my prayer come before You *and* really enter into
Your presence; incline Your ear to my cry!
[3] For I am full of troubles, and my life draws near to
Sheol (the place of the dead).
[4] I am counted among those who go down into the pit
(the grave); I am like a man who has no help *or* strength
[a mere shadow],
[5] Cast away among the dead, like the slain that lie in
a [nameless] grave, whom You [seriously] remember no
more, and they are cut off from Your hand.
[6] You have laid me in the depths of the lowest pit, in
darkness, in the deeps.
[7] Your wrath lies hard upon me, and You have afflicted
me with all Your waves. Selah [pause, and calmly think of
that]! [Ps. 42:7.]
[8] You have put my [familiar] friends far from me; You
have made me an abomination to them. I am shut up, and
I cannot come forth.
[9] My eye grows dim because of sorrow *and* affliction.
Lord, I have called daily on You; I have spread forth my
hands to You.
[10] Will You show wonders to the dead? Shall the departed arise and praise You? Selah [pause, and calmly think
of that]!
[11] Shall Your steadfast love be declared in the grave? Or
Your faithfulness in Abaddon (Sheol, as a place of ruin and
destruction)?
[12] Shall Your wonders be known in the dark? And Your
righteousness in the place of forgetfulness [where the
dead forget and are forgotten]?
[13] But to You I cry, O Lord; and in the morning shall my
prayer come to meet You.
[14] Lord, why do You cast me off? Why do You hide Your
face from me? [Matt. 27:46.]

---

[a] 3 The Hebrew has *Selah* (a word of uncertain meaning) here and
at the end of verse 6.    [b] 4 A poetic name for Egypt    [c] 4 That is,
the upper Nile region    [d] 4 Or *"I will record concerning those who
acknowledge me: / 'This one was born in Zion.' / Hear this, Rahab and
Babylon, / and you too, Philistia, Tyre and Cush."*    [e] In Hebrew texts
88:1-18 is numbered 88:2-19.    [f] Title: Possibly a tune, "The Suffering
of Affliction"    [g] Title: Probably a literary or musical term    [h] 7 The
Hebrew has *Selah* (a word of uncertain meaning) here and at the end of
verse 10.    [i] 11 Hebrew *Abaddon*

# New International Version

15 From my youth I have suffered and been close to
     death;
     I have borne your terrors and am in despair.
16 Your wrath has swept over me;
     your terrors have destroyed me.
17 All day long they surround me like a flood;
     they have completely engulfed me.
18 You have taken from me friend and neighbor—
     darkness is my closest friend.

## Psalm 89[a]

*A maskil[b] of Ethan the Ezrahite.*

1 I will sing of the LORD's great love forever;
     with my mouth I will make your faithfulness known
     through all generations.
2 I will declare that your love stands firm forever,
     that you have established your faithfulness in
     heaven itself.
3 You said, "I have made a covenant with my chosen one,
     I have sworn to David my servant,
4 'I will establish your line forever
     and make your throne firm through all
     generations.'"[c]
5 The heavens praise your wonders, LORD,
     your faithfulness too, in the assembly of the holy
     ones.
6 For who in the skies above can compare with the
     LORD?
     Who is like the LORD among the heavenly beings?
7 In the council of the holy ones God is greatly feared;
     he is more awesome than all who surround him.
8 Who is like you, LORD God Almighty?
     You, LORD, are mighty, and your faithfulness
     surrounds you.
9 You rule over the surging sea;
     when its waves mount up, you still them.
10 You crushed Rahab like one of the slain;
     with your strong arm you scattered your enemies.
11 The heavens are yours, and yours also the earth;
     you founded the world and all that is in it.
12 You created the north and the south;
     Tabor and Hermon sing for joy at your name.
13 Your arm is endowed with power;
     your hand is strong, your right hand exalted.
14 Righteousness and justice are the foundation of your
     throne;
     love and faithfulness go before you.
15 Blessed are those who have learned to acclaim you,
     who walk in the light of your presence, LORD.
16 They rejoice in your name all day long;
     they celebrate your righteousness.
17 For you are their glory and strength,
     and by your favor you exalt our horn.[d]
18 Indeed, our shield[e] belongs to the LORD,
     our king to the Holy One of Israel.

19 Once you spoke in a vision,
     to your faithful people you said:
   "I have bestowed strength on a warrior;
     I have raised up a young man from among the
     people.

# Amplified Bible

15 I was afflicted and close to death from my youth up;
while I suffer Your terrors I am distracted [I faint].
16 Your fierce wrath has swept over me; Your terrors
have destroyed me.
17 They surround me like a flood all day long; together
they have closed in upon me.
18 Lover and friend have You put far from me; my familiar friends are darkness *and* the grave.

## Psalm 89

A skillful song, *or* a didactic *or* reflective poem,
of Ethan the Ezrahite.

1 I will sing of the mercy *and* loving-kindness of the Lord
forever; with my mouth will I make known Your faithfulness from generation to generation.
2 For I have said, Mercy *and* loving-kindness shall be
built up forever; Your faithfulness will You establish in the
very heavens [unchangeable and perpetual].
3 [You have said] I have made a [a]covenant with My chosen one, I have sworn to David My servant,
4 Your Seed I will establish forever, and I will build up
your throne for all generations. Selah [pause, and calmly
think of that]! [Isa. 9:7; Luke 1:32, 33; Gal. 3:16]
5 Let heaven (the angels) praise Your wonders, O Lord,
Your faithfulness also in the assembly of the holy ones
(the holy angels).
6 For who in the heavens can be compared to the Lord?
Who among the mighty [heavenly beings] can be likened
to the Lord,
7 A God greatly feared *and* revered in the council of the
holy (angelic) ones, and to be feared *and* worshipfully revered above all those who are round about Him?
8 O Lord God of hosts, who is a mighty one like unto
You, O Lord? And Your faithfulness is round about You [an
essential part of You at all times].
9 You rule the raging of the sea; when its waves arise,
You still them.
10 You have broken Rahab (Egypt) in pieces; with Your
mighty arm You have scattered Your enemies.
11 The heavens are Yours, the earth also is Yours; the
world and all that is in it, You have founded them.
12 The north and the south, You have created them; Mount
Tabor and Mount Hermon joyously praise Your name.
13 You have a mighty arm; strong is Your hand, Your
right hand is soaring high.
14 Righteousness and justice are the foundation of Your
throne; mercy *and* loving-kindness and truth go before
Your face.
15 Blessed (happy, fortunate, to be envied) are the people who know the joyful sound [who understand and appreciate the spiritual blessings symbolized by the feasts];
they walk, O Lord, in the light *and* favor of Your countenance!
16 In Your name they rejoice all the day, and in Your righteousness they are exalted.
17 For You are the glory of their strength [their proud
adornment], and by Your favor our horn is exalted *and* we
walk with uplifted faces!
18 For our shield belongs to the Lord, and our king to the
Holy One of Israel.
19 Once You spoke in a vision to Your devoted ones and
said, I have endowed one who is mighty [a hero, giving
him the power to help—to be a champion for Israel]; I have
exalted one chosen from among the people.

---

[a] "This covenant most incontestably had Jesus Christ in view. This is
the Seed or Posterity Who would sit on the throne and reign forever and
ever. David and his family have long since become extinct; none of his
race has sat on the Jewish throne for more than two thousand years. But
the Christ . . . will reign until all His enemies are put under His feet (Ps.
110:1; I Cor. 15:25, 27; Eph. 1:22); and to this the psalmist says, Selah."
(One of many similar 19th-century comments.)

---

[a] In Hebrew texts 89:1-52 is numbered 89:2-53.   [b] Title: Probably
a literary or musical term   [c] 4 The Hebrew has *Selah* (a word of
uncertain meaning) here and at the end of verses 37, 45 and 48.
[d] 17 *Horn* here symbolizes strong one.   [e] 18 Or *sovereign*

## New International Version

20 I have found David my servant;
   with my sacred oil I have anointed him.
21 My hand will sustain him;
   surely my arm will strengthen him.
22 The enemy will not get the better of him;
   the wicked will not oppress him.
23 I will crush his foes before him
   and strike down his adversaries.
24 My faithful love will be with him,
   and through my name his horn*a* will be exalted.
25 I will set his hand over the sea,
   his right hand over the rivers.
26 He will call out to me, 'You are my Father,
   my God, the Rock my Savior.'
27 And I will appoint him to be my firstborn,
   the most exalted of the kings of the earth.
28 I will maintain my love to him forever,
   and my covenant with him will never fail.
29 I will establish his line forever,
   his throne as long as the heavens endure.

30 "If his sons forsake my law
   and do not follow my statutes,
31 if they violate my decrees
   and fail to keep my commands,
32 I will punish their sin with the rod,
   their iniquity with flogging;
33 but I will not take my love from him,
   nor will I ever betray my faithfulness.
34 I will not violate my covenant
   or alter what my lips have uttered.
35 Once for all, I have sworn by my holiness—
   and I will not lie to David—
36 that his line will continue forever
   and his throne endure before me like the sun;
37 it will be established forever like the moon,
   the faithful witness in the sky."

38 But you have rejected, you have spurned,
   you have been very angry with your anointed one.
39 You have renounced the covenant with your servant
   and have defiled his crown in the dust.
40 You have broken through all his walls
   and reduced his strongholds to ruins.
41 All who pass by have plundered him;
   he has become the scorn of his neighbors.
42 You have exalted the right hand of his foes;
   you have made all his enemies rejoice.
43 Indeed, you have turned back the edge of his sword
   and have not supported him in battle.
44 You have put an end to his splendor
   and cast his throne to the ground.
45 You have cut short the days of his youth;
   you have covered him with a mantle of shame.

46 How long, LORD? Will you hide yourself forever?
   How long will your wrath burn like fire?
47 Remember how fleeting is my life.
   For what futility you have created all humanity!
48 Who can live and not see death,
   or who can escape the power of the grave?

## Amplified Bible

20 I have found David My servant; with My holy oil have I anointed him, [Acts 13:22.]
21 With whom My hand shall be established *and* ever abide; My arm also shall strengthen him.
22 The enemy shall not exact from him *or* do him violence *or* outwit him, nor shall the wicked afflict *and* humble him.
23 I will beat down his foes before his face and smite those who hate him.
24 My faithfulness and My mercy *and* loving-kindness shall be with him, and in My name shall his horn be exalted [great power and prosperity shall be conferred upon him].
25 I will set his hand in control also on the [Mediterranean] Sea, and his right hand on the rivers [Euphrates with its tributaries].
26 He shall cry to Me, You are my Father, my God, and the Rock of my salvation!
27 Also I will make him the firstborn, the highest of the kings of the earth. [Rev. 1:5.]
28 My mercy *and* loving-kindness will I keep for him forevermore, and My covenant shall stand fast *and* be faithful with him.
29 His *a* Offspring also will I make to endure forever, and his throne as the days of heaven. [Isa. 9:7; Gal. 3:16.]
30 If his children forsake My law and walk not in My ordinances,
31 If they break *or* profane My statutes and keep not My commandments,
32 Then will I punish their transgression with the rod [of chastisement], and their iniquity with stripes. [II Sam. 7:14.]
33 Nevertheless, My loving-kindness will I not break off from him, nor allow My faithfulness to fail [to lie and be false to him].
34 My covenant will I not break *or* profane, nor alter the thing that is gone out of My lips.
35 Once [for all] have I sworn by My holiness, which cannot be violated; I will not lie to David:
36 His Offspring shall endure forever, and his throne [shall continue] as the sun before Me. [Isa. 9:7; Gal. 3:16.]
37 It shall be established forever as the moon, the faithful witness in the heavens. Selah [pause, and calmly think of that]! [Rev. 1:5; 3:14.]
38 But [in apparent contradiction to all this] You [even You the faithful Lord] have cast off and rejected; You have been full of wrath against Your anointed.
39 You have despised *and* loathed and renounced the covenant with Your servant; You have profaned his crown by casting it to the ground.
40 You have broken down all his hedges *and* his walls; You have brought his strongholds to ruin.
41 All who pass along the road spoil *and* rob him; he has become the scorn *and* reproach of his neighbors.
42 You have exalted the right hand of his foes; You have made all his enemies rejoice.
43 Moreover, You have turned back the edge of his sword and have not made him to stand in battle.
44 You have made his glory *and* splendor to cease and have hurled it to the ground his throne.
45 The days of his youth have You shortened; You have covered him with shame. Selah [pause, and calmly think of that]!
46 How long, O Lord? Will You hide Yourself forever? How long shall Your wrath burn like fire?
47 O [earnestly] remember how short my time is *and* what a mere fleeting life mine is. For what emptiness, falsity, futility, *and* frailty You have created all men!
48 What man can live and shall not see death, or can deliver himself from the [powerful] hand of Sheol (the place of the dead)? Selah [pause, and calmly consider that]!

---

*a 24 Horn* here symbolizes strength.

*a* See footnote on Ps. 89:3.

## New International Version

49 Lord, where is your former great love,
    which in your faithfulness you swore to David?
50 Remember, Lord, how your servant has[a] been mocked,
    how I bear in my heart the taunts of all the nations,
51 the taunts with which your enemies, LORD, have
        mocked,
    with which they have mocked every step of your
        anointed one.

52 Praise be to the LORD forever!
        Amen and Amen.

### BOOK IV

*Psalms 90–106*

### Psalm 90

*A prayer of Moses the man of God.*

1 Lord, you have been our dwelling place
    throughout all generations.
2 Before the mountains were born
    or you brought forth the whole world,
    from everlasting to everlasting you are God.

3 You turn people back to dust,
    saying, "Return to dust, you mortals."
4 A thousand years in your sight
    are like a day that has just gone by,
    or like a watch in the night.
5 Yet you sweep people away in the sleep of death—
    they are like the new grass of the morning:
6 In the morning it springs up new,
    but by evening it is dry and withered.

7 We are consumed by your anger
    and terrified by your indignation.
8 You have set our iniquities before you,
    our secret sins in the light of your presence.
9 All our days pass away under your wrath;
    we finish our years with a moan.
10 Our days may come to seventy years,
    or eighty, if our strength endures;
    yet the best of them are but trouble and sorrow,
    for they quickly pass, and we fly away.
11 If only we knew the power of your anger!
    Your wrath is as great as the fear that is your due.
12 Teach us to number our days,
    that we may gain a heart of wisdom.

13 Relent, LORD! How long will it be?
    Have compassion on your servants.
14 Satisfy us in the morning with your unfailing love,
    that we may sing for joy and be glad all our days.

a 50 Or *your servants have*

## Amplified Bible

49 Lord, where are Your former loving-kindnesses
[shown in the reigns of David and Solomon], which You
swore to David in Your faithfulness?
50 Remember, Lord, *and* earnestly imprint [on Your
heart] the reproach of Your servants, scorned *and* insulted, how I bear in my bosom the reproach of all the many
*and* mighty peoples,
51 With which Your enemies have taunted, O Lord, with
which they have mocked the footsteps of Your anointed.
52 Blessed be the Lord forevermore! Amen and Amen.

### BOOK FOUR

### Psalm 90

A Prayer of Moses the man of God.

1 Lord, You have been our dwelling place *and* our refuge
in all generations [says Moses].
2 Before the mountains were brought forth or ever You
had formed *and* given birth to the earth and the world,
even from everlasting to everlasting You are God.
3 You turn man back to dust *and* corruption, and say,
Return, O sons of the earthborn [to the earth]!
4 For a thousand years in Your sight are but as yesterday
when it is past, or as a watch in the night. [II Pet. 3:8.]
5 You carry away [these disobedient people, doomed to
die within forty years] as with a flood; they are as a sleep
[vague and forgotten as soon as they are gone]. In the
morning they are like grass which grows up—
6 In the morning it flourishes and springs up; in the evening it is mown down and withers.
7 For we [the Israelites in the wilderness] are consumed
by Your anger, and by Your wrath are we troubled, overwhelmed, *and* frightened away.
8 Our iniquities, our secret heart *and* its sins [which we
would so like to conceal even from ourselves], You have
set in the [revealing] light of Your countenance.
9 For all our days [out here in this wilderness, says Mo-
ses] pass away in Your wrath; we spend our years as a tale
that is told [for we adults know we are doomed to die soon,
without reaching Canaan]. [Num. 14:26-35.]
10 The days of our years are *a*threescore years and ten
(seventy years)—or even, if by reason of strength, fourscore
years (eighty years); yet is their pride [in additional years]
only labor and sorrow, for it is soon gone, and we fly away.
11 Who knows the power of Your anger? [Who worthily
connects this brevity of life with Your recognition of sin?]
And Your wrath, who connects it with the reverent *and*
worshipful fear that is due You?
12 So teach us to number our days, that we may get us a
heart of wisdom.
13 Turn, O Lord [from Your fierce anger]! How long—?
Revoke Your sentence *and* be compassionate *and* at ease
toward Your servants.
14 O satisfy us with Your mercy *and* loving-kindness in
the morning [now, before we are older], that we may rejoice and be glad all our days.

a This psalm is credited to Moses, who is interceding with God to
remove the curse which made it necessary for every Israelite over
twenty years of age (when they rebelled against God at Kadesh-barnea)
to die before reaching the promised land (Num. 14:26-35). Moses says
most of them are dying at seventy years of age. This number has often
been mistaken as a set span of life for all mankind. It was not intended
to refer to anyone except those Israelites under the curse during that
particular forty years. Seventy years never has been the average span
of life for humanity. When Jacob, the father of the twelve tribes, had
reached 130 years (Gen. 47:9), he complained that he had not attained
to the years of his immediate ancestors. In fact, Moses himself lived to
be 120 years old, Aaron 123, Miriam several years older, and Joshua 110
years of age. Note as well that in the Millennium a person dying at 100
will still be thought a child (Isa. 65:20).

## New International Version

15 Make us glad for as many days as you have afflicted us,
  for as many years as we have seen trouble.
16 May your deeds be shown to your servants,
  your splendor to their children.

17 May the favor*a* of the Lord our God rest on us;
  establish the work of our hands for us—
  yes, establish the work of our hands.

### Psalm 91

1 Whoever dwells in the shelter of the Most High
  will rest in the shadow of the Almighty.*b*
2 I will say of the LORD, "He is my refuge and my fortress,
  my God, in whom I trust."

3 Surely he will save you
  from the fowler's snare
  and from the deadly pestilence.
4 He will cover you with his feathers,
  and under his wings you will find refuge;
  his faithfulness will be your shield and rampart.
5 You will not fear the terror of night,
  nor the arrow that flies by day,
6 nor the pestilence that stalks in the darkness,
  nor the plague that destroys at midday.
7 A thousand may fall at your side,
  ten thousand at your right hand,
  but it will not come near you.
8 You will only observe with your eyes
  and see the punishment of the wicked.

9 If you say, "The LORD is my refuge,"
  and you make the Most High your dwelling,
10 no harm will overtake you,
  no disaster will come near your tent.
11 For he will command his angels concerning you
  to guard you in all your ways;
12 they will lift you up in their hands,
  so that you will not strike your foot against a stone.
13 You will tread on the lion and the cobra;
  you will trample the great lion and the serpent.

14 "Because he*c* loves me," says the LORD, "I will rescue him;
  I will protect him, for he acknowledges my name.
15 He will call on me, and I will answer him;
  I will be with him in trouble,
  I will deliver him and honor him.
16 With long life I will satisfy him
  and show him my salvation."

### Psalm 92*d*

*A psalm. A song. For the Sabbath day.*

1 It is good to praise the LORD
  and make music to your name, O Most High,
2 proclaiming your love in the morning
  and your faithfulness at night,
3 to the music of the ten-stringed lyre
  and the melody of the harp.

4 For you make me glad by your deeds, LORD;
  I sing for joy at what your hands have done.

## Amplified Bible

15 Make us glad in proportion to the days in which You have afflicted us *and* to the years in which we have suffered evil.
16 Let Your work [the signs of Your power] be revealed to Your servants, and Your [glorious] majesty to their children.
17 And let the beauty *and* delightfulness *and* favor of the Lord our God be upon us; confirm *and* establish the work of our hands—yes, the work of our hands, confirm *and* establish it.

### *a*Psalm 91

1 He who dwells in the secret place of the Most High shall remain stable *and* fixed under the shadow of the Almighty [Whose power no foe can withstand].
2 I will say of the Lord, He is my Refuge and my Fortress, my God; on Him I lean *and* rely, *and* in Him I [confidently] trust!
3 For [then] He will deliver you from the snare of the fowler and from the deadly pestilence.
4 [Then] He will cover you with His pinions, and under His wings shall you trust *and* find refuge; His truth *and* His faithfulness are a shield and a buckler.
5 You shall not be afraid of the terror of the night, nor of the arrow (the evil plots and slanders of the wicked) that flies by day,
6 Nor of the pestilence that stalks in darkness, nor of the destruction *and* sudden death that surprise *and* lay waste at noonday.
7 A thousand may fall at your side, and ten thousand at your right hand, but it shall not come near you.
8 Only a spectator shall you be [yourself inaccessible in the secret place of the Most High] as you witness the reward of the wicked.
9 Because you have made the Lord your refuge, and the Most High your dwelling place, [Ps. 91:1, 14.]
10 There shall no evil befall you, nor any plague *or* calamity come near your tent.
11 For He will give His angels [especial] charge over you to accompany *and* defend *and* preserve you in all your ways [of obedience and service].
12 They shall bear you up on their hands, lest you dash your foot against a stone. [Luke 4:10, 11; Heb. 1:14.]
13 You shall tread upon the lion and adder; the young lion and the serpent shall you trample underfoot. [Luke 10:19.]
14 Because he has set his love upon Me, therefore will I deliver him; I will set him on high, because he knows *and* understands My name [has a personal knowledge of My mercy, love, and kindness—trusts and relies on Me, knowing I will never forsake him, no, never].
15 He shall call upon Me, and I will answer him; I will be with him in trouble, I will deliver him and honor him.
16 With long life will I satisfy him and show him My salvation.

### Psalm 92

A Psalm. A song for the Sabbath day.

1 It is a good *and* delightful thing to give thanks to the Lord, to sing praises [with musical accompaniment] to Your name, O Most High,
2 To show forth Your loving-kindness in the morning and Your faithfulness by night,
3 With an instrument of ten strings and with the lute, with a solemn sound upon the lyre.
4 For You, O Lord, have made me glad by Your works; at the deeds of Your hands I joyfully sing.

---

*a 17* Or *beauty*  *b 1* Hebrew *Shaddai*  *c 14* That is, probably the king
*d* In Hebrew texts 92:1-15 is numbered 92:2-16.

*a* The rich promises of this whole chapter are dependent upon one's meeting exactly the conditions of these first two verses (see Exod. 15:26).

## New International Version

5 How great are your works, LORD,
  how profound your thoughts!
6 Senseless people do not know,
  fools do not understand,
7 that though the wicked spring up like grass
  and all evildoers flourish,
  they will be destroyed forever.

8 But you, LORD, are forever exalted.

9 For surely your enemies, LORD,
  surely your enemies will perish;
  all evildoers will be scattered.
10 You have exalted my horn[a] like that of a wild ox;
  fine oils have been poured on me.
11 My eyes have seen the defeat of my adversaries;
  my ears have heard the rout of my wicked foes.

12 The righteous will flourish like a palm tree,
  they will grow like a cedar of Lebanon;
13 planted in the house of the LORD,
  they will flourish in the courts of our God.
14 They will still bear fruit in old age,
  they will stay fresh and green,
15 proclaiming, "The LORD is upright;
  he is my Rock, and there is no wickedness in him."

### Psalm 93

1 The LORD reigns, he is robed in majesty;
  the LORD is robed in majesty and armed with
    strength;
  indeed, the world is established, firm and secure.
2 Your throne was established long ago;
  you are from all eternity.

3 The seas have lifted up, LORD,
  the seas have lifted up their voice;
  the seas have lifted up their pounding waves.
4 Mightier than the thunder of the great waters,
  mightier than the breakers of the sea—
  the LORD on high is mighty.

5 Your statutes, LORD, stand firm;
  holiness adorns your house
  for endless days.

### Psalm 94

1 The LORD is a God who avenges.
  O God who avenges, shine forth.
2 Rise up, Judge of the earth;
  pay back to the proud what they deserve.
3 How long, LORD, will the wicked,
  how long will the wicked be jubilant?

4 They pour out arrogant words;
  all the evildoers are full of boasting.
5 They crush your people, LORD;
  they oppress your inheritance.
6 They slay the widow and the foreigner;
  they murder the fatherless.
7 They say, "The LORD does not see;
  the God of Jacob takes no notice."

8 Take notice, you senseless ones among the people;
  you fools, when will you become wise?
9 Does he who fashioned the ear not hear?
  Does he who formed the eye not see?
10 Does he who disciplines nations not punish?
  Does he who teaches mankind lack knowledge?

## Amplified Bible

5 How great are Your doings, O Lord! Your thoughts are very deep.
6 A man in his rude *and* uncultivated state knows not, neither does a [self-confident] fool understand this:
7 That though the wicked spring up like grass and all evildoers flourish, they are doomed to be destroyed forever.
8 But You, Lord, are on high forever.
9 For behold, Your adversaries, O Lord, for behold, Your enemies shall perish; all the evildoers shall be scattered.
10 But my horn (emblem of excessive strength and stately grace) You have exalted like that of a wild ox; I am anointed with fresh oil.
11 My eye looks upon those who lie in wait for me; my ears hear the evildoers that rise up against me.
12 The [uncompromisingly] righteous shall flourish like the palm tree [be long-lived, stately, upright, useful, and fruitful]; they shall grow like a cedar in Lebanon [majestic, stable, durable, and incorruptible].
13 Planted in the house of the Lord, they shall flourish in the courts of our God.
14 [Growing in grace] they shall still bring forth fruit in old age; they shall be full of sap [of spiritual vitality] and [rich in the] verdure [of trust, love, and contentment].
15 [They are living memorials] to show that the Lord is upright *and* faithful to His promises; He is my Rock, and there is no unrighteousness in Him. [Rom. 9:14.]

### Psalm 93

1 The Lord reigns, He is clothed with majesty; the Lord is robed, He has girded Himself with strength *and* power; the world also is established, that it cannot be moved.
2 Your throne is established from of old; You are from everlasting.
3 The floods have lifted up, O Lord, the floods have lifted up their voice; the floods lift up the roaring of their waves.
4 The Lord on high is mightier *and* more glorious than the noise of many waters, yes, than the mighty breakers *and* waves of the sea.
5 Your testimonies are very sure; holiness [apparent in separation from sin, with simple trust and hearty obedience] is becoming to Your house, O Lord, forever.

### Psalm 94

1 O Lord God, You to Whom vengeance belongs, O God, You to Whom vengeance belongs, shine forth!
2 Rise up, O Judge of the earth; render to the proud a fit compensation!
3 Lord, how long shall the wicked, how long shall the wicked triumph *and* exult?
4 They pour out arrogant words, speaking hard things; all the evildoers boast loftily. [Jude 14, 15.]
5 They crush Your people, O Lord, and afflict Your heritage.
6 They slay the widow and the transient stranger and murder the unprotected orphan.
7 Yet they say, The Lord does not see, neither does the God of Jacob notice it.
8 Consider *and* understand, you stupid ones among the people! And you [self-confident] fools, when will you become wise?
9 He Who planted the ear, shall He not hear? He Who formed the eye, shall He not see?
10 He Who disciplines *and* instructs the nations, shall He not punish, He Who teaches man knowledge?

---

*a* 10 *Horn* here symbolizes strength.

## New International Version

[11] The LORD knows all human plans;
 he knows that they are futile.

[12] Blessed is the one you discipline, LORD,
 the one you teach from your law;
[13] you grant them relief from days of trouble,
 till a pit is dug for the wicked.
[14] For the LORD will not reject his people;
 he will never forsake his inheritance.
[15] Judgment will again be founded on righteousness,
 and all the upright in heart will follow it.

[16] Who will rise up for me against the wicked?
 Who will take a stand for me against evildoers?
[17] Unless the LORD had given me help,
 I would soon have dwelt in the silence of death.
[18] When I said, "My foot is slipping,"
 your unfailing love, LORD, supported me.
[19] When anxiety was great within me,
 your consolation brought me joy.

[20] Can a corrupt throne be allied with you—
 a throne that brings on misery by its decrees?
[21] The wicked band together against the righteous
 and condemn the innocent to death.
[22] But the LORD has become my fortress,
 and my God the rock in whom I take refuge.
[23] He will repay them for their sins
 and destroy them for their wickedness;
 the LORD our God will destroy them.

### Psalm 95

[1] Come, let us sing for joy to the LORD;
 let us shout aloud to the Rock of our salvation.
[2] Let us come before him with thanksgiving
 and extol him with music and song.

[3] For the LORD is the great God,
 the great King above all gods.
[4] In his hand are the depths of the earth,
 and the mountain peaks belong to him.
[5] The sea is his, for he made it,
 and his hands formed the dry land.

[6] Come, let us bow down in worship,
 let us kneel before the LORD our Maker;
[7] for he is our God
 and we are the people of his pasture,
 the flock under his care.

 Today, if only you would hear his voice,
[8] "Do not harden your hearts as you did at Meribah,[a]
 as you did that day at Massah[b] in the wilderness,
[9] where your ancestors tested me;
 they tried me, though they had seen what I did.
[10] For forty years I was angry with that generation;
 I said, 'They are a people whose hearts go astray,
 and they have not known my ways.'
[11] So I declared on oath in my anger,
 'They shall never enter my rest.'"

### Psalm 96

[1] Sing to the LORD a new song;
 sing to the LORD, all the earth.
[2] Sing to the LORD, praise his name;
 proclaim his salvation day after day.
[3] Declare his glory among the nations,
 his marvelous deeds among all peoples.

## Amplified Bible

[11] The Lord knows the thoughts of man, that they are vain (empty and futile—only a breath). [I Cor. 3:20.]
[12] Blessed (happy, fortunate, to be envied) is the man whom You discipline *and* instruct, O Lord, and teach out of Your law,
[13] That You may give him power to keep himself calm in the days of adversity, until the [inevitable] pit of corruption is dug for the wicked.
[14] For the Lord will not cast off *nor* spurn His people, neither will He abandon His heritage.
[15] For justice will return to the [uncompromisingly] righteous, and all the upright in heart will follow it.
[16] Who will rise up for me against the evildoers? Who will stand up for me against the workers of iniquity?
[17] Unless the Lord had been my help, I would soon have dwelt in [the land where there is] silence.
[18] When I said, My foot is slipping, Your mercy *and* loving-kindness, O Lord, held me up.
[19] In the multitude of my [anxious] thoughts within me, Your comforts cheer *and* delight my soul!
[20] Shall the throne of iniquity have fellowship with You—they who frame *and* hide their unrighteous doings under [the sacred name of] law?
[21] They band themselves together against the life of the [consistently] righteous and condemn the innocent to death.
[22] But the Lord has become my High Tower *and* Defense, and my God the Rock of my refuge.
[23] And He will turn back upon them their own iniquity and will wipe them out by means of their own wickedness; the Lord our God will wipe them out.

### Psalm 95

[1] O come, let us sing to the Lord; let us make a joyful noise to the Rock of our salvation!
[2] Let us come before His presence with thanksgiving; let us make a joyful noise to Him with songs of praise!
[3] For the Lord is a great God, and a great King above all gods.
[4] In His hand are the deep places of the earth; the heights *and* strength of the hills are His also.
[5] The sea is His, for He made it; and His hands formed the dry land.
[6] O come, let us worship and bow down, let us kneel before the Lord our Maker [in reverent praise and supplication].
[7] For He is our God and we are the people of His pasture and the sheep of His hand. Today, if you will hear His voice, [Heb. 3:7-11.]
[8] Harden not your hearts as at Meribah and as at Massah in the day of temptation in the wilderness, [Exod. 17:1-7; Num. 20:1-13; Deut. 6:16.]
[9] When your fathers tried My patience *and* tested Me, proved Me, and saw My work [of judgment].
[10] Forty years long was I grieved *and* disgusted with that generation, and I said, It is a people that do err in their hearts, and they do not approve, acknowledge, *or* regard My ways.
[11] Wherefore I swore in My wrath that they would not enter My rest [the land of promise]. [Heb. 4:3-11.]

### Psalm 96

[1] O sing to the Lord a new song; sing to the Lord, all the earth!
[2] Sing to the Lord, bless (affectionately praise) His name; show forth His salvation from day to day.
[3] Declare His glory among the nations, His marvelous works among all the peoples.

---

[a] 8 *Meribah* means *quarreling.*    [b] 8 *Massah* means *testing.*

# New International Version

4 For great is the LORD and most worthy of praise;
    he is to be feared above all gods.
5 For all the gods of the nations are idols,
    but the LORD made the heavens.
6 Splendor and majesty are before him;
    strength and glory are in his sanctuary.

7 Ascribe to the LORD, all you families of nations,
    ascribe to the LORD glory and strength.
8 Ascribe to the LORD the glory due his name;
    bring an offering and come into his courts.
9 Worship the LORD in the splendor of his*a* holiness;
    tremble before him, all the earth.
10 Say among the nations, "The LORD reigns."
    The world is firmly established, it cannot be moved;
    he will judge the peoples with equity.

11 Let the heavens rejoice, let the earth be glad;
    let the sea resound, and all that is in it.
12 Let the fields be jubilant, and everything in them;
    let all the trees of the forest sing for joy.
13 Let all creation rejoice before the LORD, for he comes,
    he comes to judge the earth.
    He will judge the world in righteousness
    and the peoples in his faithfulness.

## Psalm 97

1 The LORD reigns, let the earth be glad;
    let the distant shores rejoice.
2 Clouds and thick darkness surround him;
    righteousness and justice are the foundation of his
        throne.
3 Fire goes before him
    and consumes his foes on every side.
4 His lightning lights up the world;
    the earth sees and trembles.
5 The mountains melt like wax before the LORD,
    before the Lord of all the earth.
6 The heavens proclaim his righteousness,
    and all peoples see his glory.

7 All who worship images are put to shame,
    those who boast in idols—
    worship him, all you gods!

8 Zion hears and rejoices
    and the villages of Judah are glad
    because of your judgments, LORD.
9 For you, LORD, are the Most High over all the earth;
    you are exalted far above all gods.
10 Let those who love the LORD hate evil,
    for he guards the lives of his faithful ones
    and delivers them from the hand of the wicked.
11 Light shines*b* on the righteous
    and joy on the upright in heart.
12 Rejoice in the LORD, you who are righteous,
    and praise his holy name.

## Psalm 98

*A psalm.*

1 Sing to the LORD a new song,
    for he has done marvelous things;
    his right hand and his holy arm
    have worked salvation for him.
2 The LORD has made his salvation known
    and revealed his righteousness to the nations.

# Amplified Bible

4 For great is the Lord and greatly to be praised; He is to
be reverently feared *and* worshiped above all [so-called]
gods. [Deut. 6:5; Rev. 14:7.]
5 For all the gods of the nations are [lifeless] idols, but
the Lord made the heavens.
6 Honor and majesty are before Him; strength and beauty are in His sanctuary.
7 Ascribe to the Lord, O you families of the peoples, ascribe to the Lord glory and strength.
8 Give to the Lord the glory due His name; bring an offering and come [before Him] into His courts.
9 O worship the Lord in the beauty of holiness; tremble
before *and* reverently fear Him, all the earth.
10 Say among the nations that the Lord reigns; the world
also is established, so that it cannot be moved; He shall
judge *and* rule the people righteously *and* with justice.
[Rev. 11:15; 19:6.]
11 Let the heavens be glad, and let the earth rejoice; let
the sea roar, and all the things which fill it;
12 Let the field be exultant, and all that is in it! Then
shall all the trees of the wood sing for joy
13 Before the Lord, for He comes, for He comes to judge
*and* govern the earth! He shall judge the world with righteousness *and* justice and the peoples with His faithfulness *and* truth. [I Chron. 16:23-33; Rev. 19:11.]

## Psalm 97

1 The Lord reigns, let the earth rejoice; let the multitude
of isles *and* coastlands be glad!
2 Clouds and darkness are round about Him [as at Sinai];
righteousness and justice are the foundation of His throne.
[Exod. 19:9.]
3 Fire goes before Him and burns up His adversaries
round about.
4 His lightnings illumine the world; the earth sees and
trembles.
5 The hills melted like wax at the presence of the Lord,
at the presence of the Lord of the whole earth.
6 The heavens declare His righteousness, and all the
peoples see His glory.
7 Let all those be put to shame who serve graven images,
who boast in idols. Fall prostrate before Him, all you gods.
[Heb. 1:6.]
8 Zion heard and was glad, and the daughters of Judah
rejoiced [in relief] because of Your judgments, O Lord.
9 For You, Lord, are high above all the earth; You are
exalted far above all gods.
10 O you who love the Lord, hate evil; He preserves the
lives of His saints (the children of God), He delivers them
out of the hand of the wicked. [Rom. 8:13-17.]
11 Light is sown for the [uncompromisingly] righteous
*and* strewn along their pathway, and joy for the upright in
heart [the irrepressible joy which comes from consciousness of His favor and protection].
12 Rejoice in the Lord, you [consistently] righteous (upright and in right standing with God), and give thanks at
the remembrance of His holiness.

## Psalm 98

A Psalm.

1 O sing to the Lord a new song, for He has done marvelous things; His right hand and His holy arm have wrought
salvation for Him.
2 The Lord has made known His salvation; His righteousness has He openly shown in the sight of the nations.
[Luke 2:30, 31.]

---

*a* 9 Or LORD *with the splendor of*   *b* 11 One Hebrew manuscript and
ancient versions (see also 112:4); most Hebrew manuscripts *Light
is sown*

## New International Version

³He has remembered his love
  and his faithfulness to Israel;
all the ends of the earth have seen
  the salvation of our God.

⁴Shout for joy to the LORD, all the earth,
  burst into jubilant song with music;
⁵make music to the LORD with the harp,
  with the harp and the sound of singing,
⁶with trumpets and the blast of the ram's horn—
  shout for joy before the LORD, the King.

⁷Let the sea resound, and everything in it,
  the world, and all who live in it.
⁸Let the rivers clap their hands,
  let the mountains sing together for joy;
⁹let them sing before the LORD,
  for he comes to judge the earth.
He will judge the world in righteousness
  and the peoples with equity.

### Psalm 99

¹The LORD reigns,
  let the nations tremble;
he sits enthroned between the cherubim,
  let the earth shake.
²Great is the LORD in Zion;
  he is exalted over all the nations.
³Let them praise your great and awesome name—
  he is holy.

⁴The King is mighty, he loves justice—
  you have established equity;
in Jacob you have done
  what is just and right.
⁵Exalt the LORD our God
  and worship at his footstool;
  he is holy.

⁶Moses and Aaron were among his priests,
  Samuel was among those who called on his name;
they called on the LORD
  and he answered them.
⁷He spoke to them from the pillar of cloud;
  they kept his statutes and the decrees he gave them.

⁸LORD our God,
  you answered them;
you were to Israel a forgiving God,
  though you punished their misdeeds.ᵃ
⁹Exalt the LORD our God
  and worship at his holy mountain,
  for the LORD our God is holy.

### Psalm 100

*A psalm. For giving grateful praise.*

¹Shout for joy to the LORD, all the earth.
²  Worship the LORD with gladness;
  come before him with joyful songs.
³Know that the LORD is God.
  It is he who made us, and we are hisᵇ;
  we are his people, the sheep of his pasture.

⁴Enter his gates with thanksgiving
  and his courts with praise;
  give thanks to him and praise his name.
⁵For the LORD is good and his love endures forever;
  his faithfulness continues through all generations.

## Amplified Bible

³He has [earnestly] remembered His mercy *and* loving-kindness, His truth *and* His faithfulness toward the house of Israel; all the ends of the earth have witnessed the salvation of our God. [Acts 13:47; 28:28.]
⁴Make a joyful noise to the Lord, all the earth; break forth and sing for joy, yes, sing praises!
⁵Sing praises to the Lord with the lyre, with the lyre and the voice of melody.
⁶With trumpets and the sound of the horn make a joyful noise before the King, the Lord!
⁷Let the sea roar, and all that fills it, the world, and those who dwell in it!
⁸Let the rivers clap their hands; together let the hills sing for joy
⁹Before the Lord, for He is coming to judge [and rule] the earth; with righteousness will He judge [and rule] the world, and the peoples with equity.

### Psalm 99

¹The Lord reigns, let the peoples tremble [with reverential fear]! He sits [enthroned] above the cherubim, let the earth quake!
²The Lord is great in Zion, and He is high above all the peoples.
³Let them confess *and* praise Your great name, awesome *and* reverence inspiring! It is holy, *and* holy is He! [Rev. 15:4.]
⁴The strength of the king who loves righteousness *and* equity You establish in uprightness; You execute justice and righteousness in Jacob (Israel).
⁵Extol the Lord our God and worship at His footstool! Holy is He!
⁶Moses and Aaron were among His priests, and Samuel was among those who called upon His name; they called upon the Lord, and He answered them.
⁷He spoke to them in the pillar of cloud; they kept His testimonies and the statutes that He gave them. [Ps. 105:9, 10.]
⁸You answered them, O Lord our God; You were a forgiving God to them, although avenging their evildoing *and* wicked practices.
⁹Extol the Lord our God and worship at His holy hill, for the Lord our God is holy!

### Psalm 100

A Psalm of thanksgiving *and* for the thank offering.

¹Make a joyful noise to the Lord, all you lands!
²Serve the Lord with gladness! Come before His presence with singing!
³Know (perceive, recognize, and understand with approval) that the Lord is God! It is He Who has made us, not we ourselves [and we are His]! We are His people and the sheep of His pasture. [Eph. 2:10.]
⁴Enter into His gates with thanksgiving *and* a thank offering and into His courts with praise! Be thankful *and* say so to Him, bless *and* affectionately praise His name!
⁵For the Lord is good; His mercy *and* loving-kindness are everlasting, His faithfulness *and* truth endure to all generations.

---

ᵃ 8 Or *God, / an avenger of the wrongs done to them*   ᵇ 3 Or *and not we ourselves*

# New International Version

## Psalm 101

*Of David. A psalm.*

[1] I will sing of your love and justice;
   to you, Lord, I will sing praise.
[2] I will be careful to lead a blameless life—
   when will you come to me?

I will conduct the affairs of my house
   with a blameless heart.
[3] I will not look with approval
   on anything that is vile.

I hate what faithless people do;
   I will have no part in it.
[4] The perverse of heart shall be far from me;
   I will have nothing to do with what is evil.

[5] Whoever slanders their neighbor in secret,
   I will put to silence;
whoever has haughty eyes and a proud heart,
   I will not tolerate.

[6] My eyes will be on the faithful in the land,
   that they may dwell with me;
the one whose walk is blameless
   will minister to me.

[7] No one who practices deceit
   will dwell in my house;
no one who speaks falsely
   will stand in my presence.

[8] Every morning I will put to silence
   all the wicked in the land;
I will cut off every evildoer
   from the city of the Lord.

## Psalm 102[a]

*A prayer of an afflicted person who has grown weak and pours
   out a lament before the Lord.*

[1] Hear my prayer, Lord;
   let my cry for help come to you.
[2] Do not hide your face from me
   when I am in distress.
Turn your ear to me;
   when I call, answer me quickly.

[3] For my days vanish like smoke;
   my bones burn like glowing embers.
[4] My heart is blighted and withered like grass;
   I forget to eat my food.
[5] In my distress I groan aloud
   and am reduced to skin and bones.
[6] I am like a desert owl,
   like an owl among the ruins.
[7] I lie awake; I have become
   like a bird alone on a roof.
[8] All day long my enemies taunt me;
   those who rail against me use my name as a curse.
[9] For I eat ashes as my food
   and mingle my drink with tears
[10] because of your great wrath,
   for you have taken me up and thrown me aside.
[11] My days are like the evening shadow;
   I wither away like grass.

[12] But you, Lord, sit enthroned forever;
   your renown endures through all generations.
[13] You will arise and have compassion on Zion,
   for it is time to show favor to her;
   the appointed time has come.

# Amplified Bible

## Psalm 101

A Psalm of David.

[1] I will sing of mercy *and* loving-kindness and justice; to You, O Lord, will I sing.
[2] I will behave myself wisely *and* give heed to the blameless way—O when will You come to me? I will walk within my house in integrity *and* with a blameless heart.
[3] I will set no base *or* wicked thing before my eyes. I hate the work of them who turn aside [from the right path]; it shall not grasp hold of me.
[4] A perverse heart shall depart from me; I will know no evil person *or* thing.
[5] Whoso privily slanders his neighbor, him will I cut off [from me]; he who has a haughty look and a proud *and* arrogant heart I cannot *and* I will not tolerate.
[6] My eyes shall [look with favor] upon the faithful of the land, that they may dwell with me; he who walks blamelessly, he shall minister to me.
[7] He who works deceit shall not dwell in my house; he who tells lies shall not continue in my presence.
[8] Morning after morning I will root up all the wicked in the land, that I may eliminate all the evildoers from the city of the Lord.

## Psalm 102

A Prayer of the afflicted; when he is overwhelmed *and* faint
   and pours out his complaint to God.

[1] Hear my prayer, O Lord, and let my cry come to You.
[2] Hide not Your face from me in the day when I am in distress! Incline Your ear to me; in the day when I call, answer me speedily.
[3] For my days consume away like smoke, and my bones burn like a firebrand *or* like a hearth.
[4] My heart is smitten like grass and withered, so that [in absorption] I forget to eat my food.
[5] By reason of my loud groaning [from suffering and trouble] my flesh cleaves to my bones.
[6] I am like a melancholy pelican *or* vulture of the wilderness; I am like a [desolate] owl of the waste places.
[7] I am sleepless *and* lie awake [mourning], like a bereaved sparrow alone on the housetop.
[8] My adversaries taunt *and* reproach me all the day; and they who are angry with me use my name as a curse.
[9] For I have eaten the ashes [in which I sat] as if they were bread and have mingled my drink with weeping
[10] Because of Your indignation and Your wrath, for You have taken me up and cast me away.
[11] My days are like an evening shadow that stretches out *and* declines [with the sun]; and I am withered like grass.
[12] But You, O Lord, are enthroned forever; and the fame of Your name endures to all generations.
[13] You will arise *and* have mercy *and* loving-kindness for Zion, for it is time to have pity *and* compassion for her; yes, the set time has come [the moment designated]. [Ps. 12:5; 119:126.]

---

[a] In Hebrew texts 102:1-28 is numbered 102:2-29.

## New International Version

<sup>14</sup>For her stones are dear to your servants;
    her very dust moves them to pity.
<sup>15</sup>The nations will fear the name of the LORD,
    all the kings of the earth will revere your glory.
<sup>16</sup>For the LORD will rebuild Zion
    and appear in his glory.
<sup>17</sup>He will respond to the prayer of the destitute;
    he will not despise their plea.

<sup>18</sup>Let this be written for a future generation,
    that a people not yet created may praise the LORD:
<sup>19</sup>"The LORD looked down from his sanctuary on high,
    from heaven he viewed the earth,
<sup>20</sup>to hear the groans of the prisoners
    and release those condemned to death."
<sup>21</sup>So the name of the LORD will be declared in Zion
    and his praise in Jerusalem
<sup>22</sup>when the peoples and the kingdoms
    assemble to worship the LORD.

<sup>23</sup>In the course of my life*a* he broke my strength;
    he cut short my days.
<sup>24</sup>So I said:
    "Do not take me away, my God, in the midst of my
       days;
    your years go on through all generations.
<sup>25</sup>In the beginning you laid the foundations of the earth,
    and the heavens are the work of your hands.
<sup>26</sup>They will perish, but you remain;
    they will all wear out like a garment.
Like clothing you will change them
    and they will be discarded.
<sup>27</sup>But you remain the same,
    and your years will never end.
<sup>28</sup>The children of your servants will live in your
       presence;
    their descendants will be established before you."

### Psalm 103

*Of David.*

<sup>1</sup>Praise the LORD, my soul;
    all my inmost being, praise his holy name.
<sup>2</sup>Praise the LORD, my soul,
    and forget not all his benefits—
<sup>3</sup>who forgives all your sins
    and heals all your diseases,
<sup>4</sup>who redeems your life from the pit
    and crowns you with love and compassion,
<sup>5</sup>who satisfies your desires with good things
    so that your youth is renewed like the eagle's.

<sup>6</sup>The LORD works righteousness
    and justice for all the oppressed.

<sup>7</sup>He made known his ways to Moses,
    his deeds to the people of Israel:
<sup>8</sup>The LORD is compassionate and gracious,
    slow to anger, abounding in love.
<sup>9</sup>He will not always accuse,
    nor will he harbor his anger forever;
<sup>10</sup>he does not treat us as our sins deserve
    or repay us according to our iniquities.
<sup>11</sup>For as high as the heavens are above the earth,
    so great is his love for those who fear him;
<sup>12</sup>as far as the east is from the west,
    so far has he removed our transgressions from us.

<sup>13</sup>As a father has compassion on his children,
    so the LORD has compassion on those who fear him;

*a 23  Or By his power*

## Amplified Bible

<sup>14</sup>For Your servants take [melancholy] pleasure in the stones [of her ruins] and show pity for her dust.
<sup>15</sup>So the nations shall fear *and* worshipfully revere the name of the Lord, and all the kings of the earth Your glory. [Ps. 96:9.]
<sup>16</sup>When the Lord builds up Zion, He will appear in His glory;
<sup>17</sup>He will regard the plea of the destitute and will not despise their prayer.

<sup>18</sup>Let this be recorded for the generation yet unborn, that a people yet to be created shall praise the Lord.
<sup>19</sup>For He looked down from the height of His sanctuary, from heaven did the Lord behold the earth,
<sup>20</sup>To hear the sighing *and* groaning of the prisoner, to loose those who are appointed to death,
<sup>21</sup>So that men may declare the name of the Lord in Zion and His praise in Jerusalem
<sup>22</sup>When peoples are gathered together, and the kingdoms, to worship *and* serve the Lord.

<sup>23</sup>He has afflicted *and* weakened my strength, humbling *and* bringing me low [with sorrow] in the way; He has shortened my days [aging me prematurely].
<sup>24</sup>I said, O my God, take me not away in the midst of my days, You Whose years continue throughout all generations.
<sup>25</sup>At the beginning You existed *and* laid the foundations of the earth; the heavens are the work of Your hands.
<sup>26</sup>They shall perish, but You shall remain *and* endure; yes, all of them shall wear out *and* become old like a garment. Like clothing You shall change them, and they shall be changed *and* pass away.
<sup>27</sup>But You remain the same, and Your years shall have no end. [Heb. 1:10-12.]
<sup>28</sup>The children of Your servants shall dwell safely *and* continue, and their descendants shall be established before You.

### Psalm 103

[A Psalm] of David.

<sup>1</sup>Bless (affectionately, gratefully praise) the Lord, O my soul; and all that is [deepest] within me, bless His holy name!
<sup>2</sup>Bless (affectionately, gratefully praise) the Lord, O my soul, and forget not [one of] all His benefits—
<sup>3</sup>Who forgives [every one of] all your iniquities, Who heals [each one of] all your diseases,
<sup>4</sup>Who redeems your life from the pit *and* corruption, Who beautifies, dignifies, *and* crowns you with loving-kindness and tender mercy;
<sup>5</sup>Who satisfies your mouth [your necessity and desire at your personal age and situation] with good so that your youth, renewed, is like the eagle's [strong, overcoming, soaring]! [Isa. 40:31.]
<sup>6</sup>The Lord executes righteousness *and* justice [not for me only, but] for all who are oppressed.
<sup>7</sup>He made known His ways [of righteousness and justice] to Moses, His acts to the children of Israel.
<sup>8</sup>The Lord is merciful and gracious, slow to anger and plenteous in mercy *and* loving-kindness. [James 5:11.]
<sup>9</sup>He will not always chide *or* be contending, neither will He keep His anger forever *or* hold a grudge.
<sup>10</sup>He has not dealt with us after our sins nor rewarded us according to our iniquities.
<sup>11</sup>For as the heavens are high above the earth, so great are His mercy *and* loving-kindness toward those who reverently *and* worshipfully fear Him.
<sup>12</sup>As far as the east is from the west, so far has He removed our transgressions from us.
<sup>13</sup>As a father loves *and* pities his children, so the Lord loves *and* pities those who fear Him [with reverence, worship, and awe].

## New International Version

<sup>14</sup>for he knows how we are formed,
he remembers that we are dust.
<sup>15</sup>The life of mortals is like grass,
they flourish like a flower of the field;
<sup>16</sup>the wind blows over it and it is gone,
and its place remembers it no more.
<sup>17</sup>But from everlasting to everlasting
the LORD's love is with those who fear him,
and his righteousness with their children's
children—
<sup>18</sup>with those who keep his covenant
and remember to obey his precepts.

<sup>19</sup>The LORD has established his throne in heaven,
and his kingdom rules over all.

<sup>20</sup>Praise the LORD, you his angels,
you mighty ones who do his bidding,
who obey his word.
<sup>21</sup>Praise the LORD, all his heavenly hosts,
you his servants who do his will.
<sup>22</sup>Praise the LORD, all his works
everywhere in his dominion.

Praise the LORD, my soul.

### Psalm 104

<sup>1</sup>Praise the LORD, my soul.

LORD my God, you are very great;
you are clothed with splendor and majesty.

<sup>2</sup>The LORD wraps himself in light as with a garment;
he stretches out the heavens like a tent
<sup>3</sup>    and lays the beams of his upper chambers on their
waters.
He makes the clouds his chariot
and rides on the wings of the wind.
<sup>4</sup>He makes winds his messengers,<sup>a</sup>
flames of fire his servants.

<sup>5</sup>He set the earth on its foundations;
it can never be moved.
<sup>6</sup>You covered it with the watery depths as with a garment;
the waters stood above the mountains.
<sup>7</sup>But at your rebuke the waters fled,
at the sound of your thunder they took to flight;
<sup>8</sup>they flowed over the mountains,
they went down into the valleys,
to the place you assigned for them.
<sup>9</sup>You set a boundary they cannot cross;
never again will they cover the earth.

<sup>10</sup>He makes springs pour water into the ravines;
it flows between the mountains.
<sup>11</sup>They give water to all the beasts of the field;
the wild donkeys quench their thirst.
<sup>12</sup>The birds of the sky nest by the waters;
they sing among the branches.
<sup>13</sup>He waters the mountains from his upper chambers;
the land is satisfied by the fruit of his work.
<sup>14</sup>He makes grass grow for the cattle,
and plants for people to cultivate—
bringing forth food from the earth:
<sup>15</sup>wine that gladdens human hearts,
oil to make their faces shine,
and bread that sustains their hearts.
<sup>16</sup>The trees of the LORD are well watered,
the cedars of Lebanon that he planted.
<sup>17</sup>There the birds make their nests;
the stork has its home in the junipers.
<sup>18</sup>The high mountains belong to the wild goats;
the crags are a refuge for the hyrax.

<sup>a</sup> 4 Or *angels*

## Amplified Bible

<sup>14</sup>For He knows our frame, He [earnestly] remembers *and* imprints [on His heart] that we are dust.
<sup>15</sup>As for man, his days are as grass; as a flower of the field, so he flourishes.
<sup>16</sup>For the wind passes over it and it is gone, and its place shall know it no more.
<sup>17</sup>But the mercy *and* loving-kindness of the Lord are from everlasting to everlasting upon those who reverently *and* worshipfully fear Him, and His righteousness is to children's children—[Deut. 10:12.]
<sup>18</sup>To such as keep His covenant [hearing, receiving, loving, and obeying it] and to those who [earnestly] remember His commandments to do them [imprinting them on their hearts].
<sup>19</sup>The Lord has established His throne in the heavens, and His kingdom rules over all.
<sup>20</sup>Bless (affectionately, gratefully praise) the Lord, you His angels, you mighty ones who do His commandments, hearkening to the voice of His word.
<sup>21</sup>Bless (affectionately, gratefully praise) the Lord, all you His hosts, you His ministers who do His pleasure.
<sup>22</sup>Bless the Lord, all His works in all places of His dominion; bless (affectionately, gratefully praise) the Lord, O my soul!

### Psalm 104

<sup>1</sup>Bless (affectionately, gratefully praise) the Lord, O my soul! O Lord my God, You are very great! You are clothed with honor and majesty—
<sup>2</sup>[You are the One] Who covers Yourself with light as with a garment, Who stretches out the heavens like a curtain *or* a tent,
<sup>3</sup>Who lays the beams of the upper room of His abode in the waters [above the firmament], Who makes the clouds His chariot, Who walks on the wings of the wind,
<sup>4</sup>Who makes winds His messengers, flames of fire His ministers. [Heb. 1:7.]
<sup>5</sup>You laid the foundations of the earth, that it should not be moved forever. [Job 38:4, 6.]
<sup>6</sup>You covered it with the deep as with a garment; the waters stood above the mountains. [Gen. 1:2; II Pet. 3:5.]
<sup>7</sup>At Your rebuke they fled; at the voice of Your thunder they hastened away.
<sup>8</sup>The mountains rose, the valleys sank down to the place which You appointed for them.
<sup>9</sup>You have set a boundary [for the waters] which they may not pass over, that they turn not again to deluge the earth.
<sup>10</sup>He sends forth springs into the valleys; their waters run among the mountains.
<sup>11</sup>They give drink to every [wild] beast of the field; the wild asses quench their thirst there.
<sup>12</sup>Beside them the birds of the heavens have their nests; they sing among the branches. [Matt. 13:32.]
<sup>13</sup>He waters the mountains from His upper rooms; the earth is satisfied *and* abounds with the fruit of His works.
<sup>14</sup>He causes vegetation to grow for the cattle, and all that the earth produces for man to cultivate, that he may bring forth food out of the earth—
<sup>15</sup>And wine that gladdens the heart of man, to make his face shine more than oil, and bread to support, refresh, *and* strengthen man's heart.
<sup>16</sup>The trees of the Lord are watered abundantly *and* are filled with sap, the cedars of Lebanon which He has planted,
<sup>17</sup>Where the birds make their nests; as for the stork, the fir trees are her house.
<sup>18</sup>The high mountains are for the wild goats; the rocks are a refuge for the conies *and* badgers.

# New International Version

[19] He made the moon to mark the seasons,
and the sun knows when to go down.
[20] You bring darkness, it becomes night,
and all the beasts of the forest prowl.
[21] The lions roar for their prey
and seek their food from God.
[22] The sun rises, and they steal away;
they return and lie down in their dens.
[23] Then people go out to their work,
to their labor until evening.

[24] How many are your works, LORD!
In wisdom you made them all;
the earth is full of your creatures.
[25] There is the sea, vast and spacious,
teeming with creatures beyond number—
living things both large and small.
[26] There the ships go to and fro,
and Leviathan, which you formed to frolic there.

[27] All creatures look to you
to give them their food at the proper time.
[28] When you give it to them,
they gather it up;
when you open your hand,
they are satisfied with good things.
[29] When you hide your face,
they are terrified;
when you take away their breath,
they die and return to the dust.
[30] When you send your Spirit,
they are created,
and you renew the face of the ground.

[31] May the glory of the LORD endure forever;
may the LORD rejoice in his works—
[32] he who looks at the earth, and it trembles,
who touches the mountains, and they smoke.

[33] I will sing to the LORD all my life;
I will sing praise to my God as long as I live.
[34] May my meditation be pleasing to him,
as I rejoice in the LORD.
[35] But may sinners vanish from the earth
and the wicked be no more.

Praise the LORD, my soul.

Praise the LORD.[a]

### Psalm 105

[1] Give praise to the LORD, proclaim his name;
make known among the nations what he has done.
[2] Sing to him, sing praise to him;
tell of all his wonderful acts.
[3] Glory in his holy name;
let the hearts of those who seek the LORD rejoice.
[4] Look to the LORD and his strength;
seek his face always.

[5] Remember the wonders he has done,
his miracles, and the judgments he pronounced,
[6] you his servants, the descendants of Abraham,
his chosen ones, the children of Jacob.
[7] He is the LORD our God;
his judgments are in all the earth.

[8] He remembers his covenant forever,
the promise he made, for a thousand generations,
[9] the covenant he made with Abraham,
the oath he swore to Isaac.

[a] *35* Hebrew *Hallelu Yah*; in the Septuagint this line stands at the beginning of Psalm 105.

# Amplified Bible

[19] [The Lord] appointed the moon for the seasons; the sun knows [the exact time of] its setting.
[20] You [O Lord] make darkness and it becomes night, in which creeps forth every wild beast of the forest.
[21] The young lions roar after their prey and seek their food from God.
[22] When the sun arises, they withdraw themselves and lie down in their dens.
[23] Man goes forth to his work and remains at his task until evening.

[24] O Lord, how many *and* varied are Your works! In wisdom have You made them all; the earth is full of Your riches *and* Your creatures.
[25] Yonder is the sea, great and wide, in which are swarms of innumerable creeping things, creatures both small and great.
[26] There go the ships of the sea, and Leviathan (the sea monster), which You have formed to sport in it.

[27] These all wait *and* are dependent upon You, that You may give them their food in due season.
[28] When You give it to them, they gather it up; You open Your hand, and they are filled with good things.
[29] When You hide Your face, they are troubled *and* dismayed; when You take away their breath, they die and return to their dust.
[30] When You send forth Your Spirit *and* give them breath, they are created, and You replenish the face of the ground.

[31] May the glory of the Lord endure forever; may the Lord rejoice in His works—
[32] Who looks on the earth, and it quakes *and* trembles, Who touches the mountains, and they smoke!
[33] I will sing to the Lord as long as I live; I will sing praise to my God while I have any being.
[34] May my meditation be sweet to Him; as for me, I will rejoice in the Lord.
[35] Let sinners be consumed from the earth, and let the wicked be no more. Bless (affectionately, gratefully praise) the Lord, O my soul! Praise the Lord! (Hallelujah!)

### Psalm 105

[1] O give thanks unto the Lord, call upon His name, make known His doings among the peoples!
[2] Sing to Him, sing praises to Him; meditate on *and* talk of all His marvelous deeds *and* devoutly praise them.
[3] Glory in His holy name; let the hearts of those rejoice who seek *and* require the Lord [as their indispensable necessity].
[4] Seek, inquire of *and* for the Lord, *and* crave Him and His strength (His might and inflexibility to temptation); seek *and* require His face *and* His presence [continually] evermore.
[5] [Earnestly] remember the marvelous deeds that He has done, His miracles *and* wonders, the judgments *and* sentences which He pronounced [upon His enemies, as in Egypt]. [Ps. 78:43-51.]
[6] O you offspring of Abraham His servant, you children of Jacob, His chosen ones,
[7] He is the Lord our God; His judgments are in all the earth.
[8] He is [earnestly] mindful of His covenant *and* forever it is imprinted on His heart, the word which He commanded *and* established to a thousand generations,
[9] The covenant which He made with Abraham, and His sworn promise to Isaac, [Luke 1:72, 73.]

## New International Version

10 He confirmed it to Jacob as a decree,
to Israel as an everlasting covenant:
11 "To you I will give the land of Canaan
as the portion you will inherit."

12 When they were but few in number,
few indeed, and strangers in it,
13 they wandered from nation to nation,
from one kingdom to another.
14 He allowed no one to oppress them;
for their sake he rebuked kings:
15 "Do not touch my anointed ones;
do my prophets no harm."

16 He called down famine on the land
and destroyed all their supplies of food;
17 and he sent a man before them—
Joseph, sold as a slave.
18 They bruised his feet with shackles,
his neck was put in irons,
19 till what he foretold came to pass,
till the word of the Lord proved him true.
20 The king sent and released him,
the ruler of peoples set him free.
21 He made him master of his household,
ruler over all he possessed,
22 to instruct his princes as he pleased
and teach his elders wisdom.

23 Then Israel entered Egypt;
Jacob resided as a foreigner in the land of Ham.
24 The Lord made his people very fruitful;
he made them too numerous for their foes,
25 whose hearts he turned to hate his people,
to conspire against his servants.
26 He sent Moses his servant,
and Aaron, whom he had chosen.
27 They performed his signs among them,
his wonders in the land of Ham.
28 He sent darkness and made the land dark—
for had they not rebelled against his words?
29 He turned their waters into blood,
causing their fish to die.
30 Their land teemed with frogs,
which went up into the bedrooms of their rulers.
31 He spoke, and there came swarms of flies,
and gnats throughout their country.
32 He turned their rain into hail,
with lightning throughout their land;
33 he struck down their vines and fig trees
and shattered the trees of their country.
34 He spoke, and the locusts came,
grasshoppers without number;
35 they ate up every green thing in their land,
ate up the produce of their soil.
36 Then he struck down all the firstborn in their land,
the firstfruits of all their manhood.
37 He brought out Israel, laden with silver and gold,
and from among their tribes no one faltered.
38 Egypt was glad when they left,
because dread of Israel had fallen on them.

39 He spread out a cloud as a covering,
and a fire to give light at night.
40 They asked, and he brought them quail;
he fed them well with the bread of heaven.
41 He opened the rock, and water gushed out;
it flowed like a river in the desert.

42 For he remembered his holy promise
given to his servant Abraham.
43 He brought out his people with rejoicing,
his chosen ones with shouts of joy;

## Amplified Bible

10 Which He confirmed to Jacob as a statute, to Israel as an everlasting covenant,
11 Saying, Unto you will I give the land of Canaan as your measured portion, possession, *and* inheritance.
12 When they were but a few men in number, in fact, very few, and were temporary residents *and* strangers in it,
13 When they went from one nation to another, from one kingdom to another people,
14 He allowed no man to do them wrong; in fact, He reproved kings for their sakes, [Gen. 12:17; 20:3-7.]
15 Saying, Touch not My anointed, and do My prophets no harm. [I Chron. 16:8-22.]
16 Moreover, He called for a famine upon the land [of Egypt]; He cut off every source of bread. [Gen. 41:54.]
17 He sent a man before them, even Joseph, who was sold as a servant. [Gen. 45:5; 50:20, 21.]
18 His feet they hurt with fetters; he was laid in chains of iron *and* his soul entered into the iron,
19 Until his word [to his cruel brothers] came true, until the word of the Lord tried *and* tested him.
20 The king sent and loosed him, even the ruler of the peoples, and let him go free.
21 He made Joseph lord of his house and ruler of all his substance, [Gen. 41:40.]
22 To bind his princes at his pleasure and teach his elders wisdom.
23 Israel also came into Egypt; and Jacob sojourned in the land of Ham. [Gen. 46:6.]
24 There [the Lord] greatly increased His people and made them stronger than their oppressors.
25 He turned the hearts [of the Egyptians] to hate His people, to deal craftily with His servants.
26 He sent Moses His servant, and Aaron, whom He had chosen.
27 They showed His signs among them, wonders *and* miracles in the land of Ham (Egypt).
28 He sent [thick] darkness and made the land dark, and they [God's two servants] rebelled not against His word. [Exod. 10:22; Ps. 99:7.]
29 He turned [Egypt's] waters into blood and caused their fish to die. [Exod. 7:20, 21.]
30 Their land brought forth frogs in abundance, even in the chambers of their kings. [Exod. 8:6.]
31 He spoke, and there came swarms of beetles *and* flies and mosquitoes *and* lice in all their borders. [Exod. 8:17, 24.]
32 He gave them hail for rain, with lightning like flaming fire in their land. [Exod. 9:23, 25.]
33 He smote their vines also and their fig trees and broke the [ice-laden] trees of their borders. [Ps. 78:47.]
34 He spoke, and the locusts came, and the grasshoppers, and that without number, [Exod. 10:4, 13, 14.]
35 And ate up all the vegetation in their land and devoured the fruit of their ground.
36 He smote also all the firstborn in their land, the beginning *and* chief substance of all their strength. [Exod. 12:29; Ps. 78:51.]
37 He brought [Israel] forth also with silver and gold, and there was not one feeble person among their tribes. [Exod. 12:35.]
38 Egypt was glad when they departed, for the fear of them had fallen upon the people. [Exod. 12:33.]
39 The Lord spread a cloud for a covering [by day], and a fire to give light in the night. [Exod. 13:21.]
40 [The Israelites] asked, and He brought quails and satisfied them with the bread of heaven. [Exod. 16:12-15.]
41 He opened the rock, and water gushed out; it ran in the dry places like a river. [Exod. 17:6; Num. 20:11.]
42 For He [earnestly] remembered His holy word *and* promise to Abraham His servant. [Gen. 15:14.]
43 And He brought forth His people with joy, and His chosen ones with gladness *and* singing,

## New International Version

44he gave them the lands of the nations,
and they fell heir to what others had toiled for—
45that they might keep his precepts
and observe his laws.

Praise the LORD.[a]

### Psalm 106

1Praise the LORD.[b]

Give thanks to the LORD, for he is good;
his love endures forever.

2Who can proclaim the mighty acts of the LORD
or fully declare his praise?
3Blessed are those who act justly,
who always do what is right.

4Remember me, LORD, when you show favor to your
people,
come to my aid when you save them,
5that I may enjoy the prosperity of your chosen ones,
that I may share in the joy of your nation
and join your inheritance in giving praise.

6We have sinned, even as our ancestors did;
we have done wrong and acted wickedly.
7When our ancestors were in Egypt,
they gave no thought to your miracles;
they did not remember your many kindnesses,
and they rebelled by the sea, the Red Sea.[c]
8Yet he saved them for his name's sake,
to make his mighty power known.
9He rebuked the Red Sea, and it dried up;
he led them through the depths as through a desert.
10He saved them from the hand of the foe;
from the hand of the enemy he redeemed them.
11The waters covered their adversaries;
not one of them survived.
12Then they believed his promises
and sang his praise.

13But they soon forgot what he had done
and did not wait for his plan to unfold.
14In the desert they gave in to their craving;
in the wilderness they put God to the test.
15So he gave them what they asked for,
but sent a wasting disease among them.

16In the camp they grew envious of Moses
and of Aaron, who was consecrated to the LORD.
17The earth opened up and swallowed Dathan;
it buried the company of Abiram.
18Fire blazed among their followers;
a flame consumed the wicked.
19At Horeb they made a calf
and worshiped an idol cast from metal.
20They exchanged their glorious God
for an image of a bull, which eats grass.
21They forgot the God who saved them,
who had done great things in Egypt,
22miracles in the land of Ham
and awesome deeds by the Red Sea.
23So he said he would destroy them—
had not Moses, his chosen one,
stood in the breach before him
to keep his wrath from destroying them.

a 45 Hebrew Hallelu Yah    b 1 Hebrew Hallelu Yah; also in verse 48
c 7 Or the Sea of Reeds; also in verses 9 and 22

## Amplified Bible

44And gave them the lands of the nations [of Canaan],
and they reaped the fruits of those peoples' labor, [Deut.
6:10, 11.]
45That they might observe His statutes and keep His
laws [hearing, receiving, loving, and obeying them].
Praise the Lord! (Hallelujah!)

### Psalm 106

1Praise the Lord! (Hallelujah!) O give thanks to the
Lord, for He is good; for His mercy and loving-kindness
endure forever! [I Chron. 16:34.]
2Who can put into words and tell the mighty deeds of
the Lord? Or who can show forth all the praise [that is
due Him]?
3Blessed (happy, fortunate, to be envied) are those who
observe justice [treating others fairly] and who do right
and are in right standing with God at all times.
4[Earnestly] remember me, O Lord, when You favor
Your people! O visit me also when You deliver them, and
grant me Your salvation!—
5That I may see and share the welfare of Your chosen
ones, that I may rejoice in the gladness of Your nation, that
I may glory with Your heritage.
6We have sinned, as did also our fathers; we have committed iniquity, we have done wickedly. [Lev. 26:40-42.]
7Our fathers in Egypt understood not nor appreciated Your miracles; they did not [earnestly] remember
the multitude of Your mercies nor imprint Your loving-
kindness [on their hearts], but they were rebellious and
provoked the Lord at the sea, even at the Red Sea. [Exod.
14:21.]
8Nevertheless He saved them for His name's sake [to
prove the righteousness of the divine character], that He
might make His mighty power known.
9He rebuked the Red Sea also, and it dried up; so He
led them through the depths as through a pastureland.
[Exod. 14:21.]
10And He saved them from the hand of him that hated
them, and redeemed them from the hand of the [Egyp-
tian] enemy. [Exod. 14:30.]
11And the waters covered their adversaries; not one of
them was left. [Exod. 14:27, 28; 15:5.]
12Then [Israel] believed His words [trusting in, relying
on them]; they sang His praise.
13But they hastily forgot His works; they did not [ear-
nestly] wait for His plans [to develop] regarding them.
14But lusted exceedingly in the wilderness and tempted
and tried to restrain God [with their insistent desires] in
the desert. [Num. 11:4.]
15And He gave them their request, but sent leanness
into their souls and [thinned their numbers by] disease
and death. [Ps. 78:29-31.]
16They envied Moses also in the camp, and Aaron [the
high priest], the holy one of the Lord. [Num. 16:1-32.]
17Therefore the earth opened and swallowed up Dathan
and closed over the company of Abiram. [Num. 16:31, 32.]
18And a fire broke out in their company; the flame
burned up the wicked. [Num. 16:35, 46.]
19They made a calf in Horeb and worshiped a molten
image. [Exod. 32:4.]
20Thus they exchanged Him Who was their Glory for
the image of an ox that eats grass [they traded their Honor
for the image of a calf]!
21They forgot God their Savior, Who had done such
great things in Egypt,
22Wonders and miracles in the land of Ham, dreadful
and awesome things at the Red Sea.
23Therefore He said He would destroy them. [And
He would have done so] had not Moses, His chosen one,
stepped into the breach before Him to turn away His
threatening wrath. [Exod. 32:10, 11, 32.]

## New International Version

24 Then they despised the pleasant land;
   they did not believe his promise.
25 They grumbled in their tents
   and did not obey the LORD.
26 So he swore to them with uplifted hand
   that he would make them fall in the wilderness,
27 make their descendants fall among the nations
   and scatter them throughout the lands.

28 They yoked themselves to the Baal of Peor
   and ate sacrifices offered to lifeless gods;
29 they aroused the LORD's anger by their wicked deeds,
   and a plague broke out among them.
30 But Phinehas stood up and intervened,
   and the plague was checked.
31 This was credited to him as righteousness
   for endless generations to come.
32 By the waters of Meribah they angered the LORD,
   and trouble came to Moses because of them;
33 for they rebelled against the Spirit of God,
   and rash words came from Moses' lips.[a]

34 They did not destroy the peoples
   as the LORD had commanded them,
35 but they mingled with the nations
   and adopted their customs.
36 They worshiped their idols,
   which became a snare to them.
37 They sacrificed their sons
   and their daughters to false gods.
38 They shed innocent blood,
   the blood of their sons and daughters,
   whom they sacrificed to the idols of Canaan,
   and the land was desecrated by their blood.
39 They defiled themselves by what they did;
   by their deeds they prostituted themselves.

40 Therefore the LORD was angry with his people
   and abhorred his inheritance.
41 He gave them into the hands of the nations,
   and their foes ruled over them.
42 Their enemies oppressed them
   and subjected them to their power.
43 Many times he delivered them,
   but they were bent on rebellion
   and they wasted away in their sin.
44 Yet he took note of their distress
   when he heard their cry;
45 for their sake he remembered his covenant
   and out of his great love he relented.
46 He caused all who held them captive
   to show them mercy.

47 Save us, LORD our God,
   and gather us from the nations,
   that we may give thanks to your holy name
   and glory in your praise.

48 Praise be to the LORD, the God of Israel,
   from everlasting to everlasting.

Let all the people say, "Amen!"

Praise the LORD.

### BOOK V

*Psalms 107–150*

### Psalm 107

1 Give thanks to the LORD, for he is good;
   his love endures forever.

## Amplified Bible

24 Then they spurned *and* despised the pleasant *and* desirable land [Canaan]; they believed not His word [neither trusting in, relying on, nor holding to it];
25 But they murmured in their tents *and* hearkened not to the voice of the Lord.
26 Therefore He lifted up His hand [as if taking an oath] against them, that He would cause them to fall in the wilderness,
27 Cast out their descendants among the nations, and scatter them in the lands [of the earth].
28 They joined themselves also to the [idol] Baal of Peor and ate sacrifices [offered] to the lifeless [gods].
29 Thus they provoked the Lord to anger with their practices, and a plague broke out among them.
30 Then stood up Phinehas [the priest] and executed judgment, and so the plague was stayed. [Num. 25:7, 8.]
31 And that was credited to him for righteousness (right doing and right standing with God) to all generations forever.
32 They angered the Lord also at the waters of Meribah, so that it went ill with Moses for their sakes; [Num. 20:3-13.]
33 For they provoked [Moses'] spirit, so that he spoke unadvisedly with his lips.
34 They did not destroy the [heathen] nations as the Lord commanded them,
35 But mingled themselves with the [idolatrous] nations and learned their ways *and* works
36 And served their idols, which were a snare to them.
37 Yes, they sacrificed their sons and their daughters to demons [II Kings 16:3.]
38 And shed innocent blood, even the blood of their sons and of their daughters, whom they sacrificed to the idols of Canaan; and the land was polluted with their blood.
39 Thus were they defiled by their own works, and they played the harlot *and* practiced idolatry with their own deeds [of idolatrous rites].
40 Therefore was the wrath of the Lord kindled against His people, insomuch that He abhorred *and* rejected His own heritage. [Deut. 32:17.]
41 And He gave them into the hands of the [heathen] nations, and they that hated them ruled over them.
42 Their enemies also oppressed them, and they were brought into subjection under the hand of their foes.
43 Many times did [God] deliver them, but they were rebellious in their counsel and sank low through their iniquity.
44 Nevertheless He regarded their distress when He heard their cry;
45 And He [earnestly] remembered for their sake His covenant and relented their sentence of evil [comforting and easing Himself] according to the abundance of His mercy *and* loving-kindness [when they cried out to Him].
46 He also caused [Israel] to find sympathy among those who had carried them away captive.
47 Deliver us, O Lord our God, and gather us from among the nations, that we may give thanks to Your holy name *and* glory in praising You.
48 Blessed (affectionately and gratefully praised) be the Lord, the God of Israel, from everlasting to everlasting! And let all the people say, Amen! Praise the Lord! (Hallelujah!) [I Chron. 16:35, 36.]

### BOOK FIVE

### Psalm 107

1 O give thanks to the Lord, for He is good; for His mercy *and* loving-kindness endure forever!

---

*a* 33 Or *against his spirit, / and rash words came from his lips*

## New International Version

2 Let the redeemed of the LORD tell their story—
  those he redeemed from the hand of the foe,
3 those he gathered from the lands,
  from east and west, from north and south.<sup>a</sup>

4 Some wandered in desert wastelands,
  finding no way to a city where they could settle.
5 They were hungry and thirsty,
  and their lives ebbed away.
6 Then they cried out to the LORD in their trouble,
  and he delivered them from their distress.
7 He led them by a straight way
  to a city where they could settle.
8 Let them give thanks to the LORD for his unfailing love
  and his wonderful deeds for mankind,
9 for he satisfies the thirsty
  and fills the hungry with good things.

10 Some sat in darkness, in utter darkness,
  prisoners suffering in iron chains,
11 because they rebelled against God's commands
  and despised the plans of the Most High.
12 So he subjected them to bitter labor;
  they stumbled, and there was no one to help.
13 Then they cried to the LORD in their trouble,
  and he saved them from their distress.
14 He brought them out of darkness, the utter darkness,
  and broke away their chains.
15 Let them give thanks to the LORD for his unfailing love
  and his wonderful deeds for mankind,
16 for he breaks down gates of bronze
  and cuts through bars of iron.

17 Some became fools through their rebellious ways
  and suffered affliction because of their iniquities.
18 They loathed all food
  and drew near the gates of death.
19 Then they cried to the LORD in their trouble,
  and he saved them from their distress.
20 He sent out his word and healed them;
  he rescued them from the grave.
21 Let them give thanks to the LORD for his unfailing love
  and his wonderful deeds for mankind.
22 Let them sacrifice thank offerings
  and tell of his works with songs of joy.

23 Some went out on the sea in ships;
  they were merchants on the mighty waters.
24 They saw the works of the LORD,
  his wonderful deeds in the deep.
25 For he spoke and stirred up a tempest
  that lifted high the waves.
26 They mounted up to the heavens and went down to the depths;
  in their peril their courage melted away.
27 They reeled and staggered like drunkards;
  they were at their wits' end.
28 Then they cried out to the LORD in their trouble,
  and he brought them out of their distress.
29 He stilled the storm to a whisper;
  the waves of the sea<sup>b</sup> were hushed.
30 They were glad when it grew calm,
  and he guided them to their desired haven.

## Amplified Bible

2 Let the redeemed of the Lord say so, whom He has delivered from the hand of the adversary,
3 And gathered them out of the lands, from the east and from the west, from the north and from the [Red] Sea in the south.
4 Some wandered in the wilderness in a solitary desert track; they found no city for habitation.
5 Hungry and thirsty, they fainted; their lives were near to being extinguished.
6 Then they cried to the Lord in their trouble, and He delivered them out of their distresses.
7 He led them forth by the straight *and* right way, that they might go to a city where they could establish their homes.
8 Oh, that men would praise [and confess to] the Lord for His goodness *and* loving-kindness and His wonderful works to the children of men!
9 For He satisfies the longing soul and fills the hungry soul with good.
10 Some sat in darkness and in the shadow of death, being bound in affliction and in irons, [Luke 1:79.]
11 Because they had rebelled against the words of God and spurned the counsel of the Most High.
12 Therefore He bowed down their hearts with hard labor; they stumbled *and* fell down, and there was none to help.
13 Then they cried to the Lord in their trouble, and He saved them out of their distresses.
14 He brought them out of darkness and the shadow of death and broke apart the bonds that held them. [Ps. 68:6; Acts 12:7; 16:26.]
15 Oh, that men would praise [and confess to] the Lord for His goodness *and* loving-kindness and His wonderful works to the children of men!
16 For He has broken the gates of bronze and cut the bars of iron apart.
17 Some are fools [made ill] because of the way of their transgressions and are afflicted because of their iniquities.
18 They loathe every kind of food, and they draw near to the gates of death.
19 Then they cry to the Lord in their trouble, and He delivers them out of their distresses.
20 He sends forth His word and heals them and rescues them from the pit *and* destruction. [II Kings 20:4, 5; Matt. 8:8.]
21 Oh, that men would praise [and confess to] the Lord for His goodness *and* loving-kindness and His wonderful works to the children of men! [Heb. 13:15.]
22 And let them sacrifice the sacrifices of thanksgiving and rehearse His deeds with shouts of joy *and* singing!
23 Some go down to the sea *and* travel over it in ships to do business in great waters;
24 These see the works of the Lord and His wonders in the deep.
25 For He commands and raises up the stormy wind, which lifts up the waves of the sea.
26 [Those aboard] mount up to the heavens, they go down again to the deeps; their courage melts away because of their plight.
27 They reel to and fro and stagger like a drunken man and are at their wits' end [all their wisdom has come to nothing].
28 Then they cry to the Lord in their trouble, and He brings them out of their distresses.
29 He hushes the storm to a calm *and* to a gentle whisper, so that the waves of the sea are still. [Ps. 89:9; Matt. 8:26.]
30 Then the men are glad because of the calm, and He brings them to their desired haven.

<sup>a</sup> 3 Hebrew *north and the sea*   <sup>b</sup> 29 Dead Sea Scrolls; Masoretic Text / *their waves*

## New International Version

31 Let them give thanks to the LORD for his unfailing love
and his wonderful deeds for mankind.
32 Let them exalt him in the assembly of the people
and praise him in the council of the elders.

33 He turned rivers into a desert,
flowing springs into thirsty ground,
34 and fruitful land into a salt waste,
because of the wickedness of those who lived there.
35 He turned the desert into pools of water
and the parched ground into flowing springs;
36 there he brought the hungry to live,
and they founded a city where they could settle.
37 They sowed fields and planted vineyards
that yielded a fruitful harvest;
38 he blessed them, and their numbers greatly increased,
and he did not let their herds diminish.

39 Then their numbers decreased, and they were
humbled
by oppression, calamity and sorrow;
40 he who pours contempt on nobles
made them wander in a trackless waste.
41 But he lifted the needy out of their affliction
and increased their families like flocks.
42 The upright see and rejoice,
but all the wicked shut their mouths.

43 Let the one who is wise heed these things
and ponder the loving deeds of the LORD.

### Psalm 108[a]

*A song. A psalm of David.*

1 My heart, O God, is steadfast;
I will sing and make music with all my soul.
2 Awake, harp and lyre!
I will awaken the dawn.
3 I will praise you, LORD, among the nations;
I will sing of you among the peoples.
4 For great is your love, higher than the heavens;
your faithfulness reaches to the skies.
5 Be exalted, O God, above the heavens;
let your glory be over all the earth.

6 Save us and help us with your right hand,
that those you love may be delivered.
7 God has spoken from his sanctuary:
"In triumph I will parcel out Shechem
and measure off the Valley of Sukkoth.
8 Gilead is mine, Manasseh is mine;
Ephraim is my helmet,
Judah is my scepter.
9 Moab is my washbasin,
on Edom I toss my sandal;
over Philistia I shout in triumph."

10 Who will bring me to the fortified city?
Who will lead me to Edom?
11 Is it not you, God, you who have rejected us
and no longer go out with our armies?
12 Give us aid against the enemy,
for human help is worthless.
13 With God we will gain the victory,
and he will trample down our enemies.

## Amplified Bible

31 Oh, that men would praise [and confess to] the Lord
for His goodness *and* loving-kindness and His wonderful
works to the children of men!
32 Let them exalt Him also in the congregation of the
people and praise Him in the company of the elders.
33 He turns rivers into a wilderness, water springs into a
thirsty ground, [I Kings 17:1, 7.]
34 A fruitful land into a barren, salt waste, because of
the wickedness of those who dwell in it. [Gen. 13:10; 14:3;
19:25.]
35 He turns a wilderness into a pool of water and a dry
ground into water springs; [Isa. 41:18.]
36 And there He makes the hungry to dwell, that they
may prepare a city for habitation,
37 And sow fields, and plant vineyards which yield fruits
of increase.
38 He blesses them also, so that they are multiplied
greatly, and allows not their cattle to decrease.
39 When they are diminished and bowed down through
oppression, trouble, and sorrow,
40 He pours contempt upon princes and causes them to
wander in waste places where there is no road.
41 Yet He raises the poor *and* needy from affliction and
makes their families like a flock.
42 The upright shall see it and be glad, but all iniquity
shall shut its mouth.
43 Whoso is wise [if there be any truly wise] will observe
*and* heed these things; and they will diligently consider
the mercy *and* loving-kindness of the Lord.

### Psalm 108

A song. A Psalm of David.

1 O God, my heart is fixed (steadfast, in the confidence
of faith); I will sing, yes, I will sing praises, even with my
glory [all the faculties and powers of one created in Your
image]!
2 Awake, harp and lyre; I myself will wake very early—I
will awaken the dawn!
3 I will praise *and* give thanks to You, O Lord, among
the peoples; and I will sing praises unto You among the
nations.
4 For Your mercy *and* loving-kindness are great *and*
high as the heavens! Your truth *and* faithfulness reach to
the skies! [Ps. 57:7-11.]
5 Be exalted, O God, above the heavens, and let Your
glory be over all the earth.
6 That Your beloved [followers] may be delivered, save
with Your right hand and answer us! [or me]!
7 God has promised in His holiness [regarding the establishment of David's dynasty]: I will rejoice, I will distribute [Canaan among My people], dividing Shechem and
[the western region and allotting the eastern region which
contains] the Valley of Succoth.
8 Gilead is Mine, Manasseh is Mine; Ephraim also is My
stronghold *and* the defense of My head; Judah is My scepter *and* lawgiver. [Gen. 49:10.]
9 Moab is My washbasin; upon Edom [My slave] My
shoe I cast [to be cleaned]; over Philistia I shout [in tri-
umph].
10 Who will bring me [David] into the strong, fortified
city [of Petra]? Who will lead me into Edom?
11 Have You not cast us off, O God? And will You not go
forth, O God, with our armies?
12 Give us help against the adversary, for vain is the help
of man.
13 Through *and* with God we shall do valiantly, for He
it is Who shall tread down our adversaries. [Ps. 60:5-12.]

---

a In Hebrew texts 108:1-13 is numbered 108:2-14.

## New International Version

### Psalm 109

*For the director of music. Of David. A psalm.*

¹My God, whom I praise,
    do not remain silent,
²for people who are wicked and deceitful
    have opened their mouths against me;
    they have spoken against me with lying tongues.
³With words of hatred they surround me;
    they attack me without cause.
⁴In return for my friendship they accuse me,
    but I am a man of prayer.
⁵They repay me evil for good,
    and hatred for my friendship.

⁶Appoint someone evil to oppose my enemy;
    let an accuser stand at his right hand.
⁷When he is tried, let him be found guilty,
    and may his prayers condemn him.
⁸May his days be few;
    may another take his place of leadership.
⁹May his children be fatherless
    and his wife a widow.
¹⁰May his children be wandering beggars;
    may they be driven*ᵃ* from their ruined homes.
¹¹May a creditor seize all he has;
    may strangers plunder the fruits of his labor.
¹²May no one extend kindness to him
    or take pity on his fatherless children.
¹³May his descendants be cut off,
    their names blotted out from the next generation.
¹⁴May the iniquity of his fathers be remembered before
    the LORD;
    may the sin of his mother never be blotted out.
¹⁵May their sins always remain before the LORD,
    that he may blot out their name from the earth.

¹⁶For he never thought of doing a kindness,
    but hounded to death the poor
    and the needy and the brokenhearted.
¹⁷He loved to pronounce a curse—
    may it come back on him.
   He found no pleasure in blessing—
    may it be far from him.
¹⁸He wore cursing as his garment;
    it entered into his body like water,
    into his bones like oil.
¹⁹May it be like a cloak wrapped about him,
    like a belt tied forever around him.
²⁰May this be the LORD's payment to my accusers,
    to those who speak evil of me.

²¹But you, Sovereign LORD,
    help me for your name's sake;
    out of the goodness of your love, deliver me.
²²For I am poor and needy,
    and my heart is wounded within me.
²³I fade away like an evening shadow;
    I am shaken off like a locust.
²⁴My knees give way from fasting;
    my body is thin and gaunt.
²⁵I am an object of scorn to my accusers;
    when they see me, they shake their heads.

²⁶Help me, LORD my God;
    save me according to your unfailing love.
²⁷Let them know that it is your hand,
    that you, LORD, have done it.

## Amplified Bible

### Psalm 109

To the Chief Musician. A Psalm of David.

¹O God of my praise! Keep not silence,
²For the mouths of the wicked and the mouth of deceit are opened against me; they have spoken to me *and* against me with lying tongues.
³They have compassed me about also with words of hatred and have fought against me without a cause.
⁴In return for my love they are my adversaries, but I resort to prayer.
⁵And they have rewarded *and* laid upon me evil for good, and hatred for my love.
⁶Set a wicked man over him [as a judge], and let [a malicious] accuser stand at his right hand.
⁷When [the wicked] is judged, let him be condemned, and let his prayer [for leniency] be turned into a sin.
⁸Let his days be few; and let another take his office *and* charge. [Acts 1:20.]
⁹Let his children be fatherless and his wife a widow.
¹⁰Let his children be continual vagabonds [as was Cain] and beg; let them seek their bread *and* be driven far from their ruined homes. [Gen. 4:12.]
¹¹Let the creditor *and* extortioner seize all that he has; and let strangers (barbarians and foreigners) plunder the fruits of his labor.
¹²Let there be none to extend *or* continue mercy *and* kindness to him, neither let there be any to have pity on his fatherless children.
¹³Let his posterity be cut off, and in the generation following let their names be blotted out.
¹⁴Let the iniquity of his fathers be remembered by the Lord; and let not the sin of his mother be blotted out.
¹⁵Let them be before the Lord continually, that He may cut off the memory of them from the earth!—
¹⁶Because the man did not [earnestly] remember to show mercy, but pursued *and* persecuted the poor and needy man, and the broken in heart [he was ready] to slay.
¹⁷Yes, he loved cursing, and it came [back] upon him; he delighted not in blessing, and it was far from him.
¹⁸He clothed himself also with cursing as with his garment, and it seeped into his inward [life] like water, and like oil into his bones.
¹⁹Let it be to him as the raiment with which he covers himself and as the girdle with which he is girded continually.
²⁰Let this be the reward of my adversaries from the Lord, and of those who speak evil against my life.
²¹But You deal with me *and* act for me, O God the Lord, for Your name's sake; because Your mercy *and* loving-kindness are good, O deliver me.
²²For I am poor and needy, and my heart is wounded *and* stricken within me.
²³I am gone like the shadow when it lengthens *and* declines; I toss up and down *and* am shaken off as the locust.
²⁴My knees are weak *and* totter from fasting; and my body is gaunt *and* has no fatness.
²⁵I have become also a reproach *and* a taunt to others; when they see me, they shake their heads. [Matt. 26:39.]
²⁶Help me, O Lord my God; O save me according to Your mercy *and* loving-kindness!—
²⁷That they may know that this is Your hand, that You, Lord, have done it.

---

*ᵃ 10* Septuagint; Hebrew *sought*

## New International Version

28 While they curse, may you bless;
   may those who attack me be put to shame,
   but may your servant rejoice.
29 May my accusers be clothed with disgrace
   and wrapped in shame as in a cloak.

30 With my mouth I will greatly extol the LORD;
   in the great throng of worshipers I will praise him.
31 For he stands at the right hand of the needy,
   to save their lives from those who would condemn
   them.

### Psalm 110

*Of David. A psalm.*

1 The LORD says to my lord:[a]

"Sit at my right hand
   until I make your enemies
   a footstool for your feet."

2 The LORD will extend your mighty scepter from Zion,
   saying,
   "Rule in the midst of your enemies!"
3 Your troops will be willing
   on your day of battle.
   Arrayed in holy splendor,
   your young men will come to you
   like dew from the morning's womb.[b]

4 The LORD has sworn
   and will not change his mind:
   "You are a priest forever,
   in the order of Melchizedek."

5 The Lord is at your right hand[c];
   he will crush kings on the day of his wrath.
6 He will judge the nations, heaping up the dead
   and crushing the rulers of the whole earth.
7 He will drink from a brook along the way,[d]
   and so he will lift his head high.

### Psalm 111[e]

1 Praise the LORD.[f]

I will extol the LORD with all my heart
   in the council of the upright and in the assembly.

2 Great are the works of the LORD;
   they are pondered by all who delight in them.
3 Glorious and majestic are his deeds,
   and his righteousness endures forever.
4 He has caused his wonders to be remembered;
   the LORD is gracious and compassionate.
5 He provides food for those who fear him;
   he remembers his covenant forever.

6 He has shown his people the power of his works,
   giving them the lands of other nations.
7 The works of his hands are faithful and just;
   all his precepts are trustworthy.
8 They are established for ever and ever,
   enacted in faithfulness and uprightness.
9 He provided redemption for his people;
   he ordained his covenant forever—
   holy and awesome is his name.

10 The fear of the LORD is the beginning of wisdom;
   all who follow his precepts have good
   understanding.
   To him belongs eternal praise.

*a 1 Or Lord   b 3 The meaning of the Hebrew for this sentence is uncertain.   c 5 Or My lord is at your right hand, LORD   d 7 The meaning of the Hebrew for this clause is uncertain.   e This psalm is an acrostic poem, the lines of which begin with the successive letters of the Hebrew alphabet.   f 1 Hebrew Hallelu Yah*

## Amplified Bible

28 Let them curse, but do You bless. When adversaries arise, let them be put to shame, but let Your servant rejoice.
29 Let my adversaries be clothed with shame *and* dishonor, and let them cover themselves with their own disgrace *and* confusion as with a robe.
30 I will give great praise *and* thanks to the Lord with my mouth; yes, *and* I will praise Him among the multitude.
31 For He will stand at the right hand of the poor *and* needy, to save him from those who condemn his life.

### Psalm 110

A Psalm of David.

1 The Lord (God) says to my Lord (the Messiah), Sit at My right hand, until I make Your adversaries Your footstool. [Matt. 26:64; Acts 2:34; I Cor. 15:25; Col. 3:1; Heb. 12:2.]
2 The Lord will send forth from Zion the scepter of Your strength; rule, then, in the midst of Your foes. [Rom. 11:26, 27.]
3 Your people will offer themselves willingly in the day of Your power, in the beauty of holiness *and* in holy array out of the womb of the morning; to You [will spring forth] Your young men, who are as the dew.
4 The Lord has sworn and will not revoke *or* change it: You are a priest forever, after the manner *and* order of Melchizedek. [Heb. 5:10; 7:11, 15, 21.]
5 The Lord at Your right hand will shatter kings in the day of His indignation.
6 He will execute judgment [in overwhelming punishment] upon the nations; He will fill the valleys with the dead bodies, He will crush the [chief] heads over lands many *and* far extended. [Ezek. 38:21, 22; 39:11, 12.]
7 He will drink of the brook by the way; therefore will He lift up His head [triumphantly].

### Psalm 111

1 Praise the Lord! (Hallelujah!) I will praise *and* give thanks to the Lord with my whole heart in the council of the upright and in the congregation.
2 The works of the Lord are great, sought out by all those who have delight in them.
3 His work is honorable and glorious, and His righteousness endures forever.
4 He has made His wonderful works to be remembered; the Lord is gracious, merciful, *and* full of loving compassion.
5 He has given food *and* provision to those who reverently *and* worshipfully fear Him; He will remember His covenant forever *and* imprint it [on His mind]. [Deut. 10:12; Ps. 96:9.]
6 He has declared *and* shown to His people the power of His works in giving them the heritage of the nations [of Canaan].
7 The works of His hands are [absolute] truth and justice [faithful and right]; and all His decrees *and* precepts are sure (fixed, established, and trustworthy).
8 They stand fast *and* are established forever and ever and are done in [absolute] truth and uprightness.
9 He has sent redemption to His people; He has commanded His covenant to be forever; holy is His name, inspiring awe, reverence, *and* godly fear.
10 The reverent fear *and* worship of the Lord is the beginning of [a]Wisdom *and* skill [the preceding and the first essential, the prerequisite and the alphabet]; a good understanding, wisdom, *and* meaning have all those who do [the will of the Lord]. Their praise of Him endures forever. [Job. 28:28; Prov. 1:7; Matt. 22:37, 38; Rev. 14:7.]

*a See footnote on Job 28:12.*

# New International Version

## Psalm 112[a]

¹Praise the Lord.[b]

Blessed are those who fear the Lord,
  who find great delight in his commands.

²Their children will be mighty in the land;
  the generation of the upright will be blessed.
³Wealth and riches are in their houses,
  and their righteousness endures forever.
⁴Even in darkness light dawns for the upright,
  for those who are gracious and compassionate and
    righteous.
⁵Good will come to those who are generous and lend
  freely,
  who conduct their affairs with justice.

⁶Surely the righteous will never be shaken;
  they will be remembered forever.
⁷They will have no fear of bad news;
  their hearts are steadfast, trusting in the Lord.
⁸Their hearts are secure, they will have no fear;
  in the end they will look in triumph on their foes.
⁹They have freely scattered their gifts to the poor,
  their righteousness endures forever;
  their horn[c] will be lifted high in honor.

¹⁰The wicked will see and be vexed,
  they will gnash their teeth and waste away;
  the longings of the wicked will come to nothing.

## Psalm 113

¹Praise the Lord.[d]

Praise the Lord, you his servants;
  praise the name of the Lord.
²Let the name of the Lord be praised,
  both now and forevermore.
³From the rising of the sun to the place where it sets,
  the name of the Lord is to be praised.

⁴The Lord is exalted over all the nations,
  his glory above the heavens.
⁵Who is like the Lord our God,
  the One who sits enthroned on high,
⁶who stoops down to look
  on the heavens and the earth?

⁷He raises the poor from the dust
  and lifts the needy from the ash heap;
⁸he seats them with princes,
  with the princes of his people.
⁹He settles the childless woman in her home
  as a happy mother of children.

Praise the Lord.

## Psalm 114

¹When Israel came out of Egypt,
  Jacob from a people of foreign tongue,
²Judah became God's sanctuary,
  Israel his dominion.

³The sea looked and fled,
  the Jordan turned back;
⁴the mountains leaped like rams,
  the hills like lambs.

# Amplified Bible

## Psalm 112

¹Praise the Lord! (Hallelujah!) Blessed (happy, fortunate, to be envied) is the man who fears (reveres and worships) the Lord, who delights greatly in His commandments. [Deut. 10:12.]
²His [spiritual] offspring shall be mighty upon earth; the generation of the upright shall be blessed.
³Prosperity *and* welfare are in his house, and his righteousness endures forever.
⁴Light arises in the darkness for the upright, gracious, compassionate, *and* just [who are in right standing with God].
⁵It is well with the man who deals generously and lends, who conducts his affairs with justice. [Ps. 37:26; Luke 6:35; Col. 4:5.]
⁶He will not be moved forever; the [uncompromisingly] righteous (the upright, in right standing with God) shall be in everlasting remembrance. [Prov. 10:7.]
⁷He shall not be afraid of evil tidings; his heart is firmly fixed, trusting (leaning on and being confident) in the Lord.
⁸His heart is established *and* steady, he will not be afraid while he waits to see his desire established upon his adversaries.
⁹He has distributed freely [he has given to the poor and needy]; his righteousness (uprightness and right standing with God) endures forever; his horn shall be exalted in honor. [II Cor. 9:9.]
¹⁰The wicked man will see it and be grieved *and* angered, he will gnash his teeth and disappear [in despair]; the desire of the wicked shall perish *and* come to nothing.

## Psalm 113

¹Praise the Lord! (Hallelujah!) Praise, O servants of the Lord, praise the name of the Lord!
²Blessed be the name of the Lord from this time forth and forever
³From the rising of the sun to the going down of it *and* from east to west, the name of the Lord is to be praised!
⁴The Lord is high above all nations, and His glory above the heavens!
⁵Who is like the Lord our God, Who has His seat on high,
⁶Who humbles Himself to regard the heavens and the earth! [Ps. 138:6; Isa. 57:15.]
⁷[The Lord] raises the poor out of the dust *and* lifts the needy from the ash heap *and* the dung hill,
⁸That He may seat them with princes, even with the princes of His people.
⁹He makes the barren woman to be a homemaker *and* a joyful mother of [spiritual] children. Praise the Lord! (Hallelujah!)

## Psalm 114

¹When Israel came forth out of Egypt, the house of Jacob from a people of strange language,
²Judah became [God's] sanctuary (the Holy Place of His habitation), and Israel His dominion. [Exod. 29:45, 46; Deut. 27:9.]
³The [Red] Sea looked and fled; the Jordan [River] was turned back. [Exod. 14:21; Josh. 3:13, 16; Ps. 77:16.]
⁴The mountains skipped like rams, the little hills like lambs.

---

[a] This psalm is an acrostic poem, the lines of which begin with the successive letters of the Hebrew alphabet.   [b] 1 Hebrew *Hallelu Yah*
[c] 9 *Horn* here symbolizes dignity.   [d] 1 Hebrew *Hallelu Yah*; also in verse 9

## New International Version

⁵Why was it, sea, that you fled?
  Why, Jordan, did you turn back?
⁶Why, mountains, did you leap like rams,
  you hills, like lambs?

⁷Tremble, earth, at the presence of the Lord,
  at the presence of the God of Jacob,
⁸who turned the rock into a pool,
  the hard rock into springs of water.

### Psalm 115

¹Not to us, Lord, not to us
  but to your name be the glory,
  because of your love and faithfulness.

²Why do the nations say,
  "Where is their God?"
³Our God is in heaven;
  he does whatever pleases him.
⁴But their idols are silver and gold,
  made by human hands.
⁵They have mouths, but cannot speak,
  eyes, but cannot see.
⁶They have ears, but cannot hear,
  noses, but cannot smell.
⁷They have hands, but cannot feel,
  feet, but cannot walk,
  nor can they utter a sound with their throats.
⁸Those who make them will be like them,
  and so will all who trust in them.

⁹All you Israelites, trust in the Lord—
  he is their help and shield.
¹⁰House of Aaron, trust in the Lord—
  he is their help and shield.
¹¹You who fear him, trust in the Lord—
  he is their help and shield.

¹²The Lord remembers us and will bless us:
  He will bless his people Israel,
  he will bless the house of Aaron,
¹³he will bless those who fear the Lord—
  small and great alike.

¹⁴May the Lord cause you to flourish,
  both you and your children.
¹⁵May you be blessed by the Lord,
  the Maker of heaven and earth.

¹⁶The highest heavens belong to the Lord,
  but the earth he has given to mankind.
¹⁷It is not the dead who praise the Lord,
  those who go down to the place of silence;
¹⁸it is we who extol the Lord,
  both now and forevermore.

Praise the Lord.ᵃ

### Psalm 116

¹I love the Lord, for he heard my voice;
  he heard my cry for mercy.
²Because he turned his ear to me,
  I will call on him as long as I live.

³The cords of death entangled me,
  the anguish of the grave came over me;
  I was overcome by distress and sorrow.
⁴Then I called on the name of the Lord:
  "Lord, save me!"

⁵The Lord is gracious and righteous;
  our God is full of compassion.
⁶The Lord protects the unwary;
  when I was brought low, he saved me.

## Amplified Bible

⁵What ails you, O [Red] Sea, that you flee? O Jordan, that you turn back?
⁶You mountains, that you skip like rams, and you little hills, like lambs?
⁷Tremble, O earth, at the presence of the Lord, at the presence of the God of Jacob,
⁸Who turned the rock into a pool of water, the flint into a fountain of waters. [Exod. 17:6; Num. 20:11.]

### Psalm 115

¹Not to us, O Lord, not to us but to Your name give glory, for Your mercy and loving-kindness and for the sake of Your truth and faithfulness!
²Why should the nations say, Where is now their God?
³But our God is in heaven; He does whatever He pleases.
⁴The idols of the nations are silver and gold, the work of men's hands.
⁵They have mouths, but they speak not; eyes have they, but they see not;
⁶They have ears, but they hear not; noses have they, but they smell not;
⁷They have hands, but they handle not; feet have they, but they walk not; neither can they make a sound with their throats.
⁸They who make idols are like them; so are all who trust in and lean on them. [Ps. 135:15-18.]
⁹O Israel, trust and take refuge in the Lord! [Lean on, rely on, and be confident in Him!] He is their Help and their Shield.
¹⁰O house of Aaron [the priesthood], trust in and lean on the Lord! He is their Help and their Shield.
¹¹You who [reverently] fear the Lord, trust in and lean on the Lord! He is their Help and their Shield.
¹²The Lord has been mindful of us, He will bless us: He will bless the house of Israel, He will bless the house of Aaron [the priesthood],
¹³He will bless those who reverently and worshipfully fear the Lord, both small and great. [Ps. 103:11; Rev. 11:18; 19:5.]
¹⁴May the Lord give you increase more and more, you and your children.
¹⁵May you be blessed of the Lord, Who made heaven and earth!
¹⁶The heavens are the Lord's heavens, but the earth has He given to the children of men.
¹⁷The dead praise not the Lord, neither any who go down into silence.
¹⁸But we will bless (affectionately and gratefully praise) the Lord from this time forth and forever. Praise the Lord! (Hallelujah!)

### Psalm 116

¹I love the Lord, because He has heard [and now hears] my voice and my supplications.
²Because He has inclined His ear to me, therefore will I call upon Him as long as I live.
³The cords and sorrows of death were around me, and the terrors of Sheol (the place of the dead) had laid hold of me; I suffered anguish and grief (trouble and sorrow).
⁴Then called I upon the name of the Lord: O Lord, I beseech You, save my life and deliver me!
⁵Gracious is the Lord, and [rigidly] righteous; yes, our God is merciful.
⁶The Lord preserves the simple; I was brought low, and He helped and saved me.

---

ᵃ 18 Hebrew *Hallelu Yah*

## New International Version

7 Return to your rest, my soul,
  for the LORD has been good to you.
8 For you, LORD, have delivered me from death,
  my eyes from tears,
  my feet from stumbling,
9 that I may walk before the LORD
  in the land of the living.

10 I trusted in the LORD when I said,
  "I am greatly afflicted";
11 in my alarm I said,
  "Everyone is a liar."

12 What shall I return to the LORD
  for all his goodness to me?
13 I will lift up the cup of salvation
  and call on the name of the LORD.
14 I will fulfill my vows to the LORD
  in the presence of all his people.

15 Precious in the sight of the LORD
  is the death of his faithful servants.
16 Truly I am your servant, LORD;
  I serve you just as my mother did;
  you have freed me from my chains.

17 I will sacrifice a thank offering to you
  and call on the name of the LORD.
18 I will fulfill my vows to the LORD
  in the presence of all his people,
19 in the courts of the house of the LORD—
  in your midst, Jerusalem.

  Praise the LORD.[a]

### Psalm 117

1 Praise the LORD, all you nations;
  extol him, all you peoples.
2 For great is his love toward us,
  and the faithfulness of the LORD endures forever.

  Praise the LORD.[a]

### Psalm 118

1 Give thanks to the LORD, for he is good;
  his love endures forever.

2 Let Israel say:
  "His love endures forever."
3 Let the house of Aaron say:
  "His love endures forever."
4 Let those who fear the LORD say:
  "His love endures forever."

5 When hard pressed, I cried to the LORD;
  he brought me into a spacious place.
6 The LORD is with me; I will not be afraid.
  What can mere mortals do to me?
7 The LORD is with me; he is my helper.
  I look in triumph on my enemies.

8 It is better to take refuge in the LORD
  than to trust in humans.
9 It is better to take refuge in the LORD
  than to trust in princes.
10 All the nations surrounded me,
  but in the name of the LORD I cut them down.
11 They surrounded me on every side,
  but in the name of the LORD I cut them down.
12 They swarmed around me like bees,
  but they were consumed as quickly as burning thorns;
  in the name of the LORD I cut them down.

## Amplified Bible

7 Return to your rest, O my soul, for the Lord has dealt bountifully with you. [Matt. 11:29.]
8 For You have delivered my life from death, my eyes from tears, and my feet from stumbling and falling.
9 I will walk before the Lord in the land of the living.
10 I believed (trusted in, relied on, and clung to my God), and therefore have I spoken [even when I said], I am greatly afflicted. [II Cor. 4:13.]
11 I said in my haste, All men are deceitful and liars.
12 What shall I render to the Lord for all His benefits toward me? [How can I repay Him for all His bountiful dealings?]
13 I will lift up the cup of salvation and deliverance and call on the name of the Lord.
14 I will pay my vows to the Lord, yes, in the presence of all His people.
15 Precious (important and no light matter) in the sight of the Lord is the death of His saints (His loving ones).
16 O Lord, truly I am Your servant; I am Your servant, the son of Your handmaid; You have loosed my bonds.
17 I will offer to You the sacrifice of thanksgiving and will call on the name of the Lord.
18 I will pay my vows to the Lord, yes, in the presence of all His people,
19 In the courts of the Lord's house—in the midst of you, O Jerusalem. Praise the Lord! (Hallelujah!)

### Psalm 117

1 O praise the Lord, all you nations! Praise Him, all you people! [Rom. 15:11.]
2 For His mercy and loving-kindness are great toward us, and the truth and faithfulness of the Lord endure forever. Praise the Lord! (Hallelujah!)

### Psalm 118

1 O give thanks to the Lord, for He is good; for His mercy and loving-kindness endure forever!
2 Let Israel now say that His mercy and loving-kindness endure forever.
3 Let the house of Aaron [the priesthood] now say that His mercy and loving-kindness endure forever.
4 Let those now who reverently and worshipfully fear the Lord say that His mercy and loving-kindness endure forever.
5 Out of my distress I called upon the Lord; the Lord answered me and set me free and in a large place.
6 The Lord is on my side; I will not fear. What can man do to me? [Heb. 13:6.]
7 The Lord is on my side and takes my part, He is among those who help me; therefore shall I see my desire established upon those who hate me.
8 It is better to trust and take refuge in the Lord than to put confidence in man.
9 It is better to trust and take refuge in the Lord than to put confidence in princes.
10 All nations (the surrounding tribes) compassed me about, but in the name of the Lord I will cut them off!
11 They compassed me about, yes, they surrounded me on every side; but in the name of the Lord I will cut them off!
12 They swarmed about me like bees, they blaze up and are extinguished like a fire of thorns; in the name of the Lord I will cut them off! [Deut. 1:44.]

## New International Version

<sup>13</sup>I was pushed back and about to fall,
but the LORD helped me.
<sup>14</sup>The LORD is my strength and my defense<sup>a</sup>;
he has become my salvation.

<sup>15</sup>Shouts of joy and victory
resound in the tents of the righteous:
"The LORD's right hand has done mighty things!
<sup>16</sup>    The LORD's right hand is lifted high;
the LORD's right hand has done mighty things!"
<sup>17</sup>I will not die but live,
and will proclaim what the LORD has done.
<sup>18</sup>The LORD has chastened me severely,
but he has not given me over to death.
<sup>19</sup>Open for me the gates of the righteous;
I will enter and give thanks to the LORD.
<sup>20</sup>This is the gate of the LORD
through which the righteous may enter.
<sup>21</sup>I will give you thanks, for you answered me;
you have become my salvation.

<sup>22</sup>The stone the builders rejected
has become the cornerstone;
<sup>23</sup>the LORD has done this,
and it is marvelous in our eyes.
<sup>24</sup>The LORD has done it this very day;
let us rejoice today and be glad.

<sup>25</sup>LORD, save us!
LORD, grant us success!

<sup>26</sup>Blessed is he who comes in the name of the LORD.
From the house of the LORD we bless you.<sup>b</sup>
<sup>27</sup>The LORD is God,
and he has made his light shine on us.
With boughs in hand, join in the festal procession
up<sup>c</sup> to the horns of the altar.

<sup>28</sup>You are my God, and I will praise you;
you are my God, and I will exalt you.

<sup>29</sup>Give thanks to the LORD, for he is good;
his love endures forever.

### Psalm 119<sup>d</sup>

#### א Aleph

<sup>1</sup>Blessed are those whose ways are blameless,
who walk according to the law of the LORD.
<sup>2</sup>Blessed are those who keep his statutes
and seek him with all their heart—
<sup>3</sup>they do no wrong
but follow his ways.
<sup>4</sup>You have laid down precepts
that are to be fully obeyed.
<sup>5</sup>Oh, that my ways were steadfast
in obeying your decrees!
<sup>6</sup>Then I would not be put to shame
when I consider all your commands.
<sup>7</sup>I will praise you with an upright heart
as I learn your righteous laws.
<sup>8</sup>I will obey your decrees;
do not utterly forsake me.

#### ב Beth

<sup>9</sup>How can a young person stay on the path of purity?
By living according to your word.

## Amplified Bible

<sup>13</sup>You [my adversary] thrust sorely at me that I might
fall, but the Lord helped me.
<sup>14</sup>The Lord is my Strength and Song; and He has be-
come my Salvation.
<sup>15</sup>The voice of rejoicing and salvation is in the tents *and*
private dwellings of the [uncompromisingly] righteous:
the right hand of the Lord does valiantly *and* achieves
strength!
<sup>16</sup>The right hand of the Lord is exalted; the right hand of
the Lord does valiantly *and* achieves strength!
<sup>17</sup>I shall not die but live, and shall declare the works *and*
recount the illustrious acts of the Lord.
<sup>18</sup>The Lord has chastened me sorely, but He has not
given me over to death. [II Cor. 6:9.]
<sup>19</sup>Open to me the [temple] gates of righteousness; I
will enter through them, and I will confess *and* praise the
Lord.
<sup>20</sup>This is the gate of the Lord; the [uncompromisingly]
righteous shall enter through it. [Ps. 24:7.]
<sup>21</sup>I will confess, praise, *and* give thanks to You, for You
have heard *and* answered me; and You have become my
Salvation *and* Deliverer.
<sup>22</sup>The stone which the builders rejected has become the
chief cornerstone.
<sup>23</sup>This is from the Lord *and* is His doing; it is marvelous
in our eyes. [Matt. 21:42; Acts 4:11; I Pet. 2:7.]
<sup>24</sup>This is the day which the Lord has brought about; we
will rejoice and be glad in it.
<sup>25</sup>Save now, we beseech You, O Lord; send now prosper-
ity, O Lord, we beseech You, *and* give to us success!
<sup>26</sup>Blessed is he who comes in the name of the Lord; we
bless you from the house of the Lord [you who come into
His sanctuary under His guardianship]. [Mark 11:9, 10.]
<sup>27</sup>The Lord is God, Who has shown *and* given us light
[He has illuminated us with grace, freedom, and joy]. Decorate the festival with leafy boughs *and* bind the sacrifices
to be offered with thick cords [all over the priest's court,
right up] to the horns of the altar.
<sup>28</sup>You are my God, and I will confess, praise, *and* give
thanks to You; You are my God, I will extol You.
<sup>29</sup>O give thanks to the Lord, for He is good; for His
mercy *and* loving-kindness endure forever.

### Psalm 119

<sup>1</sup>Blessed (happy, fortunate, to be envied) are the unde-
filed (the upright, truly sincere, and blameless) in the way
[of the revealed will of God], who walk (order their conduct and conversation) in the law of the Lord (the whole of
God's revealed will).
<sup>2</sup>Blessed (happy, fortunate, to be envied) are they who
keep His testimonies, and who seek, inquire for *and* of
Him *and* crave Him with the whole heart.
<sup>3</sup>Yes, they do no unrighteousness [no willful wander-
ing from His precepts]; they walk in His ways. [I John 3:9;
5:18.]
<sup>4</sup>You have commanded us to keep Your precepts, that
we should observe them diligently.
<sup>5</sup>Oh, that my ways were directed *and* established to
observe Your statutes [hearing, receiving, loving, and
obeying them]!
<sup>6</sup>Then shall I not be put to shame [by failing to inherit
Your promises] when I have respect to all Your commandments.
<sup>7</sup>I will praise *and* give thanks to You with uprightness of
heart when I learn [by sanctified experiences] Your righteous judgments [Your decisions against and punishments
for particular lines of thought and conduct].
<sup>8</sup>I will keep Your statutes; O forsake me not utterly.
<sup>9</sup>How shall a young man cleanse his way? By taking
heed *and* keeping watch [on himself] according to Your
word [conforming his life to it].

---

<sup>a</sup> 14 Or *song*    <sup>b</sup> 26 The Hebrew is plural.    <sup>c</sup> 27 Or *Bind the festal
sacrifice with ropes / and take it*    <sup>d</sup> This psalm is an acrostic poem, the
stanzas of which begin with successive letters of the Hebrew alphabet;
moreover, the verses of each stanza begin with the same letter of the
Hebrew alphabet.

## New International Version

10 I seek you with all my heart;
    do not let me stray from your commands.
11 I have hidden your word in my heart
    that I might not sin against you.
12 Praise be to you, LORD;
    teach me your decrees.
13 With my lips I recount
    all the laws that come from your mouth.
14 I rejoice in following your statutes
    as one rejoices in great riches.
15 I meditate on your precepts
    and consider your ways.
16 I delight in your decrees;
    I will not neglect your word.

### ג Gimel

17 Be good to your servant while I live,
    that I may obey your word.
18 Open my eyes that I may see
    wonderful things in your law.
19 I am a stranger on earth;
    do not hide your commands from me.
20 My soul is consumed with longing
    for your laws at all times.
21 You rebuke the arrogant, who are accursed,
    those who stray from your commands.
22 Remove from me their scorn and contempt,
    for I keep your statutes.
23 Though rulers sit together and slander me,
    your servant will meditate on your decrees.
24 Your statutes are my delight;
    they are my counselors.

### ד Daleth

25 I am laid low in the dust;
    preserve my life according to your word.
26 I gave an account of my ways and you answered me;
    teach me your decrees.
27 Cause me to understand the way of your precepts,
    that I may meditate on your wonderful deeds.
28 My soul is weary with sorrow;
    strengthen me according to your word.
29 Keep me from deceitful ways;
    be gracious to me and teach me your law.
30 I have chosen the way of faithfulness;
    I have set my heart on your laws.
31 I hold fast to your statutes, LORD;
    do not let me be put to shame.
32 I run in the path of your commands,
    for you have broadened my understanding.

### ה He

33 Teach me, LORD, the way of your decrees,
    that I may follow it to the end.[a]
34 Give me understanding, so that I may keep your law
    and obey it with all my heart.
35 Direct me in the path of your commands,
    for there I find delight.
36 Turn my heart toward your statutes
    and not toward selfish gain.
37 Turn my eyes away from worthless things;
    preserve my life according to your word.[b]
38 Fulfill your promise to your servant,
    so that you may be feared.
39 Take away the disgrace I dread,
    for your laws are good.
40 How I long for your precepts!
    In your righteousness preserve my life.

[a] 33 Or follow it for its reward   [b] 37 Two manuscripts of the Masoretic Text and Dead Sea Scrolls; most manuscripts of the Masoretic Text life in your way

## Amplified Bible

10 With my whole heart have I sought You, inquiring for and of You and yearning for You; Oh, let me not wander or step aside [either in ignorance or willfully] from Your commandments. [II Chron. 15:15.]
11 Your word have I laid up in my heart, that I might not sin against You.
12 Blessed are You, O Lord; teach me Your statutes.
13 With my lips have I declared and recounted all the ordinances of Your mouth.
14 I have rejoiced in the way of Your testimonies as much as in all riches.
15 I will meditate on Your precepts and have respect to Your ways [the paths of life marked out by Your law]. [Ps. 104:34.]
16 I will delight myself in Your statutes; I will not forget Your word.
17 Deal bountifully with Your servant, that I may live; and I will observe Your word [hearing, receiving, loving, and obeying it]. [Ps. 119:97-101.]
18 Open my eyes, that I may behold wondrous things out of Your law.
19 I am a stranger and a temporary resident on the earth; hide not Your commandments from me. [Gen. 47:9; I Chron. 29:15; Ps. 39:12; II Cor. 5:6; Heb. 11:13.]
20 My heart is breaking with the longing that it has for Your ordinances and judgments at all times.
21 You rebuke the proud and arrogant, the accursed ones, who err and wander from Your commandments.
22 Take away from me reproach and contempt, for I keep Your testimonies.
23 Princes also sat and talked against me, but Your servant meditated on Your statutes.
24 Your testimonies also are my delight and my counselors.
25 My earthly life cleaves to the dust; revive and stimulate me according to Your word! [Ps. 143:11.]
26 I have declared my ways and opened my griefs to You, and You listened to me; teach me Your statutes.
27 Make me understand the way of Your precepts; so shall I meditate on and talk of Your wondrous works. [Ps. 145:5, 6.]
28 My life dissolves and weeps itself away for heaviness; raise me up and strengthen me according to [the promises of] Your word.
29 Remove from me the way of falsehood and unfaithfulness [to You], and graciously impart Your law to me.
30 I have chosen the way of truth and faithfulness; Your ordinances have I set before me.
31 I cleave to Your testimonies; O Lord, put me not to shame!
32 I will [not merely walk, but] run the way of Your commandments, when You give me a heart that is willing.
33 Teach me, O Lord, the way of Your statutes, and I will keep it to the end [steadfastly].
34 Give me understanding, that I may keep Your law; yes, I will observe it with my whole heart. [Prov. 2:6; James 1:5.]
35 Make me go in the path of Your commandments, for in them do I delight.
36 Incline my heart to Your testimonies and not to covetousness (robbery, sensuality, unworthy riches). [Ezek. 33:31; Mark 7:21, 22; I Tim. 6:10; Heb. 13:5.]
37 Turn away my eyes from beholding vanity (idols and idolatry); and restore me to vigorous life and health in Your ways.
38 Establish Your word and confirm Your promise to Your servant, which is for those who reverently fear and devotedly worship You. [Deut. 10:12; Ps. 96:9.]
39 Turn away my reproach which I fear and dread, for Your ordinances are good.
40 Behold, I long for Your precepts; in Your righteousness give me renewed life.

## New International Version

### ו Waw

⁴¹May your unfailing love come to me, LORD,
  your salvation, according to your promise;
⁴²then I can answer anyone who taunts me,
  for I trust in your word.
⁴³Never take your word of truth from my mouth,
  for I have put my hope in your laws.
⁴⁴I will always obey your law,
  for ever and ever.
⁴⁵I will walk about in freedom,
  for I have sought out your precepts.
⁴⁶I will speak of your statutes before kings
  and will not be put to shame,
⁴⁷for I delight in your commands
  because I love them.
⁴⁸I reach out for your commands, which I love,
  that I may meditate on your decrees.

### ז Zayin

⁴⁹Remember your word to your servant,
  for you have given me hope.
⁵⁰My comfort in my suffering is this:
  Your promise preserves my life.
⁵¹The arrogant mock me unmercifully,
  but I do not turn from your law.
⁵²I remember, LORD, your ancient laws,
  and I find comfort in them.
⁵³Indignation grips me because of the wicked,
  who have forsaken your law.
⁵⁴Your decrees are the theme of my song
  wherever I lodge.
⁵⁵In the night, LORD, I remember your name,
  that I may keep your law.
⁵⁶This has been my practice:
  I obey your precepts.

### ח Heth

⁵⁷You are my portion, LORD;
  I have promised to obey your words.
⁵⁸I have sought your face with all my heart;
  be gracious to me according to your promise.
⁵⁹I have considered my ways
  and have turned my steps to your statutes.
⁶⁰I will hasten and not delay
  to obey your commands.
⁶¹Though the wicked bind me with ropes,
  I will not forget your law.
⁶²At midnight I rise to give you thanks
  for your righteous laws.
⁶³I am a friend to all who fear you,
  to all who follow your precepts.
⁶⁴The earth is filled with your love, LORD;
  teach me your decrees.

### ט Teth

⁶⁵Do good to your servant
  according to your word, LORD.
⁶⁶Teach me knowledge and good judgment,
  for I trust your commands.
⁶⁷Before I was afflicted I went astray,
  but now I obey your word.
⁶⁸You are good, and what you do is good;
  teach me your decrees.

## Amplified Bible

⁴¹Let Your mercy *and* loving-kindness come also to me,
O Lord, even Your salvation according to Your promise;
⁴²Then shall I have an answer for those who taunt *and*
reproach me, for I lean on, rely on, *and* trust in Your word.
⁴³And take not the word of truth utterly out of my
mouth, for I hope in Your ordinances.
⁴⁴I will keep Your law continually, forever and ever
[hearing, receiving, loving, and obeying it].
⁴⁵And I will walk at liberty *and* at ease, for I have sought
and inquired for [and desperately required] Your precepts.
⁴⁶I will speak of Your testimonies also before kings and
will not be put to shame. [Ps. 138:1; Matt. 10:18, 19; Acts
26:1, 2.]
⁴⁷For I will delight myself in Your commandments,
which I love.
⁴⁸My hands also will I lift up [in fervent supplication]
to Your commandments, which I love, and I will meditate
on Your statutes.
⁴⁹Remember [fervently] the word *and* promise to Your
servant, in which You have caused me to hope.
⁵⁰This is my comfort *and* consolation in my affliction:
that Your word has revived me *and* given me life. [Rom.
15:4.]
⁵¹The proud have had me greatly in derision, yet have
I not declined in my interest in *or* turned aside from Your
law.
⁵²When I have [earnestly] recalled Your ordinances
from of old, O Lord, I have taken comfort.
⁵³Burning indignation, terror, *and* sadness seize upon
me because of the wicked, who forsake Your law.
⁵⁴Your statutes have been my songs in the house of my
pilgrimage.
⁵⁵I have [earnestly] remembered Your name, O Lord, in
the night, and I have observed Your law.
⁵⁶This I have had [as the gift of Your grace and as my
reward]: that I have kept Your precepts [hearing, receiving, loving, and obeying them].
⁵⁷You are my portion, O Lord; I have promised to keep
Your words.
⁵⁸I entreated Your favor with my whole heart; be merciful *and* gracious to me according to Your promise.
⁵⁹I considered my ways; I turned my feet to [obey] Your
testimonies.
⁶⁰I made haste and delayed not to keep Your commandments.
⁶¹Though the cords of the wicked have enclosed *and*
ensnared me, I have not forgotten Your law.
⁶²At midnight I will rise to give thanks to You because
of Your righteous ordinances.
⁶³I am a companion of all those who fear, revere, *and*
worship You, and of those who observe *and* give heed to
Your precepts.
⁶⁴The earth, O Lord, is full of Your mercy *and* loving-
kindness; teach me Your statutes.
⁶⁵You have dealt well with Your servant, O Lord, according to Your promise.
⁶⁶Teach me good judgment, wise *and* right discernment, and knowledge, for I have believed (trusted, relied
on, and clung to) Your commandments.
⁶⁷Before I was afflicted I went astray, but now Your word
do I keep [hearing, receiving, loving, and obeying it].
⁶⁸You are good *and* kind and do good; teach me Your
statutes.

## New International Version

⁶⁹Though the arrogant have smeared me with lies,
    I keep your precepts with all my heart.
⁷⁰Their hearts are callous and unfeeling,
    but I delight in your law.
⁷¹It was good for me to be afflicted
    so that I might learn your decrees.
⁷²The law from your mouth is more precious to me
    than thousands of pieces of silver and gold.

### ׳ Yodh

⁷³Your hands made me and formed me;
    give me understanding to learn your commands.
⁷⁴May those who fear you rejoice when they see me,
    for I have put my hope in your word.
⁷⁵I know, Lord, that your laws are righteous,
    and that in faithfulness you have afflicted me.
⁷⁶May your unfailing love be my comfort,
    according to your promise to your servant.
⁷⁷Let your compassion come to me that I may live,
    for your law is my delight.
⁷⁸May the arrogant be put to shame for wronging me
    without cause;
    but I will meditate on your precepts.
⁷⁹May those who fear you turn to me,
    those who understand your statutes.
⁸⁰May I wholeheartedly follow your decrees,
    that I may not be put to shame.

### כ Kaph

⁸¹My soul faints with longing for your salvation,
    but I have put my hope in your word.
⁸²My eyes fail, looking for your promise;
    I say, "When will you comfort me?"
⁸³Though I am like a wineskin in the smoke,
    I do not forget your decrees.
⁸⁴How long must your servant wait?
    When will you punish my persecutors?
⁸⁵The arrogant dig pits to trap me,
    contrary to your law.
⁸⁶All your commands are trustworthy;
    help me, for I am being persecuted without cause.
⁸⁷They almost wiped me from the earth,
    but I have not forsaken your precepts.
⁸⁸In your unfailing love preserve my life,
    that I may obey the statutes of your mouth.

### ל Lamedh

⁸⁹Your word, Lord, is eternal;
    it stands firm in the heavens.
⁹⁰Your faithfulness continues through all generations;
    you established the earth, and it endures.
⁹¹Your laws endure to this day,
    for all things serve you.
⁹²If your law had not been my delight,
    I would have perished in my affliction.
⁹³I will never forget your precepts,
    for by them you have preserved my life.
⁹⁴Save me, for I am yours;
    I have sought out your precepts.
⁹⁵The wicked are waiting to destroy me,
    but I will ponder your statutes.
⁹⁶To all perfection I see a limit,
    but your commands are boundless.

## Amplified Bible

⁶⁹The arrogant *and* godless have put together a lie against me, but I will keep Your precepts with my whole heart.
⁷⁰Their hearts are as fat as grease [their minds are dull and brutal], but I delight in Your law.
⁷¹It is good for me that I have been afflicted, that I might learn Your statutes.
⁷²The law from Your mouth is better to me than thousands of gold and silver pieces.
⁷³Your hands have made me, cunningly fashioned *and* established me; give me understanding, that I may learn Your commandments.
⁷⁴Those who reverently *and* worshipfully fear You will see me and be glad, because I have hoped in Your word *and* tarried for it.
⁷⁵I know, O Lord, that Your judgments are right *and* righteous, and that in faithfulness You have afflicted me. [Heb. 12:10.]
⁷⁶Let, I pray You, Your merciful kindness *and* steadfast love be for my comfort, according to Your promise to Your servant.
⁷⁷Let Your tender mercy *and* loving-kindness come to me that I may live, for Your law is my delight!
⁷⁸Let the proud be put to shame, for they dealt perversely with me without a cause; but I will meditate on Your precepts.
⁷⁹Let those who reverently *and* worshipfully fear You turn to me, and those who have known Your testimonies.
⁸⁰Let my heart be sound (sincere and wholehearted and blameless) in Your statutes, that I may not be put to shame.
⁸¹My soul languishes *and* grows faint for Your salvation, but I hope in Your word.
⁸²My eyes fail, watching for [the fulfillment of] Your promise. I say, When will You comfort me?
⁸³For I have become like a bottle [a wineskin blackened and shriveled] in the smoke [in which it hangs], yet do I not forget Your statutes.
⁸⁴How many are the days of Your servant [which he must endure]? When will You judge those who pursue and persecute me? [Rev. 6:10.]
⁸⁵The godless *and* arrogant have dug pitfalls for me, men who do not conform to Your law.
⁸⁶All Your commandments are faithful *and* sure. [The godless] pursue *and* persecute me with falsehood; help me [Lord]!
⁸⁷They had almost consumed me upon earth, but I forsook not Your precepts.
⁸⁸According to Your steadfast love give life to me; then I will keep the testimony of Your mouth [hearing, receiving, loving, and obeying it].
⁸⁹Forever, O Lord, Your word is settled in heaven [stands firm as the heavens]. [Ps. 89:2; Matt. 24:34, 35; I Pet. 1:25.]
⁹⁰Your faithfulness is from generation to generation; You have established the earth, and it stands fast.
⁹¹All [the whole universe] are Your servants; therefore they continue this day according to Your ordinances. [Jer. 33:25.]
⁹²Unless Your law had been my delight, I would have perished in my affliction.
⁹³I will never forget Your precepts, [how can I?] for it is by them You have quickened me (granted me life).
⁹⁴I am Yours, therefore save me [Your own]; for I have sought (inquired of and for) Your precepts *and* required them [as my urgent need]. [Ps. 42:1.]
⁹⁵The wicked wait for me to destroy me, but I will consider Your testimonies.
⁹⁶I have seen that everything [human] has its limits *and* end [no matter how extensive, noble, and excellent]; but Your commandment is exceedingly broad *and* extends without limits [into eternity]. [Rom. 3:10-19.]

## New International Version

### ב Mem

97 Oh, how I love your law!
   I meditate on it all day long.
98 Your commands are always with me
   and make me wiser than my enemies.
99 I have more insight than all my teachers,
   for I meditate on your statutes.
100 I have more understanding than the elders,
   for I obey your precepts.
101 I have kept my feet from every evil path
   so that I might obey your word.
102 I have not departed from your laws,
   for you yourself have taught me.
103 How sweet are your words to my taste,
   sweeter than honey to my mouth!
104 I gain understanding from your precepts;
   therefore I hate every wrong path.

### נ Nun

105 Your word is a lamp for my feet,
   a light on my path.
106 I have taken an oath and confirmed it,
   that I will follow your righteous laws.
107 I have suffered much;
   preserve my life, LORD, according to your word.
108 Accept, LORD, the willing praise of my mouth,
   and teach me your laws.
109 Though I constantly take my life in my hands,
   I will not forget your law.
110 The wicked have set a snare for me,
   but I have not strayed from your precepts.
111 Your statutes are my heritage forever;
   they are the joy of my heart.
112 My heart is set on keeping your decrees
   to the very end.[a]

### ס Samekh

113 I hate double-minded people,
   but I love your law.
114 You are my refuge and my shield;
   I have put my hope in your word.
115 Away from me, you evildoers,
   that I may keep the commands of my God!
116 Sustain me, my God, according to your promise, and I
      will live;
   do not let my hopes be dashed.
117 Uphold me, and I will be delivered;
   I will always have regard for your decrees.
118 You reject all who stray from your decrees,
   for their delusions come to nothing.
119 All the wicked of the earth you discard like dross;
   therefore I love your statutes.
120 My flesh trembles in fear of you;
   I stand in awe of your laws.

### ע Ayin

121 I have done what is righteous and just;
   do not leave me to my oppressors.
122 Ensure your servant's well-being;
   do not let the arrogant oppress me.
123 My eyes fail, looking for your salvation,
   looking for your righteous promise.
124 Deal with your servant according to your love
   and teach me your decrees.
125 I am your servant; give me discernment
   that I may understand your statutes.

## Amplified Bible

97 Oh, how love I Your law! It is my meditation all the day. [Ps. 1:2.]
98 You, through Your commandments, make me wiser than my enemies, for [Your words] are ever before me.
99 I have better understanding *and* deeper insight than all my teachers, because Your testimonies are my meditation. [II Tim. 3:15.]
100 I understand more than the aged, because I keep Your precepts [hearing, receiving, loving, and obeying them].
101 I have restrained my feet from every evil way, that I might keep Your word [hearing, receiving, loving, and obeying it]. [Prov. 1:15.]
102 I have not turned aside from Your ordinances, for You Yourself have taught me.
103 How sweet are Your words to my taste, sweeter than honey to my mouth! [Ps. 19:10; Prov. 8:11.]
104 Through Your precepts I get understanding; therefore I hate every false way.
105 Your word is a lamp to my feet and a light to my path. [Prov. 6:23.]
106 I have sworn [an oath] and have confirmed it, that I will keep Your righteous ordinances [hearing, receiving, loving, and obeying them]. [Neh. 10:29.]
107 I am sorely afflicted; renew *and* quicken me [give me life], O Lord, according to Your word!
108 Accept, I beseech You, the freewill offerings of my mouth, O Lord, and teach me Your ordinances. [Hos. 14:2; Heb. 13:15.]
109 My life is continually in my hand, yet I do not forget Your law.
110 The wicked have laid a snare for me, yet I do not stray from Your precepts.
111 Your testimonies have I taken as a heritage forever, for they are the rejoicing of my heart. [Deut. 33:4.]
112 I have inclined my heart to perform Your statutes forever, even to the end.
113 I hate the thoughts of undecided [in religion], double-minded people, but Your law do I love.
114 You are my hiding place and my shield; I hope in Your word. [Ps. 32:7; 91:1.]
115 Depart from me, you evildoers, that I may keep the commandments of my God [hearing, receiving, loving, and obeying them]. [Ps. 6:8; 139:19; Matt. 7:23.]
116 Uphold me according to Your promise, that I may live; and let me not be put to shame in my hope! [Ps. 25:2; Rom. 5:5; 9:33; 10:11.]
117 Hold me up, that I may be safe and have regard for Your statutes continually!
118 You spurn *and* set at nought all those who stray from Your statutes, for their own lying deceives them *and* their tricks are in vain.
119 You put away *and* count as dross all the wicked of the earth [for there is no true metal in them]; therefore I love Your testimonies.
120 My flesh trembles *and* shudders for fear *and* reverential, worshipful awe of You, and I am afraid *and* in dread of Your judgments.
121 I have done justice and righteousness; leave me not to those who would oppress me.
122 Be surety for Your servant for good [as Judah was surety for the safety of Benjamin]; let not the proud oppress me. [Gen. 43:9.]
123 My eyes fail, watching for Your salvation and for the fulfillment of Your righteous promise.
124 Deal with Your servant according to Your mercy *and* loving-kindness, and teach me Your statutes.
125 I am Your servant; give me understanding (discernment and comprehension), that I may know (discern and be familiar with the character of) Your testimonies.

---

*a* 112 Or *decrees / for their enduring reward*

## New International Version

126 It is time for you to act, LORD;
    your law is being broken.
127 Because I love your commands
    more than gold, more than pure gold,
128 and because I consider all your precepts right,
    I hate every wrong path.

### פ Pe

129 Your statutes are wonderful;
    therefore I obey them.
130 The unfolding of your words gives light;
    it gives understanding to the simple.
131 I open my mouth and pant,
    longing for your commands.
132 Turn to me and have mercy on me,
    as you always do to those who love your name.
133 Direct my footsteps according to your word;
    let no sin rule over me.
134 Redeem me from human oppression,
    that I may obey your precepts.
135 Make your face shine on your servant
    and teach me your decrees.
136 Streams of tears flow from my eyes,
    for your law is not obeyed.

### צ Tsadhe

137 You are righteous, LORD,
    and your laws are right.
138 The statutes you have laid down are righteous;
    they are fully trustworthy.
139 My zeal wears me out,
    for my enemies ignore your words.
140 Your promises have been thoroughly tested,
    and your servant loves them.
141 Though I am lowly and despised,
    I do not forget your precepts.
142 Your righteousness is everlasting
    and your law is true.
143 Trouble and distress have come upon me,
    but your commands give me delight.
144 Your statutes are always righteous;
    give me understanding that I may live.

### ק Qoph

145 I call with all my heart; answer me, LORD,
    and I will obey your decrees.
146 I call out to you; save me
    and I will keep your statutes.
147 I rise before dawn and cry for help;
    I have put my hope in your word.
148 My eyes stay open through the watches of the night,
    that I may meditate on your promises.
149 Hear my voice in accordance with your love;
    preserve my life, LORD, according to your laws.
150 Those who devise wicked schemes are near,
    but they are far from your law.
151 Yet you are near, LORD,
    and all your commands are true.
152 Long ago I learned from your statutes
    that you established them to last forever.

### ר Resh

153 Look on my suffering and deliver me,
    for I have not forgotten your law.
154 Defend my cause and redeem me;
    preserve my life according to your promise.
155 Salvation is far from the wicked,
    for they do not seek out your decrees.
156 Your compassion, LORD, is great;
    preserve my life according to your laws.

## Amplified Bible

126 It is time for the Lord to act; they have frustrated Your law.
127 Therefore I love Your commandments more than [resplendent] gold, yes, more than [perfectly] refined gold.
128 Therefore I esteem as right all, yes, all Your precepts; I hate every false way.
129 Your testimonies are wonderful [far exceeding anything conceived by man]; therefore my [penitent] self keeps them [hearing, receiving, loving, and obeying them].
130 The entrance and unfolding of Your words give light; their unfolding gives understanding (discernment and comprehension) to the simple.
131 I opened my mouth and panted [with eager desire], for I longed for Your commandments.
132 Look upon me, be merciful unto me, and show me favor, as is Your way to those who love Your name.
133 Establish my steps and direct them by [means of] Your word; let not any iniquity have dominion over me.
134 Deliver me from the oppression of man; so will I keep Your precepts [hearing, receiving, loving, and obeying them]. [Luke 1:74.]
135 Make Your face shine [with pleasure] upon Your servant, and teach me Your statutes. [Ps. 4:6.]
136 Streams of water run down my eyes, because men do not keep Your law [they hear it not, nor receive it, love it, or obey it].
137 [Rigidly] righteous are You, O Lord, and upright are Your judgments and all expressions of Your will.
138 You have commanded and appointed Your testimonies in righteousness and in great faithfulness.
139 My zeal has consumed me and cut me off, because my adversaries have forgotten Your words.
140 Your word is very pure (tried and well refined); therefore Your servant loves it.
141 I am small (insignificant) and despised, but I do not forget Your precepts.
142 Your righteousness is an everlasting righteousness, and Your law is truth. [Ps. 19:9; John 17:17.]
143 Trouble and anguish have found and taken hold on me, yet Your commandments are my delight.
144 Your righteous testimonies are everlasting and Your decrees are binding to eternity; give me understanding and I shall live [give me discernment and comprehension and I shall not die].
145 I cried with my whole heart; hear me, O Lord; I will keep Your statutes [I will hear, receive, love, and obey them].
146 I cried to You; save me, that I may keep Your testimonies [hearing, receiving, loving, and obeying them].
147 I anticipated the dawning of the morning and cried [in childlike prayer]; I hoped in Your word.
148 My eyes anticipate the night watches and I am awake before the cry of the watchman, that I may meditate on Your word.
149 Hear my voice according to Your steadfast love; O Lord, quicken me and give me life according to Your [righteous] decrees.
150 They draw near who follow after wrong thinking and persecute me with wickedness; they are far from Your law.
151 You are near, O Lord [nearer to me than my foes], and all Your commandments are truth.
152 Of old have I known Your testimonies, and for a long time, [therefore it is a thoroughly established conviction] that You have founded them forever. [Luke 21:33.]
153 Consider my affliction and deliver me, for I do not forget Your law.
154 Plead my cause and redeem me; revive me and give me life according to Your word.
155 Salvation is far from the wicked, for they seek not nor hunger for Your statutes.
156 Great are Your tender mercy and loving-kindness, O Lord; give me life according to Your ordinances.

## New International Version

157 Many are the foes who persecute me,
but I have not turned from your statutes.
158 I look on the faithless with loathing,
for they do not obey your word.
159 See how I love your precepts;
preserve my life, LORD, in accordance with your
love.
160 All your words are true;
all your righteous laws are eternal.

### ש Sin and Shin

161 Rulers persecute me without cause,
but my heart trembles at your word.
162 I rejoice in your promise
like one who finds great spoil.
163 I hate and detest falsehood
but I love your law.
164 Seven times a day I praise you
for your righteous laws.
165 Great peace have those who love your law,
and nothing can make them stumble.
166 I wait for your salvation, LORD,
and I follow your commands.
167 I obey your statutes,
for I love them greatly.
168 I obey your precepts and your statutes,
for all my ways are known to you.

### ת Taw

169 May my cry come before you, LORD;
give me understanding according to your word.
170 May my supplication come before you;
deliver me according to your promise.
171 May my lips overflow with praise,
for you teach me your decrees.
172 May my tongue sing of your word,
for all your commands are righteous.
173 May your hand be ready to help me,
for I have chosen your precepts.
174 I long for your salvation, LORD,
and your law gives me delight.
175 Let me live that I may praise you,
and may your laws sustain me.
176 I have strayed like a lost sheep.
Seek your servant,
for I have not forgotten your commands.

### Psalm 120

*A song of ascents.*

1 I call on the LORD in my distress,
and he answers me.
2 Save me, LORD,
from lying lips
and from deceitful tongues.

3 What will he do to you,
and what more besides,
you deceitful tongue?
4 He will punish you with a warrior's sharp arrows,
with burning coals of the broom bush.

5 Woe to me that I dwell in Meshek,
that I live among the tents of Kedar!
6 Too long have I lived
among those who hate peace.
7 I am for peace;
but when I speak, they are for war.

## Amplified Bible

157 Many are my persecutors and my adversaries, yet I
do not swerve from Your testimonies.
158 I behold the treacherous and am grieved *and* loathe
them, because they do not respect Your law [neither hearing, receiving, loving, nor obeying it].
159 Consider how I love Your precepts; revive me *and*
give life to me, O Lord, according to Your loving-kindness!
160 The sum of Your word is truth [the total of the full
meaning of all Your individual precepts]; and every one of
Your righteous decrees endures forever.
161 Princes pursue *and* persecute me without cause, but
my heart stands in awe of Your words [dreading violation
of them far more than the force of prince or potentate].
[I Sam. 24:11, 14; 26:18.]
162 I rejoice at Your word as one who finds great spoil.
163 I hate and abhor falsehood, but Your law do I love.
164 Seven times a day *and* all day long do I praise You
because of Your righteous decrees.
165 Great peace have they who love Your law; nothing
shall offend them *or* make them stumble. [Prov. 3:2; Isa.
32:17.]
166 I am hoping *and* waiting [eagerly] for Your salvation,
O Lord, and I do Your commandments. [Gen. 49:18.]
167 Your testimonies have I kept [hearing, receiving, loving, and obeying them]; I love them exceedingly!
168 I have observed Your precepts *and* Your testimonies,
for all my ways are [fully known] before You.
169 Let my mournful cry *and* supplication come [near]
before You, O Lord; give me understanding (discernment
and comprehension) according to Your word [of assurance
and promise].
170 Let my supplication come before You; deliver me according to Your word!
171 My lips shall pour forth praise [with thanksgiving
and renewed trust] when You teach me Your statutes.
172 My tongue shall sing [praise for the fulfillment] of
Your word, for all Your commandments are righteous.
173 Let Your hand be ready to help me, for I have chosen
Your precepts.
174 I have longed for Your salvation, O Lord, and Your
law is my delight.
175 Let me live that I may praise You, and let Your decrees help me.
176 I have gone astray like a lost sheep; seek, inquire for,
*and* demand Your servant, for I do not forget Your commandments. [Isa. 53:6; Luke 15:4; I Pet. 2:25.]

### Psalm 120

A Song of *a*Ascents.

1 In my distress I cried to the Lord, and He answered
me.
2 Deliver me, O Lord, from lying lips and from deceitful
tongues.
3 What shall be given to you? Or what more shall be
done to you, you deceitful tongue?—
4 Sharp arrows of a [mighty] warrior, with [glowing]
coals of the broom tree!
5 Woe is me that I sojourn with Meshech, that I dwell beside the tents of Kedar [as if among notoriously barbarous
people]! [Gen. 10:2; 25:13; Jer. 49:28, 29.]
6 My life has too long had its dwelling with him who
hates peace.
7 I am for peace; but when I speak, they are for war.

---

*a* It is possible that the fifteen psalms known as the "Songs of Degrees
or Ascents" were sung by the caravans of pilgrims going up to attend
the annual feasts at Jerusalem. But it is equally possible that the title
has reference to some peculiarity in connection with the music or the
manner of using it.

# New International Version

## Psalm 121

*A song of ascents.*

¹ I lift up my eyes to the mountains—
  where does my help come from?
² My help comes from the LORD,
  the Maker of heaven and earth.

³ He will not let your foot slip—
  he who watches over you will not slumber;
⁴ indeed, he who watches over Israel
  will neither slumber nor sleep.

⁵ The LORD watches over you—
  the LORD is your shade at your right hand;
⁶ the sun will not harm you by day,
  nor the moon by night.

⁷ The LORD will keep you from all harm—
  he will watch over your life;
⁸ the LORD will watch over your coming and going
  both now and forevermore.

## Psalm 122

*A song of ascents. Of David.*

¹ I rejoiced with those who said to me,
  "Let us go to the house of the LORD."
² Our feet are standing
  in your gates, Jerusalem.

³ Jerusalem is built like a city
  that is closely compacted together.
⁴ That is where the tribes go up—
  the tribes of the LORD—
to praise the name of the LORD
  according to the statute given to Israel.
⁵ There stand the thrones for judgment,
  the thrones of the house of David.

⁶ Pray for the peace of Jerusalem:
  "May those who love you be secure.
⁷ May there be peace within your walls
  and security within your citadels."
⁸ For the sake of my family and friends,
  I will say, "Peace be within you."
⁹ For the sake of the house of the LORD our God,
  I will seek your prosperity.

## Psalm 123

*A song of ascents.*

¹ I lift up my eyes to you,
  to you who sit enthroned in heaven.
² As the eyes of slaves look to the hand of their master,
  as the eyes of a female slave look to the hand of her mistress,
so our eyes look to the LORD our God,
  till he shows us his mercy.

³ Have mercy on us, LORD, have mercy on us,
  for we have endured no end of contempt.
⁴ We have endured no end
  of ridicule from the arrogant,
  of contempt from the proud.

## Psalm 124

*A song of ascents. Of David.*

¹ If the LORD had not been on our side—
  let Israel say—

# Amplified Bible

## Psalm 121

A Song of ᵃAscents.

¹ I will lift up my eyes to the hills [around Jerusalem, to sacred Mount Zion and Mount Moriah]—From whence shall my help come? [Jer. 3:23.]
² My help comes from the Lord, Who made heaven and earth.
³ He will not allow your foot to slip *or* to be moved; He Who keeps you will not slumber. [I Sam. 2:9; Ps. 127:1; Prov. 3:23, 26; Isa. 27:3.]
⁴ Behold, He who keeps Israel will neither slumber nor sleep.
⁵ The Lord is your keeper; the Lord is your shade on your right hand [the side not carrying a shield]. [Isa. 25:4.]
⁶ The sun shall not smite you by day, nor the moon by night. [Ps. 91:5; Isa. 49:10; Rev. 7:16.]
⁷ The Lord will keep you from all evil; He will keep your life.
⁸ The Lord will keep your going out and your coming in from this time forth and forevermore. [Deut. 28:6; Prov. 2:8; 3:6.]

## Psalm 122

A Song of ᵃAscents. Of David.

¹ I was glad when they said to me, Let us go to the house of the Lord! [Isa. 2:3; Zech. 8:21.]
² Our feet are standing within your gates, O Jerusalem!—
³ Jerusalem, which is built as a city that is compacted together—
⁴ To which the tribes go up, even the tribes of the Lord, as was decreed *and* as a testimony for Israel, to give thanks to the name of the Lord.
⁵ For there the thrones of judgment were set, the thrones of the house of David.
⁶ Pray for the peace of Jerusalem! May they prosper who love you [the Holy City]!
⁷ May peace be within your walls and prosperity within your palaces!
⁸ For my brethren and companions' sake, I will now say, Peace be within you!
⁹ For the sake of the house of the Lord our God, I will seek, inquire for, *and* require your good.

## Psalm 123

A Song of ᵃAscents.

¹ Unto you do I lift up my eyes, O You Who are enthroned in heaven.
² Behold, as the eyes of servants look to the hand of their master, and as the eyes of a maid to the hand of her mistress, so our eyes look to the Lord our God, until He has mercy *and* loving-kindness for us.
³ Have mercy on us, O Lord, have mercy on *and* loving-kindness for us, for we are exceedingly satiated with contempt.
⁴ Our life is exceedingly filled with the scorning *and* scoffing of those who are at ease and with the contempt of the proud (irresponsible tyrants who disregard God's law).

## Psalm 124

A Song of ᵃAscents. Of David.

¹ If it had not been the Lord Who was on our side—now may Israel say—

---

ᵃ See Psalm 120 title footnote.

## New International Version

2 if the LORD had not been on our side
    when people attacked us,
3 they would have swallowed us alive
    when their anger flared against us;
4 the flood would have engulfed us,
    the torrent would have swept over us,
5 the raging waters
    would have swept us away.

6 Praise be to the LORD,
    who has not let us be torn by their teeth.
7 We have escaped like a bird
    from the fowler's snare;
the snare has been broken,
    and we have escaped.
8 Our help is in the name of the LORD,
    the Maker of heaven and earth.

### Psalm 125

*A song of ascents.*

1 Those who trust in the LORD are like Mount Zion,
    which cannot be shaken but endures forever.
2 As the mountains surround Jerusalem,
    so the LORD surrounds his people
    both now and forevermore.

3 The scepter of the wicked will not remain
    over the land allotted to the righteous,
for then the righteous might use
    their hands to do evil.

4 LORD, do good to those who are good,
    to those who are upright in heart.
5 But those who turn to crooked ways
    the LORD will banish with the evildoers.

    Peace be on Israel.

### Psalm 126

*A song of ascents.*

1 When the LORD restored the fortunes of[a] Zion,
    we were like those who dreamed.[b]
2 Our mouths were filled with laughter,
    our tongues with songs of joy.
Then it was said among the nations,
    "The LORD has done great things for them."
3 The LORD has done great things for us,
    and we are filled with joy.

4 Restore our fortunes,[c] LORD,
    like streams in the Negev.
5 Those who sow with tears
    will reap with songs of joy.
6 Those who go out weeping,
    carrying seed to sow,
will return with songs of joy,
    carrying sheaves with them.

### Psalm 127

*A song of ascents. Of Solomon.*

1 Unless the LORD builds the house,
    the builders labor in vain.
Unless the LORD watches over the city,
    the guards stand watch in vain.
2 In vain you rise early
    and stay up late,

## Amplified Bible

2 If it had not been the Lord Who was on our side when
men rose up against us,
3 Then they would have quickly swallowed us up alive
when their wrath was kindled against us;
4 Then the waters would have overwhelmed us *and*
swept us away, the torrent would have gone over us;
5 Then the proud waters would have gone over us.
6 Blessed be the Lord, Who has not given us as prey to
their teeth!
7 We are like a bird escaped from the snare of the fowlers; the snare is broken, and we have escaped!
8 Our help is in the name of the Lord, Who made heaven
and earth.

### Psalm 125

A Song of [a]Ascents.

1 Those who trust in, lean on, *and* confidently hope in
the Lord are like Mount Zion, which cannot be moved but
abides *and* stands fast forever.
2 As the mountains are round about Jerusalem, so the
Lord is round about His people from this time forth and
forever.
3 For the scepter of wickedness shall not rest upon the
land of the [uncompromisingly] righteous, lest the righteous (God's people) stretch forth their hands to iniquity
*and* apostasy.
4 Do good, O Lord, to those who are good, and to those
who are right [with You and all people] in their hearts.
5 As for such as turn aside to their crooked ways [of indifference to God], the Lord will lead them forth with the
workers of iniquity. Peace be upon Israel!

### Psalm 126

A Song of [a]Ascents.

1 When the Lord brought back the captives [who re-
turned] to Zion, we were like those who dream [it seemed
so unreal]. [Ps. 53:6; Acts 12:9.]
2 Then were our mouths filled with laughter, and our
tongues with singing. Then they said among the nations,
The Lord has done great things for them.
3 The Lord has done great things for us! We are glad!
4 Turn to freedom our captivity *and* restore our fortunes,
O Lord, as the streams in the South (the Negeb) [are restored by the torrents].
5 They who sow in tears shall reap in joy *and* singing.
6 He who goes forth bearing seed and weeping [at needing his precious supply of grain for sowing] shall doubtless come again with rejoicing, bringing his sheaves with
him.

### Psalm 127

A Song of [a]Ascents. Of Solomon.

1 Except the Lord builds the house, they labor in vain
who build it; except the Lord keeps the city, the watchman
wakes but in vain. [Ps. 121:1, 3, 5.]
2 It is vain for you to rise up early, to take rest late, to eat

---

[a] 1 Or LORD *brought back the captives to*      [b] 1 Or *those restored to health*
[c] 4 Or *Bring back our captives*

[a] See Psalm 120 title footnote.

## New International Version

toiling for food to eat—
 for he grants sleep to[a] those he loves.
3 Children are a heritage from the LORD,
 offspring a reward from him.
4 Like arrows in the hands of a warrior
 are children born in one's youth.
5 Blessed is the man
 whose quiver is full of them.
They will not be put to shame
 when they contend with their opponents in court.

### Psalm 128

*A song of ascents.*

1 Blessed are all who fear the LORD,
 who walk in obedience to him.
2 You will eat the fruit of your labor;
 blessings and prosperity will be yours.
3 Your wife will be like a fruitful vine
 within your house;
your children will be like olive shoots
 around your table.
4 Yes, this will be the blessing
 for the man who fears the LORD.

5 May the LORD bless you from Zion;
 may you see the prosperity of Jerusalem
all the days of your life.
6 May you live to see your children's children—
 peace be on Israel.

### Psalm 129

*A song of ascents.*

1 "They have greatly oppressed me from my youth,"
 let Israel say;
2 "they have greatly oppressed me from my youth,
 but they have not gained the victory over me.
3 Plowmen have plowed my back
 and made their furrows long.
4 But the LORD is righteous;
 he has cut me free from the cords of the wicked."

5 May all who hate Zion
 be turned back in shame.
6 May they be like grass on the roof,
 which withers before it can grow;
7 a reaper cannot fill his hands with it,
 nor one who gathers fill his arms.
8 May those who pass by not say to them,
 "The blessing of the LORD be on you;
 we bless you in the name of the LORD."

### Psalm 130

*A song of ascents.*

1 Out of the depths I cry to you, LORD;
2  Lord, hear my voice.
Let your ears be attentive
 to my cry for mercy.

3 If you, LORD, kept a record of sins,
 Lord, who could stand?
4 But with you there is forgiveness,
 so that we can, with reverence, serve you.

5 I wait for the LORD, my whole being waits,
 and in his word I put my hope.

## Amplified Bible

the bread of [anxious] toil—for He gives [blessings] to His beloved in sleep.
3 Behold, children are a heritage from the Lord, the fruit of the womb a reward. [Deut. 28:4.]
4 As arrows are in the hand of a warrior, so are the children of one's youth.
5 Happy, blessed, *and* fortunate is the man whose quiver is filled with them! They will not be put to shame when they speak with their adversaries [in gatherings] at the [city's] gate.

### Psalm 128

A Song of [a]Ascents.

1 Blessed (happy, fortunate, to be envied) is everyone who fears, reveres, *and* worships the Lord, who walks in His ways *and* lives according to His commandments. [Ps. 1:1, 2.]
2 For you shall eat [the fruit] of the labor of your hands; happy (blessed, fortunate, enviable) shall you be, and it shall be well with you.
3 Your wife shall be like a fruitful vine in the innermost parts of your house; your children shall be like olive plants round about your table.
4 Behold, thus shall the man be blessed who reverently *and* worshipfully fears the Lord.
5 May the Lord bless you out of Zion [His sanctuary], and may you see the prosperity of Jerusalem all the days of your life;
6 Yes, may you see your children's children. Peace be upon Israel!

### Psalm 129

A Song of [a]Ascents.

1 Many a time *and* much have they afflicted me from my youth—let Israel now say—
2 Many a time *and* much have they afflicted me from my youth up, yet they have not prevailed against me.
3 The plowers plowed upon my back; they made long their furrows.
4 The Lord is [uncompromisingly] righteous; He has cut asunder the thick cords by which the wicked [enslaved us].
5 Let them all be put to shame and turned backward who hate Zion.
6 Let them be as the grass upon the housetops, which withers before it grows up,
7 With which the mower fills not his hand, nor the binder of sheaves his bosom—
8 While those who go by do not say, The blessing of the Lord be upon you! We bless you in the name of the Lord!

### Psalm 130

A Song of [a]Ascents.

1 Out of the depths have I cried to You, O Lord.
2 Lord, hear my voice; let Your ears be attentive to the voice of my supplications.
3 If You, Lord, should keep account of *and* treat [us according to our] sins, O Lord, who could stand? [Ps. 143:2; Rom. 3:20; Gal. 2:16.]
4 But there is forgiveness with You [just what man needs], that You may be reverently feared *and* worshiped. [Deut. 10:12.]
5 I wait for the Lord, I expectantly wait, and in His word do I hope.

---

a 2 Or *eat— / for while they sleep he provides for*

a See Psalm 120 title footnote.

# New International Version

⁶I wait for the Lord
more than watchmen wait for the morning,
more than watchmen wait for the morning.

⁷Israel, put your hope in the LORD,
for with the LORD is unfailing love
and with him is full redemption.
⁸He himself will redeem Israel
from all their sins.

## Psalm 131

*A song of ascents. Of David.*

¹My heart is not proud, LORD,
my eyes are not haughty;
I do not concern myself with great matters
or things too wonderful for me.
²But I have calmed and quieted myself,
I am like a weaned child with its mother;
like a weaned child I am content.

³Israel, put your hope in the LORD
both now and forevermore.

## Psalm 132

*A song of ascents.*

¹LORD, remember David
and all his self-denial.

²He swore an oath to the LORD,
he made a vow to the Mighty One of Jacob:
³"I will not enter my house
or go to my bed,
⁴I will allow no sleep to my eyes
or slumber to my eyelids,
⁵till I find a place for the LORD,
a dwelling for the Mighty One of Jacob."

⁶We heard it in Ephrathah,
we came upon it in the fields of Jaar:ᵃ
⁷"Let us go to his dwelling place,
let us worship at his footstool, saying,
⁸'Arise, LORD, and come to your resting place,
you and the ark of your might.
⁹May your priests be clothed with your righteousness;
may your faithful people sing for joy.'"

¹⁰For the sake of your servant David,
do not reject your anointed one.

¹¹The LORD swore an oath to David,
a sure oath he will not revoke:
"One of your own descendants
I will place on your throne.
¹²If your sons keep my covenant
and the statutes I teach them,
then their sons will sit
on your throne for ever and ever."

¹³For the LORD has chosen Zion,
he has desired it for his dwelling, saying,
¹⁴"This is my resting place for ever and ever;
here I will sit enthroned, for I have desired it.
¹⁵I will bless her with abundant provisions;
her poor I will satisfy with food.
¹⁶I will clothe her priests with salvation,
and her faithful people will ever sing for joy.

¹⁷"Here I will make a hornᵇ grow for David
and set up a lamp for my anointed one.
¹⁸I will clothe his enemies with shame,
but his head will be adorned with a radiant crown."

ᵃ 6 Or *heard of it in Ephrathah, / we found it in the fields of Jearim.*
(See 1 Chron. 13:5,6) (And no quotation marks around verses 7-9)
ᵇ 17 *Horn* here symbolizes strong one, that is, king.

# Amplified Bible

⁶I am looking *and* waiting for the Lord more than watchmen for the morning, I say, more than watchmen for the morning.
⁷O Israel, hope in the Lord! For with the Lord there is mercy *and* loving-kindness, and with Him is plenteous redemption.
⁸And He will redeem Israel from all their iniquities.

## Psalm 131

A Song of ᵃAscents. Of David.

¹Lord, my heart is not haughty, nor my eyes lofty; neither do I exercise myself in matters too great or in things too wonderful for me.
²Surely I have calmed and quieted my soul; like a weaned child with his mother, like a weaned child is my soul within me [ceased from fretting].
³O Israel, hope in the Lord from this time forth and forever.

## Psalm 132

A Song of ᵃAscents.

¹Lord, [earnestly] remember to David's credit all his humiliations *and* hardships *and* endurance—
²How he swore to the Lord and vowed to the Mighty One of Jacob:
³Surely I will not enter my dwelling house or get into my bed—
⁴I will not permit my eyes to sleep *or* my eyelids to slumber,
⁵Until I have found a place for the Lord, a habitation for the Mighty One of Jacob. [Acts 7:46.]
⁶Behold, at Ephratah we [first] heard of [the discovered ark]; we found it in the fields of the wood [at Kiriath-jearim]. [I Sam. 6:21.]
⁷Let us go into His tabernacle; let us worship at His footstool.
⁸Arise, O Lord, to Your resting-place, You and the ark [the symbol] of Your strength.
⁹Let Your priests be clothed with righteousness (right living and right standing with God); and let Your saints shout for joy!
¹⁰For Your servant David's sake, turn not away the face of Your anointed *and* reject not Your own king.
¹¹The Lord swore to David in truth; He will not turn back from it: One of the fruit of your body I will set upon your throne. [Ps. 89:3, 4; Luke 1:69; Acts 2:30, 31.]
¹²If your children will keep My covenant and My testimony that I shall teach them, their children also shall sit upon your throne forever.
¹³For the Lord has chosen Zion, He has desired it for His habitation:
¹⁴This is My resting-place forever [says the Lord]; here will I dwell, for I have desired it.
¹⁵I will surely *and* abundantly bless her provision; I will satisfy her poor with bread.
¹⁶Her priests also will I clothe with salvation, and her saints shall shout aloud for joy.
¹⁷There will I make a horn spring forth *and* bud for David; I have ordained *and* prepared a lamp for My anointed [fulfilling the promises of old]. [I Kings 11:36; 15:4; II Chron. 21:7; Luke 1:69.]
¹⁸His enemies will I clothe with shame, but upon himself shall his crown flourish.

ᵃ See Psalm 120 title footnote.

# New International Version

## Psalm 133

*A song of ascents. Of David.*

1 How good and pleasant it is
   when God's people live together in unity!
2 It is like precious oil poured on the head,
   running down on the beard,
   running down on Aaron's beard,
   down on the collar of his robe.
3 It is as if the dew of Hermon
   were falling on Mount Zion.
For there the LORD bestows his blessing,
   even life forevermore.

## Psalm 134

*A song of ascents.*

1 Praise the LORD, all you servants of the LORD
   who minister by night in the house of the LORD.
2 Lift up your hands in the sanctuary
   and praise the LORD.

3 May the LORD bless you from Zion,
   he who is the Maker of heaven and earth.

## Psalm 135

1 Praise the LORD.[a]

Praise the name of the LORD;
   praise him, you servants of the LORD,
2 you who minister in the house of the LORD,
   in the courts of the house of our God.

3 Praise the LORD, for the LORD is good;
   sing praise to his name, for that is pleasant.
4 For the LORD has chosen Jacob to be his own,
   Israel to be his treasured possession.

5 I know that the LORD is great,
   that our Lord is greater than all gods.
6 The LORD does whatever pleases him,
   in the heavens and on the earth,
   in the seas and all their depths.
7 He makes clouds rise from the ends of the earth;
   he sends lightning with the rain
   and brings out the wind from his storehouses.

8 He struck down the firstborn of Egypt,
   the firstborn of people and animals.
9 He sent his signs and wonders into your midst, Egypt,
   against Pharaoh and all his servants.
10 He struck down many nations
   and killed mighty kings—
11 Sihon king of the Amorites,
   Og king of Bashan,
   and all the kings of Canaan—
12 and he gave their land as an inheritance,
   an inheritance to his people Israel.

13 Your name, LORD, endures forever,
   your renown, LORD, through all generations.
14 For the LORD will vindicate his people
   and have compassion on his servants.

15 The idols of the nations are silver and gold,
   made by human hands.
16 They have mouths, but cannot speak,
   eyes, but cannot see.
17 They have ears, but cannot hear,
   nor is there breath in their mouths.
18 Those who make them will be like them,
   and so will all who trust in them.

# Amplified Bible

## Psalm 133

A Song of [a]Ascents. Of David.

1 Behold, how good and how pleasant it is for brethren to dwell together in unity!
2 It is like the precious ointment poured on the head, that ran down on the beard, even the beard of Aaron [the first high priest], that came down upon the collar *and* skirts of his garments [consecrating the whole body]. [Exod. 30:25, 30.]
3 It is like the dew of [lofty] Mount Hermon and the dew that comes on the hills of Zion; for there the Lord has commanded the blessing, even life forevermore [upon the high and the lowly].

## Psalm 134

A Song of [a]Ascents.

1 Behold, bless (affectionately and gratefully praise) the Lord, all you servants of the Lord, [singers] who by night stand in the house of the Lord. [I Chron. 9:33.]
2 Lift up your hands in holiness *and* to the sanctuary and bless the Lord [affectionately and gratefully praise Him]!
3 The Lord bless you out of Zion, even He Who made heaven and earth.

## Psalm 135

1 Praise the Lord! (Hallelujah!) Praise the name of the Lord; praise Him, O you servants of the Lord!
2 You who stand in the house of the Lord, in the courts of the house of our God,
3 Praise the Lord! For the Lord is good; sing praises to His name, for He is gracious *and* lovely!
4 For the Lord has chosen [the descendants of] Jacob for Himself, Israel for His peculiar possession *and* treasure. [Deut. 7:6.]
5 For I know that the Lord is great and that our Lord is above all gods.
6 Whatever the Lord pleases, that has He done in the heavens and on earth, in the seas and all deeps—
7 Who causes the vapors to arise from the ends of the earth, Who makes lightnings for the rain, Who brings the wind out of His storehouses;
8 Who smote the firstborn of Egypt, both of man and beast; [Exod. 12:12, 29; Ps. 78:51; 136:10.]
9 Who sent signs and wonders into the midst of you, O Egypt, upon Pharaoh and all his servants;
10 Who smote nations many *and* great and slew mighty kings—
11 Sihon king of the Amorites, Og king of Bashan, and all the kingdoms of Canaan.
12 [The Lord] gave their land as a heritage, a heritage to Israel His people.
13 Your name, O Lord, endures forever, Your fame, O Lord, throughout all ages.
14 For the Lord will judge *and* vindicate His people, and He will delay His judgments [manifesting His righteousness and mercy] *and* take into favor His servants [those who meet His terms of separation unto Him]. [Heb. 10:30.]
15 The idols of the nations are silver and gold, the work of men's hands.
16 [Idols] have mouths, but they speak not; eyes have they, but they see not;
17 They have ears, but they hear not, nor is there any breath in their mouths.
18 Those who make [idols] are like them; so is everyone who trusts in *and* relies on them. [Ps. 115:4-8.]

---

[a] 1 Hebrew *Hallelu Yah*; also in verses 3 and 21

[a] See Psalm 120 title footnote.

## New International Version

19 All you Israelites, praise the LORD;
   house of Aaron, praise the LORD;
20 house of Levi, praise the LORD;
   you who fear him, praise the LORD.
21 Praise be to the LORD from Zion,
   to him who dwells in Jerusalem.

Praise the LORD.

### Psalm 136

1 Give thanks to the LORD, for he is good.
   *His love endures forever.*
2 Give thanks to the God of gods.
   *His love endures forever.*
3 Give thanks to the Lord of lords:
   *His love endures forever.*

4 to him who alone does great wonders,
   *His love endures forever.*
5 who by his understanding made the heavens,
   *His love endures forever.*
6 who spread out the earth upon the waters,
   *His love endures forever.*
7 who made the great lights—
   *His love endures forever.*
8 the sun to govern the day,
   *His love endures forever.*
9 the moon and stars to govern the night;
   *His love endures forever.*

10 to him who struck down the firstborn of Egypt
   *His love endures forever.*
11 and brought Israel out from among them
   *His love endures forever.*
12 with a mighty hand and outstretched arm;
   *His love endures forever.*

13 to him who divided the Red Sea*a* asunder
   *His love endures forever.*
14 and brought Israel through the midst of it,
   *His love endures forever.*
15 but swept Pharaoh and his army into the Red Sea;
   *His love endures forever.*

16 to him who led his people through the wilderness;
   *His love endures forever.*

17 to him who struck down great kings,
   *His love endures forever.*
18 and killed mighty kings—
   *His love endures forever.*
19 Sihon king of the Amorites
   *His love endures forever.*
20 and Og king of Bashan—
   *His love endures forever.*
21 and gave their land as an inheritance,
   *His love endures forever.*
22 an inheritance to his servant Israel.
   *His love endures forever.*

23 He remembered us in our low estate
   *His love endures forever.*
24 and freed us from our enemies.
   *His love endures forever.*
25 He gives food to every creature.
   *His love endures forever.*

26 Give thanks to the God of heaven.
   *His love endures forever.*

## Amplified Bible

19 Bless (affectionately and gratefully praise) the Lord,
O house of Israel; bless the Lord, O house of Aaron [God's
ministers].
20 Bless the Lord, O house of Levi [the dedicated tribe];
you who reverently *and* worshipfully fear the Lord, bless
the Lord [affectionately and gratefully praise Him]! [Deut.
6:5; Ps. 31:23.]
21 Blessed out of Zion be the Lord, Who dwells [with us]
at Jerusalem! Praise the Lord! (Hallelujah!)

### Psalm 136

1 O give thanks to the Lord, for He is good; for His mercy
*and* loving-kindness endure forever.
2 O give thanks to the God of gods, for His mercy *and*
loving-kindness endure forever.
3 O give thanks to the Lord of lords, for His mercy *and*
loving-kindness endure forever—

4 To Him Who alone does great wonders, for His mercy
*and* loving-kindness endure forever;
5 To Him Who by wisdom *and* understanding made the
heavens, for His mercy *and* loving-kindness endure forever;
6 To Him Who stretched out the earth upon the waters,
for His mercy *and* loving-kindness endure forever;
7 To Him Who made the great lights, for His mercy *and*
loving-kindness endure forever—
8 The sun to rule over the day, for His mercy *and* loving-
kindness endure forever;
9 The moon and stars to rule by night, for His mercy *and*
loving-kindness endure forever;

10 To Him Who smote Egypt in their firstborn, for His
mercy *and* loving-kindness endure forever; [Exod. 12:29.]
11 And brought out Israel from among them, for His
mercy *and* loving-kindness endure forever; [Exod. 12:51;
13:3, 17.]
12 With a strong hand and with an outstretched arm, for
His mercy *and* loving-kindness endure forever;
13 To Him Who divided the Red Sea into parts, for His
mercy *and* loving-kindness endure forever; [Exod. 14:21,
22.]
14 And made Israel to pass through the midst of it, for
His mercy *and* loving-kindness endure forever;
15 But shook off *and* overthrew Pharaoh and his host
into the Red Sea, for His mercy *and* loving-kindness endure forever;
16 To Him Who led His people through the wilderness,
for His mercy *and* loving-kindness endure forever;
17 To Him Who smote great kings, for His mercy *and*
loving-kindness endure forever;
18 And slew famous kings, for His mercy *and* loving-
kindness endure forever—[Deut. 29:7.]
19 Sihon king of the Amorites, for His mercy *and* loving-
kindness endure forever; [Num. 21:21-24.]
20 And Og king of Bashan, for His mercy *and* loving-
kindness endure forever; [Num. 21:33-35.]
21 And gave their land as a heritage, for His mercy *and*
loving-kindness endure forever;
22 Even a heritage to Israel His servant, for His mercy
*and* loving-kindness endure forever; [Josh. 12:1.]
23 To Him Who [earnestly] remembered us in our low
estate *and* imprinted us [on His heart], for His mercy *and*
loving-kindness endure forever;
24 And rescued us from our enemies, for His mercy *and*
loving-kindness endure forever;
25 To Him Who gives food to all flesh, for His mercy *and*
loving-kindness endure forever;
26 O give thanks to the God of heaven, for His mercy *and*
loving-kindness endure forever!

---

*a 13* Or *the Sea of Reeds*; also in verse 15

# New International Version

## Psalm 137

[1] By the rivers of Babylon we sat and wept
   when we remembered Zion.
[2] There on the poplars
   we hung our harps,
[3] for there our captors asked us for songs,
   our tormentors demanded songs of joy;
   they said, "Sing us one of the songs of Zion!"

[4] How can we sing the songs of the LORD
   while in a foreign land?
[5] If I forget you, Jerusalem,
   may my right hand forget its skill.
[6] May my tongue cling to the roof of my mouth
   if I do not remember you,
   if I do not consider Jerusalem
   my highest joy.

[7] Remember, LORD, what the Edomites did
   on the day Jerusalem fell.
   "Tear it down," they cried,
   "tear it down to its foundations!"
[8] Daughter Babylon, doomed to destruction,
   happy is the one who repays you
   according to what you have done to us.
[9] Happy is the one who seizes your infants
   and dashes them against the rocks.

## Psalm 138

*Of David.*

[1] I will praise you, LORD, with all my heart;
   before the "gods" I will sing your praise.
[2] I will bow down toward your holy temple
   and will praise your name
   for your unfailing love and your faithfulness,
for you have so exalted your solemn decree
   that it surpasses your fame.
[3] When I called, you answered me;
   you greatly emboldened me.

[4] May all the kings of the earth praise you, LORD,
   when they hear what you have decreed.
[5] May they sing of the ways of the LORD,
   for the glory of the LORD is great.

[6] Though the LORD is exalted, he looks kindly on the
   lowly;
   though lofty, he sees them from afar.
[7] Though I walk in the midst of trouble,
   you preserve my life.
You stretch out your hand against the anger of my
   foes;
   with your right hand you save me.
[8] The LORD will vindicate me;
   your love, LORD, endures forever—
   do not abandon the works of your hands.

## Psalm 139

*For the director of music. Of David. A psalm.*

[1] You have searched me, LORD,
   and you know me.
[2] You know when I sit and when I rise;
   you perceive my thoughts from afar.
[3] You discern my going out and my lying down;
   you are familiar with all my ways.
[4] Before a word is on my tongue
   you, LORD, know it completely.

# Amplified Bible

## Psalm 137

[1] By the rivers of Babylon, there we [captives] sat down,
yes, we wept when we [earnestly] remembered Zion [the
city of our God imprinted on our hearts].
[2] On the willow trees in the midst of [Babylon] we hung
our harps.
[3] For there they who led us captive required of us a song
with words, and our tormentors *and* they who wasted us
required of us mirth, saying, Sing us one of the songs of
Zion.
[4] How shall we sing the Lord's song in a strange land?
[5] If I forget you, O Jerusalem, let my right hand forget its
skill [with the harp].
[6] Let my tongue cleave to the roof of my mouth if I remember you not, if I prefer not Jerusalem above my chief
joy! [Ezek. 3:26.]
[7] Remember, O Lord, against the Edomites, that they
said in the day of Jerusalem's fall, Down, down to the
ground with her!
[8] O Daughter of Babylon [you devastator, you!], who
[ought to be and] shall be destroyed, happy *and* blessed
shall he be who requites you as you have served us. [Isa.
13:1-22; Jer. 25:12, 13.]
[9] Happy *and* blessed shall he be who takes and dashes
your little ones against the rock!

## Psalm 138

[A Psalm] of David.

[1] I will confess *and* praise You [O God] with my whole
heart; before the gods will I sing praises to You.
[2] I will worship toward Your holy temple and praise
Your name for Your loving-kindness and for Your truth
*and* faithfulness; for You have exalted above all else Your
name and Your word *and* You have magnified Your word
above all Your name!
[3] In the day when I called, You answered me; and You
strengthened me with strength (might and inflexibility to
temptation) in my inner self.
[4] All the kings of the land shall give You credit *and*
praise You, O Lord, for they have heard of the promises of
Your mouth [which were fulfilled].
[5] Yes, they shall sing of the ways of the Lord *and* joyfully celebrate His mighty acts, for great is the glory of
the Lord.
[6] For though the Lord is high, yet has He respect to the
lowly [bringing them into fellowship with Him]; but the
proud *and* haughty He knows *and* recognizes [only] at a
distance. [Prov. 3:34; James 4:6; I Pet. 5:5.]
[7] Though I walk in the midst of trouble, You will revive
me; You will stretch forth Your hand against the wrath of
my enemies, and Your right hand will save me. [Ps. 23:3,
4.]
[8] The Lord will perfect that which concerns me; Your
mercy *and* loving-kindness, O Lord, endure forever—forsake not the works of Your own hands. [Ps. 57:2; Phil. 1:6.]

## Psalm 139

To the Chief Musician. A Psalm of David.

[1] O Lord, you have searched me [thoroughly] and have
known me.
[2] You know my downsitting and my uprising; You understand my thought afar off. [Matt. 9:4; John 2:24, 25.]
[3] You sift *and* search out my path and my lying down,
and You are acquainted with all my ways.
[4] For there is not a word in my tongue [still unuttered],
but, behold, O Lord, You know it altogether. [Heb. 4:13.]

## New International Version

5 You hem me in behind and before,
  and you lay your hand upon me.
6 Such knowledge is too wonderful for me,
  too lofty for me to attain.

7 Where can I go from your Spirit?
  Where can I flee from your presence?
8 If I go up to the heavens, you are there;
  if I make my bed in the depths, you are there.
9 If I rise on the wings of the dawn,
  if I settle on the far side of the sea,
10 even there your hand will guide me,
  your right hand will hold me fast.
11 If I say, "Surely the darkness will hide me
  and the light become night around me,"
12 even the darkness will not be dark to you;
  the night will shine like the day,
  for darkness is as light to you.

13 For you created my inmost being;
  you knit me together in my mother's womb.
14 I praise you because I am fearfully and wonderfully
    made;
  your works are wonderful,
  I know that full well.
15 My frame was not hidden from you
  when I was made in the secret place,
  when I was woven together in the depths of the
    earth.
16 Your eyes saw my unformed body;
  all the days ordained for me were written in your
    book
  before one of them came to be.
17 How precious to me are your thoughts,[a] God!
  How vast is the sum of them!
18 Were I to count them,
  they would outnumber the grains of sand—
  when I awake, I am still with you.

19 If only you, God, would slay the wicked!
  Away from me, you who are bloodthirsty!
20 They speak of you with evil intent;
  your adversaries misuse your name.
21 Do I not hate those who hate you, LORD,
  and abhor those who are in rebellion against you?
22 I have nothing but hatred for them;
  I count them my enemies.
23 Search me, God, and know my heart;
  test me and know my anxious thoughts.
24 See if there is any offensive way in me,
  and lead me in the way everlasting.

### Psalm 140[b]

*For the director of music. A psalm of David.*

1 Rescue me, LORD, from evildoers;
  protect me from the violent,
2 who devise evil plans in their hearts
  and stir up war every day.
3 They make their tongues as sharp as a serpent's;
  the poison of vipers is on their lips.[c]

4 Keep me safe, LORD, from the hands of the wicked;
  protect me from the violent,
  who devise ways to trip my feet.
5 The arrogant have hidden a snare for me;
  they have spread out the cords of their net
  and have set traps for me along my path.

6 I say to the LORD, "You are my God."
  Hear, LORD, my cry for mercy.

## Amplified Bible

5 You have beset me *and* shut me in—behind and before,
and You have laid Your hand upon me.
6 Your [infinite] knowledge is too wonderful for me; it is
high above me, I cannot reach it.

7 Where could I go from Your Spirit? Or where could I
flee from Your presence?
8 If I ascend up into heaven, You are there; if I make my
bed in Sheol (the place of the dead), behold, You are there.
[Rom. 11:33.]
9 If I take the wings of the morning or dwell in the uttermost parts of the sea,
10 Even there shall Your hand lead me, and Your right
hand shall hold me.
11 If I say, Surely the darkness shall cover me and the
night shall be [the only] light about me,
12 Even the darkness hides nothing from You, but the
night shines as the day; the darkness and the light are
both alike to You. [Dan. 2:22.]

13 For You did form my inward parts; You did knit me
together in my mother's womb.
14 I will confess *and* praise You *for You are fearful and
wonderful* and for the awful wonder of my birth! Wonderful
are Your works, and that my inner self knows right well.
15 My frame was not hidden from You when I was being
formed in secret [and] intricately *and* curiously wrought
[as if embroidered with various colors] in the depths of the
earth [a region of darkness and mystery].
16 Your eyes saw my unformed substance, and in Your
book all the days [of my life] were written before ever they
took shape, when as yet there was none of them.
17 How precious *and* weighty also are Your thoughts to
me, O God! How vast is the sum of them! [Ps. 40:5.]
18 If I could count them, they would be more in number
than the sand. When I awoke, [could I count to the end] I
would still be with You.

19 If You would [only] slay the wicked, O God, and the
men of blood depart from me—[Isa. 11:4.]
20 Who speak against You wickedly, Your enemies who
take Your name in vain! [Jude 15.]
21 Do I not hate them, O Lord, who hate You? And am I
not grieved *and* do I not loathe those who rise up against
You?
22 I hate them with perfect hatred; they have become
my enemies.
23 Search me [thoroughly], O God, and know my heart!
Try me and know my thoughts!
24 And see if there is any wicked *or* hurtful way in me,
and lead me in the way everlasting.

### Psalm 140

To the Chief Musician. A Psalm of David.

1 Deliver me, O Lord, from evil men; preserve me from
violent men;
2 They devise mischiefs in their heart; continually they
gather together *and* stir up wars.
3 They sharpen their tongues like a serpent's; adders'
poison is under their lips. Selah [pause, and calmly think
of that]! [Rom. 3:13.]
4 Keep me, O Lord, from the hands of the wicked; preserve me from the violent men who have purposed to
thrust aside my steps.
5 The proud have hidden a snare for me; they have
spread cords as a net by the wayside, they have set traps
for me. Selah [pause, and calmly think of that]!
6 I said to the Lord, You are my God; give ear to the voice
of my supplications, O Lord.

---

a 17 Or *How amazing are your thoughts concerning me*   b In Hebrew
texts 140:1-13 is numbered 140:2-14.   c 3 The Hebrew has *Selah* (a
word of uncertain meaning) here and at the end of verses 5 and 8.

## New International Version

7 Sovereign LORD, my strong deliverer,
  you shield my head in the day of battle.
8 Do not grant the wicked their desires, LORD;
  do not let their plans succeed.

9 Those who surround me proudly rear their heads;
  may the mischief of their lips engulf them.
10 May burning coals fall on them;
  may they be thrown into the fire,
  into miry pits, never to rise.
11 May slanderers not be established in the land;
  may disaster hunt down the violent.

12 I know that the LORD secures justice for the poor
  and upholds the cause of the needy.
13 Surely the righteous will praise your name,
  and the upright will live in your presence.

### Psalm 141

*A psalm of David.*

1 I call to you, LORD, come quickly to me;
  hear me when I call to you.
2 May my prayer be set before you like incense;
  may the lifting up of my hands be like the evening
    sacrifice.

3 Set a guard over my mouth, LORD;
  keep watch over the door of my lips.
4 Do not let my heart be drawn to what is evil
  so that I take part in wicked deeds
along with those who are evildoers;
  do not let me eat their delicacies.

5 Let a righteous man strike me—that is a kindness;
  let him rebuke me—that is oil on my head.
My head will not refuse it,
  for my prayer will still be against the deeds of
    evildoers.

6 Their rulers will be thrown down from the cliffs,
  and the wicked will learn that my words were well
    spoken.
7 They will say, "As one plows and breaks up the earth,
  so our bones have been scattered at the mouth of
    the grave."

8 But my eyes are fixed on you, Sovereign LORD;
  in you I take refuge—do not give me over to death.
9 Keep me safe from the traps set by evildoers,
  from the snares they have laid for me.
10 Let the wicked fall into their own nets,
  while I pass by in safety.

### Psalm 142[a]

*A maskil[b] of David. When he was in the cave. A prayer.*

1 I cry aloud to the LORD;
  I lift up my voice to the LORD for mercy.
2 I pour out before him my complaint;
  before him I tell my trouble.

3 When my spirit grows faint within me,
  it is you who watch over my way.
In the path where I walk
  people have hidden a snare for me.
4 Look and see, there is no one at my right hand;
  no one is concerned for me.
I have no refuge;
  no one cares for my life.

---

[a] In Hebrew texts 142:1-7 is numbered 142:2-8.   [b] Title: Probably a
literary or musical term

## Amplified Bible

7 O God the Lord, the Strength of my salvation, You have
covered my head in the day of battle.
8 Grant not, O Lord, the desires of the wicked; further
not their wicked plot *and* device, lest they exalt themselves. Selah [pause, and calmly think of that]!
9 Those who are fencing me in raise their heads; may the
mischief of their own lips *and* the very things they desire
for me come upon them.
10 Let burning coals fall upon them; let them be cast into
the fire, into floods of water *or* deep water pits, from which
they shall not rise.
11 Let not a man of slanderous tongue be established in
the earth; let evil hunt the violent man to overthrow him
[let calamity follow his evildoings].
12 I know *and* rest in confidence upon it that the Lord
will maintain the cause of the afflicted, and will secure
justice for the poor *and* needy [of His believing children].
13 Surely the [uncompromisingly] righteous shall give
thanks to Your name; the upright shall dwell in Your presence (before Your very face).

### Psalm 141

A Psalm of David.

1 Lord, I call upon You; hasten to me. Give ear to my
voice when I cry to You.
2 Let my prayer be set forth as incense before You, the
lifting up of my hands as the evening sacrifice. [I Tim. 2:8;
Rev. 8:3, 4.]
3 Set a guard, O Lord, before my mouth; keep watch at
the door of my lips.
4 Incline my heart not to submit *or* consent to any evil
thing or to be occupied in deeds of wickedness with men
who work iniquity; and let me not eat of their dainties.
5 Let the righteous man smite and correct me—it is a
kindness. Oil so choice let not my head refuse *or* discourage; for even in their evils *or* calamities shall my prayer
continue. [Prov. 9:8; 19:25; 25:12; Gal. 6:1.]
6 When their rulers are overthrown in stony places,
[their followers] shall hear my words, that they are sweet
(pleasant, mild, and just).
7 The unburied bones [of slaughtered rulers] shall lie
scattered at the mouth of Sheol, [as unregarded] as the
lumps of soil behind the plowman when he breaks open
the ground. [II Cor. 1:9.]
8 But my eyes are toward You, O God the Lord; in You
do I trust *and* take refuge; pour not out my life *nor* leave it
destitute *and* bare.
9 Keep me from the trap which they have laid for me, and
the snares of evildoers.
10 Let the wicked fall together into their own nets, while
I pass over them *and* escape.

### Psalm 142

A skillful song, *or* a didactic *or* reflective poem, of David; when
he was in the cave. A Prayer.

1 I cry to the Lord with my voice; with my voice to the
Lord do I make supplication.
2 I pour out my complaint before Him; I tell before Him
my trouble.
3 When my spirit was overwhelmed *and* fainted [throw-
ing all its weight] upon me, then You knew my path. In the
way where I walk they have hidden a snare for me.
4 Look on the right hand [the point of attack] and see; for
there is no man who knows me [to appear for me]. Refuge
has failed me *and* I have no way to flee; no man cares for
my life *or* my welfare.

## New International Version

⁵I cry to you, LORD;
 I say, "You are my refuge,
 my portion in the land of the living."

⁶Listen to my cry,
 for I am in desperate need;
rescue me from those who pursue me,
 for they are too strong for me.
⁷Set me free from my prison,
 that I may praise your name.
Then the righteous will gather about me
 because of your goodness to me.

### Psalm 143

*A psalm of David.*

¹LORD, hear my prayer,
 listen to my cry for mercy;
in your faithfulness and righteousness
 come to my relief.
²Do not bring your servant into judgment,
 for no one living is righteous before you.
³The enemy pursues me,
 he crushes my life to the ground;
he makes me dwell in the darkness
 like those long dead.
⁴So my spirit grows faint within me;
 my heart within me is dismayed.
⁵I remember the days of long ago;
 I meditate on all your works
 and consider what your hands have done.
⁶I spread out my hands to you;
 I thirst for you like a parched land.*ᵃ*

⁷Answer me quickly, LORD;
 my spirit fails.
Do not hide your face from me
 or I will be like those who go down to the pit.
⁸Let the morning bring me word of your unfailing love,
 for I have put my trust in you.
Show me the way I should go,
 for to you I entrust my life.
⁹Rescue me from my enemies, LORD,
 for I hide myself in you.
¹⁰Teach me to do your will,
 for you are my God;
may your good Spirit
 lead me on level ground.

¹¹For your name's sake, LORD, preserve my life;
 in your righteousness, bring me out of trouble.
¹²In your unfailing love, silence my enemies;
 destroy all my foes,
 for I am your servant.

### Psalm 144

*Of David.*

¹Praise be to the LORD my Rock,
 who trains my hands for war,
 my fingers for battle.
²He is my loving God and my fortress,
 my stronghold and my deliverer,
my shield, in whom I take refuge,
 who subdues peoples*ᵇ* under me.

³LORD, what are human beings that you care for them,
 mere mortals that you think of them?
⁴They are like a breath;
 their days are like a fleeting shadow.

## Amplified Bible

⁵I cried to You, O Lord; I said, You are my refuge, my portion in the land of the living.
⁶Attend to my loud cry, for I am brought very low; deliver me from my persecutors, for they are stronger than I.
⁷Bring my life out of prison, that I may confess, praise, *and* give thanks to Your name; the righteous will surround me *and* crown themselves because of me, for You will deal bountifully with me.

### Psalm 143

A Psalm of David.

¹Hear my prayer, O Lord, give ear to my supplications! In Your faithfulness answer me, and in Your righteousness.
²And enter not into judgment with Your servant, for in Your sight no man living is [in himself] righteous *or* justified. [Ps. 130:3; Rom. 3:20-26; Gal. 2:16.]
³For the enemy has pursued *and* persecuted my soul, he has crushed my life down to the ground; he has made me to dwell in dark places as those who have been long dead.
⁴Therefore is my spirit overwhelmed *and* faints within me [wrapped in gloom]; my heart within my bosom grows numb.
⁵I remember the days of old; I meditate on all Your doings; I ponder the work of Your hands.
⁶I spread forth my hands to You; my soul thirsts after You like a thirsty land [for water]. Selah [pause, and calmly think of that]!
⁷Answer me speedily, O Lord, for my spirit fails; hide not Your face from me, lest I become like those who go down into the pit (the grave).
⁸Cause me to hear Your loving-kindness in the morning, for on You do I lean *and* in You do I trust. Cause me to know the way wherein I should walk, for I lift up my inner self to You.
⁹Deliver me, O Lord, from my enemies; I flee to You to hide me.
¹⁰Teach me to do Your will, for You are my God; let Your good Spirit lead me into a level country *and* into the land of uprightness.
¹¹Save my life, O Lord, for Your name's sake; in Your righteousness, bring my life out of trouble *and* free me from distress.
¹²And in your mercy *and* loving-kindness, cut off my enemies and destroy all those who afflict my inner self, for I am Your servant.

### Psalm 144

[A Psalm] of David.

¹Blessed be the Lord, my Rock *and* my keen *and* firm Strength, Who teaches my hands to war and my fingers to fight—
²My Steadfast Love and my Fortress, my High Tower and my Deliverer, my Shield and He in Whom I trust *and* take refuge, Who subdues my people under me.
³Lord, what is man that You take notice of him? Or [the] son of man that You take account of him? [Job 7:17; Ps. 8:4; Heb. 2:6.]
⁴Man is like vanity *and* a breath; his days are as a shadow that passes away.

---

*ᵃ 6* The Hebrew has *Selah* (a word of uncertain meaning) here.
*ᵇ 2* Many manuscripts of the Masoretic Text, Dead Sea Scrolls, Aquila, Jerome and Syriac; most manuscripts of the Masoretic Text *subdues my people*

## New International Version

[5] Part your heavens, LORD, and come down;
    touch the mountains, so that they smoke.
[6] Send forth lightning and scatter the enemy;
    shoot your arrows and rout them.
[7] Reach down your hand from on high;
    deliver me and rescue me
    from the mighty waters,
    from the hands of foreigners
[8] whose mouths are full of lies,
    whose right hands are deceitful.

[9] I will sing a new song to you, my God;
    on the ten-stringed lyre I will make music to you,
[10] to the One who gives victory to kings,
    who delivers his servant David.

From the deadly sword [11] deliver me;
    rescue me from the hands of foreigners
whose mouths are full of lies,
    whose right hands are deceitful.

[12] Then our sons in their youth
    will be like well-nurtured plants,
and our daughters will be like pillars
    carved to adorn a palace.
[13] Our barns will be filled
    with every kind of provision.
Our sheep will increase by thousands,
    by tens of thousands in our fields;
[14]   our oxen will draw heavy loads. [a]
There will be no breaching of walls,
    no going into captivity,
    no cry of distress in our streets.
[15] Blessed is the people of whom this is true;
    blessed is the people whose God is the LORD.

### Psalm 145 [b]

*A psalm of praise. Of David.*

[1] I will exalt you, my God the King;
    I will praise your name for ever and ever.
[2] Every day I will praise you
    and extol your name for ever and ever.
[3] Great is the LORD and most worthy of praise;
    his greatness no one can fathom.
[4] One generation commends your works to another;
    they tell of your mighty acts.
[5] They speak of the glorious splendor of your
    majesty—
    and I will meditate on your wonderful works. [c]
[6] They tell of the power of your awesome works—
    and I will proclaim your great deeds.
[7] They celebrate your abundant goodness
    and joyfully sing of your righteousness.

[8] The LORD is gracious and compassionate,
    slow to anger and rich in love.

[9] The LORD is good to all;
    he has compassion on all he has made.
[10] All your works praise you, LORD;
    your faithful people extol you.
[11] They tell of the glory of your kingdom
    and speak of your might,
[12] so that all people may know of your mighty acts
    and the glorious splendor of your kingdom.

## Amplified Bible

[5] Bow Your heavens, O Lord, and come down; touch the mountains, and they shall smoke.
[6] Cast forth lightning and scatter [my enemies]; send out Your arrows and embarrass *and* frustrate them.
[7] Stretch forth Your hand from above; rescue me and deliver me out of great waters, from the hands of hostile aliens (tribes around us)
[8] Whose mouths speak deceit and whose right hands are right hands [raised in taking] fraudulent oaths.
[9] I will sing a new song to You, O God; upon a harp, an instrument of ten strings, will I offer praises to You.
[10] You are He Who gives salvation to kings, Who rescues David His servant from the hurtful sword [of evil].
[11] Rescue me and deliver me out of the power of [hostile] alien [tribes] whose mouths speak deceit and whose right hands are right hands [raised in taking] fraudulent oaths.
[12] When our sons shall be as plants grown large in their youth *and* our daughters as sculptured corner pillars hewn like those of a palace;
[13] When our garners are full, affording all manner of store, and our sheep bring forth thousands and ten thousands in our pastures;
[14] When our oxen are well loaded; when there is no invasion [of hostile armies] and no going forth [against besiegers—when there is no murder or manslaughter] and no outcry in our streets;
[15] Happy *and* blessed are the people who are in such a case; yes, happy (blessed, fortunate, prosperous, to be envied) are the people whose God is the Lord!

### Psalm 145

[A Psalm] of praise. Of David.

[1] I will extol You, my God, O King; and I will bless Your name forever and ever [with grateful, affectionate praise].
[2] Every day [with its new reasons] will I bless You [affectionately and gratefully praise You]; yes, I will praise Your name forever and ever.
[3] Great is the Lord and highly to be praised; and His greatness is [so vast and deep as to be] unsearchable. [Job 5:9; 9:10; Rom. 11:33.]
[4] One generation shall laud Your works to another and shall declare Your mighty acts.
[5] On the glorious splendor of Your majesty and on Your wondrous works I will meditate.
[6] Men shall speak of the might of Your tremendous *and* terrible acts, and I will declare Your greatness.
[7] They shall pour forth [like a fountain] the fame of Your great *and* abundant goodness and shall sing aloud of Your rightness *and* justice.
[8] The Lord is gracious and full of compassion, slow to anger and abounding in mercy *and* loving-kindness.
[9] The Lord is good to all, and His tender mercies are over all His works [the entirety of things created].
[10] All Your works shall praise You, O Lord, and Your loving ones shall bless You [affectionately and gratefully shall Your saints confess and praise You]!
[11] They shall speak of the glory of Your kingdom and talk of Your power,
[12] To make known to the sons of men God's mighty deeds and the glorious majesty of His kingdom.

---

[a] 14 Or *our chieftains will be firmly established*   [b] This psalm is an acrostic poem, the verses of which (including verse 13b) begin with the successive letters of the Hebrew alphabet.   [c] 5 Dead Sea Scrolls and Syriac (see also Septuagint); Masoretic Text *On the glorious splendor of your majesty / and on your wonderful works I will meditate*

# New International Version

13 Your kingdom is an everlasting kingdom,
and your dominion endures through all
generations.

The LORD is trustworthy in all he promises
and faithful in all he does.[a]
14 The LORD upholds all who fall
and lifts up all who are bowed down.
15 The eyes of all look to you,
and you give them their food at the proper time.
16 You open your hand
and satisfy the desires of every living thing.

17 The LORD is righteous in all his ways
and faithful in all he does.
18 The LORD is near to all who call on him,
to all who call on him in truth.
19 He fulfills the desires of those who fear him;
he hears their cry and saves them.
20 The LORD watches over all who love him,
but all the wicked he will destroy.

21 My mouth will speak in praise of the LORD.
Let every creature praise his holy name
for ever and ever.

## Psalm 146

1 Praise the LORD.[b]

Praise the LORD, my soul.

2 I will praise the LORD all my life;
I will sing praise to my God as long as I live.
3 Do not put your trust in princes,
in human beings, who cannot save.
4 When their spirit departs, they return to the ground;
on that very day their plans come to nothing.
5 Blessed are those whose help is the God of Jacob,
whose hope is in the LORD their God.

6 He is the Maker of heaven and earth,
the sea, and everything in them—
he remains faithful forever.
7 He upholds the cause of the oppressed
and gives food to the hungry.
The LORD sets prisoners free,
8    the LORD gives sight to the blind,
the LORD lifts up those who are bowed down,
the LORD loves the righteous.
9 The LORD watches over the foreigner
and sustains the fatherless and the widow,
but he frustrates the ways of the wicked.

10 The LORD reigns forever,
your God, O Zion, for all generations.

Praise the LORD.

## Psalm 147

1 Praise the LORD.[c]

How good it is to sing praises to our God,
how pleasant and fitting to praise him!

2 The LORD builds up Jerusalem;
he gathers the exiles of Israel.
3 He heals the brokenhearted
and binds up their wounds.
4 He determines the number of the stars
and calls them each by name.
5 Great is our Lord and mighty in power;
his understanding has no limit.

# Amplified Bible

13 Your kingdom is an everlasting kingdom, and Your
dominion endures throughout all generations.
14 The Lord upholds all those [of His own] who are falling and raises up all those who are bowed down.
15 The eyes of all wait for You [looking, watching, and
expecting] and You give them their food in due season.
16 You open Your hand and satisfy every living thing
with favor.
17 The Lord is [rigidly] righteous in all His ways and gracious and merciful in all His works.
18 The Lord is near to all who call upon Him, to all who
call upon Him sincerely and in truth.
19 He will fulfill the desires of those who reverently and
worshipfully fear Him; He also will hear their cry and will
save them.
20 The Lord preserves all those who love Him, but all the
wicked will He destroy.
21 My mouth shall speak the praise of the Lord; and let
all flesh bless (affectionately and gratefully praise) His
holy name forever and ever.

## Psalm 146

1 Praise the Lord! (Hallelujah!) Praise the Lord, O my
soul!
2 While I live will I praise the Lord; I will sing praises to
my God while I have any being.
3 Put not your trust in princes, in a son of man, in whom
there is no help.
4 When his breath leaves him, he returns to his earth; in
that very day his [previous] thoughts, plans, and purposes
perish. [I Cor. 2:6.]
5 Happy (blessed, fortunate, enviable) is he who has the
God of [special revelation to] Jacob for his help, whose
hope is in the Lord his God, [Gen. 32:30.]
6 Who made heaven and earth, the sea, and all that is in
them, Who keeps truth and is faithful forever,
7 Who executes justice for the oppressed, Who gives
food to the hungry. The Lord sets free the prisoners,
8 The Lord opens the eyes of the blind, the Lord lifts up
those who are bowed down, the Lord loves the [uncompro-
misingly] righteous (those upright in heart and in right
standing with Him). [Luke 13:13; John 9:7, 32.]
9 The Lord protects and preserves the strangers and
temporary residents, He upholds the fatherless and the
widow and sets them upright, but the way of the wicked
He makes crooked (turns upside down and brings to ruin).
10 The Lord shall reign forever, even Your God, O Zion,
from generation to generation. Praise the Lord! (Hallelujah!) [Ps. 10:16; Rev. 11:15.]

## Psalm 147

1 Praise the Lord! For it is good to sing praises to our
God, for He is gracious and lovely; praise is becoming and
appropriate.
2 The Lord is building up Jerusalem; He is gathering
together the exiles of Israel.
3 He heals the brokenhearted and binds up their wounds
[curing their pains and their sorrows]. [Ps. 34:18; Isa.
57:15; 61:1; Luke 4:18.]
4 He determines and counts the number of the stars; He
calls them all by their names.
5 Great is our Lord and of great power; His understanding is inexhaustible and boundless.

---

[a] 13 One manuscript of the Masoretic Text, Dead Sea Scrolls and Syriac
(see also Septuagint); most manuscripts of the Masoretic Text do not
have the last two lines of verse 13.   [b] 1 Hebrew Hallelu Yah; also in
verse 10   [c] 1 Hebrew Hallelu Yah; also in verse 20

# New International Version

6The LORD sustains the humble
  but casts the wicked to the ground.

7Sing to the LORD with grateful praise;
  make music to our God on the harp.

8He covers the sky with clouds;
  he supplies the earth with rain
  and makes grass grow on the hills.
9He provides food for the cattle
  and for the young ravens when they call.

10His pleasure is not in the strength of the horse,
  nor his delight in the legs of the warrior;
11the LORD delights in those who fear him,
  who put their hope in his unfailing love.

12Extol the LORD, Jerusalem;
  praise your God, Zion.

13He strengthens the bars of your gates
  and blesses your people within you.
14He grants peace to your borders
  and satisfies you with the finest of wheat.

15He sends his command to the earth;
  his word runs swiftly.
16He spreads the snow like wool
  and scatters the frost like ashes.
17He hurls down his hail like pebbles.
  Who can withstand his icy blast?
18He sends his word and melts them;
  he stirs up his breezes, and the waters flow.

19He has revealed his word to Jacob,
  his laws and decrees to Israel.
20He has done this for no other nation;
  they do not know his laws.ᵃ

  Praise the LORD.

### Psalm 148

1Praise the LORD.ᵇ

  Praise the LORD from the heavens;
    praise him in the heights above.
2Praise him, all his angels;
  praise him, all his heavenly hosts.
3Praise him, sun and moon;
  praise him, all you shining stars.
4Praise him, you highest heavens
  and you waters above the skies.

5Let them praise the name of the LORD,
  for at his command they were created,
6and he established them for ever and ever—
  he issued a decree that will never pass away.

7Praise the LORD from the earth,
  you great sea creatures and all ocean depths,
8lightning and hail, snow and clouds,
  stormy winds that do his bidding,
9you mountains and all hills,
  fruit trees and all cedars,
10wild animals and all cattle,
  small creatures and flying birds,
11kings of the earth and all nations,
  you princes and all rulers on earth,
12young men and women,
  old men and children.

13Let them praise the name of the LORD,
  for his name alone is exalted;
  his splendor is above the earth and the heavens.

# Amplified Bible

6The Lord lifts up the humble *and* downtrodden; He casts the wicked down to the ground.
7Sing to the Lord with thanksgiving; sing praises with the harp *or* the lyre to our God!—
8Who covers the heavens with clouds, Who prepares rain for the earth, Who makes grass to grow on the mountains.
9He gives to the beast his food, and to the young ravens that for which they cry.
10He delights not in the strength of the horse, nor does He take pleasure in the legs of a man.
11The Lord takes pleasure in those who reverently *and* worshipfully fear Him, in those who hope in His mercy *and* loving-kindness. [Ps. 145:20.]
12Praise the Lord, O Jerusalem! Praise your God, O Zion!
13For He has strengthened and made hard the bars of your gates, and He has blessed your children within you.
14He makes peace in your borders; He fills you with the finest of the wheat.
15He sends forth His commandment to the earth; His word runs very swiftly.
16He gives [to the earth] snow like [a blanket of] wool; He scatters the hoarfrost like ashes.
17He casts forth His ice like crumbs; who can stand before His cold?
18He sends out His word, and melts [ice and snow]; He causes His wind to blow, and the waters flow.
19He declares His word to Jacob, His statutes and His ordinances to Israel. [Mal. 4:4.]
20He has not dealt so with any [other] nation; they have not known (understood, appreciated, given heed to, and cherished) His ordinances. Praise the Lord! (Hallelujah!) [Ps. 79:6; Jer. 10:25.]

### Psalm 148

1Praise the Lord! Praise the Lord from the heavens, praise Him in the heights!
2Praise Him, all His angels, praise Him, all His hosts!
3Praise Him, sun and moon, praise Him, all you stars of light!
4Praise Him, you highest heavens and you waters above the heavens!
5Let them praise the name of the Lord, for He commanded and they were created.
6He also established them forever and ever; He made a decree which shall not pass away [He fixed their bounds which cannot be passed over].
7Praise the Lord from the earth, you sea monsters and all deeps!
8You lightning, hail, fog, *and* frost, you stormy wind fulfilling His orders!
9Mountains and all hills, fruitful trees and all cedars!
10Beasts and all cattle, creeping things and flying birds!
11Kings of the earth and all peoples, princes and all rulers *and* judges of the earth!
12Both young men and maidens, old men and children!
13Let them praise *and* exalt the name of the Lord, for His name alone is exalted *and* supreme! His glory *and* majesty are above earth and heaven!

---

ᵃ 20 Masoretic Text; Dead Sea Scrolls and Septuagint *nation; / he has not made his laws known to them*   ᵇ 1 Hebrew *Hallelu Yah*; also in verse 14

## New International Version

14 And he has raised up for his people a horn,*a*
    the praise of all his faithful servants,
    of Israel, the people close to his heart.

Praise the Lord.

### Psalm 149

1 Praise the Lord.*b*

Sing to the Lord a new song,
    his praise in the assembly of his faithful people.

2 Let Israel rejoice in their Maker;
    let the people of Zion be glad in their King.
3 Let them praise his name with dancing
    and make music to him with timbrel and harp.
4 For the Lord takes delight in his people;
    he crowns the humble with victory.
5 Let his faithful people rejoice in this honor
    and sing for joy on their beds.

6 May the praise of God be in their mouths
    and a double-edged sword in their hands,
7 to inflict vengeance on the nations
    and punishment on the peoples,
8 to bind their kings with fetters,
    their nobles with shackles of iron,
9 to carry out the sentence written against them—
    this is the glory of all his faithful people.

Praise the Lord.

### Psalm 150

1 Praise the Lord.*c*

Praise God in his sanctuary;
    praise him in his mighty heavens.
2 Praise him for his acts of power;
    praise him for his surpassing greatness.
3 Praise him with the sounding of the trumpet,
    praise him with the harp and lyre,
4 praise him with timbrel and dancing,
    praise him with the strings and pipe,
5 praise him with the clash of cymbals,
    praise him with resounding cymbals.

6 Let everything that has breath praise the Lord.

Praise the Lord.

## Amplified Bible

14 He has lifted up a horn for His people [giving them power, prosperity, dignity, and preeminence], a song of praise for all His godly ones, for the people of Israel, who are near to Him. Praise the Lord! (Hallelujah!) [Ps. 75:10; Eph. 2:17.]

### Psalm 149

1 Praise the Lord! Sing to the Lord a new song, praise Him in the assembly of His saints!
2 Let Israel rejoice in Him, their Maker; let Zion's children triumph *and* be joyful in their King! [Zech. 9:9; Matt. 21:5.]
3 Let them praise His name in chorus *and* choir *and* with the [single or group] dance; let them sing praises to Him with the tambourine and lyre!
4 For the Lord takes pleasure in His people; He will beautify the humble with salvation *and* adorn the wretched with victory.
5 Let the saints be joyful in the glory *and* beauty [which God confers upon them]; let them sing for joy upon their beds.
6 Let the high praises of God be in their throats and a two-edged sword in their hands, [Heb. 4:12; Rev. 1:16.]
7 To wreak vengeance upon the nations and chastisement upon the peoples,
8 To bind their kings with chains, and their nobles with fetters of iron,
9 To execute upon them the judgment written. He [the Lord] is the honor of all His saints. Praise the Lord! (Hallelujah!)

### Psalm 150

1 Praise the Lord! Praise God in His sanctuary; praise Him in the heavens of His power!
2 Praise Him for His mighty acts; praise Him according to the abundance of His greatness! [Deut. 3:24; Ps. 145:5, 6.]
3 Praise Him with trumpet sound; praise Him with lute and harp!
4 Praise Him with tambourine and [single or group] dance; praise Him with stringed and wind instruments *or* flutes!
5 Praise Him with resounding cymbals; praise Him with loud clashing cymbals!
6 Let everything that has breath *and* every breath of life praise the Lord! Praise the Lord! (Hallelujah!)

*a* 14 *Horn* here symbolizes strength.   *b* 1 Hebrew *Hallelu Yah*; also in verse 9   *c* 1 Hebrew *Hallelu Yah*; also in verse 6

## New International Version

# Proverbs

### Purpose and Theme

**1** The proverbs of Solomon son of David, king of Israel:

² for gaining wisdom and instruction;
    for understanding words of insight;
³ for receiving instruction in prudent behavior,
    doing what is right and just and fair;
⁴ for giving prudence to those who are simple,ᵃ
    knowledge and discretion to the young—
⁵ let the wise listen and add to their learning,
    and let the discerning get guidance—
⁶ for understanding proverbs and parables,
    the sayings and riddles of the wise.ᵇ

⁷ The fear of the LORD is the beginning of knowledge,
    but foolsᶜ despise wisdom and instruction.

### Prologue: Exhortations to Embrace Wisdom

#### Warning Against the Invitation of Sinful Men

⁸ Listen, my son, to your father's instruction
    and do not forsake your mother's teaching.
⁹ They are a garland to grace your head
    and a chain to adorn your neck.

¹⁰ My son, if sinful men entice you,
    do not give in to them.
¹¹ If they say, "Come along with us;
    let's lie in wait for innocent blood,
    let's ambush some harmless soul;
¹² let's swallow them alive, like the grave,
    and whole, like those who go down to the pit;
¹³ we will get all sorts of valuable things
    and fill our houses with plunder;
¹⁴ cast lots with us;
    we will all share the loot"—
¹⁵ my son, do not go along with them,
    do not set foot on their paths;
¹⁶ for their feet rush into evil,
    they are swift to shed blood.
¹⁷ How useless to spread a net
    where every bird can see it!
¹⁸ These men lie in wait for their own blood;
    they ambush only themselves!
¹⁹ Such are the paths of all who go after ill-gotten gain;
    it takes away the life of those who get it.

#### Wisdom's Rebuke

²⁰ Out in the open wisdom calls aloud,
    she raises her voice in the public square;
²¹ on top of the wallᵈ she cries out,
    at the city gate she makes her speech:

---

ᵃ 4 The Hebrew word rendered *simple* in Proverbs denotes a person who is gullible, without moral direction and inclined to evil. ᵇ 6 Or *understanding a proverb, namely, a parable, / and the sayings of the wise, their riddles* ᶜ 7 The Hebrew words rendered *fool* in Proverbs, and often elsewhere in the Old Testament, denote a person who is morally deficient. ᵈ 21 Septuagint; Hebrew / *at noisy street corners*

## Amplified Bible

### THE

# Proverbs

**1** The proverbs (truths obscurely expressed, maxims, and parables) of Solomon son of David, king of Israel:
²ᵃ That people may know skillful *and* godly ᵇWisdom and instruction, discern *and* comprehend the words of understanding *and* insight,
³ Receive instruction in wise dealing *and* the discipline of wise thoughtfulness, righteousness, justice, and integrity,
⁴ That prudence may be given to the simple, and knowledge, discretion, *and* discernment to the youth—
⁵ The wise also will hear and increase in learning, and the person of understanding will acquire skill *and* attain to sound counsel [so that he may be able to steer his course rightly]—[Prov. 9:9.]
⁶ That people may understand a proverb and a figure of speech *or* an enigma with its interpretation, and the words of the wise and their dark sayings *or* riddles.
⁷ The reverent *and* worshipful fear of the Lord is the beginning *and* the principal *and* choice part of knowledge [its starting point and its essence]; but fools despise skillful *and* godly Wisdom, instruction, *and* discipline. [Ps. 111:10.]
⁸ My son, hear the instruction of your father; reject not *nor* forsake the teaching of your mother.
⁹ For they are a [victor's] chaplet (garland) of grace upon your head and chains *and* pendants [of gold worn by kings] for your neck.
¹⁰ My son, if sinners entice you, do not consent. [Ps. 1:1; Eph. 5:11.]
¹¹ If they say, Come with us; let us lie in wait [to shed] blood, let us ambush the innocent without cause [and show that his piety is in vain];
¹² Let us swallow them up alive as does Sheol (the place of the dead), and whole, as those who go down into the pit [of the dead];
¹³ We shall find *and* take all kinds of precious goods [when our victims are put out of the way], we shall fill our houses with plunder;
¹⁴ Throw in your lot with us [they insist] *and* be a sworn brother *and* comrade; let us all have one purse in common—
¹⁵ My son, do not walk in the way with them; restrain your foot from their path;
¹⁶ For their feet run to evil, and they make haste to shed blood.
¹⁷ For in vain is the net spread in the sight of any bird!
¹⁸ But [when these men set a trap for others] they are lying in wait for their own blood; they set an ambush for their own lives.
¹⁹ So are the ways of everyone who is greedy of gain; such [greed for plunder] takes away the lives of its possessors. [Prov. 15:27; I Tim. 6:10.]
²⁰ᶜ Wisdom cries aloud in the street, she raises her voice in the markets;
²¹ She cries at the head of the noisy intersections [in the chief gathering places]; at the entrance of the city gates she speaks:

---

ᵃ Over the doors of the school of Plato these words were written in Greek, "Let no one enter who is not a geometrician." But Solomon opens wide the doors of his proverbs with a special message of welcome to the unlearned, the simple, the foolish, the young, and even to the wise—that all "will hear and increase in learning" (Prov. 1:5). ᵇ A key term in the book of Proverbs, "Wisdom" is capitalized throughout, as God's design for living and as a reminder of Christ, Whom the apostle Paul calls "the wisdom of God . . . in Whom are hid all the treasures of wisdom and knowledge" (I Cor. 1:24; Col. 2:3 KJV). ᶜ Wisdom here is personified. Read "the Wisdom of God" instead of "Wisdom" and see the wonderful power of this book.

## New International Version

22 "How long will you who are simple love your simple
  ways?
  How long will mockers delight in mockery
    and fools hate knowledge?
23 Repent at my rebuke!
  Then I will pour out my thoughts to you,
    I will make known to you my teachings.
24 But since you refuse to listen when I call
    and no one pays attention when I stretch out my
      hand,
25 since you disregard all my advice
    and do not accept my rebuke,
26 I in turn will laugh when disaster strikes you;
    I will mock when calamity overtakes you—
27 when calamity overtakes you like a storm,
    when disaster sweeps over you like a whirlwind,
    when distress and trouble overwhelm you.

28 "Then they will call to me but I will not answer;
    they will look for me but will not find me,
29 since they hated knowledge
    and did not choose to fear the LORD.
30 Since they would not accept my advice
    and spurned my rebuke,
31 they will eat the fruit of their ways
    and be filled with the fruit of their schemes.
32 For the waywardness of the simple will kill them,
    and the complacency of fools will destroy them;
33 but whoever listens to me will live in safety
    and be at ease, without fear of harm."

### Moral Benefits of Wisdom

2 My son, if you accept my words
    and store up my commands within you,
2 turning your ear to wisdom
    and applying your heart to understanding—
3 indeed, if you call out for insight
    and cry aloud for understanding,
4 and if you look for it as for silver
    and search for it as for hidden treasure,
5 then you will understand the fear of the LORD
    and find the knowledge of God.
6 For the LORD gives wisdom;
    from his mouth come knowledge and
      understanding.
7 He holds success in store for the upright,
    he is a shield to those whose walk is blameless,
8 for he guards the course of the just
    and protects the way of his faithful ones.

9 Then you will understand what is right and just
    and fair—every good path.
10 For wisdom will enter your heart,
    and knowledge will be pleasant to your soul.
11 Discretion will protect you,
    and understanding will guard you.

12 Wisdom will save you from the ways of wicked men,
    from men whose words are perverse,
13 who have left the straight paths
    to walk in dark ways,
14 who delight in doing wrong
    and rejoice in the perverseness of evil,
15 whose paths are crooked
    and who are devious in their ways.

16 Wisdom will save you also from the adulterous woman,
    from the wayward woman with her seductive words,

## Amplified Bible

22 How long, O simple ones [open to evil], will you love
being simple? And the scoffers delight in scoffing and
[self-confident] fools hate knowledge?
23 If you will turn (repent) *and* give heed to my reproof,
behold, I [ª Wisdom] will pour out my spirit upon you, I will
make my words known to you. [Isa. 11:2; Eph. 1:17-20.]
24 Because I have called and you have refused [to an-
swer], have stretched out my hand and no man has heeded
it, [Isa. 65:11, 12; 66:4; Jer. 7:13, 14; Zech. 7:11-13.]
25 And you treated as nothing all my counsel and would
accept none of my reproof,
26 I also will laugh at your calamity; I will mock when
the thing comes that shall cause you terror *and* panic—
27 When your panic comes as a storm *and* desolation and
your calamity comes on as a whirlwind, when distress and
anguish come upon you.
28 Then will they call upon me [Wisdom] but I will not
answer; they will seek me early *and* diligently but they will
not find me. [Job 27:9; 35:12, 13; Isa. 1:15, 16; Jer. 11:11;
Mic. 3:4; James 4:3.]
29 Because they hated knowledge and did not choose
the reverent *and* worshipful fear of the Lord, [Prov. 8:13.]
30 Would accept none of my counsel, and despised all
my reproof,
31 Therefore shall they eat of the fruit of their own way
and be satiated with their own devices.
32 For the backsliding of the simple shall slay them, and
the careless ease of [self-confident] fools shall destroy
them. [Isa. 32:6.]
33 But whoso hearkens to me [Wisdom] shall dwell securely *and* in confident trust and shall be quiet, without
fear *or* dread of evil.

2 My son, if you will receive my words and treasure up
    my commandments within you,
2 Making your ear attentive to skillful *and* godly ᵇ Wisdom *and* inclining and directing your heart *and* mind to understanding [applying all your powers to the quest for it];
3 Yes, if you cry out for insight and raise your voice for
understanding,
4 If you seek [Wisdom] as for silver and search for skillful *and* godly Wisdom as for hidden treasures,
5 Then you will understand the reverent *and* worshipful fear of the Lord and find the knowledge of [our omni-
scient] God. [Prov. 1:7.]
6 For the Lord gives skillful *and* godly Wisdom; from
His mouth come knowledge and understanding.
7 He hides away sound *and* godly Wisdom *and* stores
it for the righteous (those who are upright and in right
standing with Him); He is a shield to those who walk uprightly *and* in integrity,
8 That He may guard the paths of justice; yes, He preserves the way of His saints. [I Sam. 2:9; Ps. 66:8, 9.]
9 Then you will understand righteousness, justice, and
fair dealing [in every area and relation]; yes, you will understand every good path.
10 For skillful *and* godly Wisdom shall enter into your
heart, and knowledge shall be pleasant to you.
11 Discretion shall watch over you, understanding shall
keep you,
12 To deliver you from the way of evil *and* the evil men,
from men who speak perverse things *and* are liars,
13 Men who forsake the paths of uprightness to walk in
the ways of darkness,
14 Who rejoice to do evil and delight in the perverseness
of evil,
15 Who are crooked in their ways, wayward *and* devious
in their paths.
16 [Discretion shall watch over you, understanding shall
keep you] to deliver you from the alien woman, from the
outsider with her flattering words, [Prov. 2:11.]

ª See footnotes on Prov. 1:2 and 1:20.  ᵇ See footnote on Prov. 1:2.

# New International Version

[17] who has left the partner of her youth
and ignored the covenant she made before God.[a]
[18] Surely her house leads down to death
and her paths to the spirits of the dead.
[19] None who go to her return
or attain the paths of life.

[20] Thus you will walk in the ways of the good
and keep to the paths of the righteous.
[21] For the upright will live in the land,
and the blameless will remain in it;
[22] but the wicked will be cut off from the land,
and the unfaithful will be torn from it.

## Wisdom Bestows Well-Being

**3** My son, do not forget my teaching,
but keep my commands in your heart,
[2] for they will prolong your life many years
and bring you peace and prosperity.

[3] Let love and faithfulness never leave you;
bind them around your neck,
write them on the tablet of your heart.
[4] Then you will win favor and a good name
in the sight of God and man.

[5] Trust in the LORD with all your heart
and lean not on your own understanding;
[6] in all your ways submit to him,
and he will make your paths straight.[b]

[7] Do not be wise in your own eyes;
fear the LORD and shun evil.
[8] This will bring health to your body
and nourishment to your bones.

[9] Honor the LORD with your wealth,
with the firstfruits of all your crops;
[10] then your barns will be filled to overflowing,
and your vats will brim over with new wine.

[11] My son, do not despise the LORD's discipline,
and do not resent his rebuke,
[12] because the LORD disciplines those he loves,
as a father the son he delights in.[c]

[13] Blessed are those who find wisdom,
those who gain understanding,
[14] for she is more profitable than silver
and yields better returns than gold.
[15] She is more precious than rubies;
nothing you desire can compare with her.
[16] Long life is in her right hand;
in her left hand are riches and honor.
[17] Her ways are pleasant ways,
and all her paths are peace.
[18] She is a tree of life to those who take hold of her;
those who hold her fast will be blessed.

[19] By wisdom the LORD laid the earth's foundations,
by understanding he set the heavens in place;

# Amplified Bible

[17] Who forsakes the husband *and* guide of her youth and forgets the covenant of her God.
[18] For her house sinks down to death and her paths to the spirits [of the dead].
[19] None who go to her return again, neither do they attain *or* regain the paths of life.

[20] So may you walk in the way of good men, and keep to the paths of the [consistently] righteous (the upright, in right standing with God).
[21] For the upright shall dwell in the land, and the men of integrity, blameless *and* complete [in God's sight], shall remain in it;
[22] But the wicked shall be cut off from the earth, and the treacherous shall be rooted out of it.

**3** My son, forget not my law *or* teaching, but let your heart keep my commandments;
[2] For length of days and years of a life [worth living] and tranquility [inward and outward and continuing through old age till death], these shall they add to you.
[3] Let not mercy and kindness [shutting out all hatred and selfishness] and truth [shutting out all deliberate hypocrisy or falsehood] forsake you; bind them about your neck, write them upon the tablet of your heart. [Col. 3:9-12.]
[4] So shall you find favor, good understanding, *and* high esteem in the sight [or judgment] of God and man. [Luke 2:52.]
[5] Lean on, trust in, *and* be confident in the Lord with all your heart *and* mind and do not rely on your own insight *or* understanding.
[6] In all your ways know, recognize, *and* acknowledge Him, and He will direct *and* make straight *and* plain your paths.
[7] Be not wise in your own eyes; reverently fear *and* worship the Lord and turn [entirely] away from evil. [Prov. 8:13.]
[8] It shall be health to your nerves *and* sinews, and marrow *and* moistening to your bones.
[9] Honor the Lord with your capital *and* sufficiency [from righteous labors] and with the firstfruits of all your income; [Deut. 26:2; Mal. 3:10; Luke 14:13, 14.]
[10] So shall your storage places be filled with plenty, and your vats shall be overflowing with new wine. [Deut. 28:8.]
[11] My son, do not despise *or* shrink from the chastening of the Lord [His correction by punishment or by subjection to suffering or trial]; neither be weary of *or* impatient about *or* loathe *or* abhor His reproof, [Ps. 94:12; Heb. 12:5, 6; Rev. 3:19.]
[12] For whom the Lord loves He corrects, even as a father corrects the son in whom he delights.
[13] Happy (blessed, fortunate, enviable) is the man who finds skillful *and* godly Wisdom, and the man who gets understanding [drawing it forth from God's Word and life's experiences],
[14] For the gaining of it is better than the gaining of silver, and the profit of it better than fine gold.
[15] Skillful *and* godly [a]Wisdom is more precious than rubies; and nothing you can wish for is to be compared to her. [Job 28:12-18.]
[16] Length of days is in her right hand, and in her left hand are riches and honor. [Prov. 8:12-21; I Tim. 4:8.]
[17] Her ways are highways of pleasantness, and all her paths are peace.
[18] She is a tree of life to those who lay hold on her; and happy (blessed, fortunate, to be envied) is everyone who holds her fast.
[19] The Lord by skillful *and* godly Wisdom has founded the earth; by understanding He has established the heavens. [Col. 1:16.]

---

[a] 17 Or *covenant of her God*   [b] 6 Or *will direct your paths*
[c] 12 Hebrew; Septuagint *loves, / and he chastens everyone he accepts as his child*

[a] See footnote on Prov. 1:20.

## New International Version

20 by his knowledge the watery depths were divided,
and the clouds let drop the dew.

21 My son, do not let wisdom and understanding out of
your sight,
preserve sound judgment and discretion;
22 they will be life for you,
an ornament to grace your neck.
23 Then you will go on your way in safety,
and your foot will not stumble.
24 When you lie down, you will not be afraid;
when you lie down, your sleep will be sweet.
25 Have no fear of sudden disaster
or of the ruin that overtakes the wicked,
26 for the LORD will be at your side
and will keep your foot from being snared.

27 Do not withhold good from those to whom it is due,
when it is in your power to act.
28 Do not say to your neighbor,
"Come back tomorrow and I'll give it to you" —
when you already have it with you.
29 Do not plot harm against your neighbor,
who lives trustfully near you.
30 Do not accuse anyone for no reason —
when they have done you no harm.

31 Do not envy the violent
or choose any of their ways.

32 For the LORD detests the perverse
but takes the upright into his confidence.
33 The LORD's curse is on the house of the wicked,
but he blesses the home of the righteous.
34 He mocks proud mockers
but shows favor to the humble and oppressed.
35 The wise inherit honor,
but fools get only shame.

### Get Wisdom at Any Cost

4 Listen, my sons, to a father's instruction;
pay attention and gain understanding.
2 I give you sound learning,
so do not forsake my teaching.
3 For I too was a son to my father,
still tender, and cherished by my mother.
4 Then he taught me, and he said to me,
"Take hold of my words with all your heart;
keep my commands, and you will live.
5 Get wisdom, get understanding;
do not forget my words or turn away from them.
6 Do not forsake wisdom, and she will protect you;
love her, and she will watch over you.
7 The beginning of wisdom is this: Get[a] wisdom.
Though it cost all you have,[b] get understanding.
8 Cherish her, and she will exalt you;
embrace her, and she will honor you.

## Amplified Bible

20 By His knowledge the deeps were broken up, and the
skies distill the dew.
21 My son, let them not escape from your sight, but keep
sound *and* godly Wisdom and discretion,
22 And they will be life to your inner self, and a gracious
ornament to your neck (your outer self).
23 Then you will walk in your way securely *and* in confident trust, and you shall not dash your foot *or* stumble.
[Ps. 91:11, 12; Prov. 10:9.]
24 When you lie down, you shall not be afraid; yes, you
shall lie down, and your sleep shall be sweet.
25 Be not afraid of sudden terror *and* panic, nor of the
stormy blast *or* the storm and ruin of the wicked when it
comes [for you will be guiltless],
26 For the Lord shall be your confidence, firm *and*
strong, and shall keep your foot from being caught [in a
trap or some hidden danger].
27 Withhold not good from those to whom it is due [its
rightful owners], when it is in the power of your hand to do
it. [Rom. 13:7; Gal. 6:10.]
28 Do not say to your neighbor, Go, and come again; and
tomorrow I will give it—when you have it with you. [Lev.
19:13; Deut. 24:15.]
29 Do not contrive *or* dig up *or* cultivate evil against your
neighbor, who dwells trustingly *and* confidently beside
you.
30 Contend not with a man for no reason—when he has
done you no wrong. [Rom. 12:18.]
31 Do not resentfully envy *and* be jealous of an unscrupulous, grasping man, and choose none of his ways. [Ps.
37:1; 73:3; Prov. 24:1.]
32 For the perverse are an abomination [extremely disgusting and detestable] to the Lord; but His confidential
communion *and* secret counsel are with the [uncompro-
misingly] righteous (those who are upright and in right
standing with Him). [Ps. 25:14.]
33 The curse of the Lord is in *and* on the house of the
wicked, but He declares blessed (joyful and favored with
blessings) the home of the just *and* consistently righteous.
[Ps. 37:22; Zech. 5:4; Mal. 2:2.]
34 Though He scoffs at the scoffers *and* scorns the
scorners, yet He gives His undeserved favor to the low [in
rank], the humble, *and* the afflicted. [James 4:6; I Pet. 5:5.]
35 The wise shall inherit glory (all honor and good) but
shame is the highest rank conferred on [self-confident]
fools. [Isa. 32:6.]

4 Hear, my sons, the instruction of a father, and pay attention in order to gain *and* to know intelligent discernment, comprehension, *and* interpretation [of spiritual
matters].
2 For I give you good doctrine [what is to be received];
do not forsake my teaching.
3 When I [Solomon] was a son with my father [David],
tender and the only son in the sight of my mother [Bath-
sheba],
4 He taught me and said to me, Let your heart hold fast
my words; keep my commandments and live. [I Chron.
28:9; Eph. 6:4.]
5 Get skillful *and* godly Wisdom, get understanding
(discernment, comprehension, and interpretation); do not
forget and do not turn back from the words of my mouth.
6 Forsake not [Wisdom], and she will keep, defend, *and*
protect you; love her, and she will guard you.
7 The beginning of Wisdom is: get Wisdom (skillful and
godly Wisdom)! [For skillful *and* godly Wisdom is the
principal thing.] And with all you have gotten, get understanding (discernment, comprehension, and interpretation). [James 1:5.]
8 Prize Wisdom highly *and* exalt her, and she will exalt
*and* promote you; she will bring you to honor when you
embrace her.

---

*a* 7 Or *Wisdom is supreme; therefore get*   *b* 7 Or *wisdom. / Whatever
else you get*

## New International Version

⁹She will give you a garland to grace your head
and present you with a glorious crown."

¹⁰Listen, my son, accept what I say,
and the years of your life will be many.
¹¹I instruct you in the way of wisdom
and lead you along straight paths.
¹²When you walk, your steps will not be hampered;
when you run, you will not stumble.
¹³Hold on to instruction, do not let it go;
guard it well, for it is your life.
¹⁴Do not set foot on the path of the wicked
or walk in the way of evildoers.
¹⁵Avoid it, do not travel on it;
turn from it and go on your way.
¹⁶For they cannot rest until they do evil;
they are robbed of sleep till they make someone
stumble.
¹⁷They eat the bread of wickedness
and drink the wine of violence.

¹⁸The path of the righteous is like the morning sun,
shining ever brighter till the full light of day.
¹⁹But the way of the wicked is like deep darkness;
they do not know what makes them stumble.

²⁰My son, pay attention to what I say;
turn your ear to my words.
²¹Do not let them out of your sight,
keep them within your heart;
²²for they are life to those who find them
and health to one's whole body.
²³Above all else, guard your heart,
for everything you do flows from it.
²⁴Keep your mouth free of perversity;
keep corrupt talk far from your lips.
²⁵Let your eyes look straight ahead;
fix your gaze directly before you.
²⁶Give careful thought to theᵃ paths for your feet
and be steadfast in all your ways.
²⁷Do not turn to the right or the left;
keep your foot from evil.

### Warning Against Adultery

**5** My son, pay attention to my wisdom,
turn your ear to my words of insight,
²that you may maintain discretion
and your lips may preserve knowledge.
³For the lips of the adulterous woman drip honey,
and her speech is smoother than oil;
⁴but in the end she is bitter as gall,
sharp as a double-edged sword.
⁵Her feet go down to death;
her steps lead straight to the grave.
⁶She gives no thought to the way of life;
her paths wander aimlessly, but she does not
know it.

⁷Now then, my sons, listen to me;
do not turn aside from what I say.
⁸Keep to a path far from her,
do not go near the door of her house,
⁹lest you lose your honor to others
and your dignityᵇ to one who is cruel,
¹⁰lest strangers feast on your wealth
and your toil enrich the house of another.

## Amplified Bible

⁹She shall give to your head a wreath of gracefulness; a
crown of beauty *and* glory will she deliver to you.
¹⁰Hear, O my son, and receive my sayings, and the years
of your life shall be many.
¹¹I have taught you in the way of skillful *and* godly Wisdom [which is comprehensive insight into the ways and
purposes of God]; I have led you in paths of uprightness.
¹²When you walk, your steps shall not be hampered
[your path will be clear and open]; and when you run, you
shall not stumble.
¹³Take firm hold of instruction, do not let go; guard her,
for she is your life.
¹⁴Enter not into the path of the wicked, and go not in
the way of evil men.
¹⁵Avoid it, do not go on it; turn from it and pass on.
¹⁶For they cannot sleep unless they have caused trouble
*or* vexation; their sleep is taken away unless they have
caused someone to fall.
¹⁷For they eat the bread of wickedness and drink the
wine of violence.
¹⁸But the path of the [uncompromisingly] just *and* righteous is like the light of dawn, that shines more and more
(brighter and clearer) until [it reaches its full strength and
glory in] the perfect day [to be prepared]. [II Sam. 23:4;
Matt. 5:14; Phil. 2:15.]
¹⁹The way of the wicked is like deep darkness; they do
not know over what they stumble. [John 12:35.]
²⁰My son, attend to my words; consent *and* submit to
my sayings.
²¹Let them not depart from your sight; keep them in the
center of your heart.
²²For they are life to those who find them, healing *and*
health to all their flesh.
²³Keep *and* guard your heart with all vigilance *and*
above all that you guard, for out of it flow the springs of
life.
²⁴Put away from you false *and* dishonest speech, and
willful *and* contrary talk put far from you.
²⁵Let your eyes look right on [with fixed purpose], and
let your gaze be straight before you.
²⁶Consider well the path of your feet, and let all your
ways be established *and* ordered aright.
²⁷Turn not aside to the right hand or to the left; remove
your foot from evil.

**5** My son, be attentive to my Wisdom [godly Wisdom
learned by actual and costly experience], and incline
your ear to my understanding [of what is becoming and
prudent for you],
²That you may exercise proper discrimination *and* discretion and your lips may guard *and* keep knowledge *and*
the wise answer [to temptation].
³For the lips of a loose woman drip honey as a honeycomb, and her mouth is smoother than oil; [Ezek. 20:30;
Col. 2:8-10; II Pet. 2:14-17.]
⁴But in the end she is bitter as wormwood, sharp as a
two-edged *and* devouring sword.
⁵Her feet go down to death; her steps take hold of Sheol
(Hades, the place of the dead).
⁶She loses sight of *and* walks not in the path of life; her
ways wind about aimlessly, and you cannot know them.
⁷Now therefore, my sons, listen to me, and depart not
from the words of my mouth.
⁸Let your way in life be far from her, and come not near
the door of her house [avoid the very scenes of tempta-
tion], [Prov. 4:15; Rom. 16:17; I Thess. 5:19-22.]
⁹Lest you give your honor to others and your years to
those without mercy,
¹⁰Lest strangers [and false teachings] take their fill of
your strength *and* wealth and your labors go to the house
of an alien [from God]—

---

ᵃ 26 Or *Make level*    ᵇ 9 Or *years*

## New International Version

11 At the end of your life you will groan,
when your flesh and body are spent.
12 You will say, "How I hated discipline!
How my heart spurned correction!
13 I would not obey my teachers
or turn my ear to my instructors.
14 And I was soon in serious trouble
in the assembly of God's people."

15 Drink water from your own cistern,
running water from your own well.
16 Should your springs overflow in the streets,
your streams of water in the public squares?
17 Let them be yours alone,
never to be shared with strangers.
18 May your fountain be blessed,
and may you rejoice in the wife of your youth.
19 A loving doe, a graceful deer—
may her breasts satisfy you always,
may you ever be intoxicated with her love.
20 Why, my son, be intoxicated with another man's wife?
Why embrace the bosom of a wayward woman?

21 For your ways are in full view of the LORD,
and he examines all your paths.
22 The evil deeds of the wicked ensnare them;
the cords of their sins hold them fast.
23 For lack of discipline they will die,
led astray by their own great folly.

### Warnings Against Folly

**6** My son, if you have put up security for your neighbor,
if you have shaken hands in pledge for a stranger,
2 you have been trapped by what you said,
ensnared by the words of your mouth.
3 So do this, my son, to free yourself,
since you have fallen into your neighbor's hands:
Go—to the point of exhaustion—[a]
and give your neighbor no rest!
4 Allow no sleep to your eyes,
no slumber to your eyelids.
5 Free yourself, like a gazelle from the hand of the hunter,
like a bird from the snare of the fowler.

6 Go to the ant, you sluggard;
consider its ways and be wise!
7 It has no commander,
no overseer or ruler,
8 yet it stores its provisions in summer
and gathers its food at harvest.

9 How long will you lie there, you sluggard?
When will you get up from your sleep?
10 A little sleep, a little slumber,
a little folding of the hands to rest—
11 and poverty will come on you like a thief
and scarcity like an armed man.

12 A troublemaker and a villain,
who goes about with a corrupt mouth,

## Amplified Bible

11 And you groan *and* mourn when your end comes,
when your flesh and body are consumed,
12 And you say, How I hated instruction *and* discipline,
and my heart despised reproof!
13 I have not obeyed the voice of my teachers nor submitted *and* consented to those who instructed me.
14 [The extent and boldness of] my sin involved almost all evil [in the estimation] of the congregation *and* the community.
15 *a* Drink waters out of your own cistern [of a pure marriage relationship], and fresh running waters out of your own well.
16 Should your offspring be dispersed abroad as water brooks in the streets?
17 [Confine yourself to your own wife] let your children be for you alone, and not the children of strangers with you.
18 Let your fountain [of human life] be blessed [with the rewards of fidelity], and rejoice in the wife of your youth.
19 Let her be as the loving hind and pleasant doe [tender, gentle, attractive]—let her bosom satisfy you at all times, and always be transported with delight in her love.
20 Why should you, my son, be infatuated with a loose woman, embrace the bosom of an outsider, *and* go astray?
21 For the ways of man are directly before the eyes of the Lord, and He [Who would have us live soberly, chastely, and godly] carefully weighs all man's goings. [II Chron. 16:9; Job 31:4; 34:21; Prov. 15:3; Jer. 16:17; Hos. 7:2; Heb. 4:13.]
22 His own iniquities shall ensnare the wicked man, and he shall be held with the cords of his sin.
23 He will die for lack of discipline *and* instruction, and in the greatness of his folly he will go astray *and* be lost.

**6** My son, if you have become security for your neighbor, if you have given your pledge for a stranger *or* another,
2 You are snared with the words of your lips, you are caught by the speech of your mouth.
3 Do this now [at once and earnestly], my son, and deliver yourself when you have put yourself into the [b] power of your neighbor; go, bestir *and* humble yourself, and beg your neighbor [to pay his debt and thereby release you].
4 Give not [unnecessary] sleep to your eyes, nor slumber to your eyelids;
5 Deliver yourself, as a roe *or* gazelle from the hand of the hunter, and as a bird from the hand of the fowler.
6 Go to the ant, you sluggard; consider her ways and be wise!—[Job 12:7.]
7 Which, having no chief, overseer, or ruler,
8 Provides her food in the summer and gathers her supplies in the harvest.
9 How long will you sleep, O sluggard? When will you arise out of your sleep? [Prov. 24:33, 34.]
10 Yet a little sleep, a little slumber, a little folding of the hands to lie down *and* sleep—
11 So will your poverty come like a robber *or* one who travels [with slowly but surely approaching steps] and your want like an armed man [making you helpless]. [Prov. 10:4; 13:4; 20:4.]
12 A worthless person, a wicked man, is he who goes about with a perverse (contrary, wayward) mouth,

---

*a* All of the Ten Commandments are reflected in the book of Proverbs; here it is the seventh, "You shall not commit adultery." *b* The Bible consistently teaches that one is not to forsake a friend, and this passage is not to be otherwise construed. But it is one thing to lend a friend money, and quite another thing to promise to pay his debts for him if he fails to do so himself. It might cost one, under the rigid customary laws governing debt, his money, his land, his bed, and his clothing—and if these were not sufficient, he and his wife and children could be sold as slaves, not to be released until the next Year of Jubilee—fifty years after the previous one. God's Word is very plain on the subject of not underwriting another person's debts (see Prov. 11:15; 17:18; 22:26).

---

*a* 3 Or *Go and humble yourself,*

## New International Version

13   who winks maliciously with his eye,
    signals with his feet
    and motions with his fingers,
14   who plots evil with deceit in his heart—
    he always stirs up conflict.
15 Therefore disaster will overtake him in an instant;
    he will suddenly be destroyed—without remedy.

16 There are six things the LORD hates,
    seven that are detestable to him:
17   haughty eyes,
    a lying tongue,
    hands that shed innocent blood,
18   a heart that devises wicked schemes,
    feet that are quick to rush into evil,
19   a false witness who pours out lies
    and a person who stirs up conflict in the
    community.

### Warning Against Adultery

20 My son, keep your father's command
    and do not forsake your mother's teaching.
21 Bind them always on your heart;
    fasten them around your neck.
22 When you walk, they will guide you;
    when you sleep, they will watch over you;
    when you awake, they will speak to you.
23 For this command is a lamp,
    this teaching is a light,
  and correction and instruction
    are the way to life,
24 keeping you from your neighbor's wife,
    from the smooth talk of a wayward woman.

25 Do not lust in your heart after her beauty
    or let her captivate you with her eyes.

26 For a prostitute can be had for a loaf of bread,
    but another man's wife preys on your very life.
27 Can a man scoop fire into his lap
    without his clothes being burned?
28 Can a man walk on hot coals
    without his feet being scorched?
29 So is he who sleeps with another man's wife;
    no one who touches her will go unpunished.

30 People do not despise a thief if he steals
    to satisfy his hunger when he is starving.
31 Yet if he is caught, he must pay sevenfold,
    though it costs him all the wealth of his house.
32 But a man who commits adultery has no sense;
    whoever does so destroys himself.
33 Blows and disgrace are his lot,
    and his shame will never be wiped away.

34 For jealousy arouses a husband's fury,
    and he will show no mercy when he takes revenge.
35 He will not accept any compensation;
    he will refuse a bribe, however great it is.

### Warning Against the Adulterous Woman

**7** My son, keep my words
    and store up my commands within you.
2 Keep my commands and you will live;
    guard my teachings as the apple of your eye.
3 Bind them on your fingers;
    write them on the tablet of your heart.
4 Say to wisdom, "You are my sister,"
    and to insight, "You are my relative."
5 They will keep you from the adulterous woman,
    from the wayward woman with her seductive words.

## Amplified Bible

13 He winks with his eyes, he speaks by shuffling *or* tapping with his feet, he makes signs [to mislead and deceive] *and* teaches with his fingers.
14 Willful *and* contrary in his heart, he devises trouble, vexation, *and* evil continually; he lets loose discord *and* sows it.
15 Therefore upon him shall the crushing weight of calamity come suddenly; suddenly shall he be broken, and that without remedy.
16 These six things the Lord hates, indeed, seven are an abomination to Him:
17 A proud look [the spirit that makes one overestimate himself and underestimate others], a lying tongue, and hands that shed innocent blood, [Ps. 120:2, 3.]
18 A heart that manufactures wicked thoughts *and* plans, feet that are swift in running to evil,
19 A false witness who breathes out lies [even under oath], and he who sows discord among his brethren.
20 My son, keep your father's [God-given] commandment and forsake not the law of [God] your mother [taught you]. [Eph. 6:1-3.]
21 Bind them continually upon your heart and tie them about your neck. [Prov. 3:3; 7:3.]
22 When you go, they [the words of your parents' God] shall lead you; when you sleep, they shall keep you; and when you waken, they shall talk with you.
23 For the commandment is a lamp, and the whole teaching [of the law] is light, and reproofs of discipline are the way of life, [Ps. 19:8; 119:105.]
24 To keep you from the evil woman, from the flattery of the tongue of a loose woman.
25 Lust not after her beauty in your heart, neither let her capture you with her eyelids.
26 For on account of a harlot a man is brought to a piece of bread, and the adulteress stalks *and* snares [as with a hook] the precious life [of a man].
27 Can a man take fire in his bosom and his clothes not be burned?
28 Can one go upon hot coals and his feet not be burned?
29 So he who cohabits with his neighbor's wife [will be tortured with evil consequences and just retribution]; he who touches her shall not be innocent *or* go unpunished.
30 Men do not despise a thief if he steals to satisfy himself when he is hungry;
31 But if he is found out, he must restore seven times [what he stole]; he must give the whole substance of his house [if necessary—to meet his fine].
32 But whoever commits adultery with a woman lacks heart *and* understanding (moral principle and prudence); he who does it is destroying his own life.
33 Wounds and disgrace will he get, and his reproach will not be wiped away.
34 For jealousy makes [the wronged] man furious; therefore he will not spare in the day of vengeance [upon the detected one].
35 He will not consider any ransom [offered to buy him off from demanding full punishment]; neither will he be satisfied, though you offer him many gifts *and* bribes.

**7** My son, keep my words; lay up within you my commandments [for use when needed] *and* treasure them.
2 Keep my commandments and live, and keep my law *and* teaching as the apple (the pupil) of your eye.
3 Bind them on your fingers; write them on the tablet of your heart.
4 Say to skillful *and* godly Wisdom, You are my sister, and regard understanding *or* insight as your intimate friend—
5 That they may keep you from the loose woman, from the adventuress who flatters with *and* makes smooth her words.

## New International Version

⁶At the window of my house
  I looked down through the lattice.
⁷I saw among the simple,
  I noticed among the young men,
  a youth who had no sense.
⁸He was going down the street near her corner,
  walking along in the direction of her house
⁹at twilight, as the day was fading,
  as the dark of night set in.

¹⁰Then out came a woman to meet him,
  dressed like a prostitute and with crafty intent.
¹¹(She is unruly and defiant,
  her feet never stay at home;
¹²now in the street, now in the squares,
  at every corner she lurks.)
¹³She took hold of him and kissed him
  and with a brazen face she said:

¹⁴"Today I fulfilled my vows,
  and I have food from my fellowship offering at home.
¹⁵So I came out to meet you;
  I looked for you and have found you!
¹⁶I have covered my bed
  with colored linens from Egypt.
¹⁷I have perfumed my bed
  with myrrh, aloes and cinnamon.
¹⁸Come, let's drink deeply of love till morning;
  let's enjoy ourselves with love!
¹⁹My husband is not at home;
  he has gone on a long journey.
²⁰He took his purse filled with money
  and will not be home till full moon."

²¹With persuasive words she led him astray;
  she seduced him with her smooth talk.
²²All at once he followed her
  like an ox going to the slaughter,
  like a deer*ᵃ* stepping into a noose*ᵇ*
²³  till an arrow pierces his liver,
  like a bird darting into a snare,
  little knowing it will cost him his life.

²⁴Now then, my sons, listen to me;
  pay attention to what I say.
²⁵Do not let your heart turn to her ways
  or stray into her paths.
²⁶Many are the victims she has brought down;
  her slain are a mighty throng.
²⁷Her house is a highway to the grave,
  leading down to the chambers of death.

### Wisdom's Call

**8** Does not wisdom call out?
  Does not understanding raise her voice?
²At the highest point along the way,
  where the paths meet, she takes her stand;
³beside the gate leading into the city,
  at the entrance, she cries aloud:
⁴"To you, O people, I call out;
  I raise my voice to all mankind.
⁵You who are simple, gain prudence;
  you who are foolish, set your hearts on it.*ᶜ*
⁶Listen, for I have trustworthy things to say;
  I open my lips to speak what is right.
⁷My mouth speaks what is true,
  for my lips detest wickedness.
⁸All the words of my mouth are just;
  none of them is crooked or perverse.

## Amplified Bible

⁶For at the window of my house I looked out through my lattice.
⁷And among the simple (empty-headed and empty-hearted) ones, I perceived among the youths a young man void of good sense,
⁸Sauntering through the street near the [loose woman's] corner; and he went the way to her house
⁹In the twilight, in the evening; night black and dense was falling [over the young man's life].

¹⁰And behold, there met him a woman, dressed as a harlot and sly *and* cunning of heart.
¹¹She is turbulent *and* willful; her feet stay not in her house;
¹²Now in the streets, now in the marketplaces, she sets her ambush at every corner.
¹³So she caught him and kissed him and with impudent face she said to him,

¹⁴Sacrifices of peace offerings were due from me; this day I paid my vows.
¹⁵So I came forth to meet you [that you might share with me the feast from my offering]; diligently I sought your face, and I have found you.
¹⁶I have spread my couch with rugs *and* cushions of tapestry, with striped sheets of fine linen of Egypt.
¹⁷I have perfumed my bed with myrrh, aloes, and cinnamon.
¹⁸Come, let us take our fill of love until morning; let us console *and* delight ourselves with love.
¹⁹For the man is not at home; he is gone on a long journey;
²⁰He has taken a bag of money with him and will come home at the day appointed [at the full moon].

²¹With much justifying *and* enticing argument she persuades him, with the allurements of her lips she leads him [to overcome his conscience and his fears] *and* forces him along.
²²Suddenly he [yields and] follows her reluctantly like an ox moving to the slaughter, like one in fetters going to the correction [to be given] to a fool *or ᵃlike a dog enticed by food to the muzzle*
²³Till a dart [of passion] pierces *and* inflames his vitals; then like a bird fluttering straight into the net [he hastens], not knowing that it will cost him his life.

²⁴Listen to me now therefore, O you sons, and be attentive to the words of my mouth.
²⁵Let not your heart incline toward her ways, do not stray into her paths.
²⁶For she has cast down many wounded; indeed, all her slain are a mighty host. [Neh. 13:26.]
²⁷Her house is the way to Sheol (Hades, the place of the dead), going down to the chambers of death.

**8** Does not skillful *and* godly Wisdom cry out, and understanding raise her voice [in contrast to the loose woman]?
²On the top of the heights beside the way, where the paths meet, stands Wisdom [skillful and godly];
³At the gates at the entrance of the town, at the coming in at the doors, she cries out:
⁴To you, O men, I call, and my voice is directed to the sons of men.
⁵O you simple *and* thoughtless ones, understand prudence; you [self-confident] fools, be of an understanding heart. [Isa. 32:6.]
⁶Hear, for I will speak excellent *and* princely things; and the opening of my lips shall be for right things.
⁷For my mouth shall utter truth, and wrongdoing is detestable *and* loathsome to my lips.
⁸All the words of my mouth are righteous (upright and in right standing with God); there is nothing contrary to truth or crooked in them.

*ᵃ 22* Syriac (see also Septuagint); Hebrew *fool*    *ᵇ 22* The meaning of the Hebrew for this line is uncertain.    *ᶜ 5* Septuagint; Hebrew *foolish, instruct your minds*

*ᵃ The Septuagint* (Greek translation of the Old Testament) so reads at this point.

## New International Version

⁹To the discerning all of them are right;
    they are upright to those who have found
    knowledge.
¹⁰Choose my instruction instead of silver,
    knowledge rather than choice gold,
¹¹for wisdom is more precious than rubies,
    and nothing you desire can compare with her.

¹²"I, wisdom, dwell together with prudence;
    I possess knowledge and discretion.
¹³To fear the LORD is to hate evil;
    I hate pride and arrogance,
    evil behavior and perverse speech.
¹⁴Counsel and sound judgment are mine;
    I have insight, I have power.
¹⁵By me kings reign
    and rulers issue decrees that are just;
¹⁶by me princes govern,
    and nobles—all who rule on earth.ᵃ
¹⁷I love those who love me,
    and those who seek me find me.
¹⁸With me are riches and honor,
    enduring wealth and prosperity.
¹⁹My fruit is better than fine gold;
    what I yield surpasses choice silver.
²⁰I walk in the way of righteousness,
    along the paths of justice,
²¹bestowing a rich inheritance on those who love me
    and making their treasuries full.

²²"The LORD brought me forth as the first of his works,ᵇ,ᶜ
    before his deeds of old;
²³I was formed long ages ago,
    at the very beginning, when the world came to be.
²⁴When there were no watery depths, I was given birth,
    when there were no springs overflowing with water;
²⁵before the mountains were settled in place,
    before the hills, I was given birth,
²⁶before he made the world or its fields
    or any of the dust of the earth.
²⁷I was there when he set the heavens in place,
    when he marked out the horizon on the face of the
    deep,
²⁸when he established the clouds above
    and fixed securely the fountains of the deep,
²⁹when he gave the sea its boundary
    so the waters would not overstep his command,
    and when he marked out the foundations of the earth.
30    Then I was constantlyᵈ at his side.
    I was filled with delight day after day,
    rejoicing always in his presence,
³¹rejoicing in his whole world
    and delighting in mankind.

³²"Now then, my children, listen to me;
    blessed are those who keep my ways.
³³Listen to my instruction and be wise;
    do not disregard it.
³⁴Blessed are those who listen to me,
    watching daily at my doors,
    waiting at my doorway.
³⁵For those who find me find life
    and receive favor from the LORD.
³⁶But those who fail to find me harm themselves;
    all who hate me love death."

---

ᵃ 16 Some Hebrew manuscripts and Septuagint; other Hebrew
manuscripts *all righteous rulers*    ᵇ 22 Or *way*; or *dominion*
ᶜ 22 Or *The LORD possessed me at the beginning of his work*; or *The LORD
brought me forth at the beginning of his work*    ᵈ 30 Or *was the artisan*;
or *was a little child*

## Amplified Bible

⁹They are all plain to him who understands [and opens
his heart], and right to those who find knowledge [and
live by it].
¹⁰Receive my instruction in preference to [striving for]
silver, and knowledge rather than choice gold,
¹¹For skillful *and* godly Wisdom is better than rubies *or*
pearls, and all the things that may be desired are not to be
compared to it. [Job 28:15; Ps. 19:10; 119:127.]
¹²I, Wisdom [from God], make prudence my dwelling,
and I find out knowledge and discretion. [James 1:5.]
¹³The reverent fear *and* worshipful awe of the Lord [in-
cludes] the hatred of evil; pride, arrogance, the evil way,
and perverted *and* twisted speech I hate.
¹⁴I have counsel and sound knowledge, I have understanding, I have might *and* power.
¹⁵By me kings reign and rulers decree justice. [Dan.
2:21; Rom. 13:1.]
¹⁶By me princes rule, and nobles, even all the judges
*and* governors of the earth.
¹⁷I love those who love me, and those who seek me early
*and* diligently shall find me. [I Sam. 2:30; Ps. 91:14; John
14:21; James 1:5.]
¹⁸Riches and honor are with me, enduring wealth and
righteousness (uprightness in every area and relation, and
right standing with God). [Prov. 3:16; Matt. 6:33.]
¹⁹My fruit is better than gold, yes, than refined gold,
and my increase than choice silver.
²⁰I [Wisdom] walk in the way of righteousness (moral
and spiritual rectitude in every area and relation), in the
midst of the paths of justice,
²¹That I may cause those who love me to inherit [true]
riches and that I may fill their treasuries.
²²The Lord formed *and* brought me [Wisdom] forth at
the beginning of His way, before His acts of old.
²³I [Wisdom] was inaugurated *and* ordained from everlasting, from the beginning, before ever the earth existed.
[John 1:1; I Cor. 1:24.]
²⁴When there were no deeps, I was brought forth, when
there were no fountains laden with water.
²⁵Before the mountains were settled, before the hills, I
was brought forth, [Job 15:7, 8.]
²⁶While as yet He had not made the land or the fields or
the first of the dust of the earth.
²⁷When He prepared the heavens, I [Wisdom] was
there; when He drew a circle upon the face of the deep
*and* stretched out the firmament over it,
²⁸When He made firm the skies above, when He established the fountains of the deep,
²⁹When He gave to the sea its limit *and* His decree that
the waters should not transgress [across the boundaries
set by] His command, when He appointed the foundations
of the earth—[Job 38:10, 11; Ps. 104:6-9; Jer. 5:22.]
³⁰Then I [Wisdom] was ᵃbeside Him as a master *and*
director of the work; and I was daily His delight, rejoicing
before Him always, [Matt. 3:17; John 1:2, 18.]
³¹Rejoicing in His inhabited earth and delighting in the
sons of men. [Ps. 16:3.]
³²Now therefore listen to me, O you sons; for blessed
(happy, fortunate, to be envied) are those who keep my
ways. [Ps. 119:1, 2; 128:1, 2; Luke 11:28.]
³³Hear instruction and be wise, and do not refuse *or*
neglect it.
³⁴Blessed (happy, fortunate, to be envied) is the man
who listens to me, watching daily at my gates, waiting at
the posts of my doors.
³⁵For whoever finds me [Wisdom] finds life and draws
forth *and* obtains favor from the Lord.
³⁶But he who misses me *or* sins against me wrongs *and*
injures himself; all who hate me love *and* court death.

---

ᵃ See Wisdom here present and involved at creation as an attribute of
God.

## New International Version

### Invitations of Wisdom and Folly

**9** Wisdom has built her house;
  she has set up[a] its seven pillars.
[2] She has prepared her meat and mixed her wine;
  she has also set her table.
[3] She has sent out her servants, and she calls
  from the highest point of the city,
[4]  "Let all who are simple come to my house!"
  To those who have no sense she says,
[5]  "Come, eat my food
  and drink the wine I have mixed.
[6] Leave your simple ways and you will live;
  walk in the way of insight."

[7] Whoever corrects a mocker invites insults;
  whoever rebukes the wicked incurs abuse.
[8] Do not rebuke mockers or they will hate you;
  rebuke the wise and they will love you.
[9] Instruct the wise and they will be wiser still;
  teach the righteous and they will add to their
  learning.

[10] The fear of the LORD is the beginning of wisdom,
  and knowledge of the Holy One is understanding.
[11] For through wisdom[b] your days will be many,
  and years will be added to your life.
[12] If you are wise, your wisdom will reward you;
  if you are a mocker, you alone will suffer.

[13] Folly is an unruly woman;
  she is simple and knows nothing.
[14] She sits at the door of her house,
  on a seat at the highest point of the city,
[15] calling out to those who pass by,
  who go straight on their way,
[16]  "Let all who are simple come to my house!"
  To those who have no sense she says,
[17]  "Stolen water is sweet;
  food eaten in secret is delicious!"
[18] But little do they know that the dead are there,
  that her guests are deep in the realm of the dead.

### Proverbs of Solomon

**10** The proverbs of Solomon:

A wise son brings joy to his father,
  but a foolish son brings grief to his mother.

[2] Ill-gotten treasures have no lasting value,
  but righteousness delivers from death.

[3] The LORD does not let the righteous go hungry,
  but he thwarts the craving of the wicked.

[4] Lazy hands make for poverty,
  but diligent hands bring wealth.

[5] He who gathers crops in summer is a prudent son,
  but he who sleeps during harvest is a disgraceful son.

[6] Blessings crown the head of the righteous,
  but violence overwhelms the mouth of the wicked.[c]

[7] The name of the righteous is used in blessings,[d]
  but the name of the wicked will rot.

[8] The wise in heart accept commands,
  but a chattering fool comes to ruin.

## Amplified Bible

**9** Wisdom has built her house; she has hewn out *and* set up her seven [perfect number of] pillars.
[2] She has killed her beasts, she has mixed her [spiritual] wine; she has also set her table. [Matt. 22:2-4.]
[3] She has sent out her maids to cry from the highest places of the town:
[4] Whoever is simple (easily led astray and wavering), let him turn in here! As for him who lacks understanding, [God's] Wisdom says to him,
[5] Come, eat of my bread and drink of the [spiritual] wine which I have mixed. [Isa. 55:1; John 6:27.]
[6] Leave off, simple ones [forsake the foolish and simple-minded] and live! And walk in the way of insight *and* understanding.

[7] He who rebukes a scorner heaps upon himself abuse, and he who reproves a wicked man gets for himself bruises.
[8] Reprove not a scorner, lest he hate you; reprove a wise man, and he will love you. [Ps. 141:5.]
[9] Give instruction to a wise man and he will be yet wiser; teach a righteous man (one upright and in right standing with God) and he will increase in learning.
[10] The reverent *and* worshipful fear of the Lord is the beginning (the chief and choice part) of Wisdom, and the knowledge of the Holy One is insight *and* understanding.
[11] For by me [Wisdom from God] your days shall be multiplied, and the years of your life shall be increased.
[12] If you are wise, you are wise for yourself; if you scorn, you alone will bear it *and* pay the penalty.
[13] The foolish woman is noisy; she is simple *and* open to all forms of evil, she [willfully and recklessly] knows nothing whatever [of eternal value].
[14] For she sits at the door of her house *or* on a seat in the conspicuous places of the town,
[15] Calling to those who pass by, who go uprightly on their way:
[16] Whoever is simple (wavering and easily led astray), let him turn in here! And as for him who lacks understanding, she says to him,
[17] Stolen waters (pleasures) are sweet [because they are forbidden]; and bread eaten in secret is pleasant. [Prov. 20:17.]
[18] But he knows not that the shades of the dead are there [specters haunting the scene of past transgressions], and that her invited guests are [already sunk] in the depths of Sheol (the lower world, Hades, the place of the dead).

**10** The proverbs of Solomon: A wise son makes a glad father, but a foolish *and* self-confident son is the grief of his mother.

[2] Treasures of wickedness profit nothing, but righteousness (moral and spiritual rectitude in every area and relation) delivers from death.

[3] The Lord will not allow the [uncompromisingly] righteous to famish, but He thwarts the desire of the wicked. [Ps. 34:9, 10; 37:25.]

[4] He becomes poor who works with a slack *and* idle hand, but the hand of the diligent makes rich.

[5] He who gathers in summer is a wise son, but he who sleeps in harvest is a son who causes shame.

[6] Blessings are upon the head of the [uncompromisingly] righteous (the upright, in right standing with God) but the mouth of the wicked conceals violence.

[7] The memory of the [uncompromisingly] righteous is a blessing, but the name of the wicked shall rot. [Ps. 112:6; 9:5.]

[8] The wise in heart will accept *and* obey commandments, but the foolish of lips will fall headlong.

---

*a* 1 Septuagint, Syriac and Targum; Hebrew *has hewn out*
*b* 11 Septuagint, Syriac and Targum; Hebrew *me*   *c* 6 Or *righteous,* /
*but the mouth of the wicked conceals violence*   *d* 7 See Gen. 48:20.

## New International Version

⁹Whoever walks in integrity walks securely,
but whoever takes crooked paths will be found out.

¹⁰Whoever winks maliciously causes grief,
and a chattering fool comes to ruin.

¹¹The mouth of the righteous is a fountain of life,
but the mouth of the wicked conceals violence.

¹²Hatred stirs up conflict,
but love covers over all wrongs.

¹³Wisdom is found on the lips of the discerning,
but a rod is for the back of one who has no sense.

¹⁴The wise store up knowledge,
but the mouth of a fool invites ruin.

¹⁵The wealth of the rich is their fortified city,
but poverty is the ruin of the poor.

¹⁶The wages of the righteous is life,
but the earnings of the wicked are sin and death.

¹⁷Whoever heeds discipline shows the way to life,
but whoever ignores correction leads others astray.

¹⁸Whoever conceals hatred with lying lips
and spreads slander is a fool.

¹⁹Sin is not ended by multiplying words,
but the prudent hold their tongues.

²⁰The tongue of the righteous is choice silver,
but the heart of the wicked is of little value.

²¹The lips of the righteous nourish many,
but fools die for lack of sense.

²²The blessing of the LORD brings wealth,
without painful toil for it.

²³A fool finds pleasure in wicked schemes,
but a person of understanding delights in wisdom.

²⁴What the wicked dread will overtake them;
what the righteous desire will be granted.

²⁵When the storm has swept by, the wicked are gone,
but the righteous stand firm forever.

²⁶As vinegar to the teeth and smoke to the eyes,
so are sluggards to those who send them.

²⁷The fear of the LORD adds length to life,
but the years of the wicked are cut short.

²⁸The prospect of the righteous is joy,
but the hopes of the wicked come to nothing.

²⁹The way of the LORD is a refuge for the blameless,
but it is the ruin of those who do evil.

³⁰The righteous will never be uprooted,
but the wicked will not remain in the land.

³¹From the mouth of the righteous comes the fruit of
wisdom,
but a perverse tongue will be silenced.

³²The lips of the righteous know what finds favor,
but the mouth of the wicked only what is perverse.

## Amplified Bible

⁹He who walks uprightly walks securely, but he who
takes a crooked way shall be found out *and* punished.

¹⁰He who winks with the eye [craftily and with malice]
causes sorrow; the foolish of lips will fall headlong *but ᵃhe
who boldly reproves makes peace.*

¹¹The mouth of the [uncompromisingly] righteous man
is a well of life, but the mouth of the wicked conceals violence.

¹²Hatred stirs up contentions, but love covers all transgressions.

¹³On the lips of him who has discernment skillful *and*
godly ᵇWisdom is found, but discipline *and* the rod are for
the back of him who is without sense *and* understanding.

¹⁴Wise men store up knowledge [in mind and heart],
but the mouth of the foolish is a present destruction.

¹⁵The rich man's wealth is his strong city; the poverty of
the poor is their ruin. [Ps. 52:7; I Tim. 6:17.]

¹⁶The earnings of the righteous (the upright, in right
standing with God) lead to life, but the profit of the wicked
leads to further sin. [Rom. 6:21; I Tim. 6:10.]

¹⁷He who heeds instruction *and* correction is [not only
himself] in the way of life [but also] is a way of life for
others. And he who neglects *or* refuses reproof [not only
himself] goes astray [but also] causes to err *and* is a path
toward ruin for others.

¹⁸He who hides hatred is of lying lips, and he who utters
slander is a [self-confident] fool. [Prov. 26:24-26.]

¹⁹In a multitude of words transgression is not lacking,
but he who restrains his lips is prudent.

²⁰The tongues of those who are upright *and* in right
standing with God are as choice silver; the minds of those
who are wicked *and* out of harmony with God are of little
value.

²¹The lips of the [uncompromisingly] righteous feed
*and* guide many, but fools die for want of understanding
*and* heart.

²²The blessing of the Lord—it makes [truly] rich, and
He adds no sorrow with it [neither does toiling increase it].

²³It is as sport to a [self-confident] fool to do wickedness, but to have skillful *and* godly Wisdom is pleasure
*and* relaxation to a man of understanding.

²⁴The thing a wicked man fears shall come upon him,
but the desire of the [uncompromisingly] righteous shall
be granted.

²⁵When the whirlwind passes, the wicked are no more,
but the [uncompromisingly] righteous have an everlasting
foundation. [Ps. 125:1; Matt. 7:24-27.]

²⁶As vinegar to the teeth and as smoke to the eyes, so is
the sluggard to those who employ *and* send him.

²⁷The reverent *and* worshipful fear of the Lord prolongs
one's days, but the years of the wicked shall be made short.

²⁸The hope of the [uncompromisingly] righteous (the
upright, in right standing with God) is gladness, but the
expectation of the wicked (those who are out of harmony
with God) comes to nothing.

²⁹The way of the Lord is strength *and* a stronghold to
the upright, but it is destruction to the workers of iniquity.

³⁰The [consistently] righteous shall never be removed,
but the wicked shall not inhabit the earth [eventually].
[Ps. 37:22; 125:1.]

³¹The mouths of the righteous (those harmonious with
God) bring forth skillful *and* godly Wisdom, but the perverse tongue shall be cut down [like a barren and rotten
tree].

³²The lips of the [uncompromisingly] righteous know
[and therefore utter] what is acceptable, but the mouth
of the wicked knows [and therefore speaks only] what is
obstinately willful *and* contrary.

---

ᵃ *The Septuagint* (Greek translation of the Old Testament) so reads at
this point. ᵇ Recall that "Wisdom" is capitalized throughout the book of
Proverbs as a reminder of its divine implications. See footnotes on Prov.
1:2 and Prov. 1:20.

## New International Version

**11** The LORD detests dishonest scales,
but accurate weights find favor with him.

2 When pride comes, then comes disgrace,
but with humility comes wisdom.

3 The integrity of the upright guides them,
but the unfaithful are destroyed by their duplicity.

4 Wealth is worthless in the day of wrath,
but righteousness delivers from death.

5 The righteousness of the blameless makes their paths straight,
but the wicked are brought down by their own wickedness.

6 The righteousness of the upright delivers them,
but the unfaithful are trapped by evil desires.

7 Hopes placed in mortals die with them;
all the promise of[a] their power comes to nothing.

8 The righteous person is rescued from trouble,
and it falls on the wicked instead.

9 With their mouths the godless destroy their neighbors,
but through knowledge the righteous escape.

10 When the righteous prosper, the city rejoices;
when the wicked perish, there are shouts of joy.

11 Through the blessing of the upright a city is exalted,
but by the mouth of the wicked it is destroyed.

12 Whoever derides their neighbor has no sense,
but the one who has understanding holds their tongue.

13 A gossip betrays a confidence,
but a trustworthy person keeps a secret.

14 For lack of guidance a nation falls,
but victory is won through many advisers.

15 Whoever puts up security for a stranger will surely suffer,
but whoever refuses to shake hands in pledge is safe.

16 A kindhearted woman gains honor,
but ruthless men gain only wealth.

17 Those who are kind benefit themselves,
but the cruel bring ruin on themselves.

18 A wicked person earns deceptive wages,
but the one who sows righteousness reaps a sure reward.

19 Truly the righteous attain life,
but whoever pursues evil finds death.

20 The LORD detests those whose hearts are perverse,
but he delights in those whose ways are blameless.

21 Be sure of this: The wicked will not go unpunished,
but those who are righteous will go free.

22 Like a gold ring in a pig's snout
is a beautiful woman who shows no discretion.

23 The desire of the righteous ends only in good,
but the hope of the wicked only in wrath.

## Amplified Bible

**11** A false balance *and* unrighteous dealings are extremely offensive *and* shamefully sinful to the Lord, but a just weight is His delight. [Lev. 19:35, 36; Prov. 16:11.]

2 When swelling *and* pride come, then emptiness *and* shame come also, but with the humble (those who are lowly, who have been pruned or chiseled by trial, and renounce self) are skillful *and* godly Wisdom *and* soundness.

3 The integrity of the upright shall guide them, but the willful contrariness *and* crookedness of the treacherous shall destroy them.

4 Riches provide no security in any day of wrath *and* judgment, but righteousness (uprightness and right standing with God) delivers from death. [Prov. 10:2; Zeph. 1:18.]

5 The righteousness of the blameless shall rectify *and* make plain their way *and* keep it straight, but the wicked shall fall by their own wickedness.

6 The righteousness of the upright [their rectitude in every area and relation] shall deliver them, but the treacherous shall be taken in their own iniquity *and* greedy desire.

7 When the wicked man dies, his hope [for the future] perishes; and the expectation of the godless comes to nothing.

8 The [uncompromisingly] righteous is delivered out of trouble, and the wicked gets into it instead.

9 With his mouth the godless man destroys his neighbor, but through knowledge *and* superior discernment shall the righteous be delivered.

10 When it goes well with the [uncompromisingly] righteous, the city rejoices, but when the wicked perish, there are shouts of joy.

11 By the blessing of the influence of the upright *and* God's favor [because of them] the city is exalted, but it is overthrown by the mouth of the wicked.

12 He who belittles *and* despises his neighbor lacks sense, but a man of understanding keeps silent.

13 He who goes about as a talebearer reveals secrets, but he who is trustworthy *and* faithful in spirit keeps the matter hidden.

14 Where no wise guidance is, the people fall, but in the multitude of counselors there is safety.

15 He who becomes security for an outsider shall smart for it, but he who hates suretyship is secure [from its penalties].

16 A gracious *and* good woman wins honor [for her husband], and violent men win riches but *[a] a woman who hates righteousness is a throne of dishonor for him.*

17 The merciful, kind, *and* generous man benefits himself [for his deeds return to bless him], but he who is cruel *and* callous [to the wants of others] brings on himself retribution.

18 The wicked man earns deceitful wages, but he who sows righteousness (moral and spiritual rectitude in every area and relation) shall have a sure reward [permanent and satisfying]. [Hos. 10:12; Gal. 6:8, 9; James 3:18.]

19 He who is steadfast in righteousness (uprightness and right standing with God) attains to life, but he who pursues evil does it to his own death.

20 They who are willfully contrary in heart are extremely disgusting *and* shamefully vile in the eyes of the Lord, but such as are blameless *and* wholehearted in their ways are His delight!

21 Assuredly [I pledge it] the wicked shall not go unpunished, but the multitude of the [uncompromisingly] righteous shall be delivered.

22 As a ring of gold in a swine's snout, so is a fair woman who is without discretion.

23 The desire of the [consistently] righteous brings only good, but the expectation of the wicked brings wrath.

---

*a 7* Two Hebrew manuscripts; most Hebrew manuscripts, Vulgate, Syriac and Targum *When the wicked die, their hope perishes; / all they expected from*

*a The Septuagint* (Greek translation of the Old Testament) so reads at this point.

## New International Version

24 One person gives freely, yet gains even more;
another withholds unduly, but comes to poverty.

25 A generous person will prosper;
whoever refreshes others will be refreshed.

26 People curse the one who hoards grain,
but they pray God's blessing on the one who is
willing to sell.

27 Whoever seeks good finds favor,
but evil comes to one who searches for it.

28 Those who trust in their riches will fall,
but the righteous will thrive like a green leaf.

29 Whoever brings ruin on their family will inherit only
wind,
and the fool will be servant to the wise.

30 The fruit of the righteous is a tree of life,
and the one who is wise saves lives.

31 If the righteous receive their due on earth,
how much more the ungodly and the sinner!

**12** Whoever loves discipline loves knowledge,
but whoever hates correction is stupid.

2 Good people obtain favor from the LORD,
but he condemns those who devise wicked schemes.

3 No one can be established through wickedness,
but the righteous cannot be uprooted.

4 A wife of noble character is her husband's crown,
but a disgraceful wife is like decay in his bones.

5 The plans of the righteous are just,
but the advice of the wicked is deceitful.

6 The words of the wicked lie in wait for blood,
but the speech of the upright rescues them.

7 The wicked are overthrown and are no more,
but the house of the righteous stands firm.

8 A person is praised according to their prudence,
and one with a warped mind is despised.

9 Better to be a nobody and yet have a servant
than pretend to be somebody and have no food.

10 The righteous care for the needs of their animals,
but the kindest acts of the wicked are cruel.

11 Those who work their land will have abundant food,
but those who chase fantasies have no sense.

12 The wicked desire the stronghold of evildoers,
but the root of the righteous endures.

13 Evildoers are trapped by their sinful talk,
and so the innocent escape trouble.

14 From the fruit of their lips people are filled with good
things,
and the work of their hands brings them reward.

15 The way of fools seems right to them,
but the wise listen to advice.

16 Fools show their annoyance at once,
but the prudent overlook an insult.

## Amplified Bible

24 There are those who [generously] scatter abroad, and
yet increase more; there are those who withhold more
than is fitting *or* what is justly due, but it results only in
want.

25 The liberal person shall be enriched, and he who waters shall himself be watered. [II Cor. 9:6-10.]

26 The people curse him who holds back grain [when the
public needs it], but a blessing [from God and man] is upon
the head of him who sells it.

27 He who diligently seeks good seeks [God's] favor, but
he who searches after evil, it shall come upon him.

28 He who leans on, trusts in, *and* is confident in his
riches shall fall, but the [uncompromisingly] righteous
shall flourish like a green bough.

29 He who troubles his own house shall inherit the wind,
and the foolish shall be servant to the wise of heart.

30 The fruit of the [uncompromisingly] righteous is a
tree of life, and he who is wise captures human lives [for
God, as a fisher of men—he gathers and receives them for
eternity]. [Matt. 4:19; I Cor. 9:19; James 5:20.]

31 Behold, the [uncompromisingly] righteous shall be
recompensed on earth; how much more the wicked and
the sinner! *And* a *if the righteous are barely saved, what will
become of the ungodly and wicked?* [I Pet. 4:18.]

**12** Whoever loves instruction *and* correction loves
knowledge, but he who hates reproof is like a
brute beast, stupid *and* indiscriminating.

2 A good man obtains favor from the Lord, but a man of
wicked devices He condemns.

3 A man shall not be established by wickedness, but the
root of the [uncompromisingly] righteous shall never be
moved.

4 A virtuous *and* worthy wife [earnest and strong in
character] is a crowning joy to her husband, but she who
makes him ashamed is as rottenness in his bones. [Prov.
31:23; I Cor. 11:7.]

5 The thoughts *and* purposes of the [consistently] righteous are honest *and* reliable, but the counsels *and* designs of the wicked are treacherous.

6 The words of the wicked lie in wait for blood, but the
mouth of the upright shall deliver them *and* the innocent
ones [thus endangered].

7 The wicked are overthrown and are not, but the house
of the [uncompromisingly] righteous shall stand.

8 A man shall be commended according to his Wisdom
[godly Wisdom, which is comprehensive insight into the
ways and purposes of God], but he who is of a perverse
heart shall be despised.

9 Better is he who is lightly esteemed but works for his
own support than he who assumes honor for himself and
lacks bread.

10 A [consistently] righteous man regards the life of his
beast, but even the tender mercies of the wicked are cruel.
[Deut. 25:4.]

11 He who tills his land shall be satisfied with bread, but
he who follows worthless pursuits is lacking in sense *and*
is without understanding.

12 The wicked desire the booty of evil men, but the root of
the [uncompromisingly] righteous yields [richer fruitage].

13 The wicked is [dangerously] snared by the transgression of his lips, but the [uncompromisingly] righteous
shall come out of trouble.

14 From the fruit of his words a man shall be satisfied
with good, and the work of a man's hands shall come back
to him [as a harvest].

15 The way of a fool is right in his own eyes, but he who
listens to counsel is wise. [Prov. 3:7; 9:9; 21:2.]

16 A fool's wrath is quickly *and* openly known, but a prudent man ignores an insult.

---

a *The Septuagint* (Greek translation of the Old Testament) so reads at
this point.

## New International Version

17 An honest witness tells the truth,
but a false witness tells lies.

18 The words of the reckless pierce like swords,
but the tongue of the wise brings healing.

19 Truthful lips endure forever,
but a lying tongue lasts only a moment.

20 Deceit is in the hearts of those who plot evil,
but those who promote peace have joy.

21 No harm overtakes the righteous,
but the wicked have their fill of trouble.

22 The LORD detests lying lips,
but he delights in people who are trustworthy.

23 The prudent keep their knowledge to themselves,
but a fool's heart blurts out folly.

24 Diligent hands will rule,
but laziness ends in forced labor.

25 Anxiety weighs down the heart,
but a kind word cheers it up.

26 The righteous choose their friends carefully,
but the way of the wicked leads them astray.

27 The lazy do not roast[a] any game,
but the diligent feed on the riches of the hunt.

28 In the way of righteousness there is life;
along that path is immortality.

**13** A wise son heeds his father's instruction,
but a mocker does not respond to rebukes.

2 From the fruit of their lips people enjoy good things,
but the unfaithful have an appetite for violence.

3 Those who guard their lips preserve their lives,
but those who speak rashly will come to ruin.

4 A sluggard's appetite is never filled,
but the desires of the diligent are fully satisfied.

5 The righteous hate what is false,
but the wicked make themselves a stench
and bring shame on themselves.

6 Righteousness guards the person of integrity,
but wickedness overthrows the sinner.

7 One person pretends to be rich, yet has nothing;
another pretends to be poor, yet has great wealth.

8 A person's riches may ransom their life,
but the poor cannot respond to threatening rebukes.

9 The light of the righteous shines brightly,
but the lamp of the wicked is snuffed out.

10 Where there is strife, there is pride,
but wisdom is found in those who take advice.

11 Dishonest money dwindles away,
but whoever gathers money little by little makes it
grow.

12 Hope deferred makes the heart sick,
but a longing fulfilled is a tree of life.

13 Whoever scorns instruction will pay for it,
but whoever respects a command is rewarded.

## Amplified Bible

17 He who breathes out truth shows forth righteousness (uprightness and right standing with God), but a false witness utters deceit.

18 There are those who speak rashly, like the piercing of a sword, but the tongue of the wise brings healing.

19 Truthful lips shall be established forever, but a lying tongue is [credited] but for a moment.

20 Deceit is in the hearts of those who devise evil, but for the counselors of peace there is joy.

21 No [actual] evil, misfortune, or calamity shall come upon the righteous, but the wicked shall be filled with evil, misfortune, and calamity. [Job 5:19; Ps. 91:3; Prov. 12:13; Isa. 46:4; Jer. 1:8; Dan. 6:27; II Tim. 4:18.]

22 Lying lips are extremely disgusting and hateful to the Lord, but they who deal faithfully are His delight. [Prov. 6:17; 11:20; Rev. 22:15.]

23 A prudent man is reluctant to display his knowledge, but the heart of [self-confident] fools proclaims their folly. [Isa. 32:6.]

24 The hand of the diligent will rule, but the slothful will be put to forced labor.

25 Anxiety in a man's heart weighs it down, but an encouraging word makes it glad. [Ps. 50:4; Prov. 15:13.]

26 The [consistently] righteous man is a guide to his neighbor, but the way of the wicked causes others to go astray.

27 The slothful man does not catch his game or roast it once he kills it, but the diligent man gets precious possessions.

28 Life is in the way of righteousness (moral and spiritual rectitude in every area and relation), and in its pathway there is no death but immortality (perpetual, eternal life). [John 3:36; 4:36; 8:51; 11:26; I Cor. 15:54; Gal. 6:8.]

**13** A wise son heeds [and is the fruit of] his father's instruction and correction, but a scoffer listens not to rebuke.

2 A good man eats good from the fruit of his mouth, but the desire of the treacherous is for violence.

3 He who guards his mouth keeps his life, but he who opens wide his lips comes to ruin.

4 The appetite of the sluggard craves and gets nothing, but the appetite of the diligent is abundantly supplied. [Prov. 10:4.]

5 A [consistently] righteous man hates lying and deceit, but a wicked man is loathsome [his very breath spreads pollution] and he comes [surely] to shame.

6 Righteousness (rightness and justice in every area and relation) guards him who is upright in the way, but wickedness plunges into sin and overthrows the sinner.

7 One man considers himself rich, yet has nothing [to keep permanently]; another man considers himself poor, yet has great [and indestructible] riches. [Prov. 12:9; Luke 12:20, 21.]

8 A rich man can buy his way out of threatened death by paying a ransom, but the poor man does not even have to listen to threats [from the envious].

9 The light of the [uncompromisingly] righteous [is within him—it grows brighter and] rejoices, but the lamp of the wicked [furnishes only a derived, temporary light and] shall be put out shortly.

10 By pride and insolence comes only contention, but with the well-advised is skillful and godly Wisdom.

11 Wealth [not earned but] won in haste or unjustly or from the production of things for vain or detrimental use [such riches] will dwindle away, but he who gathers little by little will increase [his riches].

12 Hope deferred makes the heart sick, but when the desire is fulfilled, it is a tree of life.

13 Whoever despises the word and counsel [of God] brings destruction upon himself, but he who [reverently] fears and respects the commandment [of God] is rewarded.

---

a 27 The meaning of the Hebrew for this word is uncertain.

## New International Version

¹⁴The teaching of the wise is a fountain of life,
  turning a person from the snares of death.

¹⁵Good judgment wins favor,
  but the way of the unfaithful leads to their
    destruction.ᵃ

¹⁶All who are prudent act withᵇ knowledge,
  but fools expose their folly.

¹⁷A wicked messenger falls into trouble,
  but a trustworthy envoy brings healing.

¹⁸Whoever disregards discipline comes to poverty and
    shame,
  but whoever heeds correction is honored.

¹⁹A longing fulfilled is sweet to the soul,
  but fools detest turning from evil.

²⁰Walk with the wise and become wise,
  for a companion of fools suffers harm.

²¹Trouble pursues the sinner,
  but the righteous are rewarded with good things.

²²A good person leaves an inheritance for their
    children's children,
  but a sinner's wealth is stored up for the righteous.

²³An unplowed field produces food for the poor,
  but injustice sweeps it away.

²⁴Whoever spares the rod hates their children,
  but the one who loves their children is careful to
    discipline them.

²⁵The righteous eat to their hearts' content,
  but the stomach of the wicked goes hungry.

**14** The wise woman builds her house,
  but with her own hands the foolish one tears hers
    down.

²Whoever fears the LORD walks uprightly,
  but those who despise him are devious in their
    ways.

³A fool's mouth lashes out with pride,
  but the lips of the wise protect them.

⁴Where there are no oxen, the manger is empty,
  but from the strength of an ox come abundant
    harvests.

⁵An honest witness does not deceive,
  but a false witness pours out lies.

⁶The mocker seeks wisdom and finds none,
  but knowledge comes easily to the discerning.

⁷Stay away from a fool,
  for you will not find knowledge on their lips.

⁸The wisdom of the prudent is to give thought to their
    ways,
  but the folly of fools is deception.

⁹Fools mock at making amends for sin,
  but goodwill is found among the upright.

¹⁰Each heart knows its own bitterness,
  and no one else can share its joy.

¹¹The house of the wicked will be destroyed,
  but the tent of the upright will flourish.

¹²There is a way that appears to be right,
  but in the end it leads to death.

¹³Even in laughter the heart may ache,
  and rejoicing may end in grief.

## Amplified Bible

¹⁴The teaching of the wise is a fountain of life, that one
may avoid the snares of death.

¹⁵Good understanding wins favor, but the way of the
transgressor is hard [like the barren, dry soil or the im-
passable swamp].

¹⁶Every prudent man deals with knowledge, but a [self-
confident] fool exposes *and* flaunts his folly.

¹⁷A wicked messenger falls into evil, but a faithful ambassador brings healing.

¹⁸Poverty and shame come to him who refuses instruction *and* correction, but he who heeds reproof is honored.

¹⁹Satisfied desire is sweet to a person; therefore it is
hateful *and* exceedingly offensive to [self-confident] fools
to give up evil [upon which they have set their hearts].

²⁰He who walks [as a companion] with wise men is wise,
but he who associates with [self-confident] fools is [a fool
himself and] shall smart for it. [Isa. 32:6.]

²¹Evil pursues sinners, but the consistently upright *and*
in right standing with God is recompensed with good.

²²A good man leaves an inheritance [of moral stability
and goodness] to his children's children, and the wealth of
the sinner [finds its way eventually] into the hands of the
righteous, for whom it was laid up.

²³Much food is in the tilled land of the poor, but there
are those who are destroyed because of injustice.

²⁴He who spares his rod [of discipline] hates his son,
but he who loves him disciplines diligently *and* punishes
him early. [Prov. 19:18; 22:15; 23:13; 29:15, 17.]

²⁵The [uncompromisingly] righteous eats to his own
satisfaction, but the stomach of the wicked is in want.

**14** Every wise woman builds her house, but the foolish one tears it down with her own hands.

²He who walks in uprightness reverently *and* worshipfully fears the Lord, but he who is contrary *and* devious in
his ways despises Him.

³In the ᵃfool's own mouth is a rod [to shame] his pride,
but the wise men's lips preserve them.

⁴Where no oxen are, the grain crib is empty, but much
increase [of crops] comes by the strength of the ox.

⁵A faithful witness will not lie, but a false witness
breathes out falsehoods.

⁶A scoffer seeks Wisdom in vain [for his very attitude
blinds and deafens him to it], but knowledge is easy to him
who [being teachable] understands.

⁷Go from the presence of a foolish *and* self-confident
man, for you will not find knowledge on his lips.

⁸The Wisdom [godly Wisdom, which is comprehensive
insight into the ways and purposes of God] of the prudent
is to understand his way, but the folly of [self-confident]
fools is to deceive.

⁹Fools make a mock of sin *and* sin mocks the fools [who
are its victims; a sin offering made by them only mocks
them, bringing them disappointment and disfavor], but
among the upright there is the favor of God. [Prov. 10:23.]

¹⁰The heart knows its own bitterness, and no stranger
shares its joy.

¹¹The house of the wicked shall be overthrown, but the
tent of the upright shall flourish.

¹²There is a way which seems right to a man *and* appears straight before him, but at the end of it is the way
of death.

¹³Even in laughter the heart is sorrowful, and the end of
mirth is heaviness *and* grief.

## New International Version

14 The faithless will be fully repaid for their ways,
and the good rewarded for theirs.

15 The simple believe anything,
but the prudent give thought to their steps.

16 The wise fear the LORD and shun evil,
but a fool is hotheaded and yet feels secure.

17 A quick-tempered person does foolish things,
and the one who devises evil schemes is hated.

18 The simple inherit folly,
but the prudent are crowned with knowledge.

19 Evildoers will bow down in the presence of the good,
and the wicked at the gates of the righteous.

20 The poor are shunned even by their neighbors,
but the rich have many friends.

21 It is a sin to despise one's neighbor,
but blessed is the one who is kind to the needy.

22 Do not those who plot evil go astray?
But those who plan what is good find[a] love and
faithfulness.

23 All hard work brings a profit,
but mere talk leads only to poverty.

24 The wealth of the wise is their crown,
but the folly of fools yields folly.

25 A truthful witness saves lives,
but a false witness is deceitful.

26 Whoever fears the LORD has a secure fortress,
and for their children it will be a refuge.

27 The fear of the LORD is a fountain of life,
turning a person from the snares of death.

28 A large population is a king's glory,
but without subjects a prince is ruined.

29 Whoever is patient has great understanding,
but one who is quick-tempered displays folly.

30 A heart at peace gives life to the body,
but envy rots the bones.

31 Whoever oppresses the poor shows contempt for their
Maker,
but whoever is kind to the needy honors God.

32 When calamity comes, the wicked are brought down,
but even in death the righteous seek refuge in God.

33 Wisdom reposes in the heart of the discerning
and even among fools she lets herself be known.[b]

34 Righteousness exalts a nation,
but sin condemns any people.

35 A king delights in a wise servant,
but a shameful servant arouses his fury.

**15** A gentle answer turns away wrath,
but a harsh word stirs up anger.

2 The tongue of the wise adorns knowledge,
but the mouth of the fool gushes folly.

3 The eyes of the LORD are everywhere,
keeping watch on the wicked and the good.

## Amplified Bible

14 The backslider in heart [from God and from fearing God] shall be filled with [the fruit of] his own ways, and a good man shall be satisfied with [the fruit of] his ways [with the holy thoughts and actions which his heart prompts and in which he delights].

15 The simpleton believes every word he hears, but the prudent man looks *and* considers well where he is going.

16 A wise man suspects danger and cautiously avoids evil, but the fool bears himself insolently and is [presumptuously] confident.

17 He who foams up quickly *and* flies into a passion deals foolishly, and a man of wicked plots *and* plans is hated.

18 The simple acquire folly, but the prudent are crowned with knowledge.

19 The evil men bow before the good, and the wicked [stand suppliantly] at the gates of the [uncompromisingly] righteous.

20 The poor is hated even by his own neighbor, but the rich has many friends.

21 He who despises his neighbor sins [against God, his fellowman, and himself], but happy (blessed and fortunate) is he who is kind *and* merciful to the poor.

22 Do they not err who devise evil *and* wander from the way of life? But loving-kindness *and* mercy, loyalty *and* faithfulness, shall be to those who devise good.

23 In all labor there is profit, but idle talk leads only to poverty.

24 The crown of the wise is their wealth of Wisdom, but the foolishness of [self-confident] fools is [nothing but] folly.

25 A truthful witness saves lives, but a deceitful witness speaks lies [and endangers lives].

26 In the reverent *and* worshipful fear of the Lord there is strong confidence, and His children shall always have a place of refuge.

27 Reverent *and* worshipful fear of the Lord is a fountain of life, that one may avoid the snares of death. [John 4:10, 14.]

28 In a multitude of people is the king's glory, but in a lack of people is the prince's ruin.

29 He who is slow to anger has great understanding, but he who is hasty of spirit exposes *and* exalts his folly. [Prov. 16:32; James 1:19.]

30 A calm *and* undisturbed mind *and* heart are the life *and* health of the body, but envy, jealousy, *and* wrath are like rottenness of the bones.

31 He who oppresses the poor reproaches, mocks, *and* insults his Maker, but he who is kind *and* merciful to the needy honors Him. [Prov. 17:5; Matt. 25:40, 45.]

32 The wicked is overthrown through his wrongdoing *and* calamity, but the [consistently] righteous has hope *and* confidence even in death.

33 Wisdom rests [silently] in the mind *and* heart of him who has understanding, but that which is in the inward part of [self-confident] fools is made known. [Isa. 32:6.]

34 Uprightness *and* right standing with God (moral and spiritual rectitude in every area and relation) elevate a nation, but sin is a reproach to any people.

35 The king's favor is toward a wise *and* discreet servant, but his wrath is against him who does shamefully. [Matt. 24:45, 47.]

**15** A soft answer turns away wrath, but grievous words stir up anger. [Prov. 25:15.]

2 The tongue of the wise utters knowledge rightly, but the mouth of the [self-confident] fool pours out folly.

3 The eyes of the Lord are in every place, keeping watch upon the evil and the good. [Job 34:21; Prov. 5:21; Jer. 16:17; 32:19; Heb. 4:13.]

---

*a* 22 Or *show*    *b* 33 Hebrew; Septuagint and Syriac *discerning / but in the heart of fools she is not known*

## New International Version

4The soothing tongue is a tree of life,
    but a perverse tongue crushes the spirit.

5A fool spurns a parent's discipline,
    but whoever heeds correction shows prudence.

6The house of the righteous contains great treasure,
    but the income of the wicked brings ruin.

7The lips of the wise spread knowledge,
    but the hearts of fools are not upright.

8The LORD detests the sacrifice of the wicked,
    but the prayer of the upright pleases him.

9The LORD detests the way of the wicked,
    but he loves those who pursue righteousness.

10Stern discipline awaits anyone who leaves the path;
    the one who hates correction will die.

11Death and Destructiona lie open before the LORD—
    how much more do human hearts!

12Mockers resent correction,
    so they avoid the wise.

13A happy heart makes the face cheerful,
    but heartache crushes the spirit.

14The discerning heart seeks knowledge,
    but the mouth of a fool feeds on folly.

15All the days of the oppressed are wretched,
    but the cheerful heart has a continual feast.

16Better a little with the fear of the LORD
    than great wealth with turmoil.

17Better a small serving of vegetables with love
    than a fattened calf with hatred.

18A hot-tempered person stirs up conflict,
    but the one who is patient calms a quarrel.

19The way of the sluggard is blocked with thorns,
    but the path of the upright is a highway.

20A wise son brings joy to his father,
    but a foolish man despises his mother.

21Folly brings joy to one who has no sense,
    but whoever has understanding keeps a straight
    course.

22Plans fail for lack of counsel,
    but with many advisers they succeed.

23A person finds joy in giving an apt reply—
    and how good is a timely word!

24The path of life leads upward for the prudent
    to keep them from going down to the realm of the
    dead.

25The LORD tears down the house of the proud,
    but he sets the widow's boundary stones in place.

26The LORD detests the thoughts of the wicked,
    but gracious words are pure in his sight.

27The greedy bring ruin to their households,
    but the one who hates bribes will live.

28The heart of the righteous weighs its answers,
    but the mouth of the wicked gushes evil.

29The LORD is far from the wicked,
    but he hears the prayer of the righteous.

## Amplified Bible

4A gentle tongue [with its healing power] is a tree of life, but willful contrariness in it breaks down the spirit.

5A fool despises his father's instruction *and* correction, but he who regards reproof acquires prudence.

6In the house of the [uncompromisingly] righteous is great [priceless] treasure, but with the income of the wicked is trouble *and* vexation.

7The lips of the wise disperse knowledge [sifting it as chaff from the grain]; not so the minds *and* hearts of the self-confident *and* foolish.

8The sacrifice of the wicked is an abomination, hateful *and* exceedingly offensive to the Lord, but the prayer of the upright is His delight! [Isa. 1:11; Jer. 6:20; Amos 5:22.]

9The way of the wicked is an abomination, extremely disgusting *and* shamefully vile to the Lord, but He loves him who pursues righteousness (moral and spiritual rectitude in every area and relation).

10There is severe discipline for him who forsakes God's way; and he who hates reproof will die [physically, morally, and spiritually].

11Sheol (the place of the dead) and Abaddon (the abyss, the final place of the accuser Satan) are both before the Lord—how much more, then, the hearts of the children of men? [Job 26:6; Ps. 139:8; Rev. 9:2; 20:1, 2.]

12A scorner has no love for one who rebukes him; neither will he go to the wise [for counsel].

13A glad heart makes a cheerful countenance, but by sorrow of heart the spirit is broken. [Prov. 17:22.]

14The mind of him who has understanding seeks knowledge and inquires after *and* craves it, but the mouth of the [self-confident] fool feeds on folly. [Isa. 32:6.]

15All the days of the desponding *and* afflicted are made evil [by anxious thoughts and forebodings], but he who has a glad heart has a continual feast [regardless of circumstances].

16Better is little with the reverent, worshipful fear of the Lord than great *and* rich treasure and trouble with it. [Ps. 37:16; Prov. 16:8; I Tim. 6:6.]

17Better is a dinner of herbs where love is than a fatted ox and hatred with it. [Prov. 17:1.]

18A hot-tempered man stirs up strife, but he who is slow to anger appeases contention.

19The way of the sluggard is overgrown with thorns [it pricks, lacerates, and entangles him], but the way of the righteous is plain *and* raised like a highway.

20A wise son makes a glad father, but a self-confident *and* foolish man despises his mother *and* puts her to shame.

21Folly is pleasure to him who is without heart *and* sense, but a man of understanding walks uprightly [making straight his course]. [Eph. 5:15.]

22Where there is no counsel, purposes are frustrated, but with many counselors they are accomplished.

23A man has joy in making an apt answer, and a word spoken at the right moment—how good it is!

24The path of the wise leads upward to life, that he may avoid [the gloom] in the depths of Sheol (Hades, the place of the dead). [Phil. 3:20; Col. 3:1, 2.]

25The Lord tears down the house of the proud, but He makes secure the boundaries of the [consecrated] widow.

26The thoughts of the wicked are shamefully vile *and* exceedingly offensive to the Lord, but the words of the pure are pleasing words to Him.

27He who is greedy for unjust gain troubles his own household, but he who hates bribes will live. [Isa. 5:8; Jer. 17:11.]

28The mind of the [uncompromisingly] righteous studies how to answer, but the mouth of the wicked pours out evil things. [I Pet. 3:15.]

29The Lord is far from the wicked, but He hears the prayer of the [consistently] righteous (the upright, in right standing with Him).

---

a 11 Hebrew *Abaddon*

## New International Version

30 Light in a messenger's eyes brings joy to the heart,
and good news gives health to the bones.

31 Whoever heeds life-giving correction
will be at home among the wise.

32 Those who disregard discipline despise themselves,
but the one who heeds correction gains
understanding.

33 Wisdom's instruction is to fear the LORD,
and humility comes before honor.

**16** To humans belong the plans of the heart,
but from the LORD comes the proper answer of
the tongue.

2 All a person's ways seem pure to them,
but motives are weighed by the LORD.

3 Commit to the LORD whatever you do,
and he will establish your plans.

4 The LORD works out everything to its proper end—
even the wicked for a day of disaster.

5 The LORD detests all the proud of heart.
Be sure of this: They will not go unpunished.

6 Through love and faithfulness sin is atoned for;
through the fear of the LORD evil is avoided.

7 When the LORD takes pleasure in anyone's way,
he causes their enemies to make peace with them.

8 Better a little with righteousness
than much gain with injustice.

9 In their hearts humans plan their course,
but the LORD establishes their steps.

10 The lips of a king speak as an oracle,
and his mouth does not betray justice.

11 Honest scales and balances belong to the LORD;
all the weights in the bag are of his making.

12 Kings detest wrongdoing,
for a throne is established through righteousness.

13 Kings take pleasure in honest lips;
they value the one who speaks what is right.

14 A king's wrath is a messenger of death,
but the wise will appease it.

15 When a king's face brightens, it means life;
his favor is like a rain cloud in spring.

16 How much better to get wisdom than gold,
to get insight rather than silver!

17 The highway of the upright avoids evil;
those who guard their ways preserve their lives.

18 Pride goes before destruction,
a haughty spirit before a fall.

19 Better to be lowly in spirit along with the oppressed
than to share plunder with the proud.

20 Whoever gives heed to instruction prospers,[a]
and blessed is the one who trusts in the LORD.

21 The wise in heart are called discerning,
and gracious words promote instruction.[b]

## Amplified Bible

30 The light in the eyes [of him whose heart is joyful]
rejoices the hearts of others, and good news nourishes the
bones.

31 The ear that listens to the reproof [that leads to or
gives] life will remain among the wise.

32 He who refuses *and* ignores instruction *and* correction despises himself, but he who heeds reproof gets understanding.

33 The reverent *and* worshipful fear of the Lord brings
instruction in Wisdom, and humility comes before honor.

**16** The plans of the mind *and* orderly thinking belong
to man, but from the Lord comes the [wise] answer
of the tongue.

2 All the ways of a man are pure in his own eyes, but the
Lord weighs the spirits (the thoughts and intents of the
heart). [I Sam. 16:7; Heb. 4:12.]

3 Roll your works upon the Lord [commit and trust them
wholly to Him; He will cause your thoughts to become
agreeable to His will, and] so shall your plans be established *and* succeed.

4 The Lord has made everything [to accommodate itself
and contribute] to its own end *and* His own purpose—
even the wicked [are fitted for their role] for the day of
calamity *and* evil.

5 Everyone proud *and* arrogant in heart is disgusting,
hateful, *and* exceedingly offensive to the Lord; be assured
[I pledge it] they will not go unpunished. [Prov. 8:13;
11:20-21.]

6 By mercy *and* love, truth *and* fidelity [to God and
man—not by sacrificial offerings], iniquity is purged out
of the heart, and by the reverent, worshipful fear of the
Lord men depart from *and* avoid evil.

7 When a man's ways please the Lord, He makes even
his enemies to be at peace with him.

8 Better is a little with righteousness (uprightness in
every area and relation and right standing with God) than
great revenues with injustice. [Ps. 37:16; Prov. 15:16.]

9 A man's mind plans his way, but the Lord directs his
steps *and* makes them sure. [Ps. 37:23; Prov. 20:24; Jer.
10:23.]

10 Divinely directed decisions are on the lips of the king;
his mouth should not transgress in judgment.

11 A just balance *and* scales are the Lord's; all the
weights of the bag are His work [established on His eternal principles].

12 It is an abomination [to God and men] for kings to
commit wickedness, for a throne is established *and* made
secure by righteousness (moral and spiritual rectitude in
every area and relation).

13 Right *and* just lips are the delight of a king, and he
loves him who speaks what is right.

14 The wrath of a king is as messengers of death, but a
wise man will pacify it.

15 In the light of the king's countenance is life, and his
favor is as a cloud bringing the spring rain.

16 How much better it is to get skillful *and* godly Wisdom
than gold! And to get understanding is to be chosen rather
than silver! [Prov. 8:10, 19.]

17 The highway of the upright turns aside from evil; he
who guards his way preserves his life.

18 Pride goes before destruction, and a haughty spirit
before a fall.

19 Better it is to be of a humble spirit with the meek *and*
poor than to divide the spoil with the proud.

20 He who deals wisely *and* heeds [God's] word *and*
counsel shall find good, and whoever leans on, trusts in,
*and* is confident in the Lord—happy, blessed, *and* fortunate is he.

21 The wise in heart are called prudent, understanding,
*and* knowing, and winsome speech increases learning [in
both speaker and listener].

---

*a 20 Or whoever speaks prudently finds what is good    b 21 Or words
make a person persuasive*

## New International Version

22 Prudence is a fountain of life to the prudent,
  but folly brings punishment to fools.

23 The hearts of the wise make their mouths prudent,
  and their lips promote instruction.*

24 Gracious words are a honeycomb,
  sweet to the soul and healing to the bones.

25 There is a way that appears to be right,
  but in the end it leads to death.

26 The appetite of laborers works for them;
  their hunger drives them on.

27 A scoundrel plots evil,
  and on their lips it is like a scorching fire.

28 A perverse person stirs up conflict,
  and a gossip separates close friends.

29 A violent person entices their neighbor
  and leads them down a path that is not good.

30 Whoever winks with their eye is plotting perversity;
  whoever purses their lips is bent on evil.

31 Gray hair is a crown of splendor;
  it is attained in the way of righteousness.

32 Better a patient person than a warrior,
  one with self-control than one who takes a city.

33 The lot is cast into the lap,
  but its every decision is from the LORD.

**17** Better a dry crust with peace and quiet
  than a house full of feasting, with strife.

2 A prudent servant will rule over a disgraceful son
  and will share the inheritance as one of the family.

3 The crucible for silver and the furnace for gold,
  but the LORD tests the heart.

4 A wicked person listens to deceitful lips;
  a liar pays attention to a destructive tongue.

5 Whoever mocks the poor shows contempt for their
  Maker;
  whoever gloats over disaster will not go unpunished.

6 Children's children are a crown to the aged,
  and parents are the pride of their children.

7 Eloquent lips are unsuited to a godless fool—
  how much worse lying lips to a ruler!

8 A bribe is seen as a charm by the one who gives it;
  they think success will come at every turn.

9 Whoever would foster love covers over an offense,
  but whoever repeats the matter separates close
  friends.

10 A rebuke impresses a discerning person
  more than a hundred lashes a fool.

11 Evildoers foster rebellion against God;
  the messenger of death will be sent against them.

12 Better to meet a bear robbed of her cubs
  than a fool bent on folly.

13 Evil will never leave the house
  of one who pays back evil for good.

14 Starting a quarrel is like breaching a dam;
  so drop the matter before a dispute breaks out.

15 Acquitting the guilty and condemning the innocent—
  the LORD detests them both.

## Amplified Bible

22 Understanding is a wellspring of life to those who
have it, but to give instruction to fools is folly.

23 The mind of the wise instructs his mouth, and adds
learning *and* persuasiveness to his lips.

24 Pleasant words are as a honeycomb, sweet to the mind
and healing to the body.

25 There is a way that seems right to a man *and* appears
straight before him, but at the end of it is the way of death.

26 The appetite of the laborer works for him, for [the
need of] his mouth urges him on.

27 A worthless man devises *and* digs up mischief, and in
his lips there is as a scorching fire.

28 A perverse man sows strife, and a whisperer separates close friends. [Prov. 17:9.]

29 The exceedingly grasping, covetous, *and* violent man
entices his neighbor, leading him in a way that is not good.

30 He who shuts his eyes to devise perverse things and
who compresses his lips [as if in concealment] brings evil
to pass.

31 The hoary head is a crown of beauty *and* glory if it
is found in the way of righteousness (moral and spiritual
rectitude in every area and relation). [Prov. 20:29.]

32 He who is slow to anger is better than the mighty, he
who rules his [own] spirit than he who takes a city.

33 The lot is cast into the lap, but the decision is wholly of
the Lord [even the events that seem accidental are really
ordered by Him].

**17** Better is a dry morsel with quietness than a house
  full of feasting [on offered sacrifices] with strife.

2 A wise servant shall have rule over a son who causes
shame, and shall share in the inheritance among the
brothers.

3 The refining pot is for silver and the furnace for gold,
but the Lord tries the hearts. [Ps. 26:2; Prov. 27:21; Jer.
17:10; Mal. 3:3.]

4 An evildoer gives heed to wicked lips; and a liar listens
to a mischievous tongue.

5 Whoever mocks the poor reproaches his Maker, and
he who is glad at calamity shall not be held innocent *or* go
unpunished. [Job 31:29; Prov. 14:31; Obad. 12.]

6 Children's children are the crown of old men, and the
glory of children are their fathers. [Ps. 127:3; 128:3.]

7 Fine *or* arrogant speech does not befit [an empty-head-
ed] fool—much less do lying lips befit a prince.

8 A bribe is like a bright, precious stone that dazzles the
eyes *and* affects the mind of him who gives it; [as if by
magic] he prospers, whichever way he turns.

9 He who covers *and* forgives an offense seeks love, but
he who repeats *or* harps on a matter separates even close
friends.

10 A reproof enters deeper into a man of understanding
than a hundred lashes into a [self-confident] fool. [Isa.
32:6.]

11 An evil man seeks only rebellion; therefore a stern
*and* pitiless messenger shall be sent against him.

12 Let [the brute ferocity of] a bear robbed of her whelps
meet a man rather than a [self-confident] fool in his folly
[when he is in a rage]. [Hos. 13:8.]

13 Whoever rewards evil for good, evil shall not depart
from his house. [Ps. 109:4, 5; Jer. 18:20.]

14 The beginning of strife is as when water first trickles
[from a crack in a dam]; therefore stop contention before
it becomes worse *and* quarreling breaks out.

15 He who justifies the wicked and he who condemns the
righteous are both an abomination [exceedingly disgusting and hateful] to the Lord. [Exod. 23:7; Prov. 24:24; Isa.
5:23.]

---

*a* 23 Or *prudent / and make their lips persuasive*

## New International Version

<sup>16</sup>Why should fools have money in hand to buy wisdom,
　　when they are not able to understand it?

<sup>17</sup>A friend loves at all times,
　　and a brother is born for a time of adversity.

<sup>18</sup>One who has no sense shakes hands in pledge
　　and puts up security for a neighbor.

<sup>19</sup>Whoever loves a quarrel loves sin;
　　whoever builds a high gate invites destruction.

<sup>20</sup>One whose heart is corrupt does not prosper;
　　one whose tongue is perverse falls into trouble.

<sup>21</sup>To have a fool for a child brings grief;
　　there is no joy for the parent of a godless fool.

<sup>22</sup>A cheerful heart is good medicine,
　　but a crushed spirit dries up the bones.

<sup>23</sup>The wicked accept bribes in secret
　　to pervert the course of justice.

<sup>24</sup>A discerning person keeps wisdom in view,
　　but a fool's eyes wander to the ends of the earth.

<sup>25</sup>A foolish son brings grief to his father
　　and bitterness to the mother who bore him.

<sup>26</sup>If imposing a fine on the innocent is not good,
　　surely to flog honest officials is not right.

<sup>27</sup>The one who has knowledge uses words with restraint,
　　and whoever has understanding is even-tempered.

<sup>28</sup>Even fools are thought wise if they keep silent,
　　and discerning if they hold their tongues.

**18** An unfriendly person pursues selfish ends
　　and against all sound judgment starts quarrels.

<sup>2</sup>Fools find no pleasure in understanding
　　but delight in airing their own opinions.

<sup>3</sup>When wickedness comes, so does contempt,
　　and with shame comes reproach.

<sup>4</sup>The words of the mouth are deep waters,
　　but the fountain of wisdom is a rushing stream.

<sup>5</sup>It is not good to be partial to the wicked
　　and so deprive the innocent of justice.

<sup>6</sup>The lips of fools bring them strife,
　　and their mouths invite a beating.

<sup>7</sup>The mouths of fools are their undoing,
　　and their lips are a snare to their very lives.

<sup>8</sup>The words of a gossip are like choice morsels;
　　they go down to the inmost parts.

<sup>9</sup>One who is slack in his work
　　is brother to one who destroys.

<sup>10</sup>The name of the LORD is a fortified tower;
　　the righteous run to it and are safe.

<sup>11</sup>The wealth of the rich is their fortified city;
　　they imagine it a wall too high to scale.

<sup>12</sup>Before a downfall the heart is haughty,
　　but humility comes before honor.

## Amplified Bible

<sup>16</sup>Of what use is money in the hand of a [self-confident] fool to buy skillful *and* godly Wisdom—when he has no understanding *or* heart for it?

<sup>17</sup>A friend loves at all times, and is born, as is a brother, for adversity.

<sup>18</sup>A man void of good sense gives a pledge and becomes security for another in the presence of his neighbor.

<sup>19</sup>He who loves strife *and* is quarrelsome loves transgression *and* involves himself in guilt; he who raises high his gateway *and* is boastful *and* arrogant invites destruction.

<sup>20</sup>He who has a wayward *and* crooked mind finds no good, and he who has a willful *and* contrary tongue will fall into calamity. [James 3:8.]

<sup>21</sup>He who becomes the parent of a [self-confident] fool does it to his sorrow, and the father of [an empty-headed] fool has no joy [in him].

<sup>22</sup>A happy heart is good medicine *and* a cheerful mind works healing, but a broken spirit dries up the bones. [Prov. 12:25; 15:13, 15.]

<sup>23</sup>A wicked man receives a bribe out of the bosom (pocket) to pervert the ways of justice.

<sup>24</sup>A man of understanding sets skillful *and* godly Wisdom before his face, but the eyes of a [self-confident] fool are on the ends of the earth.

<sup>25</sup>A self-confident *and* foolish son is a grief to his father and bitterness to her who bore him.

<sup>26</sup>Also, to punish *or* fine the righteous is not good, nor to smite the noble for their uprightness.

<sup>27</sup>He who has knowledge spares his words, and a man of understanding has a cool spirit. [James 1:19.]

<sup>28</sup>Even a fool when he holds his peace is considered wise; when he closes his lips he is esteemed a man of understanding.

**18** He who willfully separates *and* estranges himself [from God and man] seeks his own desire *and* pretext to break out against all wise *and* sound judgment.

<sup>2</sup>A [self-confident] fool has no delight in understanding but only in revealing his personal opinions *and* himself.

<sup>3</sup>When the wicked comes in [to the depth of evil], he becomes a contemptuous despiser [of all that is pure and good], and with inner baseness comes outer shame *and* reproach.

<sup>4</sup>The words of a [discreet and wise] man's mouth are like deep waters [plenteous and difficult to fathom], and the fountain of skillful *and* godly Wisdom is like a gushing stream [sparkling, fresh, pure, and life-giving].

<sup>5</sup>To respect the person of the wicked *and* be partial to him, so as to deprive the [consistently] righteous of justice, is not good.

<sup>6</sup>A [self-confident] fool's lips bring contention, and his mouth invites a beating.

<sup>7</sup>A [self-confident] fool's mouth is his ruin, and his lips are a snare to himself.

<sup>8</sup>The words of a whisperer *or* talebearer are as dainty morsels; they go down into the innermost parts of the body.

<sup>9</sup>He who is loose *and* slack in his work is brother to him who is a destroyer *and* *he who does not use his endeavors to heal himself is brother to him who commits suicide.*

<sup>10</sup>The name of the Lord is a strong tower; the [consistently] righteous man [upright and in right standing with God] runs into it and is safe, high [above evil] *and* strong.

<sup>11</sup>The rich man's wealth is his strong city, and as a high protecting wall in his own imagination *and* conceit.

<sup>12</sup>Haughtiness comes before disaster, but humility before honor.

---

*a* This verse so reads in *The Septuagint* (Greek translation of the Old Testament). Its statement squarely addresses the problem of whether one has a moral right to neglect his body by "letting nature take its unhindered course" in illness.

## New International Version

<sup>13</sup>To answer before listening—
　　that is folly and shame.

<sup>14</sup>The human spirit can endure in sickness,
　　but a crushed spirit who can bear?

<sup>15</sup>The heart of the discerning acquires knowledge,
　　for the ears of the wise seek it out.

<sup>16</sup>A gift opens the way
　　and ushers the giver into the presence of the great.

<sup>17</sup>In a lawsuit the first to speak seems right,
　　until someone comes forward and cross-examines.

<sup>18</sup>Casting the lot settles disputes
　　and keeps strong opponents apart.

<sup>19</sup>A brother wronged is more unyielding than a fortified
　　city;
　　disputes are like the barred gates of a citadel.

<sup>20</sup>From the fruit of their mouth a person's stomach is
　　filled;
　　with the harvest of their lips they are satisfied.

<sup>21</sup>The tongue has the power of life and death,
　　and those who love it will eat its fruit.

<sup>22</sup>He who finds a wife finds what is good
　　and receives favor from the LORD.

<sup>23</sup>The poor plead for mercy,
　　but the rich answer harshly.

<sup>24</sup>One who has unreliable friends soon comes to ruin,
　　but there is a friend who sticks closer than a
　　brother.

**19** Better the poor whose walk is blameless
　　than a fool whose lips are perverse.

<sup>2</sup>Desire without knowledge is not good—
　　how much more will hasty feet miss the way!

<sup>3</sup>A person's own folly leads to their ruin,
　　yet their heart rages against the LORD.

<sup>4</sup>Wealth attracts many friends,
　　but even the closest friend of the poor person
　　deserts them.

<sup>5</sup>A false witness will not go unpunished,
　　and whoever pours out lies will not go free.

<sup>6</sup>Many curry favor with a ruler,
　　and everyone is the friend of one who gives gifts.

<sup>7</sup>The poor are shunned by all their relatives—
　　how much more do their friends avoid them!
Though the poor pursue them with pleading,
　　they are nowhere to be found.<sup>a</sup>

<sup>8</sup>The one who gets wisdom loves life;
　　the one who cherishes understanding will soon
　　prosper.

<sup>9</sup>A false witness will not go unpunished,
　　and whoever pours out lies will perish.

<sup>10</sup>It is not fitting for a fool to live in luxury—
　　how much worse for a slave to rule over princes!

<sup>11</sup>A person's wisdom yields patience;
　　it is to one's glory to overlook an offense.

<sup>12</sup>A king's rage is like the roar of a lion,
　　but his favor is like dew on the grass.

<sup>13</sup>A foolish child is a father's ruin,
　　and a quarrelsome wife is like
　　the constant dripping of a leaky roof.

## Amplified Bible

<sup>13</sup>He who answers a matter before he hears the facts—it
is folly and shame to him. [John 7:51.]

<sup>14</sup>The strong spirit of a man sustains him in bodily pain
*or* trouble, but a weak *and* broken spirit who can raise up
*or* bear?

<sup>15</sup>The mind of the prudent is ever getting knowledge,
and the ear of the wise is ever seeking (inquiring for and
craving) knowledge.

<sup>16</sup>A man's gift makes room for him and brings him
before great men. [Gen. 32:20; I Sam. 25:27; Prov. 17:8;
21:14.]

<sup>17</sup>He who states his case first seems right, until his rival
comes and cross-examines him.

<sup>18</sup>To cast lots puts an end to disputes and decides be-
tween powerful contenders.

<sup>19</sup>A brother offended is harder to be won over than a
strong city, and [their] contentions separate them like the
bars of a castle.

<sup>20</sup>A man's [moral] self shall be filled with the fruit of his
mouth; and with the consequence of his words he must be
satisfied [whether good or evil].

<sup>21</sup>Death and life are in the power of the tongue, and they
who indulge in it shall eat the fruit of it [for death or life].
[Matt. 12:37.]

<sup>22</sup>He who finds a [true] wife finds a good thing and ob-
tains favor from the Lord. [Prov. 19:14; 31:10.]

<sup>23</sup>The poor man uses entreaties, but the rich answers
roughly.

<sup>24</sup>The man of many friends [a friend of all the world] will
prove himself a bad friend, but there is a friend who sticks
closer than a brother.

**19** Better is a poor man who walks in his integrity
than a rich man who is perverse in his speech and
is a [self-confident] fool.

<sup>2</sup>Desire without knowledge is not good, and to be over-
hasty is to sin *and* miss the mark.

<sup>3</sup>The foolishness of man subverts his way [ruins his
affairs]; then his heart is resentful *and* frets against the
Lord.

<sup>4</sup>Wealth makes many friends, but the poor man is avoid-
ed by his neighbor. [Prov. 14:20.]

<sup>5</sup>A false witness shall not be unpunished, and he who
breathes out lies shall not escape. [Exod. 23:1; Deut. 19:16-
19; Prov. 6:19; 21:28.]

<sup>6</sup>Many will entreat the favor of a liberal man, and every
man is a friend to him who gives gifts.

<sup>7</sup>All the brothers of a poor man detest him—how much
more do his friends go far from him! He pursues them with
words, but they are gone.

<sup>8</sup>He who gains Wisdom loves his own life; he who keeps
understanding shall prosper *and* find good.

<sup>9</sup>A false witness shall not be unpunished, and he who
breathes forth lies shall perish.

<sup>10</sup>Luxury is not fitting for a [self-confident] fool—much
less for a slave to rule over princes.

<sup>11</sup>Good sense makes a man restrain his anger, and it is
his glory to overlook a transgression *or* an offense.

<sup>12</sup>The king's wrath is as terrifying as the roaring of a
lion, but his favor is as [refreshing as] dew upon the grass.
[Hos. 14:5.]

<sup>13</sup>A self-confident *and* foolish son is the [multiplied] ca-
lamity of his father, and the contentions of a wife are like a
continual dripping [of water through a chink in the roof].

---

<sup>a</sup> 7 The meaning of the Hebrew for this sentence is uncertain.

## New International Version

14 Houses and wealth are inherited from parents,
but a prudent wife is from the Lord.

15 Laziness brings on deep sleep,
and the shiftless go hungry.

16 Whoever keeps commandments keeps their life,
but whoever shows contempt for their ways will die.

17 Whoever is kind to the poor lends to the Lord,
and he will reward them for what they have done.

18 Discipline your children, for in that there is hope;
do not be a willing party to their death.

19 A hot-tempered person must pay the penalty;
rescue them, and you will have to do it again.

20 Listen to advice and accept discipline,
and at the end you will be counted among the wise.

21 Many are the plans in a person's heart,
but it is the Lord's purpose that prevails.

22 What a person desires is unfailing love[a];
better to be poor than a liar.

23 The fear of the Lord leads to life;
then one rests content, untouched by trouble.

24 A sluggard buries his hand in the dish;
he will not even bring it back to his mouth!

25 Flog a mocker, and the simple will learn prudence;
rebuke the discerning, and they will gain
knowledge.

26 Whoever robs their father and drives out their mother
is a child who brings shame and disgrace.

27 Stop listening to instruction, my son,
and you will stray from the words of knowledge.

28 A corrupt witness mocks at justice,
and the mouth of the wicked gulps down evil.

29 Penalties are prepared for mockers,
and beatings for the backs of fools.

**20** Wine is a mocker and beer a brawler;
whoever is led astray by them is not wise.

2 A king's wrath strikes terror like the roar of a lion;
those who anger him forfeit their lives.

3 It is to one's honor to avoid strife,
but every fool is quick to quarrel.

4 Sluggards do not plow in season;
so at harvest time they look but find nothing.

5 The purposes of a person's heart are deep waters,
but one who has insight draws them out.

6 Many claim to have unfailing love,
but a faithful person who can find?

7 The righteous lead blameless lives;
blessed are their children after them.

8 When a king sits on his throne to judge,
he winnows out all evil with his eyes.

9 Who can say, "I have kept my heart pure;
I am clean and without sin"?

10 Differing weights and differing measures—
the Lord detests them both.

11 Even small children are known by their actions,
so is their conduct really pure and upright?

## Amplified Bible

14 House and riches are the inheritance from fathers,
but a wise, understanding, *and* prudent wife is from the
Lord. [Prov. 18:22.]

15 Slothfulness casts one into a deep sleep, and the idle
person shall suffer hunger.

16 He who keeps the commandment [of the Lord] keeps
his own life, but he who despises His ways shall die. [Luke
10:28; 11:28.]

17 He who has pity on the poor lends to the Lord, and
that which he has given He will repay to him. [Prov. 28:27;
Eccl. 11:1; Matt. 10:42; 25:40; II Cor. 9:6-8; Heb. 6:10.]

18 Discipline your son while there is hope, but do not
[indulge your angry resentments by undue chastisements
and] set yourself to his ruin.

19 A man of great wrath shall suffer the penalty; for if
you deliver him [from the consequences], he will [feel free
to] cause you to do it again.

20 Hear counsel, receive instruction, *and* accept correction, that you may be wise in the time to come.

21 Many plans are in a man's mind, but it is the Lord's
purpose for him that will stand. [Job 23:13; Ps. 33:10, 11;
Isa. 14:26, 27; 46:10; Acts 5:39; Heb. 6:17.]

22 That which is desired in a man is loyalty *and* kindness
[and his glory and delight are his giving], but a poor man
is better than a liar.

23 The reverent, worshipful fear of the Lord leads to life,
and he who has it rests satisfied; he cannot be visited with
[actual] evil. [Job 5:19; Ps. 91:3; Prov. 12:13; Isa. 46:4; Jer.
1:8; Dan. 6:27; II Tim. 4:8.]

24 The sluggard buries his hand in the dish, and will not
so much as bring it to his mouth again.

25 Strike a scoffer, and the simple will learn prudence;
reprove a man of understanding, and he will increase in
knowledge.

26 He who does violence to his father and chases away
his mother is a son who causes shame and brings reproach.

27 Cease, my son, to hear instruction only to ignore it
*and* stray from the words of knowledge.

28 A worthless witness scoffs at justice, and the mouth of
the wicked swallows iniquity.

29 Judgments are prepared for scoffers, and stripes for
the backs of [self-confident] fools. [Isa. 32:6.]

**20** Wine is a mocker, strong drink a riotous brawler;
and whoever errs *or* reels because of it is not wise.
[Prov. 23:29, 30; Isa. 28:7; Hos. 4:11.]

2 The terror of a king is as the roaring of a lion; whoever
provokes him to anger *or* angers himself against him sins
against his own life.

3 It is an honor for a man to cease from strife *and* keep
aloof from it, but every fool will quarrel.

4 The sluggard does not plow when winter sets in; therefore he begs in harvest and has nothing.

5 Counsel in the heart of man is like water in a deep well,
but a man of understanding draws it out. [Prov. 18:4.]

6 Many a man proclaims his own loving-kindness *and*
goodness, but a faithful man who can find?

7 The righteous man walks in his integrity; blessed
(happy, fortunate, enviable) are his children after him.

8 A king who sits on the throne of judgment winnows out
all evil [like chaff] with his eyes.

9 Who can say, I have made my heart clean, I am pure
from my sin? [I Kings 8:46; II Chron. 6:36; Job 9:30; 14:4;
Ps. 51:5; I John 1:8.]

10 Diverse weights [one for buying and another for sell-
ing] and diverse measures—both of them are exceedingly
offensive *and* abhorrent to the Lord. [Deut. 25:13; Mic.
6:10, 11.]

11 Even a child is known by his acts, whether [or not]
what he does is pure and right.

---

*a 22 Or Greed is a person's shame*

## New International Version

<sup>12</sup> Ears that hear and eyes that see—
the LORD has made them both.

<sup>13</sup> Do not love sleep or you will grow poor;
stay awake and you will have food to spare.

<sup>14</sup> "It's no good, it's no good!" says the buyer—
then goes off and boasts about the purchase.

<sup>15</sup> Gold there is, and rubies in abundance,
but lips that speak knowledge are a rare jewel.

<sup>16</sup> Take the garment of one who puts up security for a
stranger;
hold it in pledge if it is done for an outsider.

<sup>17</sup> Food gained by fraud tastes sweet,
but one ends up with a mouth full of gravel.

<sup>18</sup> Plans are established by seeking advice;
so if you wage war, obtain guidance.

<sup>19</sup> A gossip betrays a confidence;
so avoid anyone who talks too much.

<sup>20</sup> If someone curses their father or mother,
their lamp will be snuffed out in pitch darkness.

<sup>21</sup> An inheritance claimed too soon
will not be blessed at the end.

<sup>22</sup> Do not say, "I'll pay you back for this wrong!"
Wait for the LORD, and he will avenge you.

<sup>23</sup> The LORD detests differing weights,
and dishonest scales do not please him.

<sup>24</sup> A person's steps are directed by the LORD.
How then can anyone understand their own way?

<sup>25</sup> It is a trap to dedicate something rashly
and only later to consider one's vows.

<sup>26</sup> A wise king winnows out the wicked;
he drives the threshing wheel over them.

<sup>27</sup> The human spirit is<sup>a</sup> the lamp of the LORD
that sheds light on one's inmost being.

<sup>28</sup> Love and faithfulness keep a king safe;
through love his throne is made secure.

<sup>29</sup> The glory of young men is their strength,
gray hair the splendor of the old.

<sup>30</sup> Blows and wounds scrub away evil,
and beatings purge the inmost being.

**21** In the LORD's hand the king's heart is a stream
of water
that he channels toward all who please him.

<sup>2</sup> A person may think their own ways are right,
but the LORD weighs the heart.

<sup>3</sup> To do what is right and just
is more acceptable to the LORD than sacrifice.

<sup>4</sup> Haughty eyes and a proud heart—
the unplowed field of the wicked—produce sin.

<sup>5</sup> The plans of the diligent lead to profit
as surely as haste leads to poverty.

<sup>6</sup> A fortune made by a lying tongue
is a fleeting vapor and a deadly snare.<sup>b</sup>

<sup>7</sup> The violence of the wicked will drag them away,
for they refuse to do what is right.

<sup>8</sup> The way of the guilty is devious,
but the conduct of the innocent is upright.

## Amplified Bible

<sup>12</sup> The hearing ear and the seeing eye—the Lord has
made both of them.

<sup>13</sup> Love not sleep, lest you come to poverty; open your
eyes and you will be satisfied with bread.

<sup>14</sup> It is worthless, it is worthless! says the buyer; but
when he goes his way, then he boasts [about his bargain].

<sup>15</sup> There is gold, and a multitude of pearls, but the lips
of knowledge are a vase of preciousness [the most precious
of all]. [Job 28:12, 16-19; Prov. 3:15; 8:11.]

<sup>16</sup> [The judge tells the creditor] Take the garment of
one who is security for a stranger; and hold him in pledge
when he is security for foreigners.

<sup>17</sup> Food gained by deceit is sweet to a man, but afterward
his mouth will be filled with gravel.

<sup>18</sup> Purposes *and* plans are established by counsel; and
[only] with good advice make *or* carry on war.

<sup>19</sup> He who goes about as a talebearer reveals secrets;
therefore associate not with him who talks too freely.
[Rom. 16:17, 18.]

<sup>20</sup> Whoever curses his father or his mother, his lamp
shall be put out in complete darkness.

<sup>21</sup> An inheritance hastily gotten [by greedy, unjust
means] at the beginning, in the end it will not be blessed.
[Prov. 28:20; Hab. 2:6.]

<sup>22</sup> Do not say, I will repay evil; wait [expectantly] for the
Lord, and He will rescue you. [II Sam. 16:12; Rom. 12:17-
19; I Thess. 5:15; I Pet. 3:9.]

<sup>23</sup> Diverse *and* deceitful weights are shamefully vile *and*
abhorrent to the Lord, and false scales are not good.

<sup>24</sup> Man's steps are ordered by the Lord. How then can a
man understand his way?

<sup>25</sup> It is a snare to a man to utter a vow [of consecration]
rashly and [not until] afterward inquire [whether he can
fulfill it].

<sup>26</sup> A wise king winnows out the wicked [from among the
good] and brings the threshing wheel over them [to separate the chaff from the grain].

<sup>27</sup> The spirit of man [that factor in human personality
which proceeds immediately from God] is the lamp of the
Lord, searching all his innermost parts. [I Cor. 2:11.]

<sup>28</sup> Loving-kindness *and* mercy, truth *and* faithfulness,
preserve the king, and his throne is upheld by [the people's] loyalty.

<sup>29</sup> The glory of young men is their strength, and the
beauty of old men is their gray head [suggesting wisdom
and experience].

<sup>30</sup> Blows that wound cleanse away evil, and strokes [for
correction] reach to the innermost parts.

**21** The king's heart is in the hand of the Lord, as are
the watercourses; He turns it whichever way He
wills.

<sup>2</sup> Every way of a man is right in his own eyes, but the
Lord weighs *and* tries the hearts. [Prov. 24:12; Luke
16:15.]

<sup>3</sup> To do righteousness and justice is more acceptable to
the Lord than sacrifice. [I Sam. 15:22; Prov. 15:8; Isa. 1:11;
Hos. 6:6; Mic. 6:7, 8.]

<sup>4</sup> Haughtiness of eyes and a proud heart, even the tillage
of the wicked *or* the lamp [of joy] to them [whatever it may
be], are sin [in the eyes of God].

<sup>5</sup> The thoughts of the [steadily] diligent tend only to
plenteousness, but everyone who is impatient *and* hasty
hastens only to want.

<sup>6</sup> Securing treasures by a lying tongue is a vapor driven
to and fro; those who seek them seek death.

<sup>7</sup> The violence of the wicked shall sweep them away, be-
cause they refuse to do justice.

<sup>8</sup> The way of the guilty is exceedingly crooked, but as
for the pure, his work is right *and* his conduct is straight.

---

<sup>a</sup> 27 Or *A person's words are*    <sup>b</sup> 6 Some Hebrew manuscripts,
Septuagint and Vulgate; most Hebrew manuscripts *vapor for those who
seek death*

## New International Version

9 Better to live on a corner of the roof
   than share a house with a quarrelsome wife.

10 The wicked crave evil;
    their neighbors get no mercy from them.

11 When a mocker is punished, the simple gain wisdom;
    by paying attention to the wise they get knowledge.

12 The Righteous One[a] takes note of the house of the wicked
    and brings the wicked to ruin.

13 Whoever shuts their ears to the cry of the poor
    will also cry out and not be answered.

14 A gift given in secret soothes anger,
    and a bribe concealed in the cloak pacifies great wrath.

15 When justice is done, it brings joy to the righteous
    but terror to evildoers.

16 Whoever strays from the path of prudence
    comes to rest in the company of the dead.

17 Whoever loves pleasure will become poor;
    whoever loves wine and olive oil will never be rich.

18 The wicked become a ransom for the righteous,
    and the unfaithful for the upright.

19 Better to live in a desert
    than with a quarrelsome and nagging wife.

20 The wise store up choice food and olive oil,
    but fools gulp theirs down.

21 Whoever pursues righteousness and love
    finds life, prosperity[b] and honor.

22 One who is wise can go up against the city of the mighty
    and pull down the stronghold in which they trust.

23 Those who guard their mouths and their tongues
    keep themselves from calamity.

24 The proud and arrogant person—"Mocker" is his name—
    behaves with insolent fury.

25 The craving of a sluggard will be the death of him,
    because his hands refuse to work.

26 All day long he craves for more,
    but the righteous give without sparing.

27 The sacrifice of the wicked is detestable—
    how much more so when brought with evil intent!

28 A false witness will perish,
    but a careful listener will testify successfully.

29 The wicked put up a bold front,
    but the upright give thought to their ways.

30 There is no wisdom, no insight, no plan
    that can succeed against the LORD.

31 The horse is made ready for the day of battle,
    but victory rests with the LORD.

**22** A good name is more desirable than great riches;
    to be esteemed is better than silver or gold.

2 Rich and poor have this in common:
    The LORD is the Maker of them all.

3 The prudent see danger and take refuge,
    but the simple keep going and pay the penalty.

4 Humility is the fear of the LORD;
    its wages are riches and honor and life.

## Amplified Bible

9 It is better to dwell in a corner of the housetop [on the flat oriental roof, exposed to all kinds of weather] than in a house shared with a nagging, quarrelsome, and faultfinding woman.

10 The soul or life of the wicked craves and seeks evil; his neighbor finds no favor in his eyes. [James 2:16.]

11 When the scoffer is punished, the fool gets a lesson in being wise; but men of [godly] Wisdom and good sense learn by being instructed.

12 The [uncompromisingly] righteous man considers well the house of the wicked—how the wicked are cast down to ruin.

13 Whoever stops his ears at the cry of the poor will cry himself and not be heard. [Matt. 18:30-34; James 2:13.]

14 A gift in secret pacifies and turns away anger, and a bribe in the lap, strong wrath.

15 When justice is done, it is a joy to the righteous (the upright, in right standing with God), but to the evildoers it is dismay, calamity, and ruin.

16 A man who wanders out of the way of understanding shall abide in the congregation of the spirits (of the dead).

17 He who loves pleasure will be a poor man; he who loves wine and oil will not be rich.

18 The wicked become a ransom for the [uncompromisingly] righteous, and the treacherous for the upright [because the wicked themselves fall into the traps and pits they have dug for the good].

19 It is better to dwell in a desert land than with a contentious woman and with vexation.

20 There are precious treasures and oil in the dwelling of the wise, but a self-confident and foolish man swallows it up and wastes it.

21 He who earnestly seeks after and craves righteousness, mercy, and loving-kindness will find life in addition to righteousness (uprightness and right standing with God) and honor. [Prov. 15:9; Matt. 5:6.]

22 A wise man scales the city walls of the mighty and brings down the stronghold in which they trust.

23 He who guards his mouth and his tongue keeps himself from troubles. [Prov. 12:13; 13:3; 18:21; James 3:2.]

24 The proud and haughty man—Scoffer is his name—deals and acts with overbearing pride.

25 The desire of the slothful kills him, for his hands refuse to labor.

26 He covets greedily all the day long, but the [uncompromisingly] righteous gives and does not withhold. [II Cor. 9:6-10.]

27 The sacrifice of the wicked is exceedingly disgusting and abhorrent [to the Lord]—how much more when he brings it with evil intention?

28 A false witness will perish, but the word of a man who hears attentively will endure and go unchallenged.

29 A wicked man puts on the bold, unfeeling face [of guilt], but as for the upright, he considers, directs, and establishes his way [with the confidence of integrity].

30 There is no [human] wisdom or understanding or counsel [that can prevail] against the Lord.

31 The horse is prepared for the day of battle, but deliverance and victory are of the Lord.

**22** A good name is rather to be chosen than great riches, and loving favor rather than silver and gold.

2 The rich and poor meet together; the Lord is the Maker of them all. [Job 31:15; Prov. 14:31.]

3 A prudent man sees the evil and hides himself, but the simple pass on and are punished [with suffering].

4 The reward of humility and the reverent and worshipful fear of the Lord is riches and honor and life.

---

a 12 Or The righteous person    b 21 Or righteousness

## New International Version

5 In the paths of the wicked are snares and pitfalls,
　but those who would preserve their life stay far from
　　them.

6 Start children off on the way they should go,
　and even when they are old they will not turn
　　from it.

7 The rich rule over the poor,
　and the borrower is slave to the lender.

8 Whoever sows injustice reaps calamity,
　and the rod they wield in fury will be broken.

9 The generous will themselves be blessed,
　for they share their food with the poor.

10 Drive out the mocker, and out goes strife;
　quarrels and insults are ended.

11 One who loves a pure heart and who speaks with
　　grace
　will have the king for a friend.

12 The eyes of the LORD keep watch over knowledge,
　but he frustrates the words of the unfaithful.

13 The sluggard says, "There's a lion outside!
　I'll be killed in the public square!"

14 The mouth of an adulterous woman is a deep pit;
　a man who is under the LORD's wrath falls into it.

15 Folly is bound up in the heart of a child,
　but the rod of discipline will drive it far away.

16 One who oppresses the poor to increase his wealth
　and one who gives gifts to the rich—both come to
　　poverty.

### Thirty Sayings of the Wise

*Saying 1*
17 Pay attention and turn your ear to the sayings of the
　　wise;
　apply your heart to what I teach,
18 for it is pleasing when you keep them in your heart
　and have all of them ready on your lips.
19 So that your trust may be in the LORD,
　I teach you today, even you.
20 Have I not written thirty sayings for you,
　sayings of counsel and knowledge,
21 teaching you to be honest and to speak the truth,
　so that you bring back truthful reports
　to those you serve?

*Saying 2*
22 Do not exploit the poor because they are poor
　and do not crush the needy in court,
23 for the LORD will take up their case
　and will exact life for life.

*Saying 3*
24 Do not make friends with a hot-tempered person,
　do not associate with one easily angered,
25 or you may learn their ways
　and get yourself ensnared.

*Saying 4*
26 Do not be one who shakes hands in pledge
　or puts up security for debts;
27 if you lack the means to pay,
　your very bed will be snatched from under you.

*Saying 5*
28 Do not move an ancient boundary stone
　set up by your ancestors.

## Amplified Bible

5 Thorns and snares are in the way of the obstinate *and*
willful; he who guards himself will be far from them.
6 Train up a child in the way he should go [and in keeping with his individual gift or bent], and when he is old he
will not depart from it. [Eph. 6:4; II Tim. 3:15.]
7 The rich rule over the poor, and the borrower is servant to the lender.
8 He who sows iniquity will reap calamity *and* futility,
and the rod of his wrath [with which he smites others]
will fail.
9 He who has a bountiful eye shall be blessed, for he
gives of his bread to the poor. [II Cor. 9:6-10.]
10 Drive out the scoffer, and contention will go out; yes,
strife and abuse will cease.
11 He who loves purity *and* the pure in heart *and* who is
gracious in speech—because of the grace of his lips will
he have the king for his friend.
12 The eyes of the Lord keep guard over knowledge
*and* him who has it, but He overthrows the words of the
treacherous.
13 The sluggard says, There is a lion outside! I shall be
slain in the streets!
14 The mouth of a loose woman is a deep pit [for ensnar-
ing wild animals]; he with whom the Lord is indignant *and*
who is abhorrent to Him will fall into it.
15 Foolishness is bound up in the heart of a child, but the
rod of discipline will drive it far from him.
16 He who oppresses the poor to get gain for himself *and*
he who gives to the rich—both will surely come to want.
17 Listen (consent and submit) to the words of the wise,
and apply your mind to my knowledge;
18 For it will be pleasant if you keep them in your mind
[believing them]; your lips will be accustomed to [confess-
ing] them.
19 So that your trust (belief, reliance, support, and confidence) may be in the Lord, I have made known these
things to you today, even to you.
20 Have I not written to you [long ago] excellent things
in counsels and knowledge,
21 To make you know the certainty of the words of truth,
that you may give a true answer to those who sent you?
[Luke 1:3, 4.]
22 Rob not the poor [being tempted by their helpless-
ness], neither oppress the afflicted at the gate [where the
city court is held], [Exod. 23:6; Job 31:16, 21.]
23 For the Lord will plead their cause and deprive of life
those who deprive [the poor or afflicted]. [Zech. 7:10; Mal.
3:5.]
24 Make no friendships with a man given to anger, and
with a wrathful man do not associate,
25 Lest you learn his ways and get yourself into a snare.
26 Be not one of those who strike hands *and* pledge
themselves, or of those who become security for another's
debts.
27 If you have nothing with which to pay, why should he
take your bed from under you?
28 Remove not the ancient landmark which your fathers
have set up.

## New International Version

*Saying 6*

29 Do you see someone skilled in their work?
  They will serve before kings;
  they will not serve before officials of low rank.

*Saying 7*

**23** When you sit to dine with a ruler,
  note well what*a* is before you,
2 and put a knife to your throat
  if you are given to gluttony.
3 Do not crave his delicacies,
  for that food is deceptive.

*Saying 8*

4 Do not wear yourself out to get rich;
  do not trust your own cleverness.
5 Cast but a glance at riches, and they are gone,
  for they will surely sprout wings
  and fly off to the sky like an eagle.

*Saying 9*

6 Do not eat the food of a begrudging host,
  do not crave his delicacies;
7 for he is the kind of person
  who is always thinking about the cost.*b*
"Eat and drink," he says to you,
  but his heart is not with you.
8 You will vomit up the little you have eaten
  and will have wasted your compliments.

*Saying 10*

9 Do not speak to fools,
  for they will scorn your prudent words.

*Saying 11*

10 Do not move an ancient boundary stone
  or encroach on the fields of the fatherless,
11 for their Defender is strong;
  he will take up their case against you.

*Saying 12*

12 Apply your heart to instruction
  and your ears to words of knowledge.

*Saying 13*

13 Do not withhold discipline from a child;
  if you punish them with the rod, they will not die.
14 Punish them with the rod
  and save them from death.

*Saying 14*

15 My son, if your heart is wise,
  then my heart will be glad indeed;
16 my inmost being will rejoice
  when your lips speak what is right.

*Saying 15*

17 Do not let your heart envy sinners,
  but always be zealous for the fear of the LORD.
18 There is surely a future hope for you,
  and your hope will not be cut off.

*Saying 16*

19 Listen, my son, and be wise,
  and set your heart on the right path:
20 Do not join those who drink too much wine
  or gorge themselves on meat,
21 for drunkards and gluttons become poor,
  and drowsiness clothes them in rags.

*a 1 Or who   b 7 Or for as he thinks within himself, / so he is; or for as he
puts on a feast, / so he is*

## Amplified Bible

29 Do you see a man diligent *and* skillful in his business?
He will stand before kings; he will not stand before obscure men.

**23** When you sit down to eat with a ruler, consider
  who *and* what are before you;
2 For you will put a knife to your throat if you are a man
given to desire.
3 Be not desirous of his dainties, for it is deceitful food
[offered with questionable motives].
4 Weary not yourself to be rich; cease from your own
[human] wisdom. [Prov. 28:20; I Tim. 6:9, 10.]
5 Will you set your eyes upon wealth, when [suddenly] it
is gone? For riches certainly make themselves wings, like
an eagle that flies toward the heavens.
6 Eat not the bread of him who has a hard, grudging, *and*
envious eye, neither desire his dainty foods;
7 For as he thinks in his heart, so is he. As one who reckons, he says to you, eat and drink, yet his heart is not with
you [but is grudging the cost].
8 The morsel which you have eaten you will vomit up,
and your complimentary words will be wasted.
9 Speak not in the ears of a [self-confident] fool, for he
will despise the [godly] Wisdom of your words. [Isa. 32:6.]
10 Remove not the ancient landmark and enter not into
the fields of the fatherless, [Deut. 19:14; 27:17; Prov.
22:28.]
11 For their Redeemer is mighty; He will plead their
cause against you.
12 Apply your mind to instruction *and* correction and
your ears to words of knowledge.
13 Withhold not discipline from the child; for if you strike
*and* punish him with the [reedlike] rod, he will not die.
14 You shall whip him with the rod and deliver his life
from Sheol (Hades, the place of the dead).
15 My son, if your heart is wise, my heart will be glad,
even mine;
16 Yes, my heart will rejoice when your lips speak right
things.
17 Let not your heart envy sinners, but continue in the
reverent *and* worshipful fear of the Lord all the day long.
18 For surely there is a latter end [a future and a reward],
and your hope *and* expectation shall not be cut off.
19 Hear, my son, and be wise, and direct your mind in
the way [of the Lord].
20 Do not associate with winebibbers; be not among
them *nor* among gluttonous eaters of meat, [Isa. 5:22;
Luke 21:34; Rom. 13:13; Eph. 5:18.]
21 For the drunkard and the glutton shall come to poverty, and drowsiness shall clothe a man with rags.

# New International Version

*Saying 17*

22 Listen to your father, who gave you life,
    and do not despise your mother when she is old.
23 Buy the truth and do not sell it—
    wisdom, instruction and insight as well.
24 The father of a righteous child has great joy;
    a man who fathers a wise son rejoices in him.
25 May your father and mother rejoice;
    may she who gave you birth be joyful!

*Saying 18*

26 My son, give me your heart
    and let your eyes delight in my ways,
27 for an adulterous woman is a deep pit,
    and a wayward wife is a narrow well.
28 Like a bandit she lies in wait
    and multiplies the unfaithful among men.

*Saying 19*

29 Who has woe? Who has sorrow?
    Who has strife? Who has complaints?
    Who has needless bruises? Who has bloodshot
        eyes?
30 Those who linger over wine,
    who go to sample bowls of mixed wine.
31 Do not gaze at wine when it is red,
    when it sparkles in the cup,
    when it goes down smoothly!
32 In the end it bites like a snake
    and poisons like a viper.
33 Your eyes will see strange sights,
    and your mind will imagine confusing things.
34 You will be like one sleeping on the high seas,
    lying on top of the rigging.
35 "They hit me," you will say, "but I'm not hurt!
    They beat me, but I don't feel it!
    When will I wake up
    so I can find another drink?"

*Saying 20*

**24** Do not envy the wicked,
    do not desire their company;
2 for their hearts plot violence,
    and their lips talk about making trouble.

*Saying 21*

3 By wisdom a house is built,
    and through understanding it is established;
4 through knowledge its rooms are filled
    with rare and beautiful treasures.

*Saying 22*

5 The wise prevail through great power,
    and those who have knowledge muster their
        strength.
6 Surely you need guidance to wage war,
    and victory is won through many advisers.

*Saying 23*

7 Wisdom is too high for fools;
    in the assembly at the gate they must not open their
        mouths.

*Saying 24*

8 Whoever plots evil
    will be known as a schemer.
9 The schemes of folly are sin,
    and people detest a mocker.

*Saying 25*

10 If you falter in a time of trouble,
    how small is your strength!

# Amplified Bible

22 Hearken to your father, who begot you, and despise not your mother when she is old.
23 Buy the truth and sell it not; not only that, but also get discernment *and* judgment, instruction and understanding.
24 The father of the [uncompromisingly] righteous (the upright, in right standing with God) shall greatly rejoice, and he who becomes the father of a wise child shall have joy in him.
25 Let your father and your mother be glad, and let her who bore you rejoice.
26 My son, give me your heart and let your eyes observe *and* delight in my ways,
27 For a harlot is a deep ditch, and a loose woman is a narrow pit.
28 She also lies in wait as a robber *or* as one waits for prey, and she increases the treacherous among men.
29 Who has woe? Who has sorrow? Who has strife? Who has complaining? Who has wounds without cause? Who has redness *and* dimness of eyes?
30 Those who tarry long at the wine, those who go to seek *and* try mixed wine. [Prov. 20:1; Eph. 5:18.]
31 Do not look at wine when it is red, when it sparkles in the wineglass, when it goes down smoothly.
32 At the last it bites like a serpent and stings like an adder.
33 [Under the influence of wine] your eyes will behold strange things [and loose women] and your mind will utter things turned the wrong way [untrue, incorrect, and petulant].
34 Yes, you will be [as unsteady] as he who lies down in the midst of the sea, and [as open to disaster] as he who lies upon the top of a mast.
35 You will say, They struck me, but I was not hurt! They beat me [as with a hammer], but I did not feel it! When shall I awake? I will crave *and* seek more wine again [and escape reality].

**24** Be not envious of evil men, nor desire to be with them;
2 For their minds plot oppression *and* devise violence, and their lips talk of causing trouble *and* vexation.
3 Through skillful *and* godly Wisdom is a house (a life, a home, a family) built, and by understanding it is established [on a sound and good foundation],
4 And by knowledge shall its chambers [of every area] be filled with all precious and pleasant riches.
5 A wise man is strong *and* *a is better than a strong man*, and a man of knowledge increases *and* strengthens his power; [Prov. 21:22; Eccl. 9:16.]
6 For by wise counsel you can wage your war, and in an abundance of counselors there is victory *and* safety.
7 Wisdom is too high for a *b* fool; he opens not his mouth in the gate [where the city's rulers sit in judgment].
8 He who plans to do evil will be called a mischief-maker.
9 The plans of the foolish *and* the thought of foolishness are sin, and the scoffer is an abomination to men.
10 If you faint in the day of adversity, your strength is small.

---

*a* Several other texts, including *The Septuagint* (Greek translation of the Old Testament), so read. *b* See footnote on Proverbs 14:3.

## New International Version

[11] Rescue those being led away to death;
 hold back those staggering toward slaughter.
[12] If you say, "But we knew nothing about this,"
 does not he who weighs the heart perceive it?
Does not he who guards your life know it?
 Will he not repay everyone according to what they
 have done?

*Saying 26*
[13] Eat honey, my son, for it is good;
 honey from the comb is sweet to your taste.
[14] Know also that wisdom is like honey for you:
 If you find it, there is a future hope for you,
 and your hope will not be cut off.

*Saying 27*
[15] Do not lurk like a thief near the house of the righteous,
 do not plunder their dwelling place;
[16] for though the righteous fall seven times, they rise
 again,
 but the wicked stumble when calamity strikes.

*Saying 28*
[17] Do not gloat when your enemy falls;
 when they stumble, do not let your heart rejoice,
[18] or the LORD will see and disapprove
 and turn his wrath away from them.

*Saying 29*
[19] Do not fret because of evildoers
 or be envious of the wicked,
[20] for the evildoer has no future hope,
 and the lamp of the wicked will be snuffed out.

*Saying 30*
[21] Fear the LORD and the king, my son,
 and do not join with rebellious officials,
[22] for those two will send sudden destruction on them,
 and who knows what calamities they can bring?

### Further Sayings of the Wise

[23] These also are sayings of the wise:

To show partiality in judging is not good:
[24] Whoever says to the guilty, "You are innocent,"
 will be cursed by peoples and denounced by
 nations.
[25] But it will go well with those who convict the guilty,
 and rich blessing will come on them.

[26] An honest answer
 is like a kiss on the lips.

[27] Put your outdoor work in order
 and get your fields ready;
 after that, build your house.

[28] Do not testify against your neighbor without cause—
 would you use your lips to mislead?
[29] Do not say, "I'll do to them as they have done to me;
 I'll pay them back for what they did."

[30] I went past the field of a sluggard,
 past the vineyard of someone who has no sense;
[31] thorns had come up everywhere,
 the ground was covered with weeds,
 and the stone wall was in ruins.
[32] I applied my heart to what I observed
 and learned a lesson from what I saw:
[33] A little sleep, a little slumber,
 a little folding of the hands to rest—
[34] and poverty will come on you like a thief
 and scarcity like an armed man.

## Amplified Bible

[11] Deliver those who are drawn away to death, and those
who totter to the slaughter, hold them back [from their
doom].
[12] If you [profess ignorance and] say, Behold, we did not
know this, does not He Who weighs *and* ponders the heart
perceive *and* consider it? And He Who guards your life,
does not He know it? And shall not He render to [you and]
every man according to his works?
[13] My son, eat honey, because it is good, and the drippings of the honeycomb are sweet to your taste.
[14] So shall you know skillful *and* godly Wisdom to be
thus to your life; if you find it, then shall there be a future
*and* a reward, and your hope *and* expectation shall not be
cut off.
[15] Lie not in wait as a wicked man against the dwelling
of the [uncompromisingly] righteous (the upright, in right
standing with God); destroy not his resting-place;
[16] For a righteous man falls seven times and rises again,
but the wicked are overthrown by calamity. [Job 5:19; Ps.
34:19; 37:24; Mic. 7:8.]
[17] Rejoice not when your enemy falls, and let not your
heart be glad when he stumbles *or* is overthrown,
[18] Lest the Lord see it and it be evil in His eyes *and* displease Him, and He turn away His wrath from him [to expend it upon you, the worse offender].
[19] Fret not because of evildoers, neither be envious of
the wicked,
[20] For there shall be no reward for the evil man; the lamp
of the wicked shall be put out.
[21] My son, [reverently] fear the Lord and the king, and
do not associate with those who are given to change [of
allegiance, and are revolutionary],
[22] For their calamity shall rise suddenly, and who knows
the punishment *and* ruin which both [the Lord and the
king] will bring upon [the rebellious]?
[23] These also are sayings of the wise: To discriminate
*and* show partiality, having respect of persons in judging,
is not good.
[24] He who says to the wicked, You are righteous *and*
innocent—peoples will curse him, nations will defy *and*
abhor him.
[25] But to those [upright judges] who rebuke the wicked,
it will go well with them *and* they will find delight, and a
good blessing will be upon them.
[26] He kisses the lips [and wins the hearts of men] who
give a right answer.
[27] [Put first things first.] Prepare your work outside and
get it ready for yourself in the field; and afterward build
your house *and* establish a home.
[28] Be not a witness against your neighbor without cause,
and deceive not with your lips. [Eph. 4:25.]
[29] Say not, I will do to him as he has done to me; I will
pay the man back for his deed. [Prov. 20:22; Matt. 5:39,
44; Rom. 12:17, 19.]
[30] I went by the field of the lazy man, and by the vineyard
of the man void of understanding;
[31] And, behold, it was all grown over with thorns, and
nettles were covering its face, and its stone wall was broken down.
[32] Then I beheld *and* considered it well; I looked *and* received instruction.
[33] Yet a little sleep, a little slumber, a little folding of the
hands to sleep—
[34] So shall your poverty come as a robber, and your want
as an armed man.

| New International Version | Amplified Bible |
|---|---|

## More Proverbs of Solomon

**25** These are more proverbs of Solomon, compiled by the men of Hezekiah king of Judah:

2 It is the glory of God to conceal a matter;
    to search out a matter is the glory of kings.
3 As the heavens are high and the earth is deep,
    so the hearts of kings are unsearchable.

4 Remove the dross from the silver,
    and a silversmith can produce a vessel;
5 remove wicked officials from the king's presence,
    and his throne will be established through
        righteousness.

6 Do not exalt yourself in the king's presence,
    and do not claim a place among his great men;
7 it is better for him to say to you, "Come up here,"
    than for him to humiliate you before his nobles.

What you have seen with your eyes
8     do not bring*a* hastily to court,
for what will you do in the end
    if your neighbor puts you to shame?

9 If you take your neighbor to court,
    do not betray another's confidence,
10 or the one who hears it may shame you
    and the charge against you will stand.

11 Like apples*b* of gold in settings of silver
    is a ruling rightly given.
12 Like an earring of gold or an ornament of fine gold
    is the rebuke of a wise judge to a listening ear.

13 Like a snow-cooled drink at harvest time
    is a trustworthy messenger to the one who sends
        him;
    he refreshes the spirit of his master.
14 Like clouds and wind without rain
    is one who boasts of gifts never given.

15 Through patience a ruler can be persuaded,
    and a gentle tongue can break a bone.

16 If you find honey, eat just enough—
    too much of it, and you will vomit.
17 Seldom set foot in your neighbor's house—
    too much of you, and they will hate you.

18 Like a club or a sword or a sharp arrow
    is one who gives false testimony against a neighbor.
19 Like a broken tooth or a lame foot
    is reliance on the unfaithful in a time of trouble.
20 Like one who takes away a garment on a cold day,
    or like vinegar poured on a wound,
    is one who sings songs to a heavy heart.

21 If your enemy is hungry, give him food to eat;
    if he is thirsty, give him water to drink.
22 In doing this, you will heap burning coals on his head,
    and the LORD will reward you.

23 Like a north wind that brings unexpected rain
    is a sly tongue—which provokes a horrified look.

24 Better to live on a corner of the roof
    than share a house with a quarrelsome wife.

---

**25** These are also the proverbs of Solomon, which the men of Hezekiah king of Judah copied: [I Kings 4:32.]

2 It is the glory of God to conceal a thing, but the glory of kings is to search out a thing. [Deut. 29:29; Rom. 11:33.]
3 As the heavens for height and the earth for depth, so the hearts *and* minds of kings are unsearchable.

4 Take away the dross from the silver, and there shall come forth [the material for] a vessel for the silversmith [to work up]. [II Tim. 2:21.]
5 Take away the wicked from before the king, and his throne will be established in righteousness (moral and spiritual rectitude in every area and relation).

6 Be not forward (self-assertive and boastfully ambitious) in the presence of the king, and stand not in the place of great men;
7 For better it is that it should be said to you, Come up here, than that you should be put lower in the presence of the prince, whose eyes have seen you. [Luke 14:8-10.]
8 Rush not forth soon to quarrel [before magistrates or elsewhere], lest you know not what to do in the end when your neighbor has put you to shame. [Prov. 17:14; Matt. 5:25.]
9 Argue your cause with your neighbor himself; discover not *and* disclose not another's secret, [Matt. 18:15.]
10 Lest he who hears you revile you *and* bring shame upon you and your ill repute have no end.

11 A word fitly spoken *and* in due season is like apples of gold in settings of silver. [Prov. 15:23; Isa. 50:4.]
12 Like an earring *or* nose ring of gold or an ornament of fine gold is a wise reprover to an ear that listens *and* obeys.

13 Like the cold of snow [brought from the mountains] in the time of harvest, so is a faithful messenger to those who send him; for he refreshes the life of his masters.
14 Whoever falsely boasts of gifts [he does not give] is like clouds and wind without rain. [Jude 12.]

15 By long forbearance *and* calmness of spirit a judge *or* ruler is persuaded, and soft speech breaks down the most bonelike resistance. [Gen. 32:4; I Sam. 25:24; Prov. 15:1; 16:14.]

16 Have you found [pleasure sweet like] honey? Eat only as much as is sufficient for you, lest, being filled with it, you vomit it.
17 Let your foot seldom be in your neighbor's house, lest he become tired of you and hate you.

18 A man who bears false witness against his neighbor is like a heavy sledgehammer and a sword and a sharp arrow.
19 Confidence in an unfaithful man in time of trouble is like a broken tooth or a foot out of joint.
20 He who sings songs to a heavy heart is like him who lays off a garment in cold weather *and* like vinegar upon soda. [Dan. 6:18; Rom. 12:15.]

21 If your enemy is hungry, give him bread to eat; and if he is thirsty, give him water to drink; [Matt. 5:44; Rom. 12:20.]
22 For in doing so, you will *a*heap coals of fire upon his head, and the Lord will reward you.

23 The north wind brings forth rain; so does a backbiting tongue bring forth an angry countenance.
24 It is better to dwell in the corner of the housetop than to share a house with a disagreeing, quarrelsome, *and* scolding woman. [Prov. 21:9.]

---

*a* This is not to be understood as a revengeful act intended to embarrass its victim, but just the opposite. The picture is that of the high priest (Lev. 16:12) who, on the Day of Atonement, took his censer and filled it with "coals of fire" from off the altar of burnt offering, and then put incense on the coals to create a pleasing, sweet-smelling fragrance. The cloud or smoke of the incense covered the mercy seat and was acceptable to God for atonement. Samuel Wesley wrote: / "So artists melt the sullen ore of lead, / By heaping coals of fire upon its head; / In the kind warmth the metal learns to glow, / And pure from dross the silver runs below."

---

*a* 7,8 Or *nobles / on whom you had set your eyes. / 8Do not go*
*b* 11 Or possibly *apricots*

## New International Version

25 Like cold water to a weary soul
  is good news from a distant land.
26 Like a muddied spring or a polluted well
  are the righteous who give way to the wicked.

27 It is not good to eat too much honey,
  nor is it honorable to search out matters that are too
    deep.

28 Like a city whose walls are broken through
  is a person who lacks self-control.

26 Like snow in summer or rain in harvest,
  honor is not fitting for a fool.
2 Like a fluttering sparrow or a darting swallow,
  an undeserved curse does not come to rest.
3 A whip for the horse, a bridle for the donkey,
  and a rod for the backs of fools!
4 Do not answer a fool according to his folly,
  or you yourself will be just like him.
5 Answer a fool according to his folly,
  or he will be wise in his own eyes.
6 Sending a message by the hands of a fool
  is like cutting off one's feet or drinking poison.
7 Like the useless legs of one who is lame
  is a proverb in the mouth of a fool.
8 Like tying a stone in a sling
  is the giving of honor to a fool.
9 Like a thornbush in a drunkard's hand
  is a proverb in the mouth of a fool.
10 Like an archer who wounds at random
  is one who hires a fool or any passer-by.
11 As a dog returns to its vomit,
  so fools repeat their folly.
12 Do you see a person wise in their own eyes?
  There is more hope for a fool than for them.

13 A sluggard says, "There's a lion in the road,
  a fierce lion roaming the streets!"
14 As a door turns on its hinges,
  so a sluggard turns on his bed.
15 A sluggard buries his hand in the dish;
  he is too lazy to bring it back to his mouth.
16 A sluggard is wiser in his own eyes
  than seven people who answer discreetly.

17 Like one who grabs a stray dog by the ears
  is someone who rushes into a quarrel not their own.
18 Like a maniac shooting
  flaming arrows of death
19 is one who deceives their neighbor
  and says, "I was only joking!"

20 Without wood a fire goes out;
  without a gossip a quarrel dies down.
21 As charcoal to embers and as wood to fire,
  so is a quarrelsome person for kindling strife.
22 The words of a gossip are like choice morsels;
  they go down to the inmost parts.

23 Like a coating of silver dross on earthenware
  are fervent[a] lips with an evil heart.

## Amplified Bible

25 Like cold water to a thirsty soul, so is good news from
a far [home] country.
26 Like a muddied fountain and a polluted spring is a
righteous man who yields, falls down, and compromises
his integrity before the wicked.
27 It is not good to eat much honey; so for men to seek
glory, their own glory, causes suffering and is not glory.
28 He who has no rule over his own spirit is like a city
that is broken down and without walls. [Prov. 16:32.]

26 Like snow in summer and like rain in harvest, so
honor is not fitting for a [self-confident] fool. [Isa.
32:6.]
2 Like the sparrow in her wandering, like the swallow in
her flying, so the causeless curse does not alight. [Num.
23:8.]
3 A whip for the horse, a bridle for the donkey, and a
[straight, slender] rod for the backs of [self-confident]
fools.
4 Answer not a [self-confident] fool according to his
folly, lest you also be like him.
5 Answer a [self-confident] fool according to his folly,
lest he be wise in his own eyes and conceit. [Matt. 16:1-4;
21:24-27.]
6 He who sends a message by the hand of a [a]fool cuts off
the feet [of satisfactory delivery] and drinks the damage.
[Prov. 13:17.]
7 Like the legs of a lame man which hang loose, so is a
parable in the mouth of a fool.
8 Like he who binds a stone in a sling, so is he who gives
honor to a [self-confident] fool.
9 Like a thorn that goes [without being felt] into the
hand of a drunken man, so is a proverb in the mouth of a
[self-confident] fool.
10 [But] like an archer who wounds all, so is he who
hires a fool or chance passers-by.
11 As a dog returns to his vomit, so a fool returns to his
folly.
12 Do you see a man wise in his own eyes and conceit?
There is more hope for a [self-confident] fool than for him.
[Prov. 29:20; Luke 18:11; Rom. 12:16; Rev. 3:17.]
13 The sluggard says, There is a lion in the way! A lion is
in the streets! [Prov. 22:13.]
14 As the door turns on its hinges, so does the lazy man
[move not from his place] upon his bed.
15 The slothful and self-indulgent buries his hand in his
bosom; it distresses and wearies him to bring it again to
his mouth. [Prov. 19:24.]
16 The sluggard is wiser in his own eyes and conceit than
seven men who can render a reason and answer discreetly.
17 He who, passing by, stops to meddle with strife that
is none of his business is like one who takes a dog by the
ears.
18 Like a madman who casts firebrands, arrows, and
death,
19 So is the man who deceives his neighbor and then
says, Was I not joking? [Eph. 5:4.]
20 For lack of wood the fire goes out, and where there is
no whisperer, contention ceases.
21 As coals are to hot embers and as wood to fire, so is
a quarrelsome man to inflame strife. [Prov. 15:18; 29:22.]
22 The words of a whisperer or slanderer are like dainty
morsels or words of sport [to some, but to others are like
deadly wounds]; and they go down into the innermost
parts of the body [or of the victim's nature].
23 Burning lips [uttering insincere words of love] and a
wicked heart are like an earthen vessel covered with the
scum thrown off from molten silver [making it appear to
be solid silver].

# New International Version

24 Enemies disguise themselves with their lips,
 but in their hearts they harbor deceit.
25 Though their speech is charming, do not believe them,
 for seven abominations fill their hearts.
26 Their malice may be concealed by deception,
 but their wickedness will be exposed in the
 assembly.
27 Whoever digs a pit will fall into it;
 if someone rolls a stone, it will roll back on them.
28 A lying tongue hates those it hurts,
 and a flattering mouth works ruin.

27 Do not boast about tomorrow,
 for you do not know what a day may bring.

2 Let someone else praise you, and not your own mouth;
 an outsider, and not your own lips.

3 Stone is heavy and sand a burden,
 but a fool's provocation is heavier than both.

4 Anger is cruel and fury overwhelming,
 but who can stand before jealousy?

5 Better is open rebuke
 than hidden love.

6 Wounds from a friend can be trusted,
 but an enemy multiplies kisses.

7 One who is full loathes honey from the comb,
 but to the hungry even what is bitter tastes sweet.

8 Like a bird that flees its nest
 is anyone who flees from home.

9 Perfume and incense bring joy to the heart,
 and the pleasantness of a friend
 springs from their heartfelt advice.

10 Do not forsake your friend or a friend of your family,
 and do not go to your relative's house when disaster
 strikes you —
 better a neighbor nearby than a relative far away.

11 Be wise, my son, and bring joy to my heart;
 then I can answer anyone who treats me with
 contempt.

12 The prudent see danger and take refuge,
 but the simple keep going and pay the penalty.

13 Take the garment of one who puts up security for a
 stranger;
 hold it in pledge if it is done for an outsider.

14 If anyone loudly blesses their neighbor early in the
 morning,
 it will be taken as a curse.

15 A quarrelsome wife is like the dripping
 of a leaky roof in a rainstorm;
16 restraining her is like restraining the wind
 or grasping oil with the hand.

17 As iron sharpens iron,
 so one person sharpens another.

18 The one who guards a fig tree will eat its fruit,
 and whoever protects their master will be honored.

19 As water reflects the face,
 so one's life reflects the heart.[a]

20 Death and Destruction[b] are never satisfied,
 and neither are human eyes.

21 The crucible for silver and the furnace for gold,
 but people are tested by their praise.

# Amplified Bible

24 He who hates pretends with his lips, but stores up deceit within himself.
25 When he speaks kindly, do not trust him, for seven
abominations are in his heart.
26 Though his hatred covers itself with guile, his wickedness shall be shown openly before the assembly.
27 Whoever digs a pit [for another man's feet] shall fall
into it himself, and he who rolls a stone [up a height to do
mischief], it will return upon him. [Ps. 7:15, 16; 9:15; 10:2;
57:6; Prov. 28:10; Eccl. 10:8.]
28 A lying tongue hates those it wounds *and* crushes,
and a flattering mouth works ruin.

27 Do not boast of [yourself and] tomorrow, for you
 know not what a day may bring forth. [Luke 12:19,
20; James 4:13.]

2 Let another man praise you, and not your own mouth;
a stranger, and not your own lips.

3 Stone is heavy and sand weighty, but a fool's [unrea-
soning] wrath is heavier *and* more intolerable than both
of them.

4 Wrath is cruel and anger is an overwhelming flood, but
who is able to stand before jealousy?

5 Open rebuke is better than love that is hidden. [Prov.
28:23; Gal. 2:14.]

6 Faithful are the wounds of a friend, but the kisses of an
enemy are lavish *and* deceitful.

7 He who is satiated [with sensual pleasures] loathes
*and* treads underfoot a honeycomb, but to the hungry soul
every bitter thing is sweet.

8 Like a bird that wanders from her nest, so is a man who
strays from his home.

9 Oil and perfume rejoice the heart; so does the sweetness of a friend's counsel that comes from the heart.

10 Your own friend and your father's friend, forsake
them not; neither go to your brother's house in the day of
your calamity. Better is a neighbor who is near [in spirit]
than a brother who is far off [in heart].

11 My son, be wise, and make my heart glad, that I may
answer him who reproaches me [as having failed in my
parental duty]. [Prov. 10:1; 23:15, 24.]

12 A prudent man sees the evil and hides himself, but the
simple pass on and are punished [with suffering].

13 [The judge tells the creditor] Take the garment of
one who is security for a stranger; and hold him in pledge
when he is security for foreigners. [Prov. 20:16.]

14 The flatterer who loudly praises *and* glorifies his
neighbor, rising early in the morning, it shall be counted
as cursing him [for he will be suspected of sinister pur-
poses].

15 A continual dripping on a day of violent showers and a
contentious woman are alike; [Prov. 19:13.]

16 Whoever attempts to restrain [a contentious woman]
might as well try to stop the wind—his right hand encoun-
ters oil [and she slips through his fingers].

17 Iron sharpens iron; so a man sharpens the countenance of his friend [to show rage or worthy purpose].

18 Whoever tends the fig tree shall eat its fruit; so he
who patiently *and* faithfully guards *and* heeds his master
shall be honored. [I Cor. 9:7, 13.]

19 As in water face answers to *and* reflects face, so the
heart of man to man.

20 Sheol (the place of the dead) and Abaddon (the place
of destruction) are never satisfied; so [the lust of] the eyes
of man is never satisfied. [Prov. 30:16; Hab. 2:5.]

21 As the refining pot for silver and the furnace for gold
[bring forth all the impurities of the metal], so let a man
be in his trial of praise [ridding himself of all that is base
or insincere; for a man is judged by what he praises and of
what he boasts].

---

a 19 Or *so others reflect your heart back to you*   b 20 Hebrew *Abaddon*

## New International Version

<sup>22</sup>Though you grind a fool in a mortar,
grinding them like grain with a pestle,
you will not remove their folly from them.
<sup>23</sup>Be sure you know the condition of your flocks,
give careful attention to your herds;
<sup>24</sup>for riches do not endure forever,
and a crown is not secure for all generations.
<sup>25</sup>When the hay is removed and new growth appears
and the grass from the hills is gathered in,
<sup>26</sup>the lambs will provide you with clothing,
and the goats with the price of a field.
<sup>27</sup>You will have plenty of goats' milk to feed your family
and to nourish your female servants.

**28** The wicked flee though no one pursues,
but the righteous are as bold as a lion.

<sup>2</sup>When a country is rebellious, it has many rulers,
but a ruler with discernment and knowledge
maintains order.

<sup>3</sup>A ruler<sup>a</sup> who oppresses the poor
is like a driving rain that leaves no crops.

<sup>4</sup>Those who forsake instruction praise the wicked,
but those who heed it resist them.

<sup>5</sup>Evildoers do not understand what is right,
but those who seek the Lord understand it fully.

<sup>6</sup>Better the poor whose walk is blameless
than the rich whose ways are perverse.

<sup>7</sup>A discerning son heeds instruction,
but a companion of gluttons disgraces his father.

<sup>8</sup>Whoever increases wealth by taking interest or profit
from the poor
amasses it for another, who will be kind to the poor.

<sup>9</sup>If anyone turns a deaf ear to my instruction,
even their prayers are detestable.

<sup>10</sup>Whoever leads the upright along an evil path
will fall into their own trap,
but the blameless will receive a good inheritance.

<sup>11</sup>The rich are wise in their own eyes;
one who is poor and discerning sees how deluded
they are.

<sup>12</sup>When the righteous triumph, there is great elation;
but when the wicked rise to power, people go into
hiding.

<sup>13</sup>Whoever conceals their sins does not prosper,
but the one who confesses and renounces them
finds mercy.

<sup>14</sup>Blessed is the one who always trembles before God,
but whoever hardens their heart falls into trouble.

<sup>15</sup>Like a roaring lion or a charging bear
is a wicked ruler over a helpless people.

<sup>16</sup>A tyrannical ruler practices extortion,
but one who hates ill-gotten gain will enjoy a long
reign.

<sup>17</sup>Anyone tormented by the guilt of murder
will seek refuge in the grave;
let no one hold them back.

<sup>18</sup>The one whose walk is blameless is kept safe,
but the one whose ways are perverse will fall into
the pit.<sup>b</sup>

## Amplified Bible

<sup>22</sup>Even though like grain you should pound a fool in a
mortar with a pestle, yet will not his foolishness depart
from him.
<sup>23</sup>Be diligent to know the state of your flocks, and look
well to your herds;
<sup>24</sup>For riches are not forever; does a crown endure to all
generations?
<sup>25</sup>When the hay is gone, the tender grass shows itself,
and herbs of the mountain are gathered in,
<sup>26</sup>The lambs will be for your clothing, and the goats
[will furnish you] the price of a field.
<sup>27</sup>And there will be goats' milk enough for your food,
for the food of your household, and for the maintenance
of your maids.

**28** The wicked flee when no man pursues them, but
the [uncompromisingly] righteous are bold as a
lion. [Lev. 26:17, 36; Ps. 53:5.]

<sup>2</sup>When a land transgresses, it has many rulers, but
when the ruler is a man of discernment, understanding,
*and* knowledge, its stability will long continue.

<sup>3</sup>A poor man who oppresses the poor is like a sweeping
rain which leaves no food [plundering them of their last
morsels]. [Matt. 18:28.]

<sup>4</sup>Those who forsake the law [of God and man] praise
the wicked, but those who keep the law [of God and man]
contend with them. [Prov. 29:18.]

<sup>5</sup>Evil men do not understand justice, but they who crave
*and* seek the Lord understand it fully. [John 7:17; I Cor.
2:15; I John 2:20, 27.]

<sup>6</sup>Better is the poor man who walks in his integrity than
he who willfully goes in double *and* wrong ways, though
he is rich.

<sup>7</sup>Whoever keeps the law [of God and man] is a wise son,
but he who is a companion of gluttons *and* the carousing,
self-indulgent, *and* extravagant shames his father.

<sup>8</sup>He who by charging excessive interest *and* who by un-
just efforts to get gain increases his material possession
gathers it for him [to spend] who is kind *and* generous to
the poor. [Job 27:16, 17; Prov. 13:22; Eccl. 2:26.]

<sup>9</sup>He who turns away his ear from hearing the law [of
God and man], even his prayer is an abomination, hateful
*and* revolting [to God]. [Ps. 66:18; 109:7; Prov. 15:8; Zech.
7:11.]

<sup>10</sup>Whoever leads the upright astray into an evil way, he
will himself fall into his own pit, but the blameless will
have a goodly inheritance.

<sup>11</sup>The rich man is wise in his own eyes *and* conceit, but
the poor man who has understanding will find him out.

<sup>12</sup>When the [uncompromisingly] righteous triumph,
there is great glory *and* celebration; but when the wicked
rise [to power], men hide themselves.

<sup>13</sup>He who covers his transgressions will not prosper,
but whoever confesses and forsakes his sins will obtain
mercy. [Ps. 32:3, 5; I John 1:8-10.]

<sup>14</sup>Blessed (happy, fortunate, and to be envied) is the
man who reverently *and* worshipfully fears [the Lord] at
all times [regardless of circumstances], but he who hardens his heart will fall into calamity.

<sup>15</sup>Like a roaring lion or a ravenous *and* charging bear is
a wicked ruler over a poor people.

<sup>16</sup>A ruler who lacks understanding is [like a wicked one]
a great oppressor, but he who hates covetousness *and* unjust gain shall prolong his days.

<sup>17</sup>If a man willfully sheds the blood of a person [and
keeps the guilt of murder upon his conscience], he is fleeing to the pit (the grave) *and* hastening to his own destruction; let no man stop him!

<sup>18</sup>He who walks uprightly shall be safe, but he who will-
fully goes in double *and* wrong ways shall fall in one of
them.

<sup>a</sup> 3 Or *A poor person*   <sup>b</sup> 18 Syriac (see Septuagint); Hebrew *into one*

## New International Version

19 Those who work their land will have abundant food,
but those who chase fantasies will have their fill of poverty.

20 A faithful person will be richly blessed,
but one eager to get rich will not go unpunished.

21 To show partiality is not good—
yet a person will do wrong for a piece of bread.

22 The stingy are eager to get rich
and are unaware that poverty awaits them.

23 Whoever rebukes a person will in the end gain favor
rather than one who has a flattering tongue.

24 Whoever robs their father or mother
and says, "It's not wrong,"
is partner to one who destroys.

25 The greedy stir up conflict,
but those who trust in the LORD will prosper.

26 Those who trust in themselves are fools,
but those who walk in wisdom are kept safe.

27 Those who give to the poor will lack nothing,
but those who close their eyes to them receive many curses.

28 When the wicked rise to power, people go into hiding;
but when the wicked perish, the righteous thrive.

**29** Whoever remains stiff-necked after many rebukes
will suddenly be destroyed—without remedy.

2 When the righteous thrive, the people rejoice;
when the wicked rule, the people groan.

3 A man who loves wisdom brings joy to his father,
but a companion of prostitutes squanders his wealth.

4 By justice a king gives a country stability,
but those who are greedy for*ᵃ* bribes tear it down.

5 Those who flatter their neighbors
are spreading nets for their feet.

6 Evildoers are snared by their own sin,
but the righteous shout for joy and are glad.

7 The righteous care about justice for the poor,
but the wicked have no such concern.

8 Mockers stir up a city,
but the wise turn away anger.

9 If a wise person goes to court with a fool,
the fool rages and scoffs, and there is no peace.

10 The bloodthirsty hate a person of integrity
and seek to kill the upright.

11 Fools give full vent to their rage,
but the wise bring calm in the end.

12 If a ruler listens to lies,
all his officials become wicked.

13 The poor and the oppressor have this in common:
The LORD gives sight to the eyes of both.

14 If a king judges the poor with fairness,
his throne will be established forever.

15 A rod and a reprimand impart wisdom,
but a child left undisciplined disgraces its mother.

16 When the wicked thrive, so does sin,
but the righteous will see their downfall.

*ᵃ 4 Or who give*

## Amplified Bible

19 He who cultivates his land will have plenty of bread,
but he who follows worthless people *and* pursuits will have poverty enough.

20 A faithful man shall abound with blessings, but he who makes haste to be rich [at any cost] shall not go unpunished. [Prov. 13:11; 20:21; 23:4; I Tim. 6:9.]

21 To have respect of persons *and* to show partiality is not good, neither is it good that man should transgress for a piece of bread.

22 He who has an evil *and* covetous eye hastens to be rich and knows not that want will come upon him. [Prov. 21:5; 28:20.]

23 He who rebukes a man shall afterward find more favor than he who flatters with the tongue.

24 Whoever robs his father or his mother and says, This is no sin—he is in the same class as [an open, lawless robber and] a destroyer.

25 He who is of a greedy spirit stirs up strife, but he who puts his trust in the Lord shall be enriched *and* blessed.

26 He who leans on, trusts in, *and* is confident of his own mind *and* heart is a [self-confident] fool, but he who walks in skillful *and* godly Wisdom shall be delivered. [James 1:5.]

27 He who gives to the poor will not want, but he who hides his eyes [from their want] will have many a curse. [Deut. 15:7; Prov. 19:17; 22:9.]

28 When the wicked rise [to power], men hide themselves; but when they perish, the [consistently] righteous increase *and* become many. [Prov. 28:12.]

**29** He who, being often reproved, hardens his neck shall suddenly be destroyed—and that without remedy.

2 When the [uncompromisingly] righteous are in authority, the people rejoice; but when the wicked man rules, the people groan *and* sigh.

3 Whoever loves skillful *and* godly Wisdom rejoices his father, but he who associates with harlots wastes his substance.

4 The king by justice establishes the land, but he who exacts gifts *and* tribute overthrows it.

5 A man who flatters his neighbor spreads a net for his own feet.

6 In the transgression of an evil man there is a snare, but the [uncompromisingly] righteous man sings and rejoices.

7 The [consistently] righteous man knows *and* cares for the rights of the poor, but the wicked man has no interest in such knowledge. [Job 29:16; 31:13; Ps. 41:1.]

8 Scoffers set a city afire [inflaming the minds of the people], but wise men turn away wrath.

9 If a wise man has an argument with a foolish man, the fool only rages or laughs, and there is no rest.

10 The bloodthirsty hate the blameless man, but the upright care for *and* seek [to save] his life. [Gen. 4:5, 8; I John 3:12.]

11 A [self-confident] fool utters all his anger, but a wise man holds it back and stills it.

12 If a ruler listens to falsehood, all his officials will become wicked.

13 The poor man and the oppressor meet together—the Lord gives light to the eyes of both.

14 The king who faithfully judges the poor, his throne shall be established continuously.

15 The rod and reproof give wisdom, but a child left undisciplined brings his mother to shame.

16 When the wicked are in authority, transgression increases, but the [uncompromisingly] righteous shall see the fall of the wicked.

## New International Version

¹⁷ Discipline your children, and they will give you peace;
  they will bring you the delights you desire.

¹⁸ Where there is no revelation, people cast off restraint;
  but blessed is the one who heeds wisdom's
  instruction.

¹⁹ Servants cannot be corrected by mere words;
  though they understand, they will not respond.

²⁰ Do you see someone who speaks in haste?
  There is more hope for a fool than for them.

²¹ A servant pampered from youth
  will turn out to be insolent.

²² An angry person stirs up conflict,
  and a hot-tempered person commits many sins.

²³ Pride brings a person low,
  but the lowly in spirit gain honor.

²⁴ The accomplices of thieves are their own enemies;
  they are put under oath and dare not testify.

²⁵ Fear of man will prove to be a snare,
  but whoever trusts in the LORD is kept safe.

²⁶ Many seek an audience with a ruler,
  but it is from the LORD that one gets justice.

²⁷ The righteous detest the dishonest;
  the wicked detest the upright.

### Sayings of Agur

**30** The sayings of Agur son of Jakeh—an inspired
  utterance.

This man's utterance to Ithiel:

"I am weary, God,
  but I can prevail.ᵃ
² Surely I am only a brute, not a man;
  I do not have human understanding.
³ I have not learned wisdom,
  nor have I attained to the knowledge of the Holy One.
⁴ Who has gone up to heaven and come down?
  Whose hands have gathered up the wind?
Who has wrapped up the waters in a cloak?
  Who has established all the ends of the earth?
What is his name, and what is the name of his son?
  Surely you know!

⁵ "Every word of God is flawless;
  he is a shield to those who take refuge in him.
⁶ Do not add to his words,
  or he will rebuke you and prove you a liar.

⁷ "Two things I ask of you, LORD;
  do not refuse me before I die:
⁸ Keep falsehood and lies far from me;
  give me neither poverty nor riches,
  but give me only my daily bread.
⁹ Otherwise, I may have too much and disown you
  and say, 'Who is the LORD?'
Or I may become poor and steal,
  and so dishonor the name of my God.

¹⁰ "Do not slander a servant to their master,
  or they will curse you, and you will pay for it.

¹¹ "There are those who curse their fathers
  and do not bless their mothers;
¹² those who are pure in their own eyes
  and yet are not cleansed of their filth;
¹³ those whose eyes are ever so haughty,
  whose glances are so disdainful;

## Amplified Bible

¹⁷ Correct your son, and he will give you rest; yes, he will
give delight to your heart.

¹⁸ Where there is no vision [no redemptive revelation of
God], the people perish; but he who keeps the law [of God,
which includes that of man]—blessed (happy, fortunate,
and enviable) is he. [I Sam. 3:1; Amos 8:11, 12.]

¹⁹ A servant will not be corrected by words alone; for
though he understands, he will not answer [the master
who mistreats him].

²⁰ Do you see a man who is hasty in his words? There is
more hope for a [self-confident] fool than for him.

²¹ He who pampers his servant from childhood will have
him expecting the rights of a son afterward.

²² A man of wrath stirs up strife, and a man given to anger commits and causes much transgression.

²³ A man's pride will bring him low, but he who is of a
humble spirit will obtain honor. [Prov. 15:33; 18:12; Isa.
66:2; Dan. 4:30; Matt. 23:12; James 4:6, 10; I Pet. 5:5.]

²⁴ Whoever is partner with a thief hates his own life; he
falls under the curse [pronounced upon him who knows
who the thief is] but discloses nothing.

²⁵ The fear of man brings a snare, but whoever leans on,
trusts in, and puts his confidence in the Lord is safe and
set on high.

²⁶ Many crave and seek the ruler's favor, but the wise
man [waits] for justice from the Lord.

²⁷ An unjust man is an abomination to the righteous, and
he who is upright in the way [of the Lord] is an abomination to the wicked.

**30** The words of Agur son of Jakeh of Massa: The
  man says to Ithiel, to Ithiel and to Ucal:
² Surely I am too brutish and stupid to be called a man,
and I have not the understanding of a man [for all my secular learning is as nothing].
³ I have not learned skillful and godly Wisdom, that I
should have the knowledge or burden of the Holy One.
⁴ Who has ascended into heaven and descended? Who
has gathered the wind in His fists? Who has bound the waters in His garment? Who has established all the ends of
the earth? What is His name, and what is His Son's name,
if you know? [John 3:13; Rev. 19:12.]
⁵ Every word of God is tried and purified; He is a shield
to those who trust and take refuge in Him. [Ps. 18:30;
84:11; 115:9-11.]
⁶ Add not to His Words, lest He reprove you, and you be
found a liar.
⁷ Two things have I asked of You [O Lord]; deny them
not to me before I die:
⁸ Remove far from me falsehood and lies; give me neither poverty nor riches; feed me with the food that is needful for me,
⁹ Lest I be full and deny You and say, Who is the Lord?
Or lest I be poor and steal, and so profane the name of
my God. [Deut. 8:12, 14, 17; Neh. 9:25, 26; Job 31:24; Hos.
13:6.]
¹⁰ Do not accuse and hurt a servant before his master,
lest he curse you, and you be held guilty [of adding to the
burdens of the lowly].
¹¹ There is a class of people who curse their fathers and
do not bless their mothers.
¹² There is a class of people who are pure in their own
eyes, and yet are not washed from their own filth.
¹³ There is a class of people—oh, how lofty are their
eyes and their raised eyelids!

---

ᵃ 1 With a different word division of the Hebrew; Masoretic Text
*utterance to Ithiel, / to Ithiel and Ukal:*

## New International Version

14 those whose teeth are swords
and whose jaws are set with knives
to devour the poor from the earth
and the needy from among mankind.

15 "The leech has two daughters.
'Give! Give!' they cry.

"There are three things that are never satisfied,
four that never say, 'Enough!':
16 the grave, the barren womb,
land, which is never satisfied with water,
and fire, which never says, 'Enough!'

17 "The eye that mocks a father,
that scorns an aged mother,
will be pecked out by the ravens of the valley,
will be eaten by the vultures.

18 "There are three things that are too amazing for me,
four that I do not understand:
19 the way of an eagle in the sky,
the way of a snake on a rock,
the way of a ship on the high seas,
and the way of a man with a young woman.

20 "This is the way of an adulterous woman:
She eats and wipes her mouth
and says, 'I've done nothing wrong.'

21 "Under three things the earth trembles,
under four it cannot bear up:
22 a servant who becomes king,
a godless fool who gets plenty to eat,
23 a contemptible woman who gets married,
and a servant who displaces her mistress.

24 "Four things on earth are small,
yet they are extremely wise:
25 Ants are creatures of little strength,
yet they store up their food in the summer;
26 hyraxes are creatures of little power,
yet they make their home in the crags;
27 locusts have no king,
yet they advance together in ranks;
28 a lizard can be caught with the hand,
yet it is found in kings' palaces.

29 "There are three things that are stately in their stride,
four that move with stately bearing:
30 a lion, mighty among beasts,
who retreats before nothing;
31 a strutting rooster, a he-goat,
and a king secure against revolt.*a*

32 "If you play the fool and exalt yourself,
or if you plan evil,
clap your hand over your mouth!
33 For as churning cream produces butter,
and as twisting the nose produces blood,
so stirring up anger produces strife."

### Sayings of King Lemuel

**31** The sayings of King Lemuel—an inspired utterance his mother taught him.

2 Listen, my son! Listen, son of my womb!
Listen, my son, the answer to my prayers!
3 Do not spend your strength*b* on women,
your vigor on those who ruin kings.

4 It is not for kings, Lemuel—
it is not for kings to drink wine,
not for rulers to crave beer,

*a 31* The meaning of the Hebrew for this phrase is uncertain.
*b 3* Or *wealth*

## Amplified Bible

14 There is a class of people whose teeth are as swords and whose fangs as knives, to devour the poor from the earth and the needy from among men.
15 The leech has two daughters, crying, Give, give! There are three things that are never satisfied, yes, four that do not say, It is enough:
16 Sheol (the place of the dead), the barren womb, the earth that is not satisfied with water, and the fire that says not, It is enough.
17 The eye that mocks a father and scorns to obey a mother, the ravens of the valley will pick it out, and the young vultures will devour it. [Lev. 20:9; Prov. 20:20; 23:22.]
18 There are three things which are too wonderful for me, yes, four which I do not understand:
19 The way of an eagle in the air, the way of a serpent upon a rock, the way of a ship in the midst of the sea, and the way of a man with a maid.
20 This is the way of an adulterous woman: she eats and wipes her mouth and says, I have done no wickedness.
21 Under three things the earth is disquieted, and under four it cannot bear up:
22 Under a servant when he reigns, a [empty-headed] fool when he is filled with food,
23 An unloved *and* repugnant woman when she is married, and a maidservant when she supplants her mistress.
24 There are four things which are little on the earth, but they are exceedingly wise:
25 The ants are a people not strong, yet they lay up their food in the summer; [Prov. 6:6.]
26 The conies are but a feeble folk, yet they make their houses in the rocks; [Ps. 104:18.]
27 The locusts have no king, yet they go forth all of them by bands;
28 The lizard you can seize with your hands, yet it is in kings' palaces.
29 There are three things which are stately in step, yes, four which are stately in their stride:
30 The lion, which is mightiest among beasts and turns not back before any;
31 The war horse [well-knit in the loins], the male goat also, and the king [when his army is with him and] against whom there is no uprising.
32 If you have done foolishly in exalting yourself, or if you have thought evil, lay your hand upon your mouth. [Job 21:5; 40:4.]
33 Surely the churning of milk brings forth butter, and the wringing of the nose brings forth blood; so the forcing of wrath brings forth strife.

**31** The words of Lemuel king of Massa, which his mother taught him:

2 What, my *a* son? What, son of my womb? What [shall I advise you], son of my vows *and* dedication to God?
3 Give not your strength to [loose] women, nor your ways to those who *and* that which ruin *and* destroy kings.
4 It is not for kings, O Lemuel, it is not for kings to drink wine, or for rulers to desire strong drink, [Eccl. 10:17; Hos. 4:11.]

*a* It is important to the purpose of this invaluable chapter that one realizes that it is first of all intended for young men. It is the mother's God-given task to provide youth with this information directly from its inspired source, letting them grow up with it in their consciousness.

## New International Version

⁵lest they drink and forget what has been decreed,
  and deprive all the oppressed of their rights.
⁶Let beer be for those who are perishing,
  wine for those who are in anguish!
⁷Let them drink and forget their poverty
  and remember their misery no more.

⁸Speak up for those who cannot speak for themselves,
  for the rights of all who are destitute.
⁹Speak up and judge fairly;
  defend the rights of the poor and needy.

### Epilogue: The Wife of Noble Character

¹⁰ᵃA wife of noble character who can find?
  She is worth far more than rubies.
¹¹Her husband has full confidence in her
  and lacks nothing of value.
¹²She brings him good, not harm,
  all the days of her life.
¹³She selects wool and flax
  and works with eager hands.
¹⁴She is like the merchant ships,
  bringing her food from afar.
¹⁵She gets up while it is still night;
  she provides food for her family
  and portions for her female servants.
¹⁶She considers a field and buys it;
  out of her earnings she plants a vineyard.
¹⁷She sets about her work vigorously;
  her arms are strong for her tasks.
¹⁸She sees that her trading is profitable,
  and her lamp does not go out at night.
¹⁹In her hand she holds the distaff
  and grasps the spindle with her fingers.
²⁰She opens her arms to the poor
  and extends her hands to the needy.
²¹When it snows, she has no fear for her household;
  for all of them are clothed in scarlet.
²²She makes coverings for her bed;
  she is clothed in fine linen and purple.
²³Her husband is respected at the city gate,
  where he takes his seat among the elders of the
  land.
²⁴She makes linen garments and sells them,
  and supplies the merchants with sashes.
²⁵She is clothed with strength and dignity;
  she can laugh at the days to come.
²⁶She speaks with wisdom,
  and faithful instruction is on her tongue.

ᵃ 10 Verses 10-31 are an acrostic poem, the verses of which begin with
the successive letters of the Hebrew alphabet.

## Amplified Bible

⁵Lest they drink and forget the law *and* what it decrees,
and pervert the justice due any of the afflicted.
⁶Give strong drink [as medicine] to him who is ready
to pass away, and wine to him in bitter distress of heart.
⁷Let him drink and forget his poverty and [seriously]
remember his want *and* misery no more.
⁸Open your mouth for the dumb [those unable to speak
for themselves], for the rights of all who are left desolate
*and* defenseless; [I Sam. 19:4; Esth. 4:16; Job 29:15, 16.]
⁹Open your mouth, judge righteously, and administer
justice for the poor and needy. [Lev. 19:15; Deut. 1:16; Job
29:12; Isa. 1:17; Jer. 22:16.]
¹⁰A capable, intelligent, *and* ᵃvirtuous woman—who is
he who can find her? She is far more precious than jewels
*and* her value is far above rubies *or* pearls. [Prov. 12:4;
18:22; 19:14.]
¹¹The heart of her husband trusts in her confidently *and*
relies on and believes in her securely, so that he has no
lack of [honest] gain or need of [dishonest] spoil.
¹²She comforts, encourages, *and* does him only good as
long as there is life within her.
¹³She seeks out wool and flax and works with willing
hands [to develop it].
¹⁴She is like the merchant ships loaded with foodstuffs;
she brings her household's food from a far [country].
¹⁵She rises while it is yet night and gets [spiritual] food
for her household and assigns her maids their tasks. [Job
23:12.]
¹⁶She considers a [new] field before she buys *or* accepts
it [expanding prudently and not courting neglect of her
present duties by assuming other duties]; with her sav-
ings [of time and strength] she plants fruitful vines in her
vineyard. [S. of Sol. 8:12.]
¹⁷She girds herself with strength [spiritual, mental, and
physical fitness for her God-given task] and makes her
arms strong *and* firm.
¹⁸She tastes *and* sees that her gain from work [with and
for God] is good; her lamp goes not out, but it burns on
continually through the night [of trouble, privation, or sorrow, warning away fear, doubt, and distrust].
¹⁹She lays her hands to the spindle, and her hands hold
the distaff.
²⁰She opens her hand to the poor, yes, she reaches out
her filled hands to the needy [whether in body, mind, or
spirit].
²¹She fears not the snow for her family, for all her household are doubly clothed in scarlet. [Josh. 2:18, 19; Heb.
9:19-22.]
²²She makes for herself coverlets, cushions, *and* rugs
of tapestry. Her clothing is of linen, pure *and* fine, and of
purple [such as that of which the clothing of the priests
and the hallowed cloths of the temple were made]. [Isa.
61:10; I Tim. 2:9; Rev. 3:5; 19:8, 14.]
²³Her husband is known in the [city's] gates, when he
sits among the elders of the land. [Prov. 12:4.]
²⁴She makes fine linen garments *and* leads others to
buy them; she delivers to the merchants girdles [or sashes
that free one up for service].
²⁵Strength and dignity are her clothing *and* her position
is strong and secure; she rejoices over the future [the latter day or time to come, knowing that she and her family
are in readiness for it]!
²⁶She opens her mouth in skillful and godly Wisdom,
and on her tongue is the law of kindness [giving counsel
and instruction].

ᵃ It is most unfortunate that this description of God's ideal woman is
usually confined in readers' minds merely to its literal sense—her
ability as a homemaker, as in the picture of Martha of Bethany in Luke
10:38-42. But it is obvious that far more than that is meant. When the
summary of what makes her value "far above rubies" is given (in Prov.
31:30), it is her spiritual life only that is mentioned. One can almost hear
the voice of Jesus saying, "Mary has chosen the good portion . . . which
shall not be taken away from her" (Luke 10:42).

## New International Version

27 She watches over the affairs of her household
   and does not eat the bread of idleness.
28 Her children arise and call her blessed;
   her husband also, and he praises her:
29 "Many women do noble things,
   but you surpass them all."
30 Charm is deceptive, and beauty is fleeting;
   but a woman who fears the LORD is to be praised.
31 Honor her for all that her hands have done,
   and let her works bring her praise at the city gate.

## Amplified Bible

27 She looks well to how things go in her household, and the bread of idleness (gossip, discontent, and self-pity) she will not eat. [I Tim. 5:14; Tit. 2:5.]
28 Her children rise up and call her blessed (happy, fortunate, and to be envied); and her husband boasts of *and* praises her, [saying],
29 a Many daughters have done virtuously, nobly, *and* well [with the strength of character that is steadfast in goodness], but you excel them all.
30 Charm *and* grace are deceptive, and beauty is vain [because it is not lasting], but a woman who reverently *and* worshipfully fears the Lord, she shall be praised!
31 Give her of the fruit of her hands, and let her own works praise her in the gates [of the city]! [Phil. 4:8.]

---

a "Many daughters have done . . . nobly and well . . . but you excel them all." What a glowing description here recorded of this woman in private life, this "capable, intelligent, and virtuous woman" of Prov. 31! It means she had done more than Miriam, the one who led a nation's women in praise to God (Exod. 15:20, 21); Deborah, the patriotic military advisor (Judg. 4:4-10); Ruth, the woman of constancy (Ruth 1:16); Hannah, the ideal mother (I Sam. 1:20; 2:19); the Shunammite, the hospitable woman (II Kings 4:8-10); Huldah, the woman who revealed God's secret message to national leaders (II Kings 22:14); and even more than Queen Esther, the woman who risked sacrificing her life for her people (Esth. 4:16). In what way did she "excel them all"? In her spiritual and practical devotion to God, which permeated every area and relationship of her life. All seven of the Christian virtues (II Pet. 1:5) are there, like colored threads in a tapestry. Her secret, which is open to everyone, is the Holy Spirit's climax to the story, and to this book. In Prov. 31:30, it becomes clear that the "reverent *and* worshipful fear of the Lord," which is "the beginning (the chief and choice part) of Wisdom" (Prov. 9:10), is put forth as the true foundation for a life which is valued by God and her husband as "far above rubies *or* pearls" (Prov. 31:10).

# Ecclesiastes

## Everything Is Meaningless

**1** The words of the Teacher,[a] son of David, king in Jerusalem:

² "Meaningless! Meaningless!"
    says the Teacher.
"Utterly meaningless!
    Everything is meaningless."

³ What do people gain from all their labors
    at which they toil under the sun?
⁴ Generations come and generations go,
    but the earth remains forever.
⁵ The sun rises and the sun sets,
    and hurries back to where it rises.
⁶ The wind blows to the south
    and turns to the north;
round and round it goes,
    ever returning on its course.
⁷ All streams flow into the sea,
    yet the sea is never full.
To the place the streams come from,
    there they return again.
⁸ All things are wearisome,
    more than one can say.
The eye never has enough of seeing,
    nor the ear its fill of hearing.
⁹ What has been will be again,
    what has been done will be done again;
    there is nothing new under the sun.
¹⁰ Is there anything of which one can say,
    "Look! This is something new"?
It was here already, long ago;
    it was here before our time.
¹¹ No one remembers the former generations,
    and even those yet to come
will not be remembered
    by those who follow them.

## Wisdom Is Meaningless

¹² I, the Teacher, was king over Israel in Jerusalem. ¹³ I applied my mind to study and to explore by wisdom all that is done under the heavens. What a heavy burden God has laid on mankind! ¹⁴ I have seen all the things that are done under the sun; all of them are meaningless, a chasing after the wind.

¹⁵ What is crooked cannot be straightened;
    what is lacking cannot be counted.

¹⁶ I said to myself, "Look, I have increased in wisdom more than anyone who has ruled over Jerusalem before me; I have experienced much of wisdom and knowledge." ¹⁷ Then I applied myself to the understanding of wisdom, and also of madness and folly, but I learned that this, too, is a chasing after the wind.

¹⁸ For with much wisdom comes much sorrow;
    the more knowledge, the more grief.

---

# Ecclesiastes

**1** The words of the Preacher, the son of David and king in Jerusalem.
² Vapor of vapors *and* futility of futilities, says the Preacher. Vapor of vapors *and* futility of futilities! All is vanity (emptiness, falsity, and vainglory). [Rom. 8:20.]
³ What profit does man have left from all his toil at which he toils *a*under the sun? [Is life worth living?]
⁴ One generation goes and another generation comes, but the earth remains forever. [Ps. 119:90.]
⁵ The sun also rises and the sun goes down, and hastens to the place where it rises.
⁶ The wind goes to the south and circles about to the north; it circles *and* circles about continually, and on its circuit the wind returns again. [John 3:8.]
⁷ All the rivers run into the sea, yet the sea is not full. To the place from which the rivers come, to there *and* from there they return again.
⁸ All things are weary with toil *and* all words are feeble; man cannot utter it. The eye is not satisfied with seeing, nor the ear filled with hearing. [Prov. 27:20.]
⁹ The thing that has been—it is what will be again, and that which has been done is that which will be done again; and there is nothing new under the sun.
¹⁰ Is there a thing of which it may be said, See, this is new? It has already been, in the vast ages of time [recorded or unrecorded] which were before us.
¹¹ There is no remembrance of former happenings *or* men, neither will there be any remembrance of happenings of generations that are to come by those who are to come after them.
¹² I, the Preacher, have been king over Israel in Jerusalem.
¹³ And I applied myself by heart *and* mind to seek and search out by [human] *b*wisdom all human activity under heaven. It is a miserable business which *c*God has given to the sons of man with which to busy themselves.
¹⁴ I have seen all the works that are done under the sun, and behold, all is vanity, a striving after the wind *and* a feeding on wind.
¹⁵ What is crooked cannot be made straight, and what is defective *and* lacking cannot be counted.
¹⁶ I entered into counsel with my own mind, saying, Behold, I have acquired great [human] wisdom, yes, more than all who have been over Jerusalem before me; and my mind has had great experience of [moral] wisdom and [scientific] knowledge.
¹⁷ And I gave my mind to know [practical] wisdom and to discern [the character of] madness and folly [in which men seem to find satisfaction]; I perceived that this also is a searching after wind *and* a feeding on it. [I Thess. 5:21.]
¹⁸ For in much [human] wisdom is much vexation, and he who increases knowledge increases sorrow.

---

*a* Ecclesiastes is the book of the natural man whose interests are confined to the unstable, vanishing pleasures and empty satisfactions of those who live merely "under the sun." The natural man is not aware that all the affirmative answers to life are to be found in Him Who is above, not "under," the sun. The natural man grovels in the dust and finds only earthworms, while the spiritual man may soar on wings like eagles (Isa. 40:31) above all that is futile and disappointing, and may live in the consciousness of God's companionship, favor, and incomparable, everlasting rewards. *b* The "Wisdom" of Proverbs is not the "wisdom" of Ecclesiastes. The former is Godlike, the latter is usually human. *c* Throughout this book not once is the Supreme Being recognized as "Lord" [of lords and King of kings]. The word used to designate Him is invariably the one that may be applied to God or to idols—"Elohim," the God recognized "under the sun." The wisdom which is thus limited can end only in "a miserable business" and in vexation of spirit until it finds "the wisdom that is from above" (James 3:17 KJV), "the hidden wisdom, which God ordained before the world unto our glory" (I Cor. 2:7 KJV).

## New International Version

### Pleasures Are Meaningless

**2** I said to myself, "Come now, I will test you with pleasure to find out what is good." But that also proved to be meaningless. [2]"Laughter," I said, "is madness. And what does pleasure accomplish?" [3]I tried cheering myself with wine, and embracing folly—my mind still guiding me with wisdom. I wanted to see what was good for people to do under the heavens during the few days of their lives.

[4]I undertook great projects: I built houses for myself and planted vineyards. [5]I made gardens and parks and planted all kinds of fruit trees in them. [6]I made reservoirs to water groves of flourishing trees. [7]I bought male and female slaves and had other slaves who were born in my house. I also owned more herds and flocks than anyone in Jerusalem before me. [8]I amassed silver and gold for myself, and the treasure of kings and provinces. I acquired male and female singers, and a harem[a] as well—the delights of a man's heart. [9]I became greater by far than anyone in Jerusalem before me. In all this my wisdom stayed with me.

[10]I denied myself nothing my eyes desired;
  I refused my heart no pleasure.
My heart took delight in all my labor,
  and this was the reward for all my toil.
[11]Yet when I surveyed all that my hands had done
  and what I had toiled to achieve,
everything was meaningless, a chasing after the wind;
  nothing was gained under the sun.

### Wisdom and Folly Are Meaningless

[12]Then I turned my thoughts to consider wisdom,
  and also madness and folly.
What more can the king's successor do
  than what has already been done?
[13]I saw that wisdom is better than folly,
  just as light is better than darkness.
[14]The wise have eyes in their heads,
  while the fool walks in the darkness;
but I came to realize
  that the same fate overtakes them both.

[15]Then I said to myself,

"The fate of the fool will overtake me also.
  What then do I gain by being wise?"
I said to myself,
  "This too is meaningless."
[16]For the wise, like the fool, will not be long
  remembered;
the days have already come when both have been
  forgotten.
Like the fool, the wise too must die!

### Toil Is Meaningless

[17]So I hated life, because the work that is done under the sun was grievous to me. All of it is meaningless, a chasing after the wind. [18]I hated all the things I had toiled for under the sun, because I must leave them to the one who comes after me. [19]And who knows whether that person will be wise or foolish? Yet they will have control over all the fruit of my toil into which I have poured my effort and skill under the sun. This too is meaningless. [20]So my

## Amplified Bible

**2** I said in my mind, Come now, I will prove you with mirth *and* test you with pleasure; so have a good time [enjoy pleasure]. But this also was vanity (emptiness, falsity, and futility)! [Luke 12:19, 20.]

[2]I said of laughter, It is mad, and of pleasure, What does it accomplish?

[3]I searched in my mind how to cheer my body with wine—yet at the same time having my mind hold its course *and* guide me with [human] wisdom—and how to lay hold of folly, till I might see what was good for the sons of men to do under heaven all the days of their lives.

[4]I made great works; I built myself houses, I planted vineyards.

[5]I made for myself gardens and orchards and I planted in them all kinds of fruit trees.

[6]I made for myself pools of water from which to water the forest *and* make the trees bud.

[7]I bought menservants and maidservants and had servants born in my house. Also I had great possessions of herds and flocks, more than any who had been before me in Jerusalem.

[8]I also gathered for myself silver and gold and the treasure of kings and of the provinces. I got for myself men singers and women singers, and the delights of the sons of men—[a]concubines very many. [I Kings 9:28; 10:10, 14, 21.]

[9]So I became great and increased more than all who were before me in Jerusalem. Also my wisdom remained with me *and* stood by me.

[10]And whatever my eyes desired I kept not from them; I withheld not my heart from any pleasure, for my heart rejoiced in all my labor, and this was my portion *and* reward for all my toil.

[11]Then I looked on all that my hands had done and the labor I had spent in doing it, and behold, all was vanity and a striving after the wind *and* a feeding on it, and there was no profit under the sun. [Matt. 16:26.]

[12]So I turned to consider [human] wisdom and madness and folly; for what can the man do who succeeds the king? Nothing but what has been done already.

[13]Then I saw that even [human] wisdom [that brings sorrow] is better than [the pleasures of] folly as far as light is better than darkness.

[14]The wise man's eyes are in his head, but the fool walks in darkness; and yet I perceived that [in the end] one event happens to them both. [Prov. 17:24.]

[15]Then said I in my heart, As it happens to the fool, so it will happen even to me. And of what use is it then for me to be more wise? Then I said in my heart, This also is vanity (emptiness, vainglory, and futility)!

[16]For of the wise man, the same as of the fool, there is no permanent remembrance, since in the days to come all will be long forgotten. And how does the wise man die? Even as the fool!

[17]So I hated life, because what is done under the sun was grievous to me; for all is vanity and a striving after the wind *and* a feeding on it.

[18]And I hated all my labor in which I had toiled under the sun, seeing that I must leave it to the man who will succeed me. [Ps. 49:10.]

[19]And who knows whether he will be a wise man or a fool? Yet he will have dominion over all my labor in which I have toiled and in which I have shown myself wise under the sun. This is also vanity (emptiness, falsity, and futility)!

---

[a] Solomon's reign began under most promising conditions: he "loved the Lord, walking in the statutes of David his father . . . All Israel . . . feared the king [Solomon], for they saw that the wisdom of God was in him, to do judgment" (I Kings 3:3, 28 KJV). But soon his own "wisdom" alone was guiding him. He openly affronted God by taking many wives, including even heathen women. They seduced him into tolerating and even practicing idolatry (I Kings 11:1ff.).

---

[a] 8 The meaning of the Hebrew for this phrase is uncertain.

## New International Version

heart began to despair over all my toilsome labor under the sun. <sup>21</sup>For a person may labor with wisdom, knowledge and skill, and then they must leave all they own to another who has not toiled for it. This too is meaningless and a great misfortune. <sup>22</sup>What do people get for all the toil and anxious striving with which they labor under the sun? <sup>23</sup>All their days their work is grief and pain; even at night their minds do not rest. This too is meaningless.

<sup>24</sup>A person can do nothing better than to eat and drink and find satisfaction in their own toil. This too, I see, is from the hand of God, <sup>25</sup>for without him, who can eat or find enjoyment? <sup>26</sup>To the person who pleases him, God gives wisdom, knowledge and happiness, but to the sinner he gives the task of gathering and storing up wealth to hand it over to the one who pleases God. This too is meaningless, a chasing after the wind.

### A Time for Everything

**3** There is a time for everything,
and a season for every activity under the heavens:

<sup>2</sup>    a time to be born and a time to die,
a time to plant and a time to uproot,
<sup>3</sup>    a time to kill and a time to heal,
a time to tear down and a time to build,
<sup>4</sup>    a time to weep and a time to laugh,
a time to mourn and a time to dance,
<sup>5</sup>    a time to scatter stones and a time to gather them,
a time to embrace and a time to refrain from
embracing,
<sup>6</sup>    a time to search and a time to give up,
a time to keep and a time to throw away,
<sup>7</sup>    a time to tear and a time to mend,
a time to be silent and a time to speak,
<sup>8</sup>    a time to love and a time to hate,
a time for war and a time for peace.

<sup>9</sup>What do workers gain from their toil? <sup>10</sup>I have seen the burden God has laid on the human race. <sup>11</sup>He has made everything beautiful in its time. He has also set eternity in the human heart; yet[a] no one can fathom what God has done from beginning to end. <sup>12</sup>I know that there is nothing better for people than to be happy and to do good while they live. <sup>13</sup>That each of them may eat and drink, and find satisfaction in all their toil—this is the gift of God. <sup>14</sup>I know that everything God does will endure forever; nothing can be added to it and nothing taken from it. God does it so that people will fear him.

<sup>15</sup>Whatever is has already been,
and what will be has been before;
and God will call the past to account.[b]

<sup>16</sup>And I saw something else under the sun:

In the place of judgment—wickedness was there,
in the place of justice—wickedness was there.

<sup>17</sup>I said to myself,

"God will bring into judgment
both the righteous and the wicked,
for there will be a time for every activity,
a time to judge every deed."

## Amplified Bible

<sup>20</sup>So I turned around and gave my heart up to despair over all the labor of my efforts under the sun.

<sup>21</sup>For here is a man whose labor is with wisdom and knowledge and skill; yet to a man who has not toiled for it he must leave it all as his portion. This also is vanity (emptiness, falsity, and futility) and a great evil!

<sup>22</sup>For what has a man left from all his labor and from the striving *and* vexation of his heart in which he has toiled under the sun?

<sup>23</sup>For all his days are but pain *and* sorrow, and his work is a vexation *and* grief; his mind takes no rest even at night. This is also vanity (emptiness, falsity, and futility)!

<sup>24</sup>There is nothing better for a man than that he should eat and drink and make himself enjoy good in his labor. Even this, I have seen, is from the hand of God.

<sup>25</sup>For who can eat or who can have enjoyment any more than I can—[a] *apart from Him*?

<sup>26</sup>For to the person who pleases Him God gives wisdom and knowledge and joy; but to the sinner He gives the work of gathering and heaping up, that he may give to one who pleases God. This also is vanity and a striving after the wind *and* a feeding on it.

**3** To everything there is a season, and a time for every matter *or* purpose under heaven:

<sup>2</sup>A time to be born and a time to die, a time to plant and a time to pluck up what is planted, [Heb. 9:27.]

<sup>3</sup>A time to kill and a time to heal, a time to break down and a time to build up,

<sup>4</sup>A time to weep and a time to laugh, a time to mourn and a time to dance,

<sup>5</sup>A time to cast away stones and a time to gather stones together, a time to embrace and a time to refrain from embracing,

<sup>6</sup>A time to get and a time to lose, a time to keep and a time to cast away,

<sup>7</sup>A time to rend and a time to sew, a time to keep silence and a time to speak, [Amos 5:13.]

<sup>8</sup>A time to love and a time to hate, a time for war and a time for peace. [Luke 14:26.]

<sup>9</sup>What profit remains for the worker from his toil?

<sup>10</sup>I have seen the painful labor *and* exertion *and* miserable business which God has given to the sons of men with which to exercise *and* busy themselves.

<sup>11</sup>He has made everything beautiful in its time. He also has planted eternity in men's hearts *and* minds [a divinely implanted sense of a purpose working through the ages which nothing under the sun but God alone can satisfy], yet so that men cannot find out what God has done from the beginning to the end.

<sup>12</sup>I know that there is nothing better for them than to be glad and to get *and* do good as long as they live;

<sup>13</sup>And also that every man should eat and drink and enjoy the good of all his labor—it is the gift of God.

<sup>14</sup>I know that whatever God does, it endures forever; nothing can be added to it nor anything taken from it. And God does it so that men will [reverently] fear Him [revere and worship Him, knowing that He is]. [Ps. 19:9; James 1:17.]

<sup>15</sup>That which is now already has been, and that which is to be already has been; and God seeks that which has passed by [so that history repeats itself].

<sup>16</sup>Moreover, I saw under the sun that in the place of justice there was wickedness, and that in the place of righteousness wickedness was there also.

<sup>17</sup>I said in my heart, God will judge the righteous and the wicked, for there is a time [appointed] for every matter *and* purpose and for every work.

---

[a] 11 Or *also placed ignorance in the human heart, so that* [b] 15 Or *God calls back the past*

[a] According to *The Septuagint* (Greek translation of the Old Testament) and *The Syriac* reading: Jesus recognized the unprecedented glory which Solomon's human wisdom had brought him, but He said that Solomon arrayed in all of it was not equal in glory to one tiny lily of the field—which God's wisdom had made (Matt. 6:29).

## New International Version

<sup>18</sup>I also said to myself, "As for humans, God tests them so that they may see that they are like the animals. <sup>19</sup>Surely the fate of human beings is like that of the animals; the same fate awaits them both: As one dies, so dies the other. All have the same breath<sup>a</sup>; humans have no advantage over animals. Everything is meaningless. <sup>20</sup>All go to the same place; all come from dust, and to dust all return. <sup>21</sup>Who knows if the human spirit rises upward and if the spirit of the animal goes down into the earth?"

<sup>22</sup>So I saw that there is nothing better for a person than to enjoy their work, because that is their lot. For who can bring them to see what will happen after them?

### Oppression, Toil, Friendlessness

**4** Again I looked and saw all the oppression that was taking place under the sun:

I saw the tears of the oppressed—
    and they have no comforter;
power was on the side of their oppressors—
    and they have no comforter.
<sup>2</sup>And I declared that the dead,
    who had already died,
are happier than the living,
    who are still alive.
<sup>3</sup>But better than both
    is the one who has never been born,
who has not seen the evil
    that is done under the sun.

<sup>4</sup>And I saw that all toil and all achievement spring from one person's envy of another. This too is meaningless, a chasing after the wind.

<sup>5</sup>Fools fold their hands
    and ruin themselves.
<sup>6</sup>Better one handful with tranquillity
    than two handfuls with toil
    and chasing after the wind.

<sup>7</sup>Again I saw something meaningless under the sun:

<sup>8</sup>There was a man all alone;
    he had neither son nor brother.
There was no end to his toil,
    yet his eyes were not content with his wealth.
"For whom am I toiling," he asked,
    "and why am I depriving myself of enjoyment?"
This too is meaningless—
    a miserable business!

<sup>9</sup>Two are better than one,
    because they have a good return for their labor:
<sup>10</sup>If either of them falls down,
    one can help the other up.
But pity anyone who falls
    and has no one to help them up.
<sup>11</sup>Also, if two lie down together, they will keep warm.
    But how can one keep warm alone?
<sup>12</sup>Though one may be overpowered,
    two can defend themselves.
A cord of three strands is not quickly broken.

---

<sup>a</sup> 19 Or spirit

## Amplified Bible

<sup>18</sup>I said in my heart regarding the subject of the sons of men, God is trying (separating and sifting) them, that they may see that by themselves [under the sun, without God] they are but like beasts.

<sup>19</sup>For that which befalls the sons of men befalls beasts; even [in the end] one thing befalls them both. As the one dies, so dies the other. Yes, they all have one breath *and* spirit, so that a <sup>a</sup>man has no preeminence over a beast; for all is vanity (emptiness, falsity, and futility)!

<sup>20</sup>All go to one place; all are of the dust, and all turn to dust again.

<sup>21</sup>Who knows the spirit of man, whether it goes upward, and the spirit of the beast, whether it goes downward to the earth?

<sup>22</sup>So I saw that there is nothing better than that a man should rejoice in his own works, for that is his portion. For who shall bring him back to see what will happen after he is gone?

**4** Then I returned and considered all the oppressions that are practiced under the sun: And I beheld the tears of the oppressed, and they had no comforter; and on the side of their oppressors was power, but they [too] had no comforter.

<sup>2</sup>So I praised *and* thought more fortunate those who have been long dead than the living, who are still alive.

<sup>3</sup>But better than them both [I thought] is he who has not yet been born, who has not seen the evil deeds that are done under the sun.

<sup>4</sup>Then I saw that all painful effort in labor and all skill in work comes from man's rivalry with his neighbor. This is also vanity, a vain striving after the wind *and* a feeding on it.

<sup>5</sup>The fool folds his hands together and eats his own flesh [destroying himself by indolence].

<sup>6</sup>Better is a handful with quietness than both hands full with painful effort, a vain striving after the wind *and* a feeding on it.

<sup>7</sup>Then I returned, and I saw vanity under the sun [in one of its peculiar forms].

<sup>8</sup>Here is one alone—no one with him; he neither has child nor brother. Yet there is no end to all his labor, neither is his eye satisfied with riches, neither does he ask, For whom do I labor and deprive myself of good? This is also vanity (emptiness, falsity, and futility); yes, it is a painful effort *and* an unhappy business. [Prov. 27:20; I John 2:16.]

<sup>9</sup>Two are better than one, because they have a good [more satisfying] reward for their labor:

<sup>10</sup>For if they fall, the one will lift up his fellow. But woe to him who is alone when he falls and has not another to lift him up!

<sup>11</sup>Again, if two lie down together, then they have warmth; but how can one be warm alone?

<sup>12</sup>And though a man might prevail against him who is alone, two will withstand him. A threefold cord is not quickly broken.

---

<sup>a</sup> Does the Bible really teach that "a man has no preeminence over a beast"? No! The Bible only records that the book of Ecclesiastes says it. Then why is this book in the Bible? Can it possibly be called inspired by God when it makes such "under the sun" pronouncements, some only partially true, others entirely false? Here is the tested answer: "Every scripture inspired of God is also profitable for teaching . . . reproof . . . correction, for instruction . . . in righteousness." (II Tim. 3:16 ASV.) The divine purpose in including Ecclesiastes in the Bible is obvious. It gives a startling picture of how fatal it is for even the wisest of men to substitute man's "wisdom" for God's wisdom, and to attempt to live by it. Solomon's reign began with God, gold, and glory. It ended with bafflement, brass, and bewildered acceptance of man's having "no preeminence over a beast"!—man, who was made "in the image *and* likeness of God" (Gen. 1:27) and "but little lower than God [or heavenly beings]"! (Ps. 8:5.)

## New International Version

### Advancement Is Meaningless

13 Better a poor but wise youth than an old but foolish king who no longer knows how to heed a warning. 14 The youth may have come from prison to the kingship, or he may have been born in poverty within his kingdom. 15 I saw that all who lived and walked under the sun followed the youth, the king's successor. 16 There was no end to all the people who were before them. But those who came later were not pleased with the successor. This too is meaningless, a chasing after the wind.

### Fulfill Your Vow to God

5 a Guard your steps when you go to the house of God. Go near to listen rather than to offer the sacrifice of fools, who do not know that they do wrong.

2 Do not be quick with your mouth,
  do not be hasty in your heart
    to utter anything before God.
God is in heaven
  and you are on earth,
    so let your words be few.
3 A dream comes when there are many cares,
  and many words mark the speech of a fool.

4 When you make a vow to God, do not delay to fulfill it. He has no pleasure in fools; fulfill your vow. 5 It is better not to make a vow than to make one and not fulfill it. 6 Do not let your mouth lead you into sin. And do not protest to the temple messenger, "My vow was a mistake." Why should God be angry at what you say and destroy the work of your hands? 7 Much dreaming and many words are meaningless. Therefore fear God.

### Riches Are Meaningless

8 If you see the poor oppressed in a district, and justice and rights denied, do not be surprised at such things; for one official is eyed by a higher one, and over them both are others higher still. 9 The increase from the land is taken by all; the king himself profits from the fields.

10 Whoever loves money never has enough;
  whoever loves wealth is never satisfied with their income.
    This too is meaningless.

11 As goods increase,
  so do those who consume them.
And what benefit are they to the owners
  except to feast their eyes on them?

12 The sleep of a laborer is sweet,
  whether they eat little or much,
but as for the rich, their abundance
  permits them no sleep.

13 I have seen a grievous evil under the sun:

wealth hoarded to the harm of its owners,
14    or wealth lost through some misfortune,
so that when they have children
  there is nothing left for them to inherit.
15 Everyone comes naked from their mother's womb,
  and as everyone comes, so they depart.
They take nothing from their toil
  that they can carry in their hands.

16 This too is a grievous evil:

As everyone comes, so they depart,
  and what do they gain,
    since they toil for the wind?
17 All their days they eat in darkness,
  with great frustration, affliction and anger.

a In Hebrew texts 5:1 is numbered 4:17, and 5:2-20 is numbered 5:1-19.

## Amplified Bible

13 Better is a poor and wise youth than an old and foolish king who a no longer knows how to receive counsel (friendly reproof and warning)—

14 Even though [the youth] comes out of prison to reign, while the other, born a king, becomes needy.

15 I saw all the living who walk under the sun with the youth who was to stand up in the king's stead.

16 There was no end to all the people; he was over all of them. Yet those who come later will not rejoice in him. Surely this also is vanity (emptiness, falsity, vainglory) and a striving after the wind and a feeding on it.

5 Keep your foot [give your mind to what you are doing] when you go [as Jacob to sacred Bethel] to the house of God. For to draw near to hear and obey is better than to give the sacrifice of fools [carelessly, irreverently] too ignorant to know that they are doing evil. [Gen. 35:1-4; Exod. 3:5.]

2 Be not rash with your mouth, and let not your heart be hasty to utter a word before God. For God is in heaven, and you are on earth; therefore let your words be few.

3 For a dream comes with much business and painful effort, and a fool's voice with many words.

4 When you vow a vow or make a pledge to God, do not put off paying it; for God has no pleasure in fools (those who witlessly mock Him). Pay what you vow. [Ps. 50:14; 66:13, 14; 76:11.]

5 It is better that you should not vow than that you should vow and not pay. [Prov. 20:25; Acts 5:4.]

6 Do not allow your mouth to cause your body to sin, and do not say before the messenger [the priest] that it was an error or mistake. Why should God be [made] angry at your voice and destroy the work of your hands? [Mal. 2:7.]

7 For in a multitude of dreams there is futility and worthlessness, and ruin in a flood of words. But [reverently] fear God [revere and worship Him, knowing that He is].

8 If you see the oppression of the poor and the violent taking away of justice and righteousness in the state or province, do not marvel at the matter. [Be sure that there are those who will attend to it] for a higher [official] than the high is observing, and higher ones are over them.

9 Moreover, the profit of the earth is for all; the king himself is served by the field and in all, a king is an advantage to a land with cultivated fields.

10 He who loves silver will not be satisfied with silver, nor he who loves abundance with gain. This also is vanity (emptiness, falsity, and futility)!

11 When goods increase, they who eat them increase also. And what gain is there to their owner except to see them with his eyes?

12 The sleep of a laboring man is sweet, whether he eats little or much, but the fullness of the rich will not let him sleep.

13 There is a serious and severe evil which I have seen under the sun: riches were kept by their owner to his hurt.

14 But those riches are lost in a bad venture; and he becomes the father of a son, and there is nothing in his hand [with which to support the child].

15 As [the man] came forth from his mother's womb, so he will go again, naked as he came; and he will take away nothing for all his labor which he can carry in his hand.

16 And this also is a serious and severe evil—that in all points as he came, so shall he go; and what gain has he who labors for the wind? [I Tim. 6:6.]

17 All his days also he eats in darkness [cheerlessly, with no sweetness and light in them], and much sorrow and sickness and wrath are his.

a "Christianity calls upon us to make our old age into an aspect of youth. There is to be no old age in the sense of spiritual exhaustion or moral decrepitude or misanthropic isolation; old age is to be equivalent to increase of kingliness and bounty and holy influence." "The path of the righteous is as the dawning light that shineth more and more unto the perfect day" (Prov. 4:18 ASV).

## New International Version

[18]This is what I have observed to be good: that it is appropriate for a person to eat, to drink and to find satisfaction in their toilsome labor under the sun during the few days of life God has given them—for this is their lot. [19]Moreover, when God gives someone wealth and possessions, and the ability to enjoy them, to accept their lot and be happy in their toil—this is a gift of God. [20]They seldom reflect on the days of their life, because God keeps them occupied with gladness of heart.

**6** I have seen another evil under the sun, and it weighs heavily on mankind: [2]God gives some people wealth, possessions and honor, so that they lack nothing their hearts desire, but God does not grant them the ability to enjoy them, and strangers enjoy them instead. This is meaningless, a grievous evil.

[3]A man may have a hundred children and live many years; yet no matter how long he lives, if he cannot enjoy his prosperity and does not receive proper burial, I say that a stillborn child is better off than he. [4]It comes without meaning, it departs in darkness, and in darkness its name is shrouded. [5]Though it never saw the sun or knew anything, it has more rest than does that man— [6]even if he lives a thousand years twice over but fails to enjoy his prosperity. Do not all go to the same place?

[7]Everyone's toil is for their mouth,
  yet their appetite is never satisfied.
[8]What advantage have the wise over fools?
What do the poor gain
  by knowing how to conduct themselves before
    others?
[9]Better what the eye sees
  than the roving of the appetite.
This too is meaningless,
  a chasing after the wind.

[10]Whatever exists has already been named,
  and what humanity is has been known;
no one can contend
  with someone who is stronger.
[11]The more the words,
  the less the meaning,
  and how does that profit anyone?

[12]For who knows what is good for a person in life, during the few and meaningless days they pass through like a shadow? Who can tell them what will happen under the sun after they are gone?

**Wisdom**

**7** A good name is better than fine perfume,
  and the day of death better than the day of birth.
[2]It is better to go to a house of mourning

## Amplified Bible

[18]Behold, what I have seen to be good and fitting is for one to eat and drink, and to find enjoyment in all the labor in which he labors under the sun all the days which God gives him—for this is his [allotted] part. [I Tim. 6:17.]
[19]Also, every man to whom God has given riches and possessions, and the power to enjoy them and to accept his appointed lot and to rejoice in his toil—this is the gift of God [to him].
[20]For he shall not much remember [seriously] the days of his life, because God [Himself] answers and corresponds to the joy of his heart [the tranquillity of God is mirrored in him].

**6** There is an evil which I have seen under the sun, and it lies heavily upon men:
[2]A man to whom God has given riches, possessions, and honor, so that he lacks nothing for his soul of all that he might desire, yet God does not give him the power or capacity to enjoy them [things which are gifts from God], but a stranger [in whom he has no interest succeeds him and] consumes and enjoys them. This is vanity (emptiness, falsity, and futility); it is a sore affliction! [Luke 12:20.]
[3]If a man begets a hundred children and lives many years so that the days of his years are many, but his life is not filled with good, and also he is given no burial [honors nor is laid to rest in the sepulcher of his fathers], I say that [he who had] an untimely birth [resulting in death] is better off than he, [Job 3:16.]
[4]For [the untimely one] comes in futility and goes into darkness, and in darkness his name is covered.
[5]Moreover, he has not seen the sun nor had any knowledge, yet he [the stillborn child] has rest rather than he [who is aware of all that he has missed and all that he would not have had to suffer].
[6]Even though he lives a thousand years twice over and yet has seen no good and experienced no enjoyment—do not all go to one place [the place of the dead]?
[7]All the labor of man is for his mouth [for self-preservation and enjoyment], and yet his desire is not satisfied. [Prov. 16:26.]
[8]For what advantage has the wise man over the fool [being worldly-wise is not the secret to happiness]? What advantage has the poor man who has learned how to walk before the living [publicly, with men's eyes upon him; being poor is not the secret to happiness either]?
[9]Better is the sight of the eyes [the enjoyment of what is available to one] than the cravings of wandering desire. This is also vanity (emptiness, falsity, and futility) and a striving after the wind and a feeding on it!
[10]Whatever [man] is, he has been named that long ago, and it is known that it is man *a* [Adam]; nor can he contend with Him who is mightier than he [whether God or death].
[11]Seeing that there are [all these and] many other things and words that increase the emptiness, falsity, vainglory, and futility [of living], what profit and what outcome is there for man?
[12]For who [*b* limited to human wisdom] knows what is good for man in his life, all the days of his vain life which he spends as a shadow [going through the motions but accomplishing nothing]? For who can tell a man what will happen [to his work, his treasure, his plans] under the sun after he is gone?

**7** A good name is better than precious perfume, and the day of death better than the day of one's birth.
[2]It is better to go to the house of mourning than to go to

*a* The Hebrew "Adam" means man, of the ground. The very name witnesses to his frailty. *b* How impressive throughout Ecclesiastes is the evidence that, while Solomon is doing his utmost to prove that life is futile and not worth living, the Holy Spirit is using him to show that these conclusions are the tragic effect of living "under the sun"— ignoring the Lord, dwelling away from God the Father, oblivious of the Holy Spirit—and yet face to face with the mysteries of life and nature!

## New International Version

than to go to a house of feasting,
for death is the destiny of everyone;
the living should take this to heart.
[3] Frustration is better than laughter,
because a sad face is good for the heart.
[4] The heart of the wise is in the house of mourning,
but the heart of fools is in the house of pleasure.
[5] It is better to heed the rebuke of a wise person
than to listen to the song of fools.
[6] Like the crackling of thorns under the pot,
so is the laughter of fools.
This too is meaningless.

[7] Extortion turns a wise person into a fool,
and a bribe corrupts the heart.

[8] The end of a matter is better than its beginning,
and patience is better than pride.
[9] Do not be quickly provoked in your spirit,
for anger resides in the lap of fools.

[10] Do not say, "Why were the old days better than these?"
For it is not wise to ask such questions.

[11] Wisdom, like an inheritance, is a good thing
and benefits those who see the sun.
[12] Wisdom is a shelter
as money is a shelter,
but the advantage of knowledge is this:
Wisdom preserves those who have it.

[13] Consider what God has done:

Who can straighten
what he has made crooked?
[14] When times are good, be happy;
but when times are bad, consider this:
God has made the one
as well as the other.
Therefore, no one can discover
anything about their future.

[15] In this meaningless life of mine I have seen both of
these:

the righteous perishing in their righteousness,
and the wicked living long in their wickedness.
[16] Do not be overrighteous,
neither be overwise—
why destroy yourself?
[17] Do not be overwicked,
and do not be a fool—
why die before your time?
[18] It is good to grasp the one
and not let go of the other.
Whoever fears God will avoid all extremes.[a]

[19] Wisdom makes one wise person more powerful
than ten rulers in a city.

[20] Indeed, there is no one on earth who is righteous,
no one who does what is right and never sins.

[21] Do not pay attention to every word people say,
or you may hear your servant cursing you—
[22] for you know in your heart
that many times you yourself have cursed others.

[23] All this I tested by wisdom and I said,

"I am determined to be wise"—
but this was beyond me.
[24] Whatever exists is far off and most profound—
who can discover it?
[25] So I turned my mind to understand,
to investigate and to search out wisdom and the
scheme of things

[a] 18 Or *will follow them both*

## Amplified Bible

the house of feasting, for that is the end of all men; and the
living will lay it to heart.
[3] Sorrow is better than laughter, for by the sadness of
the countenance the heart is made better *and* gains gladness. [II Cor. 7:10.]
[4] The heart of the wise is in the house of mourning, but
the heart of fools is in the house of mirth *and* sensual joy.
[5] It is better for a man to hear the rebuke of the wise than
to hear the song of fools.
[6] For like the crackling of thorns under a pot, so is the
laughter of the fool. This also is vanity (emptiness, falsity,
and futility)!
[7] Surely oppression *and* extortion make a wise man foolish, and a bribe destroys the understanding *and* judgment.
[8] Better is the end of a thing than the beginning of it,
and the patient in spirit is better than the proud in spirit.
[9] Do not be quick in spirit to be angry *or* vexed, for anger
*and* vexation lodge in the bosom of fools. [James 1:19, 20.]
[10] Do not say, Why were the old days better than these?
For it is not wise *or* because of wisdom that you ask this.
[11] Wisdom is as good as an inheritance, yes, more excellent it is for those [the living] who see the sun.
[12] For wisdom is a defense even as money is a defense,
but the excellency of knowledge is that wisdom shields
*and* preserves the life of him who has it.
[13] Consider the work of God: who can make straight
what He has made crooked?
[14] In the day of prosperity be joyful, but in the day of
adversity consider that God has made the one side by side
with the other, so that man may not find out anything that
shall be after him.
[15] I have seen everything in the days of my vanity (my
emptiness, falsity, vainglory, and futility): there is a righteous man who perishes in his righteousness, and there is
a wicked man who prolongs his life in [spite of] his evildoing.
[16] Be not [morbidly exacting and externally] righteous
overmuch, neither strive to make yourself [pretentiously
appear] overwise—why should you [get puffed up and]
destroy yourself [with presumptuous self-sufficiency]?
[17] [Although all have sinned] be not wicked overmuch
*or* willfully, neither be foolish—why should you die before
your time?
[18] It is good that you should take hold of this and from
that withdraw not your hand; for he who [reverently] fears
*and* worships God will come forth from them all.
[19] [True] wisdom is a strength to the wise man more
than ten rulers *or* valiant generals who are in the city. [Ps.
127:1; II Tim. 3:15.]
[20] Surely there is not a righteous man upon earth who
does good and never sins. [Isa. 53:6; Rom. 3:23.]
[21] Do not give heed to everything that is said, lest you
hear your servant cursing you—
[22] For often your own heart knows that you have likewise cursed others.
[23] All this have I tried *and* proved by wisdom. I said, I
will be wise [independently of God]—but it was far from
me.
[24] That which is is far off, and that which is deep is very
deep—who can find it out [true wisdom independent of the
fear of God]? [Job 28:12-28; I Cor. 2:9-16.]
[25] I turned about [penitent] and my heart was set to
know and to search out and to seek [true] wisdom and

## New International Version

and to understand the stupidity of wickedness
and the madness of folly.

26 I find more bitter than death
the woman who is a snare,
whose heart is a trap
and whose hands are chains.
The man who pleases God will escape her,
but the sinner she will ensnare.

27 "Look," says the Teacher,[a] "this is what I have discovered:

"Adding one thing to another to discover the scheme
of things—
28 while I was still searching
but not finding—
I found one upright man among a thousand,
but not one upright woman among them all.
29 This only have I found:
God created mankind upright,
but they have gone in search of many schemes."

**8** Who is like the wise?
Who knows the explanation of things?
A person's wisdom brightens their face
and changes its hard appearance.

### Obey the King

2 Obey the king's command, I say, because you took an
oath before God. 3 Do not be in a hurry to leave the king's
presence. Do not stand up for a bad cause, for he will do
whatever he pleases. 4 Since a king's word is supreme, who
can say to him, "What are you doing?"

5 Whoever obeys his command will come to no harm,
and the wise heart will know the proper time and
procedure.
6 For there is a proper time and procedure for every
matter,
though a person may be weighed down by misery.

7 Since no one knows the future,
who can tell someone else what is to come?
8 As no one has power over the wind to contain it,
so[b] no one has power over the time of their death.
As no one is discharged in time of war,
so wickedness will not release those who practice it.

9 All this I saw, as I applied my mind to everything done
under the sun. There is a time when a man lords it over
others to his own[c] hurt. 10 Then too, I saw the wicked buried—those who used to come and go from the holy place
and receive praise[d] in the city where they did this. This
too is meaningless.

11 When the sentence for a crime is not quickly carried
out, people's hearts are filled with schemes to do wrong.
12 Although a wicked person who commits a hundred
crimes may live a long time, I know that it will go better
with those who fear God, who are reverent before him.
13 Yet because the wicked do not fear God, it will not go
well with them, and their days will not lengthen like a
shadow.

14 There is something else meaningless that occurs on
earth: the righteous who get what the wicked deserve, and
the wicked who get what the righteous deserve. This too, I
say, is meaningless. 15 So I commend the enjoyment of life,

---

## Amplified Bible

the reason of things, and to know that wickedness is folly
and that foolishness is madness [and what had led me into
such wickedness and madness].
26 And I found that [of all sinful follies none has been
so ruinous in seducing one away from God as idolatrous
women] more bitter than death is the woman whose heart
is snares and nets and whose hands are bands. Whoever
pleases God shall escape from her, but the sinner shall be
taken by her.
27 Behold, this I have found, says the Preacher, while
weighing one thing after another to find out the right estimate [and the reason]—
28 Which I am still seeking but have not found—one upright man among a thousand have I found, but an upright
woman among all those [one thousand in my harem] have
I not found. [I Kings 11:3.]
29 Behold, this is the only [reason for it that] I have
found: God made man upright, but they [men and women]
have sought out many devices [for evil].

**8** Who is like the wise man? And who knows the interpretation of a thing? A man's wisdom makes his face
shine, and the hardness of his countenance is changed.

2 I counsel you to keep the king's command, and that
in regard to the oath of God [by which you swore to him
loyalty]. [II Sam. 21:7.]
3 Be not panic-stricken *and* hasty to get out of his presence. Persist not in an evil thing, for he does whatever he
pleases.
4 For the word of a king is authority *and* power, and who
can say to him, What are you doing?
5 Whoever observes the [king's] command will experience no harm, and a wise man's mind will know both when
and what to do.
6 For every purpose *and* matter has its [right] time and
judgment, although the misery *and* wickedness of man
lies heavily upon him [who rebels against the king].
7 For he does not know what is to be, for who can tell him
how *and* when it will be?
8 There is no man who has power over the spirit to retain
the breath of life, neither has he power over the day of
death; and there is no discharge in battle [against death],
neither will wickedness deliver those who are its possessors *and* given to it.
9 All this have I seen while applying my mind to every
work that is done under the sun. There is a time in which
one man has power over another to his own hurt *or* to the
other man's.
10 And so I saw the wicked buried—those who had come
and gone out of the holy place [but did not thereby escape
their doom], and they are [praised and] forgotten in the
city where they had done such things. This also is vanity
(emptiness, falsity, vainglory, and futility)!
11 Because the sentence against an evil work is not executed speedily, the hearts of the sons of men are fully
set to do evil.
12 Though a sinner does evil a hundred times and his
days [seemingly] are prolonged [in his wickedness], yet
surely I know that it will be well with those who [reverently] fear God, who revere *and* worship Him, realizing
His continual presence. [Ps. 37:11, 18, 19; Isa. 3:10, 11;
Matt. 25:34.]
13 But it will not be well with the wicked, neither will he
prolong his days like a shadow, because he does not [reverently] fear *and* worship God. [Matt. 25:41.]
14 Here also is a futility that goes on upon the earth:
there are righteous men who fare as though they were
wicked, and wicked men who fare as though they were
righteous. I say that this also is vanity (emptiness, falsity,
and futility)!
15 Then I commended enjoyment, because a man has no

---

*a* 27 Or *the leader of the assembly*    *b* 8 Or *over the human spirit to retain
it, / and so*    *c* 9 Or *to their*    *d* 10 Some Hebrew manuscripts and
Septuagint (Aquila); most Hebrew manuscripts *and are forgotten*

## New International Version

because there is nothing better for a person under the sun than to eat and drink and be glad. Then joy will accompany them in their toil all the days of the life God has given them under the sun.

16When I applied my mind to know wisdom and to observe the labor that is done on earth—people getting no sleep day or night— 17then I saw all that God has done. No one can comprehend what goes on under the sun. Despite all their efforts to search it out, no one can discover its meaning. Even if the wise claim they know, they cannot really comprehend it.

### A Common Destiny for All

**9** So I reflected on all this and concluded that the righteous and the wise and what they do are in God's hands, but no one knows whether love or hate awaits them. 2All share a common destiny—the righteous and the wicked, the good and the bad,*a* the clean and the unclean, those who offer sacrifices and those who do not.

As it is with the good,
　　so with the sinful;
as it is with those who take oaths,
　　so with those who are afraid to take them.

3This is the evil in everything that happens under the sun: The same destiny overtakes all. The hearts of people, moreover, are full of evil and there is madness in their hearts while they live, and afterward they join the dead. 4Anyone who is among the living has hope*b*—even a live dog is better off than a dead lion!

5For the living know that they will die,
　　but the dead know nothing;
they have no further reward,
　　and even their name is forgotten.
6Their love, their hate
　　and their jealousy have long since vanished;
never again will they have a part
　　in anything that happens under the sun.

7Go, eat your food with gladness, and drink your wine with a joyful heart, for God has already approved what you do. 8Always be clothed in white, and always anoint your head with oil. 9Enjoy life with your wife, whom you love, all the days of this meaningless life that God has given you under the sun—all your meaningless days. For this is your lot in life and in your toilsome labor under the sun. 10Whatever your hand finds to do, do it with all your might, for in the realm of the dead, where you are going, there is neither working nor planning nor knowledge nor wisdom.

11I have seen something else under the sun:

The race is not to the swift
　　or the battle to the strong,
nor does food come to the wise
　　or wealth to the brilliant
　　or favor to the learned;
but time and chance happen to them all.

12Moreover, no one knows when their hour will come:

As fish are caught in a cruel net,
　　or birds are taken in a snare,
so people are trapped by evil times
　　that fall unexpectedly upon them.

### Wisdom Better Than Folly

13I also saw under the sun this example of wisdom that greatly impressed me: 14There was once a small city with

## Amplified Bible

better thing under the sun [without God] than to eat and to drink and to be joyful, for that will remain with him in his toil through the days of his life which God gives him under the sun.

16When I applied my mind to know wisdom and to see the business activity *and* the painful effort that take place upon the earth—how neither day nor night some men's eyes sleep—

17Then I saw all the work of God, that man cannot find out the work that is done under the sun—because however much a man may toil in seeking, yet he will not find it out; yes, more than that, though a wise man thinks *and* claims he knows, yet will he not be able to find it out. [Deut. 29:29; Rom. 11:33.]

**9** For all this I took to heart, exploring *and* examining it all, how the righteous (the upright, in right standing with God) and the wise and their works are in the hands of God. Whether it is to be love or hatred no man knows; all that is before them.

2All things come alike to all. There is one event to the righteous and to the wicked, to the good and to the clean and to the unclean; to him who sacrifices and to him who does not sacrifice. As is the good man, so is the sinner; and he who swears is as he who fears *and* shuns an oath.

3This evil is in all that is done under the sun: one fate comes to all. Also the hearts of men are full of evil, and madness is in their hearts while they live, and after that they go to the dead.

4[There is no exemption] but he who is joined to all the living has hope—for a living dog is better than a dead lion.

5For the living know that they will die, but the dead know nothing; and they have no more reward [here], for the memory of them is forgotten.

6Their love and their hatred and their envy have already perished; neither have they any more a share in anything that is done under the sun.

7Go your way, eat your bread with joy, and drink your wine with a cheerful heart [if you are righteous, wise, and in the hands of God], for God has already accepted your works.

8Let your garments be always white [with purity], and let your head not lack [the] oil [of gladness].

9Live joyfully with the wife whom you love all the days of your vain life which He has given you under the sun—all the days of futility. For that is your portion in this life and in your work at which you toil under the sun.

10Whatever your hand finds to do, do it with all your might, for there is no work or device or knowledge or wisdom in Sheol (the place of the dead), where you are going.

11I returned and saw under the sun that the race is not to the swift nor the battle to the strong, neither is bread to the wise nor riches to men of intelligence *and* understanding nor favor to men of skill; but time and chance happen to them all. [Ps. 33:16-19; Rom. 9:16.]

12For man also knows not his time [of death]: as the fishes are taken in an evil net, and as the birds are caught in the snare, so are the sons of men snared in an evil time when [calamity] falls suddenly upon them.

13This [illustration of] wisdom have I seen also under the sun, and it seemed great to me:

14There was a little city with few men in it. And a great

---

*a* 2 Septuagint (Aquila), Vulgate and Syriac; Hebrew does not have *and the bad.* *b* 4 Or *What then is to be chosen? With all who live, there is hope*

# New International Version

only a few people in it. And a powerful king came against it, surrounded it and built huge siege works against it. [15]Now there lived in that city a man poor but wise, and he saved the city by his wisdom. But nobody remembered that poor man. [16]So I said, "Wisdom is better than strength." But the poor man's wisdom is despised, and his words are no longer heeded.

[17]The quiet words of the wise are more to be heeded
than the shouts of a ruler of fools.
[18]Wisdom is better than weapons of war,
but one sinner destroys much good.

**10** As dead flies give perfume a bad smell,
so a little folly outweighs wisdom and honor.
[2]The heart of the wise inclines to the right,
but the heart of the fool to the left.
[3]Even as fools walk along the road,
they lack sense
and show everyone how stupid they are.
[4]If a ruler's anger rises against you,
do not leave your post;
calmness can lay great offenses to rest.

[5]There is an evil I have seen under the sun,
the sort of error that arises from a ruler:
[6]Fools are put in many high positions,
while the rich occupy the low ones.
[7]I have seen slaves on horseback,
while princes go on foot like slaves.

[8]Whoever digs a pit may fall into it;
whoever breaks through a wall may be bitten by a
snake.
[9]Whoever quarries stones may be injured by them;
whoever splits logs may be endangered by them.
[10]If the ax is dull
and its edge unsharpened,
more strength is needed,
but skill will bring success.

[11]If a snake bites before it is charmed,
the charmer receives no fee.

[12]Words from the mouth of the wise are gracious,
but fools are consumed by their own lips.
[13]At the beginning their words are folly;
at the end they are wicked madness—
[14]     and fools multiply words.

No one knows what is coming—
who can tell someone else what will happen after
them?

[15]The toil of fools wearies them;
they do not know the way to town.

[16]Woe to the land whose king was a servant[a]
and whose princes feast in the morning.
[17]Blessed is the land whose king is of noble birth
and whose princes eat at a proper time—
for strength and not for drunkenness.

[18]Through laziness, the rafters sag;
because of idle hands, the house leaks.

[19]A feast is made for laughter,
wine makes life merry,
and money is the answer for everything.

[20]Do not revile the king even in your thoughts,
or curse the rich in your bedroom,
because a bird in the sky may carry your words,
and a bird on the wing may report what you say.

# Amplified Bible

king came against it and besieged it and built great bulwarks against it.

[15]But there was found in it a poor wise man, and he by his wisdom delivered the city. Yet no man [seriously] remembered that poor man.

[16]But I say that wisdom is better than might, though the poor man's wisdom is despised and his words are not heeded.

[17]The words of wise men heard in quiet are better than the shouts of him who rules among fools.

[18]Wisdom is better than weapons of war, but one sinner destroys much good.

**10** Dead flies cause the ointment of the perfumer to putrefy [and] send forth a vile odor; so does a little folly [in him who is valued for wisdom] outweigh wisdom and honor.

[2]A wise man's heart turns him toward his right hand, but a fool's heart toward his left. [Matt. 25:31-41.]

[3]Even when he who is a fool walks along the road, his heart and understanding fail him, and he says of everyone and to everyone that he is a fool.

[4]If the temper of the ruler rises up against you, do not leave your place [or show a resisting spirit]; for gentleness and calmness prevent or put a stop to great offenses.

[5]There is an evil which I have seen under the sun, like an error which proceeds from the ruler:

[6]Folly is set in great dignity and in high places, and the rich sit in low places.

[7]I have seen slaves on horses, and princes walking like slaves on the earth.

[8]He who digs a pit [for others] will fall into it, and whoever breaks through a fence or a [stone] wall, a serpent will bite him. [Ps. 57:6.]

[9]Whoever removes [landmark] stones or hews out [new ones with similar intent] will be hurt with them, and he who fells trees will be endangered by them. [Prov. 26:27.]

[10]If the ax is dull and the man does not whet the edge, he must put forth more strength; but wisdom helps him to succeed.

[11]If the serpent bites before it is charmed, then it is no use to call a charmer [and the slanderer is no better than the uncharmed snake].

[12]The words of a wise man's mouth are gracious and win him favor, but the lips of a fool consume him.

[13]The beginning of the words of his mouth is foolishness, and the end of his talk is wicked madness.

[14]A fool also multiplies words, though no man can tell what will be—and what will happen after he is gone, who can tell him?

[15]The labor of fools wearies every one of them, because [he is so ignorant of the ordinary matters that] he does not even know how to get to town.

[16]Woe to you, O land, when your king is a child or a servant and when your officials feast in the morning!

[17]Happy (fortunate and to be envied) are you, O land, when your king is a free man and of noble birth and character and when your officials feast at the proper time—for strength and not for drunkenness! [Isa. 32:8.]

[18]Through indolence the rafters [of state affairs] decay and the roof sinks in, and through idleness of the hands the house leaks.

[19][Instead of repairing the breaches, the officials] make a feast for laughter, serve wine to cheer life, and [depend on tax] money to answer for all of it.

[20]Curse not the king, no, not even in your thoughts, and curse not the rich in your bedchamber, for a bird of the air will carry the voice, and a winged creature will tell the matter. [Exod. 22:28.]

---

[a] 16 Or *king is a child*

## New International Version

### Invest in Many Ventures

**11** Ship your grain across the sea;
after many days you may receive a return.
[2] Invest in seven ventures, yes, in eight;
you do not know what disaster may come upon the
land.

[3] If clouds are full of water,
they pour rain on the earth.
Whether a tree falls to the south or to the north,
in the place where it falls, there it will lie.
[4] Whoever watches the wind will not plant;
whoever looks at the clouds will not reap.

[5] As you do not know the path of the wind,
or how the body is formed[a] in a mother's womb,
so you cannot understand the work of God,
the Maker of all things.

[6] Sow your seed in the morning,
and at evening let your hands not be idle,
for you do not know which will succeed,
whether this or that,
or whether both will do equally well.

### Remember Your Creator While Young

[7] Light is sweet,
and it pleases the eyes to see the sun.
[8] However many years anyone may live,
let them enjoy them all.
But let them remember the days of darkness,
for there will be many.
Everything to come is meaningless.

[9] You who are young, be happy while you are young,
and let your heart give you joy in the days of your
youth.
Follow the ways of your heart
and whatever your eyes see,
but know that for all these things
God will bring you into judgment.
[10] So then, banish anxiety from your heart
and cast off the troubles of your body,
for youth and vigor are meaningless.

**12** Remember your Creator
in the days of your youth,
before the days of trouble come
and the years approach when you will say,
"I find no pleasure in them"—
[2] before the sun and the light
and the moon and the stars grow dark,
and the clouds return after the rain;
[3] when the keepers of the house tremble,
and the strong men stoop,
when the grinders cease because they are few,
and those looking through the windows grow dim;
[4] when the doors to the street are closed
and the sound of grinding fades;
when people rise up at the sound of birds,
but all their songs grow faint;
[5] when people are afraid of heights
and of dangers in the streets;
when the almond tree blossoms
and the grasshopper drags itself along
and desire no longer is stirred.
Then people go to their eternal home
and mourners go about the streets.

[6] Remember him—before the silver cord is severed,
and the golden bowl is broken;
before the pitcher is shattered at the spring,
and the wheel broken at the well,

## Amplified Bible

**11** Cast your bread upon the waters, for you will find
it after many days.
[2] Give a portion to seven, yes, even [divide it] to eight,
for you know not what evil may come upon the earth.
[3] If the clouds are full of rain, they empty themselves
upon the earth; and if a tree falls toward the south or toward the north, in the place where the tree falls, there it
will lie.
[4] He who observes the wind [and waits for all conditions to be favorable] will not sow, and he who regards the
clouds will not reap.
[5] As you know not what is the way of the wind, or how the
spirit comes to the bones in the womb of a pregnant woman, even so you know not the work of God, Who does all.
[6] In the morning sow your seed, and in the evening withhold not your hands, for you know not which shall prosper,
whether this or that, or whether both alike will be good.
[7] Truly the light is sweet, and a pleasant thing it is for the
eyes to behold the sun.
[8] Yes, if a man should live many years, let him rejoice
in them all; yet let him [seriously] remember the days of
darkness, for they will be many. All that comes is vanity
(emptiness, falsity, vainglory, and futility)!
[9] Rejoice, O young man, in your adolescence, and let
your heart cheer you in the days of your [full-grown]
youth. And walk in the ways of your heart and in the sight
of your eyes, but know that for all these things God will
bring you into judgment.
[10] Therefore remove [the lusts that end in] sorrow *and*
vexation from your heart *and* mind and put away evil from
your body, for youth and the dawn of life are vanity [transi-
tory, idle, empty, and devoid of truth]. [II Cor. 7:1; II Tim.
2:22.]

**12** Remember [earnestly] also your Creator [that you
are not your own, but His property now] in the
days of your youth, before the evil days come or the years
draw near when you will say [of physical pleasures], I have
no enjoyment in them—[II Sam. 19:35.]
[2] Before the sun and the light and the moon and the
stars are darkened [sight is impaired], and the clouds [of
depression] return after the rain [of tears];
[3] In the day when the keepers of the house [the hands
and the arms] tremble, and the strong men [the feet and
the knees] bow themselves, and the grinders [the molar
teeth] cease because they are few, and those who look out
of the windows [the eyes] are darkened;
[4] When the doors [the lips] are shut in the streets and
the sound of the grinding [of the teeth] is low, and one
rises up at the voice of a bird *and* the crowing of a cock,
and all the daughters of music [the voice and the ear] are
brought low;
[5] Also when [the old] are afraid of danger from that
which is high, and fears are in the way, and the almond
tree [their white hair] blooms, and the grasshopper [a little thing] is a burden, and desire *and* appetite fail, because
man goes to his everlasting home and the mourners go
about the streets *or* marketplaces. [Job 17:13.]
[6] [Remember your Creator earnestly now] before the
silver cord [of life] is snapped apart, or the golden bowl
is broken, or the pitcher is broken at the fountain, or the
wheel broken at the cistern [and the whole circulatory system of the blood ceases to function];

---

[a] 5 Or *know how life* (or *the spirit*) / *enters the body being formed*

# New International Version

7 and the dust returns to the ground it came from,
and the spirit returns to God who gave it.

8 "Meaningless! Meaningless!" says the Teacher.[a]
"Everything is meaningless!"

## The Conclusion of the Matter

9 Not only was the Teacher wise, but he also imparted knowledge to the people. He pondered and searched out and set in order many proverbs. 10 The Teacher searched to find just the right words, and what he wrote was upright and true.

11 The words of the wise are like goads, their collected sayings like firmly embedded nails—given by one shepherd.[b] 12 Be warned, my son, of anything in addition to them.

Of making many books there is no end, and much study wearies the body.

13 Now all has been heard;
here is the conclusion of the matter:
Fear God and keep his commandments,
for this is the duty of all mankind.
14 For God will bring every deed into judgment,
including every hidden thing,
whether it is good or evil.

# Amplified Bible

7 Then shall the dust [out of which God made man's body] return to the earth as it was, and the spirit shall return to God Who gave it.

8 Vapor of vapors *and* futility of futilities, says the Preacher. All is futility (emptiness, falsity, vainglory, and transitoriness)!

9 And furthermore, because the Preacher was wise, he [Solomon] still taught the people knowledge; and he pondered and searched out and set in order many proverbs.

10 The Preacher sought acceptable words, even to write down rightly words of truth *or* correct sentiment.

11 The words of the wise are like prodding goads, and firmly fixed [in the mind] like nails are the collected sayings which are given [as proceeding] from one Shepherd. [Ezek. 37:24.]

12 But about going further [than the words given by one Shepherd], my son, be warned. Of making many books there is no end [so do not believe everything you read], and much study is a weariness of the flesh.

13 All has been heard; the end of the matter is: Fear God [revere and worship Him, knowing that He is] and keep His commandments, for this is the whole of man [the full, original purpose of his creation, the object of God's providence, the root of character, the foundation of all happiness, the adjustment to all inharmonious circumstances and conditions under the sun] *and* the whole [duty] for every man.

14 For God shall bring every work into judgment, with every secret thing, whether it is good or evil. [Matt. 12:36; Acts 17:30, 31; Rom. 2:16; I Cor. 4:5.]

---

*a* 8 Or *the leader of the assembly*; also in verses 9 and 10
*b* 11 Or *Shepherd*

# New International Version

# Song of Songs

**1** Solomon's Song of Songs.

*She*[a]

²Let him kiss me with the kisses of his mouth—
  for your love is more delightful than wine.
³Pleasing is the fragrance of your perfumes;
  your name is like perfume poured out.
  No wonder the young women love you!
⁴Take me away with you—let us hurry!
  Let the king bring me into his chambers.

*Friends*

  We rejoice and delight in you[b];
  we will praise your love more than wine.

*She*

  How right they are to adore you!

⁵Dark am I, yet lovely,
  daughters of Jerusalem,
  dark like the tents of Kedar,
  like the tent curtains of Solomon.[c]
⁶Do not stare at me because I am dark,
  because I am darkened by the sun.
  My mother's sons were angry with me
  and made me take care of the vineyards;
  my own vineyard I had to neglect.
⁷Tell me, you whom I love,
  where you graze your flock
  and where you rest your sheep at midday.
  Why should I be like a veiled woman
  beside the flocks of your friends?

*Friends*

⁸If you do not know, most beautiful of women,
  follow the tracks of the sheep
  and graze your young goats
  by the tents of the shepherds.

*He*

⁹I liken you, my darling, to a mare
  among Pharaoh's chariot horses.
¹⁰Your cheeks are beautiful with earrings,
  your neck with strings of jewels.
¹¹We will make you earrings of gold,
  studded with silver.

*She*

¹²While the king was at his table,
  my perfume spread its fragrance.
¹³My beloved is to me a sachet of myrrh
  resting between my breasts.
¹⁴My beloved is to me a cluster of henna blossoms
  from the vineyards of En Gedi.

---

*a* The main male and female speakers (identified primarily on the basis of the gender of the relevant Hebrew forms) are indicated by the captions *He* and *She* respectively. The words of others are marked *Friends*. In some instances the divisions and their captions are debatable.   *b 4* The Hebrew is masculine singular.   *c 5* Or *Salma*

# Amplified Bible

## THE

# Song of Solomon

NOTE: *Among the multitudes who read the Bible there are comparatively few who have a clear understanding of the Song of Solomon. Some have thought it to be a collection of songs, but it is more generally understood to be a sort of drama, the positive interpretation of which is impossible because the identity of the speakers and the length of the speeches are not disclosed.*

**1** The song of songs [the most excellent of them all] which is Solomon's. [I Kings 4:32.]
²Let him kiss me with the kisses of his mouth! [she cries. Then, realizing that Solomon has arrived and has heard her speech, she turns to him and adds] For your love is better than wine!
³[And she continues] The odor of your ointments is fragrant; your name is like perfume poured out. Therefore do the maidens love you.
⁴Draw me! We will run after you! The king brings me into his apartments! We will be glad and rejoice in you! We will recall [when we were favored with] your love, more fragrant than wine. The upright [are not offended at your choice, but sincerely] love you.
⁵I am so black; but [you are] lovely *and* pleasant [the ladies assured her]. O you daughters of Jerusalem, [I am as dark] as the tents of [the Bedouin tribe] Kedar, like the [beautiful] curtains of Solomon!
⁶[Please] do not look at me, [she said, for] I am swarthy. [I have worked out] in the sun *and* it has left its mark upon me. My stepbrothers were angry with me, and they made me keeper of the vineyards; but my own vineyard [my complexion] I have not kept.
⁷[Addressing her shepherd, she said] Tell me, O *a*you whom my soul loves, where you pasture your flock, you make it lie down at noon. For why should I [as I think of you] be as a veiled one straying beside the flocks of your companions? [Ps. 23:1, 2.]
⁸If you do not know [where your lover is], O you fairest among women, run along, follow the tracks of the flock, and [amuse yourself by] pasturing your kids beside the shepherds' tents.
⁹O my love [he said as he saw her], you remind me of my [favorite] mare in the chariot spans of Pharaoh.
¹⁰Your cheeks are comely with ornaments, your neck with strings of jewels.
¹¹We will make for you chains *and* ornaments of gold, studded with silver.
¹²While the king sits at his table [she said], my spikenard [my absent lover] sends forth [his] fragrance [over me].
¹³My beloved [shepherd] is to me like a [scent] bag of myrrh that lies in my bosom.
¹⁴My beloved [shepherd] is to me a cluster of henna flowers in the vineyards of En-gedi [famed for its fragrant shrubs].

---

*a* Does my spirit crave the Divine Shepherd, even in the presence of the best that the world can offer me?

## New International Version

*He*

<sup>15</sup>How beautiful you are, my darling!
  Oh, how beautiful!
  Your eyes are doves.

*She*

<sup>16</sup>How handsome you are, my beloved!
  Oh, how charming!
  And our bed is verdant.

*He*

<sup>17</sup>The beams of our house are cedars;
  our rafters are firs.

*She*<sup>a</sup>

**2** I am a rose<sup>b</sup> of Sharon,
  a lily of the valleys.

*He*

<sup>2</sup>Like a lily among thorns
  is my darling among the young women.

*She*

<sup>3</sup>Like an apple<sup>c</sup> tree among the trees of the forest
  is my beloved among the young men.
I delight to sit in his shade,
  and his fruit is sweet to my taste.
<sup>4</sup>Let him lead me to the banquet hall,
  and let his banner over me be love.
<sup>5</sup>Strengthen me with raisins,
  refresh me with apples,
  for I am faint with love.
<sup>6</sup>His left arm is under my head,
  and his right arm embraces me.
<sup>7</sup>Daughters of Jerusalem, I charge you
  by the gazelles and by the does of the field:
Do not arouse or awaken love
  until it so desires.

<sup>8</sup>Listen! My beloved!
  Look! Here he comes,
leaping across the mountains,
  bounding over the hills.
<sup>9</sup>My beloved is like a gazelle or a young stag.
  Look! There he stands behind our wall,
gazing through the windows,
  peering through the lattice.
<sup>10</sup>My beloved spoke and said to me,
  "Arise, my darling,
  my beautiful one, come with me.
<sup>11</sup>See! The winter is past;
  the rains are over and gone.
<sup>12</sup>Flowers appear on the earth;
  the season of singing has come,
the cooing of doves
  is heard in our land.
<sup>13</sup>The fig tree forms its early fruit;
  the blossoming vines spread their fragrance.
Arise, come, my darling;
  my beautiful one, come with me."

*He*

<sup>14</sup>My dove in the clefts of the rock,
  in the hiding places on the mountainside,
show me your face,
  let me hear your voice;
for your voice is sweet,
  and your face is lovely.

## Amplified Bible

<sup>15</sup>Behold, you are beautiful, my love! Behold, you are beautiful! You have doves' eyes.
<sup>16</sup>[She cried] Behold, you are beautiful, my beloved [shepherd], yes, delightful! Our arbor *and* couch are green *and* leafy.
<sup>17</sup>The beams of our house are cedars, and our rafters *and* panels are cypresses *or* pines.

**2** [She said] I am only a little rose *or* autumn crocus of the plain of Sharon, or a [humble] lily of the valleys [that grows in deep and difficult places].
<sup>2</sup>But Solomon replied, Like the lily among thorns, so are you, my love, among the daughters.
<sup>3</sup>Like an apple tree among the trees of the wood, so is my beloved [shepherd] among the sons [cried the girl]! Under his shadow I delighted to sit, and his fruit was sweet to my taste.
<sup>4</sup>He brought me to the banqueting house, and his banner over me was love [for love waved as a protecting and comforting banner over my head when I was near him].
<sup>5</sup>Sustain me with raisins, refresh me with apples, for I am sick with love.
<sup>6</sup>[I can feel] <sup>a</sup>his left hand under my head and his right hand embraces me! [Deut. 33:27; Matt. 28:20.]
<sup>7</sup>[He said] I charge you, O you daughters of Jerusalem, by the gazelles or by the hinds of the field [which are free to follow their own instincts] that you not try to stir up or awaken [my] love until it pleases.
<sup>8</sup>[Vividly she pictured it] The voice of my beloved [shepherd]! Behold, he comes, leaping upon the mountains, bounding over the hills. [John 10:27.]
<sup>9</sup>My beloved is like a gazelle or a young hart. Behold, he stands behind the wall of our house, he looks in through the windows, he glances through the lattice.
<sup>10</sup>My beloved speaks and says to me, Rise up, my love, my fair one, and come away.
<sup>11</sup>For, behold, the winter is past; the rain is over and gone.
<sup>12</sup>The flowers appear on the earth; the time of the singing [of birds] has come, and the voice of the turtledove is heard in our land.
<sup>13</sup>The fig tree puts forth *and* ripens her green figs, and the vines are in blossom and give forth their fragrance. <sup>b</sup>Arise, my love, my fair one, and come away.
<sup>14</sup>[So I went with him, and when we were climbing the rocky steps up the hillside, my beloved shepherd said to me] O my dove, [while you are here] in the seclusion of the clefts in the solid rock, in the sheltered *and* secret place of the cliff, let me see your face, <sup>c</sup>let me hear your voice; for your voice is sweet, and your face is lovely.

---

<sup>a</sup> Do I have a constant sense of my Shepherd's presence, regardless of my surroundings? <sup>b</sup> Do I take time to meet my Good Shepherd each day, letting Him tell me of His love, and cheering His heart with my interest in Him? <sup>c</sup> Do I realize that my voice lifted in praise and song is sweet to Him, or do I withhold it?

---

<sup>a</sup> Or *He*   <sup>b</sup> 1 Probably a member of the crocus family possibly *apricot*; here and elsewhere in Song of Songs   <sup>c</sup> 3 Or

## New International Version

<sup>15</sup>Catch for us the foxes,
 the little foxes
that ruin the vineyards,
 our vineyards that are in bloom.

*She*
<sup>16</sup>My beloved is mine and I am his;
 he browses among the lilies.
<sup>17</sup>Until the day breaks
 and the shadows flee,
turn, my beloved,
 and be like a gazelle
or like a young stag
 on the rugged hills.<sup>a</sup>

**3** All night long on my bed
 I looked for the one my heart loves;
 I looked for him but did not find him.
<sup>2</sup>I will get up now and go about the city,
 through its streets and squares;
I will search for the one my heart loves.
 So I looked for him but did not find him.
<sup>3</sup>The watchmen found me
 as they made their rounds in the city.
 "Have you seen the one my heart loves?"
<sup>4</sup>Scarcely had I passed them
 when I found the one my heart loves.
I held him and would not let him go
 till I had brought him to my mother's house,
 to the room of the one who conceived me.
<sup>5</sup>Daughters of Jerusalem, I charge you
 by the gazelles and by the does of the field:
Do not arouse or awaken love
 until it so desires.

<sup>6</sup>Who is this coming up from the wilderness
 like a column of smoke,
perfumed with myrrh and incense
 made from all the spices of the merchant?
<sup>7</sup>Look! It is Solomon's carriage,
 escorted by sixty warriors,
 the noblest of Israel,
<sup>8</sup>all of them wearing the sword,
 all experienced in battle,
each with his sword at his side,
 prepared for the terrors of the night.
<sup>9</sup>King Solomon made for himself the carriage;
 he made it of wood from Lebanon.
<sup>10</sup>Its posts he made of silver,
 its base of gold.
Its seat was upholstered with purple,
 its interior inlaid with love.
Daughters of Jerusalem, <sup>11</sup>come out,
 and look, you daughters of Zion.
Look<sup>b</sup> on King Solomon wearing a crown,
 the crown with which his mother crowned him
on the day of his wedding,
 the day his heart rejoiced.

*He*
**4** How beautiful you are, my darling!
 Oh, how beautiful!
 Your eyes behind your veil are doves.
Your hair is like a flock of goats
 descending from the hills of Gilead.
<sup>2</sup>Your teeth are like a flock of sheep just shorn,
 coming up from the washing.
Each has its twin;
 not one of them is alone.

## Amplified Bible

<sup>15</sup>[My heart was touched and I fervently sang to him my desire] Take for us the foxes, the <sup>a</sup>little foxes that spoil the vineyards [of our love], for our vineyards are in blossom.
<sup>16</sup>[She said distinctly] My beloved is mine and I am his! He pastures his flocks among the lilies. [Matt. 10:32; Acts 4:12.]
<sup>17</sup>[Then, longingly addressing her absent shepherd, she cried] Until the day breaks and the shadows flee away, return hastily, O my beloved, and be like a gazelle or a young hart as you cover the mountains [which separate us].

**3** In the night I dreamed that I sought the one whom I love. [She said] I looked for him but could not find him. [Isa. 26:9.]
<sup>2</sup>So I decided to go out into the city, into the streets and broad ways [which are so confusing to a country girl], and seek him whom my soul loves. I sought him, but I could not find him.
<sup>3</sup>The watchmen who go about the city found me, to whom I said, Have you seen him whom my soul loves?
<sup>4</sup>I had gone but a little way past them when I found him whom my soul loves. I held him and would not let him go until I had brought him into my mother's house, and into the chamber of her who conceived me. [Rom. 8:35; I Pet. 2:25.]
<sup>5</sup>I adjure you, O daughters of Jerusalem, by the gazelles or by the hinds of the field that you stir not up nor awaken love until it pleases.
<sup>6</sup>Who *or* what is this [she asked] that comes gliding out of the wilderness like stately pillars of smoke perfumed with myrrh, frankincense, and all the fragrant powders of the merchant?
<sup>7</sup>[Someone answered] Behold, it is the traveling litter (the bridal car) of Solomon. Sixty mighty men are around it, of the mighty men of Israel.
<sup>8</sup>They all handle the sword and are expert in war; every man has his sword upon his thigh, that fear be not excited in the night.
<sup>9</sup>King Solomon made himself a car *or* a palanquin from the [cedar] wood of Lebanon.
<sup>10</sup>He made its posts of silver, its back of gold, its seat of purple, the inside of it lovingly *and* intricately wrought in needlework by the daughters of Jerusalem.
<sup>11</sup>Go forth, O you daughters of Zion, and gaze upon King Solomon wearing the crown with which his mother [Bathsheba] crowned him on the day of his wedding, on the day of his gladness of heart.

**4** How fair you are, my love [he said], how very fair! Your eyes behind your veil [remind me] of those of a dove; your hair [makes me think of the black, wavy fleece] of a flock of [the Arabian] goats which one sees trailing down Mount Gilead [beyond the Jordan on the frontiers of the desert].
<sup>2</sup>Your teeth are like a flock of shorn ewes which have come up from the washing, of which all are in pairs, and none is missing among them.

---

<sup>a</sup> 17 Or *the hills of Bether*   <sup>b</sup> 10,11 Or *interior lovingly inlaid / by the daughters of Jerusalem. / <sup>11</sup>Come out, you daughters of Zion, / and look*

<sup>a</sup> What is my greatest concern, the thing about which most of all I want Christ's help? When He asks to hear my voice, what do I tell Him?

## New International Version

³Your lips are like a scarlet ribbon;
  your mouth is lovely.
Your temples behind your veil
  are like the halves of a pomegranate.
⁴Your neck is like the tower of David,
  built with courses of stone*;
on it hang a thousand shields,
  all of them shields of warriors.
⁵Your breasts are like two fawns,
  like twin fawns of a gazelle
  that browse among the lilies.
⁶Until the day breaks
  and the shadows flee,
I will go to the mountain of myrrh
  and to the hill of incense.
⁷You are altogether beautiful, my darling;
  there is no flaw in you.

⁸Come with me from Lebanon, my bride,
  come with me from Lebanon.
Descend from the crest of Amana,
  from the top of Senir, the summit of Hermon,
from the lions' dens
  and the mountain haunts of leopards.
⁹You have stolen my heart, my sister, my bride;
  you have stolen my heart
with one glance of your eyes,
  with one jewel of your necklace.
¹⁰How delightful is your love, my sister, my bride!
  How much more pleasing is your love than wine,
and the fragrance of your perfume
  more than any spice!
¹¹Your lips drop sweetness as the honeycomb, my bride;
  milk and honey are under your tongue.
The fragrance of your garments
  is like the fragrance of Lebanon.
¹²You are a garden locked up, my sister, my bride;
  you are a spring enclosed, a sealed fountain.
¹³Your plants are an orchard of pomegranates
  with choice fruits,
  with henna and nard,
¹⁴  nard and saffron,
  calamus and cinnamon,
  with every kind of incense tree,
  with myrrh and aloes
  and all the finest spices.
¹⁵You are* a garden fountain,
  a well of flowing water
  streaming down from Lebanon.

*She*
¹⁶Awake, north wind,
  and come, south wind!
Blow on my garden,
  that its fragrance may spread everywhere.
Let my beloved come into his garden
  and taste its choice fruits.

*He*
**5** I have come into my garden, my sister, my bride;
  I have gathered my myrrh with my spice.
I have eaten my honeycomb and my honey;
  I have drunk my wine and my milk.

*Friends*
  Eat, friends, and drink;
  drink your fill of love.

## Amplified Bible

³Your lips are like a thread of scarlet, and your mouth is lovely. Your cheeks are like halves of a pomegranate behind your veil.
⁴Your neck is like the tower of David, built for an arsenal, whereon hang a thousand bucklers, all of them shields of warriors.
⁵Your two breasts are like two fawns, like twins of a gazelle that feed among the lilies.
⁶Until the day breaks and the shadows flee away, [in my thoughts] I will get to the mountain of myrrh and the hill of frankincense [to him whom my soul adores].
⁷[He exclaimed] O my love, how beautiful you are! There is no flaw in you! [John 14:18; Eph. 5:27.]
⁸Come *ᵃaway with me from Lebanon, my [promised] bride, come with me from Lebanon. Depart from the top of Amana, from the peak of Senir and Hermon, from the lions' dens, from the mountains of the leopards. [II Cor. 11:2, 3.]
⁹You have ravished my heart *and* given me courage, my sister, my [promised] bride; you have ravished my heart *and* given me courage with one look from your eyes, with one jewel of your necklace.
¹⁰How beautiful is your love, my sister, my [promised] bride! How much better is your love than wine! And the fragrance of your ointments than all spices! [John 15:9; Rom. 8:35.]
¹¹Your lips, O my [promised] bride, drop honey as the honeycomb; honey and milk are under your tongue. And the odor of your garments is like the odor of Lebanon.
¹²A garden enclosed *and* barred is my sister, my [promised] bride—a spring shut up, a fountain sealed.
¹³Your shoots are an orchard of pomegranates *or* a paradise with precious fruits, henna with spikenard plants, [John 15:5; Eph. 5:9.]
¹⁴Spikenard and saffron, calamus and cinnamon, with all trees of frankincense, myrrh, and aloes, with all the chief spices.
¹⁵You are a fountain [springing up] in a garden, a well of living waters, and flowing streams from Lebanon. [John 4:10; 7:37, 38.]
¹⁶[You have called me a garden, she said] Oh, I pray that the [cold] *ᵇnorth wind and the [soft] south wind may blow upon my garden, that its spices may flow out [in abundance for you in whom my soul delights]. Let my beloved come into his garden and eat its choicest fruits.

**5** I have come into my garden, my sister, my [promised] bride; I have gathered my myrrh with my balsam *and* spice [from your sweet words I have gathered the richest perfumes and spices]. I have eaten my honeycomb with my honey; I have drunk my wine with my milk. Eat, O friends [feast on, O revelers of the palace; you can never make my lover disloyal to me]! Drink, yes, drink abundantly of love, O precious one [for now I know you are mine, irrevocably mine! With his confident words still thrilling her heart, through the lattice she saw her shepherd turn away and disappear into the night]. [John 16:33.]

ᵃ Do I heed Christ when He bids me to come away from the lions' den of temptation and dwell with Him? ᵇ Am I willing to have the north wind of adversity blow upon me, if it will better fit me for Christ's presence and companionship?

## New International Version

*She*
2 I slept but my heart was awake.
  Listen! My beloved is knocking:
"Open to me, my sister, my darling,
  my dove, my flawless one.
My head is drenched with dew,
  my hair with the dampness of the night."
3 I have taken off my robe—
  must I put it on again?
I have washed my feet—
  must I soil them again?
4 My beloved thrust his hand through the latch-
  opening;
  my heart began to pound for him.
5 I arose to open for my beloved,
  and my hands dripped with myrrh,
my fingers with flowing myrrh,
  on the handles of the bolt.
6 I opened for my beloved,
  but my beloved had left; he was gone.
  My heart sank at his departure.*a*
I looked for him but did not find him.
  I called him but he did not answer.
7 The watchmen found me
  as they made their rounds in the city.
They beat me, they bruised me;
  they took away my cloak,
  those watchmen of the walls!
8 Daughters of Jerusalem, I charge you—
  if you find my beloved,
what will you tell him?
  Tell him I am faint with love.

*Friends*
9 How is your beloved better than others,
  most beautiful of women?
How is your beloved better than others,
  that you so charge us?

*She*
10 My beloved is radiant and ruddy,
  outstanding among ten thousand.
11 His head is purest gold;
  his hair is wavy
  and black as a raven.
12 His eyes are like doves
  by the water streams,
washed in milk,
  mounted like jewels.
13 His cheeks are like beds of spice
  yielding perfume.
His lips are like lilies
  dripping with myrrh.
14 His arms are rods of gold
  set with topaz.
His body is like polished ivory
  decorated with lapis lazuli.
15 His legs are pillars of marble
  set on bases of pure gold.
His appearance is like Lebanon,
  choice as its cedars.
16 His mouth is sweetness itself;
  he is altogether lovely.
This is my beloved, this is my friend,
  daughters of Jerusalem.

## Amplified Bible

2 I went to sleep, but my heart stayed awake. [I dreamed that I heard] the voice of my beloved as he knocked [at the door of my mother's cottage]. Open to me, my sister, my love, my dove, my spotless one [he said], for I am wet with the [heavy] night dew; my hair is covered with it. [Job 11:13-15.]
3 [But weary from a day in the vineyards, I had already sought my rest] I had put off my garment—*a* how could I [again] put it on? I had washed my feet—how could I [again] soil them? [Isa. 32:9; Heb. 3:15.]
4 My beloved put in his hand by the hole of the door, and my heart was moved for him.
5 I rose up to open for my beloved, and my hands dripped with myrrh, and my fingers with liquid [sweet-scented] myrrh, [which he had left] upon the handles of the bolt.
6 I opened for my beloved, but my beloved had turned away *and* withdrawn himself, and was gone! My soul went forth [to him] when he spoke, but it failed me [and now he was gone]! I sought him, but I could not find him; I called him, but he gave me no answer.
7 The watchmen who go about the city found me. They struck me, they wounded me; the keepers of the walls took my veil *and* my mantle from me.
8 I charge you, O daughters of Jerusalem, if you find my beloved, that you tell him that I am sick from love [simply sick to be with him]. [Ps. 63:1.]
9 What is your beloved more than another beloved, O you fairest among women [taunted the ladies]? What is your beloved more than another beloved, that you should give us such a charge? [John 10:26.]
10 [She said] My beloved is fair and ruddy, the chief among ten thousand! [Ps. 45:2; John 1:14.]
11 His head is [as precious as] the finest gold; his locks are curly *and* bushy and black as a raven.
12 His eyes are like doves beside the water brooks, bathed in milk *and* fitly set.
13 His cheeks are like a bed of spices *or* balsam, like banks of sweet herbs yielding fragrance. His lips are like bloodred anemones or lilies distilling liquid [sweet-scented] myrrh.
14 His hands are like rods of gold set with [nails of] beryl *or* topaz. His body is a figure of bright ivory overlaid with [veins of] sapphires.
15 His legs are like strong and steady pillars of marble set upon bases of fine gold. His appearance is like Lebanon, excellent, stately, *and* majestic as the cedars.
16 His voice *and* speech are exceedingly sweet; yes, he is altogether lovely [the whole of him delights and is precious]. *b* This is my beloved, and this is my friend, O daughters of Jerusalem! [Ps. 92:15; Col. 1:15.]

---

*a* In my weariness from earthly cares, do I hesitate to answer when the Divine Shepherd knocks at my door, and so turn Him from me? *b* Is my Savior unquestionably the One altogether lovely, the One above all others most precious to me? Can I tell how and why Christ is more to me than any human being or than all earthly possessions?

---

*a* 6 Or *heart had gone out to him when he spoke*

## New International Version

**Friends**

**6** Where has your beloved gone,
   most beautiful of women?
  Which way did your beloved turn,
    that we may look for him with you?

**She**

²My beloved has gone down to his garden,
   to the beds of spices,
  to browse in the gardens
   and to gather lilies.
³I am my beloved's and my beloved is mine;
   he browses among the lilies.

**He**

⁴You are as beautiful as Tirzah, my darling,
   as lovely as Jerusalem,
   as majestic as troops with banners.
⁵Turn your eyes from me;
   they overwhelm me.
  Your hair is like a flock of goats
   descending from Gilead.
⁶Your teeth are like a flock of sheep
   coming up from the washing.
  Each has its twin,
   not one of them is missing.
⁷Your temples behind your veil
   are like the halves of a pomegranate.
⁸Sixty queens there may be,
   and eighty concubines,
   and virgins beyond number;
⁹but my dove, my perfect one, is unique,
   the only daughter of her mother,
   the favorite of the one who bore her.
  The young women saw her and called her blessed;
   the queens and concubines praised her.

**Friends**

¹⁰Who is this that appears like the dawn,
   fair as the moon, bright as the sun,
   majestic as the stars in procession?

**He**

¹¹I went down to the grove of nut trees
   to look at the new growth in the valley,
  to see if the vines had budded
   or the pomegranates were in bloom.
¹²Before I realized it,
   my desire set me among the royal chariots of my
    people.*ᵃ*

**Friends**

¹³Come back, come back, O Shulammite;
   come back, come back, that we may gaze on you!

**He**

  Why would you gaze on the Shulammite
   as on the dance of Mahanaim?*ᵇ*

**7** ᶜHow beautiful your sandaled feet,
   O prince's daughter!
  Your graceful legs are like jewels,
   the work of an artist's hands.
²Your navel is a rounded goblet
   that never lacks blended wine.
  Your waist is a mound of wheat
   encircled by lilies.
³Your breasts are like two fawns,
   like twin fawns of a gazelle.

## Amplified Bible

**6** Where has your beloved gone, O you fairest among
  women? [Again the ladies showed their interest in the
remarkable person whom the Shulammite had champi-
oned with such unstinted praise; they too wanted to know
him, they insisted.] Where is your beloved hiding himself?
For we would seek him with you.

²[She replied] My beloved has gone down to his garden,
to the beds of spices, to feed in the gardens and to gather
lilies.

³I am my beloved's [garden] and my beloved is mine! He
feeds among the lilies [which grow there].

⁴[He said] You are as beautiful as Tirzah [capital of the
northern kingdom's first king], my love, and as comely as
Jerusalem, [but you are] as terrible as a bannered host!

⁵Turn away your [flashing] eyes from me, for they have
overcome me! Your hair is like a flock of goats trailing
down from Mount Gilead.

⁶Your teeth are like a flock of ewes coming from their
washing, of which all are in pairs, and not one of them is
missing.

⁷Your cheeks are like halves of a pomegranate behind
your veil.

⁸There are sixty queens and eighty concubines, and
virgins without number;

⁹But my dove, my undefiled *and* perfect one, stands
alone [above them all]; she is the only one of her mother,
she is the choice one of her who bore her. The daughters
saw her and called her blessed *and* happy, yes, the queens
and the concubines, and they praised her. [Col. 2:8, 9.]

¹⁰[The ladies asked] Who is this that looks forth like
the dawn, fair as the moon, clear *and* pure as the sun, *and*
terrible as a bannered host?

¹¹[The Shulammite replied] I went down into the nut
orchard [one day] to look at the green plants of the valley,
to see whether the grapevine had budded and the pomegranates were in flower.

¹²Before I was aware [of what was happening], my desire [to roam about] had brought me into the area of the
princes of my people [the king's retinue].

¹³[I began to flee, but they called to me] Return, return,
O Shulammite; return, return, that we may look upon you!
[I replied] What is there for you to see in the [poor little]
Shulammite? [And they answered] As upon a dance before
two armies *or* a dance of Mahanaim.

**7** [Then her companions began noticing and comment-
  ing on the attractiveness of her person] How beautiful
are your feet in sandals, O queenly maiden! Your rounded
limbs are like jeweled chains, the work of a master hand.

²Your body is like a round goblet in which no mixed
wine is wanting. Your abdomen is like a heap of wheat set
about with lilies.

³Your two breasts are like two fawns, the twins of a gazelle.

---

*ᵃ 12* Or *among the chariots of Amminadab*; or *among the chariots of the
people of the prince*   *ᵇ 13* In Hebrew texts this verse (6:13) is numbered
7:1.   *ᶜ* In Hebrew texts 7:1-13 is numbered 7:2-14.

## New International Version

4 Your neck is like an ivory tower.
   Your eyes are the pools of Heshbon
      by the gate of Bath Rabbim.
   Your nose is like the tower of Lebanon
      looking toward Damascus.
5 Your head crowns you like Mount Carmel.
   Your hair is like royal tapestry;
      the king is held captive by its tresses.
6 How beautiful you are and how pleasing,
   my love, with your delights!
7 Your stature is like that of the palm,
   and your breasts like clusters of fruit.
8 I said, "I will climb the palm tree;
   I will take hold of its fruit."
May your breasts be like clusters of grapes on the
      vine,
   the fragrance of your breath like apples,
9     and your mouth like the best wine.

*She*

   May the wine go straight to my beloved,
      flowing gently over lips and teeth.[a]
10 I belong to my beloved,
   and his desire is for me.
11 Come, my beloved, let us go to the countryside,
   let us spend the night in the villages.[b]
12 Let us go early to the vineyards
   to see if the vines have budded,
   if their blossoms have opened,
      and if the pomegranates are in bloom—
   there I will give you my love.
13 The mandrakes send out their fragrance,
   and at our door is every delicacy,
   both new and old,
      that I have stored up for you, my beloved.

8 If only you were to me like a brother,
   who was nursed at my mother's breasts!
   Then, if I found you outside,
      I would kiss you,
      and no one would despise me.
2 I would lead you
   and bring you to my mother's house—
      she who has taught me.
   I would give you spiced wine to drink,
      the nectar of my pomegranates.
3 His left arm is under my head
   and his right arm embraces me.
4 Daughters of Jerusalem, I charge you:
   Do not arouse or awaken love
      until it so desires.

*Friends*

5 Who is this coming up from the wilderness
   leaning on her beloved?

*She*

   Under the apple tree I roused you;
      there your mother conceived you,
      there she who was in labor gave you birth.
6 Place me like a seal over your heart,
   like a seal on your arm;
   for love is as strong as death,
      its jealousy[c] unyielding as the grave.
   It burns like blazing fire,
      like a mighty flame.[d]

## Amplified Bible

4 Your neck is like a tower of ivory, your eyes like the pools of Heshbon by the gate of Bath-rabbim. Your nose is like the tower of Lebanon which looks toward Damascus.
5 Your head crowns you like Mount Carmel, and the hair of your head like purple. [Then seeing the king watching the girl in absorbed admiration, the speaker added] The king is held captive by its tresses.
6 [The king came forward, saying] How fair and how pleasant you are, O love, with your delights!
7 Your stature is like that of a palm tree, and your bosom like its clusters [of dates, declared the king].
8 I resolve that I will climb the palm tree; I will grasp its branches. Let your breasts be like clusters of the grapevine, and the scent of your breath like apples,
9 And your kisses like the best wine—[then the Shulammite interrupted] that goes down smoothly *and* sweetly for my beloved [shepherd, kisses] gliding over his lips while he sleeps!
10 [She proudly said] I am my beloved's, and his desire is toward me! [John 10:28.]
11 [She said] Come, my beloved! Let us go forth into the field, let us lodge in the villages. [Luke 14:33.]
12 Let us go out early to the vineyards and see whether the vines have budded, whether the grape blossoms have opened, and whether the pomegranates are in bloom. There I will give you my love.
13 The mandrakes give forth fragrance, and over our doors are all manner of choice fruits, new and old, which I have laid up for you, O my beloved!

8 [Looking forward to the shepherd's arrival, the eager girl pictures their meeting and says] Oh, that you were like my brother, who nursed from the breasts of my mother! If I should find you without, I would kiss you, yes, and none would despise me [for it]. [Ps. 143:6.]
2 I would lead you and bring you into the house of my mother, who would instruct me. I would cause you to drink spiced wine and of the juice of my pomegranates.
3 [Then musingly she added] Oh, that his left hand were under my head and that his right hand embraced me! [Exod. 19:4; Deut. 33:27.]
4 I adjure you, O daughters of Jerusalem, that you never [again attempt to] stir up or awaken love until it pleases.
5 Who is this who comes up from the wilderness leaning upon her beloved? [And as they sighted the home of her childhood, the bride said] Under the apple tree I awakened you; there your mother gave you birth, there she was in travail and bore you.
6 Set me like a seal upon your heart, like a seal upon your arm; for love is as strong as death, jealousy is as hard *and* cruel as Sheol (the place of the dead). Its flashes are flashes of fire, a most vehement flame [the very flame of the Lord]! [Deut. 4:24; Isa. 49:16; I Cor. 10:22.]

---

a 9 Septuagint, Aquila, Vulgate and Syriac; Hebrew *lips of sleepers*
b 11 Or *the henna bushes*    c 6 Or *ardor*    d 6 Or *fire, / like the very flame of the* Lord

## New International Version

<sup>7</sup>Many waters cannot quench love;
    rivers cannot sweep it away.
If one were to give
    all the wealth of one's house for love,
      it<sup>a</sup> would be utterly scorned.

*Friends*
<sup>8</sup>We have a little sister,
    and her breasts are not yet grown.
What shall we do for our sister
    on the day she is spoken for?
<sup>9</sup>If she is a wall,
    we will build towers of silver on her.
If she is a door,
    we will enclose her with panels of cedar.

*She*
<sup>10</sup>I am a wall,
    and my breasts are like towers.
Thus I have become in his eyes
    like one bringing contentment.
<sup>11</sup>Solomon had a vineyard in Baal Hamon;
    he let out his vineyard to tenants.
Each was to bring for its fruit
    a thousand shekels<sup>b</sup> of silver.
<sup>12</sup>But my own vineyard is mine to give;
    the thousand shekels are for you, Solomon,
    and two hundred<sup>c</sup> are for those who tend its fruit.

*He*
<sup>13</sup>You who dwell in the gardens
    with friends in attendance,
    let me hear your voice!

*She*
<sup>14</sup>Come away, my beloved,
    and be like a gazelle
or like a young stag
    on the spice-laden mountains.

## Amplified Bible

<sup>7</sup>Many waters cannot quench love, neither can floods drown it. If a man would offer all the goods of his house for love, he would be utterly scorned *and* despised.

<sup>8</sup>[Gathered with her family and the wedding guests in her mother's cottage, the bride said to her stepbrothers, When I was a little girl, you said] We have a little sister and she has no breasts. What shall we do for our sister on the day when she is spoken for in marriage?

<sup>9</sup>If she is a wall [discreet and womanly], we will build upon her a turret [a dowry] of silver; but if she is a door [bold and flirtatious], we will enclose her with boards of cedar.

<sup>10</sup>[Well] I am a wall [with battlements], and my breasts are like the towers of it. Then was I in [the king's] eyes as one [to be respected and to be allowed] to find peace.

<sup>11</sup>Solomon had a vineyard at Baal-hamon; he let out the vineyard to keepers; everyone was to bring him a thousand pieces of silver for its fruit.

<sup>12</sup>You, O Solomon, can have your thousand [pieces of silver], and those who tend the fruit of it two hundred; but my vineyard, which is mine [with all its radiant joy], is before me!

<sup>13</sup>O you who dwell in the gardens, your companions have been listening to your voice—now cause me to hear it.

<sup>14</sup>[Joyfully the radiant bride turned to him, the one altogether lovely, the chief among ten thousand to her soul, and with unconcealed eagerness to begin her life of sweet companionship with him, she answered] Make haste, my beloved, *and* come quickly, like a gazelle or a young hart [and take me to our waiting home] upon the mountains of spices!

---

<sup>a</sup> 7 Or *he*   <sup>b</sup> 11 That is, about 25 pounds or about 12 kilograms; also in verse 12   <sup>c</sup> 12 That is, about 5 pounds or about 2.3 kilograms

# Isaiah

**1** The vision concerning Judah and Jerusalem that Isaiah son of Amoz saw during the reigns of Uzziah, Jotham, Ahaz and Hezekiah, kings of Judah.

## A Rebellious Nation

²Hear me, you heavens! Listen, earth!
  For the LORD has spoken:
"I reared children and brought them up,
  but they have rebelled against me.
³The ox knows its master,
  the donkey its owner's manger,
but Israel does not know,
  my people do not understand."

⁴Woe to the sinful nation,
  a people whose guilt is great,
a brood of evildoers,
  children given to corruption!
They have forsaken the LORD;
  they have spurned the Holy One of Israel
  and turned their backs on him.

⁵Why should you be beaten anymore?
  Why do you persist in rebellion?
Your whole head is injured,
  your whole heart afflicted.
⁶From the sole of your foot to the top of your head
  there is no soundness—
only wounds and welts
  and open sores,
not cleansed or bandaged
  or soothed with olive oil.

⁷Your country is desolate,
  your cities burned with fire;
your fields are being stripped by foreigners
  right before you,
  laid waste as when overthrown by strangers.
⁸Daughter Zion is left
  like a shelter in a vineyard,
like a hut in a cucumber field,
  like a city under siege.
⁹Unless the LORD Almighty
  had left us some survivors,
we would have become like Sodom,
  we would have been like Gomorrah.

¹⁰Hear the word of the LORD,
  you rulers of Sodom;
listen to the instruction of our God,
  you people of Gomorrah!
¹¹"The multitude of your sacrifices—
  what are they to me?" says the LORD.
"I have more than enough of burnt offerings,
  of rams and the fat of fattened animals;
I have no pleasure
  in the blood of bulls and lambs and goats.
¹²When you come to appear before me,
  who has asked this of you,
  this trampling of my courts?
¹³Stop bringing meaningless offerings!
  Your incense is detestable to me.
New Moons, Sabbaths and convocations—
  I cannot bear your worthless assemblies.
¹⁴Your New Moon feasts and your appointed festivals
  I hate with all my being.
They have become a burden to me;
  I am weary of bearing them.

# Isaiah

**1** The vision [seen by spiritual perception] of Isaiah son of Amoz, which he saw concerning Judah [the kingdom] and Jerusalem [its capital] in the days of Uzziah, Jotham, Ahaz, and Hezekiah, kings of Judah.
²Hear, O heavens, and give ear, O earth! For the Lord has spoken: I have nourished and brought up sons *and* have made them great and exalted, but they have rebelled against Me *and* broken away from Me.
³The ox [instinctively] knows his owner, and the donkey his master's crib, but Israel does not know *or* recognize Me [as Lord], My people do not consider *or* understand.
⁴Ah, sinful nation, a people loaded with iniquity, offspring of evildoers, sons who deal corruptly! They have forsaken the Lord, they have despised *and* shown contempt *and* provoked the Holy One of Israel to anger, they have become utterly estranged (alienated).
⁵Why should you be stricken *and* punished any more [since it brings no correction]? You will revolt more and more. The whole head is sick, and the whole heart is faint (feeble, sick, and nauseated).
⁶From the sole of the foot even to the head there is no soundness *or* health in [the nation's body]—but wounds and bruises and fresh *and* bleeding stripes; they have not been pressed out *and* closed up or bound up or softened with oil. [No one has troubled to seek a remedy.]
⁷[Because of your detestable disobedience] your country lies desolate, your cities are burned with fire; your land—strangers devour it in your very presence, and it is desolate, as overthrown by aliens.
⁸And the Daughter of Zion [Jerusalem] is left like a [deserted] booth in a vineyard, like a lodge in a garden of cucumbers, like a besieged city [spared, but in the midst of desolation].
⁹Except the Lord of hosts had left us a very small remnant [of survivors], we should have been like Sodom, and we should have been like Gomorrah. [Gen. 19:24, 25; Rom. 9:29.]
¹⁰Hear [O Jerusalem] the word of the Lord, you rulers *or* judges of [another] Sodom! Give ear to the law *and* the teaching of our God, you people of [another] Gomorrah!
¹¹To what purpose is the multitude of your sacrifices to Me [unless they are the offering of the heart]? says the Lord. I have had enough of the burnt offerings of rams and the fat of fed beasts [without obedience]; and I do not delight in the blood of bulls or of lambs or of he-goats [without righteousness].
¹²When you come to appear before Me, who requires of you that your [unholy feet] trample My courts?
¹³Bring no more offerings of vanity (emptiness, falsity, vainglory, and futility); [your hollow offering of] incense is an abomination to Me; the New Moons and Sabbaths, the calling of assemblies, I cannot endure—[it is] iniquity *and* profanation, even the solemn meeting.
¹⁴Your New Moon festivals and your [hypocritical] appointed feasts My soul hates. They are an oppressive burden to Me; I am weary of bearing them.

# New International Version

15 When you spread out your hands in prayer,
    I hide my eyes from you;
even when you offer many prayers,
    I am not listening.

Your hands are full of blood!

16 Wash and make yourselves clean.
    Take your evil deeds out of my sight;
    stop doing wrong.
17 Learn to do right; seek justice.
    Defend the oppressed.[a]
Take up the cause of the fatherless;
    plead the case of the widow.

18 "Come now, let us settle the matter,"
    says the LORD.
"Though your sins are like scarlet,
    they shall be as white as snow;
though they are red as crimson,
    they shall be like wool.
19 If you are willing and obedient,
    you will eat the good things of the land;
20 but if you resist and rebel,
    you will be devoured by the sword."
        For the mouth of the LORD has spoken.

21 See how the faithful city
    has become a prostitute!
She once was full of justice;
    righteousness used to dwell in her—
    but now murderers!
22 Your silver has become dross,
    your choice wine is diluted with water.
23 Your rulers are rebels,
    partners with thieves;
they all love bribes
    and chase after gifts.
They do not defend the cause of the fatherless;
    the widow's case does not come before them.

24 Therefore the Lord, the LORD Almighty,
    the Mighty One of Israel, declares:
"Ah! I will vent my wrath on my foes
    and avenge myself on my enemies.
25 I will turn my hand against you;[b]
    I will thoroughly purge away your dross
    and remove all your impurities.
26 I will restore your leaders as in days of old,
    your rulers as at the beginning.
Afterward you will be called
    the City of Righteousness,
    the Faithful City."

27 Zion will be delivered with justice,
    her penitent ones with righteousness.
28 But rebels and sinners will both be broken,
    and those who forsake the LORD will perish.

29 "You will be ashamed because of the sacred oaks
    in which you have delighted;
you will be disgraced because of the gardens
    that you have chosen.
30 You will be like an oak with fading leaves,
    like a garden without water.
31 The mighty man will become tinder
    and his work a spark;
both will burn together,
    with no one to quench the fire."

# Amplified Bible

15 And when you spread forth your hands [in prayer, imploring help], I will hide My eyes from you; even though you make many prayers, I will not hear. Your hands are full of blood!
16 Wash yourselves, make yourselves clean; put away the evil of your doings from before My eyes! Cease to do evil,
17 Learn to do right! Seek justice, relieve the oppressed, *and* correct the oppressor. Defend the fatherless, plead for the widow.
18 Come now, and let us reason together, says the Lord. Though your sins are like scarlet, they shall be as white as snow; though they are red like crimson, they shall be like wool.
19 If you are willing and obedient, you shall eat the good of the land;
20 But if you refuse and rebel, you will be devoured by the sword. For the mouth of the Lord has spoken it.
21 How the faithful city has become an [idolatrous] harlot, she who was full of justice! Uprightness *and* right standing with God [once] lodged in her—but now murderers.
22 Your silver has become dross, your wine is mixed with water.
23 Your princes are rebels and companions of thieves; everyone loves bribes and runs after compensation *and* rewards. They judge not for the fatherless *nor* defend them, neither does the cause of the widow come to them [for they delay or turn a deaf ear].
24 Therefore says the Lord, the Lord of hosts, the Mighty One of Israel, Ah, I will appease Myself on My adversaries and avenge Myself on My enemies.
25 And I will bring My hand again upon you and thoroughly purge away your dross [as with lye] and take away all your tin *or* alloy.
26 And I will restore your judges as at the first, and your counselors as at the beginning; afterward you shall be called the City of Righteousness, the Faithful City.
27 Zion shall be redeemed with justice, and her [returned] converts with righteousness (uprightness and right standing with God).
28 But the crushing *and* destruction of rebels and sinners shall be together, and they who forsake the Lord shall be consumed.
29 For you will be ashamed [of the folly and degradation] of the oak *or* terebinth trees in which you found [idolatrous] pleasure, and you will blush with shame for the [idolatrous worship which you practice in the passion-inflaming] gardens which you have chosen.
30 For you shall be like an oak *or* terebinth whose leaf withers, and like a garden that has no water.
31 And the strong shall become like tow *and* become tinder, and his work like a spark, and they shall both burn together, with none to quench them.

---

*a* 17 Or *justice. / Correct the oppressor*    *b* 25 That is, against Jerusalem

## New International Version

### The Mountain of the LORD

**2** This is what Isaiah son of Amoz saw concerning Judah and Jerusalem:

² In the last days

the mountain of the LORD's temple will be established
as the highest of the mountains;
it will be exalted above the hills,
and all nations will stream to it.

³ Many peoples will come and say,

"Come, let us go up to the mountain of the LORD,
to the temple of the God of Jacob.
He will teach us his ways,
so that we may walk in his paths."
The law will go out from Zion,
the word of the LORD from Jerusalem.
⁴ He will judge between the nations
and will settle disputes for many peoples.
They will beat their swords into plowshares
and their spears into pruning hooks.
Nation will not take up sword against nation,
nor will they train for war anymore.

⁵ Come, descendants of Jacob,
let us walk in the light of the LORD.

### The Day of the LORD

⁶ You, LORD, have abandoned your people,
the descendants of Jacob.
They are full of superstitions from the East;
they practice divination like the Philistines
and embrace pagan customs.
⁷ Their land is full of silver and gold;
there is no end to their treasures.
Their land is full of horses;
there is no end to their chariots.
⁸ Their land is full of idols;
they bow down to the work of their hands,
to what their fingers have made.
⁹ So people will be brought low
and everyone humbled—
do not forgive them.ᵃ

¹⁰ Go into the rocks, hide in the ground
from the fearful presence of the LORD
and the splendor of his majesty!
¹¹ The eyes of the arrogant will be humbled
and human pride brought low;
the LORD alone will be exalted in that day.

¹² The LORD Almighty has a day in store
for all the proud and lofty,
for all that is exalted
(and they will be humbled),
¹³ for all the cedars of Lebanon, tall and lofty,
and all the oaks of Bashan,
¹⁴ for all the towering mountains
and all the high hills,
¹⁵ for every lofty tower
and every fortified wall,
¹⁶ for every trading shipᵇ
and every stately vessel.
¹⁷ The arrogance of man will be brought low
and human pride humbled;
the LORD alone will be exalted in that day,
¹⁸ and the idols will totally disappear.

¹⁹ People will flee to caves in the rocks
and to holes in the ground
from the fearful presence of the LORD
and the splendor of his majesty,
when he rises to shake the earth.

## Amplified Bible

**2** The word which Isaiah son of Amoz saw [revealed] concerning Judah and Jerusalem.

² It shall come to pass in the latter days that the mountain of the Lord's house shall be [firmly] established as the highest of the mountains and shall be exalted above the hills, and all nations shall flow to it.

³ And many people shall come and say, Come, let us go up to the mountain of the Lord, to the house of the God of Jacob, that He may teach us His ways and that we may walk in His paths. For out of Zion shall go forth the law *and* instruction, and the word of the Lord from Jerusalem.

⁴ And He shall judge between the nations and shall decide [disputes] for many peoples; and they shall beat their swords into plowshares and their spears into pruning hooks. Nation shall not lift up sword against nation, neither shall they learn war any more. [Mic. 4:1-3.]

⁵ O house of Jacob, come, let us walk in the light of the Lord.

⁶ Surely [Lord] You have rejected *and* forsaken your people, the house of Jacob, because they are filled [with customs] from the east and with soothsayers [who foretell] like the Philistines; also they strike hands *and* make pledges *and* agreements with the children of aliens. [Deut. 18:9-12.]

⁷ Their land also is full of silver and gold; neither is there any end to their treasures. Their land is also full of horses; neither is there any end to their chariots. [Deut. 17:14-17.]

⁸ Their land also is full of idols; they worship the work of their own hands, what their own fingers have made.

⁹ And the common man is bowed down [before idols], also the great man is brought low *and* humbles himself— therefore forgive them not [O Lord].

¹⁰ Enter into the rock and hide yourself in the dust from before the terror of the Lord and from the glory of His majesty.

¹¹ The proud looks of man shall be brought low, and the haughtiness of men shall be humbled; and the Lord alone shall be exalted in that day.

¹² For there shall be a day of the Lord of hosts against all who are proud and haughty and against all who are lifted up—and they shall be brought low—[Zeph. 2:3; Mal. 4:1.]

¹³ [The wrath of God will begin by coming down] against all the cedars of Lebanon [west of the Jordan] that are high and lifted up, and against all the oaks of Bashan [east of the Jordan],

¹⁴ And [after that] against all the high mountains and all the hills that are lifted up,

¹⁵ And against every high tower and every fenced wall,

¹⁶ And against all the ships of Tarshish and all the picturesque *and* desirable imagery [designed for mere ornament and luxury].

¹⁷ Then the loftiness of man shall be bowed down, and the haughtiness of men shall be brought low; and the Lord alone shall be exalted in that day.

¹⁸ And the idols shall utterly pass away (be abolished).

¹⁹ Then shall [the stricken, deprived of all in which they had trusted] go into the caves of the rocks and into the holes of the earth from before the terror *and* dread of the Lord and from before the glory of His majesty, when He arises to shake mightily *and* terribly the earth. [Luke 23:30.]

---

ᵃ 9 Or *not raise them up*    ᵇ 16 Hebrew *every ship of Tarshish*

## New International Version

[20] In that day people will throw away
   to the moles and bats
 their idols of silver and idols of gold,
   which they made to worship.
[21] They will flee to caverns in the rocks
   and to the overhanging crags
 from the fearful presence of the LORD
   and the splendor of his majesty,
   when he rises to shake the earth.

[22] Stop trusting in mere humans,
   who have but a breath in their nostrils.
   Why hold them in esteem?

### Judgment on Jerusalem and Judah

**3** See now, the Lord,
   the LORD Almighty,
 is about to take from Jerusalem and Judah
   both supply and support:
 all supplies of food and all supplies of water,
 [2]  the hero and the warrior,
 the judge and the prophet,
   the diviner and the elder,
[3] the captain of fifty and the man of rank,
   the counselor, skilled craftsman and clever
     enchanter.

[4] "I will make mere youths their officials;
   children will rule over them."

[5] People will oppress each other—
   man against man, neighbor against neighbor.
 The young will rise up against the old,
   the nobody against the honored.

[6] A man will seize one of his brothers
   in his father's house, and say,
 "You have a cloak, you be our leader;
   take charge of this heap of ruins!"
[7] But in that day he will cry out,
   "I have no remedy.
 I have no food or clothing in my house;
   do not make me the leader of the people."

[8] Jerusalem staggers,
   Judah is falling;
 their words and deeds are against the LORD,
   defying his glorious presence.
[9] The look on their faces testifies against them;
   they parade their sin like Sodom;
   they do not hide it.
 Woe to them!
   They have brought disaster upon themselves.

[10] Tell the righteous it will be well with them,
   for they will enjoy the fruit of their deeds.
[11] Woe to the wicked!
   Disaster is upon them!
 They will be paid back
   for what their hands have done.

[12] Youths oppress my people,
   women rule over them.
 My people, your guides lead you astray;
   they turn you from the path.

[13] The LORD takes his place in court;
   he rises to judge the people.
[14] The LORD enters into judgment
   against the elders and leaders of his people:
 "It is you who have ruined my vineyard;
   the plunder from the poor is in your houses.
[15] What do you mean by crushing my people
   and grinding the faces of the poor?"
     declares the Lord, the LORD Almighty.

## Amplified Bible

[20] In that day men shall cast away to the moles and to the bats their idols of silver and their idols of gold, which they made for themselves to worship,
[21] To go into the caverns of the rocks and into the clefts of the ragged rocks from before the terror *and* dread of the Lord and from before the glory of His majesty, when He rises to shake mightily *and* terribly the earth.
[22] Cease to trust in [weak, frail, and dying] man, whose breath is in his nostrils [for so short a time]; in what sense can he be counted as having intrinsic worth?

**3** For behold, the Lord, the Lord of hosts, is taking away from Jerusalem and from Judah the stay and the staff [every kind of prop], the whole stay of bread and the whole stay of water,
[2] The mighty man and the man of war, the judge *and* the [professional] prophet, the one who foretells by divination and the old man,
[3] The captain of fifty and the man of rank, the counselor and the expert craftsman and the skillful enchanter.
[4] And I will make boys their princes, and with childishness shall they rule over them [with outrage instead of justice].
[5] And the people shall be oppressed, each one by another, and each one by his neighbor; the child shall behave himself proudly *and* with insolence against the old man, and the lowborn against the honorable [person of rank].
[6] When a man shall take hold of his brother in the house of his father, saying, You have a robe, you shall be our judge *and* ruler, and this heap of ruins shall be under your control—
[7] In that day he will answer, saying, I will not be a healer *and* one who binds up; *[a] I am not a physician.* For in my house is neither bread nor clothing; you shall not make me judge *and* ruler of the people.
[8] For Jerusalem is ruined and Judah is fallen, because their speech and their deeds are against the Lord, to provoke the eyes of His glory *and* defy His glorious presence.
[9] Their respecting of persons *and* showing of partiality witnesses against them; they proclaim their sin like Sodom; they do not hide it. Woe to them! For they have brought evil [as a reward upon themselves].
[10] Say to the righteous that it shall be well with them, for they shall eat the fruit of their deeds.
[11] Woe to the wicked! It shall be ill with them, for what their hands have done shall be done to them.
[12] As for My people, children are their oppressors, and women rule over them. O My people, your leaders cause you to err, and they confuse (destroy and swallow up) the course of your paths.
[13] The Lord stands up to contend, and stands to judge the peoples *and* His people.
[14] The Lord enters into judgment with the elders of His people and their princes: For [by your exactions and oppressions you have robbed the people and ruined the country] you have devoured the vineyard; the spoil of the poor is in your houses.
[15] What do you mean by crushing My people and grinding the faces of the poor? says the Lord God of hosts.

[a] *The Latin Vulgate* rendering.

## New International Version

16 The LORD says,
"The women of Zion are haughty,
walking along with outstretched necks,
flirting with their eyes,
strutting along with swaying hips,
with ornaments jingling on their ankles.
17 Therefore the Lord will bring sores on the heads of the
women of Zion;
the LORD will make their scalps bald."

18 In that day the Lord will snatch away their finery: the
bangles and headbands and crescent necklaces, 19 the earrings and bracelets and veils, 20 the headdresses and anklets and sashes, the perfume bottles and charms, 21 the
signet rings and nose rings, 22 the fine robes and the capes
and cloaks, the purses 23 and mirrors, and the linen garments and tiaras and shawls.

24 Instead of fragrance there will be a stench;
instead of a sash, a rope;
instead of well-dressed hair, baldness;
instead of fine clothing, sackcloth;
instead of beauty, branding.
25 Your men will fall by the sword,
your warriors in battle.
26 The gates of Zion will lament and mourn;
destitute, she will sit on the ground.

**4** 1 In that day seven women
will take hold of one man
and say, "We will eat our own food
and provide our own clothes;
only let us be called by your name.
Take away our disgrace!"

### The Branch of the LORD

2 In that day the Branch of the LORD will be beautiful and
glorious, and the fruit of the land will be the pride and glory of the survivors in Israel. 3 Those who are left in Zion,
who remain in Jerusalem, will be called holy, all who are
recorded among the living in Jerusalem. 4 The Lord will
wash away the filth of the women of Zion; he will cleanse
the bloodstains from Jerusalem by a spirit[a] of judgment
and a spirit[a] of fire. 5 Then the LORD will create over all of
Mount Zion and over those who assemble there a cloud
of smoke by day and a glow of flaming fire by night; over
everything the glory[b] will be a canopy. 6 It will be a shelter
and shade from the heat of the day, and a refuge and hiding place from the storm and rain.

## Amplified Bible

16 Moreover, the Lord said, Because the daughters of
Zion are haughty and walk with outstretched necks and
with undisciplined (flirtatious and alluring) eyes, tripping
along with mincing *and* affected gait, and making a tinkling noise with [the anklets on] their feet,
17 Therefore the Lord will smite with a scab the crown
of the heads of the daughters of Zion [making them bald],
and the Lord will cause them to be [taken as captives and
to suffer the indignity of being] stripped naked.
18 In that day the Lord will take away the finery of their
tinkling anklets, the caps of network, the crescent head
ornaments,
19 The pendants, the bracelets *or* chains, and the span-
gled face veils *and* scarfs,
20 The headbands, the short ankle chains [attached
from one foot to the other to insure a measured gait], the
sashes, the perfume boxes, the amulets *or* charms [sus-
pended from the ears or neck],
21 The signet rings and nose rings,
22 The festal robes, the cloaks, the stoles *and* shawls,
and the handbags,
23 The hand mirrors, the fine linen [undergarments],
the turbans, and the [whole body-enveloping] veils.
24 And it shall come to pass that instead of the sweet
odor of spices there shall be the stench of rottenness; and
instead of a girdle, a rope; and instead of well-set hair,
baldness; and instead of a rich robe, a girding of sackcloth;
and searing [of captives by the scorching heat] instead
of beauty.
25 Your men shall fall by the sword, and your mighty
men in battle.
26 And [Jerusalem's] gates shall lament and mourn [as
those who wail for the dead]; and she, being ruined *and*
desolate, shall sit upon the ground.

**4** And in that day [a] seven women shall take hold of one
man, saying, We will eat our own bread and provide
our own apparel; only let us be called by your name to take
away our reproach [of being unmarried].
2 In that day the Branch of the Lord shall be beautiful
and glorious, and the fruit of the land shall be excellent
and lovely to those of Israel who have escaped. [Jer. 23:5;
33:15; Zech. 3:8; 6:12.]
3 And he who is left in Zion and remains in Jerusalem
will be called holy, everyone who is recorded for life in Jerusalem *and for* [b] *eternal life*, [Joel 3:17; Phil. 4:3.]
4 After the Lord has washed away the [moral] filth of
the daughters of Zion [pride, vanity, haughtiness] and has
purged the bloodstains of Jerusalem from the midst of it by
the spirit *and* blast of judgment and by the spirit *and* blast
of burning *and* sifting.
5 And the Lord will create over the whole site, over every
dwelling place of Mount Zion and over her assemblies, a
cloud and smoke by day and the shining of a flaming fire
by night; for over all the glory shall be a canopy (a defense
of divine love and protection).
6 And there shall be a pavilion for shade in the daytime
from the heat, and for a place of refuge and a shelter from
storm and from rain.

---

[a] Although more male babies are born than female babies, the number of
marriageable men in the world is constantly decreasing. Over 57 percent
of the enlisted men in World War I became casualties (according to *The
World Almanac*), and the casualties in World War II have been estimated
at 33 million. Not counting deaths in the armed forces, the ratio of
deaths between males and females was (as of 1960) nine to seven. This
had not been true in previous centuries. Isaiah here foresees a time
when the ratio between marriageable men and women will be one to
seven in Jerusalem. [b] *The Chaldee Translation* reads "eternal life."

---

[a] 4 Or *the Spirit*    [b] 5 Or *over all the glory there*

# New International Version

## The Song of the Vineyard

**5** I will sing for the one I love
a song about his vineyard:
My loved one had a vineyard
on a fertile hillside.
[2] He dug it up and cleared it of stones
and planted it with the choicest vines.
He built a watchtower in it
and cut out a winepress as well.
Then he looked for a crop of good grapes,
but it yielded only bad fruit.

[3] "Now you dwellers in Jerusalem and people of Judah,
judge between me and my vineyard.
[4] What more could have been done for my vineyard
than I have done for it?
When I looked for good grapes,
why did it yield only bad?
[5] Now I will tell you
what I am going to do to my vineyard:
I will take away its hedge,
and it will be destroyed;
I will break down its wall,
and it will be trampled.
[6] I will make it a wasteland,
neither pruned nor cultivated,
and briers and thorns will grow there.
I will command the clouds
not to rain on it."

[7] The vineyard of the LORD Almighty
is the nation of Israel,
and the people of Judah
are the vines he delighted in.
And he looked for justice, but saw bloodshed;
for righteousness, but heard cries of distress.

## Woes and Judgments

[8] Woe to you who add house to house
and join field to field
till no space is left
and you live alone in the land.

[9] The LORD Almighty has declared in my hearing:

"Surely the great houses will become desolate,
the fine mansions left without occupants.
[10] A ten-acre vineyard will produce only a bath[a] of wine;
a homer[b] of seed will yield only an ephah[c] of grain."

[11] Woe to those who rise early in the morning
to run after their drinks,
who stay up late at night
till they are inflamed with wine.
[12] They have harps and lyres at their banquets,
pipes and timbrels and wine,
but they have no regard for the deeds of the LORD,
no respect for the work of his hands.
[13] Therefore my people will go into exile
for lack of understanding;
those of high rank will die of hunger
and the common people will be parched with thirst.
[14] Therefore Death expands its jaws,
opening wide its mouth;
into it will descend their nobles and masses
with all their brawlers and revelers.
[15] So people will be brought low
and everyone humbled,
the eyes of the arrogant humbled.
[16] But the LORD Almighty will be exalted by his justice,
and the holy God will be proved holy by his
righteous acts.

---

[a] 10 That is, about 6 gallons or about 22 liters   [b] 10 That is, probably
about 360 pounds or about 160 kilograms   [c] 10 That is, probably about
36 pounds or about 16 kilograms

# Amplified Bible

**5** Let me [as God's representative] sing of and for my
greatly Beloved [God, the Son] a tender song of my
Beloved concerning His vineyard [His chosen people]. My
greatly Beloved had a vineyard on a very fruitful hill. [S. of
Sol. 6:3; Matt. 21:33-40.]
[2] And He dug and trenched the ground and gathered
out the stones from it and planted it with the choicest vine
and built a tower in the midst of it and hewed out a winepress in it. And He looked for it to bring forth grapes, and
it brought forth wild grapes.
[3] And now, O inhabitants of Jerusalem and men of Judah, judge, I pray you, between Me and My vineyard [My
people, says the Lord].
[4] What more could have been done for My vineyard that
I have not done in it? When I looked for it to bring forth
grapes, why did it yield wild grapes?
[5] And now I will tell you what I will do to My vineyard: I
will take away its hedge, and it shall be eaten and burned
up; and I will break down its wall, and it shall be trodden
down [by enemies].
[6] And I will lay it waste; it shall not be pruned or cultivated, but there shall come up briers and thorns. I will also
command the clouds that they rain no rain upon it.
[7] For the vineyard of the Lord of hosts is the house of
Israel, and the men of Judah His pleasant planting [the
plant of His delight]. And He looked for justice, but behold,
[He saw] oppression and bloodshed; [He looked] for righteousness (for uprightness and right standing with God),
but behold, [He heard] a cry [of oppression and distress]!
[8] Woe to those who join house to house [and by violently
expelling the poorer occupants enclose large acreage] and
join field to field until there is no place for others and you
are made to dwell alone in the midst of the land!
[9] In my [Isaiah's] ears the Lord of hosts said, Of a truth
many houses shall be desolate, even great and beautiful
ones shall be without inhabitant.
[10] For ten acres of vineyard shall yield only about eight
gallons, and ten bushels of seed will produce but one
bushel.
[11] Woe unto those who rise early in the morning, that
they may pursue strong drink, who tarry late into the
night till wine inflames them!
[12] They have lyre and harp, tambourine and flute and
wine at their feasts, but they do not regard the deeds of the
Lord, neither do they consider the operation of His hands
[in mercy and in judgment].
[13] Therefore My people go into captivity [to their ene-
mies] without knowing it and because they have no knowledge [of God]. And their honorable men [their glory] are
famished, and their common people are parched with
thirst.
[14] Therefore Sheol (the unseen state, the realm of the
dead) has enlarged its appetite and opened its mouth without measure; and [Jerusalem's] nobility and her multitude
and her pomp and tumult and [the drunken reveler] who
exults in her descend into it.
[15] And the common man is bowed down, and the great
man is brought low, and the eyes of the haughty are humbled.
[16] But the Lord of hosts is exalted in justice, and God,
the Holy One, shows Himself holy in righteousness and
through righteous judgments.

## New International Version

17 Then sheep will graze as in their own pasture;
  lambs will feed[a] among the ruins of the rich.

18 Woe to those who draw sin along with cords of deceit,
  and wickedness as with cart ropes,
19 to those who say, "Let God hurry;
  let him hasten his work
  so we may see it.
The plan of the Holy One of Israel—
  let it approach, let it come into view,
  so we may know it."

20 Woe to those who call evil good
  and good evil,
who put darkness for light
  and light for darkness,
who put bitter for sweet
  and sweet for bitter.

21 Woe to those who are wise in their own eyes
  and clever in their own sight.

22 Woe to those who are heroes at drinking wine
  and champions at mixing drinks,
23 who acquit the guilty for a bribe,
  but deny justice to the innocent.

24 Therefore, as tongues of fire lick up straw
  and as dry grass sinks down in the flames,
so their roots will decay
  and their flowers blow away like dust;
for they have rejected the law of the LORD Almighty
  and spurned the word of the Holy One of Israel.
25 Therefore the LORD's anger burns against his people;
  his hand is raised and he strikes them down.
The mountains shake,
  and the dead bodies are like refuse in the streets.

Yet for all this, his anger is not turned away,
  his hand is still upraised.

26 He lifts up a banner for the distant nations,
  he whistles for those at the ends of the earth.
Here they come,
  swiftly and speedily!
27 Not one of them grows tired or stumbles,
  not one slumbers or sleeps;
not a belt is loosened at the waist,
  not a sandal strap is broken.
28 Their arrows are sharp,
  all their bows are strung;
their horses' hooves seem like flint,
  their chariot wheels like a whirlwind.
29 Their roar is like that of the lion,
  they roar like young lions;
they growl as they seize their prey
  and carry it off with no one to rescue.
30 In that day they will roar over it
  like the roaring of the sea.
And if one looks at the land,
  there is only darkness and distress;
  even the sun will be darkened by clouds.

### Isaiah's Commission

**6** In the year that King Uzziah died, I saw the Lord, high and exalted, seated on a throne; and the train of his robe filled the temple. 2 Above him were seraphim, each with six wings: With two wings they covered their faces, with two they covered their feet, and with two they were flying. 3 And they were calling to one another:

"Holy, holy, holy is the LORD Almighty;
  the whole earth is full of his glory."

4 At the sound of their voices the doorposts and thresholds shook and the temple was filled with smoke.

a 17 Septuagint; Hebrew / strangers will eat

## Amplified Bible

17 Then shall the lambs feed [among the ruins] as in their own pasture, and [among] the desolate places of the [exiled] rich shall sojourners and aliens eat.

18 Woe to those who draw [calamity] with cords of iniquity and falsehood, who bring punishment to themselves with a cart rope of wickedness,

19 Who say, Let [the Holy One] make haste and speed His [prophesied] vengeance, that we may see it; and let the purpose of the Holy One of Israel draw near and come, that we may know it!

20 Woe to those who call evil good and good evil, who put darkness for light and light for darkness, who put bitter for sweet and sweet for bitter!

21 Woe to those who are wise in their own eyes and prudent and shrewd in their own sight!

22 Woe to those who are mighty heroes at drinking wine and men of strength in mixing alcoholic drinks!—

23 Who justify and acquit the guilty for a bribe, but take away the rights of the innocent and righteous from them!

24 Therefore, as the tongue of fire devours the stubble, and as the dry grass sinks down in the flame, so their root shall be like rottenness and their blossom shall go up like fine dust—because they have rejected and cast away the law and the teaching of the Lord of hosts and have not believed but have treated scornfully and have despised the word of the Holy One of Israel.

25 Therefore is the anger of the Lord kindled against His people, and He has stretched forth His hand against them and has smitten them. And the mountains trembled, and their dead bodies were like dung and sweepings in the midst of the streets. For all this, His anger is not turned away, but His hand is still stretched out [in judgment].

26 And He will lift up a signal to call together a hostile people from afar [to execute His judgment on Judea], and will hiss for them from the end of the earth [as bees are hissed from their hives], and behold, they shall come with speed, swiftly!

27 None is weary or stumbles among them, none slumbers or sleeps; nor is the girdle of their loins loosed or the latchet (thong) of their shoes broken;

28 Their arrows are sharp, and all their bows bent; their horses' hoofs seem like flint, and their wheels like a whirlwind.

29 Their roaring is like that of a lioness, they roar like young lions; they growl and seize their prey and carry it safely away, and there is none to deliver it.

30 And in that day they [the army from afar] shall roar against [the Jews] like the roaring of the sea. And if one looks to the land, behold, there is darkness and distress; and the light [itself] will be darkened by the clouds of it.

**6** In the year that King Uzziah died, [in a vision] I saw the Lord sitting upon a throne, high and lifted up, and the skirts of His train filled the [most holy part of the] temple. [John 12:41.]

2 Above Him stood the seraphim; each had six wings: with two [each] covered his [own] face, and with two [each] covered his feet, and with two [each] flew.

3 And one cried to another and said, Holy, holy, holy is the Lord of hosts; the whole earth is full of His glory!

4 And the foundations of the thresholds shook at the voice of him who cried, and the house was filled with smoke.

## New International Version

⁵"Woe to me!" I cried. "I am ruined! For I am a man of unclean lips, and I live among a people of unclean lips, and my eyes have seen the King, the LORD Almighty."
⁶Then one of the seraphim flew to me with a live coal in his hand, which he had taken with tongs from the altar. ⁷With it he touched my mouth and said, "See, this has touched your lips; your guilt is taken away and your sin atoned for."
⁸Then I heard the voice of the Lord saying, "Whom shall I send? And who will go for us?"
And I said, "Here am I. Send me!"
⁹He said, "Go and tell this people:

" 'Be ever hearing, but never understanding;
   be ever seeing, but never perceiving.'
¹⁰Make the heart of this people calloused;
   make their ears dull
   and close their eyes.ᵃ
Otherwise they might see with their eyes,
   hear with their ears,
   understand with their hearts,
and turn and be healed."

¹¹Then I said, "For how long, Lord?"
And he answered:

"Until the cities lie ruined
   and without inhabitant,
until the houses are left deserted
   and the fields ruined and ravaged,
¹²until the LORD has sent everyone far away
   and the land is utterly forsaken.
¹³And though a tenth remains in the land,
   it will again be laid waste.
But as the terebinth and oak
   leave stumps when they are cut down,
   so the holy seed will be the stump in the land."

### The Sign of Immanuel

**7** When Ahaz son of Jotham, the son of Uzziah, was king of Judah, King Rezin of Aram and Pekah son of Remaliah king of Israel marched up to fight against Jerusalem, but they could not overpower it.
²Now the house of David was told, "Aram has allied itself withᵇ Ephraim"; so the hearts of Ahaz and his people were shaken, as the trees of the forest are shaken by the wind.
³Then the LORD said to Isaiah, "Go out, you and your son Shear-Jashub,ᶜ to meet Ahaz at the end of the aqueduct of the Upper Pool, on the road to the Launderer's Field.
⁴Say to him, 'Be careful, keep calm and don't be afraid. Do not lose heart because of these two smoldering stubs of firewood—because of the fierce anger of Rezin and Aram and of the son of Remaliah. ⁵Aram, Ephraim and Remaliah's son have plotted your ruin, saying, ⁶"Let us invade Judah; let us tear it apart and divide it among ourselves, and make the son of Tabeel king over it." ⁷Yet this is what the Sovereign LORD says:

" 'It will not take place,
   it will not happen,
⁸for the head of Aram is Damascus,
   and the head of Damascus is only Rezin.
Within sixty-five years
   Ephraim will be too shattered to be a people.
⁹The head of Ephraim is Samaria,
   and the head of Samaria is only Remaliah's son.

---

ᵃ 9,10 Hebrew; Septuagint 'You will be ever hearing, but never understanding; / you will be ever seeing, but never perceiving.' / ¹⁰This people's heart has become calloused; / they hardly hear with their ears, / and they have closed their eyes   ᵇ 2 Or has set up camp in   ᶜ 3 Shear-Jashub means a remnant will return.

## Amplified Bible

⁵Then said I, Woe is me! For I am undone *and* ruined, because I am a man of unclean lips, and I dwell in the midst of a people of unclean lips; for my eyes have seen the King, the Lord of hosts!
⁶Then flew one of the seraphim [heavenly beings] to me, having a live coal in his hand which he had taken with tongs from off the altar.
⁷And with it he touched my mouth and said, Behold, this has touched your lips; your iniquity *and* guilt are taken away, and your sin is completely atoned for *and* forgiven.
⁸Also I heard the voice of the Lord, saying, Whom shall I send? And who will go for Us? Then said I, Here am I; send me.
⁹And He said, Go and tell this people, Hear *and* hear continually, but understand not; and see *and* see continually, but do not apprehend with your mind.
¹⁰Make the heart of this people fat; and make their ears heavy and shut their eyes, lest they see with their eyes and hear with their ears and understand with their hearts and turn again and be healed.
¹¹Then said I, Lord, how long? And He answered, Until cities lie waste without inhabitant and houses without man, and the land is utterly desolate,
¹²And the Lord removes [His] people far away, and the forsaken places are many in the midst of the land.
¹³And though a tenth [of the people] remain in the land, it will be for their destruction [eaten up and burned] like a terebinth tree or like an oak whose stump *and* substance remain when they are felled *or* have cast their leaves. The holy seed [the elect remnant] is the stump *and* substance [of Israel].

**7** In the days of Ahaz son of Jotham, the son of Uzziah, king of Judah, Rezin the king of Syria and Pekah son of Remaliah king of Israel went up to Jerusalem to wage war against it, but they could not conquer it.
²And the house of David [Judah] was told, Syria is allied with Ephraim [Israel]. And the heart [of Ahaz] and the hearts of his people trembled *and* shook, as the trees of the forest tremble *and* shake with the wind.
³Then said the Lord to Isaiah, Go forth now to meet *Judah's King* Ahaz, you and your son Shear-jashub [a remnant shall return], at the end of the aqueduct *or* canal of the Upper Pool on the highway to the Fuller's Field;
⁴And say to him, Take heed and be quiet; fear not, neither be fainthearted because of these two stumps of smoking firebrands—at the fierce anger of [the Syrian King] Rezin and Syria and of the son of Remaliah [Pekah, usurper of the throne of Israel].
⁵Because Syria, Ephraim [Israel], and the son of Remaliah have purposed evil against you [Judah], saying,
⁶Let us go up against Judah and harass *and* terrify it; and let us cleave it asunder [each of us taking a portion], and set a [vassal] king in the midst of it, namely the son of Tabeel,
⁷Thus says the Lord God: It shall not stand, neither shall it come to pass.
⁸For the head [the capital] of Syria is Damascus, and the head of Damascus is [King] Rezin. Within sixty-five years Ephraim will be broken to pieces so that it will no longer be a people.
⁹And the head (the capital) of Ephraim is Samaria, and the head of Samaria is Remaliah's son [Pekah]. If you will not believe *and* trust *and* rely [on God and on the words of

## New International Version

If you do not stand firm in your faith,
you will not stand at all.'"

¹⁰Again the LORD spoke to Ahaz, ¹¹"Ask the LORD your God for a sign, whether in the deepest depths or in the highest heights." ¹²But Ahaz said, "I will not ask; I will not put the LORD to the test."

¹³Then Isaiah said, "Hear now, you house of David! Is it not enough to try the patience of humans? Will you try the patience of my God also? ¹⁴Therefore the Lord himself will give you*a* a sign: The virgin*b* will conceive and give birth to a son, and*c* will call him Immanuel.*d* ¹⁵He will be eating curds and honey when he knows enough to reject the wrong and choose the right, ¹⁶for before the boy knows enough to reject the wrong and choose the right, the land of the two kings you dread will be laid waste. ¹⁷The LORD will bring on you and on your people and on the house of your father a time unlike any since Ephraim broke away from Judah—he will bring the king of Assyria."

### Assyria, the LORD's Instrument

¹⁸In that day the LORD will whistle for flies from the Nile delta in Egypt and for bees from the land of Assyria. ¹⁹They will all come and settle in the steep ravines and in the crevices in the rocks, on all the thornbushes and at all the water holes. ²⁰In that day the Lord will use a razor hired from beyond the Euphrates River—the king of Assyria—to shave your head and private parts, and to cut off your beard also. ²¹In that day, a person will keep alive a young cow and two goats. ²²And because of the abundance of the milk they give, there will be curds to eat. All who remain in the land will eat curds and honey. ²³In that day, in every place where there were a thousand vines worth a thousand silver shekels,*e* there will be only briers and thorns. ²⁴Hunters will go there with bow and arrow, for the land will be covered with briers and thorns. ²⁵As for all the hills once cultivated by the hoe, you will no longer go there for fear of the briers and thorns; they will become places where cattle are turned loose and where sheep run.

### Isaiah and His Children as Signs

**8** The LORD said to me, "Take a large scroll and write on it with an ordinary pen: Maher-Shalal-Hash-Baz."*f*

## Amplified Bible

God's prophet instead of Assyria], surely you will not be established *nor* will you remain.

¹⁰Moreover, the Lord spoke again to King Ahaz, saying, ¹¹Ask for yourself a sign (a token or proof) of the Lord your God [one that will convince you that God has spoken and will keep His word]; ask it either in the depth below or in the height above [let it be as deep as Sheol or as high as heaven]. ¹²But Ahaz said, I will not ask, neither will I tempt the Lord.

¹³And [Isaiah] said, Hear then, O house of David! Is it a small thing for you to weary *and* try the patience of men, but will you weary *and* try the patience of my God also?

¹⁴Therefore the Lord Himself shall give you a sign: Behold, the young woman who is unmarried *and* a virgin shall conceive and bear a son, and shall call his name Immanuel [God with us]. [Isa. 9:6; Jer. 31:22; Mic. 5:3-5; Matt. 1:22, 23.]

¹⁵Butter *and* curds and wild honey shall he eat when he knows [enough] to refuse the evil and choose the good.

¹⁶For before the child shall know [enough] to refuse the evil and choose the good, the land [Canaan] whose two kings you abhor *and* of whom you are in sickening dread shall be forsaken [both Ephraim and Syria]. [Isa. 7:2.]

¹⁷The Lord shall bring upon you and upon your people and upon your father's house such days as have not come since the day that Ephraim [the ten northern tribes] departed from Judah—even the king of *a*Assyria.

¹⁸And in that day the Lord shall whistle for the fly [the numerous and troublesome foe] that is in the whole extent of the canal country of Egypt and for the bee that is in the land of Assyria.

¹⁹And these [enemies like flies and bees] shall come and shall rest all of them in the desolate *and* rugged valleys *and* deep ravines and in the clefts of the rocks, and on all the thornbushes and on all the pastures.

²⁰In the same day [will the people of Judah be utterly stripped of belongings], the Lord will shave with the razor that is hired from the parts beyond the River [Euphrates]—even with the king of Assyria—[that razor will shave] the head and the hair of the legs, and it shall also consume the beard [leaving Judah with open shame and scorn]. [II Kings 16:7, 8; 18:13-16.]

²¹And [because of the desolation brought on by the invaders] in that day, a man will [be so poor that he will] keep alive only a young milk cow and two sheep.

²²And because of the abundance of milk that they will give, he will eat butter *and* curds, for [only] butter *and* curds and [wild] honey [no vegetables] shall everyone eat who is left in the land [these products provided from the extensive pastures and the plentiful wild flowers upon which the bees depend].

²³And in that day, in every place where there used to be a thousand vines worth a thousand silver shekels, there will be briers and thorns.

²⁴With arrows and with bows shall a man come [to hunt] there, because all the land will be briers and thorns.

²⁵And as for all the hills that were formerly cultivated with mattock *and* hoe, you will not go there for fear of briers and thorns; but they will become a place where oxen are let loose to pasture and where sheep tread.

**8** Then the Lord said to me, Take a large tablet [of wood, metal, or stone] and write upon it with a graving tool *and* in ordinary characters [which the humblest man can read]: Belonging to Maher-shalal-hash-baz [they (the Assyrians) hasten to the spoil (of Syria and Israel), they speed to the prey].

---

*a 14* The Hebrew is plural.   *b 14* Or *young woman*   *c 14* Masoretic Text; Dead Sea Scrolls *son, and he* or *son, and they*   *d 14* *Immanuel* means *God with us.*   *e 23* That is, about 25 pounds or about 12 kilograms   *f 1* *Maher-Shalal-Hash-Baz* means *quick to the plunder, swift to the spoil*; also in verse 3.

*a* "Jesus was actually born in a time when the Holy Land found itself under the supremacy of [Assyria, when looked upon as] the universal empire, a condition which went back to the unbelief of Ahaz as its ultimate cause" (F. Delitzsch, cited by *The New Bible Commentary*).

## New International Version

²So I called in Uriah the priest and Zechariah son of Jeberekiah as reliable witnesses for me. ³Then I made love to the prophetess, and she conceived and gave birth to a son. And the Lord said to me, "Name him Maher-Shalal-Hash-Baz. ⁴For before the boy knows how to say 'My father' or 'My mother,' the wealth of Damascus and the plunder of Samaria will be carried off by the king of Assyria."

⁵The Lord spoke to me again:

⁶"Because this people has rejected
    the gently flowing waters of Shiloah
and rejoices over Rezin
    and the son of Remaliah,
⁷therefore the Lord is about to bring against them
    the mighty floodwaters of the Euphrates—
    the king of Assyria with all his pomp.
It will overflow all its channels,
    run over all its banks
⁸and sweep on into Judah, swirling over it,
    passing through it and reaching up to the neck.
Its outspread wings will cover the breadth of your
    land,
    Immanuel*!*"
⁹Raise the war cry,*ᵇ* you nations, and be shattered!
    Listen, all you distant lands.
Prepare for battle, and be shattered!
    Prepare for battle, and be shattered!
¹⁰Devise your strategy, but it will be thwarted;
    propose your plan, but it will not stand,
    for God is with us.*ᶜ*

¹¹This is what the Lord says to me with his strong hand upon me, warning me not to follow the way of this people:

¹²"Do not call conspiracy
    everything this people calls a conspiracy;
do not fear what they fear,
    and do not dread it.
¹³The Lord Almighty is the one you are to regard as
    holy,
he is the one you are to fear,
    he is the one you are to dread.
¹⁴He will be a holy place;
    for both Israel and Judah he will be
a stone that causes people to stumble
    and a rock that makes them fall.
And for the people of Jerusalem he will be
    a trap and a snare.
¹⁵Many of them will stumble;
    they will fall and be broken,
    they will be snared and captured."

¹⁶Bind up this testimony of warning
    and seal up God's instruction among my disciples.
¹⁷I will wait for the Lord,
    who is hiding his face from the descendants of
    Jacob.
I will put my trust in him.

¹⁸Here am I, and the children the Lord has given me. We are signs and symbols in Israel from the Lord Almighty, who dwells on Mount Zion.

## Amplified Bible

²And I took faithful witnesses to record *and* attest [this prophecy] for me, Uriah the priest and Zechariah son of Jeberechiah.

³And I approached [my wife] the prophetess, and when she had conceived and borne a son, the Lord said to me, Call his name Maher-shalal-hash-baz [as a continual reminder to the people of the prophecy].

⁴For before the child knows how to say, My father or my mother, the riches of Damascus [Syria's capital] and the spoil of Samaria [Israel's capital] *ᵃ*shall be carried away before the king of Assyria.

⁵The Lord spoke to me yet again and said,

⁶Because this people [Israel and Judah] have refused *and* despised the waters of Shiloah [Siloam, the only perennial fountain of Jerusalem, and symbolic of God's protection and sustaining power] that go gently, and rejoice in *and* with Rezin [the king of Syria] and Remaliah's son [Pekah the king of Israel],

⁷Now therefore, behold, the Lord brings upon them the waters of the River [Euphrates], strong and many—even the king of Assyria and all the glory [of his gorgeous retinue]; and it will rise over all its channels, brooks, valleys, *and* canals and extend far beyond its banks; [Isa. 7:17.]

⁸And it will *ᵇ*sweep on into Judah; it will overflow *and* go over [the hills], reaching even [but only] to the neck [of which Jerusalem is the head], and the outstretched wings [of the armies of Assyria] shall fill the breadth of Your land, O Immanuel *ᶜ*[Messiah, God is with us]! [Num. 14:9; Ps. 46:7.]

⁹Make an uproar *and* be broken in pieces, O you peoples [rage, raise the war cry, do your worst, and be utterly dismayed]! Give ear, all you [our enemies] *of* far countries. Gird yourselves [for war], and be thrown into consternation! Gird yourselves, and be [utterly] dismayed!

¹⁰Take counsel together [against Judah], but it shall come to nought; speak the word, but it will not stand, for God is with us [Immanuel]!

¹¹For the Lord spoke thus to me with His strong hand [upon me], and warned *and* instructed me not to walk in the way of this people, saying,

¹²Do not call conspiracy [or hard, or holy] all that this people will call conspiracy [or hard, or holy]; neither be in fear of what they fear, nor [make others afraid and] in dread.

¹³The Lord of hosts—regard Him as holy *and* honor His holy name [by regarding Him as your only hope of safety], and let Him be your fear and let Him be your dread [lest you offend Him by your fear of man and distrust of Him].

¹⁴And He shall be a sanctuary [a sacred and indestructible asylum to those who reverently fear and trust in Him]; but He shall be a Stone of stumbling and a Rock of offense to both the houses of Israel, a trap and a snare to the inhabitants of Jerusalem. [Isa. 28:6; Rom. 9:33; I Pet. 2:6-8.]

¹⁵And many among them shall stumble thereon; and they shall fall and be broken, and be snared and taken.

¹⁶Bind up the testimony, seal the law *and* the teaching among my [Isaiah's] disciples.

¹⁷And I will wait for the Lord, Who is hiding His face from the house of Jacob; and I will look for *and* hope in Him.

¹⁸Behold, I and the children whom the Lord has given me are *ᵈ*signs and wonders [that are to take place] in Israel from the Lord of hosts, Who dwells on Mount Zion.

---

*ᵃ* Samaria was overthrown by Assyria in 722 B.C., ten years after the downfall of Damascus, fulfilling this prophecy. *ᵇ* This prophecy was literally fulfilled, and although Syria and Israel were conquered and led into captivity, the kingdom of Judah was spared and continued for over 130 years. *ᶜ* In its fullest sense 'Immanuel' [God with us] can apply only to the Messiah; the fact that Judah is His was and still is a pledge that, no matter how sorely overwhelmed, it shall be saved at last. *ᵈ* Isaiah's own name means "Salvation of the Lord." His two children's names were "signs" pointing to the coming crisis and the need for God's help: *Shearjashub* means "A remnant shall return" (Isa. 7:3), and *Maher-shalal-hash-baz* means "They hasten to the spoil; they speed to the prey," referring to the Assyrians (Isa. 8:1).

---

*ᵃ 8 Immanuel* means *God with us.*    *ᵇ 9* Or *Do your worst*
*ᶜ 10* Hebrew *Immanuel*

## New International Version

### The Darkness Turns to Light

[19]When someone tells you to consult mediums and spiritists, who whisper and mutter, should not a people inquire of their God? Why consult the dead on behalf of the living? [20]Consult God's instruction and the testimony of warning. If anyone does not speak according to this word, they have no light of dawn. [21]Distressed and hungry, they will roam through the land; when they are famished, they will become enraged and, looking upward, will curse their king and their God. [22]Then they will look toward the earth and see only distress and darkness and fearful gloom, and they will be thrust into utter darkness.

**9**[a] Nevertheless, there will be no more gloom for those who were in distress. In the past he humbled the land of Zebulun and the land of Naphtali, but in the future he will honor Galilee of the nations, by the Way of the Sea, beyond the Jordan—

[2]The people walking in darkness
　have seen a great light;
on those living in the land of deep darkness
　a light has dawned.
[3]You have enlarged the nation
　and increased their joy;
they rejoice before you
　as people rejoice at the harvest,
as warriors rejoice
　when dividing the plunder.
[4]For as in the day of Midian's defeat,
　you have shattered
the yoke that burdens them,
　the bar across their shoulders,
　the rod of their oppressor.
[5]Every warrior's boot used in battle
　and every garment rolled in blood
will be destined for burning,
　will be fuel for the fire.
[6]For to us a child is born,
　to us a son is given,
and the government will be on his shoulders.
And he will be called
　Wonderful Counselor, Mighty God,
　Everlasting Father, Prince of Peace.
[7]Of the greatness of his government and peace
　there will be no end.
He will reign on David's throne
　and over his kingdom,
establishing and upholding it
　with justice and righteousness
　from that time on and forever.
The zeal of the Lord Almighty
　will accomplish this.

### The Lord's Anger Against Israel

[8]The Lord has sent a message against Jacob;
　it will fall on Israel.
[9]All the people will know it—
　Ephraim and the inhabitants of Samaria—
who say with pride
　and arrogance of heart,
[10]"The bricks have fallen down,
　but we will rebuild with dressed stone;
the fig trees have been felled,
　but we will replace them with cedars."

## Amplified Bible

[19]And when the people [instead of putting their trust in God] shall say to you, Consult for direction mediums and wizards who chirp and mutter, should not a people seek *and* consult their God? Should they consult the dead on behalf of the living?

[20][Direct such people] to the teaching and to the testimony! If their teachings are not in accord with this word, it is surely because there is no dawn *and* no morning for them.

[21]And they [who consult mediums and wizards] shall pass through [the land] sorely distressed and hungry; and when they are hungry, they will fret, and will curse by their king and their God; and whether they look upward

[22]Or look to the earth, they will behold only distress and darkness, the gloom of anguish, and into thick darkness *and* widespread, obscure night they shall be driven away.

**9** But [in the midst of judgment there is the promise and the certainty of the Lord's deliverance and] there shall be no gloom for her who was in anguish. In the former time [the Lord] brought into contempt the land of Zebulun and the land of Naphtali, but in the latter time He will make it glorious, by the way of the Sea [of Galilee, the land] beyond the Jordan, Galilee of the nations.

[2]The people who walked in darkness have seen a great Light; those who dwelt in the land of intense darkness *and* the shadow of death, upon them has the Light shined. [Isa. 42:6; Matt. 4:15, 16.]

[3]You [O Lord] have multiplied the nation and increased their joy; they rejoice before You like the joy in harvest, as men rejoice when they divide the spoil [of battle].

[4]For the yoke of [Israel's] burden, and the staff *or* rod for [goading] their shoulders, the rod of their oppressor, You have broken as in the day of [Gideon with] Midian. [Judg. 7:8-22.]

[5]For every [tramping] warrior's war boots *and* all his armor in the battle tumult and every garment rolled in blood shall be burned as fuel for the fire.

[6]For to us a Child is born, to us a Son is given; and the government shall be upon His shoulder, and His name shall be called Wonderful Counselor, Mighty God, Everlasting Father [of Eternity], Prince of Peace. [Isa. 25:1; 40:9-11; Matt. 28:18; Luke 2:11.]

[7]Of the increase of His government and of peace there shall be no end, upon the throne of David and over his kingdom, to establish it and to uphold it with justice and with righteousness from the [latter] time forth, even forevermore. The zeal of the Lord of hosts will perform this. [Dan. 2:44; I Cor. 15:25-28; Heb. 1:8.]

[8]The Lord has sent a word against Jacob [the ten tribes], and it has lighted upon Israel [the ten tribes, the kingdom of Ephraim].

[9]And all the people shall know it—even Ephraim and the inhabitants of Samaria [its capital]—who said in pride and stoutness of heart,

[10]The bricks have fallen, but we will build [all the better] with hewn stones; the sycamores have been cut down, but we will put [costlier] cedars in their place.

[a] In Hebrew texts 9:1 is numbered 8:23, and 9:2-21 is numbered 9:1-20.

# New International Version

11 But the LORD has strengthened Rezin's foes against them
  and has spurred their enemies on.
12 Arameans from the east and Philistines from the west
  have devoured Israel with open mouth.

Yet for all this, his anger is not turned away,
  his hand is still upraised.

13 But the people have not returned to him who struck them,
  nor have they sought the LORD Almighty.
14 So the LORD will cut off from Israel both head and tail,
  both palm branch and reed in a single day;
15 the elders and dignitaries are the head,
  the prophets who teach lies are the tail.
16 Those who guide this people mislead them,
  and those who are guided are led astray.
17 Therefore the Lord will take no pleasure in the young men,
  nor will he pity the fatherless and widows,
for everyone is ungodly and wicked,
  every mouth speaks folly.

Yet for all this, his anger is not turned away,
  his hand is still upraised.

18 Surely wickedness burns like a fire;
  it consumes briers and thorns,
it sets the forest thickets ablaze,
  so that it rolls upward in a column of smoke.
19 By the wrath of the LORD Almighty
  the land will be scorched
and the people will be fuel for the fire;
  they will not spare one another.
20 On the right they will devour,
  but still be hungry;
on the left they will eat,
  but not be satisfied.
Each will feed on the flesh of their own offspring[a]:
21   Manasseh will feed on Ephraim, and Ephraim on Manasseh;
  together they will turn against Judah.

Yet for all this, his anger is not turned away,
  his hand is still upraised.

**10** Woe to those who make unjust laws,
  to those who issue oppressive decrees,
2 to deprive the poor of their rights
  and withhold justice from the oppressed of my people,
making widows their prey
  and robbing the fatherless.
3 What will you do on the day of reckoning,
  when disaster comes from afar?
To whom will you run for help?
  Where will you leave your riches?
4 Nothing will remain but to cringe among the captives
  or fall among the slain.

Yet for all this, his anger is not turned away,
  his hand is still upraised.

### God's Judgment on Assyria

5 "Woe to the Assyrian, the rod of my anger,
  in whose hand is the club of my wrath!
6 I dispatch him against a godless nation,
  I send him against a people who anger me,
to seize loot and snatch plunder,
  and to trample them down like mud in the streets.

a 20 Or arm

# Amplified Bible

11 Therefore the Lord has stirred up the adversaries [the Assyrians] of Rezin [king of Syria] against [Ephraim], and He will stir up their enemies *and* arm *and* join them together,
12 The Syrians [compelled to fight with their enemies, going] before [on the east] and the Philistines behind [on the west]; and they will devour Israel with open mouth. For all this, [God's] anger is not [then] turned away, but His hand is still stretched out [in judgment].
13 Yet the people turn not to Him Who smote them, neither do they seek [inquire for or require as their vital need] the Lord of hosts.
14 Therefore the Lord will cut off from Israel head and tail [the highest and the lowest]—[high] palm branch and [low] rush in one day;
15 The elderly and honored man, he is the head; and the prophet who teaches lies, he is the tail.
16 For they who lead this people cause them to err, and they who are led [astray] by them are swallowed up (destroyed).
17 Therefore the Lord will not rejoice over their young men, neither will He have compassion on their fatherless and widows, for everyone is profane and an evildoer, and every mouth speaks folly. For all this, [God's] anger is not turned away, but His hand is still stretched out [in judgment].
18 For wickedness burns like a fire; it devours the briers and thorns, and it kindles in the thickets of the forest; they roll upward in a column of smoke.
19 Through the wrath of the Lord of hosts the land is darkened *and* burned up, and the people are like fuel for the fire; no man spares his brother.
20 They snatch in discord on the right hand, but are still hungry [their cruelty not diminished]; and they devour *and* destroy on the left hand, but are not satisfied. Each devours *and* destroys his own flesh [and blood] *or* his neighbor's.
21 Manasseh [thirsts for the blood of his brother] Ephraim, and Ephraim [for that of] Manasseh; but together they are against Judah. For all this, [God's] anger is not turned away, but His hand is still stretched out [in judgment].

**10** Woe to those [judges] who issue unrighteous decrees, and to the magistrates who keep causing unjust *and* oppressive decisions to be recorded,
2 To turn aside the needy from justice and to make plunder of the rightful claims of the poor of My people, that widows may be their spoil, and that they may make the fatherless their prey!
3 And what will you do in the day of visitation [of God's wrath], and in the desolation which shall come from afar? To whom will you flee for help? And where will you deposit [for safekeeping] your wealth *and* with whom leave your glory?
4 Without Me they shall bow down among the prisoners, and they shall fall [overwhelmed] under the heaps of the slain [on the battlefield]. For all this, [God's] anger is not turned away, but His hand is still stretched out [in judgment].
5 Woe to the Assyrian, the rod of My anger, the staff in whose hand is My indignation *and* fury [against Israel's disobedience]!
6 I send [the Assyrian] against a hypocritical *and* godless nation and against the people of My wrath; I command him to take the spoil and to seize the prey and to tread them down like the mire in the streets.

## New International Version

7 But this is not what he intends,
    this is not what he has in mind;
his purpose is to destroy,
    to put an end to many nations.
8 'Are not my commanders all kings?' he says.
9    'Has not Kalno fared like Carchemish?
Is not Hamath like Arpad,
    and Samaria like Damascus?
10 As my hand seized the kingdoms of the idols,
    kingdoms whose images excelled those of
        Jerusalem and Samaria—
11 shall I not deal with Jerusalem and her images
    as I dealt with Samaria and her idols?'"

12 When the Lord has finished all his work against
Mount Zion and Jerusalem, he will say, "I will punish the
king of Assyria for the willful pride of his heart and the
haughty look in his eyes. 13 For he says:

"'By the strength of my hand I have done this,
    and by my wisdom, because I have understanding.
I removed the boundaries of nations,
    I plundered their treasures;
    like a mighty one I subdued*a* their kings.
14 As one reaches into a nest,
    so my hand reached for the wealth of the nations;
as people gather abandoned eggs,
    so I gathered all the countries;
not one flapped a wing,
    or opened its mouth to chirp.'"

15 Does the ax raise itself above the person who
        swings it,
    or the saw boast against the one who uses it?
As if a rod were to wield the person who lifts it up,
    or a club brandish the one who is not wood!
16 Therefore, the Lord, the LORD Almighty,
    will send a wasting disease upon his sturdy
        warriors;
under his pomp a fire will be kindled
    like a blazing flame.
17 The Light of Israel will become a fire,
    their Holy One a flame;
in a single day it will burn and consume
    his thorns and his briers.
18 The splendor of his forests and fertile fields
    it will completely destroy,
    as when a sick person wastes away.
19 And the remaining trees of his forests will be so few
    that a child could write them down.

### The Remnant of Israel

20 In that day the remnant of Israel,
    the survivors of Jacob,
will no longer rely on him
    who struck them down
but will truly rely on the LORD,
    the Holy One of Israel.
21 A remnant will return,*b* a remnant of Jacob
    will return to the Mighty God.
22 Though your people be like the sand by the sea, Israel,
    only a remnant will return.
Destruction has been decreed,
    overwhelming and righteous.
23 The Lord, the LORD Almighty, will carry out
    the destruction decreed upon the whole land.

---

*a 13 Or treasures; / I subdued the mighty,*    *b 21 Hebrew shear-jashub*
(see 7:3 and note); also in verse 22

## Amplified Bible

7 However, this is not his intention [nor is the Assyrian
aware that he is doing this at My bidding], neither does his
mind so think *and* plan; but it is in his mind to destroy and
cut off many nations.
8 For [the Assyrian] says, Are not my officers all either
[subjugated] kings *or* their equal?
9 Is not Calno [of Babylonia conquered] like Carchemish
[on the Euphrates]? Is not Hamath [in Upper Syria] like
Arpad [her neighbor]? Is not Samaria [in Israel] like Damascus [in Syria]? [Have any of these cities been able to
resist Assyria? Not one!]
10 As my hand has reached to the kingdoms of the idols
[which were unable to defend them,] whose graven images were more to be feared *and* dreaded *and* more mighty
than those of Jerusalem and of Samaria—
11 Shall I not be able to do to Jerusalem and her images
as I have done to Samaria and her idols? [says the Assyr-
ian]
12 Therefore when the Lord has completed all His
work [of chastisement and purification to be executed]
on Mount Zion and on Jerusalem, it shall be that He will
inflict punishment on the fruit [the thoughts, words, and
deeds] of the stout *and* arrogant heart of the king of Assyria and the haughtiness of his pride.
13 For [the Assyrian king] has said, I have done it solely
by the power of my own hand and wisdom, for I have insight *and* understanding. I have removed the boundaries
of the peoples and have robbed their treasures; and like
a bull I have brought down those who sat on thrones *and*
the inhabitants.
14 And my hand has found like a nest the wealth of the
people; and as one gathers eggs that are forsaken, so I
have gathered all the earth; and there was none that
moved its wing, or that opened its mouth or chirped.
15 Shall the ax boast itself against him who chops with
it? Or shall the saw magnify itself against him who wields
it back and forth? As if a rod should wield those who lift it
up, or as if a staff should lift itself up as if it were not wood
[but a man of God]!
16 Therefore instead of the trees of his fatness, send leanness among [the Assyrian's] fat ones; and instead of his
glory *or* under it He will kindle a burning like the burning
of fire.
17 And the Light of Israel shall become a fire and His
Holy One a flame, and it will *a* burn and devour [the Assyrian's] thorns and briers in one day. [II Kings 19:35-37;
Isa. 31:8-9; 37:36.]
18 [The Lord] will consume the glory of the [Assyrian's]
forest and of his fruitful field, both soul and body; and
it shall be as when a sick man pines away *or* a standard-
bearer faints.
19 And the remnant of the trees of his forest shall be few,
so that a child may make a list of them.
20 And it shall be in that day that the remnant of Israel,
and such as are escaped of the house of Jacob, shall no
more lean upon him who smote them, but will lean upon
the Lord, the Holy One of Israel, in truth.
21 A remnant will return [Shear-jashub, name of Isaiah's
son], a remnant of Jacob, to the mighty God.
22 For though your population, O Israel, be as the sand
of the sea, only a remnant of it will return [and survive].
The [fully completed] destruction is decreed (decided
upon and brought to an issue); it overflows with justice
*and* righteousness [the infliction of just punishment].
[Rom. 9:27, 28.]
23 For the Lord, the Lord of hosts, will make a full end,
whatever is determined *or* decreed [in Israel], in the midst
of all the earth.

---

*a During a single night this prophecy was fulfilled, when "the Angel of
the Lord went forth and slew 185,000 in the camp of the Assyrians; and
when the living arose early in the morning, behold, all these were dead
bodies" (II Kings 19:35)—just when their victory over God's people had
seemed certain.*

## New International Version

24Therefore this is what the Lord, the LORD Almighty, says:

"My people who live in Zion,
  do not be afraid of the Assyrians,
who beat you with a rod
  and lift up a club against you, as Egypt did.
25Very soon my anger against you will end
  and my wrath will be directed to their destruction."

26The LORD Almighty will lash them with a whip,
  as when he struck down Midian at the rock of Oreb;
and he will raise his staff over the waters,
  as he did in Egypt.
27In that day their burden will be lifted from your
      shoulders,
  their yoke from your neck;
the yoke will be broken
  because you have grown so fat.a

28They enter Aiath;
  they pass through Migron;
  they store supplies at Mikmash.
29They go over the pass, and say,
  "We will camp overnight at Geba."
  Ramah trembles;
  Gibeah of Saul flees.
30Cry out, Daughter Gallim!
  Listen, Laishah!
  Poor Anathoth!
31Madmenah is in flight;
  the people of Gebim take cover.
32This day they will halt at Nob;
  they will shake their fist
at the mount of Daughter Zion,
  at the hill of Jerusalem.

33See, the Lord, the LORD Almighty,
  will lop off the boughs with great power.
The lofty trees will be felled,
  the tall ones will be brought low.
34He will cut down the forest thickets with an ax;
  Lebanon will fall before the Mighty One.

### The Branch From Jesse

**11** A shoot will come up from the stump of Jesse;
  from his roots a Branch will bear fruit.
2The Spirit of the LORD will rest on him—
  the Spirit of wisdom and of understanding,
  the Spirit of counsel and of might,
  the Spirit of the knowledge and fear of the LORD—
3and he will delight in the fear of the LORD.

He will not judge by what he sees with his eyes,
  or decide by what he hears with his ears;
4but with righteousness he will judge the needy,
  with justice he will give decisions for the poor of the
      earth.
He will strike the earth with the rod of his mouth;
  with the breath of his lips he will slay the wicked.
5Righteousness will be his belt
  and faithfulness the sash around his waist.

6The wolf will live with the lamb,
  the leopard will lie down with the goat,
the calf and the lion and the yearlingb together;
  and a little child will lead them.
7The cow will feed with the bear,
  their young will lie down together,
  and the lion will eat straw like the ox.
8The infant will play near the cobra's den,
  and the young child will put its hand into the viper's
      nest.

## Amplified Bible

24Therefore thus says the Lord, the Lord of hosts, O My people who dwell in Zion, do not be afraid of the Assyrian, who smites you with a rod and lifts up his staff against you, as [the king of] Egypt did. [Exod. 5.]
25For yet a little while and My indignation against you shall be accomplished, and My anger shall be directed to destruction [of the Assyrian].
26And the Lord of hosts shall stir up and brandish a scourge against them as when He smote Midian at the rock of Oreb; and as His rod was over the [Red] Sea, so shall He lift it up as He did in [the flight from] Egypt. [Exod. 14:26-31; Judg. 7:24, 25.]
27And it shall be in that day that the burden of [the Assyrian] shall depart from your shoulders, and his yoke from your neck. The yoke shall be destroyed because of fatness [which prevents it from going around your neck]. [Deut. 32:15.]
28[The Assyrian with his army comes to Judah]. He arrives at Aiath; he passes through Migron; at Michmash he gets rid of his baggage [by storing it].
29They go through the pass, they make Geba their camping place for the night; Ramah is afraid and trembles, Gibeah [the city] of [King] Saul flees.
30Cry aloud [in consternation], O Daughter of Gallim! Hearken, O Laishah! [Answer her] O you poor Anathoth!
31Madmenah is in flight; the inhabitants of Gebim seize their belongings and make their households flee for safety.
32This very day [the Assyrian] will halt at Nob [the city of priests], shaking his fist at the mountain of the Daughter of Zion, at the hill of Jerusalem.
33[But just when the Assyrian is in sight of his goal] behold, the Lord, the Lord of hosts, will lop off the beautiful boughs with terrorizing force; the high in stature will be hewn down and the lofty will be brought low.
34And He will cut down the thickets of the forest with an ax, and Lebanon [the Assyrian] with its majestic trees shall fall by the Mighty One and mightily. [Gen. 49:24; Isa. 9:6.]

**11** And there shall come forth a Shoot out of the stock of Jesse [David's father], and a Branch out of his roots shall grow and bear fruit. [Isa. 4:2; Matt. 2:23; Rev. 5:5; 22:16.]
2And the Spirit of the Lord shall rest upon Him—the Spirit of wisdom and understanding, the Spirit of counsel and might, the Spirit of knowledge and of the reverential and obedient fear of the Lord—
3And shall make Him of quick understanding, and His delight shall be in the reverential and obedient fear of the Lord. And He shall not judge by the sight of His eyes, neither decide by the hearing of His ears;
4But with righteousness and justice shall He judge the poor and decide with fairness for the meek, the poor, and the downtrodden of the earth; and He shall smite the earth and the oppressor with the rod of His mouth, and with the breath of His lips He shall slay the wicked.
5And righteousness shall be the girdle of His waist and faithfulness the girdle of His loins.
6And the wolf shall dwell with the lamb, and the leopard shall lie down with the kid, and the calf and the young lion and the fatted domestic animal together; and a little child shall lead them.
7And the cow and the bear shall feed side by side, their young shall lie down together, and the lion shall eat straw like the ox.
8And the sucking child shall play over the hole of the asp, and the weaned child shall put his hand on the adder's den.

---

a 27 Hebrew; Septuagint broken / from your shoulders    b 6 Hebrew; Septuagint lion will feed

## New International Version

[9]They will neither harm nor destroy
  on all my holy mountain,
for the earth will be filled with the knowledge of the
  Lord
  as the waters cover the sea.

[10]In that day the Root of Jesse will stand as a banner for
the peoples; the nations will rally to him, and his resting
place will be glorious. [11]In that day the Lord will reach out
his hand a second time to reclaim the surviving remnant
of his people from Assyria, from Lower Egypt, from Upper
Egypt, from Cush,[a] from Elam, from Babylonia,[b] from Hamath and from the islands of the Mediterranean.

[12]He will raise a banner for the nations
  and gather the exiles of Israel;
he will assemble the scattered people of Judah
  from the four quarters of the earth.
[13]Ephraim's jealousy will vanish,
  and Judah's enemies[c] will be destroyed;
Ephraim will not be jealous of Judah,
  nor Judah hostile toward Ephraim.
[14]They will swoop down on the slopes of Philistia to the
    west;
  together they will plunder the people to the east.
They will subdue Edom and Moab,
  and the Ammonites will be subject to them.
[15]The Lord will dry up
  the gulf of the Egyptian sea;
with a scorching wind he will sweep his hand
  over the Euphrates River.
He will break it up into seven streams
  so that anyone can cross over in sandals.
[16]There will be a highway for the remnant of his people
  that is left from Assyria,
  as there was for Israel
    when they came up from Egypt.

### Songs of Praise

**12** In that day you will say:

"I will praise you, Lord.
  Although you were angry with me,
your anger has turned away
  and you have comforted me.
[2]Surely God is my salvation;
  I will trust and not be afraid.
The Lord, the Lord himself, is my strength and my
    defense[d];
  he has become my salvation."
[3]With joy you will draw water
  from the wells of salvation.

[4]In that day you will say:

"Give praise to the Lord, proclaim his name;
  make known among the nations what he has done,
  and proclaim that his name is exalted.
[5]Sing to the Lord, for he has done glorious things;
  let this be known to all the world.
[6]Shout aloud and sing for joy, people of Zion,
  for great is the Holy One of Israel among you."

### A Prophecy Against Babylon

**13** A prophecy against Babylon that Isaiah son of
Amoz saw:

## Amplified Bible

[9]They shall not hurt or destroy in all My holy mountain,
for the earth shall be full of the knowledge of the Lord as
the waters cover the sea.

[10]And it shall be in that day that the Root of Jesse shall
stand as a signal for the peoples; of Him shall the nations
inquire *and* seek knowledge, and His dwelling shall be
glory [His rest glorious]! [John 12:32.]

[11]And in that day the Lord shall again lift up His hand
a second time to recover (acquire and deliver) the remnant of His people which is left, from Assyria, from Lower
Egypt, from Pathros, from Ethiopia, from Elam [in Per-
sia], from Shinar [Babylonia], from Hamath [in Upper
Syria], and from the countries bordering on the [Mediter-
ranean] Sea. [Jer. 23:5-8.]

[12]And He will raise up a signal for the nations and will
assemble the outcasts of Israel and will gather together
the dispersed of Judah from the four corners of the earth.

[13]The envy *and* jealousy of Ephraim also shall depart,
and they who vex *and* harass Judah from outside *or* inside
shall be cut off; Ephraim shall not envy Judah, and Judah
shall not vex *and* harass Ephraim.

[14]But [with united forces Ephraim and Judah] will
swoop down upon the shoulders of the Philistines' [land
sloping] toward the west; together they will strip the people on the east [the Arabs]. They will lay their hands upon
Edom and Moab, and the Ammonites will obey them.

[15]And the Lord will utterly destroy (doom and dry up)
the tongue of the Egyptian sea [the west fork of the Red
Sea]; and with His [mighty] scorching wind He will wave
His hand over the river [Nile] and will smite it into seven
channels and will cause men to cross over dry-shod.

[16]And there shall be a highway from Assyria for the
remnant left of His people, as there was for Israel when
they came up out of the land of Egypt.

**12** And in that day you will say, I will give thanks to
You, O Lord; for though You were angry with me,
Your anger has turned away, and You comfort me.

[2]Behold, God, my salvation! I will trust and not be
afraid, for the Lord God is my strength and song; yes, He
has become my salvation.

[3]Therefore with joy will you draw water from the wells
of salvation.

[4]And in that day you will say, Give thanks to the Lord,
call upon His name *and* by means of His name [in solemn
entreaty]; declare *and* make known His deeds among the
peoples of the earth, proclaim that His name is exalted!

[5]Sing praises to the Lord, for He has done excellent
things [gloriously]; let this be made known to all the earth.

[6]Cry aloud and shout joyfully, you women *and* inhabitants of Zion, for great in your midst is the Holy One of
Israel.

**13** The mournful, inspired prediction (a burden to be
lifted up) concerning Babylon which Isaiah son of
Amoz saw [with prophetic insight]:

---

[a] 11 That is, the upper Nile region    [b] 11 Hebrew *Shinar*
[c] 13 Or *hostility*    [d] 2 Or *song*

# New International Version

2 Raise a banner on a bare hilltop,
    shout to them;
  beckon to them
    to enter the gates of the nobles.
3 I have commanded those I prepared for battle;
    I have summoned my warriors to carry out my
      wrath—
    those who rejoice in my triumph.

4 Listen, a noise on the mountains,
    like that of a great multitude!
  Listen, an uproar among the kingdoms,
    like nations massing together!
  The LORD Almighty is mustering
    an army for war.
5 They come from faraway lands,
    from the ends of the heavens—
  the LORD and the weapons of his wrath—
    to destroy the whole country.

6 Wail, for the day of the LORD is near;
    it will come like destruction from the Almighty.*a*
7 Because of this, all hands will go limp,
    every heart will melt with fear.
8 Terror will seize them,
    pain and anguish will grip them;
    they will writhe like a woman in labor.
  They will look aghast at each other,
    their faces aflame.

9 See, the day of the LORD is coming
    —a cruel day, with wrath and fierce anger—
  to make the land desolate
    and destroy the sinners within it.
10 The stars of heaven and their constellations
    will not show their light.
  The rising sun will be darkened
    and the moon will not give its light.
11 I will punish the world for its evil,
    the wicked for their sins.
  I will put an end to the arrogance of the haughty
    and will humble the pride of the ruthless.
12 I will make people scarcer than pure gold,
    more rare than the gold of Ophir.
13 Therefore I will make the heavens tremble;
    and the earth will shake from its place
  at the wrath of the LORD Almighty,
    in the day of his burning anger.

14 Like a hunted gazelle,
    like sheep without a shepherd,
  they will all return to their own people,
    they will flee to their native land.
15 Whoever is captured will be thrust through;
    all who are caught will fall by the sword.
16 Their infants will be dashed to pieces before their
      eyes;
    their houses will be looted and their wives violated.

17 See, I will stir up against them the Medes,
    who do not care for silver
    and have no delight in gold.
18 Their bows will strike down the young men;
    they will have no mercy on infants,
    nor will they look with compassion on children.
19 Babylon, the jewel of kingdoms,
    the pride and glory of the Babylonians,*b*
  will be overthrown by God
    like Sodom and Gomorrah.
20 She will never be inhabited
    or lived in through all generations;

*a 6 Hebrew Shaddai*    *b 19 Or Chaldeans*

# Amplified Bible

2 Raise up a signal banner upon the high *and* bare mountain, summon them [the Medes and Persians] with loud voice and beckoning hand that they may enter the gates of the [Babylonian] nobles.
3 I Myself [says the Lord] have commanded My designated ones and have summoned My mighty men to execute My anger, even My proudly exulting ones [the Medes and Persians]—those who are made to triumph for My honor.
4 Hark, the uproar of a multitude in the mountains, like that of a great people! The noise of the tumult of the kingdoms of the nations gathering together! The Lord of hosts is mustering the host for the battle.
5 They come from a distant country, from the uttermost part of the heavens [the far east]—even the Lord and the weapons of His indignation—to seize *and* destroy the whole land. [Ps. 19:4-6; Isa. 5:26.]
6 Wail, for the day of the Lord is at hand; as destruction from the Almighty *and* Sufficient One [Shaddai] will it come! [Gen. 17:1.]
7 Therefore will *a*all hands be feeble, and every man's heart will melt.
8 And they [of Babylon] shall be dismayed and terrified, pangs and sorrows shall take hold of them; they shall be in pain as a woman in childbirth. They will gaze stupefied *and* aghast at one another, their faces will be aflame [from the effects of the unprecedented warfare].
9 Behold, the day of the Lord is coming!—fierce, with wrath and raging anger—to make the land *and* the [whole] earth a desolation and to destroy out of it its sinners. [Isa. 2:10-22; Rev. 19:11-21.]
10 For the stars of the heavens and their constellations will not give their light; the sun will be darkened at its rising and the moon will not shed its light.
11 And I, the Lord, will punish the world for its evil, and the wicked for their guilt *and* iniquity; I will cause the arrogance of the proud to cease and will lay low the haughtiness of the terrible *and* the boasting of the violent *and* ruthless.
12 I will make a man more rare than fine gold, and mankind scarcer than the pure gold of Ophir.
13 Therefore I will make the heavens tremble; and the *b*earth shall be shaken out of its place at the wrath of the Lord of hosts in the day of His fierce anger.
14 And like the chased roe *or* gazelle, and like sheep that no man gathers, each [foreign resident] will turn to his own people, and each will flee to his own land.
15 Everyone who is found will be thrust through, and everyone who is connected with the slain *and* is caught will fall by the sword.
16 Their infants also will be dashed to pieces before their eyes; their houses will be plundered and their wives ravished.
17 Behold, I will stir up the Medes against them, who have no regard for silver and do not delight in gold [and thus cannot be bribed].
18 Their bows will cut down the young men [of Babylon]; and they will have no pity on the fruit of the womb, their eyes will not spare children.
19 And Babylon, the glory of kingdoms, the beauty of the Chaldeans' pride, shall be like Sodom and Gomorrah when God overthrew them.
20 [Babylon] shall never be inhabited or dwelt in from generation to generation; neither shall the Arab pitch his

*a Babylon was taken by surprise on the night of Belshazzar's sacrilegious feast, when Belshazzar was slain and Darius the Mede was made king over the realm of the Chaldeans (Dan. 5:30).    b "By the outbreak of [the Lord's] wrath the material universe is [to be] shaken to its foundations. Such representations are common in the descriptions of the day of the Lord, and are not to be dismissed as merely figurative" (The Cambridge Bible). See also I Thess. 5:2; II Thess. 1:7, 8; II Pet. 3:10.*

## New International Version

there no nomads will pitch their tents,
there no shepherds will rest their flocks.
21 But desert creatures will lie there,
jackals will fill her houses;
there the owls will dwell,
and there the wild goats will leap about.
22 Hyenas will inhabit her strongholds,
jackals her luxurious palaces.
Her time is at hand,
and her days will not be prolonged.

**14** The LORD will have compassion on Jacob;
once again he will choose Israel
and will settle them in their own land.
Foreigners will join them
and unite with the descendants of Jacob.
2 Nations will take them
and bring them to their own place.
And Israel will take possession of the nations
and make them male and female servants in the
LORD's land.
They will make captives of their captors
and rule over their oppressors.

3 On the day the LORD gives you relief from your suffering and turmoil and from the harsh labor forced on you, 4 you will take up this taunt against the king of Babylon:

How the oppressor has come to an end!
How his fury[a] has ended!
5 The LORD has broken the rod of the wicked,
the scepter of the rulers,
6 which in anger struck down peoples
with unceasing blows,
and in fury subdued nations
with relentless aggression.
7 All the lands are at rest and at peace;
they break into singing.
8 Even the junipers and the cedars of Lebanon
gloat over you and say,
"Now that you have been laid low,
no one comes to cut us down."

9 The realm of the dead below is all astir
to meet you at your coming;
it rouses the spirits of the departed to greet you—
all those who were leaders in the world;
it makes them rise from their thrones—
all those who were kings over the nations.
10 They will all respond,
they will say to you,
"You also have become weak, as we are;
you have become like us."
11 All your pomp has been brought down to the grave,
along with the noise of your harps;
maggots are spread out beneath you
and worms cover you.

## Amplified Bible

tent there, nor shall the shepherds make their sheepfolds there.
21 But wild beasts of the desert will lie down there, and the people's houses will be full of dolefully howling creatures; and ostriches will dwell there, and wild goats [like demons] will dance there.
22 And [a]wolves *and* howling creatures will cry *and* answer in the deserted castles, and jackals in the pleasant palaces. And [Babylon's] time has nearly come, and her days will not be prolonged.

**14** For the Lord will have mercy on Jacob [the captive Jews in Babylon] and will again choose Israel and set them in their own land; and foreigners [who are proselytes] will join them and will cleave to the house of Jacob (Israel). [Esth. 8:17.]
2 And the peoples [of Babylonia] shall [b]take them and bring them to their own country [of Judea] *and* help restore them. And the house of Israel will possess [the foreigners who prefer to stay with] them in the land of the Lord as male and female servants; and they will take captive [not by physical but by moral might] those whose captives they have been, and they will rule over their [former] oppressors. [Ezra 1.]
3 When the Lord has given you rest from your sorrow *and* pain and from your trouble *and* unrest and from the hard service with which you were made to serve,
4 You shall take up this [taunting] parable against the king of Babylon and say, How the oppressor has stilled [the restless insolence]! The golden *and* exacting city has ceased!
5 The Lord has broken the staff of the wicked, the scepter of the [tyrant] rulers,
6 Who smote the peoples in anger with incessant blows *and* trod down the nations in wrath with unrelenting persecution—[until] he who smote is persecuted and no one hinders any more.
7 The whole earth is at rest and is quiet; they break forth into singing.
8 Yes, the fir trees *and* cypresses rejoice at you [O kings of Babylon], even the cedars of Lebanon, saying, Since you have been laid low, no woodcutter comes up against us.
9 Sheol (Hades, the place of the dead) below is stirred up to meet you at your coming [O tyrant Babylonian rulers]; it stirs up the shades of the dead to greet you—even all the chief ones of the earth; it raises from their thrones [in astonishment at your humbled condition] all the kings of the nations.
10 All of them will [tauntingly] say to you, Have you also become weak as we are? Have you become like us?
11 Your pomp *and* magnificence are brought down to Sheol (the underworld), along with the sound of your harps; the maggots [which prey upon dead bodies] are spread out under you and worms cover you [O Babylonian rulers].

a This whole prophecy is generally conceded to have been written well over a century (170 years, according to archbishop James Ussher) before Babylon's downfall, when the circumstances necessary for its fulfillment seemed most improbable—but it has been literally fulfilled in detail. Human keenness of foresight could not possibly have foreseen that great Babylon would be wiped from the face of the earth (Isa. 13:19), become ruins infested by wild animals (Isa. 13:21, 22), be feared because of superstition by the Arabs (Isa. 13:20)—with only a small village near the area to mark the place where, since the days of Nimrod, mighty kings had exalted themselves above the God of heaven. Various conquerors during the centuries contributed to Babylon's downfall until, by the first century B.C., it was as utterly and hopelessly destroyed as Sodom and Gomorrah (Isa. 13:19). b This prophecy (Isa. 14:1, 2) was fulfilled literally and in detail under King Cyrus of Persia and Babylonia. (Ezra 1.)

a 4 Dead Sea Scrolls, Septuagint and Syriac; the meaning of the word in the Masoretic Text is uncertain.

## New International Version

12 How you have fallen from heaven,
  morning star, son of the dawn!
You have been cast down to the earth,
  you who once laid low the nations!
13 You said in your heart,
  "I will ascend to the heavens;
I will raise my throne
  above the stars of God;
I will sit enthroned on the mount of assembly,
  on the utmost heights of Mount Zaphon.*
14 I will ascend above the tops of the clouds;
  I will make myself like the Most High."
15 But you are brought down to the realm of the dead,
  to the depths of the pit.

16 Those who see you stare at you,
  they ponder your fate:
"Is this the man who shook the earth
  and made kingdoms tremble,
17 the man who made the world a wilderness,
  who overthrew its cities
  and would not let his captives go home?"

18 All the kings of the nations lie in state,
  each in his own tomb.
19 But you are cast out of your tomb
  like a rejected branch;
you are covered with the slain,
  with those pierced by the sword,
  those who descend to the stones of the pit.
Like a corpse trampled underfoot,
20   you will not join them in burial,
for you have destroyed your land
  and killed your people.

Let the offspring of the wicked
  never be mentioned again.
21 Prepare a place to slaughter his children
  for the sins of their ancestors;
they are not to rise to inherit the land
  and cover the earth with their cities.

22 "I will rise up against them,"
  declares the LORD Almighty.
"I will wipe out Babylon's name and survivors,
  her offspring and descendants,"
                declares the LORD.
23 "I will turn her into a place for owls
  and into swampland;
I will sweep her with the broom of destruction,"
  declares the LORD Almighty.

24 The LORD Almighty has sworn,

"Surely, as I have planned, so it will be,
  and as I have purposed, so it will happen.
25 I will crush the Assyrian in my land;
  on my mountains I will trample him down.
His yoke will be taken from my people,
  and his burden removed from their shoulders."

26 This is the plan determined for the whole world;
  this is the hand stretched out over all nations.
27 For the LORD Almighty has purposed, and who can
  thwart him?
His hand is stretched out, and who can turn it back?

*a 13 Or of the north; Zaphon was the most sacred mountain of the Canaanites.*

## Amplified Bible

12 How have you fallen from heaven, O *light-bringer and* daystar, son of the morning! How you have been cut down to the ground, you who weakened *and* laid low the nations [O blasphemous, satanic king of Babylon!]
13 And you said in your heart, I will ascend to heaven; I will exalt my throne above the stars of God; I will sit upon the mount of assembly in the uttermost north.
14 I will ascend above the heights of the clouds; I will make myself like the Most High.
15 Yet you shall be brought down to Sheol (Hades), to the innermost recesses of the pit (the region of the dead).
16 Those who see you will gaze at you *and* consider you, saying, Is this the man who made the earth tremble, who shook kingdoms?—
17 Who made the world like a wilderness and overthrew its cities, who would not permit his prisoners to return home?
18 All the kings of the nations, all of them lie sleeping in glorious array, each one in his own sepulcher.
19 But you are cast away from your tomb like a loathed growth *or* premature birth *or* an abominable branch [of the family] *and* like the raiment of the slain; and you are clothed with the slain, those thrust through with the sword, who go down to the stones of the pit [into which carcasses are thrown], like a dead body trodden underfoot.
20 You shall not be joined with them in burial, because you have destroyed your land and have slain your people. May the descendants of evildoers nevermore be named!
21 Prepare a slaughtering place for his sons because of the guilt *and* iniquity of their fathers, so that they may not rise, possess the earth, and fill the face of the world with cities.
22 And I will rise up against them, says the Lord of hosts, and cut off from Babylon name and remnant, and son and son's son, says the Lord.
23 I will also make it a possession of the hedgehog *and* porcupine, and of *marshes *and* pools of water, and I will sweep it with the broom of destruction, says the Lord of hosts.
24 The Lord of hosts has sworn, saying, Surely, as I have thought *and* planned, so shall it come to pass, and as I have purposed, so shall it stand—
25 That I will break the Assyrian in My land, and upon My mountains I will tread him underfoot. Then shall the [Assyrian's] yoke depart from [the people of Judah], and his burden depart from their shoulders.
26 This is the [Lord's] purpose that is purposed upon the whole earth [regarded as conquered and put under tribute by Assyria]; and this is [His omnipotent] hand that is stretched out over all the nations.
27 For the Lord of hosts has purposed, and who can annul it? And His hand is stretched out, and who can turn it back?

*a The Hebrew for this expression—"light-bringer" or "shining one"—is translated "Lucifer" in *The Latin Vulgate,* and is thus translated in the *King James Version.* But because of the association of that name with Satan, it is not now used in this and other translations. Some students feel that the application of the name Lucifer to Satan, in spite of the long and confident teaching to that effect, is erroneous. The application of the name to Satan has existed since the third century A.D., and is based on the supposition that Luke 10:18 is an explanation of Isa. 14:12, which many authorities believe is not true. "Lucifer," the light-bringer, is the Latin equivalent of the Greek word "Phosphoros," which is used as a title of Christ in II Pet. 1:19 and corresponds to the name "radiant *and* brilliant Morning Star" in Rev. 22:16, a name Jesus called Himself. This passage here in Isa. 14:13 clearly applies to the king of Babylon.  *b The city of Babylon was in the midst of a very fertile area, and it would have seemed reasonable to suppose that, regardless of what happened to the population, the region would always furnish pasturage for flocks. But Isaiah said it would become the possession of wild animals and would be covered with "marshes *and* pools of water." This is how that prophecy was literally fulfilled: after Babylon was taken, the whole area around the city was put under water from neglect of the canals and dikes of the Euphrates River. It became stagnant "marshes *and* pools of water" among ruins haunted by wild animals, proclaiming to any who might see it that "surely, as [the Lord has] thought *and* planned, so shall it come to pass" (Isa. 14:24).  *c The prophecy against Assyria had actually by this time already been fulfilled, but Isaiah attached it to the as yet unfulfilled prophecy against Babylon as a pledge or guarantee of the fulfillment of the latter.*

# New International Version

## A Prophecy Against the Philistines

28This prophecy came in the year King Ahaz died:

29Do not rejoice, all you Philistines,
　　that the rod that struck you is broken;
from the root of that snake will spring up a viper,
　　its fruit will be a darting, venomous serpent.
30The poorest of the poor will find pasture,
　　and the needy will lie down in safety.
But your root I will destroy by famine;
　　it will slay your survivors.
31Wail, you gate! Howl, you city!
　　Melt away, all you Philistines!
A cloud of smoke comes from the north,
　　and there is not a straggler in its ranks.
32What answer shall be given
　　to the envoys of that nation?
"The Lord has established Zion,
　　and in her his afflicted people will find refuge."

## A Prophecy Against Moab

**15** A prophecy against Moab:

Ar in Moab is ruined,
　　destroyed in a night!
Kir in Moab is ruined,
　　destroyed in a night!
2Dibon goes up to its temple,
　　to its high places to weep;
Moab wails over Nebo and Medeba.
Every head is shaved
　　and every beard cut off.
3In the streets they wear sackcloth;
　　on the roofs and in the public squares
they all wail,
　　prostrate with weeping.
4Heshbon and Elealeh cry out,
　　their voices are heard all the way to Jahaz.
Therefore the armed men of Moab cry out,
　　and their hearts are faint.
5My heart cries out over Moab;
　　her fugitives flee as far as Zoar,
　　as far as Eglath Shelishiyah.
They go up the hill to Luhith,
　　weeping as they go;
on the road to Horonaim
　　they lament their destruction.
6The waters of Nimrim are dried up
　　and the grass is withered;
the vegetation is gone
　　and nothing green is left.
7So the wealth they have acquired and stored up
　　they carry away over the Ravine of the Poplars.
8Their outcry echoes along the border of Moab;
　　their wailing reaches as far as Eglaim,
　　their lamentation as far as Beer Elim.
9The waters of Dimon*a* are full of blood,
　　but I will bring still more upon Dimon*a*—
a lion upon the fugitives of Moab
　　and upon those who remain in the land.

**16** Send lambs as tribute
　　to the ruler of the land,
from Sela, across the desert,
　　to the mount of Daughter Zion.

# Amplified Bible

28In the year that King Ahaz [of Judah] died there came this mournful, inspired prediction (a burden to be lifted up):
29Rejoice not, O Philistia, all of you, because the rod [of Judah] that smote you is broken; for out of the serpent's root shall come forth an adder [King Hezekiah of Judah], and its [the serpent's] offspring will be a fiery, flying serpent. [II Kings 18:1, 3, 8.]
30And the firstborn of the poor *and* the poorest of the poor [of Judah] shall feed on My meadows, and the needy will lie down in safety; but I will kill your root with famine, and your remnant shall be slain.
31Howl, O gate! Cry, O city! Melt away, O Philistia, all of you! For there is coming a smoke out of the north, and there is no straggler in his ranks *and* none stands aloof [in Hezekiah's battalions].
32What then shall one answer the messengers of the [Philistine] nation? That the Lord has founded Zion, and in her shall the poor *and* afflicted of His people trust *and* find refuge.

**15** The mournful, inspired prediction (a burden to be lifted up) concerning Moab: Because in a night Ar of Moab is laid waste and brought to silence! Because in a night Kir of Moab is laid waste and brought to silence!
2They are gone up to Bayith and to Dibon, to the high places to weep. Moab wails over Nebo and over Medeba; on all their heads is baldness, and every beard is cut off [as a sign of deep sorrow and humiliation]. [Jer. 48:37.]
3In their streets they gird themselves with sackcloth; on the tops of their houses and in their broad places everyone wails, weeping abundantly.
4And Heshbon and Elealeh [cities in possession of Moab] cry out; their voice is heard even to Jahaz. Therefore the armed soldiers of Moab cry out; [Moab's] life is grievous *and* trembles within him.
5My heart cries out for Moab; his nobles *and* other fugitives flee to Zoar, to Eglath-shelishiyah [like a heifer three years old]. For with weeping they go up the ascent of Luhith; for on the road to Horonaim they raise a cry of destruction. [Jer. 48:5.]
6For the waters of Nimrim are desolations, for the grass is withered away and the new growth fails; there is no green thing.
7Therefore the abundance [of possessions] they have acquired and stored away they [now] carry over the willow brook *and* to the valley of the Arabians.
8For the cry [of distress] has gone round the borders of Moab; the wailing has reached to Eglaim, and the prolonged *and* mournful cry to Beer-elim.
9For the waters of Dimon are full of blood; yet I [the Lord] will bring even more on Dimon—a lion upon those of Moab who escape and upon the remnant of the land.

**16** You [Moabites, now fugitives in Edom, which is ruled by the king of Judah] send *a*lambs to the ruler of the land, from Sela *or* Petra through the desert *and* wilderness to the mountain of the Daughter of Zion [Jerusalem]. [II Kings 3:4, 5.]

*a* As King Mesha sent 100,000 lambs each year to King Ahab of Israel (II Kings 3:4), so now the Moabites are advised to win the king's favor and protection by diverting their tribute to the king in Jerusalem, as an acknowledgment of subjection.

*a* 9 *Dimon,* a wordplay on *Dibon* (see verse 2), sounds like the Hebrew for *blood.*

## New International Version

2 Like fluttering birds
   pushed from the nest,
so are the women of Moab
   at the fords of the Arnon.

3 "Make up your mind," Moab says.
   "Render a decision.
Make your shadow like night—
   at high noon.
Hide the fugitives,
   do not betray the refugees.
4 Let the Moabite fugitives stay with you;
   be their shelter from the destroyer."

The oppressor will come to an end,
   and destruction will cease;
   the aggressor will vanish from the land.
5 In love a throne will be established;
   in faithfulness a man will sit on it—
   one from the house[a] of David—
one who in judging seeks justice
   and speeds the cause of righteousness.

6 We have heard of Moab's pride—
   how great is her arrogance!—
of her conceit, her pride and her insolence;
   but her boasts are empty.
7 Therefore the Moabites wail,
   they wail together for Moab.
Lament and grieve
   for the raisin cakes of Kir Hareseth.
8 The fields of Heshbon wither,
   the vines of Sibmah also.
The rulers of the nations
   have trampled down the choicest vines,
which once reached Jazer
   and spread toward the desert.
Their shoots spread out
   and went as far as the sea.[b]
9 So I weep, as Jazer weeps,
   for the vines of Sibmah.
Heshbon and Elealeh,
   I drench you with tears!
The shouts of joy over your ripened fruit
   and over your harvests have been stilled.
10 Joy and gladness are taken away from the orchards;
   no one sings or shouts in the vineyards;
no one treads out wine at the presses,
   for I have put an end to the shouting.
11 My heart laments for Moab like a harp,
   my inmost being for Kir Hareseth.
12 When Moab appears at her high place,
   she only wears herself out;
when she goes to her shrine to pray,
   it is to no avail.

13 This is the word the Lord has already spoken concerning Moab. 14 But now the Lord says: "Within three years, as a servant bound by contract would count them, Moab's splendor and all her many people will be despised, and her survivors will be very few and feeble."

## Amplified Bible

2 For like wandering birds, like a brood cast out *and* a scattered nest, so shall the daughters of Moab be at the fords of the [river] Arnon.
3 [Say to the ruler] Give counsel, execute justice [for Moab, O king of Judah]; make your shade [over us] like night in the midst of noonday; hide the outcasts, betray not the fugitive to his pursuer.
4 Let our outcasts of Moab dwell among you; be a sheltered hiding place to them from the destroyer. When the extortion *and* the extortioner have been brought to nought, and destruction has ceased, and the oppressors *and* they who trample men are consumed *and* have vanished out of the land,
5 Then in mercy *and* loving-kindness shall a throne be established, and *a* One shall sit upon it in truth *and* faithfulness in the tent of David, judging and seeking justice and being swift to do righteousness. [Ps. 96:13; Jer. 48:47.]
6 We have heard of the pride of Moab, that he is very proud—even of his arrogance, his conceit, his wrath, his untruthful boasting.
7 Moab therefore shall wail for Moab; everyone shall wail. For the ruins, flagons of wine, *and* the raisin cakes of Kir-hareseth you shall sigh and mourn, utterly stricken *and* discouraged.
8 For the fields of Heshbon languish *and* wither, and the vines of Sibmah; the lords of the nations have broken down [Moab's] choice vine branches, which reached even to Jazer, wandering into the wilderness; its shoots stretched out abroad, they passed over [the shores of] the [Dead] Sea.
9 Therefore I [Isaiah] will weep with the weeping of Jazer for the vines of Sibmah. I will drench you with my tears, O Heshbon and Elealeh; for upon your summer fruits and your harvest the shout [of alarm and the cry of the enemy] has fallen.
10 And gladness is taken away, and joy out of the plentiful field; and in the vineyards there is no singing, nor is there joyful sound; the treaders tread out no wine in the presses, for the shout of joy has been made to cease.
11 Wherefore my heart sounds like a harp [in mournful compassion] for Moab, and my inner being [goes out] for Kir-hareseth [for those brick-walled citadels of his].
12 It shall be that when Moab presents himself, when he wearies himself [worshiping] on the high place [of idolatry], he will come to his sanctuary [of Chemosh, god of Moab], but he will not prevail. [Then will he be ashamed of his god.] [Jer. 48:13.]
13 This is the word that the Lord has spoken concerning Moab since that time [when Moab's pride and resistance to God were first known].
14 But now the Lord has spoken, saying, Within [b]three years, as the years of a hireling [who will not serve longer than the allotted time], the glory of Moab shall be brought into contempt, in spite of all his mighty multitudes of people; and the remnant that survives will be very small, feeble, *and* of no account.

---

*a* Isaiah apparently puts these words in the mouths of the Moabite ambassadors to the king of Judah, but in "language so divinely framed as to apply to 'the latter days' under King Messiah, when the Lord shall bring again [reverse] the captivity of Moab" (Robert Jamieson, A. R. Fausset and David Brown, *A Commentary*).   *b* This prophecy was fulfilled after the death of King Ahaz of Judah (Isa. 14:28), somewhere around the third year of King Hezekiah's reign. Moab was not left completely without population at this time; there was still a "remnant." The final desolation of Moab was reserved for King Nebuchadnezzar of Babylon in around 582 B.C., some five years after the taking of Jerusalem. The ruins of Elealeh, Heshbon, Medeba, Dimon, etc., still exist to confirm through modern research the accuracy of the fulfillment of this prophecy.

*a* 5 Hebrew *tent*   *b* 8 Probably the Dead Sea

## New International Version

### A Prophecy Against Damascus

**17** A prophecy against Damascus:

"See, Damascus will no longer be a city
　　but will become a heap of ruins.
² The cities of Aroer will be deserted
　　and left to flocks, which will lie down,
　　with no one to make them afraid.
³ The fortified city will disappear from Ephraim,
　　and royal power from Damascus;
　　the remnant of Aram will be
　　like the glory of the Israelites,"
　　　　　　　declares the LORD Almighty.

⁴ "In that day the glory of Jacob will fade;
　　the fat of his body will waste away.
⁵ It will be as when reapers harvest the standing grain,
　　gathering the grain in their arms—
　　as when someone gleans heads of grain
　　in the Valley of Rephaim.
⁶ Yet some gleanings will remain,
　　as when an olive tree is beaten,
　　leaving two or three olives on the topmost branches,
　　four or five on the fruitful boughs,"
　　　　　　　declares the LORD, the God of Israel.

⁷ In that day people will look to their Maker
　　and turn their eyes to the Holy One of Israel.
⁸ They will not look to the altars,
　　the work of their hands,
　　and they will have no regard for the Asherah poles*ᵃ*
　　and the incense altars their fingers have made.

⁹ In that day their strong cities, which they left because of the Israelites, will be like places abandoned to thickets and undergrowth. And all will be desolation.

¹⁰ You have forgotten God your Savior;
　　you have not remembered the Rock, your fortress.
　　Therefore, though you set out the finest plants
　　and plant imported vines,
¹¹ though on the day you set them out, you make them grow,
　　and on the morning when you plant them, you bring
　　　　them to bud,
　　yet the harvest will be as nothing
　　in the day of disease and incurable pain.

¹² Woe to the many nations that rage—
　　they rage like the raging sea!
　　Woe to the peoples who roar—
　　they roar like the roaring of great waters!
¹³ Although the peoples roar like the roar of surging waters,
　　when he rebukes them they flee far away,
　　driven before the wind like chaff on the hills,
　　like tumbleweed before a gale.
¹⁴ In the evening, sudden terror!
　　Before the morning, they are gone!
　　This is the portion of those who loot us,
　　the lot of those who plunder us.

## Amplified Bible

**17** The mournful, inspired prediction (a burden to be lifted up) concerning Damascus [capital of Syria, and Israel's bulwark against Assyria]. Behold, Damascus will cease to be a city and will become a heap of ruins.

² The cities of Aroer [east of the Jordan] are forsaken; they shall be for flocks, which shall lie down, and none shall make them afraid.

³ His bulwark [Syria] *and* the fortress shall disappear from Ephraim, and the kingdom from Damascus; and the remnant of Syria will be like the [departed] glory of the children of Israel [her ally], says the Lord of hosts.

⁴ And in that day the former glory of Jacob [Israel—his might, his population, his prosperity] shall be enfeebled, and the fat of his flesh shall become lean.

⁵ And it shall be as when the reaper gathers the standing grain and his arm harvests the ears; yes, it shall be as when one gathers the ears of grain in the fertile Valley of Rephaim.

⁶ Yet gleanings [of grapes] shall be left in it [the land of Israel], as after the beating of an olive tree [with a stick], two or three berries in the top of the uppermost bough, four or five in the outermost branches of the fruitful tree, says the Lord, the God of Israel.

⁷ In that day will men look to their Maker, and their eyes shall regard the Holy One of Israel.

⁸ And they will not look to the [idolatrous] altars, the work of their hands, neither will they have respect for what their fingers have made—either the Asherim [symbols of the goddess Asherah] or the sun-images.

⁹ In that day will their [Syria's and Israel's] strong cities be like the forsaken places in the wood and on the mountaintop, as they [the *ᵃ*Amorites and the Hivites] forsook their [cities] because of the children of Israel; and there will be desolation.

¹⁰ Because you have forgotten the God of your salvation [O Judah] and have not been mindful of the Rock of your strength, your Stronghold—therefore, you have planted pleasant nursery grounds *and* plantings [to Adonis, pots of quickly withered flowers used to set by their doors or in the courts of temples], and have set [the grounds] with vine slips of a strange [God],

¹¹ And in the day of your planting you hedge it in, and in the morning you make your seed to blossom, yet [promising as it is] the harvest shall be a heap of ruins *and* flee away in the day of expected possession and of desperate sorrow *and* sickening, incurable pain.

¹² Hark, the uproar of a multitude of peoples! They roar *and* thunder like the noise of the seas! Ah, the roar of nations! They roar like the roaring of rushing *and* mighty waters!

¹³ The nations will rush *and* roar like the rushing *and* roaring of many waters—but [God] will rebuke them, and they will flee far off and will be chased like chaff on the mountains before the wind, and like rolling thistledown *or* whirling dust of the stubble before the storm.

¹⁴ At evening time, behold, terror! And *ᵇ*before the morning, they [the terrorizing Assyrians] are not. This is the portion of those who strip us [the Jews] of what belongs to us, and the lot of those who rob us. [Fulfilled in Isa. 37:36.]

---

*ᵃ The Septuagint* (Greek translation of the Old Testament) so reads.
*ᵇ* Isaiah foretells (in Isa. 14:25) that God will break the Assyrian conqueror and tread him underfoot. Now (in Isa. 17:14) further details seem to be furnished—"terror" (because the enemy has all but been victorious), but "before the morning, they [the terrorizing Assyrians] are not." The startling fulfillment of this prophecy (cf. also Isa. 10:33-34; 30:31; 31:8) is found in Isa. 37:36, following the repetition of the prophecy first recorded in II Kings 19:29-36. Just when an overwhelming victory by the Assyrian Sennacherib seemed inevitable, during a single night 185,000 of his army died, and Judah was spared—as the Lord through Isaiah had promised.

---

*ᵃ 8 That is, wooden symbols of the goddess Asherah*

# New International Version

## A Prophecy Against Cush

**18** Woe to the land of whirring wings[a]
along the rivers of Cush,[b]
2 which sends envoys by sea
in papyrus boats over the water.

Go, swift messengers,
to a people tall and smooth-skinned,
to a people feared far and wide,
an aggressive nation of strange speech,
whose land is divided by rivers.

3 All you people of the world,
you who live on the earth,
when a banner is raised on the mountains,
you will see it,
and when a trumpet sounds,
you will hear it.
4 This is what the LORD says to me:
"I will remain quiet and will look on from my
dwelling place,
like shimmering heat in the sunshine,
like a cloud of dew in the heat of harvest."
5 For, before the harvest, when the blossom is gone
and the flower becomes a ripening grape,
he will cut off the shoots with pruning knives,
and cut down and take away the spreading
branches.
6 They will all be left to the mountain birds of prey
and to the wild animals;
the birds will feed on them all summer,
the wild animals all winter.

7 At that time gifts will be brought to the LORD Almighty

from a people tall and smooth-skinned,
from a people feared far and wide,
an aggressive nation of strange speech,
whose land is divided by rivers—

the gifts will be brought to Mount Zion, the place of the
Name of the LORD Almighty.

## A Prophecy Against Egypt

**19** A prophecy against Egypt:

See, the LORD rides on a swift cloud
and is coming to Egypt.
The idols of Egypt tremble before him,
and the hearts of the Egyptians melt with fear.

2 "I will stir up Egyptian against Egyptian—
brother will fight against brother,
neighbor against neighbor,
city against city,
kingdom against kingdom.
3 The Egyptians will lose heart,
and I will bring their plans to nothing;
they will consult the idols and the spirits of the dead,
the mediums and the spiritists.
4 I will hand the Egyptians over
to the power of a cruel master,
and a fierce king will rule over them,"
declares the Lord, the LORD Almighty.

5 The waters of the river will dry up,
and the riverbed will be parched and dry.
6 The canals will stink;
the streams of Egypt will dwindle and dry up.
The reeds and rushes will wither,
7    also the plants along the Nile,
at the mouth of the river.
Every sown field along the Nile
will become parched, will blow away and be no more.

# Amplified Bible

**18** Woe to the land whirring with wings which is beyond the rivers of Cush or Ethiopia,
2 That sends ambassadors by the Nile, even in vessels of
papyrus upon the waters! Go, you swift messengers, to a
nation tall and polished, to a people terrible from their beginning [feared and dreaded near and far], a nation strong
and victorious, whose land the rivers divide!
3 All you inhabitants of the world, you who dwell on the
earth, when a signal is raised on the mountains—look!
When a trumpet is blown—hear!
4 For thus the Lord has said to me: I will be still and I
will look on from My dwelling place, like clear *and* glowing heat in sunshine, like a fine cloud of mist in the heat
of harvest.
5 For before the harvest, when the blossom is over and
the flower becomes a ripening grape, He will cut off the
sprigs with pruning hooks, and the spreading branches
He will remove and cut away.
6 They [the dead bodies of the slain warriors] shall be
left together to the ravenous birds of the mountains and to
the beasts of the earth; and the ravenous birds will summer upon them, and all the beasts of the earth will winter
upon them.
7 At that time shall a present be brought to the Lord of
hosts from a people tall and polished, from a people terrible from their beginning *and* feared *and* dreaded near and
far, a nation strong and victorious, whose land the rivers
*or* great channels divide—to the place [of worship] of the
[a] Name of the Lord of hosts, to Mount Zion [in Jerusalem].
[Deut. 12:5; II Chron. 32:23; Isa. 16:1; 45:14; Zeph. 3:10.]

**19** The mournful, inspired prediction (a burden to be
lifted up) concerning Egypt: Behold, the Lord is
riding on a swift cloud and comes to Egypt; and the idols
of Egypt will tremble at His presence, and the hearts of the
Egyptians will melt within them.
2 And I will stir up Egyptians against Egyptians, and
they will fight, every one against his brother and every one
against his neighbor, city against city, kingdom against
kingdom.
3 And the spirit of the Egyptians within them will become exhausted and emptied out *and* will fail, and I will
destroy their counsel *and* confound their plans; and they
will seek counsel from the idols and the sorcerers, and
from those having familiar spirits (the mediums) and the
wizards.
4 And I will give over the Egyptians into the hand of
a hard *and* cruel master, and a fierce king will rule over
them, says the Lord, the Lord of hosts.
5 And the waters shall fail from the Nile, and the river
shall be wasted and become dry.
6 And the rivers shall become foul, the streams *and* canals of Egypt shall be diminished and dried up, the reeds
and the rushes shall wither *and* rot away.
7 The meadows by the Nile, by the brink of the Nile, and
all the sown fields of the Nile shall become dry, be blown
away, and be no more.

---

[a] 1 Or *of locusts*    [b] 1 That is, the upper Nile region

[a] See footnote on Deut. 12:5.

## New International Version

8The fishermen will groan and lament,
  all who cast hooks into the Nile;
those who throw nets on the water
  will pine away.
9Those who work with combed flax will despair,
  the weavers of fine linen will lose hope.
10The workers in cloth will be dejected,
  and all the wage earners will be sick at heart.

11The officials of Zoan are nothing but fools;
  the wise counselors of Pharaoh give senseless
    advice.
How can you say to Pharaoh,
  "I am one of the wise men,
  a disciple of the ancient kings"?

12Where are your wise men now?
  Let them show you and make known
  what the LORD Almighty
    has planned against Egypt.
13The officials of Zoan have become fools,
  the leaders of Memphis are deceived;
the cornerstones of her peoples
  have led Egypt astray.
14The LORD has poured into them
  a spirit of dizziness;
they make Egypt stagger in all that she does,
  as a drunkard staggers around in his vomit.
15There is nothing Egypt can do—
  head or tail, palm branch or reed.

16In that day the Egyptians will become weaklings. They will shudder with fear at the uplifted hand that the LORD Almighty raises against them. 17And the land of Judah will bring terror to the Egyptians; everyone to whom Judah is mentioned will be terrified, because of what the LORD Almighty is planning against them.

18In that day five cities in Egypt will speak the language of Canaan and swear allegiance to the LORD Almighty. One of them will be called the City of the Sun.[a]

19In that day there will be an altar to the LORD in the heart of Egypt, and a monument to the LORD at its border. 20It will be a sign and witness to the LORD Almighty in the land of Egypt. When they cry out to the LORD because of their oppressors, he will send them a savior and defender, and he will rescue them. 21So the LORD will make himself known to the Egyptians, and in that day they will acknowledge the LORD. They will worship with sacrifices and grain offerings; they will make vows to the LORD and keep them. 22The LORD will strike Egypt with a plague; he will strike them and heal them. They will turn to the LORD, and he will respond to their pleas and heal them.

23In that day there will be a highway from Egypt to Assyria. The Assyrians will go to Egypt and the Egyptians to Assyria. The Egyptians and Assyrians will worship together. 24In that day Israel will be the third, along with Egypt and Assyria, a blessing[b] on the earth. 25The LORD Almighty will bless them, saying, "Blessed be Egypt my people, Assyria my handiwork, and Israel my inheritance."

## Amplified Bible

8The fishermen will lament, and all who cast a hook into the Nile will mourn; and they who spread nets upon the waters will languish.
9Moreover, they who work with combed flax and they who weave white [cotton] cloth will be confounded *and* in despair.
10[Those who are] the pillars *and* foundations of Egypt will be crushed, and all those who work for hire *or* who build dams will be grieved.
11The princes of Zoan [ancient capital of the Pharaohs] are utterly foolish; the counsel of the wisest counselors of Pharaoh has become witless (stupid). How can you say to Pharaoh, I am a son of the wise, a son of ancient kings?
12Where then are your wise men? Let them tell you now [if they are so wise], and let them make known what the Lord of hosts has purposed against Egypt [if they can].
13The princes of Zoan have become fools, and the princes of Memphis are confused *and* deceived; those who are the cornerstones of her tribes have led Egypt astray.
14The Lord has mingled a spirit of perverseness, error, *and* confusion within her; [her leaders] have caused Egypt to stagger in all her doings, as a drunken man staggers in his vomit.
15Neither can any work [done singly or by concerted action] accomplish anything for Egypt, whether by head or tail, palm branch or rush [high or low].
16In that day will the Egyptians be like women [timid and helpless]; and they will tremble and fear because of the shaking of the hand of the Lord of hosts which He shakes over them.
17And the land of Judah [allied to Assyria] shall become a terror to the Egyptians; everyone to whom mention of it is made will be afraid *and* everyone who mentions it—to him will they turn in fear, because of the purpose of the Lord of hosts which He purposes against Egypt.
18In that day there will be five cities in the land of Egypt that speak the language of [the Hebrews of] Canaan and swear allegiance to the Lord of hosts. One of them will be called the City of the Sun *or* Destruction.
19In that day there will be an altar to the Lord in the midst of the land of Egypt, and a pillar to the Lord at its border.
20And it will be a sign and a witness to the Lord of hosts in the land of Egypt; for they will cry to the Lord because of oppressors, and He will send them a savior, even a mighty one, and he will deliver them. [Judg. 2:18; 3:9, 15.]
21And the Lord will make Himself known to Egypt, and the Egyptians will know (have knowledge of, be acquainted with, give heed to, and cherish) the Lord in that day and will worship with sacrifices of animal *and* vegetable offerings; they will vow a vow to the Lord and perform it.
22And the Lord shall smite Egypt, smiting and healing it; and they will return to the Lord, and He will listen to their entreaties and heal them.
23In that day shall there be a highway out of Egypt to Assyria, and the Assyrian will come into Egypt and the Egyptian into Assyria; and the Egyptians will worship [the Lord] with the Assyrians.
24In that day Israel shall be the third, with Egypt and with Assyria [in a Messianic league], a blessing in the midst of the earth,
25Whom the Lord of hosts has blessed, saying, Blessed be Egypt My people and Assyria the work of My hands and Israel My heritage.

---

[a] 18 Some manuscripts of the Masoretic Text, Dead Sea Scrolls, Symmachus and Vulgate; most manuscripts of the Masoretic Text *City of Destruction*   [b] 24 Or *Assyria, whose names will be used in blessings* (see Gen. 48:20); or *Assyria, who will be seen by others as blessed*

## New International Version

### A Prophecy Against Egypt and Cush

**20** In the year that the supreme commander, sent by Sargon king of Assyria, came to Ashdod and attacked and captured it— ²at that time the LORD spoke through Isaiah son of Amoz. He said to him, "Take off the sackcloth from your body and the sandals from your feet." And he did so, going around stripped and barefoot.

³Then the LORD said, "Just as my servant Isaiah has gone stripped and barefoot for three years, as a sign and portent against Egypt and Cush,ᵃ ⁴so the king of Assyria will lead away stripped and barefoot the Egyptian captives and Cushite exiles, young and old, with buttocks bared—to Egypt's shame. ⁵Those who trusted in Cush and boasted in Egypt will be dismayed and put to shame. ⁶In that day the people who live on this coast will say, 'See what has happened to those we relied on, those we fled to for help and deliverance from the king of Assyria! How then can we escape?'"

### A Prophecy Against Babylon

**21** A prophecy against the Desert by the Sea:

Like whirlwinds sweeping through the southland,
      an invader comes from the desert,
      from a land of terror.

²A dire vision has been shown to me:
      The traitor betrays, the looter takes loot.
   Elam, attack! Media, lay siege!
      I will bring to an end all the groaning she caused.

³At this my body is racked with pain,
      pangs seize me, like those of a woman in labor;
   I am staggered by what I hear,
      I am bewildered by what I see.

⁴My heart falters,
      fear makes me tremble;
   the twilight I longed for
      has become a horror to me.

⁵They set the tables,
      they spread the rugs,
      they eat, they drink!
   Get up, you officers,
      oil the shields!

⁶This is what the Lord says to me:

"Go, post a lookout
      and have him report what he sees.
⁷When he sees chariots
      with teams of horses,
   riders on donkeys
      or riders on camels,
   let him be alert,
      fully alert."

⁸And the lookoutᵇ shouted,

"Day after day, my lord, I stand on the watchtower;
      every night I stay at my post.
⁹Look, here comes a man in a chariot
      with a team of horses.
   And he gives back the answer:
      'Babylon has fallen, has fallen!

## Amplified Bible

**20** In the year that the Tartan [Assyrian commander in chief] came to Ashdod in Philistia, sent by Sargon king of Assyria, he fought against Ashdod and took it.

²At that time the Lord spoke by Isaiah son of Amoz, saying, Go, loose the sackcloth from off your loins and take your shoes off your feet. And he had done so, walking around stripped [to his loincloth] and barefoot.

³And the Lord said, As My servant Isaiah has walked [comparatively] naked and barefoot for three years, as a sign and forewarning concerning Egypt and concerning Cush (Ethiopia),

⁴So shall the king of Assyria lead away the Egyptian captives and the Ethiopian exiles, young and old, naked and barefoot, even with buttocks uncovered—to the shame of Egypt.

⁵And they shall be dismayed and confounded because of Ethiopia their hope *and* expectation and Egypt their glory *and* boast.

⁶And the inhabitants of this coastland [the Israelites and their neighbors] will say in that day, See! This is what comes to those in whom we trusted *and* hoped, to whom we fled for help to deliver us from the king of Assyria! But we, how shall we escape [captivity and exile]?

**21** The mournful, inspired prediction (a burden to be lifted up) concerning the Desert of the Sea [which was Babylon after great dams were raised to control the waters of the Euphrates River which overflowed it like a sea—and would do so again]: As whirlwinds in the South (the Negeb) sweep through, so it [the judgment of God by hostile armies] comes from the desert, from a terrible land.

²A hard *and* grievous vision is declared to me: the treacherous dealer deals treacherously, and the destroyer destroys. Go up, O Elam! Besiege, O Media! All the sighing [caused by Babylon's ruthless oppressions] I will cause to cease [says the Lord]. [Isa. 11:11; 13:17.]

³Therefore are my [Isaiah's] loins filled with anguish, pangs have seized me like the pangs of a woman in childbirth; I am bent *and* pained so that I cannot hear, I am dismayed so that I cannot see.

⁴My mind reels *and* wanders, horror terrifies me. [In my mind's eye I am at the feast of Belshazzar. I see the defilement of the golden vessels taken from God's temple, I watch the handwriting appear on the wall—I know that Babylon's great king is to be slain.] The twilight I looked forward to with pleasure has been turned into fear *and* trembling for me. [Dan. 5.]

⁵They prepare the table, they spread the rugs, [and having] set the watchers [the revelers take no other precaution], they eat, they drink. Arise, you princes, and oil your shields [for your deadly foe is at the gates]!

⁶For thus has the Lord said to me: Go, set [yourself as] a watchman, let him declare what he sees.

⁷And when he sees a troop, horsemen in pairs, a troop of donkeys, and a troop of camels, he shall listen diligently, very diligently.

⁸And [the watchman] cried like a lion, O Lord, I stand continually on the watchtower in the daytime, and I am set in my station every night.

⁹And see! Here comes a troop of men *and* chariots, horsemen in pairs! And he [the watchman] tells [what it foretells]: Babylon has fallen, has fallen! And all the grav-

---

ᵃ 3 That is, the upper Nile region; also in verse 5    ᵇ 8 Dead Sea Scrolls and Syriac; Masoretic Text *A lion*

## New International Version

All the images of its gods
lie shattered on the ground!'"

¹⁰My people who are crushed on the threshing floor,
I tell you what I have heard
from the LORD Almighty,
from the God of Israel.

### A Prophecy Against Edom

¹¹A prophecy against Dumah[a]:

Someone calls to me from Seir,
"Watchman, what is left of the night?
Watchman, what is left of the night?"
¹²The watchman replies,
"Morning is coming, but also the night.
If you would ask, then ask;
and come back yet again."

### A Prophecy Against Arabia

¹³A prophecy against Arabia:

You caravans of Dedanites,
who camp in the thickets of Arabia,
¹⁴ bring water for the thirsty;
you who live in Tema,
bring food for the fugitives.
¹⁵They flee from the sword,
from the drawn sword,
from the bent bow
and from the heat of battle.

¹⁶This is what the Lord says to me: "Within one year, as a servant bound by contract would count it, all the splendor of Kedar will come to an end. ¹⁷The survivors of the archers, the warriors of Kedar, will be few." The LORD, the God of Israel, has spoken.

### A Prophecy About Jerusalem

**22** A prophecy against the Valley of Vision:

What troubles you now,
that you have all gone up on the roofs,
²you town so full of commotion,
you city of tumult and revelry?
Your slain were not killed by the sword,
nor did they die in battle.
³All your leaders have fled together;
they have been captured without using the bow.
All you who were caught were taken prisoner together,
having fled while the enemy was still far away.
⁴Therefore I said, "Turn away from me;
let me weep bitterly.
Do not try to console me
over the destruction of my people."

⁵The Lord, the LORD Almighty, has a day
of tumult and trampling and terror
in the Valley of Vision,
a day of battering down walls
and of crying out to the mountains.
⁶Elam takes up the quiver,
with her charioteers and horses;
Kir uncovers the shield.
⁷Your choicest valleys are full of chariots,
and horsemen are posted at the city gates.

⁸The Lord stripped away the defenses of Judah,
and you looked in that day
to the weapons in the Palace of the Forest.
⁹You saw that the walls of the City of David
were broken through in many places;
you stored up water
in the Lower Pool.

## Amplified Bible

en images of her gods lie shattered on the ground [in my vision]!
¹⁰O you my threshed and winnowed ones [my own people the Jews, who must be trodden down by Babylon], that which I have heard from the Lord of hosts, the God of Israel, I have [joyfully] announced to you [Babylon is to fall]!
¹¹The mournful, inspired prediction (a burden to be lifted up) concerning Dumah (Edom): One calls to me from Seir (Edom), Watchman, what of the night? [How far is it spent? How long till morning?] Guardian, what of the night?
¹²The watchman said, The morning comes, but also the night. [Another time, if Edom earnestly wishes to know] if you will inquire [of me], inquire; return, come again.
¹³The mournful, inspired prediction (a burden to be lifted up) concerning Arabia: In the forests *and* thickets of Arabia you shall lodge, O you caravans of Dedanites [from northern Arabia].
¹⁴To the thirsty [Dedanites] bring water, O inhabitants of the land of Tema [in Arabia]; meet the fugitive with bread [suitable] for him.
¹⁵For they have fled from the swords, from the drawn sword, from the bent bow, and from the grievousness of war [the press of battle].
¹⁶For the Lord has said this to me, Within a year, according to the years of a hireling [who will work no longer than was agreed], all the glory of Kedar [an Arabian tribe] will fail.
¹⁷And the remainder of the number of archers *and* their bows, the mighty men of the sons of Kedar, will be diminished *and* few; for the Lord, the God of Israel, has spoken it.

**22** The mournful, inspired prediction (a burden to be lifted up) concerning the Valley of Vision: What do you mean [I wonder] that you have all gone up to the housetops,
²You who are full of shouting, a tumultuous city, a joyous *and* exultant city? [O Jerusalem] your slain warriors have not met [a glorious] death with the sword or in battle.
³All your [military] leaders have fled together; without the bow [which they had thrown away] they have been taken captive *and* bound by the archers. All of you who were found were bound together [as captives], though they had fled far away.
⁴Therefore I [Isaiah] said, Look away from me; I will weep bitterly. Do not hasten *and* try to comfort me over the destruction of the daughter of my people.
⁵For it is a day of discomfiture *and* of tumult, of treading down, of confusion *and* perplexity from the Lord God of hosts in the Valley of Vision, a day of breaking down the walls and of crying to the mountains.
⁶And [in my vision I saw] Elam take up the quiver, with troops in chariots, infantry, *and* horsemen; and Kir [with Elam subject to Assyria] uncovered the shield.
⁷And it came to pass that your choicest valleys were full of chariots, and the horsemen took their station [and set themselves in offensive array at the gate of Jerusalem]. [Fulfilled in II Chron. 32; Isa. 36.]
⁸Then [God] removed the protective covering of Judah; and you looked to the weapons in the House of the Forest [the king's armory] in that day. [I Kings 7:2; 10:17, 21.]
⁹You saw that the breaches [in the walls] of the City of David [the citadel of Zion] were many; [since the water supply was still defective] you collected [within the city's walls] the waters of the Lower Pool.

---

ᵃ 11 *Dumah*, a wordplay on *Edom*, means *silence* or *stillness*.

## New International Version

[10] You counted the buildings in Jerusalem
and tore down houses to strengthen the wall.
[11] You built a reservoir between the two walls
for the water of the Old Pool,
but you did not look to the One who made it,
or have regard for the One who planned it long ago.

[12] The Lord, the LORD Almighty,
called you on that day
to weep and to wail,
to tear out your hair and put on sackcloth.
[13] But see, there is joy and revelry,
slaughtering of cattle and killing of sheep,
eating of meat and drinking of wine!
"Let us eat and drink," you say,
"for tomorrow we die!"

[14] The LORD Almighty has revealed this in my hearing:
"Till your dying day this sin will not be atoned for," says
the Lord, the LORD Almighty.

[15] This is what the Lord, the LORD Almighty, says:

"Go, say to this steward,
to Shebna the palace administrator:
[16] What are you doing here and who gave you permission
to cut out a grave for yourself here,
hewing your grave on the height
and chiseling your resting place in the rock?

[17] "Beware, the LORD is about to take firm hold of you
and hurl you away, you mighty man.
[18] He will roll you up tightly like a ball
and throw you into a large country.
There you will die
and there the chariots you were so proud of
will become a disgrace to your master's house.
[19] I will depose you from your office,
and you will be ousted from your position.

[20] "In that day I will summon my servant, Eliakim son of
Hilkiah. [21] I will clothe him with your robe and fasten your
sash around him and hand your authority over to him. He
will be a father to those who live in Jerusalem and to the
people of Judah. [22] I will place on his shoulder the key to
the house of David; what he opens no one can shut, and
what he shuts no one can open. [23] I will drive him like a peg
into a firm place; he will become a seat[a] of honor for the
house of his father. [24] All the glory of his family will hang
on him: its offspring and offshoots—all its lesser vessels,
from the bowls to all the jars.

[25] "In that day," declares the LORD Almighty, "the peg
driven into the firm place will give way; it will be sheared
off and will fall, and the load hanging on it will be cut
down." The LORD has spoken.

## A Prophecy Against Tyre

**23** A prophecy against Tyre:

Wail, you ships of Tarshish!
For Tyre is destroyed
and left without house or harbor.
From the land of Cyprus
word has come to them.

[a] 23 Or *throne*

## Amplified Bible

[10] And you numbered the houses of Jerusalem, and you
broke down the houses [to get materials] to fortify the
[city] wall.
[11] You also made a reservoir between the two walls for
the water of the Old Pool, but you did not look to the Maker
of it, nor did you recognize Him Who planned it long ago.
[12] And in that day the Lord God of hosts called you to
weeping and mourning, to the shaving off of all your hair
[in humiliation] and to the girding with sackcloth.
[13] But instead, see the pleasure and mirth, slaying oxen
and killing sheep, eating flesh and drinking wine, [with
the idea] Let us eat and drink, for tomorrow we die!
[14] And the Lord of hosts revealed Himself in my ears
[as He said], Surely this unatoned sin shall not be purged
from you until [you are punished—and the punishment
will be] death, says the Lord God of hosts.
[15] Come, go to this [contemptible] steward *and* treasurer, to Shebna, who is over the house [but who is presumptuous enough to be building himself a tomb among
those of the mighty, a tomb worthy of a king], and say to
him,
[16] What business have you here? And whom have you
entombed here, that you have the right to hew out for
yourself a tomb here? He hews out a sepulcher for himself
on the height! He carves out a dwelling for himself in the
rock!
[17] Behold, the Lord will hurl you away violently, O you
strong man; yes, He will take tight hold of you *and* He will
surely cover you [with shame].
[18] He will surely roll you up in a bundle [Shebna] and
toss you like a ball into a large country; there you will die
and there will be your splendid chariots, you disgrace to
your master's house!
[19] And I will thrust you from your office, and from your
station will you be pulled down.
[20] And in that day I will call My servant, Eliakim son
of Hilkiah.
[21] And I will clothe him with your robe and will bind your
girdle on him and will commit your authority to his hand;
he shall be a father to the inhabitants of Jerusalem and to
the house of Judah.
[22] And the key of the house of David I will lay upon his
shoulder; he shall open and no one shall shut, he shall shut
and no one shall open.
[23] And I will fasten him like a peg *or* nail in a firm place;
and he will become a throne of honor *and* glory to his father's house.
[24] And they will hang on him the honor *and* the whole
weight of [responsibility for] his father's house: the offspring and issue [of the family, high and low], every small
vessel, from the cups even to all the flasks *and* big bulging
bottles.
[25] In that day, says the Lord of hosts, the nail *or* peg
that was fastened into the sure place shall give way *and*
be moved and be hewn down and fall, and the burden that
was upon it shall be cut off; for the Lord has spoken it.

**23** The mournful, inspired prediction (a burden to
be lifted up) concerning Tyre: Wail, you ships of
[Tyre returning from trading with] Tarshish, for Tyre is
laid waste, so that there is no house, no harbor; from the
land of Kittim (Cyprus) they learn of it.

## New International Version

<sup>2</sup>Be silent, you people of the island
　　and you merchants of Sidon,
　　whom the seafarers have enriched.
<sup>3</sup>On the great waters
　　came the grain of the Shihor;
　　the harvest of the Nile*a* was the revenue of Tyre,
　　and she became the marketplace of the nations.

<sup>4</sup>Be ashamed, Sidon, and you fortress of the sea,
　　for the sea has spoken:
　　"I have neither been in labor nor given birth;
　　I have neither reared sons nor brought up
　　daughters."
<sup>5</sup>When word comes to Egypt,
　　they will be in anguish at the report from Tyre.

<sup>6</sup>Cross over to Tarshish;
　　wail, you people of the island.
<sup>7</sup>Is this your city of revelry,
　　the old, old city,
　　whose feet have taken her
　　to settle in far-off lands?
<sup>8</sup>Who planned this against Tyre,
　　the bestower of crowns,
　　whose merchants are princes,
　　whose traders are renowned in the earth?
<sup>9</sup>The Lord Almighty planned it,
　　to bring down her pride in all her splendor
　　and to humble all who are renowned on the earth.

<sup>10</sup>Till*b* your land as they do along the Nile,
　　Daughter Tarshish,
　　for you no longer have a harbor.
<sup>11</sup>The Lord has stretched out his hand over the sea
　　and made its kingdoms tremble.
He has given an order concerning Phoenicia
　　that her fortresses be destroyed.
<sup>12</sup>He said, "No more of your reveling,
　　Virgin Daughter Sidon, now crushed!

"Up, cross over to Cyprus;
　　even there you will find no rest."
<sup>13</sup>Look at the land of the Babylonians,*c*
　　this people that is now of no account!
The Assyrians have made it
　　a place for desert creatures;
they raised up their siege towers,
　　they stripped its fortresses bare
　　and turned it into a ruin.

<sup>14</sup>Wail, you ships of Tarshish;
　　your fortress is destroyed!

<sup>15</sup>At that time Tyre will be forgotten for seventy years, the span of a king's life. But at the end of these seventy years, it will happen to Tyre as in the song of the prostitute:

<sup>16</sup>"Take up a harp, walk through the city,
　　you forgotten prostitute;
play the harp well, sing many a song,
　　so that you will be remembered."

<sup>17</sup>At the end of seventy years, the Lord will deal with Tyre. She will return to her lucrative prostitution and will ply her trade with all the kingdoms on the face of the earth. <sup>18</sup>Yet her profit and her earnings will be set apart for the Lord; they will not be stored up or hoarded. Her profits will go to those who live before the Lord, for abundant food and fine clothes.

---

*a 2,3* Masoretic Text; Dead Sea Scrolls *Sidon, / who cross over the sea; / your envoys* <sup>3</sup>*are on the great waters. / The grain of the Shihor, / the harvest of the Nile,*    *b 10* Dead Sea Scrolls and some Septuagint manuscripts; Masoretic Text *Go through*    *c 13* Or *Chaldeans*

## Amplified Bible

<sup>2</sup>Be still, you inhabitants of the coast, you merchants of Sidon, *a*your *messengers* passing over the sea have replenished you [with wealth and industry].
<sup>3</sup>And were on great waters. The seed *or* grain of the Shihor, the harvest [due to the overflow] of the Nile River, was [Tyre's] revenue, and she became the merchandise of the nations.
<sup>4</sup>Be ashamed, O Sidon [mother-city of Tyre, now a widow bereaved of her children], for the sea has spoken, the stronghold of the sea, saying, I have neither travailed nor brought forth children; I have neither nourished *and* reared young men nor brought up virgins.
<sup>5</sup>When the report comes to Egypt, they will be sorely pained over the report about Tyre.
<sup>6</sup>Pass over to Tarshish [to seek safety as exiles]! Wail, you inhabitants of the [Tyre] coast!
<sup>7</sup>Is this your jubilant city, whose origin dates back into antiquity, whose own feet are accustomed to carry her far off to settle [daughter cities]?
<sup>8</sup>Who has purposed this against Tyre, the bestower of crowns, whose merchants were princes, whose traders were the honored of the earth?
<sup>9</sup>The Lord of hosts has purposed it [in accordance with a fixed principle of His government], to defile the pride of all glory and to bring into dishonor *and* contempt all the honored of the earth.
<sup>10</sup>Overflow your land like [the overflow of] the Nile River, O Daughter of Tarshish; there is no girdle of restraint [on you] any more [to make you pay tribute or customs or duties to Tyre].
<sup>11</sup>He stretched out His hand over the sea, He shook the kingdoms; the Lord has given a command concerning Canaan to destroy her strongholds *and* fortresses [Tyre, Sidon, etc.].
<sup>12</sup>And He said, You shall no more exult, you oppressed *and* crushed one, O Virgin Daughter of Sidon. Arise, pass over to Kittim (Cyprus); but even there you will have no rest.
<sup>13</sup>Look at the land of the Chaldeans! That people and not the Assyrians designed *and* assigned [Tyre] for the wild beasts *and* those who [previously] dwelt in the wilderness. They set up their siege works, they overthrew its palaces, they made it a ruin!
<sup>14</sup>Howl, you ships of Tarshish, for your stronghold [of Tyre] is laid waste [your strength has been destroyed].
<sup>15</sup>And in that day Tyre will be in obscurity *and* forgotten for seventy years, according to the days of one dynasty. After the end of seventy years will Tyre sing as a harlot [who has been forgotten but again attracts her lovers].
<sup>16</sup>Take a harp, go about the city, forgotten harlot; play skillfully *and* make sweet melody, sing many songs, that you may be remembered.
<sup>17</sup>And after the end of seventy years the Lord will remember Tyre; and she will return to her hire and will play the harlot [resume her commerce] with all the kingdoms of the world on the face of the earth.
<sup>18</sup>But her gain and her hire [the profits of Tyre's new prosperity] will be *b*dedicated to the Lord [eventually]; it will not be treasured or stored up, for her gain will be used for those who dwell in the presence of the Lord [the ministers], that they may eat sufficiently and have durable *and* stately clothing [suitable for those who minister at God's altar].

---

*a The Dead Sea Scrolls* so read.  *b* This whole prophecy (Isa. 23:14-18) was literally fulfilled in following centuries. Tyre was destroyed by Nebuchadnezzar in 572 B.C. and lay desolate for seventy years. The new city built on the island was taken by Alexander the Great in 332 B.C. (see footnotes on Ezek. 26:4, 14). Eventually the true religion prevailed at Tyre. Jesus visited there (Matt. 15:21) and so did Paul (Acts 21:3-6). Eusebius (Hist. 10:4) says that "when the church of God was founded in Tyre . . . , much of its wealth was consecrated to God . . . and was presented for the support of the ministry." Jerome, also writing in the fourth century A.D., says that the wealth of the churches of Tyre "was not treasured up or hidden but was given to those who dwelt before the Lord."

## New International Version

### The Lord's Devastation of the Earth

**24** See, the LORD is going to lay waste the earth
and devastate it;
he will ruin its face
and scatter its inhabitants—
[2] it will be the same
for priest as for people,
for the master as for his servant,
for the mistress as for her servant,
for seller as for buyer,
for borrower as for lender,
for debtor as for creditor.
[3] The earth will be completely laid waste
and totally plundered.
The LORD has spoken this word.

[4] The earth dries up and withers,
the world languishes and withers,
the heavens languish with the earth.
[5] The earth is defiled by its people;
they have disobeyed the laws,
violated the statutes
and broken the everlasting covenant.
[6] Therefore a curse consumes the earth;
its people must bear their guilt.
Therefore earth's inhabitants are burned up,
and very few are left.
[7] The new wine dries up and the vine withers;
all the merrymakers groan.
[8] The joyful timbrels are stilled,
the noise of the revelers has stopped,
the joyful harp is silent.
[9] No longer do they drink wine with a song;
the beer is bitter to its drinkers.
[10] The ruined city lies desolate;
the entrance to every house is barred.
[11] In the streets they cry out for wine;
all joy turns to gloom,
all joyful sounds are banished from the earth.
[12] The city is left in ruins,
its gate is battered to pieces.
[13] So will it be on the earth
and among the nations,
as when an olive tree is beaten,
or as when gleanings are left after the grape
harvest.

[14] They raise their voices, they shout for joy;
from the west they acclaim the LORD's majesty.
[15] Therefore in the east give glory to the LORD;
exalt the name of the LORD, the God of Israel,
in the islands of the sea.
[16] From the ends of the earth we hear singing:
"Glory to the Righteous One."

But I said, "I waste away, I waste away!
Woe to me!
The treacherous betray!
With treachery the treacherous betray!"
[17] Terror and pit and snare await you,
people of the earth.
[18] Whoever flees at the sound of terror
will fall into a pit;
whoever climbs out of the pit
will be caught in a snare.

The floodgates of the heavens are opened,
the foundations of the earth shake.
[19] The earth is broken up,
the earth is split asunder,
the earth is violently shaken.
[20] The earth reels like a drunkard,

## Amplified Bible

**24** Behold, the Lord will make the land *and* the [a] earth
empty and make it waste and turn it upside down
(twist the face of it) and scatter abroad its inhabitants.
[2] And it shall be—as [what happens] with the people, so
with the priest; as with the servant, so with his master; as
with the maid, so with her mistress; as with the buyer, so
with the seller; as with the lender, so with the borrower;
as with the creditor, so with the debtor.
[3] The land *and* the earth shall be utterly laid waste and
utterly pillaged; for the Lord has said this.
[4] The land *and* the earth mourn and wither, the world
languishes and withers, the high ones of the people [and
the heavens with the earth] languish.
[5] The land *and* the earth also are defiled by their inhabitants, because they have transgressed the laws, disregarded the statutes, and broken the everlasting covenant.
[Gen. 9:1-17; Deut. 29:20.]
[6] Therefore a curse devours the land *and* the earth, and
they who dwell in it suffer the punishment of their guilt.
Therefore the inhabitants of the land *and* the earth are
scorched *and* parched [under the curse of God's wrath],
and few people are left. [Rom. 1:20.]
[7] The new wine mourns, the vine languishes; all the
merrymakers sigh.
[8] The mirth of the timbrels is stilled, the noise of those
who rejoice ends, the joy of the lyre is stopped.
[9] No more will they drink wine with a song; strong drink
will be bitter to those who drink it.
[10] The wasted city of emptiness *and* confusion is broken
down; every house is shut up so that no one may enter.
[11] There is crying in the streets for wine; all joy is darkened, the mirth of the land is banished *and* gone into captivity.
[12] In the city is left desolation, and its gate is battered
*and* destroyed.
[13] For so shall it be in the midst of the earth among the
peoples, as the shaking *and* beating of an olive tree, or as
the gleaning when the vintage is done [and only a small
amount of the fruit remains].
[14] [But] these [who have escaped and remain] lift up
their voices, they shout; for the majesty of the Lord they
cry aloud from the [Mediterranean] Sea.
[15] Wherefore glorify the Lord in the east [whether in the
region of daybreak's lights and fires, or in the west]; [glorify] the name of the Lord, the God of Israel in the isles
*and* coasts of the [Mediterranean] Sea.
[16] From the uttermost parts of the earth have we heard
songs: Glory to the Righteous One [and to the people of
Israel]! But I say, Emaciated I pine away, I pine away. Woe
is me! The treacherous dealers deal treacherously! Yes,
the treacherous dealers deal very treacherously.
[17] Terror and pit [of destruction] and snare are upon you,
O inhabitant of the earth!
[18] And he who flees at the noise of the terror will fall into
the pit; and he who comes up out of the pit will be caught
in the snare. For the windows of the heavens are opened
[as in the deluge], and the foundations of the earth tremble
*and* shake.
[19] The earth is utterly broken, the earth is rent asunder,
the earth is shaken violently.
[20] The earth shall stagger like a drunken man and shall

---

[a] "The prophet transports himself in spirit to the end of all things. He
describes the destruction of the world. He sees, however, that this
destruction will be gradually accomplished. He here depicts the first
scene: the destruction of all that exists on the surface of the earth . . . as
even now occurs [in limited areas] as a consequence of wars . . . Jehovah
empties, devastates, depopulates the surface of the earth . . ." (Johan
P. Lange, *A Commentary*). "The writer feels that he is living in the last
days, and in the universal wretchedness and confusions of the age he
seems to discern the 'beginning of sorrows.' His thoughts glide almost
imperceptibly from the one point of view to the other, now describing the
distress and depression which exist, and now the more terrible visitation
which is imminent" (*The Cambridge Bible*).

## New International Version

it sways like a hut in the wind;
so heavy upon it is the guilt of its rebellion
that it falls—never to rise again.
²¹ In that day the LORD will punish
the powers in the heavens above
and the kings on the earth below.
²² They will be herded together
like prisoners bound in a dungeon;
they will be shut up in prison
and be punished[a] after many days.
²³ The moon will be dismayed,
the sun ashamed;
for the LORD Almighty will reign
on Mount Zion and in Jerusalem,
and before its elders—with great glory.

### Praise to the LORD

**25** LORD, you are my God;
I will exalt you and praise your name,
for in perfect faithfulness
you have done wonderful things,
things planned long ago.
² You have made the city a heap of rubble,
the fortified town a ruin,
the foreigners' stronghold a city no more;
it will never be rebuilt.
³ Therefore strong peoples will honor you;
cities of ruthless nations will revere you.
⁴ You have been a refuge for the poor,
a refuge for the needy in their distress,
a shelter from the storm
and a shade from the heat.
For the breath of the ruthless
is like a storm driving against a wall
⁵ and like the heat of the desert.
You silence the uproar of foreigners;
as heat is reduced by the shadow of a cloud,
so the song of the ruthless is stilled.

⁶ On this mountain the LORD Almighty will prepare
a feast of rich food for all peoples,
a banquet of aged wine—
the best of meats and the finest of wines.
⁷ On this mountain he will destroy
the shroud that enfolds all peoples,
the sheet that covers all nations;
⁸ he will swallow up death forever.
The Sovereign LORD will wipe away the tears
from all faces;
he will remove his people's disgrace
from all the earth.
The LORD has spoken.

⁹ In that day they will say,

"Surely this is our God;
we trusted in him, and he saved us.
This is the LORD, we trusted in him;
let us rejoice and be glad in his salvation."

¹⁰ The hand of the LORD will rest on this mountain;
but Moab will be trampled in their land
as straw is trampled down in the manure.
¹¹ They will stretch out their hands in it,
as swimmers stretch out their hands to swim.
God will bring down their pride
despite the cleverness[b] of their hands.
¹² He will bring down your high fortified walls
and lay them low;
he will bring them down to the ground,
to the very dust.

*a 22 Or released    b 11 The meaning of the Hebrew for this word is uncertain.*

## Amplified Bible

sway to and fro like a hammock; its transgression shall lie heavily upon it, and it shall fall and not rise again.
²¹ And in that day the Lord will visit *and* punish the host of the high ones on high [the host of heaven in heaven, celestial beings] and the kings of the earth on the earth. [I Cor. 15:25; Eph. 3:10; 6:12.]
²² And they will be gathered together as prisoners are gathered in a pit *or* dungeon; they will be shut up in prison, and after many days they will be visited, inspected, *and* punished *or* [a] pardoned. [Zech. 9:11, 12; II Pet. 2:4; Jude 6.]
²³ Then the moon will be confounded and the sun ashamed, when [they compare their ineffectual fire to the light of] the Lord of hosts, Who will reign on Mount Zion and in Jerusalem, and before His elders will show forth His glory.

**25** O Lord, You are my God; I will exalt You, I will praise Your name, for You have done wonderful things, even purposes planned of old [and fulfilled] in faithfulness and truth.
² For You have made a city a heap, a fortified city a ruin, a palace of aliens without a city [is no more a city]; it will never be rebuilt.
³ Therefore [many] a strong people will glorify You, [many] a city of terrible *and* ruthless nations will [reverently] fear You.
⁴ For You have been a stronghold for the poor, a stronghold for the needy in his distress, a shelter from the storm, a shade from the heat; for the blast of the ruthless ones is like a rainstorm against a wall.
⁵ As the heat in a dry land [is reduced by the shadow of a cloud, so] You will bring down the noise of aliens [exultant over their enemies]; and as the heat is brought low by the shadow of a cloud, so the song of the ruthless ones is brought low.
⁶ And on this Mount [Zion] shall the Lord of hosts make for all peoples a feast of rich things [symbolic of His coronation festival inaugurating the reign of the Lord on earth, in the wake of a background of gloom, judgment, and terror], a feast of wines on the lees—of fat things full of marrow, of wines on the lees well refined.
⁷ And He will destroy on this mountain the covering of the face that is cast over the heads of all peoples [in mourning], and the veil [of profound wretchedness] that is woven *and* spread over all nations.
⁸ He will swallow up death [in victory; He will abolish death forever]. And the Lord God will wipe away tears from all faces; and the reproach of His people He will take away from off all the earth; for the Lord has spoken it. [I Cor. 15:26, 54; II Tim. 1:10.]
⁹ It shall be said in that day, Behold our God upon Whom we have waited *and* hoped, that He might save us! This is the Lord, we have waited for Him; we will be glad and rejoice in His salvation.
¹⁰ For the hand of the Lord shall rest on this Mount [Zion], and Moab shall be threshed *and* trodden down in his place as straw is trodden down in the [filthy] water of a [primitive] cesspit.
¹¹ And though [Moab] stretches forth his hands in the midst of [the filthy water] as a swimmer stretches out his hands to swim, the Lord will bring down [Moab's] pride in spite of the skillfulness of his hands *and* together with the spoils of his hands.
¹² And the high fortifications of your walls [the Lord] will bring down, lay low, and bring to the ground, even to the dust.

*a The Hebrew word used here may mean **visit in mercy** as well as **visit in punishment**, but the context does not seem to indicate the possibility of mercy in this case.*

## New International Version

### A Song of Praise

**26** In that day this song will be sung in the land of Judah:

We have a strong city;
God makes salvation
its walls and ramparts.
²Open the gates
that the righteous nation may enter,
the nation that keeps faith.
³You will keep in perfect peace
those whose minds are steadfast,
because they trust in you.
⁴Trust in the LORD forever,
for the LORD, the LORD himself, is the Rock eternal.
⁵He humbles those who dwell on high,
he lays the lofty city low;
he levels it to the ground
and casts it down to the dust.
⁶Feet trample it down—
the feet of the oppressed,
the footsteps of the poor.

⁷The path of the righteous is level;
you, the Upright One, make the way of the righteous smooth.
⁸Yes, LORD, walking in the way of your laws,ᵃ
we wait for you;
your name and renown
are the desire of our hearts.
⁹My soul yearns for you in the night;
in the morning my spirit longs for you.
When your judgments come upon the earth,
the people of the world learn righteousness.
¹⁰But when grace is shown to the wicked,
they do not learn righteousness;
even in a land of uprightness they go on doing evil
and do not regard the majesty of the LORD.
¹¹LORD, your hand is lifted high,
but they do not see it.
Let them see your zeal for your people and be put to shame;
let the fire reserved for your enemies consume them.

¹²LORD, you establish peace for us;
all that we have accomplished you have done for us.
¹³LORD our God, other lords besides you have ruled over us,
but your name alone do we honor.
¹⁴They are now dead, they live no more;
their spirits do not rise.
You punished them and brought them to ruin;
you wiped out all memory of them.
¹⁵You have enlarged the nation, LORD;
you have enlarged the nation.
You have gained glory for yourself;
you have extended all the borders of the land.

¹⁶LORD, they came to you in their distress;
when you disciplined them,
they could barely whisper a prayer.ᵇ
¹⁷As a pregnant woman about to give birth
writhes and cries out in her pain,
so were we in your presence, LORD.
¹⁸We were with child, we writhed in labor,
but we gave birth to wind.
We have not brought salvation to the earth,
and the people of the world have not come to life.

¹⁹But your dead will live, LORD;
their bodies will rise—

---

ᵃ 8 Or *judgments*    ᵇ 16 The meaning of the Hebrew for this clause is uncertain.

## Amplified Bible

**26** In that day shall this song be sung in the land of Judah: ᵃWe have a strong city; [the Lord] sets up salvation as walls and bulwarks.
²Open the gates, that the [uncompromisingly] righteous nation which keeps her faith *and* her troth [with God] may enter in.
³You will guard him *and* keep him in perfect *and* constant peace whose mind [both its inclination and its character] is stayed on You, because he commits himself to You, leans on You, *and* hopes confidently in You.
⁴So trust in the Lord (commit yourself to Him, lean on Him, hope confidently in Him) forever; for the Lord God is an everlasting Rock [the Rock of Ages].
⁵For He has brought down the inhabitants of the height, the lofty city; He lays it low, lays it low to the ground; He brings it even to the dust.
⁶The foot has trampled it down—even the feet of the poor, and the steps of the needy.
⁷The way of the [consistently] righteous (those living in moral and spiritual rectitude in every area and relationship of their lives) is level *and* straight; You, O [Lord], Who are upright, direct aright *and* make level the path of the [uncompromisingly] just *and* righteous.
⁸Yes, in the path of Your judgments, O Lord, we wait [expectantly] for You; our heartfelt desire is for Your name and for the remembrance of You.
⁹My soul yearns for You [O Lord] in the night, yes, my spirit within me seeks You earnestly; for [only] when Your judgments are in the earth will the inhabitants of the world learn righteousness (uprightness and right standing with God).
¹⁰Though favor is shown to the wicked, yet they do not learn righteousness; in the land of uprightness they deal perversely and refuse to see the majesty of the Lord.
¹¹Though Your hand is lifted high to strike, Lord, they do not see it. Let them see Your zeal for Your people and be ashamed; yes, let the fire reserved for Your enemies consume them.
¹²Lord, You will ordain peace (God's favor and blessings, both temporal and spiritual) for us, for You have also wrought in us *and* for us all our works.
¹³O Lord, our God, other masters besides You have ruled over us, but we will acknowledge *and* mention Your name only.
¹⁴They [the former tyrant masters] are dead, they shall not live *and* reappear; they are powerless ghosts, they shall not rise *and* come back. Therefore You have visited and made an end of them and caused every memory of them [every trace of their supremacy] to perish.
¹⁵You have increased the nation, O Lord; You have increased the nation. You are glorified; You have enlarged all the borders of the land.
¹⁶Lord, when they were in trouble *and* distress, they sought *and* visited You; they poured out a prayerful whisper when Your chastening was upon them.
¹⁷As a woman with child drawing near the time of her delivery is in pain *and* writhes and cries out in her pangs, so we have been before You (at Your presence), O Lord.
¹⁸We have been with child, we have been writhing *and* in pain; we have, as it were, brought forth [only] wind. We have not wrought any deliverance in the earth, and the inhabitants of the world [of Israel] have not yet been born.
¹⁹Your dead shall live [O Lord]; the bodies of our dead

---

ᵃ *The Dead Sea Scrolls* read, "You [Lord] have been to me a strong wall."

## New International Version

let those who dwell in the dust
  wake up and shout for joy—
your dew is like the dew of the morning;
  the earth will give birth to her dead.

20 Go, my people, enter your rooms
  and shut the doors behind you;
hide yourselves for a little while
  until his wrath has passed by.
21 See, the LORD is coming out of his dwelling
  to punish the people of the earth for their sins.
The earth will disclose the blood shed on it;
  the earth will conceal its slain no longer.

### Deliverance of Israel

**27** In that day,

the LORD will punish with his sword—
  his fierce, great and powerful sword—
Leviathan the gliding serpent,
  Leviathan the coiling serpent;
he will slay the monster of the sea.

2 In that day—

"Sing about a fruitful vineyard:
3   I, the LORD, watch over it;
  I water it continually.
I guard it day and night
  so that no one may harm it.
4   I am not angry.
If only there were briers and thorns confronting me!
  I would march against them in battle;
  I would set them all on fire.
5 Or else let them come to me for refuge;
  let them make peace with me,
  yes, let them make peace with me."

6 In days to come Jacob will take root,
  Israel will bud and blossom
  and fill all the world with fruit.

7 Has the LORD struck her
  as he struck down those who struck her?
Has she been killed
  as those were killed who killed her?
8 By warfare[a] and exile you contend with her—
  with his fierce blast he drives her out,
  as on a day the east wind blows.
9 By this, then, will Jacob's guilt be atoned for,
  and this will be the full fruit of the removal of his
    sin:
When he makes all the altar stones
  to be like limestone crushed to pieces,
no Asherah poles[b] or incense altars
  will be left standing.
10 The fortified city stands desolate,
  an abandoned settlement, forsaken like the
    wilderness;
there the calves graze,
  there they lie down;
  they strip its branches bare.
11 When its twigs are dry, they are broken off
  and women come and make fires with them.
For this is a people without understanding;
  so their Maker has no compassion on them,
  and their Creator shows them no favor.

12 In that day the LORD will thresh from the flowing Euphrates to the Wadi of Egypt, and you, Israel, will be gathered up one by one. 13 And in that day a great trumpet will sound. Those who were perishing in Assyria and those

## Amplified Bible

[saints] shall rise. You who dwell in the dust, awake and sing for joy! For Your dew [O Lord] is a dew of [sparkling] light [heavenly, supernatural dew]; and the earth shall cast forth the dead [to life again; for on the land of the shades of the dead You will let Your dew fall]. [Ezek. 37:11-12.]
20 Come, my people, enter your chambers and shut your doors behind you; hide yourselves for a little while until the [Lord's] wrath is past.
21 For behold, the Lord is coming out of His place [heaven] to punish the inhabitants of the earth for their iniquity; the earth also will disclose the blood shed upon her and will no longer cover her slain and conceal her guilt.

**27** In that day [the Lord will deliver Israel from her enemies and also from the rebel powers of evil and darkness] His sharp and unrelenting, great, and strong sword will visit and punish Leviathan the swiftly fleeing serpent, Leviathan the twisting and winding serpent; and He will slay the monster that is in the sea.
2 In that day [it will be said of the redeemed nation of Israel], A vineyard beloved and lovely; sing a responsive song to it and about it!
3 I, the Lord, am its Keeper; I water it every moment; lest anyone harm it, I guard and keep it night and day.
4 Wrath is not in Me. Would that the briers and thorns [the wicked internal foe] were lined up against Me in battle! I would stride in against them; I would burn them up together.
5 Or else [if all Israel would escape being burned up together there is but one alternative], let them take hold of My strength and make complete surrender to My protection, that they may make peace with Me! Yes, let them make peace with Me!
6 In the days and generations to come Jacob shall take root; Israel shall blossom and send forth shoots and fill the whole world with fruit [of the knowledge of the true God]. [Hos. 14:1-6; Rom. 11:12.]
7 Has [the Lord] smitten [Israel] as He smote those who smote them? Or have [the Israelites] been slain as their slayers were slain?
8 By driving them out of Canaan, by exile, You contended with them in a measure [O Lord]—He removed them with His rough blast as in the day of the east wind.
9 Only on this condition shall the iniquity of Jacob (Israel) be forgiven and purged, and this shall be the full fruit [God requires] for taking away his sin: that [Israel] should make all the stones of the [idol] altars like chalk stones crushed to pieces, so that the Asherim and the sun-images shall not remain standing or rise again.
10 For the fortified city is solitary, a habitation deserted and forsaken like the wilderness; there the calf grazes, and there he lies down; he strips its branches and eats its twigs.
11 When its boughs are withered and dry, they are broken off; the women come and set them afire. For they are a people of no understanding or discernment—[a] witless folk; therefore He Who made them will not have compassion on them, and He Who formed them will show them no favor.
12 And it shall be in that day that the Lord will thresh out His grain from the flood of the River [Euphrates] to the Brook of Egypt, and you will be gathered one by one and one to another, O children of Israel!
13 And it shall be in that day that a great trumpet will be blown; and they will come who were lost and ready to perish in the land of Assyria and those who were driven

---

a 8 See Septuagint; the meaning of the Hebrew for this word is uncertain.    b 9 That is, wooden symbols of the goddess Asherah

a *The Dead Sea Scrolls* so read.

## New International Version

who were exiled in Egypt will come and worship the LORD on the holy mountain in Jerusalem.

### Woe to the Leaders of Ephraim and Judah

**28** Woe to that wreath, the pride of Ephraim's drunkards,
    to the fading flower, his glorious beauty,
    set on the head of a fertile valley—
      to that city, the pride of those laid low by wine!
[2] See, the Lord has one who is powerful and strong.
    Like a hailstorm and a destructive wind,
    like a driving rain and a flooding downpour,
      he will throw it forcefully to the ground.
[3] That wreath, the pride of Ephraim's drunkards,
    will be trampled underfoot.
[4] That fading flower, his glorious beauty,
    set on the head of a fertile valley,
    will be like figs ripe before harvest—
      as soon as people see them and take them in hand,
      they swallow them.
[5] In that day the LORD Almighty
    will be a glorious crown,
    a beautiful wreath
      for the remnant of his people.
[6] He will be a spirit of justice
    to the one who sits in judgment,
    a source of strength
      to those who turn back the battle at the gate.
[7] And these also stagger from wine
    and reel from beer:
Priests and prophets stagger from beer
    and are befuddled with wine;
they reel from beer,
    they stagger when seeing visions,
    they stumble when rendering decisions.
[8] All the tables are covered with vomit
    and there is not a spot without filth.

[9] "Who is it he is trying to teach?
    To whom is he explaining his message?
To children weaned from their milk,
    to those just taken from the breast?
[10] For it is:
    Do this, do that,
    a rule for this, a rule for that[a];
    a little here, a little there."

[11] Very well then, with foreign lips and strange tongues
    God will speak to this people,
[12] to whom he said,
    "This is the resting place, let the weary rest";
and, "This is the place of repose"—
    but they would not listen.
[13] So then, the word of the LORD to them will become:
    Do this, do that,
    a rule for this, a rule for that;
    a little here, a little there—
so that as they go they will fall backward;
    they will be injured and snared and captured.

[14] Therefore hear the word of the LORD, you scoffers
    who rule this people in Jerusalem.
[15] You boast, "We have entered into a covenant with death,
    with the realm of the dead we have made an
      agreement.
When an overwhelming scourge sweeps by,
    it cannot touch us,
for we have made a lie our refuge
    and falsehood[b] our hiding place."

## Amplified Bible

out to the land of Egypt, and they will worship the Lord on the holy mountain at Jerusalem. [Zech. 14:16; Matt. 24:31; Rev. 11:15.]

**28** Woe to [Samaria] the crown of pride of the drunkards of Ephraim [the ten tribes], and to the fading flower of its glorious beauty, which is on the head of the rich valley of those overcome *and* smitten down with wine!
[2] Behold, the Lord has a strong and mighty one [the Assyrian]; like a tempest of hail, a destroying storm, like a flood of mighty overflowing waters, he will cast it down to the earth with violent hand.
[3] With [alien] feet [Samaria] the proud crown of the drunkards of Ephraim will be trodden down.
[4] And the fading flower of its glorious beauty, which is on the head of the rich valley, will be like the early fig before the fruit harvest, which, when anyone sees it, he snatches and eats it up greedily at once. [So in an amazingly short time will the Assyrians devour Samaria, Israel's capital.]
[5] [But] in that [future [a]Messianic] day the Lord of hosts shall become a crown of glory and a diadem of beauty to the [converted] remnant of His people,
[6] And a spirit of justice to him who sits in judgment *and* administers the law, and strength to those who turn back the battle at the gate.
[7] But even these reel from wine and stagger from strong drink: the priest and the prophet reel from strong drink; they are confused from wine, they stagger *and* are gone astray through strong drink; they err in vision, they stumble when pronouncing judgment.
[8] For all the tables are full of filthy vomit, so that there is no place that is clean.
[9] To whom will He teach knowledge? [Ask the drunkards.] And whom will He make to understand the message? Those who are babies, just weaned from the milk and taken from the breasts? [Is that what He thinks we are?]
[10] For it is [His prophets repeating over and over]: precept upon precept, precept upon precept, rule upon rule, rule upon rule; here a little, there a little.
[11] No, but [the Lord will teach the rebels in a more humiliating way] by men with stammering lips and another tongue will He speak to this people [says Isaiah, and teach them His lessons].
[12] To these [complaining Jews the Lord] had said, This is the true rest [the way to true comfort and happiness] that you shall give to the weary, and, This is the [true] refreshing—yet they would not listen [to His teaching].
[13] Therefore the word of the Lord will be to them [merely monotonous repeatings of]: precept upon precept, precept upon precept, rule upon rule, rule upon rule; here a little, there a little—that they may go and fall backward, and be broken and snared and taken.
[14] Therefore hear the word of the Lord, you scoffers who rule this people in Jerusalem!
[15] Because you have said, We have made a covenant with death, and with Sheol (the place of the dead) we have an agreement—when the overflowing scourge passes through, it will not come to us, for we have made lies our refuge, and in falsehood we have taken shelter.

---

[a] 10 Hebrew / *sav lasav sav lasav / kav lakav kav lakav* (probably meaningless sounds mimicking the prophet's words); also in verse 13
[b] 15 Or *false gods*

[a] *The Bible in Aramaic: The Latter Prophets According to Targum Jonathan* reads, "In that time Messiah, the Lord of hosts, shall be a crown of joy and a diadem of praise to the residue of His people." Commentators generally agree that this is the meaning of the passage.

## New International Version

<sup>16</sup>So this is what the Sovereign Lord says:

"See, I lay a stone in Zion, a tested stone,
a precious cornerstone for a sure foundation;
the one who relies on it
will never be stricken with panic.
<sup>17</sup>I will make justice the measuring line
and righteousness the plumb line;
hail will sweep away your refuge, the lie,
and water will overflow your hiding place.
<sup>18</sup>Your covenant with death will be annulled;
your agreement with the realm of the dead will not
stand.
When the overwhelming scourge sweeps by,
you will be beaten down by it.
<sup>19</sup>As often as it comes it will carry you away;
morning after morning, by day and by night,
it will sweep through."

The understanding of this message
will bring sheer terror.
<sup>20</sup>The bed is too short to stretch out on,
the blanket too narrow to wrap around you.
<sup>21</sup>The Lord will rise up as he did at Mount Perazim,
he will rouse himself as in the Valley of Gibeon—
to do his work, his strange work,
and perform his task, his alien task.
<sup>22</sup>Now stop your mocking,
or your chains will become heavier;
the Lord, the Lord Almighty, has told me
of the destruction decreed against the whole land.

<sup>23</sup>Listen and hear my voice;
pay attention and hear what I say.
<sup>24</sup>When a farmer plows for planting, does he plow
continually?
Does he keep on breaking up and working the soil?
<sup>25</sup>When he has leveled the surface,
does he not sow caraway and scatter cumin?
Does he not plant wheat in its place,<sup>a</sup>
barley in its plot,<sup>a</sup>
and spelt in its field?
<sup>26</sup>His God instructs him
and teaches him the right way.

<sup>27</sup>Caraway is not threshed with a sledge,
nor is the wheel of a cart rolled over cumin;
caraway is beaten out with a rod,
and cumin with a stick.
<sup>28</sup>Grain must be ground to make bread;
so one does not go on threshing it forever.
The wheels of a threshing cart may be rolled over it,
but one does not use horses to grind grain.
<sup>29</sup>All this also comes from the Lord Almighty,
whose plan is wonderful,
whose wisdom is magnificent.

### Woe to David's City

**29** Woe to you, Ariel, Ariel,
the city where David settled!
Add year to year
and let your cycle of festivals go on.
<sup>2</sup>Yet I will besiege Ariel;
she will mourn and lament,
she will be to me like an altar hearth.<sup>b</sup>
<sup>3</sup>I will encamp against you on all sides;
I will encircle you with towers
and set up my siege works against you.
<sup>4</sup>Brought low, you will speak from the ground;
your speech will mumble out of the dust.
Your voice will come ghostlike from the earth;
out of the dust your speech will whisper.

## Amplified Bible

<sup>16</sup>Therefore thus says the Lord God, Behold, I am laying in Zion for a foundation a Stone, a tested Stone, a precious Cornerstone of sure foundation; he who believes (trusts in, relies on, and adheres to that Stone) will not <sup>a</sup>be ashamed or give way or hasten away [in sudden panic]. [Ps. 118:22; Matt. 21:42; Acts 4:11; Rom. 9:33; Eph. 2:20; I Pet. 2:4-6.]
<sup>17</sup>I will make justice the measuring line and righteousness the plummet; and hail will sweep away the refuge of lies, and waters will overwhelm the hiding place (the shelter).
<sup>18</sup>And your covenant with death shall be annulled, and your agreement with Sheol (the place of the dead) shall not stand; when the overwhelming scourge passes through, then you will be trodden down by it.
<sup>19</sup>As often as it passes through, it [the enemy's scourge] will take you; for morning by morning will it pass through, by day and by night. And it will be utter terror merely to hear and comprehend the report and the message of it [but only hard treatment and dispersion will make you understand God's instruction].
<sup>20</sup>For [they will find that] the bed is too short for a man to stretch himself on and the covering too narrow for him to wrap himself in. [All their sources of confidence will fail them.]
<sup>21</sup>For the Lord will rise up as on Mount Perazim, He will be wrathful as in the Valley of Gibeon, that He may do His work, His strange work, and bring to pass His act, His strange act. [II Sam. 5:20; I Chron. 14:16.]
<sup>22</sup>Now therefore do not be scoffers, lest the bands which bind you be made strong; for a decree of destruction have I heard from the Lord God of hosts upon the whole land and the whole earth.
<sup>23</sup>Give ear and hear my [Isaiah's] voice; listen and hear my words.
<sup>24</sup>Does he who plows for sowing plow continually? Does he continue to plow and harrow the ground after it is smooth?
<sup>25</sup>When he has leveled its surface, does he not cast abroad [the seed of] dill or fennel and scatter cummin [a seasoning], and put the wheat in rows, and barley in its intended place, and spelt [an inferior kind of wheat] as the border?
<sup>26</sup>[And he trains each of them correctly] for his God instructs him correctly and teaches him.
<sup>27</sup>For dill is not threshed with a sharp threshing instrument, nor is a cartwheel rolled over cummin; but dill is beaten off with a staff, and cummin with a rod [by hand].
<sup>28</sup>Does one crush bread grain? No, he does not thresh it continuously. But when he has driven his cartwheel and his horses over it, he scatters it [tossing it up to the wind] without having crushed it.
<sup>29</sup>This also comes from the Lord of hosts, Who is wonderful in counsel [and] excellent in wisdom and effectual working.

**29** Woe to Ariel [Jerusalem], to Ariel, the city where David encamped! Add yet another year; let the feasts run their round [but only one year more].
<sup>2</sup>Then will I distress Ariel; and there shall be mourning and lamentation, yet she shall be to Me like an Ariel [an altar hearth, a hearth of burning, the altar of God].
<sup>3</sup>And I will encamp against you round about; and I will hem you in with siege works and I will set up fortifications against you.
<sup>4</sup>And you shall be laid low [Jerusalem], speaking from beneath the ground, and your speech shall come humbly from the dust. And your voice shall be like that of a ghost [produced by a medium] coming from the earth, and your speech shall whisper and squeak as it chatters from the dust.

---

<sup>a</sup> 25 The meaning of the Hebrew for this word is uncertain. <sup>b</sup> 2 The Hebrew for *altar hearth* sounds like the Hebrew for *Ariel*.

<sup>a</sup> *The Septuagint* (Greek translation of the Old Testament) reads "be ashamed."

## New International Version

5 But your many enemies will become like fine dust,
  the ruthless hordes like blown chaff.
  Suddenly, in an instant,
6   the LORD Almighty will come
  with thunder and earthquake and great noise,
    with windstorm and tempest and flames of a
      devouring fire.
7 Then the hordes of all the nations that fight against
      Ariel,
    that attack her and her fortress and besiege her,
  will be as it is with a dream,
    with a vision in the night—
8 as when a hungry person dreams of eating,
    but awakens hungry still;
  as when a thirsty person dreams of drinking,
    but awakens faint and thirsty still.
  So will it be with the hordes of all the nations
    that fight against Mount Zion.

9 Be stunned and amazed,
    blind yourselves and be sightless;
  be drunk, but not from wine,
    stagger, but not from beer.
10 The LORD has brought over you a deep sleep:
    He has sealed your eyes (the prophets);
    he has covered your heads (the seers).

11 For you this whole vision is nothing but words sealed
in a scroll. And if you give the scroll to someone who can
read, and say, "Read this, please," they will answer, "I
can't; it is sealed." 12 Or if you give the scroll to someone
who cannot read, and say, "Read this, please," they will
answer, "I don't know how to read."

13 The Lord says:

"These people come near to me with their mouth
    and honor me with their lips,
  but their hearts are far from me.
  Their worship of me
    is based on merely human rules they have been
      taught.[a]
14 Therefore once more I will astound these people
    with wonder upon wonder;
  the wisdom of the wise will perish,
    the intelligence of the intelligent will vanish."
15 Woe to those who go to great depths
    to hide their plans from the LORD,
  who do their work in darkness and think,
    "Who sees us? Who will know?"
16 You turn things upside down,
    as if the potter were thought to be like the clay!
  Shall what is formed say to the one who formed it,
    "You did not make me"?
  Can the pot say to the potter,
    "You know nothing"?

17 In a very short time, will not Lebanon be turned into a
      fertile field
  and the fertile field seem like a forest?
18 In that day the deaf will hear the words of the scroll,
    and out of gloom and darkness
    the eyes of the blind will see.

## Amplified Bible

5 But the multitude of your [enemy] strangers that assail you shall be like small dust, and the multitude of the
ruthless and terrible ones like chaff that blows away. And
in an instant, suddenly,
6 You shall be visited and delivered by the Lord of hosts
with thunder and earthquake and great noise, with whirlwind and tempest and the flame of a devouring fire.
7 And the multitude of all the nations that fight against
Ariel [Jerusalem], even all that fight against her and her
stronghold and that distress her, shall be as a dream, a
vision of the night.
8 It shall be as when a hungry man dreams that he is
eating, but he wakens with his craving not satisfied; or
as when a thirsty man dreams that he is drinking, but he
wakens and is faint, and his thirst is not quenched. So shall
the multitude of all the nations be that fight against Mount
Zion.
9 Stop and wonder [at this prophecy, if you choose,
whether you understand it or not; soon you will witness
the actual event] and be confounded [reluctantly]! Blind
yourselves [now, if you choose; take your pleasure] and
then be blinded [at the actual occurrence]. They are
drunk, but not from wine; they stagger, but not from
strong drink [but from spiritual stupor].
10 For the Lord has poured out on you the spirit of deep
sleep. And He has closed your eyes, the prophets; and
your heads, the seers, He has covered and muffled.
11 And the vision of all this has become for you like the
words of a book that is sealed. When men give it to one
who can read, saying, Read this, I pray you, he says, I cannot, for it is sealed.
12 And when the book is given to him who is not learned,
saying, Read this, I pray you, he says, I cannot read.
13 And the Lord said, Forasmuch as this people draw
near Me with their mouth and honor Me with their lips
but remove their hearts and minds far from Me, and their
fear and reverence for Me are a commandment of men
that is learned by repetition [without any thought as to
the meaning],
14 Therefore, behold! I will again do marvelous things
with this people, marvelous and astonishing things; and
the wisdom of their wise men will perish, and the understanding of their discerning men will vanish or be hidden.
15 Woe to those who [seek to] hide deep from the Lord
their counsel, whose deeds are in the dark, and who say,
Who sees us? Who knows us?
16 [Oh, your perversity!] You turn things upside down!
Shall the potter be considered of no more account than the
clay? Shall the thing that is made say of its maker, He did
not make me; or the thing that is formed say of him who
formed it, He has no understanding?
17 Is it not yet a very little while until Lebanon shall be
turned into a fruitful field and the fruitful field esteemed
as a forest?
18 And in that day shall the deaf hear the words of the
book, and out of obscurity and gloom and darkness the
eyes of the blind shall see.

---

a 13 Hebrew; Septuagint *They worship me in vain; / their teachings are
merely human rules*

## New International Version

19 Once more the humble will rejoice in the LORD;
the needy will rejoice in the Holy One of Israel.
20 The ruthless will vanish,
the mockers will disappear,
and all who have an eye for evil will be cut down—
21 those who with a word make someone out to be guilty,
who ensnare the defender in court
and with false testimony deprive the innocent of
justice.

22 Therefore this is what the LORD, who redeemed Abraham, says to the descendants of Jacob:

"No longer will Jacob be ashamed;
no longer will their faces grow pale.
23 When they see among them their children,
the work of my hands,
they will keep my name holy;
they will acknowledge the holiness of the Holy One
of Jacob,
and will stand in awe of the God of Israel.
24 Those who are wayward in spirit will gain
understanding;
those who complain will accept instruction."

### Woe to the Obstinate Nation

**30** "Woe to the obstinate children,"
declares the LORD,
"to those who carry out plans that are not mine,
forming an alliance, but not by my Spirit,
heaping sin upon sin;
2 who go down to Egypt
without consulting me;
who look for help to Pharaoh's protection,
to Egypt's shade for refuge.
3 But Pharaoh's protection will be to your shame,
Egypt's shade will bring you disgrace.
4 Though they have officials in Zoan
and their envoys have arrived in Hanes,
5 everyone will be put to shame
because of a people useless to them,
who bring neither help nor advantage,
but only shame and disgrace."

6 A prophecy concerning the animals of the Negev:

Through a land of hardship and distress,
of lions and lionesses,
of adders and darting snakes,
the envoys carry their riches on donkeys' backs,
their treasures on the humps of camels,
to that unprofitable nation,
7 to Egypt, whose help is utterly useless.
Therefore I call her
Rahab the Do-Nothing.

8 Go now, write it on a tablet for them,
inscribe it on a scroll,
that for the days to come
it may be an everlasting witness.
9 For these are rebellious people, deceitful children,
children unwilling to listen to the LORD's
instruction.
10 They say to the seers,
"See no more visions!"
and to the prophets,
"Give us no more visions of what is right!
Tell us pleasant things,
prophesy illusions.
11 Leave this way,
get off this path,
and stop confronting us
with the Holy One of Israel!"

## Amplified Bible

19 The meek also shall increase their joy in the Lord, and the poor among men shall rejoice *and* exult in the Holy One of Israel.
20 For the terrible one [the Assyrian enemy] shall come to nought, and the scoffer shall cease, and all those who watch for iniquity [as an occasion for accusation] shall be cut off—
21 Those who make a man an offender *and* bring condemnation upon him with a word, and lay a trap for him who upholds justice at the city gate, and thrust aside the innocent *and* truly righteous with an empty plea.
22 Therefore thus says the Lord, Who redeemed Abraham [out of Ur and idolatry], concerning the house of Jacob: Jacob shall not then be ashamed; not then shall his face become pale [with fear and disappointment because of his children's degeneracy].
23 For when he sees his children [walking in the way of piety and virtue], the work of My hands in his midst, they will revere My name; they will revere the Holy One of Jacob and reverently fear the God of Israel.
24 Those who err in spirit will come to understanding, and those who murmur [discontentedly] will accept instruction.

**30** Woe to the rebellious children, says the Lord, who take counsel *and* carry out a plan, but not Mine, and who make a league *and* pour out a drink offering, but not of My Spirit, thus adding sin to sin;
2 Who set out to go down into Egypt, and have not asked Me—to flee to the stronghold of Pharaoh *and* to strengthen themselves in his strength and to trust in the shadow of Egypt!
3 Therefore shall the strength *and* protection of Pharaoh turn to your shame, and the refuge in the shadow of Egypt be to your humiliation *and* confusion.
4 For though [Pharaoh's] officials are at Zoan and his ambassadors arrive at Hanes [in Egypt],
5 Yet will all be ashamed because of a people [the Egyptians] who cannot profit them, who are not a help or benefit, but a shame and disgrace.
6 A mournful, inspired prediction (a burden to be lifted up) concerning the beasts of the South (the Negeb): Oh, the heavy burden, the load of treasures going to Egypt! Through a land of trouble and anguish, in which are lioness and lion, viper and fiery flying serpent, they carry their riches upon the shoulders of young donkeys, and their treasures upon the humps of camels, to a people that will not *and* cannot profit them.
7 For Egypt's help is worthless and toward no purpose. Therefore I have called her Rahab Who Sits Still.
8 Now, go, write it before them on a tablet and inscribe it in a book, that it may be as a witness for the time to come forevermore.
9 For this is a rebellious people, faithless *and* lying sons, children who will not hear the law *and* instruction of the Lord;
10 Who [virtually] say to the seers [by their conduct], See not! and to the prophets, Prophesy not to us what is right! Speak to us smooth things, prophesy deceitful illusions.
11 Get out of the true way, turn aside out of the path, cease holding up before us the Holy One of Israel.

## New International Version

12Therefore this is what the Holy One of Israel says:

"Because you have rejected this message,
    relied on oppression
    and depended on deceit,
13this sin will become for you
    like a high wall, cracked and bulging,
    that collapses suddenly, in an instant.
14It will break in pieces like pottery,
    shattered so mercilessly
that among its pieces not a fragment will be found
    for taking coals from a hearth
    or scooping water out of a cistern."

15This is what the Sovereign LORD, the Holy One of Israel, says:

"In repentance and rest is your salvation,
    in quietness and trust is your strength,
    but you would have none of it.
16You said, 'No, we will flee on horses.'
    Therefore you will flee!
You said, 'We will ride off on swift horses.'
    Therefore your pursuers will be swift!
17A thousand will flee
    at the threat of one;
at the threat of five
    you will all flee away,
till you are left
    like a flagstaff on a mountaintop,
    like a banner on a hill."

18Yet the LORD longs to be gracious to you;
    therefore he will rise up to show you compassion.
For the LORD is a God of justice.
    Blessed are all who wait for him!

19People of Zion, who live in Jerusalem, you will weep no more. How gracious he will be when you cry for help! As soon as he hears, he will answer you. 20Although the Lord gives you the bread of adversity and the water of affliction, your teachers will be hidden no more; with your own eyes you will see them. 21Whether you turn to the right or to the left, your ears will hear a voice behind you, saying, "This is the way; walk in it." 22Then you will desecrate your idols overlaid with silver and your images covered with gold; you will throw them away like a menstrual cloth and say to them, "Away with you!"

23He will also send you rain for the seed you sow in the ground, and the food that comes from the land will be rich and plentiful. In that day your cattle will graze in broad meadows. 24The oxen and donkeys that work the soil will eat fodder and mash, spread out with fork and shovel. 25In the day of great slaughter, when the towers fall, streams of water will flow on every high mountain and every lofty hill. 26The moon will shine like the sun, and the sunlight will be seven times brighter, like the light of seven full

## Amplified Bible

12Therefore thus says the Holy One of Israel: Because you despise *and* spurn this [My] word and trust in cunning *and* oppression, in crookedness *and* perverseness, and rely on them,
13Therefore this iniquity *and* guilt will be to you like a broken section of a high wall, bulging out and ready [at some distant day] to fall, whose crash will [then] come suddenly *and* swiftly, in an instant.
14And he shall break it as a potter's vessel is broken, breaking it in pieces without sparing so that there cannot be found among its pieces one large enough to carry coals of fire from the hearth or to dip water out of the cistern.
15For thus said the Lord God, the Holy One of Israel: In returning [to Me] and resting [in Me] you shall be saved; in quietness and in [trusting] confidence shall be your strength. But you would not,
16And you said, No! We will speed [our own course] on horses! Therefore you will speed [in flight from your enemies]! You said, We will ride upon swift steeds [doing our own way]! Therefore will they who pursue you be swift, [so swift that]
17One thousand of you will flee at the threat of one of them; at the threat of five you will flee till you are left like a beacon *or* a flagpole on the top of a mountain, and like a signal on a hill.
18And therefore the Lord [earnestly] waits [expecting, looking, and longing] to be gracious to you; and therefore He lifts Himself up, that He may have mercy on you *and* show loving-kindness to you. For the Lord is a God of justice. Blessed (happy, fortunate, to be envied) are all those who [earnestly] wait for Him, who expect *and* look *and* long for Him [for His victory, His favor, His love, His peace, His joy, and His matchless, unbroken companionship]! [John 14:3, 27; II Cor. 12:9; Heb. 12:2; I John 3:16; Rev. 3:5.]
19O people who dwell in Zion at Jerusalem, you will weep no more. He will surely be gracious to you at the sound of your cry; when He hears it, He will answer you.
20And though the Lord gives you the bread of adversity and the water of affliction, yet your Teacher will not hide Himself any more, but your eyes will constantly behold your Teacher.
21And your ears will hear a word behind you, saying, This is the way; walk in it, when you turn to the right hand and when you turn to the left.
22Then you will defile your carved images overlaid with silver and your molten images plated with gold; you will cast them away as a filthy bloodstained cloth, and you will say to them, Be gone!
23Then will He give you rain for the seed with which you sow the soil, and bread grain from the produce of the ground, and it will be rich and plentiful. In that day your cattle will feed in large pastures.
24The oxen likewise and the young donkeys that till the ground will eat savory *and* salted fodder, which has been winnowed with shovel and with fork.
25And upon every high mountain and upon every high hill there will be brooks and streams of water in the day of the great slaughter [the day of the Lord], when the towers fall [and all His enemies are destroyed].
26Moreover, the light of the moon will be like the light of the sun, and the light of the sun will be sevenfold, like the light of seven days [concentrated in one], in the day that

## New International Version

days, when the LORD binds up the bruises of his people
and heals the wounds he inflicted.
27 See, the Name of the LORD comes from afar,
  with burning anger and dense clouds of smoke;
his lips are full of wrath,
  and his tongue is a consuming fire.
28 His breath is like a rushing torrent,
  rising up to the neck.
He shakes the nations in the sieve of destruction;
  he places in the jaws of the peoples
  a bit that leads them astray.
29 And you will sing
  as on the night you celebrate a holy festival;
your hearts will rejoice
  as when people playing pipes go up
to the mountain of the LORD,
  to the Rock of Israel.
30 The LORD will cause people to hear his majestic voice
  and will make them see his arm coming down
with raging anger and consuming fire,
  with cloudburst, thunderstorm and hail.
31 The voice of the LORD will shatter Assyria;
  with his rod he will strike them down.
32 Every stroke the LORD lays on them
  with his punishing club
will be to the music of timbrels and harps,
  as he fights them in battle with the blows of his arm.
33 Topheth has long been prepared;
  it has been made ready for the king.
Its fire pit has been made deep and wide,
  with an abundance of fire and wood;
the breath of the LORD,
  like a stream of burning sulfur,
  sets it ablaze.

### Woe to Those Who Rely on Egypt

**31** Woe to those who go down to Egypt for help,
  who rely on horses,
who trust in the multitude of their chariots
  and in the great strength of their horsemen,
but do not look to the Holy One of Israel,
  or seek help from the LORD.
2 Yet he too is wise and can bring disaster;
  he does not take back his words.
He will rise up against that wicked nation,
  against those who help evildoers.
3 But the Egyptians are mere mortals and not God;
  their horses are flesh and not spirit.
When the LORD stretches out his hand,
  those who help will stumble,
  those who are helped will fall;
  all will perish together.
4 This is what the LORD says to me:
"As a lion growls,
  a great lion over its prey—
and though a whole band of shepherds
  is called together against it,
it is not frightened by their shouts
  or disturbed by their clamor—
so the LORD Almighty will come down
  to do battle on Mount Zion and on its heights.
5 Like birds hovering overhead,
  the LORD Almighty will shield Jerusalem;
he will shield it and deliver it,
  he will 'pass over' it and will rescue it."

## Amplified Bible

the Lord binds up the hurt of His people, and heals their
wound [inflicted by Him because of their sins].
27 Behold, the a Name of the Lord comes from afar, burning with His anger, and in thick, rising smoke. His lips are
full of indignation, and His tongue is like a consuming fire.
28 And His breath is like an overflowing stream that
reaches even to the neck, to sift the nations with the sieve
of destruction; and a bridle that causes them to err will be
in the jaws of the people.
29 You shall have a song as in the night when a holy feast
is kept, and gladness of heart as when one marches in procession with a flute to go to the temple on the mountain of
the Lord, to the Rock of Israel.
30 And the Lord shall cause His glorious voice to be
heard and the descending blow of His arm to be seen,
coming down with indignant anger and with the flame of
a devouring fire, amid crashing blast and cloudburst, tempest, and hailstones.
31 At the voice of the Lord the Assyrians will be stricken
with dismay and terror, when He smites them with His
rod.
32 And every passing stroke of the staff of punishment
and doom which the Lord lays upon them shall be to the
sound of [Israel's] timbrels and lyres, when in battle He
attacks [Assyria] with swinging and menacing arms.
33 For Topheth [a place of burning and abomination] has
already been laid out and long ago prepared; yes, for the
[Assyrian] king and [the god] Molech it has been made
ready, its pyre made deep and large, with fire and much
wood; the breath of the Lord, like a stream of brimstone,
kindles it. [Jer. 7:31, 32; Matt. 5:22; 25:41.]

**31** Woe to those who go down to Egypt for help, who
  rely on horses and trust in chariots because they
are many and in horsemen because they are very strong,
but they look not to the Holy One of Israel, nor seek and
consult the Lord!
2 And yet He is wise and brings calamity and does not
retract His words; He will arise against the house (the
whole race) of evildoers and against the helpers of those
who work iniquity.
3 Now the Egyptians are men and not God, and their
horses are flesh and not spirit; and when the Lord stretches out His hand, both [Egypt] who helps will stumble, and
[Judah] who is helped will fall, and they will all perish and
be consumed together.
4 For the Lord has said to me, As the lion or the young
lion growls over his prey—and though a large band of
shepherds is called out against him, he will not be terrified at their voice or daunted at their noise—so the Lord of
hosts will come down to fight upon Mount Zion and upon
its hills.
5 Like birds hovering, so will the Lord of hosts defend
Jerusalem; He will protect and deliver it, He will pass over
and spare and preserve it.

a The revelation of the power and glory of God.

## New International Version

⁶Return, you Israelites, to the One you have so greatly revolted against. ⁷For in that day every one of you will reject the idols of silver and gold your sinful hands have made.

⁸"Assyria will fall by no human sword;
  a sword, not of mortals, will devour them.
They will flee before the sword
  and their young men will be put to forced labor.
⁹Their stronghold will fall because of terror;
  at the sight of the battle standard their commanders
    will panic,"
declares the LORD,
  whose fire is in Zion,
  whose furnace is in Jerusalem.

### The Kingdom of Righteousness

**32** See, a king will reign in righteousness
  and rulers will rule with justice.
²Each one will be like a shelter from the wind
  and a refuge from the storm,
like streams of water in the desert
  and the shadow of a great rock in a thirsty land.
³Then the eyes of those who see will no longer be
    closed,
  and the ears of those who hear will listen.
⁴The fearful heart will know and understand,
  and the stammering tongue will be fluent and clear.
⁵No longer will the fool be called noble
  nor the scoundrel be highly respected.
⁶For fools speak folly,
  their hearts are bent on evil:
They practice ungodliness
  and spread error concerning the LORD;
the hungry they leave empty
  and from the thirsty they withhold water.
⁷Scoundrels use wicked methods,
  they make up evil schemes
to destroy the poor with lies,
  even when the plea of the needy is just.
⁸But the noble make noble plans,
  and by noble deeds they stand.

### The Women of Jerusalem

⁹You women who are so complacent,
  rise up and listen to me;
you daughters who feel secure,
  hear what I have to say!
¹⁰In little more than a year
  you who feel secure will tremble;
the grape harvest will fail,
  and the harvest of fruit will not come.
¹¹Tremble, you complacent women;
  shudder, you daughters who feel secure!
Strip off your fine clothes
  and wrap yourselves in rags.
¹²Beat your breasts for the pleasant fields,
  for the fruitful vines
¹³and for the land of my people,
  a land overgrown with thorns and briers—
yes, mourn for all houses of merriment
  and for this city of revelry.
¹⁴The fortress will be abandoned,
  the noisy city deserted;
citadel and watchtower will become a wasteland
    forever,
  the delight of donkeys, a pasture for flocks,
¹⁵till the Spirit is poured on us from on high,
  and the desert becomes a fertile field,
  and the fertile field seems like a forest.
¹⁶The LORD's justice will dwell in the desert,
  his righteousness live in the fertile field.

## Amplified Bible

⁶Return, O children of Israel, to Him against Whom you have so deeply plunged into revolt.
⁷For in that day every man of you will cast away [in contempt and disgust] his idols of silver and his idols of gold, which your own hands have sinfully made for you.
⁸Then the Assyrian shall fall by a sword not of man; and a sword, not of men [but of God], shall devour him. And he shall flee from the sword, and his young men shall be subjected to forced labor.
⁹[In his flight] he shall pass beyond his rock [refuge and stronghold] because of terror; even his officers shall desert the standard in fear and panic, says the Lord, Whose fire is in Zion and Whose furnace is in Jerusalem.

**32** Behold, a ᵃKing will reign in righteousness, and princes will rule with justice.
²And each one of them shall be like a hiding place from the wind and a shelter from the storm, like streams of water in a dry place, like the shade of a great rock in a weary land [to those who turn to them].
³Then the eyes of those who see will not be closed or dimmed, and the ears of those who hear will listen.
⁴And the mind of the rash will understand knowledge and have good judgment, and the tongue of the stammerers will speak readily and plainly.
⁵The fool (the unbeliever and the ungodly) will no more be called noble, nor the crafty and greedy [for gain] said to be bountiful and princely.
⁶For the fool speaks folly and his mind plans iniquity: practicing profane ungodliness and speaking error concerning the Lord, leaving the craving of the hungry unsatisfied and causing the drink of the thirsty to fail.
⁷The instruments and methods of the fraudulent and greedy [for gain] are evil; he devises wicked devices to ruin the poor and the lowly with lying words, even when the plea of the needy is just and right.
⁸But the noble, openhearted, and liberal man devises noble things; and he stands for what is noble, openhearted, and generous.
⁹Rise up, you women who are at ease! Hear my [Isaiah's] voice, you confident and careless daughters! Listen to what I am saying!
¹⁰In little more than a year you will be shaken with anxiety, you careless and complacent women; for the vintage will fail, and the ingathering will not come.
¹¹Tremble, you women who are at ease! Shudder with fear, you complacent ones! Strip yourselves bare and gird sackcloth upon your loins [in grief]!
¹²They shall beat upon their breasts for the pleasant fields, for the fruitful vine,
¹³For the land of my people growing over with thorns and briers—yes, for all the houses of joy in the joyous city.
¹⁴For the palace shall be forsaken, the populous city shall be deserted; the hill and the watchtower shall become dens [for wild animals] endlessly, a joy for wild donkeys, a pasture for flocks,
¹⁵Until the Spirit is poured upon us from on high, and the wilderness becomes a fruitful field, and the fruitful field is valued as a forest. [Ps. 104:30; Ezek. 36:26, 27; 39:29; Zech. 12:10.]
¹⁶Then justice will dwell in the wilderness, and righteousness (moral and spiritual rectitude in every area and relation) will abide in the fruitful field.

---

ᵃ The Messianic age is again in view (Isa. 9:7; 11:4; 16:5; 33:17).

## New International Version

17 The fruit of that righteousness will be peace;
  its effect will be quietness and confidence forever.
18 My people will live in peaceful dwelling places,
  in secure homes,
  in undisturbed places of rest.
19 Though hail flattens the forest
  and the city is leveled completely,
20 how blessed you will be,
  sowing your seed by every stream,
  and letting your cattle and donkeys range free.

### Distress and Help

**33** Woe to you, destroyer,
  you who have not been destroyed!
Woe to you, betrayer,
  you who have not been betrayed!
When you stop destroying,
  you will be destroyed;
when you stop betraying,
  you will be betrayed.

2 LORD, be gracious to us;
  we long for you.
Be our strength every morning,
  our salvation in time of distress.
3 At the uproar of your army, the peoples flee;
  when you rise up, the nations scatter.
4 Your plunder, O nations, is harvested as by young locusts;
  like a swarm of locusts people pounce on it.

5 The LORD is exalted, for he dwells on high;
  he will fill Zion with his justice and righteousness.
6 He will be the sure foundation for your times,
  a rich store of salvation and wisdom and knowledge;
  the fear of the LORD is the key to this treasure.[a]

7 Look, their brave men cry aloud in the streets;
  the envoys of peace weep bitterly.
8 The highways are deserted,
  no travelers are on the roads.
The treaty is broken,
  its witnesses[b] are despised,
  no one is respected.
9 The land dries up and wastes away,
  Lebanon is ashamed and withers;
Sharon is like the Arabah,
  and Bashan and Carmel drop their leaves.

10 "Now will I arise," says the LORD.
  "Now will I be exalted;
  now will I be lifted up.
11 You conceive chaff,
  you give birth to straw;
  your breath is a fire that consumes you.
12 The peoples will be burned to ashes;
  like cut thornbushes they will be set ablaze."

13 You who are far away, hear what I have done;
  you who are near, acknowledge my power!
14 The sinners in Zion are terrified;
  trembling grips the godless:
"Who of us can dwell with the consuming fire?
  Who of us can dwell with everlasting burning?"
15 Those who walk righteously
  and speak what is right,
who reject gain from extortion
  and keep their hands from accepting bribes,
who stop their ears against plots of murder
  and shut their eyes against contemplating evil—

a 6 Or is a treasure from him   b 8 Dead Sea Scrolls; Masoretic Text / the cities

## Amplified Bible

17 And the effect of righteousness will be peace [internal and external], and the result of righteousness will be quietness and confident trust forever.
18 My people shall dwell in a peaceable habitation, in safe dwellings, and in quiet resting-places.
19 But it [the wrath of the Lord] shall hail, coming down overpoweringly on the forest [the army of the Assyrians], and the capital [a]city shall be utterly humbled and laid prostrate.
20 Happy and fortunate are you who cast your seed upon all waters [when the river overflows its banks; for the seed will sink into the mud and when the waters subside, the plant will spring up; you will find it after many days and reap an abundant harvest], you who safely send forth the ox and the donkey [to range freely].

**33** Woe to you, O destroyer, you who were not yourself destroyed, who deal treacherously though they [your victims] did not deal treacherously with you! When you have ceased to destroy, you will be destroyed; and when you have stopped dealing treacherously, they will deal treacherously with you.
2 O Lord, be gracious to us; we have waited [expectantly] for You. Be the arm [of Your servants—their strength and defense] every morning, our salvation in the time of trouble.
3 At the noise of the tumult [caused by Your voice at which the enemy is overthrown], the peoples flee; at the lifting up of Yourself, nations are scattered.
4 And the spoil [of the Assyrians] is gathered [by the inhabitants of Jerusalem] as the caterpillar gathers; as locusts leap and run to and fro, so [the Jews spoil the Assyrians' forsaken camp as they] leap upon it.
5 The Lord is exalted, for He dwells on high; He will fill Zion with justice and righteousness (moral and spiritual rectitude in every area and relation).
6 And there shall be stability in your times, an abundance of salvation, wisdom, and knowledge; the reverent fear and worship of the Lord is your treasure and His.
7 Behold, their valiant ones cry without; the ambassadors of peace weep bitterly.
8 The highways lie waste, the wayfaring man ceases. The enemy has broken the covenant, he has despised the cities and [b]the witnesses, he regards no man.
9 The land mourns and languishes, Lebanon is confounded and [its luxuriant verdure] withers away; Sharon [a fertile pasture region south of Mount Carmel] is like a desert, and Bashan [a broad, fertile plateau east of the Jordan River] and [Mount] Carmel shake off their leaves.
10 Now will I arise, says the Lord. Now will I lift up Myself; now will I be exalted.
11 You conceive chaff, you bring forth stubble; your breath is a fire that consumes you.
12 And the people will be burned as if to lime, like thorns cut down that are burned in the fire.
13 Hear, you who are far off [says the Lord], what I have done; and you who are near, acknowledge My might!
14 The sinners in Zion are afraid; trembling seizes the godless ones. [They cry] Who among us can dwell with that devouring fire? Who among us can dwell with those everlasting burnings?
15 He who walks righteously and speaks uprightly, who despises gain from fraud and from oppression, who shakes his hand free from the taking of bribes, who stops his ears from hearing of bloodshed and shuts his eyes to avoid looking upon evil.

a Authorities find it impossible to be sure whether the "city" here means Nineveh, Jerusalem, or even Babylon. Some say it could be a composite of all the cities opposed to God.   b The Dead Sea Scrolls read "the witnesses."

## New International Version

[16] they are the ones who will dwell on the heights,
whose refuge will be the mountain fortress.
Their bread will be supplied,
and water will not fail them.

[17] Your eyes will see the king in his beauty
and view a land that stretches afar.
[18] In your thoughts you will ponder the former terror:
"Where is that chief officer?
Where is the one who took the revenue?
Where is the officer in charge of the towers?"
[19] You will see those arrogant people no more,
people whose speech is obscure,
whose language is strange and incomprehensible.

[20] Look on Zion, the city of our festivals;
your eyes will see Jerusalem,
a peaceful abode, a tent that will not be moved;
its stakes will never be pulled up,
nor any of its ropes broken.
[21] There the LORD will be our Mighty One.
It will be like a place of broad rivers and streams.
No galley with oars will ride there,
no mighty ship will sail them.
[22] For the LORD is our judge,
the LORD is our lawgiver,
the LORD is our king;
it is he who will save us.

[23] Your rigging hangs loose:
The mast is not held secure,
the sail is not spread.
Then an abundance of spoils will be divided
and even the lame will carry off plunder.
[24] No one living in Zion will say, "I am ill";
and the sins of those who dwell there will be
forgiven.

### Judgment Against the Nations

**34** Come near, you nations, and listen;
pay attention, you peoples!
Let the earth hear, and all that is in it,
the world, and all that comes out of it!
[2] The LORD is angry with all nations;
his wrath is on all their armies.
He will totally destroy[a] them,
he will give them over to slaughter.
[3] Their slain will be thrown out,
their dead bodies will stink;
the mountains will be soaked with their blood.
[4] All the stars in the sky will be dissolved
and the heavens rolled up like a scroll;
all the starry host will fall
like withered leaves from the vine,
like shriveled figs from the fig tree.

[5] My sword has drunk its fill in the heavens;
see, it descends in judgment on Edom,
the people I have totally destroyed.
[6] The sword of the LORD is bathed in blood,
it is covered with fat—
the blood of lambs and goats,
fat from the kidneys of rams.
For the LORD has a sacrifice in Bozrah
and a great slaughter in the land of Edom.
[7] And the wild oxen will fall with them,
the bull calves and the great bulls.
Their land will be drenched with blood,
and the dust will be soaked with fat.

## Amplified Bible

[16] [Such a man] will dwell on the heights; his place of
defense will be the fortresses of rocks; his bread will be
given him; water for him will be sure.
[17] Your eyes will see the King in His beauty; [your eyes]
will behold a land of wide distances that stretches afar.
[18] Your mind will meditate on the terror: [asking] Where
is he who counted? Where is he who weighed the tribute?
Where is he who counted the towers?
[19] You will see no more the fierce *and* insolent people,
a people of a speech too deep *and* obscure to be comprehended, of a strange *and* stammering tongue that you cannot understand.
[20] Look upon Zion, the city of our set feasts *and* solemni-
ties! Your eyes shall see Jerusalem, a quiet habitation, a
tent that shall not be taken down; not one of its stakes shall
ever be pulled up, neither shall any of its cords be broken.
[21] But there the Lord will be for us in majesty *and*
splendor a place of broad rivers and streams, where no
oar-propelled boat can go, and no mighty *and* stately ship
can pass.
[22] For the Lord is our Judge, the Lord is our Lawgiver,
the Lord is our King; He will save us. [Isa. 2:3-4; 11:4; 32:1;
James 4:12.]
[23] Your hoisting ropes hang loose; they cannot strength-
en *and* hold firm the foot of their mast or keep the sail
spread out. Then will prey and spoil in abundance be divided; even the lame will take the prey.
[24] And no inhabitant [of Zion] will say, I am sick; the
people who dwell there will be forgiven their iniquity *and*
guilt.

**34** Come near, you nations, to hear; and hearken, you
peoples! Let the earth hear, and all that is in it; the
world, and all things that come forth from it.
[2] For the Lord is indignant against all nations, and His
wrath is against all their host. He has utterly doomed
them, He has given them over to slaughter.
[3] Their slain also shall be cast out, and the stench of
their dead bodies shall rise, and the mountains shall flow
with their blood.
[4] All the host of the heavens shall be dissolved *and*
crumble away, and the skies shall be rolled together like
a scroll; and all their host [the stars and the planets] shall
drop like a faded leaf from the vine, and like a withered fig
from the fig tree. [Rev. 6:13, 14.]
[5] Because My sword has been bathed *and* equipped in
heaven, behold, it shall come down upon Edom [the descendants of Esau], upon the people whom I have doomed
for judgment. [Obad. 8-21.]
[6] The sword of the Lord is filled with blood [of sacrific-
es], it is gorged *and* greased with fatness—with the blood
of lambs and goats, with the fat of the kidneys of rams. For
the Lord has a sacrifice in Bozrah [capital of Edom] and a
great slaughter in the land of Edom.
[7] And the wild oxen shall fall with them, and the [young]
bullocks with the [old and mighty] bulls; and their land
shall be drunk *and* soaked with blood, and their dust made
rich with fatness.

---

[a] 2 The Hebrew term refers to the irrevocable giving over of things
or persons to the LORD, often by totally destroying them; also in
verse 5.

## New International Version

8 For the LORD has a day of vengeance,
   a year of retribution, to uphold Zion's cause.
9 Edom's streams will be turned into pitch,
   her dust into burning sulfur;
   her land will become blazing pitch!
10 It will not be quenched night or day;
   its smoke will rise forever.
From generation to generation it will lie desolate;
   no one will ever pass through it again.
11 The desert owl[a] and screech owl[a] will possess it;
   the great owl[a] and the raven will nest there.
God will stretch out over Edom
   the measuring line of chaos
   and the plumb line of desolation.
12 Her nobles will have nothing there to be called a
   kingdom,
   all her princes will vanish away.
13 Thorns will overrun her citadels,
   nettles and brambles her strongholds.
She will become a haunt for jackals,
   a home for owls.
14 Desert creatures will meet with hyenas,
   and wild goats will bleat to each other;
   there the night creatures will also lie down
   and find for themselves places of rest.
15 The owl will nest there and lay eggs,
   she will hatch them, and care for her young
   under the shadow of her wings;
   there also the falcons will gather,
   each with its mate.

16 Look in the scroll of the LORD and read:

None of these will be missing,
   not one will lack her mate.
For it is his mouth that has given the order,
   and his Spirit will gather them together.
17 He allots their portions;
   his hand distributes them by measure.
They will possess it forever
   and dwell there from generation to generation.

### Joy of the Redeemed

**35** The desert and the parched land will be glad;
   the wilderness will rejoice and blossom.
Like the crocus, 2 it will burst into bloom;
   it will rejoice greatly and shout for joy.
The glory of Lebanon will be given to it,
   the splendor of Carmel and Sharon;
they will see the glory of the LORD,
   the splendor of our God.

3 Strengthen the feeble hands,
   steady the knees that give way;
4 say to those with fearful hearts,
   "Be strong, do not fear;
your God will come,
   he will come with vengeance;
with divine retribution
   he will come to save you."

5 Then will the eyes of the blind be opened
   and the ears of the deaf unstopped.
6 Then will the lame leap like a deer,
   and the mute tongue shout for joy.
Water will gush forth in the wilderness
   and streams in the desert.
7 The burning sand will become a pool,
   the thirsty ground bubbling springs.
In the haunts where jackals once lay,
   grass and reeds and papyrus will grow.

## Amplified Bible

8 For the Lord has a day of vengeance, a year of recompense, for the cause of Zion.
9 And the streams [of Edom] will be turned into pitch and its dust into brimstone, and its land will become burning pitch.
10 [The burning of Edom] shall not be quenched night or day; its smoke shall go up forever. From generation to generation it shall lie waste; none shall pass through it forever and ever. [Rev. 19:3.]
11 But the pelican and the porcupine will possess it; the owl *and* the bittern and the raven will dwell in it. And He will stretch over it [Edom] the measuring line of confusion and the plummet stones of chaos [over its nobles].
12 They shall call its nobles to proclaim the kingdom, but nothing shall be there, and all its princes shall be no more.
13 And thorns shall come up in its palaces *and* strongholds, nettles and brambles in its fortresses; and it shall be a habitation for jackals, an abode for ostriches.
14 And the wild beasts of the desert will meet here with howling creatures [wolves and hyenas] and the [shaggy] wild goat will call to his fellow; the night monster will settle there and find a place of rest.
15 There shall the arrow snake make her nest and lay her eggs and hatch them and gather her young under her shade; there shall the kites be gathered [also to breed] every one with its mate.
16 Seek out of the book of the Lord and read: not one of these [details of prophecy] shall fail, none shall want *and* lack her mate [in fulfillment]. For the mouth [of the Lord] has commanded, and His Spirit has gathered them.
17 And He has cast the lot for them, and His hand has portioned [Edom] to [the wild beasts] by measuring line. They shall possess it forever; from generation to generation they shall dwell in it.

**35** The wilderness and the dry land shall be glad; the desert shall rejoice and blossom like the rose *and* the autumn crocus.
2 It shall blossom abundantly and rejoice even with joy and singing. The glory of Lebanon shall be given to it, the excellency of [Mount] Carmel and [the plain] of Sharon. They shall see the glory of the Lord, the majesty *and* splendor *and* excellency of our God.
3 Strengthen the weak hands and make firm the feeble *and* tottering knees. [Heb. 12:12.]
4 Say to those who are of a fearful *and* hasty heart, Be strong, fear not! Behold, your God will come with vengeance; with the recompense of God He will come and save you.
5 Then the eyes of the blind shall be opened, and the ears of the deaf shall be unstopped.
6 Then shall the lame man leap like a hart, and the tongue of the dumb shall sing for joy. For waters shall break forth in the wilderness and streams in the desert. [Matt. 11:5.]
7 And the burning sand *and* the mirage shall become a pool, and the thirsty ground springs of water; in the haunt of jackals, where they lay resting, shall be grass with reeds and rushes.

---

*a 11 The precise identification of these birds is uncertain.

## New International Version

[8]And a highway will be there;
  it will be called the Way of Holiness;
  it will be for those who walk on that Way.
The unclean will not journey on it;
  wicked fools will not go about on it.
[9]No lion will be there,
  nor any ravenous beast;
  they will not be found there.
But only the redeemed will walk there,
[10]  and those the Lord has rescued will return.
They will enter Zion with singing;
  everlasting joy will crown their heads.
Gladness and joy will overtake them,
  and sorrow and sighing will flee away.

### Sennacherib Threatens Jerusalem

**36** In the fourteenth year of King Hezekiah's reign, Sennacherib king of Assyria attacked all the fortified cities of Judah and captured them. [2]Then the king of Assyria sent his field commander with a large army from Lachish to King Hezekiah at Jerusalem. When the commander stopped at the aqueduct of the Upper Pool, on the road to the Launderer's Field, [3]Eliakim son of Hilkiah the palace administrator, Shebna the secretary, and Joah son of Asaph the recorder went out to him.

[4]The field commander said to them, "Tell Hezekiah:

"'This is what the great king, the king of Assyria, says: On what are you basing this confidence of yours? [5]You say you have counsel and might for war—but you speak only empty words. On whom are you depending, that you rebel against me? [6]Look, I know you are depending on Egypt, that splintered reed of a staff, which pierces the hand of anyone who leans on it! Such is Pharaoh king of Egypt to all who depend on him. [7]But if you say to me, "We are depending on the Lord our God"—isn't he the one whose high places and altars Hezekiah removed, saying to Judah and Jerusalem, "You must worship before this altar"?

[8]"'Come now, make a bargain with my master, the king of Assyria: I will give you two thousand horses—if you can put riders on them! [9]How then can you repulse one officer of the least of my master's officials, even though you are depending on Egypt for chariots and horsemen[a]? [10]Furthermore, have I come to attack and destroy this land without the Lord? The Lord himself told me to march against this country and destroy it.'"

[11]Then Eliakim, Shebna and Joah said to the field commander, "Please speak to your servants in Aramaic, since we understand it. Don't speak to us in Hebrew in the hearing of the people on the wall."

[12]But the commander replied, "Was it only to your master and you that my master sent me to say these things, and not to the people sitting on the wall—who, like you, will have to eat their own excrement and drink their own urine?"

[13]Then the commander stood and called out in Hebrew, "Hear the words of the great king, the king of Assyria! [14]This is what the king says: Do not let Hezekiah deceive you. He cannot deliver you! [15]Do not let Hezekiah persuade you to trust in the Lord when he says, 'The Lord will surely deliver us; this city will not be given into the hand of the king of Assyria.'

## Amplified Bible

[8]And a highway shall be there, and a way; and it shall be called the Holy Way. The unclean shall not pass over it, but it shall be for the redeemed; the wayfaring men, yes, the simple ones *and* fools, shall not err in it *and* lose their way.

[9]No lion shall be there, nor shall any ravenous beast come up on it; they shall not be found there. But the redeemed shall walk on it.

[10]And the ransomed of the Lord shall return and come to Zion with singing, and everlasting joy shall be upon their heads; they shall obtain joy and gladness, and sorrow and sighing shall flee away.

**36** Now in the fourteenth year of King Hezekiah, Sennacherib king of Assyria came up against all the fortified cities of Judah and took them. [II Kings 18:13, 17-37; II Chron. 32:9-19.]

[2]And the king of Assyria sent the Rabshakeh [the military official] from Lachish [the Judean fortress commanding the road from Egypt] to King Hezekiah at Jerusalem with a great army. And he stood by the canal of the Upper Pool on the highway to the Fuller's Field.

[3]Then came out to meet him Eliakim son of Hilkiah, who was over the [royal] household, and Shebna the secretary, and Joah son of Asaph, the recording historian.

[4]And the Rabshakeh said to them, Say to Hezekiah, Thus says the great king, the king of Assyria: What reason for confidence is this in which you trust?

[5]Do you suppose that mere words of the lips can pass for warlike counsel and strength? Now in whom do you trust *and* on whom do you rely, that you rebel against me? [II Kings 18:7.]

[6]Behold, you trust in the staff of this bruised *and* broken reed, Egypt, which will pierce the hand of any man who leans on it. So is Pharaoh king of Egypt to all who trust *and* rely on him.

[7]But if you say to me, We trust in *and* rely on the Lord our God—is it not He Whose high places and Whose altars Hezekiah has taken away, saying to Judah and to Jerusalem, You shall worship before this altar? [II Kings 18:4, 5.]

[8]Now therefore, I pray you, make a wager with my master the king of Assyria *and* give him pledges, and I will give you two thousand horses—if you are able on your part to put riders on them.

[9]How then can you repulse the attack of a single captain of the least of my master's servants, when you put your reliance on Egypt for chariots and for horsemen?

[10]Moreover, is it without the Lord that I have now come up against this land to destroy it? The Lord said to me, Go up against this land and destroy it.

[11]Then Eliakim and Shebna and Joah said to the Rabshakeh, We pray you, speak to your servants in the Aramaic *or* Syrian language, for we understand it; and do not speak to us in the language of the Jews in the hearing of the people on the wall.

[12]But the Rabshakeh said, Has my master sent me to speak these words only to your master and to you? Has he not sent me to the men sitting on the wall, who are doomed with you to eat their own dung and drink their own urine?

[13]Then the Rabshakeh stood and cried with a loud voice in the language of the Jews: Hear the words of the great king, the king of Assyria!

[14]Thus says the king: Let not Hezekiah deceive you, for he will not be able to deliver you.

[15]Nor let Hezekiah make you trust in *and* rely on the Lord, saying, The Lord will surely deliver us; this city will not be delivered into the hand of the king of Assyria.

---

[a] 9 Or *charioteers*

## New International Version

16"Do not listen to Hezekiah. This is what the king of Assyria says: Make peace with me and come out to me. Then each of you will eat fruit from your own vine and fig tree and drink water from your own cistern, 17until I come and take you to a land like your own—a land of grain and new wine, a land of bread and vineyards.

18"Do not let Hezekiah mislead you when he says, 'The LORD will deliver us.' Have the gods of any nations ever delivered their lands from the hand of the king of Assyria? 19Where are the gods of Hamath and Arpad? Where are the gods of Sepharvaim? Have they rescued Samaria from my hand? 20Who of all the gods of these countries have been able to save their lands from me? How then can the LORD deliver Jerusalem from my hand?"

21But the people remained silent and said nothing in reply, because the king had commanded, "Do not answer him."

22Then Eliakim son of Hilkiah the palace administrator, Shebna the secretary and Joah son of Asaph the recorder went to Hezekiah, with their clothes torn, and told him what the field commander had said.

### Jerusalem's Deliverance Foretold

**37** When King Hezekiah heard this, he tore his clothes and put on sackcloth and went into the temple of the LORD. 2He sent Eliakim the palace administrator, Shebna the secretary, and the leading priests, all wearing sackcloth, to the prophet Isaiah son of Amoz. 3They told him, "This is what Hezekiah says: This day is a day of distress and rebuke and disgrace, as when children come to the moment of birth and there is no strength to deliver them. 4It may be that the LORD your God will hear the words of the field commander, whom his master, the king of Assyria, has sent to ridicule the living God, and that he will rebuke him for the words the LORD your God has heard. Therefore pray for the remnant that still survives."

5When King Hezekiah's officials came to Isaiah, 6Isaiah said to them, "Tell your master, 'This is what the LORD says: Do not be afraid of what you have heard—those words with which the underlings of the king of Assyria have blasphemed me. 7Listen! When he hears a certain report, I will make him want to return to his own country, and there I will have him cut down with the sword.'"

8When the field commander heard that the king of Assyria had left Lachish, he withdrew and found the king fighting against Libnah.

9Now Sennacherib received a report that Tirhakah, the king of Cush,ᵃ was marching out to fight against him. When he heard it, he sent messengers to Hezekiah with this word: 10"Say to Hezekiah king of Judah: Do not let the god you depend on deceive you when he says, 'Jerusalem will not be given into the hands of the king of Assyria.' 11Surely you have heard what the kings of Assyria have done to all the countries, destroying them completely. And will you be delivered? 12Did the gods of the nations that were destroyed by my predecessors deliver them—the gods of Gozan, Har-

## Amplified Bible

16Do not listen to Hezekiah, for thus says the king of Assyria: Make your peace with me and come out to me; and eat every one from his own vine and every one from his own fig tree and drink every one the water of his own cistern,

17Until I come and take you away to a land like your own land, a land of grain and wine, a land of bread and vineyards.

18Beware lest Hezekiah persuade *and* mislead you by saying, The Lord will deliver us. Has any one of the gods of the nations ever delivered his land out of the hand of the king of Assyria?

19Where are the gods of Hamath and Arpad [in Syria]? Where are the gods of Sepharvaim [a place from which the Assyrians brought colonists to inhabit evacuated Samaria]? And have [the gods] delivered Samaria [capital of the ten northern tribes of Israel] out of my hand?

20Who among all the gods of these lands has delivered his land out of my hand, that [you should think that] the Lord can deliver Jerusalem out of my hand?

21But they kept still and answered him not a word, for the king's [Hezekiah's] command was, Do not answer him.

22Then Eliakim son of Hilkiah, who was over the household, and Shebna the secretary, and Joah son of Asaph, the recording historian came to Hezekiah with their clothes rent, and told him the words of the Rabshakeh [the Assyrian military official].

**37** And when King Hezekiah heard it, he rent his clothes and covered himself with sackcloth and went into the house of the Lord. [II Kings 19:1-13.]

2And he sent Eliakim, who was over the [royal] household, and Shebna the secretary, and the older priests, clothed with sackcloth, to Isaiah the prophet, the son of Amoz.

3And they said to him, Thus says Hezekiah: This day is a day of trouble *and* distress and of rebuke and of disgrace; for children have come to the birth, and there is no strength to bring them forth.

4It may be that the Lord your God will hear the words of the Rabshakeh, whom the king of Assyria, his master, has sent to mock, reproach, insult, *and* defy the living God, and will rebuke the words which the Lord your God has heard. Therefore lift up your prayer for the remnant [of His people] that is left.

5So the servants of King Hezekiah came to Isaiah.

6And Isaiah said to them, You shall say to your master, Thus says the Lord: Do not be afraid because of the words which you have heard, with which the servants of the king of Assyria have reviled *and* blasphemed Me.

7Behold, I will put a spirit in him so that he will hear a rumor and return to his own land, and I will cause him to fall by the sword in his own land.

8So the Rabshakeh returned and found the king of Assyria fighting against Libnah [a fortified city of Judah]; for he had heard that the king had departed from Lachish.

9And [Sennacherib king of Assyria] heard concerning Tirhakah king of Ethiopia, He has come forth to make war with you. And when he heard it, he sent messengers to Hezekiah, saying,

10Thus shall you speak to Hezekiah king of Judah: Let not your God in Whom you trust deceive you by saying, Jerusalem shall not be given into the hand of the king of Assyria.

11Behold, you have heard what the kings of Assyria have done to all lands, destroying them utterly. And shall you be delivered?

12Have the gods of the nations delivered those whom

---

ᵃ 9 That is, the upper Nile region

# New International Version

ran, Rezeph and the people of Eden who were in Tel Assar? [13]Where is the king of Hamath or the king of Arpad? Where are the kings of Lair, Sepharvaim, Hena and Ivvah?"

## Hezekiah's Prayer

[14]Hezekiah received the letter from the messengers and read it. Then he went up to the temple of the LORD and spread it out before the LORD. [15]And Hezekiah prayed to the LORD: [16]"LORD Almighty, the God of Israel, enthroned between the cherubim, you alone are God over all the kingdoms of the earth. You have made heaven and earth. [17]Give ear, LORD, and hear; open your eyes, LORD, and see; listen to all the words Sennacherib has sent to ridicule the living God.

[18]"It is true, LORD, that the Assyrian kings have laid waste all these peoples and their lands. [19]They have thrown their gods into the fire and destroyed them, for they were not gods but only wood and stone, fashioned by human hands. [20]Now, LORD our God, deliver us from his hand, so that all the kingdoms of the earth may know that you, LORD, are the only God.[a]"

## Sennacherib's Fall

[21]Then Isaiah son of Amoz sent a message to Hezekiah: "This is what the LORD, the God of Israel, says: Because you have prayed to me concerning Sennacherib king of Assyria, [22]this is the word the LORD has spoken against him:

"Virgin Daughter Zion
    despises and mocks you.
Daughter Jerusalem
    tosses her head as you flee.
[23]Who is it you have ridiculed and blasphemed?
    Against whom have you raised your voice
and lifted your eyes in pride?
    Against the Holy One of Israel!
[24]By your messengers
    you have ridiculed the Lord.
And you have said,
    'With my many chariots
I have ascended the heights of the mountains,
    the utmost heights of Lebanon.
I have cut down its tallest cedars,
    the choicest of its junipers.
I have reached its remotest heights,
    the finest of its forests.
[25]I have dug wells in foreign lands[b]
    and drunk the water there.
With the soles of my feet
    I have dried up all the streams of Egypt.'

[26]"Have you not heard?
    Long ago I ordained it.
In days of old I planned it;
    now I have brought it to pass,
that you have turned fortified cities
    into piles of stone.
[27]Their people, drained of power,
    are dismayed and put to shame.
They are like plants in the field,
    like tender green shoots,
like grass sprouting on the roof,
    scorched[c] before it grows up.

[28]"But I know where you are
    and when you come and go
    and how you rage against me.
[29]Because you rage against me
    and because your insolence has reached my ears,

---

[a] 20 Dead Sea Scrolls (see also 2 Kings 19:19); Masoretic Text *you alone are the LORD*    [b] 25 Dead Sea Scrolls (see also 2 Kings 19:24); Masoretic Text does not have *in foreign lands*.    [c] 27 Some manuscripts of the Masoretic Text, Dead Sea Scrolls and some Septuagint manuscripts (see also 2 Kings 19:26); most manuscripts of the Masoretic Text *roof / and terraced fields*

# Amplified Bible

my predecessors have destroyed, as [a]Gozan, Haran [of Mesopotamia], Rezeph, and the children of Eden who were in Telassar?

[13]Where is the king of Hamath, and the king of Arpad [of northern Syria], and the king of the city of Sepharvaim, the king of Hena, or the king of Ivvah?

[14]And Hezekiah received the letter from the hand of the messengers and read it. And Hezekiah went up to the house of the Lord and spread it before the Lord. [II Kings 19:14-19.]

[15]And Hezekiah prayed to the Lord:

[16]O Lord of hosts, God of Israel, Who [in symbol] are enthroned above the cherubim [of the ark in the temple], You are the God, You alone, of all the kingdoms of the earth. You have made heaven and earth.

[17]Incline Your ear, O Lord, and hear; open Your eyes, O Lord, and see; and hear all the words of Sennacherib which he has sent to mock, reproach, insult, *and* defy the living God.

[18]It is true, Lord, that the kings of Assyria have laid waste all the nations and their lands

[19]And have cast the gods of those peoples into the fire, for they were not gods but the work of men's hands, wood and stone. Therefore they have destroyed them.

[20]Now therefore, O Lord our God, save us from his hand, that all the kingdoms of the earth may know (understand and realize) that You are the Lord, even You only.

[21]Then Isaiah son of Amoz sent to Hezekiah, saying, Thus says the Lord, the God of Israel: Because you have prayed to Me against Sennacherib king of Assyria, [II Kings 19:20-37; II Chron. 32:20-21.]

[22]This is the word which the Lord has spoken concerning him: The Virgin Daughter of Zion has despised you and laughed you to scorn; the Daughter of Jerusalem has shaken her head behind you.

[23]Whom have you mocked and reviled [insulted and blasphemed]? And against Whom have you raised your voice and haughtily lifted your eyes? Against the Holy One of Israel!

[24]By your servants you have mocked, reproached, insulted, *and* defied the Lord, and you have said, With my many chariots I have gone up to the height of the mountains, to the inner recesses of Lebanon. I cut down its tallest cedars *and* its choicest cypress trees; I came to its remotest height, its most luxuriant *and* dense forest;

[25]I dug wells and drank foreign waters, and with the sole of my feet I have dried up all the rivers [the Nile streams] of Egypt.

[26][But, says the God of Israel] have you not heard that I purposed to do it long ago, that I planned it in ancient times? Now I have brought it to pass, that you [king of Assyria] should [be My instrument to] lay waste fortified cities, making them ruinous heaps.

[27]Therefore their inhabitants had little power, they were dismayed and confounded; they were like the grass of the field and like the green herb, like the grass on the housetops and like a field of grain blasted before it is grown *or* is in stalk.

[28]But I [the Lord] know your sitting down and your going out and your coming in and your raging against Me.

[29]Because your raging against Me and your arrogance *and* careless ease have come to My ears, therefore will I

---

[a] The place-names in this verse are all found on the Assyrian monuments. For further information, see E. S. Schrader, *Cuneiform Inscriptions and the Old Testament*, and his comments on II Kings 19:12.

## New International Version

I will put my hook in your nose
　　and my bit in your mouth,
and I will make you return
　　by the way you came.

30"This will be the sign for you, Hezekiah:

"This year you will eat what grows by itself,
　　and the second year what springs from that.
But in the third year sow and reap,
　　plant vineyards and eat their fruit.
31Once more a remnant of the kingdom of Judah
　　will take root below and bear fruit above.
32For out of Jerusalem will come a remnant,
　　and out of Mount Zion a band of survivors.
The zeal of the LORD Almighty
　　will accomplish this.

33"Therefore this is what the LORD says concerning the king of Assyria:

"He will not enter this city
　　or shoot an arrow here.
He will not come before it with shield
　　or build a siege ramp against it.
34By the way that he came he will return;
　　he will not enter this city,"
　　　　　　　　　　　　　　　declares the LORD.
35"I will defend this city and save it,
　　for my sake and for the sake of David my servant!"

36Then the angel of the LORD went out and put to death a hundred and eighty-five thousand in the Assyrian camp. When the people got up the next morning—there were all the dead bodies! 37So Sennacherib king of Assyria broke camp and withdrew. He returned to Nineveh and stayed there.

38One day, while he was worshiping in the temple of his god Nisrok, his sons Adrammelek and Sharezer killed him with the sword, and they escaped to the land of Ararat. And Esarhaddon his son succeeded him as king.

### Hezekiah's Illness

**38** In those days Hezekiah became ill and was at the point of death. The prophet Isaiah son of Amoz went to him and said, "This is what the LORD says: Put your house in order, because you are going to die; you will not recover."

2Hezekiah turned his face to the wall and prayed to the LORD, 3"Remember, LORD, how I have walked before you faithfully and with wholehearted devotion and have done what is good in your eyes." And Hezekiah wept bitterly.

4Then the word of the LORD came to Isaiah: 5"Go and tell Hezekiah, 'This is what the LORD, the God of your father David, says: I have heard your prayer and seen your tears; I will add fifteen years to your life. 6And I will deliv-

## Amplified Bible

put My hook in your nose and My bridle in your lips, and I will turn you back by the way you came.

30And [now, Hezekiah, says the Lord] this shall be the sign [of these things] to you: you shall eat this year what grows of itself, and in the second year that which springs from the same. And in the third year sow and reap, and plant vineyards and eat the fruit of them.

31And the remnant that has survived of the house of Judah shall again take root downward and bear fruit upward.

32For out of Jerusalem shall go forth a remnant, and a band that survives out of Mount Zion. The zeal of the Lord of hosts will perform this.

33Therefore thus says the Lord concerning the king of Assyria: He shall not come into this city or shoot an arrow here or come before it with shield or cast up a siege mound against it.

34By the way that he came, by the same way he shall return, and he shall not come into this city, says the Lord.

35For I will defend this city to save it, for My own sake and for the sake of My servant David.

36And the ªAngel of the Lord went forth, and ᵇslew 185,000 in the camp of the Assyrians; and when [the living] arose early in the morning, behold, all these were dead bodies. [II Kings 19:35.]

37So Sennacherib king of Assyria departed and returned and dwelt at Nineveh.

38And as he was worshiping in the house of Nisroch his god, Adrammelech and Sharezer his sons killed him with the sword, and they escaped into the land of Armenia or Ararat. And Esarhaddon his son reigned in his stead.

**38** In those days King Hezekiah of Judah became ill and was at the point of death. And Isaiah the prophet, the son of Amoz, came to him and said, Thus says the Lord: Set your house in order, for you shall die and not live. [II Kings 20:1-11; II Chron. 32:24-26.]

2Then Hezekiah turned his face to the wall and prayed to the Lord

3And said, Remember [earnestly] now, O Lord, I beseech You, how I have walked before You in faithfulness *and* in truth, with a whole heart [absolutely devoted to You], and have done what is good in Your sight. And Hezekiah wept bitterly.

4Then came the word of the Lord to Isaiah, saying,

5Go, and say to Hezekiah, Thus says the Lord, the God of David your father: I have heard your prayer, I have seen your tears; behold, I will ᶜadd to your life fifteen years.

ª See footnote on Gen. 16:7. ᵇ A startling, literal fulfillment of the prophecy made in Isaiah 31:8, 9. See also Isa. 10:33-34; 14:25; 17:14; 30:31. ᶜ God's time for Hezekiah to die had come (Isa. 38:1), but he had no son. It was unthinkable to him, apparently, that he should die and leave no heir to his throne. As devout as he was, he could not trust the Lord to give His faithful servant what was best for him. So he took matters into his own hands and begged to be allowed to live on. The Lord granted his request—sons were born. How immense the grief that resulted! One of his sons, Manasseh, became Hezekiah's disgraceful and ruthless successor, not for just a few years, but for fifty-five! (II Kings 21:1ff.) He undid everything reformatory that had been done, established idol worship, caused his son to go through the fire as an offering to the pagan god, defied God's prophets, and caused the slaughter of those who opposed him (including perhaps Isaiah, his father's best friend who, according to Jewish tradition, was sawed in half during Manasseh's reign). How little Hezekiah knew of what was best for him or for Judah! How presumptuous is anyone who demands that his own shortsighted vision replace the wisdom of God's plan for his own life or for that of others! See also footnote on II Kings 20:6.

## New International Version

er you and this city from the hand of the king of Assyria. I will defend this city.

7 "'This is the LORD's sign to you that the LORD will do what he has promised: 8 I will make the shadow cast by the sun go back the ten steps it has gone down on the stairway of Ahaz.'" So the sunlight went back the ten steps it had gone down.

9 A writing of Hezekiah king of Judah after his illness and recovery:

10 I said, "In the prime of my life
    must I go through the gates of death
    and be robbed of the rest of my years?"
11 I said, "I will not again see the LORD himself
    in the land of the living;
    no longer will I look on my fellow man,
    or be with those who now dwell in this world.
12 Like a shepherd's tent my house
    has been pulled down and taken from me.
    Like a weaver I have rolled up my life,
    and he has cut me off from the loom;
    day and night you made an end of me.
13 I waited patiently till dawn,
    but like a lion he broke all my bones;
    day and night you made an end of me.
14 I cried like a swift or thrush,
    I moaned like a mourning dove.
    My eyes grew weak as I looked to the heavens.
    I am being threatened; Lord, come to my aid!"

15 But what can I say?
    He has spoken to me, and he himself has done this.
    I will walk humbly all my years
    because of this anguish of my soul.
16 Lord, by such things people live;
    and my spirit finds life in them too.
    You restored me to health
    and let me live.
17 Surely it was for my benefit
    that I suffered such anguish.
    In your love you kept me
    from the pit of destruction;
    you have put all my sins
    behind your back.
18 For the grave cannot praise you,
    death cannot sing your praise;
    those who go down to the pit
    cannot hope for your faithfulness.
19 The living, the living—they praise you,
    as I am doing today;
    parents tell their children
    about your faithfulness.

20 The LORD will save me,
    and we will sing with stringed instruments
    all the days of our lives
    in the temple of the LORD.

21 Isaiah had said, "Prepare a poultice of figs and apply it to the boil, and he will recover." 22 Hezekiah had asked, "What will be the sign that I will go up to the temple of the LORD?"

### Envoys From Babylon

**39** At that time Marduk-Baladan son of Baladan king of Babylon sent Hezekiah letters and a gift, because he had heard of his illness and recovery. 2 Hezekiah received the envoys gladly and showed them what was in his storehouses—the silver, the gold, the spices, the fine olive oil—his entire armory and everything found among his treasures. There was nothing in his palace or in all his kingdom that Hezekiah did not show them.

## Amplified Bible

6 And I will deliver you and this city out of the hand of the king of Assyria; and I will defend this city [Jerusalem].

7 And this will be the sign to you from the Lord that the Lord will do this thing that He has spoken:

8 Behold, I will turn the shadow [denoting the time of day] on the steps or degrees, which has gone down on the steps or sundial of Ahaz, backward ten steps or degrees. And the sunlight turned back ten steps on the steps on which it had gone down.

9 This is the writing of Hezekiah king of Judah after he had been sick and had recovered from his sickness:

10 I said, In the noontide and tranquillity of my days I must depart; I am to pass through the gates of Sheol (the place of the dead), deprived of the remainder of my years.

11 I said, I shall not see the Lord, even the Lord, in the land of the living; I shall behold man no more among the inhabitants of the world.

12 My [fleshly] dwelling is plucked up and is removed from me like a shepherd's tent. I have rolled up my life as a weaver [rolls up the finished web]; [the Lord] cuts me free from the loom; from day to night You bring me to an end.

13 I thought and quieted myself until morning. Like a lion He breaks all my bones; from day to night You bring me to an end.

14 Like a twittering swallow or a crane, so do I chirp and chatter; I moan like a dove. My eyes are weary and dim with looking upward. O Lord, I am oppressed; take my side and be my security [as of a debtor being sent to prison].

15 But what can I say? For He has both spoken to me and He Himself has done it. I must go softly [as in solemn procession] all my years and my sleep has fled because of the bitterness of my soul.

16 O Lord, by these things men live; and in all these is the life of my spirit. O give me back my health and make me live!

17 Behold, it was for my peace that I had intense bitterness; but You have loved back my life from the pit of corruption and nothingness, for You have cast all my sins behind Your back.

18 For Sheol (the place of the dead) cannot confess and reach out the hand to You, death cannot praise and rejoice in You; they who go down to the pit cannot hope for Your faithfulness [to Your promises; their probation is at an end, their destiny is sealed].

19 The living, the living—they shall thank and praise You, as I do this day; the father shall make known to the children Your faithfulness and Your truth.

20 The Lord is ready to save (deliver) me; therefore we will sing my songs with [my] stringed instruments all the days of our lives in the house of the Lord.

21 Now Isaiah had said, Let them take a cake of figs and lay it for a plaster upon the boil, that he may recover.

22 Hezekiah also had said, What is the sign that I shall go up to the house of the Lord?

**39** At that time Merodach-baladan son of Baladan king of Babylon sent [messengers with] letters and a present to Hezekiah, for he had heard that he had been sick and had recovered. [II Kings 20:12-19.]

2 And Hezekiah was glad and welcomed them and showed them the house of his spices and precious things—the silver, the gold, the spices, the precious ointment, all the house of his armor and his jewels, and all that was found in his treasuries. There was nothing in his house nor in all his dominion that Hezekiah did not show them.

## New International Version

[3] Then Isaiah the prophet went to King Hezekiah and asked, "What did those men say, and where did they come from?"

"From a distant land," Hezekiah replied. "They came to me from Babylon."

[4] The prophet asked, "What did they see in your palace?"

"They saw everything in my palace," Hezekiah said. "There is nothing among my treasures that I did not show them."

[5] Then Isaiah said to Hezekiah, "Hear the word of the LORD Almighty: [6] The time will surely come when everything in your palace, and all that your predecessors have stored up until this day, will be carried off to Babylon. Nothing will be left, says the LORD. [7] And some of your descendants, your own flesh and blood who will be born to you, will be taken away, and they will become eunuchs in the palace of the king of Babylon."

[8] "The word of the LORD you have spoken is good," Hezekiah replied. For he thought, "There will be peace and security in my lifetime."

### Comfort for God's People

**40** Comfort, comfort my people,
   says your God.
[2] Speak tenderly to Jerusalem,
   and proclaim to her
that her hard service has been completed,
   that her sin has been paid for,
that she has received from the LORD's hand
   double for all her sins.

[3] A voice of one calling:
"In the wilderness prepare
   the way for the LORD[a];
make straight in the desert
   a highway for our God.[b]
[4] Every valley shall be raised up,
   every mountain and hill made low;
the rough ground shall become level,
   the rugged places a plain.
[5] And the glory of the LORD will be revealed,
   and all people will see it together.
      For the mouth of the LORD has spoken."

[6] A voice says, "Cry out."
   And I said, "What shall I cry?"

"All people are like grass,
   and all their faithfulness is like the flowers of the
      field.
[7] The grass withers and the flowers fall,
   because the breath of the LORD blows on them.
   Surely the people are grass.
[8] The grass withers and the flowers fall,
   but the word of our God endures forever."

[9] You who bring good news to Zion,
   go up on a high mountain.
You who bring good news to Jerusalem,[c]
   lift up your voice with a shout,
lift it up, do not be afraid;
   say to the towns of Judah,
   "Here is your God!"
[10] See, the Sovereign LORD comes with power,
   and he rules with a mighty arm.
See, his reward is with him,
   and his recompense accompanies him.
[11] He tends his flock like a shepherd:
   He gathers the lambs in his arms

## Amplified Bible

[3] Then came Isaiah the prophet to King Hezekiah and said to him, What did these men say? From where did they come to you? And Hezekiah said, They have come to me from a far country, even from Babylon.

[4] Then Isaiah said, What have they seen in your house? And Hezekiah answered, They have seen all that is in my house; there is nothing among my treasures that I have not shown them.

[5] Then said Isaiah to Hezekiah, Hear the word of the Lord of hosts:

[6] Behold, the days are coming when all that is in your house, and that which your predecessors have stored up till this day, shall be carried to Babylon. Nothing shall be left, says the Lord.

[7] And some of your own sons who are born to you shall be taken away, and they shall be eunuchs in the palace of the king of Babylon.

[8] Then said Hezekiah to Isaiah, The word of the Lord which you have spoken is good. And he added, For there will be peace and faithfulness [to His promises to us] in my days.

**40** Comfort, comfort My people, says your God.
[2] Speak tenderly to the heart of Jerusalem, and cry to her that her time of service *and* her warfare are ended, that [her punishment is accepted and] her iniquity is pardoned, that she has received [punishment] from the Lord's hand double for all her sins.

[3] A voice of one who cries: Prepare in the wilderness the way of the Lord [clear away the obstacles]; make straight *and* smooth in the desert a highway for our God! [Mark 1:3.]

[4] Every valley shall be lifted *and* filled up, and every mountain and hill shall be made low; and the crooked *and* uneven shall be made straight *and* level, and the rough places a plain.

[5] And the glory (majesty and splendor) of the Lord shall be revealed, and all flesh shall see it together; for the mouth of the Lord has spoken it. [Luke 3:5, 6.]

[6] A voice says, Cry [prophesy]! And I said, What shall I cry? [The voice answered, Proclaim:] All flesh is as frail as grass, and all that makes it attractive [its kindness, its goodwill, its mercy from God, its glory and comeliness, however good] is transitory, like the flower of the field.

[7] The grass withers, the flower fades, when the breath of the Lord blows upon it; surely [all] the people are like grass.

[8] The [a]grass withers, the flower fades, but the word of our God will stand forever. [James 1:10, 11; I Pet. 1:24, 25.]

[9] O you who bring good tidings to Zion, get up to the high mountain. O you who bring good tidings to Jerusalem, lift up your voice with strength, lift it up, be not afraid; say to the cities of Judah, Behold your God! [Acts 10:36; Rom. 10:15.]

[10] Behold, the Lord God will come with might, and His arm will rule for Him. Behold, His reward is with Him, and His recompense before Him. [Rev. 22:7, 12.]

[11] He will feed His flock like a shepherd: He will gather

---

[a] 3 Or *A voice of one calling in the wilderness: / "Prepare the way for the LORD*   [b] 3 Hebrew; Septuagint *make straight the paths of our God*   [c] 9 Or *Zion, bringer of good news, / go up on a high mountain. / Jerusalem, bringer of good news*

[a] The apostle Peter quotes this verse (I Pet. 1:24-25) and then adds, "and this Word is the good news which was preached to you"—which confirms as fact that Isaiah is here referring to the times of Christ, the Messiah, the Anointed One.

## New International Version

and carries them close to his heart;
  he gently leads those that have young.
12 Who has measured the waters in the hollow of his
    hand,
  or with the breadth of his hand marked off the
    heavens?
Who has held the dust of the earth in a basket,
  or weighed the mountains on the scales
  and the hills in a balance?
13 Who can fathom the Spirit[a] of the Lord,
  or instruct the Lord as his counselor?
14 Whom did the Lord consult to enlighten him,
  and who taught him the right way?
Who was it that taught him knowledge,
  or showed him the path of understanding?
15 Surely the nations are like a drop in a bucket;
  they are regarded as dust on the scales;
  he weighs the islands as though they were fine dust.
16 Lebanon is not sufficient for altar fires,
  nor its animals enough for burnt offerings.
17 Before him all the nations are as nothing;
  they are regarded by him as worthless
  and less than nothing.

18 With whom, then, will you compare God?
  To what image will you liken him?
19 As for an idol, a metalworker casts it,
  and a goldsmith overlays it with gold
  and fashions silver chains for it.
20 A person too poor to present such an offering
  selects wood that will not rot;
they look for a skilled worker
  to set up an idol that will not topple.

21 Do you not know?
  Have you not heard?
Has it not been told you from the beginning?
  Have you not understood since the earth was
    founded?
22 He sits enthroned above the circle of the earth,
  and its people are like grasshoppers.
He stretches out the heavens like a canopy,
  and spreads them out like a tent to live in.
23 He brings princes to naught
  and reduces the rulers of this world to nothing.
24 No sooner are they planted,
  no sooner are they sown,
  no sooner do they take root in the ground,
than he blows on them and they wither,
  and a whirlwind sweeps them away like chaff.

25 "To whom will you compare me?
  Or who is my equal?" says the Holy One.
26 Lift up your eyes and look to the heavens:
  Who created all these?
He who brings out the starry host one by one
  and calls forth each of them by name.
Because of his great power and mighty strength,
  not one of them is missing.

27 Why do you complain, Jacob?
  Why do you say, Israel,
"My way is hidden from the Lord;
  my cause is disregarded by my God"?
28 Do you not know?
  Have you not heard?
The Lord is the everlasting God,
  the Creator of the ends of the earth.
He will not grow tired or weary,
  and his understanding no one can fathom.
29 He gives strength to the weary
  and increases the power of the weak.

a 13 Or *mind*

## Amplified Bible

the lambs in His arm, He will carry them in His bosom and
will gently lead those that have their young.
12 Who has measured the waters in the hollow of his
hand, marked off the heavens with a [nine-inch] span, enclosed the dust of the earth in a measure, and weighed the
mountains in scales and the hills in a balance?
13 Who has directed the Spirit of the Lord, or as His
counselor has taught Him? [Rom. 11:34.]
14 With whom did He take counsel, that instruction
might be given Him? Who taught Him the path of justice
and taught Him knowledge and showed Him the way of
understanding?
15 Behold, the nations are like a drop from a bucket and
are counted as small dust on the scales; behold, He takes
up the isles like a very little thing.
16 And all Lebanon's [forests] cannot supply sufficient
fuel, nor all its wild beasts furnish victims enough to burn
sacrifices [worthy of the Lord].
17 All the nations are as nothing before Him; they are regarded by Him as less than nothing and emptiness (waste,
futility, and worthlessness).
18 To whom then will you liken God? Or with what likeness will you compare Him? [Acts 17:29.]
19 The graven image! A workman casts it, and a goldsmith overlays it with gold and casts silver chains for it.
20 He who is so impoverished that he has no offering *or*
oblation *or* rich gift to give [to his god is constrained to
make a wooden offering, an idol; so he] chooses a tree that
will not rot; he seeks out a skillful craftsman to carve *and*
set up an image that will not totter *or* deteriorate.
21 [You worshipers of idols, you are without excuse.] Do
you not know? Have you not heard? Has it not been told
you from the beginning? [These things ought to convince
you of God's omnipotence and of the folly of bowing to
idols.] Have you not understood from the foundations of
the earth? [Rom. 1:20, 21.]
22 It is God Who sits above the circle (the horizon) of the
earth, and its inhabitants are like grasshoppers; it is He
Who stretches out the heavens like [gauze] curtains and
spreads them out like a tent to dwell in,
23 Who brings dignitaries to nothing, Who makes the
judges *and* rulers of the earth as chaos (emptiness, falsity,
and futility).
24 Yes, these men are scarcely planted, scarcely are they
sown, scarcely does their stock take root in the earth,
when [the Lord] blows upon them and they wither, and
the whirlwind *or* tempest takes them away like stubble.
25 To whom then will you liken Me, that I should be
equal to him? says the Holy One.
26 Lift up your eyes on high and see! Who has created
these? He Who brings out their host by number and calls
them all by name; through the greatness of His might and
because He is strong in power, not one is missing *or* lacks
anything.
27 Why, O Jacob, do you say, and declare, O Israel, My
way *and* my lot are hidden from the Lord, and my right is
passed over without regard from my God?
28 Have you not known? Have you not heard? The everlasting God, the Lord, the Creator of the ends of the earth,
does not faint or grow weary; there is no searching of His
understanding.
29 He gives power to the faint *and* weary, and to him who
has no might He increases strength [causing it to multiply
and making it to abound]. [II Cor. 12:9.]

## New International Version

30 Even youths grow tired and weary,
    and young men stumble and fall;
31 but those who hope in the LORD
    will renew their strength.
They will soar on wings like eagles;
    they will run and not grow weary,
    they will walk and not be faint.

### The Helper of Israel

**41** "Be silent before me, you islands!
    Let the nations renew their strength!
Let them come forward and speak;
    let us meet together at the place of judgment.

2 "Who has stirred up one from the east,
    calling him in righteousness to his service[a]?
He hands nations over to him
    and subdues kings before him.
He turns them to dust with his sword,
    to windblown chaff with his bow.
3 He pursues them and moves on unscathed,
    by a path his feet have not traveled before.
4 Who has done this and carried it through,
    calling forth the generations from the beginning?
I, the LORD—with the first of them
    and with the last—I am he."

5 The islands have seen it and fear;
    the ends of the earth tremble.
They approach and come forward;
6    they help each other
    and say to their companions, "Be strong!"
7 The metalworker encourages the goldsmith,
    and the one who smooths with the hammer
    spurs on the one who strikes the anvil.
One says of the welding, "It is good."
    The other nails down the idol so it will not topple.

8 "But you, Israel, my servant,
    Jacob, whom I have chosen,
    you descendants of Abraham my friend,
9 I took you from the ends of the earth,
    from its farthest corners I called you.
I said, 'You are my servant';
    I have chosen you and have not rejected you.
10 So do not fear, for I am with you;
    do not be dismayed, for I am your God.
I will strengthen you and help you;
    I will uphold you with my righteous right hand.

11 "All who rage against you
    will surely be ashamed and disgraced;
those who oppose you
    will be as nothing and perish.
12 Though you search for your enemies,
    you will not find them.
Those who wage war against you
    will be as nothing at all.
13 For I am the LORD your God
    who takes hold of your right hand
and says to you, Do not fear;
    I will help you.
14 Do not be afraid, you worm Jacob,
    little Israel, do not fear,
for I myself will help you," declares the LORD,
    your Redeemer, the Holy One of Israel.
15 "See, I will make you into a threshing sledge,
    new and sharp, with many teeth.
You will thresh the mountains and crush them,
    and reduce the hills to chaff.
16 You will winnow them, the wind will pick them up,
    and a gale will blow them away.

## Amplified Bible

30 Even youths shall faint and be weary, and [selected]
young men shall feebly stumble *and* fall exhausted;
31 But those who wait for the Lord [who expect, look for,
and hope in Him] shall change *and* renew their strength
*and* power; they shall lift their wings *and* mount up [close
to God] as eagles [mount up to the sun]; they shall run
and not be weary, they shall walk and not faint *or* become
tired. [Heb. 12:1-3.]

**41** Listen in silence before Me, O islands *and* regions
bordering on the sea! And let the people gather
*and* renew their strength [for the argument; let them offer their strongest arguments]! Let them come near, then
let them speak; let us come near together for judgment
[and decide the point at issue between us concerning the
enemy advancing from the east].
2 Who has roused up one [Cyrus] from the east, whom
He calls in righteousness to His service *and* whom victory
meets at every step? He [the Lord] subdues nations before
him and makes him ruler over kings. He turns them to
dust with the sword [of Cyrus], and to driven straw *and*
chaff with his bow. [Ezra 1:2.]
3 He [Cyrus] pursues them and passes safely *and* unhindered, even by a way his feet had not trod *and* so swiftly
that his feet do not touch the ground.
4 Who has prepared and done this, calling forth *and*
guiding the destinies of the generations [of the nations]
from the beginning? I, the Lord—the first [existing before history began] and with the last [an ever-present, unchanging God]—I am He.
5 The islands *and* coastlands have seen and fear; the
ends of the earth tremble. They draw near and come;
6 They help every one his neighbor and say to his brother [in his tiresome idol making], Be of good courage!
7 So the carpenter encourages the goldsmith, *and* he
who smooths [the metal] with the hammer [encourages]
him who smites the anvil, saying of the soldering, That
is good! And he fastens it with nails so that it cannot be
moved.
8 But you, Israel, My servant, Jacob, whom I have chosen, the offspring of Abraham My friend, [Heb. 2:16;
James 2:23.]
9 You whom I [the Lord] have taken from the ends of the
earth and have called from the corners of it, and said to
you, You are My servant—I have chosen you and not cast
you off [even though you are exiled].
10 Fear not [there is nothing to fear], for I am with you;
do not look around you in terror *and* be dismayed, for I am
your God. I will strengthen *and* harden you to difficulties,
yes, I will help you; yes, I will hold you up *and* retain you
with My [victorious] right hand of rightness *and* justice.
[Acts 18:10.]
11 Behold, all they who are enraged *and* inflamed against
you shall be put to shame and confounded; they who strive
against you shall be as nothing and shall perish.
12 You shall seek those who contend with you but shall
not find them; they who war against you shall be as nothing, as nothing at all.
13 For I the Lord your God hold your right hand; I am the
Lord, Who says to you, Fear not; I will help you!
14 Fear not, you worm Jacob, you men of Israel! I will
help you, says the Lord; your Redeemer is the Holy One
of Israel.
15 Behold, I will make you to be a new, sharp, threshing
instrument which has teeth; you shall thresh the mountains and beat them small, and shall make the hills like
chaff.
16 You shall winnow them, and the wind shall carry them
away, and the tempest *or* whirlwind shall scatter them.

---

[a] 2 Or *east, / whom victory meets at every step*

## New International Version

But you will rejoice in the LORD
and glory in the Holy One of Israel.

17 "The poor and needy search for water,
but there is none;
their tongues are parched with thirst.
But I the LORD will answer them;
I, the God of Israel, will not forsake them.
18 I will make rivers flow on barren heights,
and springs within the valleys.
I will turn the desert into pools of water,
and the parched ground into springs.
19 I will put in the desert
the cedar and the acacia, the myrtle and the olive.
I will set junipers in the wasteland,
the fir and the cypress together,
20 so that people may see and know,
may consider and understand,
that the hand of the LORD has done this,
that the Holy One of Israel has created it.

21 "Present your case," says the LORD.
"Set forth your arguments," says Jacob's King.
22 "Tell us, you idols,
what is going to happen.
Tell us what the former things were,
so that we may consider them
and know their final outcome.
Or declare to us the things to come,
23    tell us what the future holds,
so we may know that you are gods.
Do something, whether good or bad,
so that we will be dismayed and filled with fear.
24 But you are less than nothing
and your works are utterly worthless;
whoever chooses you is detestable.

25 "I have stirred up one from the north, and he comes—
one from the rising sun who calls on my name.
He treads on rulers as if they were mortar,
as if he were a potter treading the clay.
26 Who told of this from the beginning, so we could
know,
or beforehand, so we could say, 'He was right'?
No one told of this,
no one foretold it,
no one heard any words from you.
27 I was the first to tell Zion, 'Look, here they are!'
I gave to Jerusalem a messenger of good news.
28 I look but there is no one—
no one among the gods to give counsel,
no one to give answer when I ask them.
29 See, they are all false!
Their deeds amount to nothing;
their images are but wind and confusion.

### The Servant of the LORD

**42** "Here is my servant, whom I uphold,
my chosen one in whom I delight;
I will put my Spirit on him,
and he will bring justice to the nations.

## Amplified Bible

And you shall rejoice in the Lord, you shall glory in the
Holy One of Israel.

17 The poor and needy are seeking water when there is
none; their tongues are parched with thirst. I the Lord will
answer them; I, the God of Israel, will not forsake them.
18 I will open rivers on the bare heights, and fountains in
the midst of the valleys; I will make the wilderness a pool
of water, and the dry land springs of water.
19 I will plant in the wilderness the cedar, the acacia, the
myrtle, and the wild olive; I will set the cypress in the desert, the plane [tree] and the pine [tree] together,
20 That men may see and know and consider and understand together that the hand of the Lord has done this,
that the Holy One of Israel has created it.
21 [You idols made by men's hands, prove your divinity!]
Produce your cause [set forth your case], says the Lord.
Bring forth your strong proofs, says the King of Jacob.
22 Let them bring them forth and tell us what is to happen. Let them tell us the former things, what they are, that
we may consider them and know the outcome of them; or
declare to us the things to come.
23 Tell us the things that are to come hereafter, that we
may know that you are gods; yes, do good or do evil [some-
thing or other], that we may stare in astonishment and be
dismayed as we behold [the miracle] together!
24 Behold, you [idols] are nothing, and your work is
nothing! The worshiper who chooses you is an abomination [extremely disgusting and shamefully vile in God's
sight]. [I Cor. 8:4.]
25 I have raised up and impelled to action one from the
north a [Cyrus], and he comes; from the rising of the sun
he calls upon My name [recognizing that his victories
have been granted to him by Me]. And he shall tread
upon rulers and deputies as upon mortar and as the potter
treads clay. [He comes with the suddenness of a comet,
but none of the idol oracles of the nations has anticipated
it.] [II Chron. 36:23; Ezra 1:1-3.]
26 [What idol] has declared this from the beginning, that
we could know? And beforetime, that we could say that he
is [unquestionably] right? Yes, there is none who declares
it, yes, there is none who proclaims it; yes, [for the truth
is, O you dumb idols] there is none who hears you speak!
27 I [the Lord] first gave to Zion the announcement,
Behold, [the Jews will be restored to their own land, and
the man Cyrus shall be raised up who will deliver them]
behold them! And to Jerusalem I gave a herald [Isaiah]
bringing the good news. [Isa. 40:9; 52:7.]
28 For I look [upon the heathen prophets and the priests
of pagan practices] and there is no man among them [who
could predict these events], and among these [idols] there
is no counselor who, when I ask of him, can answer a word.
29 Behold, these [pagan prophets and priests] are all
emptiness (falseness and futility)! Their works are worthless; their molten images are empty wind (confusion and
waste).

**42** Behold my b Servant, Whom I uphold, My elect in
Whom My soul delights! I have put My Spirit upon
Him; He will bring forth justice and right and reveal truth
to the nations. [Matt. 3:16, 17.]

---

a Cyrus came from the east (Isa. 41:2), but defeated a number of
kingdoms north of Babylon early in his reign. Palestinian authors
frequently perceived invasions as coming primarily from the north.
b This is the first of the famous prophecies concerning the great
future "Servant of the Lord" (Isa. 42:1-7; 49:1-9; 50:4-9; 52:13-53:12).
Interpreters have struggled with the question, "Who is meant by 'the
servant'?" Some think the "servant of the Lord" is the people of Israel.
Others think it makes reference to the faithful part of the people, the
"ideal" people of Israel. Still others think of the prophets as a group.
Another large group of scholars believes that the "Servant of the Lord"
is the Messiah, the One Who will establish God's kingdom on earth.

## New International Version

2 He will not shout or cry out,
    or raise his voice in the streets.
3 A bruised reed he will not break,
    and a smoldering wick he will not snuff out.
In faithfulness he will bring forth justice;
4    he will not falter or be discouraged
till he establishes justice on earth.
    In his teaching the islands will put their hope."

5 This is what God the LORD says—
    the Creator of the heavens, who stretches them out,
    who spreads out the earth with all that springs
        from it,
    who gives breath to its people,
        and life to those who walk on it:
6 "I, the LORD, have called you in righteousness;
    I will take hold of your hand.
I will keep you and will make you
    to be a covenant for the people
    and a light for the Gentiles,
7 to open eyes that are blind,
    to free captives from prison
    and to release from the dungeon those who sit in
        darkness.

8 "I am the LORD; that is my name!
    I will not yield my glory to another
    or my praise to idols.
9 See, the former things have taken place,
    and new things I declare;
before they spring into being
    I announce them to you."

### Song of Praise to the LORD
10 Sing to the LORD a new song,
    his praise from the ends of the earth,
you who go down to the sea, and all that is in it,
    you islands, and all who live in them.
11 Let the wilderness and its towns raise their voices;
    let the settlements where Kedar lives rejoice.
Let the people of Sela sing for joy;
    let them shout from the mountaintops.
12 Let them give glory to the LORD
    and proclaim his praise in the islands.
13 The LORD will march out like a champion,
    like a warrior he will stir up his zeal;
with a shout he will raise the battle cry
    and will triumph over his enemies.

14 "For a long time I have kept silent,
    I have been quiet and held myself back.
But now, like a woman in childbirth,
    I cry out, I gasp and pant.
15 I will lay waste the mountains and hills
    and dry up all their vegetation;
I will turn rivers into islands
    and dry up the pools.
16 I will lead the blind by ways they have not known,
    along unfamiliar paths I will guide them;
I will turn the darkness into light before them
    and make the rough places smooth.
These are the things I will do;
    I will not forsake them.
17 But those who trust in idols,
    who say to images, 'You are our gods,'
    will be turned back in utter shame.

### Israel Blind and Deaf
18 "Hear, you deaf;
    look, you blind, and see!
19 Who is blind but my servant,
    and deaf like the messenger I send?
Who is blind like the one in covenant with me,
    blind like the servant of the LORD?

## Amplified Bible

2 He will not cry or shout aloud or cause His voice to be heard in the street.
3 A bruised reed He will not break, and a dimly burning wick He will not quench; He will bring forth justice in truth. [Matt. 12:17-21.]
4 He will not fail or become weak or be crushed and discouraged till He has established justice in the earth; and the islands and coastal regions shall wait hopefully for Him and expect His direction and law. [Rom. 8:22-25.]
5 Thus says God the Lord—He Who created the heavens and stretched them forth, He Who spread abroad the earth and that which comes out of it, He Who gives breath to the people on it and spirit to those who walk in it:
6 I the Lord have called You [the Messiah] for a righteous purpose and in righteousness; I will take You by the hand and will keep You; I will give You for a covenant to the people [Israel], for a light to the nations [Gentiles],
7 To open the eyes of the blind, to bring out prisoners from the dungeon, and those who sit in darkness from the prison. [Matt. 12:18-21.]
8 I am the Lord; that is My name! And My glory I will not give to another, nor My praise to graven images.
9 Behold, the former things have come to pass, and new things I now declare; before they spring forth I tell you of them.
10 Sing to the Lord a new song, and His praise from the end of the earth! You who go down to the sea, and all that is in it, the islands and coastal regions and the inhabitants of them [sing a song such as has never been heard in the heathen world]!
11 Let the wilderness and its cities lift up their voices, the villages that Kedar inhabits. Let the inhabitants of the rock [Sela or Petra] sing; let them shout from the tops of the mountains!
12 Let them give glory to the Lord and declare His praise in the islands and coastal regions.
13 The Lord will go forth like a mighty man, He will rouse up His zealous indignation and vengeance like a warrior; He will cry, yes, He will shout aloud, He will do mightily against His enemies.
14 [Thus says the Lord] I have for a long time held My peace, I have been still and restrained Myself. Now I will cry out like a woman in travail, I will gasp and pant together.
15 I will lay waste the mountains and hills and dry up all their herbage; I will turn the rivers into islands, and I will dry up the pools.
16 And I will bring the blind by a way that they know not; I will lead them in paths that they have not known. I will make darkness into light before them and make uneven places into a plain. These things I have determined to do [for them]; and I will not leave them forsaken.
17 They shall be turned back, they shall be utterly put to shame, who trust in graven images, who say to molten images, You are our gods.
18 Hear, you deaf! And look, you blind, that you may see!
19 Who is blind but My servant [Israel]? Or deaf like My messenger whom I send? Who is blind like the one who is at peace with Me [who has been admitted to covenant relationship with Me]? Yes, who is blind like the Lord's servant?

## New International Version

20 You have seen many things, but you pay no attention;
  your ears are open, but you do not listen."
21 It pleased the LORD
    for the sake of his righteousness
    to make his law great and glorious.
22 But this is a people plundered and looted,
    all of them trapped in pits
    or hidden away in prisons.
  They have become plunder,
    with no one to rescue them;
  they have been made loot,
    with no one to say, "Send them back."

23 Which of you will listen to this
    or pay close attention in time to come?
24 Who handed Jacob over to become loot,
    and Israel to the plunderers?
  Was it not the LORD,
    against whom we have sinned?
  For they would not follow his ways;
    they did not obey his law.
25 So he poured out on them his burning anger,
    the violence of war.
  It enveloped them in flames, yet they did not
      understand;
    it consumed them, but they did not take it to heart.

### Israel's Only Savior

**43** But now, this is what the LORD says—
  he who created you, Jacob,
  he who formed you, Israel:
  "Do not fear, for I have redeemed you;
    I have summoned you by name; you are mine.
2 When you pass through the waters,
    I will be with you;
  and when you pass through the rivers,
    they will not sweep over you.
  When you walk through the fire,
    you will not be burned;
    the flames will not set you ablaze.
3 For I am the LORD your God,
    the Holy One of Israel, your Savior;
  I give Egypt for your ransom,
    Cush[a] and Seba in your stead.
4 Since you are precious and honored in my sight,
    and because I love you,
  I will give people in exchange for you,
    nations in exchange for your life.
5 Do not be afraid, for I am with you;
    I will bring your children from the east
    and gather you from the west.
6 I will say to the north, 'Give them up!'
    and to the south, 'Do not hold them back.'
  Bring my sons from afar
    and my daughters from the ends of the earth—
7 everyone who is called by my name,
    whom I created for my glory,
    whom I formed and made."

8 Lead out those who have eyes but are blind,
    who have ears but are deaf.
9 All the nations gather together
    and the peoples assemble.
  Which of their gods foretold this
    and proclaimed to us the former things?
  Let them bring in their witnesses to prove they were
      right,
    so that others may hear and say, "It is true."
10 "You are my witnesses," declares the LORD,
    "and my servant whom I have chosen,
  so that you may know and believe me
    and understand that I am he.

## Amplified Bible

20 You have seen many things, but you do not observe
or apprehend their true meaning. His ears are open, but
he hears not!
21 It was the Lord's pleasure for His righteousness' sake
[in accordance with a steadfast and consistent purpose]
to magnify instruction *and* revelation and glorify them.
22 But this is a people robbed and plundered; they are all
of them snared in holes and hidden in houses of bondage.
They have become a prey, with no one to deliver them, a
spoil, with no one to say, Restore them! [This shows the
condition that will ensue as Israel's punishment for not
recognizing the Servant of the Lord and the day of His
visit among them.] [Luke 19:41-44.]
23 Who is there among you who will give ear to this?
Who will listen and hear in the time to come?
24 Who gave up Jacob [the kingdom of Judah] for spoil,
and [the kingdom of] Israel to the robbers? Was it not the
Lord, He against Whom we [of Judah] have sinned and in
Whose ways they [of Israel] would not walk, neither were
they obedient to His law *or* His teaching?
25 Therefore He poured out upon [Israel] the fierceness
of His anger and the strength of battle. And it set him on
fire round about, yet he knew not [the lesson of repentance
which the Assyrian conquest was intended to teach]; it
burned him, but he did not lay it to heart.

**43** But now [in spite of past judgments for Israel's
sins], thus says the Lord, He Who created you,
O Jacob, and He Who formed you, O Israel: Fear not, for
I have redeemed you [ransomed you by paying a price instead of leaving you captives]; I have called you by your
name; you are Mine.
2 When you pass through the waters, I will be with you,
and through the rivers, they will not overwhelm you.
When you walk through the fire, you will not be burned *or*
scorched, nor will the flame kindle upon you.
3 For I am the Lord your God, the Holy One of Israel,
your Savior; I give Egypt [to the Babylonians] for your
ransom, Ethiopia and Seba [a province of Ethiopia] in exchange [for your release].
4 Because you are precious in My sight and honored,
and because I love you, I will give men in return for you
and peoples in exchange for your life.
5 Fear not, for I am with you; I will bring your offspring
from the east [where they are dispersed] and gather you
from the west. [Acts 18:10.]
6 I will say to the north, Give up! and to the south, Keep
not back. Bring My sons from afar and My daughters from
the ends of the earth—
7 Even everyone who is called by My name, whom I have
created for My glory, whom I have formed, whom I have
made.
8 Bring forth the blind people who have eyes and the
deaf who have ears.
9 Let all the nations be gathered together and let the
peoples be assembled. Who among [the idolaters] could
predict this [that Cyrus would be the deliverer of Israel]
and show us the former things? Let them bring their witnesses, that they may be justified, or let them hear and
acknowledge, It is the truth. [Ps. 123:3, 4.]
10 You are My witnesses, says the Lord, and My servant
whom I have chosen, that you may know Me, believe Me
*and* remain steadfast to Me, and understand that I am He.

---

*a* 3 That is, the upper Nile region

## New International Version

Before me no god was formed,
    nor will there be one after me.
¹¹ I, even I, am the LORD,
    and apart from me there is no savior.
¹² I have revealed and saved and proclaimed—
    I, and not some foreign god among you.
You are my witnesses," declares the LORD, "that I am
    God.
¹³   Yes, and from ancient days I am he.
No one can deliver out of my hand.
    When I act, who can reverse it?"

### God's Mercy and Israel's Unfaithfulness

¹⁴ This is what the LORD says—
    your Redeemer, the Holy One of Israel:
"For your sake I will send to Babylon
    and bring down as fugitives all the Babylonians,ᵃ
    in the ships in which they took pride.
¹⁵ I am the LORD, your Holy One,
    Israel's Creator, your King."

¹⁶ This is what the LORD says—
    he who made a way through the sea,
    a path through the mighty waters,
¹⁷ who drew out the chariots and horses,
    the army and reinforcements together,
and they lay there, never to rise again,
    extinguished, snuffed out like a wick:
¹⁸ "Forget the former things;
    do not dwell on the past.
¹⁹ See, I am doing a new thing!
    Now it springs up; do you not perceive it?
I am making a way in the wilderness
    and streams in the wasteland.
²⁰ The wild animals honor me,
    the jackals and the owls,
because I provide water in the wilderness
    and streams in the wasteland,
to give drink to my people, my chosen,
²¹   the people I formed for myself
    that they may proclaim my praise.

²² "Yet you have not called on me, Jacob,
    you have not wearied yourselves forᵇ me, Israel.
²³ You have not brought me sheep for burnt offerings,
    nor honored me with your sacrifices.
I have not burdened you with grain offerings
    nor wearied you with demands for incense.
²⁴ You have not bought any fragrant calamus for me,
    or lavished on me the fat of your sacrifices.
But you have burdened me with your sins
    and wearied me with your offenses.

²⁵ "I, even I, am he who blots out
    your transgressions, for my own sake,
    and remembers your sins no more.
²⁶ Review the past for me,
    let us argue the matter together;
    state the case for your innocence.
²⁷ Your first father sinned;
    those I sent to teach you rebelled against me.
²⁸ So I disgraced the dignitaries of your temple;
    I consigned Jacob to destructionᶜ
    and Israel to scorn.

## Amplified Bible

Before Me there was no God formed, neither shall there be after Me.
¹¹ I, even I, am the Lord, and besides Me there is no Savior.
¹² I have declared [the future] and have saved [the nation in times of danger], and I have shown [that I am God]—when there was no strange and alien god among you; therefore you are My witnesses, says the Lord, that I am God.
¹³ Yes, from the time of the first existence of day *and* from this day forth I am He; and there is no one who can deliver out of My hand. I will work, and who can hinder *or* reverse it?
¹⁴ Thus says the Lord, your Redeemer, the Holy One of Israel: For your sake I have sent [one] to Babylon, and I will bring down all of them as fugitives, [with] all their nobles, even the Chaldeans, into the ships over which they rejoiced.
¹⁵ I am the Lord, your Holy One, the Creator of Israel, your King.
¹⁶ Thus says the Lord, Who makes a way through the sea and a path through the mighty waters,
¹⁷ Who brings forth chariot and horse, army and mighty warrior. They lie down together, they cannot rise; they are extinguished, they are quenched like a lampwick:
¹⁸ Do not [earnestly] remember the former things; neither consider the things of old.
¹⁹ Behold, I am doing a new thing! Now it springs forth; do you not perceive *and* know it *and* will you not give heed to it? I will even make a way in the wilderness and rivers in the desert.
²⁰ The beasts of the field honor Me, the jackals and the ostriches, because I give waters in the wilderness *and* rivers in the desert, to give drink to My people, My chosen, [Isa. 41:17, 18; 48:21.]
²¹ The people I formed for Myself, that they may set forth My praise [and they shall do it].
²² Yet you have not called upon Me [much less toiled for Me], O Jacob; but you have been weary of Me, O Israel!
²³ You have not brought Me your sheep *and* goats for burnt offerings, or honored Me with your sacrifices. I have not required you to serve with an offering *or* treated you as a slave by demanding tribute or wearied you with offering incense.
²⁴ You have not bought Me sweet cane with money, or satiated Me with the fat of your sacrifices. But you have only burdened Me with your sins; you have wearied Me with your iniquities.
²⁵ I, even I, am He Who blots out *and* cancels your transgressions, for My own sake, and I will not remember your sins.
²⁶ Put Me in remembrance [remind Me of your merits]; let us plead *and* argue together. Set forth your case, that you may be justified (proved right).
²⁷ Your first father [Jacob, in particular] sinned, and your teachers [the priests and the prophets—your mediators] transgressed against Me.
²⁸ And so I will profane the chief ones of the sanctuary and will deliver Jacob to the curse (the ban, a solemn anathema or excommunication) and [will subject] Israel to reproaches *and* reviling.

---

ᵃ 14 Or *Chaldeans*   ᵇ 22 Or *Jacob; / surely you have grown weary of*
ᶜ 28 The Hebrew term refers to the irrevocable giving over of things or persons to the LORD, often by totally destroying them.

## New International Version

### Israel the Chosen

**44** "But now listen, Jacob, my servant,
Israel, whom I have chosen.
² This is what the LORD says—
he who made you, who formed you in the womb,
and who will help you:
Do not be afraid, Jacob, my servant,
Jeshurun,ᵃ whom I have chosen.
³ For I will pour water on the thirsty land,
and streams on the dry ground;
I will pour out my Spirit on your offspring,
and my blessing on your descendants.
⁴ They will spring up like grass in a meadow,
like poplar trees by flowing streams.
⁵ Some will say, 'I belong to the LORD';
others will call themselves by the name of Jacob;
still others will write on their hand, 'The LORD's,'
and will take the name Israel.

### The LORD, Not Idols

⁶ "This is what the LORD says—
Israel's King and Redeemer, the LORD Almighty:
I am the first and I am the last;
apart from me there is no God.
⁷ Who then is like me? Let him proclaim it.
Let him declare and lay out before me
what has happened since I established my ancient
people,
and what is yet to come—
yes, let them foretell what will come.
⁸ Do not tremble, do not be afraid.
Did I not proclaim this and foretell it long ago?
You are my witnesses. Is there any God besides me?
No, there is no other Rock; I know not one."

⁹ All who make idols are nothing,
and the things they treasure are worthless.
Those who would speak up for them are blind;
they are ignorant, to their own shame.
¹⁰ Who shapes a god and casts an idol,
which can profit nothing?
¹¹ People who do that will be put to shame;
such craftsmen are only human beings.
Let them all come together and take their stand;
they will be brought down to terror and shame.

¹² The blacksmith takes a tool
and works with it in the coals;
he shapes an idol with hammers,
he forges it with the might of his arm.
He gets hungry and loses his strength;
he drinks no water and grows faint.
¹³ The carpenter measures with a line
and makes an outline with a marker;
he roughs it out with chisels
and marks it with compasses.
He shapes it in human form,
human form in all its glory,
that it may dwell in a shrine.
¹⁴ He cut down cedars,
or perhaps took a cypress or oak.
He let it grow among the trees of the forest,
or planted a pine, and the rain made it grow.
¹⁵ It is used as fuel for burning;
some of it he takes and warms himself,
he kindles a fire and bakes bread.
But he also fashions a god and worships it;
he makes an idol and bows down to it.
¹⁶ Half of the wood he burns in the fire;
over it he prepares his meal,
he roasts his meat and eats his fill.

---

ᵃ 2 *Jeshurun* means *the upright one*, that is, Israel.

## Amplified Bible

**44** Yet now hear, O Jacob, My servant and Israel,
whom I have chosen.
² Thus says the Lord, Who made you and formed you
from the womb, Who will help you: Fear not, O Jacob, My
servant, and you Jeshurun [the upright one—applied to
Israel as a type of the Messiah], whom I have chosen.
³ For I will pour water upon him who is thirsty, and
floods upon the dry ground. I will pour My Spirit upon
your offspring, and My blessing upon your descendants.
[Isa. 32:15; 35:6, 7; Joel 2:28; John 7:37-39.]
⁴ And they shall spring up among the grass like willows
*or* poplars by the watercourses.
⁵ One will say, I am the Lord's; and another will call himself by the name of Jacob; and another will write [even
brand or tattoo] upon his hand, I am the Lord's, and surname himself by the [honorable] name of Israel.
⁶ Thus says the Lord, the King of Israel and his Redeemer, the Lord of hosts: I am the First and I am the Last;
besides Me there is no God. [Rev. 1:17; 2:8; 22:13.]
⁷ Who is like Me? Let him [stand and] proclaim it, declare it, and set [his proofs] in order before Me, since I
made *and* established the people of antiquity. [Who has
announced from of old] the things that are coming? Then
let them declare yet future things.
⁸ Fear not, nor be afraid [in the coming violent upheav-
als]; have I not told it to you from of old and declared it?
And you are My witnesses! Is there a God besides Me?
There is no [other] Rock; I know not any.
⁹ All who make graven idols are confusion, chaos, *and*
worthlessness. Their objects (idols) in which they delight
do not profit them, and their own witnesses (worshipers)
do not see or know, so that they are put to shame.
¹⁰ Who is [such a fool as] to fashion a god or cast a grav-
en image that is profitable for nothing?
¹¹ Behold, all his fellows shall be put to shame, and the
craftsmen, [how can they make a god?] they are but men.
Let them all be gathered together, let them stand forth;
they shall be terrified, they shall be put to shame together.
¹² The ironsmith sharpens *and* uses a chisel and works
it over the coals; he shapes [the core of the idol] with hammers and forges it with his strong arm. He becomes hungry and his strength fails; he drinks no water and is faint.
¹³ The carpenter stretches out a line, he marks it out
with a pencil *or* red ocher; he fashions [an idol] with planes
and marks it out with the compasses; and he shapes it to
have the figure of a man, with the beauty of a man, that it
may dwell in a house.
¹⁴ He hews for himself cedars, and takes the holm tree
and the oak and lets them grow strong for himself among
the trees of the forest; he plants a fir tree *or* an ash, and
the rain nourishes it.
¹⁵ Then it becomes fuel for a man to burn; a part of it
he takes and warms himself, yes, he kindles a fire and
bakes bread. [Then out of the remainder, the leavings]
he also makes a god and worships it! He [with his own
hands] makes it into a graven image and falls down and
worships it!
¹⁶ He burns part of the wood in the fire; with part of it
he [cooks and] eats flesh, he roasts meat and is satisfied.

## New International Version

He also warms himself and says,
"Ah! I am warm; I see the fire."
[17] From the rest he makes a god, his idol;
he bows down to it and worships.
He prays to it and says,
"Save me! You are my god!"
[18] They know nothing, they understand nothing;
their eyes are plastered over so they cannot see,
and their minds closed so they cannot understand.
[19] No one stops to think,
no one has the knowledge or understanding to say,
"Half of it I used for fuel;
I even baked bread over its coals,
I roasted meat and I ate.
Shall I make a detestable thing from what is left?
Shall I bow down to a block of wood?"
[20] Such a person feeds on ashes; a deluded heart
misleads him;
he cannot save himself, or say,
"Is not this thing in my right hand a lie?"

[21] "Remember these things, Jacob,
for you, Israel, are my servant.
I have made you, you are my servant;
Israel, I will not forget you.
[22] I have swept away your offenses like a cloud,
your sins like the morning mist.
Return to me,
for I have redeemed you."

[23] Sing for joy, you heavens, for the LORD has done this;
shout aloud, you earth beneath.
Burst into song, you mountains,
you forests and all your trees,
for the LORD has redeemed Jacob,
he displays his glory in Israel.

### Jerusalem to Be Inhabited

[24] "This is what the LORD says—
your Redeemer, who formed you in the womb:

I am the LORD,
the Maker of all things,
who stretches out the heavens,
who spreads out the earth by myself,
[25] who foils the signs of false prophets
and makes fools of diviners,
who overthrows the learning of the wise
and turns it into nonsense,
[26] who carries out the words of his servants
and fulfills the predictions of his messengers,

who says of Jerusalem, 'It shall be inhabited,'
of the towns of Judah, 'They shall be rebuilt,'
and of their ruins, 'I will restore them,'
[27] who says to the watery deep, 'Be dry,
and I will dry up your streams,'
[28] who says of Cyrus, 'He is my shepherd
and will accomplish all that I please;
he will say of Jerusalem, "Let it be rebuilt,"
and of the temple, "Let its foundations be laid."'

**45** "This is what the LORD says to his anointed,
to Cyrus, whose right hand I take hold of
to subdue nations before him
and to strip kings of their armor,
to open doors before him
so that gates will not be shut:
[2] I will go before you
and will level the mountains[a];
I will break down gates of bronze
and cut through bars of iron.

[a] 2 Dead Sea Scrolls and Septuagint; the meaning of the word in the
Masoretic Text is uncertain.

## Amplified Bible

Also he warms himself and says, Aha! I am warm, I have
seen the fire!
[17] And from what is left [of the log] he makes a god, his
graven idol. He falls down to it, he worships it and prays to
it and says, Deliver me, for you are my god!
[18] They do not know or understand, for their eyes God
has let become besmeared so that they cannot see, *and*
their minds as well so that they cannot understand.
[19] And no one considers in his mind, nor has he knowledge and understanding [enough] to say [to himself], I
have burned part of this log in the fire, and also I have
baked bread on its coals and have roasted meat and eaten
it. And shall I make the remainder of it into an abomination [the very essence of what is disgusting, detestable,
and shamefully vile in the eyes of a jealous God]? Shall I
fall down *and* worship the stock of a tree [a block of wood
without consciousness or life]?
[20] That kind of man feeds on ashes [and finds his satisfaction in ashes]! A deluded mind has led him astray, so
that he cannot release *and* save himself, or ask, Is not [this
thing I am holding] in my right hand a lie?
[21] Remember these things [earnestly], O Jacob, O Israel, for you are My servant! I formed you, you are My
servant; O Israel, you shall not be forgotten by Me.
[22] I have blotted out like a thick cloud your transgressions, and like a cloud your sins. Return to Me, for I have
redeemed you.
[23] Sing, O heavens, for the Lord has done it; shout, you
depths of the earth; break forth into singing, you mountains, O forest and every tree in it! For the Lord has redeemed Jacob, and He glorifies Himself in Israel.
[24] Thus says the Lord, your Redeemer, and He Who
formed you from the womb: I am the Lord, Who made all
things, Who alone stretched out the heavens, Who spread
out the earth by Myself [who was with Me]?—
[25] [I am the Lord] Who frustrates the signs *and* confounds the omens [upon which the false prophets' forecasts of the future are based] of the [boasting] liars and
makes fools of diviners, Who turns the wise backward and
makes their knowledge foolishness, [I Cor. 1:20.]
[26] [The Lord] Who confirms the word of His servant and
performs the counsel of His messengers, Who says of Jerusalem, She shall [again] be inhabited, and of the cities
of Judah, They shall [again] be built, and I will raise up
their ruins,
[27] Who says to the deep, Be dry, and I will dry up your
rivers,
[28] Who says of Cyrus, He is My shepherd (ruler), and he
shall perform all My pleasure *and* fulfill all My purpose—
even saying of Jerusalem, She shall [again] be built, and of
the temple, Your foundation shall [again] be laid.

**45** Thus says the Lord to His anointed, to Cyrus,
whose right hand I have held to subdue nations
before him, and I will unarm *and* ungird the loins of kings
to open doors before him, so that gates will not be shut.
[2] I will go before you and level the mountains [to make
the crooked places straight]; I will break in pieces the
doors of bronze and cut asunder the bars of iron.

## New International Version

<sup>3</sup> I will give you hidden treasures,
   riches stored in secret places,
so that you may know that I am the LORD,
   the God of Israel, who summons you by name.
<sup>4</sup> For the sake of Jacob my servant,
   of Israel my chosen,
I summon you by name
   and bestow on you a title of honor,
   though you do not acknowledge me.
<sup>5</sup> I am the LORD, and there is no other;
   apart from me there is no God.
I will strengthen you,
   though you have not acknowledged me,
<sup>6</sup> so that from the rising of the sun
   to the place of its setting
people may know there is none besides me.
   I am the LORD, and there is no other.
<sup>7</sup> I form the light and create darkness,
   I bring prosperity and create disaster;
   I, the LORD, do all these things.

<sup>8</sup> "You heavens above, rain down my righteousness;
   let the clouds shower it down.
Let the earth open wide,
   let salvation spring up,
let righteousness flourish with it;
   I, the LORD, have created it.

<sup>9</sup> "Woe to those who quarrel with their Maker,
   those who are nothing but potsherds
   among the potsherds on the ground.
Does the clay say to the potter,
   'What are you making?'
Does your work say,
   'The potter has no hands'?
<sup>10</sup> Woe to the one who says to a father,
   'What have you begotten?'
or to a mother,
   'What have you brought to birth?'

<sup>11</sup> "This is what the LORD says—
   the Holy One of Israel, and its Maker:
Concerning things to come,
   do you question me about my children,
   or give me orders about the work of my hands?
<sup>12</sup> It is I who made the earth
   and created mankind on it.
My own hands stretched out the heavens;
   I marshaled their starry hosts.
<sup>13</sup> I will raise up Cyrus<sup>a</sup> in my righteousness:
   I will make all his ways straight.
He will rebuild my city
   and set my exiles free,
but not for a price or reward,
   says the LORD Almighty."

<sup>14</sup> This is what the LORD says:

"The products of Egypt and the merchandise of Cush,<sup>b</sup>
   and those tall Sabeans—
they will come over to you
   and will be yours;
they will trudge behind you,
   coming over to you in chains.
They will bow down before you
   and plead with you, saying,
'Surely God is with you, and there is no other;
   there is no other god.'"

<sup>15</sup> Truly you are a God who has been hiding himself,
   the God and Savior of Israel.
<sup>16</sup> All the makers of idols will be put to shame and
      disgraced;
   they will go off into disgrace together.

## Amplified Bible

<sup>3</sup> And I will give you the treasures of darkness and hidden riches of secret places, that you may know that it is I, the Lord, the God of Israel, Who calls you by your name.
<sup>4</sup> For the sake of Jacob My servant, and of Israel My chosen, I have called you by your name. I have surnamed you, though you have not known Me.
<sup>5</sup> I am the Lord, and there is no one else; there is no God besides Me. I will gird *and* arm you, though you have not known Me,
<sup>6</sup> That men may know from the east *and* the rising of the sun *and* from the west *and* the setting of the sun that there is no God besides Me. I am the Lord, and no one else [is He].
<sup>7</sup> I form the light and create darkness, I make peace [national well-being] and I create [physical] <sup>a</sup>evil (calamity); I am the Lord, Who does all these things.
<sup>8</sup> Let fall in showers, you heavens, from above, and let the skies rain down righteousness [the pure, spiritual, heaven-born possibilities that have their foundation in the holy being of God]; let the earth open, and let them [skies and earth] sprout forth salvation, and let righteousness germinate *and* spring up [as plants do] together; I the Lord have created it.
<sup>9</sup> Woe to him who strives with his Maker!—a worthless piece of broken pottery among other pieces equally worthless [and yet presuming to strive with his Maker]! Shall the clay say to him who fashions it, What do you think you are making? or, Your work has no handles? [Rom. 9:20.]
<sup>10</sup> Woe to him [who complains against his parents that they have begotten him] who says to a father, What are you begetting? or to a woman, With what are you in travail?
<sup>11</sup> Thus says the Lord, the Holy One of Israel, and its Maker: Would you question Me about things to come concerning My children, and concerning the work of My hands [would you] command Me?
<sup>12</sup> I made the earth and created man upon it. I, with My hands, stretched out the heavens, and I commanded all their host.
<sup>13</sup> I will raise [Cyrus] up in righteousness [willing in every way that which is right and proper], and I will direct all his ways; he will build My city, and he will let My captives go, not for hire or for a bribe, says the Lord of hosts.
<sup>14</sup> Thus says the Lord: The labor *and* wealth of Egypt and the merchandise of Ethiopia and the Sabeans, men of stature, shall come over to you and they shall be yours; they shall follow you; in chains [of subjection to you] they shall come over, and they shall fall down before you; they shall make supplication to you, saying, Surely God is with you, and there is no other, no God besides Him. [I Cor. 14:25.]
<sup>15</sup> Truly You are a God Who hides Himself, O God of Israel, the Savior.
<sup>16</sup> They shall be put to shame, yes, confounded, all of them; they who are makers of idols shall go off into confusion together.

---

<sup>a</sup> 13 Hebrew *him*     <sup>b</sup> 14 That is, the upper Nile region

<sup>a</sup> Moral evil proceeds from the will of men, but physical evil proceeds from the will of God.

## New International Version

17 But Israel will be saved by the LORD
  with an everlasting salvation;
  you will never be put to shame or disgraced,
    to ages everlasting.

18 For this is what the LORD says—
  he who created the heavens,
    he is God;
  he who fashioned and made the earth,
    he founded it;
  he did not create it to be empty,
    but formed it to be inhabited—
  he says:
  "I am the LORD,
    and there is no other.
19 I have not spoken in secret,
    from somewhere in a land of darkness;
  I have not said to Jacob's descendants,
    'Seek me in vain.'
  I, the LORD, speak the truth;
    I declare what is right.

20 "Gather together and come;
    assemble, you fugitives from the nations.
  Ignorant are those who carry about idols of wood,
    who pray to gods that cannot save.
21 Declare what is to be, present it—
    let them take counsel together.
  Who foretold this long ago,
    who declared it from the distant past?
  Was it not I, the LORD?
    And there is no God apart from me,
  a righteous God and a Savior;
    there is none but me.

22 "Turn to me and be saved,
    all you ends of the earth;
  for I am God, and there is no other.
23 By myself I have sworn,
    my mouth has uttered in all integrity
    a word that will not be revoked:
  Before me every knee will bow;
    by me every tongue will swear.
24 They will say of me, 'In the LORD alone
    are deliverance and strength.'"
  All who have raged against him
    will come to him and be put to shame.
25 But all the descendants of Israel
    will find deliverance in the LORD
    and will make their boast in him.

### Gods of Babylon

**46** Bel bows down, Nebo stoops low;
    their idols are borne by beasts of burden.[a]
  The images that are carried about are burdensome,
    a burden for the weary.
2 They stoop and bow down together;
    unable to rescue the burden,
    they themselves go off into captivity.

3 "Listen to me, you descendants of Jacob,
    all the remnant of the people of Israel;
  you whom I have upheld since your birth,
    and have carried since you were born.
4 Even to your old age and gray hairs
    I am he, I am he who will sustain you.
  I have made you and I will carry you;
    I will sustain you and I will rescue you.

5 "With whom will you compare me or count me equal?
    To whom will you liken me that we may be
      compared?

## Amplified Bible

17 But Israel shall be saved by the Lord with an everlasting salvation; you shall not be put to shame or confounded to all eternity. [Heb. 5:9.]

18 For thus says the Lord—Who created the heavens, God Himself, Who formed the earth and made it, Who established it and did not create it to be a worthless waste; He formed it to be inhabited—I am the Lord, and there is no one else.

19 I have not spoken in secret, in a corner of the land of darkness; I did not call the descendants of Jacob [to a fruitless service], saying, Seek Me for nothing [but I promised them a just reward]. I, the Lord, speak righteousness (the truth—trustworthy, straightforward correspondence between deeds and words); I declare things that are right. [John 18:20.]

20 Assemble yourselves and come; draw near together, you survivors of the nations! They have no knowledge who carry about [in religious processions or into battle] their wooden idols and keep on praying to a god that cannot save.

21 Declare and bring forward your strong arguments [for praying to gods that cannot save]; yes, take counsel together. Who announced this [the rise of Cyrus and his conquests] beforehand (long ago)? [What god] declared it of old? Was it not I, the Lord? And there is no other God besides Me, a rigidly *and* uncompromisingly just *and* righteous God and Savior; there is none besides Me.

22 Look to Me and be saved, all the ends of the earth! For I am God, and there is no other.

23 I have sworn by Myself, the word is gone out of My mouth in righteousness and shall not return, that unto Me every knee shall bow, every tongue shall swear [allegiance]. [Rom. 14:11; Phil. 2:10, 11; Heb. 6:13.]

24 Only in the Lord shall one say, I have righteousness (salvation and victory) and strength [to achieve]. To Him shall all come who were incensed against Him, and they shall be ashamed. [I Cor. 1:30, 31.]

25 In the Lord shall all the offspring of Israel be justified (enjoy righteousness, salvation, and victory) and shall glory.

**46** Bel bows down, Nebo stoops [gods of Babylon, whose idols are being carried off]; their idols are on the beasts [of burden] and on the cattle. These things that you carry about are loaded as burdens on the weary beasts.

2 [The gods] stoop, they bow down together; they cannot save [their own idols], but are themselves going into captivity.

3 Listen to Me [says the Lord], O house of Jacob, and all the remnant of the house of Israel, you who have been borne by Me from your birth, carried from the womb:

4 Even to your old age I am He, and even to hair white with age will I carry you. I have made, and I will bear; yes, I will carry and will save you.

5 To whom will you liken Me and make Me equal and compare Me, that we may be alike? [Isa. 40:18-20.]

---

a 1 Or *are but beasts and cattle*

## New International Version

### Amplified Bible

<table>
<tr>
<td>

[6] Some pour out gold from their bags
and weigh out silver on the scales;
they hire a goldsmith to make it into a god,
and they bow down and worship it.
[7] They lift it to their shoulders and carry it;
they set it up in its place, and there it stands.
From that spot it cannot move.
Even though someone cries out to it, it cannot answer;
it cannot save them from their troubles.

[8] "Remember this, keep it in mind,
take it to heart, you rebels.
[9] Remember the former things, those of long ago;
I am God, and there is no other;
I am God, and there is none like me.
[10] I make known the end from the beginning,
from ancient times, what is still to come.
I say, 'My purpose will stand,
and I will do all that I please.'
[11] From the east I summon a bird of prey;
from a far-off land, a man to fulfill my purpose.
What I have said, that I will bring about;
what I have planned, that I will do.
[12] Listen to me, you stubborn-hearted,
you who are now far from my righteousness.
[13] I am bringing my righteousness near,
it is not far away;
and my salvation will not be delayed.
I will grant salvation to Zion,
my splendor to Israel.

</td>
<td>

[6] They lavish gold out of the cup *or* bag, weigh out silver on the scales, and hire a goldsmith, and he fashions it into a god; [then] they fall down, yes, they worship it!
[7] They bear it upon their shoulders [in religious processions or into battle]; they carry it and set it down in its place, and it cannot move from its place. Even if one cries to it for help, yet [the idol] cannot answer or save him out of his distress.
[8] [Earnestly] remember this, be ashamed *and* own yourselves guilty; bring it again to mind *and* lay it to heart, O you rebels!
[9] [Earnestly] remember the former things, [which I did] of old; for I am God, and there is no one else; I am God, and there is none like Me,
[10] Declaring the end *and* the result from the beginning, and from ancient times the things that are not yet done, saying, My counsel shall stand, and I will do all My pleasure *and* purpose,
[11] Calling a ravenous bird from the east—the man [Cyrus] who executes My counsel from a far country. Yes, I have spoken, and I will bring it to pass; I have purposed it, and I will do it.
[12] Listen to Me, you stiff-hearted *and* you who have lost heart, you who are far from righteousness (from uprightness and right standing with God, and from His righteous deliverance).
[13] I bring near My righteousness [in the deliverance of Israel], it will not be far off; and My salvation shall not tarry. And I will put salvation in Zion, for Israel My glory [yes, give salvation in Zion and My glory to Israel].

</td>
</tr>
</table>

### The Fall of Babylon

<table>
<tr>
<td>

**47** "Go down, sit in the dust,
Virgin Daughter Babylon;
sit on the ground without a throne,
queen city of the Babylonians.[a]
No more will you be called
tender or delicate.
[2] Take millstones and grind flour;
take off your veil.
Lift up your skirts, bare your legs,
and wade through the streams.
[3] Your nakedness will be exposed
and your shame uncovered.
I will take vengeance;
I will spare no one."

[4] Our Redeemer—the LORD Almighty is his name—
is the Holy One of Israel.

[5] "Sit in silence, go into darkness,
queen city of the Babylonians;
no more will you be called
queen of kingdoms.
[6] I was angry with my people
and desecrated my inheritance;
I gave them into your hand,
and you showed them no mercy.
Even on the aged
you laid a very heavy yoke.
[7] You said, 'I am forever—
the eternal queen!'
But you did not consider these things
or reflect on what might happen.

[8] "Now then, listen, you lover of pleasure,
lounging in your security
and saying to yourself,
'I am, and there is none besides me.
I will never be a widow
or suffer the loss of children.'

</td>
<td>

**47** Come down, and sit in the dust, O Virgin Daughter of Babylon; sit on the ground [in abject humiliation]; there is no throne for you, O Daughter of the Chaldeans, for you shall no longer be called dainty and delicate.
[2] Take the millstones [like the poorest female slave of the household does] and grind meal; take off your veil *and* uncover your hair. Remove your skirt, bare your leg, wade through the rivers [at the command of your captors].
[3] Your nakedness shall be exposed, and your shame shall be seen. I will take vengeance, and I will spare no man [none I encounter will be able to resist Me],
[4] [Says] our Redeemer—the Lord of hosts is His name—the Holy One of Israel.
[5] Sit in silence and go into darkness, O Daughter of the Chaldeans; for you shall no more be called the lady *and* mistress of kingdoms.
[6] I was angry with My people, I profaned My inheritance [Judah]; and I gave them into your hand [Babylon]. You showed them no mercy; upon the old people you made your yoke very heavy.
[7] And you said, I shall be the mistress forever! So you did not lay these things to heart, nor did you [seriously] remember the certain, ultimate end of such conduct.
[8] Therefore now, hear this, you who love pleasures *and* are given over to them, you who dwell safely *and* sit securely, who say in your mind, I am [the mistress] and there is no one else besides me. I shall not sit as a widow, nor shall I know the loss of children.

</td>
</tr>
</table>

---

[a] 1 Or *Chaldeans*; also in verse 5

## New International Version

⁹Both of these will overtake you
      in a moment, on a single day:
      loss of children and widowhood.
   They will come upon you in full measure,
      in spite of your many sorceries
      and all your potent spells.
¹⁰You have trusted in your wickedness
      and have said, 'No one sees me.'
   Your wisdom and knowledge mislead you
      when you say to yourself,
      'I am, and there is none besides me.'
¹¹Disaster will come upon you,
      and you will not know how to conjure it away.
   A calamity will fall upon you
      that you cannot ward off with a ransom;
   a catastrophe you cannot foresee
      will suddenly come upon you.

¹²"Keep on, then, with your magic spells
      and with your many sorceries,
      which you have labored at since childhood.
   Perhaps you will succeed,
      perhaps you will cause terror.
¹³All the counsel you have received has only worn you
         out!
      Let your astrologers come forward,
   those stargazers who make predictions month by
         month,
      let them save you from what is coming upon you.
¹⁴Surely they are like stubble;
      the fire will burn them up.
   They cannot even save themselves
      from the power of the flame.
   These are not coals for warmth;
      this is not a fire to sit by.
¹⁵That is all they are to you—
      these you have dealt with
      and labored with since childhood.
   All of them go on in their error;
      there is not one that can save you.

### Stubborn Israel

**48** "Listen to this, you descendants of Jacob,
      you who are called by the name of Israel
      and come from the line of Judah,
   you who take oaths in the name of the LORD
      and invoke the God of Israel—
      but not in truth or righteousness—
²you who call yourselves citizens of the holy city
      and claim to rely on the God of Israel—
      the LORD Almighty is his name:
³I foretold the former things long ago,
      my mouth announced them and I made them
         known;
      then suddenly I acted, and they came to pass.
⁴For I knew how stubborn you were;
      your neck muscles were iron,
      your forehead was bronze.
⁵Therefore I told you these things long ago;
      before they happened I announced them to you
   so that you could not say,
      'My images brought them about;
      my wooden image and metal god ordained them.'
⁶You have heard these things; look at them all.
      Will you not admit them?

   "From now on I will tell you of new things,
      of hidden things unknown to you.
⁷They are created now, and not long ago;
      you have not heard of them before today.
   So you cannot say,
      'Yes, I knew of them.'

## Amplified Bible

⁹But these two things shall come to you in a moment,
in one day: loss of children and widowhood. They shall
come upon you in full measure, in spite of the multitude of
[your claims to] power given you by the assistance of evil
spirits, in spite of the great abundance of your enchantments. [Rev. 18:7, 8.]
¹⁰For you [Babylon] have trusted in your wickedness;
you have said, No one sees me. Your wisdom and your
knowledge led you astray, and you said in your heart *and*
mind, I am, and there is no one besides me.
¹¹Therefore shall evil come upon you; you shall not
know the dawning of it *or* how to charm it away. And a
disaster *and* evil shall fall upon you that you shall not be
able to atone for [with all your offerings to your gods]; and
desolation shall come upon you suddenly, about which you
shall know nothing *or* how to avert it.
¹²Persist, then, with your enchantments and the multitude of your sorceries [Babylon], in which you have labored from your youth; and see if perhaps you will be able
to profit, if you will prevail *and* strike terror!
¹³You are wearied with your many counsels *and* plans.
Let now the astrologers, the stargazers, and the monthly
prognosticators stand up and make known to you *and* save
you from the things that shall come upon you [Babylon].
¹⁴Behold, they are like stubble; the fire consumes them.
They cannot even deliver themselves from the power of
the flame [much less deliver the nation]. There is no coal
for warming *or* fire before which to sit!
¹⁵Such to you shall they [the astrologers and their kind]
be, those with whom you have labored *and* such their fate,
those who have done business with you from your youth;
they will wander, every one to his own quarter *and* in his
own direction. No one will save you.

**48** Hear this, O house of Jacob, who are called by the
      name of Israel and who come forth from the seed
of Judah, you who swear allegiance by the name of the
Lord and make mention of the God of Israel—but not in
truth *and* sincerity, nor in righteousness (rightness and
moral and spiritual rectitude in every area and relation)—
²For they call themselves [citizens] of the holy city and
depend on the God of Israel—the Lord of hosts is His
name.
³I have declared from the beginning the former things
[which happened in times past to Israel]; they went forth
from My mouth and I made them known; then suddenly I
did them, and they came to pass [says the Lord].
⁴Because I knew that you were obstinate, and your neck
was an iron sinew and your brow was brass,
⁵Therefore I have declared things to come to you from
of old; before they came to pass I announced them to you,
so that you could not say, My idol has done them, and my
graven image and my molten image have commanded
them.
⁶You have heard [these things foretold], now you see
this fulfillment. And will you not bear witness to it? I show
you specified new things from this time forth, even hidden
things [kept in reserve] which you have not known.
⁷They are created now [called into being by the prophetic word], and not long ago; and before today you have
never heard of them, lest you should say, Behold, I knew
them!

## New International Version

<sup>8</sup>You have neither heard nor understood;
  from of old your ears have not been open.
Well do I know how treacherous you are;
  you were called a rebel from birth.
<sup>9</sup>For my own name's sake I delay my wrath;
  for the sake of my praise I hold it back from you,
  so as not to destroy you completely.
<sup>10</sup>See, I have refined you, though not as silver;
  I have tested you in the furnace of affliction.
<sup>11</sup>For my own sake, for my own sake, I do this.
  How can I let myself be defamed?
  I will not yield my glory to another.

### Israel Freed

<sup>12</sup>"Listen to me, Jacob,
  Israel, whom I have called:
I am he;
  I am the first and I am the last.
<sup>13</sup>My own hand laid the foundations of the earth,
  and my right hand spread out the heavens;
when I summon them,
  they all stand up together.

<sup>14</sup>"Come together, all of you, and listen:
  Which of the idols has foretold these things?
The LORD's chosen ally
  will carry out his purpose against Babylon;
  his arm will be against the Babylonians.<sup>a</sup>
<sup>15</sup>I, even I, have spoken;
  yes, I have called him.
I will bring him,
  and he will succeed in his mission.

<sup>16</sup>"Come near me and listen to this:

"From the first announcement I have not spoken in
    secret;
  at the time it happens, I am there."

And now the Sovereign LORD has sent me,
  endowed with his Spirit.

<sup>17</sup>This is what the LORD says—
  your Redeemer, the Holy One of Israel:
"I am the LORD your God,
  who teaches you what is best for you,
  who directs you in the way you should go.
<sup>18</sup>If only you had paid attention to my commands,
  your peace would have been like a river,
  your well-being like the waves of the sea.
<sup>19</sup>Your descendants would have been like the sand,
  your children like its numberless grains;
their name would never be blotted out
  nor destroyed from before me."

<sup>20</sup>Leave Babylon,
  flee from the Babylonians!
Announce this with shouts of joy
  and proclaim it.
Send it out to the ends of the earth;
  say, "The LORD has redeemed his servant Jacob."
<sup>21</sup>They did not thirst when he led them through the
    deserts;
  he made water flow for them from the rock;
he split the rock
  and water gushed out.

<sup>22</sup>"There is no peace," says the LORD, "for the wicked."

### The Servant of the LORD

**49** Listen to me, you islands;
  hear this, you distant nations:
Before I was born the LORD called me;
  from my mother's womb he has spoken my name.

<sup>a</sup> 14 Or *Chaldeans*; also in verse 20

## Amplified Bible

<sup>8</sup>Yes, you have never heard, yes, you have never known;
yes, from of old your ear has not been opened. For I, the
Lord, knew that you, O house of Israel, dealt very treacherously; you were called a transgressor *and* a rebel [in re-
volt] from your birth.
<sup>9</sup>For My name's sake I defer My anger, and for the sake
of My praise I restrain it for you, that I may not cut you off.
<sup>10</sup>Behold, I have refined you, but not as silver; I have
tried *and* chosen you in the furnace of affliction.
<sup>11</sup>For My own sake, for My own sake, I do it [I refrain
and do not utterly destroy you]; for why should I permit My
name to be polluted *and* profaned [which it would be if the
Lord completely destroyed His chosen people]? And I will
not give My glory to another [by permitting the worshipers of idols to triumph over you].
<sup>12</sup>Listen to Me, O Jacob, and Israel, My called [ones]: I
am He; I am the First, I also am the Last. [Isa. 41:4.]
<sup>13</sup>Yes, My hand has laid the foundation of the earth, and
My right hand has spread out the heavens; when I call to
them, they stand forth together [to execute My decrees].
<sup>14</sup>Assemble yourselves, all of you, and hear! Who
among them [the gods and Chaldean astrologers] has
foretold these things? The Lord has loved him [Cyrus of
Persia]; he will do His pleasure *and* purpose on Babylon,
and his arm will be against the Chaldeans.
<sup>15</sup>I, even I, have foretold it; yes, I have called him
[Cyrus]; I have brought him, and [the Lord] shall make
his way prosperous.
<sup>16</sup>Come near to me and listen to this: I have not spoken
in secret from the beginning; from the time that it happened, I was there. And now the Lord God has sent His
Spirit in *and* with me.
<sup>17</sup>Thus says the Lord, your Redeemer, the Holy One of
Israel: I am the Lord your God, Who teaches you to profit,
Who leads you in the way that you should go.
<sup>18</sup>Oh, that you had hearkened to My commandments!
Then your peace *and* prosperity would have been like a
flowing river, and your righteousness [the holiness and
purity of the nation] like the [abundant] waves of the sea.
<sup>19</sup>Your offspring would have been like the sand, and
your descendants like the offspring of the sea; their name
would not be cut off or destroyed from before Me. [Gen.
13:16; Jer. 33:22; Luke 19:42.]
<sup>20</sup>Go forth out of Babylon, flee from the Chaldeans!
With a voice of singing declare, tell this, cause it to go
forth even to the end of the earth; say, The Lord has redeemed His servant Jacob!
<sup>21</sup>And they thirsted not when He led them through the
deserts; He caused the waters to flow out of the rock for
them; He split the rock also, and the waters gushed out.
<sup>22</sup>There is no peace, says the Lord, for the wicked.

**49** Listen to me, O isles *and* coastlands, and hearken, you peoples from afar. The Lord has called
me from the womb; from the body of my mother He has
named my name.

## New International Version

2 He made my mouth like a sharpened sword,
in the shadow of his hand he hid me;
he made me into a polished arrow
and concealed me in his quiver.
3 He said to me, "You are my servant,
Israel, in whom I will display my splendor."
4 But I said, "I have labored in vain;
I have spent my strength for nothing at all.
Yet what is due me is in the LORD's hand,
and my reward is with my God."

5 And now the LORD says—
he who formed me in the womb to be his servant
to bring Jacob back to him
and gather Israel to himself,
for I am[a] honored in the eyes of the LORD
and my God has been my strength—
6 he says:
"It is too small a thing for you to be my servant
to restore the tribes of Jacob
and bring back those of Israel I have kept.
I will also make you a light for the Gentiles,
that my salvation may reach to the ends of the
earth."

7 This is what the LORD says—
the Redeemer and Holy One of Israel—
to him who was despised and abhorred by the nation,
to the servant of rulers:
"Kings will see you and stand up,
princes will see and bow down,
because of the LORD, who is faithful,
the Holy One of Israel, who has chosen you."

### Restoration of Israel

8 This is what the LORD says:

"In the time of my favor I will answer you,
and in the day of salvation I will help you;
I will keep you and will make you
to be a covenant for the people,
to restore the land
and to reassign its desolate inheritances,
9 to say to the captives, 'Come out,'
and to those in darkness, 'Be free!'

"They will feed beside the roads
and find pasture on every barren hill.
10 They will neither hunger nor thirst,
nor will the desert heat or the sun beat down on
them.
He who has compassion on them will guide them
and lead them beside springs of water.
11 I will turn all my mountains into roads,
and my highways will be raised up.
12 See, they will come from afar—
some from the north, some from the west,
some from the region of Aswan.[b]

13 Shout for joy, you heavens;
rejoice, you earth;
burst into song, you mountains!
For the LORD comforts his people
and will have compassion on his afflicted ones.

14 But Zion said, "The LORD has forsaken me,
the Lord has forgotten me."

15 "Can a mother forget the baby at her breast
and have no compassion on the child she has
borne?
Though she may forget,
I will not forget you!

## Amplified Bible

2 And He has made my mouth like a sharp sword; in the shadow of His hand has He hid me and made me a polished arrow; in His quiver has He kept me close and concealed me.
3 And [the Lord] said to me, You are My [a] servant, Israel [you who strive with God and with men and prevail], in whom I will be glorified. [Gen. 32:28; Deut. 7:6; 26:18, 19; Eph. 1:4-6.]
4 Then I said, I have labored in vain, I have spent my strength for nothing and in empty futility; yet surely my right is with the Lord, and my recompense is with my God.
5 And now, says the Lord—Who formed me from the womb to be His servant to bring Jacob back to Him and that Israel might be gathered to Him and not be swept away, for I am honorable in the eyes of the Lord and my God has become my strength—
6 He says, It is too light a thing that you should be My servant to raise up the tribes of Jacob and to restore the survivors [of the judgments] of Israel; I will also give you for a light to the nations, that My salvation may extend to the end of the earth.
7 Thus says the Lord, the Redeemer of Israel, Israel's Holy One, to him whom man rejects and despises, to him whom the nations abhor, to the servant of rulers: Kings shall see you and arise; princes, and they shall prostrate themselves, because of the Lord, Who is faithful, the Holy One of Israel, Who has chosen you.
8 Thus says the Lord, In an acceptable and favorable time I have heard and answered you, and in a day of salvation I have helped you; and I will preserve you and give you for a covenant to the people, to raise up and establish the land [from its present state of ruin] and to apportion and cause them to inherit the desolate [moral wastes of heathenism, their] heritages, [II Cor. 6:2.]
9 Saying to those who are bound, Come forth, and to those who are in [spiritual] darkness, Show yourselves [come into the light of the Sun of righteousness]. They shall feed in [b] all the ways [in which they go], and their pastures shall be [not in deserts, but] on all the bare [grass-covered] hills.
10 They will not hunger or thirst, neither will mirage [mislead] or scorching wind or sun smite them; for He Who has mercy on them will lead them, and by springs of water will He guide them. [Rev. 7:16, 17.]
11 And I will make all My mountains a way, and My highways will be raised up.
12 Behold, these shall come from afar—and, behold, these from the north and from the west, and these from the land of Sinim (China).
13 Sing for joy, O heavens, and be joyful, O earth, and break forth into singing, O mountains! For the Lord has comforted His people and will have compassion upon His afflicted.
14 But Zion [Jerusalem, her people as seen in captivity] said, The Lord has forsaken me, and my Lord has forgotten me.
15 [And the Lord answered] Can a woman forget her nursing child, that she should not have compassion on the son of her womb? Yes, they may forget, yet I will not forget you.

---

[a] It is difficult to know positively to whom the Lord is speaking in these next verses—whether (1) to the Messiah, (2) to Israel, or (3) to Isaiah. The large majority of early authorities favored interpretation (1); later scholars incline toward interpretation (2). See also footnote on Isa. 42:1.
[b] *The Septuagint* (Greek translation of the Old Testament) here reads, "In all the highways they shall be fed, and there shall be pasture for them in all the paths."

---

[a] 5 Or *him, / but Israel would not be gathered; / yet I will be*   [b] 12 Dead Sea Scrolls; Masoretic Text *Sinim*

## New International Version

[16] See, I have engraved you on the palms of my hands;
  your walls are ever before me.
[17] Your children hasten back,
  and those who laid you waste depart from you.
[18] Lift up your eyes and look around;
  all your children gather and come to you.
As surely as I live," declares the LORD,
  "you will wear them all as ornaments;
  you will put them on, like a bride.

[19] "Though you were ruined and made desolate
  and your land laid waste,
now you will be too small for your people,
  and those who devoured you will be far away.
[20] The children born during your bereavement
  will yet say in your hearing,
'This place is too small for us;
  give us more space to live in.'
[21] Then you will say in your heart,
  'Who bore me these?
I was bereaved and barren;
  I was exiled and rejected.
  Who brought these up?
I was left all alone,
  but these—where have they come from?'"

[22] This is what the Sovereign LORD says:

"See, I will beckon to the nations,
  I will lift up my banner to the peoples;
they will bring your sons in their arms
  and carry your daughters on their hips.
[23] Kings will be your foster fathers,
  and their queens your nursing mothers.
They will bow down before you with their faces to the ground;
  they will lick the dust at your feet.
Then you will know that I am the LORD;
  those who hope in me will not be disappointed."

[24] Can plunder be taken from warriors,
  or captives be rescued from the fierce[a]?

[25] But this is what the LORD says:

"Yes, captives will be taken from warriors,
  and plunder retrieved from the fierce;
I will contend with those who contend with you,
  and your children I will save.
[26] I will make your oppressors eat their own flesh;
  they will be drunk on their own blood, as with wine.
Then all mankind will know
  that I, the LORD, am your Savior,
  your Redeemer, the Mighty One of Jacob."

### Israel's Sin and the Servant's Obedience

**50** This is what the LORD says:

"Where is your mother's certificate of divorce
  with which I sent her away?
Or to which of my creditors
  did I sell you?
Because of your sins you were sold;
  because of your transgressions your mother was
    sent away.
[2] When I came, why was there no one?
  When I called, why was there no one to answer?

[a] 24 Dead Sea Scrolls, Vulgate and Syriac (see also Septuagint and
verse 25); Masoretic Text righteous

## Amplified Bible

[16] Behold, I have indelibly imprinted (tattooed a picture of) you on the palm of each of My hands; [O Zion] your walls are continually before Me.
[17] Your children *and* your builders make haste; your destroyers and those who laid you waste go forth from you.
[18] Lift up your eyes round about and see [the returning exiles, ready to rebuild Jerusalem]; all these gather together and come to you. As I live, says the Lord, you [Zion] shall surely clothe yourself with them all as with an ornament and bind them on you as a bride does.
[19] For your waste and desolate places and your land [once the scene] of destruction surely now [in coming years] will be too narrow to accommodate the population, and those who once swallowed you up will be far away.
[20] The children of your bereavement [born during your captivity] shall yet say in your ears, The place is too narrow for me; make room for me, that I may live.
[21] Then [Zion], you will say in your heart, Who has borne me all these children, seeing that I lost my offspring and am alone *and* barren *and* unfruitful, an exile put away and wandering hither and thither? And who brought them up? Behold, I was left alone [put away by the Lord, my Husband]; from where then did all these children come?
[22] Thus says the Lord God: Behold, I will lift up My hand to the Gentile nations and set up My standard *and* raise high My signal banner to the peoples; and they will bring your sons in the bosom of their garments, and your daughters will be carried upon their shoulders.
[23] And kings shall be your foster fathers *and* guardians, and their queens your nursing mothers. They shall bow down to you with their faces to the earth and lick up the dust of your feet; and you shall know [with an acquaintance and understanding based on and grounded in personal experience] that I am the Lord; for they shall not be put to shame who wait for, look for, hope for, *and* expect Me.
[24] Shall the prey be taken from the mighty, or the lawful captives of the just be delivered?
[25] For thus says the Lord: Even the captives of the mighty will be taken away, and the prey of the terrible will be delivered; for I will contend with him who contends with you, and I will give safety to your children *and* ease them.
[26] And I will make those who oppress you consume themselves [in mutually destructive wars], thus eating their own flesh; and they will be drunk with their own blood, as with sweet wine; and all flesh will know [with a knowledge grounded in personal experience] that I, the Lord, am your Savior and your Redeemer, the Mighty One of Jacob.

**50** Thus says the Lord: Where is the bill of your mother's divorce with which I put her away, O Israel? Or which of My creditors is it to whom I have sold you? Behold, for your iniquities you were sold, and for your transgressions was your mother put away.
[2] Why, when I came, was there no man? When I called, why was there no one to answer? Is My hand shortened at

## New International Version

Was my arm too short to deliver you?
  Do I lack the strength to rescue you?
By a mere rebuke I dry up the sea,
  I turn rivers into a desert;
their fish rot for lack of water
  and die of thirst.
3 I clothe the heavens with darkness
  and make sackcloth its covering."

4 The Sovereign LORD has given me a well-instructed
    tongue,
  to know the word that sustains the weary.
He wakens me morning by morning,
  wakens my ear to listen like one being instructed.
5 The Sovereign LORD has opened my ears;
  I have not been rebellious,
  I have not turned away.
6 I offered my back to those who beat me,
  my cheeks to those who pulled out my beard;
I did not hide my face
  from mocking and spitting.
7 Because the Sovereign LORD helps me,
  I will not be disgraced.
Therefore have I set my face like flint,
  and I know I will not be put to shame.
8 He who vindicates me is near.
  Who then will bring charges against me?
  Let us face each other!
Who is my accuser?
  Let him confront me!
9 It is the Sovereign LORD who helps me.
  Who will condemn me?
They will all wear out like a garment;
  the moths will eat them up.

10 Who among you fears the LORD
  and obeys the word of his servant?
Let the one who walks in the dark,
  who has no light,
trust in the name of the LORD
  and rely on their God.
11 But now, all you who light fires
  and provide yourselves with flaming torches,
go, walk in the light of your fires
  and of the torches you have set ablaze.
This is what you shall receive from my hand:
  You will lie down in torment.

### Everlasting Salvation for Zion

**51** "Listen to me, you who pursue righteousness
    and who seek the LORD:
Look to the rock from which you were cut
  and to the quarry from which you were hewn;
2 look to Abraham, your father,
  and to Sarah, who gave you birth.
When I called him he was only one man,
  and I blessed him and made him many.
3 The LORD will surely comfort Zion
  and will look with compassion on all her ruins;
he will make her deserts like Eden,
  her wastelands like the garden of the LORD.
Joy and gladness will be found in her,
  thanksgiving and the sound of singing.

4 "Listen to me, my people;
  hear me, my nation:
Instruction will go out from me;
  my justice will become a light to the nations.
5 My righteousness draws near speedily,
  my salvation is on the way,
and my arm will bring justice to the nations.
The islands will look to me
  and wait in hope for my arm.

## Amplified Bible

all, that it cannot redeem? Or have I no power to deliver? Behold, at My rebuke I dry up the sea, I make the rivers a desert; their fish stink because there is no water, and they die of thirst.

3 I clothe the heavens with [the] blackness [of murky storm clouds], and I make sackcloth [of mourning] their covering.

4 [The *a*Servant of God says] The Lord God has given Me the tongue of a disciple *and* of one who is taught, that I should know how to speak a word in season to him who is weary. He wakens Me morning by morning, He wakens My ear to hear as a disciple [as one who is taught].

5 The Lord God has opened My ear, and I have not been rebellious or turned backward.

6 I gave My back to the smiters and My cheeks to those who plucked off the hair; I hid not My face from shame and spitting. [Matt. 26:67; 27:30; John 19:1.]

7 For the Lord God helps Me; therefore have I not been ashamed *or* confounded. Therefore have I set My face like a flint, and I know that I shall not be put to shame. [Luke 9:51; Isa. 52:13; 53:10-12.]

8 He is near Who declares Me in the right. Who will contend with Me? Let us stand forth together! Who is My adversary? Let him come near to Me. [Rom. 8:33-35; I Tim. 3:16.]

9 Behold, the Lord God will help Me; who is he who will condemn Me? Behold, they all will wax old *and* be worn out as a garment; the moth will eat them up. [Heb. 1:11, 12.]

10 Who is among you who [reverently] fears the Lord, who obeys the voice of His Servant, yet who walks in darkness *and* deep trouble and has no shining splendor [in his heart]? Let him rely on, trust in, *and* be confident in the name of the Lord, and let him lean upon *and* be supported by his God.

11 Behold, all you [enemies of your own selves] who attempt to kindle your own fires [and work out your own plans of salvation], who surround *and* gird yourselves with momentary sparks, darts, *and* firebrands that you set aflame!—walk by the light of your self-made fire and of the sparks that you have kindled [for yourself, if you will]! But this shall you have from My hand: you shall lie down in grief *and* in torment. [Isa. 66:24.]

**51** Hearken to me, you who follow after rightness *and* justice, you who seek *and* inquire of [and require] the Lord [claiming Him by necessity and by right]: look to the rock from which you were hewn and to the hole in the quarry from which you were dug;

2 Look to Abraham your father and to Sarah who bore you; for I called him when he was but one, and I blessed him and made him many.

3 For the Lord will comfort Zion; He will comfort all her waste places. And He will make her wilderness like Eden, and her desert like the garden of the Lord. Joy and gladness will be found in her, thanksgiving and the voice of song *or* instrument of praise.

4 Listen to Me [the Lord], O My people, and give ear to Me, O My nation; for a [divine] law will go forth from Me, and I will establish My justice for a light to the peoples.

5 My rightness *and* justice are near, My salvation is going forth, and My arms shall rule the peoples; the islands shall wait for *and* expect Me, and on My arm shall they trust *and* wait with hope.

---

## New International Version

<sup>6</sup>Lift up your eyes to the heavens,
　look at the earth beneath;
the heavens will vanish like smoke,
　the earth will wear out like a garment
　and its inhabitants die like flies.
But my salvation will last forever,
　my righteousness will never fail.

<sup>7</sup>"Hear me, you who know what is right,
　you people who have taken my instruction to heart:
Do not fear the reproach of mere mortals
　or be terrified by their insults.
<sup>8</sup>For the moth will eat them up like a garment;
　the worm will devour them like wool.
But my righteousness will last forever,
　my salvation through all generations."

<sup>9</sup>Awake, awake, arm of the LORD,
　clothe yourself with strength!
Awake, as in days gone by,
　as in generations of old.
Was it not you who cut Rahab to pieces,
　who pierced that monster through?
<sup>10</sup>Was it not you who dried up the sea,
　the waters of the great deep,
who made a road in the depths of the sea
　so that the redeemed might cross over?
<sup>11</sup>Those the LORD has rescued will return.
　They will enter Zion with singing;
　everlasting joy will crown their heads.
Gladness and joy will overtake them,
　and sorrow and sighing will flee away.

<sup>12</sup>"I, even I, am he who comforts you.
　Who are you that you fear mere mortals,
　human beings who are but grass,
<sup>13</sup>that you forget the LORD your Maker,
　who stretches out the heavens
　and who lays the foundations of the earth,
　that you live in constant terror every day
　because of the wrath of the oppressor,
　who is bent on destruction?
For where is the wrath of the oppressor?
<sup>14</sup>　The cowering prisoners will soon be set free;
　they will not die in their dungeon,
　nor will they lack bread.
<sup>15</sup>For I am the LORD your God,
　who stirs up the sea so that its waves roar—
　the LORD Almighty is his name.
<sup>16</sup>I have put my words in your mouth
　and covered you with the shadow of my hand—
I who set the heavens in place,
　who laid the foundations of the earth,
　and who say to Zion, 'You are my people.'"

### The Cup of the LORD's Wrath

<sup>17</sup>Awake, awake!
　Rise up, Jerusalem,
you who have drunk from the hand of the LORD
　the cup of his wrath,
you who have drained to its dregs
　the goblet that makes people stagger.
<sup>18</sup>Among all the children she bore
　there was none to guide her;
among all the children she reared
　there was none to take her by the hand.
<sup>19</sup>These double calamities have come upon you—
　who can comfort you?—
ruin and destruction, famine and sword—
　who can<sup>a</sup> console you?
<sup>20</sup>Your children have fainted;
　they lie at every street corner,

## Amplified Bible

<sup>6</sup>Lift up your eyes to the heavens, and look upon the
earth beneath; for the heavens shall be dissolved *and* vanish away like smoke, and the earth shall wax old like a
garment, and they that dwell therein shall die in like manner [like gnats]. But My salvation shall be forever, and
My rightness *and* justice [and faithfully fulfilled promise]
shall not be abolished. [Matt. 24:35; Heb. 1:11; II Pet. 3:10.]

<sup>7</sup>Listen to Me, you who know rightness *and* justice *and*
right standing with God, the people in whose heart is My
law *and* My instruction: fear not the reproach of men, neither be afraid *nor* dismayed at their revilings.

<sup>8</sup>For [in comparison with the Lord they are so weak
that things as insignificant as] the moth shall eat them up
like a garment, and the worm shall eat them like wool. But
My rightness *and* justice [and faithfully fulfilled promise]
shall be forever, and My salvation to all generations.

<sup>9</sup>[Zion now cries to the Lord, the God of Israel] Awake,
awake, put on strength *and* might, O arm of the Lord;
awake, as in the ancient days, as in the generations of long
ago. Was it not You Who cut Rahab [Egypt] in pieces, Who
pierced the dragon [symbol of Egypt]? [Isa. 30:7.]

<sup>10</sup>Was it not You Who dried up the Red Sea, the waters
of the great deep, Who made the depths of the sea a way
for the redeemed to pass over? [Why then are we left so
long in captivity?]

<sup>11</sup>[The Lord God says] And the redeemed of the Lord
shall return and come with singing to Zion; everlasting
joy shall be upon their heads. They shall obtain joy and
gladness, and sorrow and sighing shall flee away. [Rev.
7:17; 21:1, 4.]

<sup>12</sup>I, even I, am He Who comforts you. Who are you, that
you should be afraid of man, who shall die, and of a son of
man, who shall be made [as destructible] as grass,

<sup>13</sup>That you should forget the Lord your Maker, Who
stretched forth the heavens and laid the foundations of the
earth, and fear continually every day because of the fury
of the oppressor, when he makes ready to destroy *or* even
though he did so? And where is the fury of the oppressor?

<sup>14</sup>The captive exile *and* he who is bent down by chains
shall speedily be released; and he shall not die and go
down to the pit of destruction, nor shall his food fail.

<sup>15</sup>For I am the Lord your God, Who stirs up the sea so
that its waves roar *and* Who by rebuke restrains it—the
Lord of hosts is His name.

<sup>16</sup>And I have put My words in your mouth and have cov-
ered you with the shadow of My hand, that I may fix the
[new] heavens as a tabernacle and lay the foundations of
a [new] earth and say to Zion, You are My people. [Isa.
65:17; 66:22; Rev. 21:1.]

<sup>17</sup>Arouse yourself, awake! Stand up, O Jerusalem, you
who have drunk at the hand of the Lord the cup of His
wrath, you who have drunk the cup of staggering *and* intoxication to the dregs.

<sup>18</sup>There is none to guide her among all the sons she
has borne; neither is there anyone to take her by the hand
among all the sons whom she has brought up.

<sup>19</sup>Two kinds of calamities have befallen you—but who
feels sorry for *and* commiserates you?—they are desolation and destruction [on the land and city], and famine
and sword [on the inhabitants]—how shall I comfort you
*or* by whom?

<sup>20</sup>Your sons have fainted; they lie [like corpses] at the
head of all the streets, like an antelope in a net; they are

---

<sup>a</sup> 19 Dead Sea Scrolls, Septuagint, Vulgate and Syriac; Masoretic Text
/ how can I

## New International Version

like antelope caught in a net.
They are filled with the wrath of the LORD,
  with the rebuke of your God.
21 Therefore hear this, you afflicted one,
  made drunk, but not with wine.
22 This is what your Sovereign LORD says,
  your God, who defends his people:
"See, I have taken out of your hand
  the cup that made you stagger;
from that cup, the goblet of my wrath,
  you will never drink again.
23 I will put it into the hands of your tormentors,
  who said to you,
  'Fall prostrate that we may walk on you.'
And you made your back like the ground,
  like a street to be walked on."

**52** Awake, awake, Zion,
  clothe yourself with strength!
Put on your garments of splendor,
  Jerusalem, the holy city.
The uncircumcised and defiled
  will not enter you again.
2 Shake off your dust;
  rise up, sit enthroned, Jerusalem.
Free yourself from the chains on your neck,
  Daughter Zion, now a captive.

3 For this is what the LORD says:

"You were sold for nothing,
  and without money you will be redeemed."

4 For this is what the Sovereign LORD says:

"At first my people went down to Egypt to live;
  lately, Assyria has oppressed them.

5 "And now what do I have here?" declares the LORD.

"For my people have been taken away for nothing,
  and those who rule them mock,[a]"
           declares the LORD.

"And all day long
  my name is constantly blasphemed.
6 Therefore my people will know my name;
  therefore in that day they will know
that it is I who foretold it.
  Yes, it is I."

7 How beautiful on the mountains
  are the feet of those who bring good news,
who proclaim peace,
  who bring good tidings,
  who proclaim salvation,
who say to Zion,
  "Your God reigns!"
8 Listen! Your watchmen lift up their voices;
  together they shout for joy.
When the LORD returns to Zion,
  they will see it with their own eyes.
9 Burst into songs of joy together,
  you ruins of Jerusalem,
for the LORD has comforted his people,
  he has redeemed Jerusalem.
10 The LORD will lay bare his holy arm
  in the sight of all the nations,
and all the ends of the earth will see
  the salvation of our God.

11 Depart, depart, go out from there!
  Touch no unclean thing!

---

## Amplified Bible

full [from drinking] of the wrath of the Lord, the rebuke of your God.
21 Therefore, now hear this, you who are afflicted, and [who are] drunk, but not with wine [but thrown down by the wrath of God].
22 Thus says your Lord, the Lord, and your God, Who pleads the cause of His people: Behold, I have taken from your hand the cup of staggering *and* intoxication; the cup of My wrath you shall drink no more.
23 And I will put it into the hands of your tormentors *and* oppressors, those who said to you, Bow down, that we may ride *or* tread over you; and you have made your back like the ground and like the street for them to pass over.

**52** Awake, awake, put on your strength, O Zion; put on your beautiful garments, O Jerusalem, the holy city; for henceforth there shall no more come into you the uncircumcised and the unclean. [Rev. 21:27.]
2 Shake yourself from the dust; arise, sit [erect in a dignified place], O Jerusalem; loose yourself from the bonds of your neck, O captive Daughter of Zion.
3 For thus says the Lord: You were sold for nothing, and you shall be redeemed without money.
4 For thus says the Lord God: My people went down at the first into Egypt to sojourn there; and [many years later Sennacherib] the Assyrian oppressed them for nothing. [Now I delivered you from both Egypt and Assyria; what then can prevent Me from delivering you from Babylon?]
5 But now what have I here, says the Lord, seeing that My people have been taken away for nothing? Those who rule over them howl [with joy], says the Lord, and My name continually is blasphemed all day long. [Rom. 2:24.]
6 Therefore My people shall know what My name is *and* what it means; therefore they shall know in that day that I am He who speaks; behold, I AM! [Exod. 3:13, 14.]
7 How beautiful upon the mountains are the feet of him who brings good tidings, who publishes peace, who brings good tidings of good, who publishes salvation, who says to Zion, Your God reigns! [Acts 10:36; Rom. 10:15; Eph. 6:14-16.]
8 Hark, your watchmen lift up their voices; together they sing for joy; for they shall see eye to eye the return of the Lord to Zion.
9 Break forth joyously, sing together, you waste places of Jerusalem, for the Lord has comforted His people, He has redeemed Jerusalem!
10 The Lord has made bare His holy arm before the eyes of all the nations [revealing Himself as the One by Whose direction the redemption of Israel from captivity is accomplished], and all the ends of the earth shall witness the salvation of our God. [Luke 2:29-32; 3:6.]
11 Depart, depart, go out from there [the lands of exile]! Touch no unclean thing! Go out of the midst of her [Bab-

---

[a] 5 Dead Sea Scrolls and Vulgate; Masoretic Text *wail*

## New International Version

Come out from it and be pure,
    you who carry the articles of the LORD's house.
12But you will not leave in haste
    or go in flight;
for the LORD will go before you,
    the God of Israel will be your rear guard.

### The Suffering and Glory of the Servant
13See, my servant will act wisely*a*;
    he will be raised and lifted up and highly exalted.
14Just as there were many who were appalled at him*b*—
    his appearance was so disfigured beyond that of any
        human being
    and his form marred beyond human likeness—
15so he will sprinkle many nations,*c*
    and kings will shut their mouths because of him.
For what they were not told, they will see,
    and what they have not heard, they will understand.

**53** Who has believed our message
    and to whom has the arm of the LORD been
        revealed?
2He grew up before him like a tender shoot,
    and like a root out of dry ground.
He had no beauty or majesty to attract us to him,
    nothing in his appearance that we should desire
        him.
3He was despised and rejected by mankind,
    a man of suffering, and familiar with pain.
Like one from whom people hide their faces
    he was despised, and we held him in low esteem.

4Surely he took up our pain
    and bore our suffering,
yet we considered him punished by God,
    stricken by him, and afflicted.
5But he was pierced for our transgressions,
    he was crushed for our iniquities;
the punishment that brought us peace was on him,
    and by his wounds we are healed.
6We all, like sheep, have gone astray,
    each of us has turned to our own way;
and the LORD has laid on him
    the iniquity of us all.

7He was oppressed and afflicted,
    yet he did not open his mouth;
he was led like a lamb to the slaughter,
    and as a sheep before its shearers is silent,
    so he did not open his mouth.
8By oppression*d* and judgment he was taken away.
    Yet who of his generation protested?
For he was cut off from the land of the living;
    for the transgression of my people he was
        punished.*e*
9He was assigned a grave with the wicked,
    and with the rich in his death,
though he had done no violence,
    nor was any deceit in his mouth.

10Yet it was the LORD's will to crush him and cause him
        to suffer,
    and though the LORD makes*f* his life an offering for
        sin,
he will see his offspring and prolong his days,
    and the will of the LORD will prosper in his hand.

## Amplified Bible

ylon]; cleanse yourselves *and* be clean, you who bear the
vessels of the Lord [on your journey from there]. [II Cor.
6:16, 17.]
12For you will not go out with haste, nor will you go in
flight [as was necessary when Israel left Egypt]; for the
Lord will go before you, and the God of Israel will be your
rear guard.
13Behold, My *a*Servant shall deal wisely *and* shall prosper; He shall be exalted and extolled and shall stand very
high.
14[For many the Servant of God became an object of
horror; many were astonished at Him.] His face *and* His
whole appearance were marred more than any man's, and
His form beyond that of the sons of men—but just as many
were astonished at Him,
15So shall He startle *and* sprinkle many nations, and
kings shall shut their mouths because of Him; for that
which has not been told them shall they see, and that
which they have not heard shall they consider *and* understand. [Rom. 15:21.]

**53** Who has believed (trusted in, relied upon, and
clung to) our message [of that which was revealed
to us]? And to whom has the arm of the Lord been disclosed? [John 12:38-41; Rom. 10:16.]
2For [the Servant of God] grew up before Him like a
tender plant, and like a root out of dry ground; He has no
form or comeliness [royal, kingly pomp], that we should
look at Him, and no beauty that we should desire Him.
3He was despised and rejected *and* forsaken by men, a
Man of sorrows *and* pains, and acquainted with grief *and*
sickness; and like One from Whom men hide their faces
He was despised, and we did not appreciate His worth *or*
have any esteem for Him.
4Surely He has borne our griefs (sicknesses, weaknesses, and distresses) and carried our sorrows *and*
pains [of punishment], yet we [ignorantly] considered
Him stricken, smitten, and afflicted by God [as if with
leprosy]. [Matt. 8:17.]
5But He was wounded for our transgressions, He was
bruised for our guilt *and* iniquities; the chastisement
[needful to obtain] peace *and* well-being for us was upon
Him, and with the stripes [that wounded] Him we are
healed *and* made whole.
6All we like sheep have gone astray, we have turned
every one to his own way; and the Lord has made to light
upon Him the guilt *and* iniquity of us all. [I Pet. 2:24, 25.]
7He was oppressed, [yet when] He was afflicted, He was
submissive *and* opened not His mouth; like a lamb that is
led to the slaughter, and as a sheep before her shearers is
dumb, so He opened not His mouth.
8By oppression and judgment He was taken away; and
as for His generation, who among them considered that
He was cut off out of the land of the living [stricken to
His death] for the transgression of my [Isaiah's] people, to
whom the stroke was due?
9And they assigned Him a grave with the wicked, and
with a rich man in His death, although He had done no violence, neither was any deceit in His mouth. [Matt. 27:57-
60; I Pet. 2:22, 23.]
10Yet it was the will of the Lord to bruise Him; He has
put Him to grief *and* made Him sick. When You *and* He
make His life an offering for sin [and He has risen from
the dead, in time to come], He shall see His [spiritual]
offspring, He shall prolong His days, and the will *and* pleasure of the Lord shall prosper in His hand.

---

*a* 13 Or *will prosper*    *b* 14 Hebrew *you*    *c* 15 Or *so will many
nations be amazed at him* (see also Septuagint)    *d* 8 Or *From
arrest*    *e* 8 Or *generation considered / that he was cut off from the land
of the living, / that he was punished for the transgression of my people?*
*f* 10 Hebrew *though you make*

*a* See footnote on Isa. 42:1.

## New International Version

11 After he has suffered,
    he will see the light of life[a] and be satisfied[b];
by his knowledge[c] my righteous servant will justify
      many,
    and he will bear their iniquities.
12 Therefore I will give him a portion among the great,[d]
    and he will divide the spoils with the strong,[e]
because he poured out his life unto death,
    and was numbered with the transgressors.
For he bore the sin of many,
    and made intercession for the transgressors.

### The Future Glory of Zion

**54** "Sing, barren woman,
    you who never bore a child;
burst into song, shout for joy,
    you who were never in labor;
because more are the children of the desolate woman
    than of her who has a husband,"
                  says the LORD.
2 "Enlarge the place of your tent,
    stretch your tent curtains wide,
      do not hold back;
lengthen your cords,
    strengthen your stakes.
3 For you will spread out to the right and to the left;
    your descendants will dispossess nations
    and settle in their desolate cities.

4 "Do not be afraid; you will not be put to shame.
    Do not fear disgrace; you will not be humiliated.
You will forget the shame of your youth
    and remember no more the reproach of your
      widowhood.
5 For your Maker is your husband—
    the LORD Almighty is his name—
the Holy One of Israel is your Redeemer;
    he is called the God of all the earth.
6 The LORD will call you back
    as if you were a wife deserted and distressed in spirit—
a wife who married young,
    only to be rejected," says your God.
7 "For a brief moment I abandoned you,
    but with deep compassion I will bring you back.
8 In a surge of anger
    I hid my face from you for a moment,
but with everlasting kindness
    I will have compassion on you,"
    says the LORD your Redeemer.

9 "To me this is like the days of Noah,
    when I swore that the waters of Noah would never
      again cover the earth.
So now I have sworn not to be angry with you,
    never to rebuke you again.
10 Though the mountains be shaken
    and the hills be removed,
yet my unfailing love for you will not be shaken
    nor my covenant of peace be removed,"
    says the LORD, who has compassion on you.

11 "Afflicted city, lashed by storms and not comforted,
    I will rebuild you with stones of turquoise,[f]
    your foundations with lapis lazuli.
12 I will make your battlements of rubies,
    your gates of sparkling jewels,
    and all your walls of precious stones.

---

a 11 Dead Sea Scrolls (see also Septuagint); Masoretic Text does not
have *the light of life.*    b 11 Or (with Masoretic Text) *11He will see the
fruit of his suffering / and will be satisfied*    c 11 Or *by knowledge of him*
d 12 Or *many*    e 12 Or *numerous*    f 11 The meaning of the Hebrew
for this word is uncertain.

## Amplified Bible

11 He shall see [the fruit] of the travail of His soul and
be satisfied; by His knowledge of Himself [which He possesses and imparts to others] shall My [uncompromis-
ingly] righteous One, My Servant, justify many *and* make
many righteous (upright and in right standing with God),
for He shall bear their iniquities *and* their guilt [with the
consequences, says the Lord].
12 Therefore will I divide Him a portion with the great
[kings and rulers], and He shall divide the spoil with the
mighty, because He poured out His life unto death, and
[He let Himself] be regarded as a criminal *and* be numbered with the transgressors; yet He bore [and took away]
the sin of many and made intercession for the transgressors (the rebellious). [Luke 22:37.]

**54** [a] Sing, O barren one, you who did not bear; break
forth into singing and cry aloud, you who did not
travail with child! For the [spiritual] children of the desolate one will be more than the children of the married wife,
says the Lord. [Gal. 4:27.]
2 Enlarge the place of your tent, and let the curtains
of your habitations be stretched out; spare not; lengthen
your cords and strengthen your stakes.
3 For you will spread abroad to the right hand and to the
left; and your offspring will possess the nations and make
the desolate cities to be inhabited.
4 Fear not, for you shall not be ashamed; neither be confounded *and* depressed, for you shall not be put to shame.
For you shall forget the shame of your youth, and you shall
not [seriously] remember the reproach of your widowhood
any more.
5 For your Maker is your Husband—the Lord of hosts is
His name—and the Holy One of Israel is your Redeemer;
the God of the whole earth He is called.
6 For the Lord has called you like a woman forsaken,
grieved in spirit, *and* heartsore—even a wife [wooed and
won] in youth, when she is [later] refused *and* scorned,
says your God.
7 For a brief moment I forsook you, but with great compassion *and* mercy I will gather you [to Me] again.
8 In a little burst of wrath I hid My face from you for a
moment, but with age-enduring love *and* kindness I will
have compassion *and* mercy on you, says the Lord, your
Redeemer.
9 For this is like the days of Noah to Me; as I swore that
the waters of Noah should no more go over the earth, so
have I sworn that I will not be angry with you or rebuke
you.
10 For though the mountains should depart and the hills
be shaken *or* removed, yet My love *and* kindness shall not
depart from you, nor shall My covenant of peace *and* completeness be removed, says the Lord, Who has compassion on you.
11 O you afflicted [city], storm-tossed and not comforted, behold, I will set your stones in fair colors [in antimony
to enhance their brilliance] and lay your foundations with
sapphires.
12 And I will make your windows *and* pinnacles of [spar-
kling] agates *or* rubies, and your gates of [shining] car-
buncles, and all your walls [of your enclosures] of precious
stones. [Rev. 21:19-21.]

---

a Although this chapter is primarily intended to express Zion's joy
over redemption, it has also a very personal, long-neglected, and often
overlooked message for women—the lonely, the disappointed, the
childless, the widow. It has all the glorious confidence and assurance,
the incentive and understanding, for which feminine hearts have longed
throughout the ages! Every woman who will read it every week for a
year with receptive heart and mind will find herself not only spiritually
prepared for her own childlessness or widowhood, should it come,
but also supplied with rich treasure with which to address the similar
needs of countless other aching hearts to whom the Holy Spirit is here
speaking.

## New International Version

<sup>13</sup>All your children will be taught by the LORD,
and great will be their peace.
<sup>14</sup>In righteousness you will be established:
Tyranny will be far from you;
you will have nothing to fear.
Terror will be far removed;
it will not come near you.
<sup>15</sup>If anyone does attack you, it will not be my doing;
whoever attacks you will surrender to you.

<sup>16</sup>"See, it is I who created the blacksmith
who fans the coals into flame
and forges a weapon fit for its work.
And it is I who have created the destroyer to wreak
havoc;
<sup>17</sup>    no weapon forged against you will prevail,
and you will refute every tongue that accuses you.
This is the heritage of the servants of the LORD,
and this is their vindication from me,"
declares the LORD.

### Invitation to the Thirsty

**55** "Come, all you who are thirsty,
come to the waters;
and you who have no money,
come, buy and eat!
Come, buy wine and milk
without money and without cost.
<sup>2</sup>Why spend money on what is not bread,
and your labor on what does not satisfy?
Listen, listen to me, and eat what is good,
and you will delight in the richest of fare.
<sup>3</sup>Give ear and come to me;
listen, that you may live.
I will make an everlasting covenant with you,
my faithful love promised to David.
<sup>4</sup>See, I have made him a witness to the peoples,
a ruler and commander of the peoples.
<sup>5</sup>Surely you will summon nations you know not,
and nations you do not know will come running to
you,
because of the LORD your God,
the Holy One of Israel,
for he has endowed you with splendor."

<sup>6</sup>Seek the LORD while he may be found;
call on him while he is near.
<sup>7</sup>Let the wicked forsake their ways
and the unrighteous their thoughts.
Let them turn to the LORD, and he will have mercy on
them,
and to our God, for he will freely pardon.

<sup>8</sup>"For my thoughts are not your thoughts,
neither are your ways my ways,"
declares the LORD.
<sup>9</sup>"As the heavens are higher than the earth,
so are my ways higher than your ways
and my thoughts than your thoughts.
<sup>10</sup>As the rain and the snow
come down from heaven,
and do not return to it
without watering the earth
and making it bud and flourish,
so that it yields seed for the sower and bread for the
eater,
<sup>11</sup>so is my word that goes out from my mouth:
It will not return to me empty,
but will accomplish what I desire
and achieve the purpose for which I sent it.

## Amplified Bible

<sup>13</sup>And all your [spiritual] children shall be disciples [taught by the Lord and obedient to His will], and great shall be the peace *and* undisturbed composure of your children. [John 6:45.]
<sup>14</sup>You shall establish yourself in righteousness (rightness, in conformity with God's will and order): you shall be far from even the thought of oppression *or* destruction, for you shall not fear, and from terror, for it shall not come near you.
<sup>15</sup>Behold, they may gather together *and* stir up strife, but it is not from Me. Whoever stirs up strife against you shall fall *and* surrender to you.
<sup>16</sup>Behold, I have created the smith who blows on the fire of coals and who produces a weapon for its purpose; and I have created the devastator to destroy.
<sup>17</sup>But no weapon that is formed against you shall prosper, and every tongue that shall rise against you in judgment you shall show to be in the wrong. This [peace, righteousness, security, triumph over opposition] is the heritage of the servants of the Lord [those in whom the ideal Servant of the Lord is reproduced]; this is the righteousness *or* the vindication which they obtain from Me [this is that which I impart to them as their justification], says the Lord.

**55** Wait *and* listen, everyone who is thirsty! Come to the waters; and he who has no money, come, buy and eat! Yes, come, buy [priceless, spiritual] wine and milk without money and without price [simply for the self-surrender that accepts the blessing]. [Rev. 21:6, 7; 22:17.]
<sup>2</sup>Why do you spend your money for that which is not bread, and your earnings for what does not satisfy? Hearken diligently to Me, and eat what is good, and let your soul delight itself in fatness [the profuseness of spiritual joy]. [Jer. 31:12-14.]
<sup>3</sup>Incline your ear [submit and consent to the divine will] and come to Me; hear, and your soul will revive; and I will make an everlasting covenant *or* league with you, even the sure mercy (kindness, goodwill, and compassion) promised to David. [II Sam. 7:8-16; Acts 13:34; Heb. 13:20.]
<sup>4</sup>Behold, I have appointed him (Him) [David, as a representative of the Messiah, or the Messiah Himself] to be a witness [one (One) who shall testify of salvation] to the nations, a prince (Prince) and commander (Commander) to the peoples.
<sup>5</sup>Behold, you *a*[Israel] shall call nations that you know not, and nations that do not know you shall run to you because of the Lord your God, and of the Holy One of Israel, for He has glorified you.
<sup>6</sup>Seek, inquire for, *and* require the Lord while He may be found [claiming Him by necessity and by right]; call upon Him while He is near.
<sup>7</sup>Let the wicked forsake his way and the unrighteous man his thoughts; and let him return to the Lord, and He will have love, pity, *and* mercy for him, and to our God, for He will multiply to him His abundant pardon.
<sup>8</sup>For My thoughts are not your thoughts, neither are your ways My ways, says the Lord.
<sup>9</sup>For as the heavens are higher than the earth, so are My ways higher than your ways and My thoughts than your thoughts.
<sup>10</sup>For as the rain and snow come down from the heavens, and return not there again, but water the earth and make it bring forth and sprout, that it may give seed to the sower and bread to the eater, [II Cor. 9:10.]
<sup>11</sup>So shall My word be that goes forth out of My mouth: it shall not return to Me void [without producing any effect, useless], but it shall accomplish that which I please *and* purpose, and it shall prosper in the thing for which I sent it.

*a* The identification of the one here addressed is uncertain. A proportionately large number of authorities believe it to be Israel, as here indicated, but other interpreters think it is the Messiah [the second David], or David as His representative.

## New International Version

¹²You will go out in joy
and be led forth in peace;
the mountains and hills
will burst into song before you,
and all the trees of the field
will clap their hands.
¹³Instead of the thornbush will grow the juniper,
and instead of briers the myrtle will grow.
This will be for the LORD's renown,
for an everlasting sign,
that will endure forever."

### Salvation for Others

**56** This is what the LORD says:

"Maintain justice
and do what is right,
for my salvation is close at hand
and my righteousness will soon be revealed.
²Blessed is the one who does this—
the person who holds it fast,
who keeps the Sabbath without desecrating it,
and keeps their hands from doing any evil."

³Let no foreigner who is bound to the LORD say,
"The LORD will surely exclude me from his people."
And let no eunuch complain,
"I am only a dry tree."

⁴For this is what the LORD says:

"To the eunuchs who keep my Sabbaths,
who choose what pleases me
and hold fast to my covenant—
⁵to them I will give within my temple and its walls
a memorial and a name
better than sons and daughters;
I will give them an everlasting name
that will endure forever.
⁶And foreigners who bind themselves to the LORD
to minister to him,
to love the name of the LORD,
and to be his servants,
all who keep the Sabbath without desecrating it
and who hold fast to my covenant—
⁷these I will bring to my holy mountain
and give them joy in my house of prayer.
Their burnt offerings and sacrifices
will be accepted on my altar;
for my house will be called
a house of prayer for all nations."
⁸The Sovereign LORD declares—
he who gathers the exiles of Israel:
"I will gather still others to them
besides those already gathered."

### God's Accusation Against the Wicked

⁹Come, all you beasts of the field,
come and devour, all you beasts of the forest!
¹⁰Israel's watchmen are blind,
they all lack knowledge;
they are all mute dogs,
they cannot bark;
they lie around and dream,
they love to sleep.
¹¹They are dogs with mighty appetites;
they never have enough.
They are shepherds who lack understanding;
they all turn to their own way,
they seek their own gain.
¹²"Come," each one cries, "let me get wine!
Let us drink our fill of beer!
And tomorrow will be like today,
or even far better."

## Amplified Bible

¹²For you shall go out [from the spiritual exile caused by sin and evil into the homeland] with joy and be led forth [by your Leader, the Lord Himself, and His word] with peace; the mountains and the hills shall break forth before you into singing, and all the trees of the field shall clap their hands.
¹³Instead of the thorn shall come up the cypress tree, and instead of the brier shall come up the myrtle tree; and it shall be to the Lord for a name of renown, for an everlasting sign [of jubilant exaltation] *and* memorial [to His praise], which shall not be cut off.

**56** Thus says the Lord: Keep justice, do *and* use righteousness (conformity to the will of God which brings salvation), for My salvation is soon to come and My righteousness (My rightness and justice) to be revealed. [Isa. 62:1, 11; Matt. 3:2; Luke 21:31; Rom. 13:11, 12.]
²Blessed, happy, *and* fortunate is the man who does this, and the son of man who lays hold of it *and* binds himself fast to it, who keeps sacred the Sabbath so as not to profane it, and keeps his hand from doing any evil.
³Let not the foreigner who has joined himself to the Lord say, The Lord will surely separate me from His people. And let not the eunuch say, Behold, I am a dry tree.
⁴For thus says the Lord: To the eunuchs who keep My Sabbaths and choose the things which please Me and hold firmly My covenant—
⁵To them I will give in My house and within My walls a memorial and a name better [and more enduring] than sons and daughters; I will give them an everlasting name that will not be cut off.
⁶Also the foreigners who join themselves to the Lord to minister to Him and to love the name of the Lord and to be His servants, everyone who keeps the Sabbath so as not to profane it and who holds fast My covenant [by conscientious obedience]—
⁷All these I will bring to My holy mountain and make them joyful in My house of prayer. Their burnt offerings and their sacrifices will be accepted on My altar; for My house will be called a house of prayer for all peoples.
⁸Thus says the Lord God, Who gathers the outcasts of Israel: I will gather yet others to [Israel] besides those already gathered.
⁹All you beasts of the field, come to devour, all you beasts (hostile nations) in the forest.
¹⁰[Israel's] watchmen are blind, they are all without knowledge; they are all dumb dogs, they cannot bark; dreaming, lying down, they love to slumber.
¹¹Yes, the dogs are greedy; they never have enough. And such are the shepherds who cannot understand; they have all turned to their own way, each one to his own gain, from every quarter [one and all].
¹²Come, say they, We will fetch wine, and we will fill ourselves with strong drink! And tomorrow shall be as this day, a day great beyond measure.

## New International Version

**57** The righteous perish,
and no one takes it to heart;
the devout are taken away,
and no one understands
that the righteous are taken away
to be spared from evil.
2 Those who walk uprightly
enter into peace;
they find rest as they lie in death.

3 "But you—come here, you children of a sorceress,
you offspring of adulterers and prostitutes!
4 Who are you mocking?
At whom do you sneer
and stick out your tongue?
Are you not a brood of rebels,
the offspring of liars?
5 You burn with lust among the oaks
and under every spreading tree;
you sacrifice your children in the ravines
and under the overhanging crags.
6 The idols among the smooth stones of the ravines are
your portion;
indeed, they are your lot.
Yes, to them you have poured out drink offerings
and offered grain offerings.
In view of all this, should I relent?
7 You have made your bed on a high and lofty hill;
there you went up to offer your sacrifices.
8 Behind your doors and your doorposts
you have put your pagan symbols.
Forsaking me, you uncovered your bed,
you climbed into it and opened it wide;
you made a pact with those whose beds you love,
and you looked with lust on their naked bodies.
9 You went to Molek[a] with olive oil
and increased your perfumes.
You sent your ambassadors[b] far away;
you descended to the very realm of the dead!
10 You wearied yourself by such going about,
but you would not say, 'It is hopeless.'
You found renewal of your strength,
and so you did not faint.

11 "Whom have you so dreaded and feared
that you have not been true to me,
and have neither remembered me
nor taken this to heart?
Is it not because I have long been silent
that you do not fear me?
12 I will expose your righteousness and your works,
and they will not benefit you.
13 When you cry out for help,
let your collection of idols save you!
The wind will carry all of them off,
a mere breath will blow them away.
But whoever takes refuge in me
will inherit the land
and possess my holy mountain."

### Comfort for the Contrite
14 And it will be said:

"Build up, build up, prepare the road!
Remove the obstacles out of the way of my people."
15 For this is what the high and exalted One says—
he who lives forever, whose name is holy:
"I live in a high and holy place,
but also with the one who is contrite and lowly in spirit,
to revive the spirit of the lowly
and to revive the heart of the contrite.

## Amplified Bible

**57** The righteous man perishes, and no one lays it
to heart; and merciful *and* devout men are taken
away, with no one considering that the uncompromisingly
upright *and* godly person is taken away from the calamity
*and* evil to come [even through wickedness].
2 He [in death] enters into peace; they rest in their beds,
each one who walks straight *and* in his uprightness.
3 But come close, you sons of a sorceress [nursed in
witchcraft and superstition], you offspring of an adulterer
and a harlot.
4 Against whom do you make sport *and* take your delight? Against whom do you open wide your mouth and
put out your tongue? Are you not yourselves the children
of transgression, the offspring of deceit—
5 You who burn with lust [inflaming yourselves with
idols] among the oaks, under every green tree, you who
slay the children [in sacrifice] in the valleys under the
clefts of the rocks?
6 Among the smooth stones of the valley is your portion;
they, they [the idols] are your lot; to them you have poured
out a drink offering, you have offered a cereal offering.
Should I be quiet in spite of all these things [and leave
them unpunished—bearing them with patience]?
7 Upon a lofty and high mountain you have openly *and*
shamelessly set your [idolatrous and adulterous] bed;
even there you went up to offer sacrifice [in spiritual unfaithfulness to your divine Husband].
8 Behind the door and the doorpost you have set up your
[idol] symbol [as a substitute for the Scripture text God
ordered]. Deserting Me, you have uncovered and ascended and enlarged your bed; and you have made a [fresh]
bargain for yourself with [the adulterers], and you loved
their bed, where you saw [a beckoning hand or a passion-inflaming image]. [Deut. 6:5, 6, 9; 11:18, 20.]
9 And you went to the king [of foreign lands with gifts]
*or* to Molech [the god] with oil and increased your perfumes *and* ointments; you sent your messengers far off
and debased yourself even to Sheol (Hades) [symbol of an
abysmal depth of degradation].
10 You were wearied with the length of your way [in trying to find rest and satisfaction in alliances apart from the
true God], yet you did not say, There is no result *or* profit.
You found quickened strength; therefore you were not
faint *or* heartsick [or penitent].
11 Of whom have you been so afraid and in dread that
you lied *and* were treacherous and did not [seriously] remember Me, did not even give Me a thought? Have I not
been silent, even for a long time, and so you do not fear
Me?
12 I will expose your [pretended] righteousness and
your doings, but they will not help you.
13 When you cry out, let your [rabble] collection of idols
deliver you! But the wind shall take them all, a breath
shall carry them away. But he who takes refuge in Me
shall possess the land [Judea] and shall inherit My holy
mountain [Zion, also the heavenly inheritance and the
spiritual Zion]. [Ps. 37:9, 11; 69:35, 36; Isa. 49:8; Matt. 5:5;
Heb. 12:22.]
14 And the word of One shall go forth, Cast up, cast up,
prepare the way! Take up the stumbling block out of the
way [of the spiritual return] of My people.
15 For thus says the high and lofty One—He Who inhabits eternity, Whose name is Holy: I dwell in the high and
holy place, but with him also who is of a thoroughly penitent and humble spirit, to revive the spirit of the humble
and to revive the heart of the thoroughly penitent [bruised
with sorrow for sin]. [Matt. 5:3.]

---

*a* 9 Or *to the king*   *b* 9 Or *idols*

## New International Version

16 I will not accuse them forever,
　　nor will I always be angry,
　for then they would faint away because of me—
　　the very people I have created.
17 I was enraged by their sinful greed;
　　I punished them, and hid my face in anger,
　　yet they kept on in their willful ways.
18 I have seen their ways, but I will heal them;
　　I will guide them and restore comfort to Israel's
　　　mourners,
19 　creating praise on their lips.
　Peace, peace, to those far and near,"
　　says the LORD. "And I will heal them."
20 But the wicked are like the tossing sea,
　　which cannot rest,
　　whose waves cast up mire and mud.
21 "There is no peace," says my God, "for the wicked."

### True Fasting

**58** "Shout it aloud, do not hold back.
　　Raise your voice like a trumpet.
　Declare to my people their rebellion
　　and to the descendants of Jacob their sins.
2 For day after day they seek me out;
　　they seem eager to know my ways,
　as if they were a nation that does what is right
　　and has not forsaken the commands of its God.
　They ask me for just decisions
　　and seem eager for God to come near them.
3 'Why have we fasted,' they say,
　　'and you have not seen it?
　Why have we humbled ourselves,
　　and you have not noticed?'

　"Yet on the day of your fasting, you do as you please
　　and exploit all your workers.
4 Your fasting ends in quarreling and strife,
　　and in striking each other with wicked fists.
　You cannot fast as you do today
　　and expect your voice to be heard on high.
5 Is this the kind of fast I have chosen,
　　only a day for people to humble themselves?
　Is it only for bowing one's head like a reed
　　and for lying in sackcloth and ashes?
　Is that what you call a fast,
　　a day acceptable to the LORD?

6 "Is not this the kind of fasting I have chosen:
　to loose the chains of injustice
　　and untie the cords of the yoke,
　to set the oppressed free
　　and break every yoke?
7 Is it not to share your food with the hungry
　　and to provide the poor wanderer with shelter—
　when you see the naked, to clothe them,
　　and not to turn away from your own flesh and blood?
8 Then your light will break forth like the dawn,
　　and your healing will quickly appear;
　then your righteousness*a* will go before you,
　　and the glory of the LORD will be your rear guard.
9 Then you will call, and the LORD will answer;
　　you will cry for help, and he will say: Here am I.

　"If you do away with the yoke of oppression,
　　with the pointing finger and malicious talk,
10 and if you spend yourselves in behalf of the hungry
　　and satisfy the needs of the oppressed,
　then your light will rise in the darkness,
　　and your night will become like the noonday.

*a 8 Or your righteous One*

## Amplified Bible

16 For I will not contend forever, neither will I be angry always, for [if I did stay angry] the spirit [of man] would faint *and* be consumed before Me, and [My purpose in] creating the souls of men would be frustrated.
17 Because of the iniquity of his [Judah's] covetousness *and* unjust gain I was angry and smote him. I hid my face and was angry, and he went on turning away *and* backsliding in the way of his [own willful] heart.
18 I have seen his [willful] ways, but I will heal him; I will lead him also and will recompense him and restore comfort to him and to those who mourn for him. [Isa. 61:1, 2; 66:10.]
19 Peace, peace, to him who is far off [both Jew and Gentile] and to him who is near! says the Lord; I create the fruit of his lips, and I will heal him [make his lips blossom anew with speech in thankful praise]. [Acts 2:39; Eph. 2:13-17, 18; Heb. 13:15.]
20 But the wicked are like the troubled sea, for it cannot rest, and its waters cast up mire and dirt.
21 There is no peace, says my God, for the wicked.

**58** Cry aloud, spare not. Lift up your voice like a trumpet and declare to My people their transgression and to the house of Jacob their sins!
2 Yet they seek, inquire for, *and* require Me daily and delight [externally] to know My ways, as [if they were in reality] a nation that did righteousness and forsook not the ordinance of their God. They ask of Me righteous judgments, they delight to draw near to God [in visible ways].
3 Why have we fasted, they say, and You do not see it? Why have we afflicted ourselves, and You take no knowledge [of it]? Behold [O Israel], on the day of your fast [when you should be grieving for your sins], you find profit in your business, and [instead of stopping all work, as the law implies you and your workmen should do] you extort from your hired servants a full amount of labor. [Lev. 16:29.]
4 [The facts are that] you fast only for strife and debate and to smite with the fist of wickedness. Fasting as you do today will not cause your voice to be heard on high.
5 Is such a fast as yours what I have chosen, a day for a man to humble himself with sorrow in his soul? [Is true fasting merely mechanical?] Is it only to bow down his head like a bulrush and to spread sackcloth and ashes under him [to indicate a condition of heart that he does not have]? Will you call this a fast and an acceptable day to the Lord?
6 [Rather] is not this the fast that I have chosen: to loose the bonds of wickedness, to undo the bands of the yoke, to let the oppressed go free, and that you break every [enslaving] yoke? [Acts 8:23.]
7 Is it not to divide your bread with the hungry and bring the homeless poor into your house—when you see the naked, that you cover him, and that you hide not yourself from [the needs of] your own flesh *and* blood?
8 Then shall your light break forth like the morning, and your healing (your restoration and the power of a new life) shall spring forth speedily; your righteousness (your rightness, your justice, and your right relationship with God) shall go before you [conducting you to peace and prosperity], and the glory of the Lord shall be your rear guard. [Exod. 14:19, 20; Isa. 52:12.]
9 Then you shall call, and the Lord will answer; you shall cry, and He will say, Here I am. If you take away from your midst yokes of oppression [wherever you find them], the finger pointed in scorn [toward the oppressed or the godly], and every form of false, harsh, unjust, *and* wicked speaking, [Exod. 3:14.]
10 And if you pour out that with which you sustain your own life for the hungry and satisfy the need of the afflicted, then shall your light rise in darkness, and your obscurity *and* gloom become like the noonday.

## New International Version

### Amplified Bible

11 The LORD will guide you always;
   he will satisfy your needs in a sun-scorched land
   and will strengthen your frame.
You will be like a well-watered garden,
   like a spring whose waters never fail.
12 Your people will rebuild the ancient ruins
   and will raise up the age-old foundations;
   you will be called Repairer of Broken Walls,
   Restorer of Streets with Dwellings.

13 "If you keep your feet from breaking the Sabbath
   and from doing as you please on my holy day,
   if you call the Sabbath a delight
   and the LORD's holy day honorable,
and if you honor it by not going your own way
   and not doing as you please or speaking idle words,
14 then you will find your joy in the LORD,
   and I will cause you to ride in triumph on the
      heights of the land
   and to feast on the inheritance of your father Jacob."
   For the mouth of the LORD has spoken.

11 And the Lord shall guide you continually and satisfy you in drought *and* in dry places and make strong your bones. And you shall be like a watered garden and like a spring of water whose waters fail not.
12 And your ancient ruins shall be rebuilt; you shall raise up the foundations of [buildings that have laid waste for] many generations; and you shall be called Repairer of the Breach, Restorer of Streets to Dwell In.
13 If you turn away your foot from [traveling unduly on] the Sabbath, from doing your own pleasure on My holy day, and call the Sabbath a [spiritual] delight, the holy day of the Lord honorable, and honor Him *and* it, not going your own way or seeking *or* finding your own pleasure or speaking with your own [idle] words,
14 Then will you delight yourself in the Lord, and I will make you to ride on the high places of the earth, and I will feed you with the heritage [promised for you] of Jacob your father; for the mouth of the Lord has spoken it. [Gen. 27:28, 29; 28:13-15.]

### Sin, Confession and Redemption

**59** Surely the arm of the LORD is not too short to save,
   nor his ear too dull to hear.
2 But your iniquities have separated
   you from your God;
   your sins have hidden his face from you,
   so that he will not hear.
3 For your hands are stained with blood,
   your fingers with guilt.
Your lips have spoken falsely,
   and your tongue mutters wicked things.
4 No one calls for justice;
   no one pleads a case with integrity.
They rely on empty arguments, they utter lies;
   they conceive trouble and give birth to evil.
5 They hatch the eggs of vipers
   and spin a spider's web.
Whoever eats their eggs will die,
   and when one is broken, an adder is hatched.
6 Their cobwebs are useless for clothing;
   they cannot cover themselves with what they make.
Their deeds are evil deeds,
   and acts of violence are in their hands.
7 Their feet rush into sin;
   they are swift to shed innocent blood.
They pursue evil schemes;
   acts of violence mark their ways.
8 The way of peace they do not know;
   there is no justice in their paths.
They have turned them into crooked roads;
   no one who walks along them will know peace.

9 So justice is far from us,
   and righteousness does not reach us.
We look for light, but all is darkness;
   for brightness, but we walk in deep shadows.
10 Like the blind we grope along the wall,
   feeling our way like people without eyes.
At midday we stumble as if it were twilight;
   among the strong, we are like the dead.
11 We all growl like bears;
   we moan mournfully like doves.
We look for justice, but find none;
   for deliverance, but it is far away.

**59** Behold, the Lord's hand is not shortened at all, that it cannot save, nor His ear dull with deafness, that it cannot hear.
2 But your iniquities have made a separation between you and your God, and your sins have hidden His face from you, so that He will not hear.
3 For your hands are defiled with blood and your fingers with iniquity; your lips have spoken lies, your tongue mutters wickedness.
4 None sues *or* calls in righteousness [but for the sake of doing injury to others—to take some undue advantage]; no one goes to law honestly *and* pleads [his case] in truth; they trust in emptiness, worthlessness *and* futility, and speaking lies! They conceive mischief and bring forth evil!
5 They hatch adders' eggs and weave the spider's web; he who eats of their eggs dies, and [from an egg] which is crushed a viper breaks out [for their nature is ruinous, deadly, evil].
6 Their webs will not serve as clothing, nor will they cover themselves with what they make; their works are works of iniquity, and the act of violence is in their hands.
7 Their feet run to evil, and they make haste to shed innocent blood. Their thoughts are thoughts of iniquity; desolation and destruction are in their paths *and* highways.
8 The way of peace they know not, and there is no justice *or* right in their goings. They have made them into crooked paths; whoever goes in them does not know peace. [Rom. 3:15-18.]
9 Therefore are justice *and* right far from us, and righteousness *and* salvation do not overtake us. We expectantly wait for light, but [only] see darkness; for brightness, but we walk in obscurity *and* gloom.
10 We grope for the wall like the blind, yes, we grope like those who have no eyes. We stumble at noonday as in the twilight; in dark places *and* among those who are full of life *and* vigor, we are as dead men.
11 We all groan *and* growl like bears and moan plaintively like doves. We look for justice, but there is none; for salvation, but it is far from us.

## New International Version

12 For our offenses are many in your sight,
　　and our sins testify against us.
　Our offenses are ever with us,
　　and we acknowledge our iniquities:
13 rebellion and treachery against the LORD,
　　turning our backs on our God,
　inciting revolt and oppression,
　　uttering lies our hearts have conceived.
14 So justice is driven back,
　　and righteousness stands at a distance;
　truth has stumbled in the streets,
　　honesty cannot enter.
15 Truth is nowhere to be found,
　　and whoever shuns evil becomes a prey.

　The LORD looked and was displeased
　　that there was no justice.
16 He saw that there was no one,
　　he was appalled that there was no one to intervene;
　so his own arm achieved salvation for him,
　　and his own righteousness sustained him.
17 He put on righteousness as his breastplate,
　　and the helmet of salvation on his head;
　he put on the garments of vengeance
　　and wrapped himself in zeal as in a cloak.
18 According to what they have done,
　　so will he repay
　wrath to his enemies
　　and retribution to his foes;
　he will repay the islands their due.
19 From the west, people will fear the name of the LORD,
　　and from the rising of the sun, they will revere his
　　　glory.
　For he will come like a pent-up flood
　　that the breath of the LORD drives along.*a*
20 "The Redeemer will come to Zion,
　　to those in Jacob who repent of their sins,"
　　　　　　　　　　　　　　　declares the LORD.

21 "As for me, this is my covenant with them," says the
LORD. "My Spirit, who is on you, will not depart from you,
and my words that I have put in your mouth will always be
on your lips, on the lips of your children and on the lips of
their descendants—from this time on and forever," says
the LORD.

### The Glory of Zion

**60** "Arise, shine, for your light has come,
　　and the glory of the LORD rises upon you.
2 See, darkness covers the earth
　　and thick darkness is over the peoples,
　but the LORD rises upon you
　　and his glory appears over you.
3 Nations will come to your light,
　　and kings to the brightness of your dawn.

4 "Lift up your eyes and look about you:
　　All assemble and come to you;
　your sons come from afar,
　　and your daughters are carried on the hip.
5 Then you will look and be radiant,
　　your heart will throb and swell with joy;

## Amplified Bible

12 For our transgressions are multiplied before You
[O Lord], and our sins testify against us; for our transgressions are with us, and as for our iniquities, we know
*and* recognize them [as]:
13 Rebelling against and denying the Lord, turning away
from following our God, speaking oppression and revolt,
conceiving in and muttering *and* moaning from the heart
words of falsehood.
14 Justice is turned away backward, and righteousness
(uprightness and right standing with God) stands far off;
for truth has fallen in the street (the city's forum), and
uprightness cannot enter [the courts of justice].
15 Yes, truth is lacking, and he who departs from evil
makes himself a prey. And the Lord saw it, and it displeased Him that there was no justice.
16 And He saw that there was no man and wondered that
there was no intercessor [no one to intervene on behalf of
truth and right]; therefore His own arm brought Him victory, and His own righteousness [having the Spirit without
measure] sustained Him. [Isa. 53:11; Col. 2:9; I John 2:1,
2.]
17 For [the Lord] put on righteousness as a breastplate
*or* coat of mail, and salvation as a helmet upon His head;
He put on garments of vengeance for clothing and was clad
with zeal [and furious divine jealousy] as a cloak. [Eph.
6:14, 17; I Thess. 5:8.]
18 According as their deeds deserve, so will He repay
wrath to His adversaries, recompense to His enemies; on
the foreign islands *and* coastlands He will make compensation.
19 So [as the result of the Messiah's intervention] they
shall [reverently] fear the name of the Lord from the west,
and His glory from the rising of the sun. When the enemy
shall come in like a flood, the Spirit of the Lord will lift up
a standard against him *and* put him to flight [for He will
come like a rushing stream which the breath of the Lord
drives]. [Matt. 8:11; Luke 13:29.]
20 He shall come as a Redeemer to Zion and to those in
Jacob (Israel) who turn from transgression, says the Lord.
21 As for Me, this is My covenant *or* league with them,
says the Lord: My Spirit, Who is upon you [and Who
writes the law of God inwardly on the heart], and My
words which I have put in your mouth shall not depart out
of your mouth, or out of the mouths of your [true, spiritual]
children, or out of the mouths of your children's children,
says the Lord, from henceforth and forever. [Jer. 31:33;
Rom. 11:26, 27; Gal. 3:29; Heb. 12:22-24.]

**60** Arise [from the depression and prostration in
　　which circumstances have kept you—rise to a new
life]! Shine (be radiant with the glory of the Lord), for your
light has come, and the glory of the Lord has risen upon
you! [Zech. 8:23.]
2 For behold, darkness shall cover the earth, and dense
darkness [all] peoples, but the Lord shall arise upon you
[O Jerusalem], and His glory shall be seen on you. [Isa.
60:19-22; Mal. 4:2; Rev. 21:2, 3.]
3 And nations shall come to your light, and kings to the
brightness of your rising. [Isa. 2:2, 3; Jer. 3:17.]
4 Lift up your eyes round about you and see! They all
gather themselves together, they come to you. Your sons
shall come from afar, and your daughters shall be carried
*and* nursed in the arms.
5 Then you shall see and be radiant, and your heart
shall thrill *and* tremble with joy [at the glorious deliver-
ance] and be enlarged; because the abundant wealth of

---

*a* 19 Or *When enemies come in like a flood, / the Spirit of the LORD will put
them to flight*

# New International Version

the wealth on the seas will be brought to you,
  to you the riches of the nations will come.
⁶Herds of camels will cover your land,
  young camels of Midian and Ephah.
And all from Sheba will come,
  bearing gold and incense
  and proclaiming the praise of the LORD.
⁷All Kedar's flocks will be gathered to you,
  the rams of Nebaioth will serve you;
they will be accepted as offerings on my altar,
  and I will adorn my glorious temple.

⁸"Who are these that fly along like clouds,
  like doves to their nests?
⁹Surely the islands look to me;
  in the lead are the ships of Tarshish,ᵃ
  bringing your children from afar,
  with their silver and gold,
to the honor of the LORD your God,
  the Holy One of Israel,
  for he has endowed you with splendor.

¹⁰"Foreigners will rebuild your walls,
  and their kings will serve you.
Though in anger I struck you,
  in favor I will show you compassion.
¹¹Your gates will always stand open,
  they will never be shut, day or night,
so that people may bring you the wealth of the
    nations—
  their kings led in triumphal procession.
¹²For the nation or kingdom that will not serve you will
    perish;
  it will be utterly ruined.

¹³"The glory of Lebanon will come to you,
  the juniper, the fir and the cypress together,
to adorn my sanctuary;
  and I will glorify the place for my feet.
¹⁴The children of your oppressors will come bowing
    before you;
  all who despise you will bow down at your feet
  and will call you the City of the LORD,
  Zion of the Holy One of Israel.

¹⁵"Although you have been forsaken and hated,
  with no one traveling through,
I will make you the everlasting pride
  and the joy of all generations.
¹⁶You will drink the milk of nations
  and be nursed at royal breasts.
Then you will know that I, the LORD, am your Savior,
  your Redeemer, the Mighty One of Jacob.
¹⁷Instead of bronze I will bring you gold,
  and silver in place of iron.
Instead of wood I will bring you bronze,
  and iron in place of stones.
I will make peace your governor
  and well-being your ruler.
¹⁸No longer will violence be heard in your land,
  nor ruin or destruction within your borders,
but you will call your walls Salvation
  and your gates Praise.
¹⁹The sun will no more be your light by day,
  nor will the brightness of the moon shine on you,
for the LORD will be your everlasting light,
  and your God will be your glory.
²⁰Your sun will never set again,
  and your moon will wane no more;
the LORD will be your everlasting light,
  and your days of sorrow will end.

ᵃ 9 Or the trading ships

# Amplified Bible

the [Dead] ᵃSea shall be turned to you, unto you shall the nations come with their treasures. [Ps. 119:32.]
⁶A multitude of camels [from the eastern trading tribes] shall cover you [Jerusalem], the young camels of Midian and Ephah; all the men from Sheba [who once came to trade] shall come, bringing gold and frankincense and proclaiming the praises of the Lord. [Matt. 2:11.]
⁷All the flocks of Kedar shall be gathered to you [as the eastern pastoral tribes join the trading tribes], the rams of Nebaioth shall minister to you; they shall come up with acceptance on My altar, and My glorious house I will glorify.
⁸Who are these who fly like a cloud, and like doves to their windows?
⁹Surely the isles and distant coastlands shall wait for and expect Me; and the ships of Tarshish [shall come] first, to bring your sons from afar, their silver and gold with them, for the name of the Lord your God, for the Holy One of Israel, because He has beautified and glorified you.
¹⁰Foreigners shall build up your walls, and their kings shall minister to you; for in My wrath I smote you, but in My favor, pleasure, and goodwill I have had mercy, love, and pity for you.
¹¹And your gates shall be open continually, they shall not be shut day or night, that men may bring to you the wealth of the nations—and their kings led in procession [your voluntary captives]. [Rev. 21:24-27.]
¹²For the nation and kingdom that will not serve you in that day [Jerusalem] shall perish; yes, those nations shall be utterly laid waste.
¹³The glory of Lebanon shall come to you, the cypress, the plane, and the pine [trees] together, to beautify the place of My sanctuary; and I will make the place of My feet glorious.
¹⁴The sons of those who afflicted you shall come bending low to you, and all those who despised you shall bow down at your feet, and they shall call you the City of the Lord, the Zion of the Holy One of Israel. [Rev. 3:9.]
¹⁵Whereas you have been forsaken and hated, so that no man passed through you, I will make you [Jerusalem] an eternal glory, a joy from age to age.
¹⁶You shall suck the milk of the [Gentile] nations and shall suck the breast of kings; and you shall recognize and know that I, the Lord, am your Savior and your Redeemer, the Mighty One of Jacob.
¹⁷Instead of bronze I will bring gold, and instead of iron I will bring silver; and instead of wood, bronze, and instead of stones, iron. [Instead of the tyranny of the present] I will appoint peace as your officers and righteousness as your taskmasters.
¹⁸Violence shall no more be heard in your land, nor devastation or destruction within your borders, but you shall call your walls Salvation and your gates Praise.
¹⁹The sun shall no more be your light by day, nor for brightness shall the moon give light to you, but the Lord shall be to you an everlasting light, and your God your glory and your beauty. [Jer. 9:23, 24; Rev. 21:23.]
²⁰Your sun shall no more go down, nor shall your moon withdraw itself, for the Lord shall be your everlasting light, and the days of your mourning shall be ended.

ᵃ Prior to well into the twentieth century, scholars could only speculate as to what Isaiah might have meant here by "the abundant wealth of the [Dead] Sea" that would one day be turned over to Jerusalem. Of course, the Dead Sea, which for ages had been considered only a place of death and desolation, was ruled out as a possible meaning. Then suddenly it was discovered that the waters of the Dead Sea contain important chemicals. In A.D. 1935 G.T. B. Davis wrote, "One is almost staggered by the computed wealth of the chemical salts of the Dead Sea. It is estimated that the potential value of the potash, bromine, and other chemical salts of its waters is . . . four times the wealth of the United States!" (G.T. B. Davis, Rebuilding Palestine) Isaiah himself did not know this, but the God who caused the Dead Sea to play a part in His program in the last days knew all about it, and He led the prophet to so prophesy here in this verse.

## New International Version

21 Then all your people will be righteous
and they will possess the land forever.
They are the shoot I have planted,
the work of my hands,
for the display of my splendor.
22 The least of you will become a thousand,
the smallest a mighty nation.
I am the LORD;
in its time I will do this swiftly."

### The Year of the LORD's Favor

**61** The Spirit of the Sovereign LORD is on me,
because the LORD has anointed me
to proclaim good news to the poor.
He has sent me to bind up the brokenhearted,
to proclaim freedom for the captives
and release from darkness for the prisoners,[a]
2 to proclaim the year of the LORD's favor
and the day of vengeance of our God,
to comfort all who mourn,
3    and provide for those who grieve in Zion—
to bestow on them a crown of beauty
instead of ashes,
the oil of joy
instead of mourning,
and a garment of praise
instead of a spirit of despair.
They will be called oaks of righteousness,
a planting of the LORD
for the display of his splendor.

4 They will rebuild the ancient ruins
and restore the places long devastated;
they will renew the ruined cities
that have been devastated for generations.
5 Strangers will shepherd your flocks;
foreigners will work your fields and vineyards.
6 And you will be called priests of the LORD,
you will be named ministers of our God.
You will feed on the wealth of nations,
and in their riches you will boast.

7 Instead of your shame
you will receive a double portion,
and instead of disgrace
you will rejoice in your inheritance.
And so you will inherit a double portion in your land,
and everlasting joy will be yours.

8 "For I, the LORD, love justice;
I hate robbery and wrongdoing.
In my faithfulness I will reward my people
and make an everlasting covenant with them.
9 Their descendants will be known among the nations
and their offspring among the peoples.
All who see them will acknowledge
that they are a people the LORD has blessed."

10 I delight greatly in the LORD;
my soul rejoices in my God.
For he has clothed me with garments of salvation
and arrayed me in a robe of his righteousness,
as a bridegroom adorns his head like a priest,
and as a bride adorns herself with her jewels.
11 For as the soil makes the sprout come up
and a garden causes seeds to grow,
so the Sovereign LORD will make righteousness
and praise spring up before all nations.

## Amplified Bible

21 Your people also shall all be [uncompromisingly and consistently] righteous; they shall possess the land forever, the branch of My planting, the work of My hands, that I may be glorified.
22 The least one shall become a thousand [a clan], and the small one a strong nation. I, the Lord, will hasten it in its [appointed] time.

**61** The Spirit of the Lord God is upon me, because the Lord has anointed *and* qualified me to preach the Gospel *of* good tidings to the meek, the poor, *and* afflicted; He has sent me to bind up *and* heal the brokenhearted, to proclaim liberty to the [physical and spiritual] captives and the opening of the prison *and* of the eyes to those who are bound, [Rom. 10:15.]
2 To proclaim the acceptable year of the Lord [the year of His favor] *a* and the day of vengeance of our God, to comfort all who mourn, [Matt. 11:2-6; Luke 4:18, 19; 7:22.]
3 To grant [consolation and joy] to those who mourn in Zion—to give them an ornament (a garland or diadem) of beauty instead of ashes, the oil of joy instead of mourning, the garment [expressive] of praise instead of a heavy, burdened, *and* failing spirit—that they may be called oaks of righteousness [lofty, strong, and magnificent, distinguished for uprightness, justice, and right standing with God], the planting of the Lord, that He may be glorified.
4 And they shall rebuild the ancient ruins; they shall raise up the former desolations and renew the ruined cities, the devastations of many generations.
5 Aliens shall stand [ready] and feed your flocks, and foreigners shall be your plowmen and your vinedressers.
6 But you shall be called the priests of the Lord; people will speak of you as the ministers of our God. You shall eat the wealth of the nations, and the glory [once that of your captors] shall be yours. [Exod. 19:6; I Pet. 2:5; Rev. 1:6; 5:10; 20:6.]
7 Instead of your [former] shame you shall have a twofold recompense; instead of dishonor *and* reproach [your people] shall rejoice in their portion. Therefore in their land they shall possess double [what they had forfeited]; everlasting joy shall be theirs.
8 For I the Lord love justice; I hate robbery *and* wrong with violence *or* a burnt offering. And I will faithfully give them their recompense in truth, and I will make an everlasting covenant *or* league with them.
9 And their offspring shall be known among the nations and their descendants among the peoples. All who see them [in their prosperity] will recognize *and* acknowledge that they are the people whom the Lord has blessed.
10 I will greatly rejoice in the Lord, my soul will exult in my God; for He has clothed me with the garments of salvation, He has covered me with the robe of righteousness, as a bridegroom decks himself with a garland, and as a bride adorns herself with her jewels.
11 For as [surely as] the earth brings forth its shoots, and as a garden causes what is sown in it to spring forth, so [surely] the Lord God will cause rightness *and* justice and praise to spring forth before all the nations [through the self-fulfilling power of His word].

---

*a* 1 Hebrew; Septuagint *the blind*

*a* See footnote on Ezek. 34:28.

## New International Version

### Zion's New Name

**62** For Zion's sake I will not keep silent,
for Jerusalem's sake I will not remain quiet,
till her vindication shines out like the dawn,
her salvation like a blazing torch.
[2] The nations will see your vindication,
and all kings your glory;
you will be called by a new name
that the mouth of the LORD will bestow.
[3] You will be a crown of splendor in the LORD's hand,
a royal diadem in the hand of your God.
[4] No longer will they call you Deserted,
or name your land Desolate.
But you will be called Hephzibah,[a]
and your land Beulah[b];
for the LORD will take delight in you,
and your land will be married.
[5] As a young man marries a young woman,
so will your Builder marry you;
as a bridegroom rejoices over his bride,
so will your God rejoice over you.

[6] I have posted watchmen on your walls, Jerusalem;
they will never be silent day or night.
You who call on the LORD,
give yourselves no rest,
[7] and give him no rest till he establishes Jerusalem
and makes her the praise of the earth.

[8] The LORD has sworn by his right hand
and by his mighty arm:
"Never again will I give your grain
as food for your enemies,
and never again will foreigners drink the new wine
for which you have toiled;
[9] but those who harvest it will eat it
and praise the LORD,
and those who gather the grapes will drink it
in the courts of my sanctuary."

[10] Pass through, pass through the gates!
Prepare the way for the people.
Build up, build up the highway!
Remove the stones.
Raise a banner for the nations.

[11] The LORD has made proclamation
to the ends of the earth:
"Say to Daughter Zion,
'See, your Savior comes!
See, his reward is with him,
and his recompense accompanies him.'"
[12] They will be called the Holy People,
the Redeemed of the LORD;
and you will be called Sought After,
the City No Longer Deserted.

### God's Day of Vengeance and Redemption

**63** Who is this coming from Edom,
from Bozrah, with his garments stained
crimson?
Who is this, robed in splendor,
striding forward in the greatness of his strength?

"It is I, proclaiming victory,
mighty to save."

[2] Why are your garments red,
like those of one treading the winepress?

[3] "I have trodden the winepress alone;
from the nations no one was with me.

## Amplified Bible

**62** For Zion's sake will I [Isaiah] not hold my peace,
and for Jerusalem's sake I will not rest until her
imputed righteousness *and* vindication go forth as brightness, and her salvation radiates as does a burning torch.
[2] And the nations shall see your righteousness *and* vindication [your rightness and justice—not your own, but
His ascribed to you], and all kings shall behold your salvation and glory; and you shall be called a new name
which the mouth of the Lord shall name. [Rev. 2:17.]
[3] You shall also be [so beautiful and prosperous as to be
thought of as] a crown of glory *and* honor in the hand of
the Lord, and a royal diadem [exceedingly beautiful] in
the hand of your God.
[4] You [Judah] shall no more be termed Forsaken, nor
shall your land be called Desolate any more. But you shall
be called Hephzibah [My delight is in her], and your land
be called Beulah [married]; for the Lord delights in you,
and your land shall be married [owned and protected by
the Lord].
[5] For as a young man marries a virgin [O Jerusalem], so
shall your sons marry you; and as the bridegroom rejoices
over the bride, so shall your God rejoice over you.
[6] I have set watchmen upon your walls, O Jerusalem,
who will never hold their peace day or night; you who [are
His servants and by your prayers] put the Lord in remembrance [of His promises], keep not silence,
[7] And give Him no rest until He establishes Jerusalem
and makes her a praise in the earth.
[8] The Lord has sworn by His right hand and by His
mighty arm: Surely I will not again give your grain as food
for your enemies, and [the invading sons of] aliens shall
not drink your new wine for which you have toiled;
[9] But they who have gathered it shall eat it and praise the
Lord, and they who have brought in the vintage shall drink
it [at the feasts celebrated] in the courts of My sanctuary
(the temple of My holiness).
[10] Go through, go through the gates! Prepare the way
for the people. Cast up, cast up the highway! Gather out
the stones. Lift up a standard *or* ensign over *and* for the
peoples.
[11] Behold, the Lord has proclaimed to the end of the
earth: Say to the Daughter of Zion, Behold, your salvation
comes [in the person of the Lord]; behold, His reward is
with Him, and His work *and* recompense before Him. [Isa.
40:10.]
[12] And they shall call them the Holy People, the Redeemed of the Lord; and you shall be called Sought Out,
a City Not Forsaken.

**63** Who is this Who comes from Edom, with crim-
son-stained garments from Bozrah [in Edom]?
This One Who is glorious in His apparel, striding triumphantly in the greatness of His might? It is I, [the One]
Who speaks in righteousness [proclaiming vindication],
mighty to save!
[2] Why is Your apparel splashed with red, and Your garments like the one who treads in the winepress?
[3] I have trodden the winepress alone, and of the peoples
there was no one with Me. I trod them in My anger and

---

[a] 4 *Hephzibah* means *my delight is in her.*     [b] 4 *Beulah* means *married.*

## New International Version

I trampled them in my anger
  and trod them down in my wrath;
their blood spattered my garments,
  and I stained all my clothing.
4 It was for me the day of vengeance;
  the year for me to redeem had come.
5 I looked, but there was no one to help,
  I was appalled that no one gave support;
so my own arm achieved salvation for me,
  and my own wrath sustained me.
6 I trampled the nations in my anger;
  in my wrath I made them drunk
  and poured their blood on the ground."

### Praise and Prayer

7 I will tell of the kindnesses of the LORD,
  the deeds for which he is to be praised,
  according to all the LORD has done for us—
yes, the many good things
  he has done for Israel,
  according to his compassion and many kindnesses.
8 He said, "Surely they are my people,
  children who will be true to me";
  and so he became their Savior.
9 In all their distress he too was distressed,
  and the angel of his presence saved them.a
In his love and mercy he redeemed them;
  he lifted them up and carried them
  all the days of old.
10 Yet they rebelled
  and grieved his Holy Spirit.
So he turned and became their enemy
  and he himself fought against them.
11 Then his people recalledb the days of old,
  the days of Moses and his people—
where is he who brought them through the sea,
  with the shepherd of his flock?
Where is he who set
  his Holy Spirit among them,
12 who sent his glorious arm of power
  to be at Moses' right hand,
who divided the waters before them,
  to gain for himself everlasting renown,
13 who led them through the depths?
Like a horse in open country,
  they did not stumble;
14 like cattle that go down to the plain,
  they were given rest by the Spirit of the LORD.
This is how you guided your people
  to make for yourself a glorious name.

15 Look down from heaven and see,
  from your lofty throne, holy and glorious.
Where are your zeal and your might?
  Your tenderness and compassion are withheld from us.
16 But you are our Father,
  though Abraham does not know us
  or Israel acknowledge us;
you, LORD, are our Father,
  our Redeemer from of old is your name.
17 Why, LORD, do you make us wander from your ways
  and harden our hearts so we do not revere you?
Return for the sake of your servants,
  the tribes that are your inheritance.

## Amplified Bible

trampled them in My wrath; and their lifeblood is sprinkled upon My garments, and I stained all My raiment.
4 For the day of vengeance was in My heart, and My year of redemption [the year of My redeemed] has come.
5 And I looked, but there was no one to help; I was amazed and appalled that there was no one to uphold [truth and right]. So My own arm brought Me victory, and My wrath upheld Me.
6 I trod down the peoples in My anger and made them drink of the cup of My wrath until they were intoxicated, and I spilled their lifeblood upon the earth.
7 I will recount the loving-kindnesses of the Lord and the praiseworthy deeds of the Lord, according to all that the Lord has bestowed on us, and the great goodness to the house of Israel, which He has granted them according to His mercy and according to the multitude of His loving-kindnesses.
8 For He said, Surely they are My people, sons who will not lie [who will not deal falsely with Me]; and so He was to them a Savior [in all their distresses].
9 In all their affliction He was afflicted, and the aAngel of His presence saved them; in His love and in His pity He redeemed them; and He lifted them up and carried them all the days of old. [Exod. 23:20-23; 33:14-15; Deut. 1:31; 32:10-12.]
10 But they rebelled and grieved His Holy Spirit; therefore He turned to become their enemy and Himself fought against them.
11 Then His people [seriously] remembered the days of old, of Moses and his people [and they said], Where is He Who brought [our fathers] up out of the [Red] Sea, with [Moses and the other] shepherds of His flock? Where is He Who put His Holy Spirit within their midst,
12 Who caused His glorious arm to go at the right hand of Moses, dividing the waters before them, to make for Himself an everlasting name,
13 Who led them through the depths, like a horse in the wilderness, so that they did not stumble?
14 Like the cattle that go down into the valley [to find better pasturage, refuge, and rest], the Spirit of the Lord caused them to rest. So did You lead Your people [Lord] to make for Yourself a beautiful and glorious name [to prepare the way for the acknowledgment of Your name by all nations].
15 Look down from heaven and see from the dwelling place of Your holiness and Your glory. Where are Your zeal and Your jealousy and Your mighty acts [which you formerly did for Your people]? Your yearning pity and the [multitude of] compassions of Your heart are restrained and withheld from me.
16 For [surely] You are our Father, even though Abraham [our ancestor] does not know us and Israel (Jacob) does not acknowledge us; You, O Lord, are [still] our Father, our Redeemer from everlasting is Your name.
17 O Lord, why have You made us [able] to err from Your ways and hardened our hearts to [reverential] fear of You? Return [to bless us] for Your servants' sake, the tribes of Your heritage.

---

a 9 Or Savior 9in their distress. / It was no envoy or angel / but his own presence that saved them    b 11 Or But may he recall

a See footnote on Genesis 16:7.

## New International Version

<sup></sup>18 For a little while your people possessed your holy
place,
    but now our enemies have trampled down your
    sanctuary.
19 We are yours from of old;
    but you have not ruled over them,
    they have not been called*a* by your name.

64 *b* Oh, that you would rend the heavens and come
down,
    that the mountains would tremble before you!
2 As when fire sets twigs ablaze
    and causes water to boil,
    come down to make your name known to your enemies
    and cause the nations to quake before you!
3 For when you did awesome things that we did not
    expect,
    you came down, and the mountains trembled before
    you.
4 Since ancient times no one has heard,
    no ear has perceived,
no eye has seen any God besides you,
    who acts on behalf of those who wait for him.
5 You come to the help of those who gladly do right,
    who remember your ways.
But when we continued to sin against them,
    you were angry.
    How then can we be saved?
6 All of us have become like one who is unclean,
    and all our righteous acts are like filthy rags;
we all shrivel up like a leaf,
    and like the wind our sins sweep us away.
7 No one calls on your name
    or strives to lay hold of you;
for you have hidden your face from us
    and have given us over to*c* our sins.

8 Yet you, LORD, are our Father.
    We are the clay, you are the potter;
    we are all the work of your hand.
9 Do not be angry beyond measure, LORD;
    do not remember our sins forever.
Oh, look on us, we pray,
    for we are all your people.
10 Your sacred cities have become a wasteland;
    even Zion is a wasteland, Jerusalem a desolation.
11 Our holy and glorious temple, where our ancestors
    praised you,
    has been burned with fire,
    and all that we treasured lies in ruins.
12 After all this, LORD, will you hold yourself back?
    Will you keep silent and punish us beyond measure?

### Judgment and Salvation

65 "I revealed myself to those who did not ask for
me;
    I was found by those who did not seek me.
To a nation that did not call on my name,
    I said, 'Here am I, here am I.'
2 All day long I have held out my hands
    to an obstinate people,
who walk in ways not good,
    pursuing their own imaginations—
3 a people who continually provoke me
    to my very face,
offering sacrifices in gardens
    and burning incense on altars of brick;

## Amplified Bible

18 Your holy people possessed Your sanctuary but a little
while; our adversaries have trodden it down.
19 We have become [to You] like those over whom You
never exercised rule, like those who were not called by
Your name.

64 Oh, that You would rend the heavens and that
You would come down, that the mountains might
quake *and* flow down at Your presence—
2 As when fire kindles the brushwood and the fire
causes the waters to boil—to make Your name known to
Your adversaries, that the nations may tremble at Your
presence!
3 When You did terrible things which we did not expect,
You came down; the mountains quaked at Your presence.
4 For from of old no one has heard nor perceived by the
ear, nor has the eye seen a God besides You, Who works
*and* shows Himself active on behalf of him who [earnestly]
waits for Him.
5 You meet *and* spare him who joyfully works righteousness (uprightness and justice), [earnestly] remembering
You in Your ways. Behold, You were angry, for we sinned;
we have long continued in our sins [prolonging Your an-
ger]. And shall we be saved?
6 For we have all become like one who is unclean [cer-
emonially, like a leper], and all our righteousness (our
best deeds of rightness and justice) is like filthy rags *or* a
polluted garment; we all fade like a leaf, and our iniquities,
like the wind, take us away [far from God's favor, hurrying
us toward destruction]. [Lev. 13:45, 46.]
7 And no one calls on Your name and awakens *and* be-
stirs himself to take *and* keep hold of You; for You have
hidden Your face from us and have delivered us into the
[consuming] power of our iniquities. [Rom. 1:21-24.]
8 Yet, O Lord, You are our Father; we are the clay, and
You our Potter, and we all are the work of Your hand.
9 Do not be exceedingly angry, O Lord, or [seriously]
remember iniquity forever. Behold, consider, we beseech
You, we are all Your people.
10 Your holy cities have become a wilderness; Zion has
become a wilderness, Jerusalem a desolation.
11 Our holy and our beautiful house, [the temple] where
our fathers praised You, is burned with fire, and all our
pleasant *and* desirable places are in ruins.
12 Considering these [calamities], will You restrain
Yourself, O Lord [and not come to our aid]? Will You keep
silent *and* not command our deliverance but humble *and*
afflict us exceedingly?

65 I was [ready to be] inquired of by those who asked
not; I was [ready to be] found by those who sought
Me not. I said, Here I am, here I am [says I AM] to a nation [Israel] that has not called on My name. [Exod. 3:14;
Isa. 58:9.]
2 I have spread out My hands all the day long to a rebellious people, who walk in a way that is not good, after their
own thoughts—
3 A people who provoke Me to My face continually, sacrificing [to idols] in gardens and burning incense upon
bricks [instead of at God's prescribed altar];

---

*a 19* Or *We are like those you have never ruled, / like those never called*
*b* In Hebrew texts 64:1 is numbered 63:19b, and 64:2-12 is numbered
64:1-11. *c 7* Septuagint, Syriac and Targum; Hebrew *have made us*
*melt because of*

## New International Version

4 who sit among the graves
   and spend their nights keeping secret vigil;
who eat the flesh of pigs,
   and whose pots hold broth of impure meat;
5 who say, 'Keep away; don't come near me,
   for I am too sacred for you!'
Such people are smoke in my nostrils,
   a fire that keeps burning all day.

6 "See, it stands written before me:
   I will not keep silent but will pay back in full;
   I will pay it back into their laps—
7 both your sins and the sins of your ancestors,"
   says the LORD.
"Because they burned sacrifices on the mountains
   and defied me on the hills,
I will measure into their laps
   the full payment for their former deeds."

8 This is what the LORD says:

"As when juice is still found in a cluster of grapes
   and people say, 'Don't destroy it,
   there is still a blessing in it,'
so will I do in behalf of my servants;
   I will not destroy them all.
9 I will bring forth descendants from Jacob,
   and from Judah those who will possess my
      mountains;
my chosen people will inherit them,
   and there will my servants live.
10 Sharon will become a pasture for flocks,
   and the Valley of Achor a resting place for herds,
   for my people who seek me.

11 "But as for you who forsake the LORD
   and forget my holy mountain,
who spread a table for Fortune
   and fill bowls of mixed wine for Destiny,
12 I will destine you for the sword,
   and all of you will fall in the slaughter;
for I called but you did not answer,
   I spoke but you did not listen.
You did evil in my sight
   and chose what displeases me."

13 Therefore this is what the Sovereign LORD says:

"My servants will eat,
   but you will go hungry;
my servants will drink,
   but you will go thirsty;
my servants will rejoice,
   but you will be put to shame.
14 My servants will sing
   out of the joy of their hearts,
but you will cry out
   from anguish of heart
   and wail in brokenness of spirit.
15 You will leave your name
   for my chosen ones to use in their curses;
the Sovereign LORD will put you to death,
   but to his servants he will give another name.
16 Whoever invokes a blessing in the land
   will do so by the one true God;
whoever takes an oath in the land
   will swear by the one true God.
For the past troubles will be forgotten
   and hidden from my eyes.

### New Heavens and a New Earth

17 "See, I will create
   new heavens and a new earth.
The former things will not be remembered,
   nor will they come to mind.

## Amplified Bible

4 Who sit among the graves [trying to talk with the dead] and lodge among the secret places [or caves where familiar spirits were thought to dwell]; who eat swine's flesh, and the broth of abominable *and* loathsome things is in their vessels;
5 Who say, Keep to yourself; do not come near me, for I am set apart from you [and lest I sanctify you]! These are smoke in My nostrils, a fire that burns all the day.
6 Behold, it is written before Me: I will not keep silence but will repay; yes, I will repay into their bosom
7 Both your own iniquities and the iniquities of your fathers, says the Lord. Because they too burned incense upon the mountains and reviled *and* blasphemed Me upon the hills, therefore will I measure *and* stretch out their former doings into their own bosom.
8 Thus says the Lord: As the juice [of the grape] is found in the cluster, and one says, Do not destroy it, for there is a blessing in it, so will I do for My servants' sake, that I may not destroy them all.
9 And I will bring forth an offspring from Jacob, and from Judah an inheritor of My mountains; My chosen *and* elect will inherit it, and My servants will dwell there.
10 And [the plain of] Sharon shall be a pasture *and* fold for flocks, and the Valley of Achor a place for herds to lie down, for My people who seek Me, inquire of Me, *and* require Me [by right of their necessity and by right of My invitation].
11 But you who forsake the Lord, who forget *and* ignore My holy Mount [Zion], who prepare a table for Gad [the Babylonian god of fortune] and who furnish mixed drinks for Meni [the god of destiny]—
12 I will destine you [says the Lord] for the sword, and you shall all bow down to the slaughter, because when I called, you did not answer; when I spoke, you did not listen *or* obey. But you did what was evil in My eyes, and you chose that in which I did not delight.
13 Therefore thus says the Lord God: Behold, My servants shall eat, but you shall be hungry; behold, My servants shall drink, but you shall be thirsty; behold, My servants shall rejoice, but you shall be put to shame.
14 Behold, My servants shall sing for joy of heart, but you shall cry out for pain *and* sorrow of heart and shall wail *and* howl for anguish, vexation, *and* breaking of spirit.
15 And you will leave your name to My chosen [to those who will use it] for a curse; and the Lord God will slay you, but He will call His servants by another name [as much greater than the former name as the name Israel was greater than the name Jacob]. [Gen. 32:28; Jer. 29:22.]
16 So [it shall be] that he who invokes a blessing on himself in the land shall do so by saying, May the God of truth *and* fidelity [the Amen] bless me; and he who takes an oath in the land shall swear by the God of truth *and* faithfulness to His promises [the Amen], because the former troubles are forgotten and because they are hidden from My eyes. [II Cor. 1:20; Rev. 3:14.]
17 For behold, I create *a*new heavens and a new earth. And the former things shall not be remembered or come into mind. [Isa. 66:22; II Pet. 3:13; Rev. 21:1.]

---

*a* A new universe is meant here. The Hebrew language has no single word to express the concept of cosmos or universe, so heavens and earth are substituted.

## New International Version

[18] But be glad and rejoice forever
  in what I will create,
for I will create Jerusalem to be a delight
  and its people a joy.
[19] I will rejoice over Jerusalem
  and take delight in my people;
the sound of weeping and of crying
  will be heard in it no more.

[20] "Never again will there be in it
  an infant who lives but a few days,
  or an old man who does not live out his years;
the one who dies at a hundred
  will be thought a mere child;
the one who fails to reach[a] a hundred
  will be considered accursed.
[21] They will build houses and dwell in them;
  they will plant vineyards and eat their fruit.
[22] No longer will they build houses and others live in
    them,
  or plant and others eat.
For as the days of a tree,
  so will be the days of my people;
my chosen ones will long enjoy
  the work of their hands.
[23] They will not labor in vain,
  nor will they bear children doomed to misfortune;
for they will be a people blessed by the Lord,
  they and their descendants with them.
[24] Before they call I will answer;
  while they are still speaking I will hear.
[25] The wolf and the lamb will feed together,
  and the lion will eat straw like the ox,
  and dust will be the serpent's food.
They will neither harm nor destroy
  on all my holy mountain,"
                      says the Lord.

### Judgment and Hope

**66** This is what the Lord says:

"Heaven is my throne,
  and the earth is my footstool.
Where is the house you will build for me?
  Where will my resting place be?
[2] Has not my hand made all these things,
  and so they came into being?"
                    declares the Lord.

"These are the ones I look on with favor:
  those who are humble and contrite in spirit,
  and who tremble at my word.
[3] But whoever sacrifices a bull
  is like one who kills a person,
and whoever offers a lamb
  is like one who breaks a dog's neck;
whoever makes a grain offering
  is like one who presents pig's blood,
and whoever burns memorial incense
  is like one who worships an idol.
They have chosen their own ways,
  and they delight in their abominations;
[4] so I also will choose harsh treatment for them
  and will bring on them what they dread.
For when I called, no one answered,
  when I spoke, no one listened.
They did evil in my sight
  and chose what displeases me."

[5] Hear the word of the Lord,
  you who tremble at his word:
"Your own people who hate you,

## Amplified Bible

[18] But be glad and rejoice forever in that which I create;
for behold, I create Jerusalem to be a rejoicing and her
people a joy.
[19] And I will rejoice in Jerusalem and be glad in My people; and the sound of weeping will no more be heard in it,
nor the cry of distress.
[20] There shall no more be in it an infant who lives but
a few days, or an old man who dies prematurely; for the
child shall die a hundred years old, and the sinner who
dies when only a hundred years old shall be [thought only
a child, cut off because he is] accursed.
[21] They shall build houses and inhabit them, and they
shall plant vineyards and eat the fruit of them.
[22] They shall not build and another inhabit; they shall
not plant and another eat [the fruit]. For as the days of a
tree, so shall be the days of My people, and My chosen
*and* elect shall long make use of *and* enjoy the work of
their hands.
[23] They shall not labor in vain or bring forth [children]
for sudden terror *or* calamity; for they shall be the descendants of the blessed of the Lord, and their offspring with
them.
[24] And it shall be that before they call I will answer; and
while they are yet speaking I will hear. [Isa. 30:19; 58:9;
Matt. 6:8.]
[25] The wolf and the lamb shall feed together, and the lion
shall eat straw like the ox; and dust shall be the serpent's
food. They shall not hurt or destroy in all My holy Mount
[Zion], says the Lord.

**66** Thus says the Lord: Heaven is My throne, and the
earth is My footstool. What kind of house would
you build for Me? And what kind can be My resting-place?
[Acts 17:24.]
[2] For all these things My hand has made, and so all
these things have come into being [by and for Me], says
the Lord. But this is the man to whom I will look *and* have
regard: he who is humble and of a broken *or* wounded
spirit, and who trembles at My word *and* reveres My commands. [John 4:24.]
[3] [The acts of the hypocrite's worship are as abominable
to God as if they were offered to idols.] He who kills an ox
[then] will be as guilty as if he slew *and* sacrificed a man;
he who sacrifices a lamb *or* a kid, as if he broke a dog's
neck *and* sacrificed him; he who offers a cereal offering,
as if he offered swine's blood; he who burns incense [to
God], as if he blessed an idol. [Such people] have chosen
their own ways, and they delight in their abominations;
[4] So I also will choose their delusions *and* mockings,
their calamities *and* afflictions, and I will bring their fears
upon them—because when I called, no one answered;
when I spoke, they did not listen *or* obey. But they did
what was evil in My sight and chose that in which I did
not delight.
[5] Hear the word of the Lord, you who tremble at His

---

*a* 20 Or *the sinner who reaches*

## New International Version

and exclude you because of my name, have said,
'Let the LORD be glorified,
  that we may see your joy!'
Yet they will be put to shame.
[6] Hear that uproar from the city,
  hear that noise from the temple!
It is the sound of the LORD
  repaying his enemies all they deserve.

[7] "Before she goes into labor,
  she gives birth;
before the pains come upon her,
  she delivers a son.
[8] Who has ever heard of such things?
  Who has ever seen things like this?
Can a country be born in a day
  or a nation be brought forth in a moment?
Yet no sooner is Zion in labor
  than she gives birth to her children.
[9] Do I bring to the moment of birth
  and not give delivery?" says the LORD.
"Do I close up the womb
  when I bring to delivery?" says your God.
[10] "Rejoice with Jerusalem and be glad for her,
  all you who love her;
rejoice greatly with her,
  all you who mourn over her.
[11] For you will nurse and be satisfied
  at her comforting breasts;
you will drink deeply
  and delight in her overflowing abundance."

[12] For this is what the LORD says:

"I will extend peace to her like a river,
  and the wealth of nations like a flooding stream;
you will nurse and be carried on her arm
  and dandled on her knees.
[13] As a mother comforts her child,
  so will I comfort you;
and you will be comforted over Jerusalem."

[14] When you see this, your heart will rejoice
  and you will flourish like grass;
the hand of the LORD will be made known to his servants,
  but his fury will be shown to his foes.
[15] See, the LORD is coming with fire,
  and his chariots are like a whirlwind;
he will bring down his anger with fury,
  and his rebuke with flames of fire.
[16] For with fire and with his sword
  the LORD will execute judgment on all people,
  and many will be those slain by the LORD.

[17] "Those who consecrate and purify themselves to go into the gardens, following one who is among those who eat the flesh of pigs, rats and other unclean things—they will meet their end together with the one they follow," declares the LORD.

[18] "And I, because of what they have planned and done, am about to come[a] and gather the people of all nations and languages, and they will come and see my glory.

[19] "I will set a sign among them, and I will send some of those who survive to the nations—to Tarshish, to the Libyans[b] and Lydians (famous as archers), to Tubal and Greece, and to the distant islands that have not heard of my fame or seen my glory. They will proclaim my glory among the nations. [20] And they will bring all your people, from all the nations, to my holy mountain in Jerusalem as an offering to the LORD—on horses, in chariots and wagons, and on mules and camels," says the LORD. "They will bring them, as the Israelites bring their grain offerings, to the temple of the LORD in ceremonially clean vessels.

[a] 18 The meaning of the Hebrew for this clause is uncertain.
[b] 19 Some Septuagint manuscripts Put (Libyans); Hebrew Pul

## Amplified Bible

word: Your brethren who hate you, who cast you out for My name's sake, have said, Let the Lord be glorified, that we may see your joy! But it is they who shall be put to shame.

[6] [Hark!] An uproar from the city! A voice from the temple! The voice of the Lord, rendering recompense to His enemies!

[7] Before [Zion] travailed, she gave birth; before her pain came upon her, she was delivered of a male child.

[8] Who has heard of such a thing? Who has seen such things? Shall a land [a] be born in one day? Or shall a nation be brought forth in a moment? For as soon as Zion was in labor, she brought forth her children.

[9] Shall I bring to the [moment of] birth and not cause to bring forth? says the Lord. Shall I Who causes to bring forth shut the womb? says your God.

[10] Rejoice with Jerusalem and be glad for her, all you who love her; rejoice for joy with her, all you who mourn over her,

[11] That you may nurse and be satisfied from her consoling breasts, that you may drink deeply and be delighted with the abundance *and* brightness of her glory.

[12] For thus says the Lord: Behold, I will extend peace to her like a river, and the glory of the nations like an overflowing stream; then you will be nursed, you will be carried on her hip and trotted [lovingly bounced up and down] on her [God's maternal] knees.

[13] As one whom his mother comforts, so will I comfort you; you shall be comforted in Jerusalem.

[14] When you see this, your heart shall rejoice; your bones shall flourish like green *and* tender grass. And the [powerful] hand of the Lord shall be revealed *and* known to be with His servants, but His indignation [shown] to be against His enemies.

[15] For behold, the Lord will come in fire, and His chariots will be like the stormy wind, to render His anger with fierceness, and His rebuke with flames of fire.

[16] For by fire and by His sword will the Lord execute judgment upon all flesh, and the slain of the Lord will be many.

[17] Those who [attempt to] sanctify themselves and cleanse themselves to enter [and sacrifice to idols] in the gardens, following after [b] one in the midst, eating hog's flesh and the abomination [creeping things] and the [mouse—their works and their thoughts] shall come to an end together, says the Lord.

[18] For I know their works and their thoughts. And the time is coming when I will gather all nations and tongues, and they will come and see My glory.

[19] And I will set up a [miraculous] sign among them, and from them I will send survivors to the nations—to Tarshish, Pul (Put) and Lud, who draw the bow, to Tubal and Javan, to the isles *and* coastlands afar off that have not heard of My fame nor seen My glory. And they will declare *and* proclaim My glory among the nations.

[20] And they shall bring all your brethren from all the nations as an offering to the Lord—upon horses and in chariots and in litters and upon mules and upon camels—to My holy mountain Jerusalem, says the Lord, just as the children of Israel bring their cereal offering in a clean vessel to the house of the Lord.

---

[a] Never in the history of the world had such a thing happened before—but God keeps His word. As definitely foretold here and in Ezekiel 37:21, 22, Israel became a recognized nation, actually "born in one day." After being away from their homeland for almost 2,000 years, the Jews were given a national homeland in Palestine by the Balfour Declaration in November, 1917. In 1922, the League of Nations gave Great Britain the mandate over Palestine. On May 14, 1948, Great Britain withdrew her mandate, and immediately Israel was declared a sovereign state, and her growth and importance among nations became astonishing. [b] Perhaps referring to the image of the Syrian god Adad. Some commentators also suggest that this may refer to the cultic leader in the center who shows by his example how to conduct the ceremonies.

## New International Version

21And I will select some of them also to be priests and Levites," says the LORD.

22"As the new heavens and the new earth that I make will endure before me," declares the LORD, "so will your name and descendants endure. 23From one New Moon to another and from one Sabbath to another, all mankind will come and bow down before me," says the LORD. 24"And they will go out and look on the dead bodies of those who rebelled against me; the worms that eat them will not die, the fire that burns them will not be quenched, and they will be loathsome to all mankind."

## Amplified Bible

21And I will also take some of them for priests and for Levites, says the Lord.

22For as the new [a]heavens and the new earth which I make shall remain before Me, says the Lord, so shall your offspring and your name remain.

23And it shall be that from one New Moon to another New Moon and from one Sabbath to another Sabbath, all flesh shall come to worship before Me, says the Lord.

24And they shall go forth and gaze upon the dead bodies of the [rebellious] men who have stepped over against Me; for their worm shall not die, their fire shall not be quenched, and they shall be an abhorrence to all mankind.

*a* See footnote on Isa. 65:17.

# Jeremiah

# Jeremiah

**1** The words of Jeremiah son of Hilkiah, one of the priests at Anathoth in the territory of Benjamin. ²The word of the LORD came to him in the thirteenth year of the reign of Josiah son of Amon king of Judah, ³and through the reign of Jehoiakim son of Josiah king of Judah, down to the fifth month of the eleventh year of Zedekiah son of Josiah king of Judah, when the people of Jerusalem went into exile.

### The Call of Jeremiah

⁴The word of the LORD came to me, saying,

⁵"Before I formed you in the womb I knew*ª* you,
  before you were born I set you apart;
I appointed you as a prophet to the nations."

⁶"Alas, Sovereign LORD," I said, "I do not know how to speak; I am too young."

⁷But the LORD said to me, "Do not say, 'I am too young.' You must go to everyone I send you to and say whatever I command you. ⁸Do not be afraid of them, for I am with you and will rescue you," declares the LORD.

⁹Then the LORD reached out his hand and touched my mouth and said to me, "I have put my words in your mouth. ¹⁰See, today I appoint you over nations and kingdoms to uproot and tear down, to destroy and overthrow, to build and to plant."

¹¹The word of the LORD came to me: "What do you see, Jeremiah?"

"I see the branch of an almond tree," I replied.

¹²The LORD said to me, "You have seen correctly, for I am watching*ᵇ* to see that my word is fulfilled."

¹³The word of the LORD came to me again: "What do you see?"

"I see a pot that is boiling," I answered. "It is tilting toward us from the north."

¹⁴The LORD said to me, "From the north disaster will be poured out on all who live in the land. ¹⁵I am about to summon all the peoples of the northern kingdoms," declares the LORD.

"Their kings will come and set up their thrones
  in the entrance of the gates of Jerusalem;
they will come against all her surrounding walls
  and against all the towns of Judah.
¹⁶I will pronounce my judgments on my people
  because of their wickedness in forsaking me,
in burning incense to other gods
  and in worshiping what their hands have made.

¹⁷"Get yourself ready! Stand up and say to them whatever I command you. Do not be terrified by them, or I will terrify you before them. ¹⁸Today I have made you a fortified city, an iron pillar and a bronze wall to stand against the whole land—against the kings of Judah, its officials, its priests and the people of the land. ¹⁹They will fight against you but will not overcome you, for I am with you and will rescue you," declares the LORD.

**1** The words of Jeremiah son of Hilkiah, of the priests who were in Anathoth in the land of Benjamin [two or three miles north of Jerusalem],

²To whom the word of the Lord came in the days of Josiah son of Amon king of Judah in the thirteenth year of his reign.

³It came also in the days of Jehoiakim son of Josiah king of Judah until the end of the eleventh year of Zedekiah son of Josiah king of Judah, until the carrying away of Jerusalem into captivity in the fifth month. [II Kings 25:8-11.]

⁴Then the word of the Lord came to me [Jeremiah], saying,

⁵Before I formed you in the womb I knew [and] approved of you [as My chosen instrument], and before you were born I separated *and* set you apart, consecrating you; [and] I appointed you as a prophet to the nations. [Exod. 33:12; Isa. 49:1, 5; Rom. 8:29.]

⁶Then said I, Ah, Lord God! Behold, I cannot speak, for I am only a youth. [Exod. 4:10; 6:12, 30; I Kings 3:7.]

⁷But the Lord said to me, Say not, I am only a youth; for you shall go to all to whom I shall send you, and whatever I command you, you shall speak.

⁸Be not afraid of them [their faces], for I am with you to deliver you, says the Lord.

⁹Then the Lord put forth His hand and touched my mouth. And the Lord said to me, Behold, I have put My words in your mouth.

¹⁰See, I have this day appointed you to the oversight of the nations and of the kingdoms to root out and pull down, to destroy and to overthrow, to build and to plant.

¹¹Moreover, the word of the Lord came to me, saying, Jeremiah, what do you see? And I said, I see a branch *or* shoot of an almond tree [the emblem of alertness and activity, blossoming in late winter].

¹²Then said the Lord to me, You have seen well, for I am alert *and* active, watching over My word to perform it.

¹³And the word of the Lord came to me the second time, saying, What do you see? And I said, I see a boiling pot, and the face of it is [tipped away] from the north [its mouth about to pour forth on the south, on Judea].

¹⁴Then the Lord said to me, Out of the north the evil [which the prophets had foretold as the result of national sin] shall disclose itself *and* break forth upon all the inhabitants of the land.

¹⁵For, behold, I will call all the tribes of the kingdoms of the north, says the Lord; and they will come and set every one his throne at the entrance of the gates of Jerusalem, against all its walls round about, and against all the cities of Judah [as God's judicial act, a consequence of Judah's wickedness].

¹⁶And I will utter My judgments against them for all the wickedness of those who have forsaken Me, burned incense to other gods, and worshiped the works of their own hands [idols].

¹⁷But you [Jeremiah], gird up your loins! Arise and tell them all that I command you. Do not be dismayed *and* break down at the sight of their faces, lest I confound you before them *and* permit you to be overcome.

¹⁸For, behold, I have made you this day a fortified city and an iron pillar and bronze walls against the whole land—against the [successive] kings of Judah, against its princes, against its priests, and against the people of the land [giving you divine strength which no hostile power can overcome]. [Isa. 50:7; 54:17; Jer. 6:27; 15:20; Luke 21:15; Acts 6:10.]

¹⁹And they shall fight against you, but they shall not [finally] prevail against you, for I am with you, says the Lord, to deliver you.

# New International Version

## Israel Forsakes God

**2** The word of the LORD came to me: ²"Go and proclaim in the hearing of Jerusalem:

"This is what the LORD says:

"'I remember the devotion of your youth,
  how as a bride you loved me
and followed me through the wilderness,
  through a land not sown.
³ Israel was holy to the LORD,
  the firstfruits of his harvest;
all who devoured her were held guilty,
  and disaster overtook them,'"
                              declares the LORD.

⁴ Hear the word of the LORD, you descendants of Jacob,
  all you clans of Israel.

⁵ This is what the LORD says:

"What fault did your ancestors find in me,
  that they strayed so far from me?
They followed worthless idols
  and became worthless themselves.
⁶ They did not ask, 'Where is the LORD,
  who brought us up out of Egypt
and led us through the barren wilderness,
  through a land of deserts and ravines,
a land of drought and utter darkness,
  a land where no one travels and no one lives?'
⁷ I brought you into a fertile land
  to eat its fruit and rich produce.
But you came and defiled my land
  and made my inheritance detestable.
⁸ The priests did not ask,
  'Where is the LORD?'
Those who deal with the law did not know me;
  the leaders rebelled against me.
The prophets prophesied by Baal,
  following worthless idols.

⁹ "Therefore I bring charges against you again,"
                              declares the LORD.
  "And I will bring charges against your children's
    children.
¹⁰ Cross over to the coasts of Cyprus and look,
  send to Kedar[a] and observe closely;
  see if there has ever been anything like this:
¹¹ Has a nation ever changed its gods?
  (Yet they are not gods at all.)
But my people have exchanged their glorious God
  for worthless idols.
¹² Be appalled at this, you heavens,
  and shudder with great horror,"
                              declares the LORD.
¹³ "My people have committed two sins:
They have forsaken me,
  the spring of living water,
and have dug their own cisterns,
  broken cisterns that cannot hold water.
¹⁴ Is Israel a servant, a slave by birth?
  Why then has he become plunder?
¹⁵ Lions have roared;
  they have growled at him.
They have laid waste his land;
  his towns are burned and deserted.
¹⁶ Also, the men of Memphis and Tahpanhes
  have cracked your skull.
¹⁷ Have you not brought this on yourselves
  by forsaking the LORD your God
  when he led you in the way?
¹⁸ Now why go to Egypt

# Amplified Bible

**2** And the word of the Lord came to me [Jeremiah], saying,
²Go and cry in the ears of Jerusalem, saying, Thus says the Lord: I [earnestly] remember the kindness *and* devotion of your youth, your love after your betrothal [in Egypt] *and* marriage [at Sinai] when you followed Me in the wilderness, in a land not sown.
³Israel was holiness [something set apart from ordinary purposes, dedicated] to the Lord, the firstfruits of His harvest [of which no stranger was allowed to partake]; all who ate of it [injuring Israel] offended *and* became guilty; evil came upon them, says the Lord.
⁴Hear the word of the Lord, O house of Jacob, and all the families of the house of Israel.
⁵Thus says the Lord: What unrighteousness did your fathers find in Me, that they went far from Me and [habitually] went after emptiness, falseness, *and* futility and themselves became fruitless *and* worthless?
⁶Nor did they say, Where is the Lord, Who brought us up out of the land of Egypt, Who led us through the wilderness, through a land of deserts and pits, through a land of drought and of the shadow of death *and* deep darkness, through a land that no man passes through and where no man dwells?
⁷And I brought you into a plentiful land to enjoy its fruits and good things. But when you entered, you defiled My land and made My heritage an abomination [detestable and loathsome].
⁸[Even] the priests did not say, Where is the Lord? And those who handle the law [given by God to Moses] knew Me not. The rulers *and* secular shepherds also transgressed against Me, and the prophets prophesied by [the authority and in the name of] Baal and followed after things that do not profit.
⁹Therefore I will still contend with you [by inflicting further judgments on you], says the Lord, and with your children's children will I contend.
¹⁰For cross over to the coasts of Cyprus [to the west] and see, and send also to Kedar [to the east] and carefully consider; and see whether there has been such a thing as this:
¹¹Has a nation [ever] changed its gods, even though they are not gods? But My people have changed their Glory [God] for that which does not profit.
¹²Be astonished *and* appalled, O heavens, at this; be shocked *and* shrivel up with horror, says the Lord [at the behavior of the people].
¹³For My people have committed two evils: they have forsaken Me, the Fountain of living waters, *and* have hewn for themselves cisterns, broken cisterns which cannot hold water.
¹⁴Is Israel a servant? Is he a homeborn slave? Why has he become a captive *and* a prey?
¹⁵The young lions have roared over him *and* made their voices heard. And they have made his land a waste; his cities are burned ruins without inhabitant.
¹⁶Moreover, the children of Memphis and Tahpanhes (Egypt) [have in times past shown their power as a foe; they] have broken *and* fed on the crown of your head [Israel]—so do not rely on them as an ally now.
¹⁷Have you not brought this upon yourself by forsaking the Lord your God when He led you in the way?
¹⁸And now what have you to gain by allying yourself

---

*a 10* In the Syro-Arabian desert

## New International Version

to drink water from the Nile[a]?
And why go to Assyria
　　to drink water from the Euphrates?
19 Your wickedness will punish you;
　　your backsliding will rebuke you.
Consider then and realize
　　how evil and bitter it is for you
when you forsake the LORD your God
　　and have no awe of me,"
　　　　　　declares the Lord, the LORD Almighty.

20 "Long ago you broke off your yoke
　　and tore off your bonds;
　　you said, 'I will not serve you!'
Indeed, on every high hill
　　and under every spreading tree
　　you lay down as a prostitute.
21 I had planted you like a choice vine
　　of sound and reliable stock.
How then did you turn against me
　　into a corrupt, wild vine?
22 Although you wash yourself with soap
　　and use an abundance of cleansing powder,
　　the stain of your guilt is still before me,"
　　　　　　declares the Sovereign LORD.
23 "How can you say, 'I am not defiled;
　　I have not run after the Baals'?
See how you behaved in the valley;
　　consider what you have done.
You are a swift she-camel
　　running here and there,
24 a wild donkey accustomed to the desert,
　　sniffing the wind in her craving—
　　in her heat who can restrain her?
Any males that pursue her need not tire themselves;
　　at mating time they will find her.
25 Do not run until your feet are bare
　　and your throat is dry.
But you said, 'It's no use!
　　I love foreign gods,
　　and I must go after them.'

26 "As a thief is disgraced when he is caught,
　　so the people of Israel are disgraced—
they, their kings and their officials,
　　their priests and their prophets.
27 They say to wood, 'You are my father,'
　　and to stone, 'You gave me birth.'
They have turned their backs to me
　　and not their faces;
yet when they are in trouble, they say,
　　'Come and save us!'
28 Where are the gods you made for yourselves?
　　Let them come if they can save you
　　when you are in trouble!
For you, Judah, have as many gods
　　as you have towns.

29 "Why do you bring charges against me?
　　You have all rebelled against me,"
　　　　　　declares the LORD.
30 "In vain I punished your people;
　　they did not respond to correction.
Your sword has devoured your prophets
　　like a ravenous lion.

31 "You of this generation, consider the word of the LORD:

"Have I been a desert to Israel
　　or a land of great darkness?
Why do my people say, 'We are free to roam;
　　we will come to you no more'?

## Amplified Bible

with Egypt *and* going her way, to drink the [black and roiled] waters of the Nile? Or what have you to gain in going the way of Assyria, to drink the waters of the Euphrates?

19 Your own wickedness shall chasten *and* correct you, and your backslidings *and* desertion of faith shall reprove you. Know therefore *and* recognize that this is an evil and bitter thing: [first,] you have forsaken the Lord your God; [second,] you are indifferent to Me *and* the fear of Me is not in you, says the Lord of hosts.

20 For long ago [in Egypt] I broke your yoke and burst your bonds [not that you might be free, but that you might serve Me] [a]*and* long ago you shattered the yoke and snapped the bonds [of My law which I put upon you]; you said, I will not serve *and* obey You! For upon every high hill and under every green tree you [eagerly] prostrated yourself [in idolatrous worship], playing the harlot.

21 Yet I had planted you [O house of Israel] a choice vine, wholly of pure seed. How then have you turned into degenerate shoots of wild vine alien to Me?

22 For though you wash yourself with lye and use much soap, yet your iniquity *and* guilt are still [upon you; you are] spotted, dirty, *and* stained before Me, says the Lord.

23 How can you say, I am not defiled; I have not gone after the Baals [other gods]? Look at your way in the valley; know what you have done. You are a restive young female camel [in the uncontrollable violence of her brute passion eagerly] running hither and thither,

24 Or [you have the untamed and reckless nature of] a wild donkey used to the desert, in her heat sniffing the wind [for the scent of a male]. In her mating season who can restrain her? No males seeking her need weary themselves; in her month they will find her [seeking them].

25 [Cease from your mad running after idols, from which you get nothing but bitter injury.] Keep your feet from being unshod and your throat from thirst. But you said, It is hopeless! For I have loved strangers *and* foreigners, and after them I will go.

26 As the thief is brought to shame when he is caught, so shall the house of Israel be brought to shame—they, their kings, their princes, their priests, and their prophets—

27 [Inasmuch as] they say to a tree, You are my father, and to a stone, You gave me birth. For they have turned their backs to Me and not their faces; but in the time of their trouble, they say, Arise [O Lord] and save us!

28 But where are your gods that you made for yourself? Let them arise if they can save you in the time of your trouble! For [as many as] the number of your cities are your gods, O Judah. [Surely so many handmade idols should be able to help you!]

29 Why do you complain *and* remonstrate against My wrath? You all have rebelled *and* revolted against Me, says the Lord.

30 In vain have I stricken your children (your people); they received no discipline (no correction). Your own sword devoured your prophets like a destroying lion.

31 O generation [that you are]! Behold, consider, *and* regard the word of the Lord: Have I been a wilderness to Israel [like a land without food]? A land of deep darkness [like a way without light]? Why do My people say, We have broken loose [we are free and will roam at large]; we will come no more to You?

---

[a] 18 Hebrew *Shihor*; that is, a branch of the Nile

[a] Another translation of the previous statement.

## New International Version

32 Does a young woman forget her jewelry,
  a bride her wedding ornaments?
Yet my people have forgotten me,
  days without number.
33 How skilled you are at pursuing love!
  Even the worst of women can learn from your ways.
34 On your clothes is found
  the lifeblood of the innocent poor,
  though you did not catch them breaking in.
Yet in spite of all this
35   you say, 'I am innocent;
  he is not angry with me.'
But I will pass judgment on you
  because you say, 'I have not sinned.'
36 Why do you go about so much,
  changing your ways?
You will be disappointed by Egypt
  as you were by Assyria.
37 You will also leave that place
  with your hands on your head,
for the LORD has rejected those you trust;
  you will not be helped by them.

**3** "If a man divorces his wife
  and she leaves him and marries another man,
should he return to her again?
  Would not the land be completely defiled?
But you have lived as a prostitute with many lovers—
  would you now return to me?"

                                   declares the LORD.
2 "Look up to the barren heights and see.
  Is there any place where you have not been
    ravished?
By the roadside you sat waiting for lovers,
  sat like a nomad in the desert.
You have defiled the land
  with your prostitution and wickedness.
3 Therefore the showers have been withheld,
  and no spring rains have fallen.
Yet you have the brazen look of a prostitute;
  you refuse to blush with shame.
4 Have you not just called to me:
  'My Father, my friend from my youth,
5 will you always be angry?
  Will your wrath continue forever?'
This is how you talk,
  but you do all the evil you can."

### Unfaithful Israel

6 During the reign of King Josiah, the LORD said to me, "Have you seen what faithless Israel has done? She has gone up on every high hill and under every spreading tree and has committed adultery there. 7 I thought that after she had done all this she would return to me but she did not, and her unfaithful sister Judah saw it. 8 I gave faithless Israel her certificate of divorce and sent her away because of all her adulteries. Yet I saw that her unfaithful sister Judah had no fear; she also went out and committed adultery. 9 Because Israel's immorality mattered so little to her, she defiled the land and committed adultery with stone and wood. 10 In spite of all this, her unfaithful sister Judah did not return to me with all her heart, but only in pretense," declares the LORD.

## Amplified Bible

32 Can a maid forget and neglect [to wear] her ornaments, or a bride her [marriage] girdle [with its significance like that of a wedding ring]? Yet My people have forgotten Me, days without number.
33 How you deck yourself and direct your way to procure [adulterous] love! Because of it even wicked women have learned [indecent] ways from you.
34 Also on your skirts is found the lifeblood of the persons of the innocent poor; you did not find them housebreaking, nor have I found it out by secret search. But it is because of [your lust for idolatry that you have done] all these things—[that is everywhere evident.]
35 Yet you keep saying, I am innocent; surely His anger has turned away from Me. Behold, I will bring you to judgment and will plead against you because you say, I have not sinned.
36 Why do you gad or wander about so much to change your way? You shall be put to shame by Egypt as you were put to shame by Assyria.
37 From [Egypt] also you will come away with your hands upon your head, for the Lord has rejected those in whom you confide, and you will not prosper with [respect to] them.

**3** That is to say, If a man puts away his wife and she goes from him and becomes another man's, will he return to her again? [Of course not!] Would not that land [where such a thing happened] be greatly polluted? But you have played the harlot [against Me] with many lovers—yet would you now return to Me? says the Lord [or do you even think to return to Me?]
2 Lift up your eyes to the bare heights and see. Where have you not been adulterously lain with? By the wayside you have sat waiting for lovers [eager for idolatry], like an Arabian [desert tribesman who waits to plunder] in the wilderness; and you have polluted the land with your vile harlotry and your wickedness (unfaithfulness and disobedience to God).
3 Therefore the showers have been withheld, and there has been no spring rain. Yet you have the brow of a prostitute; you refuse to be ashamed.
4 Have you not just now cried to Me: My Father, You were the guide and companion of my youth?
5 Will He retain His anger forever? Will He keep it to the end? Behold, you have so spoken, but you have done all the evil things you could and have had your way and have carried them through.
6 Moreover, the Lord said to me [Jeremiah] in the days of Josiah the king [of Judah], Have you seen what that faithless and backsliding Israel has done—how she went up on every high hill and under every green tree and there played the harlot?
7 And I said, After she has done all these things, she will return to Me; but she did not return, and her faithless and treacherous sister Judah saw it.
8 And I saw, even though [Judah knew] that for this very cause of committing adultery (idolatry) I [the Lord] had put faithless Israel away and given her a bill of divorce; yet her faithless and treacherous sister Judah was not afraid, but she also went and played the harlot [following after idols].
9 And through the infamy and unseemly frivolity of Israel's whoredom [because her immorality mattered little to her], she polluted and defiled the land, [by her idolatry] committing adultery with [idols of] stones and trees.
10 But in spite of all this, her faithless and treacherous sister Judah did not return to Me in sincerity and with her whole heart, but only in sheer hypocrisy [has she feigned obedience to King Josiah's reforms], says the Lord. [II Chron. 34:33; Hos. 7:13, 14.]

## New International Version

11The LORD said to me, "Faithless Israel is more righteous than unfaithful Judah. 12Go, proclaim this message toward the north:

"'Return, faithless Israel,' declares the LORD,
'I will frown on you no longer,
for I am faithful,' declares the LORD,
'I will not be angry forever.
13Only acknowledge your guilt—
you have rebelled against the LORD your God,
you have scattered your favors to foreign gods
under every spreading tree,
and have not obeyed me,'"

declares the LORD.

14"Return, faithless people," declares the LORD, "for I am your husband. I will choose you—one from a town and two from a clan—and bring you to Zion. 15Then I will give you shepherds after my own heart, who will lead you with knowledge and understanding. 16In those days, when your numbers have increased greatly in the land," declares the LORD, "people will no longer say, 'The ark of the covenant of the LORD.' It will never enter their minds or be remembered; it will not be missed, nor will another one be made. 17At that time they will call Jerusalem The Throne of the LORD, and all nations will gather in Jerusalem to honor the name of the LORD. No longer will they follow the stubbornness of their evil hearts. 18In those days the people of Judah will join the people of Israel, and together they will come from a northern land to the land I gave your ancestors as an inheritance.

19"I myself said,

"'How gladly would I treat you like my children
and give you a pleasant land,
the most beautiful inheritance of any nation.'
I thought you would call me 'Father'
and not turn away from following me.
20But like a woman unfaithful to her husband,
so you, Israel, have been unfaithful to me,"

declares the LORD.

21A cry is heard on the barren heights,
the weeping and pleading of the people of Israel,
because they have perverted their ways
and have forgotten the LORD their God.

22"Return, faithless people;
I will cure you of backsliding."

"Yes, we will come to you,
for you are the LORD our God.
23Surely the idolatrous commotion on the hills
and mountains is a deception;
surely in the LORD our God
is the salvation of Israel.
24From our youth shameful gods have consumed
the fruits of our ancestors' labor—
their flocks and herds,
their sons and daughters.
25Let us lie down in our shame,
and let our disgrace cover us.
We have sinned against the LORD our God,
both we and our ancestors;
from our youth till this day
we have not obeyed the LORD our God."

**4** "If you, Israel, will return,
then return to me,"

declares the LORD.

"If you put your detestable idols out of my sight
and no longer go astray,

## Amplified Bible

11And the Lord said to me, Backsliding *and* faithless Israel has shown herself less guilty than false *and* treacherous Judah.

12Go and proclaim these words toward the north [where the ten tribes have been taken as captives] and say, Return, faithless Israel, says the Lord, *and* I will not cause My countenance to fall *and* look in anger upon you, for I am merciful, says the Lord; I will not keep My anger forever.

13Only know, understand, *and* acknowledge your iniquity *and* guilt—that you have rebelled *and* transgressed against the Lord your God and have scattered your favors among strangers under every green tree, and you have not obeyed My voice, says the Lord.

14Return, O faithless children [of the whole twelve tribes], says the Lord, for I am Lord *and* Master *and* Husband to you, and I will take you [not as a nation, but individually]—one from a city and two from a tribal family—and I will bring you to Zion. [Luke 15:20-22.]

15And I will give you [spiritual] shepherds after My own heart [in the final time], who will feed you with knowledge and understanding *and* judgment.

16And it shall be that when you have multiplied and increased in the land in those days, says the Lord, they shall no more say, The ark of the covenant of the Lord. It shall not come to mind, nor shall they [seriously] remember it, nor shall they miss *or* visit it, nor shall it be repaired *or* made again [for instead of the ark, which represented God's presence, He will show Himself to be present throughout the city]. [Isa. 65:17; Rev. 21:3, 22, 23.]

17At that time they shall call Jerusalem The Throne of the Lord, and all the nations shall be gathered to it, in the renown *and* name of the Lord, to Jerusalem; nor shall they walk any more after the stubbornness of their own evil hearts.

18In those days the house of Judah shall walk with the house of Israel, and together they shall come out of the land of the north to the land that I gave as an inheritance to your fathers.

19And I thought how [gloriously and honorably] I would set you among My children and give you a pleasant land, a goodly heritage, the most beautiful *and* best [inheritance] among all nations! And I thought you would call Me My Father and would not turn away from following Me.

20Surely, as a wife treacherously *and* faithlessly departs from her husband, so have you dealt treacherously *and* faithlessly with Me, O house of Israel, says the Lord.

21A voice is heard on the bare heights, the weeping *and* pleading of the sons of Israel, because they have perverted their ways, they have [eagerly] forgotten the Lord their God.

22Return, O faithless sons, [says the Lord, and] I will heal your faithlessness. [And they answer] Behold, we come to You, for You are the Lord our God.

23Truly in vain is the hope of salvation from the hills and from the tumult *and* noisy throng on the mountains; truly in *and* with the Lord our God rests the salvation of Israel.

24[We have been ruined as a nation by our faithlessness and idolatry] for the shameful thing has consumed all for which our fathers toiled from our youth—their flocks and their herds, their sons and their daughters.

25Let us lie prostrate in our shame, and let our dishonor *and* confusion cover us; for we have sinned against the Lord our God, we and our fathers; from our youth even to this day we have not obeyed the voice of the Lord our God.

**4** If you will return, O Israel, says the Lord, if you will return to Me, and if you will put away your abominable false gods out of My sight and not stray *or* waver,

## New International Version

²and if in a truthful, just and righteous way
   you swear, 'As surely as the LORD lives,'
then the nations will invoke blessings by him
   and in him they will boast."

³This is what the LORD says to the people of Judah and
to Jerusalem:

"Break up your unplowed ground
   and do not sow among thorns.
⁴Circumcise yourselves to the LORD,
   circumcise your hearts,
      you people of Judah and inhabitants of Jerusalem,
or my wrath will flare up and burn like fire
   because of the evil you have done—
      burn with no one to quench it.

### Disaster From the North

⁵"Announce in Judah and proclaim in Jerusalem and
      say:
   'Sound the trumpet throughout the land!'
Cry aloud and say:
   'Gather together!
   Let us flee to the fortified cities!'
⁶Raise the signal to go to Zion!
   Flee for safety without delay!
For I am bringing disaster from the north,
   even terrible destruction."

⁷A lion has come out of his lair;
   a destroyer of nations has set out.
He has left his place
   to lay waste your land.
Your towns will lie in ruins
   without inhabitant.
⁸So put on sackcloth,
   lament and wail,
for the fierce anger of the LORD
   has not turned away from us.

⁹"In that day," declares the LORD,
   "the king and the officials will lose heart,
the priests will be horrified,
   and the prophets will be appalled."

¹⁰Then I said, "Alas, Sovereign LORD! How completely
you have deceived this people and Jerusalem by saying,
'You will have peace,' when the sword is at our throats!"

¹¹At that time this people and Jerusalem will be told,
"A scorching wind from the barren heights in the desert
blows toward my people, but not to winnow or cleanse; ¹²a
wind too strong for that comes from me. Now I pronounce
my judgments against them."

¹³Look! He advances like the clouds,
   his chariots come like a whirlwind,
his horses are swifter than eagles.
   Woe to us! We are ruined!
¹⁴Jerusalem, wash the evil from your heart and be saved.
   How long will you harbor wicked thoughts?
¹⁵A voice is announcing from Dan,
   proclaiming disaster from the hills of Ephraim.
¹⁶"Tell this to the nations,
   proclaim concerning Jerusalem:
'A besieging army is coming from a distant land,
   raising a war cry against the cities of Judah.
¹⁷They surround her like men guarding a field,
   because she has rebelled against me,'"
                              declares the LORD.

¹⁸"Your own conduct and actions
   have brought this on you.
This is your punishment.
   How bitter it is!
   How it pierces to the heart!"

## Amplified Bible

²And if you swear, As the Lord lives, in truth, in judgment *and* justice, and in righteousness (uprightness in
every area and relation), then the nations will bless themselves in Him and in Him will they glory.

³For thus says the Lord to the men of Judah and to Jerusalem: Break up your ground left uncultivated for a season, so that you may not sow among thorns.

⁴Circumcise yourselves to the Lord and take away the
foreskins of your hearts, you men of Judah and inhabitants
of Jerusalem, lest My wrath go forth like fire [consuming
all that gets in its way] and burn so that no one can quench
it because of the evil of your doings.

⁵Declare in Judah and publish in Jerusalem and say:
Blow the trumpet in the land; cry aloud and say: Assemble
yourselves, and let us go into the fortified cities.

⁶Raise a standard toward Zion [to mark out the safest
route to those seeking safety within Jerusalem's walls]!
Flee for safety, stay not, for I bring evil from the north,
and great destruction.

⁷A lion has gone up from his thicket, and a destroyer of
nations is on his way. He has gone forth from his place to
make your land a desolate waste; and your cities shall be
left in ruins without an inhabitant.

⁸For this, gird yourselves with sackcloth, lament and
wail, for the fierce anger of the Lord has not turned back
from us.

⁹And it shall be in that day, says the Lord, that the understanding *and* courage of the king shall fail (be paralyzed), and also that of the princes; the priests shall be appalled *and* the prophets astounded *and* dazed with horror.

¹⁰Then I [Jeremiah] said, ªAlas, Lord God! Surely You
have greatly deceived *and* misled this people and Jerusalem, [for the prophets represented You as] saying [to
Your people], You shall have peace, whereas the sword has
reached to [their very] life.

¹¹At that time it will be said to this people and to Jerusalem, A hot wind from the bare heights in the wilderness
[comes at My command] against the daughter of My people—not [a wind] to fan or cleanse [from chaff, as when
threshing, but]

¹²A wind too strong *and* full for winnowing comes at
My word. Now I will also speak in judgment against [My
people].

¹³Behold, [the enemy] comes up like clouds, his chariots like the whirlwind; his horses are swifter than eagles.
Woe to us, for we are ruined (destroyed)!

¹⁴O Jerusalem, wash your heart from wickedness, that
you may be saved! How long shall your iniquitous *and*
grossly offensive thoughts lodge within you?

¹⁵For a voice declares from Dan [in the north] and proclaims evil from Mount Ephraim [the range dividing Israel
from Judah].

¹⁶Warn the [neighboring] nations [that our adversary is
coming]; announce to Jerusalem that besiegers are coming from a far country, and they shout against the cities
of Judah.

¹⁷Like keepers of a field they are against her round
about, because she has been rebellious against Me, says
the Lord.

¹⁸Your ways and your doings have brought these things
upon you. This is your calamity *and* doom; surely it is bitter, for surely it reaches your very heart!

---

ª Jeremiah could not reconcile the doom he was now commanded to
pronounce either with his own previous prophecy or with what he had
read in the writings of the previous prophets. We have the apostle
Peter's comment on the perplexity of the prophets in I Pet. 1:10-12: "The
prophets, who prophesied of the grace (divine blessing) which was
intended for you, searched and inquired earnestly about this salvation.
They sought [to find out] to whom or when this was to come which the
Spirit of Christ working within them was indicating when He predicted
the sufferings of Christ and the glories that should follow [them]. It was
then disclosed to them that the services they were rendering were not
meant for themselves *and* their period of time, but for you. . . . Into these
things [the very] angels long to look!"

## New International Version

<sup>19</sup>Oh, my anguish, my anguish!
  I writhe in pain.
Oh, the agony of my heart!
  My heart pounds within me,
  I cannot keep silent.
For I have heard the sound of the trumpet;
  I have heard the battle cry.
<sup>20</sup>Disaster follows disaster;
  the whole land lies in ruins.
In an instant my tents are destroyed,
  my shelter in a moment.
<sup>21</sup>How long must I see the battle standard
  and hear the sound of the trumpet?

<sup>22</sup>"My people are fools;
  they do not know me.
They are senseless children;
  they have no understanding.
They are skilled in doing evil;
  they know not how to do good."

<sup>23</sup>I looked at the earth,
  and it was formless and empty;
and at the heavens,
  and their light was gone.
<sup>24</sup>I looked at the mountains,
  and they were quaking;
  all the hills were swaying.
<sup>25</sup>I looked, and there were no people;
  every bird in the sky had flown away.
<sup>26</sup>I looked, and the fruitful land was a desert;
  all its towns lay in ruins
  before the Lord, before his fierce anger.

<sup>27</sup>This is what the Lord says:

"The whole land will be ruined,
  though I will not destroy it completely.
<sup>28</sup>Therefore the earth will mourn
  and the heavens above grow dark,
because I have spoken and will not relent,
  I have decided and will not turn back."

<sup>29</sup>At the sound of horsemen and archers
  every town takes to flight.
Some go into the thickets;
  some climb up among the rocks.
All the towns are deserted;
  no one lives in them.

<sup>30</sup>What are you doing, you devastated one?
  Why dress yourself in scarlet
  and put on jewels of gold?
Why highlight your eyes with makeup?
  You adorn yourself in vain.
Your lovers despise you;
  they want to kill you.

<sup>31</sup>I hear a cry as of a woman in labor,
  a groan as of one bearing her first child—
the cry of Daughter Zion gasping for breath,
  stretching out her hands and saying,
"Alas! I am fainting;
  my life is given over to murderers."

### Not One Is Upright

**5** "Go up and down the streets of Jerusalem,
  look around and consider,
  search through her squares.
If you can find but one person
  who deals honestly and seeks the truth,
  I will forgive this city.
<sup>2</sup>Although they say, 'As surely as the Lord lives,'
  still they are swearing falsely."

## Amplified Bible

<sup>19</sup>[It is not only the prophet but also the people who cry out in their thoughts] My anguish, my anguish! I writhe in pain. Oh, the walls of my heart! My heart is disquieted *and* throbs aloud within me; I cannot be silent! For I have heard the sound of the trumpet, the alarm of war.
<sup>20</sup>News of one violent disaster *and* calamity comes close after another, for the whole land is laid waste; suddenly are my tents spoiled *and* destroyed, and my [tent] curtains ruined in a moment.
<sup>21</sup>[O Lord] how long must I see the flag [marking the route for flight] and hear the sound of the trumpet [urging the people to flee for refuge]?
<sup>22</sup>[Their chastisement will continue until it has accomplished its purpose] for My people are stupid, says the Lord [replying to Jeremiah]; they do not know *and* understand Me. They are thickheaded children, and they have no understanding. They are wise to do evil, but to do good they have no knowledge [and know not how].
<sup>23</sup>[In a vision Jeremiah sees Judah laid waste by conquest and captivity.] I looked at the land, and behold, it was [as at the time of creation] waste and vacant (void); and at the heavens, and they had no light.
<sup>24</sup>I looked at the mountains, and behold, they trembled, and all the hills moved lightly to and fro.
<sup>25</sup>I looked, and behold, there was no man, and all the birds of the air had fled.
<sup>26</sup>I looked, and behold, the fruitful land was a desert, and all its cities were laid waste before the Lord's presence, before His fierce anger.
<sup>27</sup>For thus says the Lord: The whole land will be a desolation, yet I will not make a full *and* complete end of it. [Jer. 5:10, 18; 30:11; 46:28.]
<sup>28</sup>For this will the earth mourn and the heavens above be black; because I have spoken, I have purposed, and I will not relent, nor will I turn back [from it].
<sup>29</sup>Every city flees because of the noise of the horsemen and bowmen. They go into the thickets and climb among the rocks; every city is forsaken, and not a man dwells in them.
<sup>30</sup>And you [plundered one], when you are made desolate, what will you do? Though you clothe yourself with scarlet, though you deck yourself with ornaments of gold, though you paint your eyelids *and* make them look farther apart, in vain you beautify yourself. Your lovers (allies) despise you; they seek your life.
<sup>31</sup>For I have heard a cry as of a woman in travail, the anguish as of one who brings forth her first child—the cry of the Daughter of Zion, who gasps for breath, who spreads her hands, saying, Woe is me now! I am fainting before the murderers.

**5** Run to and fro through the streets of Jerusalem, and see now and take notice! Seek in her broad squares to see if you can find a man [as Abraham sought in Sodom], one who does justice, who seeks truth, sincerity, *and* faithfulness; and I will pardon [Jerusalem—for one uncompromisingly righteous person]. [Gen. 18:22-32.]
<sup>2</sup>And though they say, As the Lord lives, surely they swear falsely.

## New International Version

3 LORD, do not your eyes look for truth?
   You struck them, but they felt no pain;
   you crushed them, but they refused correction.
They made their faces harder than stone
   and refused to repent.
4 I thought, "These are only the poor;
   they are foolish,
for they do not know the way of the LORD,
   the requirements of their God.
5 So I will go to the leaders
   and speak to them;
surely they know the way of the LORD,
   the requirements of their God."
But with one accord they too had broken off the yoke
   and torn off the bonds.
6 Therefore a lion from the forest will attack them,
   a wolf from the desert will ravage them,
a leopard will lie in wait near their towns
   to tear to pieces any who venture out,
for their rebellion is great
   and their backslidings many.

7 "Why should I forgive you?
   Your children have forsaken me
   and sworn by gods that are not gods.
I supplied all their needs,
   yet they committed adultery
   and thronged to the houses of prostitutes.
8 They are well-fed, lusty stallions,
   each neighing for another man's wife.
9 Should I not punish them for this?"
   declares the LORD.
"Should I not avenge myself
   on such a nation as this?

10 "Go through her vineyards and ravage them,
   but do not destroy them completely.
Strip off her branches,
   for these people do not belong to the LORD.
11 The people of Israel and the people of Judah
   have been utterly unfaithful to me,"
                         declares the LORD.

12 They have lied about the LORD;
   they said, "He will do nothing!
No harm will come to us;
   we will never see sword or famine.
13 The prophets are but wind
   and the word is not in them;
   so let what they say be done to them."

14 Therefore this is what the LORD God Almighty says:

"Because the people have spoken these words,
   I will make my words in your mouth a fire
   and these people the wood it consumes.
15 People of Israel," declares the LORD,
   "I am bringing a distant nation against you—
an ancient and enduring nation,
   a people whose language you do not know,
   whose speech you do not understand.
16 Their quivers are like an open grave;
   all of them are mighty warriors.
17 They will devour your harvests and food,
   devour your sons and daughters;
they will devour your flocks and herds,
   devour your vines and fig trees.
With the sword they will destroy
   the fortified cities in which you trust.

## Amplified Bible

3 O Lord, do not your eyes look on the truth? [They have meant to please You outwardly, but You look on their hearts.] You have stricken them, but they have not grieved; You have consumed them, but they have refused to take correction or instruction. They have made their faces harder than a rock, they have refused to repent and return to You.
4 Then I said, Surely these are only the poor; they are [sinfully] foolish and have no understanding, for they know not the way of the Lord, the judgment (the just and righteous law) of their God.
5 I will go to the great men and will speak to them, for they must know the way of the Lord, the judgment (the just and righteous law) of their God. But [I found the very reverse to be true] these had all alike broken the yoke [of God's law] and had burst the bonds [of obedience to Him].
6 Therefore a lion out of the forest shall slay them, a wolf of the desert shall destroy them, a leopard or panther shall lie in wait against their cities. Everyone who goes out of them shall be torn in pieces, because their transgressions are many, their backslidings and total desertion of faith are increased and have become great and mighty.
7 Why should I and how can I pass over this and forgive you for it? Your children have forsaken Me and sworn by those that are no gods. When I had fed them to the full and bound them to Me by oath, they committed [spiritual] adultery, assembling themselves in troops at the houses of [idol] harlots.
8 They were like fed stallions roaming at large; each one neighed after his neighbor's wife.
9 Shall I not punish them for these things? says the Lord; and shall I not avenge Myself on such a nation as this?
10 Go up within [Jerusalem's] walls and destroy [her vines], but do not make a full and complete end. Trim away the tendrils [of her vines], for they are not the Lord's.
11 For the house of Israel and the house of Judah have dealt very faithlessly and treacherously against Me, says the Lord.
12 They have lied about and denied the Lord by saying, It is not He [Who speaks through His prophets]! Evil shall not come upon us; nor shall we see war or famine.
13 And [say they] the prophets will become wind [what they prophesy will not come to pass], and the word [of God] is not in them. Thus shall it be done to them [as they threatened would be done to us].
14 Therefore thus says the Lord God of hosts: Because you [the people] have spoken this word, behold, I will make My words fire in your mouth [Jeremiah] and this people wood, and it will devour them.
15 Behold, I am bringing a nation upon you from afar, O house of Israel, says the Lord. It is a mighty and enduring nation, it is an ancient nation, a nation whose language you do not know, nor can you understand what they say.
16 Their quiver is [filled with deadly missiles] like an open sepulcher [filled with dead bodies; the foes] are all mighty men (heroes).
17 They shall consume your harvest and your food; they shall consume your sons and your daughters; they shall consume your flocks and your herds; they shall consume your vines and your fig trees. They shall break down and impoverish your fortified cities in which you trust, with the sword [they shall destroy them].

## New International Version

18"Yet even in those days," declares the LORD, "I will not destroy you completely. 19And when the people ask, 'Why has the LORD our God done all this to us?' you will tell them, 'As you have forsaken me and served foreign gods in your own land, so now you will serve foreigners in a land not your own.'

20"Announce this to the descendants of Jacob
and proclaim it in Judah:
21Hear this, you foolish and senseless people,
who have eyes but do not see,
who have ears but do not hear:
22Should you not fear me?" declares the LORD.
"Should you not tremble in my presence?
I made the sand a boundary for the sea,
an everlasting barrier it cannot cross.
The waves may roll, but they cannot prevail;
they may roar, but they cannot cross it.
23But these people have stubborn and rebellious hearts;
they have turned aside and gone away.
24They do not say to themselves,
'Let us fear the LORD our God,
who gives autumn and spring rains in season,
who assures us of the regular weeks of harvest.'
25Your wrongdoings have kept these away;
your sins have deprived you of good.

26"Among my people are the wicked
who lie in wait like men who snare birds
and like those who set traps to catch people.
27Like cages full of birds,
their houses are full of deceit;
they have become rich and powerful
28	and have grown fat and sleek.
Their evil deeds have no limit;
they do not seek justice.
They do not promote the case of the fatherless;
they do not defend the just cause of the poor.
29Should I not punish them for this?"
declares the LORD.
"Should I not avenge myself
on such a nation as this?

30"A horrible and shocking thing
has happened in the land:
31The prophets prophesy lies,
the priests rule by their own authority,
and my people love it this way.
But what will you do in the end?

### Jerusalem Under Siege

6 "Flee for safety, people of Benjamin!
Flee from Jerusalem!
Sound the trumpet in Tekoa!
Raise the signal over Beth Hakkerem!
For disaster looms out of the north,
even terrible destruction.
2I will destroy Daughter Zion,
so beautiful and delicate.
3Shepherds with their flocks will come against her;
they will pitch their tents around her,
each tending his own portion."

4"Prepare for battle against her!
Arise, let us attack at noon!
But, alas, the daylight is fading,
and the shadows of evening grow long.
5So arise, let us attack at night
and destroy her fortresses!"

## Amplified Bible

18But even in those days, says the Lord, I will not make a full and complete end of you.

19And when your people say, Why has the Lord our God done all these things to us? then you shall answer them, As you have forsaken Me, says the Lord, and have served strange gods in your land, so shall you serve strangers (gods) in a land that is not yours.

20Declare this in the house of Jacob and publish it in Judah:
21Hear now this, O foolish people without understanding or heart, who have eyes and see not, who have ears and hear not: [Isa. 6:9, 10; Matt. 13:10-15; Mark 8:17, 18.]
22Do you not fear and reverence Me? says the Lord. Do you not tremble before Me? I placed the sand for the boundary of the sea, a perpetual barrier beyond which it cannot pass and by an everlasting ordinance beyond which it cannot go? And though the waves of the sea toss and shake themselves, yet they cannot prevail [against the feeble grains of sand which God has ordained by nature to be sufficient for His purpose]; though [the billows] roar, yet they cannot pass over that [barrier]. [Is not such a God to be reverently feared and worshiped?]
23But these people have hearts that draw back from God and wills that rebel against Him; they have revolted and quit His service and have gone away [into idolatry].
24Nor do they say in their hearts, Let us now reverently fear and worship the Lord our God, Who gives rain, both the autumn and the spring rain in its season, Who reserves and keeps for us the appointed weeks of the harvest.
25Your iniquities have turned these blessings away, and your sins have kept good [harvests] from you.
26For among My people are found wicked men; they watch like fowlers who lie in wait; they set a trap, they catch men.
27As a cage is full of birds, so are their houses full of deceit and treachery; therefore they have become great and grown rich,
28They have grown fat and sleek. Yes, they surpass in deeds of wickedness; they do not judge and plead with justice the cause of the fatherless, that they may prosper, and they do not defend the rights of the needy.
29Shall I not punish them for these things? says the Lord. Shall I not avenge Myself on such a nation as this?
30An appalling and horrible thing [bringing desolation and destruction] has come to pass in the land:
31The prophets prophesy falsely, and the priests exercise rule at their own hands and by means of the prophets. And My people love to have it so! But what will you do when the end comes?

6 Flee for safety, you children of Benjamin, out of the midst of Jerusalem! And blow the trumpet in Tekoa [a town far south in Judah], and raise a [fire] signal over Beth-haccherem [a town near Jerusalem]! For evil is looking forth with eagerness from the north, and great destruction.
2The comely and delicate one, [Jerusalem] the Daughter of Zion, I will destroy. [To a pasturage, yes, a luxurious pasturage, have I likened her.]
3Shepherds with their flocks shall come against her; they shall pitch their tents round about her; they shall pasture, each one in his place [eating up all her luxurious herbage on every side].
4Prepare yourselves for war against her [they cry]; up, let us attack her at noon! But alas, the day declines, the evening shadows lengthen.
5Arise, let us go by night and destroy her palaces!

## New International Version

⁶This is what the LORD Almighty says:

"Cut down the trees
 and build siege ramps against Jerusalem.
This city must be punished;
 it is filled with oppression.
⁷As a well pours out its water,
 so she pours out her wickedness.
Violence and destruction resound in her;
 her sickness and wounds are ever before me.
⁸Take warning, Jerusalem,
 or I will turn away from you
and make your land desolate
 so no one can live in it."

⁹This is what the LORD Almighty says:

"Let them glean the remnant of Israel
 as thoroughly as a vine;
pass your hand over the branches again,
 like one gathering grapes."

¹⁰To whom can I speak and give warning?
 Who will listen to me?
Their ears are closed*a*
 so they cannot hear.
The word of the LORD is offensive to them;
 they find no pleasure in it.
¹¹But I am full of the wrath of the LORD,
 and I cannot hold it in.

"Pour it out on the children in the street
 and on the young men gathered together;
both husband and wife will be caught in it,
 and the old, those weighed down with years.
¹²Their houses will be turned over to others,
 together with their fields and their wives,
when I stretch out my hand
 against those who live in the land,"
                        declares the LORD.
¹³"From the least to the greatest,
 all are greedy for gain;
prophets and priests alike,
 all practice deceit.
¹⁴They dress the wound of my people
 as though it were not serious.
'Peace, peace,' they say,
 when there is no peace.
¹⁵Are they ashamed of their detestable conduct?
 No, they have no shame at all;
 they do not even know how to blush.
So they will fall among the fallen;
 they will be brought down when I punish them,"
                        says the LORD.

¹⁶This is what the LORD says:

"Stand at the crossroads and look;
 ask for the ancient paths,
ask where the good way is, and walk in it,
 and you will find rest for your souls.
 But you said, 'We will not walk in it.'
¹⁷I appointed watchmen over you and said,
 'Listen to the sound of the trumpet!'
 But you said, 'We will not listen.'
¹⁸Therefore hear, you nations;
 you who are witnesses,
 observe what will happen to them.
¹⁹Hear, you earth:
 I am bringing disaster on this people,
 the fruit of their schemes,
because they have not listened to my words
 and have rejected my law.

## Amplified Bible

⁶For the Lord of hosts has said, Hew down her trees and cast up a siege mound against Jerusalem. This is the city which must be punished; there is nothing but oppression within her.

⁷As a fountain wells up *and* casts forth its waters *and* keeps them fresh, so she is [continually] casting forth [fresh] wickedness. Violence and destruction are heard within her; sickness and wounds are continually before Me.

⁸Be corrected, reformed, instructed, *and* warned, O Jerusalem, lest I be alienated *and* parted from you, lest I make you a desolation, an uninhabited land.

⁹Thus says the Lord of hosts: They shall thoroughly glean as a vine what is left of Israel; turn back your hand again *and* again [O minister of destruction] into the baskets, like a grape gatherer, *and* strip the tendrils [of the vine].

¹⁰To whom shall I [Jeremiah] speak and give warning, that they may hear? Behold, their ears are uncircumcised [never brought into covenant with God or consecrated to His service], and they cannot hear *or* obey. Behold, the word of the Lord has become to them a reproach *and* the object of their scorn; they have no delight in it.

¹¹Therefore I am full of the wrath of the Lord; I am weary of restraining it. I will pour it out on the children in the street and on the gathering of young men together; for even the husband with the wife will be taken, the aged with the very old.

¹²And their houses will be turned over to others, their fields and their wives together; for I will stretch out My hand against the inhabitants of the land, says the Lord.

¹³For from the least of them even to the greatest of them, everyone is given to covetousness (to greed for unjust gain); and from the prophet even to the priest, everyone deals falsely.

¹⁴They have healed also the wound of the daughter of My people lightly *and* neglectfully, saying, Peace, peace, when there is no peace.

¹⁵Were they brought to shame because they had committed abominations (extremely disgusting and vile things)? No, they were not at all ashamed, nor could they blush [at their idolatry]. Therefore they shall fall among those who fall; at the time that I punish them they shall be overthrown, says the Lord.

¹⁶Thus says the Lord: Stand by the roads and look; and ask for the eternal paths, where the good, old way is; then walk in it, and you will find rest for your souls. But they said, We will not walk in it! [Matt. 11:29.]

¹⁷Also I set watchmen over you, saying, Hear *and* obey the sound of the trumpet! But they said, We will not listen *or* obey.

¹⁸Therefore hear, O [Gentile] nations, and know, O congregation [of believing ones], what [great things I will do] to them.

¹⁹Hear, O earth: behold, I am bringing evil upon this people, the fruit of their thoughts (their schemes and devices) because they have not listened *and* obeyed My words, and as for My law, they have rejected it.

---

*a* 10 Hebrew *uncircumcised*

## New International Version

20 What do I care about incense from Sheba
    or sweet calamus from a distant land?
Your burnt offerings are not acceptable;
    your sacrifices do not please me."

21 Therefore this is what the LORD says:

"I will put obstacles before this people.
    Parents and children alike will stumble over them;
    neighbors and friends will perish."

22 This is what the LORD says:

"Look, an army is coming
    from the land of the north;
a great nation is being stirred up
    from the ends of the earth.
23 They are armed with bow and spear;
    they are cruel and show no mercy.
They sound like the roaring sea
    as they ride on their horses;
they come like men in battle formation
    to attack you, Daughter Zion."

24 We have heard reports about them,
    and our hands hang limp.
Anguish has gripped us,
    pain like that of a woman in labor.
25 Do not go out to the fields
    or walk on the roads,
for the enemy has a sword,
    and there is terror on every side.
26 Put on sackcloth, my people,
    and roll in ashes;
mourn with bitter wailing
    as for an only son,
for suddenly the destroyer
    will come upon us.

27 "I have made you a tester of metals
    and my people the ore,
that you may observe
    and test their ways.
28 They are all hardened rebels,
    going about to slander.
They are bronze and iron;
    they all act corruptly.
29 The bellows blow fiercely
    to burn away the lead with fire,
but the refining goes on in vain;
    the wicked are not purged out.
30 They are called rejected silver,
    because the LORD has rejected them."

### False Religion Worthless

**7** This is the word that came to Jeremiah from the LORD: 2 "Stand at the gate of the LORD's house and there proclaim this message:

"'Hear the word of the LORD, all you people of Judah who come through these gates to worship the LORD. 3 This is what the LORD Almighty, the God of Israel, says: Reform your ways and your actions, and I will let you live in this place. 4 Do not trust in deceptive words and say, "This is the temple of the LORD, the temple of the LORD, the temple of the LORD!" 5 If you really change your ways and your actions and deal with each other justly, 6 if you do not oppress the foreigner, the fatherless or the widow and do not shed innocent blood in this place, and if you do not follow other gods to your own harm, 7 then I will let you live in

## Amplified Bible

20 To what purpose does frankincense come to Me from Sheba [in southwestern Arabia] and the sweet cane from a far country? Your burnt offerings are not acceptable, nor are your sacrifices sweet *or* pleasing to Me.

21 Therefore thus says the Lord: Behold, I will lay stumbling blocks before this people. And the fathers and the sons together will stumble against them; the neighbor and his friend will perish.

22 Thus says the Lord: Behold, a people is coming from the north country, and a great nation is arousing itself from the ends of the earth.

23 They lay hold on bow and spear; they are cruel (ruthless and inhuman) and have no mercy. Their voice sounds like the roaring sea; they ride on horses, every one set in array as a man for battle against you, O Daughter of Zion!

24 We have heard the report of it; our hands become feeble *and* helpless. Anguish has taken hold of us, pangs like that of a woman in childbirth.

25 Go not out into the field nor walk on the road, for the enemy is armed with the sword; terror is on every side.

26 O daughter of my people [says Jeremiah], gird yourself with sackcloth and wallow in ashes; make mourning as for an only son, a most bitter lamentation, for the destroyer will suddenly come upon us [on prophet and people].

27 I [says the Lord] have set you [Jeremiah] as an assayer *and* a prover of ore among My people, that you may know and try their doings and be like a watchtower.

28 They are all the worst [kind] of rebels *and* utter and total revolters against God, going about publishing slander. They are [not gold and silver ore, but] bronze and iron; they are all corrupters.

29 The bellows blow fiercely, the lead is consumed by the fire; in vain do they continue refining, for the wicked [the dross] are not removed.

30 Men will call them reprobate *and* rejected silver [only dross, without good metal], because the Lord has rejected them.

**7** The word that came to Jeremiah from the Lord, saying,

2 Stand in the gate of the Lord's house and proclaim there this word and say, Hear the word of the Lord, all you of Judah who enter in at these gates to worship the Lord.

3 Thus says the Lord of hosts, the God of Israel: Amend your ways and your doings, and I will cause you to dwell in this place.

4 Trust not in the lying words [of the false prophets who maintain that God will protect Jerusalem because His temple is there], saying, This is the temple of the Lord, the temple of the Lord, the temple of the Lord.

5 For if you thoroughly amend your ways and your doings, if you thoroughly *and* truly execute justice between every man and his neighbor,

6 If you do not oppress the transient *and* the alien, the fatherless, and the widow or shed innocent blood [by oppression and by judicial murders] in [Jerusalem] or go after other gods to your own hurt,

## New International Version

this place, in the land I gave your ancestors for ever and ever. ⁸But look, you are trusting in deceptive words that are worthless.

⁹"'Will you steal and murder, commit adultery and perjury,*a* burn incense to Baal and follow other gods you have not known, ¹⁰and then come and stand before me in this house, which bears my Name, and say, "We are safe"— safe to do all these detestable things? ¹¹Has this house, which bears my Name, become a den of robbers to you? But I have been watching! declares the LORD.

¹²"'Go now to the place in Shiloh where I first made a dwelling for my Name, and see what I did to it because of the wickedness of my people Israel. ¹³While you were doing all these things, declares the LORD, I spoke to you again and again, but you did not listen; I called you, but you did not answer. ¹⁴Therefore, what I did to Shiloh I will now do to the house that bears my Name, the temple you trust in, the place I gave to you and your ancestors. ¹⁵I will thrust you from my presence, just as I did all your fellow Israelites, the people of Ephraim.'

¹⁶"So do not pray for this people nor offer any plea or petition for them; do not plead with me, for I will not listen to you. ¹⁷Do you not see what they are doing in the towns of Judah and in the streets of Jerusalem? ¹⁸The children gather wood, the fathers light the fire, and the women knead the dough and make cakes to offer to the Queen of Heaven. They pour out drink offerings to other gods to arouse my anger. ¹⁹But am I the one they are provoking? declares the LORD. Are they not rather harming themselves, to their own shame?

²⁰"'Therefore this is what the Sovereign LORD says: My anger and my wrath will be poured out on this place—on man and beast, on the trees of the field and on the crops of your land—and it will burn and not be quenched.

²¹"'This is what the LORD Almighty, the God of Israel, says: Go ahead, add your burnt offerings to your other sacrifices and eat the meat yourselves! ²²For when I brought your ancestors out of Egypt and spoke to them, I did not just give them commands about burnt offerings and sacrifices, ²³but I gave them this command: Obey me, and I will be your God and you will be my people. Walk in obedience to all I command you, that it may go well with you. ²⁴But they did not listen or pay attention; instead, they followed the stubborn inclinations of their evil hearts. They went backward and not forward. ²⁵From the time your ancestors left Egypt until now, day after day, again and again I sent you my servants the prophets. ²⁶But they did not listen to me or pay attention. They were stiff-necked and did more evil than their ancestors.'

²⁷"When you tell them all this, they will not listen to you; when you call to them, they will not answer. ²⁸There-

## Amplified Bible

⁷Then I will cause you to dwell in this place, in the land that I gave of old to your fathers to dwell in forever.

⁸Behold, you trust in lying words that cannot benefit [so that you do not profit].

⁹Will you steal, murder, commit adultery, swear falsely, burn incense to Baal, and go after other gods that you have not known,

¹⁰And [then dare to] come and stand before Me in this house, which is called by My *a*Name, and say, [By the discharge of this religious formality] we are set free!—only to go on with this wickedness *and* these abominations?

¹¹Has this house, which is called by My Name, become a den of robbers in your eyes [a place of retreat for you between acts of violence]? Behold, I Myself have seen it, says the Lord.

¹²But go now to My place which was in Shiloh [in Ephraim], where I set My Name at the first, and see what I did to it for the wickedness of My people Israel. [I Sam. 4:10-18.]

¹³And now, because you have done all these things, says the Lord, and [because] when I spoke to you persistently [even rising up early and speaking], you did not listen, and when I called you, you did not answer,

¹⁴Therefore will I do to this house (the temple), which is called by My Name *and* in which you trust, to the place which I gave to you and to your fathers, as I did to Shiloh.

¹⁵And I will cast you out of My sight, as I have cast out all your brethren, even the whole posterity of Ephraim.

¹⁶Therefore do not pray for this people [of Judah] or lift up a cry or entreaty for them or make intercession to Me, for I will not listen to *or* hear you.

¹⁷Do you not see what they are doing in the cities of Judah and in the streets of Jerusalem?

¹⁸The children gather wood, the fathers kindle the fire, and the women knead the dough, to make cakes for the *b*queen of heaven; and they pour out drink offerings to other gods, that they may provoke Me to anger!

¹⁹Am I the One Whom they provoke to anger? says the Lord. Is it not themselves [whom they provoke], to their own confusion *and* vexation *and* to their own shame?

²⁰Therefore thus says the Lord God: Behold, My anger and My wrath will be poured out on this place, on man and beast, on the trees of the field and the fruit of the ground; it will burn and not be quenched.

²¹Thus says the Lord of hosts, the God of Israel: Add your burnt offerings to your sacrifices and eat the flesh [if you will. It will avail you nothing].

²²For in the day that I brought them out of the land of Egypt, I did not speak to your fathers or command them concerning burnt offerings or sacrifices.

²³But this thing I did command them: Listen to *and* obey My voice, and I will be your God and you will be My people; and walk in the whole way that I command you, that it may be well with you.

²⁴But they would not listen to *and* obey Me or bend their ear [to Me], but followed the counsels *and* the stubborn promptings of their own evil hearts *and* minds, and they turned their backs *and* went in reverse instead of forward.

²⁵Since the day that your fathers came forth out of the land of Egypt to this day, I have persistently sent to you all My servants the prophets, sending them daily, early and late.

²⁶Yet the people would not listen to *and* obey Me or bend their ears [to Me], but stiffened their necks and behaved worse than their fathers.

²⁷Speak all these words to them, but they will not listen to *and* obey you; also call to them, but they will not answer you.

---

*a* 9 Or *and swear by false gods*

*a* See footnote on Deut. 12:5. *b* A goddess of fertility, probably the Babylonian title for Ishtar. She is identified with the planet Venus. Offerings to this goddess included cakes made in the shape of a star (Jer. 44:19).

## New International Version

fore say to them, 'This is the nation that has not obeyed the LORD its God or responded to correction. Truth has perished; it has vanished from their lips.

29 "Cut off your hair and throw it away; take up a lament on the barren heights, for the LORD has rejected and abandoned this generation that is under his wrath.

### The Valley of Slaughter

30 "The people of Judah have done evil in my eyes, declares the LORD. They have set up their detestable idols in the house that bears my Name and have defiled it. 31 They have built the high places of Topheth in the Valley of Ben Hinnom to burn their sons and daughters in the fire— something I did not command, nor did it enter my mind. 32 So beware, the days are coming, declares the LORD, when people will no longer call it Topheth or the Valley of Ben Hinnom, but the Valley of Slaughter, for they will bury the dead in Topheth until there is no more room. 33 Then the carcasses of this people will become food for the birds and the wild animals, and there will be no one to frighten them away. 34 I will bring an end to the sounds of joy and gladness and to the voices of bride and bridegroom in the towns of Judah and the streets of Jerusalem, for the land will become desolate.

**8** "At that time, declares the LORD, the bones of the kings and officials of Judah, the bones of the priests and prophets, and the bones of the people of Jerusalem will be removed from their graves. 2 They will be exposed to the sun and the moon and all the stars of the heavens, which they have loved and served and which they have followed and consulted and worshiped. They will not be gathered up or buried, but will be like dung lying on the ground. 3 Wherever I banish them, all the survivors of this evil nation will prefer death to life, declares the LORD Almighty.'

### Sin and Punishment

4 "Say to them, 'This is what the LORD says:

"'When people fall down, do they not get up?
When someone turns away, do they not return?
5 Why then have these people turned away?
Why does Jerusalem always turn away?
They cling to deceit;
they refuse to return.
6 I have listened attentively,
but they do not say what is right.
None of them repent of their wickedness,
saying, "What have I done?"
Each pursues their own course
like a horse charging into battle.
7 Even the stork in the sky
knows her appointed seasons,
and the dove, the swift and the thrush
observe the time of their migration.
But my people do not know
the requirements of the LORD.

## Amplified Bible

28 Yet you shall say to them, This is the nation that did not obey the voice of the Lord their God or receive instruction *and* correction *and* warning; truth *and* faithfulness have perished and have completely vanished from their mouths.

29 Cut off your hair [your crown, O Jerusalem] and cast it away, and take up a lamentation on the bare heights, for the Lord has rejected and forsaken the generation of His wrath.

30 For the children of Judah have done evil in My sight, says the Lord; they have set their abominations (extremely disgusting and shamefully vile things) in the house which is called by My Name to defile it.

31 And they have built the high places of Topheth, which is in the Valley of Ben-hinnom [son of Hinnom], to burn their sons and their daughters in the fire [in honor of Molech, the fire god]—which I did not command, nor did it come into My mind *or* heart. [Lev. 18:21; Josh. 15:8; II Kings 16:2-3; 21:1, 6; Isa. 30:33.]

32 Therefore, behold, the days are coming, says the Lord, when it shall no more be called Topheth or the Valley of Ben-hinnom [son of Hinnom], but the Valley of Slaughter, for [in bloody warfare] they will bury in Topheth till there is no more room *and* no place else to bury. [Jer. 19:6.]

33 And the dead bodies of this people will be meat for the fowls of the air and for the beasts of the earth, and none will frighten them away.

34 Then will I cause to cease from the cities of Judah and from the streets of Jerusalem the voice of mirth and the voice of gladness, the voice of the bridegroom and the voice of the bride; for the land will become a waste.

**8** At that time, says the Lord, [the Babylonian army will break open the sepulchers, and] they shall bring out the *a* bones of the kings of Judah, the bones of its princes, the bones of the priests, the bones of the prophets, and the bones of the inhabitants of Jerusalem from their graves.

2 And they will [carelessly] scatter [the corpses] before the sun and the moon and all the host of heaven, which [the dead] have loved and which they have served and after which they have walked and which they have sought, inquired of, *and* required and which they have worshiped. They shall not be gathered, or be buried; they shall be like *b* dung upon the face of the earth.

3 And death shall be chosen rather than life by all the residue of those who remain of this evil family (nation), who remain in all the places to which I have driven them, says the Lord of hosts.

4 Moreover, you [Jeremiah] shall say to them, Thus says the Lord: Shall men fall and not rise up again? Shall one turn away [from God] and not repent *and* return [to Him]?

5 Why then is this people of Jerusalem turned away with a perpetual turning away [from Me]? They hold fast to *c* deceit (idolatry); they refuse to repent *and* return [to God].

6 I have listened and heard, but they have not spoken aright; no man repents of his wickedness, saying, What have I done? Everyone turns to his [individual] course, as the horse rushes like a torrent into battle.

7 [Even the migratory birds are punctual to their seasons.] Yes, the stork [excelling in the great height of her flight] in the heavens knows her appointed times [of migration], and the turtledove, the swallow, and the crane observe the time of their return. But My people do not know the law of the Lord [which the lower animals instinctively recognize in so far as it applies to them].

---

*a* "Of the motive of the disinterment [on the part of the Babylonian conquerors] the prophet says nothing. He had certainly no idea of its being the search for booty. He has in mind only the justice of God [which is concerned with punishment or penalties upon the rebellious people of God]" (Johan P. Lange, *A Commentary*). *b* "Observe the irony. The stars look powerlessly down on the bones of their worshipers—while these send up a stench!" (Johan P. Lange, *A Commentary*). *c* Idolatry is deceitful and false because in their idolatry men and women worship what is false, and it merely deludes the worshipers and causes them to believe a lie.

## New International Version

8 "'How can you say, "We are wise,
 for we have the law of the LORD,"
when actually the lying pen of the scribes
 has handled it falsely?
9 The wise will be put to shame;
 they will be dismayed and trapped.
Since they have rejected the word of the LORD,
 what kind of wisdom do they have?
10 Therefore I will give their wives to other men
 and their fields to new owners.
From the least to the greatest,
 all are greedy for gain;
prophets and priests alike,
 all practice deceit.
11 They dress the wound of my people
 as though it were not serious.
"Peace, peace," they say,
 when there is no peace.
12 Are they ashamed of their detestable conduct?
 No, they have no shame at all;
 they do not even know how to blush.
So they will fall among the fallen;
 they will be brought down when they are punished,
 says the LORD.

13 "'I will take away their harvest,
 declares the LORD.
 There will be no grapes on the vine.
There will be no figs on the tree,
 and their leaves will wither.
What I have given them
 will be taken from them.ᵃ'"

14 Why are we sitting here?
 Gather together!
Let us flee to the fortified cities
 and perish there!
For the LORD our God has doomed us to perish
 and given us poisoned water to drink,
 because we have sinned against him.
15 We hoped for peace
 but no good has come,
for a time of healing
 but there is only terror.
16 The snorting of the enemy's horses
 is heard from Dan;
at the neighing of their stallions
 the whole land trembles.
They have come to devour
 the land and everything in it,
 the city and all who live there.

17 "See, I will send venomous snakes among you,
 vipers that cannot be charmed,
 and they will bite you,"
 declares the LORD.

18 You who are my Comforterᵇ in sorrow,
 my heart is faint within me.
19 Listen to the cry of my people
 from a land far away:
"Is the LORD not in Zion?
 Is her King no longer there?"

"Why have they aroused my anger with their images,
 with their worthless foreign idols?"

20 "The harvest is past,
 the summer has ended,
 and we are not saved."

21 Since my people are crushed, I am crushed;
 I mourn, and horror grips me.

## Amplified Bible

8 How can you say, We are wise, and we have the written law of the Lord [and are learned in its language and teachings]? Behold, the truth is, the lying pen of the scribes has made of the law a falsehood (a mere code of ceremonial observances). [Mark 7:13.]
9 The wise men shall be put to shame; they shall be dismayed and taken [captive]. Behold, they have rejected the word of the Lord, and what wisdom and broad, full intelligence is in them?
10 Therefore will I give their wives to others and their fields to those who gain possession of them; for everyone, from the least even to the greatest, is given to covetousness (is greedy for unjust gain); from the prophet even to the priest, everyone deals falsely.
11 For they have healed the wound of the daughter of My people only lightly and slightingly, saying, Peace, peace, when there is no peace.
12 They are brought to shame because they have committed abominations (extremely disgusting and shamefully vile things). And yet they were not at all ashamed, nor could they blush. Therefore they shall fall among those who fall; at the time of their punishment they shall be overthrown, says the Lord. [Jer. 6:12-15.]
13 I will gather and sweep them away, utterly consuming them, says the Lord. [I will find] no grapes on the vine, nor figs on the fig tree, and even the leaf is withered; and the things that I have given them shall pass away from them [for I have appointed to them those who shall pass over them]. [Matt. 21:18, 19.]
14 [Then say the people to each other] Why do we sit still? Assemble yourselves, and let us enter into the fortified cities and be silent or perish there! For the Lord our God has decreed our ruin and given us bitter and poisonous water to drink, because we have sinned against the Lord.
15 We looked for peace and completeness, but no good came, and for a time of healing, but behold, dismay, trouble, and terror!
16 The snorting of [Nebuchadnezzar's] horses is heard from Dan [on the northern border of Palestine]. At the sound of the neighing of his strong war-horses the whole land quakes; for they come and devour the land and all that is in it, the city and those who dwell in it.
17 For behold, I am sending among you serpents, adders which cannot be charmed, and they shall bite you, says the Lord.
18 Oh, that I [Jeremiah] could comfort myself against sorrow, [for my grief is beyond healing], my heart is sick and faint within me!
19 Behold [says the prophet, listen to the voice of] the cry of the daughter of my people [for help] because of those who dwell in a far country: Is not the Lord in Zion? Is not her King in her? [But the Lord answers] Why have they provoked Me to anger with their carved images and with foreign idols?
20 The harvest is past, the summer has ended and the gathering of fruit is over, yet we are not saved! [comes again the voice of the people.]
21 For the hurt of the daughter of my people am I [Jeremiah] hurt; I go around mourning; dismay has taken hold on me.

---

ᵃ 13 The meaning of the Hebrew for this sentence is uncertain.
ᵇ 18 The meaning of the Hebrew for this word is uncertain.

## New International Version

<sup>22</sup>Is there no balm in Gilead?
    Is there no physician there?
Why then is there no healing
    for the wound of my people?

**9**<sup>*a* 1</sup>Oh, that my head were a spring of water
    and my eyes a fountain of tears!
I would weep day and night
    for the slain of my people.
<sup>2</sup>Oh, that I had in the desert
    a lodging place for travelers,
so that I might leave my people
    and go away from them;
for they are all adulterers,
    a crowd of unfaithful people.

<sup>3</sup>"They make ready their tongue
    like a bow, to shoot lies;
it is not by truth
    that they triumph<sup>b</sup> in the land.
They go from one sin to another;
    they do not acknowledge me,"
                       declares the LORD.
<sup>4</sup>"Beware of your friends;
    do not trust anyone in your clan.
For every one of them is a deceiver,<sup>c</sup>
    and every friend a slanderer.
<sup>5</sup>Friend deceives friend,
    and no one speaks the truth.
They have taught their tongues to lie;
    they weary themselves with sinning.
<sup>6</sup>You<sup>d</sup> live in the midst of deception;
    in their deceit they refuse to acknowledge me,"
                       declares the LORD.

<sup>7</sup>Therefore this is what the LORD Almighty says:

"See, I will refine and test them,
    for what else can I do
because of the sin of my people?
<sup>8</sup>Their tongue is a deadly arrow;
    it speaks deceitfully.
With their mouths they all speak cordially to their
    neighbors,
but in their hearts they set traps for them.
<sup>9</sup>Should I not punish them for this?"
    declares the LORD.
"Should I not avenge myself
    on such a nation as this?"

<sup>10</sup>I will weep and wail for the mountains
    and take up a lament concerning the wilderness
    grasslands.
They are desolate and untraveled,
    and the lowing of cattle is not heard.
The birds have all fled
    and the animals are gone.

<sup>11</sup>"I will make Jerusalem a heap of ruins,
    a haunt of jackals;
and I will lay waste the towns of Judah
    so no one can live there."

<sup>12</sup>Who is wise enough to understand this? Who has been instructed by the LORD and can explain it? Why has the land been ruined and laid waste like a desert that no one can cross? <sup>13</sup>The LORD said, "It is because they have forsaken my law, which I set before them; they have not obeyed me or followed my law. <sup>14</sup>Instead, they have followed the stubbornness of their hearts; they have followed the Baals, as

## Amplified Bible

<sup>22</sup>Is there no balm in Gilead? Is there no physician there? Why then is not the health of the daughter of my people restored? [Because Zion no longer enjoyed the presence of the Great Physician!] [Exod. 15:26.]

**9** Oh, that my head were waters and my eyes a reservoir of tears, that I might weep day and night for the slain of the daughter of my people!
<sup>2</sup>Oh, that I had in the wilderness a lodging place (a mere shelter) for wayfaring men, that I might leave my people and go away from them! For they are all adulterers [rendering worship to idols instead of to the Lord, Who has espoused the people to Himself]; they are a gang of treacherous men [faithless even to each other].
<sup>3</sup>And they bend their tongue, [which is] their bow for the lies [they shoot]. And not according to faithfulness do they rule *and* become strong in the land; for they proceed from evil to evil, and they do not know *and* understand *and* acknowledge Me, says the Lord.
<sup>4</sup>Let everyone beware of his neighbor and put no trust in any brother. For every brother is an utter *and* complete supplanter (one who takes by the heel and trips up, a deceiver, a Jacob), and every neighbor goes about as a slanderer. [Gen. 25:26.]
<sup>5</sup>And they deceive *and* mock every one his neighbor and do not speak the truth. They have taught their tongues to speak lies; they weary themselves committing iniquity.
<sup>6</sup>Your habitation is in the midst of deceit [oppression upon oppression and deceit upon deceit]; through deceit they refuse to know *and* understand Me, says the Lord.
<sup>7</sup>Therefore thus says the Lord of hosts: Behold, I will melt them [by the process of affliction to remove the dross] and test them, for how else should I deal with the daughter of My people?
<sup>8</sup>Their tongue is a murderous arrow; it speaks deceitfully; one speaks peaceably to his neighbor with his mouth, but in his heart he lays snares and waits in ambush for him.
<sup>9</sup>Shall I not punish them for these things? says the Lord. Shall I not avenge Myself on such a nation as this?
<sup>10</sup>For the mountains I will take up a weeping and wailing and for the pastures of the wilderness a lament, because they are burned up *and* desolated, so that no one passes through [them]; neither can men hear [any longer] the lowing of cattle. Both the fowls of the air and the beasts have fled, they are gone!
<sup>11</sup>I will make Jerusalem heaps [of ruins], a dwelling place of jackals; and I will make the cities of Judah a desolation, without inhabitant.
<sup>12</sup>Who is the wise man who may understand this? To whom has the mouth of the Lord spoken, that he may declare it? Why is the land ruined *and* laid waste like a wilderness, so that no one passes through it?
<sup>13</sup>And the Lord says, Because they have forsaken My law, which I set before them, and have not listened to *and* obeyed My voice or walked in accordance with it,
<sup>14</sup>But have walked stubbornly after their own hearts and after the Baals, as their fathers taught them,

---

<sup>a</sup> In Hebrew texts 9:1 is numbered 8:23, and 9:2-26 is numbered 9:1-25.
<sup>b</sup> 3 Or *lies; / they are not valiant for truth*    <sup>c</sup> 4 Or *a deceiving Jacob*
<sup>d</sup> 6 That is, Jeremiah (the Hebrew is singular)

## New International Version

their ancestors taught them." [15]Therefore this is what the LORD Almighty, the God of Israel, says: "See, I will make this people eat bitter food and drink poisoned water. [16]I will scatter them among nations that neither they nor their ancestors have known, and I will pursue them with the sword until I have made an end of them."

[17]This is what the LORD Almighty says:

"Consider now! Call for the wailing women to come;
    send for the most skillful of them.
[18]Let them come quickly
    and wail over us
till our eyes overflow with tears
    and water streams from our eyelids.
[19]The sound of wailing is heard from Zion:
    'How ruined we are!
    How great is our shame!
We must leave our land
    because our houses are in ruins.'"

[20]Now, you women, hear the word of the LORD;
    open your ears to the words of his mouth.
Teach your daughters how to wail;
    teach one another a lament.
[21]Death has climbed in through our windows
    and has entered our fortresses;
it has removed the children from the streets
    and the young men from the public squares.

[22]Say, "This is what the LORD declares:

"'Dead bodies will lie
    like dung on the open field,
like cut grain behind the reaper,
    with no one to gather them.'"

[23]This is what the LORD says:

"Let not the wise boast of their wisdom
    or the strong boast of their strength
    or the rich boast of their riches,
[24]but let the one who boasts boast about this:
    that they have the understanding to know me,
that I am the LORD, who exercises kindness,
    justice and righteousness on earth,
    for in these I delight,"
                      declares the LORD.

[25]"The days are coming," declares the LORD, "when I will punish all who are circumcised only in the flesh— [26]Egypt, Judah, Edom, Ammon, Moab and all who live in the wilderness in distant places.[a] For all these nations are really uncircumcised, and even the whole house of Israel is uncircumcised in heart."

### God and Idols

**10** Hear what the LORD says to you, people of Israel. [2]This is what the LORD says:

"Do not learn the ways of the nations
    or be terrified by signs in the heavens,
    though the nations are terrified by them.
[3]For the practices of the peoples are worthless;
    they cut a tree out of the forest,
    and a craftsman shapes it with his chisel.
[4]They adorn it with silver and gold;
    they fasten it with hammer and nails
    so it will not totter.
[5]Like a scarecrow in a cucumber field,
    their idols cannot speak;

[a] 26 Or *wilderness and who clip the hair by their foreheads*

## Amplified Bible

[15]Therefore thus says the Lord of hosts, the God of Israel: Behold, I will feed them, even this people, with wormwood and give them bitter *and* poisonous water to drink.

[16]I will scatter them also among nations that neither they nor their fathers have known, and I will send the sword among them *and* after them until I have consumed them.

[17]Thus says the Lord of hosts: Consider and call for the mourning women to come; send for the skillful women to come.

[18]Let them make haste and raise a wailing over us *and* for us, that our eyes may run down with tears and our eyelids gush with water.

[19]For a sound of wailing is heard [coming] out of Zion: How we are plundered *and* ruined! We are greatly confounded *and* utterly put to shame, because we have forsaken the land, because they have cast down our dwellings [our dwellings that have cast us out].

[20]Yet hear the word of the Lord, O you women, and let your ears receive the word of His mouth; teach your daughters a lament, and each one [teach] her neighbor a dirge.

[21]For death has come up into our windows; it has entered into our palaces, cutting off the children from outdoors and the young men from the streets.

[22]Speak, Thus says the Lord: The dead bodies of men shall fall like dung on the open field and like sheaves [of grain] behind the reaper, and none shall gather them. [Jer. 8:2.]

[23]Thus says the Lord: Let not the wise *and* skillful person glory *and* boast in his wisdom *and* skill; let not the mighty *and* powerful person glory *and* boast in his strength *and* power; let not the person who is rich [in physical gratification and earthly wealth] glory *and* boast in his [temporal satisfactions and earthly] riches;

[24]But let him who glories glory in this: that he understands and knows Me [personally and practically, directly discerning and recognizing My character], that I am the Lord, Who practices loving-kindness, judgment, and righteousness in the earth, for in these things I delight, says the Lord. [I Cor. 1:31; II Cor. 10:17.]

[25]Behold, the days are coming, says the Lord, when I will punish all who though circumcised [outwardly, in the flesh] are still uncircumcised [in corresponding inward purity]—[Rom. 2:25-29.]

[26]Egypt, Judah, Edom, the children of Ammon, Moab [all of whom are related except Egypt], and all who live in the desert and who clip off the corners of their hair *and* beards; for all these nations are uncircumcised [in heart], and all the house of Israel is uncircumcised in heart.

**10** Hear the word which the Lord speaks to you, O house of Israel.

[2]Thus says the Lord: Learn not the way of the [heathen] nations and be not dismayed at the signs of the heavens, though they are dismayed at them,

[3]For the customs *and* ordinances of the peoples are false, empty, *and* futile; it is but a tree which one cuts out of the forest [to make for himself a god], the work of the hands of the craftsman with the ax *or* other tool.

[4]They deck [the idol] with silver and with gold; they fasten it with nails and with hammers so it will not fall apart *or* move around.

[5][Their idols] are like pillars of turned work [as upright and stationary and immobile as a palm tree], like scarecrows in a cucumber field; they cannot speak; they have to

## New International Version

they must be carried
    because they cannot walk.
Do not fear them;
    they can do no harm
    nor can they do any good."

6 No one is like you, LORD;
    you are great,
    and your name is mighty in power.
7 Who should not fear you,
    King of the nations?
    This is your due.
Among all the wise leaders of the nations
    and in all their kingdoms,
    there is no one like you.

8 They are all senseless and foolish;
    they are taught by worthless wooden idols.
9 Hammered silver is brought from Tarshish
    and gold from Uphaz.
What the craftsman and goldsmith have made
    is then dressed in blue and purple—
    all made by skilled workers.
10 But the LORD is the true God;
    he is the living God, the eternal King.
When he is angry, the earth trembles;
    the nations cannot endure his wrath.

11 "Tell them this: 'These gods, who did not make the
heavens and the earth, will perish from the earth and from
under the heavens.'"[a]

12 But God made the earth by his power;
    he founded the world by his wisdom
    and stretched out the heavens by his understanding.
13 When he thunders, the waters in the heavens roar;
    he makes clouds rise from the ends of the earth.
He sends lightning with the rain
    and brings out the wind from his storehouses.

14 Everyone is senseless and without knowledge;
    every goldsmith is shamed by his idols.
The images he makes are a fraud;
    they have no breath in them.
15 They are worthless, the objects of mockery;
    when their judgment comes, they will perish.
16 He who is the Portion of Jacob is not like these,
    for he is the Maker of all things,
    including Israel, the people of his inheritance—
    the LORD Almighty is his name.

### Coming Destruction

17 Gather up your belongings to leave the land,
    you who live under siege.
18 For this is what the LORD says:
    "At this time I will hurl out
    those who live in this land;
I will bring distress on them
    so that they may be captured."

19 Woe to me because of my injury!
    My wound is incurable!
Yet I said to myself,
    "This is my sickness, and I must endure it."
20 My tent is destroyed;
    all its ropes are snapped.
My children are gone from me and are no more;
    no one is left now to pitch my tent
    or to set up my shelter.
21 The shepherds are senseless
    and do not inquire of the LORD;
so they do not prosper
    and all their flock is scattered.

## Amplified Bible

be carried, for they cannot walk. Do not be afraid of them,
for they cannot do evil, neither is it possible for them to do
good [and it is not in them].
6 None at all is like You, O Lord; You are great, and Your
name is great in might.
7 Who would not fear You, O King of the nations? For it
is fitting to You *and* Your due! For among all the wise [men
or gods] of the nations and in all their kingdoms, there is
none like You.
8 But they are altogether irrational *and* stupid and foolish. Their instruction is given by idols who are but wood
[it is a teaching of falsity, emptiness, futility]!
9 Silver beaten [into plates] is brought from Tarshish
and gold from Uphaz, the work of the craftsman and of
the hands of the goldsmith; the [idols'] clothing is violet
and purple—they are all the work of skillful men.
10 But the Lord is the true God *and* the God of truth (the
God Who is Truth). He is the living God and the everlasting King. At His wrath the earth quakes, and the nations
are not able to bear His indignation.
11 Thus shall you say to them: The gods, who did not
make the heavens and the earth, shall perish from the
earth and from under the heavens.
12 God made the earth by His power; He established the
world by His wisdom and by His understanding *and* skill
stretched out the heavens.
13 When He utters His voice, there is a tumult of waters
in the heavens, and He causes the vapors to ascend from
the ends of the earth. He makes lightnings for the rain and
brings forth the wind out from His treasuries *and* from
His storehouses.
14 Every man has become like a brute, irrational *and*
stupid, without knowledge [of God]; every goldsmith is
brought to shame by his graven idols; for his molten images are frauds *and* falsehood, and there is no breath in
them.
15 They are devoid of worth, usefulness, *or* truth, a work
of delusion *and* mockery; in their time of trial *and* punishment they shall [helplessly] perish.
16 The Portion of Jacob [the true God on Whom Israel
has a claim] is not like these, for He is the Fashioner *and*
Maker of all things, and Israel is the tribe of His inheritance—the Lord of hosts is His name.
17 Gather up your bundle [of baggage] from the ground,
O you who dwell under siege.
18 For thus says the Lord: Behold, I will sling out the
inhabitants of the land at this time and will bring distress
on them, that they may feel it *and* find it [to be as I have
said, and turn to Me].
19 Woe is me because of my hurt! [says Jeremiah, speaking for the nation.] My wound is grievous *and* incurable.
But I said, Surely this sickness *and* suffering *and* grief are
mine, and I must endure, tolerate, *and* bear them.
20 My tent (home) is taken by force *and* plundered, and
all my [tent] cords are broken. My children have gone
forth [as captives] from me, and they are no more; there
is no one to stretch forth my tent any more and to set up
my [tent] curtains.
21 For the shepherds [of the people] have become like
brutes, irrational *and* stupid, and have not sought the Lord
*or* inquired of Him *or* required Him [by necessity and by
right of His word]. Therefore they have not dealt prudently
*and* have not prospered, and all their flocks are scattered.

---

*a* 11 The text of this verse is in Aramaic.

# New International Version

[22] Listen! The report is coming—
    a great commotion from the land of the north!
It will make the towns of Judah desolate,
    a haunt of jackals.

### Jeremiah's Prayer

[23] LORD, I know that people's lives are not their own;
    it is not for them to direct their steps.
[24] Discipline me, LORD, but only in due measure—
    not in your anger,
    or you will reduce me to nothing.
[25] Pour out your wrath on the nations
    that do not acknowledge you,
    on the peoples who do not call on your name.
For they have devoured Jacob;
    they have devoured him completely
    and destroyed his homeland.

### The Covenant Is Broken

**11** This is the word that came to Jeremiah from the LORD: [2]"Listen to the terms of this covenant and tell them to the people of Judah and to those who live in Jerusalem. [3]Tell them that this is what the LORD, the God of Israel, says: 'Cursed is the one who does not obey the terms of this covenant— [4]the terms I commanded your ancestors when I brought them out of Egypt, out of the iron-smelting furnace.' I said, 'Obey me and do everything I command you, and you will be my people, and I will be your God. [5]Then I will fulfill the oath I swore to your ancestors, to give them a land flowing with milk and honey'—the land you possess today."

I answered, "Amen, LORD."

[6]The LORD said to me, "Proclaim all these words in the towns of Judah and in the streets of Jerusalem: 'Listen to the terms of this covenant and follow them. [7]From the time I brought your ancestors up from Egypt until today, I warned them again and again, saying, "Obey me." [8]But they did not listen or pay attention; instead, they followed the stubbornness of their evil hearts. So I brought on them all the curses of the covenant I had commanded them to follow but that they did not keep.'"

[9]Then the LORD said to me, "There is a conspiracy among the people of Judah and those who live in Jerusalem. [10]They have returned to the sins of their ancestors, who refused to listen to my words. They have followed other gods to serve them. Both Israel and Judah have broken the covenant I made with their ancestors. [11]Therefore this is what the LORD says: 'I will bring on them a disaster they cannot escape. Although they cry out to me, I will not listen to them. [12]The towns of Judah and the people of Jerusalem will go and cry out to the gods to whom they burn incense, but they will not help them at all when disaster strikes. [13]You, Judah, have as many gods as you have towns; and the altars you have set up to burn incense to that shameful god Baal are as many as the streets of Jerusalem.'

[14]"Do not pray for this people or offer any plea or petition for them, because I will not listen when they call to me in the time of their distress.

[15] "What is my beloved doing in my temple
    as she, with many others, works out her evil
      schemes?
    Can consecrated meat avert your punishment?
When you engage in your wickedness,
    then you rejoice.*"

# Amplified Bible

[22]Hark, the sound of a rumor! [The invading army] comes!—a great commotion out of the north country—to make the cities of Judah a desolation, a dwelling place of jackals.

[23]O Lord [pleads Jeremiah in the name of the people], I know that [the determination of] the way of a man is not in himself; it is not in man [even in a strong man or in a man at his best] to direct his [own] steps. [Ps. 37:23; Prov. 20:24.]

[24]O Lord, correct, instruct, *and* chastise me, but with judgment *and* in just measure—not in Your anger, lest You diminish me *and* bring me to nothing.

[25]Pour out Your wrath upon the nations that do not know *or* recognize You and upon the peoples that do not call upon Your name. For they have devoured Jacob, yes, devoured him and consumed him and made his habitation a desolate waste.

**11** The word that came to Jeremiah from the Lord: [2]Hear the words of this covenant *or* solemn pledge, and speak to the men of Judah and the inhabitants of Jerusalem.

[3]Say to them, Thus says the Lord, the God of Israel: Cursed is the man who does not heed the words of this covenant *or* solemn pledge

[4]Which I commanded your fathers at the time that I brought them out of the land of Egypt, from the iron furnace, saying, Listen to My voice and do according to all that I command you. So will you be My people, and I will be your God,

[5]That I may perform the oath which I swore to your fathers, to give them a land flowing with milk and honey, as it is this day. Then I answered, Amen (so be it), O Lord.

[6]And the Lord said to me, Proclaim all these words in the cities of Judah and in the streets of Jerusalem: Hear the words of this covenant *or* solemn pledge and do them.

[7]For I earnestly protested to *and* warned your fathers at the time that I brought them up out of the land of Egypt, even to this day, protesting to *and* warning them persistently, saying, Obey My voice.

[8]Yet they did not obey or incline their ear [to Me], but everyone walked in the stubbornness of his own evil heart. Therefore I brought upon them all [the calamities threatened in] the words of this covenant *or* solemn pledge, which I had commanded, but they did not do.

[9]And the Lord said to me, A conspiracy is found among the men of Judah and among the inhabitants of Jerusalem.

[10]They have turned back to the iniquities of their forefathers, who refused to hear My words; they have gone after other gods to serve them. The house of Israel and the house of Judah have broken My covenant *or* solemn pledge which I made with their fathers.

[11]Therefore thus says the Lord: Behold, I am bringing evil *and* calamity upon them which they will not be able to escape; though they cry to Me, I will not listen to them.

[12]Then the cities of Judah and the inhabitants of Jerusalem will go and cry out to the gods to whom they offer incense, but they cannot save them at all in the time of their evil trouble.

[13]For [as many as] the number of your cities are your gods, O Judah; and [as many as] the number of the streets of Jerusalem are the altars you have set up to the shameful thing, even altars to burn incense to Baal.

[14]Therefore do not pray for this people or lift up a cry or prayer for them, for I will not listen when they cry out to Me in the time of their evil trouble.

[15]What right has My beloved [to be] in My house when she has wrought lewdness *and* done treacherously many times? Can vows *and* the holy flesh [of your sacrifices] remove from you your wickedness *and* avert your calamity? Can you by these [escape your doom and] rejoice exultantly?

---

*a* 15 Or *Could consecrated meat avert your punishment? / Then you would rejoice*

## New International Version

16 The LORD called you a thriving olive tree
  with fruit beautiful in form.
But with the roar of a mighty storm
  he will set it on fire,
  and its branches will be broken.

17 The LORD Almighty, who planted you, has decreed disaster for you, because the people of both Israel and Judah have done evil and aroused my anger by burning incense to Baal.

### Plot Against Jeremiah

18 Because the LORD revealed their plot to me, I knew it, for at that time he showed me what they were doing. 19 I had been like a gentle lamb led to the slaughter; I did not realize that they had plotted against me, saying,

"Let us destroy the tree and its fruit;
  let us cut him off from the land of the living,
  that his name be remembered no more."
20 But you, LORD Almighty, who judge righteously
  and test the heart and mind,
let me see your vengeance on them,
  for to you I have committed my cause.

21 Therefore this is what the LORD says about the people of Anathoth who are threatening to kill you, saying, "Do not prophesy in the name of the LORD or you will die by our hands"— 22 therefore this is what the LORD Almighty says: "I will punish them. Their young men will die by the sword, their sons and daughters by famine. 23 Not even a remnant will be left to them, because I will bring disaster on the people of Anathoth in the year of their punishment."

### Jeremiah's Complaint

**12** You are always righteous, LORD,
  when I bring a case before you.
Yet I would speak with you about your justice:
  Why does the way of the wicked prosper?
  Why do all the faithless live at ease?
2 You have planted them, and they have taken root;
  they grow and bear fruit.
You are always on their lips
  but far from their hearts.
3 Yet you know me, LORD;
  you see me and test my thoughts about you.
Drag them off like sheep to be butchered!
  Set them apart for the day of slaughter!
4 How long will the land lie parched
  and the grass in every field be withered?
Because those who live in it are wicked,
  the animals and birds have perished.
Moreover, the people are saying,
  "He will not see what happens to us."

### God's Answer

5 "If you have raced with men on foot
  and they have worn you out,
  how can you compete with horses?
If you stumble[a] in safe country,
  how will you manage in the thickets by[b] the Jordan?
6 Your relatives, members of your own family—
  even they have betrayed you;
  they have raised a loud cry against you.
Do not trust them,
  though they speak well of you.

7 "I will forsake my house,
  abandon my inheritance;
I will give the one I love
  into the hands of her enemies.

---

## Amplified Bible

16 The Lord [acknowledged you once to be worthy to be] called a green olive tree, fair and of good fruit; but with the roar of a great tempest He will set fire to it, and its branches will be consumed. [Ps. 52:8; Jer. 21:14.]
17 For the Lord of hosts, Who planted you, has pronounced evil and calamity against you because of the evil which the house of Israel and the house of Judah have done against themselves in provoking Me to anger by offering incense to Baal.
18 And the Lord gave me [Jeremiah] knowledge of it [their plot], and I knew it; then You [O Lord] showed me their doings.
19 But I was like a tame lamb that is brought to the slaughter; I did not know that they had devised inventions and schemes against me, saying, Let us destroy the tree with its fruit; let us cut him off from the land of the living, that his name may be no more remembered.
20 But, O Lord of hosts, Who judges rightly and justly, Who tests the heart and the mind, let me see Your vengeance on them, for to You I have revealed and committed my cause [rolling it upon You].
21 Therefore thus says the Lord about the men of Anathoth [Jeremiah's hometown], who seek your life [Jeremiah] and say, Prophesy not in the name of the Lord, that you die not by our hands—
22 Therefore thus says the Lord of hosts: Behold, I will punish them. Their young men will die by the sword, their sons and their daughters will die by famine;
23 And there will be no remnant [of the conspirators] left, for I will bring evil and calamity upon the men of Anathoth in the year of their punishment.

**12** Uncompromisingly righteous and rigidly just are You, O Lord, when I complain against and contend with You. Yet let me plead and reason the case with You: Why does the way of the wicked prosper? Why are all they at ease and thriving who deal very treacherously and deceitfully?
2 You have planted them, yes, they have taken root; they grow, yes, they bring forth fruit. You are near in their mouths but far from their hearts.
3 But You, O Lord, know and understand me and my devotion to You; You see me and try my heart toward You. [O Lord] pull [these rebellious ones] out like sheep for the slaughter and devote and prepare them for the day of slaughter.
4 How long must the land mourn and the grass and herbs of the whole country wither? Through the wickedness of those who dwell in it, the beasts and the birds are consumed and are swept away [by the drought], because men [mocked] me, saying, He shall not [live to] see our final end.
5 [But the Lord rebukes Jeremiah's impatience, saying] If you have raced with men on foot and they have tired you out, then how can you compete with horses? And if [you take to flight] in a land of peace where you feel secure, then what will you do [when you tread the tangled maze of jungle haunted by lions] in the swelling and flooding of the Jordan?
6 For even your brethren and the house of your father— even they have dealt treacherously with you; yes, even they are [like a pack of hounds] in full cry after you. Believe them not, though they speak fair words and promise good things to you.
7 I have forsaken My house, I have cast off My heritage; I have given the dearly beloved of My life into the hands of her enemies.

---

a 5 Or you feel secure only  b 5 Or the flooding of

## New International Version

8 My inheritance has become to me
  like a lion in the forest.
She roars at me;
  therefore I hate her.
9 Has not my inheritance become to me
  like a speckled bird of prey
  that other birds of prey surround and attack?
Go and gather all the wild beasts;
  bring them to devour.
10 Many shepherds will ruin my vineyard
  and trample down my field;
they will turn my pleasant field
  into a desolate wasteland.
11 It will be made a wasteland,
  parched and desolate before me;
the whole land will be laid waste
  because there is no one who cares.
12 Over all the barren heights in the desert
  destroyers will swarm,
for the sword of the LORD will devour
  from one end of the land to the other;
  no one will be safe.
13 They will sow wheat but reap thorns;
  they will wear themselves out but gain nothing.
They will bear the shame of their harvest
  because of the LORD's fierce anger.

14 This is what the LORD says: "As for all my wicked neighbors who seize the inheritance I gave my people Israel, I will uproot them from their lands and I will uproot the people of Judah from among them. 15 But after I uproot them, I will again have compassion and will bring each of them back to their own inheritance and their own country. 16 And if they learn well the ways of my people and swear by my name, saying, 'As surely as the LORD lives'—even as they once taught my people to swear by Baal—then they will be established among my people. 17 But if any nation does not listen, I will completely uproot and destroy it," declares the LORD.

### A Linen Belt

**13** This is what the LORD said to me: "Go and buy a linen belt and put it around your waist, but do not let it touch water." 2 So I bought a belt, as the LORD directed, and put it around my waist.

3 Then the word of the LORD came to me a second time: 4 "Take the belt you bought and are wearing around your waist, and go now to Perath[a] and hide it there in a crevice in the rocks." 5 So I went and hid it at Perath, as the LORD told me.

6 Many days later the LORD said to me, "Go now to Perath and get the belt I told you to hide there." 7 So I went to Perath and dug up the belt and took it from the place where I had hidden it, but now it was ruined and completely useless.

8 Then the word of the LORD came to me: 9 "This is what the LORD says: 'In the same way I will ruin the pride of Judah and the great pride of Jerusalem. 10 These wicked people, who refuse to listen to my words, who follow the stubbornness of their hearts and go after other gods to serve and worship them, will be like this belt—completely useless! 11 For as a belt is bound around the waist, so I bound all the people of Israel and all the people of Judah

## Amplified Bible

8 My heritage has become to Me like a lion in the forest; she has uttered her voice against Me; therefore I have [treated her as if I] hated her.

9 Is My heritage to Me like a speckled bird of prey? Are the birds of prey against her round about? Go, assemble all the wild beasts of the field; bring them to devour.

10 Many shepherds [of an invading host] have destroyed My vineyard, they have trampled My portion underfoot; they have made My pleasant portion a desolate wilderness.

11 They have made it a desolation, and desolate it mourns before Me; the whole land has been made desolate, but no man lays it to heart.

12 Destroyers have come upon all the bare heights in the desert, for the sword of the Lord devours from one end of the land even to the other; no flesh has peace or can find the means to escape.

13 They have sown wheat but have reaped thorns; they have worn themselves out but without profit. And they shall be ashamed of your [lack of] harvests and revenues because of the fierce and glowing anger of the Lord.

14 Thus says the Lord against all My evil neighbor [nations] who touch the inheritance which I have caused My people Israel to inherit: Behold, I will pluck them up from their land and I will pluck up the house of Judah from among them.

15 And after I have plucked them up, I will return and have compassion on them and will bring them back again, every man to his heritage and every man to his land.

16 And if these [neighbor nations] will diligently learn the ways of My people, to swear by My name, saying, As the Lord lives—even as they taught My people to swear by Baal—then will they be built up in the midst of My people.

17 But if any nation will not hear and obey, I will utterly pluck up and destroy that nation, says the Lord.

**13** Thus the Lord said to me: Go and buy yourself a linen girdle and put it on your loins, but do not put it in water.

2 So I bought a girdle or waistcloth, according to the word of the Lord, and put it on my loins.

3 And the word of the Lord came to me the second time, saying,

4 Take the girdle which you have bought, which is on your loins, and arise, go to the [river] Euphrates, and hide it there in a cleft of the rock.

5 So I went and hid it by the Euphrates, as the Lord commanded me.

6 And after many days the Lord said to me, Arise, go to the Euphrates, and take from there the girdle which I commanded you to hide there.

7 Then I went to the Euphrates and dug and took the girdle or waistcloth from the place where I had hidden it. And behold, the girdle was decayed and spoiled; it was good for nothing.

8 Then the word of the Lord came to me, saying,

9 Thus says the Lord: After this manner will I mar the pride of Judah and the great pride of Jerusalem.

10 These evil people, who refuse to hear My words, who walk in the stubbornness of their hearts and have gone after other gods to serve them and to worship them, shall even be like this girdle or waistcloth, which is profitable for nothing.

11 For as the girdle clings to the loins of a man, so I caused the whole house of Israel and the whole house of

---

a 4 Or possibly *to the Euphrates*; similarly in verses 5-7

## New International Version

to me,' declares the LORD, 'to be my people for my renown and praise and honor. But they have not listened.'

### Wineskins

12 "Say to them: 'This is what the LORD, the God of Israel, says: Every wineskin should be filled with wine.' And if they say to you, 'Don't we know that every wineskin should be filled with wine?' 13 then tell them, 'This is what the LORD says: I am going to fill with drunkenness all who live in this land, including the kings who sit on David's throne, the priests, the prophets and all those living in Jerusalem. 14 I will smash them one against the other, parents and children alike, declares the LORD. I will allow no pity or mercy or compassion to keep me from destroying them.'"

### Threat of Captivity

15 Hear and pay attention,
    do not be arrogant,
    for the LORD has spoken.
16 Give glory to the LORD your God
    before he brings the darkness,
    before your feet stumble
    on the darkening hills.
You hope for light,
    but he will turn it to utter darkness
    and change it to deep gloom.
17 If you do not listen,
    I will weep in secret
    because of your pride;
my eyes will weep bitterly,
    overflowing with tears,
    because the LORD's flock will be taken captive.
18 Say to the king and to the queen mother,
    "Come down from your thrones,
    for your glorious crowns
    will fall from your heads."
19 The cities in the Negev will be shut up,
    and there will be no one to open them.
All Judah will be carried into exile,
    carried completely away.

20 Look up and see
    those who are coming from the north.
Where is the flock that was entrusted to you,
    the sheep of which you boasted?
21 What will you say when the LORD sets over you
    those you cultivated as your special allies?
Will not pain grip you
    like that of a woman in labor?
22 And if you ask yourself,
    "Why has this happened to me?" —
it is because of your many sins
    that your skirts have been torn off
    and your body mistreated.
23 Can an Ethiopian[a] change his skin
    or a leopard its spots?
Neither can you do good
    who are accustomed to doing evil.

24 "I will scatter you like chaff
    driven by the desert wind.
25 This is your lot,
    the portion I have decreed for you,"
                    declares the LORD,
    "because you have forgotten me
    and trusted in false gods.
26 I will pull up your skirts over your face
    that your shame may be seen—
27 your adulteries and lustful neighings,
    your shameless prostitution!

---

a 23 Hebrew Cushite (probably a person from the upper Nile region)

## Amplified Bible

Judah to cling to Me, says the Lord, that they might be for Me a people, a name, a praise, and a glory; but they would not listen or obey.
12 Therefore you shall speak to them this word: Thus says the Lord, the God of Israel: Every bottle and jar should be filled with wine. [The people] will say to you, Do we not certainly know that every bottle and jar should be filled with wine?
13 Then say to them, Thus says the Lord: Behold, I will fill with drunkenness all the inhabitants of this land, even the kings who sit upon David's throne, the priests, the prophets, and all the inhabitants of Jerusalem.
14 And I will dash them one against another, even the fathers and the sons together, says the Lord. I will not pity or spare or have compassion, that I should not destroy them.
15 Hear and give ear, do not be proud, for the Lord has spoken [says Jeremiah].
16 Give glory to the Lord your God before He brings darkness and before your feet stumble upon the dark and twilit mountains, and [before], while you are looking for light, He turns it into the shadow of death and makes it thick darkness.
17 But if you will not hear and obey, I will weep in secret for your pride; my eyes will weep bitterly and run down with tears, because the Lord's flock has been taken captive.
18 Say to the king and the queen mother, Humble yourselves and take a lowly seat, for down from your head has come your beautiful crown (the crown of your glory).
19 The cities of the South (the Negeb) have been shut up, and there is no one to open them; all Judah has been carried away captive, it has been wholly taken captive and into exile.
20 Lift up your eyes and behold those [the eruption of a hostile army] who come from the north. Where is the flock that was given to you [to shepherd], your beautiful flock?
21 What will you say [O Jerusalem] when He [the Lord] sets over you as head those [tyrannical foreign nations] whom you yourselves [at intervals] have taught to be lovers (allies) with you [instructing them, even your friends, to be head over you]? Will not pangs take hold of you like that of a woman in travail?
22 And if you say in your heart, Why have these things come upon me?—[the answer is], Because of the greatness of your iniquity has your long robe been pulled aside [showing you in the garb of a menial] and have you [barefooted and treated like a slave] suffered violence?
23 Can the Ethiopian change his skin or the leopard his spots? Then also can you do good who are accustomed and taught [even trained] to do evil.
24 Therefore I will scatter you like chaff driven away by the wind from the desert.
25 This is your lot, the portion measured to you from Me, says the Lord, because you have forgotten Me and trusted in falsehood [false gods and alliances with idolatrous nations].
26 Therefore I Myself will [retaliate], throwing your skirts up over your face, that your shame [of being clad like a slave] may be exposed.
27 I have seen your detestable acts, even your adulteries

## New International Version

I have seen your detestable acts
  on the hills and in the fields.
Woe to you, Jerusalem!
  How long will you be unclean?"

### Drought, Famine, Sword

**14** This is the word of the LORD that came to Jeremiah
  concerning the drought:

2 "Judah mourns,
  her cities languish;
they wail for the land,
  and a cry goes up from Jerusalem.
3 The nobles send their servants for water;
  they go to the cisterns
  but find no water.
They return with their jars unfilled;
  dismayed and despairing,
  they cover their heads.
4 The ground is cracked
  because there is no rain in the land;
the farmers are dismayed
  and cover their heads.
5 Even the doe in the field
  deserts her newborn fawn
  because there is no grass.
6 Wild donkeys stand on the barren heights
  and pant like jackals;
their eyes fail
  for lack of food."

7 Although our sins testify against us,
  do something, LORD, for the sake of your name.
For we have often rebelled;
  we have sinned against you.
8 You who are the hope of Israel,
  its Savior in times of distress,
why are you like a stranger in the land,
  like a traveler who stays only a night?
9 Why are you like a man taken by surprise,
  like a warrior powerless to save?
You are among us, LORD,
  and we bear your name;
  do not forsake us!

10 This is what the LORD says about this people:

"They greatly love to wander;
  they do not restrain their feet.
So the LORD does not accept them;
  he will now remember their wickedness
  and punish them for their sins."

11 Then the LORD said to me, "Do not pray for the well-being of this people. 12 Although they fast, I will not listen to their cry; though they offer burnt offerings and grain offerings, I will not accept them. Instead, I will destroy them with the sword, famine and plague."

13 But I said, "Alas, Sovereign LORD! The prophets keep telling them, 'You will not see the sword or suffer famine. Indeed, I will give you lasting peace in this place.'"

14 Then the LORD said to me, "The prophets are prophesying lies in my name. I have not sent them or appointed them or spoken to them. They are prophesying to you false visions, divinations, idolatries[a] and the delusions of their own minds. 15 Therefore this is what the LORD says about the prophets who are prophesying in my name: I did not send them, yet they are saying, 'No sword or famine will touch this land.' Those same prophets will perish by sword and famine. 16 And the people they are prophesying to will be thrown out into the streets of Jerusalem because of the famine and sword. There will be no one to

## Amplified Bible

and your lustful neighings [after idols], and the lewdness of your harlotry on the hills in the field. Woe to you, O Jerusalem! For how long a time yet will you not [meet My conditions and] be made clean?

**14** The word of the Lord that came to Jeremiah concerning the drought:

2 Judah mourns and her gates languish; [her people] sit in black [mourning garb] upon the ground, and the cry of Jerusalem goes up.

3 And their nobles send their little ones *and* their inferiors for water; they come to the cisterns and find no water. They return with empty vessels; they are put to shame and confounded and cover their heads.

4 Because the ground is cracked *and* the tillers are dismayed, since there has been no rain on the land, the plowmen are put to shame, and they cover their heads.

5 Yes, even the hind gives birth to her calf in the field and forsakes it, because there is no grass *or* herbage.

6 And the wild donkeys stand on the bare heights; they pant for air like jackals *or* crocodiles; their eyesight fails because there is no grass.

7 O Lord, though our iniquities testify against us [prays Jeremiah], deal *and* work with us for Your own name's sake [that the heathen may witness Your might and faithfulness]! For our backslidings are many; we have sinned against You.

8 O Hope of Israel, her Savior in time of trouble, why should You be like a sojourner in the land and like a wayfaring man who turns aside *and* spreads his tent to tarry [only] for a night?

9 Why should You be [hesitant and inactive] like a man stunned *and* confused, like a mighty man who cannot save? Yet You, O Lord, are in the midst of us, and we are called by Your name; do not leave us!

10 [And the Lord replied to Jeremiah] Thus says the Lord to this people [Judah]: In the manner *and* to the degree already pointed out have they loved to wander; they have not restrained their feet. Therefore the Lord does not accept them; He will now [seriously] remember their iniquity and punish them for their sins.

11 The Lord said to me, Do not pray for this people for their good.

12 Though they fast, I will not hear their cry; and though they offer burnt offering and cereal offering [without heartfelt surrender to Me, or by offering it too late], I will not accept them. But I will consume them by the sword, by famine, and by pestilence.

13 Then said I, Alas, Lord God! Behold, the [false] prophets say to them, You shall not see the sword, nor will you have famine; but I [the Lord] will give you assured peace (peace that lasts, the peace of truth) in this place.

14 Then the Lord said to me, The [false] prophets prophesy lies in My name. I sent them not, neither have I commanded them, nor have I spoken to them. They prophesy to you a false *or* pretended vision, a worthless divination [conjuring or practicing magic, trying to call forth the responses supposed to be given by idols], and the deceit of their own minds.

15 Therefore thus says the Lord concerning the [false] prophets who prophesy in My name—although I did not send them—and who say, Sword and famine shall not be in this land: By sword and famine shall those prophets be consumed.

16 And the people to whom they prophesy shall be cast out in the streets of Jerusalem, victims of famine and sword; and they shall have none to bury them—them, their wives, their sons, and their daughters. For I will pour out their wickedness upon them [and not on their false

---

a 14 Or *visions, worthless divinations*

## New International Version

bury them, their wives, their sons and their daughters. I will pour out on them the calamity they deserve.

17"Speak this word to them:

"'Let my eyes overflow with tears
  night and day without ceasing;
for the Virgin Daughter, my people,
  has suffered a grievous wound,
  a crushing blow.
18 If I go into the country,
  I see those slain by the sword;
 if I go into the city,
  I see the ravages of famine.
Both prophet and priest
  have gone to a land they know not.'"

19 Have you rejected Judah completely?
  Do you despise Zion?
Why have you afflicted us
  so that we cannot be healed?
We hoped for peace
  but no good has come,
for a time of healing
  but there is only terror.
20 We acknowledge our wickedness, LORD,
  and the guilt of our ancestors;
  we have indeed sinned against you.
21 For the sake of your name do not despise us;
  do not dishonor your glorious throne.
Remember your covenant with us
  and do not break it.
22 Do any of the worthless idols of the nations bring rain?
  Do the skies themselves send down showers?
No, it is you, LORD our God.
  Therefore our hope is in you,
  for you are the one who does all this.

**15** Then the LORD said to me: "Even if Moses and Samuel were to stand before me, my heart would not go out to this people. Send them away from my presence! Let them go! 2And if they ask you, 'Where shall we go?' tell them, 'This is what the LORD says:

"'Those destined for death, to death;
  those for the sword, to the sword;
  those for starvation, to starvation;
  those for captivity, to captivity.'

3"I will send four kinds of destroyers against them," declares the LORD, "the sword to kill and the dogs to drag away and the birds and the wild animals to devour and destroy. 4I will make them abhorrent to all the kingdoms of the earth because of what Manasseh son of Hezekiah king of Judah did in Jerusalem.

5 "Who will have pity on you, Jerusalem?
  Who will mourn for you?
  Who will stop to ask how you are?
6 You have rejected me," declares the LORD.
  "You keep on backsliding.
So I will reach out and destroy you;
  I am tired of holding back.
7 I will winnow them with a winnowing fork
  at the city gates of the land.
I will bring bereavement and destruction on my people,
  for they have not changed their ways.
8 I will make their widows more numerous
  than the sand of the sea.
At midday I will bring a destroyer
  against the mothers of their young men;

## Amplified Bible

teachers only, for the people could not have been deceived except by their own consent].

17 Therefore [Jeremiah] you shall say to them, Let my eyes run down with tears night and day, and let them not cease; for the virgin daughter of my people has been smitten with a great wound, with a very grievous blow.

18 If I go out into the field, behold, those slain with the sword! And if I enter the city, then behold, those tormented with the diseases of famine! For both prophet and priest go about not knowing what to do or as beggars [exiled] in a land that they know not, and they have no knowledge.

19 [O Lord] have You utterly rejected Judah? Do You loathe Zion? Why have You smitten us so that there is no healing for us? We looked for peace and completeness, but no good came, and for a time of healing, but behold, dismay, disaster, and terror!

20 We know and acknowledge, O Lord, our wickedness and the iniquity of our fathers; for we have sinned against You.

21 Do not abhor, condemn, and spurn us, for Your name's sake; do not dishonor, debase, and lightly esteem Your glorious throne; [earnestly] remember, break not Your covenant or solemn pledge with us.

22 Are there any among the false gods of the nations who can cause rain? Or can the heavens [of their own will] give showers? Are You [alone] not He, O Lord our God? Therefore we will wait [expectantly] for You, for You have made all these things [the heavens and the rain].

**15** Then the Lord said to me, Though Moses and Samuel stood [interceding for them] before Me, yet My mind could not be turned with favor toward this people [Judah]. Send them out of My sight and let them go!

2 And if they say to you, Where shall we go? then tell them, Thus says the Lord: Such as are [destined] for death, to death; and such as are for the sword, to the sword; and such as are for famine, to famine; and such as are for captivity, to captivity.

3 And I will appoint over them four kinds [of destroyers], says the Lord: the sword to slay, the dogs to tear and drag away, and the birds of the air and the beasts of the earth to devour and to destroy.

4 And I will cause them to be tossed to and fro among all the kingdoms of the earth and to be made a horror to all nations because of Manasseh son of Hezekiah king of Judah, for [the horrible wickedness] which he did in Jerusalem. [II Kings 21:3-7.]

5 For who will have pity on you, O Jerusalem? Or who will bemoan you? Or who will turn aside to ask about your welfare?

6 You have rejected and forsaken Me, says the Lord. You keep going in reverse. Therefore I will stretch out My hand against you and destroy you; I am weary of relenting [concerning your punishment].

7 I will winnow them with a fan and a winnowing fork in the gates of the land; I will bereave them [of children], I will destroy My people; from their [evil] ways they did not return.

8 I will increase the number of their widows more than the sand of the seas. I will bring upon them, [both] against the mother of young men and the young men [themselves],

## New International Version

suddenly I will bring down on them
 anguish and terror.
[9] The mother of seven will grow faint
 and breathe her last.
Her sun will set while it is still day;
 she will be disgraced and humiliated.
I will put the survivors to the sword
 before their enemies,"
declares the LORD.

[10] Alas, my mother, that you gave me birth,
 a man with whom the whole land strives and
 contends!
I have neither lent nor borrowed,
 yet everyone curses me.

[11] The LORD said,

"Surely I will deliver you for a good purpose;
 surely I will make your enemies plead with you
 in times of disaster and times of distress.

[12] "Can a man break iron—
 iron from the north—or bronze?

[13] "Your wealth and your treasures
 I will give as plunder, without charge,
because of all your sins
 throughout your country.
[14] I will enslave you to your enemies
 in[a] a land you do not know,
for my anger will kindle a fire
 that will burn against you."

[15] LORD, you understand;
 remember me and care for me.
 Avenge me on my persecutors.
You are long-suffering—do not take me away;
 think of how I suffer reproach for your sake.
[16] When your words came, I ate them;
 they were my joy and my heart's delight,
for I bear your name,
 LORD God Almighty.
[17] I never sat in the company of revelers,
 never made merry with them;
I sat alone because your hand was on me
 and you had filled me with indignation.
[18] Why is my pain unending
 and my wound grievous and incurable?
You are to me like a deceptive brook,
 like a spring that fails.

[19] Therefore this is what the LORD says:

"If you repent, I will restore you
 that you may serve me;
if you utter worthy, not worthless, words,
 you will be my spokesman.
Let this people turn to you,
 but you must not turn to them.
[20] I will make you a wall to this people,
 a fortified wall of bronze;
they will fight against you
 but will not overcome you,
for I am with you
 to rescue and save you,"
declares the LORD.
[21] "I will save you from the hands of the wicked
 and deliver you from the grasp of the cruel."

## Amplified Bible

a destroyer at noonday. I will cause anguish and terrors to
fall upon her [Jerusalem] suddenly.
[9] She who has borne seven languishes; she has expired.
Her sun has gone down while it was yet day; she has been
put to shame, confounded, *and* disgraced. And the rest
of them I will deliver to the sword before their enemies,
says the Lord.
[10] Woe is me, my mother, that you bore me to be a man
of strife and a man of contention to the whole earth! I have
neither loaned, nor have men loaned to me, yet everyone
curses me. [Jer. 1:18, 19.]
[11] The Lord said, Truly your release, affliction, *and*
strengthening will be for good [purposes]; surely [Jer-
emiah] I will intercede for you with the enemy *and* I will
cause the enemy to ask for your aid in the time of evil and
in the time of affliction. [Jer. 21:1, 2; 37:3; 42:2; Rom. 8:28.]
[12] Can iron break the iron from the north and the
bronze?
[13] Your [nation's] substance and your treasures will I
give as spoil, without price, and that for all your sins, even
in all your territory.
[14] And I will make [your possessions] to pass with your
enemies into a land which you do not know *and* I will make
you to serve [your conquerors] there, for a fire is kindled
in My anger which will burn upon you [Israel].
[15] [Jeremiah said] O Lord, You know *and* understand;
[earnestly] remember me and visit me and avenge me on
my persecutors. Take me not away [from joy or from life
itself] in Your long-suffering [to my enemies]; know that
for Your sake I suffer *and* bear reproach.
[16] Your words were found, and I ate them; and Your
words were to me a joy and the rejoicing of my heart, for I
am called by Your name, O Lord God of hosts.
[17] I sat not in the assembly of those who make merry, nor
did I rejoice; I sat alone because Your [powerful] hand was
upon me, for You had filled me with indignation.
[18] Why is my pain perpetual and my wound incurable,
refusing to be healed? Will you indeed be to me like a deceitful brook, like waters that fail *and* are uncertain?
[19] Therefore thus says the Lord [to Jeremiah]: If you
return [and give up this mistaken tone of distrust and de-
spair], then I will give you again a settled place of quiet
*and* safety, and you will be My minister; and if you separate the precious from the vile [cleansing your own heart
from unworthy and unwarranted suspicions concerning
God's faithfulness], you shall be My mouthpiece. [But do
not yield to them.] Let them return to you—not you to [the
people].
[20] And I will make you to this people a fortified, bronze
wall; they will fight against you, but they will not prevail
over you, for I am with you to save *and* deliver you, says
the Lord.
[21] And I will deliver you out of the hands of the wicked,
and I will redeem you out of the palms of the terrible *and*
ruthless tyrants.

---

*a* 14 Some Hebrew manuscripts, Septuagint and Syriac (see also
17:4); most Hebrew manuscripts *I will cause your enemies to bring
you / into*

## New International Version

### Day of Disaster

**16** Then the word of the LORD came to me: [2]"You must not marry and have sons or daughters in this place." [3]For this is what the LORD says about the sons and daughters born in this land and about the women who are their mothers and the men who are their fathers: [4]"They will die of deadly diseases. They will not be mourned or buried but will be like dung lying on the ground. They will perish by sword and famine, and their dead bodies will become food for the birds and the wild animals."

[5]For this is what the LORD says: "Do not enter a house where there is a funeral meal; do not go to mourn or show sympathy, because I have withdrawn my blessing, my love and my pity from this people," declares the LORD. [6]"Both high and low will die in this land. They will not be buried or mourned, and no one will cut themselves or shave their head for the dead. [7]No one will offer food to comfort those who mourn for the dead—not even for a father or a mother—nor will anyone give them a drink to console them.

[8]"And do not enter a house where there is feasting and sit down to eat and drink. [9]For this is what the LORD Almighty, the God of Israel, says: Before your eyes and in your days I will bring an end to the sounds of joy and gladness and to the voices of bride and bridegroom in this place.

[10]"When you tell these people all this and they ask you, 'Why has the LORD decreed such a great disaster against us? What wrong have we done? What sin have we committed against the LORD our God?' [11]then say to them, 'It is because your ancestors forsook me,' declares the LORD, 'and followed other gods and served and worshiped them. They forsook me and did not keep my law. [12]But you have behaved more wickedly than your ancestors. See how all of you are following the stubbornness of your evil hearts instead of obeying me. [13]So I will throw you out of this land into a land neither you nor your ancestors have known, and there you will serve other gods day and night, for I will show you no favor.'

[14]"However, the days are coming," declares the LORD, "when it will no longer be said, 'As surely as the LORD lives, who brought the Israelites up out of Egypt,' [15]but it will be said, 'As surely as the LORD lives, who brought the Israelites up out of the land of the north and out of all the countries where he had banished them.' For I will restore them to the land I gave to their ancestors.

[16]"But now I will send for many fishermen," declares the LORD, "and they will catch them. After that I will send for many hunters, and they will hunt them down on every mountain and hill and from the crevices of the rocks. [17]My eyes are on all their ways; they are not hidden from me, nor is their sin concealed from my eyes. [18]I will repay them double for their wickedness and their sin, because they have defiled my land with the lifeless forms of their vile images and have filled my inheritance with their detestable idols."

## Amplified Bible

**16** The word of the Lord came also to me, saying, [2]You shall not take a wife or have sons and daughters in this place [Jerusalem].

[3]For thus says the Lord concerning the sons and daughters who are born in this place and concerning the mothers who bore them and the fathers who begot them in this land:

[4]They shall die of deadly diseases. They shall not be lamented, nor shall they be buried, but they shall be like dung upon the face of the ground. They shall perish *and* be consumed by the sword and by famine, and their dead bodies shall be food for the fowls of the air and for the beasts of the earth.

[5]For thus says the Lord: Enter not into the house of mourning, nor go to lament or bemoan [the dead], for I have taken away My peace from this people, says the Lord, even My steadfast love *and* loving-kindness and tender mercy.

[6]Both the great and the small shall die in this land. They shall not be buried, neither shall men lament for them or cut themselves or make themselves bald for them.

[7]Neither shall men prepare food for the mourners to comfort them for the dead; nor shall men give them the cup of consolation to drink for their father or for their mother.

[8]And you [Jeremiah] shall not go into the house of feasting to sit with them to eat and drink.

[9]For thus says the Lord of hosts, the God of Israel: Behold, I will cause to cease from this place before your very eyes and in your days the voice of mirth and the voice of gladness, the voice of the bridegroom and the voice of the bride.

[10]And when you tell these people all these words and they inquire of you, Why has the Lord decreed all this enormous evil against us? Or, What is our iniquity? Or, What is the sin that we have committed against the Lord our God?

[11]Then you shall say to them, [It is] because your fathers have forsaken Me, says the Lord, and have walked after other gods and have served and worshiped them and have forsaken Me and have not kept My law,

[12]And because you have done worse than your fathers. For behold, every one of you walks after the stubbornness of his own evil heart, so that you do not listen to *and* obey Me.

[13]Therefore I will cast you out of this land [of Judah] into the land [of the Babylonians] neither you nor your fathers have known, and there you will serve other gods day and night, for I will show you no favor there.

[14]Therefore, behold, the days are coming, says the Lord, when it shall no more be said, As the Lord lives, Who brought up the children of Israel out of the land of Egypt,

[15]But, As the Lord lives, Who brought up the children of Israel from the land of the north and from all the countries to which He had driven them. And I will bring them again to their land which I gave to their fathers.

[16]Behold, I will send for many fishers, says the Lord, and they shall fish them out; and afterward I will send for many hunters, and they will hunt them from every mountain and from every hill and out of the clefts of the rocks.

[17]For My eyes are on all their ways; they are not hidden from My face, neither is their iniquity concealed from My eyes.

[18]First [before I bring them back to their land] I will doubly recompense *and* punish them for their iniquity and their sin, because they have polluted My land with the carcasses of their detestable idols and with the abominable things offered to false gods with which they have filled My inheritance.

## New International Version

19 LORD, my strength and my fortress,
    my refuge in time of distress,
to you the nations will come
    from the ends of the earth and say,
"Our ancestors possessed nothing but false gods,
    worthless idols that did them no good.
20 Do people make their own gods?
    Yes, but they are not gods!"

21 "Therefore I will teach them—
    this time I will teach them
    my power and might.
Then they will know
    that my name is the LORD.

**17** "Judah's sin is engraved with an iron tool,
    inscribed with a flint point,
on the tablets of their hearts
    and on the horns of their altars.
2 Even their children remember
    their altars and Asherah poles[a]
beside the spreading trees
    and on the high hills.
3 My mountain in the land
    and your[b] wealth and all your treasures
I will give away as plunder,
    together with your high places,
    because of sin throughout your country.
4 Through your own fault you will lose
    the inheritance I gave you.
I will enslave you to your enemies
    in a land you do not know,
for you have kindled my anger,
    and it will burn forever."

5 This is what the LORD says:

"Cursed is the one who trusts in man,
    who draws strength from mere flesh
    and whose heart turns away from the LORD.
6 That person will be like a bush in the wastelands;
    they will not see prosperity when it comes.
They will dwell in the parched places of the desert,
    in a salt land where no one lives.

7 "But blessed is the one who trusts in the LORD,
    whose confidence is in him.
8 They will be like a tree planted by the water
    that sends out its roots by the stream.
It does not fear when heat comes;
    its leaves are always green.
It has no worries in a year of drought
    and never fails to bear fruit."

9 The heart is deceitful above all things
    and beyond cure.
    Who can understand it?

10 "I the LORD search the heart
    and examine the mind,
to reward each person according to their conduct,
    according to what their deeds deserve."

11 Like a partridge that hatches eggs it did not lay
    are those who gain riches by unjust means.
When their lives are half gone, their riches will desert
    them,
    and in the end they will prove to be fools.

12 A glorious throne, exalted from the beginning,
    is the place of our sanctuary.
13 LORD, you are the hope of Israel;
    all who forsake you will be put to shame.

## Amplified Bible

19 [Then said Jeremiah] O Lord, my Strength and my Stronghold, and my Refuge in the day of affliction, to You shall the nations come from the ends of the earth and shall say, Surely our fathers have inherited nothing but lies, emptiness, *and* futility, worthless things in which there is no profit!
20 Can a man make gods for himself? Such are not gods!
21 Therefore [says the Lord] behold, I will make them know—[yes] this once I will make them know My power and My might; and they will know *and* recognize that My name is the Lord.

**17** The sin of Judah is written with a pen *or* stylus of iron and with the point of a diamond; it is engraved on the tablets of their hearts and on the horns of their altars,
2 While their children [earnestly] remember their [heathen] altars and their Asherim [wooden symbols of the goddess Asherah] beside the green trees upon the high hills.
3 O [Jerusalem] My mountain in the field, I will give your wealth *and* all your treasures to the spoil and your high places for sin [as the price of your sin] throughout all your territory.
4 And you, through your own fault, will loosen your hand *and* discontinue from your heritage which I gave you; and I will cause you to serve your enemies in a land which you do not know, for you have kindled a fire in My anger which will burn throughout the ages.
5 Thus says the Lord: Cursed [with great evil] is the strong man who trusts in *and* relies on frail man, making weak [human] flesh his arm, and whose mind *and* heart turn aside from the Lord.
6 For he shall be like a shrub *or* a person naked and destitute in the desert; and he shall not see any good come, but shall dwell in the parched places in the wilderness, in an uninhabited salt land.
7 [Most] blessed is the man who believes in, trusts in, *and* relies on the Lord, and whose hope *and* confidence the Lord is.
8 For he shall be like a tree planted by the waters that spreads out its roots by the river; and it shall not see *and* fear when heat comes; but its leaf shall be green. It shall not be anxious *and* full of care in the year of drought, nor shall it cease yielding fruit.
9 The heart is deceitful above all things, and it is exceedingly perverse *and* corrupt and severely, mortally sick! Who can know it [perceive, understand, be acquainted with his own heart and mind]? [Matt. 13:15-17; Mark 7:21-23; Eph. 4:20-24.]
10 I the Lord search the mind, I try the heart, even to give to every man according to his ways, according to the fruit of his doings.
11 Like the partridge that gathers a brood which she did not hatch *and* sits on eggs which she has not laid, so is he who gets riches by unjust means *and* not by right. He will leave them, *or* they will leave him, in the midst of his days, and at his end he will be a fool.
12 A glorious throne, set on high from the beginning, is the place of our sanctuary (the temple).
13 O Lord, the Hope of Israel, all who forsake You shall

---

*a 2* That is, wooden symbols of the goddess Asherah    *b 2,3* Or *hills /*
*3 and the mountains of the land. / Your*

## New International Version

Those who turn away from you will be written in the
dust
because they have forsaken the LORD,
the spring of living water.

14 Heal me, LORD, and I will be healed;
save me and I will be saved,
for you are the one I praise.
15 They keep saying to me,
"Where is the word of the LORD?
Let it now be fulfilled!"
16 I have not run away from being your shepherd;
you know I have not desired the day of despair.
What passes my lips is open before you.
17 Do not be a terror to me;
you are my refuge in the day of disaster.
18 Let my persecutors be put to shame,
but keep me from shame;
let them be terrified,
but keep me from terror.
Bring on them the day of disaster;
destroy them with double destruction.

### Keeping the Sabbath Day Holy

19 This is what the LORD said to me: "Go and stand at
the Gate of the People,ᵃ through which the kings of Judah
go in and out; stand also at all the other gates of Jerusalem. 20 Say to them, 'Hear the word of the LORD, you kings
of Judah and all people of Judah and everyone living in
Jerusalem who come through these gates. 21 This is what
the LORD says: Be careful not to carry a load on the Sabbath day or bring it through the gates of Jerusalem. 22 Do
not bring a load out of your houses or do any work on the
Sabbath, but keep the Sabbath day holy, as I commanded
your ancestors. 23 Yet they did not listen or pay attention;
they were stiff-necked and would not listen or respond to
discipline. 24 But if you are careful to obey me, declares the
LORD, and bring no load through the gates of this city on
the Sabbath, but keep the Sabbath day holy by not doing
any work on it, 25 then kings who sit on David's throne will
come through the gates of this city with their officials.
They and their officials will come riding in chariots and
on horses, accompanied by the men of Judah and those
living in Jerusalem, and this city will be inhabited forever.
26 People will come from the towns of Judah and the villages around Jerusalem, from the territory of Benjamin and
the western foothills, from the hill country and the Negev,
bringing burnt offerings and sacrifices, grain offerings
and incense, and bringing thank offerings to the house of
the LORD. 27 But if you do not obey me to keep the Sabbath
day holy by not carrying any load as you come through the
gates of Jerusalem on the Sabbath day, then I will kindle
an unquenchable fire in the gates of Jerusalem that will
consume her fortresses.'"

### At the Potter's House

**18** This is the word that came to Jeremiah from the
LORD: 2 "Go down to the potter's house, and there I
will give you my message." 3 So I went down to the potter's
house, and I saw him working at the wheel. 4 But the pot
he was shaping from the clay was marred in his hands; so
the potter formed it into another pot, shaping it as seemed
best to him.

5 Then the word of the LORD came to me. 6 He said, "Can
I not do with you, Israel, as this potter does?" declares the
LORD. "Like clay in the hand of the potter, so are you in

## Amplified Bible

be put to shame. They who depart from You *and* me [Your
prophet] shall [disappear like] writing upon the ground,
because they have forsaken the Lord, the Fountain of living waters.

14 Heal me, O Lord, and I shall be healed; save me, and I
shall be saved, for You are my praise.
15 Behold, they say to me, Where is the word of the Lord
[predicting the disaster that you said would befall us]? Let
it come now!
16 But as for me, I have not sought to escape from being
a shepherd after You, nor have I desired the woeful day [of
judgment]; You know that. Whatever I said was spoken in
Your presence *and* was from You.
17 Be not a terror to me; You are my refuge *and* my hope
in the day of evil.
18 Let those be put to shame who persecute me, but let
me not be put to shame; let them be dismayed, but let me
not be dismayed. Bring on them the day of evil, and destroy them with double destruction.

19 Thus said the Lord to me: Go and stand in the gate of
the sons of the people, through which the kings of Judah
enter and through which they go out, and also [stand] in
all the gates of Jerusalem.
20 Say to them, Hear the word of the Lord, you kings of
Judah, and all Judah, and all the inhabitants of Jerusalem
who enter through these gates.
21 Thus says the Lord: Take heed to yourselves *and* for
the sake of your lives bear no burden on the Sabbath day
or bring it in through the gates of Jerusalem.
22 And do not carry a burden out of your houses on the
Sabbath day or do any work, but keep the Sabbath day holy
(set apart to the worship of God), as I commanded your
fathers.
23 Yet they would not listen *and* obey or incline their
ears; but they stiffened their necks, that they might not
hear and might not receive instruction.
24 But if you diligently listen to *and* obey Me, says the
Lord, and bring in no burden through the gates of this
city on the Sabbath day, but keep the Sabbath day holy (set
apart to the worship of God), to do no work on it,
25 Then there will enter through the gates of this city
kings and princes who will sit upon the throne of David,
riding in chariots and on horses—the kings and their
princes, the men of Judah and the inhabitants of Jerusalem; and this city will be inhabited *and* last throughout
the ages.
26 And people shall come from the cities of Judah and
the places round about Jerusalem, from the land of Benjamin, from the lowland, from the hill country, and from
the South (the Negeb), bringing burnt offerings and sacrifices, cereal offerings and frankincense, and bringing
sacrifices of thanksgiving to the house of the Lord.
27 But if you will not listen to Me to keep the Sabbath
day holy (set apart to the worship of God), and not to bear
a burden and enter in at the gates of Jerusalem [with one]
on the Sabbath day, then I will kindle a fire in her gates,
and it shall devour the palaces of Jerusalem, and it shall
not be quenched.

**18** The word which came to Jeremiah from the Lord:
2 Arise and go down to the potter's house, and
there I will cause you to hear My words.
3 Then I went down to the potter's house, and behold, he
was working at the wheel.
4 And the vessel that he was making from clay was
spoiled in the hand of the potter; so he made it over, re-
working it into another vessel as it seemed good to the
potter to make it.
5 Then the word of the Lord came to me:
6 O house of Israel, can I not do with you as this potter
does? says the Lord. Behold, as the clay is in the potter's
hand, so are you in My hand, O house of Israel.

## New International Version

my hand, Israel. [7]If at any time I announce that a nation or kingdom is to be uprooted, torn down and destroyed, [8]and if that nation I warned repents of its evil, then I will relent and not inflict on it the disaster I had planned. [9]And if at another time I announce that a nation or kingdom is to be built up and planted, [10]and if it does evil in my sight and does not obey me, then I will reconsider the good I had intended to do for it.

[11]"Now therefore say to the people of Judah and those living in Jerusalem, 'This is what the LORD says: Look! I am preparing a disaster for you and devising a plan against you. So turn from your evil ways, each one of you, and reform your ways and your actions.' [12]But they will reply, 'It's no use. We will continue with our own plans; we will all follow the stubbornness of our evil hearts.'"

[13]Therefore this is what the LORD says:

"Inquire among the nations:
  Who has ever heard anything like this?
A most horrible thing has been done
  by Virgin Israel.
[14]Does the snow of Lebanon
  ever vanish from its rocky slopes?
Do its cool waters from distant sources
  ever stop flowing?[a]
[15]Yet my people have forgotten me;
  they burn incense to worthless idols,
which made them stumble in their ways,
  in the ancient paths.
They made them walk in byways,
  on roads not built up.
[16]Their land will be an object of horror
  and of lasting scorn;
all who pass by will be appalled
  and will shake their heads.
[17]Like a wind from the east,
  I will scatter them before their enemies;
I will show them my back and not my face
  in the day of their disaster."

[18]They said, "Come, let's make plans against Jeremiah; for the teaching of the law by the priest will not cease, nor will counsel from the wise, nor the word from the prophets. So come, let's attack him with our tongues and pay no attention to anything he says."

[19]Listen to me, LORD;
  hear what my accusers are saying!
[20]Should good be repaid with evil?
  Yet they have dug a pit for me.
Remember that I stood before you
  and spoke in their behalf
  to turn your wrath away from them.
[21]So give their children over to famine;
  hand them over to the power of the sword.
Let their wives be made childless and widows;
  let their men be put to death,
  their young men slain by the sword in battle.
[22]Let a cry be heard from their houses
  when you suddenly bring invaders against them,
for they have dug a pit to capture me
  and have hidden snares for my feet.
[23]But you, LORD, know
  all their plots to kill me.
Do not forgive their crimes
  or blot out their sins from your sight.
Let them be overthrown before you;
  deal with them in the time of your anger.

## Amplified Bible

[7]At one time I will suddenly speak concerning a nation or kingdom, that I will pluck up and break down and destroy it;

[8]And if [the people of] that nation concerning which I have spoken turn from their evil, I will relent *and* reverse My decision concerning the evil that I thought to do to them.

[9]At another time I will suddenly speak concerning a nation or kingdom, that I will build up and plant it;

[10]And if they do evil in My sight, obeying not My voice, then I will regret *and* reverse My decision concerning the good with which I said I would benefit them.

[11]Now therefore say to the men of Judah and to the inhabitants of Jerusalem, Thus says the Lord: Behold, I am shaping evil against you and devising a plan against you. Return now each one from his evil way; reform your [accustomed] ways *and* make your [individual] actions good *and* right.

[12]But they will say, That is in vain! For we will walk after our own devices, and we will each do as the stubbornness of his own evil heart dictates.

[13]Therefore thus says the Lord: Ask now among the nations: Who has heard such things? Virgin Israel has done a very vile *and* horrible thing.

[14]Will the snow of Mount Lebanon fail *and* vanish from its rocks [which tower above the land of Israel]? Will the cold, rushing waters of strange lands [that dash down from afar] be dried up?

[15]Yet My people have forgotten Me; they burn incense to false gods, they have been caused to stumble in their ways and in the ancient roads, to walk in bypaths, in a way not graded *and* built up [not on a highway],

[16]Making their land a desolation *and* a horror, a thing to be hissed at perpetually; everyone who passes by shall be astounded *and* horrified and shake his head.

[17]I will scatter them as with an east wind before the enemy; I will show them My back and not My face in the day of their calamity [says the Lord].

[18]Then [my enemies] said, Come and let us devise schemes against Jeremiah; for the law [of Moses] shall not perish from the priest [as this false prophet Jeremiah predicts], nor will counsel from the wise, nor the word from the prophet. Come, let us smite him with the tongue [making a charge against him to the king], and let us not pay any attention to his words.

[19]Give heed to me, Lord; listen to [what] my adversaries [are plotting to do to me—and intercede].

[20]Shall evil be recompensed for good? Yet they have dug a pit for my life. [Earnestly] remember that I stood before You to speak good for them, to turn away Your anger from them.

[21]Therefore deliver up their children to the famine; give them over to the power of the sword. And let their wives become childless and widows; let their men meet death by pestilence, their young men be slain by the sword in battle.

[22]Let a cry be heard from their houses when You suddenly bring a troop upon them, for they have dug a pit to take me and have hidden snares for my feet.

[23]Yet, Lord, You know all their plotting against me to slay me. Forgive not their iniquity, nor blot out their sin from Your sight. But let them be overthrown before You; deal with them in the time of Your anger.

---

[a] 14 The meaning of the Hebrew for this sentence is uncertain.

## New International Version

**19** This is what the LORD says: "Go and buy a clay jar from a potter. Take along some of the elders of the people and of the priests ²and go out to the Valley of Ben Hinnom, near the entrance of the Potsherd Gate. There proclaim the words I tell you, ³and say, 'Hear the word of the LORD, you kings of Judah and people of Jerusalem. This is what the LORD Almighty, the God of Israel, says: Listen! I am going to bring a disaster on this place that will make the ears of everyone who hears of it tingle. ⁴For they have forsaken me and made this a place of foreign gods; they have burned incense in it to gods that neither they nor their ancestors nor the kings of Judah ever knew, and they have filled this place with the blood of the innocent. ⁵They have built the high places of Baal to burn their children in the fire as offerings to Baal—something I did not command or mention, nor did it enter my mind. ⁶So beware, the days are coming, declares the LORD, when people will no longer call this place Topheth or the Valley of Ben Hinnom, but the Valley of Slaughter.

⁷"'In this place I will ruin*a* the plans of Judah and Jerusalem. I will make them fall by the sword before their enemies, at the hands of those who want to kill them, and I will give their carcasses as food to the birds and the wild animals. ⁸I will devastate this city and make it an object of horror and scorn; all who pass by will be appalled and will scoff because of all its wounds. ⁹I will make them eat the flesh of their sons and daughters, and they will eat one another's flesh because their enemies will press the siege so hard against them to destroy them.'

¹⁰"Then break the jar while those who go with you are watching, ¹¹and say to them, 'This is what the LORD Almighty says: I will smash this nation and this city just as this potter's jar is smashed and cannot be repaired. They will bury the dead in Topheth until there is no more room. ¹²This is what I will do to this place and to those who live here, declares the LORD. I will make this city like Topheth. ¹³The houses in Jerusalem and those of the kings of Judah will be defiled like this place, Topheth—all the houses where they burned incense on the roofs to all the starry hosts and poured out drink offerings to other gods.'"

¹⁴Jeremiah then returned from Topheth, where the LORD had sent him to prophesy, and stood in the court of the LORD's temple and said to all the people, ¹⁵"This is what the LORD Almighty, the God of Israel, says: 'Listen! I am going to bring on this city and all the villages around it every disaster I pronounced against them, because they were stiff-necked and would not listen to my words.'"

### Jeremiah and Pashhur

**20** When the priest Pashhur son of Immer, the official in charge of the temple of the LORD, heard Jeremiah prophesying these things, ²he had Jeremiah the prophet beaten and put in the stocks at the Upper Gate of Benjamin at the LORD's temple. ³The next day, when Pashhur released him from the stocks, Jeremiah said to him, "The

---

*a 7 The Hebrew for *ruin* sounds like the Hebrew for *jar* (see verses 1 and 10).

## Amplified Bible

**19** Thus says the Lord: Go and get a potter's earthen bottle, and take some of the old people and some of the elderly priests

²And go out to the Valley of Ben-hinnom [son of Hinnom], which is by the entrance of the Potsherd Gate; and proclaim there the words that I shall tell you,

³And say, Hear the word of the Lord, O kings of Judah and inhabitants of Jerusalem. Thus says the Lord of hosts, the God of Israel: Behold, I am going to bring such evil upon this place that the ears of whoever hears of it will tingle.

⁴Because the people have forsaken Me and have estranged *and* profaned this place [Jerusalem] by burning incense in it to other gods that neither they nor their fathers nor the kings of Judah ever knew, and because they have filled this place with the blood of innocents

⁵And have built the high places of Baal to burn their sons in the fire as burnt offerings to Baal, which I commanded not nor spoke of it, nor did it come into My mind *and* heart—

⁶Therefore, behold, the days are coming, says the Lord, when this place shall no more be called Topheth or the Valley of Ben-hinnom [son of Hinnom], but the Valley of Slaughter. [Jer. 7:31-32.]

⁷And I will pour out *and* make void the counsel *and* the plans of [the men of] Judah and Jerusalem in this place, and I will cause their people to fall by the sword before their enemies and by the hands of those who seek their lives, and their dead bodies I will give to be food for the birds of the air and for the beasts of the earth.

⁸And I will make this city an astonishment *and* a horror and a hissing; everyone who passes by it will be horrified and will hiss [in scorn] because of all its plagues *and* disasters.

⁹And I will cause them to eat the flesh of their sons and their daughters, and they shall eat each one the flesh of his neighbor *and* friend in the siege and in the distress with which their enemies and those who seek their lives distress them.

¹⁰Then you shall break the bottle in the sight of the men who accompany you,

¹¹And say to them, Thus said the Lord of hosts: Even so will I break this people and this city as one breaks a potter's vessel, so that it cannot be mended. Men will bury in Topheth because there will be no other place for burial *and* until there is no more room to bury.

¹²Thus will I do to this place, says the Lord, and to its inhabitants; and I will even make this city like Topheth.

¹³And the houses of Jerusalem and the houses of the kings of Judah, which are defiled, shall be like the place of Topheth—even all the houses upon whose roofs incense has been burned to all the host of the heavens and drink offerings have been poured out to other gods. [Acts 7:42, 43.]

¹⁴Then came Jeremiah from Topheth, where the Lord had sent him to prophesy, and he stood in the court of the Lord's house and said to all the people,

¹⁵Thus says the Lord of hosts, the God of Israel: Behold, I will bring upon this city and upon all its towns all the evil that I have pronounced against it, because they have stiffened their necks, refusing to hear My words.

**20** Now Pashhur son of Immer, the priest, who was [also] chief officer in the house of the Lord, heard Jeremiah prophesying these things.

²Then Pashhur beat Jeremiah the prophet and put him in the stocks that were at the upper Benjamin Gate by the house of the Lord. [Jer. 1:19; 15:15.]

³And the next day Pashhur brought Jeremiah out of the stocks. Then Jeremiah said to him, The Lord does not call

## New International Version

LORD's name for you is not Pashhur, but Terror on Every Side. ⁴For this is what the LORD says: 'I will make you a terror to yourself and to all your friends; with your own eyes you will see them fall by the sword of their enemies. I will give all Judah into the hands of the king of Babylon, who will carry them away to Babylon or put them to the sword. ⁵I will deliver all the wealth of this city into the hands of their enemies—all its products, all its valuables and all the treasures of the kings of Judah. They will take it away as plunder and carry it off to Babylon. ⁶And you, Pashhur, and all who live in your house will go into exile to Babylon. There you will die and be buried, you and all your friends to whom you have prophesied lies.'"

### Jeremiah's Complaint

⁷You deceived*ᵃ* me, LORD, and I was deceived*ᵃ*;
  you overpowered me and prevailed.
 I am ridiculed all day long;
  everyone mocks me.
⁸Whenever I speak, I cry out
  proclaiming violence and destruction.
 So the word of the LORD has brought me
  insult and reproach all day long.
⁹But if I say, "I will not mention his word
  or speak anymore in his name,"
 his word is in my heart like a fire,
  a fire shut up in my bones.
 I am weary of holding it in;
  indeed, I cannot.
¹⁰I hear many whispering,
  "Terror on every side!
  Denounce him! Let's denounce him!"
 All my friends
  are waiting for me to slip, saying,
 "Perhaps he will be deceived;
  then we will prevail over him
  and take our revenge on him."

¹¹But the LORD is with me like a mighty warrior;
  so my persecutors will stumble and not prevail.
 They will fail and be thoroughly disgraced;
  their dishonor will never be forgotten.
¹²LORD Almighty, you who examine the righteous
  and probe the heart and mind,
 let me see your vengeance on them,
  for to you I have committed my cause.

¹³Sing to the LORD!
  Give praise to the LORD!
 He rescues the life of the needy
  from the hands of the wicked.

¹⁴Cursed be the day I was born!
  May the day my mother bore me not be blessed!
¹⁵Cursed be the man who brought my father the news,
  who made him very glad, saying,
 "A child is born to you—a son!"
¹⁶May that man be like the towns
  the LORD overthrew without pity.
 May he hear wailing in the morning,
  a battle cry at noon.
¹⁷For he did not kill me in the womb,
  with my mother as my grave,
  her womb enlarged forever.
¹⁸Why did I ever come out of the womb
  to see trouble and sorrow
  and to end my days in shame?

## Amplified Bible

your name Pashhur, but Magor-missabib [terror on every side].
⁴For thus says the Lord: Behold, I will make you a terror to yourself and to all your friends; they will fall by the sword of their enemies while you look on. And I will give all Judah into the hand of the king of Babylon; he will carry them captive to Babylon and will slay them with the sword.
⁵Moreover, I will deliver all the riches of this city—all the results of its labors, all its precious things, and all the treasures of the kings of Judah—into the hand of their enemies, who will make them a prey *and* plunder them and seize them and carry them to Babylon.
⁶And you, Pashhur, and all who dwell in your house shall go into captivity; you shall go to Babylon, and there you shall die and be buried, you and all your friends to whom you have prophesied falsely.
⁷[But Jeremiah said] O Lord, You have persuaded *and* deceived me, and I was persuaded *and* deceived; You are stronger than I am and You have prevailed. I am a laughingstock all the day; everyone mocks me.
⁸For whenever I speak, I must cry out *and* complain; I shout, Violence and destruction! For the word of the Lord has become to me a reproach and a derision *and* has brought me insult all day long.
⁹If I say, I will not make mention of [the Lord] or speak any more in His name, in my mind *and* heart it is as if there were a burning fire shut up in my bones. And I am weary of enduring *and* holding it in; I cannot [contain it any longer].
¹⁰For I have heard many whispering *and* defaming, [There is] terror on every side! Denounce him! Let us denounce him! Say all my familiar friends, they who watch for my fall, Perhaps he will be persuaded *and* deceived; then we will prevail against him, and we will get our revenge on him.
¹¹But the Lord is with me as a mighty *and* terrible One; therefore my persecutors will stumble, and they will not overcome [me]. They will be utterly put to shame, for they will not deal wisely *or* prosper [in their schemes]; their eternal dishonor will never be forgotten.
¹²But, O Lord of hosts, You Who try the righteous, Who see the heart and the mind, let me see Your vengeance on them, for to You have I revealed *and* committed my cause.
¹³Sing to the Lord! Praise the Lord! For He has delivered the life of the poor *and* needy from the hands of evildoers.
¹⁴Cursed be the day on which I was born! Let not the day on which my mother bore me be blessed!
¹⁵Cursed be the man who brought the tidings to my father, saying, A son is born to you!—making him very glad.
¹⁶And let that man be like the cities which the Lord overthrew, and did not relent. Let him hear the [war] cry in the morning and the shouting of alarm at noon,
¹⁷Because he did not slay me in the womb, so that my mother might have been my grave, and her womb always great.
¹⁸Why did I come out of the womb to see labor and sorrow, that my days should be consumed in shame?

---

*ᵃ* 7 Or *persuaded*

## New International Version

### God Rejects Zedekiah's Request

**21** The word came to Jeremiah from the LORD when King Zedekiah sent to him Pashhur son of Malkijah and the priest Zephaniah son of Maaseiah. They said: [2]"Inquire now of the LORD for us because Nebuchadnezzar[a] king of Babylon is attacking us. Perhaps the LORD will perform wonders for us as in times past so that he will withdraw from us."

[3]But Jeremiah answered them, "Tell Zedekiah, [4]'This is what the LORD, the God of Israel, says: I am about to turn against you the weapons of war that are in your hands, which you are using to fight the king of Babylon and the Babylonians[b] who are outside the wall besieging you. And I will gather them inside this city. [5]I myself will fight against you with an outstretched hand and a mighty arm in furious anger and in great wrath. [6]I will strike down those who live in this city—both man and beast—and they will die of a terrible plague. [7]After that, declares the LORD, I will give Zedekiah king of Judah, his officials and the people in this city who survive the plague, sword and famine, into the hands of Nebuchadnezzar king of Babylon and to their enemies who want to kill them. He will put them to the sword; he will show them no mercy or pity or compassion.'

[8]"Furthermore, tell the people, 'This is what the LORD says: See, I am setting before you the way of life and the way of death. [9]Whoever stays in this city will die by the sword, famine or plague. But whoever goes out and surrenders to the Babylonians who are besieging you will live; they will escape with their lives. [10]I have determined to do this city harm and not good, declares the LORD. It will be given into the hands of the king of Babylon, and he will destroy it with fire.'

[11]"Moreover, say to the royal house of Judah, 'Hear the word of the LORD. [12]This is what the LORD says to you, house of David:

"'Administer justice every morning;
 rescue from the hand of the oppressor
 the one who has been robbed,
or my wrath will break out and burn like fire
 because of the evil you have done—
 burn with no one to quench it.
[13]I am against you, Jerusalem,
 you who live above this valley
 on the rocky plateau, declares the LORD—
you who say, "Who can come against us?
 Who can enter our refuge?"
[14]I will punish you as your deeds deserve,
 declares the LORD.
I will kindle a fire in your forests
 that will consume everything around you.'"

### Judgment Against Wicked Kings

**22** This is what the LORD says: "Go down to the palace of the king of Judah and proclaim this message there: [2]'Hear the word of the LORD to you, king of Judah, you who sit on David's throne—you, your officials and your people who come through these gates. [3]This is what the LORD says: Do what is just and right. Rescue from the hand of the oppressor the one who has been robbed. Do

## Amplified Bible

**21** The word which came to Jeremiah from the Lord when King Zedekiah sent to him Pashhur son of Malchiah, and Zephaniah the priest, the son of Maaseiah, saying,

[2]Inquire, I pray you, of the Lord for us, for [a]Nebuchadrezzar king of Babylon is making war against us. Perhaps the Lord will deal with us according to all His wonderful works, forcing him to withdraw from us.

[3]Then said Jeremiah to them, Say this to Zedekiah:

[4]Thus says the Lord, the God of Israel: Behold, I will turn back *and* dull the edge of the weapons of war that are in your hands, with which you fight against the king of Babylon and the Chaldeans who are besieging you outside the walls; and I will bring them into the midst of this city [Jerusalem].

[5]And I Myself will fight against you with an outstretched hand and with a strong arm in anger, in fury, and in great indignation *and* wrath.

[6]And I will smite the inhabitants of this city, both man and beast; they will die of a great pestilence.

[7]And afterward, says the Lord, I will deliver Zedekiah king of Judah and his servants and the people in this city who survive the pestilence, the sword, and the famine, into the hand of Nebuchadrezzar king of Babylon and into the hands of their enemies, into the hands of those who seek their lives. And he will smite them with the edge of the sword; he will not spare them nor have pity or mercy *and* compassion upon them.

[8]And to this people you [Jeremiah] shall say, Thus says the Lord: Behold, I set before you the way of life and the way of death.

[9]He who remains in this city [Jerusalem] shall die by the sword and by famine and by pestilence. But he who goes out and passes over to the Chaldeans who besiege you, he shall live, and his life shall be to him his only booty [as a prize of war].

[10]For I have set My face against this city for evil and not for good, says the Lord. It shall be given into the hand of the king of Babylon, and he shall burn it with fire.

[11]And concerning the royal house of the king of Judah, hear the word of the Lord:

[12]O house of David, thus says the Lord: Execute justice in the morning, and deliver from the hand of the oppressor him who has been robbed, lest My wrath go forth like fire and burn so that none can quench it—because of the evil of your doings.

[13]Behold, I am against you, O inhabitant of the valley, O rock of the plain, says the Lord—you who say, Who shall come down against us? Or, Who shall enter into our dwelling places?

[14]And I will punish you according to the fruit of your doings, says the Lord. I will kindle a fire in your forest, and it will devour all that is round about you.

**22** Thus says the Lord: Go down to the house of the king of Judah and speak there this word:

[2]Hear the word of the Lord, O king of Judah, you who sit upon the throne of David—you and your servants and your people who enter by these gates.

[3]Thus says the Lord: Execute justice and righteousness, and deliver out of the hand of the oppressor him who has been robbed. And do no wrong; do no violence to

[a] The reader will no doubt notice that the name of the Babylonian ruler Nebuchadnezzar is frequently spelled Nebuchadrezzar in the book of Jeremiah, as well as on several occasions in the book of Ezekiel (Ezek. 26:7; 29:18-19; 30:10, 24). "The two forms represent different Hebrew methods of reproducing the name" (John D. Davis, *A Dictionary of the Bible*).

[a] 2 Hebrew *Nebuchadrezzar,* of which *Nebuchadnezzar* is a variant; here and often in Jeremiah and Ezekiel    [b] 4 Or *Chaldeans*; also in verse 9

## New International Version

no wrong or violence to the foreigner, the fatherless or the widow, and do not shed innocent blood in this place. ⁴For if you are careful to carry out these commands, then kings who sit on David's throne will come through the gates of this palace, riding in chariots and on horses, accompanied by their officials and their people. ⁵But if you do not obey these commands, declares the LORD, I swear by myself that this palace will become a ruin.'"

⁶For this is what the LORD says about the palace of the king of Judah:

"Though you are like Gilead to me,
    like the summit of Lebanon,
I will surely make you like a wasteland,
    like towns not inhabited.
⁷I will send destroyers against you,
    each man with his weapons,
and they will cut up your fine cedar beams
    and throw them into the fire.

⁸"People from many nations will pass by this city and will ask one another, 'Why has the LORD done such a thing to this great city?' ⁹And the answer will be: 'Because they have forsaken the covenant of the LORD their God and have worshiped and served other gods.'"

¹⁰Do not weep for the dead king or mourn his loss;
    rather, weep bitterly for him who is exiled,
because he will never return
    nor see his native land again.

¹¹For this is what the LORD says about Shallum[a] son of Josiah, who succeeded his father as king of Judah but has gone from this place: "He will never return. ¹²He will die in the place where they have led him captive; he will not see this land again."

¹³"Woe to him who builds his palace by
        unrighteousness,
    his upper rooms by injustice,
making his own people work for nothing,
    not paying them for their labor.
¹⁴He says, 'I will build myself a great palace
    with spacious upper rooms.'
So he makes large windows in it,
    panels it with cedar
    and decorates it in red.

¹⁵"Does it make you a king
    to have more and more cedar?
Did not your father have food and drink?
    He did what was right and just,
    so all went well with him.
¹⁶He defended the cause of the poor and needy,
    and so all went well.
Is that not what it means to know me?"
    declares the LORD.
¹⁷"But your eyes and your heart
    are set only on dishonest gain,
on shedding innocent blood
    and on oppression and extortion."

¹⁸Therefore this is what the LORD says about Jehoiakim son of Josiah king of Judah:

"They will not mourn for him:
    'Alas, my brother! Alas, my sister!'
They will not mourn for him:
    'Alas, my master! Alas, his splendor!'
¹⁹He will have the burial of a donkey—
    dragged away and thrown
    outside the gates of Jerusalem."

²⁰"Go up to Lebanon and cry out,
    let your voice be heard in Bashan,

---

## Amplified Bible

the stranger *or* temporary resident, the fatherless, or the widow, nor shed innocent blood in this place.

⁴For if you will indeed obey this word, then will there enter in through the gates of this [the king's] house kings sitting [for David] upon David's throne, riding in chariots and on horses—they and their servants and their people.

⁵But if you will not hear these words, I swear by Myself, says the Lord, that this house will become a desolation.

⁶For thus says the Lord concerning the house of the king of Judah: [If you will not listen to Me, though] you are [as valuable] to Me as [the fat pastures of] Gilead [east of the Jordan] or as the [plentiful] summit of Lebanon [west of the Jordan], yet surely I will make you a wilderness and uninhabited cities.

⁷And I will prepare, solemnly set apart, *and* appoint [to execute My judgments against you] destroyers, each with his weapons, and they will cut down your [palaces built of] choicest cedars and cast them into the fire.

⁸And many nations will pass by this city, and every man will say to his neighbor, Why has the Lord done this to this great city?

⁹Then they will answer, Because [the people] forsook the covenant *or* solemn pledge with the Lord their God and worshiped other gods and served them.

¹⁰Weep not for him who is dead nor bemoan him; but weep bitterly for him who goes away [into captivity], for he shall return no more nor see his native country [again].

¹¹For thus says the Lord concerning Shallum son of Josiah king of Judah, who reigned instead of Josiah his father and who went forth out of this place: [Shallum] shall not return here any more;

¹²But he shall die in the place where they have led him captive, and he shall see this land no more.

¹³Woe to him who builds his house by unrighteousness and his [upper] chambers by injustice, who uses his neighbor's service without wages and does not give him his pay [for his work],

¹⁴Who says, I will build myself a wide house with large rooms, and he cuts himself out windows, and it is ceiled *or* paneled with cedar and painted with vermilion.

¹⁵Do you think that being a king [merely] means [self-indulgent] vying [with Solomon] *and* striving to excel in cedar [palaces]? Did not your father [Josiah], as he ate and drank, do justice and righteousness [being upright and in right standing with God]? Then it was well with him.

¹⁶He judged *and* defended the cause of the poor and needy; then it was well. Was not [all] this [what it means] to know *and* recognize Me? says the Lord.

¹⁷But your eyes and your heart are only for your covetousness *and* dishonest gain, for shedding innocent blood, for oppression and doing violence.

¹⁸Therefore thus says the Lord concerning Jehoiakim son of Josiah king of Judah: [Relatives] shall not lament for him, saying, Ah, my brother! or, Ah, sister, [how great our loss! Subjects] shall not lament for him saying, Ah, lord! or Ah, [how great was] his majesty! *or* Ah, [how great was] his glory!

¹⁹[No] he shall be buried with the burial of a donkey—dragged out and cast forth beyond the gates of Jerusalem.

²⁰Go up [north] to Lebanon and cry out, and raise your voice in [the hills] of Bashan [across the Jordan], and cry

---

*a* 11 Also called *Jehoahaz*

## New International Version

cry out from Abarim,
for all your allies are crushed.
21 I warned you when you felt secure,
but you said, 'I will not listen!'
This has been your way from your youth;
you have not obeyed me.
22 The wind will drive all your shepherds away,
and your allies will go into exile.
Then you will be ashamed and disgraced
because of all your wickedness.
23 You who live in 'Lebanon,'*a*
who are nestled in cedar buildings,
how you will groan when pangs come upon you,
pain like that of a woman in labor!

24 "As surely as I live," declares the LORD, "even if you,
Jehoiachin*b* son of Jehoiakim king of Judah, were a signet
ring on my right hand, I would still pull you off. 25 I will
deliver you into the hands of those who want to kill you,
those you fear—Nebuchadnezzar king of Babylon and the
Babylonians.*c* 26 I will hurl you and the mother who gave
you birth into another country, where neither of you was
born, and there you both will die. 27 You will never come
back to the land you long to return to."

28 Is this man Jehoiachin a despised, broken pot,
an object no one wants?
Why will he and his children be hurled out,
cast into a land they do not know?
29 O land, land, land,
hear the word of the LORD!
30 This is what the LORD says:
"Record this man as if childless,
a man who will not prosper in his lifetime,
for none of his offspring will prosper,
none will sit on the throne of David
or rule anymore in Judah."

### The Righteous Branch

**23** "Woe to the shepherds who are destroying and
scattering the sheep of my pasture!" declares the
LORD. 2 Therefore this is what the LORD, the God of Israel,
says to the shepherds who tend my people: "Because you
have scattered my flock and driven them away and have
not bestowed care on them, I will bestow punishment on
you for the evil you have done," declares the LORD. 3 "I myself will gather the remnant of my flock out of all the countries where I have driven them and will bring them back
to their pasture, where they will be fruitful and increase
in number. 4 I will place shepherds over them who will tend
them, and they will no longer be afraid or terrified, nor
will any be missing," declares the LORD.

5 "The days are coming," declares the LORD,
"when I will raise up for David*d* a righteous Branch,
a King who will reign wisely
and do what is just and right in the land.
6 In his days Judah will be saved
and Israel will live in safety.
This is the name by which he will be called:
The LORD Our Righteous Savior.

7 "So then, the days are coming," declares the LORD, "when
people will no longer say, 'As surely as the LORD lives, who
brought the Israelites up out of Egypt,' 8 but they will say,
'As surely as the LORD lives, who brought the descendants
of Israel up out of the land of the north and out of all the
countries where he had banished them.' Then they will
live in their own land."

## Amplified Bible

out from Abarim [a range of mountains southeast of Pal-
estine], for all your lovers (the king's chosen allies) are
destroyed. [Jer. 27:6-7.]
21 I spoke to you in your [times of] prosperity, but you
said, I will not listen! This has been your attitude from
your youth; you have not obeyed My voice.
22 The wind [of adversity] shall pasture upon *and* consume all your shepherds (your princes and statesmen),
and your lovers (allies) shall go into captivity. Surely then
shall you be ashamed and confounded *and* dismayed because of all your wickedness.
23 O inhabitant of Lebanon [Jerusalem, whose palaces
are made of Lebanon's trees], you who make your nest
among the cedars, how you will groan *and* how pitiable
you will be when pangs come upon you, pain like that of a
woman in childbirth! [I Kings 7:2.]
24 As I live, says the Lord, though Coniah [also called
Jeconiah and Jehoiachin] son of Jehoiakim king of Judah
were the signet [ring] upon My right hand, yet would I
tear you off.
25 And I will give you into the hands of those who seek
your life and into the hand of those of whom you are afraid,
even into the hand of Nebuchadrezzar king of Babylon and
into the hands of the Chaldeans.
26 And I will hurl you and the mother who bore you into
another country, where you were not born, and there you
will die.
27 But to the land to which they will yearn to return,
there they will not return.
28 Is this man [King] Coniah a despised, broken pot? Is
he a vessel in which no one takes pleasure? Why are they
hurled out, he and his royal offspring, and cast into a land
which they do not know, understand, *or* recognize?
29 O land, land, land, hear the word of the Lord!
30 Thus says the Lord: Write this man [Coniah] down
as childless, a man who shall not prosper in his days, for
no man of his offspring shall succeed in sitting upon the
throne of David and ruling any more in Judah.

**23** Woe to the shepherds (the civil leaders) who destroy and scatter the sheep of My pasturing! says
the Lord.
2 Therefore thus says the Lord, the God of Israel, concerning the shepherds who care for *and* feed My people:
You have scattered My flock and driven them away and
have not visited *and* attended to them; behold, I will visit
*and* attend to you for the evil of your doings, says the Lord.
3 And I will gather the remnant of My flock out of all the
countries to which I have driven them and will bring them
again to their folds *and* pastures; and they will be fruitful
and multiply.
4 And I will set up shepherds over them who will feed
them. And they will fear no more nor be dismayed, neither
will any be missing *or* lost, says the Lord.
5 Behold, the days are coming, says the Lord, when I will
raise up to David a righteous Branch (Sprout), and He will
reign as King and do wisely and will execute justice and
righteousness in the land.
6 In His days Judah shall be saved and Israel shall dwell
safely: and this is His name by which He shall be called:
The Lord Our Righteousness. [Matt. 1:21-23; Rom. 3:22.]
7 Therefore behold, the days are coming, says the Lord,
when they shall no more say, As the Lord lives, Who
brought up the children of Israel out of the land of Egypt,
8 But, As the Lord lives, Who brought up and led the
offspring of the house of Israel from the north country and
from all the countries to which I had driven them. And
they shall dwell in their own land. [Jer. 16:14-15.]

## New International Version

### Lying Prophets

⁹Concerning the prophets:

My heart is broken within me;
　all my bones tremble.
I am like a drunken man,
　like a strong man overcome by wine,
because of the LORD
　and his holy words.
¹⁰The land is full of adulterers;
　because of the curse[a] the land lies parched
　and the pastures in the wilderness are withered.
The prophets follow an evil course
　and use their power unjustly.

¹¹"Both prophet and priest are godless;
　even in my temple I find their wickedness,"
　　　　　　　　　　declares the LORD.
¹²"Therefore their path will become slippery;
　they will be banished to darkness
　and there they will fall.
I will bring disaster on them
　in the year they are punished,"
　　　　　　　　　　declares the LORD.

¹³"Among the prophets of Samaria
　I saw this repulsive thing:
They prophesied by Baal
　and led my people Israel astray.
¹⁴And among the prophets of Jerusalem
　I have seen something horrible:
They commit adultery and live a lie.
They strengthen the hands of evildoers,
　so that not one of them turns from their wickedness.
They are all like Sodom to me;
　the people of Jerusalem are like Gomorrah."

¹⁵Therefore this is what the LORD Almighty says concerning the prophets:

"I will make them eat bitter food
　and drink poisoned water,
because from the prophets of Jerusalem
　ungodliness has spread throughout the land."

¹⁶This is what the LORD Almighty says:

"Do not listen to what the prophets are prophesying to you;
　they fill you with false hopes.
They speak visions from their own minds,
　not from the mouth of the LORD.
¹⁷They keep saying to those who despise me,
　'The LORD says: You will have peace.'
And to all who follow the stubbornness of their hearts
　they say, 'No harm will come to you.'
¹⁸But which of them has stood in the council of the LORD
　to see or to hear his word?
Who has listened and heard his word?
¹⁹See, the storm of the LORD
　will burst out in wrath,
a whirlwind swirling down
　on the heads of the wicked.
²⁰The anger of the LORD will not turn back
　until he fully accomplishes
　the purposes of his heart.
In days to come
　you will understand it clearly.
²¹I did not send these prophets,
　yet they have run with their message;
I did not speak to them,
　yet they have prophesied.
²²But if they had stood in my council,
　they would have proclaimed my words to my people

## Amplified Bible

⁹Concerning the prophets: My heart [says Jeremiah] is broken within me, all my bones shake; I am like a drunken man, a man whom wine has overcome, because of the Lord and because of His holy words [which He has pronounced against unfaithful leaders].

¹⁰For the land is full of adulterers (forsakers of God, Israel's true Husband). Because of the curse [of God upon it] the land mourns, the pastures of the wilderness are dried up. They [both false prophets and people] rush into wickedness; *and* their course is evil, their might is not right.

¹¹For both [false] prophet and priest are ungodly *and* profane; even in My house have I found their wickedness, says the Lord.

¹²Therefore their way will be to them like slippery paths in the dark; they will be driven on and fall into them. For I will bring evil upon them in the year of their punishment, says the Lord.

¹³And I have seen folly in the prophets of Samaria: they prophesied by Baal and caused My people Israel to err *and* go astray.

¹⁴I have seen also in the prophets of Jerusalem a horrible thing: they commit adultery and walk in lies; they encourage *and* strengthen the hands of evildoers, so that none returns from his wickedness. They have all of them become to Me like Sodom, and her inhabitants like Gomorrah.

¹⁵Therefore thus says the Lord of hosts concerning the prophets: Behold, I will feed them with [the bitterness of] wormwood and make them drink the [poisonous] water of gall, for from the [false] prophets of Jerusalem profaneness *and* ungodliness have gone forth into all the land.

¹⁶Thus says the Lord of hosts: Do not listen to the words of the [false] prophets who prophesy to you. They teach you vanity (emptiness, falsity, and futility) *and* fill you with vain hopes; they speak a vision of their own minds and not from the mouth of the Lord.

¹⁷They are continually saying to those who despise Me *and* the word of the Lord, The Lord has said: You shall have peace; and they say to everyone who walks after the stubbornness of his own mind *and* heart, No evil shall come upon you.

¹⁸For who among them has stood in the council of the Lord, that he should perceive and hear His word? Who has marked His word [noticing and observing and giving attention to it] and has [actually] heard it?

¹⁹Behold, the tempest of the Lord has gone forth in wrath, a whirling tempest; it shall whirl *and* burst upon the heads of the wicked.

²⁰The anger of the Lord shall not turn back until He has executed *and* accomplished the thoughts *and* intents of His mind *and* heart. In the latter days you shall consider *and* understand it perfectly.

²¹I did not send these [false] prophets, yet they ran; I did not speak to them, yet they prophesied.

²²But if they had stood in My council, then they would have caused My people to hear My words, then they would

---

*a* 10 Or *because of these things*

## New International Version

and would have turned them from their evil ways
and from their evil deeds.
23 "Am I only a God nearby,"

declares the LORD,
"and not a God far away?
24 Who can hide in secret places
so that I cannot see them?"

declares the LORD.
"Do not I fill heaven and earth?"

declares the LORD.

25 "I have heard what the prophets say who prophesy
lies in my name. They say, 'I had a dream! I had a dream!'
26 How long will this continue in the hearts of these lying
prophets, who prophesy the delusions of their own minds?
27 They think the dreams they tell one another will make
my people forget my name, just as their ancestors forgot
my name through Baal worship. 28 Let the prophet who
has a dream recount the dream, but let the one who has
my word speak it faithfully. For what has straw to do with
grain?" declares the LORD. 29 "Is not my word like fire,"
declares the LORD, "and like a hammer that breaks a rock
in pieces?
30 "Therefore," declares the LORD, "I am against the
prophets who steal from one another words supposedly from me. 31 Yes," declares the LORD, "I am against the
prophets who wag their own tongues and yet declare, 'The
LORD declares.' 32 Indeed, I am against those who prophesy false dreams," declares the LORD. "They tell them and
lead my people astray with their reckless lies, yet I did not
send or appoint them. They do not benefit these people in
the least," declares the LORD.

### False Prophecy

33 "When these people, or a prophet or a priest, ask
you, 'What is the message from the LORD?' say to them,
'What message? I will forsake you, declares the LORD.'
34 If a prophet or a priest or anyone else claims, 'This is
a message from the LORD,' I will punish them and their
household. 35 This is what each of you keeps saying to
your friends and other Israelites: 'What is the LORD's answer?' or 'What has the LORD spoken?' 36 But you must not
mention 'a message from the LORD' again, because each
one's word becomes their own message. So you distort
the words of the living God, the LORD Almighty, our God.
37 This is what you keep saying to a prophet: 'What is the
LORD's answer to you?' or 'What has the LORD spoken?'
38 Although you claim, 'This is a message from the LORD,'
this is what the LORD says: You used the words, 'This is
a message from the LORD,' even though I told you that
you must not claim, 'This is a message from the LORD.'
39 Therefore, I will surely forget you and cast you out of my
presence along with the city I gave to you and your ancestors. 40 I will bring on you everlasting disgrace—everlasting shame that will not be forgotten."

## Amplified Bible

have turned them [My people] from their evil way and
from the evil of their doings.
23 Am I a God at hand, says the Lord, and not a God afar
off?
24 Can anyone hide himself in secret places so that I cannot see him? says the Lord. Do not I fill heaven and earth?
says the Lord.
25 I have heard what the prophets have said who prophesy lies in My name, saying, I have dreamed, I have
dreamed [visions on my bed at night].
26 [How long shall this state of things continue?] How
long yet shall it be in the minds of the prophets who prophesy falsehood, even the prophets of the deceit of their own
hearts,
27 Who think that they can cause My people to forget My
name by their dreams which every man tells to his neighbor, just as their fathers forgot My name because of Baal?
28 The prophet who has a dream, let him tell his dream;
but he who has My word, let him speak My word faithfully.
What has straw in common with wheat [for nourishment]?
says the Lord.
29 Is not My word like fire [that consumes all that cannot
endure the test]? says the Lord, and like a hammer that
breaks in pieces the rock [of most stubborn resistance]?
30 Therefore behold, I am against the [false] prophets,
says the Lord, [I am even now descending upon them with
punishment, these prophets] who steal My words from
one another [imitating the phrases of the true prophets].
31 Behold, I am against the prophets, says the Lord, who
use their [own deceitful] tongues and say, Thus says the
Lord.
32 Behold, I am against those who prophesy lying
dreams, says the Lord, and tell them and cause My people
to err and go astray by their lies and by their vain boasting
and recklessness—when I did not send them or command
them; nor do they profit these people at all, says the Lord.
33 And when these people, or a prophet or a priest, ask
you, What is the burden of the Lord [the thing to be lifted
up now]? then you shall say to them, What burden [indeed]! [You are the burden!] And I will disburden Myself
of you and I will cast you off, says the Lord.
34 And as for the prophet, the priest, or [any of these] the
people, whoever [in mockery calls the word of the Lord a
burden and] says, The burden of the Lord, I will even visit
in wrath and punish that man and his house.
35 [For the future, in speaking of the utterances of the
Lord] thus shall you say every one to his neighbor and
every one to his brother: What has the Lord answered? or,
What has the Lord spoken?
36 But the burden of the Lord you must mention no more,
for every man's burden is his own response and word [for
as they mockingly call all prophecies burdens, whether
good or bad, so will it prove to be to them; God will take
them at their own word]; for you pervert the words [not
of a lifeless idol, but] of the living God, the Lord of hosts,
our God!
37 Thus shall you [reverently] say to the prophet: What
has the Lord answered you? Or, What has the Lord spoken?
38 But if you say, The burden of the Lord, therefore thus
says the Lord: Because you said these words, The burden
of the Lord, when I sent to you, saying, You shall not say,
The burden of the Lord,
39 Therefore behold, I, even I, will assuredly take you up
and cast you away from My presence, you and the city [Jerusalem] which I gave to you and to your fathers.
40 And I will bring an everlasting reproach upon you and
a perpetual shame which will not be forgotten.

## New International Version

### Two Baskets of Figs

**24** After Jehoiachin[a] son of Jehoiakim king of Judah and the officials, the skilled workers and the artisans of Judah were carried into exile from Jerusalem to Babylon by Nebuchadnezzar king of Babylon, the LORD showed me two baskets of figs placed in front of the temple of the LORD. ²One basket had very good figs, like those that ripen early; the other basket had very bad figs, so bad they could not be eaten.

³Then the LORD asked me, "What do you see, Jeremiah?"

"Figs," I answered. "The good ones are very good, but the bad ones are so bad they cannot be eaten."

⁴Then the word of the LORD came to me: ⁵"This is what the LORD, the God of Israel, says: 'Like these good figs, I regard as good the exiles from Judah, whom I sent away from this place to the land of the Babylonians.[b] ⁶My eyes will watch over them for their good, and I will bring them back to this land. I will build them up and not tear them down; I will plant them and not uproot them. ⁷I will give them a heart to know me, that I am the LORD. They will be my people, and I will be their God, for they will return to me with all their heart.

⁸"'But like the bad figs, which are so bad they cannot be eaten,' says the LORD, 'so will I deal with Zedekiah king of Judah, his officials and the survivors from Jerusalem, whether they remain in this land or live in Egypt. ⁹I will make them abhorrent and an offense to all the kingdoms of the earth, a reproach and a byword, a curse[c] and an object of ridicule, wherever I banish them. ¹⁰I will send the sword, famine and plague against them until they are destroyed from the land I gave to them and their ancestors.'"

### Seventy Years of Captivity

**25** The word came to Jeremiah concerning all the people of Judah in the fourth year of Jehoiakim son of Josiah king of Judah, which was the first year of Nebuchadnezzar king of Babylon. ²So Jeremiah the prophet said to all the people of Judah and to all those living in Jerusalem: ³For twenty-three years—from the thirteenth year of Josiah son of Amon king of Judah until this very day—the word of the LORD has come to me and I have spoken to you again and again, but you have not listened.

⁴And though the LORD has sent all his servants the prophets to you again and again, you have not listened or paid any attention. ⁵They said, "Turn now, each of you, from your evil ways and your evil practices, and you can stay in the land the LORD gave to you and your ancestors for ever and ever. ⁶Do not follow other gods to serve and worship them; do not arouse my anger with what your hands have made. Then I will not harm you."

⁷"But you did not listen to me," declares the LORD, "and you have aroused my anger with what your hands have made, and you have brought harm to yourselves."

⁸Therefore the LORD Almighty says this: "Because you have not listened to my words, ⁹I will summon all the peoples of the north and my servant Nebuchadnezzar king of Babylon," declares the LORD, "and I will bring them against this land and its inhabitants and against all the surrounding nations. I will completely destroy[d] them and

---

*a 1* Hebrew *Jeconiah,* a variant of *Jehoiachin*     *b 5* Or *Chaldeans*
*c 9* That is, their names will be used in cursing (see 29:22); or, others will see that they are cursed.     *d 9* The Hebrew term refers to the irrevocable giving over of things or persons to the LORD, often by totally destroying them.

## Amplified Bible

**24** After Nebuchadrezzar king of Babylon had taken into exile Jeconiah [also called Coniah and Jehoiachin] son of Jehoiakim king of Judah and the princes of Judah, with the craftsmen and smiths from Jerusalem, and had brought them to Babylon, the Lord showed me [in a vision] two baskets of figs set before the temple of the Lord.

²One basket had very good figs, like the figs that are first ripe; but the other basket had very bad figs, so bad that they could not be eaten.

³Then the Lord said to me, What do you see, Jeremiah? And I said, Figs—the good figs very good, and the bad very bad, so bad that they cannot be eaten.

⁴Again the word of the Lord came to me, saying,

⁵Thus says the Lord, the God of Israel: Like these good figs, so will I regard the captives of Judah whom I have sent out of this place into the land of the Chaldeans for their good.

⁶For I will set My eyes upon them for good, and I will bring them again to this land; and I will build them up and not pull them down, and I will plant them and not pluck them up.

⁷And I will give them a heart to know (recognize, understand, and be acquainted with) Me, that I am the Lord; and they will be My people, and I will be their God, for they will return to Me with their whole heart.

⁸And as for the bad figs, which are so bad that they cannot be eaten, surely thus says the Lord, So will I give up Zedekiah king of Judah and his princes and the residue of Jerusalem who remains in this land and those who dwell in the land of Egypt.

⁹I will even give them up to be a dismay *and* a horror *and* to be tossed to and fro among all the kingdoms of the earth for evil, to be a reproach, a byword *or* proverb, a taunt, and a curse in all places where I will drive them.

¹⁰And I will send the sword, famine, and pestilence among them until they are consumed from off the land that I gave to them and to their fathers.

**25** The word that came to Jeremiah concerning all the people of Judah in the fourth year of the reign of Jehoiakim son of Josiah king of Judah—which was the first year of the reign of Nebuchadrezzar king of Babylon—

²Which Jeremiah the prophet spoke to all the people of Judah and to all the inhabitants of Jerusalem:

³For these twenty-three years—from the thirteenth year of Josiah son of Amon king of Judah, even to this day—the word of the Lord has come to me and I have spoken to you persistently early and late, but you have not listened *and* obeyed.

⁴Although the Lord persistently sent you all the prophets, His servants, yet you have not listened and obeyed or [even] inclined your ear to hear.

⁵[The prophets came on My behalf] saying, Turn again now every one from his evil way and wrongdoing; [that you may not forfeit the right to] dwell in the land that the Lord gave to you and to your fathers from of old *and* forevermore.

⁶Do not go after other gods to serve and worship them, and do not provoke Me to anger with the works of your hands. Then I will do you no harm.

⁷Yet you have not listened to *and* obeyed Me, says the Lord, that you might provoke Me to anger with the works (idols) made by your hands to your own hurt.

⁸Therefore thus says the Lord of hosts: Because you have not heard *and* obeyed My words,

⁹Behold, I will send for all the tribes of the north, says the Lord, and I will send for Nebuchadrezzar king of Babylon, My servant [or agent to fulfill My designs], and I will bring them against this land and its inhabitants and against all these nations round about; and I will devote

## New International Version

make them an object of horror and scorn, and an everlasting ruin. [10]I will banish from them the sounds of joy and gladness, the voices of bride and bridegroom, the sound of millstones and the light of the lamp. [11]This whole country will become a desolate wasteland, and these nations will serve the king of Babylon seventy years.

[12]"But when the seventy years are fulfilled, I will punish the king of Babylon and his nation, the land of the Babylonians,[a] for their guilt," declares the LORD, "and will make it desolate forever. [13]I will bring on that land all the things I have spoken against it, all that are written in this book and prophesied by Jeremiah against all the nations. [14]They themselves will be enslaved by many nations and great kings; I will repay them according to their deeds and the work of their hands."

### The Cup of God's Wrath

[15]This is what the LORD, the God of Israel, said to me: "Take from my hand this cup filled with the wine of my wrath and make all the nations to whom I send you drink it. [16]When they drink it, they will stagger and go mad because of the sword I will send among them."

[17]So I took the cup from the LORD's hand and made all the nations to whom he sent me drink it: [18]Jerusalem and the towns of Judah, its kings and officials, to make them a ruin and an object of horror and scorn, a curse[b]—as they are today; [19]Pharaoh king of Egypt, his attendants, his officials and all his people, [20]and all the foreign people there; all the kings of Uz; all the kings of the Philistines (those of Ashkelon, Gaza, Ekron, and the people left at Ashdod); [21]Edom, Moab and Ammon; [22]all the kings of Tyre and Sidon; the kings of the coastlands across the sea; [23]Dedan, Tema, Buz and all who are in distant places[c]; [24]all the kings of Arabia and all the kings of the foreign people who live in the wilderness; [25]all the kings of Zimri, Elam and Media; [26]and all the kings of the north, near and far, one after the other—all the kingdoms on the face of the earth. And after all of them, the king of Sheshak[d] will drink it too.

[27]"Then tell them, 'This is what the LORD Almighty, the God of Israel, says: Drink, get drunk and vomit, and fall to rise no more because of the sword I will send among you.' [28]But if they refuse to take the cup from your hand and

[a] 12 Or *Chaldeans*   [b] 18 That is, their names to be used in cursing (see 29:22); or, to be seen by others as cursed   [c] 23 Or *who clip the hair by their foreheads*   [d] 26 *Sheshak* is a cryptogram for Babylon.

## Amplified Bible

them [to God] *and* utterly destroy them and make them an amazement, a hissing, and perpetual *and* agelong desolations.

[10]Moreover, I will take from them the voice of mirth and the voice of gladness, the voice of the bridegroom and the voice of the bride, the sound of the millstones [grinding out the meal] and the light of the candle [which every home burned throughout the night]. [Jer. 7:34.]

[11]And this whole land shall be a waste and an astonishment, and these nations shall serve the king of Babylon [a]seventy years. [II Chron. 36:20-23; Jer. 4:27; 12:11, 12; Dan. 9:2.]

[12]Then when seventy years are completed, I will punish the king of Babylon and that nation, the land of the Chaldeans, says the Lord, for their iniquity, and will make the land [of the Chaldeans] a perpetual waste. [Jer. 29:10.]

[13]And I will bring upon that land all My words which I have pronounced against it, even all that is written in this book, which Jeremiah has prophesied against all the nations.

[14]For many nations and great kings shall make bondmen of them, even them [the Chaldeans who enslaved other nations]; and I will recompense [all of] them according to their deeds and according to the work of their [own] hands.

[15]For thus says the Lord, the God of Israel, to me: Take this cup of the wine of wrath from My hand and cause all the nations to whom I send you to drink it.

[16]They shall drink and reel to and fro and be crazed because of the sword that I will send among them.

[17]Then I [Jeremiah] took the cup from the Lord's hand and made all the nations drink it to whom the Lord had sent me: [that is,]

[18]Jerusalem and the cities of Judah [being most guilty because their privileges were greatest], its kings and princes, to make them a desolation, an astonishment, a hissing, and a curse, as it is to this day; [I Pet. 4:17.]

[19]Pharaoh king of Egypt, his servants, his princes, all his people,

[20]And all the mixed foreign population; all the kings of the land of Uz; and all the kings of the land of the Philistines and [their cities of] Ashkelon, Gaza, Ekron, and the remnant of Ashdod;

[21]Edom, Moab, and the children of Ammon;

[22]All the kings of Tyre, all the kings of Sidon, and the kings of the islands *and* the coastlands across the [Mediterranean] Sea;

[23]Dedan, Tema, Buz [neighboring tribes north of Arabia], and all who clip off the corners of their hair *and* beards; [Lev. 19:27; Jer. 9:26.]

[24]All the kings of Arabia and all the kings of the mixed foreign people who dwell in the desert;

[25]All the kings of Zimri, all the kings of Elam (Persia), and all the kings of Media;

[26]All the kings of the north, far and near, one after another—and all the kingdoms of the world which are on the face of the earth. And after them the king of Sheshach (Babel or Babylon) shall drink.

[27]Then you shall say to them, Thus says the Lord of hosts, the God of Israel: Drink, be drunk, vomit, and fall to rise no more because of the sword which I am sending among you.

[28]And if they refuse to take the cup from your hand to drink, then you shall say to them, Thus says the Lord of hosts: You shall surely drink!

[a] As both sacred and secular history show, this prophecy was approximately literally fulfilled, whether it refers to the duration of the Babylonian Empire (with its heyday from the beginning of Nebuchadnezzar's reign in 605 B.C. till its downfall in 539), or to the length of the Jewish captivity in Babylon (with the first deportation in 605 B.C. and the first return in 538). For the marvelous literal fulfillment of specific details concerning the destruction and perpetual desolation of Babylon, see footnotes on Isa. 13:22 and 14:23.

## New International Version

drink, tell them, 'This is what the LORD Almighty says: You must drink it! ²⁹See, I am beginning to bring disaster on the city that bears my Name, and will you indeed go unpunished? You will not go unpunished, for I am calling down a sword on all who live on the earth, declares the LORD Almighty.'

³⁰"Now prophesy all these words against them and say to them:

"'The LORD will roar from on high;
    he will thunder from his holy dwelling
    and roar mightily against his land.
He will shout like those who tread the grapes,
    shout against all who live on the earth.
³¹The tumult will resound to the ends of the earth,
    for the LORD will bring charges against the nations;
he will bring judgment on all mankind
    and put the wicked to the sword,'"
                                    declares the LORD.

³²This is what the LORD Almighty says:

"Look! Disaster is spreading
    from nation to nation;
a mighty storm is rising
    from the ends of the earth."

³³At that time those slain by the LORD will be everywhere—from one end of the earth to the other. They will not be mourned or gathered up or buried, but will be like dung lying on the ground.

³⁴Weep and wail, you shepherds;
    roll in the dust, you leaders of the flock.
For your time to be slaughtered has come;
    you will fall like the best of the rams.ᵃ
³⁵The shepherds will have nowhere to flee,
    the leaders of the flock no place to escape.
³⁶Hear the cry of the shepherds,
    the wailing of the leaders of the flock,
    for the LORD is destroying their pasture.
³⁷The peaceful meadows will be laid waste
    because of the fierce anger of the LORD.
³⁸Like a lion he will leave his lair,
    and their land will become desolate
because of the swordᵇ of the oppressor
    and because of the LORD's fierce anger.

### Jeremiah Threatened With Death

**26** Early in the reign of Jehoiakim son of Josiah king of Judah, this word came from the LORD: ²"This is what the LORD says: Stand in the courtyard of the LORD's house and speak to all the people of the towns of Judah who come to worship in the house of the LORD. Tell them everything I command you; do not omit a word. ³Perhaps they will listen and each will turn from their evil ways. Then I will relent and not inflict on them the disaster I was planning because of the evil they have done. ⁴Say to them, 'This is what the LORD says: If you do not listen to me and follow my law, which I have set before you, ⁵and if you do not listen to the words of my servants the prophets, whom I have sent to you again and again (though you have not listened), ⁶then I will make this house like Shiloh and this city a curseᶜ among all the nations of the earth.'"

⁷The priests, the prophets and all the people heard Jeremiah speak these words in the house of the LORD. ⁸But

ᵃ 34 Septuagint; Hebrew *fall and be shattered like fine pottery*
ᵇ 38 Some Hebrew manuscripts and Septuagint (see also 46:16 and 50:16); most Hebrew manuscripts *anger*    ᶜ 6 That is, its name will be used in cursing (see 29:22); or, others will see that it is cursed

## Amplified Bible

²⁹For behold, I am beginning to work evil in the city which is called by My Name, and shall you go unpunished? You shall not go unpunished, for I am calling for a sword against all the inhabitants of the earth, says the Lord of hosts. [Jer. 7:10.]

³⁰Therefore prophesy against them all these words and say to them: The Lord shall roar from on high and utter His voice from His holy habitation; He shall roar mightily against His fold *and* pasture. He shall give a shout like those who tread grapes [in the winepress, but His shout will be] against all the inhabitants of the earth.

³¹A noise will come even to the ends of the earth, for the Lord has a controversy and an indictment against the nations; He will enter into judgment with all mankind; as for the wicked, He will give them to the sword, says the Lord.

³²Thus says the Lord of hosts: Behold, evil will go forth from nation to nation, and a great whirling tempest will rise from the uttermost parts of the earth.

³³And those slain by the Lord shall be at that day from one end of the earth even to the other end of the earth. They shall not be lamented or gathered or buried; their [dead bodies] shall be dung upon the ground. [Jer. 8:2; 16:4.]

³⁴Wail, you shepherds, and cry; and roll in ashes, you principal ones of the flock. For the days of your slaughter and of your dispersions have fully come, and you shall fall *and* be dashed into pieces like a choice vessel.

³⁵And the shepherds shall have no way to flee, nor the principal ones of the flock any means of escape.

³⁶A voice! The cry of the shepherds and the wailing of the principal ones of the flock! For the Lord is laying waste *and* destroying their pasture.

³⁷And the peaceable folds are devastated *and* brought to silence because of the fierce anger of the Lord.

³⁸He has left His shelter like the lion; for their land has become a waste *and* an astonishment because of the fierceness of the oppressor and because of [the Lord's] fierce anger.

**26** In the beginning of the reign of Jehoiakim son of Josiah king of Judah came this word from the Lord:

²Thus says the Lord: Stand in the court of the Lord's house [Jeremiah] and speak to all [the people of] the cities of Judah who come to worship in the Lord's house all the words that I command you to speak to them; subtract not a word.

³It may be that they will listen and turn every man from his evil way, that I may relent *and* reverse My decision concerning the evil which I purpose to do to them because of their evil doings.

⁴And you will say to them, Thus says the Lord: If you will not listen to *and* obey Me, to walk in My law, which I have set before you,

⁵And to hear *and* obey the words of My servants the prophets, whom I have sent to you urgently *and* persistently—though you have not listened *and* obeyed—

⁶Then will I make this house [the temple] like Shiloh [the home of the Tent of Meeting, abandoned and later destroyed after the ark was captured by the Philistines], and I will make this city subject to the curses of all nations of the earth [so vile in their sight will it be]. [I Sam. 4; Jer. 7:12.]

⁷And the priests and the [false] prophets and all the people heard Jeremiah speaking these words in the house of the Lord.

## New International Version

as soon as Jeremiah finished telling all the people everything the LORD had commanded him to say, the priests, the prophets and all the people seized him and said, "You must die! ⁹Why do you prophesy in the LORD's name that this house will be like Shiloh and this city will be desolate and deserted?" And all the people crowded around Jeremiah in the house of the LORD.

¹⁰When the officials of Judah heard about these things, they went up from the royal palace to the house of the LORD and took their places at the entrance of the New Gate of the LORD's house. ¹¹Then the priests and the prophets said to the officials and all the people, "This man should be sentenced to death because he has prophesied against this city. You have heard it with your own ears!"

¹²Then Jeremiah said to all the officials and all the people: "The LORD sent me to prophesy against this house and this city all the things you have heard. ¹³Now reform your ways and your actions and obey the LORD your God. Then the LORD will relent and not bring the disaster he has pronounced against you. ¹⁴As for me, I am in your hands; do with me whatever you think is good and right. ¹⁵Be assured, however, that if you put me to death, you will bring the guilt of innocent blood on yourselves and on this city and on those who live in it, for in truth the LORD has sent me to you to speak all these words in your hearing."

¹⁶Then the officials and all the people said to the priests and the prophets, "This man should not be sentenced to death! He has spoken to us in the name of the LORD our God."

¹⁷Some of the elders of the land stepped forward and said to the entire assembly of people, ¹⁸"Micah of Moresheth prophesied in the days of Hezekiah king of Judah. He told all the people of Judah, 'This is what the LORD Almighty says:

"'Zion will be plowed like a field,
    Jerusalem will become a heap of rubble,
    the temple hill a mound overgrown with thickets.'ᵃ

¹⁹"Did Hezekiah king of Judah or anyone else in Judah put him to death? Did not Hezekiah fear the LORD and seek his favor? And did not the LORD relent, so that he did not bring the disaster he pronounced against them? We are about to bring a terrible disaster on ourselves!"

²⁰(Now Uriah son of Shemaiah from Kiriath Jearim was another man who prophesied in the name of the LORD; he prophesied the same things against this city and this land as Jeremiah did. ²¹When King Jehoiakim and all his officers and officials heard his words, the king was determined to put him to death. But Uriah heard of it and fled in fear to Egypt. ²²King Jehoiakim, however, sent Elnathan son of Akbor to Egypt, along with some other men. ²³They brought Uriah out of Egypt and took him to King Jehoia-

ᵃ 18 Micah 3:12

## Amplified Bible

⁸Now when Jeremiah had finished speaking all that the Lord had commanded him to speak to all the people, the priests and the [false] prophets and all the people seized him, saying, You shall surely die!

⁹Why have you prophesied in the name of the Lord, saying, This house shall be like Shiloh [after the ark of the Lord had been taken by our enemies] and this city [Jerusalem] shall be desolate, without inhabitant? And all the people were gathered around Jeremiah in the [outer area of the] house of the Lord.

¹⁰When the princes of Judah heard these things, they came up from the king's house to the house of the Lord and sat down in the entry of the New Gate of the house of the Lord.

¹¹Then the priests and the prophets said to the princes and to all the people, This man is deserving of death, for he has prophesied against this city, as you have heard with your own ears.

¹²Then Jeremiah said to all the princes and to all the people: The Lord sent me to prophesy against this house and against this city all the words that you have heard.

¹³Therefore now amend your ways and your doings and obey the voice of the Lord your God; then the Lord will relent *and* reverse the decision concerning the evil which He has pronounced against you.

¹⁴As for me, behold, I am in your hands; do with me as seems good and suitable to you.

¹⁵But know for certain that if you put me to death, you will bring innocent blood upon yourselves and upon this city and upon its inhabitants, for in truth the Lord has sent me to you to speak all these words in your hearing.

¹⁶Then said the princes and all the people to the priests and to the prophets: This man is not deserving of death, for he has spoken to us in the name of the Lord our God.

¹⁷Then certain of the elders of the land arose and said to all the assembly of the people,

¹⁸Micah of Moresheth prophesied in the days of Hezekiah king of Judah and said to all the people of Judah, Thus says the Lord of hosts: Zion shall be ᵃplowed like a field, and Jerusalem shall become heaps [of ruins], and the mountain of the house [of the Lord—Mount Moriah, on which stands the temple, shall become covered not with buildings, but] like a densely wooded height. [Mic. 3:12.]

¹⁹Did Hezekiah king of Judah and all Judah put [Micah] to death? Did he not [reverently] fear the Lord and entreat the Lord? And did not the Lord relent *and* reverse the decision concerning the evil which He had pronounced against them? But [here] we are thinking of committing what will be a great evil against ourselves.

²⁰And there was also a man who prophesied in the name of the Lord, Uriah son of Shemaiah of Kiriath-jearim, who prophesied against this city and against this land in words similar to those of Jeremiah.

²¹And when Jehoiakim the king, with all his mighty men and all the princes, heard his words, the king sought to put [Uriah] to death; but when Uriah heard of it, he was afraid and fled and escaped to Egypt.

²²And Jehoiakim the king sent men into Egypt, namely, Elnathan son of Achbor and certain other men [who went] with him into Egypt.

²³And they fetched Uriah from Egypt and brought him to Jehoiakim the king, who slew him [God's spokesman]

ᵃ This prophecy of Micah, made in the days of King Hezekiah, that Mount Zion would become a plowed field, was literally fulfilled. When Nebuchadnezzar and the Chaldeans took Jerusalem, they broke down the walls (II Kings 25:10). That was in 586 B.C. In A.D. 1542 the present walls of Jerusalem were built by Suleiman the Magnificent, the greatest of the sultans of the Turks. By some strange error, the part of the city known as Mount Zion was omitted from the enclosure and remained outside the walls; for centuries it was literally "plowed like a field." That Mount Zion is the only part of Jerusalem ever known to be plowed is conclusive evidence of the divine inspiration and infinite foreknowledge of the word of the Lord which came to His prophet Micah. See also footnote on Mic. 3:12.

## New International Version

kim, who had him struck down with a sword and his body thrown into the burial place of the common people.)

<sup>24</sup>Furthermore, Ahikam son of Shaphan supported Jeremiah, and so he was not handed over to the people to be put to death.

### Judah to Serve Nebuchadnezzar

**27** Early in the reign of Zedekiah<sup>a</sup> son of Josiah king of Judah, this word came to Jeremiah from the Lord: <sup>2</sup>This is what the LORD said to me: "Make a yoke out of straps and crossbars and put it on your neck. <sup>3</sup>Then send word to the kings of Edom, Moab, Ammon, Tyre and Sidon through the envoys who have come to Jerusalem to Zedekiah king of Judah. <sup>4</sup>Give them a message for their masters and say, 'This is what the LORD Almighty, the God of Israel, says: "Tell this to your masters: <sup>5</sup>With my great power and outstretched arm I made the earth and its people and the animals that are on it, and I give it to anyone I please. <sup>6</sup>Now I will give all your countries into the hands of my servant Nebuchadnezzar king of Babylon; I will make even the wild animals subject to him. <sup>7</sup>All nations will serve him and his son and his grandson until the time for his land comes; then many nations and great kings will subjugate him.

<sup>8</sup>"'If, however, any nation or kingdom will not serve Nebuchadnezzar king of Babylon or bow its neck under his yoke, I will punish that nation with the sword, famine and plague, declares the LORD, until I destroy it by his hand. <sup>9</sup>So do not listen to your prophets, your diviners, your interpreters of dreams, your mediums or your sorcerers who tell you, 'You will not serve the king of Babylon.' <sup>10</sup>They prophesy lies to you that will only serve to remove you far from your lands; I will banish you and you will perish. <sup>11</sup>But if any nation will bow its neck under the yoke of the king of Babylon and serve him, I will let that nation remain in its own land to till it and to live there, declares the LORD."'"

<sup>12</sup>I gave the same message to Zedekiah king of Judah. I said, "Bow your neck under the yoke of the king of Babylon; serve him and his people, and you will live. <sup>13</sup>Why will you and your people die by the sword, famine and plague with which the LORD has threatened any nation that will not serve the king of Babylon? <sup>14</sup>Do not listen to the words of the prophets who say to you, 'You will not serve the king of Babylon,' for they are prophesying lies to you. <sup>15</sup>'I have not sent them,' declares the LORD. 'They are prophesying lies in my name. Therefore, I will banish you and you will perish, both you and the prophets who prophesy to you.'"

<sup>16</sup>Then I said to the priests and all these people, "This is what the LORD says: Do not listen to the prophets who say, 'Very soon now the articles from the LORD's house will be brought back from Babylon.' They are prophesying lies to you. <sup>17</sup>Do not listen to them. Serve the king of Babylon, and you will live. Why should this city become

---

<sup>a</sup> 1 A few Hebrew manuscripts and Syriac (see also 27:3,12 and 28:1); most Hebrew manuscripts *Jehoiakim* (Most Septuagint manuscripts do not have this verse.)

## Amplified Bible

with the sword and cast his dead body among the graves of the common people.

<sup>24</sup>But the hand of Ahikam son of Shaphan was with Jeremiah, that he might not be given into the hands of the people to put him [also] to death.

**27** In the beginning of the reign of Zedekiah son of Josiah king of Judah, this word came to Jeremiah from the Lord:

<sup>2</sup>Thus says the Lord to me: Make for yourself thongs and yoke bars and put them on your neck,

<sup>3</sup>And send them to the king of Edom, to the king of Moab, to the king of the Ammonites, to the king of Tyre, and to the king of Sidon by the hand of the messengers who have come to Jerusalem to Zedekiah king of Judah.

<sup>4</sup>And command them to say to their masters, Thus says the Lord of hosts, the God of Israel: Thus shall you say to your masters:

<sup>5</sup>I have made the earth, the men, and the beasts that are upon the face of the earth by My great power and by My outstretched arm, and I give it to whomever it seems right *and* suitable to Me.

<sup>6</sup>And now I have given all these lands into the hand of Nebuchadnezzar king of Babylon, My servant *and* instrument, and the beasts of the field also I have given him to serve him.

<sup>7</sup>And all nations shall serve him and his son and his grandson until the [God-appointed] time [of punishment] of his own land comes; and then many nations and great kings shall make him their slave.

<sup>8</sup>But any nation or kingdom that will not serve this same Nebuchadnezzar king of Babylon and put its neck under the yoke of the king of Babylon, that nation will I punish, says the Lord, with the sword, with famine, and with pestilence, until I have consumed it by [Nebuchadnezzar's] hand.

<sup>9</sup>So do not listen to your [false] prophets, your diviners, your dreamers [and your dreams, whether your own or others'], your soothsayers, your sorcerers, who say to you, You shall not serve the king of Babylon.

<sup>10</sup>For they prophesy a lie to you which will cause you to be removed far from your land; and I will drive you out, and you will perish.

<sup>11</sup>But any nation that brings its neck under the yoke of the king of Babylon and serves him, that nation will I let remain on its own land, says the Lord, to cultivate it and dwell in it.

<sup>12</sup>I spoke also to Zedekiah king of Judah in the same way: Bring your necks under the yoke of the king of Babylon, and serve him and his people, and live.

<sup>13</sup>Why will you and your people die by the sword, by the famine, and by the pestilence, as the Lord has spoken concerning any nation that will not serve the king of Babylon?

<sup>14</sup>Do not listen to *and* believe the words of the [false] prophets who are saying to you, You shall not serve the king of Babylon, for it is a lie that they prophesy to you.

<sup>15</sup>For I have not sent them, says the Lord; but they are prophesying falsely in My name. [It will only end when] I will drive you out and to perish together with the [false] prophets who prophesy to you.

<sup>16</sup>Also I said to the priests and to all these people, Thus says the Lord: Do not listen to the words of your [false] prophets who are prophesying to you, saying, Behold, the vessels of the Lord's house shall now shortly be brought <sup>a</sup>back from Babylon; for they are prophesying a lie to you.

<sup>17</sup>Do not listen to them *or* heed them; serve the king of Babylon, and live. Why should this city be laid waste?

---

<sup>a</sup> Nebuchadnezzar besieged Jerusalem three times. The second time was during the reign of Jeconiah (Jehoiachin or Coniah), whom he took captive with all the nobles of Judah and Jerusalem (Jer. 27:20), at which time he carried away some of the sacred vessels of the temple. The third siege was now imminent.

## New International Version

a ruin? [18]If they are prophets and have the word of the LORD, let them plead with the LORD Almighty that the articles remaining in the house of the LORD and in the palace of the king of Judah and in Jerusalem not be taken to Babylon. [19]For this is what the LORD Almighty says about the pillars, the bronze Sea, the movable stands and the other articles that are left in this city, [20]which Nebuchadnezzar king of Babylon did not take away when he carried Jehoiachin[a] son of Jehoiakim king of Judah into exile from Jerusalem to Babylon, along with all the nobles of Judah and Jerusalem— [21]yes, this is what the LORD Almighty, the God of Israel, says about the things that are left in the house of the LORD and in the palace of the king of Judah and in Jerusalem: [22]'They will be taken to Babylon and there they will remain until the day I come for them,' declares the LORD. 'Then I will bring them back and restore them to this place.'"

### The False Prophet Hananiah

**28** In the fifth month of that same year, the fourth year, early in the reign of Zedekiah king of Judah, the prophet Hananiah son of Azzur, who was from Gibeon, said to me in the house of the LORD in the presence of the priests and all the people: [2]"This is what the LORD Almighty, the God of Israel, says: 'I will break the yoke of the king of Babylon. [3]Within two years I will bring back to this place all the articles of the LORD's house that Nebuchadnezzar king of Babylon removed from here and took to Babylon. [4]I will also bring back to this place Jehoiachin[a] son of Jehoiakim king of Judah and all the other exiles from Judah who went to Babylon,' declares the LORD, 'for I will break the yoke of the king of Babylon.'"

[5]Then the prophet Jeremiah replied to the prophet Hananiah before the priests and all the people who were standing in the house of the LORD. [6]He said, "Amen! May the LORD do so! May the LORD fulfill the words you have prophesied by bringing the articles of the LORD's house and all the exiles back to this place from Babylon. [7]Nevertheless, listen to what I have to say in your hearing and in the hearing of all the people: [8]From early times the prophets who preceded you and me have prophesied war, disaster and plague against many countries and great kingdoms. [9]But the prophet who prophesies peace will be recognized as one truly sent by the LORD only if his prediction comes true."

[10]Then the prophet Hananiah took the yoke off the neck of the prophet Jeremiah and broke it, [11]and he said before all the people, "This is what the LORD says: 'In the same way I will break the yoke of Nebuchadnezzar king of Babylon off the neck of all the nations within two years.'" At this, the prophet Jeremiah went on his way.

## Amplified Bible

[18]But if they are true prophets and if the word of the Lord is really spoken by them, let them now make intercession to the Lord of hosts, that the vessels which are [still] left in the house of the Lord, in the house of the king of Judah, and in Jerusalem may not go to Babylon.

[19]For thus says the Lord of hosts concerning the [bronze] pillars [each twenty-seven feet high], the [bronze] Sea [the laver at which the priests cleansed their hands and feet before ministering at the altar], the [bronze] bases [of the ten lavers in Solomon's temple used for washing animals to be offered as sacrifices], and the remainder of the vessels which are left in this city [Jerusalem], [I Kings 7:23-37; II Chron. 4:6; Jer. 52:17.]

[20]Which Nebuchadnezzar king of Babylon did not take when he carried into exile from Jerusalem to Babylon Jeconiah [also called Coniah and Jehoiachin] son of Jehoiakim king of Judah, with all the nobles of Judah and Jerusalem—

[21]Yes, thus says the Lord of hosts, the God of Israel, concerning the vessels which [still] remain in the house of the Lord, in the house of the king of Judah, and in Jerusalem:

[22]They will be [a]carried to Babylon and there will they be until the day that I visit them [with My favor], says the Lord. Then I will bring them back and restore them to this place.

**28** In that same year, in the beginning of the reign of Zedekiah king of Judah, in the fourth year and the fifth month, Hananiah son of Azzur, the [false] prophet, who was from Gibeon [one of the priests' cities], said [falsely] to me in the house of the Lord in the presence of the priests and all the people:

[2]Thus says the Lord of hosts, the God of Israel: I have broken the yoke of the king of Babylon.

[3]Within two [full] years will I bring back into this place all the vessels of the Lord's house that Nebuchadnezzar king of Babylon took away from this place and carried to Babylon.

[4]And I will also bring back to this place Jeconiah [also called Coniah and Jehoiachin] son of Jehoiakim king of Judah, with all the exiles from Judah who went to Babylon, says the Lord, for I will break the yoke of the king of Babylon. [Jer. 22:10, 24-27; 52:34]

[5]Then the prophet Jeremiah spoke to the prophet Hananiah in the presence of the priests and all the people who stood in the house of the Lord.

[6]The prophet Jeremiah said, Amen! May the Lord do so; may the Lord perform your words which you have prophesied to bring back to this place from Babylon the vessels of the Lord's house and all who were carried away captive.

[7]Nevertheless, listen now to *and* hear this word which I speak in your hearing and in the hearing of all the people:

[8]The prophets who were before me and before you from of old prophesied against many countries and against great kingdoms, of war, of evil, and of pestilence.

[9]But as for the prophet who [on the contrary] prophesies of peace, when that prophet's word comes to pass, [only] then will it be known that the Lord has truly sent him.

[10]Then Hananiah the prophet took the yoke bar off the prophet Jeremiah's neck and smashed it.

[11]And Hananiah said in the presence of all the people, Thus says the Lord: Even so will I break the yoke bars of Nebuchadnezzar king of Babylon from the neck of all the nations within the space of two [full] years. But the prophet Jeremiah went his way.

---

[a] This prophesy was literally fulfilled. The remaining sacred vessels were carried to Babylon (II Kings 25:13; II Chron. 36:18; Jer. 52:17-23), where they were kept for seventy years (II Chron. 36:21), the length of the captivity as Jeremiah had foretold it (Jer. 29:10), and then brought back to Jerusalem (Ezra 1:7; 7:19).

---

[a] 20,4 Hebrew *Jeconiah,* a variant of *Jehoiachin*

## New International Version

12After the prophet Hananiah had broken the yoke off the neck of the prophet Jeremiah, the word of the LORD came to Jeremiah: 13"Go and tell Hananiah, 'This is what the LORD says: You have broken a wooden yoke, but in its place you will get a yoke of iron. 14This is what the LORD Almighty, the God of Israel, says: I will put an iron yoke on the necks of all these nations to make them serve Nebuchadnezzar king of Babylon, and they will serve him. I will even give him control over the wild animals.'"

15Then the prophet Jeremiah said to Hananiah the prophet, "Listen, Hananiah! The LORD has not sent you, yet you have persuaded this nation to trust in lies. 16Therefore this is what the LORD says: 'I am about to remove you from the face of the earth. This very year you are going to die, because you have preached rebellion against the LORD.'"

17In the seventh month of that same year, Hananiah the prophet died.

### A Letter to the Exiles

**29** This is the text of the letter that the prophet Jeremiah sent from Jerusalem to the surviving elders among the exiles and to the priests, the prophets and all the other people Nebuchadnezzar had carried into exile from Jerusalem to Babylon. 2(This was after King Jehoiachin*a* and the queen mother, the court officials and the leaders of Judah and Jerusalem, the skilled workers and the artisans had gone into exile from Jerusalem.) 3He entrusted the letter to Elasah son of Shaphan and to Gemariah son of Hilkiah, whom Zedekiah king of Judah sent to King Nebuchadnezzar in Babylon. It said:

4This is what the LORD Almighty, the God of Israel, says to all those I carried into exile from Jerusalem to Babylon: 5"Build houses and settle down; plant gardens and eat what they produce. 6Marry and have sons and daughters; find wives for your sons and give your daughters in marriage, so that they too may have sons and daughters. Increase in number there; do not decrease. 7Also, seek the peace and prosperity of the city to which I have carried you into exile. Pray to the LORD for it, because if it prospers, you too will prosper." 8Yes, this is what the LORD Almighty, the God of Israel, says: "Do not let the prophets and diviners among you deceive you. Do not listen to the dreams you encourage them to have. 9They are prophesying lies to you in my name. I have not sent them," declares the LORD.

10This is what the LORD says: "When seventy years are completed for Babylon, I will come to you and fulfill my good promise to bring you back to this place. 11For I know the plans I have for you," declares the LORD, "plans to prosper you and not to harm you, plans to give you hope and a future. 12Then you will call on me and come and pray to me, and I will listen to you. 13You will seek me and find me when you seek me with all your heart. 14I will be found by you," declares the LORD, "and will bring you back from captivity.*b* I will gather you from all the nations and places where I have banished you," declares the LORD, "and will bring you back to the place from which I carried you into exile."

## Amplified Bible

12The word of the Lord came to Jeremiah the prophet [some time] after Hananiah the prophet had broken the yoke bar from the neck of the prophet Jeremiah: 13Go, tell Hananiah, Thus says the Lord: You have broken yoke bars of wood, but you have made in their stead bars of iron.

14For thus says the Lord of hosts, the God of Israel: I have put upon the neck of all these nations the iron yoke of servitude to Nebuchadnezzar king of Babylon, and they shall serve him. For I have given him even the beasts of the field. [Jer. 27:6-7.]

15Then said the prophet Jeremiah to Hananiah the prophet, Listen now, Hananiah, The Lord has not sent you, but you have made this people trust in a lie.

16Therefore thus says the Lord: Behold, I will cast you from the face of the earth. This year you will die, because you have uttered *and* taught rebellion against the Lord.

17So Hananiah the prophet died [two months later], the same year, in the seventh month.

**29** Now these are the words of the letter that Jeremiah the prophet sent from Jerusalem to the rest of the elders in exile and to the priests, the prophets, and all the people whom Nebuchadnezzar had carried away captive from Jerusalem to Babylon.

2This was after King Jeconiah [also called Coniah and Jehoiachin] and the queen mother, the eunuchs, the princes of Judah and Jerusalem, the craftsmen and the smiths had departed from Jerusalem.

3[The letter was sent] by the hand of Elasah son of Shaphan and Gemariah son of Hilkiah, whom Zedekiah king of Judah sent to Babylon to Nebuchadnezzar king of Babylon. It said:

4Thus says the Lord of hosts, the God of Israel, to all the captives whom I have caused to be carried into exile from Jerusalem to Babylon:

5Build yourselves houses and dwell in them; plant gardens and eat the fruit of them.

6Take wives and have sons and daughters; take wives for your sons and give your daughters in marriage, that they may bear sons and daughters; multiply there, and do not be diminished.

7And seek (inquire for, require, and request) the peace *and* welfare of the city to which I have caused you to be carried away captive; and pray to the Lord for it, for in the welfare of [the city in which you live] you will have welfare.

8For thus says the Lord of hosts, the God of Israel: Let not your [false] prophets and your diviners who are in your midst deceive you; pay no attention and attach no significance to your dreams which you dream *or* to theirs,

9For they prophesy falsely to you in My name. I have not sent them, says the Lord.

10For thus says the Lord, When seventy years are completed for Babylon, I will visit you and keep My good promise to you, causing you to return to this place.

11For I know the thoughts *and* plans that I have for you, says the Lord, thoughts *and* plans for welfare *and* peace and not for evil, to give you hope in your final outcome.

12Then you will call upon Me, and you will come and pray to Me, and I will hear *and* heed you.

13Then you will seek Me, inquire for, *and* require Me [as a vital necessity] and find Me when you search for Me with all your heart. [Deut. 4:29-30.]

14I will be found by you, says the Lord, and I will release you from captivity and gather you from all the nations and all the places to which I have driven you, says the Lord, and I will bring you back to the place from which I caused you to be carried away captive.

---

*a* 2 Hebrew *Jeconiah*, a variant of *Jehoiachin*  *b* 14 Or *will restore your fortunes*

# New International Version

[15]You may say, "The LORD has raised up prophets for us in Babylon," [16]but this is what the LORD says about the king who sits on David's throne and all the people who remain in this city, your fellow citizens who did not go with you into exile— [17]yes, this is what the LORD Almighty says: "I will send the sword, famine and plague against them and I will make them like figs that are so bad they cannot be eaten. [18]I will pursue them with the sword, famine and plague and will make them abhorrent to all the kingdoms of the earth, a curse[a] and an object of horror, of scorn and reproach, among all the nations where I drive them. [19]For they have not listened to my words," declares the LORD, "words that I sent to them again and again by my servants the prophets. And you exiles have not listened either," declares the LORD.

[20]Therefore, hear the word of the LORD, all you exiles whom I have sent away from Jerusalem to Babylon. [21]This is what the LORD Almighty, the God of Israel, says about Ahab son of Kolaiah and Zedekiah son of Maaseiah, who are prophesying lies to you in my name: "I will deliver them into the hands of Nebuchadnezzar king of Babylon, and he will put them to death before your very eyes. [22]Because of them, all the exiles from Judah who are in Babylon will use this curse: 'May the LORD treat you like Zedekiah and Ahab, whom the king of Babylon burned in the fire.' [23]For they have done outrageous things in Israel; they have committed adultery with their neighbors' wives, and in my name they have uttered lies—which I did not authorize. I know it and am a witness to it," declares the LORD.

## Message to Shemaiah

[24]Tell Shemaiah the Nehelamite, [25]"This is what the LORD Almighty, the God of Israel, says: You sent letters in your own name to all the people in Jerusalem, to the priest Zephaniah son of Maaseiah, and to all the other priests. You said to Zephaniah, [26]'The LORD has appointed you priest in place of Jehoiada to be in charge of the house of the LORD; you should put any maniac who acts like a prophet into the stocks and neck-irons. [27]So why have you not reprimanded Jeremiah from Anathoth, who poses as a prophet among you? [28]He has sent this message to us in Babylon: It will be a long time. Therefore build houses and settle down; plant gardens and eat what they produce.'"

[29]Zephaniah the priest, however, read the letter to Jeremiah the prophet. [30]Then the word of the LORD came to Jeremiah: [31]"Send this message to all the exiles: 'This is what the LORD says about Shemaiah the Nehelamite: Because Shemaiah has prophesied to you, even though I did not send him, and has persuaded you to trust in lies, [32]this is what the LORD says: I will surely punish Shemaiah the Nehelamite and his descendants. He will have no one left among this people, nor will he see the good things I will do for my people, declares the LORD, because he has preached rebellion against me.'"

# Amplified Bible

[15][But as for those still in Jerusalem] because you have said, The Lord has raised up prophets for us in Babylon, [16]Thus says the Lord concerning the king who sits upon the throne of David and concerning all the people who dwell in this city, your brethren who did not go forth with you into captivity— [17]Thus says the Lord of hosts: Behold, I am sending on them the sword, famine, and pestilence, and I will make them like vile figs which are so bad they cannot be eaten. [18]And I will pursue them with the sword, famine, and pestilence and will give them up to be tossed to and fro and to be a horror to all the kingdoms of the earth, to be a curse, an astonishment, and a terror, a hissing and a reproach among all the nations to which I have driven them, [19]Because they have not listened to and heeded My words, says the Lord, which I sent to them persistently by My servants the prophets; but you [exiles] would not listen [either], says the Lord. [Ezek. 2:5, 7.]

[20]Hear therefore the word of the Lord, all you exiles whom I have sent away from Jerusalem to Babylon. [21]Thus says the Lord of hosts, the God of Israel, concerning Ahab son of Kolaiah and concerning Zedekiah son of Maaseiah, who are prophesying lies to you in My name: Behold, I will deliver them into the hand of [a]Nebuchadrezzar king of Babylon, and he will slay them [those false prophets whom you say I have raised up for you in Babylon] before your eyes! [Jer. 29:15.] [22]And because of them, this curse shall be taken up and used by all from Judah who are in captivity in Babylon: The Lord make you like Zedekiah and like Ahab, whom the king of Babylon roasted in the fire— [23]Because they have committed folly in Israel and have committed adultery with their neighbors' wives and have spoken words in My name falsely, which I had not commanded them. I am the One Who knows and I am witness, says the Lord.

[24]Also you shall say this concerning and to Shemaiah of Nehelam [among the exiles in Babylon]: [25]Thus says the Lord of hosts, the God of Israel: Because you have sent letters in your [own] name to all the people who are in Jerusalem and to Zephaniah son of Maaseiah the priest and to all the priests, saying, [26]The Lord has made you [Zephaniah] priest instead of Jehoiada the [deputy] priest, that you should have oversight in the house of the Lord over every madman who makes himself a prophet, that you should put him in the stocks and collar. [27]Now therefore [continued the letter from Shemaiah in Babylon to Zephaniah in Jerusalem], why have you not rebuked Jeremiah of Anathoth, who makes himself a prophet to you? [28]For he has sent to us in Babylon, saying, [This captivity of yours] is to be long; build houses and dwell in them; plant gardens and eat the fruit of them. [29]And Zephaniah the priest read this letter in the hearing of Jeremiah the prophet. [30]Then came the word of the Lord to Jeremiah: [31]Send [this message] to all those in captivity, saying, Thus says the Lord concerning Shemaiah of Nehelam: Because Shemaiah has prophesied to you, though I did not send him, and has caused you to trust in a lie, [32]Therefore thus says the Lord: Behold, I will punish Shemaiah of Nehelam and his offspring. He will not have anyone [born] to dwell among this people, nor will he see the good that I will do to My people, says the Lord, because he has spoken and taught rebellion against the Lord.

---

[a] 18 That is, their names will be used in cursing (see verse 22); or, others will see that they are cursed.

[a] See footnote on Jer. 21:2.

## New International Version

### Restoration of Israel

**30** This is the word that came to Jeremiah from the LORD: ²"This is what the LORD, the God of Israel, says: 'Write in a book all the words I have spoken to you. ³The days are coming,' declares the LORD, 'when I will bring my people Israel and Judah back from captivity*a* and restore them to the land I gave their ancestors to possess,' says the LORD."

⁴These are the words the LORD spoke concerning Israel and Judah: ⁵"This is what the LORD says:

"'Cries of fear are heard—
    terror, not peace.
⁶Ask and see:
    Can a man bear children?
Then why do I see every strong man
    with his hands on his stomach like a woman in
        labor,
    every face turned deathly pale?
⁷How awful that day will be!
    No other will be like it.
It will be a time of trouble for Jacob,
    but he will be saved out of it.

⁸"'In that day,' declares the LORD Almighty,
    'I will break the yoke off their necks
and will tear off their bonds;
    no longer will foreigners enslave them.
⁹Instead, they will serve the LORD their God
    and David their king,
    whom I will raise up for them.

¹⁰"'So do not be afraid, Jacob my servant;
    do not be dismayed, Israel,'
                                    declares the LORD.
'I will surely save you out of a distant place,
    your descendants from the land of their exile.
Jacob will again have peace and security,
    and no one will make him afraid.
¹¹I am with you and will save you,'
    declares the LORD.
'Though I completely destroy all the nations
    among which I scatter you,
    I will not completely destroy you.
I will discipline you but only in due measure;
    I will not let you go entirely unpunished.'

¹²"This is what the LORD says:

"'Your wound is incurable,
    your injury beyond healing.
¹³There is no one to plead your cause,
    no remedy for your sore,
    no healing for you.
¹⁴All your allies have forgotten you;
    they care nothing for you.
I have struck you as an enemy would
    and punished you as would the cruel,
because your guilt is so great
    and your sins so many.
¹⁵Why do you cry out over your wound,
    your pain that has no cure?
Because of your great guilt and many sins
    I have done these things to you.

¹⁶"'But all who devour you will be devoured;
    all your enemies will go into exile.
Those who plunder you will be plundered;
    all who make spoil of you I will despoil.
¹⁷But I will restore you to health
    and heal your wounds,'
                                declares the LORD,
'because you are called an outcast,
    Zion for whom no one cares.'

*a 3 Or will restore the fortunes of my people Israel and Judah*

## Amplified Bible

**30** The word that came to Jeremiah from the Lord: ²Thus says the Lord, the God of Israel: Write all the words that I have spoken to you in a book.

³For, note well, the days are coming, says the Lord, when I will release from captivity My people Israel and Judah, says the Lord, and I will cause them to return to the land that I gave to their fathers, and they will possess it.

⁴And these are the words the Lord spoke concerning Israel and Judah:

⁵Thus says the Lord: We have heard a voice of trembling *and* panic—of terror, and not peace.

⁶Ask now and see whether a man can give birth to a child? Why then do I see every man with his hands on his loins like a woman in labor? Why are all faces turned pale?

⁷Alas! for that day will be great, so that none will be like it; it will be the time of Jacob's [unequaled] trouble, but he will be saved out of it. [Matt. 24:29, 30; Rev. 7:14.]

⁸For it will come to pass in that day, says the Lord of hosts, that I will break [the oppressor's] yoke from your neck, and I will burst your bonds; and strangers will no more make slaves of [the people of Israel].

⁹But they will serve the Lord their God and David's [descendant] their King, Whom I will raise up for them. [Jer. 23:5.]

¹⁰Therefore fear not, O My servant Jacob, says the Lord, nor be dismayed *or* cast down, O Israel; for behold, I will save you out of a distant land [of exile] and your posterity from the land of their captivity. Jacob will return and will be quiet and at ease, and none will make him afraid *or* cause him to be terrorized *and* to tremble.

¹¹For I am with you, says the Lord, to save you; for I will make a full *and* complete end of all the nations to which I have scattered you, but I will not make a full *and* complete end of you. But I will correct you in measure *and* with judgment and will in no sense hold you guiltless *or* leave you unpunished.

¹²For thus says the Lord: Your hurt is incurable and your wound is grievous.

¹³There is none to plead your cause; for [the pressing together of] your wound you have no healing [device], no binding plaster.

¹⁴All your lovers (allies) have forgotten you; they neither seek, inquire of, *or* require you. For I have hurt you with the wound of an enemy, with the chastisement of a cruel *and* merciless foe, because of the greatness of your perversity *and* guilt, because your sins are glaring *and* innumerable.

¹⁵Why do you cry out because of your hurt [the natural result of your sins]? Your pain is deadly (incurable). Because of the greatness of your perversity *and* guilt, because your sins are glaring *and* innumerable, I have done these things to you.

¹⁶Therefore all who devour you will be devoured; and all your adversaries, every one of them, will go into captivity. And they who despoil you will become a spoil, and all who prey upon you will I give for a prey.

¹⁷For I will restore health to you, and I will heal your wounds, says the Lord, because they have called you an outcast, saying, This is Zion, whom no one seeks after *and* for whom no one cares!

## New International Version

18"This is what the LORD says:

"'I will restore the fortunes of Jacob's tents
    and have compassion on his dwellings;
the city will be rebuilt on her ruins,
    and the palace will stand in its proper place.
19 From them will come songs of thanksgiving
    and the sound of rejoicing.
I will add to their numbers,
    and they will not be decreased;
I will bring them honor,
    and they will not be disdained.
20 Their children will be as in days of old,
    and their community will be established before me;
    I will punish all who oppress them.
21 Their leader will be one of their own;
    their ruler will arise from among them.
I will bring him near and he will come close to me—
    for who is he who will devote himself
    to be close to me?'

                                            declares the LORD.

22 "'So you will be my people,
    and I will be your God.'"

23 See, the storm of the LORD
    will burst out in wrath,
a driving wind swirling down
    on the heads of the wicked.
24 The fierce anger of the LORD will not turn back
    until he fully accomplishes
    the purposes of his heart.
In days to come
    you will understand this.

**31** "At that time," declares the LORD, "I will be the God of all the families of Israel, and they will be my people."
2 This is what the LORD says:

"The people who survive the sword
    will find favor in the wilderness;
I will come to give rest to Israel."

3 The LORD appeared to us in the past,[a] saying:

"I have loved you with an everlasting love;
    I have drawn you with unfailing kindness.
4 I will build you up again,
    and you, Virgin Israel, will be rebuilt.
Again you will take up your timbrels
    and go out to dance with the joyful.
5 Again you will plant vineyards
    on the hills of Samaria;
the farmers will plant them
    and enjoy their fruit.
6 There will be a day when watchmen cry out
    on the hills of Ephraim,
'Come, let us go up to Zion,
    to the LORD our God.'"

7 This is what the LORD says:

"Sing with joy for Jacob;
    shout for the foremost of the nations.
Make your praises heard, and say,
    'LORD, save your people,
    the remnant of Israel.'
8 See, I will bring them from the land of the north
    and gather them from the ends of the earth.
Among them will be the blind and the lame,
    expectant mothers and women in labor;
    a great throng will return.

## Amplified Bible

18 Thus says the Lord: Behold, I will release from captivity the tents of Jacob and have mercy on his dwelling places; the city will be rebuilt on its own [old] moundlike site, and the palace will be dwelt in after its former fashion.
19 Out of them [city and palace] will come songs of thanksgiving and the voices of those who make merry. And I will multiply them, and they will not be few; I will also glorify them, and they will not be small.
20 Their children too shall be as in former times, and their congregation shall be established before Me, and I will punish all who oppress them.
21 And their prince will be one of them, and their ruler will come from the midst of them. I will cause him to draw near and he will approach Me, for who is he who would have the boldness *and* would dare [on his own initiative] to approach Me? says the Lord.
22 Then you will be My people, and I will be your God. [Jer. 7:23.]
23 Behold, the tempest of the Lord has gone forth with wrath, a sweeping *and* gathering tempest; it shall whirl *and* burst upon the heads of the wicked.
24 The fierce anger *and* indignation of the Lord shall not turn back until He has executed *and* accomplished the thoughts *and* intents of His mind *and* heart. In the latter days you shall understand this.

**31** At that time, says the Lord, will I be the God of all the families of Israel, and they will be My people.
2 Thus says the Lord: The people who survived the sword found favor in the wilderness [place of exile]—when Israel sought to find rest.
3 The Lord appeared from of old to me [Israel], saying, Yes, I have loved you with an everlasting love; therefore with loving-kindness have I drawn you *and* continued My faithfulness to you. [Deut. 7:8.]
4 Again I will build you and you will be built, O Virgin Israel! You will again be adorned with your timbrels [small one-headed drums] and go forth in the dancing [chorus] of those who make merry. [Isa. 37:22; Jer. 18:13.]
5 Again you shall plant vineyards upon the mountains of Samaria; the planters shall plant and make the fruit common *and* enjoy it [undisturbed].
6 For there shall be a day when the watchmen on the hills of Ephraim shall cry out, Arise, and let us go up to Zion, to the Lord our God.
7 For thus says the Lord: Sing aloud with gladness for Jacob, and shout for the head of the nations [on account of the chosen people, Israel]. Proclaim, praise, and say, The Lord has saved His people, the remnant of Israel!
8 Behold, I will bring them from the north country and gather them from the uttermost parts of the earth, and among them will be the blind and the lame, the woman with child and she who labors in childbirth together; a great company, they will return here to Jerusalem.

*a* 3 Or LORD *has appeared to us from afar*

## New International Version

9 They will come with weeping;
  they will pray as I bring them back.
I will lead them beside streams of water
  on a level path where they will not stumble,
because I am Israel's father,
  and Ephraim is my firstborn son.

10 "Hear the word of the LORD, you nations;
  proclaim it in distant coastlands:
'He who scattered Israel will gather them
  and will watch over his flock like a shepherd.'
11 For the LORD will deliver Jacob
  and redeem them from the hand of those stronger
    than they.
12 They will come and shout for joy on the heights of
    Zion;
  they will rejoice in the bounty of the LORD—
the grain, the new wine and the olive oil,
  the young of the flocks and herds.
They will be like a well-watered garden,
  and they will sorrow no more.
13 Then young women will dance and be glad,
  young men and old as well.
I will turn their mourning into gladness;
  I will give them comfort and joy instead of sorrow.
14 I will satisfy the priests with abundance,
  and my people will be filled with my bounty,"
                                        declares the LORD.

15 This is what the LORD says:

"A voice is heard in Ramah,
  mourning and great weeping,
Rachel weeping for her children
  and refusing to be comforted,
  because they are no more."

16 This is what the LORD says:

"Restrain your voice from weeping
  and your eyes from tears,
for your work will be rewarded,"
                                        declares the LORD.
"They will return from the land of the enemy.
17 So there is hope for your descendants,"
                                        declares the LORD.
"Your children will return to their own land.

18 "I have surely heard Ephraim's moaning:
'You disciplined me like an unruly calf,
  and I have been disciplined.
Restore me, and I will return,
  because you are the LORD my God.
19 After I strayed,
  I repented;
after I came to understand,
  I beat my breast.
I was ashamed and humiliated
  because I bore the disgrace of my youth.'
20 Is not Ephraim my dear son,
  the child in whom I delight?
Though I often speak against him,
  I still remember him.
Therefore my heart yearns for him;
  I have great compassion for him,"
                                        declares the LORD.

21 "Set up road signs;
  put up guideposts.
Take note of the highway,
  the road that you take.
Return, Virgin Israel,
  return to your towns.
22 How long will you wander,
  unfaithful Daughter Israel?

## Amplified Bible

9 They will come with weeping [in penitence and for
joy], pouring out prayers [for the future]. I will lead them
back; I will cause them to walk by streams of water and
bring them in a straight way in which they will not stumble, for I am a Father to Israel, and Ephraim [Israel] is My
firstborn.

10 Hear the word of the Lord, O you nations, and declare
it in the isles and coastlands far away, and say, He Who
scattered Israel will gather him and will keep him as a
shepherd keeps his flock.

11 For the Lord has ransomed Jacob and has redeemed
him from the hand of him who was too strong for him.

12 They shall come and sing aloud on the height of Zion
and shall flow together and be radiant with joy over the
goodness of the Lord—for the corn, for the juice [of the
grape], for the oil, and for the young of the flock and the
herd. And their life shall be like a watered garden, and
they shall not sorrow or languish any more at all.

13 Then will the maidens rejoice in the dance, and the
young men and old together. For I will turn their mourning into joy and will comfort them and make them rejoice
after their sorrow.

14 I will satisfy fully the life of the priests with abundance [of offerings shared with them], and My people will
be satisfied with My goodness, says the Lord.

15 Thus says the Lord: A [a]voice is heard in Ramah, lamentation and bitter weeping. Rachel is weeping for her
children; she refuses to be comforted for her children,
because they are no more. [Matt. 2:18.]

16 Thus says the Lord: Restrain your voice from weeping
and your eyes from tears, for your work shall be rewarded,
says the Lord; and [your children] shall return from the
enemy's land.

17 And there is hope for your future, says the Lord; your
children shall come back to their own country.

18 I have surely heard Ephraim [Israel] moaning thus:
You have chastised me, and I was chastised, like a bullock
unaccustomed to the yoke; bring me back, that I may be
restored, for You are the Lord my God.

19 Surely after I [Ephraim] was turned [from You], I repented; and after I was instructed, I penitently smote my
thigh. I was ashamed, yes, even confounded, because I
bore the disgrace of my youth [as a nation].

20 Is Ephraim My dear son? Is he a darling child and beloved? For as often as I speak against him, I do [earnestly]
remember him still. Therefore My affection is stirred and
My heart yearns for him; I will surely have mercy, pity, and
loving-kindness for him, says the Lord.

21 Set up for yourselves highway markers [back to
Canaan], make for yourselves guideposts; turn your
thoughts and attention to the way by which you went [into
exile]. Retrace your steps, O Virgin Israel, return to these
your cities.

22 How long will you waver and hesitate [to return],
O you backsliding daughter? For the Lord has created a

---

[a] The mourning at Ramah is a forecast of that bitter wailing which
would be raised by the mothers of the slaughtered babes of Bethlehem
centuries later when Herod would attempt to kill the Christ Child (Matt.
2:17, 18). Rachel's name, used in the prophecy, is naturally associated
with Bethlehem by the fact that her tomb was in that neighborhood (The
Cambridge Bible).

## New International Version

The LORD will create a new thing on earth—
the woman will return to*a* the man."

23This is what the LORD Almighty, the God of Israel, says: "When I bring them back from captivity,*b* the people in the land of Judah and in its towns will once again use these words: 'The LORD bless you, you prosperous city, you sacred mountain.' 24People will live together in Judah and all its towns—farmers and those who move about with their flocks. 25I will refresh the weary and satisfy the faint."

26At this I awoke and looked around. My sleep had been pleasant to me.

27"The days are coming," declares the LORD, "when I will plant the kingdoms of Israel and Judah with the offspring of people and of animals. 28Just as I watched over them to uproot and tear down, and to overthrow, destroy and bring disaster, so I will watch over them to build and to plant," declares the LORD. 29"In those days people will no longer say,

'The parents have eaten sour grapes,
and the children's teeth are set on edge.'

30Instead, everyone will die for their own sin; whoever eats sour grapes—their own teeth will be set on edge.

31"The days are coming," declares the LORD,
"when I will make a new covenant
with the people of Israel
and with the people of Judah.
32 It will not be like the covenant
I made with their ancestors
when I took them by the hand
to lead them out of Egypt,
because they broke my covenant,
though I was a husband to*c* them,*d*"
                                        declares the LORD.
33 "This is the covenant I will make with the people of
Israel
after that time," declares the LORD.
"I will put my law in their minds
and write it on their hearts.
I will be their God,
and they will be my people.
34 No longer will they teach their neighbor,
or say to one another, 'Know the LORD,'
because they will all know me,
from the least of them to the greatest,"
                                        declares the LORD.
"For I will forgive their wickedness
and will remember their sins no more."

35This is what the LORD says,

he who appoints the sun
to shine by day,
who decrees the moon and stars
to shine by night,
who stirs up the sea
so that its waves roar—
the LORD Almighty is his name:
36 "Only if these decrees vanish from my sight,"
declares the LORD,
"will Israel ever cease
being a nation before me."

37This is what the LORD says:

"Only if the heavens above can be measured
and the foundations of the earth below be searched
out
will I reject all the descendants of Israel
because of all they have done,"
                                        declares the LORD.

*a 22 Or will protect    b 23 Or I restore their fortunes    c 32 Hebrew;
Septuagint and Syriac / and I turned away from    d 32 Or was their
master*

## Amplified Bible

*a*new thing in the land [of Israel]: a female shall compass (woo, win, and protect) a man.

23Thus says the Lord of hosts, the God of Israel: Once more they shall use these words in the land of Judah and in her cities when I release them from exile: The Lord bless you, O habitation of justice *and* righteousness, O holy mountain!

24And [the people of] Judah and all its cities shall dwell there together—[nomad] farmers and those who wander about with their flocks.

25For I will [fully] satisfy the weary soul, and I will replenish every languishing *and* sorrowful person.

26Thereupon I [Jeremiah] awoke and looked, and my [trancelike] sleep was sweet [in the assurance it gave] to me.

27Behold, the days are coming, says the Lord, when I will sow the house of Israel and the house of Judah with the seed (offspring) of man and of beast.

28And it will be that as I have watched over them to pluck up and to break down, and to overthrow, destroy, and afflict [with evil], so will I watch over them to build and to plant [with good], says the Lord.

29In those days they shall say no more, The fathers have eaten sour grapes, and the children's teeth are set on edge. [Ezek. 18:2.]

30But everyone shall die for his own iniquity [only]; every man who eats sour grapes—his [own] teeth shall be set on edge.

31Behold, the days are coming, says the Lord, when I will make a new covenant with the house of Israel and with the house of Judah, [Luke 22:20; I Cor. 11:25.]

32 Not according to the covenant which I made with their fathers in the day when I took them by the hand to bring them out of the land of Egypt, My covenant which they broke, although I was their Husband, says the Lord.

33But this is the covenant which I will make with the house of Israel: After those days, says the Lord, I will put My law within them, and on their hearts will I write it; and I will be their God, and they will be My people.

34And they will no more teach each man his neighbor and each man his brother, saying, Know the Lord, for they will all know Me [recognize, understand, and be acquainted with Me], from the least of them to the greatest, says the Lord. For I will forgive their iniquity, and I will [seriously] remember their sin no more. [Heb. 8:8-12; 10:16, 17.]

35Thus says the Lord, Who gives the sun for a light by day and the fixed order of the moon and of the stars for a light by night, Who stirs up the sea's roaring billows *or* stills the waves when they roar—the Lord of hosts is His name:

36If these ordinances [of fixed order] depart from before Me, says the Lord, then the posterity of Israel also shall cease from being a nation before Me throughout the ages.

37Thus says the Lord: If the heavens above can be measured and the foundations of the earth searched out beneath, then I will cast off all the offspring of Israel for all that they have done, says the Lord.

*a The early church fathers believed this passage had reference to the mystery of Christ's incarnation, but that interpretation is now generally rejected for various reasons. It is sufficient to say that the word "female" here used for "woman" absolutely excludes the idea that this refers to the virgin birth (for this was to be a "new thing"). To "compass" is to woo and win. That the early translators attached that meaning to it is clear from the fact that Shakespeare, their contemporary, so used it (Charles Ellicott, A Bible Commentary). Probably the implication is that Israel, the erring but deeply penitent wife, instead of going about after other lovers will devote herself to winning back and being worthy of the love of her divine Husband and Lord, Who had rejected her.*

## New International Version

38"The days are coming," declares the LORD, "when this city will be rebuilt for me from the Tower of Hananel to the Corner Gate. 39The measuring line will stretch from there straight to the hill of Gareb and then turn to Goah. 40The whole valley where dead bodies and ashes are thrown, and all the terraces out to the Kidron Valley on the east as far as the corner of the Horse Gate, will be holy to the LORD. The city will never again be uprooted or demolished."

### Jeremiah Buys a Field

**32** This is the word that came to Jeremiah from the LORD in the tenth year of Zedekiah king of Judah, which was the eighteenth year of Nebuchadnezzar. 2The army of the king of Babylon was then besieging Jerusalem, and Jeremiah the prophet was confined in the courtyard of the guard in the royal palace of Judah.

3Now Zedekiah king of Judah had imprisoned him there, saying, "Why do you prophesy as you do? You say, 'This is what the LORD says: I am about to give this city into the hands of the king of Babylon, and he will capture it. 4Zedekiah king of Judah will not escape the Babylonians*a* but will certainly be given into the hands of the king of Babylon, and will speak with him face to face and see him with his own eyes. 5He will take Zedekiah to Babylon, where he will remain until I deal with him, declares the LORD. If you fight against the Babylonians, you will not succeed.'"

6Jeremiah said, "The word of the LORD came to me: 7Hanamel son of Shallum your uncle is going to come to you and say, 'Buy my field at Anathoth, because as nearest relative it is your right and duty to buy it.'

8"Then, just as the LORD had said, my cousin Hanamel came to me in the courtyard of the guard and said, 'Buy my field at Anathoth in the territory of Benjamin. Since it is your right to redeem it and possess it, buy it for yourself.'

"I knew that this was the word of the LORD; 9so I bought the field at Anathoth from my cousin Hanamel and weighed out for him seventeen shekels*b* of silver. 10I signed and sealed the deed, had it witnessed, and weighed out the silver on the scales. 11I took the deed of purchase—the sealed copy containing the terms and conditions, as well as the unsealed copy— 12and I gave this deed to Baruch son of Neriah, the son of Mahseiah, in the presence of my cousin Hanamel and of the witnesses who

## Amplified Bible

38Behold, the days are coming, says the Lord, when the city [of Jerusalem] shall be built [again] for the Lord from the *a*Tower of Hananel to the Corner Gate.

39And the measuring line shall go out farther straight onward to the hill Gareb and shall then turn to Goah [exact location unknown].

40And the whole valley [Hinnom] of the dead bodies and [the hill] of the ashes [long dumped there from the temple sacrifices], and all the fields as far as the brook Kidron, to the corner of the Horse Gate toward the east, shall be holy to the Lord. It [the city] shall not be plucked up or overthrown any more to the end of the age. [Zech. 14:10-11.]

**32** The word that came to Jeremiah from the Lord in the tenth year of Zedekiah king of Judah, which was the eighteenth year of *b*Nebuchadrezzar.

2For the king of Babylon's army was then besieging Jerusalem, and Jeremiah the prophet was shut up in the court of the guard, which was in the house of the king of Judah.

3For Zedekiah king of Judah had locked him up, saying, Why do you prophesy and say, Thus says the Lord: Behold, I am giving this city into the hand of the king of Babylon, and he shall take it;

4And Zedekiah king of Judah shall not escape out of the hands of the Chaldeans but shall surely be delivered into the hand of the king of Babylon, and shall speak with him face to face and see him eye to eye;

5And he shall lead Zedekiah to Babylon, and there shall he be until I visit him [for evil], says the Lord; and though you fight against the Chaldeans, you shall not prosper [why do you thus prophesy]? [Jer. 21:3-7; 34:2-5; 37:17; 52:7-14.]

6And Jeremiah said, The word of the Lord came to me, saying,

7Behold, Hanamel son of Shallum your uncle shall come to you and say, Buy my field that is in Anathoth, for the right of redemption is yours to buy it.

8So Hanamel my uncle's son came to me in the court of the guard in accordance with the word of the Lord, and he said to me, I pray you, buy my field that is in Anathoth, which is in the land of Benjamin, for the right of inheritance is yours and the redemption is yours; buy it for yourself. Then I knew that this was the word of the Lord.

9And I bought the field that was in Anathoth from Hanamel my uncle's son and weighed out for him the money—seventeen shekels of silver.

10And I signed the deed and sealed it, called witnesses, and weighed for him the money on the scales.

11So I took the deed of the purchase—both that which was sealed, containing the terms and conditions, and the copy which was unsealed—

12And I gave the purchase deed to Baruch son of Neriah, the son of Mahseiah, in the sight of Hanamel my uncle's son and the witnesses who signed the purchase

---

*a* Many times after the days of the Old Testament, Jerusalem was destroyed. Travelers in recent centuries reported it to be an almost deserted city—its buildings were ruins filled with rubble, its inhabitants numbered barely enough to populate a village. Yet not only did God's word declare that it would be rebuilt, but also definitely and in detail it drew a word map of the exact outline which the future city would follow—from a well-known tower to the gate at a certain corner, then on over a particular hill, coming now outside the walls of the original city and taking in a large area definitely marked out by familiar landmarks. Eight details are unmistakably given here, and Zechariah adds another (Zech. 14:10). Moreover, the city's enlargement would be in one general direction—to the northwest. Twenty-five hundred years later, in A.D. 1935, the prophecy had been fulfilled to the letter, as if indeed with God's "measuring line" (Jer. 31:39). What a God, and what a Book! So unlikely seemed this prophecy's fulfillment that some commentators were of the opinion that it should be interpreted spiritually! *b* See footnote on Jer. 21:2.

---

*a* 4 Or *Chaldeans*; also in verses 5, 24, 25, 28, 29 and 43   *b* 9 That is, about 7 ounces or about 200 grams

## New International Version

had signed the deed and of all the Jews sitting in the court-yard of the guard.

¹³"In their presence I gave Baruch these instructions: ¹⁴'This is what the LORD Almighty, the God of Israel, says: Take these documents, both the sealed and unsealed copies of the deed of purchase, and put them in a clay jar so they will last a long time. ¹⁵For this is what the LORD Almighty, the God of Israel, says: Houses, fields and vineyards will again be bought in this land.'

¹⁶"After I had given the deed of purchase to Baruch son of Neriah, I prayed to the LORD:

¹⁷"Ah, Sovereign LORD, you have made the heavens and the earth by your great power and outstretched arm. Nothing is too hard for you. ¹⁸You show love to thousands but bring the punishment for the parents' sins into the laps of their children after them. Great and mighty God, whose name is the LORD Almighty, ¹⁹great are your purposes and mighty are your deeds. Your eyes are open to the ways of all mankind; you reward each person according to their conduct and as their deeds deserve. ²⁰You performed signs and wonders in Egypt and have continued them to this day, in Israel and among all mankind, and have gained the renown that is still yours. ²¹You brought your people Israel out of Egypt with signs and wonders, by a mighty hand and an outstretched arm and with great terror. ²²You gave them this land you had sworn to give their ancestors, a land flowing with milk and honey. ²³They came in and took possession of it, but they did not obey you or follow your law; they did not do what you commanded them to do. So you brought all this disaster on them.

²⁴"See how the siege ramps are built up to take the city. Because of the sword, famine and plague, the city will be given into the hands of the Babylonians who are attacking it. What you said has happened, as you now see. ²⁵And though the city will be given into the hands of the Babylonians, you, Sovereign LORD, say to me, 'Buy the field with silver and have the transaction witnessed.'"

²⁶Then the word of the LORD came to Jeremiah: ²⁷"I am the LORD, the God of all mankind. Is anything too hard for me? ²⁸Therefore this is what the LORD says: I am about to give this city into the hands of the Babylonians and to Nebuchadnezzar king of Babylon, who will capture it. ²⁹The Babylonians who are attacking this city will come in and set it on fire; they will burn it down, along with the houses where the people aroused my anger by burning incense on the roofs to Baal and by pouring out drink offerings to other gods.

³⁰"The people of Israel and Judah have done nothing but evil in my sight from their youth; indeed, the people of Israel have done nothing but arouse my anger with what their hands have made, declares the LORD. ³¹From the day it was built until now, this city has so aroused my anger and wrath that I must remove it from my sight. ³²The people of Israel and Judah have provoked me by all the evil they have done—they, their kings and officials, their priests and prophets, the people of Judah and those liv-

## Amplified Bible

deed, in the presence of all the Jews who were sitting in the court of the guard.

¹³And I charged Baruch before them, saying,

¹⁴Thus says the Lord of hosts, the God of Israel: Take these deeds, both this purchase deed which is sealed and this unsealed deed, and put them in an earthen vessel, that they may last a long time.

¹⁵For thus says the Lord of hosts, the God of Israel: Houses and fields and vineyards shall be purchased yet again in this land.

¹⁶Now when I had delivered the purchase deed to Baruch son of Neriah, I prayed to the Lord, saying:

¹⁷Alas, Lord God! Behold, You have made the heavens and the earth by Your great power and by Your outstretched arm! There is nothing too hard or too wonderful for You—

¹⁸You Who show loving-kindness to thousands but recompense the iniquity of the fathers into the bosoms of their children after them. The great, the mighty God; the Lord of hosts is His name—

¹⁹Great [are You] in counsel and mighty in deeds, Whose eyes are open to all the ways of the sons of men, to reward or repay each one according to his ways and according to the fruit of his doings,

²⁰Who wrought signs and wonders in the land of Egypt, and even to this day [continues to do so], both in Israel and among other men, and made for Yourself a name, as at this day.

²¹And You brought forth Your people Israel out of the land of Egypt with signs and wonders, with a strong hand and outstretched arm and with great terror;

²²And You gave them this land which You swore to their fathers to give them, a land flowing with milk and honey;

²³And they entered and took possession of it, but they obeyed not Your voice, nor walked in Your law; they have done nothing of all that You commanded them to do. Therefore You have caused all this evil to come upon them.

²⁴See the siege mounds [of earth which the foe has heaped against the walls]; they have come up to the city to take it. And the city is given into the hand of the Chaldeans who fight against it, because [the people are overcome] by the sword and the famine and the pestilence. What You have spoken has come to pass, and behold, You see it.

²⁵Yet, O Lord God, You said to me, Buy the field with money and get witnesses, even though the city is given into the hands of the Chaldeans.

²⁶Then came the word of the Lord to Jeremiah, saying,

²⁷Behold, I am the Lord, the God of all flesh; is there anything too hard for Me?

²⁸Therefore thus says the Lord: Behold, I am giving this city into the hands of the Chaldeans and into the hand of Nebuchadrezzar king of Babylon, and he shall take it;

²⁹And the Chaldeans who are fighting against this city shall come in and set this city on fire and burn it, along with the houses on whose roofs incense has been offered to Baal and drink offerings have been poured out to other gods to provoke Me to anger. [Jer. 19:13.]

³⁰For the children of Israel and the children of Judah have done only evil before Me from their youth; for the children of Israel have only provoked Me to anger with the work of their hands [the idols], says the Lord.

³¹For this city has been to Me a [such a] provocation of My anger and My wrath from the day that they [finished] building it [in the time of Solomon, who was the first Israelite king who turned to idolatry] even to this day that I must remove it from before My face—[I Kings 11:1-13.]

³²Because of all the evil of the children of Israel and of the children of Judah which they have done to provoke Me to anger—they, their kings, their princes, their priests, their prophets, the men of Judah, and the inhabitants of Jerusalem.

## New International Version

ing in Jerusalem. <sup>33</sup>They turned their backs to me and not their faces; though I taught them again and again, they would not listen or respond to discipline. <sup>34</sup>They set up their vile images in the house that bears my Name and defiled it. <sup>35</sup>They built high places for Baal in the Valley of Ben Hinnom to sacrifice their sons and daughters to Molek, though I never commanded—nor did it enter my mind—that they should do such a detestable thing and so make Judah sin.

<sup>36</sup>"You are saying about this city, 'By the sword, famine and plague it will be given into the hands of the king of Babylon'; but this is what the LORD, the God of Israel, says: <sup>37</sup>I will surely gather them from all the lands where I banish them in my furious anger and great wrath; I will bring them back to this place and let them live in safety. <sup>38</sup>They will be my people, and I will be their God. <sup>39</sup>I will give them singleness of heart and action, so that they will always fear me and that all will then go well for them and for their children after them. <sup>40</sup>I will make an everlasting covenant with them: I will never stop doing good to them, and I will inspire them to fear me, so that they will never turn away from me. <sup>41</sup>I will rejoice in doing them good and will assuredly plant them in this land with all my heart and soul.

<sup>42</sup>"This is what the LORD says: As I have brought all this great calamity on this people, so I will give them all the prosperity I have promised them. <sup>43</sup>Once more fields will be bought in this land of which you say, 'It is a desolate waste, without people or animals, for it has been given into the hands of the Babylonians.' <sup>44</sup>Fields will be bought for silver, and deeds will be signed, sealed and witnessed in the territory of Benjamin, in the villages around Jerusalem, in the towns of Judah and in the towns of the hill country, of the western foothills and of the Negev, because I will restore their fortunes,[a] declares the LORD."

### Promise of Restoration

**33** While Jeremiah was still confined in the courtyard of the guard, the word of the LORD came to him a second time: <sup>2</sup>"This is what the LORD says, he who made the earth, the LORD who formed it and established it—the LORD is his name: <sup>3</sup>'Call to me and I will answer you and tell you great and unsearchable things you do not know.' <sup>4</sup>For this is what the LORD, the God of Israel, says about the houses in this city and the royal palaces of Judah that have been torn down to be used against the siege ramps and the sword <sup>5</sup>in the fight with the Babylonians[b]: 'They will be filled with the dead bodies of the people I will slay in my anger and wrath. I will hide my face from this city because of all its wickedness.

<sup>6</sup>"'Nevertheless, I will bring health and healing to it; I will heal my people and will let them enjoy abundant peace and security. <sup>7</sup>I will bring Judah and Israel back from captivity[c] and will rebuild them as they were before. <sup>8</sup>I will cleanse them from all the sin they have committed against

## Amplified Bible

<sup>33</sup>And they have turned their backs to Me and not their faces; though I taught them persistently, yet they would not listen and receive instruction.

<sup>34</sup>But they set their abominations [of idol worship] in the house which is called by My [a]Name to defile it.

<sup>35</sup>And they built the high places [for worship] of Baal in the Valley of Ben-hinnom [son of Hinnom] to cause their sons and their daughters to pass through the fire [in worship also of and] to Molech—which I did not command them, nor did it come into My mind or heart that they should do this abomination, to cause Judah to sin. [Jer. 7:30-31.]

<sup>36</sup>And now therefore thus says the Lord, the God of Israel, concerning this city of which you say, It shall be delivered into the hand of the king of Babylon by sword and by famine and by pestilence:

<sup>37</sup>Behold, I will gather them out of all countries to which I drove them in My anger and in My wrath and in great indignation; I will bring them again to this place, and I will make them dwell safely.

<sup>38</sup>And they shall be My people, and I will be their God.

<sup>39</sup>And I will give them one heart and one way, that they may [reverently] fear Me forever for the good of themselves and of their children after them.

<sup>40</sup>And I will make an everlasting covenant with them: I will not turn away from following them to do them good, and I will put My [reverential] fear in their hearts, so that they will not depart from Me. [Jer. 31:31-34.]

<sup>41</sup>Yes, I will rejoice over them to do them good, and I will plant them in this land assuredly and in truth with My whole heart and with My whole being.

<sup>42</sup>For thus says the Lord: As I have brought all this great evil upon this people, so will I bring upon them all the good that I have promised them.

<sup>43</sup>And fields shall be bought in this land of which you say, It is desolate, without man or beast; it is given into the hands of the Chaldeans.

<sup>44</sup>Men shall buy fields for money and shall sign deeds, seal them, and call witnesses in the land of Benjamin, in the places around Jerusalem, in the cities of Judah, in the cities of the hill country, in the cities of the lowland, and in the cities of the South (the Negeb), for I will cause them to be released from their exile, says the Lord.

**33** Moreover, the word of the Lord came to Jeremiah the second time, while he was still shut up in the court of the guard, saying,

<sup>2</sup>Thus says the Lord Who made [the earth], the Lord Who formed it to establish it—the Lord is His name:

<sup>3</sup>Call to Me and I will answer you and show you great and mighty things, fenced in and hidden, which you do not know (do not distinguish and recognize, have knowledge of and understand).

<sup>4</sup>For thus says the Lord, the God of Israel, concerning the houses of this city and the houses of the kings of Judah which are torn down to make a defense against the siege mounds and before the sword: [Isa. 22:10; Jer. 6:6.]

<sup>5</sup>They [the besieged Jews] are coming in to fight against the Chaldeans, and they [the houses] will be filled with the dead bodies of men whom I shall slay in My anger and My wrath; for I have hidden My face [in indignation] from this city because of all their wickedness.

<sup>6</sup>Behold, [in the future restored Jerusalem] I will lay upon it health and healing, and I will cure them and will reveal to them the abundance of peace (prosperity, security, stability) and truth.

<sup>7</sup>And I will cause the captivity of Judah and the captivity of Israel to be reversed and will rebuild them as they were at first.

<sup>8</sup>And I will cleanse them from all the guilt and iniquity by which they have sinned against Me, and I will forgive

---

## New International Version

me and will forgive all their sins of rebellion against me. [9]Then this city will bring me renown, joy, praise and honor before all nations on earth that hear of all the good things I do for it; and they will be in awe and will tremble at the abundant prosperity and peace I provide for it.'

[10]"This is what the LORD says: 'You say about this place, "It is a desolate waste, without people or animals." Yet in the towns of Judah and the streets of Jerusalem that are deserted, inhabited by neither people nor animals, there will be heard once more [11]the sounds of joy and gladness, the voices of bride and bridegroom, and the voices of those who bring thank offerings to the house of the LORD, saying,

"Give thanks to the LORD Almighty,
    for the LORD is good;
    his love endures forever."

For I will restore the fortunes of the land as they were before,' says the LORD. [12]"This is what the LORD Almighty says: 'In this place, desolate and without people or animals—in all its towns there will again be pastures for shepherds to rest their flocks. [13]In the towns of the hill country, of the western foothills and of the Negev, in the territory of Benjamin, in the villages around Jerusalem and in the towns of Judah, flocks will again pass under the hand of the one who counts them,' says the LORD.

[14]"'The days are coming,' declares the LORD, 'when I will fulfill the good promise I made to the people of Israel and Judah.

[15]"'In those days and at that time
    I will make a righteous Branch sprout from David's
      line;
    he will do what is just and right in the land.
[16]In those days Judah will be saved
    and Jerusalem will live in safety.
This is the name by which it[a] will be called:
    The LORD Our Righteous Savior.'

[17]For this is what the LORD says: 'David will never fail to have a man to sit on the throne of Israel, [18]nor will the Levitical priests ever fail to have a man to stand before me continually to offer burnt offerings, to burn grain offerings and to present sacrifices.'"

[19]The word of the LORD came to Jeremiah: [20]"This is what the LORD says: 'If you can break my covenant with the day and my covenant with the night, so that day and night no longer come at their appointed time, [21]then my covenant with David my servant—and my covenant with the Levites who are priests ministering before me—can be broken and David will no longer have a descendant to reign on his throne. [22]I will make the descendants of David my servant and the Levites who minister before me as countless as the stars in the sky and as measureless as the sand on the seashore.'"

[23]The word of the LORD came to Jeremiah: [24]"Have you not noticed that these people are saying, 'The LORD has rejected the two kingdoms[b] he chose'? So they despise my people and no longer regard them as a nation. [25]This is what the LORD says: 'If I have not made my covenant with day and night and established the laws of heaven and earth, [26]then I will reject the descendants of Jacob and David my servant and will not choose one of his sons to

## Amplified Bible

all their guilt *and* iniquities by which they have sinned and rebelled against Me.

[9]And [Jerusalem] shall be to Me a name of joy, a praise and a glory before all the nations of the earth that hear of all the good I do for it, and they shall fear and tremble because of all the good and all the peace, prosperity, security, *and* stability I provide for it.

[10]Thus says the Lord: Yet again there shall be heard in this place of which you say, It is a desolate waste, without man and without beast—even in the cities of Judah and in the streets of Jerusalem that are desolate, without man and without inhabitant and without beast—

[11] [There shall be heard again] the voice of joy and the voice of gladness, the voice of the bridegroom and the voice of the bride, the voices of those who sing as they bring sacrifices of thanksgiving into the house of the Lord, Give praise *and* thanks to the Lord of hosts, for the Lord is good; for His mercy *and* kindness *and* steadfast love endure forever! For I will cause the captivity of the land to be reversed *and* return to be as it was at first, says the Lord.

[12]Thus says the Lord of hosts: In this place which is desolate, without man and without beast, and in all its cities, there shall again be dwellings *and* pastures of shepherds resting their flocks.

[13]In the cities of the hill country, in the cities of the lowland, in the cities of the South (the Negeb), in the land of Benjamin, in the places around Jerusalem, and in the cities of Judah shall flocks pass again under the hands of him who counts them, says the Lord.

[14]Behold, the days are coming, says the Lord, when I will fulfill the good promise I have made to the house of Israel and the house of Judah.

[15]In those days and at that time will I cause a righteous Branch [the Messiah] to grow up to David; and He shall execute justice and righteousness in the land. [Isa. 4:2; Jer. 23:5; Zech. 3:8; 6:12.]

[16]In those days Judah shall be saved and Jerusalem shall dwell safely. And this is the name by which it will be called, The Lord is Our Righteousness (our Rightness, our Justice).

[17]For thus says the Lord: David shall never fail [to have] a man [descendant] to sit on the throne of the house of Israel,

[18]Nor shall the Levitical priests fail [to have] a man [descendant] to offer burnt offerings before Me and to burn cereal offerings and to make sacrifices continually (all day long).

[19]And the word of the Lord came to Jeremiah, saying,

[20]Thus says the Lord: If you can break My covenant with the day, and My covenant with the night, so that there should not be day and night in their season,

[21]Then can also My covenant be broken with David My servant, so that he shall not have a son to reign upon his throne, and [My league be broken also] with the Levitical priests, My ministers.

[22]As the host of [the stars of] the heavens cannot be numbered nor the sand of the sea be measured, so will I multiply the offspring of David My servant and the Levites who minister to Me.

[23]Moreover, the word of the Lord came to Jeremiah, saying,

[24]Have you not noticed that these people [the Jews] are saying, The Lord has cast off the two families [Israel and Judah] which He chose? Thus My people have despised [themselves in relation to God as His covenant people], so that they are no more a nation in their [own] sight.

[25]Thus says the Lord: If My covenant with day and night does not stand, and if I have not appointed the ordinances of the heavens and the earth [the whole order of nature],

[26]Then will I also cast away the descendants of Jacob and David My servant and will not choose one of his offspring to be ruler over the descendants of Abraham, Isaac,

# New International Version

rule over the descendants of Abraham, Isaac and Jacob. For I will restore their fortunes[a] and have compassion on them.'"

## Warning to Zedekiah

**34** While Nebuchadnezzar king of Babylon and all his army and all the kingdoms and peoples in the empire he ruled were fighting against Jerusalem and all its surrounding towns, this word came to Jeremiah from the LORD: [2] "This is what the LORD, the God of Israel, says: Go to Zedekiah king of Judah and tell him, 'This is what the LORD says: I am about to give this city into the hands of the king of Babylon, and he will burn it down. [3] You will not escape from his grasp but will surely be captured and given into his hands. You will see the king of Babylon with your own eyes, and he will speak with you face to face. And you will go to Babylon.

[4] "'Yet hear the LORD's promise to you, Zedekiah king of Judah. This is what the LORD says concerning you: You will not die by the sword; [5] you will die peacefully. As people made a funeral fire in honor of your predecessors, the kings who ruled before you, so they will make a fire in your honor and lament, "Alas, master!" I myself make this promise, declares the LORD.'"

[6] Then Jeremiah the prophet told all this to Zedekiah king of Judah, in Jerusalem, [7] while the army of the king of Babylon was fighting against Jerusalem and the other cities of Judah that were still holding out—Lachish and Azekah. These were the only fortified cities left in Judah.

## Freedom for Slaves

[8] The word came to Jeremiah from the LORD after King Zedekiah had made a covenant with all the people in Jerusalem to proclaim freedom for the slaves. [9] Everyone was to free their Hebrew slaves, both male and female; no one was to hold a fellow Hebrew in bondage. [10] So all the officials and people who entered into this covenant agreed that they would free their male and female slaves and no longer hold them in bondage. They agreed, and set them free. [11] But afterward they changed their minds and took back the slaves they had freed and enslaved them again.

[12] Then the word of the LORD came to Jeremiah: [13] "This is what the LORD, the God of Israel, says: I made a covenant with your ancestors when I brought them out of Egypt, out of the land of slavery. I said, [14] 'Every seventh year each of you must free any fellow Hebrews who have sold themselves to you. After they have served you six years, you must let them go free.'[b] Your ancestors, however, did not listen to me or pay attention to me. [15] Recently you repented and did what is right in my sight: Each of you proclaimed freedom to your own people. You even made a covenant before me in the house that bears my Name. [16] But now you have turned around and profaned my name; each of you has taken back the male and female slaves you had set free to go where they wished. You have forced them to become your slaves again.

[17] "Therefore this is what the LORD says: You have not obeyed me; you have not proclaimed freedom to your own

# Amplified Bible

and Jacob. For I will cause their captivity to be reversed, and I will have mercy, kindness, *and* steadfast love on *and* for them. [Gen. 49:10.]

**34** The word that came to Jeremiah from the Lord when Nebuchadnezzar king of Babylon and all his army and all the kingdoms of the earth under his dominion and all the people were fighting against Jerusalem and all of its cities:

[2] Thus says the Lord, the God of Israel: Go and speak to Zedekiah king of Judah and tell him, Thus says the Lord: Behold, I am giving this city into the hand of the king of Babylon, and he will burn it with fire.

[3] And you will not escape out of his hand but will surely be taken and delivered into his hand; you will see the king of Babylon eye to eye, and he will speak with you face to face; and you will go to Babylon.

[4] Yet hear the word of the Lord, O Zedekiah king of Judah! Thus says the Lord concerning you: You shall not die by the sword;

[5] But you shall die in peace. And as with the burnings of [spices and perfumes on wood that were granted as suitable for and in honor of] your fathers, the former kings who were before you, so shall a burning be made for you; and [people] shall lament for you, saying, Alas, lord! For I have spoken the word, says the Lord.

[6] Then Jeremiah the prophet spoke all these words to Zedekiah king of Judah, in Jerusalem,

[7] When the army of the king of Babylon was fighting against Jerusalem and against all the cities of Judah that were left, against Lachish and Azekah, for these were the only fortified cities remaining of the cities of Judah.

[8] [This is] the word that came to Jeremiah from the Lord after King Zedekiah had made a covenant with all the people who were at Jerusalem to proclaim liberty to them:

[9] Every man should let his Hebrew slaves, male and female, go free, so that no one should make a slave of a Jew, his brother.

[10] And all the princes and all the people obeyed, who had entered into the covenant that everyone would let his manservant and his maidservant go free, so that none should make bondmen of them any more; they obeyed, and let them go.

[11] But afterward they turned around and caused the servants and the handmaids whom they had let go free to return [to their former masters] and brought them into subjection for servants and for handmaids.

[12] Therefore the word of the Lord came to Jeremiah from the Lord, saying,

[13] Thus says the Lord, the God of Israel: I made a covenant with your fathers in the day that I brought them forth out of the land of Egypt, out of the house of bondage, saying,

[14] At the end of seven years you shall let every man his brother who is a Hebrew go free who has sold himself *or* has been sold to you and has served you six years; but your fathers did not listen to *and* obey Me or incline their ear [submitting and consenting to Me]. [Deut. 15:12.]

[15] And you recently turned around *and* repented, doing what was right in My sight by proclaiming liberty each one to his neighbor [who was his bond servant]; and you made a covenant *or* pledge before Me in the house which is called by My [a] Name;

[16] But then you turned around and defiled My name; each of you caused to return to you your servants, male and female, whom you had set free as they might desire; and you brought them into subjection again to be your slaves.

[17] Therefore thus says the Lord: You have not listened to Me *and* obeyed Me in proclaiming liberty each one to

---

[a] 26 Or *will bring them back from captivity*   [b] 14 Deut. 15:12   [a] See footnote on Deut. 12:5.

## New International Version

people. So I now proclaim 'freedom' for you, declares the LORD—'freedom' to fall by the sword, plague and famine. I will make you abhorrent to all the kingdoms of the earth. [18]Those who have violated my covenant and have not fulfilled the terms of the covenant they made before me, I will treat like the calf they cut in two and then walked between its pieces. [19]The leaders of Judah and Jerusalem, the court officials, the priests and all the people of the land who walked between the pieces of the calf, [20]I will deliver into the hands of their enemies who want to kill them. Their dead bodies will become food for the birds and the wild animals.

[21]"I will deliver Zedekiah king of Judah and his officials into the hands of their enemies who want to kill them, to the army of the king of Babylon, which has withdrawn from you. [22]I am going to give the order, declares the LORD, and I will bring them back to this city. They will fight against it, take it and burn it down. And I will lay waste the towns of Judah so no one can live there."

### The Rekabites

**35** This is the word that came to Jeremiah from the LORD during the reign of Jehoiakim son of Josiah king of Judah: [2]"Go to the Rekabite family and invite them to come to one of the side rooms of the house of the LORD and give them wine to drink."

[3]So I went to get Jaazaniah son of Jeremiah, the son of Habazziniah, and his brothers and all his sons—the whole family of the Rekabites. [4]I brought them into the house of the LORD, into the room of the sons of Hanan son of Igdaliah the man of God. It was next to the room of the officials, which was over that of Maaseiah son of Shallum the doorkeeper. [5]Then I set bowls full of wine and some cups before the Rekabites and said to them, "Drink some wine."

[6]But they replied, "We do not drink wine, because our forefather Jehonadab[a] son of Rekab gave us this command: 'Neither you nor your descendants must ever drink wine. [7]Also you must never build houses, sow seed or plant vineyards; you must never have any of these things, but must always live in tents. Then you will live a long time in the land where you are nomads.' [8]We have obeyed everything our forefather Jehonadab son of Rekab commanded us. Neither we nor our wives nor our sons and daughters have ever drunk wine [9]or built houses to live in or had vineyards, fields or crops. [10]We have lived in tents and have fully obeyed everything our forefather Jehonadab commanded us. [11]But when Nebuchadnezzar king of Babylon invaded this land, we said, 'Come, we must go to Jerusalem to escape the Babylonian[b] and Aramean armies.' So we have remained in Jerusalem."

[12]Then the word of the LORD came to Jeremiah, saying: [13]"This is what the LORD Almighty, the God of Israel, says: Go and tell the people of Judah and those living in Jerusalem, 'Will you not learn a lesson and obey my words?'

## Amplified Bible

his brother and neighbor. Behold, I proclaim to you liberty—to the sword, to pestilence, and to famine, says the Lord; and I will make you to be tossed to and fro *and* to be a horror among all the kingdoms of the earth!

[18]And the men who have transgressed My covenant, who have not kept the terms of the covenant *or* solemn pledge which they had made before Me, I will make them [like] the [sacrificial] calf which they cut in two and then passed between its separated parts [solemnizing their pledge to Me]—I will make those men the calf! [Gen. 15:9, 10, 17.]

[19]The princes of Judah, the princes of Jerusalem, the eunuchs, the priests, and all the people of the land who passed between the parts of the calf,

[20]I will give them into the hands of their enemies and into the hands of those who seek their life. And their dead bodies will be food for the birds of the heavens and the beasts of the earth.

[21]And Zedekiah king of Judah and his princes will I give into the hands of their enemies and into the hands of those who seek their life, and into the hand of the king of Babylon's army which has withdrawn from you.

[22]Behold, I will command, says the Lord, and cause them [the Chaldeans] to return to this city; and they shall fight against it and take it and burn it with fire. I will make the cities of Judah a desolation without inhabitant.

**35** The word that came to Jeremiah from the Lord in the days of Jehoiakim son of Josiah king of Judah: [2]Go to the house of the Rechabites and speak to them and bring them into the house of the Lord, into one of the chambers; then give them [who are pledged to drink no wine] some wine to drink.

[3]So I took Jaazaniah son of Jeremiah, the son of Habazziniah, and his brothers and all his sons, and the whole house of the Rechabites,

[4]And I brought them into the house of the Lord, into the chamber of the sons of Hanan son of Igdaliah the man of God, which was by the chamber of the princes, above the chamber of Maaseiah son of Shallum the keeper of the door.

[5]And I set before the sons of the house of the Rechabites pitchers full of wine, and cups, and I said to them, Drink wine.

[6]But they said, We will drink no wine, for Jonadab son of Rechab, our father, commanded us: You shall not drink wine, neither you nor your sons, forever.

[7]Neither shall you build a house or sow seed or plant a vineyard or have them; but you shall dwell all your days in tents, that you may live many days in the land where you are temporary residents.

[8]And we have obeyed the voice of Jonadab son of Rechab, our father, in all that he charged us, to drink no wine all our days—we, our wives, our sons, and our daughters—

[9]And not to build ourselves houses to live in; nor do we have vineyard or field or seed.

[10]But we have dwelt in tents and have obeyed and done according to all that Jonadab our ancestor commanded us.

[11]But when [a]Nebuchadrezzar king of Babylon came up against the land, we said, Come and let us go to Jerusalem for fear of the army of the Chaldeans and the army of the Syrians. So we are living in Jerusalem.

[12]Then came the word of the Lord to Jeremiah:

[13]Thus says the Lord of hosts, the God of Israel: Go and say to the men of Judah and the inhabitants of Jerusalem, Will you not receive instruction and listen to My words *and* obey them? says the Lord.

---

[a] 6 Hebrew *Jonadab*, a variant of *Jehonadab*; here and often in this chapter   [b] 11 Or *Chaldean*

[a] See footnote on Jer. 21:2.

## New International Version

declares the LORD. 14'Jehonadab son of Rekab ordered his descendants not to drink wine and this command has been kept. To this day they do not drink wine, because they obey their forefather's command. But I have spoken to you again and again, yet you have not obeyed me. 15Again and again I sent all my servants the prophets to you. They said, "Each of you must turn from your wicked ways and reform your actions; do not follow other gods to serve them. Then you will live in the land I have given to you and your ancestors." But you have not paid attention or listened to me. 16The descendants of Jehonadab son of Rekab have carried out the command their forefather gave them, but these people have not obeyed me.'

17"Therefore this is what the LORD God Almighty, the God of Israel, says: 'Listen! I am going to bring on Judah and on everyone living in Jerusalem every disaster I pronounced against them. I spoke to them, but they did not listen; I called to them, but they did not answer.'"

18Then Jeremiah said to the family of the Rekabites, "This is what the LORD Almighty, the God of Israel, says: 'You have obeyed the command of your forefather Jehonadab and have followed all his instructions and have done everything he ordered.' 19Therefore this is what the LORD Almighty, the God of Israel, says: 'Jehonadab son of Rekab will never fail to have a descendant to serve me.'"

### Jehoiakim Burns Jeremiah's Scroll

**36** In the fourth year of Jehoiakim son of Josiah king of Judah, this word came to Jeremiah from the LORD: 2"Take a scroll and write on it all the words I have spoken to you concerning Israel, Judah and all the other nations from the time I began speaking to you in the reign of Josiah till now. 3Perhaps when the people of Judah hear about every disaster I plan to inflict on them, they will each turn from their wicked ways; then I will forgive their wickedness and their sin."

4So Jeremiah called Baruch son of Neriah, and while Jeremiah dictated all the words the LORD had spoken to him, Baruch wrote them on the scroll. 5Then Jeremiah told Baruch, "I am restricted; I am not allowed to go to the LORD's temple. 6So you go to the house of the LORD on a day of fasting and read to the people from the scroll the words of the LORD that you wrote as I dictated. Read them to all the people of Judah who come in from their towns. 7Perhaps they will bring their petition before the LORD and will each turn from their wicked ways, for the anger and wrath pronounced against this people by the LORD are great."

8Baruch son of Neriah did everything Jeremiah the prophet told him to do; at the LORD's temple he read the words of the LORD from the scroll. 9In the ninth month of the fifth year of Jehoiakim son of Josiah king of Judah, a time of fasting before the LORD was proclaimed for all the people in Jerusalem and those who had come from the towns of Judah. 10From the room of Gemariah son of Shaphan the secretary, which was in the upper courtyard at the entrance of the New Gate of the temple, Baruch read to all the people at the LORD's temple the words of Jeremiah from the scroll.

## Amplified Bible

14The command which Jonadab son of Rechab gave to his sons not to drink wine, has been carried out and established [as a custom for more than two hundred years]. To this day they drink no wine, but they have obeyed their father's command. But I, even I, have persistently spoken to you, but you have not listened to and obeyed Me.

15I have sent also to you all My servants the prophets earnestly and persistently, saying, Return now every man from his evil way and amend your doings and go not after other gods to serve them; and then you shall dwell in the land which I have given to you and to your fathers. But you did not submit and consent to Me or listen to and obey Me.

16Since the sons of Jonadab son of Rechab have fulfilled and established the command of their father which he commanded them, but these people have not listened to and obeyed Me,

17Therefore thus says the Lord God of hosts, the God of Israel: Behold, I am bringing upon Judah and all the inhabitants of Jerusalem all the evil that I have pronounced against them, because I have spoken to them, but they have not listened, and I have called to them, but they have not answered.

18And Jeremiah said to the house of the Rechabites, Thus says the Lord of hosts, the God of Israel: Because you have obeyed the command of Jonadab your father and have kept all his precepts and have done according to all that he commanded you,

19Therefore thus says the Lord of hosts, the God of Israel: Jonadab son of Rechab shall never fail [to have] a man [descendant] to stand before Me.

**36** In the fourth year of Jehoiakim son of Josiah king of Judah, this word came to Jeremiah from the Lord:

2Take a scroll [of parchment] for a book and write on it all the words I have spoken to you against Israel and Judah and all the nations from the day I spoke to you in the days of [King] Josiah until this day.

3It may be that the house of Judah will hear all the evil which I purpose to do to them, so that each one may turn from his evil way, that I may forgive their iniquity and their sin. [Jer. 18:7-10; 26:3.]

4Then Jeremiah called Baruch son of Neriah, and Baruch wrote upon the scroll of the book all the words which Jeremiah dictated, [words] that the Lord had spoken to him.

5And Jeremiah commanded Baruch, saying, I am [in hiding, virtually] restrained and shut up; I cannot go into the house of the Lord.

6Therefore you go, and on a day of fasting, in the hearing of all the people in the Lord's house, you shall read the words of the Lord which you have written on the scroll at my dictation. Also you shall read them in the hearing of all who come out of the cities of Judah.

7It may be that they will make their supplication [for mercy] before the Lord, and each one will turn back from his evil way, for great is the anger and the wrath that the Lord has pronounced against this people.

8And Baruch son of Neriah did according to all that Jeremiah the prophet commanded him, reading from [Jeremiah's] book the words of the Lord in the Lord's house.

9And in the fifth year of Jehoiakim son of Josiah king of Judah, in the ninth month, a fast was proclaimed before the Lord for all the people in Jerusalem and all the people who came to Jerusalem from the cities of Judah.

10Then Baruch read in the hearing of all the people the words of Jeremiah from the scroll of the book in the house of the Lord, in the chamber of Gemariah son of Shaphan the scribe, in the upper court at the entry of the New Gate of the Lord's house.

## New International Version

[11]When Micaiah son of Gemariah, the son of Shaphan, heard all the words of the LORD from the scroll, [12]he went down to the secretary's room in the royal palace, where all the officials were sitting: Elishama the secretary, Delaiah son of Shemaiah, Elnathan son of Akbor, Gemariah son of Shaphan, Zedekiah son of Hananiah, and all the other officials. [13]After Micaiah told them everything he had heard Baruch read to the people from the scroll, [14]all the officials sent Jehudi son of Nethaniah, the son of Shelemiah, the son of Cushi, to say to Baruch, "Bring the scroll from which you have read to the people and come." So Baruch son of Neriah went to them with the scroll in his hand. [15]They said to him, "Sit down, please, and read it to us."

So Baruch read it to them. [16]When they heard all these words, they looked at each other in fear and said to Baruch, "We must report all these words to the king." [17]Then they asked Baruch, "Tell us, how did you come to write all this? Did Jeremiah dictate it?"

[18]"Yes," Baruch replied, "he dictated all these words to me, and I wrote them in ink on the scroll."

[19]Then the officials said to Baruch, "You and Jeremiah, go and hide. Don't let anyone know where you are."

[20]After they put the scroll in the room of Elishama the secretary, they went to the king in the courtyard and reported everything to him. [21]The king sent Jehudi to get the scroll, and Jehudi brought it from the room of Elishama the secretary and read it to the king and all the officials standing beside him. [22]It was the ninth month and the king was sitting in the winter apartment, with a fire burning in the firepot in front of him. [23]Whenever Jehudi had read three or four columns of the scroll, the king cut them off with a scribe's knife and threw them into the firepot, until the entire scroll was burned in the fire. [24]The king and all his attendants who heard all these words showed no fear, nor did they tear their clothes. [25]Even though Elnathan, Delaiah and Gemariah urged the king not to burn the scroll, he would not listen to them. [26]Instead, the king commanded Jerahmeel, a son of the king, Seraiah son of Azriel and Shelemiah son of Abdeel to arrest Baruch the scribe and Jeremiah the prophet. But the LORD had hidden them.

[27]After the king burned the scroll containing the words that Baruch had written at Jeremiah's dictation, the word of the LORD came to Jeremiah: [28]"Take another scroll and write on it all the words that were on the first scroll, which Jehoiakim king of Judah burned up. [29]Also tell Jehoiakim king of Judah, 'This is what the LORD says: You burned that scroll and said, "Why did you write on it that the king of Babylon would certainly come and destroy this land and wipe from it both man and beast?" [30]Therefore this is what the LORD says about Jehoiakim king of Judah: He

## Amplified Bible

[11]When Micaiah son of Gemariah, the son of Shaphan, had heard out of the book all the words of the Lord,

[12]He went down to the king's house into the scribe's chamber, and behold, all the princes were sitting there: Elishama the scribe, Delaiah son of Shemaiah, Elnathan son of Achbor, Gemariah son of Shaphan, Zedekiah son of Hananiah, and all the [other] princes.

[13]Then Micaiah declared to them all the words that he had heard when Baruch read the book in the hearing of the people.

[14]Therefore all the princes sent Jehudi son of Nethaniah, the son of Shelemiah, the son of Cushi, to Baruch, saying, Take in your hand the scroll from which you have read in the hearing of the people and come [to us]. So Baruch son of Neriah took the scroll in his hand and came to them.

[15]And they said to him, Sit down now and read it in our hearing. So Baruch read it in their hearing.

[16]Now when they had heard all the words, they turned one to another in fear and said to Baruch, We must surely tell the king of all these words.

[17]And they asked Baruch, Tell us now, how did you write all these words? At [Jeremiah's] dictation?

[18]Then Baruch answered them, He dictated all these words to me, and I wrote them with ink in the book.

[19]Then the princes said to Baruch, Go and hide, you and Jeremiah, and let no one know where you are.

[20]Then they went into the court to the king, but they [first] put the scroll in the chamber of Elishama the scribe; then they reported all the words to the king.

[21]So the king sent Jehudi to get the scroll, and he took it out of the chamber of Elishama the scribe. And Jehudi read it in the hearing of the king and of all the princes who stood beside the king.

[22]Now it was the ninth month, and the king was sitting in the winter house, and a fire was burning there before him in the brazier.

[23]And [each time] when Jehudi had read three or four columns [of the scroll], he [King Jehoiakim] would cut them off with a penknife and cast them into the fire that was in the brazier, until the entire scroll was consumed in the fire that was in the brazier.

[24]Yet they were not afraid, nor did they rend their garments—neither the king, nor any of his servants who heard all these words.

[25]Even though Elnathan and Delaiah and Gemariah tried to persuade the king not to burn the scroll, he would not listen to them.

[26]And the king commanded Jerahmeel the king's son and Seraiah son of Azriel and Shelemiah son of Abdeel to seize Baruch the scribe and Jeremiah the prophet, but the Lord hid them.

[27]Now the word of the Lord came to Jeremiah after the king had burned the scroll with the words which Baruch wrote at the dictation of Jeremiah, [and the Lord] said:

[28]Take another scroll and write on it all the former words that were on the first scroll, which Jehoiakim the king of Judah burned.

[29]And concerning Jehoiakim king of Judah you shall say, Thus says the Lord: You have burned this scroll, saying, Why have you written on it that the king of Babylon shall surely come and destroy this land and shall cut off man and beast from it?

[30]Therefore thus says the Lord concerning Jehoiakim king of Judah: [a]He shall have no [heir] to sit upon the

[a] This prophecy against King Jehoiakim was literally fulfilled. Several years after these events, the king rebelled against Babylon (II Kings 24:1) and was attacked by numerous bands from various nations subject to Babylon (II Kings 24:2). He thus came to a violent death and a disgraceful burial such as Jeremiah had foretold several chapters before this one (Jer. 22:13-19). There, after a stern and scathing censure of the king, the Lord foretells through his prophet that Jehoiakim will "be buried with the burial of a donkey—dragged out and cast forth beyond the gates of Jerusalem" (Jer. 22:19). How could Jeremiah possibly have foreseen these events except by divine inspiration?

## New International Version

will have no one to sit on the throne of David; his body will be thrown out and exposed to the heat by day and the frost by night. ³¹I will punish him and his children and his attendants for their wickedness; I will bring on them and those living in Jerusalem and the people of Judah every disaster I pronounced against them, because they have not listened.'"

³²So Jeremiah took another scroll and gave it to the scribe Baruch son of Neriah, and as Jeremiah dictated, Baruch wrote on it all the words of the scroll that Jehoiakim king of Judah had burned in the fire. And many similar words were added to them.

### Jeremiah in Prison

**37** Zedekiah son of Josiah was made king of Judah by Nebuchadnezzar king of Babylon; he reigned in place of Jehoiachin*ᵃ* son of Jehoiakim. ²Neither he nor his attendants nor the people of the land paid any attention to the words the Lᴏʀᴅ had spoken through Jeremiah the prophet.

³King Zedekiah, however, sent Jehukal son of Shelemiah with the priest Zephaniah son of Maaseiah to Jeremiah the prophet with this message: "Please pray to the Lᴏʀᴅ our God for us."

⁴Now Jeremiah was free to come and go among the people, for he had not yet been put in prison. ⁵Pharaoh's army had marched out of Egypt, and when the Babylonians*ᵇ* who were besieging Jerusalem heard the report about them, they withdrew from Jerusalem.

⁶Then the word of the Lᴏʀᴅ came to Jeremiah the prophet: ⁷"This is what the Lᴏʀᴅ, the God of Israel, says: Tell the king of Judah, who sent you to inquire of me, 'Pharaoh's army, which has marched out to support you, will go back to its own land, to Egypt. ⁸Then the Babylonians will return and attack this city; they will capture it and burn it down.'

⁹"This is what the Lᴏʀᴅ says: Do not deceive yourselves, thinking, 'The Babylonians will surely leave us.' They will not! ¹⁰Even if you were to defeat the entire Babylonian*ᶜ* army that is attacking you and only wounded men were left in their tents, they would come out and burn this city down."

¹¹After the Babylonian army had withdrawn from Jerusalem because of Pharaoh's army, ¹²Jeremiah started to leave the city to go to the territory of Benjamin to get his share of the property among the people there. ¹³But when he reached the Benjamin Gate, the captain of the guard, whose name was Irijah son of Shelemiah, the son of Hananiah, arrested him and said, "You are deserting to the Babylonians!"

¹⁴"That's not true!" Jeremiah said. "I am not deserting to the Babylonians." But Irijah would not listen to him; instead, he arrested Jeremiah and brought him to the officials. ¹⁵They were angry with Jeremiah and had him beaten and imprisoned in the house of Jonathan the secretary, which they had made into a prison.

¹⁶Jeremiah was put into a vaulted cell in a dungeon, where he remained a long time. ¹⁷Then King Zedekiah sent for him and had him brought to the palace, where he asked him privately, "Is there any word from the Lᴏʀᴅ?"

"Yes," Jeremiah replied, "you will be delivered into the hands of the king of Babylon."

## Amplified Bible

throne of David, and his dead body shall be cast out to the heat by day and to the frost by night. ³¹And I will punish him and his offspring and his servants for their iniquity; and I will bring upon them the inhabitants of Jerusalem and the men of Judah all the evil that I have pronounced against them—but they would not hear.

³²Then Jeremiah took another scroll and gave it to Baruch the scribe, the son of Neriah, who wrote on it at the dictation of Jeremiah all the words of the book which Jehoiakim king of Judah had burned in the fire; and besides them many similar words were added.

**37** And Zedekiah son of Josiah, whom *ᵃ*Nebuchadrezzar king of Babylon made king in the land of Judah, reigned instead of Coniah [also called Jeconiah and Jehoiachin] son of Jehoiakim.

²But neither he nor his servants nor the people of the land listened to *and* obeyed the words of the Lord which He spoke through the prophet Jeremiah.

³Zedekiah the king sent Jehucal son of Shelemiah with Zephaniah son of Maaseiah, the priest, to the prophet Jeremiah, saying, Pray now to the Lord our God for us.

⁴Now Jeremiah was coming in and going out among the people, for they had not [yet] put him in prison.

⁵And Pharaoh's army had come forth out of Egypt, and when the Chaldeans who were besieging Jerusalem heard the news about them, they withdrew from Jerusalem *and* departed.

⁶Then came the word of the Lord to the prophet Jeremiah:

⁷Thus says the Lord, the God of Israel: Thus shall you say to the king of Judah, who sent you to Me to inquire of Me: Behold, Pharaoh's army, which has come forth to help you, will return to Egypt, to their own land.

⁸And the Chaldeans shall come again and fight against this city, and they shall take it and burn it with fire.

⁹Thus says the Lord: Do not deceive yourselves, saying, The Chaldeans will surely stay away from us—for they will not stay away.

¹⁰For though you should defeat the whole army of the Chaldeans who fight against you, and there remained only the wounded *and* men stricken through among them, every man confined to his tent, yet they would rise up and burn this city with fire.

¹¹And when the army of the Chaldeans had departed from Jerusalem for fear of Pharaoh's approaching army,

¹²Jeremiah went forth out of Jerusalem to go into the land of Benjamin [to slip away during the brief lull in the Chaldean invasion] to receive [the title to] his portion [of land, which the Lord had promised would eventually be valuable] there among the people.

¹³And when he was at the Gate of Benjamin, a sentry was [on guard] there, whose name was Irijah son of Shelemiah, the son of Hananiah; and he seized Jeremiah the prophet, saying, You are deserting to the Chaldeans.

¹⁴Then said Jeremiah, It is false! I am not deserting to the Chaldeans. But the sentry would not listen to him. So Irijah took Jeremiah and brought him to the princes.

¹⁵Therefore the princes were enraged with Jeremiah and beat him and put him in prison in the house of Jonathan the scribe—for they had made that the prison.

¹⁶When Jeremiah had come into *ᵇ*the cells in the dungeon and had remained there many days,

¹⁷Zedekiah the king sent and brought him out; and the king asked him secretly in his house, Is there any word from the Lord? And Jeremiah said, There is! And he said also, You shall be delivered into the hand of the king of Babylon.

---

*ᵃ 1* Hebrew *Koniah,* a variant of *Jehoiachin*   *ᵇ 5* Or *Chaldeans;* also in verses 8, 9, 13 and 14   *ᶜ 10* Or *Chaldean;* also in verse 11

*ᵃ* See footnote on Jer. 21:2.   *ᵇ* Literally, "the house of the cistern."

## New International Version

18Then Jeremiah said to King Zedekiah, "What crime have I committed against you or your attendants or this people, that you have put me in prison? 19Where are your prophets who prophesied to you, 'The king of Babylon will not attack you or this land'? 20But now, my lord the king, please listen. Let me bring my petition before you: Do not send me back to the house of Jonathan the secretary, or I will die there."

21King Zedekiah then gave orders for Jeremiah to be placed in the courtyard of the guard and given a loaf of bread from the street of the bakers each day until all the bread in the city was gone. So Jeremiah remained in the courtyard of the guard.

### Jeremiah Thrown Into a Cistern

**38** Shephatiah son of Mattan, Gedaliah son of Pashhur, Jehukal[a] son of Shelemiah, and Pashhur son of Malkijah heard what Jeremiah was telling all the people when he said, 2"This is what the LORD says: 'Whoever stays in this city will die by the sword, famine or plague, but whoever goes over to the Babylonians[b] will live. They will escape with their lives; they will live.' 3And this is what the LORD says: 'This city will certainly be given into the hands of the army of the king of Babylon, who will capture it.'"

4Then the officials said to the king, "This man should be put to death. He is discouraging the soldiers who are left in this city, as well as all the people, by the things he is saying to them. This man is not seeking the good of these people but their ruin."

5"He is in your hands," King Zedekiah answered. "The king can do nothing to oppose you."

6So they took Jeremiah and put him into the cistern of Malkijah, the king's son, which was in the courtyard of the guard. They lowered Jeremiah by ropes into the cistern; it had no water in it, only mud, and Jeremiah sank down into the mud.

7But Ebed-Melek, a Cushite,[c] an official[d] in the royal palace, heard that they had put Jeremiah into the cistern. While the king was sitting in the Benjamin Gate, 8Ebed-Melek went out of the palace and said to him, 9"My lord the king, these men have acted wickedly in all they have done to Jeremiah the prophet. They have thrown him into a cistern, where he will starve to death when there is no longer any bread in the city."

10Then the king commanded Ebed-Melek the Cushite, "Take thirty men from here with you and lift Jeremiah the prophet out of the cistern before he dies."

11So Ebed-Melek took the men with him and went to a room under the treasury in the palace. He took some old rags and worn-out clothes from there and let them down with ropes to Jeremiah in the cistern. 12Ebed-Melek the Cushite said to Jeremiah, "Put these old rags and worn-out clothes under your arms to pad the ropes." Jeremiah did so, 13and they pulled him up with the ropes and lifted him out of the cistern. And Jeremiah remained in the courtyard of the guard.

### Zedekiah Questions Jeremiah Again

14Then King Zedekiah sent for Jeremiah the prophet and had him brought to the third entrance to the temple of the LORD. "I am going to ask you something," the king said to Jeremiah. "Do not hide anything from me."

## Amplified Bible

18Moreover, Jeremiah said to King Zedekiah, In what have I sinned against you or against your servants or against this people, that you have put me in prison?

19Where now are your prophets who prophesied to you, saying, The king of Babylon shall not come against you or against this land?

20Therefore hear now, I pray you, O my lord the king. Let my supplication, I pray you, come before you *and* be acceptable, that you do not cause me to return to the house of Jonathan the scribe, lest I die there.

21Then Zedekiah the king commanded, and they committed Jeremiah to the court of the guard, and a round loaf of bread from the bakers' street was given to him daily until all the bread in the city was gone. So Jeremiah remained [imprisoned] in the court of the guard.

**38** Now Shephatiah son of Mattan, Gedaliah son of Pashhur, Jucal [also called Jehucal] son of Shelemiah, and Pashhur son of Malchiah heard the words that Jeremiah spoke to all the people, saying,

2Thus says the Lord: He who remains in this city shall die by the sword, by famine, and by pestilence, but he who goes out to the Chaldeans shall live; for he shall have his life as his only booty [as a prize of war], and he shall live. [Jer. 21:9.]

3Thus says the Lord: This city shall surely be given into the hand of the army of the king of Babylon, and he shall take it.

4Therefore the princes said to the king, We beseech you, let this man [Jeremiah] be put to death; for [talking] thus he weakens the hands of the soldiers who remain in this city and the hands of all the people by speaking such words to them. For this man is not seeking the welfare of these people, but [to do them] harm.

5Then Zedekiah the king said, Behold, he is in your hands; for the king is in no position to do anything against you.

6So they took Jeremiah and cast him into the dungeon *or* cistern pit [in the charge] of Malchiah the king's son, which was in the court of the guard; and they let Jeremiah down [into the pit] with ropes. And in the dungeon *or* cistern pit there was no water, but only mire, and Jeremiah sank in the mire.

7Now when Ebed-melech the Ethiopian [a Cushite], one of the eunuchs who was in the king's house, heard that they had put Jeremiah in the dungeon *or* cistern pit; and while the king was then sitting in the Gate of Benjamin,

8Ebed-melech went out of the king's house and spoke to the king, saying,

9My lord the king, these men have done evil in all that they have done to Jeremiah the prophet, whom they have cast into the dungeon *or* cistern pit; and he is liable to die of hunger *and* is [as good as] dead in the place where he is, for there is no more bread left in the city.

10Then the king commanded Ebed-melech the Ethiopian, saying, Take from here thirty men with you and raise Jeremiah the prophet out of the dungeon *or* cistern pit before he dies.

11So Ebed-melech took the men with him and went into the house of the king [to a room] under the treasury, and took along from there old rags and worn-out garments and let them down by ropes into the dungeon *or* cistern pit to Jeremiah.

12And Ebed-melech the Ethiopian said to Jeremiah, Put now these old rags and worn-out garments under your armpits under the ropes. And Jeremiah did so.

13So they drew up Jeremiah with the ropes and took him up out of the dungeon *or* cistern pit; and Jeremiah remained in the court of the guard.

14Then Zedekiah the king sent and brought Jeremiah the prophet to him into the third entrance that is in the house of the Lord. And the king said to Jeremiah, I am going to ask you something; hide nothing from me.

---

[a] 1 Hebrew *Jukal*, a variant of *Jehukal*   [b] 2 Or *Chaldeans*; also in verses 18, 19 and 23   [c] 7 Probably from the upper Nile region   [d] 7 Or *a eunuch*

# New International Version

[15]Jeremiah said to Zedekiah, "If I give you an answer, will you not kill me? Even if I did give you counsel, you would not listen to me."

[16]But King Zedekiah swore this oath secretly to Jeremiah: "As surely as the LORD lives, who has given us breath, I will neither kill you nor hand you over to those who want to kill you."

[17]Then Jeremiah said to Zedekiah, "This is what the LORD God Almighty, the God of Israel, says: 'If you surrender to the officers of the king of Babylon, your life will be spared and this city will not be burned down; you and your family will live. [18]But if you will not surrender to the officers of the king of Babylon, this city will be given into the hands of the Babylonians and they will burn it down; you yourself will not escape from them.'"

[19]King Zedekiah said to Jeremiah, "I am afraid of the Jews who have gone over to the Babylonians, for the Babylonians may hand me over to them and they will mistreat me."

[20]"They will not hand you over," Jeremiah replied. "Obey the LORD by doing what I tell you. Then it will go well with you, and your life will be spared. [21]But if you refuse to surrender, this is what the LORD has revealed to me: [22]All the women left in the palace of the king of Judah will be brought out to the officials of the king of Babylon. Those women will say to you:

"'They misled you and overcame you—
  those trusted friends of yours.
Your feet are sunk in the mud;
  your friends have deserted you.'

[23]"All your wives and children will be brought out to the Babylonians. You yourself will not escape from their hands but will be captured by the king of Babylon; and this city will[a] be burned down."

[24]Then Zedekiah said to Jeremiah, "Do not let anyone know about this conversation, or you may die. [25]If the officials hear that I talked with you, and they come to you and say, 'Tell us what you said to the king and what the king said to you; do not hide it from us or we will kill you,' [26]then tell them, 'I was pleading with the king not to send me back to Jonathan's house to die there.'"

[27]All the officials did come to Jeremiah and question him, and he told them everything the king had ordered him to say. So they said no more to him, for no one had heard his conversation with the king.

[28]And Jeremiah remained in the courtyard of the guard until the day Jerusalem was captured.

## The Fall of Jerusalem

**39** This is how Jerusalem was taken: [1]In the ninth year of Zedekiah king of Judah, in the tenth month, Nebuchadnezzar king of Babylon marched against Jerusalem with his whole army and laid siege to it. [2]And on the ninth day of the fourth month of Zedekiah's eleventh year, the city wall was broken through. [3]Then all the officials of the king of Babylon came and took seats in the Middle Gate: Nergal-Sharezer of Samgar, Nebo-Sarsekim a chief officer, Nergal-Sharezer a high official and all the other officials of the king of Babylon. [4]When Zedekiah king of

# Amplified Bible

[15]Then Jeremiah said to Zedekiah, If I tell you, will you not surely put me to death? And even if I did give you counsel, you would not listen to me.

[16]So Zedekiah the king swore secretly to Jeremiah, As the Lord lives, Who made our lives, I will not put you to death or give you into the hands of these men who seek your life.

[17]Then said Jeremiah to Zedekiah, Thus says the Lord God of hosts, the God of Israel: If you will go forth *and* surrender to the princes of the king of Babylon, then you will live and this city will not be burned with fire; and you will live—you and your house.

[18]But if you will not go forth *and* surrender to the princes of the king of Babylon, then this city will be given into the hands of the Chaldeans and they will burn it with fire; and you will not escape out of their hands.

[19]And Zedekiah the king said to Jeremiah, I am afraid of the Jews who have deserted to the Chaldeans, lest the enemy deliver me into their [these former subjects'] hands and they mock me *and* abuse me.

[20]But Jeremiah said, They will not deliver you [to them]. Obey, I beg of you, the voice of the Lord, Who speaks to you through me. Then it will be well with you, and you will live.

[21]But if you refuse to go forth *and* surrender to them, this is the word [the vision] that the Lord has shown me:

[22]Behold, [in it] all the women who are left in the house of the king of Judah will be brought forth to the king of Babylon's princes and will say [to you, King Zedekiah], Your friends have prevailed against your better judgment *and* have deceived you. Now when your feet are sunk in the mire [of trouble], they have turned their backs.

[23]All your wives and your children will be brought out to the Chaldeans; and you [yourself] will not escape out of their hands, but you will be seized by the king of Babylon, and you will cause this city [Jerusalem] to be burned with fire.

[24]Then Zedekiah said to Jeremiah, Let no man know of this conversation and you will not die.

[25]But if the princes hear that I have talked with you, and they come to you and say, Tell us what you said to the king and what he said to you; hide it not from us and we will not put you to death,

[26]Then you shall say to them, I was presenting to the king my humble plea that he would not send me back to Jonathan's house to die there.

[27]Then came all the princes to Jeremiah and asked him [just what King Zedekiah had anticipated they would ask], and he told them all that the king had commanded. So they left off speaking with him, for what the conversation [with the king] had been was not discovered.

[28]So Jeremiah remained in the court of the guard until the day that Jerusalem was taken [by the Chaldeans].

**39** In the ninth year of Zedekiah king of Judah, in the tenth month, [a]Nebuchadrezzar king of Babylon and all his army came against Jerusalem and besieged it. [Jer. 52:4-27.]

[2]And in the eleventh year of Zedekiah, in the fourth month, on the ninth day of the month, they broke into the city.

[3][b]When Jerusalem was taken] all the princes of the king of Babylon came in and sat in the Middle Gate: Nergal-sharezer, Samgar-nebo, Sarsechim [the Rabsaris] a chief of the eunuchs, and Nergal-sharezer [II, the Rabmag] a chief of the magicians, with all the rest of the officials of the king of Babylon.

*a* See footnote on Jer. 21:2. *b* This clause has been supplied from the end of chapter 38, where, according to many authorities, many translations have wrongly placed it.

*a 23 Or and you will cause this city to*

## New International Version

Judah and all the soldiers saw them, they fled; they left the city at night by way of the king's garden, through the gate between the two walls, and headed toward the Arabah.[a] [5]But the Babylonian[b] army pursued them and overtook Zedekiah in the plains of Jericho. They captured him and took him to Nebuchadnezzar king of Babylon at Riblah in the land of Hamath, where he pronounced sentence on him. [6]There at Riblah the king of Babylon slaughtered the sons of Zedekiah before his eyes and also killed all the nobles of Judah. [7]Then he put out Zedekiah's eyes and bound him with bronze shackles to take him to Babylon.

[8]The Babylonians[c] set fire to the royal palace and the houses of the people and broke down the walls of Jerusalem. [9]Nebuzaradan commander of the imperial guard carried into exile to Babylon the people who remained in the city, along with those who had gone over to him, and the rest of the people. [10]But Nebuzaradan the commander of the guard left behind in the land of Judah some of the poor people, who owned nothing; and at that time he gave them vineyards and fields.

[11]Now Nebuchadnezzar king of Babylon had given these orders about Jeremiah through Nebuzaradan commander of the imperial guard: [12]"Take him and look after him; don't harm him but do for him whatever he asks." [13]So Nebuzaradan the commander of the guard, Nebushazban a chief officer, Nergal-Sharezer a high official and all the other officers of the king of Babylon [14]sent and had Jeremiah taken out of the courtyard of the guard. They turned him over to Gedaliah son of Ahikam, the son of Shaphan, to take him back to his home. So he remained among his own people.

[15]While Jeremiah had been confined in the courtyard of the guard, the word of the LORD came to him: [16]"Go and tell Ebed-Melek the Cushite, 'This is what the LORD Almighty, the God of Israel, says: I am about to fulfill my words against this city—words concerning disaster, not prosperity. At that time they will be fulfilled before your eyes. [17]But I will rescue you on that day, declares the LORD; you will not be given into the hands of those you fear. [18]I will save you; you will not fall by the sword but will escape with your life, because you trust in me, declares the LORD.'"

### Jeremiah Freed

**40** The word came to Jeremiah from the LORD after Nebuzaradan commander of the imperial guard had released him at Ramah. He had found Jeremiah bound in chains among all the captives from Jerusalem and Judah who were being carried into exile to Babylon. [2]When the commander of the guard found Jeremiah, he said to him, "The LORD your God decreed this disaster for this place. [3]And now the LORD has brought it about; he has done just as he said he would. All this happened because you people sinned against the LORD and did not obey him. [4]But today I am freeing you from the chains on your wrists. Come with me to Babylon, if you like, and I will look after you;

## Amplified Bible

[4]And when Zedekiah king of Judah and all the men of war saw them, they fled and went forth out of the city at night by way of the king's garden, through the gate between the two walls, and [the king] went out toward the Arabah (the Jordan Valley). [5]But the Chaldean army pursued them and overtook Zedekiah in the plains of Jericho. And when they had taken him, they brought him up to Nebuchadrezzar king of Babylon at Riblah in the [Syrian] land of Hamath, where he pronounced sentence upon him. [6]Then the king of Babylon slew the sons of Zedekiah at Riblah before his eyes; also the king of Babylon slew all the nobles of Judah.

[7]Moreover, he put out Zedekiah's eyes and bound him with shackles to take him to Babylon. [Ezek. 12:13.]

[8]And the Chaldeans burned the king's house and the houses of the people and broke down the walls of Jerusalem.

[9]Then Nebuzaradan the [chief executioner and] captain of the guard carried away captive to Babylon the rest of the people who remained in the city, along with those who deserted to him, and the remainder of the [so-called better class of] people who were left.

[10]But Nebuzaradan the [Babylonian] captain of the guard left in the land of Judah some of the poor of the people who had nothing, giving them vineyards and fields at the same time.

[11]Nebuchadrezzar king of Babylon gave command concerning Jeremiah to Nebuzaradan the captain of the guard, saying,

[12]Take him and look after him well; do him no harm but deal with him as he may ask of you.

[13]So Nebuzaradan the captain of the guard, Nebushasban [the Rabsaris] a chief of the eunuchs, Nergal-sharezer [II, the Rabmag] a chief of the magicians, and all the chief officers of the king of Babylon

[14]Sent and took Jeremiah out of the court of the guard and entrusted him to Gedaliah [a prominent man whose father had once saved the prophet's life] son of Ahikam, the son of Shaphan, that he should take him home [with him to Mizpah]. So Jeremiah was released and dwelt among the people. [Jer. 26:24.]

[15]Now the word of the Lord came to Jeremiah while he was [still] shut up in the court of the guard, saying,

[16]Go and say to Ebed-melech the Ethiopian, Thus says the Lord of hosts, the God of Israel: Behold, I will bring to pass My words against this city for evil and not for good; and they will be accomplished before you on that day.

[17]But I will deliver you [Ebed-melech] on that day, says the Lord, and you will not be given into the hands of the men of whom you are afraid. [Jer. 38:7-13.]

[18]For I will surely deliver you; and you will not fall by the sword, but your life will be [as your only booty and] as a reward of battle to you, because you have put your trust in Me, says the Lord.

**40** The word that came to Jeremiah from the Lord after Nebuzaradan the captain of the guard had let him go from Ramah, when he had taken him bound in chains among all who were carried away captive from Jerusalem and Judah, who were taken as exiles to Babylon.

[2]And the captain of the guard took Jeremiah and said to him, The Lord your God pronounced evil upon this place.

[3]Now the Lord has brought it about and has done as He said: [It is] because you [of Judah] have sinned against the Lord and have not obeyed His voice, therefore this thing has come upon you.

[4]Now, see, I am freeing you today [Jeremiah] from the chains upon your hands. If it seems good to you to come with me to Babylon, come, and I will keep an eye on you and look after you well. But if it seems bad to you to come

## New International Version

but if you do not want to, then don't come. Look, the whole country lies before you; go wherever you please." [5]However, before Jeremiah turned to go,[a] Nebuzaradan added, "Go back to Gedaliah son of Ahikam, the son of Shaphan, whom the king of Babylon has appointed over the towns of Judah, and live with him among the people, or go anywhere else you please."

Then the commander gave him provisions and a present and let him go. [6]So Jeremiah went to Gedaliah son of Ahikam at Mizpah and stayed with him among the people who were left behind in the land.

### Gedaliah Assassinated

[7]When all the army officers and their men who were still in the open country heard that the king of Babylon had appointed Gedaliah son of Ahikam as governor over the land and had put him in charge of the men, women and children who were the poorest in the land and who had not been carried into exile to Babylon, [8]they came to Gedaliah at Mizpah—Ishmael son of Nethaniah, Johanan and Jonathan the sons of Kareah, Seraiah son of Tanhumeth, the sons of Ephai the Netophathite, and Jaazaniah[b] the son of the Maakathite, and their men. [9]Gedaliah son of Ahikam, the son of Shaphan, took an oath to reassure them and their men. "Do not be afraid to serve the Babylonians,[c]" he said. "Settle down in the land and serve the king of Babylon, and it will go well with you. [10]I myself will stay at Mizpah to represent you before the Babylonians who come to us, but you are to harvest the wine, summer fruit and olive oil, and put them in your storage jars, and live in the towns you have taken over."

[11]When all the Jews in Moab, Ammon, Edom and all the other countries heard that the king of Babylon had left a remnant in Judah and had appointed Gedaliah son of Ahikam, the son of Shaphan, as governor over them, [12]they all came back to the land of Judah, to Gedaliah at Mizpah, from all the countries where they had been scattered. And they harvested an abundance of wine and summer fruit.

[13]Johanan son of Kareah and all the army officers still in the open country came to Gedaliah at Mizpah [14]and said to him, "Don't you know that Baalis king of the Ammonites has sent Ishmael son of Nethaniah to take your life?" But Gedaliah son of Ahikam did not believe them.

[15]Then Johanan son of Kareah said privately to Gedaliah in Mizpah, "Let me go and kill Ishmael son of Nethaniah, and no one will know it. Why should he take your life and cause all the Jews who are gathered around you to be scattered and the remnant of Judah to perish?"

[16]But Gedaliah son of Ahikam said to Johanan son of Kareah, "Don't do such a thing! What you are saying about Ishmael is not true."

**41** In the seventh month Ishmael son of Nethaniah, the son of Elishama, who was of royal blood and had been one of the king's officers, came with ten men to Gedaliah son of Ahikam at Mizpah. While they were eating together there, [2]Ishmael son of Nethaniah and the ten men who were with him got up and struck down Gedaliah son of Ahikam, the son of Shaphan, with the sword, killing the one whom the king of Babylon had appointed as governor over the land. [3]Ishmael also killed all the men

## Amplified Bible

with me to Babylon, then do not do it. Behold, all the land is before you; wherever it seems good, right, *and* convenient for you to go, go there.

[5]While [Jeremiah] was hesitating, [the captain of the guard] said, Go back then to Gedaliah son of Ahikam, the son of Shaphan, whom the king of Babylon made governor over the cities of Judah, and dwell with him among the people; or go wherever it seems right for you to go. So the captain of the guard gave him an allowance of food and a present and let him go.

[6]Then Jeremiah went to Gedaliah son of Ahikam at Mizpah and dwelt with him among the people who were left in the land.

[7]Now when all the captains of the forces that were in the open country [of Judah] and their men heard that the king of Babylon had made Gedaliah son of Ahikam governor in the land [of Judah] and had committed to him men, women, and children, those of the poorest of the land who had not been taken into exile to Babylon,

[8]They went to Gedaliah at Mizpah—Ishmael son of Nethaniah, Johanan and Jonathan the sons of Kareah, Seraiah son of Tanhumeth, the sons of Ephai the Netophathite, and Jezaniah the son of the Maacathite, they and their men.

[9]And Gedaliah son of Ahikam, the son of Shaphan, swore to them and their men, saying, Do not be afraid to serve the Chaldeans; dwell in [this] land and serve the king of Babylon, and it shall be well with you.

[10]As for me, I will dwell at Mizpah to stand [for you] before the Chaldeans who come to us [ministering to them and looking after the king's interests]; but as for you, gather the juice [of the grape], summer fruits and oil, and store them in your utensils [chosen for such purposes], and dwell in your cities that you have seized.

[11]Likewise, when all the Jews who were in Moab and among the people of Ammon and in Edom and who were in all the other countries heard that the king of Babylon had left a remnant in Judah and had set over them [as governor] Gedaliah son of Ahikam, the son of Shaphan,

[12]Then all the Jews returned from all the places to which they had been driven and came to the land of Judah, to Gedaliah at Mizpah, and gathered a great abundance of juice [of the grape] and summer fruits.

[13]Moreover, Johanan son of Kareah and all the captains of the forces that were in the open country came to Gedaliah at Mizpah

[14]And said to him, Do you know that Baalis king of the Ammonites has sent Ishmael son of Nethaniah to take your life? But Gedaliah son of Ahikam did not believe them.

[15]Then Johanan son of Kareah spoke to Gedaliah in Mizpah secretly, saying, Let me go, I pray you, and I will slay Ishmael son of Nethaniah, and no man will know it. Why should he slay you and cause all the Jews who are gathered to you to be scattered and the remnant of Judah to perish?

[16]But Gedaliah son of Ahikam said to Johanan son of Kareah, You shall not do this thing, for you speak falsely of Ishmael.

**41** Now in the seventh month [of that year] Ishmael son of Nethaniah, the son of Elishama, of the royal descendants and one of the princes of the king, came [at the instigation of the Ammonites] with ten men to Gedaliah son of Ahikam in Mizpah. As they were eating a meal together there in Mizpah,

[2]Ishmael son of Nethaniah and the ten men who were with him arose and struck down Gedaliah son of Ahikam, the son of Shaphan, with the sword and killed him, the one whom the king of Babylon had made governor over the land. [II Kings 25:25.]

---

[a] 5 Or *Jeremiah answered*   [b] 8 Hebrew *Jezaniah*, a variant of *Jaazaniah*
[c] 9 Or *Chaldeans*; also in verse 10

## New International Version

of Judah who were with Gedaliah at Mizpah, as well as the Babylonian[a] soldiers who were there.

[4]The day after Gedaliah's assassination, before anyone knew about it, [5]eighty men who had shaved off their beards, torn their clothes and cut themselves came from Shechem, Shiloh and Samaria, bringing grain offerings and incense with them to the house of the LORD. [6]Ishmael son of Nethaniah went out from Mizpah to meet them, weeping as he went. When he met them, he said, "Come to Gedaliah son of Ahikam." [7]When they went into the city, Ishmael son of Nethaniah and the men who were with him slaughtered them and threw them into a cistern. [8]But ten of them said to Ishmael, "Don't kill us! We have wheat and barley, olive oil and honey, hidden in a field." So he let them alone and did not kill them with the others. [9]Now the cistern where he threw all the bodies of the men he had killed along with Gedaliah was the one King Asa had made as part of his defense against Baasha king of Israel. Ishmael son of Nethaniah filled it with the dead.

[10]Ishmael made captives of all the rest of the people who were in Mizpah—the king's daughters along with all the others who were left there, over whom Nebuzaradan commander of the imperial guard had appointed Gedaliah son of Ahikam. Ishmael son of Nethaniah took them captive and set out to cross over to the Ammonites.

[11]When Johanan son of Kareah and all the army officers who were with him heard about all the crimes Ishmael son of Nethaniah had committed, [12]they took all their men and went to fight Ishmael son of Nethaniah. They caught up with him near the great pool in Gibeon. [13]When all the people Ishmael had with him saw Johanan son of Kareah and the army officers who were with him, they were glad. [14]All the people Ishmael had taken captive at Mizpah turned and went over to Johanan son of Kareah. [15]But Ishmael son of Nethaniah and eight of his men escaped from Johanan and fled to the Ammonites.

### Flight to Egypt

[16]Then Johanan son of Kareah and all the army officers who were with him led away all the people of Mizpah who had survived, whom Johanan had recovered from Ishmael son of Nethaniah after Ishmael had assassinated Gedaliah son of Ahikam—the soldiers, women, children and court officials he had recovered from Gibeon. [17]And they went on, stopping at Geruth Kimham near Bethlehem on their way to Egypt [18]to escape the Babylonians.[b] They were afraid of them because Ishmael son of Nethaniah had killed Gedaliah son of Ahikam, whom the king of Babylon had appointed as governor over the land.

**42** Then all the army officers, including Johanan son of Kareah and Jezaniah[c] son of Hoshaiah, and all the people from the least to the greatest approached [2]Jeremiah the prophet and said to him, "Please hear our petition and pray to the LORD your God for this entire remnant.

## Amplified Bible

[3]Ishmael [manipulated by the Ammonites] also slew all the Jews who were with Gedaliah at Mizpah, and the Chaldean soldiers who were found there.

[4]And the second day after the slaying of Gedaliah, before anyone knew about it,

[5]There came eighty men from Shechem, from Shiloh, and from Samaria, having their beards shaved off and their clothes torn and having cut themselves, bringing cereal offerings and incense, going up [to Jerusalem] to present them in the house of the Lord.

[6]And Ishmael son of Nethaniah went out from Mizpah to meet them, weeping all the way as he went. As he met them, he said to them, Come to Gedaliah son of Ahikam.

[7]And when they came into the city, Ishmael son of Nethaniah slew them, and cast them into the midst of the [city] cistern pit—he and the men with him.

[8]But ten men were among them who said to Ishmael, Do not kill us! For we have stores hidden in the field—of wheat and barley and oil and honey. So he refrained and did not slay them with their brethren.

[9]Now the cistern pit into which Ishmael had cast all the dead bodies of the men whom he had slain in addition to Gedaliah was the one which Asa the king [of Judah] had once made for fear of Baasha king of Israel [should Baasha lay siege to Mizpah]. Ishmael son of Nethaniah filled it with those who were slain.

[10]Then Ishmael carried away captive all the rest of the people who were in Mizpah—even the king's daughters and all the people who remained in Mizpah, whom Nebuzaradan the captain of the guard had committed to Gedaliah son of Ahikam. Ishmael son of Nethaniah carried them away captive and departed to cross over [the Jordan] to the Ammonites.

[11]But when Johanan son of Kareah and all the captains of the forces that were with him heard of all the evil that Ishmael son of Nethaniah had done,

[12]They took all their men and went to fight with Ishmael son of Nethaniah and found him by the great pool that is in Gibeon.

[13]Now when all the people who were [captives] with Ishmael saw Johanan son of Kareah and all the captains of the forces that were with him, they were glad.

[14]So all the people whom Ishmael had carried away captive from Mizpah turned around and came back, and went to Johanan son of Kareah.

[15]But Ishmael son of Nethaniah escaped from Johanan with eight men and went to the Ammonites.

[16]Then Johanan son of Kareah and all the captains of the forces that were with him took from Mizpah all the remainder of the people whom he had recovered from Ishmael son of Nethaniah after he had slain Gedaliah son of Ahikam: [they were] the soldiers, the women, the children, and the eunuchs whom [Johanan] had brought back from Gibeon.

[17]And they departed and stayed at the lodging place of Chimham, which is near Bethlehem, [intending] to go to Egypt

[18]Because of the Chaldeans; for they were afraid of them because Ishmael son of Nethaniah had slain Gedaliah son of Ahikam, whom the king of Babylon had made governor over the land [and whose death the king could avenge without much discrimination].

**42** Then all the captains of the forces, and Johanan son of Kareah and Jezaniah [Azariah] son of Hoshaiah, and all the people from the least even to the greatest came near

[2]And said to Jeremiah the prophet, We beseech you that you will let our supplication be presented before you and that you will pray to the Lord your God for us, even for all this remnant [of the people of Judah]; for whereas we were

---

*a 3* Or *Chaldean*   *b 18* Or *Chaldeans*   *c 1* Hebrew; Septuagint (see also 43:2) *Azariah*

## New International Version

For as you now see, though we were once many, now only a few are left. ³Pray that the LORD your God will tell us where we should go and what we should do."

⁴"I have heard you," replied Jeremiah the prophet. "I will certainly pray to the LORD your God as you have requested; I will tell you everything the LORD says and will keep nothing back from you."

⁵Then they said to Jeremiah, "May the LORD be a true and faithful witness against us if we do not act in accordance with everything the LORD your God sends you to tell us. ⁶Whether it is favorable or unfavorable, we will obey the LORD our God, to whom we are sending you, so that it will go well with us, for we will obey the LORD our God."

⁷Ten days later the word of the LORD came to Jeremiah. ⁸So he called together Johanan son of Kareah and all the army officers who were with him and all the people from the least to the greatest. ⁹He said to them, "This is what the LORD, the God of Israel, to whom you sent me to present your petition, says: ¹⁰'If you stay in this land, I will build you up and not tear you down; I will plant you and not uproot you, for I have relented concerning the disaster I have inflicted on you. ¹¹Do not be afraid of the king of Babylon, whom you now fear. Do not be afraid of him, declares the LORD, for I am with you and will save you and deliver you from his hands. ¹²I will show you compassion so that he will have compassion on you and restore you to your land.'

¹³"However, if you say, 'We will not stay in this land,' and so disobey the LORD your God, ¹⁴and if you say, 'No, we will go and live in Egypt, where we will not see war or hear the trumpet or be hungry for bread,' ¹⁵then hear the word of the LORD, you remnant of Judah. This is what the LORD Almighty, the God of Israel, says: 'If you are determined to go to Egypt and you do go to settle there, ¹⁶then the sword you fear will overtake you there, and the famine you dread will follow you into Egypt, and there you will die. ¹⁷Indeed, all who are determined to go to Egypt to settle there will die by the sword, famine and plague; not one of them will survive or escape the disaster I will bring on them.' ¹⁸This is what the LORD Almighty, the God of Israel, says: 'As my anger and wrath have been poured out on those who lived in Jerusalem, so will my wrath be poured out on you when you go to Egypt. You will be a curse*ᵃ* and an object of horror, a curse*ᵃ* and an object of reproach; you will never see this place again.'

¹⁹"Remnant of Judah, the LORD has told you, 'Do not go to Egypt.' Be sure of this: I warn you today ²⁰that you made a fatal mistake when you sent me to the LORD your God and said, 'Pray to the LORD our God for us; tell us everything he says and we will do it.' ²¹I have told you today, but you still have not obeyed the LORD your God in all he

## Amplified Bible

once many, there are but a few of us left, as you see with your [own] eyes.

³[Pray] that the Lord your God may show us the way in which we should walk and the thing that we should do.

⁴Then Jeremiah the prophet said to them, I have heard you. Behold, I will pray to the Lord your God according to your words; and it will be that whatever thing the Lord will answer you, I will declare it to you; I will keep nothing back from you.

⁵Then they said to Jeremiah, May the Lord be a true and faithful witness against us if we fail to do according to all the things that the Lord your God sends you to tell us.

⁶Whether it is good or evil, we will obey the voice of the Lord our God, to Whom we are sending you [to inquire], that it may be well with us when we obey the voice of the Lord our God.

⁷And after ten days the word of the Lord came to Jeremiah.

⁸Then he called Johanan son of Kareah and all the captains of the forces that were with him and all the people from the least even to the greatest,

⁹And said to them, Thus says the Lord, the God of Israel, to Whom you sent me to present your supplication before Him:

¹⁰If you will remain in this land, then I will build you up and not pull you down, and I will plant you and not pull you up; for I will relent *and* comfort *and* ease Myself concerning the evil that [in chastisement] I have done to you [and I will substitute mercy and loving-kindness for judgment]. [Jer. 31:4, 28.]

¹¹Be not afraid of the king of Babylon, of whom you are fearful [with the profound and reverent dread inspired by deity]; be not afraid of him, says the Lord, for [he is a mere man, while I am the all-wise, all-powerful, and ever-present God] I [the Lord] am with you to save you and to deliver you from his hand.

¹²And I will grant mercy to you, that he may have mercy on you and permit you to remain in your own land.

¹³But if you say, We will not dwell in this land, and so disobey the voice of the Lord your God,

¹⁴Saying, No, but we will go to the land of Egypt, where we will not see war or hear the sound of the trumpet or be hungry for bread, and we will dwell there,

¹⁵Then hear the word of the Lord, O remnant of Judah. Thus says the Lord of hosts, the God of Israel: If you are fully determined to go to Egypt and you do go to dwell there temporarily,

¹⁶Then the sword which you fear shall overtake you there in the land of Egypt, and the famine of which you are afraid shall follow close after you to Egypt *and* in it, and there you shall die.

¹⁷So will it be with all the men who set their faces to go to Egypt to dwell there temporarily; they will die by the sword, by famine, and by pestilence; none of them will remain or survive the evil that I will bring upon them.

¹⁸For thus says the Lord of hosts, the God of Israel: As My anger and My wrath have been poured forth upon the inhabitants of Jerusalem, so shall My wrath be poured forth upon you when you enter Egypt. You shall be a detested thing, an astonishment *and* horror, a curse, a thing lightly esteemed *and* a taunt *and* a reproach; you shall see this place no more.

¹⁹The Lord has said to you, O remnant of Judah, Do not go to Egypt. Know for a certainty that I [Jeremiah] have warned *and* testified to you this day

²⁰That you have dealt deceitfully against your own lives; for you sent me [Jeremiah] to the Lord your God, saying, Pray for us to the Lord our God; and whatever the Lord our God says, declare it to us and we will do it.

²¹And I have this day declared it to you, but you have not obeyed the voice of the Lord your God in anything that He sent me to tell you.

---

*ᵃ 18* That is, your name will be used in cursing (see 29:22); or, others will see that you are cursed.

## New International Version

sent me to tell you. ²²So now, be sure of this: You will die by the sword, famine and plague in the place where you want to go to settle."

**43** When Jeremiah had finished telling the people all the words of the LORD their God—everything the LORD had sent him to tell them— ²Azariah son of Hoshaiah and Johanan son of Kareah and all the arrogant men said to Jeremiah, "You are lying! The LORD our God has not sent you to say, 'You must not go to Egypt to settle there.' ³But Baruch son of Neriah is inciting you against us to hand us over to the Babylonians,ᵃ so they may kill us or carry us into exile to Babylon."

⁴So Johanan son of Kareah and all the army officers and all the people disobeyed the LORD's command to stay in the land of Judah. ⁵Instead, Johanan son of Kareah and all the army officers led away all the remnant of Judah who had come back to live in the land of Judah from all the nations where they had been scattered. ⁶They also led away all those whom Nebuzaradan commander of the imperial guard had left with Gedaliah son of Ahikam, the son of Shaphan—the men, the women, the children and the king's daughters. And they took Jeremiah the prophet and Baruch son of Neriah along with them. ⁷So they entered Egypt in disobedience to the LORD and went as far as Tahpanhes.

⁸In Tahpanhes the word of the LORD came to Jeremiah: ⁹"While the Jews are watching, take some large stones with you and bury them in clay in the brick pavement at the entrance to Pharaoh's palace in Tahpanhes. ¹⁰Then say to them, 'This is what the LORD Almighty, the God of Israel, says: I will send for my servant Nebuchadnezzar king of Babylon, and I will set his throne over these stones I have buried here; he will spread his royal canopy above them. ¹¹He will come and attack Egypt, bringing death to those destined for death, captivity to those destined for captivity, and the sword to those destined for the sword. ¹²He will set fire to the temples of the gods of Egypt; he will burn their temples and take their gods captive. As a shepherd picks his garment clean of lice, so he will pick Egypt clean and depart. ¹³There in the temple of the sunᵇ in Egypt he will demolish the sacred pillars and will burn down the temples of the gods of Egypt.'"

### Disaster Because of Idolatry

**44** This word came to Jeremiah concerning all the Jews living in Lower Egypt—in Migdol, Tahpanhes and Memphis—and in Upper Egypt: ²"This is what the LORD Almighty, the God of Israel, says: You saw the great disaster I brought on Jerusalem and on all the towns of Judah. Today they lie deserted and in ruins ³because of the evil they have done. They aroused my anger by burning incense to and worshiping other gods that neither they nor you nor your ancestors ever knew. ⁴Again and again I

## Amplified Bible

²²Now therefore know for a certainty that you shall die by the sword, by famine, and by pestilence in the place [Egypt] where you desire to go to dwell temporarily.

**43** And when Jeremiah had finished speaking to all the people all these words of the Lord their God—everything for which the Lord their God had sent him to them—

²Then Azariah son of Hoshaiah and Johanan son of Kareah and all the proud *and* insolent men said to Jeremiah, You are not telling the truth! The Lord our God has not sent you to say, Do not go into Egypt to dwell there temporarily.

³But Baruch son of Neriah is setting you against us to deliver us into the hands of the Chaldeans, so they may put us to death or carry us away captive to Babylon.

⁴So Johanan son of Kareah and all the captains of the forces and all the people did not obey the voice of the Lord to remain in the land of Judah.

⁵But Johanan son of Kareah and all the captains of the forces took all the remnant of Judah who had returned to dwell in the land of Judah from all the nations to which they had been driven—

⁶Even men, women, and children, the king's daughters, and every person whom Nebuzaradan the captain of the guard had left with Gedaliah son of Ahikam, the son of Shaphan; also he took Jeremiah the prophet and Baruch son of Neriah.

⁷So they came into the land of Egypt—for they obeyed not the voice of the Lord. And they came to Tahpanhes.

⁸Then came the word of the Lord to Jeremiah in Tahpanhes, saying,

⁹Take large stones in your hands and hide them in the mortar in the pavement of brick which is at the entrance of Pharaoh's house in Tahpanhes, in the sight of the men of Judah;

¹⁰And say to them, Thus says the Lord of hosts, the God of Israel: Behold, I will send and take ᵃNebuchadrezzar king of Babylon, My servant [because he works for Me], and I [through him] will set his throne upon these stones that I have hidden; and his [glittering, royal] canopy will be stretched over them. [Ezek. 29:19, 20.]

¹¹And he shall come and smite the land of Egypt, giving such as are [destined] for death, to death, and such as are [destined] for captivity, to captivity, and such as are [destined] for the sword, to the sword.

¹²And I [through him] will kindle a fire in the temples of the gods of Egypt; and he will burn [the houses] and carry [the people] away captive. And he will array himself with the land of Egypt, as a shepherd puts on his garment [as he wills and when he chooses]; and he will go away from there in peace.

¹³[Nebuchadrezzar] shall break also the images *and* obelisks of Heliopolis [called On or Beth-shemesh—house of the sun] in the land of Egypt, and the temples of the gods of Egypt shall he burn with fire.

**44** The word that came to Jeremiah concerning all the Jews who were dwelling in the land of Egypt—at Migdol, at Tahpanhes, at Memphis—and in the country of Pathros, saying,

²Thus says the Lord of hosts, the God of Israel: You have seen all the evil that I brought upon Jerusalem and upon all the cities of Judah; and see, this day they are a desolation and no man dwells in them

³Because of the wickedness which they committed, provoking Me to anger in that they went to burn incense to serve other gods that they did not know—neither they, nor you, nor your fathers.

⁴Yet I sent to you all My servants the prophets earnestly

---

ᵃ 3 Or *Chaldeans*   ᵇ 13 Or *in Heliopolis*        ᵃ See footnote on Jer. 21:2.

## New International Version

sent my servants the prophets, who said, 'Do not do this detestable thing that I hate!' ⁵But they did not listen or pay attention; they did not turn from their wickedness or stop burning incense to other gods. ⁶Therefore, my fierce anger was poured out; it raged against the towns of Judah and the streets of Jerusalem and made them the desolate ruins they are today.

⁷"Now this is what the LORD God Almighty, the God of Israel, says: Why bring such great disaster on yourselves by cutting off from Judah the men and women, the children and infants, and so leave yourselves without a remnant? ⁸Why arouse my anger with what your hands have made, burning incense to other gods in Egypt, where you have come to live? You will destroy yourselves and make yourselves a curse*a* and an object of reproach among all the nations on earth. ⁹Have you forgotten the wickedness committed by your ancestors and by the kings and queens of Judah and the wickedness committed by you and your wives in the land of Judah and the streets of Jerusalem? ¹⁰To this day they have not humbled themselves or shown reverence, nor have they followed my law and the decrees I set before you and your ancestors.

¹¹"Therefore this is what the LORD Almighty, the God of Israel, says: I am determined to bring disaster on you and to destroy all Judah. ¹²I will take away the remnant of Judah who were determined to go to Egypt to settle there. They will all perish in Egypt; they will fall by the sword or die from famine. From the least to the greatest, they will die by sword or famine. They will become a curse and an object of horror, a curse and an object of reproach. ¹³I will punish those who live in Egypt with the sword, famine and plague, as I punished Jerusalem. ¹⁴None of the remnant of Judah who have gone to live in Egypt will escape or survive to return to the land of Judah, to which they long to return and live; none will return except a few fugitives."

¹⁵Then all the men who knew that their wives were burning incense to other gods, along with all the women who were present—a large assembly—and all the people living in Lower and Upper Egypt, said to Jeremiah, ¹⁶"We will not listen to the message you have spoken to us in the name of the LORD! ¹⁷We will certainly do everything we said we would: We will burn incense to the Queen of Heaven and will pour out drink offerings to her just as we and our ancestors, our kings and our officials did in the towns of Judah and in the streets of Jerusalem. At that time we had plenty of food and were well off and suffered no harm. ¹⁸But ever since we stopped burning incense to the Queen of Heaven and pouring out drink offerings to her, we have had nothing and have been perishing by sword and famine."

¹⁹The women added, "When we burned incense to the Queen of Heaven and poured out drink offerings to her,

## Amplified Bible

*and* persistently, saying, Oh, do not do this loathsome *and* shamefully vile thing that I hate *and* abhor!

⁵But they did not listen *and* obey or submit *and* consent to turn from their wickedness and burn no incense to other gods.

⁶Therefore My wrath and My anger were poured out and were kindled in the cities of Judah and in the streets of Jerusalem; and they became wasted and desolate, as it is this day.

⁷Therefore now thus says the Lord God of hosts, the God of Israel: Why do you commit this great evil against yourselves that will cut off from you man and woman, infant and weaned child, out of Judah, to leave yourselves with none remaining?

⁸Why do you provoke Me to anger with the works (idols) of your own hands, burning incense to other gods in the land of Egypt, where you [of your own accord] have come to dwell temporarily, that you might be cut off and become a curse and a reproach (an object of reviling and taunts) among all the nations of the earth?

⁹Have you forgotten the wickedness of your fathers, the wickedness of the kings of Judah, the wickedness of their wives [who clung to their foreign gods], your own wickedness, and the wickedness of your wives [who imitated their queens], which they committed in the land of Judah and in the streets of Jerusalem?

¹⁰They are not humbled (contrite, penitent, and bruised for their guilt and iniquities) even to this day, neither have they feared *and* revered [Me] nor walked in My law or My statutes which I set before you and before your fathers. [Jer. 6:15; 26:4-6; 44:23.]

¹¹Therefore thus says the Lord of hosts, the God of Israel: Behold, I will set My face against you for evil—even to cut off all Judah [from the land].

¹²And I will take away the remnant of Judah who have set their faces to come into the land of Egypt to dwell here temporarily [fleeing to Egypt instead of surrendering to the Chaldeans as directed by the Lord through Jeremiah], and they will all be consumed and fall in the land of Egypt; they will be consumed by the sword and by famine. From the least even to the greatest, they shall die by the sword and by famine. And they will be a detestable thing, an astonishment, a curse, and a reproach (an object of horror, reviling, and taunts).

¹³For I will punish all the inhabitants of the land of Egypt as I have punished Jerusalem—by the sword, by famine, and by pestilence—

¹⁴So that none of the remnant of Judah who have come to the land of Egypt to dwell temporarily shall escape or survive or return to the land of Judah, to which they desire *and* lift up their souls to return to dwell there; for none shall return except [a few] fugitives.

¹⁵Then all the men who knew that their wives were burning incense to other gods, and all the women who stood by—a great assembly—even all the people who dwelt in Pathros in the land of Egypt, answered Jeremiah:

¹⁶As for the word that you have spoken to us in the name of the Lord, we will not listen to *or* obey you.

¹⁷But we will certainly perform every word of the vows we have made: to burn incense to the *a*queen of heaven and to pour out drink offerings to her as we have done—we and our fathers, our kings and our princes—in the cities of Judah and in the streets of Jerusalem; for then we had plenty of food and were well off *and* prosperous and saw no evil.

¹⁸But since we stopped burning incense to the queen of heaven and pouring out drink offerings to her, we have lacked everything and have been consumed by the sword and by famine.

¹⁹[And the wives said] When we burned incense to the queen of heaven and poured out drink offerings to her, did

---

*a* 8 That is, your name will be used in cursing (see 29:22); or, others will see that you are cursed; also in verse 12; similarly in verse 22.

*a* See footnote on Jer. 7:18.

## New International Version

did not our husbands know that we were making cakes impressed with her image and pouring out drink offerings to her?"

²⁰Then Jeremiah said to all the people, both men and women, who were answering him, ²¹"Did not the LORD remember and call to mind the incense burned in the towns of Judah and the streets of Jerusalem by you and your ancestors, your kings and your officials and the people of the land? ²²When the LORD could no longer endure your wicked actions and the detestable things you did, your land became a curse and a desolate waste without inhabitants, as it is today. ²³Because you have burned incense and have sinned against the LORD and have not obeyed him or followed his law or his decrees or his stipulations, this disaster has come upon you, as you now see."

²⁴Then Jeremiah said to all the people, including the women, "Hear the word of the LORD, all you people of Judah in Egypt. ²⁵This is what the LORD Almighty, the God of Israel, says: You and your wives have done what you said you would do when you promised, 'We will certainly carry out the vows we made to burn incense and pour out drink offerings to the Queen of Heaven.'

"Go ahead then, do what you promised! Keep your vows! ²⁶But hear the word of the LORD, all you Jews living in Egypt: 'I swear by my great name,' says the LORD, 'that no one from Judah living anywhere in Egypt will ever again invoke my name or swear, "As surely as the Sovereign LORD lives." ²⁷For I am watching over them for harm, not for good; the Jews in Egypt will perish by sword and famine until they are all destroyed. ²⁸Those who escape the sword and return to the land of Judah from Egypt will be very few. Then the whole remnant of Judah who came to live in Egypt will know whose word will stand—mine or theirs.

²⁹"This will be the sign to you that I will punish you in this place,' declares the LORD, 'so that you will know that my threats of harm against you will surely stand.' ³⁰This is what the LORD says: 'I am going to deliver Pharaoh Hophra king of Egypt into the hands of his enemies who want to kill him, just as I gave Zedekiah king of Judah into the hands of Nebuchadnezzar king of Babylon, the enemy who wanted to kill him.'"

### A Message to Baruch

**45** When Baruch son of Neriah wrote on a scroll the words Jeremiah the prophet dictated in the fourth year of Jehoiakim son of Josiah king of Judah, Jeremiah said this to Baruch: ²"This is what the LORD, the God of Israel, says to you, Baruch: ³You said, 'Woe to me! The LORD has added sorrow to my pain; I am worn out with groaning and find no rest.' ⁴But the LORD has told me to say to you, 'This is what the LORD says: I will overthrow what I have built and uproot what I have planted, throughout the earth.

## Amplified Bible

we make cakes [in the shape of a star] to represent *and* honor her and pour out drink offerings to her without [the knowledge and approval of] our husbands?

²⁰Then Jeremiah said to all the people—to the men and to the women and to all the people who had given him that answer—

²¹The incense that you burned in the cities of Judah and in the streets of Jerusalem—you and your fathers, your kings and your princes, and the people of the land—did not the Lord [earnestly] remember [your idolatrous wickedness] and did it not come into His mind?

²²The Lord could no longer endure the evil of your doings and the abominations which you have committed; because of them therefore has your land become a desolation and an [astonishing] waste and a curse, without inhabitants, as it is this day.

²³Because you have burned incense [to idols] and because you have sinned against the Lord and have not obeyed the voice of the Lord or walked in His law and in His statutes and in His testimonies, therefore this evil has fallen upon you, as it is this day.

²⁴Moreover, Jeremiah said to all the people, including all the women, Hear the word of the Lord, all you of Judah who are in the land of Egypt,

²⁵Thus says the Lord of hosts, the God of Israel: You and your wives have both declared with your mouths and fulfilled it with your hands, saying, We will surely perform our vows that we have vowed to burn incense to the queen of heaven and to pour out drink offerings to her. [Surely] then confirm your vows and [surely] perform your vows! [If you will defy all My warnings to you, then, by all means, go ahead!]

²⁶Therefore hear the word of the Lord, all [you people of] Judah who dwell in the land of Egypt: Behold, I have sworn by My great name, says the Lord, that My name shall no more be invoked by the mouth of any man of Judah in all the land of Egypt, saying, As the Lord God lives.

²⁷Behold, I am watching over them for evil and not for good; and all the men of Judah who are in the land of Egypt shall be consumed by the sword and by famine until there is an end of them *and* they are all destroyed.

²⁸Yet a small number who escape the sword shall return out of the land of Egypt to the land of Judah; and all the remnant of Judah who came to the land of Egypt to dwell temporarily shall know whose words shall stand, Mine or theirs.

²⁹And this will be the sign to you, says the Lord, that I will punish you in this place, so that you may know that My words will surely stand against you for evil.

³⁰Thus says the Lord: Behold, I will give Pharaoh Hophra king of Egypt into the hands of his enemies and into the hands of those who seek his life, just as I gave Zedekiah king of Judah into the hand of ᵃNebuchadrezzar king of Babylon, who was his enemy and was seeking his life.

**45** The word that Jeremiah the prophet spoke to Baruch son of Neriah, when he had written these words in a book at the dictation of Jeremiah, in the fourth year of Jehoiakim son of Josiah king of Judah, saying,

²Thus says the Lord, the God of Israel, unto you, O Baruch:

³You said, Woe is me now! For the Lord has added sorrow to my pain; I am weary with my groaning *and* sighing and I find no rest.

⁴Say this to him: The Lord speaks thus: Behold, what I have built I will break down, and that which I have planted I will pluck up—and this means the whole land.

ᵃ See footnote on Jer. 21:2

## New International Version

⁵Should you then seek great things for yourself? Do not seek them. For I will bring disaster on all people, declares the LORD, but wherever you go I will let you escape with your life.'"

### A Message About Egypt

**46** This is the word of the LORD that came to Jeremiah the prophet concerning the nations:

²Concerning Egypt:

This is the message against the army of Pharaoh Necho king of Egypt, which was defeated at Carchemish on the Euphrates River by Nebuchadnezzar king of Babylon in the fourth year of Jehoiakim son of Josiah king of Judah:

³"Prepare your shields, both large and small,
and march out for battle!
⁴Harness the horses,
mount the steeds!
Take your positions
with helmets on!
Polish your spears,
put on your armor!
⁵What do I see?
They are terrified,
they are retreating,
their warriors are defeated.
They flee in haste
without looking back,
and there is terror on every side,"
declares the LORD.
⁶"The swift cannot flee
nor the strong escape.
In the north by the River Euphrates
they stumble and fall.

⁷"Who is this that rises like the Nile,
like rivers of surging waters?
⁸Egypt rises like the Nile,
like rivers of surging waters.
She says, 'I will rise and cover the earth;
I will destroy cities and their people.'
⁹Charge, you horses!
Drive furiously, you charioteers!
March on, you warriors—men of Cush[a] and Put who
carry shields,
men of Lydia who draw the bow.
¹⁰But that day belongs to the Lord, the LORD
Almighty—
a day of vengeance, for vengeance on his foes.
The sword will devour till it is satisfied,
till it has quenched its thirst with blood.
For the Lord, the LORD Almighty, will offer sacrifice
in the land of the north by the River Euphrates.

¹¹"Go up to Gilead and get balm,
Virgin Daughter Egypt.
But you try many medicines in vain;
there is no healing for you.
¹²The nations will hear of your shame;
your cries will fill the earth.
One warrior will stumble over another;
both will fall down together."

¹³This is the message the LORD spoke to Jeremiah the prophet about the coming of Nebuchadnezzar king of Babylon to attack Egypt:

¹⁴"Announce this in Egypt, and proclaim it in Migdol;
proclaim it also in Memphis and Tahpanhes:
'Take your positions and get ready,
for the sword devours those around you.'

---

*a 9 That is, the upper Nile region*

## Amplified Bible

⁵And should you *a* seek great things for yourself? Seek them not; for behold, I will bring evil upon all flesh, says the Lord, but your life I will give to you [as your only booty and] as a [snatched] prize of war wherever you go.

**46** The word of the Lord that came to Jeremiah the prophet concerning *and* against the [Gentile] nations.

²Concerning *and* against Egypt: against the army of Pharaoh Necho king of Egypt, which was by the river Euphrates at Carchemish, which *b* Nebuchadrezzar king of Babylon smote *and* defeated in the fourth year of Jehoiakim son of Josiah king of Judah: [Isa. 19-20; Ezek. 29-32; Zech. 14:18, 19.]
³Put in order the buckler and shield, and advance for battle!
⁴Harness the horses, and mount, you horsemen! Stand forth with your helmets! Polish the spears, put on the coats of mail!
⁵Why have I seen it? They are dismayed and have turned backward, and their mighty warriors are beaten down. They flee in haste and look not back; terror is on every side! says the Lord. [Ps. 31:13; Jer. 6:25; 20:3, 10; 49:29.]
⁶Let not the swift flee nor the mighty man escape; in the north by the river Euphrates they stumble and fall.
⁷Who is this that rises up like the Nile [River], like the branches [of the Nile in the delta of Egypt] whose waters surge *and* toss?
⁸Egypt rises like the Nile, like the rivers whose waters surge *and* toss. She says, I will rise, I will cover the earth; I will destroy cities and their inhabitants.
⁹Go up, you horses, and drive furiously, you chariots! Let the warriors go forth—men of Ethiopia and Put who handle the shield, men of Lud who are skilled in handling and stringing the bow.
¹⁰But that day is a day of the Lord, the Lord of hosts—a day of vengeance, that He may avenge Himself on His adversaries. And the sword shall devour, and it shall be satiated and shall drink its fill of their blood; for the Lord, the Lord of hosts has a sacrifice [like that of a great sin offering] in the north country by the river Euphrates.
¹¹Go up into Gilead and take [healing] balm, O Virgin Daughter of Egypt! In vain do you use many medicines; for you there is no healing *or* remedy.
¹²The nations have heard of your disgrace *and* shame, and your cry has filled the earth. For warrior has stumbled against *and* thrown down warrior, and they have fallen both of them together.
¹³The word that the Lord spoke to Jeremiah the prophet concerning the coming of *b* Nebuchadrezzar king of Babylon and his smiting of the land of Egypt:
¹⁴Declare in Egypt and proclaim in Migdol; and publish in Memphis and in Tahpanhes; say, Stand forth and get yourself ready, for the sword devours round about you.

---

*a Baruch plays a role familiar in normal human life today—that of having to take second place, having to play second fiddle. He was of high birth; his grandfather Maaseiah was governor of Jerusalem in the days of King Josiah (II Chron. 34:8). Considering all that Baruch was doing to make Jeremiah's prophecies permanent by recording them for posterity, it is not surprising that he seems to have expected to share the prophet's rewards. "To play a prominent part in the impending crisis, to be the hero of a national revival, to gain the favor of the conqueror he announced," seems to have been his high ideal, his glorious dream. When its realization was denied him, "he sank in despair at the seeming fruitlessness of his efforts" (Sir William Smith, A Dictionary of the Bible). Yet Baruch is an excellent illustration of how little the gift of prophecy depended on men, and how completely it remained for God to grant or deny prominence and recognition to His perhaps equally deserving servants. But each man's eternal rewards are proportioned according to his faithfulness, and not according to his earthly recognition or the lack of it (Matt. 25:14-30). b See footnote on Jer. 21:2.*

## New International Version

15 Why will your warriors be laid low?
They cannot stand, for the LORD will push them
down.
16 They will stumble repeatedly;
they will fall over each other.
They will say, 'Get up, let us go back
to our own people and our native lands,
away from the sword of the oppressor.'
17 There they will exclaim,
'Pharaoh king of Egypt is only a loud noise;
he has missed his opportunity.'

18 "As surely as I live," declares the King,
whose name is the LORD Almighty,
"one will come who is like Tabor among the
mountains,
like Carmel by the sea.
19 Pack your belongings for exile,
you who live in Egypt,
for Memphis will be laid waste
and lie in ruins without inhabitant.

20 "Egypt is a beautiful heifer,
but a gadfly is coming
against her from the north.
21 The mercenaries in her ranks
are like fattened calves.
They too will turn and flee together,
they will not stand their ground,
for the day of disaster is coming upon them,
the time for them to be punished.
22 Egypt will hiss like a fleeing serpent
as the enemy advances in force;
they will come against her with axes,
like men who cut down trees.
23 They will chop down her forest,"
declares the LORD,
"dense though it be.
They are more numerous than locusts,
they cannot be counted.
24 Daughter Egypt will be put to shame,
given into the hands of the people of the north."

25 The LORD Almighty, the God of Israel, says: "I am
about to bring punishment on Amon god of Thebes, on
Pharaoh, on Egypt and her gods and her kings, and on
those who rely on Pharaoh. 26 I will give them into the
hands of those who want to kill them—Nebuchadnezzar
king of Babylon and his officers. Later, however, Egypt
will be inhabited as in times past," declares the LORD.

27 "Do not be afraid, Jacob my servant;
do not be dismayed, Israel.
I will surely save you out of a distant place,
your descendants from the land of their exile.
Jacob will again have peace and security,
and no one will make him afraid.
28 Do not be afraid, Jacob my servant,
for I am with you," declares the LORD.
"Though I completely destroy all the nations
among which I scatter you,
I will not completely destroy you.
I will discipline you but only in due measure;
I will not let you go entirely unpunished."

## Amplified Bible

15 Why is your strong one [the sacred bull-god Apis]
swept and dragged away? He stood not, because the Lord
drove him and thrust him down.
16 [The Lord] made many to stumble and fall; yes, they
fell one upon another. And they said, Arise, and let us go
back to our own people and to the land of our birth, away
from the sword of the oppressor.
17 They cried there, Pharaoh king of Egypt is destroyed
and is only a noise; he has let the appointed time [in which
God had him on probation] pass by!
18 As I live, says the King, Whose name is the Lord of
hosts, surely like Tabor among the mountains and like
Carmel by the sea, so shall he [the king of Babylon, standing out above other rulers] come.
19 O you daughter who dwells in Egypt and you who
dwell with her, furnish yourselves [with all you will need]
to go into exile, for Memphis will be waste, desolate, and
burned up, without inhabitant.
20 Egypt is a very fair heifer [like Apis the bull-god, to
which the country is, so to speak, espoused], but destruction [a gadfly] is coming—out of the north it is coming
[against her]!
21 Also her hired troops in the midst of her are like fatted calves [in the stall], for they also are turned back and
are fleeing together; they do not stand, because the day
of their calamity is coming upon them, the time of their
visitation (their inspection and punishment).
22 The sound [of Egypt fleeing from the enemy] is like
the rustling of an escaping serpent, for her foes advance
with a mighty army and come against her with axes, like
those who fell trees and cut wood.
23 They shall cut down her forest, says the Lord, though
it is impenetrable, because they [the invading army] are
more numerous than locusts and cannot be counted.
24 The Daughter of Egypt shall be disgraced; she shall
be delivered into the hands of the people of the north [the
Chaldeans].
25 The Lord of hosts, the God of Israel, says: Behold, I
will visit punishment upon Amon [the chief god of the sacred city, the capital of Upper Egypt] of No or Thebes, and
upon Pharaoh and Egypt, with her gods and her kings—
even Pharaoh and all those [Jews and others] who put
their trust in [Pharaoh as a support against Babylon].
26 And I will deliver them into the hands of those who
seek their lives, and into the hand of Nebuchadrezzar king
of Babylon, and into the hands of his servants. Afterward
[Egypt] will be *a* inhabited as in the days of old, says the
Lord.
27 But fear not, O My servant Jacob, and be not dismayed, O Israel. For behold, I will save you from afar, and
your offspring from the land of their exile; and Jacob will
return and be quiet and at ease, and none will make him
afraid.
28 Fear not, O Jacob My servant, says the Lord, for I am
with you. For I will make a full and complete end of all the
nations to which I have driven you; yet I will not make a
full end of you. But I will chasten and correct you in just
measure, and I will not hold you guiltless by any means or
leave you unpunished.

*a* It is startling to realize that God, through His prophets, accurately
foretold in detail the future of every one of the prominent nations of Old
Testament times, often specifying the fate of particular rulers and chief
cities as well. It will greatly increase the reader's interest if he or she will
look up the literal fulfillment of these prophecies as he or she comes to
them, as indicated in the textual references or the footnotes. Notice how
definite and specific the prophecies are; what was said of Babylon, for
instance, would not have been applicable to Egypt or Ammon or Sidon.
And history proves their fulfillment. If there was no other evidence that
there is a God and that the Bible is inspired by Him, the fulfillment of
prophecy in history should be sufficient proof for any person capable
of thinking it through. Nor are the prophecies against some nations
recorded by only one writer, but a number of them, widely separated
by time and circumstances, set down in writing. Let us approach
these records with awe and awakened vision; we are on holy ground.

## New International Version

### A Message About the Philistines

**47** This is the word of the LORD that came to Jeremiah the prophet concerning the Philistines before Pharaoh attacked Gaza:

2 This is what the LORD says:

"See how the waters are rising in the north;
they will become an overflowing torrent.
They will overflow the land and everything in it,
the towns and those who live in them.
The people will cry out;
all who dwell in the land will wail
3 at the sound of the hooves of galloping steeds,
at the noise of enemy chariots
and the rumble of their wheels.
Parents will not turn to help their children;
their hands will hang limp.
4 For the day has come
to destroy all the Philistines
and to remove all survivors
who could help Tyre and Sidon.
The LORD is about to destroy the Philistines,
the remnant from the coasts of Caphtor.a
5 Gaza will shave her head in mourning;
Ashkelon will be silenced.
You remnant on the plain,
how long will you cut yourselves?

6 "'Alas, sword of the LORD,
how long till you rest?
Return to your sheath;
cease and be still.'
7 But how can it rest
when the LORD has commanded it,
when he has ordered it
to attack Ashkelon and the coast?"

### A Message About Moab

**48** Concerning Moab:

This is what the LORD Almighty, the God of Israel, says:

"Woe to Nebo, for it will be ruined.
Kiriathaim will be disgraced and captured;
the strongholdb will be disgraced and shattered.
2 Moab will be praised no more;
in Heshbonc people will plot her downfall:
'Come, let us put an end to that nation.'
You, the people of Madmen,d will also be silenced;
the sword will pursue you.
3 Cries of anguish arise from Horonaim,
cries of great havoc and destruction.
4 Moab will be broken;
her little ones will cry out.e
5 They go up the hill to Luhith,
weeping bitterly as they go;
on the road down to Horonaim
anguished cries over the destruction are heard.
6 Flee! Run for your lives;
become like a bushf in the desert.
7 Since you trust in your deeds and riches,
you too will be taken captive,
and Chemosh will go into exile,
together with his priests and officials.
8 The destroyer will come against every town,
and not a town will escape.
The valley will be ruined
and the plateau destroyed,
because the LORD has spoken.

## Amplified Bible

**47** The word of the Lord that came to Jeremiah the prophet concerning the Philistines before Pharaoh smote [the Philistine city] Gaza. [Isa. 14:29-31; Ezek. 25:15-17; Amos 1:6-8; Zeph. 2:4-7; Zech. 9:5-7.]

2 Thus says the Lord: Behold, waters are rising out of the north and shall become an overflowing stream and shall overflow the land and all that is in it, the city and those who dwell in it. Then the men shall cry, and all the inhabitants of the land [of Philistia] shall wail.

3 At the noise of the stamping of the hoofs of [the Chaldean king's] war-horses, at the rattling of his chariots, and at the rumbling of his wheels, the fathers do not look back to their children, so feeble are their hands [with terror].

4 Because of the day that is coming to destroy all the Philistines and to cut off from Tyre and Sidon every helper who remains. For the Lord is destroying the Philistines, the remnant [still surviving] of the isle or coastland of Caphtor [where the Philistines originated]. [Amos 9:7.]

5 Baldness [as a token of mourning] will come upon Gaza; Ashkelon will be cut off and be dumb. O remnant of their valley and of the giants, how long will you gash yourselves [as a token of mourning]?

6 O you sword of the Lord, how long will it be before you are quiet? Put yourself into your scabbard; rest and be still.

7 How can it [the sword of the Lord] be quiet when the Lord has given it an assignment to discharge? Against Ashkelon and against the [whole Philistine] seashore He has appointed it.

**48** Concerning Moab: Thus says the Lord of hosts, the God of Israel: Woe to [the city of] Nebo, for it is laid waste! Kiriathaim is put to shame and taken; Misgab [the high fortress] is put to shame, broken down, and crushed. [Isa. 15-16; 25:10-12; Ezek. 25:8-11; Amos 2:1-3; Zeph. 2:8-11.]

2 The glory of Moab is no more; in Heshbon [a border town between Reuben and Gad, east of the Jordan River] they planned evil against her, saying, Come, let us cut her off from being a nation. You also, O [town of] Madmen, shall be brought to silence; the sword shall pursue you.

3 The sound of a cry from Horonaim, [a cry of] desolation and great destruction!

4 Moab is destroyed; her little ones have caused a cry to be heard [as far as] Zoar.

5 For the ascent of Luhith will be climbed [by successive bands of fugitives] with continual weeping; for on the descent of Horonaim they have heard the distress of the cry of destruction.

6 Flee! Save your lives! But they shall be like a destitute and forsaken person in the wilderness.

7 For because you have trusted in your works [your bungling idol images] and in your treasures [instead of in God], you shall also be taken. And Chemosh [your god] shall go into captivity, his priests and his princes together.

8 And the destroyer shall come upon every city; no city shall escape. The [Jordan] valley also shall perish, and the plain shall be devastated, as the Lord has said.

---

a 4 That is, Crete   b 1 Or captured; / Misgab   c 2 The Hebrew for Heshbon sounds like the Hebrew for plot.   d 2 The name of the Moabite town Madmen sounds like the Hebrew for be silenced.   e 4 Hebrew; Septuagint / proclaim it to Zoar   f 6 Or like Aroer

## New International Version

⁹Put salt on Moab,
for she will be laid waste*a*;
her towns will become desolate,
with no one to live in them.

¹⁰"A curse on anyone who is lax in doing the Lᴏʀᴅ's
work!
A curse on anyone who keeps their sword from
bloodshed!

¹¹"Moab has been at rest from youth,
like wine left on its dregs,
not poured from one jar to another—
she has not gone into exile.
So she tastes as she did,
and her aroma is unchanged.

¹²But days are coming,"
declares the Lᴏʀᴅ,
"when I will send men who pour from pitchers,
and they will pour her out;
they will empty her pitchers
and smash her jars.

¹³Then Moab will be ashamed of Chemosh,
as Israel was ashamed
when they trusted in Bethel.

¹⁴"How can you say, 'We are warriors,
men valiant in battle'?

¹⁵Moab will be destroyed and her towns invaded;
her finest young men will go down in the
slaughter,"
declares the King, whose name is the Lᴏʀᴅ
Almighty.

¹⁶"The fall of Moab is at hand;
her calamity will come quickly.

¹⁷Mourn for her, all who live around her,
all who know her fame;
say, 'How broken is the mighty scepter,
how broken the glorious staff!'

¹⁸"Come down from your glory
and sit on the parched ground,
you inhabitants of Daughter Dibon,
for the one who destroys Moab
will come up against you
and ruin your fortified cities.

¹⁹Stand by the road and watch,
you who live in Aroer.
Ask the man fleeing and the woman escaping,
ask them, 'What has happened?'

²⁰Moab is disgraced, for she is shattered.
Wail and cry out!
Announce by the Arnon
that Moab is destroyed.

²¹Judgment has come to the plateau—
to Holon, Jahzah and Mephaath,

²² to Dibon, Nebo and Beth Diblathaim,

²³ to Kiriathaim, Beth Gamul and Beth Meon,

²⁴ to Kerioth and Bozrah—
to all the towns of Moab, far and near.

²⁵Moab's horn*b* is cut off;
her arm is broken,"
declares the Lᴏʀᴅ.

²⁶"Make her drunk,
for she has defied the Lᴏʀᴅ.
Let Moab wallow in her vomit;
let her be an object of ridicule.

²⁷Was not Israel the object of your ridicule?
Was she caught among thieves,
that you shake your head in scorn
whenever you speak of her?

*a 9* Or *Give wings to Moab, / for she will fly away*     *b 25 Horn* here
symbolizes strength.

## Amplified Bible

⁹Give wings to Moab, for [by that means only] she will
flee and get away; her cities will be desolate, without any
to dwell in them.

¹⁰Cursed be he who does the work of the Lord negli-
gently [with slackness, deceitfully]; and cursed be he who
keeps back his sword from blood [in executing judgment
pronounced by the Lord].

¹¹Moab has been at ease from his youth, and he has
settled on his lees [like wine] and has not been drawn off
from one vessel to another, neither has he gone into exile.
Therefore his taste remains in him, and his scent has not
changed.

¹²Therefore behold, the days are coming, says the Lord,
when I shall send to [Moab] tilters who shall tilt him up
and shall empty his vessels and break his bottles (earthenware) in pieces.

¹³And Moab shall be ashamed of Chemosh [his god],
as the house of Israel was ashamed of Bethel, their confidence. [I Kings 12:28, 29.]

¹⁴How can you say, We are heroes and mighty men in
the war?

¹⁵Moab has been made desolate, and his cities have
gone up [in smoke and flame]; and his chosen young men
have gone down to the slaughter, says the King, Whose
name is the Lord of hosts.

¹⁶The destruction of Moab is coming near, and his calamity hastens swiftly.

¹⁷Bemoan him, all you [nations] who are around him,
and all you [nations more remote] who know his name;
say, How broken is the mighty scepter [of national power]
and the splendid rod [of glory]!

¹⁸Come down from your glory, you inhabitant of the
Daughter of *a*Dibon, and sit on the ground among the
thirsty! For the destroyer of Moab is advancing against
you; he will destroy your strongholds.

¹⁹O inhabitant of Aroer, stand by the way and watch!
Ask him who flees and her who escapes, What has happened?

²⁰Moab is put to shame, for she is broken down. Wail
and cry out! Tell by [the banks of] the Arnon that Moab is
laid waste (destroyed).

²¹Judgment has come upon the land of the plain—upon
Holon and Jahzah and Mephaath,

²²And upon Dibon and Nebo and Beth-diblathaim,

²³And upon Kiriathaim and Beth-gamul and Beth-
meon,

²⁴And upon Kerioth and Bozrah—and all the cities of
the land of Moab, far and near.

²⁵The horn (strength) of Moab is cut off, and his arm [of
authority] is shattered, says the Lord.

²⁶Make him drunk, for he has magnified himself
against the Lord [by resisting Reuben's occupation of the
land the Lord had assigned him]. Moab also shall splash
in his vomit, and he too shall be held in derision. [Num.
22:1-7.]

²⁷For was not Israel [an object of] derision to you? Was
he found among thieves—since whenever you speak of
him you wag your head [in scorn]?

*a* Dibon, known today as Dhiban, stands on two hills. The "Moabite
Stone," which contains a record of Moabite history, was found among the
ruins of Dibon. The Aroer mentioned in this chapter (Jer. 48:19) stood
on the north side of the river Arnon (Jer. 48:20), just south of Dibon.
Mesha records on the "Moabite Stone" that he "built [restored] the city
[Aroer] and made the road over the Arnon" (*The Cambridge Bible*).

## New International Version

28 Abandon your towns and dwell among the rocks,
    you who live in Moab.
Be like a dove that makes its nest
    at the mouth of a cave.

29 "We have heard of Moab's pride—
    how great is her arrogance!—
of her insolence, her pride, her conceit
    and the haughtiness of her heart.
30 I know her insolence but it is futile,"
                                        declares the LORD,
    "and her boasts accomplish nothing.
31 Therefore I wail over Moab,
    for all Moab I cry out,
    I moan for the people of Kir Hareseth.
32 I weep for you, as Jazer weeps,
    you vines of Sibmah.
Your branches spread as far as the sea*a*;
    they reached as far as*b* Jazer.
The destroyer has fallen
    on your ripened fruit and grapes.
33 Joy and gladness are gone
    from the orchards and fields of Moab.
I have stopped the flow of wine from the presses;
    no one treads them with shouts of joy.
Although there are shouts,
    they are not shouts of joy.

34 "The sound of their cry rises
    from Heshbon to Elealeh and Jahaz,
from Zoar as far as Horonaim and Eglath Shelishiyah,
    for even the waters of Nimrim are dried up.
35 In Moab I will put an end
    to those who make offerings on the high places
    and burn incense to their gods,"
                                        declares the LORD.
36 "So my heart laments for Moab like the music of a pipe;
    it laments like a pipe for the people of Kir Hareseth.
    The wealth they acquired is gone.
37 Every head is shaved
    and every beard cut off;
every hand is slashed
    and every waist is covered with sackcloth.
38 On all the roofs in Moab
    and in the public squares
there is nothing but mourning,
    for I have broken Moab
    like a jar that no one wants,"
                                        declares the LORD.
39 "How shattered she is! How they wail!
    How Moab turns her back in shame!
Moab has become an object of ridicule,
    an object of horror to all those around her."

40 This is what the LORD says:

"Look! An eagle is swooping down,
    spreading its wings over Moab.
41 Kerioth*c* will be captured
    and the strongholds taken.
In that day the hearts of Moab's warriors
    will be like the heart of a woman in labor.
42 Moab will be destroyed as a nation
    because she defied the LORD.
43 Terror and pit and snare await you,
    you people of Moab,"
                                        declares the LORD.
44 "Whoever flees from the terror
    will fall into a pit,
whoever climbs out of the pit
    will be caught in a snare;

*a 32* Probably the Dead Sea   *b 32* Two Hebrew manuscripts and
Septuagint; most Hebrew manuscripts *as far as the Sea of*   *c 41* Or *The
cities*

## Amplified Bible

28 O you inhabitants of Moab, leave the cities and dwell
among the rocks, and be like the dove that makes her nest
in the walls of the yawning ravine.
29 We have heard of the [giddy] pride of Moab, the extremely proud one—his loftiness, his arrogance, his conceit, and the haughtiness of his heart.
30 I know his insolent wrath, says the Lord, and the nothingness of his boastings *and* his deeds; they are false *and*
have accomplished nothing.
31 Therefore I will wail over Moab, and I will cry out
over the whole of Moab. Over the men of Kir-heres (Kir-
hareseth) there will be sighing *and* mourning. [Isa. 15:1;
16:7, 11.]
32 O vines of Sibmah, I weep for you more than the weeping of Jazer [over its ruins and wasted vineyards]. Your
tendrils [of influence] have gone over the sea, reaching
even to Jazer. The destroyer has fallen upon your summer
fruit harvest and your [season's] crop of grapes.
33 Joy and gladness are taken away from the fruitful orchards *and* fields and from the land of Moab. And I have
made the juice [of the grape] to fail from what is pressed
out in the vats; no one treads [the grapes] with shouting.
Their shouting is no shouting [of joy, but is a battle cry].
34 From the cry of Heshbon even to Elealeh even to Jahaz have they uttered their voice, from Zoar even to Horonaim and Eglath-shelishiyah [like a three-year-old heifer],
for even the waters of Nimrim have become desolations.
35 Moreover, I will cause to cease in Moab, says the
Lord, the one who ascends *and* offers in the high place and
the one who burns incense to his gods.
36 Therefore My heart moans *and* sighs for Moab like
flutes, and My heart moans *and* sighs like flutes for the
men of Kir-heres (Kir-hareseth); therefore [the remnant
of] the abundant riches they gained has perished.
37 For every head is shaven bald and every beard cut off:
upon all the hands are cuts (slashes) and upon the loins is
sackcloth [all to express mourning]. [Isa. 15:2, 3.]
38 On all the housetops of Moab and in its streets there
is lamentation everywhere, for I have broken Moab like a
vessel in which there is no pleasure, says the Lord.
39 How it is broken down! How they wail! How Moab has
turned his back in shame! So Moab has become [an object
of] a derision and a [horrifying] terror to all who are round
about him.
40 For thus says the Lord: Behold, he [Babylon] shall fly
swiftly like an eagle and shall spread out his wings against
Moab. [Ezek. 17:3.]
41 Kerioth [and the cities] shall be taken and the strongholds seized; and the hearts of the mighty warriors of
Moab in that day shall be as the heart of a woman in her
pangs [in childbirth].
42 And Moab shall be *a*destroyed from being a nation,
because he has magnified himself against the Lord.
43 Terror and pit and snare are before you, O inhabitant
of Moab, says the Lord. [Isa. 24:7.]
44 He who flees from the terror will fall into the pit, and
he who gets up out of the pit will be taken *and* caught in

*a* Nebuchadnezzar (605-562 B.C.) subjugated the Moabites, but they
continued to exist as a race into the first century A.D. (though the
national existence of both Moab and Ammon seems to have ended long
before the time of Christ). This in itself is a remarkable fulfillment of
prophecy; but the fact that Moab's fortunes are to be restored "in the
latter days" (Jer. 48:47), and have proceeded toward that end before our
very eyes, is even more startling. Yet Moab is only one of the numerous
nations whose fate was accurately written down in advance by the
ancient prophets of God.

## New International Version

for I will bring on Moab
the year of her punishment,"
declares the LORD.

45 "In the shadow of Heshbon
the fugitives stand helpless,
for a fire has gone out from Heshbon,
a blaze from the midst of Sihon;
it burns the foreheads of Moab,
the skulls of the noisy boasters.
46 Woe to you, Moab!
The people of Chemosh are destroyed;
your sons are taken into exile
and your daughters into captivity.

47 "Yet I will restore the fortunes of Moab
in days to come,"
declares the LORD.

Here ends the judgment on Moab.

### A Message About Ammon

**49** Concerning the Ammonites:

This is what the LORD says:

"Has Israel no sons?
Has Israel no heir?
Why then has Molek[a] taken possession of Gad?
Why do his people live in its towns?
2 But the days are coming,"
declares the LORD,
"when I will sound the battle cry
against Rabbah of the Ammonites;
it will become a mound of ruins,
and its surrounding villages will be set on fire.
Then Israel will drive out
those who drove her out,"
says the LORD.

3 "Wail, Heshbon, for Ai is destroyed!
Cry out, you inhabitants of Rabbah!
Put on sackcloth and mourn;
rush here and there inside the walls,
for Molek will go into exile,
together with his priests and officials.
4 Why do you boast of your valleys,
boast of your valleys so fruitful?
Unfaithful Daughter Ammon,
you trust in your riches and say,
'Who will attack me?'
5 I will bring terror on you
from all those around you,"
declares the Lord, the LORD Almighty.
"Every one of you will be driven away,
and no one will gather the fugitives.

6 "Yet afterward, I will restore the fortunes of the
Ammonites,"
declares the LORD.

### A Message About Edom

7 Concerning Edom:

This is what the LORD Almighty says:

"Is there no longer wisdom in Teman?
Has counsel perished from the prudent?
Has their wisdom decayed?

---

a 1 Or their king; also in verse 3

## Amplified Bible

the trap or snare; for I will bring upon it, even upon Moab,
the year of their visitation (their inspection and infliction
of punishment), says the Lord.

45 In the shadow of Heshbon the fugitives stand powerless (stopped in their tracks, helpless and without
strength), for a fire has gone forth from Heshbon, a flame
from the midst of Sihon; it has destroyed the corner of
Moab and the crowns of the heads of the ones in tumult
[the proud Moabites].

46 Woe to you, O Moab! The people of [the god] Chemosh *are* undone; for your sons are taken away captive and
your daughters into captivity.

47 Yet will I reverse the captivity *and* [a]restore the fortunes of Moab in the latter days, says the Lord. Thus far is
the judgment on Moab.

**49** Concerning *and* against the Ammonites: Thus
says the Lord: Has Israel no sons [to return after
their captivity and claim the territory of Gad east of the
Jordan which the Ammonites have taken over]? Has [Is-
rael's Gad] no heir? Why then has Milcom [the god the
Ammonites call their king] dispossessed *and* inherited
Gad, and [why do] his people dwell in Gad's cities?

2 Therefore behold, the days are coming, says the Lord,
when I will cause an alarm of war to be heard against Rabbah of the Ammonites; and it [the high ground on which
it stands] will become a desolate heap, and its daughter
[villages] will be burned with fire. Then will Israel dispossess those who dispossessed him, says the Lord. [Ezek.
21:28-32; 25:1-7, 11; Amos 1:13-15; Zeph. 2:8-11.]

3 Wail, O Heshbon [in Moab, just south of Ammon], for
Ai [in Ammon] is laid waste! Cry out, you daughter [vil-
lages] of Rabbah! Gird yourselves with sackcloth, lament,
and run to and fro inside the [sheepfold] enclosures; for
Milcom [the god-king] shall go into exile, together with
his priests and his princes.

4 Why do you boast of your valleys? Your valley flows
away, O [Ammon] rebellious *and* faithless daughter, who
trusted in her treasures, who said, Who can come against
me?

5 Behold, I will bring terror upon you, says the Lord, the
Lord of hosts, from all who are round about you; and you
will be driven out, each man fleeing straight before him
[without thought of his neighbor], and there will be no one
to gather together the fugitives.

6 And [b]afterward I will reverse the captivity of the children of Ammon *and* restore their fortunes, says the Lord.

7 Concerning *and* against Edom: Thus says the Lord
of hosts: Is there no longer wisdom in Teman [a district
in Edom]? Has counsel vanished from the intelligent *and*
prudent? Is their wisdom all poured out *and* used up? [Isa.
34; 63:1-6; Ezek. 25:12-14; 35; Amos 1:11, 12; Obad. 1-16;
Mal. 1:2-5.]

---

a Nebuchadnezzar (605-562 B.C.) subjugated the Moabites, but they
continued to exist as a race into the first century A.D. (though the
national existence of both Moab and Ammon seems to have ended long
before the time of Christ). This in itself is a remarkable fulfillment of
prophecy; but the fact that Moab's fortunes are to be restored "in the
latter days" (Jer. 48:47), and have proceeded toward that end before
our very eyes, is even more startling. Yet Moab is only one of the
numerous nations whose fate was accurately written down in advance
by the ancient prophets of God.   b As complete and continuous as the
desolation of Moab and Ammon was for so many long centuries, yet
God is keeping His word for their restoration "in the latter days" (Jer.
48:47) in a remarkable manner. For instance, Amman, the capital of the
Hashemite Kingdom of Jordan (formerly called Transjordania, and in
Bible times the ancient Rabbah of Ammon), was a mere village in 1900,
but by 1960 it was a city of 200,000 inhabitants. One can only stand in
awe and reverent amazement at the precision with which the prophecies
of the Word of God are being carried out in the present day and age.

## New International Version

⁸Turn and flee, hide in deep caves,
  you who live in Dedan,
for I will bring disaster on Esau
  at the time when I punish him.
⁹If grape pickers came to you,
  would they not leave a few grapes?
If thieves came during the night,
  would they not steal only as much as they wanted?
¹⁰But I will strip Esau bare;
  I will uncover his hiding places,
  so that he cannot conceal himself.
His armed men are destroyed,
  also his allies and neighbors,
  so there is no one to say,
¹¹'Leave your fatherless children; I will keep them alive.
  Your widows too can depend on me.'"

¹²This is what the LORD says: "If those who do not deserve to drink the cup must drink it, why should you go unpunished? You will not go unpunished, but must drink it. ¹³I swear by myself," declares the LORD, "that Bozrah will become a ruin and a curse,ᵃ an object of horror and reproach; and all its towns will be in ruins forever."

¹⁴I have heard a message from the LORD;
  an envoy was sent to the nations to say,
"Assemble yourselves to attack it!
  Rise up for battle!"

¹⁵"Now I will make you small among the nations,
  despised by mankind.
¹⁶The terror you inspire
  and the pride of your heart have deceived you,
you who live in the clefts of the rocks,
  who occupy the heights of the hill.
Though you build your nest as high as the eagle's,
  from there I will bring you down,"
                    declares the LORD.
¹⁷"Edom will become an object of horror;
  all who pass by will be appalled and will scoff
  because of all its wounds.
¹⁸As Sodom and Gomorrah were overthrown,
  along with their neighboring towns,"
                    says the LORD,
"so no one will live there;
  no people will dwell in it.

¹⁹"Like a lion coming up from Jordan's thickets
  to a rich pastureland,
I will chase Edom from its land in an instant.
  Who is the chosen one I will appoint for this?
Who is like me and who can challenge me?
  And what shepherd can stand against me?"
²⁰Therefore, hear what the LORD has planned against Edom,
  what he has purposed against those who live in Teman:
The young of the flock will be dragged away;
  their pasture will be appalled at their fate.
²¹At the sound of their fall the earth will tremble;
  their cry will resound to the Red Sea.ᵇ

## Amplified Bible

⁸Flee, turn back, dwell deep [in the deserts to escape the Chaldeans], O inhabitants of Dedan [neighbor of Edom]! For I will bring the calamity *and* destruction of Esau upon him [Edom] when I inspect *and* punish him.
⁹If grape gatherers came to you, would they not leave some ungleaned grapes? If thieves came by night, would they not destroy only what is enough [for them]?
¹⁰But I have stripped Esau (Edom) bare; I have uncovered his hiding places, and he cannot hide himself. His offspring will be destroyed, with his brethren and his neighbors; and he will be no more.
¹¹Leave your fatherless children; I will [do what is necessary to] preserve them alive. And let [those who have been made] your widows trust *and* confide in Me.
¹²For thus says the Lord: Behold, they [Israel] whose rule was not to drink the cup [of wrath] shall assuredly drink—and are you to remain unpunished? You shall not go unpunished, but you shall surely drink. [Jer. 25:28, 29.]
¹³For I have sworn by Myself, says the Lord, that Bozrah [in Edom, between Petra and the Dead Sea] shall become a horror, a reproach, a waste, and a curse; and all its cities shall be ᵃperpetual wastes.
¹⁴I have heard a report from the Lord, and a messenger is sent to the nations, saying, Gather together and come against her! And rise up for the battle.
¹⁵For, behold, I will make you [Edom] small among the nations and despised among men. [Ezek. 35:9.]
¹⁶Your [object of] horror (your idol) has deceived you, and the pride of your heart [has deceived you], O you who dwell in the clefts of the rock [Sela or ᵇPetra], who hold *and* occupy the height of the hill. Though you make your nest as high as the eagle's, I will bring you down from there, says the Lord.
¹⁷And Edom shall be an astonishment *and* a horror; everyone who goes by it shall be astonished *and* shall hiss with horror at all its plagues *and* disasters.
¹⁸As [it was] in the overthrow of Sodom and Gomorrah and their neighboring cities, says the Lord, no man shall dwell there; neither shall a son of man live in it temporarily.
¹⁹See, there comes up one [Nebuchadnezzar] like a lion from [lurking in] the jungles (the pride) of the Jordan against the strong habitation [of Edom] *and* into the permanent pastures; for in a twinkling I will drive him [Edom] from there. And I will appoint over him the one whom I choose. For who is like Me? And who will appoint for Me the time *and* prosecute Me for this proceeding? And what [earthly, national] shepherd can stand before Me *and* defy Me?
²⁰Therefore hear the plan of the Lord which He has made against Edom, and His purposes which He has formed against the inhabitants of Teman: Surely they shall be dragged away [by Nebuchadnezzar], even the little ones of the flock; surely He shall make their habitation desolate because of them *and* their fold shocked at their fate.
²¹At the sound of their fall the earth shall tremble; at their crying the sound shall be heard at the Red Sea.

---

ᵃ How except by divine inspiration could the prophets have foretold that Edom's desolation would be perpetual? After 2,500 years the statement is so literally true that in the land of Edom, where millions once lived, there are only a few people barely existing, and the land is in ruins. For there was no prophecy that Edom would recover "in the latter days" (Jer. 48:47), as was predicted for Moab and Ammon, but Edom's desolation was to be lasting. The short book of Obadiah presents an interesting further clarification of God's reason for this exceptional treatment of Edom. It was all the outcome of a mere quarrel, a family feud, between two brothers, Jacob and Esau, which erupted into acts of violence and which continued from Genesis to the Gospels. (Gen. 27 and footnote on Gen. 27:41). ᵇ Petra, once an important Roman province in Edom, was lost for many centuries but rediscovered in 1812. On the height above its ruins is the great high place, and other evidences of idolatry stand on neighboring heights.

---

ᵃ 13 That is, its name will be used in cursing (see 29:22); or, others will see that it is cursed.  ᵇ 21 Or *the Sea of Reeds*

## New International Version

22 Look! An eagle will soar and swoop down,
    spreading its wings over Bozrah.
In that day the hearts of Edom's warriors
    will be like the heart of a woman in labor.

### A Message About Damascus

23 Concerning Damascus:

"Hamath and Arpad are dismayed,
    for they have heard bad news.
They are disheartened,
    troubled like<sup>a</sup> the restless sea.
24 Damascus has become feeble,
    she has turned to flee
    and panic has gripped her;
anguish and pain have seized her,
    pain like that of a woman in labor.
25 Why has the city of renown not been abandoned,
    the town in which I delight?
26 Surely, her young men will fall in the streets;
    all her soldiers will be silenced in that day,"
                        declares the LORD Almighty.
27 "I will set fire to the walls of Damascus;
    it will consume the fortresses of Ben-Hadad."

### A Message About Kedar and Hazor

28 Concerning Kedar and the kingdoms of Hazor, which Nebuchadnezzar king of Babylon attacked:

This is what the LORD says:

"Arise, and attack Kedar
    and destroy the people of the East.
29 Their tents and their flocks will be taken;
    their shelters will be carried off
    with all their goods and camels.
People will shout to them,
    'Terror on every side!'

30 "Flee quickly away!
    Stay in deep caves, you who live in Hazor,"
                        declares the LORD.
"Nebuchadnezzar king of Babylon has plotted against you;
    he has devised a plan against you.

31 "Arise and attack a nation at ease,
    which lives in confidence,"
                        declares the LORD,
"a nation that has neither gates nor bars;
    its people live far from danger.
32 Their camels will become plunder,
    and their large herds will be spoils of war.
I will scatter to the winds those who are in distant places<sup>b</sup>
    and will bring disaster on them from every side,"
                        declares the LORD.
33 "Hazor will become a haunt of jackals,
    a desolate place forever.
No one will live there;
    no people will dwell in it."

### A Message About Elam

34 This is the word of the LORD that came to Jeremiah the prophet concerning Elam, early in the reign of Zedekiah king of Judah:

35 This is what the LORD Almighty says:

"See, I will break the bow of Elam,
    the mainstay of their might.
36 I will bring against Elam the four winds
    from the four quarters of heaven;
I will scatter them to the four winds,

## Amplified Bible

22 Behold, one will come up and fly swiftly like an eagle and spread his wings against [the Edomite city of] Bozrah; and in that day the hearts of the mighty warriors of Edom will be like the heart of a woman in her pangs [in childbirth]. [Jer. 48:41.]

23 Concerning *and* against Damascus [in Syria]: Hamath and Arpad are confounded *and* put to shame, for they have heard bad news; they are fainthearted *and* wasting away; there is trouble *and* anxiety [like] on a [storm-tossed] sea which cannot rest.

24 Damascus has become feeble; she has turned to flee, and terror *and* panic have seized her; anguish and sorrow have taken hold of her, like a woman in childbirth.

25 How [remarkable that] the renowned city is not deserted, the city of my joy! [exclaims one from Damascus].

26 Therefore her young men shall fall in her streets, and all her soldiers shall be destroyed in that day, says the Lord of hosts. [Isa. 17:1-3; Amos 1:3-5; Zech. 9:1.]

27 And I will kindle a fire in the wall of Damascus, and it will consume the palaces of Ben-hadad [title of several kings of Syria].

28 Concerning Kedar [a tribe of nomad Arabs] and concerning the kingdoms of <sup>a</sup>Hazor, which Nebuchadrezzar king of Babylon shall smite: Thus says the Lord [to him]: Arise, go up against Kedar and destroy the sons of the east.

29 Their tents and their flocks shall they [the Chaldeans] take—their tent hangings and all their utensils and their camels. And men shall cry to them, Terror on every side! [Ps. 31:13; Jer. 6:25; 20:3, 10; 46:5.]

30 Flee, wander far off, dwell deep [in the deserts], O you inhabitants of Hazor [in the Arabian Desert] says the Lord, for <sup>b</sup>Nebuchadrezzar king of Babylon has planned a course against you and has conceived a purpose against you.

31 Arise [Nebuchadrezzar], get up into a nation which is at ease, which dwells without care, says the Lord, [a nation] which has neither gates nor bars, which dwells apart *and* alone.

32 And their camels will be booty, and their herds of cattle a spoil; and I will scatter to all [the four] winds those who [as evidence of their idolatry] clip off the corners of their hair, and I will bring their calamity from every side, says the Lord. [Lev. 19:27.]

33 And Hazor shall become a dwelling place of jackals, a desolation forever; no man shall dwell there; neither shall a son of man live in it temporarily.

34 The word of the Lord that came to Jeremiah the prophet concerning *and* against Elam, in the beginning of the reign of Zedekiah king of Judah, saying,

35 Thus says the Lord of hosts: Behold, I will break the bow of Elam, the chief [weapon and part] of their strength.

36 And upon Elam will I bring the four winds from the four corners of heaven; and I will scatter them toward all

---

<sup>a</sup> 23 Hebrew *on* or *by*    <sup>b</sup> 32 Or *who clip the hair by their foreheads*

<sup>a</sup> This Hazor is not to be confused with three others mentioned elsewhere (Josh. 11:1; 15:23; Neh. 11:33). It was a region in the Arabian Desert east of Palestine. Jeremiah's prophecy concerning it was literally fulfilled. Nebuchadnezzar conquered Arabia, according to historians, and Hazor's exact situation is long since unknown. Hazor is also known as that part of the Arab nation which used fixed dwellings in unwalled towns, in contrast to nomad Arabs.   <sup>b</sup> See footnote on Jer. 21:2.

## New International Version

and there will not be a nation
where Elam's exiles do not go.
37 I will shatter Elam before their foes,
before those who want to kill them;
I will bring disaster on them,
even my fierce anger,"
declares the LORD.
"I will pursue them with the sword
until I have made an end of them.
38 I will set my throne in Elam
and destroy her king and officials,"
declares the LORD.
39 "Yet I will restore the fortunes of Elam
in days to come,"
declares the LORD.

### A Message About Babylon

**50** This is the word the LORD spoke through Jeremiah the prophet concerning Babylon and the land of the Babylonians[a]:

2 "Announce and proclaim among the nations,
lift up a banner and proclaim it;
keep nothing back, but say,
'Babylon will be captured;
Bel will be put to shame,
Marduk filled with terror.
Her images will be put to shame
and her idols filled with terror.'
3 A nation from the north will attack her
and lay waste her land.
No one will live in it;
both people and animals will flee away.

4 "In those days, at that time,"
declares the LORD,
"the people of Israel and the people of Judah together
will go in tears to seek the LORD their God.
5 They will ask the way to Zion
and turn their faces toward it.
They will come and bind themselves to the LORD
in an everlasting covenant
that will not be forgotten.

6 "My people have been lost sheep;
their shepherds have led them astray
and caused them to roam on the mountains.
They wandered over mountain and hill
and forgot their own resting place.
7 Whoever found them devoured them;
their enemies said, 'We are not guilty,
for they sinned against the LORD, their verdant pasture,
the LORD, the hope of their ancestors.'

## Amplified Bible

those winds, and there will be no nation to which the outcasts of Elam will not come.
37 And I will cause ªElam to be dismayed *and* terrified before their enemies and before those who seek *and* demand their lives; and I will bring evil *and* disaster upon them, even My fierce anger, says the Lord. And I will send the sword after them until I have consumed them.
38 And I will set My throne [of judgment] in Elam [whose capital city was Shushan, from which God wrought wonders through Nehemiah, Esther, and Daniel]; and I will destroy from their king and princes, says the Lord. [Neh. 1:1; Esth. 1:2; Dan. 8:1, 2.]
39 But it shall be ªin the latter days (the end of days) that I will reverse the captivity and restore the fortunes of Elam, says the Lord.

**50** The word that the Lord spoke concerning *and* against Babylon and concerning *and* against the land of the Chaldeans through Jeremiah the prophet: [Isa. 13:1-14:23; 47; Hab. 1, 2.]

2 Declare it among the nations and publish it and set up a signal [to spread the news]—publish and conceal it not; say, Babylon has been taken; Bel [the patron god] is put to shame, Merodach (Bel) is dismayed *and* broken down. [Babylon's] images are put to shame, her [senseless] idols are thrown down!

3 For out of the north there has come up a nation [Media] against her which will make her land desolate, and none will dwell there. They will have fled, they will be gone—from man even to beast.

4 In those days and at that time, says the Lord, the children of Israel shall come, they and the children of Judah together; they shall come up weeping as they come and seek the Lord their God [inquiring for and of Him and requiring Him, both by right of necessity and of the promises of God's Word].

5 They shall ask the way to Zion, with their faces in that direction, saying, Come, let us join ourselves to the Lord in a perpetual covenant that shall not be forgotten.

6 My people have been lost sheep; their shepherds have led them astray [to favorite places of idolatry] on mountains [that seduce]. They have gone from [one sin to another] mountain to hill; they have forgotten their [own] resting-place. [Isa. 53:6; I Pet. 2:25.]

7 All who found them devoured them; and their adversaries said, We are not guilty, because they have sinned against the Lord [and are no longer holy to Him], their true habitation of righteousness *and* justice, even the Lord, the hope of their fathers.

---

ª Elam was a region beyond the Tigris River. After a long period of subjugation to foreign powers, it joined with Media and ultimately captured Babylon (Isa. 21:2, 9). Elam became a province of the Persian Empire. Elamites had been settled as colonists in Samaria long before the return of the Jews from Babylon, and they joined with others in attempting to prevent the rebuilding of Jerusalem and the temple (Ezra 4:9). There were also Elamites present on the Day of Pentecost (Acts 2:9), but they became extinct in the eleventh century. Elam in modern times is a province of modern Iran, bearing the name Khuzistan. Thus this prophecy of that nation's destruction is long since fulfilled, with the restoration of Elam's fortunes predicted in Jer. 49:39, the fulfillment of which we anticipate and await.

---

ª 1 Or *Chaldeans*; also in verses 8, 25, 35 and 45

## New International Version

⁸"Flee out of Babylon;
  leave the land of the Babylonians,
  and be like the goats that lead the flock.
⁹For I will stir up and bring against Babylon
  an alliance of great nations from the land of the
    north.
  They will take up their positions against her,
  and from the north she will be captured.
  Their arrows will be like skilled warriors
  who do not return empty-handed.
¹⁰So Babylonia*ᵃ* will be plundered;
  all who plunder her will have their fill,"
                                        declares the LORD.

¹¹"Because you rejoice and are glad,
  you who pillage my inheritance,
  because you frolic like a heifer threshing grain
  and neigh like stallions,
¹²your mother will be greatly ashamed;
  she who gave you birth will be disgraced.
  She will be the least of the nations—
  a wilderness, a dry land, a desert.
¹³Because of the LORD's anger she will not be inhabited
  but will be completely desolate.
  All who pass Babylon will be appalled;
  they will scoff because of all her wounds.

¹⁴"Take up your positions around Babylon,
  all you who draw the bow.
  Shoot at her! Spare no arrows,
  for she has sinned against the LORD.
¹⁵Shout against her on every side!
  She surrenders, her towers fall,
  her walls are torn down.
  Since this is the vengeance of the LORD,
  take vengeance on her;
  do to her as she has done to others.
¹⁶Cut off from Babylon the sower,
  and the reaper with his sickle at harvest.
  Because of the sword of the oppressor
  let everyone return to their own people,
  let everyone flee to their own land.

¹⁷"Israel is a scattered flock
  that lions have chased away.
  The first to devour them
  was the king of Assyria;
  the last to crush their bones
  was Nebuchadnezzar king of Babylon."

¹⁸Therefore this is what the LORD Almighty, the God
of Israel, says:

"I will punish the king of Babylon and his land
  as I punished the king of Assyria.
¹⁹But I will bring Israel back to their own pasture,
  and they will graze on Carmel and Bashan;
  their appetite will be satisfied
  on the hills of Ephraim and Gilead.
²⁰In those days, at that time,"
                                        declares the LORD,
"search will be made for Israel's guilt,
  but there will be none,
  and for the sins of Judah,
  but none will be found,
  for I will forgive the remnant I spare.

²¹"Attack the land of Merathaim
  and those who live in Pekod.
  Pursue, kill and completely destroy*ᵇ* them,"
                                        declares the LORD.
  "Do everything I have commanded you.

## Amplified Bible

⁸Flee out of the midst of Babylon, and go forth out of the
land of the Chaldeans; and be as the he-goats [who serve
as examples and as leaders in the flight] before the flocks.
[Jer. 51:6, 9, 45; II Cor. 6:17; Rev. 18:4.]
⁹For behold, I will raise and cause to come up against
Babylon an assembly of great nations from the north country. They will equip *and* set themselves against her; from
there she will be taken. Their arrows will be like [both]
an expert, mighty warrior *and* like his arrows—none [of
them] will return in vain.
¹⁰And Chaldea shall become plunder; all who plunder
her shall be satisfied, says the Lord.
¹¹Though you are glad, though you rejoice, O you who
plunder My heritage, though you are wanton *and* skip
about like a heifer at grass and neigh like strong stallions,
¹²Your mother [Babylon] shall be put to great shame;
she who bore you shall blush *and* be disgraced. Behold, she shall be at the rear of the nations [least of the
nations]—a wilderness, waste, and desert.
¹³Because of the wrath of the Lord she shall not be inhabited but shall be wholly desolate; everyone who goes
by Babylon shall be appalled and hiss *and* mock at all her
wounds *and* plagues.
¹⁴Set yourselves in array against Babylon round about,
all you archers. Shoot at her! Spare not the arrows, for she
has sinned against the Lord.
¹⁵Raise the battle cry against her round about! She
gives her hand [in agreement] *and* surrenders; her supports *and* battlements fall, her walls are thrown down. For
this is the vengeance of the Lord: take vengeance on her;
as she has done [to others], do to her.
¹⁶Exterminate the sower from Babylon, and the one
who handles the sickle in the time of harvest. For fear of
the sword of the oppressor everyone shall return to his
people, and everyone shall flee to his own land.
¹⁷Israel is a hunted *and* scattered sheep [driven hither
and thither and preyed upon by savage beasts]; the lions
have chased him. First the king of Assyria devoured him,
and now at last ᵃNebuchadrezzar king of Babylon has broken *and* gnawed his bones.
¹⁸Therefore thus says the Lord of hosts, the God of Israel: Behold, I will visit *and* punish the king of Babylon and
his land, just as I visited *and* punished the king of Assyria.
¹⁹And I will bring Israel [home] again to his fold *and*
pasturage, and he will feed on Carmel and Bashan [in the
most fertile districts both west and east], and his soul will
be satisfied upon the hills of Ephraim and Gilead.
²⁰In those days and at that time, says the Lord, the iniquity of Israel will be sought, but there will be none, and the
sins of Judah [will be sought], but none will be found, for
I will pardon those whom I cause to remain as a remnant
(the preserved ones who come forth after a long tribulation). [Isa. 1:9; 43:25; Jer. 31:34; 33:8; Rom. 9:27.]
²¹Go up against [Babylon] the land of Merathaim [two
rebellions, double or intense defiance], even against it and
against the inhabitants of Pekod [visitation and punish-
ment]. Slay and utterly destroy them, says the Lord, and
do according to all that I have commanded you.

---

*ᵃ 10* Or *Chaldea*    *ᵇ 21* The Hebrew term refers to the irrevocable
giving over of things or persons to the LORD, often by totally destroying
them; also in verse 26.

*ᵃ* See footnote on Jer. 21:2.

## New International Version

22 The noise of battle is in the land,
the noise of great destruction!
23 How broken and shattered
is the hammer of the whole earth!
How desolate is Babylon
among the nations!
24 I set a trap for you, Babylon,
and you were caught before you knew it;
you were found and captured
because you opposed the LORD.
25 The LORD has opened his arsenal
and brought out the weapons of his wrath,
for the Sovereign LORD Almighty has work to do
in the land of the Babylonians.
26 Come against her from afar.
Break open her granaries;
pile her up like heaps of grain.
Completely destroy her
and leave her no remnant.
27 Kill all her young bulls;
let them go down to the slaughter!
Woe to them! For their day has come,
the time for them to be punished.
28 Listen to the fugitives and refugees from Babylon
declaring in Zion
how the LORD our God has taken vengeance,
vengeance for his temple.

29 "Summon archers against Babylon,
all those who draw the bow.
Encamp all around her;
let no one escape.
Repay her for her deeds;
do to her as she has done.
For she has defied the LORD,
the Holy One of Israel.
30 Therefore, her young men will fall in the streets;
all her soldiers will be silenced in that day,"
declares the LORD.
31 "See, I am against you, you arrogant one,"
declares the Lord, the LORD Almighty,
"for your day has come,
the time for you to be punished.
32 The arrogant one will stumble and fall
and no one will help her up;
I will kindle a fire in her towns
that will consume all who are around her."

33 This is what the LORD Almighty says:

"The people of Israel are oppressed,
and the people of Judah as well.
All their captors hold them fast,
refusing to let them go.
34 Yet their Redeemer is strong;
the LORD Almighty is his name.
He will vigorously defend their cause
so that he may bring rest to their land,
but unrest to those who live in Babylon.

35 "A sword against the Babylonians!"
declares the LORD —
"against those who live in Babylon
and against her officials and wise men!
36 A sword against her false prophets!
They will become fools.
A sword against her warriors!
They will be filled with terror.
37 A sword against her horses and chariots

## Amplified Bible

22 The cry *and* noise of battle is in the land, and [the noise] of great destruction.
23 How the hammer of the whole earth is crushed and broken! How Babylon has become a horror of desolation among the nations!
24 I set a trap for you, and you also were taken, O Babylon, and you did not know it; you were found and also caught because you have struggled *and* contended against the Lord.
25 The Lord has opened His armory and has brought forth [the nations who unknowingly are] the weapons of His indignation *and* wrath, for the Lord God of hosts has work to do in the land of the Chaldeans.
26 Come against her from every quarter *and* from the utmost border. Open her granaries *and* storehouses; pile up [their contents] like heaps of rubbish. Burn *and* destroy her utterly; let nothing be left of her.
27 Slay all her bullocks (her choice youths, the strength of her army); let them go down to the slaughter! Woe to [the Chaldeans]! For their day has come, the time of their visitation (their inspection and punishment).
28 Listen! The voice of those [Jews] who flee and escape out of the land of Babylon proclaiming in Zion the vengeance of the Lord our God, the vengeance [of the Lord upon the Chaldeans] for [the plundering and destruction of] His temple.
29 Call together [many] archers against Babylon, all those who bend the bow. Encamp against her round about; let none from there escape. Recompense her according to her deeds; just as she has done, do to her. For against the Lord, against the Holy One of Israel, has she been proudly defiant *and* presumptuous.
30 Therefore shall her young men fall in her streets *and* squares, and all her soldiers shall be destroyed on that day, says the Lord.
31 Behold, I am against you, O Babylon [you who are pride and presumption personified], says the Lord, the Lord of hosts, for your day has come, the time when I will visit *and* punish you.
32 And Pride (the arrogant one) shall stumble (totter) and fall, and none shall raise him up. And I will kindle a fire in his cities, and it shall devour all who are round about him.
33 Thus says the Lord of hosts: The children of Israel and the children of Judah are oppressed together; all who took them captive have held them fast; they refuse to let them go.
34 Their Redeemer is strong; the Lord of hosts is His name. He will surely *and* thoroughly plead their case *and* defend their cause, that He may give rest to [the land of Israel and to the Babylonian-enslaved nations of] the earth, but unrest to the inhabitants of Babylon.
35 A sword upon the Chaldeans, says the Lord—upon the inhabitants of Babylon and upon her princes (rulers in civic matters) and upon her wise men (the astrologers and rulers in religious affairs)!
36 A sword upon the babbling liars (the diviners), that they may become fools! A sword upon her mighty warriors, that they may be dismayed *and* destroyed!
37 A sword upon their horses and upon their chariots

## New International Version

and all the foreigners in her ranks!
They will become weaklings.
A sword against her treasures!
They will be plundered.
³⁸A drought on*ᵃ* her waters!
They will dry up.
For it is a land of idols,
idols that will go mad with terror.

³⁹"So desert creatures and hyenas will live there,
and there the owl will dwell.
It will never again be inhabited
or lived in from generation to generation.
⁴⁰As I overthrew Sodom and Gomorrah
along with their neighboring towns,"
declares the LORD,
"so no one will live there;
no people will dwell in it.

⁴¹"Look! An army is coming from the north;
a great nation and many kings
are being stirred up from the ends of the earth.
⁴²They are armed with bows and spears;
they are cruel and without mercy.
They sound like the roaring sea
as they ride on their horses;
they come like men in battle formation
to attack you, Daughter Babylon.
⁴³The king of Babylon has heard reports about them,
and his hands hang limp.
Anguish has gripped him,
pain like that of a woman in labor.
⁴⁴Like a lion coming up from Jordan's thickets
to a rich pastureland,
I will chase Babylon from its land in an instant.
Who is the chosen one I will appoint for this?
Who is like me and who can challenge me?
And what shepherd can stand against me?"

⁴⁵Therefore, hear what the LORD has planned against
Babylon,
what he has purposed against the land of the
Babylonians:
The young of the flock will be dragged away;
their pasture will be appalled at their fate.
⁴⁶At the sound of Babylon's capture the earth will
tremble;
its cry will resound among the nations.

## 51

**51** This is what the LORD says:

"See, I will stir up the spirit of a destroyer
against Babylon and the people of Leb Kamai.*ᵇ*
²I will send foreigners to Babylon
to winnow her and to devastate her land;
they will oppose her on every side
in the day of her disaster.
³Let not the archer string his bow,
nor let him put on his armor.
Do not spare her young men;
completely destroy*ᶜ* her army.
⁴They will fall down slain in Babylon,*ᵈ*
fatally wounded in her streets.
⁵For Israel and Judah have not been forsaken
by their God, the LORD Almighty,
though their land*ᵉ* is full of guilt
before the Holy One of Israel.

---

*ᵃ 38* Or *A sword against*    *ᵇ 1* *Leb Kamai* is a cryptogram for Chaldea,
that is, Babylonia.    *ᶜ 3* The Hebrew term refers to the irrevocable
giving over of things or persons to the LORD, often by totally destroying
them.    *ᵈ 4* Or *Chaldea*    *ᵉ 5* Or *Almighty, / and the land of the*
*Babylonians*

## Amplified Bible

and upon all the mixed foreign troops that are in the midst
of her, that they may become [as weak and defenseless
as] women! A sword upon her treasures, that they may
be plundered!
³⁸A sword *and* a drought upon her waters, that they may
be dried up! For it is a land of images, and they are mad
over idols (objects of terror in which they foolishly trust).
³⁹Therefore *ᵃ*wild beasts of the desert shall dwell [in
Babylon] with the jackals, and ostriches shall dwell there.
And it shall never again be inhabited with people, even
from generation to generation. [Isa. 13:20-22.]
⁴⁰As when God overthrew Sodom and Gomorrah and
their neighboring cities, says the Lord, so no man shall
dwell there; neither shall any son of man live there temporarily. [Jer. 49:18.]
⁴¹Behold, a people is coming from the north; and a great
nation and many kings are stirring from the uttermost
parts of the earth.
⁴²They lay hold of bow, lance, *and* spear; they are cruel
*and* have no mercy *or* compassion. They sound like the
roaring of the sea; they ride upon horses, every man
equipped like a man [ready] for the battle against you,
O Daughter of Babylon!
⁴³The king of Babylon has heard the news about them,
and his hands fall feeble *and* helpless; anguish has seized
him, and pangs like that of a woman in childbirth.
⁴⁴See, there comes up one like a lion from the jungles
(the pride) of the Jordan against the strong habitation [of
Babylon] *and* into the permanent pasturage *and* sheepfold;
for in a twinkling I will drive him [Babylon] from there.
And I will appoint over him the one whom I choose. For
who is like Me? And who will challenge Me *and* prosecute
Me for this proceeding? And what [earthly, national] shepherd can stand before Me *and* defy Me? [Jer. 49:19.]
⁴⁵Therefore hear the plan of the Lord which He has
made against Babylon, and His purposes which He has
formed against the land of the Chaldeans: Surely they
shall be dragged away, even the little ones of the flock;
surely He shall make their habitation desolate because of
them *and* their fold amazed *and* appalled at their fate.
⁴⁶At the cry, Babylon has been taken! the earth shall
tremble, and the cry shall be heard among the nations.

## 51

**51** Thus says the Lord: Behold, I will raise up against
Babylon and against those who dwell among those
rebelling against Me a destroying wind *and* spirit;
²And I will send to Babylon strangers *or* winnowers who
will winnow her and will empty her land; for in the day of
calamity they will be against her on every side.
³Against him who bends let the archer bend his bow,
and against him who lifts himself up in his coat of mail.
And spare not her young men; devote [to God] and utterly
destroy her entire host.
⁴Thus they shall fall down slain in the land of the Chaldeans, and wounded in her streets.
⁵For Israel has not been widowed *and* forsaken, nor has
Judah, by his God, the Lord of hosts, though their land is
full of guilt against the Holy One of Israel.

---

*ᵃ* See footnote on Isa. 13:22 for this prophecy's fulfillment.

## New International Version

6 "Flee from Babylon!
     Run for your lives!
  Do not be destroyed because of her sins.
  It is time for the LORD's vengeance;
     he will repay her what she deserves.
7 Babylon was a gold cup in the LORD's hand;
     she made the whole earth drunk.
  The nations drank her wine;
     therefore they have now gone mad.
8 Babylon will suddenly fall and be broken.
     Wail over her!
  Get balm for her pain;
     perhaps she can be healed.
9 "'We would have healed Babylon,
     but she cannot be healed;
  let us leave her and each go to our own land,
     for her judgment reaches to the skies,
     it rises as high as the heavens.'
10 "'The LORD has vindicated us;
     come, let us tell in Zion
     what the LORD our God has done.'
11 "Sharpen the arrows,
     take up the shields!
  The LORD has stirred up the kings of the Medes,
     because his purpose is to destroy Babylon.
  The LORD will take vengeance,
     vengeance for his temple.
12 Lift up a banner against the walls of Babylon!
     Reinforce the guard,
  station the watchmen,
     prepare an ambush!
  The LORD will carry out his purpose,
     his decree against the people of Babylon.
13 You who live by many waters
     and are rich in treasures,
  your end has come,
     the time for you to be destroyed.
14 The LORD Almighty has sworn by himself:
     I will surely fill you with troops, as with a swarm of
        locusts,
     and they will shout in triumph over you.
15 "He made the earth by his power;
     he founded the world by his wisdom
     and stretched out the heavens by his understanding.
16 When he thunders, the waters in the heavens roar;
     he makes clouds rise from the ends of the earth.
  He sends lightning with the rain
     and brings out the wind from his storehouses.
17 "Everyone is senseless and without knowledge;
     every goldsmith is shamed by his idols.
  The images he makes are a fraud;
     they have no breath in them.
18 They are worthless, the objects of mockery;
     when their judgment comes, they will perish.
19 He who is the Portion of Jacob is not like these,
     for he is the Maker of all things,
  including the people of his inheritance—
     the LORD Almighty is his name.
20 "You are my war club,
     my weapon for battle—
  with you I shatter nations,
     with you I destroy kingdoms,
21 with you I shatter horse and rider,
     with you I shatter chariot and driver,
22 with you I shatter man and woman,
     with you I shatter old man and youth,

## Amplified Bible

6 Flee out of the midst of Babylon! Let every man save his life! Let not destruction come upon you through her [punishment for] sin and guilt. For it is the time of the Lord's vengeance; He will render to her a recompense. [Jer. 50:28; II Cor. 6:17; Rev. 18:4.]
7 Babylon was a golden cup in the Lord's hand, making all the earth drunken. The nations drank of her wine; therefore the nations have gone mad. [Rev. 14:8; 17:4.]
8 Babylon has suddenly fallen and is shattered (destroyed)! Wail for her [if you care to]! Get balm for her [incurable] pain; if [you do] so she may [possibly] be healed! [Jer. 25:15; Rev. 14:8-10; 16:19; 18:2, 3.]
9 We would have healed Babylon, but she is not healed. Forsake her and let us each go to his own country, for her guilt and the judgment against her reach to heaven and are lifted even to the skies. [Gen. 18:20, 21.]
10 The Lord has brought forth and made known the righteousness [of our cause]; come and let us declare in Zion the work of the Lord our God.
11 Make clean and sharp the arrows, take up the shields or coats of armor [and cover your bodies with them]! The Lord has stirred up the spirit of the kings of the Medes [who with the Persians will destroy the Babylonian Empire], for His purpose concerning Babylon is to destroy it; for that is the vengeance of the Lord, the vengeance [upon Babylon for the plundering and destruction] of His temple.
12 Set up a standard or signal [to spread the news] upon the walls of Babylon! Make the watch and blockade strong, set the guards, prepare the ambushes! For the Lord has both purposed and done that which He spoke against the inhabitants of Babylon.
13 O [Babylon] you who dwell by many waters, rich in treasures, your end has come, and the line measuring your life is cut. [Rev. 17:1-6.]
14 The Lord of hosts has sworn by Himself, saying, Surely I will fill you with men, as with [a swarm of] locusts [who strip a land clean], and they will lift up a song and shout [of victory] over you.
15 He made the earth by His power; He established the world by His wisdom and stretched out the heavens by His understanding.
16 When He utters His voice, there is a tumult of waters in the heavens, and He causes the vapors to ascend from the ends of the earth. He makes lightnings for the rain and brings forth the wind from His treasuries.
17 Every man has become stupid and brutelike, without knowledge [of God]; every goldsmith is put to shame by the images he has made; for his molten idols are a lie, and there is no breath [of life] in them.
18 They are worthless (emptiness, falsity, futility), a work of delusion and worthy of derision; in the time of their inspection and punishment they shall [helplessly] perish.
19 Not like these [gods] is He Who is the Portion of Jacob [the true God on Whom Israel has a claim], for He is the One Who formed all things, and Israel is the tribe of His inheritance—the Lord of hosts is His name. [Jer. 10:12-16.]
20 You [Cyrus of Persia, soon to conquer Babylon] are My battle-ax or maul and weapon of war—for with you I break nations in pieces, with you I destroy kingdoms,
21 With you I break in pieces the horse and his rider, with you I break in pieces the chariot and the charioteer,
22 With you I break in pieces man and woman, with you

## New International Version

with you I shatter young man and young woman,
23 with you I shatter shepherd and flock,
with you I shatter farmer and oxen,
with you I shatter governors and officials.

24 "Before your eyes I will repay Babylon and all who live
in Babylonia[a] for all the wrong they have done in Zion,"
declares the LORD.

25 "I am against you, you destroying mountain,
you who destroy the whole earth,"
declares the LORD.

"I will stretch out my hand against you,
roll you off the cliffs,
and make you a burned-out mountain.
26 No rock will be taken from you for a cornerstone,
nor any stone for a foundation,
for you will be desolate forever,"
declares the LORD.

27 "Lift up a banner in the land!
Blow the trumpet among the nations!
Prepare the nations for battle against her;
summon against her these kingdoms:
Ararat, Minni and Ashkenaz.
Appoint a commander against her;
send up horses like a swarm of locusts.
28 Prepare the nations for battle against her—
the kings of the Medes,
their governors and all their officials,
and all the countries they rule.
29 The land trembles and writhes,
for the LORD's purposes against Babylon stand—
to lay waste the land of Babylon
so that no one will live there.
30 Babylon's warriors have stopped fighting;
they remain in their strongholds.
Their strength is exhausted;
they have become weaklings.
Her dwellings are set on fire;
the bars of her gates are broken.
31 One courier follows another
and messenger follows messenger
to announce to the king of Babylon
that his entire city is captured,
32 the river crossings seized,
the marshes set on fire,
and the soldiers terrified."

33 This is what the LORD Almighty, the God of Israel,
says:

"Daughter Babylon is like a threshing floor
at the time it is trampled;
the time to harvest her will soon come."

34 "Nebuchadnezzar king of Babylon has devoured us,
he has thrown us into confusion,
he has made us an empty jar.
Like a serpent he has swallowed us
and filled his stomach with our delicacies,
and then has spewed us out.
35 May the violence done to our flesh[b] be on Babylon,"
say the inhabitants of Zion.
"May our blood be on those who live in Babylonia,"
says Jerusalem.

36 Therefore this is what the LORD says:

"See, I will defend your cause
and avenge you;
I will dry up her sea
and make her springs dry.
37 Babylon will be a heap of ruins,
a haunt of jackals,

## Amplified Bible

I break in pieces old man and youth, with you I break in
pieces young man and maiden,
23 With you I break in pieces the shepherd and his flock,
with you I break in pieces the farmer and his yoke of oxen,
and with you I break in pieces governors and commanders.
24 And I will [completely] repay Babylon and all the inhabitants of Chaldea for all the evil that they have done in
Zion—before your very eyes [I will do it], says the Lord.
25 Behold, I am against you, says the Lord, O destroying
mountain [which is burning out, you who will be as barren
and desolate as an extinct volcano], you who [would] destroy the whole earth. I will stretch out My hand over and
against you and roll you down from the [burnt] crags and
will make you a burnt-out mountain [of combustive fires].
26 And [O Babylon] they shall not take your cracked
stones for a cornerstone, or any stone for foundations, but
you shall be waste and [a] desolate forever, says the Lord.
27 Set up a standard or signal in the land [to spread the
news]! Blow the trumpet among the nations! Prepare and
dedicate the nations for war against her; call against her
the kingdoms of Ararat, Minni, and Ashkenaz. Appoint a
marshal against her; cause the horses to come up like [a
swarm of] locusts [when their wings are not yet released
from their horny cases].
28 Prepare and dedicate the nations for war against
her—the kings of Media, with their governors and commanders (deputies), and every land of their dominion.
29 [I foresee this:] The land trembles and writhes in pain
and sorrow, for the purposes of the Lord against Babylon
stand—to make the land of Babylon a desolation without
inhabitant.
30 The mighty warriors of Babylon have ceased to fight;
they have remained in their holds. Their might has failed;
they have become [weak and helpless] like women. Her
dwelling places are burned up; her bars [and defenses gen-
erally] are broken.
31 One post shall run to meet another and one messenger to meet another to show the king of Babylon that his
city is taken on every side and to its farthest end,
32 And that the passages [or ferries across the Euphra-
tes] are stopped, and the great marshes they [the Medes]
have burned with fire, and the men of war are frightened.
33 For thus says the Lord of hosts, the God of Israel: The
Daughter of Babylon is like a threshing floor at the time it
is [being prepared]; yet a little while and the time of harvest shall come to her.
34 [The inhabitants of Zion say] [b] Nebuchadrezzar king
of Babylon has devoured us, he has crushed us, he has
made us an empty vessel. Like a monster he has swallowed
us up, he has filled his belly with our delicacies; he has
rinsed us out and cast us away.
35 May the violence done to me and to my flesh and
blood be upon Babylon, will the inhabitant of Zion say;
and, May my blood be upon the inhabitants of Chaldea,
will Jerusalem say.
36 Therefore thus says the Lord: Behold, I will plead
your cause and take vengeance for you. I will dry up her
lake or great reservoir and make her fountain dry.
37 And Babylon shall become heaps [of ruins], a dwell-

---

[a] 24 Or *Chaldea*; also in verse 35    [b] 35 Or *done to us and to our children*

[a] See footnote on Isa. 13:22 for this prophecy's fulfillment.    [b] See
footnote on Jer. 21:2.

## New International Version

an object of horror and scorn,
 a place where no one lives.
<sup>38</sup>Her people all roar like young lions,
 they growl like lion cubs.
<sup>39</sup>But while they are aroused,
 I will set out a feast for them
 and make them drunk,
 so that they shout with laughter—
 then sleep forever and not awake,"
 declares the LORD.
<sup>40</sup>"I will bring them down
 like lambs to the slaughter,
 like rams and goats.

<sup>41</sup>"How Sheshak<sup>a</sup> will be captured,
 the boast of the whole earth seized!
 How desolate Babylon will be
 among the nations!
<sup>42</sup>The sea will rise over Babylon;
 its roaring waves will cover her.
<sup>43</sup>Her towns will be desolate,
 a dry and desert land,
 a land where no one lives,
 through which no one travels.
<sup>44</sup>I will punish Bel in Babylon
 and make him spew out what he has swallowed.
 The nations will no longer stream to him.
 And the wall of Babylon will fall.

<sup>45</sup>"Come out of her, my people!
 Run for your lives!
 Run from the fierce anger of the LORD.
<sup>46</sup>Do not lose heart or be afraid
 when rumors are heard in the land;
 one rumor comes this year, another the next,
 rumors of violence in the land
 and of ruler against ruler.
<sup>47</sup>For the time will surely come
 when I will punish the idols of Babylon;
 her whole land will be disgraced
 and her slain will all lie fallen within her.
<sup>48</sup>Then heaven and earth and all that is in them
 will shout for joy over Babylon,
 for out of the north
 destroyers will attack her,"
 declares the LORD.

<sup>49</sup>"Babylon must fall because of Israel's slain,
 just as the slain in all the earth
 have fallen because of Babylon.
<sup>50</sup>You who have escaped the sword,
 leave and do not linger!
 Remember the LORD in a distant land,
 and call to mind Jerusalem."

<sup>51</sup>"We are disgraced,
 for we have been insulted
 and shame covers our faces,
 because foreigners have entered
 the holy places of the LORD's house."

<sup>52</sup>"But days are coming," declares the LORD,
 "when I will punish her idols,
 and throughout her land
 the wounded will groan.
<sup>53</sup>Even if Babylon ascends to the heavens
 and fortifies her lofty stronghold,
 I will send destroyers against her,"
 declares the LORD.

<sup>54</sup>"The sound of a cry comes from Babylon,
 the sound of great destruction
 from the land of the Babylonians.<sup>b</sup>

<sup>a</sup> 41 Sheshak is a cryptogram for Babylon.  <sup>b</sup> 54 Or Chaldeans

## Amplified Bible

ing place of jackals, a horror (an astonishing desolation) and a hissing [of amazement], without inhabitant.
<sup>38</sup>They [the Chaldean lords] shall be roaring together [before their sudden capture] like young lions [over their prey], they [the princes] shall be growling like lions' whelps.
<sup>39</sup>When the revelers are <sup>a</sup>inflamed [with wine and lust during their drinking bouts], I will prepare them a feast [of My wrath] and make them drunk, that they may rejoice and fall asleep to a perpetual sleep and not waken, says the Lord.
<sup>40</sup>I will bring them down like lambs to the slaughter, like rams together with he-goats.
<sup>41</sup>How Sheshach [Babylon] is taken! And the praise of the whole earth is surprised *and* seized! How Babylon has become an astonishing desolation *and* a horror among the nations!
<sup>42</sup>The sea has come up upon Babylon; she is covered with the tumult *and* multitude of its waves.
<sup>43</sup>Her cities have become a desolation *and* a horror, a land of drought and a wilderness, a land in which no one lives, nor does any son of man pass through it.
<sup>44</sup>And I will punish *and* execute judgment upon Bel [the god] in Babylon and take out of his mouth what he has swallowed up [the sacred vessels and the people of Judah and elsewhere who were taken captive]. The nations will not flow any more to him. Yes, the wall of Babylon has fallen!
<sup>45</sup>My people, come out of the midst of her! And let every man save his life from the fierce anger of the Lord! [Jer. 50:8; II Cor. 6:17; Rev. 18:4.]
<sup>46</sup>And beware, lest your heart faint and you be afraid at the report (rumor) heard in the land; for in one year shall one report come and in another year another report, and violence shall be in the land, ruler against ruler.
<sup>47</sup>Therefore behold, the days will come when I will execute judgment *and* punishment upon the idols of Babylon; her whole land will be confounded *and* put to shame, and all her slain will fall in the midst of her.
<sup>48</sup>Then heaven and earth and all that is in them shall sing for joy over Babylon, for the [Median] destroyers shall come against her from the north, says the Lord. [Isa. 44:23; Jer. 51:11; Rev. 12:12; 18:20.]
<sup>49</sup>As Babylon caused the slain of Israel to fall, so at Babylon shall fall the slain of all [her] land.
<sup>50</sup>You who have escaped the sword, go away, stand not still! [Seriously and earnestly] remember the Lord from afar [Babylon], and let [desolate] Jerusalem come into your mind.
<sup>51</sup>We are confounded *and* ashamed, for we have heard reproach; confusion *and* shame have covered our faces, for strangers have come into the [most] sacred parts of the sanctuary of the Lord [even those forbidden for entrance by all but the high priest or the appointed priests].
<sup>52</sup>Therefore behold, the days are coming, says the Lord, when I will execute judgment upon [Babylon's] idols *and* images, and throughout all her land the wounded will groan.
<sup>53</sup>Though Babylon should mount up to heaven, and though she should fortify her strong height (her lofty stronghold), yet destroyers will come upon her from Me, says the Lord.
<sup>54</sup>The sound of a cry [comes] from Babylon, and [the sound of] great destruction *and* ruin from the land of the Chaldeans!

<sup>a</sup> Here is God's forecast through Jeremiah of what was going to happen to great Babylon, of whom Herodotus said she had been "embellished with ornaments more than any city" of his acquaintance. The fact that all of the details of the prophecy were carried out is recorded by Daniel (5:1-30), and becomes more and more amazing and awe-inspiring as one reflects on it all after twenty-five verifying centuries. Truly only an "[empty-headed] fool" could say in his heart, "There is no God" (Ps. 14:1).

## New International Version

55 The LORD will destroy Babylon;
  he will silence her noisy din.
Waves of enemies will rage like great waters;
  the roar of their voices will resound.
56 A destroyer will come against Babylon;
  her warriors will be captured,
  and their bows will be broken.
For the LORD is a God of retribution;
  he will repay in full.
57 I will make her officials and wise men drunk,
  her governors, officers and warriors as well;
  they will sleep forever and not awake,"
    declares the King, whose name is the LORD
    Almighty.
58 This is what the LORD Almighty says:

"Babylon's thick wall will be leveled
  and her high gates set on fire;
the peoples exhaust themselves for nothing,
  the nations' labor is only fuel for the flames."

59 This is the message Jeremiah the prophet gave to the staff officer Seraiah son of Neriah, the son of Mahseiah, when he went to Babylon with Zedekiah king of Judah in the fourth year of his reign. 60 Jeremiah had written on a scroll about all the disasters that would come upon Babylon—all that had been recorded concerning Babylon. 61 He said to Seraiah, "When you get to Babylon, see that you read all these words aloud. 62 Then say, 'LORD, you have said you will destroy this place, so that neither people nor animals will live in it; it will be desolate forever.' 63 When you finish reading this scroll, tie a stone to it and throw it into the Euphrates. 64 Then say, 'So will Babylon sink to rise no more because of the disaster I will bring on her. And her people will fall.'"

The words of Jeremiah end here.

### The Fall of Jerusalem

**52** Zedekiah was twenty-one years old when he became king, and he reigned in Jerusalem eleven years. His mother's name was Hamutal daughter of Jeremiah; she was from Libnah. 2 He did evil in the eyes of the LORD, just as Jehoiakim had done. 3 It was because of the LORD's anger that all this happened to Jerusalem and Judah, and in the end he thrust them from his presence.

Now Zedekiah rebelled against the king of Babylon.

4 So in the ninth year of Zedekiah's reign, on the tenth day of the tenth month, Nebuchadnezzar king of Babylon marched against Jerusalem with his whole army. They encamped outside the city and built siege works all around it. 5 The city was kept under siege until the eleventh year of King Zedekiah.

6 By the ninth day of the fourth month the famine in the city had become so severe that there was no food for the people to eat. 7 Then the city wall was broken through, and the whole army fled. They left the city at night through the gate between the two walls near the king's garden, though the Babylonians*a* were surrounding the city. They fled to-

## Amplified Bible

55 For the Lord is destroying Babylon *and* laying her waste and stilling her great voice [the hum of the city's life]. And the waves [of her conquerors] roar like great waters, the noise of their voices is raised up [like the tramping of an army].
56 For the destroyer is coming upon her, upon Babylon; and her mighty warriors are taken, their bows are broken in pieces; for the Lord is a God of recompense; He will surely requite.
57 And I will make drunk her princes and her wise men, her governors and her commanders (deputies) and her mighty warriors; and they will sleep a perpetual sleep and not waken, says the King—the Lord of hosts is His name.
58 Thus says the Lord of hosts: The broad walls of Babylon shall be utterly overthrown *and* [the foundations] made bare, and her high gates shall be burned with fire; the peoples shall labor in vain, and the nations [only] to satisfy the fire, and they shall be weary. [Hab. 2:13.]
59 The word that Jeremiah the prophet commanded Seraiah son of Neriah, the son of Mahseiah, when he went with Zedekiah king of Judah to Babylon in the fourth year of his reign. Now this Seraiah was chief chamberlain *or* quartermaster [and brother of Baruch].
60 So Jeremiah wrote in a book all the evil that would come upon Babylon—even all these words that are written against Babylon.
61 And Jeremiah said to Seraiah, When you come to Babylon, see to it that you read all these words.
62 Then say, O Lord, You have spoken concerning this place that it shall be cut off, so that nothing shall remain and dwell in it, neither man nor beast; but it shall be desolate forever.
63 And it shall be that when you have finished reading this book, you shall bind a stone to it and cast it into the midst of the Euphrates.
64 Then say, Thus will Babylon sink and not rise because of the evil that I will bring upon her; and [the Babylonians] will be weary (hopelessly exhausted). Thus far are the words of Jeremiah. [Rev. 18:21.]

**52** Zedekiah was twenty-one years old when he began to reign, and he reigned eleven years in Jerusalem. And his mother's name was Hamutal daughter of Jeremiah [not the prophet] of Libnah. [II Kings 24:18-25:21.]
2 And he did that which was evil in the sight of the Lord, according to all that Jehoiakim had done.
3 For all this came to pass in Jerusalem and Judah because of the anger of the Lord, and [in the end] He cast them out from His presence. And Zedekiah rebelled against the king of Babylon.
4 And in the ninth year of his reign, in the tenth month, on the tenth day of the month, *a* Nebuchadrezzar king of Babylon came, he and all his army, against Jerusalem; and they pitched against it and built moveable towers *and* siege mounds against it round about. [Jer. 39:1-10.]
5 So the city was besieged until the eleventh year of King Zedekiah. [II Chron. 36:11-13.]
6 And in the fourth month, on the ninth day of the month, the famine was so severe in the city that there was no bread for the people of the land.
7 Then the city [wall] was broken through, so that all the men of war might flee, and they went forth out of the city by night [as Ezekiel had foretold] by way of the gate between the two walls by the king's garden, though the Chaldeans were round about the city. And they [the Jewish soldiers fled] by way of the Arabah (the Jordan Valley). [Ezek. 12:12.]

---

*a* 7 Or *Chaldeans*; also in verse 17

*a* See footnote on Jer. 21:2.

# New International Version

ward the Arabah,[a] [8]but the Babylonian[b] army pursued King Zedekiah and overtook him in the plains of Jericho. All his soldiers were separated from him and scattered, [9]and he was captured.

He was taken to the king of Babylon at Riblah in the land of Hamath, where he pronounced sentence on him. [10]There at Riblah the king of Babylon killed the sons of Zedekiah before his eyes; he also killed all the officials of Judah. [11]Then he put out Zedekiah's eyes, bound him with bronze shackles and took him to Babylon, where he put him in prison till the day of his death.

[12]On the tenth day of the fifth month, in the nineteenth year of Nebuchadnezzar king of Babylon, Nebuzaradan commander of the imperial guard, who served the king of Babylon, came to Jerusalem. [13]He set fire to the temple of the LORD, the royal palace and all the houses of Jerusalem. Every important building he burned down. [14]The whole Babylonian army, under the commander of the imperial guard, broke down all the walls around Jerusalem. [15]Nebuzaradan the commander of the guard carried into exile some of the poorest people and those who remained in the city, along with the rest of the craftsmen[c] and those who had deserted to the king of Babylon. [16]But Nebuzaradan left behind the rest of the poorest people of the land to work the vineyards and fields.

[17]The Babylonians broke up the bronze pillars, the movable stands and the bronze Sea that were at the temple of the LORD and they carried all the bronze to Babylon. [18]They also took away the pots, shovels, wick trimmers, sprinkling bowls, dishes and all the bronze articles used in the temple service. [19]The commander of the imperial guard took away the basins, censers, sprinkling bowls, pots, lampstands, dishes and bowls used for drink offerings—all that were made of pure gold or silver.

[20]The bronze from the two pillars, the Sea and the twelve bronze bulls under it, and the movable stands, which King Solomon had made for the temple of the LORD, was more than could be weighed. [21]Each pillar was eighteen cubits high and twelve cubits in circumference[d]; each was four fingers thick, and hollow. [22]The bronze capital on top of one pillar was five cubits[e] high and was decorated with a network and pomegranates of bronze all around. The other pillar, with its pomegranates, was similar. [23]There were ninety-six pomegranates on the sides; the total number of pomegranates above the surrounding network was a hundred.

# Amplified Bible

[8]But the army of the Chaldeans pursued the king and overtook Zedekiah in the plains of Jericho; and all his army was scattered from him.

[9]Then they seized the king and brought him up to the king of Babylon at Riblah in the [Syrian] land of Hamath [on the northern border of Israel], where he pronounced sentence upon him.

[10]And the king of Babylon slew the sons of Zedekiah before his eyes; he slew also all the princes of Judah at Riblah.

[11]Then he put out the eyes of Zedekiah; and the king of Babylon bound him with shackles and carried him to Babylon and put him in prison [a][mill] till the day of his death. [Ezek. 12:13.]

[12]Now in the fifth month, on the tenth day of the month, which was the nineteenth year of Nebuchadrezzar king of Babylon, there came to Jerusalem Nebuzaradan captain of the guard, who stood *and* served before the king of Babylon.

[13]And he burned the house of the Lord and the king's house and all the houses of Jerusalem; every great house he consumed with fire.

[14]And all the army of the Chaldeans who were with the captain of the guard broke down all the walls round about Jerusalem.

[15]Then Nebuzaradan the captain of the guard carried away captive some of the poorest of the people and those who were left in the city [at the time it was captured], along with those who went out to the king of Babylon [during the siege] and the remnant of the multitude [the country's working people].

[16]But Nebuzaradan the captain of the guard left some of the poorest of the land to be vinedressers and tillers of the soil.

[17]Also the pillars of bronze that belonged to the house of the Lord, and the bronze bases *or* pedestals [which supported the ten basins] and the bronze Sea *or* huge laver that were in the house of the Lord, the Chaldeans broke into pieces and carried all the bronze of them to Babylon.

[18]The pots [for carrying away ashes] also and the shovels and the snuffers and the bowls and the spoons and all the vessels of bronze used in the temple service they took away.

[19]Also the small bowls and the firepans and the basins and the pots and the lampstands and the incense cups and the bowls for the drink offerings—whatever was of gold the captain of the guard took away as gold, and whatever was of silver as silver.

[20]The two pillars, one Sea *or* huge laver, and [b]twelve bronze bulls *or* oxen under the Sea, which King Solomon had made in the house of the Lord—the bronze of all these things was beyond weighing.

[21]Concerning the pillars, the height of the one pillar was eighteen cubits (twenty-seven feet), and an ornamental molding of twelve cubits (eighteen feet) went around its circumference; it was four fingers thick, and it [the pillar] was hollow.

[22]An upper part *or* capital of bronze was on top of it. The height of one capital was five cubits (seven and one-half feet), with a network and pomegranates around it, all of bronze. The second pillar also, with its pomegranates, was similar to these.

[23]And there were ninety-six pomegranates on the sides; and all the pomegranates upon the network were a hundred round about.

[a] *The Septuagint* (Greek translation of the Old Testament) renders this word "mill." Hence it has been inferred that the Chaldeans ascribed to Zedekiah in his old age the same fate as that to which the Philistines assigned Samson (Judg. 16:21) (*The Cambridge Bible*). [b] King Ahaz had previously removed the twelve bronze bulls or oxen (I Kings 7:25) from under the big laver and had replaced them with a substructure of stone (II Kings 16:17), but obviously he had not put them beyond the reach of the Chaldeans when they set their minds to find them.

---

[a] 7 Or *the Jordan Valley*    [b] 8 Or *Chaldean*; also in verse 14
[c] 15 Or *the populace*    [d] 21 That is, about 27 feet high and 18 feet in circumference or about 8.1 meters high and 5.4 meters in circumference    [e] 22 That is, about 7 1/2 feet or about 2.3 meters

## New International Version

24The commander of the guard took as prisoners Seraiah the chief priest, Zephaniah the priest next in rank and the three doorkeepers. 25Of those still in the city, he took the officer in charge of the fighting men, and seven royal advisers. He also took the secretary who was chief officer in charge of conscripting the people of the land, sixty of whom were found in the city. 26Nebuzaradan the commander took them all and brought them to the king of Babylon at Riblah. 27There at Riblah, in the land of Hamath, the king had them executed.

So Judah went into captivity, away from her land. 28This is the number of the people Nebuchadnezzar carried into exile:

in the seventh year, 3,023 Jews;
29in Nebuchadnezzar's eighteenth year,
  832 people from Jerusalem;
30in his twenty-third year,
  745 Jews taken into exile by Nebuzaradan the commander of the imperial guard.
There were 4,600 people in all.

### Jehoiachin Released

31In the thirty-seventh year of the exile of Jehoiachin king of Judah, in the year Awel-Marduk became king of Babylon, on the twenty-fifth day of the twelfth month, he released Jehoiachin king of Judah and freed him from prison. 32He spoke kindly to him and gave him a seat of honor higher than those of the other kings who were with him in Babylon. 33So Jehoiachin put aside his prison clothes and for the rest of his life ate regularly at the king's table. 34Day by day the king of Babylon gave Jehoiachin a regular allowance as long as he lived, till the day of his death.

## Amplified Bible

24And the captain of the guard took [as prisoners] Seraiah the chief priest and Zephaniah the second priest and the three keepers of the door.
25He took also out of the city a court officer who had been overseer of the soldiers, and seven men of them who were next to the king [as advisers] *and* saw his face, who were found in the city, and the scribe of the prince *or* captain of the army who mustered the people of the land, and sixty men of the people of the land who were found in the midst of the city.
26And Nebuzaradan the captain of the guard took them and brought them to the king of Babylon at Riblah.
27And the king of Babylon smote them and put them to death at Riblah in the land of Hamath. Thus Judah was carried away captive out of his own land.
28This is the number of people whom Nebuchadrezzar carried away captive: in the seventh year, 3,023 Jews;
29In the eighteenth year of Nebuchadrezzar, he carried away captive from Jerusalem 832 persons;
30In the twenty-third year of Nebuchadrezzar, Nebuzaradan the captain of the [Babylonian] guard carried away captive of the Jews 745 persons. All the persons were 4,600.
31And in the thirty-seventh year of the captivity of Jehoiachin [also called Coniah and Jeconiah] king of Judah, in the twelfth month, on the twenty-fifth day of the month, Evil-merodach king of Babylon in the first year of his reign lifted up the head of Jehoiachin king of Judah [and showed favor to him] and brought him out of prison. [II Kings 25:27-30.]
32He spoke kindly to him and gave him a seat above the seats of the kings who were [captives] with him in Babylon,
33Jehoiachin put off his prison garments, and he dined regularly at the king's table all the days of his life.
34And his allowance, a continual one, was given him by the king of Babylon, a portion according to his requirements until the day of his death, *a*all the days of his life.

---

*a* The latter of these clauses is probably an afterthought in order to prevent ending the book with the word "death." The general object too of the paragraph [the last four verses] seems to have been to leave the reader with a parting ray of comfort and encouragement in the thought that even in exile the Lord remembered His people and softened the heart of the heathen tyrant toward David's seed (*The Cambridge Bible*). Note also the contrast between Zedekiah, who remained in prison till the day he died (Jer. 52:11), and Jehoiachin, who was released from prison and treated well by the Babylonian kings till the day he died.

# Lamentations

**1** *a* How deserted lies the city,
  once so full of people!
How like a widow is she,
  who once was great among the nations!
She who was queen among the provinces
  has now become a slave.

2 Bitterly she weeps at night,
  tears are on her cheeks.
Among all her lovers
  there is no one to comfort her.
All her friends have betrayed her;
  they have become her enemies.

3 After affliction and harsh labor,
  Judah has gone into exile.
She dwells among the nations;
  she finds no resting place.
All who pursue her have overtaken her
  in the midst of her distress.

4 The roads to Zion mourn,
  for no one comes to her appointed festivals.
All her gateways are desolate,
  her priests groan,
her young women grieve,
  and she is in bitter anguish.

5 Her foes have become her masters;
  her enemies are at ease.
The LORD has brought her grief
  because of her many sins.
Her children have gone into exile,
  captive before the foe.

6 All the splendor has departed
  from Daughter Zion.
Her princes are like deer
  that find no pasture;
in weakness they have fled
  before the pursuer.

7 In the days of her affliction and wandering
  Jerusalem remembers all the treasures
  that were hers in days of old.
When her people fell into enemy hands,
  there was no one to help her.
Her enemies looked at her
  and laughed at her destruction.

8 Jerusalem has sinned greatly
  and so has become unclean.
All who honored her despise her,
  for they have all seen her naked;
she herself groans
  and turns away.

9 Her filthiness clung to her skirts;
  she did not consider her future.
Her fall was astounding;
  there was none to comfort her.
"Look, LORD, on my affliction,
  for the enemy has triumphed."

10 The enemy laid hands
  on all her treasures;

---

# Lamentations

**1** How solitary *and* lonely sits the city [Jerusalem] that was [once] full of people! How like a widow has she become! She who was *a* great among the nations and princess among the provinces has become a tributary [in servitude]!
2 She weeps bitterly in the night, and her tears are [constantly] on her cheeks. Among all her lovers (allies) she has no one to comfort her. All her friends have dealt treacherously with her; they have become her enemies. [Jer. 3:1; 4:30.]
3 Judah has gone into exile [to escape] from the affliction and laborious servitude [of the homeland]. She dwells among the [heathen] nations, but she finds no rest; all her persecutors overtook her amid the [dire] straits [of her distress].
4 The roads to Zion mourn, because no one comes to the solemn assembly *or* the appointed feasts. All her gates are desolate, her priests sigh *and* groan, her maidens are grieved *and* vexed, and she herself is in bitterness.
5 Her adversaries have become the head; her enemies prosper. For the Lord has afflicted her for the multitude of her transgressions; her young children have gone into captivity before the enemy. [Jer. 30:14, 15; 52:28; Dan. 9:7-14.]
6 From the Daughter of Zion all her beauty *and* majesty have departed. Her princes have become like harts that find no pasture; they have fled without strength before the pursuer.
7 Jerusalem [earnestly] remembers in the days of her affliction, in the days of her [compulsory] wanderings *and* her bitterness, all the pleasant *and* precious things that she had from the days of old. When her people fell into *and* at the hands of the adversary, and there was none to help her, the enemy [gloated as they] looked at her, and they mocked at her desolations *and* downfall.
8 Jerusalem has grievously sinned; therefore she has become an unclean thing *and* has been removed. All who honored her despise her, because they have seen her nakedness; yes, she herself groans *and* sighs and turns [her face] away.
9 Her filthiness was in *and* on her skirts; she did not [seriously and earnestly] consider her final end. Therefore she has come down [from throne to slavery] singularly *and* astonishingly; she has no comforter. O Lord [cries Jerusalem], look at my affliction, for the enemy has magnified himself [in triumph]!
10 The adversary has spread out his hand upon all her precious *and* desirable things; for she has seen the na-

---

*a* It is possible to read the writings of the prophets only as valuable contributions to Old Testament history. And the reader may be enriched by familiarity with their forecasts of events which have been startlingly fulfilled, thus proclaiming the divine inspiration of the books and the wisdom and power of the God Who prompted their writings. But to stop there is by no means to grasp their full and outstanding purpose for today. Through the prophets God is speaking definitely and definitively to every individual and nation on earth, even right now demanding that we see ourselves as He sees us—a world of nations and individuals tobogganing toward disaster; and He declares that there is no alternative unless we repent and come to terms with Him.

---

*a* This chapter is an acrostic poem, the verses of which begin with the successive letters of the Hebrew alphabet.

## New International Version

she saw pagan nations
  enter her sanctuary—
those you had forbidden
  to enter your assembly.

¹¹ All her people groan
  as they search for bread;
they barter their treasures for food
  to keep themselves alive.
"Look, LORD, and consider,
  for I am despised."

¹² "Is it nothing to you, all you who pass by?
  Look around and see.
Is any suffering like my suffering
  that was inflicted on me,
that the LORD brought on me
  in the day of his fierce anger?

¹³ "From on high he sent fire,
  sent it down into my bones.
He spread a net for my feet
  and turned me back.
He made me desolate,
  faint all the day long.

¹⁴ "My sins have been bound into a yoke*ᵃ*;
  by his hands they were woven together.
They have been hung on my neck,
  and the Lord has sapped my strength.
He has given me into the hands
  of those I cannot withstand.

¹⁵ "The Lord has rejected
  all the warriors in my midst;
he has summoned an army against me
  to*ᵇ* crush my young men.
In his winepress the Lord has trampled
  Virgin Daughter Judah.

¹⁶ "This is why I weep
  and my eyes overflow with tears.
No one is near to comfort me,
  no one to restore my spirit.
My children are destitute
  because the enemy has prevailed."

¹⁷ Zion stretches out her hands,
  but there is no one to comfort her.
The LORD has decreed for Jacob
  that his neighbors become his foes;
Jerusalem has become
  an unclean thing among them.

¹⁸ "The LORD is righteous,
  yet I rebelled against his command.
Listen, all you peoples;
  look on my suffering.
My young men and young women
  have gone into exile.

¹⁹ "I called to my allies
  but they betrayed me.
My priests and my elders
  perished in the city
while they searched for food
  to keep themselves alive.

²⁰ "See, LORD, how distressed I am!
  I am in torment within,
and in my heart I am disturbed,
  for I have been most rebellious.
Outside, the sword bereaves;
  inside, there is only death.

*ᵃ 14 Most Hebrew manuscripts; many Hebrew manuscripts and Septuagint* He kept watch over my sins    *ᵇ 15 Or* has set a time for me / when he will

## Amplified Bible

tions enter her sanctuary [of the temple]—*ᵃ*when You commanded that they should not even enter Your congregation [in the outer courts]. [Deut. 23:3; Jer. 51:51; Ezek. 44:7, 9.]

¹¹ All her people groan *and* sigh, seeking for bread; they have given their desirable *and* precious things [in exchange] for food to revive their strength *and* bring back life. See, O Lord, and consider how wretched *and* lightly esteemed, how vile *and* abominable, I have become!

¹² Is it nothing to you, all you who pass by? Look and see if there is any sorrow like my sorrow which was dealt out to me, with which the Lord has afflicted me in the day of His fierce anger!

¹³ From above He has sent fire into my bones, and it prevailed against them. He has spread a net for my feet; He has turned me back. He has made me hopelessly miserable and faint all the day long.

¹⁴ The yoke of my transgressions is bound by His hand; they were twined together; they were set upon my neck. He has made my strength fail *and* [me to] stumble; the Lord has delivered me into the hands of those I am unable to resist *or* withstand. [Deut. 28:48.]

¹⁵ The Lord has made of no account all my [Jerusalem's] mighty men in the midst of me; He has proclaimed a set time against me to crush my young men. The Lord has trodden as in a winepress the Virgin Daughter of Judah.

¹⁶ For these things I weep; my eyes overflow with tears, because a comforter, one who could refresh *and* restore my soul, is far from me. My children are desolate *and* perishing, for the enemy has prevailed. [Lam. 1:21.]

¹⁷ Zion stretches forth her hands, but there is no comforter for her. The Lord has commanded concerning *and* against Jacob that his neighbors should be his adversaries; Jerusalem has become a filthy thing among them [an object of contempt].

¹⁸ The Lord is righteous (just and in the right); for I have rebelled against His commandment (His word). Hear, I pray you, all you peoples, and look at my sorrow *and* suffering; my maidens and my young men have gone into captivity.

¹⁹ I [Jerusalem] called to my lovers [allies], but they deceived me. My priests and my elders expired in the city while they sought food to save their lives.

²⁰ Behold, O Lord, how distressed I am! My vital parts (emotions) are in tumult *and* are deeply disturbed; my heart cannot rest *and* is violently agitated within me, for I have grievously rebelled. Outside the house the sword bereaves, at home there is [famine, pestilence] death!

*ᵃ The Ammonites and Moabites, descendants of Lot and kinsmen of Israel, were forbidden to enter the congregation of the Lord, "even to their tenth generation," because they refused assistance to the Israelites when they were fleeing from Egypt, and because they hired Balaam to curse Israel (Deut. 23:3, 4). The Israelites themselves never assembled any closer to the sanctuary of the temple than in the court outside its door. No Jew—not even David or Jesus Himself or any of His apostles—ever ventured into the sanctuary or temple proper except for certain Levites to whom such service was assigned. Two Greek words have customarily been translated "temple" in the New Testament. One (hieron) always means the temple enclosure (the porches, courts, chambers, and the like); the other word (naos) means the sanctuary proper—the Holy Place and the Holy of Holies—into which none but the authorized priests might go, and then only at stated times. But now, Jeremiah says, the forbidden heathen nations enter the very Holy of Holies for plunder! Nothing more humiliating could happen for a Jew than this.*

## New International Version

21 "People have heard my groaning,
    but there is no one to comfort me.
All my enemies have heard of my distress;
    they rejoice at what you have done.
May you bring the day you have announced
    so they may become like me.

22 "Let all their wickedness come before you;
    deal with them
as you have dealt with me
    because of all my sins.
My groans are many
    and my heart is faint."

**2** *a* How the Lord has covered Daughter Zion
    with the cloud of his anger*b*!
He has hurled down the splendor of Israel
    from heaven to earth;
he has not remembered his footstool
    in the day of his anger.

2 Without pity the Lord has swallowed up
    all the dwellings of Jacob;
in his wrath he has torn down
    the strongholds of Daughter Judah.
He has brought her kingdom and its princes
    down to the ground in dishonor.

3 In fierce anger he has cut off
    every horn*c,d* of Israel.
He has withdrawn his right hand
    at the approach of the enemy.
He has burned in Jacob like a flaming fire
    that consumes everything around it.

4 Like an enemy he has strung his bow;
    his right hand is ready.
Like a foe he has slain
    all who were pleasing to the eye;
he has poured out his wrath like fire
    on the tent of Daughter Zion.

5 The Lord is like an enemy;
    he has swallowed up Israel.
He has swallowed up all her palaces
    and destroyed her strongholds.
He has multiplied mourning and lamentation
    for Daughter Judah.

6 He has laid waste his dwelling like a garden;
    he has destroyed his place of meeting.
The LORD has made Zion forget
    her appointed festivals and her Sabbaths;
in his fierce anger he has spurned
    both king and priest.

7 The Lord has rejected his altar
    and abandoned his sanctuary.
He has given the walls of her palaces
    into the hands of the enemy;
they have raised a shout in the house of the LORD
    as on the day of an appointed festival.

8 The LORD determined to tear down
    the wall around Daughter Zion.
He stretched out a measuring line
    and did not withhold his hand from destroying.
He made ramparts and walls lament;
    together they wasted away.

9 Her gates have sunk into the ground;
    their bars he has broken and destroyed.

*a* This chapter is an acrostic poem, the verses of which begin with the
successive letters of the Hebrew alphabet.   *b 1* Or *How the Lord in
his anger / has treated Daughter Zion with contempt*   *c 3* Or *off / all the
strength*; or *every king*   *d 3* *Horn* here symbolizes strength.

## Amplified Bible

21 [My foes] have heard that I [Jerusalem] sigh *and*
groan, that I have no comforter [in You]. All my enemies
have heard of my trouble; they are glad [O Lord] that You
have done it. You will bring the day [of Judah's punish-
ment] that you have foretold *and* proclaimed; [it involves
also my foes' punishment] and they will become like me.
[Isa. 14:5, 6; Jer. 30:16.]
22 Let all their wickedness come before You; and deal
with them as You have dealt with me because of all my
transgressions; for my sighs *and* groans are many and my
heart is faint.

**2** How the Lord has covered the Daughter of Zion with
a cloud in His anger! He has cast down from heaven
to the earth the beauty *and* splendor of Israel and has not
[earnestly] remembered His footstool in the day of His
anger!
2 The Lord has swallowed up all the country places *and*
habitations of Jacob and has spared not *nor* pitied; He has
demolished in His wrath the strongholds of the Daughter
of Judah. He has cast down to the ground the kingdom
and its rulers, polluting them *and* depriving them of their
sanctity.
3 He has broken off in His fierce anger every horn
(means of defense) of Israel. He has drawn back His right
hand from before the enemy. And He has burned amidst
Jacob like a flaming fire consuming all around.
4 He has bent His bow like an enemy; He has stood with
His right hand set like a foe and has slain all the delights
*and* pride of the eye; on *and* in the tent of the Daughter of
Zion He has poured out His wrath like fire.
5 The Lord has become like an enemy; He has destroyed
Israel. He has destroyed all its palaces, has laid in ruins its
strongholds, and has multiplied in the Daughter of Judah
groaning and moaning and lamentation.
6 And He has violently broken down His temple like a
booth *or* hedge of a garden; He has destroyed the place of
His appointed assembly. The Lord has caused the solemn
appointed feasts and Sabbaths to be forgotten in Zion and
has spurned *and* rejected in the indignation of His anger
the king and the priest.
7 The Lord has scorned, rejected, *and* cast off His altar;
He has abhorred *and* disowned His sanctuary. He has giv-
en into the hand of the enemy the walls of her palaces [and
high buildings]; they have raised a clamor in the house of
the Lord as on a day of a solemn appointed feast.
8 The Lord purposed to lay in ruins the [city] wall of the
Daughter of Zion. He marked it off by measuring line; He
restrained not His hand from destroying. He made rampart and wall lament; they languished together.
9 Her gates have sunk into the ground; He has destroyed

## New International Version

Her king and her princes are exiled among the
nations,
the law is no more,
and her prophets no longer find
visions from the LORD.

¹⁰The elders of Daughter Zion
sit on the ground in silence;
they have sprinkled dust on their heads
and put on sackcloth.
The young women of Jerusalem
have bowed their heads to the ground.

¹¹My eyes fail from weeping,
I am in torment within;
my heart is poured out on the ground
because my people are destroyed,
because children and infants faint
in the streets of the city.

¹²They say to their mothers,
"Where is bread and wine?"
as they faint like the wounded
in the streets of the city,
as their lives ebb away
in their mothers' arms.

¹³What can I say for you?
With what can I compare you,
Daughter Jerusalem?
To what can I liken you,
that I may comfort you,
Virgin Daughter Zion?
Your wound is as deep as the sea.
Who can heal you?

¹⁴The visions of your prophets
were false and worthless;
they did not expose your sin
to ward off your captivity.
The prophecies they gave you
were false and misleading.

¹⁵All who pass your way
clap their hands at you;
they scoff and shake their heads
at Daughter Jerusalem:
"Is this the city that was called
the perfection of beauty,
the joy of the whole earth?"

¹⁶All your enemies open their mouths
wide against you;
they scoff and gnash their teeth
and say, "We have swallowed her up.
This is the day we have waited for;
we have lived to see it."

¹⁷The LORD has done what he planned;
he has fulfilled his word,
which he decreed long ago.
He has overthrown you without pity,
he has let the enemy gloat over you,
he has exalted the horn[a] of your foes.

¹⁸The hearts of the people
cry out to the Lord.
You walls of Daughter Zion,
let your tears flow like a river
day and night;
give yourself no relief,
your eyes no rest.

¹⁹Arise, cry out in the night,
as the watches of the night begin;

---

[a] 17 *Horn* here symbolizes strength.

## Amplified Bible

and broken her bars. Her king and her princes are [exiled]
among the nations; the law is no more; her prophets also
obtain no vision from the Lord.

¹⁰The elders of the Daughter of Zion sit on the ground
keeping silent; they have cast dust on their heads, they
have girded themselves with sackcloth. The maidens of
Jerusalem have bowed their heads to the ground [says
Jeremiah].

¹¹My eyes fail from weeping, my emotions are deeply
disturbed, my heart is poured out upon the ground [in
grief] because of the destruction of the daughter of my
people, because infants and nurslings faint in the streets
of the city.

¹²They keep crying to their mothers, Where is corn
and wine [food and drink]? as they faint like wounded men
in the streets of the city, as their lives ebb away on their
mothers' bosom.

¹³What [example of suffering in the past] is sufficient
for me to remind you for your [comfort]? To what shall
I liken you, O Daughter of Jerusalem? With what shall I
compare you, that I may comfort you, O Virgin Daughter
of Zion? For your ruin is as measureless as the sea! Who
can heal you? [Lam. 1:12; Dan. 9:12.]

¹⁴Your prophets have predicted for you falsehood and
delusion *and* foolish things; and they have not exposed
your iniquity *and* guilt to avert your captivity [by causing
you to repent]. But they have divined *and* declared to you
false *and* deceptive prophecies, worthless *and* misleading.

¹⁵All who pass by clap their hands at you; they hiss and
wag their heads at the Daughter of Jerusalem, saying, Is
this the city which was called the perfection of beauty, the
joy of all the earth?

¹⁶All your enemies have opened wide their mouths
against you; they scornfully hiss and gnash their teeth.
They cry, We have swallowed her up! Certainly this is the
day we have looked for; we have it, we see it!

¹⁷The Lord has done what He planned; He has carried
out *and* finished His word which He threatened *and* decreed [a] in the days of old. He has demolished without pity;
He has made the enemy rejoice over you and has exalted
the might of your foes. [Lev. 26:14-39; Deut. 28:15-68.]

¹⁸The hearts [of the inhabitants of Jerusalem] cried to
the Lord. [Then to the congregation, I, Jeremiah, cried,
addressing the wall as its symbol] O wall of the Daughter
of Zion, let tears run down like a river day and night; give
yourself no rest, let not your eyes stop [shedding tears].

¹⁹Arise [from your bed], cry out in the night, at the
beginning of the watches; pour out your heart like water

---

[a] "This reference to the ancient predictions of judgment against Israel
for their sins is of great importance, both because it shows that these
prophecies were then extant and well known among the Jews, and
because it shows that they were understood by the pious remnant
exactly as we now explain them" (Johan P. Lange, *A Commentary*).

## New International Version

pour out your heart like water
  in the presence of the Lord.
Lift up your hands to him
  for the lives of your children,
who faint from hunger
  at every street corner.

20 "Look, LORD, and consider:
  Whom have you ever treated like this?
Should women eat their offspring,
  the children they have cared for?
Should priest and prophet be killed
  in the sanctuary of the Lord?

21 "Young and old lie together
  in the dust of the streets;
my young men and young women
  have fallen by the sword.
You have slain them in the day of your anger;
  you have slaughtered them without pity.

22 "As you summon to a feast day,
  so you summoned against me terrors on every side.
In the day of the LORD's anger
  no one escaped or survived;
those I cared for and reared
  my enemy has destroyed."

**3**[a] I am the man who has seen affliction
  by the rod of the LORD's wrath.
2 He has driven me away and made me walk
  in darkness rather than light;
3 indeed, he has turned his hand against me
  again and again, all day long.

4 He has made my skin and my flesh grow old
  and has broken my bones.
5 He has besieged me and surrounded me
  with bitterness and hardship.
6 He has made me dwell in darkness
  like those long dead.

7 He has walled me in so I cannot escape;
  he has weighed me down with chains.
8 Even when I call out or cry for help,
  he shuts out my prayer.
9 He has barred my way with blocks of stone;
  he has made my paths crooked.

10 Like a bear lying in wait,
  like a lion in hiding,
11 he dragged me from the path and mangled me
  and left me without help.
12 He drew his bow
  and made me the target for his arrows.

13 He pierced my heart
  with arrows from his quiver.
14 I became the laughingstock of all my people;
  they mock me in song all day long.
15 He has filled me with bitter herbs
  and given me gall to drink.

16 He has broken my teeth with gravel;
  he has trampled me in the dust.
17 I have been deprived of peace;
  I have forgotten what prosperity is.
18 So I say, "My splendor is gone
  and all that I had hoped from the LORD."

19 I remember my affliction and my wandering,
  the bitterness and the gall.
20 I well remember them,
  and my soul is downcast within me.

a This chapter is an acrostic poem; the verses of each stanza begin with
the successive letters of the Hebrew alphabet, and the verses within
each stanza begin with the same letter.

## Amplified Bible

before the face of the Lord. Lift up your hands toward Him for the lives of your young children, who faint from hunger at the head of every street. [Ps. 62:8.]

20 Behold, O Lord, and consider [carefully] to whom You have done this. Should *and* shall women eat the fruit of their own bodies, the children whom they have tended *and* swaddled with their hands? Should *and* shall priest and prophet be slain in the place set apart [for the worship] of the Lord?

21 The young and the old lie on the ground in the streets; my maidens and my young men have fallen by the sword. You have slain them in the day of Your anger, slaughtering them without pity.

22 You [Lord] called together, as on an appointed feast day of solemn assembly, my terrors (dangers) from every side. And there was not one in the day of God's wrath who escaped or survived; those I have nursed and brought up, my enemy has destroyed.

**3** I am [Jeremiah] the man who has seen affliction under the rod of His wrath.

2 He has led me and brought me into darkness and not light.

3 Surely He has turned away from me; His hand is against me all the day.

4 My flesh and my skin has He worn out *and* made old; He has shattered my bones.

5 He has built up [siege mounds] against me and surrounded me with bitterness, tribulation, *and* anguish.

6 He has caused me to dwell in dark places like those long dead.

7 He walled me in so that I cannot get out; He has weighted down my chain.

8 Even when I cry and shout for help, He shuts out my prayer.

9 He has enclosed my ways with hewn stone; He has made my paths crooked.

10 He is to me like a bear lying in wait, and like a lion [hiding] in secret places.

11 He has turned me off my ways and pulled me in pieces; He has made me desolate.

12 He has bent His bow and set me as a mark for the arrow.

13 He has caused the arrows of His quiver to enter into my heart [the seat of my affections and desires].

14 I have become a derision to all my people, and [the subject of] their singsong all the day.

15 He has filled me with bitterness; He has made me drink to excess *and* until drunken with wormwood [bitterness].

16 He has also broken my teeth with gravel (stones); He has covered me with ashes.

17 And You have bereaved my soul *and* cast it off far from peace; I have forgotten what good *and* happiness *are*.

18 And I say, Perished is my strength and my expectation from the Lord.

19 [O Lord] remember [earnestly] my affliction and my misery, my wandering *and* my outcast state, the wormwood and the gall.

20 My soul has them continually in remembrance and is bowed down within me.

## New International Version

21 Yet this I call to mind
   and therefore I have hope:

22 Because of the LORD's great love we are not consumed,
   for his compassions never fail.
23 They are new every morning;
   great is your faithfulness.
24 I say to myself, "The LORD is my portion;
   therefore I will wait for him."

25 The LORD is good to those whose hope is in him,
   to the one who seeks him;
26 it is good to wait quietly
   for the salvation of the LORD.
27 It is good for a man to bear the yoke
   while he is young.

28 Let him sit alone in silence,
   for the LORD has laid it on him.
29 Let him bury his face in the dust—
   there may yet be hope.
30 Let him offer his cheek to one who would strike him,
   and let him be filled with disgrace.

31 For no one is cast off
   by the Lord forever.
32 Though he brings grief, he will show compassion,
   so great is his unfailing love.
33 For he does not willingly bring affliction
   or grief to anyone.

34 To crush underfoot
   all prisoners in the land,
35 to deny people their rights
   before the Most High,
36 to deprive them of justice—
   would not the Lord see such things?

37 Who can speak and have it happen
   if the Lord has not decreed it?
38 Is it not from the mouth of the Most High
   that both calamities and good things come?
39 Why should the living complain
   when punished for their sins?

40 Let us examine our ways and test them,
   and let us return to the LORD.
41 Let us lift up our hearts and our hands
   to God in heaven, and say:
42 "We have sinned and rebelled
   and you have not forgiven.

43 "You have covered yourself with anger and pursued us;
   you have slain without pity.
44 You have covered yourself with a cloud
   so that no prayer can get through.
45 You have made us scum and refuse
   among the nations.

46 "All our enemies have opened their mouths
   wide against us.
47 We have suffered terror and pitfalls,
   ruin and destruction."
48 Streams of tears flow from my eyes
   because my people are destroyed.

49 My eyes will flow unceasingly,
   without relief,
50 until the LORD looks down
   from heaven and sees.
51 What I see brings grief to my soul
   because of all the women of my city.

## Amplified Bible

21 But this I recall and therefore have I hope *and* expectation:
22 It is because of the Lord's mercy *and* loving-kindness that we are not consumed, because His [tender] compassions fail not. [Mal. 3:6.]
23 They are new every morning; great *and* abundant is Your stability *and* faithfulness. [Isa. 33:2.]
24 The Lord is my portion *or* share, says my living being (my inner self); therefore will I hope in Him *and* wait expectantly for Him. [Num. 18:20.]
25 The Lord is good to those who wait hopefully *and* expectantly for Him, to those who seek Him [inquire of and for Him and require Him by right of necessity and on the authority of God's word].
26 It is good that one should hope in *and* wait quietly for the salvation (the safety and ease) of the Lord.
27 It is good for a man that he should bear the yoke [of divine disciplinary dealings] in his youth.
28 Let him sit alone uncomplaining *and* keeping silent [in hope], because [God] has laid [the yoke] upon him [for his benefit]. [Rom. 8:28.]
29 Let him put his mouth in the dust [in abject recognition of his unworthiness]—there may yet be hope. [Mic. 7:17.]
30 Let him give his cheek to the One Who smites him [even through His human agents]; let him be filled [full] with [men's] reproach [in meekness].
31 For the Lord will not cast off forever! [Ps. 94:14.]
32 But though He causes grief, yet will He be moved to compassion according to the multitude of His loving-kindness *and* tender mercy.
33 For He does not willingly *and* from His heart afflict or grieve the children of men. [Ezek. 18:23, 32; Hos. 11:8; Heb. 12:5-10; II Pet. 3:9.]
34 To trample *and* crush underfoot all the prisoners of the earth,
35 To turn aside *and* deprive a man of his rights before the face of the Most High *or* a superior [acting as God's representative],
36 To subvert a man in his cause—[of these things] the Lord does not approve.
37 Who is he who speaks and it comes to pass, if the Lord has not authorized *and* commanded it?
38 Is it not out of the mouth of the Most High that evil and good both proceed [adversity and prosperity, physical evil or misfortune and physical good or happiness]?
39 Why does a living man sigh [one who is still in this life's school of discipline]? [And why does] a man complain for the punishment of his sins?
40 Let us test and examine our ways, and let us return to the Lord!
41 Let us lift up our hearts and our hands [and then with them mount up in prayer] to God in heaven:
42 We have transgressed and rebelled and You have not pardoned.
43 You have covered Yourself with wrath and pursued *and* afflicted us; You have slain without pity.
44 You have covered Yourself with a cloud so that no prayer can pass through.
45 You have made us offscouring and refuse among the nations.
46 All our enemies have gaped at us *and* railed against us.
47 Fear and pitfall have come upon us, devastation and destruction.
48 My eyes overflow with streams of tears because of the destruction of the daughter of my people.
49 My eyes overflow continually and will not cease
50 Until the Lord looks down and sees from heaven.
51 My eyes cause me grief at the fate of all the maidens [and the daughter-towns] of my city [Jerusalem].

## New International Version

52 Those who were my enemies without cause
  hunted me like a bird.
53 They tried to end my life in a pit
  and threw stones at me;
54 the waters closed over my head,
  and I thought I was about to perish.

55 I called on your name, LORD,
  from the depths of the pit.
56 You heard my plea: "Do not close your ears
  to my cry for relief."
57 You came near when I called you,
  and you said, "Do not fear."

58 You, Lord, took up my case;
  you redeemed my life.
59 LORD, you have seen the wrong done to me.
  Uphold my cause!
60 You have seen the depth of their vengeance,
  all their plots against me.

61 LORD, you have heard their insults,
  all their plots against me—
62 what my enemies whisper and mutter
  against me all day long.
63 Look at them! Sitting or standing,
  they mock me in their songs.

64 Pay them back what they deserve, LORD,
  for what their hands have done.
65 Put a veil over their hearts,
  and may your curse be on them!
66 Pursue them in anger and destroy them
  from under the heavens of the LORD.

4 *a* How the gold has lost its luster,
  the fine gold become dull!
The sacred gems are scattered
  at every street corner.

2 How the precious children of Zion,
  once worth their weight in gold,
are now considered as pots of clay,
  the work of a potter's hands!

3 Even jackals offer their breasts
  to nurse their young,
but my people have become heartless
  like ostriches in the desert.

4 Because of thirst the infant's tongue
  sticks to the roof of its mouth;
the children beg for bread,
  but no one gives it to them.

5 Those who once ate delicacies
  are destitute in the streets.
Those brought up in royal purple
  now lie on ash heaps.

6 The punishment of my people
  is greater than that of Sodom,
which was overthrown in a moment
  without a hand turned to help her.

7 Their princes were brighter than snow
  and whiter than milk,
their bodies more ruddy than rubies,
  their appearance like lapis lazuli.

8 But now they are blacker than soot;
  they are not recognized in the streets.
Their skin has shriveled on their bones;
  it has become as dry as a stick.

## Amplified Bible

52 I have been hunted down like a bird by those who
were my enemies without cause.
53 They [thought they had] destroyed my life in the dungeon (pit) and cast a stone [over it] above me. [Jer. 38.]
54 The waters ran down on my head; I said, I am gone.
55 I called upon Your name, O Lord, out of the depths [of the mire] of the dungeon. [Jer. 38:6.]
56 You heard my voice [then]: [Oh] hide not Your ear [now] at my prayer for relief.
57 You drew near on the day I called to You; You said, Fear not. [James 4:8.]
58 O Lord, You have pleaded the causes of my soul [You have managed my affairs and You have protected my person and my rights]; You have rescued *and* redeemed my life!
59 O Lord, You have seen my wrong [done to me]; judge *and* maintain my cause.
60 You have seen all their vengeance, all their devices against me.
61 You have heard their reproach *and* revilings, O Lord, and all their devices against me—
62 The lips *and* thoughts of my assailants are against me all day long.
63 Look at their sitting down and their rising up [their movements, doings, and secret counsels]; I am their singsong [the subject of their derision and merriment]. [Ps. 139:2; Isa. 37:28.]
64 Render to them a recompense, O Lord, according to the work of their hands.
65 You will give them hardness *and* blindness of heart; Your curse will be upon them.
66 You will pursue *and* afflict them in anger and destroy them from under Your heavens, O Lord.

4 How the gold has become dim! How the most pure gold has changed! The hallowed stones [of the temple] are poured out at the head of every street.
2 The noble *and* precious sons of Zion, [once] worth their weight in fine gold—how they are esteemed [merely] as earthen pots *or* pitchers, the work of the hands of the potter! [Isa. 30:14; Jer. 19:11; II Cor. 4:7.]
3 Even the jackals draw out the breast, they give suck to their young ones, but the daughter of my people has become cruel like ostriches in the wilderness [that desert their young].
4 The tongue of the nursing babe cleaves to the roof of its mouth because of thirst; the young children beg for food, but no one gives it to them.
5 Those who feasted on dainties are perishing in the streets; those who were brought up in purple lie cleaving to refuse *and* ash heaps.
6 For the punishment of the iniquity of the daughter of my people is greater than the punishment of the sin of Sodom, which was overthrown in a moment, and no hands had come against her *or* been laid on her. [Gen. 19:25.]
7 [In physical appearance] her princes were purer than snow, they were whiter than milk; they were more ruddy in body than rubies *or* corals, their shapely figures [suggested a carefully cut] sapphire.
8 [Prolonged famine has made] them look blacker than soot and darkness; they are not recognized in the streets. Their skin clings to their bones; it is withered and it has become [dry] like a stick.

*a* This chapter is an acrostic poem, the verses of which begin with the successive letters of the Hebrew alphabet.

## New International Version

9 Those killed by the sword are better off
  than those who die of famine;
racked with hunger, they waste away
  for lack of food from the field.

10 With their own hands compassionate women
  have cooked their own children,
who became their food
  when my people were destroyed.

11 The LORD has given full vent to his wrath;
  he has poured out his fierce anger.
He kindled a fire in Zion
  that consumed her foundations.

12 The kings of the earth did not believe,
  nor did any of the peoples of the world,
that enemies and foes could enter
  the gates of Jerusalem.

13 But it happened because of the sins of her prophets
  and the iniquities of her priests,
who shed within her
  the blood of the righteous.

14 Now they grope through the streets
  as if they were blind.
They are so defiled with blood
  that no one dares to touch their garments.

15 "Go away! You are unclean!" people cry to them.
  "Away! Away! Don't touch us!"
When they flee and wander about,
  people among the nations say,
  "They can stay here no longer."

16 The LORD himself has scattered them;
  he no longer watches over them.
The priests are shown no honor,
  the elders no favor.

17 Moreover, our eyes failed,
  looking in vain for help;
from our towers we watched
  for a nation that could not save us.

18 People stalked us at every step,
  so we could not walk in our streets.
Our end was near, our days were numbered,
  for our end had come.

19 Our pursuers were swifter
  than eagles in the sky;
they chased us over the mountains
  and lay in wait for us in the desert.

20 The LORD's anointed, our very life breath,
  was caught in their traps.
We thought that under his shadow
  we would live among the nations.

21 Rejoice and be glad, Daughter Edom,
  you who live in the land of Uz.
But to you also the cup will be passed;
  you will be drunk and stripped naked.

22 Your punishment will end, Daughter Zion;
  he will not prolong your exile.
But he will punish your sin, Daughter Edom,
  and expose your wickedness.

5 Remember, LORD, what has happened to us;
  look, and see our disgrace.
2 Our inheritance has been turned over to strangers,
  our homes to foreigners.
3 We have become fatherless,
  our mothers are widows.

## Amplified Bible

9 Those who are slain with the sword are more fortunate than those who are the victims of hunger [slain by the famine]; for they [the hungry] pine and ebb away, stricken through for want of the fruits of the field.

10 The hands of [heretofore] compassionate women have boiled their own children; they were their food during the destruction of the daughter of my people [Judah].

11 The Lord has fulfilled His wrath; He has poured out His fierce anger and has kindled a fire in Zion that has consumed her foundations.

12 The kings of the earth did not believe, nor did any of the inhabitants of the earth, that the oppressor and enemy could enter the gates of Jerusalem.

13 [But this happened] because of the sins of her [false] prophets and the iniquities of her priests, who shed the blood of the just and righteous in the midst of her.

14 [The false prophets and priests] wandered [staggering] in the streets as if blind; they had so polluted themselves with blood it was not [lawful] for men to touch their garments.

15 [People] cried to them, Go away! Unclean! Depart! Depart! Touch not! When they fled away, then they wandered [as fugitives]; men said among the nations, They shall not stay here any longer.

16 The anger of the Lord has scattered [and divided them among the nations]; He will no longer look after them. They did not respect the persons of the priests; they did not favor the elders.

17 As for us, our eyes yet failed and wasted away in looking for our worthless help. In our watching [on our watchtower] we have watched and waited expectantly for a nation [Egypt or some other one to come to our rescue] that could not save us. [Ezek. 29:16.]

18 [The missiles of the enemy] dog our steps, so that we cannot go into our streets; our end is near, our days are fulfilled—yes, our end has come.

19 Our pursuers were swifter than the eagles of the sky; they pursued us on the mountains, they lay in wait for us in the wilderness.

20 The breath of our nostrils, the anointed of the Lord [our king], was taken in their snares—he of whom we said, Under his shadow we shall live among the nations.

21 Rejoice and be glad, O Daughter of Edom, you who dwell in the land of Uz. But the cup [of the wine of God's wrath] also shall pass to you; you shall become drunk and make yourself naked. [Jer. 25:17.]

22 The punishment of your iniquity will be accomplished and completed, O Daughter of Zion; [the Lord] will no more carry you away or keep you in exile. But He will inspect and punish your iniquity and guilt, O Daughter of Edom; He will uncover your sins. [Ps. 137:7.]

5 O Lord, [earnestly] remember what has come upon us! Look down and see our reproach (our national disgrace)!
2 Our inheritance has fallen over to strangers, our houses to foreigners.
3 We have become orphans and fatherless; our mothers are like widows.

## New International Version

4 We must buy the water we drink;
  our wood can be had only at a price.
5 Those who pursue us are at our heels;
  we are weary and find no rest.
6 We submitted to Egypt and Assyria
  to get enough bread.
7 Our ancestors sinned and are no more,
  and we bear their punishment.
8 Slaves rule over us,
  and there is no one to free us from their hands.
9 We get our bread at the risk of our lives
  because of the sword in the desert.
10 Our skin is hot as an oven,
  feverish from hunger.
11 Women have been violated in Zion,
  and virgins in the towns of Judah.
12 Princes have been hung up by their hands;
  elders are shown no respect.
13 Young men toil at the millstones;
  boys stagger under loads of wood.
14 The elders are gone from the city gate;
  the young men have stopped their music.
15 Joy is gone from our hearts;
  our dancing has turned to mourning.
16 The crown has fallen from our head.
  Woe to us, for we have sinned!
17 Because of this our hearts are faint,
  because of these things our eyes grow dim
18 for Mount Zion, which lies desolate,
  with jackals prowling over it.

19 You, LORD, reign forever;
  your throne endures from generation to generation.
20 Why do you always forget us?
  Why do you forsake us so long?
21 Restore us to yourself, LORD, that we may return;
  renew our days as of old
22 unless you have utterly rejected us
  and are angry with us beyond measure.

## Amplified Bible

4 We have had to pay money to drink the water that belongs to us; our [own] wood is sold to us.
5 Our pursuers are upon our necks [like a yoke]; we are weary and are allowed no rest.
6 We have given the hand [as a pledge of fidelity and submission] to the Egyptians and to the Assyrians [merely] to get food to satisfy [our hunger].
7 Our fathers sinned and are no more, and *a* we have borne their iniquities. [Isa. 65:7; Jer. 16:11-12; 31:29; Ezek. 18:2-4.]
8 Servants *and* slaves rule over us; there is none to deliver us out of their hands. [Neh. 5:15.]
9 We get our bread at the peril of our lives because of the sword of the wilderness [the wild Arabs, who may attack if we venture into the fields to reap our harvests].
10 Our skin glows *and* is parched as from [the heat of] an oven because of the burning heat of [the fever of] famine.
11 They ravished the women in Zion, the virgins in the cities of Judah.
12 They hung princes by their hands; the persons of elders were not respected.
13 Young men carried millstones, and boys fell [staggering] under [burdens of] wood.
14 The elders have ceased from [congregating at] the city's gate, the young men from their music.
15 Ceased is the joy of our hearts; our dancing has turned into mourning.
16 The crown has fallen from our head [our honor is brought to the dust]! Woe to us, for we have sinned!
17 Because of this our hearts are faint *and* sick; because of these things our eyes are dim *and* see darkly.
18 As for Mount Zion, which lies desolate, the jackals prowl over it!
19 But You, O Lord, remain *and* reign forever; Your throne endures from generation to [all] generations.
20 Why do You forget us forever? Why do You forsake us so long?
21 Turn us to Yourself, O Lord, and we shall be turned *and* restored! Renew our days as of old!—
22 Or have You utterly rejected us? *b* Or are You exceedingly angry with us [still]?

---

*a* Fathers and sons alike are responsible for the calamity that has befallen Jerusalem. The truth of the matter is: this generation too deserved their punishment. "Woe to us, for we have sinned! Because of this our hearts are faint and sick; because of these things our eyes are dim *and* see darkly" (Lam. 5:16, 17).  *b* "The Book of Lamentations, like so many of even the saddest of the psalms, does in fact end with the language of hope, a hope that is so little apparent on the first reading of the conclusion to Lamentations that in many Hebrew manuscripts the words of Lam. 5:21 are repeated at the end, right after Lam. 5:22, so that its words of hope and restoration rather than the somber ending of "Or are You exceedingly angry with us [still]?" may be the last to fall upon the ear. A similar expedient is used in the case of Ecclesiastes, Isaiah, and Malachi" (*The Cambridge Bible*). See also footnote on Jer. 52:34.

# Ezekiel

# Ezekiel

## Ezekiel's Inaugural Vision

**1** In my thirtieth year, in the fourth month on the fifth day, while I was among the exiles by the Kebar River, the heavens were opened and I saw visions of God.

2 On the fifth of the month—it was the fifth year of the exile of King Jehoiachin— 3 the word of the LORD came to Ezekiel the priest, the son of Buzi, by the Kebar River in the land of the Babylonians.[a] There the hand of the LORD was on him.

4 I looked, and I saw a windstorm coming out of the north—an immense cloud with flashing lightning and surrounded by brilliant light. The center of the fire looked like glowing metal, 5 and in the fire was what looked like four living creatures. In appearance their form was human, 6 but each of them had four faces and four wings. 7 Their legs were straight; their feet were like those of a calf and gleamed like burnished bronze. 8 Under their wings on their four sides they had human hands. All four of them had faces and wings, 9 and the wings of one touched the wings of another. Each one went straight ahead; they did not turn as they moved.

10 Their faces looked like this: Each of the four had the face of a human being, and on the right side each had the face of a lion, and on the left the face of an ox; each also had the face of an eagle. 11 Such were their faces. They each had two wings spreading out upward, each wing touching that of the creature on either side; and each had two other wings covering its body. 12 Each one went straight ahead. Wherever the spirit would go, they would go, without turning as they went. 13 The appearance of the living creatures was like burning coals of fire or like torches. Fire moved back and forth among the creatures; it was bright, and lightning flashed out of it. 14 The creatures sped back and forth like flashes of lightning.

15 As I looked at the living creatures, I saw a wheel on the ground beside each creature with its four faces. 16 This was the appearance and structure of the wheels: They sparkled like topaz, and all four looked alike. Each appeared to be made like a wheel intersecting a wheel. 17 As they moved, they would go in any one of the four directions the creatures faced; the wheels did not change direction as the creatures went. 18 Their rims were high and awesome, and all four rims were full of eyes all around.

19 When the living creatures moved, the wheels beside them moved; and when the living creatures rose from the

**1** Now [when I was] in [my] thirtieth year, in the fourth month, in the fifth day of the month, as I was in the midst of captivity beside the river Chebar [in Babylonia], the heavens were opened and I saw visions of God.

2 On the fifth day of the month, which was in the fifth year of King Jehoiachin's captivity,

3 The word of the Lord came expressly to Ezekiel the priest, the son of Buzi, in the land of the Chaldeans by the river Chebar; and the hand of the Lord was there upon him. [I Kings 18:46; II Kings 3:15.]

4 As I looked, behold, a stormy wind came out of the north, and a great cloud with a fire enveloping it *and* flashing continually; a brightness was about it and out of the midst of it there seemed to glow amber metal, out of the midst of the fire.

5 And out of the midst of it came the likeness of four living creatures [or cherubim]. And this was their appearance: they had the likeness of a man,

6 But each one had four faces and each one had four wings.

7 And their legs were straight legs, and the sole of their feet was like the sole of a calf's foot, and they sparkled like burnished bronze.

8 And they had the hands of a man under their wings on their four sides. And the four of them had their faces and their wings thus:

9 Their wings touched one another; they turned not when they went but went every one straight forward.

10 As for the [a] likeness of their faces, they each had the face of a man [in front], and each had the face of a lion on the right side and the face of an ox on the left side; the four also had the face of an eagle [at the back of their heads]. [Rev. 4:7.]

11 Such were their faces. And their wings were stretched out upward [each creature had four wings]; two wings of each one were touching the [adjacent] wing of the creatures on either side of it, and [the remaining] two wings of each creature covered its body.

12 And they went every one straight forward; wherever the spirit would go, they went, and they turned not when they went.

13 In the midst of the living creatures there was what looked like burning coals of fire, like torches moving to and fro among the living creatures; the fire was bright and out of the fire went forth lightning.

14 And the living creatures darted back and forth like a flash of lightning.

15 Now as I was still looking at the living creatures, I saw one wheel upon the ground beside each of the living creatures with its four faces.

16 As to the appearance of the wheels and their construction: in appearance they gleamed like chrysolite; and the four were formed alike, and their construction work was as it were a wheel within a wheel.

17 When they went, they went in one of their four directions without turning [for they were faced that way].

18 As for their rims, they were so high that they were dreadful, and the four had their rims full of eyes round about.

19 And when the living creatures went, the wheels went beside them; and when the living creatures were lifted up from the earth, the wheels were lifted up.

---

*a* It is noteworthy that the four faces of the living creatures as here described are symbolic of "the four portraits of Jesus" as given in the four Gospels. Matthew represents our Lord as the King (the lion), Mark portrays Him as the Servant (the ox), Luke emphasizes His humanity (man), and John proclaims especially His deity (the eagle).

# New International Version

ground, the wheels also rose. 20Wherever the spirit would go, they would go, and the wheels would rise along with them, because the spirit of the living creatures was in the wheels. 21When the creatures moved, they also moved; when the creatures stood still, they also stood still; and when the creatures rose from the ground, the wheels rose along with them, because the spirit of the living creatures was in the wheels.

22Spread out above the heads of the living creatures was what looked something like a vault, sparkling like crystal, and awesome. 23Under the vault their wings were stretched out one toward the other, and each had two wings covering its body. 24When the creatures moved, I heard the sound of their wings, like the roar of rushing waters, like the voice of the Almighty,[a] like the tumult of an army. When they stood still, they lowered their wings.

25Then there came a voice from above the vault over their heads as they stood with lowered wings. 26Above the vault over their heads was what looked like a throne of lapis lazuli, and high above on the throne was a figure like that of a man. 27I saw that from what appeared to be his waist up he looked like glowing metal, as if full of fire, and that from there down he looked like fire; and brilliant light surrounded him. 28Like the appearance of a rainbow in the clouds on a rainy day, so was the radiance around him.

This was the appearance of the likeness of the glory of the LORD. When I saw it, I fell facedown, and I heard the voice of one speaking.

## Ezekiel's Call to Be a Prophet

**2** He said to me, "Son of man,[b] stand up on your feet and I will speak to you." 2As he spoke, the Spirit came into me and raised me to my feet, and I heard him speaking to me.

3He said: "Son of man, I am sending you to the Israelites, to a rebellious nation that has rebelled against me; they and their ancestors have been in revolt against me to this very day. 4The people to whom I am sending you are obstinate and stubborn. Say to them, 'This is what the Sovereign LORD says.' 5And whether they listen or fail to listen—for they are a rebellious people—they will know that a prophet has been among them. 6And you, son of man, do not be afraid of them or their words. Do not be afraid, though briers and thorns are all around you and you live among scorpions. Do not be afraid of what they say or be terrified by them, though they are a rebellious people. 7You must speak my words to them, whether they listen or fail to listen, for they are rebellious. 8But you, son of man, listen to what I say to you. Do not rebel like that rebellious people; open your mouth and eat what I give you."

9Then I looked, and I saw a hand stretched out to me. In it was a scroll, 10which he unrolled before me. On both sides of it were written words of lament and mourning and woe.

# Amplified Bible

20Wherever the spirit went, the creatures went and the wheels rose along with them, for the spirit or life of the [four living creatures acting as one] living creature was in the wheels.

21When those went, these went; and when those stood, these stood; and when those were lifted up from the earth, the wheels were lifted up high beside them, for the spirit or life of the [combined] living creature was in the wheels.

22Over the head of the [combined] living creature there was the likeness of a firmament, looking the terrible and awesome [dazzling of shining] crystal or ice stretched across the expanse of sky over their heads.

23And under the firmament their wings were stretched out straight, one toward another. Every living creature had two wings which covered its body on this side and two which covered it on that side.

24And when they went, I heard the sound of their wings like the noise of great waters, like the voice of the Almighty, the sound of tumult like the noise of a host. When they stood, they let down their wings.

25And there was a voice above the firmament that was over their heads; when they stood, they let down their wings.

26And above the firmament that was over their heads was the likeness of a throne in appearance like a sapphire stone, and seated above the likeness of a throne was a likeness with the appearance of a Man. [Phil. 2:5-8.]

27From what had the appearance of His waist upward, I saw a lustre as it were glowing metal with the appearance of fire enclosed round about within it; and from the appearance of His waist downward, I saw as it were the appearance of fire, and there was brightness [of a halo] round about Him.

28Like the appearance of the bow that is in the cloud on the day of rain, so was the appearance of the brightness round about. This was the appearance of the likeness of the glory of the Lord. And when I saw it, I fell upon my face and I heard a voice of One speaking. [Rev. 4:3.]

**2** And he said to me [Ezekiel], Son of man, stand upon your feet and I will speak to you.

2And the Spirit entered into me when He spoke to me and set me upon my feet, and I heard Him speaking to me.

3And He said to me, I send you, son of man, to the children of Israel, two rebellious nations that have rebelled against Me. They and their fathers have transgressed against Me even to this very day.

4And the children are impudent and hard of heart. I send you to them and you shall say to them, Thus says the Lord God.

5And they, whether they will hear or refuse to hear—for they are a rebellious house—yet shall they know and realize that there has been a prophet among them.

6And you, son of man, be not afraid of them, neither be afraid of their words; though briers and thorns are all around you and you dwell and sit among scorpions, be not afraid of their words nor be dismayed at their looks, for they are a rebellious house.

7And you shall speak My words to them whether they will hear or refuse to hear, for they are most rebellious.

8As for you, son of man, hear what I say to you; be not rebellious like that rebellious house; open your mouth and eat what I give you.

9And when I looked, behold, a hand was stretched out to me and behold, a scroll of a book was in it.

10And He spread it before me and it was written within and on the back, and written on it were words of lamentation and mourning and woe.

---

[a] 24 Hebrew *Shaddai*   [b] 1 The Hebrew phrase *ben adam* means *human being*. The phrase *son of man* is retained as a form of address here and throughout Ezekiel because of its possible association with "Son of Man" in the New Testament.

## New International Version

**3** And he said to me, "Son of man, eat what is before you, eat this scroll; then go and speak to the people of Israel." ²So I opened my mouth, and he gave me the scroll to eat.

³Then he said to me, "Son of man, eat this scroll I am giving you and fill your stomach with it." So I ate it, and it tasted as sweet as honey in my mouth.

⁴He then said to me: "Son of man, go now to the people of Israel and speak my words to them. ⁵You are not being sent to a people of obscure speech and strange language, but to the people of Israel— ⁶not to many peoples of obscure speech and strange language, whose words you cannot understand. Surely if I had sent you to them, they would have listened to you. ⁷But the people of Israel are not willing to listen to you because they are not willing to listen to me, for all the Israelites are hardened and obstinate. ⁸But I will make you as unyielding and hardened as they are. ⁹I will make your forehead like the hardest stone, harder than flint. Do not be afraid of them or terrified by them, though they are a rebellious people."

¹⁰And he said to me, "Son of man, listen carefully and take to heart all the words I speak to you. ¹¹Go now to your people in exile and speak to them. Say to them, 'This is what the Sovereign LORD says,' whether they listen or fail to listen."

¹²Then the Spirit lifted me up, and I heard behind me a loud rumbling sound as the glory of the LORD rose from the place where it was standing.ᵃ ¹³It was the sound of the wings of the living creatures brushing against each other and the sound of the wheels beside them, a loud rumbling sound. ¹⁴The Spirit then lifted me up and took me away, and I went in bitterness and in the anger of my spirit, with the strong hand of the LORD on me. ¹⁵I came to the exiles who lived at Tel Aviv near the Kebar River. And there, where they were living, I sat among them for seven days— deeply distressed.

### Ezekiel's Task as Watchman

¹⁶At the end of seven days the word of the LORD came to me: ¹⁷"Son of man, I have made you a watchman for the people of Israel; so hear the word I speak and give them warning from me. ¹⁸When I say to a wicked person, 'You will surely die,' and you do not warn them or speak out to dissuade them from their evil ways in order to save their life, that wicked person will die forᵇ their sin, and I will hold you accountable for their blood. ¹⁹But if you do warn the wicked person and they do not turn from their wickedness or from their evil ways, they will die for their sin; but you will have saved yourself.

²⁰"Again, when a righteous person turns from their righteousness and does evil, and I put a stumbling block before them, they will die. Since you did not warn them, they will die for their sin. The righteous things that person did will not be remembered, and I will hold you accountable for their blood. ²¹But if you do warn the righteous person not to sin and they do not sin, they will surely live because they took warning, and you will have saved yourself."

## Amplified Bible

**3** He said to me, Son of man, eat what you find [in this book]; eat this scroll; then go and speak to the house of Israel.

²So I opened my mouth, and He caused me to eat the scroll.

³And He said to me, Son of man, eat this scroll that I give you and fill your stomach with it. Then I ate it, and it was as sweet as honey in my mouth.

⁴And He said to me, Son of man, go, get you to the house of Israel and speak to them with My words.

⁵For you are not sent to a people of a foreign speech and of a difficult language but to the house of Israel;

⁶Not to many peoples of foreign speech and of a hard language, whose words you cannot understand. Surely, had I sent you to such people, they would have listened to you *and* heeded My words.

⁷But the house of Israel will not listen to you *and* obey you since they will not listen to Me *and* obey Me, for all the house of Israel are impudent and stubborn of heart.

⁸Behold, I have made your face strong *and* hard against their faces and your forehead strong *and* hard against their foreheads.

⁹Like an adamant harder than flint *or* a diamond point have I made your forehead; fear them not, neither be dismayed at their looks, for they are a rebellious house. [Isa. 50:7; Jer. 1:18; 15:20; Mic. 3:8.]

¹⁰Moreover, He said to me, Son of man, all My words that I shall speak to you, receive in your heart and hear with your ears.

¹¹And go, get you to the [Jewish] captives [in Babylon], to the children of your people, and speak to them and tell them, Thus says the Lord God, whether they will hear or refuse to hear.

¹²Then the Spirit lifted me up, and I heard behind me a voice of a great rushing [saying], Blessed be the glory of the Lord from His place [above the firmament].

¹³I heard the noise of the wings of the living creatures as they touched *and* joined each one the other [its sister wing], and I heard the noise of the wheels beside them and the noise of a great rushing.

¹⁴So the Spirit lifted me up and took me away [in the vision], and I went in bitterness [of discouragement] in the heat of my spirit; and the hand of the Lord was strong upon me.

¹⁵Then I came to them of the captivity at Tel-abib, who sat *and* dwelt by the river of Chebar, and I sat where they sat and remained there among them seven days, overwhelmed with astonishment *and* silent.

¹⁶And at the end of seven days, the word of the Lord came to me:

¹⁷Son of man, I have made you a watchman to the house of Israel; therefore hear the word at My mouth and give them warning from Me. [Isa. 52:8; 56:10; 62:6; Jer. 6:17.]

¹⁸If I say to the wicked, You shall surely die, and you do not give him warning or speak to warn the wicked to turn from his wicked way, to save his life, the same wicked man shall die in his iniquity, but his blood will I require at your hand.

¹⁹Yet if you warn the wicked and he turn not from his wickedness or from his wicked way, he shall die in his iniquity, but you have delivered yourself.

²⁰Again, if a righteous man turns from his righteousness (right doing and right standing with God) and some gift or providence which I lay before him he perverts into an occasion to sin and he commits iniquity, he shall die; because you have not given him warning, he shall die in his sin and his righteous deeds which he has done shall not be remembered, but his blood will I require at your hand.

²¹Nevertheless if you warn the righteous man not to sin and he does not sin, he shall surely live because he is warned; also you have delivered yourself from guilt.

---

ᵃ *12* Probable reading of the original Hebrew text; Masoretic Text
*sound—may the glory of the LORD be praised from his place*  ᵇ *18* Or *in*;
also in verses 19 and 20

## New International Version

²²The hand of the LORD was on me there, and he said to me, "Get up and go out to the plain, and there I will speak to you." ²³So I got up and went out to the plain. And the glory of the LORD was standing there, like the glory I had seen by the Kebar River, and I fell facedown.

²⁴Then the Spirit came into me and raised me to my feet. He spoke to me and said: "Go, shut yourself inside your house. ²⁵And you, son of man, they will tie with ropes; you will be bound so that you cannot go out among the people. ²⁶I will make your tongue stick to the roof of your mouth so that you will be silent and unable to rebuke them, for they are a rebellious people. ²⁷But when I speak to you, I will open your mouth and you shall say to them, 'This is what the Sovereign LORD says.' Whoever will listen let them listen, and whoever will refuse let them refuse; for they are a rebellious people.

### Siege of Jerusalem Symbolized

**4** "Now, son of man, take a block of clay, put it in front of you and draw the city of Jerusalem on it. ²Then lay siege to it: Erect siege works against it, build a ramp up to it, set up camps against it and put battering rams around it. ³Then take an iron pan, place it as an iron wall between you and the city and turn your face toward it. It will be under siege, and you shall besiege it. This will be a sign to the people of Israel.

⁴"Then lie on your left side and put the sin of the people of Israel upon yourself.ᵃ You are to bear their sin for the number of days you lie on your side. ⁵I have assigned you the same number of days as the years of their sin. So for 390 days you will bear the sin of the people of Israel.

⁶"After you have finished this, lie down again, this time on your right side, and bear the sin of the people of Judah. I have assigned you 40 days, a day for each year. ⁷Turn your face toward the siege of Jerusalem and with bared arm prophesy against her. ⁸I will tie you up with ropes so that you cannot turn from one side to the other until you have finished the days of your siege.

⁹"Take wheat and barley, beans and lentils, millet and spelt; put them in a storage jar and use them to make bread for yourself. You are to eat it during the 390 days you lie on your side. ¹⁰Weigh out twenty shekelsᵇ of food to eat each day and eat it at set times. ¹¹Also measure out a sixth of a hinᶜ of water and drink it at set times. ¹²Eat the food as you would a loaf of barley bread; bake it in the sight of the people, using human excrement for fuel." ¹³The LORD said, "In this way the people of Israel will eat defiled food among the nations where I will drive them."

¹⁴Then I said, "Not so, Sovereign LORD! I have never defiled myself. From my youth until now I have never eaten anything found dead or torn by wild animals. No impure meat has ever entered my mouth."

¹⁵"Very well," he said, "I will let you bake your bread over cow dung instead of human excrement."

## Amplified Bible

²²And the hand of the Lord was there upon me, and He said to me, Arise, go forth into the plain and I will talk with you there.

²³Then I arose and went forth into the plain, and behold, the glory of the Lord stood there, like the glory I had seen by the river Chebar, and I fell on my face.

²⁴Then the Spirit entered into me and set me on my feet; He spoke and said to me, Go, shut yourself up in your house.

²⁵But you, O son of man, behold, ropes will be put upon you and you will be bound with them, and you cannot go out among people.

²⁶And I will make your tongue cleave to the roof of your mouth so that you cannot talk and be a reprover of the people, for they are a rebellious house.

²⁷But when I speak with you, I will open your mouth and you shall say to the people, Thus says the Lord God; he who hears, let him hear, and he who refuses to hear, let him refuse; for they are a rebellious house.

**4** And you, son of man, take a tile and lay it before you, and make upon it a drawing of a city, even Jerusalem.

²And put siege works against it, build a siege wall against it, and cast up a mound against it; set camps also against it and set battering rams against it round about.

³Moreover, take a plate of iron and place it for an iron wall between you and the city; and set your face toward it and it shall be besieged, and you shall press the siege against it. This is a sign to the house of Israel.

⁴Then [bound as you are] lie upon your left [and north] side to bear symbolically the iniquity of the house of the ten tribes of Israel upon that side. According to the number of days that you shall lie upon it you shall bear their iniquity.

⁵For I have laid upon you the years of their iniquity, according to the number of the days, 390 days [representing 390 years]; so you shall bear the iniquity of the house of Israel.

⁶And when you have fulfilled the days for Israel, lie again, but on your right [and south] side, and you shall bear the iniquity of the house of Judah forty days. I have appointed you one day for each year.

⁷Therefore you shall set your face toward the siege of Jerusalem and your arm shall be uncovered [ready for battle], and you shall prophesy against [the city].

⁸And, behold, I will lay bands upon you and you shall not turn yourself from one side to another till you have ended the days of your siege.

⁹Also take wheat, barley, beans, lentils, millet, and spelt, and put them into one vessel and make bread of them. According to the number of the days that you shall lie upon your side, 390 days you shall eat of it.

¹⁰And the food you eat shall be by weight, twenty shekels *or* a full half pound a day, to be eaten at a fixed time each day.

¹¹You shall drink water by measure also, about one quart *or* the sixth part of a hin; you shall drink at a fixed time each day.

¹²And you shall eat your food as barley cakes and you shall bake it with human dung as fuel in the sight of the people.

¹³And the Lord said, Even thus shall the children of Israel eat their defiled bread among the nations to whom I will drive them. [Hos. 9:3.]

¹⁴Then said I, Ah, Lord God! Behold, I have never defiled myself. From my youth up even till now have I not eaten of that which dies of itself or is torn in pieces; neither did there ever come abominable flesh into my mouth. [Acts 10:14.]

¹⁵Then He said to me, Behold, I will let you use cow's dung instead of human dung, and you shall prepare your food with it.

---

ᵃ 4 Or *upon your side*    ᵇ 10 That is, about 8 ounces or about 230 grams    ᶜ 11 That is, about 2/3 quart or about 0.6 liter

## New International Version

16He then said to me: "Son of man, I am about to cut off the food supply in Jerusalem. The people will eat rationed food in anxiety and drink rationed water in despair, 17for food and water will be scarce. They will be appalled at the sight of each other and will waste away because of[a] their sin.

### God's Razor of Judgment

**5** "Now, son of man, take a sharp sword and use it as a barber's razor to shave your head and your beard. Then take a set of scales and divide up the hair. 2When the days of your siege come to an end, burn a third of the hair inside the city. Take a third and strike it with the sword all around the city. And scatter a third to the wind. For I will pursue them with drawn sword. 3But take a few hairs and tuck them away in the folds of your garment. 4Again, take a few of these and throw them into the fire and burn them up. A fire will spread from there to all Israel.

5"This is what the Sovereign LORD says: This is Jerusalem, which I have set in the center of the nations, with countries all around her. 6Yet in her wickedness she has rebelled against my laws and decrees more than the nations and countries around her. She has rejected my laws and has not followed my decrees.

7"Therefore this is what the Sovereign LORD says: You have been more unruly than the nations around you and have not followed my decrees or kept my laws. You have not even[b] conformed to the standards of the nations around you.

8"Therefore this is what the Sovereign LORD says: I myself am against you, Jerusalem, and I will inflict punishment on you in the sight of the nations. 9Because of all your detestable idols, I will do to you what I have never done before and will never do again. 10Therefore in your midst parents will eat their children, and children will eat their parents. I will inflict punishment on you and will scatter all your survivors to the winds. 11Therefore as surely as I live, declares the Sovereign LORD, because you have defiled my sanctuary with all your vile images and detestable practices, I myself will shave you; I will not look on you with pity or spare you. 12A third of your people will die of the plague or perish by famine inside you; a third will fall by the sword outside your walls; and a third I will scatter to the winds and pursue with drawn sword.

13"Then my anger will cease and my wrath against them will subside, and I will be avenged. And when I have spent my wrath on them, they will know that I the LORD have spoken in my zeal.

14"I will make you a ruin and a reproach among the nations around you, in the sight of all who pass by. 15You will be a reproach and a taunt, a warning and an object of horror to the nations around you when I inflict punishment on

*a 17* Or *away in*   *b 7* Most Hebrew manuscripts; some Hebrew manuscripts and Syriac *You have*

## Amplified Bible

16Moreover, He said to me, Son of man, behold, I will break the staff of bread [by which life is supported] in Jerusalem; and they shall eat bread rationed by weight and with fearfulness, and they shall drink water rationed by measure and with dismay (silent, speechless grief caused by the impending starvation), [Lev. 26:26; Ps. 105:16; Isa. 3:1.]

17In order that they may lack bread and water and look at one another in dismay and waste away [in their punishment] for their iniquity.

**5** And you, son of man [Ezekiel], take a sharp sword and use it as a barber's razor and shave your head and your beard. Then take balances for weighing and divide the hair into three parts.

2You shall burn one part with fire in the midst of the city, when the days of the siege are fulfilled; and you shall take a second part and strike with the sword round about it; and a third part you shall scatter to the wind, and I will draw out a sword after them.

3You shall also take from these a small number of hairs and bind them in the skirts of your robe.

4And of these again take some hairs and cast them into the midst of the fire and burn them in the fire; from there a fire shall come forth into all the house of Israel.

5Thus says the Lord God: This is Jerusalem; in the center of the nations I have set her, and countries are round about her.

6And she has changed *and* rebelled against My ordinances more wickedly than the [heathen] nations, and against My statutes more than the countries that are round about her; for [Israel] rejected My ordinances, and as for My statutes, they have not walked in them. [Rom. 2:14, 15.]

7Therefore thus says the Lord God: Because you were more turbulent *and* raged [against Me] more than the nations that are round about you and have not walked in My statutes, neither have kept My ordinances, nor have done according to the ordinances [concerning] the nations that are round about you; [Deut. 7:2-6; Josh. 23:7; Judg. 2:2.]

8Therefore thus says the Lord God: Behold, I, even I, am against you, and I will execute judgments in the midst of you in the sight of the nations.

9And because of all your abominations, I will do in you that which I have not done and the like of which I will never do again. [Lam. 4:6; Dan. 9:12; Amos 3:2.]

10Therefore fathers shall eat their sons in your midst, and sons shall eat their fathers; and I will execute judgments on you and all who are left of you I will scatter to all the winds. [Lev. 26:33; Deut. 28:64; Ezek. 12:14; Zech. 2:6.]

11Therefore, as I live, says the Lord God, surely because you have defiled My sanctuary with all your detestable things and with all your abominations, therefore will I also diminish you *and* withdraw My eye that it shall not spare you. And I also will have no pity.

12And a third of you shall die of pestilence and be consumed by famine in the midst of you; a third shall fall by the sword round about you; and I will scatter a third to all the winds and will draw out a sword after them.

13Thus shall My anger be spent and I will cause My wrath toward them to rest and I will be eased *and* comforted. And they shall know, understand, *and* realize that I the Lord have spoken in My zeal, when I have accomplished My wrath upon them. [Ezek. 36:6; 38:19.]

14Moreover, I will make you a desolation and a reproach among the nations that are round about you and in the sight of all who pass by. [Lev. 26:31, 32; Neh. 2:17.]

15So it shall be a reproach and a taunt, a warning and a horror *and* an astonishment to the [heathen] nations around you when I shall execute judgments upon you in anger and in wrath and in furious chastisements *and*

## New International Version

you in anger and in wrath and with stinging rebuke. I the LORD have spoken. ¹⁶When I shoot at you with my deadly and destructive arrows of famine, I will shoot to destroy you. I will bring more and more famine upon you and cut off your supply of food. ¹⁷I will send famine and wild beasts against you, and they will leave you childless. Plague and bloodshed will sweep through you, and I will bring the sword against you. I the LORD have spoken."

### Doom for the Mountains of Israel

**6** The word of the LORD came to me: ²"Son of man, set your face against the mountains of Israel; prophesy against them ³and say: 'You mountains of Israel, hear the word of the Sovereign LORD. This is what the Sovereign LORD says to the mountains and hills, to the ravines and valleys: I am about to bring a sword against you, and I will destroy your high places. ⁴Your altars will be demolished and your incense altars will be smashed; and I will slay your people in front of your idols. ⁵I will lay the dead bodies of the Israelites in front of their idols, and I will scatter your bones around your altars. ⁶Wherever you live, the towns will be laid waste and the high places demolished, so that your altars will be laid waste and devastated, your idols smashed and ruined, your incense altars broken down, and what you have made wiped out. ⁷Your people will fall slain among you, and you will know that I am the LORD.

⁸"But I will spare some, for some of you will escape the sword when you are scattered among the lands and nations. ⁹Then in the nations where they have been carried captive, those who escape will remember me—how I have been grieved by their adulterous hearts, which have turned away from me, and by their eyes, which have lusted after their idols. They will loathe themselves for the evil they have done and for all their detestable practices. ¹⁰And they will know that I am the LORD; I did not threaten in vain to bring this calamity on them.

¹¹"This is what the Sovereign LORD says: Strike your hands together and stamp your feet and cry out "Alas!" because of all the wicked and detestable practices of the people of Israel, for they will fall by the sword, famine and plague. ¹²One who is far away will die of the plague, and one who is near will fall by the sword, and anyone who survives and is spared will die of famine. So will I pour out my wrath on them. ¹³And they will know that I am the LORD, when their people lie slain among their idols around their altars, on every high hill and on all the mountaintops, under every spreading tree and every leafy oak—places where they offered fragrant incense to all their

## Amplified Bible

rebukes—I the Lord have spoken it. [Deut. 28:37; Ps. 79:4; Jer. 24:9.]

¹⁶When I shall loose against them the evil arrows of hunger that are for destruction, which I will send to destroy you, then I will increase the famine upon you and will break your staff of bread.

¹⁷And I will send upon you hunger and wild beasts, and they shall bereave you [of your loved ones]; and pestilence and blood shall pass through you, and I will bring the sword upon you. I the Lord have spoken it.

**6** And the word of the Lord came to me, saying, ²Son of man, set your face toward the mountains of Israel and prophesy against them,

³And say, You mountains of Israel, hear the word of the Lord God! Thus says the Lord God to the mountains and the hills, to the river ravines and the valleys: Behold, I, even I, will bring a sword upon you, and I will destroy your high places [of idolatrous worship],

⁴And your altars shall be made desolate and your sun-pillars shall be broken in pieces, and I will cast down your slain before your idols. [Lev. 26:30.]

⁵And I will lay the dead bodies of the children of Israel before their idols, and I will scatter your bones round about your altars.

⁶In all your dwelling places the cities shall be laid waste and the high places shall be made desolate, that your altars may bear their guilt *and* be laid waste and made desolate, your idols may be broken and destroyed, your sun-images may be hewn down, and your handiworks may be wiped away *and* blotted out.

⁷And the slain shall fall in the midst of you, and you shall ᵃknow, understand, *and* realize that I am the Lord.

⁸Yet will I leave some of you alive. When you have some that shall escape the sword among the nations, when you shall be scattered through the countries,

⁹Then those of you who escape shall [earnestly] remember Me among the nations to which they shall be carried captive, how that I have been broken by their lewdness *and* have Myself broken their wanton heart which has departed from Me and blinded their eyes which turn after their idols wantonly; and they shall be loathsome in their own sight for the evils which they have committed in all their abominations.

¹⁰And they shall know, understand, *and* realize that I am the Lord. I have not said in vain that I would bring this evil calamity [in punishment] upon them.

¹¹Thus says the Lord God: Strike with your fist, stamp with your foot, and say, Alas! over all the vile abominations of the house of Israel for which [Israel] shall fall by sword, by famine, and by pestilence.

¹²He who is far off shall die of the pestilence, and he that is near shall fall by the sword, and he who remains and is preserved shall die by the famine. Thus will I accomplish My wrath upon them.

¹³Then shall you know, understand, *and* realize that I am the Lord, when their slain shall lie among their idols round about their altars upon every high hill, on all the tops of the mountains, under every green tree, and under every thickly leafed oak, the places where they were accustomed to offer sweet incense to all their idols.

---

ᵃ On the basis of the fact that God uses it more often than any other important word in the Bible, the word "Lord" becomes the most essential term in any language for the welfare of any person. It is not enough that one knows that God is God, and that He is, for only a fool would deny that (Ps. 53:1), but God demands of every person who is to be recognized by Him that he accepts Him as Lord of his life, his Sovereign Ruler, to Whom he yields implicit obedience. When Thomas was able to say of Jesus, "My Lord and my God!" (John 20:28), his doubts ceased to exist. Nothing short of that kind of expression of Christ's lordship meets God's demands. Watch for the word "Lord" in the Bible; it occurs around 5,000 times. Watch also for this phrase ("you shall know, understand, *and* realize that I am the Lord") throughout the book of Ezekiel.

## New International Version

idols. ¹⁴And I will stretch out my hand against them and make the land a desolate waste from the desert to Diblah[a]—wherever they live. Then they will know that I am the LORD.'"

### The End Has Come

**7** The word of the LORD came to me: ²"Son of man, this is what the Sovereign LORD says to the land of Israel:

"'The end! The end has come
　upon the four corners of the land!
³The end is now upon you,
　and I will unleash my anger against you.
I will judge you according to your conduct
　and repay you for all your detestable practices.
⁴I will not look on you with pity;
　I will not spare you.
I will surely repay you for your conduct
　and for the detestable practices among you.

"'Then you will know that I am the LORD.'

⁵"This is what the Sovereign LORD says:

"'Disaster! Unheard-of[b] disaster!
　See, it comes!
⁶The end has come!
　The end has come!
It has roused itself against you.
　See, it comes!
⁷Doom has come upon you,
　upon you who dwell in the land.
The time has come! The day is near!
　There is panic, not joy, on the mountains.
⁸I am about to pour out my wrath on you
　and spend my anger against you.
I will judge you according to your conduct
　and repay you for all your detestable practices.
⁹I will not look on you with pity;
　I will not spare you.
I will repay you for your conduct
　and for the detestable practices among you.

"'Then you will know that it is I the LORD who strikes you.

¹⁰"'See, the day!
　See, it comes!
Doom has burst forth,
　the rod has budded,
　arrogance has blossomed!
¹¹Violence has arisen,[c]
　a rod to punish the wicked.
None of the people will be left,
　none of that crowd—
none of their wealth,
　nothing of value.
¹²The time has come!
　The day has arrived!
Let not the buyer rejoice
　nor the seller grieve,
　for my wrath is on the whole crowd.
¹³The seller will not recover
　the property that was sold—
　as long as both buyer and seller live.
For the vision concerning the whole crowd
　will not be reversed.
Because of their sins, not one of them
　will preserve their life.

¹⁴"'They have blown the trumpet,
　they have made all things ready,
but no one will go into battle,
　for my wrath is on the whole crowd.

## Amplified Bible

¹⁴And I will stretch out My hand upon them and make the land desolate and waste, yes, more desolate than the wilderness toward Diblah [a Moabite city], throughout all their dwelling places; and they shall know, understand, *and* realize that I am the Lord.

**7** Moreover, the word of the Lord came to me, saying, ²Also, son of man, thus says the Lord God to the land of Israel: An end! The end has come upon the four corners of the land. [Ezek. 11:13; Amos 8:2.]
³Now is the end upon you, and I will send My anger upon you and will judge you according to your ways and will bring upon you retribution for all your abominations.
⁴And My eye will not spare you, neither will I have pity; but I will bring recompense for your evil ways upon you, while your abominations are in the midst of you [calling down punishment from a righteous God]; and you shall know (recognize, understand, and realize) that I am the Lord.
⁵Thus says the Lord God: Behold, an evil is coming, [an evil so destructive and injurious, so sudden and violent, that it stands alone, not as a succession but as] only one evil.
⁶An end has come! The end has come! [The end—after sleeping so long] awakes against you. See, it has come!
⁷Your turn (your doom) has come upon you, O inhabitant of the land; the time has come, the day is near, a day not of joyful shouting, but a day of tumult upon the mountains.
⁸Now will I shortly pour out My wrath upon you and finish spending My anger against you, and I will judge you according to your ways and will recompense you with punishment for all your abominations.
⁹And My eye will not spare, nor will I have pity. I will punish you according to your ways while your abominations are right in the midst of you. And you shall know, understand, *and* realize that it is I the Lord Who smites you.
¹⁰Behold, the day! Behold, it has come! Your doom has gone forth, the rod has blossomed, pride has budded.
¹¹Violence has grown up into a rod of wickedness; none of [Israel] shall remain, none of their abundance, none of their wealth; neither shall there be preeminence among them *or* wailing for them.
¹²The time has come, the day draws near. Let not the buyer rejoice nor the seller mourn, for wrath is upon all their multitude.
¹³For the seller shall not return to that which is sold, even were they yet alive. For the vision [of punishment] is touching [Israel's] whole multitude; he shall not come back, neither shall any strengthen himself whose life is in his iniquity.
¹⁴They have blown the trumpet and have made all ready, but none goes to the battle, for My wrath is upon all their multitude.

---

*a* 14 Most Hebrew manuscripts; a few Hebrew manuscripts *Riblah*
*b* 5 Most Hebrew manuscripts; some Hebrew manuscripts and Syriac
*Disaster after*　*c* 11 Or *The violent one has become*

## New International Version

15Outside is the sword;
    inside are plague and famine.
  Those in the country
    will die by the sword;
  those in the city
    will be devoured by famine and plague.
16The fugitives who escape
    will flee to the mountains.
  Like doves of the valleys,
    they will all moan,
    each for their own sins.
17Every hand will go limp;
    every leg will be wet with urine.
18They will put on sackcloth
    and be clothed with terror.
  Every face will be covered with shame,
    and every head will be shaved.

19"'They will throw their silver into the streets,
    and their gold will be treated as a thing unclean.
  Their silver and gold
    will not be able to deliver them
    in the day of the LORD's wrath.
  It will not satisfy their hunger
    or fill their stomachs,
    for it has caused them to stumble into sin.
20They took pride in their beautiful jewelry
    and used it to make their detestable idols.
  They made it into vile images;
    therefore I will make it a thing unclean for them.
21I will give their wealth as plunder to foreigners
    and as loot to the wicked of the earth,
    who will defile it.
22I will turn my face away from the people,
    and robbers will desecrate the place I treasure.
  They will enter it
    and will defile it.

23"'Prepare chains!
  For the land is full of bloodshed,
    and the city is full of violence.
24I will bring the most wicked of nations
    to take possession of their houses.
  I will put an end to the pride of the mighty,
    and their sanctuaries will be desecrated.
25When terror comes,
    they will seek peace in vain.
26Calamity upon calamity will come,
    and rumor upon rumor.
  They will go searching for a vision from the prophet,
    priestly instruction in the law will cease,
    the counsel of the elders will come to an end.
27The king will mourn,
    the prince will be clothed with despair,
    and the hands of the people of the land will tremble.
  I will deal with them according to their conduct,
    and by their own standards I will judge them.

"'Then they will know that I am the LORD.'"

### Idolatry in the Temple

**8** In the sixth year, in the sixth month on the fifth day, while I was sitting in my house and the elders of Judah were sitting before me, the hand of the Sovereign LORD came on me there. 2I looked, and I saw a figure like that of a man.[a] From what appeared to be his waist down he was like fire, and from there up his appearance was as bright as glowing metal. 3He stretched out what looked like a hand and took me by the hair of my head. The Spirit lifted me up between earth and heaven and in visions of God he

## Amplified Bible

15The sword is without and pestilence and famine are within. He who is in the field shall die by the sword, and him who is in the city shall famine and pestilence devour.
16But those of them that escape shall escape, but shall be on the mountains like doves of the valleys, all of them moaning, every one in his iniquity's [punishment].
17All hands shall be feeble and all knees shall be weak as water. [Isa. 13:7; Jer. 6:24; Ezek. 21:7.]
18They shall also gird themselves with sackcloth; horror and dismay shall cover them, and shame shall be upon all faces and baldness upon all their heads [as evidence of grief].
19They shall cast their silver into the streets, and their gold shall be [discarded] like an unclean thing or rubbish; their silver and their gold shall not be able to deliver them in the day of the wrath of the Lord; they shall not satisfy their animal cravings nor fill their stomachs with them, for [wealth] has been the stumbling block of their iniquity. [Prov. 11:4; Zeph. 1:18.]
20As for the beauty of gold for ornament, they turned it to pride and made of it the images of their abominations (idols) and of their detestable things. Therefore I will make it to them as an unclean thing.
21And I will give it for plunder into the hands of strangers and to the wicked of the earth for a spoil, and they shall profane it.
22Also I will turn My face from them and they shall profane My secret treasure [the temple]; and robbers shall enter into it and profane it.
23Prepare the chain [of imprisonment], for the land is full of bloodguiltiness [murders committed with pretended formalities of justice] and the city is full of violence.
24Therefore I will bring in the worst of the [heathen] nations, who will take possession of the houses [of the people of Judah]; I will also silence their strongholds and put an end to their proud might, and their holy places and those who sanctify them shall be profaned.
25Distress, panic, and destruction shall come, and they [of Judah] shall seek peace, and there shall be none.
26Calamity shall come upon calamity and rumor shall be upon rumor, and they shall seek a vision of the prophet; and the law and instruction shall cease from the [distracted] priest and counsel from the [dismayed] elders. [Ps. 74:9; Lam. 2:9.]
27The king [of Judah] shall wear mourning and the prince shall clothe himself with garments of despair and desolation, while the hands of the people of the land shall tremble [palsied by terror]; for I will do to them in accordance with their ways, and according to their deserts will I judge them; and they shall know, recognize, and realize that I am the Lord.

**8** And in the sixth year [of the capitivity of King Jehoiachin], in the sixth month, on the fifth day of the month, as I sat in my house [a captive of the Babylonians] with the elders of Judah sitting before me, the hand of the Lord God fell there upon me.
2Then I beheld, and lo, a likeness of a Man with the appearance of fire; from His waist downward He was like fire, and from His waist upward He had the appearance of brightness like gleaming bronze.
3And He put forth the form of a hand and took me by a lock of my head; and the Spirit lifted me up between the earth and the heavens and brought me in the visions of

---

a 2 Or saw a fiery figure

## New International Version

took me to Jerusalem, to the entrance of the north gate of the inner court, where the idol that provokes to jealousy stood. [4]And there before me was the glory of the God of Israel, as in the vision I had seen in the plain.

[5]Then he said to me, "Son of man, look toward the north." So I looked, and in the entrance north of the gate of the altar I saw this idol of jealousy.

[6]And he said to me, "Son of man, do you see what they are doing—the utterly detestable things the Israelites are doing here, things that will drive me far from my sanctuary? But you will see things that are even more detestable."

[7]Then he brought me to the entrance to the court. I looked, and I saw a hole in the wall. [8]He said to me, "Son of man, now dig into the wall." So I dug into the wall and saw a doorway there.

[9]And he said to me, "Go in and see the wicked and detestable things they are doing here." [10]So I went in and looked, and I saw portrayed all over the walls all kinds of crawling things and unclean animals and all the idols of Israel. [11]In front of them stood seventy elders of Israel, and Jaazaniah son of Shaphan was standing among them. Each had a censer in his hand, and a fragrant cloud of incense was rising.

[12]He said to me, "Son of man, have you seen what the elders of Israel are doing in the darkness, each at the shrine of his own idol? They say, 'The LORD does not see us; the LORD has forsaken the land.'" [13]Again, he said, "You will see them doing things that are even more detestable."

[14]Then he brought me to the entrance of the north gate of the house of the LORD, and I saw women sitting there, mourning the god Tammuz. [15]He said to me, "Do you see this, son of man? You will see things that are even more detestable than this."

[16]He then brought me into the inner court of the house of the LORD, and there at the entrance to the temple, between the portico and the altar, were about twenty-five men. With their backs toward the temple of the LORD and their faces toward the east, they were bowing down to the sun in the east.

[17]He said to me, "Have you seen this, son of man? Is it a trivial matter for the people of Judah to do the detestable things they are doing here? Must they also fill the land with violence and continually arouse my anger? Look at them putting the branch to their nose! [18]Therefore I will deal with them in anger; I will not look on them with pity or spare them. Although they shout in my ears, I will not listen to them."

### Judgment on the Idolaters

**9** Then I heard him call out in a loud voice, "Bring near those who are appointed to execute judgment on the city, each with a weapon in his hand." [2]And I saw six men coming from the direction of the upper gate, which faces north, each with a deadly weapon in his hand. With them was a man clothed in linen who had a writing kit at his side. They came in and stood beside the bronze altar.

[3]Now the glory of the God of Israel went up from above the cherubim, where it had been, and moved to the thresh-

## Amplified Bible

God to Jerusalem, to the entrance of the door of the inner [court] which faces toward the north, where was the seat of the idol (image) of jealousy, which provokes to jealousy. [II Kings 16:10-16; 21:4, 5.]

[4]And behold, there was the glory of the God of Israel [Who had loved and chosen them], like the vision I saw in the plain. [Ezek. 1:28; 3:22, 23.]

[5]Then He [the Spirit] said to me, Son of man, now lift up your eyes toward the north. So I lifted up my eyes toward the north, and behold, on the north of the altar gate was that idol (image) of jealousy in the entrance.

[6]Furthermore, [the Spirit] said to me, Son of man, do you see what they are doing? The great abominations that the house of Israel is committing here to drive Me far from My sanctuary? But you shall again see greater abominations.

[7]And He brought me to the door of the court; and when I looked, behold, there was a hole in the wall.

[8]Then He said to me, Son of man, dig now in the wall. And when I had dug in the wall, behold, there was a door.

[9]And He said to me, Go in and see the wicked abominations that they do here.

[10]So I went in and saw there pictures of every form of creeping things and loathsome beasts and all the idols of the house of Israel, painted round about on the wall.

[11]And there stood before these [pictures] seventy men of the elders of the house of Israel, and in the midst of them stood Jaazaniah the son of Shaphan [the scribe], with every man his censer in his hand, and a thick cloud of incense was going up [in prayer to these their gods].

[12]Then said He to me, Son of man, have you seen what the elders of the house of Israel do in the dark, every man in his [secret] chambers of [idol] pictures? For they say, The Lord does not see us; the Lord has forsaken the land.

[13]He also said to me, Yet again you shall see greater abominations which they are committing.

[14]Then He brought me to the entrance of the north gate of the Lord's house; and behold, there sat women weeping for Tammuz [a Babylonian god, who was supposed to die annually and subsequently be resurrected].

[15]Then said [the Spirit] to me, Have you seen this, O son of man? Yet again you shall see greater abominations that they are committing.

[16]And He brought me to the inner court of the Lord's house; and behold, at the door of the temple of the Lord, between the porch and the bronze altar, were about twenty-five men with their backs to the temple of the Lord and their faces toward the east, and they were bowing themselves toward the east *and* worshiping the sun.

[17]Then [the Spirit] said to me, Have you seen this, O son of man? Is it too slight a thing to the house of Judah to commit the abominations which they commit here, that they must fill the land with violence and turn back afresh to provoke Me to anger? And behold, they put the branch to their nose [actually, before their mouths, in superstitious worship]!

[18]Therefore I will deal in wrath; My eye will not spare, nor will I have pity; and though they cry in My ears with a loud voice, yet will I not hear them. [Prov. 1:28; Isa. 1:15; Jer. 11:11; 14:12; Mic. 3:4; Zech. 7:13.]

**9** [The Spirit] cried in my ears [in the vision] with a loud voice, saying, Cause those to draw near who have charge over the city [as executioners], every man with his destroying weapon in his hand.

[2]And behold, six men came from the direction of the Upper Gate, which faces north, every man with his battle-ax in his hand; and one man among them was clothed in linen, with a writer's ink bottle at his side. And they went in and stood beside the bronze altar.

[3]And the glory of the God of Israel [the Shekinah, cloud] had gone up from the cherubim upon which it had rested

## New International Version

old of the temple. Then the LORD called to the man clothed in linen who had the writing kit at his side ⁴and said to him, "Go throughout the city of Jerusalem and put a mark on the foreheads of those who grieve and lament over all the detestable things that are done in it."

⁵As I listened, he said to the others, "Follow him through the city and kill, without showing pity or compassion. ⁶Slaughter the old men, the young men and women, the mothers and children, but do not touch anyone who has the mark. Begin at my sanctuary." So they began with the old men who were in front of the temple.

⁷Then he said to them, "Defile the temple and fill the courts with the slain. Go!" So they went out and began killing throughout the city. ⁸While they were killing and I was left alone, I fell facedown, crying out, "Alas, Sovereign LORD! Are you going to destroy the entire remnant of Israel in this outpouring of your wrath on Jerusalem?"

⁹He answered me, "The sin of the people of Israel and Judah is exceedingly great; the land is full of bloodshed and the city is full of injustice. They say, 'The LORD has forsaken the land; the LORD does not see.' ¹⁰So I will not look on them with pity or spare them, but I will bring down on their own heads what they have done."

¹¹Then the man in linen with the writing kit at his side brought back word, saying, "I have done as you commanded."

### God's Glory Departs From the Temple

**10** I looked, and I saw the likeness of a throne of lapis lazuli above the vault that was over the heads of the cherubim. ²The LORD said to the man clothed in linen, "Go in among the wheels beneath the cherubim. Fill your hands with burning coals from among the cherubim and scatter them over the city." And as I watched, he went in.

³Now the cherubim were standing on the south side of the temple when the man went in, and a cloud filled the inner court. ⁴Then the glory of the LORD rose from above the cherubim and moved to the threshold of the temple. The cloud filled the temple, and the court was full of the radiance of the glory of the LORD. ⁵The sound of the wings of the cherubim could be heard as far away as the outer court, like the voice of God Almighty[a] when he speaks.

⁶When the LORD commanded the man in linen, "Take fire from among the wheels, from among the cherubim," the man went in and stood beside a wheel. ⁷Then one of the cherubim reached out his hand to the fire that was among them. He took up some of it and put it into the hands of the man in linen, who took it and went out. ⁸ (Under the wings of the cherubim could be seen what looked like human hands.)

⁹I looked, and I saw beside the cherubim four wheels, one beside each of the cherubim; the wheels sparkled like topaz. ¹⁰As for their appearance, the four of them looked alike; each was like a wheel intersecting a wheel. ¹¹As they

## Amplified Bible

to [stand above] the threshold of the [Lord's] house. And [the Lord] called to the man clothed with linen, who had the writer's ink bottle at his side.

⁴And the Lord said to him, Go through the midst of the city, through the midst of Jerusalem, and set a mark upon the foreheads of the men who sigh and groan over all the abominations that are committed in the midst of it.

⁵And to the others He said in my hearing, Follow [the man with the ink bottle] through the city and smite; let not your eye spare, neither have any pity.

⁶Slay outright the elderly, the young man and the virgin, the infant and the women; but do not touch *or* go near anyone on whom is the mark. Begin at My sanctuary. So they began with the old men who were in front of the temple [who did not have the Lord's mark on their foreheads]. [I Pet. 4:17.]

⁷And He said to [the executioners], Defile the temple and fill its courts with the slain. Go forth! And they went forth and slew in the city.

⁸And while they were slaying them and I was left, I fell upon my face and cried, Ah, Lord God! Will You destroy all that is left of Israel in Your pouring out of Your wrath *and* indignation upon Jerusalem?

⁹Then said He to me, The iniquity *and* guilt of the house of Israel and Judah are exceedingly great; the land is full of blood and the city full of injustice *and* perverseness; for they say, The Lord has forsaken the land; the Lord does not see [what we are doing].

¹⁰And as for Me, My eye will not spare, neither will I have pity, but I will recompense their wicked doings upon their own heads.

¹¹And behold, the man clothed in linen, who had the ink bottle at his side, reported the matter, saying, I have done as You have commanded me.

**10** Then I looked and behold, in the firmament that was over the heads of the cherubim there appeared above them something looking like a sapphire stone, in form resembling a throne.

²And [the Lord] spoke to the man clothed in linen and said, Go in among the whirling wheels under the cherubim; fill your hands with coals of fire from between the cherubim and scatter them over the city. And he went in before my eyes. [Rev. 8:5.]

³Now the cherubim stood on the south side of the house when the man went in; and the cloud [the Shekinah] filled the inner court.

⁴Then the glory of the Lord mounted up from the cherubim to stand over the threshold of the [Lord's] house; and the house was filled with the cloud, and the court was full of the brightness of the Lord's glory. [I Kings 8:10, 11; Ezek. 43:5.]

⁵And the sound of the wings of the cherubim was heard even to the outer court, like the voice of God Almighty when He speaks. [Ps. 29:3, 4.]

⁶And when He commanded the man clothed in linen, saying, Take fire from between the whirling wheels, from between the cherubim, [the man] went in and stood beside a wheel.

⁷And a cherub stretched forth his hand from between the cherubim to the fire that was between the cherubim, and took some of it and put it into the hands of the man clothed in linen, who took it and went out.

⁸And the cherubim seemed to have the form of a man's hand under their wings.

⁹And I looked and behold, there were four wheels beside the cherubim, one wheel beside one cherub and another wheel beside another cherub; and the appearance of the wheels was like sparkling chrysolite.

¹⁰And as for their appearance, they four looked alike, as if a wheel had been within a wheel.

---

ᵃ 5 Hebrew *El-Shaddai*

## New International Version

moved, they would go in any one of the four directions the cherubim faced; the wheels did not turn about[a] as the cherubim went. The cherubim went in whatever direction the head faced, without turning as they went. [12]Their entire bodies, including their backs, their hands and their wings, were completely full of eyes, as were their four wheels. [13]I heard the wheels being called "the whirling wheels." [14]Each of the cherubim had four faces: One face was that of a cherub, the second the face of a human being, the third the face of a lion, and the fourth the face of an eagle.

[15]Then the cherubim rose upward. These were the living creatures I had seen by the Kebar River. [16]When the cherubim moved, the wheels beside them moved; and when the cherubim spread their wings to rise from the ground, the wheels did not leave their side. [17]When the cherubim stood still, they also stood still; and when the cherubim rose, they rose with them, because the spirit of the living creatures was in them.

[18]Then the glory of the LORD departed from over the threshold of the temple and stopped above the cherubim. [19]While I watched, the cherubim spread their wings and rose from the ground, and as they went, the wheels went with them. They stopped at the entrance of the east gate of the LORD's house, and the glory of the God of Israel was above them.

[20]These were the living creatures I had seen beneath the God of Israel by the Kebar River, and I realized that they were cherubim. [21]Each had four faces and four wings, and under their wings was what looked like human hands. [22]Their faces had the same appearance as those I had seen by the Kebar River. Each one went straight ahead.

### God's Sure Judgment on Jerusalem

**11** Then the Spirit lifted me up and brought me to the gate of the house of the LORD that faces east. There at the entrance of the gate were twenty-five men, and I saw among them Jaazaniah son of Azzur and Pelatiah son of Benaiah, leaders of the people. [2]The LORD said to me, "Son of man, these are the men who are plotting evil and giving wicked advice in this city. [3]They say, 'Haven't our houses been recently rebuilt? This city is a pot, and we are the meat in it.' [4]Therefore prophesy against them; prophesy, son of man."

[5]Then the Spirit of the LORD came on me, and he told me to say: "This is what the LORD says: That is what you are saying, you leaders in Israel, but I know what is going through your mind. [6]You have killed many people in this city and filled its streets with the dead.

[7]"Therefore this is what the Sovereign LORD says: The bodies you have thrown there are the meat and this city is the pot, but I will drive you out of it. [8]You fear the sword, and the sword is what I will bring against you, declares the Sovereign LORD. [9]I will drive you out of the city and deliver you into the hands of foreigners and inflict punishment on

## Amplified Bible

[11]When they went, they went in any one of the four directions [in which their four individual faces were turned]; they did not turn as they went, but to the place to which the front wheel faced the others followed; they turned not as they went.

[12]And their whole body, their backs, their hands, and their wings, and the wheels, were full of eyes round about, even the wheels that each had.

[13]As regarding the wheels [attached to them], they were called in my hearing the whirling wheels.

[14]And every one had four faces: the first face was the face of the cherub, the second the face of a man, the third the face of a lion, and the fourth the face of an eagle.

[15]And the cherubim mounted upward. This is the [same] living creature [the four regarded as one] that I saw by the river Chebar [in Babylonia]. [Ezek. 1:5.]

[16]And when the cherubim went, the wheels went beside them; and when the cherubim lifted up their wings to mount up from the earth, the wheels did not turn from beside them.

[17]When those stood still, these stood still; and when those mounted up, these [the wheels] mounted up also, for the spirit of life was in these [wheels]. [Ezek. 1:21.]

[18]Then the glory of the Lord [the Shekinah, cloud] went forth from above the threshold of the temple and stood over the cherubim.

[19]And the cherubim lifted up their wings and mounted up from the earth in my sight, and they went forth with the wheels beside them; and they stood at the entrance of the East Gate of the house of the Lord, and the glory of the God of Israel [the Shekinah, cloud] was over them.

[20]This is the living creature [of four combined creatures] that I saw beneath the God of Israel by the river Chebar, and I knew that they were cherubim.

[21]Each one had four faces and each one had four wings, and what looked like the hands of a man was under their wings.

[22]And as for the likeness of their faces, they were the same faces which I saw by the river Chebar, with regard to their appearances and themselves; they went every one straight forward.

**11** Moreover, the Spirit lifted me up and brought me to the East Gate of the Lord's house, which faces east. And behold, at the door of the gateway there were twenty-five men; and I saw in the midst of them Jaazaniah the son of Azzur and Pelatiah the son of Benaiah, princes of the people.

[2]Then [the Spirit] said to me, Son of man, these are the men who devise iniquity and give wicked counsel in this city,

[3]Who say, [The time] is not near to build houses; this city is the boiling pot and we are the flesh.

[4]Therefore prophesy against them; prophesy, O son of man!

[5]And the Spirit of the Lord fell upon me, and He said to me, Speak. Say, Thus says the Lord: This is what you thought, O house of Israel, for I know the things that come into your mind.

[6]You have multiplied your slain in this city and you have filled its streets with the slain.

[7]Therefore thus says the Lord God: Your slain whom you have laid in your midst; they are the flesh and this city is the boiling pot, but you shall be brought forth out of the midst of it.

[8]You have feared the sword, and I will bring a sword upon you, says the Lord God.

[9]And I will bring you forth out of the midst of it and deliver you into the hands of foreigners and execute judgments among you.

## New International Version

you. [10]You will fall by the sword, and I will execute judgment on you at the borders of Israel. Then you will know that I am the LORD. [11]This city will not be a pot for you, nor will you be the meat in it; I will execute judgment on you at the borders of Israel. [12]And you will know that I am the LORD, for you have not followed my decrees or kept my laws but have conformed to the standards of the nations around you."

[13]Now as I was prophesying, Pelatiah son of Benaiah died. Then I fell facedown and cried out in a loud voice, "Alas, Sovereign LORD! Will you completely destroy the remnant of Israel?"

### The Promise of Israel's Return

[14]The word of the LORD came to me: [15]"Son of man, the people of Jerusalem have said of your fellow exiles and all the other Israelites, 'They are far away from the LORD; this land was given to us as our possession.'

[16]"Therefore say: 'This is what the Sovereign LORD says: Although I sent them far away among the nations and scattered them among the countries, yet for a little while I have been a sanctuary for them in the countries where they have gone.'

[17]"Therefore say: 'This is what the Sovereign LORD says: I will gather you from the nations and bring you back from the countries where you have been scattered, and I will give you back the land of Israel again.'

[18]"They will return to it and remove all its vile images and detestable idols. [19]I will give them an undivided heart and put a new spirit in them; I will remove from them their heart of stone and give them a heart of flesh. [20]Then they will follow my decrees and be careful to keep my laws. They will be my people, and I will be their God. [21]But as for those whose hearts are devoted to their vile images and detestable idols, I will bring down on their own heads what they have done, declares the Sovereign LORD."

[22]Then the cherubim, with the wheels beside them, spread their wings, and the glory of the God of Israel was above them. [23]The glory of the LORD went up from within the city and stopped above the mountain east of it. [24]The Spirit lifted me up and brought me to the exiles in Babylonia[a] in the vision given by the Spirit of God.

Then the vision I had seen went up from me, [25]and I told the exiles everything the LORD had shown me.

### The Exile Symbolized

**12** The word of the LORD came to me: [2]"Son of man, you are living among a rebellious people. They have eyes to see but do not see and ears to hear but do not hear, for they are a rebellious people.

[3]"Therefore, son of man, pack your belongings for exile and in the daytime, as they watch, set out and go from where you are to another place. Perhaps they will understand, though they are a rebellious people. [4]During the daytime, while they watch, bring out your belongings packed for exile. Then in the evening, while they are watching, go out like those who go into exile. [5]While they

## Amplified Bible

[10]You shall fall by the sword; I will judge *and* punish you [before your neighbors] at the border *or* outside the land of Israel, and you shall know (understand and realize) that I am the Lord.

[11]This city shall not be your boiling pot, neither shall you be the flesh in the midst of it; I will judge you at the border *or* outside of Israel.

[12]And you shall know (understand and realize) that I am the Lord; for you have not walked in My statutes nor executed My ordinances, but have acted according to the ordinances of the nations around you.

[13]And while I was prophesying, Pelatiah the son of Benaiah died. Then I fell down upon my face and cried with a loud voice, Ah, Lord God! Will You make a complete end of the remnant of Israel?

[14]And the word of the Lord came to me, saying,

[15]Son of man, your brethren, even your kindred, your fellow exiles, and all the house of Israel, all of them, are they of whom the [present] inhabitants of Jerusalem have said, They have gone far from the Lord [and from this land]; therefore this land is given to us for a possession.

[16]Therefore say, Thus says the Lord God: Whereas I have removed [Israel] far off among the nations, and whereas I have scattered them among the countries, yet I have been to them a sanctuary for a little while in the countries to which they have come.

[17]Therefore say, Thus says the Lord God: I will gather you from the peoples and assemble you out of the countries where you have been scattered, and I will give back to you the land of Israel.

[18]And when they return there, they shall take away from it all traces of its detestable things and all its abominations (sex impurities and heathen religious practices).

[19]And I will give them one heart [a new heart] and I will put a new spirit within them; and I will take the stony [unnaturally hardened] heart out of their flesh, and will give them a heart of flesh [sensitive and responsive to the touch of their God], [Ezek. 18:31; 36:26; II Cor. 3:3.]

[20]That they may walk in My statutes and keep My ordinances, and do them. And they shall be My people, and I will be their God.

[21]But as for those whose heart yearns for *and* goes after their detestable things and their loathsome abominations [associated with idolatry], I will repay their deeds upon their own heads, says the Lord God.

[22]Then the cherubim lifted up their wings with the wheels which were beside them, and the glory of the God of Israel [the Shekinah, cloud] was over them.

[23]Then the glory of the Lord rose up from over the midst of the city and stood over the mountain which is on the east side of the city.

[24]And the Spirit lifted me up and brought me in a vision by the Spirit of God into Chaldea, to the exiles. Then the vision that I had seen went up from me.

[25]And I told the exiles everything that the Lord had shown me.

**12** The word of the Lord also came to me, saying, [2]Son of man, you dwell in the midst of the house of the rebellious, who have eyes to see and see not, who have ears to hear and hear not, for they are a rebellious house. [Mark 8:18.]

[3]Therefore, son of man, prepare your belongings for removing *and* going into exile, and move out by day in their sight; and you shall remove from your place to another place in their sight. It may be they will consider *and* perceive that they are a rebellious house.

[4]And you shall bring forth your baggage by day in their sight, as baggage for removing into exile; and you shall go forth yourself at evening in their sight, as those who go forth into exile.

[a] 24 Or *Chaldea*

## New International Version

watch, dig through the wall and take your belongings out through it. [6]Put them on your shoulder as they are watching and carry them out at dusk. Cover your face so that you cannot see the land, for I have made you a sign to the Israelites."

[7]So I did as I was commanded. During the day I brought out my things packed for exile. Then in the evening I dug through the wall with my hands. I took my belongings out at dusk, carrying them on my shoulders while they watched.

[8]In the morning the word of the Lord came to me: [9]"Son of man, did not the Israelites, that rebellious people, ask you, 'What are you doing?'

[10]"Say to them, 'This is what the Sovereign Lord says: This prophecy concerns the prince in Jerusalem and all the Israelites who are there.' [11]Say to them, 'I am a sign to you.'

"As I have done, so it will be done to them. They will go into exile as captives.

[12]"The prince among them will put his things on his shoulder at dusk and leave, and a hole will be dug in the wall for him to go through. He will cover his face so that he cannot see the land. [13]I will spread my net for him, and he will be caught in my snare; I will bring him to Babylonia, the land of the Chaldeans, but he will not see it, and there he will die. [14]I will scatter to the winds all those around him — his staff and all his troops — and I will pursue them with drawn sword.

[15]"They will know that I am the Lord, when I disperse them among the nations and scatter them through the countries. [16]But I will spare a few of them from the sword, famine and plague, so that in the nations where they go they may acknowledge all their detestable practices. Then they will know that I am the Lord."

[17]The word of the Lord came to me: [18]"Son of man, tremble as you eat your food, and shudder in fear as you drink your water. [19]Say to the people of the land: 'This is what the Sovereign Lord says about those living in Jerusalem and in the land of Israel: They will eat their food in anxiety and drink their water in despair, for their land will be stripped of everything in it because of the violence of all who live there. [20]The inhabited towns will be laid waste and the land will be desolate. Then you will know that I am the Lord.'"

### There Will Be No Delay

[21]The word of the Lord came to me: [22]"Son of man, what is this proverb you have in the land of Israel: 'The days go by and every vision comes to nothing'? [23]Say to them, 'This is what the Sovereign Lord says: I am going to put an end to this proverb, and they will no longer quote it in Israel.' Say to them, 'The days are near when every vision will be fulfilled. [24]For there will be no more false visions or flattering divinations among the people of Israel. [25]But I the Lord will speak what I will, and it shall be fulfilled

## Amplified Bible

[5]Dig through the wall in their sight and carry the stuff out through the hole.

[6]In their sight you shall bear your baggage upon your shoulder and carry it forth in the dark; you shall cover your face so that you cannot see the land, for I have set you as a sign for the house of Israel.

[7]And I did as I was commanded. I brought forth my baggage by day, as baggage for exile, and in the evening I dug through the wall with my own hands. I brought out my baggage in the dark, carrying it upon my shoulder in their sight.

[8]And in the morning came the word of the Lord to me, saying,

[9]Son of man, has not the house of Israel, the rebellious house, asked you what you are doing?

[10]Say to them, Thus says the Lord God: This oracle or revelation concerns the prince in Jerusalem and all the house of Israel who are in it.

[11]Say, I am your sign; as I have done, so shall it be done to them; into banishment, into captivity, they shall go.

[12]And the prince who is in their midst shall lift up his luggage to his shoulder in the dark; then shall he go forth. They shall dig through the wall to carry out through the hole in it. He shall cover his face so that he will [a]not see with his eyes the land.

[13]My net also will I spread over him, and he shall be taken in My snare, and I will bring him to Babylonia, to the land of the Chaldeans; yet shall he [b]not see it, though he shall die there. [II Kings 25:1-7; 39:5; Jer. 52:7-11.]

[14]And I will scatter toward every wind all who are about him to help him, even all his bands; and I will draw out the sword after them.

[15]And they shall know (recognize, understand, and realize) that I am the Lord, when I shall scatter them among the nations and disperse them in the countries.

[16]But I will leave a few survivors who will escape the sword, the famine, and the pestilence, that they may declare and confess all their [idolatrous] abominations among the nations to which they go, and [thus God's punishment of them will be justified before everyone and] they shall know (understand and realize) that I am the Lord.

[17]Moreover, the word of the Lord came to me, saying,

[18]Son of man, eat your bread with shaking, and drink water with trembling and with fearfulness;

[19]And say to the people of the land, Thus says the Lord God concerning the inhabitants of Jerusalem in the land of Israel: They shall eat their bread with fearfulness and drink water with dismay, for their land will be stripped and plundered of all its fullness, because of the violence of all those who dwell in it.

[20]And the cities that are inhabited shall be laid waste, and the land shall be deserted and become a desolation; and you shall know (understand and realize) that I am the Lord.

[21]And the word of the Lord came to me, saying,

[22]Son of man, what is this proverb that you have in the land of Israel, saying, The days drag on and every vision comes to nothing and is not fulfilled?

[23]Tell them therefore, Thus says the Lord God: I will put an end to this proverb, and they shall use it no more as a proverb in Israel. But say to them, The days are at hand and the fulfillment of every vision.

[24]For there shall be no more any false, empty, and fruitless vision or flattering divination in the house of Israel.

[25]For I am the Lord; I will speak, and the word that I shall speak shall be performed (come to pass); it shall be no more delayed or prolonged, for in your days, O rebel-

*a* This prophecy was literally fulfilled as recorded in Jer. 52:7-11. King Zedekiah's eyes were put out in Riblah, Palestine, before he was carried to Babylon, where he died. Thus he did "not see it," even though he died there. *b* This prophecy was literally fulfilled as recorded in several Old Testament passages (see textual references).

## New International Version

without delay. For in your days, you rebellious people, I will fulfill whatever I say, declares the Sovereign LORD.'"

26The word of the LORD came to me: 27"Son of man, the Israelites are saying, 'The vision he sees is for many years from now, and he prophesies about the distant future.'

28"Therefore say to them, 'This is what the Sovereign LORD says: None of my words will be delayed any longer; whatever I say will be fulfilled, declares the Sovereign LORD.'"

### False Prophets Condemned

**13** The word of the LORD came to me: 2"Son of man, prophesy against the prophets of Israel who are now prophesying. Say to those who prophesy out of their own imagination: 'Hear the word of the LORD! 3This is what the Sovereign LORD says: Woe to the foolish*a* prophets who follow their own spirit and have seen nothing! 4Your prophets, Israel, are like jackals among ruins. 5You have not gone up to the breaches in the wall to repair it for the people of Israel so that it will stand firm in the battle on the day of the LORD. 6Their visions are false and their divinations a lie. Even though the LORD has not sent them, they say, "The LORD declares," and expect him to fulfill their words. 7Have you not seen false visions and uttered lying divinations when you say, "The LORD declares," though I have not spoken?

8"'Therefore this is what the Sovereign LORD says: Because of your false words and lying visions, I am against you, declares the Sovereign LORD. 9My hand will be against the prophets who see false visions and utter lying divinations. They will not belong to the council of my people or be listed in the records of Israel, nor will they enter the land of Israel. Then you will know that I am the Sovereign LORD.

10"'Because they lead my people astray, saying, "Peace," when there is no peace, and because, when a flimsy wall is built, they cover it with whitewash, 11therefore tell those who cover it with whitewash that it is going to fall. Rain will come in torrents, and I will send hailstones hurtling down, and violent winds will burst forth. 12When the wall collapses, will people not ask you, "Where is the whitewash you covered it with?"

13"'Therefore this is what the Sovereign LORD says: In my wrath I will unleash a violent wind, and in my anger hailstones and torrents of rain will fall with destructive fury. 14I will tear down the wall you have covered with whitewash and will level it to the ground so that its foundation will be laid bare. When it*b* falls, you will be destroyed in it; and you will know that I am the LORD. 15So I will pour out my wrath against the wall and against those who covered it with whitewash. I will say to you, "The wall is gone and so are those who whitewashed it, 16those prophets of Israel who prophesied to Jerusalem and saw visions of peace for her when there was no peace, declares the Sovereign LORD."'

17"Now, son of man, set your face against the daughters of your people who prophesy out of their own imagination.

## Amplified Bible

lious house, I will speak the word and will perform it, says the Lord God.

26Again the word of the Lord came to me, saying, 27Son of man, behold, they of the house of Israel say, The vision that [Ezekiel] sees is for many days to come, and he prophesies of the times that are far off.

28Therefore say to them, Thus says the Lord God: There shall none of My words be deferred any more, but the word which I have spoken shall be performed, says the Lord God.

**13** And the word of the Lord came to me, saying, 2Son of man, prophesy against the prophets of Israel who prophesy, and say to those who prophesy out of their own mind *and* heart, Hear the word of the Lord!

3Thus says the Lord God: Woe to the foolish prophets who follow their own spirit [and things they have not seen] and have seen nothing!

4O Israel, your prophets have been like foxes among ruins *and* in waste places.

5You have not gone up into the gaps *or* breeches, nor built up the wall for the house of Israel that it might stand in the battle in the day of the Lord.

6They have seen falsehood and lying divination, saying, The Lord says; but the Lord has not sent them. Yet they have hoped *and* made men to hope for the confirmation of their word.

7Have you not seen a false vision and have you not spoken a lying divination when you say, The Lord says, although I have not spoken?

8Therefore thus says the Lord God: Because you have spoken empty, false, *and* delusive words and have seen lies, therefore behold, I am against you, says the Lord God.

9And My hand shall be against the prophets who see empty, false, *and* delusive visions and who give lying prophecies. They shall not be in the secret council of My people, nor shall they be recorded in the register of the house of Israel, nor shall they enter into the land of Israel; and you shall know (understand and realize) that I am the Lord God.

10Because, even because they have seduced My people, saying, Peace, when there is no peace, and because when one builds a [flimsy] wall, behold, [these prophets] daub it over with whitewash,

11Say to them who daub it with whitewash that it shall fall! There shall be a downpour of rain; and you, O great hailstones, shall fall, and a violent wind shall tear apart [the whitewashed, flimsy wall].

12Behold, when the wall is fallen, will you not be asked, Where is the coating with which you [prophets] daubed it?

13Therefore thus says the Lord God: I will even rend it with a stormy wind in My wrath, and there shall be an overwhelming rain in My anger and great hailstones in wrath to destroy [that wall].

14So will I break down the wall that you have daubed with whitewash and bring it down to the ground, so that its foundations will be exposed; when it falls, you will perish *and* be consumed in the midst of it. And you will know (understand and realize) that I am the Lord.

15Thus will I accomplish My wrath upon the wall and upon those who have daubed it with whitewash, and I will say to you, The wall is no more, neither are they who daubed it,

16The [false] prophets of Israel who prophesied deceitfully about Jerusalem, seeing visions of peace for her when there is no peace, says the Lord God.

17And you, son of man, set your face against the daughters of your people who prophesy out of [the wishful thinking of] their own minds *and* hearts; prophesy against them,

*a 3 Or wicked    b 14 Or the city*

## New International Version

Prophesy against them [18]and say, 'This is what the Sovereign LORD says: Woe to the women who sew magic charms on all their wrists and make veils of various lengths for their heads in order to ensnare people. Will you ensnare the lives of my people but preserve your own? [19]You have profaned me among my people for a few handfuls of barley and scraps of bread. By lying to my people, who listen to lies, you have killed those who should not have died and have spared those who should not live.

[20]"'Therefore this is what the Sovereign LORD says: I am against your magic charms with which you ensnare people like birds and I will tear them from your arms; I will set free the people that you ensnare like birds. [21]I will tear off your veils and save my people from your hands, and they will no longer fall prey to your power. Then you will know that I am the LORD. [22]Because you disheartened the righteous with your lies, when I had brought them no grief, and because you encouraged the wicked not to turn from their evil ways and so save their lives, [23]therefore you will no longer see false visions or practice divination. I will save my people from your hands. And then you will know that I am the LORD.'"

### Idolaters Condemned

**14** Some of the elders of Israel came to me and sat down in front of me. [2]Then the word of the LORD came to me: [3]"Son of man, these men have set up idols in their hearts and put wicked stumbling blocks before their faces. Should I let them inquire of me at all? [4]Therefore speak to them and tell them, 'This is what the Sovereign LORD says: When any of the Israelites set up idols in their hearts and put a wicked stumbling block before their faces and then go to a prophet, I the LORD will answer them myself in keeping with their great idolatry. [5]I will do this to recapture the hearts of the people of Israel, who have all deserted me for their idols.'

[6]"Therefore say to the people of Israel, 'This is what the Sovereign LORD says: Repent! Turn from your idols and renounce all your detestable practices!

[7]"'When any of the Israelites or any foreigner residing in Israel separate themselves from me and set up idols in their hearts and put a wicked stumbling block before their faces and then go to a prophet to inquire of me, I the LORD will answer them myself. [8]I will set my face against them and make them an example and a byword. I will remove them from my people. Then you will know that I am the LORD.

[9]"'And if the prophet is enticed to utter a prophecy, I the LORD have enticed that prophet, and I will stretch out my hand against him and destroy him from among my people Israel. [10]They will bear their guilt—the prophet will be as guilty as the one who consults him. [11]Then the peo-

## Amplified Bible

[18]And say, Thus says the Lord God: Woe to the women who sew pillows to all armholes and fasten magic, protective charms to all wrists, and deceptive veils upon the heads of those of every stature to hunt *and* capture human lives! Will you snare the lives of My people to keep your own selves alive?

[19]You have profaned Me among My people [in payment] for handfuls of barley and for pieces of bread, slaying persons who should not die and giving [a guaranty of] life to those who should not live, by your lying to My people, who give heed to lies.

[20]Therefore thus says the Lord God: Behold, I am against your pillows *and* charms *and* veils with which you snare human lives like birds, and I will tear them from your arms; and I will let the lives you hunt go free, the lives you are snaring like birds.

[21]Your [deceptive] veils also will I tear and deliver My people out of your hand, and they shall be no more in your hand to be hunted *and* snared. Then you shall know (understand and realize) that I am the Lord.

[22]Because with lies you have made the righteous sad *and* disheartened, whom I have not made sad *or* disheartened, and because you have encouraged *and* strengthened the hands of the wicked, that he should not return from his wicked way and be saved [in that you falsely promised him life],

[23]Therefore you will no more see false visions or practice divinations, and I will deliver My people out of your hand. Then you will know (understand and realize) that I am the Lord.

**14** Then came certain of the elders of Israel to me and sat before me.

[2]And the word of the Lord came to me:

[3]Son of man, these men have set up their idols in their hearts and put the stumbling block of their iniquity *and* guilt before their faces; should I permit Myself to be inquired of at all by them?

[4]Therefore speak to them and say to them, Thus says the Lord God: Every man of the house of Israel who takes his idols [of self-will and unsubmissiveness] into his heart and puts the stumbling block of his iniquity [idols of silver and gold] before his face, and yet comes to the prophet [to inquire of him], I the Lord will answer him, answer him according to the multitude of his idols,

[5]That I may lay hold of the house of Israel in the thoughts of their own mind *and* heart, because they are all estranged from Me through their idols.

[6]Therefore say to the house of Israel, Thus says the Lord God: Repent *and* turn away from your idols, and turn away your faces from all your abominations.

[7]For anyone of the house of Israel or of the strangers who sojourn in Israel who separates himself from Me, taking his idols into his heart and putting the stumbling block of his iniquity *and* guilt before his face, and [yet] comes to the prophet to inquire for himself of Me, I the Lord will answer him Myself!

[8]And I will set My face against that [false worshiper] and will make him a sign and a byword, and I will cut him off from the midst of My people; and you shall know (understand and realize) that I am the Lord.

[9][The prophet has not been granted permission to give an answer to the hypocritical inquirer] but if the prophet does give the man the answer he desires [thus allowing himself to be a party to the inquirer's sin], I the Lord will see to it that the prophet is deceived in his answer, and I will stretch out My hand against him and will destroy him from the midst of My people Israel.

[10]And they both shall bear the punishment of their iniquity: the iniquity of the [presumptuous] prophet shall be the same as the iniquity of the [hypocritical] inquirer,

## New International Version

ple of Israel will no longer stray from me, nor will they defile themselves anymore with all their sins. They will be my people, and I will be their God, declares the Sovereign LORD.'"

### Jerusalem's Judgment Inescapable

[12] The word of the LORD came to me: [13] "Son of man, if a country sins against me by being unfaithful and I stretch out my hand against it to cut off its food supply and send famine upon it and kill its people and their animals, [14] even if these three men—Noah, Daniel[a] and Job—were in it, they could save only themselves by their righteousness, declares the Sovereign LORD.

[15] "Or if I send wild beasts through that country and they leave it childless and it becomes desolate so that no one can pass through it because of the beasts, [16] as surely as I live, declares the Sovereign LORD, even if these three men were in it, they could not save their own sons or daughters. They alone would be saved, but the land would be desolate.

[17] "Or if I bring a sword against that country and say, 'Let the sword pass throughout the land,' and I kill its people and their animals, [18] as surely as I live, declares the Sovereign LORD, even if these three men were in it, they could not save their own sons or daughters. They alone would be saved.

[19] "Or if I send a plague into that land and pour out my wrath on it through bloodshed, killing its people and their animals, [20] as surely as I live, declares the Sovereign LORD, even if Noah, Daniel and Job were in it, they could save neither son nor daughter. They would save only themselves by their righteousness.

[21] "For this is what the Sovereign LORD says: How much worse will it be when I send against Jerusalem my four dreadful judgments—sword and famine and wild beasts and plague—to kill its men and their animals! [22] Yet there will be some survivors—sons and daughters who will be brought out of it. They will come to you, and when you see their conduct and their actions, you will be consoled regarding the disaster I have brought on Jerusalem—every disaster I have brought on it. [23] You will be consoled when you see their conduct and their actions, for you will know that I have done nothing in it without cause, declares the Sovereign LORD."

### Jerusalem as a Useless Vine

**15** The word of the LORD came to me: [2] "Son of man, how is the wood of a vine different from that of a branch from any of the trees in the forest? [3] Is wood ever taken from it to make anything useful? Do they make pegs from it to hang things on? [4] And after it is thrown on the fire as fuel and the fire burns both ends and chars the middle, is it then useful for anything? [5] If it was not useful for anything when it was whole, how much less can it be made into something useful when the fire has burned it and it is charred?

[6] "Therefore this is what the Sovereign LORD says: As I have given the wood of the vine among the trees of the forest as fuel for the fire, so will I treat the people living in Jerusalem. [7] I will set my face against them. Although they have come out of the fire, the fire will yet consume them. And when I set my face against them, you will know that I am the LORD. [8] I will make the land desolate because they have been unfaithful, declares the Sovereign LORD."

## Amplified Bible

[11] That the house of Israel may go no more astray from Me, neither defile themselves any more with all their transgressions, but that they may be My people, and I may be their God, says the Lord God.

[12] The word of the Lord came [again] to me, saying,

[13] Son of man, when a land sins against Me by committing a trespass, and I stretch out My hand against it and break its staff of bread and send famine upon it and cut off from it man and beast,

[14] Even if these three men, Noah, Daniel, and Job were in it, they would save but their own lives by their righteousness (their uprightness and right standing with Me), says the Lord God.

[15] If I cause ferocious *and* evil wild animals to pass through the land and they ravage *and* bereave it, and it becomes desolate so that no man may pass through because of the beasts;

[16] Though these three men were in it, as I live, says the Lord God, they would deliver neither sons nor daughters; they themselves alone would be delivered but the land would be desolate (laid waste and deserted).

[17] Or if I bring a sword upon that land and say, Sword, go through the land, so that I cut off man and beast from it,

[18] Though these three men were in it, as I live, says the Lord God, they would deliver neither sons nor daughters, but they themselves alone would be delivered.

[19] Or if I send a pestilence into that land and pour out My wrath upon it in blood, to cut off from it man and beast,

[20] Though Noah, Daniel, and Job were in it, as I live, says the Lord God, they would deliver neither son nor daughter; they would but deliver their own lives by their righteousness (their moral and spiritual rectitude in every area and relation).

[21] For thus says the Lord God: How much more when I send My four sore acts of judgment upon Jerusalem—the sword, the famine, the evil wild beasts, and the pestilence—to cut off from it man and beast! [Lev. 26:21-33.]

[22] And yet, behold, in it shall be left a remnant (an escaped portion), both sons and daughters. They shall be carried forth to you [in Babylon], and when you see their [ungodly] walk and their [wicked] doings, you will be consoled for the evil that I have brought upon Jerusalem, even concerning all that I have brought upon it.

[23] And they shall console you when you see their evil ways and their rebellious actions. Then you shall know (understand and realize) that I have not done without cause all that I have done in Jerusalem, says the Lord God.

**15** And the word of the Lord came to me, saying, [2] Son of man, How is the wood of the grapevine [Israel] more than that of any tree, the vine branch which was among the trees of the forest? [Ps. 80:8-13; Jer. 2:21.]

[3] Shall wood be taken from it to do any work? Or will men take a peg of it on which to hang any vessel?

[4] Behold, it is cast into the fire for fuel; the fire consumes both ends of it and the middle of it is charred. Is it suitable *or* profitable for any work?

[5] Notice, even when it was whole, it was good for no work; how much less shall it be useful *and* profitable when the fire has devoured it and it is charred?

[6] Therefore thus says the Lord God: Like the wood of the grapevine among the trees of the forest, which I have given to the fire for fuel, so will I give up the inhabitants of Jerusalem.

[7] And I will set My face against them; they shall go out from one fire and another fire shall devour them, and you shall know (understand and realize) that I am the Lord, when I set My face against them.

[8] And I will make the land desolate (laid waste and deserted) because they have acted faithlessly [through their idolatry], says the Lord.

---

[a] 14 Or *Danel*, a man of renown in ancient literature; also in verse 20

## New International Version

### Jerusalem as an Adulterous Wife

**16** The word of the LORD came to me: [2]"Son of man, confront Jerusalem with her detestable practices [3]and say, 'This is what the Sovereign LORD says to Jerusalem: Your ancestry and birth were in the land of the Canaanites; your father was an Amorite and your mother a Hittite. [4]On the day you were born your cord was not cut, nor were you washed with water to make you clean, nor were you rubbed with salt or wrapped in cloths. [5]No one looked on you with pity or had compassion enough to do any of these things for you. Rather, you were thrown out into the open field, for on the day you were born you were despised.

[6]"'Then I passed by and saw you kicking about in your blood, and as you lay there in your blood I said to you, "Live!"[a] [7]I made you grow like a plant of the field. You grew and developed and entered puberty. Your breasts had formed and your hair had grown, yet you were stark naked.

[8]"'Later I passed by, and when I looked at you and saw that you were old enough for love, I spread the corner of my garment over you and covered your naked body. I gave you my solemn oath and entered into a covenant with you, declares the Sovereign LORD, and you became mine.

[9]"'I bathed you with water and washed the blood from you and put ointments on you. [10]I clothed you with an embroidered dress and put sandals of fine leather on you. I dressed you in fine linen and covered you with costly garments. [11]I adorned you with jewelry: I put bracelets on your arms and a necklace around your neck, [12]and I put a ring on your nose, earrings on your ears and a beautiful crown on your head. [13]So you were adorned with gold and silver; your clothes were of fine linen and costly fabric and embroidered cloth. Your food was honey, olive oil and the finest flour. You became very beautiful and rose to be a queen. [14]And your fame spread among the nations on account of your beauty, because the splendor I had given you made your beauty perfect, declares the Sovereign LORD.

[15]"'But you trusted in your beauty and used your fame to become a prostitute. You lavished your favors on anyone who passed by and your beauty became his. [16]You took some of your garments to make gaudy high places, where you carried on your prostitution. You went to him, and he possessed your beauty.[b] [17]You also took the fine jewelry I gave you, the jewelry made of my gold and silver, and you made for yourself male idols and engaged in prostitution with them. [18]And you took your embroidered clothes to put on them, and you offered my oil and incense before them. [19]Also the food I provided for you—the flour, olive oil and honey I gave you to eat—you offered as fragrant incense before them. That is what happened, declares the Sovereign LORD.

[20]"'And you took your sons and daughters whom you bore to me and sacrificed them as food to the idols. Was your prostitution not enough? [21]You slaughtered my chil-

## Amplified Bible

**16** Again the word of the Lord came to me, saying, [2]Son of man, cause Jerusalem to know, understand, *and* realize her [idolatrous] abominations [that they] are disgusting, detestable, and shamefully vile.

[3]And say, Thus says the Lord God to Jerusalem [representing Israel]: Your [spiritual] origin and your birth are thoroughly Canaanitish; your [spiritual] father was an Amorite and your [spiritual] mother a Hittite. [Ezek. 16:45; John 8:44.]

[4]And as for your birth, on the day you were born your navel cord was not cut, nor were you washed with water to cleanse you, nor rubbed with salt or swaddled with bands at all.

[5]No eye pitied you to do any of these things for you, to have compassion on you; but you were cast out in the open field, for your person was abhorrent *and* loathsome on the day that you were born.

[6]And when I passed by you and saw you rolling about in your blood, I said to you in your blood, Live! Yes, I said to you still in your natal blood, Live!

[7]I caused you [Israel] to multiply as the bud which grows in the field, and you increased and became tall and you came to full maidenhood *and* beauty; your breasts were formed and your hair had grown, yet you were naked and bare.

[8]Now I passed by you again and looked upon you; behold, you were maturing *and* at the time for love, and I spread My skirt over you and covered your nakedness. Yes, I plighted My troth to you and entered into a covenant with you, says the Lord, and you became Mine.

[9]Then I washed you with water; yes, I thoroughly washed away your [clinging] blood from you and I anointed you with oil.

[10]I clothed you also with embroidered cloth and shod you with [fine seal] leather; and I girded you about with fine linen and covered you with silk.

[11]I decked you also with ornaments and I put bracelets on your wrists and a chain on your neck.

[12]And I put a ring on your nostril and earrings in your ears and a beautiful crown upon your head!

[13]Thus you were decked with gold and silver, and your raiment was of fine linen and silk and embroidered cloth; you ate fine flour and honey and oil. And you were exceedingly beautiful and you prospered into royal estate.

[14]And your renown went forth among the nations for your beauty, for it was perfect through My majesty *and* splendor which I had put upon you, says the Lord God.

[15]But you trusted in *and* relied on your own beauty and were unfaithful to God *and* played the harlot [in idolatry] because of your renown, and you poured out your fornications upon anyone who passed by [as you worshiped the idols of every nation which prevailed over you] and your beauty was his.

[16]And you took some of your garments and made for yourself gaily decorated high places *or* shrines and played the harlot on them—things which should not come and that which should not take place.

[17]You did also take your fair jewels *and* beautiful vessels of My gold and My silver which I had given you and made for yourself images of men, and you played the harlot with them;

[18]And you took your embroidered garments and covered them and set My oil and My incense before them.

[19]My bread also which I gave you—fine flour and oil and honey with which I fed you—you have even set it before the idols for a sweet odor. Thus it was, says the Lord God.

[20]Moreover, you have taken your sons and your daughters whom you have borne to Me, and you have sacrificed them [to your idols] to be destroyed. Were your harlotries too little,

---

[a] 6 A few Hebrew manuscripts, Septuagint and Syriac; most Hebrew manuscripts repeat *and as you lay there in your blood I said to you, "Live!"*
[b] 16 The meaning of the Hebrew for this sentence is uncertain.

# New International Version

dren and sacrificed them to the idols. [22]In all your detestable practices and your prostitution you did not remember the days of your youth, when you were naked and bare, kicking about in your blood.

[23]"'Woe! Woe to you, declares the Sovereign LORD. In addition to all your other wickedness, [24]you built a mound for yourself and made a lofty shrine in every public square. [25]At every street corner you built your lofty shrines and degraded your beauty, spreading your legs with increasing promiscuity to anyone who passed by. [26]You engaged in prostitution with the Egyptians, your neighbors with large genitals, and aroused my anger with your increasing promiscuity. [27]So I stretched out my hand against you and reduced your territory; I gave you over to the greed of your enemies, the daughters of the Philistines, who were shocked by your lewd conduct. [28]You engaged in prostitution with the Assyrians too, because you were insatiable; and even after that, you still were not satisfied. [29]Then you increased your promiscuity to include Babylonia,[a] a land of merchants, but even with this you were not satisfied.

[30]"'I am filled with fury against you,[b] declares the Sovereign LORD, when you do all these things, acting like a brazen prostitute! [31]When you built your mounds at every street corner and made your lofty shrines in every public square, you were unlike a prostitute, because you scorned payment.

[32]"'You adulterous wife! You prefer strangers to your own husband! [33]All prostitutes receive gifts, but you give gifts to all your lovers, bribing them to come to you from everywhere for your illicit favors. [34]So in your prostitution you are the opposite of others; no one runs after you for your favors. You are the very opposite, for you give payment and none is given to you.

[35]"'Therefore, you prostitute, hear the word of the LORD! [36]This is what the Sovereign LORD says: Because you poured out your lust and exposed your naked body in your promiscuity with your lovers, and because of all your detestable idols, and because you gave them your children's blood, [37]therefore I am going to gather all your lovers, with whom you found pleasure, those you loved as well as those you hated. I will gather them against you from all around and will strip you in front of them, and they will see you stark naked. [38]I will sentence you to the punishment of women who commit adultery and who shed blood; I will bring on you the blood vengeance of my wrath and jealous anger. [39]Then I will deliver you into the

# Amplified Bible

[21]That you have slain My children and delivered them up, in setting them apart *and* causing them to pass through the fire for [your idols]?

[22]And in all your abominations and idolatrous whoredoms you have not [earnestly] remembered the days of your youth when you were naked and bare, rolling about in your natal blood.

[23]And after all your wickedness—Woe, woe to you! says the Lord God—

[24]You have built also for yourself a vaulted chamber (brothel) and have made a high place [of idol worship] in every street.

[25]At every crossway you built your high place [for idol worship] and have made your beauty an abomination [abhorrent, loathsome, extremely disgusting, and detestable]; and you have made your body available to every passerby and multiplied your [idolatry and spiritual] harlotry.

[26]You have also played the harlot with the Egyptians, your neighbors, [by adopting their idolatries] whose worship is thoroughly sensuous, and you have multiplied your harlotry to provoke Me to anger.

[27]Behold therefore, I have stretched out My hand against you, diminished your ordinary allowance of food, and delivered you over to the will of those who hate *and* despise you, the daughters of the Philistines, who turned away in shame from your despicable policy *and* lewd behavior [for they are faithful to their gods]!

[28]You played the harlot also with the Assyrians because you were unsatiable; yes, you played the harlot with them, and yet you were not satisfied.

[29]Moreover, you multiplied your harlotry with the land of trade, with Chaldea, and yet even with this you were not satisfied.

[30]How weak *and* spent with longing *and* lust is your heart *and* mind, says the Lord God, seeing you do all these things, the work of a bold, domineering harlot,

[31]In that you build your vaulted place (brothel) at the head of every street and make your high place at every crossing. But you were not like a harlot because you scorned pay.

[32]Rather, you were as an adulterous wife who receives strangers instead of her husband!

[33]Men give gifts to all harlots, but you give your gifts to all your lovers and hire them, bribing [the nations to ally themselves with you], that they may come to you on every side for your harlotries (your idolatrous unfaithfulnesses to God).

[34]And you are different [the reverse] from other women in your harlotries, in that nobody follows you to lure you into harlotry and in that you give hire when no hire is given you; and so you are different.

[35]Therefore, O harlot [Israel], hear the word of the Lord!

[36]Thus says the Lord God: Because your brass [coins and gifts] *and* your filthiness were emptied out and your nakedness uncovered through your harlotries with your lovers, and because of all the [filthy] idols of your abominations, and the blood of your children that you gave to them,

[37]Therefore behold, I will gather all your lovers with whom you have taken pleasure, and all those whom you have loved with all those whom you have hated; I will even gather them [the allies you have courted] against you on every side and will uncover your nakedness to them, that they may see all your nakedness [making you, Israel, an object of loathing and of mockery, a spectacle among the nations].

[38]And I the Lord will judge you as women who break wedlock and shed blood are judged, and I will bring upon you the blood of [your divine Husband's] wrath and jealousy. [Num. 5:18.]

## New International Version

hands of your lovers, and they will tear down your mounds and destroy your lofty shrines. They will strip you of your clothes and take your fine jewelry and leave you stark naked. <sup>40</sup>They will bring a mob against you, who will stone you and hack you to pieces with their swords. <sup>41</sup>They will burn down your houses and inflict punishment on you in the sight of many women. I will put a stop to your prostitution, and you will no longer pay your lovers. <sup>42</sup>Then my wrath against you will subside and my jealous anger will turn away from you; I will be calm and no longer angry.

<sup>43</sup>"Because you did not remember the days of your youth but enraged me with all these things, I will surely bring down on your head what you have done, declares the Sovereign LORD. Did you not add lewdness to all your other detestable practices?

<sup>44</sup>"Everyone who quotes proverbs will quote this proverb about you: "Like mother, like daughter." <sup>45</sup>You are a true daughter of your mother, who despised her husband and her children; and you are a true sister of your sisters, who despised their husbands and their children. Your mother was a Hittite and your father an Amorite. <sup>46</sup>Your older sister was Samaria, who lived to the north of you with her daughters; and your younger sister, who lived to the south of you with her daughters, was Sodom. <sup>47</sup>You not only followed their ways and copied their detestable practices, but in all your ways you soon became more depraved than they. <sup>48</sup>As surely as I live, declares the Sovereign LORD, your sister Sodom and her daughters never did what you and your daughters have done.

<sup>49</sup>"Now this was the sin of your sister Sodom: She and her daughters were arrogant, overfed and unconcerned; they did not help the poor and needy. <sup>50</sup>They were haughty and did detestable things before me. Therefore I did away with them as you have seen. <sup>51</sup>Samaria did not commit half the sins you did. You have done more detestable things than they, and have made your sisters seem righteous by all these things you have done. <sup>52</sup>Bear your disgrace, for you have furnished some justification for your sisters. Because your sins were more vile than theirs, they appear more righteous than you. So then, be ashamed and bear your disgrace, for you have made your sisters appear righteous.

<sup>53</sup>"However, I will restore the fortunes of Sodom and her daughters and of Samaria and her daughters, and your fortunes along with them, <sup>54</sup>so that you may bear your disgrace and be ashamed of all you have done in giving them comfort. <sup>55</sup>And your sisters, Sodom with her daugh-

## Amplified Bible

<sup>39</sup>And I will also give you into the hand of those [your enemies], and they shall throw down your vaulted place (brothel) and shall demolish your high places [of idolatry]; they shall strip you of your clothes and shall take your splendid jewels and leave you naked and bare.

<sup>40</sup>They shall also bring up a company against you, and they shall stone you with stones and hew down *and* thrust you through with their swords.

<sup>41</sup>And they shall burn your houses with fire and execute judgments upon you before the eyes of many women spectators [the nations]. And I will cause you to cease playing the harlot, and you also shall give hire no more.

<sup>42</sup>So will I make My wrath toward you to rest and My jealousy shall depart from you [My adulterous wife], and I will be quiet and will be no more angry.

<sup>43</sup>Because you have not [earnestly] remembered the days of your youth but have enraged Me with all these things, therefore behold, I also will bring your deeds down on your own head, says the Lord God. Did you not commit this lewdness above *and* in addition to all your other abominations?

<sup>44</sup>Behold, everyone who uses proverbs will use this proverb against you: As is the mother, so is her daughter.

<sup>45</sup>You are your [spiritual] mother's daughter who loathed her husband and her children, and you are the sister of your sisters who loathed their husbands and their children. Your mother was a Hittite and your father an Amorite.

<sup>46</sup>And your elder sister is Samaria, she and her daughters who dwelt in the north *and* at your left hand; and your younger sister who dwelt in the south *and* at your right hand is Sodom and her daughters.

<sup>47</sup>Yet you were not satisfied to walk after their ways or to do after their abominations, but very soon you were more corrupt in all your ways than they were [for your sin, as those taught of God, is far blacker than theirs]. [Matt. 11:20-24.]

<sup>48</sup>As I live, says the Lord God, Sodom your sister has not done, she nor her daughters, as you have done, you and your daughters.

<sup>49</sup>Behold, this was the iniquity of your sister Sodom: pride, overabundance of food, prosperous ease, *and* idleness were hers and her daughters'; neither did she strengthen the hand of the poor and needy.

<sup>50</sup>And they were haughty and committed abominable offenses before Me; therefore I removed them when I saw it *and* I saw fit. [Gen. 13:13; 18:20; 19:5.]

<sup>51</sup>Neither has Samaria committed half of your sins, but you have multiplied your [idolatrous] abominations more than they and have seemed to justify your sisters [Samaria and Sodom] in all their wickedness by all the abominable things which you have done—you even make them appear righteous in comparison with you.

<sup>52</sup>Take upon you *and* bear your own shame *and* disgrace [in your punishment], you also who called in question *and* judged your sisters, for you have virtually absolved them by your sins in which you behaved more abominably than they; they are more right than you. Yes, be ashamed *and* confounded and bear your shame *and* disgrace, you also, for you have seemed to justify your sisters *and* make them appear righteous.

<sup>53</sup>I will restore them again from their captivity, restore the fortunes of Sodom and her daughters and the fortunes of Samaria and her daughters, and I will restore your own fortunes in the midst of them [in the day of the Lord], [Isa. 1:9.]

<sup>54</sup>That you [Judah], amid your shame *and* disgrace, may be compelled to recognize your wickedness *and* be thoroughly ashamed *and* confounded at all you have done, becoming [converted and bringing] consolation *and* comfort to [your sisters.]

<sup>55</sup>And your sisters, Sodom and her daughters shall re-

# New International Version

ters and Samaria with her daughters, will return to what they were before; and you and your daughters will return to what you were before. ⁵⁶You would not even mention your sister Sodom in the day of your pride, ⁵⁷before your wickedness was uncovered. Even so, you are now scorned by the daughters of Edom*a* and all her neighbors and the daughters of the Philistines—all those around you who despise you. ⁵⁸You will bear the consequences of your lewdness and your detestable practices, declares the LORD.

⁵⁹"'This is what the Sovereign LORD says: I will deal with you as you deserve, because you have despised my oath by breaking the covenant. ⁶⁰Yet I will remember the covenant I made with you in the days of your youth, and I will establish an everlasting covenant with you. ⁶¹Then you will remember your ways and be ashamed when you receive your sisters, both those who are older than you and those who are younger. I will give them to you as daughters, but not on the basis of my covenant with you. ⁶²So I will establish my covenant with you, and you will know that I am the LORD. ⁶³Then, when I make atonement for you for all you have done, you will remember and be ashamed and never again open your mouth because of your humiliation, declares the Sovereign LORD.'"

## Two Eagles and a Vine

**17** The word of the LORD came to me: ²"Son of man, set forth an allegory and tell it to the Israelites as a parable. ³Say to them, 'This is what the Sovereign LORD says: A great eagle with powerful wings, long feathers and full plumage of varied colors came to Lebanon. Taking hold of the top of a cedar, ⁴he broke off its topmost shoot and carried it away to a land of merchants, where he planted it in a city of traders.

⁵"'He took one of the seedlings of the land and put it in fertile soil. He planted it like a willow by abundant water, ⁶and it sprouted and became a low, spreading vine. Its branches turned toward him, but its roots remained under it. So it became a vine and produced branches and put out leafy boughs.

⁷"'But there was another great eagle with powerful wings and full plumage. The vine now sent out its roots toward him from the plot where it was planted and stretched out its branches to him for water. ⁸It had been planted in good soil by abundant water so that it would produce branches, bear fruit and become a splendid vine.'

⁹"Say to them, 'This is what the Sovereign LORD says: Will it thrive? Will it not be uprooted and stripped of its fruit so that it withers? All its new growth will wither. It will not take a strong arm or many people to pull it up by the roots. ¹⁰It has been planted, but will it thrive? Will it not wither completely when the east wind strikes it—wither away in the plot where it grew?'"

¹¹Then the word of the LORD came to me: ¹²"Say to this rebellious people, 'Do you not know what these things mean?' Say to them: 'The king of Babylon went to Jeru-

# Amplified Bible

turn to their former estate, and Samaria and her daughters shall return to their former estate; then you and your daughters shall return to your former estate.

⁵⁶For was your sister Sodom not mentioned by you [except] as a byword in the day of your pride,

⁵⁷Before your own wickedness was uncovered? Now you have become like her, an object of reproach *and* a byword for the daughters of Syria *and* of Edom and for all who are round about them and for the daughters of the Philistines—those round about who despise you.

⁵⁸You bear the penalty of your lewdness and your [idolatrous] abominations, says the Lord.

⁵⁹Yes, thus says the Lord God: I will even deal with you as you have done, who have despised the oath in breaking the covenant;

⁶⁰Nevertheless, I will [earnestly] remember My covenant with you in the days of your youth and I will establish with you an everlasting covenant. [Ps. 106:45.]

⁶¹Then you will [earnestly] remember your ways and be ashamed *and* confounded when you shall receive your sisters, both your elder and your younger; I will give them to you as daughters, but not on account of your covenant [with Me]. [John 10:16.]

⁶²And I will establish My covenant with you, and you shall know (understand and realize) that I am the Lord, [Hos. 2:19, 20.]

⁶³That you may [earnestly] remember and be ashamed *and* confounded and never open your mouth again because of your shame, when I have forgiven you all that you have done, says the Lord God.

**17** And the word of the Lord came to me, saying, ²Son of man, put forth a riddle and speak a parable *or* allegory to the house of Israel;

³Say, Thus says the Lord God: A great eagle [Nebuchadnezzar] with great wings and long pinions, rich in feathers of various colors, came to Lebanon [symbolic of Jerusalem] and took the top of the cedar [tree].

⁴He broke off the topmost of its young twigs [the youthful King Jehoiachin] and carried it into a land of trade [Babylon]; he set it in a city of merchants.

⁵He took also of the seedlings of the land [Zedekiah, one of the native royal family] and planted it in fertile soil *and* a fruitful field; he placed it beside abundant waters and set it as a willow tree [to succeed Zedekiah's nephew Jehoiachin in Judah as vassal king].

⁶And it grew and became a spreading vine of low [not Davidic] stature, whose branches turned [in submission] toward him, and its roots remained under *and* subject to him [the king of Babylon]; so it became a vine and brought forth branches and shot forth leafy twigs.

⁷There was also another great eagle [the Egyptian king] with great wings and many feathers; and behold, this vine [Zedekiah] bent its roots [languishingly] toward him and shot forth its branches toward him, away from the beds of its planting, for him to water.

⁸Though it was planted in good soil where water was plentiful for it to produce leaves and to bear fruit, it was transplanted, that it might become a splendid vine.

⁹Thus says the Lord God: Ask, Will it thrive? Will he [the insulted Nebuchadnezzar] not pluck up its roots and strip off its fruit so that all its fresh sprouting leaves will wither? It will not take a strong arm or many people to pluck it up by its roots [totally ending Israel's national existence]. [II Kings 25:1-7.]

¹⁰Yes, behold, though transplanted, will it prosper? Will it not utterly wither when the east wind touches it? It will wither in the furrows *and* beds where it sprouted *and* grew. [Hos. 13:9-12, 15.]

¹¹Moreover, the word of the Lord came to me, saying,

¹²Say now to the rebellious house, Do you not know *and* realize what these things mean? Tell them, Behold, the

---

*a* 57 Many Hebrew manuscripts and Syriac; most Hebrew manuscripts, Septuagint and Vulgate *Aram*

## New International Version

salem and carried off her king and her nobles, bringing them back with him to Babylon. ¹³Then he took a member of the royal family and made a treaty with him, putting him under oath. He also carried away the leading men of the land, ¹⁴so that the kingdom would be brought low, unable to rise again, surviving only by keeping his treaty. ¹⁵But the king rebelled against him by sending his envoys to Egypt to get horses and a large army. Will he succeed? Will he who does such things escape? Will he break the treaty and yet escape?

¹⁶"'As surely as I live, declares the Sovereign LORD, he shall die in Babylon, in the land of the king who put him on the throne, whose oath he despised and whose treaty he broke. ¹⁷Pharaoh with his mighty army and great horde will be of no help to him in war, when ramps are built and siege works erected to destroy many lives. ¹⁸He despised the oath by breaking the covenant. Because he had given his hand in pledge and yet did all these things, he shall not escape.

¹⁹"'Therefore this is what the Sovereign LORD says: As surely as I live, I will repay him for despising my oath and breaking my covenant. ²⁰I will spread my net for him, and he will be caught in my snare. I will bring him to Babylon and execute judgment on him there because he was unfaithful to me. ²¹All his choice troops will fall by the sword, and the survivors will be scattered to the winds. Then you will know that I the LORD have spoken.

²²"'This is what the Sovereign LORD says: I myself will take a shoot from the very top of a cedar and plant it; I will break off a tender sprig from its topmost shoots and plant it on a high and lofty mountain. ²³On the mountain heights of Israel I will plant it; it will produce branches and bear fruit and become a splendid cedar. Birds of every kind will nest in it; they will find shelter in the shade of its branches. ²⁴All the trees of the forest will know that I the LORD bring down the tall tree and make the low tree grow tall. I dry up the green tree and make the dry tree flourish.

"'I the LORD have spoken, and I will do it.'"

### The One Who Sins Will Die

**18** The word of the LORD came to me: ²"What do you people mean by quoting this proverb about the land of Israel:

"'The parents eat sour grapes,
    and the children's teeth are set on edge'?

³"As surely as I live, declares the Sovereign LORD, you will no longer quote this proverb in Israel. ⁴For everyone belongs to me, the parent as well as the child—both alike belong to me. The one who sins is the one who will die.

⁵"Suppose there is a righteous man
    who does what is just and right.
⁶He does not eat at the mountain shrines
    or look to the idols of Israel.
He does not defile his neighbor's wife
    or have sexual relations with a woman during her
        period.

## Amplified Bible

king of Babylon came to Jerusalem and took its king [Jehoiachin] and its princes and brought them with him to Babylon. [II Kings 24:11-16.]

¹³And he took one of the royal family [the king's uncle, Zedekiah] and made a covenant with him, putting him under oath. He also took the mighty *and* chief men of the land, [II Kings 24:17.]

¹⁴That the kingdom might become low *and* base and be unable to lift itself up, but that by keeping his [Nebuchadnezzar's] covenant it might stand.

¹⁵But he [Zedekiah] rebelled against him [Nebuchadnezzar] in sending his ambassadors into Egypt, that they might give him horses and much people. Will he prosper? Will he escape who does such things? Can he break the covenant with [Babylon] and yet escape?

¹⁶As I live, says the Lord God, surely in the place where the king [Nebuchadnezzar] dwells who made [Zedekiah as vassal] king, whose oath [Zedekiah] despised and whose covenant he broke, even with him in the midst of Babylon shall [Zedekiah] die.

¹⁷Neither shall Pharaoh with his mighty army and great company help him in the war when the [Babylonians] cast up mounds and build forts to destroy many lives.

¹⁸For [Zedekiah] despised the oath and broke the covenant and behold, he had given his hand, and yet has done all these things; he shall not escape.

¹⁹Therefore thus says the Lord God: As I live, surely My oath [made for Me by Nebuchadnezzar] that [Zedekiah] has despised and My covenant with him that he has broken, I will even bring down on his own head.

²⁰And I will spread My net over him, and he shall be taken in My snare; and I will bring him to Babylon and will enter into judgment *and* punishment with him there for his trespass *and* treason that he has committed against Me.

²¹And all his fugitives [from Judah] in all his bands shall fall by the sword, and they that remain shall be scattered toward every wind. And you shall know (understand and realize) that I the Lord have spoken it.

²²Thus says the Lord God: I Myself will take a twig from the lofty top of the cedar and will set it out; I will crop off from the topmost of its young twigs a tender one and will plant it upon a mountain high and exalted. [Isa. 11:1, 10; 53:2; Jer. 23:5; Zech. 3:8.]

²³On the mountain height of Israel will I plant it, that it may bring forth boughs and bear fruit and be a noble cedar, and under it shall dwell all birds of every feather; in the shade of its branches they shall nestle *and* find rest.

²⁴And all the trees of the field shall know (understand and realize) that I the Lord have brought low the high tree, have exalted the low tree, have dried up the green tree, and have made the dry tree flourish. I the Lord have spoken, and I will do it.

**18** The word of the Lord came to me again, saying, ²What do you mean by using this proverb concerning the land of Israel, The fathers have eaten sour grapes, and the children's teeth are set on edge?

³As I live, says the Lord God, you shall not have occasion any more to use this proverb in Israel.

⁴Behold, all souls are Mine; as the soul of the father, so also the soul of the son is Mine; the soul that sins, it shall die. [Rom. 6:23.]

⁵But if a man is [uncompromisingly] righteous (upright and in right standing with God) and does what is lawful and right,

⁶And has not eaten [at the idol shrines] upon the mountains nor lifted up his eyes to the idols of the house of Israel, has not defiled his neighbor's wife nor come near to a woman in her time of impurity,

## New International Version

7 He does not oppress anyone,
but returns what he took in pledge for a loan.
He does not commit robbery
but gives his food to the hungry
and provides clothing for the naked.
8 He does not lend to them at interest
or take a profit from them.
He withholds his hand from doing wrong
and judges fairly between two parties.
9 He follows my decrees
and faithfully keeps my laws.
That man is righteous;
he will surely live,
declares the Sovereign LORD.

10 "Suppose he has a violent son, who sheds blood or does any of these other things*a* 11 (though the father has done none of them):

"He eats at the mountain shrines.
He defiles his neighbor's wife.
12 He oppresses the poor and needy.
He commits robbery.
He does not return what he took in pledge.
He looks to the idols.
He does detestable things.
13 He lends at interest and takes a profit.

Will such a man live? He will not! Because he has done all these detestable things, he is to be put to death; his blood will be on his own head.

14 "But suppose this son has a son who sees all the sins his father commits, and though he sees them, he does not do such things:

15 "He does not eat at the mountain shrines
or look to the idols of Israel.
He does not defile his neighbor's wife.
16 He does not oppress anyone
or require a pledge for a loan.
He does not commit robbery
but gives his food to the hungry
and provides clothing for the naked.
17 He withholds his hand from mistreating the poor
and takes no interest or profit from them.
He keeps my laws and follows my decrees.

He will not die for his father's sin; he will surely live. 18 But his father will die for his own sin, because he practiced extortion, robbed his brother and did what was wrong among his people.

19 "Yet you ask, 'Why does the son not share the guilt of his father?' Since the son has done what is just and right and has been careful to keep all my decrees, he will surely live. 20 The one who sins is the one who will die. The child will not share the guilt of the parent, nor will the parent share the guilt of the child. The righteousness of the righteous will be credited to them, and the wickedness of the wicked will be charged against them.

21 "But if a wicked person turns away from all the sins they have committed and keeps all my decrees and does what is just and right, that person will surely live; they will not die. 22 None of the offenses they have committed will be remembered against them. Because of the righteous things they have done, they will live. 23 Do I take any pleasure in the death of the wicked? declares the Sovereign LORD. Rather, am I not pleased when they turn from their ways and live?

24 "But if a righteous person turns from their righteousness and commits sin and does the same detestable things the wicked person does, will they live? None of the righteous things that person has done will be remembered. Because of the unfaithfulness they are guilty of and because of the sins they have committed, they will die.

*a 10* Or *things to a brother*

## Amplified Bible

7 And has not wronged anyone but has restored to the debtor his pledge, has taken nothing by robbery but has given his bread to the hungry and has covered the naked with a garment,
8 Who does not charge interest or percentage of increase on what he lends [in compassion], who withholds his hand from iniquity, who executes true justice between man and man,
9 Who has walked in My statutes and kept My ordinances, to deal justly; [then] he is [truly] righteous; he shall surely live, says the Lord God. [Ezek. 20:11; Amos 5:4.]
10 If he begets a son who is a robber or a shedder of blood, who does to a brother either of these sins of violence,
11 And leaves undone all of the duties [of a righteous man], and has even eaten [the food set before idols] on the mountains and defiled his neighbor's wife,
12 Has wronged the poor and needy, has taken by robbery, has not restored [to the debtor] his pledge, has lifted up his eyes to the idols, has committed abomination (things hateful and exceedingly vile in the eyes of God),
13 And has charged interest or percentage of increase on what he has loaned [in supposed compassion]; shall he then live? He shall not live! He has done all these abominations; he shall surely die; his blood shall be upon him.
14 But if this wicked man begets a son who sees all the sins which his father has committed, and considers *and* fears [God] and does not do like his father,
15 Who has not eaten [food set before idols] upon the mountains nor has lifted up his eyes to the idols of the house of Israel, has not defiled his neighbor's wife,
16 Nor wronged anyone, nor has taken anything in pledge, nor has taken by robbery but has given his bread to the hungry and has covered the naked with a garment,
17 Who has withdrawn his hand from [oppressing] the poor, who has not received interest or increase [from the needy] but has executed My ordinances and has walked in My statutes; he shall not die for the iniquity of his father; he shall surely live.
18 As for his father, because he cruelly oppressed, robbed his brother, and did that which is not good among his people, behold, he shall die for his iniquity *and* guilt.
19 Yet do you say, Why does not the son bear the iniquity of the father? When the son has done that which is lawful and right and has kept all My statutes and has done them, he shall surely live.
20 The soul that sins, it [is the one that] shall die. The son shall not bear *and* be punished for the iniquity of the father, neither shall the father bear *and* be punished for the iniquity of the son; the righteousness of the righteous shall be upon him only, and the wickedness of the wicked shall be upon the wicked only.
21 But if the wicked man turns from all his sins that he has committed and keeps all My statutes and does that which is lawful and right, he shall surely live; he shall not die.
22 None of his transgressions which he has committed shall be remembered against him; for his righteousness which he has executed [for his moral and spiritual rectitude in every area and relation], he shall live.
23 Have I any pleasure in the death of the wicked? says the Lord, and not rather that he should turn from his evil way *and* return [to his God] and live?
24 But if the righteous man turns away from his righteousness and commits iniquity and does according to all the abominations that the wicked man does, shall he live? None of his righteous deeds which he has done shall be remembered. In his trespass that he has trespassed and in his sin that he has sinned, in them shall he die.

## New International Version

<sup>25</sup>"Yet you say, 'The way of the Lord is not just.' Hear, you Israelites: Is my way unjust? Is it not your ways that are unjust? <sup>26</sup>If a righteous person turns from their righteousness and commits sin, they will die for it; because of the sin they have committed they will die. <sup>27</sup>But if a wicked person turns away from the wickedness they have committed and does what is just and right, they will save their life. <sup>28</sup>Because they consider all the offenses they have committed and turn away from them, that person will surely live; they will not die. <sup>29</sup>Yet the Israelites say, 'The way of the Lord is not just.' Are my ways unjust, people of Israel? Is it not your ways that are unjust?

<sup>30</sup>"Therefore, you Israelites, I will judge each of you according to your own ways, declares the Sovereign LORD. Repent! Turn away from all your offenses; then sin will not be your downfall. <sup>31</sup>Rid yourselves of all the offenses you have committed, and get a new heart and a new spirit. Why will you die, people of Israel? <sup>32</sup>For I take no pleasure in the death of anyone, declares the Sovereign LORD. Repent and live!

### A Lament Over Israel's Princes

**19** <sup>"</sup>Take up a lament concerning the princes of Israel <sup>2</sup>and say:

"'What a lioness was your mother
     among the lions!
She lay down among them
     and reared her cubs.
<sup>3</sup>She brought up one of her cubs,
     and he became a strong lion.
He learned to tear the prey
     and he became a man-eater.
<sup>4</sup>The nations heard about him,
     and he was trapped in their pit.
They led him with hooks
     to the land of Egypt.

<sup>5</sup>"'When she saw her hope unfulfilled,
     her expectation gone,
she took another of her cubs
     and made him a strong lion.
<sup>6</sup>He prowled among the lions,
     for he was now a strong lion.
He learned to tear the prey
     and he became a man-eater.
<sup>7</sup>He broke down<sup>a</sup> their strongholds
     and devastated their towns.
The land and all who were in it
     were terrified by his roaring.
<sup>8</sup>Then the nations came against him,
     those from regions round about.
They spread their net for him,
     and he was trapped in their pit.
<sup>9</sup>With hooks they pulled him into a cage
     and brought him to the king of Babylon.
They put him in prison,
     so his roar was heard no longer
     on the mountains of Israel.

<sup>10</sup>"'Your mother was like a vine in your vineyard<sup>b</sup>
     planted by the water;
it was fruitful and full of branches
     because of abundant water.
<sup>11</sup>Its branches were strong,
     fit for a ruler's scepter.

<sup>a</sup> 7 Targum (see Septuagint); Hebrew *He knew*     <sup>b</sup> 10 Two Hebrew manuscripts; most Hebrew manuscripts *your blood*

## Amplified Bible

<sup>25</sup>Yet you say, The way of the Lord is not fair *and* just. Hear now, O house of Israel: Is not My way fair *and* just? Are not your ways unfair *and* unjust?

<sup>26</sup>When a righteous man turns away from his righteousness and commits iniquity and dies in his sins, for his iniquity that he has done he shall die.

<sup>27</sup>Again, when the wicked man turns away from his wickedness which he has committed and does that which is lawful and right, he shall save his life.

<sup>28</sup>Because he considers and turns away from all his transgressions which he has committed, he shall surely live; he shall not die.

<sup>29</sup>Yet says the house of Israel, The way of the Lord is not fair and just! O house of Israel, are not My ways fair and just? Are not your ways unfair and unjust?

<sup>30</sup>Therefore I will judge you, O house of Israel, every one according to his ways, says the Lord God. Repent and turn from all your transgressions, lest iniquity be your ruin *and* so shall they not be a stumbling block to you. [Matt. 3:2; Rev. 2:5.]

<sup>31</sup>Cast away from you all your transgressions by which you have transgressed against Me, and make you a new mind *and* heart and a new spirit. For why will you die, O house of Israel? [Eph. 4:22, 23.]

<sup>32</sup>For I have no pleasure in the death of him who dies, says the Lord God. Therefore turn (be converted) and live!

**19** Moreover, take up a lamentation for the princes of Israel,

<sup>2</sup>And say, What a lioness was your mother [Jerusalem-Judah]! She couched among lions; in the midst of young lions she nourished her cubs.

<sup>3</sup>And she [the royal mother-city] brought up one of her cubs [Jehoahaz]; he became a young lion and he learned to catch the prey; he devoured men. [II Kings 23:30, 32.]

<sup>4</sup>The nations also heard of him; he was taken in their pit, and they brought him with hooks to the land of Egypt. [II Chron. 36:1, 4.]

<sup>5</sup>Now when she had waited, she saw her hope was lost. Then she took another of her cubs [Jehoiachin] and made him a young lion. [II Kings 23:34; 24:1, 6.]

<sup>6</sup>And he [Jehoiachin] went up and down among the lions; he became a young lion and learned to catch prey, and he devoured men.

<sup>7</sup>And he knew *and* ravaged their strongholds and he laid waste their cities, and the land was appalled and all who were in it by the noise of his roaring.

<sup>8</sup>Then the nations set against [the king] on every side from the provinces, and they spread their net over him [Jehoiachin]; he was taken in their pit. [II Kings 24:8-15.]

<sup>9</sup>With hooks they put him in a cage and brought him to the king of Babylon; they brought him into custody *and* put him in strongholds, that his voice should no more be heard upon the mountains of Israel.

<sup>10</sup>Your mother [the mother-city Jerusalem] was like a vine [like you, Zedekiah, and in your blood] planted by the waters; it was fruitful and full of branches by reason of abundant water. [II Kings 24:17; Ezek. 17:7.]

<sup>11</sup>And it had strong rods for the scepters of those who

## New International Version

It towered high
    above the thick foliage,
conspicuous for its height
    and for its many branches.
¹²But it was uprooted in fury
    and thrown to the ground.
The east wind made it shrivel,
    it was stripped of its fruit;
its strong branches withered
    and fire consumed them.
¹³Now it is planted in the desert,
    in a dry and thirsty land.
¹⁴Fire spread from one of its main[a] branches
    and consumed its fruit.
No strong branch is left on it
    fit for a ruler's scepter.'

"This is a lament and is to be used as a lament."

### Rebellious Israel Purged

**20** In the seventh year, in the fifth month on the tenth day, some of the elders of Israel came to inquire of the LORD, and they sat down in front of me. ²Then the word of the LORD came to me: ³"Son of man, speak to the elders of Israel and say to them, 'This is what the Sovereign LORD says: Have you come to inquire of me? As surely as I live, I will not let you inquire of me, declares the Sovereign LORD.'

⁴"Will you judge them? Will you judge them, son of man? Then confront them with the detestable practices of their ancestors ⁵and say to them: 'This is what the Sovereign LORD says: On the day I chose Israel, I swore with uplifted hand to the descendants of Jacob and revealed myself to them in Egypt. With uplifted hand I said to them, "I am the LORD your God." ⁶On that day I swore to them that I would bring them out of Egypt into a land I had searched out for them, a land flowing with milk and honey, the most beautiful of all lands. ⁷And I said to them, "Each of you, get rid of the vile images you have set your eyes on, and do not defile yourselves with the idols of Egypt. I am the LORD your God."

⁸"But they rebelled against me and would not listen to me; they did not get rid of the vile images they had set their eyes on, nor did they forsake the idols of Egypt. So I said I would pour out my wrath on them and spend my anger against them in Egypt. ⁹But for the sake of my name, I brought them out of Egypt. I did it to keep my name from being profaned in the eyes of the nations among whom they lived and in whose sight I had revealed myself to the Israelites. ¹⁰Therefore I led them out of Egypt and brought them into the wilderness. ¹¹I gave them my decrees and made known to them my laws, by which the person who obeys them will live. ¹²Also I gave them my Sabbaths as a sign between us, so they would know that I the LORD made them holy.

¹³"Yet the people of Israel rebelled against me in the wilderness. They did not follow my decrees but rejected my laws—by which the person who obeys them will live—and they utterly desecrated my Sabbaths. So I said I would pour out my wrath on them and destroy them in the wil-

## Amplified Bible

bore rule and its height was exalted among the thick branches *and* into the clouds, and it was seen in its height among the multitude of its branches *and* was conspicuous. ¹²But the vine was plucked up in God's wrath [by His agent the Babylonian king] and it was cast down to the ground; the east wind dried up its fruit; its strong rods were broken off and withered; the fire [of God's judgment] consumed them.

¹³And now it is transplanted in the wilderness, in a dry and thirsty land [Babylon].

¹⁴And fire went out of a rod [Zedekiah] of its branches which has consumed the vine's fruit, so that it has in it no [longer a] strong rod to be a scepter for ruling. This is a lamentation and shall be for a lamentation *and* a dirge.

**20** In the seventh year, in the fifth [month], on the tenth [day] of the month [after the beginning of the Babylonian captivity, which was to last seventy years], certain of the elders of Israel came to inquire of the Lord and sat down before me [Ezekiel, in Babylonia]. [Jer. 25:11; 29:10.]

²Then came the word of the Lord to me, saying, ³Son of man, speak to the elders of Israel and say to them, Thus says the Lord God: Have you come to inquire of Me? As I live, says the Lord God, I will not be inquired of by you!

⁴Will you judge them, son of man [Ezekiel], will you judge them? Then cause them to know, understand, *and* realize the abominations of their fathers. [Matt. 23:29-33; Acts 7:51, 52.]

⁵And say to them, Thus says the Lord God: In the day when I chose Israel and lifted up My hand *and* swore to the offspring of the house of Jacob and made Myself known to them in the land of Egypt, when I lifted up My hand *and* swore to them, saying, I am the Lord your God,

⁶On that day I lifted up My hand *and* swore to them to bring them out of the land of Egypt to a land that I had searched out for them, flowing with milk and honey, [a land] which is an ornament *and* a glory to all lands.

⁷Then said I to them, Let every man cast away the abominable things on which he feasts his eyes, and defile not yourselves with the idols of Egypt; I am the Lord your God.

⁸But they rebelled against Me and would not listen to Me; they did not every man cast away the abominable things on which they feasted their eyes, nor did they forsake the idols of Egypt. Then I [thought], I will pour out My wrath upon them and finish My anger against them in the midst of the land of Egypt.

⁹But I acted for My name's sake, that it should not be profaned in the sight of the [heathen] nations among whom they dwelt, in whose sight I made Myself known to them by bringing them out of the land of Egypt.

¹⁰So I caused them to go out from the land of Egypt and brought them into the wilderness.

¹¹And I gave them My statutes and showed *and* made known to them My judgments, which, if a man keeps, he must live in *and* by them.

¹²Moreover, also I gave them My Sabbaths to be a sign between Me and them, that they might understand *and* realize that I am the Lord Who sanctifies them [separates and sets them apart].

¹³But the house of Israel rebelled against Me in the wilderness; they walked not in My statutes and they despised *and* cast away My judgments, which, if a man keeps, he must even live in *and* by them; and they grievously profaned My Sabbaths. Then I thought I would pour out My wrath on them in the wilderness and uproot *and* consume them.

---

*a* 14 Or *from under its*

## New International Version

derness. ¹⁴But for the sake of my name I did what would keep it from being profaned in the eyes of the nations in whose sight I had brought them out. ¹⁵Also with uplifted hand I swore to them in the wilderness that I would not bring them into the land I had given them—a land flowing with milk and honey, the most beautiful of all lands—¹⁶because they rejected my laws and did not follow my decrees and desecrated my Sabbaths. For their hearts were devoted to their idols. ¹⁷Yet I looked on them with pity and did not destroy them or put an end to them in the wilderness. ¹⁸I said to their children in the wilderness, "Do not follow the statutes of your parents or keep their laws or defile yourselves with their idols. ¹⁹I am the LORD your God; follow my decrees and be careful to keep my laws. ²⁰Keep my Sabbaths holy, that they may be a sign between us. Then you will know that I am the LORD your God."

²¹'But the children rebelled against me: They did not follow my decrees, they were not careful to keep my laws, of which I said, "The person who obeys them will live by them," and they desecrated my Sabbaths. So I said I would pour out my wrath on them and spend my anger against them in the wilderness. ²²But I withheld my hand, and for the sake of my name I did what would keep it from being profaned in the eyes of the nations in whose sight I had brought them out. ²³Also with uplifted hand I swore to them in the wilderness that I would disperse them among the nations and scatter them through the countries, ²⁴because they had not obeyed my laws but had rejected my decrees and desecrated my Sabbaths, and their eyes lusted after their parents' idols. ²⁵So I gave them other statutes that were not good and laws through which they could not live; ²⁶I defiled them through their gifts—the sacrifice of every firstborn—that I might fill them with horror so they would know that I am the LORD.'

²⁷"Therefore, son of man, speak to the people of Israel and say to them, 'This is what the Sovereign LORD says: In this also your ancestors blasphemed me by being unfaithful to me: ²⁸When I brought them into the land I had sworn to give them and they saw any high hill or any leafy tree, there they offered their sacrifices, made offerings that aroused my anger, presented their fragrant incense and poured out their drink offerings. ²⁹Then I said to them: What is this high place you go to?'" (It is called Bamah[a] to this day.)

### Rebellious Israel Renewed

³⁰"Therefore say to the Israelites: 'This is what the Sovereign LORD says: Will you defile yourselves the way your ancestors did and lust after their vile images? ³¹When you offer your gifts—the sacrifice of your children in the fire—you continue to defile yourselves with all your idols to this day. Am I to let you inquire of me, you Israelites? As surely as I live, declares the Sovereign LORD, I will not let you inquire of me.

## Amplified Bible

¹⁴But I acted for My name's sake, that it should not be profaned before the [heathen] nations in whose sight I brought them out.

¹⁵Yet also I lifted up My hand to swear to them in the wilderness that I would not bring them into the land which I had given them, flowing with milk and honey, which is the ornament and glory of all lands—

¹⁶Because they despised and rejected My ordinances and walked not in My statutes and profaned My Sabbaths, for their hearts went after their idols.

¹⁷Yet My eye pitied them instead of destroying them, and I did not make a full end of them in the wilderness.

¹⁸But I said to their sons in the wilderness, You shall not walk in the statutes of your fathers nor observe their ordinances nor defile yourselves with their idols.

¹⁹I the Lord am your God; walk in My statutes and keep My ordinances,

²⁰And hallow (separate and keep holy) My Sabbaths, and they shall be a sign between Me and you, that you may know, understand, and realize that I am the Lord your God.

²¹Yet the sons rebelled against Me; they walked not in My statutes, neither kept My ordinances which, if a man does, he must live in and by them; they profaned My Sabbaths. Then I thought I would pour out My wrath on them and finish My anger against them in the wilderness.

²²Yet I withheld My hand and acted for My name's sake, that it should not be debased and profaned in the sight of the [heathen] nations, in whose sight I had brought them forth [from bondage].

²³Moreover, I lifted up My hand and swore to them in the wilderness that I would scatter them among the [heathen] nations and disperse them in the countries,

²⁴Because they had not executed My ordinances but had despised and rejected My statutes and had profaned My Sabbaths, and their eyes were set on their fathers' idols.

²⁵Wherefore also I gave them [over to] statutes that were not good and ordinances whereby they should not live and could not have life, [Ps. 81:12; Isa. 66:4; Rom. 1:21-25, 28.]

²⁶And I [let them] pollute and make themselves unclean in their own offerings [to their idols], in that they caused to pass through the fire all the firstborn, that I might make them desolate, to the end that they might know, understand, and realize that I am the Lord. [Lev. 20:2-5.]

²⁷Therefore, son of man, speak to the house of Israel and say to them, Thus says the Lord God: Again in this your fathers blasphemed Me, in that they dealt faithlessly and treacherously with Me and committed a treasonous trespass against Me.

²⁸For when I had brought them into the land which I lifted up My hand and swore to give to them, then they saw every high hill and every dark and leafy tree [as a place for idol worship], and they offered there their sacrifices and there they presented their offering that provoked My anger and sadness; there also they made their sweet-smelling savor and poured out there their drink offerings.

²⁹Then I said to them, What is the high place to which you go? And the name of it is called Bamah [high place] to this day.

³⁰Therefore say to the house of Israel, Thus says the Lord God: Do you [exiles] debase and defile yourselves after the manner of your fathers? And do you play the harlot after their loathsome and detestable things?

³¹And when you offer your gifts, when you make your sons pass through the fire, do you not debase and defile yourselves with all your idols to this day? And shall I be inquired of by you, O house of Israel? As I live, says the Lord God, I will not be inquired of by you!

---

*a 29 Bamah* means *high place.*

## New International Version

³²"'You say, "We want to be like the nations, like the peoples of the world, who serve wood and stone." But what you have in mind will never happen. ³³As surely as I live, declares the Sovereign LORD, I will reign over you with a mighty hand and an outstretched arm and with outpoured wrath. ³⁴I will bring you from the nations and gather you from the countries where you have been scattered—with a mighty hand and an outstretched arm and with outpoured wrath. ³⁵I will bring you into the wilderness of the nations and there, face to face, I will execute judgment upon you. ³⁶As I judged your ancestors in the wilderness of the land of Egypt, so I will judge you, declares the Sovereign LORD. ³⁷I will take note of you as you pass under my rod, and I will bring you into the bond of the covenant. ³⁸I will purge you of those who revolt and rebel against me. Although I will bring them out of the land where they are living, yet they will not enter the land of Israel. Then you will know that I am the LORD.

³⁹"'As for you, people of Israel, this is what the Sovereign LORD says: Go and serve your idols, every one of you! But afterward you will surely listen to me and no longer profane my holy name with your gifts and idols. ⁴⁰For on my holy mountain, the high mountain of Israel, declares the Sovereign LORD, there in the land all the people of Israel will serve me, and there I will accept them. There I will require your offerings and your choice gifts,ᵃ along with all your holy sacrifices. ⁴¹I will accept you as fragrant incense when I bring you out from the nations and gather you from the countries where you have been scattered, and I will be proved holy through you in the sight of the nations. ⁴²Then you will know that I am the LORD, when I bring you into the land of Israel, the land I had sworn with uplifted hand to give to your ancestors. ⁴³There you will remember your conduct and all the actions by which you have defiled yourselves, and you will loathe yourselves for all the evil you have done. ⁴⁴You will know that I am the LORD, when I deal with you for my name's sake and not according to your evil ways and your corrupt practices, you people of Israel, declares the Sovereign LORD.'"

### Prophecy Against the South

⁴⁵The word of the LORD came to me: ⁴⁶"Son of man, set your face toward the south; preach against the south and prophesy against the forest of the southland. ⁴⁷Say to the southern forest: 'Hear the word of the LORD. This is what the Sovereign LORD says: I am about to set fire to you, and it will consume all your trees, both green and dry. The blazing flame will not be quenched, and every face from south to north will be scorched by it. ⁴⁸Everyone will see that I the LORD have kindled it; it will not be quenched.'"

⁴⁹Then I said, "Sovereign LORD, they are saying of me, 'Isn't he just telling parables?'"ᵇ

## Amplified Bible

³²And that which has come up in your mind shall never happen, in that you think, We will be as the nations, as the tribes of the countries, to serve idols of wood and stone.

³³As I live, says the Lord God, surely with a mighty hand and an outstretched arm and with wrath poured out will I be King over you.

³⁴And I will bring you out from the peoples and will gather you out of the countries in which you are scattered, with a mighty hand and an outstretched arm and with wrath poured out.

³⁵And I will bring you into the wilderness of the peoples, and there will I enter into judgment with you *and* contend with you face to face.

³⁶As I entered into judgment *and* contended with your fathers in the wilderness of the land of Egypt, so will I enter into judgment *and* contend with you, says the Lord God. [Num. 11; Ps. 106:15; I Cor. 10:5-10.]

³⁷And I will cause you to pass under the rod [as the shepherd does his sheep when he counts them, and I will count you as Mine and I will constrain you] and bring you into the covenant to which you are permanently bound. [Lev. 27:32.]

³⁸And I will purge out *and* separate from among you the rebels and those who transgress against Me; I will bring them out of the country where they temporarily dwell, but they shall not enter the land of Israel. Then you shall know, understand, *and* realize that I am the Lord. [Heb. 4:2, 3.]

³⁹As for you, O house of Israel, thus says the Lord God: Go, serve every one of you his idols, now and hereafter, if you will not listen to Me! But you shall not profane My holy name any more with your sacrificial gifts and your idols!

⁴⁰For on My holy mountain, on the mountain height of Israel, says the Lord God, there all the house of Israel, all of them in the land, shall serve Me. There will I [graciously] accept them, and there will I require your offerings and the firstfruits *and* the choicest of your contributions, with all your sacred things.

⁴¹I will accept you [graciously] as a pleasant odor when I lead you out from the peoples and gather you out of the countries in which you have been scattered, and I will manifest My holiness among you in the sight of the nations [who will seek Me because of My power displayed in you]. [Eph. 5:2; Phil. 4:18.]

⁴²And you shall know, understand, *and* realize that I am the Lord, when I bring you into the land of Israel, into the country which I lifted up My hand *and* swore to give to your fathers.

⁴³And there you shall [earnestly] remember your ways and all your doings with which you have defiled yourselves, and you shall loathe yourselves in your own sight for all your evil deeds which you have done.

⁴⁴And you shall know, understand, *and* realize that I am the Lord, when I deal with you for My name's sake, not according to your evil ways nor according to your corrupt doings, O house of Israel, says the Lord God.

⁴⁵Moreover, the word of the Lord came to me, saying,

⁴⁶Son of man, set your face toward the south, preach against the south, and prophesy against the forest land of the South (the Negeb).

⁴⁷And say to the forest of the South (the Negeb), Hear the word of the Lord; Thus says the Lord God: Behold, I will kindle a fire in you and it shall devour every green tree in you and every dry tree. The blazing flame shall not be quenched, and all faces from the south to the north shall be scorched by it.

⁴⁸All flesh shall see that I the Lord have kindled it; it shall not be quenched.

⁴⁹Then said I, Ah, Lord God! They are saying of me, Does he not speak in parables *and* make allegories?

ᵃ 40 Or *and the gifts of your firstfruits*    ᵇ 49 In Hebrew texts 20:45-49 is numbered 21:1-5.

## New International Version

### Babylon as God's Sword of Judgment

**21** *a* The word of the LORD came to me: ²"Son of man, set your face against Jerusalem and preach against the sanctuary. Prophesy against the land of Israel ³and say to her: 'This is what the LORD says: I am against you. I will draw my sword from its sheath and cut off from you both the righteous and the wicked. ⁴Because I am going to cut off the righteous and the wicked, my sword will be unsheathed against everyone from south to north. ⁵Then all people will know that I the LORD have drawn my sword from its sheath; it will not return again.'

⁶"Therefore groan, son of man! Groan before them with broken heart and bitter grief. ⁷And when they ask you, 'Why are you groaning?' you shall say, 'Because of the news that is coming. Every heart will melt with fear and every hand go limp; every spirit will become faint and every leg will be wet with urine.' It is coming! It will surely take place, declares the Sovereign LORD."

⁸The word of the LORD came to me: ⁹"Son of man, prophesy and say, 'This is what the Lord says:

"'A sword, a sword,
    sharpened and polished—
¹⁰sharpened for the slaughter,
    polished to flash like lightning!

"'Shall we rejoice in the scepter of my royal son? The sword despises every such stick.

¹¹"'The sword is appointed to be polished,
    to be grasped with the hand;
it is sharpened and polished,
    made ready for the hand of the slayer.
¹²Cry out and wail, son of man,
    for it is against my people;
    it is against all the princes of Israel.
They are thrown to the sword
    along with my people.
Therefore beat your breast.

¹³"'Testing will surely come. And what if even the scepter, which the sword despises, does not continue? declares the Sovereign LORD.'

¹⁴"So then, son of man, prophesy
    and strike your hands together.
Let the sword strike twice,
    even three times.
It is a sword for slaughter—
    a sword for great slaughter,
    closing in on them from every side.
¹⁵So that hearts may melt with fear
    and the fallen be many,
I have stationed the sword for slaughter*b*
    at all their gates.
Look! It is forged to strike like lightning,
    it is grasped for slaughter.
¹⁶Slash to the right, you sword,
    then to the left,
    wherever your blade is turned.
¹⁷I too will strike my hands together,
    and my wrath will subside.
I the LORD have spoken."

¹⁸The word of the LORD came to me: ¹⁹"Son of man, mark out two roads for the sword of the king of Babylon to take, both starting from the same country. Make a signpost where the road branches off to the city. ²⁰Mark out one road for the sword to come against Rabbah of the Ammonites and another against Judah and fortified Jerusalem. ²¹For the king of Babylon will stop at the fork in the road, at the junction of the two roads, to seek an omen: He will cast lots with arrows, he will consult his idols, he

## Amplified Bible

**21** And the word of the Lord came to me, saying, ²Son of man, set your face toward Jerusalem and direct your [prophetic] word against the holy places; prophesy against the land of Israel

³And say to the land of Israel, Thus says the Lord: Behold, I am against you and will draw forth My sword out of its sheath and will cut off from you both the righteous and the wicked.

⁴Because I will cut off from you both the righteous and the wicked, therefore shall My sword go out of its sheath against all flesh from the south to the north,

⁵And all living shall know, understand, *and* realize that I the Lord have drawn My sword out of its sheath; it shall not be sheathed any more.

⁶Sigh therefore, son of man! With breaking heart and with bitterness shall you sigh before their eyes.

⁷And it shall be that when they say to you, Why do you sigh? that you shall answer, Because of the tidings. When it comes, every heart will melt and all hands will be feeble, and every spirit will faint and all knees will be weak as water. Behold, it comes and it shall be fulfilled, says the Lord God.

⁸Again the word of the Lord came to me, saying,

⁹Son of man, prophesy and say, Thus says the Lord: Say, A sword, a sword is sharpened and also polished;

¹⁰It [the sword of Babylon] is sharpened that it may make a slaughter, polished that it may flash *and* glitter like lightning! Shall we then rejoice *and* make mirth [when such a calamity is impending]? But the rod *or* scepter of My son [Judah] rejects *and* views with contempt every tree [that is, since God's promise long ago to Judah is certain, he believes Judah's scepter must remain no matter what power arises against it]! [Gen. 49:9, 10; II Sam. 7:23.]

¹¹And the sword [of Babylon] is given to be polished that it may be put to use; the sword is sharpened and polished to be given into the hand of the slayer.

¹²Cry and wail, son of man, for it is against My people; it is against all the princes of Israel; they are thrown to the sword along with My people, *and* terrors by reason of the sword are upon My people. Therefore smite your thigh [in dismay].

¹³For this sword has been tested *and* proved [on others], and what if the rejecting *and* despising rod *or* scepter of Judah shall be no more but completely swept away? says the Lord God.

¹⁴Therefore, son of man, prophesy and smite your hands together and let the sword be doubled, yes, trebled in intensity—the sword for those to be overthrown *and* pierced through; it is the sword of great slaughter which encompasses them [so that none can escape, even by entering into their inner chambers].

¹⁵I have set the threatening *and* glittering sword against all their gates, that their hearts may melt and their stumblings be multiplied. Ah! It is made [to flash] like lightning; it is pointed *and* sharpened for slaughter.

¹⁶Turn [O sword] and cut right or cut left, whichever way your lust for blood *and* your edge direct you.

¹⁷I will also clap My hands, and I will cause My wrath to rest. I the Lord have said it.

¹⁸The word of the Lord came to me again, saying,

¹⁹Also, son of man, mark out two ways by which the sword of the king of Babylon may come; both shall come forth from the same land. And make a signpost (a hand); make it at the head of the way to a city.

²⁰You shall point out a way for the [Babylonian] sword to come to Rabbah [the capital] of the sons of Ammon and to Judah with Jerusalem, the fortified *and* inaccessible.

²¹For the king of Babylon stands at the parting of the way, at the fork of the two ways, to use divination. He shakes the arrows to and fro, he consults the teraphim (household gods), he looks at the liver.

---

*a* In Hebrew texts 21:1-32 is numbered 21:6-37.   *b* 15 Septuagint; the meaning of the Hebrew for this word is uncertain.

## New International Version

will examine the liver. <sup>22</sup>Into his right hand will come the lot for Jerusalem, where he is to set up battering rams, to give the command to slaughter, to sound the battle cry, to set battering rams against the gates, to build a ramp and to erect siege works. <sup>23</sup>It will seem like a false omen to those who have sworn allegiance to him, but he will remind them of their guilt and take them captive.

<sup>24</sup>"Therefore this is what the Sovereign Lord says: 'Because you people have brought to mind your guilt by your open rebellion, revealing your sins in all that you do—because you have done this, you will be taken captive.

<sup>25</sup>"'You profane and wicked prince of Israel, whose day has come, whose time of punishment has reached its climax, <sup>26</sup>this is what the Sovereign Lord says: Take off the turban, remove the crown. It will not be as it was: The lowly will be exalted and the exalted will be brought low. <sup>27</sup>A ruin! A ruin! I will make it a ruin! The crown will not be restored until he to whom it rightfully belongs shall come; to him I will give it.'

<sup>28</sup>"And you, son of man, prophesy and say, 'This is what the Sovereign Lord says about the Ammonites and their insults:

"'A sword, a sword,
    drawn for the slaughter,
polished to consume
    and to flash like lightning!
<sup>29</sup>Despite false visions concerning you
    and lying divinations about you,
it will be laid on the necks
    of the wicked who are to be slain,
whose day has come,
    whose time of punishment has reached its climax.

<sup>30</sup>"'Let the sword return to its sheath.
In the place where you were created,
in the land of your ancestry,
    I will judge you.
<sup>31</sup>I will pour out my wrath on you
    and breathe out my fiery anger against you;
I will deliver you into the hands of brutal men,
    men skilled in destruction.
<sup>32</sup>You will be fuel for the fire,
    your blood will be shed in your land,
you will be remembered no more;
    for I the Lord have spoken.'"

### Judgment on Jerusalem's Sins

**22** The word of the Lord came to me:

<sup>2</sup>"Son of man, will you judge her? Will you judge this city of bloodshed? Then confront her with all her detestable practices <sup>3</sup>and say: 'This is what the Sovereign Lord says: You city that brings on herself doom by shedding blood in her midst and defiles herself by making idols, <sup>4</sup>you have become guilty because of the blood you have shed and have become defiled by the idols you have made. You have brought your days to a close, and the end of your years has come. Therefore I will make you an object of scorn to the nations and a laughingstock to all the countries. <sup>5</sup>Those who are near and those who are far away will mock you, you infamous city, full of turmoil.

<sup>6</sup>"'See how each of the princes of Israel who are in you uses his power to shed blood. <sup>7</sup>In you they have treated father and mother with contempt; in you they have oppressed the foreigner and mistreated the fatherless and

## Amplified Bible

<sup>22</sup>In his right hand is the lot marked for Jerusalem: to set battering rams, to open the mouth calling for slaughter, to lift up the voice with a war cry, to set battering rams against the gates, to cast up siege mounds, and to build siege towers.

<sup>23</sup>And it shall seem like a lying divination to them who have sworn oaths [of allegiance to Nebuchadnezzar]. [Will he now fight against their homeland?] But he will remind them of their guilt *and* iniquity [in violating those oaths], that they may be caught. [II Chron. 36:10, 13; Ezek. 17:15, 18-21.]

<sup>24</sup>Therefore thus says the Lord God: Because you have made your guilt *and* iniquity to be remembered, in that your transgressions are uncovered, so that in all your doings your sins appear—because, I say, you have come to remembrance, you shall be taken with the [enemy's] hand.

<sup>25</sup>And you, O dishonored and wicked one [Zedekiah], the prince of Israel, whose day will come at the time of your final reckoning *and* punishment,

<sup>26</sup>Thus says the Lord God: Remove the [high priest's] miter *or* headband and take off the [king's] crown; things shall not remain as they have been; the low is to be exalted and the high is to be brought low.

<sup>27</sup>I will overthrow, overthrow, overthrow it; this also shall be no more until He comes Whose right it is [to reign in judgment and in righteousness], and I will give it to Him. [Gen. 49:10; Isa. 9:6, 7; 11:1-4; Dan. 7:14; Luke 1:31-33.]

<sup>28</sup>And you, son of man, prophesy and say, Thus says the Lord God concerning the sons of Ammon and concerning their reproach: Say, A sword, a sword is drawn for the slaughter; it is polished to cause it to devour to the uttermost *and* to flash like lightning,

<sup>29</sup>While they see for you false visions, while they divine lies for you to lay you [of Ammon] upon the headless trunks of those who are slain, of the wicked whose day is coming at the time of the final reckoning *and* punishment.

<sup>30</sup>Return [the sword] to its sheath. In the place where you were created, in the land of your origin *and* of your birth, I will judge you.

<sup>31</sup>And I will pour out My indignation upon you [O sons of Ammon]; I will blow upon you with the fire of My wrath and will deliver you into the hand of brutish men, skillful to destroy.

<sup>32</sup>You shall be for fuel to the fire; your blood shall be in the midst of the land; you shall be no more remembered, for I the Lord have spoken it. [Jer. 49:1-6; Ezek. 25:1-7; Amos 1:13-15; Zeph. 2:8-11.]

**22** Moreover, the word of the Lord came to me, saying,

<sup>2</sup>And you son of man [Ezekiel], will you judge, will you judge the bloodshedding city? Then cause her to know all her abominations,

<sup>3</sup>And say, Thus says the Lord God: A city that sheds blood in the midst of her so that her time [of doom] will come, and makes idols [over those who worship them] to defile her!

<sup>4</sup>In your blood which you have shed you have become guilty, and you are defiled by the idols which you have made, and you have caused your time [of judgment and punishment] to draw near and have arrived at the full measure of your years. Therefore have I made you a reproach to the [heathen] nations and a mocking to all countries.

<sup>5</sup>Those who are near and those who are far from you will mock you, you infamous one, full of tumult.

<sup>6</sup>Behold, the princes of Israel in you, every one according to his power, have been intending to shed blood.

<sup>7</sup>In you have they treated father and mother lightly; in the midst of you they have dealt unjustly *and* by oppression in relation to the stranger; in you they have wronged the fatherless and the widow.

## New International Version

the widow. [8]You have despised my holy things and desecrated my Sabbaths. [9]In you are slanderers who are bent on shedding blood; in you are those who eat at the mountain shrines and commit lewd acts. [10]In you are those who dishonor their father's bed; in you are those who violate women during their period, when they are ceremonially unclean. [11]In you one man commits a detestable offense with his neighbor's wife, another shamefully defiles his daughter-in-law, and another violates his sister, his own father's daughter. [12]In you are people who accept bribes to shed blood; you take interest and make a profit from the poor. You extort unjust gain from your neighbors. And you have forgotten me, declares the Sovereign LORD.

[13]"'I will surely strike my hands together at the unjust gain you have made and at the blood you have shed in your midst. [14]Will your courage endure or your hands be strong in the day I deal with you? I the LORD have spoken, and I will do it. [15]I will disperse you among the nations and scatter you through the countries; and I will put an end to your uncleanness. [16]When you have been defiled[a] in the eyes of the nations, you will know that I am the LORD.'"

[17]Then the word of the LORD came to me: [18]"Son of man, the people of Israel have become dross to me; all of them are the copper, tin, iron and lead left inside a furnace. They are but the dross of silver. [19]Therefore this is what the Sovereign LORD says: 'Because you have all become dross, I will gather you into Jerusalem. [20]As silver, copper, iron, lead and tin are gathered into a furnace to be melted with a fiery blast, so will I gather you in my anger and my wrath and put you inside the city and melt you. [21]I will gather you and I will blow on you with my fiery wrath, and you will be melted inside her. [22]As silver is melted in a furnace, so you will be melted inside her, and you will know that I the LORD have poured out my wrath on you.'"

[23]Again the word of the LORD came to me: [24]"Son of man, say to the land, 'You are a land that has not been cleansed or rained on in the day of wrath.' [25]There is a conspiracy of her princes[b] within her like a roaring lion tearing its prey; they devour people, take treasures and precious things and make many widows within her. [26]Her priests do violence to my law and profane my holy things; they do not distinguish between the holy and the common; they teach that there is no difference between the unclean and the clean; and they shut their eyes to the keeping of my Sabbaths, so that I am profaned among them. [27]Her officials within her are like wolves tearing their prey; they shed blood and kill people to make unjust gain. [28]Her prophets whitewash these deeds for them by false visions and lying divinations. They say, 'This is what the Sovereign LORD says'—when the LORD has not spoken. [29]The people of the land practice extortion and commit robbery;

## Amplified Bible

[8]You have despised *and* scorned My sacred things and have profaned My Sabbaths.

[9]In you are slanderous men who arouse suspicions to shed blood, and in you are they who have eaten [food offered to idols] upon the mountains; in the midst of you they have committed lewdness.

[10]In you men have uncovered their fathers' nakedness [the nakedness of mother or stepmother]; in you they have humbled women who are [ceremonially] unclean [during their periods or because of childbirth].

[11]And one has committed abomination with his neighbor's wife, another has lewdly defiled his daughter-in-law, and another in you has humbled his sister, his father's daughter.

[12]In you they have accepted bribes to shed blood; you have taken [forbidden] interest and [percentage of] increase, and you have greedily gained from your neighbors by oppression *and* extortion and have forgotten Me, says the Lord God.

[13]Behold therefore, I have struck My hands together at your dishonest gain which you have made and at the blood which has been in the midst of you.

[14]Can your heart *and* courage endure or can your hands be strong in the days that I shall deal with you? I the Lord have spoken it, and I will do it.

[15]And I will scatter you among the nations and disperse you through the countries, and I will consume your filthiness out of you.

[16]And you shall be dishonored *and* profane yourself in the sight of the nations, and you shall know (understand and realize) that I am the Lord.

[17]And the word of the Lord came to me, saying,

[18]Son of man, the house of Israel has become to Me scum *and* waste matter. All of them are bronze and tin and iron and lead in the midst of the furnace; they are dross of silver.

[19]Therefore thus says the Lord God: Because you have all become scum *and* waste matter, behold therefore, I will gather you [O Israel] into the midst of Jerusalem.

[20]As they gather silver and bronze and iron and lead and tin into the midst of the furnace, to blow the fire upon it in order to melt it, so will I gather you in My anger and in My wrath, and I will put you in and melt you.

[21]Yes, I will gather you and blow upon you with the fire of My wrath, and you shall be melted in the midst of it.

[22]As silver is melted in the midst of the furnace, so shall you be melted in the midst of it, and you shall know, understand, *and* realize that I the Lord have poured out My wrath upon you [O Israel].

[23]And the word of the Lord came to me, saying,

[24]Son of man, say to her, You are a land that is not cleansed nor rained upon in the day of indignation.

[25]There is a conspiracy of [Israel's false] prophets in the midst of her, like a roaring lion tearing the prey; they have devoured human lives; they have taken [in their greed] treasure and precious things; they have made many widows in the midst of her.

[26]Her priests have done violence to My law and have profaned My holy things. They have made no distinction between the sacred and the secular, neither have they taught people the difference between the unclean and the clean and have hid their eyes from My Sabbaths, and I am profaned among them.

[27]Her princes in the midst of her are like wolves rending *and* devouring the prey, shedding blood and destroying lives to get dishonest gain.

[28]And her prophets have daubed them over with whitewash, seeing false visions and divining lies to them, saying, Thus says the Lord God—when the Lord has not spoken.

[29]The people of the land have used oppression *and* extortion and have committed robbery; yes, they have

---

*a* 16 Or *When I have allotted you your inheritance*    *b* 25 Septuagint; Hebrew *prophets*

## New International Version

they oppress the poor and needy and mistreat the foreigner, denying them justice.

³⁰"I looked for someone among them who would build up the wall and stand before me in the gap on behalf of the land so I would not have to destroy it, but I found no one. ³¹So I will pour out my wrath on them and consume them with my fiery anger, bringing down on their own heads all they have done, declares the Sovereign LORD."

### Two Adulterous Sisters

**23** The word of the LORD came to me: ²"Son of man, there were two women, daughters of the same mother. ³They became prostitutes in Egypt, engaging in prostitution from their youth. In that land their breasts were fondled and their virgin bosoms caressed. ⁴The older was named Oholah, and her sister was Oholibah. They were mine and gave birth to sons and daughters. Oholah is Samaria, and Oholibah is Jerusalem.

⁵"Oholah engaged in prostitution while she was still mine; and she lusted after her lovers, the Assyrians—warriors ⁶clothed in blue, governors and commanders, all of them handsome young men, and mounted horsemen. ⁷She gave herself as a prostitute to all the elite of the Assyrians and defiled herself with all the idols of everyone she lusted after. ⁸She did not give up the prostitution she began in Egypt, when during her youth men slept with her, caressed her virgin bosom and poured out their lust on her.

⁹"Therefore I delivered her into the hands of her lovers, the Assyrians, for whom she lusted. ¹⁰They stripped her naked, took away her sons and daughters and killed her with the sword. She became a byword among women, and punishment was inflicted on her.

¹¹"Her sister Oholibah saw this, yet in her lust and prostitution she was more depraved than her sister. ¹²She too lusted after the Assyrians—governors and commanders, warriors in full dress, mounted horsemen, all handsome young men. ¹³I saw that she too defiled herself; both of them went the same way.

¹⁴"But she carried her prostitution still further. She saw men portrayed on a wall, figures of Chaldeansᵃ portrayed in red, ¹⁵with belts around their waists and flowing turbans on their heads; all of them looked like Babylonian chariot officers, natives of Chaldea.ᵇ ¹⁶As soon as she saw them, she lusted after them and sent messengers to them in Chaldea. ¹⁷Then the Babylonians came to her, to the bed of love, and in their lust they defiled her. After she had been defiled by them, she turned away from them in disgust. ¹⁸When she carried on her prostitution openly and exposed her naked body, I turned away from her in disgust, just as I had turned away from her sister. ¹⁹Yet she became more and more promiscuous as she recalled the days of her youth, when she was a prostitute in Egypt. ²⁰There she lusted after her lovers, whose genitals were like those of donkeys and whose emission was like that of horses. ²¹So you longed for the lewdness of your youth, when in Egypt your bosom was caressed and your young breasts fondled.ᶜ

²²"Therefore, Oholibah, this is what the Sovereign

---

## Amplified Bible

wronged *and* vexed the poor and needy; yes, they have oppressed the stranger *and* temporary resident wrongfully. ³⁰And I sought a man among them who should build up the wall and stand in the gap before Me for the land, that I should not destroy it, but I found none. ³¹Therefore have I poured out My indignation upon them; I have consumed them with the fire of My wrath; their own way have I repaid [by bringing it] upon their own heads, says the Lord God.

**23** The word of the Lord came again to me, saying, ²Son of man, there were two women, the daughters of one mother; ³And they played the harlot in Egypt. There they played the harlot in their youth; there their bosoms were pressed and there their virgin breasts were handled.

⁴And the names of them were Aholah the elder and Aholibah her sister, and they became Mine and they bore sons and daughters. As for the identity of their names, Aholah is Samaria and Aholibah is Jerusalem.

⁵And Aholah played the harlot when she was Mine, and she was foolishly fond of her lovers *and* doted on the Assyrians her neighbors,

⁶Who were clothed with blue, governors and deputies, all of them attractive young men, horsemen riding upon horses.

⁷And she bestowed her harlotries upon them, the choicest men of Assyria all of them; and on whomever she doted, with all their idols she defiled herself.

⁸Neither has she left her harlotries since the days of Egypt [from where she brought them], for in her youth men there lay with her and handled her girlish bosom, and they poured out their sinful desire upon her.

⁹Wherefore I delivered her into the hand of her lovers, into the hand of the Assyrians upon whom she doted.

¹⁰These uncovered her nakedness *and* shame; they took her sons and her daughters and they slew her with the sword, and her name became notorious *and* a byword among women when judgments were executed upon her.

¹¹And her sister Aholibah saw this; yet she was more corrupt in her foolish fondness than she, and in her harlotries she was more wanton than her sister in her harlotries.

¹²She doted upon the Assyrians—governors and deputies, her neighbors, clothed most gorgeously, horsemen riding upon horses, all of them desirable young men.

¹³And I saw that she was defiled, that both [of the sisters] took one way.

¹⁴But [Aholibah] carried her harlotries further, for she saw men pictured upon the wall, the pictures of the Chaldeans sketched in bright red pigment,

¹⁵Girded with girdles on their loins, with flowing turbans on their heads, all of them looking like officers, a picture of Babylonian men whose native land was Chaldea,

¹⁶Then as soon as she saw [the sketches of] them, she doted on them and sent messengers to them in Chaldea.

¹⁷And the Babylonians came to her into the bed of love, and they defiled her with their evil desire; and when she was polluted by them, she [Jerusalem] broke the relationship *and* pushed them away from her in disgust.

¹⁸So she flaunted her harlotries and exposed her nakedness, and I was disgusted and turned from her, as I had turned in disgust from her sister.

¹⁹Yet she multiplied her harlotries, remembering the days of her youth in which she had played the harlot in the land of Egypt.

²⁰For she doted upon her paramours there, whose lust was sensuous *and* vulgar like that of asses *or* stallions.

²¹Thus you yearned for the lewdness of your youth, when those of Egypt handled your bosom on account of your girlish breasts.

²²Therefore, O Aholibah, thus says the Lord God: Be-

---

ᵃ 14 Or *Babylonians*   ᵇ 15 Or *Babylonia*; also in verse 16   ᶜ 21 Syriac (see also verse 3); Hebrew *caressed because of your young breasts*

## New International Version

LORD says: I will stir up your lovers against you, those you turned away from in disgust, and I will bring them against you from every side— ²³the Babylonians and all the Chaldeans, the men of Pekod and Shoa and Koa, and all the Assyrians with them, handsome young men, all of them governors and commanders, chariot officers and men of high rank, all mounted on horses. ²⁴They will come against you with weapons,ᵃ chariots and wagons and with a throng of people; they will take up positions against you on every side with large and small shields and with helmets. I will turn you over to them for punishment, and they will punish you according to their standards. ²⁵I will direct my jealous anger against you, and they will deal with you in fury. They will cut off your noses and your ears, and those of you who are left will fall by the sword. They will take away your sons and daughters, and those of you who are left will be consumed by fire. ²⁶They will also strip you of your clothes and take your fine jewelry. ²⁷So I will put a stop to the lewdness and prostitution you began in Egypt. You will not look on these things with longing or remember Egypt anymore.

²⁸"For this is what the Sovereign LORD says: I am about to deliver you into the hands of those you hate, to those you turned away from in disgust. ²⁹They will deal with you in hatred and take away everything you have worked for. They will leave you stark naked, and the shame of your prostitution will be exposed. Your lewdness and promiscuity ³⁰have brought this on you, because you lusted after the nations and defiled yourself with their idols. ³¹You have gone the way of your sister; so I will put her cup into your hand.

³²"This is what the Sovereign LORD says:

"You will drink your sister's cup,
  a cup large and deep;
it will bring scorn and derision,
  for it holds so much.
³³You will be filled with drunkenness and sorrow,
  the cup of ruin and desolation,
  the cup of your sister Samaria.
³⁴You will drink it and drain it dry
  and chew on its pieces—
  and you will tear your breasts.

I have spoken, declares the Sovereign LORD.

³⁵"Therefore this is what the Sovereign LORD says: Since you have forgotten me and turned your back on me, you must bear the consequences of your lewdness and prostitution."

³⁶The LORD said to me: "Son of man, will you judge Oholah and Oholibah? Then confront them with their detestable practices, ³⁷for they have committed adultery and blood is on their hands. They committed adultery with their idols; they even sacrificed their children, whom they bore to me, as food for them. ³⁸They have also done this to me: At that same time they defiled my sanctuary and desecrated my Sabbaths. ³⁹On the very day they sacrificed their children to their idols, they entered my sanctuary and desecrated it. That is what they did in my house.

⁴⁰"They even sent messengers for men who came from far away, and when they arrived you bathed yourself for them, applied eye makeup and put on your jewelry. ⁴¹You

ᵃ 24 The meaning of the Hebrew for this word is uncertain.

## Amplified Bible

hold, I will rouse up your lovers against you, from whom you turned in disgust, and I will bring them against you on every side:

²³The Babylonians and all the Chaldeans, Pekod and Shoa and Koa, and all the Assyrians with them, desirable young men, governors and officers all of them, princes, men of renown *and* counselors, all of them riding on horses.

²⁴And they shall come against you with weapons, chariots, wagons *and* wheels, and with a host of infantry which shall array themselves against you with buckler and shield and helmet round about; and I will commit the judgment *and* punishment to them, and they shall judge *and* punish you according to their [heathen] customs in such matters.

²⁵And I will set My jealous indignation against you, and they shall deal with you in fury; they shall take away your nose and your ears, and those who are left of you shall fall by the sword; they shall take your sons and your daughters, and the remainder shall be devoured by the fire.

²⁶They shall also strip you [Judah] of your clothes and take away your fine jewels.

²⁷Thus I will put an end to your lewdness and your harlotry brought from the land of Egypt, so that you will not lift up your eyes to them nor [earnestly] remember Egypt any more.

²⁸For thus says the Lord God: Behold, I will deliver you into the hands of those whom you hate, into the hands of those from whom you turned away in disgust.

²⁹They shall deal with you in hatred and shall take away all [the earnings of] your labor and shall leave you naked and bare, and the nakedness of your harlotry shall be uncovered, both your lewdness and your wanton ways.

³⁰These things shall be done to you, because you have played the harlot after the nations and because you have defiled yourself with their idols.

³¹You have walked in the way of your sister [Samaria, Israel's capital]; therefore I will give her cup into your hand.

³²Thus says the Lord God: You shall drink of your sister's cup which is deep and wide *and* brimful; you shall be laughed to scorn and held in derision, for it contains much [too much to endure].

³³You shall be filled with drunkenness and sorrow, with the cup of wasting astonishment *and* horror and desolation, with the cup of your sister Samaria.

³⁴You shall drink it and drain it out, and then gnaw the pieces of it [which in your drunkenness you have broken] and shall tear your [own] breasts; for I have spoken it, says the Lord God.

³⁵Therefore thus says the Lord God: Because you have forgotten Me [your divine Husband] and cast Me behind your back, therefore bear also [the consequences of] your lewdness and your harlotry.

³⁶The Lord said, moreover, to me: Son of man, will you judge Aholah and Aholibah? Then declare *and* show to them their abominations (the detestable, loathsome, and shamefully vile things they do),

³⁷For they have committed adultery and blood is on their hands, even with their idols have they committed adultery [against Me]. And they have also caused their sons, whom they bore to Me, to pass through the fire to their images [as an offering of food] to be devoured [by them].

³⁸Moreover, this they have done to Me: they have defiled My sanctuary on the same day [of their idolatries] and have profaned My Sabbaths.

³⁹For when they had slain their children [as offerings] to their idols, then they came the same day into My sanctuary to profane it [by daring to offer sacrifice there also]! And behold, thus have they done in the midst of My house!

⁴⁰And furthermore, you have sent for men to come from afar, to whom a messenger was sent; and behold, they came—those for whom you washed yourself, painted your eyelids, and decked yourself with ornaments;

## New International Version

sat on an elegant couch, with a table spread before it on which you had placed the incense and olive oil that belonged to me.

⁴²"The noise of a carefree crowd was around her; drunkards were brought from the desert along with men from the rabble, and they put bracelets on the wrists of the woman and her sister and beautiful crowns on their heads. ⁴³Then I said about the one worn out by adultery, 'Now let them use her as a prostitute, for that is all she is.' ⁴⁴And they slept with her. As men sleep with a prostitute, so they slept with those lewd women, Oholah and Oholibah. ⁴⁵But righteous judges will sentence them to the punishment of women who commit adultery and shed blood, because they are adulterous and blood is on their hands.

⁴⁶"This is what the Sovereign LORD says: Bring a mob against them and give them over to terror and plunder. ⁴⁷The mob will stone them and cut them down with their swords; they will kill their sons and daughters and burn down their houses.

⁴⁸"So I will put an end to lewdness in the land, that all women may take warning and not imitate you. ⁴⁹You will suffer the penalty for your lewdness and bear the consequences of your sins of idolatry. Then you will know that I am the Sovereign LORD."

### Jerusalem as a Cooking Pot

**24** In the ninth year, in the tenth month on the tenth day, the word of the LORD came to me: ²"Son of man, record this date, this very date, because the king of Babylon has laid siege to Jerusalem this very day. ³Tell this rebellious people a parable and say to them: 'This is what the Sovereign LORD says:

"'Put on the cooking pot; put it on
    and pour water into it.
⁴Put into it the pieces of meat,
    all the choice pieces—the leg and the shoulder.
Fill it with the best of these bones;
⁵    take the pick of the flock.
Pile wood beneath it for the bones;
    bring it to a boil
    and cook the bones in it.

⁶"'For this is what the Sovereign LORD says:

"'Woe to the city of bloodshed,
    to the pot now encrusted,
    whose deposit will not go away!
Take the meat out piece by piece
    in whatever order it comes.

⁷"'For the blood she shed is in her midst:
    She poured it on the bare rock;
she did not pour it on the ground,
    where the dust would cover it.
⁸To stir up wrath and take revenge
    I put her blood on the bare rock,
    so that it would not be covered.

⁹"'Therefore this is what the Sovereign LORD says:

"'Woe to the city of bloodshed!
    I, too, will pile the wood high.
¹⁰So heap on the wood
    and kindle the fire.
Cook the meat well,
    mixing in the spices;
    and let the bones be charred.
¹¹Then set the empty pot on the coals
    till it becomes hot and its copper glows,
so that its impurities may be melted
    and its deposit burned away.

## Amplified Bible

⁴¹And you sat upon a stately couch with a table spread before it upon which you set My incense and My oil.

⁴²And with the sound of a careless crowd was with her, and with men of the common sort were brought drunkards from the wilderness, who put bracelets upon the hands of both sisters and beautiful crowns upon their heads.

⁴³Then I said of the one [Aholah] worn out with adulteries, Will they now play the harlot with her [now that she is old] and she with them?

⁴⁴Yet they went in to her as they go in to a woman who plays the harlot; so they went in to Aholah and to Aholibah [Israel and Judah], the lewd women.

⁴⁵And the righteous men, they shall judge *and* condemn them to the punishment due to adulteresses, to women who shed blood, for they are adulteresses and blood is upon their hands.

⁴⁶For thus says the Lord God: I will bring up a host upon them and will give them over to be tossed to and fro and robbed,

⁴⁷And the host shall stone them with stones and cut them down with their swords; they shall slay their sons and their daughters and burn up their houses with fire.

⁴⁸Thus will I cause lewdness to cease out of the land, that all women may be taught not to do after your lewdness.

⁴⁹Thus your lewdness shall be recompensed upon you and you shall suffer the penalty for your sinful idolatry; and you shall know (understand and realize) that I am the Lord God.

**24** Again in the ninth year [of King Jehoiachin's captivity by Nebuchadnezzar of Babylon], in the tenth month, on the tenth day of the month, the word of the Lord came to me, saying,

²Son of man, record the name of the day, even of this same day; the king of Babylon set himself against *and* assailed Jerusalem this same day.

³And utter a parable against the rebellious house [of Judah] and say to them, Thus says the Lord God: Put on a pot; put it on and also pour water into it.

⁴Put into it the pieces [of meat], all the good pieces, the thigh and the shoulder; fill it with the choice of the bones.

⁵Take the choicest of the flock and burn also the unused bones under it, and make it boil well and seethe its bones in [the pot].

⁶Therefore thus says the Lord God: Woe to the bloody city, to the pot whose rust *and* scum are in it and whose rust *and* scum have not gone out of it! Take out of it piece by piece, without making any choice.

⁷For the blood she has shed remains in the midst of her; she put it upon the bare rock; she did not pour it on the ground to cover it with dust.

⁸That it may cause wrath to come up to take vengeance, I have put her blood [guilt for her children sacrificed to Molech] upon the bare rock, that it would not be covered.

⁹Therefore thus says the Lord God: Woe to the blood-guilty city! Also I will make the pile [of fuel] great.

¹⁰Heap on wood, kindle the fire *and* make it hot, boil well the meat *and* mix the spices, pour out the broth when thick, and let the bones be burned up.

¹¹Then set [the pot Jerusalem] back empty upon the coals, that the bronze of it may be hot and may glow and the filthiness of it may be melted in it and the rust *and* scum of it may be consumed.

## New International Version

12 It has frustrated all efforts;
its heavy deposit has not been removed,
not even by fire.

13 "'Now your impurity is lewdness. Because I tried to cleanse you but you would not be cleansed from your impurity, you will not be clean again until my wrath against you has subsided.

14 "'I the LORD have spoken. The time has come for me to act. I will not hold back; I will not have pity, nor will I relent. You will be judged according to your conduct and your actions, declares the Sovereign LORD.'"

### Ezekiel's Wife Dies

15 The word of the LORD came to me: 16 "Son of man, with one blow I am about to take away from you the delight of your eyes. Yet do not lament or weep or shed any tears. 17 Groan quietly; do not mourn for the dead. Keep your turban fastened and your sandals on your feet; do not cover your mustache and beard or eat the customary food of mourners."

18 So I spoke to the people in the morning, and in the evening my wife died. The next morning I did as I had been commanded.

19 Then the people asked me, "Won't you tell us what these things have to do with us? Why are you acting like this?"

20 So I said to them, "The word of the LORD came to me: 21 Say to the people of Israel, 'This is what the Sovereign LORD says: I am about to desecrate my sanctuary—the stronghold in which you take pride, the delight of your eyes, the object of your affection. The sons and daughters you left behind will fall by the sword. 22 And you will do as I have done. You will not cover your mustache and beard or eat the customary food of mourners. 23 You will keep your turbans on your heads and your sandals on your feet. You will not mourn or weep but will waste away because of*a* your sins and groan among yourselves. 24 Ezekiel will be a sign to you; you will do just as he has done. When this happens, you will know that I am the Sovereign LORD.'

25 "And you, son of man, on the day I take away their stronghold, their joy and glory, the delight of their eyes, their heart's desire, and their sons and daughters as well— 26 on that day a fugitive will come to tell you the news. 27 At that time your mouth will be opened; you will speak with him and will no longer be silent. So you will be a sign to them, and they will know that I am the LORD."

### A Prophecy Against Ammon

**25** The word of the LORD came to me: 2 "Son of man, set your face against the Ammonites and prophesy against them. 3 Say to them, 'Hear the word of the Sovereign LORD. This is what the Sovereign LORD says: Because you said "Aha!" over my sanctuary when it was desecrated and over the land of Israel when it was laid waste and over the people of Judah when they went into exile, 4 therefore I am going to give you to the people of the East as a possession. They will set up their camps and pitch their tents

*a 23 Or away in*

## Amplified Bible

12 She has wearied herself *and* Me with toil; yet her great rust *and* scum go not forth out of her, for however hotly the fire burns, her thick rust *and* filth will not go out of her by fire.

13 In your filthiness is abomination; [and therefore] because I would have cleansed you and you were not cleansed, you shall not be cleansed from your filthiness any more until I have satisfied My wrath against *and* upon you.

14 I the Lord have spoken it; it shall come to pass and I will do it; I will not go back, neither will I spare, neither will I relent; according to your ways and according to your doings shall they judge *and* punish you, says the Lord God.

15 Also the word of the Lord came to me, saying,

16 Son of man [Ezekiel], behold, I take away from you the desire of your eyes [your wife] at a single stroke. Yet you shall neither mourn nor weep, neither shall your tears flow.

17 Sigh *and* groan, but not aloud [be silent]; make no mourning for the dead; bind your turban upon your head and put your shoes on your feet, and do not cover your beard or eat the bread of mourners [furnished by others].

18 So I spoke to the people in the morning and in the evening my wife died, and I did the next morning as I was commanded.

19 And the people said to me, Will you not tell us what these things are supposed to mean to us, that you are acting as you do?

20 Then I answered them, The word of the Lord came to me, saying,

21 Speak to the house of Israel, Thus says the Lord God: Behold, I will profane My sanctuary—[in which you take] pride as your strength, the desire of your eyes, and the pity *and* sympathy of your soul [that you would spare with your life]; and your sons and your daughters whom you have left behind shall fall by the sword.

22 And you shall do as I [Ezekiel] have done; you shall not cover your beard nor eat the bread of mourning [brought to you by others],

23 And your turbans shall be upon your heads and your shoes upon your feet; you shall not mourn or weep, but you shall pine away for your iniquities (your guilt) and sigh *and* groan to one another. [Lev. 26:39.]

24 Thus Ezekiel is to you for a sign; according to all that he has done you shall do. And when this [destruction of the temple] comes, you shall know, understand, *and* realize that I am the Lord God [the Sovereign Ruler, Who calls forth loyalty and obedient service].

25 And you, son of man, on the day when I take from them [My temple] their strength *and* their stronghold, their joy and their glory, the delight of their eyes and their hearts' chief desire, and also [take] their sons and their daughters—

26 On that day an escaped fugitive shall come to you to cause you to hear of it [the destruction of Jerusalem] with your own ears.

27 In that day your mouth shall be open to him who has escaped, and you shall speak and be no more speechless, and you shall be a sign to them and they shall know, understand, *and* realize that I am the Lord.

**25** The word of the Lord came again to me, saying, 2 Son of man, set your face toward the Ammonites and prophesy against them.

3 And say to the Ammonites, Hear the word of the Lord God, for thus says the Lord God: Because you said Aha! over My sanctuary when it was profaned and over the land of Israel when it was made desolate and over the house of Judah when it went into captivity *and* exile,

4 Therefore behold, I am delivering you to the people of the East for a possession, and they shall set their encamp-

## New International Version

among you; they will eat your fruit and drink your milk. [5]I will turn Rabbah into a pasture for camels and Ammon into a resting place for sheep. Then you will know that I am the LORD. [6]For this is what the Sovereign LORD says: Because you have clapped your hands and stamped your feet, rejoicing with all the malice of your heart against the land of Israel, [7]therefore I will stretch out my hand against you and give you as plunder to the nations. I will wipe you out from among the nations and exterminate you from the countries. I will destroy you, and you will know that I am the LORD.'"

### A Prophecy Against Moab

[8]"This is what the Sovereign LORD says: 'Because Moab and Seir said, "Look, Judah has become like all the other nations," [9]therefore I will expose the flank of Moab, beginning at its frontier towns—Beth Jeshimoth, Baal Meon and Kiriathaim—the glory of that land. [10]I will give Moab along with the Ammonites to the people of the East as a possession, so that the Ammonites will not be remembered among the nations; [11]and I will inflict punishment on Moab. Then they will know that I am the LORD.'"

### A Prophecy Against Edom

[12]"This is what the Sovereign LORD says: 'Because Edom took revenge on Judah and became very guilty by doing so, [13]therefore this is what the Sovereign LORD says: I will stretch out my hand against Edom and kill both man and beast. I will lay it waste, and from Teman to Dedan they will fall by the sword. [14]I will take vengeance on Edom by the hand of my people Israel, and they will deal with Edom in accordance with my anger and my wrath; they will know my vengeance, declares the Sovereign LORD.'"

### A Prophecy Against Philistia

[15]"This is what the Sovereign LORD says: 'Because the Philistines acted in vengeance and took revenge with malice in their hearts, and with ancient hostility sought to destroy Judah, [16]therefore this is what the Sovereign LORD says: I am about to stretch out my hand against the Philistines, and I will wipe out the Kerethites and destroy those remaining along the coast. [17]I will carry out great vengeance on them and punish them in my wrath. Then they will know that I am the LORD, when I take vengeance on them.'"

### A Prophecy Against Tyre

**26** In the eleventh month of the twelfth[a] year, on the first day of the month, the word of the LORD came to me: [2]"Son of man, because Tyre has said of Jerusalem, 'Aha! The gate to the nations is broken, and its doors have swung open to me; now that she lies in ruins I will prosper,' [3]therefore this is what the Sovereign LORD says: I am against you, Tyre, and I will bring many nations against you, like the sea casting up its waves. [4]They will destroy

---

[a] 1 Probable reading of the original Hebrew text; Masoretic Text does not have *month of the twelfth*.

## Amplified Bible

ments among you and make their dwellings in your midst; they shall eat your fruit and they shall drink your milk.
[5]And I will make Rabbah [your chief city] a stable for camels and [the cities of] the Ammonites a fold for flocks. And you shall know (understand and realize) that I am the Lord [the Sovereign Ruler, Who calls forth loyalty and obedient service].
[6]For thus says the Lord God: Because you have clapped your hands and stamped with the feet and rejoiced [in heart] with all the contempt, malice, *and* spite that is in you against the land of Israel,
[7]Therefore behold, I have stretched out My hand against you and will hand you over for a prey *and* a spoil to the nations, and I will cut you off from the peoples and will cause you to perish *and* be lost out of the countries; I will destroy you. Then will you know (understand and realize) that I am the Lord [the Sovereign Ruler, Who calls forth loyalty and obedient service]. [Jer. 49:1-6; Ezek. 21:28-32; Amos 1:13-15; Zeph. 2:8-11.]
[8]Thus says the Lord God: Because Moab says, as does Seir [Edom], Behold, the house of Judah is like all the [heathen] nations,
[9]Therefore behold, I will lay open the flank of Moab from the cities, from its cities on its frontiers *and* in every quarter, the glory of the country, Beth-jeshimoth, Baal-meon, and Kiriathaim.
[10]I will give it along with the children of Ammon to the people of the East for a possession, that it *and* the children of Ammon may not be [any more seriously] remembered among the nations.
[11]And I will execute judgments *and* punishments upon Moab, and they shall know (understand and realize) that I am the Lord [the Sovereign Ruler, Who calls forth loyalty and obedient service]. [Isa. 15, 16; Jer. 48; Amos 2:1-3; Zeph. 2:8-11.]
[12]Thus says the Lord God: Because Edom has dealt against the house of Judah by taking vengeance and has greatly offended *and* has become doubly guilty by taking revenge upon them,
[13]Therefore thus says the Lord God: I will also stretch out My hand against Edom and will cut off *and* root out man and beast from it, and I will make it desolate; from Teman even to Dedan they shall fall by the sword.
[14]And I will lay My vengeance upon Edom by the hand of My people Israel, and they shall do upon Edom according to My anger and according to My wrath, and they shall know My vengeance, says the Lord God. [Isa. 34; Ezek. 35; Amos 1:11, 12; Obad.]
[15]Thus says the Lord God: Because the Philistines have dealt revengefully and have taken vengeance contemptuously, with malice *and* spite in their hearts, to destroy in perpetual enmity,
[16]Therefore thus says the Lord God: Behold, I will stretch out My hand against the Philistines, and I will cut off the Cherethites [an immigration in Philistia] and destroy the remainder of the seacoast.
[17]And I will execute great vengeance upon them with wrathful rebukes *and* chastisements, and they shall know (understand and realize) that I am the Lord, when I lay My vengeance upon them. [Isa. 14:29-31; Jer. 47; Amos 1:6-8; Zeph. 2:4-7; Zech. 9:5-7.]

**26** And in the eleventh year, on the first day of the month [after the carrying away of King Jehoiachin], the word of the Lord came to me, saying,
[2]Son of man, because Tyre has said against Jerusalem, Aha! She is broken that has been the gate of the people; she is open to me [Tyre]; I shall become full now that she is desolate *and* a wasteland,
[3]Therefore thus says the Lord God: Behold, I am against you, O Tyre, and will cause many nations to come up against you as the sea mounts up by its waves.

## New International Version

the walls of Tyre and pull down her towers; I will scrape away her rubble and make her a bare rock. ⁵Out in the sea she will become a place to spread fishnets, for I have spoken, declares the Sovereign LORD. She will become plunder for the nations, ⁶and her settlements on the mainland will be ravaged by the sword. Then they will know that I am the LORD.

⁷"For this is what the Sovereign LORD says: From the north I am going to bring against Tyre Nebuchadnezzar*ᵃ* king of Babylon, king of kings, with horses and chariots, with horsemen and a great army. ⁸He will ravage your settlements on the mainland with the sword; he will set up siege works against you, build a ramp up to your walls and raise his shields against you. ⁹He will direct the blows of his battering rams against your walls and demolish your towers with his weapons. ¹⁰His horses will be so many that they will cover you with dust. Your walls will tremble at the noise of the warhorses, wagons and chariots when he enters your gates as men enter a city whose walls have been broken through. ¹¹The hooves of his horses will trample all your streets; he will kill your people with the sword, and your strong pillars will fall to the ground. ¹²They will plunder your wealth and loot your merchandise; they will break down your walls and demolish your fine houses and throw your stones, timber and rubble into the sea. ¹³I will put an end to your noisy songs, and the music of your harps will be heard no more. ¹⁴I will make you a bare rock, and you will become a place to spread fishnets. You will never be rebuilt, for I the LORD have spoken, declares the Sovereign LORD.

¹⁵"This is what the Sovereign LORD says to Tyre: Will not the coastlands tremble at the sound of your fall, when the wounded groan and the slaughter takes place in you? ¹⁶Then all the princes of the coast will step down from their thrones and lay aside their robes and take off their

## Amplified Bible

⁴And they shall destroy the walls of Tyre and break down her towers; I will also ᵃscrape her dust from her and make her bare like the top of a rock.

⁵Her island in the midst of the sea shall become a place for the spreading of nets, for I have spoken it, says the Lord God; and she shall become a prey *and* a spoil to the nations.

⁶And Tyre's daughters [her towns and villages on the mainland] in the level place shall be slain by the sword, and they shall know (understand and realize) that I am the Lord [the Sovereign Ruler, Who calls forth loyalty and obedient service].

⁷For thus says the Lord God: Behold, I will bring from the north upon Tyre ᵇNebuchadrezzar king of Babylon, a king of kings, with horses and chariots and with horsemen and a host of many people.

⁸He shall slay with the sword your daughters [the towns and villages] in the level area [on the mainland], and he shall make a fortified wall against you and cast up a siege mound against you and raise up a roof of bucklers *and* shields as a defense against you.

⁹And he shall set his battering engines in shock against your walls, and with his axes he will break down your towers.

¹⁰Because of the great number of [Nebuchadrezzar's] horses, their dust will cover you; your walls [O Tyre] will shake at the noise of the horsemen and of the wagon wheels and of the chariots, when he enters into your gates as men enter into the city in whose walls there has been made a breach.

¹¹With the hoofs of his horses [Nebuchadrezzar] will trample all your streets; he will slay your people with the sword and your strong pillars *or* obelisks will fall to the ground.

¹²And [your adversaries] shall make a spoil of your riches and make booty of your merchandise. And they shall break down your walls and destroy your pleasant houses, and they shall lay the stones and the timber and the very dust from your demolished city out in the midst of the water [between the island and the mainland city site to make a causeway].

¹³And I will cause the noise of your songs to cease, and the sound of your lyres shall be no more heard.

¹⁴And I will make you [Tyre] a ᶜbare rock; you shall be a place upon which to spread nets; you shall never be rebuilt, for I the Lord have spoken it, says the Lord God.

¹⁵Thus says the Lord God to Tyre: Shall not the isles *and* coastlands shake at the sound of your fall when the wounded groan, when the slaughter is made in the midst of you?

¹⁶Then all the princes of the sea shall come down from their thrones and lay aside their robes and strip off their

ᵃ To prevent Nebuchadnezzar from getting her valuables, Tyre transported herself to an island a half mile out in the sea. The conqueror destroyed the city on the mainland and left. But more than two centuries later, Alexander the Great took the ruins of the old city, even scraping up the dust, and made a causeway to the island, thus fulfilling the prophecy exactly.  ᵇ See footnote on Jer. 21:2.  ᶜ According to Herodotus, Tyre's history began in 2750 B.C. It was a fortified city in Joshua's time (Josh. 19:29), and later became a great maritime commercial center (Isa. 23:8). Yet Jeremiah (27:2-7; 47:4) and Ezekiel (26:3-21; 28:6-10) foretold utter destruction for Tyre, naming not less than twenty-five separate details, each of which in the following centuries came true literally. Mathematicians have estimated, according to the "Law of Compound Probabilities," that if a prophecy concerning a person, place, or event has twenty-five details beyond the possibility of human collusion, calculation, coincidence, and comprehension, there is only one chance in more than thirty-three and one-half million of its accidental fulfillment. Yet Tyre's history at the hands of Nebuchadnezzar, and then more than two centuries later at the hands of Alexander the Great, and centuries after that at the hands of the Crusaders, was the striking fulfillment of each detail of the prophets' forecasts. No other city in the world's history could have fulfilled them. The authenticity and credibility of God's Word leaves no chance for sane denial. See footnote on Zeph. 2:7 for information about a similar fulfillment of details of Bible prophecy with regard to Palestine and to the end of Christ's life.

ᵃ 7 Hebrew *Nebuchadrezzar,* of which *Nebuchadnezzar* is a variant; here and often in Ezekiel and Jeremiah

## New International Version

embroidered garments. Clothed with terror, they will sit on the ground, trembling every moment, appalled at you. [17]Then they will take up a lament concerning you and say to you:

"'How you are destroyed, city of renown,
    peopled by men of the sea!
You were a power on the seas,
    you and your citizens;
you put your terror
    on all who lived there.
[18]Now the coastlands tremble
    on the day of your fall;
the islands in the sea
    are terrified at your collapse.'

[19]"This is what the Sovereign LORD says: When I make you a desolate city, like cities no longer inhabited, and when I bring the ocean depths over you and its vast waters cover you, [20]then I will bring you down with those who go down to the pit, to the people of long ago. I will make you dwell in the earth below, as in ancient ruins, with those who go down to the pit, and you will not return or take your place[a] in the land of the living. [21]I will bring you to a horrible end and you will be no more. You will be sought, but you will never again be found, declares the Sovereign LORD."

### A Lament Over Tyre

**27** The word of the LORD came to me: [2]"Son of man, take up a lament concerning Tyre. [3]Say to Tyre, situated at the gateway to the sea, merchant of peoples on many coasts, 'This is what the Sovereign LORD says:

"'You say, Tyre,
    "I am perfect in beauty."
[4]Your domain was on the high seas;
    your builders brought your beauty to perfection.
[5]They made all your timbers
    of juniper from Senir[b];
they took a cedar from Lebanon
    to make a mast for you.
[6]Of oaks from Bashan
    they made your oars;
of cypress wood[c] from the coasts of Cyprus
    they made your deck, adorned with ivory.
[7]Fine embroidered linen from Egypt was your sail
    and served as your banner;
your awnings were of blue and purple
    from the coasts of Elishah.
[8]Men of Sidon and Arvad were your oarsmen;
    your skilled men, Tyre, were aboard as your sailors.
[9]Veteran craftsmen of Byblos were on board
    as shipwrights to caulk your seams.
All the ships of the sea and their sailors
    came alongside to trade for your wares.

[10]"'Men of Persia, Lydia and Put
    served as soldiers in your army.
They hung their shields and helmets on your walls,
    bringing you splendor.
[11]Men of Arvad and Helek
    guarded your walls on every side;
men of Gammad
    were in your towers.
They hung their shields around your walls;
    they brought your beauty to perfection.

[12]"'Tarshish did business with you because of your great wealth of goods; they exchanged silver, iron, tin and lead for your merchandise.

## Amplified Bible

embroidered garments; they shall clothe themselves with tremblings; they shall sit upon the ground and shall tremble every moment and be astonished at you *and* appalled.

[17]They shall take up a lamentation over you and say to you, How you are destroyed *and* vanished, O renowned city that was won from the seas *and* inhabited by seafaring men, renowned city that was mighty on the sea, she and her inhabitants who caused their terror to fall upon all who dwell there!

[18]Now the isles *and* coastlands tremble in the day of your fall; yes, the isles that are in the sea are troubled *and* dismayed at your departure.

[19]For thus says the Lord God: When I make you a desolate city like the cities that are not inhabited, when I bring up the deep over you and great waters cover you,

[20]Then I will thrust you down with those who descend into the pit (the place of the dead) to the people of olden times, and I will make you [Tyre] to dwell in the lower world like the places that were desolate of old, with those who go down to the pit, that you be not inhabited or shed forth your glory *and* renown in the land of the living.

[21]I will make you a terror [bring you to a dreadful end] and you shall be no more. Though you be sought, yet you shall never be found again, says the Lord God.

**27** The word of the Lord came again to me, saying, [2]Now you, son of man, take up a lamentation over Tyre,

[3]And say to Tyre, O you who dwell at the entrance to the sea, who are merchant of the peoples of many islands *and* coastlands, thus says the Lord God: O Tyre, you have thought *and* said, I am perfect in beauty.

[4]Your borders are in the heart of the seas; your builders have perfected your beauty.

[5]They have made all your planks *and* boards of fir trees from Senir [a peak of Mount Hermon]; they have taken a cedar from Lebanon to make a mast for you.

[6]Of the oaks of Bashan they have made your oars; they have made your deck *and* benches of boxwood from the coasts of Cyprus, inlaid with ivory.

[7]Of fine linen with embroidered work from Egypt was your sail, that it might be an ensign for you; blue and purple from the coasts of Elishah [of Asia Minor] was the [ship's] awning which covered you.

[8]The inhabitants of Sidon and [the island] of Arvad were your oarsmen; your skilled *and* wise men, O Tyre, were in you; they were your pilots.

[9]The old men of Gebal [a city north of Sidon] and its skilled *and* wise men in you were your calkers; all the ships of the sea with their mariners were in you to deal in your merchandise *and* trading.

[10]Persia and Lud and Put were in your army as your men of war; they hung the shield and helmet in you; they gave you beauty *and* splendor.

[11]The men of Arvad with your army were upon your walls round about and valorous men [of Gamad] were in your towers; they hung their shields upon your walls round about; they have perfected your beauty *and* splendor.

[12]Tarshish [in Spain] carried on traffic with you because of the abundance of your riches of all kinds; with silver, iron, tin, and lead they traded for your wares.

[a] 20 Septuagint; Hebrew *return, and I will give glory*  [b] 5 That is, Mount Hermon  [c] 6 Targum; the Masoretic Text has a different division of the consonants.

## New International Version

13 "'Greece, Tubal and Meshek did business with you; they traded human beings and articles of bronze for your wares.

14 "'Men of Beth Togarmah exchanged chariot horses, cavalry horses and mules for your merchandise.

15 "'The men of Rhodes*a* traded with you, and many coastlands were your customers; they paid you with ivory tusks and ebony.

16 "'Aram*b* did business with you because of your many products; they exchanged turquoise, purple fabric, embroidered work, fine linen, coral and rubies for your merchandise.

17 "'Judah and Israel traded with you; they exchanged wheat from Minnith and confections,*c* honey, olive oil and balm for your wares.

18 "'Damascus did business with you because of your many products and great wealth of goods. They offered wine from Helbon, wool from Zahar 19 and casks of wine from Izal in exchange for your wares: wrought iron, cassia and calamus.

20 "'Dedan traded in saddle blankets with you.

21 "'Arabia and all the princes of Kedar were your customers; they did business with you in lambs, rams and goats.

22 "'The merchants of Sheba and Raamah traded with you; for your merchandise they exchanged the finest of all kinds of spices and precious stones, and gold.

23 "'Harran, Kanneh and Eden and merchants of Sheba, Ashur and Kilmad traded with you. 24 In your marketplace they traded with you beautiful garments, blue fabric, embroidered work and multicolored rugs with cords twisted and tightly knotted.

25 "'The ships of Tarshish serve
    as carriers for your wares.
You are filled with heavy cargo
    as you sail the sea.
26 Your oarsmen take you
    out to the high seas.
But the east wind will break you to pieces
    far out at sea.
27 Your wealth, merchandise and wares,
    your mariners, sailors and shipwrights,
your merchants and all your soldiers,
    and everyone else on board
will sink into the heart of the sea
    on the day of your shipwreck.
28 The shorelands will quake
    when your sailors cry out.
29 All who handle the oars
    will abandon their ships;
the mariners and all the sailors
    will stand on the shore.
30 They will raise their voice
    and cry bitterly over you;
they will sprinkle dust on their heads
    and roll in ashes.
31 They will shave their heads because of you
    and will put on sackcloth.
They will weep over you with anguish of soul
    and with bitter mourning.
32 As they wail and mourn over you,
    they will take up a lament concerning you:
"Who was ever silenced like Tyre,
    surrounded by the sea?"
33 When your merchandise went out on the seas,
    you satisfied many nations;
with your great wealth and your wares
    you enriched the kings of the earth.

## Amplified Bible

13 Javan (Greece), Tubal, and Meshech [in the mountainous region between the Black and Caspian Seas] traded with you. They exchanged the lives of men [taken as slaves] and vessels of bronze for your merchandise.

14 They of the house of Togarmah (Armenia) traded for your wares with [chariot] horses, cavalry horses, and mules.

15 The men of Dedan [in Arabia] traded with you; many islands *and* coastlands were your own markets; they brought you in payment *or* as presents ivory tusks and ebony.

16 Aram (Syria or Mesopotamia) *and Edom* traded with you because of the multitude of the wares of your making. They exchanged for your merchandise emeralds, purple, embroidered work, fine linen, coral, and agate *or* rubies.

17 Judah and the land of Israel, they were your traders; they exchanged in your market wheat of Minnith [in Ammon], olives *or* early figs, honey, oil, and balm.

18 Damascus traded with you because of the abundance of supplies of your handiworks and the immense wealth of every kind, with wine of Helbon [Aleppo] and white wool [of Sachar in Syria].

19 Vedan also and [Arabic] Javan traded with yarn from Uzal [in Arabia] for your wares; wrought iron, cassia, and calamus were exchanged for your merchandise.

20 Dedan supplied you with precious [saddle] cloths for riding.

21 Arabia and all the princes of Kedar, they were the merchants in lambs, rams, and goats favored by you; in these they traded with you.

22 The merchants of Sheba and Raamah [in Arabia] traded with you; they exchanged for your wares the choicest of all kinds of spices and all precious stones and gold.

23 Haran and Canneh and Eden [in Mesopotamia], the merchants of Sheba [on the Euphrates], Asshur, and Chilmad [near Bagdad] were your traders.

24 These traded with you in choice fabrics, in bales of garments of blue and embroidered work, and in treasures of many colored rich damask *and* carpets bound with cords and made firm; in these they traded with you.

25 The ships of Tarshish were your caravans for your merchandise, and you were replenished [Tyre] and were heavily loaded *and* made an imposing fleet [in your location] in the heart of the seas.

26 Your rowers have brought you out into great *and* deep waters; the east wind has broken *and* wrecked you in the heart of the seas.

27 Your riches, your wares, your merchandise, your oarsmen and your pilots, your caulkers, your dealers in merchandise, and all your men of war who are in you, with all your company which is in your midst, sink in the heart of the seas on the day of your ruin!

28 The waves *and* the countryside shake at the [piercing] sound of the [hopeless, wailing] cry of your pilots.

29 And down from their ships come all who handle the oar. The mariners and all the pilots of the sea stand upon the shore

30 And are heard wailing loudly over you, and they cry bitterly. They cast up dust on their heads; they wallow in ashes,

31 And they make themselves [utterly] bald for you and gird themselves with sackcloth, and they weep over you in bitterness of heart and with bitter mourning *and* wailing.

32 And in their wailing they take up a lamentation for you and lament over you, saying, Who was ever like Tyre, the destroyed (the annihilated), [who has become so still] in the heart of the sea?

33 When your wares came forth from the seas, you met the desire, the demand, *and* the necessities of many people; you enriched the kings of the earth with your abundant wealth and merchandise.

---

*a* 15 Septuagint; Hebrew *Dedan*    *b* 16 Most Hebrew manuscripts; some Hebrew manuscripts and Syriac *Edom*    *c* 17 The meaning of the Hebrew for this word is uncertain.

## New International Version

34 Now you are shattered by the sea
    in the depths of the waters;
  your wares and all your company
    have gone down with you.
35 All who live in the coastlands
    are appalled at you;
  their kings shudder with horror
    and their faces are distorted with fear.
36 The merchants among the nations scoff at you;
    you have come to a horrible end
    and will be no more.'"

### A Prophecy Against the King of Tyre

**28** The word of the LORD came to me: 2 "Son of man, say to the ruler of Tyre, 'This is what the Sovereign LORD says:

"'In the pride of your heart
    you say, "I am a god;
  I sit on the throne of a god
    in the heart of the seas."
  But you are a mere mortal and not a god,
    though you think you are as wise as a god.
3 Are you wiser than Daniel[a]?
    Is no secret hidden from you?
4 By your wisdom and understanding
    you have gained wealth for yourself
  and amassed gold and silver
    in your treasuries.
5 By your great skill in trading
    you have increased your wealth,
  and because of your wealth
    your heart has grown proud.

6 "'Therefore this is what the Sovereign LORD says:

"'Because you think you are wise,
    as wise as a god,
7 I am going to bring foreigners against you,
    the most ruthless of nations;
  they will draw their swords against your beauty and
      wisdom
    and pierce your shining splendor.
8 They will bring you down to the pit,
    and you will die a violent death
    in the heart of the seas.
9 Will you then say, "I am a god,"
    in the presence of those who kill you?
  You will be but a mortal, not a god,
    in the hands of those who slay you.
10 You will die the death of the uncircumcised
    at the hands of foreigners.

I have spoken, declares the Sovereign LORD.'"

11 The word of the LORD came to me: 12 "Son of man, take up a lament concerning the king of Tyre and say to him: 'This is what the Sovereign LORD says:

"'You were the seal of perfection,
    full of wisdom and perfect in beauty.
13 You were in Eden,
    the garden of God;
  every precious stone adorned you:
    carnelian, chrysolite and emerald,
    topaz, onyx and jasper,
    lapis lazuli, turquoise and beryl.[b]
  Your settings and mountings[c] were made of gold;
    on the day you were created they were prepared.
14 You were anointed as a guardian cherub,
    for so I ordained you.

---

[a] 3 Or *Danel*, a man of renown in ancient literature    [b] 13 The precise identification of some of these precious stones is uncertain.
[c] 13 The meaning of the Hebrew for this phrase is uncertain.

## Amplified Bible

34 Now you are shattered by the seas in the depths of the waters; your merchandise and all your crew have gone down with you.
35 All the inhabitants of the isles *and* coastlands are astonished *and* appalled at you, and their kings are horribly frightened *and* shudder greatly; their faces quiver.
36 The merchants among the people hiss over you [with malicious joy]; you have become a horror *and* a source of terrors. You shall be [a]no more [forever].

**28** The word of the Lord came again to me, saying, 2 Son of man, say to the prince of Tyre, Thus says the Lord God: Because your heart is lifted up and you have said *and* thought, I am a god, I sit in the seat of the gods, in the heart of the seas; yet you are only man [weak, feeble, made of earth] and not God, though you imagine yourself to be almost more than mortal with your mind as the mind of God;
3 Indeed, you are [imagining yourself] wiser than Daniel; there is no secret [you think] that is hidden from you;
4 With your own wisdom and with your own understanding you have gotten you riches *and* power and have brought gold and silver into your treasuries;
5 By your great wisdom and by your traffic you have increased your riches *and* power, and your heart is proud *and* lifted up because of your wealth;
6 Therefore thus says the Lord God: Because you have imagined your mind as the mind of God [having thoughts and purposes suitable only to God Himself], [Obad. 3.]
7 Behold therefore, I am bringing strangers upon you, the most terrible of the nations, and they shall draw their swords against the beauty of your wisdom [O Tyre], and they shall defile your splendor.
8 They shall bring you down to the pit [of destruction] and you shall die the [many] deaths of all the Tyrians that are slain in the heart of the seas.
9 Will you still say, I am a god, before him who slays you? But you are only a man [made of earth] and no god in the hand of him who wounds *and* profanes you.
10 You shall die the death of the uncircumcised by the hand of strangers, for I have spoken it, says the Lord God.
11 Moreover, the word of the Lord came to me, saying,
12 Son of man, take up a lamentation over the king of Tyre and say to him, Thus says the Lord God: You are the full measure *and* pattern of exactness [giving the finishing touch to all that constitutes completeness], full of wisdom and perfect in beauty.
13 You were in [b]Eden, the garden of God; every precious stone was your covering, the carnelian, topaz, jasper, chrysolite, beryl, onyx, sapphire, carbuncle, and emerald; and your settings and your sockets *and* engravings were wrought in gold. On the day that you were created they were prepared. [Gen. 3:14, 15; Isa. 14:12-15; Matt. 16:23.]
14 You were the anointed cherub that covers with overshadowing [wings], and I set you so. You were upon the holy mountain of God; you walked up and down in the

---

[a] Down to the thirteenth century A.D. the grandeur of the ancient city of Tyre was still visible. But God's Word does not fail. Soon Tyre had become an almost uninhabited pile of ruins. A large part of the western section of "the island" became covered by the sea, and early travelers told of seeing "houses, towers, and streets far down in the deep." In modern times the population of Tyre, made up largely of fishermen who spread their nets on its beaches, has increased to around 6,000, but the city as such was never been revived, and the original site has long since become obliterated.    [b] This speech, though not addressed to Satan in and of himself, seems to be ironically spoken against his evil genius fulfilling itself in and through the human ruler who appropriates to himself the honors due only to God, as in the case of the king of Babylon (Isa. 14:12-15). Here is to be seen a foreshadowing of "the beast" who is to attribute to himself divine rights in the time of the end (Dan. 7:8-28; II Thess. 2:1-12; Rev. 13; 19:20).

## New International Version

You were on the holy mount of God;
  you walked among the fiery stones.
15 You were blameless in your ways
  from the day you were created
  till wickedness was found in you.
16 Through your widespread trade
  you were filled with violence,
  and you sinned.
So I drove you in disgrace from the mount of God,
  and I expelled you, guardian cherub,
  from among the fiery stones.
17 Your heart became proud
  on account of your beauty,
and you corrupted your wisdom
  because of your splendor.
So I threw you to the earth;
  I made a spectacle of you before kings.
18 By your many sins and dishonest trade
  you have desecrated your sanctuaries.
So I made a fire come out from you,
  and it consumed you,
and I reduced you to ashes on the ground
  in the sight of all who were watching.
19 All the nations who knew you
  are appalled at you;
you have come to a horrible end
  and will be no more.'"

### A Prophecy Against Sidon

20 The word of the LORD came to me: 21 "Son of man, set your face against Sidon; prophesy against her 22 and say: 'This is what the Sovereign LORD says:

"'I am against you, Sidon,
  and among you I will display my glory.
You will know that I am the LORD,
  when I inflict punishment on you
  and within you am proved to be holy.
23 I will send a plague upon you
  and make blood flow in your streets.
The slain will fall within you,
  with the sword against you on every side.
Then you will know that I am the LORD.

24 "'No longer will the people of Israel have malicious neighbors who are painful briers and sharp thorns. Then they will know that I am the Sovereign LORD.

25 "'This is what the Sovereign LORD says: When I gather the people of Israel from the nations where they have been scattered, I will be proved holy through them in the sight of the nations. Then they will live in their own land, which I gave to my servant Jacob. 26 They will live there in safety and will build houses and plant vineyards; they will live in safety when I inflict punishment on all their neighbors who maligned them. Then they will know that I am the LORD their God.'"

### A Prophecy Against Egypt

*Judgment on Pharaoh*

**29** In the tenth year, in the tenth month on the twelfth day, the word of the LORD came to me: 2 "Son of man, set your face against Pharaoh king of Egypt and prophesy against him and against all Egypt. 3 Speak to him and say: 'This is what the Sovereign LORD says:

"'I am against you, Pharaoh king of Egypt,
  you great monster lying among your streams.

## Amplified Bible

midst of the stones of fire [like the paved work of gleaming sapphire stone upon which the God of Israel walked on Mount Sinai]. [Exod. 24:10.]

15 You were blameless in your ways from the day you were created until iniquity *and* guilt were found in you.

16 Through the abundance of your commerce you were filled with lawlessness *and* violence, and you sinned; therefore I cast you out as a profane thing from the mountain of God and the guardian cherub drove you out from the midst of the stones of fire.

17 Your heart was proud *and* lifted up because of your beauty; you corrupted your wisdom for the sake of your splendor. I cast you to the ground; I lay you before kings, that they might gaze at you.

18 You have profaned your sanctuaries by the multitude of your iniquities *and* the enormity of your guilt, by the unrighteousness of your trade. Therefore I have brought forth a fire from your midst; it has consumed you, and I have reduced you to ashes upon the earth in the sight of all who looked at you.

19 All who know you among the people are astonished and appalled at you; you have come to a horrible end and shall never return to being. [Isa. 23; Joel 3:4-8; Amos 1:9, 10; Zech. 9:3, 4.]

20 Again the word of the Lord came to me, saying,

21 Son of man, set your face toward Sidon and prophesy against her.

22 And say, Thus says the Lord God: Behold, I am against you, O Sidon, and I will show forth My glory *and* be glorified in the midst of you. And they shall know (understand and realize) that I am the Lord when I execute judgments *and* punishments in her, and am set apart *and* separated *and* My holiness is manifested in her.

23 For I will send pestilence into her and blood into her streets, and the wounded shall be judged *and* fall by the sword in the midst of her on every side, and they shall know (understand and realize) that I am the Lord [the Sovereign Ruler, Who calls forth loyalty and obedient service].

24 And there shall be no more a brier to prick the house of Israel or a hurting thorn of all those around them who have treated them with contempt, and they shall know (understand and realize) that I am the Lord God [the Sovereign Ruler, Who calls forth loyalty and obedient service].

25 Thus says the Lord God: When I gather the house of Israel from the peoples among whom they are scattered, and I shall be set apart *and* separated *and* My holiness made apparent in them in the sight of the nations, then shall they dwell in their own land which I gave to My servant Jacob.

26 And they shall dwell safely in it and shall build houses and plant vineyards; yes, they shall dwell securely *and* with confidence when I have executed judgments *and* punishments upon all those round about them who have despised *and* trodden upon them *and* pushed them away, and they shall know (understand and realize) that I am the Lord their God [their Sovereign Ruler, Who calls forth loyalty and obedient service].

**29** In the tenth year [of the captivity of King Jehoiachin by the king of Babylon], in the tenth [month], on the twelfth [day] of the month, the word of the Lord came to me, saying,

2 Son of man, set your face toward Pharaoh king of Egypt and prophesy against him and against all Egypt.

3 Say, Thus says the Lord God: Behold, I am against you, Pharaoh king of Egypt, the great monster [of sluggish and unwieldy strength] that lies in the midst of his [delta]

## New International Version

You say, "The Nile belongs to me;
  I made it for myself."
⁴But I will put hooks in your jaws
  and make the fish of your streams stick to your
    scales.
I will pull you out from among your streams,
  with all the fish sticking to your scales.
⁵I will leave you in the desert,
  you and all the fish of your streams.
You will fall on the open field
  and not be gathered or picked up.
I will give you as food
  to the beasts of the earth and the birds of the sky.

⁶Then all who live in Egypt will know that I am the LORD.

"'You have been a staff of reed for the people of Israel.
⁷When they grasped you with their hands, you splintered
and you tore open their shoulders; when they leaned on
you, you broke and their backs were wrenched.ᵃ

⁸"'Therefore this is what the Sovereign LORD says: I will
bring a sword against you and kill both man and beast.
⁹Egypt will become a desolate wasteland. Then they will
know that I am the LORD.

"'Because you said, "The Nile is mine; I made it,"
¹⁰therefore I am against you and against your streams,
and I will make the land of Egypt a ruin and a desolate
waste from Migdol to Aswan, as far as the border of Cush.ᵇ
¹¹The foot of neither man nor beast will pass through it; no
one will live there for forty years. ¹²I will make the land of
Egypt desolate among devastated lands, and her cities will
lie desolate forty years among ruined cities. And I will disperse the Egyptians among the nations and scatter them
through the countries.

¹³"'Yet this is what the Sovereign LORD says: At the end
of forty years I will gather the Egyptians from the nations
where they were scattered. ¹⁴I will bring them back from
captivity and return them to Upper Egypt, the land of their
ancestry. There they will be a lowly kingdom. ¹⁵It will be
the lowliest of kingdoms and will never again exalt itself
above the other nations. I will make it so weak that it will
never again rule over the nations. ¹⁶Egypt will no longer
be a source of confidence for the people of Israel but will
be a reminder of their sin in turning to her for help. Then
they will know that I am the Sovereign LORD.'"

### Nebuchadnezzar's Reward

¹⁷In the twenty-seventh year, in the first month on the
first day, the word of the LORD came to me: ¹⁸"Son of man,
Nebuchadnezzar king of Babylon drove his army in a hard
campaign against Tyre; every head was rubbed bare and

## Amplified Bible

streams, [boastfully] declaring, My river Nile is my own
and I have made it for myself.
⁴But I will put hooks in your jaws [O Egyptian dragon]
and I will cause the fish of your rivers to stick to your
scales, and I will draw you up out of the midst of your
streams with all the fish of your streams which stick to
your scales.
⁵And I will cast you forth into the wilderness, you and
all the fish of your rivers; you shall fall upon the open
field and not be gathered up or buried. I have given you
for food to the [wild] beasts of the earth and the birds of
the heavens.
⁶And all the inhabitants of Egypt shall know (understand and realize) that I am the Lord [the Sovereign Ruler, Who calls forth loyalty and obedient service], because
they have been a [deceitful] staff [made of fragile] reeds
to the house of Israel.
⁷When they grasped you with the hand *and* leaned upon
you, you broke and tore their whole shoulder, and [by injuring their muscles made them so stiff and rigid that]
they could do no more than stand.
⁸Therefore thus says the Lord God: Behold, I will bring
a sword upon you and cut off man and beast from you,
⁹And the land of Egypt shall be a desolation and a
waste. And they shall know (understand and realize) that
I am the Lord [the Sovereign Ruler, Who calls forth loyalty
and obedient service]. Because you have said, The river is
mine and I have made it,
¹⁰Behold therefore, I am against you and against your
streams, and I will make the land of Egypt an utter [plun-
dered] waste and desolation [of subjection] from [north-
ern] Migdol to [southern] Syene, even as far as the border
of Ethiopia.
¹¹No foot of man shall pass through it [in travel], no foot
of beast shall pass through it [in trade with other coun-
tries], neither shall [Egypt] be [truly] inhabited [again]
for forty years.
¹²And I will make the land of Egypt a desolation [plun-
dered and reduced to subjection] in the midst of desolated
(plundered and reduced to subjection) countries, and her
cities among the cities that are laid waste shall be a desolation forty years. I will scatter the Egyptians among the
nations and will disperse them through the countries.
¹³Yet thus says the Lord God: At the end of [their] forty
years will I gather the Egyptians from the peoples among
whom they were scattered, [Jer. 46:25, 26.]
¹⁴And I will reverse the captivity of Egypt [as I will that
of Israel] and will cause them to return into the land of
Pathros [under Egypt], the land of their origin, and they
shall be there a lowly kingdom.
¹⁵It shall be the lowliest of the kingdoms, neither shall
it ᵃexalt itself any more above the nations; I will diminish
[the Egyptians] so they shall never again rule over the
nations.
¹⁶And never again shall Egypt have the confidence *and*
be the reliance of the house of Israel; their iniquity will be
brought to remembrance whenever [Israel] looks toward
them [for help]. They shall know (understand and realize) that I am the Lord God [Who demands loyalty and
obedient service].
¹⁷In the twenty-seventh year [after King Jehoiachin was
taken to Babylon], in the first month, on the first day of the
month, the word of the Lord came to me, saying,
¹⁸Son of man, ᵇNebuchadrezzar king of Babylon caused
his army to render heavy service [at My bidding] against
Tyre; every [soldier's] head became bald and every shoulder was worn *and* peeled [with carrying loads of earth and

---

ᵃ For a little while Egypt struggled against its oppressors, but its power
was already broken. From the time of its conquest by Cambyses, it has
never been for any length of time independent. There are few stronger
contrasts in any inhabited country than between the ancient glory,
dignity, power, and wealth of Egypt and its later [lack of] significance
(Charles J. Ellicott, *A Bible Commentary*). ᵇ See footnote on Jer. 21:2.

---

ᵃ 7 Syriac (see also Septuagint and Vulgate); Hebrew *and you caused
their backs to stand*   ᵇ 10 That is, the upper Nile region

## New International Version

every shoulder made raw. Yet he and his army got no reward from the campaign he led against Tyre. [19]Therefore this is what the Sovereign LORD says: I am going to give Egypt to Nebuchadnezzar king of Babylon, and he will carry off its wealth. He will loot and plunder the land as pay for his army. [20]I have given him Egypt as a reward for his efforts because he and his army did it for me, declares the Sovereign LORD.

[21]"On that day I will make a horn[a] grow for the Israelites, and I will open your mouth among them. Then they will know that I am the LORD."

### A Lament Over Egypt

**30** The word of the LORD came to me: [2]"Son of man, prophesy and say: 'This is what the Sovereign LORD says:

"'Wail and say,
"Alas for that day!"
[3]For the day is near,
the day of the LORD is near—
a day of clouds,
a time of doom for the nations.
[4]A sword will come against Egypt,
and anguish will come upon Cush.[b]
When the slain fall in Egypt,
her wealth will be carried away
and her foundations torn down.

[5]Cush and Libya, Lydia and all Arabia, Kub and the people of the covenant land will fall by the sword along with Egypt.

[6]"This is what the LORD says:

"'The allies of Egypt will fall
and her proud strength will fail.
From Migdol to Aswan
they will fall by the sword within her,
declares the Sovereign LORD.
[7]"They will be desolate
among desolate lands,
and their cities will lie
among ruined cities.
[8]Then they will know that I am the LORD,
when I set fire to Egypt
and all her helpers are crushed.

[9]"'On that day messengers will go out from me in ships to frighten Cush out of her complacency. Anguish will take hold of them on the day of Egypt's doom, for it is sure to come.

[10]"'This is what the Sovereign LORD says:

"'I will put an end to the hordes of Egypt
by the hand of Nebuchadnezzar king of Babylon.
[11]He and his army—the most ruthless of nations—
will be brought in to destroy the land.
They will draw their swords against Egypt
and fill the land with the slain.
[12]I will dry up the waters of the Nile
and sell the land to an evil nation;
by the hand of foreigners
I will lay waste the land and everything in it.

I the LORD have spoken.

## Amplified Bible

stones for siege works]. Yet he had no remuneration from Tyre [in proportion to the time and labor expended in the thirteen years' siege], either for himself or his army, for the work that he had done against it [for Me].

[19]Therefore thus says the Lord God: Behold, I will give the land of Egypt to Nebuchadrezzar king of Babylon, and he shall carry off her great mass of people *and* of things (her riches) and take her spoil and take her prey, and it shall be the wages for his army.

[20]I have given him the land of Egypt for his labor with which he served [against Tyre] because they did it for Me, says the Lord God.

[21]In that day will I cause a horn to spring forth to the house of Israel and I will open your lips among them, and they shall know (understand and realize) that I am the Lord [the Sovereign Ruler, Who calls forth loyalty and obedient service].

**30** The word of the Lord came again to me, saying, [2]Son of man, prophesy and say, Thus says the Lord God: Wail, Alas for the day!

[3]For the day is near, even the day of the Lord is near, a cloudy day; it shall be the time [of doom] for the nations.

[4]And a sword shall come upon Egypt, and anguish *and* great sorrow shall be in Ethiopia (Cush), when the slain fall in Egypt and they [of Babylon] carry away her great mass of people *and* of things and her foundations are broken down.

[5]Ethiopia (Cush) and Put, Lud and all the mingled people [foreigners living in Egypt], Cub (Lub, Libya) and the children of the land of the covenant [the Jews who had taken refuge in Egypt] shall fall with [the Egyptians] by the sword.

[6]Thus says the Lord: They also who uphold *or* lean upon *and* are supported by Egypt shall fall, and the pride of her power shall come down; from Migdol [in the north] to Syene [in the south] they shall fall within her by the sword, says the Lord God.

[7]And they shall be desolated in the midst of countries that are desolated, and her cities shall be in the midst of cities that are wasted [by plunder and subjection].

[8]And they shall know (understand and realize) that I am the Lord [the Sovereign Ruler, Who calls forth loyalty and obedient service], when I have set a fire in Egypt and all her helpers are broken *and* destroyed.

[9]In that day shall [swift] messengers go forth from Me in ships to terrify the careless *and* unsuspecting Ethiopians, and there shall be anguish *and* great sorrow upon them as in the day of Egypt's [doom], for behold, [their day] comes!

[10]Thus says the Lord God: I will also make the tumult *and* the wealth *and* the large population of Egypt to cease by the hand of [a]Nebuchadrezzar king of Babylon.

[11]He and his people with him, the [most] terrible of the nations, shall be brought in to destroy the land, and they shall draw their swords against Egypt and fill the land with the slain.

[12]And I will make the [artificial] streams [of the Nile delta] dry and will sell the land into the hand of evil men, and I will make the land desolate, and all that is in it, by the hand of strangers. I the Lord [the Sovereign Ruler, Who calls forth loyalty and obedient service] have spoken it.

---

[a] *21 Horn* here symbolizes strength.    [b] *4* That is, the upper Nile region; also in verses 5 and 9

[a] See footnote on Jer. 21:2.

## New International Version

13"'This is what the Sovereign Lord says:

"'I will destroy the idols
    and put an end to the images in Memphis.
No longer will there be a prince in Egypt,
    and I will spread fear throughout the land.
14 I will lay waste Upper Egypt,
    set fire to Zoan
    and inflict punishment on Thebes.
15 I will pour out my wrath on Pelusium,
    the stronghold of Egypt,
    and wipe out the hordes of Thebes.
16 I will set fire to Egypt;
    Pelusium will writhe in agony.
Thebes will be taken by storm;
    Memphis will be in constant distress.
17 The young men of Heliopolis and Bubastis
    will fall by the sword,
    and the cities themselves will go into captivity.
18 Dark will be the day at Tahpanhes
    when I break the yoke of Egypt;
    there her proud strength will come to an end.
She will be covered with clouds,
    and her villages will go into captivity.
19 So I will inflict punishment on Egypt,
    and they will know that I am the Lord.'"

### Pharaoh's Arms Are Broken

20 In the eleventh year, in the first month on the seventh day, the word of the Lord came to me: 21"Son of man, I have broken the arm of Pharaoh king of Egypt. It has not been bound up to be healed or put in a splint so that it may become strong enough to hold a sword. 22 Therefore this is what the Sovereign Lord says: I am against Pharaoh king of Egypt. I will break both his arms, the good arm as well as the broken one, and make the sword fall from his hand. 23 I will disperse the Egyptians among the nations and scatter them through the countries. 24 I will strengthen the arms of the king of Babylon and put my sword in his hand, but I will break the arms of Pharaoh, and he will groan before him like a mortally wounded man. 25 I will strengthen the arms of the king of Babylon, but the arms of Pharaoh will fall limp. Then they will know that I am the Lord, when I put my sword into the hand of the king of Babylon and he brandishes it against Egypt. 26 I will disperse the Egyptians among the nations and scatter them through the countries. Then they will know that I am the Lord."

### Pharaoh as a Felled Cedar of Lebanon

**31** In the eleventh year, in the third month on the first day, the word of the Lord came to me: 2"Son of man, say to Pharaoh king of Egypt and to his hordes:

"'Who can be compared with you in majesty?
3 Consider Assyria, once a cedar in Lebanon,
    with beautiful branches overshadowing the forest;
it towered on high,
    its top above the thick foliage.
4 The waters nourished it,
    deep springs made it grow tall;
their streams flowed
    all around its base
and sent their channels
    to all the trees of the field.

## Amplified Bible

13 Thus says the Lord God: I will also destroy the idols and I will put an end to the images in Noph or Memphis, and there shall be no longer a prince of the land of Egypt. And I will put fear in the land of Egypt.

14 And I will make Pathros desolate and will set fire to Zoan and will execute judgments and punishments upon No or Thebes.

15 And I will pour My wrath upon Pelusium, the stronghold of Egypt, and I will cut off the tumult, the prosperity and the population of No or Thebes.

16 And I will set fire to Egypt; Pelusium shall have great anguish and No or Thebes shall be torn open and Noph or Memphis shall have adversaries in the daytime and all the day long.

17 The young men of Aven or On and of Pibeseth shall fall by the sword, and the [women and children] shall go into captivity.

18 At Tehaphnehes also the day shall withdraw itself and be dark when I break there the yokes and dominion of Egypt, and the pride of her power shall come to an end. As for her, a cloud [of calamities] shall cover her and her daughters shall go into captivity.

19 Thus will I execute judgments and punishments upon Egypt. Then shall they know (understand and realize) that I am the Lord [the Sovereign Ruler, Who calls forth loyalty and obedient service].

20 And in the eleventh year [after King Jehoiachin was taken to Babylon], in the first month, on the seventh day of the month, the word of the Lord came to me, saying,

21 Son of man, I have broken the arm of Pharaoh king of Egypt, and behold, it has not been bound up to heal it by binding it with a bandage, to make it strong to hold and wield the sword.

22 Therefore thus says the Lord God: Behold, I am against Pharaoh king of Egypt and will break his arms, both the strong one and the one which was broken, and I will cause the sword to fall from his hand.

23 And I will scatter the Egyptians among the nations and will disperse them throughout the countries.

24 And I will strengthen the arms of the king of Babylon and put My sword in his hand, but I will break Pharaoh's arms and he will groan before [Nebuchadrezzar] with the groanings of a mortally wounded man.

25 But I will strengthen and hold up the arms of the king of Babylon and the arms of Pharaoh shall fall down, and they [of Egypt] shall know (understand and realize) that I am the Lord [the Sovereign Ruler, Who calls forth loyalty and obedient service], when I put My sword into the hand of the king of Babylon and he shall stretch it out upon the land of Egypt.

26 And I will scatter the Egyptians among the nations and disperse them through the countries, and they shall know (understand and realize) that I am the Lord [the Sovereign Ruler, Who calls forth loyalty and obedient service].

**31** And in the eleventh year [after King Jehoiachin was taken captive to Babylon], in the third month, on the first day of the month, the word of the Lord came to me, saying,

2 Son of man, say to Pharaoh king of Egypt and to his multitude: Whom are you like in your greatness?

3 Behold, [I will liken you to] Assyria, a cedar in Lebanon, with fair branches and with forestlike shade and of high stature, with its top among the thick boughs [even among the clouds].

4 The waters nourished it; the deep made it grow tall; its rivers ran round about its planting, sending out its streams to all the trees of the forest [the other nations].

## New International Version

5So it towered higher
    than all the trees of the field;
  its boughs increased
    and its branches grew long,
    spreading because of abundant waters.
6All the birds of the sky
    nested in its boughs,
  all the animals of the wild
    gave birth under its branches;
  all the great nations
    lived in its shade.
7It was majestic in beauty,
    with its spreading boughs,
  for its roots went down
    to abundant waters.
8The cedars in the garden of God
    could not rival it,
  nor could the junipers
    equal its boughs,
  nor could the plane trees
    compare with its branches—
  no tree in the garden of God
    could match its beauty.
9I made it beautiful
    with abundant branches,
  the envy of all the trees of Eden
    in the garden of God.

10"'Therefore this is what the Sovereign LORD says: Because the great cedar towered over the thick foliage, and because it was proud of its height, 11I gave it into the hands of the ruler of the nations, for him to deal with according to its wickedness. I cast it aside, 12and the most ruthless of foreign nations cut it down and left it. Its boughs fell on the mountains and in all the valleys; its branches lay broken in all the ravines of the land. All the nations of the earth came out from under its shade and left it. 13All the birds settled on the fallen tree, and all the wild animals lived among its branches. 14Therefore no other trees by the waters are ever to tower proudly on high, lifting their tops above the thick foliage. No other trees so well-watered are ever to reach such a height; they are all destined for death, for the earth below, among mortals who go down to the realm of the dead.

15"'This is what the Sovereign LORD says: On the day it was brought down to the realm of the dead I covered the deep springs with mourning for it; I held back its streams, and its abundant waters were restrained. Because of it I clothed Lebanon with gloom, and all the trees of the field withered away. 16I made the nations tremble at the sound of its fall when I brought it down to the realm of the dead to be with those who go down to the pit. Then all the trees of Eden, the choicest and best of Lebanon, the well-watered trees, were consoled in the earth below. 17They too, like the great cedar, had gone down to the realm of the dead, to those killed by the sword, along with the armed men who lived in its shade among the nations.

18"Which of the trees of Eden can be compared with you in splendor and majesty? Yet you, too, will be brought

## Amplified Bible

5Therefore it towered higher than all the trees of the forest; its boughs were multiplied and its branches became long, because there was much water when they were shot forth.
6All the birds of the heavens made their nests in its boughs, and under its branches all the wild beasts of the field brought forth their young and under its shadow dwelt all of the great nations.
7Thus was it beautiful in its greatness, in the length of its branches, for its root was by many and great waters.
8The cedars in the garden of God could not hide or rival it; the cypress trees did not have boughs like it and the plane trees did not have branches like it, nor was any tree in the garden of God like it in its beauty.
9I made it beautiful with the multitude of its branches, so that all the trees of aEden that were in the garden of God envied it [Assyria].
10Therefore thus said the Lord God: Because it is exalted in stature and has set its top among the thick boughs and the clouds, and its heart is proud of its height, [II Kings 18:31-35.]
11I will even bdeliver it into the hand of a mighty one of the nations; he shall surely deal with it. I have driven it out for its wickedness and lawlessness.
12And strangers, the most terrible of the nations, will cut it off and leave it; upon the mountains and in all the valleys its branches will fall and its boughs will lie broken by all the watercourses of the land, and all the peoples of the earth will go down out of its shade and leave it.
13Upon its ruins all the birds of the heavens will dwell, and all the wild beasts of the field will be upon [Assyria's fallen] branches.
14All this is so that none of the trees by the waters may exalt themselves because of their height or shoot up their top among the thick boughs and the clouds, and that none of their mighty ones should stand upon [their own estimate of] themselves for their height, all that drink water. For they are all delivered over to death, to the lower world, in the midst of the children of men, with those who go down to the pit (the grave).
15Thus says the Lord God: When [Assyria] goes down to Sheol (the place of the dead), I will cause a mourning; I will cover the deep for it and I will restrain its floods, and the many waters [that contributed to its prosperity] will be stayed; and I will cause Lebanon to be in black gloom and to mourn for it, and all the trees of the field, dismayed, will faint because of it.
16I will make the nations quake at the sound of its fall when I cast it down to Sheol with those who descend into the pit, and all the trees of Eden, the choice and best of Lebanon, all [the trees] that drink water, will be comforted in the netherworld [at Assyria's downfall].
17They also shall go down into Sheol with it to those who were slain by the sword—yes, those who were its arm, who dwelt under its shadow in the midst of the nations.
18To whom [O Egypt] among the trees of Eden are you thus like in glory and in greatness? Yet you [also] shall be brought down with the trees of Eden to the netherworld.

---

a The traditional site of Eden was within the bounds of the Assyrian Empire. However, this in no sense implies that Assyria was in the garden of God told about in Gen. 2:8.  b The effectiveness of this comparison [of Egypt] with Assyria becomes clear when it is remembered that Assyria had conquered and held Egypt in vassalage, and had then herself been conquered and annihilated only thirty-seven years before the date of this prophecy—by the same Chaldean [Babylonian] power [then controlled by the father of Nebuchadnezzar, which is] now foretold as about to execute judgment upon Egypt. Egypt could not hope to resist the conqueror of her conqueror (Charles Ellicott, A Bible Commentary).

## New International Version

down with the trees of Eden to the earth below; you will lie among the uncircumcised, with those killed by the sword. "'This is Pharaoh and all his hordes, declares the Sovereign LORD.'"

### A Lament Over Pharaoh

**32** In the twelfth year, in the twelfth month on the first day, the word of the LORD came to me: ²"Son of man, take up a lament concerning Pharaoh king of Egypt and say to him:

"'You are like a lion among the nations;
 you are like a monster in the seas
thrashing about in your streams,
 churning the water with your feet
 and muddying the streams.

³"'This is what the Sovereign LORD says:

"'With a great throng of people
 I will cast my net over you,
 and they will haul you up in my net.
⁴I will throw you on the land
 and hurl you on the open field.
I will let all the birds of the sky settle on you
 and all the animals of the wild gorge themselves on
 you.
⁵I will spread your flesh on the mountains
 and fill the valleys with your remains.
⁶I will drench the land with your flowing blood
 all the way to the mountains,
 and the ravines will be filled with your flesh.
⁷When I snuff you out, I will cover the heavens
 and darken their stars;
I will cover the sun with a cloud,
 and the moon will not give its light.
⁸All the shining lights in the heavens
 I will darken over you;
I will bring darkness over your land,
 declares the Sovereign LORD.
⁹I will trouble the hearts of many peoples
 when I bring about your destruction among the
 nations,
 among*a* lands you have not known.
¹⁰I will cause many peoples to be appalled at you,
 and their kings will shudder with horror because of
 you
 when I brandish my sword before them.
On the day of your downfall
 each of them will tremble
 every moment for his life.

¹¹"'For this is what the Sovereign LORD says:

"'The sword of the king of Babylon
 will come against you.
¹²I will cause your hordes to fall
 by the swords of mighty men—
 the most ruthless of all nations.
They will shatter the pride of Egypt,
 and all her hordes will be overthrown.
¹³I will destroy all her cattle
 from beside abundant waters
no longer to be stirred by the foot of man
 or muddied by the hooves of cattle.
¹⁴Then I will let her waters settle
 and make her streams flow like oil,
 declares the Sovereign LORD.
¹⁵When I make Egypt desolate
 and strip the land of everything in it,
when I strike down all who live there,
 then they will know that I am the LORD.'

---

*a* 9 Hebrew; Septuagint *bring you into captivity among the nations, / to*

## Amplified Bible

You shall lie among the *a*uncircumcised heathen with those who are slain by the sword. This is *b*how it shall be with Pharaoh and all the multitude of his strength, his tumult, *and* his store [of wealth and glory], says the Lord God. [Ezek. 28:10; 32:19.]

**32** In the twelfth year [after King Jehoiachin of Judah was taken into exile by the king of Babylon], in the twelfth month, on the first day of the month, the word of the Lord came to me, saying,

²Son of man, take up a lamentation over Pharaoh king of Egypt and say to him, You have likened [yourself] to a young lion, leader of the nations, but you are like a [monster] dragon in the seas; you break forth in your rivers and trouble the waters with your feet, and you make foul their rivers [the sources of their prosperity].

³Thus says the Lord God: I will therefore throw out My net over you with a host of many peoples, and they shall bring you up in My dragnet.

⁴Then I will leave you [Egypt] upon the shore; I will cast you on the open field and will cause all the birds of the heavens to settle upon you, and I will fill the beasts of the whole earth with you.

⁵And I will scatter your flesh upon the mountains and fill the valleys with your high heap of corpses *and* their worms.

⁶I will also water with your flowing blood the land, even to the mountains, and the hollows *and* water channels shall be full of you.

⁷And when I have extinguished you, I will cover the heavens [of Egypt] and make their stars dark; I will cover the sun with a cloud and the moon shall not give her light.

⁸All the bright lights of the heavens I will make dark over you and set darkness upon your land, says the Lord God.

⁹I will also trouble *and* vex the hearts of many peoples when I bring your breaking *and* trembling *and* destruction *and* carry you captive among the nations, into the countries which you have not known.

¹⁰I will make many peoples amazed *and* appalled at you [Egypt], and their kings shall shudder *and* be horribly afraid because of you when I brandish My sword before them; they shall tremble every moment, every man for his own life, in the day of your downfall.

¹¹For thus says the Lord God: The sword of the king of Babylon shall come upon you.

¹²I will cause your multitude, your tumult, *and* your store [of wealth, strength, and glory] to fall by the swords of the mighty—the most terrible among the nations are they all. And they shall bring to nothing the pomp *and* pride of Egypt, and all its multitude [with its activity and its wealth in every sphere] shall be destroyed.

¹³I will destroy also all its beasts from beside many *and* great waters, and no foot of man shall trouble them any more, nor shall the hoofs of beasts trouble them.

¹⁴Then will I make their waters sink down (subside, be quiet, and become clear); their rivers I will cause to run [slowly and smoothly] like oil, says the Lord God.

¹⁵When I make the land of Egypt desolate, and the country is stripped *and* destitute of all that of which it was full when I smite all those who dwell in it, then will they know, understand, *and* realize that I am the Lord [the Sovereign Ruler, Who requires and calls forth loyalty and obedient service].

---

*a* Though there were other circumcised peoples besides the Hebrews, especially the Egyptians (and they as early as 3000 B.C.), yet the Philistines, the Moabites, the Ammonites, the Syrians, the Assyrians, the Babylonians, and various other nationalities with whom the Jews were in contact were uncircumcised, so that the word "uncircumcised" as a term of reproach meant practically (though not etymologically) almost the same thing as heathen (John D. Davis, *A Dictionary of the Bible*). *b* The Septuagint (Greek translation of the Old Testament) so reads at this point.

## New International Version

16"This is the lament they will chant for her. The daughters of the nations will chant it; for Egypt and all her hordes they will chant it, declares the Sovereign Lord."

### Egypt's Descent Into the Realm of the Dead

17In the twelfth year, on the fifteenth day of the month, the word of the Lord came to me: 18"Son of man, wail for the hordes of Egypt and consign to the earth below both her and the daughters of mighty nations, along with those who go down to the pit. 19Say to them, 'Are you more favored than others? Go down and be laid among the uncircumcised.' 20They will fall among those killed by the sword. The sword is drawn; let her be dragged off with all her hordes. 21From within the realm of the dead the mighty leaders will say of Egypt and her allies, 'They have come down and they lie with the uncircumcised, with those killed by the sword.'

22"Assyria is there with her whole army; she is surrounded by the graves of all her slain, all who have fallen by the sword. 23Their graves are in the depths of the pit and her army lies around her grave. All who had spread terror in the land of the living are slain, fallen by the sword.

24"Elam is there, with all her hordes around her grave. All of them are slain, fallen by the sword. All who had spread terror in the land of the living went down uncircumcised to the earth below. They bear their shame with those who go down to the pit. 25A bed is made for her among the slain, with all her hordes around her grave. All of them are uncircumcised, killed by the sword. Because their terror had spread in the land of the living, they bear their shame with those who go down to the pit; they are laid among the slain.

26"Meshek and Tubal are there, with all their hordes around their graves. All of them are uncircumcised, killed by the sword because they spread their terror in the land of the living. 27But they do not lie with the fallen warriors of old,*a* who went down to the realm of the dead with their weapons of war—their swords placed under their heads and their shields*b* resting on their bones—though these warriors also had terrorized the land of the living.

28"You too, Pharaoh, will be broken and will lie among the uncircumcised, with those killed by the sword.

29"Edom is there, her kings and all her princes; despite their power, they are laid with those killed by the sword. They lie with the uncircumcised, with those who go down to the pit.

30"All the princes of the north and all the Sidonians are there; they went down with the slain in disgrace despite the terror caused by their power. They lie uncircumcised with those killed by the sword and bear their shame with those who go down to the pit.

31"Pharaoh—he and all his army—will see them and he will be consoled for all his hordes that were killed by the sword, declares the Sovereign Lord. 32Although I had him spread terror in the land of the living, Pharaoh and

## Amplified Bible

16This is the lamentation with which they shall intone *or* chant the lament for her; the daughters of the nations shall chant their lament with it; over Egypt and over all her multitude, her tumult, *and* her wealth in every sphere shall they chant it, says the Lord God.

17In the twelfth year [after King Jehoiachin of Judah was taken into exile], on the fifteenth day of the month, the word of the Lord came to me, saying,

18Son of man, wail over the multitude of Egypt and cast them down, even her and the daughters of the famous *and* majestic nations, to the netherworld, with those who go down to the pit.

19Whom [among them] do you surpass in beauty? Go down and be laid with the uncircumcised (the heathen).

20They shall fall in the midst of those who are slain by the sword; she [Egypt] is delivered to the sword; they draw her down [to her judgment], and all her multitudes [with their noise and stores].

21The strong among the mighty shall speak of [Pharaoh] out of the midst of Sheol (the place of the dead, the netherworld) with those who helped him; they are gone down; they lie still, even the uncircumcised (the heathen) slain by the sword.

22Assyria is there and all her company; their graves are round about her, all of them slain, fallen by the sword,

23Whose graves are set in the uttermost parts of the pit and whose company is round about her grave, all of them slain, fallen by the sword, who caused terror to spread in the land of the living.

24Elam [an auxiliary of Assyria] is there and all her multitude round about her grave, all of them slain, fallen by the sword, who have gone down uncircumcised into the netherworld, who caused their terror to spread in the land of the living and have borne their shame with those who go down to the pit.

25They have set her a bed (a sepulcher) among the slain with all her multitude—their graves round about her, all of them uncircumcised, slain by the sword, for their terror had spread in the land of the living, and they henceforth bear their shame with those who go down to the pit; they are laid in the midst of the slain.

26Meshech, Tubal, and all their multitude are there; their graves are round about [Pharaoh], all of them uncircumcised, slain by the sword, for they caused their terror to be spread in the land of the living.

27And they shall not lie with the mighty who have fallen of the uncircumcised [and] who have gone down to Sheol (the place of the dead, the netherworld) with their weapons of war, whose swords were laid [with honors] under their heads and whose iniquities are upon their bones, for they caused their terror to spread in the land of the living.

28But you [Meshech and Tubal] shall be broken in the midst of the uncircumcised and shall lie [without honors] with those who are slain with the sword.

29Edom is there, her kings and all her princes, who for all their might are laid with those who were slain by the sword; they shall lie with the *a*uncircumcised (the heathen) and with those who go down to the pit.

30The princes of the north are there, all of them, and all the Sidonians, who have gone down with the slain; for all the terror which they caused by their might they are put to shame, and they lie uncircumcised with those who are slain by the sword and henceforth bear their shame with those who go down to the pit.

31When Pharaoh sees them, he will comfort himself for all his multitude—even Pharaoh and all his army, slain by the sword, says the Lord God.

32For I have put his *and* My terror in the land of the liv-

---

*a* 27 Septuagint; Hebrew *warriors who were uncircumcised*
*b* 27 Probable reading of the original Hebrew text; Masoretic Text *punishment*

---

*a* The Edomites observed the rite of circumcision, but they were not spared because of that.

## New International Version

all his hordes will be laid among the uncircumcised, with those killed by the sword, declares the Sovereign LORD."

### Renewal of Ezekiel's Call as Watchman

**33** The word of the LORD came to me: [2]"Son of man, speak to your people and say to them: 'When I bring the sword against a land, and the people of the land choose one of their men and make him their watchman, [3]and he sees the sword coming against the land and blows the trumpet to warn the people, [4]then if anyone hears the trumpet but does not heed the warning and the sword comes and takes their life, their blood will be on their own head. [5]Since they heard the sound of the trumpet but did not heed the warning, their blood will be on their own head. If they had heeded the warning, they would have saved themselves. [6]But if the watchman sees the sword coming and does not blow the trumpet to warn the people and the sword comes and takes someone's life, that person's life will be taken because of their sin, but I will hold the watchman accountable for their blood.'

[7]"Son of man, I have made you a watchman for the people of Israel; so hear the word I speak and give them warning from me. [8]When I say to the wicked, 'You wicked person, you will surely die,' and you do not speak out to dissuade them from their ways, that wicked person will die for[a] their sin, and I will hold you accountable for their blood. [9]But if you do warn the wicked person to turn from their ways and they do not do so, they will die for their sin, though you yourself will be saved.

[10]"Son of man, say to the Israelites, 'This is what you are saying: "Our offenses and sins weigh us down, and we are wasting away because of[b] them. How then can we live?"' [11]Say to them, 'As surely as I live, declares the Sovereign LORD, I take no pleasure in the death of the wicked, but rather that they turn from their ways and live. Turn! Turn from your evil ways! Why will you die, people of Israel?'

[12]"Therefore, son of man, say to your people, 'If someone who is righteous disobeys, that person's former righteousness will count for nothing. And if someone who is wicked repents, that person's former wickedness will not bring condemnation. The righteous person who sins will not be allowed to live even though they were formerly righteous.' [13]If I tell a righteous person that they will surely live, but then they trust in their righteousness and do evil, none of the righteous things that person has done will be remembered; they will die for the evil they have done. [14]And if I say to a wicked person, 'You will surely die,' but they then turn away from their sin and do what is just and right— [15]if they give back what they took in pledge for a loan, return what they had stolen, follow the decrees that give life, and do no evil—that person will surely live; they will not die. [16]None of the sins that person has committed will be remembered against them. They have done what is just and right; they will surely live.

[17]"Yet your people say, 'The way of the Lord is not just.' But it is their way that is not just. [18]If a righteous person turns from their righteousness and does evil, they will

## Amplified Bible

ing, and he shall be laid in the midst of the uncircumcised (the heathen) with those slain by the sword, even Pharaoh and all his multitude, says the Lord God. [Isa. 19; Jer. 46; Zech. 14:18, 19.]

**33** And the word of the Lord came to me, saying, [2]Son of man, speak to your people [the Israelite captives in Babylon] and say to them, When I bring the sword upon a land and the people of the land take a man from among them and make him their watchman,

[3]If when he sees the sword coming upon the land, he blows the trumpet and warns the people,

[4]Then whoever hears the sound of the trumpet and does not take warning, and the sword comes and takes him away, his blood shall be upon his own head.

[5]He heard the sound of the trumpet and did not take warning; his blood shall be upon himself. But he who takes warning shall save his life.

[6]But if the watchman sees the sword coming and does not blow the trumpet and the people are not warned, and the sword comes and takes any one of them, he is taken away in *and* for his perversity *and* iniquity, but his blood will I require at the watchman's hand.

[7]So you, son of man, I have made you a watchman for the house of Israel; therefore hear the word at My mouth and give them warning from Me.

[8]When I say to the wicked, O wicked man, you shall surely die, and you do not speak to warn the wicked from his way, that wicked man shall die in his perversity *and* iniquity, but his blood will I require at your hand.

[9]But if you warn the wicked to turn from his evil way and he does not turn from his evil way, he shall die in his iniquity, but you shall have saved your life.

[10]And you, son of man, say to the house of Israel, Thus you have said: Truly our transgressions and our sins are upon us, and we waste away because of them; how then can we live?

[11]Say to them, As I live, says the Lord God, I have no pleasure in the death of the wicked, but rather that the wicked turn from his way and live. Turn back, turn back from your evil ways, for why will you die, O house of Israel?

[12]And you, son of man, say to your people, The uprightness *and* justice of the [uncompromisingly] righteous shall not deliver him in the day of his transgression; and as for the wicked lawlessness of the wicked lawless, he shall not fall because of it in the day that he turns from his wickedness, neither shall the rigidly upright *and* just be able to live because of his past righteousness in the day that he sins *and* misses the mark [in keeping in harmony and right standing with God].

[13]When I shall say to the [uncompromisingly] righteous that he shall surely live, and he trusts to his own righteousness [to save him] and commits iniquity (heinous sin), all his righteous deeds shall not be [seriously] remembered; but for his perversity *and* iniquity that he has committed he shall die.

[14]Again, when I have said to the wicked, You shall surely die, if he turns from his sin and does that which is lawful and right—

[15]If the wicked restores [what he took in] pledge, gives back what he had taken in robbery, walks in the statutes of life [right relationship with God], without committing iniquity, he shall surely live; he shall not die.

[16]None of his sins that he has committed shall be [seriously] remembered against him; he has done that which is lawful and right; he shall surely live.

[17]Yet your people say, The way of the Lord is not perfect *or* even just; but as for them, it is their own way that is not perfect *or* even just.

[18]When the righteous turns back from his [uncompromising] righteousness and commits perverseness *and* iniquity, he shall even die in *and* because of it.

---

[a] 8 Or *in*; also in verse 9   [b] 10 Or *away in*

## New International Version

die for it. [19]And if a wicked person turns away from their wickedness and does what is just and right, they will live by doing so. [20]Yet you Israelites say, 'The way of the Lord is not just.' But I will judge each of you according to your own ways."

### Jerusalem's Fall Explained

[21]In the twelfth year of our exile, in the tenth month on the fifth day, a man who had escaped from Jerusalem came to me and said, "The city has fallen!" [22]Now the evening before the man arrived, the hand of the LORD was on me, and he opened my mouth before the man came to me in the morning. So my mouth was opened and I was no longer silent.

[23]Then the word of the LORD came to me: [24]"Son of man, the people living in those ruins in the land of Israel are saying, 'Abraham was only one man, yet he possessed the land. But we are many; surely the land has been given to us as our possession.' [25]Therefore say to them, 'This is what the Sovereign LORD says: Since you eat meat with the blood still in it and look to your idols and shed blood, should you then possess the land? [26]You rely on your sword, you do detestable things, and each of you defiles his neighbor's wife. Should you then possess the land?'

[27]"Say this to them: 'This is what the Sovereign LORD says: As surely as I live, those who are left in the ruins will fall by the sword, those out in the country I will give to the wild animals to be devoured, and those in strongholds and caves will die of a plague. [28]I will make the land a desolate waste, and her proud strength will come to an end, and the mountains of Israel will become desolate so that no one will cross them. [29]Then they will know that I am the LORD, when I have made the land a desolate waste because of all the detestable things they have done.'

[30]"As for you, son of man, your people are talking together about you by the walls and at the doors of the houses, saying to each other, 'Come and hear the message that has come from the LORD.' [31]My people come to you, as they usually do, and sit before you to hear your words, but they do not put them into practice. Their mouths speak of love, but their hearts are greedy for unjust gain. [32]Indeed, to them you are nothing more than one who sings love songs with a beautiful voice and plays an instrument well, for they hear your words but do not put them into practice.

[33]"When all this comes true—and it surely will—then they will know that a prophet has been among them."

### The LORD Will Be Israel's Shepherd

**34** The word of the LORD came to me: [2]"Son of man, prophesy against the shepherds of Israel; prophesy and say to them: 'This is what the Sovereign LORD says: Woe to you shepherds of Israel who only take care of yourselves! Should not shepherds take care of the flock? [3]You eat the curds, clothe yourselves with the wool and slaughter the choice animals, but you do not take care of the flock. [4]You have not strengthened the weak or healed the sick or bound up the injured. You have not brought back the strays or searched for the lost. You have ruled them harshly and brutally. [5]So they were scattered because

## Amplified Bible

[19]But if the wicked turns back from his wickedness and does what is lawful and right, he shall live because of it.

[20]Yet you say, The way of the Lord is not perfect *or* [even] just. O you house of Israel, I will judge you, every one according to his own ways!

[21]In the twelfth year of our captivity [in Babylon], in the tenth [month], on the fifth [day] of the month, a man who had escaped out of Jerusalem came to me [Ezekiel], saying, The city [Jerusalem] is taken.

[22]Now the hand of the Lord had been upon me in the evening before this one who had escaped came, and He had opened my mouth [in readiness for the fugitives] coming to me in the morning, and my mouth was opened and I was no longer dumb.

[23]Then the word of the Lord came to me, saying,

[24]Son of man, those [back in Palestine] who inhabit those wastes of the ground of Israel are saying, Abraham was only one man and he inherited the land, but we are many; the land is surely given to us to possess as our inheritance.

[25]Therefore say to them, Thus says the Lord God: You eat meat with the blood [as an idolatrous rite] and lift up your eyes to your [filthy] idols and shed blood; shall you then possess the land? [Gen. 9:4; Lev. 3:17; 7:27; Acts 15:28, 29.]

[26]You stand upon your sword [as your dependence]; you commit abominations and each of you defiles your neighbor's wife; shall you then possess the land?

[27]Say this to them, Thus says the Lord God: As I live, surely those who are in the waste places shall fall by the sword, and him that is in the open field will I give to the beasts to be devoured, and those who are in strongholds and in caves shall die by pestilence.

[28]And I will make the land [of Israel] a desolation and a waste, and her proud might shall cease, and the mountains of Israel shall be so desolate that no one will pass through them.

[29]Then shall they know, understand, *and* realize that I am the Lord, when I have made the land a desolation and a waste because of all their abominations which they have committed.

[30]As for you, son of man, your people who talk of you by the walls and in the doors of the houses say one to another, every one to his brother, Come and hear what the word is that comes forth from the Lord.

[31]And they come to you as people come, and they sit before you as My people, and they hear the words you say, but they will not do them; for with their mouths they show much love, but their hearts go after *and* are set on their [idolatrous greed for] gain.

[32]Behold, you are to them as a very lovely [love] song of one who has a pleasant voice and can play well on an instrument, for they hear your words but do not do them.

[33]When this comes to pass—for behold, it will come!—then shall they know, understand, *and* realize that a prophet has been among them.

**34** And the word of the Lord came to me, saying, [2]Son of man, prophesy against the shepherds of Israel; prophesy and say to them, even to the [spiritual] shepherds, Thus says the Lord God: Woe to the [spiritual] shepherds of Israel who feed themselves! Should not the shepherds feed the sheep?

[3]You eat the fat, you clothe yourselves with the wool, you kill the fatlings, but you do not feed the sheep.

[4]The diseased *and* weak you have not strengthened, the sick you have not healed, the hurt *and* crippled you have not bandaged, those gone astray you have not brought back, the lost you have not sought to find, but with force and hardhearted harshness you have ruled them.

[5]And they were scattered because there was no shep-

## New International Version

there was no shepherd, and when they were scattered they became food for all the wild animals. [6]My sheep wandered over all the mountains and on every high hill. They were scattered over the whole earth, and no one searched or looked for them.

[7]"'Therefore, you shepherds, hear the word of the LORD: [8]As surely as I live, declares the Sovereign LORD, because my flock lacks a shepherd and so has been plundered and has become food for all the wild animals, and because my shepherds did not search for my flock but cared for themselves rather than for my flock, [9]therefore, you shepherds, hear the word of the LORD: [10]This is what the Sovereign LORD says: I am against the shepherds and will hold them accountable for my flock. I will remove them from tending the flock so that the shepherds can no longer feed themselves. I will rescue my flock from their mouths, and it will no longer be food for them.

[11]"'For this is what the Sovereign LORD says: I myself will search for my sheep and look after them. [12]As a shepherd looks after his scattered flock when he is with them, so will I look after my sheep. I will rescue them from all the places where they were scattered on a day of clouds and darkness. [13]I will bring them out from the nations and gather them from the countries, and I will bring them into their own land. I will pasture them on the mountains of Israel, in the ravines and in all the settlements in the land. [14]I will tend them in a good pasture, and the mountain heights of Israel will be their grazing land. There they will lie down in good grazing land, and there they will feed in a rich pasture on the mountains of Israel. [15]I myself will tend my sheep and have them lie down, declares the Sovereign LORD. [16]I will search for the lost and bring back the strays. I will bind up the injured and strengthen the weak, but the sleek and the strong I will destroy. I will shepherd the flock with justice.

[17]"'As for you, my flock, this is what the Sovereign LORD says: I will judge between one sheep and another, and between rams and goats. [18]Is it not enough for you to feed on the good pasture? Must you also trample the rest of your pasture with your feet? Is it not enough for you to drink clear water? Must you also muddy the rest with your feet? [19]Must my flock feed on what you have trampled and drink what you have muddied with your feet?

[20]"'Therefore this is what the Sovereign LORD says to them: See, I myself will judge between the fat sheep and the lean sheep. [21]Because you shove with flank and shoulder, butting all the weak sheep with your horns until you have driven them away, [22]I will save my flock, and they will no longer be plundered. I will judge between one sheep and another. [23]I will place over them one shepherd, my

## Amplified Bible

herd, and when they were scattered they became food for all the wild beasts of the field.

[6]My sheep wandered through all the mountains and upon every high hill; yes, My sheep were scattered upon all the face of the earth and no one searched or sought for them. [Matt. 9:36.]

[7]Therefore, you [spiritual] shepherds, hear the word of the Lord:

[8]As I live, says the Lord God, surely because My sheep became a prey, and My sheep became food for every beast of the field because there was no shepherd—neither did My shepherds search for My sheep, but the shepherds fed themselves and fed not My sheep—

[9]Therefore, O you [spiritual] shepherds, hear the word of the Lord:

[10]Thus says the Lord God: Behold, I am against the shepherds, and I will require My sheep at their hand and cause them to cease feeding the sheep, neither shall the shepherds feed themselves any more. I will rescue My sheep from their mouths, that they may not be food for them.

[11]For thus says the Lord God: Behold, I, I Myself, will search for My sheep and will seek them out.

[12]As a shepherd seeks out his sheep in the day that he is among his flock that are scattered, so will I seek out My sheep; and I will rescue them out of all places where they have been scattered in the day of clouds and thick darkness.

[13]And I will bring them out from the peoples and gather them from the countries and will bring them to their own land; and I will feed them upon the mountains of Israel, by the watercourses, and in all the inhabited places of the country.

[14]I will feed them with good pasture, and upon the high mountains of Israel shall their fold be; there shall they lie down in a good fold, and in a fat pasture shall they feed upon the mountains of Israel.

[15]I will feed My sheep and I will cause them to lie down, says the Lord God.

[16]I will seek that which was lost and bring back that which has strayed, and I will bandage the hurt *and* the crippled and will strengthen the weak *and* the sick, but I will destroy the fat and the strong [who have become hardhearted and perverse]; I will feed them with judgment *and* punishment. [Luke 19:10.]

[17]And as for you, O My flock, thus says the Lord God: Behold, I judge between sheep and sheep, between the rams and the great he-goats [the malicious and the tyrants of the pasture].

[18]Is it too little for you that you feed on the best pasture, but you must tread down with your feet the rest of your pasture? And to have drunk of the waters clarified by subsiding, but you must foul the rest of the water with your feet?

[19]And My flock, must they feed on what your feet have trodden and drink what your feet have fouled?

[20]Therefore thus says the Lord God to them: Behold, I, I Myself, will judge between fat sheep and impoverished sheep, *or* fat goats and lean goats.

[21]Because you push with side and with shoulder and thrust with your horns all those that have become weak *and* diseased, till you have scattered them abroad,

[22]Therefore will I rescue My flock, and they shall no more be a prey; and I will judge between sheep and sheep.

[23]And I will raise up over them one Shepherd and He shall feed them, even My Servant [a]David; He shall feed

---

[a] The name of David is here put simply, as well as in Ezek. 34:24; Ezek. 37:24, 25; Jer. 30:9; Hos. 3:5, instead of the more usual designations of the Messiah as the Son (Matt. 1:1), the Branch (Jer. 23:5), the Offspring of David (Rev. 22:16). But there can be no possible doubt as to the meaning . . . . David, as the head of the theocracy and the ancestor of our Lord according to the flesh, constantly appears in the Scriptures as a type of the Messiah, and there can be no reasonable doubt that the prophecy would have been so understood, even at the time it was uttered (Charles Ellicott, *A Bible Commentary*).

## New International Version

servant David, and he will tend them; he will tend them and be their shepherd. 24I the LORD will be their God, and my servant David will be prince among them. I the LORD have spoken.

25"'I will make a covenant of peace with them and rid the land of savage beasts so that they may live in the wilderness and sleep in the forests in safety. 26I will make them and the places surrounding my hill a blessing.*a* I will send down showers in season; there will be showers of blessing. 27The trees will yield their fruit and the ground will yield its crops; the people will be secure in their land. They will know that I am the LORD, when I break the bars of their yoke and rescue them from the hands of those who enslaved them. 28They will no longer be plundered by the nations, nor will wild animals devour them. They will live in safety, and no one will make them afraid. 29I will provide for them a land renowned for its crops, and they will no longer be victims of famine in the land or bear the scorn of the nations. 30Then they will know that I, the LORD their God, am with them and that they, the Israelites, are my people, declares the Sovereign LORD. 31You are my sheep, the sheep of my pasture, and I am your God, declares the Sovereign LORD.'"

### A Prophecy Against Edom

**35** The word of the LORD came to me: 2"Son of man, set your face against Mount Seir; prophesy against it 3and say: 'This is what the Sovereign LORD says: I am against you, Mount Seir, and I will stretch out my hand against you and make you a desolate waste. 4I will turn your towns into ruins and you will be desolate. Then you will know that I am the LORD.

5"'Because you harbored an ancient hostility and delivered the Israelites over to the sword at the time of their calamity, the time their punishment reached its climax, 6therefore as surely as I live, declares the Sovereign LORD, I will give you over to bloodshed and it will pursue you. Since you did not hate bloodshed, bloodshed will pursue you. 7I will make Mount Seir a desolate waste and cut off from it all who come and go. 8I will fill your mountains with the slain; those killed by the sword will fall on your hills and in your valleys and in all your ravines. 9I will

*a 26 Or I will cause them and the places surrounding my hill to be named in blessings (see Gen. 48:20); or I will cause them and the places surrounding my hill to be seen as blessed*

## Amplified Bible

them and He shall be their Shepherd. [Ezek. 37:24; John 10:14-18.]

24And I the Lord will be their God and My Servant David a Prince among them; I the Lord have spoken it.

25And I will confirm with them a covenant of peace and will cause the evil beasts to cease out of the land, and [My people] shall dwell safely in the wilderness, desert, *or* pastureland and sleep [confidently] in the woods. [Ps. 127:2b; Isa. 11:6-9; John 14:27; 16:33.]

26And I will make them and the places round about My hill a blessing, and I will cause the showers to come down in their season; there shall be showers of blessing [of good insured by God's favor].

27And the tree of the field shall yield its fruit and the earth shall yield its increase; and [My people] shall be secure in their land, and they shall be confident *and* know (understand and realize) that I am the Lord, when I have broken the bars of their yoke and delivered them out of the hand of those who made slaves of them.

28And they shall no more be a prey to the nations, nor shall the beasts of the earth devour them, but they shall dwell safely and none shall make them afraid [in the *a* day of the Messiah's reign]. [Isa. 60:21; 61:3.]

29And I will raise up for them a planting of crops for renown, and they shall be no more consumed with hunger in the land nor bear the reproach of the nations any longer.

30Then shall they know [positively] that I, the Lord their God, am with them and that they, the house of Israel, are My people, says the Lord God,

31And that you, My sheep, the sheep of My pasture, are [only] men and I am your God, says the Lord God.

**35** Moreover, the word of the Lord came to me, saying,

2Son of man, set your face against the mountain [range of] Seir [in Edom] and prophesy against it,

3And say to it, Thus says the Lord God: Behold, O Mount Seir, I am against you, and I will stretch out My hand against you and I will make you a desolation and an astonishment.

4I will lay your cities waste and you shall be desolate, and you shall know, understand, *and* realize that I am the Lord [the Sovereign Ruler, Who calls forth loyalty and obedient service].

5Because you [of Esau] have had a perpetual enmity [for Jacob] and you gave over the sons of Israel to the power of the sword at the time of their calamity, when they were suffering their final punishment [the Babylonian conquest], [Ezek. 25:12-14; 36:5.]

6Therefore, as I live, says the Lord God, I will expose you to slaughter and slaughter shall pursue you; since you could not bear to live without bloodshed, therefore bloodshed shall pursue you.

7Thus will I make Mount Seir an astonishment and a desolation, and I will cut off from it him who passes through it and him who returns [that way].

8And I will fill [Edom's] mountains with his slain men; on your hills and in your valleys and in all your ravines shall those fall who are slain with the sword.

*a* One day when Jesus visited the synagogue in Nazareth (Luke 4:16-21), He was handed the roll of the book of Isaiah to read aloud. He deliberately turned to Isaiah 61, which tells in its eleven verses what His coming to the world would mean. But Jesus read only a few lines of the chapter, stopping in the midst of a sentence, and said, "This day is this scripture fulfilled in your ears" (Luke 4:21 KJV). He had just read of His coming to preach the Gospel, to proclaim release to the captives [of Satan], to give sight to the blind, to set at liberty the bruised, and to proclaim the acceptable year of the Lord. But He had to stop there, for the rest of the chapter could not be fulfilled until His second coming, of which Isaiah's prophecy tells. This section before us in Ezekiel (34:24-31) is telling of the same Messianic reign of which so many Scripture passages speak, the Messianic reign for which Jesus definitely promised to return to earth. [Matt. 25:31-34; 24:30; Rev. 1:7, 8. (See also Luke 1:32, 33; Acts 1:10, 11).]

## New International Version

make you desolate forever; your towns will not be inhabited. Then you will know that I am the LORD.

¹⁰"'Because you have said, "These two nations and countries will be ours and we will take possession of them," even though I the LORD was there, ¹¹therefore as surely as I live, declares the Sovereign LORD, I will treat you in accordance with the anger and jealousy you showed in your hatred of them and I will make myself known among them when I judge you. ¹²Then you will know that I the LORD have heard all the contemptible things you have said against the mountains of Israel. You said, "They have been laid waste and have been given over to us to devour." ¹³You boasted against me and spoke against me without restraint, and I heard it. ¹⁴This is what the Sovereign LORD says: While the whole earth rejoices, I will make you desolate. ¹⁵Because you rejoiced when the inheritance of Israel became desolate, that is how I will treat you. You will be desolate, Mount Seir, you and all of Edom. Then they will know that I am the LORD.'"

### Hope for the Mountains of Israel

**36** "Son of man, prophesy to the mountains of Israel and say, 'Mountains of Israel, hear the word of the LORD. ²This is what the Sovereign LORD says: The enemy said of you, "Aha! The ancient heights have become our possession."' ³Therefore prophesy and say, 'This is what the Sovereign LORD says: Because they ravaged and crushed you from every side so that you became the possession of the rest of the nations and the object of people's malicious talk and slander, ⁴therefore, mountains of Israel, hear the word of the Sovereign LORD: This is what the Sovereign LORD says to the mountains and hills, to the ravines and valleys, to the desolate ruins and the deserted towns that have been plundered and ridiculed by the rest of the nations around you— ⁵this is what the Sovereign LORD says: In my burning zeal I have spoken against the rest of the nations, and against all Edom, for with glee and with malice in their hearts they made my land their own possession so that they might plunder its pastureland.' ⁶Therefore prophesy concerning the land of Israel and say to the mountains and hills, to the ravines and valleys: 'This is what the Sovereign LORD says: I speak in my jealous wrath because you have suffered the scorn of the na-

## Amplified Bible

⁹I will make you a perpetual desolation and your ᵃcities shall not be inhabited. Then you will know, understand, and realize that I am the Lord [the Sovereign Ruler, Who calls forth loyalty and obedient service].

¹⁰Because you [Edom] said, These two nations [Israel and Judah] and these two countries shall be mine and we will take possession of them—although the Lord was there,

¹¹Therefore, as I live, says the Lord God, I will deal with you according to the anger and envy you showed because of your enmity for them, and I will make Myself known among them [as He Who will judge and punish] when I judge and punish you.

¹²And you shall know, understand, and realize that I am the Lord [the Sovereign Ruler, Who calls forth loyalty and obedient service], and that I have heard all your revilings and scornful speeches that you have uttered against the mountains of Israel, saying, They are laid waste and desolate; they are given to us to devour.

¹³Thus you have boasted and magnified yourselves against Me with your mouth, multiplying your words against Me; I have heard it.

¹⁴Thus says the Lord God: While the whole earth rejoices, I will make you a waste and desolation.

¹⁵As you rejoiced over the inheritance of the house of Israel because it was desolate, so will I deal with you; you shall be a waste and desolation, O Mount Seir and all Edom, all of it. Then they shall know, understand, and realize that I am the Lord [the Sovereign Ruler, Who calls forth loyalty and obedient service].

**36** Also you, son of man, prophesy to the mountains of Israel and say, You mountains of Israel, hear the word of the Lord.

²Thus says the Lord God: Because the enemy has said over you, Aha! and, The ancient heights have become our possession,

³Therefore prophesy and say, Thus says the Lord God: Because, yes, because they made you a desolation, and they snapped after and crushed you from every side so that you became the possession of the rest of the nations and you became the talk and evil gossip of the people,

⁴Therefore, O mountains of Israel, hear the word of the Lord God: Thus says the Lord God to the mountains and hills, to the ravines and valleys, to the desolate wastes and the cities that are forsaken, that have become a prey and derision to the rest of the nations that are round about;

⁵Therefore thus says the Lord God: Surely in the fire of My hot jealousy have I spoken against the rest of the nations and against all Edom, who have given to themselves My land with wholehearted joy and with uttermost contempt, that they might empty it out and possess it for a prey and a spoil.

⁶Prophesy therefore concerning the land of Israel and say to the mountains and hills, to the ravines and valleys, Thus says the Lord God: Behold, I have spoken in My jealousy and in My wrath because you have suffered the shame and reproach of the nations;

---

ᵃ The Edomites gave whatever help they could to Nebuchadnezzar when he captured Judah (Ps. 137:7; Obad. 11-14). Later these cousins of the Israelites were pushed out of their own country into southern Judea; Hebron became their chief city. When in A.D. 70 the Romans under Titus besieged Jerusalem, Josephus says that the Edomites joined the Jews in rebellion against the attackers, and 20,000 were admitted into the city as defenders of the Holy City. But once in, they pillaged the city, raping and killing, not even sparing the priests—though these traitors themselves had been previously forced to become circumcised and recognized as Jews. The Roman conqueror slew them, and Edom ceased to be. The forecasts of the prophets regarding Edom are in striking contrast to those of their neighbors, Moab and Ammon. The latter two countries were to suffer great and severe judgments, as was Edom. But restoration and renewed prosperity were promised to them "in the latter days" (Jer. 48:47; 49:6), while Edom was never to be rebuilt. This is all obviously nearing fulfillment in the twentieth century. Truly Edom is the scene of "a perpetual desolation," with no hint of restoration.

## New International Version

tions. ⁷Therefore this is what the Sovereign LORD says: I swear with uplifted hand that the nations around you will also suffer scorn.

⁸"But you, mountains of Israel, will produce branches and fruit for my people Israel, for they will soon come home. ⁹I am concerned for you and will look on you with favor; you will be plowed and sown, ¹⁰and I will cause many people to live on you—yes, all of Israel. The towns will be inhabited and the ruins rebuilt. ¹¹I will increase the number of people and animals living on you, and they will be fruitful and become numerous. I will settle people on you as in the past and will make you prosper more than before. Then you will know that I am the LORD. ¹²I will cause people, my people Israel, to live on you. They will possess you, and you will be their inheritance; you will never again deprive them of their children.

¹³"This is what the Sovereign LORD says: Because some say to you, "You devour people and deprive your nation of its children," ¹⁴therefore you will no longer devour people or make your nation childless, declares the Sovereign LORD. ¹⁵No longer will I make you hear the taunts of the nations, and no longer will you suffer the scorn of the peoples or cause your nation to fall, declares the Sovereign LORD.'"

### Israel's Restoration Assured

¹⁶Again the word of the LORD came to me: ¹⁷"Son of man, when the people of Israel were living in their own land, they defiled it by their conduct and their actions. Their conduct was like a woman's monthly uncleanness in my sight. ¹⁸So I poured out my wrath on them because they had shed blood in the land and because they had defiled it with their idols. ¹⁹I dispersed them among the nations, and they were scattered through the countries; I judged them according to their conduct and their actions. ²⁰And wherever they went among the nations they profaned my holy name, for it was said of them, 'These are the LORD's people, and yet they had to leave his land.' ²¹I had concern for my holy name, which the people of Israel profaned among the nations where they had gone.

²²"Therefore say to the Israelites, 'This is what the Sovereign LORD says: It is not for your sake, people of Israel, that I am going to do these things, but for the sake of my holy name, which you have profaned among the nations where you have gone. ²³I will show the holiness of my great name, which has been profaned among the nations, the name you have profaned among them. Then the nations will know that I am the LORD, declares the Sovereign LORD, when I am proved holy through you before their eyes.

## Amplified Bible

⁷Therefore thus says the Lord God: I have lifted up My hand *and* sworn, Surely the nations that are round about you shall themselves suffer shame and reproach.

⁸But you, O mountains of Israel, shall shoot forth your branches and yield your fruit to My people Israel, for they are soon to come [home].

⁹For behold, I am for you and I will turn to you; and you shall be tilled and sown,

¹⁰And I will multiply men upon you, the whole house of Israel, even all of it; the cities shall be inhabited and the waste places shall be rebuilt,

¹¹And I will multiply upon you man and beast, and they shall increase and be fruitful. And I will cause you to be inhabited according to your former estate and I will do better for you than at your beginnings; and you shall know, understand, *and* realize that I am the Lord [the Sovereign Ruler, Who calls forth loyalty and obedient service].

¹²Yes, [O mountains of Israel] I will cause men to walk upon you, even My people Israel, and they shall possess you, and you shall be their inheritance; and you shall no more after this bereave them of children [for idol sacrifices].

¹³Thus says the Lord God: Because they say to you, You [O land] are a devourer of men and have bereaved your nation of children [offered to idols],

¹⁴Therefore you shall devour men no more, neither bereave your nation *or* cause it to stumble any more, says the Lord God.

¹⁵Neither will I let you hear any more the reproach of the nations, nor shall you suffer the dishonor of the peoples any more, nor shall you cause your nation to stumble *and* fall any more [through idolatry], says Lord God.

¹⁶Moreover, the word of the Lord came to me, saying,

¹⁷Son of man, when the house of Israel dwelt in their own land, they defiled it by [doing] their [own] way and by their [idolatrous] doings. Their conduct before Me was like the uncleanness of a woman during her [physical] impurity.

¹⁸So I poured out My wrath upon them for the blood that they had shed upon the land and for their idols with which they had defiled it.

¹⁹And I scattered them among the nations, and they were dispersed through the countries; according to their conduct and their [idolatrous] deeds I judged *and* punished them.

²⁰And when they came to the nations to which they went, they profaned My holy name in that men said of them, These are the people of the Lord, and yet they had to go forth out of His land.

²¹But I had regard, concern, *and* compassion for My holy name, which the house of Israel had profaned among the nations to which they went.

²²Therefore say to the house of Israel, Thus says the Lord God: I do not do this for your sakes, O house of Israel, but for My holy name's sake, which you have profaned among the nations to which you went.

²³And I will vindicate the holiness of My great name *and* separate it for its holy purpose from all that defiles it—My name, which has been profaned among the nations, which you have profaned among them—and the nations will know, understand, *and* realize that I am the Lord [the Sovereign Ruler, Who calls forth loyalty and obedient service], when I shall be set apart by you *and* My holiness vindicated in you before their eyes *and* yours.

## New International Version

[24]"'For I will take you out of the nations; I will gather you from all the countries and bring you back into your own land. [25]I will sprinkle clean water on you, and you will be clean; I will cleanse you from all your impurities and from all your idols. [26]I will give you a new heart and put a new spirit in you; I will remove from you your heart of stone and give you a heart of flesh. [27]And I will put my Spirit in you and move you to follow my decrees and be careful to keep my laws. [28]Then you will live in the land I gave your ancestors; you will be my people, and I will be your God. [29]I will save you from all your uncleanness. I will call for the grain and make it plentiful and will not bring famine upon you. [30]I will increase the fruit of the trees and the crops of the field, so that you will no longer suffer disgrace among the nations because of famine. [31]Then you will remember your evil ways and wicked deeds, and you will loathe yourselves for your sins and detestable practices. [32]I want you to know that I am not doing this for your sake, declares the Sovereign LORD. Be ashamed and disgraced for your conduct, people of Israel!

[33]"'This is what the Sovereign LORD says: On the day I cleanse you from all your sins, I will resettle your towns, and the ruins will be rebuilt. [34]The desolate land will be cultivated instead of lying desolate in the sight of all who pass through it. [35]They will say, "This land that was laid waste has become like the garden of Eden; the cities that were lying in ruins, desolate and destroyed, are now fortified and inhabited." [36]Then the nations around you that remain will know that I the LORD have rebuilt what was destroyed and have replanted what was desolate. I the LORD have spoken, and I will do it.'

[37]"This is what the Sovereign LORD says: Once again I will yield to Israel's plea and do this for them: I will make their people as numerous as sheep, [38]as numerous as the flocks for offerings at Jerusalem during her appointed festivals. So will the ruined cities be filled with flocks of people. Then they will know that I am the LORD."

### The Valley of Dry Bones

**37** The hand of the LORD was on me, and he brought me out by the Spirit of the LORD and set me in the middle of a valley; it was full of bones. [2]He led me back and forth among them, and I saw a great many bones on the floor of the valley, bones that were very dry. [3]He asked me, "Son of man, can these bones live?"

I said, "Sovereign LORD, you alone know."

[4]Then he said to me, "Prophesy to these bones and say to them, 'Dry bones, hear the word of the LORD! [5]This is what the Sovereign LORD says to these bones: I will make breath[a] enter you, and you will come to life. [6]I will attach

---

[a] 5 The Hebrew for this word can also mean *wind* or *spirit* (see verses 6-14).

## Amplified Bible

[24]For I will [a]take you from among the nations and gather you out of all countries and bring you into your own land.

[25]Then will I sprinkle clean water upon you, and you shall be clean from all your uncleanness; and from all your idols will I cleanse you.

[26]A new heart will I give you and a new spirit will I put within you, and I will take away the stony heart out of your flesh and give you a heart of flesh.

[27]And I will put my Spirit within you and cause you to walk in My statutes, and you shall heed My ordinances and do them.

[28]And you shall dwell in the land that I gave to your fathers; and you shall be My people, and I will be your God.

[29]I will also save you from all your uncleannesses, and I will call forth the grain and make it abundant and lay no famine on you.

[30]And I will multiply the fruit of the tree and the increase of the field, that you may no more suffer the reproach *and* disgrace of famine among the nations.

[31]Then you shall [earnestly] remember your own evil ways and your doings that were not good, and shall loathe yourselves in your own sight for your iniquities and for your abominable deeds.

[32]Not for your sake do I do this, says the Lord God; let that be known to you. Be ashamed and confounded for your [own] wicked ways, O house of Israel!

[33]Thus says the Lord God: In the day that I cleanse you from all your iniquities I will [also] cause [Israel's] cities to be inhabited, and the waste places shall be rebuilt.

[34]And the desolate land shall be tilled, that which had lain desolate in the sight of all who passed by.

[35]And they shall say, This land that was desolate has become like the garden of Eden, and the waste and desolate and ruined cities are fortified and inhabited.

[36]Then the nations that are left round about you shall know that I the Lord have rebuilt the ruined places and replanted that which was desolate. I the Lord have spoken it, and I will do it.

[37]Thus says the Lord God: For this also I will let the house of Israel inquire of Me to do it for them; I will increase their men like a flock.

[38]Like the flock of holy things for sacrifice, like the flock of Jerusalem in her [solemn] appointed feasts, so shall the waste cities be filled with flocks of men; and they shall know, understand, *and* realize that I am the Lord [the Sovereign Ruler, Who calls forth loyalty and obedient service].

**37** The hand of the Lord was upon me, and He brought me out in the Spirit of the Lord and set me down in the midst of the valley; and it was full of bones.

[2]And He caused me to pass round about among them, and behold, there were very many [human bones] in the open valley *or* plain, and behold, they were very dry.

[3]And He said to me, Son of man, can these bones live? And I answered, O Lord God, You know! [I Cor. 15:35.]

[4]Again He said to me, Prophesy to these bones and say to them, O you dry bones, hear the word of the Lord. [John 5:28.]

[5]Thus says the Lord God to these bones: Behold, I will cause breath *and* spirit to enter you, and you shall live;

---

[a] No person needs to be reminded of the startling way in which this prophecy has been in the process of fulfillment since World War II. The Jews have for centuries been dispersed among all the nations with only a few left in the homeland which lay waste and desolate. It was said that travelers in Palestine had no difficulty in recognizing the appropriateness of Ezekiel's label for the country: a "valley . . . full of bones" (Ezek. 37:1). But by A.D. 1960 one-sixth of the Jewish population of the world was in Palestine. Already they had been made "one nation" (Ezek. 37:22a)—between sunrise of one day and sunset of the next—"a nation born in one day" (Isa. 66:8)! But the greatest event of all is yet to come (Ezek. 37:22b-25). This prophecy will be fulfilled in its entirety.

## New International Version

tendons to you and make flesh come upon you and cover you with skin; I will put breath in you, and you will come to life. Then you will know that I am the LORD.'"

⁷So I prophesied as I was commanded. And as I was prophesying, there was a noise, a rattling sound, and the bones came together, bone to bone. ⁸I looked, and tendons and flesh appeared on them and skin covered them, but there was no breath in them.

⁹Then he said to me, "Prophesy to the breath; prophesy, son of man, and say to it, 'This is what the Sovereign LORD says: Come, breath, from the four winds and breathe into these slain, that they may live.'" ¹⁰So I prophesied as he commanded me, and breath entered them; they came to life and stood up on their feet—a vast army.

¹¹Then he said to me: "Son of man, these bones are the people of Israel. They say, 'Our bones are dried up and our hope is gone; we are cut off.' ¹²Therefore prophesy and say to them: 'This is what the Sovereign LORD says: My people, I am going to open your graves and bring you up from them; I will bring you back to the land of Israel. ¹³Then you, my people, will know that I am the LORD, when I open your graves and bring you up from them. ¹⁴I will put my Spirit in you and you will live, and I will settle you in your own land. Then you will know that I the LORD have spoken, and I have done it, declares the LORD.'"

### One Nation Under One King

¹⁵The word of the LORD came to me: ¹⁶"Son of man, take a stick of wood and write on it, 'Belonging to Judah and the Israelites associated with him.' Then take another stick of wood, and write on it, 'Belonging to Joseph (that is, to Ephraim) and all the Israelites associated with him.' ¹⁷Join them together into one stick so that they will become one in your hand.

¹⁸"When your people ask you, 'Won't you tell us what you mean by this?' ¹⁹say to them, 'This is what the Sovereign LORD says: I am going to take the stick of Joseph—which is in Ephraim's hand—and of the Israelite tribes associated with him, and join it to Judah's stick. I will make them into a single stick of wood, and they will become one in my hand.' ²⁰Hold before their eyes the sticks you have written on ²¹and say to them, 'This is what the Sovereign LORD says: I will take the Israelites out of the nations where they have gone. I will gather them from all around and bring them back into their own land. ²²I will make them one nation in the land, on the mountains of Israel. There will be one king over all of them and they will never again be two nations or be divided into two kingdoms. ²³They will no longer defile themselves with their idols and vile images or with any of their offenses, for I will save them from all their sinful backsliding,ᵃ and I will cleanse them. They will be my people, and I will be their God.

²⁴"My servant David will be king over them, and they will all have one shepherd. They will follow my laws and be careful to keep my decrees. ²⁵They will live in the land

## Amplified Bible

⁶And I will lay sinews upon you and bring up flesh upon you and cover you with skin, and I will put breath *and* spirit in you, and you [dry bones] shall live; and you shall know, understand, *and* realize that I am the Lord [the Sovereign Ruler, Who calls forth loyalty and obedient service].

⁷So I prophesied as I was commanded; and as I prophesied, there was a [thundering] noise and behold, a shaking *and* trembling *and* a rattling, and the bones came together, bone to its bone.

⁸And I looked and behold, there were sinews upon [the bones] and flesh came upon them and skin covered them over, but there was no breath *or* spirit in them.

⁹Then said He to me, Prophesy to the breath *and* spirit, son of man, and say to the breath *and* spirit, Thus says the Lord God: Come from the four winds, O breath *and* spirit, and breathe upon these slain that they may live.

¹⁰So I prophesied as He commanded me, and the breath *and* spirit came into [the bones], and they lived and stood up upon their feet, an exceedingly great host. [Rev. 11:11.]

¹¹Then He said to me, Son of man, these bones are the whole house of Israel. Behold, they say, Our bones are dried up and our hope is lost; we are completely cut off.

¹²Therefore prophesy and say to them, Thus says the Lord God: Behold, I will open your graves and cause you to come up out of your graves, O My people; and I will bring you [back home] to the land of Israel. [Hos. 13:14.]

¹³And you shall know that I am the Lord [your Sovereign Ruler], when I have opened your graves and caused you to come up out of your graves, O My people.

¹⁴And I shall put My Spirit in you and you shall live, and I shall place you in your own land. Then you shall know, understand, *and* realize that I the Lord have spoken it and performed it, says the Lord.

¹⁵The word of the Lord came again to me, saying,

¹⁶Son of man, take a stick and write on it, For Judah and the children of Israel his companions; then take another stick and write upon it, For Joseph, the stick of Ephraim, and all the house of Israel his companions;

¹⁷And join them together into one stick that they may become one in your hand.

¹⁸And when your people say to you, Will you not show us what you mean by these?

¹⁹Say to them, Thus says the Lord God: Behold, I will take the stick of Joseph—which is in the hand of Ephraim—and the tribes of Israel his associates, and will join with it the stick of Judah and make them one stick, and they shall be one in My hand.

²⁰When the sticks on which you write shall be in your hand before their eyes,

²¹Then say to them, Thus says the Lord God: Behold, I will take the children of Israel from among the nations to which they have gone, and will ᵃgather them from every side and bring them into their own land.

²²And I will make them one nation in the land, upon the mountains of Israel, and one ᵇKing shall be King over them all; and they shall be no longer two nations, neither be divided into two kingdoms any more. [Jer. 50:4.]

²³They shall not defile themselves any more with their idols and their detestable things or with any of their transgressions, but I will save them out of all their dwelling places *and* from all their backslidings in which they have sinned, and I will cleanse them. So shall they be My people, and I will be their God.

²⁴And ᶜDavid My Servant shall be King over them, and they all shall have one Shepherd. They shall also walk in My ordinances and heed My statutes and do them.

---

ᵃ 23 Many Hebrew manuscripts (see also Septuagint); most Hebrew manuscripts *all their dwelling places where they sinned*

ᵃ See footnote on Ezek. 36:24. ᵇ Reference to the coming Messianic ruler, Who would achieve for Israel what David had—only more fully. See also footnote on Ezek. 34:23. ᶜ See footnote on Ezek. 34:23.

## New International Version

I gave to my servant Jacob, the land where your ancestors lived. They and their children and their children's children will live there forever, and David my servant will be their prince forever. 26 I will make a covenant of peace with them; it will be an everlasting covenant. I will establish them and increase their numbers, and I will put my sanctuary among them forever. 27 My dwelling place will be with them; I will be their God, and they will be my people. 28 Then the nations will know that I the LORD make Israel holy, when my sanctuary is among them forever.'"

### The LORD's Great Victory Over the Nations

**38** The word of the LORD came to me: 2 "Son of man, set your face against Gog, of the land of Magog, the chief prince ofᵃ Meshek and Tubal; prophesy against him 3 and say: 'This is what the Sovereign LORD says: I am against you, Gog, chief prince ofᵇ Meshek and Tubal. 4 I will turn you around, put hooks in your jaws and bring you out with your whole army—your horses, your horsemen fully armed, and a great horde with large and small shields, all of them brandishing their swords. 5 Persia, Cushᶜ and Put will be with them, all with shields and helmets, 6 also Gomer with all its troops, and Beth Togarmah from the far north with all its troops—the many nations with you.

7 "'Get ready; be prepared, you and all the hordes gathered about you, and take command of them. 8 After many days you will be called to arms. In future years you will invade a land that has recovered from war, whose people were gathered from many nations to the mountains of Israel, which had long been desolate. They had been brought out from the nations, and now all of them live in safety. 9 You and all your troops and the many nations with you will go up, advancing like a storm; you will be like a cloud covering the land.

10 "'This is what the Sovereign LORD says: On that day thoughts will come into your mind and you will devise an evil scheme. 11 You will say, "I will invade a land of unwalled villages; I will attack a peaceful and unsuspecting people—all of them living without walls and without gates and bars. 12 I will plunder and loot and turn my hand against the resettled ruins and the people gathered from the nations, rich in livestock and goods, living at the center of the land.ᵈ" 13 Sheba and Dedan and the merchants of Tarshish and all her villagesᵉ will say to you, "Have you come to plunder? Have you gathered your hordes to loot, to carry off silver and gold, to take away livestock and goods and to seize much plunder?"'

14 "Therefore, son of man, prophesy and say to Gog: 'This is what the Sovereign LORD says: In that day, when my people Israel are living in safety, will you not take notice of it? 15 You will come from your place in the far north,

## Amplified Bible

25 They shall dwell in the land in which your fathers dwelt, that I gave to My servant Jacob, and they shall dwell there, they and their children and their children's children, forever; and My Servant David shall be their Prince forever. [Isa. 60:21; Joel 3:20; Amos 9:15.]
26 I will make a covenant of peace with them; it shall be an everlasting covenant with them, and I will give blessings to them and multiply them and will set My sanctuary in the midst of them forevermore.
27 My tabernacle or dwelling place also shall be with them; and I will be their God, and they shall be My people.
28 Then the nations shall know, understand, and realize that I the Lord do set apart and consecrate Israel for holy use, when My sanctuary shall be in their midst forevermore.

**38** And the word of the Lord came to me, saying, 2 Son of man, set your face against Gog, of the land of ᵃMagog, the prince of Rosh, of Meshech, and of Tubal, and prophesy against him,
3 And say, Thus says the Lord God: Behold, I am against you, O Gog, chief prince (ruler) of Rosh, of Meshech, and of Tubal.
4 And I will turn you back and put hooks into your jaws, and I will bring you forth and all your army, horses and horsemen, all of them clothed in full armor, a great company with buckler and shield, all of them handling swords—
5 Persia, Cush, and Put or Libya with them, all of them with shield and helmet,
6 Gomer and all his hordes, the house of Togarmah in the uttermost parts of the north and all his hordes—many people are with you.
7 You [Gog] be prepared; yes, prepare yourself, you and all your companies that are assembled about you, and you be a guard and a commander for them.
8 After many days you shall be visited and mustered [for service]; in the latter years you shall go against the land that is restored from the ravages of the sword, where people are gathered out of many nations upon the mountains of Israel, which had been a continual waste; but its [people] are brought forth out of the nations and they shall dwell securely, all of them. [Isa. 24:22.]
9 You shall ascend and come like a storm; you shall be like a cloud to cover the land, you and all your hosts and many people with you.
10 Thus says the Lord God: At the same time thoughts shall come into your mind, and you will devise an evil plan.
11 And you will say, I will go up against an open country [the land of unwalled villages]; I will fall upon those who are at rest, who dwell securely, all of them dwelling without walls and having neither bars nor gates,
12 To take spoil and prey, to turn your hand upon the desolate places now inhabited and assail the people gathered out of the nations, who have obtained livestock and goods, who dwell at the center of the earth [Palestine].
13 Sheba and Dedan and the merchants of Tarshish, with all their lionlike cubs [or satellite areas], shall say to you, Have you come to take spoil? Have you gathered your hosts to take the prey? To carry away silver and gold, to take away livestock and goods, to take a great spoil?
14 Therefore, son of man, prophesy and say to Gog, Thus says the Lord God: In that day when My people Israel dwell securely, will you not know it and be aroused?
15 And you will come from your place out of the utter-

---

ᵃ 2 Or *the prince of Rosh,* ᵇ 3 Or *Gog, prince of Rosh,* ᶜ 5 That is, the upper Nile region ᵈ 12 The Hebrew for this phrase means *the navel of the earth.* ᵉ 13 Or *her strong lions*

ᵃ Gog is a symbolic name, representing the leader of the world powers antagonistic to God (see also Rev. 20:8). Meshech and Tubal are understood to have been the same as the Moschi and Tibareni of the Greeks—tribes that inhabited regions in the Caucasus. Rosh, which some would identify with Russia, must have designated a land and people somewhere in the same area. And therefore the Gog of Ezekiel must be viewed as in some sense the head of the high regions in the northwest of Asia. (Patrick Fairbairn, *The Imperial Bible-dictionary*).

## New International Version

you and many nations with you, all of them riding on horses, a great horde, a mighty army. 16You will advance against my people Israel like a cloud that covers the land. In days to come, Gog, I will bring you against my land, so that the nations may know me when I am proved holy through you before their eyes.

17"'This is what the Sovereign LORD says: You are the one I spoke of in former days by my servants the prophets of Israel. At that time they prophesied for years that I would bring you against them. 18This is what will happen in that day: When Gog attacks the land of Israel, my hot anger will be aroused, declares the Sovereign LORD. 19In my zeal and fiery wrath I declare that at that time there shall be a great earthquake in the land of Israel. 20The fish in the sea, the birds in the sky, the beasts of the field, every creature that moves along the ground, and all the people on the face of the earth will tremble at my presence. The mountains will be overturned, the cliffs will crumble and every wall will fall to the ground. 21I will summon a sword against Gog on all my mountains, declares the Sovereign LORD. Every man's sword will be against his brother. 22I will execute judgment on him with plague and bloodshed; I will pour down torrents of rain, hailstones and burning sulfur on him and on his troops and on the many nations with him. 23And so I will show my greatness and my holiness, and I will make myself known in the sight of many nations. Then they will know that I am the LORD.'

**39** "Son of man, prophesy against Gog and say: 'This is what the Sovereign LORD says: I am against you, Gog, chief prince of*a* Meshek and Tubal. 2I will turn you around and drag you along. I will bring you from the far north and send you against the mountains of Israel. 3Then I will strike your bow from your left hand and make your arrows drop from your right hand. 4On the mountains of Israel you will fall, you and all your troops and the nations with you. I will give you as food to all kinds of carrion birds and to the wild animals. 5You will fall in the open field, for I have spoken, declares the Sovereign LORD. 6I will send fire on Magog and on those who live in safety in the coastlands, and they will know that I am the LORD.

7"'I will make known my holy name among my people Israel. I will no longer let my holy name be profaned, and the nations will know that I the LORD am the Holy One in Israel. 8It is coming! It will surely take place, declares the Sovereign LORD. This is the day I have spoken of.

9"'Then those who live in the towns of Israel will go out and use the weapons for fuel and burn them up—the small and large shields, the bows and arrows, the war clubs and spears. For seven years they will use them for fuel. 10They will not need to gather wood from the fields or cut it from the forests, because they will use the weapons for fuel.

## Amplified Bible

most parts of the north, you and many peoples with you, all of them riding on horses, a great host, a mighty army.

16And you shall come up against My people Israel like a cloud to cover the land. In the latter days I will bring you against My land, that the nations may know, understand, *and* realize Me when My holiness shall be vindicated through you [vindicated and honored in your overwhelming destruction], O Gog, before their eyes.

17Thus says the Lord God: Are you he of whom I have spoken in olden times by My servants the prophets of Israel, who prophesied in those days for years that I would bring you [Gog] against them?

18But in that day when Gog shall come against the land of Israel, says the Lord God, My wrath shall come up into My nostrils.

19For in My jealousy and in the fire of My wrath have I said, Surely in that day there shall be a great shaking *or* cosmic catastrophe in the land of Israel,

20So that the fishes of the sea and the birds of the heavens, the beasts of the field and all creeping things that creep upon the earth, and all the men that are upon the face of the earth, shall tremble *and* shake at My presence; and the mountains shall be thrown down and the steep places shall fall and every wall [natural or artificial] shall fall to the ground.

21And I will call for a sword against [Gog] throughout all My mountains, says the Lord God, every man's sword shall be against his brother [over the dividing of booty].

22And with pestilence and with bloodshed will I enter into judgment with [Gog], and I will rain upon him and upon his hordes and upon the many peoples that are with him torrents of rain and great hailstones, fire and brimstone. [Ps. 11:6.]

23Thus will I demonstrate My greatness and My holiness, and I will be recognized, understood, *and* known in the eyes of many nations; yes, they shall know that I am the Lord [the Sovereign Ruler, Who calls forth loyalty and obedient service].

**39** And you, son of man, prophesy against Gog, Thus says the Lord God: Behold, I am against you, O Gog, chief prince (ruler) of Rosh, of Meshech, and of Tubal.

2And I will turn you about and will lead you on, and will cause you to come up from the uttermost parts of the north and will lead you against the mountains of Israel;

3And I will smite your bow from your left hand and will cause your arrows to fall out of your right hand.

4You shall fall [dead] upon the mountains of Israel, you and all your hosts and the peoples who are with you. I will give you to the ravenous birds of every sort and to the beasts of the field to be devoured.

5You shall fall in the open field, for I have spoken [it], says the Lord God.

6I will send fire on Magog and upon those who dwell securely in the coastlands, and they shall know, understand, *and* realize that I am the Lord [the Sovereign Ruler, Who calls forth loyalty and obedient service].

7And I will make My holy name known in the midst of My people Israel, and I will not let them profane My holy name any more; and the nations shall know, understand, *and* realize that I am the Lord, the Holy One of Israel.

8Behold, it is coming and it will be done, says the Lord God; that is the day of which I have spoken.

9And [when you, Gog, are no longer] they who dwell in the cities of Israel shall go forth and shall set on fire and burn the battle gear, the shields and the bucklers, the bows and the arrows, the handspikes *or* riding whips and the spears; and they shall burn them as fuel for seven years,

10So that My people shall take no firewood out of the field or cut down any out of the forests, for they shall make

## New International Version

And they will plunder those who plundered them and loot those who looted them, declares the Sovereign LORD.

[11]"'On that day I will give Gog a burial place in Israel, in the valley of those who travel east of the Sea. It will block the way of travelers, because Gog and all his hordes will be buried there. So it will be called the Valley of Hamon Gog.[a]

[12]"'For seven months the Israelites will be burying them in order to cleanse the land. [13]All the people of the land will bury them, and the day I display my glory will be a memorable day for them, declares the Sovereign LORD. [14]People will be continually employed in cleansing the land. They will spread out across the land and, along with others, they will bury any bodies that are lying on the ground.

"'After the seven months they will carry out a more detailed search. [15]As they go through the land, anyone who sees a human bone will leave a marker beside it until the gravediggers bury it in the Valley of Hamon Gog, [16]near a town called Hamonah.[b] And so they will cleanse the land.'

[17]"Son of man, this is what the Sovereign LORD says: Call out to every kind of bird and all the wild animals: 'Assemble and come together from all around to the sacrifice I am preparing for you, the great sacrifice on the mountains of Israel. There you will eat flesh and drink blood. [18]You will eat the flesh of mighty men and drink the blood of the princes of the earth as if they were rams and lambs, goats and bulls—all of them fattened animals from Bashan. [19]At the sacrifice I am preparing for you, you will eat fat till you are glutted and drink blood till you are drunk. [20]At my table you will eat your fill of horses and riders, mighty men and soldiers of every kind,' declares the Sovereign LORD.

[21]"I will display my glory among the nations, and all the nations will see the punishment I inflict and the hand I lay on them. [22]From that day forward the people of Israel will know that I am the LORD their God. [23]And the nations will know that the people of Israel went into exile for their sin, because they were unfaithful to me. So I hid my face from them and handed them over to their enemies, and they all fell by the sword. [24]I dealt with them according to their uncleanness and their offenses, and I hid my face from them.

[25]"Therefore this is what the Sovereign LORD says: I will now restore the fortunes of Jacob[c] and will have compassion on all the people of Israel, and I will be zealous for my holy name. [26]They will forget their shame and all the

## Amplified Bible

their fires of the weapons. And they shall despoil those who despoiled them and plunder those who plundered them, says the Lord God.

[11]And in that day, I will give to Gog a place for burial there in Israel, the valley of those who pass through on the east side in front of the [Dead] Sea [the highway between Syria, Petra, and Egypt], and it will delay *and* stop those who pass through. And there shall they [a]bury Gog and all his multitude, and they shall call it the Valley of Hamon-gog [multitude of Gog].

[12]For seven months the house of Israel will be burying them, that they may cleanse the land.

[13]Yes, all the people of the land will bury them, and it shall bring them renown in the day that I shall be glorified, says the Lord God.

[14]And they shall set apart men to work continually who shall pass through the land, men commissioned to bury, with the help of those who are passing by, those bodies that lie unburied on the face of the ground, in order to cleanse the land. After the end of seven months they shall make their search.

[15]And when these pass through the land and anyone sees a human bone, he shall set up a marker by it as a sign to the buriers, until they have buried it in the Valley of Hamon-gog *or* of Gog's multitude.

[16]And Hamonah [multitude] shall also be the name of the city [of the dead]. Thus shall they cleanse the land.

[17]And you, son of man, thus says the Lord God: Say to the birds of prey of every sort and to every beast of the field, Assemble yourselves and come, gather from every side to the sacrificial feast that I am preparing for you, even a great sacrificial feast on the mountains of Israel at which you may eat flesh and drink blood.

[18]You shall eat the flesh of the mighty and drink the blood of the princes of the earth, of rams, of lambs, of goats, and of bullocks, all of them fatlings of Bashan [east of the Jordan].

[19]And you shall eat fat till you are filled and drink blood till you are drunk at the sacrificial feast which I am preparing for you.

[20]And you shall be filled at My table with horses and riders, with mighty men, and with soldiers of every kind, says the Lord God.

[21]And I will manifest My honor *and* glory among the nations, and all the nations shall see My judgment *and* justice [in the punishment] which I have executed and My hand which I have laid on them.

[22]So the house of Israel shall know, understand, *and* realize beyond all question that I am the Lord their God from that day forward.

[23]And the nations shall know, understand, *and* realize positively that the house of Israel went into captivity for their iniquity, because they trespassed against Me; and I hid My face from them. So I gave them into the hand of their enemies and they all fell [into captivity or were slain] by the power of the sword. [Deut. 31:17.]

[24]According to their uncleanness and according to their transgressions I dealt with them and hid My face from them.

[25]Therefore thus says the Lord God: Now will I reverse the captivity of Jacob and have mercy upon the whole house of Israel and will be jealous for My holy name.

[26]They shall forget their shame *and* self-reproach and

---

[a] The number of dead bodies left after the great catastrophe which God will send upon Gog and his hosts would necessarily amount to several millions. Their graves would naturally interfere with traffic on the interstate highway. The dead will not be slain in battle. God will slay them by a great "cosmic catastrophe" (Ezek. 38:18-23). And not just some, but "all" of Gog's multitude will die then (Ezek. 39:4, 11); before they have had a chance to use their weapons, God will strike them from their hands (Ezek. 39:3). That one-sixth of the horde from the north will be left alive, as the *King James Version* says (Ezek. 39:2), is without noted exception conceded to be a mistaken translation by all authorities of modern times.

---

[a] 11 *Hamon Gog* means *hordes of Gog.*    [b] 16 *Hamonah* means *horde.*
[c] 25 Or *now bring Jacob back from captivity*

## New International Version

unfaithfulness they showed toward me when they lived in safety in their land with no one to make them afraid. [27]When I have brought them back from the nations and have gathered them from the countries of their enemies, I will be proved holy through them in the sight of many nations. [28]Then they will know that I am the LORD their God, for though I sent them into exile among the nations, I will gather them to their own land, not leaving any behind. [29]I will no longer hide my face from them, for I will pour out my Spirit on the people of Israel, declares the Sovereign LORD."

### The Temple Area Restored

**40** In the twenty-fifth year of our exile, at the beginning of the year, on the tenth of the month, in the fourteenth year after the fall of the city—on that very day the hand of the LORD was on me and he took me there. [2]In visions of God he took me to the land of Israel and set me on a very high mountain, on whose south side were some buildings that looked like a city. [3]He took me there, and I saw a man whose appearance was like bronze; he was standing in the gateway with a linen cord and a measuring rod in his hand. [4]The man said to me, "Son of man, look carefully and listen closely and pay attention to everything I am going to show you, for that is why you have been brought here. Tell the people of Israel everything you see."

*The East Gate to the Outer Court*

[5]I saw a wall completely surrounding the temple area. The length of the measuring rod in the man's hand was six long cubits,[a] each of which was a cubit and a handbreadth. He measured the wall; it was one measuring rod thick and one rod high.

[6]Then he went to the east gate. He climbed its steps and measured the threshold of the gate; it was one rod deep. [7]The alcoves for the guards were one rod long and one rod wide, and the projecting walls between the alcoves were five cubits[b] thick. And the threshold of the gate next to the portico facing the temple was one rod deep.

[8]Then he measured the portico of the gateway; [9]it[c] was eight cubits[d] deep and its jambs were two cubits[e] thick. The portico of the gateway faced the temple.

[10]Inside the east gate were three alcoves on each side; the three had the same measurements, and the faces of the projecting walls on each side had the same measurements. [11]Then he measured the width of the entrance of the gateway; it was ten cubits and its length was thirteen cubits.[f] [12]In front of each alcove was a wall one cubit high, and the alcoves were six cubits square. [13]Then he measured the gateway from the top of the rear wall of one alcove to the top of the opposite one; the distance was twenty-five cubits[g] from one parapet opening to the opposite

---

*a 5 That is, about 11 feet or about 3.2 meters; also in verse 12. The long cubit of about 21 inches or about 53 centimeters is the basic unit of measurement of length throughout chapters 40–48. b 7 That is, about 8 3/4 feet or about 2.7 meters; also in verse 48 c 8,9 Many Hebrew manuscripts, Septuagint, Vulgate and Syriac; most Hebrew manuscripts gateway facing the temple; it was one rod deep. 9Then he measured the portico of the gateway; it d 9 That is, about 14 feet or about 4.2 meters e 9 That is, about 3 1/2 feet or about 1 meter f 11 That is, about 18 feet wide and 23 feet long or about 5.3 meters wide and 6.9 meters long g 13 That is, about 44 feet or about 13 meters; also in verses 21, 25, 29, 30, 33 and 36*

## Amplified Bible

all their treachery *and* unfaithfulness in which they have transgressed against Me, when they dwell securely in their land and there is none who makes them afraid.

[27]When I have brought them again from the peoples and gathered them out of their enemies' lands, and My justice *and* holiness are set apart *and* vindicated through them in the sight of many nations, [28]Then shall they know, understand, *and* realize positively that I am the Lord their God, because I sent them into captivity *and* exile among the nations and then gathered them to their own land. I will leave none of them remaining among the nations any more [in the latter days]. [29]Neither will I hide My face any more then from them, when I have poured out My Spirit upon the house of Israel, says the Lord God.

**40** In the twenty-fifth year of our captivity [by Babylon], in the beginning of the year, on the tenth day of the month, in the fourteenth year after the city [of Jerusalem] was taken, on the very same day the hand of the Lord was upon me and He brought me to that place.

[2]In the visions of God He brought me into the land of Israel and set me down upon a very high mountain, on the south side of which there was what seemed to be the structure of a city.

[3]He brought me there, and behold, there was a man [an angel] whose appearance was like bronze, with a line of flax and a measuring reed in his hand, and he stood in the gateway.

[4]And the man said to me, Son of man, look with your eyes and hear with your ears and set your heart *and* mind on all that I will show you, for you are brought here that I may show them to you. Declare all that you see to the house of Israel.

[5]And behold, there was a wall all around the outside area of the house [of the Lord], and in the man's hand a measuring reed six long cubits in length, each cubit being longer [than the usual one] by a handbreadth; so he measured the thickness of the wall, one reed, and the height, one reed.

[6]Then he came to the gate which faced the east and went up its [seven] steps and measured the threshold of the gateway, one reed broad, and the other threshold of the gateway [inside the thick wall], one reed broad.

[7]And every room for the guards was one reed long and one reed broad, and the space between the guardrooms *or* lodges was five cubits. And the threshold of the gate by the porch *or* vestibule of the gateway within was one reed.

[8]He measured also the porch *or* vestibule of the gate toward the house [of the Lord], one reed.

[9]Then he measured the porch *or* vestibule of the gateway, eight cubits, and its posts *or* jambs, two cubits. And the porch *or* vestibule of the gate was inside [toward the house of the Lord].

[10]And the guardrooms *or* lodges of the east gateway were three on this side and three on that side; the three were the same size, and the posts *or* jambs were the same size on either side.

[11]And he measured the breadth of the opening of the gateway, ten cubits, and the length of the gateway, thirteen cubits.

[12]And a border *or* barrier before the guardrooms was one cubit on this side, and a border *or* barrier, one cubit on that side. And the guardrooms *or* lodges were six cubits on this side and six cubits on that side.

[13]And *a*the man [an angel] measured the gate from the outer wall of one chamber *or* guardroom to the outer wall of another—a breadth of twenty-five cubits from door to door.

---

*a As The Septuagint (Greek translation of the Old Testament) renders these verses. The Hebrew is obscure.*

## New International Version

one. [14] He measured along the faces of the projecting walls all around the inside of the gateway—sixty cubits.[a] The measurement was up to the portico[b] facing the courtyard.[c] [15] The distance from the entrance of the gateway to the far end of its portico was fifty cubits.[d] [16] The alcoves and the projecting walls inside the gateway were surmounted by narrow parapet openings all around, as was the portico; the openings all around faced inward. The faces of the projecting walls were decorated with palm trees.

### The Outer Court

[17] Then he brought me into the outer court. There I saw some rooms and a pavement that had been constructed all around the court; there were thirty rooms along the pavement. [18] It abutted the sides of the gateways and was as wide as they were long; this was the lower pavement. [19] Then he measured the distance from the inside of the lower gateway to the outside of the inner court; it was a hundred cubits[e] on the east side as well as on the north.

### The North Gate

[20] Then he measured the length and width of the north gate, leading into the outer court. [21] Its alcoves—three on each side—its projecting walls and its portico had the same measurements as those of the first gateway. It was fifty cubits long and twenty-five cubits wide. [22] Its openings, its portico and its palm tree decorations had the same measurements as those of the gate facing east. Seven steps led up to it, with its portico opposite them. [23] There was a gate to the inner court facing the north gate, just as there was on the east. He measured from one gate to the opposite one; it was a hundred cubits.

### The South Gate

[24] Then he led me to the south side and I saw the south gate. He measured its jambs and its portico, and they had the same measurements as the others. [25] The gateway and its portico had narrow openings all around, like the openings of the others. It was fifty cubits long and twenty-five cubits wide. [26] Seven steps led up to it, with its portico opposite them; it had palm tree decorations on the faces of the projecting walls on each side. [27] The inner court also had a gate facing south, and he measured from this gate to the outer gate on the south side; it was a hundred cubits.

### The Gates to the Inner Court

[28] Then he brought me into the inner court through the south gate, and he measured the south gate; it had the same measurements as the others. [29] Its alcoves, its projecting walls and its portico had the same measurements as the others. The gateway and its portico had openings all around. It was fifty cubits long and twenty-five cubits wide. [30] (The porticoes of the gateways around the inner court were twenty-five cubits wide and five cubits deep.) [31] Its portico faced the outer court; palm trees decorated its jambs, and eight steps led up to it.

[32] Then he brought me to the inner court on the east side, and he measured the gateway; it had the same measurements as the others. [33] Its alcoves, its projecting walls and its portico had the same measurements as the others. The gateway and its portico had openings all around. It was fifty cubits long and twenty-five cubits wide. [34] Its por-

[a] 14 That is, about 105 feet or about 32 meters    [b] 14 Septuagint;
Hebrew *projecting wall*    [c] 14 The meaning of the Hebrew for this
verse is uncertain.    [d] 15 That is, about 88 feet or about 27 meters; also
in verses 21, 25, 29, 33 and 36    [e] 19 That is, about 175 feet or about 53
meters; also in verses 23, 27 and 47

## Amplified Bible

[14] And [a] the open part of the porch *or* vestibule of the gateway on the outside was twenty cubits, the chambers *or* guardrooms of the gate being round about.

[15] And including this porch *or* vestibule of the gate on the outside and the porch *or* vestibule on the inside, the extent was fifty cubits.

[16] And there were closed windows to the guardrooms *or* chambers and to their posts *or* pillars within the gate round about, and likewise to the archway *or* vestibule; and windows were round about facing into the court, and upon each post *or* pillar were palm tree [decorations].

[17] Then he brought me into the outward court, and behold, there were chambers and a pavement round about the court; thirty chambers fronted on the pavement.

[18] And the pavement was along by the side of the gates, answerable to the length of the gateways; this was the lower pavement.

[19] Then *the man* measured the distance from the inner front before the lower gate to the outer front of the inner court, a hundred cubits, both on the east and on the north.

[20] And the gate of the outward court which faced the north, of it he measured both the length and the breadth.

[21] And its guardrooms *or* lodges, three on this side and three on that side, and its posts *or* pillars and archway *or* vestibule were the same size as those of the first gate; the length was fifty cubits and the breadth twenty-five cubits.

[22] And its windows and its archway *or* vestibule and its palm trees were of the same size as those of the gate that faces toward the east. It was reached by going up seven steps, and the archway of its vestibule was on the inner side.

[23] Opposite the gate on the north and on the east was a gate to the inner court, and he [the man with the measuring rod of reed] measured from gate to gate, a hundred cubits.

[24] After that *the man* brought me toward the south, and behold, there was a gate on the south, and he measured its posts *or* pillars and its archway *or* vestibule; they measured as the others did.

[25] And there were windows round about in it and in its archway *or* vestibule, like those windows in the other gateways; its length was fifty cubits and its breadth twenty-five cubits.

[26] And there were seven steps going up to the gate, and its archway *or* vestibule was on the inside. And it had palm trees, one on this side and another on that side, carved on its posts *or* pillars.

[27] And there was a gate to the inner court on the south, and he measured from gate to gate toward the south, a hundred cubits.

[28] And *the man* [an angel] brought me into the inner court by the south gate, and he measured the south gate; its measurements were the same as those of the other gateways.

[29] And its guardrooms *or* chambers and its posts *or* pillars and its archway *or* vestibule measured as did the others. And there were windows in the gateway and in its archway *or* vestibule round about; its length was fifty cubits and its breadth twenty-five cubits.

[30] And there was an archway *or* a vestibule round about, twenty-five cubits long and five cubits wide.

[31] And its [arched] vestibule faced the outer court; and palm trees were carved upon its posts *or* pillars, and the steps going up to it were eight.

[32] And he brought me into the inner court toward the east and he measured the gate; it measured the same as the others.

[33] And its guardrooms *or* chambers and its posts *or* pillars and its archway *or* vestibule measured as did the others. And there were windows in it and in its [arched] vestibule round about; the gateway was fifty cubits long and twenty-five cubits wide.

[a] As *The Septuagint* (Greek translation of the Old Testament) renders
these verses. The Hebrew is obscure.

# New International Version

tico faced the outer court; palm trees decorated the jambs on either side, and eight steps led up to it.

[35] Then he brought me to the north gate and measured it. It had the same measurements as the others, [36] as did its alcoves, its projecting walls and its portico, and it had openings all around. It was fifty cubits long and twenty-five cubits wide. [37] Its portico[a] faced the outer court; palm trees decorated the jambs on either side, and eight steps led up to it.

## The Rooms for Preparing Sacrifices

[38] A room with a doorway was by the portico in each of the inner gateways, where the burnt offerings were washed. [39] In the portico of the gateway were two tables on each side, on which the burnt offerings, sin offerings[b] and guilt offerings were slaughtered. [40] By the outside wall of the portico of the gateway, near the steps at the entrance of the north gateway were two tables, and on the other side of the steps were two tables. [41] So there were four tables on one side of the gateway and four on the other—eight tables in all—on which the sacrifices were slaughtered. [42] There were also four tables of dressed stone for the burnt offerings, each a cubit and a half long, a cubit and a half wide and a cubit high.[c] On them were placed the utensils for slaughtering the burnt offerings and the other sacrifices. [43] And double-pronged hooks, each a handbreadth[d] long, were attached to the wall all around. The tables were for the flesh of the offerings.

## The Rooms for the Priests

[44] Outside the inner gate, within the inner court, were two rooms, one[e] at the side of the north gate and facing south, and another at the side of the south[f] gate and facing north. [45] He said to me, "The room facing south is for the priests who guard the temple, [46] and the room facing north is for the priests who guard the altar. These are the sons of Zadok, who are the only Levites who may draw near to the Lord to minister before him."

[47] Then he measured the court: It was square—a hundred cubits long and a hundred cubits wide. And the altar was in front of the temple.

## The New Temple

[48] He brought me to the portico of the temple and measured the jambs of the portico; they were five cubits wide on either side. The width of the entrance was fourteen cubits[g] and its projecting walls were[h] three cubits[i] wide on either side. [49] The portico was twenty cubits[j] wide, and twelve[k] cubits[l] from front to back. It was reached by a flight of stairs,[m] and there were pillars on each side of the jambs.

# Amplified Bible

[34] And its [arched] vestibule faced the outer court; and palm trees were carved upon its posts or pillars on either side, and the steps leading to it were eight.

[35] And the man [an angel] brought me to the north gate and measured it; the measurements were the same as those of the other gates.

[36] Its guardrooms or chambers, its posts or pillars, its [arched] vestibule, and the windows to it round about [were of the same size as the others]. The length of the gateway was fifty cubits and the width was twenty-five cubits.

[37] And its posts or pillars were toward the outer court, and palm trees were carved upon them on either side. And the approach to it had eight steps.

[38] There was an attached chamber with its door beside the posts or pillars of the gates where the burnt offering was to be washed.

[39] And in the porch or vestibule of the gate were two tables on this side and two tables on that side, on which to slay the burnt offering and the sin offering and the trespass or guilt offering.

[40] And on the one side without, as one goes up to the entrance of the gate to the north, were two tables; and on the other side at the vestibule of the gate were two tables.

[41] Four tables were on the inside and four tables on the outside of the side of the gate, eight tables upon which the sacrifices were to be slain.

[42] Moreover, there were four tables of hewn stone for the burnt offering, a cubit and a half long, a cubit and a half broad, and one cubit high. Upon them were to be laid the instruments with which were slain the burnt offering and the sacrifice.

[43] And slabs or hooks a handbreadth long were fastened within [the room] round about. Upon the tables was to be placed the flesh of the offering.

[44] [a] Then the man [an angel] led me [from without] into the inner court, and behold, there were two chambers in the inner court: one beside the north gate but facing the south, and one beside the south gate but looking toward the north.

[45] And the man [an angel who was guiding me] said, This chamber with its view to the south is for the priests who have charge of the house [of the Lord],

[46] And the chamber with its view to the north is for the priests who have charge of the altar. These are the sons of Zadok, who alone among the sons of Levi may come near to the Lord to minister to Him.

[47] And he measured the court, a hundred cubits long and a hundred cubits broad, foursquare; and the altar was in front of the house [of the Lord].

[48] Then he brought me to the porch or vestibule of the temple proper, and he measured each post or pillar of the porch, five cubits on either side. And the width of the gate was three cubits for this [leaf] and three cubits for that one.

[49] And the length of the porch or vestibule was twenty cubits and the breadth eleven cubits; and he brought me by the steps by which it was reached, and there were two pillars standing on the posts [as bases] or beside them, one on either side of the entrance.

---

[a] 37 Septuagint (see also verses 31 and 34); Hebrew *jambs*
[b] 39 Or *purification offerings*   [c] 42 That is, about 2 2/3 feet long and wide and 21 inches high or about 80 centimeters long and wide and 53 centimeters high   [d] 43 That is, about 3 1/2 inches or about 9 centimeters   [e] 44 Septuagint; Hebrew *were rooms for singers, which were*   [f] 44 Septuagint; Hebrew *east*   [g] 48 That is, about 25 feet or about 7.4 meters   [h] 48 Septuagint; Hebrew *entrance was*   [i] 48 That is, about 5 1/4 feet or about 1.6 meters   [j] 49 That is, about 35 feet or about 11 meters   [k] 49 Septuagint; Hebrew *eleven*   [l] 49 That is, about 21 feet or about 6.4 meters   [m] 49 Hebrew; Septuagint *Ten steps led up to it*

---

[a] Taken from *The Septuagint* (Greek translation of the Old Testament) for a clearer description.

## New International Version

**41** Then the man brought me to the main hall and measured the jambs; the width of the jambs was six cubits[a] on each side.[b] [2]The entrance was ten cubits[c] wide, and the projecting walls on each side of it were five cubits[d] wide. He also measured the main hall; it was forty cubits long and twenty cubits wide.[e]

[3]Then he went into the inner sanctuary and measured the jambs of the entrance; each was two cubits[f] wide. The entrance was six cubits wide, and the projecting walls on each side of it were seven cubits[g] wide. [4]And he measured the length of the inner sanctuary; it was twenty cubits, and its width was twenty cubits across the end of the main hall. He said to me, "This is the Most Holy Place."

[5]Then he measured the wall of the temple; it was six cubits thick, and each side room around the temple was four cubits[h] wide. [6]The side rooms were on three levels, one above another, thirty on each level. There were ledges all around the wall of the temple to serve as supports for the side rooms, so that the supports were not inserted into the wall of the temple. [7]The side rooms all around the temple were wider at each successive level. The structure surrounding the temple was built in ascending stages, so that the rooms widened as one went upward. A stairway went up from the lowest floor to the top floor through the middle floor.

[8]I saw that the temple had a raised base all around it, forming the foundation of the side rooms. It was the length of the rod, six long cubits. [9]The outer wall of the side rooms was five cubits thick. The open area between the side rooms of the temple [10]and the priests' rooms was twenty cubits wide all around the temple. [11]There were entrances to the side rooms from the open area, one on the north and another on the south; and the base adjoining the open area was five cubits wide all around.

[12]The building facing the temple courtyard on the west side was seventy cubits[i] wide. The wall of the building was five cubits thick all around, and its length was ninety cubits.[j]

[13]Then he measured the temple; it was a hundred cubits[k] long, and the temple courtyard and the building with its walls were also a hundred cubits long. [14]The width of the temple courtyard on the east, including the front of the temple, was a hundred cubits.

[15]Then he measured the length of the building facing the courtyard at the rear of the temple, including its galleries on each side; it was a hundred cubits.

The main hall, the inner sanctuary and the portico facing the court, [16]as well as the thresholds and the narrow windows and galleries around the three of them—everything beyond and including the threshold was covered with wood. The floor, the wall up to the windows, and the windows were covered. [17]In the space above the outside of the entrance to the inner sanctuary and on the walls at regular intervals all around the inner and outer sanctuary

---

[a] *1* That is, about 11 feet or about 3.2 meters; also in verses 3, 5 and 8
[b] *1* One Hebrew manuscript and Septuagint; most Hebrew manuscripts *side, the width of the tent*   [c] *2* That is, about 18 feet or about 5.3 meters   [d] *2* That is, about 8 3/4 feet or about 2.7 meters; also in verses 9, 11 and 12   [e] *2* That is, about 70 feet long and 35 feet wide or about 21 meters long and 11 meters wide   [f] *3* That is, about 3 1/2 feet or about 1.1 meters; also in verse 22   [g] *3* That is, about 12 feet or about 3.7 meters   [h] *5* That is, about 7 feet or about 2.1 meters   [i] *12* That is, about 123 feet or about 37 meters   [j] *12* That is, about 158 feet or about 48 meters   [k] *13* That is, about 175 feet or about 53 meters; also in verses 14 and 15

## Amplified Bible

**41** And *the man* [an angel] brought me to [the Holy Place of] the temple and measured the wall pillars, six cubits broad on one side [of the ten-cubit door] and six cubits broad on the other side, [a]which was the breadth of the tabernacle *or* tent [later called the temple].

[2]And the breadth of the entrance was ten cubits, and the leaves of the door were five cubits on the one side and five cubits on the other side; and he measured its length, forty cubits, and its breadth, twenty cubits.

[3]Then *the man* [being an angel, and unrestricted] went inside [the inner room, but went alone] and measured each post of the door, two cubits, the doorway, six cubits, and the breadth of the entrance, seven cubits. [Heb. 9:6, 7; 10:19-25.]

[4]And he measured the length [of the interior of the second room] in the temple proper, twenty cubits, and the breadth, twenty cubits; and he [came out and] said to me, This is the Most Holy Place (the Holy of Holies).

[5]Then he measured the wall of the temple, six cubits thick [to accommodate side chambers]; and the breadth of every side chamber, four cubits, round about the temple proper on every side.

[6]These side chambers were three stories high, one over another and thirty in each story; and they entered into the wall which belonged to the house for the side chambers round about, that they might have hold of the wall [of the house], but they did not have hold of the wall of the temple.

[7]And the side rooms became broader as they encompassed the temple higher and higher, for the encircling of the house went higher and higher round about the temple; therefore the breadth of the house continued upward, and so one went up from the lowest story to the highest one by way of the middle story [on a winding stairway].

[8]I saw also that the temple had an elevation *or* foundation platform round about it. The foundations of the side chambers measured a full reed measure of six long cubits.

[9]The thickness of the outer wall of the side chamber was five cubits, as was the width of that part of the foundation that was left free of the side chambers that belonged to the house.

[10]And between [the free space of the foundation platform and] the chambers was a breadth of twenty cubits round about the temple on every side.

[11]And the doors of the attached side chambers opened on the free space that was left, one door toward the north and another door toward the south; and the breadth of the space on the foundation platform that was left free was five cubits round about.

[12]And the building that faced the temple yard on the west side was seventy cubits broad, and the wall of the building was five cubits thick round about, and its length ninety cubits.

[13]And *the man* [an angel in my vision] measured the temple, a hundred cubits long; and the yard and the building with its walls, a hundred cubits long;

[14]Also the breadth of the east front of the temple and yard, a hundred cubits.

[15]Then *the man* [an angel] measured the length of the building on the west side of the yard with its walls on either side, a hundred cubits. The Holy Place of the temple, the inner Holy of Holies, and the outer vestibule

[16]Were roofed over, and all three had latticed windows all around. The inside walls of the temple were paneled with wood round about from the floor up to the windows and from the windows to the roof,

[17]Including the space above the door leading to the inner room, inside and out. And on the walls round about in the inner room and the Holy Place were carvings,

---

[a] *The Septuagint* (Greek translation of the Old Testament) does not contain this phrase, "which was the breadth of the tabernacle," but most Hebrew manuscripts do contain it.

## New International Version

[18]were carved cherubim and palm trees. Palm trees alternated with cherubim. Each cherub had two faces: [19]the face of a human being toward the palm tree on one side and the face of a lion toward the palm tree on the other. They were carved all around the whole temple. [20]From the floor to the area above the entrance, cherubim and palm trees were carved on the wall of the main hall.

[21]The main hall had a rectangular doorframe, and the one at the front of the Most Holy Place was similar. [22]There was a wooden altar three cubits[a] high and two cubits square[b]; its corners, its base[c] and its sides were of wood. The man said to me, "This is the table that is before the LORD." [23]Both the main hall and the Most Holy Place had double doors. [24]Each door had two leaves—two hinged leaves for each door. [25]And on the doors of the main hall were carved cherubim and palm trees like those carved on the walls, and there was a wooden overhang on the front of the portico. [26]On the sidewalls of the portico were narrow windows with palm trees carved on each side. The side rooms of the temple also had overhangs.

### The Rooms for the Priests

**42** Then the man led me northward into the outer court and brought me to the rooms opposite the temple courtyard and opposite the outer wall on the north side. [2]The building whose door faced north was a hundred cubits long and fifty cubits wide.[d] [3]Both in the section twenty cubits[e] from the inner court and in the section opposite the pavement of the outer court, gallery faced gallery at the three levels. [4]In front of the rooms was an inner passageway ten cubits wide and a hundred cubits[f] long.[g] Their doors were on the north. [5]Now the upper rooms were narrower, for the galleries took more space from them than from the rooms on the lower and middle floors of the building. [6]The rooms on the top floor had no pillars, as the courts had; so they were smaller in floor space than those on the lower and middle floors. [7]There was an outer wall parallel to the rooms and the outer court; it extended in front of the rooms for fifty cubits. [8]While the row of rooms on the side next to the outer court was fifty cubits long, the row on the side nearest the sanctuary was a hundred cubits long. [9]The lower rooms had an entrance on the east side as one enters them from the outer court.

[10]On the south side[h] along the length of the wall of the outer court, adjoining the temple courtyard and opposite the outer wall, were rooms [11]with a passageway in front of them. These were like the rooms on the north; they had the same length and width, with similar exits and dimensions. Similar to the doorways on the north [12]were the doorways of the rooms on the south. There was a doorway at the beginning of the passageway that was parallel to the corresponding wall extending eastward, by which one enters the rooms.

[13]Then he said to me, "The north and south rooms facing the temple courtyard are the priests' rooms, where the priests who approach the LORD will eat the most holy

---

[a] 22 That is, about 5 1/4 feet or about 1.5 meters  [b] 22 Septuagint; Hebrew *long*  [c] 22 Septuagint; Hebrew *length*  [d] 2 That is, about 175 feet long and 88 feet wide or about 53 meters long and 27 meters wide  [e] 3 That is, about 35 feet or about 11 meters  [f] 4 Septuagint and Syriac; Hebrew *and one cubit*  [g] 4 That is, about 18 feet wide and 175 feet long or about 5.3 meters wide and 53 meters long  [h] 10 Septuagint; Hebrew *Eastward*

## Amplified Bible

[18]With figures of cherubim and palm trees, so that a palm tree was between a cherub and a cherub; and every cherub had two faces,

[19]So that the face of a man was toward the palm tree on the one side, and the face of a young lion toward the palm tree on the other side. It was made this way through all the house round about.

[20]From the floor to above the entrance were cherubim and palm trees made, and also on the wall of the temple [the Holy Place].

[21]The door frames of the temple were squared, and in front [outside of the sanctuary or Holy of Holies] was what appeared to be

[22]An altar of wood, three cubits high and two cubits long [and wide]; and its corners, its base, and its sides were of wood. And *the man* [an angel] said to me, This is the table that is before the Lord.

[23]And the temple *or* Holy Place and the sanctuary *or* Holy of Holies, had two doors [one for each of them].

[24]And the doors had two leaves apiece, two folding leaves—two leaves for the one door and two leaves for the other door.

[25]And there were carved on them, on the doors of the temple, cherubim and palm trees, like those carved upon the walls; and there was also a canopy of wood in front of the porch outside.

[26]And there were recessed windows and palm trees on the one side and on the other side of the porch. Thus were the side chambers and the canopies of the house.

**42** Then *the man* [an angel] brought me forth into the outer court northward, and he brought me to the attached chambers that were opposite the temple yard and were opposite the building on the north.

[2]Before the long side of one hundred cubits was the door toward the north, and the breadth was fifty cubits.

[3]Adjoining the twenty cubits which belonged to the inner court, and opposite the pavement which belonged to the outer court, was balcony facing balcony in three stories.

[4]And before the attached chambers was a walk inward of ten cubits breadth and a hundred cubits long, and their doors were on the north.

[5]Now the upper chambers were shorter, for the balconies took off from these more than from the lower and middle chambers of the building.

[6]For they were in three stories, but did not have pillars as the pillars of the [outer] court; therefore the upper chambers were set back more than the lower and middle ones from the ground.

[7]And the wall *or* fence that was outside, opposite *and* parallel to the chambers, toward the outer court before the chambers, was fifty cubits long,

[8]For the length of the [combined] chambers that were on the outer court was fifty cubits, while [the length] of those opposite the temple was a hundred cubits.

[9]And under these chambers was the entrance on the east side, as one approached them from the outer court.

[10]In the breadth of the wall of the court going toward the east, before the yard and before the building, were chambers

[11]With a passage before them that gave the appearance of the attached chambers on the north, of the same length and breadth, with similar exits and arrangements and doors.

[12]And like the doors of the chambers that were toward the south there was an entrance at the head of the way, the way before the dividing wall toward the east, as one enters them.

[13]Then said *the man* [an angel] to me, The north chambers and the south chambers, which are opposite the yard, are the holy chambers where the priests who approach the

## New International Version

offerings. There they will put the most holy offerings—the grain offerings, the sin offerings[a] and the guilt offerings—for the place is holy. 14Once the priests enter the holy precincts, they are not to go into the outer court until they leave behind the garments in which they minister, for these are holy. They are to put on other clothes before they go near the places that are for the people."

15When he had finished measuring what was inside the temple area, he led me out by the east gate and measured the area all around: 16He measured the east side with the measuring rod; it was five hundred cubits.[b,c] 17He measured the north side; it was five hundred cubits[d] by the measuring rod. 18He measured the south side; it was five hundred cubits by the measuring rod. 19Then he turned to the west side and measured; it was five hundred cubits by the measuring rod. 20So he measured the area on all four sides. It had a wall around it, five hundred cubits long and five hundred cubits wide, to separate the holy from the common.

### God's Glory Returns to the Temple

**43** Then the man brought me to the gate facing east, 2and I saw the glory of the God of Israel coming from the east. His voice was like the roar of rushing waters, and the land was radiant with his glory. 3The vision I saw was like the vision I had seen when he[e] came to destroy the city and like the visions I had seen by the Kebar River, and I fell facedown. 4The glory of the LORD entered the temple through the gate facing east. 5Then the Spirit lifted me up and brought me into the inner court, and the glory of the LORD filled the temple.

6While the man was standing beside me, I heard someone speaking to me from inside the temple. 7He said: "Son of man, this is the place of my throne and the place for the soles of my feet. This is where I will live among the Israelites forever. The people of Israel will never again defile my holy name—neither they nor their kings—by their prostitution and the funeral offerings[f] for their kings at their death.[g] 8When they placed their threshold next to my threshold and their doorposts beside my doorposts, with only a wall between me and them, they defiled my holy name by their detestable practices. So I destroyed them in my anger. 9Now let them put away from me their prostitution and the funeral offerings for their kings, and I will live among them forever.

10"Son of man, describe the temple to the people of Israel, that they may be ashamed of their sins. Let them consider its perfection, 11and if they are ashamed of all they have done, make known to them the design of the temple—its arrangement, its exits and entrances—its whole design and all its regulations[h] and laws. Write these down before them so that they may be faithful to its design and follow all its regulations.

12"This is the law of the temple: All the surrounding

---

a 13 Or purification offerings   b 16 See Septuagint of verse 17;
Hebrew rods; also in verses 18 and 19.   c 16 Five hundred cubits
equal about 875 feet or about 265 meters; also in verses 17, 18 and 19.
d 17 Septuagint; Hebrew rods   e 3 Some Hebrew manuscripts and
Vulgate; most Hebrew manuscripts I   f 7 Or the memorial monuments;
also in verse 9   g 7 Or their high places   h 11 Some Hebrew
manuscripts and Septuagint; most Hebrew manuscripts regulations and
its whole design

## Amplified Bible

Lord shall eat the most holy offerings; there shall they lay the most holy things—the meal offering, the sin offering, and the trespass or guilt offering—for the place is holy.

14When the priests enter the Holy Place, they shall not go out of it into the outer court unless they lay aside there the garments in which they minister, for these are holy, separate, and set apart. They shall put on other garments before they approach that which is for the people.

15Now when he had finished measuring the inner temple area, he brought me forth toward the gate which faces east and measured it [the outer area] round about.

16He measured the east side with the measuring reed, five hundred reeds with the measuring reed round about.

17He measured the north side, five hundred reeds with the measuring reed round about.

18He measured the south side, five hundred reeds with the measuring reed.

19He turned about to the west side and measured five hundred reeds with the measuring reed.

20He measured it on the four sides; it had a wall round about, the length five hundred reeds and the breadth five hundred, to make a separation between that which was holy [the temple proper] and that which was common [the outer area].

**43** Afterward the man [an angel] brought me to the gate, the gate that faces east.

2And behold, the glory of the God of Israel came from the east and His voice was like the sound of many waters, and the earth shone with His glory. [Rev. 1:15; 14:2.]

3And the vision which I saw was like the vision I had seen when I came to foretell the destruction of the city and like the vision I had seen beside the river Chebar [near Babylon]; and I fell on my face. [Ezek. 1:4; 3:23; 10:15, 22.]

4And the glory of the Lord entered the temple by the gate facing east.

5Then the Spirit caught me up and brought me into the inner court, and behold, the glory of the Lord filled the temple.

6And I heard One speaking to me out of the temple, and a Man stood by me.

7And He [the Lord] said to me, Son of man, this is the place of My throne and the place of the soles of My feet, where I will dwell in the midst of the children of Israel forever; and My holy name the house of Israel shall no more profane, neither they nor their kings, by their [idolatrous] harlotry, nor by the dead bodies and monuments of their kings,

8Nor by setting their threshold by My thresholds and their doorposts by My doorposts, with a mere wall between Me and them. They have profaned My holy name by their abominations which they have committed; therefore I have consumed them in My anger.

9Now let them put away their [idolatrous] harlotry and the dead bodies and monuments of their kings far from Me, and I will dwell in their midst forever.

10Son of man, show the temple by your description of it to the house of Israel, that they may be ashamed of their iniquities; and let them measure accurately its appearance and plan.

11And if they are ashamed of all that they have done, make known to them the form of the temple and the arrangement of it—its exits and its entrances and the whole form of it—all its ordinances and all its forms and all its laws. And write it down in their sight so that they may keep the whole form of it and all the ordinances of it and do them.

12This is the law of the house [of the Lord]: The whole area round about on the top of the mountain a [Mount Mo-

---

a Moriah is identified in Gen. 22:2 as the region where Abraham
prepared to sacrifice Isaac, and is identified in II Chron. 3:1 as the site of
the temple built by Solomon.

## New International Version

area on top of the mountain will be most holy. Such is the law of the temple.

### The Great Altar Restored

13"These are the measurements of the altar in long cubits,ᵃ that cubit being a cubit and a handbreadth: Its gutter is a cubit deep and a cubit wide, with a rim of one spanᵇ around the edge. And this is the height of the altar: 14From the gutter on the ground up to the lower ledge that goes around the altar it is two cubits high, and the ledge is a cubit wide.ᶜ From this lower ledge to the upper ledge that goes around the altar it is four cubits high, and that ledge is also a cubit wide.ᵈ 15Above that, the altar hearth is four cubits high, and four horns project upward from the hearth. 16The altar hearth is square, twelve cubitsᵉ long and twelve cubits wide. 17The upper ledge also is square, fourteen cubitsᶠ long and fourteen cubits wide. All around the altar is a gutter of one cubit with a rim of half a cubit.ᵇ The steps of the altar face east."

18Then he said to me, "Son of man, this is what the Sovereign LORD says: These will be the regulations for sacrificing burnt offerings and splashing blood against the altar when it is built: 19You are to give a young bull as a sin offeringᵍ to the Levitical priests of the family of Zadok, who come near to minister before me, declares the Sovereign LORD. 20You are to take some of its blood and put it on the four horns of the altar and on the four corners of the upper ledge and all around the rim, and so purify the altar and make atonement for it. 21You are to take the bull for the sin offering and burn it in the designated part of the temple area outside the sanctuary.

22"On the second day you are to offer a male goat without defect for a sin offering, and the altar is to be purified as it was purified with the bull. 23When you have finished purifying it, you are to offer a young bull and a ram from the flock, both without defect. 24You are to offer them before the LORD, and the priests are to sprinkle salt on them and sacrifice them as a burnt offering to the LORD.

25"For seven days you are to provide a male goat daily for a sin offering; you are also to provide a young bull and a ram from the flock, both without defect. 26For seven days they are to make atonement for the altar and cleanse it; thus they will dedicate it. 27At the end of these days, from the eighth day on, the priests are to present your burnt offerings and fellowship offerings on the altar. Then I will accept you, declares the Sovereign LORD."

### The Priesthood Restored

**44** Then the man brought me back to the outer gate of the sanctuary, the one facing east, and it was shut. 2The LORD said to me, "This gate is to remain shut. It must not be opened; no one may enter through it. It is to remain shut because the LORD, the God of Israel, has entered through it. 3The prince himself is the only one who

## Amplified Bible

riah] shall be most holy, separated, *and* set apart. Behold, this is the law of the house [of the Lord].

13And these are the measurements of the altar [of burnt offering] in cubits. The cubit is a royal cubit [the length of a forearm and a palm of the hand]; the bottom *or* gutter shall be a cubit deep and a cubit wide, with a rim or lip round about it of a span's breadth. And this shall be the height of the altar:

14From the bottom *or* gutter on the ground to the lower ledge *or* brim shall be two cubits, and the breadth one cubit; and from the lesser ledge to the greater ledge shall be four cubits, and the breadth one cubit.

15And the altar hearth shall be four cubits high, and from the altar hearth reaching upward there shall be four horns one cubit high.

16And the altar hearth shall be square—twelve cubits long, twelve cubits broad, square in its four sides.

17And the ledge shall be fourteen cubits long and fourteen cubits broad on its four sides, and the border about it shall be half a cubit; and its bottom *or* gutter shall be a cubit deep and wide, and its ascent [not steps] shall face the east. [Exod. 20:26.]

18And [the Lord] said to me, Son of man, thus says the Lord God: These are the regulations for the use of the altar in the day that it is erected, upon which to offer burnt offerings and to sprinkle blood against it:

19You shall give to the priests, the Levites who are of the offspring of Zadok, who are near to Me to minister to Me, says the Lord God, a young bull for a sin offering.

20And you shall take of its blood and put it on the four horns of [the altar of burnt offering] and on the four corners of the ledge and on the rim *or* border round about. Thus shall you cleanse *and* make atonement for [the altar].

21You shall also take the bullock of the sin offering, and it shall be burned in the appointed place of the temple, outside the sacred enclosure. [Heb. 13:11.]

22And on the second day you shall offer a male goat without blemish for a sin offering. Thus the altar shall be cleansed, as it was cleansed with the bullock.

23When you have finished cleansing it, you shall offer a young bull without blemish and a ram out of the flock without blemish.

24And you shall bring them near before the Lord, and the priests shall cast salt upon them and they shall offer them up for a burnt offering to the Lord.

25Seven days you shall prepare every day a goat for a sin offering; also a young bull and a ram out of the flock, without blemish, shall be prepared.

26For seven days shall they make atonement for the altar and purify it; so the priests shall consecrate, separate, *and* set it apart to receive offerings. [Exod. 29:37.]

27And when these days have been accomplished, on the eighth day and from then on, the priests shall offer your burnt offerings upon the altar and your peace offerings; and I will accept you, says the Lord God. [Rom. 12:1; I Pet. 2:5.]

**44** Then *the man* [an angel] brought me back the way of the outer gate of the sanctuary which faces the east, and it was shut. 2Then the Lord said to me, This gate shall be ᵃshut; it shall not be opened and no man shall enter in by it, for the Lord, the God of Israel, has entered in by it; therefore it shall remain shut.

3As for the prince, being the prince, he shall sit in it

---

ᵃ 13 That is, about 21 inches or about 53 centimeters; also in verses 14 and 17. The long cubit is the basic unit for linear measurement throughout Ezekiel 40–48.   ᵇ 13,17 That is, about 11 inches or about 27 centimeters   ᶜ 14 That is, about 3 1/2 feet high and 1 3/4 feet wide or about 105 centimeters high and 53 centimeters wide   ᵈ 14 That is, about 7 feet high and 1 3/4 feet wide or about 2.1 meters high and 53 centimeters wide   ᵉ 16 That is, about 21 feet or about 6.4 meters   ᶠ 17 That is, about 25 feet or about 7.4 meters   ᵍ 19 Or *purification offering*; also in verses 21, 22 and 25

---

ᵃ In Christ's time the Golden Gate was the principal eastside thoroughfare. Through it the Prince of Peace would naturally make His triumphal entry. But by A.D. 1542-3, when Sultan Suleiman the Magnificent rebuilt the wall of Jerusalem, tradition says that the road which once led to this gate had fallen into disuse, and what is now St. Stephen's Gate was the accepted entrance. So the Sultan walled up the Golden Gate with its double entrance, and it has remained so ever since.

## New International Version

may sit inside the gateway to eat in the presence of the LORD. He is to enter by way of the portico of the gateway and go out the same way."

⁴Then the man brought me by way of the north gate to the front of the temple. I looked and saw the glory of the LORD filling the temple of the LORD, and I fell facedown.

⁵The LORD said to me, "Son of man, look carefully, listen closely and give attention to everything I tell you concerning all the regulations and instructions regarding the temple of the LORD. Give attention to the entrance to the temple and all the exits of the sanctuary. ⁶Say to rebellious Israel, 'This is what the Sovereign LORD says: Enough of your detestable practices, people of Israel! ⁷In addition to all your other detestable practices, you brought foreigners uncircumcised in heart and flesh into my sanctuary, desecrating my temple while you offered me food, fat and blood, and you broke my covenant. ⁸Instead of carrying out your duty in regard to my holy things, you put others in charge of my sanctuary. ⁹This is what the Sovereign LORD says: No foreigner uncircumcised in heart and flesh is to enter my sanctuary, not even the foreigners who live among the Israelites.

¹⁰"'The Levites who went far from me when Israel went astray and who wandered from me after their idols must bear the consequences of their sin. ¹¹They may serve in my sanctuary, having charge of the gates of the temple and serving in it; they may slaughter the burnt offerings and sacrifices for the people and stand before the people and serve them. ¹²But because they served them in the presence of their idols and made the people of Israel fall into sin, therefore I have sworn with uplifted hand that they must bear the consequences of their sin, declares the Sovereign LORD. ¹³They are not to come near to serve me as priests or come near any of my holy things or my most holy offerings; they must bear the shame of their detestable practices. ¹⁴And I will appoint them to guard the temple for all the work that is to be done in it.

¹⁵"'But the Levitical priests, who are descendants of Zadok and who guarded my sanctuary when the Israelites went astray from me, are to come near to minister before me; they are to stand before me to offer sacrifices of fat and blood, declares the Sovereign LORD. ¹⁶They alone are to enter my sanctuary; they alone are to come near my table to minister before me and serve me as guards.

¹⁷"'When they enter the gates of the inner court, they are to wear linen clothes; they must not wear any woolen garment while ministering at the gates of the inner court or inside the temple. ¹⁸They are to wear linen turbans on their heads and linen undergarments around their waists. They must not wear anything that makes them perspire. ¹⁹When they go out into the outer court where the people are, they are to take off the clothes they have been ministering in and are to leave them in the sacred rooms, and

## Amplified Bible

to eat bread before the Lord; he shall enter by way of the porch *or* vestibule of the gate and shall go out the same way.

⁴Then he brought me by way of the north gate to the front of the temple; I looked, and behold, the glory of the Lord filled the house of the Lord, and I fell upon my face. [Rev. 15:8.]

⁵And the Lord said to me, Son of man, mark well *and* set your heart to see with your eyes and hear with your ears all that I say to you concerning all the ordinances of the house of the Lord and all its laws, and mark well *and* set your heart to know who are allowed to enter the temple and all those who are excluded from the sanctuary.

⁶And you shall say to the rebellious, even to the house of Israel, Thus says the Lord God: O you house of Israel, let all your previous abominations be enough for you! [Do not repeat them!]

⁷You have brought into My sanctuary aliens, uncircumcised in heart and uncircumcised in flesh, to be in My sanctuary to pollute *and* profane it, even My house, when you offer My bread, the fat and the blood; and through it all *and* in addition to all your abominations, they *and* you have broken My covenant.

⁸And you have not kept charge of My holy things, but you have chosen foreign keepers to please yourselves and have set them in charge of My sanctuary.

⁹Therefore thus says the Lord God: No foreigner uncircumcised in heart and flesh shall enter into My sanctuary [where no one but the priests might enter], of any foreigners who are among the children of Israel.

¹⁰But the Levites who went far away from Me when Israel went astray, who went astray from Me after their idols, they shall bear [the punishment for] their iniquity *and* guilt.

¹¹They shall minister in My sanctuary, having oversight as guards at the gates of the temple and ministering in the temple. They shall slay the burnt offering and the sacrifice for the people, and they shall attend the people to serve them.

¹²Because [the priests] ministered to [the people] before their idols and became a stumbling block of iniquity *and* guilt to the house of Israel, therefore I have lifted up My hand *and* have sworn against them, says the Lord God, that they shall bear the punishment for their iniquity *and* guilt.

¹³And they shall not come near to Me to do the office of a priest to Me, nor come near to any of My holy things that are most sacred; but they shall bear their shame *and* their punishment for the abominations which they have committed.

¹⁴Yet I will appoint them as caretakers to have charge of the temple, for all the service of the temple and for all that will be done in it.

¹⁵But the Levitical priests, the sons of Zadok, who kept the charge of My sanctuary when the children of Israel went astray from Me, shall come near to Me to minister to Me, and they shall attend Me to offer to Me the fat and the blood, says the Lord God.

¹⁶They shall enter into My sanctuary; and they shall come near to My table to minister to Me, and they shall keep My charge.

¹⁷When they enter the gates of the inner court, they shall be clothed in linen garments; no wool shall be on them while they minister at the gates of the inner court and within the temple.

¹⁸They shall have linen turbans on their heads and linen breeches upon their loins; they shall not gird themselves with anything that causes [them to] sweat.

¹⁹And when they go out into the outer court to the people, they shall put off the garments in which they ministered and lay them in the holy chambers, and they shall put on other garments, lest by contact of their garments

## New International Version

put on other clothes, so that the people are not consecrated through contact with their garments.

[20]"They must not shave their heads or let their hair grow long, but they are to keep the hair of their heads trimmed. [21]No priest is to drink wine when he enters the inner court. [22]They must not marry widows or divorced women; they may marry only virgins of Israelite descent or widows of priests. [23]They are to teach my people the difference between the holy and the common and show them how to distinguish between the unclean and the clean.

[24]"In any dispute, the priests are to serve as judges and decide it according to my ordinances. They are to keep my laws and my decrees for all my appointed festivals, and they are to keep my Sabbaths holy.

[25]"A priest must not defile himself by going near a dead person; however, if the dead person was his father or mother, son or daughter, brother or unmarried sister, then he may defile himself. [26]After he is cleansed, he must wait seven days. [27]On the day he goes into the inner court of the sanctuary to minister in the sanctuary, he is to offer a sin offering[a] for himself, declares the Sovereign LORD.

[28]"I am to be the only inheritance the priests have. You are to give them no possession in Israel; I will be their possession. [29]They will eat the grain offerings, the sin offerings and the guilt offerings; and everything in Israel devoted[b] to the LORD will belong to them. [30]The best of all the firstfruits and of all your special gifts will belong to the priests. You are to give them the first portion of your ground meal so that a blessing may rest on your household. [31]The priests must not eat anything, whether bird or animal, found dead or torn by wild animals.

### Israel Fully Restored

**45** "When you allot the land as an inheritance, you are to present to the LORD a portion of the land as a sacred district, 25,000 cubits[c] long and 20,000[d] cubits[e] wide; the entire area will be holy. [2]Of this, a section 500 cubits[f] square is to be for the sanctuary, with 50 cubits[g] around it for open land. [3]In the sacred district, measure off a section 25,000 cubits long and 10,000 cubits[h] wide. In it will be the sanctuary, the Most Holy Place. [4]It will be the sacred portion of the land for the priests, who minister in the sanctuary and who draw near to minister before the LORD. It will be a place for their houses as well as a holy place for the sanctuary. [5]An area 25,000 cubits long and 10,000 cubits wide will belong to the Levites, who serve in the temple, as their possession for towns to live in.[i]

[6]"You are to give the city as its property an area 5,000

## Amplified Bible

with the people they should consecrate (separate and set apart for holy use) such persons [unintentionally and unfittingly].

[20]Neither shall they shave their heads or allow their locks to grow long; they shall only cut short or trim the hair of their heads.

[21]Neither shall any priest drink wine when he enters the inner court.

[22]Neither shall they take for their wives a widow or a woman separated or divorced from her husband; but they shall marry maidens [who are virgins] of the offspring of the house of Israel or a widow previously married to a priest.

[23]The priests shall teach My people the difference between the holy and the common or profane, and cause them to distinguish between the unclean and the clean.

[24]And in a controversy they shall act as judges, and they shall judge according to My judgments; and they shall keep My laws and My statutes in all My appointed feasts, and they shall keep My Sabbaths holy.

[25]And they shall go near to no dead person to defile themselves, except for father or for mother, for son or for daughter, for brother or for sister who has had no husband; for them they may defile themselves. [Lev. 21:1, 2.]

[26]And after he is cleansed [from the defilement of a dead body] they shall reckon to him seven days more before returning to the temple.

[27]And on the day that he goes into the sanctuary, into the inner court to minister in the sanctuary, he shall offer his sin offering, says the Lord God.

[28]This [their ministry to Me] shall be to them as an inheritance, for I am their inheritance; and you shall give them no possession in Israel, for I am their possession. [Josh. 13:14, 33.]

[29]They shall eat the meal offering and the sin offering and the trespass offering, and every offering in Israel dedicated by a solemn vow to God shall be theirs.

[30]And the first of all the firstfruits of all kinds, and every offering of all kinds from all your offerings, shall belong to the priests. You shall also give to the priest the first of your coarse meal and bread dough, that a blessing may rest on your house.

[31]The priests shall not eat of anything that has died of itself or is torn, whether it be bird or beast.

**45** Moreover, when you shall divide the land by apportioned and assigned lots for inheritance, you shall set apart as an offering to the Lord a portion of the land to be used for holy purposes. The length shall be 25,000 [a]cubits, and the breadth 20,000. It shall be holy (set apart and consecrated to sacred use) in its every area. [Ezek. 48:9, 12, 13.]

[2]Of this there shall belong to the sanctuary a square plot 500 by 500, and 50 cubits for the open space around it.

[3]And in this sacred section you shall measure off a portion 25,000 [a]cubits in length and 10,000 cubits in breadth. And in it shall be the sanctuary which is most holy.

[4]It is a holy portion of the land; it shall be for the priests, the ministers of the sanctuary, who come near to minister to the Lord; and it shall be a place for their houses and a holy place (set apart as sacred) for the sanctuary.

[5]And another portion of land, 25,000 cubits long and 10,000 cubits wide, shall also be for the Levites, the ministers of the temple, and they shall possess it as a place in which to live.

[6]And you shall appoint for the possession of the city an

---

[a] 27 Or purification offering; also in verse 29   [b] 29 The Hebrew term refers to the irrevocable giving over of things or persons to the LORD.   [c] 1 That is, about 8 miles or about 13 kilometers; also in verses 3, 5 and 6   [d] 1 Septuagint (see also verses 3 and 5 and 48:9); Hebrew 10,000   [e] 1 That is, about 6 1/2 miles or about 11 kilometers   [f] 2 That is, about 875 feet or about 265 meters   [g] 2 That is, about 88 feet or about 27 meters   [h] 3 That is, about 3 1/3 miles or about 5.3 kilometers; also in verse 5   [i] 5 Septuagint; Hebrew temple; they will have as their possession 20 rooms

[a] The Septuagint (Greek translation of the Old Testament) so reads. The term "cubits" rather than "reeds" is supplied throughout this chapter only as the more probable reading. Neither is definitely designated in the Hebrew.

## New International Version

cubits*a* wide and 25,000 cubits long, adjoining the sacred portion; it will belong to all Israel.

7 "The prince will have the land bordering each side of the area formed by the sacred district and the property of the city. It will extend westward from the west side and eastward from the east side, running lengthwise from the western to the eastern border parallel to one of the tribal portions. 8 This land will be his possession in Israel. And my princes will no longer oppress my people but will allow the people of Israel to possess the land according to their tribes.

9 "This is what the Sovereign LORD says: You have gone far enough, princes of Israel! Give up your violence and oppression and do what is just and right. Stop dispossessing my people, declares the Sovereign LORD. 10 You are to use accurate scales, an accurate ephah*b* and an accurate bath.*c* 11 The ephah and the bath are to be the same size, the bath containing a tenth of a homer and the ephah a tenth of a homer; the homer is to be the standard measure for both. 12 The shekel*d* is to consist of twenty gerahs. Twenty shekels plus twenty-five shekels plus fifteen shekels equal one mina.*e*

13 "This is the special gift you are to offer: a sixth of an ephah*f* from each homer of wheat and a sixth of an ephah*g* from each homer of barley. 14 The prescribed portion of olive oil, measured by the bath, is a tenth of a bath*h* from each cor (which consists of ten baths or one homer, for ten baths are equivalent to a homer). 15 Also one sheep is to be taken from every flock of two hundred from the well-watered pastures of Israel. These will be used for the grain offerings, burnt offerings and fellowship offerings to make atonement for the people, declares the Sovereign LORD. 16 All the people of the land will be required to give this special offering to the prince in Israel. 17 It will be the duty of the prince to provide the burnt offerings, grain offerings and drink offerings at the festivals, the New Moons and the Sabbaths—at all the appointed festivals of Israel. He will provide the sin offerings,*i* grain offerings, burnt offerings and fellowship offerings to make atonement for the Israelites.

18 "This is what the Sovereign LORD says: In the first month on the first day you are to take a young bull without defect and purify the sanctuary. 19 The priest is to take some of the blood of the sin offering and put it on the doorposts of the temple, on the four corners of the upper ledge of the altar and on the gateposts of the inner court. 20 You are to do the same on the seventh day of the month for anyone who sins unintentionally or through ignorance; so you are to make atonement for the temple.

21 "In the first month on the fourteenth day you are to observe the Passover, a festival lasting seven days, during which you shall eat bread made without yeast. 22 On that day the prince is to provide a bull as a sin offering for himself and for all the people of the land. 23 Every day during the seven days of the festival he is to provide seven bulls and seven rams without defect as a burnt offering to the LORD, and a male goat for a sin offering. 24 He is to provide

## Amplified Bible

area of 5,000 *cubits* wide and 25,000 *cubits* long, along beside the portion set aside as a holy section. It shall belong to the whole house of Israel.

7 And to the prince shall belong the land on the one side and on the other side of the portion set aside as a holy section and the property of the city, in front of the holy section and the property of the city, from the west side westward and from the east side eastward; and the length shall be answerable to that of one of the tribal portions *and* parallel to it from the western boundary to the eastern boundary of the land.

8 It shall be for the prince—his possession in Israel. And My princes shall no more oppress My people, but they shall give the rest of the land to the house of Israel according to their tribes.

9 Thus says the Lord God: That is enough for you, O princes of Israel! Stop the violence and plundering *and* oppression [that you did when you were given no property], and do justice and righteousness, and take away your exactions *and* cease your evictions of My people, says the Lord God.

10 You shall have just weights on your scales and just measures—both a just ephah measure and a just bath measure.

11 The ephah and the bath measures shall both be the same size, the bath containing one tenth of a homer and the ephah one tenth of a homer; the standard measure shall be the homer.

12 And the shekel shall be twenty gerahs; twenty shekels and twenty-five shekels and fifteen shekels shall be your maneh.

13 This is the offering which you shall make: a sixth of an ephah from each homer of wheat and a sixth of an ephah from each homer of barley.

14 And as to the set portion of oil, you shall offer the tenth part of a bath of oil out of each cor, which is a homer of ten baths, for ten baths make [both a cor and] a homer.

15 And [you shall offer] one lamb out of every flock of two hundred, out of the well-watered pastures of Israel *and* from all the families of Israel, to provide for a meal offering and for a burnt offering and for peace offerings, to make atonement for those who brought them, says the Lord God.

16 All the people of the land shall give this offering for the prince in Israel.

17 And it shall be the prince's part to furnish [from the contributions of the people] the burnt offerings, meal offerings, and drink offerings at the feasts and on the New Moons and on the Sabbaths, at all the appointed feasts of the house of Israel. He shall prepare *and* make the sin offering, the meal offering, the burnt offering, and the peace offerings to make atonement for, bringing forgiveness *and* reconciliation to, the house of Israel.

18 Thus says the Lord God: In the first [month], on the first [day] of the month, you shall take a young bull without blemish and you shall cleanse the sanctuary.

19 And the priest shall take some of the blood of the sin offering and put it upon the doorposts of the temple and upon the four corners of the ledge of the altar and upon the posts of the gate of the inner court.

20 You shall do this on the seventh day of the month for everyone who has sinned through error *or* ignorance and for him who is simple-minded. So shall you make atonement for the temple.

21 In the first month on the fourteenth day of the [month]; you shall have the Passover, a feast of seven days; unleavened bread shall be eaten.

22 Upon that day the prince shall prepare for himself and for all the people of the land a bullock for a sin offering.

23 And for the seven days of the feast he shall prepare a burnt offering to the Lord, seven bullocks and seven rams without blemish daily for the seven days, and a he-goat daily for a sin offering.

## New International Version

as a grain offering an ephah for each bull and an ephah for each ram, along with a hin[a] of olive oil for each ephah.

25 "'During the seven days of the festival, which begins in the seventh month on the fifteenth day, he is to make the same provision for sin offerings, burnt offerings, grain offerings and oil.

# 46

"'This is what the Sovereign LORD says: The gate of the inner court facing east is to be shut on the six working days, but on the Sabbath day and on the day of the New Moon it is to be opened. 2The prince is to enter from the outside through the portico of the gateway and stand by the gatepost. The priests are to sacrifice his burnt offering and his fellowship offerings. He is to bow down in worship at the threshold of the gateway and then go out, but the gate will not be shut until evening. 3On the Sabbaths and New Moons the people of the land are to worship in the presence of the LORD at the entrance of that gateway. 4The burnt offering the prince brings to the LORD on the Sabbath day is to be six male lambs and a ram, all without defect. 5The grain offering given with the ram is to be an ephah,[b] and the grain offering with the lambs is to be as much as he pleases, along with a hin[c] of olive oil for each ephah. 6On the day of the New Moon he is to offer a young bull, six lambs and a ram, all without defect. 7He is to provide as a grain offering one ephah with the bull, one ephah with the ram, and with the lambs as much as he wants to give, along with a hin of oil for each ephah. 8When the prince enters, he is to go in through the portico of the gateway, and he is to come out the same way.

9 "'When the people of the land come before the LORD at the appointed festivals, whoever enters by the north gate to worship is to go out the south gate; and whoever enters by the south gate is to go out the north gate. No one is to return through the gate by which they entered, but each is to go out the opposite gate. 10The prince is to be among them, going in when they go in and going out when they go out. 11At the feasts and the appointed festivals, the grain offering is to be an ephah with a bull, an ephah with a ram, and with the lambs as much as he pleases, along with a hin of oil for each ephah.

12 "'When the prince provides a freewill offering to the LORD—whether a burnt offering or fellowship offerings—the gate facing east is to be opened for him. He shall offer his burnt offering or his fellowship offerings as he does on the Sabbath day. Then he shall go out, and after he has gone out, the gate will be shut.

13 "'Every day you are to provide a year-old lamb without defect for a burnt offering to the LORD; morning by morning you shall provide it. 14You are also to provide with it morning by morning a grain offering, consisting of a sixth of an ephah[d] with a third of a hin[e] of oil to moisten the flour. The presenting of this grain offering to the LORD is a lasting ordinance. 15So the lamb and the grain offering and the oil shall be provided morning by morning for a regular burnt offering.

16 "'This is what the Sovereign LORD says: If the prince makes a gift from his inheritance to one of his sons, it will also belong to his descendants; it is to be their property

## Amplified Bible

24 And he shall prepare as a meal offering to be offered with each bullock an ephah of meal, an ephah for each ram, and a hin of oil for each ephah of meal.

25 In the seventh [month], on the fifteenth day of the month, he shall make the same provision and preparation for the seven days of the feast, for sin offerings, burnt offerings, bloodless or meal offerings, and for the oil.

# 46

Thus says the Lord God: The gate of the inner court that faces east shall be shut during the six working days, but on the Sabbath it shall be opened, and also on the day of the New Moon it shall be opened.

2 And the prince shall enter by the porch or vestibule of the gate from without and shall stand by the sidepost of the gate. The priests shall prepare and offer his burnt offering and his peace offerings, and he shall worship at the threshold of the gate. Then he shall go out, but the gate shall not be shut until evening.

3 The people of the land shall worship at the entrance of that gate before the Lord on the Sabbaths and on the New Moons.

4 And the burnt offering that the prince shall offer to the Lord on the Sabbath day shall be six lambs without blemish and a ram without blemish.

5 And the bloodless or meal offering with the ram shall be an ephah, and the meal offering with the lambs shall be as much as he is able and willing to give, and a hin of oil with each ephah.

6 And on the day of the New Moon the offering shall be a young bull without blemish and six lambs and a ram without blemish.

7 And the prince shall provide and make a meal or bloodless offering, an ephah for the bullock and an ephah for the ram, and for the lambs as he is able and willing according to what has been made available to his hand, and a hin of oil to each ephah.

8 And when the prince shall enter, he shall go in by the porch or vestibule of that gate and he shall go out by way of it.

9 But when the people of the land shall come before the Lord at the appointed solemn feasts, he who enters the north gate to worship shall go out by the south gate, and he who enters by the south gate shall go out by the north gate; he shall not return by the gate by which he came in but shall go out by the opposite gate [straight ahead]. [Phil. 3:13.]

10 And the prince, when they go in, shall go in with them, and when they go out, he shall go out.

11 And in the appointed and solemn feasts the meal or bloodless offering shall be with a bullock an ephah, and with a ram an ephah, and with the lambs as much as the prince is willing and able to give [from what has been made available to him], and a hin of oil with each ephah.

12 When the prince shall prepare and make a freewill burnt offering or peace offerings voluntarily to the Lord, the gate that faces east shall be opened for him, and he shall offer his burnt offering and his peace offerings as he does on the Sabbath day. Then he shall go out, and after he has gone out, the gate shall be shut.

13 And a lamb a year old without blemish shall you [the priests, for the congregation] offer daily to the Lord; you shall prepare and offer it every morning.

14 And you [the priests] shall prepare a meal offering to go with it every morning, one-sixth of an ephah with one-third of a hin of oil to moisten the fine flour. This is a perpetual ordinance for a continual meal offering to the Lord.

15 Thus shall they prepare and offer the lamb and the meal offering and the oil every morning for a continual burnt offering.

16 Thus says the Lord God: If the prince gives a gift to any of his sons out of his inheritance, it shall belong to his sons; it is their property by inheritance.

---

[a] 24 That is, about 1 gallon or about 3.8 liters    [b] 5 That is, probably about 35 pounds or about 16 kilograms; also in verses 7 and 11    [c] 5 That is, about 1 gallon or about 3.8 liters; also in verses 7 and 11    [d] 14 That is, probably about 6 pounds or about 2.7 kilograms    [e] 14 That is, about 1 1/2 quarts or about 1.3 liters

## New International Version

by inheritance. [17] If, however, he makes a gift from his inheritance to one of his servants, the servant may keep it until the year of freedom; then it will revert to the prince. His inheritance belongs to his sons only; it is theirs. [18] The prince must not take any of the inheritance of the people, driving them off their property. He is to give his sons their inheritance out of his own property, so that not one of my people will be separated from their property.' "

[19] Then the man brought me through the entrance at the side of the gate to the sacred rooms facing north, which belonged to the priests, and showed me a place at the western end. [20] He said to me, "This is the place where the priests are to cook the guilt offering and the sin offering[a] and bake the grain offering, to avoid bringing them into the outer court and consecrating the people."

[21] He then brought me to the outer court and led me around to its four corners, and I saw in each corner another court. [22] In the four corners of the outer court were enclosed[b] courts, forty cubits long and thirty cubits wide;[c] each of the courts in the four corners was the same size. [23] Around the inside of each of the four courts was a ledge of stone, with places for fire built all around under the ledge. [24] He said to me, "These are the kitchens where those who minister at the temple are to cook the sacrifices of the people."

### The River From the Temple

**47** The man brought me back to the entrance to the temple, and I saw water coming out from under the threshold of the temple toward the east (for the temple faced east). The water was coming down from under the south side of the temple, south of the altar. [2] He then brought me out through the north gate and led me around the outside to the outer gate facing east, and the water was trickling from the south side.

[3] As the man went eastward with a measuring line in his hand, he measured off a thousand cubits[d] and then led me through water that was ankle-deep. [4] He measured off another thousand cubits and led me through water that was knee-deep. He measured off another thousand and led me through water that was up to the waist. [5] He measured off another thousand, but now it was a river that I could not cross, because the water had risen and was deep enough to swim in—a river that no one could cross. [6] He asked me, "Son of man, do you see this?"

Then he led me back to the bank of the river. [7] When I arrived there, I saw a great number of trees on each side of the river. [8] He said to me, "This water flows toward the eastern region and goes down into the Arabah,[e] where it enters the Dead Sea. When it empties into the sea, the salty water there becomes fresh. [9] Swarms of living creatures will live wherever the river flows. There will be large numbers of fish, because this water flows there and makes the salt water fresh; so where the river flows everything

## Amplified Bible

[17] But if he gives a gift out of his inheritance to one of his servants, then it shall be his until the year of liberty [the Year of Jubilee]; after that it shall be returned to the prince; only his sons may keep a gift from his inheritance [permanently].

[18] Moreover, the prince shall not take of the people's inheritance by oppression, thrusting them out of their property; what he gives to his sons he shall take out of his own possession, so that none of My people shall be separated from his [inherited] possession.

[19] Then he [my guide] led me through the entrance which was at the side of the gate into the holy chambers for the priests, which faced the north; and behold, there was a place at the extreme western end of them.

[20] And he said to me, This is the place where the priests shall boil the guilt offering and the sin offering, and where they shall bake the [bloodless] meal offering, to prevent their having to bring them into the outer court, lest they should thereby wrongfully sanctify (separate and consecrate for holy service) the people who are there.

[21] And he brought me out into the outer court and caused me to pass by the four corners of the court, and behold, in every corner of the court there was a court.

[22] In the four corners of the court there were courts joined on *and* enclosed, forty cubits long and thirty broad; these four in the corners were the same size.

[23] And there was a row of masonry inside them, round about [each of] the four courts, and it was made with hearths for boiling at the bottom of the rows round about.

[24] Then said he to me, These are the kitchens of those who do the boiling, where the ministers [the Levites] of the temple shall boil the sacrifices of the people.

**47** Then he [my guide] brought me again to the door of the house [of the Lord—the temple], and behold, waters issued out from under the threshold of the temple toward the east, for the front of the temple was toward the east; and the waters came down from under, from the right side of the temple, on the south side of the altar.

[2] Then he brought me out by way of the north gate and led me around outside to the outer gate by the way that faces east, and behold, waters were running out on the right side. [Zech. 14:8; Rev. 22:1, 2.]

[3] And when the man went eastward with the measuring line in his hand, he measured a thousand cubits, and he caused me to pass through the waters, waters that were ankle-deep.

[4] Again he measured a thousand cubits and caused me to pass through the waters, waters that reached to the knees. Again he measured a thousand cubits and caused me to pass through the waters, waters that reached to the loins.

[5] Afterward he measured a thousand, and it was a river that I could not pass through, for the waters had risen, waters to swim in, a river that could not be passed over *or* through.

[6] And he said to me, Son of man, have you seen this? Then he led me and caused me to return to the bank of the river.

[7] Now when I had returned, behold, on the bank of the river were very many trees on the one side and on the other.

[8] Then he said to me, These waters pour out toward the eastern region and go down into the Arabah (the Jordan Valley) and on into the Dead Sea. And when they shall enter into the sea [the sea of putrid waters], the waters shall be healed *and* made fresh.

[9] And wherever the double river shall go, every living creature which swarms shall live. And there shall be a very great number of fish, because these waters go there that [the waters of the sea] may be healed *and* made fresh; and everything shall live wherever the river goes.

---

[a] 20 Or *purification offering*   [b] 22 The meaning of the Hebrew for this word is uncertain.   [c] 22 That is, about 70 feet long and 53 feet wide or about 21 meters long and 16 meters wide   [d] 3 That is, about 1,700 feet or about 530 meters   [e] 8 Or *the Jordan Valley*

## New International Version

will live. [10]Fishermen will stand along the shore; from En Gedi to En Eglaim there will be places for spreading nets. The fish will be of many kinds—like the fish of the Mediterranean Sea. [11]But the swamps and marshes will not become fresh; they will be left for salt. [12]Fruit trees of all kinds will grow on both banks of the river. Their leaves will not wither, nor will their fruit fail. Every month they will bear fruit, because the water from the sanctuary flows to them. Their fruit will serve for food and their leaves for healing."

### The Boundaries of the Land

[13]This is what the Sovereign LORD says: "These are the boundaries of the land that you will divide among the twelve tribes of Israel as their inheritance, with two portions for Joseph. [14]You are to divide it equally among them. Because I swore with uplifted hand to give it to your ancestors, this land will become your inheritance.

[15]"This is to be the boundary of the land:

"On the north side it will run from the Mediterranean Sea by the Hethlon road past Lebo Hamath to Zedad, [16]Berothah[a] and Sibraim (which lies on the border between Damascus and Hamath), as far as Hazer Hattikon, which is on the border of Hauran. [17]The boundary will extend from the sea to Hazar Enan,[b] along the northern border of Damascus, with the border of Hamath to the north. This will be the northern boundary.
[18]"On the east side the boundary will run between Hauran and Damascus, along the Jordan between Gilead and the land of Israel, to the Dead Sea and as far as Tamar.[c] This will be the eastern boundary.
[19]"On the south side it will run from Tamar as far as the waters of Meribah Kadesh, then along the Wadi of Egypt to the Mediterranean Sea. This will be the southern boundary.
[20]"On the west side, the Mediterranean Sea will be the boundary to a point opposite Lebo Hamath. This will be the western boundary.

[21]"You are to distribute this land among yourselves according to the tribes of Israel. [22]You are to allot it as an inheritance for yourselves and for the foreigners residing among you and who have children. You are to consider them as native-born Israelites; along with you they are to be allotted an inheritance among the tribes of Israel. [23]In whatever tribe a foreigner resides, there you are to give them their inheritance," declares the Sovereign LORD.

### The Division of the Land

**48** "These are the tribes, listed by name: At the northern frontier, Dan will have one portion; it will follow the Hethlon road to Lebo Hamath; Hazar Enan and the northern border of Damascus next to Hamath will be part of its border from the east side to the west side.

[2]"Asher will have one portion; it will border the territory of Dan from east to west.
[3]"Naphtali will have one portion; it will border the territory of Asher from east to west.
[4]"Manasseh will have one portion; it will border the territory of Naphtali from east to west.
[5]"Ephraim will have one portion; it will border the territory of Manasseh from east to west.
[6]"Reuben will have one portion; it will border the territory of Ephraim from east to west.

## Amplified Bible

[10]The fishermen shall stand on [the banks of the Dead Sea]; from En-gedi even to En-eglaim shall be a place to spread nets; their fish shall be of very many kinds, as the fish of the Great or Mediterranean Sea.
[11]But its swamps and marshes shall not become wholesome for animal life; they shall [as the river subsides] be left encrusted with salt and given over to it.
[12]And on the banks of the river on both its sides, there shall grow all kinds of trees for food; their leaf shall not fade nor shall their fruit fail [to meet the demand]. Each tree shall bring forth new fruit every month, [these supernatural qualities being] because their waters came from out of the sanctuary. And their fruit shall be for food and their leaves for healing.
[13]Thus says the Lord God: These shall be the boundaries by which you shall divide the land among the twelve tribes of Israel: Joseph shall have two portions.
[14]And you shall divide it equally. I lifted up My hand and swore to give it to your fathers, and this land shall fall to you as your inheritance.
[15]And this shall be the boundary of the land on the north side: from the Great or Mediterranean Sea by way of Hethlon to the entrance of Zedad,
[16]Hamath, Berothah, Sibraim, which is on the border between Damascus and Hamath, as far as Hazer-hatticon on the border of Hauran.
[17]So the boundary shall extend from the [Mediterranean] Sea to Hazar-enan, at the boundary of Damascus on the north, together with the boundary of Hamath to the north. This is the north side.
[18]And on the east side you shall measure the boundary from between Hauran and Damascus, and Gilead on one side and the land of Israel on the other, with the Jordan forming the boundary down to the East or Dead Sea. And this [from Damascus to the Dead Sea and including it] is the east side.
[19]And the south side [boundary] southward, from Tamar [near the Dead Sea] shall run as far as the waters of Meribath-kadesh, then along the Brook of Egypt to the Great or Mediterranean Sea. And this is the south side.
[20]On the west side [the boundary] shall be the Great or Mediterranean Sea to a point opposite the entrance of Hamath [north of Mount Hermon]. This is the west side.
[21]So you shall divide this land among you according to the tribes of Israel.
[22]You shall divide it by allotment as an inheritance for yourselves and for the foreigners who reside among you and shall have children born among you. They shall be to you as those born in the country among the children of Israel; they shall inherit with you among the tribes of Israel.
[23]In whatever tribe the foreigner resides, there shall you give him his inheritance, says the Lord God.

**48** Now these are the names of the tribes: From the north end, beside the way of Hethlon to the entrance of Hamath as far as Hazar-enan, which is on the northern border of Damascus opposite Hamath, and reaching from the east border to the west, Dan, one [portion].
[2]And beside the border of Dan, from the east side to the west side, Asher, one [portion].
[3]And beside the border of Asher, from the east side to the west side, Naphtali, one [portion].
[4]And beside the border of Naphtali, from the east side to the west side, Manasseh, one [portion].
[5]And beside the border of Manasseh, from the east side to the west side, Ephraim, one [portion].
[6]And beside the border of Ephraim, from the east side to the west side, Reuben, one [portion].

---

[a] 15,16 See Septuagint and 48:1; Hebrew road to go into Zedad, [16]Hamath, Berothah.    [b] 17 Hebrew Enon, a variant of Enan    [c] 18 See Syriac; Hebrew Israel. You will measure to the Dead Sea.

## New International Version

7"Judah will have one portion; it will border the territory of Reuben from east to west.

8"Bordering the territory of Judah from east to west will be the portion you are to present as a special gift. It will be 25,000 cubits*a* wide, and its length from east to west will equal one of the tribal portions; the sanctuary will be in the center of it.

9"The special portion you are to offer to the LORD will be 25,000 cubits long and 10,000 cubits*b* wide. 10This will be the sacred portion for the priests. It will be 25,000 cubits long on the north side, 10,000 cubits wide on the west side, 10,000 cubits wide on the east side and 25,000 cubits long on the south side. In the center of it will be the sanctuary of the LORD. 11This will be for the consecrated priests, the Zadokites, who were faithful in serving me and did not go astray as the Levites did when the Israelites went astray. 12It will be a special gift to them from the sacred portion of the land, a most holy portion, bordering the territory of the Levites.

13"Alongside the territory of the priests, the Levites will have an allotment 25,000 cubits long and 10,000 cubits wide. Its total length will be 25,000 cubits and its width 10,000 cubits. 14They must not sell or exchange any of it. This is the best of the land and must not pass into other hands, because it is holy to the LORD.

15"The remaining area, 5,000 cubits*c* wide and 25,000 cubits long, will be for the common use of the city, for houses and for pastureland. The city will be in the center of it 16and will have these measurements: the north side 4,500 cubits,*d* the south side 4,500 cubits, the east side 4,500 cubits, and the west side 4,500 cubits. 17The pastureland for the city will be 250 cubits*e* on the north, 250 cubits on the south, 250 cubits on the east, and 250 cubits on the west. 18What remains of the area, bordering on the sacred portion and running the length of it, will be 10,000 cubits on the east side and 10,000 cubits on the west side. Its produce will supply food for the workers of the city. 19The workers from the city who farm it will come from all the tribes of Israel. 20The entire portion will be a square, 25,000 cubits on each side. As a special gift you will set aside the sacred portion, along with the property of the city.

21"What remains on both sides of the area formed by the sacred portion and the property of the city will belong to the prince. It will extend eastward from the 25,000 cubits of the sacred portion to the eastern border, and westward from the 25,000 cubits to the western border. Both these areas running the length of the tribal portions will belong to the prince, and the sacred portion with the temple sanctuary will be in the center of them. 22So the property of the Levites and the property of the city will lie in the center of the area that belongs to the prince. The area belonging to the prince will lie between the border of Judah and the border of Benjamin.

23"As for the rest of the tribes: Benjamin will have one portion; it will extend from the east side to the west side.

24"Simeon will have one portion; it will border the territory of Benjamin from east to west.

25"Issachar will have one portion; it will border the territory of Simeon from east to west.

26"Zebulun will have one portion; it will border the territory of Issachar from east to west.

## Amplified Bible

7And beside the border of Reuben, from the east side to the west side, Judah, one [portion].

8And beside the border of Judah, from the east side to the west side, shall be the offering of land which you shall offer: 25,000 reeds in breadth, and in length as one of the tribal portions from the east side to the west side; and the sanctuary shall be in the midst of it.

9The portion of land that you shall set apart and offer to the Lord shall be 25,000 [measures] in length and 10,000 in breadth [for each of the two districts].

10And for these, even for the priests, shall be this holy offering of land: toward the north 25,000 [measures] in length, and toward the west 10,000 in breadth, and toward the east 10,000 in breadth, and toward the south 25,000 in length, and the sanctuary of the Lord shall be in the midst of it.

11The set-apart *and* sacred portion shall be for the consecrated priests of the sons of Zadok, who have kept My charge and who did not go astray when the children of Israel went astray, as the other Levites did.

12And this land offering shall be for the priests as a thing most holy beside the border of the [other] Levites.

13And opposite the border of the priests the [other] Levites shall have 25,000 [measures] in length and 10,000 in breadth. The whole length shall be 25,000 and the breadth 10,000.

14And they shall not sell any of it or exchange it; they shall not convey *or* transfer this the firstfruits of the land, for it has been offered to the Lord and is holy to Him.

15And the remaining strip of 5,000 [measures] in breadth and 25,000 in length shall be for the city's secular use, for a place in which to dwell and for open country *or* suburbs. The city shall be in the midst of the plot.

16And these shall be the dimensions of it: the north side 4,500 [measures] and the south side 4,500, the east side 4,500 and the west side 4,500. [Rev. 21:16.]

17And the city shall have suburbs *or* open country: toward the north 250 [measures] and toward the south 250, toward the east 250 and toward the west 250.

18The remainder of the length along beside the holy portion shall be 10,000 [measures] to the east and 10,000 to the west, and it shall be along beside the holy portion. The produce from it shall be for food for those who work in the city.

19And the workers of the city from all the tribes of Israel shall till the open land.

20The whole portion that you shall set apart as an offering to God shall be 25,000 [measures] by 25,000; you shall set apart the holy portion foursquare, together with the property of the city.

21And what is left unallotted, on both sides of the holy portion and of that possessed by the city, shall belong to the prince. Reaching eastward from the 25,000 [measures] of the holy portion to the east border, and westward from the 25,000 [measures] to the west border, parallel to the tribal allotments, it belongs to the prince. The holy portion with the sanctuary of the temple in its midst,

22And the possession of the Levites and the property of the city [of Jerusalem] shall be in the midst of that which belongs to the prince. What lies between the border of Judah and the border of Benjamin shall be for the prince.

23As for the rest of the tribes, from the east side to the west side, Benjamin, one [portion].

24And beside the border of Benjamin, from the east side to the west side, Simeon, one [portion].

25And beside the border of Simeon, from the east side to the west side, Issachar, one [portion].

26And beside the border of Issachar, from the east side to the west side, Zebulun, one [portion].

---

*a 8* That is, about 8 miles or about 13 kilometers; also in verses 9, 10, 13, 15, 20 and 21    *b 9* That is, about 3 1/3 miles or about 5.3 kilometers; also in verses 10, 13 and 18    *c 15* That is, about 1 2/3 miles or about 2.7 kilometers    *d 16* That is, about 1 1/2 miles or about 2.4 kilometers; also in verses 30, 32, 33 and 34    *e 17* That is, about 440 feet or about 135 meters

## New International Version

27"Gad will have one portion; it will border the territory of Zebulun from east to west.

28"The southern boundary of Gad will run south from Tamar to the waters of Meribah Kadesh, then along the Wadi of Egypt to the Mediterranean Sea.

29"This is the land you are to allot as an inheritance to the tribes of Israel, and these will be their portions," declares the Sovereign LORD.

### The Gates of the New City

30"These will be the exits of the city: Beginning on the north side, which is 4,500 cubits long, 31the gates of the city will be named after the tribes of Israel. The three gates on the north side will be the gate of Reuben, the gate of Judah and the gate of Levi.

32"On the east side, which is 4,500 cubits long, will be three gates: the gate of Joseph, the gate of Benjamin and the gate of Dan.

33"On the south side, which measures 4,500 cubits, will be three gates: the gate of Simeon, the gate of Issachar and the gate of Zebulun.

34"On the west side, which is 4,500 cubits long, will be three gates: the gate of Gad, the gate of Asher and the gate of Naphtali.

35"The distance all around will be 18,000 cubits.*a*

"And the name of the city from that time on will be:

THE LORD IS THERE."

## Amplified Bible

27And beside the border of Zebulun, from the east side to the west side, Gad, one [portion].

28And beside the border of Gad, at the south side southward, the border shall extend from Tamar to the waters of Meribath-kadesh and on along the Brook [of Egypt] to the Great *or* Mediterranean Sea.

29This is the land which you shall divide by allotment among the tribes of Israel as their inheritance, and these are their several portions, says the Lord God.

30And these shall be the exits of the city: On the north side, which is to extend 4,500 measures,

31Three gates: one gate of Reuben, one gate of Judah, one gate of Levi, the gates of the city being called after the names of the tribes of Israel;

32And on the east side's 4,500 measures, three gates: one gate of Joseph, one gate of Benjamin, one gate of Dan;

33And on the south side's 4,500 measures, three gates: one gate of Simeon, one gate of Issachar, one gate of Zebulun;

34On the west side's 4,500 measures, three gates: one gate of Gad, one gate of Asher, one gate of Naphtali.

35The distance around the city shall be 18,000 [4 x 4,500] measures; and the name of the city from that day *and* ever after shall be, THE LORD IS THERE. [Rev. 21:12, 13, 16.]

*a 35 That is, about 6 miles or about 9.5 kilometers

# Daniel

# Daniel

### Daniel's Training in Babylon

**1** In the third year of the reign of Jehoiakim king of Judah, Nebuchadnezzar king of Babylon came to Jerusalem and besieged it. ²And the Lord delivered Jehoiakim king of Judah into his hand, along with some of the articles from the temple of God. These he carried off to the temple of his god in Babylonia*a* and put in the treasure house of his god.

³Then the king ordered Ashpenaz, chief of his court officials, to bring into the king's service some of the Israelites from the royal family and the nobility— ⁴young men without any physical defect, handsome, showing aptitude for every kind of learning, well informed, quick to understand, and qualified to serve in the king's palace. He was to teach them the language and literature of the Babylonians.*b* ⁵The king assigned them a daily amount of food and wine from the king's table. They were to be trained for three years, and after that they were to enter the king's service.

⁶Among those who were chosen were some from Judah: Daniel, Hananiah, Mishael and Azariah. ⁷The chief official gave them new names: to Daniel, the name Belteshazzar; to Hananiah, Shadrach; to Mishael, Meshach; and to Azariah, Abednego.

⁸But Daniel resolved not to defile himself with the royal food and wine, and he asked the chief official for permission not to defile himself this way. ⁹Now God had caused the official to show favor and compassion to Daniel, ¹⁰but the official told Daniel, "I am afraid of my lord the king, who has assigned your*c* food and drink. Why should he see you looking worse than the other young men your age? The king would then have my head because of you."

¹¹Daniel then said to the guard whom the chief official had appointed over Daniel, Hananiah, Mishael and Azariah, ¹²"Please test your servants for ten days: Give us nothing but vegetables to eat and water to drink. ¹³Then compare our appearance with that of the young men who eat the royal food, and treat your servants in accordance with what you see." ¹⁴So he agreed to this and tested them for ten days.

¹⁵At the end of the ten days they looked healthier and better nourished than any of the young men who ate the royal food. ¹⁶So the guard took away their choice food and the wine they were to drink and gave them vegetables instead.

¹⁷To these four young men God gave knowledge and understanding of all kinds of literature and learning. And Daniel could understand visions and dreams of all kinds.

¹⁸At the end of the time set by the king to bring them into his service, the chief official presented them to Nebuchadnezzar. ¹⁹The king talked with them, and he found

**1** In the third year of the reign of Jehoiakim king of Judah, Nebuchadnezzar king of Babylon came to Jerusalem and besieged it.

²And the Lord gave Jehoiakim king of Judah into his hand, along with a part of the vessels of the house of God; and he carried them into the land of Shinar [Babylonia] to the house of his god and placed the vessels in the treasury of his god. [II Chron. 36:5-7; Jer. 27:19, 20; Dan. 5:1-3.]

³And the [Babylonian] king told Ashpenaz, the master of his eunuchs, to bring in some of the children of Israel, both of the royal family and of the nobility—[II Kings 20:17, 18.]

⁴Youths without blemish, well-favored in appearance and skillful in all wisdom, discernment, *and* understanding, apt in learning knowledge, competent to stand *and* serve in the king's palace—and to teach them the literature and language of the Chaldeans.

⁵And the king assigned for them a daily portion of his own rich *and* dainty food and of the wine which he drank. They were to be so educated *and* so nourished for three years that at the end of that time they might stand before the king.

⁶Among these were of the children of Judah: Daniel, Hananiah, Mishael, and Azariah.

⁷The chief of the eunuchs gave them names: Daniel he called Belteshazzar [the king's attendant], Hananiah he called Shadrach, Mishael he called Meshach, and Azariah he called Abednego.

⁸But Daniel determined in his heart that he would not defile himself by [eating his portion of] the king's rich *and* dainty food or by [drinking] the wine which he drank; therefore he requested of the chief of the eunuchs that he might [be allowed] not to defile himself. [Num. 6:1-4; I Cor. 10:21.]

⁹Now God made Daniel to find favor, compassion, *and* loving-kindness with the chief of the eunuchs.

¹⁰And the chief of the eunuchs said to Daniel, I fear, lest my lord the king, who has appointed your food and your drink, should see your faces worse looking *or* more sad than the other youths of your age. Then you would endanger my head with the king.

¹¹Then said Daniel to the steward whom the chief of the eunuchs had set over Daniel, Hananiah, Mishael, and Azariah,

¹²Prove your servants, I beseech you, for ten days and let us be given a vegetable diet and water to drink.

¹³Then let our appearance and the appearance of the youths who eat of the king's [rich] dainties be observed *and* compared by you, and deal with us your servants according to what you see.

¹⁴So [the man] consented to them in this matter and proved them ten days.

¹⁵And at the end of ten days it was seen that they were looking better and had taken on more flesh than all the youths who ate of the king's rich dainties.

¹⁶So the steward took away their [rich] dainties and the wine they were to drink and gave them vegetables.

¹⁷As for these four youths, God gave them knowledge and skill in all learning and wisdom, and Daniel had understanding in all [kinds of] visions and dreams. [Luke 21:15; James 1:5-7.]

¹⁸Now at the end of the time which the king had set for bringing [all the young men in], the chief of the eunuchs brought them before Nebuchadnezzar.

¹⁹And the king conversed with them, and among them all

---

*a*2 Hebrew *Shinar*    *b*4 Or *Chaldeans*    *c*10 The Hebrew for *your* and *you* in this verse is plural.

## New International Version

none equal to Daniel, Hananiah, Mishael and Azariah; so they entered the king's service. [20]In every matter of wisdom and understanding about which the king questioned them, he found them ten times better than all the magicians and enchanters in his whole kingdom.

[21]And Daniel remained there until the first year of King Cyrus.

### Nebuchadnezzar's Dream

**2** In the second year of his reign, Nebuchadnezzar had dreams; his mind was troubled and he could not sleep. [2]So the king summoned the magicians, enchanters, sorcerers and astrologers[a] to tell him what he had dreamed. When they came in and stood before the king, [3]he said to them, "I have had a dream that troubles me and I want to know what it means.[b]"

[4]Then the astrologers answered the king,[c] "May the king live forever! Tell your servants the dream, and we will interpret it."

[5]The king replied to the astrologers, "This is what I have firmly decided: If you do not tell me what my dream was and interpret it, I will have you cut into pieces and your houses turned into piles of rubble. [6]But if you tell me the dream and explain it, you will receive from me gifts and rewards and great honor. So tell me the dream and interpret it for me."

[7]Once more they replied, "Let the king tell his servants the dream, and we will interpret it."

[8]Then the king answered, "I am certain that you are trying to gain time, because you realize that this is what I have firmly decided: [9]If you do not tell me the dream, there is only one penalty for you. You have conspired to tell me misleading and wicked things, hoping the situation will change. So then, tell me the dream, and I will know that you can interpret it for me."

[10]The astrologers answered the king, "There is no one on earth who can do what the king asks! No king, however great and mighty, has ever asked such a thing of any magician or enchanter or astrologer. [11]What the king asks is too difficult. No one can reveal it to the king except the gods, and they do not live among humans."

[12]This made the king so angry and furious that he ordered the execution of all the wise men of Babylon. [13]So the decree was issued to put the wise men to death, and men were sent to look for Daniel and his friends to put them to death.

[14]When Arioch, the commander of the king's guard, had gone out to put to death the wise men of Babylon, Daniel spoke to him with wisdom and tact. [15]He asked the king's officer, "Why did the king issue such a harsh decree?" Arioch then explained the matter to Daniel. [16]At this, Daniel went in to the king and asked for time, so that he might interpret the dream for him.

[17]Then Daniel returned to his house and explained the matter to his friends Hananiah, Mishael and Azariah. [18]He urged them to plead for mercy from the God of heaven concerning this mystery, so that he and his friends might

---

[a] 2 Or *Chaldeans*; also in verses 4, 5 and 10   [b] 3 Or *was*   [c] 4 At this point the Hebrew text has *in Aramaic*, indicating that the text from here through the end of chapter 7 is in Aramaic.

## Amplified Bible

none was found like Daniel, Hananiah, Mishael, and Azariah; therefore they were assigned to stand before the king.

[20]And in all matters of wisdom and understanding concerning which the king asked them, he found them ten times better than all the [learned] magicians and enchanters who were in his whole realm.

[21]And Daniel continued there even to the first year of King Cyrus [at the close of the seventy years' exile of Judah in Babylonia, which Jeremiah had foretold]. [Ezra 1:1-3; Jer. 25:11, 12; 29:10.]

**2** In the second year of the reign of Nebuchadnezzar, Nebuchadnezzar had dreams by which his spirit was troubled *and* agitated and his sleep went from him. [2]Then the king commanded to call the magicians, the enchanters *or* soothsayers, the sorcerers, and the Chaldeans [diviners], to tell the king his dreams. So they came and stood before the king.

[3]And the king said to them, I had a dream and my spirit is troubled to know the dream.

[4]Then said the Chaldeans [diviners] to the king in Aramaic [the Syrian language], O king, live forever! Tell your servants the dream, and we will show the interpretation.

[5]The king answered the Chaldeans, The thing is gone from me! And the decree goes forth from me *and* I say it with all emphasis: if you do not make known to me the dream with its interpretation, you shall be cut in pieces and your houses shall be made a dunghill!

[6]But if you show the dream and its interpretation, you shall receive from me gifts and rewards and great honor. So show me the dream and the interpretation of it.

[7]They answered again, Let the king tell his servants the dream, and we will show the interpretation of it.

[8]The king answered, I know with certainty that you are trying to gain time, because you see the thing is gone from me *and* because you see that my word [against you] is sure:

[9]If you will not make known to me the dream, there is but one sentence for you; for you have prepared lying and corrupt words to speak before me [hoping to delay your execution] until the time is changed. Therefore tell me the dream, and I will know that you can tell me the interpretation of it.

[10]The Chaldeans [diviners] answered before the king and said, There is not a man on earth who can show the king this matter, for no king, lord, or ruler has [ever] asked such a thing of any magician or enchanter or Chaldean.

[11]A rare *and* weighty thing indeed the king requires! None except the gods can reveal it to the king, and their dwelling is not with [human] flesh.

[12]For this cause the king was angry and very furious and commanded that all the wise men of Babylon be destroyed.

[13]So the decree went forth that the wise men were to be killed, and [the officers] sought Daniel and his companions to be slain.

[14]Then Daniel returned an answer which was full of prudence and wisdom to Arioch the captain *or* executioner of the king's guard, who had gone forth to slay the wise men of Babylon.

[15]He said to Arioch, the king's captain, Why is the decree so urgent *and* hasty from the king? Then Arioch explained the matter to Daniel.

[16]And Daniel went in and desired of the king that he would set a date *and* give him time, and he would show the king the interpretation.

[17]Then Daniel went to his house and made the thing known to Hananiah, Mishael, and Azariah, his companions,

[18]So that they would desire *and* request mercy of the God of heaven concerning this secret, that Daniel and his

## New International Version

not be executed with the rest of the wise men of Babylon. [19]During the night the mystery was revealed to Daniel in a vision. Then Daniel praised the God of heaven [20]and said:

"Praise be to the name of God for ever and ever;
    wisdom and power are his.
[21]He changes times and seasons;
    he deposes kings and raises up others.
He gives wisdom to the wise
    and knowledge to the discerning.
[22]He reveals deep and hidden things;
    he knows what lies in darkness,
    and light dwells with him.
[23]I thank and praise you, God of my ancestors:
    You have given me wisdom and power,
you have made known to me what we asked of you,
    you have made known to us the dream of the king."

### Daniel Interprets the Dream

[24]Then Daniel went to Arioch, whom the king had appointed to execute the wise men of Babylon, and said to him, "Do not execute the wise men of Babylon. Take me to the king, and I will interpret his dream for him."

[25]Arioch took Daniel to the king at once and said, "I have found a man among the exiles from Judah who can tell the king what his dream means."

[26]The king asked Daniel (also called Belteshazzar), "Are you able to tell me what I saw in my dream and interpret it?"

[27]Daniel replied, "No wise man, enchanter, magician or diviner can explain to the king the mystery he has asked about, [28]but there is a God in heaven who reveals mysteries. He has shown King Nebuchadnezzar what will happen in days to come. Your dream and the visions that passed through your mind as you were lying in bed are these:

[29]"As Your Majesty was lying there, your mind turned to things to come, and the revealer of mysteries showed you what is going to happen. [30]As for me, this mystery has been revealed to me, not because I have greater wisdom than anyone else alive, but so that Your Majesty may know the interpretation and that you may understand what went through your mind.

[31]"Your Majesty looked, and there before you stood a large statue—an enormous, dazzling statue, awesome in appearance. [32]The head of the statue was made of pure gold, its chest and arms of silver, its belly and thighs of bronze, [33]its legs of iron, its feet partly of iron and partly of baked clay. [34]While you were watching, a rock was cut out, but not by human hands. It struck the statue on its feet of iron and clay and smashed them. [35]Then the iron, the clay, the bronze, the silver and the gold were all broken to pieces and became like chaff on a threshing floor in the summer. The wind swept them away without leaving a trace. But the rock that struck the statue became a huge mountain and filled the whole earth.

## Amplified Bible

companions should not perish with the rest of the wise men of Babylon.

[19]Then the secret was revealed to Daniel in a vision of the night, and Daniel blessed the God of heaven.

[20]Daniel answered, Blessed be the name of God forever and ever! For wisdom and might are His!

[21]He changes the times and the seasons; He removes kings and sets up kings. He gives wisdom to the wise and knowledge to those who have understanding! [Dan. 4:35.]

[22]He reveals the deep and secret things; He knows what is in the darkness, and the light dwells with Him! [Job 15:8; Ps. 25:14; Matt. 6:6.]

[23]I thank You and praise You, O God of my fathers, Who has given me wisdom and might and has made known to me now what we desired of You, for You have made known to us the solution to the king's problem.

[24]Therefore Daniel went to Arioch, whom the king had appointed to destroy the wise men of Babylon; he went and said thus to him: Do not destroy the wise men of Babylon! Bring me in before the king, and I will show to the king the interpretation.

[25]Then Arioch brought in Daniel before the king in haste and said thus to him: I have found a man of the captives of Judah who will make known to the king the interpretation [of his dream].

[26]The king said to Daniel, whose name was Belteshazzar, Are you able to make known to me the dream which I have seen and the interpretation of it?

[27]Daniel answered the king, The [mysterious] secret which the king has demanded neither the wise men, enchanters, magicians, nor astrologers can show the king,

[28]But there is a God in heaven Who reveals secrets, and He has made known to King Nebuchadnezzar what it is that shall be in the latter days (at the end of days). Your dream and the visions in your head upon your bed are these:

[29]As for you, O king, as you were lying upon your bed thoughts came into your mind about what should come to pass hereafter, and He Who reveals secrets was making known to you what shall come to pass.

[30]But as for me, this secret is not revealed to me for any wisdom that I have more than anyone else living, but in order that the interpretation may be made known to the king and that you may know the thoughts of your heart and mind.

[31]You, O king, saw, and behold, [there was] a great image. This image which was mighty and of exceedingly great brightness stood before you, and the appearance of it was frightening and terrible.

[32]As for this [a]image, its head was of fine gold, its breast and its arms of silver, its belly and its thighs of bronze,

[33]Its legs of iron, its feet partly of iron and partly of clay [the baked clay of the potter].

[34]As you looked, a [b]Stone was cut out without human hands, which smote the image on its feet of iron and [baked] clay [of the potter] and broke them to pieces. [I Pet. 2:3-8.]

[35]Then the iron, the [baked] clay [of the potter], the bronze, the silver, and the gold were broken and crushed together and became like the chaff of the summer threshing floors, and the wind carried them away so that not a trace of them could be found. And the Stone that smote the image became a great mountain or rock and filled the whole earth.

---

[a] Daniel's interpretation of Nebuchadnezzar's dream outlines the further history of Gentile world power. The four metals of which the image was made represented four successive empires, each with the power to possess the whole inhabited earth—though each stopped short of that. They were: (1) Babylon (Jer. 51:7) (2) Medo-Persia (3) Greece under Alexander (4) Rome. The latter power was divided first into the two legs, corresponding to the eastern and western Roman empires, and then (after a very long time apparently) into the ten toes, a confederacy made up largely of European nations (Dan. 7:24-27). [b] The eternal kingdom of God, the Messianic kingdom, will extend over "the whole earth," and all who reject Jesus, the Messiah, the Stone, will be crushed. See also Ps. 118:22-23; Isa. 8:14; Matt. 21:44; Luke 2:34; 20:18; I Pet. 2:3-8.

## New International Version

36"This was the dream, and now we will interpret it to the king. 37Your Majesty, you are the king of kings. The God of heaven has given you dominion and power and might and glory; 38in your hands he has placed all mankind and the beasts of the field and the birds in the sky. Wherever they live, he has made you ruler over them all. You are that head of gold.

39"After you, another kingdom will arise, inferior to yours. Next, a third kingdom, one of bronze, will rule over the whole earth. 40Finally, there will be a fourth kingdom, strong as iron—for iron breaks and smashes everything—and as iron breaks things to pieces, so it will crush and break all the others. 41Just as you saw that the feet and toes were partly of baked clay and partly of iron, so this will be a divided kingdom; yet it will have some of the strength of iron in it, even as you saw iron mixed with clay. 42As the toes were partly iron and partly clay, so this kingdom will be partly strong and partly brittle. 43And just as you saw the iron mixed with baked clay, so the people will be a mixture and will not remain united, any more than iron mixes with clay.

44"In the time of those kings, the God of heaven will set up a kingdom that will never be destroyed, nor will it be left to another people. It will crush all those kingdoms and bring them to an end, but it will itself endure forever. 45This is the meaning of the vision of the rock cut out of a mountain, but not by human hands—a rock that broke the iron, the bronze, the clay, the silver and the gold to pieces.

"The great God has shown the king what will take place in the future. The dream is true and its interpretation is trustworthy."

46Then King Nebuchadnezzar fell prostrate before Daniel and paid him honor and ordered that an offering and incense be presented to him. 47The king said to Daniel, "Surely your God is the God of gods and the Lord of kings and a revealer of mysteries, for you were able to reveal this mystery."

48Then the king placed Daniel in a high position and lavished many gifts on him. He made him ruler over the entire province of Babylon and placed him in charge of all its wise men. 49Moreover, at Daniel's request the king appointed Shadrach, Meshach and Abednego administrators over the province of Babylon, while Daniel himself remained at the royal court.

### The Image of Gold and the Blazing Furnace

**3** King Nebuchadnezzar made an image of gold, sixty cubits high and six cubits wide,[a] and set it up on the plain of Dura in the province of Babylon. 2He then summoned the satraps, prefects, governors, advisers, treasurers, judges, magistrates and all the other provincial officials to come to the dedication of the image he had set up.

---

a 1 That is, about 90 feet high and 9 feet wide or about 27 meters high and 2.7 meters wide

## Amplified Bible

36This was the dream, and we will tell the interpretation of it to the king.

37You, O king, are king of the [earthly] kings to whom the God of heaven has given the kingdom, the power, the might, and the glory. [Jer. 25:9; 27:6; 28:14.]

38And wherever the children of men dwell, and the beasts of the field, and the birds of the heavens—He has given them into your hand and has made you to rule over them all. You [king of Babylon] are the head of gold.

39And after you shall arise another kingdom [the Medo-Persian], inferior to you, and still a third kingdom of bronze [Greece under Alexander the Great] which shall bear rule over all the earth.

40And the fourth kingdom [Rome] shall be strong as iron, since iron breaks to pieces and subdues all things; and like iron which crushes, it shall break and crush all these. [Dan. 7:7, 23.]

41And as you saw the feet and toes, partly of [baked] clay [of the potter] and partly of iron, it shall be a divided kingdom; but there shall be in it some of the firmness and strength of iron, just as you saw the iron mixed with miry [earthen] clay.

42And as the toes of the feet were partly of iron and partly of [baked] clay [of the potter], so the kingdom shall be partly strong and partly brittle and broken.

43And as you saw the iron mixed with miry and earthen clay, so they shall mingle themselves in the seed of men [in marriage bonds]; but they will not hold together [for two such elements or ideologies can never harmonize], even as iron does not mingle itself with clay.

44And in the days of these [final ten] kings shall the God of heaven set up a kingdom which shall never be destroyed, nor shall its sovereignty be left to another people; but it shall break and crush and consume all these kingdoms and it shall stand forever. [Dan. 7:14-17; Luke 1:31-33; Rev. 11:15.]

45Just as you saw that the Stone was cut out of the mountain without hands and that it broke in pieces the iron, the bronze, the clay, the silver, and the gold, the great God has made known to the king what shall come to pass hereafter. The dream is certain and the interpretation of it is sure.

46Then King Nebuchadnezzar fell on his face and paid homage to Daniel [as a great prophet of the highest God] and ordered that an offering and incense should be offered up to him [in honor of his God].

47The king answered Daniel, Of a truth your God is the God of gods and the Lord of kings and a Revealer of secret mysteries, seeing that you could reveal this secret mystery! [Prov. 3:32; Rev. 19:16.]

48Then the king made Daniel great and gave him many great gifts, and he made him to rule over the whole province of Babylon and to be chief governor over all the wise men of Babylon.

49And Daniel requested of the king and he appointed Shadrach, Meshach, and Abednego over the affairs of the province of Babylon. But Daniel remained in the gate of the king [at the king's court].

**3** Nebuchadnezzar the king [caused to be] made an image of gold, whose height was sixty cubits or ninety feet and its breadth six cubits or nine feet. He set it up on the plain of Dura in the province of Babylon.

2Then Nebuchadnezzar the king sent to gather together the satraps, the deputies, the governors, the judges and chief stargazers, the treasurers, the counselors, the sheriffs and lawyers, and all the chief officials of the provinces to come to the dedication of the image which King Nebuchadnezzar had [caused to be] set up.

## New International Version

³So the satraps, prefects, governors, advisers, treasurers, judges, magistrates and all the other provincial officials assembled for the dedication of the image that King Nebuchadnezzar had set up, and they stood before it.

⁴Then the herald loudly proclaimed, "Nations and peoples of every language, this is what you are commanded to do: ⁵As soon as you hear the sound of the horn, flute, zither, lyre, harp, pipe and all kinds of music, you must fall down and worship the image of gold that King Nebuchadnezzar has set up. ⁶Whoever does not fall down and worship will immediately be thrown into a blazing furnace."

⁷Therefore, as soon as they heard the sound of the horn, flute, zither, lyre, harp and all kinds of music, all the nations and peoples of every language fell down and worshiped the image of gold that King Nebuchadnezzar had set up.

⁸At this time some astrologers*a* came forward and denounced the Jews. ⁹They said to King Nebuchadnezzar, "May the king live forever! ¹⁰Your Majesty has issued a decree that everyone who hears the sound of the horn, flute, zither, lyre, harp, pipe and all kinds of music must fall down and worship the image of gold, ¹¹and that whoever does not fall down and worship will be thrown into a blazing furnace. ¹²But there are some Jews whom you have set over the affairs of the province of Babylon—Shadrach, Meshach and Abednego—who pay no attention to you, Your Majesty. They neither serve your gods nor worship the image of gold you have set up."

¹³Furious with rage, Nebuchadnezzar summoned Shadrach, Meshach and Abednego. So these men were brought before the king, ¹⁴and Nebuchadnezzar said to them, "Is it true, Shadrach, Meshach and Abednego, that you do not serve my gods or worship the image of gold I have set up? ¹⁵Now when you hear the sound of the horn, flute, zither, lyre, harp, pipe and all kinds of music, if you are ready to fall down and worship the image I made, very good. But if you do not worship it, you will be thrown immediately into a blazing furnace. Then what god will be able to rescue you from my hand?"

¹⁶Shadrach, Meshach and Abednego replied to him, "King Nebuchadnezzar, we do not need to defend ourselves before you in this matter. ¹⁷If we are thrown into the blazing furnace, the God we serve is able to deliver us from it, and he will deliver us*b* from Your Majesty's hand. ¹⁸But even if he does not, we want you to know, Your Majesty, that we will not serve your gods or worship the image of gold you have set up."

¹⁹Then Nebuchadnezzar was furious with Shadrach, Meshach and Abednego, and his attitude toward them changed. He ordered the furnace heated seven times hotter than usual ²⁰and commanded some of the strongest soldiers in his army to tie up Shadrach, Meshach and Abednego and throw them into the blazing furnace. ²¹So these men, wearing their robes, trousers, turbans and oth-

## Amplified Bible

³Then the satraps, the deputies, the governors, the judges *and* chief stargazers, the treasurers, the counselors, the sheriffs *and* lawyers, and all the chief officials of the provinces were gathered together for the dedication of the image that King Nebuchadnezzar had set up, and they stood before the image that Nebuchadnezzar had set up.

⁴Then the herald cried aloud, You are commanded, O peoples, nations, and languages,

⁵That when you hear the sound of the horn, pipe, lyre, trigon, harp, dulcimer *or* bagpipe, and every kind of music, you are to fall down and worship the golden image that King Nebuchadnezzar has set up.

⁶And whoever does not fall down and worship shall that very hour be cast into the midst of a burning fiery furnace.

⁷Therefore, when all the peoples heard the sound of the horn, pipe, lyre, trigon, dulcimer *or* bagpipe, and every kind of music, all the peoples, nations, and languages fell down and worshiped the golden image that King Nebuchadnezzar had set up.

⁸Therefore at that time certain men of Chaldean descent came near and brought [malicious] accusations against the Jews.

⁹They said to King Nebuchadnezzar, O king, live forever!

¹⁰You, O king, have made a decree that every man who hears the sound of the horn, pipe, lyre, trigon, harp, dulcimer *or* bagpipe, and every kind of music shall fall down and worship the golden image,

¹¹And that whoever does not fall down and worship shall be cast into the midst of a burning fiery furnace.

¹²There are certain Jews whom you have appointed *and* set over the affairs of the province of Babylon—Shadrach, Meshach, and Abednego. These men, O king, pay no attention to you; they do not serve your gods or worship the golden image which you have set up.

¹³Then Nebuchadnezzar in rage and fury commanded to bring Shadrach, Meshach, and Abednego; and these men were brought before the king.

¹⁴[Then] Nebuchadnezzar said to them, Is it true, O Shadrach, Meshach, and Abednego, that you do not serve my gods or worship the golden image which I have set up?

¹⁵Now if you are ready when you hear the sound of the horn, pipe, lyre, trigon, harp, dulcimer *or* bagpipe, and every kind of music to fall down and worship the image which I have made, very good. But if you do not worship, you shall be cast at once into the midst of a burning fiery furnace, and who is that god who can deliver you out of my hands?

¹⁶Shadrach, Meshach, and Abednego answered the king, O Nebuchadnezzar, it is not necessary for us to answer you on this point.

¹⁷If our God Whom we serve is able to deliver us from the burning fiery furnace, He will deliver us out of your hand, O king.

¹⁸But if not, let it be known to you, O king, that we will not serve your gods or worship the golden image which you have set up! [Job 13:15; Acts 4:19, 20.]

¹⁹Then Nebuchadnezzar was full of fury and his facial expression was changed [to antagonism] against Shadrach, Meshach, and Abednego. Therefore he commanded that the furnace should be heated seven times hotter than it was usually heated.

²⁰And he commanded the strongest men in his army to bind Shadrach, Meshach, and Abednego and to cast them into the burning fiery furnace.

²¹Then these [three] men were bound in their cloaks,

---

*a* 8 Or *Chaldeans*   *b* 17 Or *If the God we serve is able to deliver us, then he will deliver us from the blazing furnace and*

## New International Version

er clothes, were bound and thrown into the blazing furnace. ²²The king's command was so urgent and the furnace so hot that the flames of the fire killed the soldiers who took up Shadrach, Meshach and Abednego, ²³and these three men, firmly tied, fell into the blazing furnace.

²⁴Then King Nebuchadnezzar leaped to his feet in amazement and asked his advisers, "Weren't there three men that we tied up and threw into the fire?"

They replied, "Certainly, Your Majesty."

²⁵He said, "Look! I see four men walking around in the fire, unbound and unharmed, and the fourth looks like a son of the gods."

²⁶Nebuchadnezzar then approached the opening of the blazing furnace and shouted, "Shadrach, Meshach and Abednego, servants of the Most High God, come out! Come here!"

So Shadrach, Meshach and Abednego came out of the fire, ²⁷and the satraps, prefects, governors and royal advisers crowded around them. They saw that the fire had not harmed their bodies, nor was a hair of their heads singed; their robes were not scorched, and there was no smell of fire on them.

²⁸Then Nebuchadnezzar said, "Praise be to the God of Shadrach, Meshach and Abednego, who has sent his angel and rescued his servants! They trusted in him and defied the king's command and were willing to give up their lives rather than serve or worship any god except their own God. ²⁹Therefore I decree that the people of any nation or language who say anything against the God of Shadrach, Meshach and Abednego be cut into pieces and their houses be turned into piles of rubble, for no other god can save in this way."

³⁰Then the king promoted Shadrach, Meshach and Abednego in the province of Babylon.

### Nebuchadnezzar's Dream of a Tree

**4** ᵃ King Nebuchadnezzar,

To the nations and peoples of every language, who live in all the earth:

May you prosper greatly!

²It is my pleasure to tell you about the miraculous signs and wonders that the Most High God has performed for me.

³How great are his signs,
how mighty his wonders!
His kingdom is an eternal kingdom;
his dominion endures from generation to
generation.

⁴I, Nebuchadnezzar, was at home in my palace, contented and prosperous. ⁵I had a dream that made me afraid. As I was lying in bed, the images and visions that passed through my mind terrified me. ⁶So I commanded that all the wise men of Babylon be brought before me to interpret the dream for me. ⁷When the magicians, enchanters, astrologersᵇ and diviners came, I told them the dream, but they could not interpret it for me. ⁸Finally, Daniel came into my presence and I told him the dream. (He is called Belteshazzar, after the name of my god, and the spirit of the holy gods is in him.)

## Amplified Bible

their tunics or undergarments, their turbans, and their other clothing, and they were cast into the midst of the burning fiery furnace.

²²Therefore because the king's commandment was urgent and the furnace exceedingly hot, the flame and sparks from the fire killed those men who handled Shadrach, Meshach, and Abednego.

²³And these three men, Shadrach, Meshach, and Abednego, fell down bound into the burning fiery furnace.

²⁴Then Nebuchadnezzar the king [saw and] was astounded, and he jumped up and said to his counselors, Did we not cast three men bound into the midst of the fire? They answered, True, O king.

²⁵He answered, Behold, I see four men loose, walking in the midst of the fire, and they are not hurt! And the form of the fourth is like a son of the gods! [Phil. 2:5-8.]

²⁶Then Nebuchadnezzar came near to the mouth of the burning fiery furnace and said, Shadrach, Meshach, and Abednego, you servants of the Most High God, come out and come here. Then Shadrach, Meshach, and Abednego came out from the midst of the fire.

²⁷And the satraps, the deputies, the governors, and the king's counselors gathered around together and saw these men—that the fire had no power upon their bodies, nor was the hair of their head singed; neither were their garments scorched or changed in color or condition, nor had even the smell of smoke clung to them.

²⁸Then Nebuchadnezzar said, Blessed be the God of Shadrach, Meshach, and Abednego, Who has sent His angel and delivered His servants who believed in, trusted in, and relied on Him! And they set aside the king's command and yielded their bodies rather than serve or worship any god except their own God.

²⁹Therefore I make a decree that any people, nation, and language that speaks anything amiss against the God of Shadrach, Meshach, and Abednego shall be cut in pieces and their houses be made a dunghill; for there is no other God who can deliver in this way!

³⁰Then the king promoted Shadrach, Meshach, and Abednego in the province of Babylon.

**4** Nebuchadnezzar the king, to all people, nations, and languages that dwell on all the earth: May peace be multiplied to you!

²It seemed good to me to show the signs and wonders that the Most High God has performed toward me.

³How great are His signs! And how mighty His wonders! His kingdom is an everlasting kingdom, and His dominion is from generation to generation. [Dan. 7:13, 14; Luke 1:31-33.]

⁴I, Nebuchadnezzar, was at rest in my house and prospering in my palace.

⁵I had a dream which made me afraid, and the thoughts and imaginations and the visions of my head as I was lying upon my bed troubled and agitated me.

⁶Therefore I made a decree to bring in all the wise men of Babylon before me, that they might make known to me the interpretation of the dream.

⁷Then the magicians, the enchanters, the Chaldeans, and the astrologers came in, and I told them the dream, but they could not make known to me the interpretation of it.

⁸But at last Daniel came in before me—he who was named Belteshazzar, after the name of my god, and in whom is the Spirit of the Holy God—and I told the dream before him, saying,

---

ᵃ In Aramaic texts 4:1-3 is numbered 3:31-33, and 4:4-37 is numbered 4:1-34.   ᵇ 7 Or *Chaldeans*

## New International Version

⁹I said, "Belteshazzar, chief of the magicians, I know that the spirit of the holy gods is in you, and no mystery is too difficult for you. Here is my dream; interpret it for me. ¹⁰These are the visions I saw while lying in bed: I looked, and there before me stood a tree in the middle of the land. Its height was enormous. ¹¹The tree grew large and strong and its top touched the sky; it was visible to the ends of the earth. ¹²Its leaves were beautiful, its fruit abundant, and on it was food for all. Under it the wild animals found shelter, and the birds lived in its branches; from it every creature was fed.

¹³"In the visions I saw while lying in bed, I looked, and there before me was a holy one, a messenger,ᵃ coming down from heaven. ¹⁴He called in a loud voice: 'Cut down the tree and trim off its branches; strip off its leaves and scatter its fruit. Let the animals flee from under it and the birds from its branches. ¹⁵But let the stump and its roots, bound with iron and bronze, remain in the ground, in the grass of the field.

"'Let him be drenched with the dew of heaven, and let him live with the animals among the plants of the earth. ¹⁶Let his mind be changed from that of a man and let him be given the mind of an animal, till seven timesᵇ pass by for him.

¹⁷"'The decision is announced by messengers, the holy ones declare the verdict, so that the living may know that the Most High is sovereign over all kingdoms on earth and gives them to anyone he wishes and sets over them the lowliest of people.'

¹⁸"This is the dream that I, King Nebuchadnezzar, had. Now, Belteshazzar, tell me what it means, for none of the wise men in my kingdom can interpret it for me. But you can, because the spirit of the holy gods is in you."

### Daniel Interprets the Dream

¹⁹Then Daniel (also called Belteshazzar) was greatly perplexed for a time, and his thoughts terrified him. So the king said, "Belteshazzar, do not let the dream or its meaning alarm you."

Belteshazzar answered, "My lord, if only the dream applied to your enemies and its meaning to your adversaries! ²⁰The tree you saw, which grew large and strong, with its top touching the sky, visible to the whole earth, ²¹with beautiful leaves and abundant fruit, providing food for all, giving shelter to the wild animals, and having nesting places in its branches— ²²Your Majesty, you are that tree! You have become great and strong; your greatness has grown until it reaches the sky, and your dominion extends to distant parts of the earth.

²³"Your Majesty saw a holy one, a messenger, coming down from heaven and saying, 'Cut down the tree and destroy it, but leave the stump, bound with iron and bronze, in the grass of the field, while its roots remain in the ground. Let him be drenched with the dew of heaven; let him live with the wild animals, until seven times pass by for him.'

²⁴"This is the interpretation, Your Majesty, and

## Amplified Bible

⁹O Belteshazzar, chief of the magicians, because I know that the Spirit of the Holy God is in you and no secret mystery is a burden or troubles you, tell me the visions of my dream that I have seen and the interpretation of it.

¹⁰The visions of my head [as I lay] on my bed were these: I saw, and behold, [there was] a tree in the midst of the earth, and its height was great.

¹¹The tree grew and was strong and its height reached to the heavens, and the sight of it reached to the end of the whole earth.

¹²Its leaves were fair and its fruit abundant, and in it was food for all. The living creatures of the field found shade under it, and the birds of the sky dwelt in its branches; and all flesh was fed from it.

¹³I saw in the visions of my head [as I lay] on my bed, and behold, a watcher, a holy one, came down from heaven.

¹⁴He cried aloud [with might] and said, Cut down the tree and cut off its branches; shake off its leaves and scatter its fruit. Let the living creatures flee from under it and the fowls from its branches.

¹⁵Nevertheless leave the stump of its roots in the earth, bound with a band of iron and bronze, in the midst of the tender grass of the field. Let him be wet with the dew of the heavens, and let him share the lot of the living creatures in the grass of the earth.

¹⁶Let his nature and understanding be changed from a man's and let a beast's nature and understanding be given him, and let seven times [or years] pass over him.

¹⁷This sentence is by the decree of the [heavenly] watchers and the decision is by the word of the holy ones, to the intent that the living may know that the Most High [God] rules the kingdom of mankind and gives it to whomever He will and sets over it the humblest and lowliest of men. [Dan. 2:21; 5:21.]

¹⁸This dream I, King Nebuchadnezzar, have seen. And you, O Belteshazzar [Daniel], declare now its interpretation, since all the wise men of my kingdom are not able to make known to me the interpretation; but you are able, for the Spirit of the Holy God is in you.

¹⁹Then Daniel, whose name was Belteshazzar, was astonished and dismayed and stricken dumb for a while [concerned about the king's destiny], and his thoughts troubled, agitated, and alarmed him. The king said, Belteshazzar, let not the dream or its interpretation trouble or alarm you. Belteshazzar answered, My lord, may the dream be for those who hate you and its message for your enemies.

²⁰The tree that you saw, which grew [great] and was strong, whose height reached to the heavens and which was visible to all the earth,

²¹Whose foliage was beautiful and its fruit abundant, on which was food for all, under which the living creatures of the field dwelt, and on whose branches the birds of the sky had their nests—

²²It is you, O king, who have grown and become strong; your greatness has increased and it reaches to the heavens, and your dominion to the ends of the earth.

²³And whereas the king saw a watcher, a holy one, coming down from heaven and saying, Cut the tree down and destroy it, but leave the stump of its roots in the earth with a band of iron and bronze around it, in the tender grass of the field; and let him be wet with the dew of the heavens, and let his portion be with the living creatures of the field until seven times [or years] pass over him—

²⁴This is the interpretation, O king: It is the decree of

---

ᵃ 13 Or *watchman*; also in verses 17 and 23    ᵇ 16 Or *years*; also in verses 23, 25 and 32

## New International Version

this is the decree the Most High has issued against my lord the king: ²⁵You will be driven away from people and will live with the wild animals; you will eat grass like the ox and be drenched with the dew of heaven. Seven times will pass by for you until you acknowledge that the Most High is sovereign over all kingdoms on earth and gives them to anyone he wishes. ²⁶The command to leave the stump of the tree with its roots means that your kingdom will be restored to you when you acknowledge that Heaven rules. ²⁷Therefore, Your Majesty, be pleased to accept my advice: Renounce your sins by doing what is right, and your wickedness by being kind to the oppressed. It may be that then your prosperity will continue."

### The Dream Is Fulfilled

²⁸All this happened to King Nebuchadnezzar. ²⁹Twelve months later, as the king was walking on the roof of the royal palace of Babylon, ³⁰he said, "Is not this the great Babylon I have built as the royal residence, by my mighty power and for the glory of my majesty?"

³¹Even as the words were on his lips, a voice came from heaven, "This is what is decreed for you, King Nebuchadnezzar: Your royal authority has been taken from you. ³²You will be driven away from people and will live with the wild animals; you will eat grass like the ox. Seven times will pass by for you until you acknowledge that the Most High is sovereign over all kingdoms on earth and gives them to anyone he wishes."

³³Immediately what had been said about Nebuchadnezzar was fulfilled. He was driven away from people and ate grass like the ox. His body was drenched with the dew of heaven until his hair grew like the feathers of an eagle and his nails like the claws of a bird.

³⁴At the end of that time, I, Nebuchadnezzar, raised my eyes toward heaven, and my sanity was restored. Then I praised the Most High; I honored and glorified him who lives forever.

His dominion is an eternal dominion;
    his kingdom endures from generation to generation.
³⁵All the peoples of the earth
    are regarded as nothing.
He does as he pleases
    with the powers of heaven
    and the peoples of the earth.
No one can hold back his hand
    or say to him: "What have you done?"

³⁶At the same time that my sanity was restored, my honor and splendor were returned to me for the glory of my kingdom. My advisers and nobles sought me out, and I was restored to my throne and became even greater than before. ³⁷Now I, Nebuchadnezzar, praise and exalt and glorify the King of heaven, because everything he does is right and all his ways are just. And those who walk in pride he is able to humble.

### The Writing on the Wall

**5** King Belshazzar gave a great banquet for a thousand of his nobles and drank wine with them. ²While Belshazzar was drinking his wine, he gave orders to bring in the gold and silver goblets that Nebuchadnezzar his fa-

## Amplified Bible

the Most High [God] which has come upon my lord the king:

²⁵You shall be driven from among men and your dwelling shall be with the beasts of the field; you shall be made to eat grass as do the oxen and you shall be wet with the dew of the heavens; and seven times [or years] shall pass over you until you learn *and* know *and* recognize that the Most High [God] rules the kingdom of mankind and gives it to whomever He will.

²⁶And in that it was commanded to leave the stump of the roots of the tree, your kingdom shall be sure to you after you have learned *and* know that [the God of] heaven rules.

²⁷Therefore, O king, let my counsel be acceptable to you; break off your sins *and* show the reality of your repentance by righteousness (right standing with God and moral and spiritual rectitude and rightness in every area and relation) *and* liberate yourself from your iniquities by showing mercy *and* loving-kindness to the poor *and* oppressed, that [if the king will repent] there may possibly be a continuance *and* lengthening of your peace *and* tranquility *and* a healing of your error.

²⁸All this was fulfilled *and* came upon King Nebuchadnezzar.

²⁹At the end of twelve months he was walking in the royal palace of Babylon.

³⁰The king said, Is not this the great Babylon that I have built as the royal residence *and* seat of government by the might of my power and for the honor *and* glory of my majesty?

³¹While the words were still in the king's mouth, there fell a voice from heaven, saying, O King Nebuchadnezzar, to you it is spoken: The kingdom has departed from you,

³²And you shall be driven from among men and your dwelling will be with the living creatures of the field. You will be made to eat grass like the oxen, and seven times [or years] shall pass over you until you have learned *and* know that the Most High [God] rules in the kingdom of men and gives it to whomever He will.

³³That very hour the thing was [in process of] being fulfilled upon Nebuchadnezzar. He was driven from among men and did eat grass like oxen [as Daniel had said he would], and his body was wet with the dew of the heavens until his hair grew like eagles' [feathers] and his nails [were] like birds' [claws].

³⁴And at the end of the days [seven years], I, Nebuchadnezzar, lifted up my eyes to heaven, and my understanding *and* the right use of my mind returned to me; and I blessed the Most High [God] and I praised and honored *and* glorified Him Who lives forever, Whose dominion is an everlasting dominion; and His kingdom endures from generation to generation.

³⁵And all the inhabitants of the earth are accounted as nothing. And He does according to His will in the host of heaven and among the inhabitants of the earth, and none can stay His hand or say to Him, What are You doing?

³⁶Now at the same time my reason *and* understanding returned to me; and for the glory of my kingdom, my majesty and splendor returned to me, and my counselors and my lords sought me out; I was reestablished in my kingdom, and still more greatness [than before] was added to me.

³⁷Now I, Nebuchadnezzar, praise and extol and honor the King of heaven, Whose works are all faithful *and* right and Whose ways are just. And those who walk in pride He is able to abase *and* humble.

**5** Belshazzar the king [descendant of Nebuchadnezzar] made a great feast for a thousand of his lords, and he drank his wine in the presence of the thousand.

²Belshazzar, while he was tasting the wine, commanded that the gold and silver vessels which his father Nebu-

## New International Version

ther[a] had taken from the temple in Jerusalem, so that the king and his nobles, his wives and his concubines might drink from them. [3]So they brought in the gold goblets that had been taken from the temple of God in Jerusalem, and the king and his nobles, his wives and his concubines drank from them. [4]As they drank the wine, they praised the gods of gold and silver, of bronze, iron, wood and stone.

[5]Suddenly the fingers of a human hand appeared and wrote on the plaster of the wall, near the lampstand in the royal palace. The king watched the hand as it wrote. [6]His face turned pale and he was so frightened that his legs became weak and his knees were knocking.

[7]The king summoned the enchanters, astrologers[b] and diviners. Then he said to these wise men of Babylon, "Whoever reads this writing and tells me what it means will be clothed in purple and have a gold chain placed around his neck, and he will be made the third highest ruler in the kingdom."

[8]Then all the king's wise men came in, but they could not read the writing or tell the king what it meant. [9]So King Belshazzar became even more terrified and his face grew more pale. His nobles were baffled.

[10]The queen,[c] hearing the voices of the king and his nobles, came into the banquet hall. "May the king live forever!" she said. "Don't be alarmed! Don't look so pale! [11]There is a man in your kingdom who has the spirit of the holy gods in him. In the time of your father he was found to have insight and intelligence and wisdom like that of the gods. Your father, King Nebuchadnezzar, appointed him chief of the magicians, enchanters, astrologers and diviners. [12]He did this because Daniel, whom the king called Belteshazzar, was found to have a keen mind and knowledge and understanding, and also the ability to interpret dreams, explain riddles and solve difficult problems. Call for Daniel, and he will tell you what the writing means."

[13]So Daniel was brought before the king, and the king said to him, "Are you Daniel, one of the exiles my father the king brought from Judah? [14]I have heard that the spirit of the gods is in you and that you have insight, intelligence and outstanding wisdom. [15]The wise men and enchanters were brought before me to read this writing and tell me what it means, but they could not explain it. [16]Now I have heard that you are able to give interpretations and to solve difficult problems. If you can read this writing and tell me what it means, you will be clothed in purple and have a gold chain placed around your neck, and you will be made the third highest ruler in the kingdom."

[17]Then Daniel answered the king, "You may keep your gifts for yourself and give your rewards to someone else. Nevertheless, I will read the writing for the king and tell him what it means.

[18]"Your Majesty, the Most High God gave your father Nebuchadnezzar sovereignty and greatness and glory and

## Amplified Bible

chadnezzar had taken out of the temple [out of the sacred area—the Holy Place and the Holy of Holies] which was in Jerusalem be brought, that the king and his lords, his wives, and his concubines might drink from them. [3]Then they brought in the gold *and* silver vessels which had been taken out of the temple, the house of God which was in Jerusalem; and the king and his lords, his wives, and his concubines drank from them. [4]They drank wine and praised the gods of gold and silver, of bronze, iron, wood, and stone.

[5]Immediately *and* suddenly there appeared the fingers of a man's hand and wrote on the plaster of the wall opposite the candlestick [so exposed especially to the light] in the king's palace, and the king saw the part of the hand that wrote.

[6]Then the color *and* the [drunken] hilarious brightness of the king's face was changed, and his [terrifying] thoughts troubled *and* alarmed him; the joints *and* muscles of his hips *and* back gave way and his knees smote together.

[7]The king cried aloud [mightily] to bring in the enchanters *or* soothsayers, the Chaldeans [diviners], and the astrologers. The king said to the wise men of Babylon, Whoever will read this writing and show me the interpretation of it will be clothed with purple and have a chain of gold put about his neck and will be the third ruler in the kingdom.

[8]And all the king's wise men came in, but they could not read the writing or make known to the king the interpretation of it.

[9]Then King Belshazzar was greatly perplexed *and* alarmed and the color faded from his face, and his lords were puzzled *and* astounded.

[10]Now the queen [mother], overhearing the exciting words of the king and his lords, came into the banquet house. The queen [mother] said, O king, live forever! Do not be alarmed at your thoughts or let your cheerful expression *and* the color of your face be changed.

[11]There is a man in your kingdom in whom is the Spirit of the holy God [or gods], and in the days of your father light and understanding and wisdom like the wisdom of the gods were found in him; and King Nebuchadnezzar, your father—the king, I say, your father—appointed him master of the magicians, enchanters *or* soothsayers, Chaldeans, and astrologers,

[12]Because an excellent spirit, knowledge, and understanding to interpret dreams, clarify riddles, and solve knotty problems were found in this same Daniel, whom the king named Belteshazzar. Now let Daniel be called, and he will show the interpretation.

[13]Then Daniel was brought in before the king. And the king said to Daniel, Are you that Daniel of the children of the captivity of Judah, whom the king my father brought out of Judah?

[14]I have heard of you, that the Spirit of the holy God [or gods] is in you and that light and understanding and superior wisdom are found in you.

[15]Now the wise men, the enchanters, have been brought in before me that they might read this writing and make known to me the interpretation of it, but they could not show the interpretation of the matter.

[16]But I have heard of you, that you can make interpretations and solve knotty problems. Now if you can read the writing and make known to me its interpretation, you shall be clothed with purple and have a chain of gold put around your neck and shall be the third ruler in the kingdom.

[17]Then Daniel answered before the king, Let your gifts be for yourself and give your rewards to another. However, I will read the writing to the king and make known to him the interpretation.

[18]O king, the Most High God gave Nebuchadnezzar your father a kingdom and greatness and glory and majesty;

---

[a] 2 Or *ancestor*; or *predecessor*; also in verses 11, 13 and 18
[b] 7 Or *Chaldeans*; also in verse 11   [c] 10 Or *queen mother*

## New International Version

splendor. [19]Because of the high position he gave him, all the nations and peoples of every language dreaded and feared him. Those the king wanted to put to death, he put to death; those he wanted to spare, he spared; those he wanted to promote, he promoted; and those he wanted to humble, he humbled. [20]But when his heart became arrogant and hardened with pride, he was deposed from his royal throne and stripped of his glory. [21]He was driven away from people and given the mind of an animal; he lived with the wild donkeys and ate grass like the ox; and his body was drenched with the dew of heaven, until he acknowledged that the Most High God is sovereign over all kingdoms on earth and sets over them anyone he wishes. [22]"But you, Belshazzar, his son,[a] have not humbled yourself, though you knew all this. [23]Instead, you have set yourself up against the Lord of heaven. You had the goblets from his temple brought to you, and you and your nobles, your wives and your concubines drank wine from them. You praised the gods of silver and gold, of bronze, iron, wood and stone, which cannot see or hear or understand. But you did not honor the God who holds in his hand your life and all your ways. [24]Therefore he sent the hand that wrote the inscription.

[25]"This is the inscription that was written:

MENE, MENE, TEKEL, PARSIN

[26]"Here is what these words mean:

*Mene*[b]: God has numbered the days of your reign and brought it to an end.
[27] *Tekel*[c]: You have been weighed on the scales and found wanting.
[28] *Peres*[d]: Your kingdom is divided and given to the Medes and Persians."

[29]Then at Belshazzar's command, Daniel was clothed in purple, a gold chain was placed around his neck, and he was proclaimed the third highest ruler in the kingdom.

[30]That very night Belshazzar, king of the Babylonians,[e] was slain, [31]and Darius the Mede took over the kingdom, at the age of sixty-two.[f]

### Daniel in the Den of Lions

**6**[g] It pleased Darius to appoint 120 satraps to rule throughout the kingdom, [2]with three administrators over them, one of whom was Daniel. The satraps were made accountable to them so that the king might not suffer loss. [3]Now Daniel so distinguished himself among the administrators and the satraps by his exceptional qualities that the king planned to set him over the whole kingdom. [4]At this, the administrators and the satraps tried to find grounds for charges against Daniel in his conduct of government affairs, but they were unable to do so. They could find no corruption in him, because he was trustworthy and neither corrupt nor negligent. [5]Finally these men

---

*a 22* Or *descendant; or successor*    *b 26 Mene* can mean *numbered* or *mina* (a unit of money).    *c 27 Tekel* can mean *weighed* or *shekel.*    *d 28 Peres* (the singular of *Parsin*) can mean *divided* or *Persia* or *a half mina* or *a half shekel.*    *e 30* Or *Chaldeans*    *f 31* In Aramaic texts this verse (5:31) is numbered 6:1.    *g* In Aramaic texts 6:1-28 is numbered 6:2-29.

## Amplified Bible

[19]And because of the greatness that He gave him, all peoples, nations, and languages trembled and feared before him. Whom he would he slew, and whom he would he kept alive; whom he would he set up, and whom he would he put down. [20]But when his heart was lifted up and his mind *and* spirit were hardened so that he dealt proudly, he was deposed from his kingly throne and his glory was taken from him; [21]He was driven from among men, and his heart *or* mind was made like the beasts, and his dwelling was with the wild asses. He was fed with grass like oxen, and his body was wet with the dew of the heavens until he learned *and* knew that the Most High God rules in the kingdom of men and that He appoints *and* sets over it whomever He will. [22]And you his son, O Belshazzar, have not humbled your heart *and* mind, though you knew all this [knew it and were defiant]. [23]And you have lifted yourself up against the Lord of heaven, and the vessels of His house have been brought before you, and you and your lords, your wives, and your concubines have drunk wine from them; and you have praised the gods of silver and gold, of bronze, iron, wood, and stone, which do not see or hear or know; but the God in Whose hand your breath is and Whose are all your ways you have not honored *and* glorified [but have dishonored and disgraced]. [24]Then was the part of the hand sent from the presence of [the Most High God], and this writing was inscribed. [25]And this is the *a* inscription that was written, MENE, MENE, TEKEL, UPHARSIN—numbered, numbered, weighed, divisions. [26]This is the interpretation of the matter: MENE, God has numbered the days of your kingship and brought them to an end; [27]TEKEL, You are weighed in the balances and are found wanting; [28]*b* PERES, Your kingdom *and* your kingship are divided and given to the Medes and Persians. [Foretold in Isa. 21:2, 5, 9.] [29]Then Belshazzar commanded, and Daniel was clothed with purple and a chain of gold put about his neck, and a proclamation was made concerning him that he should be the third ruler in the kingdom. [30]During that night Belshazzar the king of the Chaldeans was slain, [31]And Darius the Mede took the kingdom; he was about sixty-two years old.

**6** It pleased [King] Darius [successor to Belshazzar] to set over the kingdom 120 satraps who should be [in charge] throughout all the kingdom, [2]And over them three presidents—of whom Daniel was one—that these satraps might give account to them and that the king should have no loss *or* damage. [3]Then this Daniel was distinguished above the presidents and the satraps because an excellent spirit was in him, and the king thought to set him over the whole realm. [4]Then the presidents and satraps sought to find occasion [to bring accusation] against Daniel concerning the kingdom, but they could find no occasion or fault, for he was faithful, nor was there any error or fault found in him.

---

*a* For many people it may be difficult to understand why all the wise men, the magicians, the soothsayers, the Chaldeans, and the astrologers were unable to translate a few simple words, especially when Daniel's prescribed education in languages was the same as their own—and he had no difficulty translating. The answer is that any wise man who was present there probably could recognize the four inscribed words, but only the uncompromising man of God—who knew God through daily fellowship and communion with Him, who was so dedicated to Him that God could speak to him and through him—only such a man could tell what the words really meant. Blessed (happy, fortunate, prosperous, and enviable) are those who dare to be a Daniel! *b* The singular of UPHARSIN (see Dan. 5:25).

## New International Version

said, "We will never find any basis for charges against this man Daniel unless it has something to do with the law of his God."

6So these administrators and satraps went as a group to the king and said: "May King Darius live forever! 7The royal administrators, prefects, satraps, advisers and governors have all agreed that the king should issue an edict and enforce the decree that anyone who prays to any god or human being during the next thirty days, except to you, Your Majesty, shall be thrown into the lions' den. 8Now, Your Majesty, issue the decree and put it in writing so that it cannot be altered—in accordance with the law of the Medes and Persians, which cannot be repealed." 9So King Darius put the decree in writing.

10Now when Daniel learned that the decree had been published, he went home to his upstairs room where the windows opened toward Jerusalem. Three times a day he got down on his knees and prayed, giving thanks to his God, just as he had done before. 11Then these men went as a group and found Daniel praying and asking God for help. 12So they went to the king and spoke to him about his royal decree: "Did you not publish a decree that during the next thirty days anyone who prays to any god or human being except to you, Your Majesty, would be thrown into the lions' den?"

The king answered, "The decree stands—in accordance with the law of the Medes and Persians, which cannot be repealed."

13Then they said to the king, "Daniel, who is one of the exiles from Judah, pays no attention to you, Your Majesty, or to the decree you put in writing. He still prays three times a day." 14When the king heard this, he was greatly distressed; he was determined to rescue Daniel and made every effort until sundown to save him.

15Then the men went as a group to King Darius and said to him, "Remember, Your Majesty, that according to the law of the Medes and Persians no decree or edict that the king issues can be changed."

16So the king gave the order, and they brought Daniel and threw him into the lions' den. The king said to Daniel, "May your God, whom you serve continually, rescue you!"

17A stone was brought and placed over the mouth of the den, and the king sealed it with his own signet ring and with the rings of his nobles, so that Daniel's situation might not be changed. 18Then the king returned to his palace and spent the night without eating and without any entertainment being brought to him. And he could not sleep.

19At the first light of dawn, the king got up and hurried to the lions' den. 20When he came near the den, he called to Daniel in an anguished voice, "Daniel, servant of the living God, has your God, whom you serve continually, been able to rescue you from the lions?"

21Daniel answered, "May the king live forever! 22My God sent his angel, and he shut the mouths of the lions. They have not hurt me, because I was found innocent in his sight. Nor have I ever done any wrong before you, Your Majesty."

23The king was overjoyed and gave orders to lift Daniel out of the den. And when Daniel was lifted from the den,

## Amplified Bible

5Then said these men, We shall not find any occasion [to bring accusation] against this Daniel except we find it against him concerning the law of his God. [Acts 24:13-21; I Pet. 4:12-16.]

6Then these presidents and satraps came [tumultuously] together to the king and said to him, King Darius, live forever!

7All the presidents of the kingdom, the deputies and the satraps, the counselors and the governors, have consulted and agreed that the king should establish a royal statute and make a firm decree that whoever shall ask a petition of any god or man for thirty days, except of you, O king, shall be cast into the den of lions.

8Now, O king, establish the decree and sign the writing that it may not be changed, according to the law of the Medes and Persians, which cannot be altered.

9So King Darius signed the writing and the decree.

10Now when Daniel knew that the writing was signed, he went into his house, and his windows being open in his chamber toward Jerusalem, he got down upon his knees three times a day and prayed and gave thanks before his God, as he had done previously. [Ps. 5:7.]

11Then these men came thronging [by agreement] and found Daniel praying and making supplication before his God.

12Then they came near and said before the king concerning his prohibitory decree, Have you not signed an edict that any man who shall make a petition to any god or man within thirty days, except of you, O king, shall be cast into the den of lions? The king answered and said, The thing is true, according to the law of the Medes and Persians, which cannot be changed or repealed.

13Then they said before the king, That Daniel, who is one of the exiles from Judah, does not regard or pay any attention to you, O king, or to the decree that you have signed, but makes his petition three times a day.

14Then the king, when he heard these words, was much distressed [over what he had done] and set his mind on Daniel to deliver him; and he labored until the sun went down to rescue him.

15Then these same men came thronging [by agreement] to the king and said, Know, O king, that it is a law of the Medes and Persians that no decree or statute which the king establishes may be changed or repealed.

16Then the king commanded, and Daniel was brought and cast into the den of lions. The king said to Daniel, May your God, Whom you are serving continually, deliver you! [Ps. 34:7, 19; 37:39, 40; 50:15.]

17And a stone was brought and laid upon the mouth of the den, and the king sealed it with his own signet and with the signet of his lords, that there might be no change of purpose concerning Daniel.

18Then the king went to his palace and passed the night fasting, neither were instruments of music or dancing girls brought before him; and his sleep fled from him.

19Then the king arose very early in the morning and went in haste to the den of lions.

20And when he came to the den and to Daniel, he cried out in a voice of anguish. The king said to Daniel, O Daniel, servant of the living God, is your God, Whom you serve continually, able to deliver you from the lions?

21Then Daniel said to the king, O king, live forever!

22My God has sent His angel and has shut the lions' mouths so that they have not hurt me, because I was found innocent and blameless before Him; and also before you, O king, [as you very well know] I have done no harm or wrong. [II Tim. 4:17.]

23Then the king was exceedingly glad and commanded that Daniel should be taken up out of the den. So Daniel

## New International Version

no wound was found on him, because he had trusted in his God.

²⁴At the king's command, the men who had falsely accused Daniel were brought in and thrown into the lions' den, along with their wives and children. And before they reached the floor of the den, the lions overpowered them and crushed all their bones.

²⁵Then King Darius wrote to all the nations and peoples of every language in all the earth:

"May you prosper greatly!

²⁶"I issue a decree that in every part of my kingdom people must fear and reverence the God of Daniel.

"For he is the living God
and he endures forever;
his kingdom will not be destroyed,
his dominion will never end.
²⁷He rescues and he saves;
he performs signs and wonders
in the heavens and on the earth.
He has rescued Daniel
from the power of the lions."

²⁸So Daniel prospered during the reign of Darius and the reign of Cyrus[a] the Persian.

### Daniel's Dream of Four Beasts

**7** In the first year of Belshazzar king of Babylon, Daniel had a dream, and visions passed through his mind as he was lying in bed. He wrote down the substance of his dream.

²Daniel said: "In my vision at night I looked, and there before me were the four winds of heaven churning up the great sea. ³Four great beasts, each different from the others, came up out of the sea.

⁴"The first was like a lion, and it had the wings of an eagle. I watched until its wings were torn off and it was lifted from the ground so that it stood on two feet like a human being, and the mind of a human was given to it.

⁵"And there before me was a second beast, which looked like a bear. It was raised up on one of its sides, and it had three ribs in its mouth between its teeth. It was told, 'Get up and eat your fill of flesh!'

⁶"After that, I looked, and there before me was another beast, one that looked like a leopard. And on its back it had four wings like those of a bird. This beast had four heads, and it was given authority to rule.

⁷"After that, in my vision at night I looked, and there before me was a fourth beast—terrifying and frightening and very powerful. It had large iron teeth; it crushed and devoured its victims and trampled underfoot whatever was left. It was different from all the former beasts, and it had ten horns.

⁸"While I was thinking about the horns, there before me was another horn, a little one, which came up among them; and three of the first horns were uprooted before it.

## Amplified Bible

was taken up out of the den, and no hurt of any kind was found on him because he believed in (relied on, adhered to, and trusted in) his God.

²⁴And the king commanded, and those men who had accused Daniel were brought and cast into the den of lions, they, their children, and their wives; and before they ever reached the bottom of the den, the lions had overpowered them and had broken their bones in pieces.

²⁵Then King Darius wrote to all peoples, nations, and languages [in his realm] that dwelt in all the earth: May peace be multiplied to you!

²⁶I make a decree that in all my royal dominion men must tremble and fear before the God of Daniel, for He is the living God, enduring *and* steadfast forever, and His kingdom shall not be destroyed and His dominion shall be even to the end [of the world].

²⁷He is a Savior and Deliverer, and He works signs and wonders in the heavens and on the earth—He Who has delivered Daniel from the power of the lions.

²⁸So this [man] Daniel prospered in the reign of Darius and in the reign of Cyrus the Persian.

**7** ᵃIn the first year of Belshazzar king of Babylon Daniel had a dream and visions in his head as he was lying upon his bed. Then he wrote down the dream and told the gist of the matter.

²Daniel said, I saw in my vision by night, and behold, the four winds of the heavens [political and social agitations] were stirring up the great sea [the nations of the world].

³And four great beasts came up out of the sea in succession, and different from one another.

⁴The first [the Babylonian empire under Nebuchadnezzar] was like a lion and had eagle's wings. I looked till the wings of it were plucked, and it was lifted up from the earth and made to stand upon two feet as a man, and a man's heart was given to it. [Dan. 2:37, 38.]

⁵And behold another beast, a second one [the Medo-Persian empire], was like a bear, and it raised up itself on one side [or one dominion] and three ribs were in its mouth between its teeth; and it was told, Arise, devour much flesh.

⁶After this I looked, and behold, another [the Grecian empire of Alexander the Great], like a leopard which had four wings of a bird on its back. The beast had also four heads [Alexander's generals, his successors], and dominion was given to it. [Dan. 2:39; 8:20-22.]

⁷After this I saw in the night visions, and behold, a fourth beast [the Roman empire]—terrible, powerful *and* dreadful, and exceedingly strong. And it had great iron teeth; it devoured and crushed and trampled what was left with its feet. And it was different from all the beasts that came before it, and it had ten horns [symbolizing ten kings]. [Dan. 2:40-43; 7:23.]

⁸I considered the horns, and behold, there came up among them another horn, a little one, before which three of the first horns were plucked up by the roots; and behold,

ᵃ This chapter, in its subject matter as well as its position in the central part of the book, is to the book of Daniel what the eighth chapter of Romans is to that epistle. Next to the fifty-third chapter of Isaiah (and perhaps the ninth chapter also), we have here the most precious and prominent portion of the sure word of prophecy concerning the coming of the Messiah. The chapter is worthy of the most careful prayer and study. It is referred to directly or indirectly by Christ and His apostles perhaps more than other portions of the Old Testament of similar extent. It appears to have been regarded by the Old Testament saints in the centuries preceding the Messiah's first advent as preeminently the "word of prophecy" (*Homiletical Commentary*).

## New International Version

This horn had eyes like the eyes of a human being and a mouth that spoke boastfully. [9]"As I looked,

"thrones were set in place,
    and the Ancient of Days took his seat.
His clothing was as white as snow;
    the hair of his head was white like wool.
His throne was flaming with fire,
    and its wheels were all ablaze.
[10] A river of fire was flowing,
    coming out from before him.
Thousands upon thousands attended him;
    ten thousand times ten thousand stood before him.
The court was seated,
    and the books were opened.

[11]"Then I continued to watch because of the boastful words the horn was speaking. I kept looking until the beast was slain and its body destroyed and thrown into the blazing fire. [12] (The other beasts had been stripped of their authority, but were allowed to live for a period of time.)

[13]"In my vision at night I looked, and there before me was one like a son of man,[a] coming with the clouds of heaven. He approached the Ancient of Days and was led into his presence. [14] He was given authority, glory and sovereign power; all nations and peoples of every language worshiped him. His dominion is an everlasting dominion that will not pass away, and his kingdom is one that will never be destroyed.

### The Interpretation of the Dream

[15]"I, Daniel, was troubled in spirit, and the visions that passed through my mind disturbed me. [16] I approached one of those standing there and asked him the meaning of all this.

"So he told me and gave me the interpretation of these things: [17]'The four great beasts are four kings that will rise from the earth. [18] But the holy people of the Most High will receive the kingdom and will possess it forever—yes, for ever and ever.'

[19]"Then I wanted to know the meaning of the fourth beast, which was different from all the others and most terrifying, with its iron teeth and bronze claws—the beast that crushed and devoured its victims and trampled underfoot whatever was left. [20] I also wanted to know about the ten horns on its head and about the other horn that came up, before which three of them fell—the horn that looked more imposing than the others and that had eyes and a mouth that spoke boastfully. [21] As I watched, this horn was waging war against the holy people and defeating them, [22] until the Ancient of Days came and pronounced judgment in favor of the holy people of the Most High, and the time came when they possessed the kingdom.

[23]"He gave me this explanation: 'The fourth beast is a fourth kingdom that will appear on earth. It will be different from all the other kingdoms and will devour the whole earth, trampling it down and crushing it. [24] The ten

## Amplified Bible

in this horn were eyes like the eyes of a man and a mouth speaking great things.

[9] I kept looking until thrones were placed [for the assessors with the Judge], and the Ancient of Days [God, the eternal Father] took His seat, Whose garment was white as snow and the hair of His head like pure wool. His throne was like the fiery flame; its wheels were burning fire. [I Kings 22:19; Ps. 90:2; Ezek. 1:26-28; Dan. 7:13, 22; Matt. 19:28; Rev. 20:4.]

[10] A stream of fire came forth from before Him; a thousand thousands ministered to Him and ten thousand times ten thousand rose up *and* stood before Him; the Judge was seated [the court was in session] and the books were opened.

[11] I looked then because of the sound of the great words which the horn was speaking. I watched until the beast was slain and its body destroyed and given over to be burned with fire.

[12] And as for the rest of the beasts, their power of dominion was taken away; yet their lives were prolonged [for the duration of their lives was fixed] for a season and a time.

[13] I saw in the night visions, and behold, [a] on the clouds of the heavens came One like a Son of man, and He came to the Ancient of Days and was presented before Him.

[14] And there was given Him [the Messiah] dominion and glory and kingdom, that all peoples, nations, and languages should serve Him. His dominion is an everlasting dominion which shall not pass away, and His kingdom is one which shall not be destroyed. [Rev. 5:1-10.]

[15] As for me, Daniel, my spirit was grieved *and* anxious within me, and the visions of my head alarmed *and* agitated me.

[16] I came near to one of those who stood there and asked him the truth of all this. So he told me and made known to me the interpretation of the things.

[17] These four great beasts are four kings who shall arise out of the earth.

[18] But the saints of the Most High [God] shall receive the kingdom and possess the kingdom forever, even forever and ever. [Rom. 8:17; I Pet. 2:9; Rev. 3:21.]

[19] Then I wished to know the truth about the fourth beast—which was different from all the others, exceedingly terrible *and* shocking, whose teeth were of iron and its nails of bronze, which devoured, broke *and* crushed, and trampled what was left with its feet—

[20] And about the ten horns [representing kings] that were on its head, and the other horn which came up later and before which three of [the horns] fell, the horn which had eyes and a mouth that spoke great things and which looked greater than the others.

[21] As I looked, this horn made war with the saints and prevailed over them [Rev. 13:7-9.]

[22] Until the Ancient of Days came, and judgment was given to the saints of the Most High [God], and the time came when the saints possessed the kingdom.

[23] Thus [the angel] said, The fourth beast shall be a fourth kingdom on earth, which shall be different from all other kingdoms and shall devour the whole earth, tread it down, and break it in pieces *and* crush it.

---

[a] Notice that the four beasts of this seventh chapter of Daniel symbolize the same world kingdoms that were pictured by the images in Dan. 2, and the ten horns of the last beast correspond to the ten toes of the legs of iron (Dan. 2:41-42). Much of both prophecies has been fulfilled, and at this writing "the blessed hope" (Tit. 2:13) of the ages is also showing every evidence of nearing realization. Both visions portray the end of Gentile world power. View the events of the present in the light of these disclosures, and they fall into focus and make sense. The individual child of God is challenged as never before in the world's history to let go of the trivial and the transient, and to yield himself unreservedly to Him Who is coming back to fulfill the longings of every true believer—forever and ever!

---

[a] 13 The Aramaic phrase *bar enash* means *human being*. The phrase *son of man* is retained here because of its use in the New Testament as a title of Jesus, probably based largely on this verse.

## New International Version

horns are ten kings who will come from this kingdom. After them another king will arise, different from the earlier ones; he will subdue three kings. ²⁵He will speak against the Most High and oppress his holy people and try to change the set times and the laws. The holy people will be delivered into his hands for a time, times and half a time.ᵃ

²⁶"But the court will sit, and his power will be taken away and completely destroyed forever. ²⁷Then the sovereignty, power and greatness of all the kingdoms under heaven will be handed over to the holy people of the Most High. His kingdom will be an everlasting kingdom, and all rulers will worship and obey him.'

²⁸"This is the end of the matter. I, Daniel, was deeply troubled by my thoughts, and my face turned pale, but I kept the matter to myself."

### Daniel's Vision of a Ram and a Goat

**8** In the third year of King Belshazzar's reign, I, Daniel, had a vision, after the one that had already appeared to me. ²In my vision I saw myself in the citadel of Susa in the province of Elam; in the vision I was beside the Ulai Canal. ³I looked up, and there before me was a ram with two horns, standing beside the canal, and the horns were long. One of the horns was longer than the other but grew up later. ⁴I watched the ram as it charged toward the west and the north and the south. No animal could stand against it, and none could rescue from its power. It did as it pleased and became great.

⁵As I was thinking about this, suddenly a goat with a prominent horn between its eyes came from the west, crossing the whole earth without touching the ground. ⁶It came toward the two-horned ram I had seen standing beside the canal and charged at it in great rage. ⁷I saw it attack the ram furiously, striking the ram and shattering its two horns. The ram was powerless to stand against it; the goat knocked it to the ground and trampled on it, and none could rescue the ram from its power. ⁸The goat became very great, but at the height of its power the large horn was broken off, and in its place four prominent horns grew up toward the four winds of heaven.

## Amplified Bible

²⁴And as for the ten horns, out of this kingdom ten kings shall arise; and another shall arise after them, and he shall be different from the former ones, and he shall subdue *and* put down three kings.

²⁵And he shall speak words against the Most High [God] and shall wear out the saints of the Most High and think to change the time [of sacred feasts and holy days] and the law; and the saints shall be given into his hand for a time, two times, and half a time [three and one-half years]. [Rev. 13:1-6.]

²⁶But the judgment shall be set [by the court of the Most High], and they shall take away his dominion to consume it [gradually] and to destroy it [suddenly] in the end.

²⁷And the kingdom and the dominion and the greatness of the kingdom under the whole heavens shall be given to the people of the saints of the Most High; His kingdom is an everlasting kingdom, and all the dominions shall serve and obey Him.

²⁸Here is the end of the matter. As for me, Daniel, my [waking] thoughts troubled and alarmed me much and my cheerfulness of countenance was changed in me; but I kept the matter [of the interpreting angel's information] in my heart *and* mind.

**8** In the third year of the reign of King Belshazzar a vision appeared to me, Daniel, after the one that appeared to me at the first.

²And I saw in the vision and it seemed that I was at Shushan the palace *or* fortress [in Susa, the capital of Persia], which is in the province of Elam, and I saw in the vision and I was by the river of Ulai.

³And I lifted up my eyes and saw, and behold, there stood before the river a [single] ram which had two horns [representing two kings of Medo-Persia: Darius the Mede, then Cyrus]; and the two horns were high, but one [Persia] was higher than the other, and the higher one came up last.

⁴I looked *and* saw the ram [Medo-Persia] pushing *and* charging westward and northward and southward; no beast could stand before him, neither could any rescue from his power, but he did according to his [own] will *and* pleasure and magnified himself. [Dan. 8:20.]

⁵As I was considering, behold, a he-goat [the king of Greece] came from the west across the face of the whole earth without touching the ground, and the goat had a conspicuous *and* remarkable horn between his eyes [symbolizing Alexander the Great]. [Dan. 8:21.]

⁶And he came to the ram that had the two horns which I had seen standing on the bank of the river and ran at him in the heat of his power.

⁷[In my vision] I saw him come close to the ram [Medo-Persia], and he was moved with anger against him and he [Alexander the Great] struck the ram and broke his two horns; and there was no power in the ram to stand before him, but the goat threw him to the ground and trampled on him. And there was no one who could rescue the ram from his power.

⁸And the he-goat [Alexander the Great] magnified himself exceedingly, and when he was [young and] strong, the ᵃgreat horn [he] was [suddenly] broken; and instead of [him] there came up four notable horns [to whom the kingdom was divided, one] toward [each of] the four winds of the heavens.

---

ᵃ Alexander the Great suddenly died at the height of his power, and his empire was divided into four parts—east, west, north, and south—ruled over by his four generals.

ᵃ 25 Or *for a year, two years and half a year*

## New International Version

⁹Out of one of them came another horn, which started small but grew in power to the south and to the east and toward the Beautiful Land. ¹⁰It grew until it reached the host of the heavens, and it threw some of the starry host down to the earth and trampled on them. ¹¹It set itself up to be as great as the commander of the army of the LORD; it took away the daily sacrifice from the LORD, and his sanctuary was thrown down. ¹²Because of rebellion, the LORD's people[a] and the daily sacrifice were given over to it. It prospered in everything it did, and truth was thrown to the ground.

¹³Then I heard a holy one speaking, and another holy one said to him, "How long will it take for the vision to be fulfilled—the vision concerning the daily sacrifice, the rebellion that causes desolation, the surrender of the sanctuary and the trampling underfoot of the LORD's people?"

¹⁴He said to me, "It will take 2,300 evenings and mornings; then the sanctuary will be reconsecrated."

### The Interpretation of the Vision

¹⁵While I, Daniel, was watching the vision and trying to understand it, there before me stood one who looked like a man. ¹⁶And I heard a man's voice from the Ulai calling, "Gabriel, tell this man the meaning of the vision."

¹⁷As he came near the place where I was standing, I was terrified and fell prostrate. "Son of man,"[b] he said to me, "understand that the vision concerns the time of the end."

¹⁸While he was speaking to me, I was in a deep sleep, with my face to the ground. Then he touched me and raised me to my feet.

¹⁹He said: "I am going to tell you what will happen later in the time of wrath, because the vision concerns the appointed time of the end.[c] ²⁰The two-horned ram that you saw represents the kings of Media and Persia. ²¹The shaggy goat is the king of Greece, and the large horn between its eyes is the first king. ²²The four horns that replaced the one that was broken off represent four kingdoms that will emerge from his nation but will not have the same power.

²³"In the latter part of their reign, when rebels have become completely wicked, a fierce-looking king, a master of intrigue, will arise. ²⁴He will become very strong, but not by his own power. He will cause astounding devastation and will succeed in whatever he does. He will destroy those who are mighty, the holy people. ²⁵He will cause

## Amplified Bible

⁹Out of littleness *and* small beginnings one of them came forth [Antiochus Epiphanes], a ᵃhorn whose [impious presumption and pride] grew exceedingly great toward the south and toward the east and toward the ornament [the precious, blessed land of Israel]. [Dan. 8:23.]

¹⁰And [in my vision this horn] grew great, even against the host of heaven [God's true people, the saints], and some of the host and of the stars [priests] it cast down to the ground and trampled on them,

¹¹Yes, [this horn] magnified itself, even [matching itself] against the Prince of the host [of heaven]; and from Him the continual [burnt offering] was taken away and the place of [God's] sanctuary was cast down *and* profaned.

¹²And the host [the chosen people] was given [to the wicked horn] together with the continual burnt offering because of the transgression [of God's people—their abounding irreverence, ungodliness, and lack of piety]. And righteousness *and* truth were cast down to the ground, and it [the wicked horn] accomplished this [by divine permission] and prospered.

¹³Then I heard a holy one speaking, and another holy one said to the one that spoke, For how long is the vision concerning the continual offering, the transgression that makes desolate, and the giving over of both the sanctuary and the host [of the people] to be trampled underfoot? [Luke 21:24.]

¹⁴And he said to him *and* to me, For 2,300 evenings and mornings; then the sanctuary shall be cleansed *and* restored.

¹⁵When I, even I, Daniel, had seen the vision, I sought to understand it; then behold, there stood before me one [Gabriel] with the appearance of a man.

¹⁶And I heard a man's voice between the banks of the [river] Ulai which called and said, Gabriel, make this man [Daniel] understand the vision. [Dan. 9:21; Luke 1:19, 26.]

¹⁷So he came near where I stood, and when he came, I was frightened and fell on my face. But he said to me, Understand, O son of man, for the [fulfillment of the] vision belongs to [events that shall occur in] the time of the end.

¹⁸Now as he [Gabriel] was speaking with me, I fell stunned *and* in deep unconsciousness with my face to the ground; but he touched me and set me upright [where I had stood].

¹⁹And he said, Behold, I will make you know what will be in the latter time of the indignation [of God upon the ungodly], for it has to do with the time of the end.

²⁰The ram you saw having two horns, they are the kings of Media and Persia.

²¹And the shaggy *and* rough he-goat is the king of Greece, and the great horn between his eyes is the first king [who consolidated the whole realm, Alexander the Great].

²²And as for the horn which was shattered, in whose place four others arose, four kingdoms shall arise out of his nation but not having his [Alexander's] power.

²³And at the latter end of their kingdom, when the transgressors [the apostate Jews] have reached the fullness [of their wickedness, taxing the limits of God's mercy], a king of fierce countenance and understanding dark trickery *and* craftiness shall stand up.

²⁴And his power shall be mighty, but not by his own power; and he shall corrupt *and* destroy astonishingly and shall prosper and do his own pleasure, and he shall corrupt *and* destroy the mighty men and the holy people (the people of the saints). [Dan. 8:9-12; II Thess. 2:3-10; Rev. 13:4-10.]

ᵃ This horn of Dan. 8:9-12 is not to be confused with the "little horn" of Dan. 7:8. This one is a prophetic forecast of Antiochus Epiphanes, who came out of Syria, one of the four dynasties into which Alexander's empire was divided, and became a great conqueror. Hating God, he profaned the temple and persecuted the Jews terribly. However, he serves as a type of the "little horn" of Dan. 7:8, the even more ruthless beast of the last days (Rev. 13:4-9).

---

ᵃ 12 Or *rebellion, the armies*   ᵇ 17 The Hebrew phrase *ben adam* means *human being.* The phrase *son of man* is retained as a form of address here because of its possible association with "Son of Man" in the New Testament.   ᶜ 19 Or *because the end will be at the appointed time*

## New International Version

deceit to prosper, and he will consider himself superior. When they feel secure, he will destroy many and take his stand against the Prince of princes. Yet he will be destroyed, but not by human power.

26"The vision of the evenings and mornings that has been given you is true, but seal up the vision, for it concerns the distant future."

27I, Daniel, was worn out. I lay exhausted for several days. Then I got up and went about the king's business. I was appalled by the vision; it was beyond understanding.

### Daniel's Prayer

**9** In the first year of Darius son of Xerxes*a* (a Mede by descent), who was made ruler over the Babylonian*b* kingdom— 2in the first year of his reign, I, Daniel, understood from the Scriptures, according to the word of the LORD given to Jeremiah the prophet, that the desolation of Jerusalem would last seventy years. 3So I turned to the Lord God and pleaded with him in prayer and petition, in fasting, and in sackcloth and ashes.

4I prayed to the LORD my God and confessed:

"Lord, the great and awesome God, who keeps his covenant of love with those who love him and keep his commandments, 5we have sinned and done wrong. We have been wicked and have rebelled; we have turned away from your commands and laws. 6We have not listened to your servants the prophets, who spoke in your name to our kings, our princes and our ancestors, and to all the people of the land.

7"Lord, you are righteous, but this day we are covered with shame—the people of Judah and the inhabitants of Jerusalem and all Israel, both near and far, in all the countries where you have scattered us because of our unfaithfulness to you. 8We and our kings, our princes and our ancestors are covered with shame, LORD, because we have sinned against you. 9The Lord our God is merciful and forgiving, even though we have rebelled against him; 10we have not obeyed the LORD our God or kept the laws he gave us through his servants the prophets. 11All Israel has transgressed your law and turned away, refusing to obey you.

"Therefore the curses and sworn judgments written in the Law of Moses, the servant of God, have been poured out on us, because we have sinned against you. 12You have fulfilled the words spoken against us and against our rulers by bringing on us great disaster. Under the whole heaven nothing has ever been done like what has been done to Jerusalem. 13Just as it is written in the Law of Moses, all this disaster has come on us, yet we have not sought the favor of the LORD our God by turning from our sins and giving attention to your truth. 14The LORD did not hesitate to bring the disaster on us, for the LORD our

## Amplified Bible

25And through his policy he shall cause trickery to prosper in his hand; he shall magnify himself in his heart *and* mind, and in their security he will corrupt *and* destroy many. He shall also stand up against the Prince of princes, but he shall be broken and that by no [human] hand. [Rev. 19:19, 20.]

26The vision of the evenings and the mornings which has been told you is true. But seal up the vision, for it has to do with *and* belongs to the [now] distant future.

27And I, Daniel, fainted and was sick [for several] days. Afterward I rose up and did the king's business; and I wondered at the vision, but there was no one who understood it *or* could make it understood.

**9** In the first year of Darius son of Ahasuerus, of the offspring of the Medes, who was made king over the realm of the Chaldeans—

2In the first year of his reign, I, Daniel, understood from the books the number of years which, according to the word of the Lord to Jeremiah the prophet, must pass by before the desolations [which had been] pronounced on Jerusalem should end; and it was seventy years. [Jer. 25:11, 12; 29:10.]

3And I set my face to the Lord God to seek Him by prayer and supplications, with fasting and sackcloth and ashes;

4And I prayed to the Lord my God and made confession and said, O Lord, the great and dreadful God, Who keeps covenant, mercy, *and* loving-kindness with those who love Him and keep His commandments,

5We have sinned and dealt perversely and done wickedly and have rebelled, turning aside from Your commandments and ordinances.

6Neither have we listened to *and* heeded Your servants the prophets, who spoke in Your name to our kings, our princes and our fathers, and to all the people of the land.

7O Lord, righteousness belongs to You, but to us confusion *and* shame of face, as at this day—to the men of Judah, to the inhabitants of Jerusalem, and to all Israel, to those who are near and those who are far off, through all the countries to which You have driven them because of the [treacherous] trespass which they have committed against You.

8O Lord, to us belong confusion *and* shame of face—to our kings, to our princes, and to our fathers—because we have sinned against You.

9To the Lord our God belong mercy *and* loving-kindness and forgiveness, for we have rebelled against Him;

10And we have not obeyed the voice of the Lord our God by walking in His laws which He set before us through His servants the prophets.

11Yes, all Israel has transgressed Your law, even turning aside that they might not obey Your voice. Therefore the curse has been poured out on us and the oath that is written in the Law of Moses the servant of God, because we have sinned against Him. [Lev. 26:14-45; Deut. 28:15-68.]

12And He has carried out intact His [threatening] words which He threatened against us and against our judges [the kings, princes, and rulers generally] who ruled us, and He has brought upon us a great evil; for under the whole heavens there has not been done before [anything so dreadful] as [He has caused to be] done against Jerusalem.

13Just as it is written in the Law of Moses as to all this evil [that would surely come upon transgressors], so it has come upon us. Yet we have not earnestly begged for forgiveness *and* entreated the favor of the Lord our God, that we might turn from our iniquities and have understanding *and* become wise in Your truth. [Deut. 4:29; 28:15ff.]

14Therefore the Lord has kept ready the calamity

---

*a* 1 Hebrew *Ahasuerus*   *b* 1 Or *Chaldean*

## New International Version

God is righteous in everything he does; yet we have not obeyed him.

[15] "Now, Lord our God, who brought your people out of Egypt with a mighty hand and who made for yourself a name that endures to this day, we have sinned, we have done wrong. [16] Lord, in keeping with all your righteous acts, turn away your anger and your wrath from Jerusalem, your city, your holy hill. Our sins and the iniquities of our ancestors have made Jerusalem and your people an object of scorn to all those around us.

[17] "Now, our God, hear the prayers and petitions of your servant. For your sake, Lord, look with favor on your desolate sanctuary. [18] Give ear, our God, and hear; open your eyes and see the desolation of the city that bears your Name. We do not make requests of you because we are righteous, but because of your great mercy. [19] Lord, listen! Lord, forgive! Lord, hear and act! For your sake, my God, do not delay, because your city and your people bear your Name."

### The Seventy "Sevens"

[20] While I was speaking and praying, confessing my sin and the sin of my people Israel and making my request to the Lord my God for his holy hill— [21] while I was still in prayer, Gabriel, the man I had seen in the earlier vision, came to me in swift flight about the time of the evening sacrifice. [22] He instructed me and said to me, "Daniel, I have now come to give you insight and understanding. [23] As soon as you began to pray, a word went out, which I have come to tell you, for you are highly esteemed. Therefore, consider the word and understand the vision:

[24] "Seventy 'sevens'[a] are decreed for your people and your holy city to finish[b] transgression, to put an end to sin, to atone for wickedness, to bring in everlasting righteousness, to seal up vision and prophecy and to anoint the Most Holy Place.[c]

[25] "Know and understand this: From the time the word goes out to restore and rebuild Jerusalem until the Anointed One,[d] the ruler, comes, there will be seven 'sevens,' and sixty-two 'sevens.' It will be rebuilt with streets and a trench, but in times of trouble. [26] After the sixty-two 'sevens,' the Anointed One will be put to death and will have nothing.[e] The people of the ruler who will come will destroy the city and the sanctuary. The end will come like a flood: War will continue until the end, and desolations have been decreed. [27] He will confirm a covenant with many for one 'seven.'[f] In the middle of the 'seven'[f] he will put an end to sacrifice and offering. And at the temple[g] he will set up an abomination that causes desolation, until the end that is decreed is poured out on him.[h]"[i]

## Amplified Bible

(evil) and has brought it upon us, for the Lord our God is [uncompromisingly] righteous *and* rigidly just in all His works which He does [keeping His Word]; and we have not obeyed His voice.

[15] And now, O Lord our God, Who brought Your people forth out of the land of Egypt with a mighty hand and secured Yourself renown *and* a name as at this day, we have sinned, we have done wickedly!

[16] O Lord, according to all Your rightness *and* justice, I beseech You, let Your anger and Your wrath be turned away from Your city Jerusalem, Your holy mountain. Because of our sins and the iniquities of our fathers, Jerusalem and Your people have become a reproach *and* a byword to all who are around about us.

[17] Now therefore, O our God, listen to *and* heed the prayer of Your servant [a][Daniel] and his supplications, and for Your own sake cause Your face to shine upon Your sanctuary which is desolate.

[18] O my God, incline Your ear and hear; open Your eyes and look at our desolations and the city which is called by Your name; for we do not present our supplications before You for our own righteousness *and* justice, but for Your great mercy *and* loving-kindness.

[19] O Lord, hear! O Lord, forgive! O Lord, give heed and act! Do not delay, for Your own sake, O my God, because Your city and Your people are called by Your name.

[20] While I was speaking and praying, confessing my sin and the sin of my people Israel, and presenting my supplication before the Lord my God for the holy hill of my God—

[21] Yes, while I was speaking in prayer, the man Gabriel, whom I had seen in the former vision, being caused to fly swiftly, came near to me *and* touched me about the time of the evening sacrifice. [Dan. 8:16.]

[22] He instructed me *and* made me understand; he talked with me and said, O Daniel, I am now come forth to give you skill *and* wisdom and understanding.

[23] At the beginning of your prayers, the word [giving an answer] went forth, and I have come to tell you, for you are greatly beloved. Therefore consider the matter and understand the vision.

[24] Seventy weeks [of years, or 490 years] are decreed upon your people and upon your holy city [Jerusalem], to finish *and* put an end to transgression, to seal up *and* make full the measure of sin, to purge away *and* make expiation *and* reconciliation for sin, to bring in everlasting righteousness (permanent moral and spiritual rectitude in every area and relation) and to seal up vision and prophecy *and* prophet, and to anoint a Holy of Holies.

[25] Know therefore and understand that from the going forth of the commandment to restore and to build Jerusalem until [the coming of] the Anointed One, a Prince, shall be seven weeks [of years] and sixty-two weeks [of years]; it shall be built again with [city] square and moat, but in troublous times.

[26] And after the sixty-two weeks [of years] shall the Anointed One be cut off *or* killed and shall have nothing [and no one] belonging to [and defending] Him. And the people of the [other] prince who will come will destroy the city and the sanctuary. Its end shall come with a flood; and even to the end there shall be war, and desolations are decreed. [Isa. 53:7-9; Nah. 1:8; Matt. 24:6-14.]

[27] And he shall enter into a strong *and* firm covenant with the many for one week [seven years]. And in the midst of the week he shall cause the sacrifice and offering to cease [for the remaining three and one-half years]; and upon the wing *or* pinnacle of abominations [shall come] one who makes desolate, until the full determined end is poured out on the desolator.

---

[a] 24 Or 'weeks'; also in verses 25 and 26   [b] 24 Or *restrain*
[c] 24 Or *the most holy One*   [d] 25 Or *an anointed one*; also in verse 26   [e] 26 Or *death and will have no one*; or *death, but not for himself*   [f] 27 Or 'week'   [g] 27 Septuagint and Theodotion; Hebrew *wing*   [h] 27 Or *it*   [i] 27 Or *And one who causes desolation will come upon the wing of the abominable temple, until the end that is decreed is poured out on the desolated city*

---

[a] Compare this verse with Ezek. 14:12-20.

## New International Version

### Daniel's Vision of a Man

**10** In the third year of Cyrus king of Persia, a revelation was given to Daniel (who was called Belteshazzar). Its message was true and it concerned a great war.[a] The understanding of the message came to him in a vision.

² At that time I, Daniel, mourned for three weeks. ³ I ate no choice food; no meat or wine touched my lips; and I used no lotions at all until the three weeks were over.

⁴ On the twenty-fourth day of the first month, as I was standing on the bank of the great river, the Tigris, ⁵ I looked up and there before me was a man dressed in linen, with a belt of fine gold from Uphaz around his waist. ⁶ His body was like topaz, his face like lightning, his eyes like flaming torches, his arms and legs like the gleam of burnished bronze, and his voice like the sound of a multitude.

⁷ I, Daniel, was the only one who saw the vision; those who were with me did not see it, but such terror overwhelmed them that they fled and hid themselves. ⁸ So I was left alone, gazing at this great vision; I had no strength left, my face turned deathly pale and I was helpless. ⁹ Then I heard him speaking, and as I listened to him, I fell into a deep sleep, my face to the ground.

¹⁰ A hand touched me and set me trembling on my hands and knees. ¹¹ He said, "Daniel, you who are highly esteemed, consider carefully the words I am about to speak to you, and stand up, for I have now been sent to you." And when he said this to me, I stood up trembling.

¹² Then he continued, "Do not be afraid, Daniel. Since the first day that you set your mind to gain understanding and to humble yourself before your God, your words were heard, and I have come in response to them. ¹³ But the prince of the Persian kingdom resisted me twenty-one days. Then Michael, one of the chief princes, came to help me, because I was detained there with the king of Persia. ¹⁴ Now I have come to explain to you what will happen to your people in the future, for the vision concerns a time yet to come."

¹⁵ While he was saying this to me, I bowed with my face toward the ground and was speechless. ¹⁶ Then one who looked like a man[b] touched my lips, and I opened my mouth and began to speak. I said to the one standing before me, "I am overcome with anguish because of the vision, my lord, and I feel very weak. ¹⁷ How can I, your servant, talk with you, my lord? My strength is gone and I can hardly breathe."

¹⁸ Again the one who looked like a man touched me and gave me strength. ¹⁹ "Do not be afraid, you who are highly esteemed," he said. "Peace! Be strong now; be strong."

When he spoke to me, I was strengthened and said, "Speak, my lord, since you have given me strength."

²⁰ So he said, "Do you know why I have come to you? Soon I will return to fight against the prince of Persia, and when I go, the prince of Greece will come; ²¹ but first I

---

## Amplified Bible

**10** In the third year of Cyrus king of Persia a word was revealed to Daniel, who was called Belteshazzar. And the word was true and it referred to great tribulation (conflict and wretchedness). And he understood the word and had understanding of the vision. [Dan. 8:26; Rev. 19:9.]

² In those days I, Daniel, was mourning for three whole weeks.

³ I ate no pleasant *or* desirable food, nor did any meat or wine come into my mouth; and I did not anoint myself at all for the full three weeks.

⁴ On the twenty-fourth day of the first month, as I was on the bank of the great river Hiddekel [which is the Tigris],

⁵ I lifted up my eyes and looked, and behold, a man clothed in linen, whose loins were girded with pure gold of Uphaz.

⁶ His body also was [a golden luster] like beryl, his face had the appearance of lightning, his eyes were like flaming torches, his arms and his feet like glowing burnished bronze, and the sound of his words was like the noise of a multitude [of people or the roaring of the sea]. [Rev. 1:12-16; 19:6.]

⁷ And I, Daniel, alone saw the vision [of this heavenly being], for the men who were with me did not see the vision, but a great trembling fell upon them so that they fled to hide themselves.

⁸ So I was left alone and saw this great vision, and no strength was left in me, for my fresh appearance was turned to pallor; I grew weak *and* faint [with fright].

⁹ Then I heard the sound of his words; and when I heard the sound of his words, I fell on my face in a deep sleep, with my face [sunk] to the ground.

¹⁰ And behold, a hand touched me, which set me [unsteadily] upon my knees and upon the palms of my hands.

¹¹ And [the angel] said to me, O Daniel, you greatly beloved man, understand the words that I speak to you and stand upright, for to you I am now sent. And while he was saying this word to me, I stood up trembling.

¹² Then he said to me, Fear not, Daniel, for from the first day that you set your mind *and* heart to understand and to humble yourself before your God, your words were heard, and I have come as a consequence of [and in response to] your words.

¹³ But the prince of the kingdom of Persia withstood me for twenty-one days. Then Michael, one of the chief [of the celestial] princes, came to help me, for I remained there with the kings of Persia.

¹⁴ Now I have come to make you understand what is to befall your people in the latter days, for the vision is for [many] days yet to come.

¹⁵ When he had spoken to me according to these words, I turned my face toward the ground and was dumb.

¹⁶ And behold, one in the likeness of the sons of men touched my lips. Then I opened my mouth and spoke. I said to him who stood before me, O my lord, by reason of the vision sorrows *and* pains have come upon me, and I retain no strength.

¹⁷ For how can my lord's servant [who is so feeble] talk with this my lord? For now no strength remains in me, nor is there any breath left in me.

¹⁸ Then there touched me again one whose appearance was like that of a man, and he strengthened me.

¹⁹ And he said, O man greatly beloved, fear not! Peace be to you! Be strong, yes, be strong. And when he had spoken to me, I was strengthened and said, Let my lord speak, for you have strengthened me.

²⁰ Then he said, Do you know why I have come to you? And now I will return to fight with the [hostile] prince of Persia; and when I have gone, behold, the [hostile] prince of Greece will come.

## New International Version

will tell you what is written in the Book of Truth. (No one supports me against them except Michael, your prince.

**11** ¹And in the first year of Darius the Mede, I took my stand to support and protect him.)

### The Kings of the South and the North

²"Now then, I tell you the truth: Three more kings will arise in Persia, and then a fourth, who will be far richer than all the others. When he has gained power by his wealth, he will stir up everyone against the kingdom of Greece. ³Then a mighty king will arise, who will rule with great power and do as he pleases. ⁴After he has arisen, his empire will be broken up and parceled out toward the four winds of heaven. It will not go to his descendants, nor will it have the power he exercised, because his empire will be uprooted and given to others.

⁵"The king of the South will become strong, but one of his commanders will become even stronger than he and will rule his own kingdom with great power. ⁶After some years, they will become allies. The daughter of the king of the South will go to the king of the North to make an alliance, but she will not retain her power, and he and his power*ᵃ* will not last. In those days she will be betrayed, together with her royal escort and her father*ᵇ* and the one who supported her.

⁷"One from her family line will arise to take her place. He will attack the forces of the king of the North and enter his fortress; he will fight against them and be victorious. ⁸He will also seize their gods, their metal images and their valuable articles of silver and gold and carry them off to Egypt. For some years he will leave the king of the North alone. ⁹Then the king of the North will invade the realm of the king of the South but will retreat to his own country. ¹⁰His sons will prepare for war and assemble a great army, which will sweep on like an irresistible flood and carry the battle as far as his fortress.

¹¹"Then the king of the South will march out in a rage and fight against the king of the North, who will raise a large army, but it will be defeated. ¹²When the army is carried off, the king of the South will be filled with pride and will slaughter many thousands, yet he will not remain triumphant. ¹³For the king of the North will muster another army, larger than the first; and after several years, he will advance with a huge army fully equipped.

## Amplified Bible

²¹But I will tell you what is inscribed in the writing of truth *or* the Book of Truth. There is no one who holds with me *and* strengthens himself against these [hostile spirit forces] except Michael, your prince [national guardian angel].

**11** Also I [the angel], in the first year of Darius the Mede, even I, stood up to confirm and to strengthen him [Michael, the angelic prince].

²And now I will show you the truth. Behold, there shall arise three more kings in Persia, and a fourth shall be far richer than they all. And when he has become strong through his riches he shall stir up *and* stake all against the realm of Greece.

³Then a *ᵃ*mighty [warlike, threatening] king shall arise who shall rule with great dominion and do according to his [own] will.

⁴And as soon as he has fully arisen, his [Alexander the Great's] kingdom shall be broken [by his death] and divided toward the four winds [the east, west, north, and south] of the heavens, but not to his posterity, nor according to the [Grecian] dominion which he ruled, for his kingdom shall be torn out *and* uprooted and go to others [to his four generals] to the exclusion of these.

⁵Then the king of the South (Egypt) shall be strong, but one of his princes shall be stronger than he is and have dominion; his dominion shall be a great dominion.

⁶At the end of some years they [the king of the North, Syria, and the king of the South, Egypt] shall make an alliance; the daughter of the king of the South shall come to the king of the North to make [a just and peaceful marriage] agreement; but she shall not retain the power of her might, neither shall he and his might endure. She shall be handed over with her attendants, her child, and him who strengthened her in those times.

⁷But out of a branch of the [same ancestral] roots as hers shall one [her brother] stand up in his place *or* office, who shall come against the [Syrian] army and shall enter into the fortress of the king of the North and shall deal against them and shall prevail.

⁸And also he shall carry off to Egypt their [Syria's] gods with their molten images and with their precious vessels of silver and of gold, and he shall refrain for some years from [waging war against] the king of the North.

⁹And he [the king of Syria] shall come into the kingdom of the king of the South but shall return to his own land.

¹⁰But his sons shall be stirred up *and* shall prepare for war and shall assemble a multitude of great forces, which shall come on and overflow and pass through and again shall make war even to the fortress [of the king of the South].

¹¹And the king of the South (Egypt) shall be moved with anger and shall come forth and fight with the king of the North (Syria); and he [the Syrian king] shall set forth a great multitude, but the multitude shall be given into his [the Egyptian king's] hand.

¹²When the multitude is taken *and* carried away, the heart *and* mind [of the Egyptian king] shall be exalted, and he shall cast down tens of thousands, but he shall not prevail.

¹³For the king of the North shall raise a multitude greater than [he had] before, and after some years shall certainly return, coming with a great army and much substance *and* equipment.

---

*ᵃ* There are many good reasons for identifying this mighty king as Alexander the Great, as well as identifying the other characters according to their relationship to the events of those times. "But the mere similarity which exists between certain things predicted here and what actually occurred in the times of the Ptolemies of Egypt is not sufficient to limit the fulfillment of the prophecy to those times—certainly [we find here what] was characteristic of Alexander, but there is nothing in the context which makes it necessary to limit the passage to him. Some autocrat may arise 'in the latter days' to whom it will apply with greater force than it did to Alexander." (Charles Ellicott, *A Bible Commentary*).

---

*ᵃ* 6 Or *offspring*    *ᵇ* 6 Or *child* (see Vulgate and Syriac)

## New International Version

14"In those times many will rise against the king of the South. Those who are violent among your own people will rebel in fulfillment of the vision, but without success. 15Then the king of the North will come and build up siege ramps and will capture a fortified city. The forces of the South will be powerless to resist; even their best troops will not have the strength to stand. 16The invader will do as he pleases; no one will be able to stand against him. He will establish himself in the Beautiful Land and will have the power to destroy it. 17He will determine to come with the might of his entire kingdom and will make an alliance with the king of the South. And he will give him a daughter in marriage in order to overthrow the kingdom, but his plans*a* will not succeed or help him. 18Then he will turn his attention to the coastlands and will take many of them, but a commander will put an end to his insolence and will turn his insolence back on him. 19After this, he will turn back toward the fortresses of his own country but will stumble and fall, to be seen no more.

20"His successor will send out a tax collector to maintain the royal splendor. In a few years, however, he will be destroyed, yet not in anger or in battle.

21"He will be succeeded by a contemptible person who has not been given the honor of royalty. He will invade the kingdom when its people feel secure, and he will seize it through intrigue. 22Then an overwhelming army will be swept away before him; both it and a prince of the covenant will be destroyed. 23After coming to an agreement with him, he will act deceitfully, and with only a few people he will rise to power. 24When the richest provinces feel secure, he will invade them and will achieve what neither his fathers nor his forefathers did. He will distribute plunder, loot and wealth among his followers. He will plot the overthrow of fortresses—but only for a time.

25"With a large army he will stir up his strength and courage against the king of the South. The king of the South will wage war with a large and very powerful army, but he will not be able to stand because of the plots devised against him. 26Those who eat from the king's provisions will try to destroy him; his army will be swept away, and many will fall in battle. 27The two kings, with their hearts

## Amplified Bible

14In those times many shall rise up against the king of the South (Egypt); also the men of violence among your own people shall lift themselves up in order to fulfill the visions [of Dan. 8 and 9], but they shall fail *and* fall. 15Then the king of the North shall come and cast up siege works and take a well-fortified city, and the forces of the South shall not stand, or even his chosen troops, for there shall be no strength to stand [against the Syrian king]. 16But he [Antiochus the Great] who comes against him [from Syria] shall do according to his own will, and none shall stand before him; he shall stand in the glorious land [of Israel], and in his hand shall be destruction *and* all the land shall be in his power. 17He [Antiochus the Great] shall set his face to come with the strength of his whole kingdom, and with him upright conditions *and* terms of peace, and he shall perform them [by making an agreement with the king of the South]. He shall give him [his] daughter to corrupt *and* destroy it [his league with Egypt] *and* the kingdom, but it shall not succeed or be to his advantage. 18After this he shall turn his attention to the islands *and* coastlands and shall take over many of them. But a prince *or* commander shall teach him [Antiochus the Great] to put an end to the insults offered by him; in fact he shall turn his insolence *and* reproaches back upon him. 19Then he shall turn his face back toward the fortresses of his own land [of Syria], but he shall stumble and fall and not be found. 20Then shall *a*stand up in his place *or* office one who shall send an exactor of tribute to pass through the glory of the kingdom, but within a few days he shall be destroyed, [yet] neither in anger nor in battle. 21And in his place *or* office [in Syria] shall arise a *b*contemptuous *and* contemptible person, to whom royal majesty *and* honor of the kingdom have not been given. But he shall come in without warning in time of security and shall obtain the kingdom by flatteries, intrigues, *and* cunning hypocritical conduct. [Dan. 8:9-12, 23-25.] 22Before him the overwhelming forces of invading armies shall be broken *and* utterly swept away; yes, and a prince of the covenant [with those who were at peace with him] also [shall be broken and swept away]. 23And from the time that an alliance is made with him he shall work deceitfully, and he shall come up unexpectedly and shall become strong with a small people. 24Without warning *and* stealthily he shall come into the most productive places of a province *or* among the richest men of a province [of Egypt], and he shall do that which his fathers have not done nor his fathers' fathers; he shall distribute among them plunder, spoil, and goods. He shall devise plans against strongholds—but only for a time [the period decreed by God]. 25And he shall stir up his power and his courage against the king of the South [Egypt] with a great army; and the king of the South shall wage war with an exceedingly great and mighty army, but he shall not stand, for schemes shall be devised against [the king of the South]. 26Yes, those who eat of his rich *and* dainty food shall break *and* destroy him, and his army shall drift *or* turn away to flee, and many shall fall down slain. 27And as for both of these kings, their hearts *and* minds

---

*a* The reference here is undoubtedly to Seleucus Philopator [a king of Syria], the eldest son of Antiochus the Great and his immediate successor (Albert Barnes, *Notes on the Old Testament*). *b* This contemptible conqueror is generally identified as Antiochus Epiphanes, the younger son of Antiochus the Great, king of Syria, and is a type of the final antichrist referred to in Dan. 11:36; II Thess. 2:3-12; I John 4:3; II John 7; and Rev. 13:5-8. "He [Antiochus Epiphanes] stirred up the Jews by robbing the temple and setting up a statue of Jupiter in the Holy of Holies. He also pulled down the walls of Jerusalem, commanded the sacrifice of [forbidden] swine, forbade circumcision, and destroyed all the sacred books that could be found" (John D. Davis, *A Dictionary of the Bible*).

*a* 17 Or *but she*

## New International Version

bent on evil, will sit at the same table and lie to each other, but to no avail, because an end will still come at the appointed time. [28]The king of the North will return to his own country with great wealth, but his heart will be set against the holy covenant. He will take action against it and then return to his own country.

[29]"At the appointed time he will invade the South again, but this time the outcome will be different from what it was before. [30]Ships of the western coastlands will oppose him, and he will lose heart. Then he will turn back and vent his fury against the holy covenant. He will return and show favor to those who forsake the holy covenant.

[31]"His armed forces will rise up to desecrate the temple fortress and will abolish the daily sacrifice. Then they will set up the abomination that causes desolation. [32]With flattery he will corrupt those who have violated the covenant, but the people who know their God will firmly resist him.

[33]"Those who are wise will instruct many, though for a time they will fall by the sword or be burned or captured or plundered. [34]When they fall, they will receive a little help, and many who are not sincere will join them. [35]Some of the wise will stumble, so that they may be refined, purified and made spotless until the time of the end, for it will still come at the appointed time.

### The King Who Exalts Himself

[36]"The king will do as he pleases. He will exalt and magnify himself above every god and will say unheard-of things against the God of gods. He will be successful until the time of wrath is completed, for what has been determined must take place. [37]He will show no regard for the gods of his ancestors or for the one desired by women, nor will he regard any god, but will exalt himself above them all. [38]Instead of them, he will honor a god of fortresses; a god unknown to his ancestors he will honor with gold and silver, with precious stones and costly gifts. [39]He will attack the mightiest fortresses with the help of a foreign god and will greatly honor those who acknowledge him. He will make them rulers over many people and will distribute the land at a price.[a]

[40]"At the time of the end the king of the South will engage him in battle, and the king of the North will storm out against him with chariots and cavalry and a great fleet of ships. He will invade many countries and sweep through them like a flood. [41]He will also invade the Beautiful Land. Many countries will fall, but Edom, Moab and the leaders of Ammon will be delivered from his hand. [42]He will extend his power over many countries; Egypt will not es-

## Amplified Bible

shall be set on doing mischief; they shall speak lies over the same table, but it will not succeed, for the end is yet to be at the time appointed.

[28]Then shall [the vile conqueror from the North] return into his land with much booty; and his heart *and* purpose shall be set against [God's] holy covenant [with His people], and he shall accomplish [his malicious intention] and return to his own land [Syria].

[29]At the time appointed [God's own time] he shall return and come into the South, but it shall not be successful as were the former invasions [of Egypt].

[30]For the ships of Kittim [or Cyprus, in Roman hands] shall come against him; therefore he shall be grieved *and* discouraged and turn back [to Palestine] and carry out his rage *and* indignation against the holy covenant *and* God's people, and he shall do his own pleasure; he shall even turn back and make common cause with those [Jews] who abandon the holy covenant [with God].

[31]And armed forces of his shall appear [in the holy land] and they shall pollute the sanctuary, the [spiritual] stronghold, and shall take away the continual [daily burnt offering]; and they shall set up [in the sanctuary] the abomination that astonishes *and* makes desolate [probably an altar to a pagan god].

[32]And such as violate the covenant he shall pervert *and* seduce with flatteries, but the people who know their God shall prove themselves strong *and* shall stand firm and do exploits [for God].

[33]And they who are wise *and* understanding among the people shall instruct many *and* make them understand, though some [of them and their followers] shall fall by the sword and flame, by captivity and plunder, for many days.

[34]Now when they fall, they shall receive a little help. Many shall join themselves to them with flatteries *and* hypocrisies.

[35]And some of those who are wise, prudent, *and* understanding shall be weakened *and* fall, [thus, then, the insincere among the people will lose courage and become deserters. It will be a test] to refine, to purify, and to make those among [God's people] white, even to the time of the end, because it is yet for the time [God] appointed.

[36]And the [a]king shall do according to his will; he shall exalt himself and magnify himself above every god and shall speak astonishing things against the God of gods and shall prosper till the indignation be accomplished, for that which is determined [by God] shall be done.

[37]He shall not regard the gods of his fathers or Him [to Whom] women desire [to give birth—the Messiah] or any other god, for he shall magnify himself above all.

[38]But in their place he shall honor the god of fortresses; a god whom his fathers knew not shall he honor with gold and silver, with precious stones, and with pleasant *and* expensive things.

[39]And he shall deal with the strongest fortresses by the help of a foreign god. Those who acknowledge him he shall magnify with glory *and* honor, and he shall cause them to rule over many and shall divide the land for a price.

[40]And at the time of the end the king of the South shall push at *and* attack him, and the king of the North shall come against him like a whirlwind, with chariots and horsemen and with many ships; and he shall enter into the countries and shall overflow and pass through.

[41]He shall enter into the Glorious Land [Palestine] and many shall be overthrown, but these shall be delivered out of his hand: Edom, Moab, and the main [core] of the people of Ammon.

[42]He shall stretch out his hand also against the [other] countries, but the land of Egypt shall not be among the escaped ones.

---

*a* The antichrist is in view from this point in the prophecy to the end of the chapter. The details listed here do not fit what is known of Antiochus Epiphanes. See II Thess. 2:4; Rev. 13:5-8.

*a 39 Or land for a reward*

## New International Version

cape. 43He will gain control of the treasures of gold and silver and all the riches of Egypt, with the Libyans and Cushites*a* in submission. 44But reports from the east and the north will alarm him, and he will set out in a great rage to destroy and annihilate many. 45He will pitch his royal tents between the seas at*b* the beautiful holy mountain. Yet he will come to his end, and no one will help him.

### The End Times

**12** "At that time Michael, the great prince who protects your people, will arise. There will be a time of distress such as has not happened from the beginning of nations until then. But at that time your people—everyone whose name is found written in the book—will be delivered. 2Multitudes who sleep in the dust of the earth will awake: some to everlasting life, others to shame and everlasting contempt. 3Those who are wise*c* will shine like the brightness of the heavens, and those who lead many to righteousness, like the stars for ever and ever. 4But you, Daniel, roll up and seal the words of the scroll until the time of the end. Many will go here and there to increase knowledge."

5Then I, Daniel, looked, and there before me stood two others, one on this bank of the river and one on the opposite bank. 6One of them said to the man clothed in linen, who was above the waters of the river, "How long will it be before these astonishing things are fulfilled?"

7The man clothed in linen, who was above the waters of the river, lifted his right hand and his left hand toward heaven, and I heard him swear by him who lives forever, saying, "It will be for a time, times and half a time.*d* When the power of the holy people has been finally broken, all these things will be completed."

8I heard, but I did not understand. So I asked, "My lord, what will the outcome of all this be?"

9He replied, "Go your way, Daniel, because the words are rolled up and sealed until the time of the end. 10Many will be purified, made spotless and refined, but the wicked will continue to be wicked. None of the wicked will understand, but those who are wise will understand.

11"From the time that the daily sacrifice is abolished and the abomination that causes desolation is set up, there will be 1,290 days. 12Blessed is the one who waits for and reaches the end of the 1,335 days.

13"As for you, go your way till the end. You will rest, and then at the end of the days you will rise to receive your allotted inheritance."

## Amplified Bible

43But he shall have power over the treasures of gold and of silver and over all the precious things of Egypt, and the Libyans and the Ethiopians shall accompany him [compelled to follow his steps].

44But rumors from the east and from the north shall alarm *and* hasten him. And he shall go forth with great fury to destroy and utterly to sweep away many.

45And he shall pitch his palatial tents between the seas and the glorious holy Mount [Zion]; yet he shall come to his end with none to help him. [II Thess. 2:4; Rev. 13:5-8.]

**12** And at that time [of the end] Michael shall arise, the great [angelic] prince who defends *and* has charge of your [Daniel's] people. And there shall be a time of trouble, straitness, *and* distress such as never was since there was a nation till that time. But at that time your people shall be delivered, everyone whose name shall be found written in the Book [of God's plan for His own].

2And many of those who sleep in the dust of the earth shall awake: some to everlasting life and some to shame and everlasting contempt *and* abhorrence. [John 5:29.]

3And the teachers *and* those who are wise shall shine like the brightness of the firmament, and those who turn many to righteousness (to uprightness and right standing with God) [shall give forth light] like the stars forever and ever. [Matt. 13:43.]

4But you, O Daniel, shut up the words and seal the Book until the time of the end. [Then] many shall run to and fro *and* search anxiously [through the Book], and knowledge [of God's purposes as revealed by His prophets] shall be increased *and* become great. [Amos 8:12.]

5Then I, Daniel, looked, and behold, there stood two others, the one on the brink of the river on this side and the other on the brink of the river on that side.

6And one said to the man clothed in linen, who was above the waters of the river, How long shall it be to the end of these wonders? [Dan. 10:5.]

7And I heard the man clothed in linen, who was above the waters of the river, when he held up his right hand and his left hand toward the heavens and swore by Him Who lives forever that it shall be for a time, times, and a half a time [or three and one-half years]; and when they have made an end of shattering *and* crushing the power of the holy people, all these things shall be finished.

8And I heard, but I did not understand. Then I said, O my lord, what shall be the issue *and* final end of these things?

9And he [the angel] said, Go your way, Daniel, for the words are shut up and sealed till the time of the end.

10Many shall purify themselves and make themselves white and be tried, smelted, *and* refined, but the wicked shall do wickedly. And none of the wicked shall understand, but the teachers *and* those who are wise shall understand. [Dan. 11:33-35.]

11And from the time that the continual burnt offering is taken away and the abomination that makes desolate is set up, there shall be 1,290 days. [Dan. 11:31.]

12Blessed, happy, fortunate, spiritually prosperous, *and* to be envied is he who waits expectantly *and* earnestly [who endures without wavering beyond the period of tribulation] and comes to the 1,335 days!

13But you [Daniel, who was now over ninety years of age], go your way until the end; for you shall rest and shall stand [fast] in your allotted place at the end of the days. [Heb. 11:32-40.]

---

*a* 43 That is, people from the upper Nile region    *b* 45 Or *the sea and*
*c* 3 Or *who impart wisdom*    *d* 7 Or *a year, two years and half a year*

## New International Version

# Hosea

**1** The word of the LORD that came to Hosea son of Beeri during the reigns of Uzziah, Jotham, Ahaz and Hezekiah, kings of Judah, and during the reign of Jeroboam son of Jehoash[a] king of Israel:

### Hosea's Wife and Children

[2] When the LORD began to speak through Hosea, the LORD said to him, "Go, marry a promiscuous woman and have children with her, for like an adulterous wife this land is guilty of unfaithfulness to the LORD." [3] So he married Gomer daughter of Diblaim, and she conceived and bore him a son.

[4] Then the LORD said to Hosea, "Call him Jezreel, because I will soon punish the house of Jehu for the massacre at Jezreel, and I will put an end to the kingdom of Israel. [5] In that day I will break Israel's bow in the Valley of Jezreel."

[6] Gomer conceived again and gave birth to a daughter. Then the LORD said to Hosea, "Call her Lo-Ruhamah (which means "not loved"), for I will no longer show love to Israel, that I should at all forgive them. [7] Yet I will show love to Judah; and I will save them—not by bow, sword or battle, or by horses and horsemen, but I, the LORD their God, will save them."

[8] After she had weaned Lo-Ruhamah, Gomer had another son. [9] Then the LORD said, "Call him Lo-Ammi (which means "not my people"), for you are not my people, and I am not your God.[b]

[10] "Yet the Israelites will be like the sand on the seashore, which cannot be measured or counted. In the place where it was said to them, 'You are not my people,' they will be called 'children of the living God.' [11] The people of Judah and the people of Israel will come together; they will appoint one leader and will come up out of the land, for great will be the day of Jezreel.[c]

**2**[d] "Say of your brothers, 'My people,' and of your sisters, 'My loved one.'

### Israel Punished and Restored

[2] "Rebuke your mother, rebuke her,
  for she is not my wife,
  and I am not her husband.
Let her remove the adulterous look from her face
  and the unfaithfulness from between her breasts.
[3] Otherwise I will strip her naked
  and make her as bare as on the day she was born;
I will make her like a desert,
  turn her into a parched land,
  and slay her with thirst.
[4] I will not show my love to her children,
  because they are the children of adultery.
[5] Their mother has been unfaithful
  and has conceived them in disgrace.
She said, 'I will go after my lovers,
  who give me my food and my water,
  my wool and my linen, my olive oil and my drink.'

## Amplified Bible

### THE BOOK OF

# Hosea

**1** The word of the Lord that came to Hosea son of Beeri in the days of Uzziah, Jotham, Ahaz, and Hezekiah, kings of Judah, and in the days of Jeroboam son of Joash king of Israel.

[2] When the Lord first spoke with *and* through Hosea, the Lord said to him, Go, take to yourself a wife of harlotry and have children of [her] harlotry, for the land commits great whoredom by departing from the Lord.

[3] So he went and took Gomer the daughter of Diblaim, and she became pregnant and bore him a son.

[4] And the Lord said to him, Call his name Jezreel *or* God-sows, for yet a little while and I will avenge the blood of Jezreel *and* visit the punishment for it upon the house of Jehu, and I will put an end to the kingdom of the house of Israel. [II Kings 10:11.]

[5] And on that day I will break the bow of Israel in the Valley of Jezreel.

[6] And [Gomer] conceived again and bore a daughter. And the Lord said to Hosea, Call her name Lo-Ruhamah *or* Not-pitied, for I will no more have love, pity, *and* mercy on the house of Israel, that I should in any way pardon them.

[7] But I will have love, pity, *and* mercy on the house of Judah and will deliver them by the Lord their God and will [a] not save them by bow, nor by sword, nor by equipment of war, nor by horses, nor by horsemen. [Isa. 31:8; 37:33-35.]

[8] Now when [Gomer] had weaned Lo-Ruhamah [Not-pitied], she became pregnant [again] and bore a son.

[9] And the Lord said, Call his name Lo-Ammi [Not-my-people], for you are not My people and I am not your God.

[10] Yet the number of the children of Israel shall be as the sand of the sea, which cannot be measured or numbered; and instead of it being said to them, You are not My people, it shall be said to them, Sons of the Living God! [Rom. 9:26.]

[11] Then shall the children of Judah and the children of Israel be gathered together and appoint themselves one head, and they shall go up out of the land, for great shall be the day of Jezreel [for the spiritually reborn Israel, a divine offspring, the people whom the Lord has blessed.] [Isa. 11:12, 13; Ezek. 37:15-28.]

**2** [Hosea], say to your brethren, Ammi [or You-are-my-people], and to your sisters, Ruhamah [or You-have-been-pitied-and-have-obtained-mercy].

[2] Plead with your mother [your nation]; plead, for she is not My wife and I am not her Husband; [plead] that she put away her [marks of] harlotry from her face and her adulteries from between her breasts, [Isa. 50:1.]

[3] Lest I strip her naked and make her as in the day she was born, and make her as a wilderness and set her like a parched land and slay her with thirst.

[4] Yes, for her children I will have no love *nor* pity *nor* mercy, for they are the children of harlotry.

[5] For their mother has played the harlot; she who conceived them has done shamefully, for she said, I will go after my lovers that give me my food and my water, my wool and my flax, my oil and my refreshing drinks.

[a] 1 Hebrew *Joash,* a variant of *Jehoash*  [b] 9 Or *your I AM*  [c] 11 In Hebrew texts 1:10,11 is numbered 2:1,2.  [d] In Hebrew texts 2:1-23 is numbered 2:3-25.

[a] Isaiah also made this prophecy (Isa. 31:8-9) and both he and Hosea lived to see its remarkable, literal fulfillment (Isa. 37:36). See also II Kings 19:35-37.

## New International Version

6 Therefore I will block her path with thornbushes;
  I will wall her in so that she cannot find her way.
7 She will chase after her lovers but not catch them;
  she will look for them but not find them.
Then she will say,
  'I will go back to my husband as at first,
  for then I was better off than now.'
8 She has not acknowledged that I was the one
  who gave her the grain, the new wine and oil,
  who lavished on her the silver and gold—
  which they used for Baal.

9 "Therefore I will take away my grain when it ripens,
  and my new wine when it is ready.
I will take back my wool and my linen,
  intended to cover her naked body.
10 So now I will expose her lewdness
  before the eyes of her lovers;
  no one will take her out of my hands.
11 I will stop all her celebrations:
  her yearly festivals, her New Moons,
  her Sabbath days—all her appointed festivals.
12 I will ruin her vines and her fig trees,
  which she said were her pay from her lovers;
I will make them a thicket,
  and wild animals will devour them.
13 I will punish her for the days
  she burned incense to the Baals;
she decked herself with rings and jewelry,
  and went after her lovers,
  but me she forgot,"
                                    declares the LORD.

14 "Therefore I am now going to allure her;
  I will lead her into the wilderness
  and speak tenderly to her.
15 There I will give her back her vineyards,
  and will make the Valley of Achor[a] a door of hope.
There she will respond[b] as in the days of her youth,
  as in the day she came up out of Egypt.

16 "In that day," declares the LORD,
  "you will call me 'my husband';
  you will no longer call me 'my master.'[c]
17 I will remove the names of the Baals from her lips;
  no longer will their names be invoked.
18 In that day I will make a covenant for them
  with the beasts of the field, the birds in the sky
  and the creatures that move along the ground.
Bow and sword and battle
  I will abolish from the land,
  so that all may lie down in safety.
19 I will betroth you to me forever;
  I will betroth you in[d] righteousness and justice,
  in[d] love and compassion.
20 I will betroth you in[d] faithfulness,
  and you will acknowledge the LORD.

21 "In that day I will respond,"
  declares the LORD—
"I will respond to the skies,
  and they will respond to the earth;
22 and the earth will respond to the grain,
  the new wine and the olive oil,
  and they will respond to Jezreel.[e]

## Amplified Bible

6 Therefore, behold, I [the Lord God] will hedge up her way [even yours, O Israel] with thorns; and I will build a wall against her that she shall not find her paths.
7 And she shall follow after her lovers but she shall not overtake them; and she shall seek them [inquiring for and requiring them], but shall not find them. Then shall she say, Let me go and return to my first husband, for then was it better with me than now.
8 For she has not noticed, understood, or realized that it was I [the Lord God] Who gave her the grain and the new wine and the fresh oil, and Who lavished upon her silver and gold which they used for Baal and made into his image.
9 Therefore will I return and take back My grain in the time for it and My new wine in the season for it, and will pluck away and recover My wool and My flax which were to cover her [Israel's] nakedness.
10 And now will I uncover her lewdness and her shame in the sight of her lovers, and no one shall rescue her out of My hand.
11 I will also cause to cease all her mirth, her feastmaking, her New Moons, her Sabbaths, and all her solemn feasts and appointed festive assemblies.
12 And I will lay waste and destroy her vines and her fig trees of which she has said, These are my reward or loose woman's hire that my lovers have given me; and I will make [her plantations] an inaccessible forest, and the wild beasts of the open country shall eat them.
13 And I will visit [punishment] upon her for the feast days of the Baals, when she burned incense to them and decked herself with her earrings and nose rings and her jewelry and went after her lovers and forgot Me, says the Lord.
14 Therefore, behold, I will allure her [Israel] and bring her into the wilderness, and I will speak tenderly and to her heart.
15 There I will give her her vineyards and make the Valley of Achor [troubling] to be for her a door of hope and expectation. And she shall sing there and respond as in the days of her youth and as at the time when she came up out of the land of Egypt. [Exod. 15:2; Josh. 7:24-26.]
16 And it shall be in that day, says the Lord, that you will call Me Ishi [my Husband], and you shall no more call Me Baali [my Baal].
17 For I will take away the names of Baalim [the Baals] out of her mouth, and they shall no more be mentioned or seriously remembered by their name.
18 And in that day will I make a covenant for Israel with the living creatures of the open country and with the birds of the heavens and with the creeping things of the ground. And I will break the bow and the sword and [abolish battle equipment and] conflict out of the land and will make you lie down safely.
19 And I will betroth you to Me forever; yes, I will betroth you to Me in righteousness and justice, in steadfast love, and in mercy.
20 I will even betroth you to Me in stability and in faithfulness, and you shall know (recognize, be acquainted with, appreciate, give heed to, and cherish) the Lord.
21 And in that day I will respond, says the Lord; I will respond to the heavens [which ask for rain to pour on the earth], and they shall respond to the earth [which begs for the rain it needs],
22 And the earth shall respond to the grain and the wine and the oil [which beseech it to bring them forth], and these shall respond to Jezreel [restored Israel, who prays for a supply of them].

---

a 15 Achor means trouble.   b 15 Or sing   c 16 Hebrew baal
d 19,20 Or with   e 22 Jezreel means God plants.

## New International Version

23 I will plant her for myself in the land;
  I will show my love to the one I called 'Not my loved
  one.'*a*'
I will say to those called 'Not my people,*b*' 'You are my
  people';
  and they will say, 'You are my God.'"

### Hosea's Reconciliation With His Wife

**3** The LORD said to me, "Go, show your love to your
wife again, though she is loved by another man and
is an adulteress. Love her as the LORD loves the Israelites,
though they turn to other gods and love the sacred raisin
cakes."

2 So I bought her for fifteen shekels*c* of silver and about
a homer and a lethek*d* of barley. 3 Then I told her, "You are
to live with me many days; you must not be a prostitute or
be intimate with any man, and I will behave the same way
toward you."

4 For the Israelites will live many days without king or
prince, without sacrifice or sacred stones, without ephod
or household gods. 5 Afterward the Israelites will return
and seek the LORD their God and David their king. They
will come trembling to the LORD and to his blessings in
the last days.

### The Charge Against Israel

**4** Hear the word of the LORD, you Israelites,
  because the LORD has a charge to bring
    against you who live in the land:
"There is no faithfulness, no love,
  no acknowledgment of God in the land.
2 There is only cursing,*e* lying and murder,
  stealing and adultery;
they break all bounds,
  and bloodshed follows bloodshed.
3 Because of this the land dries up,
  and all who live in it waste away;
the beasts of the field, the birds in the sky
  and the fish in the sea are swept away.

4 "But let no one bring a charge,
  let no one accuse another,
for your people are like those
  who bring charges against a priest.
5 You stumble day and night,
  and the prophets stumble with you.
So I will destroy your mother—
6   my people are destroyed from lack of knowledge.

"Because you have rejected knowledge,
  I also reject you as my priests;
because you have ignored the law of your God,
  I also will ignore your children.
7 The more priests there were,
  the more they sinned against me;
they exchanged their glorious God*f* for something
  disgraceful.
8 They feed on the sins of my people
  and relish their wickedness.
9 And it will be: Like people, like priests.
  I will punish both of them for their ways
  and repay them for their deeds.

## Amplified Bible

23 And I will sow her for Myself anew in the land, and
I will have love, pity, *and* mercy for her who had not obtained love, pity, *and* mercy; and I will say to those who
were not My people, You are My people, and they shall say,
You are my God! [I Pet. 2:9, 10.]

**3** Then said the Lord to me, Go again, love [the same]
woman [Gomer] who is beloved of a paramour and is
an adulteress, even as the Lord loves the children of Israel,
though they turn to other gods and love cakes of raisins
[used in the sacrificial feasts in idol worship].

2 So I bought her for *a*fifteen pieces of silver and a homer
and a half of barley [the price of a slave].

3 And I said to her, You shall be [betrothed] to me for
many days; you shall not play the harlot and you shall not
belong to another man. So will I also be to you [until you
have proved your loyalty to me and our marital relations
may be resumed].

4 For the children of Israel shall dwell *and* sit deprived
many days, without king or prince, without sacrifice or
[idolatrous] pillar, and without ephod [a garment worn by
priests when seeking divine counsel] or teraphim (household gods).

5 Afterward shall the children of Israel return and seek
the Lord their God, [inquiring of and requiring Him] and
[from the line of] David, their King [of kings]; and they
shall come in [anxious] fear to the Lord and to His goodness *and* His good things in the latter days. [Jer. 30:9;
Ezek. 34:24.]

**4** Hear the word of the Lord, you children of Israel, for
the Lord has a controversy (a pleading contention)
with the inhabitants of the land, because there is no faithfulness, love, pity *and* mercy, or knowledge of God [from
personal experience with Him] in the land.

2 There is nothing but [false] swearing and breaking
faith and killing and stealing and committing adultery;
they break out [into violence], one [deed of] bloodshed
following close on another.

3 Therefore shall the land [continually] mourn, and
all who dwell in it shall languish, together with the wild
beasts of the open country and the birds of the heavens;
yes, the fishes of the sea also shall [perish because of the
drought] be collected *and* taken away.

4 Yet let no man strive, neither let any man reprove [an-
other—do not waste your time in mutual recriminations],
for with you is My contention, O priest!

5 And you shall stumble in the daytime, and the [false]
prophet also shall stumble with you in the night; and I will
destroy your mother [the priestly nation]. [Exod. 19:6.]

6 My people are destroyed for lack of knowledge; because you [the priestly nation] have rejected knowledge,
I will also reject you that you shall be no priest to Me;
seeing you have forgotten the law of your God, I will also
forget your children.

7 The more they increased *and* multiplied [in prosperity and power], the more they sinned against Me; I will
change their glory into shame.

8 They feed on the sin of My people and set their heart
on their iniquity.

9 And it shall be: Like people, like priest; I will punish
them for their ways and repay them for their doings.

---

*a 23* Hebrew *Lo-Ruhamah* (see 1:6)   *b 23* Hebrew *Lo-Ammi* (see
1:9)   *c 2* That is, about 6 ounces or about 170 grams   *d 2* A homer
and a lethek possibly weighed about 430 pounds or about 195 kilograms.
*e 2* That is, to pronounce a curse on   *f 7* Syriac (see also an ancient
Hebrew scribal tradition); Masoretic Text *me; / I will exchange their glory*

---

*a* Hosea bought Gomer back after she had become a slave. The
combination of fifteen pieces of silver and a homer and a half of barley
totaled the standard price of a slave (30 pieces of silver). See Exod. 21:7,
32; II Kings 7:1, 16, 18.

## New International Version

10 "They will eat but not have enough;
   they will engage in prostitution but not flourish,
because they have deserted the LORD
   to give themselves 11 to prostitution;
old wine and new wine
   take away their understanding.
12 My people consult a wooden idol,
   and a diviner's rod speaks to them.
A spirit of prostitution leads them astray;
   they are unfaithful to their God.
13 They sacrifice on the mountaintops
   and burn offerings on the hills,
under oak, poplar and terebinth,
   where the shade is pleasant.
Therefore your daughters turn to prostitution
   and your daughters-in-law to adultery.

14 "I will not punish your daughters
   when they turn to prostitution,
nor your daughters-in-law
   when they commit adultery,
because the men themselves consort with harlots
   and sacrifice with shrine prostitutes—
   a people without understanding will come to ruin!

15 "Though you, Israel, commit adultery,
   do not let Judah become guilty.

"Do not go to Gilgal;
   do not go up to Beth Aven.ᵃ
   And do not swear, 'As surely as the LORD lives!'
16 The Israelites are stubborn,
   like a stubborn heifer.
How can the LORD pasture them
   like lambs in a meadow?
17 Ephraim is joined to idols;
   leave him alone!
18 Even when their drinks are gone,
   they continue their prostitution;
   their rulers dearly love shameful ways.
19 A whirlwind will sweep them away,
   and their sacrifices will bring them shame.

### Judgment Against Israel

**5** "Hear this, you priests!
   Pay attention, you Israelites!
Listen, royal house!
   This judgment is against you:
You have been a snare at Mizpah,
   a net spread out on Tabor.
2 The rebels are knee-deep in slaughter.
   I will discipline all of them.
3 I know all about Ephraim;
   Israel is not hidden from me.
Ephraim, you have now turned to prostitution;
   Israel is corrupt.

4 "Their deeds do not permit them
   to return to their God.
A spirit of prostitution is in their heart;
   they do not acknowledge the LORD.
5 Israel's arrogance testifies against them;
   the Israelites, even Ephraim, stumble in their sin;
   Judah also stumbles with them.
6 When they go with their flocks and herds
   to seek the LORD,
they will not find him;
   he has withdrawn himself from them.
7 They are unfaithful to the LORD;

## Amplified Bible

10 For they shall eat and not have enough; they shall play the harlot and beget no increase, because they have forsaken the Lord for harlotry;
11 Harlotry and wine and new wine take away the heart and the mind and the spiritual understanding.
12 My people [habitually] ask counsel of their [senseless] wood [idols], and their staff [of wood] gives them oracles and instructs them. For the spirit of harlotry has led them astray and they have played the harlot, withdrawing themselves from subjection to their God.
13 They sacrifice on the tops of the mountains, and they burn incense upon the hills and under oaks, poplars, and terebinths, because the shade is good. Therefore your daughters play the harlot and your sons' wives commit adultery.
14 I will not punish your daughters when they play the harlot nor your daughters-in-law when they commit adultery, for [the fathers and husbands] themselves go aside in order to be alone with women who prostitute themselves for gain, and they sacrifice at the altar with dedicated harlots [who surrender their chastity in honor of the goddess]. Therefore the people without understanding shall stumble and fall and come to ruin.
15 Though you, Israel, play the harlot and worship idols, let not Judah offend and become guilty; come not to Gilgal, neither go up to Beth-aven [contemptuous reference to Bethel, then noted for idolatry], nor swear [in idolatrous service, saying], As the Lord lives.
16 For Israel has behaved stubbornly, like a stubborn heifer. How then should he expect to be fed and treated by the Lord like a lamb in a large pasture?
17 Ephraim is joined [fast] to idols, [so] let him alone [to take the consequences].
18 Their drinking carousal over, they go habitually to play the harlot; [Ephraim's] rulers [continue to] love shame more than her glory [which is the Lord, Israel's God].
19 The resistless wind [of God's wrath] has bound up [Israel] in its wings or skirts, and [in captivity] they and their altars shall be put to shame because of their sacrifices [to calves, to sun, moon, and stars, and to heathen gods].

**5** Hear this, O you priests! And listen, O house of Israel! And give ear, O house of the king! For the judgment pronounced pertains to you and is meant for you, because you have been a snare at Mizpah and a net spread upon Tabor [military strongholds on either side of the Jordan River].
2 The revolters are deeply sunk in corruption and slaughter, but I [the Lord God] am a rebuke and a chastisement for them all.
3 I know Ephraim, and Israel is not hid from Me; for now, O Ephraim, you have played the harlot and have worshiped idols; Israel is defiled.
4 Their doings will not permit them to return to their God, for the spirit of harlotry is within them and they know not the Lord [they do not recognize, appreciate, give heed to, or cherish the Lord].
5 But the pride and self-reliance of Israel testifies before his [own] face. Therefore shall [all] Israel, and [especially] Ephraim [the northern ten tribes], totter and fall in their iniquity and guilt, and Judah shall stumble and fall with them.
6 They shall go with their flocks and with their herds to seek the Lord [inquiring for and requiring Him], but they will not find Him; He has withdrawn Himself from them.
7 They have dealt faithlessly and treacherously with the

---

ᵃ 15 Beth Aven means house of wickedness (a derogatory name for Bethel, which means house of God).

## New International Version

they give birth to illegitimate children.
When they celebrate their New Moon feasts,
he will devour*a* their fields.

8 "Sound the trumpet in Gibeah,
the horn in Ramah.
Raise the battle cry in Beth Aven*b*;
lead on, Benjamin.
9 Ephraim will be laid waste
on the day of reckoning.
Among the tribes of Israel
I proclaim what is certain.
10 Judah's leaders are like those
who move boundary stones.
I will pour out my wrath on them
like a flood of water.
11 Ephraim is oppressed,
trampled in judgment,
intent on pursuing idols.*c*
12 I am like a moth to Ephraim,
like rot to the people of Judah.

13 "When Ephraim saw his sickness,
and Judah his sores,
then Ephraim turned to Assyria,
and sent to the great king for help.
But he is not able to cure you,
not able to heal your sores.
14 For I will be like a lion to Ephraim,
like a great lion to Judah.
I will tear them to pieces and go away;
I will carry them off, with no one to rescue them.
15 Then I will return to my lair
until they have borne their guilt
and seek my face—
in their misery
they will earnestly seek me."

### Israel Unrepentant

**6** "Come, let us return to the LORD.
He has torn us to pieces
but he will heal us;
he has injured us
but he will bind up our wounds.
2 After two days he will revive us;
on the third day he will restore us,
that we may live in his presence.
3 Let us acknowledge the LORD;
let us press on to acknowledge him.
As surely as the sun rises,
he will appear;
he will come to us like the winter rains,
like the spring rains that water the earth."

4 "What can I do with you, Ephraim?
What can I do with you, Judah?
Your love is like the morning mist,
like the early dew that disappears.
5 Therefore I cut you in pieces with my prophets,
I killed you with the words of my mouth—
then my judgments go forth like the sun.*d*
6 For I desire mercy, not sacrifice,
and acknowledgment of God rather than burnt offerings.
7 As at Adam,*e* they have broken the covenant;
they were unfaithful to me there.
8 Gilead is a city of evildoers,
stained with footprints of blood.
9 As marauders lie in ambush for a victim,

## Amplified Bible

Lord [their espoused Husband], for they have borne alien children. Now shall a [single] New Moon (one month) devour them with their fields.

8 Blow the horn in Gibeah and the trumpet in Ramah [both lofty hills on Benjamin's northern border]. Sound the alarm at Beth-aven: [the enemy is] behind you *and* after you, O Benjamin [be on your guard]!

9 Ephraim shall become a desolation in the day of rebuke *and* punishment. Among the tribes of Israel I declare what shall surely be.

10 The princes of Judah are like those who remove the landmark [the barrier between right and wrong]; I will pour out My wrath upon them like water. [Deut. 19:14; Prov. 22:28.]

11 Ephraim is oppressed; he is broken *and* crushed by [divine] judgment, because he was content to walk after idols (images) *and* man's [evil] command *a* (vanities and filth).

12 Therefore I am like a moth to Ephraim and like dry rot to the house of Judah [in My judgment against them].

13 When Ephraim saw his sickness and Judah saw his wound, then Ephraim went to Assyria and sent to [Assyria's] great King Jareb [for help]. Yet he cannot heal you nor will he cure you of your wound [received in divine judgment].

14 For I will be to Ephraim like a lion, and like a young lion to the house of Judah. I, even I, will rend and go on [rending]; I will carry off and there will be no one to deliver.

15 I will return to My place [on high] until they acknowledge their offense *and* feel their guilt and seek My face; in their affliction *and* distress they will seek, inquire for, *and* require Me earnestly, saying,

**6** Come and let us return to the Lord, for He has torn so that He may heal us; He has stricken so that He may bind us up.

2 After two days He will revive us (quicken us, give us life); on the third day He will raise us up that we may live before Him. [Isa. 26:19; Ezek. 37:1-10.]

3 Yes, let us know (recognize, be acquainted with, and understand) Him; let us be zealous to know the Lord [to appreciate, give heed to, and cherish Him]. His going forth is prepared *and* certain as the dawn, and He will come to us as the [heavy] rain, as the latter rain that waters the earth.

4 O Ephraim, what shall I do with you? [says the Lord] O Judah, what shall I do with you? For your [wavering] love *and* kindness are like the night mist *or* like the dew that goes early away.

5 Therefore have I hewn down *and* smitten them by means of the prophets; I have slain them by the words of My mouth; My judgments [pronounced upon them by you prophets] are like the light that goes forth.

6 For I desire *and* delight in dutiful steadfast love *and* goodness, not sacrifice, and the knowledge of *and* acquaintance with God more than burnt offerings. [Matt. 9:13; 12:7.]

7 But they, like [less-privileged] men *and* like Adam, have transgressed the covenant; there have they dealt faithlessly *and* treacherously with Me.

8 Gilead is a city of evildoers; it is tracked with bloody [footprints].

9 And as troops of robbers lie in wait for a man, so the

---

*a* 7 Or *Now their New Moon feasts / will devour them and*    *b* 8 *Beth Aven* means *house of wickedness* (a derogatory name for Bethel, which means *house of God*).    *c* 11 The meaning of the Hebrew for this word is uncertain.    *d* 5 The meaning of the Hebrew for this line is uncertain.    *e* 7 Or *Like Adam*; or *Like human beings*

*a* "Vanities" is the rendering of *The Septuagint* (Greek translation of the Old Testament); "filth," the rendering of *The Dead Sea Scrolls*.

## New International Version

    so do bands of priests;
  they murder on the road to Shechem,
    carrying out their wicked schemes.
¹⁰ I have seen a horrible thing in Israel:
  There Ephraim is given to prostitution,
  Israel is defiled.

¹¹ "Also for you, Judah,
  a harvest is appointed.

"Whenever I would restore the fortunes of my people,

**7** ¹ whenever I would heal Israel,
    the sins of Ephraim are exposed
  and the crimes of Samaria revealed.
They practice deceit,
  thieves break into houses,
  bandits rob in the streets;
² but they do not realize
  that I remember all their evil deeds.
Their sins engulf them;
  they are always before me.

³ "They delight the king with their wickedness,
  the princes with their lies.
⁴ They are all adulterers,
  burning like an oven
whose fire the baker need not stir
from the kneading of the dough till it rises.
⁵ On the day of the festival of our king
  the princes become inflamed with wine,
  and he joins hands with the mockers.
⁶ Their hearts are like an oven;
  they approach him with intrigue.
Their passion smolders all night;
  in the morning it blazes like a flaming fire.
⁷ All of them are as an oven;
  they devour their rulers.
All their kings fall,
  and none of them calls on me.

⁸ "Ephraim mixes with the nations;
  Ephraim is a flat loaf not turned over.
⁹ Foreigners sap his strength,
  but he does not realize it.
His hair is sprinkled with gray,
  but he does not notice.
¹⁰ Israel's arrogance testifies against him,
  but despite all this
he does not return to the LORD his God
  or search for him.

¹¹ "Ephraim is like a dove,
  easily deceived and senseless—
now calling to Egypt,
  now turning to Assyria.
¹² When they go, I will throw my net over them;
  I will pull them down like the birds in the sky.
When I hear them flocking together,
  I will catch them.
¹³ Woe to them,
  because they have strayed from me!
Destruction to them,
  because they have rebelled against me!
I long to redeem them
  but they speak about me falsely.
¹⁴ They do not cry out to me from their hearts
  but wail on their beds.
They slash themselves,ᵃ appealing to their gods
  for grain and new wine,
  but they turn away from me.
¹⁵ I trained them and strengthened their arms,
  but they plot evil against me.

## Amplified Bible

company of priests murder on the road toward Shechem; yes, they commit villainy *and* outrages.
¹⁰ I have seen a horrible thing in the house of Israel! There harlotry *and* idolatry are found in Ephraim; Israel is defiled.
¹¹ Also, O Judah, there is a harvest [of divine judgment] appointed for you; when I would return My people from their captivity [in which they are slaves to the misery brought on by their own sins],

**7** When I would heal Israel, then Ephraim's guilt is uncovered, and the wickedness of Samaria; how they practice falsehood, and the thief enters and the troop of bandits ravage *and* raid without.
² But they do not consider *and* say to their minds *and* hearts that I [earnestly] remember all their wickedness. Now their own doings surround and entangle them; they are before My face.
³ They make the king glad with their wickedness, and the princes with their lies.
⁴ They are all [idolatrous] adulterers; their passion smolders like heat of an oven when the baker ceases to stir the fire from the kneading of the dough until it is leavened.
⁵ On the [special] day of our king the princes made themselves *and* him sick with the heat of wine; [the king] stretched out his hand with scoffers *and* lawless men.
⁶ For they have made ready their heart, *and* their mind burns [with intrigue] like an oven while they lie in wait. Their anger smolders all night; in the morning it blazes forth as a flaming fire.
⁷ They are all hot as an oven and devour their judges; all their kings are fallen; there is none among them who calls to Me.
⁸ Ephraim mixes himself among the peoples [courting the favor of first one country, then another]; Ephraim is a cake not turned.
⁹ Strangers have devoured his strength, and he knows it not; yes, gray hairs are sprinkled here and there upon him, and he does not know it.
¹⁰ And the pride of Israel testifies against him *and* to his face. But they do not return to the Lord their God, nor seek *nor* inquire of *nor* require Him in spite of all this.
¹¹ Ephraim also is like a silly dove without heart *or* understanding; they call to Egypt; they go to Assyria.
¹² As they go, I will spread My net over them; I will bring them down like birds of the heavens. I will chastise them according to the announcement [or prediction made] to their congregation [in the Scriptures]. [Lev. 26:14-39.]
¹³ Woe to them, for they have wandered from Me! Destruction to them, because they have rebelled *and* trespassed against Me! Though I would redeem them, yet they have spoken lies against Me.
¹⁴ They do not cry to Me from their heart, but they wail upon their beds; they gash *and* distress *and* assemble themselves [in mourning] for grain and new wine; they rebel against Me.
¹⁵ Although I have chastened them *and* trained and strengthened their arms, yet they think *and* devise evil against Me.

---

ᵃ *14* Some Hebrew manuscripts and Septuagint; most Hebrew manuscripts *They gather together*

## New International Version

16They do not turn to the Most High;
  they are like a faulty bow.
Their leaders will fall by the sword
  because of their insolent words.
For this they will be ridiculed
  in the land of Egypt.

### Israel to Reap the Whirlwind

**8** "Put the trumpet to your lips!
  An eagle is over the house of the LORD
because the people have broken my covenant
  and rebelled against my law.
2Israel cries out to me,
  'Our God, we acknowledge you!'
3But Israel has rejected what is good;
  an enemy will pursue him.
4They set up kings without my consent;
  they choose princes without my approval.
With their silver and gold
  they make idols for themselves
  to their own destruction.
5Samaria, throw out your calf-idol!
  My anger burns against them.
How long will they be incapable of purity?
6  They are from Israel!
This calf—a metalworker has made it;
  it is not God.
It will be broken in pieces,
  that calf of Samaria.
7"They sow the wind
  and reap the whirlwind.
The stalk has no head;
  it will produce no flour.
Were it to yield grain,
  foreigners would swallow it up.
8Israel is swallowed up;
  now she is among the nations
  like something no one wants.
9For they have gone up to Assyria
  like a wild donkey wandering alone.
Ephraim has sold herself to lovers.
10Although they have sold themselves among the
    nations,
  I will now gather them together.
They will begin to waste away
  under the oppression of the mighty king.

11"Though Ephraim built many altars for sin offerings,
  these have become altars for sinning.
12I wrote for them the many things of my law,
  but they regarded them as something foreign.
13Though they offer sacrifices as gifts to me,
  and though they eat the meat,
  the LORD is not pleased with them.
Now he will remember their wickedness
  and punish their sins:
  They will return to Egypt.
14Israel has forgotten their Maker
  and built palaces;
  Judah has fortified many towns.
But I will send fire on their cities
  that will consume their fortresses."

### Punishment for Israel

**9** Do not rejoice, Israel;
  do not be jubilant like the other nations.
For you have been unfaithful to your God;
  you love the wages of a prostitute
  at every threshing floor.
2Threshing floors and winepresses will not feed the
    people;
  the new wine will fail them.

## Amplified Bible

16They turn back, shift, *or* change, but not upwards
[to the Most High]. They are like a deceitful bow; their
princes shall fall by the sword for the insolence *and* rage
of their tongue. This shall be [cause for] their derision *and*
scorning in the land of Egypt.

**8** Set the trumpet to your lips! [The enemy] comes as a
  [great] vulture against the house of the Lord, because
they have broken My covenant and transgressed against
My law.
2Then they will cry to Me, My God, we [of Israel] know
You!
3Israel has rejected the good [with loathing]; the enemy
shall pursue him.
4They set up kings, but not from Me [therefore without
My blessing]; they have made princes or removed them
[without consulting Me; therefore], I knew *and* recognized [them] not. With their silver and their gold they
made idols for themselves, that they [the silver and the
gold] may be destroyed.
5Your calf [idol], O Samaria, is loathsome *and* I have
spurned it. My wrath burns against them. How long will it
be before they attain purity?
6For this [calf] too is from Israel; a craftsman made it;
therefore it is not God. The calf of Samaria shall be broken
to shivers *and* go up in flames.
7For they sow the wind and they shall reap the whirlwind. The standing grain has no heads; it shall yield no
meal; if it were to yield, strangers *and* aliens would eat
it up.
8Israel is [as if] swallowed up. Already they have become among the nations as a vessel [of cheap, coarse pottery] that is useless.
9For they are gone up to Assyria, a wild ass taking her
own way by herself; Ephraim has hired lovers.
10Yes, though with presents they hire [allies] among the
nations, now will I gather them up, and in a little while they
will sorrow *and* begin to diminish [their gifts] because of
the burden (tribute) imposed by the king of princes [the
king of Assyria].
11For Ephraim has multiplied altars for sinning; yes, to
him altars are intended for sinning.
12I wrote for him the ten thousand things of My law, but
they are counted as a strange thing [as something which
does not concern him].
13My sacrificial gifts they sacrifice [as a mere form];
yes, they sacrifice flesh and eat it, but the Lord does not
accept them. Now He will [earnestly] remember their
guilt *and* iniquity and will punish their sins. They shall
return to [another] Egypt [Assyria]. [Deut. 28:68.]
14For Israel has forgotten his Maker and built palaces
*and* idol temples, and Judah has multiplied fortified cities;
but I will send a fire upon his cities and it shall devour
his palaces *and* fortified buildings. [Amos 1:4, 7, 10, 12,
14; 2:2, 5.]

**9** Rejoice not, O Israel, with exultation as do the peoples, for you have played the harlot, forsaking your
God. You have loved [a harlot's] hire upon every threshing
floor [ascribing the harvest to the Baals instead of to God].
2The threshing floor and the winevat shall not feed
them, and the new wine shall fail them.

## New International Version

3 They will not remain in the LORD's land;
  Ephraim will return to Egypt
    and eat unclean food in Assyria.
4 They will not pour out wine offerings to the LORD,
    nor will their sacrifices please him.
  Such sacrifices will be to them like the bread of
      mourners;
    all who eat them will be unclean.
  This food will be for themselves;
    it will not come into the temple of the LORD.

5 What will you do on the day of your appointed
      festivals,
    on the feast days of the LORD?
6 Even if they escape from destruction,
    Egypt will gather them,
    and Memphis will bury them.
  Their treasures of silver will be taken over by briers,
    and thorns will overrun their tents.
7 The days of punishment are coming,
    the days of reckoning are at hand.
  Let Israel know this.
  Because your sins are so many
    and your hostility so great,
  the prophet is considered a fool,
    the inspired person a maniac.
8 The prophet, along with my God,
    is the watchman over Ephraim,[a]
  yet snares await him on all his paths,
    and hostility in the house of his God.
9 They have sunk deep into corruption,
    as in the days of Gibeah.
  God will remember their wickedness
    and punish them for their sins.

10 "When I found Israel,
    it was like finding grapes in the desert;
  when I saw your ancestors,
    it was like seeing the early fruit on the fig tree.
  But when they came to Baal Peor,
    they consecrated themselves to that shameful idol
    and became as vile as the thing they loved.
11 Ephraim's glory will fly away like a bird—
    no birth, no pregnancy, no conception.
12 Even if they rear children,
    I will bereave them of every one.
  Woe to them
    when I turn away from them!
13 I have seen Ephraim, like Tyre,
    planted in a pleasant place.
  But Ephraim will bring out
    their children to the slayer."

14 Give them, LORD—
    what will you give them?
  Give them wombs that miscarry
    and breasts that are dry.

15 "Because of all their wickedness in Gilgal,
    I hated them there.
  Because of their sinful deeds,
    I will drive them out of my house.
  I will no longer love them;
    all their leaders are rebellious.
16 Ephraim is blighted,
    their root is withered,
    they yield no fruit.
  Even if they bear children,
    I will slay their cherished offspring."

17 My God will reject them
    because they have not obeyed him;
    they will be wanderers among the nations.

## Amplified Bible

3 They shall not remain in the Lord's land, but Ephraim shall return to [another] Egypt and they shall eat unclean food in Assyria. [Ezek. 4:13.]
4 They shall not pour out wine offerings to the Lord, neither shall they be pleasing to Him. Their sacrifices shall be to them as the bread of mourners; all who eat of them shall be defiled, for their bread shall be [only] for their appetite; it shall not come into the house of the Lord [to be offered first to Him].
5 What will you do on the day of the appointed solemn assembly or festival and on the day of the feast of the Lord [when you are in exile]?
6 For behold, they are gone away from devastation and destruction; Egypt shall gather them in; Memphis shall bury them. Their precious things of silver shall be in the possession of nettles; thorns shall be [growing] in their tents.
7 The days of visitation and punishment have come; the days of recompense have come; Israel shall know it. The prophet is [considered] a crazed fool and the man who is inspired is [treated as if] mad or a fanatic, because of the abundance of your iniquity and because the enmity, hostility, and persecution are great. [Luke 21:22.]
8 Ephraim was [intended to be] a watchman with my God [and a prophet to the surrounding nations]; but he, that prophet, has become a fowler's snare in all his ways. There is enmity, hostility, and persecution in the house of his God.
9 They have deeply corrupted themselves as in the days of Gibeah. The Lord will [earnestly] remember their iniquity; He will punish their sins. [Judg. 20.]
10 I found Israel like grapes in the wilderness; I saw your fathers as the first ripe fruit on the fig tree in its first season, but they went to Baal-peor and consecrated themselves to that shameful thing [Baal], and they became detestable and loathsome like that which they loved.
11 As for Ephraim, their glory shall fly away like a bird; there shall be no birth, no being with child, and [because of their impurity] no becoming pregnant.
12 Though they bring up their children, yet will I bereave them so that not a man shall be left; yes, woe also to them when I look away and depart from them!
13 Ephraim, as I have seen with Tyre, is planted in a pleasant place, but Ephraim shall bring out his children to the slayer.
14 Give them [their due], O Lord! [But] what will You give? Give them a miscarrying womb and dry breasts.
15 All their wickedness [says the Lord] is focused in Gilgal, for there I hated them; for the wickedness of their [idolatrous] doings I will drive them out of My house [the Holy Land]; I will love them no more; all their princes are rebels. [Hos. 4:15; 12:11.]
16 Ephraim is smitten, their root is dried up, they shall bear no fruit. Yes, though they bring forth, yet will I slay even their beloved children.
17 My God will cast them away because they did not listen to and obey Him, and they shall be wanderers and fugitives among the nations.

---

a 8 Or *The prophet is the watchman over Ephraim, / the people of my God*

## New International Version

## Amplified Bible

**10** Israel was a spreading vine;
he brought forth fruit for himself.
As his fruit increased,
he built more altars;
as his land prospered,
he adorned his sacred stones.
² Their heart is deceitful,
and now they must bear their guilt.
The Lᴏʀᴅ will demolish their altars
and destroy their sacred stones.

³ Then they will say, "We have no king
because we did not revere the Lᴏʀᴅ.
But even if we had a king,
what could he do for us?"
⁴ They make many promises,
take false oaths
and make agreements;
therefore lawsuits spring up
like poisonous weeds in a plowed field.
⁵ The people who live in Samaria fear
for the calf-idol of Beth Aven.ᵃ
Its people will mourn over it,
and so will its idolatrous priests,
those who had rejoiced over its splendor,
because it is taken from them into exile.
⁶ It will be carried to Assyria
as tribute for the great king.
Ephraim will be disgraced;
Israel will be ashamed of its foreign alliances.
⁷ Samaria's king will be destroyed,
swept away like a twig on the surface of the waters.
⁸ The high places of wickednessᵇ will be destroyed—
it is the sin of Israel.
Thorns and thistles will grow up
and cover their altars.
Then they will say to the mountains, "Cover us!"
and to the hills, "Fall on us!"

⁹ "Since the days of Gibeah, you have sinned, Israel,
and there you have remained.ᶜ
Will not war again overtake
the evildoers in Gibeah?
¹⁰ When I please, I will punish them;
nations will be gathered against them
to put them in bonds for their double sin.
¹¹ Ephraim is a trained heifer
that loves to thresh;
so I will put a yoke
on her fair neck.
I will drive Ephraim,
Judah must plow,
and Jacob must break up the ground.
¹² Sow righteousness for yourselves,
reap the fruit of unfailing love,
and break up your unplowed ground;
for it is time to seek the Lᴏʀᴅ,
until he comes
and showers his righteousness on you.
¹³ But you have planted wickedness,
you have reaped evil,
you have eaten the fruit of deception.
Because you have depended on your own strength
and on your many warriors,
¹⁴ the roar of battle will rise against your people,
so that all your fortresses will be devastated—
as Shalman devastated Beth Arbel on the day of battle,
when mothers were dashed to the ground with their children.

**10** Israel is a luxuriant vine that puts forth its [material] fruit. According to the abundance of his fruit he has multiplied his altars [to idols]; according to the goodness *and* prosperity of their land they have made goodly pillars *or* obelisks [to false gods].
²Their heart is divided *and* deceitful; now shall they be found guilty *and* suffer punishment. The Lord will smite *and* break down [the horns of] their altars; He will destroy their [idolatrous] pillars.
³Surely now they shall say, We have no [actual] king because we fear not the Lord; and as for the king, what can he do for us?
⁴They have spoken mere words of the lips, swearing falsely in making covenants; therefore judgment springs up like hemlock [or other poisonous plants] in the furrows of the field.
⁵The inhabitants of Samaria shall be in terror for the calf [idol] of Beth-aven [the house of idolatry, contemptuously meaning Bethel], for its people shall mourn over it and its [idolatrous] priests who rejoiced over it [shall tremble] for the glory of [their calf god], because it is departed from it.
⁶[The golden calf] shall also be carried into Assyria as a tribute-gift to the fighting King Jareb; Ephraim shall be put to shame and Israel shall be ashamed of his own counsel [to set up calf worship and detach Israel from Judah].
⁷As for Samaria, her king *and* her whole monarchy are cut off like twigs *or* foam upon the water.
⁸The high places also of Aven [once Beth(el), house of God, now (Beth-)aven, house of idolatry], the sin of Israel, shall be destroyed; the thorn and the thistle shall come up on their [idol] altars, and they shall say to the mountains, Cover us! And to the hills, Fall on us! [Luke 23:30; Rev. 6:16; 9:6.]
⁹O Israel, you have [willfully] sinned from the days of Gibeah [when you all but wiped out the tribe of Benjamin]! There [Israel] stood [then, only] that the battle against the sons of unrighteousness might not overtake *and* turn against them at Gibeah [but now the kingdom of the ten tribes and the name of Ephraim shall be utterly blotted out]. [Judg. 20.]
¹⁰When I please I will chastise them, and hostile peoples shall be gathered against them when I shall bind *and* yoke them for their two transgressions [revolt from the Lord their God and the worship of idols]. [Jer. 2:13; Lam. 3:31-33.]
¹¹Ephraim indeed is a heifer broken in *and* loving to tread out the grain, but I have [heretofore] spared the beauty of her fair neck. I will now set a rider upon Ephraim *and* make him to draw; Judah shall plow and Jacob shall break his clods.
¹²Sow for yourselves according to righteousness (uprightness and right standing with God); reap according to mercy *and* loving-kindness. Break up your uncultivated ground, for it is time to seek the Lord, to inquire for *and* of Him, *and* to require His favor, till He comes and teaches you righteousness *and* rains His righteous gift of salvation upon you. [II Cor. 9:10.]
¹³You have plowed *and* plotted wickedness, you have reaped the [willful] injustice [of oppressors], you have eaten the fruit of lies. Because you have trusted in your [own] way *and* your chariots, in the multitude of your mighty men,
¹⁴Therefore shall a tumult arise against your people and all your fortresses shall be wasted *and* destroyed, as Shalmaneser wasted *and* destroyed Beth-arbel on the day of battle; the mother was dashed in pieces with her children. [II Kings 17:3.]

---

ᵃ 5 *Beth Aven* means *house of wickedness* (a derogatory name for Bethel, which means *house of God*).   ᵇ 8 Hebrew *aven,* a reference to Beth Aven (a derogatory name for Bethel); see verse 5.   ᶜ 9 Or *there a stand was taken*

## New International Version

<sup>15</sup> So will it happen to you, Bethel,
　　because your wickedness is great.
When that day dawns,
　　the king of Israel will be completely destroyed.

### God's Love for Israel

**11** "When Israel was a child, I loved him,
　　and out of Egypt I called my son.
<sup>2</sup> But the more they were called,
　　the more they went away from me.*ᵃ*
They sacrificed to the Baals
　　and they burned incense to images.
<sup>3</sup> It was I who taught Ephraim to walk,
　　taking them by the arms;
but they did not realize
　　it was I who healed them.
<sup>4</sup> I led them with cords of human kindness,
　　with ties of love.
To them I was like one who lifts
　　a little child to the cheek,
　　and I bent down to feed them.

<sup>5</sup> "Will they not return to Egypt
　　and will not Assyria rule over them
　　because they refuse to repent?
<sup>6</sup> A sword will flash in their cities;
　　it will devour their false prophets
　　and put an end to their plans.
<sup>7</sup> My people are determined to turn from me.
　　Even though they call me God Most High,
　　I will by no means exalt them.

<sup>8</sup> "How can I give you up, Ephraim?
　　How can I hand you over, Israel?
How can I treat you like Admah?
　　How can I make you like Zeboyim?
My heart is changed within me;
　　all my compassion is aroused.
<sup>9</sup> I will not carry out my fierce anger,
　　nor will I devastate Ephraim again.
For I am God, and not a man—
　　the Holy One among you.
　　I will not come against their cities.
<sup>10</sup> They will follow the Lord;
　　he will roar like a lion.
When he roars,
　　his children will come trembling from the west.
<sup>11</sup> They will come from Egypt,
　　trembling like sparrows,
　　from Assyria, fluttering like doves.
I will settle them in their homes,"
　　declares the Lord.

### Israel's Sin

<sup>12</sup> Ephraim has surrounded me with lies,
　　Israel with deceit.
And Judah is unruly against God,
　　even against the faithful Holy One.*ᵇ*

**12**ᶜ <sup>1</sup> Ephraim feeds on the wind;
　　he pursues the east wind all day
and multiplies lies and violence.
He makes a treaty with Assyria
　　and sends olive oil to Egypt.
<sup>2</sup> The Lord has a charge to bring against Judah;
　　he will punish Jacob*ᵈ* according to his ways
　　and repay him according to his deeds.
<sup>3</sup> In the womb he grasped his brother's heel;
　　as a man he struggled with God.
<sup>4</sup> He struggled with the angel and overcame him;

---

*ᵃ 2 Septuagint; Hebrew them    ᵇ 12 In Hebrew texts this verse (11:12)
is numbered 12:1.    ᶜ In Hebrew texts 12:1-14 is numbered 12:2-15.
ᵈ 2 Jacob means he grasps the heel, a Hebrew idiom for he takes advantage
of or he deceives.*

## Amplified Bible

<sup>15</sup> So shall it be done to you at [idolatrous] Bethel because of your great wickedness; at daybreak shall the king of Israel be utterly cut off.

**11** When Israel was a child, then I loved him and called My son out of Egypt. [Matt. 2:15.]
<sup>2</sup> The more [the prophets] called to them, the more they went from them; they kept sacrificing to the Baals and burning incense to the graven images.
<sup>3</sup> Yet I taught Ephraim to walk, taking them by their arms or taking them up in My arms, but they did not know that I healed them.
<sup>4</sup> I drew them with cords of a man, with bands of love, and I was to them as one who lifts up and eases the yoke over their cheeks, and I bent down to them and gently laid food before them.
<sup>5</sup> They shall not [literally] return into [another bondage in] the land of Egypt, but the Assyrian shall be their king because they refused to return to Me.
<sup>6</sup> And the sword shall rage against and fall upon their cities and shall consume the bars of their gates and shall make an end [of their defenses], because of their own counsels and devices.
<sup>7</sup> My people are bent on backsliding from Me; though [the prophets] call them to Him Who is on high, none at all will exalt Him or lift himself up [to come to Him].
<sup>8</sup> How can I give you up, O Ephraim! How can I surrender you and cast you off, O Israel! How can I make you as Admah or how can I treat you as Zeboiim [both destroyed with Sodom]! My heart recoils within Me; My compassions are kindled together. [Deut. 29:23.]
<sup>9</sup> I will not execute the fierceness of My anger; I will not bring back Ephraim to nothing or again destroy him. For I am God and not man, the Holy One in the midst of you, and I will not come in wrath or enter into the city.
<sup>10</sup> They shall walk after the Lord, Who will roar like a lion; He Himself will roar and [His] sons shall come trembling and eagerly from the west.
<sup>11</sup> They shall come trembling but hurriedly like a bird out of Egypt and like a dove out of the land of Assyria, and I will cause them to dwell in their houses, says the Lord.
<sup>12</sup> Ephraim surrounds Me with lies and the house of Israel with deceit, and Judah is not yet steadfast with God, with the faithful Holy One.

**12** Ephraim herds and feeds on the wind and pursues the [parching] east wind; every day he increases lies and violence, and a covenant is made with Assyria and oil is carried to Egypt. [Isa. 30:6, 7.]
<sup>2</sup> The Lord has also a controversy (a pleading contention) with Judah, and will punish Jacob by visiting upon him according to his ways; according to his doings will He recompense him.
<sup>3</sup> He took his brother by the heel in [their mother's] womb, and in the strength [of his manhood] he contended and had power with God. [Gen. 25:26; 27:36.]
<sup>4</sup> Yes, he had power over the *ᵃ*Angel [of the Lord] and

---

*ᵃ See footnotes on Gen. 16:7 and Gen. 32:28.*

## New International Version

he wept and begged for his favor.
He found him at Bethel
and talked with him there—
⁵the Lord God Almighty,
the Lord is his name!
⁶But you must return to your God;
maintain love and justice,
and wait for your God always.

⁷The merchant uses dishonest scales
and loves to defraud.
⁸Ephraim boasts,
"I am very rich; I have become wealthy.
With all my wealth they will not find in me
any iniquity or sin."

⁹"I have been the Lord your God
ever since you came out of Egypt;
I will make you live in tents again,
as in the days of your appointed festivals.
¹⁰I spoke to the prophets,
gave them many visions
and told parables through them."

¹¹Is Gilead wicked?
Its people are worthless!
Do they sacrifice bulls in Gilgal?
Their altars will be like piles of stones
on a plowed field.
¹²Jacob fled to the country of Aram*a*;
Israel served to get a wife,
and to pay for her he tended sheep.
¹³The Lord used a prophet to bring Israel up from Egypt,
by a prophet he cared for him.
¹⁴But Ephraim has aroused his bitter anger;
his Lord will leave on him the guilt of his bloodshed
and will repay him for his contempt.

### The Lord's Anger Against Israel

**13** When Ephraim spoke, people trembled;
he was exalted in Israel.
But he became guilty of Baal worship and died.
²Now they sin more and more;
they make idols for themselves from their silver,
cleverly fashioned images,
all of them the work of craftsmen.
It is said of these people,
"They offer human sacrifices!
They kiss*b* calf-idols!"
³Therefore they will be like the morning mist,
like the early dew that disappears,
like chaff swirling from a threshing floor,
like smoke escaping through a window.

⁴"But I have been the Lord your God
ever since you came out of Egypt.
You shall acknowledge no God but me,
no Savior except me.
⁵I cared for you in the wilderness,
in the land of burning heat.
⁶When I fed them, they were satisfied;
when they were satisfied, they became proud;
then they forgot me.
⁷So I will be like a lion to them,
like a leopard I will lurk by the path.
⁸Like a bear robbed of her cubs,
I will attack them and rip them open;
like a lion I will devour them—
a wild animal will tear them apart.

⁹"You are destroyed, Israel,
because you are against me, against your helper.

## Amplified Bible

prevailed; he wept and sought His favor. He met Him in
Bethel, and there [God] spoke with [him and through him
with] us—[Gen. 28:12-19; 32:28; Gen. 35:1-15.]
⁵Even the Lord the God of hosts, the name of Him [Who
spoke with Jacob] is the Lord.
⁶Therefore return to your God! Hold fast to love *and*
mercy, to righteousness *and* justice, and wait [expectant-
ly] for your God continually!
⁷Canaan [Israel—whose ideals have sunk to those of
Canaan] is a trader; the balances of deceit are in his hand;
he loves to oppress *and* defraud.
⁸Ephraim has said, Ah, but I have become rich; I have
gained for myself wealth. All my profits shall bring on
me no iniquity that would be sin. [But all his profits will
never offset nor suffice to expiate the guilt which he has
incurred.] [Rev. 3:17.]
⁹But I [Who] am the Lord your God from [when you
became a nation in] the land of Egypt will yet make you to
dwell in tents, as in the days of the appointed *and* solemn
Feast [of Tabernacles]. [Lev. 23:39-43.]
¹⁰I have also spoken to [you by] the prophets, and I have
multiplied visions [for you] and [have appealed to you]
through parables acted out by the prophets.
¹¹If Gilead is given over to idolatry, they shall come to
nought *and* be mere waste; if they [insult God by] sacrificing bullocks in Gilgal [on heathen altars], their altars shall
be like heaps in the furrows of the fields.
¹²Jacob fled into the open country of Aram *or* Padan-
aram, and [there] Israel served for a wife, and for a wife he
herded sheep. [Gen. 29:18-20; 30:31; 31:38-41.]
¹³And by a prophet the Lord brought Israel out of Egypt,
and by a prophet was [Israel] preserved.
¹⁴Ephraim has provoked most bitter anger; therefore
shall his blood [guilt] be left upon him, and his disgrace
*and* reproach shall his Lord return upon him.

**13** When Ephraim spoke with trembling, he exalted
himself in Israel; but when he offended *and* became guilty in Baal worship, he died [spiritually, and then
outward ruin came also, sealing Israel's doom as a nation].
²And now they sin more and more and have made for
themselves molten images of their silver, even idols according to their own understanding [as it pleased them],
all of them the work of the craftsmen. To these [very
works of their hands] they speak *or* pray who sacrifice to
them; they kiss *and* show homage to the calves [as if they
were alive]!
³Therefore they shall be like the morning mist or like
the dew that passes early away, like the chaff that swirls
with the whirlwind from the threshing floor and as the
smoke out of the chimney *or* through the window.
⁴Yet I am the Lord your God from [the time you became
a nation in] the land of Egypt, and you shall know *or* recognize no God but Me, for there is no Savior besides Me.
⁵I knew (recognized, understood, and had regard for)
you in the wilderness, in the land of great drought.
⁶According to their pasture, so were they filled [when
they fed, they grew full], and their heart was lifted up;
therefore have they forgotten Me.
⁷Therefore I have become to them like a lion; like a leopard I will lurk by the way [to Assyria] *and* watch them.
⁸I will meet them like a bear that is robbed of her cubs,
and I will rend the covering of their heart, and there will
I devour them like a lioness, as a wild beast would tear
them.
⁹It is your destruction, O Israel, that you have been
against Me, for in Me is your help.

---

*a* 12 That is, Northwest Mesopotamia   *b* 2 Or *"Men who sacrifice / kiss*

## New International Version

10 Where is your king, that he may save you?
   Where are your rulers in all your towns,
of whom you said,
   'Give me a king and princes'?
11 So in my anger I gave you a king,
   and in my wrath I took him away.
12 The guilt of Ephraim is stored up,
   his sins are kept on record.
13 Pains as of a woman in childbirth come to him,
   but he is a child without wisdom;
when the time arrives,
   he doesn't have the sense to come out of the womb.

14 "I will deliver this people from the power of the grave;
   I will redeem them from death.
Where, O death, are your plagues?
   Where, O grave, is your destruction?

"I will have no compassion,
15   even though he thrives among his brothers.
An east wind from the LORD will come,
   blowing in from the desert;
his spring will fail
   and his well dry up.
His storehouse will be plundered
   of all its treasures.
16 The people of Samaria must bear their guilt,
   because they have rebelled against their God.
They will fall by the sword;
   their little ones will be dashed to the ground,
   their pregnant women ripped open."[a]

### Repentance to Bring Blessing

**14** [b] Return, Israel, to the LORD your God.
   Your sins have been your downfall!
2 Take words with you
   and return to the LORD.
Say to him:
   "Forgive all our sins
and receive us graciously,
   that we may offer the fruit of our lips.[c]
3 Assyria cannot save us;
   we will not mount warhorses.
We will never again say 'Our gods'
   to what our own hands have made,
   for in you the fatherless find compassion."

4 "I will heal their waywardness
   and love them freely,
   for my anger has turned away from them.
5 I will be like the dew to Israel;
   he will blossom like a lily.
Like a cedar of Lebanon
   he will send down his roots;
6   his young shoots will grow.
His splendor will be like an olive tree,
   his fragrance like a cedar of Lebanon.
7 People will dwell again in his shade;
   they will flourish like the grain,
they will blossom like the vine—
   Israel's fame will be like the wine of Lebanon.
8 Ephraim, what more have I[d] to do with idols?
   I will answer him and care for him.
I am like a flourishing juniper;
   your fruitfulness comes from me."

9 Who is wise? Let them realize these things.
   Who is discerning? Let them understand.
The ways of the LORD are right;
   the righteous walk in them,
   but the rebellious stumble in them.

## Amplified Bible

10 Where now is your king that he may save you in all
your cities? And your judges of whom you said, Give me a
king and princes?
11 I have given you a king in My anger, and I have taken
him away in My wrath.
12 The iniquity of Ephraim [not fully punished yet] is
bound up [as in a bag]; his sin is laid up in store [for judgment and destruction].
13 The pains of a woman in childbirth are coming on for
him [to be born]; but he is an unwise son, for now when it
is time [to be born], he comes not to the place where [un-
born] children break forth [he needs new birth but makes
no effort to acquire it].
14 Should I ransom them from the power of Sheol (the
place of the dead)? Should I redeem them from death?
[a] O death, where are your plagues? O Sheol, where is your
destruction? Relenting *and* compassion are hidden from
My eyes. [I Cor. 15:55.]
15 For though among his brethren [his fellow tribes]
he may be fruitful, an east wind [Assyria] will come, the
breath of the Lord rising from the desert; and Ephraim's
spring shall become dry and his fountain be dried up. [As-
syria] shall plunder his treasury of every precious vessel.
16 Samaria shall bear her guilt *and* become desolate, for
she rebelled against her God; they shall fall by the sword,
their infants shall be dashed in pieces, and their pregnant
women shall be ripped up.

**14** O Israel, return to the Lord your God, for you have
stumbled *and* fallen, [visited by calamity] due to
your iniquity.
2 Take with you words and return to the Lord. Say to
Him, Take away all *our* iniquity; accept what is good *and*
receive us graciously; so will we render [our thanks] as
bullocks [to be sacrificed] *and* pay the confession of our
lips. [Heb. 13:15.]
3 Assyria shall not save us; we will not ride upon horses,
neither will we say any more to the work of our hands
[idols], You are our gods. For in You [O Lord] the fatherless find love, pity, *and* mercy.
4 I will heal their faithlessness; I will love them freely,
for My anger is turned away from [Israel].
5 I will be like the dew *and* the night mist to Israel; he
shall grow *and* blossom like the lily and cast forth his roots
like [the sturdy evergreens of] Lebanon.
6 His suckers *and* shoots shall spread, and his beauty
shall be like the olive tree and his fragrance like [the cedars and aromatic shrubs of] Lebanon.
7 They that dwell under his shade shall return; they
shall revive like the grain and blossom like the vine; the
scent of it shall be like the wine of Lebanon.
8 Ephraim shall say, What have I to do any more with
idols? I have answered [him] and will regard *and* watch
over him; I am like a green fir *or* cypress tree; with Me is
the fruit found [which is to nourish you].
9 Who is wise, that he may understand these things?
Prudent, that he may know them? For the ways of the Lord
are right, and the [uncompromisingly] just shall walk in
them, but transgressors shall stumble *and* fall in them.
[Ps. 107:43; Isa. 26:7; Jer. 9:12; Dan. 12:10.]

---

[a] 16 In Hebrew texts this verse (13:16) is numbered 14:1.   [b] In Hebrew
texts 14:1-9 is numbered 14:2-10.   [c] 2 Or *offer our lips as sacrifices of
bulls*   [d] 8 Or Hebrew; Septuagint *What more has Ephraim*

[a] The apostle Paul in I Cor. 15:55 brings to mind this passage—but
with a triumphal reversal of meaning made possible by our Lord's
resurrection.

# Joel

**1** The word of the LORD that came to Joel son of Pethuel.

### An Invasion of Locusts

2 Hear this, you elders;
  listen, all who live in the land.
Has anything like this ever happened in your days
  or in the days of your ancestors?
3 Tell it to your children,
  and let your children tell it to their children,
  and their children to the next generation.
4 What the locust swarm has left
  the great locusts have eaten;
what the great locusts have left
  the young locusts have eaten;
what the young locusts have left
  other locusts*a* have eaten.

5 Wake up, you drunkards, and weep!
  Wail, all you drinkers of wine;
wail because of the new wine,
  for it has been snatched from your lips.
6 A nation has invaded my land,
  a mighty army without number;
it has the teeth of a lion,
  the fangs of a lioness.
7 It has laid waste my vines
  and ruined my fig trees.
It has stripped off their bark
  and thrown it away,
  leaving their branches white.

8 Mourn like a virgin in sackcloth
  grieving for the betrothed of her youth.
9 Grain offerings and drink offerings
  are cut off from the house of the LORD.
The priests are in mourning,
  those who minister before the LORD.
10 The fields are ruined,
  the ground is dried up;
the grain is destroyed,
  the new wine is dried up,
  the olive oil fails.

11 Despair, you farmers,
  wail, you vine growers;
grieve for the wheat and the barley,
  because the harvest of the field is destroyed.
12 The vine is dried up
  and the fig tree is withered;
the pomegranate, the palm and the apple*b* tree—
  all the trees of the field—are dried up.
Surely the people's joy
  is withered away.

### A Call to Lamentation

13 Put on sackcloth, you priests, and mourn;
  wail, you who minister before the altar.
Come, spend the night in sackcloth,
  you who minister before my God;
for the grain offerings and drink offerings
  are withheld from the house of your God.
14 Declare a holy fast;
  call a sacred assembly.
Summon the elders
  and all who live in the land

# Joel

**1** The word of the Lord that came to *a*Joel the son of Pethuel.
2 Hear this, you aged men, and give ear, all you inhabitants of the land! Has such a thing as this occurred in your days or even in the days of your fathers?
3 Tell your children of it, and let your children tell their children, and their children another generation.
4 What the crawling locust left, the swarming locust has eaten; and what the swarming locust left, the hopping locust has eaten; and what the hopping locust left, the stripping locust has eaten.
5 Awake, you drunkards, and weep; wail, all you drinkers of wine, because of the [fresh] sweet juice [of the grape], for it is cut off *and* removed from your mouth.
6 For a [heathen and hostile] nation [of locusts, illustrative of a human foe] has invaded My land, mighty and without number; its teeth are the teeth of a lion, and it has the jaw teeth of a lioness. [Rev. 9:7, 8.]
7 It has laid waste My vine [symbol of God's people] and barked *and* broken My fig tree; it has made them completely bare and thrown them down; their branches are made white. [Isa. 5:5, 6.]
8 Lament like a virgin [bride] girded with sackcloth for the husband of her youth [who has died].
9 The meal *or* cereal offering and the drink offering are cut off from the house of the Lord; the priests, the Lord's ministers, mourn.
10 The field is laid waste, the ground mourns; for the grain is destroyed, the new juice [of the grape] is dried up, the oil fails.
11 Be ashamed, O you tillers of the soil; wail, O you vinedressers, for the wheat and for the barley, because the harvest of the field has perished.
12 The vine is dried up and the fig tree fails; the pomegranate tree, the palm tree also, and the apple *or* quince tree, even all the trees of the field are withered, so that joy has withered *and* fled away from the sons of men.
13 Gird yourselves and lament, you priests; wail, you ministers of the altar; come, lie all night in sackcloth, you ministers of my [Joel's] God, for the cereal *or* meal offering and the drink offering are withheld from the house of your God.
14 Sanctify a fast, call a solemn assembly, gather the elders and all the inhabitants of the land in the house of

---

*a 4* The precise meaning of the four Hebrew words used here for locusts is uncertain.   *b 12* Or possibly *apricot*

*a* Joel was a prophet of Judah and possibly a contemporary of Elisha.

## New International Version

to the house of the LORD your God,
and cry out to the LORD.

[15] Alas for that day!
For the day of the LORD is near;
it will come like destruction from the Almighty.[a]

[16] Has not the food been cut off
before our very eyes—
joy and gladness
from the house of our God?
[17] The seeds are shriveled
beneath the clods.[b]
The storehouses are in ruins,
the granaries have been broken down,
for the grain has dried up.
[18] How the cattle moan!
The herds mill about
because they have no pasture;
even the flocks of sheep are suffering.

[19] To you, LORD, I call,
for fire has devoured the pastures in the wilderness
and flames have burned up all the trees of the field.
[20] Even the wild animals pant for you;
the streams of water have dried up
and fire has devoured the pastures in the
wilderness.

### An Army of Locusts

**2** Blow the trumpet in Zion;
sound the alarm on my holy hill.

Let all who live in the land tremble,
for the day of the LORD is coming.
It is close at hand—
[2]    a day of darkness and gloom,
a day of clouds and blackness.
Like dawn spreading across the mountains
a large and mighty army comes,
such as never was in ancient times
nor ever will be in ages to come.

[3] Before them fire devours,
behind them a flame blazes.
Before them the land is like the garden of Eden,
behind them, a desert waste—
nothing escapes them.
[4] They have the appearance of horses;
they gallop along like cavalry.
[5] With a noise like that of chariots
they leap over the mountaintops,
like a crackling fire consuming stubble,
like a mighty army drawn up for battle.

[6] At the sight of them, nations are in anguish;
every face turns pale.
[7] They charge like warriors;
they scale walls like soldiers.
They all march in line,
not swerving from their course.
[8] They do not jostle each other;
each marches straight ahead.
They plunge through defenses
without breaking ranks.
[9] They rush upon the city;
they run along the wall.
They climb into the houses;
like thieves they enter through the windows.

[10] Before them the earth shakes,
the heavens tremble,
the sun and moon are darkened,
and the stars no longer shine.

## Amplified Bible

the Lord, your God, and cry to the Lord [in penitent pleadings].

[15] Alas for the day! For the day of [the judgment of] the Lord is at hand, and as a destructive tempest from the Almighty will it come. [Zeph. 1:14-18.]

[16] Is not the food cut off before our eyes, joy and gladness from the house of our God?

[17] The seed [grain] rots *and* shrivels under the clods, the garners are desolate *and* empty, the barns are in ruins because the grain has failed.

[18] How the beasts groan! The herds of cattle are perplexed *and* huddle together because they have no pasture; even the flocks of sheep suffer punishment (are forsaken and made wretched).

[19] O Lord, to You will I cry, for the fire has devoured the pastures *and* folds of the plain *and* the wilderness, and flame has burned all the trees of the field.

[20] Even the wild beasts of the field pant *and* cry to You, for the water brooks are dried up and fire has consumed the pastures *and* folds of the wilderness *and* the plain.

**2** Blow the trumpet in Zion; sound an alarm on My holy Mount [Zion]. Let all the inhabitants of the land tremble, for the day of [the judgment of] the Lord is coming; it is close at hand—[Ezek. 7:2-4; Amos 5:16-20.]

[2] A day of darkness and gloom, a day of clouds and of thick mists *and* darkness, like the morning dawn spread upon the mountains; so there comes a [heathen, hostile] people numerous and mighty, the like of which has never been before and shall not be again even to the years of many generations.

[3] A fire devours before them, and behind them a flame burns; the land is as the garden of Eden before them, and behind them a desolate wilderness; yes, and none has escaped [the ravages of the devouring hordes].

[4] Their appearance is like the appearance of horses, and like war horses *and* horsemen, so do they run.

[5] Like the noise of chariots on the tops of the mountains they leap—like the noise of a flame of fire devouring the stubble, like a mighty people set in battle array. [Rev. 9:7, 9.]

[6] Before them the peoples are in anguish; all faces become pale.

[7] They run like mighty men; they climb the wall like men of war. They march each one [straight ahead] on his ways, and they do not break their ranks.

[8] Neither does one thrust upon another; they walk every one in his path. And they burst through *and* upon the weapons, yet they are not wounded *and* do not change their course.

[9] They leap upon the city; they run upon the wall; They climb up on *and* into the houses; they enter in at the windows like a thief.

[10] The earth quakes before them; the heavens tremble. The sun and the moon are darkened and the stars withdraw their shining. [Rev. 9:2-4; 16:14.]

[a] 15 Hebrew *Shaddai*    [b] 17 The meaning of the Hebrew for this word is uncertain.

# New International Version

11 The LORD thunders
    at the head of his army;
his forces are beyond number,
    and mighty is the army that obeys his command.
The day of the LORD is great;
    it is dreadful.
    Who can endure it?

## Rend Your Heart

12 "Even now," declares the LORD,
    "return to me with all your heart,
    with fasting and weeping and mourning."

13 Rend your heart
    and not your garments.
Return to the LORD your God,
    for he is gracious and compassionate,
slow to anger and abounding in love,
    and he relents from sending calamity.
14 Who knows? He may turn and relent
    and leave behind a blessing—
grain offerings and drink offerings
    for the LORD your God.

15 Blow the trumpet in Zion,
    declare a holy fast,
    call a sacred assembly.
16 Gather the people,
    consecrate the assembly;
bring together the elders,
    gather the children,
    those nursing at the breast.
Let the bridegroom leave his room
    and the bride her chamber.
17 Let the priests, who minister before the LORD,
    weep between the portico and the altar.
Let them say, "Spare your people, LORD.
    Do not make your inheritance an object of scorn,
    a byword among the nations.
Why should they say among the peoples,
    'Where is their God?'"

## The LORD's Answer

18 Then the LORD was jealous for his land
    and took pity on his people.

19 The LORD replied[a] to them:

"I am sending you grain, new wine and olive oil,
    enough to satisfy you fully;
never again will I make you
    an object of scorn to the nations.

20 "I will drive the northern horde far from you,
    pushing it into a parched and barren land;
its eastern ranks will drown in the Dead Sea
    and its western ranks in the Mediterranean Sea.
And its stench will go up;
    its smell will rise."

Surely he has done great things!
21     Do not be afraid, land of Judah;
    be glad and rejoice.
Surely the LORD has done great things!
22     Do not be afraid, you wild animals,
    for the pastures in the wilderness are becoming green.
The trees are bearing their fruit;
    the fig tree and the vine yield their riches.
23 Be glad, people of Zion,
    rejoice in the LORD your God,
for he has given you the autumn rains
    because he is faithful.
He sends you abundant showers,
    both autumn and spring rains, as before.

a 18,19 Or LORD will be jealous . . . / and take pity . . . / 19The LORD will reply

# Amplified Bible

11 And the Lord utters His voice before His army, for His host is very great, and [they are] strong and powerful who execute [God's] word. For the day of the Lord is great and very terrible, and who can endure it? [Isa. 26:20, 21; 34:1-4, 8; Rev. 6:16, 17.]

12 Therefore also now, says the Lord, turn and keep on coming to Me with all your heart, with fasting and weeping, and with mourning [until every hindrance is removed and the broken fellowship is restored].

13 Rend your hearts and not your garments and return to the Lord, your God, for He is gracious and merciful, slow to anger, and abounding in loving-kindness; and He revokes His sentence of evil [when His conditions are met].

14 Who knows but what He will turn, revoke your sentence [of evil], and leave a blessing behind Him [giving you the means with which to serve Him], even a cereal or meal offering and a drink offering for the Lord, your God?

15 Blow the trumpet in Zion; set apart a fast [a day of restraint and humility]; call a solemn assembly.

16 Gather the people, sanctify the congregation; assemble the elderly people, gather the children and the nursing infants; let the bridegroom [who is legally exempt from attending] go forth from his chamber and the bride out of her closet. [None is exempt from the humiliation.]

17 Let the priests, the ministers of the Lord, weep between the porch and the altar; and let them say, Have pity and spare Your people, O Lord, and give not Your heritage to reproach, that the [heathen] nations should rule over them or use a byword against them. Why should they say among the peoples, Where is their God?

18 Then was the Lord jealous for His land and had pity on His people.

19 Yes, the Lord answered and said to His people, Behold, I am sending you grain and juice [of the grape] and oil, and you shall be satisfied with them; and I will no more make you a reproach among the [heathen] nations.

20 But I will remove far off from you the northern [destroyer's] army and will drive it into a land barren and desolate, with its front toward the eastern [Dead] Sea and with its rear toward the western [Mediterranean] Sea. And its stench shall come up [like that of a decaying mass of locusts, a symbol and forecast of the fate of the northern army in the final day of the Lord], and its foul odor shall come up, because a He has done great things [the Lord will have destroyed the invaders]! [Isa. 34:1-4, 8; Jer. 25:31-35; Joel 2:11.]

21 Fear not, O land; be glad and rejoice, for the Lord has done great things! [Zech. 12:8-10.]

22 Be not afraid, you wild beasts of the field, for the pastures of the wilderness have sprung up and are green; the tree bears its fruit, and the fig tree and the vine yield their [full] strength.

23 Be glad then, you children of Zion, and rejoice in the Lord, your God; for He gives you the former or early rain in just measure and in righteousness, and He causes to come down for you the rain, the former rain and the latter rain, as before.

a The capitalization here is suppositional. Interpreters are divided as to whether it is the northern destroyer who has "done great things," or the Lord; either, in different senses, is true. However, the latter view is strongly supported by the parallel phrase to the same effect in the next verse (Joel 2:21).

## New International Version

24 The threshing floors will be filled with grain;
 the vats will overflow with new wine and oil.

25 "I will repay you for the years the locusts have eaten—
 the great locust and the young locust,
 the other locusts and the locust swarm[a]—
 my great army that I sent among you.
26 You will have plenty to eat, until you are full,
 and you will praise the name of the LORD your God,
 who has worked wonders for you;
 never again will my people be shamed.
27 Then you will know that I am in Israel,
 that I am the LORD your God,
 and that there is no other;
 never again will my people be shamed.

### The Day of the LORD
28 "And afterward,
 I will pour out my Spirit on all people.
 Your sons and daughters will prophesy,
 your old men will dream dreams,
 your young men will see visions.
29 Even on my servants, both men and women,
 I will pour out my Spirit in those days.
30 I will show wonders in the heavens
 and on the earth,
 blood and fire and billows of smoke.
31 The sun will be turned to darkness
 and the moon to blood
 before the coming of the great and dreadful day of
 the LORD.
32 And everyone who calls
 on the name of the LORD will be saved;
 for on Mount Zion and in Jerusalem
 there will be deliverance,
 as the LORD has said,
 even among the survivors
 whom the LORD calls.[b]

### The Nations Judged
**3**[c] "In those days and at that time,
 when I restore the fortunes of Judah and Jerusalem,
2 I will gather all nations
 and bring them down to the Valley of Jehoshaphat.[d]
 There I will put them on trial
 for what they did to my inheritance, my people
 Israel,
 because they scattered my people among the nations
 and divided up my land.
3 They cast lots for my people
 and traded boys for prostitutes;
 they sold girls for wine to drink.

4 "Now what have you against me, Tyre and Sidon and all you regions of Philistia? Are you repaying me for something I have done? If you are paying me back, I will swiftly and speedily return on your own heads what you have done. 5 For you took my silver and my gold and carried off my finest treasures to your temples.[e] 6 You sold the people of Judah and Jerusalem to the Greeks, that you might send them far from their homeland.

7 "See, I am going to rouse them out of the places to which you sold them, and I will return on your own heads what you have done. 8 I will sell your sons and daughters to

## Amplified Bible

24 And the [threshing] floors shall be full of grain and the vats shall overflow with juice [of the grape] and oil.

25 And I will restore or replace for you the years that the locust has eaten—the hopping locust, the stripping locust, and the crawling locust, My great army which I sent among you.

26 And you shall eat in plenty and be satisfied and praise the name of the Lord, your God, Who has dealt wondrously with you. And My people shall never be put to shame.

27 And you shall know, understand, and realize that I am in the midst of Israel and that I the Lord am your God and there is none else. My people shall never be put to shame.

28 And afterward I will pour out My Spirit upon all flesh; and your sons and your daughters shall prophesy, your old men shall dream dreams, your young men shall see visions.

29 Even upon the menservants and upon the maidservants in those days will I pour out My Spirit.

30 And I will show signs and wonders in the heavens, and on the earth, blood and fire and columns of smoke.

31 The sun shall be turned to darkness and the moon to blood before the great and terrible day of the Lord comes. [Isa. 13:6, 9-11; 24:21-23; Ezek. 32:7-10; Matt. 24:29, 30; Rev. 6:12-17.]

32 And whoever shall call on the name of the Lord shall be delivered and saved, for in Mount Zion and in Jerusalem there shall be those who escape, as the Lord has said, and among the remnant [of survivors] shall be those whom the Lord calls. [Acts 2:17-21; Rom. 10:13.]

**3** For behold, in those days and at that time when I shall reverse the captivity and restore the fortunes of Judah and Jerusalem,

2 I will gather all nations and will bring them down into the Valley of Jehoshaphat, and there will I deal with and execute judgment upon them for [their treatment of] My people and of My heritage Israel, whom they have scattered among the nations and [because] they have divided My land.

3 And they have cast lots for My people, and have given a boy for a harlot and have sold a girl for juice [of the grape] and have drunk it.

4 Yes, and what are you to Me, O Tyre and Sidon and all the [five small] divisions of Philistia? Will you pay Me back for something? Even if you pay Me back, swiftly and speedily I will return your deed [of retaliation] upon your own head, [Isa. 23; Ezek. 26:1-18; Amos 1:6-10; Zeph. 2:4-7; Zech. 9:2-7.]

5 Because you have taken My silver and My gold and have carried into your temples and palaces My precious treasures,

6 And have sold the children of Judah and the children of Jerusalem to the sons of the Grecians, that you may remove them far from their border.

7 Behold, I will stir them up out of the place to which you have sold them and will return your deed [of retaliation] upon your own head.

8 I will sell your sons and your daughters into the hand

---

a 25 The precise meaning of the four Hebrew words used here for locusts is uncertain.   b 32 In Hebrew texts 2:28-32 is numbered 3:1-5.
c In Hebrew texts 3:1-21 is numbered 4:1-21.   d 2 Jehoshaphat means the LORD judges; also in verse 12.   e 5 Or palaces

## New International Version

the people of Judah, and they will sell them to the Sabeans, a nation far away." The Lord has spoken.

⁹Proclaim this among the nations:
  Prepare for war!
Rouse the warriors!
  Let all the fighting men draw near and attack.
¹⁰Beat your plowshares into swords
  and your pruning hooks into spears.
Let the weakling say,
  "I am strong!"
¹¹Come quickly, all you nations from every side,
  and assemble there.

Bring down your warriors, Lord!

¹²"Let the nations be roused;
  let them advance into the Valley of Jehoshaphat,
for there I will sit
  to judge all the nations on every side.
¹³Swing the sickle,
  for the harvest is ripe.
Come, trample the grapes,
  for the winepress is full
  and the vats overflow—
so great is their wickedness!"

¹⁴Multitudes, multitudes
  in the valley of decision!
For the day of the Lord is near
  in the valley of decision.
¹⁵The sun and moon will be darkened,
  and the stars no longer shine.
¹⁶The Lord will roar from Zion
  and thunder from Jerusalem;
  the earth and the heavens will tremble.
But the Lord will be a refuge for his people,
  a stronghold for the people of Israel.

### Blessings for God's People

¹⁷"Then you will know that I, the Lord your God,
  dwell in Zion, my holy hill.
Jerusalem will be holy;
  never again will foreigners invade her.

¹⁸"In that day the mountains will drip new wine,
  and the hills will flow with milk;
all the ravines of Judah will run with water.
  A fountain will flow out of the Lord's house
  and will water the valley of acacias.ᵃ
¹⁹But Egypt will be desolate,
  Edom a desert waste,
because of violence done to the people of Judah,
  in whose land they shed innocent blood.
²⁰Judah will be inhabited forever
  and Jerusalem through all generations.
²¹Shall I leave their innocent blood unavenged?
  No, I will not."

The Lord dwells in Zion!

## Amplified Bible

of the children of Judah, and they will sell them to the Sabeans, to a nation far off, for the Lord has spoken it. [Isa. 14:2; 60:14.]
⁹Proclaim this among the nations: Prepare war! Stir up the mighty men! Let all the men of war draw near, let them come up.
¹⁰Beat your plowshares into swords, and your pruning hooks into spears; let the weak say, I am strong [a warrior]! [Isa. 2:4; Mic. 4:3.]
¹¹Hasten and come, all you nations round about, and assemble yourselves; there You, O Lord, will bring down Your mighty ones (Your warriors).
¹²Let the nations bestir themselves and come up to the Valley of Jehoshaphat, for there will I sit to judge all the nations round about.
¹³Put in the sickle, for the [vintage] harvest is ripe; come, get down *and* tread the grapes, for the winepress is full; the vats overflow, for the wickedness [of the peoples] is great. [Mark 4:29; Rev. 14:15, 18-20.]
¹⁴Multitudes, multitudes in the valley of decision! For the day of the Lord is near in the valley of decision. [Zech. 14:1-9.]
¹⁵The sun and the moon are darkened and the stars withdraw their shining.
¹⁶The Lord will thunder *and* roar from Zion and utter His voice from Jerusalem, and the heavens and the earth shall shake; but the Lord will be a refuge for His people and a stronghold to the children of Israel. [Amos 9:11-15; Mic. 4:1-3; 5:2; Zech. 6:12, 13; 12:8, 9.]
¹⁷So shall you know, understand, *and* realize that I am the Lord your God, dwelling in Zion, My holy mountain. Then shall Jerusalem be holy, and strangers *and* foreigners [not born into the family of God] shall no more pass through it.
¹⁸And in that day, the mountains shall drip with fresh juice [of the grape] and the hills shall flow with milk; and all the brooks *and* riverbeds of Judah shall flow with water, and a fountain shall come forth from the house of the Lord and shall water the Valley of Shittim. [Ezek. 47:1-12; Amos 9:13; Zech. 14:8.]
¹⁹Egypt shall be a desolation and Edom shall be a desolate wilderness for their violence against the children of Judah, because they have shed innocent blood in their land.
²⁰But Judah shall remain *and* be inhabited forever, and Jerusalem from generation to generation.
²¹And I will cleanse *and* hold as innocent their blood *and* avenge it, blood which I have not cleansed, held innocent, *and* avenged, for the Lord dwells in Zion.

---

ᵃ 18 Or *Valley of Shittim*

# Amos

# Amos

**1** The words of Amos, one of the shepherds of Tekoa—the vision he saw concerning Israel two years before the earthquake, when Uzziah was king of Judah and Jeroboam son of Jehoash[a] was king of Israel.

²He said:

"The LORD roars from Zion
   and thunders from Jerusalem;
the pastures of the shepherds dry up,
   and the top of Carmel withers."

## Judgment on Israel's Neighbors

³This is what the LORD says:

"For three sins of Damascus,
   even for four, I will not relent.
Because she threshed Gilead
   with sledges having iron teeth,
⁴I will send fire on the house of Hazael
   that will consume the fortresses of Ben-Hadad.
⁵I will break down the gate of Damascus;
   I will destroy the king who is in[b] the Valley of Aven[c]
and the one who holds the scepter in Beth Eden.
   The people of Aram will go into exile to Kir,"
                                        says the LORD.

⁶This is what the LORD says:

"For three sins of Gaza,
   even for four, I will not relent.
Because she took captive whole communities
   and sold them to Edom,
⁷I will send fire on the walls of Gaza
   that will consume her fortresses.
⁸I will destroy the king[d] of Ashdod
   and the one who holds the scepter in Ashkelon.
I will turn my hand against Ekron,
   till the last of the Philistines are dead,"
                              says the Sovereign LORD.

⁹This is what the LORD says:

"For three sins of Tyre,
   even for four, I will not relent.
Because she sold whole communities of captives to
      Edom,
   disregarding a treaty of brotherhood,
¹⁰I will send fire on the walls of Tyre
   that will consume her fortresses."

¹¹This is what the LORD says:

"For three sins of Edom,
   even for four, I will not relent.
Because he pursued his brother with a sword
   and slaughtered the women of the land,
because his anger raged continually
   and his fury flamed unchecked,
¹²I will send fire on Teman
   that will consume the fortresses of Bozrah."

¹³This is what the LORD says:

"For three sins of Ammon,
   even for four, I will not relent.
Because he ripped open the pregnant women of Gilead
   in order to extend his borders,

**1** The words of Amos, who was among the herdsmen *and* sheep masters of Tekoa, which he saw [in divine revelation] concerning Israel in the days of Uzziah king of Judah and in the days of Jeroboam the son of Joash, king of Israel, two years before the earthquake. [Zech. 14:5.]

²And he said, The Lord roars out of Zion and utters His voice from Jerusalem; then the pastures of the shepherds mourn and the top of [Mount] Carmel dries up. [Isa. 42:13; Jer. 25:30; Joel 3:16.]

³Thus says the Lord: For three transgressions of Damascus [the capital of Syria] and for four [for multiplied delinquencies], I will not reverse the punishment of it *or* revoke My word concerning it, because they have threshed Gilead [east of the Jordan River] with iron sledges. [II Kings 10:32, 33.]

⁴So I will send a fire [of war, conquest, and destruction] upon the house of Hazael [who killed and succeeded King Ben-hadad] which shall devour the palaces *and* strongholds of Ben-hadad.

⁵I will break also the bar [of the gate] of Damascus and cut off the inhabitant from the plain of Aven *or* On, and him who holds the scepter from Beth-eden; and the people of Syria [conquered by the Assyrians] shall go into exile to Kir, says the Lord. [Ezek. 30:17.]

⁶Thus says the Lord: For three transgressions of Gaza [a city in Philistia] and for four [for multiplied delinquencies], I will not reverse the punishment of it *or* revoke My word concerning it, because [as slave traders] they carried away captive the whole [Jewish] population [of defenseless Judean border villages, of which none was spared, none left behind] and delivered them up to Edom [for the slave trade]. [Joel 3:6.]

⁷So I will send a fire on the wall of Gaza which shall devour its strongholds.

⁸And I will cut off the inhabitants from Ashdod and him who holds the scepter from Ashkelon, and I will turn My hand against Ekron; and the rest of the Philistines [in Gath and the towns dependent on these four Philistine cities] shall perish, says the Lord God. [Josh. 13:3.]

⁹Thus says the Lord: For three transgressions of Tyre and for four [for multiplied delinquencies], I will not reverse the punishment of it *or* revoke My word concerning it, because they [as middlemen] delivered up a whole [Jewish] population to Edom and did not [seriously] remember their brotherly covenant. [I Kings 5:1, 12; 9:12, 13.]

¹⁰So I will send a fire on the wall of Tyre which shall devour its strongholds.

¹¹Thus says the Lord: For three transgressions of Edom [descendants of Esau] and for four [for multiplied delinquencies], I will not reverse the punishment of it *or* revoke My word concerning it, because he pursued his brother Jacob (Israel) with the sword, corrupting his compassions *and* casting off all pity, and his anger tore perpetually and his wrath he kept *and* heeded forever.

¹²So I will send a fire upon Teman which shall devour the strongholds of Bozrah [in Edom].

¹³Thus says the Lord: For three transgressions of the children of Ammon [descendants of Lot] and for four [for multiplied delinquencies], I will not reverse the punishment of it *or* revoke My word concerning it, because [the Ammonites] have ripped up women with child in Gilead, that they might enlarge their border.

---

ᵃ 1 Hebrew *Joash,* a variant of *Jehoash*   ᵇ 5 Or *the inhabitants of*
ᶜ 5 *Aven* means *wickedness.*   ᵈ 8 Or *inhabitants*

## New International Version

<sup>14</sup> I will set fire to the walls of Rabbah
    that will consume her fortresses
amid war cries on the day of battle,
    amid violent winds on a stormy day.
<sup>15</sup> Her king<sup>a</sup> will go into exile,
    he and his officials together,"
                           says the LORD.

**2** This is what the LORD says:

"For three sins of Moab,
    even for four, I will not relent.
Because he burned to ashes
    the bones of Edom's king,
<sup>2</sup> I will send fire on Moab
    that will consume the fortresses of Kerioth.<sup>b</sup>
Moab will go down in great tumult
    amid war cries and the blast of the trumpet.
<sup>3</sup> I will destroy her ruler
    and kill all her officials with him,"
                           says the LORD.

<sup>4</sup> This is what the LORD says:

"For three sins of Judah,
    even for four, I will not relent.
Because they have rejected the law of the LORD
    and have not kept his decrees,
because they have been led astray by false gods,<sup>c</sup>
    the gods<sup>d</sup> their ancestors followed,
<sup>5</sup> I will send fire on Judah
    that will consume the fortresses of Jerusalem."

### Judgment on Israel

<sup>6</sup> This is what the LORD says:

"For three sins of Israel,
    even for four, I will not relent.
They sell the innocent for silver,
    and the needy for a pair of sandals.
<sup>7</sup> They trample on the heads of the poor
    as on the dust of the ground
    and deny justice to the oppressed.
Father and son use the same girl
    and so profane my holy name.
<sup>8</sup> They lie down beside every altar
    on garments taken in pledge.
In the house of their god
    they drink wine taken as fines.

<sup>9</sup> "Yet I destroyed the Amorites before them,
    though they were tall as the cedars
    and strong as the oaks.
I destroyed their fruit above
    and their roots below.
<sup>10</sup> I brought you up out of Egypt
    and led you forty years in the wilderness
    to give you the land of the Amorites.

<sup>11</sup> "I also raised up prophets from among your children
    and Nazirites from among your youths.
Is this not true, people of Israel?"
                     declares the LORD.
<sup>12</sup> "But you made the Nazirites drink wine
    and commanded the prophets not to prophesy.

<sup>13</sup> "Now then, I will crush you
    as a cart crushes when loaded with grain.
<sup>14</sup> The swift will not escape,
    the strong will not muster their strength,
    and the warrior will not save his life.
<sup>15</sup> The archer will not stand his ground,
    the fleet-footed soldier will not get away,
    and the horseman will not save his life.

## Amplified Bible

<sup>14</sup> So I will kindle a fire in the wall of Rabbah [in Ammon] and it shall devour the strongholds of it, with shouting in the day of battle, with a tempest in the day of the whirlwind;

<sup>15</sup> And their king shall go into exile, he and his princes together, says the Lord.

**2** Thus says the Lord: For three transgressions of Moab [descendants of Lot] and for four [for multiplied delinquencies], I will not reverse the punishment of it *or* revoke My word concerning it, because he burned the bones of the king of Edom [Esau's descendant] into lime.

<sup>2</sup> So I will send a fire upon Moab and it shall devour the strongholds of Kerioth, and Moab shall die amid uproar, shouting, and the sound of the trumpet.

<sup>3</sup> And I will cut off the ruler from its midst and will slay all its princes with him, says the Lord.

<sup>4</sup> Thus says the Lord: For three transgressions of Judah and for four [for multiplied delinquencies], I will not reverse the punishment of it *or* revoke My word concerning it, because they have despised *and* rejected the law of the Lord and have not kept His commandments, but their lies, after which their fathers have walked, caused them to err *and* go astray.

<sup>5</sup> So I will send a fire upon Judah and it shall devour the strongholds of Jerusalem.

<sup>6</sup> Thus says the Lord: For three transgressions of Israel and for four [for multiplied delinquencies], I will not reverse the punishment of it *or* revoke My word concerning it, because they have sold the [strictly] just *and* uncompromisingly righteous for silver and the needy for a pair of sandals;

<sup>7</sup> They pant after [the sight of] the poor [reduced to such misery that they will be throwing] dust of the earth on their heads [in token of their grief]; they defraud *and* turn aside the humble [who are too meek to defend themselves]; and a man and his father will have sexual relations with the same maiden, so that My holy name is profaned.

<sup>8</sup> And they lay themselves down beside every [pagan] altar upon clothes they have taken in pledge [for indebtedness], and in the house of their God [in daring contempt of Him] they frivolously drink the wine which has been exacted from those [unjustly] fined.

<sup>9</sup> Yet I destroyed the Amorite before them, whose height was like the height of the cedars and he was strong as the oaks; yet I destroyed his fruit from above and his roots from beneath.

<sup>10</sup> Also I brought you up out of the land of Egypt and led you forty years through the wilderness to possess the land of the Amorite.

<sup>11</sup> And I raised up some of your sons for prophets and some of your young men for dedicated ones [Nazirites]. Is this not true, O you children of Israel? says the Lord. [Num. 6:1-8.]

<sup>12</sup> But you gave the dedicated ones [the Nazirites] wine to drink and commanded the prophets, saying, Prophesy not.

<sup>13</sup> Behold, I am pressed under you *and* I will press you down in your place as a cart presses that is full of sheaves.

<sup>14</sup> And flight shall be lost to the swift *and* refuge shall fail him; the strong shall not retain *and* confirm his strength, neither shall the mighty deliver himself.

<sup>15</sup> Neither shall he stand who handles the bow, and he who is swift of foot shall not deliver himself; neither shall he who rides the horse deliver his life.

---

<sup>a</sup> 15 Or / Molek   <sup>b</sup> 2 Or *of her cities*   <sup>c</sup> 4 Or *by lies*   <sup>d</sup> 4 Or *lies*

## New International Version

<sup>16</sup>Even the bravest warriors
　　will flee naked on that day,"
　　　　　　　　　　declares the LORD.

### Witnesses Summoned Against Israel

**3** Hear this word, people of Israel, the word the LORD
has spoken against you—against the whole family I
brought up out of Egypt:

<sup>2</sup>"You only have I chosen
　　of all the families of the earth;
　therefore I will punish you
　　for all your sins."

<sup>3</sup>Do two walk together
　　unless they have agreed to do so?
<sup>4</sup>Does a lion roar in the thicket
　　when it has no prey?
　Does it growl in its den
　　when it has caught nothing?
<sup>5</sup>Does a bird swoop down to a trap on the ground
　　when no bait is there?
　Does a trap spring up from the ground
　　if it has not caught anything?
<sup>6</sup>When a trumpet sounds in a city,
　　do not the people tremble?
　When disaster comes to a city,
　　has not the LORD caused it?

<sup>7</sup>Surely the Sovereign LORD does nothing
　　without revealing his plan
　to his servants the prophets.

<sup>8</sup>The lion has roared—
　　who will not fear?
　The Sovereign LORD has spoken—
　　who can but prophesy?

<sup>9</sup>Proclaim to the fortresses of Ashdod
　　and to the fortresses of Egypt:
"Assemble yourselves on the mountains of Samaria;
　　see the great unrest within her
　　and the oppression among her people."

<sup>10</sup>"They do not know how to do right," declares the
　　LORD,
　　"who store up in their fortresses
　　what they have plundered and looted."

<sup>11</sup>Therefore this is what the Sovereign LORD says:

"An enemy will overrun your land,
　　pull down your strongholds
　　and plunder your fortresses."

<sup>12</sup>This is what the LORD says:

"As a shepherd rescues from the lion's mouth
　　only two leg bones or a piece of an ear,
　so will the Israelites living in Samaria be rescued,
　　with only the head of a bed
　　and a piece of fabric<sup>a</sup> from a couch.<sup>b</sup>"

<sup>13</sup>"Hear this and testify against the descendants of Ja-
cob," declares the Lord, the LORD God Almighty.

<sup>14</sup>"On the day I punish Israel for her sins,
　　I will destroy the altars of Bethel;
　the horns of the altar will be cut off
　　and fall to the ground.
<sup>15</sup>I will tear down the winter house
　　along with the summer house;
　the houses adorned with ivory will be destroyed
　　and the mansions will be demolished,"
　　　　　　　　　　declares the LORD.

---

<sup>a</sup> 12 The meaning of the Hebrew for this phrase is uncertain.
<sup>b</sup> 12 Or Israelites be rescued, / those who sit in Samaria / on the edge of
their beds / and in Damascus on their couches.

## Amplified Bible

<sup>16</sup>And he who is courageous among the mighty shall
flee away naked on that day, says the Lord.

**3** Hear this word that the Lord has spoken against you,
O children of Israel, against the whole family which I
brought up from the land of Egypt:

<sup>2</sup>You only have I known (chosen, sympathized with, and
loved) of all the families of the earth; therefore I will visit
upon you all your wickedness *and* punish you for all your
iniquities.

<sup>3</sup>Do two walk together except they make an appoint-
ment *and* have agreed?

<sup>4</sup>Will a lion roar in the forest when he has no prey? Will
a young lion cry out of his den if he has taken nothing?

<sup>5</sup>Can a bird fall in a snare upon the earth where there
is no trap for him? Does a trap spring up from the ground
when nothing at all has sprung it?

<sup>6</sup>Shall a trumpet be blown in the city and the people not
be alarmed *and* afraid? Shall misfortune *or* evil occur [as
punishment] and the Lord has not caused it?

<sup>7</sup>Surely the Lord God will do nothing <sup>a</sup>without reveal-
ing His secret to His servants the prophets. [Rev. 10:7.]

<sup>8</sup>The lion has roared; who will not fear? The Lord God
has spoken; who can but prophesy? [Acts 4:20; 5:20, 29;
I Cor. 9:16.]

<sup>9</sup>Publish to the strongholds in Ashdod [Philistia] and
to the strongholds in the land of Egypt, and say, Assemble
yourselves upon the mountains of Samaria, and behold
what great tumults (confusion and disorder) are in her
and what oppressions are in the midst of her.

<sup>10</sup>For they know not how to do right, says the Lord, they
who store up violence and robbery in their strongholds.

<sup>11</sup>Therefore thus says the Lord God: An adversary shall
surround the land, and he shall bring down your defenses
from you and your strongholds shall be plundered.

<sup>12</sup>Thus says the Lord: As the shepherd rescues out of
the mouth of the lion two legs or a piece of an ear [of a
sheep], so shall the children of Israel who dwell in Samaria
be rescued with the corner of a couch and [part of] the
damask covering of a bed.

<sup>13</sup>Hear and bear witness in the house of Jacob, says the
Lord God, the God of hosts,

<sup>14</sup>That in the day when I visit Israel's transgressions
upon him I will also visit [with punishment] the altars of
Bethel [with its golden calf], and the horns of the altar
shall be cut off and fall to the ground.

<sup>15</sup>And I will smite the winter house with the summer
house, and the houses of ivory shall perish and the many
*and* great houses shall come to an end, says the Lord.

---

<sup>a</sup> God has always warned the world of coming judgments in order that
it may not bring them upon itself. He warned Noah of the coming flood
(Gen. 6:13ff.); Abraham and Lot of the future destruction of Sodom
(Gen. 18:17; 19:14); Joseph of the seven-year famine (Gen. 41:30); Moses
of the ten plagues on Egypt (Exod. 7:1ff.); Jonah of the destruction
of Nineveh (Jonah 1:2; 3:4); Amos of the downfall of Syria, Philistia,
Tyre, Edom, Ammon, Moab, Judah, and Israel (Amos 1 and 2). Various
prophets were told in detail about the final events in connection with the
captivities of the chosen people, and in every case the warnings were
startlingly executed. Jonah announced the destruction of Nineveh, but
judgment was postponed following repentance. When later generations
of Ninevites backslid and reverted to extreme wickedness, the warning
of Nahum was carried out completely against them. Christ's coming
was foretold throughout the Old Testament, from Genesis to Malachi.
Equally plain and inevitable of fulfillment are the warnings of Jesus and
the prophets concerning the future that each day comes nearer to every
nation on earth.

## New International Version

### Israel Has Not Returned to God

**4** Hear this word, you cows of Bashan on Mount
Samaria,
you women who oppress the poor and crush the
needy
and say to your husbands, "Bring us some drinks!"
[2] The Sovereign LORD has sworn by his holiness:
"The time will surely come
when you will be taken away with hooks,
the last of you with fishhooks.[a]
[3] You will each go straight out
through breaches in the wall,
and you will be cast out toward Harmon,[b]"
declares the LORD.
[4] "Go to Bethel and sin;
go to Gilgal and sin yet more.
Bring your sacrifices every morning,
your tithes every three years.[c]
[5] Burn leavened bread as a thank offering
and brag about your freewill offerings—
boast about them, you Israelites,
for this is what you love to do,"
declares the Sovereign LORD.

[6] "I gave you empty stomachs in every city
and lack of bread in every town,
yet you have not returned to me,"
declares the LORD.

[7] "I also withheld rain from you
when the harvest was still three months away.
I sent rain on one town,
but withheld it from another.
One field had rain;
another had none and dried up.
[8] People staggered from town to town for water
but did not get enough to drink,
yet you have not returned to me,"
declares the LORD.

[9] "Many times I struck your gardens and vineyards,
destroying them with blight and mildew.
Locusts devoured your fig and olive trees,
yet you have not returned to me,"
declares the LORD.

[10] "I sent plagues among you
as I did to Egypt.
I killed your young men with the sword,
along with your captured horses.
I filled your nostrils with the stench of your camps,
yet you have not returned to me,"
declares the LORD.

[11] "I overthrew some of you
as I overthrew Sodom and Gomorrah.
You were like a burning stick snatched from the fire,
yet you have not returned to me,"
declares the LORD.

[12] "Therefore this is what I will do to you, Israel,
and because I will do this to you, Israel,
prepare to meet your God."

[13] He who forms the mountains,
who creates the wind,
and who reveals his thoughts to mankind,
who turns dawn to darkness,
and treads on the heights of the earth—
the LORD God Almighty is his name.

## Amplified Bible

**4** Hear this word, you cows [women] of Bashan who are
in the mountain of Samaria, who oppress the poor,
who crush the needy, who say to their husbands, Bring
and let us drink! [Ps. 22:12; Ezek. 39:18.]
[2] The Lord God has sworn by His holiness that behold,
the days shall come upon you when they shall take you
away with hooks and the last of you with fishhooks. [Ps.
89:35.]
[3] And you shall go out through the breaches [made in
the city's wall], every [woman] straight before her, and
you shall be cast forth into Harmon [an unknown place of
exile], says the Lord.
[4] Come to Bethel [where the golden calf is] and transgress; at Gilgal [another idol worship center] multiply
transgression; and bring your sacrifices every morning
and your tithes every three days.
[5] And offer [by burning] a sacrifice of thanksgiving of
that which is leavened, and proclaim and publish freewill
offerings, for this you like to do, O children of Israel! says
the Lord God.
[6] I also gave you cleanness of teeth in all your cities and
want of bread in all your places; yet you did not return to
Me, says the Lord.
[7] And also I withheld the rain from you when there
were yet three months to the harvest. I caused it to rain
upon one city and caused it not to rain upon another city;
one piece of ground was rained upon, and the piece upon
which it did not rain withered.
[8] So [the people of] two or three cities wandered *and*
staggered into one city to drink water, but they were not
satisfied; yet you did not return to Me, says the Lord.
[9] I smote you with blight [from the poisonous east wind]
and with mildew; I laid waste the multitude of your gardens and your vineyards; your fig trees and your olive
trees the palmerworm [a form of locust] devoured; yet you
did not return to Me, says the Lord.
[10] I have sent among you the pestilence [which I made]
epidemic in Egypt; your young men I slew with the sword
and I took into exile your horses, and I made the stench
of your camp come up into your nostrils; yet you did not
return to Me, says the Lord. [II Kings 8:12; 13:3, 7.]
[11] I have overthrown some among you as when God
overthrew Sodom and Gomorrah, and you were as a brand
plucked out of the burning; yet you did not return to Me,
says the Lord. [Gen. 19:24, 25; Isa. 13:19; Jer. 49:18.]
[12] Therefore thus will I do to you, O Israel; and because
I will do this to you, prepare to meet your God, O Israel!
[13] For behold, He Who forms the mountains and creates
the wind and declares to man what is his thought, Who
makes the morning darkness and treads on the heights of
the earth—the Lord, the God of hosts, is His name! [Ps.
139:2; Dan. 2:28.]

---

[a] 2 Or *away in baskets, / the last of you in fish baskets*    [b] 3 Masoretic
Text; with a different word division of the Hebrew (see Septuagint) *out,
you mountain of oppression*    [c] 4 Or *days*

## New International Version

### A Lament and Call to Repentance

**5** Hear this word, Israel, this lament I take up concerning you:

[2] "Fallen is Virgin Israel,
never to rise again,
deserted in her own land,
with no one to lift her up."

[3] This is what the Sovereign LORD says to Israel:

"Your city that marches out a thousand strong
will have only a hundred left;
your town that marches out a hundred strong
will have only ten left."

[4] This is what the LORD says to Israel:

"Seek me and live;
[5]    do not seek Bethel,
do not go to Gilgal,
do not journey to Beersheba.
For Gilgal will surely go into exile,
and Bethel will be reduced to nothing.[a]"

[6] Seek the LORD and live,
or he will sweep through the tribes of Joseph like a
fire;
it will devour them,
and Bethel will have no one to quench it.

[7] There are those who turn justice into bitterness
and cast righteousness to the ground.

[8] He who made the Pleiades and Orion,
who turns midnight into dawn
and darkens day into night,
who calls for the waters of the sea
and pours them out over the face of the land—
the LORD is his name.

[9] With a blinding flash he destroys the stronghold
and brings the fortified city to ruin.

[10] There are those who hate the one who upholds justice
in court
and detest the one who tells the truth.

[11] You levy a straw tax on the poor
and impose a tax on their grain.
Therefore, though you have built stone mansions,
you will not live in them;
though you have planted lush vineyards,
you will not drink their wine.

[12] For I know how many are your offenses
and how great your sins.

There are those who oppress the innocent and take
bribes
and deprive the poor of justice in the courts.

[13] Therefore the prudent keep quiet in such times,
for the times are evil.

[14] Seek good, not evil,
that you may live.
Then the LORD God Almighty will be with you,
just as you say he is.

[15] Hate evil, love good;
maintain justice in the courts.
Perhaps the LORD God Almighty will have mercy
on the remnant of Joseph.

[16] Therefore this is what the Lord, the LORD God Almighty, says:

"There will be wailing in all the streets
and cries of anguish in every public square.
The farmers will be summoned to weep
and the mourners to wail.

[a] 5 Hebrew *aven*, a reference to Beth Aven (a derogatory name for
Bethel); see Hosea 4:15.

## Amplified Bible

**5** Hear this word which I take up concerning you in lamentation, O house of Israel:

[2] The Virgin of Israel has fallen; she shall no more rise;
she lies cast down *and* forsaken on her land; there is no
one to raise her up.

[3] For thus says the Lord God: The city that went forth a
thousand shall have a hundred left, and that which went
forth a hundred shall have ten left to the house of Israel.

[4] For thus says the Lord to the house of Israel: Seek Me
[inquire for and of Me and require Me as you require food]
and you shall live! [II Chron. 15:2; Jer. 29:13.]

[5] But seek not [the golden calf at] Bethel nor enter into
[idolatrous] Gilgal, and pass not over to [the idols of]
Beersheba; for Gilgal shall surely go into captivity *and*
exile, and Bethel [house of God] shall become Beth-aven
[house of vanity, emptiness, falsity, and futility] and come
to nothing.

[6] Seek the Lord [inquire for and of Him and require
Him] and you shall live, lest He rush down like fire upon
the house of Joseph [representing the ten tribes] and devour it, and there be none to quench it in Bethel [the center
of their idol hopes].

[7] You who turn justice into [the bitterness of] wormwood and cast righteousness (uprightness and right
standing with God) down to the ground,

[8] Seek Him Who made the [cluster of stars called] Pleiades and [the constellation] Orion, Who turns the shadow
of death *or* deep darkness into the morning and darkens
the day into night, Who calls for the waters of the sea and
pours them out upon the face of the earth—the Lord is
His name—

[9] Who causes sudden destruction to flash forth upon the
strong so that destruction comes upon the fortress.

[10] They hate him who reproves in the [city] gate [holding him as an abomination and rejecting his rebuke], and
they abhor him who speaks uprightly.

[11] Therefore because you tread upon the poor and take
from him exactions of wheat, you have built houses of
hewn stone, but you shall not dwell in them; you have
planted pleasant vineyards, but you shall not drink their
wine.

[12] For I know how manifold are your transgressions and
how mighty are your sins—you who afflict the [uncompromisingly] righteous, who take a bribe, and who turn aside
the needy in the [court of the city] gate from their right.

[13] Therefore he who is prudent will keep silence in such
a time, for it is an evil time.

[14] Seek (inquire for and require) good and not evil that
you may live, and so the Lord, the God of hosts, will be
with you, as you have said.

[15] Hate the evil and love the good and establish justice in
the [court of the city's] gate. It may be that the Lord, the
God of hosts, will be gracious to the remnant of Joseph
[the northern kingdom].

[16] Therefore thus says the Lord, the God of hosts, the
Lord: There shall be wailing in all the broad ways, and
in all the streets they shall say, Alas! Alas! And they shall
call the farmers to mourning and such as are skilled in
lamentation to wailing.

## New International Version

17 There will be wailing in all the vineyards,
    for I will pass through your midst,"
                                    says the LORD.

### The Day of the LORD
18 Woe to you who long
    for the day of the LORD!
  Why do you long for the day of the LORD?
    That day will be darkness, not light.
19 It will be as though a man fled from a lion
    only to meet a bear,
  as though he entered his house
    and rested his hand on the wall
    only to have a snake bite him.
20 Will not the day of the LORD be darkness, not light—
    pitch-dark, without a ray of brightness?
21 "I hate, I despise your religious festivals;
    your assemblies are a stench to me.
22 Even though you bring me burnt offerings and grain
        offerings,
    I will not accept them.
  Though you bring choice fellowship offerings,
    I will have no regard for them.
23 Away with the noise of your songs!
    I will not listen to the music of your harps.
24 But let justice roll on like a river,
    righteousness like a never-failing stream!
25 "Did you bring me sacrifices and offerings
    forty years in the wilderness, people of Israel?
26 You have lifted up the shrine of your king,
    the pedestal of your idols,
    the star of your god[a]—
    which you made for yourselves.
27 Therefore I will send you into exile beyond
        Damascus,"
    says the LORD, whose name is God Almighty.

### Woe to the Complacent
**6** Woe to you who are complacent in Zion,
    and to you who feel secure on Mount Samaria,
  you notable men of the foremost nation,
    to whom the people of Israel come!
2 Go to Kalneh and look at it;
    go from there to great Hamath,
    and then go down to Gath in Philistia.
  Are they better off than your two kingdoms?
    Is their land larger than yours?
3 You put off the day of disaster
    and bring near a reign of terror.
4 You lie on beds adorned with ivory
    and lounge on your couches.
  You dine on choice lambs
    and fattened calves.
5 You strum away on your harps like David
    and improvise on musical instruments.
6 You drink wine by the bowlful
    and use the finest lotions,
    but you do not grieve over the ruin of Joseph.
7 Therefore you will be among the first to go into exile;
    your feasting and lounging will end.

### The LORD Abhors the Pride of Israel
8 The Sovereign LORD has sworn by himself—the LORD
God Almighty declares:

  "I abhor the pride of Jacob
    and detest his fortresses;
  I will deliver up the city
    and everything in it."

a 26 Or lifted up Sakkuth your king / and Kaiwan your idols, / your star-gods; Septuagint lifted up the shrine of Molek / and the star of your god Rephan, / their idols

## Amplified Bible

17 And in all vineyards there shall be wailing, for I will pass through the midst of you, says the Lord.
18 Woe to you who desire the day of the Lord! Why would you want the day of the Lord? It is darkness and not light;
19 It is as if a man fled from a lion and a bear met him, or went into the house and leaned with his hand against the wall and a serpent bit him.
20 Shall not the day of the Lord be darkness, not light? Even very dark with no brightness in it?
21 I hate, I despise your feasts, and I will not smell a savor or take delight in your solemn assemblies.
22 Though you offer Me your burnt offerings and your cereal offerings, I will not accept them, neither will I look upon the peace or thank offerings of your fatted beasts.
23 Take away from Me the noise of your songs, for I will not listen to the melody of your harps.
24 But let justice run down like waters and righteousness as a mighty and ever-flowing stream.
25 Did you bring to Me sacrifices and cereal offerings during those forty years in the wilderness, O house of Israel?
26 [No] but [instead of bringing Me the appointed sacrifices] you carried about the tent of your king Sakkuth and Kaiwan [names for the gods of the planet Saturn], your images of your star-god which you made for yourselves [and you will do so again].
27 Therefore I will cause you to go into exile beyond Damascus, says the Lord, whose name is the God of hosts. [Acts 7:42, 43.]

**6** Woe to those who are at ease in Zion and to those on the mountain of Samaria who are careless and feel secure, the notable men of the chief [because chosen by God] of the nations, to whom the house of Israel comes! [Luke 6:24, 25.]
2 Pass over to Calneh and see, and from there to Hamath the great [city, north of Damascus]; then go down to Gath of the Philistines. Are they better than these [your] kingdoms? Or are their boundaries greater than your boundaries,
3 O you who put far away the evil day [of punishment], yet cause the sitting of violence [upon you] to come near?
4 Woe to those who lie upon beds of ivory and stretch themselves upon their couches, and eat the lambs out of the flock and the calves out of the midst of the stall,
5 Who sing idle songs to the sound of the harp and invent for themselves instruments of music like David's, [I Chron. 23:5.]
6 Who drink wine in bowls and anoint themselves with the finest oils, but are not grieved and sick at heart over the affliction and ruin of Joseph (Israel)! [Gen. 49:22, 23.]
7 Therefore now shall they go captive with the first who go into exile, and the revelry and banqueting of those who stretch themselves shall be ended.
8 The Lord God has sworn by Himself—the Lord, the God of hosts, says: I abhor, reject, and despise the pride and false, futile glory of Jacob (Israel), and I hate his palaces and strongholds; and I will deliver up the city [idol-worshiping Samaria] with all that is in it.

## New International Version

⁹If ten people are left in one house, they too will die. ¹⁰And if the relative who comes to carry the bodies out of the house to burn them*ᵃ* asks anyone who might be hiding there, "Is anyone else with you?" and he says, "No," then he will go on to say, "Hush! We must not mention the name of the LORD."

¹¹For the LORD has given the command,
    and he will smash the great house into pieces
    and the small house into bits.

¹²Do horses run on the rocky crags?
    Does one plow the sea*ᵇ* with oxen?
But you have turned justice into poison
    and the fruit of righteousness into bitterness—
¹³you who rejoice in the conquest of Lo Debar*ᶜ*
    and say, "Did we not take Karnaim*ᵈ* by our own strength?"

¹⁴For the LORD God Almighty declares,
    "I will stir up a nation against you, Israel,
that will oppress you all the way
    from Lebo Hamath to the valley of the Arabah."

### Locusts, Fire and a Plumb Line

**7** This is what the Sovereign LORD showed me: He was preparing swarms of locusts after the king's share had been harvested and just as the late crops were coming up. ²When they had stripped the land clean, I cried out, "Sovereign LORD, forgive! How can Jacob survive? He is so small!"

³So the LORD relented.

"This will not happen," the LORD said.

⁴This is what the Sovereign LORD showed me: The Sovereign LORD was calling for judgment by fire; it dried up the great deep and devoured the land. ⁵Then I cried out, "Sovereign LORD, I beg you, stop! How can Jacob survive? He is so small!"

⁶So the LORD relented.

"This will not happen either," the Sovereign LORD said.

⁷This is what he showed me: The Lord was standing by a wall that had been built true to plumb,*ᵉ* with a plumb line*ᶠ* in his hand. ⁸And the LORD asked me, "What do you see, Amos?"

"A plumb line," I replied.

Then the Lord said, "Look, I am setting a plumb line among my people Israel; I will spare them no longer.

⁹"The high places of Isaac will be destroyed
    and the sanctuaries of Israel will be ruined;
with my sword I will rise against the house of Jeroboam."

### Amos and Amaziah

¹⁰Then Amaziah the priest of Bethel sent a message to Jeroboam king of Israel: "Amos is raising a conspiracy against you in the very heart of Israel. The land cannot bear all his words. ¹¹For this is what Amos is saying:

"'Jeroboam will die by the sword,
    and Israel will surely go into exile,
    away from their native land.'"

¹²Then Amaziah said to Amos, "Get out, you seer! Go back to the land of Judah. Earn your bread there and do your prophesying there. ¹³Don't prophesy anymore at

## Amplified Bible

⁹And it shall come to pass that if there remain ten men in one house, they shall die [by the pestilence that comes with war].

¹⁰And then a man's uncle *or* kinsman, he who is to make a burning to cremate *and* dispose [of his pestilence-infected body], comes in to bring the bones out of the house, and he shall say to another still alive in the farthest parts of the house, Is there anyone else with you? and he shall say, No. Then shall the newcomer say, Hush! Hold your [cursing] tongue! We dare not so mention the name of the Lord [lest we invoke more punishment]. [I Sam. 31:12.]

¹¹For behold, the Lord commands and He will smite the great house into ruins and the little house into fragments.

¹²Do horses run upon rocks? Do men plow the ocean with oxen? But you have turned justice into [the poison of] gall and the fruit of righteousness into [the bitterness of] wormwood—

¹³You who rejoice in Lo-debar [a thing of nought], who say, Have we not by our own strength taken Karnaim *or* horns [of resistance] for ourselves?

¹⁴For behold, I will raise up against you a nation, O house of Israel, says the Lord, the God of hosts; and they shall afflict *and* oppress you [to the entire limits of Israel] from the entrance of Hamath to the brook of the Arabah.

**7** Thus the Lord God showed me [Amos], and behold, He formed locusts in the beginning of the shooting up of the second crop, and behold, it was the second crop after the king's mowings.

²And when [the locusts] had finished eating the plants of the land, then I said, O Lord God, forgive, I pray You. How can Jacob stand? For he is so small!

³The Lord relented *and* revoked this sentence: It shall not take place, said the Lord [and He was eased and comforted concerning it].

⁴Thus the Lord God showed me, and behold, the Lord God called for punishment with fire, and it devoured the great deep and would have eaten up the land.

⁵Then said I, O Lord God, cease, I pray You! How can Jacob stand? He is so little!

⁶The Lord relented *and* revoked this sentence: This also shall not be, said the Lord [and He was eased and comforted concerning it].

⁷Thus He showed me, and behold, the Lord stood upon a wall with a plumb line, with a plumb line in His hand. [II Kings 21:13; Isa. 34:11.]

⁸And the Lord said to me, Amos, what do you see? And I said, A plumb line. Then said the Lord, Behold, I am setting a plumb line as a standard in the midst of My people Israel. I will not pass by *and* spare them any more [the door of mercy is shut].

⁹And the [idolatrous] high places of Isaac (Israel) shall be desolate and the sanctuaries of Israel shall be laid waste, and I will rise with the sword against the house of King Jeroboam [who set up the golden calf shrines].

¹⁰Then Amaziah the priest of [the golden calf shrine at] Bethel sent to Jeroboam king of Israel, saying, Amos has conspired against you in the midst of the house of Israel; the land is not able to bear all his words. [I Kings 12:31, 32.]

¹¹For thus Amos has said, Jeroboam shall die by the sword and Israel shall surely be led away captive out of his land.

¹²Also Amaziah said to Amos, O you seer, go! Flee back to the land of Judah [your own country], and eat your bread and live out your profession as a prophet there [as I perform my duties here].

---

*ᵃ 10 Or to make a funeral fire in honor of the dead*     *ᵇ 12 With a different word division of the Hebrew; Masoretic Text plow there*     *ᶜ 13 Lo Debar means nothing.*     *ᵈ 13 Karnaim means horns; horn here symbolizes strength.*     *ᵉ 7 The meaning of the Hebrew for this phrase is uncertain.*     *ᶠ 7 The meaning of the Hebrew for this phrase is uncertain; also in verse 8.*

## New International Version

Bethel, because this is the king's sanctuary and the temple of the kingdom."

[14]Amos answered Amaziah, "I was neither a prophet nor the son of a prophet, but I was a shepherd, and I also took care of sycamore-fig trees. [15]But the LORD took me from tending the flock and said to me, 'Go, prophesy to my people Israel.' [16]Now then, hear the word of the LORD. You say,

"'Do not prophesy against Israel,
   and stop preaching against the descendants of
      Isaac.'

[17]"Therefore this is what the LORD says:

"'Your wife will become a prostitute in the city,
   and your sons and daughters will fall by the sword.
Your land will be measured and divided up,
   and you yourself will die in a pagan[a] country.
And Israel will surely go into exile,
   away from their native land.'"

### A Basket of Ripe Fruit

**8** This is what the Sovereign LORD showed me: a basket of ripe fruit. [2]"What do you see, Amos?" he asked.
"A basket of ripe fruit," I answered.
Then the LORD said to me, "The time is ripe for my people Israel; I will spare them no longer.
[3]"In that day," declares the Sovereign LORD, "the songs in the temple will turn to wailing.[b] Many, many bodies—flung everywhere! Silence!"

[4]Hear this, you who trample the needy
   and do away with the poor of the land,

[5]saying,

"When will the New Moon be over
   that we may sell grain,
and the Sabbath be ended
   that we may market wheat?"—
skimping on the measure,
   boosting the price
   and cheating with dishonest scales,
[6]buying the poor with silver
   and the needy for a pair of sandals,
   selling even the sweepings with the wheat.

[7]The LORD has sworn by himself, the Pride of Jacob: "I will never forget anything they have done.

[8]"Will not the land tremble for this,
   and all who live in it mourn?
The whole land will rise like the Nile;
   it will be stirred up and then sink
   like the river of Egypt.

[9]"In that day," declares the Sovereign LORD,

"I will make the sun go down at noon
   and darken the earth in broad daylight.
[10]I will turn your religious festivals into mourning
   and all your singing into weeping.
I will make all of you wear sackcloth
   and shave your heads.
I will make that time like mourning for an only son
   and the end of it like a bitter day.

[11]"The days are coming," declares the Sovereign LORD,
   "when I will send a famine through the land—
not a famine of food or a thirst for water,
   but a famine of hearing the words of the LORD.
[12]People will stagger from sea to sea
   and wander from north to east,
searching for the word of the LORD,
   but they will not find it.

## Amplified Bible

[13]But do not prophesy any more at Bethel, for it is the king's sanctuary and a seat of his kingdom. [Luke 10:10-12.]

[14]Then Amos said to Amaziah, I was no prophet [by profession]! Neither was I a prophet's son; [but I had my occupation] I was a herdsman and a dresser of sycamore trees and a gatherer of sycamore figs.

[15]And the Lord took me as I followed the flock and the Lord said to me, Go, prophesy to My people Israel.

[16]Now therefore listen to the word of the Lord: You say, Do not prophesy against Israel and drop no statements not complimentary to the house of Isaac.

[17]Therefore thus says the Lord: Your wife shall be a harlot in the city and your sons and your daughters shall fall by the sword, and your land shall be divided up by line; you yourself shall die in an unclean *and* defiled land, and Israel shall surely go forth out of his land into exile.

**8** Thus the Lord God showed to me, and behold, a basket of [ripe and therefore soon to perish] summer fruit.

[2]And He said, Amos, what do you see? And I said, A basket of summer fruit. Then said the Lord to me, The end has come upon My people Israel; I will not pass by *and* spare them any more.

[3]And the songs of the temple shall become wailings in that day, says the Lord God. The dead bodies shall be many; in every place they shall be cast forth in silence.

[4]Hear this, O you who would swallow up *and* trample down the needy, even to make the poor of the land to fail *and* come to an end,

[5]Saying, When will the New Moon festival be past that we may sell grain? And the Sabbath that we may offer wheat for sale, making the ephah [measure] small and the shekel [measure] great and falsifying the scales by deceit,

[6]That we may buy [into slavery] the poor for silver and the needy for a pair of sandals; yes, and sell the refuse of the wheat [as if it were good grade]?

[7]The Lord has sworn by [Himself Who is] the Glory *and* Pride of Jacob, Surely I will never forget any of their [rebellious] deeds.

[8]Shall not the land tremble on this account, and everyone mourn who dwells in it? Yes, it shall rise like the river [Nile], all of it, and it shall be tossed about and sink back again to normal level, as does the Nile of Egypt.

[9]And in that day, says the Lord God, I will cause the sun to go down at noon, and I will darken the earth in the broad daylight. [Ezek. 32:7-10.]

[10]And I will turn your feasts into mourning and all your songs into lamentation, and I will cause sackcloth to be put upon all loins and baldness [for mourning] shall come on every head; and I will make that time as the mourning for an only son, and the end of it as a bitter day.

[11]Behold, the days are coming, says the Lord God, when I will send a famine in the land, not a famine of bread, nor a thirst for water, but [a famine] for hearing the words of the Lord.

[12]And [the people] shall wander from sea to sea and from the north even to the east; they shall run to and fro to seek the word of the Lord [inquiring for and requiring it as one requires food], but shall not find it.

---

[a] 17 Hebrew *an unclean*   [b] 3 Or *"the temple singers will wail"*

## New International Version

13 "In that day

"the lovely young women and strong young men
will faint because of thirst.
14 Those who swear by the sin of Samaria—
who say, 'As surely as your god lives, Dan,'
or, 'As surely as the god*a* of Beersheba lives'—
they will fall, never to rise again."

### Israel to Be Destroyed

9 I saw the Lord standing by the altar, and he said:

"Strike the tops of the pillars
so that the thresholds shake.
Bring them down on the heads of all the people;
those who are left I will kill with the sword.
Not one will get away,
none will escape.
2 Though they dig down to the depths below,
from there my hand will take them.
Though they climb up to the heavens above,
from there I will bring them down.
3 Though they hide themselves on the top of Carmel,
there I will hunt them down and seize them.
Though they hide from my eyes at the bottom of the
sea,
there I will command the serpent to bite them.
4 Though they are driven into exile by their enemies,
there I will command the sword to slay them.

"I will keep my eye on them
for harm and not for good."

5 The Lord, the LORD Almighty—
he touches the earth and it melts,
and all who live in it mourn;
the whole land rises like the Nile,
then sinks like the river of Egypt;
6 he builds his lofty palace*b* in the heavens
and sets its foundation*c* on the earth;
he calls for the waters of the sea
and pours them out over the face of the land—
the LORD is his name.

7 "Are not you Israelites
the same to me as the Cushites*d*?"
declares the LORD.

"Did I not bring Israel up from Egypt,
the Philistines from Caphtor*e*
and the Arameans from Kir?

8 "Surely the eyes of the Sovereign LORD
are on the sinful kingdom.
I will destroy it
from the face of the earth.
Yet I will not totally destroy
the descendants of Jacob,"
declares the LORD.

9 "For I will give the command,
and I will shake the people of Israel
among all the nations
as grain is shaken in a sieve,
and not a pebble will reach the ground.
10 All the sinners among my people
will die by the sword,
all those who say,
'Disaster will not overtake or meet us.'

## Amplified Bible

13 In that day shall the fair virgins and young men faint
for thirst.
14 Those who swear by Ashimah *or* the sin of Samaria
and say, By the life of your god [the golden calf], O Dan!
and [swear], By the life of the way of [idolatrous] Beersheba, they shall fall and rise no more.

9 I saw the Lord standing at the altar, and He said,
Smite the tops of the pillars until the thresholds tremble, and shatter them on the heads of all of the people; and
the remainder of them I will slay with the sword. He who
flees of them shall not get away, and he who escapes of
them shall not be delivered.
2 Though they dig into Sheol (Hades, the dark abode of
the gathered dead), from there shall My hand take them;
though they climb up to heaven [the abode of light], from
there will I bring them down;
3 And though they hide themselves on the top of
[Mount] Carmel, from there I will search out and take
them; and though they [try to] hide from My sight at the
bottom of the sea, there I will command the serpent and
it shall bite them.
4 And though they go into captivity before their enemies, there will I command the sword and it shall slay
them, and I will set My eyes upon them for evil and not
for good.
5 The Lord God of hosts, it is He Who touches the earth
and it melts, and all who dwell in it mourn; it shall rise like
the [river] Nile, all of it, and it shall sink again like the
Nile of Egypt.
6 It is He Who builds His upper chambers in the heavens
and Who founds His vault over the earth, Who calls to the
waters of the sea and pours them out on the face of the
earth—The Lord is His name.
7 You [O degenerate children of Israel] are no more
to Me than these [despised] Cushites, says the Lord. I
brought up Israel out of the land of Egypt, but have I not
[also] brought the Philistines out of Caphtor and the Syrians from Kir?
8 Behold, the eyes of the Lord God are upon the sinful
kingdom [of Israel's ten tribes] and I will destroy it from
the surface of the ground, except that I will not utterly
destroy the house of Jacob, says the Lord.
9 For behold, I will command, and I will sift the house of
Israel among all nations *and* cause it to move to and fro as
grain is sifted in a sieve, yet shall not the least kernel fall
upon the earth *and* be lost [from My sight]. [Lev. 26:33;
Deut. 28:64; Hos. 9:17.]
10 All the sinners of My people shall die by the sword,
who say, The evil shall not overtake or meet [and assail]
us.

---

*a* 14 Hebrew *the way*   *b* 6 The meaning of the Hebrew for this phrase is
uncertain.   *c* 6 The meaning of the Hebrew for this word is uncertain.
*d* 7 That is, people from the upper Nile region   *e* 7 That is, Crete

# New International Version

### Israel's Restoration

¹¹ "In that day

"I will restore David's fallen shelter —
  I will repair its broken walls
  and restore its ruins —
  and will rebuild it as it used to be,
¹² so that they may possess the remnant of Edom
  and all the nations that bear my name,ᵃ"
    declares the LORD, who will do these things.

¹³ "The days are coming," declares the LORD,

"when the reaper will be overtaken by the plowman
  and the planter by the one treading grapes.
New wine will drip from the mountains
  and flow from all the hills,
¹⁴  and I will bring my people Israel back from exile.ᵇ

"They will rebuild the ruined cities and live in them.
  They will plant vineyards and drink their wine;
  they will make gardens and eat their fruit.
¹⁵ I will plant Israel in their own land,
  never again to be uprooted
  from the land I have given them,"

       says the LORD your God.

# Amplified Bible

¹¹ In that day will I raise up the tabernacle of David, the fallen hut *or* booth, and close up its breaches; and I will raise up its ruins, and I will build it as in the days of old,
¹² That they may possess the remnant of Edom and of all the nations that are called by My name, says the Lord Who does this. [Acts 15:15-17.]
¹³ Behold, the days are coming, says the Lord, that the plowman shall overtake the reaper, and the treader of grapes him who sows the seed; and the mountains shall drop sweet wine and all the hills shall melt [that is, everything heretofore barren and unfruitful shall overflow with spiritual blessing]. [Lev. 26:5; Joel 3:18.]
¹⁴ And I will bring back the exiles of My people Israel, and they shall build the waste cities and inhabit them; and they shall plant vineyards and drink the wine from them; they shall also make gardens and eat the fruit of them.
¹⁵ And I will plant them upon their land, and they shall no more be torn up out of their land which I gave them, says the Lord your God.

---

ᵃ 12 Hebrew; Septuagint *so that the remnant of people / and all the nations that bear my name may seek me*  ᵇ 14 Or *will restore the fortunes of my people Israel*

# New International Version

# Obadiah

## Obadiah's Vision

¹The vision of Obadiah.

This is what the Sovereign Lord says about Edom—

We have heard a message from the Lord:
  An envoy was sent to the nations to say,
"Rise, let us go against her for battle"—

²"See, I will make you small among the nations;
  you will be utterly despised.
³The pride of your heart has deceived you,
  you who live in the clefts of the rocks[a]
  and make your home on the heights,
you who say to yourself,
  'Who can bring me down to the ground?'
⁴Though you soar like the eagle
  and make your nest among the stars,
  from there I will bring you down,"
                              declares the Lord.

⁵"If thieves came to you,
  if robbers in the night—
oh, what a disaster awaits you!—
  would they not steal only as much as they wanted?
If grape pickers came to you,
  would they not leave a few grapes?
⁶But how Esau will be ransacked,
  his hidden treasures pillaged!
⁷All your allies will force you to the border;
  your friends will deceive and overpower you;
  those who eat your bread will set a trap for you,[b]
  but you will not detect it.

⁸"In that day," declares the Lord,
  "will I not destroy the wise men of Edom,
  those of understanding in the mountains of Esau?
⁹Your warriors, Teman, will be terrified,
  and everyone in Esau's mountains
  will be cut down in the slaughter.
¹⁰Because of the violence against your brother Jacob,
  you will be covered with shame;
  you will be destroyed forever.
¹¹On the day you stood aloof
  while strangers carried off his wealth
and foreigners entered his gates
  and cast lots for Jerusalem,
  you were like one of them.
¹²You should not gloat over your brother
  in the day of his misfortune,
nor rejoice over the people of Judah
  in the day of their destruction,
nor boast so much
  in the day of their trouble.
¹³You should not march through the gates of my people
  in the day of their disaster,
nor gloat over them in their calamity
  in the day of their disaster,
nor seize their wealth
  in the day of their disaster.
¹⁴You should not wait at the crossroads
  to cut down their fugitives,
nor hand over their survivors
  in the day of their trouble.

¹⁵"The day of the Lord is near
  for all nations.
As you have done, it will be done to you;
  your deeds will return upon your own head.

*a* 3 Or *of Sela*    *b* 7 The meaning of the Hebrew for this clause is uncertain.

# Amplified Bible

## THE BOOK OF

# Obadiah

**1** The vision of Obadiah. Thus says the Lord God concerning *a* Edom: We have heard tidings from the Lord, and an ambassador is sent forth among the nations [saying], Arise, and let us rise up against [Edom] for battle! [Ps. 137:7; Isa. 34:1-15; 63:1-6; Jer. 49:7-22; Ezek. 25:8-14.]

²Behold, I will make you small among the nations [Edom]; you shall be despised exceedingly. [Ezek. 35.]

³The pride of your heart has deceived you, you dweller in the refuges of the rock [Petra, Edom's capital], whose habitation is high, who says in his heart, Who can bring me down to the ground?

⁴Though you mount on high as the eagle and though you set your nest among the stars, I will bring you down from there, says the Lord.

⁵If thieves came to you, if robbers by night—how you are brought to nothing!—would they not steal only enough for themselves? If grape gatherers came to you, would they not leave some grapes for gleaning? [But this ravaging was done by God, not men.] [Jer. 49:9.]

⁶How are the things of Esau [Edom] searched out! How are his hidden treasures sought out!

⁷All the men of your confederacy (your allies) have brought you on your way, even to the border; the men who were at peace with you have deceived you and prevailed against you; they who eat your bread have laid a snare under you. There is no understanding [in Edom, or] of it.

⁸Will not I in that day, says the Lord, destroy the wise men out of Edom and [men of] understanding out of Mount Esau [Idumea, a mountainous region]?

⁹And your mighty men, O Teman, shall be dismayed, to the end that everyone from Mount Esau will be cut off by slaughter.

¹⁰For the violence you did against your brother Jacob, shame shall cover you, and you shall be cut off forever.

¹¹On the day that you stood aloof [from your brother Jacob]—on the day that strangers took captive his forces *and* carried off his wealth, and foreigners entered into his gates and cast lots for Jerusalem—you were even as one of them. [Num. 20:18-20; Amos 1:11, 12.]

¹²But you should not have gloated over your brother's day, the day when his misfortune came *and* he was made a stranger; you should not have rejoiced over the sons of Judah in the day of their ruin; you should not have spoken arrogantly in the day of their distress.

¹³You should not have entered the gate of My people in the day of their calamity *and* ruin; yes, you should not have looked [with delight] on their misery in the day of their calamity *and* ruin, and not have reached after their army *and* their possessions in the day of their calamity *and* ruin.

¹⁴And you should not have stood at the crossway to cut off those of Judah who escaped, neither should you have delivered up those [of Judah] who remained in the day of distress.

¹⁵For the day of the Lord is near upon all the nations. As you have done, it shall be done to you; your dealings will return upon your own head. [Isa. 2:10-22; Zeph. 3:8-20; Zech. 12:1-14; Rev. 19:11-21.]

*a* Edom, or Seir, was the country southeast of Judah extending from the Dead Sea to the eastern arm of the Red Sea. It included the city of Petra. The country of Moab formed Edom's boundary on the north, and the descendants of Esau constituted its population. Edom and Moab have a remarkably prominent place in prophecy as "the scene of the final destruction of Gentile world power in the day of the Lord," as revealed in the Scripture references accompanying Obad. 1 (which are important for the full, vivid picture of what lies ahead for the nations of the world).

## New International Version

16 Just as you drank on my holy hill,
so all the nations will drink continually;
they will drink and drink
and be as if they had never been.
17 But on Mount Zion will be deliverance;
it will be holy,
and Jacob will possess his inheritance.
18 Jacob will be a fire
and Joseph a flame;
Esau will be stubble,
and they will set him on fire and destroy him.
There will be no survivors
from Esau."

The LORD has spoken.

19 People from the Negev will occupy
the mountains of Esau,
and people from the foothills will possess
the land of the Philistines.
They will occupy the fields of Ephraim and Samaria,
and Benjamin will possess Gilead.
20 This company of Israelite exiles who are in Canaan
will possess the land as far as Zarephath;
the exiles from Jerusalem who are in Sepharad
will possess the towns of the Negev.
21 Deliverers will go up on*a* Mount Zion
to govern the mountains of Esau.
And the kingdom will be the LORD's.

## Amplified Bible

16 For as you [Edom] have drunk upon the mountain of My holiness [desecrating it in the wild revelry of the destroyers], so shall all the nations drink continually [in turn, of My wrath]; yes, they shall drink, talk foolishly, *and* swallow down [the full measure of punishment] and they shall be [destroyed] as though they had not been. [Rev. 16:14-16.]
17 But on Mount Zion [in Jerusalem] there shall be deliverance [for those who escape], and it shall be holy; and the house of Jacob shall possess its [own former] possessions. [Ezek. 36; Joel 2:32.]
18 The house of Jacob shall be a fire and the house of Joseph a flame, but the house of Esau shall be stubble; they shall kindle *and* burn them and consume them, and there shall be no survivor of the house of Esau, for the Lord has spoken it. [Ezek. 25:12-14.]
19 They of the South (the Negeb) shall possess Mount Esau, and they of the lowland the land of the Philistines; they shall possess the land of Ephraim and the fields of Samaria, and Benjamin shall possess Gilead [across the Jordan River]. [Amos 9:12; Zeph. 2:7.]
20 And the exiles of this host of the children of Israel who are among the Canaanites shall possess [Phoenicia] as far as Zarephath, and the exiles of Jerusalem who are in Sepharad shall possess the cities of the South (the Negeb).
21 And deliverers shall go up on Mount Zion to rule *and* judge Mount Esau, and the kingdom *and* the kingship shall be the Lord's. [Zech. 12:8, 9; Mal. 1:2-5; Matt. 24:27-30; Luke 1:31-33; Acts 15:14-17.]

*a 21 Or from*

# Jonah

# Jonah

## Jonah Flees From the LORD

**1** The word of the LORD came to Jonah son of Amittai: ²"Go to the great city of Nineveh and preach against it, because its wickedness has come up before me."

³But Jonah ran away from the LORD and headed for Tarshish. He went down to Joppa, where he found a ship bound for that port. After paying the fare, he went aboard and sailed for Tarshish to flee from the LORD.

⁴Then the LORD sent a great wind on the sea, and such a violent storm arose that the ship threatened to break up. ⁵All the sailors were afraid and each cried out to his own god. And they threw the cargo into the sea to lighten the ship.

But Jonah had gone below deck, where he lay down and fell into a deep sleep. ⁶The captain went to him and said, "How can you sleep? Get up and call on your god! Maybe he will take notice of us so that we will not perish."

⁷Then the sailors said to each other, "Come, let us cast lots to find out who is responsible for this calamity." They cast lots and the lot fell on Jonah. ⁸So they asked him, "Tell us, who is responsible for making all this trouble for us? What kind of work do you do? Where do you come from? What is your country? From what people are you?"

⁹He answered, "I am a Hebrew and I worship the LORD, the God of heaven, who made the sea and the dry land."

¹⁰This terrified them and they asked, "What have you done?" (They knew he was running away from the LORD, because he had already told them so.)

¹¹The sea was getting rougher and rougher. So they asked him, "What should we do to you to make the sea calm down for us?"

¹²"Pick me up and throw me into the sea," he replied, "and it will become calm. I know that it is my fault that this great storm has come upon you."

¹³Instead, the men did their best to row back to land. But they could not, for the sea grew even wilder than before. ¹⁴Then they cried out to the LORD, "Please, LORD, do not let us die for taking this man's life. Do not hold us accountable for killing an innocent man, for you, LORD, have done as you pleased." ¹⁵Then they took Jonah and threw him overboard, and the raging sea grew calm. ¹⁶At this the

**1** Now the word of the Lord came to [a]Jonah son of Amittai, saying,

²Arise, go to [b]Nineveh, that great city, and proclaim against it, for their wickedness has come up before Me. [Gen. 10:11, 12.]

³But Jonah rose up to flee to Tarshish from being in the presence of the Lord [as His prophet] and went down to Joppa and found a ship going to Tarshish [the most remote of the Phoenician trading places then known]. So he paid the appointed fare and went down into the ship to go with them to Tarshish from being in the presence of the Lord [as His servant and minister]. [Gen. 4:16; Job 1:12; 2:7.]

⁴But the Lord sent out a great wind upon the sea, and there was a violent tempest on the sea so that the ship was about to be broken. [Ps. 107:23-27.]

⁵Then the mariners were afraid, and each man cried to his god; and they cast the goods that were in the ship into the sea to lighten it for them. But Jonah had gone down into the inner part of the ship and had lain down and was fast asleep.

⁶So the captain came and said to him, What do you mean, you sleeper? Arise, call upon your God! Perhaps your God will give a thought to us so that we shall not perish.

⁷And they each said to one another, Come, let us cast lots, that we may know on whose account this evil has come upon us. So they cast lots and the lot fell on Jonah.

⁸Then they said to him, Tell us, we pray you, on whose account has this evil come upon us? What is your occupation? Where did you come from? And what is your country and nationality?

⁹And he said to them, I am a Hebrew, and I [reverently] fear *and* worship the Lord, the God of heaven, Who made the sea and the dry land.

¹⁰Then the men were exceedingly afraid and said to him, What is this that you have done? For the men knew that he fled from being in the presence of the Lord [as His prophet and servant], because he had told them.

¹¹Then they said to him, What shall we do to you, that the sea may subside *and* be calm for us? For the sea became more and more [violently] tempestuous.

¹²And [Jonah] said to them, Take me up and cast me into the sea; so shall the sea become calm for you, for I know that it is because of me that this great tempest has come upon you.

¹³Nevertheless the men rowed hard to bring the ship to the land, but they could not, for the sea became more and more violent against them.

¹⁴Therefore they cried to the Lord, We beseech You, O Lord, we beseech You, let us not perish for this man's life, and lay not upon us innocent blood; for You, O Lord, have done as it pleased You.

¹⁵So they took up Jonah and cast him into the sea, and the sea ceased from its raging.

---

[a] That Jonah was a historical character is evidenced beyond question by the reference to him in II Kings 14:25: "Jeroboam restored Israel's border . . . according to the word of the Lord . . . which He spoke through His servant Jonah son of Amittai, the prophet from Gath-hepher." [b] In spite of the fact that Nineveh is called a "great city" three times in the Old Testament (Gen. 10:11, 12; Jonah 1:2; 3:3) and once in the Apocrypha (Judith 1:1), skeptical Bible critics long believed the statement to be greatly exaggerated. When the walled city was first excavated, it was found to be less than nine miles in circumference. That sparked cynical claims that the author, Jonah, did not know what he was talking about. But the real author, the Holy Spirit, was being overlooked. Later excavations have revealed that Nineveh had many suburbs, three of which are mentioned along with Nineveh in Gen. 10:11, 12. One first-century writer (Diodorus of Sicily) justifiably says that Nineveh was a quadrangle measuring about sixty miles in circuit—a "great city" indeed.

## New International Version

men greatly feared the LORD, and they offered a sacrifice to the LORD and made vows to him.

### Jonah's Prayer

¹⁷Now the LORD provided a huge fish to swallow Jonah, and Jonah was in the belly of the fish three days and three

**2**ᵃ nights. ¹From inside the fish Jonah prayed to the LORD his God. ²He said:

"In my distress I called to the LORD,
   and he answered me.
From deep in the realm of the dead I called for help,
   and you listened to my cry.
³You hurled me into the depths,
   into the very heart of the seas,
   and the currents swirled about me;
all your waves and breakers
   swept over me.
⁴I said, 'I have been banished
   from your sight;
yet I will look again
   toward your holy temple.'
⁵The engulfing waters threatened me,ᵇ
   the deep surrounded me;
   seaweed was wrapped around my head.
⁶To the roots of the mountains I sank down;
   the earth beneath barred me in forever.
But you, LORD my God,
   brought my life up from the pit.

⁷"When my life was ebbing away,
   I remembered you, LORD,
and my prayer rose to you,
   to your holy temple.

⁸"Those who cling to worthless idols
   turn away from God's love for them.
⁹But I, with shouts of grateful praise,
   will sacrifice to you.
What I have vowed I will make good.
   I will say, 'Salvation comes from the LORD.'"

¹⁰And the LORD commanded the fish, and it vomited Jonah onto dry land.

### Jonah Goes to Nineveh

**3** Then the word of the LORD came to Jonah a second time: ²"Go to the great city of Nineveh and proclaim to it the message I give you."

³Jonah obeyed the word of the LORD and went to Nineveh. Now Nineveh was a very large city; it took three days to go through it. ⁴Jonah began by going a day's journey into the city, proclaiming, "Forty more days and Nineveh will be overthrown." ⁵The Ninevites believed God. A fast was proclaimed, and all of them, from the greatest to the least, put on sackcloth.

⁶When Jonah's warning reached the king of Nineveh, he rose from his throne, took off his royal robes, covered himself with sackcloth and sat down in the dust. ⁷This is the proclamation he issued in Nineveh:

"By the decree of the king and his nobles:

Do not let people or animals, herds or flocks, taste anything; do not let them eat or drink. ⁸But let people and animals be covered with sackcloth. Let everyone call urgently on God. Let them give up their evil ways and their violence. ⁹Who knows? God may yet relent and with compassion turn from his fierce anger so that we will not perish."

ᵃ In Hebrew texts 2:1 is numbered 1:17, and 2:1-10 is numbered 2:2-11.
ᵇ 5 Or *waters were at my throat*

## Amplified Bible

¹⁶Then the men [reverently and worshipfully] feared the Lord exceedingly, and they offered a sacrifice to the Lord and made vows.

¹⁷Now the Lord had prepared *and* appointed a great fish to swallow up Jonah. And Jonah was in the belly of the fish three days and three nights. [Matt. 12:40.]

**2** Then Jonah prayed to the Lord his God from the fish's belly,

²And said, I cried out of my distress to the Lord, and He heard me; out of the belly of Sheol cried I, and You heard my voice. [Ps. 120:1; 130:1; 142:1; Lam. 3:55-58.]

³For You cast me into the deep, into the heart of the seas, and the floods surrounded me; all Your waves and Your billows passed over me. [Ps. 42:7.]

⁴Then I said, I have been cast out of Your presence *and* Your sight; yet I will look again toward Your holy temple. [Ps. 31:22.]

⁵The waters compassed me about, even to [the extinction of] life; the abyss surrounded me, the seaweed was wrapped about my head. [Ps. 69:1; Lam. 3:54.]

⁶I went down to the bottoms *and* the very roots of the mountains; the earth with its bars closed behind me forever. Yet You have brought up my life from the pit *and* corruption, O Lord my God.

⁷When my soul fainted upon me [crushing me], I earnestly *and* seriously remembered the Lord; and my prayer came to You, into Your holy temple.

⁸Those who pay regard to false, useless, *and* worthless idols forsake their own [Source of] mercy *and* lovingkindness.

⁹But as for me, I will sacrifice to You with the voice of thanksgiving; I will pay that which I have vowed. Salvation *and* deliverance belong to the Lord!

¹⁰And the Lord spoke to the fish, and it vomited out Jonah upon the dry land.

**3** And the word of the Lord came to Jonah the second time, saying,

²Arise, go to Nineveh, that great city, and preach *and* cry out to it the preaching that I tell you.

³So Jonah arose and went to Nineveh according to the word of the Lord. Now Nineveh was an exceedingly great city of three days' journey [sixty miles in circumference].

⁴And Jonah began to enter into the city a day's journey, and he cried, Yet forty days and Nineveh shall be overthrown!

⁵So the people of Nineveh believed in God and proclaimed a fast and put on sackcloth [in penitent mourning], from the greatest of them even to the least of them.

⁶For word came to the king of Nineveh [of all that had happened to Jonah, and his terrifying message from God], and he arose from his throne and he laid his robe aside, covered himself with sackcloth, and sat in ashes.

⁷And he made proclamation and published through Nineveh, By the decree of the king and his nobles: Let neither man nor beast, herd nor flock, taste anything; let them not feed nor drink water.

⁸But let man and beast be covered with sackcloth and let them cry mightily to God. Yes, let every one turn from his evil way and from the violence that is in his hands.

⁹Who can tell, God may turn and revoke His sentence against us [when we have met His terms], and turn away from His fierce anger so that we perish not. [Joel 2:13, 14.]

## New International Version

[10]When God saw what they did and how they turned from their evil ways, he relented and did not bring on them the destruction he had threatened.

### Jonah's Anger at the LORD's Compassion

**4** But to Jonah this seemed very wrong, and he became angry. [2]He prayed to the LORD, "Isn't this what I said, LORD, when I was still at home? That is what I tried to forestall by fleeing to Tarshish. I knew that you are a gracious and compassionate God, slow to anger and abounding in love, a God who relents from sending calamity. [3]Now, LORD, take away my life, for it is better for me to die than to live."

[4]But the LORD replied, "Is it right for you to be angry?"

[5]Jonah had gone out and sat down at a place east of the city. There he made himself a shelter, sat in its shade and waited to see what would happen to the city. [6]Then the LORD God provided a leafy plant[a] and made it grow up over Jonah to give shade for his head to ease his discomfort, and Jonah was very happy about the plant. [7]But at dawn the next day God provided a worm, which chewed the plant so that it withered. [8]When the sun rose, God provided a scorching east wind, and the sun blazed on Jonah's head so that he grew faint. He wanted to die, and said, "It would be better for me to die than to live."

[9]But God said to Jonah, "Is it right for you to be angry about the plant?"

"It is," he said. "And I'm so angry I wish I were dead."

[10]But the LORD said, "You have been concerned about this plant, though you did not tend it or make it grow. It sprang up overnight and died overnight. [11]And should I not have concern for the great city of Nineveh, in which there are more than a hundred and twenty thousand people who cannot tell their right hand from their left—and also many animals?"

## Amplified Bible

[10]And God saw their works, that they turned from their evil way; and God revoked His [sentence of] evil that He had said that He would do to them and He did not do it [for He was comforted and eased concerning them].

**4** But it displeased Jonah exceedingly and he was very angry. [2]And he prayed to the Lord and said, I pray You, O Lord, is not this just what I said when I was still in my country? That is why I fled to Tarshish, for I knew that You are a gracious God and merciful, slow to anger and of great kindness, and [when sinners turn to You and meet Your conditions] You revoke the [sentence of] evil against them. [Exod. 34:6.]

[3]Therefore now, O Lord, I beseech You, take my life from me, for it is better for me to die than to live.

[4]Then said the Lord, Do you do well to be angry?

[5]So Jonah went out of the city and sat to the east of the city, and he made a booth there for himself. He sat there under it in the shade till he might see what would become of the city.

[6]And the Lord God prepared a gourd and made it to come up over Jonah, that it might be a shade over his head, to deliver him from his evil situation. So Jonah was exceedingly glad [to have the protection] of the gourd.

[7]But God prepared a cutworm when the morning dawned the next day, and it smote the gourd so that it withered.

[8]And when the sun arose, God prepared a sultry east wind, and the sun beat upon the head of Jonah so that he fainted and wished in himself to die and said, It is better for me to die than to live.

[9]And God said to Jonah, Do you do well to be angry for the loss of the gourd? And he said, I do well to be angry, angry enough to die!

[10]Then said the Lord, You have had pity on the gourd, for which you have not labored nor made it grow, which came up in a night and perished in a night.

[11]And should not I spare Nineveh, that great city, in which there are more than 120,000 persons not [yet old enough to] know their right hand from their left, and also many cattle [not accountable for sin]?

---

[a] 6 The precise identification of this plant is uncertain; also in verses 7, 9 and 10.

# Micah

# Micah

**1** The word of the LORD that came to Micah of Moresh-eth during the reigns of Jotham, Ahaz and Hezekiah, kings of Judah—the vision he saw concerning Samaria and Jerusalem.

² Hear, you peoples, all of you,
  listen, earth and all who live in it,
  that the Sovereign LORD may bear witness against you,
  the Lord from his holy temple.

### Judgment Against Samaria and Jerusalem
³ Look! The LORD is coming from his dwelling place;
  he comes down and treads on the heights of the
    earth.
⁴ The mountains melt beneath him
  and the valleys split apart,
like wax before the fire,
  like water rushing down a slope.
⁵ All this is because of Jacob's transgression,
  because of the sins of the people of Israel.
What is Jacob's transgression?
  Is it not Samaria?
What is Judah's high place?
  Is it not Jerusalem?

⁶ "Therefore I will make Samaria a heap of rubble,
  a place for planting vineyards.
I will pour her stones into the valley
  and lay bare her foundations.
⁷ All her idols will be broken to pieces;
  all her temple gifts will be burned with fire;
  I will destroy all her images.
Since she gathered her gifts from the wages of
    prostitutes,
  as the wages of prostitutes they will again be used."

### Weeping and Mourning
⁸ Because of this I will weep and wail;
  I will go about barefoot and naked.
I will howl like a jackal
  and moan like an owl.
⁹ For Samaria's plague is incurable;
  it has spread to Judah.
It has reached the very gate of my people,
  even to Jerusalem itself.
¹⁰ Tell it not in Gath*a*;
  weep not at all.
In Beth Ophrah*b*
  roll in the dust.
¹¹ Pass by naked and in shame,
  you who live in Shaphir.*c*
Those who live in Zaanan*d*
  will not come out.
Beth Ezel is in mourning;
  it no longer protects you.
¹² Those who live in Maroth*e* writhe in pain,
  waiting for relief,
because disaster has come from the LORD,
  even to the gate of Jerusalem.
¹³ You who live in Lachish,
  harness fast horses to the chariot.
You are where the sin of Daughter Zion began,
  for the transgressions of Israel were found in you.

---

*a 10 Gath* sounds like the Hebrew for *tell.*     *b 10 Beth Ophrah* means
*house of dust.*     *c 11 Shaphir* means *pleasant.*     *d 11 Zaanan* sounds
like the Hebrew for *come out.*     *e 12 Maroth* sounds like the Hebrew
for *bitter.*

**1** The word of the Lord that came to Micah of Mo-resheth in the days of Jotham, Ahaz, and Hezekiah, kings of Judah, which he saw [through divine revelation] concerning Samaria and Jerusalem.

² Hear, all you people; listen closely, O earth and all that is in it, and let the Lord God be witness among you *and* against you, the Lord from His holy temple. [I Kings 22:28.]

³ For behold, the Lord comes forth out of His place and will come down and tread upon the high places of the earth. [Zech. 14:3, 4; Mal. 4:2, 3; Matt. 24:27-30; Rev. 1:7; 19:11-16.]

⁴ And the mountains shall melt under Him and the valleys shall be cleft like wax before the fire, like waters poured down a steep road.

⁵ All this is because of the transgression of Jacob and the sins of the house of Israel. What is the transgression of Jacob? Is it not [the idol worship of] Samaria? And what are the high places [of idolatry] in Judah? Are they not Jerusalem?

⁶ Therefore I [the Lord] will make Samaria a *a*heap in the open country, a place for planting vineyards; and I will pour down into the ravine her stones and lay bare her foundations. [II Kings 19:25; Ezek. 13:14.]

⁷ And all her carved images shall be broken in pieces, and all her hires [all that man would gain from desertion of God] shall be burned with fire, and all her idols will be laid waste; for from the hire of [one] harlot she gathered them, and to the hire of [another] harlot they shall return.

⁸ Therefore I [Micah] will lament and wail; I will go stripped and [virtually] naked; I will make a wailing like the jackals and a lamentation like the ostriches.

⁹ For [Samaria's] wounds are incurable and they come even to Judah; He [the Lord] has reached to the gate of my people, to Jerusalem.

¹⁰ In Gath [a city in Philistia] announce it not; *in b*Acco weep not at all, [betraying your grief to foreigners; but among your own people] in Beth-le-aphrah [house of dust] roll yourself in the dust.

¹¹ Pass on your way [into exile], dwellers of Shaphir, in shameful nakedness. The dwellers of Zaanan dare not come forth; the wailing of Beth-ezel takes away from you the place on which it stands.

¹² For the inhabitant of Maroth [bitterness] writhes in pain [at its losses] and waits anxiously for good, because evil comes down from the Lord to the gate of Jerusalem.

¹³ Bind the chariot to the swift steed, O lady inhabitant of Lachish; you were the beginning of sin to the Daughter of Zion, for the transgressions of Israel were found in you.

---

*a* Samaria was captured by the king of Assyria around 722 B.C. (II Kings
17:6), and was besieged and demolished by John Hyrcanus around 128
B.C. In his book *Syria and Palestine,* written in the nineteenth century,
Van de Velde, after visiting Sebaste or Samaria, wrote: "Samaria, a
heap of stones! Her foundations discovered, her streets plowed up and
covered with corn fields and olive gardens! Samaria has been destroyed;
her rubbish has been thrown down into the valley; her foundation stones
lie scattered about on the slope of the hill." Through the inspiration of
the omniscient and omnipotent God, Micah was able to foretell all this
more than 2,000 years before.     *b The Septuagint* (Greek translation of
the Old Testament) suggests this rendering: "in Acco weep not at all."
Acco was a coastal city about 25 miles south of Tyre.

## New International Version

14 Therefore you will give parting gifts
  to Moresheth Gath.
The town of Akzib*a* will prove deceptive
  to the kings of Israel.
15 I will bring a conqueror against you
  who live in Mareshah.*b*
The nobles of Israel
  will flee to Adullam.
16 Shave your head in mourning
  for the children in whom you delight;
make yourself as bald as the vulture,
  for they will go from you into exile.

### Human Plans and God's Plans

2 Woe to those who plan iniquity,
  to those who plot evil on their beds!
At morning's light they carry it out
  because it is in their power to do it.
2 They covet fields and seize them,
  and houses, and take them.
They defraud people of their homes,
  they rob them of their inheritance.

3 Therefore, the LORD says:

"I am planning disaster against this people,
  from which you cannot save yourselves.
You will no longer walk proudly,
  for it will be a time of calamity.
4 In that day people will ridicule you;
  they will taunt you with this mournful song:
'We are utterly ruined;
  my people's possession is divided up.
He takes it from me!
  He assigns our fields to traitors.'"

5 Therefore you will have no one in the assembly of the
  LORD
  to divide the land by lot.

### False Prophets

6 "Do not prophesy," their prophets say.
  "Do not prophesy about these things;
  disgrace will not overtake us."
7 You descendants of Jacob, should it be said,
  "Does the LORD become*c* impatient?
  Does he do such things?"

"Do not my words do good
  to the one whose ways are upright?
8 Lately my people have risen up
  like an enemy.
You strip off the rich robe
  from those who pass by without a care,
  like men returning from battle.
9 You drive the women of my people
  from their pleasant homes.
You take away my blessing
  from their children forever.
10 Get up, go away!
  For this is not your resting place,
because it is defiled,
  it is ruined, beyond all remedy.
11 If a liar and deceiver comes and says,
  'I will prophesy for you plenty of wine and beer,'
  that would be just the prophet for this people!

### Deliverance Promised

12 "I will surely gather all of you, Jacob;
  I will surely bring together the remnant of Israel.
I will bring them together like sheep in a pen,

## Amplified Bible

14 Therefore you must give parting gifts to Moresheth-
gath [Micah's home town]; the houses of Achzib [place of
deceit] shall be a deception to the kings of Israel.
15 Yet will I bring a conqueror upon you, O lady inhabitant of Mareshah, who shall possess you; the glory *and* nobility of Israel shall come to Adullam [to hide in the caves,
as did David]. [I Sam. 22:1.]
16 Make yourself bald in mourning and cut off your hair
for the children of your delight; enlarge your baldness as
the eagle, for [your children] shall be carried from you
into exile.

2 Woe to those who devise iniquity and work out evil
  upon their beds! When the morning is light, they perform *and* practice it because it is in their power.
2 They covet fields and seize them, and houses and take
them away; they oppress *and* crush a man and his house,
a man and his inheritance. [Isa. 5:8.]
3 Therefore thus says the Lord: Behold, against this
family I am planning a disaster from which you cannot
remove your necks, nor will you be able to walk erect; for
it will be an evil time.
4 In that day shall they take up a [taunting] parable
against you and wail with a doleful *and* bitter lamentation and say, We are utterly ruined *and* laid waste! [God]
changes the portion of my people. How He removes it from
me! He divides our fields [to the rebellious, our captors].
5 Therefore you shall have no one to cast a line by lot
upon a plot [of ground] in the assembly of the Lord. [Rev.
21:27.]
6 Do not preach, say the prophesying false prophets; one
should not babble *and* harp on such things; disgrace will
not overtake us [the reviling has no end].
7 O house of Jacob, shall it be said, Is the Spirit of the
Lord restricted, impatient, *and* shortened? Or are these
[prophesied plagues] His doings? Do not My words do
good to him who walks uprightly?
8 But lately (yesterday) My people have stood up as an
enemy [and have made Me their antagonist]. Off from the
garment you strip the cloak of those who pass by in secure
confidence of safety *and* are averse to war.
9 The women of My people you cast out from their pleasant houses; from their young children you take away My
glory forever.
10 Arise and depart, for this is not the rest [which was
promised to the righteous in Canaan], because of uncleanness that works destruction, even a sharp *and* grievous
destruction.
11 If a man walking in a spirit [of vanity] and in falsehood should lie and say, I will prophesy to you of wine and
strong drink, O Israel, he would even be the acceptable
prophet of this people! [Jer. 5:31.]
12 I will surely gather all of you, O Jacob; I will surely
collect the remnant of Israel. I will bring them [Israel] together like sheep in a fold, like a flock in the midst of their

---

*a 14 Akzib* means *deception.*  *b 15 Mareshah* sounds like the Hebrew
for *conqueror.*  *c 7* Or *Is the Spirit of the* LORD

## New International Version

like a flock in its pasture;
the place will throng with people.
¹³The One who breaks open the way will go up before
them;
they will break through the gate and go out.
Their King will pass through before them,
the LORD at their head."

### Leaders and Prophets Rebuked

**3** Then I said,

"Listen, you leaders of Jacob,
you rulers of Israel.
Should you not embrace justice,
² you who hate good and love evil;
who tear the skin from my people
and the flesh from their bones;
³who eat my people's flesh,
strip off their skin
and break their bones in pieces;
who chop them up like meat for the pan,
like flesh for the pot?"

⁴Then they will cry out to the LORD,
but he will not answer them.
At that time he will hide his face from them
because of the evil they have done.

⁵This is what the LORD says:

"As for the prophets
who lead my people astray,
they proclaim 'peace'
if they have something to eat,
but prepare to wage war against anyone
who refuses to feed them.
⁶Therefore night will come over you, without visions,
and darkness, without divination.
The sun will set for the prophets,
and the day will go dark for them.
⁷The seers will be ashamed
and the diviners disgraced.
They will all cover their faces
because there is no answer from God."
⁸But as for me, I am filled with power,
with the Spirit of the LORD,
and with justice and might,
to declare to Jacob his transgression,
to Israel his sin.

⁹Hear this, you leaders of Jacob,
you rulers of Israel,
who despise justice
and distort all that is right;
¹⁰who build Zion with bloodshed,
and Jerusalem with wickedness.
¹¹Her leaders judge for a bribe,
her priests teach for a price,
and her prophets tell fortunes for money.
Yet they look for the LORD's support and say,
"Is not the LORD among us?
No disaster will come upon us."
¹²Therefore because of you,
Zion will be plowed like a field,
Jerusalem will become a heap of rubble,
the temple hill a mound overgrown with thickets.

## Amplified Bible

pasture. They [the fold and the pasture] shall swarm with men *and* hum with much noise.
¹³The ᵃBreaker [the Messiah] will go up before them. They will break through, pass in through the gate and go out through it, and their King will pass on before them, the Lord at their head. [Exod. 23:20, 21; 33:14; Isa. 63:8, 9; Hos. 3:5; Amos 9:11.]

**3** And I [Micah] said, Hear, I pray you, you heads of Jacob and rulers of the house of Israel! Is it not for you to know justice?—
²You who hate the good and love the evil, who pluck *and* steal the skin from off [My people] and their flesh from off their bones;
³Yes, you who eat the flesh of my people and strip their skin from off them, who break their bones and chop them in pieces as for the pot, like meat in a big kettle.
⁴Then will they cry to the Lord, but He will not answer them; He will even hide His face from them at that time, because they have made their deeds evil. [Isa. 1:15.]
⁵Thus says the Lord: Concerning the false prophets who make My people err, when they have anything good to bite with their teeth they cry, Peace; and whoever gives them nothing to chew, against him they declare a sanctified war.
⁶Therefore it shall be night to you, so that you shall have no vision; yes, it shall be dark to you without divination. And the sun shall go down over the false prophets, and the day shall be black over them.
⁷And the seers shall be put to shame and the diviners shall blush *and* be confounded; yes, they shall all cover their lips, for there is no answer from God.
⁸But truly I [Micah] am full of power, of the Spirit of the Lord, and of justice and might, to declare to Jacob his transgression and to Israel his sin.
⁹Hear this, I pray you, you heads of the house of Jacob and rulers of the house of Israel, who abhor *and* reject justice and pervert all equity,
¹⁰Who build up Zion with blood and Jerusalem with iniquity.
¹¹Its heads judge for reward *and* a bribe and its priests teach for hire and its prophets divine for money; yet they lean on the Lord and say, Is not the Lord among us? No evil can come upon us. [Isa. 1:10-15.]
¹²Therefore shall Zion on your account be ᵇplowed like a field, Jerusalem shall become heaps [of ruins], and the mountain of the house [of the Lord] like a densely wooded height. [Jer. 26:17-19.]

---

ᵃ Over and over again the prophets unveiled the full dimensions of God's judgment and salvation. God must punish His rebellious people but will afterward redeem them. Israel will be carried into captivity, yet a remnant will return. The Messiah, the One who breaks open the way, will lead them back home, and will restore the kingdom of David. ᵇ In his book *The Land and the Book*, Dr. William Thomson wrote, "Mount Zion is now [in the eighteenth century], for the most part, a rough field. From the tomb of David I passed on through the fields of ripe grain. It is the only part of Jerusalem that is now or ever has been plowed." When Sultan Suleiman the Magnificent rebuilt the walls of Jerusalem in A.D. 1542, the architect omitted Mount Zion, the City of David, from the area he enclosed, and strangely enough it was only partly built up again. How, except by divine inspiration, could Micah have foretold that this particular part of Jerusalem would be "plowed like a field"?

## New International Version

### The Mountain of the Lord

**4** In the last days

the mountain of the Lord's temple will be established
as the highest of the mountains;
it will be exalted above the hills,
and peoples will stream to it.
2 Many nations will come and say,

"Come, let us go up to the mountain of the Lord,
to the temple of the God of Jacob.
He will teach us his ways,
so that we may walk in his paths."
The law will go out from Zion,
the word of the Lord from Jerusalem.
3 He will judge between many peoples
and will settle disputes for strong nations far and
wide.
They will beat their swords into plowshares
and their spears into pruning hooks.
Nation will not take up sword against nation,
nor will they train for war anymore.
4 Everyone will sit under their own vine
and under their own fig tree,
and no one will make them afraid,
for the Lord Almighty has spoken.
5 All the nations may walk
in the name of their gods,
but we will walk in the name of the Lord
our God for ever and ever.

### The Lord's Plan

6 "In that day," declares the Lord,

"I will gather the lame;
I will assemble the exiles
and those I have brought to grief.
7 I will make the lame my remnant,
those driven away a strong nation.
The Lord will rule over them in Mount Zion
from that day and forever.
8 As for you, watchtower of the flock,
stronghold*a* of Daughter Zion,
the former dominion will be restored to you;
kingship will come to Daughter Jerusalem."

9 Why do you now cry aloud—
have you no king*b*?
Has your ruler*c* perished,
that pain seizes you like that of a woman in labor?
10 Writhe in agony, Daughter Zion,
like a woman in labor,
for now you must leave the city
to camp in the open field.
You will go to Babylon;
there you will be rescued.
There the Lord will redeem you
out of the hand of your enemies.

11 But now many nations
are gathered against you.
They say, "Let her be defiled,
let our eyes gloat over Zion!"
12 But they do not know
the thoughts of the Lord;
they do not understand his plan,
that he has gathered them like sheaves to the
threshing floor.
13 "Rise and thresh, Daughter Zion,
for I will give you horns of iron;
I will give you hooves of bronze,
and you will break to pieces many nations."

*a 8 Or hill*   *b 9 Or King*   *c 9 Or Ruler*

## Amplified Bible

**4** But in the latter days it shall come to pass that the
mountain of the house of the Lord shall be established
as the highest of the mountains; and it shall be exalted
above the hills, and peoples shall flow to it.
2 And many nations shall come and say, Come, let us go
up to the mountain of the Lord, to the house of the God of
Jacob, that He may teach us His ways, and we may walk
in His paths. For the law shall go forth out of Zion and the
word of the Lord from Jerusalem.
3 And He shall judge between many peoples and shall
decide for strong nations afar off, and they shall beat their
swords into plowshares and their spears into pruning
hooks; nation shall not lift up sword against nation, neither shall they learn war any more. [Isa. 2:2-4; Joel 3:10.]
4 But they shall sit every man under his vine and under his fig tree, and none shall make them afraid, for the
mouth of the Lord of hosts has spoken it. [Zech. 3:10.]
5 For all the peoples [now] walk every man in the name
of his god, but we will walk in the name of the Lord our
God forever and ever.
6 In that day, says the Lord, I will assemble the lame, and
I will gather those who have been driven away and those
whom I have afflicted.
7 And I will make the lame a remnant, and those who
were cast off a strong nation; and the Lord shall reign over
them in Mount Zion from this time forth and forever.
8 And you, O tower of the flock, the hill *and* stronghold
of the Daughter of Zion, unto you the former dominion
shall come, the kingdom of the Daughter of Jerusalem.
9 Now why do you cry aloud? Is there no king among
you? Has your counselor perished, that pains have taken
you like a woman in labor?
10 Writhe in pain and labor to bring forth, O Daughter
of Zion, like a woman in childbirth; for now you shall go
forth out of the city and you shall live in the open country.
You shall go to Babylon; there you shall be rescued. There
the Lord shall redeem you from the hand of your enemies.
11 Now many nations are assembled against you, saying,
Let her be profaned and let our eyes gaze upon Zion.
12 But they know not the thoughts of the Lord, neither
do they understand His plan, for He shall gather them as
the sheaves to the threshing floor.
13 Arise and thresh, O Daughter of Zion! For I will make
your horn iron and I will make your hoofs bronze; you
shall beat in pieces many peoples, and I will devote their

| New International Version | Amplified Bible |
|---|---|

**New International Version**

You will devote their ill-gotten gains to the LORD,
their wealth to the Lord of all the earth.

### A Promised Ruler From Bethlehem

**5**[a] Marshal your troops now, city of troops,
for a siege is laid against us.
They will strike Israel's ruler
on the cheek with a rod.

2 "But you, Bethlehem Ephrathah,
though you are small among the clans[b] of Judah,
out of you will come for me
one who will be ruler over Israel,
whose origins are from of old,
from ancient times."

3 Therefore Israel will be abandoned
until the time when she who is in labor bears a son,
and the rest of his brothers return
to join the Israelites.

4 He will stand and shepherd his flock
in the strength of the LORD,
in the majesty of the name of the LORD his God.
And they will live securely, for then his greatness
will reach to the ends of the earth.

5 And he will be our peace
when the Assyrians invade our land
and march through our fortresses.
We will raise against them seven shepherds,
even eight commanders.

6 who will rule[c] the land of Assyria with the sword,
the land of Nimrod with drawn sword.[d]
He will deliver us from the Assyrians
when they invade our land
and march across our borders.

7 The remnant of Jacob will be
in the midst of many peoples
like dew from the LORD,
like showers on the grass,
which do not wait for anyone
or depend on man.

8 The remnant of Jacob will be among the nations,
in the midst of many peoples,
like a lion among the beasts of the forest,
like a young lion among flocks of sheep,
which mauls and mangles as it goes,
and no one can rescue.

9 Your hand will be lifted up in triumph over your
enemies,
and all your foes will be destroyed.

10 "In that day," declares the LORD,

"I will destroy your horses from among you
and demolish your chariots.

11 I will destroy the cities of your land
and tear down all your strongholds.

12 I will destroy your witchcraft
and you will no longer cast spells.

13 I will destroy your idols
and your sacred stones from among you;
you will no longer bow down
to the work of your hands.

14 I will uproot from among you your Asherah poles[e]
when I demolish your cities.

15 I will take vengeance in anger and wrath
on the nations that have not obeyed me."

**Amplified Bible**

gain to the Lord and their treasure to the Lord of all the
earth. [Zech. 12:1-8; 14:14.]

**5** Now gather yourself in troops, O daughter of troops;
a state of siege has been placed against us. They
shall smite the ruler of Israel with a rod (a scepter) on
the cheek.

2 But you, Bethlehem Ephrath, you are little to be
among the clans of Judah; [yet] out of you shall One come
forth for Me Who is to be Ruler in Israel, Whose goings
forth have been from of old, from ancient days (eternity).
[Gen. 49:10; Matt. 2:5-12; John 7:42.]

3 Therefore shall He give them up until the time that
she who travails has brought forth; then what is left of His
brethren shall return to the children of Israel.

4 And He shall stand and feed His flock in the strength
of the Lord, in the majesty of the name of the Lord His
God; and they shall dwell [secure], for then shall He be
great [even] to the ends of the earth. [Ps. 72:8; Isa. 40:11;
Zech. 9:10; Luke 1:32, 33.]

5 And this [One] shall be our peace. When the Assyrian
comes into our land and treads upon our soil *and* in our
palaces, then will we raise against him seven shepherds
and eight princes among men. [Isa. 9:6; Eph. 2:14.]

6 And they shall rule and waste the land of Assyria with
the sword and the land of Nimrod within her [Assyria's
own] gates. Thus shall He [the Messiah] deliver us from
the Assyrian [representing the opposing powers] when he
comes into our land and when he treads on our borders.

7 Then the remnant of Jacob shall be in the midst of
many peoples like dew from the Lord, like showers upon
the grass which [come suddenly and] tarry not for man
nor wait for the sons of men. [Ps. 72:6; 110:3.]

8 And the remnant of Jacob shall be among the nations
in the midst of many peoples like a lion among the beasts
of the forest, like a young lion [suddenly appearing]
among the flocks of sheep which, when it goes through,
treads down and tears in pieces, and there is no deliverer.

9 Your hand will be lifted up above your adversaries, and
all your enemies shall be cut off.

10 And in that day, says the Lord, I will cut off your
horses [on which you depend] from among you and will
destroy your chariots. [Ps. 20:7, 8; Zech. 9:10.]

11 And I will cut off the cities of your land and throw
down all your strongholds.

12 And I will cut off witchcrafts *and* sorceries from your
hand, and you shall have no more soothsayers.

13 Your carved images also I will cut off and your statues
*or* pillars out of your midst, and you shall no more worship
the work of your hands.

14 And I will root out your Asherim [symbols of the goddess Asherah] and I will destroy your cities [the seats of
false worship]. [Deut. 16:21.]

15 And in anger and wrath I will execute vengeance upon
the nations which would not obey [vengeance such as they
have not heard of before].

---

[a] In Hebrew texts 5:1 is numbered 4:14, and 5:2-15 is numbered 5:1-14.
[b] 2 Or *rulers*    [c] 6 Or *crush*    [d] 6 Or *Nimrod in its gates*    [e] 14 That is,
wooden symbols of the goddess Asherah

## New International Version

### The Lord's Case Against Israel

**6** Listen to what the Lord says:

"Stand up, plead my case before the mountains;
    let the hills hear what you have to say.

2 "Hear, you mountains, the Lord's accusation;
    listen, you everlasting foundations of the earth.
For the Lord has a case against his people;
    he is lodging a charge against Israel.

3 "My people, what have I done to you?
    How have I burdened you? Answer me.
4 I brought you up out of Egypt
    and redeemed you from the land of slavery.
I sent Moses to lead you,
    also Aaron and Miriam.
5 My people, remember
    what Balak king of Moab plotted
    and what Balaam son of Beor answered.
Remember your journey from Shittim to Gilgal,
    that you may know the righteous acts of the Lord."

6 With what shall I come before the Lord
    and bow down before the exalted God?
Shall I come before him with burnt offerings,
    with calves a year old?
7 Will the Lord be pleased with thousands of rams,
    with ten thousand rivers of olive oil?
Shall I offer my firstborn for my transgression,
    the fruit of my body for the sin of my soul?
8 He has shown you, O mortal, what is good.
    And what does the Lord require of you?
To act justly and to love mercy
    and to walk humbly[a] with your God.

### Israel's Guilt and Punishment

9 Listen! The Lord is calling to the city—
    and to fear your name is wisdom—
    "Heed the rod and the One who appointed it.[b]
10 Am I still to forget your ill-gotten treasures, you
        wicked house,
    and the short ephah,[c] which is accursed?
11 Shall I acquit someone with dishonest scales,
    with a bag of false weights?
12 Your rich people are violent;
    your inhabitants are liars
    and their tongues speak deceitfully.
13 Therefore, I have begun to destroy you,
    to ruin[d] you because of your sins.
14 You will eat but not be satisfied;
    your stomach will still be empty.[e]
You will store up but save nothing,
    because what you save[f] I will give to the sword.
15 You will plant but not harvest;
    you will press olives but not use the oil,
    you will crush grapes but not drink the wine.
16 You have observed the statutes of Omri
    and all the practices of Ahab's house;
    you have followed their traditions.
Therefore I will give you over to ruin
    and your people to derision;
    you will bear the scorn of the nations.[g]"

## Amplified Bible

**6** Hear now what the Lord says: Arise, contend *and* plead your case before the mountains, and let the hills hear your voice.

2 Hear, O mountains, the Lord's controversy, and you strong *and* enduring foundations of the earth, for the Lord has a controversy (a pleading contention) with His people, and He will [pleadingly] contend with Israel.

3 O My people, what have I done to you? And in what have I wearied you? Testify against Me [answer Me]!

4 For I brought you up out of the land of Egypt and redeemed you out of the house where you were bond servants, and I sent before you Moses, Aaron, and Miriam.

5 O My people, [earnestly] remember now what Balak king of Moab devised and what Balaam the son of Beor answered him; [remember] what the Lord did for you] from *a* Shittim to Gilgal, that you may know the righteous *and* saving acts of the Lord. [Num. 23:7-24; 24:3-24; Josh. 3:1; 4:19.]

6 With what shall I come before the Lord and bow myself before God on high? Shall I come before Him with burnt offerings, with calves a year old?

7 Will the Lord be pleased with thousands of rams or with ten thousands of rivers of oil? Shall I give my firstborn for my transgression, the fruit of my body for the sin of my soul?

8 He has showed you, O man, what is good. And what does the Lord require of you but to do justly, and to love kindness *and* mercy, and to humble yourself *and* walk humbly with your God? [Deut. 10:12, 13.]

9 The voice of the Lord calls to the city [Jerusalem]— and it is sound wisdom to hear *and* fear Your name—Hear (heed) the rod and Him Who has appointed it.

10 Are there not still treasures gained by wickedness in the house of the wicked, and a scant measure [a false measure for grain] that is abominable *and* accursed?

11 Can I be pure [Myself, and acquit the man] with wicked scales and with a bag of deceitful weights? [I Thess. 4:6.]

12 For [the city's] rich men are full of violence; her inhabitants have spoken lies and their tongues are deceitful in their mouths.

13 Therefore I have also smitten you with a deadly wound *and* made you sick, laying you desolate, waste, *and* deserted because of your sins.

14 You shall eat but not be satisfied, and your emptiness *and* hunger shall remain in you; you shall carry away [goods and those you love] but fail to save them, and those you do deliver I will give to the sword.

15 You shall sow but not reap; you shall tread olives but not anoint yourselves with oil, and [you shall extract juice from] the grapes but not drink the wine.

16 For the statutes of [idolatrous] Omri you have kept, and all the works of the house of [wicked] Ahab, and you walk in their counsels. Therefore I will make you a desolation *and* an astonishment and your [city's] inhabitants a hissing, and you shall bear the reproach *and* scorn of My people.

---

*a* 8 Or *prudently*    *b* 9 The meaning of the Hebrew for this line is uncertain.    *c* 10 An ephah was a dry measure.    *d* 13 Or *Therefore, I will make you ill and destroy you; / I will ruin*    *e* 14 The meaning of the Hebrew for this word is uncertain.    *f* 14 Or *You will press toward birth but not give birth, / and what you bring to birth*    *g* 16 Septuagint; Hebrew *scorn due my people*

*a* God reminds His people of His gracious acts in their behalf—how Balak sought to oppose Israel through pagan divination, sending for Balaam to put a curse on the Israelites; how God saved Israel by causing Balaam to bless instead of curse; and how God later led them across the Jordan River into the promised land, from Shittim (Josh. 3:1) to Gilgal (Josh. 4:19).

## New International Version

### Israel's Misery

**7** What misery is mine!
    I am like one who gathers summer fruit
        at the gleaning of the vineyard;
    there is no cluster of grapes to eat,
        none of the early figs that I crave.
[2] The faithful have been swept from the land;
        not one upright person remains.
    Everyone lies in wait to shed blood;
        they hunt each other with nets.
[3] Both hands are skilled in doing evil;
        the ruler demands gifts,
    the judge accepts bribes,
        the powerful dictate what they desire—
        they all conspire together.
[4] The best of them is like a brier,
        the most upright worse than a thorn hedge.
    The day God visits you has come,
        the day your watchmen sound the alarm.
    Now is the time of your confusion.
[5] Do not trust a neighbor;
        put no confidence in a friend.
    Even with the woman who lies in your embrace
        guard the words of your lips.
[6] For a son dishonors his father,
        a daughter rises up against her mother,
    a daughter-in-law against her mother-in-law—
        a man's enemies are the members of his own
            household.
[7] But as for me, I watch in hope for the LORD,
        I wait for God my Savior;
    my God will hear me.

### Israel Will Rise

[8] Do not gloat over me, my enemy!
        Though I have fallen, I will rise.
    Though I sit in darkness,
        the LORD will be my light.
[9] Because I have sinned against him,
        I will bear the LORD's wrath,
    until he pleads my case
        and upholds my cause.
    He will bring me out into the light;
        I will see his righteousness.
[10] Then my enemy will see it
        and will be covered with shame,
    she who said to me,
        "Where is the LORD your God?"
    My eyes will see her downfall;
        even now she will be trampled underfoot
            like mire in the streets.

[11] The day for building your walls will come,
        the day for extending your boundaries.
[12] In that day people will come to you
        from Assyria and the cities of Egypt,
    even from Egypt to the Euphrates
        and from sea to sea
        and from mountain to mountain.
[13] The earth will become desolate because of its
            inhabitants,
        as the result of their deeds.

### Prayer and Praise

[14] Shepherd your people with your staff,
        the flock of your inheritance,
    which lives by itself in a forest,
        in fertile pasturelands.[a]
    Let them feed in Bashan and Gilead
        as in days long ago.

*a 14 Or in the middle of Carmel*

## Amplified Bible

**7** Woe is me! For I am as when the summer fruits have been gathered, as when the vintage grapes have been gleaned and there is no cluster to eat, no first-ripe fig for which my appetite craves.

[2] The godly man has perished from the earth, and there is none upright among men. They all lie in wait for blood; each hunts his brother with a net.

[3] Both their hands are put forth *and* are upon what is evil to do it diligently; the prince and the judge ask for a bribe, and the great man utters his evil desire. Thus they twist between them [the course of justice].

[4] The best of them is like a brier; the most upright *or* the straightest is like a thorn hedge. The day of your watchmen, even of [God's] judgment *and* your punishment, has come; now shall be their perplexity *and* confusion.

[5] Trust not in a neighbor; put no confidence in a friend. Keep the doors of your mouth from her who lies in your bosom. [Luke 12:51-53.]

[6] For the son dishonors the father, the daughter rises up against her mother, the daughter-in-law against her mother-in-law—a man's enemies are the men (members) of his own house. [Matt. 10:21, 35, 36; Mark 13:12, 13.]

[7] But as for me, I will look to the Lord *and* confident in Him I will keep watch; I will wait with hope *and* expectancy for the God of my salvation; my God will hear me.

[8] Rejoice not against me, O my enemy! When I fall, I shall arise; when I sit in darkness, the Lord shall be a light to me.

[9] I will bear the indignation of the Lord because I have sinned against Him, until He pleads my cause and executes judgment for me. He will bring me forth to the light, and I shall behold His righteous deliverance. [Rom. 10:1-4; 11:23-27.]

[10] Then my enemy will see it, and shame will cover her who said to me, Where is the Lord your God? My eyes will see my desire upon her; now she will be trodden down as the mire of the streets.

[11] In the day that your walls are to be built [a day for building], in that day shall the boundary [of Israel] be far extended *and* the decree [against her] be far removed. [Isa. 33:17; Amos 9:11.]

[12] In that day they will come to you from Assyria and from the cities of Matzor [Egypt] and from Egypt even to the river [Euphrates], from sea to sea and from mountain to mountain.

[13] Yet shall the earth be desolate because of those who dwell in it, for the fruit of their doings.

[14] Rule *and* feed Your people with Your rod *and* scepter, the flock of Your inheritance who dwell alone in a forest in the midst of Carmel [a garden land]; they shall feed in Bashan and Gilead, as in the days of old.

## New International Version

15 "As in the days when you came out of Egypt,
    I will show them my wonders."

16 Nations will see and be ashamed,
    deprived of all their power.
They will put their hands over their mouths
    and their ears will become deaf.
17 They will lick dust like a snake,
    like creatures that crawl on the ground.
They will come trembling out of their dens;
    they will turn in fear to the LORD our God
    and will be afraid of you.
18 Who is a God like you,
    who pardons sin and forgives the transgression
    of the remnant of his inheritance?
You do not stay angry forever
    but delight to show mercy.
19 You will again have compassion on us;
    you will tread our sins underfoot
    and hurl all our iniquities into the depths of the sea.
20 You will be faithful to Jacob,
    and show love to Abraham,
as you pledged on oath to our ancestors
    in days long ago.

## Amplified Bible

15 As in the days of your coming forth from the land of Egypt, I will show them marvelous things.
16 The nations shall see [God's deliverance] and be ashamed of all their might [which cannot be compared to His]. They shall lay their hands upon their mouths in consternation; their ears shall be deaf.
17 They shall lick the dust like a serpent; like crawling things of the earth they shall come trembling out of their strongholds and close places. They shall turn and come with fear and dread to the Lord our God and shall be afraid and stand in awe because of You [O Lord]. [Jer. 33:9.]
18 Who is a God like You, Who forgives iniquity and passes over the transgression of the remnant of His heritage? He retains not His anger forever, because He delights in mercy and loving-kindness.
19 He will again have compassion on us; He will subdue and tread underfoot our iniquities. You will cast all our sins into the depths of the sea. [Ps. 103:12.]
20 You will show Your faithfulness and perform the sure promise to Jacob and loving-kindness and mercy to Abraham, as You have sworn to our fathers from the days of old. [Luke 1:54, 55.]

THE BOOK OF

# Nahum

# Nahum

**1** A prophecy concerning Nineveh. The book of the vision of Nahum the Elkoshite.

**1** The burden *or* oracle (the thing to be lifted up) concerning *a*Nineveh [the capital of Assyria]. The book of the vision of Nahum of Elkosh.

### The Lord's Anger Against Nineveh

<sup>2</sup>The Lord is a jealous and avenging God;
the Lord takes vengeance and is filled with wrath.
The Lord takes vengeance on his foes
and vents his wrath against his enemies.
<sup>3</sup>The Lord is slow to anger but great in power;
the Lord will not leave the guilty unpunished.
His way is in the whirlwind and the storm,
and clouds are the dust of his feet.
<sup>4</sup>He rebukes the sea and dries it up;
he makes all the rivers run dry.
Bashan and Carmel wither
and the blossoms of Lebanon fade.
<sup>5</sup>The mountains quake before him
and the hills melt away.
The earth trembles at his presence,
the world and all who live in it.
<sup>6</sup>Who can withstand his indignation?
Who can endure his fierce anger?
His wrath is poured out like fire;
the rocks are shattered before him.

<sup>7</sup>The Lord is good,
a refuge in times of trouble.
He cares for those who trust in him,
<sup>8</sup>  but with an overwhelming flood
he will make an end of Nineveh;
he will pursue his foes into the realm of darkness.

<sup>9</sup>Whatever they plot against the Lord
he will bring*a* to an end;
trouble will not come a second time.
<sup>10</sup>They will be entangled among thorns
and drunk from their wine;
they will be consumed like dry stubble.*b*
<sup>11</sup>From you, Nineveh, has one come forth
who plots evil against the Lord
and devises wicked plans.

<sup>12</sup>This is what the Lord says:

"Although they have allies and are numerous,
they will be destroyed and pass away.
Although I have afflicted you, Judah,
I will afflict you no more.
<sup>13</sup>Now I will break their yoke from your neck
and tear your shackles away."

<sup>2</sup>The Lord is a jealous God and avenging; the Lord avenges and He is full of wrath. The Lord takes vengeance on His adversaries and reserves wrath for His enemies. [Exod. 20:5.]
<sup>3</sup>The Lord is slow to anger and great in power and will by no means clear the guilty. The Lord has His way in the whirlwind and in the storm, and the clouds are the dust of His feet. [Exod. 34:6, 7.]
<sup>4</sup>He rebukes *and* threatens the sea and makes it dry, and dries up all the rivers. Bashan [on the east] and Mount Carmel [on the west] wither, and [in the north] the blossom of Lebanon fades.
<sup>5</sup>The mountains tremble *and* quake before Him and the hills melt away, and the earth is upheaved at His presence—yes, the world and all that dwell in it.
<sup>6</sup>Who can stand before His indignation? And who can stand up *and* endure the fierceness of His anger? His wrath is poured out like fire, and the rocks are broken asunder by Him.
<sup>7</sup>The Lord is good, a Strength *and* Stronghold in the day of trouble; He knows (recognizes, has knowledge of, and understands) those who take refuge *and* trust in Him. [Ps. 1:6; Hos. 13:5; John 10:14, 27.]
<sup>8</sup>But with an *b*overrunning flood He will make a full end of [Nineveh's very] site and pursue His enemies into darkness.
<sup>9</sup>What do you devise *and* [how mad is your attempt to] plot against the Lord? He will make a full end [of Nineveh]; affliction [which My people shall suffer from Assyria] shall not rise up the second time.
<sup>10</sup>For [the Ninevites] are as bundles of thorn branches [for fuel], and even while drowned in their drunken [carousing] they shall be consumed like stubble fully dry [in the day of the Lord's wrath]. [Mal. 4:1.]
<sup>11</sup>There is one gone forth out of you [O Nineveh] who plots evil against the Lord, a villainous *c*counselor [the king of Assyria, who counsels for wickedness and worthlessness]. [II Kings 19:20-23; Isa. 10:5-7; 36:15-20.]
<sup>12</sup>Thus says the Lord: Though they be in full strength and likewise many, even so shall [the Assyrians] be cut down when [their evil counselor] shall pass away. Though I have afflicted you [Jerusalem], I will not cause you to be afflicted [for your past sins] any more. [II Kings 19:35-37; John 5:14.]
<sup>13</sup>For now will I break his yoke from off you and will burst your bonds asunder. [Isa. 14:25.]

---

*a* Under the preaching of Jonah, the king of Nineveh and all its people repented (Jonah 3:5). They must not only have heard his startling testimony of the terrible suffering which running away from obedience to God had cost him, but they must have been terrified at the evidence of the truth of his near-death experience in the belly of the great fish. So the whole city turned to God. But when Nahum came to Nineveh some 150 years later, all that was forgotten, and the later generations had become hopelessly godless. God's wrath was not to be turned away this time. Jonah had been sent to preach, "Repent!" But Nahum's one "burden (the thing to be lifted up)" is the message that Nineveh is to be destroyed—utterly. *b* Countless authorities confirm the literal accuracy of this reference. Diodorus of Sicily refers to a legend that Nineveh could never be taken until the river became its enemy. Arbaces the Scythian had besieged the city in vain for two years, but in the third year, the river Khoser during a flood season washed away a considerable section of the very great wall, and through this opening the besiegers gained entrance. Nah. 2:6 refers to the devastating flood, and 3:13, 15 probably to the destruction of Nineveh by fire. The vivid descriptions of chapter 3 "are true to their records and their sculptures." *c* The reference here may be to Sennacherib, who reigned over Assyria from 705-681 B.C.

---

*a* 9 Or *What do you foes plot against the Lord? / He will bring it*
*b* 10 The meaning of the Hebrew for this verse is uncertain.

## New International Version

[14] The Lord has given a command concerning you,
  Nineveh:
"You will have no descendants to bear your name.
I will destroy the images and idols
  that are in the temple of your gods.
I will prepare your grave,
  for you are vile."

[15] Look, there on the mountains,[a]
  the feet of one who brings good news,
  who proclaims peace!
Celebrate your festivals, Judah,
  and fulfill your vows.
No more will the wicked invade you;
  they will be completely destroyed.[a]

### Nineveh to Fall

**2**[b] An attacker advances against you, Nineveh.
  Guard the fortress,
  watch the road,
  brace yourselves,
  marshal all your strength!

[2] The Lord will restore the splendor of Jacob
  like the splendor of Israel,
though destroyers have laid them waste
  and have ruined their vines.

[3] The shields of the soldiers are red;
  the warriors are clad in scarlet.
The metal on the chariots flashes
  on the day they are made ready;
  the spears of juniper are brandished.[c]
[4] The chariots storm through the streets,
  rushing back and forth through the squares.
They look like flaming torches;
  they dart about like lightning.
[5] Nineveh summons her picked troops,
  yet they stumble on their way.
They dash to the city wall;
  the protective shield is put in place.
[6] The river gates are thrown open
  and the palace collapses.
[7] It is decreed[d] that Nineveh
  be exiled and carried away.
Her female slaves moan like doves
  and beat on their breasts.
[8] Nineveh is like a pool
  whose water is draining away.
"Stop! Stop!" they cry,
  but no one turns back.
[9] Plunder the silver!
  Plunder the gold!
The supply is endless,
  the wealth from all its treasures!
[10] She is pillaged, plundered, stripped!
  Hearts melt, knees give way,
  bodies tremble, every face grows pale.

[11] Where now is the lions' den,
  the place where they fed their young,
where the lion and lioness went,
  and the cubs, with nothing to fear?
[12] The lion killed enough for his cubs
  and strangled the prey for his mate,
filling his lairs with the kill
  and his dens with the prey.

[13] "I am against you,"
  declares the Lord Almighty.

## Amplified Bible

[14] And the Lord has given a commandment concerning you [evil Assyrian counselor], that no more of your name shall be born nor shall your name be perpetuated. Out of the house of your gods I will cut off the graven and molten images; I will make [their temple] your tomb, for you are vile and despised. [Isa. 37:38.]
[15] Behold! upon the mountains the feet of him who brings good tidings [telling of the Assyrian's death], who publishes peace! Celebrate your feasts, O Judah; perform your vows. For the wicked counselor [the king of Assyria] shall no more come against you or pass through your land; he is utterly cut off. [Isa. 52:7; Rom. 10:15.] [Then the prophet Nahum sarcastically addresses his message to Nineveh:]

**2** He who dashes in pieces [that is, the king of Medo-Babylon] is come up before your face [Nineveh]. Keep the fortress and ramparts manned, watch the road, gird your loins, collect and fortify all your strength and power mightily.
[2] For the Lord restores the excellency of Jacob as the excellency of [ancient] Israel, for plunderers have plundered them and emptied them out and [outrageously] destroyed their vine branches. [Isa. 10:12.]
[3] The shields of the mighty men [of Media and Babylon] are [dyed] red; the valiant men are [clothed] in dyed scarlet. The chariots blaze with fire of steel on the day of his preparation [for battle], and the officers' horses prance like a cypress forest [reeling in the wind].
[4] The chariots rage in confusion in the streets; they run to and fro [in wild terror] in the broad ways. They flash with steel [making them appear like torches]; they rush [in various directions] like forked lightnings.
[5] [The Assyrian leader] remembers and summons his bravest men; they stumble in their march. They hasten to the city's wall, and their movable defense shelter is prepared and set up.
[6] The gates or dams of the rivers [surrounding and guarding Nineveh] are opened and the [imperial] palace [of sun-dried brick] is dissolved [by the torrents] and is in dismay.
[7] It is decreed. She [Nineveh] is stripped and removed, and her maids are lamenting and moaning like doves [softly for fear], beating upon their breasts [and hearts].
[8] And Nineveh, like a standing pool are her waters and [her inhabitants] are fleeing away! Stand! Stand [firm! a few cry], but no one looks back or causes them to return.
[9] Take the spoil of silver; take the spoil of gold! For there is no end of the treasure, the glory and wealth of all the precious furnishings.
[10] Emptiness! Desolation! Utter waste! Hearts faint and knees smite together, and anguish is in all loins, and the faces of all grow pale! [Isa. 13:7, 8.]
[11] Where is the den of the lions which was the feeding place of the young lions, where the lion and the lioness walked, and the lion's whelp, and none made them afraid?
[12] The lion tore in pieces enough for his whelps and strangled [prey] for his lionesses; he filled his caves with prey and his dens with what he had seized and carried off.
[13] Behold, I am against you [Nineveh], says the Lord of

---

[a] 15 In Hebrew texts this verse (1:15) is numbered 2:1.   [b] In Hebrew texts 2:1-13 is numbered 2:2-14.   [c] 3 Hebrew; Septuagint and Syriac ready; / the horsemen rush to and fro.   [d] 7 The meaning of the Hebrew for this word is uncertain.

## New International Version

"I will burn up your chariots in smoke,
  and the sword will devour your young lions.
I will leave you no prey on the earth.
The voices of your messengers
  will no longer be heard."

### Woe to Nineveh

**3** Woe to the city of blood,
  full of lies,
full of plunder,
  never without victims!
[2] The crack of whips,
  the clatter of wheels,
galloping horses
  and jolting chariots!
[3] Charging cavalry,
  flashing swords
  and glittering spears!
Many casualties,
  piles of dead,
bodies without number,
  people stumbling over the corpses—
[4] all because of the wanton lust of a prostitute,
  alluring, the mistress of sorceries,
who enslaved nations by her prostitution
  and peoples by her witchcraft.

[5] "I am against you," declares the LORD Almighty.
  "I will lift your skirts over your face.
I will show the nations your nakedness
  and the kingdoms your shame.
[6] I will pelt you with filth,
  I will treat you with contempt
  and make you a spectacle.
[7] All who see you will flee from you and say,
  'Nineveh is in ruins—who will mourn for her?'
Where can I find anyone to comfort you?"

[8] Are you better than Thebes,
  situated on the Nile,
  with water around her?
The river was her defense,
  the waters her wall.
[9] Cush[a] and Egypt were her boundless strength;
  Put and Libya were among her allies.
[10] Yet she was taken captive
  and went into exile.
Her infants were dashed to pieces
  at every street corner.
Lots were cast for her nobles,
  and all her great men were put in chains.
[11] You too will become drunk;
  you will go into hiding
  and seek refuge from the enemy.

[12] All your fortresses are like fig trees
  with their first ripe fruit;
when they are shaken,
  the figs fall into the mouth of the eater.
[13] Look at your troops—
  they are all weaklings.
The gates of your land
  are wide open to your enemies;
  fire has consumed the bars of your gates.

[14] Draw water for the siege,
  strengthen your defenses!
Work the clay,
  tread the mortar,
  repair the brickwork!

## Amplified Bible

hosts, and I will burn *your* chariots in the smoke, and the sword shall devour your young lions. And I will cut off your prey from the earth, and the voice of your messengers shall no more be heard.

**3** Woe to the bloody city! It is full of lies and booty and [there is] no end to the plunder! [Ezek. 24:6, 9, 10; Hab. 2:12.]
[2] The cracking of the whip, the noise of the rattling of wheels, and prancing horses and chariots rumbling *and* bounding,
[3] Horsemen mounting *and* charging, the flashing sword, the gleaming spear, a multitude of slain and a great number of corpses, no end of corpses! [The horsemen] stumble over the corpses!
[4] All because of the multitude of the harlotries [of Nineveh], the well-favored harlot, the mistress of deadly charms who betrays *and* sells nations through her whoredoms [idolatry] and peoples through her enchantments.
[5] Behold, I am against you, says the Lord of hosts, and I will lift up your skirts over your face, and I will let the nations look on your nakedness [O Nineveh] and the kingdoms on your shame.
[6] I will cast abominable things at you *and* make you filthy, treat you with contempt, and make you a gazingstock.
[7] And all who look on you will shrink *and* flee from you and say, Nineveh is laid waste; who will pity *and* bemoan her? Where [then] shall I seek comforters for you?
[8] Are you better than No-amon [Thebes, capital of Upper Egypt], that dwelt by the rivers *or* canals, that had the waters round about her, whose rampart was a sea [the Nile] and water her wall?
[9] Ethiopia and Egypt were her strength, and that without limit. Put and the Libyans were *her* helpers.
[10] Yet she was carried away; she went into captivity. Her young children also were dashed in pieces at all the street corners; lots were cast [by the Assyrian officers] for her nobles, and all her great men were bound with chains.
[11] You will be drunk [Nineveh, with the cup of God's wrath]; you will be dazed. You will seek *and* require a refuge because of the enemy.
[12] All your fortresses are fig trees with early figs; if they are shaken they will fall into the mouth of the eater.
[13] Behold, your troops in the midst of you are [as weak and helpless as] women; the gates of your land are set wide open to your enemies [without effort]; fire consumes your bars.
[14] Draw for yourself the water [necessary] for a [long continued] siege, make strong your fortresses! Go down into the clay pits and trample the mortar; make ready the brickkiln [to burn bricks for the bulwarks]!

---

*a* 9 That is, the upper Nile region

## New International Version

<sup>15</sup>There the fire will consume you;
the sword will cut you down—
they will devour you like a swarm of locusts.
Multiply like grasshoppers,
multiply like locusts!
<sup>16</sup>You have increased the number of your merchants
till they are more numerous than the stars in the
sky,
but like locusts they strip the land
and then fly away.
<sup>17</sup>Your guards are like locusts,
your officials like swarms of locusts
that settle in the walls on a cold day—
but when the sun appears they fly away,
and no one knows where.
<sup>18</sup>King of Assyria, your shepherds<sup>a</sup> slumber;
your nobles lie down to rest.
Your people are scattered on the mountains
with no one to gather them.
<sup>19</sup>Nothing can heal you;
your wound is fatal.
All who hear the news about you
clap their hands at your fall,
for who has not felt
your endless cruelty?

## Amplified Bible

<sup>15</sup>[But] there [in the very midst of these preparations] will the fire devour you; the sword will cut you off; it will destroy you as the locusts [destroy]. Multiply yourselves like the licking locusts; make yourselves many like the swarming locusts!
<sup>16</sup>You increased your merchants more than the [visible] stars of the heavens. The swarming locust spreads itself *and* destroys, and then flies away.
<sup>17</sup>Your princes are like the grasshoppers and your marshals like the swarms of locusts which encamp in the hedges on a cold day—but when the sun rises, they fly away, and no one knows where they are.
<sup>18</sup>Your shepherds are asleep, O king of Assyria; your nobles are lying still [in death]. Your people are scattered on the mountains and there is no one to gather them.
<sup>19</sup>There is no healing of your hurt; your wound is grievous. All who hear the news about you clap their hands over [what has happened to] you. For upon whom has not your [unceasing] evil come continually?

# New International Version

## Habakkuk

**1** The prophecy that Habakkuk the prophet received.

### Habakkuk's Complaint

[2] How long, LORD, must I call for help,
   but you do not listen?
Or cry out to you, "Violence!"
   but you do not save?
[3] Why do you make me look at injustice?
   Why do you tolerate wrongdoing?
Destruction and violence are before me;
   there is strife, and conflict abounds.
[4] Therefore the law is paralyzed,
   and justice never prevails.
The wicked hem in the righteous,
   so that justice is perverted.

### The LORD's Answer

[5] "Look at the nations and watch—
   and be utterly amazed.
For I am going to do something in your days
   that you would not believe,
   even if you were told.
[6] I am raising up the Babylonians,[a]
   that ruthless and impetuous people,
who sweep across the whole earth
   to seize dwellings not their own.
[7] They are a feared and dreaded people;
   they are a law to themselves
   and promote their own honor.
[8] Their horses are swifter than leopards,
   fiercer than wolves at dusk.
Their cavalry gallops headlong;
   their horsemen come from afar.
They fly like an eagle swooping to devour;
[9]   they all come intent on violence.
Their hordes[b] advance like a desert wind
   and gather prisoners like sand.
[10] They mock kings
   and scoff at rulers.
They laugh at all fortified cities;
   by building earthen ramps they capture them.
[11] Then they sweep past like the wind and go on—
   guilty people, whose own strength is their god."

### Habakkuk's Second Complaint

[12] LORD, are you not from everlasting?
   My God, my Holy One, you[c] will never die.
You, LORD, have appointed them to execute judgment;
   you, my Rock, have ordained them to punish.
[13] Your eyes are too pure to look on evil;
   you cannot tolerate wrongdoing.
Why then do you tolerate the treacherous?
   Why are you silent while the wicked
swallow up those more righteous than themselves?
[14] You have made people like the fish in the sea,
   like the sea creatures that have no ruler.
[15] The wicked foe pulls all of them up with hooks,
   he catches them in his net,
he gathers them up in his dragnet;
   and so he rejoices and is glad.
[16] Therefore he sacrifices to his net
   and burns incense to his dragnet,
for by his net he lives in luxury
   and enjoys the choicest food.

[a] 6 Or *Chaldeans*   [b] 9 The meaning of the Hebrew for this word is
uncertain.   [c] 12 An ancient Hebrew scribal tradition; Masoretic
Text *we*

# Amplified Bible

## Habakkuk

**1** The burden *or* oracle (the thing to be lifted up) which Habakkuk the prophet saw.

[2] O Lord, how long shall I cry for help and You will not hear? Or cry out to You of violence and You will not save?

[3] Why do You show me iniquity *and* wrong, and Yourself look upon *or* cause me to see perverseness *and* trouble? For destruction and violence are before me; and there is strife, and contention arises.

[4] Therefore the law is slackened and justice *and* a righteous sentence never go forth, for the [hostility of the] wicked surrounds the [uncompromisingly] righteous; therefore justice goes forth perverted.

[5] Look around [you, Habakkuk, replied the Lord] among the nations and see! Be astonished! Astounded! For I am putting into effect a work in your days [such] that you would not believe it if it were told you. [Acts 13:40, 41.]

[6] For behold, I am rousing up the Chaldeans, that bitter and impetuous nation who march through the breadth of the earth to take possession of dwelling places that do not belong to them. [II Kings 24:2.]

[7] [The Chaldeans] are terrible and dreadful; their justice and dignity proceed [only] from themselves.

[8] Their horses also are swifter than leopards and are fiercer than the evening wolves, and their horsemen spread themselves *and* press on proudly; yes, their horsemen come from afar; they fly like an eagle that hastens to devour.

[9] They all come for violence; their faces turn eagerly forward, and they gather prisoners together like sand.

[10] They scoff at kings, and rulers are a derision to them; they ridicule every stronghold, for they heap up dust [for earth mounds] and take it.

[11] Then they sweep by like a wind and pass on, and they load themselves with guilt, [as do all men] whose own power is their god.

[12] Are not You from everlasting, O Lord my God, my Holy One? We shall not die. O Lord, You have appointed [the Chaldean] to execute [Your] judgment, and You, O Rock, have established him for chastisement *and* correction. [Deut. 32:4.]

[13] You are of purer eyes than to behold evil and can not look [inactively] upon injustice. Why then do You look upon the plunderer? Why are you silent when the wicked one destroys him who is more righteous than [the Chaldean oppressor] is?

[14] Why do You make men like the fish of the sea, like reptiles *and* creeping things that have no ruler [and are defenseless against their foes]?

[15] [The Chaldean] brings all of them up with his hook; he catches and drags them out with his net, he gathers them in his dragnet; so he rejoices and is in high spirits.

[16] Therefore he sacrifices [offerings] to his net and burns incense to his dragnet, because from them he lives luxuriously and his food is plentiful *and* rich.

## New International Version

17 Is he to keep on emptying his net,
    destroying nations without mercy?

**2** I will stand at my watch
    and station myself on the ramparts;
I will look to see what he will say to me,
    and what answer I am to give to this complaint.*a*

### The LORD's Answer

2 Then the LORD replied:

"Write down the revelation
    and make it plain on tablets
    so that a herald*b* may run with it.
3 For the revelation awaits an appointed time;
    it speaks of the end
    and will not prove false.
Though it linger, wait for it;
    it*c* will certainly come
    and will not delay.

4 "See, the enemy is puffed up;
    his desires are not upright—
    but the righteous person will live by his
        faithfulness*d*—
5 indeed, wine betrays him;
    he is arrogant and never at rest.
Because he is as greedy as the grave
    and like death is never satisfied,
he gathers to himself all the nations
    and takes captive all the peoples.

6 "Will not all of them taunt him with ridicule and scorn,
saying,

"'Woe to him who piles up stolen goods
    and makes himself wealthy by extortion!
    How long must this go on?'
7 Will not your creditors suddenly arise?
    Will they not wake up and make you tremble?
    Then you will become their prey.
8 Because you have plundered many nations,
    the peoples who are left will plunder you.
For you have shed human blood;
    you have destroyed lands and cities and everyone in
        them.

9 "Woe to him who builds his house by unjust gain,
    setting his nest on high
    to escape the clutches of ruin!
10 You have plotted the ruin of many peoples,
    shaming your own house and forfeiting your life.
11 The stones of the wall will cry out,
    and the beams of the woodwork will echo it.

12 "Woe to him who builds a city with bloodshed
    and establishes a town by injustice!
13 Has not the LORD Almighty determined
    that the people's labor is only fuel for the fire,
    that the nations exhaust themselves for nothing?
14 For the earth will be filled with the knowledge of the
        glory of the LORD
    as the waters cover the sea.

## Amplified Bible

17 Shall he therefore continue to empty his net and mer-
cilessly go on slaying the nations forever?

**2** [Oh, I know, I have been rash to talk out plainly this
    way to God!] I will [in my thinking] stand upon my
post of observation and station myself on the tower *or* fortress, and will watch to see what He will say within me
and what answer I will make [as His mouthpiece] to the
perplexities of my complaint against Him.
2 And the Lord answered me and said, Write the vision
and engrave it so plainly upon tablets that everyone who
passes may [be able to] read [it easily and quickly] as he
hastens by.
3 For the vision is yet for an appointed time and it hastens to the end [fulfillment]; it will not deceive *or* disap-
point. Though it tarry, wait [earnestly] for it, because it
will surely come; it will not be behindhand on its appointed
day. [Heb. 10:37, 38.]
4 Look at the proud; his soul is not straight *or* right within him, but the [rigidly] just *and* the [uncompromisingly]
righteous man shall *a*live by his faith *and* in his faithfulness. [Rom. 1:17; Gal. 3:11.]
5 Moreover, wine *and* *b*wealth are treacherous; the proud
man [the Chaldean invader] is restless *and* cannot stay
at home. His appetite is large like that of Sheol and [his
greed] is like death and cannot be satisfied; he gathers to
himself all nations and collects all people as if he owned
them.
6 Shall not all these [victims of his greed] take up a taunt
against him and in scoffing derision of him say, Woe to
him who piles up that which is not his! [How long will
he possess it?] And [woe to him] who loads himself with
promissory notes for usury!
7 Shall [your debtors] not rise up suddenly who shall
bite you, exacting usury of you, and those awake who will
vex you [toss you to and fro and make you tremble vio-
lently]? Then you will be booty for them.
8 Because you [king of Babylon] have plundered
many nations, all who are left of the people shall plunder you—because of men's blood and for the violence
done to the earth, to the city and all the people who live
in each city.
9 Woe to him who obtains wicked gain for his house,
[who thinks by so doing] to set his nest on high that he
may be preserved from calamity *and* delivered from the
power of evil!
10 You have devised shame to your house by cutting off
*and* putting an end to many peoples, and you have sinned
against *and* forfeited your own life.
11 For the stone shall cry out of the wall [built in sin,
to accuse you], and the beam out of the woodwork will
answer it [agreeing with its charge against you].
12 Woe to him who builds a town with blood and establishes a city by iniquity!
13 Behold, is it not by appointment of the Lord of hosts
that the nations toil only to satisfy the fire [that will consume their work], and the peoples weary themselves only
for emptiness, falsity, *and* futility?
14 But [the time is coming when] the earth shall be filled
with the knowledge of the glory of the Lord as the waters
cover the sea. [Isa. 11:9.]

*a* There is a curious passage in the Talmud [the body of Jewish civil and
religious law] which says that Moses gave six hundred injunctions to
the Israelites. As these commands might prove too numerous to commit
to memory, David brought them down to eleven in Psalm 15. Isaiah
reduced these eleven to six in [his] chapter 33:15. Micah (6:8) further
reduced them to three; and Isaiah (56:1) once more brought them down
to two. These two Amos (5:4) reduced to one. However, lest it might be
supposed from this that God could be found only in the fulfillment of the
law, Habakkuk (2:4 KJV) said, "The just shall live by his faith" (William
H. Saulez, *The Romance of the Hebrew Language*). *b* The Dead Sea Scrolls
read "wealth."

*a* 1 Or *and what to answer when I am rebuked*   *b* 2 Or *so that whoever
reads it*   *c* 3 Or *Though he linger, wait for him; / he*   *d* 4 Or *faith*

## New International Version

15 "Woe to him who gives drink to his neighbors,
   pouring it from the wineskin till they are drunk,
   so that he can gaze on their naked bodies!
16 You will be filled with shame instead of glory.
   Now it is your turn! Drink and let your nakedness be
      exposed[a]!
The cup from the LORD's right hand is coming around
      to you,
   and disgrace will cover your glory.
17 The violence you have done to Lebanon will
      overwhelm you,
   and your destruction of animals will terrify you.
For you have shed human blood;
   you have destroyed lands and cities and everyone in
      them.

18 "Of what value is an idol carved by a craftsman?
   Or an image that teaches lies?
For the one who makes it trusts in his own creation;
   he makes idols that cannot speak.
19 Woe to him who says to wood, 'Come to life!'
   Or to lifeless stone, 'Wake up!'
Can it give guidance?
   It is covered with gold and silver;
   there is no breath in it."

20 The LORD is in his holy temple;
   let all the earth be silent before him.

### Habakkuk's Prayer

**3** A prayer of Habakkuk the prophet. On *shigionoth*.[b]

2 LORD, I have heard of your fame;
   I stand in awe of your deeds, LORD.
Repeat them in our day,
   in our time make them known;
   in wrath remember mercy.

3 God came from Teman,
   the Holy One from Mount Paran.[c]
His glory covered the heavens
   and his praise filled the earth.
4 His splendor was like the sunrise;
   rays flashed from his hand,
   where his power was hidden.
5 Plague went before him;
   pestilence followed his steps.
6 He stood, and shook the earth;
   he looked, and made the nations tremble.
The ancient mountains crumbled
   and the age-old hills collapsed—
   but he marches on forever.
7 I saw the tents of Cushan in distress,
   the dwellings of Midian in anguish.

8 Were you angry with the rivers, LORD?
   Was your wrath against the streams?
Did you rage against the sea
   when you rode your horses
   and your chariots to victory?
9 You uncovered your bow,
   you called for many arrows.
You split the earth with rivers;
10    the mountains saw you and writhed.
Torrents of water swept by;
   the deep roared
   and lifted its waves on high.

## Amplified Bible

15 Woe to him who gives his neighbors drink, who pours out your bottle to them *and* adds to it your poisonous *and* blighting wrath and also makes them drunk, that you may look on their stripped condition *and* pour out foul shame [on their glory]!
16 You [yourself] will be filled with shame *and* contempt instead of glory. Drink also and be like an uncircumcised [heathen]! The cup [of wrath] in the Lord's right hand will come around to you [O destroyer], and foul shame shall be upon your own glory! [Rev. 16:19.]
17 For the violence done to Lebanon will cover *and* overwhelm you; the destruction of the animals [which the violence frightened away] will terrify you on account of men's blood and the violence done to the land, to the city and all its inhabitants.
18 What profit is the graven image when its maker has formed it? It is only a molten image and a teacher of lies. For the maker trusts in his own creations [as his gods] when he makes dumb idols.
19 Woe to him who says to the wooden image, Awake! and to the dumb stone, Arise, teach! [Yet, it cannot, for] behold, it is laid over with gold and silver and there is no breath at all inside it!
20 But the Lord is in His holy temple; let all the earth hush *and* keep silence before Him. [Zeph. 1:7; Zech. 2:13.]

**3** A prayer of Habakkuk the prophet, set to wild, enthusiastic, *and* triumphal music.

2 O Lord, I have heard the report of You and was afraid. O Lord, revive Your work in the midst of the years, in the midst of the years make [Yourself] known! In wrath [earnestly] remember love, pity, *and* mercy.
3 God [approaching from Sinai] came from Teman [which represents Edom] and the Holy One from Mount Paran [in the Sinai region]. Selah [pause, and calmly think of that]! His glory covered the heavens and the earth was full of His praise.
4 And His brightness was like the sunlight; rays streamed from His hand, and there [in the sunlike splendor] was the hiding place of His power.
5 Before Him went the pestilence [as in Egypt], and burning plague followed His feet [as in Sennacherib's army]. [Exod. 7:2-4; II Kings 19:32-35.]
6 He stood and measured the earth; He looked and shook the nations, and the eternal mountains were scattered and the perpetual hills bowed low. His ways are everlasting *and* His goings are of old.
7 I [Habakkuk, in vision] saw the tents of Cushan [probably Ethiopia] in affliction; the [tent] curtains of the land of Midian trembled.
8 Were You displeased with the rivers, O Lord? Or was Your anger against the rivers [You divided]? Was Your wrath against the [Red] Sea, that You rode [before] upon Your horses and Your chariots of victory *and* deliverance?
9 Your bow was made quite bare; sworn to the tribes [of Israel] by Your sure word were the rods of chastisement, scourges, *and* calamities. Selah [pause, and calmly think of that]! With rivers You cleaved the earth [bringing forth waters in dry places]. [Exod. 17:6; Num. 20:11.]
10 The mountains saw You; they trembled *and* writhed [as if in pain]. The overflowing of the water passed by [as at the deluge]; the deep uttered its voice and lifted its hands on high.

---

a 16 Masoretic Text; Dead Sea Scrolls, Aquila, Vulgate and Syriac (see also Septuagint) *and stagger*   b 1 Probably a literary or musical term
c 3 The Hebrew has *Selah* (a word of uncertain meaning) here and at the middle of verse 9 and at the end of verse 13.

## New International Version

11 Sun and moon stood still in the heavens
   at the glint of your flying arrows,
   at the lightning of your flashing spear.
12 In wrath you strode through the earth
   and in anger you threshed the nations.
13 You came out to deliver your people,
   to save your anointed one.
   You crushed the leader of the land of wickedness,
   you stripped him from head to foot.
14 With his own spear you pierced his head
   when his warriors stormed out to scatter us,
   gloating as though about to devour
   the wretched who were in hiding.
15 You trampled the sea with your horses,
   churning the great waters.

16 I heard and my heart pounded,
   my lips quivered at the sound;
   decay crept into my bones,
   and my legs trembled.
   Yet I will wait patiently for the day of calamity
   to come on the nation invading us.
17 Though the fig tree does not bud
   and there are no grapes on the vines,
   though the olive crop fails
   and the fields produce no food,
   though there are no sheep in the pen
   and no cattle in the stalls,
18 yet I will rejoice in the LORD,
   I will be joyful in God my Savior.

19 The Sovereign LORD is my strength;
   he makes my feet like the feet of a deer,
   he enables me to tread on the heights.

   For the director of music. On my stringed
   instruments.

## Amplified Bible

11 The sun and moon stood back [as before Joshua] in their habitation at the light of Your arrows as they sped, at the flash of Your glittering spear. [Josh. 10:12, 13.]
12 You marched through the land in indignation; You trampled *and* threshed the nations in anger.
13 You went forth *and* have come for the salvation of Your people, for the deliverance *and* victory of Your anointed [people Israel]; You smote the head of the house of the wicked, laying bare the foundation even to the neck. Selah [pause, and calmly think of that]!
14 You pierced with his own arrows the head of [the enemy's] hordes; they came out as a whirlwind to scatter me [the people], rejoicing as if to devour the poor [Israel] secretly.
15 You have trodden the sea with Your horses, [beside] the heap of great *and* surging waters. [Exod. 15:8.]
16 I heard and my [whole inner self] trembled; my lips quivered at the sound. Rottenness enters into my bones and under me [down to my feet]; I tremble. I will wait quietly for the day of trouble and distress when there shall come up against [my] people him who is about to invade *and* oppress them.
17 Though the fig tree does not blossom and there is no fruit on the vines, [though] the product of the olive fails and the fields yield no food, though the flock is cut off from the fold and there are no cattle in the stalls,
18 Yet I will rejoice in the Lord; I will exult in the [victorious] God of my salvation! [Rom. 8:37.]
19 The Lord God is my Strength, my personal bravery, *and* my invincible army; He makes my feet like hinds' feet and will make me to walk [not to stand still in terror, but to walk] *and* make [spiritual] progress upon my high places [of trouble, suffering, or responsibility]!

For the Chief Musician; with my stringed instruments.

# Zephaniah

# Zephaniah

**1** The word of the LORD that came to Zephaniah son of Cushi, the son of Gedaliah, the son of Amariah, the son of Hezekiah, during the reign of Josiah son of Amon king of Judah:

## Judgment on the Whole Earth in the Day of the LORD

² "I will sweep away everything
　　from the face of the earth,"
　　　　　　　　　　declares the LORD.
³ "I will sweep away both man and beast;
　　I will sweep away the birds in the sky
　　and the fish in the sea—
　　and the idols that cause the wicked to stumble."ᵃ

"When I destroy all mankind
　　on the face of the earth,"
　　　　　　　　　　declares the LORD,
⁴ "I will stretch out my hand against Judah
　　and against all who live in Jerusalem.
I will destroy every remnant of Baal worship in this place,
　　the very names of the idolatrous priests—
⁵ those who bow down on the roofs
　　to worship the starry host,
those who bow down and swear by the LORD
　　and who also swear by Molek,ᵇ
⁶ those who turn back from following the LORD
　　and neither seek the LORD nor inquire of him."

⁷ Be silent before the Sovereign LORD,
　　for the day of the LORD is near.
The LORD has prepared a sacrifice;
　　he has consecrated those he has invited.

⁸ "On the day of the LORD's sacrifice
　　I will punish the officials
　　and the king's sons
and all those clad
　　in foreign clothes.
⁹ On that day I will punish
　　all who avoid stepping on the threshold,ᶜ
who fill the temple of their gods
　　with violence and deceit.

¹⁰ "On that day,"
　　declares the LORD,
"a cry will go up from the Fish Gate,
　　wailing from the New Quarter,
　　and a loud crash from the hills.
¹¹ Wail, you who live in the market districtᵈ;
　　all your merchants will be wiped out,
　　all who trade withᵉ silver will be destroyed.
¹² At that time I will search Jerusalem with lamps
　　and punish those who are complacent,
　　who are like wine left on its dregs,
who think, 'The LORD will do nothing,
　　either good or bad.'
¹³ Their wealth will be plundered,
　　their houses demolished.
Though they build houses,
　　they will not live in them;
though they plant vineyards,
　　they will not drink the wine."

¹⁴ The great day of the LORD is near—
　　near and coming quickly.
The cry on the day of the LORD is bitter;
　　the Mighty Warrior shouts his battle cry.

**1** The word of the Lord which came to Zephaniah son of Cushi, the son of Gedaliah, the son of Amariah, the son of Hezekiah, in the days of Josiah king of Judah and son of Amon.

² By taking away I will make an end *and* I will utterly consume *and* sweep away all things from the face of the earth, says the Lord.

³ I will consume *and* sweep away man and beast; I will consume *and* sweep away the birds of the air and the fish of the sea. I will overthrow the stumbling blocks (the idols) with the wicked [worshipers], and I will cut off mankind from the face of the earth, says the Lord.

⁴ I will also stretch out My hand over Judah and over all the inhabitants of Jerusalem, and I will cut off the remnant of Baal from this place and the name of the idol priests with the [false] priests,

⁵ And those who worship the starry host of the heavens upon their housetops and those who [pretend to] worship the Lord and swear by *and* to Him and yet swear by *and* to [the heathen god Molech or] Malcam [their idol king],

⁶ And those who have drawn back from following the Lord and those who have not sought the Lord nor inquired for, inquired of, *and* required the Lord [as their first necessity].

⁷ [Hush!] Be silent before the Lord God, for the day [of the vengeance] of the Lord is near; for the Lord has prepared a sacrifice, and He has set apart [for His use] those who have accepted His invitation. [Hab. 2:20.]

⁸ And on the day of the Lord's sacrifice, I will punish the officials and the king's sons and all who are clothed in [lavish] foreign apparel [instead of the Jewish dress, with its reminders to obey God's commandments]. [Num. 15:38, 39.]

⁹ In the same day also will I punish all those who leap swiftly on *or* over the threshold [upon entering houses to steal], who fill their master's house with violence and deceit *and* fraud.

¹⁰ And in that day, says the Lord, there shall be heard the voice of crying from the Fish Gate [in the wall of Jerusalem] and a wailing from the Second Quarter *or* Lower City and a great crashing *and* sound of destruction from the hills.

¹¹ Wail, you inhabitants of the Mortar [those located in the hollow part of the city]! For all the merchant people, like the people of Canaan, will be silent [entirely destroyed]; all those who weighed out silver *and* were loaded with it will be cut off.

¹² And at that time I will search Jerusalem with lamps and punish the men who [like old wine] are thickening *and* settling on their lees, who say in their hearts, The Lord will not do good, nor will He do evil.

¹³ And their wealth shall become plunder and their houses a desolation. Though they build houses, they shall not inhabit them; though they plant vineyards, they shall not drink the wine from them. [Deut. 28:30, 39; Amos 5:11, 12.]

¹⁴ The great day of the Lord is near—near and hastening fast. Hark! the voice of the day of the Lord! The mighty man [unable to fight or to flee] will cry then bitterly.

---

ᵃ 3 The meaning of the Hebrew for this line is uncertain.　　ᵇ 5 Hebrew *Malkam*　　ᶜ 9 See 1 Samuel 5:5.　　ᵈ 11 Or *the Mortar*　　ᵉ 11 Or *in*

## New International Version

[15]That day will be a day of wrath—
  a day of distress and anguish,
    a day of trouble and ruin,
  a day of darkness and gloom,
    a day of clouds and blackness—
[16] a day of trumpet and battle cry
against the fortified cities
  and against the corner towers.

[17] "I will bring such distress on all people
  that they will grope about like those who are blind,
  because they have sinned against the LORD.
Their blood will be poured out like dust
  and their entrails like dung.
[18]Neither their silver nor their gold
  will be able to save them
  on the day of the LORD's wrath."

In the fire of his jealousy
  the whole earth will be consumed,
for he will make a sudden end
  of all who live on the earth.

### Judah and Jerusalem Judged Along With the Nations

*Judah Summoned to Repent*

**2** Gather together, gather yourselves together,
  you shameful nation,
[2] before the decree takes effect
  and that day passes like windblown chaff,
  before the LORD's fierce anger
    comes upon you,
  before the day of the LORD's wrath
    comes upon you.
[3] Seek the LORD, all you humble of the land,
  you who do what he commands.
Seek righteousness, seek humility;
  perhaps you will be sheltered
  on the day of the LORD's anger.

*Philistia*

[4] Gaza will be abandoned
  and Ashkelon left in ruins.
At midday Ashdod will be emptied
  and Ekron uprooted.
[5] Woe to you who live by the sea,
  you Kerethite people;
the word of the LORD is against you,
  Canaan, land of the Philistines.
He says, "I will destroy you,
  and none will be left."
[6] The land by the sea will become pastures
  having wells for shepherds
  and pens for flocks.
[7] That land will belong
  to the remnant of the people of Judah;
  there they will find pasture.
In the evening they will lie down
  in the houses of Ashkelon.

## Amplified Bible

[15]That day is a day of wrath, a day of distress and anguish, a day of ruin and devastation, a day of darkness and gloom, a day of clouds and thick darkness, [Jer. 30:7; Joel 2:11; Amos 5:18.]
[16]A day of the blast of trumpet and battle cry against the fortified cities and against the high towers *and* battlements.
[17]And I will bring distress upon men, so that they shall walk like blind men, because they have sinned against the Lord; their blood shall be poured out like dust and their flesh like dung.
[18]Neither their silver nor their gold shall be able to deliver them in the day of the Lord's indignation *and* wrath. But the whole earth shall be consumed in the fire of His jealous [a]wrath, for a full, yes, a sudden, end will He make of all the inhabitants of the earth. [Luke 21:35, 36; II Pet. 3:10-13.]

**2** Collect your thoughts, yes, unbend yourselves [in submission and see if there is no sense of shame and no consciousness of sin left in you], O shameless nation [not desirous or desired]!
[2] [The time for repentance is speeding by like chaff whirled before the wind!] Therefore consider, before God's decree brings forth [the curse upon you], before the time [to repent] is gone like the drifting chaff, before the fierce anger of the Lord comes upon you—yes, before the day of the wrath of the Lord comes upon you!
[3] Seek the Lord [inquire for Him, inquire of Him, and require Him as the foremost necessity of your life], all you humble of the land who have acted in compliance with His revealed will *and* have kept His commandments; seek righteousness, seek humility [inquire for them, require them as vital]. It may be you will be hidden in the day of the Lord's anger.
[4] For [hear the fate of the Philistines:] Gaza shall be forsaken and Ashkelon shall become a desolation; the people of Ashdod shall be driven out at noonday and Ekron shall be uprooted.
[5] Woe to the inhabitants of the seacoast, the nation of the Cherethites [in Philistia]! The word of the Lord is against you, O Canaan, land of the Philistines; I will destroy you until no inhabitant is left.
[6] And the seacoast shall be pastures, with [deserted] dwelling places *and* caves for shepherds and folds for flocks.
[7] The [b]seacoast shall belong to the remnant of the house of Judah; they shall pasture their flocks upon it; in the houses of [deserted Philistine] Ashkelon shall they of

[a] God's judgment, God's mercy—the twin themes of the prophets. In this dramatic passage, the Lord describes the destruction that will sweep the earth in the day of God's wrath. Yet the Lord is true to His promises—the remnant will be restored (Zeph. 3:18-20); the last day is also "the day of redemption" (Eph. 4:30). See also Matt. 24:31; John 14:3; I Thess. 4:15-17. [b] This is one of the more than twenty-five details of Bible prophecy concerning the land of Palestine that has been literally fulfilled. Probability computers estimate that if a prophecy concerning a person, place, or event has twenty-five details, there is one chance in more than thirty-three million of its accidental fulfillment. And such prophecy must be (1) above the possibility of human collusion; (2) beyond the ability of human calculation; (3) proof against human coincidence; (4) above all possibility of human comprehension. What inconceivable omniscience was behind the writing of the Bible! Twenty-five details also concerning the betrayal, trial, death, and burial of our Lord were fulfilled, fulfilled within twenty-four hours! And the fulfillment of the most remarkable prophecies of all time is predicted in the Bible for the rapidly approaching future! See footnote on Ezek. 26:14 for information about a similar fulfillment of details of Bible prophecy with regard to Tyre.

# New International Version

The LORD their God will care for them;
  he will restore their fortunes.*

## Moab and Ammon

8 "I have heard the insults of Moab
    and the taunts of the Ammonites,
  who insulted my people
    and made threats against their land.
9 Therefore, as surely as I live,"
    declares the LORD Almighty,
    the God of Israel,
  "surely Moab will become like Sodom,
    the Ammonites like Gomorrah—
  a place of weeds and salt pits,
    a wasteland forever.
  The remnant of my people will plunder them;
    the survivors of my nation will inherit their land."

10 This is what they will get in return for their pride,
    for insulting and mocking
      the people of the LORD Almighty.
11 The LORD will be awesome to them
    when he destroys all the gods of the earth.
  Distant nations will bow down to him,
    all of them in their own lands.

## Cush

12 "You Cushites,* too,
    will be slain by my sword."

## Assyria

13 He will stretch out his hand against the north
    and destroy Assyria,
  leaving Nineveh utterly desolate
    and dry as the desert.
14 Flocks and herds will lie down there,
    creatures of every kind.
  The desert owl and the screech owl
    will roost on her columns.
  Their hooting will echo through the windows,
    rubble will fill the doorways,
    the beams of cedar will be exposed.
15 This is the city of revelry
    that lived in safety.
  She said to herself,
    "I am the one! And there is none besides me."
  What a ruin she has become,
    a lair for wild beasts!
  All who pass by her scoff
    and shake their fists.

## Jerusalem

3 Woe to the city of oppressors,
    rebellious and defiled!
2 She obeys no one,
    she accepts no correction.
  She does not trust in the LORD,
    she does not draw near to her God.
3 Her officials within her
    are roaring lions;
  her rulers are evening wolves,
    who leave nothing for the morning.
4 Her prophets are unprincipled;
    they are treacherous people.
  Her priests profane the sanctuary
    and do violence to the law.
5 The LORD within her is righteous;
    he does no wrong.
  Morning by morning he dispenses his justice,
    and every new day he does not fail,
    yet the unrighteous know no shame.

*7 Or *will bring back their captives*   *12 That is, people from the upper Nile region*

# Amplified Bible

Judah lie down in the evening. For the Lord their [Judah's] God shall visit them [for their relief] and restore them from their captivity. [Isa. 14:29-31; Amos 1:6-8.]
8 I have heard the taunts of Moab and the revilings of the Ammonites by which they have reproached My people, and magnified themselves *and* made boasts against their territory.
9 Therefore, as I live, says the Lord of hosts, the God of Israel, Moab shall become like Sodom and the Ammonites like Gomorrah, a land possessed by nettles *and* wild vetches and salt pits, and a perpetual desolation. The remnant of My people shall make a prey of them and what is left of My nation shall possess them.
10 This shall they have for their pride, because they have taunted and boasted against the people of the Lord of hosts.
11 The Lord will be terrible to them, for He will make lean *and* famish all the gods of the earth; and men shall worship Him, every one from his place, even all the isles *and* coastlands of the nations. [Joel 2:11; Zeph. 1:4; 3:9.]
12 You Ethiopians also, you shall be slain by My sword. [Isa. 18.]
13 And [the Lord] will stretch out His hand against the north and destroy Assyria and will make Nineveh a desolation, dry as the desert. [Isa. 10:12; Nah. 1:1.]
14 Herds shall lie down in the midst of [Nineveh], all the [wild] beasts of the nations *and* of every kind; both the pelican and the hedgehog shall lodge on the upper part of her [fallen] pillars; the voice [of the nesting bird] shall sing in the windows; desolation *and* drought shall be on the thresholds, for her cedar paneling will He lay bare.
15 This is the joyous *and* exultant city that dwelt carelessly [feeling so secure], that said in her heart, I am and there is none beside me. What a desolation she has become, a lair for [wild] beasts! Everyone who passes by her shall hiss and wave his hand [indicating his gratification]. [Isa. 10:5-34; 47:8, 10.]

3 Woe to her that is rebellious and polluted, the oppressing city [Jerusalem]!
2 She did not listen to *and* heed the voice [of God]; she accepted no correction *or* instruction; she trusted not in the Lord [nor leaned on or was confident in Him, but was confident in her own wealth]; she drew not near to her God [but to the god of Baal or Molech].
3 Her officials in the midst of her are roaring lions; her judges are evening wolves; they gnaw not the bones on the morrow, for nothing is left by morning.
4 Her prophets are light [lacking truth, gravity, and steadiness] and men of treachery; her priests have profaned the sanctuary; [defrauding God and man by pretending their own word is God's word] they have done violence to the law. [Jer. 23:11; Ezek. 22:26; Hos. 9:7.]
5 The Lord in the midst of her is [uncompromisingly] righteous; He will not do iniquity. Every morning He brings His justice to light; He fails not, but the unjust [person] knows no shame.

## New International Version

*Jerusalem Remains Unrepentant*

⁶"I have destroyed nations;
  their strongholds are demolished.
I have left their streets deserted,
  with no one passing through.
Their cities are laid waste;
  they are deserted and empty.
⁷Of Jerusalem I thought,
  'Surely you will fear me
  and accept correction!'
Then her place of refuge*ᵃ* would not be destroyed,
  nor all my punishments come upon*ᵇ* her.
But they were still eager
  to act corruptly in all they did.
⁸Therefore wait for me,"
  declares the LORD,
  "for the day I will stand up to testify.*ᶜ*
I have decided to assemble the nations,
  to gather the kingdoms
and to pour out my wrath on them—
  all my fierce anger.
The whole world will be consumed
  by the fire of my jealous anger.

### Restoration of Israel's Remnant

⁹"Then I will purify the lips of the peoples,
  that all of them may call on the name of the LORD
  and serve him shoulder to shoulder.
¹⁰From beyond the rivers of Cush*ᵈ*
  my worshipers, my scattered people,
  will bring me offerings.
¹¹On that day you, Jerusalem, will not be put to shame
  for all the wrongs you have done to me,
because I will remove from you
  your arrogant boasters.
Never again will you be haughty
  on my holy hill.
¹²But I will leave within you
  the meek and humble.
The remnant of Israel
  will trust in the name of the LORD.
¹³They will do no wrong;
  they will tell no lies.
A deceitful tongue
  will not be found in their mouths.
They will eat and lie down
  and no one will make them afraid."

¹⁴Sing, Daughter Zion;
  shout aloud, Israel!
Be glad and rejoice with all your heart,
  Daughter Jerusalem!
¹⁵The LORD has taken away your punishment,
  he has turned back your enemy.
The LORD, the King of Israel, is with you;
  never again will you fear any harm.
¹⁶On that day
  they will say to Jerusalem,
  "Do not fear, Zion;
  do not let your hands hang limp.
¹⁷The LORD your God is with you,
  the Mighty Warrior who saves.
He will take great delight in you;
  in his love he will no longer rebuke you,
  but will rejoice over you with singing."

¹⁸"I will remove from you
  all who mourn over the loss of your appointed
  festivals,
  which is a burden and reproach for you.

## Amplified Bible

⁶I [the Lord] have cut off nations; their battlements *and* corner towers are desolate *and* in ruins. I laid their streets waste so that none passes over them; their cities are destroyed so that there is no man, there is no inhabitant.

⁷I said, Only let her [reverently and worshipfully] fear Me, receive correction and instruction, and [Jerusalem's] dwelling shall not be cut off. However, I have punished her [according to all that I have appointed concerning her in the way of punishment], but all the more they are eager to make all their doings corrupt *and* infamous.

⁸Therefore [earnestly] wait for Me, says the Lord, [waiting] for the day when I rise up to the attack [as a witness, accuser, or judge, and a testimony]. For My decision *and* determination *and* right it is to gather the nations together, to assemble the kingdoms, to pour upon them My indignation, even all [the heat of] My fierce anger; for [in that day] all the earth shall be consumed with the fire of My zeal *and* jealousy.

⁹For then [changing their impure language] I will give to the people a clear *and* pure speech from pure lips, that they may all call upon the name of the Lord, to serve Him with one unanimous consent *and* one united shoulder [bearing the yoke of the Lord].

¹⁰From beyond the rivers of Cush *or* Ethiopia those who pray to Me, the daughter of My dispersed people, will bring *and* present My offering.

¹¹In that day you [the congregation of Israel] shall not be put to shame for all your deeds by which you have rebelled *and* transgressed against Me, for then I will take away out of your midst those who exult in your majesty *and* pride; and you shall no more be haughty [and carry yourselves arrogantly on or] because of My holy mountain.

¹²For I will leave in the midst of you a people afflicted and poor, and they shall trust, seek refuge, *and* be confident in the name of the Lord.

¹³What is left of Israel shall not do iniquity or speak lies, neither shall a deceitful tongue be found in their mouth, for they shall feed and lie down and none shall make them afraid.

¹⁴Sing, O Daughter of Zion; shout, O Israel! Rejoice, be in high spirits *and* glory with all your heart, O Daughter of Jerusalem [in that day].

¹⁵[For then it will be that] the Lord has taken away the judgments against you; He has cast out your enemy. The King of Israel, even the Lord [Himself], is in the midst of you; [and after He has come to you] you shall not experience *or* fear evil any more.

¹⁶In that day it shall be said to Jerusalem, Fear not, O Zion. Let not your hands sink down *or* be slow *and* listless.

¹⁷The Lord your God is in the midst of you, a Mighty One, a Savior [Who saves]! He will rejoice over you with joy; He will rest [in silent satisfaction] and in His love He will be silent *and* make no mention [of past sins, or even recall them]; He will exult over you with singing.

¹⁸I will gather those belonging to you [those Israelites in captivity] who yearn *and* grieve for the solemn assembly [and the festivals], on whom [their exile and inability to attend services at Jerusalem have brought derision and] the reproach of it is a burden.

---

*ᵃ* 7 Or *her sanctuary*   *ᵇ* 7 Or *all those I appointed over*   *ᶜ* 8 Septuagint and Syriac; Hebrew *will rise up to plunder*   *ᵈ* 10 That is, the upper Nile region

## New International Version

19 At that time I will deal
  with all who oppressed you.
I will rescue the lame;
  I will gather the exiles.
I will give them praise and honor
  in every land where they have suffered shame.
20 At that time I will gather you;
  at that time I will bring you home.
I will give you honor and praise
  among all the peoples of the earth
when I restore your fortunes[a]
  before your very eyes,"

says the Lord.

## Amplified Bible

19 Behold, at that time I will deal with all those who afflict you; I will save the limping [ones] and gather the outcasts and will make them a praise and a name in every land of their shame. [Mic. 4:6, 7.]
20 At that time I will bring you in; yes, at that time I will gather you, for I will make you a name and a praise among all the nations of the earth when I reverse your captivity before your eyes, says the Lord.

[a] 20 Or I bring back your captives

# Haggai

## A Call to Build the House of the Lord

**1** In the second year of King Darius, on the first day of the sixth month, the word of the Lord came through the prophet Haggai to Zerubbabel son of Shealtiel, governor of Judah, and to Joshua son of Jozadak,[a] the high priest:

[2] This is what the Lord Almighty says: "These people say, 'The time has not yet come to rebuild the Lord's house.'"

[3] Then the word of the Lord came through the prophet Haggai: [4] "Is it a time for you yourselves to be living in your paneled houses, while this house remains a ruin?"

[5] Now this is what the Lord Almighty says: "Give careful thought to your ways. [6] You have planted much, but harvested little. You eat, but never have enough. You drink, but never have your fill. You put on clothes, but are not warm. You earn wages, only to put them in a purse with holes in it."

[7] This is what the Lord Almighty says: "Give careful thought to your ways. [8] Go up into the mountains and bring down timber and build my house, so that I may take pleasure in it and be honored," says the Lord. [9] "You expected much, but see, it turned out to be little. What you brought home, I blew away. Why?" declares the Lord Almighty. "Because of my house, which remains a ruin, while each of you is busy with your own house. [10] Therefore, because of you the heavens have withheld their dew and the earth its crops. [11] I called for a drought on the fields and the mountains, on the grain, the new wine, the olive oil and everything else the ground produces, on people and livestock, and on all the labor of your hands."

[12] Then Zerubbabel son of Shealtiel, Joshua son of Jozadak, the high priest, and the whole remnant of the people obeyed the voice of the Lord their God and the message of the prophet Haggai, because the Lord their God had sent him. And the people feared the Lord. [13] Then Haggai, the Lord's messenger, gave this message of the Lord to the people: "I am with you," declares the Lord. [14] So the Lord stirred up the spirit of Zerubbabel son of Shealtiel, governor of Judah, and the spirit of Joshua son of Jozadak, the high priest, and the spirit of the whole remnant of the people. They came and began to work on the house of the Lord Almighty, their God, [15] on the twenty-fourth day of the sixth month.

## The Promised Glory of the New House

**2** In the second year of King Darius, [1] on the twenty-first day of the seventh month, the word of the Lord came through the prophet Haggai: [2] "Speak to Zerubbabel son of Shealtiel, governor of Judah, to Joshua son of Jozadak,[b] the high priest, and to the remnant of the people. Ask them, [3] 'Who of you is left who saw this house in its former glory? How does it look to you now? Does it not seem to you like

---

[a] 1 Hebrew *Jehozadak*, a variant of *Jozadak*; also in verses 12 and 14
[b] 2 Hebrew *Jehozadak*, a variant of *Jozadak*; also in verse 4

## THE BOOK OF

# Haggai

**1** In the second year of Darius king [of Persia], in the sixth month, on the first day of the month, the word of the Lord came by means of Haggai the prophet [in Jerusalem after the Babylonian captivity] to Zerubbabel son of Shealtiel, governor of Judah, and to Joshua son of Jehozadak, the high priest, saying,

[2] Thus says the Lord of hosts: These people say, The time is not yet come that the [a] Lord's house should be rebuilt [although Cyrus had ordered it done eighteen years before]. [Ezra 1:1-6; 4:1-6, 24; 5:1-3.]

[3] Then came the word of the Lord by Haggai the prophet, saying,

[4] Is it time for you yourselves to dwell in your paneled houses while this house [of the Lord] lies in ruins?

[5] Now therefore thus says the Lord of hosts: Consider your ways *and* set your mind on what has come to you.

[6] You have sown much, but you have reaped little; you eat, but you do not have enough; you drink, but you do not have your fill; you clothe yourselves, but no one is warm; and he who earns wages has earned them to put them in a bag with holes in it.

[7] Thus says the Lord of hosts: Consider your ways (your previous and present conduct) *and* how you have fared.

[8] Go up to the hill country and bring lumber and rebuild [My] house, and I will take pleasure in it and I will be glorified, says the Lord [by accepting it as done for My glory and by displaying My glory in it].

[9] You looked for much [harvest], and behold, it came to little; and even when you brought that home, I blew it away. Why? says the Lord of hosts. Because of My house, which lies waste while you yourselves run each man to his own house [eager to build and adorn it].

[10] Therefore the heavens above you [for your sake] withhold the dew, and the earth withholds its produce.

[11] And I have called for a drought upon the land and the hill country, upon the grain, the fresh wine, the oil, upon what the ground brings forth, upon men and cattle, and upon all the [wearisome] toil of [men's] hands.

[12] Then Zerubbabel son of Shealtiel and Joshua son of Jehozadak, the high priest, with all the remnant of the people [who had returned from captivity], listened to *and* obeyed the voice of the Lord their God [not vaguely or partly, but completely, according to] the words of Haggai the prophet, since the Lord their God had sent him, and the people [reverently] feared *and* [worshipfully] turned to the Lord.

[13] Then Haggai, the Lord's messenger, spoke the Lord's message to the people saying, I am with you, says the Lord.

[14] And the Lord aroused the spirit of Zerubbabel son of Shealtiel, governor of Judah, and the spirit of Joshua son of Jehozadak, the high priest, and the spirit of all the remnant of the people, so that they came and labored on the house of the Lord of hosts, their God,

[15] On the twenty-fourth day of the sixth month.

**2** In the seventh month, on the twenty-first day of the month, in the second year of Darius king [of Persia], came the word of the Lord by the prophet Haggai, saying,

[2] Speak now to Zerubbabel son of Shealtiel, governor of Judah, and to Joshua son of Jehozadak, the high priest, and to the remainder of the people, saying,

[3] Who is left among you who saw this house in its former glory? And how do you see it now? Is not this in your sight as nothing in comparison to that?

---

[a] See footnote on Ezra 4:24.

## New International Version

nothing? ⁴But now be strong, Zerubbabel,' declares the LORD. 'Be strong, Joshua son of Jozadak, the high priest. Be strong, all you people of the land,' declares the LORD, 'and work. For I am with you,' declares the LORD Almighty. ⁵'This is what I covenanted with you when you came out of Egypt. And my Spirit remains among you. Do not fear.'

⁶"This is what the LORD Almighty says: 'In a little while I will once more shake the heavens and the earth, the sea and the dry land. ⁷I will shake all nations, and what is desired by all nations will come, and I will fill this house with glory,' says the LORD Almighty. ⁸'The silver is mine and the gold is mine,' declares the LORD Almighty. ⁹'The glory of this present house will be greater than the glory of the former house,' says the LORD Almighty. 'And in this place I will grant peace,' declares the LORD Almighty."

### Blessings for a Defiled People

¹⁰On the twenty-fourth day of the ninth month, in the second year of Darius, the word of the LORD came to the prophet Haggai: ¹¹"This is what the LORD Almighty says: 'Ask the priests what the law says: ¹²If someone carries consecrated meat in the fold of their garment, and that fold touches some bread or stew, some wine, olive oil or other food, does it become consecrated?'"

The priests answered, "No."

¹³Then Haggai said, "If a person defiled by contact with a dead body touches one of these things, does it become defiled?"

"Yes," the priests replied, "it becomes defiled."

¹⁴Then Haggai said, "'So it is with this people and this nation in my sight,' declares the LORD. 'Whatever they do and whatever they offer there is defiled.

¹⁵"'Now give careful thought to this from this day on[a]— consider how things were before one stone was laid on another in the LORD's temple. ¹⁶When anyone came to a heap of twenty measures, there were only ten. When anyone went to a wine vat to draw fifty measures, there were only twenty. ¹⁷I struck all the work of your hands with blight, mildew and hail, yet you did not return to me,' declares the LORD. ¹⁸'From this day on, from this twenty-fourth day of the ninth month, give careful thought to the day when the foundation of the LORD's temple was laid. Give careful thought: ¹⁹Is there yet any seed left in the barn? Until now, the vine and the fig tree, the pomegranate and the olive tree have not borne fruit.

"'From this day on I will bless you.'"

## Amplified Bible

⁴Yet now be strong, alert, *and* courageous, O Zerubbabel, says the Lord; be strong, alert, *and* courageous, O Joshua son of Jehozadak, the high priest; and be strong, alert, *and* courageous, all you people of the land, says the Lord, and work! For I am with you, says the Lord of hosts.

⁵According to the promise that I covenanted with you when you came out of Egypt, so My Spirit stands *and* abides in the midst of you; fear not.

⁶For thus says the Lord of hosts: Yet once more, in a little while, I will shake *and* make tremble the [starry] heavens, the earth, the sea, and the dry land; [Heb. 12:26.]

⁷And I will shake all nations and the *ᵃ*desire *and* the precious things of all nations shall come in, and I will fill this house with splendor, says the Lord of hosts. [Isa. 60:5; Matt. 2:1-12.]

⁸The silver is Mine and the gold is Mine, says the Lord of hosts.

⁹The latter glory of this house [with its successor, to which Jesus came] shall be greater than the former, says the Lord of hosts; and in this place will I give peace *and* prosperity, says the Lord of hosts.

¹⁰On the twenty-fourth day of the ninth month, in the second year of Darius, came the word of the Lord by Haggai the prophet, saying,

¹¹Thus says the Lord of hosts: Ask now the priests to decide this question of law:

¹²If one carries in the skirt of his garment flesh that is holy [because it has been offered in sacrifice to God], and with his skirt *or* the flaps of his garment he touches bread, or pottage, or wine, or oil, or any kind of food, does what he touches become holy [dedicated to God's service exclusively]? And the priests answered, No! [Holiness is not infectious.]

¹³Then said Haggai, If one who is [ceremonially] unclean because he has come in contact with a dead body should touch any of these articles of food, shall it be [ceremonially] unclean? And the priests answered, It shall be unclean. [Unholiness is infectious.]

¹⁴Then answered Haggai, So is this people and so is this nation before Me, says the Lord; and so is every work of their hands, and what they offer there [on the altar] is unclean [because they who offer it are themselves unclean].

¹⁵And now, I pray you, consider what will happen from this day onward. Since the time before a stone was laid upon a stone in the temple of the Lord, how have you fared?

¹⁶Through all that time [the harvests have not fulfilled expectations, for] when one has gone expecting to find a heap [of sheaves] of twenty measures, there were but ten; when he has gone to the wine vat to draw out fifty bucketfuls from the press, there were only twenty.

¹⁷I smote you with blight and with mildew and with hail in all [the products of] the labors of your hands; yet you returned not *nor* were converted to Me, says the Lord.

¹⁸Consider, I pray you, from this day onward, from the twenty-fourth day of the ninth month, even from the day that the foundation of the Lord's temple was [re]laid, consider this:

¹⁹Is the harvested grain any longer in the barn? As to the grapevine, the fig tree, the pomegranate, and the olive tree—they have not yet borne. From this day on I will bless you.

---

*ᵃ* It is with great reluctance that we refrain from capitalizing the word "desire" here, thus making the phrase point directly to the Messiah, as has been the accepted interpretation through many centuries until modern times. But the verb "shall come" has a plural referent, and, as many commentators agree, refers to the most desired treasures that all nations will bring as gifts to adorn the temple where the Messiah will one day come. Thus the Messianic reference of the prophecy is neither questioned nor obscured, but the picture presented is like that of the coming of the Magi (Matt. 2:1-12) to find the Babe of Bethlehem, the Desire of all of them; and when they found Him they fell down and worshiped Him, bringing Him their most desirable treasures—gold, frankincense, and myrrh.

---

*ᵃ 15 Or to the days past*

## New International Version

### Zerubbabel the Lord's Signet Ring

[20]The word of the Lord came to Haggai a second time on the twenty-fourth day of the month: [21]"Tell Zerubbabel governor of Judah that I am going to shake the heavens and the earth. [22]I will overturn royal thrones and shatter the power of the foreign kingdoms. I will overthrow chariots and their drivers; horses and their riders will fall, each by the sword of his brother.

[23]"'On that day,' declares the Lord Almighty, 'I will take you, my servant Zerubbabel son of Shealtiel,' declares the Lord, 'and I will make you like my signet ring, for I have chosen you,' declares the Lord Almighty."

## Amplified Bible

[20]And again the word of the Lord came to Haggai on the twenty-fourth *day* of the month, saying,

[21]Speak to Zerubbabel [the representative of the Davidic monarchy and covenant and in direct line of the ancestry of Jesus Christ] governor of Judah, saying, I will shake the heavens and the earth; [Hag. 2:6; Matt. 1:12, 13.]

[22]And I will [in the distant future] overthrow the throne of kingdoms and I will destroy the strength of the kingdoms of the [ungodly] nations, and I will overthrow the chariots and those who ride in them, and the horses and their riders shall go down, every one by the sword of his brother. [Dan. 2:34, 35, 44, 45; Rev. 19:11-21.]

[23]In that day, says the Lord of hosts, will I take you, O Zerubbabel, My servant, the son of Shealtiel, says the Lord, and will make you [through the Messiah, your descendant] *My* signet ring; for I have chosen you [as the one with whom to renew My covenant to David's line], says the Lord of hosts. [II Sam. 7:12, 16.]

# New International Version

## Zechariah

### A Call to Return to the Lord

**1** In the eighth month of the second year of Darius, the word of the Lord came to the prophet Zechariah son of Berekiah, the son of Iddo:

²"The Lord was very angry with your ancestors. ³Therefore tell the people: This is what the Lord Almighty says: 'Return to me,' declares the Lord Almighty, 'and I will return to you,' says the Lord Almighty. ⁴Do not be like your ancestors, to whom the earlier prophets proclaimed: This is what the Lord Almighty says: 'Turn from your evil ways and your evil practices.' But they would not listen or pay attention to me, declares the Lord. ⁵Where are your ancestors now? And the prophets, do they live forever? ⁶But did not my words and my decrees, which I commanded my servants the prophets, overtake your ancestors?

"Then they repented and said, 'The Lord Almighty has done to us what our ways and practices deserve, just as he determined to do.'"

### The Man Among the Myrtle Trees

⁷On the twenty-fourth day of the eleventh month, the month of Shebat, in the second year of Darius, the word of the Lord came to the prophet Zechariah son of Berekiah, the son of Iddo.

⁸During the night I had a vision, and there before me was a man mounted on a red horse. He was standing among the myrtle trees in a ravine. Behind him were red, brown and white horses.

⁹I asked, "What are these, my lord?"

The angel who was talking with me answered, "I will show you what they are."

¹⁰Then the man standing among the myrtle trees explained, "They are the ones the Lord has sent to go throughout the earth."

¹¹And they reported to the angel of the Lord who was standing among the myrtle trees, "We have gone throughout the earth and found the whole world at rest and in peace."

¹²Then the angel of the Lord said, "Lord Almighty, how long will you withhold mercy from Jerusalem and from the towns of Judah, which you have been angry with these seventy years?" ¹³So the Lord spoke kind and comforting words to the angel who talked with me.

¹⁴Then the angel who was speaking to me said, "Proclaim this word: This is what the Lord Almighty says: 'I am very jealous for Jerusalem and Zion, ¹⁵and I am very angry with the nations that feel secure. I was only a little angry, but they went too far with the punishment.'

¹⁶"Therefore this is what the Lord says: 'I will return to Jerusalem with mercy, and there my house will be rebuilt. And the measuring line will be stretched out over Jerusalem,' declares the Lord Almighty.

# Amplified Bible

## THE BOOK OF

## Zechariah

**1** In the eighth month, in the second year [of the reign] of Darius, came the word of the Lord to Zechariah son of Berechiah, the son of Iddo, the prophet, saying, [Ezra 5:1.]

²The Lord was very angry with your fathers.

³Therefore say to them [the Jews of this day], Thus says the Lord of hosts: Return to Me, says the Lord of hosts, and I will return to you; it is the utterance of the Lord of hosts.

⁴Be not as your fathers to whom the former prophets cried, Thus says the Lord of hosts: Return now from your evil ways and your evil doings; but they would not hear or listen to Me, says the Lord. [II Kings 17:13; Isa. 45:22; Jer. 18:11; Ezek. 33:11.]

⁵Your fathers, where are they? And the prophets, do they live forever?

⁶But My words and My statutes, which I commanded My servants the prophets, did they not overtake *and* take hold of your fathers? So they repented and said, As the Lord of hosts planned *and* purposed to do to us, according to our ways and according to our doings, so has He dealt with us.

⁷Upon the twenty-fourth day of the eleventh month, which is the month of Shebat, in the second year of the reign of Darius, the word of the Lord came to Zechariah son of Berechiah, the son of Iddo, the prophet. Zechariah said,

⁸I saw in the night [vision] and behold, a *ᵃ*Man riding upon a red horse, and He stood among the myrtle trees that were in a low valley *or* bottom, and behind Him there were horses, red, bay *or* flame-colored, and white.

⁹Then said I, O my lord, what are these? And the *ᵇ*angel who talked with me said, I will show you what these are.

¹⁰And the Man who stood among the myrtle trees answered and said, These are they whom the Lord has sent to walk to and fro through the earth *and* patrol it.

¹¹And the men on the horses answered *ᶜ*the Angel of the Lord Who stood among the myrtle trees and said, We have walked to and fro through the earth [patrolling it] and behold, all the earth sits at rest [in peaceful security].

¹²Then the Angel of the Lord said, O Lord of hosts, how long will You not have mercy *and* lovingkindness for Jerusalem and the cities of Judah, against which You have had indignation these seventy years [of the Babylonian captivity]?

¹³And the Lord answered the angel who talked with me with gracious and comforting words.

¹⁴So the angel who talked with me said to me, Cry out, Thus says the Lord of hosts: I am jealous for Jerusalem and for Zion with a great jealousy.

¹⁵And I am very angry with the nations that are at ease; for while I was but a little displeased, they helped forward the affliction *and* disaster.

¹⁶Therefore thus says the Lord: I have returned to Jerusalem with compassion (lovingkindness and mercy). My house shall be built in it, says the Lord of hosts, and a measuring line shall be stretched out over Jerusalem [with a view to rebuilding its walls].

---

ᵃ The Angel of the Lord of Zech. 1:11. ᵇ The interpreting angel, mentioned in Zech. 1:9, 13-14; 2:3; 4:1, 4-5; 5:5, 10; 6:4-5, not to be confused with the Man of Zech. 1:8 or the Angel of the Lord of Zech. 1:11. ᶜ That the Angel of the Lord is an uncreated angel distinguished from other angels, and in many places identified with the Lord God, is undeniable. On the other hand there are passages in which He seems to be distinguished from God the Father. The simplest way of reconciling these two classes is to adopt the old view that this Angel is Christ, the second person of the Godhead, even at that early period appearing as the Revealer of the Father (Johan P. Lange, *A Commentary*). See also footnote on Gen. 16:7.

## New International Version

[17]"Proclaim further: This is what the LORD Almighty says: 'My towns will again overflow with prosperity, and the LORD will again comfort Zion and choose Jerusalem.'"

### Four Horns and Four Craftsmen

[18]Then I looked up, and there before me were four horns. [19]I asked the angel who was speaking to me, "What are these?"

He answered me, "These are the horns that scattered Judah, Israel and Jerusalem."

[20]Then the LORD showed me four craftsmen. [21]I asked, "What are these coming to do?"

He answered, "These are the horns that scattered Judah so that no one could raise their head, but the craftsmen have come to terrify them and throw down these horns of the nations who lifted up their horns against the land of Judah to scatter its people."[a]

### A Man With a Measuring Line

**2**[b] Then I looked up, and there before me was a man with a measuring line in his hand. [2]I asked, "Where are you going?"

He answered me, "To measure Jerusalem, to find out how wide and how long it is."

[3]While the angel who was speaking to me was leaving, another angel came to meet him [4]and said to him: "Run, tell that young man, 'Jerusalem will be a city without walls because of the great number of people and animals in it. [5]And I myself will be a wall of fire around it,' declares the LORD, 'and I will be its glory within.'

[6]"Come! Come! Flee from the land of the north," declares the LORD, "for I have scattered you to the four winds of heaven," declares the LORD.

[7]"Come, Zion! Escape, you who live in Daughter Babylon!" [8]For this is what the LORD Almighty says: "After the Glorious One has sent me against the nations that have plundered you—for whoever touches you touches the apple of his eye— [9]I will surely raise my hand against them so that their slaves will plunder them.[c] Then you will know that the LORD Almighty has sent me.

[10]"Shout and be glad, Daughter Zion. For I am coming, and I will live among you," declares the LORD. [11]"Many nations will be joined with the LORD in that day and will become my people. I will live among you and you will know that the LORD Almighty has sent me to you. [12]The LORD will inherit Judah as his portion in the holy land and will again choose Jerusalem. [13]Be still before the LORD, all mankind, because he has roused himself from his holy dwelling."

### Clean Garments for the High Priest

**3** Then he showed me Joshua the high priest standing before the angel of the LORD, and Satan[d] standing at his right side to accuse him. [2]The LORD said to Satan, "The LORD rebuke you, Satan! The LORD, who has chosen Jerusalem, rebuke you! Is not this man a burning stick snatched from the fire?"

## Amplified Bible

[17]Cry yet again, saying, Thus says the Lord of hosts: My cities shall yet again overflow with prosperity, and the Lord shall yet comfort Zion and shall yet choose Jerusalem.

[18]Then I lifted up my eyes and saw, and behold, four horns [symbols of strength].

[19]And I said to the angel who talked with me, What are these? And he answered me, These are the horns or powers which have scattered Judah, Israel, and Jerusalem.

[20]Then the Lord showed me four smiths or workmen [one for each enemy horn, to beat it down].

[21]Then said I, What are these [horns and smiths] coming to do? And he said, These are the horns or powers that scattered Judah so that no man lifted up his head. But these smiths or workmen have come to terrorize them and cause them to be panic-stricken, to cast out the horns or powers of the nations who lifted up their horn against the land of Judah to scatter it.

**2** And I lifted up my eyes and saw, and behold, a man with a measuring line in his hand.

[2]Then said I, Where are you going? And he said to me, To measure Jerusalem, to see what is its breadth and what is its length.

[3]And behold, the angel who talked with me went forth and another angel went out to meet him,

[4]And he said to the second angel, Run, speak to this young man, saying, Jerusalem shall be inhabited and dwell as villages without walls, because of the multitude of people and livestock in it.

[5]For I, says the Lord, will be to her a wall of fire round about, and I will be the glory in the midst of her.

[6]Ho! ho! [Hear and] flee from the land of the north, says the Lord, and from the four winds of the heavens, for to them have I scattered you, says the Lord.

[7]Ho! Escape to Zion, you who dwell with the daughter of Babylon!

[8]For thus said the Lord of hosts, after [His] glory had sent me [His messenger] to the nations who plundered you—for he who touches you touches the apple or pupil of His eye:

[9]Behold, I will swing my hand over them and they shall become plunder for those who served them. Then you shall know (recognize and understand) that the Lord of hosts has sent me [His messenger].

[10]Sing and rejoice, O Daughter of Zion; for behold, I come, and I will dwell in the midst of you, says the Lord.

[11]And many nations shall join themselves to the Lord in that day and shall be My people. And I will dwell in the midst of you, and you shall know (recognize and understand) that the Lord of hosts has sent me [His messenger] to you. [Isa. 2:3; Mic. 4:2.]

[12]And the Lord shall inherit Judah as His portion in the holy land and shall again choose Jerusalem.

[13]Be still, all flesh, before the Lord, for He is aroused and risen from His holy habitation. [Hab. 2:20; Zeph. 1:7.]

**3** Then [the guiding angel] showed me Joshua the high priest standing before [a]the Angel of the Lord, and Satan standing at Joshua's right hand to be his adversary and to accuse him.

[2]And the Lord said to Satan, The Lord rebuke you, O Satan! Even the Lord, Who [now and habitually] chooses Jerusalem, rebuke you! Is not this [returned captive Joshua] a brand plucked out of the fire? [Jude 9.]

---

[a] 21 In Hebrew texts 1:18-21 is numbered 2:1-4.   [b] In Hebrew texts 2:1-13 is numbered 2:5-17.   [c] 8,9 Or says after . . . eye: [9]"I . . . plunder them."   [d] 1 Hebrew satan means adversary.

[a] See footnote on Zechariah 1:11.

## New International Version

3Now Joshua was dressed in filthy clothes as he stood before the angel. 4The angel said to those who were standing before him, "Take off his filthy clothes."

Then he said to Joshua, "See, I have taken away your sin, and I will put fine garments on you."

5Then I said, "Put a clean turban on his head." So they put a clean turban on his head and clothed him, while the angel of the LORD stood by.

6The angel of the LORD gave this charge to Joshua: 7"This is what the LORD Almighty says: 'If you will walk in obedience to me and keep my requirements, then you will govern my house and have charge of my courts, and I will give you a place among these standing here.

8"'Listen, High Priest Joshua, you and your associates seated before you, who are men symbolic of things to come: I am going to bring my servant, the Branch. 9See, the stone I have set in front of Joshua! There are seven eyes*a* on that one stone, and I will engrave an inscription on it,' says the LORD Almighty, 'and I will remove the sin of this land in a single day.

10"'In that day each of you will invite your neighbor to sit under your vine and fig tree,' declares the LORD Almighty."

### The Gold Lampstand and the Two Olive Trees

4 Then the angel who talked with me returned and woke me up, like someone awakened from sleep. 2He asked me, "What do you see?"

I answered, "I see a solid gold lampstand with a bowl at the top and seven lamps on it, with seven channels to the lamps. 3Also there are two olive trees by it, one on the right of the bowl and the other on its left."

4I asked the angel who talked with me, "What are these, my lord?"

5He answered, "Do you not know what these are?"

"No, my lord," I replied.

6So he said to me, "This is the word of the LORD to Zerubbabel: 'Not by might nor by power, but by my Spirit,' says the LORD Almighty.

7"What are you, mighty mountain? Before Zerubbabel you will become level ground. Then he will bring out the capstone to shouts of 'God bless it! God bless it!'"

8Then the word of the LORD came to me: 9"The hands of Zerubbabel have laid the foundation of this temple; his hands will also complete it. Then you will know that the LORD Almighty has sent me to you.

10"Who dares despise the day of small things, since the seven eyes of the LORD that range throughout the earth will rejoice when they see the chosen capstone*b* in the hand of Zerubbabel?"

## Amplified Bible

3Now Joshua was clothed with filthy garments and was standing before the Angel [of the Lord].

4And He spoke to those who stood before Him, saying, Take away the filthy garments from him. And He said to [Joshua], Behold, I have caused your iniquity to pass from you, and I will clothe you with rich apparel.

5And I [Zechariah] said, Let them put a clean turban on his head. So they put a clean turban on his head and clothed him with [rich] garments. And the Angel of the Lord stood by.

6And the Angel of the Lord [solemnly and earnestly] protested *and* affirmed to Joshua, saying,

7Thus says the Lord of hosts: If you will walk in My ways and keep My charge, then also you shall rule My house and have charge of My courts, and I will give you access [to My presence] *and* places to walk among these who stand here.

8Hear now, O Joshua the high priest, you and your colleagues who [usually] sit before you—for they are men who are a sign *or* omen [types of what is to come]—for behold, I will bring forth My servant the *a*Branch. [Isa. 4:2; Jer. 23:5; 33:15; Zech. 6:12.]

9For behold, upon the stone which I have set before Joshua, upon that one stone are seven eyes *or* facets [the all-embracing providence of God and the sevenfold radiations of the Spirit of God]. Behold, I will carve upon it its inscription, says the Lord of hosts, and I will remove the iniquity *and* guilt of this land in a single day. [II Chron. 16:9; Jer. 50:20; Zech. 4:10.]

10In that day, says the Lord of hosts, you shall invite each man his neighbor under his own vine and his own fig tree. [Mic. 4:1-4.]

4 And the angel who talked with me came again and awakened me, like a man who is wakened out of his sleep.

2And said to me, What do you see? I said, I see, and behold, a lampstand all of gold, with its bowl [for oil] on the top of it and its seven lamps on it, and [there are] seven pipes to each of the seven lamps which are upon the top of it. [Matt. 5:14, 16; Luke 12:35; Phil. 2:15; Rev. 1:20.]

3And there are two olive trees by it, one upon the right side of the bowl and the other upon the left side of it [feeding it continuously with oil]. [Rev. 11:4-13.]

4So I asked the angel who talked with me, What are these, my lord?

5Then the angel who talked with me answered me, Do you not know what these are? And I said, No, my lord.

6Then he said to me, This [addition of the bowl to the candlestick, causing it to yield a ceaseless supply of oil from the olive trees] is the word of the Lord to Zerubbabel, saying, Not by might, nor by power, but by My Spirit [of Whom the oil is a symbol], says the Lord of hosts.

7For who are you, O great mountain [of human obstacles]? Before Zerubbabel [who with Joshua had led the return of the exiles from Babylon and was undertaking the rebuilding of the temple, before him] you shall become a plain [a mere *b*molehill]! And he shall bring forth the finishing gable stone [of the new temple] with loud shoutings of the people, crying, Grace, grace to it! [Ezra 4:1-5, 24; Isa. 40:4.]

8Moreover, the word of the Lord came to me, saying,

9The hands of Zerubbabel have laid the foundations of this house; his hands shall also finish it. Then you shall know (recognize and understand) that the Lord of hosts has sent me [His messenger] to you.

10Who [with reason] despises the day of small things? For these seven shall rejoice when they see the plummet in the hand of Zerubbabel. [These seven] are the eyes of the Lord which run to and fro throughout the whole earth. [Rev. 5:6.]

---

*a* 9 Or *facets*    *b* 10 Or *the plumb line*

*a* A Messianic title.   *b* This recalls the familiar proverb about "making mountains out of molehills," with a surprising twist.

## New International Version

¹¹Then I asked the angel, "What are these two olive trees on the right and the left of the lampstand?"

¹²Again I asked him, "What are these two olive branches beside the two gold pipes that pour out golden oil?"

¹³He replied, "Do you not know what these are?"

"No, my lord," I said.

¹⁴So he said, "These are the two who are anointed to<sup>a</sup> serve the Lord of all the earth."

### The Flying Scroll

**5** I looked again, and there before me was a flying scroll. ²He asked me, "What do you see?"

I answered, "I see a flying scroll, twenty cubits long and ten cubits wide.<sup>b</sup>"

³And he said to me, "This is the curse that is going out over the whole land; for according to what it says on one side, every thief will be banished, and according to what it says on the other, everyone who swears falsely will be banished. ⁴The Lord Almighty declares, 'I will send it out, and it will enter the house of the thief and the house of anyone who swears falsely by my name. It will remain in that house and destroy it completely, both its timbers and its stones.'"

### The Woman in a Basket

⁵Then the angel who was speaking to me came forward and said to me, "Look up and see what is appearing."

⁶I asked, "What is it?"

He replied, "It is a basket." And he added, "This is the iniquity<sup>c</sup> of the people throughout the land."

⁷Then the cover of lead was raised, and there in the basket sat a woman! ⁸He said, "This is wickedness," and he pushed her back into the basket and pushed its lead cover down on it.

⁹Then I looked up—and there before me were two women, with the wind in their wings! They had wings like those of a stork, and they lifted up the basket between heaven and earth.

¹⁰"Where are they taking the basket?" I asked the angel who was speaking to me.

¹¹He replied, "To the country of Babylonia<sup>d</sup> to build a house for it. When the house is ready, the basket will be set there in its place."

### Four Chariots

**6** I looked up again, and there before me were four chariots coming out from between two mountains—mountains of bronze. ²The first chariot had red horses, the second black, ³the third white, and the fourth dappled—all of them powerful. ⁴I asked the angel who was speaking to me, "What are these, my lord?"

⁵The angel answered me, "These are the four spirits<sup>e</sup> of heaven, going out from standing in the presence of the

## Amplified Bible

¹¹Then I said to him [the angel who talked with me], What are these two olive trees on the right side of the lampstand and on the left side of it?

¹²And a second time I said to him, What are these two olive branches which are beside the two golden tubes *or* spouts by which the golden oil is emptied out?

¹³And he answered me, Do you not know what these are? And I said, No, my lord.

¹⁴Then said he, These are the two <sup>a</sup>sons of oil [Joshua the high priest and Zerubbabel the prince of Judah, the two anointed ones] who stand before the Lord of the whole earth [as His anointed instruments]. [Rev. 11:4.]

**5** Again I lifted up my eyes and behold, I saw a scroll flying *or* floating in the air!

²And the angel said to me, What do you see? And I answered, I see a flying scroll; its length is twenty cubits *or* thirty feet and its breadth is ten cubits *or* fifteen feet.

³Then he said to me, This is the curse that goes out over the face of the whole land; for everyone who steals shall be cut off from henceforth according to it [the curse written on this subject on the scroll], and everyone who swears falsely shall be cut off from henceforth according to it. [Isa. 24:6; Mal. 3:8, 9.]

⁴I will bring [the curse] forth, says the Lord of hosts, and it shall enter into the house of the thief and into the house of him who swears falsely by My name; and it shall abide in the midst of his house and shall consume it, both its timber and its stones.

⁵Then the angel who talked with me came forward and said to me, Lift up now your eyes and see what this is that goes forth.

⁶And I said, What is it? [What does it symbolize?] And he said, This that goes forth is an ephah[-sized vessel for separate grains all collected together]. This, he continued, is the symbol of the sinners mentioned above *and* is the resemblance of their iniquity throughout the whole land. [Amos 8:5.]

⁷And behold, a round, flat weight of lead was lifted and there sat a woman in the midst of the ephah[-sized vessel].

⁸And he said, This is lawlessness (wickedness)! And he thrust her back into the ephah[-sized vessel] and he cast the weight of lead upon the mouth of it!

⁹Then lifted I up my eyes and looked, and behold, there were two women coming forward! The wind was in their wings, for they had wings like the wings of a stork, and they lifted up the ephah[-sized vessel] between the earth and the heavens.

¹⁰Then said I to the angel who talked with me, Where are they taking the ephah[-sized vessel]?

¹¹And he said to me, To the land of Shinar [Babylonia] to build it a house, and when it is finished, to set up the ephah[-sized vessel—the symbol of such sinners and their guilt] there upon its own base.

**6** And again I lifted up my eyes and saw, and behold, four chariots came out from between two mountains; and the mountains were mountains of firm, immovable bronze.

²The first chariot had red *or* bay horses, the second chariot had black horses,

³The third chariot had white horses, and the fourth chariot had dappled, active, *and* strong horses.

⁴Then I said to the angel who talked with me, What are these, my lord?

⁵And the angel answered me, These are the four winds *or* spirits of the heavens, which go forth from presenting themselves before the Lord of all the earth. [Ps. 104:4; Matt. 24:31.]

---

<sup>a</sup> 14 Or *two who bring oil and*    <sup>b</sup> 2 That is, about 30 feet long and 15 feet wide or about 9 meters long and 4.5 meters wide    <sup>c</sup> 6 Or *appearance*    <sup>d</sup> 11 Hebrew *Shinar*    <sup>e</sup> 5 Or *winds*

---

<sup>a</sup> The oil used in anointing symbolizes the Holy Spirit (Zech. 4:6). The combination of priest and ruler points ultimately to the Messianic Priest-King (Ps. 110; Zech. 6:13; Heb. 7).

## New International Version

Lord of the whole world. 6The one with the black horses is going toward the north country, the one with the white horses toward the west,a and the one with the dappled horses toward the south."

7When the powerful horses went out, they were straining to go throughout the earth. And he said, "Go throughout the earth!" So they went throughout the earth.

8Then he called to me, "Look, those going toward the north country have given my Spiritb rest in the land of the north."

### A Crown for Joshua

9The word of the LORD came to me: 10"Take silver and gold from the exiles Heldai, Tobijah and Jedaiah, who have arrived from Babylon. Go the same day to the house of Josiah son of Zephaniah. 11Take the silver and gold and make a crown, and set it on the head of the high priest, Joshua son of Jozadak.c 12Tell him this is what the LORD Almighty says: 'Here is the man whose name is the Branch, and he will branch out from his place and build the temple of the LORD. 13It is he who will build the temple of the LORD, and he will be clothed with majesty and will sit and rule on his throne. And hed will be a priest on his throne. And there will be harmony between the two.' 14The crown will be given to Heldai,e Tobijah, Jedaiah and Henf son of Zephaniah as a memorial in the temple of the LORD. 15Those who are far away will come and help to build the temple of the LORD, and you will know that the LORD Almighty has sent me to you. This will happen if you diligently obey the LORD your God."

### Justice and Mercy, Not Fasting

**7** In the fourth year of King Darius, the word of the LORD came to Zechariah on the fourth day of the ninth month, the month of Kislev. 2The people of Bethel had sent Sharezer and Regem-Melek, together with their men, to entreat the LORD 3by asking the priests of the house of the LORD Almighty and the prophets, "Should I mourn and fast in the fifth month, as I have done for so many years?"

4Then the word of the LORD Almighty came to me: 5"Ask all the people of the land and the priests, 'When you fasted and mourned in the fifth and seventh months for the past seventy years, was it really for me that you fasted? 6And when you were eating and drinking, were you not just feasting for yourselves? 7Are these not the words the LORD proclaimed through the earlier prophets when Jerusalem and its surrounding towns were at rest and prosperous, and the Negev and the western foothills were settled?'"

8And the word of the LORD came again to Zechariah: 9"This is what the LORD Almighty said: 'Administer true justice; show mercy and compassion to one another. 10Do

## Amplified Bible

6The chariot with the black horses is going forth into the north country, and the white ones are going forth after them [because there are two northern powers to overcome], and the dappled ones are going forth toward the south country.

7And [the chariots with] the strong [horses] went forth and sought to go that they might patrol the earth. And [the Lord] said to them, Go, walk to and fro through the earth and patrol it. So they walked about through the earth [watching and protecting it].

8Then He summoned me and said to me, Behold, these that go toward the north country have quieted My Spirit [of wrath] and have caused it to rest in the north country.

9And the word of the Lord came to me, saying,

10Accept donations and offerings from these [as representatives of the] exiles, from Heldai, from Tobijah, and from Jedaiah, who have come from Babylon; and come the same day and go to the house of Josiah the son of Zephaniah.

11Yes, take from them silver and gold, and make crowns and set [one] upon the head of Joshua the son of Jehozadak, the high priest,

12And say to him, Thus says the Lord of hosts: [You, Joshua] behold (look at, keep in sight, watch) the Man [the Messiah] whose name is the Branch, for He shall grow up in His place and He shall build the [true] temple of the Lord. [Isa. 4:2; Jer. 23:5; 33:15; Zech. 3:8.]

13Yes, [you are building a temple of the Lord, but] it is He Who shall build the [true] temple of the Lord, and He shall bear the honor and glory [as of the only begotten of the Father] and shall sit and rule upon His throne. And He shall be a aPriest upon His throne, and the counsel of peace shall be between the two [offices—Priest and King]. [John 1:14; 17:5; Heb. 2:9.]

14And the [other] crown shall be [credited] to Helem (Heldai), to Tobijah, and to Jedaiah, and to the kindness and favor of Josiah the son of Zephaniah, and shall be in the temple of the Lord for a reminder and memorial. [Matt. 10:41.]

15And those who are far off shall come and help build the temple of the Lord, and you shall know (recognize and understand) that the Lord sent me [Zechariah] to you. And [your part in this] shall come to pass if you will diligently obey the voice of the Lord your God.

**7** And in the fourth year of the reign of King Darius, the word of the Lord came to Zechariah on the fourth day of the ninth month, Chislev.

2Now the people of Bethel had sent Sharezer and Regem-melech and their men to pray and entreat the favor of the Lord

3And to speak to the priests of the house of the Lord of hosts and to the prophets, saying, [Now that I am returned from exile] should I weep in the fifth month, separating myself as I have done these so many years [in Babylon]?

4Then came the word of the Lord of hosts to me [Zechariah], saying,

5Speak to all the people of the land and to the priests, saying, When you fasted and mourned in the fifth and seventh months, even those seventy years you were in exile, was it for Me that you fasted, for Me?

6And when you ate and when you drank, did you not eat for yourselves and drink for yourselves?

7Should you not hear the words which the Lord cried by the former prophets when Jerusalem was inhabited and in prosperity with her cities round about her, and the South (the Negeb) and the lowlands were inhabited?

8And the word of the Lord came to Zechariah, saying,

9Thus has the Lord of hosts spoken: Execute true judgment and show mercy and kindness and tender compassion, every man to his brother;

---

a 6 Or horses after them   b 8 Or spirit   c 11 Hebrew Jehozadak, a variant of Jozadak   d 13 Or there   e 14 Syriac; Hebrew Helem   f 14 Or and the gracious one, the

a The coming Davidic King will also be a Priest.

## New International Version

not oppress the widow or the fatherless, the foreigner or the poor. Do not plot evil against each other.'

¹¹"But they refused to pay attention; stubbornly they turned their backs and covered their ears. ¹²They made their hearts as hard as flint and would not listen to the law or to the words that the LORD Almighty had sent by his Spirit through the earlier prophets. So the LORD Almighty was very angry.

¹³"'When I called, they did not listen; so when they called, I would not listen,' says the LORD Almighty. ¹⁴'I scattered them with a whirlwind among all the nations, where they were strangers. The land they left behind them was so desolate that no one traveled through it. This is how they made the pleasant land desolate.'"

### The LORD Promises to Bless Jerusalem

**8** The word of the LORD Almighty came to me. ²This is what the LORD Almighty says: "I am very jealous for Zion; I am burning with jealousy for her."

³This is what the LORD says: "I will return to Zion and dwell in Jerusalem. Then Jerusalem will be called the Faithful City, and the mountain of the LORD Almighty will be called the Holy Mountain."

⁴This is what the LORD Almighty says: "Once again men and women of ripe old age will sit in the streets of Jerusalem, each of them with cane in hand because of their age. ⁵The city streets will be filled with boys and girls playing there."

⁶This is what the LORD Almighty says: "It may seem marvelous to the remnant of this people at that time, but will it seem marvelous to me?" declares the LORD Almighty.

⁷This is what the LORD Almighty says: "I will save my people from the countries of the east and the west. ⁸I will bring them back to live in Jerusalem; they will be my people, and I will be faithful and righteous to them as their God."

⁹This is what the LORD Almighty says: "Now hear these words, 'Let your hands be strong so that the temple may be built.' This is also what the prophets said who were present when the foundation was laid for the house of the LORD Almighty. ¹⁰Before that time there were no wages for people or hire for animals. No one could go about their business safely because of their enemies, since I had turned everyone against their neighbor. ¹¹But now I will not deal with the remnant of this people as I did in the past," declares the LORD Almighty.

¹²"The seed will grow well, the vine will yield its fruit, the ground will produce its crops, and the heavens will drop their dew. I will give all these things as an inheritance to the remnant of this people. ¹³Just as you, Judah and Israel, have been a curse*a* among the nations, so I will save you, and you will be a blessing.*b* Do not be afraid, but let your hands be strong."

¹⁴This is what the LORD Almighty says: "Just as I had

## Amplified Bible

¹⁰And oppress not the widow or the fatherless, the temporary resident or the poor, and let none of you devise or imagine or think evil against his brother in your heart.

¹¹But they refused to listen and turned a rebellious and stubborn shoulder and made heavy and dull their ears that they might not hear.

¹²Yes, they made their hearts as an adamant stone or diamond point, lest they should hear the law and the words which the Lord of hosts had sent by His Spirit through the former prophets. Therefore there came great wrath from the Lord of hosts.

¹³So it came to pass that as He cried and they would not hear [He said], So they shall cry and I will not answer, says the Lord of hosts,

¹⁴But I will scatter them with a whirlwind among all the nations whom they know not and who know not them. Thus the land was desolate after they had gone, so that no man passed through or returned, for they [the Jews by their sins] had [caused to be] laid waste and forsaken the pleasant land (the land of desire).

**8** And the word of the Lord of hosts came to me, saying, ²Thus says the Lord of hosts: I am jealous for Zion with great jealousy, and I am jealous for her with great wrath [against her enemies].

³Thus says the Lord: I shall return to Zion and will dwell in the midst of Jerusalem, and Jerusalem shall be called the [faithful] City of Truth, and the mountain of the Lord of hosts, the Holy Mountain.

⁴Thus says the Lord of hosts: Old men and old women shall again dwell in Jerusalem and sit out in the streets, every man with his staff in his hand for very [advanced] age.

⁵And the streets of the city shall be full of boys and girls playing in its streets.

⁶Thus says the Lord of hosts: Because it will be marvelous in the eyes of the remnant of this people in those days [in which it comes to pass], should it also be marvelous in My eyes? says the Lord of hosts. [Gen. 18:14; Jer. 32:17, 27; Luke 18:27.]

⁷Thus says the Lord of hosts: Behold, I will save My people from the east country and from the west [the country of the going down of the sun]. [Isa. 43:5, 6.]

⁸And I will bring them [home] and they shall dwell in the midst of Jerusalem; and they shall be My people, and I will be their God in truth and faithfulness and in righteousness.

⁹Thus says the Lord of hosts: Let your hands be strong and hardened, you who in these days hear these words from the mouths of the prophets who on the day that the foundation of the house of the Lord of hosts was laid foretold that the temple should be rebuilt.

¹⁰For before those days there was no hire for man nor any hire for beast, neither was there any peace or success to him who went out or came in because of the adversary and oppressor, for I set (let loose) all men, every one against his neighbor.

¹¹But now [in this period since you began to build] I am not to the remnant of this people as in the former days, says the Lord of hosts.

¹²For there shall the seed produce peace and prosperity; the vine shall yield her fruit and the ground shall give its increase and the heavens shall give their dew; and I will cause the remnant of this people to inherit and possess all these things.

¹³And as you have been a curse and a byword among the nations, O house of Judah and house of Israel, so will I save you, and you shall be a blessing. Fear not, but let your hands be strong and hardened. [Jer. 22:8, 9.]

¹⁴For thus says the Lord of hosts: As I thought to bring

---

*a 13* That is, your name has been used in cursing (see Jer. 29:22); or, you have been regarded as under a curse.    *b 13* Or *and your name will be used in blessings* (see Gen. 48:20); or *and you will be seen as blessed*

## New International Version

determined to bring disaster on you and showed no pity when your ancestors angered me," says the LORD Almighty, [15]"so now I have determined to do good again to Jerusalem and Judah. Do not be afraid. [16]These are the things you are to do: Speak the truth to each other, and render true and sound judgment in your courts; [17]do not plot evil against each other, and do not love to swear falsely. I hate all this," declares the LORD.

[18]The word of the LORD Almighty came to me. [19]This is what the LORD Almighty says: "The fasts of the fourth, fifth, seventh and tenth months will become joyful and glad occasions and happy festivals for Judah. Therefore love truth and peace."

[20]This is what the LORD Almighty says: "Many peoples and the inhabitants of many cities will yet come, [21]and the inhabitants of one city will go to another and say, 'Let us go at once to entreat the LORD and seek the LORD Almighty. I myself am going.' [22]And many peoples and powerful nations will come to Jerusalem to seek the LORD Almighty and to entreat him."

[23]This is what the LORD Almighty says: "In those days ten people from all languages and nations will take firm hold of one Jew by the hem of his robe and say, 'Let us go with you, because we have heard that God is with you.'"

### Judgment on Israel's Enemies

**9** A prophecy:

The word of the LORD is against the land of Hadrak
  and will come to rest on Damascus—
for the eyes of all people and all the tribes of Israel
  are on the LORD— [a]
[2]and on Hamath too, which borders on it,
  and on Tyre and Sidon, though they are very
    skillful.
[3]Tyre has built herself a stronghold;
  she has heaped up silver like dust,
  and gold like the dirt of the streets.
[4]But the Lord will take away her possessions
  and destroy her power on the sea,
  and she will be consumed by fire.
[5]Ashkelon will see it and fear;
  Gaza will writhe in agony,
  and Ekron too, for her hope will wither.
Gaza will lose her king
  and Ashkelon will be deserted.

---

## Amplified Bible

calamity upon you when your fathers provoked Me to wrath, says the Lord of hosts, and I did not relent or revoke your sentence,

[15]So again have I purposed in these days to do good to Jerusalem and to the house of Judah. Fear not! [16]These are the things that you shall do: speak every man the truth with his neighbor; render the truth and pronounce the judgment or verdict that makes for peace in [the courts at] your gates. [Eph. 4:25.]

[17]And let none of you think or imagine or devise evil or injury in your hearts against his neighbor, and love no false oath, for all these things I hate, says the Lord.

[18]And the word of the Lord of hosts came to me [Zechariah], saying,

[19]Thus says the Lord of hosts: The fast of the fourth month and the fast of the fifth, the fast of the seventh and the fast of the tenth, shall be to the house of Judah times of joy and gladness and cheerful, appointed seasons; therefore [in order that this may happen to you, as the condition of fulfilling the promise] love truth and peace.

[20]Thus says the Lord of hosts: It shall yet come to pass that there shall come [to Jerusalem] peoples and the inhabitants of many and great cities,

[21]And the inhabitants of one city shall go to them of another, saying, Let us go speedily to pray and entreat the favor of the Lord and to seek, inquire of, and require [to meet our own most essential need] the Lord of hosts. I will go also.

[22]Yes, many people and strong nations shall come to Jerusalem to seek, inquire of, and require [to fill their own urgent need] the Lord of hosts and to pray to the Lord for His favor.

[23]Thus says the Lord of hosts: In those days ten men out of all languages of the nations shall take hold of the robe of him who is a Jew, saying, Let us go with you, for we have heard that God is with you.

**9** The burden or oracle (the thing to be lifted up) of the word of the Lord is against the land of Hadrach [in Syria], and Damascus shall be its resting place, for the Lord has an eye upon mankind as upon all the tribes of Israel,

[2]And Hamath also, which borders on [Damascus], Tyre with Sidon, though they are very wise.

[3]And Tyre has built herself a stronghold [on an island a half mile from the shore, which seems impregnable], and heaped up silver like dust and fine gold like the mire of the streets.

[4]Behold, the Lord will [a]cast her out and dispossess her; He will smite her power in the sea and into it and [Tyre] shall be devoured by fire.

[5][The strong cities of Philistia] shall see it and fear; [b]Ashkelon, Gaza also, and be sorely pained, and Ekron, for her confidence and expectation shall be put to shame, and a king [monarchial government] shall perish from Gaza, and Ashkelon shall not be inhabited.

---

[a] Tyre was utterly destroyed by Alexander the Great and has never been rebuilt. History records that after he had slain everyone except those who had fled to the temples, Alexander ordered the houses to be set afire. Yet Sidon, Tyre's sister city (Zech. 9:2), though meeting with many adversities, has survived and has kept her identity (modern Saida) for an estimated 4,000 years (Gen. 10:15, 19). How did Zechariah know that it was Tyre, not Sidon, that was to be permanently destroyed? Ezekiel wrote of Tyre, after telling the details of her destruction, "You shall never be rebuilt, for I the Lord have spoken it, says the Lord God" (Ezek. 26:14). [b] Ashkelon was one of the five strong, leading Philistine cities (Josh. 13:3)—Gath and Ashdod being the ones not named here in this verse. Ashkelon was the birthplace of Herod the Great, and the residence of his sister Salome. It was not until A.D. 1270 that Zechariah's prophecy of its total destruction was fulfilled, when the Sultan Bibars reduced it to ruins and filled the harbor with stones. Nearly 700 years later the city is still uninhabited, and the seacoast has been and continues to be the site of "dwellings and cottages for shepherds and folds for flocks" (Zeph. 2:6 KJV).

---

[a] 1 Or Damascus. / For the eye of the LORD is on all people, / as well as on the tribes of Israel,

## New International Version

6A mongrel people will occupy Ashdod,
and I will put an end to the pride of the Philistines.
7I will take the blood from their mouths,
the forbidden food from between their teeth.
Those who are left will belong to our God
and become a clan in Judah,
and Ekron will be like the Jebusites.
8But I will encamp at my temple
to guard it against marauding forces.
Never again will an oppressor overrun my people,
for now I am keeping watch.

### The Coming of Zion's King

9Rejoice greatly, Daughter Zion!
Shout, Daughter Jerusalem!
See, your king comes to you,
righteous and victorious,
lowly and riding on a donkey,
on a colt, the foal of a donkey.
10I will take away the chariots from Ephraim
and the warhorses from Jerusalem,
and the battle bow will be broken.
He will proclaim peace to the nations.
His rule will extend from sea to sea
and from the River*a* to the ends of the earth.
11As for you, because of the blood of my covenant with you,
I will free your prisoners from the waterless pit.
12Return to your fortress, you prisoners of hope;
even now I announce that I will restore twice as
much to you.
13I will bend Judah as I bend my bow
and fill it with Ephraim.
I will rouse your sons, Zion,
against your sons, Greece,
and make you like a warrior's sword.

### The Lord Will Appear

14Then the Lord will appear over them;
his arrow will flash like lightning.
The Sovereign Lord will sound the trumpet;
he will march in the storms of the south,
15    and the Lord Almighty will shield them.
They will destroy
and overcome with slingstones.
They will drink and roar as with wine;
they will be full like a bowl
used for sprinkling*b* the corners of the altar.
16The Lord their God will save his people on that day
as a shepherd saves his flock.
They will sparkle in his land
like jewels in a crown.
17How attractive and beautiful they will be!
Grain will make the young men thrive,
and new wine the young women.

### The Lord Will Care for Judah

**10** Ask the Lord for rain in the springtime;
it is the Lord who sends the thunderstorms.
He gives showers of rain to all people,
and plants of the field to everyone.
2The idols speak deceitfully,
diviners see visions that lie;
they tell dreams that are false,
they give comfort in vain.
Therefore the people wander like sheep
oppressed for lack of a shepherd.
3"My anger burns against the shepherds,
and I will punish the leaders;

## Amplified Bible

6And a mongrel people shall dwell in Ashdod, and I will put an end to the pride of the Philistines.
7And I will take out of [the Philistines'] mouths and from between their teeth the abominable idolatrous sacrifices eaten with the blood. And they too shall remain *and* be a remnant for our God, and they shall be like chieftains (the head over a thousand) in Judah, and Ekron shall be like one of the Jebusites [who at last were merged and had lost their identity in Israel].
8Then I will encamp about My house as a guard *or* a garrison so that none shall march back and forth, and no oppressor *or* demanding collector shall again overrun them, for now My eyes are upon them.
9Rejoice greatly, O Daughter of Zion! Shout aloud, O Daughter of Jerusalem! Behold, your King comes to you; He is [uncompromisingly] just and having salvation [triumphant and victorious], patient, meek, lowly, and riding on a donkey, upon a colt, the foal of a donkey. [Matt. 21:5; John 12:14, 15.]
10And I will cut off *and* exterminate the war chariot from Ephraim and the [war] horse from Jerusalem, and the battle bow shall be cut off; and He shall speak the word and peace shall come to the nations, and His dominion shall be from the [Mediterranean] Sea to [any other] sea, and from the River [Euphrates] to the ends of the earth! [Ps. 72:8.]
11As for you also, because of *and* for the sake of the [covenant of the Lord with His people, which was sealed with sprinkled] covenant blood, I have released *and* sent forth your imprisoned people out of the waterless pit. [Gen. 37:24; Exod. 24:4-8; Heb. 9:16.]
12Return to the stronghold [of security and prosperity], you prisoners of hope; even today do I declare that I will restore double your former prosperity to you. [Ps. 40:2; Isa. 40:2.]
13For I have bent Judah for Myself as My bow, filled the bow with Ephraim as My arrow, and will stir up your sons, O Zion, against your sons, O Greece, and will make you [Israel] as the sword of a mighty man.
14And the Lord shall be seen over them and His arrow shall go forth as the lightning, and the Lord God will blow the trumpet and will go forth in the windstorms of the south.
15The Lord of hosts shall defend *and* protect them; and they shall devour and they shall tread on [their fallen enemies] as on slingstones [that have missed their aim], and they shall drink [of victory] and be noisy *and* turbulent as from wine and become full like bowls [used to catch the sacrificial blood], like the corners of the [sacrificial] altar.
16And the Lord their God will save them on that day as the flock of His people, for they shall be as the [precious] jewels of a crown, lifted high over *and* shining glitteringly upon His land.
17For how great is God's goodness and how great is His beauty! And how great [He will make Israel's] goodliness and [Israel's] beauty! Grain shall make the young men thrive and fresh wine the maidens.

**10** Ask of the Lord rain in the time of the latter *or* spring rain. It is the Lord Who makes lightnings which usher in the rain *and* give men showers, and grass to everyone in the field.
2For the teraphim (household idols) have spoken vanity (emptiness, falsity, and futility) and the diviners have seen a lie and the dreamers have told false dreams; they comfort in vain. Therefore the people go their way like sheep; they are afflicted *and* hurt because there is no shepherd.
3My anger is kindled against the shepherds [who are not true shepherds] and I will punish the goat leaders, for

---

*a 10* That is, the Euphrates    *b 15* Or *bowl, / like*

## New International Version

for the Lord Almighty will care
    for his flock, the people of Judah,
    and make them like a proud horse in battle.
[4] From Judah will come the cornerstone,
    from him the tent peg,
from him the battle bow,
    from him every ruler.
[5] Together they[a] will be like warriors in battle
    trampling their enemy into the mud of the streets.
They will fight because the Lord is with them,
    and they will put the enemy horsemen to shame.

[6] "I will strengthen Judah
    and save the tribes of Joseph.
I will restore them
    because I have compassion on them.
They will be as though
    I had not rejected them,
for I am the Lord their God
    and I will answer them.
[7] The Ephraimites will become like warriors,
    and their hearts will be glad as with wine.
Their children will see it and be joyful;
    their hearts will rejoice in the Lord.
[8] I will signal for them
    and gather them in.
Surely I will redeem them;
    they will be as numerous as before.
[9] Though I scatter them among the peoples,
    yet in distant lands they will remember me.
They and their children will survive,
    and they will return.
[10] I will bring them back from Egypt
    and gather them from Assyria.
I will bring them to Gilead and Lebanon,
    and there will not be room enough for them.
[11] They will pass through the sea of trouble;
    the surging sea will be subdued
    and all the depths of the Nile will dry up.
Assyria's pride will be brought down
    and Egypt's scepter will pass away.
[12] I will strengthen them in the Lord
    and in his name they will live securely,"
                                    declares the Lord.

**11** Open your doors, Lebanon,
        so that fire may devour your cedars!
[2] Wail, you juniper, for the cedar has fallen;
    the stately trees are ruined!
Wail, oaks of Bashan;
    the dense forest has been cut down!
[3] Listen to the wail of the shepherds;
    their rich pastures are destroyed!
Listen to the roar of the lions;
    the lush thicket of the Jordan is ruined!

### Two Shepherds

[4] This is what the Lord my God says: "Shepherd the flock marked for slaughter. [5] Their buyers slaughter them and go unpunished. Those who sell them say, 'Praise the Lord, I am rich!' Their own shepherds do not spare them. [6] For I will no longer have pity on the people of the land," declares the Lord. "I will give everyone into the hands of their neighbors and their king. They will devastate the land, and I will not rescue anyone from their hands."

## Amplified Bible

the Lord of hosts has visited His flock, the house of Judah, and will make them as His beautiful *and* majestic horse in the battle. [Ezek. 34:1-10.]
[4] Out of him [Judah] shall come forth the [a] Cornerstone, out of him the tent peg, out of him the battle bow; every ruler shall proceed from him. [Jer. 30:21.]
[5] And they shall be like mighty men treading down their enemies in the mire of the streets in the battle, and they shall fight because the Lord is with them, and the [oppressor's] riders on horses shall be confounded *and* put to shame.
[6] And I will strengthen the house of Judah and I will save the house of Joseph [Ephraim]. I will bring them back *and* cause them to dwell securely, for I have mercy, loving-kindness, *and* compassion for them. They shall be as though I had not cast them off, for I am the Lord their God, and I will hear them.
[7] Then Ephraim [the ten tribes] shall become like a mighty warrior, and their hearts shall rejoice as through wine; yes, their children shall see it and rejoice; their hearts shall feel great delight *and* glory triumphantly in the Lord!
[8] I will hiss for them [as the keeper does for his bees] and gather them in, for I have redeemed them, and they shall increase [again] as they have increased [before, in Egypt]. [Ezek. 36:10, 11.]
[9] And though I sow them among the nations, yet they shall [earnestly] remember Me in far countries, and with their children they shall live and shall return [to God and the land He gave them].
[10] I will bring them [all Israel] home again from the land of Egypt and gather them out of Assyria, and I will bring them into the land [on the east and on the west of the Jordan, into] Gilead and Lebanon, and room enough shall not be found for them.
[11] And [the Lord] will pass through the sea of distress *and* affliction [at the head of His people, as He did at the Red Sea]; and He will smite down the waves of the sea, and all the depths of the [river] Nile shall be dried up *and* put to shame; and the pride of Assyria shall be brought down and the scepter *or* rod [of the taskmasters of Egypt] shall pass away.
[12] And I will strengthen [Israel] in the Lord, and they shall walk up and down *and* glory in His name, says the Lord.

**11** Open your doors, O Lebanon, that the fire may
        devour your cedars!
[2] Wail, O fir tree *and* cypress, for the cedar has fallen, because the glorious *and* lofty trees are laid waste! Wail, O you oaks of Bashan, for the thick *and* inaccessible forest [on the steep mountainside] has in flames been felled!
[3] A voice of the wailing of the shepherds, for their glory, the broad pasturage, is laid waste! A voice of the roaring of young lions, for the pride of the Jordan [the jungle or thickets] is ruined!
[4] Thus says the Lord my God: Shepherd the flock [destined] for slaughter,
[5] Whose buyers *or* possessors slay them and hold themselves not guilty; and they who sell them say, Blessed be the Lord, for I have become rich! And their own shepherds neither pity *nor* spare them [from the wolves].
[6] For I will no more pity *or* spare the inhabitants of the land, says the Lord; but behold, I will deliver every man into his neighbor's hand and into the hand of his [foreign] king. And [the enemy] shall lay waste the land, and I will not deliver [the people] out of the hand [of the foreign oppressor].

---

[a] 4,5 Or *ruler, all of them together. / 5They*

[a] This Messianic referent reminds one of the "Cornerstone" imagery of Ps. 118:22-23; Isa. 28:16; Matt. 21:42; Acts 4:11; Eph. 2:19-22; I Pet. 2:6-8.

## New International Version

⁷So I shepherded the flock marked for slaughter, particularly the oppressed of the flock. Then I took two staffs and called one Favor and the other Union, and I shepherded the flock. ⁸In one month I got rid of the three shepherds.

The flock detested me, and I grew weary of them ⁹and said, "I will not be your shepherd. Let the dying die, and the perishing perish. Let those who are left eat one another's flesh."

¹⁰Then I took my staff called Favor and broke it, revoking the covenant I had made with all the nations. ¹¹It was revoked on that day, and so the oppressed of the flock who were watching me knew it was the word of the LORD.

¹²I told them, "If you think it best, give me my pay; but if not, keep it." So they paid me thirty pieces of silver.

¹³And the LORD said to me, "Throw it to the potter"—the handsome price at which they valued me! So I took the thirty pieces of silver and threw them to the potter at the house of the LORD.

¹⁴Then I broke my second staff called Union, breaking the family bond between Judah and Israel.

¹⁵Then the LORD said to me, "Take again the equipment of a foolish shepherd. ¹⁶For I am going to raise up a shepherd over the land who will not care for the lost, or seek the young, or heal the injured, or feed the healthy, but will eat the meat of the choice sheep, tearing off their hooves.

¹⁷"Woe to the worthless shepherd,
　who deserts the flock!
May the sword strike his arm and his right eye!
　May his arm be completely withered,
　his right eye totally blinded!"

### Jerusalem's Enemies to Be Destroyed

**12** A prophecy: The word of the LORD concerning Israel.

The LORD, who stretches out the heavens, who lays the foundation of the earth, and who forms the human spirit within a person, declares: ²"I am going to make Jerusalem a cup that sends all the surrounding peoples reeling. Judah will be besieged as well as Jerusalem. ³On that day, when all the nations of the earth are gathered against her, I will make Jerusalem an immovable rock for all the nations. All who try to move it will injure themselves. ⁴On that day I will strike every horse with panic and its rider with madness," declares the LORD. "I will keep a watchful eye over Judah, but I will blind all the horses of the nations. ⁵Then the clans of Judah will say in their hearts, 'The people of Jerusalem are strong, because the LORD Almighty is their God.'

## Amplified Bible

⁷So I [Zechariah] shepherded the flock of slaughter, truly [as the name implies] the most miserable of sheep. And I took two [shepherd's] staffs, the one I called Beauty or Grace and the other I called Bands or Union; and I fed and shepherded the flock.

⁸And I cut off the three shepherds [the civil authorities, the priests, and the prophets] in one month, for I was weary and impatient with them, and they also loathed me. [Jer. 2:8, 26; 18:18.]

⁹So I [Zechariah] said, I will not be your shepherd. What is to die, let it die, and what is to be destroyed, let it be destroyed; and let the survivors devour one another's flesh.

¹⁰And I took my staff, Beauty or Grace, and broke it in pieces to show that I was annulling the covenant or agreement which I had made with all the peoples [not to molest them].

¹¹So the covenant was annulled on that day, and thus the most wretched of the flock and the traffickers in the sheep who were watching me knew (recognized and understood) that it was truly the word of the Lord.

¹²And I said to them, If it seems just and right to you, give me my wages; but if not, withhold them. So they weighed out for my price thirty pieces of silver.

¹³And the Lord said to me, Cast it to the potter [as if He said, To the dogs!]—the munificently [miserable] sum at which I [and My shepherd] am priced by them! And I [Zechariah] took the thirty pieces of silver and cast them to the potter in the house of the Lord. [Matt. 26:14, 15; 27:3-10.]

¹⁴Then I broke into pieces my other staff, Bands or Union, indicating that I was annulling the brotherhood between Judah and Israel.

¹⁵And the Lord said to me, Take up once more the implements [the staff and rod of a shepherd, but this time] of a worthless and wicked shepherd. [Ezek. 34:2-6.]

¹⁶For behold, I will raise up a false shepherd in the land; the lost and perishing he will not miss or visit, the young and scattered he will not go to seek, the wounded and broken he will not heal, nor will he feed those that are sound and strong; but he will eat the flesh of the fat ones and break off their hoofs [to consume all the flesh].

¹⁷Woe to the worthless and foolish shepherd who deserts the flock! The sword shall smite his arm and his right eye; his arm shall be utterly withered and his right eye utterly blinded. [Jer. 23:1; John 10:12, 13.]

**12** The burden or oracle (the thing to be lifted up) of the word of the Lord concerning Israel: Thus says the Lord, Who stretches out the heavens and lays the foundation of the earth and forms the spirit of man within him:

²Behold, I am about to make Jerusalem a cup or bowl of reeling to all the peoples round about, and in the siege against Jerusalem will there also be a siege against and upon Judah.

³And in that day I will make Jerusalem a burdensome stone for all peoples; all who lift it or burden themselves with it shall be sorely wounded. And all the nations of the earth shall come and gather together against it.

⁴In that day, says the Lord, I will smite every horse [of the armies that contend against Jerusalem] with terror and panic and his rider with madness; and I will open My eyes and regard with favor the house of Judah and will smite every horse of the opposing nations with blindness.

⁵And the chiefs of Judah shall say in their hearts, The inhabitants of Jerusalem are our strength in the Lord of hosts, their God.

## New International Version

⁶"On that day I will make the clans of Judah like a fire-pot in a woodpile, like a flaming torch among sheaves. They will consume all the surrounding peoples right and left, but Jerusalem will remain intact in her place.

⁷"The LORD will save the dwellings of Judah first, so that the honor of the house of David and of Jerusalem's in-habitants may not be greater than that of Judah. ⁸On that day the LORD will shield those who live in Jerusalem, so that the feeblest among them will be like David, and the house of David will be like God, like the angel of the LORD going before them. ⁹On that day I will set out to destroy all the nations that attack Jerusalem.

### Mourning for the One They Pierced

¹⁰"And I will pour out on the house of David and the in-habitants of Jerusalem a spirit*ᵃ* of grace and supplication. They will look on*ᵇ* me, the one they have pierced, and they will mourn for him as one mourns for an only child, and grieve bitterly for him as one grieves for a firstborn son. ¹¹On that day the weeping in Jerusalem will be as great as the weeping of Hadad Rimmon in the plain of Megiddo. ¹²The land will mourn, each clan by itself, with their wives by themselves: the clan of the house of David and their wives, the clan of the house of Nathan and their wives, ¹³the clan of the house of Levi and their wives, the clan of Shimei and their wives, ¹⁴and all the rest of the clans and their wives.

### Cleansing From Sin

**13** "On that day a fountain will be opened to the house of David and the inhabitants of Jerusalem, to cleanse them from sin and impurity.

²"On that day, I will banish the names of the idols from the land, and they will be remembered no more," declares the LORD Almighty. "I will remove both the prophets and the spirit of impurity from the land. ³And if anyone still prophesies, their father and mother, to whom they were born, will say to them, 'You must die, because you have told lies in the LORD's name.' Then their own parents will stab the one who prophesies.

⁴"On that day every prophet will be ashamed of their prophetic vision. They will not put on a prophet's garment of hair in order to deceive. ⁵Each will say, 'I am not a proph-et. I am a farmer; the land has been my livelihood since my youth.'*ᶜ* ⁶If someone asks, 'What are these wounds on your body*ᵈ*?' they will answer, 'The wounds I was given at the house of my friends.'

## Amplified Bible

⁶In that day will I make the chiefs of Judah like a big, blazing pot among [sticks of] wood and like a flaming torch among sheaves [of grain], and they shall devour all the peoples round about, on the right hand and on the left; and they of Jerusalem shall yet again dwell *and* sit securely in their own place, in Jerusalem.

⁷And the Lord shall save *and* give victory to the tents of Judah first, that the glory of the house of David and the glory of the inhabitants of Jerusalem may not be magni-fied *and* exalted above Judah.

⁸In that day will the Lord guard *and* defend the inhabi-tants of Jerusalem, and he who is [spiritually] feeble *and* stumbles among them in that day [of persecution] shall become [strong and noble] like David; and the house of David [shall maintain its supremacy] like God, like the *ᵃ*Angel of the Lord Who is before them.

⁹And it shall be in that day that I will make it My aim to destroy all the nations that come against Jerusalem.

¹⁰And I will pour out upon the house of David and upon the inhabitants of Jerusalem the Spirit of grace *or* unmer-ited favor and supplication. And they shall look [earnestly] upon Me Whom they have pierced, and they shall mourn for Him as one mourns for his only son, and shall be in bitterness for Him as one who is in bitterness for his first-born. [John 19:37; Rev. 1:7.]

¹¹In that day shall there be a great mourning in Jerusa-lem, as the mourning of [the city of] Hadadrimmon in the Valley of Megiddo [over beloved King *ᵇ*Josiah]. [II Chron. 35:22-25.]

¹²And the land shall mourn, every family apart: the [kingly] family of the house of David apart and their wives apart; the family of the house of Nathan [David's son] apart and their wives apart;

¹³The [priestly] family of the house of Levi apart and their wives apart; the family of Shimei [grandson of Levi] apart and their wives apart;

¹⁴All the families that are left, each by itself, and their wives by themselves [each with an overwhelming indi-vidual sorrow over having blindly rejected their unrecog-nized Messiah].

**13** In that day there shall be a fountain opened for the house of David and for the inhabitants of Jerusa-lem [to cleanse them from] sin and uncleanness.

²And in that day, says the Lord of hosts, I will cut off the names of the idols from the land, and they shall no more be remembered; and also I will remove from the land the [false] prophets and the unclean spirit.

³And if anyone again appears [falsely] as a prophet, then his father and his mother who bore him shall say to him, You shall not live, for you speak lies in the name of the Lord; and his father and his mother who bore him shall thrust him through when he prophesies.

⁴And in that day the [false] prophets shall each be ashamed of his vision when he prophesies, nor will he wear a hairy *or* rough garment to deceive,

⁵But he will [deny his identity and] say, I am no prophet. I am a tiller of the ground, for I have been made a bond servant from my youth.

⁶And one shall say to him, What are these wounds on your breast *or* between your hands? Then he will answer, Those with which I was wounded [when disciplined] in the house of my [loving] friends.

## New International Version

### The Shepherd Struck, the Sheep Scattered

7 "Awake, sword, against my shepherd,
  against the man who is close to me!"
    declares the LORD Almighty.
"Strike the shepherd,
  and the sheep will be scattered,
  and I will turn my hand against the little ones.
8 In the whole land," declares the LORD,
  "two-thirds will be struck down and perish;
  yet one-third will be left in it.
9 This third I will put into the fire;
  I will refine them like silver
  and test them like gold.
They will call on my name
  and I will answer them;
I will say, 'They are my people,'
  and they will say, 'The LORD is our God.'"

### The LORD Comes and Reigns

**14** A day of the LORD is coming, Jerusalem, when your possessions will be plundered and divided up within your very walls.

2 I will gather all the nations to Jerusalem to fight against it; the city will be captured, the houses ransacked, and the women raped. Half of the city will go into exile, but the rest of the people will not be taken from the city. 3 Then the LORD will go out and fight against those nations, as he fights on a day of battle. 4 On that day his feet will stand on the Mount of Olives, east of Jerusalem, and the Mount of Olives will be split in two from east to west, forming a great valley, with half of the mountain moving north and half moving south. 5 You will flee by my mountain valley, for it will extend to Azel. You will flee as you fled from the earthquake[a] in the days of Uzziah king of Judah. Then the LORD my God will come, and all the holy ones with him.

6 On that day there will be neither sunlight nor cold, frosty darkness. 7 It will be a unique day—a day known only to the LORD—with no distinction between day and night. When evening comes, there will be light.

8 On that day living water will flow out from Jerusalem, half of it east to the Dead Sea and half of it west to the Mediterranean Sea, in summer and in winter.

9 The LORD will be king over the whole earth. On that day there will be one LORD, and his name the only name.

10 The whole land, from Geba to Rimmon, south of Jerusalem, will become like the Arabah. But Jerusalem will be raised up high from the Benjamin Gate to the site of the First Gate, to the Corner Gate, and from the Tower of Hananel to the royal winepresses, and will remain in its place.

## Amplified Bible

7 Awake, O sword, against My shepherd and against the man who is My associate, says the Lord of hosts; smite the shepherd and the sheep [of the flock] shall be scattered, and I will turn back My hand *and* stretch it out again upon the little ones [of the flock]. [Matt. 26:31, 32.]

8 And in all the land, says the Lord, two-thirds shall be cut off and perish, but one-third shall be left alive. [Hos. 2:23; Rom. 11:5.]

9 And I will bring the third part through the fire, and will refine them as silver is refined and will test them as gold is tested. They will call on My name, and I will hear *and* answer them. I will say, It is My people; and they will say, The Lord is my God.

**14** Behold, a day of the Lord is coming when the spoil [taken from you] shall be divided [among the victors] in the midst of you.

2 For I will gather all nations against Jerusalem to battle, and the city shall be taken and the houses rifled and the women ravished; and half of the city shall go into exile, but the rest of the people shall not be cut off from the city.

3 Then shall the Lord go forth and fight against those nations, as when He fought in the day of battle.

4 And His feet shall stand in that day upon the Mount of Olives, which lies before Jerusalem on the east, and the Mount of Olives shall be split in two from the east to the west by a very great valley; and half of the mountain shall remove toward the north and half of it toward the south. [Isa. 64:1, 2.]

5 And you shall flee by the valley of My mountains, for the valley of the mountains shall reach to Azal; and you shall flee as you fled from before the earthquake in the days of Uzziah king of Judah; and the Lord my [Zechariah's] *a* God shall come, and all the holy ones [saints and angels] with *Him*. [Amos 1:1; Col. 3:4; I Thess. 4:14; Jude 14, 15.]

6 And it shall come to pass in that day that there shall not be light; the glorious *and* bright ones [the heavenly bodies] shall be darkened.

7 But it shall be one continuous day, known to the Lord—not day and not night, but at evening time there shall be light.

8 And it shall be in that day that living waters shall go out from Jerusalem, half of them to the eastern [Dead] Sea and half of them to the western [Mediterranean] Sea; in summer and in winter shall it be.

9 And the Lord shall be King over all the earth; in that day the Lord shall be one [in the recognition and worship of men] and His name one.

10 All the land shall be turned into a plain from Geba to Rimmon, [the Rimmon that is] south of Jerusalem. But Jerusalem shall remain lifted up on its site and dwell in its place, from Benjamin's gate to the place of the First Gate, to the Corner Gate, and from the Tower of Hananel to the king's winepresses.

---

*a* The second advent of Christ is the coming of **God** to earth—hence the emphasis placed upon it in the Scriptures. It is heralded not just once, but many times—plainly, without opportunity for misinterpretation, such as in Deut. 30:3; Zech. 14:3, 4; Matt. 16:27; 24:3-14, 27, 36-39; 25:31, 32; 26:64; Luke 21:25-28; Acts 1:9-11; I Cor. 1:7, 8; 4:5; I Tim. 6:14; II Tim. 4:1; Tit. 2:13; Heb. 9:28; I John 2:28; Rev. 3:11; 16:15; 22:7, 20.

*a* 5 Or 5*My mountain valley will be blocked and will extend to Azel. It will be blocked as it was blocked because of the earthquake*

## New International Version

[11]It will be inhabited; never again will it be destroyed. Jerusalem will be secure.

[12]This is the plague with which the LORD will strike all the nations that fought against Jerusalem: Their flesh will rot while they are still standing on their feet, their eyes will rot in their sockets, and their tongues will rot in their mouths. [13]On that day people will be stricken by the LORD with great panic. They will seize each other by the hand and attack one another. [14]Judah too will fight at Jerusalem. The wealth of all the surrounding nations will be collected—great quantities of gold and silver and clothing. [15]A similar plague will strike the horses and mules, the camels and donkeys, and all the animals in those camps.

[16]Then the survivors from all the nations that have attacked Jerusalem will go up year after year to worship the King, the LORD Almighty, and to celebrate the Festival of Tabernacles. [17]If any of the peoples of the earth do not go up to Jerusalem to worship the King, the LORD Almighty, they will have no rain. [18]If the Egyptian people do not go up and take part, they will have no rain. The LORD[a] will bring on them the plague he inflicts on the nations that do not go up to celebrate the Festival of Tabernacles. [19]This will be the punishment of Egypt and the punishment of all the nations that do not go up to celebrate the Festival of Tabernacles.

[20]On that day HOLY TO THE LORD will be inscribed on the bells of the horses, and the cooking pots in the LORD's house will be like the sacred bowls in front of the altar. [21]Every pot in Jerusalem and Judah will be holy to the LORD Almighty, and all who come to sacrifice will take some of the pots and cook in them. And on that day there will no longer be a Canaanite[b] in the house of the LORD Almighty.

## Amplified Bible

[11]And it shall be inhabited, for there shall be no more curse *or* ban of utter destruction, but Jerusalem shall dwell securely. [Rev. 22:3.]

[12]And this shall be the plague wherewith the Lord will smite all the peoples that have warred against Jerusalem: their flesh shall rot away while they stand upon their feet and their eyes shall corrode away in their sockets and their tongue shall decay away in their mouth.

[13]And in that day there shall be a great confusion, discomfiture, *and* panic among them from the Lord; and they shall seize each his neighbor's hand, and the hand of the one shall be raised against the hand of the other.

[14]And Judah also shall fight at Jerusalem, and the wealth of all the nations round about shall be gathered together—gold and silver and apparel in great abundance.

[15]And as that plague on men, so shall be the plague on the horse, on the mule, on the camel, on the donkey, and on all the livestock *and* beasts that may be in those camps.

[16]And everyone who is left of all the nations which came against Jerusalem shall even go up from year to year to worship the King, the Lord of hosts, and to keep the Feast of Tabernacles *or* Booths.

[17]And it shall be that whoso of the families of the earth shall not go up to Jerusalem to worship the King, the Lord of hosts, upon them there shall be no rain.

[18]And if the family of Egypt does not go up to Jerusalem and present themselves, upon them there shall be no rain, but there shall be the plague with which the Lord will smite the nations that go not up to keep the Feast of Tabernacles.

[19]This shall be the consequent punishment of the sin of Egypt and the consequent punishment of the sin of all the nations that do not go up to keep the Feast of Tabernacles.

[20]In that day there shall be [written] upon the [little] bells on the horses, HOLY TO THE LORD, and the pots in the Lord's house shall be holy to the Lord like the bowls before the altar.

[21]Yes, every pot in all the houses of Jerusalem and in Judah shall be dedicated *and* holy to the Lord of hosts, and all who sacrifice may come and take of them and boil their sacrifices in them [and traders in such wares will no longer be seen at the temple]. And in that day there shall be no more a Canaanite [that is, any godless or unclean person, whether Jew or Gentile] in the house of the Lord of hosts. [Eph. 2:19-22.]

---

[a] 18 Or *part, then the* LORD    [b] 21 Or *merchant*

# Malachi

**1** A prophecy: The word of the LORD to Israel through Malachi.ᵃ

## Israel Doubts God's Love

2"I have loved you," says the LORD.

"But you ask, 'How have you loved us?'

"Was not Esau Jacob's brother?" declares the LORD. "Yet I have loved Jacob, 3but Esau I have hated, and I have turned his hill country into a wasteland and left his inheritance to the desert jackals."

4Edom may say, "Though we have been crushed, we will rebuild the ruins."

But this is what the LORD Almighty says: "They may build, but I will demolish. They will be called the Wicked Land, a people always under the wrath of the LORD. 5You will see it with your own eyes and say, 'Great is the LORD—even beyond the borders of Israel!'

## Breaking Covenant Through Blemished Sacrifices

6"A son honors his father, and a slave his master. If I am a father, where is the honor due me? If I am a master, where is the respect due me?" says the LORD Almighty.

"It is you priests who show contempt for my name.

"But you ask, 'How have we shown contempt for your name?'

7"By offering defiled food on my altar.

"But you ask, 'How have we defiled you?'

"By saying that the LORD's table is contemptible. 8When you offer blind animals for sacrifice, is that not wrong? When you sacrifice lame or diseased animals, is that not wrong? Try offering them to your governor! Would he be pleased with you? Would he accept you?" says the LORD Almighty.

9"Now plead with God to be gracious to us. With such offerings from your hands, will he accept you?"—says the LORD Almighty.

10"Oh, that one of you would shut the temple doors, so that you would not light useless fires on my altar! I am not pleased with you," says the LORD Almighty, "and I will accept no offering from your hands. 11My name will be great among the nations, from where the sun rises to where it sets. In every place incense and pure offerings will be brought to me, because my name will be great among the nations," says the LORD Almighty.

12"But you profane it by saying, 'The Lord's table is defiled,' and, 'Its food is contemptible.' 13And you say, 'What a burden!' and you sniff at it contemptuously," says the LORD Almighty.

"When you bring injured, lame or diseased animals and offer them as sacrifices, should I accept them from your hands?" says the LORD. 14"Cursed is the cheat who has an acceptable male in his flock and vows to give it, but then sacrifices a blemished animal to the Lord. For I am a great king," says the LORD Almighty, "and my name is to be feared among the nations.

# Malachi

**1** The burden *or* oracle (the thing to be lifted up) of the word of the Lord to Israel by Malachi [My messenger].

2I have loved you, says the Lord. Yet you say, How *and* in what way have You loved us? Was not Esau Jacob's brother? says the Lord; yet I loved Jacob (Israel),

3But [in comparison with the degree of love I have for Jacob] I have hated Esau [Edom] and have laid waste his mountains, and his heritage I have given to the jackals of the wilderness. [Rom. 9:13, 16.]

4Though [impoverished] Edom should say, We are beaten down, but we will return and build the waste places—thus says the Lord of hosts: They may build, but I will tear *and* throw down; and men will call them the Wicked Country, the people against whom the Lord has indignation forever.

5Your own eyes shall see this and you shall say, The Lord is great *and* will be magnified over *and* beyond the border of Israel! [Isa. 34; 63:1-6; Jer. 49:7-22; Ezek. 25:12-14; Obad. 1.]

6A son honors his father, and a servant his master. If then I am a Father, where is My honor? And if I am a Master, where is the [reverent] fear due Me? says the Lord of hosts to you, O priests, who despise My name. You say, How *and* in what way have we despised Your name?

7By offering polluted food upon My altar. And you ask, How have we polluted it *and* profaned You? By thinking that the table of the Lord is contemptible *and* may be despised.

8When you [priests] offer blind [animals] for sacrifice, is it not evil? And when you offer the lame and the sick, is it not evil? Present such a thing [a blind or lame or sick animal] now to your governor [in payment of your taxes, and see what will happen]. Will he be pleased with you? Or will he receive you graciously? says the Lord of hosts.

9Now then, I [Malachi] beg [you priests], entreat God [earnestly] that He will be gracious to us. With such a gift from your hand [as a defective animal for sacrifice], will He accept it *or* show favor to any of you? says the Lord of hosts.

10Oh, that there were even one among you [whose duty it is to minister to Me] who would shut the doors, that you might not kindle fire on My altar to no purpose [an empty, futile, fruitless pretense]! I have no pleasure in you, says the Lord of hosts, nor will I accept an offering from your hand.

11For from the rising of the sun to its setting My name shall be great among the nations, and in every place incense shall be offered to My name, and indeed a pure offering; for My name shall be great among the nations, says the Lord of hosts.

12But you [priests] profane it when [by your actions] you say, The table of the Lord is polluted, and the fruit of it, its food, is contemptible *and* may be despised.

13You say also, Behold, what a drudgery *and* weariness this is! And you have sniffed at it, says the Lord of hosts. And you have brought that which was ᵃtaken by violence, or the lame or the sick; this you bring as an offering! Shall I accept this from your hand? says the Lord. [Lev. 1:3; Deut. 15:21.]

14But cursed is the [cheating] deceiver who has a male in his flock and vows to offer it, yet sacrifices to the [sovereign] Lord a blemished *or* diseased thing! For I am a great King, says the Lord of hosts, and My name is terrible *and* to be [reverently] feared among the nations.

---

ᵃ *1 Malachi* means *my messenger.*

ᵃ Animals with defects or serious flaws were unacceptable as sacrifices.

## New International Version

### Additional Warning to the Priests

**2** "And now, you priests, this warning is for you. ²If you do not listen, and if you do not resolve to honor my name," says the LORD Almighty, "I will send a curse on you, and I will curse your blessings. Yes, I have already cursed them, because you have not resolved to honor me. ³"Because of you I will rebuke your descendants[a]; I will smear on your faces the dung from your festival sacrifices, and you will be carried off with it. ⁴And you will know that I have sent you this warning so that my covenant with Levi may continue," says the LORD Almighty. ⁵"My covenant was with him, a covenant of life and peace, and I gave them to him; this called for reverence and he revered me and stood in awe of my name. ⁶True instruction was in his mouth and nothing false was found on his lips. He walked with me in peace and uprightness, and turned many from sin.

⁷"For the lips of a priest ought to preserve knowledge, because he is the messenger of the LORD Almighty and people seek instruction from his mouth. ⁸But you have turned from the way and by your teaching have caused many to stumble; you have violated the covenant with Levi," says the LORD Almighty. ⁹"So I have caused you to be despised and humiliated before all the people, because you have not followed my ways but have shown partiality in matters of the law."

### Breaking Covenant Through Divorce

¹⁰Do we not all have one Father[b]? Did not one God create us? Why do we profane the covenant of our ancestors by being unfaithful to one another?

¹¹Judah has been unfaithful. A detestable thing has been committed in Israel and in Jerusalem: Judah has desecrated the sanctuary the LORD loves by marrying women who worship a foreign god. ¹²As for the man who does this, whoever he may be, may the LORD remove him from the tents of Jacob[c]—even though he brings an offering to the LORD Almighty.

¹³Another thing you do: You flood the LORD's altar with tears. You weep and wail because he no longer looks with favor on your offerings or accepts them with pleasure from your hands. ¹⁴You ask, "Why?" It is because the LORD is the witness between you and the wife of your youth. You have been unfaithful to her, though she is your partner, the wife of your marriage covenant.

¹⁵Has not the one God made you? You belong to him in body and spirit. And what does the one God seek? Godly offspring.[d] So be on your guard, and do not be unfaithful to the wife of your youth.

¹⁶"The man who hates and divorces his wife," says

## Amplified Bible

**2** And now, O you priests, this commandment is for you. ²If you will not hear and if you will not lay it to heart to give glory to My name, says the Lord of hosts, then I will send the curse upon you, and I will curse your blessings; yes, I have already turned them to curses because you do not lay it to heart.

³Behold, I will rebuke your seed [grain—which will prevent due harvest], and I will spread the ᵃdung from the festival offerings upon your faces, and you shall be taken away with it.

⁴And you shall know, recognize, *and* understand that I have sent this [new] decree to you priests, to be My [new] covenant with Levi [the priestly tribe], says the Lord of hosts.

⁵My covenant [on My part with Levi] was to give him life and peace, because [on his part] of the [reverent and worshipful] fear with which [the priests] would revere Me and stand in awe of My name.

⁶The law of truth was in [Levi's] mouth, and unrighteousness was not found in his lips; he walked with Me in peace and uprightness and turned many away from iniquity.

⁷For the priest's lips should guard *and* keep pure the knowledge [of My law], and the people should seek (inquire for and require) instruction at his mouth; for he is the messenger of the Lord of hosts.

⁸But you have turned aside out of the way; you have caused many to stumble by your instruction [in the law]; you have corrupted the covenant of Levi [with Me], says the Lord of hosts.

⁹Therefore have I also made you despised and abased before all the people, inasmuch as you have not kept My ways but have shown favoritism to persons in your administration of the law [of God].

¹⁰Have we not all one Father? Has not one God created us? Why then do we deal faithlessly and treacherously each against his brother, profaning the covenant of [God with] our fathers?

¹¹Judah has been faithless *and* dealt treacherously, and an abomination has been committed in Israel and in Jerusalem; for Judah [that is, Jewish men] has profaned the holy sanctuary of the Lord which He loves, and has married the daughter of a foreign god [having divorced his Jewish wife]. [Ezra 9:2; Jer. 2:3.]

¹²The Lord will cast out of the tents of Jacob to the last man those who do this [evil thing], the master and the servant [or the pupil] alike, even him who brings an offering to the Lord of hosts.

¹³And this you do with double guilt; you cover the altar of the Lord with tears [shed by your unoffending wives, divorced by you that you might take heathen wives], and with [your own] weeping and crying out because the Lord does not regard your offering any more or accept it with favor at your hand.

¹⁴Yet you ask, Why does He reject it? Because the Lord was witness [to the covenant made at your marriage] between you and the wife of your youth, against whom you have dealt treacherously *and* to whom you were faithless. Yet she is your companion and the wife of your covenant [made by your marriage vows].

¹⁵And did not God make [you and your wife] one [flesh]? Did not One make you and preserve your spirit alive? And why [did God make you two] one? Because He sought a godly offspring [from your union]. Therefore take heed to yourselves, and let no one deal treacherously *and* be faithless to the wife of his youth.

¹⁶For the Lord, the God of Israel, says: I hate divorce

---

ᵃ 3 Or *will blight your grain*    ᵇ 10 Or *father*    ᶜ 12 Or *¹²May the LORD remove from the tents of Jacob anyone who gives testimony in behalf of the man who does this*    ᵈ 15 The meaning of the Hebrew for the first part of this verse is uncertain.

ᵃ Instead of the edible portions of the sacrificed animals—the shoulder, cheeks, and stomach—which were the wages for the work of the priests (Deut. 18:3).

## New International Version

the Lord, the God of Israel, "does violence to the one he should protect,"[a] says the Lord Almighty.

So be on your guard, and do not be unfaithful.

### Breaking Covenant Through Injustice

17You have wearied the Lord with your words.

"How have we wearied him?" you ask.

By saying, "All who do evil are good in the eyes of the Lord, and he is pleased with them" or "Where is the God of justice?"

**3** "I will send my messenger, who will prepare the way before me. Then suddenly the Lord you are seeking will come to his temple; the messenger of the covenant, whom you desire, will come," says the Lord Almighty. 2But who can endure the day of his coming? Who can stand when he appears? For he will be like a refiner's fire or a launderer's soap. 3He will sit as a refiner and purifier of silver; he will purify the Levites and refine them like gold and silver. Then the Lord will have men who will bring offerings in righteousness, 4and the offerings of Judah and Jerusalem will be acceptable to the Lord, as in days gone by, as in former years.

5"So I will come to put you on trial. I will be quick to testify against sorcerers, adulterers and perjurers, against those who defraud laborers of their wages, who oppress the widows and the fatherless, and deprive the foreigners among you of justice, but do not fear me," says the Lord Almighty.

### Breaking Covenant by Withholding Tithes

6"I the Lord do not change. So you, the descendants of Jacob, are not destroyed. 7Ever since the time of your ancestors you have turned away from my decrees and have not kept them. Return to me, and I will return to you," says the Lord Almighty.

"But you ask, 'How are we to return?'

8"Will a mere mortal rob God? Yet you rob me.

"But you ask, 'How are we robbing you?'

"In tithes and offerings. 9You are under a curse—your whole nation—because you are robbing me. 10Bring the whole tithe into the storehouse, that there may be food in my house. Test me in this," says the Lord Almighty, "and see if I will not throw open the floodgates of heaven and pour out so much blessing that there will not be room enough to store it. 11I will prevent pests from devouring your crops, and the vines in your fields will not drop their fruit before it is ripe," says the Lord Almighty. 12"Then all the nations will call you blessed, for yours will be a delightful land," says the Lord Almighty.

### Israel Speaks Arrogantly Against God

13"You have spoken arrogantly against me," says the Lord.

"Yet you ask, 'What have we said against you?'

## Amplified Bible

and marital separation and him who covers his garment [his wife] with violence. Therefore keep a watch upon your spirit [that it may be controlled by My Spirit], that you deal not treacherously and faithlessly [with your marriage mate].

17You have wearied the Lord with your words. Yet you say, In what way have we wearied Him? [You do it when by your actions] you say, Everyone who does evil is good in the sight of the Lord and He delights in them. Or [by asking], Where is the God of justice?

**3** Behold, I send My [a]messenger, and he shall prepare the way before Me. And the Lord [the Messiah], Whom you seek, will suddenly come to His temple; the [b]Messenger or Angel of the covenant, Whom you desire, behold, He shall come, says the Lord of hosts. [Matt. 11:10; Luke 1:13-17, 76.] 2But who can endure the day of His coming? And who can stand when He appears? For He is like a refiner's fire and like fullers' soap; [Rev. 6:12-17.] 3He will sit as a refiner and purifier of silver, and He will purify the priests, the sons of Levi, and refine them like gold and silver, that they may offer to the Lord offerings in righteousness.

4Then will the offering of Judah and Jerusalem be pleasing to the Lord as in the days of old and as in ancient years. 5Then I will draw near to you for judgment; I will be a swift witness against the sorcerers, against the adulterers, against the false swearers, and against those who oppress the hireling in his wages, the widow and the fatherless, and who turn aside the temporary resident from his right and fear not Me, says the Lord of hosts.

6For I am the Lord, I do not change; that is why you, O sons of Jacob, are not consumed. 7Even from the days of your fathers you have turned aside from My ordinances and have not kept them. Return to me, and I will return to you, says the Lord of hosts. But you say, How shall we return?

8Will a man rob or defraud God? Yet you rob and defraud Me. But you say, In what way do we rob or defraud You? [You have withheld your] tithes and offerings. 9You are cursed with the curse, for you are robbing Me, even this whole nation. [Lev. 26:14-17.] 10Bring all the tithes (the whole tenth of your income) into the storehouse, that there may be food in My house, and prove Me now by it, says the Lord of hosts, if I will not open the windows of heaven for you and pour you out a blessing, that there shall not be room enough to receive it. [Mal. 2:2.] 11And I will rebuke the devourer [insects and plagues] for your sakes and he shall not destroy the fruits of your ground, neither shall your vine drop its fruit before the time in the field, says the Lord of hosts. 12And all nations shall call you happy and blessed, for you shall be a land of delight, says the Lord of hosts.

13Your words have been strong and hard against Me, says the Lord. Yet you say, What have we spoken against You?

---

a 16 Or "I hate divorce," says the Lord, the God of Israel, "because the man who divorces his wife covers his garment with violence,"

---

a This is fulfilled in John the Baptist (Matt. 11:10; Mark 1:2; Luke 1:76).
b The Messiah as God's representative will confirm and establish the covenant (see Isa. 42:6).

# New International Version

## Amplified Bible

¹⁴"You have said, 'It is futile to serve God. What do we gain by carrying out his requirements and going about like mourners before the LORD Almighty? ¹⁵But now we call the arrogant blessed. Certainly evildoers prosper, and even when they put God to the test, they get away with it.'"

### The Faithful Remnant

¹⁶Then those who feared the LORD talked with each other, and the LORD listened and heard. A scroll of remembrance was written in his presence concerning those who feared the LORD and honored his name.

¹⁷"On the day when I act," says the LORD Almighty, "they will be my treasured possession. I will spare them, just as a father has compassion and spares his son who serves him. ¹⁸And you will again see the distinction between the righteous and the wicked, between those who serve God and those who do not.

### Judgment and Covenant Renewal

**4** ᵃ "Surely the day is coming; it will burn like a furnace. All the arrogant and every evildoer will be stubble, and the day that is coming will set them on fire," says the LORD Almighty. "Not a root or a branch will be left to them. ²But for you who revere my name, the sun of righteousness will rise with healing in its rays. And you will go out and frolic like well-fed calves. ³Then you will trample on the wicked; they will be ashes under the soles of your feet on the day when I act," says the LORD Almighty.

⁴"Remember the law of my servant Moses, the decrees and laws I gave him at Horeb for all Israel.

⁵"See, I will send the prophet Elijah to you before that great and dreadful day of the LORD comes. ⁶He will turn the hearts of the parents to their children, and the hearts of the children to their parents; or else I will come and strike the land with total destruction."

---

¹⁴You have said, It is useless to serve God, and what profit is it if we keep His ordinances and walk gloomily *and* as if in mourning apparel before the Lord of hosts?

¹⁵And now we consider the proud *and* arrogant to be happy *and* favored; evildoers are exalted *and* prosper; yes, and when they test God, they escape [unpunished].

¹⁶Then those who feared the Lord talked often one to another; and the Lord listened and heard it, and a book of remembrance was written before Him of those who reverenced *and* worshipfully feared the Lord and who thought on His name.

¹⁷And they shall be Mine, says the Lord of hosts, in that day when I publicly recognize *and* openly declare them to be My jewels (My special possession, My peculiar treasure). And I will spare them, as a man spares his own son who serves him.

¹⁸Then shall you return and discern between the righteous and the wicked, between him who serves God and him who does not serve Him.

**4** For behold, the day comes that shall burn like an oven, and all the proud *and* arrogant, yes, and all that do wickedly *and* are lawless, shall be stubble; the day that comes shall burn them up, says the Lord of hosts, so that it will leave them neither root nor branch. [Isa. 5:21-25; Matt. 3:12.]

²But unto you who revere *and* worshipfully fear My name shall the Sun of Righteousness arise with healing in His wings *and* His beams, and you shall go forth and gambol like calves [released] from the stall *and* leap for joy.

³And you shall tread down the lawless *and* wicked, for they shall be ashes under the soles of your feet in the day that I shall do this, says the Lord of hosts.

⁴[Earnestly] remember the law of Moses, My servant, the statutes and the ordinances which I commanded him on [Mount] Horeb [to give] to all Israel.

⁵Behold, I will send you Elijah the prophet before the great and terrible day of the Lord comes. [Matt. 11:14; 17:10-13.]

⁶And he shall turn *and* reconcile the hearts of the [estranged] fathers to the [ungodly] children, and the hearts of the [rebellious] children to [the piety of] their fathers [a reconciliation produced by repentance of the ungodly], lest I come and smite the land with a curse *and* a ban of utter destruction. [Luke 1:17.]

---

ᵃ In Hebrew texts 4:1-6 is numbered 3:19-24.

# THE
# New Testament

# Matthew

## The Genealogy of Jesus the Messiah

**1** This is the genealogy[a] of Jesus the Messiah[b] the son of David, the son of Abraham:

2 Abraham was the father of Isaac,
Isaac the father of Jacob,
Jacob the father of Judah and his brothers,
3 Judah the father of Perez and Zerah, whose mother was Tamar,
Perez the father of Hezron,
Hezron the father of Ram,
4 Ram the father of Amminadab,
Amminadab the father of Nahshon,
Nahshon the father of Salmon,
5 Salmon the father of Boaz, whose mother was Rahab,
Boaz the father of Obed, whose mother was Ruth,
Obed the father of Jesse,
6 and Jesse the father of King David.

David was the father of Solomon, whose mother had been Uriah's wife,
7 Solomon the father of Rehoboam,
Rehoboam the father of Abijah,
Abijah the father of Asa,
8 Asa the father of Jehoshaphat,
Jehoshaphat the father of Jehoram,
Jehoram the father of Uzziah,
9 Uzziah the father of Jotham,
Jotham the father of Ahaz,
Ahaz the father of Hezekiah,
10 Hezekiah the father of Manasseh,
Manasseh the father of Amon,
Amon the father of Josiah,
11 and Josiah the father of Jeconiah[c] and his brothers at the time of the exile to Babylon.

12 After the exile to Babylon:
Jeconiah was the father of Shealtiel,
Shealtiel the father of Zerubbabel,
13 Zerubbabel the father of Abihud,
Abihud the father of Eliakim,
Eliakim the father of Azor,
14 Azor the father of Zadok,
Zadok the father of Akim,
Akim the father of Elihud,
15 Elihud the father of Eleazar,
Eleazar the father of Matthan,
Matthan the father of Jacob,
16 and Jacob the father of Joseph, the husband of Mary, and Mary was the mother of Jesus who is called the Messiah.

17 Thus there were fourteen generations in all from Abraham to David, fourteen from David to the exile to Babylon, and fourteen from the exile to the Messiah.

## Joseph Accepts Jesus as His Son

18 This is how the birth of Jesus the Messiah came about[d]: His mother Mary was pledged to be married to Joseph, but before they came together, she was found to be pregnant through the Holy Spirit. 19 Because Joseph her husband was faithful to the law, and yet[e] did not want to expose her to public disgrace, he had in mind to divorce her quietly.

---

# Matthew

**1** The book of the ancestry (genealogy) of Jesus Christ (the Messiah, the Anointed), the son (descendant) of David, the son (descendant) of Abraham. [Ps. 132:11; Isa. 11:1.]

2 Abraham was the father of Isaac, Isaac the father of Jacob, Jacob the father of Judah and his brothers,

3 Judah the father of Perez and Zerah, whose mother was Tamar, Perez the father of Hezron, Hezron the father of Aram,

4 Aram the father of Aminadab, Aminadab the father of Nahshon, Nahshon the father of Salmon,

5 Salmon the father of Boaz, whose mother was Rahab, Boaz the father of Obed, whose mother was Ruth, Obed the father of Jesse,

6 Jesse the father of King David, King David the father of Solomon, whose mother had been the wife of Uriah, [Ruth 4:18-22; I Chron. 2:13-15.]

7 Solomon the father of Rehoboam, Rehoboam the father of Abijah, Abijah the father of Asa,

8 Asa the father of Jehoshaphat, Jehoshaphat the father of Joram [Jehoram], Joram the father of Uzziah,

9 Uzziah the father of Jotham, Jotham the father of Ahaz, Ahaz the father of Hezekiah,

10 Hezekiah the father of Manasseh, Manasseh the father of Amon, Amon the father of Josiah,

11 And Josiah became the father of Jeconiah [also called Coniah and Jehoiachin] and his brothers about the time of the removal (deportation) to Babylon. [II Kings 24:14; I Chron. 3:15, 16.]

12 After the exile to Babylon, Jeconiah became the father of Shealtiel [Salathiel], Shealtiel the father of Zerubbabel,

13 Zerubbabel the father of Abiud, Abiud the father of Eliakim, Eliakim the father of Azor,

14 Azor the father of Sadoc, Sadoc the father of Achim, Achim the father of Eliud,

15 Eliud the father of Eleazar, Eleazar the father of Matthan, Matthan the father of Jacob,

16 Jacob the father of Joseph, the husband of Mary, of whom was born Jesus, Who is called the Christ. (the Messiah, the Anointed)

17 So all the generations from Abraham to David are fourteen, from David to the Babylonian exile (deportation) fourteen generations, from the Babylonian exile to the Christ fourteen generations.

18 Now the birth of Jesus Christ took place under these circumstances: When His mother Mary had been promised in marriage to Joseph, before they came together, she was found to be pregnant [through the power] of the Holy Spirit.

19 And her [promised] husband Joseph, being a just *and* upright man and not willing to expose her publicly *and* to shame *and* disgrace her, decided to repudiate *and* dismiss (divorce) her quietly *and* secretly.

---

## New International Version

20 But after he had considered this, an angel of the Lord appeared to him in a dream and said, "Joseph son of David, do not be afraid to take Mary home as your wife, because what is conceived in her is from the Holy Spirit. 21 She will give birth to a son, and you are to give him the name Jesus,ᵃ because he will save his people from their sins."

22 All this took place to fulfill what the Lord had said through the prophet: 23 "The virgin will conceive and give birth to a son, and they will call him Immanuel"ᵇ (which means "God with us").

24 When Joseph woke up, he did what the angel of the Lord had commanded him and took Mary home as his wife. 25 But he did not consummate their marriage until she gave birth to a son. And he gave him the name Jesus.

### The Magi Visit the Messiah

**2** After Jesus was born in Bethlehem in Judea, during the time of King Herod, Magiᶜ from the east came to Jerusalem 2 and asked, "Where is the one who has been born king of the Jews? We saw his star when it rose and have come to worship him."

3 When King Herod heard this he was disturbed, and all Jerusalem with him. 4 When he had called together all the people's chief priests and teachers of the law, he asked them where the Messiah was to be born. 5 "In Bethlehem in Judea," they replied, "for this is what the prophet has written:

6 "'But you, Bethlehem, in the land of Judah,
  are by no means least among the rulers of Judah;
  for out of you will come a ruler
  who will shepherd my people Israel.'ᵈ"

7 Then Herod called the Magi secretly and found out from them the exact time the star had appeared. 8 He sent them to Bethlehem and said, "Go and search carefully for the child. As soon as you find him, report to me, so that I too may go and worship him."

9 After they had heard the king, they went on their way, and the star they had seen when it rose went ahead of them until it stopped over the place where the child was. 10 When they saw the star, they were overjoyed. 11 On coming to the house, they saw the child with his mother Mary, and they bowed down and worshiped him. Then they opened their treasures and presented him with gifts of gold, frankincense and myrrh. 12 And having been warned in a dream not to go back to Herod, they returned to their country by another route.

### The Escape to Egypt

13 When they had gone, an angel of the Lord appeared to Joseph in a dream. "Get up," he said, "take the child and his mother and escape to Egypt. Stay there until I tell you, for Herod is going to search for the child to kill him."

## Amplified Bible

20 But as he was thinking this over, behold, an angel of the Lord appeared to him in a dream, saying, Joseph, descendant of David, do not be afraid to take Mary [as] your wife, for that which is conceived in her is of (from, out of) the Holy Spirit.

21 She will bear a Son, and you shall call His name Jesus [the Greek form of the Hebrew Joshua, which means Savior], for He will save His people from their sins [that is, prevent them from ᵃfailing and missing the true end and scope of life, which is God].

22 All this took place that it might be fulfilled which the Lord had spoken through the prophet,

23 Behold, the virgin shall become pregnant and give birth to a Son, and they shall call His name Emmanuel—which, when translated, means, God with us. [Isa. 7:14.]

24 Then Joseph, being aroused from his sleep, did as the angel of the Lord had commanded him: he took [her to his side as] his wife.

25 But he had no union with her as her husband until she had borne *her firstborn* Son; and he called His name Jesus.

**2** Now when Jesus was born in Bethlehem of Judea in the days of Herod the king, behold, wise men [astrologers] from the east came to Jerusalem, asking,

2 Where is He Who has been born King of the Jews? For we have seen His star in the east ᵇat its rising and have come to worship Him. [Num. 24:17; Jer. 23:5; Zech. 9:9.]

3 When Herod the king heard this, he was disturbed *and* troubled, and the whole of Jerusalem with him.

4 So he called together all the chief priests and learned men (scribes) of the people and ᶜanxiously asked them where the Christ was to be born.

5 They replied to him, In Bethlehem of Judea, for so it is written by the prophet:

6 And you Bethlehem, in the land of Judah, you are not in any way least *or* insignificant among the ᵈchief cities of Judah; for from you shall come a Ruler (ᵉLeader) Who will govern *and* ᶠshepherd My people Israel. [Mic. 5:2.]

7 Then Herod sent for the wise men [astrologers] secretly, and ᶠaccurately to the last point ascertained from them the time of the appearing of the star [that is, ᶠhow long the star had made itself visible since its rising in the east].

8 Then he sent them to Bethlehem, saying, Go and search for the Child carefully *and* diligently, and when you have found ᵍHim, bring me word, that I too may come and worship Him.

9 When they had listened to the king, they went their way, and behold, the star which had been seen in the east ʰin its rising went before them until it came and stood over the place where the young Child was.

10 When they saw the star, they were thrilled with ecstatic joy.

11 And on going into the house, they saw the Child with Mary His mother, and they fell down and worshiped Him. Then opening their treasure bags, they presented to Him gifts—gold and frankincense and myrrh.

12 And ᶠreceiving an answer to their asking, they were divinely instructed *and* warned in a dream not to go back to Herod; so they departed to their own country by a different way.

13 Now after they had gone, behold, an angel of the Lord appeared to Joseph in a dream and said, Get up! [ⁱTenderly] take *unto you* the young Child and His mother and flee to Egypt; and remain there till I tell you [otherwise], for Herod intends to search for the Child in order to destroy Him.

---

ᵃ Marvin Vincent, *Word Studies in the New Testament.* ᵇ Alternate translation. ᶜ Charles B. Williams, *The New Testament: A Translation in the Language of the People.* ᵈ Joseph Henry Thayer, *A Greek-English Lexicon of the New Testament.* ᵉ James Hope Moulton and George Milligan, *The Vocabulary of the Greek Testament.* ᶠ Marvin Vincent, *Word Studies.* ᵍ Capitalized because of what He is, the spotless Son of God, not what the speaker may have thought He was. ʰ Alternate translation. ⁱ Charles B. Williams, *The New Testament: A Translation.*

---

ᵃ 21 *Jesus* is the Greek form of *Joshua,* which means *the LORD saves.*
ᵇ 23 Isaiah 7:14    ᶜ 1 Traditionally *wise men*    ᵈ 6 Micah 5:2,4

## New International Version

[14]So he got up, took the child and his mother during the night and left for Egypt, [15]where he stayed until the death of Herod. And so was fulfilled what the Lord had said through the prophet: "Out of Egypt I called my son."[a]

[16]When Herod realized that he had been outwitted by the Magi, he was furious, and he gave orders to kill all the boys in Bethlehem and its vicinity who were two years old and under, in accordance with the time he had learned from the Magi. [17]Then what was said through the prophet Jeremiah was fulfilled:

[18]"A voice is heard in Ramah,
    weeping and great mourning,
Rachel weeping for her children
    and refusing to be comforted,
    because they are no more."[b]

### The Return to Nazareth

[19]After Herod died, an angel of the Lord appeared in a dream to Joseph in Egypt [20]and said, "Get up, take the child and his mother and go to the land of Israel, for those who were trying to take the child's life are dead."

[21]So he got up, took the child and his mother and went to the land of Israel. [22]But when he heard that Archelaus was reigning in Judea in place of his father Herod, he was afraid to go there. Having been warned in a dream, he withdrew to the district of Galilee, [23]and he went and lived in a town called Nazareth. So was fulfilled what was said through the prophets, that he would be called a Nazarene.

### John the Baptist Prepares the Way

**3** In those days John the Baptist came, preaching in the wilderness of Judea [2]and saying, "Repent, for the kingdom of heaven has come near." [3]This is he who was spoken of through the prophet Isaiah:

"A voice of one calling in the wilderness,
'Prepare the way for the Lord,
    make straight paths for him.'"[c]

[4]John's clothes were made of camel's hair, and he had a leather belt around his waist. His food was locusts and wild honey. [5]People went out to him from Jerusalem and all Judea and the whole region of the Jordan. [6]Confessing their sins, they were baptized by him in the Jordan River.

[7]But when he saw many of the Pharisees and Sadducees coming to where he was baptizing, he said to them: "You brood of vipers! Who warned you to flee from the coming wrath? [8]Produce fruit in keeping with repentance. [9]And do not think you can say to yourselves, 'We have Abraham as our father.' I tell you that out of these stones God can raise up children for Abraham. [10]The ax is already at the root of the trees, and every tree that does not produce good fruit will be cut down and thrown into the fire.

[11]"I baptize you with[d] water for repentance. But after

## Amplified Bible

[14]And having risen, he took the Child and His mother by night and withdrew to Egypt

[15]And remained there until Herod's death. This was to fulfill what the Lord had spoken by the prophet, Out of Egypt have I called My Son. [Hos. 11:1.]

[16]Then Herod, when he realized that he had been misled by the wise men, was furiously enraged, and he sent and put to death all the male children in Bethlehem and in all that territory who were two years old and under, reckoning according to the date which he had investigated diligently and had learned exactly from the wise men.

[17]Then was fulfilled what was spoken by the prophet Jeremiah:

[18]A voice was heard in Ramah, wailing and loud lamentation, Rachel weeping for her children; she refused to be comforted, because they were no more. [Jer. 31:15.]

[19]But when Herod died, behold, an angel of the Lord appeared in a dream to Joseph in Egypt

[20]And said, Rise, [a]tenderly] take unto you the Child and His mother and go to the land of Israel, for those who sought the Child's life are dead.

[21]Then he awoke and arose and [a]tenderly] took the Child and His mother and came into the land of Israel.

[22]But because he heard that Archelaus was ruling over Judea in the place of his father Herod, he was afraid to go there. And being divinely warned in a dream, he withdrew to the region of Galilee.

[23]He went and dwelt in a town called Nazareth, so that what was spoken through the prophets might be fulfilled: He shall be called a Nazarene [Branch, Separated One]. [Isa. 11:1.]

**3** In those days there appeared John the Baptist, preaching in the Wilderness (Desert) of Judea

[2]And saying, Repent ([b]think differently; change your mind, regretting your sins and changing your conduct), for the kingdom of heaven is at hand.

[3]This is he who was mentioned by the prophet Isaiah when he said, The voice of one crying in the wilderness (shouting in the desert), Prepare the road for the Lord, make His highways straight (level, [c]direct). [Isa. 40:3.]

[4]This same John's garments were made of camel's hair, and he wore a leather girdle about his waist; and his food was locusts and wild honey. [Lev. 11:22; II Kings 1:8; Zech. 13:4.]

[5]Then Jerusalem and all Judea and all the country round about the Jordan went out to him;

[6]And they were baptized in the Jordan by him, confessing their sins.

[7]But when he saw many of the Pharisees and Sadducees coming for baptism, he said to them, You brood of vipers! Who warned you and escape from the wrath and indignation [of God against disobedience] that is coming?

[8]Bring forth fruit that is consistent with repentance [let your lives prove your change of heart];

[9]And do not presume to say to yourselves, We have Abraham for our forefather; for I tell you, God is able to raise up descendants for Abraham from these stones!

[10]And already the ax is lying at the root of the trees; every tree therefore that does not bear good fruit is cut down and thrown into the fire.

[11]I indeed baptize you [d]in (with) water [a]because of re-

---

[a] Charles B. Williams, *The New Testament: A Translation.* [b] Marvin Vincent, *Word Studies.* [c] G. Abbott-Smith, *Manual Greek Lexicon of the New Testament.* [d] *En,* the preposition used here, is translated both "in" and "with" in the Greek lexicons and concordances generally. The *King James Version* (the *Authorized Version*) gives preference to "with," putting "in" in the margin; the *American Standard Version* gives preference to "in," putting "with" in the margin. Many modern versions choose one or the other about equally.

[a] 15 Hosea 11:1    [b] 18 Jer. 31:15    [c] 3 Isaiah 40:3    [d] 11 Or *in*

## New International Version

me comes one who is more powerful than I, whose sandals I am not worthy to carry. He will baptize you with[a] the Holy Spirit and fire. [12]His winnowing fork is in his hand, and he will clear his threshing floor, gathering his wheat into the barn and burning up the chaff with unquenchable fire."

### The Baptism of Jesus

[13]Then Jesus came from Galilee to the Jordan to be baptized by John. [14]But John tried to deter him, saying, "I need to be baptized by you, and do you come to me?"

[15]Jesus replied, "Let it be so now; it is proper for us to do this to fulfill all righteousness." Then John consented.

[16]As soon as Jesus was baptized, he went up out of the water. At that moment heaven was opened, and he saw the Spirit of God descending like a dove and alighting on him. [17]And a voice from heaven said, "This is my Son, whom I love; with him I am well pleased."

### Jesus Is Tested in the Wilderness

**4** Then Jesus was led by the Spirit into the wilderness to be tempted[b] by the devil. [2]After fasting forty days and forty nights, he was hungry. [3]The tempter came to him and said, "If you are the Son of God, tell these stones to become bread."

[4]Jesus answered, "It is written: 'Man shall not live on bread alone, but on every word that comes from the mouth of God.'[c]"

[5]Then the devil took him to the holy city and had him stand on the highest point of the temple. [6]"If you are the Son of God," he said, "throw yourself down. For it is written:

"'He will command his angels concerning you,
    and they will lift you up in their hands,
  so that you will not strike your foot against a
    stone.'[d]"

[7]Jesus answered him, "It is also written: 'Do not put the Lord your God to the test.'[e]"

[8]Again, the devil took him to a very high mountain and showed him all the kingdoms of the world and their splendor. [9]"All this I will give you," he said, "if you will bow down and worship me."

[10]Jesus said to him, "Away from me, Satan! For it is written: 'Worship the Lord your God, and serve him only.'[f]"

[11]Then the devil left him, and angels came and attended him.

### Jesus Begins to Preach

[12]When Jesus heard that John had been put in prison, he withdrew to Galilee. [13]Leaving Nazareth, he went and lived in Capernaum, which was by the lake in the area of Zebulun and Naphtali— [14]to fulfill what was said through the prophet Isaiah:

## Amplified Bible

pentance [that is, because of your [a]changing your minds for the better, heartily amending your ways, with abhorrence of your past sins]. But He Who is coming after me is mightier than I, Whose sandals I am not worthy or fit to take off or carry; He will baptize you with the Holy Spirit and with fire.

[12]His winnowing fan (shovel, fork) is in His hand, and He will thoroughly clear out and clean His threshing floor and gather and store His wheat in His barn, but the chaff He will burn up with fire that cannot be put out.

[13]Then Jesus came from Galilee to the Jordan to John to be baptized by him.

[14]But John [b]protested strenuously, having in mind to prevent Him, saying, It is I who have need to be baptized by You, and do You come to me?

[15]But Jesus replied to him, [a]Permit it just now; for this is the fitting way for [both of] us to fulfill all righteousness [that is, to [a]perform completely whatever is right]. Then he permitted Him.

[16]And when Jesus was baptized, He went up at once out of the water; and behold, the heavens were opened, and he [John] saw the Spirit of God descending like a dove and alighting on Him.

[17]And behold, a voice from heaven said, This is My Son, My Beloved, in Whom I delight! [Ps. 2:7; Isa. 42:1.]

**4** Then Jesus was led (guided) by the [Holy] Spirit into the wilderness (desert) to be tempted (tested and tried) by the devil.

[2]And He went without food for forty days and forty nights, and later He was hungry. [Exod. 34:28; I Kings 19:8.]

[3]And the tempter came and said to Him, If You are God's Son, command these stones to be made [c]loaves of] bread.

[4]But He replied, It has been written, Man shall not live and be upheld and sustained by bread alone, but by every word that comes forth from the mouth of God. [Deut. 8:3.]

[5]Then the devil took Him into the holy city and placed Him on [d]a turret (pinnacle, [e]gable) of the temple [f]sanctuary. [Neh. 11:1; Dan. 9:24.]

[6]And he said to Him, If You are the Son of God, throw Yourself down; for it is written, He will give His angels charge over you, and they will bear you up on their hands, lest you strike your foot against a stone. [Ps. 91:11, 12.]

[7]Jesus said to him, [b]On the other hand, it is written also, You shall not tempt, [a]test thoroughly, or [g]try exceedingly the Lord your God. [Deut. 6:16.]

[8]Again, the devil took Him up on a very high mountain and showed Him all the kingdoms of the world and the glory (the splendor, magnificence, preeminence, and excellence) of them.

[9]And he said to Him, These things, all taken together, I will give You, if You will prostrate Yourself before me and do homage and worship me.

[10]Then Jesus said to him, Begone, Satan! For it has been written, You shall worship the Lord your God, and Him alone shall you serve. [Deut. 6:13.]

[11]Then the devil departed from Him, and behold, angels came and ministered to Him.

[12]Now when Jesus heard that John had been arrested and put in prison, He withdrew into Galilee.

[13]And leaving Nazareth, He went and dwelt in Capernaum by the sea, in the country of Zebulun and Naphtali—

[14]That what was spoken by the prophet Isaiah might be brought to pass:

[a] Joseph Thayer, *A Greek-English Lexicon.* [b] Marvin Vincent, *Word Studies.* [c] John Wycliffe, *The Wycliffe Bible.* [d] G. Abbott-Smith, *Manual Greek Lexicon.* [e] James Moulton and George Milligan, *The Vocabulary.* [f] Richard Trench, *Synonyms of the New Testament.* [g] Robert Young, *Analytical Concordance to the Bible.*

[a] 11 Or *in*   [b] 1 The Greek for *tempted* can also mean *tested.*
[c] 4 Deut. 8:3   [d] 6 Psalm 91:11,12   [e] 7 Deut. 6:16   [f] 10 Deut. 6:13

## New International Version

15"Land of Zebulun and land of Naphtali,
the Way of the Sea, beyond the Jordan,
Galilee of the Gentiles—
16the people living in darkness
have seen a great light;
on those living in the land of the shadow of death
a light has dawned."[a]

17From that time on Jesus began to preach, "Repent, for the kingdom of heaven has come near."

### Jesus Calls His First Disciples

18As Jesus was walking beside the Sea of Galilee, he saw two brothers, Simon called Peter and his brother Andrew. They were casting a net into the lake, for they were fishermen. 19"Come, follow me," Jesus said, "and I will send you out to fish for people." 20At once they left their nets and followed him.

21Going on from there, he saw two other brothers, James son of Zebedee and his brother John. They were in a boat with their father Zebedee, preparing their nets. Jesus called them, 22and immediately they left the boat and their father and followed him.

### Jesus Heals the Sick

23Jesus went throughout Galilee, teaching in their synagogues, proclaiming the good news of the kingdom, and healing every disease and sickness among the people. 24News about him spread all over Syria, and people brought to him all who were ill with various diseases, those suffering severe pain, the demon-possessed, those having seizures, and the paralyzed; and he healed them. 25Large crowds from Galilee, the Decapolis,[b] Jerusalem, Judea and the region across the Jordan followed him.

### Introduction to the Sermon on the Mount

5 Now when Jesus saw the crowds, he went up on a mountainside and sat down. His disciples came to him, 2and he began to teach them.

### The Beatitudes

He said:

3"Blessed are the poor in spirit,
for theirs is the kingdom of heaven.
4Blessed are those who mourn,
for they will be comforted.
5Blessed are the meek,
for they will inherit the earth.
6Blessed are those who hunger and thirst for
righteousness,
for they will be filled.
7Blessed are the merciful,
for they will be shown mercy.

## Amplified Bible

15The land of Zebulun and the land of Naphtali, in the [a]way to the sea, beyond the Jordan, Galilee of the Gentiles [of the [a]peoples who are not of Israel]—[Isa. 9:1-2.]
16The people who sat [b](dwelt enveloped) in darkness have seen a great Light, and for those who sat in the land and shadow of death Light has dawned.
17From that time Jesus began to preach, [c]crying out, Repent ([d]change your mind for the better, heartily amend your ways, with abhorrence of your past sins), for the kingdom of heaven is at hand.
18As He was walking by the Sea of Galilee, He noticed two brothers, Simon who is called Peter and Andrew his brother, throwing a dragnet into the sea, for they were fishermen.
19And He said to them, Come [d]after Me [as disciples—letting Me be your Guide], follow Me, and I will make you fishers of men!
20At once they left their nets and [d]became His disciples [sided with His party and followed Him].
21And going on further from there He noticed two other brothers, James son of Zebedee and his brother John, in the boat with their father Zebedee, mending their nets and putting them right; and He called them.
22At once they left the boat and their father and [d]joined Jesus as disciples [sided with His party and followed Him].
23And He went about all Galilee, teaching in their synagogues and preaching the good news (Gospel) of the kingdom, and healing every disease and every weakness and infirmity among the people.
24So the report of Him spread throughout all Syria, and they brought Him all who were sick, those afflicted with various diseases and torments, those under the power of demons, and epileptics, and paralyzed people, and He healed them.
25And great crowds joined and accompanied Him about, coming from Galilee and Decapolis [the district of the ten cities east of the Sea of Galilee] and Jerusalem and Judea and from the other [the east] side of the Jordan.

5 Seeing the crowds, He went up on the mountain; and when He was seated, His disciples came to Him.
2Then He opened His mouth and taught them, saying:
3Blessed (happy, [e]to be envied, and [c]spiritually prosperous—[f]with life-joy and satisfaction in God's favor and salvation, regardless of their outward conditions) are the poor in spirit (the humble, who rate themselves insignificant), for theirs is the kingdom of heaven!
4Blessed and enviably happy [with a [f]happiness produced by the experience of God's favor and especially conditioned by the revelation of His matchless grace] are those who mourn, for they shall be comforted! [Isa. 61:2.]
5Blessed (happy, blithesome, joyous, [c]spiritually prosperous—[f]with life-joy and satisfaction in God's favor and salvation, regardless of their outward conditions) are the meek (the mild, patient, long-suffering), for they shall inherit the earth! [Ps. 37:11.]
6Blessed and fortunate and happy and [c]spiritually prosperous (in that state in which the born-again child of God [f]enjoys His favor and salvation) are those who hunger and thirst for righteousness (uprightness and right standing with God), for they shall be [c]completely satisfied! [Isa. 55:1, 2.]
7Blessed (happy, [g]to be envied, and [c]spiritually prosperous—[a]with life-joy and satisfaction in God's favor and salvation, regardless of their outward conditions) are the merciful, for they shall obtain mercy!

---

a Hermann Cremer, *Biblico-Theological Lexicon of New Testament Greek.* b John Wycliffe, *The Wycliffe Bible.* c Marvin Vincent, *Word Studies.* d Joseph Thayer, *A Greek-English Lexicon.* e Alexander Souter, *Pocket Lexicon of the Greek New Testament.* f Hermann Cremer, *Biblico-Theological Lexicon.* g Alexander Souter, *Pocket Lexicon.*

a 16 Isaiah 9:1,2    b 25 That is, the Ten Cities

## New International Version

8 Blessed are the pure in heart,
for they will see God.
9 Blessed are the peacemakers,
for they will be called children of God.
10 Blessed are those who are persecuted because of
righteousness,
for theirs is the kingdom of heaven.

11 "Blessed are you when people insult you, persecute
you and falsely say all kinds of evil against you because of
me. 12 Rejoice and be glad, because great is your reward in
heaven, for in the same way they persecuted the prophets
who were before you.

### Salt and Light

13 "You are the salt of the earth. But if the salt loses its
saltiness, how can it be made salty again? It is no longer
good for anything, except to be thrown out and trampled
underfoot.

14 "You are the light of the world. A town built on a hill
cannot be hidden. 15 Neither do people light a lamp and
put it under a bowl. Instead they put it on its stand, and it
gives light to everyone in the house. 16 In the same way,
let your light shine before others, that they may see your
good deeds and glorify your Father in heaven.

### The Fulfillment of the Law

17 "Do not think that I have come to abolish the Law
or the Prophets; I have not come to abolish them but to
fulfill them. 18 For truly I tell you, until heaven and earth
disappear, not the smallest letter, not the least stroke of a
pen, will by any means disappear from the Law until everything is accomplished. 19 Therefore anyone who sets aside
one of the least of these commands and teaches others accordingly will be called least in the kingdom of heaven, but
whoever practices and teaches these commands will be
called great in the kingdom of heaven. 20 For I tell you that
unless your righteousness surpasses that of the Pharisees
and the teachers of the law, you will certainly not enter the
kingdom of heaven.

### Murder

21 "You have heard that it was said to the people long
ago, 'You shall not murder,a and anyone who murders
will be subject to judgment.' 22 But I tell you that anyone
who is angry with a brother or sisterb,c will be subject to
judgment. Again, anyone who says to a brother or sister,
'Raca,'d is answerable to the court. And anyone who says,
'You fool!' will be in danger of the fire of hell.

## Amplified Bible

8 Blessed (happy, aenviably fortunate, and bspiritually
prosperous—possessing the chappiness produced by the
experience of God's favor and especially conditioned by
the revelation of His grace, regardless of their outward
conditions) are the pure in heart, for they shall see God!
[Ps. 24:3, 4.]
9 Blessed (enjoying aenviable happiness, bspiritually
prosperous—cwith life-joy and satisfaction in God's favor
and salvation, regardless of their outward conditions) are
the makers and dmaintainers of peace, for they shall be
called the sons of God!
10 Blessed and happy and aenviably fortunate and bspiritually prosperous c (in the state in which the born-again
child of God enjoys and finds satisfaction in God's favor
and salvation, regardless of his outward conditions) are
those who are persecuted for righteousness' sake (for being and doing right), for theirs is the kingdom of heaven!
11 Blessed (happy, ato be envied, and bspiritually prosperous—cwith life-joy and satisfaction in God's favor and
salvation, regardless of your outward conditions) are you
when people revile you and persecute you and say all
kinds of evil things against you falsely on My account.
12 Be glad and supremely joyful, for your reward in
heaven is great (strong and intense), for in this same way
people persecuted the prophets who were before you.
[II Chron. 36:16.]
13 You are the salt of the earth, but if salt has lost its taste
(its strength, its quality), how can its saltness be restored?
It is not good for anything any longer but to be thrown out
and trodden underfoot by men.
14 You are the light of the world. A city set on a hill cannot be hidden.
15 Nor do men light a lamp and put it under a peck measure, but on a lampstand, and it gives light to all in the house.
16 Let your light so shine before men that they may see
your cmoral excellence and your praiseworthy, noble, and
good deeds and crecognize and honor and praise and glorify your Father Who is in heaven.
17 Do not think that I have come to do away with or eundo
the Law or the Prophets; I have come not to do away with
or undo but to complete and fulfill them.
18 For truly I tell you, until the sky and earth pass away
and perish, not one smallest letter nor one little hook
[identifying certain Hebrew letters] will pass from the
Law until all things [it foreshadows] are accomplished.
19 Whoever then breaks or does away with or relaxes
one of the least [important] of these commandments
and teaches men so shall be called least [important] in
the kingdom of heaven, but he who practices them and
teaches others to do so shall be called great in the kingdom of heaven.
20 For I tell you, unless your righteousness (your uprightness and your right standing with God) is more than
that of the scribes and Pharisees, you will never enter the
kingdom of heaven.
21 You have heard that it was said to the men of old, You
shall not kill, and whoever kills shall be fliable to and
unable to escape the punishment imposed by the court.
[Exod. 20:13; Deut. 5:17; 16:18.]
22 But I say to you that everyone who continues to be gan-
gry with his brother or harbors malice (enmity of heart)
against him shall be fliable to and unable to escape the
punishment imposed by the court; and whoever speaks
contemptuously and insultingly to his brother shall be fliable to and unable to escape the punishment imposed by
the Sanhedrin, and whoever says, You hcursed fool! [You
empty-headed idiot!] shall be fliable to and unable to escape the hell (Gehenna) of fire.

---

a 21 Exodus 20:13    b 22 The Greek word for brother or sister
(adelphos) refers here to a fellow disciple, whether man or woman; also
in verse 23.    c 22 Some manuscripts brother or sister without cause
d 22 An Aramaic term of contempt

a Alexander Souter, Pocket Lexicon.  b Marvin Vincent, Word Studies.
c Hermann Cremer, Biblico-Theological Lexicon.  d William Tyndale, The
Tyndale Bible.  e John Wycliffe, The Wycliffe Bible.  f Joseph Thayer,
A Greek-English Lexicon.  g Some manuscripts insert here: "without
cause."  h Charles B. Williams, The New Testament: A Translation.

## New International Version

23"Therefore, if you are offering your gift at the altar and there remember that your brother or sister has something against you, 24leave your gift there in front of the altar. First go and be reconciled to them; then come and offer your gift.

25"Settle matters quickly with your adversary who is taking you to court. Do it while you are still together on the way, or your adversary may hand you over to the judge, and the judge may hand you over to the officer, and you may be thrown into prison. 26Truly I tell you, you will not get out until you have paid the last penny.

### Adultery

27"You have heard that it was said, 'You shall not commit adultery.'ᵃ 28But I tell you that anyone who looks at a woman lustfully has already committed adultery with her in his heart. 29If your right eye causes you to stumble, gouge it out and throw it away. It is better for you to lose one part of your body than for your whole body to be thrown into hell. 30And if your right hand causes you to stumble, cut it off and throw it away. It is better for you to lose one part of your body than for your whole body to go into hell.

### Divorce

31"It has been said, 'Anyone who divorces his wife must give her a certificate of divorce.'ᵇ 32But I tell you that anyone who divorces his wife, except for sexual immorality, makes her the victim of adultery, and anyone who marries a divorced woman commits adultery.

### Oaths

33"Again, you have heard that it was said to the people long ago, 'Do not break your oath, but fulfill to the Lord the vows you have made.' 34But I tell you, do not swear an oath at all: either by heaven, for it is God's throne; 35or by the earth, for it is his footstool; or by Jerusalem, for it is the city of the Great King. 36And do not swear by your head, for you cannot make even one hair white or black. 37All you need to say is simply 'Yes' or 'No'; anything beyond this comes from the evil one.ᶜ

### Eye for Eye

38"You have heard that it was said, 'Eye for eye, and tooth for tooth.'ᵈ 39But I tell you, do not resist an evil person. If anyone slaps you on the right cheek, turn to them the other cheek also. 40And if anyone wants to sue you and take your shirt, hand over your coat as well. 41If anyone forces you to go one mile, go with them two miles. 42Give to the one who asks you, and do not turn away from the one who wants to borrow from you.

### Love for Enemies

43"You have heard that it was said, 'Love your neighborᵉ and hate your enemy.' 44But I tell you, love your enemies and pray for those who persecute you, 45that you may be children of your Father in heaven. He causes his sun to rise on the evil and the good, and sends rain on the righteous and the unrighteous. 46If you love those who love you, what reward will you get? Are not even the tax collectors doing that? 47And if you greet only your own people, what are you doing more than others? Do not even pagans

## Amplified Bible

23So if when you are offering your gift at the altar you there remember that your brother has any [grievance] against you,

24Leave your gift at the altar and go. First make peace with your brother, and then come back *and* present your gift.

25Come to terms quickly with your accuser while you are on the way traveling with him, lest your accuser hand you over to the judge, and the judge to the guard, and you be put in prison.

26Truly I say to you, you will not be released until you have paid the last fraction of a penny.

27You have heard that it was said, You shall not commit adultery. [Exod. 20:14; Deut. 5:18.]

28But I say to you that everyone who so much as looks at a woman with evil desire for her has already committed adultery with her in his heart.

29If your right eye serves as a trap to ensnare you *or* is an occasion for you to stumble *and* sin, pluck it out and throw it away. It is better that you lose one of your members than that your whole body be cast into hell (Gehenna).

30And if your right hand serves as a trap to ensnare you *or* is an occasion for you to stumble *and* sin, cut it off and cast it from you. It is better that you lose one of your members than that your entire body should be cast into hell (Gehenna).

31It has also been said, Whoever divorces his wife must give her a certificate of divorce.

32But I tell you, Whoever dismisses *and* repudiates *and* divorces his wife, except on the grounds of unfaithfulness (sexual immorality), causes her to commit adultery, and whoever marries a woman who has been divorced commits adultery. [Deut. 24:1-4.]

33Again, you have heard that it was said to the men of old, You shall not swear falsely, but you shall perform your oaths to the Lord [as a religious duty].

34But I tell you, Do not bind yourselves by an oath at all: either by heaven, for it is the throne of God;

35Or by the earth, for it is the footstool of His feet; or by Jerusalem, for it is the city of the Great King. [Ps. 48:2; Isa. 66:1.]

36And do not swear by your head, for you are not able to make a single hair white or black.

37Let your Yes be simply Yes, and your No be simply No; anything more than that comes from the evil one. [Lev. 19:12; Num. 30:2; Deut. 23:21.]

38You have heard that it was said, An eye for an eye, and a tooth for a tooth. [Exod. 21:24; Lev. 24:20; Deut. 19:21.]

39But I say to you, Do not resist the evil man [who injures you]; but if anyone strikes you on the right jaw *or* cheek, turn to him the other one too.

40And if anyone wants to sue you and take your undershirt (tunic), let him have your coat also.

41And if anyone forces you to go one mile, go with him two [miles].

42Give to him who keeps on begging from you, and do not turn away from him who would borrow [ᵃat interest] from you. [Deut. 15:8; Prov. 24:29.]

43You have heard that it was said, You shall love your neighbor and hate your enemy; [Lev. 19:18; Ps. 139:21, 22.]

44But I tell you, Love your enemies and pray for those who persecute you, [Prov. 25:21, 22.]

45ᵇTo show that you are the children of your Father Who is in heaven; for He makes His sun rise on the wicked and on the good, and makes the rain fall upon the upright and the wrongdoers [alike].

46For if you love those who love you, what reward can you have? Do not even the tax collectors do that?

47And if you greet only your brethren, what more than others are you doing? Do not even the Gentiles (the heathen) do that?

---

ᵃ 27 Exodus 20:14    ᵇ 31 Deut. 24:1    ᶜ 37 Or *from evil*
ᵈ 38 Exodus 21:24; Lev. 24:20; Deut. 19:21    ᵉ 43 Lev. 19:18

ᵃ Marvin Vincent, *Word Studies.*    ᵇ Joseph Thayer, *A Greek-English Lexicon.*

## New International Version

do that? [48]Be perfect, therefore, as your heavenly Father is perfect.

### Giving to the Needy

**6** "Be careful not to practice your righteousness in front of others to be seen by them. If you do, you will have no reward from your Father in heaven.

[2]"So when you give to the needy, do not announce it with trumpets, as the hypocrites do in the synagogues and on the streets, to be honored by others. Truly I tell you, they have received their reward in full. [3]But when you give to the needy, do not let your left hand know what your right hand is doing, [4]so that your giving may be in secret. Then your Father, who sees what is done in secret, will reward you.

### Prayer

[5]"And when you pray, do not be like the hypocrites, for they love to pray standing in the synagogues and on the street corners to be seen by others. Truly I tell you, they have received their reward in full. [6]But when you pray, go into your room, close the door and pray to your Father, who is unseen. Then your Father, who sees what is done in secret, will reward you. [7]And when you pray, do not keep on babbling like pagans, for they think they will be heard because of their many words. [8]Do not be like them, for your Father knows what you need before you ask him.

[9]"This, then, is how you should pray:

"'Our Father in heaven,
hallowed be your name,
[10]your kingdom come,
your will be done,
on earth as it is in heaven.
[11]Give us today our daily bread.
[12]And forgive us our debts,
as we also have forgiven our debtors.
[13]And lead us not into temptation,[a]
but deliver us from the evil one.[b]'

[14]For if you forgive other people when they sin against you, your heavenly Father will also forgive you. [15]But if you do not forgive others their sins, your Father will not forgive your sins.

### Fasting

[16]"When you fast, do not look somber as the hypocrites do, for they disfigure their faces to show others they are fasting. Truly I tell you, they have received their reward in full. [17]But when you fast, put oil on your head and wash your face, [18]so that it will not be obvious to others that you are fasting, but only to your Father, who is unseen; and your Father, who sees what is done in secret, will reward you.

### Treasures in Heaven

[19]"Do not store up for yourselves treasures on earth, where moths and vermin destroy, and where thieves

## Amplified Bible

[48]You, therefore, must be perfect [growing into complete [a]maturity of godliness in mind and character, [b]having reached the proper height of virtue and integrity], as your heavenly Father is perfect. [Lev. 19:2, 18.]

**6** Take care not to do your good deeds publicly or before men, in order to be seen by them; otherwise you will have no reward [[c]reserved for and awaiting you] with and from your Father Who is in heaven.

[2]Thus, whenever you give to the poor, do not blow a trumpet before you, as the hypocrites in the synagogues and in the streets like to do, that they may be [d]recognized and honored and praised by men. Truly I tell you, they have their reward [c]in full already.

[3]But when you give to charity, do not let your left hand know what your right hand is doing,

[4]So that your deeds of charity may be in secret; and your Father Who sees in secret will reward you openly.

[5]Also when you pray, you must not be like the hypocrites, for they love to pray standing in the synagogues and on the corners of the streets, that they may be seen by people. Truly I tell you, they have their reward [c]in full already.

[6]But when you pray, go into your [most] private room, and, closing the door, pray to your Father, Who is in secret; and your Father, Who sees in secret, will reward you in the open.

[7]And when you pray, do not heap up phrases (multiply words, repeating the same ones over and over) as the Gentiles do, for they think they will be heard for their much speaking. [I Kings 18:25-29.]

[8]Do not be like them, for your Father knows what you need before you ask Him.

[9]Pray, therefore, like this: Our Father Who is in heaven, hallowed (kept holy) be Your name.

[10]Your kingdom come, Your will be done on earth as it is in heaven.

[11]Give us this day our daily bread.

[12]And forgive us our debts, as we also have forgiven ([e]left, remitted, and let go of the debts, and have [f]given up resentment against) our debtors.

[13]And lead (bring) us not into temptation, but deliver us from the evil one. For Yours is the kingdom and the power and the glory forever. Amen.

[14]For if you forgive people their trespasses [their [c]reckless and willful sins, [e]leaving them, letting them go, and [f]giving up resentment], your heavenly Father will also forgive you.

[15]But if you do not forgive others their trespasses [their [c]reckless and willful sins, [e]leaving them, letting them go, and [f]giving up resentment], neither will your Father forgive your trespasses.

[16]And whenever you are fasting, do not look gloomy and [g]sour and [h]dreary like the hypocrites, for they put on a dismal countenance, that their fasting may be apparent to and seen by men. Truly I say to you, they have their reward [c]in full already. [Isa. 58:5.]

[17]But when you fast, perfume your head and wash your face,

[18]So that your fasting may not be noticed by men but by your Father, Who sees in secret; and your Father, Who sees in secret, will reward you in the open.

[19]Do not [b]gather and heap up and store up for yourselves treasures on earth, where moth and rust and worm consume and destroy, and where thieves break through and steal.

[a] Kenneth Wuest, Word Studies in the New Testament. [b] Joseph Thayer, A Greek-English Lexicon. [c] Marvin Vincent, Word Studies. [d] Hermann Cremer, Biblico-Theological Lexicon. [e] James Moulton and George Milligan, The Vocabulary. [f] Webster's New International Dictionary offers this phrase as a definition of the word "forgive." [g] Martin Luther, cited by Marvin Vincent, Word Studies. [h] Richard Trench, Synonyms of the New Testament.

[a] 13 The Greek for temptation can also mean testing.    [b] 13 Or from evil; some late manuscripts one, / for yours is the kingdom and the power and the glory forever. Amen.

## New International Version

break in and steal. [20]But store up for yourselves treasures in heaven, where moths and vermin do not destroy, and where thieves do not break in and steal. [21]For where your treasure is, there your heart will be also.

[22]"The eye is the lamp of the body. If your eyes are healthy,[a] your whole body will be full of light. [23]But if your eyes are unhealthy,[b] your whole body will be full of darkness. If then the light within you is darkness, how great is that darkness!

[24]"No one can serve two masters. Either you will hate the one and love the other, or you will be devoted to the one and despise the other. You cannot serve both God and money.

### Do Not Worry

[25]"Therefore I tell you, do not worry about your life, what you will eat or drink; or about your body, what you will wear. Is not life more than food, and the body more than clothes? [26]Look at the birds of the air; they do not sow or reap or store away in barns, and yet your heavenly Father feeds them. Are you not much more valuable than they? [27]Can any one of you by worrying add a single hour to your life[c]?

[28]"And why do you worry about clothes? See how the flowers of the field grow. They do not labor or spin. [29]Yet I tell you that not even Solomon in all his splendor was dressed like one of these. [30]If that is how God clothes the grass of the field, which is here today and tomorrow is thrown into the fire, will he not much more clothe you—you of little faith? [31]So do not worry, saying, 'What shall we eat?' or 'What shall we drink?' or 'What shall we wear?' [32]For the pagans run after all these things, and your heavenly Father knows that you need them. [33]But seek first his kingdom and his righteousness, and all these things will be given to you as well. [34]Therefore do not worry about tomorrow, for tomorrow will worry about itself. Each day has enough trouble of its own.

### Judging Others

**7** "Do not judge, or you too will be judged. [2]For in the same way you judge others, you will be judged, and with the measure you use, it will be measured to you.

[3]"Why do you look at the speck of sawdust in your brother's eye and pay no attention to the plank in your own eye? [4]How can you say to your brother, 'Let me take the speck out of your eye,' when all the time there is a plank in

## Amplified Bible

[20]But [a]gather and heap up and store for yourselves treasures in heaven, where neither moth nor rust nor worm consume and destroy, and where thieves do not break through and steal;

[21]For where your treasure is, there will your heart be also.

[22]The eye is the lamp of the body. So if your eye is sound, your entire body will be full of light.

[23]But if your eye is unsound, your whole body will be full of darkness. If then the very light in you [your [b]conscience] is darkened, how dense is that darkness!

[24]No one can serve two masters; for either he will hate the one and love the other, or he will stand by and be devoted to the one and despise and be [c]against the other. You cannot serve God and mammon ([b]deceitful riches, money, possessions, or [a]whatever is trusted in).

[25]Therefore I tell you, stop being [d]perpetually uneasy (anxious and worried) about your life, what you shall eat or *what you shall drink;* or about your body, what you shall put on. Is not life greater [in quality] than food, and the body [far above and more excellent] than clothing?

[26]Look at the birds of the air; they neither sow nor reap nor gather into barns, and yet your heavenly Father keeps feeding them. Are you not worth much more than they?

[27]And who of you by worrying and being anxious can add one unit of measure (cubit) to his stature or to the [e]span of his life? [Ps. 39:5-7.]

[28]And why should you be anxious about clothes? Consider the lilies of the field and [a]learn thoroughly how they grow; they neither toil nor spin.

[29]Yet I tell you, even Solomon in all his [a]magnificence (excellence, dignity, and grace) was not arrayed like one of these. [I Kings 10:4-7.]

[30]But if God so clothes the grass of the field, which today is alive and green and tomorrow is tossed into the furnace, will He not much more surely clothe you, O you of little faith?

[31]Therefore do not worry and be anxious, saying, What are we going to have to eat? or, What are we going to have to drink? or, What are we going to have to wear?

[32]For the Gentiles (heathen) wish for and crave and diligently seek all these things, and your heavenly Father knows well that you need them all.

[33]But seek ([a]aim at and strive after) first of all His kingdom and His righteousness ([f]His way of doing and being right), and then all these things [a]taken together will be given you besides.

[34]So do not worry or be anxious about tomorrow, for tomorrow will have worries and anxieties of its own. Sufficient for each day is its own trouble.

**7** Do not judge and criticize and condemn others, so that you may not be judged and criticized and condemned yourselves.

[2]For just as you judge and criticize and condemn others, you will be judged and criticized and condemned, and in accordance with the measure you [use to] deal out to others, it will be dealt out again to you.

[3]Why do you [g]stare from without at the [g]very small particle that is in your brother's eye but do not become aware of and consider the beam [h]of timber that is in your own eye?

[4]Or how can you say to your brother, Let me get the tiny particle out of your eye, when there is the beam [h]of timber in your own eye?

[a] Joseph Thayer, *A Greek-English Lexicon.*   [b] Hermann Cremer, *Biblico-Theological Lexicon.*   [c] Marvin Vincent, *Word Studies.*   [d] Kenneth Wuest, *Word Studies.*   [e] Alexander Souter, *Pocket Lexicon:* the word translated "cubit" is used as a measurement of time, as well as a measurement of length.   [f] Charles B. Williams, *The New Testament: A Translation.*   [g] James Moulton and George Milligan, *The Vocabulary.*   [h] G. Abbott-Smith, *Manual Greek Lexicon.*

[a] 22 The Greek for *healthy* here implies *generous.*   [b] 23 The Greek for *unhealthy* here implies *stingy.*   [c] 27 Or *single cubit to your height*

## New International Version

your own eye? ⁵You hypocrite, first take the plank out of your own eye, and then you will see clearly to remove the speck from your brother's eye.

⁶"Do not give dogs what is sacred; do not throw your pearls to pigs. If you do, they may trample them under their feet, and turn and tear you to pieces.

### Ask, Seek, Knock

⁷"Ask and it will be given to you; seek and you will find; knock and the door will be opened to you. ⁸For everyone who asks receives; the one who seeks finds; and to the one who knocks, the door will be opened.

⁹"Which of you, if your son asks for bread, will give him a stone? ¹⁰Or if he asks for a fish, will give him a snake? ¹¹If you, then, though you are evil, know how to give good gifts to your children, how much more will your Father in heaven give good gifts to those who ask him! ¹²So in everything, do to others what you would have them do to you, for this sums up the Law and the Prophets.

### The Narrow and Wide Gates

¹³"Enter through the narrow gate. For wide is the gate and broad is the road that leads to destruction, and many enter through it. ¹⁴But small is the gate and narrow the road that leads to life, and only a few find it.

### True and False Prophets

¹⁵"Watch out for false prophets. They come to you in sheep's clothing, but inwardly they are ferocious wolves. ¹⁶By their fruit you will recognize them. Do people pick grapes from thornbushes, or figs from thistles? ¹⁷Likewise, every good tree bears good fruit, but a bad tree bears bad fruit. ¹⁸A good tree cannot bear bad fruit, and a bad tree cannot bear good fruit. ¹⁹Every tree that does not bear good fruit is cut down and thrown into the fire. ²⁰Thus, by their fruit you will recognize them.

### True and False Disciples

²¹"Not everyone who says to me, 'Lord, Lord,' will enter the kingdom of heaven, but only the one who does the will of my Father who is in heaven. ²²Many will say to me on that day, 'Lord, Lord, did we not prophesy in your name and in your name drive out demons and in your name perform many miracles?' ²³Then I will tell them plainly, 'I never knew you. Away from me, you evildoers!'

### The Wise and Foolish Builders

²⁴"Therefore everyone who hears these words of mine and puts them into practice is like a wise man who built his house on the rock. ²⁵The rain came down, the streams rose, and the winds blew and beat against that house; yet it did not fall, because it had its foundation on the rock. ²⁶But everyone who hears these words of mine and does not put them into practice is like a foolish man who built his house on sand. ²⁷The rain came down, the streams rose, and the winds blew and beat against that house, and it fell with a great crash."

²⁸When Jesus had finished saying these things, the crowds were amazed at his teaching, ²⁹because he taught as one who had authority, and not as their teachers of the law.

## Amplified Bible

⁵You hypocrite, first get the beam of timber out of your own eye, and then you will see clearly to take the tiny particle out of your brother's eye.

⁶Do not give that which is holy (the sacred thing) to the dogs, and do not throw your pearls before hogs, lest they trample upon them with their feet and turn *and* tear you in pieces.

⁷ᵃKeep on asking and it will be given you; ᵈkeep on seeking and you will find; ᵃkeep on knocking [reverently] and [the door] will be opened to you.

⁸For everyone who keeps on asking receives; and he who keeps on seeking finds; and to him who keeps on knocking, [the door] will be opened.

⁹Or what man is there of you, if his son asks him for a loaf of bread, will hand him a stone?

¹⁰Or if he asks for a fish, will hand him a serpent?

¹¹If you then, evil as you are, know how to give good *and* ᵇadvantageous gifts to your children, how much more will your Father Who is in heaven [perfect as He is] give good *and* ᵇadvantageous things to those who ᵃkeep on asking Him!

¹²So then, whatever you desire that others would do to *and* for you, even so do also to *and* for them, for this is (sums up) the Law and the Prophets.

¹³Enter through the narrow gate; for wide is the gate and spacious *and* broad is the way that leads away to destruction, and many are those who are entering through it.

¹⁴But the gate is narrow (contracted ᶜby pressure) and the way is straitened *and* compressed that leads away to life, and few are those who find it. [Deut. 30:19; Jer. 21:8.]

¹⁵Beware of false prophets, who come to you dressed as sheep, but inside they are devouring wolves. [Ezek. 22:27.]

¹⁶You will ᵈfully recognize them by their fruits. Do people pick grapes from thorns, or figs from thistles?

¹⁷Even so, every healthy (sound) tree bears good fruit [ᵇworthy of admiration], but the sickly (decaying, worthless) tree bears bad (worthless) fruit.

¹⁸A good (healthy) tree cannot bear bad (worthless) fruit, nor can a bad (diseased) tree bear ᵇexcellent fruit [worthy of admiration].

¹⁹Every tree that does not bear good fruit is cut down and cast into the fire.

²⁰Therefore, you will ᵈfully know them by their fruits.

²¹Not everyone who says to Me, Lord, Lord, will enter the kingdom of heaven, but he who does the will of My Father Who is in heaven.

²²Many will say to Me on that day, Lord, Lord, have we not prophesied in Your name and driven out demons in Your name and done many mighty works in Your name?

²³And then I will say to them openly (publicly), I never knew you; depart from Me, you who act wickedly [disregarding My commands]. [Ps. 6:8.]

²⁴So everyone who hears these words of Mine and acts upon them [obeying them] will be like a ᵉsensible (prudent, practical, wise) man who built his house upon the rock.

²⁵And the rain fell and the floods came and the winds blew and beat against that house; yet it did not fall, because it had been founded on the rock.

²⁶And everyone who hears these words of Mine and does not do them will be like a stupid (foolish) man who built his house upon the sand.

²⁷And the rain fell and the floods came and the winds blew and beat against that house, and it fell—and great *and* complete was the fall of it.

²⁸When Jesus had finished these sayings [the Sermon on the Mount], the crowds were astonished *and* overwhelmed with bewildered wonder at His teaching,

²⁹For He was teaching as *One* Who had [and was] authority, and not as [did] the scribes.

---

ᵃ Kenneth Wuest, *Word Studies.* ᵇ Hermann Cremer, *Biblico-Theological Lexicon.* ᶜ Alexander Souter, *Pocket Lexicon.* ᵈ Marvin Vincent, *Word Studies.* ᵉ G. Abbott-Smith, *Manual Greek Lexicon.*

## New International Version

### Jesus Heals a Man With Leprosy

**8** When Jesus came down from the mountainside, large crowds followed him. ²A man with leprosy[a] came and knelt before him and said, "Lord, if you are willing, you can make me clean."

³Jesus reached out his hand and touched the man. "I am willing," he said. "Be clean!" Immediately he was cleansed of his leprosy. ⁴Then Jesus said to him, "See that you don't tell anyone. But go, show yourself to the priest and offer the gift Moses commanded, as a testimony to them."

### The Faith of the Centurion

⁵When Jesus had entered Capernaum, a centurion came to him, asking for help. ⁶"Lord," he said, "my servant lies at home paralyzed, suffering terribly."

⁷Jesus said to him, "Shall I come and heal him?"

⁸The centurion replied, "Lord, I do not deserve to have you come under my roof. But just say the word, and my servant will be healed. ⁹For I myself am a man under authority, with soldiers under me. I tell this one, 'Go,' and he goes; and that one, 'Come,' and he comes. I say to my servant, 'Do this,' and he does it."

¹⁰When Jesus heard this, he was amazed and said to those following him, "Truly I tell you, I have not found anyone in Israel with such great faith. ¹¹I say to you that many will come from the east and the west, and will take their places at the feast with Abraham, Isaac and Jacob in the kingdom of heaven. ¹²But the subjects of the kingdom will be thrown outside, into the darkness, where there will be weeping and gnashing of teeth."

¹³Then Jesus said to the centurion, "Go! Let it be done just as you believed it would." And his servant was healed at that moment.

### Jesus Heals Many

¹⁴When Jesus came into Peter's house, he saw Peter's mother-in-law lying in bed with a fever. ¹⁵He touched her hand and the fever left her, and she got up and began to wait on him.

¹⁶When evening came, many who were demon-possessed were brought to him, and he drove out the spirits with a word and healed all the sick. ¹⁷This was to fulfill what was spoken through the prophet Isaiah:

"He took up our infirmities
   and bore our diseases."[b]

### The Cost of Following Jesus

¹⁸When Jesus saw the crowd around him, he gave orders to cross to the other side of the lake. ¹⁹Then a teacher of the law came to him and said, "Teacher, I will follow you wherever you go."

²⁰Jesus replied, "Foxes have dens and birds have nests, but the Son of Man has no place to lay his head."

²¹Another disciple said to him, "Lord, first let me go and bury my father."

²²But Jesus told him, "Follow me, and let the dead bury their own dead."

### Jesus Calms the Storm

²³Then he got into the boat and his disciples followed him. ²⁴Suddenly a furious storm came up on the lake, so

## Amplified Bible

**8** When Jesus came down from the mountain, great throngs followed Him.

²And behold, a leper came up to Him and, prostrating himself, worshiped Him, saying, Lord, if You are willing, You are able to ᵃcleanse me by curing me.

³And He reached out His hand and touched him, saying, I am willing; be cleansed ᵃby being cured. And instantly his leprosy was cured *and* cleansed.

⁴And Jesus said to him, See that you tell nothing about this to anyone; but go, show yourself to the priest and present the offering that Moses commanded, for a testimony [to your healing] *and* as an evidence to the people. [Lev. 14:2.]

⁵As Jesus went into Capernaum, a centurion came up to Him, begging Him,

⁶And saying, Lord, my servant boy is lying at the house paralyzed *and* ᵃdistressed with intense pains.

⁷And Jesus said to him, I will come and restore him.

⁸But the centurion replied to Him, Lord, I am not worthy *or* fit to have You come under my roof; but only speak the word, and my servant boy will be cured.

⁹For I also am a man subject to authority, with soldiers subject to me. And I say to one, Go, and he goes; and to another, Come, and he comes; and to my slave, Do this, and he does it.

¹⁰When Jesus heard him, He marveled and said to those who followed Him [ᵃwho adhered steadfastly to Him, conforming to His example in living and, if need be, in dying also], I tell you truly, I have not found so much faith as this ᵇwith anyone, even in Israel.

¹¹I tell you, many will come from east and west, and will sit at table with Abraham, Isaac, and Jacob in the kingdom of heaven,

¹²While the sons *and* heirs of the kingdom will be driven out into the darkness outside, where there will be weeping and grinding of teeth. [Ps. 107:2, 3; Isa. 49:12; 59:19; Mal. 1:11.]

¹³Then to the centurion Jesus said, Go; it shall be done for you as you have believed. And the servant boy was restored to health at that very ᶜmoment.

¹⁴And when Jesus went into Peter's house, He saw his mother-in-law lying ill with a fever.

¹⁵He touched her hand and the fever left her; and she got up and began waiting on Him.

¹⁶When evening came, they brought to Him many who were ᵃunder the power of demons, and He drove out the spirits with a word and restored to health all who were sick.

¹⁷And thus He fulfilled what was spoken by the prophet Isaiah, He Himself took [ᵃin order to carry away] our weaknesses *and* infirmities and bore ᵈaway our diseases. [Isa. 53:4.]

¹⁸Now Jesus, when He saw the great throngs around Him, gave orders to cross to the other side [of the lake].

¹⁹And a scribe came up and said to Him, Master, I will accompany You wherever You go.

²⁰And Jesus replied to him, Foxes have holes and the birds of the air have lodging places, but the Son of Man has nowhere to lay His head.

²¹Another of the disciples said to Him, Lord, let me first go and bury [ᵉcare for till death] my father.

²²But Jesus said to him, Follow Me, and leave the dead [ᶠin sin] to bury their own dead.

²³And after He got into the boat, His disciples followed Him.

²⁴And ᵍsuddenly, behold, there arose a violent storm

---

ᵃ Joseph Thayer, *A Greek-English Lexicon.* ᵇ Some manuscripts add "with anyone." ᶜ James Moulton and George Milligan, *The Vocabulary.* ᵈ G. Abbott-Smith, *Manual Greek Lexicon*; George Ricker Berry, *Greek-English New Testament Lexicon*; Alexander Souter, *Pocket Lexicon*; Joseph Thayer, *A Greek-English Lexicon*; W. J. Hickie, *Greek-English Lexicon.* ᵉ Many commentators interpret it thus. ᶠ Albert Barnes, *Notes on the New Testament.* ᵍ Marvin Vincent, *Word Studies.*

---

ᵃ 2 The Greek word traditionally translated *leprosy* was used for various diseases affecting the skin.   ᵇ 17 Isaiah 53:4 (see Septuagint)

## New International Version

that the waves swept over the boat. But Jesus was sleeping. [25]The disciples went and woke him, saying, "Lord, save us! We're going to drown!"

[26]He replied, "You of little faith, why are you so afraid?" Then he got up and rebuked the winds and the waves, and it was completely calm.

[27]The men were amazed and asked, "What kind of man is this? Even the winds and the waves obey him!"

### Jesus Restores Two Demon-Possessed Men

[28]When he arrived at the other side in the region of the Gadarenes,[a] two demon-possessed men coming from the tombs met him. They were so violent that no one could pass that way. [29]"What do you want with us, Son of God?" they shouted. "Have you come here to torture us before the appointed time?"

[30]Some distance from them a large herd of pigs was feeding. [31]The demons begged Jesus, "If you drive us out, send us into the herd of pigs."

[32]He said to them, "Go!" So they came out and went into the pigs, and the whole herd rushed down the steep bank into the lake and died in the water. [33]Those tending the pigs ran off, went into the town and reported all this, including what had happened to the demon-possessed men. [34]Then the whole town went out to meet Jesus. And when they saw him, they pleaded with him to leave their region.

### Jesus Forgives and Heals a Paralyzed Man

**9** Jesus stepped into a boat, crossed over and came to his own town. [2]Some men brought to him a paralyzed man, lying on a mat. When Jesus saw their faith, he said to the man, "Take heart, son; your sins are forgiven."

[3]At this, some of the teachers of the law said to themselves, "This fellow is blaspheming!"

[4]Knowing their thoughts, Jesus said, "Why do you entertain evil thoughts in your hearts? [5]Which is easier: to say, 'Your sins are forgiven,' or to say, 'Get up and walk'? [6]But I want you to know that the Son of Man has authority on earth to forgive sins." So he said to the paralyzed man, "Get up, take your mat and go home." [7]Then the man got up and went home. [8]When the crowd saw this, they were filled with awe; and they praised God, who had given such authority to man.

### The Calling of Matthew

[9]As Jesus went on from there, he saw a man named Matthew sitting at the tax collector's booth. "Follow me," he told him, and Matthew got up and followed him.

[10]While Jesus was having dinner at Matthew's house, many tax collectors and sinners came and ate with him and his disciples. [11]When the Pharisees saw this, they asked his disciples, "Why does your teacher eat with tax collectors and sinners?"

[12]On hearing this, Jesus said, "It is not the healthy who need a doctor, but the sick. [13]But go and learn what this

## Amplified Bible

on the sea, so that the boat was being covered up by the waves; but He was sleeping.

[25]And they went and awakened Him, saying, Lord, rescue *and* preserve us! We are perishing!

[26]And He said to them, Why are you timid *and* afraid, O you of little faith? Then He got up and rebuked the winds and the sea, and there was a great *and* wonderful calm (*a* perfect peaceableness).

[27]And the men were stunned with bewildered wonder *and* marveled, saying, What kind of Man is this, that even the winds and the sea obey Him!

[28]And when He arrived at the other side in the country of the Gadarenes, two men under the control of demons went to meet Him, coming out of the tombs, so fierce *and* savage that no one was able to pass that way.

[29]And behold, they shrieked *and* screamed, What have You to do with us, *Jesus,* Son of God? Have You come to torment us before the appointed time? [Judg. 11:12; II Sam. 16:10.]

[30]Now at some distance from there a drove of many hogs was grazing.

[31]And the demons begged Him, If You drive us out, send us into the drove of hogs.

[32]And He said to them, Begone! So they came out and went into the hogs, and behold, the whole drove rushed down the steep bank into the sea and died in the water.

[33]The herdsmen fled and went into the town and reported everything, including what had happened to the men under the power of demons.

[34]And behold, the whole town went out to meet Jesus; and as soon as they saw Him, they begged Him to depart from their locality.

**9** And Jesus, getting into a boat, crossed to the other side and came to His own town [Capernaum].

[2]And behold, they brought to Him a man paralyzed *and* prostrated by illness, lying on a sleeping pad; and when Jesus saw their faith, He said to the paralyzed man, Take courage, son; your sins are forgiven *and* the *b*penalty remitted.

[3]And behold, some of the scribes said to themselves, This man blasphemes [He claims the rights and prerogatives of God]!

[4]But Jesus, knowing (*c*seeing) their thoughts, said, Why do you think evil *and* harbor *b*malice in your hearts?

[5]For which is easier: to say, Your sins are forgiven *and* the *b*penalty remitted, or to say, Get up and walk?

[6]But in order that you may know that the Son of Man has authority on earth to forgive sins *and* *b*remit the penalty, He then said to the paralyzed man, Get up! Pick up your sleeping pad and go to your own house.

[7]And he got up and went away to his own house.

[8]When the crowds saw it, they were struck with fear *and* awe; and they *d*recognized God *and* praised *and* thanked Him, Who had given such power *and* authority to men.

[9]As Jesus passed on from there, He saw a man named Matthew sitting at the tax collector's office; and He said to him, *b*Be My disciple [side with My party and follow Me]. And he rose and followed Him.

[10]And as Jesus reclined at table in the house, behold, many tax collectors and *e*[especially wicked] sinners came and sat (reclined) with Him and His disciples.

[11]And when the Pharisees saw this, they said to His disciples, Why does your Master eat with tax collectors and those [preeminently] sinful?

[12]But when Jesus heard it, He replied, Those who are strong *and* well (healthy) have no need of a physician, but those who are weak *and* sick.

[13]Go and learn what this means: I desire mercy [that

*a* John Wycliffe, *The Wycliffe Bible.*  *b* Joseph Thayer, *A Greek-English Lexicon.*  *c* Many manuscripts so read.  *d* Hermann Cremer, *Biblico-Theological Lexicon.*  *e* G. Abbott-Smith, *Manual Greek Lexicon.*

*a 28* Some manuscripts *Gergesenes*; other manuscripts *Gerasenes*

## New International Version

means: 'I desire mercy, not sacrifice.'[a] For I have not come to call the righteous, but sinners."

### Jesus Questioned About Fasting

14Then John's disciples came and asked him, "How is it that we and the Pharisees fast often, but your disciples do not fast?"

15Jesus answered, "How can the guests of the bridegroom mourn while he is with them? The time will come when the bridegroom will be taken from them; then they will fast.

16"No one sews a patch of unshrunk cloth on an old garment, for the patch will pull away from the garment, making the tear worse. 17Neither do people pour new wine into old wineskins. If they do, the skins will burst; the wine will run out and the wineskins will be ruined. No, they pour new wine into new wineskins, and both are preserved."

### Jesus Raises a Dead Girl and Heals a Sick Woman

18While he was saying this, a synagogue leader came and knelt before him and said, "My daughter has just died. But come and put your hand on her, and she will live." 19Jesus got up and went with him, and so did his disciples.

20Just then a woman who had been subject to bleeding for twelve years came up behind him and touched the edge of his cloak. 21She said to herself, "If I only touch his cloak, I will be healed."

22Jesus turned and saw her. "Take heart, daughter," he said, "your faith has healed you." And the woman was healed at that moment.

23When Jesus entered the synagogue leader's house and saw the noisy crowd and people playing pipes, 24he said, "Go away. The girl is not dead but asleep." But they laughed at him. 25After the crowd had been put outside, he went in and took the girl by the hand, and she got up. 26News of this spread through all that region.

### Jesus Heals the Blind and the Mute

27As Jesus went on from there, two blind men followed him, calling out, "Have mercy on us, Son of David!"

28When he had gone indoors, the blind men came to him, and he asked them, "Do you believe that I am able to do this?"

"Yes, Lord," they replied.

29Then he touched their eyes and said, "According to your faith let it be done to you"; 30and their sight was restored. Jesus warned them sternly, "See that no one knows about this." 31But they went out and spread the news about him all over that region.

32While they were going out, a man who was demon-possessed and could not talk was brought to Jesus. 33And when the demon was driven out, the man who had been mute spoke. The crowd was amazed and said, "Nothing like this has ever been seen in Israel."

34But the Pharisees said, "It is by the prince of demons that he drives out demons."

### The Workers Are Few

35Jesus went through all the towns and villages, teaching in their synagogues, proclaiming the good news of the kingdom and healing every disease and sickness. 36When he saw the crowds, he had compassion on them, because

## Amplified Bible

is, [a]readiness to help those in trouble] and not sacrifice and sacrificial victims. For I came not to call and invite [to repentance] the righteous (those who are upright and in right standing with God), but sinners (the erring ones and all those not free from sin). [Hos. 6:6.]

14Then the disciples of John came to Jesus, inquiring, Why is it that we and the Pharisees fast [b]often, [that is, abstain from food and drink as a religious exercise], but Your disciples do not fast?

15And Jesus replied to them, Can the wedding guests mourn while the bridegroom is still with them? The days will come when the bridegroom is taken away from them, and then they will fast.

16And no one puts a piece of cloth that has not been shrunk on an old garment, for such a patch tears away from the garment and a worse rent (tear) is made.

17Neither is new wine put in old wineskins; for if it is, the skins burst and are [a]torn in pieces, and the wine is spilled and the skins are ruined. But new wine is put into fresh wineskins, and so both are preserved.

18While He was talking this way to them, behold, a ruler entered and, kneeling down, worshiped Him, saying, My daughter has just [c]now died; but come and lay Your hand on her, and she will come to life.

19And Jesus got up and accompanied him, with His disciples.

20And behold, a woman who had suffered from a flow of blood for twelve years came up behind Him and touched the fringe of His garment; [Matt. 14:36.]

21For she kept saying to herself, If I only touch His garment, I shall be restored to health.

22Jesus turned around and, seeing her, He said, Take courage, daughter! Your faith has made you well. And at once the woman was restored to health.

23And when Jesus came to the ruler's house and saw the flute players and the crowd making an uproar and din,

24He said, Go away; for the girl is not dead but sleeping. And they laughed and jeered at Him.

25But when the crowd had been ordered to go outside, He went in and took her by the hand, and the girl arose.

26And the news about this spread through all that district.

27As Jesus passed on from there, two blind men followed Him, shouting loudly, Have pity and mercy on us, Son of David!

28When He reached the house and went in, the blind men came to Him, and Jesus said to them, Do you believe that I am able to do this? They said to Him, Yes, Lord.

29Then He touched their eyes, saying, According to your faith and trust and reliance [on the power invested in Me] be it done to you;

30And their eyes were opened. And Jesus earnestly and sternly charged them, See that you let no one know about this.

31But they went off and blazed and spread His fame abroad throughout that whole district.

32And while they were going away, behold, a dumb man under the power of a demon was brought to Jesus.

33And when the demon was driven out, the dumb man spoke; and the crowds were stunned with bewildered wonder, saying, Never before has anything like this been seen in Israel.

34But the Pharisees said, He drives out demons through and with the help of the prince of demons.

35And Jesus went about all the cities and villages, teaching in their synagogues and proclaiming the good news (the Gospel) of the kingdom and curing all kinds of disease and every weakness and infirmity.

36When He saw the throngs, He was moved with pity and sympathy for them, because they were bewildered

---

a 13 Hosea 6:6

a Joseph Thayer, A Greek-English Lexicon. b Many manuscripts so read.
c Marvin Vincent, Word Studies.

## New International Version

they were harassed and helpless, like sheep without a shepherd. [37]Then he said to his disciples, "The harvest is plentiful but the workers are few. [38]Ask the Lord of the harvest, therefore, to send out workers into his harvest field."

### Jesus Sends Out the Twelve

**10** Jesus called his twelve disciples to him and gave them authority to drive out impure spirits and to heal every disease and sickness.

[2]These are the names of the twelve apostles: first, Simon (who is called Peter) and his brother Andrew; James son of Zebedee, and his brother John; [3]Philip and Bartholomew; Thomas and Matthew the tax collector; James son of Alphaeus, and Thaddaeus; [4]Simon the Zealot and Judas Iscariot, who betrayed him.

[5]These twelve Jesus sent out with the following instructions: "Do not go among the Gentiles or enter any town of the Samaritans. [6]Go rather to the lost sheep of Israel. [7]As you go, proclaim this message: 'The kingdom of heaven has come near.' [8]Heal the sick, raise the dead, cleanse those who have leprosy,[a] drive out demons. Freely you have received; freely give.

[9]"Do not get any gold or silver or copper to take with you in your belts— [10]no bag for the journey or extra shirt or sandals or a staff, for the worker is worth his keep. [11]Whatever town or village you enter, search there for some worthy person and stay at their house until you leave. [12]As you enter the home, give it your greeting. [13]If the home is deserving, let your peace rest on it; if it is not, let your peace return to you. [14]If anyone will not welcome you or listen to your words, leave that home or town and shake the dust off your feet. [15]Truly I tell you, it will be more bearable for Sodom and Gomorrah on the day of judgment than for that town.

[16]"I am sending you out like sheep among wolves. Therefore be as shrewd as snakes and as innocent as doves. [17]Be on your guard; you will be handed over to the local councils and be flogged in the synagogues. [18]On my account you will be brought before governors and kings as witnesses to them and to the Gentiles. [19]But when they arrest you, do not worry about what to say or how to say it. At that time you will be given what to say, [20]for it will not be you speaking, but the Spirit of your Father speaking through you.

[21]"Brother will betray brother to death, and a father his child; children will rebel against their parents and have

## Amplified Bible

(harassed and distressed and dejected and helpless), like sheep without a shepherd. [Zech. 10:2.]

[37]Then He said to His disciples, The harvest is indeed plentiful, but the laborers are few.

[38]So pray to the Lord of the harvest to [a]force out and thrust laborers into His harvest.

**10** And Jesus summoned to Him His twelve disciples and gave them power and authority over unclean spirits, to drive them out, and to cure all kinds of disease and all kinds of weakness and infirmity.

[2]Now these are the names of the twelve apostles (special messengers): first, Simon, who is called Peter, and Andrew his brother; James son of Zebedee, and John his brother;

[3]Philip and Bartholomew [Nathaniel]; Thomas and Matthew the tax collector; James son of Alphaeus, and Thaddaeus [Judas, not Iscariot];

[4]Simon the Cananaean, and Judas Iscariot, who also betrayed Him.

[5]Jesus sent out these twelve, charging them, Go nowhere among the Gentiles and do not go into any town of the Samaritans;

[6]But go rather to the lost sheep of the house of Israel.

[7]And as you go, preach, saying, The kingdom of heaven is at hand!

[8]Cure the sick, raise the dead, cleanse the lepers, drive out demons. Freely (without pay) you have received, freely (without charge) give.

[9]Take no gold nor silver nor [even] copper money in your purses (belts);

[10]And do not take a provision bag or a [b]wallet for a collection bag for your journey, nor two undergarments, nor sandals, nor a staff; for the workman deserves his support (his living, his food).

[11]And into whatever town or village you go, inquire who in it is deserving, and stay there [at his house] until you leave [that vicinity].

[12]As you go into the house, give your greetings and wish it well.

[13]Then if indeed that house is deserving, let come upon it your peace [that is, [c]freedom from all the distresses that are experienced as the result of sin]. But if it is not deserving, let your peace return to you.

[14]And whoever will not receive and accept and welcome you nor listen to your message, as you leave that house or town, shake the dust [of it] from your feet.

[15]Truly I tell you, it shall be more tolerable on the day of judgment for the land of Sodom and Gomorrah than for that town.

[16]Behold, I am sending you out like sheep in the midst of wolves; be [d]wary and wise as serpents, and be innocent (harmless, guileless, and [e]without falsity) as doves. [Gen. 3:1.]

[17]Be on guard against men [whose [c]way or nature is to act in opposition to God]; for they will deliver you up to councils and flog you in their synagogues,

[18]And you will be brought before governors and kings for My sake, as a witness to bear testimony before them and to the Gentiles (the nations).

[19]But when they deliver you up, do not be anxious about how or what you are to speak; for what you are to say will be given you in that very hour and [b]moment,

[20]For it is not you who are speaking, but the Spirit of your Father speaking through you.

[21]Brother will deliver up brother to death, and the father his child; and children will take a stand against their parents and will have them put to death.

[a] Marvin Vincent, *Word Studies*. [b] James Moulton and George Milligan, *The Vocabulary*. [c] Hermann Cremer, *Biblico-Theological Lexicon*. [d] John Wycliffe, *The Wycliffe Bible*. [e] Martin Luther, cited by Marvin Vincent, *Word Studies*.

[a] 8 The Greek word traditionally translated *leprosy* was used for various diseases affecting the skin.

## New International Version

them put to death. 22You will be hated by everyone because of me, but the one who stands firm to the end will be saved. 23When you are persecuted in one place, flee to another. Truly I tell you, you will not finish going through the towns of Israel before the Son of Man comes.

24"The student is not above the teacher, nor a servant above his master. 25It is enough for students to be like their teachers, and servants like their masters. If the head of the house has been called Beelzebul, how much more the members of his household!

26"So do not be afraid of them, for there is nothing concealed that will not be disclosed, or hidden that will not be made known. 27What I tell you in the dark, speak in the daylight; what is whispered in your ear, proclaim from the roofs. 28Do not be afraid of those who kill the body but cannot kill the soul. Rather, be afraid of the One who can destroy both soul and body in hell. 29Are not two sparrows sold for a penny? Yet not one of them will fall to the ground outside your Father's care.a 30And even the very hairs of your head are all numbered. 31So don't be afraid; you are worth more than many sparrows.

32"Whoever acknowledges me before others, I will also acknowledge before my Father in heaven. 33But whoever disowns me before others, I will disown before my Father in heaven.

34"Do not suppose that I have come to bring peace to the earth. I did not come to bring peace, but a sword. 35For I have come to turn

> "'a man against his father,
> a daughter against her mother,
> a daughter-in-law against her mother-in-law—
> 36 a man's enemies will be the members of his own
> household.'b

37"Anyone who loves their father or mother more than me is not worthy of me; anyone who loves their son or daughter more than me is not worthy of me. 38Whoever does not take up their cross and follow me is not worthy of me. 39Whoever finds their life will lose it, and whoever loses their life for my sake will find it.

40"Anyone who welcomes you welcomes me, and anyone who welcomes me welcomes the one who sent me. 41Whoever welcomes a prophet as a prophet will receive a prophet's reward, and whoever welcomes a righteous person as a righteous person will receive a righteous person's reward. 42And if anyone gives even a cup of cold water to one of these little ones who is my disciple, truly I tell you, that person will certainly not lose their reward."

## Amplified Bible

22And you will be hated by all for My name's sake, but he who perseveres and endures to the end will be saved [afrom spiritual disease and death in the world to come].

23When they persecute you in one town [that is, pursue you in a manner that would injure you and cause you to suffer because of your belief], flee to another town; for truly I tell you, you will not have gone through all the towns of Israel before bthe Son of Man comes.

24A disciple is not above his teacher, nor is a servant or slave above his master.

25It is sufficient for the disciple to be like his teacher, and the servant or slave like his master. If they have called the Master of the house Beelzebub [cmaster of the dwelling], how much more will they speak evil of those of His household. [II Kings 1:2.]

26So have no fear of them; for nothing is concealed that will not be revealed, or kept secret that will not become known.

27What I say to you in the dark, tell in the light; and what you hear whispered in the ear, proclaim upon the housetops.

28And do not be afraid of those who kill the body but cannot kill the soul; but rather be afraid of Him who can destroy both soul and body in hell (Gehenna).

29Are not two dlittle sparrows sold for a penny? And yet not one of them will fall to the ground without your Father's leave (consent) and notice.

30But even the very hairs of your head are all numbered.

31Fear not, then; you are of more value than many sparrows.

32Therefore, everyone who acknowledges Me before men and confesses Me [dout of a state of oneness with Me], I will also acknowledge him before My Father Who is in heaven and dconfess [that I am abiding in] him.

33But whoever denies and disowns Me before men, I also will deny and disown him before My Father Who is in heaven.

34Do not think that I have come to bring peace upon the earth; I have not come to bring peace, but a sword.

35For I have come to part asunder a man from his father, and a daughter from her mother, and a dnewly married wife from her mother-in-law—

36And a man's foes will be they of his own household. [Mic. 7:6.]

37He who loves [and etakes more pleasure in] father or mother more than [in] Me is not worthy of Me; and he who loves [and takes more pleasure in] son or daughter more than [in] Me is not worthy of Me;

38And he who does not take up his cross and follow Me [fcleave steadfastly to Me, conforming wholly to My example in living and, if need be, in dying also] is not worthy of Me.

39Whoever finds his [elower] life will lose it [the higher life], and whoever loses his [lower] life on My account will find it [the higher life].

40He who receives and welcomes and accepts you receives and welcomes and accepts Me, and he who receives and welcomes and accepts Me receives and welcomes and accepts Him Who sent Me.

41He who receives and welcomes and accepts a prophet because he is a prophet shall receive a prophet's reward, and he who receives and welcomes and accepts a righteous man because he is a righteous man shall receive a righteous man's reward.

42And whoever gives to one of these little ones [in rank or influence] even a cup of cold water because he is My disciple, surely I declare to you, he shall not lose his reward.

---

a G. Abbott-Smith, *Manual Greek Lexicon.* b Believed by many to mean the coming of the Holy Spirit at Pentecost. Other commentators observe that the saying seems to teach that the Gospel will continue to be preached to the Jews until Christ's second coming. c John D. Davis, *A Dictionary of the Bible.* d Marvin Vincent, *Word Studies.* e Kenneth Wuest, *Word Studies.* f Joseph Thayer, *A Greek-English Lexicon.*

---

a 29 Or *will*; or *knowledge*    b 36 Micah 7:6

## New International Version

### Jesus and John the Baptist

**11** After Jesus had finished instructing his twelve disciples, he went on from there to teach and preach in the towns of Galilee.[a]

[2] When John, who was in prison, heard about the deeds of the Messiah, he sent his disciples [3] to ask him, "Are you the one who is to come, or should we expect someone else?"

[4] Jesus replied, "Go back and report to John what you hear and see: [5] The blind receive sight, the lame walk, those who have leprosy[b] are cleansed, the deaf hear, the dead are raised, and the good news is proclaimed to the poor. [6] Blessed is anyone who does not stumble on account of me."

[7] As John's disciples were leaving, Jesus began to speak to the crowd about John: "What did you go out into the wilderness to see? A reed swayed by the wind? [8] If not, what did you go out to see? A man dressed in fine clothes? No, those who wear fine clothes are in kings' palaces. [9] Then what did you go out to see? A prophet? Yes, I tell you, and more than a prophet. [10] This is the one about whom it is written:

"'I will send my messenger ahead of you,
    who will prepare your way before you.'[c]

[11] Truly I tell you, among those born of women there has not risen anyone greater than John the Baptist; yet whoever is least in the kingdom of heaven is greater than he. [12] From the days of John the Baptist until now, the kingdom of heaven has been subjected to violence,[d] and violent people have been raiding it. [13] For all the Prophets and the Law prophesied until John. [14] And if you are willing to accept it, he is the Elijah who was to come. [15] Whoever has ears, let them hear.

[16] "To what can I compare this generation? They are like children sitting in the marketplaces and calling out to others:

[17] "'We played the pipe for you,
    and you did not dance;
we sang a dirge,
    and you did not mourn.'

[18] For John came neither eating nor drinking, and they say, 'He has a demon.' [19] The Son of Man came eating and drinking, and they say, 'Here is a glutton and a drunkard, a friend of tax collectors and sinners.' But wisdom is proved right by her deeds."

### Woe on Unrepentant Towns

[20] Then Jesus began to denounce the towns in which most of his miracles had been performed, because they did not repent. [21] "Woe to you, Chorazin! Woe to you, Bethsaida! For if the miracles that were performed in you had been performed in Tyre and Sidon, they would have repented long ago in sackcloth and ashes. [22] But I tell you, it will be more bearable for Tyre and Sidon on the day of

## Amplified Bible

**11** When Jesus had finished His charge to His twelve disciples, He left there to teach and to preach in their [Galilean] cities.

[2] Now when John in prison heard about the activities of Christ, he sent a message by his disciples

[3] And asked Him, Are You the One Who was to come, or should we keep on expecting a different one? [Gen. 49:10; Num. 24:17.]

[4] And Jesus replied to them, Go and report to John what you hear and see:

[5] The blind receive their sight and the lame walk, lepers are cleansed (by healing) and the deaf hear, the dead are raised up and the poor have good news (the Gospel) preached to them. [Isa. 35:5, 6; 61:1.]

[6] And blessed (happy, fortunate, and [a] to be envied) is he who takes no offense at Me *and* finds no cause for stumbling in *or* through Me *and* is not hindered from seeing the Truth.

[7] Then as these men went their way, Jesus began to speak to the crowds about John: What did you go out in the wilderness (desert) to see? A reed swayed by the wind?

[8] What did you go out to see then? A man clothed in soft garments? Behold, those who wear soft clothing are in the houses of kings.

[9] But what did you go out to see? A prophet? Yes, I tell you, and one [[b] out of the common, more eminent, more remarkable, and] [b] superior to a prophet.

[10] This is the one of whom it is written, Behold, I send My messenger ahead of You, who shall make ready Your way before You. [Mal. 3:1.]

[11] Truly I tell you, among those born of women there has not risen anyone greater than John the Baptist; yet he who is least in the kingdom of heaven is greater than he.

[12] And from the days of John the Baptist until the present time, the kingdom of heaven has endured violent assault, and violent men seize it by force [as a precious prize—a [c] share in the heavenly kingdom is sought with most ardent zeal and intense exertion].

[13] For all the Prophets and the Law prophesied up until John.

[14] And if you are willing to receive *and* accept it, John himself is Elijah who was to come [before the kingdom]. [Mal. 4:5.]

[15] He who has ears to hear, let him be listening *and* let him consider *and* [b] perceive *and* comprehend by hearing.

[16] But to what shall I liken this generation? It is like little children sitting in the marketplaces who call to their playmates,

[17] We piped to you [playing wedding], and you did not dance; we wailed dirges [playing funeral], and you did not mourn *and* beat your breasts *and* weep aloud.

[18] For John came neither eating nor drinking [with others], and they say, He has a demon!

[19] The Son of Man came eating and drinking [with others], and they say, Behold, a glutton and a wine drinker, a friend of tax collectors *and* [[b] especially wicked] sinners! Yet wisdom is justified *and* vindicated by what she does (her deeds) *and by* [d] her children.

[20] Then He began to censure *and* reproach the cities in which most of His mighty works had been performed, because they did not repent [and their hearts were not changed].

[21] Woe to you, Chorazin! Woe to you, Bethsaida! For if the mighty works done in you had been done in Tyre and Sidon, they would long ago have repented in sackcloth and ashes [and their hearts would have been changed].

[22] I tell you [further], it shall be more endurable for Tyre and Sidon on the day of judgment than for you.

---

[a] 1 Greek *in their towns*    [b] 5 The Greek word traditionally translated *leprosy* was used for various diseases affecting the skin.    [c] 10 Mal. 3:1
[d] 12 Or *been forcefully advancing*

[a] Alexander Souter, *Pocket Lexicon*.   [b] G. Abbott-Smith, *Manual Greek Lexicon*.   [c] Joseph Thayer, *A Greek-English Lexicon*.   [d] Many manuscripts read "children" here, as in Luke 7:35.

## New International Version

judgment than for you. 23And you, Capernaum, will you be lifted to the heavens? No, you will go down to Hades.ᵃ For if the miracles that were performed in you had been performed in Sodom, it would have remained to this day. 24But I tell you that it will be more bearable for Sodom on the day of judgment than for you."

### The Father Revealed in the Son

25At that time Jesus said, "I praise you, Father, Lord of heaven and earth, because you have hidden these things from the wise and learned, and revealed them to little children. 26Yes, Father, for this is what you were pleased to do.

27"All things have been committed to me by my Father. No one knows the Son except the Father, and no one knows the Father except the Son and those to whom the Son chooses to reveal him.

28"Come to me, all you who are weary and burdened, and I will give you rest. 29Take my yoke upon you and learn from me, for I am gentle and humble in heart, and you will find rest for your souls. 30For my yoke is easy and my burden is light."

### Jesus Is Lord of the Sabbath

**12** At that time Jesus went through the grainfields on the Sabbath. His disciples were hungry and began to pick some heads of grain and eat them. 2When the Pharisees saw this, they said to him, "Look! Your disciples are doing what is unlawful on the Sabbath."

3He answered, "Haven't you read what David did when he and his companions were hungry? 4He entered the house of God, and he and his companions ate the consecrated bread—which was not lawful for them to do, but only for the priests. 5Or haven't you read in the Law that the priests on Sabbath duty in the temple desecrate the Sabbath and yet are innocent? 6I tell you that something greater than the temple is here. 7If you had known what these words mean, 'I desire mercy, not sacrifice,'ᵇ you would not have condemned the innocent. 8For the Son of Man is Lord of the Sabbath."

9Going on from that place, he went into their synagogue, 10and a man with a shriveled hand was there. Looking for a reason to bring charges against Jesus, they asked him, "Is it lawful to heal on the Sabbath?"

11He said to them, "If any of you has a sheep and it falls into a pit on the Sabbath, will you not take hold of it and lift it out? 12How much more valuable is a person than a sheep! Therefore it is lawful to do good on the Sabbath."

13Then he said to the man, "Stretch out your hand." So he stretched it out and it was completely restored, just as

## Amplified Bible

23And you, Capernaum, are you to be lifted up to heaven? You shall be brought down to Hades [the region of the dead]! For if the mighty works done in you had been done in Sodom, it would have continued until today.

24But I tell you, it shall be more endurable for the land of Sodom on the day of judgment than for you.

25At that time Jesus began to say, I thank You, Father, Lord of heaven and earth [and ᵃI acknowledge openly and joyfully to Your honor], that You have hidden these things from the wise and clever and learned, and revealed them to babies [to the ᵃchildish, untaught, and unskilled].

26Yes, Father, [I praise You that] such was Your gracious will and good pleasure.

27All things have been entrusted and delivered to Me by My Father; and no one ᵇfully knows and ᵃaccurately understands the Son except the Father, and no one ᵇfully knows and ᵃaccurately understands the Father except the Son and anyone to whom the Son ᵃdeliberately wills to make Him known.

28Come to Me, all you who labor and are heavy-laden and overburdened, and I will cause you to rest. [I will ᶜease and relieve and ᵈrefresh ᵃyour souls.]

29Take My yoke upon you and learn of Me, for I am gentle (meek) and humble (lowly) in heart, and you will find rest (ᵉrelief and ease and refreshment and ᵃrecreation and blessed quiet) for your souls. [Jer. 6:16.]

30For My yoke is wholesome (useful, ᶠgood—not harsh, hard, sharp, or pressing, but comfortable, gracious, and pleasant), and My burden is light and easy to be borne.

**12** At that ᵇparticular time Jesus went through the fields of standing grain on the Sabbath; and His disciples were hungry, and they began to pick off the spikes of grain to eat. [Deut. 23:25.]

2And when the Pharisees saw it, they said to Him, See there! Your disciples are doing what is unlawful and not permitted on the Sabbath.

3He said to them, Have you not even read what David did when he was hungry, and those who accompanied him—[Lev. 24:9; I Sam. 21:1-6.]

4How he went into the house of God and ate the loaves of the showbread—which was not lawful for him to eat, nor for the men who accompanied him, but for the priests only?

5Or have you never read in the Law that on the Sabbath the priests in the temple violate the sanctity of the Sabbath [breaking it] and yet are guiltless? [Num. 28:9, 10.]

6But I tell you, Something greater and ᵃmore exalted and more majestic than the temple is here!

7And if you had only known what this saying means, I desire mercy [readiness to help, to spare, to forgive] rather than sacrifice and sacrificial victims, you would not have condemned the guiltless. [Hos. 6:6; Matt. 9:13.]

8For the Son of Man is Lord [even] of the Sabbath.

9And going on from there, He went into their synagogue.

10And behold, a man was there with one withered hand. And they said to Him, Is it lawful or allowable to cure people on the Sabbath days?—that they might accuse Him.

11But He said to them, What man is there among you, if he has only one sheep and it falls into a pit or ditch on the Sabbath, will not take hold of it and lift it out?

12How much better and of more value is a man than a sheep! So it is lawful and allowable to do good on the Sabbath days.

13Then He said to the man, Reach out your hand. And the man reached it out and it was restored, as sound as the other one.

---

ᵃ Joseph Thayer, *A Greek-English Lexicon*. ᵇ Marvin Vincent, *Word Studies*. ᶜ William Tyndale, *The Tyndale Bible*. ᵈ John Wycliffe, *The Wycliffe Bible*. ᵉ Alexander Souter, *Pocket Lexicon*. ᶠ James Moulton and George Milligan, *The Vocabulary*.

ᵃ 23 That is, the realm of the dead    ᵇ 7 Hosea 6:6

## New International Version

sound as the other. ¹⁴But the Pharisees went out and plotted how they might kill Jesus.

### God's Chosen Servant

¹⁵Aware of this, Jesus withdrew from that place. A large crowd followed him, and he healed all who were ill. ¹⁶He warned them not to tell others about him. ¹⁷This was to fulfill what was spoken through the prophet Isaiah:

¹⁸"Here is my servant whom I have chosen,
 the one I love, in whom I delight;
I will put my Spirit on him,
 and he will proclaim justice to the nations.
¹⁹He will not quarrel or cry out;
 no one will hear his voice in the streets.
²⁰A bruised reed he will not break,
 and a smoldering wick he will not snuff out,
 till he has brought justice through to victory.
²¹ In his name the nations will put their hope."ᵃ

### Jesus and Beelzebul

²²Then they brought him a demon-possessed man who was blind and mute, and Jesus healed him, so that he could both talk and see. ²³All the people were astonished and said, "Could this be the Son of David?"

²⁴But when the Pharisees heard this, they said, "It is only by Beelzebul, the prince of demons, that this fellow drives out demons."

²⁵Jesus knew their thoughts and said to them, "Every kingdom divided against itself will be ruined, and every city or household divided against itself will not stand. ²⁶If Satan drives out Satan, he is divided against himself. How then can his kingdom stand? ²⁷And if I drive out demons by Beelzebul, by whom do your people drive them out? So then, they will be your judges. ²⁸But if it is by the Spirit of God that I drive out demons, then the kingdom of God has come upon you.

²⁹"Or again, how can anyone enter a strong man's house and carry off his possessions unless he first ties up the strong man? Then he can plunder his house.

³⁰"Whoever is not with me is against me, and whoever does not gather with me scatters. ³¹And so I tell you, every kind of sin and slander can be forgiven, but blasphemy against the Spirit will not be forgiven. ³²Anyone who speaks a word against the Son of Man will be forgiven, but anyone who speaks against the Holy Spirit will not be forgiven, either in this age or in the age to come.

³³"Make a tree good and its fruit will be good, or make a tree bad and its fruit will be bad, for a tree is recognized by its fruit. ³⁴You brood of vipers, how can you who are evil say anything good? For the mouth speaks what the heart

## Amplified Bible

¹⁴But the Pharisees went out and held a consultation against Him, how they might do away with Him.

¹⁵But being aware of this, Jesus went away from there. And many people ᵃjoined *and* accompanied Him, and He cured all of them,

¹⁶And strictly charged them *and* sharply warned them not to make Him ᵇpublicly known.

¹⁷This was in fulfillment of what was spoken by the prophet Isaiah,

¹⁸Behold, My Servant Whom I have chosen, My Beloved in *and* with Whom My soul is well pleased *and* ᵇhas found its delight. I will put My Spirit upon Him, and He shall proclaim *and* ᵇshow forth justice to the nations.

¹⁹He will not strive *or* wrangle *or* cry out loudly; nor will anyone hear His voice in the streets;

²⁰A bruised reed He will not break, and a smoldering (dimly burning) wick He will not quench, till He brings ᵃjustice *and* a just cause to victory.

²¹And in *and* on His name will the Gentiles (the ᶜpeoples outside of Israel) set their hopes. [Isa. 42:1-4.]

²²Then a blind and dumb man under the power of a demon was brought to Jesus, and He cured him, so that the blind and dumb man both spoke and saw.

²³And all the [crowds of] people were stunned with bewildered wonder and said, This cannot be the Son of David, can it?

²⁴But the Pharisees, hearing it, said, This ᵈMan drives out demons only by *and* with the help of Beelzebub, the prince of demons.

²⁵And knowing their thoughts, He said to them, Any kingdom that is divided against itself is being brought to desolation *and* laid waste, and no city *or* house divided against itself will last *or* continue to stand.

²⁶And if Satan drives out Satan, he has become divided against himself *and* disunified; how then will his kingdom last *or* continue to stand?

²⁷And if I drive out the demons by [help of] Beelzebub, by whose [help] do your sons drive them out? ᵇFor this reason they shall be your judges.

²⁸But if it is by the Spirit of God that I drive out the demons, then the kingdom of God has come upon you [ᵉbefore you expected it].

²⁹Or how can a person go into a strong man's house and carry off his goods (the entire equipment of his house) without first binding the strong man? Then indeed he may plunder his house.

³⁰He who is not with Me [definitely ᵃon My side] is against Me, and he who does not [definitely] gather with Me *and* for ᵃMy side scatters.

³¹Therefore I tell you, every sin and blasphemy (every evil, abusive, ᶠinjurious speaking, or indignity against sacred things) can be forgiven men, but blasphemy against the [Holy] Spirit shall not *and* ᶠcannot be forgiven.

³²And whoever speaks a word against the Son of Man will be forgiven, but whoever speaks against the Spirit, the Holy One, will not be forgiven, either in this world *and* age or in the world *and* age to come.

³³Either make the tree sound (healthy and good), and its fruit sound (healthy and good), or make the tree rotten (diseased and bad), and its fruit rotten (diseased and bad); for the tree is known *and* recognized *and* judged by its fruit.

³⁴You offspring of vipers! How can you speak good things when you are evil (wicked)? For out of the fullness (the overflow, the ᵍsuperabundance) of the heart the mouth speaks.

ᵃ Joseph Thayer, *A Greek-English Lexicon*. ᵇ John Darby, *The New Testament, a New Translation*. ᶜ Hermann Cremer, *Biblico-Theological Lexicon*. ᵈ Capitalized because of what He is, the spotless Son of God, not what the speakers may have thought He was. ᵉ Marvin Vincent, *Word Studies*. ᶠ Charles B. Williams, *The New Testament: A Translation*. ᵍ Alexander Souter, *Pocket Lexicon*.

## New International Version

is full of. 35 A good man brings good things out of the good stored up in him, and an evil man brings evil things out of the evil stored up in him. 36 But I tell you that everyone will have to give account on the day of judgment for every empty word they have spoken. 37 For by your words you will be acquitted, and by your words you will be condemned."

### The Sign of Jonah

38 Then some of the Pharisees and teachers of the law said to him, "Teacher, we want to see a sign from you." 39 He answered, "A wicked and adulterous generation asks for a sign! But none will be given it except the sign of the prophet Jonah. 40 For as Jonah was three days and three nights in the belly of a huge fish, so the Son of Man will be three days and three nights in the heart of the earth. 41 The men of Nineveh will stand up at the judgment with this generation and condemn it; for they repented at the preaching of Jonah, and now something greater than Jonah is here. 42 The Queen of the South will rise at the judgment with this generation and condemn it; for she came from the ends of the earth to listen to Solomon's wisdom, and now something greater than Solomon is here.

43 "When an impure spirit comes out of a person, it goes through arid places seeking rest and does not find it. 44 Then it says, 'I will return to the house I left.' When it arrives, it finds the house unoccupied, swept clean and put in order. 45 Then it goes and takes with it seven other spirits more wicked than itself, and they go in and live there. And the final condition of that person is worse than the first. That is how it will be with this wicked generation."

### Jesus' Mother and Brothers

46 While Jesus was still talking to the crowd, his mother and brothers stood outside, wanting to speak to him. 47 Someone told him, "Your mother and brothers are standing outside, wanting to speak to you." 48 He replied to him, "Who is my mother, and who are my brothers?" 49 Pointing to his disciples, he said, "Here are my mother and my brothers. 50 For whoever does the will of my Father in heaven is my brother and sister and mother."

### The Parable of the Sower

**13** That same day Jesus went out of the house and sat by the lake. 2 Such large crowds gathered around him that he got into a boat and sat in it, while all the people stood on the shore. 3 Then he told them many things in parables, saying: "A farmer went out to sow his seed. 4 As he was scattering the seed, some fell along the path, and the birds came and ate it up. 5 Some fell on rocky places, where it did not have much soil. It sprang up quickly, because the soil was shallow. 6 But when the sun came up, the plants were scorched, and they withered because they had

## Amplified Bible

35 The good man from his inner good treasure *a* flings forth good things, and the evil man out of his inner evil storehouse *a* flings forth evil things.

36 But I tell you, on the day of judgment men will have to give account for every *a* idle (inoperative, nonworking) word they speak.

37 For by your words you will be justified *and* acquitted, and by your words you will be condemned *and* sentenced.

38 Then some of the scribes and Pharisees said to Him, Teacher, we desire to see a sign *or* miracle from You [proving that You are what You claim to be].

39 But He replied to them, An evil and adulterous generation (a generation *a* morally unfaithful to God) seeks *and* demands a sign; but no sign shall be given to it except the sign of the prophet Jonah.

40 For even as Jonah was three days and three nights in the belly of the sea monster, so will the Son of Man be three days and three nights in the heart of the earth. [Jonah 1:17.]

41 The men of Nineveh will stand up at the judgment with this generation and condemn it; for they repented at the preaching of Jonah, and behold, Someone more *and* greater than Jonah is here! [Jonah 3:5.]

42 The queen of the South will stand up at the judgment with this generation and condemn it; for she came from the ends of the earth to listen to the wisdom of Solomon, and behold, Someone more *and* greater than Solomon is here. [I Kings 10:1; II Chron. 9:1.]

43 But when the unclean spirit has gone out of a man, it roams through dry [arid] places in search of rest, but it does not find any.

44 Then it says, I will go back to my house from which I came out. And when it arrives, it finds the place unoccupied, swept, put in order, *and* decorated.

45 Then it goes and brings with it seven other spirits more wicked than itself, and they go in and make their home there. And the last condition of that man becomes worse than the first. So also shall it be with this wicked generation.

46 Jesus was still speaking to the people when behold, His mother and brothers stood outside, seeking to speak to Him.

47 *b* *Someone said to Him, Listen! Your mother and Your brothers are standing outside, seeking to speak to You.*

48 But He replied to the man who told Him, Who is My mother, and who are My brothers?

49 And stretching out His hand toward [not only the twelve disciples but all] *c* His adherents, He said, Here are My mother and My brothers.

50 For whoever does the will of My Father in heaven is My brother and sister and mother!

**13** That same day Jesus went out of the house and was sitting beside the sea.

2 But such great crowds gathered about Him that He got into a boat and remained sitting there, while all the throng stood on the shore.

3 And He told them many things in parables (stories by way of illustration and comparison), saying, A sower went out to sow.

4 And as he sowed, some seeds fell by the roadside, and the birds came and ate them up.

5 Other seeds fell on rocky ground, where they had not much soil; and at once they sprang up, because they had no depth of soil.

6 But when the sun rose, they were scorched, and because they had no root, they dried up *and* withered away.

---

*a* Marvin Vincent, *Word Studies.*  *b* Some manuscripts omit verse 47.
*c* Hermann Cremer, *Biblico-Theological Lexicon.*

## New International Version

no root. [7]Other seed fell among thorns, which grew up and choked the plants. [8]Still other seed fell on good soil, where it produced a crop—a hundred, sixty or thirty times what was sown. [9]Whoever has ears, let them hear."

[10]The disciples came to him and asked, "Why do you speak to the people in parables?"

[11]He replied, "Because the knowledge of the secrets of the kingdom of heaven has been given to you, but not to them. [12]Whoever has will be given more, and they will have an abundance. Whoever does not have, even what they have will be taken from them. [13]This is why I speak to them in parables:

"Though seeing, they do not see;
  though hearing, they do not hear or understand.

[14]In them is fulfilled the prophecy of Isaiah:

"'You will be ever hearing but never understanding;
  you will be ever seeing but never perceiving.
[15]For this people's heart has become calloused;
  they hardly hear with their ears,
  and they have closed their eyes.
Otherwise they might see with their eyes,
  hear with their ears,
  understand with their hearts
and turn, and I would heal them.'[a]

[16]But blessed are your eyes because they see, and your ears because they hear. [17]For truly I tell you, many prophets and righteous people longed to see what you see but did not see it, and to hear what you hear but did not hear it.

[18]"Listen then to what the parable of the sower means: [19]When anyone hears the message about the kingdom and does not understand it, the evil one comes and snatches away what was sown in their heart. This is the seed sown along the path. [20]The seed falling on rocky ground refers to someone who hears the word and at once receives it with joy. [21]But since they have no root, they last only a short time. When trouble or persecution comes because of the word, they quickly fall away. [22]The seed falling among the thorns refers to someone who hears the word, but the worries of this life and the deceitfulness of wealth choke the word, making it unfruitful. [23]But the seed falling on good soil refers to someone who hears the word and understands it. This is the one who produces a crop, yielding a hundred, sixty or thirty times what was sown."

### The Parable of the Weeds

[24]Jesus told them another parable: "The kingdom of heaven is like a man who sowed good seed in his field. [25]But while everyone was sleeping, his enemy came and sowed weeds among the wheat, and went away. [26]When the wheat sprouted and formed heads, then the weeds also appeared.

## Amplified Bible

[7]Other seeds fell among thorns, and the thorns grew up and choked them out.

[8]Other seeds fell on good soil, and yielded grain—some a hundred times as much as was sown, some sixty times as much, and some thirty.

[9]He who has ears [to hear], let him be listening *and* let him *a* consider *and* *b* perceive *and* comprehend by hearing.

[10]Then the disciples came to Him and said, Why do You speak to them in parables?

[11]And He replied to them, To you it has been given to know the secrets *and* mysteries of the kingdom of heaven, but to them it has not been given.

[12]For whoever has [spiritual knowledge], to him will more be given *and* he will *a* be furnished richly so that he will have abundance; but from him who has not, even what he has will be taken away.

[13]This is the reason that I speak to them in parables: because *a* having the power of seeing, they do not see; and *a* having the power of hearing, they do not hear, nor do they grasp *and* understand.

[14]In them indeed is *c* the process of fulfillment of the prophecy of Isaiah, which says: You shall indeed hear *and* hear but never grasp *and* understand; and you shall indeed look *and* look but never see *and* perceive.

[15]For this nation's heart has grown gross (fat and dull), and their ears heavy *and* difficult of hearing, and their eyes they have tightly closed, lest they see *and* perceive with their eyes, and hear *and* comprehend the sense with their ears, and grasp *and* understand with their heart, and turn *and* I should heal them. [Isa. 6:9, 10.]

[16]But blessed (happy, fortunate, and *d* to be envied) are your eyes because they do see, and your ears because they do hear.

[17]Truly I tell you, many prophets and righteous men [men who were upright and in right standing with God] yearned to see what you see, and did not see it, and to hear what you hear, and did not hear it.

[18]Listen then to the [meaning of the] parable of the sower:

[19]*c* While anyone is hearing the Word of the kingdom and does not grasp *and* comprehend it, the evil one comes and snatches away what was sown in his heart. This is what was sown along the roadside.

[20]As for what was sown on thin (rocky) soil, this is he who hears the Word and at once welcomes *and* accepts it with joy;

[21]Yet it has no real root in him, but is temporary (inconstant, *c* lasts but a little while); and when affliction *or* trouble *or* persecution comes on account of the Word, at once he is caused to stumble [he is repelled and *a* begins to distrust and desert Him Whom he ought to trust and obey] and he falls away.

[22]As for what was sown among thorns, this is he who hears the Word, but the cares of the world and the pleasure *and* delight *and* glamour *and* deceitfulness of riches choke *and* suffocate the Word, and it yields no fruit.

[23]As for what was sown on good soil, this is he who hears the Word and grasps *and* comprehends it; he indeed bears fruit and yields in one case a hundred times as much as was sown, in another sixty times as much, and in another thirty.

[24]Another parable He set forth before them, saying, The kingdom of heaven is like a man who sowed good seed in his field.

[25]But while he was sleeping, his enemy came and sowed also darnel (weeds resembling wheat) among the wheat, and went on his way.

[26]So when the plants sprouted and formed grain, the darnel (weeds) appeared also.

*a* Joseph Thayer, *A Greek-English Lexicon.* *b* G. Abbott-Smith, *Manual Greek Lexicon.* *c* Marvin Vincent, *Word Studies.* *d* Alexander Souter, *Pocket Lexicon.* *e* John Wycliffe, *The Wycliffe Bible.*

*a* 15 Isaiah 6:9,10 (see Septuagint)

## New International Version

27"The owner's servants came to him and said, 'Sir, didn't you sow good seed in your field? Where then did the weeds come from?'

28"'An enemy did this,' he replied.

"The servants asked him, 'Do you want us to go and pull them up?'

29"'No,' he answered, 'because while you are pulling the weeds, you may uproot the wheat with them. 30Let both grow together until the harvest. At that time I will tell the harvesters: First collect the weeds and tie them in bundles to be burned; then gather the wheat and bring it into my barn.'"

### The Parables of the Mustard Seed and the Yeast

31He told them another parable: "The kingdom of heaven is like a mustard seed, which a man took and planted in his field. 32Though it is the smallest of all seeds, yet when it grows, it is the largest of garden plants and becomes a tree, so that the birds come and perch in its branches."

33He told them still another parable: "The kingdom of heaven is like yeast that a woman took and mixed into about sixty pounds[a] of flour until it worked all through the dough."

34Jesus spoke all these things to the crowd in parables; he did not say anything to them without using a parable. 35So was fulfilled what was spoken through the prophet:

"I will open my mouth in parables,
    I will utter things hidden since the creation of the world."[b]

### The Parable of the Weeds Explained

36Then he left the crowd and went into the house. His disciples came to him and said, "Explain to us the parable of the weeds in the field."

37He answered, "The one who sowed the good seed is the Son of Man. 38The field is the world, and the good seed stands for the people of the kingdom. The weeds are the people of the evil one, 39and the enemy who sows them is the devil. The harvest is the end of the age, and the harvesters are angels.

40"As the weeds are pulled up and burned in the fire, so it will be at the end of the age. 41The Son of Man will send out his angels, and they will weed out of his kingdom everything that causes sin and all who do evil. 42They will throw them into the blazing furnace, where there will be weeping and gnashing of teeth. 43Then the righteous will shine like the sun in the kingdom of their Father. Whoever has ears, let them hear.

### The Parables of the Hidden Treasure and the Pearl

44"The kingdom of heaven is like treasure hidden in a field. When a man found it, he hid it again, and then in his joy went and sold all he had and bought that field.

45"Again, the kingdom of heaven is like a merchant looking for fine pearls. 46When he found one of great value, he went away and sold everything he had and bought it.

### The Parable of the Net

47"Once again, the kingdom of heaven is like a net that was let down into the lake and caught all kinds of fish. 48When it was full, the fishermen pulled it up on the shore. Then they sat down and collected the good fish in baskets,

## Amplified Bible

27And the servants of the owner came to him and said, Sir, did you not sow good seed in your field? Then how does it have darnel shoots in it?

28He replied to them, An enemy has done this. The servants said to him, Then do you want us to go and weed them out?

29But he said, No, lest in gathering the wild wheat (weeds resembling wheat), you root up the [true] wheat along with it.

30Let them grow together until the harvest; and at harvest time I will say to the reapers, Gather the darnel first and bind it in bundles to be burned, but gather the wheat into my granary.

31Another story by way of comparison He set forth before them, saying, The kingdom of heaven is like a grain of mustard seed, which a man took and sowed in his field.

32Of all the seeds it is the smallest, but when it has grown it is the largest of the garden herbs and becomes a tree, so that the birds of the air come and find shelter in its branches.

33He told them another parable: The kingdom of heaven is like leaven (ªsour dough) which a woman took and covered over in three measures of meal or flour till all of it was leavened. [Gen. 18:6.]

34These things ᵇall taken together Jesus said to the crowds in parables; indeed, without a parable He said nothing to them.

35This was in fulfillment of what was spoken by the prophet: I will open My mouth in parables; I will utter things that have been hidden since the foundation of the world. [Ps. 78:2.]

36Then He left the throngs and went into the house. And His disciples came to Him saying, Explain to us the parable of the darnel in the field.

37He answered, He Who sows the good seed is the Son of Man.

38The field is the world, and the good seed means the children of the kingdom; the darnel is the children of the evil one,

39And the enemy who sowed it is the devil. The harvest is the close and consummation of the age, and the reapers are angels.

40Just as the darnel (weeds resembling wheat) is gathered and burned with fire, so it will be at the close of the age.

41The Son of Man will send forth His angels, and they will gather out of His kingdom all causes of offense [ᵇpersons by whom others are drawn into error or sin] and all who do iniquity and act wickedly,

42And will cast them into the furnace of fire; there will be weeping and wailing and grinding of teeth.

43Then will the righteous (those who are upright and in right standing with God) shine forth like the sun in the kingdom of their Father. Let him who has ears [to hear] be listening, and let him ᵇconsider and perceive and understand by hearing. [Dan. 12:3.]

44The kingdom of heaven is like ᵇsomething precious buried in a field, which a man found and hid again; then in his joy he goes and sells all he has and buys that field.

45Again the kingdom of heaven is like a man who is a dealer in search of fine and ᵇprecious pearls,

46Who, on finding a single pearl of great price, went and sold all he had and bought it.

47Again, the kingdom of heaven is like a ᶜdragnet which was cast into the sea and gathered in fish of every sort.

48When it was full, men dragged it up on the beach, and sat down and sorted out the good fish into baskets, but the worthless ones they threw away.

---

a 33 Or about 27 kilograms    b 35 Psalm 78:2

ª John Wycliffe, *The Wycliffe Bible.* ᵇ Joseph Thayer, *A Greek-English Lexicon.* ᶜ Marvin Vincent, *Word Studies.*

## New International Version

but threw the bad away. [49]This is how it will be at the end of the age. The angels will come and separate the wicked from the righteous [50]and throw them into the blazing furnace, where there will be weeping and gnashing of teeth.

[51]"Have you understood all these things?" Jesus asked.
"Yes," they replied.

[52]He said to them, "Therefore every teacher of the law who has become a disciple in the kingdom of heaven is like the owner of a house who brings out of his storeroom new treasures as well as old."

### A Prophet Without Honor

[53]When Jesus had finished these parables, he moved on from there. [54]Coming to his hometown, he began teaching the people in their synagogue, and they were amazed. "Where did this man get this wisdom and these miraculous powers?" they asked. [55]"Isn't this the carpenter's son? Isn't his mother's name Mary, and aren't his brothers James, Joseph, Simon and Judas? [56]Aren't all his sisters with us? Where then did this man get all these things?" [57]And they took offense at him.

But Jesus said to them, "A prophet is not without honor except in his own town and in his own home."

[58]And he did not do many miracles there because of their lack of faith.

### John the Baptist Beheaded

**14** At that time Herod the tetrarch heard the reports about Jesus, [2]and he said to his attendants, "This is John the Baptist; he has risen from the dead! That is why miraculous powers are at work in him."

[3]Now Herod had arrested John and bound him and put him in prison because of Herodias, his brother Philip's wife, [4]for John had been saying to him: "It is not lawful for you to have her." [5]Herod wanted to kill John, but he was afraid of the people, because they considered John a prophet.

[6]On Herod's birthday the daughter of Herodias danced for the guests and pleased Herod so much [7]that he promised with an oath to give her whatever she asked. [8]Prompted by her mother, she said, "Give me here on a platter the head of John the Baptist." [9]The king was distressed, but because of his oaths and his dinner guests, he ordered that her request be granted [10]and had John beheaded in the prison. [11]His head was brought in on a platter and given to the girl, who carried it to her mother. [12]John's disciples came and took his body and buried it. Then they went and told Jesus.

### Jesus Feeds the Five Thousand

[13]When Jesus heard what had happened, he withdrew by boat privately to a solitary place. Hearing of this, the crowds followed him on foot from the towns. [14]When Jesus landed and saw a large crowd, he had compassion on them and healed their sick.

[15]As evening approached, the disciples came to him and said, "This is a remote place, and it's already getting late.

## Amplified Bible

[49]So it will be at the close and consummation of the age. The angels will go forth and separate the wicked from the righteous (those who are upright and in right standing with God)

[50]And cast them [the wicked] into the furnace of fire; there will be weeping and wailing and grinding of teeth.

[51]Have you understood [a]all these things [parables] taken together? They said to Him, Yes, Lord.

[52]He said to them, Therefore every [a]teacher and interpreter of the Sacred Writings who has been instructed about and trained for the kingdom of heaven and [b]become a disciple is like a householder who brings forth out of his storehouse treasure that is new and [treasure that is] old [the fresh as well as the familiar].

[53]When Jesus had finished these parables (these comparisons), He left there.

[54]And coming to His own country [Nazareth], He taught in their synagogue so that they were amazed with bewildered wonder, and said, Where did this [c]Man get this wisdom and these miraculous powers?

[55]Is not this the carpenter's Son? Is not His mother called Mary? And are not His brothers James and Joseph and Simon and Judas?

[56]And do not all His sisters live here among us? Where then did this Man get all this?

[57]And they took offense at Him [they were repelled and hindered from acknowledging His authority, and caused to stumble]. But Jesus said to them, A prophet is not without honor except in his own country and in his own house.

[58]And He did not do many works of power there, because of their unbelief (their lack of faith [b]in the divine mission of Jesus).

**14** At that time Herod the governor heard the reports about Jesus,

[2]And he said to his attendants, This is John the Baptist; He has been raised from the dead, and that is why the powers [b]of performing miracles are at work in Him.

[3]For Herod had arrested John and bound him and put him in prison [to [d]stow him out of the way] on account and for the sake of Herodias, his brother Philip's wife,

[4]For John had said to him, It is not lawful or right for you to have her. [Lev. 18:16; 20:21.]

[5]Although he wished to have him put to death, he was afraid of the people, for they regarded John as a prophet.

[6]But when Herod's birthday came, the daughter of Herodias danced in the midst [before the company] and pleased and fascinated Herod,

[7]And so he promised with an oath to give her whatever she might ask.

[8]And she, being put forward and prompted by her mother, said, Give me the head of John the Baptist right here on a [e]platter.

[9]And the king was distressed and sorry, but because of his oaths and his guests, he ordered it to be given her;

[10]He sent and had John beheaded in the prison.

[11]And his head was brought in on a [e]platter and given [f]to the little maid, and she brought it to her mother.

[12]And John's disciples came and took up the body and buried it. Then they went and told Jesus.

[13]When Jesus heard it, He withdrew from there privately in a boat to a solitary place. But when the crowds heard of it, they followed Him [by land] on foot from the towns.

[14]When He went ashore and saw a great throng of people, He had compassion (pity and deep sympathy) for them and cured their sick.

[15]When evening came, the disciples came to Him and said, This is a remote and barren place, and the day is now

[a] Joseph Thayer, A Greek-English Lexicon.  [b] Marvin Vincent, Word Studies.  [c] See footnote on Matt. 2:8.  [d] G. Abbott-Smith, Manual Greek Lexicon.  [e] William Tyndale, The Tyndale Bible.  [f] Martin Luther, cited by Marvin Vincent, Word Studies.

## New International Version

Send the crowds away, so they can go to the villages and buy themselves some food."

[16]Jesus replied, "They do not need to go away. You give them something to eat."

[17]"We have here only five loaves of bread and two fish," they answered.

[18]"Bring them here to me," he said. [19]And he directed the people to sit down on the grass. Taking the five loaves and the two fish and looking up to heaven, he gave thanks and broke the loaves. Then he gave them to the disciples, and the disciples gave them to the people. [20]They all ate and were satisfied, and the disciples picked up twelve basketfuls of broken pieces that were left over. [21]The number of those who ate was about five thousand men, besides women and children.

### Jesus Walks on the Water

[22]Immediately Jesus made the disciples get into the boat and go on ahead of him to the other side, while he dismissed the crowd. [23]After he had dismissed them, he went up on a mountainside by himself to pray. Later that night, he was there alone, [24]and the boat was already a considerable distance from land, buffeted by the waves because the wind was against it.

[25]Shortly before dawn Jesus went out to them, walking on the lake. [26]When the disciples saw him walking on the lake, they were terrified. "It's a ghost," they said, and cried out in fear.

[27]But Jesus immediately said to them: "Take courage! It is I. Don't be afraid."

[28]"Lord, if it's you," Peter replied, "tell me to come to you on the water."

[29]"Come," he said.

Then Peter got down out of the boat, walked on the water and came toward Jesus. [30]But when he saw the wind, he was afraid and, beginning to sink, cried out, "Lord, save me!"

[31]Immediately Jesus reached out his hand and caught him. "You of little faith," he said, "why did you doubt?"

[32]And when they climbed into the boat, the wind died down. [33]Then those who were in the boat worshiped him, saying, "Truly you are the Son of God."

[34]When they had crossed over, they landed at Gennesaret. [35]And when the men of that place recognized Jesus, they sent word to all the surrounding country. People brought all their sick to him [36]and begged him to let the sick just touch the edge of his cloak, and all who touched it were healed.

### That Which Defiles

**15** Then some Pharisees and teachers of the law came to Jesus from Jerusalem and asked, [2]"Why do your disciples break the tradition of the elders? They don't wash their hands before they eat!"

[3]Jesus replied, "And why do you break the command of God for the sake of your tradition? [4]For God said, 'Honor your father and mother'[a] and 'Anyone who curses their father or mother is to be put to death.'[b] [5]But you say that

## Amplified Bible

over; send the throngs away into the villages to buy food for themselves.

[16]Jesus said, They do not need to go away; you give them something to eat.

[17]They said to Him, We have nothing here but five loaves and two fish.

[18]He said, Bring them here to Me.

[19]Then He ordered the crowds to recline on the grass; and He took the five loaves and the two fish and, looking up to heaven, He gave thanks *and* blessed and broke the loaves and handed the pieces to the disciples, and the disciples gave them to the people.

[20]And they all ate and were satisfied. And they picked up twelve [a]small hand] baskets full of the broken pieces left over.

[21]And those who ate were about 5,000 men, not including women and children.

[22]Then He directed the disciples to get into the boat and go before Him to the other side, while He sent away the crowds.

[23]And after He had dismissed the multitudes, He went up into the hills by Himself to pray. When it was evening, He was still there alone.

[24]But the boat was by this time out on the sea, *many furlongs* [a furlong is one-eighth of a mile] *distant from the land,* beaten and tossed by the waves, for the wind was against them.

[25]And in the fourth watch [between 3:00—6:00 A.M.] of the night, Jesus came to them, walking on the sea.

[26]And when the disciples saw Him walking on the sea, they were terrified and said, It is a ghost! And they screamed out with fright.

[27]But instantly He spoke to them, saying, Take courage! I AM! Stop being afraid! [Exod. 3:14.]

[28]And Peter answered Him, Lord, if it is You, command me to come to You on the water.

[29]He said, Come! So Peter got out of the boat and walked on the water, and he came toward Jesus.

[30]But when he perceived *and* felt the strong wind, he was frightened, and as he began to sink, he cried out, Lord, save me [from death]!

[31]Instantly Jesus reached out His hand and caught *and* held him, saying to him, O you of little faith, why did you doubt?

[32]And when they got into the boat, the wind ceased.

[33]And those in the boat knelt and worshiped Him, saying, Truly You are the Son of God!

[34]And when they had crossed over to the other side, they went ashore at Gennesaret.

[35]And when the men of that place recognized Him, they sent around into all the surrounding country and brought to Him all who were sick

[36]And begged Him to let them merely touch the fringe of His garment; and as many as touched it were perfectly restored. [Matt. 9:20.]

**15** Then from Jerusalem came scribes and Pharisees and said,

[2]Why do Your disciples transgress *and* violate the rules handed down by the elders of the past? For they do not practice [ceremonially] washing their hands before they eat.

[3]He replied to them, And why also do you transgress *and* violate the commandment of God for the sake of the rules handed down to you by your forefathers (the elders)?

[4]For God commanded, Honor your father and your mother, and, He who curses *or* reviles *or* speaks evil of *or* abuses *or* treats improperly his father or mother, let him surely come to his end by death. [Exod. 20:12; 21:17; Lev. 20:9; Deut. 5:16.]

---

[a] Marvin Vincent, *Word Studies.* But according to James Moulton and George Milligan, *The Vocabulary,* the term refers to the type of material of which the basket is constructed (perhaps a wicker basket) and not necessarily the size of the basket.

---

[a] 4 Exodus 20:12; Deut. 5:16    [b] 4 Exodus 21:17; Lev. 20:9

## New International Version

if anyone declares that what might have been used to help their father or mother is 'devoted to God,' [6]they are not to 'honor their father or mother' with it. Thus you nullify the word of God for the sake of your tradition. [7]You hypocrites! Isaiah was right when he prophesied about you:

[8]"'These people honor me with their lips,
 but their hearts are far from me.
[9]They worship me in vain;
 their teachings are merely human rules.'[a]"

[10]Jesus called the crowd to him and said, "Listen and understand. [11]What goes into someone's mouth does not defile them, but what comes out of their mouth, that is what defiles them."

[12]Then the disciples came to him and asked, "Do you know that the Pharisees were offended when they heard this?"

[13]He replied, "Every plant that my heavenly Father has not planted will be pulled up by the roots. [14]Leave them; they are blind guides.[b] If the blind lead the blind, both will fall into a pit."

[15]Peter said, "Explain the parable to us."

[16]"Are you still so dull?" Jesus asked them. [17]"Don't you see that whatever enters the mouth goes into the stomach and then out of the body? [18]But the things that come out of a person's mouth come from the heart, and these defile them. [19]For out of the heart come evil thoughts—murder, adultery, sexual immorality, theft, false testimony, slander. [20]These are what defile a person; but eating with unwashed hands does not defile them."

### The Faith of a Canaanite Woman

[21]Leaving that place, Jesus withdrew to the region of Tyre and Sidon. [22]A Canaanite woman from that vicinity came to him, crying out, "Lord, Son of David, have mercy on me! My daughter is demon-possessed and suffering terribly."

[23]Jesus did not answer a word. So his disciples came to him and urged him, "Send her away, for she keeps crying out after us."

[24]He answered, "I was sent only to the lost sheep of Israel."

[25]The woman came and knelt before him. "Lord, help me!" she said.

[26]He replied, "It is not right to take the children's bread and toss it to the dogs."

[27]"Yes it is, Lord," she said. "Even the dogs eat the crumbs that fall from their master's table."

## Amplified Bible

[5]But you say, If anyone tells his father or mother, What you would have gained from me [that is, the money and whatever I have that might be used for helping you] is already dedicated as a gift to God, then he is exempt *and* no longer under obligation to honor *and* help his father *or his mother*.

[6]So for the sake of your tradition (the rules handed down by your forefathers), you have set aside the Word of God [depriving it of force and authority and making it of no effect].

[7]You pretenders (hypocrites)! Admirably *and* truly did Isaiah prophesy of you when he said:

[8]These people *draw near Me with their mouths and* honor Me with their lips, but their hearts hold off *and* are far away from Me.

[9]Uselessly do they worship Me, for they teach as doctrines the commands of men. [Isa. 29:13.]

[10]And Jesus called the people to Him and said to them, Listen and grasp *and* comprehend this:

[11]It is not what goes into the mouth of a man that makes him unclean *and* defiled, but what comes out of the mouth; this makes a man unclean *and* defiles [him].

[12]Then the disciples came and said to Him, Do You know that the Pharisees were displeased *and* offended *and* indignant when they heard this saying?

[13]He answered, Every plant which My heavenly Father has not planted will be torn up by the roots. [Isa. 60:21.]

[14]Let them alone *and* disregard them; they are blind guides *and* teachers. And if a blind man leads a blind man, both will fall into a ditch.

[15]But Peter said to Him, Explain this [a]proverb (this [b]maxim) to us.

[16]And He said, Are you also even yet dull *and* ignorant [without understanding and [c]unable to put things together]?

[17]Do you not see *and* understand that whatever goes into the mouth passes into the [d]abdomen and so passes on into the place where discharges are deposited?

[18]But whatever comes out of the mouth comes from the heart, and this is what makes a man unclean *and* defiles [him].

[19]For out of the heart come evil thoughts (reasonings and disputings and designs) such as murder, adultery, sexual vice, theft, false witnessing, slander, *and* irreverent speech.

[20]These are what make a man unclean *and* defile [him]; but eating with unwashed hands does not make him unclean *or* defile [him].

[21]And going away from there, Jesus withdrew to the district of Tyre and Sidon.

[22]And behold, a woman who was a Canaanite from that district came out and, with a [loud, troublesomely urgent] cry, begged, Have mercy on me, O Lord, Son of David! My daughter is miserably *and* distressingly *and* cruelly possessed by a demon!

[23]But He did not answer her a word. And His disciples came and implored Him, saying, Send her away, for she is crying out after us.

[24]He answered, I was sent only to the lost sheep of the house of Israel.

[25]But she came and, kneeling, worshiped Him and kept praying, Lord, help me!

[26]And He answered, It is not right (proper, becoming, or fair) to take the children's bread and throw it to the [e]little dogs.

[27]She said, Yes, Lord, yet even the little pups ([f]little whelps) eat the crumbs that fall from their [young] masters' table.

---

[a] G. Abbott-Smith, *Manual Greek Lexicon.* [b] Joseph Thayer, *A Greek-English Lexicon.* [c] Hermann Cremer, *Biblico-Theological Lexicon.* [d] James Moulton and George Milligan, *The Vocabulary.* [e] Marvin Vincent, *Word Studies.* [f] John Wycliffe, *The Wycliffe Bible.*

# New International Version

[28] Then Jesus said to her, "Woman, you have great faith! Your request is granted." And her daughter was healed at that moment.

## Jesus Feeds the Four Thousand

[29] Jesus left there and went along the Sea of Galilee. Then he went up on a mountainside and sat down. [30] Great crowds came to him, bringing the lame, the blind, the crippled, the mute and many others, and laid them at his feet; and he healed them. [31] The people were amazed when they saw the mute speaking, the crippled made well, the lame walking and the blind seeing. And they praised the God of Israel.

[32] Jesus called his disciples to him and said, "I have compassion for these people; they have already been with me three days and have nothing to eat. I do not want to send them away hungry, or they may collapse on the way."

[33] His disciples answered, "Where could we get enough bread in this remote place to feed such a crowd?"

[34] "How many loaves do you have?" Jesus asked.

"Seven," they replied, "and a few small fish."

[35] He told the crowd to sit down on the ground. [36] Then he took the seven loaves and the fish, and when he had given thanks, he broke them and gave them to the disciples, and they in turn to the people. [37] They all ate and were satisfied. Afterward the disciples picked up seven basketfuls of broken pieces that were left over. [38] The number of those who ate was four thousand men, besides women and children. [39] After Jesus had sent the crowd away, he got into the boat and went to the vicinity of Magadan.

## The Demand for a Sign

**16** The Pharisees and Sadducees came to Jesus and tested him by asking him to show them a sign from heaven.

[2] He replied, "When evening comes, you say, 'It will be fair weather, for the sky is red,' [3] and in the morning, 'Today it will be stormy, for the sky is red and overcast.' You know how to interpret the appearance of the sky, but you cannot interpret the signs of the times.[a] [4] A wicked and adulterous generation looks for a sign, but none will be given it except the sign of Jonah." Jesus then left them and went away.

## The Yeast of the Pharisees and Sadducees

[5] When they went across the lake, the disciples forgot to take bread. [6] "Be careful," Jesus said to them. "Be on your guard against the yeast of the Pharisees and Sadducees."

[7] They discussed this among themselves and said, "It is because we didn't bring any bread."

[8] Aware of their discussion, Jesus asked, "You of little faith, why are you talking among yourselves about having no bread? [9] Do you still not understand? Don't you remember the five loaves for the five thousand, and how many

# Amplified Bible

[28] Then Jesus answered her, O woman, great is your faith! Be it done for you as you wish. And her daughter was cured from that [a]moment.

[29] And Jesus went on from there and passed along the shore of the Sea of Galilee. Then He went up into the hills and kept sitting there.

[30] And a great multitude came to Him, bringing with them the lame, the maimed, the blind, the dumb, and many others, and they put them down at His feet; and He cured them,

[31] So that the crowd was amazed when they saw the dumb speaking, the maimed made whole, the lame walking, and the blind seeing; and they [b]recognized and praised and thanked and glorified the God of Israel.

[32] Then Jesus called His disciples to Him and said, I have pity and sympathy and am deeply moved for the crowd, because they have been with Me now three days and they have nothing [at all left] to eat; and I am not willing to send them away hungry, lest they faint or become exhausted on the way.

[33] And the disciples said to Him, Where are we to get bread sufficient to feed so great a crowd in this isolated and desert place?

[34] And Jesus asked them, How many loaves of bread do you have? They replied, Seven, and a few small fish.

[35] And ordering the crowd to recline on the ground,

[36] He took the seven loaves and the fish, and when He had given thanks, He broke them and gave them to the disciples, and the disciples gave them to the people.

[37] And they all ate and were satisfied. And they gathered up seven [c]large provision] baskets full of the broken pieces that were left over.

[38] Those who ate were 4,000 men, not including the women and the children.

[39] Then He dismissed the crowds, got into the boat, and went to the district of Magadan.

**16** Now the Pharisees and Sadducees came up to Jesus, and they asked Him to show them a sign (spectacular miracle) from heaven [attesting His divine authority].

[2] He replied to them, [d]When it is evening you say, It will be fair weather, for the sky is red,

[3] And in the morning, It will be stormy today, for the sky is red and has a gloomy and threatening look. You know how to interpret the appearance of the sky, but you cannot interpret the signs of the times.

[4] A wicked and morally unfaithful generation craves a sign, but no sign shall be given to it except the sign of the prophet Jonah. Then He left them and went away. [Jonah 3:4, 5.]

[5] When the disciples reached the other side of the sea, they found that they had forgotten to bring any bread.

[6] Jesus said to them, Be careful and on your guard against the leaven (ferment) of the Pharisees and Sadducees.

[7] And they reasoned among themselves about it, saying, It is because we did not bring any bread.

[8] But Jesus, aware of this, asked, Why are you discussing among yourselves the fact that you have no bread? O you [men, how little trust you have in Me, how] little faith!

[9] Do you not yet discern (perceive and understand)? Do you not remember the five loaves of the five thousand, and how many [c]small hand] baskets you gathered?

---

[a] James Moulton and George Milligan, *The Vocabulary.* [b] Hermann Cremer, *Biblico-Theological Lexicon.* [c] Marvin Vincent, *Word Studies.* See also footnote on Matt. 14:20. [d] Some manuscripts do not have the rest of verse 2 and all of verse 3.

[a] 2,3 Some early manuscripts do not have *When evening comes . . . of the times.*

## New International Version

basketfuls you gathered? [10]Or the seven loaves for the four thousand, and how many basketfuls you gathered? [11]How is it you don't understand that I was not talking to you about bread? But be on your guard against the yeast of the Pharisees and Sadducees." [12]Then they understood that he was not telling them to guard against the yeast used in bread, but against the teaching of the Pharisees and Sadducees.

### Peter Declares That Jesus Is the Messiah

[13]When Jesus came to the region of Caesarea Philippi, he asked his disciples, "Who do people say the Son of Man is?"

[14]They replied, "Some say John the Baptist; others say Elijah; and still others, Jeremiah or one of the prophets."

[15]"But what about you?" he asked. "Who do you say I am?"

[16]Simon Peter answered, "You are the Messiah, the Son of the living God."

[17]Jesus replied, "Blessed are you, Simon son of Jonah, for this was not revealed to you by flesh and blood, but by my Father in heaven. [18]And I tell you that you are Peter,[a] and on this rock I will build my church, and the gates of Hades[b] will not overcome it. [19]I will give you the keys of the kingdom of heaven; whatever you bind on earth will be[c] bound in heaven, and whatever you loose on earth will be[c] loosed in heaven." [20]Then he ordered his disciples not to tell anyone that he was the Messiah.

### Jesus Predicts His Death

[21]From that time on Jesus began to explain to his disciples that he must go to Jerusalem and suffer many things at the hands of the elders, the chief priests and the teachers of the law, and that he must be killed and on the third day be raised to life.

[22]Peter took him aside and began to rebuke him. "Never, Lord!" he said. "This shall never happen to you!"

[23]Jesus turned and said to Peter, "Get behind me, Satan! You are a stumbling block to me; you do not have in mind the concerns of God, but merely human concerns."

[24]Then Jesus said to his disciples, "Whoever wants to be my disciple must deny themselves and take up their cross and follow me. [25]For whoever wants to save their life[d] will lose it, but whoever loses their life for me will find it. [26]What good will it be for someone to gain the whole world, yet forfeit their soul? Or what can anyone give in exchange for their soul? [27]For the Son of Man is going to come in his Father's glory with his angels, and then he will reward each person according to what they have done.

## Amplified Bible

[10]Nor the seven loaves for the four thousand, and how many [a]large provision] baskets you took up?

[11]How is it that you fail to understand that I was not talking to you about bread? But beware of the leaven (ferment) of the Pharisees and Sadducees.

[12]Then they discerned that He did not tell them to beware of the leaven of bread, but of the teaching of the Pharisees and Sadducees.

[13]Now when Jesus went into the region of Caesarea Philippi, He asked His disciples, Who do people say that the Son of Man is?

[14]And they answered, Some say John the Baptist; others say Elijah; and others Jeremiah or one of the prophets.

[15]He said to them, But who do you [yourselves] say that I am?

[16]Simon Peter replied, You are the Christ, the Son of the living God.

[17]Then Jesus answered him, Blessed (happy, fortunate, and [b]to be envied) are you, Simon Bar-Jonah. For flesh and blood [men] have not revealed this to you, but My Father Who is in heaven.

[18]And I tell you, you are [c]Peter [Greek, *Petros*—a large piece of rock], and on this rock [Greek, *petra*—a [d]huge rock like Gibraltar] I will build My church, and the gates of Hades (the powers of the [d]infernal region) shall [e]not overpower it [or be strong to its detriment or hold out against it].

[19]I will give you the keys of the kingdom of heaven; and whatever you bind (declare to be improper and unlawful) on earth [f]must be what is already bound in heaven; and whatever you loose (declare lawful) on earth [f]must be what is already loosed in heaven. [Isa. 22:22.]

[20]Then He sternly *and* strictly charged *and* warned the disciples to tell no one that He was *Jesus* the Christ.

[21]From that time forth Jesus began [clearly] to show His disciples that He must go to Jerusalem and suffer many things at the hands of the elders and the high priests and scribes, and be killed, and on the third day be raised [g]from death.

[22]Then Peter took Him aside [a]to speak to Him privately and began to reprove and [e]charge Him sharply, saying, God forbid, Lord! This must never happen to You!

[23]But Jesus turned [a]away from Peter and said to him, Get behind Me, Satan! You are in My way [an offense and a hindrance and a snare to Me]; for you are [e]minding what partakes not of the nature *and* quality of God, but of men.

[24]Then Jesus said to His disciples, If anyone desires to be My disciple, let him deny himself [disregard, lose sight of, and forget himself and his own interests] and take up his cross and follow Me [e]cleave steadfastly to Me, conform wholly to My example in living and, if need be, in dying, also].

[25]For whoever is bent on saving his [temporal] life [his comfort and security here] shall lose it [eternal life]; and whoever loses his life [his comfort and security here] for My sake shall find it [life everlasting].

[26]For what will it profit a man if he gains the whole world and forfeits his life [his blessed [e]life in the kingdom of God]? Or what would a man give as an exchange for his [blessed] [e]life [in the kingdom of God]?

[27]For the Son of Man is going to come in the glory (majesty, splendor) of His Father with His angels, and then He will render account *and* reward every man in accordance with what he has done.

---

[a] Marvin Vincent, *Word Studies*. See also footnote on Matt. 14:20. [b] Alexander Souter, *Pocket Lexicon*. [c] The rock on which the church is built is traditionally interpreted as either Peter's inspired confession of faith in Jesus as the Messiah, or it may be Peter himself (see Eph. 2:20). [d] Kenneth Wuest, *Word Studies*. [e] Joseph Thayer, *A Greek-English Lexicon*. [f] Charles B. Williams, *The New Testament: A Translation*: "The perfect passive participle, here referring to a state of having been already forbidden [or permitted]." [g] Hermann Cremer, *Biblico-Theological Lexicon*.

---

[a] 18 The Greek word for *Peter* means *rock*.  [b] 18 That is, the realm of the dead  [c] 19 Or *will have been*  [d] 25 The Greek word means either *life* or *soul*; also in verse 26.

## New International Version

28"Truly I tell you, some who are standing here will not taste death before they see the Son of Man coming in his kingdom."

### The Transfiguration

**17** After six days Jesus took with him Peter, James and John the brother of James, and led them up a high mountain by themselves. 2There he was transfigured before them. His face shone like the sun, and his clothes became as white as the light. 3Just then there appeared before them Moses and Elijah, talking with Jesus.

4Peter said to Jesus, "Lord, it is good for us to be here. If you wish, I will put up three shelters—one for you, one for Moses and one for Elijah."

5While he was still speaking, a bright cloud covered them, and a voice from the cloud said, "This is my Son, whom I love; with him I am well pleased. Listen to him!"

6When the disciples heard this, they fell facedown to the ground, terrified. 7But Jesus came and touched them. "Get up," he said. "Don't be afraid." 8When they looked up, they saw no one except Jesus.

9As they were coming down the mountain, Jesus instructed them, "Don't tell anyone what you have seen, until the Son of Man has been raised from the dead."

10The disciples asked him, "Why then do the teachers of the law say that Elijah must come first?"

11Jesus replied, "To be sure, Elijah comes and will restore all things. 12But I tell you, Elijah has already come, and they did not recognize him, but have done to him everything they wished. In the same way the Son of Man is going to suffer at their hands." 13Then the disciples understood that he was talking to them about John the Baptist.

### Jesus Heals a Demon-Possessed Boy

14When they came to the crowd, a man approached Jesus and knelt before him. 15"Lord, have mercy on my son," he said. "He has seizures and is suffering greatly. He often falls into the fire or into the water. 16I brought him to your disciples, but they could not heal him."

17"You unbelieving and perverse generation," Jesus replied, "how long shall I stay with you? How long shall I put up with you? Bring the boy here to me." 18Jesus rebuked the demon, and it came out of the boy, and he was healed at that moment.

19Then the disciples came to Jesus in private and asked, "Why couldn't we drive it out?"

20He replied, "Because you have so little faith. Truly I tell you, if you have faith as small as a mustard seed, you can say to this mountain, 'Move from here to there,' and it will move. Nothing will be impossible for you." [21]a

## Amplified Bible

28Truly I tell you, there are some standing here who will not taste death before they see the Son of Man coming in (into) His kingdom.

**17** And six days after this, Jesus took with Him Peter and James and John his brother, and led them up on a high mountain by themselves.

2And His appearance underwent a change in their presence; and His face shone aclear and bright like the sun, and His clothing became as white as light.

3And behold, there appeared to them Moses and Elijah, who kept talking with Him.

4Then Peter began to speak and said to Jesus, Lord, it is good and delightful that we are here; if You approve, I will put up three booths here—one for You and one for Moses and one for Elijah.

5While he was still speaking, behold, a shining cloud [bcomposed of light] overshadowed them, and a voice from the cloud said, This is My Son, My Beloved, with Whom I am [and chave always been] delighted. Listen to Him! [Ps. 2:7; Isa. 42:1.]

6When the disciples heard it, they fell on their faces and were bseized with alarm and struck with fear.

7But Jesus came and touched them and said, Get up, and do not be afraid.

8And when they raised their eyes, they saw no one but Jesus only.

9And as they were going down the mountain, Jesus cautioned and commanded them, Do not mention to anyone what you have seen, until the Son of Man has been raised from the dead.

10The disciples asked Him, Then why do the scribes say that Elijah must come first?

11He replied, Elijah does come and will get everything restored and ready.

12But I tell you that Elijah has come already, and they did not know or recognize him, but did to him as they liked. So also the Son of Man is going to be treated and suffer at their hands.

13Then the disciples understood that He spoke to them about John the Baptist. [Mal. 4:5.]

14And when they approached the multitude, a man came up to Him, kneeling before Him and saying,

15Lord, do pity and have mercy on my son, for he has epilepsy (is dmoonstruck) and he suffers terribly; for frequently he falls into the fire and many times into the water.

16And I brought him to Your disciples, and they were not able to cure him.

17And Jesus answered, O you unbelieving (ewarped, wayward, rebellious) and fthoroughly perverse generation! How long am I to remain with you? How long am I to bear with you? Bring him here to Me.

18And Jesus rebuked the demon, and it came out of him, and the boy was cured instantly.

19Then the disciples came to Jesus and asked privately, Why could we not drive it out?

20He said to them, Because of the littleness of your faith [that is, your lack of afirmly relying trust]. For truly I say to you, if you have faith [gthat is living] like a grain of mustard seed, you can say to this mountain, Move from here to yonder place, and it will move; and nothing will be impossible to you.

21hBut this kind does not go out except by prayer and fasting.

---

a Hermann Cremer, *Biblico-Theological Lexicon.* b Joseph Thayer, *A Greek-English Lexicon.* c Charles B. Williams, *The New Testament: A Translation.*: "suggested by the aorist (past) tense." d Joseph Thayer, *A Greek-English Lexicon*: "Epilepsy is supposed to return and increase with the increase of the moon." e Marvin Vincent, *Word Studies.* f Literally, "throughout" *(dia).* g Charles B. Williams, *The New Testament: A Translation.* h Some manuscripts do not contain this verse.

---

a 21 Some manuscripts include here words similar to Mark 9:29.

## New International Version

### Jesus Predicts His Death a Second Time

22When they came together in Galilee, he said to them, "The Son of Man is going to be delivered into the hands of men. 23They will kill him, and on the third day he will be raised to life." And the disciples were filled with grief.

### The Temple Tax

24After Jesus and his disciples arrived in Capernaum, the collectors of the two-drachma temple tax came to Peter and asked, "Doesn't your teacher pay the temple tax?"

25"Yes, he does," he replied.

When Peter came into the house, Jesus was the first to speak. "What do you think, Simon?" he asked. "From whom do the kings of the earth collect duty and taxes—from their own children or from others?"

26"From others," Peter answered.

"Then the children are exempt," Jesus said to him. 27"But so that we may not cause offense, go to the lake and throw out your line. Take the first fish you catch; open its mouth and you will find a four-drachma coin. Take it and give it to them for my tax and yours."

### The Greatest in the Kingdom of Heaven

**18** At that time the disciples came to Jesus and asked, "Who, then, is the greatest in the kingdom of heaven?"

2He called a little child to him, and placed the child among them. 3And he said: "Truly I tell you, unless you change and become like little children, you will never enter the kingdom of heaven. 4Therefore, whoever takes the lowly position of this child is the greatest in the kingdom of heaven. 5And whoever welcomes one such child in my name welcomes me.

### Causing to Stumble

6"If anyone causes one of these little ones—those who believe in me—to stumble, it would be better for them to have a large millstone hung around their neck and to be drowned in the depths of the sea. 7Woe to the world because of the things that cause people to stumble! Such things must come, but woe to the person through whom they come! 8If your hand or your foot causes you to stumble, cut it off and throw it away. It is better for you to enter life maimed or crippled than to have two hands or two feet and be thrown into eternal fire. 9And if your eye causes you to stumble, gouge it out and throw it away. It is better for you to enter life with one eye than to have two eyes and be thrown into the fire of hell.

### The Parable of the Wandering Sheep

10"See that you do not despise one of these little ones. For I tell you that their angels in heaven always see the face of my Father in heaven. [11]a

12"What do you think? If a man owns a hundred sheep, and one of them wanders away, will he not leave the nine-

## Amplified Bible

22When they were going about here and there in Galilee, Jesus said to them, The Son of Man is going to be turned over into the hands of men.

23And they will kill Him, and He will be raised [to life] again on the third day. And they were deeply and exceedingly grieved and distressed.

24When they arrived in Capernaum, the collectors of the half shekel [the temple tax] went up to Peter and said, Does not your Teacher pay the half shekel? [Exod. 30:13; 38:26.]

25He answered, Yes. And when he came home, Jesus spoke to him [about it] first, saying, What do you think, Simon? From whom do earthly rulers collect duties or tribute—from their own sons or from others anot of their own family?

26And when Peter said, From other people anot of their own family, Jesus said to him, Then the sons are exempt.

27However, in order not to give offense and cause them to stumble [that is, to cause them ato judge unfavorably and unjustly] go down to the sea and throw in a hook. Take the first fish that comes up, and when you open its mouth you will find there a shekel. Take it and give it to them to pay the temple tax for Me and for yourself.

**18** At that time the disciples came up and asked Jesus, Who then is [really] the greatest in the kingdom of heaven?

2And He called a little child to Himself and put him in the midst of them,

3And said, Truly I say to you, unless you repent (change, turn about) and become like little children [trusting, lowly, loving, forgiving], you can never enter the kingdom of heaven [at all].

4Whoever will humble himself therefore and become like this little child [trusting, lowly, loving, forgiving] is greatest in the kingdom of heaven.

5And whoever receives and accepts and welcomes one little child like this for My sake and in My name receives and accepts and welcomes Me.

6But whoever causes one of these little ones who believe in and backnowledge and cleave to Me to stumble and sin [that is, who entices him or hinders him in right conduct or thought], it would be better (cmore expedient and profitable or advantageous) for him to have a great millstone fastened around his neck and to be sunk in the depth of the sea.

7Woe to the world for such temptations to sin and influences to do wrong! It is necessary that temptations come, but woe to the person on whose account or by whom the temptation comes!

8And if your hand or your foot causes you to stumble and sin, cut it off and throw it away from you; it is better (more profitable and wholesome) for you to enter life maimed or lame than to have two hands or two feet and be thrown into everlasting fire.

9And if your eye causes you to stumble and sin, pluck it out and throw it away from you; it is better (more profitable and wholesome) for you to enter life with only one eye than to have two eyes and be thrown into the hell (Gehenna) of fire.

10Beware that you do not despise or feel scornful toward or think little of one of these little ones, for I tell you that in heaven their angels always are in the presence of and look upon the face of My Father Who is in heaven.

11dFor the Son of man came to save [bfrom the penalty of eternal death] that which was lost.

12What do you think? If a man has a hundred sheep, and one of them has gone astray and gets lost, will he not

a Joseph Thayer, A Greek-English Lexicon. b Hermann Cremer, Biblico-Theological Lexicon. c G. Abbott-Smith, Manual Greek Lexicon. d Many manuscripts do not contain this verse.

---

a 11 Some manuscripts include here the words of Luke 19:10.

## New International Version

ty-nine on the hills and go to look for the one that wandered off? [13]And if he finds it, truly I tell you, he is happier about that one sheep than about the ninety-nine that did not wander off. [14]In the same way your Father in heaven is not willing that any of these little ones should perish.

### Dealing With Sin in the Church

[15]"If your brother or sister[a] sins,[b] go and point out their fault, just between the two of you. If they listen to you, you have won them over. [16]But if they will not listen, take one or two others along, so that 'every matter may be established by the testimony of two or three witnesses.'[c] [17]If they still refuse to listen, tell it to the church; and if they refuse to listen even to the church, treat them as you would a pagan or a tax collector.

[18]"Truly I tell you, whatever you bind on earth will be[d] bound in heaven, and whatever you loose on earth will be[d] loosed in heaven.

[19]"Again, truly I tell you that if two of you on earth agree about anything they ask for, it will be done for them by my Father in heaven. [20]For where two or three gather in my name, there am I with them."

### The Parable of the Unmerciful Servant

[21]Then Peter came to Jesus and asked, "Lord, how many times shall I forgive my brother or sister who sins against me? Up to seven times?"

[22]Jesus answered, "I tell you, not seven times, but seventy-seven times.[e]

[23]"Therefore, the kingdom of heaven is like a king who wanted to settle accounts with his servants. [24]As he began the settlement, a man who owed him ten thousand bags of gold[f] was brought to him. [25]Since he was not able to pay, the master ordered that he and his wife and his children and all that he had be sold to repay the debt.

[26]"At this the servant fell on his knees before him. 'Be patient with me,' he begged, 'and I will pay back everything.' [27]The servant's master took pity on him, canceled the debt and let him go.

[28]"But when that servant went out, he found one of his fellow servants who owed him a hundred silver coins.[g] He grabbed him and began to choke him. 'Pay back what you owe me!' he demanded.

[29]"His fellow servant fell to his knees and begged him, 'Be patient with me, and I will pay it back.'

[30]"But he refused. Instead, he went off and had the man thrown into prison until he could pay the debt. [31]When the other servants saw what had happened, they were outraged and went and told their master everything that had happened.

[32]"Then the master called the servant in. 'You wicked servant,' he said, 'I canceled all that debt of yours because you begged me to. [33]Shouldn't you have had mercy on your fellow servant just as I had on you?' [34]In anger his master handed him over to the jailers to be tortured, until he should pay back all he owed.

[35]"This is how my heavenly Father will treat each of you unless you forgive your brother or sister from your heart."

## Amplified Bible

leave the ninety-nine on the mountain and go in search of the one that is lost?

[13]And if it should be that he finds it, truly I say to you, he rejoices more over it than over the ninety-nine that did not get lost.

[14]Just so it is not the will of My Father Who is in heaven that one of these little ones should be lost and perish.

[15]If your brother wrongs you, go and show him his fault, between you and him privately. If he listens to you, you have won back your brother.

[16]But if he does not listen, take along with you one or two others, so that every word may be confirmed and upheld by the testimony of two or three witnesses.

[17]If he pays no attention to them [refusing to listen and obey], tell it to the church; and if he refuses to listen even to the church, let him be to you as a pagan and a tax collector. [Lev. 19:17; Deut. 19:15.]

[18]Truly I tell you, whatever you forbid and declare to be improper and unlawful on earth must be [a]what is already forbidden in heaven, and whatever you permit and declare proper and lawful on earth must be [a]what is already permitted in heaven.

[19]Again I tell you, if two of you on earth agree (harmonize together, make a symphony together) about whatever [anything and [b]everything] they may ask, it will come to pass and be done for them by My Father in heaven.

[20]For wherever two or three are gathered (drawn together as My followers) in (into) My name, there I AM in the midst of them. [Exod. 3:14.]

[21]Then Peter came up to Him and said, Lord, how many times may my brother sin against me and I forgive him and [c]let it go? [As many as] up to seven times?

[22]Jesus answered him, I tell you, not up to seven times, but seventy times seven! [Gen. 4:24.]

[23]Therefore the kingdom of heaven is like a human king who wished to settle accounts with his attendants.

[24]When he began the accounting, one was brought to him who owed him 10,000 talents [probably about $10,000,000],

[25]And because he could not pay, his master ordered him to be sold, with his wife and his children and everything that he possessed, and payment to be made.

[26]So the attendant fell on his knees, begging him, Have patience with me and I will pay you everything.

[27]And his master's heart was moved with compassion, and he released him and forgave him [cancelling] the debt.

[28]But that same attendant, as he went out, found one of his fellow attendants who owed him a hundred denarii [about twenty dollars]; and he caught him by the throat and said, Pay what you owe!

[29]So his fellow attendant fell down and begged him earnestly, Give me time, and I will pay you all!

[30]But he was unwilling, and he went out and had him put in prison till he should pay the debt.

[31]When his fellow attendants saw what had happened, they were greatly distressed, and they went and told everything that had taken place to their master.

[32]Then his master called him and said to him, You contemptible and wicked attendant! I forgave and cancelled all that [great] debt of yours because you begged me to.

[33]And should you not have had pity and mercy on your fellow attendant, as I had pity and mercy on you?

[34]And in wrath his master turned him over to the torturers (the jailers), till he should pay all that he owed.

[35]So also My heavenly Father will deal with every one of you if you do not freely forgive your brother from your heart his offenses.

---

[a] 15 The Greek word for *brother or sister* (*adelphos*) refers here to a fellow disciple, whether man or woman; also in verses 21 and 35.   [b] 15 Some manuscripts *sins against you*   [c] 16 Deut. 19:15   [d] 18 Or *will have been*   [e] 22 Or *seventy times seven*   [f] 24 Greek *ten thousand talents*; a talent was worth about 20 years of a day laborer's wages.   [g] 28 Greek *a hundred denarii*; a denarius was the usual daily wage of a day laborer (see 20:2).

---

[a] See footnote on Matt. 16:19.   [b] John Wycliffe, *The Wycliffe Bible*.   [c] Joseph Thayer, *A Greek-English Lexicon*.

## New International Version

### Divorce

**19** When Jesus had finished saying these things, he left Galilee and went into the region of Judea to the other side of the Jordan. ²Large crowds followed him, and he healed them there.

³Some Pharisees came to him to test him. They asked, "Is it lawful for a man to divorce his wife for any and every reason?"

⁴"Haven't you read," he replied, "that at the beginning the Creator 'made them male and female,'ᵃ ⁵and said, 'For this reason a man will leave his father and mother and be united to his wife, and the two will become one flesh'ᵇ? ⁶So they are no longer two, but one flesh. Therefore what God has joined together, let no one separate."

⁷"Why then," they asked, "did Moses command that a man give his wife a certificate of divorce and send her away?"

⁸Jesus replied, "Moses permitted you to divorce your wives because your hearts were hard. But it was not this way from the beginning. ⁹I tell you that anyone who divorces his wife, except for sexual immorality, and marries another woman commits adultery."

¹⁰The disciples said to him, "If this is the situation between a husband and wife, it is better not to marry."

¹¹Jesus replied, "Not everyone can accept this word, but only those to whom it has been given. ¹²For there are eunuchs who were born that way, and there are eunuchs who have been made eunuchs by others—and there are those who choose to live like eunuchs for the sake of the kingdom of heaven. The one who can accept this should accept it."

### The Little Children and Jesus

¹³Then people brought little children to Jesus for him to place his hands on them and pray for them. But the disciples rebuked them.

¹⁴Jesus said, "Let the little children come to me, and do not hinder them, for the kingdom of heaven belongs to such as these." ¹⁵When he had placed his hands on them, he went on from there.

### The Rich and the Kingdom of God

¹⁶Just then a man came up to Jesus and asked, "Teacher, what good thing must I do to get eternal life?"

¹⁷"Why do you ask me about what is good?" Jesus replied. "There is only One who is good. If you want to enter life, keep the commandments."

¹⁸"Which ones?" he inquired.

Jesus replied, "'You shall not murder, you shall not commit adultery, you shall not steal, you shall not give false testimony, ¹⁹honor your father and mother,'ᶜ and 'love your neighbor as yourself.'ᵈ"

²⁰"All these I have kept," the young man said. "What do I still lack?"

²¹Jesus answered, "If you want to be perfect, go, sell

## Amplified Bible

**19** Now when Jesus had finished saying these things, He left Galilee and went into the part of Judea that is beyond the Jordan;

²And great throngs accompanied Him, and He cured them there.

³And Pharisees came to Him and put Him to the test by asking, Is it lawful and right to dismiss and repudiate and divorce one's wife for any and ᵃevery cause?

⁴He replied, Have you never read that He Who made them from the beginning made them male and female,

⁵And said, For this reason a man shall leave his father and mother and shall be united firmly (joined inseparably) to his wife, and the two shall become one flesh? [Gen. 1:27; 2:24.]

⁶So they are no longer two, but one flesh. What therefore God has joined together, let not man put asunder (separate).

⁷They said to Him, Why then did Moses command [us] to give a certificate of divorce and thus to dismiss and repudiate a wife? [Deut. 24:1-4.]

⁸He said to them, Because of the hardness (stubbornness and perversity) of your hearts Moses permitted you to dismiss and repudiate and divorce your wives; but from the beginning it has not been ᵇso [ordained].

⁹I say to you: whoever dismisses (repudiates, divorces) his wife, except for unchastity, and marries another commits adultery, ᶜand he who marries a divorced woman commits adultery.

¹⁰The disciples said to Him, If the case of a man with his wife is like this, it is neither profitable nor advisable to marry.

¹¹But He said to them, Not all men can accept this saying, but it is for those to whom [the capacity to receive] it has been given.

¹²For there are eunuchs who have been born incapable of marriage; and there are eunuchs who have been made so by men; and there are eunuchs who have made themselves incapable of marriage for the sake of the kingdom of heaven. Let him who is able to accept this accept it.

¹³Then little children were brought to Jesus, that He might put His hands on them and pray; but the disciples rebuked those who brought them.

¹⁴But He said, Leave the children alone! Allow the little ones to come to Me, and do not forbid or restrain or hinder them, for of such [as these] is the kingdom of heaven composed.

¹⁵And He put His hands upon them, and then went on His way.

¹⁶And behold, there came a man up to Him, saying, Teacher, what excellent and perfectly and essentially good deed must I do to possess eternal life? [Lev. 18:5.]

¹⁷And He said to him, Why do you ask Me about the perfectly and essentially good? There is only One Who is good [perfectly and essentially]—God. If you would enter into the Life, you must continually keep the commandments.

¹⁸He said to Him, What ᵈsort of commandments? [Or, which ones?] And Jesus answered, You shall not kill, You shall not commit adultery, You shall not steal, You shall not bear false witness, [Exod. 20:12-16; Deut. 5:16-20.]

¹⁹Honor your father and your mother, and, You shall love your neighbor as [you do] yourself. [Lev. 19:18; Matt. 22:39.]

²⁰The young man said, I have observed all these from my youth; what still do I lack?

²¹Jesus answered him, If you would be perfect [that is, ᵉhave that spiritual maturity which accompanies self-sac-

---

ᵃ 4 Gen. 1:27   ᵇ 5 Gen. 2:24   ᶜ 19 Exodus 20:12-16; Deut. 5:16-20
ᵈ 19 Lev. 19:18

ᵃ Marvin Vincent, *Word Studies.*   ᵇ Joseph Thayer, *A Greek-English Lexicon.*   ᶜ Some manuscripts do not contain this phrase.   ᵈ Charles B. Williams, *The New Testament: A Translation:* "Interrogative of quality."
ᵉ Kenneth Wuest, *Word Studies.*

## New International Version

your possessions and give to the poor, and you will have treasure in heaven. Then come, follow me."

²²When the young man heard this, he went away sad, because he had great wealth.

²³Then Jesus said to his disciples, "Truly I tell you, it is hard for someone who is rich to enter the kingdom of heaven. ²⁴Again I tell you, it is easier for a camel to go through the eye of a needle than for someone who is rich to enter the kingdom of God."

²⁵When the disciples heard this, they were greatly astonished and asked, "Who then can be saved?"

²⁶Jesus looked at them and said, "With man this is impossible, but with God all things are possible."

²⁷Peter answered him, "We have left everything to follow you! What then will there be for us?"

²⁸Jesus said to them, "Truly I tell you, at the renewal of all things, when the Son of Man sits on his glorious throne, you who have followed me will also sit on twelve thrones, judging the twelve tribes of Israel. ²⁹And everyone who has left houses or brothers or sisters or father or mother or wife*a* or children or fields for my sake will receive a hundred times as much and will inherit eternal life. ³⁰But many who are first will be last, and many who are last will be first.

### The Parable of the Workers in the Vineyard

**20** "For the kingdom of heaven is like a landowner who went out early in the morning to hire workers for his vineyard. ²He agreed to pay them a denarius*b* for the day and sent them into his vineyard.

³"About nine in the morning he went out and saw others standing in the marketplace doing nothing. ⁴He told them, 'You also go and work in my vineyard, and I will pay you whatever is right.' ⁵So they went.

"He went out again about noon and about three in the afternoon and did the same thing. ⁶About five in the afternoon he went out and found still others standing around. He asked them, 'Why have you been standing here all day long doing nothing?'

⁷"'Because no one has hired us,' they answered.

"He said to them, 'You also go and work in my vineyard.'

⁸"When evening came, the owner of the vineyard said to his foreman, 'Call the workers and pay them their wages, beginning with the last ones hired and going on to the first.'

⁹"The workers who were hired about five in the afternoon came and each received a denarius. ¹⁰So when those came who were hired first, they expected to receive more. But each one of them also received a denarius. ¹¹When they received it, they began to grumble against the landowner. ¹²'These who were hired last worked only one hour,' they said, 'and you have made them equal to us who have borne the burden of the work and the heat of the day.'

¹³"But he answered one of them, 'I am not being unfair to you, friend. Didn't you agree to work for a denarius? ¹⁴Take your pay and go. I want to give the one who was hired last the same as I gave you. ¹⁵Don't I have the right

## Amplified Bible

rificing character], go and sell what you have and give to the poor, and you will have riches in heaven; and come, *a*be My disciple [side with My party and follow Me].

²²But when the young man heard this, he went away sad (grieved and in much distress), for he had great possessions.

²³And Jesus said to His disciples, Truly I say to you, it will be difficult for a rich man to get into the kingdom of heaven.

²⁴Again I tell you, it is easier for a camel to go through the eye of a needle than for a rich man to go into the kingdom of heaven.

²⁵When the disciples heard this, they were utterly puzzled (astonished, bewildered), saying, Who then can be saved [*b*from eternal death]?

²⁶But Jesus looked at them and said, With men this is impossible, but all things are possible with God. [Gen. 18:14; Job 42:2.]

²⁷Then Peter answered Him, saying, Behold, we have left [our] all and have become *a*Your disciples [sided with Your party and followed You]. What then shall we receive?

²⁸Jesus said to them, Truly I say to you, in the new age [the *c*Messianic rebirth of the world], when the Son of Man shall sit down on the throne of His glory, you who have [become My disciples, sided with My party and] followed Me will also sit on twelve thrones and judge the twelve tribes of Israel.

²⁹And anyone *and* everyone who has left houses or brothers or sisters or father or mother or children or lands for My name's sake will receive *d*many [even a hundred] times more and will inherit eternal life.

³⁰But many who [now] are first will be last [then], and many who [now] are last will be first [then].

**20** For the kingdom of heaven is like the owner of an estate who went out in the morning *e*along with the dawn to hire workmen for his vineyard.

²After agreeing with the laborers for a denarius a day, he sent them into his vineyard.

³And going out about the third hour (nine o'clock), he saw others standing idle in the marketplace;

⁴And he said to them, You go also into the vineyard, and whatever is right I will pay you. And they went.

⁵He went out again about the sixth hour (noon), and the ninth hour (three o'clock) he did the same.

⁶And about the eleventh hour (five o'clock) he went out and found still others standing around, and said to them, Why do you stand here idle all day?

⁷They answered him, Because nobody has hired us. He told them, You go out into the vineyard also *f*and you will get whatever is just and fair.

⁸When evening came, the owner of the vineyard said to his manager, Call the workmen and pay them their wages, beginning with the last and ending with the first. [Lev. 19:13; Deut. 24:15.]

⁹And those who had been hired at the eleventh hour (five o'clock) came and received a denarius each.

¹⁰Now when the first came, they supposed they would get more, but each of them also received a denarius.

¹¹And when they received it, they grumbled at the owner of the estate,

¹²Saying, These [men] who came last worked no more than an hour, and yet you have made them rank with us who have borne the burden and the *e*scorching heat of the day.

¹³But he answered one of them, Friend, I am doing you no injustice. Did you not agree with me for a denarius?

¹⁴Take what belongs to you and go. I choose to give to this man hired last the same as I give to you.

*a* Joseph Thayer, *A Greek-English Lexicon.* *b* Hermann Cremer, *Biblico-Theological Lexicon.* *c* James Moulton and George Milligan, *The Vocabulary.* *d* Some manuscripts read "manifold." *e* Marvin Vincent, *Word Studies.* *f* Some manuscripts do not contain this phrase.

*a* 29 Some manuscripts do not have *or wife.* *b* 2 A denarius was the usual daily wage of a day laborer.

## New International Version

to do what I want with my own money? Or are you envious because I am generous?'

16"So the last will be first, and the first will be last."

### Jesus Predicts His Death a Third Time

17Now Jesus was going up to Jerusalem. On the way, he took the Twelve aside and said to them, 18"We are going up to Jerusalem, and the Son of Man will be delivered over to the chief priests and the teachers of the law. They will condemn him to death 19and will hand him over to the Gentiles to be mocked and flogged and crucified. On the third day he will be raised to life!"

### A Mother's Request

20Then the mother of Zebedee's sons came to Jesus with her sons and, kneeling down, asked a favor of him.

21"What is it you want?" he asked.

She said, "Grant that one of these two sons of mine may sit at your right and the other at your left in your kingdom."

22"You don't know what you are asking," Jesus said to them. "Can you drink the cup I am going to drink?"

"We can," they answered.

23Jesus said to them, "You will indeed drink from my cup, but to sit at my right or left is not for me to grant. These places belong to those for whom they have been prepared by my Father."

24When the ten heard about this, they were indignant with the two brothers. 25Jesus called them together and said, "You know that the rulers of the Gentiles lord it over them, and their high officials exercise authority over them. 26Not so with you. Instead, whoever wants to become great among you must be your servant, 27and whoever wants to be first must be your slave— 28just as the Son of Man did not come to be served, but to serve, and to give his life as a ransom for many."

### Two Blind Men Receive Sight

29As Jesus and his disciples were leaving Jericho, a large crowd followed him. 30Two blind men were sitting by the roadside, and when they heard that Jesus was going by, they shouted, "Lord, Son of David, have mercy on us!"

31The crowd rebuked them and told them to be quiet, but they shouted all the louder, "Lord, Son of David, have mercy on us!"

32Jesus stopped and called them. "What do you want me to do for you?" he asked.

33"Lord," they answered, "we want our sight."

34Jesus had compassion on them and touched their eyes. Immediately they received their sight and followed him.

### Jesus Comes to Jerusalem as King

**21** As they approached Jerusalem and came to Bethphage on the Mount of Olives, Jesus sent two disciples, 2saying to them, "Go to the village ahead of you, and at once you will find a donkey tied there, with her colt by her. Untie them and bring them to me. 3If anyone says anything to you, say that the Lord needs them, and he will send them right away."

4This took place to fulfill what was spoken through the prophet:

5"Say to Daughter Zion,
    'See, your king comes to you,

## Amplified Bible

15Am I not permitted to do what I choose with what is mine? [Or do you begrudge my being generous?] Is your eye evil because I am good?

16So those who [now] are last will be first [then], and those who [now] are first will be last [then]. ªFor many are called, but few chosen.

17And as Jesus was going up to Jerusalem, He took the twelve disciples aside along the way and said to them,

18Behold, we are going up to Jerusalem, and the Son of Man will be handed over to the chief priests and scribes; and they will sentence Him to death

19And deliver Him over to the Gentiles to be mocked and whipped and crucified, and He will be raised [to life] on the third day.

20Then the mother of Zebedee's children came up to Him with her sons and, kneeling, worshiped Him and asked a favor of Him.

21And He asked her, What do you wish? She answered Him, Give orders that these two sons of mine may sit, one at Your right hand and one at Your left in Your kingdom.

22But Jesus replied, You do not realize what you are asking. Are you able to drink the cup that I am about to drink ªand to be baptized with the baptism with which I am baptized? They answered, We are able.

23He said to them, You will drink My cup, but seats at My right hand and at My left are not Mine to give, but they are for those for whom they have been ᵇordained and prepared by My Father.

24But when the ten [other disciples] heard this, they were indignant at the two brothers.

25And Jesus called them to Him and said, You know that the rulers of the Gentiles lord it over them, and their great men hold them in subjection [tyrannizing over them].

26Not so shall it be among you; but whoever wishes to be great among you must be your servant,

27And whoever desires to be first among you must be your slave—

28Just as the Son of Man came not to be waited on but to serve, and to give His life as a ransom for many [the price paid to set them free].

29And as they were going out of Jericho, a great throng accompanied Him.

30And behold, two blind men were sitting by the roadside, and when they heard that Jesus was passing by, they cried out, Lord, have pity and mercy on us, [You] Son of David!

31The crowds reproved them and told them to keep still; but they cried out all the more, Lord, have pity and mercy on us, [You] Son of David!

32And Jesus stopped and called them, and asked, What do you want Me to do for you?

33They answered Him, Lord, we want our eyes to be opened!

34And Jesus, in pity, touched their eyes; and instantly they received their sight and followed Him.

**21** And when they came near Jerusalem and had reached Bethphage at the Mount of Olives, Jesus sent two disciples on ahead,

2Saying to them, Go into the village that is opposite you, and at once you will find a donkey tied, and a colt with her; untie [them] and bring [them] to Me.

3If anyone says anything to you, you shall reply, The Lord needs them, and he will let them go without delay.

4This happened that what was spoken by the prophet might be fulfilled, saying,

5Say to the Daughter of Zion [inhabitants of Jerusalem], Behold, your King is coming to you, lowly and riding on

---

ª Some manuscripts do not contain this phrase. ᵇ Joseph Thayer, *A Greek-English Lexicon.*

# New International Version

gentle and riding on a donkey,
and on a colt, the foal of a donkey.' "*a*

⁶The disciples went and did as Jesus had instructed them. ⁷They brought the donkey and the colt and placed their cloaks on them for Jesus to sit on. ⁸A very large crowd spread their cloaks on the road, while others cut branches from the trees and spread them on the road. ⁹The crowds that went ahead of him and those that followed shouted,

"Hosanna*b* to the Son of David!"

"Blessed is he who comes in the name of the Lord!"*c*

"Hosanna*b* in the highest heaven!"

¹⁰When Jesus entered Jerusalem, the whole city was stirred and asked, "Who is this?"

¹¹The crowds answered, "This is Jesus, the prophet from Nazareth in Galilee."

## Jesus at the Temple

¹²Jesus entered the temple courts and drove out all who were buying and selling there. He overturned the tables of the money changers and the benches of those selling doves. ¹³"It is written," he said to them, "'My house will be called a house of prayer,'*d* but you are making it 'a den of robbers.'*e*"

¹⁴The blind and the lame came to him at the temple, and he healed them. ¹⁵But when the chief priests and the teachers of the law saw the wonderful things he did and the children shouting in the temple courts, "Hosanna to the Son of David," they were indignant.

¹⁶"Do you hear what these children are saying?" they asked him.

"Yes," replied Jesus, "have you never read,

"'From the lips of children and infants
you, Lord, have called forth your praise'*f*?"

¹⁷And he left them and went out of the city to Bethany, where he spent the night.

## Jesus Curses a Fig Tree

¹⁸Early in the morning, as Jesus was on his way back to the city, he was hungry. ¹⁹Seeing a fig tree by the road, he went up to it but found nothing on it except leaves. Then he said to it, "May you never bear fruit again!" Immediately the tree withered.

²⁰When the disciples saw this, they were amazed. "How did the fig tree wither so quickly?" they asked.

²¹Jesus replied, "Truly I tell you, if you have faith and do not doubt, not only can you do what was done to the fig tree, but also you can say to this mountain, 'Go, throw yourself into the sea,' and it will be done. ²²If you believe, you will receive whatever you ask for in prayer."

## The Authority of Jesus Questioned

²³Jesus entered the temple courts, and, while he was teaching, the chief priests and the elders of the people came to him. "By what authority are you doing these things?" they asked. "And who gave you this authority?"

²⁴Jesus replied, "I will also ask you one question. If you answer me, I will tell you by what authority I am doing

# Amplified Bible

a donkey, and on a colt, the foal of a donkey [a beast of burden]. [Isa. 62:11; Zech. 9:9.]

⁶Then the disciples went and did as Jesus had directed them.

⁷They brought the donkey and the colt and laid their coats upon them, and He seated Himself on them [the clothing].

⁸And most of the crowd kept spreading their garments on the road, and others kept cutting branches from the trees and scattering them on the road.

⁹And the crowds that went ahead of Him and those that followed Him kept shouting, Hosanna (*a*O be propitious, graciously inclined) to the Son of David, [*a*the Messiah]! Blessed (praised, glorified) is He Who comes in the name of the Lord! Hosanna (O be favorably disposed) in the highest [heaven]! [Ps. 118:26.]

¹⁰And when He entered Jerusalem, all the city became agitated and *b*[trembling with excitement] said, Who is *c*This?

¹¹And the crowds replied, This is the prophet Jesus from Nazareth of Galilee.

¹²And Jesus went into the temple (*d*whole temple enclosure) and drove out all who bought and sold in the *a*sacred place, and He turned over the *e*four-footed tables of the money changers and the chairs of those who sold doves.

¹³He said to them, The Scripture says, My house shall be called a house of prayer; but you have made it a den of robbers. [Isa. 56:7; Jer. 7:11.]

¹⁴And the blind and the lame came to Him in the *d*porches *and* courts of the temple, and He cured them.

¹⁵But when the chief priests and the scribes saw the wonderful things that He did and the boys *and* the girls *and* the *f*youths *and* the maidens crying out in the *d*porches *and* courts of the temple, Hosanna (O be propitious, graciously inclined) to the Son of David! they were indignant.

¹⁶And they said to Him, Do You hear what these are saying? And Jesus replied to them, Yes; have you never read, Out of the mouths of babes and unweaned infants You have made (provided) perfect praise? [Ps. 8:2.]

¹⁷And leaving them, He departed from the city and went out to Bethany and lodged there.

¹⁸In the early dawn the next morning, as He was coming back to the city, He was hungry.

¹⁹And as He saw *g*one single leafy fig tree *a*above the roadside, He went to it but He found nothing but leaves on it [*h*seeing that in the fig tree the fruit appears at the same time as the leaves]. And He said to it, Never again shall fruit grow on you! And the fig tree withered up at once.

²⁰When the disciples saw it, they marveled greatly and asked, How is it that the fig tree has withered away all at once?

²¹And Jesus answered them, Truly I say to you, if you have faith (a *i*firm relying trust) and do not doubt, you will not only do what has been done to the fig tree, but even if you say to this mountain, Be taken up and cast into the sea, it will be done.

²²And whatever you ask for in prayer, having faith *and* [really] believing, you will receive.

²³And when He entered the sacred *d*enclosure of the temple, the chief priests and elders of the people came up to Him as He was teaching and said, By what *a*power of authority are You doing these things, and who gave You this power of authority?

²⁴Jesus answered them, I also will ask you a question, and if you give Me the answer, then I also will tell you by what *a*power of authority I do these things.

*a* Joseph Thayer, *A Greek-English Lexicon.* *b* Literal meaning. *c* Capitalized because of what He is, the spotless Son of God, not what the speakers may have thought He was. *d* Richard Trench, *Synonyms of the New Testament.* *e* James Moulton and George Milligan, *The Vocabulary.* *f* G. Abbott-Smith, *Manual Greek Lexicon.* *g* Literal meaning. *h* James Orr et al., eds., *International Standard Bible Encyclopedia.* *i* Hermann Cremer, *Biblico-Theological Lexicon.*

*a 5* Zech. 9:9    *b 9* A Hebrew expression meaning "Save!" which became an exclamation of praise; also in verse 15    *c 9* Psalm 118:25,26    *d 13* Isaiah 56:7    *e 13* Jer. 7:11    *f 16* Psalm 8:2 (see Septuagint)

## New International Version

these things. 25John's baptism—where did it come from? Was it from heaven, or of human origin?"

They discussed it among themselves and said, "If we say, 'From heaven,' he will ask, 'Then why didn't you believe him?' 26But if we say, 'Of human origin'—we are afraid of the people, for they all hold that John was a prophet."

27So they answered Jesus, "We don't know."

Then he said, "Neither will I tell you by what authority I am doing these things.

### The Parable of the Two Sons

28"What do you think? There was a man who had two sons. He went to the first and said, 'Son, go and work today in the vineyard.'

29"'I will not,' he answered, but later he changed his mind and went.

30"Then the father went to the other son and said the same thing. He answered, 'I will, sir,' but he did not go.

31"Which of the two did what his father wanted?"

"The first," they answered.

Jesus said to them, "Truly I tell you, the tax collectors and the prostitutes are entering the kingdom of God ahead of you. 32For John came to you to show you the way of righteousness, and you did not believe him, but the tax collectors and the prostitutes did. And even after you saw this, you did not repent and believe him.

### The Parable of the Tenants

33"Listen to another parable: There was a landowner who planted a vineyard. He put a wall around it, dug a winepress in it and built a watchtower. Then he rented the vineyard to some farmers and moved to another place. 34When the harvest time approached, he sent his servants to the tenants to collect his fruit.

35"The tenants seized his servants; they beat one, killed another, and stoned a third. 36Then he sent other servants to them, more than the first time, and the tenants treated them the same way. 37Last of all, he sent his son to them. 'They will respect my son,' he said.

38"But when the tenants saw the son, they said to each other, 'This is the heir. Come, let's kill him and take his inheritance.' 39So they took him and threw him out of the vineyard and killed him.

40"Therefore, when the owner of the vineyard comes, what will he do to those tenants?"

41"He will bring those wretches to a wretched end," they replied, "and he will rent the vineyard to other tenants, who will give him his share of the crop at harvest time."

42Jesus said to them, "Have you never read in the Scriptures:

"'The stone the builders rejected
  has become the cornerstone;
the Lord has done this,
  and it is marvelous in our eyes'a?

43"Therefore I tell you that the kingdom of God will be taken away from you and given to a people who will produce its fruit. 44Anyone who falls on this stone will be broken to pieces; anyone on whom it falls will be crushed."b

45When the chief priests and the Pharisees heard Jesus' parables, they knew he was talking about them. 46They looked for a way to arrest him, but they were afraid of the crowd because the people held that he was a prophet.

## Amplified Bible

25The baptism of John—from where was it? From heaven or from men? And they reasoned and argued with one another, If we say, From heaven, aHe will ask us, Why then did you not believe him?

26But if we say, From men—we are afraid of and must reckon with the multitude, for they all regard John as a prophet.

27So they answered Jesus, We do not know. And He said to them, Neither will I tell you by what bpower of authority I do these things.

28What do you think? There was a man who had two sons. He came to the first and said, Son, go and work today in the vineyard.

29And he answered, I will not; but afterward he changed his mind and went.

30Then the man came to the second and said the same [thing]. And he replied, I will [go], sir; but he did not go.

31Which of the two did the will of the father? They replied, The first one. Jesus said to them, Truly I tell you, the tax collectors and the harlots will get into the kingdom of heaven before you.

32For John came to you walking in the way of an upright man in right standing with God, and you did not believe him, but the tax collectors and the harlots did believe him; and you, even when you saw that, did not afterward change your minds and believe him [adhere to, trust in, and rely on what he told you].

33Listen to another parable: There was a master of a house who planted a vineyard and put a hedge around it and dug a wine vat in it and built a watchtower. Then he let it out [for rent] to tenants and went into another country.

34When the fruit season drew near, he sent his servants to the tenants to get his [share of the] fruit.

35But the tenants took his servants and beat one, killed another, and stoned another.

36Again he sent other servants, more than the first time, and they treated them the same way.

37Finally he sent his own son to them, saying, They will respect and give heed to my son.

38But when the tenants saw the son, they said to themselves, This is the heir; come on, let us kill him and have his inheritance.

39And they took him and threw him out of the vineyard and killed him.

40Now when the owner of the vineyard comes back, what will he do to those tenants?

41They said to Him, He will put those wretches to a miserable death and rent the vineyard to other tenants cof such a character that they will give him the fruits promptly in their season. [Isa. 5:1-7.]

42Jesus asked them, Have you never read in the Scriptures: The very Stone which the builders rejected and threw away has become the Cornerstone; this is the Lord's doing, and it is marvelous in our eyes? [Ps. 118:22, 23.]

43I tell you, for this reason the kingdom of God will be taken away from you and given to a people who will produce the fruits of it.

44dAnd whoever falls on this Stone will be broken to pieces, but he on whom It falls will be crushed to powder [and It will bwinnow him, cscattering him like dust]. [Isa. 8:14; Dan. 2:34, 35.]

45And when the chief priests and the Pharisees heard His parables (comparisons, stories used to illustrate and explain), they perceived that He was talking about them.

46And although they were trying to arrest Him, they feared the throngs because they regarded Him as a prophet.

a Capitalized because of what He is, the spotless Son of God, not what the speakers may have thought He was.  b Joseph Thayer, A Greek-English Lexicon.  c Marvin Vincent, Word Studies.  d Some manuscripts do not contain verse 44.

a 42 Psalm 118:22,23    b 44 Some manuscripts do not have verse 44.

## New International Version

### The Parable of the Wedding Banquet

**22** Jesus spoke to them again in parables, saying: 2 "The kingdom of heaven is like a king who prepared a wedding banquet for his son. 3 He sent his servants to those who had been invited to the banquet to tell them to come, but they refused to come.

4 "Then he sent some more servants and said, 'Tell those who have been invited that I have prepared my dinner: My oxen and fattened cattle have been butchered, and everything is ready. Come to the wedding banquet.'

5 "But they paid no attention and went off—one to his field, another to his business. 6 The rest seized his servants, mistreated them and killed them. 7 The king was enraged. He sent his army and destroyed those murderers and burned their city.

8 "Then he said to his servants, 'The wedding banquet is ready, but those I invited did not deserve to come. 9 So go to the street corners and invite to the banquet anyone you find.' 10 So the servants went out into the streets and gathered all the people they could find, the bad as well as the good, and the wedding hall was filled with guests.

11 "But when the king came in to see the guests, he noticed a man there who was not wearing wedding clothes. 12 He asked, 'How did you get in here without wedding clothes, friend?' The man was speechless.

13 "Then the king told the attendants, 'Tie him hand and foot, and throw him outside, into the darkness, where there will be weeping and gnashing of teeth.'

14 "For many are invited, but few are chosen."

### Paying the Imperial Tax to Caesar

15 Then the Pharisees went out and laid plans to trap him in his words. 16 They sent their disciples to him along with the Herodians. "Teacher," they said, "we know that you are a man of integrity and that you teach the way of God in accordance with the truth. You aren't swayed by others, because you pay no attention to who they are. 17 Tell us then, what is your opinion? Is it right to pay the imperial tax[a] to Caesar or not?"

18 But Jesus, knowing their evil intent, said, "You hypocrites, why are you trying to trap me? 19 Show me the coin used for paying the tax." They brought him a denarius, 20 and he asked them, "Whose image is this? And whose inscription?"

21 "Caesar's," they replied.

Then he said to them, "So give back to Caesar what is Caesar's, and to God what is God's."

22 When they heard this, they were amazed. So they left him and went away.

### Marriage at the Resurrection

23 That same day the Sadducees, who say there is no resurrection, came to him with a question. 24 "Teacher," they said, "Moses told us that if a man dies without having children, his brother must marry the widow and raise up

## Amplified Bible

**22** And again Jesus spoke to them in parables (comparisons, stories used to illustrate and explain), saying,

2 The kingdom of heaven is like a king who gave a wedding banquet for his son

3 And sent his servants to summon those who had been invited to the wedding banquet, but they refused to come.

4 Again he sent other servants, saying, Tell those who are invited, Behold, I have prepared my banquet; my bullocks and my fat calves are killed, and everything is prepared; come to the wedding feast.

5 But they were not concerned *and* paid no attention [they ignored and made light of the summons, treating it with contempt] and they went away—one to his farm, another to his business,

6 While the others seized his servants, treated them shamefully, and put them to death.

7 [Hearing this] the king was infuriated; and he sent his soldiers and put those murderers to death and burned their city.

8 Then he said to his servants, The wedding [feast] is prepared, but those invited were not worthy.

9 So go to the thoroughfares where they leave the city [where the main roads and those from the country end] and invite to the wedding feast as many as you find.

10 And those servants went out on the crossroads and got together as many as they found, both bad and good, so [the room in which] the wedding feast [was held] was filled with guests.

11 But when the king came in to view the guests, he looked intently at a man there who had on no wedding garment.

12 And he said, Friend, how did you come in here without putting on the [appropriate] wedding garment? And he was speechless (*a*muzzled, gagged).

13 Then the king said to the attendants, Tie him hand and foot, and throw him into the darkness outside; there will be weeping and grinding of teeth.

14 For many are called (invited and summoned), but few *are* chosen.

15 Then the Pharisees went and consulted *and* plotted together how they might entangle Jesus in His talk.

16 And they sent their disciples to Him along with the Herodians, saying, Teacher, we know that You are *b*sincere *and* what You profess to be and that You teach the way of God truthfully, regardless of consequences *and* being afraid of no man; for You are impartial *and* do not regard either the person *or* the position of anyone.

17 Tell us then what You think about this: Is it lawful to pay tribute [levied on individuals and to be paid yearly] to Caesar or not?

18 But Jesus, aware of their malicious plot, asked, Why do you put Me to the test *and* try to entrap Me, you pretenders (hypocrites)?

19 Show me the money *used* for the tribute. And they brought Him a denarius.

20 And Jesus said to them, Whose likeness and title are these?

21 They said, Caesar's. Then He said to them, Pay therefore to Caesar the things that are due to Caesar, and pay to God the things that are due to God.

22 When they heard it they were amazed *and* marveled; and they left Him and departed.

23 The same day some Sadducees, who say that there is no resurrection [of the dead], came to Him and they asked Him a question,

24 Saying, Teacher, Moses said, If a man dies, leaving no children, his brother shall marry the widow and raise up a family for his brother. [Deut. 25:5.]

---

*a* 17 A special tax levied on subject peoples, not on Roman citizens

*a* Literal translation. *b* Hermann Cremer, *Biblico-Theological Lexicon*.

## New International Version

offspring for him. 25Now there were seven brothers among us. The first one married and died, and since he had no children, he left his wife to his brother. 26The same thing happened to the second and third brother, right on down to the seventh. 27Finally, the woman died. 28Now then, at the resurrection, whose wife will she be of the seven, since all of them were married to her?"

29Jesus replied, "You are in error because you do not know the Scriptures or the power of God. 30At the resurrection people will neither marry nor be given in marriage; they will be like the angels in heaven. 31But about the resurrection of the dead—have you not read what God said to you, 32'I am the God of Abraham, the God of Isaac, and the God of Jacob'ᵃ? He is not the God of the dead but of the living."

33When the crowds heard this, they were astonished at his teaching.

### The Greatest Commandment

34Hearing that Jesus had silenced the Sadducees, the Pharisees got together. 35One of them, an expert in the law, tested him with this question: 36"Teacher, which is the greatest commandment in the Law?"

37Jesus replied: "'Love the Lord your God with all your heart and with all your soul and with all your mind.'ᵇ 38This is the first and greatest commandment. 39And the second is like it: 'Love your neighbor as yourself.'ᶜ 40All the Law and the Prophets hang on these two commandments."

### Whose Son Is the Messiah?

41While the Pharisees were gathered together, Jesus asked them, 42"What do you think about the Messiah? Whose son is he?"

"The son of David," they replied.

43He said to them, "How is it then that David, speaking by the Spirit, calls him 'Lord'? For he says,

44 "'The Lord said to my Lord:
   "Sit at my right hand
until I put your enemies
   under your feet."'ᵈ

45If then David calls him 'Lord,' how can he be his son?" 46No one could say a word in reply, and from that day on no one dared to ask him any more questions.

### A Warning Against Hypocrisy

**23** Then Jesus said to the crowds and to his disciples: 2"The teachers of the law and the Pharisees sit in Moses' seat. 3So you must be careful to do everything they tell you. But do not do what they do, for they do not practice what they preach. 4They tie up heavy, cumbersome loads and put them on other people's shoulders, but they themselves are not willing to lift a finger to move them.

5"Everything they do is done for people to see: They make their phylacteriesᵉ wide and the tassels on their garments long; 6they love the place of honor at banquets and the most important seats in the synagogues; 7they love to be greeted with respect in the marketplaces and to be called 'Rabbi' by others.

8"But you are not to be called 'Rabbi,' for you have one Teacher, and you are all brothers. 9And do not call any-

## Amplified Bible

25Now there were seven brothers among us; the first married and died, and, having no children, left his wife to his brother.

26The second also died childless, and the third, down to the seventh.

27Last of all, the woman died also.

28Now, in the resurrection, to which of the seven will she be wife? For they all had her.

29But Jesus replied to them, You are wrong because you know neither the Scriptures nor God's power.

30For in the resurrected state neither do [men] marry nor are [women] given in marriage, but they are like the angels in heaven.

31But as to the resurrection of the dead—have you never read what was said to you by God,

32I am the God of Abraham, and the God of Isaac, and the God of Jacob? He is not the God of the dead but of the living! [Exod. 3:6.]

33And when the throng heard it, they were astonished *and* filled with [ᵃglad] amazement at His teaching.

34Now when the Pharisees heard that He had silenced (ᵇmuzzled) the Sadducees, they gathered together.

35And one of their number, a lawyer, asked Him a question to test Him.

36Teacher, which ᶜkind of commandment is great and important (the principal kind) in the Law? [Some commandments are light—which are heavy?]

37And He replied to him, You shall love the Lord your God with all your heart and with all your soul and with all your mind (intellect). [Deut. 6:5.]

38This is the great (most important, principal) and first commandment.

39And a second is like it: You shall love your neighbor as [you do] yourself. [Lev. 19:18.]

40These two commandments ᵃsum up *and* upon them depend all the Law and the Prophets.

41Now while the Pharisees were still assembled there, Jesus asked them a question,

42Saying, What do you think of the Christ? Whose Son is He? They said to Him, The Son of David.

43He said to them, How is it then that David, under the influence of the [Holy] Spirit, calls Him Lord, saying,

44The Lord said to My Lord, Sit at My right hand until I put Your enemies under Your feet? [Ps. 110:1.]

45If then David thus calls Him Lord, how is He his Son?

46And no one was able to answer Him a word, nor from that day did anyone venture *or* dare to question Him.

**23** Then Jesus said to the multitudes and to His disciples,

2The scribes and Pharisees sit on Moses' seat [of authority].

3So observe and practice all they tell you; but do not do what they do, for they preach, but do not practice.

4They tie up heavy loads, *hard to bear,* and place them on men's shoulders, but they themselves will not lift a finger to help bear them.

5They do all their works to be seen of men; for they make wide their phylacteries (ᵈsmall cases enclosing certain Scripture passages, worn during prayer on the left arm and forehead) and make long their fringes [worn by all male Israelites, according to the command]. [Exod. 13:9; Num. 15:38; Deut. 6:8.]

6And they ᵉtake pleasure in *and* [thus] love the place of honor at feasts and the best seats in the synagogues,

7And to be greeted with honor in the marketplaces and to have people call them rabbi.

8But you are not to be called rabbi (teacher), for you have one Teacher and you are all brothers.

---

ᵃ 32 Exodus 3:6   ᵇ 37 Deut. 6:5   ᶜ 39 Lev. 19:18   ᵈ 44 Psalm 110:1
ᵉ 5 That is, boxes containing Scripture verses, worn on forehead and arm

ᵃ Joseph Thayer, *A Greek-English Lexicon.*   ᵇ Literal translation.
ᶜ Marvin Vincent, *Word Studies.*   ᵈ John D. Davis, *A Dictionary of the Bible.*   ᵉ Kenneth Wuest, *Word Studies.*

## New International Version

one on earth 'father,' for you have one Father, and he is in heaven. ¹⁰Nor are you to be called instructors, for you have one Instructor, the Messiah. ¹¹The greatest among you will be your servant. ¹²For those who exalt themselves will be humbled, and those who humble themselves will be exalted.

### Seven Woes on the Teachers of the Law and the Pharisees

¹³"Woe to you, teachers of the law and Pharisees, you hypocrites! You shut the door of the kingdom of heaven in people's faces. You yourselves do not enter, nor will you let those enter who are trying to. [14]ᵃ

¹⁵"Woe to you, teachers of the law and Pharisees, you hypocrites! You travel over land and sea to win a single convert, and when you have succeeded, you make them twice as much a child of hell as you are.

¹⁶"Woe to you, blind guides! You say, 'If anyone swears by the temple, it means nothing; but anyone who swears by the gold of the temple is bound by that oath.' ¹⁷You blind fools! Which is greater: the gold, or the temple that makes the gold sacred? ¹⁸You also say, 'If anyone swears by the altar, it means nothing; but anyone who swears by the gift on the altar is bound by that oath.' ¹⁹You blind men! Which is greater: the gift, or the altar that makes the gift sacred? ²⁰Therefore, anyone who swears by the altar swears by it and by everything on it. ²¹And anyone who swears by the temple swears by it and by the one who dwells in it. ²²And anyone who swears by heaven swears by God's throne and by the one who sits on it.

²³"Woe to you, teachers of the law and Pharisees, you hypocrites! You give a tenth of your spices—mint, dill and cumin. But you have neglected the more important matters of the law—justice, mercy and faithfulness. You should have practiced the latter, without neglecting the former. ²⁴You blind guides! You strain out a gnat but swallow a camel.

²⁵"Woe to you, teachers of the law and Pharisees, you hypocrites! You clean the outside of the cup and dish, but inside they are full of greed and self-indulgence. ²⁶Blind Pharisee! First clean the inside of the cup and dish, and then the outside also will be clean.

²⁷"Woe to you, teachers of the law and Pharisees, you hypocrites! You are like whitewashed tombs, which look beautiful on the outside but on the inside are full of the bones of the dead and everything unclean. ²⁸In the same way, on the outside you appear to people as righteous but on the inside you are full of hypocrisy and wickedness.

²⁹"Woe to you, teachers of the law and Pharisees, you hypocrites! You build tombs for the prophets and decorate the graves of the righteous. ³⁰And you say, 'If we had lived in the days of our ancestors, we would not have taken part with them in shedding the blood of the prophets.' ³¹So you

## Amplified Bible

⁹And do not call anyone [in the church] on earth father, for you have one Father, Who is in heaven.

¹⁰And you must not be called masters (leaders), for you have one Master (Leader), the Christ.

¹¹He who is greatest among you shall be your servant.

¹²Whoever exalts himself [ᵃwith haughtiness and empty pride] shall be humbled (brought low), and whoever humbles himself [whoever has a modest opinion of himself and behaves accordingly] shall be ᵃraised to honor.

¹³But woe to you, scribes and Pharisees, pretenders (hypocrites)! For you shut the kingdom of heaven in men's faces; for you neither enter yourselves, nor do you allow those who are about to go in to do so.

¹⁴ᵇ*Woe to you, scribes and Pharisees, pretenders (hypocrites)! For you swallow up widows' houses and for a pretense to cover it up make long prayers; therefore you will receive the greater condemnation and the heavier sentence.*

¹⁵Woe to you, scribes and Pharisees, pretenders (hypocrites)! For you travel over sea and land to make a single proselyte, and when he becomes one [a proselyte], you make him doubly as much a child of hell (Gehenna) as you are.

¹⁶Woe to you, blind guides, who say, If anyone swears by the ᶜsanctuary of the temple, it is nothing; but if anyone swears by the gold of the ᶜsanctuary, he is a debtor [bound by his oath].

¹⁷You blind fools! For which is greater: the gold, or the ᶜsanctuary of the temple that has made the gold sacred? [Exod. 30:29.]

¹⁸You say too, Whoever swears by the altar is not duty bound; but whoever swears by the offering on the altar, his oath is binding.

¹⁹You blind men! Which is greater: the gift, or the altar which makes the gift sacred?

²⁰So whoever swears by the altar swears by it and by everything on it.

²¹And he who swears by the ᶜsanctuary of the temple swears by it and by Him Who dwells in it. [I Kings 8:13; Ps. 26:8.]

²²And whoever swears by heaven swears by the throne of God and by Him Who sits upon it.

²³Woe to you, scribes and Pharisees, pretenders (hypocrites)! For you give a tenth of your mint and dill and cummin, and have neglected *and* omitted the weightier (more important) matters of the Law—right *and* justice and mercy and fidelity. These you ought [particularly] to have done, without neglecting the others.

²⁴You blind guides, filtering out a gnat and gulping down a ᵈcamel! [Lev. 27:30; Mic. 6:8.]

²⁵Woe to you, scribes and Pharisees, pretenders (hypocrites)! For you clean the outside of the cup and of the plate, but within they are full of extortion (prey, spoil, plunder) and grasping self-indulgence.

²⁶You blind Pharisee! First clean the inside of the cup and of the plate, so that the outside may be clean also.

²⁷Woe to you, scribes and Pharisees, pretenders (hypocrites)! For you are like tombs that have been whitewashed, which look beautiful on the outside but inside are full of dead men's bones and everything impure.

²⁸Just so, you also outwardly seem to people to be just *and* upright but inside you are full of pretense and lawlessness *and* iniquity. [Ps. 5:9.]

²⁹Woe to you, scribes and Pharisees, pretenders (hypocrites)! For you build tombs for the prophets and decorate the monuments of the righteous,

³⁰Saying, If we had lived in the days of our forefathers, we would not have aided them in shedding the blood of the prophets.

---

ᵃ 14 Some manuscripts include here words similar to Mark 12:40 and Luke 20:47.

ᵃ Joseph Thayer, *A Greek-English Lexicon.* ᵇ Some manuscripts do not contain verse 14. ᶜ Richard Trench, *Synonyms of the New Testament.* ᵈ The camel was also unclean, one of the largest of unclean animals, whereas the gnat was the smallest of unclean animals (Lev. 11:4).

## New International Version

testify against yourselves that you are the descendants of those who murdered the prophets. [32]Go ahead, then, and complete what your ancestors started!

[33]"You snakes! You brood of vipers! How will you escape being condemned to hell? [34]Therefore I am sending you prophets and sages and teachers. Some of them you will kill and crucify; others you will flog in your synagogues and pursue from town to town. [35]And so upon you will come all the righteous blood that has been shed on earth, from the blood of righteous Abel to the blood of Zechariah son of Berekiah, whom you murdered between the temple and the altar. [36]Truly I tell you, all this will come on this generation.

[37]"Jerusalem, Jerusalem, you who kill the prophets and stone those sent to you, how often I have longed to gather your children together, as a hen gathers her chicks under her wings, and you were not willing. [38]Look, your house is left to you desolate. [39]For I tell you, you will not see me again until you say, 'Blessed is he who comes in the name of the Lord.'[a]"

### The Destruction of the Temple and Signs of the End Times

**24** Jesus left the temple and was walking away when his disciples came up to him to call his attention to its buildings. [2]"Do you see all these things?" he asked. "Truly I tell you, not one stone here will be left on another; every one will be thrown down."

[3]As Jesus was sitting on the Mount of Olives, the disciples came to him privately. "Tell us," they said, "when will this happen, and what will be the sign of your coming and of the end of the age?"

[4]Jesus answered: "Watch out that no one deceives you. [5]For many will come in my name, claiming, 'I am the Messiah,' and will deceive many. [6]You will hear of wars and rumors of wars, but see to it that you are not alarmed. Such things must happen, but the end is still to come. [7]Nation will rise against nation, and kingdom against kingdom. There will be famines and earthquakes in various places. [8]All these are the beginning of birth pains.

[9]"Then you will be handed over to be persecuted and put to death, and you will be hated by all nations because of me. [10]At that time many will turn away from the faith and will betray and hate each other, [11]and many false prophets will appear and deceive many people. [12]Because of the increase of wickedness, the love of most will grow cold, [13]but the one who stands firm to the end will be

## Amplified Bible

[31]Thus you are testifying against yourselves that you are the descendants of those who murdered the prophets.

[32]Fill up, then, the measure of your fathers' sins to the brim [so [a]that nothing may be wanting to a full measure].

[33]You serpents! You spawn of vipers! How can you escape the [a]penalty to be suffered in hell (Gehenna)?

[34]Because of this, take notice: I am sending you prophets and wise men (interpreters and teachers) and scribes (men learned in the Mosaic Law and the Prophets); some of them you will kill, even crucify, and some you will flog in your synagogues and pursue and persecute from town to town,

[35]So that upon your heads may come all the blood of the righteous ([b]those who correspond to the divine standard of right) shed on earth, from the blood of the righteous Abel to the blood of Zechariah son of Barachiah, whom you murdered between the sanctuary and the altar [of burnt offering]. [Gen. 4:8; II Chron. 24:21.]

[36]Truly I declare to you, all these [[a]evil, calamitous times] will come upon this generation. [II Chron. 36:15, 16.]

[37]O Jerusalem, Jerusalem, murdering the prophets and stoning those who are sent to you! How often would I have gathered your children together as a mother fowl gathers her brood under her wings, and you refused!

[38]Behold, your house is forsaken and desolate (abandoned and left destitute of God's help). [I Kings 9:7; Jer. 22:5.]

[39]For I declare to you, you will not see Me again until you say, Blessed (magnified in worship, adored, and exalted) is He Who comes in the name of the Lord! [Ps. 118:26.]

**24** Jesus departed from the temple [c]area and was going on His way when His disciples came up to Him to call His attention to the buildings of the temple and point them out to Him.

[2]But He answered them, Do you see all these? Truly I tell you, there will not be left here one stone upon another that will not be thrown down.

[3]While He was seated on the Mount of Olives, the disciples came to Him privately and said, Tell us, when will this take place, and what will be the sign of Your coming and of the end (the completion, the consummation) of the age?

[4]Jesus answered them, Be careful that no one misleads you [deceiving you and leading you into error].

[5]For many will come in (on the strength of) My name, [[a]appropriating the name which belongs to Me], saying, I am the Christ (the Messiah), and they will lead many astray.

[6]And you will hear of wars and rumors of wars; see that you are not frightened or troubled, for this must take place, but the end is not yet.

[7]For nation will rise against nation, and kingdom against kingdom, and there will be famines and earthquakes in place after place;

[8]All this is but the beginning [the early pains] of the [d]birth pangs [of the [a]intolerable anguish].

[9]Then they will hand you over to suffer affliction and tribulation and put you to death, and you will be hated by all nations for My name's sake.

[10]And then many will be offended and repelled and will [a]begin to distrust and desert [Him Whom they ought to trust and obey] and will stumble and fall away and betray one another and pursue one another with hatred.

[11]And many false prophets will rise up and deceive and lead many into error.

[12]And the love of [e]the great body of people will grow cold because of the multiplied lawlessness and iniquity,

[13]But he who endures to the end will be saved.

[a] Joseph Thayer, *A Greek-English Lexicon.* [b] G. Abbott-Smith, *Manual Greek Lexicon.* [c] Richard Trench, *Synonyms of the New Testament.* [d] Literal translation. [e] Marvin Vincent, *Word Studies.*

## New International Version

saved. [14]And this gospel of the kingdom will be preached in the whole world as a testimony to all nations, and then the end will come.

[15]"So when you see standing in the holy place 'the abomination that causes desolation,'[a] spoken of through the prophet Daniel—let the reader understand— [16]then let those who are in Judea flee to the mountains. [17]Let no one on the housetop go down to take anything out of the house. [18]Let no one in the field go back to get their cloak. [19]How dreadful it will be in those days for pregnant women and nursing mothers! [20]Pray that your flight will not take place in winter or on the Sabbath. [21]For then there will be great distress, unequaled from the beginning of the world until now—and never to be equaled again.

[22]"If those days had not been cut short, no one would survive, but for the sake of the elect those days will be shortened. [23]At that time if anyone says to you, 'Look, here is the Messiah!' or, 'There he is!' do not believe it. [24]For false messiahs and false prophets will appear and perform great signs and wonders to deceive, if possible, even the elect. [25]See, I have told you ahead of time.

[26]"So if anyone tells you, 'There he is, out in the wilderness,' do not go out; or, 'Here he is, in the inner rooms,' do not believe it. [27]For as lightning that comes from the east is visible even in the west, so will be the coming of the Son of Man. [28]Wherever there is a carcass, there the vultures will gather.

[29]"Immediately after the distress of those days

"'the sun will be darkened,
    and the moon will not give its light;
the stars will fall from the sky,
    and the heavenly bodies will be shaken.'[b]

[30]"Then will appear the sign of the Son of Man in heaven. And then all the peoples of the earth[c] will mourn when they see the Son of Man coming on the clouds of heaven, with power and great glory.[d] [31]And he will send his angels with a loud trumpet call, and they will gather his elect from the four winds, from one end of the heavens to the other.

[32]"Now learn this lesson from the fig tree: As soon as its twigs get tender and its leaves come out, you know that summer is near. [33]Even so, when you see all these things, you know that it[e] is near, right at the door. [34]Truly I tell you, this generation will certainly not pass away until all these things have happened. [35]Heaven and earth will pass away, but my words will never pass away.

### The Day and Hour Unknown

[36]"But about that day or hour no one knows, not even the angels in heaven, nor the Son,[f] but only the Father.

## Amplified Bible

[14]And this good news of the kingdom (the Gospel) will be preached throughout the whole world as a testimony to all the nations, and then will come the end.

[15]So when you see the appalling sacrilege [the abomination that astonishes and makes desolate], spoken of by the prophet Daniel, standing in the Holy Place—let the reader take notice and *ponder and consider and heed [this]— [Dan. 9:27; 11:31; 12:11.]

[16]Then let those who are in Judea flee to the mountains;

[17]Let him who is on the housetop not come down *and go into the house to take anything;

[18]And let him who is in the field not turn back to get his overcoat.

[19]And alas for the women who are pregnant and for those who have nursing babies in those days!

[20]Pray that your flight may not be in winter or on a Sabbath.

[21]For then there will be great tribulation (affliction, distress, and oppression) such as has not been from the beginning of the world until now—no, and never will be [again]. [Dan. 12:1; Joel 2:2.]

[22]And if those days had not been shortened, no human being would endure *and survive, but for the sake of the elect (God's chosen ones) those days will be shortened.

[23]If anyone says to you then, Behold, here is the Christ (the Messiah)! or, There He is!—do not believe it.

[24]For false Christs and false prophets will arise, and they will show great signs and wonders so as to deceive *and lead astray, if possible, even the elect (God's chosen ones).

[25]See, I have warned you beforehand.

[26]So if they say to you, Behold, He is in the wilderness (desert)—do not go out there; if they tell you, Behold, He is in the secret places *or inner rooms—do not believe it.

[27]For just as the lightning flashes from the east and shines *and [b]is seen as far as the west, so will the coming of the Son of Man be.

[28]Wherever there is a fallen body (a corpse), there the vultures (or eagles) will flock together. [Job 39:30.]

[29]Immediately after the tribulation of those days the sun will be darkened, and the moon will not shed its light, and the stars will fall from the sky, and the powers of the heavens will be shaken. [Isa. 13:10; 34:4; Joel 2:10, 11; Zeph. 1:15.]

[30]Then the sign of the Son of Man will appear in the sky, and then all the tribes of the earth will mourn *and [b]beat their breasts *and lament in anguish, and they will see the Son of Man coming on the clouds of heaven with power and great glory [in brilliancy and splendor]. [Dan. 7:13; Rev. 1:7.]

[31]And He will send out His angels with a loud trumpet call, and they will gather His elect (His chosen ones) from the four winds, [even] from one end of the [c]universe to the other. [Isa. 27:13; Zech. 9:14.]

[32]From the fig tree learn this lesson: as soon as its [b]young shoots become soft and tender and it puts out its leaves, you know [a]of a surety that summer is near.

[33]So also when you see these signs, [a]all taken together, coming to pass, you may know [a]of a surety that He is near, at the very doors.

[34]Truly I tell you, this generation ([a]the whole multitude of people living at the same time, [d]in a definite, [c]given period) will not pass away till all these things [a]taken together take place.

[35][e]Sky and earth will pass away, but My words will not pass away.

[36]But of that [exact] day and hour no one knows, not even the angels of heaven, nor the Son, but only the Father.

---

[a] 15 Daniel 9:27; 11:31; 12:11   [b] 29 Isaiah 13:10; 34:4   [c] 30 Or the tribes of the land   [d] 30 See Daniel 7:13-14.   [e] 33 Or he   [f] 36 Some manuscripts do not have *nor the Son*.

[a] Joseph Thayer, *A Greek-English Lexicon*.   [b] Marvin Vincent, *Word Studies*.   [c] G. Abbott-Smith, *Manual Greek Lexicon*.   [d] Hermann Cremer, *Biblico-Theological Lexicon*.   [e] James Moulton and George Milligan, *The Vocabulary*.

## New International Version

37As it was in the days of Noah, so it will be at the coming of the Son of Man. 38For in the days before the flood, people were eating and drinking, marrying and giving in marriage, up to the day Noah entered the ark; 39and they knew nothing about what would happen until the flood came and took them all away. That is how it will be at the coming of the Son of Man. 40Two men will be in the field; one will be taken and the other left. 41Two women will be grinding with a hand mill; one will be taken and the other left.

42"Therefore keep watch, because you do not know on what day your Lord will come. 43But understand this: If the owner of the house had known at what time of night the thief was coming, he would have kept watch and would not have let his house be broken into. 44So you also must be ready, because the Son of Man will come at an hour when you do not expect him.

45"Who then is the faithful and wise servant, whom the master has put in charge of the servants in his household to give them their food at the proper time? 46It will be good for that servant whose master finds him doing so when he returns. 47Truly I tell you, he will put him in charge of all his possessions. 48But suppose that servant is wicked and says to himself, 'My master is staying away a long time,' 49and he then begins to beat his fellow servants and to eat and drink with drunkards. 50The master of that servant will come on a day when he does not expect him and at an hour he is not aware of. 51He will cut him to pieces and assign him a place with the hypocrites, where there will be weeping and gnashing of teeth.

### The Parable of the Ten Virgins

**25** "At that time the kingdom of heaven will be like ten virgins who took their lamps and went out to meet the bridegroom. 2Five of them were foolish and five were wise. 3The foolish ones took their lamps but did not take any oil with them. 4The wise ones, however, took oil in jars along with their lamps. 5The bridegroom was a long time in coming, and they all became drowsy and fell asleep.

6"At midnight the cry rang out: 'Here's the bridegroom! Come out to meet him!'

7"Then all the virgins woke up and trimmed their lamps. 8The foolish ones said to the wise, 'Give us some of your oil; our lamps are going out.'

9"'No,' they replied, 'there may not be enough for both us and you. Instead, go to those who sell oil and buy some for yourselves.'

10"But while they were on their way to buy the oil, the bridegroom arrived. The virgins who were ready went in with him to the wedding banquet. And the door was shut.

11"Later the others also came. 'Lord, Lord,' they said, 'open the door for us!'

## Amplified Bible

37As were the days of Noah, so will be the coming of the Son of Man.

38For just as in those days before the flood they were eating and drinking, [men] marrying and [women] being given in marriage, until the [very] day when Noah went into the ark,

39And they did not know or understand until the flood came and swept them all away—so will be the coming of the Son of Man. [Gen. 6:5-8; 7:6-24.]

40At that time two men will be in the field; one will be taken and one will be left.

41Two women will be grinding at the hand mill; one will be taken and one will be left.

42Watch therefore [[a]give strict attention, be cautious and active], for you do not know in what kind of a day [[b]whether a near or remote one] your Lord is coming.

43But understand this: had the householder known in what [part of the night, whether in a [b]night or a morning] watch the thief was coming, he would have watched and would not have allowed his house to be [c]undermined and broken into.

44You also must be ready therefore, for the Son of Man is coming at an hour when you do not expect Him.

45Who then is the faithful, thoughtful, and wise servant, whom his master has put in charge of his household to give to the others the food and supplies at the proper time?

46Blessed (happy, fortunate, and [d]to be envied) is that servant whom, when his master comes, he will find so doing.

47I solemnly declare to you, he will set him over all his possessions.

48But if that servant is wicked and says to himself, My master is delayed and is going to be gone a long time,

49And begins to beat his fellow servants and to eat and drink with the drunken,

50The master of that servant will come on a day when he does not expect him and at an hour of which he is not aware,

51And will punish him [[a]cut him up by scourging] and put him with the pretenders (hypocrites); there will be weeping and grinding of teeth.

**25** Then the kingdom of heaven shall be likened to ten virgins who took their lamps and went to meet the bridegroom.

2Five of them were foolish (thoughtless, without forethought) and five were wise (sensible, intelligent, and prudent).

3For when the foolish took their lamps, they did not take any [extra] oil with them;

4But the wise took flasks of oil along with them [also] with their lamps.

5While the bridegroom lingered and was slow in coming, they all began nodding their heads, and they fell asleep.

6But at midnight there was a shout, Behold, the bridegroom! Go out to meet him!

7Then all those virgins got up and put their own lamps in order.

8And the foolish said to the wise, Give us some of your oil, for our lamps are going out.

9But the wise replied, There will not be enough for us and for you; go instead to the dealers and buy for yourselves.

10But while they were going away to buy, the bridegroom came, and those who were prepared went in with him to the marriage feast; and the door was shut.

11Later the other virgins also came and said, Lord, Lord, open [the door] to us!

[a] Joseph Thayer, *A Greek-English Lexicon*. [b] Marvin Vincent, *Word Studies*. [c] John Wycliffe, *The Wycliffe Bible*. [d] Alexander Souter, *Pocket Lexicon*.

## New International Version

<sup>12</sup>"But he replied, 'Truly I tell you, I don't know you.'
<sup>13</sup>"Therefore keep watch, because you do not know the day or the hour.

### The Parable of the Bags of Gold

<sup>14</sup>"Again, it will be like a man going on a journey, who called his servants and entrusted his wealth to them. <sup>15</sup>To one he gave five bags of gold, to another two bags, and to another one bag,[a] each according to his ability. Then he went on his journey. <sup>16</sup>The man who had received five bags of gold went at once and put his money to work and gained five bags more. <sup>17</sup>So also, the one with two bags of gold gained two more. <sup>18</sup>But the man who had received one bag went off, dug a hole in the ground and hid his master's money.

<sup>19</sup>"After a long time the master of those servants returned and settled accounts with them. <sup>20</sup>The man who had received five bags of gold brought the other five. 'Master,' he said, 'you entrusted me with five bags of gold. See, I have gained five more.'

<sup>21</sup>"His master replied, 'Well done, good and faithful servant! You have been faithful with a few things; I will put you in charge of many things. Come and share your master's happiness!'

<sup>22</sup>"The man with two bags of gold also came. 'Master,' he said, 'you entrusted me with two bags of gold; see, I have gained two more.'

<sup>23</sup>"His master replied, 'Well done, good and faithful servant! You have been faithful with a few things; I will put you in charge of many things. Come and share your master's happiness!'

<sup>24</sup>"Then the man who had received one bag of gold came. 'Master,' he said, 'I knew that you are a hard man, harvesting where you have not sown and gathering where you have not scattered seed. <sup>25</sup>So I was afraid and went out and hid your gold in the ground. See, here is what belongs to you.'

<sup>26</sup>"His master replied, 'You wicked, lazy servant! So you knew that I harvest where I have not sown and gather where I have not scattered seed? <sup>27</sup>Well then, you should have put my money on deposit with the bankers, so that when I returned I would have received it back with interest.

<sup>28</sup>"So take the bag of gold from him and give it to the one who has ten bags. <sup>29</sup>For whoever has will be given more, and they will have an abundance. Whoever does not have, even what they have will be taken from them. <sup>30</sup>And throw that worthless servant outside, into the darkness, where there will be weeping and gnashing of teeth.'

### The Sheep and the Goats

<sup>31</sup>"When the Son of Man comes in his glory, and all the angels with him, he will sit on his glorious throne. <sup>32</sup>All the nations will be gathered before him, and he will separate the people one from another as a shepherd separates the sheep from the goats. <sup>33</sup>He will put the sheep on his right and the goats on his left.

<sup>34</sup>"Then the King will say to those on his right, 'Come, you who are blessed by my Father; take your inheritance, the kingdom prepared for you since the creation of the

## Amplified Bible

<sup>12</sup>But He replied, I solemnly declare to you, I do not know you [I am not acquainted with you].

<sup>13</sup>Watch therefore [give strict attention and be cautious and active], for you know neither the day nor the hour *when the Son of Man will come.*

<sup>14</sup>For it is like a man who was about to take a long journey, and he called his servants together and entrusted them with his property.

<sup>15</sup>To one he gave five talents [probably about $5,000], to another two, to another one—to each in proportion to his own [a]personal ability. Then he departed *and* left the country.

<sup>16</sup>He who had received the five talents went at once and traded with them, and he gained five talents more.

<sup>17</sup>And likewise he who had received the two talents—he also gained two talents more.

<sup>18</sup>But he who had received the one talent went and dug a hole in the ground and hid his master's money.

<sup>19</sup>Now after a long time the master of those servants returned and settled accounts with them.

<sup>20</sup>And he who had received the five talents came and brought him five more, saying, Master, you entrusted to me five talents; see, here I have gained five talents more.

<sup>21</sup>His master said to him, Well done, you upright (honorable, [b]admirable) and faithful servant! You have been faithful *and* trustworthy over a little; I will put you in charge of much. Enter into *and* share the joy (the delight, the [c]blessedness) which your master enjoys.

<sup>22</sup>And he also who had the two talents came forward, saying, Master, you entrusted two talents to me; here I have gained two talents more.

<sup>23</sup>His master said to him, Well done, you upright (honorable, [b]admirable) and faithful servant! You have been faithful *and* trustworthy over a little; I will put you in charge of much. Enter into *and* share the joy (the delight, the [c]blessedness) which your master enjoys.

<sup>24</sup>He who had received one talent also came forward, saying, Master, I knew you to be a harsh *and* hard man, reaping where you did not sow, and gathering where you had not winnowed [the grain].

<sup>25</sup>So I was afraid, and I went and hid your talent in the ground. Here you have what is your own.

<sup>26</sup>But his master answered him, You wicked *and* lazy *and* idle servant! Did you indeed know that I reap where I have not sowed and gather [grain] where I have not winnowed?

<sup>27</sup>Then you should have invested my money with the bankers, and at my coming I would have received what was my own with interest.

<sup>28</sup>So take the talent away from him and give it to the one who has the ten talents.

<sup>29</sup>For to everyone who has will more be given, and he will be [c]furnished richly so that he will have an abundance; but from the one who does not have, even what he does have will be taken away.

<sup>30</sup>And throw the good-for-nothing servant into the outer darkness; there will be weeping and grinding of teeth.

<sup>31</sup>When the Son of Man comes in His glory (His majesty and splendor), and all the *holy* angels with Him, then He will sit on the throne of His glory.

<sup>32</sup>All nations will be gathered before Him, and He will separate them [the people] from one another as a shepherd separates his sheep from the goats; [Ezek. 34:17.]

<sup>33</sup>And He will cause the sheep to stand at His right hand, but the goats at His left.

<sup>34</sup>Then the King will say to those at His right hand, Come, you blessed of My Father [you [c]favored of God and appointed to eternal salvation], inherit (receive as your own) the kingdom prepared for you from the foundation of the world.

---

[a] 15 Greek *five talents . . . two talents . . . one talent*; also throughout this parable; a talent was worth about 20 years of a day laborer's wage.

[a] Marvin Vincent, *Word Studies.* [b] Hermann Cremer, *Biblico-Theological Lexicon.* [c] Joseph Thayer, *A Greek-English Lexicon.*

## New International Version

world. <sup>35</sup>For I was hungry and you gave me something to eat, I was thirsty and you gave me something to drink, I was a stranger and you invited me in, <sup>36</sup>I needed clothes and you clothed me, I was sick and you looked after me, I was in prison and you came to visit me.'

<sup>37</sup>"Then the righteous will answer him, 'Lord, when did we see you hungry and feed you, or thirsty and give you something to drink? <sup>38</sup>When did we see you a stranger and invite you in, or needing clothes and clothe you? <sup>39</sup>When did we see you sick or in prison and go to visit you?'

<sup>40</sup>"The King will reply, 'Truly I tell you, whatever you did for one of the least of these brothers and sisters of mine, you did for me.'

<sup>41</sup>"Then he will say to those on his left, 'Depart from me, you who are cursed, into the eternal fire prepared for the devil and his angels. <sup>42</sup>For I was hungry and you gave me nothing to eat, I was thirsty and you gave me nothing to drink, <sup>43</sup>I was a stranger and you did not invite me in, I needed clothes and you did not clothe me, I was sick and in prison and you did not look after me.'

<sup>44</sup>"They also will answer, 'Lord, when did we see you hungry or thirsty or a stranger or needing clothes or sick or in prison, and did not help you?'

<sup>45</sup>"He will reply, 'Truly I tell you, whatever you did not do for one of the least of these, you did not do for me.'

<sup>46</sup>"Then they will go away to eternal punishment, but the righteous to eternal life."

### The Plot Against Jesus

**26** When Jesus had finished saying all these things, he said to his disciples, <sup>2</sup>"As you know, the Passover is two days away—and the Son of Man will be handed over to be crucified."

<sup>3</sup>Then the chief priests and the elders of the people assembled in the palace of the high priest, whose name was Caiaphas, <sup>4</sup>and they schemed to arrest Jesus secretly and kill him. <sup>5</sup>"But not during the festival," they said, "or there may be a riot among the people."

### Jesus Anointed at Bethany

<sup>6</sup>While Jesus was in Bethany in the home of Simon the Leper, <sup>7</sup>a woman came to him with an alabaster jar of very expensive perfume, which she poured on his head as he was reclining at the table.

<sup>8</sup>When the disciples saw this, they were indignant. "Why this waste?" they asked. <sup>9</sup>"This perfume could have been sold at a high price and the money given to the poor."

<sup>10</sup>Aware of this, Jesus said to them, "Why are you bothering this woman? She has done a beautiful thing to me. <sup>11</sup>The poor you will always have with you,[a] but you will not always have me. <sup>12</sup>When she poured this perfume on my body, she did it to prepare me for burial. <sup>13</sup>Truly I tell you, wherever this gospel is preached throughout the world, what she has done will also be told, in memory of her."

### Judas Agrees to Betray Jesus

<sup>14</sup>Then one of the Twelve—the one called Judas Iscariot—went to the chief priests <sup>15</sup>and asked, "What are you

## Amplified Bible

<sup>35</sup>For I was hungry and you gave Me food, I was thirsty and you gave Me something to drink, I was a stranger and you <sup>a</sup>brought Me together with yourselves *and* welcomed *and* entertained *and* <sup>b</sup>lodged Me,

<sup>36</sup>I was naked and you clothed Me, I was sick and you visited Me <sup>c</sup>with help *and* ministering care, I was in prison and you came to see Me. [Isa. 58:7.]

<sup>37</sup>Then the just *and* upright will answer Him, Lord, when did we see You hungry and gave You food, or thirsty and gave You something to drink?

<sup>38</sup>And when did we see You a stranger and welcomed *and* entertained You, or naked and clothed You?

<sup>39</sup>And when did we see You sick or in prison and came to visit You?

<sup>40</sup>And the King will reply to them, Truly I tell you, in so far as you did it for one of the least [<sup>d</sup>in the estimation of men] of these My brethren, you did it for Me. [Prov. 19:17.]

<sup>41</sup>Then He will say to those at His left hand, Begone from Me, you cursed, into the eternal fire prepared for the devil and his angels!

<sup>42</sup>For I was hungry and you gave Me no food, I was thirsty and you gave Me nothing to drink,

<sup>43</sup>I was a stranger and you did not welcome Me *and* entertain Me, I was naked and you did not clothe Me, I was sick and in prison and you did not visit Me <sup>c</sup>with help *and* ministering care.

<sup>44</sup>Then they also [in their turn] will answer, Lord, when did we see You hungry or thirsty or a stranger or naked or sick or in prison, and did not minister to You?

<sup>45</sup>And He will reply to them, Solemnly I declare to you, in so far as you failed to do it for the least [<sup>d</sup>in the estimation of men] of these, you failed to do it for Me. [Prov. 14:31; 17:5.]

<sup>46</sup>Then they will go away into eternal punishment, but those who are just *and* upright *and* in right standing with God into eternal life. [Dan. 12:2.]

**26** When Jesus had ended this discourse, He said to His disciples,

<sup>2</sup>You know that the Passover is in two days—and the Son of Man will be delivered up <sup>d</sup>treacherously to be crucified.

<sup>3</sup>Then the chief priests and the elders of the people gathered in the [<sup>e</sup>open] court of the palace of the high priest, whose name was Caiaphas,

<sup>4</sup>And consulted together in order to arrest Jesus by stratagem secretly and put Him to death.

<sup>5</sup>But they said, It must not be during the Feast, for fear that there will be a riot among the people.

<sup>6</sup>Now when Jesus came back to Bethany and was in the house of Simon the leper,

<sup>7</sup>A woman came up to Him with an alabaster flask of very precious perfume, and she poured it on His head as He reclined at table.

<sup>8</sup>And when the disciples saw it, they were indignant, saying, For what purpose is all this waste?

<sup>9</sup>For this perfume might have been sold for a large sum and the money given to the poor.

<sup>10</sup>But Jesus, fully aware of this, said to them, Why do you bother the woman? She has done a noble (praiseworthy and beautiful) thing to Me.

<sup>11</sup>For you always have the poor among you, but you will not always have Me. [Deut. 15:11.]

<sup>12</sup>In pouring this perfume on My body she has done something to prepare Me for My burial.

<sup>13</sup>Truly I tell you, wherever this good news (the Gospel) is preached in the whole world, what this woman has done will be told also, in memory of her.

<sup>14</sup>Then one of the Twelve [apostles], who was called Judas Iscariot, went to the chief priests

*a* Literal meaning. *b* William Tyndale, *The Tyndale Bible*. *c* Kenneth Wuest, *Word Studies*. *d* Joseph Thayer, *A Greek-English Lexicon*. *e* Marvin Vincent, *Word Studies*.

## New International Version

willing to give me if I deliver him over to you?" So they counted out for him thirty pieces of silver. [16]From then on Judas watched for an opportunity to hand him over.

### The Last Supper

[17]On the first day of the Festival of Unleavened Bread, the disciples came to Jesus and asked, "Where do you want us to make preparations for you to eat the Passover?"

[18]He replied, "Go into the city to a certain man and tell him, 'The Teacher says: My appointed time is near. I am going to celebrate the Passover with my disciples at your house.'" [19]So the disciples did as Jesus had directed them and prepared the Passover.

[20]When evening came, Jesus was reclining at the table with the Twelve. [21]And while they were eating, he said, "Truly I tell you, one of you will betray me."

[22]They were very sad and began to say to him one after the other, "Surely you don't mean me, Lord?"

[23]Jesus replied, "The one who has dipped his hand into the bowl with me will betray me. [24]The Son of Man will go just as it is written about him. But woe to that man who betrays the Son of Man! It would be better for him if he had not been born."

[25]Then Judas, the one who would betray him, said, "Surely you don't mean me, Rabbi?"

Jesus answered, "You have said so."

[26]While they were eating, Jesus took bread, and when he had given thanks, he broke it and gave it to his disciples, saying, "Take and eat; this is my body."

[27]Then he took a cup, and when he had given thanks, he gave it to them, saying, "Drink from it, all of you. [28]This is my blood of the[a] covenant, which is poured out for many for the forgiveness of sins. [29]I tell you, I will not drink from this fruit of the vine from now on until that day when I drink it new with you in my Father's kingdom."

[30]When they had sung a hymn, they went out to the Mount of Olives.

### Jesus Predicts Peter's Denial

[31]Then Jesus told them, "This very night you will all fall away on account of me, for it is written:

"'I will strike the shepherd,
   and the sheep of the flock will be scattered.'[b]

[32]But after I have risen, I will go ahead of you into Galilee."

[33]Peter replied, "Even if all fall away on account of you, I never will."

[34]"Truly I tell you," Jesus answered, "this very night, before the rooster crows, you will disown me three times."

[35]But Peter declared, "Even if I have to die with you, I will never disown you." And all the other disciples said the same.

### Gethsemane

[36]Then Jesus went with his disciples to a place called Gethsemane, and he said to them, "Sit here while I go over there and pray." [37]He took Peter and the two sons of Zebedee along with him, and he began to be sorrowful and troubled. [38]Then he said to them, "My soul is overwhelmed with sorrow to the point of death. Stay here and keep watch with me."

## Amplified Bible

[15]And said, What are you willing to give me if I hand Him over to you? And they weighed out for and paid to him thirty pieces of silver [about twenty-one dollars and sixty cents]. [Exod. 21:32; Zech. 11:12.]

[16]And from that moment he sought a fitting opportunity to betray Him.

[17]Now on the first day of Unleavened Bread [Passover week], the disciples came to Jesus and said to Him, Where do You wish us to prepare for You to eat the Passover supper?

[18]He said, Go into the city to a certain man and say to him, The Master says: My time is near; I will keep the Passover at your house with My disciples.

[19]And accordingly the disciples did as Jesus had directed them, and they made ready the Passover supper. [Deut. 16:5-8.]

[20]When it was evening, He was reclining at table with the twelve disciples.

[21]And as they were eating, He said, Solemnly I say to you, one of you will betray Me!

[22]They were exceedingly pained and distressed and deeply hurt and sorrowful and began to say to Him one after another, [a]Surely it cannot be I, Lord, can it?

[23]He replied, He who has [just] dipped his hand in the same dish with Me will betray Me!

[24]The Son of Man is going just as it is written of Him; but woe to that man by whom the Son of Man is betrayed! It would have been better (more profitable and wholesome) for that man if he had never been born! [Ps. 41:9.]

[25]Judas, the betrayer, said, [a]Surely it is not I, is it, Master? He said to him, You have stated [the fact].

[26]Now as they were eating, Jesus took bread and, [b]praising God, gave thanks and asked Him to bless it to their use, and when He had broken it, He gave it to the disciples and said, Take, eat; this is My body.

[27]And He took a cup, and when He had given thanks, He gave it to them, saying, Drink of it, all of you;

[28]For this is My blood of the new covenant, which [[b]ratifies the agreement and] is [a]being poured out for many for the forgiveness of sins. [Exod. 24:6-8.]

[29]I say to you, I shall not drink again of this fruit of the vine until that day when I drink it with you new and [b]of superior quality in My Father's kingdom.

[30]And when they had sung a hymn, they went out to the Mount of Olives.

[31]Then Jesus said to them, You will all be offended and stumble and fall away because of Me this night [distrusting and deserting Me], for it is written, I will strike the Shepherd, and the sheep of the flock will be scattered. [Zech. 13:7.]

[32]But after I am raised up [to life again], I will go ahead of you to Galilee.

[33]Peter declared to Him, Though they all are offended and stumble and fall away because of You [and distrust and desert You], I will never do so.

[34]Jesus said to him, Solemnly I declare to you, this very night, before a [a]single rooster crows, you will deny and disown Me three times.

[35]Peter said to Him, Even if I must die with You, I will not deny or disown You! And all the disciples said the same thing.

[36]Then Jesus went with them to a place called Gethsemane, and He told His disciples, Sit down here while I go over yonder and pray.

[37]And taking with Him Peter and the two sons of Zebedee, He began to [a]show grief and distress of mind and was [c]deeply depressed.

[38]Then He said to them, My soul is very sad and deeply grieved, so that [b]I am almost dying of sorrow. Stay here and keep awake and keep watch with Me.

---

*a* 28 Some manuscripts *the new*   *b* 31 Zech. 13:7

*a* Marvin Vincent, *Word Studies*.   *b* Joseph Thayer, *A Greek-English Lexicon*.   *c* George R. Berry, *Greek-English New Testament Lexicon*.

## New International Version

39Going a little farther, he fell with his face to the ground and prayed, "My Father, if it is possible, may this cup be taken from me. Yet not as I will, but as you will."
40Then he returned to his disciples and found them sleeping. "Couldn't you men keep watch with me for one hour?" he asked Peter. 41"Watch and pray so that you will not fall into temptation. The spirit is willing, but the flesh is weak."
42He went away a second time and prayed, "My Father, if it is not possible for this cup to be taken away unless I drink it, may your will be done."
43When he came back, he again found them sleeping, because their eyes were heavy. 44So he left them and went away once more and prayed the third time, saying the same thing.
45Then he returned to the disciples and said to them, "Are you still sleeping and resting? Look, the hour has come, and the Son of Man is delivered into the hands of sinners. 46Rise! Let us go! Here comes my betrayer!"

### Jesus Arrested

47While he was still speaking, Judas, one of the Twelve, arrived. With him was a large crowd armed with swords and clubs, sent from the chief priests and the elders of the people. 48Now the betrayer had arranged a signal with them: "The one I kiss is the man; arrest him." 49Going at once to Jesus, Judas said, "Greetings, Rabbi!" and kissed him.
50Jesus replied, "Do what you came for, friend."a
Then the men stepped forward, seized Jesus and arrested him. 51With that, one of Jesus' companions reached for his sword, drew it out and struck the servant of the high priest, cutting off his ear.
52"Put your sword back in its place," Jesus said to him, "for all who draw the sword will die by the sword. 53Do you think I cannot call on my Father, and he will at once put at my disposal more than twelve legions of angels? 54But how then would the Scriptures be fulfilled that say it must happen in this way?"
55In that hour Jesus said to the crowd, "Am I leading a rebellion, that you have come out with swords and clubs to capture me? Every day I sat in the temple courts teaching, and you did not arrest me. 56But this has all taken place that the writings of the prophets might be fulfilled." Then all the disciples deserted him and fled.

### Jesus Before the Sanhedrin

57Those who had arrested Jesus took him to Caiaphas the high priest, where the teachers of the law and the elders had assembled. 58But Peter followed him at a distance, right up to the courtyard of the high priest. He entered and sat down with the guards to see the outcome.
59The chief priests and the whole Sanhedrin were looking for false evidence against Jesus so that they could put him to death. 60But they did not find any, though many false witnesses came forward.

## Amplified Bible

39And going a little farther, He threw Himself upon the ground on His face and prayed saying, My Father, if it is possible, let this cup pass away from Me; nevertheless, not what I will [not what I desire], but as You will and desire.
40And He came to the disciples and found them sleeping, and He said to Peter, What! Are you so utterly unable to stay awake and keep watch with Me for one hour?
41All of you must keep awake (give strict attention, be cautious and active) and watch and pray, that you may not come into temptation. The spirit indeed is willing, but the flesh is weak.
42Again a second time He went away and prayed, My Father, if this cannot pass by unless I drink it, Your will be done.
43And again He came and found them sleeping, for their eyes were weighed down with sleep.
44So, leaving them again, He went away and prayed for the third time, using the same words.
45Then He returned to the disciples and said to them, Are you still sleeping and taking your rest? Behold, the hour is at hand, and the Son of Man is betrayed into the hands of aespecially wicked sinners [bwhose way or nature it is to act in opposition to God].
46Get up, let us be going! See, My betrayer is at hand!
47As He was still speaking, Judas, one of the Twelve [apostles], came up, and with him a great crowd with swords and clubs, from the chief priests and elders of the people.
48Now the betrayer had given them a sign, saying, The One I shall kiss is the Man; seize Him.
49And he came up to Jesus at once and said, Hail (greetings, good health to You, long life to You), Master! And he cembraced Him and kissed Him dwith [pretended] warmth and devotion.
50Jesus said to him, Friend, for what are you here? Then they came up and laid hands on Jesus and arrested Him.
51And behold, one of those who were with Jesus reached out his hand and drew his sword and, striking the body servant of the high priest, cut off his ear.
52Then Jesus said to him, Put your sword back into its place, for all who draw the sword will die by the sword. [Gen. 9:6.]
53Do you suppose that I cannot appeal to My Father, and He will immediately provide Me with more than twelve legions [emore than 80,000] of angels?
54But how then would the Scriptures be fulfilled, that it must come about this way?
55At that moment Jesus said to the crowds, Have you come out with swords and clubs as [you would] against a robber to capture Me? Day after day I was faccustomed to sit in the gporches and courts of the temple teaching, and you did not arrest Me.
56But all this has taken place in order that the Scriptures of the prophets might be fulfilled. Then all the disciples deserted Him and, fleeing, escaped.
57But those who had seized Jesus took Him away to Caiaphas, the high priest, where the scribes and the elders had assembled.
58But Peter followed Him at a distance, as far as the courtyard of the high priest's home; he even went inside and sat with the guards to see the end.
59Now the chief priests and the whole council (the Sanhedrin) sought to get false witnesses to testify against Jesus, so that they might put Him to death;
60But they found none, though many witnesses came forward [to testify]. At last two men came forward

---

a G. Abbott-Smith, *Manual Greek Lexicon*. b Hermann Cremer, *Biblico-Theological Lexicon*. c H.A. W. Meyer, *Critical and Exegetical Handbook to the Gospel of Matthew*. d Kenneth Wuest, *Word Studies*. e Joseph Thayer, *A Greek-English Lexicon*. f Marvin Vincent, *Word Studies*. g Richard Trench, *Synonyms of the New Testament*.

---

a 50 Or *"Why have you come, friend?"*

## New International Version

Finally two came forward [61]and declared, "This fellow said, 'I am able to destroy the temple of God and rebuild it in three days.'"

[62]Then the high priest stood up and said to Jesus, "Are you not going to answer? What is this testimony that these men are bringing against you?" [63]But Jesus remained silent.

The high priest said to him, "I charge you under oath by the living God: Tell us if you are the Messiah, the Son of God."

[64]"You have said so," Jesus replied. "But I say to all of you: From now on you will see the Son of Man sitting at the right hand of the Mighty One and coming on the clouds of heaven."[a]

[65]Then the high priest tore his clothes and said, "He has spoken blasphemy! Why do we need any more witnesses? Look, now you have heard the blasphemy. [66]What do you think?"

"He is worthy of death," they answered.

[67]Then they spit in his face and struck him with their fists. Others slapped him [68]and said, "Prophesy to us, Messiah. Who hit you?"

### Peter Disowns Jesus

[69]Now Peter was sitting out in the courtyard, and a servant girl came to him. "You also were with Jesus of Galilee," she said.

[70]But he denied it before them all. "I don't know what you're talking about," he said.

[71]Then he went out to the gateway, where another servant girl saw him and said to the people there, "This fellow was with Jesus of Nazareth."

[72]He denied it again, with an oath: "I don't know the man!"

[73]After a little while, those standing there went up to Peter and said, "Surely you are one of them; your accent gives you away."

[74]Then he began to call down curses, and he swore to them, "I don't know the man!"

Immediately a rooster crowed. [75]Then Peter remembered the word Jesus had spoken: "Before the rooster crows, you will disown me three times." And he went outside and wept bitterly.

### Judas Hangs Himself

**27** Early in the morning, all the chief priests and the elders of the people made their plans how to have Jesus executed. [2]So they bound him, led him away and handed him over to Pilate the governor.

[3]When Judas, who had betrayed him, saw that Jesus was condemned, he was seized with remorse and returned the thirty pieces of silver to the chief priests and the elders. [4]"I have sinned," he said, "for I have betrayed innocent blood."

"What is that to us?" they replied. "That's your responsibility."

[5]So Judas threw the money into the temple and left. Then he went away and hanged himself.

[6]The chief priests picked up the coins and said, "It is against the law to put this into the treasury, since it is blood money." [7]So they decided to use the money to buy the potter's field as a burial place for foreigners. [8]That is

## Amplified Bible

[61]And testified, This [a]Fellow said, I am able to tear down the [b]sanctuary of the temple of God and to build it up again in three days.

[62]And the high priest stood up and said, Have You no answer to make? What about this that these men testify against You?

[63]But Jesus kept silent. And the high priest said to Him, [c]I call upon you to swear by the living God, and tell us whether you are the Christ, the Son of God.

[64]Jesus said to him, [c]You have stated [the fact]. More than that, I tell you: You will in the future see the Son of Man seated at the right hand of [d]the Almighty and coming on the clouds of the sky. [Ps. 110:1; Dan. 7:13.]

[65]Then the high priest tore his clothes and exclaimed, He has uttered blasphemy! What need have we of further evidence? You have now heard His blasphemy. [Lev. 24:16; Num. 14:6.]

[66]What do you think now? They answered, He deserves to be put to death.

[67]Then they spat in His face and struck Him with their fists; and some [d]slapped Him in the face, [Isa. 50:6.]

[68]Saying, Prophesy to us, You Christ (the Messiah)! Who was it that struck You?

[69]Now Peter was sitting outside in the courtyard, and [c]one maid came up to him and said, You were also with Jesus the Galilean!

[70]But he denied it [e]falsely before them all, saying, I do not know what you mean.

[71]And when he had gone out to the porch, another maid saw him, and she said to the bystanders, This fellow was with Jesus the Nazarene!

[72]And again he denied it and [e]disowned Him with an oath, saying, I do not know the Man!

[73]After a little while, the bystanders came up and said to Peter, You certainly are one of them too, for even your accent betrays you.

[74]Then Peter began to invoke a curse on himself and to swear, I do not even know the Man! And at that moment a rooster crowed.

[75]And Peter remembered Jesus' words, when He had said, Before a [c]single rooster crows, you will deny *and* disown Me three times. And he went outside and wept bitterly.

**27** When it was morning, all the chief priests and the elders of the people held a consultation against Jesus to put Him to death;

[2]And they bound Him and led Him away and handed Him over to Pilate the governor.

[3]When Judas, His betrayer, saw that [Jesus] was condemned, [Judas was [f]afflicted in mind and troubled for his former folly; and] with remorse [with little more than a selfish dread of the consequences] he brought back the thirty pieces of silver to the chief priests and the elders, [Exod. 21:32.]

[4]Saying, I have sinned in betraying innocent blood. They replied, What is that to us? See to that yourself.

[5]And casting the pieces of silver [forward] into the [Holy Place of the [b]sanctuary of the] temple, he departed; and he went off and hanged himself.

[6]But the chief priests, picking up the pieces of silver, said, It is not legal to put these in the [consecrated] treasury, for it is the price of blood.

[7]So after consultation they bought with them [the pieces of silver] the potter's field [as a place] in which to bury strangers.

---

[a]64 See Psalm 110:1; Daniel 7:13.

[a] Capitalized because of what He is, the spotless Son of God, not what the speakers may have thought He was. [b] Richard Trench, *Synonyms of the New Testament.* [c] Marvin Vincent, *Word Studies.* [d] Joseph Thayer, *A Greek-English Lexicon.* [e] Hermann Cremer, *Biblico-Theological Lexicon.* [f] Jeremy Taylor and Aristotle, cited by Richard Trench, *Synonyms of the New Testament.*

## New International Version

why it has been called the Field of Blood to this day. ⁹Then what was spoken by Jeremiah the prophet was fulfilled: "They took the thirty pieces of silver, the price set on him by the people of Israel, ¹⁰and they used them to buy the potter's field, as the Lord commanded me."ᵃ

### Jesus Before Pilate

¹¹Meanwhile Jesus stood before the governor, and the governor asked him, "Are you the king of the Jews?"

"You have said so," Jesus replied.

¹²When he was accused by the chief priests and the elders, he gave no answer. ¹³Then Pilate asked him, "Don't you hear the testimony they are bringing against you?" ¹⁴But Jesus made no reply, not even to a single charge—to the great amazement of the governor.

¹⁵Now it was the governor's custom at the festival to release a prisoner chosen by the crowd. ¹⁶At that time they had a well-known prisoner whose name was Jesusᵇ Barabbas. ¹⁷So when the crowd had gathered, Pilate asked them, "Which one do you want me to release to you: Jesus Barabbas, or Jesus who is called the Messiah?" ¹⁸For he knew it was out of self-interest that they had handed Jesus over to him.

¹⁹While Pilate was sitting on the judge's seat, his wife sent him this message: "Don't have anything to do with that innocent man, for I have suffered a great deal today in a dream because of him."

²⁰But the chief priests and the elders persuaded the crowd to ask for Barabbas and to have Jesus executed.

²¹"Which of the two do you want me to release to you?" asked the governor.

"Barabbas," they answered.

²²"What shall I do, then, with Jesus who is called the Messiah?" Pilate asked.

They all answered, "Crucify him!"

²³"Why? What crime has he committed?" asked Pilate. But they shouted all the louder, "Crucify him!"

²⁴When Pilate saw that he was getting nowhere, but that instead an uproar was starting, he took water and washed his hands in front of the crowd. "I am innocent of this man's blood," he said. "It is your responsibility!"

²⁵All the people answered, "His blood is on us and on our children!"

²⁶Then he released Barabbas to them. But he had Jesus flogged, and handed him over to be crucified.

### The Soldiers Mock Jesus

²⁷Then the governor's soldiers took Jesus into the Praetorium and gathered the whole company of soldiers around him. ²⁸They stripped him and put a scarlet robe on him, ²⁹and then twisted together a crown of thorns and set it on his head. They put a staff in his right hand. Then they knelt in front of him and mocked him. "Hail, king of the Jews!" they said. ³⁰They spit on him, and took the staff and struck him on the head again and again. ³¹After they had mocked him, they took off the robe and put his own clothes on him. Then they led him away to crucify him.

### The Crucifixion of Jesus

³²As they were going out, they met a man from Cyrene, named Simon, and they forced him to carry the cross. ³³They came to a place called Golgotha (which means "the

## Amplified Bible

⁸Therefore that piece of ground has been called the Field of Blood to the present day.

⁹Then were fulfilled the words spoken by Jeremiah the prophet when he said, And they took the thirty pieces of silver, the price of Him on Whom a price had been set by some of the sons of Israel, [Zech. 11:12, 13.]

¹⁰And they gave them for the potter's field, as the Lord directed me.

¹¹Now Jesus stood before the governor [Pilate], and the governor asked Him, Are you the King of the Jews? Jesus said to him, You have stated [the fact].

¹²But when the charges were made against Him by the chief priests and elders, He made no answer. [Isa. 53:7.]

¹³Then Pilate said to Him, Do You not hear how many *and* how serious are the things they are testifying against You?

¹⁴But He made no reply to him, not even to a single accusation, so that the governor marveled greatly.

¹⁵Now at the Feast [of the Passover] the governor was in the habit of setting free for the people any one prisoner whom they chose.

¹⁶And at that time they had a notorious prisoner whose name was Barabbas.

¹⁷So when they had assembled for this purpose, Pilate said to them, Whom do you want me to set free for you, Barabbas, or Jesus Who is called Christ?

¹⁸For he knew that it was because of envy that they had handed Him over to him.

¹⁹Also, while he was seated on the judgment bench, his wife sent him a message, saying, Have nothing to do with that just *and* upright Man, for I have had a painful experience today in a dream because of Him.

²⁰But the chief priests and the elders prevailed on the people to ask for Barabbas, and put Jesus to death.

²¹Again the governor said to them, Which of the two do you wish me to release for you? And they said, Barabbas!

²²Pilate said to them, Then what shall I do with Jesus Who is called Christ?

²³They all replied, Let Him be crucified! And he said, Why? What has He done that is evil? But they shouted all the louder, Let Him be crucified!

²⁴So when Pilate saw that he was getting nowhere, but rather that a riot was about to break out, he took water and washed his hands in the presence of the crowd, saying, I am not guilty of *nor* responsible for this ᵃrighteous Man's blood; see to it yourselves. [Deut. 21:6-9; Ps. 26:6.]

²⁵And all the people answered, Let His blood be on us and on our children! [Josh. 2:19.]

²⁶So he set free for them Barabbas; and he [had] Jesus whipped, and delivered Him up to be crucified.

²⁷Then the governor's soldiers took Jesus into the palace, and they gathered the whole battalion about Him.

²⁸And they stripped off His clothes and put a scarlet robe (ᵇgarment of dignity and office worn by Roman officers of rank) upon Him,

²⁹And, weaving a crown of thorns, they put it on His head and put a reed (staff) in His right hand. And kneeling before Him, they made sport of Him, saying, Hail (greetings, good health to You, long life to You), King of the Jews!

³⁰And they spat on Him, and took the reed (staff) and struck Him on the head.

³¹And when they finished making sport of Him, they stripped Him of the robe and put His own garments on Him and led Him away to be crucified.

³²As they were marching forth, they came upon a man of Cyrene named Simon; this man they forced to carry the cross of Jesus.

³³And when they came to a place called Golgotha [Latin: Calvary], which means The Place of a Skull,

---

ᵃ 10 See Zech. 11:12,13; Jer. 19:1-13; 32:6-9.    ᵇ 16 Many manuscripts do not have *Jesus*; also in verse 17.

ᵃ Some manuscripts so read.    ᵇ Richard Trench, *Synonyms of the New Testament.*

## New International Version

place of the skull"). [34]There they offered Jesus wine to drink, mixed with gall; but after tasting it, he refused to drink it. [35]When they had crucified him, they divided up his clothes by casting lots. [36]And sitting down, they kept watch over him there. [37]Above his head they placed the written charge against him: THIS IS JESUS, THE KING OF THE JEWS.

[38]Two rebels were crucified with him, one on his right and one on his left. [39]Those who passed by hurled insults at him, shaking their heads [40]and saying, "You who are going to destroy the temple and build it in three days, save yourself! Come down from the cross, if you are the Son of God!" [41]In the same way the chief priests, the teachers of the law and the elders mocked him. [42]"He saved others," they said, "but he can't save himself! He's the king of Israel! Let him come down now from the cross, and we will believe in him. [43]He trusts in God. Let God rescue him now if he wants him, for he said, 'I am the Son of God.'" [44]In the same way the rebels who were crucified with him also heaped insults on him.

### The Death of Jesus

[45]From noon until three in the afternoon darkness came over all the land. [46]About three in the afternoon Jesus cried out in a loud voice, *"Eli, Eli,[a] lema sabachthani?"* (which means "My God, my God, why have you forsaken me?").[b]

[47]When some of those standing there heard this, they said, "He's calling Elijah."

[48]Immediately one of them ran and got a sponge. He filled it with wine vinegar, put it on a staff, and offered it to Jesus to drink. [49]The rest said, "Now leave him alone. Let's see if Elijah comes to save him."

[50]And when Jesus had cried out again in a loud voice, he gave up his spirit.

[51]At that moment the curtain of the temple was torn in two from top to bottom. The earth shook, the rocks split [52]and the tombs broke open. The bodies of many holy people who had died were raised to life. [53]They came out of the tombs after Jesus' resurrection and[c] went into the holy city and appeared to many people.

[54]When the centurion and those with him who were guarding Jesus saw the earthquake and all that had happened, they were terrified, and exclaimed, "Surely he was the Son of God!"

[55]Many women were there, watching from a distance. They had followed Jesus from Galilee to care for his needs. [56]Among them were Mary Magdalene, Mary the mother of James and Joseph,[d] and the mother of Zebedee's sons.

### The Burial of Jesus

[57]As evening approached, there came a rich man from Arimathea, named Joseph, who had himself become a dis-

## Amplified Bible

[34]They offered Him wine mingled with gall to drink; but when He tasted it, He refused to drink it.

[35]And when they had crucified Him, they divided *and* distributed His garments [among them] by casting lots [a]*so that the prophet's saying was fulfilled, They parted My garments among them and over My apparel they cast lots.* [Ps. 22:18.]

[36]Then they sat down there and kept watch over Him.

[37]And over His head they put the accusation against Him ([b]the cause of His death), which read, This is Jesus, the King of the Jews.

[38]At the same time two robbers were crucified with Him, one on the right hand and one on the left.

[39]And those who passed by spoke reproachfully *and* abusively *and* jeered at Him, wagging their heads, [Ps. 22:7, 8; 109:25.]

[40]And they said, You Who would tear down the [c]sanctuary of the temple and rebuild it in three days, rescue Yourself [d]from death. If You are the Son of God, come down from the cross.

[41]In the same way the chief priests, with the scribes and elders, made sport of Him, saying,

[42]He rescued others [d]from death; Himself He cannot rescue [d]from death. He is the King of Israel? Let Him come down from the cross now, and we will believe in *and* [d]acknowledge *and* cleave to Him.

[43]He trusts in God; let God deliver Him now if He cares for Him *and* will have Him, for He said, I am the Son of God.

[44]And the robbers who were crucified with Him also abused *and* reproached *and* made sport of Him in the same way.

[45]Now from the sixth hour (noon) there was darkness over all the land until the ninth hour (three o'clock).

[46]And about the ninth hour (three o'clock) Jesus cried with a loud voice, Eli, Eli, lama sabachthani?—that is, My God, My God, why have You abandoned Me [leaving Me [e]helpless, forsaking and failing Me in My need]? [Ps. 22:1.]

[47]And some of the bystanders, when they heard it, said, This Man is calling for Elijah!

[48]And one of them immediately ran and took a sponge, soaked it with vinegar (a sour wine), and put it on a reed (staff), and was [f]about to give it to Him to drink. [Ps. 69:21.]

[49]But the others said, Wait! Let us see whether Elijah will come to save Him [f]from death.

[50]And Jesus cried again with a loud voice and gave up His spirit.

[51]And at once the curtain of the [c]sanctuary of the temple was torn in two from top to bottom; the earth shook and the rocks were split. [Exod. 26:31-35.]

[52]The tombs were opened and many bodies of the saints who had fallen asleep [d]in death were raised [to life];

[53]And coming out of the tombs after His resurrection, they went into the holy city and appeared to many people.

[54]When the centurion and those who were with him keeping watch over Jesus observed the earthquake and all that was happening, they were terribly frightened *and* filled with awe, and said, Truly this was God's Son!

[55]There were also numerous women there, looking on from a distance, who were of those who had accompanied Jesus from Galilee, ministering to Him.

[56]Among them were Mary of Magdala, and Mary the mother of James and Joseph, and the mother of Zebedee's sons.

[57]When it was evening, there came a rich man from Arimathea, named Joseph, who also was a disciple of Jesus.

[a] 46 Some manuscripts *Eli, Eli* and after Jesus' resurrection they    [b] 46 Psalm 22:1    [c] 53 Or *tombs,*    [d] 56 Greek *Joses,* a variant of *Joseph*

[a] Many manuscripts do not contain this part of verse 35.    [b] William Tyndale, *The Tyndale Bible.*    [c] Richard Trench, *Synonyms of the New Testament.*    [d] Hermann Cremer, *Biblico-Theological Lexicon.*    [e] Kenneth Wuest, *Word Studies.*    [f] Marvin Vincent, *Word Studies.*

## New International Version

ciple of Jesus. [58] Going to Pilate, he asked for Jesus' body, and Pilate ordered that it be given to him. [59] Joseph took the body, wrapped it in a clean linen cloth, [60] and placed it in his own new tomb that he had cut out of the rock. He rolled a big stone in front of the entrance to the tomb and went away. [61] Mary Magdalene and the other Mary were sitting there opposite the tomb.

### The Guard at the Tomb

[62] The next day, the one after Preparation Day, the chief priests and the Pharisees went to Pilate. [63] "Sir," they said, "we remember that while he was still alive that deceiver said, 'After three days I will rise again.' [64] So give the order for the tomb to be made secure until the third day. Otherwise, his disciples may come and steal the body and tell the people that he has been raised from the dead. This last deception will be worse than the first."

[65] "Take a guard," Pilate answered. "Go, make the tomb as secure as you know how." [66] So they went and made the tomb secure by putting a seal on the stone and posting the guard.

### Jesus Has Risen

**28** After the Sabbath, at dawn on the first day of the week, Mary Magdalene and the other Mary went to look at the tomb.

[2] There was a violent earthquake, for an angel of the Lord came down from heaven and, going to the tomb, rolled back the stone and sat on it. [3] His appearance was like lightning, and his clothes were white as snow. [4] The guards were so afraid of him that they shook and became like dead men.

[5] The angel said to the women, "Do not be afraid, for I know that you are looking for Jesus, who was crucified. [6] He is not here; he has risen, just as he said. Come and see the place where he lay. [7] Then go quickly and tell his disciples: 'He has risen from the dead and is going ahead of you into Galilee. There you will see him.' Now I have told you."

[8] So the women hurried away from the tomb, afraid yet filled with joy, and ran to tell his disciples. [9] Suddenly Jesus met them. "Greetings," he said. They came to him, clasped his feet and worshiped him. [10] Then Jesus said to them, "Do not be afraid. Go and tell my brothers to go to Galilee; there they will see me."

### The Guards' Report

[11] While the women were on their way, some of the guards went into the city and reported to the chief priests everything that had happened. [12] When the chief priests had met with the elders and devised a plan, they gave the soldiers a large sum of money, [13] telling them, "You are to say, 'His disciples came during the night and stole him away while we were asleep.' [14] If this report gets to the governor, we will satisfy him and keep you out of trouble." [15] So the soldiers took the money and did as they were instructed. And this story has been widely circulated among the Jews to this very day.

### The Great Commission

[16] Then the eleven disciples went to Galilee, to the mountain where Jesus had told them to go. [17] When they

## Amplified Bible

[58] He went to Pilate and asked for the body of Jesus, and Pilate ordered that it be given to him.

[59] And Joseph took the body and *a* rolled it up in a clean linen cloth *b* used for swathing dead bodies

[60] And laid it in his own fresh (*c* undefiled) tomb, which he had hewn in the rock; and he rolled a big boulder over the door of the tomb and went away.

[61] And Mary of Magdala and the other Mary kept sitting there opposite the tomb.

[62] The next day, that is, the day after the day of Preparation [for the Sabbath], the chief priests and the Pharisees assembled before Pilate

[63] And said, Sir, we have just remembered how that *c* vagabond Imposter said while He was still alive, After three days I will rise again.

[64] Therefore give an order to have the tomb made secure *and* safeguarded until the third day, for fear that His disciples will come and steal Him away and tell the people that He has risen from the dead, and the last deception *and* fraud will be worse than the first.

[65] Pilate said to them, You have a guard [of soldiers; take them and] go, make it as secure as you can.

[66] So they went off and made the tomb secure by sealing the boulder, a guard of soldiers being with them *and* remaining to watch.

**28** Now after the Sabbath, near dawn of the first day of the week, Mary of Magdala and the other Mary went to take a look at the tomb.

[2] And behold, there was a great earthquake, for an angel of the Lord descended from heaven and came and rolled the boulder back and sat upon it.

[3] His appearance was like lightning, and his garments as white as snow.

[4] And those keeping guard were so frightened at the sight of him that they were agitated *and* they trembled and became like dead men.

[5] But the angel said to the women, Do not be alarmed *and* frightened, for I know that you are looking for Jesus, Who was crucified.

[6] He is not here; He has risen, as He said [He would do]. Come, see the place where He lay.

[7] Then go quickly and tell His disciples, He has risen from the dead, and behold, He is going before you to Galilee; there you will see Him. Behold, I have told you.

[8] So they left the tomb hastily with fear and great joy and ran to tell the disciples.

[9] And *as they went,* behold, Jesus met them and said, Hail (greetings)! And they went up to Him and clasped His feet and worshiped Him.

[10] Then Jesus said to them, Do not be alarmed *and* afraid; go and tell My brethren to go into Galilee, and there they will see Me.

[11] While they were on their way, behold, some of the guards went into the city and reported to the chief priests everything that had occurred.

[12] And when they [the chief priests] had gathered with the elders and had consulted together, they gave a sufficient sum of money to the soldiers,

[13] And said, Tell people, His disciples came at night and stole Him away while we were sleeping.

[14] And if the governor hears of it, we will appease him and make you safe *and* free from trouble *and* care.

[15] So they took the money and did as they were instructed; and this story has been current among the Jews to the present day.

[16] Now the eleven disciples went to Galilee, to the mountain to which Jesus had directed *and* made appointment with them.

---

*a* Robert Young, *Analytical Concordance.* *b* James Moulton and George Milligan, *The Vocabulary.* *c* Marvin Vincent, *Word Studies.*

## New International Version

saw him, they worshiped him; but some doubted. [18]Then Jesus came to them and said, "All authority in heaven and on earth has been given to me. [19]Therefore go and make disciples of all nations, baptizing them in the name of the Father and of the Son and of the Holy Spirit, [20]and teaching them to obey everything I have commanded you. And surely I am with you always, to the very end of the age."

## Amplified Bible

[17]And when they saw Him, they fell down and worshiped Him; but some doubted.

[18]Jesus approached and, [a]breaking the silence, said to them, All authority (all power of rule) in heaven and on earth has been given to Me.

[19]Go then and make disciples of all the nations, baptizing them [a]into the name of the Father and of the Son and of the Holy Spirit,

[20]Teaching them to observe everything that I have commanded you, and behold, I am with you [b]all the days ([c]perpetually, uniformly, and on every occasion), to the [very] close *and* consummation of the age. [d]*Amen (so let it be).*

*a* Marvin Vincent, *Word Studies.* *b* John Wycliffe, *The Wycliffe Bible.* *c* *Webster's New International Dictionary* offers this phrase as a definition of "always." *d* Some manuscripts do not contain this ending.

## New International Version

# Mark

### John the Baptist Prepares the Way

**1** The beginning of the good news about Jesus the Messiah,[a] the Son of God,[b] 2 as it is written in Isaiah the prophet:

"I will send my messenger ahead of you,
who will prepare your way"[c]—
3 "a voice of one calling in the wilderness,
'Prepare the way for the Lord,
make straight paths for him.'"[d]

4 And so John the Baptist appeared in the wilderness, preaching a baptism of repentance for the forgiveness of sins. 5 The whole Judean countryside and all the people of Jerusalem went out to him. Confessing their sins, they were baptized by him in the Jordan River. 6 John wore clothing made of camel's hair, with a leather belt around his waist, and he ate locusts and wild honey. 7 And this was his message: "After me comes the one more powerful than I, the straps of whose sandals I am not worthy to stoop down and untie. 8 I baptize you with[e] water, but he will baptize you with[e] the Holy Spirit."

### The Baptism and Testing of Jesus

9 At that time Jesus came from Nazareth in Galilee and was baptized by John in the Jordan. 10 Just as Jesus was coming up out of the water, he saw heaven being torn open and the Spirit descending on him like a dove. 11 And a voice came from heaven: "You are my Son, whom I love; with you I am well pleased."

12 At once the Spirit sent him out into the wilderness, 13 and he was in the wilderness forty days, being tempted[f] by Satan. He was with the wild animals, and angels attended him.

### Jesus Announces the Good News

14 After John was put in prison, Jesus went into Galilee, proclaiming the good news of God. 15 "The time has come," he said. "The kingdom of God has come near. Repent and believe the good news!"

### Jesus Calls His First Disciples

16 As Jesus walked beside the Sea of Galilee, he saw Simon and his brother Andrew casting a net into the lake, for they were fishermen. 17 "Come, follow me," Jesus said, "and I will send you out to fish for people." 18 At once they left their nets and followed him.

19 When he had gone a little farther, he saw James son of Zebedee and his brother John in a boat, preparing their

---

## Amplified Bible

### THE GOSPEL ACCORDING TO

# Mark

**1** The beginning [of the facts] of the good news (the Gospel) of Jesus Christ, [a]the Son of God.

2 b Just as it is written in the prophet Isaiah: Behold, I send My messenger before Your face, who will make ready Your way—[Mal. 3:1.]

3 A voice of one crying in the wilderness [shouting in the desert], Prepare the way of the Lord, make His [c]beaten tracks straight (level and passable)! [Isa. 40:3.]

4 John the Baptist appeared in the wilderness (desert), preaching a baptism [d]obligating] repentance ([e]a change of one's mind for the better, heartily amending one's ways, with abhorrence of his past sins) in order [f]to obtain forgiveness of and release from sins.

5 And there kept going out to him [continuously] all the country of Judea and all the inhabitants of Jerusalem; and they were baptized by him in the river Jordan, [d]as they were confessing their sins.

6 And John wore clothing woven of camel's hair and had a leather girdle around his loins and ate locusts and wild honey.

7 And he preached, saying, After me comes He Who is stronger (more powerful and more valiant) than I, the strap of Whose sandals I am not worthy or fit to stoop down and unloose.

8 I have baptized you with water, but He will baptize you with the Holy Spirit.

9 In those days Jesus came from Nazareth of Galilee and was baptized by John in the Jordan.

10 And when He came up out of the water, at once he [John] saw the heavens torn open and the [Holy] Spirit like a dove coming down [d]to enter] [g]into Him. [John 1:32.]

11 And there came a voice [d]out from within heaven, You are My Beloved Son; in You I am well pleased. [Ps. 2:7; Isa. 42:1.]

12 Immediately the [Holy] Spirit [from within] drove Him out into the wilderness (desert),

13 And He stayed in the wilderness (desert) forty days, being tempted [all the while] by Satan; and He was with the wild beasts, and the angels ministered to Him [continually].

14 Now after John was arrested and put in prison, Jesus came into Galilee, preaching the good news (the Gospel) of the kingdom of God,

15 And saying, The [appointed period of] time is fulfilled (completed), and the kingdom of God is at hand; repent ([h]have a change of mind which issues in regret for past sins and in change of conduct for the better) and believe (trust in, rely on, and adhere to) the good news (the Gospel).

16 And passing along the shore of the Sea of Galilee, He saw Simon [Peter] and Andrew the brother of Simon casting a net [to and fro] in the sea, for they were fishermen.

17 And Jesus said to them, Come after Me and [e]be My disciples, and I will make you to become fishers of men.

18 And at once they left their nets and [e]yielding up all claim to them] followed [with] Him [e]joining Him as disciples and siding with His party].

19 He went on a little farther and saw James the son of Zebedee, and John his brother, who were in [their] boat putting their nets in order.

---

a 1 Or *Jesus Christ*. *Messiah* (Hebrew) and *Christ* (Greek) both mean *Anointed One.* b 1 Some manuscripts do not have *the Son of God.* c 2 Mal. 3:1 d 3 Isaiah 40:3 e 8 Or *in* f 13 The Greek for *tempted* can also mean *tested.*

a Some manuscripts do not contain this phrase. b Kenneth Wuest, *Word Studies in the Greek New Testament.* c James Moulton and George Milligan, *The Vocabulary of the Greek Testament.* d Kenneth Wuest, *Word Studies.* e Joseph Thayer, *A Greek-English Lexicon of the New Testament.* f Charles B. Williams, *The New Testament: A Translation in the Language of the People.* g Literal translation of *eis.* h Marvin Vincent, *Word Studies in the New Testament.*

## New International Version

nets. [20]Without delay he called them, and they left their father Zebedee in the boat with the hired men and followed him.

### Jesus Drives Out an Impure Spirit

[21]They went to Capernaum, and when the Sabbath came, Jesus went into the synagogue and began to teach. [22]The people were amazed at his teaching, because he taught them as one who had authority, not as the teachers of the law. [23]Just then a man in their synagogue who was possessed by an impure spirit cried out, [24]"What do you want with us, Jesus of Nazareth? Have you come to destroy us? I know who you are—the Holy One of God!"

[25]"Be quiet!" said Jesus sternly. "Come out of him!" [26]The impure spirit shook the man violently and came out of him with a shriek.

[27]The people were all so amazed that they asked each other, "What is this? A new teaching—and with authority! He even gives orders to impure spirits and they obey him." [28]News about him spread quickly over the whole region of Galilee.

### Jesus Heals Many

[29]As soon as they left the synagogue, they went with James and John to the home of Simon and Andrew. [30]Simon's mother-in-law was in bed with a fever, and they immediately told Jesus about her. [31]So he went to her, took her hand and helped her up. The fever left her and she began to wait on them.

[32]That evening after sunset the people brought to Jesus all the sick and demon-possessed. [33]The whole town gathered at the door, [34]and Jesus healed many who had various diseases. He also drove out many demons, but he would not let the demons speak because they knew who he was.

### Jesus Prays in a Solitary Place

[35]Very early in the morning, while it was still dark, Jesus got up, left the house and went off to a solitary place, where he prayed. [36]Simon and his companions went to look for him, [37]and when they found him, they exclaimed: "Everyone is looking for you!"

[38]Jesus replied, "Let us go somewhere else—to the nearby villages—so I can preach there also. That is why I have come." [39]So he traveled throughout Galilee, preaching in their synagogues and driving out demons.

### Jesus Heals a Man With Leprosy

[40]A man with leprosy[a] came to him and begged him on his knees, "If you are willing, you can make me clean."

[41]Jesus was indignant.[b] He reached out his hand and touched the man. "I am willing," he said. "Be clean!" [42]Immediately the leprosy left him and he was cleansed.

[43]Jesus sent him away at once with a strong warning:

## Amplified Bible

[20]And immediately He called out to them, and [a abandoning all mutual claims] they left their father Zebedee in the boat with the hired men and went off after Him [a to be His disciples, side with His party, and follow Him].

[21]And they entered into Capernaum, and immediately on the Sabbath He went into the synagogue and began to teach.

[22]And they were completely astonished at His teaching, for He was teaching as One Who possessed authority, and not as the scribes.

[23]Just at that time there was in their synagogue a man [who was in the power] of an unclean spirit; and now [immediately] he raised a deep *and* terrible cry from the depths of his throat, saying,

[24]What have You to do with us, Jesus of Nazareth? Have You come to destroy us? I know who You are—the Holy One of God!

[25]And Jesus rebuked him, saying, Hush up (be muzzled, gagged), and come out of him!

[26]And the unclean spirit, throwing the man into convulsions and [b]screeching with a loud voice, came out of him.

[27]And they were all so amazed *and* [c]almost terrified that they kept questioning *and* demanding one of another, saying, What is this? What new (fresh) teaching! With authority He gives orders even to the unclean spirits and they obey Him!

[28]And immediately rumors concerning Him spread [everywhere] throughout all the region surrounding Galilee.

[29]And at once He left the synagogue and went into the house of Simon [Peter] and Andrew, accompanied by James and John.

[30]Now Simon's mother-in-law [d]had for some time been lying sick with a fever, and at once they told Him about her.

[31]And He went up to her and took her by the hand and raised her up; and the fever left her, and she began to wait on them.

[32]Now when it was evening, after the sun had set, they brought to Him all who were sick and those under the power of demons,

[33]Until the whole town was gathered together about the door.

[34]And He cured many who were afflicted with various diseases; and He drove out many demons, but would not allow the demons to talk because they knew Him [e intuitively].

[35]And in the morning, long before daylight, He got up and went out to a [f]deserted place, and there He prayed.

[36]And Simon [Peter] and those who were with him followed Him [g pursuing Him eagerly and hunting Him out],

[37]And they found Him and said to Him, Everybody is looking for You.

[38]And He said to them, Let us be going on into the neighboring country towns, that I may preach there also; for that is why I came out.

[39][So] He went throughout the whole of Galilee, preaching in their synagogues and driving out demons.

[40]And a leper came to Him, begging Him on his knees and saying to Him, If You are willing, You are able to make me clean.

[41]And being moved with pity *and* sympathy, Jesus reached out His hand and touched him, and said to him, I am willing; be made clean!

[42]And at once the leprosy [completely] left him and he was made clean [by being healed].

[43]And Jesus charged him sternly (sharply and threateningly, and with earnest admonition) and [acting with deep feeling thrust him forth and] sent him away at once,

*a* Joseph Thayer, *A Greek-English Lexicon.* *b* A. T. Robertson, *Word Pictures in the New Testament.* *c* Alexander Souter, *Pocket Lexicon of the Greek New Testament.* *d* Kenneth Wuest, *Word Studies.* *e* Charles B. Williams, *The New Testament: A Translation.* *f* James Moulton and George Milligan, *The Vocabulary.* *g* Marvin Vincent, *Word Studies.*

*a 40* The Greek word traditionally translated *leprosy* was used for various diseases affecting the skin.   *b 41* Many manuscripts *Jesus was filled with compassion*

## New International Version

44"See that you don't tell this to anyone. But go, show yourself to the priest and offer the sacrifices that Moses commanded for your cleansing, as a testimony to them." 45Instead he went out and began to talk freely, spreading the news. As a result, Jesus could no longer enter a town openly but stayed outside in lonely places. Yet the people still came to him from everywhere.

### Jesus Forgives and Heals a Paralyzed Man

2 A few days later, when Jesus again entered Capernaum, the people heard that he had come home. 2They gathered in such large numbers that there was no room left, not even outside the door, and he preached the word to them. 3Some men came, bringing to him a paralyzed man, carried by four of them. 4Since they could not get him to Jesus because of the crowd, they made an opening in the roof above Jesus by digging through it and then lowered the mat the man was lying on. 5When Jesus saw their faith, he said to the paralyzed man, "Son, your sins are forgiven."

6Now some teachers of the law were sitting there, thinking to themselves, 7"Why does this fellow talk like that? He's blaspheming! Who can forgive sins but God alone?"

8Immediately Jesus knew in his spirit that this was what they were thinking in their hearts, and he said to them, "Why are you thinking these things? 9Which is easier: to say to this paralyzed man, 'Your sins are forgiven,' or to say, 'Get up, take your mat and walk'? 10But I want you to know that the Son of Man has authority on earth to forgive sins." So he said to the man, 11"I tell you, get up, take your mat and go home." 12He got up, took his mat and walked out in full view of them all. This amazed everyone and they praised God, saying, "We have never seen anything like this!"

### Jesus Calls Levi and Eats With Sinners

13Once again Jesus went out beside the lake. A large crowd came to him, and he began to teach them. 14As he walked along, he saw Levi son of Alphaeus sitting at the tax collector's booth. "Follow me," Jesus told him, and Levi got up and followed him.

15While Jesus was having dinner at Levi's house, many tax collectors and sinners were eating with him and his disciples, for there were many who followed him. 16When the teachers of the law who were Pharisees saw him eating with the sinners and tax collectors, they asked his disciples: "Why does he eat with tax collectors and sinners?"

## Amplified Bible

44And said to him, See that you tell nothing [of this] to anyone; but begone, show yourself to the priest, and offer for your purification what Moses commanded, as a proof (an evidence and witness) to the people [that you are really healed]. [Lev. 13:49; 14:2-32.]

45But he went out and began to talk so freely about it and blaze abroad the news [spreading it everywhere] that [Jesus] could no longer openly go into a town but was outside in [lonely] desert places. But the people kept on coming to Him from ªall sides and every quarter.

2 And Jesus having returned to Capernaum, after some days it was rumored about that He was in the house [probably Peter's].

2And so many people gathered together there that there was no longer room [for them], not even around the door; and He was discussing the Word.

3Then they came, bringing a paralytic to Him, who had been picked up and was being carried by four men.

4And when they could not get him to a place in front of Jesus because of the throng, they dug through the roof above Him; and when they had ᵇscooped out an opening, they let down the [ᵇthickly padded] quilt or mat upon which the paralyzed man lay.

5And when Jesus saw their faith [their confidence in God through Him], He said to the paralyzed man, Son, your sins are forgiven [you] and put away [that is, the ᶜpenalty is remitted, the sense of guilt removed, and you are made upright and in right standing with God].

6Now some of the scribes were sitting there, holding a dialogue with themselves as they questioned in their hearts,

7Why does this ᵈMan talk like this? He is blaspheming! Who can forgive sins [ᶜremove guilt, remit the penalty, and bestow righteousness instead] except God alone?

8And at once Jesus, becoming fully aware in His spirit that they thus debated within themselves, said to them, Why do you argue (debate, reason) about all this in your hearts?

9Which is easier: to say to the paralyzed man, Your sins are forgiven and ᶜput away, or to say, Rise, take up your sleeping pad or mat, and start walking about [and ᶜkeep on walking]?

10But that you may know positively and beyond a doubt that the Son of Man has right and authority and power on earth to forgive sins—He said to the paralyzed man,

11I say to you, arise, pick up and carry your sleeping pad or mat, and be going on home.

12And he arose at once and picked up the sleeping pad or mat and went out before them all, so that they were all amazed and ᵉrecognized and praised and thanked God, saying, We have never seen anything like this before!

13[Jesus] went out again along the seashore; and all the multitude kept gathering about Him, and He kept teaching them.

14And as He was passing by, He saw Levi (Matthew) son of Alphaeus sitting at the tax office, and He said to him, Follow Me! [Be ᶠjoined to Me as a disciple, side with My party!] And he arose and joined Him as His disciple and sided with His party and accompanied Him.

15And as Jesus, together with His disciples, sat at table in his [Levi's] house, many tax collectors and persons [ᶠdefinitely stained] with sin were dining with Him, for there were many who walked the same road (followed) with Him.

16And the scribes [belonging to the party] of the Pharisees, when they saw that He was eating with [those ᶠdefinitely known to be especially wicked] sinners and tax collectors, said to His disciples, Why does He eat and drink with tax collectors and [notorious] sinners?

ª James Moulton and George Milligan, *The Vocabulary.* ᵇ Marvin Vincent, *Word Studies.* ᶜ Kenneth Wuest, *Word Studies.* ᵈ Capitalized because of what He is, the spotless Son of God, not what the speakers may have thought He was. ᵉ Hermann Cremer, *Biblico-Theological Lexicon.* ᶠ Joseph Thayer, *A Greek-English Lexicon.*

# New International Version

17On hearing this, Jesus said to them, "It is not the healthy who need a doctor, but the sick. I have not come to call the righteous, but sinners."

## Jesus Questioned About Fasting

18Now John's disciples and the Pharisees were fasting. Some people came and asked Jesus, "How is it that John's disciples and the disciples of the Pharisees are fasting, but yours are not?"

19Jesus answered, "How can the guests of the bridegroom fast while he is with them? They cannot, so long as they have him with them. 20But the time will come when the bridegroom will be taken from them, and on that day they will fast.

21"No one sews a patch of unshrunk cloth on an old garment. Otherwise, the new piece will pull away from the old, making the tear worse. 22And no one pours new wine into old wineskins. Otherwise, the wine will burst the skins, and both the wine and the wineskins will be ruined. No, they pour new wine into new wineskins."

## Jesus Is Lord of the Sabbath

23One Sabbath Jesus was going through the grainfields, and as his disciples walked along, they began to pick some heads of grain. 24The Pharisees said to him, "Look, why are they doing what is unlawful on the Sabbath?"

25He answered, "Have you never read what David did when he and his companions were hungry and in need? 26In the days of Abiathar the high priest, he entered the house of God and ate the consecrated bread, which is lawful only for priests to eat. And he also gave some to his companions."

27Then he said to them, "The Sabbath was made for man, not man for the Sabbath. 28So the Son of Man is Lord even of the Sabbath."

## Jesus Heals on the Sabbath

3 Another time Jesus went into the synagogue, and a man with a shriveled hand was there. 2Some of them were looking for a reason to accuse Jesus, so they watched him closely to see if he would heal him on the Sabbath. 3Jesus said to the man with the shriveled hand, "Stand up in front of everyone."

4Then Jesus asked them, "Which is lawful on the Sabbath: to do good or to do evil, to save life or to kill?" But they remained silent.

5He looked around at them in anger and, deeply distressed at their stubborn hearts, said to the man, "Stretch out your hand." He stretched it out, and his hand was completely restored. 6Then the Pharisees went out and began to plot with the Herodians how they might kill Jesus.

## Crowds Follow Jesus

7Jesus withdrew with his disciples to the lake, and a large crowd from Galilee followed. 8When they heard about all he was doing, many people came to him from Judea, Jerusalem, Idumea, and the regions across the Jordan and around Tyre and Sidon. 9Because of the crowd he told his disciples to have a small boat ready for him, to keep the people from crowding him. 10For he had healed

# Amplified Bible

17And when Jesus heard it, He said to them, Those who are strong *and* well have no need of a physician, but those who are weak *and* sick; I came not to call the righteous ones *to repentance,* but sinners (the *a*erring ones and *b*all those not free from sin).

18Now John's disciples and the Pharisees were observing a fast; and [some people] came and asked Jesus, Why are John's disciples and the disciples of the Pharisees fasting, but Your disciples are not doing so?

19Jesus answered them, Can the wedding guests fast (abstain from food and drink) while the bridegroom is with them? As long as they have the bridegroom with them, they cannot fast.

20But the days will come when the bridegroom will be taken away from them, and they will fast in that day.

21No one sews a patch of unshrunken (new) goods on an old garment; if he does, the patch tears away from it, the new from the old, and the rent (tear) becomes bigger *and* worse [than it was before].

22And no one puts new wine into old wineskins; if he does, the wine will burst the skins, and the wine is lost and the bottles destroyed; but new wine is to be put in new (fresh) wineskins.

23One Sabbath He was going along beside the fields of standing grain, and as they made their way, His disciples began to *c*pick off the grains. [Deut. 23:25.]

24And the Pharisees said to Him, Look! Why are they doing what is not permitted *or* lawful on the Sabbath?

25And He said to them, Have you never [even] read what David did when he was in need and was hungry, he and those who were accompanying him?—

26How he went into the house of God when Abiathar was the high priest, and ate the sacred loaves set forth [before God], which it is not permitted *or* lawful for any but the priests to eat, and [how he] also gave [them] to those who were with him? [I Sam. 21:1-6; II Sam. 8:17.]

27And Jesus said to them, The Sabbath was made on account *and* for the sake of man, not man for the Sabbath; [Exod. 23:12; Deut. 5:14.]

28So the Son of Man is Lord even of the Sabbath.

3 Again Jesus went into a synagogue, and a man was there who had one withered hand [*d*as the result of accident or disease].

2And [the Pharisees] kept watching Jesus [closely] to see whether He would cure him on the Sabbath, so that they might get a charge to bring against Him [*e*formally].

3And He said to the man who had the withered hand, Get up [and stand here] in the midst.

4And He said to them, Is it lawful *and* right on the Sabbath to do good or to do evil, to save life or to take it? But they kept silence.

5And He glanced around at them with vexation *and* anger, grieved at the hardening of their hearts, and said to the man, Hold out your hand. He held it out, and his hand was [completely] restored.

6Then the Pharisees went out and immediately held a consultation with the Herodians against Him, how they might [devise some means to] put Him to death.

7And Jesus retired with His disciples to the lake, and a great throng from Galilee followed Him. Also from Judea

8And from Jerusalem and Idumea and from beyond the Jordan and from about Tyre and Sidon—a vast multitude, hearing all the many things that He was doing, came to Him.

9And He told His disciples to have a little boat in [constant] readiness for Him because of the crowd, lest they press hard upon Him *and* crush Him.

*a* Robert Young, *Analytical Concordance to the Bible.* *b* Joseph Thayer, *A Greek-English Lexicon.* *c* Kenneth Wuest, *Word Studies.* *d* Marvin Vincent, *Word Studies.*

## New International Version

many, so that those with diseases were pushing forward to touch him. [11]Whenever the impure spirits saw him, they fell down before him and cried out, "You are the Son of God." [12]But he gave them strict orders not to tell others about him.

### Jesus Appoints the Twelve

[13]Jesus went up on a mountainside and called to him those he wanted, and they came to him. [14]He appointed twelve[a] that they might be with him and that he might send them out to preach [15]and to have authority to drive out demons. [16]These are the twelve he appointed: Simon (to whom he gave the name Peter), [17]James son of Zebedee and his brother John (to them he gave the name Boanerges, which means "sons of thunder"), [18]Andrew, Philip, Bartholomew, Matthew, Thomas, James son of Alphaeus, Thaddaeus, Simon the Zealot [19]and Judas Iscariot, who betrayed him.

### Jesus Accused by His Family and by Teachers of the Law

[20]Then Jesus entered a house, and again a crowd gathered, so that he and his disciples were not even able to eat. [21]When his family[b] heard about this, they went to take charge of him, for they said, "He is out of his mind."

[22]And the teachers of the law who came down from Jerusalem said, "He is possessed by Beelzebul! By the prince of demons he is driving out demons."

[23]So Jesus called them over to him and began to speak to them in parables: "How can Satan drive out Satan? [24]If a kingdom is divided against itself, that kingdom cannot stand. [25]If a house is divided against itself, that house cannot stand. [26]And if Satan opposes himself and is divided, he cannot stand; his end has come. [27]In fact, no one can enter a strong man's house without first tying him up. Then he can plunder the strong man's house. [28]Truly I tell you, people can be forgiven all their sins and every slander they utter, [29]but whoever blasphemes against the Holy Spirit will never be forgiven; they are guilty of an eternal sin."

[30]He said this because they were saying, "He has an impure spirit."

[31]Then Jesus' mother and brothers arrived. Standing outside, they sent someone in to call him. [32]A crowd was sitting around him, and they told him, "Your mother and brothers are outside looking for you."

[33]"Who are my mother and my brothers?" he asked.

[34]Then he looked at those seated in a circle around him and said, "Here are my mother and my brothers! [35]Whoever does God's will is my brother and sister and mother."

## Amplified Bible

[10]For He had healed so many that all who had distressing bodily diseases kept falling upon Him *and* pressing upon Him in order that they might touch Him.

[11]And the spirits, the unclean ones, *a*as often as they might see Him, fell down before Him and kept screaming out, You are the Son of God!

[12]And He charged them strictly *and* severely under penalty again *and* again that they should not make Him known.

[13]And He went up on the hillside and called to Him [*b*for Himself] those whom He wanted *and* chose, and they came to Him.

[14]And He appointed twelve to *b*continue to be with Him, and that He might send them out to preach [as apostles or special messengers]

[15]And to have authority *and* power to *heal the sick and to* drive out demons:

[16][They were] Simon, and He surnamed [him] Peter;

[17]James son of Zebedee and John the brother of James, and He surnamed them Boanerges, that is, Sons of Thunder;

[18]And Andrew, and Philip, and Bartholomew (Nathaniel), and Matthew, and Thomas, and James son of Alphaeus, and Thaddaeus (Judas, not Iscariot), and Simon the Cananaean [also called Zelotes],

[19]And Judas Iscariot, he who betrayed Him.

[20]Then He went to a house [probably Peter's], but a throng came together again, so that Jesus and His disciples could not even take food.

[21]And when those *c*who belonged to Him (*d*His kinsmen) heard it, they went out to take Him by force, for they kept saying, He is out of *e*His mind (beside Himself, deranged)!

[22]And the scribes who came down from Jerusalem said, He is possessed by Beelzebub, and, By [the help of] the prince of demons He is casting out demons.

[23]And He summoned them to Him and said to them in parables (illustrations or comparisons put beside truths to explain them), How can Satan drive out Satan?

[24]And if a kingdom is divided *and* rebelling against itself, that kingdom cannot stand.

[25]And if a house is divided (split into factions and rebelling) against itself, that house will not be able to last.

[26]And if Satan has raised an insurrection against himself and is divided, he cannot stand but is [surely] coming to an end.

[27]But no one can go into a strong man's house and ransack his household goods right and left *and* seize them as plunder unless he first binds the strong man; then indeed he may [thoroughly] plunder his house. [Isa. 49:24, 25.]

[28]Truly *and* solemnly I say to you, all sins will be forgiven the sons of men, and whatever abusive *and* blasphemous things they utter;

[29]But whoever speaks abusively against *or* maliciously misrepresents the Holy Spirit can never get forgiveness, but is guilty of *and* is in the grasp of *d*an everlasting trespass.

[30]For they *a*persisted in saying, *e*He has an unclean spirit.

[31]Then His mother and His brothers came and, standing outside, they sent word to Him, calling [for] Him.

[32]And a crowd was sitting around Him, and they said to Him, Your mother and Your brothers *and Your sisters* are outside asking for You.

[33]And He replied, Who are My mother and My brothers?

[34]And looking around on those who sat in a circle about Him, He said, See! Here are My mother and My brothers;

[35]For whoever does the things God wills is My brother and sister and mother!

---

*a* Marvin Vincent, *Word Studies.*  *b* Kenneth Wuest, *Word Studies.*
*c* William Tyndale, *The Tyndale Bible.*  *d* John Wycliffe, *The Wycliffe Bible.*  *e* Capitalized for what He is, the spotless Son of God, not what the speakers may have thought He was.

---

*a 14* Some manuscripts *twelve—designating them apostles—*
*b 21* Or *his associates*

## New International Version

### The Parable of the Sower

**4** Again Jesus began to teach by the lake. The crowd that gathered around him was so large that he got into a boat and sat in it out on the lake, while all the people were along the shore at the water's edge. ²He taught them many things by parables, and in his teaching said: ³"Listen! A farmer went out to sow his seed. ⁴As he was scattering the seed, some fell along the path, and the birds came and ate it up. ⁵Some fell on rocky places, where it did not have much soil. It sprang up quickly, because the soil was shallow. ⁶But when the sun came up, the plants were scorched, and they withered because they had no root. ⁷Other seed fell among thorns, which grew up and choked the plants, so that they did not bear grain. ⁸Still other seed fell on good soil. It came up, grew and produced a crop, some multiplying thirty, some sixty, some a hundred times."

⁹Then Jesus said, "Whoever has ears to hear, let them hear."

¹⁰When he was alone, the Twelve and the others around him asked him about the parables. ¹¹He told them, "The secret of the kingdom of God has been given to you. But to those on the outside everything is said in parables ¹²so that,

"'they may be ever seeing but never perceiving,
    and ever hearing but never understanding;
otherwise they might turn and be forgiven!'ᵃ"

¹³Then Jesus said to them, "Don't you understand this parable? How then will you understand any parable? ¹⁴The farmer sows the word. ¹⁵Some people are like seed along the path, where the word is sown. As soon as they hear it, Satan comes and takes away the word that was sown in them. ¹⁶Others, like seed sown on rocky places, hear the word and at once receive it with joy. ¹⁷But since they have no root, they last only a short time. When trouble or persecution comes because of the word, they quickly fall away. ¹⁸Still others, like seed sown among thorns, hear the word; ¹⁹but the worries of this life, the deceitfulness of wealth and the desires for other things come in and choke the word, making it unfruitful. ²⁰Others, like seed sown on good soil, hear the word, accept it, and produce a crop—some thirty, some sixty, some a hundred times what was sown."

### A Lamp on a Stand

²¹He said to them, "Do you bring in a lamp to put it under a bowl or a bed? Instead, don't you put it on its stand?

## Amplified Bible

**4** Again Jesus began to teach beside the lake. And a very great crowd gathered about Him, so that He got into a ship in order to sit in it on the sea, and the whole crowd was at the lakeside on the shore.

²And He taught them many things in parables (illustrations or comparisons put beside truths to explain them), and in His teaching He said to them:

³Give attention to this! Behold, a sower went out to sow.

⁴And as he was sowing, some seed fell along the path, and the birds came and ate it up.

⁵Other seed [of the same kind] fell on ground full of rocks, where it had not much soil; and at once it sprang up, because it had no depth of soil;

⁶And when the sun came up, it was scorched, and because it had not taken root, it withered away.

⁷Other seed [of the same kind] fell among thorn plants, and the thistles grew *and* pressed together *and* utterly choked *and* suffocated it, and it yielded no grain.

⁸And other seed [of the same kind] fell into good (well-adapted) soil and brought forth grain, growing up and increasing, and yielded up to thirty times as much, and sixty times as much, and even a hundred times as much as had been sown.

⁹And He said, He who has ears to hear, let him be hearing [and let him ᵃconsider, and comprehend].

¹⁰And as soon as He was alone, those who were around Him, with the Twelve [apostles], began to ask Him about the parables.

¹¹And He said to them, To you has been entrusted the mystery of the kingdom of God [that is, ᵇthe secret counsels of God which are hidden from the ungodly]; but for those outside [ᶜof our circle] everything becomes a parable,

¹²In order that they may [indeed] look *and* look but not see *and* perceive, and may hear *and* hear but not grasp *and* comprehend, ᵈlest haply they should turn again, and it [ᵇtheir willful rejection of the truth] should be forgiven them. [Isa. 6:9, 10; Matt. 13:13-15.]

¹³And He said to them, Do you not discern *and* understand this parable? How then is it possible for you to discern *and* understand all the parables?

¹⁴The sower sows the Word.

¹⁵The ones along the path are those who have the Word sown [in their hearts], but when they hear, Satan comes at once and [by force] takes away the message which is sown in them.

¹⁶And in the same way the ones sown upon stony ground are those who, when they hear the Word, at once receive *and* accept *and* welcome it with joy;

¹⁷And they have no real root in themselves, and so they endure for a little while; then when trouble or persecution arises on account of the Word, they immediately are offended (become displeased, indignant, resentful) *and* they stumble *and* fall away.

¹⁸And the ones sown among the thorns are others who hear the Word;

¹⁹Then the cares *and* anxieties of the world *and* distractions of the age, and the pleasure *and* delight *and* false glamour *and* deceitfulness of riches, and the craving *and* passionate desire for other things creep in and choke *and* suffocate the Word, and it becomes fruitless.

²⁰And those sown on the good (well-adapted) soil are the ones who hear the Word and receive *and* accept *and* welcome it and bear fruit—some thirty times as much as was sown, some sixty times as much, and some [even] a hundred times as much.

²¹And He said to them, Is the lamp brought in to be put under a ᵉpeck measure or under a bed, and not [to be put] on the lampstand?

## New International Version

22For whatever is hidden is meant to be disclosed, and whatever is concealed is meant to be brought out into the open. 23If anyone has ears to hear, let them hear."

24"Consider carefully what you hear," he continued. "With the measure you use, it will be measured to you— and even more. 25Whoever has will be given more; whoever does not have, even what they have will be taken from them."

### The Parable of the Growing Seed

26He also said, "This is what the kingdom of God is like. A man scatters seed on the ground. 27Night and day, whether he sleeps or gets up, the seed sprouts and grows, though he does not know how. 28All by itself the soil produces grain—first the stalk, then the head, then the full kernel in the head. 29As soon as the grain is ripe, he puts the sickle to it, because the harvest has come."

### The Parable of the Mustard Seed

30Again he said, "What shall we say the kingdom of God is like, or what parable shall we use to describe it? 31It is like a mustard seed, which is the smallest of all seeds on earth. 32Yet when planted, it grows and becomes the largest of all garden plants, with such big branches that the birds can perch in its shade."

33With many similar parables Jesus spoke the word to them, as much as they could understand. 34He did not say anything to them without using a parable. But when he was alone with his own disciples, he explained everything.

### Jesus Calms the Storm

35That day when evening came, he said to his disciples, "Let us go over to the other side." 36Leaving the crowd behind, they took him along, just as he was, in the boat. There were also other boats with him. 37A furious squall came up, and the waves broke over the boat, so that it was nearly swamped. 38Jesus was in the stern, sleeping on a cushion. The disciples woke him and said to him, "Teacher, don't you care if we drown?"

39He got up, rebuked the wind and said to the waves, "Quiet! Be still!" Then the wind died down and it was completely calm.

40He said to his disciples, "Why are you so afraid? Do you still have no faith?"

41They were terrified and asked each other, "Who is this? Even the wind and the waves obey him!"

### Jesus Restores a Demon-Possessed Man

**5** They went across the lake to the region of the Gerasenes.a 2When Jesus got out of the boat, a man with an impure spirit came from the tombs to meet him.

## Amplified Bible

22[aThings are hidden temporarily only as a means to revelation.] For there is nothing hidden except to be revealed, nor is anything [temporarily] kept secret except in order that it may be made known.

23If any man has ears to hear, let him be listening and let him perceive and comprehend.

24And He said to them, Be careful what you are hearing. The measure b [of thought and study] you give [to cthe truth you hear] will be the measure b [of virtue and knowledge] that comes back to you—and more [besides] will be given to you who hear.

25For to him who has will more be given; and from him who has nothing, even what he has will be taken away [dby force],

26And He said, The kingdom of God is like a man who scatters seed upon the ground,

27And then continues sleeping and rising night and day while the seed sprouts and grows and dincreases—he knows not how.

28The earth produces [acting] by itself—first the blade, then the ear, then the full grain in the ear.

29But when the grain is ripe and permits, immediately he esends forth [the reapers] and puts in the sickle, because the harvest stands ready.

30And He said, With what can we compare the kingdom of God, or what parable shall we use to illustrate and explain it?

31It is like a grain of mustard seed, which, when sown upon the ground, is the smallest of all seeds upon the earth;

32Yet after it is sown, it grows up and becomes the greatest of all garden herbs and puts out large branches, so that the birds of the air are able to make nests and dwell in its shade.

33With many such parables [Jesus] spoke the Word to them, as they were able to hear and dto comprehend and understand.

34He did not tell them anything without a parable; but privately to His disciples (fthose who were peculiarly His own) He explained everything [fully].

35On that same day [when] evening had come, He said to them, Let us go over to the other side [of the lake].

36And leaving the throng, they took Him with them, [just] as He was, in the boat [in which He was sitting]. And other boats were with Him.

37And a furious storm of wind [fof hurricane proportions] arose, and the waves kept beating into the boat, so that it was already becoming filled.

38But He [Himself] was in the stern [of the boat], asleep on the [leather] cushion; and they awoke Him and said to Him, Master, do You not care that we are perishing?

39And He arose and rebuked the wind and said to the sea, Hush now! Be still (muzzled)! And the wind ceased (esank to rest as if exhausted by its beating) and there was [immediately] a great calm (ga perfect peacefulness).

40He said to them, Why are you so timid and fearful? How is it that you have no faith (no hfirmly relying trust)?

41And they were filled with great awe and efeared exceedingly and said one to another, Who then is this, that even wind and sea obey Him?

**5** They came to the other side of the sea to the region of the Gerasenes.

2And as soon as He got out of the boat, there met Him out of the tombs a man [under the power] of an unclean spirit.

---

a Henry Swete, *The Gospel According to Saint Mark*; A. T. Robertson, *Word Pictures*; Marvin Vincent, *Word Studies*; and others. b W. Robertson Nicoll, ed., *The Expositor's Greek New Testament*. c James C. Gray and George M. Adams, *Bible Commentary*; Kenneth Wuest, *Word Studies*; Albert Barnes, *Notes on the New Testament*; and others. d Joseph Thayer, *A Greek-English Lexicon*. e Marvin Vincent, *Word Studies*. f Kenneth Wuest, *Word Studies*. g John Wycliffe, *The Wycliffe Bible*. h Hermann Cremer, *Biblico-Theological Lexicon*.

---

a 1 Some manuscripts *Gadarenes*; other manuscripts *Gergesenes*

## New International Version

³This man lived in the tombs, and no one could bind him anymore, not even with a chain. ⁴For he had often been chained hand and foot, but he tore the chains apart and broke the irons on his feet. No one was strong enough to subdue him. ⁵Night and day among the tombs and in the hills he would cry out and cut himself with stones.

⁶When he saw Jesus from a distance, he ran and fell on his knees in front of him. ⁷He shouted at the top of his voice, "What do you want with me, Jesus, Son of the Most High God? In God's name don't torture me!" ⁸For Jesus had said to him, "Come out of this man, you impure spirit!"

⁹Then Jesus asked him, "What is your name?"

"My name is Legion," he replied, "for we are many." ¹⁰And he begged Jesus again and again not to send them out of the area.

¹¹A large herd of pigs was feeding on the nearby hillside. ¹²The demons begged Jesus, "Send us among the pigs; allow us to go into them." ¹³He gave them permission, and the impure spirits came out and went into the pigs. The herd, about two thousand in number, rushed down the steep bank into the lake and were drowned.

¹⁴Those tending the pigs ran off and reported this in the town and countryside, and the people went out to see what had happened. ¹⁵When they came to Jesus, they saw the man who had been possessed by the legion of demons, sitting there, dressed and in his right mind; and they were afraid. ¹⁶Those who had seen it told the people what had happened to the demon-possessed man—and told about the pigs as well. ¹⁷Then the people began to plead with Jesus to leave their region.

¹⁸As Jesus was getting into the boat, the man who had been demon-possessed begged to go with him. ¹⁹Jesus did not let him, but said, "Go home to your own people and tell them how much the Lord has done for you, and how he has had mercy on you." ²⁰So the man went away and began to tell in the Decapolis[a] how much Jesus had done for him. And all the people were amazed.

### Jesus Raises a Dead Girl and Heals a Sick Woman

²¹When Jesus had again crossed over by boat to the other side of the lake, a large crowd gathered around him while he was by the lake. ²²Then one of the synagogue leaders, named Jairus, came, and when he saw Jesus, he fell at his feet. ²³He pleaded earnestly with him, "My little daughter is dying. Please come and put your hands on her so that she will be healed and live." ²⁴So Jesus went with him.

A large crowd followed and pressed around him. ²⁵And a woman was there who had been subject to bleeding for twelve years. ²⁶She had suffered a great deal under the

## Amplified Bible

³This man ᵃcontinually lived among the tombs, and no one could subdue him any more, even with a chain;

⁴For he had been bound often with shackles for the feet and ᵇhandcuffs, but the handcuffs of [light] chains he wrenched apart, and the shackles he rubbed and ground together and broke in pieces; and no one had strength enough to restrain or tame him.

⁵Night and day among the tombs and on the mountains he was always ᵇshrieking and screaming and ᶜbeating and bruising and ᵈcutting himself with stones.

⁶And when from a distance he saw Jesus, he ran and fell on his knees before Him in homage,

⁷And crying out with a loud voice, he said, What have You to do with me, Jesus, Son of the Most High God? [What is there in common between us?] I ᵃsolemnly implore you by God, do not begin to torment me!

⁸For Jesus was commanding, Come out of the man, you unclean spirit!

⁹And He asked him, What is your name? He replied, My name is Legion, for we are many.

¹⁰And he kept begging Him urgently not to send them [himself and the other demons] away out of that region.

¹¹Now a great herd of hogs was grazing there on the hillside.

¹²And the demons begged Him, saying, Send us to the hogs, that we may go into them!

¹³So He gave them permission. And the unclean spirits came out [of the man] and entered into the hogs; and the herd, numbering about 2,000, rushed headlong down the steep slope into the sea and were drowned in the sea.

¹⁴The hog feeders ran away, and told [it] in the town and in the country. And [the people] came to see what it was that had taken place.

¹⁵And they came to Jesus and looked intently and searchingly at the man who had been a demoniac, sitting there, clothed and in his right mind, [the same man] who had had the legion [of demons]; and they were ᵇseized with alarm and struck with fear.

¹⁶And those who had seen it related in full what had happened to the man possessed by demons and to the hogs.

¹⁷And they began to beg [Jesus] to leave their neighborhood.

¹⁸And when He had stepped into the boat, the man who had been controlled by the unclean spirits kept begging Him that he might be with Him.

¹⁹But Jesus refused to permit him, but said to him, Go home to your own [family and relatives and friends] and bring back word to them of how much the Lord has done for you, and [how He has] had sympathy for you and mercy on you.

²⁰And he departed and began to publicly proclaim in Decapolis [the region of the ten cities] how much Jesus had done for him, and all the people were astonished and marveled. [Matt. 4:25.]

²¹And when Jesus had recrossed in the boat to the other side, a great throng gathered about Him, and He was at the lakeshore.

²²Then one of the rulers of the synagogue came up, Jairus by name; and seeing Him, he prostrated himself at His feet

²³And begged Him earnestly, saying, My little daughter is at the point of death. Come and lay Your hands on her, so that she may be healed and live.

²⁴And Jesus went with him; and a great crowd kept following Him and pressed Him ᵇfrom all sides [so as almost to suffocate Him].

²⁵And there was a woman who had had a flow of blood for twelve years,

²⁶And who had endured much ᶜsuffering under [the

ᵃ Kenneth Wuest, Word Studies. ᵇ Joseph Thayer, A Greek-English Lexicon. ᶜ James Moulton and George Milligan, The Vocabulary. ᵈ G. Abbott-Smith, Manual Greek Lexicon. ᵉ Marvin Vincent, Word Studies.

## New International Version

care of many doctors and had spent all she had, yet instead of getting better she grew worse. <sup>27</sup>When she heard about Jesus, she came up behind him in the crowd and touched his cloak, <sup>28</sup>because she thought, "If I just touch his clothes, I will be healed." <sup>29</sup>Immediately her bleeding stopped and she felt in her body that she was freed from her suffering.

<sup>30</sup>At once Jesus realized that power had gone out from him. He turned around in the crowd and asked, "Who touched my clothes?"

<sup>31</sup>"You see the people crowding against you," his disciples answered, "and yet you can ask, 'Who touched me?'"

<sup>32</sup>But Jesus kept looking around to see who had done it. <sup>33</sup>Then the woman, knowing what had happened to her, came and fell at his feet and, trembling with fear, told him the whole truth. <sup>34</sup>He said to her, "Daughter, your faith has healed you. Go in peace and be freed from your suffering."

<sup>35</sup>While Jesus was still speaking, some people came from the house of Jairus, the synagogue leader. "Your daughter is dead," they said. "Why bother the teacher anymore?"

<sup>36</sup>Overhearing[a] what they said, Jesus told him, "Don't be afraid; just believe."

<sup>37</sup>He did not let anyone follow him except Peter, James and John the brother of James. <sup>38</sup>When they came to the home of the synagogue leader, Jesus saw a commotion, with people crying and wailing loudly. <sup>39</sup>He went in and said to them, "Why all this commotion and wailing? The child is not dead but asleep." <sup>40</sup>But they laughed at him.

After he put them all out, he took the child's father and mother and the disciples who were with him, and went in where the child was. <sup>41</sup>He took her by the hand and said to her, "Talitha koum!" (which means "Little girl, I say to you, get up!"). <sup>42</sup>Immediately the girl stood up and began to walk around (she was twelve years old). At this they were completely astonished. <sup>43</sup>He gave strict orders not to let anyone know about this, and told them to give her something to eat.

### A Prophet Without Honor

**6** Jesus left there and went to his hometown, accompanied by his disciples. <sup>2</sup>When the Sabbath came, he began to teach in the synagogue, and many who heard him were amazed.

"Where did this man get these things?" they asked. "What's this wisdom that has been given him? What are these remarkable miracles he is performing? <sup>3</sup>Isn't this the carpenter? Isn't this Mary's son and the brother of James, Joseph,[b] Judas and Simon? Aren't his sisters here with us?" And they took offense at him.

a 36 Or *Ignoring*  b 3 Greek *Joses*, a variant of *Joseph*

## Amplified Bible

hands of] many physicians and had spent all that she had, and was no better but instead grew worse.

<sup>27</sup>She had heard the reports concerning Jesus, and she came up behind Him in the throng and touched His garment,

<sup>28</sup>For she kept saying, If I only touch His garments, I shall be restored to health.

<sup>29</sup>And immediately her flow of blood was dried up at the source, and [<sup>a</sup>suddenly] she felt in her body that she was healed of her [<sup>b</sup>distressing] ailment.

<sup>30</sup>And Jesus, recognizing in Himself that the power proceeding from Him had gone forth, turned around immediately in the crowd and said, Who touched My clothes?

<sup>31</sup>And the disciples kept saying to Him, You see the crowd pressing hard around You <sup>b</sup>from all sides, and You ask, Who touched Me?

<sup>32</sup>Still He kept looking around to see her who had done it.

<sup>33</sup>But the woman, knowing what had been done for her, though alarmed *and* frightened and trembling, fell down before Him and told Him the whole truth.

<sup>34</sup>And He said to her, Daughter, your faith (your <sup>b</sup>trust and confidence in Me, springing from faith in God) has restored you to health. Go in <sup>a</sup>(into) peace and be continually healed *and* freed from your [<sup>b</sup>distressing bodily] disease.

<sup>35</sup>While He was still speaking, there came some from the ruler's house, who said [to Jairus], Your daughter has died. Why bother *and* distress the Teacher any further?

<sup>36</sup><sup>c</sup>Overhearing but ignoring what they said, Jesus said to the ruler of the synagogue, Do not be seized with alarm *and* struck with fear; only keep on believing.

<sup>37</sup>And He permitted no one to accompany Him except Peter and James and John the brother of James.

<sup>38</sup>When they arrived at the house of the ruler of the synagogue, He <sup>a</sup>looked [carefully and with understanding] at [the] tumult and *the people* weeping and wailing loudly.

<sup>39</sup>And when He had gone in, He said to them, Why do you make an uproar and weep? The little girl is not dead but is sleeping.

<sup>40</sup>And they laughed *and* <sup>d</sup>jeered at Him. But He put them all out, and, taking the child's father and mother and those who were with Him, He went in where the little girl was *lying*.

<sup>41</sup>Gripping her [firmly] by the hand, He said to her, Talitha cumi—which translated is, Little girl, I say to you, arise [<sup>b</sup>from the sleep of death]!

<sup>42</sup>And instantly the girl got up and started walking around—for she was twelve years old. And they were utterly astonished *and* overcome with amazement.

<sup>43</sup>And He strictly commanded *and* warned them that no one should know this, and He [<sup>b</sup>expressly] told them to give her [something] to eat.

**6** Jesus went away from there and came to His [own] country *and* hometown [Nazareth], and His disciples followed [with] Him.

<sup>2</sup>And on the Sabbath He began to teach in the synagogue; and many who listened to Him were utterly astonished, saying, Where did this <sup>e</sup>Man acquire all this? What is the wisdom [the broad and full intelligence which has been] given to Him? What mighty works *and* exhibitions of power are wrought by His hands!

<sup>3</sup>Is not this the Carpenter, the son of Mary and the brother of James and Joses and Judas and Simon? And are not His sisters here among us? And they took offense at Him *and* <sup>f</sup>were hurt [that is, they <sup>a</sup>disapproved of Him, and it hindered them from acknowledging His authority] *and* they were caused to stumble *and* fall.

a Kenneth Wuest, *Word Studies*.  b Joseph Thayer, *A Greek-English Lexicon*.  c Some manuscripts so read.  d G. Abbott-Smith, *Manual Greek Lexicon*.  e Capitalized because of what He is, the spotless Son of God, not what the speakers may have thought He was.  f William Tyndale, *The Tyndale Bible*.

## New International Version

[4]Jesus said to them, "A prophet is not without honor except in his own town, among his relatives and in his own home." [5]He could not do any miracles there, except lay his hands on a few sick people and heal them. [6]He was amazed at their lack of faith.

### Jesus Sends Out the Twelve

Then Jesus went around teaching from village to village. [7]Calling the Twelve to him, he began to send them out two by two and gave them authority over impure spirits.

[8]These were his instructions: "Take nothing for the journey except a staff—no bread, no bag, no money in your belts. [9]Wear sandals but not an extra shirt. [10]Whenever you enter a house, stay there until you leave that town. [11]And if any place will not welcome you or listen to you, leave that place and shake the dust off your feet as a testimony against them."

[12]They went out and preached that people should repent. [13]They drove out many demons and anointed many sick people with oil and healed them.

### John the Baptist Beheaded

[14]King Herod heard about this, for Jesus' name had become well known. Some were saying,[a] "John the Baptist has been raised from the dead, and that is why miraculous powers are at work in him."

[15]Others said, "He is Elijah."

And still others claimed, "He is a prophet, like one of the prophets of long ago."

[16]But when Herod heard this, he said, "John, whom I beheaded, has been raised from the dead!"

[17]For Herod himself had given orders to have John arrested, and he had him bound and put in prison. He did this because of Herodias, his brother Philip's wife, whom he had married. [18]For John had been saying to Herod, "It is not lawful for you to have your brother's wife." [19]So Herodias nursed a grudge against John and wanted to kill him. But she was not able to, [20]because Herod feared John and protected him, knowing him to be a righteous and holy man. When Herod heard John, he was greatly puzzled[b]; yet he liked to listen to him.

[21]Finally the opportune time came. On his birthday Herod gave a banquet for his high officials and military commanders and the leading men of Galilee. [22]When the daughter of[c] Herodias came in and danced, she pleased Herod and his dinner guests.

The king said to the girl, "Ask me for anything you want, and I'll give it to you." [23]And he promised her with an oath, "Whatever you ask I will give you, up to half my kingdom."

[24]She went out and said to her mother, "What shall I ask for?"

"The head of John the Baptist," she answered.

[25]At once the girl hurried in to the king with the request: "I want you to give me right now the head of John the Baptist on a platter."

## Amplified Bible

[4]But Jesus said to them, A prophet is not without honor (deference, reverence) except in his [own] country and among [his] relatives and in his [own] house.

[5]And He was not able to do [a]even one work of power there, except that He laid His hands on a few sickly people [and] cured them.

[6]And He marveled because of their unbelief (their lack of faith in Him). And He went about among the surrounding villages and continued teaching.

[7]And He called to Him the Twelve [apostles] and began to send them out [as His ambassadors] two by two and gave them authority *and* power over the unclean spirits.

[8]He charged them to take nothing for their journey except a walking stick—no bread, [b]no wallet for a collection bag, no money in their belts (girdles, purses)—

[9]But to go with sandals on their feet and not to put on two tunics (undergarments).

[10]And He told them, Wherever you go into a house, stay there until you leave that place.

[11]And if any community will not receive *and* accept *and* welcome you, and they refuse to listen to you, when you depart, shake off the dust that is on your feet, for a testimony against them. [c]Truly I tell you, it will be more tolerable for Sodom and Gomorrah in the judgment day than for that town.

[12]So they went out and preached that men should repent [[d]that they should change their minds for the better and heartily amend their ways, with abhorrence of their past sins].

[13]And they drove out many unclean spirits and anointed with oil many who were sick and cured them.

[14]King Herod heard of it, for [Jesus'] name had become well known. [e]He *and* they [of his court] said, John the Baptist has been raised from the dead; that is why these mighty powers [[f]of performing miracles] are at work in Him.

[15][But] others kept saying, It is Elijah! And others said, It is a prophet, like one of the prophets [of old].

[16]But when Herod heard [of it], he said, [g]This very John, whom I beheaded, has been raised [from the dead].

[17]For [this] Herod himself had sent and seized John and bound him in prison for the sake of Herodias, his brother Philip's wife, because he [Herod] had married her.

[18]For John had told Herod, It is not lawful *and* you have no right to have your brother's wife.

[19]And Herodias was angry (enraged) with him *and* held a grudge against him and wanted to kill him; but she could not,

[20]For Herod had [[f]a reverential] fear of John, knowing that he was a righteous and holy man, and [continually] kept him safe [[g]under guard]. When he heard [John speak], he was much perplexed; and [yet] he heard him gladly.

[21]But an opportune time came [for Herodias] when Herod on his birthday gave a banquet for his nobles and the high military commanders and chief men of Galilee.

[22]For when the daughter [a]of Herodias herself came in and danced, she pleased *and* [a]fascinated Herod and his guests; and the king said to the girl, Ask me for whatever you desire, and I will give it to you.

[23]And he put himself under oath to her, Whatever you ask me, I will give it to you, even to the half of my kingdom. [Esth. 5:3, 6.]

[24]Then she left the room and said to her mother, What shall I ask for [myself]? And she replied, The head of John the Baptist!

[25]And she rushed back instantly to the king and requested, saying, I wish you to give me right now the head of John the Baptist on a platter.

---

[a] 14 Some early manuscripts *He was saying*   [b] 20 Some early manuscripts *he did many things*   [c] 22 Some early manuscripts *When his daughter*

[a] Kenneth Wuest, *Word Studies.*   [b] James Moulton and George Milligan, *The Vocabulary.*   [c] Some manuscripts do not contain the last section of verse 11.   [d] Joseph Thayer, *A Greek-English Lexicon.*   [e] Some ancient manuscripts read "he," while others read "they."   [f] G. Abbott-Smith, *Manual Greek Lexicon.*   [g] Marvin Vincent, *Word Studies.*

## New International Version

26The king was greatly distressed, but because of his oaths and his dinner guests, he did not want to refuse her. 27So he immediately sent an executioner with orders to bring John's head. The man went, beheaded John in the prison, 28and brought back his head on a platter. He presented it to the girl, and she gave it to her mother. 29On hearing of this, John's disciples came and took his body and laid it in a tomb.

### Jesus Feeds the Five Thousand

30The apostles gathered around Jesus and reported to him all they had done and taught. 31Then, because so many people were coming and going that they did not even have a chance to eat, he said to them, "Come with me by yourselves to a quiet place and get some rest."

32So they went away by themselves in a boat to a solitary place. 33But many who saw them leaving recognized them and ran on foot from all the towns and got there ahead of them. 34When Jesus landed and saw a large crowd, he had compassion on them, because they were like sheep without a shepherd. So he began teaching them many things.

35By this time it was late in the day, so his disciples came to him. "This is a remote place," they said, "and it's already very late. 36Send the people away so that they can go to the surrounding countryside and villages and buy themselves something to eat."

37But he answered, "You give them something to eat." They said to him, "That would take more than half a year's wages*a*! Are we to go and spend that much on bread and give it to them to eat?"

38"How many loaves do you have?" he asked. "Go and see."

When they found out, they said, "Five—and two fish."

39Then Jesus directed them to have all the people sit down in groups on the green grass. 40So they sat down in groups of hundreds and fifties. 41Taking the five loaves and the two fish and looking up to heaven, he gave thanks and broke the loaves. Then he gave them to his disciples to distribute to the people. He also divided the two fish among them all. 42They all ate and were satisfied, 43and the disciples picked up twelve basketfuls of broken pieces of bread and fish. 44The number of the men who had eaten was five thousand.

### Jesus Walks on the Water

45Immediately Jesus made his disciples get into the boat and go on ahead of him to Bethsaida, while he dismissed the crowd. 46After leaving them, he went up on a mountainside to pray.

47Later that night, the boat was in the middle of the lake, and he was alone on land. 48He saw the disciples straining at the oars, because the wind was against them. Shortly before dawn he went out to them, walking on the lake. He was about to pass by them, 49but when they saw him walking on the lake, they thought he was a ghost. They cried out, 50because they all saw him and were terrified.

## Amplified Bible

26And the king was deeply pained *and* grieved *and* exceedingly sorry, but because of his oaths and his guests, he did not want to slight her [by breaking faith with her].

27And immediately the king sent off one [of the soldiers] of his bodyguard and gave him orders to bring [John's] head. He went and beheaded him in the prison

28And brought his head on a platter and handed it to the girl, and the girl gave it to her mother.

29When his disciples learned of it, they came and took [John's] body and laid it in a tomb.

30The apostles [sent out as missionaries] came back *and* gathered together to Jesus, and told Him all that they had done and taught.

31And He said to them, [*a*As for you] come away by yourselves to a deserted place, and rest a while—for many were [continually] coming and going, and they had not even leisure enough to eat.

32And they went away in a boat to a solitary place by themselves.

33Now many [people] saw them going and recognized them, and they ran there on foot from all the surrounding towns, and they got there ahead [of those in the boat].

34As Jesus landed, He saw a great crowd waiting, and He was moved with compassion for them, because they were like sheep without a shepherd; and He began to teach them many things.

35And when *a*the day was already far gone, His disciples came to Him and said, This is a desolate *and* isolated place, and the hour is now late.

36Send the crowds away to go into the country and villages round about and buy themselves something to eat.

37But He replied to them, Give them something to eat yourselves. And they said to Him, Shall we go and buy 200 *b*denarii [about forty dollars] worth of bread and give it to them to eat? [II Kings 4:42-44.]

38And He said to them, How many loaves do you have? Go and see. And when they [had looked and] knew, they said, Five [loaves] and two fish.

39Then He commanded the people all to recline on the green grass by companies.

40So they threw themselves down in ranks of hundreds and fifties [with the *c*regularity of an arrangement of beds of herbs, looking *d*like so many garden plots].

41And taking the five loaves and two fish, He looked up to heaven and, praising God, gave thanks and broke the loaves and kept on giving them to the disciples to set before the people; and He [also] divided the two fish among [them] all.

42And they all ate and were satisfied.

43And they took up twelve [*e*small hand] baskets full of broken pieces [from the loaves] and of the fish.

44And those who ate the loaves were 5,000 men.

45And at once He insisted that the disciples get into the boat and go ahead of Him to the other side to Bethsaida, while He was sending the throng away.

46And after He had taken leave of them, He went off into the hills to pray.

47Now when evening had come, the boat was out in the middle of the lake, and He was by Himself on the land.

48And having seen that they were troubled *and* tormented in [their] rowing, for the wind was against them, about the fourth watch of the night [between 3:00-6:00 a.m.] He came to them, walking [directly] on the sea. And He acted as if He meant to pass by them,

49But when they saw Him walking on the sea they thought it was a ghost, and *f*raised a [deep, throaty] shriek of terror.

50For they all saw Him and were agitated (troubled and

---

*a* Kenneth Wuest, *Word Studies*. *b* The usual pay for a day's work was one denarius. *c* James Moulton and George Milligan, *The Vocabulary*. *d* Richard Trench, *Notes on the Miracles of our Lord*. *e* Marvin Vincent, *Word Studies*. See also footnote on Matt. 14:20. *f* Joseph Thayer, *A Greek-English Lexicon*.

## New International Version

Immediately he spoke to them and said, "Take courage! It is I. Don't be afraid." ⁵¹Then he climbed into the boat with them, and the wind died down. They were completely amazed, ⁵²for they had not understood about the loaves; their hearts were hardened.

⁵³When they had crossed over, they landed at Gennesaret and anchored there. ⁵⁴As soon as they got out of the boat, people recognized Jesus. ⁵⁵They ran throughout that whole region and carried the sick on mats to wherever they heard he was. ⁵⁶And wherever he went—into villages, towns or countryside—they placed the sick in the marketplaces. They begged him to let them touch even the edge of his cloak, and all who touched it were healed.

### That Which Defiles

**7** The Pharisees and some of the teachers of the law who had come from Jerusalem gathered around Jesus ²and saw some of his disciples eating food with hands that were defiled, that is, unwashed. ³(The Pharisees and all the Jews do not eat unless they give their hands a ceremonial washing, holding to the tradition of the elders. ⁴When they come from the marketplace they do not eat unless they wash. And they observe many other traditions, such as the washing of cups, pitchers and kettles.ᵃ)

⁵So the Pharisees and teachers of the law asked Jesus, "Why don't your disciples live according to the tradition of the elders instead of eating their food with defiled hands?"

⁶He replied, "Isaiah was right when he prophesied about you hypocrites; as it is written:

"'These people honor me with their lips,
  but their hearts are far from me.
⁷They worship me in vain;
  their teachings are merely human rules.'ᵇ

⁸You have let go of the commands of God and are holding on to human traditions."

⁹And he continued, "You have a fine way of setting aside the commands of God in order to observeᶜ your own traditions! ¹⁰For Moses said, 'Honor your father and mother,'ᵈ and, 'Anyone who curses their father or mother is to be

## Amplified Bible

filled with fear and dread). But immediately He talked with them and said, Take heart! I AM! Stop being alarmed *and* afraid. [Exod. 3:14.]

⁵¹And He went up into the boat with them, and the wind ceased (ᵃsank to rest as if exhausted by its own beating). And they were astonished exceedingly [beyond measure],

⁵²For they failed to consider *or* understand [the teaching and meaning of the miracle of] the loaves; [in fact] their hearts had ᵇgrown callous [had become dull and had ᵇlost the power of understanding].

⁵³And when they had crossed over, they reached the land of Gennesaret and ᵇcame to [anchor at] the shore.

⁵⁴As soon as they got out of the boat, [the people] recognized Him,

⁵⁵And they ran about the whole countryside, and began to carry around sick people on their sleeping pads *or* mats to any place where they heard that He was.

⁵⁶And wherever He came into villages or cities or the country, they would lay the sick in the marketplaces and beg Him that they might touch even the fringe of His outer garment, and as many as touched Him were restored to health.

**7** Now there gathered together to [Jesus] the Pharisees and some of the scribes who had come from Jerusalem,

²For they had seen that some of His disciples ate with ᶜcommon hands, that is, unwashed [with hands defiled and unhallowed, because they had not given them a ᵈceremonial washing]—

³For the Pharisees and all of the Jews do not eat unless [merely for ceremonial reasons] they wash their hands [diligently ᵉup to the elbow] with clenched fist, adhering [carefully and faithfully] to the tradition of [practices and customs handed down to them by] their forefathers [to be observed],

⁴And [when they come] from the marketplace, they do not eat unless they purify themselves; and there are many other traditions [oral, man-made laws handed down to them, which they observe faithfully and diligently, such as], the washing of cups and wooden pitchers and wide-mouthed jugs and utensils of copper and ᶠbeds—

⁵And the Pharisees and scribes kept asking [Jesus], Why do Your disciples not order their way of living according to the tradition handed down by the forefathers [to be observed], but eat with hands unwashed *and* ceremonially not purified?

⁶But He said to them, Excellently *and* truly [ᵇso that there will be no room for blame] did Isaiah prophesy of you, the pretenders *and* hypocrites, as it stands written: These people [constantly] honor Me with their lips, but their hearts hold off *and* are far distant from Me.

⁷In vain (fruitlessly and without profit) do they worship Me, ordering *and* teaching [to be obeyed] as doctrines the commandments *and* precepts of men. [Isa. 29:13.]

⁸You disregard *and* give up *and* ask to depart from you the commandment of God and cling to the tradition of men [keeping it carefully and faithfully].

⁹And He said to them, You have a fine way of rejecting [thus thwarting and nullifying and doing away with] the commandment of God in order to keep your tradition (your own human regulations)!

¹⁰For Moses said, Honor (revere with tenderness of feeling and deference) your father and your mother, and, He who curses *or* reviles *or* speaks evil of *or* abuses *or* treats improperly his father or mother, let him surely die. [Exod. 20:12; 21:17; Lev. 20:9; Deut. 5:16.]

ᵃ Marvin Vincent, *Word Studies*. ᵇ Joseph Thayer, *A Greek-English Lexicon*. ᶜ William Tyndale, *The Tyndale Bible*. ᵈ Charles B. Williams, *The New Testament: A Translation*. ᵉ G. Abbott-Smith, *Manual Greek Lexicon*. ᶠ James Moulton and George Milligan, *The Vocabulary* and Robert Young, *Analytical Concordance* agree with most lexicons in reading "beds" here. Some manuscripts end verse 4 after "utensils of copper."

---

ᵃ 4 Some early manuscripts *pitchers, kettles and dining couches*
ᵇ 6,7 Isaiah 29:13    ᶜ 9 Some manuscripts *set up*    ᵈ 10 Exodus 20:12;
Deut. 5:16

## New International Version

put to death.'[a] [11]But you say that if anyone declares that what might have been used to help their father or mother is Corban (that is, devoted to God) — [12]then you no longer let them do anything for their father or mother. [13]Thus you nullify the word of God by your tradition that you have handed down. And you do many things like that."

[14]Again Jesus called the crowd to him and said, "Listen to me, everyone, and understand this. [15]Nothing outside a person can defile them by going into them. Rather, it is what comes out of a person that defiles them." [16][b]

[17]After he had left the crowd and entered the house, his disciples asked him about this parable. [18]"Are you so dull?" he asked. "Don't you see that nothing that enters a person from the outside can defile them? [19]For it doesn't go into their heart but into their stomach, and then out of the body." (In saying this, Jesus declared all foods clean.)

[20]He went on: "What comes out of a person is what defiles them. [21]For it is from within, out of a person's heart, that evil thoughts come — sexual immorality, theft, murder, [22]adultery, greed, malice, deceit, lewdness, envy, slander, arrogance and folly. [23]All these evils come from inside and defile a person."

### Jesus Honors a Syrophoenician Woman's Faith

[24]Jesus left that place and went to the vicinity of Tyre.[c] He entered a house and did not want anyone to know it; yet he could not keep his presence secret. [25]In fact, as soon as she heard about him, a woman whose little daughter was possessed by an impure spirit came and fell at his feet. [26]The woman was a Greek, born in Syrian Phoenicia. She begged Jesus to drive the demon out of her daughter.

[27]"First let the children eat all they want," he told her, "for it is not right to take the children's bread and toss it to the dogs."

[28]"Lord," she replied, "even the dogs under the table eat the children's crumbs."

[29]Then he told her, "For such a reply, you may go; the demon has left your daughter."

[30]She went home and found her child lying on the bed, and the demon gone.

### Jesus Heals a Deaf and Mute Man

[31]Then Jesus left the vicinity of Tyre and went through Sidon, down to the Sea of Galilee and into the region of

## Amplified Bible

[11]But [as for you] you say, A man is exempt if he tells [his] father or [his] mother, What you would otherwise have gained from me [everything I have that would have been of use to you] is Corban, that is, is a gift [already given as an offering to God],

[12]Then you no longer are permitting him to do anything for [his] father or mother [but are letting him off from helping them].

[13]Thus you are nullifying and making void and of no effect [the authority of] the Word of God through your tradition, which you [in turn] hand on. And many things of this kind you are doing.

[14]And He called the people to [Him] again and said to them, Listen to Me, all of you, and understand [what I say].

[15]There is not [even] one thing outside a man which by going into him can pollute and defile him; but the things which come out of a man are what defile him and make him unhallowed and unclean.

[16][a] If any man has ears to hear, let him be listening [and let him [b]perceive and comprehend by hearing].

[17]And when He had left the crowd and had gone into the house, His disciples began asking Him about the parable.

[18]And He said to them, Then are you also unintelligent and dull and without understanding? Do you not discern and see that whatever goes into a man from the outside cannot make him unhallowed or unclean,

[19]Since it does not reach and enter his heart but [only his] digestive tract, and so passes on [into the place designed to receive waste]? Thus He was making and declaring all foods [ceremonially] clean [that is, [c]abolishing the ceremonial distinctions of the Levitical Law].

[20]And He said, What comes out of a man is what makes a man unclean and renders [him] unhallowed.

[21]For from within, [that is] out of the hearts of men, come base and wicked thoughts, sexual immorality, stealing, murder, adultery,

[22]Coveting (a greedy desire to have more wealth), dangerous and destructive wickedness, deceit; [d]unrestrained (indecent) conduct; an evil eye (envy), slander (evil speaking, malicious misrepresentation, abusiveness), pride ([e]the sin of an uplifted heart against God and man), foolishness (folly, lack of sense, recklessness, thoughtlessness).

[23]All these evil [purposes and desires] come from within, and they make the man unclean and render him unhallowed.

[24]And Jesus arose and went away from there to the region of Tyre and Sidon. And He went into a house and did not want anyone to know [that He was there]; but it was not possible for Him to be hidden [from public notice].

[25]Instead, at once, a woman whose little daughter had (was under the control of) an unclean spirit heard about Him and came and flung herself down at His feet.

[26]Now the woman was a Greek (Gentile), a Syrophoenician by nationality. And she kept begging Him to drive the demon out of her little daughter.

[27]And He said to her, First let the children be fed, for it is not becoming or proper or right to take the children's bread and throw it to the [little house] dogs.

[28]But she answered Him, Yes, Lord, yet even the small pups under the table eat the little children's scraps of food.

[29]And He said to her, Because of this saying, you may go your way; the demon has gone out of your daughter [permanently].

[30]And she went home and found the child thrown on the couch, and the demon departed.

[31]Soon after this, Jesus, coming back from the region of Tyre, passed through Sidon on to the Sea of Galilee, through the region of Decapolis [the ten cities].

---

[a] Many manuscripts do not contain this verse. [b] G. Abbott-Smith, *Manual Greek Lexicon.* [c] W. Robertson Nicoll, ed., *The Expositor's Greek New Testament.* [d] Alexander Souter, *Pocket Lexicon of the Greek New Testament.* [e] Marvin Vincent, *Word Studies.*

---

[a] 10 Exodus 21:17; Lev. 20:9   [b] 16 Some manuscripts include here the words of 4:23.   [c] 24 Many early manuscripts *Tyre and Sidon*

## New International Version

the Decapolis.[a] [32]There some people brought to him a man who was deaf and could hardly talk, and they begged Jesus to place his hand on him.

[33]After he took him aside, away from the crowd, Jesus put his fingers into the man's ears. Then he spit and touched the man's tongue. [34]He looked up to heaven and with a deep sigh said to him, *"Ephphatha!"* (which means "Be opened!"). [35]At this, the man's ears were opened, his tongue was loosened and he began to speak plainly.

[36]Jesus commanded them not to tell anyone. But the more he did so, the more they kept talking about it. [37]People were overwhelmed with amazement. "He has done everything well," they said. "He even makes the deaf hear and the mute speak."

### Jesus Feeds the Four Thousand

**8** During those days another large crowd gathered. Since they had nothing to eat, Jesus called his disciples to him and said, [2]"I have compassion for these people; they have already been with me three days and have nothing to eat. [3]If I send them home hungry, they will collapse on the way, because some of them have come a long distance."

[4]His disciples answered, "But where in this remote place can anyone get enough bread to feed them?"

[5]"How many loaves do you have?" Jesus asked.

"Seven," they replied.

[6]He told the crowd to sit down on the ground. When he had taken the seven loaves and given thanks, he broke them and gave them to his disciples to distribute to the people, and they did so. [7]They had a few small fish as well; he gave thanks for them also and told the disciples to distribute them. [8]The people ate and were satisfied. Afterward the disciples picked up seven basketfuls of broken pieces that were left over. [9]About four thousand were present. After he had sent them away, [10]he got into the boat with his disciples and went to the region of Dalmanutha.

[11]The Pharisees came and began to question Jesus. To test him, they asked him for a sign from heaven. [12]He sighed deeply and said, "Why does this generation ask for a sign? Truly I tell you, no sign will be given to it." [13]Then he left them, got back into the boat and crossed to the other side.

### The Yeast of the Pharisees and Herod

[14]The disciples had forgotten to bring bread, except for one loaf they had with them in the boat. [15]"Be careful," Jesus warned them. "Watch out for the yeast of the Pharisees and that of Herod."

[16]They discussed this with one another and said, "It is because we have no bread."

[17]Aware of their discussion, Jesus asked them: "Why are you talking about having no bread? Do you still not see or understand? Are your hearts hardened? [18]Do you have

## Amplified Bible

[32]And they brought to Him a man who was deaf and had difficulty in speaking, and they begged Jesus to place His hand upon him.

[33]And taking him aside from the crowd [privately], He thrust His fingers into the man's ears and spat and touched his tongue;

[34]And looking up to heaven, He sighed as He said, Ephphatha, which means, Be opened!

[35]And his ears were opened, his tongue was loosed, and he began to speak distinctly *and* as he should.

[36]And Jesus [ain His own interest] admonished *and* ordered them sternly *and* expressly to tell no one; but the more He commanded them, the more zealously they proclaimed it.

[37]And they were overwhelmingly astonished, saying, He has done everything excellently (commendably and nobly)! He even makes the deaf to hear and the dumb to speak!

**8** In those days when [again] an immense crowd had gathered and they had nothing to eat, Jesus called His disciples to Him and told them,

[2]I have pity *and* sympathy for the people *and* My heart goes out to them, for they have been with Me now three days and have nothing [left] to eat;

[3]And if I send them away to their homes hungry, they will be feeble through exhaustion *and* faint along the road; and some of them have come a long way.

[4]And His disciples replied to Him, How can anyone fill *and* satisfy [these people] with loaves of bread here in [this] desolate *and* uninhabited region?

[5]And He asked them, How many loaves have you? They said, Seven.

[6]And He commanded the multitude to recline upon the ground, and He [then] took the seven loaves [of bread] and, having given thanks, He broke them and kept on giving them to His disciples to put before [the people], and they placed them before the crowd.

[7]And they had a few small fish; and when He had [b]praised God *and* given thanks *and* asked Him to bless them [to their use], He ordered that these also should be set before [them].

[8]And they ate and were satisfied; and they took up seven [clarge provision] baskets full of the broken pieces left over.

[9]And there were about 4,000 people. And He dismissed them,

[10]And at once He got into the boat with His disciples and went to the district of Dalmanutha (or Magdala).

[11]The Pharisees came and began to argue with *and* question Him, demanding from Him a sign (an attesting miracle from heaven) [maliciously] to test Him.

[12]And He groaned *and* sighed deeply in His spirit and said, Why does this generation demand a sign? Positively I say to you, no sign shall be given this generation.

[13]And He went away *and* left them and, getting into the boat again, He departed to the other side.

[14]Now they had [dcompletely] forgotten to bring bread, and they had only one loaf with them in the boat.

[15]And Jesus [repeatedly and expressly] charged *and* admonished them, saying, Look out; keep on your guard *and* beware of the leaven of the Pharisees and the leaven of Herod [eand the Herodians].

[16]And they discussed it *and* reasoned with one another, It is because we have no bread.

[17]And being aware [of it], Jesus said to them, Why are you reasoning *and* saying it is because you have no bread? Do you not yet discern or understand? Are your hearts in [a settled state of] hardness? [Isa. 6:9, 10; Jer. 5:21.]

## New International Version

eyes but fail to see, and ears but fail to hear? And don't you remember? [19]When I broke the five loaves for the five thousand, how many basketfuls of pieces did you pick up?"

"Twelve," they replied.

[20]"And when I broke the seven loaves for the four thousand, how many basketfuls of pieces did you pick up?"

They answered, "Seven."

[21]He said to them, "Do you still not understand?"

### Jesus Heals a Blind Man at Bethsaida

[22]They came to Bethsaida, and some people brought a blind man and begged Jesus to touch him. [23]He took the blind man by the hand and led him outside the village. When he had spit on the man's eyes and put his hands on him, Jesus asked, "Do you see anything?"

[24]He looked up and said, "I see people; they look like trees walking around."

[25]Once more Jesus put his hands on the man's eyes. Then his eyes were opened, his sight was restored, and he saw everything clearly. [26]Jesus sent him home, saying, "Don't even go into[a] the village."

### Peter Declares That Jesus Is the Messiah

[27]Jesus and his disciples went on to the villages around Caesarea Philippi. On the way he asked them, "Who do people say I am?"

[28]They replied, "Some say John the Baptist; others say Elijah; and still others, one of the prophets."

[29]"But what about you?" he asked. "Who do you say I am?"

Peter answered, "You are the Messiah."

[30]Jesus warned them not to tell anyone about him.

### Jesus Predicts His Death

[31]He then began to teach them that the Son of Man must suffer many things and be rejected by the elders, the chief priests and the teachers of the law, and that he must be killed and after three days rise again. [32]He spoke plainly about this, and Peter took him aside and began to rebuke him.

[33]But when Jesus turned and looked at his disciples, he rebuked Peter. "Get behind me, Satan!" he said. "You do not have in mind the concerns of God, but merely human concerns."

### The Way of the Cross

[34]Then he called the crowd to him along with his disciples and said: "Whoever wants to be my disciple must deny themselves and take up their cross and follow me. [35]For whoever wants to save their life[b] will lose it, but whoever loses their life for me and for the gospel will save it. [36]What good is it for someone to gain the whole world, yet forfeit their soul? [37]Or what can anyone give in exchange

## Amplified Bible

[18]Having eyes, do you not see [with them], and having ears, do you not hear *and* perceive *and* understand the sense of what is said? And do you not remember?

[19]When I broke the five loaves for the 5,000, how many [a small hand] baskets full of broken pieces did you take up? They said to Him, Twelve.

[20]And [when I broke] the seven loaves for the 4,000, how many [a large provision] baskets full of broken pieces did you take up? And they said to Him, Seven.

[21]And He [b]kept repeating, Do you not yet understand?

[22]And they came to Bethsaida. And [people] brought to Him a blind man and begged Him to touch him.

[23]And He [c]caught the blind man by the hand and led him out of the village; and when He had spit on his eyes and put His hands upon him, He asked him, Do you [b possibly] see anything?

[24]And he looked up and said, I see people, but [they look] like trees, walking.

[25]Then He put His hands on his eyes again; and the man looked intently [that is, fixed his eyes on definite objects], and he was restored and saw everything distinctly [even what was [d]at a distance].

[26]And He sent him away to his house, telling [him], Do not [even] enter the village [e]or tell anyone there.

[27]And Jesus went on with His disciples to the villages of Caesarea Philippi; and on the way He asked His disciples, Who do people say that I am?

[28]And they answered [Him], John the Baptist; and others [say], Elijah; but others, one of the prophets.

[29]And He asked them, But who do you yourselves say that I am? Peter replied to Him, You are the Christ (the Messiah, the Anointed One).

[30]And He charged them sharply to tell no one about Him.

[31]And He began to teach them that the Son of Man must of necessity suffer many things and be tested *and* disapproved *and* rejected by the elders and the chief priests and the scribes, and be put to death, and after three days rise again [[f]from death].

[32]And He said this freely (frankly, plainly, and explicitly, making it unmistakable). And Peter took Him [d]by the hand *and* led Him aside and then [facing Him] began to rebuke Him.

[33]But turning around [His back to Peter] and seeing His disciples, He rebuked Peter, saying, Get behind Me, Satan! For you do not have a mind [d]intent on promoting what God wills, but what pleases men [you are not on God's side, but that of men].

[34]And Jesus called [to Him] the throng with His disciples and said to them, If anyone intends to come after Me, let him deny himself [forget, ignore, disown, and [d]lose sight of himself and his own interests] and take up his cross, and [d]joining Me as a disciple and siding with My party] follow [g]with Me [continually, cleaving steadfastly to Me].

[35]For whoever wants to save his [h]higher, spiritual, eternal] life, will lose it [the [h]lower, natural, temporal life [d]which is lived only on earth]; and whoever gives up his life [which is lived only on earth] for My sake and the Gospel's will save it [his [h]higher, spiritual life [d]in the eternal kingdom of God].

[36]For what does it profit a man to gain the whole world, and forfeit his life [d]in the eternal kingdom of God]?

[37]For what can a man give as an exchange ([f]a compensation, a ransom, in return) for his [blessed] life [d]in the eternal kingdom of God]?

*a* Marvin Vincent, *Word Studies*. See also footnote on Matt. 14:20.  *b* W. Robertson Nicoll, ed., *The Expositor's Greek New Testament*.  *c* William Tyndale, *The Tyndale Bible*.  *d* Joseph Thayer, *A Greek-English Lexicon*.  *e* Some manuscripts add this phrase.  *f* Hermann Cremer, *Biblico-Theological Lexicon*.  *g* Kenneth Wuest, *Word Studies*.  *h* Robert Jamieson, A. R. Fausett and David Brown, *A Commentary on the Old and New Testaments*.

*a 26* Some manuscripts *go and tell anyone in*     *b 35* The Greek word means either *life* or *soul*; also in verses 36 and 37.

## New International Version

for their soul? ³⁸If anyone is ashamed of me and my words in this adulterous and sinful generation, the Son of Man will be ashamed of them when he comes in his Father's glory with the holy angels."

**9** And he said to them, "Truly I tell you, some who are standing here will not taste death before they see that the kingdom of God has come with power."

### The Transfiguration
²After six days Jesus took Peter, James and John with him and led them up a high mountain, where they were all alone. There he was transfigured before them. ³His clothes became dazzling white, whiter than anyone in the world could bleach them. ⁴And there appeared before them Elijah and Moses, who were talking with Jesus.
⁵Peter said to Jesus, "Rabbi, it is good for us to be here. Let us put up three shelters—one for you, one for Moses and one for Elijah." ⁶(He did not know what to say, they were so frightened.)
⁷Then a cloud appeared and covered them, and a voice came from the cloud: "This is my Son, whom I love. Listen to him!"
⁸Suddenly, when they looked around, they no longer saw anyone with them except Jesus.
⁹As they were coming down the mountain, Jesus gave them orders not to tell anyone what they had seen until the Son of Man had risen from the dead. ¹⁰They kept the matter to themselves, discussing what "rising from the dead" meant.
¹¹And they asked him, "Why do the teachers of the law say that Elijah must come first?"
¹²Jesus replied, "To be sure, Elijah does come first, and restores all things. Why then is it written that the Son of Man must suffer much and be rejected? ¹³But I tell you, Elijah has come, and they have done to him everything they wished, just as it is written about him."

### Jesus Heals a Boy Possessed by an Impure Spirit
¹⁴When they came to the other disciples, they saw a large crowd around them and the teachers of the law arguing with them. ¹⁵As soon as all the people saw Jesus, they were overwhelmed with wonder and ran to greet him.
¹⁶"What are you arguing with them about?" he asked.
¹⁷A man in the crowd answered, "Teacher, I brought you my son, who is possessed by a spirit that has robbed him of speech. ¹⁸Whenever it seizes him, it throws him to the ground. He foams at the mouth, gnashes his teeth and becomes rigid. I asked your disciples to drive out the spirit, but they could not."
¹⁹"You unbelieving generation," Jesus replied, "how long shall I stay with you? How long shall I put up with you? Bring the boy to me."

## Amplified Bible

³⁸For whoever ᵃis ashamed [here and now] of Me and My words in this adulterous (unfaithful) and [preeminently] sinful generation, of him will the Son of Man also be ashamed when He comes in the glory (splendor and majesty) of His Father with the holy angels.

**9** And Jesus said to them, Truly *and* solemnly I say to you, there are some standing here who will in no way taste death before they see the kingdom of God come in [its] power.
²Six days after this, Jesus took with Him Peter and James and John and led them up on a high mountain apart by themselves. And He was transfigured before them *and* became resplendent with divine brightness.
³And His garments became glistening, intensely white, as no fuller (cloth dresser, launderer) on earth could bleach them.
⁴And Elijah appeared [there] to them, accompanied by Moses, and they were ᵇholding [a protracted] conversation with Jesus.
⁵And ᶜPeter took up the conversation, saying, Master, it is good *and* suitable *and* beautiful for us to be here. Let us make three booths (tents)—one for You and one for Moses and one for Elijah.
⁶For he did not [really] know what to say, for they were in a violent fright (ᵈaghast with dread).
⁷And a cloud threw a shadow upon them, and a voice came out of the cloud, saying, This is My Son, the [ᵈmost dearworthy] Beloved One. Be ᵇconstantly listening to *and* obeying Him!
⁸And looking around, they suddenly no longer saw anyone with them except Jesus only.
⁹And as they were coming back down the mountain, He admonished *and* ᵉexpressly ordered them to tell no one what they had seen until the Son of Man should rise from among the dead.
¹⁰So they carefully *and* faithfully kept the matter to themselves, questioning *and* disputing with one another about what rising from among the dead meant.
¹¹And they asked Him, Why do the scribes say that it is necessary for Elijah to come first? [Mal. 4:5, 6.]
¹²And He said to them, Elijah, it is true, does come first to restore all things *and* ᶠset them to rights. And how is it written of the Son of Man that He will suffer many things *and* be utterly despised *and* be treated with contempt *and* rejected? [Isa. 53:3.]
¹³But I tell you that Elijah has already come, and [people] did to him whatever they desired, as it is written of him.
¹⁴And when they came to the [nine] disciples, they saw a great crowd around them and scribes questioning *and* disputing with them.
¹⁵And immediately all the crowd, when they saw Jesus [ᵍreturning from the holy mount, His face and person yet glistening], they were greatly amazed and ran up to Him [and] greeted Him.
¹⁶And He asked them, About what are you questioning *and* discussing with them?
¹⁷And one of the throng replied to Him, Teacher, I brought my son to You, for he has a dumb spirit.
¹⁸And wherever it lays hold of him [so as to make him its own], it dashes him down *and* convulses him, and he foams [at the mouth] and grinds his teeth, *and* he [ᵇfalls into a motionless stupor and] is wasting away. And I asked Your disciples to drive it out, and they were not able [to do it].
¹⁹And He answered them, O unbelieving generation [without any faith]! How long ᵇshall I [have to do] with you? How long am I to bear with you? Bring him to Me.

ᵃ A. T. Robertson, *Word Pictures*. ᵇ Kenneth Wuest, *Word Studies*.
ᶜ H.A. A. Kennedy, *Sources of New Testament Greek*. ᵈ John Wycliffe, *The Wycliffe Bible*. ᵉ G. Abbott-Smith, *Manual Greek Lexicon*. ᶠ Matthew Henry, *Commentary on the Holy Bible*. ᵍ Richard Trench, *Notes on the Miracles*.

## New International Version

20So they brought him. When the spirit saw Jesus, it immediately threw the boy into a convulsion. He fell to the ground and rolled around, foaming at the mouth.

21Jesus asked the boy's father, "How long has he been like this?"

"From childhood," he answered. 22"It has often thrown him into fire or water to kill him. But if you can do anything, take pity on us and help us."

23"'If you can'?" said Jesus. "Everything is possible for one who believes."

24Immediately the boy's father exclaimed, "I do believe; help me overcome my unbelief!"

25When Jesus saw that a crowd was running to the scene, he rebuked the impure spirit. "You deaf and mute spirit," he said, "I command you, come out of him and never enter him again."

26The spirit shrieked, convulsed him violently and came out. The boy looked so much like a corpse that many said, "He's dead." 27But Jesus took him by the hand and lifted him to his feet, and he stood up.

28After Jesus had gone indoors, his disciples asked him privately, "Why couldn't we drive it out?"

29He replied, "This kind can come out only by prayer.a"

### Jesus Predicts His Death a Second Time

30They left that place and passed through Galilee. Jesus did not want anyone to know where they were, 31because he was teaching his disciples. He said to them, "The Son of Man is going to be delivered into the hands of men. They will kill him, and after three days he will rise." 32But they did not understand what he meant and were afraid to ask him about it.

33They came to Capernaum. When he was in the house, he asked them, "What were you arguing about on the road?" 34But they kept quiet because on the way they had argued about who was the greatest.

35Sitting down, Jesus called the Twelve and said, "Anyone who wants to be first must be the very last, and the servant of all."

36He took a little child whom he placed among them. Taking the child in his arms, he said to them, 37"Whoever welcomes one of these little children in my name welcomes me; and whoever welcomes me does not welcome me but the one who sent me."

### Whoever Is Not Against Us Is for Us

38"Teacher," said John, "we saw someone driving out demons in your name and we told him to stop, because he was not one of us."

39"Do not stop him," Jesus said. "For no one who does a miracle in my name can in the next moment say anything bad about me, 40for whoever is not against us is for us. 41Truly I tell you, anyone who gives you a cup of water in my name because you belong to the Messiah will certainly not lose their reward.

### Causing to Stumble

42"If anyone causes one of these little ones—those who believe in me—to stumble, it would be better for them if a large millstone were hung around their neck and they were thrown into the sea. 43If your hand causes you to

## Amplified Bible

20So they brought [the boy] to Him, and when the spirit saw Him, at once it completely convulsed the boy, and he fell to the ground and kept rolling about, foaming [at the mouth].

21And [Jesus] asked his father, How long has he had this? And he answered, From the time he was a little boy.

22And it has often thrown him both into fire and into water, intending to kill him. But if You can do anything, do have pity on us and help us.

23And Jesus said, [You say to Me], If You can do anything? [Why,] all things can be (are possible) to him who believes!

24At once the father of the boy gave [an aeager, bpiercing, inarticulate] cry with tears, and he said, Lord, I believe! [Constantly] help my cweakness of faith!

25But when Jesus noticed that a crowd [of people] came running together, He rebuked the unclean spirit, saying to it, You dumb and deaf spirit, I charge you to come out of him and never go into him again.

26And after giving a [hoarse, clamoring, fear-stricken] shriek of anguish and convulsing him terribly, it came out; and the boy lay [pale and motionless] like a corpse, so that many of them said, He is dead.

27But Jesus took [da strong grip of] his hand and began lifting him up, and he stood.

28And when He had gone indoors, His disciples asked Him privately, Why could not we drive it out?

29And He replied to them, This kind cannot be driven out by anything but prayer eand fasting.

30They went on from there and passed along through Galilee. And He did not wish to have anyone know it,

31For He was [engaged for the time being in] teaching His disciples. He said to them, The Son of Man is being delivered into the hands of men, and they will put Him to death; and when He has been killed, after three days He will rise [ffrom death].

32But they did not comprehend what He was saying, and they were afraid to ask Him [what this statement meant].

33And they arrived at Capernaum; and when [they were] in the house, He asked them, What were you discussing and arguing about on the road?

34But they kept still, for on the road they had discussed and disputed with one another as to who was the greatest.

35And He sat down and called the Twelve [apostles], and He said to them, If anyone desires to be first, he must be last of all, and servant of all.

36And He took a little child and put him in the center of their group; and taking him in [His] arms, He said to them,

37Whoever in My name and for My sake accepts and receives and welcomes one such child also accepts and receives and welcomes Me; and whoever so receives Me receives not only Me but Him Who sent Me.

38John said to Him, Teacher, we saw a man who does not follow along with us driving out demons in Your name, and we forbade him to do it, because he cis not one of our band [of Your disciples].

39But Jesus said, Do not restrain or hinder or forbid him; for no one who does a mighty work in My name will soon afterward be able to speak evil of Me.

40For he who is not against us is for us. [Num. 11:27-29.]

41For I tell you truly, whoever gives you a cup of water to drink because you belong to and bear the name of Christ will by no means fail to get his reward.

42And whoever causes one of these little ones (these believers) who facknowledge and cleave to Me to stumble and sin, it would be better (more profitable and wholesome) for him if a [huge] millstone were hung about his neck, and he were thrown into the sea.

---

a W. Robertson Nicoll, ed., *The Expositor's Greek New Testament.* b Henry Swete, *The Gospel According to Saint Mark.* c Joseph Thayer, *A Greek-English Lexicon.* d Kenneth Wuest, *Word Studies.* e Some manuscripts add "and fasting." f Hermann Cremer, *Biblico-Theological Lexicon.*

a 29 Some manuscripts *prayer and fasting*

## New International Version

stumble, cut it off. It is better for you to enter life maimed than with two hands to go into hell, where the fire never goes out. [44]a 45And if your foot causes you to stumble, cut it off. It is better for you to enter life crippled than to have two feet and be thrown into hell. [46]a 47And if your eye causes you to stumble, pluck it out. It is better for you to enter the kingdom of God with one eye than to have two eyes and be thrown into hell, 48where

"'the worms that eat them do not die,
    and the fire is not quenched.'b

49Everyone will be salted with fire. 50"Salt is good, but if it loses its saltiness, how can you make it salty again? Have salt among yourselves, and be at peace with each other."

### Divorce

**10** Jesus then left that place and went into the region of Judea and across the Jordan. Again crowds of people came to him, and as was his custom, he taught them.

2Some Pharisees came and tested him by asking, "Is it lawful for a man to divorce his wife?"

3"What did Moses command you?" he replied.

4They said, "Moses permitted a man to write a certificate of divorce and send her away."

5"It was because your hearts were hard that Moses wrote you this law," Jesus replied. 6"But at the beginning of creation God 'made them male and female.'c 7'For this reason a man will leave his father and mother and be united to his wife,d 8and the two will become one flesh.'e So they are no longer two, but one flesh. 9Therefore what God has joined together, let no one separate."

10When they were in the house again, the disciples asked Jesus about this. 11He answered, "Anyone who divorces his wife and marries another woman commits adultery against her. 12And if she divorces her husband and marries another man, she commits adultery."

### The Little Children and Jesus

13People were bringing little children to Jesus for him to place his hands on them, but the disciples rebuked them. 14When Jesus saw this, he was indignant. He said to them, "Let the little children come to me, and do not hinder them, for the kingdom of God belongs to such as these. 15Truly I tell you, anyone who will not receive the kingdom of God like a little child will never enter it." 16And he took the children in his arms, placed his hands on them and blessed them.

## Amplified Bible

43And if your hand puts a stumbling block before you *and* causes you to sin, cut it off! It is more profitable *and* wholesome for you to go into life [athat is really worthwhile] maimed than with two hands to go to hell (Gehenna), into the fire that cannot be put out.b

45And if your foot is a cause of stumbling *and* sin to you, cut it off! It is more profitable *and* wholesome for you to enter into life [that is really worthwhile] crippled than, having two feet, to be cast into hell (Gehenna)c.

47And if your eye causes you to stumble *and* sin, pluck it out! It is more profitable *and* wholesome for you to enter the kingdom of God with one eye than with two eyes to be thrown into hell (Gehenna),

48Where their worm [dwhich preys on the inhabitants and is a symbol of the wounds inflicted on the man himself by his sins] does not die, and the fire is not put out. [Isa. 66:24.]

49For everyone shall be salted with fire.

50Salt is good (beneficial), but if salt has lost its saltness, how will you restore [the saltness to] it? Have salt within yourselves, and be at peace *and* live in harmony with one another.

**10** And [Jesus] left there [Capernaum] and went to the region of Judea and beyond [east of] the Jordan; and crowds [constantly] gathered around Him again, and as was His custom, He began to teach them again.

2And some Pharisees came up, and, in order to test Him *and* try to find a weakness in Him, asked, Is it lawful for a man to edismiss *and* repudiate *and* divorce his wife?

3He answered them, What did Moses command you?

4They replied, Moses allowed a man to write a bill of divorce and to put her away. [Deut. 24:1-4.]

5But Jesus said to them, Because of your hardness of heart [/your condition of insensibility to the call of God] he wrote you this eprecept in your Law.

6But from the beginning of creation God made them male and female. [Gen. 1:27; 5:2.]

7For this reason a man shall leave [behind] his father and his mother gand be hjoined to his wife and cleave closely to her permanently,

8And the two shall become one flesh, so that they are no longer two, but one flesh. [Gen. 2:24.]

9What therefore God has united (joined together), let not man separate *or* divide.

10And indoors the disciples questioned Him again about this subject.

11And He said to them, Whoever fdismisses (repudiates and divorces) his wife and marries another commits adultery against her;

12And if a woman dismisses (repudiates and divorces) her husband and marries another, she commits adultery.

13And they kept bringing young children to Him that He might touch them, and the disciples were reproving them [for it].

14But when Jesus saw [it], He was indignant *and* ipained and said to them, Allow the children to come to Me—do not forbid *or* prevent *or* hinder them—for to such belongs the kingdom of God.

15Truly I tell you, whoever does not receive *and* accept *and* welcome the kingdom of God like a little child [does] positively shall not enter it at all.

16And He took them [the children up jone by one] in His arms and [kfervently invoked a] blessing, placing His hands upon them.

a Kenneth Wuest, *Word Studies*. b Verses 44 and 46, which are identical with verse 48, are not found in the best ancient manuscripts. cSee footnote on Mark 9:43. d Ezra Palmer Gould, cited by A. T. Robertson, *Word Pictures* and Henry Swete, *The Gospel According to Saint Mark*. eJoseph Thayer, *A Greek-English Lexicon*. fHenry Swete, *The Gospel According to Saint Mark*. gSome manuscripts do not contain this last section of verse 7. h James Moulton and George Milligan, *The Vocabulary*. iA. T. Robertson, *Word Pictures*. jW. Robertson Nicoll, ed., *The Expositor's Greek New Testament*. kHenry Alford, *The Greek New Testament*.

a 44,46 Some manuscripts include here the words of verse 48.
b 48 Isaiah 66:24    c 6 Gen. 1:27    d 7 Some early manuscripts do not have *and be united to his wife*.    e 8 Gen. 2:24

## New International Version

### The Rich and the Kingdom of God

¹⁷As Jesus started on his way, a man ran up to him and fell on his knees before him. "Good teacher," he asked, "what must I do to inherit eternal life?"

¹⁸"Why do you call me good?" Jesus answered. "No one is good—except God alone. ¹⁹You know the commandments: 'You shall not murder, you shall not commit adultery, you shall not steal, you shall not give false testimony, you shall not defraud, honor your father and mother.'ᵃ"

²⁰"Teacher," he declared, "all these I have kept since I was a boy."

²¹Jesus looked at him and loved him. "One thing you lack," he said. "Go, sell everything you have and give to the poor, and you will have treasure in heaven. Then come, follow me."

²²At this the man's face fell. He went away sad, because he had great wealth.

²³Jesus looked around and said to his disciples, "How hard it is for the rich to enter the kingdom of God!"

²⁴The disciples were amazed at his words. But Jesus said again, "Children, how hard it isᵇ to enter the kingdom of God! ²⁵It is easier for a camel to go through the eye of a needle than for someone who is rich to enter the kingdom of God."

²⁶The disciples were even more amazed, and said to each other, "Who then can be saved?"

²⁷Jesus looked at them and said, "With man this is impossible, but not with God; all things are possible with God."

²⁸Then Peter spoke up, "We have left everything to follow you!"

²⁹"Truly I tell you," Jesus replied, "no one who has left home or brothers or sisters or mother or father or children or fields for me and the gospel ³⁰will fail to receive a hundred times as much in this present age: homes, brothers, sisters, mothers, children and fields—along with persecutions—and in the age to come eternal life. ³¹But many who are first will be last, and the last first."

### Jesus Predicts His Death a Third Time

³²They were on their way up to Jerusalem, with Jesus leading the way, and the disciples were astonished, while those who followed were afraid. Again he took the Twelve aside and told them what was going to happen to him. ³³"We are going up to Jerusalem," he said, "and the Son of Man will be delivered over to the chief priests and the teachers of the law. They will condemn him to death and will hand him over to the Gentiles, ³⁴who will mock him and spit on him, flog him and kill him. Three days later he will rise."

### The Request of James and John

³⁵Then James and John, the sons of Zebedee, came to him. "Teacher," they said, "we want you to do for us whatever we ask."

## Amplified Bible

¹⁷And as He was setting out on His journey, a man ran up and knelt before Him and asked Him, Teacher, [You are ᵃessentially and perfectly ᵇmorally] good, what must I do to inherit eternal life [that is, ᵃto partake of eternal salvation in the Messiah's kingdom]?

¹⁸And Jesus said to him, Why do you call Me [ᵃessentially and perfectly ᵇmorally] good? There is no one [ᵃessentially and perfectly ᵇmorally] good—except God alone.

¹⁹You know the commandments: Do not kill, do not commit adultery, do not steal, do not bear false witness, do not defraud, honor your father and mother. [Exod. 20:12-16; Deut. 5:16-20.]

²⁰And he replied to Him, Teacher, I have carefully guarded *and* observed all these *and* taken care not to violate them from my boyhood.

²¹And Jesus, looking upon him, loved him, and He said to him, You lack one thing; go and sell all you have and give [the money] to the poor, and you will have treasure in heaven; and come [and] accompany Me [ᶜwalking the same road that I walk].

²²At that saying the man's countenance fell *and* was gloomy, and he went away grieved *and* sorrowing, for he was holding great possessions.

²³And Jesus looked around and said to His disciples, With what difficulty will those who possess wealth *and* ᵈkeep on holding it enter the kingdom of God!

²⁴And the disciples were amazed *and* bewildered *and* perplexed at His words. But Jesus said to them again, Children, how hard it is ᵉfor those who trust (place their confidence, their sense of safety) in riches to enter the kingdom of God!

²⁵It is easier for a camel to go through the eye of a needle than for a rich man to enter the kingdom of God.

²⁶And they were shocked *and* exceedingly astonished, and said to Him *and*ᶠto one another, Then who can be saved?

²⁷Jesus glanced around at them and said, With men [it is] impossible, but not with God; for all things are possible with God.

²⁸Peter started to say to Him, Behold, we have ᵈyielded up *and* abandoned everything [once and for all and ᵃjoined You as Your disciples, siding with Your party] and accompanied You [ᶜwalking the same road that You walk].

²⁹Jesus said, Truly I tell you, there is no one who has given up *and* left house or brothers or sisters or mother or father or children or lands for My sake and for the Gospel's

³⁰Who will not receive a hundred times as much now in this time—houses and brothers and sisters and mothers and children and lands, with persecutions—and in the age to come, eternal life.

³¹But many [who are now] first will be last [then], and many [who are now] last will be first [then].

³²They were on the way going up to Jerusalem, and Jesus was walking on in front of them; and they were bewildered *and* perplexed *and* greatly astonished, and those [who were still] following were seized with alarm *and* were afraid. And He took the Twelve [apostles] again and began to tell them what was about to happen to Him,

³³ [Saying], Behold, we are going up to Jerusalem, and the Son of Man will be turned over to the chief priests and the scribes; and they will condemn *and* sentence Him to death and turn Him over to the Gentiles.

³⁴And they will mock Him and spit on Him, and whip Him and put Him to death; but after three days He will rise again [ᵇfrom death].

³⁵And James and John, the sons of Zebedee, approached Him and said to Him, Teacher, we desire You to do for us whatever we ask of You.

ᵃ 19 Exodus 20:12-16; Deut. 5:16-20    ᵇ 24 Some manuscripts *is for those who trust in riches*

ᵃ Joseph Thayer, *A Greek-English Lexicon.*  ᵇ Hermann Cremer, *Biblico-Theological Lexicon.*  ᶜ Literal translation.  ᵈ Kenneth Wuest, *Word Studies.*  ᵉ Some manuscripts do not contain this phrase.  ᶠ Many ancient manuscripts add "to one another."

## New International Version

36"What do you want me to do for you?" he asked.
37They replied, "Let one of us sit at your right and the other at your left in your glory."
38"You don't know what you are asking," Jesus said. "Can you drink the cup I drink or be baptized with the baptism I am baptized with?"
39"We can," they answered.
Jesus said to them, "You will drink the cup I drink and be baptized with the baptism I am baptized with, 40but to sit at my right or left is not for me to grant. These places belong to those for whom they have been prepared."
41When the ten heard about this, they became indignant with James and John. 42Jesus called them together and said, "You know that those who are regarded as rulers of the Gentiles lord it over them, and their high officials exercise authority over them. 43Not so with you. Instead, whoever wants to become great among you must be your servant, 44and whoever wants to be first must be slave of all. 45For even the Son of Man did not come to be served, but to serve, and to give his life as a ransom for many."

### Blind Bartimaeus Receives His Sight

46Then they came to Jericho. As Jesus and his disciples, together with a large crowd, were leaving the city, a blind man, Bartimaeus (which means "son of Timaeus"), was sitting by the roadside begging. 47When he heard that it was Jesus of Nazareth, he began to shout, "Jesus, Son of David, have mercy on me!"
48Many rebuked him and told him to be quiet, but he shouted all the more, "Son of David, have mercy on me!"
49Jesus stopped and said, "Call him."
So they called to the blind man, "Cheer up! On your feet! He's calling you." 50Throwing his cloak aside, he jumped to his feet and came to Jesus.
51"What do you want me to do for you?" Jesus asked him.
The blind man said, "Rabbi, I want to see."
52"Go," said Jesus, "your faith has healed you." Immediately he received his sight and followed Jesus along the road.

### Jesus Comes to Jerusalem as King

11 As they approached Jerusalem and came to Bethphage and Bethany at the Mount of Olives, Jesus sent two of his disciples, 2saying to them, "Go to the village ahead of you, and just as you enter it, you will find a colt tied there, which no one has ever ridden. Untie it and bring it here. 3If anyone asks you, 'Why are you doing this?' say, 'The Lord needs it and will send it back here shortly.'"
4They went and found a colt outside in the street, tied at a doorway. As they untied it, 5some people standing there asked, "What are you doing, untying that colt?" 6They answered as Jesus had told them, and the people let them go. 7When they brought the colt to Jesus and threw their cloaks over it, he sat on it. 8Many people spread their

## Amplified Bible

36And He replied to them, What do you desire Me to do for you?
37And they said to Him, Grant that we may sit, one at Your right hand and one at [Your] left hand, in Your glory (Your majesty and splendor).
38But Jesus said to them, You do not know what you are asking. Are you able to drink the cup that I drink or be baptized with the baptism [of affliction] with which I am baptized?
39And they replied to Him, We are able. And Jesus told them, The cup that I drink you will drink, and you will be baptized with the baptism with which I am baptized,
40But to sit at My right hand or at My left hand is not Mine to give; but [it will be given to those] for whom it is ordained and prepared.
41And when the other ten [apostles] heard it, they began to be indignant with James and John.
42But Jesus called them to [Him] and said to them, You know that those who are recognized as governing and are supposed to rule the Gentiles (the nations) lord it over them [ruling with absolute power, holding them in subjection], and their great men exercise authority and dominion over them.
43But this is not to be so among you; instead, whoever desires to be great among you must be your servant,
44And whoever wishes to be most important and first in rank among you must be slave of all.
45For even the Son of Man came not to have service rendered to Him, but to serve, and to give His life as a ransom for (ainstead of) many.
46Then they came to Jericho. And as He was leaving Jericho with His disciples and a great crowd, Bartimaeus, a blind beggar, a son of Timaeus, was sitting by the roadside.
47And when he heard that it was Jesus of Nazareth, he began to shout, saying, Jesus, Son of David, have pity and mercy on me [bnow]!
48And many cseverely censured and reproved him, telling him to keep still, but he kept on shouting out all the more, You Son of David, have pity and mercy on me [now]!
49And Jesus stopped and said, Call him. And they called the blind man, telling him, Take courage! Get up! He is calling you.
50And throwing off his outer garment, he leaped up and came to Jesus.
51And Jesus said to him, What do you want Me to do for you? And the blind man said to Him, Master, let me receive my sight.
52And Jesus said to him, Go your way; your faith has healed you. And at once he received his sight and accompanied Jesus on the road. [Isa. 42:6, 7.]

11 When they were getting near to Jerusalem, to Bethphage and Bethany at the Mount of Olives, He sent ahead two of His disciples
2And instructed them, Go into the village in front of you, and as soon as you enter it, you will find a colt tied, which has never been ridden by anyone; unfasten it and bring it [here].
3If anyone asks you, Why are you doing this? answer, The Lord needs it, and He will send it back here presently.
4So they went away and found a colt tied at the door out in the [winding] open street, and they loosed it.
5And some who were standing there said to them, What are you doing, untying the colt?
6And they replied as Jesus had directed them, and they allowed them to go.
7And they brought the colt to Jesus and threw their outer garments upon it, and He sat on it.

a Marvin Vincent, *Word Studies.* b Kenneth Wuest, *Word Studies*: The Greek aorist (past tense) imperative. c Joseph Thayer, *A Greek-English Lexicon.*

## New International Version

cloaks on the road, while others spread branches they had cut in the fields. 9Those who went ahead and those who followed shouted,

"Hosanna!a"

"Blessed is he who comes in the name of the Lord!"b

10"Blessed is the coming kingdom of our father David!"

"Hosanna in the highest heaven!"

11Jesus entered Jerusalem and went into the temple courts. He looked around at everything, but since it was already late, he went out to Bethany with the Twelve.

### Jesus Curses a Fig Tree and Clears the Temple Courts

12The next day as they were leaving Bethany, Jesus was hungry. 13Seeing in the distance a fig tree in leaf, he went to find out if it had any fruit. When he reached it, he found nothing but leaves, because it was not the season for figs. 14Then he said to the tree, "May no one ever eat fruit from you again." And his disciples heard him say it.

15On reaching Jerusalem, Jesus entered the temple courts and began driving out those who were buying and selling there. He overturned the tables of the money changers and the benches of those selling doves, 16and would not allow anyone to carry merchandise through the temple courts. 17And as he taught them, he said, "Is it not written: 'My house will be called a house of prayer for all nations'c? But you have made it 'a den of robbers.'d"

18The chief priests and the teachers of the law heard this and began looking for a way to kill him, for they feared him, because the whole crowd was amazed at his teaching.

19When evening came, Jesus and his disciplese went out of the city.

20In the morning, as they went along, they saw the fig tree withered from the roots. 21Peter remembered and said to Jesus, "Rabbi, look! The fig tree you cursed has withered!"

22"Have faith in God," Jesus answered. 23"Trulyf I tell you, if anyone says to this mountain, 'Go, throw yourself into the sea,' and does not doubt in their heart but believes that what they say will happen, it will be done for them. 24Therefore I tell you, whatever you ask for in prayer, believe that you have received it, and it will be yours. 25And when you stand praying, if you hold anything against anyone, forgive them, so that your Father in heaven may forgive you your sins." [26]g

### The Authority of Jesus Questioned

27They arrived again in Jerusalem, and while Jesus was walking in the temple courts, the chief priests, the teachers of the law and the elders came to him. 28"By what au-

---

a 9 A Hebrew expression meaning "Save!" which became an exclamation of praise; also in verse 10    b 9 Psalm 118:25,26    c 17 Isaiah 56:7    d 17 Jer. 7:11    e 19 Some early manuscripts came, Jesus    f 22,23 Some early manuscripts "If you have faith in God," Jesus answered, 23"truly    g 26 Some manuscripts include here words similar to Matt. 6:15.

## Amplified Bible

8And many [of the people] spread their garments on the road, and others [scattered a layer of] leafy branches which they had cut from the fields.

9And those who went before and those who followed cried out [awith a cry of happiness], Hosanna! [Be graciously inclined and propitious to Him!] Praised and blessed is He Who comes in the name of the Lord! [Ps. 118:26.]

10Praised and blessed in the name of the Lord is the coming kingdom of our father David! Hosanna (O save us) in the highest [heaven]!

11And Jesus went into Jerusalem and entered the temple [benclosure]; and when He had looked around, surveying and observing everything, as it was already late, He went out to Bethany together with the Twelve [apostles].

12On the day following, when they had come away from Bethany, He was hungry.

13And seeing in the distance a fig tree [covered] with leaves, He went to see if He could find any [fruit] on it [cfor in the fig tree the fruit appears at the same time as the leaves]. But when He came up to it, He found nothing but leaves, for the fig season had not yet come.

14And He said to it, No one ever again shall eat fruit from you. And His disciples were listening [to what He said].

15And they came to Jerusalem. And He went into the temple [area, the bporches and courts] and began to drive out those who sold and bought in the temple area, and He overturned the [dfour-footed] tables of the money changers and the seats of those who dealt in doves;

16And He would not permit anyone to carry any household equipment through the temple enclosure [thus making the temple area a short-cut traffic lane].

17And He taught and said to them, Is it not written, My house shall be called a house of prayer for all the nations? But you have turned it into a den of robbers. [Isa. 56:7; Jer. 7:11.]

18And the chief priests and the scribes heard [of this] and kept seeking some way to destroy Him, for they feared Him, because the entire multitude was struck with astonishment at His teaching.

19And when evening came on, He and eHis disciples, as accustomed, went out of the city.

20In the morning, when they were passing along, they noticed that the fig tree was withered [completely] away to its roots.

21And Peter remembered and said to Him, Master, look! The fig tree which You doomed has withered away!

22And Jesus, replying, said to them, Have faith in God [constantly].

23Truly I tell you, whoever says to this mountain, Be lifted up and thrown into the sea! and does not doubt at all in his heart but believes that what he says will take place, it will be done for him.

24For this reason I am telling you, whatever you ask for in prayer, believe (trust and be confident) that it is granted to you, and you will [get it].

25And whenever you stand praying, if you have anything against anyone, forgive him and dlet it drop (leave it, let it go), in order that your Father Who is in heaven may also forgive you your [own] failings and shortcomings and let them drop.

26fBut if you do not forgive, neither will your Father in heaven forgive your failings and shortcomings.

27And they came again to Jerusalem. And when Jesus was walking about in the [bcourts and porches of the] temple, the chief priests and the scribes and the elders came to Him,

---

a Alexander Souter, Pocket Lexicon.    b Richard Trench, Synonyms of the New Testament.    c James Orr et al., eds., The International Standard Bible Encyclopedia.    d James Moulton and George Milligan, The Vocabulary.    e Some manuscripts read "they."    f Some manuscripts do not contain verse 26.

## New International Version

thority are you doing these things?" they asked. "And who gave you authority to do this?"

²⁹Jesus replied, "I will ask you one question. Answer me, and I will tell you by what authority I am doing these things. ³⁰John's baptism—was it from heaven, or of human origin? Tell me!"

³¹They discussed it among themselves and said, "If we say, 'From heaven,' he will ask, 'Then why didn't you believe him?' ³²But if we say, 'Of human origin' . . ." (They feared the people, for everyone held that John really was a prophet.)

³³So they answered Jesus, "We don't know."

Jesus said, "Neither will I tell you by what authority I am doing these things."

### The Parable of the Tenants

**12** Jesus then began to speak to them in parables: "A man planted a vineyard. He put a wall around it, dug a pit for the winepress and built a watchtower. Then he rented the vineyard to some farmers and moved to another place. ²At harvest time he sent a servant to the tenants to collect from them some of the fruit of the vineyard. ³But they seized him, beat him and sent him away empty-handed. ⁴Then he sent another servant to them; they struck this man on the head and treated him shamefully. ⁵He sent still another, and that one they killed. He sent many others; some of them they beat, others they killed.

⁶"He had one left to send, a son, whom he loved. He sent him last of all, saying, 'They will respect my son.'

⁷"But the tenants said to one another, 'This is the heir. Come, let's kill him, and the inheritance will be ours.' ⁸So they took him and killed him, and threw him out of the vineyard.

⁹"What then will the owner of the vineyard do? He will come and kill those tenants and give the vineyard to others. ¹⁰Haven't you read this passage of Scripture:

"'The stone the builders rejected
    has become the cornerstone;
¹¹the Lord has done this,
    and it is marvelous in our eyes'ᵃ?"

¹²Then the chief priests, the teachers of the law and the elders looked for a way to arrest him because they knew he had spoken the parable against them. But they were afraid of the crowd; so they left him and went away.

### Paying the Imperial Tax to Caesar

¹³Later they sent some of the Pharisees and Herodians to Jesus to catch him in his words. ¹⁴They came to him and said, "Teacher, we know that you are a man of integrity. You aren't swayed by others, because you pay no attention to who they are; but you teach the way of God in accordance with the truth. Is it right to pay the imperial taxᵇ to Caesar or not? ¹⁵Should we pay or shouldn't we?"

But Jesus knew their hypocrisy. "Why are you trying to trap me?" he asked. "Bring me a denarius and let me

## Amplified Bible

²⁸And they kept saying to Him, By what [sort of] authority are You doing these things, or who gave You this authority to do them?

²⁹Jesus told them, I will ask you a question. Answer Me, and then I will tell you by what [sort of] authority I do these things.

³⁰Was the baptism of John from heaven or from men? Answer Me.

³¹And they reasoned *and* argued with one another, If we say, From heaven, He will say, Why then did you not believe him?

³²But [on the other hand] can we say, From men? For they were afraid of the people, because everybody considered *and* held John actually to be a prophet.

³³So they replied to Jesus, We do not know. And Jesus said to them, Neither am I going to tell you what [sort of] authority I have for doing these things.

**12** And [Jesus] started to speak to them in parables [with comparisons and illustrations]. A man planted a vineyard and put a hedge around it and dug a pit for the winepress and built a tower and let it out [for rent] to vinedressers and went into another country.

²When the season came, he sent a bond servant to the tenants to collect from them some of the fruit of the vineyard.

³But they took him and beat him and sent him away without anything.

⁴Again he sent to them another bond servant, and they *stoned him and* wounded him in the head and treated him shamefully [sending him away with insults].

⁵And he sent another, and that one they killed; then many others—some they beat, and some they put to death.

⁶He had still one left [to send], a beloved son; last of all he sent him to them, saying, They will respect my son.

⁷But those tenants said to one another, Here is the heir; come on, let us put him to death, and [then] the inheritance will be ours.

⁸And they took him and killed him, and threw [his body] outside the vineyard.

⁹Now what will the owner of the vineyard do? He will come and destroy the tenants, and give the vineyard to others.

¹⁰Have you not even read this [passage of] Scripture: The very Stone which [ᵃafter putting It to the test] the builders rejected has become the Head of the corner [Cornerstone];

¹¹This is from the Lord *and* is His doing, and it is marvelous in our eyes? [Ps. 118:22, 23.]

¹²And they were trying to get hold of Him, but they were afraid of the people, for they knew that He spoke this parable with reference to *and* against them. So they left Him and departed. [Isa. 5:1-7.]

¹³But they sent some of the Pharisees and of the Herodians to Him for the purpose of entrapping Him in His speech.

¹⁴And they came up and said to Him, Teacher, we know that You are ᵇsincere *and* what You profess to be, that You cannot lie, *and* that You have no personal bias for anyone; for You are not influenced by partiality *and* have no ᶜregard for anyone's external condition *or* position, but in [and on the basis of] truth You teach the way of God. Is it lawful (permissible and right) to give tribute (ᶜpoll taxes) to Caesar or not?

¹⁵Should we pay [them] or should we not pay [them]? But knowing their hypocrisy, He asked them, Why do you put Me to the test? Bring Me a coin (a denarius), so I may see it.

---

ᵃ 11 Psalm 118:22,23   ᵇ 14 A special tax levied on subject peoples, not on Roman citizens

ᵃ Kenneth Wuest, *Word Studies.*   ᵇ Hermann Cremer, *Biblico-Theological Lexicon.*   ᶜ Joseph Thayer, *A Greek-English Lexicon.*

## New International Version

look at it." [16]They brought the coin, and he asked them, "Whose image is this? And whose inscription?"

"Caesar's," they replied.

[17]Then Jesus said to them, "Give back to Caesar what is Caesar's and to God what is God's."

And they were amazed at him.

### Marriage at the Resurrection

[18]Then the Sadducees, who say there is no resurrection, came to him with a question. [19]"Teacher," they said, "Moses wrote for us that if a man's brother dies and leaves a wife but no children, the man must marry the widow and raise up offspring for his brother. [20]Now there were seven brothers. The first one married and died without leaving any children. [21]The second one married the widow, but he also died, leaving no child. It was the same with the third. [22]In fact, none of the seven left any children. Last of all, the woman died too. [23]At the resurrection[a] whose wife will she be, since the seven were married to her?"

[24]Jesus replied, "Are you not in error because you do not know the Scriptures or the power of God? [25]When the dead rise, they will neither marry nor be given in marriage; they will be like the angels in heaven. [26]Now about the dead rising—have you not read in the Book of Moses, in the account of the burning bush, how God said to him, 'I am the God of Abraham, the God of Isaac, and the God of Jacob'[b]? [27]He is not the God of the dead, but of the living. You are badly mistaken!"

### The Greatest Commandment

[28]One of the teachers of the law came and heard them debating. Noticing that Jesus had given them a good answer, he asked him, "Of all the commandments, which is the most important?"

[29]"The most important one," answered Jesus, "is this: 'Hear, O Israel: The Lord our God, the Lord is one.[c] [30]Love the Lord your God with all your heart and with all your soul and with all your mind and with all your strength.'[d] [31]The second is this: 'Love your neighbor as yourself.'[e] There is no commandment greater than these."

[32]"Well said, teacher," the man replied. "You are right in saying that God is one and there is no other but him. [33]To love him with all your heart, with all your understanding and with all your strength, and to love your neighbor as yourself is more important than all burnt offerings and sacrifices."

[34]When Jesus saw that he had answered wisely, he said to him, "You are not far from the kingdom of God." And from then on no one dared ask him any more questions.

### Whose Son Is the Messiah?

[35]While Jesus was teaching in the temple courts, he asked, "Why do the teachers of the law say that the Messiah is the son of David? [36]David himself, speaking by the Holy Spirit, declared:

"'The Lord said to my Lord:
  "Sit at my right hand
  until I put your enemies
    under your feet."'[f]

## Amplified Bible

[16]And they brought [Him one]. Then He asked them, Whose image (picture) is this? And whose superscription ([a]title)? They said to Him, Caesar's.

[17]Jesus said to them, Pay to Caesar the things that are Caesar's and to [b]God the things that are God's. And they [a]stood marveling and greatly amazed at Him.

[18]And [some] Sadducees came to Him, [of that party] who say there is no resurrection, and they asked Him a question, saying,

[19]Teacher, Moses gave us [a law] that if a man's brother died, leaving a wife but no child, the man must marry the widow and raise up offspring for his brother. [Deut. 25:5.]

[20]Now there were seven brothers; the first one took a wife and died, leaving no children.

[21]And the second [brother] married her, and died, leaving no children; and the third did the same;

[22]And all seven, leaving no children. Last of all, the woman died also.

[23]Now in the resurrection, whose wife will she be? For the seven were married to her.

[24]Jesus said to them, Is not this where you wander out of the way and go wrong, because you know neither the Scriptures nor the power of God?

[25]For when they arise from among the dead, [men] do not marry nor are [women] given in marriage, but are like the angels in heaven.

[26]But concerning the dead being raised—have you not read in the book of Moses, [in the passage] about the [burning] bush, how God said to him, I am the God of Abraham and the God of Isaac and the God of Jacob? [Exod. 3:2-6.]

[27]He is not the God of [the] dead, but of [the] living! You are very wrong.

[28]Then one of the scribes came up and listened to them disputing with one another, and, noticing that Jesus answered them fitly and admirably, he asked Him, Which commandment is first and most important of all [[c]in its nature]?

[29]Jesus answered, The first and principal one of all commands is: Hear, O Israel, The Lord our God is one Lord;

[30]And you shall love the Lord your God [c]out of and with all your whole heart and out of and with all your soul (your [d]life) and out of and with all your mind (with [c]your faculty of thought and your moral understanding) and out of and with all your strength. [e]This is the first and principal commandment. [Deut. 6:4, 5.]

[31]The second is like it and is this, You shall love your neighbor as yourself. There is no other commandment greater than these. [Lev. 19:18.]

[32]And the scribe said to Him, Excellently and fitly and admirably answered, Teacher! You have said truly that He is One, and there is no other but Him;

[33]And to love Him out of and with all the heart and with all the understanding [with the [c]faculty of quick apprehension and intelligence and keenness of discernment] and with all the strength, and to love one's neighbor as oneself, is much more than all the whole burnt offerings and sacrifices. [I Sam. 15:22; Hos. 6:6; Mic. 6:6-8; Heb. 10:8.]

[34]And when Jesus saw that he answered intelligently (discreetly and [c]having his wits about him), He said to him, You are not far from the kingdom of God. And after that no one ventured or dared to ask Him any further question.

[35]And as Jesus taught in [a [f]porch or court of] the temple, He said, How can the scribes say that the Christ is David's Son?

[36]David himself, [inspired] in the Holy Spirit, declared, The Lord said to my Lord, Sit at My right hand until I make Your enemies [a footstool] under Your feet. [Ps. 110:1.]

---

[a] 23 Some manuscripts *resurrection, when people rise from the dead,*
[b] 26 Exodus 3:6    [c] 29 Or *The Lord our God is one Lord*    [d] 30 Deut.
6:4,5    [e] 31 Lev. 19:18    [f] 36 Psalm 110:1

[a] Kenneth Wuest, *Word Studies.*  [b] A rebuke of emperor worship.
[c] Marvin Vincent, *Word Studies.*  [d] Hermann Cremer, *A Biblico-Theological Lexicon.*  [e] Some manuscripts do not contain this part of verse 30.  [f] Richard Trench, *Synonyms of the New Testament.*

## New International Version

37David himself calls him 'Lord.' How then can he be his son?"

The large crowd listened to him with delight.

### Warning Against the Teachers of the Law

38As he taught, Jesus said, "Watch out for the teachers of the law. They like to walk around in flowing robes and be greeted with respect in the marketplaces, 39and have the most important seats in the synagogues and the places of honor at banquets. 40They devour widows' houses and for a show make lengthy prayers. These men will be punished most severely."

### The Widow's Offering

41Jesus sat down opposite the place where the offerings were put and watched the crowd putting their money into the temple treasury. Many rich people threw in large amounts. 42But a poor widow came and put in two very small copper coins, worth only a few cents.

43Calling his disciples to him, Jesus said, "Truly I tell you, this poor widow has put more into the treasury than all the others. 44They all gave out of their wealth; but she, out of her poverty, put in everything—all she had to live on."

### The Destruction of the Temple and Signs of the End Times

**13** As Jesus was leaving the temple, one of his disciples said to him, "Look, Teacher! What massive stones! What magnificent buildings!"

2"Do you see all these great buildings?" replied Jesus. "Not one stone here will be left on another; every one will be thrown down."

3As Jesus was sitting on the Mount of Olives opposite the temple, Peter, James, John and Andrew asked him privately, 4"Tell us, when will these things happen? And what will be the sign that they are all about to be fulfilled?"

5Jesus said to them: "Watch out that no one deceives you. 6Many will come in my name, claiming, 'I am he,' and will deceive many. 7When you hear of wars and rumors of wars, do not be alarmed. Such things must happen, but the end is still to come. 8Nation will rise against nation, and kingdom against kingdom. There will be earthquakes in various places, and famines. These are the beginning of birth pains.

9"You must be on your guard. You will be handed over to the local councils and flogged in the synagogues. On account of me you will stand before governors and kings as witnesses to them. 10And the gospel must first be preached to all nations. 11Whenever you are arrested and brought to trial, do not worry beforehand about what to say. Just say whatever is given you at the time, for it is not you speaking, but the Holy Spirit.

12"Brother will betray brother to death, and a father his child. Children will rebel against their parents and have

## Amplified Bible

37David himself calls Him Lord; so how can it be that He is his Son? Now the great mass of the people heard [Jesus] gladly [listening to Him with delight].

38And in [the course of] His teaching, He said, Beware of the scribes, who like to go around in long robes and [to get] greetings in the marketplaces [public forums],

39And [have] the front seats in the synagogues and the *a*chief couches (places of honor) at feasts,

40Who devour widows' houses and to cover it up make long prayers. They will receive the heavier [sentence of] condemnation.

41And He sat down opposite the treasury and saw how the crowd was casting money into the treasury. Many rich [people] were throwing in large sums.

42And a widow who was poverty-stricken came and put in two copper mites [the smallest of coins], which together make *b*half of a cent.

43And He called His disciples [to Him] and said to them, Truly *and* surely I tell you, this widow, [she who is] poverty-stricken, has put in more than all those contributing to the treasury.

44For they all threw in out of their abundance; but she, out of her deep poverty, has put in everything that she had—[even] all she had on which to live.

**13** And as [Jesus] was coming out of the temple [*a*area], one of His disciples said to Him, Look, Teacher! Notice the sort *and* quality of these stones and buildings!

2And Jesus replied to him, You see these great buildings? There will not be left here one stone upon another that will not be loosened *and* torn down.

3And as He sat on the Mount of Olives opposite the temple [*a*enclosure], Peter and James and John and Andrew asked Him privately,

4Tell us when is this to take place and what will be the sign when these things, all [of them], are about to be accomplished?

5And Jesus began to tell them, Be careful *and* watchful that no one misleads you [about it].

6Many will come in [*c*appropriating to themselves] the name [of Messiah] which belongs to Me [*d*basing their claims on the use of My name], saying, I am [He]! And they will mislead many.

7And when you hear of wars and rumors of wars, do not get alarmed (troubled and frightened); it is necessary [that these things] take place, but the end is not yet.

8For nation will rise against nation, and kingdom against kingdom. There will be earthquakes in various places; there will be famines *and calamities*. This is but the beginning of the *c*intolerable anguish *and* suffering [only the first of the *e*birth pangs].

9But look to yourselves; for they will turn you over to councils, and you will be beaten in the synagogues, and you will stand before governors and kings for My sake as a testimony to them.

10And the good news (the Gospel) must first be preached to all nations.

11Now when they take you [to court] and put you under arrest, do not be anxious beforehand about what you are to say *f*nor [*even*] *meditate about it;* but say whatever is given you in that hour *and* at *g*the moment, for it is not you who will be speaking, but the Holy Spirit.

12And brother will hand over brother to death, and the father his child; and children will take a stand against their parents and [have] them put to death.

*a* Richard Trench, *Synonyms of the New Testament.* *b* John D. Davis, *A Dictionary of the Bible.* *c* Joseph Thayer, *A Greek-English Lexicon.* *d* Marvin Vincent, *Word Studies.* *e* Literal meaning. *f* Most manuscripts do not contain this phrase. *g* James Moulton and George Milligan, *The Vocabulary.*

## New International Version

them put to death. ¹³Everyone will hate you because of me, but the one who stands firm to the end will be saved.

¹⁴"When you see 'the abomination that causes desolation'[a] standing where it[b] does not belong—let the reader understand—then let those who are in Judea flee to the mountains. ¹⁵Let no one on the housetop go down or enter the house to take anything out. ¹⁶Let no one in the field go back to get their cloak. ¹⁷How dreadful it will be in those days for pregnant women and nursing mothers! ¹⁸Pray that this will not take place in winter, ¹⁹because those will be days of distress unequaled from the beginning, when God created the world, until now—and never to be equaled again.

²⁰"If the Lord had not cut short those days, no one would survive. But for the sake of the elect, whom he has chosen, he has shortened them. ²¹At that time if anyone says to you, 'Look, here is the Messiah!' or, 'Look, there he is!' do not believe it. ²²For false messiahs and false prophets will appear and perform signs and wonders to deceive, if possible, even the elect. ²³So be on your guard; I have told you everything ahead of time.

²⁴"But in those days, following that distress,

"'the sun will be darkened,
    and the moon will not give its light;
²⁵ the stars will fall from the sky,
    and the heavenly bodies will be shaken.'[c]

²⁶"At that time people will see the Son of Man coming in clouds with great power and glory. ²⁷And he will send his angels and gather his elect from the four winds, from the ends of the earth to the ends of the heavens.

²⁸"Now learn this lesson from the fig tree: As soon as its twigs get tender and its leaves come out, you know that summer is near. ²⁹Even so, when you see these things happening, you know that it[b] is near, right at the door. ³⁰Truly I tell you, this generation will certainly not pass away until all these things have happened. ³¹Heaven and earth will pass away, but my words will never pass away.

### The Day and Hour Unknown

³²"But about that day or hour no one knows, not even the angels in heaven, nor the Son, but only the Father. ³³Be on guard! Be alert[d]! You do not know when that time will come. ³⁴It's like a man going away: He leaves his house and puts his servants in charge, each with their assigned task, and tells the one at the door to keep watch.

³⁵"Therefore keep watch because you do not know when the owner of the house will come back—whether in the evening, or at midnight, or when the rooster crows,

## Amplified Bible

¹³And you will be hated *and* detested by everybody for My name's sake, but he who patiently perseveres *and* endures to the end will be saved ([a]made a partaker of the salvation by Christ, and delivered [a]from spiritual death).

¹⁴But when you see the abomination of desolation *mentioned by Daniel the prophet* standing where it ought not to be—[and] let the one who reads take notice *and* consider *and* understand *and* heed [this]—then let those who are in Judea flee to the mountains. [Dan. 9:27; 11:31; 12:11.]

¹⁵Let him who is on the housetop not go down *into the house* nor go inside to take anything out of his house;

¹⁶And let him who is in the field not turn back again to get his mantle (cloak).

¹⁷And alas for those who are pregnant and for those who have nursing babies in those days!

¹⁸Pray that it may not occur in winter,

¹⁹For at that time there will be such affliction (oppression and tribulation) as has not been from the beginning of the creation which God created until this particular time—and [b]positively never will be [again].

²⁰And unless the Lord had shortened the days, no human being would be saved (rescued); but for the sake of the elect, His chosen ones (those whom He [c]picked out for Himself), He has shortened the days. [Dan. 12:1.]

²¹And then if anyone says to you, See, here is the Christ (the Messiah)! or, Look, there He is! do not believe it.

²²False Christs (Messiahs) and false prophets will arise and show signs and [work] miracles to deceive *and* lead astray, if possible, even the elect (those God has chosen out for Himself).

²³But look to yourselves *and* be on your guard; I have told you everything beforehand.

²⁴But in those days, after [the affliction and oppression and distress of] that tribulation, the sun will be darkened, and the moon will not give its light; [Isa. 13:10.]

²⁵And the stars will be falling from the sky, and the powers in the heavens will be shaken. [Isa. 34:4.]

²⁶And then they will see the Son of Man coming in clouds with great (kingly) power and glory (majesty and splendor). [Dan. 7:13, 14.]

²⁷And then He will send out the angels and will gather together His elect (those He has [c]picked out for Himself) from the four winds, from the farthest bounds of the earth to the farthest bounds of heaven.

²⁸Now learn a lesson from the fig tree: as soon as its branch becomes tender and it puts forth its leaves, you recognize *and* know that summer is near.

²⁹So also, when you see these things happening, you may recognize *and* know that He is near, at [the very] door.

³⁰Surely I say to you, this generation ([d]the whole multitude of people living at that one time) positively will not perish *or* pass away before all these things take place.

³¹Heaven and earth will perish *and* pass away, but My words will not perish *or* pass away.

³²But of that day or that hour not a [single] person knows, not even the angels in heaven, nor the Son, but only the Father.

³³Be on your guard [constantly alert], and watch [e]*and pray*; for you do not know when the time will come.

³⁴It is like a man [f]already] going on a journey; when he leaves home, he puts his servants in charge, each with his particular task, and he gives orders to the doorkeeper to be constantly alert *and* on the watch.

³⁵Therefore watch (give strict attention, be cautious and alert), for you do not know when the Master of the house is coming—in the evening, or at midnight, or at cockcrowing, or in the morning—

[a] Joseph Thayer, *A Greek-English Lexicon.* [b] Kenneth Wuest, *Word Studies.* [c] G. Abbott-Smith, *Manual Greek Lexicon.* [d] Hermann Cremer, *Biblico-Theological Lexicon*; Joseph Thayer, *A Greek-English Lexicon*; and G. Abbott-Smith, *Manual Greek Lexicon.* [e] Some manuscripts add "and pray." [f] John Wycliffe, *The Wycliffe Bible*; William Tyndale, *The Tyndale Bible.*

[a] 14 Daniel 9:27; 11:31; 12:11    [b] 14,29 Or *he*    [c] 25 Isaiah 13:10; 34:4    [d] 33 Some manuscripts *alert and pray*

# New International Version

or at dawn. ³⁶If he comes suddenly, do not let him find you sleeping. ³⁷What I say to you, I say to everyone: 'Watch!'"

## Jesus Anointed at Bethany

**14** Now the Passover and the Festival of Unleavened Bread were only two days away, and the chief priests and the teachers of the law were scheming to arrest Jesus secretly and kill him. ²"But not during the festival," they said, "or the people may riot."

³While he was in Bethany, reclining at the table in the home of Simon the Leper, a woman came with an alabaster jar of very expensive perfume, made of pure nard. She broke the jar and poured the perfume on his head.

⁴Some of those present were saying indignantly to one another, "Why this waste of perfume? ⁵It could have been sold for more than a year's wages*ᵃ* and the money given to the poor." And they rebuked her harshly.

⁶"Leave her alone," said Jesus. "Why are you bothering her? She has done a beautiful thing to me. ⁷The poor you will always have with you,*ᵇ* and you can help them any time you want. But you will not always have me. ⁸She did what she could. She poured perfume on my body beforehand to prepare for my burial. ⁹Truly I tell you, wherever the gospel is preached throughout the world, what she has done will also be told, in memory of her."

¹⁰Then Judas Iscariot, one of the Twelve, went to the chief priests to betray Jesus to them. ¹¹They were delighted to hear this and promised to give him money. So he watched for an opportunity to hand him over.

## The Last Supper

¹²On the first day of the Festival of Unleavened Bread, when it was customary to sacrifice the Passover lamb, Jesus' disciples asked him, "Where do you want us to go and make preparations for you to eat the Passover?"

¹³So he sent two of his disciples, telling them, "Go into the city, and a man carrying a jar of water will meet you. Follow him. ¹⁴Say to the owner of the house he enters, 'The Teacher asks: Where is my guest room, where I may eat the Passover with my disciples?' ¹⁵He will show you a large room upstairs, furnished and ready. Make preparations for us there."

¹⁶The disciples left, went into the city and found things just as Jesus had told them. So they prepared the Passover.

¹⁷When evening came, Jesus arrived with the Twelve. ¹⁸While they were reclining at the table eating, he said, "Truly I tell you, one of you will betray me—one who is eating with me."

¹⁹They were saddened, and one by one they said to him, "Surely you don't mean me?"

²⁰"It is one of the Twelve," he replied, "one who dips bread into the bowl with me. ²¹The Son of Man will go just as it is written about him. But woe to that man who betrays the Son of Man! It would be better for him if he had not been born."

# Amplified Bible

³⁶[Watch, I say] lest He come suddenly *and* unexpectedly and find you asleep.

³⁷And what I say to you I say to everybody: Watch (give strict attention, be cautious, active, and alert)!

**14** It was now two days before the Passover and the Feast of Unleavened Bread, and the chief priests and the scribes were all the while seeking to arrest [Jesus] by secrecy *and* deceit and put [Him] to death,

²For they kept saying, It must not be during the Feast, for fear that there might be a riot of the people.

³And while He was in Bethany, [a guest] in the house of Simon the leper, as He was reclining [at table], a woman came with an alabaster jar of ointment (*ᵃ*perfume) of pure nard, very costly *and* precious; and she broke the jar and poured [the perfume] over His head.

⁴But there were some who were moved with indignation and said to themselves, To what purpose was the ointment (*ᵃ*perfume) thus wasted?

⁵For it was possible to have sold this [perfume] for more than 300 denarii [a laboring man's wages for a year] and to have given [the money] to the poor. And they censured *and* reproved her.

⁶But Jesus said, Let her alone; why are you troubling her? She has done a good *and* beautiful thing to Me [praiseworthy and noble].

⁷For you always have the poor with you, and whenever you wish you can do good to them; but you will not always have Me. [Deut. 15:11.]

⁸She has done what she could; she came beforehand to anoint My body for the burial.

⁹And surely I tell you, wherever the good news (the Gospel) is proclaimed in the entire world, what she has done will be told in memory of her.

¹⁰Then Judas Iscariot, who was one of the Twelve [apostles], went off to the chief priests in order to betray *and* hand Him over to them.

¹¹And when they heard it, they rejoiced *and* were delighted, and they promised to give him money. And he [busying himself continually] sought an opportunity to betray Him.

¹²On the first day [of the Feast] of Unleavened Bread, when [as was customary] they killed the Passover lamb, [Jesus'] disciples said to Him, Where do You wish us to go [and] prepare the Passover [supper] for You to eat?

¹³And He sent two of His disciples and said to them, Go into the city, and a man carrying an [earthen] jar *or* pitcher of water will meet you; follow him.

¹⁴And whatever [house] he enters, say to the master of the house, The Teacher says: Where is My guest room, where I may eat the Passover [supper] with My disciples?

¹⁵And he [himself] show you a large upper room, furnished [with carpets and with dining couches properly spread] and ready; there prepare for us.

¹⁶Then the disciples set out and came to the city and found [everything] just as He had told them; and they prepared the Passover.

¹⁷And when it was evening, He came with the Twelve [apostles].

¹⁸And while they were at the table eating, Jesus said, Surely I say to you, one of you will betray Me, [one] who is eating [here] with Me. [Ps. 41:9.]

¹⁹And they began to show that they were sad *and* hurt, and to say to Him one after another, Is it I? *or,* It is not I, is it?

²⁰He replied to them, It is one of the Twelve [apostles], one who is dipping [bread] into the [same deep] dish with Me.

²¹For the Son of Man is going as it stands written concerning Him; but woe to that man by whom the Son of Man is betrayed! It would have been good (profitable and wholesome) for that man if he had never been born. [Ps. 41:9.]

---

*ᵃ* 5 Greek *than three hundred denarii*    *ᵇ* 7 See Deut. 15:11.

*ᵃ* James Moulton and George Milligan, *The Vocabulary.*

# New International Version

## Amplified Bible

**22**While they were eating, Jesus took bread, and when he had given thanks, he broke it and gave it to his disciples, saying, "Take it; this is my body."

**23**Then he took a cup, and when he had given thanks, he gave it to them, and they all drank from it.

**24**"This is my blood of the[a] covenant, which is poured out for many," he said to them. **25**"Truly I tell you, I will not drink again from the fruit of the vine until that day when I drink it new in the kingdom of God."

**26**When they had sung a hymn, they went out to the Mount of Olives.

### Jesus Predicts Peter's Denial

**27**"You will all fall away," Jesus told them, "for it is written:

"'I will strike the shepherd,
and the sheep will be scattered.'[b]

**28**But after I have risen, I will go ahead of you into Galilee."

**29**Peter declared, "Even if all fall away, I will not."

**30**"Truly I tell you," Jesus answered, "today—yes, tonight—before the rooster crows twice[c] you yourself will disown me three times."

**31**But Peter insisted emphatically, "Even if I have to die with you, I will never disown you." And all the others said the same.

### Gethsemane

**32**They went to a place called Gethsemane, and Jesus said to his disciples, "Sit here while I pray." **33**He took Peter, James and John along with him, and he began to be deeply distressed and troubled. **34**"My soul is overwhelmed with sorrow to the point of death," he said to them. "Stay here and keep watch."

**35**Going a little farther, he fell to the ground and prayed that if possible the hour might pass from him. **36**"Abba,[d] Father," he said, "everything is possible for you. Take this cup from me. Yet not what I will, but what you will."

**37**Then he returned to his disciples and found them sleeping. "Simon," he said to Peter, "are you asleep? Couldn't you keep watch for one hour? **38**Watch and pray so that you will not fall into temptation. The spirit is willing, but the flesh is weak."

**39**Once more he went away and prayed the same thing. **40**When he came back, he again found them sleeping, because their eyes were heavy. They did not know what to say to him.

**41**Returning the third time, he said to them, "Are you still sleeping and resting? Enough! The hour has come. Look, the Son of Man is delivered into the hands of sinners. **42**Rise! Let us go! Here comes my betrayer!"

### Jesus Arrested

**43**Just as he was speaking, Judas, one of the Twelve, appeared. With him was a crowd armed with swords and clubs, sent from the chief priests, the teachers of the law, and the elders.

**44**Now the betrayer had arranged a signal with them: "The one I kiss is the man; arrest him and lead him away

---

**22**And while they were eating, He took a loaf [of bread], praised God *and* gave thanks *and* asked Him to bless it to their use. [Then] He broke [it] and gave to them and said, Take. *Eat.* This is My body.

**23**He also took a cup [of the juice of grapes], and when He had given thanks, He gave [it] to them, and they all drank of it.

**24**And He said to them, This is My blood [which ratifies] the *new* covenant, [the blood] which is being poured out for (on account of) many. [Exod. 24:8.]

**25**Solemnly *and* surely I tell you, I shall not again drink of the fruit of the vine till that day when I drink it[d] of a new *and* a higher quality in God's kingdom.

**26**And when they had sung a hymn, they went out to the Mount of Olives.

**27**And Jesus said to them, You will all fall away *this night* [that is, you will be caused to stumble and will begin to distrust and desert Me], for it stands written, I will strike the Shepherd, and the sheep will be scattered. [Zech. 13:7.]

**28**But after I am raised [to life], I will go before you into Galilee.

**29**But Peter said to Him, Even if they all fall away *and* are caused to stumble *and* distrust *and* desert You, yet I will not [do so]!

**30**And Jesus said to him, Truly I tell you, this very night, before a cock crows twice, you will utterly deny Me [disclaiming all connection with Me] three times.

**31**But [Peter] said more vehemently *and* repeatedly, [Even] if it should be necessary for me to die with You, I will not deny *or* disown You! And they all kept saying the same thing.

**32**Then they went to a place called Gethsemane, and He said to His disciples, Sit down here while I pray.

**33**And He took with Him Peter and James and John, and began to be[b]struck with terror *and* amazement and deeply troubled *and* depressed.

**34**And He said to them, My soul is exceedingly sad (overwhelmed with grief) so that it almost kills Me! Remain here and keep awake *and* be watching.

**35**And going a little farther, He fell on the ground and kept praying that if it were possible the [b]fatal] hour might pass from Him.

**36**And He was saying, Abba, [which means] Father, everything is possible for You. Take away this cup from Me; yet not what I will, but what You [will].

**37**And He came back and found them sleeping, and He said to Peter, Simon, are you asleep? Have you not the strength to keep awake *and* watch [with Me for] one hour?

**38**Keep awake *and* watch and pray [constantly], that you may not enter into temptation; the spirit indeed is willing, but the flesh is weak.

**39**He went away again and prayed, saying the same words.

**40**And again He came back and found them sleeping, for their eyes were very heavy; and they did not know what answer to give Him.

**41**And He came back a third time and said to them, Are you still sleeping and resting? It is enough [of that]! The hour has come. The Son of Man is betrayed into the hands of sinful men (men[c]whose way or nature is to act in opposition to God).

**42**Get up, let us be going! See, My betrayer is at hand!

**43**And at once, while He was still speaking, Judas came, one of the Twelve [apostles], and with him a crowd of men with swords and clubs, [who came] from the chief priests and the scribes and the elders [of the Sanhedrin].

**44**Now the betrayer had given them a signal, saying, The One I shall kiss is [the Man]; seize Him and lead [Him] away safely [so as to prevent His escape].

---

*a* 24 Some manuscripts *the new*     *b* 27 Zech. 13:7     *c* 30 Some early manuscripts do not have *twice*.     *d* 36 Aramaic for *father*

*a* Marvin Vincent, *Word Studies.*     *b* Joseph Thayer, *A Greek-English Lexicon.*     *c* Hermann Cremer, *Biblico-Theological Lexicon.*

## New International Version

under guard." ⁴⁵Going at once to Jesus, Judas said, "Rabbi!" and kissed him. ⁴⁶The men seized Jesus and arrested him. ⁴⁷Then one of those standing near drew his sword and struck the servant of the high priest, cutting off his ear.

⁴⁸"Am I leading a rebellion," said Jesus, "that you have come out with swords and clubs to capture me? ⁴⁹Every day I was with you, teaching in the temple courts, and you did not arrest me. But the Scriptures must be fulfilled." ⁵⁰Then everyone deserted him and fled.

⁵¹A young man, wearing nothing but a linen garment, was following Jesus. When they seized him, ⁵²he fled naked, leaving his garment behind.

### Jesus Before the Sanhedrin

⁵³They took Jesus to the high priest, and all the chief priests, the elders and the teachers of the law came together. ⁵⁴Peter followed him at a distance, right into the courtyard of the high priest. There he sat with the guards and warmed himself at the fire.

⁵⁵The chief priests and the whole Sanhedrin were looking for evidence against Jesus so that they could put him to death, but they did not find any. ⁵⁶Many testified falsely against him, but their statements did not agree.

⁵⁷Then some stood up and gave this false testimony against him: ⁵⁸"We heard him say, 'I will destroy this temple made with human hands and in three days will build another, not made with hands.'" ⁵⁹Yet even then their testimony did not agree.

⁶⁰Then the high priest stood up before them and asked Jesus, "Are you not going to answer? What is this testimony that these men are bringing against you?" ⁶¹But Jesus remained silent and gave no answer.

Again the high priest asked him, "Are you the Messiah, the Son of the Blessed One?"

⁶²"I am," said Jesus. "And you will see the Son of Man sitting at the right hand of the Mighty One and coming on the clouds of heaven."

⁶³The high priest tore his clothes. "Why do we need any more witnesses?" he asked. ⁶⁴"You have heard the blasphemy. What do you think?"

They all condemned him as worthy of death. ⁶⁵Then some began to spit at him; they blindfolded him, struck him with their fists, and said, "Prophesy!" And the guards took him and beat him.

### Peter Disowns Jesus

⁶⁶While Peter was below in the courtyard, one of the servant girls of the high priest came by. ⁶⁷When she saw Peter warming himself, she looked closely at him.

"You also were with that Nazarene, Jesus," she said.

⁶⁸But he denied it. "I don't know or understand what you're talking about," he said, and went out into the entryway.ᵃ

⁶⁹When the servant girl saw him there, she said again to those standing around, "This fellow is one of them." ⁷⁰Again he denied it.

## Amplified Bible

⁴⁵And when he came, he went up to Jesus immediately and said, Master! *Master!* and he ᵃembraced Him *and* kissed Him fervently.

⁴⁶And they threw their hands on Him and arrested Him.

⁴⁷But one of the bystanders drew his sword and struck the bond servant of the high priest and cut off his ear.

⁴⁸And Jesus said to them, Have you come out with swords and clubs as [you would] against a robber to capture Me?

⁴⁹I was with you daily in the temple [ᵇporches and courts] teaching, and you did not seize Me; but [this has happened] that the Scriptures might be fulfilled.

⁵⁰Then [His disciples], forsaking Him, fled, all [of them].

⁵¹And a young man was following Him, with nothing but a linen cloth (ᶜsheet) thrown about [his] naked [body]; and they laid hold of him,

⁵²But, leaving behind the linen cloth (ᶜsheet), he fled from them naked.

⁵³And they led Jesus away to the high priest, and all the chief priests and the elders and the scribes were gathered together.

⁵⁴And Peter followed Him at a distance, even right into the courtyard of the high priest. And he was sitting [ᵈin the firelight] with the guards and warming himself at the fire.

⁵⁵Now the chief priests and the entire council (the Sanhedrin) were constantly seeking [to get] testimony against Jesus with a view to condemning Him *and* putting Him to death, but they did not find any.

⁵⁶For many were repeatedly bearing false witness against Him, but their testimonies did not agree.

⁵⁷And some stood up and were bearing false witness against Him, saying,

⁵⁸We heard Him say, I will destroy this temple (sanctuary) which is made with hands, and in three days I will build another, made without hands.

⁵⁹Still not even [in this] did their testimony agree.

⁶⁰And the high priest stood up in the midst and asked Jesus, Have You not even one answer to make? What [about this which] these [men] are testifying against You?

⁶¹But He kept still and did not answer at all. Again the high priest asked Him, Are You the Christ (the Messiah, the Anointed One), the Son of the Blessed?

⁶²And Jesus said, I AM; and you will [all] see the Son of Man seated at the right hand of Power (ᶜthe Almighty) and coming on the clouds of heaven. [Ps. 110:1; Dan. 7:13.]

⁶³Then the high priest tore his garments and said, What need have we for more witnesses? [Num. 14:6.]

⁶⁴You have heard His blasphemy. What is your decision? And they all condemned Him as being guilty *and* deserving of death. [Lev. 24:16.]

⁶⁵And some of them began to spit on Him and to blindfold Him and to strike Him with their fists, saying to Him, Prophesy! And the guards received Him with blows *and* by slapping Him.

⁶⁶While Peter was down below in the courtyard, one of the [serving] maids of the high priest came;

⁶⁷And when she saw Peter warming himself, she gazed intently at him and said, You were with Jesus of Nazareth too.

⁶⁸But he denied it ᶠfalsely *and* disowned Him, saying, I neither know nor understand what you say. Then he went outside [the courtyard and was] into the ᵈvestibule. ᵍ*And a cock crowed.*

⁶⁹And the maidservant saw him, and began again to say to the bystanders, This [man] is [one] of them.

⁷⁰But again he denied it ᶠfalsely *and* disowned Him. And

---

ᵃ H.A. W. Meyer, *Critical and Exegetical Handbook to the Gospel of Mark.* ᵇ Richard Trench, *Synonyms of the New Testament.* ᶜ Alexander Souter, *Pocket Lexicon.* ᵈ Marvin Vincent, *Word Studies.* ᵉ Joseph Thayer, *A Greek-English Lexicon.* ᶠ Hermann Cremer, *Biblico-Theological Lexicon.* ᵍ Some manuscripts add this sentence.

---

ᵃ 68 Some early manuscripts *entryway and the rooster crowed*

## New International Version

After a little while, those standing near said to Peter, "Surely you are one of them, for you are a Galilean."

[71] He began to call down curses, and he swore to them, "I don't know this man you're talking about."

[72] Immediately the rooster crowed the second time.[a] Then Peter remembered the word Jesus had spoken to him: "Before the rooster crows twice[b] you will disown me three times." And he broke down and wept.

### Jesus Before Pilate

**15** Very early in the morning, the chief priests, with the elders, the teachers of the law and the whole Sanhedrin, made their plans. So they bound Jesus, led him away and handed him over to Pilate.

[2] "Are you the king of the Jews?" asked Pilate.

"You have said so," Jesus replied.

[3] The chief priests accused him of many things. [4] So again Pilate asked him, "Aren't you going to answer? See how many things they are accusing you of."

[5] But Jesus still made no reply, and Pilate was amazed.

[6] Now it was the custom at the festival to release a prisoner whom the people requested. [7] A man called Barabbas was in prison with the insurrectionists who had committed murder in the uprising. [8] The crowd came up and asked Pilate to do for them what he usually did.

[9] "Do you want me to release to you the king of the Jews?" asked Pilate, [10] knowing it was out of self-interest that the chief priests had handed Jesus over to him. [11] But the chief priests stirred up the crowd to have Pilate release Barabbas instead.

[12] "What shall I do, then, with the one you call the king of the Jews?" Pilate asked them.

[13] "Crucify him!" they shouted.

[14] "Why? What crime has he committed?" asked Pilate. But they shouted all the louder, "Crucify him!"

[15] Wanting to satisfy the crowd, Pilate released Barabbas to them. He had Jesus flogged, and handed him over to be crucified.

### The Soldiers Mock Jesus

[16] The soldiers led Jesus away into the palace (that is, the Praetorium) and called together the whole company of soldiers. [17] They put a purple robe on him, then twisted together a crown of thorns and set it on him. [18] And they began to call out to him, "Hail, king of the Jews!" [19] Again and again they struck him on the head with a staff and spat on him. Falling on their knees, they paid homage to him. [20] And when they had mocked him, they took off the purple robe and put his own clothes on him. Then they led him out to crucify him.

### The Crucifixion of Jesus

[21] A certain man from Cyrene, Simon, the father of Alexander and Rufus, was passing by on his way in from the country, and they forced him to carry the cross. [22] They brought Jesus to the place called Golgotha (which means

## Amplified Bible

after a short while, again the bystanders said to Peter, [a] Really, you are one of them, for you are a Galilean [b] and your dialect shows it.

[71] Then he commenced invoking a curse on himself [should he not be telling the truth] and swearing, I do not know the Man about Whom you are talking!

[72] And at once for the second time a cock crowed. And Peter remembered how Jesus said to him, Before a cock crows twice, you will [c] utterly deny Me [disclaiming all connection with Me] three times. And [d] having put his thought upon it [and remembering], he broke down and wept aloud and [e] lamented.

**15** And immediately when it was morning, the chief priests, with the elders and scribes and the whole council, held a consultation; and when they had bound Jesus, they took Him away [[e] violently] and handed Him over to Pilate. [Isa. 53:8.]

[2] And Pilate inquired of Him, Are You the King of the Jews? And He replied, It is as you say.

[3] And the chief priests kept accusing Him of many things.

[4] And Pilate again asked Him, Have [f] You no answer to make? See how many charges they are bringing against You!

[5] But Jesus made no further answer at all, so that Pilate wondered and marveled. [Isa. 53:7.]

[6] Now at the Feast he [was accustomed to] set free for them any one prisoner whom they requested.

[7] And among the rioters in the prison who had committed murder in the insurrection there was a man named Barabbas.

[8] And the throng came up and began asking Pilate to do as he usually did for them.

[9] And he replied to them, Do you wish me to set free for you the King of the Jews?

[10] For he was aware that it was [e] because they were prompted] by envy that the chief priests had delivered Him up.

[11] But the chief priests stirred up the crowd to get him to release for them Barabbas instead.

[12] And again Pilate said to them, Then what shall I do with the Man Whom you call the King of the Jews?

[13] And they shouted back again, Crucify Him!

[14] But Pilate said to them, Why? What has He done that is evil? But they shouted with all their might all the more, Crucify Him [[d] at once]!

[15] So Pilate, wishing to satisfy the crowd, set Barabbas free for them; and after having Jesus whipped, he handed [Him] over to be crucified. [Isa. 53:5.]

[16] Then the soldiers led Him away to the courtyard inside the palace, that is, the Praetorium, and they called the entire detachment of soldiers together.

[17] And they dressed Him in [a] purple [robe], and, weaving together a crown of thorns, they placed it on Him.

[18] And they began to salute Him, Hail (greetings, good health to You, long life to You), King of the Jews!

[19] And they struck His head with a staff made of a [bamboo-like] reed and spat on Him and kept bowing their knees in homage to Him. [Isa. 50:6.]

[20] And when they had [finished] making sport of Him, they took the purple [robe] off of Him and put His own clothes on Him. And they led Him out [of the city] to crucify Him.

[21] And they forced a passerby, Simon of Cyrene, the father of Alexander and Rufus, who was coming in from the field (country), to carry His cross.

[22] And they led Him to Golgotha [in Latin: Calvary], meaning The Place of a Skull.

---

[a] Hermann Cremer, *Biblico-Theological Lexicon.* [b] Some manuscripts contain this phrase instead. [c] Marvin Vincent, *Word Studies.* [d] Kenneth Wuest, *Word Studies.* [e] Joseph Thayer, *A Greek-English Lexicon.* [f] Capitalized because of what He is, the spotless Son of God, not what the speaker may have thought He was.

---

[a] 72 Some early manuscripts do not have *the second time.* [b] 72 Some early manuscripts do not have *twice.*

## New International Version

"the place of the skull"). ²³Then they offered him wine mixed with myrrh, but he did not take it. ²⁴And they crucified him. Dividing up his clothes, they cast lots to see what each would get.

²⁵It was nine in the morning when they crucified him. ²⁶The written notice of the charge against him read: THE KING OF THE JEWS.

²⁷They crucified two rebels with him, one on his right and one on his left. [²⁸]ᵃ ²⁹Those who passed by hurled insults at him, shaking their heads and saying, "So! You who are going to destroy the temple and build it in three days, ³⁰come down from the cross and save yourself!" ³¹In the same way the chief priests and the teachers of the law mocked him among themselves. "He saved others," they said, "but he can't save himself! ³²Let this Messiah, this king of Israel, come down now from the cross, that we may see and believe." Those crucified with him also heaped insults on him.

### The Death of Jesus

³³At noon, darkness came over the whole land until three in the afternoon. ³⁴And at three in the afternoon Jesus cried out in a loud voice, *"Eloi, Eloi, lema sabachthani?"* (which means "My God, my God, why have you forsaken me?").ᵇ

³⁵When some of those standing near heard this, they said, "Listen, he's calling Elijah."

³⁶Someone ran, filled a sponge with wine vinegar, put it on a staff, and offered it to Jesus to drink. "Now leave him alone. Let's see if Elijah comes to take him down," he said.

³⁷With a loud cry, Jesus breathed his last.

³⁸The curtain of the temple was torn in two from top to bottom. ³⁹And when the centurion, who stood there in front of Jesus, saw how he died,ᶜ he said, "Surely this man was the Son of God!"

⁴⁰Some women were watching from a distance. Among them were Mary Magdalene, Mary the mother of James the younger and of Joseph,ᵈ and Salome. ⁴¹In Galilee these women had followed him and cared for his needs. Many other women who had come up with him to Jerusalem were also there.

### The Burial of Jesus

⁴²It was Preparation Day (that is, the day before the Sabbath). So as evening approached, ⁴³Joseph of Arimathea, a prominent member of the Council, who was himself waiting for the kingdom of God, went boldly to Pilate and asked for Jesus' body. ⁴⁴Pilate was surprised to hear that he was already dead. Summoning the centurion, he asked him if Jesus had already died. ⁴⁵When he learned from the centurion that it was so, he gave the body to Joseph.

## Amplified Bible

²³And they [attempted to] give Him wine mingled with myrrh, but He would not take it.

²⁴And they crucified Him; and they divided His garments *and* distributed them among themselves, throwing lots for them to decide who should take what. [Ps. 22:18.]

²⁵And it was the third hour (about nine o'clock in the morning) when they crucified Him. [Ps. 22:14-16.]

²⁶And the inscription of the accusation against Him was written above, The King of the Jews.

²⁷And with Him they crucified two robbers, one on [His] right hand and one on His left.

²⁸ᵃ*And the Scripture was fulfilled which says, He was counted among the transgressors.* [Isa. 53:12.]

²⁹And those who passed by kept reviling Him *and* reproaching Him abusively in harsh *and* insolent language, wagging their heads and saying, Aha! You Who would destroy the temple and build it in three days,

³⁰Now rescue ᵇYourself [ᶜfrom death], coming down from the cross!

³¹So also the chief priests, with the scribes, made sport of Him to one another, saying, He rescued others [ᶜfrom death]; Himself He is unable to rescue. [Ps. 22:7, 8.]

³²Let the Christ (the Messiah), the King of Israel, come down now from the cross, that we may see [it] and trust in *and* rely on Him *and* adhere to Him! Those who were crucified with Him also reviled *and* reproached Him [speaking abusively, harshly, and insolently].

³³And when the sixth hour (about midday) had come, there was darkness over the whole land until the ninth hour (about three o'clock).

³⁴And at the ninth hour Jesus cried with a loud voice, Eloi, Eloi, lama sabachthani?—which means, My God, My God, why have You forsaken Me [ᵈdeserting Me and leaving Me helpless and abandoned]? [Ps. 22:1.]

³⁵And some of those standing by, [and] hearing it, said, See! He is calling Elijah!

³⁶And one man ran, and, filling a sponge with vinegar (a ᵈmixture of sour wine and water), put it on a staff made of a [bamboo-like] reed and gave it to Him to drink, saying, Hold off! Let us see whether Elijah [does] come to take Him down. [Ps. 69:21.]

³⁷And Jesus uttered a loud cry, and breathed out His life.

³⁸And the curtain [of the Holy of Holies] of the temple was torn in two from top to bottom.

³⁹And when the centurion who stood facing Him saw Him expire this way, he said, ᶜReally, this Man was God's Son!

⁴⁰Now some women were there also, looking on from a distance, among whom were Mary Magdalene, and Mary the mother of James the younger and of Joses, and Salome,

⁴¹Who, when [Jesus] was in Galilee, were in the habit of accompanying and ministering to Him; and [there were] also many other [women] who had come up with Him to Jerusalem.

⁴²As evening had already come, since it was the day of Preparation, that is, [the day] before the Sabbath, [Deut. 21:22, 23.]

⁴³Joseph, he of Arimathea, noble *and* honorable in rank *and* a respected member of the council (Sanhedrin), who was himself waiting for the kingdom of God, daring the consequences, took courage *and* ventured to go to Pilate and asked for the body of Jesus.

⁴⁴But Pilate wondered whether He was dead so soon, and, having called the centurion, he asked him whether [Jesus] was already dead.

⁴⁵And when he learned from the centurion [that He was indeed dead], he gave the body to Joseph.

---

ᵃ 28 Some manuscripts include here words similar to Luke 22:37.
ᵇ 34 Psalm 22:1   ᶜ 39 Some manuscripts *saw that he died with such a cry*   ᵈ 40 Greek *Joses,* a variant of *Joseph;* also in verse 47

ᵃ Many manuscripts do not contain this verse.   ᵇ Capitalized because of what He is, the spotless Son of God, not what the speakers may have thought He was.   ᶜ Hermann Cremer, *Biblico-Theological Lexicon.*   ᵈ Joseph Thayer, *A Greek-English Lexicon.*

## New International Version

[46]So Joseph bought some linen cloth, took down the body, wrapped it in the linen, and placed it in a tomb cut out of rock. Then he rolled a stone against the entrance of the tomb. [47]Mary Magdalene and Mary the mother of Joseph saw where he was laid.

### Jesus Has Risen

**16** When the Sabbath was over, Mary Magdalene, Mary the mother of James, and Salome bought spices so that they might go to anoint Jesus' body. [2]Very early on the first day of the week, just after sunrise, they were on their way to the tomb [3]and they asked each other, "Who will roll the stone away from the entrance of the tomb?"

[4]But when they looked up, they saw that the stone, which was very large, had been rolled away. [5]As they entered the tomb, they saw a young man dressed in a white robe sitting on the right side, and they were alarmed.

[6]"Don't be alarmed," he said. "You are looking for Jesus the Nazarene, who was crucified. He has risen! He is not here. See the place where they laid him. [7]But go, tell his disciples and Peter, 'He is going ahead of you into Galilee. There you will see him, just as he told you.'"

[8]Trembling and bewildered, the women went out and fled from the tomb. They said nothing to anyone, because they were afraid.[a]

---

[The earliest manuscripts and some other ancient witnesses do not have verses 9–20.]

[9]*When Jesus rose early on the first day of the week, he appeared first to Mary Magdalene, out of whom he had driven seven demons.* [10]*She went and told those who had been with him and who were mourning and weeping.* [11]*When they heard that Jesus was alive and that she had seen him, they did not believe it.*

[12]*Afterward Jesus appeared in a different form to two of them while they were walking in the country.* [13]*These returned and reported it to the rest; but they did not believe them either.*

[14]*Later Jesus appeared to the Eleven as they were eating; he rebuked them for their lack of faith and their stubborn refusal to believe those who had seen him after he had risen.*

[15]*He said to them, "Go into all the world and preach the gospel to all creation.* [16]*Whoever believes and is baptized will be saved, but whoever does not believe will be condemned.* [17]*And these signs will accompany those who believe: In my name they will drive out demons; they will speak in new tongues;* [18]*they will pick up snakes with their hands; and when they drink deadly poison, it will not hurt them at all; they will place their hands on sick people, and they will get well."*

---

[a] 8 Some manuscripts have the following ending between verses 8 and 9, and one manuscript has it after verse 8 (omitting verses 9-20): *Then they quickly reported all these instructions to those around Peter. After this, Jesus himself also sent out through them from east to west the sacred and imperishable proclamation of eternal salvation. Amen.*

## Amplified Bible

[46]And Joseph bought a [fine] linen cloth [[a]for swathing dead bodies], and, taking Him down from the cross, he [b]rolled Him up in the [fine] linen cloth and placed Him in a tomb which had been hewn out of a rock. Then he rolled a [very large] stone against the door of the tomb. [Isa. 53:9; Matt. 16:4.]

[47]And Mary Magdalene and Mary [the mother] of Joses were [[c]attentively] observing where He was laid.

**16** And when the Sabbath was past [that is, after the sun had set], Mary Magdalene, and Mary [the mother] of James, and Salome purchased sweet-smelling spices, so that they might go and anoint [Jesus' body].

[2]And very early on the first day of the week they came to the tomb; [by then] the sun had risen.

[3]And they said to one another, Who will roll back the stone for us out of [the groove across the floor at] the door of the tomb?

[4]And when they looked up, they [distinctly] saw that the stone was already rolled back, for it was very large.

[5]And going into the tomb, they saw a young man sitting [there] on the right [side], clothed in a [[d]long, stately, sweeping] robe of white, and they were utterly amazed *and* struck with terror.

[6]And he said to them, Do not be amazed *and* terrified; you are looking for Jesus of Nazareth, Who was crucified. He has risen; He is not here. See the place where they laid Him. [Ps. 16:10.]

[7]But be going; tell the disciples and Peter, He goes before you into Galilee; you will see Him there, [just] as He told you. [Mark 14:28.]

[8]Then they went out [and] fled from the tomb, for trembling and bewilderment *and* consternation had seized them. And they said nothing about it to anyone, for they were held by alarm *and* fear.

[9][e]Now Jesus, having risen [[f]from death] early on the first day of the week, appeared first to Mary Magdalene, from whom He had driven out seven demons.

[10]She went and reported it to those who had been with Him, as they grieved and wept.

[11]And when they heard that He was alive and that she had seen Him, they did not believe it.

[12]After this, He appeared in a different form to two of them as they were walking [along the way] into the country.

[13]And they returned [to Jerusalem] and told the others, but they did not believe them either.

[14]Afterward He appeared to the Eleven [apostles themselves] as they reclined at table; and He reproved *and* reproached them for their unbelief (their lack of faith) and their hardness of heart, because they had refused to believe those who had seen Him *and* looked at Him attentively after He had risen [[f]from death].

[15]And He said to them, Go into all the world and preach *and* publish openly the good news (the Gospel) to every creature [of the whole [g]human race].

[16]He who believes [who adheres to and trusts in and relies on the Gospel and Him Whom it sets forth] and is baptized will be saved [[f]from the penalty of eternal death]; but he who does not believe [who does not adhere to and trust in and rely on the Gospel and Him Whom it sets forth] will be condemned.

[17]And these attesting signs will accompany those who believe: in My name they will drive out demons; they will speak in new languages;

[18]They will pick up serpents; and [even] if they drink anything deadly, it will not hurt them; they will lay their hands on the sick, and they will get well.

---

[a] James Moulton and George Milligan, *The Vocabulary.* [b] Robert Young, *Analytical Concordance.* [c] Marvin Vincent, *Word Studies.* [d] Richard Trench, *Synonyms of the New Testament.* [e] Some of the earliest manuscripts do not contain verses 9-20. [f] Hermann Cremer, *Biblico-Theological Lexicon.* [g] Joseph Thayer, *A Greek-English Lexicon.*

## New International Version

[19] *After the Lord Jesus had spoken to them, he was taken up into heaven and he sat at the right hand of God. [20] Then the disciples went out and preached everywhere, and the Lord worked with them and confirmed his word by the signs that accompanied it.*

## Amplified Bible

[19] So then the Lord Jesus, after He had spoken to them, was taken up into heaven and He sat down at the right hand of God. [Ps. 110:1.]

[20] And they went out and preached everywhere, while the Lord kept working with them and confirming the message by the attesting signs *and* miracles that closely accompanied [it]. Amen (so be it).

# Luke

# Luke

## Introduction

**1** Many have undertaken to draw up an account of the things that have been fulfilled[a] among us, [2]just as they were handed down to us by those who from the first were eyewitnesses and servants of the word. [3]With this in mind, since I myself have carefully investigated everything from the beginning, I too decided to write an orderly account for you, most excellent Theophilus, [4]so that you may know the certainty of the things you have been taught.

### The Birth of John the Baptist Foretold

[5]In the time of Herod king of Judea there was a priest named Zechariah, who belonged to the priestly division of Abijah; his wife Elizabeth was also a descendant of Aaron. [6]Both of them were righteous in the sight of God, observing all the Lord's commands and decrees blamelessly. [7]But they were childless because Elizabeth was not able to conceive, and they were both very old.

[8]Once when Zechariah's division was on duty and he was serving as priest before God, [9]he was chosen by lot, according to the custom of the priesthood, to go into the temple of the Lord and burn incense. [10]And when the time for the burning of incense came, all the assembled worshipers were praying outside.

[11]Then an angel of the Lord appeared to him, standing at the right side of the altar of incense. [12]When Zechariah saw him, he was startled and was gripped with fear. [13]But the angel said to him: "Do not be afraid, Zechariah; your prayer has been heard. Your wife Elizabeth will bear you a son, and you are to call him John. [14]He will be a joy and delight to you, and many will rejoice because of his birth, [15]for he will be great in the sight of the Lord. He is never to take wine or other fermented drink, and he will be filled with the Holy Spirit even before he is born. [16]He will bring back many of the people of Israel to the Lord their God. [17]And he will go on before the Lord, in the spirit and power of Elijah, to turn the hearts of the parents to their children and the disobedient to the wisdom of the righteous—to make ready a people prepared for the Lord."

[18]Zechariah asked the angel, "How can I be sure of this? I am an old man and my wife is well along in years."

**1** Since [[a]as is well known] many have undertaken to put in order and draw up a [[a]thorough] narrative of the surely established deeds which have been accomplished and fulfilled [b]in and among us,

[2]Exactly as they were handed down to us by those who from the [[a]official] beginning [of Jesus' ministry] were eyewitnesses and ministers of the Word [that is, of [c]the doctrine concerning the attainment through Christ of salvation in the kingdom of God],

[3]It seemed good and desirable to me, [and so I have determined] also after [d]having searched out diligently and followed all things closely and traced accurately the course from the highest to the minutest detail from the very first, to write an orderly account for you, most excellent Theophilus, [Acts 1:1.]

[4][My purpose is] that you may know the full truth and understand with certainty and security against error the accounts (histories) and doctrines of the faith of which you have been informed and in which you have been [a]orally instructed.

[5]In the days when Herod was king of Judea there was a certain priest whose name was Zachariah, [a]of the daily service (the division) of Abia; and his wife was also a descendant of Aaron, and her name was Elizabeth.

[6]And they both were righteous in the sight of God, walking blamelessly in all the commandments and requirements of the Lord.

[7]But they had no child, for Elizabeth was barren; and both were [b]far advanced in years.

[8]Now while on duty, serving as priest before God in the order of his division,

[9]As was the custom of the priesthood, it fell to him by lot to enter [the [c]sanctuary of] the temple of the Lord and burn incense. [Exod. 30:7.]

[10]And all the throng of people were praying outside [in the court] at the hour of incense [burning].

[11]And there appeared to him an angel of the Lord, standing at the right side of the altar of incense.

[12]And when Zachariah saw him, he was troubled, and fear took possession of him.

[13]But the angel said to him, Do not be afraid, Zachariah, because your petition [d]was heard, and your wife Elizabeth will bear you a son, and you must call his name John [God is favorable].

[14]And you shall have joy and exultant delight, and many will rejoice over his birth,

[15]For he will be great and distinguished in the sight of the Lord. And he must drink no wine nor strong drink, and he will be filled with and controlled by the Holy Spirit even [d]in and from his mother's womb. [Num. 6:3.]

[16]And he will turn back and cause to return many of the sons of Israel to the Lord their God,

[17]And he will [himself] go before Him in the spirit and power of Elijah, to turn back the hearts of the fathers to the children, and the disobedient and incredulous and unpersuadable to the wisdom of the upright [which is [f]the knowledge and holy love of the will of God]—in order to make ready for the Lord a people [perfectly] prepared [in spirit, [g]adjusted and disposed and placed in the right moral state]. [Isa. 40:3; Mal. 4:5, 6.]

[18]And Zachariah said to the angel, By what shall I know and be sure of this? For I am an old man, and my wife is well advanced in years.

[a] Marvin Vincent, *Word Studies in the New Testament.*  [b] John Wycliffe, *The Wycliffe Bible.*  [c] Joseph Thayer, *A Greek-English Lexicon of the New Testament.*  [d] William Tyndale, *The Tyndale Bible.*  [e] Richard Trench, *Synonyms of the New Testament.*  [f] Joseph Thayer, *A Greek-English Lexicon.*  [g] Marvin Vincent, *Word Studies.*

[a] 1 Or *been surely believed*

## New International Version

[19]The angel said to him, "I am Gabriel. I stand in the presence of God, and I have been sent to speak to you and to tell you this good news. [20]And now you will be silent and not able to speak until the day this happens, because you did not believe my words, which will come true at their appointed time."

[21]Meanwhile, the people were waiting for Zechariah and wondering why he stayed so long in the temple. [22]When he came out, he could not speak to them. They realized he had seen a vision in the temple, for he kept making signs to them but remained unable to speak.

[23]When his time of service was completed, he returned home. [24]After this his wife Elizabeth became pregnant and for five months remained in seclusion. [25]"The Lord has done this for me," she said. "In these days he has shown his favor and taken away my disgrace among the people."

### The Birth of Jesus Foretold

[26]In the sixth month of Elizabeth's pregnancy, God sent the angel Gabriel to Nazareth, a town in Galilee, [27]to a virgin pledged to be married to a man named Joseph, a descendant of David. The virgin's name was Mary. [28]The angel went to her and said, "Greetings, you who are highly favored! The Lord is with you."

[29]Mary was greatly troubled at his words and wondered what kind of greeting this might be. [30]But the angel said to her, "Do not be afraid, Mary; you have found favor with God. [31]You will conceive and give birth to a son, and you are to call him Jesus. [32]He will be great and will be called the Son of the Most High. The Lord God will give him the throne of his father David, [33]and he will reign over Jacob's descendants forever; his kingdom will never end."

[34]"How will this be," Mary asked the angel, "since I am a virgin?"

[35]The angel answered, "The Holy Spirit will come on you, and the power of the Most High will overshadow you. So the holy one to be born will be called[a] the Son of God. [36]Even Elizabeth your relative is going to have a child in her old age, and she who was said to be unable to conceive is in her sixth month. [37]For no word from God will ever fail."

[38]"I am the Lord's servant," Mary answered. "May your word to me be fulfilled." Then the angel left her.

### Mary Visits Elizabeth

[39]At that time Mary got ready and hurried to a town in the hill country of Judea, [40]where she entered Zechariah's home and greeted Elizabeth. [41]When Elizabeth heard Mary's greeting, the baby leaped in her womb, and Elizabeth was filled with the Holy Spirit. [42]In a loud voice she

## Amplified Bible

[19]And the angel replied to him, I am Gabriel. I stand in the [very] presence of God, and I have been sent to speak to you and to bring you this good news. [Dan. 8:16; 9:21.]

[20]Now behold, you will be and [a]will continue to be silent and not able to speak till the day when these things take place, because you have not believed what I told you; but my words are [a]of a kind which will be fulfilled in the appointed and proper time.

[21]Now the people kept waiting for Zachariah, and they wondered at his delaying [so long] in the [b]sanctuary.

[22]But when he did come out, he was unable to speak to them; and they [[a]clearly] perceived that he had seen a vision in the [b]sanctuary; and he kept making signs to them, still he remained dumb.

[23]And when his time of performing priestly functions was ended, he returned to his [own] house.

[24]Now after this his wife Elizabeth became pregnant, and for five months she secluded herself [b]entirely, saying, [I have hid myself]

[25][a]Because thus the Lord has dealt with me in the days when He deigned to look on me to take away my reproach among men. [Gen. 30:23; Isa. 4:1.]

[26]Now in the sixth month [after that], the angel Gabriel was sent from God to a town of Galilee named Nazareth,

[27]To a girl never having been married and a [c]virgin engaged to be married to a man whose name was Joseph, a descendant of the house of David; and the virgin's name was Mary.

[28]And he came to her and said, Hail, O favored one [[d]endued with grace]! The Lord is with you! [e]Blessed (favored of God) are you before all other women!

[29]But when she saw him, she was greatly troubled and disturbed and confused at what he said and kept revolving in her mind what such a greeting might mean.

[30]And the angel said to her, Do not be afraid, Mary, for you have found grace ([a]free, spontaneous, absolute favor and loving-kindness) with God.

[31]And listen! You will become pregnant and will give birth to a Son, and you shall call His name Jesus.

[32]He will be great (eminent) and will be called the Son of the Most High; and the Lord God will give to Him the throne of His forefather David,

[33]And He will reign over the house of Jacob throughout the ages; and of His reign there will be no end. [Isa. 9:6, 7; Dan. 2:44.]

[34]And Mary said to the angel, How can this be, since I have no [intimacy with any man as a] husband?

[35]Then the angel said to her, The Holy Spirit will come upon you, and the power of the Most High will overshadow you [like a shining cloud]; and so the holy (pure, sinless) Thing (Offspring) which shall be born of you will be called the Son of God. [Exod. 40:34; Isa. 7:14.]

[36]And listen! Your relative Elizabeth in her old age has also conceived a son, and this is now the sixth month with her who was called barren.

[37]For with God nothing is ever impossible and no word from God shall be without power or impossible of fulfillment.

[38]Then Mary said, Behold, I am the handmaiden of the Lord; let it be done to me according to what you have said. And the angel left her.

[39]And at that time Mary arose and went with haste into the hill country to a town of Judah,

[40]And she went to the house of Zachariah and, entering it, saluted Elizabeth.

[41]And it occurred that when Elizabeth heard Mary's greeting, the baby leaped in her womb, and Elizabeth was filled with and controlled by the Holy Spirit.

[a] 35 Or *So the child to be born will be called holy,*

## New International Version

exclaimed: "Blessed are you among women, and blessed is the child you will bear! [43]But why am I so favored, that the mother of my Lord should come to me? [44]As soon as the sound of your greeting reached my ears, the baby in my womb leaped for joy. [45]Blessed is she who has believed that the Lord would fulfill his promises to her!"

### Mary's Song

[46]And Mary said:

"My soul glorifies the Lord
[47] and my spirit rejoices in God my Savior,
[48]for he has been mindful
of the humble state of his servant.
From now on all generations will call me blessed,
[49] for the Mighty One has done great things for me—
holy is his name.
[50]His mercy extends to those who fear him,
from generation to generation.
[51]He has performed mighty deeds with his arm;
he has scattered those who are proud in their
inmost thoughts.
[52]He has brought down rulers from their thrones
but has lifted up the humble.
[53]He has filled the hungry with good things
but has sent the rich away empty.
[54]He has helped his servant Israel,
remembering to be merciful
[55]to Abraham and his descendants forever,
just as he promised our ancestors."

[56]Mary stayed with Elizabeth for about three months and then returned home.

### The Birth of John the Baptist

[57]When it was time for Elizabeth to have her baby, she gave birth to a son. [58]Her neighbors and relatives heard that the Lord had shown her great mercy, and they shared her joy.

[59]On the eighth day they came to circumcise the child, and they were going to name him after his father Zechariah, [60]but his mother spoke up and said, "No! He is to be called John."

[61]They said to her, "There is no one among your relatives who has that name."

[62]Then they made signs to his father, to find out what he would like to name the child. [63]He asked for a writing tablet, and to everyone's astonishment he wrote, "His name is John." [64]Immediately his mouth was opened and his tongue set free, and he began to speak, praising God. [65]All the neighbors were filled with awe, and throughout the hill country of Judea people were talking about all these things. [66]Everyone who heard this wondered about it, asking, "What then is this child going to be?" For the Lord's hand was with him.

### Zechariah's Song

[67]His father Zechariah was filled with the Holy Spirit and prophesied:

[68]"Praise be to the Lord, the God of Israel,
because he has come to his people and redeemed
them.

## Amplified Bible

[42]And she cried out with a loud cry, and then exclaimed, Blessed (favored of God) above all other women are you! And blessed (favored of God) is the Fruit of your womb!

[43]And how [have I deserved that this honor should] be granted to me, that the mother of my Lord should come to me?

[44]For behold, the instant the sound of your salutation reached my ears, the baby in my womb leaped for joy.

[45]And blessed (happy, [a]to be envied) is she who believed that there would be a fulfillment of the things that were spoken to her from the Lord.

[46]And Mary said, My soul magnifies *and* extols the Lord,

[47]And my spirit rejoices in God my Savior,

[48]For He has looked upon the low station *and* humiliation of His handmaiden. For behold, from now on all generations [of all ages] will call me blessed *and* declare me happy *and* [b]to be envied!

[49]For He Who is almighty has done great things for me—and holy is His name [to be venerated in His purity, majesty and glory]!

[50]And His mercy (His compassion and kindness toward the miserable and afflicted) is on those who fear Him with godly reverence, from generation to generation *and* age to age. [Ps. 103:17.]

[51]He has shown strength *and* [c]made might with His arm; He has scattered the proud *and* haughty in *and* by the imagination *and* purpose *and* designs of their hearts.

[52]He has put down the mighty from their thrones and exalted those of low degree.

[53]He has filled *and* satisfied the hungry with good things, and the rich He has sent away empty-handed [without a gift].

[54]He has laid hold on His servant Israel [to help him, to espouse his cause], in remembrance of His mercy,

[55]Even as He promised to our forefathers, to Abraham and to his descendants forever. [Gen. 17:7; 18:18; 22:17; I Sam. 2:1-10; Mic. 7:20.]

[56]And Mary remained with her [Elizabeth] for about three months and [then] returned to her [own] home.

[57]Now the time that Elizabeth should be delivered came, and she gave birth to a son.

[58]And her neighbors and relatives heard that the Lord had shown great mercy on her, and they rejoiced with her.

[59]And it occurred that on the eighth day, when they came to circumcise the child, they were intending to call him Zachariah after his father, [Gen. 17:12; Lev. 12:3.]

[60]But his mother answered, Not so! But he shall be called John.

[61]And they said to her, None of your relatives is called by that name.

[62]And they inquired with signs to his father [as to] what he wanted to have him called.

[63]Then Zachariah asked for a writing tablet and wrote, His name is John. And they were all astonished.

[64]And at once his mouth was opened and his tongue loosed, and he began to speak, blessing *and* praising *and* thanking God.

[65]And awe *and* reverential fear came on all their neighbors; and all these things were discussed throughout the hill country of Judea.

[66]And all who heard them laid them up in their hearts, saying, Whatever will this little boy be then? For the hand of the Lord was [d]so evidently] with him [protecting and aiding him].

[67]Now Zachariah his father was filled with *and* controlled by the Holy Spirit and prophesied, saying,

[68]Blessed (praised and extolled and thanked) be the Lord, the God of Israel, because He has come and brought deliverance *and* redemption to His people!

[a] Alexander Souter, *Pocket Lexicon of the Greek New Testament.*
[b] Alexander Souter, *Pocket Lexicon.* [c] John Wycliffe, *The Wycliffe Bible.*
[d] Albert Barnes, *Notes on the New Testament.*

## New International Version

69 He has raised up a horn[a] of salvation for us
　　in the house of his servant David
70 (as he said through his holy prophets of long ago),
71 salvation from our enemies
　　and from the hand of all who hate us—
72 to show mercy to our ancestors
　　and to remember his holy covenant,
73 　the oath he swore to our father Abraham:
74 to rescue us from the hand of our enemies,
　　and to enable us to serve him without fear
75 　in holiness and righteousness before him all our
　　days.

76 And you, my child, will be called a prophet of the Most
　　High;
　　for you will go on before the Lord to prepare the way
　　for him,
77 to give his people the knowledge of salvation
　　through the forgiveness of their sins,
78 because of the tender mercy of our God,
　　by which the rising sun will come to us from heaven
79 to shine on those living in darkness
　　and in the shadow of death,
　　to guide our feet into the path of peace."

80 And the child grew and became strong in spirit[b]; and
he lived in the wilderness until he appeared publicly to
Israel.

### The Birth of Jesus

2 In those days Caesar Augustus issued a decree that
a census should be taken of the entire Roman world.
2 (This was the first census that took place while[c] Quirinius was governor of Syria.) 3 And everyone went to their
own town to register.

4 So Joseph also went up from the town of Nazareth in
Galilee to Judea, to Bethlehem the town of David, because
he belonged to the house and line of David. 5 He went there
to register with Mary, who was pledged to be married to
him and was expecting a child. 6 While they were there,
the time came for the baby to be born, 7 and she gave birth
to her firstborn, a son. She wrapped him in cloths and
placed him in a manger, because there was no guest room
available for them.

8 And there were shepherds living out in the fields nearby, keeping watch over their flocks at night. 9 An angel
of the Lord appeared to them, and the glory of the Lord
shone around them, and they were terrified. 10 But the angel said to them, "Do not be afraid. I bring you good news
that will cause great joy for all the people. 11 Today in the
town of David a Savior has been born to you; he is the Messiah, the Lord. 12 This will be a sign to you: You will find a
baby wrapped in cloths and lying in a manger."

## Amplified Bible

69 And He has raised up a Horn of salvation [a mighty
and valiant Helper, the Author of salvation] for us in the
house of David His servant—
70 This is as He promised by the mouth of His holy
prophets from the most ancient times [in the memory of
man]—
71 That we should have deliverance and be saved from
our enemies and from the hand of all who detest and pursue us with hatred;
72 To make true and show the mercy and compassion
and kindness [promised] to our forefathers and to remember and carry out His holy covenant [to bless, which is
a all the more sacred because it is made by God Himself],
73 That covenant He sealed by oath to our forefather
Abraham:
74 To grant us that we, being delivered from the hand of
our foes, might serve Him fearlessly
75 In holiness (divine consecration) and righteousness
[in accordance with the everlasting principles of right]
within His presence all the days of our lives.
76 And you, little one, shall be called a prophet of the
Most High; for you shall go on before the face of the Lord
to make ready His ways, [Isa. 40:3; Mal. 4:5.]
77 To bring and give the knowledge of salvation to His
people in the forgiveness and remission of their sins.
78 Because of and through the heart of tender mercy
and loving-kindness of our God, a Light from on high will
dawn upon us and visit [us] [Mal. 4:2.]
79 To shine upon and give light to those who sit in darkness and in the shadow of death, to direct and guide our
feet in a straight line into the way of peace. [Isa. 9:2.]
80 And the little boy grew and became strong in spirit;
and he was in the deserts (wilderness) until the day of
his appearing to Israel [the commencement of his public
ministry].

2 In those days it occurred that a decree went out from
Caesar Augustus that the whole b Roman empire
should be registered.
2 This was the first enrollment, and it was made when
Quirinius was governor of Syria.
3 And all the people were going to be registered, each to
his own city or town.
4 And Joseph also went up from Galilee from the town
of Nazareth to Judea, to the town of David, which is called
Bethlehem, because he was of the house and family of
David,
5 To be enrolled with Mary, his espoused (c married)
wife, who was about to become a mother. [Matt. 1:18-25.]
6 And while they were there, the time came for her delivery,
7 And she gave birth to her Son, her Firstborn; and she
wrapped Him in swaddling clothes and laid Him in a manger, because there was no room or place for them in the
inn.
8 And in that vicinity there were shepherds living [out
under the open sky] in the field, watching [in shifts] over
their flock by night.
9 And behold, an angel of the Lord stood by them, and
the glory of the Lord flashed and shone all about them,
and they were terribly frightened.
10 But the angel said to them, Do not be afraid; for behold, I bring you good news of a great joy which will come
to all the people.
11 For to you is born this day in the town of David a Savior, Who is Christ (the Messiah) the Lord! [Mic. 5:2.]
12 And this will be a sign for you [by which you will
recognize Him]: you will find [a after searching] a Baby
wrapped in swaddling clothes and lying in a manger.
[I Sam. 2:34; II Kings 19:29; Isa. 7:14.]

---

a 69 Horn here symbolizes a strong king.　　b 80 Or in the Spirit
c 2 Or This census took place before

a Joseph Thayer, A Greek-English Lexicon.　b George R. Berry, Greek-
English New Testament Lexicon.　c Marvin Vincent, Word Studies.

## New International Version

### Amplified Bible

**New International Version**

13Suddenly a great company of the heavenly host appeared with the angel, praising God and saying,

14"Glory to God in the highest heaven,
and on earth peace to those on whom his favor rests."

15When the angels had left them and gone into heaven, the shepherds said to one another, "Let's go to Bethlehem and see this thing that has happened, which the Lord has told us about."

16So they hurried off and found Mary and Joseph, and the baby, who was lying in the manger. 17When they had seen him, they spread the word concerning what had been told them about this child, 18and all who heard it were amazed at what the shepherds said to them. 19But Mary treasured up all these things and pondered them in her heart. 20The shepherds returned, glorifying and praising God for all the things they had heard and seen, which were just as they had been told.

21On the eighth day, when it was time to circumcise the child, he was named Jesus, the name the angel had given him before he was conceived.

### Jesus Presented in the Temple

22When the time came for the purification rites required by the Law of Moses, Joseph and Mary took him to Jerusalem to present him to the Lord 23 (as it is written in the Law of the Lord, "Every firstborn male is to be consecrated to the Lord"ᵃ), 24and to offer a sacrifice in keeping with what is said in the Law of the Lord: "a pair of doves or two young pigeons."ᵇ

25Now there was a man in Jerusalem called Simeon, who was righteous and devout. He was waiting for the consolation of Israel, and the Holy Spirit was on him. 26It had been revealed to him by the Holy Spirit that he would not die before he had seen the Lord's Messiah. 27Moved by the Spirit, he went into the temple courts. When the parents brought in the child Jesus to do for him what the custom of the Law required, 28Simeon took him in his arms and praised God, saying:

29"Sovereign Lord, as you have promised,
you may now dismissᶜ your servant in peace.
30For my eyes have seen your salvation,
31    which you have prepared in the sight of all nations:
32a light for revelation to the Gentiles,
and the glory of your people Israel."

33The child's father and mother marveled at what was said about him. 34Then Simeon blessed them and said to Mary, his mother: "This child is destined to cause the falling and rising of many in Israel, and to be a sign that will be spoken against, 35so that the thoughts of many hearts will be revealed. And a sword will pierce your own soul too."

36There was also a prophet, Anna, the daughter of Pe-

**Amplified Bible**

13Then suddenly there appeared with the angel an army of the troops of heaven (ᵃa heavenly knighthood), praising God and saying,

14Glory to God in the highest [heaven], and on earth peace among men with whom He is well pleased [ᵃmen of goodwill, of His favor].

15When the angels went away from them into heaven, the shepherds said one to another, Let us go over to Bethlehem and see this thing (ᵇsaying) that has come to pass, which the Lord has made known to us.

16So they went with haste and [ᶜby searching] found Mary and Joseph, and the Baby lying in a manger.

17And when they saw it, they made known what had been told them concerning this Child,

18And all who heard it were astounded and marveled at what the shepherds told them.

19But Mary was keeping ᵇwithin herself all these things (ᵇsayings), weighing and pondering them in her heart.

20And the shepherds returned, glorifying and praising God for all the things they had heard and seen, just as it had been told them.

21And at the end of eight days, when [the Baby] was to be circumcised, He was called Jesus, the name given by the angel before He was conceived in the womb.

22And when the time for their purification [the mother's purification and the Baby's dedication] came according to the Law of Moses, they brought Him up to Jerusalem to present Him to the Lord—[Lev. 12:1-4.]

23As it is written in the Law of the Lord, Every [firstborn] male that opens the womb shall be set apart and dedicated and called holy to the Lord—[Exod. 13:1, 2, 12; Num. 8:17.]

24And [they came also] to offer a sacrifice according to what is said in the Law of the Lord: a pair of turtledoves or two young pigeons. [Lev. 12:6-8.]

25Now there was a man in Jerusalem whose name was Simeon, and this man was righteous and devout [cautiously and carefully observing the divine Law], and looking for the Consolation of Israel; and the Holy Spirit was upon him.

26And it had been divinely revealed (communicated) to him by the Holy Spirit that he would not see death before he had seen the Lord's Christ (the Messiah, the Anointed One).

27And prompted by the [Holy] Spirit, he came into the temple [ᵈenclosure]; and when the parents brought in the little child Jesus to do for Him what was customary according to the Law,

28[Simeon] took Him up in his arms and praised and thanked God and said,

29And now, Lord, You are releasing Your servant to depart (leave this world) in peace, according to Your word.

30For with my [own] eyes I have seen Your Salvation, [Isa. 52:10.]

31Which You have ordained and prepared before (in the presence of) all peoples,

32A Light for ᵇrevelation to the Gentiles [to disclose what was before unknown] and [to bring] praise and honor and glory to Your people Israel. [Isa. 42:6; 49:6.]

33And His [legal] father and [His] mother were marveling at what was said about Him.

34And Simeon blessed them and said to Mary His mother, Behold, this Child is appointed and destined for the fall and rising of many in Israel, and for a sign that is spoken against—[Isa. 8:14, 15.]

35And a sword will pierce through your own soul also— that the secret thoughts and purposes of many hearts may be brought out and disclosed.

36And there was also a prophetess, Anna, the daughter

ᵃ John Wycliffe, *The Wycliffe Bible.*  ᵇ Marvin Vincent, *Word Studies.*
ᶜ Joseph Thayer, *A Greek-English Lexicon.*  ᵈ Richard Trench, *Synonyms of the New Testament.*

ᵃ 23 Exodus 13:2,12    ᵇ 24 Lev. 12:8    ᶜ 29 Or *promised, / now dismiss*

## New International Version

nuel, of the tribe of Asher. She was very old; she had lived with her husband seven years after her marriage, <sup>37</sup>and then was a widow until she was eighty-four.<sup>a</sup> She never left the temple but worshiped night and day, fasting and praying. <sup>38</sup>Coming up to them at that very moment, she gave thanks to God and spoke about the child to all who were looking forward to the redemption of Jerusalem.

<sup>39</sup>When Joseph and Mary had done everything required by the Law of the Lord, they returned to Galilee to their own town of Nazareth. <sup>40</sup>And the child grew and became strong; he was filled with wisdom, and the grace of God was on him.

### The Boy Jesus at the Temple

<sup>41</sup>Every year Jesus' parents went to Jerusalem for the Festival of the Passover. <sup>42</sup>When he was twelve years old, they went up to the festival, according to the custom. <sup>43</sup>After the festival was over, while his parents were returning home, the boy Jesus stayed behind in Jerusalem, but they were unaware of it. <sup>44</sup>Thinking he was in their company, they traveled on for a day. Then they began looking for him among their relatives and friends. <sup>45</sup>When they did not find him, they went back to Jerusalem to look for him. <sup>46</sup>After three days they found him in the temple courts, sitting among the teachers, listening to them and asking them questions. <sup>47</sup>Everyone who heard him was amazed at his understanding and his answers. <sup>48</sup>When his parents saw him, they were astonished. His mother said to him, "Son, why have you treated us like this? Your father and I have been anxiously searching for you."

<sup>49</sup>"Why were you searching for me?" he asked. "Didn't you know I had to be in my Father's house?"<sup>b</sup> <sup>50</sup>But they did not understand what he was saying to them.

<sup>51</sup>Then he went down to Nazareth with them and was obedient to them. But his mother treasured all these things in her heart. <sup>52</sup>And Jesus grew in wisdom and stature, and in favor with God and man.

### John the Baptist Prepares the Way

**3** In the fifteenth year of the reign of Tiberius Caesar— when Pontius Pilate was governor of Judea, Herod tetrarch of Galilee, his brother Philip tetrarch of Iturea and Traconitis, and Lysanias tetrarch of Abilene— <sup>2</sup>during the high-priesthood of Annas and Caiaphas, the word of God came to John son of Zechariah in the wilderness. <sup>3</sup>He went into all the country around the Jordan, preaching a baptism of repentance for the forgiveness of sins. <sup>4</sup>As it is written in the book of the words of Isaiah the prophet:

"A voice of one calling in the wilderness,
'Prepare the way for the Lord,
    make straight paths for him.

## Amplified Bible

of Phanuel, of the tribe of Asher. She was very old, having lived with her husband seven years from her maidenhood, [Josh. 19:24.]

<sup>37</sup>And as a widow even for eighty-four years. She did not go out from the temple <sup>a</sup>enclosure, but was worshiping night and day with fasting and prayer.

<sup>38</sup>And she too came up at that same hour, and she returned thanks to God and talked of [Jesus] to all who were looking for the redemption (deliverance) of Jerusalem.

<sup>39</sup>And when they had done everything according to the Law of the Lord, they went back into Galilee to their own town, Nazareth.

<sup>40</sup>And the Child grew and became strong *in spirit,* filled with wisdom; and the grace (favor and spiritual blessing) of God was upon Him. [Judg. 13:24; I Sam. 2:26.]

<sup>41</sup>Now His parents went to Jerusalem every year to the Passover Feast. [Deut. 16:1-8; Exod. 23:15.]

<sup>42</sup>And when He was twelve years [old], they went up, as was their custom.

<sup>43</sup>And when the Feast was ended, as they were returning, the boy Jesus remained behind in Jerusalem. Now His parents did not know this,

<sup>44</sup>But, supposing Him to be in the caravan, they traveled on a day's journey; and [then] they sought Him [diligently, looking up and down for Him] among their kinsfolk and acquaintances.

<sup>45</sup>And when they failed to find Him, they went back to Jerusalem, looking for Him [up and down] all the way.

<sup>46</sup>After three days they found Him [came upon Him] in the <sup>a</sup>[court of the] temple, sitting among the teachers, listening to them and asking them questions.

<sup>47</sup>And all who heard Him were astonished *and* overwhelmed with bewildered wonder at His intelligence *and* understanding and His replies.

<sup>48</sup>And when they [Joseph and Mary] saw Him, they were amazed; and His mother said to Him, Child, why have You treated us like this? Here Your father and I have been anxiously looking for You [distressed and tormented].

<sup>49</sup>And He said to them, How is it that you had to look for Me? Did you not see *and* know that it is necessary [as a duty] for Me <sup>b</sup>to be in My Father's house *and* [occupied] about My Father's business?

<sup>50</sup>But they did not comprehend what He was saying to them.

<sup>51</sup>And He went down with them and came to Nazareth and was [habitually] obedient to them; and His mother kept *and* closely and persistently guarded all these things in her heart.

<sup>52</sup>And Jesus increased in wisdom (in broad and full understanding) and in stature *and* years, and in favor with God and man.

**3** In the fifteenth year of Tiberius Caesar's reign—when Pontius Pilate was governor of Judea, and Herod was tetrarch of Galilee, and his brother Philip tetrarch of the region of Ituraea and Trachonitis, and Lysanias tetrarch of Abilene—

<sup>2</sup>In the high priesthood of Annas and Caiaphas, the Word of God [<sup>c</sup>concerning the attainment through Christ of salvation in the kingdom of God] came to John son of Zechariah in the wilderness (desert).

<sup>3</sup>And he went into all the country round about the Jordan, preaching a baptism of repentance (<sup>c</sup>of hearty amending of their ways, with abhorrence of past wrongdoing) unto the forgiveness of sin.

<sup>4</sup>As it is written in the book of the words of Isaiah the prophet, The voice of one crying in the wilderness [shouting in the desert]: Prepare the way of the Lord, make His beaten paths straight.

## New International Version

⁵Every valley shall be filled in,
   every mountain and hill made low.
The crooked roads shall become straight,
   the rough ways smooth.
⁶And all people will see God's salvation.'"ᵃ

⁷John said to the crowds coming out to be baptized by him, "You brood of vipers! Who warned you to flee from the coming wrath? ⁸Produce fruit in keeping with repentance. And do not begin to say to yourselves, 'We have Abraham as our father.' For I tell you that out of these stones God can raise up children for Abraham. ⁹The ax is already at the root of the trees, and every tree that does not produce good fruit will be cut down and thrown into the fire."

¹⁰"What should we do then?" the crowd asked.

¹¹John answered, "Anyone who has two shirts should share with the one who has none, and anyone who has food should do the same."

¹²Even tax collectors came to be baptized. "Teacher," they asked, "what should we do?"

¹³"Don't collect any more than you are required to," he told them.

¹⁴Then some soldiers asked him, "And what should we do?"

He replied, "Don't extort money and don't accuse people falsely—be content with your pay."

¹⁵The people were waiting expectantly and were all wondering in their hearts if John might possibly be the Messiah. ¹⁶John answered them all, "I baptize you withᵇ water. But one who is more powerful than I will come, the straps of whose sandals I am not worthy to untie. He will baptize you withᵇ the Holy Spirit and fire. ¹⁷His winnowing fork is in his hand to clear his threshing floor and to gather the wheat into his barn, but he will burn up the chaff with unquenchable fire." ¹⁸And with many other words John exhorted the people and proclaimed the good news to them.

¹⁹But when John rebuked Herod the tetrarch because of his marriage to Herodias, his brother's wife, and all the other evil things he had done, ²⁰Herod added this to them all: He locked John up in prison.

### The Baptism and Genealogy of Jesus

²¹When all the people were being baptized, Jesus was baptized too. And as he was praying, heaven was opened ²²and the Holy Spirit descended on him in bodily form like a dove. And a voice came from heaven: "You are my Son, whom I love; with you I am well pleased."

²³Now Jesus himself was about thirty years old when he began his ministry. He was the son, so it was thought, of Joseph,

the son of Heli, ²⁴the son of Matthat,
the son of Levi, the son of Melki,
the son of Jannai, the son of Joseph,
²⁵the son of Mattathias, the son of Amos,
the son of Nahum, the son of Esli,
the son of Naggai, ²⁶the son of Maath,
the son of Mattathias, the son of Semein,
the son of Josek, the son of Joda,
²⁷the son of Joanan, the son of Rhesa,
the son of Zerubbabel, the son of Shealtiel,

## Amplified Bible

⁵Every valley *and* ravine shall be filled up, and every mountain and hill shall be leveled; and the crooked places shall be made straight, and the rough roads shall be made smooth;

⁶And all mankind shall see (behold and ᵃunderstand and at last acknowledge) the salvation of God (the deliverance from eternal death ᵇdecreed by God). [Isa. 40:3-5.]

⁷So he said to the crowds who came out to be baptized by him, You offspring of vipers! Who ᶜsecretly warned you to flee from the coming wrath?

⁸Bear fruits that are deserving *and* consistent with [your] repentance [that is, ᵇconduct worthy of a heart changed, a heart abhorring sin]. And do not begin to say to yourselves, We have Abraham as our father; for I tell you that God is able from these stones to raise up descendants for Abraham.

⁹Even now the ax is laid to the root of the trees, so that every tree that does not bear good fruit is cut down and cast into the fire.

¹⁰And the multitudes asked him, Then what shall we do?

¹¹And he replied to them, He who has two tunics (undergarments), let him share with him who has none; and he who has food, let him do it the same way.

¹²Even tax collectors came to be baptized, and they said to him, Teacher, what shall we do?

¹³And he said to them, Exact *and* collect no more than the fixed amount appointed you.

¹⁴Those serving as soldiers also asked him, And we, what shall we do? And he replied to them, Never demand *or* enforce ᵈby terrifying people or by accusing wrongfully, and always be satisfied with your rations (supplies) *and* with your allowance (wages).

¹⁵As the people were in suspense *and* waiting expectantly, and everybody reasoned *and* questioned in their hearts concerning John, whether he perhaps might be the Christ (the Messiah, the Anointed One).

¹⁶John answered them all by saying, I baptize you with water; but He Who is mightier than I is coming, the strap of Whose sandals I am not fit to unfasten. He will baptize you with the Holy Spirit and fire.

¹⁷His winnowing shovel (fork) is in His hand to thoroughly clear *and* cleanse His [threshing] floor and to gather the wheat *and* store it in His granary, but the chaff He will burn with fire that cannot be extinguished.

¹⁸So with many other [various] appeals and admonitions he preached the good news (the Gospel) to the people.

¹⁹But Herod the tetrarch, who had been [repeatedly] told about his fault *and* reproved with rebuke ᵈproducing conviction by [John] for [having] Herodias, his brother's wife, and for all the wicked things that Herod had done,

²⁰Added this to them all—that he shut up John in prison.

²¹Now when all the people were baptized, and when Jesus also had been baptized, and [while He was still] praying, the [visible] heaven was opened

²²And the Holy Spirit descended upon Him in bodily form like a dove, and a voice came from heaven, *saying*, You are My Son, My Beloved! In You I am well pleased *and* find delight! [Ps. 2:7; Isa. 42:1.]

²³Jesus Himself, when He began [His ministry], was about thirty years of age, being the Son, as was supposed, of Joseph, the son of Heli,

²⁴The son of Matthat, the son of Levi, the son of Melchi, the son of Jannai, the son of Joseph,

²⁵The son of Mattathias, the son of Amos, the son of Nahum, the son of Esli, the son of Naggai,

²⁶The son of Maath, the son of Mattathias, the son of Semein, the son of Josech, the son of Joda,

²⁷The son of Joanan, the son of Rhesa, the son of Zerubbabel, the son of Shealtiel, the son of Neri,

ᵃ James Gray and George Adams, *Bible Commentary.*  ᵇ Joseph Thayer, *A Greek-English Lexicon.*  ᶜ Literal translation.  ᵈ Marvin Vincent, *Word Studies.*

## New International Version

the son of Neri, 28the son of Melki,
the son of Addi, the son of Cosam,
the son of Elmadam, the son of Er,
29the son of Joshua, the son of Eliezer,
the son of Jorim, the son of Matthat,
the son of Levi, 30the son of Simeon,
the son of Judah, the son of Joseph,
the son of Jonam, the son of Eliakim,
31the son of Melea, the son of Menna,
the son of Mattatha, the son of Nathan,
the son of David, 32the son of Jesse,
the son of Obed, the son of Boaz,
the son of Salmon,a the son of Nahshon,
33the son of Amminadab, the son of Ram,b
the son of Hezron, the son of Perez,
the son of Judah, 34the son of Jacob,
the son of Isaac, the son of Abraham,
the son of Terah, the son of Nahor,
35the son of Serug, the son of Reu,
the son of Peleg, the son of Eber,
the son of Shelah, 36the son of Cainan,
the son of Arphaxad, the son of Shem,
the son of Noah, the son of Lamech,
37the son of Methuselah, the son of Enoch,
the son of Jared, the son of Mahalalel,
the son of Kenan, 38the son of Enosh,
the son of Seth, the son of Adam,
the son of God.

### Jesus Is Tested in the Wilderness

**4** Jesus, full of the Holy Spirit, left the Jordan and was led by the Spirit into the wilderness, 2where for forty days he was temptedc by the devil. He ate nothing during those days, and at the end of them he was hungry.
3The devil said to him, "If you are the Son of God, tell this stone to become bread."
4Jesus answered, "It is written: 'Man shall not live on bread alone.'d"
5The devil led him up to a high place and showed him in an instant all the kingdoms of the world. 6And he said to him, "I will give you all their authority and splendor; it has been given to me, and I can give it to anyone I want to. 7If you worship me, it will all be yours."
8Jesus answered, "It is written: 'Worship the Lord your God and serve him only.'e"
9The devil led him to Jerusalem and had him stand on the highest point of the temple. "If you are the Son of God," he said, "throw yourself down from here. 10For it is written:

"'He will command his angels concerning you
    to guard you carefully;
11they will lift you up in their hands,
    so that you will not strike your foot against a
    stone.'f"

## Amplified Bible

28The son of Melchi, the son of Addi, the son of Cosam, the son of Elmadam, the son of Er,
29The son of Jesus, the son of Eliezer, the son of Jorim, the son of Matthat, the son of Levi,
30The son of Simeon, the son of Judah, the son of Joseph, the son of Jonam, the son of Eliakim,
31The son of Melea, the son of Menna, the son of Mattatha, the son of Nathan, the son of David,
32The son of Jesse, the son of Obed, the son of Boaz, the son of Salmon (Sala), the son of Nahshon,
33The son of Aminadab, the son of Admin, the son of Arni, the son of Hezron, the son of Perez, the son of Judah,
34The son of Jacob, the son of Isaac, the son of Abraham, the son of Terah, the son of Nahor,
35The son of Serug, the son of Reu, the son of Peleg, the son of Eber, the son of Shelah,
36The son of Cainan, the son of Arphaxad, the son of Shem, the son of Noah, the son of Lamech,
37The son of Methuselah, the son of Enoch, the son of Jared, the son of Mahalaleel, the son of Cainan,
38The son of Enos, the son of Seth, the son of Adam, the son of God. [Gen. 5:3-32; 11:10-26; Ruth 4:18-22; I Chron. 1:1-4, 24-28; 2:1-15.]

**4** Then Jesus, full of *and* controlled by the Holy Spirit, returned from the Jordan and was led in [by] the [Holy] Spirit
2For (during) forty days in the wilderness (desert), where He was tempted (atried, tested exceedingly) by the devil. And He ate nothing during those days, and when they were completed, He was hungry. [Deut. 9:9; I Kings 19:8.]
3Then the devil said to Him, If You are the Son of God, order this stone to turn into a loaf [of bread].
4And Jesus replied to him, It is written, Man shall not live *and* be sustained by (on) bread alone, b*but by every word and expression of God.* [Deut. 8:3.]
5Then the devil took Him up to a high mountain and showed Him all the kingdoms of the habitable world in a moment of time [cin the twinkling of an eye].
6And he said to Him, To You I will give all this power *and* authority and their glory (all their magnificence, excellence, preeminence, dignity, and grace), for it has been turned over to me, and I give it to whomever I will.
7Therefore if You will do homage to *and* worship me [djust once], it shall all be Yours.
8And Jesus replied to him, eGet behind Me, Satan! It is written, You shall do homage to *and* worship the Lord your God, and Him only shall you serve. [Deut. 6:13; 10:20.]
9Then he took Him to Jerusalem and set Him on fa gable of the temple, and said to Him, If You are the Son of God, cast Yourself down from here;
10For it is written, He will give His angels charge over you to guard *and* watch over you closely *and* carefully;
11And on their hands they will bear you up, lest you strike your foot against a stone. [Ps. 91:11, 12.]

---

a 32 Some early manuscripts *Sala*    b 33 Some manuscripts *Amminadab, the son of Admin, the son of Arni*; other manuscripts vary widely.    c 2 The Greek for *tempted* can also mean *tested.*
d 4 Deut. 8:3    e 8 Deut. 6:13    f 11 Psalm 91:11,12

---

a Robert Young, *Analytical Concordance to the Bible.*  b Some manuscripts add this phrase.  c William Tyndale, *The Tyndale Bible.*  d Charles B. Williams, *The New Testament: A Translation in the Language of the People:* "expressed by the Greek aorist tense."  e Some manuscripts add this phrase.  f James Moulton and George Milligan, *The Vocabulary of the Greek Testament.*

## New International Version

[12]Jesus answered, "It is said: 'Do not put the Lord your God to the test.'[a]"

[13]When the devil had finished all this tempting, he left him until an opportune time.

### Jesus Rejected at Nazareth

[14]Jesus returned to Galilee in the power of the Spirit, and news about him spread through the whole countryside. [15]He was teaching in their synagogues, and everyone praised him.

[16]He went to Nazareth, where he had been brought up, and on the Sabbath day he went into the synagogue, as was his custom. He stood up to read, [17]and the scroll of the prophet Isaiah was handed to him. Unrolling it, he found the place where it is written:

[18]"The Spirit of the Lord is on me,
　　because he has anointed me
　　　to proclaim good news to the poor.
He has sent me to proclaim freedom for the prisoners
　　and recovery of sight for the blind,
　　to set the oppressed free,
[19]　to proclaim the year of the Lord's favor."[b]

[20]Then he rolled up the scroll, gave it back to the attendant and sat down. The eyes of everyone in the synagogue were fastened on him. [21]He began by saying to them, "Today this scripture is fulfilled in your hearing."

[22]All spoke well of him and were amazed at the gracious words that came from his lips. "Isn't this Joseph's son?" they asked.

[23]Jesus said to them, "Surely you will quote this proverb to me: 'Physician, heal yourself!' And you will tell me, 'Do here in your hometown what we have heard that you did in Capernaum.'"

[24]"Truly I tell you," he continued, "no prophet is accepted in his hometown. [25]I assure you that there were many widows in Israel in Elijah's time, when the sky was shut for three and a half years and there was a severe famine throughout the land. [26]Yet Elijah was not sent to any of them, but to a widow in Zarephath in the region of Sidon. [27]And there were many in Israel with leprosy[c] in the time of Elisha the prophet, yet not one of them was cleansed—only Naaman the Syrian."

[28]All the people in the synagogue were furious when they heard this. [29]They got up, drove him out of the town, and took him to the brow of the hill on which the town was built, in order to throw him off the cliff. [30]But he walked right through the crowd and went on his way.

### Jesus Drives Out an Impure Spirit

[31]Then he went down to Capernaum, a town in Galilee, and on the Sabbath he taught the people. [32]They were amazed at his teaching, because his words had authority.

## Amplified Bible

[12]And Jesus replied to him, [The Scripture] says, You shall not tempt (try, [a]test exceedingly) the Lord your God. [Deut. 6:16.]

[13]And when the devil had ended every [the complete cycle of] temptation, he [temporarily] left Him [that is, [b]stood off from Him] until another more opportune and favorable time.

[14]Then Jesus went back full of and under the power of the [Holy] Spirit into Galilee, and the fame of Him spread through the whole region round about.

[15]And He Himself conducted [[c]a course of] teaching in their synagogues, being [d]recognized and honored and praised by all.

[16]So He came to Nazareth, [[e]that Nazareth] where He had been brought up, and He entered the synagogue, as was His custom on the Sabbath day. And He stood up to read.

[17]And there was handed to Him [the roll of] the book of the prophet Isaiah. He opened (unrolled) the book and found the place where it was written, [Isa. 61:1, 2.]

[18]The Spirit of the Lord [is] upon Me, because He has anointed Me [the Anointed One, the Messiah] to preach the good news (the Gospel) to the poor; He has sent Me to announce release to the captives and recovery of sight to the blind, to send forth as delivered those who are oppressed [who are downtrodden, bruised, crushed, and broken down by calamity],

[19]To proclaim the accepted and acceptable year of the Lord [the day [f]when salvation and the free favors of God profusely abound]. [Isa. 61:1, 2.]

[20]Then He rolled up the book and gave it back to the attendant and sat down; and the eyes of all in the synagogue were gazing [attentively] at Him.

[21]And He began to speak to them: Today this Scripture has been fulfilled [f]while you are present and hearing.

[22]And all spoke well of Him and marveled at the words of grace that came forth from His mouth; and they said, Is not this Joseph's [g]Son?

[23]So He said to them, You will doubtless quote to Me this proverb: Physician, heal Yourself! What we have learned by hearsay that You did in Capernaum, do here also in Your [own] town.

[24]Then He said, Solemnly I say to you, no prophet is acceptable and welcome in his [own] town (country).

[25]But in truth I tell you, there were many widows in Israel in the days of Elijah, when the heavens were closed up for three years and six months, so that there came a great famine over all the land;

[26]And yet Elijah was not sent to a single one of them, but only to Zarephath in the country of Sidon, to a woman who was a widow. [I Kings 17:1, 8-16; 18:1.]

[27]And there were many lepers in Israel in the time of Elisha the prophet, and yet not one of them was cleansed [by being healed]—but only Naaman the Syrian. [II Kings 5:1-14.]

[28]When they heard these things, all the people in the synagogue were filled with rage.

[29]And rising up, they pushed and drove Him out of the town, and [laying hold of Him] they led Him to the [projecting] upper part of the hill on which their town was built, that they might hurl Him headlong down [over the cliff].

[30]But passing through their midst, He went on His way.

[31]And He descended to Capernaum, a town of Galilee, and there He continued to teach the people on the Sabbath days.

[32]And they were amazed at His teaching, for His word was with authority and ability and weight and power.

---

[a] 12 Deut. 6:16　[b] 19 Isaiah 61:1,2 (see Septuagint); Isaiah 58:6
[c] 27 The Greek word traditionally translated leprosy was used for various diseases affecting the skin.

[a] Robert Young, Analytical Concordance. [b] Kenneth Wuest, Word Studies in the Greek New Testament. [c] Marvin Vincent, Word Studies: in Greek imperfect tense. [d] Hermann Cremer, Biblico-Theological Lexicon of New Testament Greek. [e] James Moulton and George Milligan, The Vocabulary of the Greek Testament. [f] Joseph Thayer, A Greek-English Lexicon.
[g] Capitalized because of what He is, the spotless Son of God, not what the speakers may have thought He was.

## New International Version

³³In the synagogue there was a man possessed by a demon, an impure spirit. He cried out at the top of his voice, ³⁴"Go away! What do you want with us, Jesus of Nazareth? Have you come to destroy us? I know who you are—the Holy One of God!"

³⁵"Be quiet!" Jesus said sternly. "Come out of him!" Then the demon threw the man down before them all and came out without injuring him.

³⁶All the people were amazed and said to each other, "What words these are! With authority and power he gives orders to impure spirits and they come out!" ³⁷And the news about him spread throughout the surrounding area.

### Jesus Heals Many

³⁸Jesus left the synagogue and went to the home of Simon. Now Simon's mother-in-law was suffering from a high fever, and they asked Jesus to help her. ³⁹So he bent over her and rebuked the fever, and it left her. She got up at once and began to wait on them.

⁴⁰At sunset, the people brought to Jesus all who had various kinds of sickness, and laying his hands on each one, he healed them. ⁴¹Moreover, demons came out of many people, shouting, "You are the Son of God!" But he rebuked them and would not allow them to speak, because they knew he was the Messiah.

⁴²At daybreak, Jesus went out to a solitary place. The people were looking for him and when they came to where he was, they tried to keep him from leaving them. ⁴³But he said, "I must proclaim the good news of the kingdom of God to the other towns also, because that is why I was sent." ⁴⁴And he kept on preaching in the synagogues of Judea.

### Jesus Calls His First Disciples

**5** One day as Jesus was standing by the Lake of Gennesaret,ᵃ the people were crowding around him and listening to the word of God. ²He saw at the water's edge two boats, left there by the fishermen, who were washing their nets. ³He got into one of the boats, the one belonging to Simon, and asked him to put out a little from shore. Then he sat down and taught the people from the boat.

⁴When he had finished speaking, he said to Simon, "Put out into deep water, and let down the nets for a catch."

⁵Simon answered, "Master, we've worked hard all night and haven't caught anything. But because you say so, I will let down the nets."

⁶When they had done so, they caught such a large number of fish that their nets began to break. ⁷So they signaled their partners in the other boat to come and help them, and they came and filled both boats so full that they began to sink.

⁸When Simon Peter saw this, he fell at Jesus' knees and said, "Go away from me, Lord; I am a sinful man!" ⁹For he and all his companions were astonished at the catch of fish

## Amplified Bible

³³Now in the synagogue there was a man who was possessed by the foul spirit of a demon; and he cried out with a loud (deep, terrible) cry, ³⁴Ah, ᵃlet us alone! What have You to do with us [What have ᵇwe in common], Jesus of Nazareth? Have You come to destroy us? I know Who You are—the Holy One of God!

³⁵But Jesus rebuked him, saying, Be silent (muzzled, gagged), and come out of him! And when the demon had thrown the man down in their midst, he came out of him without injuring him in any ᶜpossible way.

³⁶And they were all amazed and said to one another, What kind of talk is this? For with authority and power He commands the foul spirits and they come out!

³⁷And a rumor about Him spread into every place in the surrounding country.

³⁸Then He arose and left the synagogue and went into Simon's (Peter's) house. Now Simon's mother-in-law was suffering in the grip of a burning fever, and they pleaded with Him for her.

³⁹And standing over her, He rebuked the fever, and it left her; and immediately she got up and began waiting on them.

⁴⁰Now at the setting of the sun [indicating the end of the Sabbath], all those who had any [who were] sick with various diseases brought them to Him, and He laid His hands upon every one of them and cured them.

⁴¹And demons even came out of many people, screaming and crying out, You are the Son of God! But He rebuked them and would not permit them to speak, because they knew that He was the Christ (the Messiah).

⁴²And when daybreak came, He left [Peter's house] and went into an isolated [desert] place. And the people looked for Him until they came up to Him and tried to prevent Him from leaving them.

⁴³But He said to them, I must preach the good news (the Gospel) of the kingdom of God to the other cities [and towns] also, for I was sent for this [purpose].

⁴⁴And He continued to preach in the synagogues of Galilee.

**5** Now it occurred that while the people pressed upon Jesus to hear the message of God, He was standing by the Lake of Gennesaret (Sea of Galilee).

²And He saw two boats drawn up by the lake, but the fishermen had gone down from them and were washing their nets.

³And getting into one of the boats, [the one] that belonged to Simon (Peter), He requested him to draw away a little from the shore. Then He sat down and continued to teach the crowd [of people] from the boat.

⁴When He had stopped speaking, He said to Simon (Peter), Put out into the deep [water], and lower your nets for a haul.

⁵And Simon (Peter) answered, Master, we toiled all night [ᵈexhaustingly] and caught nothing [in our nets]. But ᵈon the ground of Your word, I will lower the nets [again].

⁶And when they had done this, they caught a great number of fish; and as their nets were [ᵉat the point of] breaking,

⁷They signaled to their partners in the other boat to come and take hold with them. And they came and filled both the boats, so that they began to sink.

⁸But when Simon Peter saw this, he fell down at Jesus' knees, saying, Depart from me, for I am a sinful man, O Lord.

⁹For he was gripped with bewildering amazement [allied to terror], and all who were with him, at the haul of fish which they had made;

---

ᵃ Some manuscripts so read.  ᵇ John Wycliffe, *The Wycliffe Bible.*
ᶜ Literal translation.  ᵈ Marvin Vincent, *Word Studies.*  ᵉ Richard Trench, *Synonyms of the New Testament.*

ᵃ 1 That is, the Sea of Galilee

# New International Version

they had taken, 10and so were James and John, the sons of Zebedee, Simon's partners.

Then Jesus said to Simon, "Don't be afraid; from now on you will fish for people." 11So they pulled their boats up on shore, left everything and followed him.

## Jesus Heals a Man With Leprosy

12While Jesus was in one of the towns, a man came along who was covered with leprosy.a When he saw Jesus, he fell with his face to the ground and begged him, "Lord, if you are willing, you can make me clean."

13Jesus reached out his hand and touched the man. "I am willing," he said. "Be clean!" And immediately the leprosy left him.

14Then Jesus ordered him, "Don't tell anyone, but go, show yourself to the priest and offer the sacrifices that Moses commanded for your cleansing, as a testimony to them."

15Yet the news about him spread all the more, so that crowds of people came to hear him and to be healed of their sicknesses. 16But Jesus often withdrew to lonely places and prayed.

## Jesus Forgives and Heals a Paralyzed Man

17One day Jesus was teaching, and Pharisees and teachers of the law were sitting there. They had come from every village of Galilee and from Judea and Jerusalem. And the power of the Lord was with Jesus to heal the sick. 18Some men came carrying a paralyzed man on a mat and tried to take him into the house to lay him before Jesus. 19When they could not find a way to do this because of the crowd, they went up on the roof and lowered him on his mat through the tiles into the middle of the crowd, right in front of Jesus.

20When Jesus saw their faith, he said, "Friend, your sins are forgiven."

21The Pharisees and the teachers of the law began thinking to themselves, "Who is this fellow who speaks blasphemy? Who can forgive sins but God alone?"

22Jesus knew what they were thinking and asked, "Why are you thinking these things in your hearts? 23Which is easier: to say, 'Your sins are forgiven,' or to say, 'Get up and walk'? 24But I want you to know that the Son of Man has authority on earth to forgive sins." So he said to the paralyzed man, "I tell you, get up, take your mat and go home." 25Immediately he stood up in front of them, took what he had been lying on and went home praising God. 26Everyone was amazed and gave praise to God. They were filled with awe and said, "We have seen remarkable things today."

## Jesus Calls Levi and Eats With Sinners

27After this, Jesus went out and saw a tax collector by the name of Levi sitting at his tax booth. "Follow me," Jesus said to him, 28and Levi got up, left everything and followed him.

29Then Levi held a great banquet for Jesus at his house, and a large crowd of tax collectors and others were eating with them. 30But the Pharisees and the teachers of the

# Amplified Bible

10And so also were James and John, the sons of Zebedee, who were partners with Simon (Peter). And Jesus said to Simon, Have no fear; from now on you will be catching men!

11And after they had run their boats on shore, they left everything and ajoined Him as His disciples and sided with His party and accompanied Him.

12While He was in one of the towns, there came a man full of (covered with) leprosy; and when he saw Jesus, he fell on his face and implored Him, saying, Lord, if You are willing, You are able to cure me and make me clean.

13And [Jesus] reached out His hand and touched him, saying, I am willing; be cleansed! And immediately the leprosy left him.

14And [Jesus] charged him to tell no one [bthat he might chance to meet], cuntil [He said] you go and show yourself to the priest, and make an offering for your purification, as Moses commanded, for a testimony and proof to the people, that they may have evidence [of your healing]. [Lev. 13:49; 14:2-32.]

15But so much the more the news spread abroad concerning Him, and great crowds kept coming together to hear [Him] and to be healed by Him of their infirmities.

16But He Himself withdrew [in retirement] to the wilderness (desert) and prayed.

17One of those days, as He was teaching, there were Pharisees and teachers of the Law sitting by, who had come from every village and town of Galilee and Judea and from Jerusalem. And the power of the Lord was [present] with Him to heal dthem.

18And behold, some men were bringing on a stretcher a man who was paralyzed, and they tried to carry him in and lay him before [Jesus].

19But finding no way to bring him in because of the crowd, they went up on the roof and lowered him with his stretcher through the tiles into the midst, in front of Jesus.

20And when He saw [their confidence in Him, springing from] their faith, He said, Man, your sins are forgiven you!

21And the scribes and the Pharisees began to reason and question and argue, saying, Who is this [Man] Who speaks blasphemies? Who can forgive sins but God alone?

22But Jesus, knowing their thoughts and questionings, answered them, Why do you question in your hearts?

23Which is easier: to say, Your sins are forgiven you, or to say, Arise and walk [about]?

24But that you may know that the Son of Man has the [apower of] authority and right on earth to forgive sins, He said to the paralyzed man, I say to you, arise, pick up your litter (stretcher), and go to your own house!

25And instantly [the man] stood up before them and picked up what he had been lying on and went away to his house, erecognizing and praising and thanking God.

26And overwhelming astonishment and ecstasy seized them all, and they erecognized and praised and thanked God; and they were filled with and controlled by reverential fear and kept saying, We have seen wonderful and strange and incredible and unthinkable things today!

27And after this, Jesus went out and looked [attentively] at a tax collector named Levi sitting at the tax office; and He said to him, aJoin Me as a disciple and side with My party and accompany Me.

28And he forsook everything and got up and followed Him [becoming His disciple and siding with His party].

29And Levi (Matthew) made a great banquet for Him in his own house, and there was a large company of tax collectors and others who were reclining [at the table] with them.

30Now the Pharisees and their scribes were grumbling

---

a 12 The Greek word traditionally translated leprosy was used for various diseases affecting the skin.

a Joseph Thayer, A Greek-English Lexicon. b Marvin Vincent, Word Studies. c Richard Trench, Notes on the Miracles of our Lord. d Some ancient manuscripts so read. e Hermann Cremer, Biblico-Theological Lexicon.

## New International Version

law who belonged to their sect complained to his disciples, "Why do you eat and drink with tax collectors and sinners?"

[31] Jesus answered them, "It is not the healthy who need a doctor, but the sick. [32] I have not come to call the righteous, but sinners to repentance."

### Jesus Questioned About Fasting

[33] They said to him, "John's disciples often fast and pray, and so do the disciples of the Pharisees, but yours go on eating and drinking."

[34] Jesus answered, "Can you make the friends of the bridegroom fast while he is with them? [35] But the time will come when the bridegroom will be taken from them; in those days they will fast."

[36] He told them this parable: "No one tears a piece out of a new garment to patch an old one. Otherwise, they will have torn the new garment, and the patch from the new will not match the old. [37] And no one pours new wine into old wineskins. Otherwise, the new wine will burst the skins; the wine will run out and the wineskins will be ruined. [38] No, new wine must be poured into new wineskins. [39] And no one after drinking old wine wants the new, for they say, 'The old is better.'"

### Jesus Is Lord of the Sabbath

**6** One Sabbath Jesus was going through the grainfields, and his disciples began to pick some heads of grain, rub them in their hands and eat the kernels. [2] Some of the Pharisees asked, "Why are you doing what is unlawful on the Sabbath?"

[3] Jesus answered them, "Have you never read what David did when he and his companions were hungry? [4] He entered the house of God, and taking the consecrated bread, he ate what is lawful only for priests to eat. And he also gave some to his companions." [5] Then Jesus said to them, "The Son of Man is Lord of the Sabbath."

[6] On another Sabbath he went into the synagogue and was teaching, and a man was there whose right hand was shriveled. [7] The Pharisees and the teachers of the law were looking for a reason to accuse Jesus, so they watched him closely to see if he would heal on the Sabbath. [8] But Jesus knew what they were thinking and said to the man with the shriveled hand, "Get up and stand in front of everyone." So he got up and stood there.

[9] Then Jesus said to them, "I ask you, which is lawful on the Sabbath: to do good or to do evil, to save life or to destroy it?"

[10] He looked around at them all, and then said to the man, "Stretch out your hand." He did so, and his hand was completely restored. [11] But the Pharisees and the teachers of the law were furious and began to discuss with one another what they might do to Jesus.

### The Twelve Apostles

[12] One of those days Jesus went out to a mountainside to pray, and spent the night praying to God. [13] When morning

## Amplified Bible

against Jesus' disciples, saying, Why are you eating and drinking with tax collectors and [preeminently] sinful people?

[31] And Jesus replied to them, It is not those who are healthy who need a physician, but those who are sick.

[32] I have not come to arouse *and* invite *and* call the righteous, but [a]the erring ones ([b]those not free from sin) to repentance [[b]to change their minds for the better and heartily to amend their ways, with abhorrence of their past sins].

[33] Then they said to Him, The disciples of John practice fasting often and offer up prayers of [special] petition, and so do [the disciples] of the Pharisees also, but Yours eat and drink.

[34] And Jesus said to them, Can you make the wedding guests fast as long as the bridegroom is with them?

[35] But the days will come when the bridegroom will be taken from them; and then they will fast in those days.

[36] He told them a [c]proverb also: No one puts a patch from a new garment on an old garment; if he does, he will both tear the new one, and the patch from the new [one] will not match the old [garment].

[37] And no one pours new wine into old wineskins; if he does, the fresh wine will burst the skins and it will be spilled and the skins will be ruined (destroyed).

[38] But new wine must be put into fresh wineskins.

[39] And no one after drinking old wine immediately desires new wine, for he says, The old is good *or* [d]better.

**6** One sabbath while Jesus was passing through the fields of standing grain, it occurred that His disciples picked some of the spikes and ate [of the grain], rubbing it out in their hands. [Deut. 23:25.]

[2] But some of the Pharisees asked them, Why are you doing what is not permitted to be done on the Sabbath days? [Exod. 20:10; 23:12; Deut. 5:14.]

[3] And Jesus replied to them, saying, Have you never so much as read what David did when he was hungry, he and those who were with him?—[I Sam. 21:1-6.]

[4] How he went into the house of God and took and ate the [sacred] loaves of the showbread, which it is not permitted for any except only the priests to eat, and also gave to those [who were] with him? [Lev. 24:9.]

[5] And He said to them, The Son of Man is Lord even of the Sabbath.

[6] And it occurred on another Sabbath that when He went into the synagogue and taught, a man was present whose right hand was withered.

[7] And the scribes and the Pharisees kept watching Jesus to see whether He would [actually] heal on the Sabbath, in order that they might get [some ground for] accusation against Him.

[8] But He was aware all along of their thoughts, and He said to the man with the withered hand, Come and stand here in the midst. And he arose and stood there.

[9] Then Jesus said to them, I ask you, is it lawful *and* right on the Sabbath to do good [e]so that someone derives advantage from it] or to do evil, to save a life [and [f]make a soul safe] or to destroy it?

[10] Then He glanced around at them all and said to the man, Stretch out your hand! And he did so, and his hand was fully restored [g]like the other one.

[11] But they were filled with lack of understanding *and* senseless rage and discussed (consulted) with one another what they might do to Jesus.

[12] Now in those days it occurred that He went up into a mountain to pray, and spent the whole night in prayer to God.

---

[a] Robert Young, *Analytical Concordance.* [b] Joseph Thayer, *A Greek-English Lexicon.* [c] G. Abbott-Smith, *Manual Greek Lexicon of the New Testament.* [d] Many ancient manuscripts read "better." [e] Hermann Cremer, *Biblico-Theological Lexicon.* [f] John Wycliffe, *The Wycliffe Bible.* [g] Some manuscripts add this phrase.

## New International Version

came, he called his disciples to him and chose twelve of them, whom he also designated apostles: [14]Simon (whom he named Peter), his brother Andrew, James, John, Philip, Bartholomew, [15]Matthew, Thomas, James son of Alphaeus, Simon who was called the Zealot, [16]Judas son of James, and Judas Iscariot, who became a traitor.

### Blessings and Woes

[17]He went down with them and stood on a level place. A large crowd of his disciples was there and a great number of people from all over Judea, from Jerusalem, and from the coastal region around Tyre and Sidon, [18]who had come to hear him and to be healed of their diseases. Those troubled by impure spirits were cured, [19]and the people all tried to touch him, because power was coming from him and healing them all.

[20]Looking at his disciples, he said:

"Blessed are you who are poor,
for yours is the kingdom of God.
[21]Blessed are you who hunger now,
for you will be satisfied.
Blessed are you who weep now,
for you will laugh.
[22]Blessed are you when people hate you,
when they exclude you and insult you
and reject your name as evil,
because of the Son of Man.

[23]"Rejoice in that day and leap for joy, because great is your reward in heaven. For that is how their ancestors treated the prophets.

[24]"But woe to you who are rich,
for you have already received your comfort.
[25]Woe to you who are well fed now,
for you will go hungry.
Woe to you who laugh now,
for you will mourn and weep.
[26]Woe to you when everyone speaks well of you,
for that is how their ancestors treated the false
prophets.

### Love for Enemies

[27]"But to you who are listening I say: Love your enemies, do good to those who hate you, [28]bless those who curse you, pray for those who mistreat you. [29]If someone slaps you on one cheek, turn to them the other also. If

## Amplified Bible

[13]And when it was day, He summoned His disciples and selected from them twelve, whom He named apostles (special messengers):

[14]They were Simon, whom He named Peter, and his brother Andrew; and James and John; and Philip and Bartholomew;

[15]And Matthew and Thomas; and James son of Alphaeus, and Simon who was called the Zealot,

[16]And Judas son of James, and Judas Iscariot, who became a traitor (a treacherous, basely faithless person).

[17]And Jesus came down with them and took His stand on a level spot, with a great crowd of His disciples and a vast throng of people from all over Judea and Jerusalem and the seacoast of Tyre and Sidon, who came to listen to Him and to be cured of their diseases—

[18]Even those who were disturbed *and* troubled with unclean spirits, and they were being healed [also].

[19]And all the multitude were seeking to touch Him, for healing power was all the while going forth from Him and curing them all [[a]saving them from severe illnesses or calamities].

[20]And solemnly lifting up His eyes on His disciples, He said: Blessed (happy—[b]with life-joy and satisfaction in God's favor and salvation, apart from your outward condition—and [c]to be envied) are you poor *and* [d]lowly *and* afflicted (destitute of wealth, influence, position, and honor), for the kingdom of God is yours!

[21]Blessed (happy—[b]with life-joy and satisfaction in God's favor and salvation, apart from your outward condition—and [c]to be envied) are you who hunger *and* seek with eager desire now, for you shall be filled *and* completely satisfied! Blessed (happy—[b]with life-joy and satisfaction in God's favor and salvation, apart from your outward condition—and [c]to be envied) are you who weep *and* sob now, for you shall laugh!

[22]Blessed (happy—[b]with life-joy and satisfaction in God's favor and salvation, apart from your outward condition—and [c]to be envied) are you when people despise (hate) you, and when they exclude *and* excommunicate you [as disreputable] and revile *and* denounce you and defame *and* cast out and spurn your name as evil (wicked) on account of the Son of Man.

[23]Rejoice *and* be glad at such a time and exult *and* leap for joy, for behold, your reward is rich *and* great *and* strong *and* intense *and* abundant in heaven; for even so their forefathers treated the prophets.

[24]But woe to (alas for) you who are rich ([d]abounding in material resources), for you already are receiving your consolation (the solace and sense of strengthening and cheer that come from prosperity) *and* have taken and enjoyed your comfort in full [having nothing left to be awarded you].

[25]Woe to (alas for) you who are full now (completely filled, luxuriously gorged and satiated), for you shall hunger *and* suffer want! Woe to (alas for) you who laugh now, for you shall mourn and weep *and* wail!

[26]Woe to (alas for) you when everyone speaks fairly *and* handsomely of you *and* praises you, for even so their forefathers did to the false prophets.

[27]But I say to you who are listening now to Me: [[a]in order to heed, make it a practice to] love your enemies, treat well (do good to, act nobly toward) those who detest you *and* pursue you with hatred,

[28]Invoke blessings upon *and* pray for the happiness of those who curse you, implore God's blessing (favor) upon those who abuse you [who revile, reproach, disparage, and high-handedly misuse you].

[29]To the one who strikes you on the [d]jaw *or* cheek, offer the other [d]jaw *or* cheek also; and from him who takes away

---

[a] Marvin Vincent, *Word Studies.* [b] Hermann Cremer, *Biblico-Theological Lexicon.* [c] Alexander Souter, *Pocket Lexicon.* [d] Joseph Thayer, *A Greek-English Lexicon.*

## New International Version

someone takes your coat, do not withhold your shirt from them. [30]Give to everyone who asks you, and if anyone takes what belongs to you, do not demand it back. [31]Do to others as you would have them do to you.

[32]"If you love those who love you, what credit is that to you? Even sinners love those who love them. [33]And if you do good to those who are good to you, what credit is that to you? Even sinners do that. [34]And if you lend to those from whom you expect repayment, what credit is that to you? Even sinners lend to sinners, expecting to be repaid in full. [35]But love your enemies, do good to them, and lend to them without expecting to get anything back. Then your reward will be great, and you will be children of the Most High, because he is kind to the ungrateful and wicked. [36]Be merciful, just as your Father is merciful.

### Judging Others

[37]"Do not judge, and you will not be judged. Do not condemn, and you will not be condemned. Forgive, and you will be forgiven. [38]Give, and it will be given to you. A good measure, pressed down, shaken together and running over, will be poured into your lap. For with the measure you use, it will be measured to you."

[39]He also told them this parable: "Can the blind lead the blind? Will they not both fall into a pit? [40]The student is not above the teacher, but everyone who is fully trained will be like their teacher.

[41]"Why do you look at the speck of sawdust in your brother's eye and pay no attention to the plank in your own eye? [42]How can you say to your brother, 'Brother, let me take the speck out of your eye,' when you yourself fail to see the plank in your own eye? You hypocrite, first take the plank out of your eye, and then you will see clearly to remove the speck from your brother's eye.

### A Tree and Its Fruit

[43]"No good tree bears bad fruit, nor does a bad tree bear good fruit. [44]Each tree is recognized by its own fruit. People do not pick figs from thornbushes, or grapes from briers. [45]A good man brings good things out of the good stored up in his heart, and an evil man brings evil things out of the evil stored up in his heart. For the mouth speaks what the heart is full of.

## Amplified Bible

your outer garment, do not withhold your undergarment as well.

[30]Give away to everyone who begs of you [who is [a]in want of necessities], and of him who takes away from you your goods, do not demand or require them back again.

[31]And as you would like and desire that men would do to you, do exactly so to them.

[32]If you [merely] love those who love you, what [b]quality of credit and thanks is that to you? For even [c]the [very] sinners love their lovers (those who love them).

[33]And if you are kind and good and do favors to and benefit those who are kind and good and do favors to and benefit you, what [b]quality of credit and thanks is that to you? For even [a]the preeminently sinful do the same.

[34]And if you lend money [b]at interest to those from whom you hope to receive, what [b]quality of credit and thanks is that to you? Even notorious sinners lend money [b]at interest to sinners, so as to recover as much again.

[35]But love your enemies and be kind and do good [doing favors [d]so that someone derives benefit from them] and lend, expecting and hoping for nothing in return but [b]considering nothing as lost and despairing of no one; and then your recompense (your reward) will be great (rich, strong, intense, and abundant), and you will be sons of the Most High, for He is kind and charitable and good to the ungrateful and the selfish and wicked.

[36]So be merciful (sympathetic, tender, responsive, and compassionate) even as your Father is [all these].

[37]Judge not [neither pronouncing judgment nor subjecting to censure], and you will not be judged; do not condemn and pronounce guilty, and you will not be condemned and pronounced guilty; acquit and forgive and [e]release (give up resentment, let it drop), and you will be acquitted and forgiven and [f]released.

[38]Give, and [gifts] will be given to you; good measure, pressed down, shaken together, and running over, will they pour [b]into [the pouch formed by] the bosom [of your robe and used as a bag]. For with the measure you deal out [with the measure you use when you confer benefits on others], it will be measured back to you.

[39]He further told them [g]a proverb: Can a blind [man] guide and direct a blind [man]? Will they not both stumble into a ditch or a [h]hole in the ground?

[40]A pupil is not superior to his teacher, but everyone [when he is] completely trained (readjusted, restored, set to rights, and perfected) will be like his teacher.

[41]Why do you see the speck that is in your brother's eye but do not notice or consider the beam [of timber] that is in your own eye?

[42]Or how can you say to your brother, Brother, allow me to take out the speck that is in your eye, when you yourself do not see the beam that is in your own eye? You actor (pretender, hypocrite)! First take the beam out of your own eye, and then you will see clearly to take out the speck that is in your brother's eye.

[43]For there is no good (healthy) tree that bears decayed (worthless, stale) fruit, nor on the other hand does a decayed (worthless, sickly) tree bear good fruit.

[44]For each tree is known and identified by its own fruit; for figs are not gathered from thornbushes, nor is a cluster of grapes picked from a bramblebush.

[45]The upright (honorable, intrinsically good) man out of the good treasure [stored] in his heart produces what is upright (honorable and intrinsically good), and the evil man out of the evil storehouse brings forth that which is depraved (wicked and intrinsically evil); for out of the abundance (overflow) of the heart his mouth speaks.

[a] Joseph Thayer, A Greek-English Lexicon. [b] Marvin Vincent, Word Studies. [c] William Tyndale, The Tyndale Bible. [d] Hermann Cremer, Biblico-Theological Lexicon. [e] Literal translation. [f] Literal meaning. [g] G. Abbott-Smith, Manual Greek Lexicon. [h] Alexander Souter, Pocket Lexicon.

| New International Version | Amplified Bible |

## The Wise and Foolish Builders

46 "Why do you call me, 'Lord, Lord,' and do not do what I say? 47 As for everyone who comes to me and hears my words and puts them into practice, I will show you what they are like. 48 They are like a man building a house, who dug down deep and laid the foundation on rock. When a flood came, the torrent struck that house but could not shake it, because it was well built. 49 But the one who hears my words and does not put them into practice is like a man who built a house on the ground without a foundation. The moment the torrent struck that house, it collapsed and its destruction was complete."

## The Faith of the Centurion

**7** When Jesus had finished saying all this to the people who were listening, he entered Capernaum. 2 There a centurion's servant, whom his master valued highly, was sick and about to die. 3 The centurion heard of Jesus and sent some elders of the Jews to him, asking him to come and heal his servant. 4 When they came to Jesus, they pleaded earnestly with him, "This man deserves to have you do this, 5 because he loves our nation and has built our synagogue." 6 So Jesus went with them.

He was not far from the house when the centurion sent friends to say to him: "Lord, don't trouble yourself, for I do not deserve to have you come under my roof. 7 That is why I did not even consider myself worthy to come to you. But say the word, and my servant will be healed. 8 For I myself am a man under authority, with soldiers under me. I tell this one, 'Go,' and he goes; and that one, 'Come,' and he comes. I say to my servant, 'Do this,' and he does it."

9 When Jesus heard this, he was amazed at him, and turning to the crowd following him, he said, "I tell you, I have not found such great faith even in Israel." 10 Then the men who had been sent returned to the house and found the servant well.

## Jesus Raises a Widow's Son

11 Soon afterward, Jesus went to a town called Nain, and his disciples and a large crowd went along with him. 12 As he approached the town gate, a dead person was being carried out—the only son of his mother, and she was a widow. And a large crowd from the town was with her. 13 When the Lord saw her, his heart went out to her and he said, "Don't cry."

14 Then he went up and touched the bier they were carrying him on, and the bearers stood still. He said, "Young man, I say to you, get up!" 15 The dead man sat up and began to talk, and Jesus gave him back to his mother.

16 They were all filled with awe and praised God. "A great prophet has appeared among us," they said. "God

---

46 Why do you call Me, Lord, Lord, and do not [practice] what I tell you?

47 For everyone who comes to Me and listens to My words [in order to heed their teaching] and does them, I will show you what he is like:

48 He is like a man building a house, who dug and went down deep and laid a foundation upon the rock; and when a flood arose, the torrent broke against that house and could not shake or move it, because it had been securely built or *a founded on a rock.*

49 But he who merely hears and does not practice doing My words is like a man who built a house on the ground without a foundation, against which the torrent burst, and immediately it collapsed *and* fell, and the breaking *and* ruin of that house was great.

**7** After Jesus had finished all that He had to say in the hearing of the people [on the mountain], He entered Capernaum.

2 Now a centurion had a bond servant who was held in honor *and* highly valued by him, who was sick and at the point of death.

3 And when the centurion heard of Jesus, he sent some Jewish elders to Him, requesting Him to come and make his bond servant well.

4 And when they reached Jesus, they begged Him earnestly, saying, He is worthy that You should do this for him,

5 For he loves our nation and he built us our synagogue [at his own expense].

6 And Jesus went with them. But when He was not far from the house, the centurion sent [some] friends to Him, saying, Lord, do not trouble [Yourself], for I am not *b suf-ficiently* worthy to have You come under my roof;

7 Neither did I consider myself worthy to come to You. But [just] speak a word, and my servant boy will be healed.

8 For I also am a man [daily] subject to authority, with soldiers under me. And I say to one, Go, and he goes; and to another, Come, and he comes; and to my bond servant, Do this, and he does it.

9 Now when Jesus heard this, He marveled at him, and He turned and said to the crowd that followed Him, I tell you, not even in [all] Israel have I found such great faith [as this].

10 And when the messengers who had been sent returned to the house, they found the bond servant *c who had been ill* quite well again.

11 *d Soon* afterward, Jesus went to a town called Nain, and His disciples and a great throng accompanied Him.

12 [Just] as He drew near the gate of the town, behold, a man who had died was being carried out—the only son of his mother, and she was a widow; and a large gathering from the town was accompanying her.

13 And when the Lord saw her, He had compassion on her and said to her, Do not weep.

14 And He went forward and touched the funeral bier, and the pallbearers stood still. And He said, Young man, I say to you, arise [*e from death*]!

15 And the man [who was] dead sat up and began to speak. And [Jesus] gave him [back] to his mother.

16 Profound *and* reverent fear seized them all, and they began *f* to recognize God *and* praise *and* give thanks, saying, A great *g* Prophet has appeared among us! And God has visited His people [in order to help and care for and provide for them]!

---

*a* Some manuscripts so read. *b* Literal translation: "sufficient." *c* Some manuscripts add this phrase. *d* Many ancient manuscripts read "the next day." *e* Hermann Cremer, *Biblico-Theological Lexicon.* *f* Joseph Thayer, *A Greek-English Lexicon.* *g* Capitalized because of what He is, the spotless Son of God, not what the speakers may have thought He was.

## New International Version

has come to help his people." [17]This news about Jesus spread throughout Judea and the surrounding country.

### Jesus and John the Baptist

[18]John's disciples told him about all these things. Calling two of them, [19]he sent them to the Lord to ask, "Are you the one who is to come, or should we expect someone else?"

[20]When the men came to Jesus, they said, "John the Baptist sent us to you to ask, 'Are you the one who is to come, or should we expect someone else?'"

[21]At that very time Jesus cured many who had diseases, sicknesses and evil spirits, and gave sight to many who were blind. [22]So he replied to the messengers, "Go back and report to John what you have seen and heard: The blind receive sight, the lame walk, those who have leprosy[a] are cleansed, the deaf hear, the dead are raised, and the good news is proclaimed to the poor. [23]Blessed is anyone who does not stumble on account of me."

[24]After John's messengers left, Jesus began to speak to the crowd about John: "What did you go out into the wilderness to see? A reed swayed by the wind? [25]If not, what did you go out to see? A man dressed in fine clothes? No, those who wear expensive clothes and indulge in luxury are in palaces. [26]But what did you go out to see? A prophet? Yes, I tell you, and more than a prophet. [27]This is the one about whom it is written:

"'I will send my messenger ahead of you,
    who will prepare your way before you.'[b]

[28]I tell you, among those born of women there is no one greater than John; yet the one who is least in the kingdom of God is greater than he."

[29](All the people, even the tax collectors, when they heard Jesus' words, acknowledged that God's way was right, because they had been baptized by John. [30]But the Pharisees and the experts in the law rejected God's purpose for themselves, because they had not been baptized by John.)

[31]Jesus went on to say, "To what, then, can I compare the people of this generation? What are they like? [32]They are like children sitting in the marketplace and calling out to each other:

"'We played the pipe for you,
    and you did not dance;
we sang a dirge,
    and you did not cry.'

[33]For John the Baptist came neither eating bread nor drinking wine, and you say, 'He has a demon.' [34]The Son of Man came eating and drinking, and you say, 'Here is a glutton and a drunkard, a friend of tax collectors and sinners.' [35]But wisdom is proved right by all her children."

### Jesus Anointed by a Sinful Woman

[36]When one of the Pharisees invited Jesus to have dinner with him, he went to the Pharisee's house and reclined at the table. [37]A woman in that town who lived a sinful life learned that Jesus was eating at the Pharisee's house, so she came there with an alabaster jar of perfume. [38]As she

## Amplified Bible

[17]And this report concerning [Jesus] spread through the whole of Judea and all the country round about. [I Kings 17:17-24; II Kings 4:32-37.]

[18]And John's disciples brought him [who was now in prison] word of all these things.

[19]And John summoned to him a certain two of his disciples and sent them to the Lord, saying, Are You He Who is to come, or shall we [continue to] look for another?

[20]So the men came to Jesus and said, John the Baptist sent us to You to ask, Are You the One Who is to come, or shall we [continue to] look for another?

[21]In that very hour Jesus was healing many [people] of sicknesses and distressing bodily plagues and evil spirits, and to many who were blind He gave [[a] free, gracious, joy-giving gift of] sight.

[22]So He replied to them, Go and tell John what you have seen and heard: the blind receive their sight, the lame walk, the lepers are cleansed, the deaf hear, the dead are raised up, and the poor have the good news (the Gospel) preached to them. [Isa. 29:18, 19; 35:5, 6; 61:1.]

[23]And blessed (happy—[b]with life-joy and satisfaction in God's favor and salvation, apart from outward conditions—and [c]to be envied) is he who takes no offense in Me and who is not hurt or resentful or annoyed or repelled or made to stumble [[a]whatever may occur].

[24]And the messengers of John having departed, Jesus began to speak to the crowds about John: What did you go out into the desert to gaze on? A reed shaken and swayed by the wind?

[25]Then what did you go out to see? A man dressed up in soft garments? Behold, those who wear fine apparel and live in luxury are in the courts or palaces of kings.

[26]What then did you go out to see? A prophet (a forthteller)? Yes, I tell you, and far more than a prophet.

[27]This is the one of whom it is written, Behold, I send My messenger before Your face, who shall make ready Your way before You. [Mal. 3:1.]

[28]I tell you, among those born of women there is no one greater than John; but [d]he that is inferior [to the other citizens] in the kingdom of God is greater [in incomparable privilege] than he.

[29]And all the people who heard Him, even the tax collectors, acknowledged the justice of God [in [d]calling them to repentance and in pronouncing future wrath on the impenitent], being baptized with the baptism of John.

[30]But the Pharisees and the lawyers [of the Mosaic Law] annulled and rejected and brought to nothing God's purpose concerning themselves, by [refusing and] not being baptized by him [John].

[31]So to what shall I compare the men of this generation? And what are they like?

[32]They are like little children sitting in the marketplace, calling to one another and saying, We piped to you [playing wedding], and you did not dance; we sang dirges and wailed [playing funeral], and you did not weep.

[33]For John the Baptist has come neither eating bread nor drinking wine, and you say, He has a demon.

[34]The Son of Man has come eating and drinking, and you say, Behold, a Man Who is a glutton and a wine drinker, a friend of tax collectors and notorious sinners.

[35]Yet wisdom is vindicated ([e]shown to be true and divine) by all her children [[e]by their life, character, and deeds].

[36]One of the Pharisees asked Jesus to dine with him, and He went into the Pharisee's house and reclined at table.

[37]And behold, a woman of the town who was [d]an especially wicked sinner, when she learned that He was reclining at table in the Pharisee's house, brought an alabaster flask of ointment (perfume).

---

[a] 22 The Greek word traditionally translated *leprosy* was used for various diseases affecting the skin.    [b] 27 Mal. 3:1

[a] Marvin Vincent, *Word Studies*.   [b] Hermann Cremer, *Biblico-Theological Lexicon*.   [c] Alexander Souter, *Pocket Lexicon*.   [d] Joseph Thayer, *A Greek-English Lexicon*.   [e] Albert Barnes, *Notes on the New Testament*.

## New International Version

stood behind him at his feet weeping, she began to wet his feet with her tears. Then she wiped them with her hair, kissed them and poured perfume on them. [39]When the Pharisee who had invited him saw this, he said to himself, "If this man were a prophet, he would know who is touching him and what kind of woman she is—that she is a sinner." [40]Jesus answered him, "Simon, I have something to tell you."

"Tell me, teacher," he said.

[41]"Two people owed money to a certain moneylender. One owed him five hundred denarii,[a] and the other fifty. [42]Neither of them had the money to pay him back, so he forgave the debts of both. Now which of them will love him more?"

[43]Simon replied, "I suppose the one who had the bigger debt forgiven."

"You have judged correctly," Jesus said.

[44]Then he turned toward the woman and said to Simon, "Do you see this woman? I came into your house. You did not give me any water for my feet, but she wet my feet with her tears and wiped them with her hair. [45]You did not give me a kiss, but this woman, from the time I entered, has not stopped kissing my feet. [46]You did not put oil on my head, but she has poured perfume on my feet. [47]Therefore, I tell you, her many sins have been forgiven—as her great love has shown. But whoever has been forgiven little loves little."

[48]Then Jesus said to her, "Your sins are forgiven."

[49]The other guests began to say among themselves, "Who is this who even forgives sins?"

[50]Jesus said to the woman, "Your faith has saved you; go in peace."

### The Parable of the Sower

**8** After this, Jesus traveled about from one town and village to another, proclaiming the good news of the kingdom of God. The Twelve were with him, [2]and also some women who had been cured of evil spirits and diseases: Mary (called Magdalene) from whom seven demons had come out; [3]Joanna the wife of Chuza, the manager of Herod's household; Susanna; and many others. These women were helping to support them out of their own means.

[4]While a large crowd was gathering and people were coming to Jesus from town after town, he told this parable: [5]"A farmer went out to sow his seed. As he was scattering the seed, some fell along the path; it was trampled on, and the birds ate it up. [6]Some fell on rocky ground, and when it came up, the plants withered because they had no moisture. [7]Other seed fell among thorns, which grew up with it and choked the plants. [8]Still other seed fell on good soil. It came up and yielded a crop, a hundred times more than was sown."

When he said this, he called out, "Whoever has ears to hear, let them hear."

[9]His disciples asked him what this parable meant. [10]He said, "The knowledge of the secrets of the kingdom of God has been given to you, but to others I speak in parables, so that,

## Amplified Bible

[38]And standing behind Him at His feet weeping, she began to wet His feet with [her] tears; and she wiped them with the hair of her head and kissed His feet [affectionately] and anointed them with the ointment (perfume). [39]Now when the Pharisee who had invited Him saw it, he said to himself, If this Man were a prophet, He would surely know who and what sort of woman this is who is touching Him—for she is a notorious sinner (a social outcast, devoted to sin).

[40]And Jesus, replying, said to him, Simon, I have something to say to you. And he answered, Teacher, say it.

[41]A certain lender of money [at interest] had two debtors: one owed him five hundred denarii, and the other fifty. [42]When they had no means of paying, he freely forgave them both. Now which of them will love him more?

[43]Simon answered, The one, I take it, for whom he forgave and cancelled more. And Jesus said to him, You have decided correctly.

[44]Then turning toward the woman, He said to Simon, Do you see this woman? When I came into your house, you gave Me no water for My feet, but she has wet My feet with her tears and wiped them with her hair. [45]You gave Me no kiss, but she from the moment I came in has not ceased [a]intermittently] to kiss My feet tenderly and caressingly.

[46]You did not anoint My head with [b][cheap, ordinary] oil, but she has anointed My feet with [b][costly, rare] perfume.

[47]Therefore I tell you, her sins, many [as they are], are forgiven her—because she has loved much. But he who is forgiven little loves little.

[48]And He said to her, Your sins are forgiven!

[49]Then those who were at table with Him began to say among themselves, Who is this Who even forgives sins?

[50]But Jesus said to the woman, Your faith has saved you; go (enter) [a]into peace [[b]in freedom from all the distresses that are experienced as the result of sin].

**8** Soon afterward, [Jesus] went on through towns and villages, preaching and bringing the good news (the Gospel) of the kingdom of God. And the Twelve [apostles] were with Him,

[2]And also some women who had been cured of evil spirits and diseases: Mary, called Magdalene, from whom seven demons had been expelled;

[3]And Joanna, the wife of Chuza, Herod's household manager; and Susanna; and many others, who ministered to and provided for [c]Him and them out of their property and personal belongings.

[4]And when a very great throng was gathering together and people from town after town kept coming to Jesus, He said in a parable:

[5]A sower went out to sow seed; and as he sowed, some fell along the traveled path and was trodden underfoot, and the birds of the air ate it up.

[6]And some [seed] fell on the rock, and as soon as it sprouted, it withered away because it had no moisture.

[7]And other [seed] fell in the midst of the thorns, and the thorns grew up with it and choked it [off].

[8]And some seed fell into good soil, and grew and yielded a crop a hundred times [as great]. As He said these things, He called out, He who has ears to hear, let him be listening and let him [d]consider and understand by hearing!

[9]And when His disciples asked Him the meaning of this parable,

[10]He said to them, To you it has been given to [come progressively to] know (to recognize and understand more strongly and clearly) the mysteries and secrets of the kingdom of God, but for others they are in parables,

---

[a] 41 A denarius was the usual wage of a day laborer (see Matt. 20:2).

[a] Marvin Vincent, Word Studies. [b] Hermann Cremer, Biblico-Theological Lexicon. [c] Some ancient manuscripts read "Him" instead of "them." [d] Joseph Thayer, A Greek-English Lexicon.

## New International Version

"'though seeing, they may not see;
though hearing, they may not understand.'[a]

11"This is the meaning of the parable: The seed is the word of God. 12Those along the path are the ones who hear, and then the devil comes and takes away the word from their hearts, so that they may not believe and be saved. 13Those on the rocky ground are the ones who receive the word with joy when they hear it, but they have no root. They believe for a while, but in the time of testing they fall away. 14The seed that fell among thorns stands for those who hear, but as they go on their way they are choked by life's worries, riches and pleasures, and they do not mature. 15But the seed on good soil stands for those with a noble and good heart, who hear the word, retain it, and by persevering produce a crop.

### A Lamp on a Stand

16"No one lights a lamp and hides it in a clay jar or puts it under a bed. Instead, they put it on a stand, so that those who come in can see the light. 17For there is nothing hidden that will not be disclosed, and nothing concealed that will not be known or brought out into the open. 18Therefore consider carefully how you listen. Whoever has will be given more; whoever does not have, even what they think they have will be taken from them."

### Jesus' Mother and Brothers

19Now Jesus' mother and brothers came to see him, but they were not able to get near him because of the crowd. 20Someone told him, "Your mother and brothers are standing outside, wanting to see you."

21He replied, "My mother and brothers are those who hear God's word and put it into practice."

### Jesus Calms the Storm

22One day Jesus said to his disciples, "Let us go over to the other side of the lake." So they got into a boat and set out. 23As they sailed, he fell asleep. A squall came down on the lake, so that the boat was being swamped, and they were in great danger.

24The disciples went and woke him, saying, "Master, Master, we're going to drown!"

He got up and rebuked the wind and the raging waters; the storm subsided, and all was calm. 25"Where is your faith?" he asked his disciples.

In fear and amazement they asked one another, "Who is this? He commands even the winds and the water, and they obey him."

### Jesus Restores a Demon-Possessed Man

26They sailed to the region of the Gerasenes,[b] which is across the lake from Galilee. 27When Jesus stepped ashore, he was met by a demon-possessed man from the town. For a long time this man had not worn clothes or lived in a house, but had lived in the tombs. 28When he saw Jesus, he cried out and fell at his feet, shouting at the

## Amplified Bible

so that, [though] looking, they may not see; and hearing, they may not comprehend. [Isa. 6:9, 10; Jer. 5:21; Ezek. 12:2.]

11Now the meaning of the parable is this: The seed is the Word of God.

12Those along the traveled road are the people who have heard; then the devil comes and carries away the message out of their hearts, that they may not believe (aacknowledge Me as their Savior and devote themselves to Me) and be saved [here and hereafter].

13And those upon the rock [are the people] who, when they hear [the Word], receive and welcome it with joy; but these have no root. They believe for a while, and in time of trial and temptation fall away (withdraw and stand aloof).

14And as for what fell among the thorns, these are [the people] who hear, but as they go on their way they are choked and suffocated with the anxieties and cares and riches and pleasures of life, and their fruit does not ripen (come to maturity and perfection).

15But as for that [seed] in the good soil, these are [the people] who, hearing the Word, hold it fast in a just (bnoble, virtuous) and worthy heart, and steadily bring forth fruit with patience.

16No one after he has lighted a lamp covers it with a vessel or puts it under a [dining table] couch; but he puts it on a lampstand, that those who come in may see the light.

17For there is nothing hidden that shall not be disclosed, nor anything secret that shall not be known and come out into the open.

18Be careful therefore how you listen. For to him who has [spiritual knowledge] will more be given; and from him who does not have [spiritual knowledge], even what he thinks and cguesses and dsupposes that he has will be taken away.

19Then Jesus' mother and His brothers came along toward Him, but they could not get to Him because of the crowd.

20And it was told Him, Your mother and Your brothers are standing outside, desiring to have an interview with You.

21But He answered them, My mother and My brothers are those who listen to the Word of God and do it!

22One of those days He and His disciples got into a boat, and He said to them, Let us go across to the other side of the lake. So they put out to sea.

23But as they were sailing, He fell off to sleep. And a ewhirlwind revolving from below upwards swept down on the lake, and the boat was filling with water, and they were in great danger.

24And the disciples came and woke Him, saying, Master, Master, we are perishing! And He, being thoroughly awakened, fcensured and erebuked the wind and the raging waves; and they ceased, and there came a calm.

25And He said to them, [Why are you so fearful?] Where is your faith (your trust, your confidence in Me—in My veracity and My integrity)? And they were seized with alarm and profound and reverent dread, and they marveled, saying to one another, Who then is this, that He commands even wind and sea, and they obey Him?

26Then they came to the country of the Gerasenes, which is opposite Galilee.

27Now when Jesus stepped out on land, there met Him a certain man out of the town who had [was possessed by] demons. For a long time he had worn no clothes, and he lived not in a house but in the tombs.

28And when he saw Jesus, he raised a deep (terrible) cry [from the depths of his throat] and fell down before Him

a Joseph Thayer, A Greek-English Lexicon. b Marvin Vincent, Word Studies. c John Wycliffe, The Wycliffe Bible. d William Tyndale, The Tyndale Bible. e J. H. Heinrich Schmidt, cited by Joseph Thayer, A Greek-English Lexicon. f James Moulton and George Milligan, The Vocabulary.

a 10 Isaiah 6:9    b 26 Some manuscripts Gadarenes; other manuscripts Gergesenes; also in verse 37

## New International Version

top of his voice, "What do you want with me, Jesus, Son of the Most High God? I beg you, don't torture me!" 29For Jesus had commanded the impure spirit to come out of the man. Many times it had seized him, and though he was chained hand and foot and kept under guard, he had broken his chains and had been driven by the demon into solitary places.

30Jesus asked him, "What is your name?"

"Legion," he replied, because many demons had gone into him. 31And they begged Jesus repeatedly not to order them to go into the Abyss.

32A large herd of pigs was feeding there on the hillside. The demons begged Jesus to let them go into the pigs, and he gave them permission. 33When the demons came out of the man, they went into the pigs, and the herd rushed down the steep bank into the lake and was drowned.

34When those tending the pigs saw what had happened, they ran off and reported this in the town and countryside, 35and the people went out to see what had happened. When they came to Jesus, they found the man from whom the demons had gone out, sitting at Jesus' feet, dressed and in his right mind; and they were afraid. 36Those who had seen it told the people how the demon-possessed man had been cured. 37Then all the people of the region of the Gerasenes asked Jesus to leave them, because they were overcome with fear. So he got into the boat and left.

38The man from whom the demons had gone out begged to go with him, but Jesus sent him away, saying, 39"Return home and tell how much God has done for you." So the man went away and told all over town how much Jesus had done for him.

### Jesus Raises a Dead Girl and Heals a Sick Woman

40Now when Jesus returned, a crowd welcomed him, for they were all expecting him. 41Then a man named Jairus, a synagogue leader, came and fell at Jesus' feet, pleading with him to come to his house 42because his only daughter, a girl of about twelve, was dying.

As Jesus was on his way, the crowds almost crushed him. 43And a woman was there who had been subject to bleeding for twelve years,a but no one could heal her. 44She came up behind him and touched the edge of his cloak, and immediately her bleeding stopped.

45"Who touched me?" Jesus asked.

When they all denied it, Peter said, "Master, the people are crowding and pressing against you."

46But Jesus said, "Someone touched me; I know that power has gone out from me."

47Then the woman, seeing that she could not go unnoticed, came trembling and fell at his feet. In the presence of all the people, she told why she had touched him and how she had been instantly healed. 48Then he said to her, "Daughter, your faith has healed you. Go in peace."

## Amplified Bible

[in terror] and shouted loudly, What have You [to do] with me, Jesus, Son of the Most High God? [aWhat have we in common?] I beg You, do not torment me!

29For Jesus was already commanding the unclean spirit to come out of the man. For many times it had snatched and held him; he was kept under guard and bound with chains and fetters, but he would break the bonds and be driven by the demon into the wilderness (desert).

30Jesus then asked him, What is your name? And he answered, Legion; for many demons had entered him.

31And they begged [Jesus] not to command them to depart into the Abyss (bottomless pit). [Rev. 9:1.]

32Now a great herd of swine was there feeding on the hillside; and [the demons] begged Him to give them leave to enter these. And He allowed them [to do so].

33Then the demons came out of the man and entered into the swine, and the herd rushed down the steep cliff into the lake and were drowned.

34When the herdsmen saw what had happened, they ran away and told it in the town and in the country.

35And [people] went out to see what had occurred, and they came to Jesus and found the man from whom the demons had gone out, sitting at the feet of Jesus, clothed and in his right (sound) mind; and they were seized with alarm and fear.

36And those [also] who had seen it told them how he who had been possessed with demons was restored [to health].

37Then all the people of the country surrounding the Gerasenes' district asked [Jesus] to depart from them, for they were possessed and suffering with dread and terror; so He entered a boat and returned [to the west side of the Sea of Galilee].

38But the man from whom the demons had gone out kept begging and bpraying that he might accompany Him and be with Him, but [Jesus] sent him away, saying,

39Return to your home, and recount [the story] of how many and great things God has done for you. And [the man] departed, proclaiming throughout the whole city how much Jesus had done for him.

40Now when Jesus came back [to Galilee], the crowd received and welcomed Him gladly, for they were all waiting and looking for Him.

41And there came a man named Jairus, who had [for a clong time] been a director of the synagogue; and falling at the feet of Jesus, he begged Him to come to his house,

42For he had an only daughter, about twelve years of age, and she was dying. As [Jesus] went, the people pressed together around Him [almost suffocating Him].

43And a woman who had suffered from a flow of blood for twelve years dand had spent all her living upon physicians, and could not be healed by anyone,

44Came up behind Him and touched the fringe of His garment, and immediately her flow of blood ceased.

45And Jesus said, Who is it who touched Me? When all were denying it, Peter eand those who were with him said, Master, the multitudes surround You and press You on every side!

46But Jesus said, Someone did touch Me; for I perceived that [healing] power has gone forth from Me.

47And when the woman saw that she had not escaped notice, she came up trembling, and, falling down before Him, she declared in the presence of all the people for what reason she had touched Him and how she had been instantly cured.

48And He said to her, Daughter, your faith (your confidence and trust in Me) has made you well! Go (enter) finto peace (guntroubled, undisturbed well-being).

a John Wycliffe, The Wycliffe Bible. b Marvin Vincent, Word Studies. c Charles B. Williams, The New Testament: A Translation: "The Greek imperfect tense expresses this idea of duration." d Many manuscripts add this phrase. e Some manuscripts add this phrase. f Richard Trench, Synonyms of the New Testament. g Hermann Cremer, Biblico-Theological Lexicon.

a 43 Many manuscripts years, and she had spent all she had on doctors

## New International Version

49While Jesus was still speaking, someone came from the house of Jairus, the synagogue leader. "Your daughter is dead," he said. "Don't bother the teacher anymore."

50Hearing this, Jesus said to Jairus, "Don't be afraid; just believe, and she will be healed."

51When he arrived at the house of Jairus, he did not let anyone go in with him except Peter, John and James, and the child's father and mother. 52Meanwhile, all the people were wailing and mourning for her. "Stop wailing," Jesus said. "She is not dead but asleep."

53They laughed at him, knowing that she was dead. 54But he took her by the hand and said, "My child, get up!" 55Her spirit returned, and at once she stood up. Then Jesus told them to give her something to eat. 56Her parents were astonished, but he ordered them not to tell anyone what had happened.

### Jesus Sends Out the Twelve

**9** When Jesus had called the Twelve together, he gave them power and authority to drive out all demons and to cure diseases, 2and he sent them out to proclaim the kingdom of God and to heal the sick. 3He told them: "Take nothing for the journey—no staff, no bag, no bread, no money, no extra shirt. 4Whatever house you enter, stay there until you leave that town. 5If people do not welcome you, leave their town and shake the dust off your feet as a testimony against them." 6So they set out and went from village to village, proclaiming the good news and healing people everywhere.

7Now Herod the tetrarch heard about all that was going on. And he was perplexed because some were saying that John had been raised from the dead, 8others that Elijah had appeared, and still others that one of the prophets of long ago had come back to life. 9But Herod said, "I beheaded John. Who, then, is this I hear such things about?" And he tried to see him.

### Jesus Feeds the Five Thousand

10When the apostles returned, they reported to Jesus what they had done. Then he took them with him and they withdrew by themselves to a town called Bethsaida, 11but the crowds learned about it and followed him. He welcomed them and spoke to them about the kingdom of God, and healed those who needed healing.

12Late in the afternoon the Twelve came to him and said, "Send the crowd away so they can go to the surrounding villages and countryside and find food and lodging, because we are in a remote place here."

13He replied, "You give them something to eat."

They answered, "We have only five loaves of bread and two fish—unless we go and buy food for all this crowd." 14(About five thousand men were there.)

But he said to his disciples, "Have them sit down in

## Amplified Bible

49While He was still speaking, a man from the house of the director of the synagogue came and said [to Jairus], Your daughter is dead; do not ªweary *and* trouble the Teacher any further.

50But Jesus, on hearing this, answered him, Do not be seized with alarm *or* struck with fear; simply believe [ᵇin Me as able to do this], and she shall be made well.

51And when He came to the house, He permitted no one to enter with Him except Peter and John and James, and the girl's father and mother.

52And all were weeping for and bewailing her; but He said, Do not weep, for she is not dead but sleeping.

53And they laughed Him to scorn, knowing full well that she was dead.

54And grasping her hand, He called, saying, Child, arise [ᵇfrom the sleep of death]!

55And her spirit returned [ᶜfrom death], and she arose immediately; and He directed that she should be given something to eat.

56And her parents were amazed, but He charged them to tell no one what had occurred.

**9** Then Jesus called together the Twelve [apostles] and gave them power and authority over all demons, and to cure diseases,

2And He sent them out to announce *and* preach the kingdom of God and to bring healing.

3And He said to them, Do not take anything for your journey—neither walking stick, nor ᵈwallet [for a collection bag], nor food of any kind, nor money, and do not have two undergarments (tunics).

4And whatever house you enter, stay there until you go away [from that place].

5And wherever they do not receive *and* accept *and* welcome you, when you leave that town shake off [even] the dust from your feet, as a testimony against them.

6And departing, they went about from village to village, preaching the Gospel and restoring the afflicted to health everywhere.

7Now Herod the tetrarch heard of all that was being done by [Jesus], and he was [thoroughly] perplexed *and* troubled, because it was said by some that John [the Baptist] had been raised from the dead,

8And by others that Elijah had appeared, and by others that one of the prophets of old had come back to life.

9But Herod said, John I beheaded; but Who is this about Whom I [learn] such things by hearsay? And he sought to see Him.

10Upon their return, the apostles reported to Jesus all that they had done. And He took them [along with Him] and withdrew into privacy near a town called Bethsaida.

11But when the crowds learned of it, [they] followed Him; and He welcomed them and talked to them about the kingdom of God, and healed those who needed restoration to health.

12Now the day began to decline, and the Twelve came and said to Him, Dismiss the crowds *and* send them away, so that they may go to the neighboring hamlets *and* villages and the surrounding country and find lodging and get a ᵉsupply of provisions, for we are here in an uninhabited (barren, solitary) place.

13But He said to them, You [yourselves] give them [food] to eat. They said, We have no more than five loaves and two fish—unless we are to go and buy food for all this crowd, [II Kings 4:42-44.]

14For there were about 5,000 men. And [Jesus] said to His disciples, Have them [sit down] reclining in table groups (companies) of about fifty each.

ª Richard Trench, *Synonyms of the New Testament.* ᵇ Joseph Thayer, *A Greek-English Lexicon.* ᶜ Hermann Cremer, *Biblico-Theological Lexicon.* ᵈ James Moulton and George Milligan, *The Vocabulary.* ᵉ Marvin Vincent, *Word Studies.*

## New International Version

groups of about fifty each." 15The disciples did so, and everyone sat down. 16Taking the five loaves and the two fish and looking up to heaven, he gave thanks and broke them. Then he gave them to the disciples to distribute to the people. 17They all ate and were satisfied, and the disciples picked up twelve basketfuls of broken pieces that were left over.

### Peter Declares That Jesus Is the Messiah

18Once when Jesus was praying in private and his disciples were with him, he asked them, "Who do the crowds say I am?"

19They replied, "Some say John the Baptist; others say Elijah; and still others, that one of the prophets of long ago has come back to life."

20"But what about you?" he asked. "Who do you say I am?"

Peter answered, "God's Messiah."

### Jesus Predicts His Death

21Jesus strictly warned them not to tell this to anyone. 22And he said, "The Son of Man must suffer many things and be rejected by the elders, the chief priests and the teachers of the law, and he must be killed and on the third day raised to life."

23Then he said to them all: "Whoever wants to be my disciple must deny themselves and take up their cross daily and follow me. 24For whoever wants to save their life will lose it, but whoever loses their life for me will save it. 25What good is it for someone to gain the whole world, and yet lose or forfeit their very self? 26Whoever is ashamed of me and my words, the Son of Man will be ashamed of them when he comes in his glory and in the glory of the Father and of the holy angels.

27"Truly I tell you, some who are standing here will not taste death before they see the kingdom of God."

### The Transfiguration

28About eight days after Jesus said this, he took Peter, John and James with him and went up onto a mountain to pray. 29As he was praying, the appearance of his face changed, and his clothes became as bright as a flash of lightning. 30Two men, Moses and Elijah, appeared in glorious splendor, talking with Jesus. 31They spoke about his departure,[a] which he was about to bring to fulfillment at Jerusalem. 32Peter and his companions were very sleepy, but when they became fully awake, they saw his glory and the two men standing with him. 33As the men were leaving Jesus, Peter said to him, "Master, it is good for us to be here. Let us put up three shelters—one for you, one for Moses and one for Elijah." (He did not know what he was saying.)

34While he was speaking, a cloud appeared and covered them, and they were afraid as they entered the cloud. 35A voice came from the cloud, saying, "This is my Son, whom I have chosen; listen to him." 36When the voice had spo-

## Amplified Bible

15And they did so, and made them all recline.

16And taking the five loaves and the two fish, He looked up to heaven and [praising God] gave thanks and asked Him to bless them [to their use]. Then He broke them and gave them to the disciples to place before the multitude.

17And all the people ate and were satisfied. And they gathered up what remained over—twelve [a small hand] baskets of broken pieces.

18Now it occurred that as Jesus was praying privately, the disciples were with Him, and He asked them, Who do men say that I am?

19And they answered, John the Baptist; but some say, Elijah; and others, that one of the ancient prophets has come back to life.

20And He said to them, But who do you [yourselves] say that I am? And Peter replied, The Christ of God!

21But He strictly charged and sharply commanded them [under penalty] to tell this to no one [no one, b whoever he might be],

22Saying, The Son of Man must suffer many things and be [b deliberately] disapproved and repudiated and rejected on the part of the elders and chief priests and scribes, and be put to death and on the third day be raised [again].

23And He said to all, If any person wills to come after Me, let him deny himself [c disown himself, d forget, lose sight of himself and his own interests, e refuse and give up himself] and take up his cross daily and follow Me [d cleave steadfastly to Me, conform wholly to My example in living and, if need be, in dying also].

24For whoever would preserve his life and save it will lose and destroy it, but whoever loses his life for My sake, he will preserve and save it [e from the penalty of eternal death].

25For what does it profit a man, if he gains the whole world and ruins or forfeits (loses) himself?

26Because whoever is ashamed of Me and of My teachings, of him will the Son of Man be ashamed when He comes in the [b threefold] glory (the splendor and majesty) of Himself and of the Father and of the holy angels.

27However I tell you truly, there are some of those standing here who will not taste death before they see the kingdom of God.

28Now about eight days after these teachings, Jesus took with Him Peter and John and James and went up on the mountain to pray.

29And as He was praying, the appearance of His countenance became altered (different), and His raiment became dazzling white [b flashing with the brilliance of lightning].

30And behold, two men were conversing with Him—Moses and Elijah,

31Who appeared in splendor and majesty and brightness and were speaking of His exit [from life], which He was about to bring to realization at Jerusalem.

32Now Peter and those with him were weighed down with sleep, but when they fully awoke, they saw His glory (splendor and majesty and brightness) and the two men who stood with Him.

33And it occurred as the men were parting from Him that Peter said to Jesus, Master, it is delightful and good that we are here; and let us construct three booths or huts—one for You and one for Moses and one for Elijah! not noticing or knowing what he was saying.

34But even as he was saying this, a cloud came and began to overshadow them, and they were seized with alarm and struck with fear as they entered into the cloud.

35Then there came a voice out of the cloud, saying, This is My Son, My Chosen One or f My Beloved; listen to and yield to and obey Him!

---

a Marvin Vincent, Word Studies. See also footnote on Matt. 14:20.
b Marvin Vincent, Word Studies. c James Moulton and George Milligan, The Vocabulary. d Joseph Thayer, A Greek-English Lexicon. e Hermann Cremer, Biblico-Theological Lexicon. f Many ancient manuscripts so read.

---

## New International Version

ken, they found that Jesus was alone. The disciples kept this to themselves and did not tell anyone at that time what they had seen.

### Jesus Heals a Demon-Possessed Boy

³⁷The next day, when they came down from the mountain, a large crowd met him. ³⁸A man in the crowd called out, "Teacher, I beg you to look at my son, for he is my only child. ³⁹A spirit seizes him and he suddenly screams; it throws him into convulsions so that he foams at the mouth. It scarcely ever leaves him and is destroying him. ⁴⁰I begged your disciples to drive it out, but they could not."

⁴¹"You unbelieving and perverse generation," Jesus replied, "how long shall I stay with you and put up with you? Bring your son here."

⁴²Even while the boy was coming, the demon threw him to the ground in a convulsion. But Jesus rebuked the impure spirit, healed the boy and gave him back to his father. ⁴³And they were all amazed at the greatness of God.

### Jesus Predicts His Death a Second Time

While everyone was marveling at all that Jesus did, he said to his disciples, ⁴⁴"Listen carefully to what I am about to tell you: The Son of Man is going to be delivered into the hands of men." ⁴⁵But they did not understand what this meant. It was hidden from them, so that they did not grasp it, and they were afraid to ask him about it.

⁴⁶An argument started among the disciples as to which of them would be the greatest. ⁴⁷Jesus, knowing their thoughts, took a little child and had him stand beside him. ⁴⁸Then he said to them, "Whoever welcomes this little child in my name welcomes me; and whoever welcomes me welcomes the one who sent me. For it is the one who is least among you all who is the greatest."

⁴⁹"Master," said John, "we saw someone driving out demons in your name and we tried to stop him, because he is not one of us."

⁵⁰"Do not stop him," Jesus said, "for whoever is not against you is for you."

### Samaritan Opposition

⁵¹As the time approached for him to be taken up to heaven, Jesus resolutely set out for Jerusalem. ⁵²And he sent messengers on ahead, who went into a Samaritan village to get things ready for him; ⁵³but the people there did not welcome him, because he was heading for Jerusalem. ⁵⁴When the disciples James and John saw this, they asked, "Lord, do you want us to call fire down from heaven to destroy themᵃ?" ⁵⁵But Jesus turned and rebuked them. ⁵⁶Then he and his disciples went to another village.

### The Cost of Following Jesus

⁵⁷As they were walking along the road, a man said to him, "I will follow you wherever you go."

## Amplified Bible

³⁶And when the voice had died away, Jesus was found there alone. And they kept still, and told no one at that time any of these things that they had seen.

³⁷Now it occurred the next day, when they had come down from the mountain, that a great multitude met Him.

³⁸And behold, a man from the crowd shouted out, Master, I implore You to look at my son, for he is my only child.

³⁹And behold, a spirit seizes him and suddenly he cries out; it convulses him so that he foams at the mouth; and he is sorely shattered, and it will scarcely leave him.

⁴⁰And I implored Your disciples to drive it out, but they could not.

⁴¹Jesus answered, O [faithless ones] unbelieving *and* without trust in God, a perverse (ᵃwayward, ᵇcrooked and ᶜwarped) generation! Until when *and* how long am I to be with you and bear with you? Bring your son here [to Me].

⁴²And even while he was coming, the demon threw him down and [completely] convulsed him. But Jesus censured *and* severely rebuked the unclean spirit and healed the child and restored him to his father.

⁴³And all were astounded at the evidence of God's mighty power *and* His majesty *and* magnificence. But [while] they were all marveling at everything Jesus was doing, He said to His disciples,

⁴⁴Let these words sink into your ears: the Son of Man is about to be delivered into the hands of men [ᵈwhose conduct is opposed to God].

⁴⁵However, they did not comprehend this saying; and it was kept hidden from them, so that they should not grasp it *and* understand, and they were afraid to ask Him about the statement.

⁴⁶But a controversy arose among them as to which of them might be the greatest [surpassing the others in excellence, worth, and authority].

⁴⁷But Jesus, as He perceived the thoughts of their hearts, took a little child and put him at His side

⁴⁸And told them, Whoever receives *and* accepts *and* welcomes this child in My name *and* for My sake receives *and* accepts *and* welcomes Me; and whoever so receives Me so also receives Him Who sent Me. For he who is least *and* lowliest among you all—he is [the one who is truly] great.

⁴⁹John said, Master, we saw a man driving out demons in Your name and we commanded him to stop it, for he does not follow along with us.

⁵⁰But Jesus told him, Do not forbid [such people]; for whoever is not against you is for you.

⁵¹Now when the time was almost come for Jesus to be received up [to heaven], He steadfastly *and* determinedly set His face to go to Jerusalem.

⁵²And He sent messengers before Him; and they reached and entered a Samaritan village to make [things] ready for Him;

⁵³But [the people] would not welcome *or* receive *or* accept Him, because His face was [set as if He was] going to Jerusalem.

⁵⁴And when His disciples James and John observed this, they said, Lord, do You wish us to command fire to come down from heaven and consume them, ᵉ*even as Elijah did*? [II Kings 1:9-16.]

⁵⁵But He turned and rebuked *and* severely censured them. ᶠ*He said, You do not know of what sort of spirit you are,*

⁵⁶*For the Son of Man did not come to destroy men's lives, but to save them* ᵈ*[from the penalty of eternal death].* And they journeyed on to another village.

⁵⁷And it occurred that as they were going along the road, a man said to Him, *Lord,* I will follow You wherever You go.

ᵃ John Wycliffe, *The Wycliffe Bible.* ᵇ William Tyndale, *The Tyndale Bible.* ᶜ Marvin Vincent, *Word Studies.* ᵈ Hermann Cremer, *Biblico-Theological Lexicon.* ᵉ Some manuscripts add this phrase. ᶠ Some manuscripts add this to verse 55 and continue into verse 56.

---

ᵃ 54 Some manuscripts *them, just as Elijah did*

## New International Version

58Jesus replied, "Foxes have dens and birds have nests, but the Son of Man has no place to lay his head."

59He said to another man, "Follow me."

But he replied, "Lord, first let me go and bury my father."

60Jesus said to him, "Let the dead bury their own dead, but you go and proclaim the kingdom of God."

61Still another said, "I will follow you, Lord; but first let me go back and say goodbye to my family."

62Jesus replied, "No one who puts a hand to the plow and looks back is fit for service in the kingdom of God."

### Jesus Sends Out the Seventy-Two

**10** After this the Lord appointed seventy-two[a] others and sent them two by two ahead of him to every town and place where he was about to go. 2He told them, "The harvest is plentiful, but the workers are few. Ask the Lord of the harvest, therefore, to send out workers into his harvest field. 3Go! I am sending you out like lambs among wolves. 4Do not take a purse or bag or sandals; and do not greet anyone on the road.

5"When you enter a house, first say, 'Peace to this house.' 6If someone who promotes peace is there, your peace will rest on them; if not, it will return to you. 7Stay there, eating and drinking whatever they give you, for the worker deserves his wages. Do not move around from house to house.

8"When you enter a town and are welcomed, eat what is offered to you. 9Heal the sick who are there and tell them, 'The kingdom of God has come near to you.' 10But when you enter a town and are not welcomed, go into its streets and say, 11'Even the dust of your town we wipe from our feet as a warning to you. Yet be sure of this: The kingdom of God has come near.' 12I tell you, it will be more bearable on that day for Sodom than for that town.

13"Woe to you, Chorazin! Woe to you, Bethsaida! For if the miracles that were performed in you had been performed in Tyre and Sidon, they would have repented long ago, sitting in sackcloth and ashes. 14But it will be more bearable for Tyre and Sidon at the judgment than for you. 15And you, Capernaum, will you be lifted to the heavens? No, you will go down to Hades.[b]

16"Whoever listens to you listens to me; whoever rejects you rejects me; but whoever rejects me rejects him who sent me."

17The seventy-two returned with joy and said, "Lord, even the demons submit to us in your name."

18He replied, "I saw Satan fall like lightning from heaven. 19I have given you authority to trample on snakes and

## Amplified Bible

58And Jesus told him, Foxes have lurking holes and the birds of the air have roosts *and* nests, but the Son of Man has no place to lay His head.

59And He said to another, *a*Become My disciple, side with My party, and accompany Me! But he replied, *Lord,* permit me first to go and bury (*b*await the death of) my father.

60But Jesus said to him, Allow the dead to bury their own dead; but as for you, go *and* publish abroad *c*throughout all regions of the kingdom of God.

61Another also said, I will follow You, Lord, *and* become Your disciple *and* side with Your party; but let me first say good-bye to those at my home.

62Jesus said to him, No one who puts his hand to the plow and looks back [to the things behind] is fit for the kingdom of God.

**10** Now after this the Lord chose *and* appointed seventy others and sent them out ahead of Him, two by two, into every town and place where He Himself was about to come (visit).

2And He said to them, The harvest indeed is abundant [*d*there is much ripe grain], but the farmhands are few. Pray therefore the Lord of the harvest to send out laborers into His harvest.

3Go your way; behold, I send you out like lambs into the midst of wolves.

4Carry no purse, no provisions bag, no [change of] sandals; refrain from [retarding your journey by] saluting *and* wishing anyone well along the way.

5Whatever house you enter, first say, Peace be to this household! [*e*Freedom from all the distresses that result from sin be with this family].

6And if anyone [worthy] of peace *and* blessedness is there, the peace *and* blessedness you wish shall come upon him; but if not, it shall come back to you.

7And stay on in the same house, eating and drinking what they provide, for the laborer is worthy of his wages. Do not keep moving from house to house. [Deut. 24:15.]

8Whenever you go into a town and they receive *and* accept *and* welcome you, eat what is set before you;

9And heal the sick in it and say to them, The kingdom of God has come close to you.

10But whenever you go into a town and they do not receive *and* accept *and* welcome you, go out into its streets and say,

11Even the dust of your town that clings to our feet we are wiping off against you; yet know *and* understand this: the kingdom of God has come near *you.*

12I tell you, it shall be more tolerable in that day for Sodom than for that town. [Gen. 19:24-28.]

13Woe to you, Chorazin! Woe to you, Bethsaida! For if the mighty miracles performed in you had been performed in Tyre and Sidon, they would have repented long ago, sitting in sackcloth and ashes.

14However, it shall be more tolerable in the judgment for Tyre and Sidon than for you.

15And you, Capernaum, will you be exalted unto heaven? You shall be brought down to Hades (the regions of the dead).

16He who hears *and* heeds you [disciples] hears *and* heeds Me; and he who slights *and* rejects you slights *and* rejects Me; and he who slights *and* rejects Me slights *and* rejects Him who sent Me.

17The seventy returned with joy, saying, Lord, even the demons are subject to us in Your name!

18And He said to them, I saw Satan falling like a lightning [flash] from heaven.

19Behold! I have given you authority *and* power to tram-

---

## New International Version

scorpions and to overcome all the power of the enemy; nothing will harm you. [20]However, do not rejoice that the spirits submit to you, but rejoice that your names are written in heaven."

[21]At that time Jesus, full of joy through the Holy Spirit, said, "I praise you, Father, Lord of heaven and earth, because you have hidden these things from the wise and learned, and revealed them to little children. Yes, Father, for this is what you were pleased to do.

[22]"All things have been committed to me by my Father. No one knows who the Son is except the Father, and no one knows who the Father is except the Son and those to whom the Son chooses to reveal him."

[23]Then he turned to his disciples and said privately, "Blessed are the eyes that see what you see. [24]For I tell you that many prophets and kings wanted to see what you see but did not see it, and to hear what you hear but did not hear it."

### The Parable of the Good Samaritan

[25]On one occasion an expert in the law stood up to test Jesus. "Teacher," he asked, "what must I do to inherit eternal life?"

[26]"What is written in the Law?" he replied. "How do you read it?"

[27]He answered, "'Love the Lord your God with all your heart and with all your soul and with all your strength and with all your mind'[a]; and, 'Love your neighbor as yourself.'[b]"

[28]"You have answered correctly," Jesus replied. "Do this and you will live."

[29]But he wanted to justify himself, so he asked Jesus, "And who is my neighbor?"

[30]In reply Jesus said: "A man was going down from Jerusalem to Jericho, when he was attacked by robbers. They stripped him of his clothes, beat him and went away, leaving him half dead. [31]A priest happened to be going down the same road, and when he saw the man, he passed by on the other side. [32]So too, a Levite, when he came to the place and saw him, passed by on the other side. [33]But a Samaritan, as he traveled, came where the man was; and when he saw him, he took pity on him. [34]He went to him and bandaged his wounds, pouring on oil and wine. Then he put the man on his own donkey, brought him to an inn and took care of him. [35]The next day he took out two denarii[c] and gave them to the innkeeper. 'Look after him,' he said, 'and when I return, I will reimburse you for any extra expense you may have.'

[36]"Which of these three do you think was a neighbor to the man who fell into the hands of robbers?"

[37]The expert in the law replied, "The one who had mercy on him."

Jesus told him, "Go and do likewise."

### At the Home of Martha and Mary

[38]As Jesus and his disciples were on their way, he came to a village where a woman named Martha opened her home to him. [39]She had a sister called Mary, who sat at the Lord's feet listening to what he said. [40]But Martha was distracted by all the preparations that had to be made. She came to him and asked, "Lord, don't you care that my

## Amplified Bible

ple upon serpents and scorpions, and [physical and mental strength and ability] over all the power that the enemy [possesses]; and nothing shall in any way harm you.

[20]Nevertheless, do not rejoice at this, that the spirits are subject to you, but rejoice that your names are enrolled in heaven. [Exod. 32:32; Ps. 69:28; Dan. 12:1.]

[21]In that same hour He rejoiced *and* gloried in the Holy Spirit and said, I thank You, Father, Lord of heaven and earth, that You have concealed these things [relating to salvation] from the wise and understanding *and* learned, and revealed them to babes (the childish, unskilled, and untaught). Yes, Father, for such was Your gracious *a*will *and* choice *and* good pleasure.

[22]All things have been given over into My power by My Father; and no one knows Who the Son is except the Father, or Who the Father is except the Son and anyone to whom the Son may choose to reveal *and* make Him known.

[23]Then turning to His disciples, He said privately, Blessed (happy, *b*to be envied) are those whose eyes see what you see!

[24]For I tell you that many prophets and kings longed to see what you see and they did not see it, and to hear what you hear and they did not hear it.

[25]And then a certain lawyer arose to try (test, tempt) Him, saying, Teacher, what am I to do to inherit everlasting life [that is, to partake of eternal salvation in the Messiah's kingdom]?

[26]Jesus said to him, What is written in the Law? How do you read it?

[27]And he replied, You must love the Lord your God with all your heart and with all your soul and with all your strength and with all your mind; and your neighbor as yourself. [Lev. 19:18; Deut. 6:5.]

[28]And Jesus said to him, You have answered correctly; do this, and you will live [enjoy active, blessed, endless life in the kingdom of God].

[29]And he, *c*determined to acquit himself of reproach, said to Jesus, And who is my neighbor?

[30]Jesus, *c*taking him up, replied, A certain man was going from Jerusalem down to Jericho, and he fell among robbers, who stripped him of his clothes and belongings and beat him and went their way, [*c*unconcernedly] leaving him half dead, as it happened.

[31]Now by *c*coincidence a certain priest was going down along that road, and when he saw him, he passed by on the other side.

[32]A Levite likewise came down to the place and saw him, and passed by on the other side [of the road].

[33]But a certain Samaritan, as he traveled along, came down to where he was; and when he saw him, he was moved with pity *and* sympathy [for him],

[34]And went to him and dressed his wounds, pouring on [them] oil and wine. Then he set him on his own beast and brought him to an inn and took care of him.

[35]And the next day he took out two denarii [two day's wages] and gave [them] to the innkeeper, saying, Take care of him; and whatever more you spend, I [myself] will repay you when I return.

[36]Which of these three do you think proved himself a neighbor to him who fell among the robbers?

[37]He answered, The one who showed pity *and* mercy to him. And Jesus said to him, Go and do likewise.

[38]Now while they were on their way, it occurred that Jesus entered a certain village, and a woman named Martha received *and* welcomed Him into her house.

[39]And she had a sister named Mary, who seated herself at the Lord's feet and was listening to His teaching.

[40]But Martha [overly occupied and too busy] was distracted with much serving; and she came up to Him and said, Lord, is it nothing to You that my sister has left me to

*a 27* Deut. 6:5   *b 27* Lev. 19:18   *c 35* A denarius was the usual daily wage of a day laborer (see Matt. 20:2).

*a* Joseph Thayer, *A Greek-English Lexicon.*   *b* Alexander Souter, *Pocket Lexicon.*   *c* Marvin Vincent, *Word Studies.*

## New International Version

sister has left me to do the work by myself? Tell her to help me!"

<sup>41</sup>"Martha, Martha," the Lord answered, "you are worried and upset about many things, <sup>42</sup>but few things are needed—or indeed only one.<sup>a</sup> Mary has chosen what is better, and it will not be taken away from her."

### Jesus' Teaching on Prayer

**11** One day Jesus was praying in a certain place. When he finished, one of his disciples said to him, "Lord, teach us to pray, just as John taught his disciples."

<sup>2</sup>He said to them, "When you pray, say:

"'Father,<sup>b</sup>
hallowed be your name,
   your kingdom come.<sup>c</sup>
<sup>3</sup>Give us each day our daily bread.
<sup>4</sup>Forgive us our sins,
   for we also forgive everyone who sins against us.<sup>d</sup>
And lead us not into temptation.<sup>e</sup>'"

<sup>5</sup>Then Jesus said to them, "Suppose you have a friend, and you go to him at midnight and say, 'Friend, lend me three loaves of bread; <sup>6</sup>a friend of mine on a journey has come to me, and I have no food to offer him.' <sup>7</sup>And suppose the one inside answers, 'Don't bother me. The door is already locked, and my children and I are in bed. I can't get up and give you anything.' <sup>8</sup>I tell you, even though he will not get up and give you the bread because of friendship, yet because of your shameless audacity<sup>f</sup> he will surely get up and give you as much as you need.

<sup>9</sup>"So I say to you: Ask and it will be given to you; seek and you will find; knock and the door will be opened to you. <sup>10</sup>For everyone who asks receives; the one who seeks finds; and to the one who knocks, the door will be opened.

<sup>11</sup>"Which of you fathers, if your son asks for<sup>g</sup> a fish, will give him a snake instead? <sup>12</sup>Or if he asks for an egg, will give him a scorpion? <sup>13</sup>If you then, though you are evil, know how to give good gifts to your children, how much more will your Father in heaven give the Holy Spirit to those who ask him!"

### Jesus and Beelzebul

<sup>14</sup>Jesus was driving out a demon that was mute. When the demon left, the man who had been mute spoke, and the crowd was amazed. <sup>15</sup>But some of them said, "By Beelzebul, the prince of demons, he is driving out demons." <sup>16</sup>Others tested him by asking for a sign from heaven.

<sup>17</sup>Jesus knew their thoughts and said to them: "Any kingdom divided against itself will be ruined, and a house divided against itself will fall. <sup>18</sup>If Satan is divided against himself, how can his kingdom stand? I say this because you claim that I drive out demons by Beelzebul. <sup>19</sup>Now if I

## Amplified Bible

serve alone? Tell her then to help me [to lend a hand and do her part along with me]!

<sup>41</sup>But the Lord replied to her by saying, Martha, Martha, you are anxious and troubled about many things;

<sup>42</sup>There is need of only one *or but <sup>a</sup>a few things.* Mary has chosen the good portion [<sup>b</sup>that which is to her advantage], which shall not be taken away from her.

**11** Then he was praying in a certain place; and when He stopped, one of His disciples said to Him, Lord, teach us to pray, [just] as John taught his disciples.

<sup>2</sup>And He said to them, When you pray, say: *Our* Father *Who is in heaven,* hallowed be Your name, Your kingdom come. *Your will be done [held holy and revered] on earth as it is in heaven.*

<sup>3</sup>Give us daily our bread [<sup>c</sup>food for the morrow].

<sup>4</sup>And forgive us our sins, for we ourselves also forgive everyone who is indebted to us [who has offended us or done us wrong]. And bring us not into temptation *but rescue us from evil.*

<sup>5</sup>And He said to them, Which of you who has a friend will go to him at midnight and will say to him, Friend, lend me three loaves [of bread],

<sup>6</sup>For a friend of mine who is on a journey has just come, and I have nothing to put before him;

<sup>7</sup>And he from within will answer, Do not disturb me; the door is now closed, and my children are with me in bed; I cannot get up and supply you [with anything]?

<sup>8</sup>I tell you, although he will not get up and supply him anything because he is his friend, yet because of his shameless persistence *and* insistence he will get up and give him as much as he needs.

<sup>9</sup>So I say to you, Ask *and* <sup>d</sup>keep on asking and it shall be given you; seek *and* <sup>d</sup>keep on seeking and you shall find; knock *and* <sup>d</sup>keep on knocking and the door shall be opened to you.

<sup>10</sup>For everyone who asks *and* <sup>d</sup>keeps on asking receives; and he who seeks *and* <sup>d</sup>keeps on seeking finds; and to him who knocks *and* <sup>d</sup>keeps on knocking, the door shall be opened.

<sup>11</sup>What father among you, if his son asks for *<sup>e</sup>a loaf of bread, will give him a stone; or if he asks for* a fish, will instead of a fish give him a serpent?

<sup>12</sup>Or if he asks for an egg, will give him a scorpion?

<sup>13</sup>If you then, evil as you are, know how to give good gifts [gifts <sup>b</sup>that are to their advantage] to your children, how much more will your heavenly Father give the Holy Spirit to those who ask *and* <sup>d</sup>continue to ask Him!

<sup>14</sup>Now Jesus was driving out a demon that was dumb; and it occurred that when the demon had gone out, the dumb man spoke. And the crowds marveled.

<sup>15</sup>But some of them said, He drives out demons [because He is in league with and] by Beelzebub, the prince of demons,

<sup>16</sup>While others, to try *and* test *and* tempt Him, demanded a sign of Him from heaven.

<sup>17</sup>But He, [well] aware of their intent *and* purpose, said to them, Every kingdom split up against itself is doomed *and* brought to desolation, and so house falls upon house. [The disunited household will collapse.]

<sup>18</sup>And if Satan also is divided against himself, how will his kingdom last? For you say that I expel demons with the help of *and* by Beelzebub.

---

<sup>a</sup> 42 Some manuscripts *but only one thing is needed*    <sup>b</sup> 2 Some manuscripts *Our Father in heaven*    <sup>c</sup> 2 Some manuscripts *come. May your will be done on earth as it is in heaven.*    <sup>d</sup> 4 Greek *everyone who is indebted to us*    <sup>e</sup> 4 Some manuscripts *temptation, but deliver us from the evil one*    <sup>f</sup> 8 Or *yet to preserve his good name*    <sup>g</sup> 11 Some manuscripts *for bread, will give him a stone? Or if he asks for*

<sup>a</sup> Some ancient manuscripts read "a few things," while others read "only one," and still others read "a few and only one."    <sup>b</sup> Hermann Cremer, *Biblico-Theological Lexicon.*    <sup>c</sup> James Moulton and George Milligan, *The Vocabulary.*    <sup>d</sup> Charles B. Williams, *The New Testament: A Translation*: The idea of continuing or repeated action is often carried by the present imperative and present participles in Greek.    <sup>e</sup> Some manuscripts contain this portion within verse 11.

## New International Version

drive out demons by Beelzebul, by whom do your followers drive them out? So then, they will be your judges. ²⁰But if I drive out demons by the finger of God, then the kingdom of God has come upon you.

²¹"When a strong man, fully armed, guards his own house, his possessions are safe. ²²But when someone stronger attacks and overpowers him, he takes away the armor in which the man trusted and divides up his plunder.

²³"Whoever is not with me is against me, and whoever does not gather with me scatters.

²⁴"When an impure spirit comes out of a person, it goes through arid places seeking rest and does not find it. Then it says, 'I will return to the house I left.' ²⁵When it arrives, it finds the house swept clean and put in order. ²⁶Then it goes and takes seven other spirits more wicked than itself, and they go in and live there. And the final condition of that person is worse than the first."

²⁷As Jesus was saying these things, a woman in the crowd called out, "Blessed is the mother who gave you birth and nursed you."

²⁸He replied, "Blessed rather are those who hear the word of God and obey it."

### The Sign of Jonah

²⁹As the crowds increased, Jesus said, "This is a wicked generation. It asks for a sign, but none will be given it except the sign of Jonah. ³⁰For as Jonah was a sign to the Ninevites, so also will the Son of Man be to this generation. ³¹The Queen of the South will rise at the judgment with the people of this generation and condemn them, for she came from the ends of the earth to listen to Solomon's wisdom; and now something greater than Solomon is here. ³²The men of Nineveh will stand up at the judgment with this generation and condemn it, for they repented at the preaching of Jonah; and now something greater than Jonah is here.

### The Lamp of the Body

³³"No one lights a lamp and puts it in a place where it will be hidden, or under a bowl. Instead they put it on its stand, so that those who come in may see the light. ³⁴Your eye is the lamp of your body. When your eyes are healthy,ᵃ your whole body also is full of light. But when they are unhealthy,ᵇ your body also is full of darkness. ³⁵See to it, then, that the light within you is not darkness. ³⁶Therefore, if your whole body is full of light, and no part of it dark, it will be just as full of light as when a lamp shines its light on you."

### Woes on the Pharisees and the Experts in the Law

³⁷When Jesus had finished speaking, a Pharisee invited him to eat with him; so he went in and reclined at the table. ³⁸But the Pharisee was surprised when he noticed that Jesus did not first wash before the meal.

³⁹Then the Lord said to him, "Now then, you Pharisees clean the outside of the cup and dish, but inside you are full of greed and wickedness. ⁴⁰You foolish people! Did not

## Amplified Bible

¹⁹Now if I expel demons with the help of *and* by Beelzebub, with whose help *and* by whom do your sons drive them out? Therefore they shall be your judges.

²⁰But if I drive out the demons by the finger of God, then the kingdom of God has [already] come upon you.

²¹When the strong man, fully armed, [ᵃfrom his courtyard] guards his own dwelling, his belongings are undisturbed [his property is at peace and is secure].

²²But when one stronger than he attacks him and conquers him, he robs him of his whole armor on which he had relied and divides up *and* distributes all his goods as plunder (spoil).

²³He who is not with Me [siding and believing with Me] is against Me, and he who does not gather with Me [engage in My interest], scatters.

²⁴When the unclean spirit has gone out of a person, it roams through waterless places in search [of a place] of rest (release, refreshment, ease); and finding none it says, I will go back to my house from which I came.

²⁵And when it arrives, it finds [the place] swept *and* put in order and furnished *and* decorated.

²⁶And it goes and brings other spirits, seven [of them], more evil than itself, and they enter in, settle down, *and* dwell there; and the last state of that person is worse than the first.

²⁷Now it occurred that as He was saying these things, a certain woman in the crowd raised her voice and said to Him, Blessed (happy and ᵇto be envied) is the womb that bore You and the breasts that You sucked!

²⁸But He said, Blessed (happy and ᵇto be envied) rather are those who hear the Word of God and obey *and* practice it!

²⁹Now as the crowds were [increasingly] thronging Him, He began to say, This present generation is a wicked one; it seeks *and* demands a sign (miracle), but no sign shall be given to it except the sign of Jonah [the prophet]. [Jonah 1:17; Matt. 12:40.]

³⁰For [just] as Jonah became a sign to the people of Nineveh, so will also the Son of Man be [a sign] to this age *and* generation. [Jonah 3:4-10.]

³¹The queen of the South will arise in the judgment with the people of this age *and* generation and condemn them; for she came from the ends of the [inhabited] earth to listen to the wisdom of Solomon, and notice, ᶜhere is more than Solomon. [I Kings 10:1-13; II Chron. 9:1-12.]

³²The men of Nineveh will appear as witnesses at the judgment with this generation and will condemn it; for they repented at the preaching of Jonah, and behold, ᶜhere is more than Jonah. [Jonah 3:4-10.]

³³No one after lighting a lamp puts it in a cellar *or* crypt or under a bushel measure, but on a lampstand, that those who are coming in may see the light.

³⁴Your eye is the lamp of your body; when your eye (ᵈyour conscience) is sound *and* fulfilling its office, your whole body is full of light; but when it is not sound *and* is not fulfilling its office, your body is full of darkness.

³⁵Be careful, therefore, that the light that is in you is not darkness.

³⁶If then your entire body is illuminated, having no part dark, it will be wholly bright [with light], as when a lamp with its bright rays gives you light.

³⁷Now while Jesus was speaking, a Pharisee invited Him to take dinner with him, so He entered and reclined at table.

³⁸The Pharisee noticed and was astonished [to see] that Jesus did not first wash before dinner.

³⁹But the Lord said to him, Now you Pharisees cleanse the outside of the cup and of the plate, but inside you yourselves are full of greed *and* robbery *and* extortion and malice *and* wickedness.

---

ᵃ 34 The Greek for *healthy* here implies *generous*.   ᵇ 34 The Greek for *unhealthy* here implies *stingy*.

ᵃ Marvin Vincent, *Word Studies*.   ᵇ Alexander Souter, *Pocket Lexicon*.
ᶜ John Wycliffe, *The Wycliffe Bible*.   ᵈ Hermann Cremer, *Biblico-Theological Lexicon*.

## New International Version

the one who made the outside make the inside also? [41]But now as for what is inside you—be generous to the poor, and everything will be clean for you.

[42]"Woe to you Pharisees, because you give God a tenth of your mint, rue and all other kinds of garden herbs, but you neglect justice and the love of God. You should have practiced the latter without leaving the former undone.

[43]"Woe to you Pharisees, because you love the most important seats in the synagogues and respectful greetings in the marketplaces.

[44]"Woe to you, because you are like unmarked graves, which people walk over without knowing it."

[45]One of the experts in the law answered him, "Teacher, when you say these things, you insult us also."

[46]Jesus replied, "And you experts in the law, woe to you, because you load people down with burdens they can hardly carry, and you yourselves will not lift one finger to help them.

[47]"Woe to you, because you build tombs for the prophets, and it was your ancestors who killed them. [48]So you testify that you approve of what your ancestors did; they killed the prophets, and you build their tombs. [49]Because of this, God in his wisdom said, 'I will send them prophets and apostles, some of whom they will kill and others they will persecute.' [50]Therefore this generation will be held responsible for the blood of all the prophets that has been shed since the beginning of the world, [51]from the blood of Abel to the blood of Zechariah, who was killed between the altar and the sanctuary. Yes, I tell you, this generation will be held responsible for it all.

[52]"Woe to you experts in the law, because you have taken away the key to knowledge. You yourselves have not entered, and you have hindered those who were entering."

[53]When Jesus went outside, the Pharisees and the teachers of the law began to oppose him fiercely and to besiege him with questions, [54]waiting to catch him in something he might say.

### Warnings and Encouragements

**12** Meanwhile, when a crowd of many thousands had gathered, so that they were trampling on one another, Jesus began to speak first to his disciples, saying: "Be[a] on your guard against the yeast of the Pharisees, which is hypocrisy. [2]There is nothing concealed that will not be disclosed, or hidden that will not be made known. [3]What you have said in the dark will be heard in the daylight, and what you have whispered in the ear in the inner rooms will be proclaimed from the roofs.

[4]"I tell you, my friends, do not be afraid of those who kill the body and after that can do no more. [5]But I will show you whom you should fear: Fear him who, after your body has been killed, has authority to throw you into hell. Yes, I

## Amplified Bible

[40]You senseless (foolish, stupid) ones [acting without reflection or intelligence]! Did not He Who made the outside make the inside also?

[41]But [dedicate your inner self and] give as donations to the poor of those things which are within [of inward righteousness] and behold, everything is purified and clean for you.

[42]But woe to you, Pharisees! For you tithe mint and rue and every [little] herb, but disregard and neglect justice and the love of God. These you ought to have done without leaving the others undone. [Lev. 27:30; Mic. 6:8.]

[43]Woe to you, Pharisees! For you love the best seats in the synagogues and [you love] to be greeted and bowed down to in the [public] marketplaces.

[44]Woe to you! For you are like graves which are not marked or seen, and men walk over them without being aware of it [and are ceremonially defiled].

[45]One of the experts in the [Mosaic] Law answered Him, Teacher, in saying this, You reproach and outrage and affront even us!

[46]But He said, Woe to you, the lawyers, also! For you load men with oppressive burdens hard to bear, and you do not personally [even [a]gently] touch the burdens with one of your fingers.

[47]Woe to you! For you are [b]rebuilding and repairing the tombs of the prophets, whom your fathers killed (destroyed).

[48]So you bear witness and give your full approval and consent to the deeds of your fathers; for they actually killed them, and you rebuild and repair monuments to them.

[49]For this reason also the wisdom of God said, I will send them prophets and apostles, [some] of whom they will put to death and persecute,

[50]So that the blood of all the prophets shed from the foundation of the world may be charged against and required of this age and generation,

[51]From the blood of Abel to the blood of Zechariah, who was slain between the altar and the sanctuary. Yes, I tell you, it shall be charged against and required of this age and generation. [Gen. 4:8; II Chron. 24:20, 21; Zech. 1:1.]

[52]Woe to you, lawyers (experts in the Mosaic Law)! For you have taken away the key to knowledge; you did not go in yourselves, and you hindered and prevented those who were entering.

[53]As He left there, the scribes and the Pharisees [followed Him closely, and they] began [b]to be enraged with and set themselves violently against Him and to draw Him out and provoke Him to speak of many things,

[54]Secretly watching and plotting and lying in wait for Him, to seize upon something He might say [that they might accuse Him].

**12** In the meanwhile, when so many thousands of the people had gathered that they were trampling on one another, Jesus commenced by saying primarily to His disciples, Be on your guard against the leaven (ferment) of the Pharisees, which is hypocrisy [producing unrest and violent agitation].

[2]Nothing is [so closely] covered up that it will not be revealed, or hidden that it will not be known.

[3]Whatever you have spoken in the darkness shall be heard and listened to in the light, and what you have whispered in [people's] ears and behind closed doors will be proclaimed upon the housetops.

[4]I tell you, My friends, do not dread and be afraid of those who kill the body and after that have nothing more that they can do.

[5]But I will warn you whom you should fear: fear Him Who, after killing, has power to hurl into hell (Gehenna); yes, I say to you, fear Him!

---

[a] 1 Or *speak to his disciples, saying: "First of all, be*

[a] Marvin Vincent, *Word Studies.*  [b] Joseph Thayer, *A Greek-English Lexicon.*

## New International Version

tell you, fear him. [6]Are not five sparrows sold for two pennies? Yet not one of them is forgotten by God. [7]Indeed, the very hairs of your head are all numbered. Don't be afraid; you are worth more than many sparrows.

[8]"I tell you, whoever publicly acknowledges me before others, the Son of Man will also acknowledge before the angels of God. [9]But whoever disowns me before others will be disowned before the angels of God. [10]And everyone who speaks a word against the Son of Man will be forgiven, but anyone who blasphemes against the Holy Spirit will not be forgiven.

[11]"When you are brought before synagogues, rulers and authorities, do not worry about how you will defend yourselves or what you will say, [12]for the Holy Spirit will teach you at that time what you should say."

### The Parable of the Rich Fool

[13]Someone in the crowd said to him, "Teacher, tell my brother to divide the inheritance with me."

[14]Jesus replied, "Man, who appointed me a judge or an arbiter between you?" [15]Then he said to them, "Watch out! Be on your guard against all kinds of greed; life does not consist in an abundance of possessions."

[16]And he told them this parable: "The ground of a certain rich man yielded an abundant harvest. [17]He thought to himself, 'What shall I do? I have no place to store my crops.'

[18]"Then he said, 'This is what I'll do. I will tear down my barns and build bigger ones, and there I will store my surplus grain. [19]And I'll say to myself, "You have plenty of grain laid up for many years. Take life easy; eat, drink and be merry."'

[20]"But God said to him, 'You fool! This very night your life will be demanded from you. Then who will get what you have prepared for yourself?'

[21]"This is how it will be with whoever stores up things for themselves but is not rich toward God."

### Do Not Worry

[22]Then Jesus said to his disciples: "Therefore I tell you, do not worry about your life, what you will eat; or about your body, what you will wear. [23]For life is more than food, and the body more than clothes. [24]Consider the ravens: They do not sow or reap, they have no storeroom or barn; yet God feeds them. And how much more valuable you are than birds! [25]Who of you by worrying can add a single

## Amplified Bible

[6]Are not five sparrows sold for two pennies? And [yet] not one of them is forgotten or uncared for in the presence of God.

[7]But [even] the very hairs of your head are all numbered. Do not be struck with fear or seized with alarm; you are of greater worth than many [flocks] of sparrows.

[8]And I tell you, Whoever declares openly [speaking out freely] and confesses that he is My worshiper and acknowledges Me before men, the Son of Man also will declare and confess and acknowledge him before the angels of God.

[9]But he who disowns and denies and rejects and refuses to acknowledge Me before men will be disowned and denied and rejected and refused acknowledgement in the presence of the angels of God.

[10]And everyone who makes a statement or speaks a word against the Son of Man, it will be forgiven him; but he who blasphemes against the Holy Spirit [that is, whoever [a]intentionally comes short of the reverence due the Holy Spirit], it will not be forgiven him [for him there is no forgiveness].

[11]And when they bring you before the synagogues and the magistrates and the authorities, do not be anxious [beforehand] how you shall reply in defense or what you are to say.

[12]For the Holy Spirit will teach you in that very hour and [b]moment what [you] ought to say.

[13]Someone from the crowd said to Him, Master, order my brother to divide the inheritance and share it with me.

[14]But He told him, Man, who has appointed Me a judge or umpire and divider over you?

[15]And He said to them, Guard yourselves and keep free from all covetousness (the immoderate desire for wealth, the greedy longing to have more); for a man's life does not consist in and is not derived from possessing [c]overflowing abundance or that which is [d]over and above his needs.

[16]Then He told them a parable, saying, The land of a rich man was fertile and yielded plentifully.

[17]And he considered and debated within himself, What shall I do? I have no place [in which] to gather together my harvest.

[18]And he said, I will do this: I will pull down my storehouses and build larger ones, and there I will store all [e]my grain or produce and my goods.

[19]And I will say to my soul, Soul, you have many good things laid up, [enough] for many years. Take your ease; eat, drink, and enjoy yourself merrily.

[20]But God said to him, You fool! This very night [f]they [the messengers of God] will demand your soul of you; and all the things that you have prepared, whose will they be? [Job 27:8; Jer. 17:11.]

[21]So it is with the one who continues to lay up and hoard possessions for himself and is not rich [in his relation] to God [this is how he fares].

[22]And [Jesus] said to His disciples, Therefore I tell you, do not be anxious and troubled [with cares] about your life, as to what you will [have to] eat; or about your body, as to what you will [have to] wear.

[23]For life is more than food, and the body [more] than clothes.

[24]Observe and consider the ravens; for they neither sow nor reap, they have neither storehouse nor barn; and [yet] God feeds them. Of how much more worth are you than the birds!

[25]And which of you by being overly anxious and troubled with cares can add a [g]cubit to his stature or a moment [unit] of time to his [g]age [the length of his life]?

[a] Joseph Thayer, *A Greek-English Lexicon.* [b] James Moulton and George Milligan, *The Vocabulary.* [c] Alexander Souter, *Pocket Lexicon.* [d] G. Abbott-Smith, *Manual Greek Lexicon.* [e] Some ancient manuscripts read "grain;" some read "produce" or "fruits." [f] Marvin Vincent, *Word Studies*: "The indefiniteness is impressive." [g] G. Abbott-Smith, *Manual Greek Lexicon*: "A stage of growth, whether measured by age or stature."

## New International Version

hour to your life*? ²⁶Since you cannot do this very little thing, why do you worry about the rest?

²⁷"Consider how the wild flowers grow. They do not labor or spin. Yet I tell you, not even Solomon in all his splendor was dressed like one of these. ²⁸If that is how God clothes the grass of the field, which is here today, and tomorrow is thrown into the fire, how much more will he clothe you—you of little faith! ²⁹And do not set your heart on what you will eat or drink; do not worry about it. ³⁰For the pagan world runs after all such things, and your Father knows that you need them. ³¹But seek his kingdom, and these things will be given to you as well.

³²"Do not be afraid, little flock, for your Father has been pleased to give you the kingdom. ³³Sell your possessions and give to the poor. Provide purses for yourselves that will not wear out, a treasure in heaven that will never fail, where no thief comes near and no moth destroys. ³⁴For where your treasure is, there your heart will be also.

### Watchfulness

³⁵"Be dressed ready for service and keep your lamps burning, ³⁶like servants waiting for their master to return from a wedding banquet, so that when he comes and knocks they can immediately open the door for him. ³⁷It will be good for those servants whose master finds them watching when he comes. Truly I tell you, he will dress himself to serve, will have them recline at the table and will come and wait on them. ³⁸It will be good for those servants whose master finds them ready, even if he comes in the middle of the night or toward daybreak. ³⁹But understand this: If the owner of the house had known at what hour the thief was coming, he would not have let his house be broken into. ⁴⁰You also must be ready, because the Son of Man will come at an hour when you do not expect him."

⁴¹Peter asked, "Lord, are you telling this parable to us, or to everyone?"

⁴²The Lord answered, "Who then is the faithful and wise manager, whom the master puts in charge of his servants to give them their food allowance at the proper time? ⁴³It will be good for that servant whom the master finds doing so when he returns. ⁴⁴Truly I tell you, he will put him in charge of all his possessions. ⁴⁵But suppose the servant says to himself, 'My master is taking a long time in coming,' and he then begins to beat the other servants, both men and women, and to eat and drink and get drunk. ⁴⁶The master of that servant will come on a day when he does not expect him and at an hour he is not aware of. He will cut him to pieces and assign him a place with the unbelievers.

⁴⁷"The servant who knows the master's will and does not get ready or does not do what the master wants will be

## Amplified Bible

²⁶If then you are not able to do such a little thing as that, why are you anxious *and* troubled with cares about the rest?

²⁷Consider the lilies, how they grow. They neither [wearily] toil nor spin *nor ᵃweave;* yet I tell you, even Solomon in all his glory (his splendor and magnificence) was not arrayed like one of these. [I Kings 10:4-7.]

²⁸But if God so clothes the grass in the field, which is alive today, and tomorrow is thrown into the furnace, how much more will He clothe you, O you [people] of little faith?

²⁹And you, do not seek [by meditating and reasoning to inquire into] what you are to eat and what you are to drink; nor be of anxious (troubled) mind [ᵇunsettled, excited, worried, and ᶜin suspense];

³⁰For all the pagan world is [greedily] seeking these things, and your Father knows that you need them.

³¹Only aim at *and* strive for *and* seek His kingdom, and all these things shall be supplied to you also.

³²Do not be seized with alarm *and* struck with fear, little flock, for it is your Father's good pleasure to give you the kingdom!

³³Sell what you possess and give donations to the poor; provide yourselves with purses *and* handbags that do not grow old, an unfailing *and* inexhaustible treasure in the heavens, where no thief comes near and no moth destroys.

³⁴For where your treasure is, there will your heart be also.

³⁵Keep your loins girded and your lamps burning,

³⁶And be like men who are waiting for their master to return home from the marriage feast, so that when he returns from the wedding and comes and knocks, they may open to him immediately.

³⁷Blessed (happy, fortunate, and ᵈto be envied) are those servants whom the master finds awake *and* alert *and* watching when he comes. Truly I say to you, he will gird himself and have them recline at table and will come and serve them!

³⁸If he comes in the second watch (before midnight) or the third watch (after midnight), and finds them so, blessed (happy, fortunate, and ᵈto be envied) are those servants!

³⁹But of this be assured: if the householder had known at what time the burglar was coming, he would have been awake *and* alert *and* watching and would not have permitted his house to be dug through *and* broken into.

⁴⁰You also must be ready, for the Son of Man is coming at an hour *and* a ᵉmoment when you do not anticipate it.

⁴¹Peter said, Lord, are You telling this parable for us, or for all alike?

⁴²And the Lord said, Who then is that faithful steward, the wise man whom his master will set over those in his household service to supply them their allowance of food at the appointed time?

⁴³Blessed (happy and ᵈto be envied) is that servant whom his master finds so doing when he arrives.

⁴⁴Truly I tell you, he will set him in charge over all his possessions.

⁴⁵But if that servant says in his heart, My master is late in coming, and begins to strike the menservants and the maids and to eat and drink and get drunk,

⁴⁶The master of that servant will come on a day when he does not expect him and at an hour of which he does not know, and will punish him *and* cut him off and assign his lot with ᶠthe unfaithful.

⁴⁷And that servant who knew his master's will but did not get ready or act as he would wish him to act shall be beaten with many [lashes].

---

ᵃ Some ancient manuscripts read "weave." ᵇ Marvin Vincent, *Word Studies.* ᶜ G. Abbott-Smith, *Manual Greek Lexicon.* ᵈ Alexander Souter, *Pocket Lexicon.* ᵉ James Moulton and George Milligan, *The Vocabulary.* ᶠ John Wycliffe, *The Wycliffe Bible.*

---

ᵃ 25 Or *single cubit to your height*

## New International Version

beaten with many blows. [48]But the one who does not know and does things deserving punishment will be beaten with few blows. From everyone who has been given much, much will be demanded; and from the one who has been entrusted with much, much more will be asked.

### Not Peace but Division

[49]"I have come to bring fire on the earth, and how I wish it were already kindled! [50]But I have a baptism to undergo, and what constraint I am under until it is completed! [51]Do you think I came to bring peace on earth? No, I tell you, but division. [52]From now on there will be five in one family divided against each other, three against two and two against three. [53]They will be divided, father against son and son against father, mother against daughter and daughter against mother, mother-in-law against daughter-in-law and daughter-in-law against mother-in-law."

### Interpreting the Times

[54]He said to the crowd: "When you see a cloud rising in the west, immediately you say, 'It's going to rain,' and it does. [55]And when the south wind blows, you say, 'It's going to be hot,' and it is. [56]Hypocrites! You know how to interpret the appearance of the earth and the sky. How is it that you don't know how to interpret this present time?

[57]"Why don't you judge for yourselves what is right? [58]As you are going with your adversary to the magistrate, try hard to be reconciled on the way, or your adversary may drag you off to the judge, and the judge turn you over to the officer, and the officer throw you into prison. [59]I tell you, you will not get out until you have paid the last penny."

### Repent or Perish

**13** Now there were some present at that time who told Jesus about the Galileans whose blood Pilate had mixed with their sacrifices. [2]Jesus answered, "Do you think that these Galileans were worse sinners than all the other Galileans because they suffered this way? [3]I tell you, no! But unless you repent, you too will all perish. [4]Or those eighteen who died when the tower in Siloam fell on them—do you think they were more guilty than all the others living in Jerusalem? [5]I tell you, no! But unless you repent, you too will all perish."

[6]Then he told this parable: "A man had a fig tree growing in his vineyard, and he went to look for fruit on it but did not find any. [7]So he said to the man who took care of the vineyard, 'For three years now I've been coming to look for fruit on this fig tree and haven't found any. Cut it down! Why should it use up the soil?'

[8]"'Sir,' the man replied, 'leave it alone for one more year, and I'll dig around it and fertilize it. [9]If it bears fruit next year, fine! If not, then cut it down.'"

## Amplified Bible

[48]But he who did not know and did things worthy of a beating shall be beaten with few [lashes]. For everyone to whom much is given, of him shall much be required; and of him to whom men entrust much, they will require *and* demand all the more. [Num. 15:29, 30; Deut. 25:2, 3.]

[49]I have come to cast fire upon the earth, and how I wish that it were already kindled!

[50]I have a baptism with which to be baptized, and how greatly *and* sorely I am urged on (impelled, [a]constrained) until it is accomplished!

[51]Do you suppose that I have come to give peace upon earth? No, I say to you, but rather division;

[52]For from now on in one house there will be five divided [among themselves], three against two and two against three.

[53]They will be divided, father against son and son against father, mother against daughter and daughter against mother, mother-in-law against her daughter-in-law and daughter-in-law against her mother-in-law. [Mic. 7:6.]

[54]He also said to the crowds of people, When you see a cloud rising in the west, at once you say, It is going to rain! And so it does.

[55]And when [you see that] a south wind is blowing, you say, There will be severe heat! And it occurs.

[56]You playactors (hypocrites)! You know how [intelligently] to discern *and* interpret *and* [a]prove the looks of the earth and sky; but how is it that you do not know how to discern *and* interpret *and* apply the proof to this present time?

[57]And why do you not judge what is just *and* personally decide what is right?

[58]Then as you go with your accuser before a magistrate, on the way make a diligent effort to settle *and* be quit (free) of him, lest he drag you to the judge, and the judge turn you over to the officer, and the officer put you in prison.

[59]I tell you, you will never get out until you have paid the very last [fraction of a] cent.

**13** Just at that time there [arrived] some people who informed Jesus about the Galileans whose blood Pilate had mixed with their sacrifices.

[2]And He replied by saying to them, Do you think that these Galileans were greater sinners than all the other Galileans because they have suffered in this way?

[3]I tell you, No; but unless you repent ([b]change your mind for the better and heartily amend your ways, with abhorrence of your past sins), you will all likewise perish *and* be lost [c]eternally.

[4]Or those eighteen on whom the tower in Siloam fell and killed them—do you think that they were more guilty offenders (debtors) than all the others who dwelt in Jerusalem?

[5]I tell you, No; but unless you repent ([b]change your mind for the better and heartily amend your ways, with abhorrence of your past sins), you will all likewise perish *and* be lost [c]eternally.

[6]And He told them this parable: A certain man had a fig tree, planted in his vineyard, and he came looking for fruit on it, but did not find [any].

[7]So he said to the vinedresser, See here! For these three years I have come looking for fruit on this fig tree and I find none. Cut it down! Why should it continue also to use up the ground [to [d]deplete the soil, intercept the sun, and take up room]?

[8]But he replied to him, Leave it alone, sir, [just] this one more year, till I dig around it and put manure [on the soil].

[9]Then perhaps it will bear fruit after this; but if not, you can cut it down *and* out.

[a] John Wycliffe, *The Wycliffe Bible*. [b] Joseph Thayer, *A Greek-English Lexicon*. [c] Robert Jamieson, A. R. Fausett and David Brown, *A Commentary on the Old and New Testaments*. [d] Johann Bengel, cited by Marvin Vincent, *Word Studies*.

## New International Version

### Jesus Heals a Crippled Woman on the Sabbath

[10] On a Sabbath Jesus was teaching in one of the synagogues, [11] and a woman was there who had been crippled by a spirit for eighteen years. She was bent over and could not straighten up at all. [12] When Jesus saw her, he called her forward and said to her, "Woman, you are set free from your infirmity." [13] Then he put his hands on her, and immediately she straightened up and praised God.

[14] Indignant because Jesus had healed on the Sabbath, the synagogue leader said to the people, "There are six days for work. So come and be healed on those days, not on the Sabbath."

[15] The Lord answered him, "You hypocrites! Doesn't each of you on the Sabbath untie your ox or donkey from the stall and lead it out to give it water? [16] Then should not this woman, a daughter of Abraham, whom Satan has kept bound for eighteen long years, be set free on the Sabbath day from what bound her?"

[17] When he said this, all his opponents were humiliated, but the people were delighted with all the wonderful things he was doing.

### The Parables of the Mustard Seed and the Yeast

[18] Then Jesus asked, "What is the kingdom of God like? What shall I compare it to? [19] It is like a mustard seed, which a man took and planted in his garden. It grew and became a tree, and the birds perched in its branches."

[20] Again he asked, "What shall I compare the kingdom of God to? [21] It is like yeast that a woman took and mixed into about sixty pounds[a] of flour until it worked all through the dough."

### The Narrow Door

[22] Then Jesus went through the towns and villages, teaching as he made his way to Jerusalem. [23] Someone asked him, "Lord, are only a few people going to be saved?"

He said to them, [24] "Make every effort to enter through the narrow door, because many, I tell you, will try to enter and will not be able to. [25] Once the owner of the house gets up and closes the door, you will stand outside knocking and pleading, 'Sir, open the door for us.'

"But he will answer, 'I don't know you or where you come from.'

[26] "Then you will say, 'We ate and drank with you, and you taught in our streets.'

[27] "But he will reply, 'I don't know you or where you come from. Away from me, all you evildoers!'

[28] "There will be weeping there, and gnashing of teeth, when you see Abraham, Isaac and Jacob and all the prophets in the kingdom of God, but you yourselves thrown out. [29] People will come from east and west and north and south, and will take their places at the feast in the kingdom of God. [30] Indeed there are those who are last who will be first, and first who will be last."

## Amplified Bible

[10] Now Jesus was teaching in one of the synagogues on the Sabbath.

[11] And there was a woman there who for eighteen years had had an [a]infirmity caused by a spirit ([b]a demon of sickness). She was [c]bent completely forward and utterly unable to straighten herself up or to [d]look upward.

[12] And when Jesus saw her, He called [her to Him] and said to her, Woman, you are released from your infirmity!

[13] Then He laid [His] hands on her, and instantly she was made straight, and she [e]recognized and thanked and praised God.

[14] But the [d]leader of the synagogue, indignant because Jesus had healed on the Sabbath, said to the crowd, There are six days on which work ought to be done; so come on those days and be cured, and not on the Sabbath day. [Exod. 20:9, 10.]

[15] But the Lord replied to him, saying, You playactors (hypocrites)! Does not each one of you on the Sabbath loose his ox or his donkey from the stall and lead it out to water it?

[16] And ought not this woman, a daughter of Abraham, whom Satan has kept bound for eighteen years, be loosed from this bond on the Sabbath day?

[17] Even as He said this, all His opponents were put to shame, and all the people were rejoicing over all the glorious things that were being done by Him.

[18] This led Him to say, What is the kingdom of God like? And to what shall I compare it?

[19] It is like a grain of mustard seed, which a man took and planted in his own garden; and it grew and became a tree, and the wild birds [f]found shelter and roosted and nested in its branches.

[20] And again He said, To what shall I liken the kingdom of God?

[21] It is like leaven which a woman took and hid in three measures of wheat flour or meal until it was all leavened (fermented).

[22] [Jesus] journeyed on through towns and villages, teaching, and making His way toward Jerusalem.

[23] And someone asked Him, Lord, will only a few be saved (rescued, delivered from the penalties of the last judgment, and made partakers of the salvation by Christ)? And He said to them,

[24] Strive to enter by the narrow door [force yourselves through it], for many, I tell you, will try to enter and will not be able.

[25] When once the Master of the house gets up and closes the door, and you begin to stand outside and to knock at the door [again and again], saying, Lord, open to us! He will answer you, I do not know where [a]what household—certainly not Mine] you come from.

[26] Then you will begin to say, We ate and drank in Your presence, and You taught in our streets.

[27] But He will say, I tell you, I do not know where [a]what household—certainly not Mine] you come from; depart from Me, all you wrongdoers!

[28] There will be weeping and grinding of teeth when you see Abraham and Isaac and Jacob and all the prophets in the kingdom of God, but you yourselves being cast forth (banished, driven away).

[29] And [people] will come from east and west, and from north and south, and sit down (feast at table) in the kingdom of God.

[30] And behold, there are some [now] last who will be first [then], and there are some [now] first who will be last [then].

---

[a] Marvin Vincent, *Word Studies.*  [b] Hermann Cremer, *Biblico-Theological Lexicon.*  [c] Joseph Thayer, *A Greek-English Lexicon.*  [d] Alexander Souter, *Pocket Lexicon.*  [e] Johann Bengel, cited by Marvin Vincent, *Word Studies.*  [f] James Moulton and George Milligan, *The Vocabulary.*

---

[a] 21 Or about 27 kilograms

## New International Version

### Jesus' Sorrow for Jerusalem

[31] At that time some Pharisees came to Jesus and said to him, "Leave this place and go somewhere else. Herod wants to kill you."

[32] He replied, "Go tell that fox, 'I will keep on driving out demons and healing people today and tomorrow, and on the third day I will reach my goal.' [33] In any case, I must press on today and tomorrow and the next day—for surely no prophet can die outside Jerusalem!

[34] "Jerusalem, Jerusalem, you who kill the prophets and stone those sent to you, how often I have longed to gather your children together, as a hen gathers her chicks under her wings, and you were not willing. [35] Look, your house is left to you desolate. I tell you, you will not see me again until you say, 'Blessed is he who comes in the name of the Lord.'[a]"

### Jesus at a Pharisee's House

**14** One Sabbath, when Jesus went to eat in the house of a prominent Pharisee, he was being carefully watched. [2] There in front of him was a man suffering from abnormal swelling of his body. [3] Jesus asked the Pharisees and experts in the law, "Is it lawful to heal on the Sabbath or not?" [4] But they remained silent. So taking hold of the man, he healed him and sent him on his way.

[5] Then he asked them, "If one of you has a child[b] or an ox that falls into a well on the Sabbath day, will you not immediately pull it out?" [6] And they had nothing to say.

[7] When he noticed how the guests picked the places of honor at the table, he told them this parable: [8] "When someone invites you to a wedding feast, do not take the place of honor, for a person more distinguished than you may have been invited. [9] If so, the host who invited both of you will come and say to you, 'Give this person your seat.' Then, humiliated, you will have to take the least important place. [10] But when you are invited, take the lowest place, so that when your host comes, he will say to you, 'Friend, move up to a better place.' Then you will be honored in the presence of all the other guests. [11] For all those who exalt themselves will be humbled, and those who humble themselves will be exalted."

[12] Then Jesus said to his host, "When you give a luncheon or dinner, do not invite your friends, your brothers or sisters, your relatives, or your rich neighbors; if you do, they may invite you back and so you will be repaid. [13] But when you give a banquet, invite the poor, the crippled, the lame, the blind, [14] and you will be blessed. Although they cannot repay you, you will be repaid at the resurrection of the righteous."

### The Parable of the Great Banquet

[15] When one of those at the table with him heard this, he said to Jesus, "Blessed is the one who will eat at the feast in the kingdom of God."

## Amplified Bible

[31] At that very hour some Pharisees came up and said to Him, Go away from here, for Herod is determined to kill You.

[32] And He said to them, Go and tell that fox [sly and crafty, skulking and cowardly], Behold, I drive out demons and perform healings today and tomorrow, and on the third day I finish (complete) My course.

[33] Nevertheless, I must continue on My way today and tomorrow and the day after that—for it will never do for a prophet to be destroyed away from Jerusalem!

[34] O Jerusalem, Jerusalem, you who continue to kill the prophets and to stone those who are sent to you! How often I have desired *and* yearned to gather your children together [around Me], as a hen [gathers] her young under her wings, but you would not!

[35] Behold, your house is forsaken (abandoned, left to you destitute of God's help)! And I tell you, you will not see Me again until the time comes when you shall say, Blessed (to be celebrated with praises) is He Who comes in the name of the Lord! [Ps. 118:26; Jer. 22:5.]

**14** It occurred one Sabbath, when [Jesus] went for a meal at the house of one of the ruling Pharisees, that they were [engaged in] watching Him [closely].

[2] And behold, [just] in front of Him there was a man who had dropsy.

[3] And Jesus asked the lawyers and the Pharisees, Is it lawful *and* right to cure on the Sabbath or not?

[4] But they kept silent. Then He took hold [of the man] and cured him and [a] sent him away.

[5] And He said to them, Which of you, having a son [b] *or a donkey* or an ox that has fallen into a well, will not at once pull him out on the Sabbath day?

[6] And they were unable to reply to this.

[7] Now He told a parable to those who were invited, [when] He noticed how they were selecting the places of honor, saying to them,

[8] When you are invited by anyone to a marriage feast, do not recline on the chief seat [in the place of honor], lest a more distinguished person than you has been invited by him, [Prov. 25:6, 7.]

[9] And he who invited both of you will come to you and say, Let this man have the place [you have taken]. Then, with humiliation *and* a guilty sense of impropriety, you will begin to take the lowest place.

[10] But when you are invited, go and recline in the lowest place, so that when your host comes in, he may say to you, Friend, go up higher! Then you will be honored in the presence of all who sit [at table] with you.

[11] For everyone who exalts himself will be humbled (ranked below others who are honored or rewarded), and he who humbles himself (keeps a modest opinion of himself and behaves accordingly) will be exalted (elevated in rank).

[12] Jesus also said to the man who had invited Him, When you give a dinner or a supper, do not invite your friends or your brothers or your relatives or your wealthy neighbors, lest perhaps they also invite you in return, and so you are paid back.

[13] But when you give a banquet *or* a reception, invite the poor, the disabled, the lame, and the blind.

[14] Then you will be blessed (happy, fortunate, and [c] to be envied), because they have no way of repaying you, and you will be recompensed at the resurrection of the just (upright).

[15] When one of those who reclined [at the table] with Him heard this, he said to Him, Blessed (happy, fortunate, and [c] to be envied) is he who shall eat bread in the kingdom of God!

---

[a] 35 Psalm 118:26   [b] 5 Some manuscripts *donkey*

[a] Joseph Thayer, *A Greek-English Lexicon*.   [b] Many ancient manuscripts so read.   [c] Alexander Souter, *Pocket Lexicon*.

## New International Version

[16]Jesus replied: "A certain man was preparing a great banquet and invited many guests. [17]At the time of the banquet he sent his servant to tell those who had been invited, 'Come, for everything is now ready.'

[18]"But they all alike began to make excuses. The first said, 'I have just bought a field, and I must go and see it. Please excuse me.'

[19]"Another said, 'I have just bought five yoke of oxen, and I'm on my way to try them out. Please excuse me.'

[20]"Still another said, 'I just got married, so I can't come.'

[21]"The servant came back and reported this to his master. Then the owner of the house became angry and ordered his servant, 'Go out quickly into the streets and alleys of the town and bring in the poor, the crippled, the blind and the lame.'

[22]"'Sir,' the servant said, 'what you ordered has been done, but there is still room.'

[23]"Then the master told his servant, 'Go out to the roads and country lanes and compel them to come in, so that my house will be full. [24]I tell you, not one of those who were invited will get a taste of my banquet.'"

### The Cost of Being a Disciple

[25]Large crowds were traveling with Jesus, and turning to them he said: [26]"If anyone comes to me and does not hate father and mother, wife and children, brothers and sisters—yes, even their own life—such a person cannot be my disciple. [27]And whoever does not carry their cross and follow me cannot be my disciple.

[28]"Suppose one of you wants to build a tower. Won't you first sit down and estimate the cost to see if you have enough money to complete it? [29]For if you lay the foundation and are not able to finish it, everyone who sees it will ridicule you, [30]saying, 'This person began to build and wasn't able to finish.'

[31]"Or suppose a king is about to go to war against another king. Won't he first sit down and consider whether he is able with ten thousand men to oppose the one coming against him with twenty thousand? [32]If he is not able, he will send a delegation while the other is still a long way off and will ask for terms of peace. [33]In the same way, those of you who do not give up everything you have cannot be my disciples.

[34]"Salt is good, but if it loses its saltiness, how can it be made salty again? [35]It is fit neither for the soil nor for the manure pile; it is thrown out.

"Whoever has ears to hear, let them hear."

### The Parable of the Lost Sheep

**15** Now the tax collectors and sinners were all gathering around to hear Jesus. [2]But the Pharisees and the teachers of the law muttered, "This man welcomes sinners and eats with them."

## Amplified Bible

[16]But Jesus said to him, A man was once giving a great supper and invited many;

[17]And at the hour for the supper he sent his servant to say to those who had been invited, Come, for all is now ready.

[18]But they all alike began to make excuses *and* to beg off. The first said to him, I have bought a piece of land, and I have to go out and see it; I beg you, have me excused.

[19]And another said, I have bought five yoke of oxen, and I am going to examine *and* [a]put my approval on them; I beg you, have me excused.

[20]And another said, I have married a wife, and because of this I am unable to come. [Deut. 24:5.]

[21]So the servant came and reported these [answers] to his master. Then the master of the house said in wrath to his servant, Go quickly into the [b]great streets and the small streets of the city and bring in here the poor and the disabled and the blind and the lame.

[22]And the servant [returning] said, Sir, what you have commanded me to do has been done, and yet there is room.

[23]Then the master said to the servant, Go out into the highways and hedges and urge *and* constrain [them] to yield *and* come in, so that my house may be filled.

[24]For I tell you, not one of those who were invited shall taste my supper.

[25]Now huge crowds were going along with [Jesus], and He turned and said to them,

[26]If anyone comes to Me and does not hate his [own] father and mother [c]in the sense of indifference to or relative disregard for them in comparison with his attitude toward God] and [likewise] his wife and children and brothers and sisters—[yes] and even his own life also—he cannot be My disciple.

[27]Whoever does not persevere *and* carry his own cross and come after (follow) Me cannot be My disciple.

[28]For which of you, wishing to build a [d]farm building, does not first sit down and calculate the cost [to see] whether he has sufficient means to finish it?

[29]Otherwise, when he has laid the foundation and is unable to complete [the building], all who see it will begin to mock *and* jeer at him,

[30]Saying, This man began to build and was not able ([e]worth enough) to finish.

[31]Or what king, going out to engage in conflict with another king, will not first sit down and consider *and* take counsel whether he is able with ten thousand [men] to meet him who comes against him with twenty thousand?

[32]And if he cannot [do so], when the other king is still a great way off, he sends an envoy and asks the terms of peace.

[33]So then, any of you who does not forsake (renounce, surrender claim to, give up, [e]say good-bye to) all that he has cannot be My disciple.

[34]Salt is good [an excellent thing], but if salt has lost its strength *and* has become saltless (insipid, flat), how shall its saltness be restored?

[35]It is fit neither for the land nor for the manure heap; men throw it away. He who has ears to hear, let him listen *and* consider *and* comprehend by hearing!

**15** Now the tax collectors and [notorious and [f]especially wicked] sinners were all coming near to [Jesus] to listen to Him.

[2]And the Pharisees and the scribes kept muttering *and* indignantly complaining, saying, This man accepts *and* receives *and* welcomes [[f]preeminently wicked] sinners and eats with them.

[a] Kenneth Wuest, *Word Studies.* [b] John Wycliffe, *The Wycliffe Bible.*
[c] G. Abbott-Smith, *Manual Greek Lexicon.* [d] James Moulton and George Milligan, *The Vocabulary.* [e] Marvin Vincent, *Word Studies.* [f] Joseph Thayer, *A Greek-English Lexicon.*

## New International Version

³Then Jesus told them this parable: ⁴"Suppose one of you has a hundred sheep and loses one of them. Doesn't he leave the ninety-nine in the open country and go after the lost sheep until he finds it? ⁵And when he finds it, he joyfully puts it on his shoulders ⁶and goes home. Then he calls his friends and neighbors together and says, 'Rejoice with me; I have found my lost sheep.' ⁷I tell you that in the same way there will be more rejoicing in heaven over one sinner who repents than over ninety-nine righteous persons who do not need to repent.

### The Parable of the Lost Coin

⁸"Or suppose a woman has ten silver coins*a* and loses one. Doesn't she light a lamp, sweep the house and search carefully until she finds it? ⁹And when she finds it, she calls her friends and neighbors together and says, 'Rejoice with me; I have found my lost coin.' ¹⁰In the same way, I tell you, there is rejoicing in the presence of the angels of God over one sinner who repents."

### The Parable of the Lost Son

¹¹Jesus continued: "There was a man who had two sons. ¹²The younger one said to his father, 'Father, give me my share of the estate.' So he divided his property between them.

¹³"Not long after that, the younger son got together all he had, set off for a distant country and there squandered his wealth in wild living. ¹⁴After he had spent everything, there was a severe famine in that whole country, and he began to be in need. ¹⁵So he went and hired himself out to a citizen of that country, who sent him to his fields to feed pigs. ¹⁶He longed to fill his stomach with the pods that the pigs were eating, but no one gave him anything.

¹⁷"When he came to his senses, he said, 'How many of my father's hired servants have food to spare, and here I am starving to death! ¹⁸I will set out and go back to my father and say to him: Father, I have sinned against heaven and against you. ¹⁹I am no longer worthy to be called your son; make me like one of your hired servants.' ²⁰So he got up and went to his father.

"But while he was still a long way off, his father saw him and was filled with compassion for him; he ran to his son, threw his arms around him and kissed him.

²¹"The son said to him, 'Father, I have sinned against heaven and against you. I am no longer worthy to be called your son.'

²²"But the father said to his servants, 'Quick! Bring the best robe and put it on him. Put a ring on his finger and sandals on his feet. ²³Bring the fattened calf and kill it. Let's have a feast and celebrate. ²⁴For this son of mine was

## Amplified Bible

³So He told them this parable:

⁴What man of you, if he has a hundred sheep and should lose one of them, does not leave the ninety-nine in the wilderness (desert) and go after the one that is lost until he finds it?

⁵And when he has found it, he lays it on his [own] shoulders, rejoicing.

⁶And when he gets home, he summons together [his] friends and [his] neighbors, saying to them, Rejoice with me, because I have found my sheep which was lost.

⁷Thus, I tell you, there will be more joy in heaven over one [*a*especially] wicked person who repents (*a*changes his mind, abhorring his errors and misdeeds, and determines to enter upon a better course of life) than over ninety-nine righteous persons who have no need of repentance.

⁸Or what woman, having ten [silver] drachmas [each one equal to a day's wages], if she loses one coin, does not light a lamp and sweep the house and look carefully *and* diligently until she finds it?

⁹And when she has found it, she summons her [women] friends and neighbors, saying, Rejoice with me, for I have found the silver coin which I had lost.

¹⁰Even so, I tell you, there is joy among *and* in the presence of the angels of God over one [*a*especially] wicked person who repents (*a*changes his mind for the better, heartily amending his ways, with abhorrence of his past sins).

¹¹And He said, There was a certain man who had two sons;

¹²And the younger of them said to his father, Father, give me the part of the property that falls [to me]. And he divided the estate between them. [Deut. 21:15-17.]

¹³And not many days after that, the younger son gathered up all that he had and journeyed into a distant country, and there he wasted his fortune in reckless *and* loose [from restraint] living.

¹⁴And when he had spent all he had, a *b*mighty famine came upon that country, and he began to fall behind *and* be in want.

¹⁵So he went and forced (glued) himself upon one of the citizens of that country, who sent him into his fields to feed hogs.

¹⁶And he would gladly have fed on *and* *c*filled his belly *with* the *b*carob pods that the hogs were eating, but [they could not satisfy his hunger and] nobody gave him anything [better]. [Jer. 30:14.]

¹⁷Then when he came to himself, he said, How many hired servants of my father have enough food, and [even food] to spare, but I am perishing (dying) here of hunger!

¹⁸I will get up and go to my father, and I will say to him, Father, I have sinned against heaven and in your sight.

¹⁹I am no longer worthy to be called your son; [just] make me like one of your hired servants.

²⁰So he got up and came to his [own] father. But while he was still a long way off, his father saw him and was moved with pity *and* tenderness [for him]; and he ran and embraced him and kissed him [*b*fervently].

²¹And the son said to him, Father, I have sinned against heaven and in your sight; I am no longer worthy to be called your son [I no longer deserve to be recognized as a son of yours]!

²²But the father said to his bond servants, Bring quickly the best robe (the festive robe of honor) and put it on him; and give him a ring for his hand and sandals for his feet. [Gen. 41:42; Zech. 3:4.]

²³And bring out *d*that [wheat-]fattened calf and kill it; and let us *e*revel *and* feast *and* be happy *and* make merry,

---

*a* Joseph Thayer, *A Greek-English Lexicon.*  *b* G. Abbott-Smith, *Manual Greek Lexicon.*  *c* Many ancient manuscripts so read.  *d* William Tyndale, *The Tyndale Bible.*  *e* Alexander Souter, *Pocket Lexicon.*

## New International Version

dead and is alive again; he was lost and is found.' So they began to celebrate.

25"Meanwhile, the older son was in the field. When he came near the house, he heard music and dancing. 26So he called one of the servants and asked him what was going on. 27'Your brother has come,' he replied, 'and your father has killed the fattened calf because he has him back safe and sound.'

28"The older brother became angry and refused to go in. So his father went out and pleaded with him. 29But he answered his father, 'Look! All these years I've been slaving for you and never disobeyed your orders. Yet you never gave me even a young goat so I could celebrate with my friends. 30But when this son of yours who has squandered your property with prostitutes comes home, you kill the fattened calf for him!'

31"'My son,' the father said, 'you are always with me, and everything I have is yours. 32But we had to celebrate and be glad, because this brother of yours was dead and is alive again; he was lost and is found.'"

### The Parable of the Shrewd Manager

**16** Jesus told his disciples: "There was a rich man whose manager was accused of wasting his possessions. 2So he called him in and asked him, 'What is this I hear about you? Give an account of your management, because you cannot be manager any longer.'

3"The manager said to himself, 'What shall I do now? My master is taking away my job. I'm not strong enough to dig, and I'm ashamed to beg— 4I know what I'll do so that, when I lose my job here, people will welcome me into their houses.'

5"So he called in each one of his master's debtors. He asked the first, 'How much do you owe my master?'

6"'Nine hundred gallonsᵃ of olive oil,' he replied.

"The manager told him, 'Take your bill, sit down quickly, and make it four hundred and fifty.'

7"Then he asked the second, 'And how much do you owe?'

"'A thousand bushelsᵇ of wheat,' he replied.

"He told him, 'Take your bill and make it eight hundred.'

8"The master commended the dishonest manager because he had acted shrewdly. For the people of this world are more shrewd in dealing with their own kind than are the people of the light. 9I tell you, use worldly wealth to gain friends for yourselves, so that when it is gone, you will be welcomed into eternal dwellings.

10"Whoever can be trusted with very little can also be trusted with much, and whoever is dishonest with very little will also be dishonest with much. 11So if you have not been trustworthy in handling worldly wealth, who

## Amplified Bible

24Because this my son was dead and is alive again; he was lost and is found! And they began to ᵃrevel and feast and make merry.

25But his older son was in the field; and as he returned and came near the house, he heard music and dancing.

26And having called one of the servant [boys] to him, he began to ask what this meant.

27And he said to him, Your brother has come, and your father has killed ᵇthat [wheat-]fattened calf, because he has received him back safe and well.

28But [the elder brother] was angry [with deep-seated wrath] and resolved not to go in. Then his father came out and began to plead with him,

29But he answered his father, Look! These many years I have served you, and I have never disobeyed your command. Yet you never gave me [so much as] a [little] kid, that I might ᵃrevel and feast and be happy and make merry with my friends;

30But when this son of yours arrived, who has devoured your estate with immoral women, you have killed for him ᵇthat [wheat-] fattened calf!

31And the father said to him, Son, you are always with me, and all that is mine is yours.

32But it was fitting to make merry, to ᵃrevel and feast and rejoice, for this brother of yours was dead and is alive again! He was lost and is found!

**16** Also [Jesus] said to the disciples, There was a certain rich man who had a ᶜmanager of his estate, and accusations [against this man] were brought to him, that he was squandering his [master's] possessions.

2And he called him and said to him, What is this that I hear about you? Turn in the account of your management [of my affairs], for you can be [my] manager no longer.

3And the manager of the estate said to himself, What shall I do, seeing that my master is taking the management away from me? I am not able to dig, and I am ashamed to beg.

4I have come to know what I will do, so that they [my master's debtors] may accept and welcome me into their houses when I am put out of the management.

5So he summoned his master's debtors one by one, and he said to the first, How much do you owe my master?

6He said, A hundred measures [about 900 gallons] of oil. And he said to him, Take back your written acknowledgement of ᵈobligation, and sit down quickly and write fifty [about 450 gallons].

7After that he said to another, And how much do you owe? He said, A hundred measures [about 900 bushels] of wheat. He said to him, Take back your written acknowledgement of ᵈobligation, and write eighty [about 700 bushels].

8And [his] master praised the dishonest (unjust) manager for acting ᵉshrewdly and ᵈprudently; for the sons of this age are shrewder and more prudent and wiser in [ᵉrelation to] their own generation [to their own age and ᵇkind] than are the sons of light.

9And I tell you, make friends for yourselves by means of unrighteous mammon (ᵃdeceitful riches, money, possessions), so that when it fails, they [those you have favored] may receive and welcome you into the everlasting habitations (dwellings).

10He who is faithful in a very little [thing] is faithful also in much, and he who is dishonest and unjust in a very little [thing] is dishonest and unjust also in much.

11Therefore if you have not been faithful in the [case of] unrighteous mammon (ᵃdeceitful riches, money, possessions), who will entrust to you the true riches?

---

ᵃ Alexander Souter, *Pocket Lexicon.*  ᵇ William Tyndale, *The Tyndale Bible.*  ᶜ James Moulton and George Milligan, *The Vocabulary.*  ᵈ John Wycliffe, *The Wycliffe Bible.*  ᵉ Marvin Vincent, *Word Studies.*

---

ᵃ 6 Or about 3,000 liters    ᵇ 7 Or about 30 tons

## New International Version

will trust you with true riches? <sup>12</sup>And if you have not been trustworthy with someone else's property, who will give you property of your own?

<sup>13</sup>"No one can serve two masters. Either you will hate the one and love the other, or you will be devoted to the one and despise the other. You cannot serve both God and money."

<sup>14</sup>The Pharisees, who loved money, heard all this and were sneering at Jesus. <sup>15</sup>He said to them, "You are the ones who justify yourselves in the eyes of others, but God knows your hearts. What people value highly is detestable in God's sight.

### Additional Teachings

<sup>16</sup>"The Law and the Prophets were proclaimed until John. Since that time, the good news of the kingdom of God is being preached, and everyone is forcing their way into it. <sup>17</sup>It is easier for heaven and earth to disappear than for the least stroke of a pen to drop out of the Law.

<sup>18</sup>"Anyone who divorces his wife and marries another woman commits adultery, and the man who marries a divorced woman commits adultery.

### The Rich Man and Lazarus

<sup>19</sup>"There was a rich man who was dressed in purple and fine linen and lived in luxury every day. <sup>20</sup>At his gate was laid a beggar named Lazarus, covered with sores <sup>21</sup>and longing to eat what fell from the rich man's table. Even the dogs came and licked his sores.

<sup>22</sup>"The time came when the beggar died and the angels carried him to Abraham's side. The rich man also died and was buried. <sup>23</sup>In Hades, where he was in torment, he looked up and saw Abraham far away, with Lazarus by his side. <sup>24</sup>So he called to him, 'Father Abraham, have pity on me and send Lazarus to dip the tip of his finger in water and cool my tongue, because I am in agony in this fire.'

<sup>25</sup>"But Abraham replied, 'Son, remember that in your lifetime you received your good things, while Lazarus received bad things, but now he is comforted here and you are in agony. <sup>26</sup>And besides all this, between us and you a great chasm has been set in place, so that those who want to go from here to you cannot, nor can anyone cross over from there to us.'

<sup>27</sup>"He answered, 'Then I beg you, father, send Lazarus to my family, <sup>28</sup>for I have five brothers. Let him warn them, so that they will not also come to this place of torment.'

<sup>29</sup>"Abraham replied, 'They have Moses and the Prophets; let them listen to them.'

<sup>30</sup>"'No, father Abraham,' he said, 'but if someone from the dead goes to them, they will repent.'

<sup>31</sup>"He said to him, 'If they do not listen to Moses and the Prophets, they will not be convinced even if someone rises from the dead.'"

## Amplified Bible

<sup>12</sup>And if you have not proved faithful in that which belongs to another [whether God or man], who will give you that which is your own [that is, <sup>a</sup>the true riches]?

<sup>13</sup>No servant is able to serve two masters; for either he will hate the one and love the other, or he will stand by *and* be devoted to the one and despise the other. You cannot serve God and mammon (riches, or <sup>b</sup>anything in which you trust and on which you rely).

<sup>14</sup>Now the Pharisees, who were covetous *and* lovers of money, heard all these things [taken together], and they began to sneer at *and* ridicule *and* scoff at Him.

<sup>15</sup>But He said to them, You are the ones who declare yourselves just *and* upright before men, but God knows your hearts. For what is exalted *and* highly thought of among men is detestable *and* abhorrent (an abomination) in the sight of God. [I Sam. 16:7; Prov. 21:2.]

<sup>16</sup>Until John came, there were the Law and the Prophets; since then the good news (the Gospel) of the kingdom of God is being preached, and everyone strives violently to go in [would force his <sup>c</sup>own way rather than God's way into it].

<sup>17</sup>Yet it is easier for heaven and earth to pass away than for one dot of the Law to fail *and* become void.

<sup>18</sup>Whoever divorces (dismisses and repudiates) his wife and marries another commits adultery, and he who marries a woman who is divorced from her husband commits adultery.

<sup>19</sup>There was a certain rich man who [habitually] clothed himself in purple and fine linen and <sup>d</sup>reveled *and* feasted *and* made merry in splendor every day.

<sup>20</sup>And at his gate there <sup>a</sup>was [carelessly] dropped down *and* left a certain <sup>a</sup>utterly destitute man named Lazarus, [reduced to begging alms and] covered with [<sup>a</sup>ulcerated] sores.

<sup>21</sup>He [eagerly] desired to be satisfied with what fell from the rich man's table; moreover, the dogs even came and licked his sores.

<sup>22</sup>And it occurred that the man [reduced to] begging died and was carried by the angels to Abraham's bosom. The rich man also died and was buried.

<sup>23</sup>And in Hades (the realm of the dead), being in torment, he lifted up his eyes and saw Abraham far away, and Lazarus in his bosom.

<sup>24</sup>And he cried out and said, Father Abraham, have pity *and* mercy on me and send Lazarus to dip the tip of his finger in water and cool my tongue, for I am in anguish in this flame.

<sup>25</sup>But Abraham said, Child, remember that you in your lifetime fully received [what is due you in] comforts *and* delights, and Lazarus in like manner the discomforts *and* distresses; but now he is comforted here and you are in anguish.

<sup>26</sup>And besides all this, between us and you a great chasm has been fixed, in order that those who want to pass from this [place] to you may not be able, and no one may pass from there to us.

<sup>27</sup>And [the man] said, Then, father, I beseech you to send him to my father's house—

<sup>28</sup>For I have five brothers—so that he may give [solemn] testimony *and* warn them, lest they too come into this place of torment.

<sup>29</sup>But Abraham said, They have Moses and the Prophets; let them hear *and* listen to them.

<sup>30</sup>But he answered, No, father Abraham, but if someone from the dead goes to them, they will repent (<sup>b</sup>change their minds for the better and heartily amend their ways, with abhorrence of their past sins).

<sup>31</sup>He said to him, If they do not hear *and* listen to Moses and the Prophets, neither will they be persuaded *and* convinced *and* believe [even] if someone should rise from the dead.

<sup>a</sup> Marvin Vincent, *Word Studies.* <sup>b</sup> Joseph Thayer, *A Greek-English Lexicon.* <sup>c</sup> Gerrit Verkuyl, *The Berkeley Version in Modern English.* <sup>d</sup> Alexander Souter, *Pocket Lexicon.*

## New International Version

### Sin, Faith, Duty

**17** Jesus said to his disciples: "Things that cause people to stumble are bound to come, but woe to anyone through whom they come. ²It would be better for them to be thrown into the sea with a millstone tied around their neck than to cause one of these little ones to stumble. ³So watch yourselves.

"If your brother or sister[a] sins against you, rebuke them; and if they repent, forgive them. ⁴Even if they sin against you seven times in a day and seven times come back to you saying 'I repent,' you must forgive them."

⁵The apostles said to the Lord, "Increase our faith!"

⁶He replied, "If you have faith as small as a mustard seed, you can say to this mulberry tree, 'Be uprooted and planted in the sea,' and it will obey you.

⁷"Suppose one of you has a servant plowing or looking after the sheep. Will he say to the servant when he comes in from the field, 'Come along now and sit down to eat'? ⁸Won't he rather say, 'Prepare my supper, get yourself ready and wait on me while I eat and drink; after that you may eat and drink'? ⁹Will he thank the servant because he did what he was told to do? ¹⁰So you also, when you have done everything you were told to do, should say, 'We are unworthy servants; we have only done our duty.'"

### Jesus Heals Ten Men With Leprosy

¹¹Now on his way to Jerusalem, Jesus traveled along the border between Samaria and Galilee. ¹²As he was going into a village, ten men who had leprosy[b] met him. They stood at a distance ¹³and called out in a loud voice, "Jesus, Master, have pity on us!"

¹⁴When he saw them, he said, "Go, show yourselves to the priests." And as they went, they were cleansed.

¹⁵One of them, when he saw he was healed, came back, praising God in a loud voice. ¹⁶He threw himself at Jesus' feet and thanked him—and he was a Samaritan.

¹⁷Jesus asked, "Were not all ten cleansed? Where are the other nine? ¹⁸Has no one returned to give praise to God except this foreigner?" ¹⁹Then he said to him, "Rise and go; your faith has made you well."

### The Coming of the Kingdom of God

²⁰Once, on being asked by the Pharisees when the kingdom of God would come, Jesus replied, "The coming of the kingdom of God is not something that can be observed, ²¹nor will people say, 'Here it is,' or 'There it is,' because the kingdom of God is in your midst."[c]

²²Then he said to his disciples, "The time is coming when you will long to see one of the days of the Son of Man, but you will not see it. ²³People will tell you, 'There he is!' or 'Here he is!' Do not go running off after them.

## Amplified Bible

**17** And [Jesus] said to His disciples, Temptations (snares, traps set to entice to sin) are sure to come, but woe to him by or through whom they come!

²It would be more profitable for him if a millstone were hung around his neck and he were hurled into the sea than that he should cause to sin or be a snare to one of these little ones [a lowly in rank or influence].

³ᵇPay attention and always be on your guard [looking out for one another]. If your brother sins (misses the mark), solemnly tell him so and reprove him, and if he repents (feels sorry for having sinned), forgive him.

⁴And even if he sins against you seven times in a day, and turns to you seven times and says, I repent [I am sorry], you must forgive him (give up resentment and consider the offense as recalled and annulled].

⁵The apostles said to the Lord, Increase our faith (that trust and confidence that spring from our belief in God).

⁶And the Lord answered, If you had faith (trust and confidence in God) even [so small] like a grain of mustard seed, you could say to this mulberry tree, Be pulled up by the roots, and be planted in the sea, and it would obey you.

⁷Will any man of you who has a servant plowing or tending sheep say to him when he has come in from the field, Come at once and take your place at the table?

⁸Will he not instead tell him, Get my supper ready and gird yourself and serve me while I eat and drink; then afterward you yourself shall eat and drink?

⁹Is he grateful and does he praise the servant because he did what he was ordered to do?

¹⁰Even so on your part, when you have done everything that was assigned and commanded you, say, We are unworthy servants [possessing no merit, for we have not gone beyond our obligation]; we have [merely] done what was our duty to do.

¹¹As He went on His way to Jerusalem, it occurred that [Jesus] was passing [along the border] between Samaria and Galilee.

¹²And as He was going into one village, He was met by ten lepers, who stood at a distance.

¹³And they raised up their voices and called, Jesus, Master, take pity and have mercy on us!

¹⁴And when He saw them, He said to them, Go [at once] and show yourselves to the priests. And as they went, they were cured and made clean. [Lev. 14:2-32.]

¹⁵Then one of them, upon seeing that he was cured, turned back, ᶜrecognizing and thanking and praising God with a loud voice;

¹⁶And he fell prostrate at Jesus' feet, thanking Him [over and over]. And he was a Samaritan.

¹⁷Then Jesus asked, Were not [all] ten cleansed? Where are the nine?

¹⁸Was there no one found to return and to ᶜrecognize and give thanks and praise to God except this alien?

¹⁹And He said to him, Get up and go on your way. Your faith (your trust and confidence that spring from your belief in God) has restored you to health.

²⁰Asked by the Pharisees when the kingdom of God would come, He replied to them by saying, The kingdom of God does not come with signs to be observed or with visible display,

²¹Nor will people say, Look! Here [it is]! or, See, [it is] there! For behold, the kingdom of God is within you [in your hearts] and among you [surrounding you].

²²And He said to the disciples, The time is coming when you will long to see [even] one of the days of the Son of Man, and you will not see [it].

²³And they will say to you, Look! [He is] there! or, Look! [He is] here! But do not go out or follow [them].

---

a 3 The Greek word for brother or sister (adelphos) refers here to a fellow disciple, whether man or woman.   b 12 The Greek word traditionally translated leprosy was used for various diseases affecting the skin.
c 21 Or is within you

a G. Abbott-Smith, Manual Greek Lexicon.   b James Moulton and George Milligan, The Vocabulary.   c Hermann Cremer, Biblico-Theological Lexicon.

## New International Version

24For the Son of Man in his day*a* will be like the lightning, which flashes and lights up the sky from one end to the other. 25But first he must suffer many things and be rejected by this generation.

26"Just as it was in the days of Noah, so also will it be in the days of the Son of Man. 27People were eating, drinking, marrying and being given in marriage up to the day Noah entered the ark. Then the flood came and destroyed them all.

28"It was the same in the days of Lot. People were eating and drinking, buying and selling, planting and building. 29But the day Lot left Sodom, fire and sulfur rained down from heaven and destroyed them all.

30"It will be just like this on the day the Son of Man is revealed. 31On that day no one who is on the housetop, with possessions inside, should go down to get them. Likewise, no one in the field should go back for anything. 32Remember Lot's wife! 33Whoever tries to keep their life will lose it, and whoever loses their life will preserve it. 34I tell you, on that night two people will be in one bed; one will be taken and the other left. 35Two women will be grinding grain together; one will be taken and the other left." [36]*b*

37"Where, Lord?" they asked.

He replied, "Where there is a dead body, there the vultures will gather."

### The Parable of the Persistent Widow

**18** Then Jesus told his disciples a parable to show them that they should always pray and not give up. 2He said: "In a certain town there was a judge who neither feared God nor cared what people thought. 3And there was a widow in that town who kept coming to him with the plea, 'Grant me justice against my adversary.'

4"For some time he refused. But finally he said to himself, 'Even though I don't fear God or care what people think, 5yet because this widow keeps bothering me, I will see that she gets justice, so that she won't eventually come and attack me!'"

6And the Lord said, "Listen to what the unjust judge says. 7And will not God bring about justice for his chosen ones, who cry out to him day and night? Will he keep putting them off? 8I tell you, he will see that they get justice, and quickly. However, when the Son of Man comes, will he find faith on the earth?"

### The Parable of the Pharisee and the Tax Collector

9To some who were confident of their own righteousness and looked down on everyone else, Jesus told this parable: 10"Two men went up to the temple to pray, one a Pharisee and the other a tax collector. 11The Pharisee

## Amplified Bible

24For like the lightning, that flashes and lights up the sky from one end to the other, so will the Son of Man be in His [own] day.

25But first He must suffer many things and be disapproved *and* repudiated *and* rejected by this age *and* generation.

26And [just] as it was in the days of Noah, so will it be in the time of the Son of Man.

27[People] ate, they drank, they married, they were given in marriage, right up to the day when Noah went into the ark, and the flood came and destroyed them all. [Gen. 6:5-8; 7:6-24.]

28So also [it was the same] as it was in the days of Lot. [People] ate, they drank, they bought, they sold, they planted, they built;

29But on the [very] day that Lot went out of Sodom, it rained fire and brimstone from heaven and destroyed [them] all.

30That is the way it will be on the day that the Son of Man is revealed. [Gen. 18:20-33; 19:24, 25.]

31On that day let him who is on the housetop, with his belongings in the house, not come down [and go inside] to carry them away; and likewise let him who is in the field not turn back.

32Remember Lot's wife! [Gen. 19:26.]

33Whoever tries to preserve his life will lose it, but whoever loses his life will preserve and *a* quicken it.

34I tell you, in that night there will be two men in one bed; one will be taken and the other will be left.

35There will be two women grinding together; one will be taken and the other will be left.

36*b Two men will be in the field; one will be taken and the other will be left.*

37Then they asked Him, Where, Lord? He said to them, Wherever the dead body is, there will the vultures *or* eagles be gathered together.

**18** Also [Jesus] told them a parable to the effect that they ought always to pray and not to *c*turn coward (faint, lose heart, and give up).

2He said, In a certain city there was a judge who neither reverenced *and* feared God nor respected *or* considered man.

3And there was a widow in that city who kept coming to him and saying, Protect *and* defend *and* give me justice against my adversary.

4And for a time he would not; but later he said to himself, Though I have neither reverence *or* fear for God nor respect *or* consideration for man,

5Yet because this widow continues to bother me, I will defend *and* protect *and* avenge her, lest she give me *d*intolerable annoyance *and* wear me out by her continual coming *or* *e*at the last she come and rail on me *or* *c*assault me *or* *e*strangle me.

6Then the Lord said, Listen to what the unjust judge says!

7And will not [our just] God defend *and* protect *and* avenge His elect (His chosen ones), who cry to Him day and night? Will He *e*defer them *and* *c*delay help on their behalf?

8I tell you, He will defend *and* protect *and* avenge them speedily. However, when the Son of Man comes, will He find [*c*persistence in] faith on the earth?

9He also told this parable to some people who trusted in themselves *and* were confident that they were righteous [that they were upright and in right standing with God] and scorned *and* made nothing of all the rest of men:

10Two men went up into the temple [*f*enclosure] to pray, the one a Pharisee and the other a tax collector.

---

## New International Version

stood by himself and prayed: 'God, I thank you that I am not like other people—robbers, evildoers, adulterers—or even like this tax collector. ¹²I fast twice a week and give a tenth of all I get.'

¹³"But the tax collector stood at a distance. He would not even look up to heaven, but beat his breast and said, 'God, have mercy on me, a sinner.'

¹⁴"I tell you that this man, rather than the other, went home justified before God. For all those who exalt themselves will be humbled, and those who humble themselves will be exalted."

### The Little Children and Jesus

¹⁵People were also bringing babies to Jesus for him to place his hands on them. When the disciples saw this, they rebuked them. ¹⁶But Jesus called the children to him and said, "Let the little children come to me, and do not hinder them, for the kingdom of God belongs to such as these. ¹⁷Truly I tell you, anyone who will not receive the kingdom of God like a little child will never enter it."

### The Rich and the Kingdom of God

¹⁸A certain ruler asked him, "Good teacher, what must I do to inherit eternal life?"

¹⁹"Why do you call me good?" Jesus answered. "No one is good—except God alone. ²⁰You know the commandments: 'You shall not commit adultery, you shall not murder, you shall not steal, you shall not give false testimony, honor your father and mother.'ᵃ"

²¹"All these I have kept since I was a boy," he said.

²²When Jesus heard this, he said to him, "You still lack one thing. Sell everything you have and give to the poor, and you will have treasure in heaven. Then come, follow me."

²³When he heard this, he became very sad, because he was very wealthy. ²⁴Jesus looked at him and said, "How hard it is for the rich to enter the kingdom of God! ²⁵Indeed, it is easier for a camel to go through the eye of a needle than for someone who is rich to enter the kingdom of God."

²⁶Those who heard this asked, "Who then can be saved?"

²⁷Jesus replied, "What is impossible with man is possible with God."

²⁸Peter said to him, "We have left all we had to follow you!"

²⁹"Truly I tell you," Jesus said to them, "no one who has left home or wife or brothers or sisters or parents or children for the sake of the kingdom of God ³⁰will fail to receive many times as much in this age, and in the age to come eternal life."

### Jesus Predicts His Death a Third Time

³¹Jesus took the Twelve aside and told them, "We are going up to Jerusalem, and everything that is written by the prophets about the Son of Man will be fulfilled. ³²He will be delivered over to the Gentiles. They will mock him, insult him and spit on him; ³³they will flog him and kill him. On the third day he will rise again."

³⁴The disciples did not understand any of this. Its meaning was hidden from them, and they did not know what he was talking about.

## Amplified Bible

¹¹The Pharisee ᵃtook his stand ostentatiously and began to pray thus before and with himself: God, I thank You that I am not like the rest of men—extortioners (robbers), swindlers [unrighteous in heart and life], adulterers—or even like this tax collector here.

¹²I fast twice a week; I give tithes of all that I gain.

¹³But the tax collector, [merely] standing at a distance, would not even lift up his eyes to heaven, but kept striking his breast, saying, O God, be favorable (be gracious, be merciful) to me, the ᵇespecially wicked sinner that I am!

¹⁴I tell you, this man went down to his home justified (forgiven and made upright and in right standing with God), rather than the other man; for everyone who exalts himself will be humbled, but he who humbles himself will be exalted.

¹⁵Now they were also bringing [even] babies to Him that He might touch them, and when the disciples noticed it, they reproved them.

¹⁶But Jesus called them [ᶜthe parents] to Him, saying, Allow the little children to come to Me, and do not hinder them, for to such [as these] belongs the kingdom of God.

¹⁷Truly I say to you, whoever does not accept and receive and welcome the kingdom of God like a little child [does] shall not in any way enter it [at all].

¹⁸And a certain ruler asked Him, Good Teacher [You who are ᵇessentially and perfectly ᵈmorally good], what shall I do to inherit eternal life [to partake of eternal salvation in the Messiah's kingdom]?

¹⁹Jesus said to him, Why do you call Me [ᵇessentially and perfectly ᵈmorally] good? No one is [ᵇessentially and perfectly ᵈmorally] good—except God only.

²⁰You know the commandments: Do not commit adultery, do not kill, do not steal, do not witness falsely, honor your father and your mother. [Exod. 20:12-16; Deut. 5:16-20.]

²¹And he replied, All these I have kept from my youth.

²²And when Jesus heard it, He said to him, One thing you still lack. Sell everything that you have and ᵇdivide [the money] among the poor, and you will have [rich] treasure in heaven; and come back [and] follow Me [become My disciple, join My party, and accompany Me].

²³But when he heard this, he became distressed and very sorrowful, for he was rich—exceedingly so.

²⁴Jesus, observing him, said, How difficult it is for those who have wealth to enter the kingdom of God!

²⁵For it is easier for a camel to enter through a needle's eye than [for] a rich man to enter the kingdom of God.

²⁶And those who heard it said, Then who can be saved?

²⁷But He said, What is impossible with men is possible with God. [Gen. 18:14; Jer. 32:17.]

²⁸And Peter said, See, we have left our own [things—home, family, and business] and have followed You.

²⁹And He said to them, I say to you truly, there is no one who has left house or wife or brothers or parents or children for the sake of the kingdom of God

³⁰Who will not receive in return many times more in this world and, in the coming age, eternal life.

³¹Then taking the Twelve [apostles] aside, He said to them, Listen! We are going up to Jerusalem, and all things that are written about the Son of Man through and by the prophets will be fulfilled. [Isa. 53:1-12.]

³²For He will be handed over to the Gentiles and will be made sport of and scoffed and jeered at and insulted and spit upon. [Isa. 50:6.]

³³They will flog Him and kill Him; and on the third day He will rise again. [Ps. 16:10.]

³⁴But they understood nothing of these things; His words were a mystery and hidden from them, and they did not comprehend what He was telling them.

---

ᵃ Marvin Vincent, *Word Studies.* ᵇ Joseph Thayer, *A Greek-English Lexicon.* ᶜ Matthew Henry, *Commentary on the Holy Bible.* ᵈ Hermann Cremer, *Biblico-Theological Lexicon.*

| New International Version | Amplified Bible |

## A Blind Beggar Receives His Sight

<sup>35</sup>As Jesus approached Jericho, a blind man was sitting by the roadside begging. <sup>36</sup>When he heard the crowd going by, he asked what was happening. <sup>37</sup>They told him, "Jesus of Nazareth is passing by."

<sup>38</sup>He called out, "Jesus, Son of David, have mercy on me!"

<sup>39</sup>Those who led the way rebuked him and told him to be quiet, but he shouted all the more, "Son of David, have mercy on me!"

<sup>40</sup>Jesus stopped and ordered the man to be brought to him. When he came near, Jesus asked him, <sup>41</sup>"What do you want me to do for you?"

"Lord, I want to see," he replied.

<sup>42</sup>Jesus said to him, "Receive your sight; your faith has healed you." <sup>43</sup>Immediately he received his sight and followed Jesus, praising God. When all the people saw it, they also praised God.

## Zacchaeus the Tax Collector

**19** Jesus entered Jericho and was passing through. <sup>2</sup>A man was there by the name of Zacchaeus; he was a chief tax collector and was wealthy. <sup>3</sup>He wanted to see who Jesus was, but because he was short he could not see over the crowd. <sup>4</sup>So he ran ahead and climbed a sycamore-fig tree to see him, since Jesus was coming that way.

<sup>5</sup>When Jesus reached the spot, he looked up and said to him, "Zacchaeus, come down immediately. I must stay at your house today." <sup>6</sup>So he came down at once and welcomed him gladly.

<sup>7</sup>All the people saw this and began to mutter, "He has gone to be the guest of a sinner."

<sup>8</sup>But Zacchaeus stood up and said to the Lord, "Look, Lord! Here and now I give half of my possessions to the poor, and if I have cheated anybody out of anything, I will pay back four times the amount."

<sup>9</sup>Jesus said to him, "Today salvation has come to this house, because this man, too, is a son of Abraham. <sup>10</sup>For the Son of Man came to seek and to save the lost."

## The Parable of the Ten Minas

<sup>11</sup>While they were listening to this, he went on to tell them a parable, because he was near Jerusalem and the people thought that the kingdom of God was going to appear at once. <sup>12</sup>He said: "A man of noble birth went to a distant country to have himself appointed king and then to return. <sup>13</sup>So he called ten of his servants and gave them ten minas.<sup>a</sup> 'Put this money to work,' he said, 'until I come back.'

<sup>14</sup>"But his subjects hated him and sent a delegation after him to say, 'We don't want this man to be our king.'

<sup>15</sup>"He was made king, however, and returned home.

## Amplified Bible

<sup>35</sup>As He came near to Jericho, it occurred that a blind man was sitting by the roadside begging.

<sup>36</sup>And hearing a crowd going by, he asked what it meant.

<sup>37</sup>They told him, Jesus of Nazareth is passing by.

<sup>38</sup>And he shouted, saying, Jesus, Son of David, take pity *and* have mercy on me!

<sup>39</sup>But those who were in front reproved him, telling him to keep quiet; yet he <sup>a</sup>screamed *and* shrieked so much the more, Son of David, take pity *and* have mercy on me!

<sup>40</sup>Then Jesus stood still and ordered that he be led to Him; and when he came near, Jesus asked him,

<sup>41</sup>What do you want Me to do for you? He said, Lord, let me receive my sight!

<sup>42</sup>And Jesus said to him, Receive your sight! Your faith (<sup>b</sup>your trust and confidence that spring from your faith in God) has healed you.

<sup>43</sup>And instantly he received his sight and began to follow Jesus, <sup>c</sup>recognizing, praising, *and* honoring God; and all the people, when they saw it, praised God.

**19** And [Jesus] entered Jericho and was passing through it.

<sup>2</sup>And there was a man called Zacchaeus, a chief tax collector, and [he was] rich.

<sup>3</sup>And he was trying to see Jesus, which One He was, but he could not on account of the crowd, because he was small in stature.

<sup>4</sup>So he ran on ahead and climbed up in a sycamore tree in order to see Him, for He was about to pass that way.

<sup>5</sup>And when Jesus reached the place, He looked up and said to him, Zacchaeus, hurry and come down; for I must stay at your house today.

<sup>6</sup>So he hurried and came down, and he received *and* welcomed Him joyfully.

<sup>7</sup>And when the people saw it, they all <sup>d</sup>muttered among themselves *and* indignantly complained, He has gone in to be the guest of *and* lodge with a man who is devoted to sin *and* preeminently a sinner.

<sup>8</sup>So then Zacchaeus stood up and solemnly declared to the Lord, See, Lord, the half of my goods I [now] give [by way of restoration] to the poor, and if I have cheated anyone out of anything, I [now] restore four times as much. [Exod. 22:1; Lev. 6:5; Num. 5:6, 7.]

<sup>9</sup>And Jesus said to him, Today is [<sup>e</sup>Messianic and spiritual] salvation come to [all the members of] this household, since Zacchaeus too is a [real spiritual] son of Abraham;

<sup>10</sup>For the Son of Man came to seek and to save that which was lost.

<sup>11</sup>Now as they were listening to these things, He proceeded to tell a parable, because He was approaching Jerusalem and because they thought that the kingdom of God was going to be brought to light *and* shown forth immediately.

<sup>12</sup>He therefore said, A certain nobleman went into a distant country to obtain for himself a kingdom and then to return.

<sup>13</sup>Calling ten of his [own] bond servants, he gave them ten minas [each equal to about one hundred days' wages or nearly twenty dollars] and said to them, <sup>f</sup>Buy *and* sell with these <sup>a</sup>while I go *and* then return.

<sup>14</sup>But his citizens detested him and sent an embassy after him to say, We do not want this man to become ruler over us.

<sup>15</sup>When he returned after having received the kingdom,

<sup>a</sup> Marvin Vincent, *Word Studies.*  <sup>b</sup> Joseph Thayer, *A Greek-English Lexicon.*  <sup>c</sup> Hermann Cremer, *Biblico-Theological Lexicon.*  <sup>d</sup> G. Abbott-Smith, *Manual Greek Lexicon.*  <sup>e</sup> James Moulton and George Milligan, *The Vocabulary.*  <sup>f</sup> William Tyndale, *The Tyndale Bible.*

<sup>a</sup> 13 A mina was about three months' wages.

## New International Version

Then he sent for the servants to whom he had given the money, in order to find out what they had gained with it.

¹⁶"The first one came and said, 'Sir, your mina has earned ten more.'

¹⁷"'Well done, my good servant!' his master replied. 'Because you have been trustworthy in a very small matter, take charge of ten cities.'

¹⁸"The second came and said, 'Sir, your mina has earned five more.'

¹⁹"His master answered, 'You take charge of five cities.'

²⁰"Then another servant came and said, 'Sir, here is your mina; I have kept it laid away in a piece of cloth. ²¹I was afraid of you, because you are a hard man. You take out what you did not put in and reap what you did not sow.'

²²"His master replied, 'I will judge you by your own words, you wicked servant! You knew, did you, that I am a hard man, taking out what I did not put in, and reaping what I did not sow? ²³Why then didn't you put my money on deposit, so that when I came back, I could have collected it with interest?'

²⁴"Then he said to those standing by, 'Take his mina away from him and give it to the one who has ten minas.'

²⁵"'Sir,' they said, 'he already has ten!'

²⁶"He replied, 'I tell you that to everyone who has, more will be given, but as for the one who has nothing, even what they have will be taken away. ²⁷But those enemies of mine who did not want me to be king over them—bring them here and kill them in front of me.'"

### Jesus Comes to Jerusalem as King

²⁸After Jesus had said this, he went on ahead, going up to Jerusalem. ²⁹As he approached Bethphage and Bethany at the hill called the Mount of Olives, he sent two of his disciples, saying to them, ³⁰"Go to the village ahead of you, and as you enter it, you will find a colt tied there, which no one has ever ridden. Untie it and bring it here. ³¹If anyone asks you, 'Why are you untying it?' say, 'The Lord needs it.'"

³²Those who were sent ahead went and found it just as he had told them. ³³As they were untying the colt, its owners asked them, "Why are you untying the colt?"

³⁴They replied, "The Lord needs it."

³⁵They brought it to Jesus, threw their cloaks on the colt and put Jesus on it. ³⁶As he went along, people spread their cloaks on the road.

³⁷When he came near the place where the road goes down the Mount of Olives, the whole crowd of disciples began joyfully to praise God in loud voices for all the miracles they had seen:

³⁸"Blessed is the king who comes in the name of the Lord!"ᵃ

"Peace in heaven and glory in the highest!"

³⁹Some of the Pharisees in the crowd said to Jesus, "Teacher, rebuke your disciples!"

⁴⁰"I tell you," he replied, "if they keep quiet, the stones will cry out."

⁴¹As he approached Jerusalem and saw the city, he wept

---

## Amplified Bible

he ordered these bond servants to whom he had given the money to be called to him, that he might know how much each one had made by ᵃbuying and selling.

¹⁶The first one came before him, and he said, Lord, your mina has made ten [additional] minas.

¹⁷And he said to him, Well done, excellent bond servant! Because you have been faithful and trustworthy in a very little [thing], you shall have authority over ten cities.

¹⁸The second one also came and said, Lord, your mina has made five more minas.

¹⁹And he said also to him, And you will take charge over five cities.

²⁰Then another came and said, Lord, here is your mina, which I have kept laid up in a ᵇhandkerchief.

²¹For I was [constantly] afraid of you, because you are a stern (hard, severe) man; you pick up what you did not lay down, and you reap what you did not sow.

²²He said to the servant, I will judge and condemn you out of your own mouth, you wicked slave! You knew [did you] that I was a stern (hard, severe) man, picking up what I did not lay down, and reaping what I did not sow?

²³Then why did you not put my money in a bank, so that on my return, I might have collected it with interest?

²⁴And he said to the bystanders, Take the mina away from him and give it to him who has the ten minas.

²⁵And they said to him, Lord, he has ten minas [already]!

²⁶And [said Jesus,] I tell you that to everyone who gets and has will more be given, but from the man who does not get and does not have, even what he has will be taken away.

²⁷[The indignant king ended by saying] But as for these enemies of mine who did not want me to reign over them—bring them here and ᶜslaughter them in my presence!

²⁸And after saying these things, Jesus went on ahead of them, going up to Jerusalem.

²⁹When He came near Bethphage and Bethany at the mount called [the Mount of] Olives, He sent two of His disciples,

³⁰Telling [them], Go into the village yonder; there, as you go in, you will find a donkey's colt tied, on which no man has ever yet sat. Loose it and bring [it here].

³¹If anybody asks you, Why are you untying [it]? you shall say this: Because the Lord has need of it.

³²So those who were sent went away and found it [just] as He had told them.

³³And as they were loosening the colt, its owners said to them, Why are you untying the colt?

³⁴And they said, The Lord has need of it.

³⁵And they brought it to Jesus; then they threw their garments over the colt and set Jesus upon it. [Zech. 9:9.]

³⁶And as He rode along, the people kept spreading their garments on the road. [II Kings 9:13.]

³⁷As He was approaching [the city], at the descent of the Mount of Olives, the whole crowd of the disciples began to rejoice and to praise God [extolling Him exultantly and] loudly for all the mighty miracles and works of power that they had witnessed,

³⁸Crying, Blessed (celebrated with praises) is the King Who comes in the name of the Lord! Peace in heaven [ᵈfreedom there from all the distresses that are experienced as the result of sin] and glory (majesty and splendor) in the highest [heaven]! [Ps. 118:26.]

³⁹And some of the Pharisees from the throng said to Jesus, Teacher, reprove Your disciples!

⁴⁰He replied, I tell you that if these keep silent, the very stones will cry out. [Hab. 2:11.]

⁴¹And as He approached, He saw the city, and He wept [ᶜaudibly] over it,

---

ᵃ William Tyndale, *The Tyndale Bible*. ᵇ James Moulton and George Milligan, *The Vocabulary*. ᶜ Marvin Vincent, *Word Studies*. ᵈ Hermann Cremer, *Biblico-Theological Lexicon*.

---

ᵃ 38 Psalm 118:26

## New International Version

over it [42]and said, "If you, even you, had only known on this day what would bring you peace—but now it is hidden from your eyes. [43]The days will come upon you when your enemies will build an embankment against you and encircle you and hem you in on every side. [44]They will dash you to the ground, you and the children within your walls. They will not leave one stone on another, because you did not recognize the time of God's coming to you."

### Jesus at the Temple

[45]When Jesus entered the temple courts, he began to drive out those who were selling. [46]"It is written," he said to them, "'My house will be a house of prayer'[a]; but you have made it 'a den of robbers.'[b]"

[47]Every day he was teaching at the temple. But the chief priests, the teachers of the law and the leaders among the people were trying to kill him. [48]Yet they could not find any way to do it, because all the people hung on his words.

### The Authority of Jesus Questioned

**20** One day as Jesus was teaching the people in the temple courts and proclaiming the good news, the chief priests and the teachers of the law, together with the elders, came up to him. [2]"Tell us by what authority you are doing these things," they said. "Who gave you this authority?"

[3]He replied, "I will also ask you a question. Tell me: [4]John's baptism—was it from heaven, or of human origin?"

[5]They discussed it among themselves and said, "If we say, 'From heaven,' he will ask, 'Why didn't you believe him?' [6]But if we say, 'Of human origin,' all the people will stone us, because they are persuaded that John was a prophet."

[7]So they answered, "We don't know where it was from."

[8]Jesus said, "Neither will I tell you by what authority I am doing these things."

### The Parable of the Tenants

[9]He went on to tell the people this parable: "A man planted a vineyard, rented it to some farmers and went away for a long time. [10]At harvest time he sent a servant to the tenants so they would give him some of the fruit of the vineyard. But the tenants beat him and sent him away empty-handed. [11]He sent another servant, but that one also they beat and treated shamefully and sent away empty-handed. [12]He sent still a third, and they wounded him and threw him out.

[13]"Then the owner of the vineyard said, 'What shall I do? I will send my son, whom I love; perhaps they will respect him.'

## Amplified Bible

[42]Exclaiming, Would that you had known personally, even at least in this your day, the things that make for peace (for [a]freedom from all the distresses that are experienced as the result of sin and upon which your peace—your [b]security, safety, prosperity, and happiness—depends)! But now they are hidden from your eyes.

[43]For a time is coming upon you when your enemies will throw up a [c]bank [with pointed stakes] about you and surround you and shut you in on every side. [Isa. 29:3; Jer. 6:6; Ezek. 4:2.]

[44]And they will dash you down to the ground, you [Jerusalem] and your children within you; and they will not leave in you one stone upon another, [all] because you did not come progressively to recognize *and* know *and* understand [from observation and experience] the time of your visitation [that is, when God was visiting you, the time [b]in which God showed Himself gracious toward you and offered you salvation through Christ],

[45]Then He went into the temple [[d]enclosure] and began to drive out those who were selling,

[46]Telling them, It is written, My house shall be a house of prayer; but you have made it a [e]cave of robbers. [Isa. 56:7; Jer. 7:11.]

[47]And He continued to teach day after day in the temple [[d]porches and courts]. The chief priests and scribes and the leading men of the people were seeking to put Him to death,

[48]But they did not discover anything they could do, for all the people hung upon His words *and* [f]stuck by Him.

**20** One day as Jesus was instructing the people in the temple [[d]porches] and preaching the good news (the Gospel), the chief priests and the scribes came up with the elders (members of the Sanhedrin)

[2]And said to Him, Tell us by what [sort of] authority You are doing these things? Or who is it who gave You this authority?

[3]He replied to them, I will also ask you a question. Now answer Me:

[4]Was the baptism of John from heaven, or from men?

[5]And they argued *and* discussed [it] *and* reasoned together [c]with themselves, saying, If we reply, From heaven, He will say, Why then did you not believe him?

[6]But if we answer, From men, all the people will stone us [c]to death, for they are [c]long since firmly convinced that John was a prophet.

[7]So they replied that they did not know from where it came.

[8]Then Jesus said to them, Neither will I tell you by what authority I do these things.

[9]Then He began to relate to the people this parable ([b]this story to figuratively portray what He had to say): A man planted a vineyard and leased it to some vinedressers and went into another country for a long stay. [Isa. 5:1-7.]

[10]When the [right] season came, he sent a bond servant to the tenants, that they might give him [his part] of the fruit of the vineyard; but the tenants beat ([b]thrashed) him and sent him away empty-handed.

[11]And he sent still another servant; him they also beat ([b]thrashed) and dishonored *and* insulted him [g]disgracefully and sent him away empty-handed.

[12]And he sent yet a third; this one they wounded and threw out [of the vineyard].

[13]Then the owner of the vineyard said, What shall I do? I will send my beloved son; it is [c]probable that they will respect him.

[a] Hermann Cremer, *Biblico-Theological Lexicon.* [b] Joseph Thayer, *A Greek-English Lexicon.* [c] Marvin Vincent, *Word Studies.* [d] Richard Trench, *Synonyms of the New Testament.* [e] James Moulton and George Milligan, *The Vocabulary.* [f] William Tyndale, *The Tyndale Bible.* [g] Alexander Souter, *Pocket Lexicon.*

[a] 46 Isaiah 56:7   [b] 46 Jer. 7:11

## New International Version

14"But when the tenants saw him, they talked the matter over. 'This is the heir,' they said. 'Let's kill him, and the inheritance will be ours.' 15So they threw him out of the vineyard and killed him.

"What then will the owner of the vineyard do to them? 16He will come and kill those tenants and give the vineyard to others."

When the people heard this, they said, "God forbid!"

17Jesus looked directly at them and asked, "Then what is the meaning of that which is written:

"'The stone the builders rejected
has become the cornerstone'*a*?

18Everyone who falls on that stone will be broken to pieces; anyone on whom it falls will be crushed."

19The teachers of the law and the chief priests looked for a way to arrest him immediately, because they knew he had spoken this parable against them. But they were afraid of the people.

### Paying Taxes to Caesar

20Keeping a close watch on him, they sent spies, who pretended to be sincere. They hoped to catch Jesus in something he said, so that they might hand him over to the power and authority of the governor. 21So the spies questioned him: "Teacher, we know that you speak and teach what is right, and that you do not show partiality but teach the way of God in accordance with the truth. 22Is it right for us to pay taxes to Caesar or not?"

23He saw through their duplicity and said to them, 24"Show me a denarius. Whose image and inscription are on it?"

"Caesar's," they replied.

25He said to them, "Then give back to Caesar what is Caesar's, and to God what is God's."

26They were unable to trap him in what he had said there in public. And astonished by his answer, they became silent.

### The Resurrection and Marriage

27Some of the Sadducees, who say there is no resurrection, came to Jesus with a question. 28"Teacher," they said, "Moses wrote for us that if a man's brother dies and leaves a wife but no children, the man must marry the widow and raise up offspring for his brother. 29Now there were seven brothers. The first one married a woman and died childless. 30The second 31and then the third married her, and in the same way the seven died, leaving no children. 32Finally, the woman died too. 33Now then, at the resurrection whose wife will she be, since the seven were married to her?"

34Jesus replied, "The people of this age marry and are given in marriage. 35But those who are considered worthy of taking part in the age to come and in the resurrection from the dead will neither marry nor be given in marriage, 36and they can no longer die; for they are like the angels. They are God's children, since they are children of the resurrection. 37But in the account of the burning bush, even Moses showed that the dead rise, for he calls the Lord 'the God of Abraham, and the God of Isaac, and the God of Ja-

## Amplified Bible

14But when the tenants saw him, they argued among themselves, saying, This is the heir; let us kill him, so that the inheritance may be ours.

15So they drove him out of the vineyard and killed him. What then will the owner of the vineyard do to them?

16He will come and [*a*utterly] put an end to those tenants and will give the vineyard to others. When they [the chief priests and the scribes and the elders] heard this, they said, May it never be!

17But [Jesus] looked at them and said, What then is [the meaning of] this that is written: The [very] Stone that the builders rejected has become the chief Stone of the corner [Cornerstone]? [Ps. 118:22, 23.]

18Everyone who falls on that Stone will be broken [in pieces]; but upon whomever It falls, It will crush him [winnow him and *b*scatter him as dust]. [Isa. 8:14, 15; Dan. 2:34, 35.]

19The scribes and the chief priests desired *and* tried to find a way to arrest Him at that very hour, but they were afraid of the people; for they discerned that He had related this parable against them.

20So they watched [for an opportunity to ensnare] Him, and sent spies who pretended to be upright (honest and sincere), that they might lay hold of something He might say, so as to turn Him over to the control and authority of the governor.

21They asked Him, Teacher, we know that You speak and teach what is right, and that You show no partiality to anyone but teach the way of God honestly *and* in truth.

22Is it lawful for us to give tribute to Caesar or not?

23But He recognized *and* understood their cunning *and* *c*unscrupulousness and said to them,

24Show Me a denarius (a coin)! Whose image and inscription does it have? They answered, Caesar's.

25He said to them, Then render to Caesar the things that are Caesar's, *d*and to God the things that are God's.

26So they could not in the presence of the people take hold of anything He said to turn it against Him; but marveling at His reply, they were silent.

27Also there came to Him some Sadducees, those who say that there is no resurrection.

28And they asked Him a question, saying, Teacher, Moses wrote for us [a law] that if a man's brother dies, leaving a wife and no children, the man shall take the woman and raise up offspring for his brother. [Deut. 25:5, 6.]

29Now there were seven brothers; and the first took a wife and died without [having any] children.

30And the second

31And then the third took her, and in like manner all seven, and they died, leaving no children.

32Last of all, the woman died also.

33Now in the resurrection whose wife will the woman be? For the seven married her.

34And Jesus said to them, The people of this world *and* present age marry and are given in marriage;

35But those who are considered worthy to gain that other world *and* that future age and to attain to the resurrection from the dead neither marry nor are given in marriage;

36For they cannot die again, but they are *e*angel-like *and* *f*equal to angels. And being sons of *and* *a*sharers in the resurrection, they are sons of God.

37But that the dead are raised [*a*from death]—even Moses made known *and* showed in the passage concerning the [burning] bush, where he calls the Lord, The God of Abraham, the God of Isaac, and the God of Jacob. [Exod. 3:6.]

*a* Joseph Thayer, *A Greek-English Lexicon.* *b* James Moulton and George Milligan, *The Vocabulary.* *c* Marvin Vincent, *Word Studies.* *d* A rebuke of emperor worship. *e* Hermann Cremer, *Biblico-Theological Lexicon.* *f* G. Abbott-Smith, *Manual Greek Lexicon.*

## New International Version

cob.'*ᵃ* ³⁸He is not the God of the dead, but of the living, for to him all are alive."

³⁹Some of the teachers of the law responded, "Well said, teacher!" ⁴⁰And no one dared to ask him any more questions.

### Whose Son Is the Messiah?

⁴¹Then Jesus said to them, "Why is it said that the Messiah is the son of David? ⁴²David himself declares in the Book of Psalms:

"'The Lord said to my Lord:
"Sit at my right hand
⁴³until I make your enemies
a footstool for your feet."'*ᵇ*

⁴⁴David calls him 'Lord.' How then can he be his son?"

### Warning Against the Teachers of the Law

⁴⁵While all the people were listening, Jesus said to his disciples, ⁴⁶"Beware of the teachers of the law. They like to walk around in flowing robes and love to be greeted with respect in the marketplaces and have the most important seats in the synagogues and the places of honor at banquets. ⁴⁷They devour widows' houses and for a show make lengthy prayers. These men will be punished most severely."

### The Widow's Offering

**21** As Jesus looked up, he saw the rich putting their gifts into the temple treasury. ²He also saw a poor widow put in two very small copper coins. ³"Truly I tell you," he said, "this poor widow has put in more than all the others. ⁴All these people gave their gifts out of their wealth; but she out of her poverty put in all she had to live on."

### The Destruction of the Temple and Signs of the End Times

⁵Some of his disciples were remarking about how the temple was adorned with beautiful stones and with gifts dedicated to God. But Jesus said, ⁶"As for what you see here, the time will come when not one stone will be left on another; every one of them will be thrown down."

⁷"Teacher," they asked, "when will these things happen? And what will be the sign that they are about to take place?"

⁸He replied: "Watch out that you are not deceived. For many will come in my name, claiming, 'I am he,' and, 'The time is near.' Do not follow them. ⁹When you hear of wars and uprisings, do not be frightened. These things must happen first, but the end will not come right away."

¹⁰Then he said to them: "Nation will rise against nation, and kingdom against kingdom. ¹¹There will be great earthquakes, famines and pestilences in various places, and fearful events and great signs from heaven.

¹²"But before all this, they will seize you and persecute you. They will hand you over to synagogues and put you in prison, and you will be brought before kings and governors, and all on account of my name. ¹³And so you will bear testimony to me. ¹⁴But make up your mind not to worry beforehand how you will defend yourselves. ¹⁵For

## Amplified Bible

³⁸Now He is not the God of the dead, but of the living, for to Him all men are alive [whether in the body or out of it] *and* they are alive [not dead] unto Him [in definite relationship to Him].

³⁹And some of the scribes replied, Teacher, you have spoken well *and* expertly [*ᵃ*so that there is no room for blame].

⁴⁰For they did not dare to question Him further.

⁴¹But He asked them, How can people say that the Christ (the Messiah, the Anointed One) is David's Son?

⁴²For David himself says in [the] Book of Psalms, The Lord said to my Lord, Sit at My right hand

⁴³Until I make Your enemies a footstool for Your feet. [Ps. 110:1.]

⁴⁴So David calls Him Lord; how then is He his Son?

⁴⁵And with all the people listening, He said to His disciples,

⁴⁶Beware of the scribes, who like to walk about in long robes and love to be saluted [with honor] in places where people congregate and love the front *and* best seats in the synagogues and places of distinction at feasts,

⁴⁷Who make away with *and* devour widows' houses, and [to cover it up] with pretense make long prayers. They will receive the greater condemnation (the heavier sentence, the severer punishment).

**21** Looking up, [Jesus] saw the rich people putting their gifts into the treasury.

²And He saw also a poor widow putting in two mites (copper coins).

³And He said, Truly I say to you, this poor widow has put in more than all of them;

⁴For they all gave out of their abundance (their surplus); but she has contributed out of her lack *and* her want, putting in all that she had on which to live.

⁵And as some were saying of the temple that it was decorated with handsome (shapely and magnificent) stones and consecrated offerings [*ᵃ*laid up to be kept], He said,

⁶As for all this that you [thoughtfully] look at, the time will come when there shall not be left here one stone upon another that will not be thrown down.

⁷And they asked Him, Teacher, when will this happen? And what sign will there be when this is about to occur?

⁸And He said, Be on your guard *and* be careful that you are not led astray; for many will come in My name [*ᵃ*appropriating to themselves the name Messiah which belongs to Me], saying, I am He! and, The time is at hand! Do not go out after them.

⁹And when you hear of wars and insurrections (disturbances, disorder, and confusion), do not become alarmed *and* panic-stricken *and* terrified; for all this must take place first, but the end will not [come] immediately.

¹⁰Then He told them, Nation will rise against nation, and kingdom against kingdom. [II Chron. 15:6; Isa. 19:2.]

¹¹There will be mighty *and* violent earthquakes, and in various places famines and pestilences (plagues: *ᵇ*malignant and contagious or infectious epidemic diseases which are deadly and devastating); and there will be sights of terror and great signs from heaven.

¹²But previous to all this, they will lay their hands on you and persecute you, turning you over to the synagogues and prisons, and you will be led away before kings and governors for My name's sake.

¹³This will be a time (an opportunity) for you to bear testimony.

¹⁴Resolve *and* settle it in your minds not to meditate *and* prepare beforehand how you are to make your defense *and* how you will answer.

---

*ᵃ 37* Exodus 3:6     *ᵇ 43* Psalm 110:1

*ᵃ* Joseph Thayer, *A Greek-English Lexicon.* *ᵇ Webster's New International Dictionary* offers this phrase as a definition of "plague" and "pestilence."

## New International Version

I will give you words and wisdom that none of your adversaries will be able to resist or contradict. ¹⁶You will be betrayed even by parents, brothers and sisters, relatives and friends, and they will put some of you to death. ¹⁷Everyone will hate you because of me. ¹⁸But not a hair of your head will perish. ¹⁹Stand firm, and you will win life.

²⁰"When you see Jerusalem being surrounded by armies, you will know that its desolation is near. ²¹Then let those who are in Judea flee to the mountains, let those in the city get out, and let those in the country not enter the city. ²²For this is the time of punishment in fulfillment of all that has been written. ²³How dreadful it will be in those days for pregnant women and nursing mothers! There will be great distress in the land and wrath against this people. ²⁴They will fall by the sword and will be taken as prisoners to all the nations. Jerusalem will be trampled on by the Gentiles until the times of the Gentiles are fulfilled.

²⁵"There will be signs in the sun, moon and stars. On the earth, nations will be in anguish and perplexity at the roaring and tossing of the sea. ²⁶People will faint from terror, apprehensive of what is coming on the world, for the heavenly bodies will be shaken. ²⁷At that time they will see the Son of Man coming in a cloud with power and great glory. ²⁸When these things begin to take place, stand up and lift up your heads, because your redemption is drawing near."

²⁹He told them this parable: "Look at the fig tree and all the trees. ³⁰When they sprout leaves, you can see for yourselves and know that summer is near. ³¹Even so, when you see these things happening, you know that the kingdom of God is near.

³²"Truly I tell you, this generation will certainly not pass away until all these things have happened. ³³Heaven and earth will pass away, but my words will never pass away.

³⁴"Be careful, or your hearts will be weighed down with carousing, drunkenness and the anxieties of life, and that day will close on you suddenly like a trap. ³⁵For it will come on all those who live on the face of the whole earth. ³⁶Be always on the watch, and pray that you may be able

## Amplified Bible

¹⁵For I [Myself] will give you a mouth *and* such utterance and wisdom that all of your foes combined will be unable to stand against or refute.

¹⁶You will be delivered up *and* betrayed even by parents and brothers and relatives and friends, and [some] of you they will put to death.

¹⁷And you will be hated (despised) by everyone because [you bear] My name *and* for its sake.

¹⁸But not a hair of your head shall perish. [I Sam. 14:45.]

¹⁹By your steadfastness *and* patient endurance you *ᵃ*shall win the *ᵇ*true life of your souls.

²⁰But when you see Jerusalem surrounded by armies, then know *and* understand that its desolation has come near.

²¹Then let those who are in Judea flee to the mountains, and let those who are inside [the city] get out of it, and let not those who are out in the country come into it;

²²For those are days of vengeance [of rendering full justice or satisfaction], that all things that are written may be fulfilled.

²³Alas for those who are pregnant and for those who have babies which they are nursing in those days! For great misery *and* anguish *and* distress shall be upon the land and indignation *and* punishment *and* retribution upon this people.

²⁴They will fall by *ᶜ*the mouth *and* the edge of the sword and will be led away as captives to *and* among all nations; and Jerusalem will be trodden down by the Gentiles until the times of the Gentiles are fulfilled (completed). [Isa. 63:18; Dan. 8:13.]

²⁵And there will be signs in the sun and moon and stars; and upon the earth [there will be] distress (trouble and anguish) of nations in bewilderment *and* perplexity [*ᵇ*without resources, left wanting, embarrassed, in doubt, not knowing which way to turn] at the roaring (*ᵃ*the echo) of the tossing of the sea, [Isa. 13:10; Joel 2:10; Zeph. 1:15.]

²⁶Men swooning away *or* expiring with fear *and* dread *and* apprehension and expectation of the things that are coming on the world; for the [very] powers of the heavens will be shaken *and* *ᵇ*caused to totter.

²⁷And then they will see the Son of Man coming in a cloud with great (transcendent and overwhelming) power and [all His kingly] glory (majesty and splendor). [Dan. 7:13, 14.]

²⁸Now when these things begin to occur, look up and lift up your heads, because your redemption (deliverance) is drawing near.

²⁹And He told them a parable: Look at the fig tree and all the trees;

³⁰When they put forth their buds *and* come out in leaf, you see for yourselves and perceive *and* know that summer is already near.

³¹Even so, when you see these things taking place, understand *and* know that the kingdom of God is at hand.

³²Truly I tell you, this generation (*ᵈ*those living at that definite period of time) will not perish *and* pass away until all has taken place.

³³The *ᵉ*sky and the earth (*ᵇ*the universe, the world) will pass away, but My words will not pass away.

³⁴But take heed to yourselves *and* be on your guard, lest your hearts be overburdened *and* depressed (weighed down) with the *ᵇ*giddiness *and* headache *and* *ᶠ*nausea of self-indulgence, drunkenness, and worldly worries *and* cares pertaining to [the business of] this life, and [lest] that day come upon you suddenly like a trap *or* a noose;

³⁵For it will come upon all who live upon the face of the entire earth.

³⁶Keep awake then *and* watch at all times [be discreet,

*ᵃ* Marvin Vincent, *Word Studies.* *ᵇ* Joseph Thayer, *A Greek-English Lexicon.* *ᶜ* John Wycliffe, *The Wycliffe Bible.* *ᵈ* Hermann Cremer, *Biblico-Theological Lexicon.* *ᵉ* James Moulton and George Milligan, *The Vocabulary.* *ᶠ* G. Abbott-Smith, *Manual Greek Lexicon.*

## New International Version

to escape all that is about to happen, and that you may be able to stand before the Son of Man."

[37] Each day Jesus was teaching at the temple, and each evening he went out to spend the night on the hill called the Mount of Olives, [38] and all the people came early in the morning to hear him at the temple.

### Judas Agrees to Betray Jesus

**22** Now the Festival of Unleavened Bread, called the Passover, was approaching, [2] and the chief priests and the teachers of the law were looking for some way to get rid of Jesus, for they were afraid of the people. [3] Then Satan entered Judas, called Iscariot, one of the Twelve. [4] And Judas went to the chief priests and the officers of the temple guard and discussed with them how he might betray Jesus. [5] They were delighted and agreed to give him money. [6] He consented, and watched for an opportunity to hand Jesus over to them when no crowd was present.

### The Last Supper

[7] Then came the day of Unleavened Bread on which the Passover lamb had to be sacrificed. [8] Jesus sent Peter and John, saying, "Go and make preparations for us to eat the Passover."

[9] "Where do you want us to prepare for it?" they asked.

[10] He replied, "As you enter the city, a man carrying a jar of water will meet you. Follow him to the house that he enters, [11] and say to the owner of the house, 'The Teacher asks: Where is the guest room, where I may eat the Passover with my disciples?' [12] He will show you a large room upstairs, all furnished. Make preparations there."

[13] They left and found things just as Jesus had told them. So they prepared the Passover.

[14] When the hour came, Jesus and his apostles reclined at the table. [15] And he said to them, "I have eagerly desired to eat this Passover with you before I suffer. [16] For I tell you, I will not eat it again until it finds fulfillment in the kingdom of God."

[17] After taking the cup, he gave thanks and said, "Take this and divide it among you. [18] For I tell you I will not drink again from the fruit of the vine until the kingdom of God comes."

[19] And he took bread, gave thanks and broke it, and gave it to them, saying, "This is my body given for you; do this in remembrance of me."

[20] In the same way, after the supper he took the cup, saying, "This cup is the new covenant in my blood, which is poured out for you.[a] [21] But the hand of him who is going to betray me is with mine on the table. [22] The Son of Man will go as it has been decreed. But woe to that man who betrays him!" [23] They began to question among themselves which of them it might be who would do this.

[24] A dispute also arose among them as to which of them was considered to be greatest. [25] Jesus said to them, "The

## Amplified Bible

attentive, and ready], praying that you may have the full strength *and* ability *and* be accounted worthy to escape all these things [taken together] that will take place, and to stand in the presence of the Son of Man.

[37] Now in the daytime Jesus was teaching in [a the porches and courts of] the temple, but at night He would go out and stay on the mount called Olivet.

[38] And early in the morning all the people came to Him in the temple [a porches or courts] to listen to Him.

**22** Now the Festival of Unleavened Bread was drawing near, which is called the Passover.

[2] And the chief priests and the scribes were seeking how to do away with [Jesus], for they feared the people.

[3] But [then] Satan entered into Judas, called Iscariot, who was one of the Twelve [apostles].

[4] And he went away and discussed with the chief priests and captains how he might betray Him *and* deliver Him up to them.

[5] And they were delighted and pledged [themselves] to give him money.

[6] So he agreed [to this], and sought an opportunity to betray Him to them [without an uprising] in the absence of the throng.

[7] Then came the day of Unleavened Bread on which the Passover [lamb] had to be slain. [Exod. 12:18-20; Deut. 16:5-8.]

[8] So Jesus sent Peter and John, saying, Go and prepare for us the Passover meal, that we may eat it.

[9] They said to Him, Where do You want us to prepare [it]?

[10] He said to them, Behold, when you have gone into the city, a man carrying an earthen jug *or* pitcher of water will meet you; follow him into the house which he enters,

[11] And say to the master of the house, The Teacher asks you, Where is the guest room, where I may eat the Passover [meal] with My disciples?

[12] And he will show you a large room upstairs, furnished [with carpets and with couches properly spread]; there make [your] preparations.

[13] And they went and found it [just] as He had said to them; and they made ready the Passover [supper].

[14] And when the hour came, [Jesus] reclined at table, and the apostles with Him.

[15] And He said to them, I have earnestly *and* intensely desired to eat this Passover with you before I suffer;

[16] For I say to you, I shall eat it no more until it is fulfilled in the kingdom of God.

[17] And He took a cup, and when He had given thanks, He said, Take this and divide *and* distribute it among yourselves;

[18] For I say to you that from now on I shall not drink of the fruit of the vine at all until the kingdom of God comes.

[19] Then He took a loaf [of bread], and when He had given thanks, He broke [it] and gave it to them saying, This is My body which is given for you; do this in remembrance of Me.

[20] And in like manner, He took the cup after supper, saying, This cup is the new testament *or* covenant [ratified] in My blood, which is shed (poured out) for you.

[21] But, behold, the hand of him who [b] is now engaged in betraying Me is with Me on the table. [Ps. 41:9.]

[22] For the Son of Man is going as it has been determined *and* appointed, but woe to that man by whom He is betrayed *and* delivered up!

[23] And they began to inquire among themselves which of them it was who was about to do this. [Ps. 41:9.]

[24] Now [b] an eager contention arose among them [as to] which of them was considered *and* reputed to be the greatest.

---

[a] 19,20 Some manuscripts do not have *given for you . . . poured out for you.*

[a] Richard Trench, *Synonyms of the New Testament.* [b] Marvin Vincent, *Word Studies.*

## New International Version

kings of the Gentiles lord it over them; and those who exercise authority over them call themselves Benefactors. 26But you are not to be like that. Instead, the greatest among you should be like the youngest, and the one who rules like the one who serves. 27For who is greater, the one who is at the table or the one who serves? Is it not the one who is at the table? But I am among you as one who serves. 28You are those who have stood by me in my trials. 29And I confer on you a kingdom, just as my Father conferred one on me, 30so that you may eat and drink at my table in my kingdom and sit on thrones, judging the twelve tribes of Israel.

31"Simon, Simon, Satan has asked to sift all of you as wheat. 32But I have prayed for you, Simon, that your faith may not fail. And when you have turned back, strengthen your brothers."

33But he replied, "Lord, I am ready to go with you to prison and to death."

34Jesus answered, "I tell you, Peter, before the rooster crows today, you will deny three times that you know me."

35Then Jesus asked them, "When I sent you without purse, bag or sandals, did you lack anything?"

"Nothing," they answered.

36He said to them, "But now if you have a purse, take it, and also a bag; and if you don't have a sword, sell your cloak and buy one. 37It is written: 'And he was numbered with the transgressors'a; and I tell you that this must be fulfilled in me. Yes, what is written about me is reaching its fulfillment."

38The disciples said, "See, Lord, here are two swords."

"That's enough!" he replied.

### Jesus Prays on the Mount of Olives

39Jesus went out as usual to the Mount of Olives, and his disciples followed him. 40On reaching the place, he said to them, "Pray that you will not fall into temptation." 41He withdrew about a stone's throw beyond them, knelt down and prayed, 42"Father, if you are willing, take this cup from me; yet not my will, but yours be done." 43An angel from heaven appeared to him and strengthened him. 44And being in anguish, he prayed more earnestly, and his sweat was like drops of blood falling to the ground.b

45When he rose from prayer and went back to the disciples, he found them asleep, exhausted from sorrow. 46"Why are you sleeping?" he asked them. "Get up and pray so that you will not fall into temptation."

### Jesus Arrested

47While he was still speaking a crowd came up, and the man who was called Judas, one of the Twelve, was leading them. He approached Jesus to kiss him, 48but Jesus asked him, "Judas, are you betraying the Son of Man with a kiss?"

49When Jesus' followers saw what was going to happen, they said, "Lord, should we strike with our swords?" 50And

## Amplified Bible

25But Jesus said to them, The kings of the Gentiles aare deified by them and exercise lordship [aruling as emperor-gods] over them; and those in authority over them are called benefactors and well-doers.

26But this is not to be so with you; on the contrary, let him who is the greatest among you become like the youngest, and him who is the chief and leader like one who serves.

27For who is the greater, the one who reclines at table (the master), or the one who serves? Is it not the one who reclines at table? But I am in your midst as One Who serves.

28And you are those who have remained [throughout] and persevered with Me in My trials;

29And as My Father has appointed a kingdom and conferred it on Me, so do I confer on you [the privilege and decree],

30That you may eat and drink at My table in My kingdom and sit on thrones, judging the twelve tribes of Israel.

31Simon, Simon (Peter), listen! Satan bhas asked excessively that [all of] you be given up to him [out of the power and keeping of God], that he might sift [all of] you like grain, [Job 1:6-12; Amos 9:9.]

32But I have prayed especially for you [Peter], that your [own] faith may not fail; and when you yourself have turned again, strengthen and establish your brethren.

33And [Simon Peter] said to Him, Lord, I am ready to go with You both to prison and to death.

34But Jesus said, I tell you, Peter, before a [single] cock shall crow this day, you will three times [utterly] deny that you know Me.

35And He said to them, When I sent you out with no purse or [provision] bag or sandals, did you lack anything? They answered, Nothing!

36Then He said to them, But now let him who has a purse take it, and also [his provision] bag; and let him who has no sword sell his mantle and buy a sword.

37For I tell you that this Scripture must yet be fulfilled in Me: And He was counted and classed among the wicked (the outlaws, the criminals); for what is written about Me has its fulfillment [has reached its end and is finally settled]. [Isa. 53:12.]

38And they said, Look, Lord! Here are two swords. And He said to them, It is enough.

39And He came out and went, as was His habit, to the Mount of Olives, and the disciples also followed Him.

40And when He came to the place, He said to them, Pray that you may not [at all] enter into temptation.

41And He withdrew from them about a stone's throw and knelt down and prayed,

42Saying, Father, if You are willing, remove this cup from Me; yet not My will, but [calways] Yours be done.

43And there appeared to Him an angel from heaven, strengthening Him in spirit.

44And being in an agony [of mind], He prayed [all the] more earnestly and intently, and His sweat became like great dclots of blood dropping down upon the ground.

45And when He got up from prayer, He came to the disciples and found them sleeping from grief,

46And He said to them, Why do you sleep? Get up and pray that you may not enter [at all] into temptation.

47And while He was still speaking, behold, there came a crowd, and the man called Judas, one of the Twelve [apostles], was going before [leading] them. He drew near to Jesus to kiss Him,

48But Jesus said to him, Judas! Would you betray and deliver up the Son of Man with a kiss?

49And when those who were around Him saw what was about to happen, they said, Lord, shall we strike with the sword?

---

a 37 Isaiah 53:12    b 43,44 Many early manuscripts do not have verses 43 and 44.

a Kenneth Wuest, Word Studies. b Joseph Thayer, A Greek-English Lexicon. c Charles B. Williams, The New Testament: A Translation: "in the Greek present imperative, denoting continued action." d Marvin Vincent, Word Studies.

## New International Version

one of them struck the servant of the high priest, cutting off his right ear.

⁵¹But Jesus answered, "No more of this!" And he touched the man's ear and healed him.

⁵²Then Jesus said to the chief priests, the officers of the temple guard, and the elders, who had come for him, "Am I leading a rebellion, that you have come with swords and clubs? ⁵³Every day I was with you in the temple courts, and you did not lay a hand on me. But this is your hour—when darkness reigns."

### Peter Disowns Jesus

⁵⁴Then seizing him, they led him away and took him into the house of the high priest. Peter followed at a distance. ⁵⁵And when some there had kindled a fire in the middle of the courtyard and had sat down together, Peter sat down with them. ⁵⁶A servant girl saw him seated there in the firelight. She looked closely at him and said, "This man was with him."

⁵⁷But he denied it. "Woman, I don't know him," he said.

⁵⁸A little later someone else saw him and said, "You also are one of them."

"Man, I am not!" Peter replied.

⁵⁹About an hour later another asserted, "Certainly this fellow was with him, for he is a Galilean."

⁶⁰Peter replied, "Man, I don't know what you're talking about!" Just as he was speaking, the rooster crowed. ⁶¹The Lord turned and looked straight at Peter. Then Peter remembered the word the Lord had spoken to him: "Before the rooster crows today, you will disown me three times." ⁶²And he went outside and wept bitterly.

### The Guards Mock Jesus

⁶³The men who were guarding Jesus began mocking and beating him. ⁶⁴They blindfolded him and demanded, "Prophesy! Who hit you?" ⁶⁵And they said many other insulting things to him.

### Jesus Before Pilate and Herod

⁶⁶At daybreak the council of the elders of the people, both the chief priests and the teachers of the law, met together, and Jesus was led before them. ⁶⁷"If you are the Messiah," they said, "tell us."

Jesus answered, "If I tell you, you will not believe me, ⁶⁸and if I asked you, you would not answer. ⁶⁹But from now on, the Son of Man will be seated at the right hand of the mighty God."

⁷⁰They all asked, "Are you then the Son of God?"

He replied, "You say that I am."

⁷¹Then they said, "Why do we need any more testimony? We have heard it from his own lips."

**23** Then the whole assembly rose and led him off to Pilate. ²And they began to accuse him, saying, "We have found this man subverting our nation. He opposes payment of taxes to Caesar and claims to be Messiah, a king."

## Amplified Bible

⁵⁰And one of them struck the bond servant of the high priest and cut off his ear, the right one.

⁵¹But Jesus said, Permit ᵃthem to go so far [as to seize Me]. And He touched the ᵇlittle (insignificant) ear and healed him.

⁵²Then Jesus said to those who had come out against Him—the chief priests and captains of the temple and elders [of the Sanhedrin]—Have you come out with swords and clubs as [you would] against a robber?

⁵³When I was with you day after day in the temple [ᶜenclosure], you did not stretch forth [your] hands against Me. But this is your hour—and the power [which] darkness [gives you has its way].

⁵⁴Then they seized Him and led Him away, bringing Him into the house of the high priest. Peter was following at a distance.

⁵⁵And when they had kindled a fire in the middle of the courtyard and were seated together, Peter sat among them.

⁵⁶Then a servant girl, seeing him as he sat in the firelight and gazing [intently] at him, said, This man too was with ᵈHim.

⁵⁷But he denied it and said, Woman, I do not know Him!

⁵⁸And a little later someone else saw him and said, You are one of them also. But Peter said, Man, I am not!

⁵⁹And when about an hour more had elapsed, still another emphatically insisted, It is the truth that this man also was with Him, for he too is a Galilean!

⁶⁰But Peter said, Man, I do not know what you are talking about. And instantly, while he was still speaking, the cock crowed.

⁶¹And the Lord turned and looked at Peter. And Peter recalled the Lord's words, how He had told him, Before the cock crows today, you will deny Me thrice.

⁶²And he went out and wept bitterly [that is, with painfully moving grief].

⁶³Now the men who had Jesus in custody treated Him with contempt and scoffed at and ridiculed Him and beat Him;

⁶⁴They blindfolded Him also and asked Him, Prophesy! Who is it that struck ᵈYou?

⁶⁵And they said many other evil and slanderous and insulting words against Him, reviling Him.

⁶⁶As soon as it was day, the assembly of the elders of the people gathered together, both chief priests and scribes; and they led Him into their council (the Sanhedrin), and they said,

⁶⁷If You are the Christ (the Messiah), tell us. But He said to them, If I tell you, you will not believe (trust in, cleave to, and rely on what I say),

⁶⁸And if I question you, you will not answer.

⁶⁹But hereafter (from this time on), the Son of Man shall be seated at the right hand of the power of God. [Ps. 110:1.]

⁷⁰And they all said, You are the Son of God, then? And He said to them, ᵉIt is just as you say; I AM.

⁷¹And they said, What further evidence do we need? For we have heard [it] ourselves from His own mouth!

**23** Then the whole assembly of them got up and conducted [Jesus] before Pilate.

²And they began to accuse Him, asserting, We found this ᵈMan perverting (misleading, corrupting, and turning away) our nation and forbidding to pay tribute to Caesar, saying that He Himself is Christ (the Messiah, the Anointed One), a King!

---

ᵃ Marvin Vincent, *Word Studies.* ᵇ John Wycliffe, *The Wycliffe Bible.* ᶜ Richard Trench, *Synonyms of the New Testament.* ᵈ Capitalized because of what He is, the spotless Son of God, not what the speaker may have thought He was. ᵉ Joseph Thayer, *A Greek-English Lexicon.*

## New International Version

³So Pilate asked Jesus, "Are you the king of the Jews?"

"You have said so," Jesus replied.

⁴Then Pilate announced to the chief priests and the crowd, "I find no basis for a charge against this man."

⁵But they insisted, "He stirs up the people all over Judea by his teaching. He started in Galilee and has come all the way here."

⁶On hearing this, Pilate asked if the man was a Galilean. ⁷When he learned that Jesus was under Herod's jurisdiction, he sent him to Herod, who was also in Jerusalem at that time.

⁸When Herod saw Jesus, he was greatly pleased, because for a long time he had been wanting to see him. From what he had heard about him, he hoped to see him perform a sign of some sort. ⁹He plied him with many questions, but Jesus gave him no answer. ¹⁰The chief priests and the teachers of the law were standing there, vehemently accusing him. ¹¹Then Herod and his soldiers ridiculed and mocked him. Dressing him in an elegant robe, they sent him back to Pilate. ¹²That day Herod and Pilate became friends—before this they had been enemies.

¹³Pilate called together the chief priests, the rulers and the people, ¹⁴and said to them, "You brought me this man as one who was inciting the people to rebellion. I have examined him in your presence and have found no basis for your charges against him. ¹⁵Neither has Herod, for he sent him back to us; as you can see, he has done nothing to deserve death. ¹⁶Therefore, I will punish him and then release him." [17]ᵃ

¹⁸But the whole crowd shouted, "Away with this man! Release Barabbas to us!" ¹⁹(Barabbas had been thrown into prison for an insurrection in the city, and for murder.)

²⁰Wanting to release Jesus, Pilate appealed to them again. ²¹But they kept shouting, "Crucify him! Crucify him!"

²²For the third time he spoke to them: "Why? What crime has this man committed? I have found in him no grounds for the death penalty. Therefore I will have him punished and then release him."

²³But with loud shouts they insistently demanded that he be crucified, and their shouts prevailed. ²⁴So Pilate decided to grant their demand. ²⁵He released the man who had been thrown into prison for insurrection and murder, the one they asked for, and surrendered Jesus to their will.

### The Crucifixion of Jesus

²⁶As the soldiers led him away, they seized Simon from Cyrene, who was on his way in from the country, and put the cross on him and made him carry it behind Jesus. ²⁷A large number of people followed him, including women who mourned and wailed for him. ²⁸Jesus turned and said

## Amplified Bible

³So Pilate asked Him, Are You the King of the Jews? And He answered him, [ᵃIt is just as] you say. [I AM.]

⁴And Pilate said to the chief priests and the throngs, I find no guilt or crime in this Man.

⁵But they were urgent and emphatic, saying, He stirs up and excites the people, teaching throughout all Judea—from Galilee, where He began, even to this place.

⁶Upon hearing this, Pilate asked whether the Man was a Galilean.

⁷And when he found out [certainly] that He belonged to Herod's jurisdiction, he sent Him up to Herod [a higher authority], who was also in Jerusalem in those days.

⁸Now when Herod saw Jesus, he was exceedingly glad, for he had eagerly desired to see Him for a long time because of what he had heard concerning Him, and he was hoping to witness some sign (some striking evidence or spectacular performance) done by Him.

⁹So he asked Him many questions, but He made no reply. [Isa. 53:7.]

¹⁰Meanwhile, the chief priests and the scribes stood by, continuing vehemently and violently to accuse Him.

¹¹And Herod, with his soldiers, treated Him with contempt and scoffed at and ridiculed Him; then, dressing Him up in bright and gorgeous apparel, he sent Him back to Pilate. [Isa. 53:8.]

¹²And that very day Herod and Pilate became friends with each other—[though] they had been at enmity before this.

¹³Pilate then called together the chief priests and the rulers and the people,

¹⁴And said to them, You brought this Man before me as One Who was perverting and misleading and ᵇturning away and corrupting the people; and behold, after examining Him before you, I have not found any offense (crime or guilt) in this Man in regard to your accusations against Him;

¹⁵No, nor indeed did Herod, for he sent Him back to us; behold, He has done nothing deserving of death.

¹⁶I will therefore chastise Him and ᵇdeliver Him amended (reformed, taught His lesson) and release Him.

¹⁷ᶜFor it was necessary for him to release to them one prisoner at the Feast.

¹⁸But they all together raised a deep cry [from the depths of their throats], saying, Away with this Man! Release to us Barabbas!

¹⁹He was a man who had been thrown into prison for raising a riot in the city, and for murder.

²⁰Once more Pilate called to them, wishing to release Jesus;

²¹But they kept shouting out, Crucify, crucify Him!

²²A third time he said to them, Why? What wrong has He done? I have found [no offense or crime or guilt] in Him nothing deserving of death; I will therefore chastise Him [ᵈin order to teach Him better] and release Him.

²³But they were insistent and urgent, demanding with loud cries that He should be crucified. And their voices prevailed (accomplished their purpose).

²⁴And Pilate gave sentence, that what they asked should be done.

²⁵So he released the man who had been thrown into prison for riot and murder, for whom they continued to ask, but Jesus he delivered up to be done with as they willed.

²⁶And as they led Him away, they seized one Simon of Cyrene, who was coming in from the country, and laid on him the cross and made him carry it behind Jesus.

²⁷And there accompanied [Jesus] a great multitude of the people, [including] women who bewailed and lamented Him.

---

ᵃ 17 Some manuscripts include here words similar to Matt. 27:15 and Mark 15:6.

ᵃ Joseph Thayer, A Greek-English Lexicon.  ᵇ John Wycliffe, The Wycliffe Bible.  ᶜ Many manuscripts do not contain this verse.  ᵈ Marvin Vincent, Word Studies.

## New International Version

to them, "Daughters of Jerusalem, do not weep for me; weep for yourselves and for your children. ²⁹For the time will come when you will say, 'Blessed are the childless women, the wombs that never bore and the breasts that never nursed!' ³⁰Then

"'they will say to the mountains, "Fall on us!"
and to the hills, "Cover us!"'ᵃ

³¹For if people do these things when the tree is green, what will happen when it is dry?"

³²Two other men, both criminals, were also led out with him to be executed. ³³When they came to the place called the Skull, they crucified him there, along with the criminals—one on his right, the other on his left. ³⁴Jesus said, "Father, forgive them, for they do not know what they are doing."ᵇ And they divided up his clothes by casting lots.

³⁵The people stood watching, and the rulers even sneered at him. They said, "He saved others; let him save himself if he is God's Messiah, the Chosen One."

³⁶The soldiers also came up and mocked him. They offered him wine vinegar ³⁷and said, "If you are the king of the Jews, save yourself."

³⁸There was a written notice above him, which read: THIS IS THE KING OF THE JEWS.

³⁹One of the criminals who hung there hurled insults at him: "Aren't you the Messiah? Save yourself and us!"

⁴⁰But the other criminal rebuked him. "Don't you fear God," he said, "since you are under the same sentence? ⁴¹We are punished justly, for we are getting what our deeds deserve. But this man has done nothing wrong."

⁴²Then he said, "Jesus, remember me when you come into your kingdom.ᶜ"

⁴³Jesus answered him, "Truly I tell you, today you will be with me in paradise."

### The Death of Jesus

⁴⁴It was now about noon, and darkness came over the whole land until three in the afternoon, ⁴⁵for the sun stopped shining. And the curtain of the temple was torn in two. ⁴⁶Jesus called out with a loud voice, "Father, into your hands I commit my spirit."ᵈ When he had said this, he breathed his last.

⁴⁷The centurion, seeing what had happened, praised God and said, "Surely this was a righteous man." ⁴⁸When all the people who had gathered to witness this sight saw what took place, they beat their breasts and went away. ⁴⁹But all those who knew him, including the women who had followed him from Galilee, stood at a distance, watching these things.

## Amplified Bible

²⁸But Jesus, turning toward them, said, Daughters of Jerusalem, do not weep for Me, but weep for yourselves and for your children.

²⁹For behold, the days are coming during which they will say, Blessed (happy, fortunate, and ᵃto be envied) are the barren, and the wombs that have not borne, and the breasts that have never nursed [babies]!

³⁰Then they will begin to say to the mountains, Fall on us! and to the hills, Cover (conceal, hide) us!

³¹For if they do these things when the timber is green, what will happen when it is dry?

³²Two others also, who were criminals, were led away to be executed with Him. [Isa. 53:12.]

³³And when they came to the place which is called The Skull [Latin: Calvary; Hebrew: Golgotha], there they crucified Him, and [along with] the criminals, one on the right and one on the left.

³⁴And Jesus prayed, Father, forgive them, for they know not what they do. And they divided His garments and distributed them by casting lots for them. [Ps. 22:18.]

³⁵Now the people stood by [ᵇcalmly and leisurely] watching; but the rulers scoffed and sneered (ᶜturned up their noses) at Him, saying, He rescued others [ᵈfrom death]; let Him now rescue Himself, if He is the Christ (the Messiah) of God, His Chosen One!

³⁶The soldiers also ridiculed and made sport of Him, coming up and offering Him vinegar (a sour wine mixed with water) [Ps. 69:21.]

³⁷And saying, If You are the King of the Jews, save (rescue) Yourself [ᵈfrom death].

³⁸For there was also an inscription above Him ᵉin letters of Greek and Latin and Hebrew: This is the King of the Jews.

³⁹One of the criminals who was suspended kept up a railing at Him, saying, Are You not the Christ (the Messiah)? Rescue Yourself and us [ᵈfrom death]!

⁴⁰But the other one reproved him, saying, Do you not even fear God, seeing you yourself are under the same sentence of condemnation and suffering the same penalty?

⁴¹And we indeed suffer it justly, receiving the due reward of our actions; but this Man has done nothing out of the way [nothing ᵇstrange or eccentric or perverse or unreasonable].

⁴²Then he said to Jesus, Lord, remember me when You come ᵇin Your kingly glory!

⁴³And He answered him, Truly I tell you, today you shall be with Me in Paradise.

⁴⁴It was now about the sixth hour (midday), and darkness enveloped the whole land and earth until the ninth hour (about three o'clock in the afternoon),

⁴⁵While the sun's light faded or ᶠwas darkened; and the curtain [of the Holy of Holies] of the temple was torn in two. [Exod. 26:31-35.]

⁴⁶And Jesus, crying out with a loud voice, said, Father, into Your hands I commit My spirit! And with these words, He expired. [Ps. 31:5.]

⁴⁷Now the centurion, having seen what had taken place, ᵈrecognized God and thanked and praised Him, and said, Indeed, without question, this Man was upright (just and innocent)!

⁴⁸And all the throngs that had gathered to see this spectacle, when they saw what had taken place, returned to their homes, beating their breasts.

⁴⁹And all the acquaintances of [Jesus] and the women who had followed Him from Galilee stood at a distance and watched these things.

---

ᵃ 30 Hosea 10:8    ᵇ 34 Some early manuscripts do not have this sentence.    ᶜ 42 Some manuscripts *come with your kingly power*
ᵈ 46 Psalm 31:5

ᵃ Alexander Souter, *Pocket Lexicon*.   ᵇ Marvin Vincent, *Word Studies*.
ᶜ Literal translation.   ᵈ Hermann Cremer, *Biblico-Theological Lexicon*.
ᵉ Some manuscripts add this phrase.   ᶠ Many ancient manuscripts so read.

## New International Version

### The Burial of Jesus

⁵⁰Now there was a man named Joseph, a member of the Council, a good and upright man, ⁵¹who had not consented to their decision and action. He came from the Judean town of Arimathea, and he himself was waiting for the kingdom of God. ⁵²Going to Pilate, he asked for Jesus' body. ⁵³Then he took it down, wrapped it in linen cloth and placed it in a tomb cut in the rock, one in which no one had yet been laid. ⁵⁴It was Preparation Day, and the Sabbath was about to begin.

⁵⁵The women who had come with Jesus from Galilee followed Joseph and saw the tomb and how his body was laid in it. ⁵⁶Then they went home and prepared spices and perfumes. But they rested on the Sabbath in obedience to the commandment.

### Jesus Has Risen

**24** On the first day of the week, very early in the morning, the women took the spices they had prepared and went to the tomb. ²They found the stone rolled away from the tomb, ³but when they entered, they did not find the body of the Lord Jesus. ⁴While they were wondering about this, suddenly two men in clothes that gleamed like lightning stood beside them. ⁵In their fright the women bowed down with their faces to the ground, but the men said to them, "Why do you look for the living among the dead? ⁶He is not here; he has risen! Remember how he told you, while he was still with you in Galilee: ⁷'The Son of Man must be delivered over to the hands of sinners, be crucified and on the third day be raised again.' " ⁸Then they remembered his words.

⁹When they came back from the tomb, they told all these things to the Eleven and to all the others. ¹⁰It was Mary Magdalene, Joanna, Mary the mother of James, and the others with them who told this to the apostles. ¹¹But they did not believe the women, because their words seemed to them like nonsense. ¹²Peter, however, got up and ran to the tomb. Bending over, he saw the strips of linen lying by themselves, and he went away, wondering to himself what had happened.

### On the Road to Emmaus

¹³Now that same day two of them were going to a village called Emmaus, about seven miles[a] from Jerusalem. ¹⁴They were talking with each other about everything that had happened. ¹⁵As they talked and discussed these things with each other, Jesus himself came up and walked along with them; ¹⁶but they were kept from recognizing him.

¹⁷He asked them, "What are you discussing together as you walk along?"

They stood still, their faces downcast. ¹⁸One of them,

## Amplified Bible

⁵⁰Now notice, there was a man named Joseph from the Jewish town of Arimathea. He was a member of the council (the Sanhedrin), and a good (upright, ᵃadvantageous) man, and righteous (in right standing with God and man),

⁵¹Who had not agreed with *or* assented to the purpose and action of the others; and he was expecting *and* waiting for the kingdom of God.

⁵²This man went to Pilate and asked for the body of Jesus.

⁵³Then he took it down and ᵇrolled it up in a linen cloth ᶜfor swathing dead bodies and laid Him in a rock-hewn tomb, where no one had ever yet been laid.

⁵⁴It was the day of Preparation [for the Sabbath], and the Sabbath was dawning (approaching).

⁵⁵The women who had come with [Jesus] from Galilee followed closely and saw the tomb and how His body was laid.

⁵⁶Then they went back and made ready spices and ointments (perfumes). On the Sabbath day they rested in accordance with the commandment. [Exod. 12:16; 20:10.]

**24** But on the first day of the week, at early dawn, [the women] went to the tomb, taking the spices which they had made ready.

²And they found the stone rolled back from the tomb,

³But when they went inside, they did not find the body of the Lord Jesus.

⁴And while they were perplexed *and* wondering what to do about this, behold, two men in dazzling raiment suddenly stood beside them.

⁵And as [the women] were frightened and were bowing their faces to the ground, the men said to them, Why do you look for the living among [those who are] dead?

⁶He is not here, but has risen! Remember how He told you while He was still in Galilee

⁷That the Son of Man must be given over into the hands of sinful men (men ᵃwhose way or nature is to act in opposition to God) and be crucified and on the third day rise [ᵃfrom death]. [Ps. 16:10.]

⁸And they remembered His words.

⁹And having returned from the tomb, they reported all these things [taken together] to the eleven apostles and to all the rest.

¹⁰Now it was Mary Magdalene and Joanna and Mary the mother of James, and the other women with them, who reported these things to the apostles.

¹¹But these reports seemed to the men an idle tale (ᵈmadness, ᵉfeigned things, ᶜnonsense), and they did not believe the women.

¹²But Peter got up and ran to the tomb; and stooping down and looking in, he saw the linen cloths alone by themselves, and he went away, wondering about *and* marveling at what had happened.

¹³And behold, that very day two of [the disciples] were going to a village called Emmaus, [which is] about seven miles from Jerusalem.

¹⁴And they were talking with each other about all these things that had occurred.

¹⁵And while they were conversing and discussing together, Jesus Himself caught up with them and was already accompanying them.

¹⁶But their eyes were held, so that they did not recognize Him.

¹⁷And He said to them, What is this discussion that you are exchanging (ᶠthrowing back and forth) between yourselves as you walk along? And they stood still, looking sad *and* downcast.

---

ᵃ Hermann Cremer, *Biblico-Theological Lexicon.* ᵇ Robert Young, *Analytical Concordance.* ᶜ James Moulton and George Milligan, *The Vocabulary.* ᵈ John Wycliffe, *The Wycliffe Bible.* ᵉ William Tyndale, *The Tyndale Bible.* ᶠ Literal translation.

---

ᵃ 13 Or about 11 kilometers

## New International Version

named Cleopas, asked him, "Are you the only one visiting Jerusalem who does not know the things that have happened there in these days?"

[19]"What things?" he asked.

"About Jesus of Nazareth," they replied. "He was a prophet, powerful in word and deed before God and all the people. [20]The chief priests and our rulers handed him over to be sentenced to death, and they crucified him; [21]but we had hoped that he was the one who was going to redeem Israel. And what is more, it is the third day since all this took place. [22]In addition, some of our women amazed us. They went to the tomb early this morning [23]but didn't find his body. They came and told us that they had seen a vision of angels, who said he was alive. [24]Then some of our companions went to the tomb and found it just as the women had said, but they did not see Jesus."

[25]He said to them, "How foolish you are, and how slow to believe all that the prophets have spoken! [26]Did not the Messiah have to suffer these things and then enter his glory?" [27]And beginning with Moses and all the Prophets, he explained to them what was said in all the Scriptures concerning himself.

[28]As they approached the village to which they were going, Jesus continued on as if he were going farther. [29]But they urged him strongly, "Stay with us, for it is nearly evening; the day is almost over." So he went in to stay with them.

[30]When he was at the table with them, he took bread, gave thanks, broke it and began to give it to them. [31]Then their eyes were opened and they recognized him, and he disappeared from their sight. [32]They asked each other, "Were not our hearts burning within us while he talked with us on the road and opened the Scriptures to us?"

[33]They got up and returned at once to Jerusalem. There they found the Eleven and those with them, assembled together [34]and saying, "It is true! The Lord has risen and has appeared to Simon." [35]Then the two told what had happened on the way, and how Jesus was recognized by them when he broke the bread.

### Jesus Appears to the Disciples

[36]While they were still talking about this, Jesus himself stood among them and said to them, "Peace be with you."

[37]They were startled and frightened, thinking they saw a ghost. [38]He said to them, "Why are you troubled, and why do doubts rise in your minds? [39]Look at my hands and my feet. It is I myself! Touch me and see; a ghost does not have flesh and bones, as you see I have."

[40]When he had said this, he showed them his hands and

## Amplified Bible

[18]Then one of them, named Cleopas, answered Him, Do you alone dwell as a stranger in Jerusalem and not know the things that have occurred there in these days?

[19]And He said to them, What [kind of] things? And they said to Him, About Jesus of Nazareth, Who was a Prophet mighty in work and word before God and all the people—

[20]And how our chief priests and rulers gave Him up to be sentenced to death, and crucified Him.

[21]But we were hoping that it was He Who would redeem *and* set Israel free. Yes, and besides all this, it is now the third day since these things occurred.

[22]And moreover, some women of our company astounded us *and* ᵃdrove us out of our senses. They were at the tomb early [in the morning]

[23]But did not find His body; and they returned saying that they had [even] seen a vision of angels, who said that He was alive!

[24]So some of those [who were] with us went to the tomb and they found it just as the women had said, but Him they did not see.

[25]And [Jesus] said to them, O foolish ones [sluggish in mind, dull of perception] and slow of heart to believe (adhere to and trust in and rely on) everything that the prophets have spoken!

[26]Was it not necessary *and* ᵇessentially fitting that the Christ (the Messiah) should suffer all these things before entering into His glory (His majesty and splendor)?

[27]Then beginning with Moses and [throughout] all the Prophets, He went on explaining *and* interpreting to them in all the Scriptures the things concerning *and* referring to Himself.

[28]Then they drew near the village to which they were going, and He acted as if He would go further.

[29]But they urged *and* insisted, saying to Him, Remain with us, for it is toward evening, and the day is now far spent. So He went in to stay with them.

[30]And it occurred that as He reclined at table with them, He took [a loaf of] bread and praised [God] *and* gave thanks *and* asked a blessing, and then broke it and was giving it to them

[31]When their eyes were [instantly] opened and they [clearly] recognized Him, and He vanished (ᵇdeparted invisibly).

[32]And they said to one another, Were not our hearts greatly moved *and* burning within us while He was talking with us on the road and as He opened *and* explained to us [the sense of] the Scriptures?

[33]And rising up that very hour, they went back to Jerusalem, where they found the Eleven [apostles] gathered together and those who were with them,

[34]Who said, The Lord really has risen and has appeared to Simon (Peter)!

[35]Then they [themselves] ᵇrelated [in full] what had happened on the road, and how He was known *and* recognized by them in the breaking of bread.

[36]Now while they were talking about this, Jesus Himself took His stand among them and said to them, Peace (ᶜfreedom from all the distresses that are experienced as the result of sin) be to you!

[37]But they were so startled and terrified that they thought they saw a spirit.

[38]And He said to them, Why are you disturbed *and* troubled, and why do such doubts *and* questionings arise in your hearts?

[39]See My hands and My feet, that it is I Myself! Feel *and* handle Me and see, for a spirit does not have flesh and bones, as you see that I have.

[40]And when He had said this, He showed them His hands and His feet.

---

ᵃ Literal translation. ᵇ Marvin Vincent, *Word Studies*. ᶜ Hermann Cremer, *Biblico-Theological Lexicon*.

## New International Version

feet. 41And while they still did not believe it because of joy and amazement, he asked them, "Do you have anything here to eat?" 42They gave him a piece of broiled fish, 43and he took it and ate it in their presence.

44He said to them, "This is what I told you while I was still with you: Everything must be fulfilled that is written about me in the Law of Moses, the Prophets and the Psalms."

45Then he opened their minds so they could understand the Scriptures. 46He told them, "This is what is written: The Messiah will suffer and rise from the dead on the third day, 47and repentance for the forgiveness of sins will be preached in his name to all nations, beginning at Jerusalem. 48You are witnesses of these things. 49I am going to send you what my Father has promised; but stay in the city until you have been clothed with power from on high."

### The Ascension of Jesus

50When he had led them out to the vicinity of Bethany, he lifted up his hands and blessed them. 51While he was blessing them, he left them and was taken up into heaven. 52Then they worshiped him and returned to Jerusalem with great joy. 53And they stayed continually at the temple, praising God.

## Amplified Bible

41And while [since] they still could not believe it for sheer joy and marveled, He said to them, Have you anything here to eat?

42They gave Him a piece of broiled fish,

43And He took [it] and ate [it] before them.

44Then He said to them, This is what I told you while I was still with you: everything which is written concerning Me in the Law of Moses and the Prophets and the Psalms must be fulfilled.

45Then He [thoroughly] opened up their minds to understand the Scriptures,

46And said to them, Thus it is written that the Christ (the Messiah) should suffer and on the third day rise from (*among) the dead, [Hos. 6:2.]

47And that repentance [with a view to and as the condition of] forgiveness of sins should be preached in His name to all nations, beginning from Jerusalem.

48You are witnesses of these things.

49And behold, I will send forth upon you what My Father has promised; but remain in the city [Jerusalem] until you are clothed with power from on high.

50Then He conducted them out as far as Bethany, and, lifting up His hands, He invoked a blessing on them.

51And it occurred that while He was blessing them, He parted from them and was taken up into heaven.

52And they, worshiping Him, went back to Jerusalem with great joy;

53And they were continually in the temple *celebrating with praises and* blessing *and* extolling God. *Amen (so be it).*

---

*a* George Ricker Berry, *Greek-English New Testament Lexicon.*

# John

# John

## NIV

### The Word Became Flesh

**1** In the beginning was the Word, and the Word was with God, and the Word was God. ²He was with God in the beginning. ³Through him all things were made; without him nothing was made that has been made. ⁴In him was life, and that life was the light of all mankind. ⁵The light shines in the darkness, and the darkness has not overcome*ᵃ* it.

⁶There was a man sent from God whose name was John. ⁷He came as a witness to testify concerning that light, so that through him all might believe. ⁸He himself was not the light; he came only as a witness to the light.

⁹The true light that gives light to everyone was coming into the world. ¹⁰He was in the world, and though the world was made through him, the world did not recognize him. ¹¹He came to that which was his own, but his own did not receive him. ¹²Yet to all who did receive him, to those who believed in his name, he gave the right to become children of God— ¹³children born not of natural descent, nor of human decision or a husband's will, but born of God.

¹⁴The Word became flesh and made his dwelling among us. We have seen his glory, the glory of the one and only Son, who came from the Father, full of grace and truth.

¹⁵(John testified concerning him. He cried out, saying, "This is the one I spoke about when I said, 'He who comes after me has surpassed me because he was before me.'") ¹⁶Out of his fullness we have all received grace in place of grace already given. ¹⁷For the law was given through Moses; grace and truth came through Jesus Christ. ¹⁸No one has ever seen God, but the one and only Son, who is himself God and*ᵇ* is in closest relationship with the Father, has made him known.

## Amplified

**1** In the beginning [before all time] was the Word (ᵃChrist), and the Word was with God, and the Word was God ᵇHimself. [Isa. 9:6.]

²He was present originally with God.

³All things were made *and* came into existence through Him; and without Him was not even one thing made that has come into being.

⁴In Him was Life, and the Life was the Light of men.

⁵And the Light shines on in the darkness, for the darkness has never overpowered it [put it out or absorbed it or appropriated it, and is unreceptive to it].

⁶There came a man sent from God, whose name was John. [Mal. 3:1.]

⁷This man came to witness, that he might testify of the Light, that all men might believe in it [adhere to it, trust it, and rely upon it] through him.

⁸He was not the Light himself, but came that he might bear witness regarding the Light.

⁹There it was—the true Light [was then] coming into the world [the genuine, perfect, steadfast Light] that illumines every person. [Isa. 49:6.]

¹⁰He came into the world, and though the world was made through Him, the world did not recognize Him [did not know Him].

¹¹He came to that which belonged to Him [to His own— His domain, creation, things, world], and they who were His own did not receive Him *and* did not welcome Him.

¹²But to as many as did receive *and* welcome Him, He gave the authority (power, privilege, right) to become the children of God, that is, to those who believe in (adhere to, trust in, and rely on) His name—[Isa. 56:5.]

¹³Who owe their birth neither to ᶜbloods nor to the will of the flesh [that of physical impulse] nor to the will of man [that of a natural father], but to God. [They are born of God!]

¹⁴And the Word (Christ) became flesh (human, incarnate) and tabernacled (fixed His tent of flesh, lived awhile) among us; and we [actually] saw His glory (His honor, His majesty), such glory as an only begotten son receives from his father, full of grace (favor, loving-kindness) and truth. [Isa. 40:5.]

¹⁵John testified about Him and cried out, This was He of Whom I said, He Who comes after me has priority over me, for He was before me. [He takes rank above me, for He existed before I did. He has advanced before me, because He is my Chief.]

¹⁶For out of His fullness (abundance) we have all received [all had a share and we were all supplied with] one grace after another *and* spiritual blessing upon spiritual blessing *and* even favor upon favor *and* gift [heaped] upon gift.

¹⁷For while the Law was given through Moses, grace (ᵈunearned, undeserved favor and spiritual blessing) and truth came through Jesus Christ. [Exod. 20:1.]

¹⁸No man has ever seen God at any time; *the only ᵉunique Son, or ᶠthe only begotten God,* Who is in the bosom [in the intimate presence] of the Father, He has declared Him [He has revealed Him and brought Him out where He can be seen; He has interpreted Him and He has made Him known]. [Prov. 8:30.]

---

ᵃ In John's vision (Rev. 19), he sees Christ returning as Warrior-Messiah-King, and "the title by which He is called is The Word of God . . . and Lord of lords" (Rev. 19:13, 16). ᵇ Charles B. Williams, *The New Testament: A Translation in the Language of the People*: "God" appears first in the Greek word order in this phrase, denoting emphasis óso "God Himself." ᶜ Literal translation. ᵈ Richard Trench, *Synonyms of the New Testament.* ᵉ James Moulton and George Milligan, *The Vocabulary of the Greek Testament.* ᶠ Marvin Vincent, *Word Studies in the New Testament*: This reading is supported by "a great mass of ancient evidence."

## New International Version

### John the Baptist Denies Being the Messiah

[19]Now this was John's testimony when the Jewish leaders[a] in Jerusalem sent priests and Levites to ask him who he was. [20]He did not fail to confess, but confessed freely, "I am not the Messiah."

[21]They asked him, "Then who are you? Are you Elijah?"

He said, "I am not."

"Are you the Prophet?"

He answered, "No."

[22]Finally they said, "Who are you? Give us an answer to take back to those who sent us. What do you say about yourself?"

[23]John replied in the words of Isaiah the prophet, "I am the voice of one calling in the wilderness, 'Make straight the way for the Lord.'"[b]

[24]Now the Pharisees who had been sent [25]questioned him, "Why then do you baptize if you are not the Messiah, nor Elijah, nor the Prophet?"

[26]"I baptize with[c] water," John replied, "but among you stands one you do not know. [27]He is the one who comes after me, the straps of whose sandals I am not worthy to untie."

[28]This all happened at Bethany on the other side of the Jordan, where John was baptizing.

### John Testifies About Jesus

[29]The next day John saw Jesus coming toward him and said, "Look, the Lamb of God, who takes away the sin of the world! [30]This is the one I meant when I said, 'A man who comes after me has surpassed me because he was before me.' [31]I myself did not know him, but the reason I came baptizing with water was that he might be revealed to Israel."

[32]Then John gave this testimony: "I saw the Spirit come down from heaven as a dove and remain on him. [33]And I myself did not know him, but the one who sent me to baptize with water told me, 'The man on whom you see the Spirit come down and remain is the one who will baptize with the Holy Spirit.' [34]I have seen and I testify that this is God's Chosen One."[d]

### John's Disciples Follow Jesus

[35]The next day John was there again with two of his disciples. [36]When he saw Jesus passing by, he said, "Look, the Lamb of God!"

[37]When the two disciples heard him say this, they followed Jesus. [38]Turning around, Jesus saw them following and asked, "What do you want?"

They said, "Rabbi" (which means "Teacher"), "where are you staying?"

[39]"Come," he replied, "and you will see."

So they went and saw where he was staying, and they spent that day with him. It was about four in the afternoon.

[40]Andrew, Simon Peter's brother, was one of the two who heard what John had said and who had followed Jesus. [41]The first thing Andrew did was to find his brother Simon and tell him, "We have found the Messiah" (that is, the Christ). [42]And he brought him to Jesus.

## Amplified Bible

[19]And this is the testimony of John when the Jews sent priests and Levites to him from Jerusalem to ask him, Who are you?

[20]He confessed (admitted the truth) and did not try to conceal it, but acknowledged, I am not the Christ!

[21]They asked him, What then? Are you Elijah? And he said, I am not! Are you the Prophet? And he answered, No! [Deut. 18:15, 18; Mal. 4:5.]

[22]Then they said to him, Who are you? Tell us, so that we may give an answer to those who sent us. What do you say about yourself?

[23]He said, I am the voice of one crying aloud in the wilderness [the voice of one shouting in the desert], Prepare the way of the Lord [level, straighten out, the path of the Lord], as the prophet Isaiah said. [Isa. 40:3.]

[24]The messengers had been sent from the Pharisees.

[25]And they asked him, Why then are you baptizing if you are not the Christ, nor Elijah, nor the Prophet?

[26]John answered them, I [only] baptize[a]in (with) water. Among you there stands One Whom you do not recognize and with Whom you are not acquainted and of Whom you know nothing. [Mal. 3:1.]

[27]It is He Who, coming after me, is preferred before me, the string of Whose sandal I am not worthy to unloose.

[28]These things occurred in Bethany (Bethabara) across the Jordan [b]at the Jordan crossing], where John was then baptizing.

[29]The next day John saw Jesus coming to him and said, Look! There is the Lamb of God, Who takes away the sin of the world! [Exod. 12:3; Isa. 53:7.]

[30]This is He of Whom I said, After me comes a Man Who has priority over me [Who takes rank above me] because He was before me and existed before I did.

[31]And I did not know Him and did not recognize Him [myself]; but it is in order that He should be made manifest and be revealed to Israel [be brought out where we can see Him] that I came baptizing[c]in (with) water.

[32]John gave further evidence, saying, I have seen the Spirit descending as a dove out of heaven, and it dwelt on Him [never to depart].

[33]And I did not know Him nor recognize Him, but He Who sent me to baptize[c]in (with) water said to me, Upon Him Whom you shall see the Spirit descend and remain, that One is He Who baptizes with the Holy Spirit.

[34]And I have seen [that happen—I actually did see it] and my testimony is that this is the Son of God!

[35]Again the next day John was standing with two of his disciples,

[36]And he looked at Jesus as He walked along, and said, Look! There is the Lamb of God!

[37]The two disciples heard him say this, and they followed Jesus.

[38]But Jesus turned, and as He saw them following Him, He said to them, What are you looking for? [And what is it you wish?] And they answered Him, Rabbi—which translated is Teacher—where are You staying?

[39]He said to them, Come and see. So they went and saw where He was staying, and they remained with Him [d]that day. It was then about the tenth hour (about four o'clock in the afternoon).

[40]One of the two who heard what John said and followed Jesus was Andrew, Simon Peter's brother.

[41]He first sought out and found his own brother Simon and said to him, We have found (discovered) the Messiah!—which translated is the Christ (the Anointed One).

[42]Andrew then led (brought) Simon to Jesus. Jesus

---

[a] 19 The Greek term traditionally translated the Jews (hoi Ioudaioi) refers here and elsewhere in John's Gospel to those Jewish leaders who opposed Jesus; also in 5:10, 15, 16; 7:1, 11, 13; 9:22; 18:14, 28, 36; 19:7, 12, 31, 38; 20:19.   [b] 23 Isaiah 40:3   [c] 26 Or in; also in verses 31 and 33 (twice)   [d] 34 See Isaiah 42:1; many manuscripts is the Son of God.

[a] The Greek can be translated "with" or "in;" also in verses 31 and 33. The KJV prefers "with," while the ASV prefers "in."   [b] George M. Lamsa, The New Testament According to the Ancient Text.   [c] See footnote on John 1:26.   [d] George M. Lamsa, Gospel Light from the Aramaic: In accordance with Oriental hospitality, the guests would be invited to remain that night also.

## New International Version

Jesus looked at him and said, "You are Simon son of John. You will be called Cephas" (which, when translated, is Peter[a]).

### Jesus Calls Philip and Nathanael

[43] The next day Jesus decided to leave for Galilee. Finding Philip, he said to him, "Follow me."

[44] Philip, like Andrew and Peter, was from the town of Bethsaida. [45] Philip found Nathanael and told him, "We have found the one Moses wrote about in the Law, and about whom the prophets also wrote—Jesus of Nazareth, the son of Joseph."

[46] "Nazareth! Can anything good come from there?" Nathanael asked.

"Come and see," said Philip.

[47] When Jesus saw Nathanael approaching, he said of him, "Here truly is an Israelite in whom there is no deceit."

[48] "How do you know me?" Nathanael asked.

Jesus answered, "I saw you while you were still under the fig tree before Philip called you."

[49] Then Nathanael declared, "Rabbi, you are the Son of God; you are the king of Israel."

[50] Jesus said, "You believe[b] because I told you I saw you under the fig tree. You will see greater things than that." [51] He then added, "Very truly I tell you,[c] you[c] will see 'heaven open, and the angels of God ascending and descending on'[d] the Son of Man."

### Jesus Changes Water Into Wine

**2** On the third day a wedding took place at Cana in Galilee. Jesus' mother was there, [2] and Jesus and his disciples had also been invited to the wedding. [3] When the wine was gone, Jesus' mother said to him, "They have no more wine."

[4] "Woman,[e] why do you involve me?" Jesus replied. "My hour has not yet come."

[5] His mother said to the servants, "Do whatever he tells you."

[6] Nearby stood six stone water jars, the kind used by the Jews for ceremonial washing, each holding from twenty to thirty gallons.[f]

[7] Jesus said to the servants, "Fill the jars with water"; so they filled them to the brim.

[8] Then he told them, "Now draw some out and take it to the master of the banquet."

They did so, [9] and the master of the banquet tasted the water that had been turned into wine. He did not realize where it had come from, though the servants who had drawn the water knew. Then he called the bridegroom aside [10] and said, "Everyone brings out the choice wine first and then the cheaper wine after the guests have had too much to drink; but you have saved the best till now."

[11] What Jesus did here in Cana of Galilee was the first of the signs through which he revealed his glory; and his disciples believed in him.

[12] After this he went down to Capernaum with his mother and brothers and his disciples. There they stayed for a few days.

### Jesus Clears the Temple Courts

[13] When it was almost time for the Jewish Passover, Jesus went up to Jerusalem. [14] In the temple courts he found people selling cattle, sheep and doves, and others sitting at tables exchanging money. [15] So he made a whip

---

## Amplified Bible

looked at him and said, You are Simon son of John. You shall be called Cephas—which translated is Peter [Stone].

[43] The next day Jesus desired *and* decided to go into Galilee; and He found Philip and said to him, Join Me as My attendant *and* follow Me.

[44] Now Philip was from Bethsaida, of the same city as Andrew and Peter.

[45] Philip sought *and* found Nathanael and told him, We have found (discovered) the One Moses in the Law and also the Prophets wrote about—Jesus from Nazareth, the [legal] son of Joseph!

[46] Nathanael answered him, [Nazareth!] Can anything good come out of Nazareth? Philip replied, Come and see!

[47] Jesus saw Nathanael coming toward Him and said concerning him, See! Here is an Israelite indeed [a true descendant of Jacob], in whom there is no guile *nor* deceit *nor* falsehood *nor* duplicity!

[48] Nathanael said to Jesus, How do You know me? [How is it that You know these things about me?] Jesus answered him, Before [ever] Philip called you, when you were still under the fig tree, I saw you.

[49] Nathanael answered, Teacher, You are the Son of God! You are the King of Israel!

[50] Jesus replied, Because I said to you, I saw you beneath the fig tree, do you believe in *and* rely on *and* trust in Me? You shall see greater things than this!

[51] Then He said to him, I assure you, most solemnly I tell you all, you shall see heaven opened, and the angels of God ascending and descending upon the Son of Man! [Gen. 28:12; Dan. 7:13.]

**2** On the third day there was a wedding at Cana of Galilee, and the mother of Jesus was there.

[2] Jesus also was invited with His disciples to the wedding.

[3] And when the wine was all gone, the mother of Jesus said to Him, They have no more wine!

[4] Jesus said to her, [a Dear] woman, what is that to you and to Me? [What do we have in common? Leave it to Me.] My time (hour to act) has not yet come. [Eccl. 3:1.]

[5] His mother said to the servants, Whatever He says to you, do it.

[6] Now there were six waterpots of stone standing there, as the Jewish custom of purification (ceremonial washing) demanded, holding twenty to thirty gallons apiece.

[7] Jesus said to them, Fill the waterpots with water. So they filled them up to the brim.

[8] Then He said to them, Draw some out now and take it to the manager of the feast [to the one presiding, the superintendent of the banquet]. So they took him some.

[9] And when the manager tasted the water just now turned into wine, not knowing where it came from—though the servants who had drawn the water knew—he called the bridegroom

[10] And said to him, Everyone else serves his best wine first, and when people have drunk freely, then he serves that which is not so good; but you have kept back the good wine until now!

[11] This, the first of His signs (miracles, wonderworks), Jesus performed in Cana of Galilee, and manifested His glory [by it He displayed His greatness and His power openly], and His disciples believed in Him [adhered to, trusted in, and relied on Him]. [Deut. 5:24; Ps. 72:19.]

[12] After that He went down to Capernaum with His mother and brothers and disciples, and they stayed there only a few days.

[13] Now the Passover of the Jews was approaching, so Jesus went up to Jerusalem.

[14] There He found in the temple [b enclosure] those who were selling oxen and sheep and doves, and the money changers sitting there [also at their stands].

---

[a] 42 *Cephas* (Aramaic) and *Peter* (Greek) both mean *rock.*     [b] 50 Or *Do you believe . . . ?*     [c] 51 The Greek is plural.     [d] 51 Gen. 28:12     [e] 4 The Greek for *Woman* does not denote any disrespect.     [f] 6 Or from about 75 to about 115 liters

[a] G. Abbott-Smith, *Manual Greek Lexicon of the New Testament:* "a term of respect and endearment."     [b] Richard Trench, *Synonyms of the New Testament.*

## New International Version

out of cords, and drove all from the temple courts, both sheep and cattle; he scattered the coins of the money changers and overturned their tables. ¹⁶To those who sold doves he said, "Get these out of here! Stop turning my Father's house into a market!" ¹⁷His disciples remembered that it is written: "Zeal for your house will consume me."ᵃ

¹⁸The Jews then responded to him, "What sign can you show us to prove your authority to do all this?"

¹⁹Jesus answered them, "Destroy this temple, and I will raise it again in three days."

²⁰They replied, "It has taken forty-six years to build this temple, and you are going to raise it in three days?" ²¹But the temple he had spoken of was his body. ²²After he was raised from the dead, his disciples recalled what he had said. Then they believed the scripture and the words that Jesus had spoken.

²³Now while he was in Jerusalem at the Passover Festival, many people saw the signs he was performing and believed in his name.ᵇ ²⁴But Jesus would not entrust himself to them, for he knew all people. ²⁵He did not need any testimony about mankind, for he knew what was in each person.

### Jesus Teaches Nicodemus

**3** Now there was a Pharisee, a man named Nicodemus who was a member of the Jewish ruling council. ²He came to Jesus at night and said, "Rabbi, we know that you are a teacher who has come from God. For no one could perform the signs you are doing if God were not with him."

³Jesus replied, "Very truly I tell you, no one can see the kingdom of God unless they are born again.ᶜ"

⁴"How can someone be born when they are old?" Nicodemus asked. "Surely they cannot enter a second time into their mother's womb to be born!"

⁵Jesus answered, "Very truly I tell you, no one can enter the kingdom of God unless they are born of water and the Spirit. ⁶Flesh gives birth to flesh, but the Spiritᵈ gives birth to spirit. ⁷You should not be surprised at my saying, 'Youᵉ must be born again.' ⁸The wind blows wherever it pleases. You hear its sound, but you cannot tell where it comes from or where it is going. So it is with everyone born of the Spirit.ᶠ"

⁹"How can this be?" Nicodemus asked.

¹⁰"You are Israel's teacher," said Jesus, "and do you not

## Amplified Bible

¹⁵And having made a lash (a whip) of cords, He drove them all out of the temple [ᵃenclosure]—both the sheep and the oxen—spilling *and* scattering the brokers' money and upsetting *and* tossing around their trays (their stands).

¹⁶Then to those who sold the doves He said, Take these things away (out of here)! Make not My Father's house a house of merchandise (a marketplace, a sales shop)! [Ps. 93:5.]

¹⁷And His disciples remembered that it is written [in the Holy Scriptures], Zeal (the fervor of love) for Your house will eat Me up. [I will be consumed with jealousy for the honor of Your house.] [Ps. 69:9.]

¹⁸Then the Jews retorted, What sign can ᵇYou show us, seeing You do these things? [What sign, miracle, token, indication can You give us as evidence that You have authority and are commissioned to act in this way?]

¹⁹Jesus answered them, Destroy (undo) this temple, and in three days I will raise it up again.

²⁰Then the Jews replied, It took forty-six years to build this temple (sanctuary), and will You raise it up in three days?

²¹But He had spoken of the temple which was His body.

²²When therefore He had risen from the dead, His disciples remembered that He said this. And so they believed *and* trusted *and* relied on the Scripture and the word (message) Jesus had spoken. [Ps. 16:10.]

²³But when He was in Jerusalem during the Passover Feast, many believed in His name [identified themselves with His party] after seeing His signs (wonders, miracles) which He was doing.

²⁴But Jesus [for His part] did not trust Himself to them, because He knew all [men];

²⁵And He did not need anyone to bear witness concerning man [needed no evidence from anyone about men], for He Himself knew what was in human nature. [He could read men's hearts.] [I Sam. 16:7.]

**3** Now there was a certain man among the Pharisees named Nicodemus, a ruler (a leader, an authority) among the Jews,

²Who came to Jesus at night and said to Him, Rabbi, we know *and* are certain that You have come from God [as] a Teacher; for no one can do these signs (these wonderworks, these miracles—and produce the proofs) that You do unless God is with him.

³Jesus answered him, I assure you, most solemnly I tell you, that unless a person is born again (anew, from above), he cannot ever see (know, be acquainted with, and experience) the kingdom of God.

⁴Nicodemus said to Him, How can a man be born when he is old? Can he enter his mother's womb again and be born?

⁵Jesus answered, I assure you, most solemnly I tell you, unless a man is born of water and [ᶜeven] the Spirit, he cannot [ever] enter the kingdom of God. [Ezek. 36:25-27.]

⁶What is born of [from] the flesh is flesh [of the physical is physical]; and what is born of the Spirit is spirit.

⁷Marvel not [do not be surprised, astonished] at My telling you, You must all be born anew (from above).

⁸The wind blows (breathes) where it wills; and though you hear its sound, yet you neither know where it comes from nor where it is going. So it is with everyone who is born of the Spirit.

⁹Nicodemus answered by asking, How can all this be possible?

¹⁰Jesus replied, Are you the teacher of Israel, and yet do not know *nor* understand these things? [Are they strange to you?]

---

ᵃ 17 Psalm 69:9   ᵇ 23 Or *in him*   ᶜ 3 The Greek for *again* also means *from above*; also in verse 7.   ᵈ 6 Or *but spirit*   ᵉ 7 The Greek is plural.   ᶠ 8 The Greek for *Spirit* is the same as that for *wind*.

ᵃ Richard Trench, *Synonyms of the New Testament*.   ᵇ Capitalized because of what He is, the spotless Son of God, not what the speaker may have thought He was.   ᶜ The Greek "kai" ("and") may be rendered "even."

## New International Version

understand these things? [11] Very truly I tell you, we speak of what we know, and we testify to what we have seen, but still you people do not accept our testimony. [12] I have spoken to you of earthly things and you do not believe; how then will you believe if I speak of heavenly things? [13] No one has ever gone into heaven except the one who came from heaven—the Son of Man.[a] [14] Just as Moses lifted up the snake in the wilderness, so the Son of Man must be lifted up,[b] [15] that everyone who believes may have eternal life in him."[c]

[16] For God so loved the world that he gave his one and only Son, that whoever believes in him shall not perish but have eternal life. [17] For God did not send his Son into the world to condemn the world, but to save the world through him. [18] Whoever believes in him is not condemned, but whoever does not believe stands condemned already because they have not believed in the name of God's one and only Son. [19] This is the verdict: Light has come into the world, but people loved darkness instead of light because their deeds were evil. [20] Everyone who does evil hates the light, and will not come into the light for fear that their deeds will be exposed. [21] But whoever lives by the truth comes into the light, so that it may be seen plainly that what they have done has been done in the sight of God.

### John Testifies Again About Jesus

[22] After this, Jesus and his disciples went out into the Judean countryside, where he spent some time with them, and baptized. [23] Now John also was baptizing at Aenon near Salim, because there was plenty of water, and people were coming and being baptized. [24] (This was before John was put in prison.) [25] An argument developed between some of John's disciples and a certain Jew over the matter of ceremonial washing. [26] They came to John and said to him, "Rabbi, that man who was with you on the other side of the Jordan—the one you testified about—look, he is baptizing, and everyone is going to him."

[27] To this John replied, "A person can receive only what is given them from heaven. [28] You yourselves can testify

## Amplified Bible

[11] I assure you, most solemnly I tell you, We speak only of what we know [we know absolutely what we are talking about]; we have actually seen what we are testifying to [we were eyewitnesses of it]. And still you do not receive our testimony [you reject and refuse our evidence—that of Myself and of all those who are born of the Spirit].

[12] If I have told you of things that happen right here on the earth and yet none of you believes Me, how can you believe (trust Me, adhere to Me, rely on Me) if I tell you of heavenly things?

[13] And yet no one has ever gone up to heaven, but there is One Who has come down from heaven—the Son of Man [Himself], *a Who is (dwells, has His home) in heaven.*

[14] And just as Moses lifted up the serpent in the desert [on a pole], so must [so it is necessary that] the Son of Man be lifted up [on the cross], [Num. 21:9.]

[15] In order that everyone who believes in Him [who cleaves to Him, trusts Him, and relies on Him] may *a not perish, but* have eternal life *and* [actually] live forever!

[16] For God so greatly loved *and* dearly prized the world that He [even] gave up His only begotten (*b* unique) Son, so that whoever believes in (trusts in, clings to, relies on) Him shall not perish (come to destruction, be lost) but have eternal (everlasting) life.

[17] For God did not send the Son into the world in order to judge (to reject, to condemn, to pass sentence on) the world, but that the world might find salvation *and* be made safe *and* sound through Him.

[18] He who believes in Him [who clings to, trusts in, relies on Him] is not judged [he who trusts in Him never comes up for judgment; for him there is no rejection, no condemnation—he incurs no damnation]; but he who does not believe (cleave to, rely on, trust in Him) is judged already [he has already been convicted and has already received his sentence] because he has not believed in *and* trusted in the name of the only begotten Son of God. [He is condemned for refusing to let his trust rest in Christ's name.]

[19] The [basis of the] judgment (indictment, the test by which men are judged, the ground for the sentence) lies in this: the Light has come into the world, and people have loved the darkness rather than *and* more than the Light, for their works (deeds) were evil. [Isa. 5:20.]

[20] For every wrongdoer hates (loathes, detests) the Light, and will not come out into the Light *but* shrinks from it, lest his works (his deeds, his activities, his conduct) be exposed *and* reproved.

[21] But he who practices truth [who does what is right] comes out into the Light; so that his works may be plainly shown to be what they are—wrought with God [divinely prompted, done with God's help, in dependence upon Him].

[22] After this, Jesus and His disciples went into the land (the countryside) of Judea, where He remained with them, and baptized.

[23] But John also was baptizing at Aenon near Salim, for there was an abundance of water there, and the people kept coming and being baptized.

[24] For John had not yet been thrown into prison.

[25] Therefore there arose a controversy between some of John's disciples and a Jew in regard to purification.

[26] So they came to John and reported to him, Rabbi, the Man Who was with you on the other side of the Jordan [*c* at the Jordan crossing]—and to Whom you yourself have borne testimony—notice, here He is baptizing too, and everybody is flocking to Him!

[27] John answered, A man can receive nothing [he can claim nothing, he can *d* take unto himself nothing] except as it has been granted to him from heaven. [A man must be content to receive the gift which is given him from heaven; there is no other source.]

---

*a* 13 Some manuscripts *Man, who is in heaven*    *b* 14 The Greek for *lifted up* also means *exalted.*    *c* 15 Some interpreters end the quotation with verse 21.

*a* Some manuscripts add this phrase.    *b* James Moulton and George Milligan, *The Vocabulary.*    *c* George M. Lamsa, *The New Testament.*    *d* Joseph Thayer, *A Greek-English Lexicon of the New Testament.*

## New International Version

that I said, 'I am not the Messiah but am sent ahead of him.' <sup>29</sup>The bride belongs to the bridegroom. The friend who attends the bridegroom waits and listens for him, and is full of joy when he hears the bridegroom's voice. That joy is mine, and it is now complete. <sup>30</sup>He must become greater; I must become less."<sup>a</sup>

<sup>31</sup>The one who comes from above is above all; the one who is from the earth belongs to the earth, and speaks as one from the earth. The one who comes from heaven is above all. <sup>32</sup>He testifies to what he has seen and heard, but no one accepts his testimony. <sup>33</sup>Whoever has accepted it has certified that God is truthful. <sup>34</sup>For the one whom God has sent speaks the words of God, for God<sup>b</sup> gives the Spirit without limit. <sup>35</sup>The Father loves the Son and has placed everything in his hands. <sup>36</sup>Whoever believes in the Son has eternal life, but whoever rejects the Son will not see life, for God's wrath remains on them.

### Jesus Talks With a Samaritan Woman

**4** Now Jesus learned that the Pharisees had heard that he was gaining and baptizing more disciples than John— <sup>2</sup>although in fact it was not Jesus who baptized, but his disciples. <sup>3</sup>So he left Judea and went back once more to Galilee.

<sup>4</sup>Now he had to go through Samaria. <sup>5</sup>So he came to a town in Samaria called Sychar, near the plot of ground Jacob had given to his son Joseph. <sup>6</sup>Jacob's well was there, and Jesus, tired as he was from the journey, sat down by the well. It was about noon.

<sup>7</sup>When a Samaritan woman came to draw water, Jesus said to her, "Will you give me a drink?" <sup>8</sup>(His disciples had gone into the town to buy food.)

<sup>9</sup>The Samaritan woman said to him, "You are a Jew and I am a Samaritan woman. How can you ask me for a drink?" (For Jews do not associate with Samaritans.<sup>c</sup>)

<sup>10</sup>Jesus answered her, "If you knew the gift of God and who it is that asks you for a drink, you would have asked him and he would have given you living water."

<sup>11</sup>"Sir," the woman said, "you have nothing to draw with and the well is deep. Where can you get this living water? <sup>12</sup>Are you greater than our father Jacob, who gave us the well and drank from it himself, as did also his sons and his livestock?"

## Amplified Bible

<sup>28</sup>You yourselves are my witnesses [you personally bear me out] that I stated, I am not the Christ (the Anointed One, the Messiah), but I have [only] been sent before Him [in advance of Him, to be His appointed forerunner, His messenger, His announcer]. [Mal. 3:1.]

<sup>29</sup>He who has the bride is the bridegroom; but the groomsman who stands by and listens to him rejoices greatly *and* heartily on account of the bridegroom's voice. This then is my pleasure *and* joy, and it is now complete. [S. of Sol. 5:1.]

<sup>30</sup>He must increase, but I must decrease. [He must grow more prominent; I must grow less so.] [Isa. 9:7.]

<sup>31</sup>He Who comes from above (heaven) is [far] above all [others]; he who comes from the earth belongs to the earth, and talks the language of earth [his words are from an earthly standpoint]. He Who comes from heaven is [far] above all others [far superior to all others in prominence and in excellence].

<sup>32</sup>It is to what He has [actually] seen and heard that He bears testimony, and yet no one accepts His testimony [no one receives His evidence as true].

<sup>33</sup>Whoever receives His testimony has set his seal of approval to this: God is true. [That man has definitely certified, acknowledged, declared once and for all, and is himself assured that it is divine truth that God cannot lie].

<sup>34</sup>For since He Whom God has sent speaks the words of God [proclaims God's own message], God does not give Him His Spirit sparingly *or* by measure, *but* boundless is the gift God makes of His Spirit! [Deut. 18:18.]

<sup>35</sup>The Father loves the Son and has given (entrusted, committed) everything into His hand. [Dan. 7:14.]

<sup>36</sup>And he who believes in (has faith in, clings to, relies on) the Son has (now possesses) eternal life. But whoever disobeys (is unbelieving toward, refuses to trust in, disregards, is not subject to) the Son will never see (experience) life, but [instead] the wrath of God abides on him. [God's displeasure remains on him; His indignation hangs over him continually.] [Hab. 2:4.]

**4** Now when the Lord knew (learned, became aware) that the Pharisees had been told that Jesus was winning and baptizing more disciples than John— <sup>2</sup>Though Jesus Himself did not baptize, but His disciples— <sup>3</sup>He left Judea and returned to Galilee.

<sup>4</sup>It was necessary for Him to go through Samaria. <sup>5</sup>And in doing so, He arrived at a Samaritan town called Sychar, near the tract of land that Jacob gave to his son Joseph.

<sup>6</sup>And Jacob's well was there. So Jesus, tired as He was from His journey, sat down [to rest] by the well. It was then about the sixth hour (about noon).

<sup>7</sup>Presently, when a woman of Samaria came along to draw water, Jesus said to her, Give Me a drink— <sup>8</sup>For His disciples had gone off into the town to buy food—

<sup>9</sup>The Samaritan woman said to Him, How is it that <sup>a</sup>You, being a Jew, ask me, a Samaritan [and a] woman, for a drink?—For the Jews have nothing to do with the Samaritans—

<sup>10</sup>Jesus answered her, If you had only known *and* had recognized God's gift and Who this is that is saying to you, Give Me a drink, you would have asked Him [instead] and He would have given you living water.

<sup>11</sup>She said to Him, Sir, You have nothing to draw with [no drawing bucket] and the well is deep; how then can You provide living water? [Where do You get Your living water?]

<sup>12</sup>Are You greater than *and* superior to our ancestor Jacob, who gave us this well and who used to drink from it himself, and his sons and his cattle also?

<sup>a</sup> 30 Some interpreters end the quotation with verse 36.　<sup>b</sup> 34 Greek *he*
<sup>c</sup> 9 Or *do not use dishes Samaritans have used*

<sup>a</sup> Capitalized because of what He is, the spotless Son of God, not what the speaker may have thought He was.

## New International Version

13Jesus answered, "Everyone who drinks this water will be thirsty again, 14but whoever drinks the water I give them will never thirst. Indeed, the water I give them will become in them a spring of water welling up to eternal life."

15The woman said to him, "Sir, give me this water so that I won't get thirsty and have to keep coming here to draw water."

16He told her, "Go, call your husband and come back."

17"I have no husband," she replied.

Jesus said to her, "You are right when you say you have no husband. 18The fact is, you have had five husbands, and the man you now have is not your husband. What you have just said is quite true."

19"Sir," the woman said, "I can see that you are a prophet. 20Our ancestors worshiped on this mountain, but you Jews claim that the place where we must worship is in Jerusalem."

21"Woman," Jesus replied, "believe me, a time is coming when you will worship the Father neither on this mountain nor in Jerusalem. 22You Samaritans worship what you do not know; we worship what we do know, for salvation is from the Jews. 23Yet a time is coming and has now come when the true worshipers will worship the Father in the Spirit and in truth, for they are the kind of worshipers the Father seeks. 24God is spirit, and his worshipers must worship in the Spirit and in truth."

25The woman said, "I know that Messiah" (called Christ) "is coming. When he comes, he will explain everything to us."

26Then Jesus declared, "I, the one speaking to you—I am he."

### The Disciples Rejoin Jesus

27Just then his disciples returned and were surprised to find him talking with a woman. But no one asked, "What do you want?" or "Why are you talking with her?"

28Then, leaving her water jar, the woman went back to the town and said to the people, 29"Come, see a man who told me everything I ever did. Could this be the Messiah?" 30They came out of the town and made their way toward him.

31Meanwhile his disciples urged him, "Rabbi, eat something."

32But he said to them, "I have food to eat that you know nothing about."

33Then his disciples said to each other, "Could someone have brought him food?"

34"My food," said Jesus, "is to do the will of him who sent me and to finish his work. 35Don't you have a saying, 'It's still four months until harvest'? I tell you, open your eyes and look at the fields! They are ripe for harvest. 36Even now the one who reaps draws a wage and harvests a crop for eternal life, so that the sower and the reaper may be glad together. 37Thus the saying 'One sows and

## Amplified Bible

13Jesus answered her, All who drink of this water will be thirsty again.

14But whoever takes a drink of the water that I will give him shall never, no never, be thirsty any more. But the water that I will give him shall become a spring of water welling up (flowing, bubbling) [continually] within him unto (into, for) eternal life.

15The woman said to Him, Sir, give me this water, so that I may never get thirsty nor have to come [continually all the way] here to draw.

16At this, Jesus said to her, Go, call your husband and come back here.

17The woman answered, I have no husband. Jesus said to her, You have spoken truly in saying, I have no husband.

18For you have had five husbands, and the man you are now living with is not your husband. In this you have spoken truly.

19The woman said to Him, Sir, I see *and* understand that You are a prophet.

20Our forefathers worshiped on this mountain, but you [Jews] say that Jerusalem is the place where it is necessary *and* proper to worship.

21Jesus said to her, Woman, believe Me, a time is coming when you will worship the Father neither [merely] in this mountain nor [merely] in Jerusalem.

22You [Samaritans] do not know what you are worshiping [you worship what you do not comprehend]. We do know what we are worshiping [we worship what we have knowledge of and understand], for [after all] salvation comes from [among] the Jews.

23A time will come, however, indeed it is already here, when the true (genuine) worshipers will worship the Father in spirit and in truth (reality); for the Father is seeking just such people as these as His worshipers.

24God is a Spirit (a spiritual Being) and those who worship Him must worship *Him* in spirit and in truth (reality).

25The woman said to Him, I know that Messiah is coming, He Who is called the Christ (the Anointed One); and when He arrives, He will tell us everything we need to know *and* make it clear to us.

26Jesus said to her, I Who now speak with you am He.

27Just then His disciples came and they wondered (were surprised, astonished) to find Him talking with a woman [a married woman]. However, not one of them asked Him, What are You inquiring about? *or* What do You want? or, Why do You speak with her?

28Then the woman left her water jar and went away to the town. And she began telling the people,

29Come, see a Man Who has told me everything that I ever did! Can this be [is not this] the Christ? [Must not this be the Messiah, the Anointed One?]

30So the people left the town and set out to go to Him.

31Meanwhile, the disciples urged Him saying, Rabbi, eat something.

32But He assured them, I have food (nourishment) to eat of which you know nothing *and* have no idea.

33So the disciples said one to another, Has someone brought Him something to eat?

34Jesus said to them, My food (nourishment) is to do the will (pleasure) of Him Who sent Me and to accomplish *and* completely finish His work.

35Do you not say, It is still four months until harvest time comes? Look! I tell you, raise your eyes and observe the fields *and* see how they are already white for harvesting.

36Already the reaper is getting his wages [he who does the cutting now has his reward], for he is gathering fruit (crop) unto life eternal, so that he who does the planting and he who does the reaping may rejoice together.

37For in this the saying holds true, One sows and another reaps.

## New International Version

another reaps' is true. <sup>38</sup>I sent you to reap what you have not worked for. Others have done the hard work, and you have reaped the benefits of their labor."

### Many Samaritans Believe

<sup>39</sup>Many of the Samaritans from that town believed in him because of the woman's testimony, "He told me everything I ever did." <sup>40</sup>So when the Samaritans came to him, they urged him to stay with them, and he stayed two days. <sup>41</sup>And because of his words many more became believers.

<sup>42</sup>They said to the woman, "We no longer believe just because of what you said; now we have heard for ourselves, and we know that this man really is the Savior of the world."

### Jesus Heals an Official's Son

<sup>43</sup>After the two days he left for Galilee. <sup>44</sup>(Now Jesus himself had pointed out that a prophet has no honor in his own country.) <sup>45</sup>When he arrived in Galilee, the Galileans welcomed him. They had seen all that he had done in Jerusalem at the Passover Festival, for they also had been there.

<sup>46</sup>Once more he visited Cana in Galilee, where he had turned the water into wine. And there was a certain royal official whose son lay sick at Capernaum. <sup>47</sup>When this man heard that Jesus had arrived in Galilee from Judea, he went to him and begged him to come and heal his son, who was close to death.

<sup>48</sup>"Unless you people see signs and wonders," Jesus told him, "you will never believe."

<sup>49</sup>The royal official said, "Sir, come down before my child dies."

<sup>50</sup>"Go," Jesus replied, "your son will live."

The man took Jesus at his word and departed. <sup>51</sup>While he was still on the way, his servants met him with the news that his boy was living. <sup>52</sup>When he inquired as to the time when his son got better, they said to him, "Yesterday, at one in the afternoon, the fever left him."

<sup>53</sup>Then the father realized that this was the exact time at which Jesus had said to him, "Your son will live." So he and his whole household believed.

<sup>54</sup>This was the second sign Jesus performed after coming from Judea to Galilee.

### The Healing at the Pool

**5** Some time later, Jesus went up to Jerusalem for one of the Jewish festivals. <sup>2</sup>Now there is in Jerusalem near the Sheep Gate a pool, which in Aramaic is called Bethesda<sup>a</sup> and which is surrounded by five covered colonnades. <sup>3</sup>Here a great number of disabled people used to lie—the blind, the lame, the paralyzed. <sup>[4]b</sup> <sup>5</sup>One who was there had been an invalid for thirty-eight years. <sup>6</sup>When Jesus saw him lying there and learned that he had been in this condition for a long time, he asked him, "Do you want to get well?"

---

<sup>a</sup> 2 Some manuscripts *Bethzatha*; other manuscripts *Bethsaida*
<sup>b</sup> 3,4 Some manuscripts include here, wholly or in part, *paralyzed—and they waited for the moving of the waters.* *4From time to time an angel of the Lord would come down and stir up the waters. The first one into the pool after each such disturbance would be cured of whatever disease they had.*

## Amplified Bible

<sup>38</sup>I sent you to reap a crop for which you have not toiled. Other men have labored and you have stepped in to reap the results of their work.

<sup>39</sup>Now numerous Samaritans from that town believed in *and* trusted in Him because of what the woman said when she declared *and* testified, He told me everything that I ever did.

<sup>40</sup>So when the Samaritans arrived, they asked Him to remain with them, and He did stay there two days.

<sup>41</sup>Then many more believed in *and* adhered to *and* relied on Him because of His personal message [what He Himself said].

<sup>42</sup>And they told the woman, Now we no longer believe (trust, have faith) just because of what you said; for we have heard Him ourselves [personally], and we know that He truly is the Savior of the world, *the Christ.*

<sup>43</sup>But after these two days Jesus went on from there into Galilee—

<sup>44</sup>Although He Himself declared that a prophet has no honor in his own country.

<sup>45</sup>However, when He came into Galilee, the Galileans also welcomed Him *and* took Him to their hearts eagerly, for they had seen everything that He did in Jerusalem during the Feast; for they too had attended the Feast.

<sup>46</sup>So Jesus came again to Cana of Galilee, where He had turned the water into wine. And there was a certain royal official whose son was lying ill in Capernaum.

<sup>47</sup>Having heard that Jesus had come back from Judea into Galilee, he went away to meet Him and began to beg Him to come down and cure his son, for he was lying at the point of death.

<sup>48</sup>Then Jesus said to him, Unless you see signs and miracles happen, you [people] never will believe (trust, have faith) at all.

<sup>49</sup>The king's officer pleaded with Him, Sir, do come down at once before my little child is dead!

<sup>50</sup>Jesus answered him, Go in peace; your son will live! And the man put his trust in what Jesus said and started home.

<sup>51</sup>But even as he was on the road going down, his servants met him and reported, saying, Your son lives!

<sup>52</sup>So he asked them at what time he had begun to get better. They said, Yesterday during the seventh hour (about one o'clock in the afternoon) the fever left him.

<sup>53</sup>Then the father knew that it was at that very hour when Jesus had said to him, Your son will live. And he and his entire household believed (adhered to, trusted in, and relied on Jesus).

<sup>54</sup>This is the second sign (wonderwork, miracle) that Jesus performed after He had come out of Judea into Galilee.

**5** Later on there was a Jewish festival (feast) for which Jesus went up to Jerusalem.

<sup>2</sup>Now there is in Jerusalem a pool near the Sheep Gate. This pool in the Hebrew is called Bethesda, having five porches (alcoves, colonnades, doorways).

<sup>3</sup>In these lay a great number of sick folk—some blind, some crippled, and some paralyzed (shriveled up)—<sup>a</sup>*waiting for the bubbling up of the water.*

<sup>4</sup>*For an angel of the Lord went down at appointed seasons into the pool and moved and stirred up the water; whoever then first, after the stirring up of the water, stepped in was cured of whatever disease with which he was afflicted.*

<sup>5</sup>There was a certain man there who had suffered with a deep-seated *and* lingering disorder for thirty-eight years.

<sup>6</sup>When Jesus noticed him lying there [helpless], knowing that he had already been a long time in that condition, He said to him, Do you want to become well? [Are you really in earnest about getting well?]

---

<sup>a</sup> Many manuscripts omit the last part of verse 3 and all of verse 4.

## New International Version

[7]"Sir," the invalid replied, "I have no one to help me into the pool when the water is stirred. While I am trying to get in, someone else goes down ahead of me."

[8]Then Jesus said to him, "Get up! Pick up your mat and walk." [9]At once the man was cured; he picked up his mat and walked.

The day on which this took place was a Sabbath, [10]and so the Jewish leaders said to the man who had been healed, "It is the Sabbath; the law forbids you to carry your mat."

[11]But he replied, "The man who made me well said to me, 'Pick up your mat and walk.' "

[12]So they asked him, "Who is this fellow who told you to pick it up and walk?"

[13]The man who was healed had no idea who it was, for Jesus had slipped away into the crowd that was there.

[14]Later Jesus found him at the temple and said to him, "See, you are well again. Stop sinning or something worse may happen to you." [15]The man went away and told the Jewish leaders that it was Jesus who had made him well.

### The Authority of the Son

[16]So, because Jesus was doing these things on the Sabbath, the Jewish leaders began to persecute him. [17]In his defense Jesus said to them, "My Father is always at his work to this very day, and I too am working." [18]For this reason they tried all the more to kill him; not only was he breaking the Sabbath, but he was even calling God his own Father, making himself equal with God.

[19]Jesus gave them this answer: "Very truly I tell you, the Son can do nothing by himself; he can do only what he sees his Father doing, because whatever the Father does the Son also does. [20]For the Father loves the Son and shows him all he does. Yes, and he will show him even greater works than these, so that you will be amazed. [21]For just as the Father raises the dead and gives them life, even so the Son gives life to whom he is pleased to give it. [22]Moreover, the Father judges no one, but has entrusted all judgment to the Son, [23]that all may honor the Son just as they honor the Father. Whoever does not honor the Son does not honor the Father, who sent him.

[24]"Very truly I tell you, whoever hears my word and believes him who sent me has eternal life and will not be judged but has crossed over from death to life. [25]Very truly I tell you, a time is coming and has now come when the dead will hear the voice of the Son of God and those who

## Amplified Bible

[7]The invalid answered, Sir, I have nobody when the water is moving to put me into the pool; but while I am trying to come [into it] myself, somebody else steps down ahead of me.

[8]Jesus said to him, Get up! Pick up your bed (sleeping pad) and walk!

[9]Instantly the man became well *and* recovered his strength and picked up his bed and walked. But that happened on the Sabbath.

[10]So the Jews kept saying to the man who had been healed, It is the Sabbath, and you have no right to pick up your bed [it is not lawful].

[11]He answered them, The [a]Man Who healed me *and* gave me back my strength, He Himself said to me, Pick up your bed and walk!

[12]They asked him, Who is the Man Who told you, Pick up your bed and walk?

[13]Now the invalid who had been healed did not know who it was, for Jesus had quietly gone away [had passed on unnoticed], since there was a crowd in the place.

[14]Afterward, when Jesus found him in the temple, He said to him, See, you are well! Stop sinning or something worse may happen to you.

[15]The man went away and told the Jews that it was Jesus Who had made him well.

[16]For this reason the Jews began to persecute (annoy, torment) Jesus [b]*and sought to kill Him,* because He was doing these things on the Sabbath.

[17]But Jesus answered them, My Father has worked [even] until now, [He has never ceased working; He is still working] and I, too, must be at [divine] work.

[18]This made the Jews more determined than ever to kill Him [to do away with Him]; because He not only was breaking (weakening, violating) the Sabbath, but He actually was speaking of God as being [in a special sense] His own Father, making Himself equal [putting Himself on a level] with God.

[19]So Jesus answered them by saying, I assure you, most solemnly I tell you, the Son is able to do nothing of Himself (of His own accord); but He is able to do only what He sees the Father doing, for whatever the Father does is what the Son does in the same way [in His turn].

[20]The Father dearly loves the Son and discloses to (shows) Him everything that He Himself does. And He will disclose to Him (let Him see) greater things than these, so that you may marvel *and* be full of wonder *and* astonishment.

[21]Just as the Father raises up the dead and gives them life [makes them live on], even so the Son also gives life to whomever He wills *and* is pleased to give it.

[22]Even the Father judges no one, for He has given all judgment (the last judgment and the whole business of judging) entirely into the hands of the Son,

[23]So that all men may give honor (reverence, homage) to the Son just as they give honor to the Father. [In fact] whoever does not honor the Son does not honor the Father, Who has sent Him.

[24]I assure you, most solemnly I tell you, the person whose ears are open to My words [who listens to My message] and believes *and* trusts in *and* clings to *and* relies on Him Who sent Me has (possesses now) eternal life. And he does not come into judgment [does not incur sentence of judgment, will not come under condemnation], but he has already passed over out of death into life.

[25]Believe Me when I assure you, most solemnly I tell you, the time is coming and is here now when the dead shall hear the voice of the Son of God and those who hear it shall live.

---

[a] Capitalized because of what He is, the spotless Son of God, not what the speaker may have thought He was.   [b] Some manuscripts add this phrase.

## New International Version

hear will live. ²⁶For as the Father has life in himself, so he has granted the Son also to have life in himself. ²⁷And he has given him authority to judge because he is the Son of Man.

²⁸"Do not be amazed at this, for a time is coming when all who are in their graves will hear his voice ²⁹and come out—those who have done what is good will rise to live, and those who have done what is evil will rise to be condemned. ³⁰By myself I can do nothing; I judge only as I hear, and my judgment is just, for I seek not to please myself but him who sent me.

### Testimonies About Jesus

³¹"If I testify about myself, my testimony is not true. ³²There is another who testifies in my favor, and I know that his testimony about me is true.

³³"You have sent to John and he has testified to the truth. ³⁴Not that I accept human testimony; but I mention it that you may be saved. ³⁵John was a lamp that burned and gave light, and you chose for a time to enjoy his light.

³⁶"I have testimony weightier than that of John. For the works that the Father has given me to finish—the very works that I am doing—testify that the Father has sent me. ³⁷And the Father who sent me has himself testified concerning me. You have never heard his voice nor seen his form, ³⁸nor does his word dwell in you, for you do not believe the one he sent. ³⁹You studyᵃ the Scriptures diligently because you think that in them you have eternal life. These are the very Scriptures that testify about me, ⁴⁰yet you refuse to come to me to have life.

⁴¹"I do not accept glory from human beings, ⁴²but I know you. I know that you do not have the love of God in your hearts. ⁴³I have come in my Father's name, and you do not accept me; but if someone else comes in his own name, you will accept him. ⁴⁴How can you believe since you accept glory from one another but do not seek the glory that comes from the only Godᵇ?

## Amplified Bible

²⁶For even as the Father has life in Himself *and* is self-existent, so He has given to the Son to have life in Himself *and* be self-existent.

²⁷And He has given Him authority *and* granted Him power to execute (exercise, practice) judgment because He is ᵃa Son of man [very man].

²⁸Do not be surprised *and* wonder at this, for the time is coming when all those who are in the tombs shall hear His voice,

²⁹And they shall come out—those who have practiced doing good [will come out] to the resurrection of [new] life, and those who have done evil will be raised for judgment [raised to meet their sentence]. [Dan. 12:2.]

³⁰I am able to do nothing from Myself [independently, of My own accord—but only as I am taught by God and as I get His orders]. Even as I hear, I judge [I decide as I am bidden to decide. As the voice comes to Me, so I give a decision], and My judgment is right (just, righteous), because I do not seek *or* consult My own will [I have no desire to do what is pleasing to Myself, My own aim, My own purpose] but only the will *and* pleasure of the Father Who sent Me.

³¹If I alone testify in My behalf, My testimony is not valid *and* cannot be worth anything.

³²There is Another Who testifies concerning Me, and I know *and* am certain that His evidence on My behalf is true and valid.

³³You yourselves have sent [an inquiry] to John and he has been a witness to the truth.

³⁴But I do not receive [a mere] human witness [the evidence which I accept on My behalf is not from man]; but I simply mention all these things in order that you may be saved (made and kept safe and sound).

³⁵John was the lamp that kept on burning and shining [to show you the way], and you were willing for a while to delight (sun) yourselves in his light.

³⁶But I have as My witness something greater (weightier, higher, better) than that of John; for the works that the Father has appointed Me to accomplish *and* finish, the very same works that I am now doing, are a witness *and* proof that the Father has sent Me.

³⁷And the Father Who sent Me has Himself testified concerning Me. Not one of you has ever given ear to His voice or seen His form (His face—what He is like). [You have always been deaf to His voice and blind to the vision of Him.]

³⁸And you have not His word (His thought) living in your hearts, because you do not believe *and* adhere to *and* trust in *and* rely on Him Whom He has sent. [That is why you do not keep His message living in you, because you do not believe in the Messenger Whom He has sent.]

³⁹You search *and* investigate *and* pore over the Scriptures diligently, because you suppose *and* trust that you have eternal life through them. And these [very Scriptures] testify about Me!

⁴⁰And still you are not willing [but refuse] to come to Me, so that you might have life.

⁴¹I receive not glory from men [I crave no human honor, I look for no mortal fame],

⁴²But I know you and recognize *and* understand that you have not the love of God in you.

⁴³I have come in My Father's name *and* with His power, and you do not receive Me [your hearts are not open to Me, you give Me no welcome]; but if another comes in his own name *and* his own power *and* with no other authority but himself, you will receive him *and* give him your approval.

⁴⁴How is it possible for you to believe [how can you learn to believe], you who [are content to seek and] receive praise *and* honor *and* glory from one another, and yet do not seek the praise *and* honor *and* glory which come from Him Who alone is God?

---

ᵃ 39 Or ³⁹*Study*   ᵇ 44 Some early manuscripts *the Only One*

ᵃ Marvin Vincent, *Word Studies*.

## New International Version

45"But do not think I will accuse you before the Father. Your accuser is Moses, on whom your hopes are set. 46If you believed Moses, you would believe me, for he wrote about me. 47But since you do not believe what he wrote, how are you going to believe what I say?"

### Jesus Feeds the Five Thousand

**6** Some time after this, Jesus crossed to the far shore of the Sea of Galilee (that is, the Sea of Tiberias), 2and a great crowd of people followed him because they saw the signs he had performed by healing the sick. 3Then Jesus went up on a mountainside and sat down with his disciples. 4The Jewish Passover Festival was near.

5When Jesus looked up and saw a great crowd coming toward him, he said to Philip, "Where shall we buy bread for these people to eat?" 6He asked this only to test him, for he already had in mind what he was going to do.

7Philip answered him, "It would take more than half a year's wages*a* to buy enough bread for each one to have a bite!"

8Another of his disciples, Andrew, Simon Peter's brother, spoke up, 9"Here is a boy with five small barley loaves and two small fish, but how far will they go among so many?"

10Jesus said, "Have the people sit down." There was plenty of grass in that place, and they sat down (about five thousand men were there). 11Jesus then took the loaves, gave thanks, and distributed to those who were seated as much as they wanted. He did the same with the fish.

12When they had all had enough to eat, he said to his disciples, "Gather the pieces that are left over. Let nothing be wasted." 13So they gathered them and filled twelve baskets with the pieces of the five barley loaves left over by those who had eaten.

14After the people saw the sign Jesus performed, they began to say, "Surely this is the Prophet who is to come into the world." 15Jesus, knowing that they intended to come and make him king by force, withdrew again to a mountain by himself.

### Jesus Walks on the Water

16When evening came, his disciples went down to the lake, 17where they got into a boat and set off across the lake for Capernaum. By now it was dark, and Jesus had not yet joined them. 18A strong wind was blowing and the waters grew rough. 19When they had rowed about three or four miles,*b* they saw Jesus approaching the boat, walking on the water; and they were frightened. 20But he said to them, "It is I; don't be afraid." 21Then they were willing to take him into the boat, and immediately the boat reached the shore where they were heading.

## Amplified Bible

45Put out of your minds the thought *and* do not suppose [as some of you are supposing] that I will accuse you before the Father. There is one who accuses you—it is Moses, the very one on whom you have built your hopes [in whom you trust].

46For if you believed *and* relied on Moses, you would believe *and* rely on Me, for he wrote about Me [personally].

47But if you do not believe *and* trust his writings, how then will you believe *and* trust My teachings? [How shall you cleave to and rely on My words?]

**6** After this, Jesus went to the farther side of the Sea of Galilee—that is, the Sea of Tiberias.

2And a great crowd was following Him because they had seen the signs (miracles) which He [continually] performed upon those who were sick.

3And Jesus walked up the mountainside and sat down there with His disciples.

4Now the Passover, the feast of the Jews, was approaching.

5Jesus looked up then, and seeing that a vast multitude was coming toward Him, He said to Philip, Where are we to buy bread, so that all these people may eat?

6But He said this to prove (test) him, for He well knew what He was about to do.

7Philip answered Him, Two hundred pennies' (forty dollars) worth of bread is not enough that everyone may receive even a little.

8Another of His disciples, Andrew, Simon Peter's brother, said to Him,

9There is a little boy here, who has [with him] five barley loaves, and two small fish; but what are they among so many people?

10Jesus said, Make all the people recline (sit down). Now the ground (a pasture) was covered with thick grass at the spot, so the men threw themselves down, about 5,000 in number.

11Jesus took the loaves, and when He had given thanks, He distributed *a to the disciples and the disciples* to the reclining people; so also [He did] with the fish, as much as they wanted.

12When they had all had enough, He said to His disciples, Gather up now the fragments (the broken pieces that are left over), so that nothing may be lost *and* wasted.

13So accordingly they gathered them up, and they filled twelve [*b* small hand] baskets with fragments left over by those who had eaten from the five barley loaves.

14When the people saw the sign (miracle) that Jesus had performed, they began saying, Surely *and* beyond a doubt this is the Prophet Who is to come into the world! [Deut. 18:15, 18; John 1:21; Acts 3:22.]

15Then Jesus, knowing that they meant to come and seize Him that they might make Him king, withdrew again to the hillside by Himself alone.

16When evening came, His disciples went down to the sea,

17And they took a boat and were going across the sea to Capernaum. It was now dark, and still Jesus had not [yet] come back to them.

18Meanwhile, the sea was getting rough *and* rising high because of a great *and* violent wind that was blowing.

19[However] when they had rowed three or four miles, they saw Jesus walking on the sea and approaching the boat. And they were afraid (terrified).

20But Jesus said to them, It is I; be not afraid! [I AM; stop being frightened!] [Exod. 3:14.]

21Then they were quite willing *and* glad for Him to come into the boat. And now the boat went at once to the land they had steered toward. [And immediately they reached the shore toward which they had been slowly making their way.]

---

*a* 7 Greek *take two hundred denarii*    *b* 19 Or about 5 or 6 kilometers

*a* Some manuscripts add this phrase.  *b* G. Abbott-Smith, *Manual Greek Lexicon.* See also footnote on Matt. 14:20.

## New International Version

22The next day the crowd that had stayed on the opposite shore of the lake realized that only one boat had been there, and that Jesus had not entered it with his disciples, but that they had gone away alone. 23Then some boats from Tiberias landed near the place where the people had eaten the bread after the Lord had given thanks. 24Once the crowd realized that neither Jesus nor his disciples were there, they got into the boats and went to Capernaum in search of Jesus.

### Jesus the Bread of Life

25When they found him on the other side of the lake, they asked him, "Rabbi, when did you get here?"

26Jesus answered, "Very truly I tell you, you are looking for me, not because you saw the signs I performed but because you ate the loaves and had your fill. 27Do not work for food that spoils, but for food that endures to eternal life, which the Son of Man will give you. For on him God the Father has placed his seal of approval."

28Then they asked him, "What must we do to do the works God requires?"

29Jesus answered, "The work of God is this: to believe in the one he has sent."

30So they asked him, "What sign then will you give that we may see it and believe you? What will you do? 31Our ancestors ate the manna in the wilderness; as it is written: 'He gave them bread from heaven to eat.'*a*"

32Jesus said to them, "Very truly I tell you, it is not Moses who has given you the bread from heaven, but it is my Father who gives you the true bread from heaven. 33For the bread of God is the bread that comes down from heaven and gives life to the world."

34"Sir," they said, "always give us this bread."

35Then Jesus declared, "I am the bread of life. Whoever comes to me will never go hungry, and whoever believes in me will never be thirsty. 36But as I told you, you have seen me and still you do not believe. 37All those the Father gives me will come to me, and whoever comes to me I will never drive away. 38For I have come down from heaven not to do my will but to do the will of him who sent me. 39And this is the will of him who sent me, that I shall lose none of all those he has given me, but raise them up at the last day. 40For my Father's will is that everyone who looks to the Son and believes in him shall have eternal life, and I will raise them up at the last day."

41At this the Jews there began to grumble about him because he said, "I am the bread that came down from heaven." 42They said, "Is this not Jesus, the son of Joseph,

## Amplified Bible

22The next day the crowd [that still remained] standing on the other side of the sea realized that there had been only one small boat there, and that Jesus had not gone into it with His disciples, but that His disciples had gone away by themselves.

23But now some other boats from Tiberias had come in near the place where they ate the bread after the Lord had given thanks.

24So the people, finding that neither Jesus nor His disciples were there, themselves got into the small boats and came to Capernaum looking for Jesus.

25And when they found Him on the other side of the lake, they said to Him, Rabbi! When did You come here?

26Jesus answered them, I assure you, most solemnly I tell you, you have been searching for Me, not because you saw the miracles *and* signs but because you were fed with the loaves and were filled *and* satisfied.

27Stop toiling *and* doing *and* producing for the food that perishes *and* decomposes [in the using], but strive *and* work *and* produce rather for the [lasting] food which endures [continually] unto life eternal; the Son of Man will give (furnish) you that, for God the Father has authorized *and* certified Him *and* put His seal of endorsement upon Him.

28They then said, What are we to do, that we may [habitually] be working the works of God? [What are we to do to carry out what God requires?]

29Jesus replied, This is the work (service) that God asks of you: that you believe in the One Whom He has sent [that you cleave to, trust, rely on, and have faith in His Messenger].

30Therefore they said to Him, What sign (miracle, wonderwork) will *a*You perform then, so that we may see it and believe *and* rely on *and* adhere to You? What [supernatural] work have You [to show what You can do]?

31Our forefathers ate the manna in the wilderness; as the Scripture says, He gave them bread out of heaven to eat. [Exod. 16:15; Neh. 9:15; Ps. 78:24.]

32Jesus then said to them, I assure you, most solemnly I tell you, Moses did not give you the Bread from heaven [what Moses gave you was not the Bread from heaven], but it is My Father Who gives you the true heavenly Bread.

33For the Bread of God is He Who comes down out of heaven and gives life to the world.

34Then they said to Him, Lord, give us this bread always (all the time)!

35Jesus replied, I am the Bread of Life. He who comes to Me will never be hungry, and he who believes in *and* cleaves to *and* trusts in *and* relies on Me will never thirst any more (at any time).

36But [as] I told you, although you have seen Me, still you do not believe *and* trust *and* have faith.

37All whom My Father gives (entrusts) to Me will come to Me; and the one who comes to Me I will most certainly not cast out [I will never, no never, reject one of them who comes to Me].

38For I have come down from heaven not to do My own will *and* purpose but to do the will *and* purpose of Him Who sent Me.

39And this is the will of Him Who sent Me, that I should not lose any of all that He has given Me, but that I should give new life *and* raise [them all] up at the last day.

40For this is My Father's will *and* His purpose, that everyone who sees the Son and believes in *and* cleaves to *and* trusts in *and* relies on Him should have eternal life, and I will raise him up [from the dead] at the last day.

41Now the Jews murmured *and* found fault with *and* grumbled about Jesus because He said, I am [Myself] the Bread that came down from heaven.

42They kept asking, Is not this Jesus, the *a*Son of Jo-

*a* Capitalized because of what He is, the spotless Son of God, not what the speaker may have thought He was.

## New International Version

whose father and mother we know? How can he now say, 'I came down from heaven'?"

⁴³"Stop grumbling among yourselves," Jesus answered. ⁴⁴"No one can come to me unless the Father who sent me draws them, and I will raise them up at the last day. ⁴⁵It is written in the Prophets: 'They will all be taught by God.'ᵃ Everyone who has heard the Father and learned from him comes to me. ⁴⁶No one has seen the Father except the one who is from God; only he has seen the Father. ⁴⁷Very truly I tell you, the one who believes has eternal life. ⁴⁸I am the bread of life. ⁴⁹Your ancestors ate the manna in the wilderness, yet they died. ⁵⁰But here is the bread that comes down from heaven, which anyone may eat and not die. ⁵¹I am the living bread that came down from heaven. Whoever eats this bread will live forever. This bread is my flesh, which I will give for the life of the world."

⁵²Then the Jews began to argue sharply among themselves, "How can this man give us his flesh to eat?"

⁵³Jesus said to them, "Very truly I tell you, unless you eat the flesh of the Son of Man and drink his blood, you have no life in you. ⁵⁴Whoever eats my flesh and drinks my blood has eternal life, and I will raise them up at the last day. ⁵⁵For my flesh is real food and my blood is real drink. ⁵⁶Whoever eats my flesh and drinks my blood remains in me, and I in them. ⁵⁷Just as the living Father sent me and I live because of the Father, so the one who feeds on me will live because of me. ⁵⁸This is the bread that came down from heaven. Your ancestors ate manna and died, but whoever feeds on this bread will live forever." ⁵⁹He said this while teaching in the synagogue in Capernaum.

### Many Disciples Desert Jesus

⁶⁰On hearing it, many of his disciples said, "This is a hard teaching. Who can accept it?"

⁶¹Aware that his disciples were grumbling about this, Jesus said to them, "Does this offend you? ⁶²Then what if you see the Son of Man ascend to where he was before! ⁶³The Spirit gives life; the flesh counts for nothing. The words I have spoken to you—they are full of the Spiritᵇ and life. ⁶⁴Yet there are some of you who do not believe." For Jesus had known from the beginning which of them did not believe and who would betray him. ⁶⁵He went on

## Amplified Bible

seph, Whose father and mother we know? How then can He say, I have come down from heaven?

⁴³So Jesus answered them, Stop grumbling *and* saying things against Me to one another.

⁴⁴No one is able to come to Me unless the Father Who sent Me attracts *and* draws him *and* gives him the desire to come to Me, and [then] I will raise him up [from the dead] at the last day.

⁴⁵It is written in [the book of] the Prophets, And they shall all be taught of God [have Him in person for their Teacher]. Everyone who has listened to and learned from the Father comes to Me—[Isa. 54:13.]

⁴⁶Which does not imply that anyone has seen the Father [not that anyone has ever seen Him] except He [Who was with the Father] Who comes from God; He [alone] has seen the Father.

⁴⁷I assure you, most solemnly I tell you, he who believes *in Me* [who adheres to, trusts in, relies on, and has faith in Me] has (now possesses) eternal life.

⁴⁸I am the Bread of Life [that gives life—the Living Bread].

⁴⁹Your forefathers ate the manna in the wilderness, and [yet] they died.

⁵⁰[But] this is the Bread that comes down from heaven, so that [any]one may eat of it and never die.

⁵¹I [Myself] am this Living Bread that came down from heaven. If anyone eats of this Bread, he will live forever; and also the Bread that I shall give for the life of the world is My flesh (body).

⁵²Then the Jews angrily contended with one another, saying, How is He able to give us His flesh to eat?

⁵³And Jesus said to them, I assure you, most solemnly I tell you, you cannot have any life in you unless you eat the flesh of the Son of Man and drink His blood [unless you appropriate His life and the saving merit of His blood].

⁵⁴He who feeds on My flesh and drinks My blood has (possesses now) eternal life, and I will raise him up [from the dead] on the last day.

⁵⁵For My flesh is true *and* genuine food, and My blood is true *and* genuine drink.

⁵⁶He who feeds on My flesh and drinks My blood dwells continually in Me, and I [in like manner dwell continually] in him.

⁵⁷Just as the living Father sent Me and I live by (through, because of) the Father, even so whoever continues to feed on Me [whoever takes Me for his food *and* is nourished by Me] shall [in his turn] live through *and* because of Me.

⁵⁸This is the Bread that came down from heaven. It is not like the manna which our forefathers ate, and yet died; he who takes this Bread for his food shall live forever.

⁵⁹He said these things in a synagogue while He was teaching at Capernaum.

⁶⁰When His disciples heard this, many of them said, This is a hard *and* difficult *and* strange saying (an offensive and unbearable message). Who can stand to hear it? [Who can be expected to listen to such teaching?]

⁶¹But Jesus, knowing within Himself that His disciples were complaining *and* protesting *and* grumbling about it, said to them: Is this a stumbling block *and* an offense to you? [Does this upset and displease and shock and scandalize you?]

⁶²What then [will be your reaction] if you should see the Son of Man ascending to [the place] where He was before?

⁶³It is the Spirit Who gives life [He is the Life-giver]; the flesh conveys no benefit whatever [there is no profit in it]. The words (truths) that I have been speaking to you are spirit and life.

⁶⁴But [still] some of you fail to believe *and* trust *and* have faith. For Jesus knew from the first who did not believe *and* had no faith and who would betray Him *and* be false to Him.

---

ᵃ 45 Isaiah 54:13   ᵇ 63 Or *are Spirit*; or *are spirit*

## New International Version

to say, "This is why I told you that no one can come to me unless the Father has enabled them."

66From this time many of his disciples turned back and no longer followed him.

67"You do not want to leave too, do you?" Jesus asked the Twelve.

68Simon Peter answered him, "Lord, to whom shall we go? You have the words of eternal life. 69We have come to believe and to know that you are the Holy One of God."

70Then Jesus replied, "Have I not chosen you, the Twelve? Yet one of you is a devil!" 71 (He meant Judas, the son of Simon Iscariot, who, though one of the Twelve, was later to betray him.)

### Jesus Goes to the Festival of Tabernacles

7 After this, Jesus went around in Galilee. He did not want[a] to go about in Judea because the Jewish leaders there were looking for a way to kill him. 2But when the Jewish Festival of Tabernacles was near, 3Jesus' brothers said to him, "Leave Galilee and go to Judea, so that your disciples there may see the works you do. 4No one who wants to become a public figure acts in secret. Since you are doing these things, show yourself to the world." 5For even his own brothers did not believe in him.

6Therefore Jesus told them, "My time is not yet here; for you any time will do. 7The world cannot hate you, but it hates me because I testify that its works are evil. 8You go to the festival. I am not[b] going up to this festival, because my time has not yet fully come." 9After he had said this, he stayed in Galilee.

10However, after his brothers had left for the festival, he went also, not publicly, but in secret. 11Now at the festival the Jewish leaders were watching for Jesus and asking, "Where is he?"

12Among the crowds there was widespread whispering about him. Some said, "He is a good man."

Others replied, "No, he deceives the people." 13But no one would say anything publicly about him for fear of the leaders.

### Jesus Teaches at the Festival

14Not until halfway through the festival did Jesus go up to the temple courts and begin to teach. 15The Jews were amazed and asked, "How did this man get such learning without having been taught?"

16Jesus answered, "My teaching is not my own. It comes from the one who sent me. 17Anyone who chooses to do the will of God will find out whether my teaching comes from God or whether I speak on my own. 18Whoever

## Amplified Bible

65And He said, This is why I told you that no one can come to Me unless it is granted him [unless he is enabled to do so] by the Father.

66After this, many of His disciples drew back (returned to their old associations) and no longer accompanied Him.

67Jesus said to the Twelve, Will you also go away? [And do you too desire to leave Me?]

68Simon Peter answered, Lord, to whom shall we go? You have the words (the message) of eternal life.

69And we have learned to believe and trust, and [more] we have come to know [surely] that You are the Holy One of God, the Christ (the Anointed One), the Son of the living God.

70Jesus answered them, Did I not choose you, the Twelve? And [yet] one of you is a devil (of the evil one and a false accuser).

71He was speaking of Judas, the son of Simon Iscariot, for he was about to betray Him, [although] he was one of the Twelve.

7 After this, Jesus went from place to place in Galilee, for He would not travel in Judea because the Jews were seeking to kill Him.

2Now the Jewish Feast of Tabernacles was drawing near.

3So His brothers said to Him, Leave here and go into Judea, so that aYour disciples [there] may also see the works that You do. [This is no place for You.]

4For no one does anything in secret when he wishes to be conspicuous and secure publicity. If You [must] do these things [if You must act like this], show Yourself openly and make Yourself known to the world!

5For [even] His brothers did not believe in or adhere to or trust in or rely on Him either.

6Whereupon Jesus said to them, My time (opportunity) has not come yet; but any time is suitable for you and your opportunity is ready any time [is always here].

7The world cannot [be expected to] hate you, but it does hate Me because I denounce it for its wicked works and reveal that its doings are evil.

8Go to the Feast yourselves. I am not [yet] going up to the Festival, because My time is not ripe. [My term is not yet completed; it is not time for Me to go.]

9Having said these things to them, He stayed behind in Galilee.

10But afterward, when His brothers had gone up to the Feast, He went up also, not publicly [not with a caravan], but by Himself quietly and as if He did not wish to be observed.

11Therefore the Jews kept looking for Him at the Feast and asking, Where can He be? [Where is that Fellow?]

12And there was among the mass of the people much whispered discussion and hot disputing about Him. Some were saying, He is good! [He is a good Man!] Others said, No, He misleads and deceives the people [gives them false ideas]!

13But no one dared speak out boldly about Him for fear of [the leaders of] the Jews.

14When the Feast was already half over, Jesus went up into the temple [bcourt] and began to teach.

15The Jews were astonished. They said, How is it that this Man has learning [is so versed in the sacred Scriptures and in theology] when He has never studied?

16Jesus answered them by saying, My teaching is not My own, but His Who sent Me.

17If any man desires to do His will (God's pleasure), he will know (have the needed illumination to recognize, and can tell for himself) whether the teaching is from God or whether I am speaking from Myself and of My own accord and on My own authority.

---

a 1 Some manuscripts not have authority    b 8 Some manuscripts not yet

a Capitalized because of what He is, the spotless Son of God, not what the speaker may have thought He was.    b Richard Trench, Synonyms of the New Testament.

## New International Version

speaks on their own does so to gain personal glory, but he who seeks the glory of the one who sent him is a man of truth; there is nothing false about him. ¹⁹Has not Moses given you the law? Yet not one of you keeps the law. Why are you trying to kill me?"

²⁰"You are demon-possessed," the crowd answered. "Who is trying to kill you?"

²¹Jesus said to them, "I did one miracle, and you are all amazed. ²²Yet, because Moses gave you circumcision (though actually it did not come from Moses, but from the patriarchs), you circumcise a boy on the Sabbath. ²³Now if a boy can be circumcised on the Sabbath so that the law of Moses may not be broken, why are you angry with me for healing a man's whole body on the Sabbath? ²⁴Stop judging by mere appearances, but instead judge correctly."

### Division Over Who Jesus Is

²⁵At that point some of the people of Jerusalem began to ask, "Isn't this the man they are trying to kill? ²⁶Here he is, speaking publicly, and they are not saying a word to him. Have the authorities really concluded that he is the Messiah? ²⁷But we know where this man is from; when the Messiah comes, no one will know where he is from."

²⁸Then Jesus, still teaching in the temple courts, cried out, "Yes, you know me, and you know where I am from. I am not here on my own authority, but he who sent me is true. You do not know him, ²⁹but I know him because I am from him and he sent me."

³⁰At this they tried to seize him, but no one laid a hand on him, because his hour had not yet come. ³¹Still, many in the crowd believed in him. They said, "When the Messiah comes, will he perform more signs than this man?"

³²The Pharisees heard the crowd whispering such things about him. Then the chief priests and the Pharisees sent temple guards to arrest him.

³³Jesus said, "I am with you for only a short time, and then I am going to the one who sent me. ³⁴You will look for me, but you will not find me; and where I am, you cannot come."

³⁵The Jews said to one another, "Where does this man intend to go that we cannot find him? Will he go where our people live scattered among the Greeks, and teach the Greeks? ³⁶What did he mean when he said, 'You will look for me, but you will not find me,' and 'Where I am, you cannot come'?"

³⁷On the last and greatest day of the festival, Jesus stood and said in a loud voice, "Let anyone who is thirsty come to me and drink. ³⁸Whoever believes in me, as Scripture has said, rivers of living water will flow from within them."ᵃ

## Amplified Bible

¹⁸He who speaks on his own authority seeks to win honor for himself. [He whose teaching originates with himself seeks his own glory.] But He Who seeks the glory *and* is eager for the honor of Him Who sent Him, He is true; and there is no unrighteousness *or* falsehood *or* deception in Him.

¹⁹Did not Moses give you the Law? And yet not one of you keeps the Law. [If that is the truth] why do you seek to kill Me [for not keeping it]?

²⁰The crowd answered Him, You are possessed by a demon! [You are raving!] Who seeks to kill You?

²¹Jesus answered them, I did one work, and you all are astounded. [John 5:1-9.]

²²Now Moses established circumcision among you— though it did not originate with Moses but with the previous patriarchs—and you circumcise a person [even] on the Sabbath day.

²³If, to avoid breaking the Law of Moses, a person undergoes circumcision on the Sabbath day, have you any cause to be angry with (indignant with, bitter against) Me for making a man's whole body well on the Sabbath?

²⁴Be honest in your judgment *and* do not decide at a glance (superficially and by appearances); but judge fairly *and* righteously.

²⁵Then some of the Jerusalem people said, Is not this the Man they seek to kill?

²⁶And here He is speaking openly, and they say nothing to Him! Can it be possible that the rulers have discovered *and* know that this is truly the Christ?

²⁷No, we know where this Man comes from; when the Christ arrives, no one is to know from what place He comes.

²⁸Whereupon Jesus called out as He taught in the temple [ᵃporches], Do you know Me, and do you know where I am from? I have not come on My own authority *and* of My own accord *and* as self-appointed, but the One Who sent Me is true (real, genuine, steadfast); and Him you do not know!

²⁹I know Him [Myself] because I come from His [very] presence, and it was He [personally] Who sent Me.

³⁰Therefore they were eager to arrest Him, but no one laid a hand on Him, for His hour (time) had not yet come.

³¹And besides, many of the multitude believed in Him [adhered to Him, trusted in Him, relied on Him]. And they kept saying, When the Christ comes, will He do [can He be expected to do] more miracles *and* produce more proofs *and* signs than what this Man has done?

³²The Pharisees learned how the people were saying these things about Him under their breath; and the chief priests and Pharisees sent attendants (guards) to arrest Him.

³³Therefore Jesus said, For a little while I am [still] with you, and then I go back to Him Who sent Me.

³⁴You will look for Me, but you will not [be able to] find Me; where I am, you cannot come.

³⁵Then the Jews said among themselves, Where does this Man intend to go that we shall not find Him? Will He go to the Jews who are scattered in the Dispersion among the Greeks, and teach the Greeks?

³⁶What does this statement of His mean, You will look for Me and not be able to find Me, and, Where I am, you cannot come?

³⁷Now on the final and most important day of the Feast, Jesus stood, and He cried in a loud voice, If any man is thirsty, let him come to Me and drink!

³⁸He who believes in Me [who cleaves to *and* trusts in *and* relies on Me] as the Scripture has said, From his innermost being shall flow [continuously] springs *and* rivers of living water.

---

ᵃ 37,38 Or *me. And let anyone drink* ³⁸*who believes in me." As Scripture has said, "Out of him* (or *them*) *will flow rivers of living water."*

ᵃ Richard Trench, *Synonyms of the New Testament.*

## New International Version

39By this he meant the Spirit, whom those who believed in him were later to receive. Up to that time the Spirit had not been given, since Jesus had not yet been glorified.

40On hearing his words, some of the people said, "Surely this man is the Prophet."

41Others said, "He is the Messiah."

Still others asked, "How can the Messiah come from Galilee? 42Does not Scripture say that the Messiah will come from David's descendants and from Bethlehem, the town where David lived?" 43Thus the people were divided because of Jesus. 44Some wanted to seize him, but no one laid a hand on him.

### Unbelief of the Jewish Leaders

45Finally the temple guards went back to the chief priests and the Pharisees, who asked them, "Why didn't you bring him in?"

46"No one ever spoke the way this man does," the guards replied.

47"You mean he has deceived you also?" the Pharisees retorted. 48"Have any of the rulers or of the Pharisees believed in him? 49No! But this mob that knows nothing of the law—there is a curse on them."

50Nicodemus, who had gone to Jesus earlier and who was one of their own number, asked, 51"Does our law condemn a man without first hearing him to find out what he has been doing?"

52They replied, "Are you from Galilee, too? Look into it, and you will find that a prophet does not come out of Galilee."

---

[The earliest manuscripts and many other ancient witnesses do not have John 7:53—8:11. A few manuscripts include these verses, wholly or in part, after John 7:36, John 21:25, Luke 21:38 or Luke 24:53.]

**8** *53Then they all went home, 1but Jesus went to the Mount of Olives.*

*2At dawn he appeared again in the temple courts, where all the people gathered around him, and he sat down to teach them. 3The teachers of the law and the Pharisees brought in a woman caught in adultery. They made her stand before the group 4and said to Jesus, "Teacher, this woman was caught in the act of adultery. 5In the Law Moses commanded us to stone such women. Now what do you say?" 6They were using this question as a trap, in order to have a basis for accusing him.*

*But Jesus bent down and started to write on the ground with his finger. 7When they kept on questioning him, he straightened up and said to them, "Let any one of you who is without sin be the first to throw a stone at her." 8Again he stooped down and wrote on the ground.*

*9At this, those who heard began to go away one at a time, the older ones first, until only Jesus was left, with the woman still standing there. 10Jesus straightened up and asked her, "Woman, where are they? Has no one condemned you?"*

## Amplified Bible

39But He was speaking here of the Spirit, Whom those who believed (trusted, had faith) in Him were afterward to receive. For the [Holy] Spirit had not yet been given, because Jesus was not yet glorified (raised to honor).

40Listening to those words, some of the multitude said, This is certainly *and* beyond doubt the Prophet! [Deut. 18:15, 18; John 1:21; 6:14; Acts 3:22.]

41Others said, This is the Christ (the Messiah, Anointed One)! But some said, What? Does the Christ come out of Galilee?

42Does not the Scripture tell us that the Christ will come from the offspring of David and from Bethlehem, the village where David lived? [Ps. 89:3, 4; Mic. 5:2.]

43So there arose a division *and* dissension among the people concerning Him.

44Some of them wanted to arrest Him, but no one [ventured and] laid hands on Him.

45Meanwhile the attendants (guards) had gone back to the chief priests and Pharisees, who asked them, Why have you not brought Him here with you?

46The attendants replied, Never has a man talked as this Man talks! [No mere man has ever spoken as He speaks!]

47The Pharisees said to them, Are you also deluded *and* led astray? [Are you also swept off your feet?]

48Has any of the authorities or of the Pharisees believed in Him?

49As for this multitude (rabble) that does not know the Law, they are contemptible *and* doomed *and* accursed!

50Then Nicodemus, who came to Jesus before at night and was one of them, asked,

51Does our Law convict a man without giving him a hearing and finding out what he has done?

52They answered him, Are you too from Galilee? Search [the Scriptures yourself], and you will see that no prophet comes (will rise to prominence) from Galilee.

53a And they went [back], each to his own house.

**8** But Jesus went to the Mount of Olives.

2Early in the morning (at dawn), He came back into the temple [b court], and the people came to Him in crowds. He sat down and was teaching them,

3When the scribes and Pharisees brought a woman who had been caught in adultery. They made her stand in the middle of the court and put the case before Him.

4Teacher, they said, This woman has been caught in the very act of adultery.

5Now Moses in the Law commanded us that such [women—offenders] shall be stoned to death. But what do You say [to do with her—what is Your sentence]? [Deut. 22:22-24.]

6This they said to try (test) Him, hoping they might find a charge on which to accuse Him. But Jesus stooped down and wrote on the ground with His finger.

7However, when they persisted with their question, He raised Himself up and said, Let him who is without sin among you be the first to throw a stone at her.

8Then He bent down and went on writing on the ground with His finger.

9They listened to Him, and then they began going out, conscience-stricken, one by one, from the oldest down to the last one of them, till Jesus was left alone, with the woman standing there before Him in the center of the court.

10When Jesus raised Himself up, He said to her, Woman, where are your accusers? Has no man condemned you?

---

a John 7:53 to 8:11 is absent from most of the older manuscripts, and those that have it sometimes place it elsewhere. The story may well be authentic. Indeed, Christ's response of compassion and mercy is so much in keeping with His character that we accept it as authentic, and feel that to omit it would be most unfortunate. b Richard Trench, *Synonyms of the New Testament.*

## New International Version

*11 "No one, sir," she said.*

*"Then neither do I condemn you," Jesus declared. "Go now and leave your life of sin."*

### Dispute Over Jesus' Testimony

12 When Jesus spoke again to the people, he said, "I am the light of the world. Whoever follows me will never walk in darkness, but will have the light of life."

13 The Pharisees challenged him, "Here you are, appearing as your own witness; your testimony is not valid."

14 Jesus answered, "Even if I testify on my own behalf, my testimony is valid, for I know where I came from and where I am going. But you have no idea where I come from or where I am going. 15 You judge by human standards; I pass judgment on no one. 16 But if I do judge, my decisions are true, because I am not alone. I stand with the Father, who sent me. 17 In your own Law it is written that the testimony of two witnesses is true. 18 I am one who testifies for myself; my other witness is the Father, who sent me."

19 Then they asked him, "Where is your father?"

"You do not know me or my Father," Jesus replied. "If you knew me, you would know my Father also." 20 He spoke these words while teaching in the temple courts near the place where the offerings were put. Yet no one seized him, because his hour had not yet come.

### Dispute Over Who Jesus Is

21 Once more Jesus said to them, "I am going away, and you will look for me, and you will die in your sin. Where I go, you cannot come."

22 This made the Jews ask, "Will he kill himself? Is that why he says, 'Where I go, you cannot come'?"

23 But he continued, "You are from below; I am from above. You are of this world; I am not of this world. 24 I told you that you would die in your sins; if you do not believe that I am he, you will indeed die in your sins."

25 "Who are you?" they asked.

"Just what I have been telling you from the beginning," Jesus replied. 26 "I have much to say in judgment of you. But he who sent me is trustworthy, and what I have heard from him I tell the world."

27 They did not understand that he was telling them about his Father. 28 So Jesus said, "When you have lifted up*a* the Son of Man, then you will know that I am he and that I do nothing on my own but speak just what the Father has taught me. 29 The one who sent me is with me; he has not left me alone, for I always do what pleases him." 30 Even as he spoke, many believed in him.

### Dispute Over Whose Children Jesus' Opponents Are

31 To the Jews who had believed him, Jesus said, "If you hold to my teaching, you are really my disciples. 32 Then you will know the truth, and the truth will set you free."

## Amplified Bible

11 She answered, No one, Lord! And Jesus said, I do not condemn you either. Go on your way and from now on sin no more.

12 Once more Jesus addressed the crowd. He said, I am the Light of the world. He who follows Me will not be walking in the dark, but will have the Light which is Life.

13 Whereupon the Pharisees told Him, You are testifying on Your own behalf; Your testimony is not valid *and* is worthless.

14 Jesus answered, Even if I do testify on My own behalf, My testimony is true *and* reliable *and* valid, for I know where I came from and where I am going; but you do not know where I come from or where I am going.

15 You [set yourselves up to] judge according to the flesh (by what you see). [You condemn by external, human standards.] I do not [set Myself up to] judge *or* condemn *or* sentence anyone.

16 Yet even if I do judge, My judgment is true [My decision is right]; for I am not alone [in making it], but [there are two of Us] I and the Father, Who sent Me.

17 In your [own] Law it is written that the testimony (evidence) of two persons is reliable *and* valid. [Deut. 19:15.]

18 I am One [of the Two] bearing testimony concerning Myself; and My Father, Who sent Me, He also testifies about Me.

19 Then they said to Him, Where is this *a* Father of Yours? Jesus answered, You know My Father as little as you know Me. If you knew Me, you would know My Father also.

20 Jesus said these things in the treasury while He was teaching in the temple [*b* court]; but no one ventured to arrest Him, because His hour had not yet come.

21 Therefore He said again to them, I am going away, and you will be looking for Me, and you will die in (under the curse of) your sin. Where I am going, it is not possible for you to come.

22 At this the Jews began to ask among themselves, Will He kill Himself? Is that why He says, Where I am going, it is not possible for you to come?

23 He said to them, You are from below; I am from above. You are of this world (of this earthly order); I am not of this world.

24 That is why I told you that you will die in (under the curse of) your sins; for if you do not believe that I am He [Whom I claim to be—if you do not adhere to, trust in, and rely on Me], you will die in your sins.

25 Then they said to Him, Who are You anyway? Jesus replied, [Why do I even speak to you!] I am exactly what I have been telling you from the first.

26 I have much to say about you and to judge *and* condemn. But He Who sent Me is true (reliable), and I tell the world [only] the things that I have heard from Him.

27 They did not perceive (know, understand) that He was speaking to them about the Father.

28 So Jesus added, When you have lifted up the Son of Man [on the cross], you will realize (know, understand) that I am He [for Whom you look] and that I do nothing of Myself (of My own accord or on My own authority), but I say [exactly] what My Father has taught Me.

29 And He Who sent Me is ever with Me; My Father has not left Me alone, for I always do what pleases Him.

30 As He said these things, many believed in Him [trusted, relied on, and adhered to Him].

31 So Jesus said to those Jews who had believed in Him, If you abide in My word [hold fast to My teachings and live in accordance with them], you are truly My disciples.

32 And you will know the Truth, and the Truth will set you free.

---

*a Capitalized because of Who He is, the everlasting Father, not who the speaker may have thought He was.  b Richard Trench, Synonyms of the New Testament.*

---

*a 28 The Greek for lifted up also means exalted.*

## New International Version

³³They answered him, "We are Abraham's descendants and have never been slaves of anyone. How can you say that we shall be free?"

³⁴Jesus replied, "Very truly I tell you, everyone who sins is a slave to sin. ³⁵Now a slave has no permanent place in the family, but a son belongs to it forever. ³⁶So if the Son sets you free, you will be free indeed. ³⁷I know that you are Abraham's descendants. Yet you are looking for a way to kill me, because you have no room for my word. ³⁸I am telling you what I have seen in the Father's presence, and you are doing what you have heard from your father.ᵃ"

³⁹"Abraham is our father," they answered.

"If you were Abraham's children," said Jesus, "then you wouldᵇ do what Abraham did. ⁴⁰As it is, you are looking for a way to kill me, a man who has told you the truth that I heard from God. Abraham did not do such things. ⁴¹You are doing the works of your own father."

"We are not illegitimate children," they protested. "The only Father we have is God himself."

⁴²Jesus said to them, "If God were your Father, you would love me, for I have come here from God. I have not come on my own; God sent me. ⁴³Why is my language not clear to you? Because you are unable to hear what I say. ⁴⁴You belong to your father, the devil, and you want to carry out your father's desires. He was a murderer from the beginning, not holding to the truth, for there is no truth in him. When he lies, he speaks his native language, for he is a liar and the father of lies. ⁴⁵Yet because I tell the truth, you do not believe me! ⁴⁶Can any of you prove me guilty of sin? If I am telling the truth, why don't you believe me? ⁴⁷Whoever belongs to God hears what God says. The reason you do not hear is that you do not belong to God."

### Jesus' Claims About Himself

⁴⁸The Jews answered him, "Aren't we right in saying that you are a Samaritan and demon-possessed?"

⁴⁹"I am not possessed by a demon," said Jesus, "but I honor my Father and you dishonor me. ⁵⁰I am not seeking glory for myself; but there is one who seeks it, and he is the judge. ⁵¹Very truly I tell you, whoever obeys my word will never see death."

⁵²At this they exclaimed, "Now we know that you are demon-possessed! Abraham died and so did the prophets, yet you say that whoever obeys your word will never taste

## Amplified Bible

³³They answered Him, We are Abraham's offspring (descendants) and have never been in bondage to anybody. What do You mean by saying, You will be set free?

³⁴Jesus answered them, I assure you, most solemnly I tell you, Whoever commits *and* practices sin is the slave of sin.

³⁵Now a slave does not remain in a household permanently (forever); the son [of the house] does remain forever.

³⁶So if the Son liberates you [makes you free men], then you are really *and* unquestionably free.

³⁷[Yes] I know that you are Abraham's offspring; yet you plan to kill Me, because My word has no entrance (makes no progress, does not find any place) in you.

³⁸I tell the things which I have seen *and* learned at My Father's side, and your actions also reflect what you have heard *and* learned from your father.

³⁹They retorted, Abraham is our father. Jesus said, If you were [truly] Abraham's children, then you would do the works of Abraham [follow his example, do as Abraham did].

⁴⁰But now [instead] you are wanting *and* seeking to kill Me, a Man Who has told you the truth which I have heard from God. This is not the way Abraham acted.

⁴¹You are doing the works of your [own] father. They said to Him, We are not illegitimate children *and* born out of fornication; we have one Father, even God.

⁴²Jesus said to them, If God were your Father, you would love Me *and* respect Me *and* welcome Me gladly, for I proceeded (came forth) from God [out of His very presence]. I did not even come on My own authority *or* of My own accord (as self-appointed); but He sent Me.

⁴³Why do you misunderstand what I say? It is because you are unable to hear what I am saying. [You cannot bear to listen to My message; your ears are shut to My teaching.]

⁴⁴You are of your father, the devil, and it is your will to practice the lusts *and* gratify the desires [which are characteristic] of your father. He was a murderer from the beginning and does not stand in the truth, because there is no truth in him. When he speaks a falsehood, he speaks what is natural to him, for he is a liar [himself] and the father of lies *and* of all that is false.

⁴⁵But because I speak the truth, you do not believe Me [do not trust Me, do not rely on Me, or adhere to Me].

⁴⁶Who of you convicts Me of wrongdoing *or* finds Me guilty of sin? Then if I speak truth, why do you not believe Me [trust Me, rely on, and adhere to Me]?

⁴⁷Whoever is of God listens to God. [Those who belong to God hear the words of God.] This is the reason that you do not listen [to those words, to Me]: because you do not belong to God *and* are not of God *or* in harmony with Him.

⁴⁸The Jews answered Him, Are we not right when we say You are a Samaritan and that You have a demon [that You are under the power of an evil spirit]?

⁴⁹Jesus answered, I am not possessed by a demon. On the contrary, I honor *and* reverence My Father and you dishonor (despise, vilify, and scorn) Me.

⁵⁰However, I am not in search of honor for Myself. [I do not seek and am not aiming for My own glory.] There is One Who [looks after that; He] seeks [My glory], and He is the Judge.

⁵¹I assure you, most solemnly I tell you, if anyone observes My teaching [lives in accordance with My message, keeps My word], he will by no means ever see *and* experience death.

⁵²The Jews said to Him, Now we know that You are under the power of a demon (ᵃinsane). Abraham died, and also the prophets, yet You say, If a man keeps My word, he will never taste of death into all eternity.

---

ᵃ 38 Or *presence. Therefore do what you have heard from the Father.*
ᵇ 39 Some early manuscripts *"If you are Abraham's children," said Jesus, "then*

ᵃ Joseph Thayer, *A Greek-English Lexicon.*

## New International Version

death. [53]Are you greater than our father Abraham? He died, and so did the prophets. Who do you think you are?"

[54]Jesus replied, "If I glorify myself, my glory means nothing. My Father, whom you claim as your God, is the one who glorifies me. [55]Though you do not know him, I know him. If I said I did not, I would be a liar like you, but I do know him and obey his word. [56]Your father Abraham rejoiced at the thought of seeing my day; he saw it and was glad."

[57]"You are not yet fifty years old," they said to him, "and you have seen Abraham!"

[58]"Very truly I tell you," Jesus answered, "before Abraham was born, I am!" [59]At this, they picked up stones to stone him, but Jesus hid himself, slipping away from the temple grounds.

### Jesus Heals a Man Born Blind

**9** As he went along, he saw a man blind from birth. [2]His disciples asked him, "Rabbi, who sinned, this man or his parents, that he was born blind?"

[3]"Neither this man nor his parents sinned," said Jesus, "but this happened so that the works of God might be displayed in him. [4]As long as it is day, we must do the works of him who sent me. Night is coming, when no one can work. [5]While I am in the world, I am the light of the world."

[6]After saying this, he spit on the ground, made some mud with the saliva, and put it on the man's eyes. [7]"Go," he told him, "wash in the Pool of Siloam" (this word means "Sent"). So the man went and washed, and came home seeing.

[8]His neighbors and those who had formerly seen him begging asked, "Isn't this the same man who used to sit and beg?" [9]Some claimed that he was.

Others said, "No, he only looks like him."

But he himself insisted, "I am the man."

[10]"How then were your eyes opened?" they asked.

[11]He replied, "The man they call Jesus made some mud and put it on my eyes. He told me to go to Siloam and wash. So I went and washed, and then I could see."

[12]"Where is this man?" they asked him.

"I don't know," he said.

### The Pharisees Investigate the Healing

[13]They brought to the Pharisees the man who had been blind. [14]Now the day on which Jesus had made the mud and opened the man's eyes was a Sabbath. [15]Therefore the Pharisees also asked him how he had received his sight. "He put mud on my eyes," the man replied, "and I washed, and now I see."

[16]Some of the Pharisees said, "This man is not from God, for he does not keep the Sabbath."

But others asked, "How can a sinner perform such signs?" So they were divided.

[17]Then they turned again to the blind man, "What have you to say about him? It was your eyes he opened."

The man replied, "He is a prophet."

[18]They still did not believe that he had been blind and had received his sight until they sent for the man's par-

## Amplified Bible

[53]Are You greater than our father Abraham? He died, and all the prophets died! Who do You make Yourself out to be?

[54]Jesus answered, If I were to glorify Myself (magnify, praise, and honor Myself), I would have no real glory, for My glory would be nothing *and* worthless. [My honor must come to Me from My Father.] It is My Father Who glorifies Me [Who extols Me, magnifies, and praises Me], of Whom you say that He is your God.

[55]Yet you do not know Him *or* recognize Him *and* are not acquainted with Him, but I know Him. If I should say that I do not know Him, I would be a liar like you. But I know Him and keep His word [obey His teachings, am faithful to His message].

[56]Your forefather Abraham was extremely happy at the hope *and* prospect of seeing My day (My incarnation); and he did see it and was delighted. [Heb. 11:13.]

[57]Then the Jews said to Him, You are not yet fifty years old, and have You seen Abraham?

[58]Jesus replied, I assure you, most solemnly I tell you, before Abraham was born, I AM. [Exod. 3:14.]

[59]So they took up stones to throw at Him, but Jesus, by mixing with the crowd, concealed Himself and went out of the temple [[a]enclosure].

**9** As he passed along, He noticed a man blind from his birth.

[2]His disciples asked Him, Rabbi, who sinned, this man or his parents, that he should be born blind?

[3]Jesus answered, It was not that this man or his parents sinned, but he was born blind in order that the workings of God should be manifested (displayed and illustrated) in him.

[4]We must work the works of Him Who sent Me *and* be busy with His business while it is daylight; night is coming on, when no man can work.

[5]As long as I am in the world, I am the world's Light.

[6]When He had said this, He spat on the ground and made clay (mud) with His saliva, and He spread it [as ointment] on the man's eyes.

[7]And He said to him, Go, wash in the Pool of Siloam— which means Sent. So he went and washed, and came back seeing.

[8]When the neighbors and those who used to know him by sight as a beggar saw him, they said, Is not this the man who used to sit and beg?

[9]Some said, It is he. Others said, No, but he looks very much like him. But he said, Yes, I am the man.

[10]So they said to him, How were your eyes opened?

[11]He replied, The Man called Jesus made mud and smeared it on my eyes and said to me, Go to Siloam and wash. So I went and washed, and I obtained my sight!

[12]They asked him, Where is He? He said, I do not know.

[13]Then they conducted to the Pharisees the man who had formerly been blind.

[14]Now it was on the Sabbath day that Jesus mixed the mud and opened the man's eyes.

[15]So now again the Pharisees asked him how he received his sight. And he said to them, He smeared mud on my eyes, and I washed, and now I see.

[16]Then some of the Pharisees said, This Man [Jesus] is not from God, because He does not observe the Sabbath. But others said, How can a man who is a sinner (a bad man) do such signs *and* miracles? So there was a difference of opinion among them.

[17]Accordingly they said to the blind man again, What do you say about Him, seeing that He opened your eyes? And he said, He is [He must be] a prophet!

[18]However, the Jews did not believe that he had [really] been blind and that he had received his sight until they called (summoned) the parents of the man.

[a] Richard Trench, *Synonyms of the New Testament.*

## New International Version

ents. ¹⁹"Is this your son?" they asked. "Is this the one you say was born blind? How is it that now he can see?"

²⁰"We know he is our son," the parents answered, "and we know he was born blind. ²¹But how he can see now, or who opened his eyes, we don't know. Ask him. He is of age; he will speak for himself." ²²His parents said this because they were afraid of the Jewish leaders, who already had decided that anyone who acknowledged that Jesus was the Messiah would be put out of the synagogue. ²³That was why his parents said, "He is of age; ask him."

²⁴A second time they summoned the man who had been blind. "Give glory to God by telling the truth," they said. "We know this man is a sinner."

²⁵He replied, "Whether he is a sinner or not, I don't know. One thing I do know. I was blind but now I see!"

²⁶Then they asked him, "What did he do to you? How did he open your eyes?"

²⁷He answered, "I have told you already and you did not listen. Why do you want to hear it again? Do you want to become his disciples too?"

²⁸Then they hurled insults at him and said, "You are this fellow's disciple! We are disciples of Moses! ²⁹We know that God spoke to Moses, but as for this fellow, we don't even know where he comes from."

³⁰The man answered, "Now that is remarkable! You don't know where he comes from, yet he opened my eyes. ³¹We know that God does not listen to sinners. He listens to the godly person who does his will. ³²Nobody has ever heard of opening the eyes of a man born blind. ³³If this man were not from God, he could do nothing."

³⁴To this they replied, "You were steeped in sin at birth; how dare you lecture us!" And they threw him out.

### Spiritual Blindness

³⁵Jesus heard that they had thrown him out, and when he found him, he said, "Do you believe in the Son of Man?"

³⁶"Who is he, sir?" the man asked. "Tell me so that I may believe in him."

³⁷Jesus said, "You have now seen him; in fact, he is the one speaking with you."

³⁸Then the man said, "Lord, I believe," and he worshiped him.

³⁹Jesus said,[a] "For judgment I have come into this world, so that the blind will see and those who see will become blind."

⁴⁰Some Pharisees who were with him heard him say this and asked, "What? Are we blind too?"

⁴¹Jesus said, "If you were blind, you would not be guilty of sin; but now that you claim you can see, your guilt remains."

## Amplified Bible

¹⁹They asked them, Is this your son, whom you reported as having been born blind? How then does he see now?

²⁰His parents answered, We know that this is our son, and that he was born blind.

²¹But as to how he can now see, we do not know; or who has opened his eyes, we do not know. He is of age. Ask him; let him speak for himself *and* give his own account of it.

²²His parents said this because they feared [the leaders of] the Jews; for the Jews had already agreed that if anyone should acknowledge Jesus to be the Christ, he should be expelled *and* excluded from the synagogue.

²³On that account his parents said, He is of age; ask him.

²⁴So the second time they summoned the man who had been born blind, and said to him, Now give God the glory (praise). This ᵃFellow we know is only a sinner (a wicked person).

²⁵Then he answered, I do not know whether He is a sinner *and* wicked or not. But one thing I do know, that whereas I was blind before, now I see.

²⁶So they said to him, What did He [actually] do to you? How did He open your eyes?

²⁷He answered, I already told you and you would not listen. Why do you want to hear it again? Can it be that you wish to become His disciples also?

²⁸And they stormed at him [they jeered, they sneered, they reviled him] and retorted, You are His disciple yourself, but we are the disciples of Moses.

²⁹We know for certain that God spoke with Moses, but as for this Fellow, we know nothing about where He hails from.

³⁰The man replied, Well, this is astonishing! Here a Man has opened my eyes, and yet you do not know where He comes from. [That is amazing!]

³¹We know that God does not listen to sinners; but if anyone is God-fearing *and* a worshiper of Him and does His will, He listens to him.

³²Since the beginning of time it has never been heard that anyone opened the eyes of a man born blind.

³³If this Man were not from God, He would not be able to do anything like this.

³⁴They retorted, You were wholly born in sin [from head to foot]; and do you [presume to] teach us? So they cast him out [threw him clear outside the synagogue].

³⁵Jesus heard that they had put him out, and meeting him He said, Do you believe in *and* adhere to the Son of Man ᵇ*or the Son of God*?

³⁶He answered, Who is He, Sir? Tell me, that I may believe in *and* adhere to Him.

³⁷Jesus said to him, You have seen Him; [in fact] He is talking to you right now.

³⁸He called out, Lord, I believe! [I rely on, I trust, I cleave to You!] And he worshiped Him.

³⁹Then Jesus said, I came into this world for judgment [as a Separator, in order that there may be ᶜseparation between those who believe on Me and those who reject Me], to make the sightless see and to make those who see become blind.

⁴⁰Some Pharisees who were near, hearing this remark, said to Him, Are we also blind?

⁴¹Jesus said to them, If you were blind, you would have no sin; but because you now claim to have sight, your sin remains. [If you were blind, you would not be guilty of sin; but because you insist, We do see clearly, you are unable to escape your guilt.]

---

ᵃ 38,39 Some early manuscripts do not have *Then the man said . . . ³⁹Jesus said.*

ᵃ Capitalized because of what He is, the spotless Son of God, not what the speaker may have thought He was. ᵇ Many ancient manuscripts read "the Son of God." ᶜ Marvin Vincent, *Word Studies.*

## New International Version

### The Good Shepherd and His Sheep

**10** "Very truly I tell you Pharisees, anyone who does not enter the sheep pen by the gate, but climbs in by some other way, is a thief and a robber. ²The one who enters by the gate is the shepherd of the sheep. ³The gatekeeper opens the gate for him, and the sheep listen to his voice. He calls his own sheep by name and leads them out. ⁴When he has brought out all his own, he goes on ahead of them, and his sheep follow him because they know his voice. ⁵But they will never follow a stranger; in fact, they will run away from him because they do not recognize a stranger's voice." ⁶Jesus used this figure of speech, but the Pharisees did not understand what he was telling them.

⁷Therefore Jesus said again, "Very truly I tell you, I am the gate for the sheep. ⁸All who have come before me are thieves and robbers, but the sheep have not listened to them. ⁹I am the gate; whoever enters through me will be saved.ᵃ They will come in and go out, and find pasture. ¹⁰The thief comes only to steal and kill and destroy; I have come that they may have life, and have it to the full.

¹¹"I am the good shepherd. The good shepherd lays down his life for the sheep. ¹²The hired hand is not the shepherd and does not own the sheep. So when he sees the wolf coming, he abandons the sheep and runs away. Then the wolf attacks the flock and scatters it. ¹³The man runs away because he is a hired hand and cares nothing for the sheep.

¹⁴"I am the good shepherd; I know my sheep and my sheep know me— ¹⁵just as the Father knows me and I know the Father—and I lay down my life for the sheep. ¹⁶I have other sheep that are not of this sheep pen. I must bring them also. They too will listen to my voice, and there shall be one flock and one shepherd. ¹⁷The reason my Father loves me is that I lay down my life—only to take it up again. ¹⁸No one takes it from me, but I lay it down of my own accord. I have authority to lay it down and authority to take it up again. This command I received from my Father."

¹⁹The Jews who heard these words were again divided. ²⁰Many of them said, "He is demon-possessed and raving mad. Why listen to him?"

²¹But others said, "These are not the sayings of a man possessed by a demon. Can a demon open the eyes of the blind?"

### Further Conflict Over Jesus' Claims

²²Then came the Festival of Dedicationᵇ at Jerusalem. It was winter, ²³and Jesus was in the temple courts walking

## Amplified Bible

**10** I assure you, most solemnly I tell you, he who does not enter by the door into the sheepfold, but climbs up some other way (elsewhere, from some other quarter) is a thief and a robber.

²But he who enters by the door is the shepherd of the sheep.

³The watchman opens the door for this man, and the sheep listen to his voice *and* heed it; and he calls his own sheep by name and brings (leads) them out.

⁴When he has brought out his own sheep outside, he walks on before them, and the sheep follow him because they know his voice.

⁵They will never [on any account] follow a stranger, but will run away from him because they do not know the voice of strangers *or* recognize their call.

⁶Jesus used this parable (illustration) with them, but they did not understand what He was talking about.

⁷So Jesus said again, I assure you, most solemnly I tell you, that I Myself am the Door ᵃfor the sheep.

⁸All others who came [as such] before Me are thieves and robbers, but the [true] sheep did not listen to *and* obey them.

⁹I am the Door; anyone who enters in through Me will be saved (will live). He will come in and he will go out [freely], and will find pasture.

¹⁰The thief comes only in order to steal and kill and destroy. I came that they may have *and* enjoy life, and have it in abundance (to the full, till it ᵇoverflows).

¹¹I am the Good Shepherd. The Good Shepherd risks *and* lays down His [own] life for the sheep. [Ps. 23.]

¹²But the hired servant (he who merely serves for wages) who is neither the shepherd nor the owner of the sheep, when he sees the wolf coming, deserts the flock and runs away. And the wolf chases *and* snatches them and scatters [the flock].

¹³Now the hireling flees because he merely serves for wages and is not himself concerned about the sheep [cares nothing for them].

¹⁴I am the Good Shepherd; and I know *and* recognize My own, and My own know *and* recognize Me—

¹⁵Even as [truly as] the Father knows Me and I also know the Father—and I am giving My [very own] life *and* laying it down on behalf of the sheep.

¹⁶And I have other sheep [beside these] that are not of this fold. I must bring *and* ᶜimpel those also; and they will listen to My voice *and* heed My call, and so there will be [they will become] one flock under one Shepherd. [Ezek. 34:23.]

¹⁷For this [reason] the Father loves Me, because I lay down My [own] life—to take it back again.

¹⁸No one takes it away from Me. On the contrary, I lay it down voluntarily. [I put it from Myself.] I am authorized *and* have power to lay it down (to resign it) and I am authorized *and* have power to take it back again. These are the instructions (orders) which I have received [as My charge] from My Father.

¹⁹Then a fresh division of opinion arose among the Jews because of His saying these things.

²⁰And many of them said, He has a demon and He is mad (insane—He raves, He rambles). Why do you listen to Him?

²¹Others argued, These are not the thoughts *and* the language of one possessed. Can a demon-possessed person open blind eyes?

²²After this the Feast of Dedication [of the reconsecration of the temple] was taking place at Jerusalem. It was winter,

²³And Jesus was walking in Solomon's Porch in the temple area.

---

ᵃ 9 Or *kept safe*   ᵇ 22 That is, Hanukkah

ᵃ Marvin Vincent, *Word Studies.*   ᵇ Alexander Souter, *Pocket Lexicon of the Greek New Testament.*   ᶜ G. Abbott-Smith, *Manual Greek Lexicon.*

## New International Version

in Solomon's Colonnade. 24The Jews who were there gathered around him, saying, "How long will you keep us in suspense? If you are the Messiah, tell us plainly."

25Jesus answered, "I did tell you, but you do not believe. The works I do in my Father's name testify about me, 26but you do not believe because you are not my sheep. 27My sheep listen to my voice; I know them, and they follow me. 28I give them eternal life, and they shall never perish; no one will snatch them out of my hand. 29My Father, who has given them to me, is greater than all*a*; no one can snatch them out of my Father's hand. 30I and the Father are one."

31Again his Jewish opponents picked up stones to stone him, 32but Jesus said to them, "I have shown you many good works from the Father. For which of these do you stone me?"

33"We are not stoning you for any good work," they replied, "but for blasphemy, because you, a mere man, claim to be God."

34Jesus answered them, "Is it not written in your Law, 'I have said you are "gods"'*b*? 35If he called them 'gods,' to whom the word of God came—and Scripture cannot be set aside— 36what about the one whom the Father set apart as his very own and sent into the world? Why then do you accuse me of blasphemy because I said, 'I am God's Son'? 37Do not believe me unless I do the works of my Father. 38But if I do them, even though you do not believe me, believe the works, that you may know and understand that the Father is in me, and I in the Father." 39Again they tried to seize him, but he escaped their grasp.

40Then Jesus went back across the Jordan to the place where John had been baptizing in the early days. There he stayed, 41and many people came to him. They said, "Though John never performed a sign, all that John said about this man was true." 42And in that place many believed in Jesus.

### The Death of Lazarus

**11** Now a man named Lazarus was sick. He was from Bethany, the village of Mary and her sister Martha. 2(This Mary, whose brother Lazarus now lay sick, was the same one who poured perfume on the Lord and wiped his feet with her hair.) 3So the sisters sent word to Jesus, "Lord, the one you love is sick."

4When he heard this, Jesus said, "This sickness will not end in death. No, it is for God's glory so that God's Son

## Amplified Bible

24So the Jews surrounded Him and began asking Him, How long are You going to keep us in doubt *and* suspense? If You are really the Christ (the Messiah), tell us so plainly *and* openly.

25Jesus answered them, I have told you so, yet you do not believe Me [you do not trust Me *and* rely on Me]. The very works that I do by the power of My Father *and* in My Father's name bear witness concerning Me [they are My credentials and evidence in support of Me].

26But you do not believe *and* trust *and* rely on Me because you do not belong to My fold [you are no sheep of Mine].

27The sheep that are My own hear *and* are listening to My voice; and I know them, and they follow Me.

28And I give them eternal life, and they shall never lose it *or* perish throughout the ages. [To all eternity they shall never by any means be destroyed.] And no one is able to snatch them out of My hand.

29My Father, Who has given them to Me, is greater *and* mightier than all [else]; and no one is able to snatch [them] out of the Father's hand.

30I and the Father are One.

31Again the Jews *a*brought up stones to stone Him.

32Jesus said to them, My Father has enabled Me to do many good deeds. [I have shown many acts of mercy in your presence.] For which of these do you mean to stone Me?

33The Jews replied, We are not going to stone You for a good act, but for blasphemy, because You, a mere *b*Man, make Yourself [out to be] God.

34Jesus answered, Is it not written in your Law, I said, You are gods? [Ps. 82:6.]

35So men are called gods [by the Law], men to whom God's message came—and the Scripture cannot be set aside *or* cancelled *or* broken *or* annulled—

36[If that is true] do you say of the One Whom the Father consecrated *and* dedicated *and* set apart for Himself and sent into the world, You are blaspheming, because I said, I am the Son of God?

37If I am not doing the works [performing the deeds] of My Father, then do not believe Me [do not adhere to Me and trust Me and rely on Me].

38But if I do them, even though you do not believe Me *or* have faith in Me, [at least] believe the works *and* have faith in what I do, in order that you may know and understand [clearly] that the Father is in Me, and I am in the Father [One with Him].

39They sought again to arrest Him, but He escaped from their hands.

40He went back again across the Jordan to the locality where John was when he first baptized, and there He remained.

41And many came to Him, and they kept saying, John did not perform a [single] sign *or* miracle, but everything John said about this Man was true.

42And many [people] there became believers in Him. [They adhered to *and* trusted in *and* relied on Him.]

**11** Now a certain man named Lazarus was ill. He was of Bethany, the village where Mary and her sister Martha lived.

2This Mary was the one who anointed the Lord with perfume and wiped His feet with her hair. It was her brother Lazarus who was [now] sick.

3So the sisters sent to Him, saying, Lord, he whom You love [so well] is sick.

4When Jesus received the message, He said, This sickness is not to end in death; but [on the contrary] it is to honor God *and* to promote His glory, that the Son of God may be glorified through (by) it.

---

*a* 29 Many early manuscripts *What my Father has given me is greater than all*   *b* 34 Psalm 82:6

*a* Marvin Vincent, *Word Studies.*   *b* Capitalized because of what He is, the spotless Son of God, not what the speaker may have thought He was.

## New International Version

may be glorified through it." [5] Now Jesus loved Martha and her sister and Lazarus. [6] So when he heard that Lazarus was sick, he stayed where he was two more hours, [7] and then he said to his disciples, "Let us go back to Judea."

[8] "But Rabbi," they said, "a short while ago the Jews there tried to stone you, and yet you are going back?"

[9] Jesus answered, "Are there not twelve hours of daylight? Anyone who walks in the daytime will not stumble, for they see by this world's light. [10] It is when a person walks at night that they stumble, for they have no light."

[11] After he had said this, he went on to tell them, "Our friend Lazarus has fallen asleep; but I am going there to wake him up."

[12] His disciples replied, "Lord, if he sleeps, he will get better." [13] Jesus had been speaking of his death, but his disciples thought he meant natural sleep.

[14] So then he told them plainly, "Lazarus is dead, [15] and for your sake I am glad I was not there, so that you may believe. But let us go to him."

[16] Then Thomas (also known as Didymus[a]) said to the rest of the disciples, "Let us also go, that we may die with him."

### Jesus Comforts the Sisters of Lazarus

[17] On his arrival, Jesus found that Lazarus had already been in the tomb for four days. [18] Now Bethany was less than two miles[b] from Jerusalem, [19] and many Jews had come to Martha and Mary to comfort them in the loss of their brother. [20] When Martha heard that Jesus was coming, she went out to meet him, but Mary stayed at home.

[21] "Lord," Martha said to Jesus, "if you had been here, my brother would not have died. [22] But I know that even now God will give you whatever you ask."

[23] Jesus said to her, "Your brother will rise again."

[24] Martha answered, "I know he will rise again in the resurrection at the last day."

[25] Jesus said to her, "I am the resurrection and the life. The one who believes in me will live, even though they die; [26] and whoever lives by believing in me will never die. Do you believe this?"

[27] "Yes, Lord," she replied, "I believe that you are the Messiah, the Son of God, who is to come into the world."

[28] After she had said this, she went back and called her sister Mary aside. "The Teacher is here," she said, "and is asking for you." [29] When Mary heard this, she got up quickly and went to him. [30] Now Jesus had not yet entered the village, but was still at the place where Martha had met him. [31] When the Jews who had been with Mary in the house, comforting her, noticed how quickly she got up and went out, they followed her, supposing she was going to the tomb to mourn there.

[32] When Mary reached the place where Jesus was and saw him, she fell at his feet and said, "Lord, if you had been here, my brother would not have died."

## Amplified Bible

[5] Now Jesus loved Martha and her sister and Lazarus. [They were His dear friends, and He held them in loving esteem.]

[6] Therefore [even] when He heard that Lazarus was sick, He still stayed two days longer in the same place where He was.

[7] Then after that interval He said to His disciples, Let us go back again to Judea.

[8] The disciples said to Him, Rabbi, the Jews only recently were intending *and* trying to stone You, and are You [thinking of] going back there again?

[9] Jesus answered, Are there not twelve hours in the day? Anyone who walks about in the daytime does not stumble, because he sees [by] the light of this world.

[10] But if anyone walks about in the night, he does stumble, because there is no light in him [the light is lacking to him].

[11] He said these things, and then added, Our friend Lazarus is at rest *and* sleeping; but I am going there that I may awaken him out of his sleep.

[12] The disciples answered, Lord, if he is sleeping, he will recover.

[13] However, Jesus had spoken of his death, but they thought that He referred to falling into a refreshing *and* natural sleep.

[14] So then Jesus told them plainly, Lazarus is dead,

[15] And for your sake I am glad that I was not there; it will help you to believe (to trust and rely on Me). However, let us go to him.

[16] Then Thomas, who was called the Twin, said to his fellow disciples, Let us go too, that we may die [be killed] along with Him.

[17] So when Jesus arrived, He found that he [Lazarus] had already been in the tomb four days.

[18] Bethany was near Jerusalem, only about two miles away,

[19] And a considerable number of the Jews had gone out to see Martha and Mary to console them concerning their brother.

[20] When Martha heard that Jesus was coming, she went to meet Him, while Mary remained sitting in the house.

[21] Martha then said to Jesus, Master, if You had been here, my brother would not have died.

[22] And even now I know that whatever You ask from God, He will grant it to You.

[23] Jesus said to her, Your brother shall rise again.

[24] Martha replied, I know that he will rise again in the resurrection at the last day.

[25] Jesus said to her, I am [Myself] the Resurrection and the Life. Whoever believes in (adheres to, trusts in, and relies on) Me, although he may die, yet he shall live;

[26] And whoever continues to live and believes in (has faith in, cleaves to, and relies on) Me shall never [actually] die at all. Do you believe this?

[27] She said to Him, Yes, Lord, I have believed [I do believe] that You are the Christ (the Messiah, the Anointed One), the Son of God, [even He] Who was to come into the world. [It is for Your coming that the world has waited.]

[28] After she had said this, she went back and called her sister Mary, privately whispering to her, The Teacher is close at hand and is asking for you.

[29] When she heard this, she sprang up quickly and went to Him.

[30] Now Jesus had not yet entered the village, but was still at the same spot where Martha had met Him.

[31] When the Jews who were sitting with her in the house and consoling her saw how hastily Mary had arisen and gone out, they followed her, supposing that she was going to the tomb to pour out her grief there.

[32] When Mary came to the place where Jesus was and saw Him, she dropped down at His feet, saying to Him, Lord, if You had been here, my brother would not have died.

[a] 16 *Thomas* (Aramaic) and *Didymus* (Greek) both mean *twin*.
[b] 18 Or about 3 kilometers

## New International Version

33When Jesus saw her weeping, and the Jews who had come along with her also weeping, he was deeply moved in spirit and troubled. 34"Where have you laid him?" he asked.

"Come and see, Lord," they replied.

35Jesus wept.

36Then the Jews said, "See how he loved him!"

37But some of them said, "Could not he who opened the eyes of the blind man have kept this man from dying?"

### Jesus Raises Lazarus From the Dead

38Jesus, once more deeply moved, came to the tomb. It was a cave with a stone laid across the entrance. 39"Take away the stone," he said.

"But, Lord," said Martha, the sister of the dead man, "by this time there is a bad odor, for he has been there four days."

40Then Jesus said, "Did I not tell you that if you believe, you will see the glory of God?"

41So they took away the stone. Then Jesus looked up and said, "Father, I thank you that you have heard me. 42I knew that you always hear me, but I said this for the benefit of the people standing here, that they may believe that you sent me."

43When he had said this, Jesus called in a loud voice, "Lazarus, come out!" 44The dead man came out, his hands and feet wrapped with strips of linen, and a cloth around his face.

Jesus said to them, "Take off the grave clothes and let him go."

### The Plot to Kill Jesus

45Therefore many of the Jews who had come to visit Mary, and had seen what Jesus did, believed in him. 46But some of them went to the Pharisees and told them what Jesus had done. 47Then the chief priests and the Pharisees called a meeting of the Sanhedrin.

"What are we accomplishing?" they asked. "Here is this man performing many signs. 48If we let him go on like this, everyone will believe in him, and then the Romans will come and take away both our temple and our nation."

49Then one of them, named Caiaphas, who was high priest that year, spoke up, "You know nothing at all! 50You do not realize that it is better for you that one man die for the people than that the whole nation perish."

51He did not say this on his own, but as high priest that year he prophesied that Jesus would die for the Jewish nation, 52and not only for that nation but also for the scattered children of God, to bring them together and make them one. 53So from that day on they plotted to take his life.

54Therefore Jesus no longer moved about publicly among the people of Judea. Instead he withdrew to a region near the wilderness, to a village called Ephraim, where he stayed with his disciples.

55When it was almost time for the Jewish Passover, many went up from the country to Jerusalem for their ceremonial cleansing before the Passover. 56They kept looking for Jesus, and as they stood in the temple courts they asked one another, "What do you think? Isn't he coming

## Amplified Bible

33When Jesus saw her sobbing, and the Jews who came with her [also] sobbing, He was deeply moved in spirit and troubled. [He chafed in spirit and sighed and was disturbed.]

34And He said, Where have you laid him? They said to Him, Lord, come and see.

35Jesus wept.

36The Jews said, See how [tenderly] He loved him!

37But some of them said, Could not He Who opened a blind man's eyes have prevented this man from dying?

38Now Jesus, again sighing repeatedly and deeply disquieted, approached the tomb. It was a cave (a hole in the rock), and a boulder lay against [the entrance to close] it.

39Jesus said, Take away the stone. Martha, the sister of the dead man, exclaimed, But Lord, by this time he [is decaying and] throws off an offensive odor, for he has been dead four days!

40Jesus said to her, Did I not tell you and *a*promise you that if you would believe and rely on Me, you would see the glory of God?

41So they took away the stone. And Jesus lifted up His eyes and said, Father, I thank You that You have heard Me.

42Yes, I know You always hear and listen to Me, but I have said this on account of and for the benefit of the people standing around, so that they may believe that You did send Me [that You have made Me Your Messenger].

43When He had said this, He shouted with a loud voice, Lazarus, come out!

44And out walked the man who had been dead, his hands and feet wrapped in burial cloths (linen strips), and with a [burial] napkin bound around his face. Jesus said to them, Free him of the burial wrappings and let him go.

45Upon seeing what Jesus had done, many of the Jews who had come with Mary believed in Him. [They trusted in Him and adhered to Him and relied on Him.]

46But some of them went back to the Pharisees and told them what Jesus had done.

47So the chief priests and Pharisees called a meeting of the council (the Sanhedrin) and said, What are we to do? For this Man performs many signs (evidences, miracles).

48If we let Him alone to go on like this, everyone will believe in Him and adhere to Him, and the Romans will come and suppress and destroy and take away our [holy] place and our nation [*b*our temple and city and our civil organization].

49But one of them, Caiaphas, who was the high priest that year, declared, You know nothing at all!

50Nor do you understand or reason out that it is expedient and better for your own welfare that one man should die on behalf of the people than that the whole nation should perish (be destroyed, ruined).

51Now he did not say this simply of his own accord [he was not self-moved]; but being the high priest that year, he prophesied that Jesus was to die for the nation, [Isa. 53:8.]

52And not only for the nation but also for the purpose of uniting into one body the children of God who have been scattered far and wide. [Isa. 49:6.]

53So from that day on they took counsel and plotted together how they might put Him to death.

54For that reason Jesus no longer appeared publicly among the Jews, but left there and retired to the district that borders on the wilderness (the desert), to a village called Ephraim, and there He stayed with the disciples.

55Now the Jewish Passover was at hand, and many from the country went up to Jerusalem in order that they might purify and consecrate themselves before the Passover.

56So they kept looking for Jesus and questioned among themselves as they were standing about in the temple [*c*area], What do you think? Will He not come to the Feast at all?

---

*a* Charles B. Williams, *The New Testament: A Translation.* *b* Marvin Vincent, *Word Studies.* *c* Richard Trench, *Synonyms of the New Testament.*

## New International Version

to the festival at all?" [57] But the chief priests and the Pharisees had given orders that anyone who found out where Jesus was should report it so that they might arrest him.

### Jesus Anointed at Bethany

**12** Six days before the Passover, Jesus came to Bethany, where Lazarus lived, whom Jesus had raised from the dead. [2] Here a dinner was given in Jesus' honor. Martha served, while Lazarus was among those reclining at the table with him. [3] Then Mary took about a pint[a] of pure nard, an expensive perfume; she poured it on Jesus' feet and wiped his feet with her hair. And the house was filled with the fragrance of the perfume.

[4] But one of his disciples, Judas Iscariot, who was later to betray him, objected, [5] "Why wasn't this perfume sold and the money given to the poor? It was worth a year's wages.[b]" [6] He did not say this because he cared about the poor but because he was a thief; as keeper of the money bag, he used to help himself to what was put into it.

[7] "Leave her alone," Jesus replied. "It was intended that she should save this perfume for the day of my burial. [8] You will always have the poor among you,[c] but you will not always have me."

[9] Meanwhile a large crowd of Jews found out that Jesus was there and came, not only because of him but also to see Lazarus, whom he had raised from the dead. [10] So the chief priests made plans to kill Lazarus as well, [11] for on account of him many of the Jews were going over to Jesus and believing in him.

### Jesus Comes to Jerusalem as King

[12] The next day the great crowd that had come for the festival heard that Jesus was on his way to Jerusalem. [13] They took palm branches and went out to meet him, shouting,

"Hosanna![d]"

"Blessed is he who comes in the name of the Lord!"[e]

"Blessed is the king of Israel!"

[14] Jesus found a young donkey and sat on it, as it is written:

[15] "Do not be afraid, Daughter Zion;
see, your king is coming,
seated on a donkey's colt."[f]

[16] At first his disciples did not understand all this. Only after Jesus was glorified did they realize that these things had been written about him and that these things had been done to him.

[17] Now the crowd that was with him when he called Lazarus from the tomb and raised him from the dead continued to spread the word. [18] Many people, because they had heard that he had performed this sign, went out to meet him. [19] So the Pharisees said to one another, "See, this is getting us nowhere. Look how the whole world has gone after him!"

### Jesus Predicts His Death

[20] Now there were some Greeks among those who went up to worship at the festival. [21] They came to Philip, who was from Bethsaida in Galilee, with a request. "Sir," they said, "we would like to see Jesus." [22] Philip went to tell Andrew; Andrew and Philip in turn told Jesus.

---

*a 3* Or about 0.5 liter    *b 5* Greek *three hundred denarii*    *c 8* See Deut. 15:11.    *d 13* A Hebrew expression meaning "Save!" which became an exclamation of praise    *e 13* Psalm 118:25,26    *f 15* Zech. 9:9

## Amplified Bible

[57] Now the chief priests and Pharisees had given orders that if anyone knew where He was, he should report it to them, so that they might arrest Him.

**12** So six days before the Passover Feast, Jesus came to Bethany, where Lazarus was, who had died and whom He had raised from the dead.

[2] So they made Him a supper; and Martha served, but Lazarus was one of those at the table with Him.

[3] Mary took a pound of ointment of pure liquid nard [a rare perfume] that was very expensive, and she poured it on Jesus' feet and wiped them with her hair. And the whole house was filled with the fragrance of the perfume.

[4] But Judas Iscariot, the one of His disciples who was about to betray Him, said,

[5] Why was this perfume not sold for 300 denarii [a year's wages for an ordinary workman] and that [money] given to the poor (the destitute)?

[6] Now he did not say this because he cared for the poor but because he was a thief; and having the bag (the money box, the purse of the Twelve), he took for himself what was put into it [pilfering the collections).

[7] But Jesus said, Let her alone. It was [intended] that she should keep it for the time of My preparation for burial. [She has kept it that she might have it for the time of My *a* embalming.]

[8] You always have the poor with you, but you do not always have Me.

[9] Now a great crowd of the Jews heard that He was at Bethany, and they came there, not only because of Jesus but that they also might see Lazarus, whom He had raised from the dead.

[10] So the chief priests planned to put Lazarus to death also,

[11] Because on account of him many of the Jews were going away [were withdrawing from and leaving the Judeans] and believing in *and* adhering to Jesus.

[12] The next day a vast crowd of those who had come to the Passover Feast heard that Jesus was coming to Jerusalem.

[13] So they took branches of palm trees and went out to meet Him. And as they went, they kept shouting, Hosanna! Blessed is He *and* praise to Him Who comes in the name of the Lord, even the King of Israel! [Ps. 118:26.]

[14] And Jesus, having found a young donkey, rode upon it, [just] as it is written in the Scriptures,

[15] Do not fear, O Daughter of Zion! Look! Your King is coming, sitting on a donkey's colt! [Zech. 9:9.]

[16] His disciples did not understand *and* could not comprehend the meaning of these things at first; but when Jesus was glorified *and* exalted, they remembered that these things had been written about Him and had been done to Him.

[17] The group that had been with Jesus when He called Lazarus out of the tomb and raised him from among the dead kept telling it [bearing witness] to others.

[18] It was for this reason that the crowd went out to meet Him, because they had heard that He had performed this sign (proof, miracle).

[19] Then the Pharisees said among themselves, You see how futile your efforts are *and* how you accomplish nothing. See! The whole world is running after Him!

[20] Now among those who went up to worship at the Feast were some Greeks.

[21] These came to Philip, who was from Bethsaida in Galilee, and they made this request, Sir, we desire to see Jesus.

[22] Philip came and told Andrew; then Andrew and Philip together [went] and told Jesus.

---

*a* Marvin Vincent, *Word Studies.*

## New International Version

23Jesus replied, "The hour has come for the Son of Man to be glorified. 24Very truly I tell you, unless a kernel of wheat falls to the ground and dies, it remains only a single seed. But if it dies, it produces many seeds. 25Anyone who loves their life will lose it, while anyone who hates their life in this world will keep it for eternal life. 26Whoever serves me must follow me; and where I am, my servant also will be. My Father will honor the one who serves me.

27"Now my soul is troubled, and what shall I say? 'Father, save me from this hour'? No, it was for this very reason I came to this hour. 28Father, glorify your name!"

Then a voice came from heaven, "I have glorified it, and will glorify it again." 29The crowd that was there and heard it said it had thundered; others said an angel had spoken to him.

30Jesus said, "This voice was for your benefit, not mine. 31Now is the time for judgment on this world; now the prince of this world will be driven out. 32And I, when I am lifted up*a* from the earth, will draw all people to myself." 33He said this to show the kind of death he was going to die.

34The crowd spoke up, "We have heard from the Law that the Messiah will remain forever, so how can you say, 'The Son of Man must be lifted up'? Who is this 'Son of Man'?"

35Then Jesus told them, "You are going to have the light just a little while longer. Walk while you have the light, before darkness overtakes you. Whoever walks in the dark does not know where they are going. 36Believe in the light while you have the light, so that you may become children of light." When he had finished speaking, Jesus left and hid himself from them.

### Belief and Unbelief Among the Jews

37Even after Jesus had performed so many signs in their presence, they still would not believe in him. 38This was to fulfill the word of Isaiah the prophet:

"Lord, who has believed our message
　　and to whom has the arm of the Lord been
　　　　revealed?"*b*

39For this reason they could not believe, because, as Isaiah says elsewhere:

40"He has blinded their eyes
　　and hardened their hearts,
so they can neither see with their eyes,
　　nor understand with their hearts,
　　nor turn—and I would heal them."*c*

41Isaiah said this because he saw Jesus' glory and spoke about him.

42Yet at the same time many even among the leaders believed in him. But because of the Pharisees they would not openly acknowledge their faith for fear they would be

## Amplified Bible

23And Jesus answered them, The time has come for the Son of Man to be glorified *and* exalted.

24I assure you, most solemnly I tell you, Unless a grain of wheat falls into the earth and dies, it remains [just one grain; it never becomes more but lives] by itself alone. But if it dies, it produces many others *and* yields a rich harvest.

25Anyone who loves his life loses it, but anyone who hates his life in this world will keep it to life eternal. [Whoever has no love for, no concern for, no regard for his life here on earth, but despises it, preserves his life forever and ever.]

26If anyone serves Me, he must continue to follow Me [*a*to cleave steadfastly to Me, conform wholly to My example in living and, if need be, in dying] and wherever I am, there will My servant be also. If anyone serves Me, the Father will honor him.

27Now My soul is troubled *and* distressed, and what shall I say? Father, save Me from this hour [of trial and agony]? But it was for this very purpose that I have come to this hour [that I might undergo it].

28[Rather, I will say,] Father, glorify (honor and extol) Your [own] name! Then there came a voice out of heaven saying, I have already glorified it, and I will glorify it again.

29The crowd of bystanders heard the sound and said that it had thundered; others said, An angel has spoken to Him!

30Jesus answered, This voice has not come for My sake, but for your sake.

31Now the judgment (crisis) of this world is coming on [sentence is now being passed on this world]. Now the ruler (evil genius, prince) of this world shall be cast out (expelled).

32And I, if *and* when I am lifted up from the earth [on the cross], will draw *and* attract all men [Gentiles as well as Jews] to Myself.

33He said this to signify in what manner He would die.

34At this the people answered Him, We have learned from the Law that the Christ is to remain forever; how then can You say, The Son of Man must be lifted up [on the cross]? Who is this Son of Man? [Ps. 110:4.]

35So Jesus said to them, You will have the Light only a little while longer. Walk while you have the Light [keep on living by it], so that darkness may not overtake *and* overcome you. He who walks about in the dark does not know where he goes [he is drifting].

36While you have the Light, believe in the Light [have faith in it, hold to it, rely on it], that you may become sons of the Light *and* be filled with Light. Jesus said these things, and then He went away and hid Himself from them [was lost to their view].

37Even though He had done so many miracles before them (right before their eyes), yet they still did not trust in Him *and* failed to believe in Him—

38So that what Isaiah the prophet said was fulfilled: Lord, who has believed our report *and* our message? And to whom has the arm (the power) of the Lord been shown (unveiled and revealed)? [Isa. 53:1.]

39Therefore they could not believe [they were unable to believe]. For Isaiah has also said,

40He has blinded their eyes and hardened *and* benumbed their [callous, degenerated] hearts [He has made their minds dull], to keep them from seeing with their eyes and understanding with their hearts *and* minds and repenting *and* turning to Me to heal them.

41Isaiah said this because he saw His glory and spoke of Him. [Isa. 6:9, 10.]

42And yet [in spite of all this] many even of the leading men (the authorities and the nobles) believed *and* trusted in Him. But because of the Pharisees they did not confess it, for fear that [if they should acknowledge Him] they would be expelled from the synagogue;

---

*a 32* The Greek for *lifted up* also means *exalted.*　　*b 38* Isaiah 53:1
*c 40* Isaiah 6:10

*a* Joseph Thayer, *A Greek-English Lexicon.*

## New International Version

put out of the synagogue; 43for they loved human praise more than praise from God.

44Then Jesus cried out, "Whoever believes in me does not believe in me only, but in the one who sent me. 45The one who looks at me is seeing the one who sent me. 46I have come into the world as a light, so that no one who believes in me should stay in darkness.

47"If anyone hears my words but does not keep them, I do not judge that person. For I did not come to judge the world, but to save the world. 48There is a judge for the one who rejects me and does not accept my words; the very words I have spoken will condemn them at the last day. 49For I did not speak on my own, but the Father who sent me commanded me to say all that I have spoken. 50I know that his command leads to eternal life. So whatever I say is just what the Father has told me to say."

### Jesus Washes His Disciples' Feet

**13** It was just before the Passover Festival. Jesus knew that the hour had come for him to leave this world and go to the Father. Having loved his own who were in the world, he loved them to the end. 2The evening meal was in progress, and the devil had already prompted Judas, the son of Simon Iscariot, to betray Jesus. 3Jesus knew that the Father had put all things under his power, and that he had come from God and was returning to God; 4so he got up from the meal, took off his outer clothing, and wrapped a towel around his waist. 5After that, he poured water into a basin and began to wash his disciples' feet, drying them with the towel that was wrapped around him.

6He came to Simon Peter, who said to him, "Lord, are you going to wash my feet?"

7Jesus replied, "You do not realize now what I am doing, but later you will understand."

8"No," said Peter, "you shall never wash my feet."

Jesus answered, "Unless I wash you, you have no part with me."

9"Then, Lord," Simon Peter replied, "not just my feet but my hands and my head as well!"

10Jesus answered, "Those who have had a bath need only to wash their feet; their whole body is clean. And you are clean, though not every one of you." 11For he knew who was going to betray him, and that was why he said not every one was clean.

12When he had finished washing their feet, he put on his clothes and returned to his place. "Do you understand what I have done for you?" he asked them. 13"You call me 'Teacher' and 'Lord,' and rightly so, for that is what I am. 14Now that I, your Lord and Teacher, have washed your feet, you also should wash one another's feet. 15I have set

## Amplified Bible

43For they loved the approval *and* the praise *and* the glory that come from men [instead of and] more than the glory that comes from God. [They valued their credit with men more than their credit with God.]

44But Jesus loudly declared, The one who believes in Me does not [only] believe in *and* trust in *and* rely on Me, but [in believing in Me he believes] in Him Who sent Me.

45And whoever sees Me sees Him Who sent Me.

46I have come as a Light into the world, so that whoever believes in Me [whoever cleaves to *and* trusts in *and* relies on Me] may not continue to live in darkness.

47If anyone hears My teachings and fails to observe them [does not keep them, but disregards them], it is not I who judges him. For I have not come to judge *and* to condemn *and* to pass sentence *and* to inflict penalty on the world, but to save the world.

48Anyone who rejects Me *and* persistently sets Me at naught, refusing to accept My teachings, has his judge [however]; for the [very] message that I have spoken will itself judge *and* convict him at the last day.

49This is because I have never spoken on My own authority *or* of My own accord *or* as self-appointed, but the Father Who sent Me has Himself given Me orders [concerning] what to say and what to tell. [Deut. 18:18, 19.]

50And I know that His commandment is (means) eternal life. So whatever I speak, I am saying [exactly] what My Father has told Me to say *and* in accordance with His instructions.

**13** [Now] before the Passover Feast began, Jesus knew (was fully aware) that the time had come for Him to leave this world *and* return to the Father. And as He had loved those who were His own in the world, He loved them to the last *and* *a*to the highest degree.

2So [it was] during supper, Satan having already put the thought of betraying Jesus in the heart of Judas Iscariot, Simon's son,

3[That] Jesus, knowing (fully aware) that the Father had put everything into His hands, and that He had come from God and was [now] returning to God,

4Got up from supper, took off His garments, and taking a [servant's] towel, He fastened it around His waist.

5Then He poured water into the washbasin and began to wash the disciples' feet and to wipe them with the [servant's] towel with which He was girded.

6When He came to Simon Peter, [Peter] said to Him, Lord, are my feet to be washed by You? [Is it for You to wash my feet?]

7Jesus said to him, You do not understand now what I am doing, but you will understand later on.

8Peter said to Him, You shall never wash my feet! Jesus answered him, Unless I wash you, you have no part with (*b*in) Me [you have no share in companionship with Me].

9Simon Peter said to Him, Lord, [wash] not only my feet, but my hands and my head too!

10Jesus said to him, Anyone who has bathed needs only to wash his feet, but is clean all over. And you [My disciples] are clean, but not all of you.

11For He knew who was going to betray Him; that was the reason He said, Not all of you are clean.

12So when He had finished washing their feet and had put on His garments and had sat down again, He said to them, Do you understand what I have done to you?

13You call Me the Teacher (Master) and the Lord, and you are right in doing so, for that is what I am.

14If I then, your Lord and Teacher (Master), have washed your feet, you ought [it is your duty, you are under obligation, you owe it] to wash one another's feet.

*a* Saint John Chrysostom, cited by Joseph Thayer, *A Greek-English Lexicon.* *b* Origen (the greatest theologian of the early Greek Church); Adam Clarke, *The Holy Bible with A Commentary*; and others so interpret this passage. Notice the "in Me" emphasis in John 15, especially in verses 4-9, words spoken concerning the same subject, and on the same evening.

## New International Version

you an example that you should do as I have done for you. [16]Very truly I tell you, no servant is greater than his master, nor is a messenger greater than the one who sent him. [17]Now that you know these things, you will be blessed if you do them.

### Jesus Predicts His Betrayal

[18]"I am not referring to all of you; I know those I have chosen. But this is to fulfill this passage of Scripture: 'He who shared my bread has turned[a] against me.'[b]

[19]"I am telling you now before it happens, so that when it does happen you will believe that I am who I am. [20]Very truly I tell you, whoever accepts anyone I send accepts me; and whoever accepts me accepts the one who sent me."

[21]After he had said this, Jesus was troubled in spirit and testified, "Very truly I tell you, one of you is going to betray me."

[22]His disciples stared at one another, at a loss to know which of them he meant. [23]One of them, the disciple whom Jesus loved, was reclining next to him. [24]Simon Peter motioned to this disciple and said, "Ask him which one he means."

[25]Leaning back against Jesus, he asked him, "Lord, who is it?"

[26]Jesus answered, "It is the one to whom I will give this piece of bread when I have dipped it in the dish." Then, dipping the piece of bread, he gave it to Judas, the son of Simon Iscariot. [27]As soon as Judas took the bread, Satan entered into him.

So Jesus told him, "What you are about to do, do quickly." [28]But no one at the meal understood why Jesus said this to him. [29]Since Judas had charge of the money, some thought Jesus was telling him to buy what was needed for the festival, or to give something to the poor. [30]As soon as Judas had taken the bread, he went out. And it was night.

### Jesus Predicts Peter's Denial

[31]When he was gone, Jesus said, "Now the Son of Man is glorified and God is glorified in him. [32]If God is glorified in him,[c] God will glorify the Son in himself, and will glorify him at once.

[33]"My children, I will be with you only a little longer. You will look for me, and just as I told the Jews, so I tell you now: Where I am going, you cannot come.

[34]"A new command I give you: Love one another. As I have loved you, so you must love one another. [35]By this everyone will know that you are my disciples, if you love one another."

[36]Simon Peter asked him, "Lord, where are you going?"

Jesus replied, "Where I am going, you cannot follow now, but you will follow later."

[37]Peter asked, "Lord, why can't I follow you now? I will lay down my life for you."

## Amplified Bible

[15]For I have given you this as an example, so that you should do [in your turn] what I have done to you.

[16]I assure you, most solemnly I tell you, A servant is not greater than his master, and no one who is sent is superior to the one who sent him.

[17]If you know these things, blessed and happy and [a]to be envied are you if you practice them [if you act accordingly and really do them].

[18]I am not speaking of and I do not mean all of you. I know whom I have chosen; but it is that the Scripture may be fulfilled, He who eats [b]My bread with Me has raised up his heel against Me. [Ps. 41:9.]

[19]I tell you this now before it occurs, so that when it does take place you may be persuaded and believe that I am He [Who I say I am—the Christ, the Anointed One, the Messiah].

[20]I assure you, most solemnly I tell you, he who receives and welcomes and takes into his heart any messenger of Mine receives Me [in just that way]; and he who receives and welcomes and takes Me into his heart receives Him Who sent Me [in that same way].

[21]After Jesus had said these things, He was troubled (disturbed, agitated) in spirit and said, I assure you, most solemnly I tell you, one of you will deliver Me up [one of you will be false to Me and betray Me]!

[22]The disciples kept looking at one another, puzzled as to whom He could mean.

[23]One of His disciples, whom Jesus loved [whom He esteemed and delighted in], was reclining [next to Him] on Jesus' bosom.

[24]So Simon Peter motioned to him to ask of whom He was speaking.

[25]Then leaning back against Jesus' breast, he asked Him, Lord, who is it?

[26]Jesus answered, It is the one to whom I am going to give this morsel (bit) of food after I have dipped it. So when He had dipped the morsel of bread [into the dish], He gave it to Judas, Simon Iscariot's son.

[27]Then after [he had taken] the bit of food, Satan entered into and took possession of [Judas]. Jesus said to him, What you are going to do, do [d]more swiftly than you seem to intend and [d]make quick work of it.

[28]But nobody reclining at the table knew why He spoke to him or what He meant by telling him this.

[29]Some thought that, since Judas had the money box (the purse), Jesus was telling him, Buy what we need for the Festival, or that he should give something to the poor.

[30]So after receiving the bit of bread, he went out immediately. And it was night.

[31]When he had left, Jesus said, Now is the Son of Man glorified! [Now He has achieved His glory, His honor, His exaltation!] And God has been glorified through and in Him.

[32]And if God is glorified through and in Him, God will also glorify Him in Himself, and He will glorify Him at once and not delay.

[33][Dear] little children, I am to be with you only a little longer. You will look for Me and, as I told the Jews, so I tell you now: you are not able to come where I am going.

[34]I give you a new commandment: that you should love one another. Just as I have loved you, so you too should love one another.

[35]By this shall all [men] know that you are My disciples, if you love one another [if you keep on showing love among yourselves].

[36]Simon Peter said to Him, Lord, where are You going? Jesus answered, You are not able to follow Me now where I am going, but you shall follow Me afterwards.

[37]Peter said to Him, Lord, why cannot I follow You now? I will lay down my life for You.

---

[a] 18 Greek has lifted up his heel   [b] 18 Psalm 41:9   [c] 32 Many early manuscripts do not have If God is glorified in him.

[a] Alexander Souter, Pocket Lexicon.   [b] Many ancient manuscripts read "with Me."   [c] Joseph Thayer, A Greek-English Lexicon.   [d] Charles B. Williams, The New Testament: A Translation.

## New International Version

38Then Jesus answered, "Will you really lay down your life for me? Very truly I tell you, before the rooster crows, you will disown me three times!

### Jesus Comforts His Disciples

**14** "Do not let your hearts be troubled. You believe in God[a]; believe also in me. 2My Father's house has many rooms; if that were not so, would I have told you that I am going there to prepare a place for you? 3And if I go and prepare a place for you, I will come back and take you to be with me that you also may be where I am. 4You know the way to the place where I am going."

### Jesus the Way to the Father

5Thomas said to him, "Lord, we don't know where you are going, so how can we know the way?"

6Jesus answered, "I am the way and the truth and the life. No one comes to the Father except through me. 7If you really know me, you will know[b] my Father as well. From now on, you do know him and have seen him."

8Philip said, "Lord, show us the Father and that will be enough for us."

9Jesus answered: "Don't you know me, Philip, even after I have been among you such a long time? Anyone who has seen me has seen the Father. How can you say, 'Show us the Father'? 10Don't you believe that I am in the Father, and that the Father is in me? The words I say to you I do not speak on my own authority. Rather, it is the Father, living in me, who is doing his work. 11Believe me when I say that I am in the Father and the Father is in me; or at least believe on the evidence of the works themselves. 12Very truly I tell you, whoever believes in me will do the works I have been doing, and they will do even greater things than these, because I am going to the Father. 13And I will do whatever you ask in my name, so that the Father may be glorified in the Son. 14You may ask me for anything in my name, and I will do it.

### Jesus Promises the Holy Spirit

15"If you love me, keep my commands. 16And I will ask the Father, and he will give you another advocate to help you and be with you forever— 17the Spirit of truth. The world cannot accept him, because it neither sees him nor knows him. But you know him, for he lives with you and will be[c] in you. 18I will not leave you as orphans; I will come to you. 19Before long, the world will not see me anymore, but you will see me. Because I live, you also will live. 20On that day you will realize that I am in my Father, and you are in me, and I am in you. 21Whoever has my commands and keeps them is the one who loves me. The one who loves

## Amplified Bible

38Jesus answered, Will you [really] lay down your life for Me? I assure you, most solemnly I tell you, before a rooster crows, you will deny Me [completely disown Me] three times.

**14** Do not let your hearts be troubled (distressed, agitated). You believe in and adhere to and trust in and rely on God; believe in and adhere to and trust in and rely also on Me.

2In My Father's house there are many dwelling places (homes). If it were not so, I would have told you; for I am going away to prepare a place for you.

3And when (if) I go and make ready a place for you, I will come back again and will take you to Myself, that where I am you may be also.

4And [to the place] where I am going, you know the way.

5Thomas said to Him, Lord, we do not know where You are going, so how can we know the way?

6Jesus said to him, I am the Way and the Truth and the Life; no one comes to the Father except by (through) Me.

7If you had known Me [had learned to recognize Me], you would also have known My Father. From now on, you know Him and have seen Him.

8Philip said to Him, Lord, show us the Father [cause us to see the Father—that is all we ask]; then we shall be satisfied.

9Jesus replied, Have I been with all of you for so long a time, and do you not recognize and know Me yet, Philip? Anyone who has seen Me has seen the Father. How can you say then, Show us the Father?

10Do you not believe that I am in the Father, and that the Father is in Me? What I am telling you I do not say on My own authority and of My own accord; but the Father Who lives continually in Me does the ([a]His) works (His own miracles, deeds of power).

11Believe Me that I am in the Father and the Father in Me; or else believe Me for the sake of the [very] works themselves. [If you cannot trust Me, at least let these works that I do in My Father's name convince you.]

12I assure you, most solemnly I tell you, if anyone steadfastly believes in Me, he will himself be able to do the things that I do; and he will do even greater things than these, because I go to the Father.

13And I will do [I Myself will grant] whatever you ask in My Name [as [b]presenting all that I AM], so that the Father may be glorified and extolled in (through) the Son. [Exod. 3:14.]

14[Yes] I will grant [I Myself will do for you] whatever you shall ask in My Name [as [b]presenting all that I AM].

15If you [really] love Me, you will keep (obey) My commands.

16And I will ask the Father, and He will give you another Comforter (Counselor, Helper, Intercessor, Advocate, Strengthener, and Standby), that He may remain with you forever—

17The Spirit of Truth, Whom the world cannot receive (welcome, take to its heart), because it does not see Him or know and recognize Him. But you know and recognize Him, for He lives with you [constantly] and will be in you.

18I will not leave you as orphans [comfortless, desolate, bereaved, forlorn, helpless]; I will come [back] to you.

19Just a little while now, and the world will not see Me any more, but you will see Me; because I live, you will live also.

20At that time [when that day comes] you will know [for yourselves] that I am in My Father, and you [are] in Me, and I [am] in you.

21The person who has My commands and keeps them is the one who [really] loves Me; and whoever [really] loves Me will be loved by My Father, and I [too] will love him and

---

a 1 Or Believe in God   b 7 Some manuscripts If you really knew me, you would know   c 17 Some early manuscripts and is

a Several ancient manuscripts read "His works."   b Hermann Cremer, Biblico-Theological Lexicon.

## New International Version

me will be loved by my Father, and I too will love them and show myself to them."

22Then Judas (not Judas Iscariot) said, "But, Lord, why do you intend to show yourself to us and not to the world?"

23Jesus replied, "Anyone who loves me will obey my teaching. My Father will love them, and we will come to them and make our home with them. 24Anyone who does not love me will not obey my teaching. These words you hear are not my own; they belong to the Father who sent me.

25"All this I have spoken while still with you. 26But the Advocate, the Holy Spirit, whom the Father will send in my name, will teach you all things and will remind you of everything I have said to you. 27Peace I leave with you; my peace I give you. I do not give to you as the world gives. Do not let your hearts be troubled and do not be afraid.

28"You heard me say, 'I am going away and I am coming back to you.' If you loved me, you would be glad that I am going to the Father, for the Father is greater than I. 29I have told you now before it happens, so that when it does happen you will believe. 30I will not say much more to you, for the prince of this world is coming. He has no hold over me, 31but he comes so that the world may learn that I love the Father and do exactly what my Father has commanded me.

"Come now; let us leave.

### The Vine and the Branches

**15** "I am the true vine, and my Father is the gardener. 2He cuts off every branch in me that bears no fruit, while every branch that does bear fruit he prunes*a* so that it will be even more fruitful. 3You are already clean because of the word I have spoken to you. 4Remain in me, as I also remain in you. No branch can bear fruit by itself; it must remain in the vine. Neither can you bear fruit unless you remain in me.

5"I am the vine; you are the branches. If you remain in me and I in you, you will bear much fruit; apart from me you can do nothing. 6If you do not remain in me, you are like a branch that is thrown away and withers; such branches are picked up, thrown into the fire and burned. 7If you remain in me and my words remain in you, ask whatever you wish, and it will be done for you. 8This is to my Father's glory, that you bear much fruit, showing yourselves to be my disciples.

## Amplified Bible

will show (reveal, manifest) Myself to him. [I will let Myself be clearly seen by him and make Myself real to him.]

22Judas, not Iscariot, asked Him, Lord, how is it that You will reveal Yourself [make Yourself real] to us and not to the world?

23Jesus answered, If a person [really] loves Me, he will keep My word [obey My teaching]; and My Father will love him, and We will come to him and make Our home (abode, special dwelling place) with him.

24Anyone who does not [really] love Me does not observe *and* obey My teaching. And the teaching which you hear *and* heed is not Mine, but [comes] from the Father Who sent Me.

25I have told you these things while I am still with you.

26But the Comforter (Counselor, Helper, Intercessor, Advocate, Strengthener, Standby), the Holy Spirit, Whom the Father will send in My name [in My place, to represent Me and act on My behalf], He will teach you all things. And He will cause you to recall (will remind you of, bring to your remembrance) everything I have told you.

27Peace I leave with you; My [own] peace I now give *and* bequeath to you. Not as the world gives do I give to you. Do not let your hearts be troubled, neither let them be afraid. [Stop allowing yourselves to be agitated and disturbed; and do not permit yourselves to be fearful and intimidated and cowardly and unsettled.]

28You heard Me tell you, I am going away and I am coming [back] to you. If you [really] loved Me, you would have been glad, because I am going to the Father; for the Father is greater *and* mightier than I am.

29And now I have told you [this] before it occurs, so that when it does take place you may believe *and* have faith in *and* rely on Me.

30I will not talk with you much more, for the prince (evil genius, ruler) of the world is coming. And he has no claim on Me. [He has nothing in common with Me; there is nothing in Me that belongs to him, and he has no power over Me.]

31But [*a*Satan is coming and] I do as the Father has commanded Me, so that the world may know (be convinced) that I love the Father and that I do only what the Father has instructed Me to do. [I act in full agreement with His orders.] Rise, let us go away from here.

**15** I am the True Vine, and My Father is the Vinedresser.

2Any branch in Me that does not bear fruit [that stops bearing] He cuts away (trims off, takes away); and He cleanses *and* repeatedly prunes every branch that continues to bear fruit, to make it bear more *and* richer *and* more excellent fruit.

3You are cleansed *and* pruned already, because of the word which I have given you [the teachings I have discussed with you].

4Dwell in Me, and I will dwell in you. [Live in Me, and I will live in you.] Just as no branch can bear fruit of itself without abiding in (being vitally united to) the vine, neither can you bear fruit unless you abide in Me.

5I am the Vine; you are the branches. Whoever lives in Me and I in him bears much (abundant) fruit. However, apart from Me [cut off from vital union with Me] you can do nothing.

6If a person does not dwell in Me, he is thrown out like a [broken-off] branch, and withers; such branches are gathered up and thrown into the fire, and they are burned.

7If you live in Me [abide vitally united to Me] and My words remain in you *and* continue to live in your hearts, ask whatever you will, and it shall be done for you.

8When you bear (produce) much fruit, My Father is honored *and* glorified, and you show *and* prove yourselves to be true followers of Mine.

---

*a* 2 The Greek for *he prunes* also means *he cleans*.

*a* Marvin Vincent, *Word Studies*.

## New International Version

[9]"As the Father has loved me, so have I loved you. Now remain in my love. [10]If you keep my commands, you will remain in my love, just as I have kept my Father's commands and remain in his love. [11]I have told you this so that my joy may be in you and that your joy may be complete. [12]My command is this: Love each other as I have loved you. [13]Greater love has no one than this: to lay down one's life for one's friends. [14]You are my friends if you do what I command. [15]I no longer call you servants, because a servant does not know his master's business. Instead, I have called you friends, for everything that I learned from my Father I have made known to you. [16]You did not choose me, but I chose you and appointed you so that you might go and bear fruit—fruit that will last—and so that whatever you ask in my name the Father will give you. [17]This is my command: Love each other.

### The World Hates the Disciples

[18]"If the world hates you, keep in mind that it hated me first. [19]If you belonged to the world, it would love you as its own. As it is, you do not belong to the world, but I have chosen you out of the world. That is why the world hates you. [20]Remember what I told you: 'A servant is not greater than his master.'[a] If they persecuted me, they will persecute you also. If they obeyed my teaching, they will obey yours also. [21]They will treat you this way because of my name, for they do not know the one who sent me. [22]If I had not come and spoken to them, they would not be guilty of sin; but now they have no excuse for their sin. [23]Whoever hates me hates my Father as well. [24]If I had not done among them the works no one else did, they would not be guilty of sin. As it is, they have seen, and yet they have hated both me and my Father. [25]But this is to fulfill what is written in their Law: 'They hated me without reason.'[b]

### The Work of the Holy Spirit

[26]"When the Advocate comes, whom I will send to you from the Father—the Spirit of truth who goes out from the Father—he will testify about me. [27]And you also must testify, for you have been with me from the beginning.

**16** "All this I have told you so that you will not fall away. [2]They will put you out of the synagogue; in fact, the time is coming when anyone who kills you will think they are offering a service to God. [3]They will do

## Amplified Bible

[9]I have loved you, [just] as the Father has loved Me; abide in My love [[a]continue in His love with Me].

[10]If you keep My commandments [if you continue to obey My instructions], you will abide in My love *and* live on in it, just as I have obeyed My Father's commandments and live on in His love.

[11]I have told you these things, that My joy *and* delight may be in you, and that your joy *and* gladness may be of full measure *and* complete *and* overflowing.

[12]This is My commandment: that you love one another [just] as I have loved you.

[13]No one has greater love [no one has shown stronger affection] than to lay down (give up) his own life for his friends.

[14]You are My friends if you keep on doing the things which I command you to do.

[15]I do not call you servants (slaves) any longer, for the servant does not know what his master is doing (working out). But I have called you My friends, because I have made known to you everything that I have heard from My Father. [I have revealed to you everything that I have learned from Him.]

[16]You have not chosen Me, but I have chosen you and I have appointed you [I have planted you], that you might go and bear fruit *and* keep on bearing, and that your fruit may be lasting [that it may remain, abide], so that whatever you ask the Father in My Name [as [a]presenting all that I AM], He may give it to you.

[17]This is what I command you: that you love one another.

[18]If the world hates you, know that it hated Me before it hated you.

[19]If you belonged to the world, the world would treat you with affection *and* would love you as its own. But because you are not of the world [no longer one with it], but I have chosen (selected) you out of the world, the world hates (detests) you.

[20]Remember that I told you, A servant is not greater than his master [is not superior to him]. If they persecuted Me, they will also persecute you; if they kept My word *and* obeyed My teachings, they will also keep *and* obey yours.

[21]But they will do all this to you [inflict all this suffering on you] because of [your bearing] My name *and* on My account, for they do not know *or* understand the One Who sent Me.

[22]If I had not come and spoken to them, they would not be guilty of sin [would be blameless]; but now they have no excuse for their sin.

[23]Whoever hates Me also hates My Father.

[24]If I had not done (accomplished) among them the works which no one else ever did, they would not be guilty of sin. But [the fact is] now they have both seen [these works] and have hated both Me and My Father.

[25]But [this is so] that the word written in their Law might be fulfilled, They hated Me without a cause. [Ps. 35:19; 69:4.]

[26]But when the Comforter (Counselor, Helper, Advocate, Intercessor, Strengthener, Standby) comes, Whom I will send to you from the Father, the Spirit of Truth Who comes (proceeds) from the Father, He [Himself] will testify regarding Me.

[27]But you also will testify *and* be My witnesses, because you have been with Me from the beginning.

**16** I have told you all these things, so that you should not be offended (taken unawares and falter, or be caused to stumble and fall away). [I told you to keep you from being scandalized and repelled.]

[2]They will put you out of (expel you from) the synagogues; but an hour is coming when whoever kills you will think *and* claim that he has offered service to God.

[a] Hermann Cremer, *Biblico-Theological Lexicon.*

## New International Version

such things because they have not known the Father or me. [4]I have told you this, so that when their time comes you will remember that I warned you about them. I did not tell you this from the beginning because I was with you, [5]but now I am going to him who sent me. None of you asks me, 'Where are you going?' [6]Rather, you are filled with grief because I have said these things. [7]But very truly I tell you, it is for your good that I am going away. Unless I go away, the Advocate will not come to you; but if I go, I will send him to you. [8]When he comes, he will prove the world to be in the wrong about sin and righteousness and judgment: [9]about sin, because people do not believe in me; [10]about righteousness, because I am going to the Father, where you can see me no longer; [11]and about judgment, because the prince of this world now stands condemned.

[12]"I have much more to say to you, more than you can now bear. [13]But when he, the Spirit of truth, comes, he will guide you into all the truth. He will not speak on his own; he will speak only what he hears, and he will tell you what is yet to come. [14]He will glorify me because it is from me that he will receive what he will make known to you. [15]All that belongs to the Father is mine. That is why I said the Spirit will receive from me what he will make known to you."

### The Disciples' Grief Will Turn to Joy

[16]Jesus went on to say, "In a little while you will see me no more, and then after a little while you will see me."

[17]At this, some of his disciples said to one another, "What does he mean by saying, 'In a little while you will see me no more, and then after a little while you will see me,' and 'Because I am going to the Father'?" [18]They kept asking, "What does he mean by 'a little while'? We don't understand what he is saying."

[19]Jesus saw that they wanted to ask him about this, so he said to them, "Are you asking one another what I meant when I said, 'In a little while you will see me no more, and then after a little while you will see me'? [20]Very truly I tell you, you will weep and mourn while the world rejoices. You will grieve, but your grief will turn to joy. [21]A woman giving birth to a child has pain because her time has come; but when her baby is born she forgets the anguish because of her joy that a child is born into the world. [22]So with you: Now is your time of grief, but I will see you again and you

## Amplified Bible

[3]And they will do this because they have not known the Father or Me.

[4]But I have told you these things now, so that when they occur you will remember that I told you of them. I did not say these things to you from the beginning, because I was with you.

[5]But now I am going to Him Who sent Me, yet none of you asks Me, Where are You going?

[6]But because I have said these things to you, sorrow has filled your hearts [taken complete possession of them].

[7]However, I am telling you nothing but the truth when I say it is profitable (good, expedient, advantageous) for you that I go away. Because if I do not go away, the Comforter (Counselor, Helper, Advocate, Intercessor, Strengthener, Standby) will not come to you [into close fellowship with you]; but if I go away, I will send Him to you [to be in close fellowship with you].

[8]And when He comes, He will convict *and* convince the world *and* bring demonstration to it about sin and about righteousness (uprightness of heart and right standing with God) and about judgment:

[9]About sin, because they do not believe in Me [trust in, rely on, and adhere to Me];

[10]About righteousness (uprightness of heart and right standing with God), because I go to My Father, and you will see Me no longer;

[11]About judgment, because the ruler (evil genius, prince) of this world [Satan] is judged *and* condemned *and* sentence already is passed upon him.

[12]I have still many things to say to you, but you are not able to bear them *or* to take them upon you *or* to grasp them now.

[13]But when He, the Spirit of Truth (the Truth-giving Spirit) comes, He will guide you into all the Truth (the whole, full Truth). For He will not speak His own message [on His own authority]; but He will tell whatever He hears [from the Father; He will give the message that has been given to Him], and He will announce *and* declare to you the things that are to come [that will happen in the future].

[14]He will honor *and* glorify Me, because He will take of (receive, draw upon) what is Mine and will reveal (declare, disclose, transmit) it to you.

[15]Everything that the Father has is Mine. That is what I meant when I said that He [the Spirit] will take the things that are Mine and will reveal (declare, disclose, transmit) it to you.

[16]In a little while you will no longer see Me, and again after a short while you will see Me.

[17]So some of His disciples questioned among themselves, What does He mean when He tells us, In a little while you will no longer see Me, and again after a short while you will see Me, and, Because I go to My Father?

[18]What does He mean by a little while? We do not know *or* understand what He is talking about.

[19]Jesus knew that they wanted to ask Him, so He said to them, Are you wondering *and* inquiring among yourselves what I meant when I said, In a little while you will no longer see Me, and again after a short while you will see Me?

[20]I assure you, most solemnly I tell you, that you shall weep and grieve, but the world will rejoice. You will be sorrowful, but your sorrow will be turned into joy.

[21]A woman, when she gives birth to a child, has grief (anguish, agony) because her time has come. But when she has delivered the child, she no longer remembers her pain (trouble, anguish) because she is so glad that a man (a child, a human being) has been born into the world.

[22]So for the present you are also in sorrow (in distress and depressed); but I will see you again and [then] your

## New International Version

will rejoice, and no one will take away your joy. ²³In that day you will no longer ask me anything. Very truly I tell you, my Father will give you whatever you ask in my name. ²⁴Until now you have not asked for anything in my name. Ask and you will receive, and your joy will be complete.

²⁵"Though I have been speaking figuratively, a time is coming when I will no longer use this kind of language but will tell you plainly about my Father. ²⁶In that day you will ask in my name. I am not saying that I will ask the Father on your behalf. ²⁷No, the Father himself loves you because you have loved me and have believed that I came from God. ²⁸I came from the Father and entered the world; now I am leaving the world and going back to the Father."

²⁹Then Jesus' disciples said, "Now you are speaking clearly and without figures of speech. ³⁰Now we can see that you know all things and that you do not even need to have anyone ask you questions. This makes us believe that you came from God."

³¹"Do you now believe?" Jesus replied. ³²"A time is coming and in fact has come when you will be scattered, each to your own home. You will leave me all alone. Yet I am not alone, for my Father is with me.

³³"I have told you these things, so that in me you may have peace. In this world you will have trouble. But take heart! I have overcome the world."

### Jesus Prays to Be Glorified

**17** After Jesus said this, he looked toward heaven and prayed:

"Father, the hour has come. Glorify your Son, that your Son may glorify you. ²For you granted him authority over all people that he might give eternal life to all those you have given him. ³Now this is eternal life: that they know you, the only true God, and Jesus Christ, whom you have sent. ⁴I have brought you glory on earth by finishing the work you gave me to do. ⁵And now, Father, glorify me in your presence with the glory I had with you before the world began.

### Jesus Prays for His Disciples

⁶"I have revealed youᵃ to those whom you gave me out of the world. They were yours; you gave them to me and they have obeyed your word. ⁷Now they know that everything you have given me comes from you. ⁸For I gave them the words you gave me and they ac-

ᵃ 6 Greek *your name*

## Amplified Bible

hearts will rejoice, and no one can take from you your joy (gladness, delight).

²³And when that time comes, you will ask nothing of Me [you will need to ask Me no questions]. I assure you, most solemnly I tell you, that My Father will grant you whatever you ask in My Name [as ᵃpresenting all that I AM]. [Exod. 3:14.]

²⁴Up to this time you have not asked a [single] thing in My Name [as ᵃpresenting all that I AM]; but now ask *and* keep on asking and you will receive, so that your joy (gladness, delight) may be full *and* complete.

²⁵I have told you these things in parables (veiled language, allegories, dark sayings); the hour is now coming when I shall no longer speak to you in figures of speech, but I shall tell you about the Father in plain words *and* openly (without reserve).

²⁶At that time you will ask (pray) in My Name; and I am not saying that I will ask the Father on your behalf [for it will be unnecessary].

²⁷For the Father Himself [tenderly] loves you because you have loved Me and have believed that I came out from the Father.

²⁸I came out from the Father and have come into the world; again, I am leaving the world and going to the Father.

²⁹His disciples said, Ah, now You are speaking plainly to us and not in parables (veiled language and figures of speech)!

³⁰Now we know that You are acquainted with everything and have no need to be asked questions. Because of this we believe that you [really] came from God.

³¹Jesus answered them, Do you now believe? [Do you believe it at last?]

³²But take notice, the hour is coming, and it has arrived, when you will all be dispersed *and* scattered, every man to his own home, leaving Me alone. Yet I am not alone, because the Father is with Me.

³³I have told you these things, so that in Me you may have [perfect] peace *and* confidence. In the world you have tribulation *and* trials *and* distress *and* frustration; but be of good cheer [take courage; be confident, certain, undaunted]! For I have overcome the world. [I have deprived it of power to harm you and have conquered it for you.]

**17** When Jesus had spoken these things, He lifted up His eyes to heaven and said, Father, the hour has come. Glorify *and* exalt *and* honor *and* magnify Your Son, so that Your Son may glorify *and* extol *and* honor *and* magnify You.

²[Just as] You have granted Him power *and* authority over all flesh (all humankind), [now glorify Him] so that He may give eternal life to all whom You have given Him.

³And this is eternal life: [it means] to know (to perceive, recognize, become acquainted with, and understand) You, the only true *and* real God, and [likewise] to know Him, Jesus [as the] Christ (the Anointed One, the Messiah), Whom You have sent.

⁴I have glorified You down here on the earth by completing the work that You gave Me to do.

⁵And now, Father, glorify Me along with Yourself *and* restore Me to such majesty *and* honor in Your presence as I had with You before the world existed.

⁶I have manifested Your Name [I have revealed Your very Self, Your real Self] to the people whom You have given Me out of the world. They were Yours, and You gave them to Me, and they have obeyed *and* kept Your word.

⁷Now [at last] they know *and* understand that all You have given Me belongs to You [is really and truly Yours].

⁸For the [uttered] words that You gave Me I have given them; and they have received *and* accepted [them] and have come to know positively *and* in reality [to believe

ᵃ Hermann Cremer, *Biblico-Theological Lexicon*.

## New International Version

cepted them. They knew with certainty that I came from you, and they believed that you sent me. ⁹I pray for them. I am not praying for the world, but for those you have given me, for they are yours. ¹⁰All I have is yours, and all you have is mine. And glory has come to me through them. ¹¹I will remain in the world no longer, but they are still in the world, and I am coming to you. Holy Father, protect them by the power of*ᵃ* your name, the name you gave me, so that they may be one as we are one. ¹²While I was with them, I protected them and kept them safe byᵇ that name you gave me. None has been lost except the one doomed to destruction so that Scripture would be fulfilled.

¹³"I am coming to you now, but I say these things while I am still in the world, so that they may have the full measure of my joy within them. ¹⁴I have given them your word and the world has hated them, for they are not of the world any more than I am of the world. ¹⁵My prayer is not that you take them out of the world but that you protect them from the evil one. ¹⁶They are not of the world, even as I am not of it. ¹⁷Sanctify them byᶜ the truth; your word is truth. ¹⁸As you sent me into the world, I have sent them into the world. ¹⁹For them I sanctify myself, that they too may be truly sanctified.

### Jesus Prays for All Believers

²⁰"My prayer is not for them alone. I pray also for those who will believe in me through their message, ²¹that all of them may be one, Father, just as you are in me and I am in you. May they also be in us so that the world may believe that you have sent me. ²²I have given them the glory that you gave me, that they may be one as we are one— ²³I in them and you in me—so that they may be brought to complete unity. Then the world will know that you sent me and have loved them even as you have loved me.

²⁴"Father, I want those you have given me to be with me where I am, and to see my glory, the glory you have given me because you loved me before the creation of the world.

²⁵"Righteous Father, though the world does not know you, I know you, and they know that you have sent me. ²⁶I have made youᵈ known to them, and will continue to make you known in order that the love you have for me may be in them and that I myself may be in them."

## Amplified Bible

with absolute assurance] that I came forth from Your presence, and they have believed *and* are convinced that You did send Me.

⁹I am praying for them. I am not praying (requesting) for the world, but for those You have given Me, for they belong to You.

¹⁰All [things that *are*] Mine are Yours, and all [things that *are*] Yours belong to Me; and I am glorified in (through) them. [They have done Me honor; in them My glory is achieved.]

¹¹And [now] I am no more in the world, but these are [still] in the world, and I am coming to You. Holy Father, keep in Your Name [ᵃin the knowledge of Yourself] those whom You have given Me, that they may be one as We [are one].

¹²While I was with them, I kept *and* preserved them in Your Name [ᵃin the knowledge and worship of You]. Those You have given Me I guarded *and* protected, and not one of them has perished *or* is lost except the son of perdition [Judas Iscariot—the one who is now doomed to destruction, destined to be lost], that the Scripture might be fulfilled. [Ps. 41:9; John 6:70.]

¹³And now I am coming to You; I say these things while I am still in the world, so that My joy may be made full *and* complete *and* perfect in them [that they may experience My delight fulfilled in them, that My enjoyment may be perfected in their own souls, that they may have My gladness within them, filling their hearts].

¹⁴I have given *and* delivered to them Your word (message) and the world has hated them, because they are not of the world [do not belong to the world], just as I am not of the world.

¹⁵I do not ask that You will take them out of the world, but that You will keep *and* protect them from the evil one.

¹⁶They are not of the world (worldly, belonging to the world), [just] as I am not of the world.

¹⁷Sanctify them [purify, consecrate, separate them for Yourself, make them holy] by the Truth; Your Word is Truth.

¹⁸Just as You sent Me into the world, I also have sent them into the world.

¹⁹And so for their sake *and* on their behalf I sanctify (dedicate, consecrate) Myself, that they also may be sanctified (dedicated, consecrated, made holy) in the Truth.

²⁰Neither for these alone do I pray [it is not for their sake only that I make this request], but also for all those who will ever come to believe in (trust in, cling to, rely on) Me through their word *and* teaching,

²¹That they all may be one, [just] as You, Father, are in Me and I in You, that they also may be one in Us, so that the world may believe *and* be convinced that You have sent Me.

²²I have given to them the glory *and* honor which You have given Me, that they may be one [even] as We are one:

²³I in them and You in Me, in order that they may become one *and* perfectly united, that the world may know *and* [definitely] recognize that You sent Me and that You have loved them [even] as You have loved Me.

²⁴Father, I desire that they also whom You have entrusted to Me [as Your gift to Me] may be with Me where I am, so that they may see My glory, which You have given Me [Your love gift to Me]; for You loved Me before the foundation of the world.

²⁵O just *and* righteous Father, although the world has not known You *and* has failed to recognize You *and* has never acknowledged You, I have known You [continually]; and these men understand *and* know that You have sent Me.

²⁶I have made Your Name known to them *and* revealed Your character *and* Your very ᵇSelf, and I will continue to make [You] known, that the love which You have bestowed upon Me may be in them [felt in their hearts] and that I [Myself] may be in them.

---

ᵃ 11 Or *Father, keep them faithful to*    ᵇ 12 Or *kept them faithful to*
ᶜ 17 Or *them to live in accordance with*    ᵈ 26 Greek *your name*

ᵃ Albert Barnes, *Notes on the New Testament.*    ᵇ Joseph Thayer, *A Greek-English Lexicon.*

## New International Version

### Jesus Arrested

**18** When he had finished praying, Jesus left with his disciples and crossed the Kidron Valley. On the other side there was a garden, and he and his disciples went into it.

2 Now Judas, who betrayed him, knew the place, because Jesus had often met there with his disciples. 3 So Judas came to the garden, guiding a detachment of soldiers and some officials from the chief priests and the Pharisees. They were carrying torches, lanterns and weapons.

4 Jesus, knowing all that was going to happen to him, went out and asked them, "Who is it you want?"

5 "Jesus of Nazareth," they replied.

"I am he," Jesus said. (And Judas the traitor was standing there with them.) 6 When Jesus said, "I am he," they drew back and fell to the ground.

7 Again he asked them, "Who is it you want?"

"Jesus of Nazareth," they said.

8 Jesus answered, "I told you that I am he. If you are looking for me, then let these men go." 9 This happened so that the words he had spoken would be fulfilled: "I have not lost one of those you gave me."[a]

10 Then Simon Peter, who had a sword, drew it and struck the high priest's servant, cutting off his right ear. (The servant's name was Malchus.)

11 Jesus commanded Peter, "Put your sword away! Shall I not drink the cup the Father has given me?"

12 Then the detachment of soldiers with its commander and the Jewish officials arrested Jesus. They bound him 13 and brought him first to Annas, who was the father-in-law of Caiaphas, the high priest that year. 14 Caiaphas was the one who had advised the Jewish leaders that it would be good if one man died for the people.

### Peter's First Denial

15 Simon Peter and another disciple were following Jesus. Because this disciple was known to the high priest, he went with Jesus into the high priest's courtyard, 16 but Peter had to wait outside at the door. The other disciple, who was known to the high priest, came back, spoke to the servant girl on duty there and brought Peter in.

17 "You aren't one of this man's disciples too, are you?" she asked Peter.

He replied, "I am not."

18 It was cold, and the servants and officials stood around a fire they had made to keep warm. Peter also was standing with them, warming himself.

### The High Priest Questions Jesus

19 Meanwhile, the high priest questioned Jesus about his disciples and his teaching.

20 "I have spoken openly to the world," Jesus replied. "I always taught in synagogues or at the temple, where all the Jews come together. I said nothing in secret. 21 Why question me? Ask those who heard me. Surely they know what I said."

22 When Jesus said this, one of the officials nearby slapped him in the face. "Is this the way you answer the high priest?" he demanded.

## Amplified Bible

**18** Having said these things, Jesus went out with His disciples beyond (across) the winter torrent of the Kidron [in the ravine]. There was a garden there, which He and His disciples entered.

2 And Judas, who was betraying Him *and* delivering Him up, also knew the place, because Jesus had often retired there with His disciples.

3 So Judas, obtaining *and* taking charge of the band of soldiers and some guards (attendants) of the high priests and Pharisees, came there with lanterns and torches and weapons.

4 Then Jesus, knowing all that was about to befall Him, went out to them and said, Whom are you seeking? [Whom do you want?]

5 They answered Him, Jesus the Nazarene. Jesus said to them, I am He. Judas, who was betraying Him, was also standing with them.

6 When Jesus said to them, I am He, they went backwards (drew back, lurched backward) and fell to the ground.

7 Then again He asked them, Whom are you seeking? And they said, Jesus the Nazarene.

8 Jesus answered, I told you that I am He. So, if you want Me [if it is only I for Whom you are looking], let these men go their way.

9 Thus what He had said was fulfilled *and* verified, Of those whom You have given Me, I have not lost even one. [John 6:39; 17:12.]

10 Then Simon Peter, who had a sword, drew it and struck the high priest's servant and cut off his right ear. The servant's name was Malchus.

11 Therefore, Jesus said to Peter, Put the sword [back] into the sheath! The cup which My Father has given Me, shall I not drink it?

12 So the troops and their captain and the guards (attendants) of the Jews seized Jesus and bound Him,

13 And they brought Him first to Annas, for he was the father-in-law of Caiaphas, who was the high priest that year.

14 It was Caiaphas who had counseled the Jews that it was expedient *and* for their welfare that one man should die for (instead of, in behalf of) the people. [John 11:49, 50.]

15 Now Simon Peter and another disciple were following Jesus. And that disciple was known to the high priest, and so he entered along with Jesus into the court of the palace of the high priest;

16 But Peter was standing outside at the door. So the other disciple, who was known to the high priest, went out and spoke to the maid who kept the door and brought Peter inside.

17 Then the maid who was in charge at the door said to Peter, You are not also one of the disciples of this *a*Man, are you? He said, I am not!

18 Now the servants and the guards (the attendants) had made a fire of coals, for it was cold, and they were standing and warming themselves. And Peter was with them, standing and warming himself.

19 Then the high priest questioned Jesus about His disciples and about His teaching.

20 Jesus answered him, I have spoken openly to the world. I have always taught in a synagogue and in the temple [area], where the Jews [habitually] congregate (assemble); and I have spoken nothing secretly.

21 Why do you ask Me? Ask those who have heard [Me] what I said to them. See! They know what I said.

22 But when He said this, one of the attendants who stood by struck Jesus, saying, Is that how *a*You answer the high priest?

---

a 9 John 6:39

a Capitalized because of what He is, the spotless Son of God, not what the speaker may have thought He was.

## New International Version

23"If I said something wrong," Jesus replied, "testify as to what is wrong. But if I spoke the truth, why did you strike me?" 24Then Annas sent him bound to Caiaphas the high priest.

### Peter's Second and Third Denials

25Meanwhile, Simon Peter was still standing there warming himself. So they asked him, "You aren't one of his disciples too, are you?"

He denied it, saying, "I am not."

26One of the high priest's servants, a relative of the man whose ear Peter had cut off, challenged him, "Didn't I see you with him in the garden?" 27Again Peter denied it, and at that moment a rooster began to crow.

### Jesus Before Pilate

28Then the Jewish leaders took Jesus from Caiaphas to the palace of the Roman governor. By now it was early morning, and to avoid ceremonial uncleanness they did not enter the palace, because they wanted to be able to eat the Passover. 29So Pilate came out to them and asked, "What charges are you bringing against this man?"

30"If he were not a criminal," they replied, "we would not have handed him over to you."

31Pilate said, "Take him yourselves and judge him by your own law."

"But we have no right to execute anyone," they objected. 32This took place to fulfill what Jesus had said about the kind of death he was going to die.

33Pilate then went back inside the palace, summoned Jesus and asked him, "Are you the king of the Jews?"

34"Is that your own idea," Jesus asked, "or did others talk to you about me?"

35"Am I a Jew?" Pilate replied. "Your own people and chief priests handed you over to me. What is it you have done?"

36Jesus said, "My kingdom is not of this world. If it were, my servants would fight to prevent my arrest by the Jewish leaders. But now my kingdom is from another place."

37"You are a king, then!" said Pilate.

Jesus answered, "You say that I am a king. In fact, the reason I was born and came into the world is to testify to the truth. Everyone on the side of truth listens to me."

38"What is truth?" retorted Pilate. With this he went out again to the Jews gathered there and said, "I find no basis for a charge against him. 39But it is your custom for me to release to you one prisoner at the time of the Passover. Do you want me to release 'the king of the Jews'?"

40They shouted back, "No, not him! Give us Barabbas!" Now Barabbas had taken part in an uprising.

### Jesus Sentenced to Be Crucified

**19** Then Pilate took Jesus and had him flogged. 2The soldiers twisted together a crown of thorns and put it on his head. They clothed him in a purple robe 3and went up to him again and again, saying, "Hail, king of the Jews!" And they slapped him in the face.

4Once more Pilate came out and said to the Jews gathered there, "Look, I am bringing him out to you to let you know that I find no basis for a charge against him." 5When

## Amplified Bible

23Jesus replied, If I have said anything wrong [if I have spoken abusively, if there was evil in what I said] tell what was wrong with it. But if I spoke rightly *and* properly, why do you strike Me?

24Then Annas sent Him bound to Caiaphas the high priest.

25But Simon Peter [still] was standing and was warming himself. They said to him, You are not also one of His disciples, are you? He denied it and said, I am not!

26One of the high priest's servants, a relative of the man whose ear Peter cut off, said, Did I not see you in the garden with Him?

27And again Peter denied it. And immediately a rooster crowed.

28Then they brought Jesus from Caiaphas into the Praetorium (judgment hall, governor's palace). And it was early. They themselves did not enter the Praetorium, that they might not be defiled (become ceremonially unclean), but might be fit to eat the Passover [supper].

29So Pilate went out to them and said, What accusation do you bring against this *a* Man?

30They retorted, If He were not an evildoer (criminal), we would not have handed Him over to you.

31Pilate said to them, Take Him yourselves and judge *and* sentence *and* punish Him according to your [own] law. The Jews answered, It is not lawful for us to put anyone to death.

32This was to fulfill the word which Jesus had spoken to show (indicate, predict) by what manner of death He was to die. [John 12:32-34.]

33So Pilate went back again into the judgment hall and called Jesus and asked Him, Are You the King of the Jews?

34Jesus replied, Are you saying this of yourself [on your own initiative], or have others told you about Me?

35Pilate answered, Am I a Jew? Your [own] people *and* nation and their chief priests have delivered You to me. What have You done?

36Jesus answered, My kingdom (kingship, royal power) belongs not to this world. If My kingdom were of this world, My followers would have been fighting to keep Me from being handed over to the Jews. But as it is, My kingdom is not from here (this world); [it has no such origin or source].

37Pilate said to Him, Then You are a King? Jesus answered, You say it! [You speak correctly!] For I am a King. [Certainly I am a King!] This is why I was born, and for this I have come into the world, to bear witness to the Truth. Everyone who is of the Truth [who is a friend of the Truth, who belongs to the Truth] hears *and* listens to My voice.

38Pilate said to Him, What is Truth? On saying this he went out to the Jews again and told them, I find no fault in Him.

39But it is your custom that I release one [prisoner] for you at the Passover. So shall I release for you the King of the Jews?

40Then they all shouted back again, Not Him [not this Man], but Barabbas! Now Barabbas was a robber.

**19** So then Pilate took Jesus and scourged (flogged, whipped) Him.

2And the soldiers, having twisted together a crown of thorns, put it on His head, and threw a purple cloak around Him.

3And they kept coming to Him and saying, Hail, King of the Jews! [Good health to you! Peace to you! Long life to you, King of the Jews!] And they struck Him with the palms of their hands. [Isa. 53:3, 5, 7.]

4Then Pilate went out again and said to them, See, I bring Him out to you, so that you may know that I find no fault (crime, cause for accusation) in Him.

---

*a* Capitalized because of what He is, the spotless Son of God, not what the speaker may have thought He was.

## New International Version

Jesus came out wearing the crown of thorns and the purple robe, Pilate said to them, "Here is the man!"

⁶As soon as the chief priests and their officials saw him, they shouted, "Crucify! Crucify!"

But Pilate answered, "You take him and crucify him. As for me, I find no basis for a charge against him."

⁷The Jewish leaders insisted, "We have a law, and according to that law he must die, because he claimed to be the Son of God."

⁸When Pilate heard this, he was even more afraid, ⁹and he went back inside the palace. "Where do you come from?" he asked Jesus, but Jesus gave him no answer. ¹⁰"Do you refuse to speak to me?" Pilate said. "Don't you realize I have power either to free you or to crucify you?"

¹¹Jesus answered, "You would have no power over me if it were not given to you from above. Therefore the one who handed me over to you is guilty of a greater sin."

¹²From then on, Pilate tried to set Jesus free, but the Jewish leaders kept shouting, "If you let this man go, you are no friend of Caesar. Anyone who claims to be a king opposes Caesar."

¹³When Pilate heard this, he brought Jesus out and sat down on the judge's seat at a place known as the Stone Pavement (which in Aramaic is Gabbatha). ¹⁴It was the day of Preparation of the Passover; it was about noon.

"Here is your king," Pilate said to the Jews.

¹⁵But they shouted, "Take him away! Take him away! Crucify him!"

"Shall I crucify your king?" Pilate asked.

"We have no king but Caesar," the chief priests answered.

¹⁶Finally Pilate handed him over to them to be crucified.

### The Crucifixion of Jesus

So the soldiers took charge of Jesus. ¹⁷Carrying his own cross, he went out to the place of the Skull (which in Aramaic is called Golgotha). ¹⁸There they crucified him, and with him two others—one on each side and Jesus in the middle.

¹⁹Pilate had a notice prepared and fastened to the cross. It read: JESUS OF NAZARETH, THE KING OF THE JEWS. ²⁰Many of the Jews read this sign, for the place where Jesus was crucified was near the city, and the sign was written in Aramaic, Latin and Greek. ²¹The chief priests of the Jews protested to Pilate, "Do not write 'The King of the Jews,' but that this man claimed to be king of the Jews."

²²Pilate answered, "What I have written, I have written."

²³When the soldiers crucified Jesus, they took his clothes, dividing them into four shares, one for each of them, with the undergarment remaining. This garment was seamless, woven in one piece from top to bottom.

²⁴"Let's not tear it," they said to one another. "Let's decide by lot who will get it."

This happened that the scripture might be fulfilled that said,

"They divided my clothes among them
   and cast lots for my garment."ᵃ

So this is what the soldiers did.

²⁵Near the cross of Jesus stood his mother, his mother's sister, Mary the wife of Clopas, and Mary Magdalene. ²⁶When Jesus saw his mother there, and the disciple whom he loved standing nearby, he said to her, "Woman,ᵇ

## Amplified Bible

⁵So Jesus came out wearing the thorny crown and purple cloak, and Pilate said to them, See, [here is] the ᵃMan!

⁶When the chief priests and attendants (guards) saw Him, they cried out, Crucify Him! Crucify Him! Pilate said to them, Take Him yourselves and crucify Him, for I find no fault (crime) in Him.

⁷The Jews answered him, We have a law, and according to that law He should die, because He has claimed *and* made Himself out to be the Son of God.

⁸So, when Pilate heard this said, he was more alarmed *and* awestricken *and* afraid than before.

⁹He went into the judgment hall again and said to Jesus, Where are You from? [To what world do You belong?] But Jesus did not answer him.

¹⁰So Pilate said to Him, Will You not speak [even] to me? Do You not know that I have power (authority) to release You and I have power to crucify You?

¹¹Jesus answered, You would not have any power *or* authority whatsoever against (over) Me if it were not given you from above. For this reason the sin *and* guilt of the one who delivered Me over to you is greater.

¹²Upon this, Pilate wanted (sought, was anxious) to release Him, but the Jews kept shrieking, If you release this Man, you are no friend of Caesar! Anybody who makes himself [out to be] a king sets himself up against Caesar [is a rebel against the emperor]!

¹³Hearing this, Pilate brought Jesus out and sat down on the judgment seat at a place called the Pavement [the Mosaic Pavement, the Stone Platform]—in Hebrew, Gabbatha.

¹⁴Now it was the day of Preparation for the Passover, and it was about the sixth hour (about twelve o'clock noon). He said to the Jews, See, [here is] your King!

¹⁵But they shouted, Away with Him! Away with Him! Crucify Him! Pilate said to them, Crucify your King? The chief priests answered, We have no king but Caesar!

¹⁶Then he delivered Him over to them to be crucified.

¹⁷And they took Jesus *and* led [Him] away; so He went out, bearing His own cross, to the spot called The Place of the Skull—in Hebrew it is called Golgotha.

¹⁸There they crucified Him, and with Him two others—one on either side and Jesus between them. [Isa. 53:12.]

¹⁹And Pilate also wrote a title (an inscription on a placard) and put it on the cross. And the writing was: Jesus the Nazarene, the King of the Jews.

²⁰And many of the Jews read this title, for the place where Jesus was crucified was near the city, and it was written in Hebrew, in Latin, [and] in Greek.

²¹Then the chief priests of the Jews said to Pilate, Do not write, The King of the Jews, but, He said, I am King of the Jews.

²²Pilate replied, What I have written, I have written.

²³Then the soldiers, when they had crucified Jesus, took His garments and made four parts, one share for each soldier, and also the tunic (the long shirtlike undergarment). But the tunic was seamless, woven [in one piece] from the top throughout.

²⁴So they said to one another, Let us not tear it, but let us cast lots to decide whose it shall be. This was to fulfill the Scripture, They parted My garments among them, and for My clothing they cast lots. So the soldiers did these things. [Ps. 22:18.]

²⁵But by the cross of Jesus stood His mother, His mother's sister, Mary the [wife] of Clopas, and Mary Magdalene.

²⁶So Jesus, seeing His mother there, and the disciple whom He loved standing near, said to His mother, [ᵇDear] woman, See, [here is] your son!

---

ᵃ 24 Psalm 22:18   ᵇ 26 The Greek for *Woman* does not denote any disrespect.

ᵃ Capitalized because of what He is, the spotless Son of God, not what the speaker may have thought He was.   ᵇ G. Abbott-Smith, *Manual Greek Lexicon:* "A term of respect and endearment."

## New International Version

here is your son," 27 and to the disciple, "Here is your mother." From that time on, this disciple took her into his home.

### The Death of Jesus

28 Later, knowing that everything had now been finished, and so that Scripture would be fulfilled, Jesus said, "I am thirsty." 29 A jar of wine vinegar was there, so they soaked a sponge in it, put the sponge on a stalk of the hyssop plant, and lifted it to Jesus' lips. 30 When he had received the drink, Jesus said, "It is finished." With that, he bowed his head and gave up his spirit.

31 Now it was the day of Preparation, and the next day was to be a special Sabbath. Because the Jewish leaders did not want the bodies left on the crosses during the Sabbath, they asked Pilate to have the legs broken and the bodies taken down. 32 The soldiers therefore came and broke the legs of the first man who had been crucified with Jesus, and then those of the other. 33 But when they came to Jesus and found that he was already dead, they did not break his legs. 34 Instead, one of the soldiers pierced Jesus' side with a spear, bringing a sudden flow of blood and water. 35 The man who saw it has given testimony, and his testimony is true. He knows that he tells the truth, and he testifies so that you also may believe. 36 These things happened so that the scripture would be fulfilled: "Not one of his bones will be broken,"ᵃ 37 and, as another scripture says, "They will look on the one they have pierced."ᵇ

### The Burial of Jesus

38 Later, Joseph of Arimathea asked Pilate for the body of Jesus. Now Joseph was a disciple of Jesus, but secretly because he feared the Jewish leaders. With Pilate's permission, he came and took the body away. 39 He was accompanied by Nicodemus, the man who earlier had visited Jesus at night. Nicodemus brought a mixture of myrrh and aloes, about seventy-five pounds.ᶜ 40 Taking Jesus' body, the two of them wrapped it, with the spices, in strips of linen. This was in accordance with Jewish burial customs. 41 At the place where Jesus was crucified, there was a garden, and in the garden a new tomb, in which no one had ever been laid. 42 Because it was the Jewish day of Preparation and since the tomb was nearby, they laid Jesus there.

### The Empty Tomb

**20** Early on the first day of the week, while it was still dark, Mary Magdalene went to the tomb and saw that the stone had been removed from the entrance. 2 So she came running to Simon Peter and the other disciple, the one Jesus loved, and said, "They have taken the Lord out of the tomb, and we don't know where they have put him!"

3 So Peter and the other disciple started for the tomb. 4 Both were running, but the other disciple outran Peter and reached the tomb first. 5 He bent over and looked in at the strips of linen lying there but did not go in. 6 Then Simon Peter came along behind him and went straight into the tomb. He saw the strips of linen lying there, 7 as well as the cloth that had been wrapped around Jesus' head. The cloth was still lying in its place, separate from the lin-

## Amplified Bible

27 Then He said to the disciple, See, [here is] your mother! And from that hour, the disciple took her into his own [keeping, own home].

28 After this, Jesus, knowing that all was now finished (ended), said in fulfillment of the Scripture, I thirst. [Ps. 69:21.]

29 A vessel (jar) full of sour wine (vinegar) was placed there, so they put a sponge soaked in the sour wine on [a stalk, reed of] hyssop, and held it to [His] mouth.

30 When Jesus had received the sour wine, He said, It is finished! And He bowed His head and gave up His spirit.

31 Since it was the day of Preparation, in order to prevent the bodies from hanging on the cross on the Sabbath—for that Sabbath was a very solemn *and* important one—the Jews requested Pilate to have the legs broken and the bodies taken away.

32 So the soldiers came and broke the legs of the first one, and of the other who had been crucified with Him.

33 But when they came to Jesus and they saw that He was already dead, they did not break His legs.

34 But one of the soldiers pierced His side with a spear, and immediately blood and water came (flowed) out.

35 And he who saw it (the eyewitness) gives this evidence, and his testimony is true; and he knows that he tells the truth, that you may believe also.

36 For these things took place, that the Scripture might be fulfilled (verified, carried out), Not one of His bones shall be broken; [Exod. 12:46; Num. 9:12; Ps. 34:20.]

37 And again another Scripture says, They shall look on Him Whom they have pierced. [Zech. 12:10.]

38 And after this, Joseph of Arimathea—a disciple of Jesus, but secretly for fear of the Jews—asked Pilate to let him take away the body of Jesus. And Pilate granted him permission. So he came and took away His body.

39 And Nicodemus also, who first had come to Jesus by night, came bringing a mixture of myrrh and aloes, [weighing] about a hundred pounds.

40 So they took Jesus' body and bound it in linen cloths with the spices (aromatics), as is the Jews' customary way to prepare for burial.

41 Now there was a garden in the place where He was crucified, and in the garden a new tomb, in which no one had ever [yet] been laid.

42 So there, because of the Jewish day of Preparation [and] since the tomb was near by, they laid Jesus.

**20** Now on the first day of the week, Mary Magdalene came to the tomb early, while it was still dark, and saw that the stone had been removed from (lifted out of the groove across the entrance of) the tomb.

2 So she ran and went to Simon Peter and the other disciple, whom Jesus [tenderly] loved, and said to them, They have taken away the Lord out of the tomb, and we do not know where they have laid Him!

3 Upon this, Peter and the other disciple came out and they went toward the tomb.

4 And they came running together, but the other disciple outran Peter and arrived at the tomb first.

5 And stooping down, he saw the linen cloths lying there, but he did not enter.

6 Then Simon Peter came up, following him, and went into the tomb and saw the linen cloths lying there;

7 But the burial napkin (kerchief) which had been around Jesus' head, was not lying with the other linen cloths, but was [still] ᵃrolled up (wrapped round and round) in a place by itself.

---

ᵃ 36 Exodus 12:46; Num. 9:12; Psalm 34:20    ᵇ 37 Zech. 12:10
ᶜ 39 Or about 34 kilograms

ᵃ Marvin Vincent, *Word Studies.*

## New International Version

en. ⁸Finally the other disciple, who had reached the tomb first, also went inside. He saw and believed. ⁹(They still did not understand from Scripture that Jesus had to rise from the dead.) ¹⁰Then the disciples went back to where they were staying.

### Jesus Appears to Mary Magdalene

¹¹Now Mary stood outside the tomb crying. As she wept, she bent over to look into the tomb ¹²and saw two angels in white, seated where Jesus' body had been, one at the head and the other at the foot.

¹³They asked her, "Woman, why are you crying?"

"They have taken my Lord away," she said, "and I don't know where they have put him." ¹⁴At this, she turned around and saw Jesus standing there, but she did not realize that it was Jesus.

¹⁵He asked her, "Woman, why are you crying? Who is it you are looking for?"

Thinking he was the gardener, she said, "Sir, if you have carried him away, tell me where you have put him, and I will get him."

¹⁶Jesus said to her, "Mary."

She turned toward him and cried out in Aramaic, "Rabboni!" (which means "Teacher").

¹⁷Jesus said, "Do not hold on to me, for I have not yet ascended to the Father. Go instead to my brothers and tell them, 'I am ascending to my Father and your Father, to my God and your God.'"

¹⁸Mary Magdalene went to the disciples with the news: "I have seen the Lord!" And she told them that he had said these things to her.

### Jesus Appears to His Disciples

¹⁹On the evening of that first day of the week, when the disciples were together, with the doors locked for fear of the Jewish leaders, Jesus came and stood among them and said, "Peace be with you!" ²⁰After he said this, he showed them his hands and side. The disciples were overjoyed when they saw the Lord.

²¹Again Jesus said, "Peace be with you! As the Father has sent me, I am sending you." ²²And with that he breathed on them and said, "Receive the Holy Spirit. ²³If you forgive anyone's sins, their sins are forgiven; if you do not forgive them, they are not forgiven."

### Jesus Appears to Thomas

²⁴Now Thomas (also known as Didymus*ᵃ*), one of the Twelve, was not with the disciples when Jesus came. ²⁵So the other disciples told him, "We have seen the Lord!"

But he said to them, "Unless I see the nail marks in his hands and put my finger where the nails were, and put my hand into his side, I will not believe."

²⁶A week later his disciples were in the house again, and Thomas was with them. Though the doors were locked, Jesus came and stood among them and said, "Peace be with you!" ²⁷Then he said to Thomas, "Put your finger here; see my hands. Reach out your hand and put it into my side. Stop doubting and believe."

²⁸Thomas said to him, "My Lord and my God!"

²⁹Then Jesus told him, "Because you have seen me, you have believed; blessed are those who have not seen and yet have believed."

## Amplified Bible

⁸Then the other disciple, who had reached the tomb first, went in too; and he saw and was convinced *and* believed.

⁹For as yet they did not know (understand) the statement of Scripture that He must rise again from the dead. [Ps. 16:10.]

¹⁰Then the disciples went back again to their homes (lodging places).

¹¹But Mary remained standing outside the tomb sobbing. As she wept, she stooped down [and looked] into the tomb.

¹²And she saw two angels in white sitting there, one at the head and one at the feet, where the body of Jesus had lain.

¹³And they said to her, Woman, why are you sobbing? She told them, Because they have taken away my Lord, and I do not know where they have laid Him.

¹⁴On saying this, she turned around and saw Jesus standing [there], but she did not know (recognize) that it was Jesus.

¹⁵Jesus said to her, Woman, why are you crying [so]? For Whom are you looking? Supposing that it was the gardener, she replied, Sir, if you carried Him away from here, tell me where you have put Him and I will take Him away.

¹⁶Jesus said to her, Mary! Turning around she said to Him in Hebrew, Rabboni!—which means Teacher *or* Master.

¹⁷Jesus said to her, Do not cling to Me [do not hold Me], for I have not yet ascended to the Father. But go to My brethren and tell them, I am ascending to My Father and your Father, and to My God and your God.

¹⁸Away came Mary Magdalene, bringing the disciples news (word) that she had seen the Lord and that He had said these things to her.

¹⁹Then on that same first day of the week, when it was evening, though the disciples were behind closed doors for fear of the Jews, Jesus came and stood among them and said, Peace to you!

²⁰So saying, He showed them His hands and His side. And when the disciples saw the Lord, they were filled with joy (delight, exultation, ecstasy, rapture).

²¹Then Jesus said to them again, Peace to you! [Just] as the Father has sent Me forth, so I am sending you.

²²And having said this, He breathed on them and said to them, Receive the Holy Spirit!

²³[Now having received the Holy Spirit, and being *ᵃ*led and directed by Him] if you forgive the sins of anyone, they are forgiven; if you retain the sins of anyone, they are retained.

²⁴But Thomas, one of the Twelve, called the Twin, was not with them when Jesus came.

²⁵So the other disciples kept telling him, We have seen the Lord! But he said to them, Unless I see in His hands the marks made by the nails and put my finger into the nail prints, and put my hand into His side, I will never believe [it].

²⁶Eight days later His disciples were again in the house, and Thomas was with them. Jesus came, though they were behind closed doors, and stood among them and said, Peace to you!

²⁷Then He said to Thomas, Reach out your finger here, and see My hands; and put out your hand and place [it] in My side. Do not be faithless *and* incredulous, but [stop your unbelief and] believe!

²⁸Thomas answered Him, My Lord and my God!

²⁹Jesus said to him, Because you have seen Me, *Thomas,* do you now believe (trust, have faith)? Blessed *and* happy *and* ᵇto be envied are those who have never seen Me and yet have believed *and* adhered to *and* trusted *and* relied on Me.

---

ᵃ 24 *Thomas* (Aramaic) and *Didymus* (Greek) both mean *twin.*

ᵃ Matthew Henry, *Commentary on the Holy Bible.* ᵇ Alexander Souter, *Pocket Lexicon.*

## New International Version

### The Purpose of John's Gospel

30 Jesus performed many other signs in the presence of his disciples, which are not recorded in this book. 31 But these are written that you may believe*a* that Jesus is the Messiah, the Son of God, and that by believing you may have life in his name.

### Jesus and the Miraculous Catch of Fish

**21** Afterward Jesus appeared again to his disciples, by the Sea of Galilee.*b* It happened this way: 2 Simon Peter, Thomas (also known as Didymus*c*), Nathanael from Cana in Galilee, the sons of Zebedee, and two other disciples were together. 3 "I'm going out to fish," Simon Peter told them, and they said, "We'll go with you." So they went out and got into the boat, but that night they caught nothing.

4 Early in the morning, Jesus stood on the shore, but the disciples did not realize that it was Jesus.

5 He called out to them, "Friends, haven't you any fish?"

"No," they answered.

6 He said, "Throw your net on the right side of the boat and you will find some." When they did, they were unable to haul the net in because of the large number of fish.

7 Then the disciple whom Jesus loved said to Peter, "It is the Lord!" As soon as Simon Peter heard him say, "It is the Lord," he wrapped his outer garment around him (for he had taken it off) and jumped into the water. 8 The other disciples followed in the boat, towing the net full of fish, for they were not far from shore, about a hundred yards.*d* 9 When they landed, they saw a fire of burning coals there with fish on it, and some bread.

10 Jesus said to them, "Bring some of the fish you have just caught." 11 So Simon Peter climbed back into the boat and dragged the net ashore. It was full of large fish, 153, but even with so many the net was not torn. 12 Jesus said to them, "Come and have breakfast." None of the disciples dared ask him, "Who are you?" They knew it was the Lord. 13 Jesus came, took the bread and gave it to them, and did the same with the fish. 14 This was now the third time Jesus appeared to his disciples after he was raised from the dead.

### Jesus Reinstates Peter

15 When they had finished eating, Jesus said to Simon Peter, "Simon son of John, do you love me more than these?"

"Yes, Lord," he said, "you know that I love you."

Jesus said, "Feed my lambs."

16 Again Jesus said, "Simon son of John, do you love me?"

He answered, "Yes, Lord, you know that I love you."

Jesus said, "Take care of my sheep."

17 The third time he said to him, "Simon son of John, do you love me?"

## Amplified Bible

30 There are also many other signs *and* miracles which Jesus performed in the presence of the disciples which are not written in this book.

31 But these are written (recorded) in order that you may believe that Jesus is the Christ (the Anointed One), the Son of God, and that through believing *and* trusting *and* relying upon Him you may have life through (in) His name [*a* through Who He is]. [Ps. 2:7, 12.]

**21** After this, Jesus let Himself be seen *and* revealed [Himself] again to the disciples, at the Sea of Tiberias. And He did it in this way:

2 There were together Simon Peter, and Thomas, called the Twin, and Nathanael from Cana of Galilee, also the sons of Zebedee, and two others of His disciples.

3 Simon Peter said to them, I am going fishing! They said to him, And we are coming with you! So they went out and got into the boat, and throughout that night they caught nothing.

4 Morning was already breaking when Jesus came to the beach and stood there. However, the disciples did not know that it was Jesus.

5 So Jesus said to them, *b* Boys (children), you do not have any meat (fish), do you? [Have you caught anything to eat along with your bread?] They answered Him, No!

6 And He said to them, Cast the net on the right side of the boat and you will find [some]. So they cast the net, and now they were not able to haul it in for such a big catch (mass, quantity) of fish [was in it].

7 Then the disciple whom Jesus loved said to Peter, It is the Lord! Simon Peter, hearing him say that it was the Lord, put (girded) on his upper garment (his fisherman's coat, his outer tunic)—for he was stripped [for work]—and sprang into the sea.

8 And the other disciples came in the small boat, for they were not far from shore, only some hundred yards away, dragging the net full of fish.

9 When they got out on land (the beach), they saw a fire of coals there and fish lying on it [cooking], and bread.

10 Jesus said to them, Bring some of the fish which you have just caught.

11 So Simon Peter went aboard and hauled the net to land, full of large fish, 153 of them; and [though] there were so many of them, the net was not torn.

12 Jesus said to them, Come [and] have breakfast. But none of the disciples ventured *or* dared to ask Him, Who are You? because they [well] knew that it was the Lord.

13 Jesus came and took the bread and gave it to them, and so also [with] the fish.

14 This was now the third time that Jesus revealed Himself (appeared, was manifest) to the disciples after He had risen from the dead.

15 When they had eaten, Jesus said to Simon Peter, Simon, son of John, do you love Me more than these [others do—with reasoning, intentional, spiritual devotion, as one loves the Father]? He said to Him, Yes, Lord, You know that I love You [that I have deep, instinctive, personal affection for You, as for a close friend]. He said to him, Feed My lambs.

16 Again He said to him the second time, Simon, son of John, do you love Me [with reasoning, intentional, spiritual devotion, as one loves the Father]? He said to Him, Yes, Lord, You know that I love You [that I have a deep, instinctive, personal affection for You, as for a close friend]. He said to him, Shepherd (tend) My sheep.

17 He said to him the third time, Simon, son of John, do you love Me [with a deep, instinctive, personal affection for Me, as for a close friend]? Peter was grieved (was saddened and hurt) that He should ask him the third time, Do

---

*a* 31 Or *may continue to believe*    *b* 1 Greek *Tiberias*    *c* 2 *Thomas* (Aramaic) and *Didymus* (Greek) both mean *twin.*    *d* 8 Or about 90 meters

*a* Hermann Cremer, *Biblico-Theological Lexicon.*    *b* Alexander Souter, *Pocket Lexicon.*

## New International Version

Peter was hurt because Jesus asked him the third time, "Do you love me?" He said, "Lord, you know all things; you know that I love you."

Jesus said, "Feed my sheep. [18]Very truly I tell you, when you were younger you dressed yourself and went where you wanted; but when you are old you will stretch out your hands, and someone else will dress you and lead you where you do not want to go." [19]Jesus said this to indicate the kind of death by which Peter would glorify God. Then he said to him, "Follow me!"

[20]Peter turned and saw that the disciple whom Jesus loved was following them. (This was the one who had leaned back against Jesus at the supper and had said, "Lord, who is going to betray you?") [21]When Peter saw him, he asked, "Lord, what about him?"

[22]Jesus answered, "If I want him to remain alive until I return, what is that to you? You must follow me." [23]Because of this, the rumor spread among the believers that this disciple would not die. But Jesus did not say that he would not die; he only said, "If I want him to remain alive until I return, what is that to you?"

[24]This is the disciple who testifies to these things and who wrote them down. We know that his testimony is true.

[25]Jesus did many other things as well. If every one of them were written down, I suppose that even the whole world would not have room for the books that would be written.

## Amplified Bible

you love Me? And he said to Him, Lord, You know everything; You know that I love You [that I have a deep, instinctive, personal affection for You, as for a close friend]. Jesus said to him, Feed My sheep.

[18]I assure you, most solemnly I tell you, when you were young you girded yourself [put on your own belt or girdle] and you walked about wherever you pleased to go. But when you grow old you will stretch out your hands, and someone else will put a girdle around you and carry you where you do not wish to go.

[19]He said this to indicate by what kind of death Peter would glorify God. And after this, He said to him, Follow Me!

[20]But Peter turned and saw the disciple whom Jesus loved, following—the one who also had leaned back on His breast at the supper and had said, Lord, who is it that is going to betray You?

[21]When Peter saw him, he said to Jesus, Lord, what about this man?

[22]Jesus said to him, If I want him to stay (survive, live) until I come, what is that to you? [What concern is it of yours?] You follow Me!

[23]So word went out among the brethren that this disciple was not going to die; yet Jesus did not say to him that he was not going to die, but, If I want him to stay (survive, live) till I come, what is that to you?

[24]It is this same disciple who is bearing witness to these things and who has recorded (written) them; and we [well] know that his testimony is true.

[25]And there are also many other things which Jesus did. If they should be all recorded one by one [in detail], I suppose that even the world itself could not contain (have room for) the books that would be written.

# Acts

## Jesus Taken Up Into Heaven

**1** In my former book, Theophilus, I wrote about all that Jesus began to do and to teach ²until the day he was taken up to heaven, after giving instructions through the Holy Spirit to the apostles he had chosen. ³After his suffering, he presented himself to them and gave many convincing proofs that he was alive. He appeared to them over a period of forty days and spoke about the kingdom of God. ⁴On one occasion, while he was eating with them, he gave them this command: "Do not leave Jerusalem, but wait for the gift my Father promised, which you have heard me speak about. ⁵For John baptized with*a* water, but in a few days you will be baptized with*a* the Holy Spirit."

⁶Then they gathered around him and asked him, "Lord, are you at this time going to restore the kingdom to Israel?"

⁷He said to them: "It is not for you to know the times or dates the Father has set by his own authority. ⁸But you will receive power when the Holy Spirit comes on you; and you will be my witnesses in Jerusalem, and in all Judea and Samaria, and to the ends of the earth."

⁹After he said this, he was taken up before their very eyes, and a cloud hid him from their sight.

¹⁰They were looking intently up into the sky as he was going, when suddenly two men dressed in white stood beside them. ¹¹"Men of Galilee," they said, "why do you stand here looking into the sky? This same Jesus, who has been taken from you into heaven, will come back in the same way you have seen him go into heaven."

## Matthias Chosen to Replace Judas

¹²Then the apostles returned to Jerusalem from the hill called the Mount of Olives, a Sabbath day's walk*b* from the city. ¹³When they arrived, they went upstairs to the room where they were staying. Those present were Peter, John, James and Andrew; Philip and Thomas, Bartholomew and Matthew; James son of Alphaeus and Simon the Zealot, and Judas son of James. ¹⁴They all joined together constantly in prayer, along with the women and Mary the mother of Jesus, and with his brothers.

¹⁵In those days Peter stood up among the believers (a group numbering about a hundred and twenty) ¹⁶and said, "Brothers and sisters,*c* the Scripture had to be fulfilled in which the Holy Spirit spoke long ago through David concerning Judas, who served as guide for those who ar-

**1** In the former account [which I prepared], O Theophilus, I made [a continuous report] dealing with all the things which Jesus began to do and to teach [Luke 1:1-4.]

²Until the day when He ascended, after He through the Holy Spirit had instructed *and* commanded the apostles (special messengers) whom He had chosen.

³To them also He showed Himself alive after His passion (His suffering in the garden and on the cross) by [a series of] many convincing demonstrations [unquestionable evidences and infallible proofs], appearing to them during forty days and talking [to them] about the things of the kingdom of God.

⁴And while being in their company *and* eating with them, He commanded them not to leave Jerusalem but to wait for what the Father had promised, Of which [He said] you have heard Me speak. [John 14:16, 26; 15:26.]

⁵For John baptized with water, but not many days from now you shall be baptized with (*a*placed in, introduced into) the Holy Spirit.

⁶So when they were assembled, they asked Him, Lord, is this the time when You will reestablish the kingdom *and* restore it to Israel?

⁷He said to them, It is not for you to become acquainted with *and* know *b*what time brings [the things and events of time and their definite periods] or fixed *c*years and seasons (their critical niche in time), which the Father has appointed (fixed and reserved) by His own choice *and* authority *and* personal power.

⁸But you shall receive power (ability, efficiency, and might) when the Holy Spirit has come upon you, and you shall be My witnesses in Jerusalem and all Judea and Samaria and to the ends (the very bounds) of the earth.

⁹And when He had said this, even as they were looking [at Him], He was caught up, and a cloud received *and* carried Him away out of their sight.

¹⁰And while they were gazing intently into heaven as He went, behold, two men [dressed] in white robes suddenly stood beside them,

¹¹Who said, Men of Galilee, why do you stand gazing into heaven? This same Jesus, Who was caught away *and* lifted up from among you into heaven, will return in [just] the same way in which you saw Him go into heaven.

¹²Then [the disciples] went back to Jerusalem from the hill called Olivet, which is near Jerusalem, [only] a Sabbath day's journey (three-quarters of a mile) away.

¹³And when they had entered [the city], they mounted [the stairs] to the upper room where they were [*d*indefinitely] staying—Peter and John and James and Andrew; Philip and Thomas, Bartholomew and Matthew; James son of Alphaeus and Simon the Zealot, and Judas [son] of James.

¹⁴All of these with their minds in full agreement devoted themselves steadfastly to prayer, [waiting together] with the women and Mary the mother of Jesus, and with His brothers.

¹⁵Now on one of those days Peter arose among the brethren, the whole number of whom gathered together was about a hundred and twenty.

¹⁶Brethren, he said, it was necessary that the Scripture be fulfilled which the Holy Spirit foretold by the lips of David, about Judas who acted as guide to those who arrested Jesus.

---

*a* 5 Or *in*   *b* 12 That is, about 5/8 mile or about 1 kilometer   *c* 16 The Greek word for *brothers and sisters (adelphoi)* refers here to believers, both men and women, as part of God's family; also in 6:3; 11:29; 12:17; 16:40; 18:18, 27; 21:7, 17; 28:14, 15.

*a* Kenneth Wuest, *Word Studies in the Greek New Testament.* *b* Joseph Thayer, *A Greek-English Lexicon of the New Testament.* *c* Richard Trench, *Synonyms of the New Testament.* *d* James Moulton and George Milligan, *The Vocabulary of the Greek Testament.*

## New International Version

rested Jesus. [17] He was one of our number and shared in our ministry."

[18] (With the payment he received for his wickedness, Judas bought a field; there he fell headlong, his body burst open and all his intestines spilled out. [19] Everyone in Jerusalem heard about this, so they called that field in their language Akeldama, that is, Field of Blood.)

[20] "For," said Peter, "it is written in the Book of Psalms:

"'May his place be deserted;
    let there be no one to dwell in it,'[a]

and,

"'May another take his place of leadership.'[b]

[21] Therefore it is necessary to choose one of the men who have been with us the whole time the Lord Jesus was living among us, [22] beginning from John's baptism to the time when Jesus was taken up from us. For one of these must become a witness with us of his resurrection."

[23] So they nominated two men: Joseph called Barsabbas (also known as Justus) and Matthias. [24] Then they prayed, "Lord, you know everyone's heart. Show us which of these two you have chosen [25] to take over this apostolic ministry, which Judas left to go where he belongs." [26] Then they cast lots, and the lot fell to Matthias; so he was added to the eleven apostles.

### The Holy Spirit Comes at Pentecost

2 When the day of Pentecost came, they were all together in one place. [2] Suddenly a sound like the blowing of a violent wind came from heaven and filled the whole house where they were sitting. [3] They saw what seemed to be tongues of fire that separated and came to rest on each of them. [4] All of them were filled with the Holy Spirit and began to speak in other tongues[c] as the Spirit enabled them.

[5] Now there were staying in Jerusalem God-fearing Jews from every nation under heaven. [6] When they heard this sound, a crowd came together in bewilderment, because each one heard their own language being spoken. [7] Utterly amazed, they asked: "Aren't all these who are speaking Galileans? [8] Then how is it that each of us hears them in our native language? [9] Parthians, Medes and Elamites; residents of Mesopotamia, Judea and Cappadocia, Pontus and Asia,[d] [10] Phrygia and Pamphylia, Egypt and the parts of Libya near Cyrene; visitors from Rome [11] (both Jews and converts to Judaism); Cretans and Arabs—we hear them declaring the wonders of God in our own tongues!"

## Amplified Bible

[17] For he was counted among us and received [by divine allotment] his portion in this ministry.

[18] Now this man obtained a piece of land with the [money paid him as a] reward for his treachery *and* wickedness, and falling headlong he burst open in the middle [of his body] and all his intestines poured forth.

[19] And all the residents of Jerusalem became acquainted with the facts, so that they called the piece of land in their own dialect—Akeldama, that is, Field of Blood.

[20] For in the book of Psalms it is written, Let his place of residence become deserted *and* gloomy, and let there be no one to live in it; and [again], Let another take his position *or* overseership. [Ps. 69:25; 109:8.]

[21] So one of the [other] men who have accompanied us [apostles] during all the time that the Lord Jesus went in and out among us,

[22] From the baptism of John at the outset until the day when He was taken up from among us—one of these men must join with us and become a witness to testify to His resurrection.

[23] And they accordingly proposed (nominated) two men, Joseph called Barsabbas, who was surnamed Justus, and Matthias.

[24] And they prayed and said, You, Lord, Who know all hearts (a their thoughts, passions, desires, appetites, purposes, and endeavors), indicate to us which one of these two You have chosen

[25] To take the place in this ministry and receive the position of an apostle, from which Judas fell away *and* went astray to go [where he belonged] to his own [proper] place.

[26] And they drew lots [between the two], and the lot fell on Matthias; and he was added to *and* counted with the eleven apostles (special messengers).

2 And when the day of Pentecost had fully come, they were all assembled together in one place,

[2] When suddenly there came a sound from heaven like the rushing of a violent tempest blast, and it filled the whole house in which they were sitting.

[3] And there appeared to them tongues resembling fire, which were separated *and* distributed and which settled on each one of them.

[4] And they were all filled (diffused throughout their souls) with the Holy Spirit and began to speak in other (different, foreign) languages (tongues), as the Spirit *b* kept giving them clear *and* loud expression [in each tongue in appropriate words].

[5] Now there were then residing in Jerusalem Jews, devout *and* God-fearing men from every country under heaven.

[6] And when this sound was heard, the multitude came together and they were astonished *and* bewildered, because each one heard them [the apostles] speaking in his own [particular] dialect.

[7] And they were beside themselves with amazement, saying, Are not all these who are talking Galileans?

[8] Then how is it that we hear, each of us, in our own (particular) dialect to which we were born?

[9] Parthians and Medes and Elamites and inhabitants of Mesopotamia, Judea and Cappadocia, Pontus and [the province of] Asia,

[10] Phrygia and Pamphylia, Egypt and the parts of Libya about Cyrene, and the transient residents from Rome, both Jews and the proselytes [to Judaism from other religions],

[11] Cretans and Arabians too—we all hear them speaking in our own native tongues [and telling of] the mighty works of God!

---

*a* 20 Psalm 69:25    *b* 20 Psalm 109:8    *c* 4 Or *languages*; also in verse 11    *d* 9 That is, the Roman province by that name

*a* Joseph Thayer, *A Greek-English Lexicon.*  *b* Marvin Vincent, *Word Studies in the New Testament.*

## New International Version

¹²Amazed and perplexed, they asked one another, "What does this mean?"

¹³Some, however, made fun of them and said, "They have had too much wine."

### Peter Addresses the Crowd

¹⁴Then Peter stood up with the Eleven, raised his voice and addressed the crowd: "Fellow Jews and all of you who live in Jerusalem, let me explain this to you; listen carefully to what I say. ¹⁵These people are not drunk, as you suppose. It's only nine in the morning! ¹⁶No, this is what was spoken by the prophet Joel:

¹⁷"'In the last days, God says,
    I will pour out my Spirit on all people.
Your sons and daughters will prophesy,
    your young men will see visions,
    your old men will dream dreams.
¹⁸Even on my servants, both men and women,
    I will pour out my Spirit in those days,
    and they will prophesy.
¹⁹I will show wonders in the heavens above
    and signs on the earth below,
    blood and fire and billows of smoke.
²⁰The sun will be turned to darkness
    and the moon to blood
    before the coming of the great and glorious day of
        the Lord.
²¹And everyone who calls
    on the name of the Lord will be saved.'ᵃ

²²"Fellow Israelites, listen to this: Jesus of Nazareth was a man accredited by God to you by miracles, wonders and signs, which God did among you through him, as you yourselves know. ²³This man was handed over to you by God's deliberate plan and foreknowledge; and you, with the help of wicked men,ᵇ put him to death by nailing him to the cross. ²⁴But God raised him from the dead, freeing him from the agony of death, because it was impossible for death to keep its hold on him. ²⁵David said about him:

"'I saw the Lord always before me.
    Because he is at my right hand,
    I will not be shaken.
²⁶Therefore my heart is glad and my tongue rejoices;
    my body also will rest in hope,
²⁷because you will not abandon me to the realm of the
        dead,
    you will not let your holy one see decay.
²⁸You have made known to me the paths of life;
    you will fill me with joy in your presence.'ᶜ

²⁹"Fellow Israelites, I can tell you confidently that the patriarch David died and was buried, and his tomb is here to this day. ³⁰But he was a prophet and knew that God had promised him on oath that he would place one of his descendants on his throne. ³¹Seeing what was to come, he spoke of the resurrection of the Messiah, that he was not abandoned to the realm of the dead, nor did his body see

## Amplified Bible

¹²And all were beside themselves with amazement and were puzzled *and* bewildered, saying one to another, What can this mean?

¹³But others made a joke of it *and* derisively said, They are simply drunk *and* full of sweet [intoxicating] wine.

¹⁴But Peter, standing with the eleven, raised his voice and addressed them: You Jews and all you residents of Jerusalem, let this be [explained] to you so that you will know *and* understand; listen closely to what I have to say.

¹⁵For these men are not drunk, as you imagine, for it is [only] the third hour (about 9:00 a.m.) of the day;

¹⁶But [instead] this is [the beginning of] what was spoken through the prophet Joel:

¹⁷And it shall come to pass in the last days, God declares, that I will pour out of My Spirit upon all mankind, and your sons and your daughters shall prophesy [ᵃtelling forth the divine counsels] and your young men shall see visions (ᵇ divinely granted appearances), and your old men shall dream [ᵇdivinely suggested] dreams.

¹⁸Yes, and on My menservants also and on My maidservants in those days I will pour out of My Spirit, and they shall prophesy [ᵃtelling forth the divine counsels and ᵇpredicting future events pertaining especially to God's kingdom].

¹⁹And I will show wonders in the sky above and signs on the earth beneath, blood and fire and smoking vapor;

²⁰The sun shall be turned into darkness and the moon into blood before the obvious day of the Lord comes—that great and notable *and* conspicuous and renowned [day].

²¹And it shall be that whoever shall call upon the name of the Lord [ᵇinvoking, adoring, and worshiping the Lord—Christ] shall be saved. [Joel 2:28-32.]

²²You men of Israel, listen to what I have to say: Jesus of Nazareth, a Man accredited *and* pointed out *and* shown forth *and* commended *and* attested to you by God by the mighty works and [the power of performing] wonders and signs which God worked through Him [right] in your midst, as you yourselves know—

²³This Jesus, when delivered up according to the definite *and* fixed purpose *and* settled plan and foreknowledge of God, you crucified *and* put out of the way [killing Him] by the hands of lawless *and* wicked men.

²⁴[But] God raised Him up, liberating Him from the pangs of death, seeing that it was not possible for Him to continue to be controlled *or* retained by it.

²⁵For David says in regard to Him, I saw the Lord constantly before me, for He is at my right hand that I may not be shaken *or* overthrown *or* cast down [from my secure and happy state].

²⁶Therefore my heart rejoiced and my tongue exulted exceedingly; moreover, my flesh also will dwell in hope [will encamp, pitch its tent, and dwell in hope in anticipation of the resurrection].

²⁷For You will not abandon my soul, leaving it helpless in Hades (the state of departed spirits), nor let Your Holy One know decay *or* see destruction [of the body after death].

²⁸You have made known to me the ways of life; You will enrapture me [diffusing my soul with joy] with *and* in Your presence. [Ps. 16:8-11.]

²⁹Brethren, it is permitted me to tell you confidently *and* with freedom concerning the patriarch David that he both died and was buried, and his tomb is with us to this day.

³⁰Being however a prophet, and knowing that God had sealed to him with an oath that He would set one of his descendants on his throne, [II Sam. 7:12-16; Ps. 132:11.]

³¹He, foreseeing this, spoke [by foreknowledge] of the resurrection of the Christ (the Messiah) that He was not deserted [in death] *and* left in Hades (the state of departed spirits), nor did His body know decay *or* see destruction. [Ps. 16:10.]

---

ᵃ *21* Joel 2:28-32    ᵇ *23* Or *of those not having the law* (that is, Gentiles)
ᶜ *28* Psalm 16:8-11 (see Septuagint)

ᵃ G. Abbott-Smith, *Manual Greek Lexicon of the New Testament.*    ᵇ Joseph Thayer, *A Greek-English Lexicon.*

## New International Version

decay. <sup>32</sup>God has raised this Jesus to life, and we are all witnesses of it. <sup>33</sup>Exalted to the right hand of God, he has received from the Father the promised Holy Spirit and has poured out what you now see and hear. <sup>34</sup>For David did not ascend to heaven, and yet he said,

"'The Lord said to my Lord:
"Sit at my right hand
<sup>35</sup>until I make your enemies
a footstool for your feet."'<sup>a</sup>

<sup>36</sup>"Therefore let all Israel be assured of this: God has made this Jesus, whom you crucified, both Lord and Messiah."

<sup>37</sup>When the people heard this, they were cut to the heart and said to Peter and the other apostles, "Brothers, what shall we do?"

<sup>38</sup>Peter replied, "Repent and be baptized, every one of you, in the name of Jesus Christ for the forgiveness of your sins. And you will receive the gift of the Holy Spirit. <sup>39</sup>The promise is for you and your children and for all who are far off—for all whom the Lord our God will call."

<sup>40</sup>With many other words he warned them; and he pleaded with them, "Save yourselves from this corrupt generation." <sup>41</sup>Those who accepted his message were baptized, and about three thousand were added to their number that day.

### The Fellowship of the Believers

<sup>42</sup>They devoted themselves to the apostles' teaching and to fellowship, to the breaking of bread and to prayer. <sup>43</sup>Everyone was filled with awe at the many wonders and signs performed by the apostles. <sup>44</sup>All the believers were together and had everything in common. <sup>45</sup>They sold property and possessions to give to anyone who had need. <sup>46</sup>Every day they continued to meet together in the temple courts. They broke bread in their homes and ate together with glad and sincere hearts, <sup>47</sup>praising God and enjoying the favor of all the people. And the Lord added to their number daily those who were being saved.

### Peter Heals a Lame Beggar

**3** One day Peter and John were going up to the temple at the time of prayer—at three in the afternoon. <sup>2</sup>Now a man who was lame from birth was being carried to the temple gate called Beautiful, where he was put every day to beg from those going into the temple courts. <sup>3</sup>When he saw Peter and John about to enter, he asked them for money. <sup>4</sup>Peter looked straight at him, as did John. Then Peter

## Amplified Bible

<sup>32</sup>This Jesus God raised up, and of that all we [His disciples] are witnesses.

<sup>33</sup>Being therefore lifted high by *and* to the right hand of God, and having received from the Father <sup>a</sup>the promised [blessing which is the] Holy Spirit, He has made this outpouring which you yourselves both see and hear.

<sup>34</sup>For David did not ascend into the heavens; yet he himself says, The Lord said to my Lord, Sit at My right hand *and* share My throne

<sup>35</sup>Until I make Your enemies a footstool for Your feet. [Ps. 110:1.]

<sup>36</sup>Therefore let the whole house of Israel recognize beyond all doubt *and* acknowledge assuredly that God has made Him both Lord and Christ (the Messiah)—this Jesus Whom you crucified.

<sup>37</sup>Now when they heard this they were stung (cut) to the heart, and they said to Peter and the rest of the apostles (special messengers), Brethren, what shall we do?

<sup>38</sup>And Peter answered them, Repent (change your views and purpose to accept the will of God in your inner selves instead of rejecting it) and be baptized, every one of you, in the name of Jesus Christ for the forgiveness of *and* release from your sins; and you shall receive the gift of the Holy Spirit.

<sup>39</sup>For the promise [of the Holy Spirit] is to *and* for you and your children, and to *and* for all that are far away, [even] to *and* for as many as the Lord our God invites *and* bids to come to Himself. [Isa. 57:19; Joel 2:32.]

<sup>40</sup>And [Peter] <sup>b</sup>solemnly *and* earnestly witnessed (testified) and admonished (exhorted) with much more continuous speaking *and* warned (reproved, advised, encouraged) them, saying, Be saved from this crooked (perverse, wicked, unjust) generation.

<sup>41</sup>Therefore those who accepted *and* welcomed his message were baptized, and there were added that day about 3,000 souls.

<sup>42</sup>And they steadfastly persevered, devoting themselves constantly to the instruction and fellowship of the apostles, to the breaking of bread [including the Lord's Supper] and prayers.

<sup>43</sup>And a sense of awe (reverential fear) came upon every soul, and many wonders and signs were performed through the apostles (the special messengers).

<sup>44</sup>And all who believed (who adhered to and trusted in and relied on Jesus Christ) were united and [together] they had everything in common;

<sup>45</sup>And they sold their possessions (both their landed property and their movable goods) and distributed the price among all, according as any had need.

<sup>46</sup>And day after day they regularly assembled in the temple with united purpose, and in their homes they broke bread [including the Lord's Supper]. They partook of their food with gladness and simplicity *and* generous hearts,

<sup>47</sup>Constantly praising God and being in favor *and* goodwill with all the people; and the Lord kept adding [to their number] daily those who were being saved [from spiritual death].

**3** Now Peter and John were going up to the temple at the hour of prayer, the ninth hour (three o'clock in the afternoon),

<sup>2</sup>[When] a certain man crippled from his birth was being carried along, who was laid each day at that gate of the temple [which is] called Beautiful, so that he might beg for charitable gifts from those who entered the temple.

<sup>3</sup>So when he saw Peter and John about to go into the temple, he asked them to give him a gift.

<sup>4</sup>And Peter directed his gaze intently at him, and so did John, and said, Look at us!

---

<sup>a</sup> 35 Psalm 110:1

<sup>a</sup> Joseph Thayer, *A Greek-English Lexicon.* <sup>b</sup> Marvin Vincent, *Word Studies:* The preposition *dia* gives this force.

## New International Version

said, "Look at us!" 5So the man gave them his attention, expecting to get something from them.

6Then Peter said, "Silver or gold I do not have, but what I do have I give you. In the name of Jesus Christ of Nazareth, walk." 7Taking him by the right hand, he helped him up, and instantly the man's feet and ankles became strong. 8He jumped to his feet and began to walk. Then he went with them into the temple courts, walking and jumping, and praising God. 9When all the people saw him walking and praising God, 10they recognized him as the same man who used to sit begging at the temple gate called Beautiful, and they were filled with wonder and amazement at what had happened to him.

### Peter Speaks to the Onlookers

11While the man held on to Peter and John, all the people were astonished and came running to them in the place called Solomon's Colonnade. 12When Peter saw this, he said to them: "Fellow Israelites, why does this surprise you? Why do you stare at us as if by our own power or godliness we had made this man walk? 13The God of Abraham, Isaac and Jacob, the God of our fathers, has glorified his servant Jesus. You handed him over to be killed, and you disowned him before Pilate, though he had decided to let him go. 14You disowned the Holy and Righteous One and asked that a murderer be released to you. 15You killed the author of life, but God raised him from the dead. We are witnesses of this. 16By faith in the name of Jesus, this man whom you see and know was made strong. It is Jesus' name and the faith that comes through him that has completely healed him, as you can all see.

17"Now, fellow Israelites, I know that you acted in ignorance, as did your leaders. 18But this is how God fulfilled what he had foretold through all the prophets, saying that his Messiah would suffer. 19Repent, then, and turn to God, so that your sins may be wiped out, that times of refreshing may come from the Lord, 20and that he may send the Messiah, who has been appointed for you—even Jesus. 21Heaven must receive him until the time comes for God to restore everything, as he promised long ago through his holy prophets. 22For Moses said, 'The Lord your God will raise up for you a prophet like me from among your own people; you must listen to everything he tells you. 23Anyone who does not listen to him will be completely cut off from their people.'a

24"Indeed, beginning with Samuel, all the prophets who

## Amplified Bible

5And [the man] paid attention to them, expecting that he was going to get something from them.

6But Peter said, Silver and gold (money) I do not have; but what I do have, that I give to you: in [the ause of] the name of Jesus Christ of Nazareth, walk!

7Then he took hold of the man's right hand with a firm grip and raised him up. And at once his feet and ankle bones became strong and steady,

8And leaping forth he stood and bbegan to walk, and he went into the temple with them, walking and leaping and praising God.

9And all the people saw him walking about and praising God,

10And they recognized him as the man who usually sat [begging] for alms at the Beautiful Gate of the temple; and they were filled with wonder and amazement (bewilderment, consternation) over what had occurred to him.

11Now while he [still] firmly clung to Peter and John, all the people in utmost amazement ran together and crowded around them in the covered porch (walk) called Solomon's.

12And Peter, seeing it, answered the people, You men of Israel, why are you so surprised and wondering at this? Why do you keep staring at us, as though by our [own individual] power or [active] piety we had made this man [able] to walk?

13The God of Abraham and of Isaac and of Jacob, the God of our forefathers, has glorified His Servant and cSon Jesus [doing Him this honor], Whom you indeed delivered up and denied and rejected and disowned in the presence of Pilate, when he had determined to let Him go. [Exod. 3:6; Isa. 52:13.]

14But you denied and rejected and disowned the Pure and Holy, the Just and Blameless One, and demanded [the pardon of] a murderer to be granted to you.

15But you killed the very Source (the Author) of life, Whom God raised from the dead. To this we are witnesses.

16And His name, through and by faith in His name, has made this man whom you see and recognize well and strong. [Yes] the faith which is through and by Him [Jesus] has given the man this perfect soundness [of body] before all of you.

17And now, brethren, I know that you acted in ignorance [not aware of what you were doing], as did your rulers also.

18Thus has God fulfilled what He foretold by the mouth of all the prophets, that His Christ (the Messiah) should undergo ill treatment and be afflicted and suffer.

19So repent (change your mind and purpose); turn around and return [to God], that your sins may be erased (blotted out, wiped clean), that times of refreshing (of recovering from the effects of heat, of breviving with fresh air) may come from the presence of the Lord;

20And that He may send [to you] the Christ (the Messiah), Who before was designated and appointed for you—even Jesus,

21Whom heaven must receive [and retain] until the time for the complete restoration of all that God spoke by the mouth of all His holy prophets for ages past [from the most ancient time in the memory of man].

22Thus Moses said to the forefathers, The Lord God will raise up for you a Prophet from among your brethren as [He raised up] me; Him you shall listen to and understand by hearing and heed in all things whatever He tells you.

23And it shall be that every soul that does not listen to and understand by hearing and heed that Prophet shall be utterly dexterminated from among the people. [Deut. 18:15-19.]

24Indeed, all the prophets from Samuel and those who

---

a Joseph Thayer, A Greek-English Lexicon. b Marvin Vincent, Word Studies. c The Greek word used here means both "Servant" and "Child" ("Son"). d Alexander Souter, Pocket Lexicon of the Greek New Testament.

# New International Version

have spoken have foretold these days. 25And you are heirs of the prophets and of the covenant God made with your fathers. He said to Abraham, 'Through your offspring all peoples on earth will be blessed.'*a* 26When God raised up his servant, he sent him first to you to bless you by turning each of you from your wicked ways."

## Peter and John Before the Sanhedrin

**4** The priests and the captain of the temple guard and the Sadducees came up to Peter and John while they were speaking to the people. 2They were greatly disturbed because the apostles were teaching the people, proclaiming in Jesus the resurrection of the dead. 3They seized Peter and John and, because it was evening, they put them in jail until the next day. 4But many who heard the message believed; so the number of men who believed grew to about five thousand.

5The next day the rulers, the elders and the teachers of the law met in Jerusalem. 6Annas the high priest was there, and so were Caiaphas, John, Alexander and others of the high priest's family. 7They had Peter and John brought before them and began to question them: "By what power or what name did you do this?"

8Then Peter, filled with the Holy Spirit, said to them: "Rulers and elders of the people! 9If we are being called to account today for an act of kindness shown to a man who was lame and are being asked how he was healed, 10then know this, you and all the people of Israel: It is by the name of Jesus Christ of Nazareth, whom you crucified but whom God raised from the dead, that this man stands before you healed. 11Jesus is

"'the stone you builders rejected,
   which has become the cornerstone.'*b*

12Salvation is found in no one else, for there is no other name under heaven given to mankind by which we must be saved."

13When they saw the courage of Peter and John and realized that they were unschooled, ordinary men, they were astonished and they took note that these men had been with Jesus. 14But since they could see the man who had been healed standing there with them, there was nothing they could say. 15So they ordered them to withdraw from the Sanhedrin and then conferred together. 16"What are we going to do with these men?" they asked. "Everyone living in Jerusalem knows they have performed a notable sign, and we cannot deny it. 17But to stop this thing from spreading any further among the people, we must warn them to speak no longer to anyone in this name."

# Amplified Bible

came afterwards, as many as have spoken, also promised *and* foretold *and* proclaimed these days.

25You are the descendants (sons) of the prophets and the heirs of the covenant which God made *and* gave to your forefathers, saying to Abraham, And in your Seed (Heir) shall all the families of the earth be blessed *and* benefited. [Gen. 22:18; Gal. 3:16.]

26It was to you first that God sent His Servant *and* Son *Jesus,* when He raised Him up [*a*provided and gave Him for us], to bless you in turning every one of you from your wickedness *and* evil ways. [Acts 2:24; 3:22.]

**4** And while they [Peter and John] were talking to the people, the high priests and the military commander of the temple and the Sadducees came upon them,

2Being vexed *and* indignant through *and* through because they were teaching the people *and* proclaiming in [the case of] Jesus the resurrection from the dead.

3So they laid hands on them (arrested them) and put them in prison until the following day, for it was already evening.

4But many of those who heard the message believed (adhered to and trusted in and relied on Jesus as the Christ). And their number grew *and* came to about 5,000.

5Then on the following day, their magistrates and elders and scribes were assembled in Jerusalem,

6Including Annas the high priest and Caiaphas and John and Alexander and all others who belonged to the high priestly relationship.

7And they set the men in their midst and repeatedly demanded, By what sort of power or by what kind of authority did [such people as] you do this [healing]?

8Then Peter, [because he was] filled with [and controlled by] the Holy Spirit, said to them, Rulers of the people and members of the council (the Sanhedrin),

9If we are being put on trial [here] today *and* examined concerning a good deed done to benefit a feeble (helpless) cripple, by what means this man has been restored to health,

10Let it be known *and* understood by all of you, and by the whole house of Israel, that in the name and through the power *and* authority of Jesus Christ of Nazareth, Whom you crucified, [but] Whom God raised from the dead, in Him *and* by means of Him this man is standing here before you well *and* sound in body.

11This [Jesus] is the Stone which was despised *and* rejected by you, the builders, but which has become the Head of the corner [the Cornerstone]. [Ps. 118:22.]

12And there is salvation in *and* through no one else, for there is no other name under heaven given among men by *and* in which we must be saved.

13Now when they saw the boldness *and* unfettered eloquence of Peter and John and perceived that they were unlearned *and* untrained in the schools [common men with no educational advantages], they marveled; and they recognized that they had been with Jesus.

14And since they saw the man who had been cured standing there beside them, they could not contradict the fact *or* say anything in opposition.

15But having ordered [the prisoners] to go aside out of the council [chamber], they conferred (debated) among themselves,

16Saying, What are we to do with these men? For that an extraordinary miracle has been performed by (through) them is plain to all the residents of Jerusalem, and we cannot deny it.

17But in order that it may not spread further among the people *and* the nation, let us warn *and* forbid them with a stern threat to speak any more to anyone in this name [or about this Person].

*a* Robert Jamieson, A. R. Fausett and David Brown, *A Commentary on the Old and New Testaments.*

*a 25* Gen. 22:18; 26:4    *b 11* Psalm 118:22

## New International Version

[18]Then they called them in again and commanded them not to speak or teach at all in the name of Jesus. [19]But Peter and John replied, "Which is right in God's eyes: to listen to you, or to him? You be the judges! [20]As for us, we cannot help speaking about what we have seen and heard."

[21]After further threats they let them go. They could not decide how to punish them, because all the people were praising God for what had happened. [22]For the man who was miraculously healed was over forty years old.

### The Believers Pray

[23]On their release, Peter and John went back to their own people and reported all that the chief priests and the elders had said to them. [24]When they heard this, they raised their voices together in prayer to God. "Sovereign Lord," they said, "you made the heavens and the earth and the sea, and everything in them. [25]You spoke by the Holy Spirit through the mouth of your servant, our father David:

"'Why do the nations rage
    and the peoples plot in vain?
[26]The kings of the earth rise up
    and the rulers band together
against the Lord
    and against his anointed one.[a][b]

[27]Indeed Herod and Pontius Pilate met together with the Gentiles and the people of Israel in this city to conspire against your holy servant Jesus, whom you anointed. [28]They did what your power and will had decided beforehand should happen. [29]Now, Lord, consider their threats and enable your servants to speak your word with great boldness. [30]Stretch out your hand to heal and perform signs and wonders through the name of your holy servant Jesus."

[31]After they prayed, the place where they were meeting was shaken. And they were all filled with the Holy Spirit and spoke the word of God boldly.

### The Believers Share Their Possessions

[32]All the believers were one in heart and mind. No one claimed that any of their possessions was their own, but they shared everything they had. [33]With great power the apostles continued to testify to the resurrection of the Lord Jesus. And God's grace was so powerfully at work in them all [34]that there were no needy persons among them. For from time to time those who owned land or houses sold them, brought the money from the sales [35]and put it at the apostles' feet, and it was distributed to anyone who had need.

[36]Joseph, a Levite from Cyprus, whom the apostles called Barnabas (which means "son of encouragement"), [37]sold a field he owned and brought the money and put it at the apostles' feet.

## Amplified Bible

[18][So] they summoned them and imperatively instructed them not to converse in any way or teach at all in or about the name of Jesus.

[19]But Peter and John replied to them, Whether it is right in the sight of God to listen to you and obey you rather than God, you must decide (judge).

[20]But we [ourselves] cannot help telling what we have seen and heard.

[21]Then when [the rulers and council members] had further threatened them, they let them go, not seeing how they could secure a conviction against them because of the people; for everybody was praising and glorifying God for what had occurred.

[22]For the man on whom this sign (miracle) of healing was performed was more than forty years old.

[23]After they were permitted to go, [the apostles] returned to their own [company] and told all that the chief priests and elders had said to them.

[24]And when they heard it, lifted their voices together with one united mind to God and said, O Sovereign Lord, You are He Who made the heaven and the earth and the sea and everything that is in them, [Exod. 20:11; Ps. 146:6.]

[25]Who by the mouth of our forefather David, Your servant and child, said through the Holy Spirit, Why did the heathen (Gentiles) become wanton and insolent and rage, and the people imagine and study and plan vain (fruitless) things [that will not succeed]?

[26]The kings of the earth took their stand in array [for attack] and the rulers were assembled and combined together against the Lord and against His Anointed (Christ, the Messiah). [Ps. 2:1, 2.]

[27]For in this city there actually met and plotted together against Your holy Child and Servant Jesus, Whom You consecrated by anointing, both Herod and Pontius Pilate with the Gentiles and peoples of Israel, [Ps. 2:1, 2.]

[28]To carry out all that Your hand and Your will and purpose had predestined (predetermined) should occur.

[29]And now, Lord, observe their threats and grant to Your bond servants [full freedom] to declare Your message fearlessly,

[30]While You stretch out Your hand to cure and to perform signs and wonders through the authority and by the power of the name of Your holy Child and Servant Jesus.

[31]And when they had prayed, the place in which they were assembled was shaken; and they were all filled with the Holy Spirit, and they continued to speak the Word of God with freedom and boldness and courage.

[32]Now the company of believers was of one heart and soul, and not one of them claimed that anything which he possessed was [exclusively] his own, but everything they had was in common and for the use of all.

[33]And with great strength and ability and power the apostles delivered their testimony to the resurrection of the Lord Jesus, and great grace (loving-kindness and favor and goodwill) rested richly upon them all.

[34]Nor was there a destitute or needy person among them, for as many as were owners of lands or houses proceeded to sell them, and one by one they brought (gave back) the amount received from the sales

[35]And laid it at the feet of the apostles (special messengers). Then distribution was made according as anyone had need.

[36]Now Joseph, a Levite and native of Cyprus who was surnamed Barnabas by the apostles, which interpreted means Son of Encouragement,

[37]Sold a field which belonged to him and brought the sum of money and laid it at the feet of the apostles.

---

[a] 26 That is, Messiah or Christ    [b] 26 Psalm 2:1,2

## New International Version

### Ananias and Sapphira

**5** Now a man named Ananias, together with his wife Sapphira, also sold a piece of property. ²With his wife's full knowledge he kept back part of the money for himself, but brought the rest and put it at the apostles' feet.

³Then Peter said, "Ananias, how is it that Satan has so filled your heart that you have lied to the Holy Spirit and have kept for yourself some of the money you received for the land? ⁴Didn't it belong to you before it was sold? And after it was sold, wasn't the money at your disposal? What made you think of doing such a thing? You have not lied just to human beings but to God."

⁵When Ananias heard this, he fell down and died. And great fear seized all who heard what had happened. ⁶Then some young men came forward, wrapped up his body, and carried him out and buried him.

⁷About three hours later his wife came in, not knowing what had happened. ⁸Peter asked her, "Tell me, is this the price you and Ananias got for the land?"

"Yes," she said, "that is the price."

⁹Peter said to her, "How could you conspire to test the Spirit of the Lord? Listen! The feet of the men who buried your husband are at the door, and they will carry you out also."

¹⁰At that moment she fell down at his feet and died. Then the young men came in and, finding her dead, carried her out and buried her beside her husband. ¹¹Great fear seized the whole church and all who heard about these events.

### The Apostles Heal Many

¹²The apostles performed many signs and wonders among the people. And all the believers used to meet together in Solomon's Colonnade. ¹³No one else dared join them, even though they were highly regarded by the people. ¹⁴Nevertheless, more and more men and women believed in the Lord and were added to their number. ¹⁵As a result, people brought the sick into the streets and laid them on beds and mats so that at least Peter's shadow might fall on some of them as he passed by. ¹⁶Crowds gathered also from the towns around Jerusalem, bringing their sick and those tormented by impure spirits, and all of them were healed.

### The Apostles Persecuted

¹⁷Then the high priest and all his associates, who were members of the party of the Sadducees, were filled with jealousy. ¹⁸They arrested the apostles and put them in the public jail. ¹⁹But during the night an angel of the Lord opened the doors of the jail and brought them out. ²⁰"Go, stand in the temple courts," he said, "and tell the people all about this new life."

²¹At daybreak they entered the temple courts, as they had been told, and began to teach the people.

When the high priest and his associates arrived, they

## Amplified Bible

**5** But a certain man named Ananias with his wife Sapphira sold a piece of property,

²And with his wife's knowledge *and* connivance he kept back *and* wrongfully appropriated some of the proceeds, bringing only a part and putting it at the feet of the apostles.

³But Peter said, Ananias, why has Satan filled your heart that you should lie to *and* attempt to deceive the Holy Spirit, and should [in violation of your promise] withdraw secretly *and* appropriate to your own use part of the price from the sale of the land?

⁴As long as it remained unsold, was it not still your own? And [even] after it was sold, was not [the money] at your disposal *and* under your control? Why then, is it that you have proposed *and* purposed in your heart to do this thing? [How could you have the heart to do such a deed?] You have not [simply] lied to men [playing false and showing yourself utterly deceitful] but to God.

⁵Upon hearing these words, Ananias fell down and died. And great dread *and* terror took possession of all who heard of it.

⁶And the young men arose and wrapped up [the body] and carried it out and buried it.

⁷Now after an interval of about three hours his wife came in, not having learned of what had happened.

⁸And Peter said to her, Tell me, did you sell the land for so much? Yes, she said, for so much.

⁹Then Peter said to her, How could you two have agreed *and* conspired together to try to deceive the Spirit of the Lord? Listen! The feet of those who have buried your husband are at the door, and they will carry you out [also].

¹⁰And instantly she fell down at his feet and died; and the young men entering found her dead, and they carried her out and buried her beside her husband.

¹¹And the whole church and all others who heard of these things were appalled [great awe and strange terror and dread seized them].

¹²Now by the hands of the apostles (special messengers) numerous *and* startling signs *and* wonders were being performed among the people. And by common consent they all met together [at the temple] in the covered porch (walk) called Solomon's.

¹³And none of those who were not of their number dared to join *and* associate with them, but the people held them in high regard *and* praised *and* made much of them.

¹⁴More *and* more there were being added to the Lord those who believed [those who acknowledged Jesus as their Savior and devoted themselves to Him joined and gathered with them], crowds both of men and of women,

¹⁵So that they [even] kept carrying out the sick into the streets and placing them on couches and sleeping pads, [in the hope] that as Peter passed by, at least his shadow might fall on some of them.

¹⁶And the people gathered also from the towns *and* hamlets around Jerusalem, bringing the sick and those troubled with foul spirits, and they were all cured.

¹⁷But the high priest rose up and all who were his supporters, that is, the party of the Sadducees, and being filled with *a*jealousy *and* indignation *and* rage,

¹⁸They seized and arrested the apostles (special messengers) and put them in the public jail.

¹⁹But during the night an angel of the Lord opened the prison doors and, leading them out, said,

²⁰Go, take your stand in the temple courts and declare to the people the whole doctrine concerning this Life (the eternal life which Christ revealed).

²¹And when they heard this, they accordingly went into the temple about daybreak and began to teach. Now the high priest and his supporters who were with him arrived and called together the council (Sanhedrin), even all the

---

*a* G. Abbott-Smith, *Manual Greek Lexicon.*

## New International Version

called together the Sanhedrin—the full assembly of the elders of Israel—and sent to the jail for the apostles. ²²But on arriving at the jail, the officers did not find them there. So they went back and reported, ²³"We found the jail securely locked, with the guards standing at the doors; but when we opened them, we found no one inside." ²⁴On hearing this report, the captain of the temple guard and the chief priests were at a loss, wondering what this might lead to.

²⁵Then someone came and said, "Look! The men you put in jail are standing in the temple courts teaching the people." ²⁶At that, the captain went with his officers and brought the apostles. They did not use force, because they feared that the people would stone them.

²⁷The apostles were brought in and made to appear before the Sanhedrin to be questioned by the high priest. ²⁸"We gave you strict orders not to teach in this name," he said. "Yet you have filled Jerusalem with your teaching and are determined to make us guilty of this man's blood."

²⁹Peter and the other apostles replied: "We must obey God rather than human beings! ³⁰The God of our ancestors raised Jesus from the dead—whom you killed by hanging him on a cross. ³¹God exalted him to his own right hand as Prince and Savior that he might bring Israel to repentance and forgive their sins. ³²We are witnesses of these things, and so is the Holy Spirit, whom God has given to those who obey him."

³³When they heard this, they were furious and wanted to put them to death. ³⁴But a Pharisee named Gamaliel, a teacher of the law, who was honored by all the people, stood up in the Sanhedrin and ordered that the men be put outside for a little while. ³⁵Then he addressed the Sanhedrin: "Men of Israel, consider carefully what you intend to do to these men. ³⁶Some time ago Theudas appeared, claiming to be somebody, and about four hundred men rallied to him. He was killed, all his followers were dispersed, and it all came to nothing. ³⁷After him, Judas the Galilean appeared in the days of the census, and led a band of people in revolt. He too was killed, and all his followers were scattered. ³⁸Therefore, in the present case I advise you: Leave these men alone! Let them go! For if their purpose or activity is of human origin, it will fail. ³⁹But if it is from God, you will not be able to stop these men; you will only find yourselves fighting against God."

⁴⁰His speech persuaded them. They called the apostles in and had them flogged. Then they ordered them not to speak in the name of Jesus, and let them go.

⁴¹The apostles left the Sanhedrin, rejoicing because they had been counted worthy of suffering disgrace for

## Amplified Bible

senate of the sons of Israel, and they sent to the prison to have [the apostles] brought.

²²But when the attendants arrived there, they failed to find them in the jail; so they came back and reported,

²³We found the prison quite safely locked up and the guards were on duty outside the doors, but when we opened [it], we found no one on the inside.

²⁴Now when the military leader of the temple area and the chief priests heard these facts, they were much perplexed *and* thoroughly at a loss about them, wondering into what this might grow.

²⁵But some man came and reported to them, saying, Listen! The men whom you put in jail are standing [right here] in the temple and teaching the people!

²⁶Then the military leader went with the attendants and brought [the prisoners], but without violence, for they dreaded the people lest they be stoned by them.

²⁷So they brought them and set them before the council (Sanhedrin). And the high priest examined them by questioning,

²⁸Saying, We definitely commanded *and* strictly charged you not to teach in *or* about this Name; yet here you have flooded Jerusalem with your doctrine and you intend to bring this ᵃMan's blood upon us.

²⁹Then Peter and the apostles replied, We must obey God rather than men.

³⁰The God of our forefathers raised up Jesus, Whom you killed by hanging Him on a tree (cross). [Deut. 21:22, 23.]

³¹God exalted Him to His right hand to be Prince *and* Leader and Savior *and* Deliverer *and* Preserver, in order to grant repentance to Israel and to bestow forgiveness *and* release from sins.

³²And we are witnesses of these things, and the Holy Spirit is also, Whom God has bestowed on those who obey Him.

³³Now when they heard this, they were cut to the heart *and* infuriated and wanted to kill the disciples.

³⁴But a certain Pharisee in the council (Sanhedrin) named Gamaliel, a teacher of the Law, highly esteemed by all the people, standing up, ordered that the apostles be taken outside for a little while.

³⁵Then he addressed them [the council, saying]: Men of Israel, take care in regard to what you propose to do concerning these men.

³⁶For before our time there arose Theudas, asserting himself to be a person of importance, with whom a number of men allied themselves, about 400; but he was killed and all who had listened to *and* adhered to him were scattered and brought to nothing.

³⁷And after this one rose up Judas the Galilean, [who led an uprising] during the time of the census, and drew away a popular following after him; he also perished and all his adherents were scattered.

³⁸Now in the present case let me say to you, stand off (withdraw) from these men and let them alone. For if this doctrine *or* purpose or undertaking *or* movement is of human origin, it will fail (be overthrown and come to nothing);

³⁹But if it is of God, you will not be able to stop *or* overthrow *or* destroy them; you might even be found fighting against God!

⁴⁰So, convinced by him, they took his advice; and summoning the apostles, they flogged them and sternly forbade them to speak in *or* about the name of Jesus, and allowed them to go.

⁴¹So they went out from the presence of the council (Sanhedrin), rejoicing that they were being counted worthy [dignified by the indignity] to suffer shame *and* be exposed to disgrace for [the sake of] His name.

---

ᵃ Capitalized because of what He is, the spotless Son of God, not what the speakers may have thought He was.

## New International Version

the Name. [42]Day after day, in the temple courts and from house to house, they never stopped teaching and proclaiming the good news that Jesus is the Messiah.

### The Choosing of the Seven

**6** In those days when the number of disciples was increasing, the Hellenistic Jews[a] among them complained against the Hebraic Jews because their widows were being overlooked in the daily distribution of food. [2]So the Twelve gathered all the disciples together and said, "It would not be right for us to neglect the ministry of the word of God in order to wait on tables. [3]Brothers and sisters, choose seven men from among you who are known to be full of the Spirit and wisdom. We will turn this responsibility over to them [4]and will give our attention to prayer and the ministry of the word."

[5]This proposal pleased the whole group. They chose Stephen, a man full of faith and of the Holy Spirit; also Philip, Procorus, Nicanor, Timon, Parmenas, and Nicolas from Antioch, a convert to Judaism. [6]They presented these men to the apostles, who prayed and laid their hands on them.

[7]So the word of God spread. The number of disciples in Jerusalem increased rapidly, and a large number of priests became obedient to the faith.

### Stephen Seized

[8]Now Stephen, a man full of God's grace and power, performed great wonders and signs among the people. [9]Opposition arose, however, from members of the Synagogue of the Freedmen (as it was called) — Jews of Cyrene and Alexandria as well as the provinces of Cilicia and Asia — who began to argue with Stephen. [10]But they could not stand up against the wisdom the Spirit gave him as he spoke. [11]Then they secretly persuaded some men to say, "We have heard Stephen speak blasphemous words against Moses and against God."

[12]So they stirred up the people and the elders and the teachers of the law. They seized Stephen and brought him before the Sanhedrin. [13]They produced false witnesses, who testified, "This fellow never stops speaking against this holy place and against the law. [14]For we have heard him say that this Jesus of Nazareth will destroy this place and change the customs Moses handed down to us."

[15]All who were sitting in the Sanhedrin looked intently at Stephen, and they saw that his face was like the face of an angel.

### Stephen's Speech to the Sanhedrin

**7** Then the high priest asked Stephen, "Are these charges true?"

[2]To this he replied: "Brothers and fathers, listen to me! The God of glory appeared to our father Abraham while he was still in Mesopotamia, before he lived in Harran. [3]'Leave your country and your people,' God said, 'and go to the land I will show you.'[b]

---

[a] 1 That is, Jews who had adopted the Greek language and culture
[b] 3 Gen. 12:1

## Amplified Bible

[42]Yet [in spite of the threats] they never ceased for a single day, both in the temple area and at home, to teach *and* to proclaim the good news (Gospel) of Jesus [as] the Christ (the Messiah).

**6** Now about this time, when the number of the disciples was greatly increasing, complaint was made by the Hellenists (the Greek-speaking Jews) against the [native] Hebrews because their widows were being overlooked *and* neglected in the daily ministration (distribution of relief). [2]So the Twelve [apostles] convened the multitude of the disciples and said, It is not seemly *or* desirable *or* right that we should have to give up *or* neglect [preaching] the Word of God in order to attend to serving at tables *and* superintending the distribution of food.

[3]Therefore select out from among yourselves, brethren, seven men of good *and* attested character *and* repute, full of the [Holy] Spirit and wisdom, whom we may assign to look after this business *and* duty.

[4]But we will continue to devote ourselves steadfastly to prayer and the ministry of the Word.

[5]And the suggestion pleased the whole assembly, and they selected Stephen, a man full of faith (a strong and welcome belief that Jesus is the Messiah) and full of *and* controlled by the Holy Spirit, and Philip, and Prochorus, and Nicanor, and Timon, and Parmenas, and Nicolaus, a proselyte (convert) from Antioch.

[6]These they presented to the apostles, who after prayer laid their hands on them.

[7]And the message of God kept on spreading, and the number of disciples multiplied greatly in Jerusalem; and [besides] a large number of the priests were obedient to the faith [in Jesus as the Messiah, through Whom is obtained eternal salvation in the kingdom of God].

[8]Now Stephen, full of grace (divine blessing and favor) and power (strength and ability) worked great wonders and signs (miracles) among the people.

[9]However, some of those who belonged to the synagogue of the Freedmen (freed Jewish slaves), as it was called, and [of the synagogues] of the Cyrenians and of the Alexandrians and of those from Cilicia and [the province of] Asia, arose [and undertook] to debate *and* dispute with Stephen.

[10]But they were not able to resist the intelligence *and* the wisdom and [the inspiration of] the Spirit with which *and* by Whom he spoke.

[11]So they [secretly] instigated *and* instructed men to say, We have heard this man speak, using slanderous *and* abusive *and* blasphemous language against Moses and God.

[12][Thus] they incited the people as well as the elders and the scribes, and they came upon Stephen and arrested him and took him before the council (Sanhedrin).

[13]And they brought forward false witnesses who asserted, This man never stops making statements against this sacred place and the Law [of Moses].

[14]For we have heard him say that this Jesus the Nazarene will tear down *and* destroy this place, and will alter the institutions *and* usages which Moses transmitted to us.

[15]Then all who sat in the council (Sanhedrin), as they gazed intently at Stephen, saw that his face had the appearance of the face of an angel.

**7** And the high priest asked [Stephen], Are these charges true?

[2]And he answered, Brethren and fathers, listen to me! The God of glory appeared to our forefather Abraham when he was still in Mesopotamia, before he [went to] live in Haran, [Gen. 11:31; 15:7; Ps. 29:3.]

[3]And He said to him, Leave your own country and your relatives and come into the land (region) that I will point out to you. [Gen. 12:1.]

## New International Version

4"So he left the land of the Chaldeans and settled in Harran. After the death of his father, God sent him to this land where you are now living. 5He gave him no inheritance here, not even enough ground to set his foot on. But God promised him that he and his descendants after him would possess the land, even though at that time Abraham had no child. 6God spoke to him in this way: 'For four hundred years your descendants will be strangers in a country not their own, and they will be enslaved and mistreated. 7But I will punish the nation they serve as slaves,' God said, 'and afterward they will come out of that country and worship me in this place.'*a* 8Then he gave Abraham the covenant of circumcision. And Abraham became the father of Isaac and circumcised him eight days after his birth. Later Isaac became the father of Jacob, and Jacob became the father of the twelve patriarchs.

9"Because the patriarchs were jealous of Joseph, they sold him as a slave into Egypt. But God was with him 10and rescued him from all his troubles. He gave Joseph wisdom and enabled him to gain the goodwill of Pharaoh king of Egypt. So Pharaoh made him ruler over Egypt and all his palace.

11"Then a famine struck all Egypt and Canaan, bringing great suffering, and our ancestors could not find food. 12When Jacob heard that there was grain in Egypt, he sent our forefathers on their first visit. 13On their second visit, Joseph told his brothers who he was, and Pharaoh learned about Joseph's family. 14After this, Joseph sent for his father Jacob and his whole family, seventy-five in all. 15Then Jacob went down to Egypt, where he and our ancestors died. 16Their bodies were brought back to Shechem and placed in the tomb that Abraham had bought from the sons of Hamor at Shechem for a certain sum of money.

17"As the time drew near for God to fulfill his promise to Abraham, the number of our people in Egypt had greatly increased. 18Then 'a new king, to whom Joseph meant nothing, came to power in Egypt.'*b* 19He dealt treacherously with our people and oppressed our ancestors by forcing them to throw out their newborn babies so that they would die. 20"At that time Moses was born, and he was no ordinary child.*c* For three months he was cared for by his family. 21When he was placed outside, Pharaoh's daughter took him and brought him up as her own son. 22Moses was edu-

## Amplified Bible

4So then he went forth from the land of the Chaldeans and settled in Haran. And from there, after his father died, [God] transferred him to this country in which you are now dwelling. [Gen. 11:31; 12:5; 15:7.]

5Yet He gave him no inheritable property in it, [no] not even enough ground to set his foot on; but He promised that He would give it to Him for a *a*permanent possession and to his descendants after him, even though [as yet] he had no child. [Gen. 12:7; 17:8; Deut. 2:5.]

6And this is [in effect] what God told him: That his descendants would be aliens (strangers) in a land belonging to other people, who would bring them into bondage and ill-treat them 400 years.

7But I will judge the nation to whom they will be slaves, said God, and after that they will escape *and* come forth and worship Me in this [very] place. [Gen. 15:13, 14; Exod. 3:12.]

8And [God] made with Abraham a covenant (an agreement to be religiously observed) *a*of which circumcision was the seal. And under these circumstances [Abraham] became the father of Isaac and circumcised him on the eighth day; and Isaac [did so] when he became the father of Jacob, and Jacob [when each of his sons was born], the twelve patriarchs. [Gen. 17:10-14; 21:2-4; 25:26; 29:31-35; 30:1-24; 35:16-26.]

9And the patriarchs [Jacob's sons], boiling with envy *and* hatred *and* anger, sold Joseph into slavery in Egypt; but God was with him, [Gen. 37:11, 28; 45:4.]

10And delivered him from all his distressing afflictions and won him goodwill *and* favor and wisdom *and* understanding in the sight of Pharaoh, king of Egypt, who made him governor over Egypt and all his house. [Gen. 39:2, 3, 21; 41:40-46; Ps. 105:21.]

11Then there came a famine over all of Egypt and Canaan, with great distress, and our forefathers could find no fodder [for the cattle] *or* vegetable sustenance [for their households]. [Gen. 41:54, 55; 42:5.]

12But when Jacob heard that there was grain in Egypt, he sent forth our forefathers [to go there on their] first trip. [Gen. 42:2.]

13And on their second visit Joseph revealed himself to his brothers, and the family of Joseph became known to Pharaoh *and* his origin *and* race. [Gen. 45:1-4.]

14And Joseph sent an invitation calling to himself Jacob his father and all his kindred, seventy-five persons in all. [Gen. 45:9, 10.]

15And Jacob went down into Egypt, where he himself died, as did [also] our forefathers; [Deut. 10:22.]

16And their *b*bodies [Jacob's and Joseph's] were taken back to Shechem and laid in the tomb which Abraham had purchased for a sum of [silver] money from the sons of Hamor in Shechem. [Gen. 50:13; Josh. 24:32.]

17But as the time for the fulfillment of the promise drew near which God had made to Abraham, the [Hebrew] people increased and multiplied in Egypt,

18Until [the time when] there arose over Egypt another *and* a different king who did not know Joseph [neither knowing his history and services nor recognizing his merits]. [Exod. 1:7, 8.]

19He dealt treacherously with *and* defrauded our race; he abused *and* oppressed our forefathers, forcing them to expose their babies so that they might not be kept alive. [Exod. 1:7-11, 15-22.]

20At this juncture Moses was born, and was exceedingly beautiful in God's sight. For three months he was nurtured in his father's house; [Exod. 2:2.]

21Then when he was exposed [to perish], the daughter of Pharaoh rescued him and took him *and* reared him as her own son. [Exod. 2:5, 6, 10.]

---

*a* 7 Gen. 15:13,14    *b 18* Exodus 1:8    *c 20* Or *was fair in the sight of God*

*a* Marvin Vincent, *Word Studies.* *b* Stephen greatly compresses Old Testament accounts of two land purchases and two burial places (at Hebron and Shechem). See Gen. 23:17-18 and Gen. 33:19.

## New International Version

cated in all the wisdom of the Egyptians and was powerful in speech and action. [23] "When Moses was forty years old, he decided to visit his own people, the Israelites. [24] He saw one of them being mistreated by an Egyptian, so he went to his defense and avenged him by killing the Egyptian. [25] Moses thought that his own people would realize that God was using him to rescue them, but they did not. [26] The next day Moses came upon two Israelites who were fighting. He tried to reconcile them by saying, 'Men, you are brothers; why do you want to hurt each other?'

[27] "But the man who was mistreating the other pushed Moses aside and said, 'Who made you ruler and judge over us? [28] Are you thinking of killing me as you killed the Egyptian yesterday?'[a] [29] When Moses heard this, he fled to Midian, where he settled as a foreigner and had two sons.

[30] "After forty years had passed, an angel appeared to Moses in the flames of a burning bush in the desert near Mount Sinai. [31] When he saw this, he was amazed at the sight. As he went over to get a closer look, he heard the Lord say: [32] 'I am the God of your fathers, the God of Abraham, Isaac and Jacob.'[b] Moses trembled with fear and did not dare to look.

[33] "Then the Lord said to him, 'Take off your sandals, for the place where you are standing is holy ground. [34] I have indeed seen the oppression of my people in Egypt. I have heard their groaning and have come down to set them free. Now come, I will send you back to Egypt.'[c]

[35] "This is the same Moses they had rejected with the words, 'Who made you ruler and judge?' He was sent to be their ruler and deliverer by God himself, through the angel who appeared to him in the bush. [36] He led them out of Egypt and performed wonders and signs in Egypt, at the Red Sea and for forty years in the wilderness.

[37] "This is the Moses who told the Israelites, 'God will raise up for you a prophet like me from your own people.'[d] [38] He was in the assembly in the wilderness, with the angel who spoke to him on Mount Sinai, and with our ancestors; and he received living words to pass on to us.

[39] "But our ancestors refused to obey him. Instead, they rejected him and in their hearts turned back to Egypt. [40] They told Aaron, 'Make us gods who will go before us. As for this fellow Moses who led us out of Egypt—we don't know what has happened to him!'[e] [41] That was the time

## Amplified Bible

[22] So Moses was educated in all the wisdom and culture of the Egyptians, and he was mighty (powerful) in his speech and deeds.

[23] And when he was in his fortieth year, it came into his heart to visit his kinsmen the children of Israel [a to help them and to care for them].

[24] And on seeing one of them being unjustly treated, he defended the oppressed man and avenged him by striking down the Egyptian and slaying [him].

[25] He expected his brethren to understand that God was granting them deliverance by his hand [taking it for granted that they would accept him]; but they did not understand.

[26] Then on the next day he b suddenly appeared to some who were quarreling and fighting among themselves, and he urged them to make peace and become reconciled, saying, Men, you are brethren; why do you abuse and wrong one another?

[27] Whereupon the man who was abusing his neighbor pushed [Moses] aside, saying, Who appointed you a ruler (umpire) and a judge over us?

[28] Do you intend to slay me as you slew the Egyptian yesterday?

[29] At that reply Moses sought safety by flight and he was an exile and an alien in the country of Midian, where he became the father of two sons. [Exod. 2:11-15, 22; 18:3, 4.]

[30] And when forty years had gone by, there appeared to him in the wilderness (desert) of Mount Sinai an angel, in the flame of a burning bramblebush.

[31] When Moses saw it, he was astonished and marveled at the sight; but when he went close to investigate, there came to him the voice of the Lord, saying,

[32] I am the God of your forefathers, the God of Abraham and of Isaac and of Jacob. And Moses trembled and was so terrified that he did not venture to look.

[33] Then the Lord said to him, Remove the sandals from your feet, for the place where you are standing is holy ground and worthy of veneration.

[34] Because I have most assuredly seen the abuse and oppression of My people in Egypt and have heard their sighing and groaning, I have come down to rescue them. So, now come! I will send you back to Egypt [as My messenger]. [Exod. 3:1-10.]

[35] It was this very Moses whom they had denied (disowned and rejected), saying, Who made you our ruler (referee) and judge? whom God sent to be a ruler and deliverer and redeemer, by and with the [protecting and helping] hand of the Angel that appeared to him in the bramblebush. [Exod. 2:14.]

[36] He it was who led them forth, having worked wonders and signs in Egypt and at the Red Sea and during the forty years in the wilderness (desert). [Exod. 7:3; 14:21; Num. 14:33.]

[37] It was this [very] Moses who said to the children of Israel, God will raise up for you a Prophet from among your brethren as He raised me up. [Deut. 18:15, 18.]

[38] This is he who in the assembly in the wilderness (desert) was the go-between for the Angel who spoke to him on Mount Sinai and our forefathers, and he received living oracles (words that still live) to be handed down to us. [Exod. 19.]

[39] [And yet] our forefathers determined not to be subject to him [refusing to listen to or obey him]; but thrusting him aside they rejected him, and in their hearts yearned for and turned back to Egypt. [Num. 14:3, 4.]

[40] And they said to Aaron, Make us gods who shall [be our leaders and] go before us; as for this Moses who led us forth from the land of Egypt—we have no knowledge of what has happened to him. [Exod. 32:1, 23.]

---

[a] 28 Exodus 2:14  [b] 32 Exodus 3:6  [c] 34 Exodus 3:5,7,8,10
[d] 37 Deut. 18:15  [e] 40 Exodus 32:1

[a] G. Abbott-Smith, *Manual Greek Lexicon*.  [b] Marvin Vincent, *Word Studies*.

## New International Version

they made an idol in the form of a calf. They brought sacrifices to it and reveled in what their own hands had made. [42]But God turned away from them and gave them over to the worship of the sun, moon and stars. This agrees with what is written in the book of the prophets:

"'Did you bring me sacrifices and offerings
  forty years in the wilderness, people of Israel?
[43]You have taken up the tabernacle of Molek
  and the star of your god Rephan,
  the idols you made to worship.
Therefore I will send you into exile'[a] beyond Babylon.

[44]"Our ancestors had the tabernacle of the covenant law with them in the wilderness. It had been made as God directed Moses, according to the pattern he had seen. [45]After receiving the tabernacle, our ancestors under Joshua brought it with them when they took the land from the nations God drove out before them. It remained in the land until the time of David, [46]who enjoyed God's favor and asked that he might provide a dwelling place for the God of Jacob.[b] [47]But it was Solomon who built a house for him.

[48]"However, the Most High does not live in houses made by human hands. As the prophet says:

[49]"'Heaven is my throne,
  and the earth is my footstool.
What kind of house will you build for me?
                                  says the Lord.
  Or where will my resting place be?
[50]Has not my hand made all these things?'[c]

[51]"You stiff-necked people! Your hearts and ears are still uncircumcised. You are just like your ancestors: You always resist the Holy Spirit! [52]Was there ever a prophet your ancestors did not persecute? They even killed those who predicted the coming of the Righteous One. And now you have betrayed and murdered him— [53]you who have received the law that was given through angels but have not obeyed it."

### The Stoning of Stephen

[54]When the members of the Sanhedrin heard this, they were furious and gnashed their teeth at him. [55]But Stephen, full of the Holy Spirit, looked up to heaven and saw the glory of God, and Jesus standing at the right hand of God. [56]"Look," he said, "I see heaven open and the Son of Man standing at the right hand of God."

[57]At this they covered their ears and, yelling at the top of their voices, they all rushed at him, [58]dragged him out of the city and began to stone him. Meanwhile, the witnesses laid their coats at the feet of a young man named Saul.

[59]While they were stoning him, Stephen prayed, "Lord Jesus, receive my spirit." [60]Then he fell on his knees and cried out, "Lord, do not hold this sin against them." When he had said this, he fell asleep.

## Amplified Bible

[41]And they [even] made a calf in those days, and offered sacrifice to the idol and made merry *and* exulted in the work of their [own] hands. [Exod. 32:4, 6.]

[42]But God turned [away from them] and delivered them up to worship *and* serve the host (stars) of heaven, as it is written in the book of the prophets: Did you [really] offer to Me slain beasts and sacrifices for forty years in the wilderness (desert), O house of Israel? [Jer. 19:13.]

[43][No!] You took up the tent (the portable temple) of Moloch *and* carried it [with you], and the star of the god Rephan, the images which you [yourselves] made that you might worship them; and I will remove you [carrying you away into exile] beyond Babylon. [Amos 5:25-27.]

[44]Our forefathers had the tent (tabernacle) of witness in the wilderness, even as He Who directed Moses to make it had ordered, according to the pattern *and* model he had seen. [Exod. 25:9-40.]

[45]Our forefathers in turn brought it [this tent of witness] in [with them into the land] with Joshua when they dispossessed the nations which God drove out before the face of our forefathers. [So it remained here] until the time of David, [Deut. 32:49; Josh. 3:14-17.]

[46]Who found grace (favor and spiritual blessing) in the sight of God and prayed that he might be allowed to find a dwelling place for the God of Jacob. [II Sam. 7:8-16; Ps. 132:1-5.]

[47]But it was Solomon who built a house for Him. [I Kings 6.]

[48]However, the Most High does not dwell in houses *and* temples made with hands; as the prophet says, [Isa. 66:1, 2.]

[49]Heaven [is] My throne, and earth the footstool for My feet. What [kind of] house can you build for Me, says the Lord, or what is the place in which I can rest?

[50]Was it not My hand that made all these things? [Isa. 66:1, 2.]

[51]You stubborn *and* stiff-necked people, still heathen *and* uncircumcised in heart and ears, you are always [a]actively resisting the Holy Spirit. As your forefathers [were], so you [are and so you do]! [Exod. 33:3, 5; Num. 27:14; Isa. 63:10; Jer. 6:10; 9:26.]

[52]Which of the prophets did your forefathers not persecute? And they slew those who proclaimed beforehand the coming of the Righteous One, Whom you now have betrayed and murdered—

[53]You who received the Law as it was ordained *and* set in order *and* delivered by angels, and [yet] you did not obey it!

[54]Now upon hearing these things, they [the Jews] were cut to the heart *and* infuriated, and they ground their teeth against [Stephen].

[55]But he, full of the Holy Spirit *and* controlled by Him, gazed into heaven and saw the glory (the splendor and majesty) of God, and Jesus standing at God's right hand;

[56]And he said, Look! I see the heavens opened, and the Son of man standing at God's right hand!

[57]But they raised a great shout and put their hands over their ears and rushed together upon him.

[58]Then they dragged him out of the city and began to stone him, and the witnesses placed their garments at the feet of a young man named Saul. [Acts 22:20.]

[59]And while they were stoning Stephen, he prayed, Lord Jesus, receive *and* accept *and* welcome my spirit!

[60]And falling on his knees, he cried out loudly, Lord, fix not this sin upon them [lay it not to their charge]! And when he had said this, he fell asleep [b][in death].

---

[a] 43 Amos 5:25-27 (see Septuagint)   [b] 46 Some early manuscripts *the house of Jacob*   [c] 50 Isaiah 66:1,2

[a] Marvin Vincent, *Word Studies.*   [b] Hermann Cremer, *Biblico-Theological Lexicon of New Testament Greek.*

## New International Version

**8** And Saul approved of their killing him.

### The Church Persecuted and Scattered

On that day a great persecution broke out against the church in Jerusalem, and all except the apostles were scattered throughout Judea and Samaria. ²Godly men buried Stephen and mourned deeply for him. ³But Saul began to destroy the church. Going from house to house, he dragged off both men and women and put them in prison.

### Philip in Samaria

⁴Those who had been scattered preached the word wherever they went. ⁵Philip went down to a city in Samaria and proclaimed the Messiah there. ⁶When the crowds heard Philip and saw the signs he performed, they all paid close attention to what he said. ⁷For with shrieks, impure spirits came out of many, and many who were paralyzed or lame were healed. ⁸So there was great joy in that city.

### Simon the Sorcerer

⁹Now for some time a man named Simon had practiced sorcery in the city and amazed all the people of Samaria. He boasted that he was someone great, ¹⁰and all the people, both high and low, gave him their attention and exclaimed, "This man is rightly called the Great Power of God." ¹¹They followed him because he had amazed them for a long time with his sorcery. ¹²But when they believed Philip as he proclaimed the good news of the kingdom of God and the name of Jesus Christ, they were baptized, both men and women. ¹³Simon himself believed and was baptized. And he followed Philip everywhere, astonished by the great signs and miracles he saw.

¹⁴When the apostles in Jerusalem heard that Samaria had accepted the word of God, they sent Peter and John to Samaria. ¹⁵When they arrived, they prayed for the new believers there that they might receive the Holy Spirit, ¹⁶because the Holy Spirit had not yet come on any of them; they had simply been baptized in the name of the Lord Jesus. ¹⁷Then Peter and John placed their hands on them, and they received the Holy Spirit.

¹⁸When Simon saw that the Spirit was given at the laying on of the apostles' hands, he offered them money ¹⁹and said, "Give me also this ability so that everyone on whom I lay my hands may receive the Holy Spirit."

²⁰Peter answered: "May your money perish with you, because you thought you could buy the gift of God with money! ²¹You have no part or share in this ministry, because your heart is not right before God. ²²Repent of this

## Amplified Bible

**8** And Saul was [not only] consenting to [Stephen's] death [he was ªpleased and ᵇentirely approving]. On that day a great *and* severe persecution broke out against the church which was in Jerusalem; and they were all scattered throughout the regions of Judea and Samaria, except the apostles (special messengers).

²[A party of] devout men ªwith others helped to carry out *and* bury Stephen and made great lamentation over him.

³But Saul shamefully treated *and* laid waste the church continuously [with cruelty and violence]; and entering house after house, he dragged out men and women and committed them to prison.

⁴Now those who were scattered abroad went about [through the land from place to place] preaching the glad tidings, the Word [ªthe doctrine concerning the attainment through Christ of salvation in the kingdom of God].

⁵Philip [the deacon, not the apostle] went down to the city of Samaria and proclaimed the Christ (the Messiah) to them [the people]; [Acts 6:5.]

⁶And great crowds of people with one accord listened to *and* heeded what was said by Philip, as they heard him *and* watched the miracles *and* wonders which he kept performing [from time to time].

⁷For foul spirits came out of many who were possessed by them, screaming *and* shouting with a loud voice, and many who were suffering from palsy or were crippled were restored to health.

⁸And there was great rejoicing in that city.

⁹But there was a man named Simon, who had formerly practiced magic arts in the city to the utter amazement of the Samaritan nation, claiming that he himself was an extraordinary *and* distinguished person.

¹⁰They all paid earnest attention to him, from the least to the greatest, saying, This man is that exhibition of the power of God which is called great (intense).

¹¹And they were attentive *and* made much of him, because for a long time he had amazed *and* bewildered *and* dazzled them with his skill in magic arts.

¹²But when they believed the good news (the Gospel) about the kingdom of God and the name of Jesus Christ (the Messiah) as Philip preached it, they were baptized, both men and women.

¹³Even Simon himself believed [he adhered to, trusted in, and relied on the teaching of Philip], and after being baptized, devoted himself constantly to him. And seeing signs *and* miracles of great power which were being performed, he was utterly amazed.

¹⁴Now when the apostles (special messengers) at Jerusalem heard that [the country of] Samaria had accepted *and* welcomed the Word of God, they sent Peter and John to them,

¹⁵And they came down and prayed for them that the Samaritans might receive the Holy Spirit;

¹⁶For He had not yet fallen upon any of them, but they had only been baptized into the name of the Lord Jesus.

¹⁷Then [the apostles] laid their hands on them one by one, and they received the Holy Spirit.

¹⁸However, when Simon saw that the [Holy] Spirit was imparted through the laying on of the apostles' hands, he brought money *and* offered it to them,

¹⁹Saying, Grant me also this power *and* authority, in order that anyone on whom I place my hands may receive the Holy Spirit.

²⁰But Peter said to him, Destruction overtake your money and you, because you imagined you could obtain the [free] gift of God with money!

²¹You have neither part nor lot in this matter, for your heart is all wrong in God's sight [it is not straightforward or right or true before God]. [Ps. 78:37.]

---

ª Joseph Thayer, *A Greek-English Lexicon.*  ᵇ Alexander Souter, *Pocket Lexicon.*

# New International Version

wickedness and pray to the Lord in the hope that he may forgive you for having such a thought in your heart. [23]For I see that you are full of bitterness and captive to sin."

[24]Then Simon answered, "Pray to the Lord for me so that nothing you have said may happen to me."

[25]After they had further proclaimed the word of the Lord and testified about Jesus, Peter and John returned to Jerusalem, preaching the gospel in many Samaritan villages.

## Philip and the Ethiopian

[26]Now an angel of the Lord said to Philip, "Go south to the road—the desert road—that goes down from Jerusalem to Gaza." [27]So he started out, and on his way he met an Ethiopian[d] eunuch, an important official in charge of all the treasury of the Kandake (which means "queen of the Ethiopians"). This man had gone to Jerusalem to worship, [28]and on his way home was sitting in his chariot reading the Book of Isaiah the prophet. [29]The Spirit told Philip, "Go to that chariot and stay near it."

[30]Then Philip ran up to the chariot and heard the man reading Isaiah the prophet. "Do you understand what you are reading?" Philip asked.

[31]"How can I," he said, "unless someone explains it to me?" So he invited Philip to come up and sit with him.

[32]This is the passage of Scripture the eunuch was reading:

"He was led like a sheep to the slaughter,
    and as a lamb before its shearer is silent,
    so he did not open his mouth.
[33]In his humiliation he was deprived of justice.
    Who can speak of his descendants?
    For his life was taken from the earth."[b]

[34]The eunuch asked Philip, "Tell me, please, who is the prophet talking about, himself or someone else?" [35]Then Philip began with that very passage of Scripture and told him the good news about Jesus.

[36]As they traveled along the road, they came to some water and the eunuch said, "Look, here is water. What can stand in the way of my being baptized?" [37]c [38]And he gave orders to stop the chariot. Then both Philip and the eunuch went down into the water and Philip baptized him. [39]When they came up out of the water, the Spirit of the Lord suddenly took Philip away, and the eunuch did not see him again, but went on his way rejoicing. [40]Philip, however, appeared at Azotus and traveled about, preaching the gospel in all the towns until he reached Caesarea.

# Amplified Bible

[22]So repent of this depravity *and* wickedness of yours and pray to the Lord that, if possible, this [a]contriving thought *and* purpose of your heart may be removed *and* disregarded *and* forgiven you.

[23]For I see that you are in the gall of bitterness and in [b]a bond forged by iniquity [to fetter souls]. [Isa. 58:6.]

[24]And Simon answered, Pray for me [beseech the Lord, both of you], that nothing of what you have said may befall me!

[25]Now when [the apostles] had borne their testimony and preached the message of the Lord, they went back to Jerusalem, proclaiming the glad tidings (Gospel) to many villages of the Samaritans [on the way].

[26]But an angel of the Lord said to Philip, Rise and proceed southward *or* at midday on the road that runs from Jerusalem down to Gaza. This is the desert [a route].

[27]So he got up and went. And behold, an Ethiopian, a eunuch of great authority under Candace the queen of the Ethiopians, who was in charge of all her treasure, had come to Jerusalem to worship.

[28]And he was [now] returning, and sitting in his chariot he was reading the book of the prophet Isaiah.

[29]Then the [Holy] Spirit said to Philip, Go forward and join yourself to this chariot.

[30]Accordingly Philip, running up to him, heard [the man] reading the prophet Isaiah and asked, Do you really understand what you are reading?

[31]And he said, How is it possible for me to do so unless someone explains it to me *and* guides me [in the right way]? And he earnestly requested Philip to come up and sit beside him.

[32]Now this was the passage of Scripture which he was reading: Like a sheep He was led to the slaughter, and as a lamb before its shearer is dumb, so He opens not His mouth.

[33]In His humiliation [c]He was taken away by distressing *and* oppressive judgment *and* justice was denied Him [caused to cease]. Who can describe *or* relate in full [a]the wickedness of His contemporaries (generation)? For His life is taken from the earth *and* [b]a bloody death inflicted upon Him. [Isa. 53:7, 8.]

[34]And the eunuch said to Philip, I beg of you, tell me about whom does the prophet say this, about himself or about someone else?

[35]Then Philip opened his mouth, and beginning with this portion of Scripture he announced to him the glad tidings (Gospel) of Jesus *and* about Him.

[36]And as they continued along on the way, they came to some water, and the eunuch exclaimed, See, [here is] water! What is to hinder my being baptized?

[37][d]And Philip said, If you believe with all your heart [if you have [b]a conviction, full of joyful trust, that Jesus is the Messiah and accept Him as the Author of your salvation in the kingdom of God, giving Him your obedience, then] you may. And he replied, I do believe that Jesus Christ is the Son of God.

[38]And he ordered that the chariot be stopped; and both Philip and the eunuch went down into the water, and [Philip] baptized him.

[39]And when they came up out of the water, the Spirit of the Lord [a suddenly] caught away Philip; and the eunuch saw him no more, and he went on his way rejoicing.

[40]But Philip was found at Azotus, and passing on he preached the good news (Gospel) to all the towns until he reached Caesarea.

---

[a] 27 That is, from the southern Nile region   [b] 33 Isaiah 53:7,8 (see Septuagint)   [c] 37 Some manuscripts include here *Philip said, "If you believe with all your heart, you may." The eunuch answered, "I believe that Jesus Christ is the Son of God."*

[a] Marvin Vincent, *Word Studies.*   [b] Joseph Thayer, *A Greek-English Lexicon.*   [c] Adam Clarke, *The Holy Bible with A Commentary.*   [d] Many manuscripts do not contain this verse.

## New International Version

### Saul's Conversion

**9** Meanwhile, Saul was still breathing out murderous threats against the Lord's disciples. He went to the high priest ²and asked him for letters to the synagogues in Damascus, so that if he found any there who belonged to the Way, whether men or women, he might take them as prisoners to Jerusalem. ³As he neared Damascus on his journey, suddenly a light from heaven flashed around him. ⁴He fell to the ground and heard a voice say to him, "Saul, Saul, why do you persecute me?"

⁵"Who are you, Lord?" Saul asked.

"I am Jesus, whom you are persecuting," he replied. ⁶"Now get up and go into the city, and you will be told what you must do."

⁷The men traveling with Saul stood there speechless; they heard the sound but did not see anyone. ⁸Saul got up from the ground, but when he opened his eyes he could see nothing. So they led him by the hand into Damascus. ⁹For three days he was blind, and did not eat or drink anything.

¹⁰In Damascus there was a disciple named Ananias. The Lord called to him in a vision, "Ananias!"

"Yes, Lord," he answered.

¹¹The Lord told him, "Go to the house of Judas on Straight Street and ask for a man from Tarsus named Saul, for he is praying. ¹²In a vision he has seen a man named Ananias come and place his hands on him to restore his sight."

¹³"Lord," Ananias answered, "I have heard many reports about this man and all the harm he has done to your holy people in Jerusalem. ¹⁴And he has come here with authority from the chief priests to arrest all who call on your name."

¹⁵But the Lord said to Ananias, "Go! This man is my chosen instrument to proclaim my name to the Gentiles and their kings and to the people of Israel. ¹⁶I will show him how much he must suffer for my name."

¹⁷Then Ananias went to the house and entered it. Placing his hands on Saul, he said, "Brother Saul, the Lord—Jesus, who appeared to you on the road as you were coming here—has sent me so that you may see again and be filled with the Holy Spirit." ¹⁸Immediately, something like scales fell from Saul's eyes, and he could see again. He got up and was baptized, ¹⁹and after taking some food, he regained his strength.

### Saul in Damascus and Jerusalem

Saul spent several days with the disciples in Damascus. ²⁰At once he began to preach in the synagogues that Jesus is the Son of God. ²¹All those who heard him were astonished and asked, "Isn't he the man who raised havoc in Jerusalem among those who call on this name? And hasn't he come here to take them as prisoners to the chief priests?" ²²Yet Saul grew more and more powerful and baffled the Jews living in Damascus by proving that Jesus is the Messiah.

## Amplified Bible

**9** Meanwhile Saul, ᵃstill drawing his breath hard from threatening and murderous desire against the disciples of the Lord, went to the high priest

²And requested of him letters to the synagogues at Damascus [authorizing him], so that if he found any men or women belonging to the Way [of life as determined by faith in Jesus Christ], he might bring them bound [with chains] to Jerusalem.

³Now as he traveled on, he came near to Damascus, and suddenly a light from heaven flashed around him,

⁴And he fell to the ground. Then he heard a voice saying to him, Saul, Saul, why are you persecuting Me [harassing, troubling, and molesting Me]?

⁵And Saul said, Who are You, Lord? And He said, I am Jesus, Whom you are persecuting. ᵇ*It is dangerous and it will turn out badly for you to keep kicking against the goad [to offer vain and perilous resistance].*

⁶*Trembling and astonished he asked, Lord, what do You desire me to do? The Lord said to him,* But arise and go into the city, and you will be told what you must do.

⁷The men who were accompanying him were unable to speak [for terror], hearing the voice but seeing no one.

⁸Then Saul got up from the ground, but though his eyes were opened, he could see nothing; so they led him by the hand and brought him into Damascus.

⁹And he was unable to see for three days, and he neither ate nor drank [anything].

¹⁰Now there was in Damascus a disciple named Ananias. The Lord said to him in a vision, Ananias. And he answered, Here am I, Lord.

¹¹And the Lord said to him, Get up and go to the street called Straight and ask at the house of Judas for a man of Tarsus named Saul, for behold, he is praying [there].

¹²And he has seen *in a vision* a man named Ananias enter and lay his hands on him so that he might regain his sight.

¹³But Ananias answered, Lord, I have heard many people tell about this man, especially how much evil *and* what great suffering he has brought on Your saints at Jerusalem;

¹⁴Now he is here and has authority from the high priests to put in chains all who call upon Your name.

¹⁵But the Lord said to him, Go, for this man is a chosen instrument of Mine to bear My name before the Gentiles and kings and the descendants of Israel;

¹⁶For I will make clear to him how much he will be afflicted *and* must endure *and* suffer for My name's sake.

¹⁷So Ananias left and went into the house. And he laid his hands on Saul and said, Brother Saul, the Lord Jesus, Who appeared to you along the way by which you came here, has sent me that you may recover your sight and be filled with the Holy Spirit.

¹⁸And instantly something like scales fell from [Saul's] eyes, and he recovered his sight. Then he arose and was baptized,

¹⁹And after he took some food, he was strengthened. For several days [afterward] he remained with the disciples at Damascus.

²⁰And immediately in the synagogues he proclaimed Jesus, saying, He is the Son of God!

²¹And all who heard him were amazed and said, Is not this the very man who harassed *and* overthrew *and* destroyed in Jerusalem those who called upon this Name? And he has come here for the express purpose of arresting them *and* bringing them in chains before the chief priests.

²²But Saul increased all the more in strength, and continued to confound *and* put to confusion the Jews who lived in Damascus by comparing *and* examining evidence *and* proving that Jesus is the Christ (the Messiah).

---

ᵃ Marvin Vincent, *Word Studies.* ᵇ Many manuscripts do not contain this portion of verse 5 and the first part of verse 6.

## New International Version

23After many days had gone by, there was a conspiracy among the Jews to kill him, 24but Saul learned of their plan. Day and night they kept close watch on the city gates in order to kill him. 25But his followers took him by night and lowered him in a basket through an opening in the wall.

26When he came to Jerusalem, he tried to join the disciples, but they were all afraid of him, not believing that he really was a disciple. 27But Barnabas took him and brought him to the apostles. He told them how Saul on his journey had seen the Lord and that the Lord had spoken to him, and how in Damascus he had preached fearlessly in the name of Jesus. 28So Saul stayed with them and moved about freely in Jerusalem, speaking boldly in the name of the Lord. 29He talked and debated with the Hellenistic Jews,*a* but they tried to kill him. 30When the believers learned of this, they took him down to Caesarea and sent him off to Tarsus.

31Then the church throughout Judea, Galilee and Samaria enjoyed a time of peace and was strengthened. Living in the fear of the Lord and encouraged by the Holy Spirit, it increased in numbers.

### Aeneas and Dorcas

32As Peter traveled about the country, he went to visit the Lord's people who lived in Lydda. 33There he found a man named Aeneas, who was paralyzed and had been bedridden for eight years. 34"Aeneas," Peter said to him, "Jesus Christ heals you. Get up and roll up your mat." Immediately Aeneas got up. 35All those who lived in Lydda and Sharon saw him and turned to the Lord.

36In Joppa there was a disciple named Tabitha (in Greek her name is Dorcas); she was always doing good and helping the poor. 37About that time she became sick and died, and her body was washed and placed in an upstairs room. 38Lydda was near Joppa; so when the disciples heard that Peter was in Lydda, they sent two men to him and urged him, "Please come at once!"

39Peter went with them, and when he arrived he was taken upstairs to the room. All the widows stood around him, crying and showing him the robes and other clothing that Dorcas had made while she was still with them.

40Peter sent them all out of the room; then he got down on his knees and prayed. Turning toward the dead woman, he said, "Tabitha, get up." She opened her eyes, and seeing Peter she sat up. 41He took her by the hand and helped her to her feet. Then he called for the believers, especially the widows, and presented her to them alive. 42This became known all over Joppa, and many people believed in the Lord. 43Peter stayed in Joppa for some time with a tanner named Simon.

### Cornelius Calls for Peter

**10** At Caesarea there was a man named Cornelius, a centurion in what was known as the Italian Regiment. 2He and all his family were devout and God-fearing; he gave generously to those in need and prayed to God

## Amplified Bible

23After considerable time had elapsed, the Jews conspired to put Saul out of the way by slaying him,

24But [the knowledge of] their plot was made known to Saul. They were guarding the [city's] gates day and night to kill him,

25But his disciples took him at night and let him down through the [city's] wall, lowering him in a basket *or* hamper.

26And when he had arrived in Jerusalem, he tried to associate himself with the disciples; but they were all afraid of him, for they did not believe he really was a disciple.

27However, Barnabas took him and brought him to the apostles, and he explained to them how along the way he had seen the Lord, Who spoke to him, and how at Damascus he had preached freely *and* confidently *and* courageously in the name of Jesus.

28So he went in and out [as one] among them at Jerusalem,

29Preaching freely *and* confidently *and* boldly in the name of the Lord. And he spoke and discussed with *and* disputed against the Hellenists (the Grecian Jews), but they were seeking to slay him.

30And when the brethren found it out, they brought him down to Caesarea and sent him off to Tarsus [his home town].

31So the church throughout the whole of Judea and Galilee and Samaria had peace and was edified [growing in wisdom, virtue, and piety] and walking in the respect *and* reverential fear of the Lord and in the consolation *and* exhortation of the Holy Spirit, continued to increase *and* was multiplied.

32Now as Peter went here and there among them all, he went down also to the saints who lived at Lydda.

33There he found a man named Aeneas, who had been bedfast for eight years and was paralyzed.

34And Peter said to him, Aeneas, Jesus Christ (the Messiah) [now] makes you whole. Get up and make your bed! And immediately [Aeneas] stood up.

35Then all the inhabitants of Lydda and the plain of Sharon saw [what had happened to] him and they turned to the Lord.

36Now there was at Joppa a disciple [a woman] named [in Aramaic] Tabitha, which [in Greek] means Dorcas. She was abounding in good deeds and acts of charity.

37About that time she fell sick and died, and when they had cleansed her, they laid [her] in an upper room.

38Since Lydda was near Joppa [however], the disciples, hearing that Peter was there, sent two men to him begging him, Do come to us without delay.

39So Peter [immediately] rose and accompanied them. And when he had arrived, they took him to the upper room. All the widows stood around him, crying and displaying undershirts (tunics) and [other] garments such as Dorcas was accustomed to make while she was with them.

40But Peter put them all out [of the room] and knelt down and prayed; then turning to the body he said, Tabitha, get up! And she opened her eyes; and when she saw Peter, she raised herself *and* sat upright.

41And he gave her his hand and lifted her up. Then calling in God's people and the widows, he presented her to them alive.

42And this became known throughout all Joppa, and many came to believe on the Lord [to adhere to and trust in and rely on Him as the Christ and as their Savior].

43And Peter remained in Joppa for considerable time with a certain Simon a tanner.

**10** Now [living] at Caesarea there was a man whose name was Cornelius, a centurion (captain) of what was known as the Italian Regiment,

2A devout man who venerated God *and* treated Him with reverential obedience, as did all his household; and he gave much alms to the people and prayed continually to God.

---

*a 29* That is, Jews who had adopted the Greek language and culture

## New International Version

regularly. [3]One day at about three in the afternoon he had a vision. He distinctly saw an angel of God, who came to him and said, "Cornelius!"

[4]Cornelius stared at him in fear. "What is it, Lord?" he asked.

The angel answered, "Your prayers and gifts to the poor have come up as a memorial offering before God. [5]Now send men to Joppa to bring back a man named Simon who is called Peter. [6]He is staying with Simon the tanner, whose house is by the sea."

[7]When the angel who spoke to him had gone, Cornelius called two of his servants and a devout soldier who was one of his attendants. [8]He told them everything that had happened and sent them to Joppa.

### Peter's Vision

[9]About noon the following day as they were on their journey and approaching the city, Peter went up on the roof to pray. [10]He became hungry and wanted something to eat, and while the meal was being prepared, he fell into a trance. [11]He saw heaven opened and something like a large sheet being let down to earth by its four corners. [12]It contained all kinds of four-footed animals, as well as reptiles and birds. [13]Then a voice told him, "Get up, Peter. Kill and eat."

[14]"Surely not, Lord!" Peter replied. "I have never eaten anything impure or unclean."

[15]The voice spoke to him a second time, "Do not call anything impure that God has made clean."

[16]This happened three times, and immediately the sheet was taken back to heaven.

[17]While Peter was wondering about the meaning of the vision, the men sent by Cornelius found out where Simon's house was and stopped at the gate. [18]They called out, asking if Simon who was known as Peter was staying there.

[19]While Peter was still thinking about the vision, the Spirit said to him, "Simon, three[a] men are looking for you. [20]So get up and go downstairs. Do not hesitate to go with them, for I have sent them."

[21]Peter went down and said to the men, "I'm the one you're looking for. Why have you come?"

[22]The men replied, "We have come from Cornelius the centurion. He is a righteous and God-fearing man, who is respected by all the Jewish people. A holy angel told him to ask you to come to his house so that he could hear what you have to say." [23]Then Peter invited the men into the house to be his guests.

### Peter at Cornelius's House

The next day Peter started out with them, and some of the believers from Joppa went along. [24]The following day he arrived in Caesarea. Cornelius was expecting them and had called together his relatives and close friends. [25]As Peter entered the house, Cornelius met him and fell at his

## Amplified Bible

[3]About the ninth hour (about 3:00 p.m.) of the day he saw clearly in a vision an angel of God entering and saying to him, Cornelius!

[4]And he, gazing intently at him, became frightened and said, What is it, Lord? And the angel said to him, Your prayers and your [generous] gifts to the poor have come up [as a sacrifice] to God *and* have been remembered by Him.

[5]And now send men to Joppa and have them call for *and* invite here a certain Simon whose surname is Peter;

[6]He is lodging with Simon a tanner, whose house is by the seaside.

[7]When the angel who spoke to him had left, Cornelius called two of his servants and a God-fearing soldier from among his own personal attendants.

[8]And having rehearsed everything to them, he sent them to Joppa.

[9]The next day as they were still on their way and were approaching the town, Peter went up to the roof of the house to pray, about the sixth hour (noon).

[10]But he became very hungry, and wanted something to eat; and while the meal was being prepared a trance came over him,

[11]And he saw the sky opened and something like a great sheet lowered by the four corners, descending to the earth.

[12]It contained all kinds of quadrupeds *and wild beasts* and creeping things of the earth and birds of the air.

[13]And there came a voice to him, saying, Rise up, Peter, kill and eat.

[14]But Peter said, No, by no means, Lord; for I have never eaten anything that is common *and* unhallowed or [ceremonially] unclean.

[15]And the voice came to him again a second time, What God has cleansed *and* pronounced clean, do not you defile *and* profane by regarding *and* calling common *and* unhallowed or unclean.

[16]This occurred three times; then immediately the sheet was taken up to heaven.

[17]Now Peter was still inwardly perplexed *and* doubted as to what the vision which he had seen could mean, when [just then] behold the messengers that were sent by Cornelius, who had made inquiry for Simon's house, stopped *and* stood before the gate.

[18]And they called out to inquire whether Simon who was surnamed Peter was staying there.

[19]And while Peter was [a]earnestly revolving the vision in his mind *and* meditating on it, the [Holy] Spirit said to him, Behold, three men are looking for you!

[20]Get up and go below and accompany them without any doubt [about its legality] *or* any discrimination *or* hesitation, for I have sent them.

[21]Then Peter went down to the men and said, I am the man you seek; what is the purpose of your coming?

[22]And they said, Cornelius, a centurion (captain) who is just *and* upright in right standing with God, being God-fearing *and* obedient and well spoken of by the whole Jewish nation, has been instructed by a holy angel to send for you to come to his house; and he [a]has received in answer [to prayer] a warning to listen to *and* act upon what you have to say.

[23]So Peter invited them in to be his guests [for the night]. The next day he arose and went away with them, and some of the brethren from Joppa accompanied him.

[24]And on the following day they entered Caesarea. Cornelius was waiting for *and* expecting them, and he had invited together his relatives and his intimate friends.

[25]As Peter arrived, Cornelius met him, and falling down at his feet he made obeisance *and* paid worshipful reverence to him.

---

[a] 19 One early manuscript *two*; other manuscripts do not have the number.

[a] Marvin Vincent, *Word Studies.*

## New International Version

feet in reverence. 26But Peter made him get up. "Stand up," he said, "I am only a man myself."

27While talking with him, Peter went inside and found a large gathering of people. 28He said to them: "You are well aware that it is against our law for a Jew to associate with or visit a Gentile. But God has shown me that I should not call anyone impure or unclean. 29So when I was sent for, I came without raising any objection. May I ask why you sent for me?"

30Cornelius answered: "Three days ago I was in my house praying at this hour, at three in the afternoon. Suddenly a man in shining clothes stood before me 31and said, 'Cornelius, God has heard your prayer and remembered your gifts to the poor. 32Send to Joppa for Simon who is called Peter. He is a guest in the home of Simon the tanner, who lives by the sea.' 33So I sent for you immediately, and it was good of you to come. Now we are all here in the presence of God to listen to everything the Lord has commanded you to tell us."

34Then Peter began to speak: "I now realize how true it is that God does not show favoritism 35but accepts from every nation the one who fears him and does what is right. 36You know the message God sent to the people of Israel, announcing the good news of peace through Jesus Christ, who is Lord of all. 37You know what has happened throughout the province of Judea, beginning in Galilee after the baptism that John preached— 38how God anointed Jesus of Nazareth with the Holy Spirit and power, and how he went around doing good and healing all who were under the power of the devil, because God was with him.

39"We are witnesses of everything he did in the country of the Jews and in Jerusalem. They killed him by hanging him on a cross, 40but God raised him from the dead on the third day and caused him to be seen. 41He was not seen by all the people, but by witnesses whom God had already chosen—by us who ate and drank with him after he rose from the dead. 42He commanded us to preach to the people and to testify that he is the one whom God appointed as judge of the living and the dead. 43All the prophets testify about him that everyone who believes in him receives forgiveness of sins through his name."

44While Peter was still speaking these words, the Holy Spirit came on all who heard the message. 45The circumcised believers who had come with Peter were astonished that the gift of the Holy Spirit had been poured out even

## Amplified Bible

26But Peter raised him up, saying, Get up; I myself am also a man.

27And as [Peter] spoke with him, he entered the house and found a large group of persons assembled;

28And he said to them, You yourselves are aware how it is not lawful or permissible for a Jew to keep company with or to visit or [even] to come near or to speak first to anyone of another nationality, but God has shown and taught me by words that I should not call any human being common or unhallowed or [ceremonially] unclean.

29Therefore when I was sent for, I came without hesitation or objection or misgivings. So now I ask for what reason you sent for me.

30And Cornelius said, This is now the fourth day since about this time I was observing the ninth hour (three o'clock in the afternoon) of prayer in my lodging place; [suddenly] a man stood before me in dazzling apparel,

31And he said, Cornelius, your prayer has been heard and harkened to, and your donations to the poor have been known and ᵃpreserved before God [so that He heeds and is about to help you].

32Send therefore to Joppa and ask for Simon who is surnamed Peter; he is staying in the house of Simon the tanner by the seaside.

33So at once I sent for you, and you [being a Jew] have done a kind and ᵇcourteous and handsome thing in coming. Now then, we are all present in the sight of God to listen to all that you have been instructed by the Lord to say.

34And Peter opened his mouth and said: Most certainly and thoroughly I now perceive and understand that God shows no partiality and is no respecter of persons,

35But in every nation he who venerates and has a reverential fear for God, treating Him with worshipful obedience and living uprightly, is acceptable to Him and ᶜsure of being received and welcomed [by Him].

36You know the contents of the message which He sent to Israel, announcing the good news (Gospel) of peace by Jesus Christ, Who is Lord of all—

37The [same] message which was proclaimed throughout all Judea, starting from Galilee after the baptism preached by John—

38How God anointed and consecrated Jesus of Nazareth with the [Holy] Spirit and with strength and ability and power; how He went about doing good and, ᵇin particular, curing all who were harassed and oppressed by [the power of] the devil, for God was with Him.

39And we are [eye and ear] witnesses of everything that He did both in the land of the Jews and in Jerusalem. And [yet] they put Him out of the way (murdered Him) by hanging Him on a tree;

40But God raised Him to life on the third day and caused Him to be manifest (to be plainly seen),

41Not by all the people but to us who were chosen (designated) beforehand by God as witnesses, who ate and drank with Him after He arose from the dead.

42And He charged us to preach to the people and to bear solemn testimony that He is the God-appointed and God-ordained Judge of the living and the dead.

43To Him all the prophets testify (bear witness) that everyone who believes in Him [who adheres to, trusts in, and relies on Him, giving himself up to Him] receives forgiveness of sins through His name.

44While Peter was still speaking these words, the Holy Spirit fell on all who were listening to the message.

45And the believers from among the circumcised [the Jews] who came with Peter were surprised and amazed, because the free gift of the Holy Spirit had been bestowed and poured out largely even on the Gentiles.

ᵃ Joseph Thayer, *A Greek-English Lexicon.* ᵇ Marvin Vincent, *Word Studies.* ᶜ *Webster's New International Dictionary* offers this phrase as a definition of "acceptable."

## New International Version

on Gentiles. [46]For they heard them speaking in tongues[a] and praising God.

Then Peter said, [47]"Surely no one can stand in the way of their being baptized with water. They have received the Holy Spirit just as we have." [48]So he ordered that they be baptized in the name of Jesus Christ. Then they asked Peter to stay with them for a few days.

### Peter Explains His Actions

**11** The apostles and the believers throughout Judea heard that the Gentiles also had received the word of God. [2]So when Peter went up to Jerusalem, the circumcised believers criticized him [3]and said, "You went into the house of uncircumcised men and ate with them."

[4]Starting from the beginning, Peter told them the whole story: [5]"I was in the city of Joppa praying, and in a trance I saw a vision. I saw something like a large sheet being let down from heaven by its four corners, and it came down to where I was. [6]I looked into it and saw four-footed animals of the earth, wild beasts, reptiles and birds. [7]Then I heard a voice telling me, 'Get up, Peter. Kill and eat.'

[8]"I replied, 'Surely not, Lord! Nothing impure or unclean has ever entered my mouth.'

[9]"The voice spoke from heaven a second time, 'Do not call anything impure that God has made clean.' [10]This happened three times, and then it was all pulled up to heaven again.

[11]"Right then three men who had been sent to me from Caesarea stopped at the house where I was staying. [12]The Spirit told me to have no hesitation about going with them. These six brothers also went with me, and we entered the man's house. [13]He told us how he had seen an angel appear in his house and say, 'Send to Joppa for Simon who is called Peter. [14]He will bring you a message through which you and all your household will be saved.'

[15]"As I began to speak, the Holy Spirit came on them as he had come on us at the beginning. [16]Then I remembered what the Lord had said: 'John baptized with[b] water, but you will be baptized with[b] the Holy Spirit.' [17]So if God gave them the same gift as he gave us who believed in the Lord Jesus Christ, who was I to think that I could stand in God's way?"

[18]When they heard this, they had no further objections and praised God, saying, "So then, even to Gentiles God has granted repentance that leads to life."

## Amplified Bible

[46]For they heard them talking in [unknown] tongues (languages) and extolling *and* magnifying God. Then Peter asked,

[47]Can anyone forbid *or* refuse water for baptizing these people, seeing that they have received the Holy Spirit just as we have?

[48]And he ordered that they be baptized in the name of Jesus Christ (the Messiah). Then they begged him to stay on there for some days.

**11** Now the apostles (special messengers) and the brethren who were throughout Judea heard [with astonishment] that the Gentiles (heathen) also had received *and* accepted *and* welcomed the Word of God [the doctrine concerning the attainment through Christ of salvation in the kingdom of God].

[2]So when Peter went up to Jerusalem, the circumcision party [certain Jewish Christians] found fault with him [separating themselves from him in a hostile spirit, opposing and disputing and contending with him],

[3]Saying, Why did you go to uncircumcised men and [even] eat with them?

[4]But Peter began [at the beginning] and narrated *and* explained to them step by step [the whole list of events]. He said:

[5]I was in the town of Joppa praying, and [falling] in a trance I saw a vision of something coming down from heaven, like a huge sheet lowered by the four corners; and it descended until it came to me.

[6]Gazing intently *and* closely at it, I observed in it [a variety of] four-footed animals and wild beasts and reptiles of the earth and birds of the air,

[7]And I heard a voice saying to me, Get up, Peter; kill and eat.

[8]But I said, No, by no means, Lord; for nothing common *or* unhallowed or [ceremonially] unclean has ever entered my mouth.

[9]But the voice answered a second time from heaven, What God has cleansed *and* pronounced clean, do not you defile *and* profane by regarding *or* calling it common *or* unhallowed *or* unclean.

[10]This occurred three times, and then all was drawn up again into heaven.

[11]And right then the three men sent to me from Caesarea arrived at the house in which we were.

[12]And the [Holy] Spirit instructed me to accompany them without [the least] hesitation *or* misgivings *or* discrimination. So these six brethren accompanied me also, and we went into the man's house.

[13]And he related to us how he had seen the angel in his house which stood and said to him, Send men to Joppa and bring Simon who is surnamed Peter;

[14]He will give *and* explain to you a message by means of which you and all your household [as well] will be saved [[a]from eternal death].

[15]When I began to speak, the Holy Spirit fell on them just as He did on us at the beginning. [Acts 2:1-4.]

[16]Then I recalled the declaration of the Lord, how He said, John indeed baptized with water, but you shall be baptized with ([b]be placed in, introduced into) the Holy Spirit.

[17]If then God gave to them the same Gift [equally] as He gave to us when we believed in (adhered to, trusted in, and relied on) the Lord Jesus Christ, who was I *and* what power *or* authority had I to interfere *or* hinder *or* forbid *or* withstand God?

[18]When they heard this, they were quieted *and* made no further objection. And they glorified God, saying, Then God has also granted to the Gentiles repentance [c]unto [real] life [after resurrection].

---

[a] Hermann Cremer, *Biblico-Theological Lexicon.*   [b] Kenneth Wuest, *Word Studies.*   [c] Joseph Thayer, *A Greek-English Lexicon.*

## New International Version

### The Church in Antioch

[19] Now those who had been scattered by the persecution that broke out when Stephen was killed traveled as far as Phoenicia, Cyprus and Antioch, spreading the word only among Jews. [20] Some of them, however, men from Cyprus and Cyrene, went to Antioch and began to speak to Greeks also, telling them the good news about the Lord Jesus. [21] The Lord's hand was with them, and a great number of people believed and turned to the Lord.

[22] News of this reached the church in Jerusalem, and they sent Barnabas to Antioch. [23] When he arrived and saw what the grace of God had done, he was glad and encouraged them all to remain true to the Lord with all their hearts. [24] He was a good man, full of the Holy Spirit and faith, and a great number of people were brought to the Lord.

[25] Then Barnabas went to Tarsus to look for Saul, [26] and when he found him, he brought him to Antioch. So for a whole year Barnabas and Saul met with the church and taught great numbers of people. The disciples were called Christians first at Antioch.

[27] During this time some prophets came down from Jerusalem to Antioch. [28] One of them, named Agabus, stood up and through the Spirit predicted that a severe famine would spread over the entire Roman world. (This happened during the reign of Claudius.) [29] The disciples, as each one was able, decided to provide help for the brothers and sisters living in Judea. [30] This they did, sending their gift to the elders by Barnabas and Saul.

### Peter's Miraculous Escape From Prison

**12** It was about this time that King Herod arrested some who belonged to the church, intending to persecute them. [2] He had James, the brother of John, put to death with the sword. [3] When he saw that this met with approval among the Jews, he proceeded to seize Peter also. This happened during the Festival of Unleavened Bread. [4] After arresting him, he put him in prison, handing him over to be guarded by four squads of four soldiers each. Herod intended to bring him out for public trial after the Passover.

[5] So Peter was kept in prison, but the church was earnestly praying to God for him.

[6] The night before Herod was to bring him to trial, Peter was sleeping between two soldiers, bound with two chains, and sentries stood guard at the entrance. [7] Suddenly an angel of the Lord appeared and a light shone in the cell. He struck Peter on the side and woke him up. "Quick, get up!" he said, and the chains fell off Peter's wrists.

## Amplified Bible

[19] Meanwhile those who were scattered because of the persecution that arose in connection with Stephen had traveled as far away as Phoenicia and Cyprus and Antioch, without delivering the message [concerning [a] the attainment through Christ of salvation in the kingdom of God] to anyone except Jews.

[20] But there were some of them, men of Cyprus and Cyrene, who on returning to Antioch spoke to the Greeks also, proclaiming [to them] the good news (the Gospel) about the Lord Jesus.

[21] And the presence of the Lord was with them with power, so that a great number [learned] to believe (to adhere to and trust in and rely on the Lord) and turned *and* surrendered themselves to Him.

[22] The rumors of this came to the ears of the church (assembly) in Jerusalem, and they sent Barnabas to Antioch.

[23] When he arrived and saw what grace (favor) God was bestowing upon them, he was full of joy; and he continuously exhorted (warned, urged, and encouraged) them all to cleave unto *and* remain faithful to *and* devoted to the Lord with [resolute and steady] purpose of heart.

[24] For he was a good man [[b] good in himself and also at once for the good and the advantage of other people], full of *and* controlled by the Holy Spirit and full of faith (of his [a] belief that Jesus is the Messiah, through Whom we obtain eternal salvation). And a large company was added to the Lord.

[25] [Barnabas] went on to Tarsus to hunt for Saul.

[26] And when he had found him, he brought him back to Antioch. For a whole year they assembled together with *and* [c] were guests of the church and instructed a large number of people; and in Antioch the disciples were first called Christians.

[27] And during these days prophets (inspired teachers and interpreters of the divine will and purpose) came down from Jerusalem to Antioch.

[28] And one of them named Agabus stood up and prophesied through the [Holy] Spirit that a great *and* severe famine would come upon the whole world. And this did occur during the reign of Claudius.

[29] So the disciples resolved to send relief, each according to his individual ability [in proportion as he had prospered], to the brethren who lived in Judea.

[30] And so they did, sending [their contributions] to the elders by the hand of Barnabas and Saul.

**12** About that time Herod the king stretched forth his hands to afflict *and* oppress *and* torment some who belonged to the church (assembly).

[2] And he killed James the brother of John with a sword;

[3] And when he saw that it was pleasing to the Jews, he proceeded further and arrested Peter also. This was during the days of Unleavened Bread [the Passover week].

[4] And when he had seized [Peter], he put him in prison and delivered him to four squads of soldiers of four each to guard him, purposing after the Passover to bring him forth to the people.

[5] So Peter was kept in prison, but fervent prayer for him was persistently made to God by the church (assembly).

[6] The very night before Herod was about to bring him forth, Peter was sleeping between two soldiers, fastened with two chains, and sentries before the door were guarding the prison.

[7] And suddenly an angel of the Lord appeared [standing beside him], and a light shone in the place where he was. And the angel gently smote Peter on the side and awakened him, saying, Get up quickly! And the chains fell off his hands.

---

[a] Joseph Thayer, *A Greek-English Lexicon.* [b] Hermann Cremer, *Biblico-Theological Lexicon.* [c] Alternate translation.

## New International Version

[8]Then the angel said to him, "Put on your clothes and sandals." And Peter did so. "Wrap your cloak around you and follow me," the angel told him. [9]Peter followed him out of the prison, but he had no idea that what the angel was doing was really happening; he thought he was seeing a vision. [10]They passed the first and second guards and came to the iron gate leading to the city. It opened for them by itself, and they went through it. When they had walked the length of one street, suddenly the angel left him.

[11]Then Peter came to himself and said, "Now I know without a doubt that the Lord has sent his angel and rescued me from Herod's clutches and from everything the Jewish people were hoping would happen."

[12]When this had dawned on him, he went to the house of Mary the mother of John, also called Mark, where many people had gathered and were praying. [13]Peter knocked at the outer entrance, and a servant named Rhoda came to answer the door. [14]When she recognized Peter's voice, she was so overjoyed she ran back without opening it and exclaimed, "Peter is at the door!"

[15]"You're out of your mind," they told her. When she kept insisting that it was so, they said, "It must be his angel."

[16]But Peter kept on knocking, and when they opened the door and saw him, they were astonished. [17]Peter motioned with his hand for them to be quiet and described how the Lord had brought him out of prison. "Tell James and the other brothers and sisters about this," he said, and then he left for another place.

[18]In the morning, there was no small commotion among the soldiers as to what had become of Peter. [19]After Herod had a thorough search made for him and did not find him, he cross-examined the guards and ordered that they be executed.

### Herod's Death

Then Herod went from Judea to Caesarea and stayed there. [20]He had been quarreling with the people of Tyre and Sidon; they now joined together and sought an audience with him. After securing the support of Blastus, a trusted personal servant of the king, they asked for peace, because they depended on the king's country for their food supply.

[21]On the appointed day Herod, wearing his royal robes, sat on his throne and delivered a public address to the people. [22]They shouted, "This is the voice of a god, not of a man." [23]Immediately, because Herod did not give praise to God, an angel of the Lord struck him down, and he was eaten by worms and died.

[24]But the word of God continued to spread and flourish.

### Barnabas and Saul Sent Off

[25]When Barnabas and Saul had finished their mission, they returned from[a] Jerusalem, taking with them John, **13** also called Mark. [1]Now in the church at Antioch there were prophets and teachers: Barnabas, Simeon called Niger, Lucius of Cyrene, Manaen (who had been brought up with Herod the tetrarch) and Saul. [2]While they were worshiping the Lord and fasting, the Holy Spirit said, "Set apart for me Barnabas and Saul for the work to which I have called them." [3]So after they had

[a] 25 Some manuscripts *to*

## Amplified Bible

[8]And the angel said to him, Tighten your belt and bind on your sandals. And he did so. And he said to him, Wrap your outer garment around you and follow me.

[9]And [Peter] went out [along] following him, and he was not conscious that what was apparently being done by the angel was real, but thought he was seeing a vision.

[10]When they had passed through the first guard and the second, they came to the iron gate which leads into the city. Of its own accord [the gate] swung open, and they went out and passed on through one street; and at once the angel left him.

[11]Then Peter came to himself and said, Now I really know *and* am sure that the Lord has sent His angel and delivered me from the hand of Herod and from all that the Jewish people were expecting [to do to me].

[12]When he, at a glance, became aware of this [[a]comprehending all the elements of the case], he went to the house of Mary the mother of John, whose surname was Mark, where a large number were assembled together and were praying.

[13]And when he knocked at the gate of the porch, a maid named Rhoda came to answer.

[14]And recognizing Peter's voice, in her joy she failed to open the gate, but ran in and told the people that Peter was standing before the porch gate.

[15]They said to her, You are crazy! But she persistently *and* strongly *and* confidently affirmed that it was the truth. They said, It is his angel!

[16]But meanwhile Peter continued knocking, and when they opened the gate and saw him, they were amazed.

[17]But motioning to them with his hand to keep quiet *and* listen, he related to them how the Lord had delivered him out of the prison. And he said, Report all this to James [the Less] and to the brethren. Then he left and went to some other place.

[18]Now as soon as it was day, there was no small disturbance among the soldiers over what had become of Peter.

[19]And when Herod had looked for him and could not find him, he placed the guards on trial and commanded that they should be led away [to execution]. Then [Herod] went down from Judea to Caesarea and stayed on there.

[20]Now [Herod] cherished bitter animosity *and* hostility for the people of Tyre and Sidon; and [their deputies] came to him in a united body, and having made Blastus the king's chamberlain their friend, they asked for peace, because their country was nourished by *and* depended on the king's [country] for food.

[21]On an appointed day Herod arrayed himself in his royal robes, took his seat upon [his] throne, and addressed an oration to them.

[22]And the assembled people shouted, It is the voice of a god, and not of a man!

[23]And at once an angel of the Lord smote him *and* cut him down, because he did not give God the glory (the preeminence and kingly majesty that belong to Him as the supreme Ruler); and he was eaten by worms and died.

[24]But the Word of the Lord [concerning the attainment through Christ of salvation in the kingdom of God] continued to grow and spread.

[25]And Barnabas and Saul came back from Jerusalem when they had completed their mission, bringing with them John whose surname was Mark. [Acts 11:28-30.]

**13** Now in the church (assembly) at Antioch there were prophets (inspired interpreters of the will and purposes of God) and teachers: Barnabas, Symeon who was called Niger [Black], Lucius of Cyrene, Manaen a member of the court of Herod the tetrarch, and Saul. [2]While they were worshiping the Lord and fasting, the Holy Spirit said, Separate now for Me Barnabas and Saul for the work to which I have called them.

[a] Marvin Vincent, *Word Studies.*

## New International Version

fasted and prayed, they placed their hands on them and sent them off.

### On Cyprus

4The two of them, sent on their way by the Holy Spirit, went down to Seleucia and sailed from there to Cyprus. 5When they arrived at Salamis, they proclaimed the word of God in the Jewish synagogues. John was with them as their helper.

6They traveled through the whole island until they came to Paphos. There they met a Jewish sorcerer and false prophet named Bar-Jesus, 7who was an attendant of the proconsul, Sergius Paulus. The proconsul, an intelligent man, sent for Barnabas and Saul because he wanted to hear the word of God. 8But Elymas the sorcerer (for that is what his name means) opposed them and tried to turn the proconsul from the faith. 9Then Saul, who was also called Paul, filled with the Holy Spirit, looked straight at Elymas and said, 10"You are a child of the devil and an enemy of everything that is right! You are full of all kinds of deceit and trickery. Will you never stop perverting the right ways of the Lord? 11Now the hand of the Lord is against you. You are going to be blind for a time, not even able to see the light of the sun."

Immediately mist and darkness came over him, and he groped about, seeking someone to lead him by the hand. 12When the proconsul saw what had happened, he believed, for he was amazed at the teaching about the Lord.

### In Pisidian Antioch

13From Paphos, Paul and his companions sailed to Perga in Pamphylia, where John left them to return to Jerusalem. 14From Perga they went on to Pisidian Antioch. On the Sabbath they entered the synagogue and sat down. 15After the reading from the Law and the Prophets, the leaders of the synagogue sent word to them, saying, "Brothers, if you have a word of exhortation for the people, please speak."

16Standing up, Paul motioned with his hand and said: "Fellow Israelites and you Gentiles who worship God, listen to me! 17The God of the people of Israel chose our ancestors; he made the people prosper during their stay in Egypt; with mighty power he led them out of that country; 18for about forty years he endured their conduct[a] in the wilderness; 19and he overthrew seven nations in Canaan, giving their land to his people as their inheritance. 20All this took about 450 years.

"After this, God gave them judges until the time of Samuel the prophet. 21Then the people asked for a king, and he gave them Saul son of Kish, of the tribe of Benjamin, who ruled forty years. 22After removing Saul, he made David their king. God testified concerning him: 'I have found David son of Jesse, a man after my own heart; he will do everything I want him to do.'

## Amplified Bible

3Then after fasting and praying, they put their hands on them and sent them away.

4So then, being sent out by the Holy Spirit, they went down to Seleucia, and from [that port] they sailed away to Cyprus.

5When they arrived at Salamis, they preached the Word of God [concerning the attainment through Christ of salvation in the kingdom of God] in the synagogues of the Jews. And they had John [Mark] as an attendant to assist them.

6When they had passed through the entire island of Cyprus as far as Paphos, they came upon a certain Jewish wizard or sorcerer, a false prophet named Bar-Jesus.

7He was closely associated with the proconsul, Sergius Paulus, who was an intelligent and sensible man of sound understanding; he summoned to him Barnabas and Saul and sought to hear the Word of God [concerning salvation in the kingdom of God attained through Christ].

8But Elymas [a]the wise man—for that is the translation of his name [[b]which he had given himself]—opposed them, seeking to keep the proconsul from accepting the faith.

9But Saul, who is also called Paul, filled with and controlled by the Holy Spirit, looked steadily at [Elymas]

10And said, You master in every form of deception and recklessness, unscrupulousness, and wickedness, you son of the devil, you enemy of everything that is upright and good, will you never stop perverting and making crooked the straight paths of the Lord and plotting against His saving purposes? [Hos. 14:9.]

11And now, behold, the hand of the Lord is upon you, and you will be blind, [so blind that you will be] unable to see the sun for a time. Instantly there fell upon him a mist and a darkness, and he groped about seeking persons who would lead him by the hand.

12Then the proconsul believed (became a Christian) when he saw what had occurred, for he was astonished and deeply touched at the teaching concerning the Lord and from Him.

13Now Paul and his companions sailed from Paphos and came to Perga in Pamphylia. And John [Mark] separated himself from them and went back to Jerusalem,

14But they [themselves] came on from Perga and arrived at Antioch in Pisidia. And on the Sabbath day they went into the synagogue there and sat down.

15After the reading of the Law and the Prophets, the leaders [of the worship] of the synagogue sent to them saying, Brethren, if you have any word of exhortation or consolation or encouragement for the people, say it.

16So Paul arose, and motioning with his hand said, Men of Israel and you who reverence and fear God, listen!

17The God of this people Israel selected our forefathers and made this people great and important during their stay in the land of Egypt, and then with an uplifted arm He led them out from there. [Exod. 6:1, 6.]

18And for about forty years [c]like a fatherly nurse He cared for them in the wilderness and endured their behavior. [Deut. 1:31.]

19When He had destroyed seven nations in the land of Canaan, He gave them [the Hebrews] their land as an inheritance [distributing it to them by lot; all of which took] about 450 years. [Deut. 7:1; Josh. 14:1.]

20After that, He gave them judges until the prophet Samuel.

21Then they asked for a king; and God gave them Saul son of Kish, a man of the tribe of Benjamin, for forty years.

22And when He had deposed him, He raised up David to be their king; of him He bore witness and said, I have found David son of Jesse a man after My own heart, who will do all My will and carry out My program fully. [I Sam. 13:14; Ps. 89:20; Isa. 44:28.]

---

[a] 18 Some manuscripts he cared for them

[a] G. Abbott-Smith, Manual Greek Lexicon. [b] Henry Alford, The Greek New Testament, with Notes. [c] Some ancient manuscripts so read.

# New International Version

[23]"From this man's descendants God has brought to Israel the Savior Jesus, as he promised. [24]Before the coming of Jesus, John preached repentance and baptism to all the people of Israel. [25]As John was completing his work, he said: 'Who do you suppose I am? I am not the one you are looking for. But there is one coming after me whose sandals I am not worthy to untie.'

[26]"Fellow children of Abraham and you God-fearing Gentiles, it is to us that this message of salvation has been sent. [27]The people of Jerusalem and their rulers did not recognize Jesus, yet in condemning him they fulfilled the words of the prophets that are read every Sabbath. [28]Though they found no proper ground for a death sentence, they asked Pilate to have him executed. [29]When they had carried out all that was written about him, they took him down from the cross and laid him in a tomb. [30]But God raised him from the dead, [31]and for many days he was seen by those who had traveled with him from Galilee to Jerusalem. They are now his witnesses to our people.

[32]"We tell you the good news: What God promised our ancestors [33]he has fulfilled for us, their children, by raising up Jesus. As it is written in the second Psalm:

"'You are my son;
today I have become your father.'[a]

[34]God raised him from the dead so that he will never be subject to decay. As God has said,

"'I will give you the holy and sure blessings promised to David.'[b]

[35]So it is also stated elsewhere:

"'You will not let your holy one see decay.'[c]

[36]"Now when David had served God's purpose in his own generation, he fell asleep; he was buried with his ancestors and his body decayed. [37]But the one whom God raised from the dead did not see decay.

[38]"Therefore, my friends, I want you to know that through Jesus the forgiveness of sins is proclaimed to you. [39]Through him everyone who believes is set free from every sin, a justification you were not able to obtain under the law of Moses. [40]Take care that what the prophets have said does not happen to you:

[41]"'Look, you scoffers,
wonder and perish,
for I am going to do something in your days
that you would never believe,
even if someone told you.'[d]"

[42]As Paul and Barnabas were leaving the synagogue, the people invited them to speak further about these

# Amplified Bible

[23]Of this man's descendants God has brought to Israel a Savior [in the person of Jesus], according to His promise. [24]Before His coming John had [already] preached baptism of repentance to all the people of Israel.

[25]And as John was ending his course, he asked, What or [a]who do you secretly think that I am? I am not He [the Christ. No], but note that after me One is coming, the sandals of Whose feet I am not worthy to untie!

[26]Brethren, sons of the family of Abraham, and all those others among you who reverence and fear God, to us has been sent the message of this salvation [the salvation obtained through Jesus Christ]. [Ps. 107:20.]

[27]For those who dwell in Jerusalem and their rulers, because they did not know or recognize Him or understand the utterances of the prophets which are read every Sabbath, have actually fulfilled these very predictions by condemning and sentencing [Him].

[28]And although they could find no cause deserving death with which to charge Him, yet they asked Pilate to have Him executed and put out of the way.

[29]And when they had finished and fulfilled everything that was written about Him, they took Him down from the tree and laid Him in a tomb.

[30]But God raised Him from the dead.

[31]And for many days He appeared to those who came up with Him from Galilee to Jerusalem, and they are His witnesses to the people.

[32]So now we are bringing you the good news (Gospel) that what God promised to our forefathers,

[33]This He has [b]completely fulfilled for us, their children, by raising up Jesus, as it is written in the second psalm, You are My Son; today I have begotten You [caused You to arise, to be born; [c]formally shown You to be the Messiah by the resurrection]. [Ps. 2:7.]

[34]And as to His having raised Him from among the dead, now no more to return to [undergo] putrefaction and dissolution [of the grave], He spoke in this way, I will fulfill and give to you the holy and sure mercy and blessings [that were promised and assured] to David. [Isa. 55:3.]

[35]For this reason He says also in another psalm, You will not allow Your Holy One to see corruption [to undergo putrefaction and dissolution of the grave]. [Ps. 16:10.]

[36]For David, after he had served God's will and purpose and counsel in his own generation, fell asleep [d]in death] and was buried among his forefathers, and he did see corruption and undergo putrefaction and dissolution [of the grave].

[37]But He Whom God raised up [to life] saw no corruption [did not experience putrefaction and dissolution of the grave].

[38]So let it be clearly known and understood by you, brethren, that through this Man forgiveness and removal of sins is now proclaimed to you;

[39]And that through Him everyone who believes [who [c]acknowledges Jesus as his Savior and devotes himself to Him] is absolved (cleared and freed) from every charge from which he could not be justified and freed by the Law of Moses and given right standing with God.

[40]Take care, therefore, lest there come upon you what is spoken in the prophets:

[41]Look, you scoffers and scorners, and marvel and perish and vanish away; for I am doing a deed in your days, a deed which you will never have confidence in or believe, [even] if someone [b]clearly describing it in detail] declares it to you. [Hab. 1:5.]

[42]As they [Paul and Barnabas] went out [of the synagogue], the people earnestly begged that these things might be told to them [further] the next Sabbath.

---

[a] 33 Psalm 2:7    [b] 34 Isaiah 55:3    [c] 35 Psalm 16:10 (see Septuagint)
[d] 41 Hab. 1:5

[a] Some manuscripts so read.  [b] Marvin Vincent, Word Studies.  [c] Joseph Thayer, A Greek-English Lexicon.  [d] Hermann Cremer, Biblico-Theological Lexicon.

## New International Version

things on the next Sabbath. ⁴³When the congregation was dismissed, many of the Jews and devout converts to Judaism followed Paul and Barnabas, who talked with them and urged them to continue in the grace of God.

⁴⁴On the next Sabbath almost the whole city gathered to hear the word of the Lord. ⁴⁵When the Jews saw the crowds, they were filled with jealousy. They began to contradict what Paul was saying and heaped abuse on him.

⁴⁶Then Paul and Barnabas answered them boldly: "We had to speak the word of God to you first. Since you reject it and do not consider yourselves worthy of eternal life, we now turn to the Gentiles. ⁴⁷For this is what the Lord has commanded us:

"'I have made you*a* a light for the Gentiles,
    that you*a* may bring salvation to the ends of the
        earth.'*b*"

⁴⁸When the Gentiles heard this, they were glad and honored the word of the Lord; and all who were appointed for eternal life believed.

⁴⁹The word of the Lord spread through the whole region. ⁵⁰But the Jewish leaders incited the God-fearing women of high standing and the leading men of the city. They stirred up persecution against Paul and Barnabas, and expelled them from their region. ⁵¹So they shook the dust off their feet as a warning to them and went to Iconium. ⁵²And the disciples were filled with joy and with the Holy Spirit.

### In Iconium

**14** At Iconium Paul and Barnabas went as usual into the Jewish synagogue. There they spoke so effectively that a great number of Jews and Greeks believed. ²But the Jews who refused to believe stirred up the other Gentiles and poisoned their minds against the brothers. ³So Paul and Barnabas spent considerable time there, speaking boldly for the Lord, who confirmed the message of his grace by enabling them to perform signs and wonders. ⁴The people of the city were divided; some sided with the Jews, others with the apostles. ⁵There was a plot afoot among both Gentiles and Jews, together with their leaders, to mistreat them and stone them. ⁶But they found out about it and fled to the Lycaonian cities of Lystra and Derbe and to the surrounding country, ⁷where they continued to preach the gospel.

### In Lystra and Derbe

⁸In Lystra there sat a man who was lame. He had been that way from birth and had never walked. ⁹He listened to Paul as he was speaking. Paul looked directly at him, saw that he had faith to be healed ¹⁰and called out, "Stand up on your feet!" At that, the man jumped up and began to walk.

## Amplified Bible

⁴³And when the congregation of the synagogue dispersed, many of the Jews and the devout converts to Judaism followed Paul and Barnabas, who talked to them and urged them to continue [to trust themselves to and to stand fast] in the grace (the unmerited favor and blessing) of God.

⁴⁴The next Sabbath almost the entire city gathered together to hear the Word of God [concerning *a*the attainment through Christ of salvation in the kingdom of God].

⁴⁵But when the Jews saw the crowds, filled with envy *and* jealousy they contradicted what was said by Paul and talked abusively [reviling and slandering him].

⁴⁶And Paul and Barnabas spoke out plainly *and* boldly, saying, It was necessary that God's message [concerning *a*salvation through Christ] should be spoken to you first. But since you thrust it from you, you pass this judgment on yourselves that you are unworthy of eternal life *and* out of your own mouth you will be judged. [Now] behold, we turn to the Gentiles (the heathen).

⁴⁷For so the Lord has charged us, saying, I have set you to be a light for the Gentiles (the heathen), that you may bring [eternal] salvation to the uttermost parts of the earth. [Isa. 49:6.]

⁴⁸And when the Gentiles heard this, they rejoiced and glorified (praised and gave thanks for) the Word of God; and as many as were destined (appointed and ordained) to eternal life believed (adhered to, trusted in, and relied on Jesus as the Christ and their Savior).

⁴⁹And so the Word of the Lord [concerning eternal salvation through Christ] scattered *and* spread throughout the whole region.

⁵⁰But the Jews stirred up the devout women of high rank and the outstanding men of the town, and instigated persecution against Paul and Barnabas and drove them out of their boundaries.

⁵¹But [the apostles] shook off the dust from their feet against them and went to Iconium.

⁵²And the disciples were continually filled [throughout their souls] with joy and the Holy Spirit.

**14** Now at Iconium [also Paul and Barnabas] went into the Jewish synagogue together and spoke with such power that a great number both of Jews and of Greeks believed (became Christians);

²But the unbelieving Jews [who rejected their message] aroused the Gentiles and embittered their minds against the brethren.

³So [Paul and Barnabas] stayed on there for a long time, speaking freely *and* fearlessly *and* boldly in the Lord, Who continued to bear testimony to the Word of His grace, granting signs and wonders to be performed by their hands.

⁴But the residents of the town were divided, some siding with the Jews and some with the apostles.

⁵When there was an attempt both on the part of the Gentiles and the Jews together with their rulers, to insult *and* abuse *and* molest [Paul and Barnabas] and to stone them,

⁶They, aware of the situation, made their escape to Lystra and Derbe, cities of Lycaonia, and the neighboring districts;

⁷And there they continued to preach the glad tidings (Gospel).

⁸Now at Lystra a man sat who found it impossible to use his feet, for he was a cripple from birth and had never walked.

⁹He was listening to Paul as he talked, and [Paul] gazing intently at him and observing that he had faith to be healed,

¹⁰Shouted at him, saying, Stand erect on your feet! And he leaped up and walked.

---

*a* 47 The Greek is singular.   *b* 47 Isaiah 49:6.

*a* Joseph Thayer, *A Greek-English Lexicon*.

## New International Version

[11]When the crowd saw what Paul had done, they shouted in the Lycaonian language, "The gods have come down to us in human form!" [12]Barnabas they called Zeus, and Paul they called Hermes because he was the chief speaker. [13]The priest of Zeus, whose temple was just outside the city, brought bulls and wreaths to the city gates because he and the crowd wanted to offer sacrifices to them.

[14]But when the apostles Barnabas and Paul heard of this, they tore their clothes and rushed out into the crowd, shouting: [15]"Friends, why are you doing this? We too are only human, like you. We are bringing you good news, telling you to turn from these worthless things to the living God, who made the heavens and the earth and the sea and everything in them. [16]In the past, he let all nations go their own way. [17]Yet he has not left himself without testimony: He has shown kindness by giving you rain from heaven and crops in their seasons; he provides you with plenty of food and fills your hearts with joy." [18]Even with these words, they had difficulty keeping the crowd from sacrificing to them.

[19]Then some Jews came from Antioch and Iconium and won the crowd over. They stoned Paul and dragged him outside the city, thinking he was dead. [20]But after the disciples had gathered around him, he got up and went back into the city. The next day he and Barnabas left for Derbe.

### The Return to Antioch in Syria

[21]They preached the gospel in that city and won a large number of disciples. Then they returned to Lystra, Iconium and Antioch, [22]strengthening the disciples and encouraging them to remain true to the faith. "We must go through many hardships to enter the kingdom of God," they said. [23]Paul and Barnabas appointed elders[a] for them in each church and, with prayer and fasting, committed them to the Lord, in whom they had put their trust. [24]After going through Pisidia, they came into Pamphylia, [25]and when they had preached the word in Perga, they went down to Attalia.

[26]From Attalia they sailed back to Antioch, where they had been committed to the grace of God for the work they had now completed. [27]On arriving there, they gathered the church together and reported all that God had done through them and how he had opened a door of faith to the Gentiles. [28]And they stayed there a long time with the disciples.

### The Council at Jerusalem

**15** Certain people came down from Judea to Antioch and were teaching the believers: "Unless you are circumcised, according to the custom taught by Moses, you cannot be saved." [2]This brought Paul and Barnabas into sharp dispute and debate with them. So Paul and Barnabas were appointed, along with some other believers, to go up to Jerusalem to see the apostles and elders about

## Amplified Bible

[11]And the crowds, when they saw what Paul had done, lifted up their voices, shouting in the Lycaonian language, The gods have come down to us in human form!

[12]They called Barnabas Zeus, and they called Paul, because he led in the discourse, Hermes [god of speech].

[13]And the priest of Zeus, whose [temple] was at the entrance of the town, brought bulls and garlands to the [city's] gates and wanted to join the people in offering sacrifice.

[14]But when the apostles Barnabas and Paul heard of it, they tore their clothing and dashed out among the crowd, shouting,

[15]Men, why are you doing this? We also are [only] human beings, of nature like your own, and we bring you the good news (Gospel) that you should turn away from these foolish *and* vain things to the living God, Who made heaven and the earth and the sea and everything that they contain. [Exod. 20:11; Ps. 146:6.]

[16]In generations past He permitted all the nations to walk in their own ways;

[17]Yet He did not neglect to leave some witness of Himself, for He did you good *and* [showed you] kindness and gave you rains from heaven and fruitful seasons, satisfying your hearts with nourishment and happiness.

[18]Even in [the light of] these words they with difficulty prevented the people from offering sacrifice to them.

[19]But some Jews arrived there from Antioch and Iconium; and having persuaded the people *and* won them over, they stoned Paul and [a afterward] dragged him out of the town, thinking that he was dead.

[20]But the disciples formed a circle about him, and he got up and went back into the town; and on the morrow he went on with Barnabas to Derbe.

[21]When they had preached the good news (Gospel) to that town and made disciples of many of the people, they went back to Lystra and Iconium and Antioch,

[22]Establishing *and* strengthening the souls *and* the hearts of the disciples, urging *and* warning *and* encouraging them to stand firm in the faith, and [telling them] that it is through many hardships *and* tribulations we must enter the kingdom of God.

[23]And when they had appointed *and* ordained elders for them in each church with prayer and fasting, they committed them to the Lord in Whom they had come to believe [being full of joyful trust that He is the Christ, the Messiah].

[24]Then they went through Pisidia and arrived at Pamphylia.

[25]And when they had spoken the Word in Perga [the doctrine concerning the attainment through Christ of salvation in the kingdom of God], they went down to Attalia;

[26]And from there they sailed back to Antioch, where they had [first] been commended to the grace of God for the work which they had [now] completed.

[27]Arriving there, they gathered the church together and declared all that God had accomplished with them and how He had opened to the Gentiles a door of faith [in Jesus as the Messiah, through Whom we obtain salvation in the kingdom of God].

[28]And there they stayed no little time with the disciples.

**15** But some men came down from Judea and were instructing the brethren, Unless you are circumcised in accordance with the Mosaic custom, you cannot be saved. [Gen. 17:9-14.]

[2]And when Paul and Barnabas had no small disagreement and discussion with them, it was decided that Paul and Barnabas and some of the others of their number should go up to Jerusalem [and confer] with the apostles (special messengers) and the elders about this matter.

---

[a] 23 Or *Barnabas ordained elders*; or *Barnabas had elders elected*

[a] Henry Alford, *The Greek New Testament*.

## New International Version

this question. ³The church sent them on their way, and as they traveled through Phoenicia and Samaria, they told how the Gentiles had been converted. This news made all the believers very glad. ⁴When they came to Jerusalem, they were welcomed by the church and the apostles and elders, to whom they reported everything God had done through them.

⁵Then some of the believers who belonged to the party of the Pharisees stood up and said, "The Gentiles must be circumcised and required to keep the law of Moses."

⁶The apostles and elders met to consider this question. ⁷After much discussion, Peter got up and addressed them: "Brothers, you know that some time ago God made a choice among you that the Gentiles might hear from my lips the message of the gospel and believe. ⁸God, who knows the heart, showed that he accepted them by giving the Holy Spirit to them, just as he did to us. ⁹He did not discriminate between us and them, for he purified their hearts by faith. ¹⁰Now then, why do you try to test God by putting on the necks of Gentiles a yoke that neither we nor our ancestors have been able to bear? ¹¹No! We believe it is through the grace of our Lord Jesus that we are saved, just as they are."

¹²The whole assembly became silent as they listened to Barnabas and Paul telling about the signs and wonders God had done among the Gentiles through them. ¹³When they finished, James spoke up. "Brothers," he said, "listen to me. ¹⁴Simon*a* has described to us how God first intervened to choose a people for his name from the Gentiles. ¹⁵The words of the prophets are in agreement with this, as it is written:

¹⁶ "'After this I will return
    and rebuild David's fallen tent.
  Its ruins I will rebuild,
    and I will restore it,
¹⁷ that the rest of mankind may seek the Lord,
    even all the Gentiles who bear my name,
  says the Lord, who does these things'*b*—
¹⁸    things known from long ago.*c*

¹⁹"It is my judgment, therefore, that we should not make it difficult for the Gentiles who are turning to God. ²⁰Instead we should write to them, telling them to abstain from food polluted by idols, from sexual immorality, from the meat of strangled animals and from blood. ²¹For the law of Moses has been preached in every city from the earliest times and is read in the synagogues on every Sabbath."

### The Council's Letter to Gentile Believers

²²Then the apostles and elders, with the whole church, decided to choose some of their own men and send them to Antioch with Paul and Barnabas. They chose Judas (called Barsabbas) and Silas, men who were leaders among the believers. ²³With them they sent the following letter:

## Amplified Bible

³So, being *a*fitted out *and* sent on their way by the church, they went through both Phoenicia and Samaria telling of the conversion of the Gentiles (the heathen), and they caused great rejoicing among all the brethren.

⁴When they arrived in Jerusalem, they were heartily welcomed by the church and the apostles and the elders, and they told them all that God had accomplished through them.

⁵But some who believed [who *a*acknowledged Jesus as their Savior and devoted themselves to Him] belonged to the sect of the Pharisees, and they rose up and said, It is necessary to circumcise [the Gentile converts] and to charge them to obey the Law of Moses.

⁶The apostles and the elders were assembled together to look into *and* consider this matter.

⁷And after there had been a long debate, Peter got up and said to them, Brethren, you know that quite a while ago God made a choice *or* selection from among you, that by my mouth the Gentiles should hear the message of the Gospel [concerning the *a*attainment through Christ of salvation in the kingdom of God] and believe (credit and place their confidence in it).

⁸And God, Who is acquainted with *and* understands the heart, bore witness to them, giving them the Holy Spirit as He also did to us;

⁹And He made no difference between us and them, but cleansed their hearts by faith (*a*by a strong and welcome conviction that Jesus is the Messiah, through Whom we obtain eternal salvation in the kingdom of God).

¹⁰Now then, why do you try to test God by putting a yoke on the necks of the disciples, such as neither our forefathers nor we [ourselves] were able to endure?

¹¹But we believe that we are saved through the grace (the undeserved favor and mercy) of the Lord Jesus, just as they [are].

¹²Then the whole assembly remained silent, and they listened [attentively] as Barnabas and Paul rehearsed what signs and wonders God had performed through them among the Gentiles.

¹³When they had finished talking, James replied, Brethren, listen to me.

¹⁴Simeon [Peter] has rehearsed how God first visited the Gentiles, to take out of them a people [to bear and honor] His name.

¹⁵And with this the predictions of the prophets agree, as it is written,

¹⁶After this I will come back, and will rebuild the house of David, which has fallen; I will rebuild its [very] ruins, and I will set it up again,

¹⁷So that the rest of men may seek the Lord, and all the Gentiles upon whom My name has been invoked,

¹⁸Says the Lord, Who has been making these things known from the beginning of the world. [Isa. 45:21; Jer. 12:15; Amos 9:11, 12.]

¹⁹Therefore it is my opinion that we should not put obstacles in the way of *and* annoy *and* disturb those of the Gentiles who turn to God,

²⁰But we should send word to them in writing to abstain from *and* avoid anything that has been polluted by being offered to idols, and all sexual impurity, and [eating meat of animals] that have been strangled, and [tasting of] blood.

²¹For from ancient generations Moses has had his preachers in every town, for he is read [aloud] every Sabbath in the synagogues.

²²Then the apostles and the elders, together with the whole church, resolved to select men from among their number and send them to Antioch with Paul and Barnabas. They chose Judas called Barsabbas, and Silas, [both] leading men among the brethren, *and* sent them.

²³With [them they sent] the following letter: The breth-

*a* 14 Greek *Simeon*, a variant of *Simon*; that is, Peter    *b* 17 Amos 9:11,12 (see Septuagint)    *c* 17,18 Some manuscripts *things'— / ¹⁸the Lord's work is known to him from long ago*

*a* Joseph Thayer, *A Greek-English Lexicon*.

## New International Version

The apostles and elders, your brothers,

To the Gentile believers in Antioch, Syria and Cilicia:

Greetings.

24We have heard that some went out from us without our authorization and disturbed you, troubling your minds by what they said. 25So we all agreed to choose some men and send them to you with our dear friends Barnabas and Paul— 26men who have risked their lives for the name of our Lord Jesus Christ. 27Therefore we are sending Judas and Silas to confirm by word of mouth what we are writing. 28It seemed good to the Holy Spirit and to us not to burden you with anything beyond the following requirements: 29You are to abstain from food sacrificed to idols, from blood, from the meat of strangled animals and from sexual immorality. You will do well to avoid these things.

Farewell.

30So the men were sent off and went down to Antioch, where they gathered the church together and delivered the letter. 31The people read it and were glad for its encouraging message. 32Judas and Silas, who themselves were prophets, said much to encourage and strengthen the believers. 33After spending some time there, they were sent off by the believers with the blessing of peace to return to those who had sent them. [34]a 35But Paul and Barnabas remained in Antioch, where they and many others taught and preached the word of the Lord.

### Disagreement Between Paul and Barnabas

36Some time later Paul said to Barnabas, "Let us go back and visit the believers in all the towns where we preached the word of the Lord and see how they are doing." 37Barnabas wanted to take John, also called Mark, with them, 38but Paul did not think it wise to take him, because he had deserted them in Pamphylia and had not continued with them in the work. 39They had such a sharp disagreement that they parted company. Barnabas took Mark and sailed for Cyprus, 40but Paul chose Silas and left, commended by the believers to the grace of the Lord. 41He went through Syria and Cilicia, strengthening the churches.

### Timothy Joins Paul and Silas

**16** Paul came to Derbe and then to Lystra, where a disciple named Timothy lived, whose mother was Jewish and a believer but whose father was a Greek. 2The believers at Lystra and Iconium spoke well of him. 3Paul wanted to take him along on the journey, so he circumcised him because of the Jews who lived in that area, for they all knew that his father was a Greek. 4As they

## Amplified Bible

ren, both the apostles and the elders, to the brethren who are of the Gentiles in Antioch and Syria and Cilicia, greetings:

24As we have heard that some persons from our number have disturbed you with their teaching, unsettling your minds and athrowing you into confusion, although we gave them no express orders or instructions [on the points in question],

25It has been resolved by us in assembly to select men and send them [as messengers] to you with our beloved Barnabas and Paul,

26Men who have hazarded their lives for the sake of our Lord Jesus Christ.

27So we have sent Judas and Silas, who themselves will bring you the same message by word of mouth.

28For it has seemed good to the Holy Spirit and to us not to lay upon you any greater burden than these indispensable requirements:

29That you abstain from what has been sacrificed to idols and from [tasting] blood and from [eating the meat of animals] that have been strangled and from sexual impurity. If you keep yourselves from these things, you will do well. Farewell [be strong]!

30So when [the messengers] were sent off, they went down to Antioch; and having assembled the congregation, they delivered the letter.

31And when they read it, the people rejoiced at the consolation and encouragement [it brought them].

32And Judas and Silas, who were themselves prophets (inspired interpreters of the will and purposes of God), urged and warned and consoled and encouraged the brethren with many words and strengthened them.

33And after spending some time there, they were sent back by the brethren with [the greeting] peace to those who had sent them.

34However, Silas decided to stay on there.

35But Paul and Barnabas remained in Antioch and with many others also continued teaching and proclaiming the good news, the Word of the Lord [concerning the battainment through Christ of eternal salvation in God's kingdom].

36And after some time Paul said to Barnabas, Come, let us go back and again visit and help and minister to the brethren in every town where we made known the message of the Lord, and see how they are getting along.

37Now Barnabas wanted to take with them John called Mark [his near relative].

38But Paul did not think it best to have along with them the one who had quit and deserted them in Pamphylia and had not gone on with them to the work.

39And there followed a sharp disagreement between them, so that they separated from each other, and Barnabas took Mark with him and sailed away to Cyprus.

40But Paul selected Silas and set out, being commended by the brethren to the grace (the favor and mercy) of the Lord.

41And he passed through Syria and Cilicia, establishing and strengthening the churches.

**16** And [Paul] went down to Derbe and also to Lystra. A disciple named Timothy was there, the son of a Jewish woman who was a believer [she had become bconvinced that Jesus is the Messiah and the Author of eternal salvation, and yielded obedience to Him]; but [Timothy's] father was a Greek.

2He [Timothy] had a good reputation among the brethren at Lystra and Iconium.

3Paul desired Timothy to go with him [aas a missionary]; and he took him and circumcised him because of the Jews that were in those places, all of whom knew that his father was a Greek.

a Marvin Vincent, Word Studies.  b Joseph Thayer, A Greek-English Lexicon.

---

a 34 Some manuscripts include here But Silas decided to remain there.

# New International Version

traveled from town to town, they delivered the decisions reached by the apostles and elders in Jerusalem for the people to obey. [5]So the churches were strengthened in the faith and grew daily in numbers.

## Paul's Vision of the Man of Macedonia

[6]Paul and his companions traveled throughout the region of Phrygia and Galatia, having been kept by the Holy Spirit from preaching the word in the province of Asia. [7]When they came to the border of Mysia, they tried to enter Bithynia, but the Spirit of Jesus would not allow them to. [8]So they passed by Mysia and went down to Troas. [9]During the night Paul had a vision of a man of Macedonia standing and begging him, "Come over to Macedonia and help us." [10]After Paul had seen the vision, we got ready at once to leave for Macedonia, concluding that God had called us to preach the gospel to them.

## Lydia's Conversion in Philippi

[11]From Troas we put out to sea and sailed straight for Samothrace, and the next day we went on to Neapolis. [12]From there we traveled to Philippi, a Roman colony and the leading city of that district[a] of Macedonia. And we stayed there several days.

[13]On the Sabbath we went outside the city gate to the river, where we expected to find a place of prayer. We sat down and began to speak to the women who had gathered there. [14]One of those listening was a woman from the city of Thyatira named Lydia, a dealer in purple cloth. She was a worshiper of God. The Lord opened her heart to respond to Paul's message. [15]When she and the members of her household were baptized, she invited us to her home. "If you consider me a believer in the Lord," she said, "come and stay at my house." And she persuaded us.

## Paul and Silas in Prison

[16]Once when we were going to the place of prayer, we were met by a female slave who had a spirit by which she predicted the future. She earned a great deal of money for her owners by fortune-telling. [17]She followed Paul and the rest of us, shouting, "These men are servants of the Most High God, who are telling you the way to be saved." [18]She kept this up for many days. Finally Paul became so annoyed that he turned around and said to the spirit, "In the name of Jesus Christ I command you to come out of her!" At that moment the spirit left her.

[19]When her owners realized that their hope of making money was gone, they seized Paul and Silas and dragged them into the marketplace to face the authorities. [20]They brought them before the magistrates and said, "These men are Jews, and are throwing our city into an uproar [21]by advocating customs unlawful for us Romans to accept or practice."

[22]The crowd joined in the attack against Paul and Silas, and the magistrates ordered them to be stripped and beaten with rods. [23]After they had been severely flogged, they were thrown into prison, and the jailer was commanded to guard them carefully. [24]When he received these orders, he put them in the inner cell and fastened their feet in the stocks.

# Amplified Bible

[4]As they went on their way from town to town, they delivered over [to the assemblies] for their observance the regulations decided upon by the apostles and elders who were at Jerusalem.

[5]So the churches were strengthened *and* made firm in the faith, and they increased in number day after day.

[6]And Paul and Silas passed through the territory of Phrygia and Galatia, having been forbidden by the Holy Spirit to proclaim the Word in [the province of] Asia.

[7]And when they had come opposite Mysia, they tried to go into Bithynia, but the Spirit of Jesus did not permit them.

[8]So passing by Mysia, they went down to Troas.

[9][There] a vision appeared to Paul in the night: a man from Macedonia stood pleading with him and saying, Come over to Macedonia and help us!

[10]And when he had seen the vision, we [including Luke] at once endeavored to go on into Macedonia, confidently inferring that God had called us to proclaim the glad tidings (Gospel) to them.

[11]Therefore, setting sail from Troas, we came in a direct course to Samothrace, and the next day went on to Neapolis.

[12]And from there [we came] to Philippi, which is the chief city of the district of Macedonia and a [Roman] colony. We stayed on in this place some days;

[13]And on the Sabbath day we went outside the [city's] gate to the bank of the river where we supposed there was an [accustomed] place of prayer, and we sat down and addressed the women who had assembled there.

[14]One of those who listened to us was a woman named Lydia, from the city of Thyatira, a dealer in fabrics dyed in purple. She was [already] a worshiper of God, and the Lord opened her heart to pay attention to what was said by Paul.

[15]And when she was baptized along with her household, she earnestly entreated us, saying, If in your opinion I am one really convinced [that Jesus is the Messiah and the Author of salvation] *and* that I will be faithful to the Lord, come to my house and stay. And she induced us [to do it].

[16]As we were on our way to the place of prayer, we were met by a slave girl who was possessed by a spirit of divination [claiming to foretell future events and to discover hidden knowledge], and she brought her owners much gain by her fortunetelling.

[17]She kept following Paul and [the rest of] us, shouting loudly, These men are the servants of the Most High God! They announce to you the way of salvation!

[18]And she did this for many days. Then Paul, being sorely annoyed *and* worn out, turned and said to the spirit within her, I charge you in the name of Jesus Christ to come out of her! And it came out that very [a]moment.

[19]But when her owners discovered that their hope of profit was gone, they caught hold of Paul and Silas and dragged them before the authorities in the forum (marketplace), [where trials are held].

[20]And when they had brought them before the magistrates, they declared, These fellows are Jews and they are throwing our city into great confusion.

[21]They encourage the practice of customs which it is unlawful for us Romans to accept or observe!

[22]The crowd [also] joined in the attack upon them, and the rulers tore the clothes off of them and commanded that they be beaten with rods.

[23]And when they had struck them with many blows, they threw them into prison, charging the jailer to keep them safely.

[24]He, having received [so strict a] charge, put them into the inner prison (the dungeon) and fastened their feet in the stocks.

---

[a] 12 The text and meaning of the Greek for *the leading city of that district* are uncertain.

[a] James Moulton and George Milligan, *The Vocabulary*.

## New International Version

[25] About midnight Paul and Silas were praying and singing hymns to God, and the other prisoners were listening to them. [26] Suddenly there was such a violent earthquake that the foundations of the prison were shaken. At once all the prison doors flew open, and everyone's chains came loose. [27] The jailer woke up, and when he saw the prison doors open, he drew his sword and was about to kill himself because he thought the prisoners had escaped. [28] But Paul shouted, "Don't harm yourself! We are all here!"

[29] The jailer called for lights, rushed in and fell trembling before Paul and Silas. [30] He then brought them out and asked, "Sirs, what must I do to be saved?"

[31] They replied, "Believe in the Lord Jesus, and you will be saved—you and your household." [32] Then they spoke the word of the Lord to him and to all the others in his house. [33] At that hour of the night the jailer took them and washed their wounds; then immediately he and all his household were baptized. [34] The jailer brought them into his house and set a meal before them; he was filled with joy because he had come to believe in God—he and his whole household.

[35] When it was daylight, the magistrates sent their officers to the jailer with the order: "Release those men." [36] The jailer told Paul, "The magistrates have ordered that you and Silas be released. Now you can leave. Go in peace."

[37] But Paul said to the officers: "They beat us publicly without a trial, even though we are Roman citizens, and threw us into prison. And now do they want to get rid of us quietly? No! Let them come themselves and escort us out."

[38] The officers reported this to the magistrates, and when they heard that Paul and Silas were Roman citizens, they were alarmed. [39] They came to appease them and escorted them from the prison, requesting them to leave the city. [40] After Paul and Silas came out of the prison, they went to Lydia's house, where they met with the brothers and sisters and encouraged them. Then they left.

### In Thessalonica

**17** When Paul and his companions had passed through Amphipolis and Apollonia, they came to Thessalonica, where there was a Jewish synagogue. [2] As was his custom, Paul went into the synagogue, and on three Sabbath days he reasoned with them from the Scriptures, [3] explaining and proving that the Messiah had to suffer and rise from the dead. "This Jesus I am proclaiming to you is the Messiah," he said. [4] Some of the Jews were persuaded and joined Paul and Silas, as did a large number of God-fearing Greeks and quite a few prominent women.

## Amplified Bible

[25] But about midnight, as Paul and Silas were praying and singing hymns of praise to God, and the [other] prisoners were listening to them,

[26] Suddenly there was a great earthquake, so that the very foundations of the prison were shaken; and at once all the doors were opened and everyone's shackles were unfastened.

[27] When the jailer, startled out of his sleep, saw that the prison doors were open, he drew his sword and was on the point of killing himself, because he supposed that the prisoners had escaped.

[28] But Paul shouted, Do not harm yourself, for we are all here!

[29] Then [the jailer] called for lights and rushed in, and trembling *and* terrified he fell down before Paul and Silas.

[30] And he brought them out [of the dungeon] and said, Men, what is it necessary for me to do that I may be saved?

[31] And they answered, Believe in the Lord Jesus *Christ* [[a]give yourself up to Him, [b]take yourself out of your own keeping and entrust yourself into His keeping] and you will be saved, [and this applies both to] you and your household as well.

[32] And they declared the Word of the Lord [the doctrine concerning the [a]attainment through Christ of eternal salvation in the kingdom of God] to him and to all who were in his house.

[33] And he took them the same hour of the night and [c]bathed [them because of their bloody] wounds, and he was baptized immediately and all [the members of] his [household].

[34] Then he took them up into his house and set food before them; and he [d]leaped much for joy *and* exulted with all his family that he believed in God [accepting and joyously welcoming what He had made known through Christ].

[35] But when it was day, the magistrates sent policemen, saying, Release those fellows *and* let them go.

[36] And the jailer repeated the words to Paul, saying, The magistrates have sent to release you *and* let you go; now therefore come out and go in peace.

[37] But Paul answered them, They have beaten us openly *and* publicly, without a trial *and* uncondemned, men who are Roman citizens, and have thrown us into prison; and do they now thrust us out secretly? No, indeed! Let them come here themselves and conduct us out!

[38] The police reported this message to the magistrates, and they were frightened when they heard that the prisoners were Roman citizens;

[39] So they came themselves and [striving to appease them by entreaty] apologized to them. And they brought them out and asked them to leave the city.

[40] So [Paul and Silas] left the prison and went to Lydia's house; and when they had seen the brethren, they warned *and* urged *and* consoled *and* encouraged them and departed.

**17** Now after [Paul and Silas] had passed through Amphipolis and Apollonia, they came to Thessalonica, where there was a synagogue of the Jews.

[2] And Paul entered, as he usually did, and for three Sabbaths he reasoned *and* argued with them from the Scriptures,

[3] Explaining [them] *and* [quoting passages] setting forth *and* proving that it was necessary for the Christ to suffer and to rise from the dead, and saying, This Jesus, Whom I proclaim to you, is the Christ (the Messiah).

[4] And some of them [accordingly] were induced to believe and associated themselves with Paul and Silas, as did a great number of the devout Greeks and not a few of the leading women.

[a] Joseph Thayer, *A Greek-English Lexicon.*  [b] Kenneth Wuest, *Word Studies.*  [c] Marvin Vincent, *Word Studies.*  [d] Robert Young, *Analytical Concordance to the Bible.*

## New International Version

[5] But other Jews were jealous; so they rounded up some bad characters from the marketplace, formed a mob and started a riot in the city. They rushed to Jason's house in search of Paul and Silas in order to bring them out to the crowd.[a] [6] But when they did not find them, they dragged Jason and some other believers before the city officials, shouting: "These men who have caused trouble all over the world have now come here, [7] and Jason has welcomed them into his house. They are all defying Caesar's decrees, saying that there is another king, one called Jesus." [8] When they heard this, the crowd and the city officials were thrown into turmoil. [9] Then they made Jason and the others post bond and let them go.

### In Berea

[10] As soon as it was night, the believers sent Paul and Silas away to Berea. On arriving there, they went to the Jewish synagogue. [11] Now the Berean Jews were of more noble character than those in Thessalonica, for they received the message with great eagerness and examined the Scriptures every day to see if what Paul said was true. [12] As a result, many of them believed, as did also a number of prominent Greek women and many Greek men.

[13] But when the Jews in Thessalonica learned that Paul was preaching the word of God at Berea, some of them went there too, agitating the crowds and stirring them up. [14] The believers immediately sent Paul to the coast, but Silas and Timothy stayed at Berea. [15] Those who escorted Paul brought him to Athens and then left with instructions for Silas and Timothy to join him as soon as possible.

### In Athens

[16] While Paul was waiting for them in Athens, he was greatly distressed to see that the city was full of idols. [17] So he reasoned in the synagogue with both Jews and God-fearing Greeks, as well as in the marketplace day by day with those who happened to be there. [18] A group of Epicurean and Stoic philosophers began to debate with him. Some of them asked, "What is this babbler trying to say?" Others remarked, "He seems to be advocating foreign gods." They said this because Paul was preaching the good news about Jesus and the resurrection. [19] Then they took him and brought him to a meeting of the Areopagus, where they said to him, "May we know what this new teaching is that you are presenting? [20] You are bringing some strange ideas to our ears, and we would like to know what they mean." [21] (All the Athenians and the foreigners who lived there spent their time doing nothing but talking about and listening to the latest ideas.)

[22] Paul then stood up in the meeting of the Areopagus and said: "People of Athens! I see that in every way you are

## Amplified Bible

[5] But the unbelieving Jews were aroused to jealousy, and, getting hold of some wicked men (ruffians and rascals) and loungers in the marketplace, they gathered together a mob, set the town in an uproar, and attacked the house of Jason, seeking to bring [Paul and Silas] out to the people.

[6] But when they failed to find them, they dragged Jason and some of the brethren before the city authorities, crying, These men who have turned the world upside down have come here also,

[7] And Jason has received them to his house and privately protected them! And they are all ignoring and acting contrary to the decrees of Caesar, [actually] asserting that there is another king, one Jesus!

[8] And both the crowd and the city authorities, on hearing this, were irritated (stirred up and troubled).

[9] And when they had taken security [bail] from Jason and the others, they let them go.

[10] Now the brethren at once sent Paul and Silas away by night to Beroea; and when they arrived, they entered the synagogue of the Jews.

[11] Now these [Jews] were better disposed and more noble than those in Thessalonica, for they were entirely ready and accepted and welcomed the message [a concerning the attainment through Christ of eternal salvation in the kingdom of God] with inclination of mind and eagerness, searching and examining the Scriptures daily to see if these things were so.

[12] Many of them therefore became believers, together with not a few prominent Greeks, women as well as men.

[13] But when the Jews of Thessalonica learned that the Word of God [a concerning the attainment through Christ of eternal salvation in the kingdom of God] was also preached by Paul at Beroea, they came there too, disturbing and inciting the masses.

[14] At once the brethren sent Paul off on his way to the sea, but Silas and Timothy remained behind.

[15] Those who escorted Paul brought him as far as Athens; and receiving instructions for Silas and Timothy that they should come to him as soon as possible, they departed.

[16] Now while Paul was awaiting them at Athens, his spirit was grieved and roused to anger as he saw that the city was full of idols.

[17] So he reasoned and argued in the synagogue with the Jews and those who worshiped there, and in the marketplace [where assemblies are held] day after day with any who chanced to be there.

[18] And some also of the Epicurean and Stoic philosophers encountered him and began to engage in discussion. And some said, What is this babbler with his scrapheap learning trying to say? Others said, He seems to be an announcer of foreign deities—because he preached Jesus and the resurrection.

[19] And they took hold of him and brought him to the [b] Areopagus [Mars Hill meeting place], saying, May we know what this novel (unheard of and unprecedented) teaching is which you are openly declaring?

[20] For you set forth some startling things, foreign and strange to our ears; we wish to know therefore just what these things mean—

[21] For the Athenians, all of them, and the foreign residents and visitors among them spent all their leisure time in nothing except telling or hearing something newer than the last—

[22] So Paul, standing in the center of the Areopagus [Mars Hill meeting place], said: Men of Athens, I perceive in every way [on every hand and with every turn I make] that you are most religious or very reverent to demons.

---

[a] Joseph Thayer, *A Greek-English Lexicon*. [b] Many modern interpreters note that the Areopagus may also have been a reference to the Council of the Areopagus, the supreme court of Athens, custodians of teachings that introduced new religions and foreign gods. See also Acts 17:34.

[a] 5 Or *the assembly of the people*

## New International Version

very religious. 23 For as I walked around and looked carefully at your objects of worship, I even found an altar with this inscription: TO AN UNKNOWN GOD. So you are ignorant of the very thing you worship—and this is what I am going to proclaim to you.

24 "The God who made the world and everything in it is the Lord of heaven and earth and does not live in temples built by human hands. 25 And he is not served by human hands, as if he needed anything. Rather, he himself gives everyone life and breath and everything else. 26 From one man he made all the nations, that they should inhabit the whole earth; and he marked out their appointed times in history and the boundaries of their lands. 27 God did this so that they would seek him and perhaps reach out for him and find him, though he is not far from any one of us. 28 'For in him we live and move and have our being.'ᵃ As some of your own poets have said, 'We are his offspring.'ᵇ

29 "Therefore since we are God's offspring, we should not think that the divine being is like gold or silver or stone—an image made by human design and skill. 30 In the past God overlooked such ignorance, but now he commands all people everywhere to repent. 31 For he has set a day when he will judge the world with justice by the man he has appointed. He has given proof of this to everyone by raising him from the dead."

32 When they heard about the resurrection of the dead, some of them sneered, but others said, "We want to hear you again on this subject." 33 At that, Paul left the Council. 34 Some of the people became followers of Paul and believed. Among them was Dionysius, a member of the Areopagus, also a woman named Damaris, and a number of others.

### In Corinth

**18** After this, Paul left Athens and went to Corinth. 2 There he met a Jew named Aquila, a native of Pontus, who had recently come from Italy with his wife Priscilla, because Claudius had ordered all Jews to leave Rome. Paul went to see them, 3 and because he was a tentmaker as they were, he stayed and worked with them. 4 Every Sabbath he reasoned in the synagogue, trying to persuade Jews and Greeks.

5 When Silas and Timothy came from Macedonia, Paul devoted himself exclusively to preaching, testifying to the Jews that Jesus was the Messiah. 6 But when they opposed Paul and became abusive, he shook out his clothes in protest and said to them, "Your blood be on your own heads! I am innocent of it. From now on I will go to the Gentiles."

7 Then Paul left the synagogue and went next door to the house of Titius Justus, a worshiper of God. 8 Crispus, the synagogue leader, and his entire household believed

## Amplified Bible

23 For as I passed along and carefully observed your objects of worship, I came also upon an altar with this inscription, To the unknown god. Now what you are already worshiping as unknown, this I set forth to you.

24 The God Who produced *and* formed the world and all things in it, being Lord of heaven and earth, does not dwell in handmade shrines.

25 Neither is He served by human hands, as though He lacked anything, for it is He Himself Who gives life and breath and all things to all [people]. [Isa. 42:5.]

26 And He made from one [common origin, one source, one blood] all nations of men to settle on the face of the earth, having definitely determined [their] allotted periods of time and the fixed boundaries of their habitation (their settlements, lands, and abodes),

27 So that they should seek God, in the hope that they might feel after Him and find Him, although He is not far from each one of us.

28 For in Him we live and move and have our being; as even some of your [own] poets have said, For we are also His offspring.

29 Since then we are God's offspring, we ought not to suppose that Deity (the Godhead) is like gold or silver or stone, [of the nature of] a representation by human art and imagination, *or* anything constructed *or* invented.

30 Such [former] ages of ignorance God, it is true, ignored *and* allowed to pass unnoticed; but now He charges all people everywhere to repent (ᵃto change their minds for the better and heartily to amend their ways, with abhorrence of their past sins),

31 Because He has fixed a day when He will judge the world righteously (justly) by a Man Whom He has destined *and* appointed for that task, and He has made this credible *and* given conviction *and* assurance *and* evidence to everyone by raising Him from the dead. [Ps. 9:8; 96:13; 98:9.]

32 Now when they had heard [that there had been] a resurrection from the dead, some scoffed; but others said, We will hear you again about this matter.

33 So Paul went out from among them.

34 But some men were on his side *and* joined him and believed (became Christians); among them were Dionysius, a judge of the Areopagus, and a woman named Damaris, and some others with them.

**18** After this [Paul] departed from Athens and went to Corinth. 2 There he met a Jew named Aquila, a native of Pontus, recently arrived from Italy with Priscilla his wife, due to the fact that Claudius had issued an edict that all the Jews were to leave Rome. And [Paul] went to see them,

3 And because he was of the same occupation, he stayed with them; and they worked [together], for they were tentmakers by trade.

4 But he discoursed *and* argued in the synagogue every Sabbath and won over [both] Jews and Greeks.

5 By the time Silas and Timothy arrived from Macedonia, Paul was completely engrossed with preaching, earnestly arguing *and* testifying to the Jews that Jesus [is] the Christ.

6 But since they kept opposing *and* abusing *and* reviling him, he shook out his clothing [against them] and said to them, Your blood be upon your [own] heads! I am innocent [of it]. From now on I will go to the Gentiles (the heathen). [Acts 13:46.]

7 He then left there and went to the house of a man named Titus Justus, who worshiped God and whose house was next door to the synagogue.

8 But Crispus, the leader of the synagogue, believed [that Jesus is the Messiah and acknowledged Him with

---

ᵃ 28 From the Cretan philosopher Epimenides    ᵇ 28 From the Cilician Stoic philosopher Aratus

ᵃ Joseph Thayer, *A Greek-English Lexicon.*

## New International Version

in the Lord; and many of the Corinthians who heard Paul believed and were baptized.

⁹One night the Lord spoke to Paul in a vision: "Do not be afraid; keep on speaking, do not be silent. ¹⁰For I am with you, and no one is going to attack and harm you, because I have many people in this city." ¹¹So Paul stayed in Corinth for a year and a half, teaching them the word of God.

¹²While Gallio was proconsul of Achaia, the Jews of Corinth made a united attack on Paul and brought him to the place of judgment. ¹³"This man," they charged, "is persuading the people to worship God in ways contrary to the law."

¹⁴Just as Paul was about to speak, Gallio said to them, "If you Jews were making a complaint about some misdemeanor or serious crime, it would be reasonable for me to listen to you. ¹⁵But since it involves questions about words and names and your own law—settle the matter yourselves. I will not be a judge of such things." ¹⁶So he drove them off. ¹⁷Then the crowd there turned on Sosthenes the synagogue leader and beat him in front of the proconsul; and Gallio showed no concern whatever.

### Priscilla, Aquila and Apollos

¹⁸Paul stayed on in Corinth for some time. Then he left the brothers and sisters and sailed for Syria, accompanied by Priscilla and Aquila. Before he sailed, he had his hair cut off at Cenchreae because of a vow he had taken. ¹⁹They arrived at Ephesus, where Paul left Priscilla and Aquila. He himself went into the synagogue and reasoned with the Jews. ²⁰When they asked him to spend more time with them, he declined. ²¹But as he left, he promised, "I will come back if it is God's will." Then he set sail from Ephesus. ²²When he landed at Caesarea, he went up to Jerusalem and greeted the church and then went down to Antioch.

²³After spending some time in Antioch, Paul set out from there and traveled from place to place throughout the region of Galatia and Phrygia, strengthening all the disciples.

²⁴Meanwhile a Jew named Apollos, a native of Alexandria, came to Ephesus. He was a learned man, with a thorough knowledge of the Scriptures. ²⁵He had been instructed in the way of the Lord, and he spoke with great fervor*a* and taught about Jesus accurately, though he knew only the baptism of John. ²⁶He began to speak boldly in the synagogue. When Priscilla and Aquila heard him, they invited him to their home and explained to him the way of God more adequately.

²⁷When Apollos wanted to go to Achaia, the brothers and sisters encouraged him and wrote to the disciples there to welcome him. When he arrived, he was a great help to those who by grace had believed. ²⁸For he vigorously refuted his Jewish opponents in public debate, proving from the Scriptures that Jesus was the Messiah.

## Amplified Bible

joyful trust as Savior and Lord], together with his entire household; and many of the Corinthians who listened [to Paul also] believed and were baptized.

⁹And one night the Lord said to Paul in a vision, Have no fear, but speak and do not keep silent;

¹⁰For I am with you, and no man shall assault you to harm you, for I have many people in this city. [Isa. 43:5; Jer. 1:8.]

¹¹So he settled down among them for a year and six months, teaching the Word of God [concerning the *a*attainment through Christ of eternal salvation in the kingdom of God].

¹²But when Gallio was proconsul of Achaia (most of Greece), the Jews unitedly made an attack upon Paul and brought him before the judge's seat,

¹³Declaring, This fellow is advising *and* inducing *and* inciting people to worship God in violation of the *b*Law [of Rome and of Moses].

¹⁴But when Paul was about to open his mouth to reply, Gallio said to the Jews, If it were a matter of some misdemeanor or villainy, O Jews, I should have cause to bear with you *and* listen;

¹⁵But since it is merely a question [of doctrine] about words and names and your own law, see to it yourselves; I decline to be a judge of such matters *and* I have no intention of trying such cases.

¹⁶And he drove them away from the judgment seat.

¹⁷Then they [the Greeks] all seized Sosthenes, the leader of the synagogue, and beat him right in front of the judgment seat. But Gallio paid no attention to any of this.

¹⁸Afterward Paul remained many days longer, and then told the brethren farewell and sailed for Syria; and he was accompanied by Priscilla and Aquila. At Cenchreae he [*c*Paul] cut his hair, for he had made a vow.

¹⁹Then they arrived at Ephesus, and [Paul] left the others there; but he himself entered the synagogue and discoursed *and* argued with the Jews.

²⁰When they asked him to remain for a longer time, he would not consent;

²¹But when he was leaving them he said, I will return to you if God is willing, and he set sail from Ephesus.

²²When he landed at Caesarea, he went up and saluted the church [at Jerusalem], and then went down to Antioch.

²³After staying there some time, he left and went from place to place in an orderly journey through the territory of Galatia and Phrygia, establishing the disciples *and* imparting new strength to them.

²⁴Meanwhile, there was a Jew named Apollos, a native of Alexandria, who came to Ephesus. He was a cultured *and* eloquent man, well versed *and* mighty in the Scriptures.

²⁵He had been instructed in the way of the Lord, and burning with spiritual zeal, he spoke and taught diligently *and* accurately the things concerning Jesus, though he was acquainted only with the baptism of John.

²⁶He began to speak freely (fearlessly and boldly) in the synagogue; but when Priscilla and Aquila heard him, they took him with them and expounded to him the way of God more definitely *and* accurately.

²⁷And when [Apollos] wished to cross to Achaia (most of Greece), the brethren wrote to the disciples there, urging *and* encouraging them to accept *and* welcome him heartily. When he arrived, he proved a great help to those who through grace (God's unmerited favor and mercy) had believed (adhered to, trusted in, and relied on Christ as Lord and Savior).

²⁸For with great power he refuted the Jews in public [discussions], showing *and* proving by the Scriptures that Jesus is the Christ (the Messiah).

---

*a* Joseph Thayer, *A Greek-English Lexicon.* *b* The Jews were claiming that Paul was advocating a religion not recognized by Roman law as Judaism was. *c* Some commentators (such as Marvin Vincent, *Word Studies* and Henry Alford, *The Greek New Testament*) believe Paul is the one who made the vow, while others think Aquila is meant.

---

*a* 25 Or *with fervor in the Spirit*

## New International Version

### Paul in Ephesus

**19** While Apollos was at Corinth, Paul took the road through the interior and arrived at Ephesus. There he found some disciples ²and asked them, "Did you receive the Holy Spirit when*a* you believed?"

They answered, "No, we have not even heard that there is a Holy Spirit."

³So Paul asked, "Then what baptism did you receive?"

"John's baptism," they replied.

⁴Paul said, "John's baptism was a baptism of repentance. He told the people to believe in the one coming after him, that is, in Jesus." ⁵On hearing this, they were baptized in the name of the Lord Jesus. ⁶When Paul placed his hands on them, the Holy Spirit came on them, and they spoke in tongues*b* and prophesied. ⁷There were about twelve men in all.

⁸Paul entered the synagogue and spoke boldly there for three months, arguing persuasively about the kingdom of God. ⁹But some of them became obstinate; they refused to believe and publicly maligned the Way. So Paul left them. He took the disciples with him and had discussions daily in the lecture hall of Tyrannus. ¹⁰This went on for two years, so that all the Jews and Greeks who lived in the province of Asia heard the word of the Lord.

¹¹God did extraordinary miracles through Paul, ¹²so that even handkerchiefs and aprons that had touched him were taken to the sick, and their illnesses were cured and the evil spirits left them.

¹³Some Jews who went around driving out evil spirits tried to invoke the name of the Lord Jesus over those who were demon-possessed. They would say, "In the name of the Jesus whom Paul preaches, I command you to come out." ¹⁴Seven sons of Sceva, a Jewish chief priest, were doing this. ¹⁵One day the evil spirit answered them, "Jesus I know, and Paul I know about, but who are you?" ¹⁶Then the man who had the evil spirit jumped on them and overpowered them all. He gave them such a beating that they ran out of the house naked and bleeding.

¹⁷When this became known to the Jews and Greeks living in Ephesus, they were all seized with fear, and the name of the Lord Jesus was held in high honor. ¹⁸Many of those who believed now came and openly confessed what they had done. ¹⁹A number who had practiced sorcery brought their scrolls together and burned them publicly. When they calculated the value of the scrolls, the total came to fifty thousand drachmas.*c* ²⁰In this way the word of the Lord spread widely and grew in power.

²¹After all this had happened, Paul decided*d* to go to Jerusalem, passing through Macedonia and Achaia. "After

## Amplified Bible

**19** While Apollos was in Corinth, Paul went through the upper inland districts and came down to Ephesus. There he found some disciples.

²And he asked them, Did you receive the Holy Spirit when you believed [on Jesus as the Christ]? And they said, No, we have not even heard that there is a Holy Spirit.

³And he asked, Into what [baptism] then were you baptized? They said, Into John's baptism.

⁴And Paul said, John baptized with the baptism of repentance, continually telling the people that they should believe in the One Who was to come after him, that is, in Jesus [having a conviction full of joyful trust that He is Christ, the Messiah, and being obedient to Him].

⁵On hearing this they were baptized [again, this time] in the name of the Lord Jesus.

⁶And as Paul laid his hands upon them, the Holy Spirit came on them; and they spoke in [foreign, unknown] tongues (languages) and prophesied.

⁷There were about twelve of them in all.

⁸And he went into the synagogue and for three months spoke boldly, persuading *and* arguing and pleading about the kingdom of God.

⁹But when some became more and more stubborn (hardened and unbelieving), discrediting *and* reviling *and* speaking evil of the Way [of the Lord] before the congregation, he separated himself from them, taking the disciples with him, and went on holding daily discussions in the lecture room of Tyrannus *from about ten o'clock till three.*

¹⁰This continued for two years, so that all the inhabitants of [the province of] Asia, Jews as well as Greeks, heard the Word of the Lord [concerning the *a*attainment through Christ of eternal salvation in the kingdom of God].

¹¹And God did unusual *and* extraordinary miracles by the hands of Paul,

¹²So that handkerchiefs *or* towels or aprons which had touched his skin were carried away *and* put upon the sick, and their diseases left them and the evil spirits came out of them.

¹³Then some of the traveling Jewish exorcists (men who adjure evil spirits) also undertook to call the name of the Lord Jesus over those who had evil spirits, saying, I solemnly implore *and* charge you by the Jesus Whom Paul preaches!

¹⁴Seven sons of a certain Jewish chief priest named Sceva were doing this.

¹⁵But [one] evil spirit retorted, Jesus I know, and Paul I know *b*about, but who are you?

¹⁶Then the man in whom the evil spirit dwelt leaped upon them, mastering *c*two of them, and was so violent against them that they dashed out of that house [in fear], stripped naked and wounded.

¹⁷This became known to all who lived in Ephesus, both Jews and Greeks, and alarm *and* terror fell upon them all; and the name of the Lord Jesus was extolled *and* magnified.

¹⁸Many also of those who were now believers came making *d*full confession *and* thoroughly exposing their [former deceptive and evil] practices.

¹⁹And many of those who had practiced curious, magical arts collected their books and [throwing them, *d*book after book, on the pile] burned them in the sight of everybody. When they counted the value of them, they found it amounted to 50,000 pieces of silver (*d*about $9,300).

²⁰Thus the Word of the Lord [concerning the *a*attainment through Christ of eternal salvation in the kingdom of God] grew *and* spread *and* intensified, prevailing mightily.

²¹Now after these events Paul determined in the [Holy] Spirit that he would travel through Macedonia and Achaia

---

*a 2* Or *after* 　*b 6* Or *other languages* 　*c 19* A drachma was a silver coin worth about a day's wages. 　*d 21* Or *decided in the Spirit*

*a* Joseph Thayer, *A Greek-English Lexicon.* 　*b* A weaker verb. 　*c* The best texts read "both of them." 　*d* Marvin Vincent, *Word Studies.*

# New International Version

I have been there," he said, "I must visit Rome also." 22 He sent two of his helpers, Timothy and Erastus, to Macedonia, while he stayed in the province of Asia a little longer.

## The Riot in Ephesus

23 About that time there arose a great disturbance about the Way. 24 A silversmith named Demetrius, who made silver shrines of Artemis, brought in a lot of business for the craftsmen there. 25 He called them together, along with the workers in related trades, and said: "You know, my friends, that we receive a good income from this business. 26 And you see and hear how this fellow Paul has convinced and led astray large numbers of people here in Ephesus and in practically the whole province of Asia. He says that gods made by human hands are no gods at all. 27 There is danger not only that our trade will lose its good name, but also that the temple of the great goddess Artemis will be discredited; and the goddess herself, who is worshiped throughout the province of Asia and the world, will be robbed of her divine majesty."

28 When they heard this, they were furious and began shouting: "Great is Artemis of the Ephesians!" 29 Soon the whole city was in an uproar. The people seized Gaius and Aristarchus, Paul's traveling companions from Macedonia, and all of them rushed into the theater together. 30 Paul wanted to appear before the crowd, but the disciples would not let him. 31 Even some of the officials of the province, friends of Paul, sent him a message begging him not to venture into the theater.

32 The assembly was in confusion: Some were shouting one thing, some another. Most of the people did not even know why they were there. 33 The Jews in the crowd pushed Alexander to the front, and they shouted instructions to him. He motioned for silence in order to make a defense before the people. 34 But when they realized he was a Jew, they all shouted in unison for about two hours: "Great is Artemis of the Ephesians!"

35 The city clerk quieted the crowd and said: "Fellow Ephesians, doesn't all the world know that the city of Ephesus is the guardian of the temple of the great Artemis and of her image, which fell from heaven? 36 Therefore, since these facts are undeniable, you ought to calm down and not do anything rash. 37 You have brought these men here, though they have neither robbed temples nor blasphemed our goddess. 38 If, then, Demetrius and his fellow craftsmen have a grievance against anybody, the courts are open and there are proconsuls. They can press charges. 39 If there is anything further you want to bring up, it must be settled in a legal assembly. 40 As it is, we are in danger of being charged with rioting because of what happened today. In that case we would not be able to account for this commotion, since there is no reason for it." 41 After he had said this, he dismissed the assembly.

# Amplified Bible

(most of Greece) and go to Jerusalem, saying, After I have been there, I must visit Rome also.

22 And having sent two of his assistants, Timothy and Erastus, into Macedonia, he himself stayed on in [the province of] Asia for a while.

23 But as time went on, there arose no little disturbance concerning the Way [of the Lord].

24 For a man named Demetrius, a silversmith, who made silver shrines of [the goddess] Artemis *a* [Diana], brought no small income to his craftsmen.

25 These he called together, along with the workmen of similar trades, and said, Men, you are acquainted with the facts *and* understand that from this business we derive our wealth *and* livelihood.

26 Now you notice and hear that not only at Ephesus but almost all over [the province of] Asia this Paul has persuaded *and* induced people to believe his teaching and has alienated a considerable company of them, saying that gods that are made with hands are not really gods at all.

27 Now there is danger not merely that this trade of ours may be discredited, but also that the temple of the great goddess Artemis may come into disrepute *and* count for nothing, and that her glorious magnificence may be degraded and fall into contempt—she whom all [the province of] Asia and the wide world worship.

28 As they listened to this, they were filled with rage and they continued to shout, Great is Artemis of the Ephesians!

29 Then the city was filled with confusion; and they rushed together into the amphitheater, dragging along with them Gaius and Aristarchus, Macedonians who were fellow travelers with Paul.

30 Paul wished to go in among the crowd, but the disciples would not permit him to do it.

31 Even some of the Asiarchs (political or religious officials in Asia) who were his friends also sent to him and warned him not to risk venturing into the theater.

32 Now some shouted one thing and some another, for the gathering was in a tumult and most of them did not know why they had come together.

33 Some of the crowd called upon Alexander [to speak], since the Jews had pushed *and* urged him forward. And Alexander motioned with his hand, wishing to make a defense *and* [planning] to apologize to the people.

34 But as soon as they saw him *and* recognized that he was a Jew, a shout went up from them as the voice of one man, as for about two hours they cried, Great is Artemis of the Ephesians!

35 And when the town clerk had calmed the crowd down, he said, Men of Ephesus, what man is there who does not know that the city of the Ephesians is guardian of the temple of the great Artemis and of the sacred stone [image of her] that fell from the sky?

36 Seeing then that these things cannot be denied, you ought to be quiet (keep yourselves in check) and do nothing rashly.

37 For you have brought these men here, who are [guilty of] neither temple robberies nor blasphemous speech about our goddess.

38 Now then, if Demetrius and his fellow tradesmen who are with him have a grievance against anyone, the courts are open and proconsuls are [available]; let them bring charges against one another [legally].

39 But if you require anything further about this *or about other matters*, it must be decided *and* cleared up in the regular assembly.

40 For we are in danger of being called to render an account *and* of being accused of rioting because of [this commotion] today, there being no reason that we can offer to justify this disorder.

41 And when he had said these things, he dismissed the assembly.

---

*a* Artemis is the Greek name for the Roman goddess Diana.

## New International Version

### Through Macedonia and Greece

**20** When the uproar had ended, Paul sent for the disciples and, after encouraging them, said goodbye and set out for Macedonia. ²He traveled through that area, speaking many words of encouragement to the people, and finally arrived in Greece, ³where he stayed three months. Because some Jews had plotted against him just as he was about to sail for Syria, he decided to go back through Macedonia. ⁴He was accompanied by Sopater son of Pyrrhus from Berea, Aristarchus and Secundus from Thessalonica, Gaius from Derbe, Timothy also, and Tychicus and Trophimus from the province of Asia. ⁵These men went on ahead and waited for us at Troas. ⁶But we sailed from Philippi after the Festival of Unleavened Bread, and five days later joined the others at Troas, where we stayed seven days.

### Eutychus Raised From the Dead at Troas

⁷On the first day of the week we came together to break bread. Paul spoke to the people and, because he intended to leave the next day, kept on talking until midnight. ⁸There were many lamps in the upstairs room where we were meeting. ⁹Seated in a window was a young man named Eutychus, who was sinking into a deep sleep as Paul talked on and on. When he was sound asleep, he fell to the ground from the third story and was picked up dead. ¹⁰Paul went down, threw himself on the young man and put his arms around him. "Don't be alarmed," he said. "He's alive!" ¹¹Then he went upstairs again and broke bread and ate. After talking until daylight, he left. ¹²The people took the young man home alive and were greatly comforted.

### Paul's Farewell to the Ephesian Elders

¹³We went on ahead to the ship and sailed for Assos, where we were going to take Paul aboard. He had made this arrangement because he was going there on foot. ¹⁴When he met us at Assos, we took him aboard and went on to Mitylene. ¹⁵The next day we set sail from there and arrived off Chios. The day after that we crossed over to Samos, and on the following day arrived at Miletus. ¹⁶Paul had decided to sail past Ephesus to avoid spending time in the province of Asia, for he was in a hurry to reach Jerusalem, if possible, by the day of Pentecost. ¹⁷From Miletus, Paul sent to Ephesus for the elders of the church. ¹⁸When they arrived, he said to them: "You know how I lived the whole time I was with you, from the first day I came into the province of Asia. ¹⁹I served the Lord with great humility and with tears and in the midst of severe testing by the plots of my Jewish opponents. ²⁰You know that I have not hesitated to preach anything that would be helpful to you but have taught you publicly and from house to house. ²¹I have declared to both Jews and Greeks that they must turn to God in repentance and have faith in our Lord Jesus.

## Amplified Bible

**20** After the uproar had ceased, Paul sent for the disciples and warned *and* consoled *and* urged *and* encouraged them; then he embraced them *and* told them farewell and set forth on his journey to Macedonia.

²Then after he had gone through those districts and had warned *and* consoled *and* urged *and* encouraged the brethren with much discourse, he came to Greece.

³Having spent three months there, when a plot was formed against him by the Jews as he was about to set sail for Syria, he resolved to go back through Macedonia.

⁴He was accompanied by Sopater the son of Pyrrhus from Beroea, and by the Thessalonians Aristarchus and Secundus, and Gaius of Derbe and Timothy, and the Asians Tychicus and Trophimus.

⁵These went on ahead and were waiting for us [including Luke] at Troas,

⁶But we [ourselves] sailed from Philippi after the days of Unleavened Bread [the Passover week], and in five days we joined them at Troas, where we remained for seven days.

⁷And on the first day of the week, when we were assembled together to break bread [ᵃthe Lord's Supper], Paul discoursed with them, intending to leave the next morning; and he kept on with his message until midnight.

⁸Now there were numerous lights in the upper room where we were assembled,

⁹And there was a young man named Eutychus sitting in the window. He was borne down with deep sleep as Paul kept on talking still longer, and [finally] completely overcome by sleep, he fell down from the third story and was picked up dead.

¹⁰But Paul went down and bent over him and embraced him, saying, Make no ado; his life is within him.

¹¹When Paul had gone back upstairs and had broken bread and eaten [with them], and after he had talked confidentially *and* communed with them for a considerable time—until daybreak [in fact]—he departed.

¹²They took the youth home alive, and were not a little comforted *and* cheered *and* refreshed *and* encouraged.

¹³But going on ahead to the ship, the rest of us set sail for Assos, intending to take Paul aboard there, for that was what he had directed, intending himself to go by land [on foot].

¹⁴So when he met us at Assos, we took him aboard and sailed on to Mitylene.

¹⁵And sailing from there, we arrived the day after at a point opposite Chios; the following day we struck across to Samos, and the next day we arrived at Miletus.

¹⁶For Paul had determined to sail on past Ephesus, lest he might have to spend time [unnecessarily] in [the province of] Asia; for he was hastening on so that he might reach Jerusalem, if at all possible, by the day of Pentecost.

¹⁷However, from Miletus he sent to Ephesus and summoned the elders of the church [to come to him there].

¹⁸And when they arrived he said to them: You yourselves are well acquainted with my manner of living among you from the first day that I set foot in [the province of] Asia, and how I continued afterward,

¹⁹Serving the Lord with all humility in tears and in the midst of adversity (affliction and trials) which befell me, due to the plots of the Jews [against me];

²⁰How I did not shrink from telling you anything that was for your benefit and teaching you in public meetings and from house to house,

²¹But constantly *and* earnestly I bore testimony both to Jews and Greeks, urging them to turn in repentance [ᵇthat is due] to God and to have faith in our Lord Jesus Christ [ᵇthat is due Him].

---

ᵃ Joseph Thayer, *A Greek-English Lexicon.* ᵇ Marvin Vincent, *Word Studies.*

## New International Version

22"And now, compelled by the Spirit, I am going to Jerusalem, not knowing what will happen to me there. 23I only know that in every city the Holy Spirit warns me that prison and hardships are facing me. 24However, I consider my life worth nothing to me; my only aim is to finish the race and complete the task the Lord Jesus has given me—the task of testifying to the good news of God's grace.

25"Now I know that none of you among whom I have gone about preaching the kingdom will ever see me again. 26Therefore, I declare to you today that I am innocent of the blood of any of you. 27For I have not hesitated to proclaim to you the whole will of God. 28Keep watch over yourselves and all the flock of which the Holy Spirit has made you overseers. Be shepherds of the church of God,*a* which he bought with his own blood.*b* 29I know that after I leave, savage wolves will come in among you and will not spare the flock. 30Even from your own number men will arise and distort the truth in order to draw away disciples after them. 31So be on your guard! Remember that for three years I never stopped warning each of you night and day with tears.

32"Now I commit you to God and to the word of his grace, which can build you up and give you an inheritance among all those who are sanctified. 33I have not coveted anyone's silver or gold or clothing. 34You yourselves know that these hands of mine have supplied my own needs and the needs of my companions. 35In everything I did, I showed you that by this kind of hard work we must help the weak, remembering the words the Lord Jesus himself said: 'It is more blessed to give than to receive.'"

36When Paul had finished speaking, he knelt down with all of them and prayed. 37They all wept as they embraced him and kissed him. 38What grieved them most was his statement that they would never see his face again. Then they accompanied him to the ship.

### On to Jerusalem

**21** After we had torn ourselves away from them, we put out to sea and sailed straight to Kos. The next day we went to Rhodes and from there to Patara. 2We found a ship crossing over to Phoenicia, went on board and set sail. 3After sighting Cyprus and passing to the south of it, we sailed on to Syria. We landed at Tyre, where our ship

## Amplified Bible

22And now, you see, I am going to Jerusalem, bound by the [Holy] Spirit *and* obligated *and* compelled by the [convictions of my own] spirit, not knowing what will befall me there—

23Except that the Holy Spirit clearly *and* emphatically affirms to me in city after city that imprisonment and suffering await me.

24But *none of these things move me;* neither do I esteem my life dear to myself, if only I may finish my course *with joy* and the ministry which I have obtained from [which was entrusted to me by] the Lord Jesus, faithfully to attest to the good news (Gospel) of God's grace (His unmerited favor, spiritual blessing, and mercy).

25And now, observe, I perceive that all of you, among whom I have gone in and out proclaiming the kingdom, will see my face no more.

26Therefore I testify *and* protest to you on this [our parting] day that I am clean *and* innocent *and* not responsible for the blood of any of you.

27For I never shrank *or* kept back *or* fell short from declaring to you the whole purpose *and* plan *and* counsel of God.

28Take care *and* be on guard for yourselves and the whole flock over which the Holy Spirit has appointed you bishops and guardians, to shepherd (tend and feed and guide) the church of the Lord *or* *a*of God which He obtained for Himself [buying it and saving it for Himself] with His own blood.

29I know that after I am gone, ferocious wolves will get in among you, not sparing the flock;

30Even from among your own selves men will come to the front who, by saying perverse (distorted and corrupt) things, will endeavor to draw away the disciples after them [to their own party].

31Therefore be always alert *and* on your guard, being mindful that for three years I never stopped night or day seriously to admonish *and* advise *and* exhort you one by one with tears.

32And now [brethren], I commit you to God [I deposit you in His charge, entrusting you to His protection and care]. And I commend you to the Word of His grace [to the commands and counsels and promises of His unmerited favor]. It is able to build you up and to give you [your rightful] inheritance among all God's set-apart ones (those consecrated, purified, and transformed of soul).

33I coveted no man's silver or gold or [costly] garments.

34You yourselves know personally that these hands ministered to my own needs and those [of the persons] who were with me.

35In everything I have pointed out to you [by example] that, by working diligently in this manner, we ought to assist the weak, being mindful of the words of the Lord Jesus, how He Himself said, It is more blessed (makes one happier and more *b*to be envied) to give than to receive.

36Having spoken thus, he knelt down with them all and prayed.

37And they all wept freely and threw their arms around Paul's neck and kissed him fervently *and* repeatedly,

38Being especially distressed *and* sorrowful because he had stated that they were about to see his face no more. And they accompanied him to the ship.

**21** And when we had torn ourselves away from them *and* withdrawn, we set sail and made a straight run to Cos, and on the following [day came] to Rhodes and from there to Patara.

2There we found a ship crossing over to Phoenicia; so we went aboard and sailed away.

3After we had sighted Cyprus, leaving it on our left we sailed on to Syria and put in at Tyre, for there the ship was to unload her cargo.

---

*a* 28 Many manuscripts *of the Lord*   *b* 28 Or *with the blood of his own Son.*

*a* Many ancient manuscripts read "of God."   *b* Alexander Souter, *Pocket Lexicon.*

## New International Version

was to unload its cargo. ⁴We sought out the disciples there and stayed with them seven days. Through the Spirit they urged Paul not to go on to Jerusalem. ⁵When it was time to leave, we left and continued on our way. All of them, including wives and children, accompanied us out of the city, and there on the beach we knelt to pray. ⁶After saying goodbye to each other, we went aboard the ship, and they returned home.

⁷We continued our voyage from Tyre and landed at Ptolemais, where we greeted the brothers and sisters and stayed with them for a day. ⁸Leaving the next day, we reached Caesarea and stayed at the house of Philip the evangelist, one of the Seven. ⁹He had four unmarried daughters who prophesied.

¹⁰After we had been there a number of days, a prophet named Agabus came down from Judea. ¹¹Coming over to us, he took Paul's belt, tied his own hands and feet with it and said, "The Holy Spirit says, 'In this way the Jewish leaders in Jerusalem will bind the owner of this belt and will hand him over to the Gentiles.'"

¹²When we heard this, we and the people there pleaded with Paul not to go up to Jerusalem. ¹³Then Paul answered, "Why are you weeping and breaking my heart? I am ready not only to be bound, but also to die in Jerusalem for the name of the Lord Jesus." ¹⁴When he would not be dissuaded, we gave up and said, "The Lord's will be done."

¹⁵After this, we started on our way up to Jerusalem. ¹⁶Some of the disciples from Caesarea accompanied us and brought us to the home of Mnason, where we were to stay. He was a man from Cyprus and one of the early disciples.

### Paul's Arrival at Jerusalem

¹⁷When we arrived at Jerusalem, the brothers and sisters received us warmly. ¹⁸The next day Paul and the rest of us went to see James, and all the elders were present. ¹⁹Paul greeted them and reported in detail what God had done among the Gentiles through his ministry.

²⁰When they heard this, they praised God. Then they said to Paul: "You see, brother, how many thousands of Jews have believed, and all of them are zealous for the law. ²¹They have been informed that you teach all the Jews who live among the Gentiles to turn away from Moses, telling them not to circumcise their children or live according to our customs. ²²What shall we do? They will certainly hear that you have come, ²³so do what we tell you. There are four men with us who have made a vow. ²⁴Take these men, join in their purification rites and pay their expenses, so that they can have their heads shaved. Then everyone will know there is no truth in these reports about you, but that you yourself are living in obedience to the law. ²⁵As for the Gentile believers, we have written to them our deci-

## Amplified Bible

⁴And having looked up the disciples there, we remained with them for seven days. Prompted by the [Holy] Spirit, they kept telling Paul not to set foot in Jerusalem.

⁵But when our time there was ended, we left and proceeded on our journey; and all of them with their wives and children accompanied us on our way till we were outside the city. There we knelt down on the beach and prayed.

⁶Then when we had told one another farewell, we went on board the ship, and they returned to their own homes.

⁷When we had completed the voyage from Tyre, we landed at Ptolemais, where we paid our respects to the brethren and remained with them for one day.

⁸On the morrow we left there and came to Caesarea; and we went into the house of Philip the evangelist, who was one of the Seven [first deacons], and stayed with him. [Acts 6:5.]

⁹And he had four maiden daughters who had the gift of prophecy.

¹⁰While we were remaining there for some time, a prophet named Agabus came down from Judea.

¹¹And coming to [see] us, he took Paul's belt and with it bound his own feet and hands and said, Thus says the Holy Spirit: The Jews at Jerusalem shall bind like this the man who owns this belt, and they shall deliver him into the hands of the Gentiles (heathen).

¹²When we heard this, both we and the residents of that place pleaded with him not to go up to Jerusalem.

¹³Then Paul replied, What do you mean by weeping and breaking my heart like this? For I hold myself in readiness not only to be arrested and bound and imprisoned at Jerusalem, but also [even] to die for the name of the Lord Jesus.

¹⁴And when he would not yield to [our] persuading, we stopped [urging and imploring him], saying, The Lord's will be done!

¹⁵After these days we packed our baggage and went up to Jerusalem.

¹⁶And some of the disciples from Caesarea came with us, conducting us to the house of Mnason, a man from Cyprus, one of the disciples of long standing, with whom we were to lodge.

¹⁷When we arrived in Jerusalem, the brethren received and welcomed us gladly.

¹⁸On the next day Paul went in with us to [see] James, and all the elders of the church were present [also].

¹⁹After saluting them, Paul gave a detailed account of the things God had done among the Gentiles through his ministry.

²⁰And upon hearing it, they adored and exalted and praised and thanked God. And they said to [Paul], You see, brother, how many thousands of believers there are among the Jews, and all of them are enthusiastic upholders of the [Mosaic] Law.

²¹Now they have been informed about you that you continually teach all the Jews who live among the Gentiles to turn back from and forsake Moses, advising them not to circumcise their children or pay any attention to the observance of the [Mosaic] customs.

²²What then [is best that] should be done? A multitude will come together, for they will surely hear that you have arrived.

²³Therefore do just what we tell you. With us are four men who have taken a vow upon themselves.

²⁴Take these men and purify yourself along with them and pay their expenses [for the temple offering], so that they may have their heads shaved. Thus everybody will know that there is no truth in what they have been told about you, but that you yourself walk in observance of the Law.

²⁵But with regard to the Gentiles who have believed (adhered to, trusted in, and relied on Christ), we have

## New International Version

sion that they should abstain from food sacrificed to idols, from blood, from the meat of strangled animals and from sexual immorality."

26The next day Paul took the men and purified himself along with them. Then he went to the temple to give notice of the date when the days of purification would end and the offering would be made for each of them.

### Paul Arrested

27When the seven days were nearly over, some Jews from the province of Asia saw Paul at the temple. They stirred up the whole crowd and seized him, 28shouting, "Fellow Israelites, help us! This is the man who teaches everyone everywhere against our people and our law and this place. And besides, he has brought Greeks into the temple and defiled this holy place." 29(They had previously seen Trophimus the Ephesian in the city with Paul and assumed that Paul had brought him into the temple.)

30The whole city was aroused, and the people came running from all directions. Seizing Paul, they dragged him from the temple, and immediately the gates were shut. 31While they were trying to kill him, news reached the commander of the Roman troops that the whole city of Jerusalem was in an uproar. 32He at once took some officers and soldiers and ran down to the crowd. When the rioters saw the commander and his soldiers, they stopped beating Paul.

33The commander came up and arrested him and ordered him to be bound with two chains. Then he asked who he was and what he had done. 34Some in the crowd shouted one thing and some another, and since the commander could not get at the truth because of the uproar, he ordered that Paul be taken into the barracks. 35When Paul reached the steps, the violence of the mob was so great he had to be carried by the soldiers. 36The crowd that followed kept shouting, "Get rid of him!"

### Paul Speaks to the Crowd

37As the soldiers were about to take Paul into the barracks, he asked the commander, "May I say something to you?"

"Do you speak Greek?" he replied. 38"Aren't you the Egyptian who started a revolt and led four thousand terrorists out into the wilderness some time ago?"

39Paul answered, "I am a Jew, from Tarsus in Cilicia, a citizen of no ordinary city. Please let me speak to the people."

40After receiving the commander's permission, Paul stood on the steps and motioned to the crowd. When they were all silent, he said to them in Aramaic*a*:

**22** 1"Brothers and fathers, listen now to my defense." 2When they heard him speak to them in Aramaic, they became very quiet.

Then Paul said: 3"I am a Jew, born in Tarsus of Cilicia, but brought up in this city. I studied under Gamaliel and was thoroughly trained in the law of our ancestors. I was just as zealous for God as any of you are today. 4I persecuted the followers of this Way to their death, arresting both men and women and throwing them into prison, 5as the

*a 40* Or possibly *Hebrew*; also in 22:2

## Amplified Bible

sent them a letter with our decision that they should keep themselves free from anything that has been sacrificed to idols and from [tasting] blood and [eating the meat of animals] which have been strangled and from all impurity *and* sexual immorality.

26Then Paul took the [four] men with him and the following day [he went through the rites of] purifying himself along with them. And they entered the temple to give notice when the days of purification (the ending of each vow) would be fulfilled and the usual offering could be presented on behalf of each of them.

27When the seven days were drawing to a close, some of the Jews from [the province of] Asia, who had caught sight of Paul in the temple, incited all the rabble and laid hands on him,

28Shouting, Men of Israel, help! [Help!] This is the man who is teaching everybody everywhere against the people and the Law and this place! Moreover, he has also [actually] brought Greeks into the temple; he has desecrated *and* polluted this holy place!

29For they had previously seen Trophimus the Ephesian in the city with Paul and they supposed that he had brought the man into the temple [into the inner court forbidden to Gentiles].

30Then the whole city was aroused *and* thrown into confusion, and the people rushed together; they laid hands on Paul and dragged him outside the temple, and immediately the gates were closed.

31Now while they were trying to kill him, word came to the commandant of the regular Roman garrison that the whole of Jerusalem was in a state of ferment.

32So immediately he took soldiers and centurions and hurried down among them; and when the people saw the commandant and the troops, they stopped beating Paul.

33Then the commandant approached and arrested Paul and ordered that he be secured with two chains. He then inquired who he was and what he had done.

34Some in the crowd kept shouting back one thing and others something else, and since he could not ascertain the facts because of the furor, he ordered that Paul be removed to the barracks.

35And when [Paul] came to mount the steps, he was actually being carried by the soldiers because of the violence of the mob;

36For the mass of the people kept following them, shouting, Away with him! [Kill him!]

37Just as Paul was about to be taken into the barracks, he asked the commandant, May I say something to you? And the man replied, Can you speak Greek?

38Are you not then [as I supposed] the Egyptian who not long ago stirred up a rebellion and led those 4,000 men who were cutthroats out into the wilderness (desert)?

39Paul answered, I am a Jew, from Tarsus in Cilicia, a citizen of no insignificant *or* undistinguished city. I beg you, allow me to address the people.

40And when the man had granted him permission, Paul, standing on the steps, gestured with his hand to the people; and there was a great hush. Then he spoke to them in the Hebrew dialect, saying:

**22** Brethren and fathers, listen to the defense which I now make in your presence.

2And when they heard that he addressed them in the Hebrew tongue, they were all the more quiet. And he continued,

3I am a Jew, born in Tarsus of Cilicia but reared in this city. At the feet of Gamaliel I was educated according to the strictest care in the Law of our fathers, being ardent [even a zealot] for God, as all of you are today.

4[Yes] I harassed (troubled, molested, and persecuted) this Way [of the Lord] to the death, putting in chains and committing to prison both men and women,

## New International Version

high priest and all the Council can themselves testify. I even obtained letters from them to their associates in Damascus, and went there to bring these people as prisoners to Jerusalem to be punished.

⁶"About noon as I came near Damascus, suddenly a bright light from heaven flashed around me. ⁷I fell to the ground and heard a voice say to me, 'Saul! Saul! Why do you persecute me?'

⁸"'Who are you, Lord?' I asked.

"'I am Jesus of Nazareth, whom you are persecuting,' he replied. ⁹My companions saw the light, but they did not understand the voice of him who was speaking to me.

¹⁰"'What shall I do, Lord?' I asked.

"'Get up,' the Lord said, 'and go into Damascus. There you will be told all that you have been assigned to do.' ¹¹My companions led me by the hand into Damascus, because the brilliance of the light had blinded me.

¹²"A man named Ananias came to see me. He was a devout observer of the law and highly respected by all the Jews living there. ¹³He stood beside me and said, 'Brother Saul, receive your sight!' And at that very moment I was able to see him.

¹⁴"Then he said: 'The God of our ancestors has chosen you to know his will and to see the Righteous One and to hear words from his mouth. ¹⁵You will be his witness to all people of what you have seen and heard. ¹⁶And now what are you waiting for? Get up, be baptized and wash your sins away, calling on his name.'

¹⁷"When I returned to Jerusalem and was praying at the temple, I fell into a trance ¹⁸and saw the Lord speaking to me. 'Quick!' he said. 'Leave Jerusalem immediately, because the people here will not accept your testimony about me.'

¹⁹"'Lord,' I replied, 'these people know that I went from one synagogue to another to imprison and beat those who believe in you. ²⁰And when the blood of your martyr[a] Stephen was shed, I stood there giving my approval and guarding the clothes of those who were killing him.'

²¹"Then the Lord said to me, 'Go; I will send you far away to the Gentiles.' "

### Paul the Roman Citizen

²²The crowd listened to Paul until he said this. Then they raised their voices and shouted, "Rid the earth of him! He's not fit to live!"

²³As they were shouting and throwing off their cloaks and flinging dust into the air, ²⁴the commander ordered that Paul be taken into the barracks. He directed that he be flogged and interrogated in order to find out why the people were shouting at him like this. ²⁵As they stretched

## Amplified Bible

⁵As the high priest and whole council of elders (Sanhedrin) can testify; for from them indeed I received letters with which I was on my way to the brethren in Damascus in order to take also those [believers] who were there, and bring them in chains to Jerusalem that they might be punished.

⁶But as I was on my journey and approached Damascus, about noon a great blaze of light flashed suddenly from heaven and shone about me.

⁷And I fell to the ground and heard a voice saying to me, Saul, Saul, why do you persecute Me [harass and trouble and molest Me]?

⁸And I replied, Who are You, Lord? And He said to me, I am Jesus the Nazarene, Whom you are persecuting.

⁹Now the men who were with me saw the light, but they did not hear [ᵃthe sound of the uttered words of] the voice of the One Who was speaking to me [so that they could ᵇunderstand it].

¹⁰And I asked, What shall I do, Lord? And the Lord answered me, Get up and go into Damascus, and there it will be told you all that it is destined *and* appointed for you to do.

¹¹And since I could not see because [of the dazzlingly glorious intensity] of the brightness of that light, I was led by the hand by those who were with me, and [thus] I arrived in Damascus.

¹²And one Ananias, a devout man according to the Law, well spoken of by all the Jews who resided there,

¹³Came to see me, and standing by my side said to me, Brother Saul, ᵃlook up *and* receive back your sight. And in that very ᶜinstant I [recovered my sight and] looking up saw him.

¹⁴And he said, The God of our forefathers has destined *and* appointed you to come progressively to know His will [to perceive, to recognize more strongly and clearly, and to become better and more intimately acquainted with His will], and to see the Righteous One (Jesus Christ, the Messiah), and to hear a voice from His [own] mouth *and* a message from His [own] lips;

¹⁵For you will be His witness unto all men of everything that you have seen and heard.

¹⁶And now, why do you delay? Rise and be baptized, and ᵈby calling upon His name, wash away your sins.

¹⁷Then when I had come back to Jerusalem and was praying in the temple [ᵉenclosure], I fell into a trance (an ecstasy);

¹⁸And I saw Him as He said to me, Hurry, get quickly out of Jerusalem, because they will not receive your testimony about Me.

¹⁹And I said, Lord, they themselves well know that throughout all the synagogues I cast into prison and flogged those who believed on (adhered to and trusted in and relied on) You.

²⁰And when the blood of Your witness (martyr) Stephen was shed, I also was personally standing by and consenting *and* approving and guarding the garments of those who slew him.

²¹And the Lord said to me, Go, for I will send you far away unto the Gentiles (nations).

²²Up to the moment that Paul made this last statement, the people listened to him; but now they raised their voices and shouted, Away with such a fellow from the earth! He is not fit to live!

²³And as they were shouting and tossing *and* waving their garments and throwing dust into the air,

²⁴The commandant ordered that Paul be brought into the barracks, and that he be examined by scourging in order that [the commandant] might learn why the people cried out thus against him.

ᵃ Joseph Thayer, *A Greek-English Lexicon*. ᵇ Marvin Vincent, *Word Studies*. ᶜ James Moulton and George Milligan, *The Vocabulary*. ᵈ Charles B. Williams, *The New Testament: A Translation in the Language of the People*: Circumstantial participle expressing manner or means. ᵉ Richard Trench, *Synonyms of the New Testament*.

ᵃ 20 Or *witness*

## New International Version

him out to flog him, Paul said to the centurion standing there, "Is it legal for you to flog a Roman citizen who hasn't even been found guilty?"

²⁶When the centurion heard this, he went to the commander and reported it. "What are you going to do?" he asked. "This man is a Roman citizen."

²⁷The commander went to Paul and asked, "Tell me, are you a Roman citizen?"

"Yes, I am," he answered.

²⁸Then the commander said, "I had to pay a lot of money for my citizenship."

"But I was born a citizen," Paul replied.

²⁹Those who were about to interrogate him withdrew immediately. The commander himself was alarmed when he realized that he had put Paul, a Roman citizen, in chains.

### Paul Before the Sanhedrin

³⁰The commander wanted to find out exactly why Paul was being accused by the Jews. So the next day he released him and ordered the chief priests and all the members of the Sanhedrin to assemble. Then he brought Paul and had him stand before them.

**23** Paul looked straight at the Sanhedrin and said, "My brothers, I have fulfilled my duty to God in all good conscience to this day." ²At this the high priest Ananias ordered those standing near Paul to strike him on the mouth. ³Then Paul said to him, "God will strike you, you whitewashed wall! You sit there to judge me according to the law, yet you yourself violate the law by commanding that I be struck!"

⁴Those who were standing near Paul said, "How dare you insult God's high priest!"

⁵Paul replied, "Brothers, I did not realize that he was the high priest; for it is written: 'Do not speak evil about the ruler of your people.'ᵃ"

⁶Then Paul, knowing that some of them were Sadducees and the others Pharisees, called out in the Sanhedrin, "My brothers, I am a Pharisee, descended from Pharisees. I stand on trial because of the hope of the resurrection of the dead." ⁷When he said this, a dispute broke out between the Pharisees and the Sadducees, and the assembly was divided. ⁸(The Sadducees say that there is no resurrection, and that there are neither angels nor spirits, but the Pharisees believe all these things.)

⁹There was a great uproar, and some of the teachers of the law who were Pharisees stood up and argued vigorously. "We find nothing wrong with this man," they said. "What if a spirit or an angel has spoken to him?" ¹⁰The dispute became so violent that the commander was afraid Paul would be torn to pieces by them. He ordered the troops to go down and take him away from them by force and bring him into the barracks.

¹¹The following night the Lord stood near Paul and said, "Take courage! As you have testified about me in Jerusalem, so you must also testify in Rome."

### The Plot to Kill Paul

¹²The next morning some Jews formed a conspiracy and bound themselves with an oath to not eat or drink until they had killed Paul. ¹³More than forty men were involved in this plot. ¹⁴They went to the chief priests and the elders

## Amplified Bible

²⁵But when they had stretched him out with the thongs (leather straps), Paul asked the centurion who was standing by, Is it legal for you to flog a man who is a Roman citizen and uncondemned [without a trial]?

²⁶When the centurion heard that, he went to the commandant and said to him, What are you about to do? This man is a Roman citizen!

²⁷So the commandant came and said to [Paul], Tell me, are you a Roman citizen? And he said, Yes [indeed]!

²⁸The commandant replied, I purchased this citizenship [as a capital investment] for a big price. Paul said, But I was born [Roman]!

²⁹Instantly those who were about to examine *and* flog him withdrew from him; and the commandant also was frightened, for he realized that [Paul] was a Roman citizen and he had put him in chains.

³⁰But the next day, desiring to know the real cause for which the Jews accused him, he unbound him and ordered the chief priests and all the council (Sanhedrin) to assemble; and he brought Paul down and placed him before them.

**23** Then Paul, gazing earnestly at the council (Sanhedrin), said, Brethren, I have lived before God, doing my duty with a perfectly good conscience until this very day [ᵃ as a citizen, a true and loyal Jew].

²At this the high priest Ananias ordered those who stood near him to strike him on the mouth.

³Then Paul said to him, God is about to strike you, you whitewashed wall! Do you sit as a judge to try me in accordance with the Law, and yet in defiance of the Law you order me to be struck?

⁴Those who stood near exclaimed, Do you rail at *and* insult the high priest of God?

⁵And Paul said, I was not conscious, brethren, that he was a high priest; for the Scripture says, You shall not speak ill of a ruler of your people. [Exod. 22:28.]

⁶But Paul, when he perceived that one part of them were Sadducees and the other part Pharisees, cried out to the council (Sanhedrin), Brethren, I am a Pharisee, a son of Pharisees; it is with regard to the hope and the resurrection of the dead that I am indicted *and* being judged.

⁷So when he had said this, an angry dispute arose between the Pharisees and the Sadducees; and the whole [crowded] assemblage was divided [into two factions].

⁸For the Sadducees hold that there is no resurrection, nor angel nor spirit, but the Pharisees declare openly *and* speak out freely, acknowledging [their belief in] them both.

⁹Then a great uproar ensued, and some of the scribes of the Pharisees' party stood up and thoroughly fought the case, [contending fiercely] and declaring, We find nothing evil *or* wrong in this man. But if a spirit or an angel [really] spoke to him—? *Let us not fight against God!*

¹⁰And when the strife became more and more tense *and* violent, the commandant, fearing that Paul would be torn in pieces by them, ordered the troops to go down and take him forcibly from among them and conduct him back into the barracks.

¹¹And [that same] following night the Lord stood beside Paul and said, Take courage, *Paul,* for as you have borne faithful witness concerning Me at Jerusalem, so you must also bear witness at Rome.

¹²Now when daylight came, the Jews formed a plot and bound themselves by an oath *and* under a curse neither to eat nor drink till they had done away with Paul.

¹³There were more than forty [men of them], who formed this conspiracy [swearing together this oath and curse].

¹⁴And they went to the chief priests and elders, saying,

ᵃ 5 Exodus 22:28

ᵃ Marvin Vincent, *Word Studies.*

## New International Version

and said, "We have taken a solemn oath not to eat anything until we have killed Paul. ¹⁵Now then, you and the Sanhedrin petition the commander to bring him before you on the pretext of wanting more accurate information about his case. We are ready to kill him before he gets here."

¹⁶But when the son of Paul's sister heard of this plot, he went into the barracks and told Paul.

¹⁷Then Paul called one of the centurions and said, "Take this young man to the commander; he has something to tell him." ¹⁸So he took him to the commander.

The centurion said, "Paul, the prisoner, sent for me and asked me to bring this young man to you because he has something to tell you."

¹⁹The commander took the young man by the hand, drew him aside and asked, "What is it you want to tell me?"

²⁰He said: "Some Jews have agreed to ask you to bring Paul before the Sanhedrin tomorrow on the pretext of wanting more accurate information about him. ²¹Don't give in to them, because more than forty of them are waiting in ambush for him. They have taken an oath not to eat or drink until they have killed him. They are ready now, waiting for your consent to their request."

²²The commander dismissed the young man with this warning: "Don't tell anyone that you have reported this to me."

### Paul Transferred to Caesarea

²³Then he called two of his centurions and ordered them, "Get ready a detachment of two hundred soldiers, seventy horsemen and two hundred spearmen[a] to go to Caesarea at nine tonight. ²⁴Provide horses for Paul so that he may be taken safely to Governor Felix."

²⁵He wrote a letter as follows:

²⁶Claudius Lysias,

To His Excellency, Governor Felix:

Greetings.

²⁷This man was seized by the Jews and they were about to kill him, but I came with my troops and rescued him, for I had learned that he is a Roman citizen. ²⁸I wanted to know why they were accusing him, so I brought him to their Sanhedrin. ²⁹I found that the accusation had to do with questions about their law, but there was no charge against him that deserved death or imprisonment. ³⁰When I was informed of a plot to be carried out against the man, I sent him to you at once. I also ordered his accusers to present to you their case against him.

³¹So the soldiers, carrying out their orders, took Paul with them during the night and brought him as far as Antipatris. ³²The next day they let the cavalry go on with him, while they returned to the barracks. ³³When the cavalry arrived in Caesarea, they delivered the letter to the governor and handed Paul over to him. ³⁴The governor read the letter and asked what province he was from. Learning that he was from Cilicia, ³⁵he said, "I will hear your case when your accusers get here." Then he ordered that Paul be kept under guard in Herod's palace.

## Amplified Bible

We have strictly bound ourselves by an oath *and* under a curse not to taste any food until we have slain Paul.

¹⁵So now you, along with the council (Sanhedrin), give notice to the commandant to bring [Paul] down to you, as if you were going to investigate his case more accurately. But we [ourselves] are ready to slay him before he comes near.

¹⁶But the son of Paul's sister heard of their intended attack, and he went and got into the barracks and told Paul.

¹⁷Then Paul, calling in one of the centurions, said, Take this young man to the commandant, for he has something to report to him.

¹⁸So he took him and conducted him to the commandant and said, Paul the prisoner called me to him and requested me to conduct this young man to you, for he has something to report to you.

¹⁹The commandant took him by the hand, and going aside with him, asked privately, What is it that you have to report to me?

²⁰And he replied, The Jews have agreed to ask you to bring Paul down to the council (Sanhedrin) tomorrow, as if [they were] intending to examine him more exactly.

²¹But do not yield to their persuasion, for more than forty of their men are lying in ambush waiting for him, having bound themselves by an oath *and* under a curse neither to eat nor drink till they have killed him; and even now they are all ready, [just] waiting for your promise.

²²So the commandant sent the youth away, charging him, Do not disclose to anyone that you have given me this information.

²³Then summoning two of the centurions, he said, Have two hundred footmen ready by the third hour of the night (about 9:00 p.m.) to go as far as Caesarea, with seventy horsemen and two hundred spearmen.

²⁴Also provide beasts for mounts for Paul to ride, and bring him in safety to Felix the governor.

²⁵And he wrote a letter having this message:

²⁶Claudius Lysias sends greetings to His Excellency Felix the governor.

²⁷This man was seized [as prisoner] by the Jews, and was about to be killed by them when I came upon them with the troops and rescued him, because I learned that he is a Roman citizen.

²⁸And wishing to know the exact accusation which they were making against him, I brought him down before their council (Sanhedrin),

²⁹[Where] I found that he was charged in regard to questions of their own law, but he was accused of nothing that would call for death or [even] for imprisonment.

³⁰[However] when it was pointed out to me that there would be a conspiracy against the man, I sent him to you immediately, directing his accusers also to present before you their charge against him.

³¹So the soldiers, in compliance with their instructions, took Paul and conducted him during the night to Antipatris.

³²And the next day they returned to the barracks, leaving the mounted men to proceed with him.

³³When these came to Caesarea and gave the letter to the governor, they also presented Paul before him.

³⁴Having read the letter, he asked to what province [Paul] belonged. When he discovered that he was from Cilicia [an imperial province],

³⁵He said, I will hear your case *a*fully when your accusers also have come. And he ordered that an eye be kept on him in Herod's palace (the Praetorium).

---

*a* 23 The meaning of the Greek for this word is uncertain.    *a* Marvin Vincent, *Word Studies.*

## New International Version

### Paul's Trial Before Felix

**24** Five days later the high priest Ananias went down to Caesarea with some of the elders and a lawyer named Tertullus, and they brought their charges against Paul before the governor. [2] When Paul was called in, Tertullus presented his case before Felix: "We have enjoyed a long period of peace under you, and your foresight has brought about reforms in this nation. [3] Everywhere and in every way, most excellent Felix, we acknowledge this with profound gratitude. [4] But in order not to weary you further, I would request that you be kind enough to hear us briefly.

[5] "We have found this man to be a troublemaker, stirring up riots among the Jews all over the world. He is a ringleader of the Nazarene sect [6] and even tried to desecrate the temple; so we seized him. [7]a [8] By examining him yourself you will be able to learn the truth about all these charges we are bringing against him."

[9] The other Jews joined in the accusation, asserting that these things were true.

[10] When the governor motioned for him to speak, Paul replied: "I know that for a number of years you have been a judge over this nation; so I gladly make my defense. [11] You can easily verify that no more than twelve days ago I went up to Jerusalem to worship. [12] My accusers did not find me arguing with anyone at the temple, or stirring up a crowd in the synagogues or anywhere else in the city. [13] And they cannot prove to you the charges they are now making against me. [14] However, I admit that I worship the God of our ancestors as a follower of the Way, which they call a sect. I believe everything that is in accordance with the Law and that is written in the Prophets, [15] and I have the same hope in God as these men themselves have, that there will be a resurrection of both the righteous and the wicked. [16] So I strive always to keep my conscience clear before God and man.

[17] "After an absence of several years, I came to Jerusalem to bring my people gifts for the poor and to present offerings. [18] I was ceremonially clean when they found me in the temple courts doing this. There was no crowd with me, nor was I involved in any disturbance. [19] But there are some Jews from the province of Asia, who ought to be here before you and bring charges if they have anything against me. [20] Or these who are here should state what crime they found in me when I stood before the Sanhedrin— [21] unless

## Amplified Bible

**24** Five days later, the high priest Ananias came down [from Jerusalem to Caesarea] with some elders and a certain forensic advocate Tertullus [acting as spokesman and counsel]. They presented to the governor their evidence against Paul.

[2] And when he was called, Tertullus began the complaint [against him] by saying: Since through you we obtain and enjoy much peace, and since by your foresight and provision wonderful reforms (amendments and improvements) are introduced and effected on behalf of this nation,

[3] In every way and in every place, most excellent Felix, we accept and acknowledge this with deep appreciation and with all gratitude.

[4] But not to hinder or detain you too long, I beg you in your clemency and courtesy and kindness to grant us a brief and a concise hearing.

[5] For we have found this man a perfect pest (a real plague), an agitator and source of disturbance to all the Jews throughout the world, and a ringleader of the [heretical, a division-producing] sect of the Nazarenes.

[6] He also [even] tried to desecrate and defile the temple, but we laid hands on him b and would have sentenced him by our Law,

[7] But the commandant Lysias came and took him from us with violence and force,

[8] And ordered his accusers to present themselves to you. By examining and cross-questioning him yourself, you will be able to ascertain the truth from him about all these things with which we charge him.

[9] The Jews also agreed and joined in the accusation, declaring that all these things were exactly so.

[10] And when the governor had beckoned to Paul to speak, he answered: Because I know that for many years you have been a judge over this nation, I find it easier to make my defense and do it cheerfully and with good courage.

[11] As you can readily verify, it is not more than twelve days since I went up to Jerusalem to worship;

[12] And neither in the temple nor in the synagogues nor in the city did they find me disputing with anybody or bringing together a seditious crowd.

[13] Neither can they present argument or evidence to prove to you what they now bring against me.

[14] But this I confess to you, however, that in accordance with the Way [of the Lord], which they call a [heretical, division-producing] sect, I worship (serve) the God of our fathers, still persuaded of the truth of and believing in and placing full confidence in everything laid down in the Law [of Moses] or written in the prophets;

[15] Having [the same] hope in God which these themselves hold and look for, that there is to be a resurrection both of the righteous and the unrighteous (the just and the unjust).

[16] Therefore I always exercise and discipline myself [mortifying my body, deadening my carnal affections, bodily appetites, and worldly desires, endeavoring in all respects] to have a clear (unshaken, blameless) conscience, void of offense toward God and toward men.

[17] Now after several years I came up [to Jerusalem] to bring to my people contributions of charity and offerings.

[18] While I was engaged in presenting these, they found me [occupied in the rites of purification] in the temple, without any crowd or uproar. But some Jews from [the province of] Asia [were there],

[19] Who ought to be here before you and to present their charges, if they have anything against me.

[20] Or else let these men themselves tell of what crime or wrongdoing they found me guilty when I appeared before the council (Sanhedrin),

---

a 6-8 Some manuscripts include here *him, and we would have judged him in accordance with our law.* 7*But the commander Lysias came and took him from us with much violence,* 8*ordering his accusers to come before you.*

a Marvin Vincent, *Word Studies.* b Many manuscripts do not contain the remainder of verse 6, all of verse 7, and the first part of verse 8.

# New International Version

it was this one thing I shouted as I stood in their presence: 'It is concerning the resurrection of the dead that I am on trial before you today.'"

²²Then Felix, who was well acquainted with the Way, adjourned the proceedings. "When Lysias the commander comes," he said, "I will decide your case." ²³He ordered the centurion to keep Paul under guard but to give him some freedom and permit his friends to take care of his needs.

²⁴Several days later Felix came with his wife Drusilla, who was Jewish. He sent for Paul and listened to him as he spoke about faith in Christ Jesus. ²⁵As Paul talked about righteousness, self-control and the judgment to come, Felix was afraid and said, "That's enough for now! You may leave. When I find it convenient, I will send for you." ²⁶At the same time he was hoping that Paul would offer him a bribe, so he sent for him frequently and talked with him.

²⁷When two years had passed, Felix was succeeded by Porcius Festus, but because Felix wanted to grant a favor to the Jews, he left Paul in prison.

## Paul's Trial Before Festus

**25** Three days after arriving in the province, Festus went up from Caesarea to Jerusalem, ²where the chief priests and the Jewish leaders appeared before him and presented the charges against Paul. ³They requested Festus, as a favor to them, to have Paul transferred to Jerusalem, for they were preparing an ambush to kill him along the way. ⁴Festus answered, "Paul is being held at Caesarea, and I myself am going there soon. ⁵Let some of your leaders come with me, and if the man has done anything wrong, they can press charges against him there."

⁶After spending eight or ten days with them, Festus went down to Caesarea. The next day he convened the court and ordered that Paul be brought before him. ⁷When Paul came in, the Jews who had come down from Jerusalem stood around him. They brought many serious charges against him, but they could not prove them.

⁸Then Paul made his defense: "I have done nothing wrong against the Jewish law or against the temple or against Caesar."

⁹Festus, wishing to do the Jews a favor, said to Paul, "Are you willing to go up to Jerusalem and stand trial before me there on these charges?"

¹⁰Paul answered: "I am now standing before Caesar's court, where I ought to be tried. I have not done any wrong to the Jews, as you yourself know very well. ¹¹If, however, I am guilty of doing anything deserving death, I do not refuse to die. But if the charges brought against me by these Jews are not true, no one has the right to hand me over to them. I appeal to Caesar!"

¹²After Festus had conferred with his council, he declared: "You have appealed to Caesar. To Caesar you will go!"

# Amplified Bible

²¹Unless it be this one sentence which I cried out as I stood among them, In regard to the resurrection of the dead I am indicted and on trial before you this day!

²²But Felix, having a rather accurate understanding of the Way [of the Lord], put them off and adjourned the trial, saying, When Lysias the commandant comes down, I will determine your case more fully.

²³Then he ordered the centurion to keep [Paul] in custody, but to treat him with indulgence [giving him some liberty] and not to hinder his friends from ministering to his needs and serving him.

²⁴Some days later Felix came with his wife Drusilla, who was a Jewess; and he sent for Paul and listened to him [talk] about faith in Christ Jesus.

²⁵But as he continued to argue about uprightness, purity of life (the control of the passions), and the judgment to come, Felix became alarmed and terrified and said, Go away for the present; when I have a convenient opportunity, I will send for you.

²⁶At the same time he hoped to get money from Paul, for which reason he continued to send for him and was in his company and conversed with him often.

²⁷But when two years had gone by, Felix was succeeded in office by Porcius Festus; and wishing to gain favor with the Jews, Felix left Paul still a prisoner in chains.

**25** Now when Festus had entered into his own province, after three days he went up from Caesarea to Jerusalem.

²And [there] the chief priests and the principal men of the Jews laid charges before him against Paul, and they kept begging and urging him,

³Asking as a favor that he would have him brought to Jerusalem; [meanwhile] they were planning an ambush to slay him on the way.

⁴Festus answered that Paul was in custody in Caesarea and that he himself planned to leave for there soon.

⁵So, said he, let those who are in a position of authority and are influential among you go down with me, and if there is anything amiss or criminal about the man, let them so charge him.

⁶So when Festus had remained among them not more than eight or ten days, he went down to Caesarea, took his seat the next day on the judgment bench, and ordered Paul to be brought before him.

⁷And when he arrived, the Jews who had come down from Jerusalem stood all around him, bringing many grave accusations against him which they were not able to prove.

⁸Paul declared in [his own] defense, Neither against the Law of the Jews, nor against the temple, nor against Caesar have I offended in any way.

⁹But Festus, wishing to ingratiate himself with the Jews, answered Paul, Are you willing to go up to Jerusalem and there be put on trial [ᵃbefore the Jewish Sanhedrin] in my presence concerning these charges?

¹⁰But Paul replied, I am standing before Caesar's judgment seat, where I ought to be tried. To the Jews I have done no wrong, as you know ᵃbetter [than your question implies].

¹¹If then I am a wrongdoer and a criminal and have committed anything for which I deserve to die, I do not beg off and seek to escape death; but if there is no ground for their accusations against me, no one can give me up and make a present of me [ᵇgive me up freely] to them. I appeal to Caesar.

¹²Then Festus, when he had consulted with the [ᵃmen who formed his] council, answered, You have appealed to Caesar; to Caesar you shall go.

---

ᵃ Marvin Vincent, *Word Studies.* ᵇ G. Abbott-Smith, *Manual Greek Lexicon.*

## New International Version

### Festus Consults King Agrippa

<sup>13</sup>A few days later King Agrippa and Bernice arrived at Caesarea to pay their respects to Festus. <sup>14</sup>Since they were spending many days there, Festus discussed Paul's case with the king. He said: "There is a man here whom Felix left as a prisoner. <sup>15</sup>When I went to Jerusalem, the chief priests and the elders of the Jews brought charges against him and asked that he be condemned.

<sup>16</sup>"I told them that it is not the Roman custom to hand over anyone before they have faced their accusers and have had an opportunity to defend themselves against the charges. <sup>17</sup>When they came here with me, I did not delay the case, but convened the court the next day and ordered the man to be brought in. <sup>18</sup>When his accusers got up to speak, they did not charge him with any of the crimes I had expected. <sup>19</sup>Instead, they had some points of dispute with him about their own religion and about a dead man named Jesus who Paul claimed was alive. <sup>20</sup>I was at a loss how to investigate such matters; so I asked if he would be willing to go to Jerusalem and stand trial there on these charges. <sup>21</sup>But when Paul made his appeal to be held over for the Emperor's decision, I ordered him held until I could send him to Caesar."

<sup>22</sup>Then Agrippa said to Festus, "I would like to hear this man myself."

He replied, "Tomorrow you will hear him."

### Paul Before Agrippa

<sup>23</sup>The next day Agrippa and Bernice came with great pomp and entered the audience room with the high-ranking military officers and the prominent men of the city. At the command of Festus, Paul was brought in. <sup>24</sup>Festus said: "King Agrippa, and all who are present with us, you see this man! The whole Jewish community has petitioned me about him in Jerusalem and here in Caesarea, shouting that he ought not to live any longer. <sup>25</sup>I found he had done nothing deserving of death, but because he made his appeal to the Emperor I decided to send him to Rome. <sup>26</sup>But I have nothing definite to write to His Majesty about him. Therefore I have brought him before all of you, and especially before you, King Agrippa, so that as a result of this investigation I may have something to write. <sup>27</sup>For I think it is unreasonable to send a prisoner on to Rome without specifying the charges against him."

**26** Then Agrippa said to Paul, "You have permission to speak for yourself."

So Paul motioned with his hand and began his defense: <sup>2</sup>"King Agrippa, I consider myself fortunate to stand before you today as I make my defense against all the accusations of the Jews, <sup>3</sup>and especially so because you are well acquainted with all the Jewish customs and controversies. Therefore, I beg you to listen to me patiently.

<sup>4</sup>"The Jewish people all know the way I have lived ever since I was a child, from the beginning of my life in my own country, and also in Jerusalem. <sup>5</sup>They have known me for a long time and can testify, if they are willing, that I conformed to the strictest sect of our religion, living as a

## Amplified Bible

<sup>13</sup>Now after an interval of some days, Agrippa the king and Bernice arrived at Caesarea to pay their respects to Festus [to welcome him and wish him well].

<sup>14</sup>And while they remained there for many days, Festus acquainted the king with Paul's case, telling him, There is a man left a prisoner in chains by Felix;

<sup>15</sup>And when I was at Jerusalem, the chief priests and the elders of the Jews informed me about him, petitioning for a judicial hearing *and* condemnation of him.

<sup>16</sup>But I replied to them that it was not the custom of the Romans to <sup>a</sup>give up freely any man for punishment before the accused had met the accusers face to face and had opportunity to defend himself concerning the charge brought against him.

<sup>17</sup>So when they came here together, I did not delay, but on the morrow took my place on the judgment seat and ordered that the man be brought before me.

<sup>18</sup>[But] when the accusers stood up, they brought forward no accusation [in his case] of any such misconduct as I was expecting.

<sup>19</sup>Instead they had some points of controversy with him about their own religion *or* superstition and concerning one Jesus, Who had died but Whom Paul kept asserting [over and over] to be alive.

<sup>20</sup>And I, being puzzled to know how to make inquiries into such questions, asked whether he would be willing to go to Jerusalem and there be tried regarding them.

<sup>21</sup>But when Paul had appealed to have his case retained for examination *and* decision by the emperor, I ordered that he be detained until I could send him to Caesar.

<sup>22</sup>Then Agrippa said to Festus, I also desire to hear the man myself. Tomorrow, [Festus] replied, you shall hear him.

<sup>23</sup>So the next day Agrippa and Bernice approached with great display, and they went into the audience hall accompanied by the military commandants and the prominent citizens of the city. At the order of Festus Paul was brought in.

<sup>24</sup>Then Festus said, King Agrippa and all the men present with us, you see this man about whom the whole Jewish people came to me *and* complained, both at Jerusalem and here, insisting *and* shouting that he ought not to live any longer.

<sup>25</sup>But I found nothing that he had done deserving of death. Still, as he himself appealed to the emperor, I determined to send him to Rome.

<sup>26</sup>[However] I have nothing in particular *and* definite to write to my lord concerning him. So I have brought him before all of you, and especially before you, King Agrippa, so that after [further] examination has been made, I may have something to put in writing.

<sup>27</sup>For it seems to me senseless *and* absurd to send a prisoner and not state the accusations against him.

**26** Then Agrippa said to Paul, You are permitted to speak on your own behalf. At that Paul stretched forth his hand and made his defense [as follows]:

<sup>2</sup>I consider myself fortunate, King Agrippa, that it is before you that I am to make my defense today in regard to all the charges brought against me by [the] Jews,

<sup>3</sup>[Especially] because you are so fully *and* unusually conversant with all the Jewish customs and controversies; therefore, I beg you to hear me patiently.

<sup>4</sup>My behavior *and* manner of living from my youth up is known by all the Jews; [they are aware] that from [its] commencement my youth was spent among my own race in Jerusalem.

<sup>5</sup>They have had knowledge of me for a long time, if they are willing to testify to it, that in accordance with the strictest sect of our religion I have lived as a Pharisee.

<sup>a</sup> G. Abbott-Smith, *Manual Greek Lexicon.*

## New International Version

Pharisee. ⁶And now it is because of my hope in what God has promised our ancestors that I am on trial today. ⁷This is the promise our twelve tribes are hoping to see fulfilled as they earnestly serve God day and night. King Agrippa, it is because of this hope that these Jews are accusing me. ⁸Why should any of you consider it incredible that God raises the dead?

⁹"I too was convinced that I ought to do all that was possible to oppose the name of Jesus of Nazareth. ¹⁰And that is just what I did in Jerusalem. On the authority of the chief priests I put many of the Lord's people in prison, and when they were put to death, I cast my vote against them. ¹¹Many a time I went from one synagogue to another to have them punished, and I tried to force them to blaspheme. I was so obsessed with persecuting them that I even hunted them down in foreign cities.

¹²"On one of these journeys I was going to Damascus with the authority and commission of the chief priests. ¹³About noon, King Agrippa, as I was on the road, I saw a light from heaven, brighter than the sun, blazing around me and my companions. ¹⁴We all fell to the ground, and I heard a voice saying to me in Aramaic,ᵃ 'Saul, Saul, why do you persecute me? It is hard for you to kick against the goads.'

¹⁵"Then I asked, 'Who are you, Lord?'

"'I am Jesus, whom you are persecuting,' the Lord replied. ¹⁶'Now get up and stand on your feet. I have appeared to you to appoint you as a servant and as a witness of what you have seen and will see of me. ¹⁷I will rescue you from your own people and from the Gentiles. I am sending you to them ¹⁸to open their eyes and turn them from darkness to light, and from the power of Satan to God, so that they may receive forgiveness of sins and a place among those who are sanctified by faith in me.'

¹⁹"So then, King Agrippa, I was not disobedient to the vision from heaven. ²⁰First to those in Damascus, then to those in Jerusalem and in all Judea, and then to the Gentiles, I preached that they should repent and turn to God and demonstrate their repentance by their deeds. ²¹That is why some Jews seized me in the temple courts and tried to kill me. ²²But God has helped me to this very day; so I stand here and testify to small and great alike. I am saying nothing beyond what the prophets and Moses said would happen— ²³that the Messiah would suffer and, as the first to rise from the dead, would bring the message of light to his own people and to the Gentiles."

²⁴At this point Festus interrupted Paul's defense. "You are out of your mind, Paul!" he shouted. "Your great learning is driving you insane."

²⁵"I am not insane, most excellent Festus," Paul replied. "What I am saying is true and reasonable. ²⁶The king is familiar with these things, and I can speak freely to him.

## Amplified Bible

⁶And now I stand here on trial [to be judged on the ground] of the hope of that promise made to our forefathers by God, [Acts 13:32, 33.]

⁷Which hope [of the Messiah and the resurrection] our twelve tribes confidently expect to realize as they fervently worship [without ceasing] night and day. And for that hope, O king, I am accused by Jews *and* considered a criminal!

⁸Why is it thought incredible by any of you that God raises the dead?

⁹I myself indeed was [once] persuaded that it was my duty to do many things contrary to *and* in defiance of the name of Jesus of Nazareth.

¹⁰And that is what I did in Jerusalem; I [not only] locked up many of the [faithful] saints (holy ones) in prison by virtue of authority received from the chief priests, but when they were being condemned to death, I cast my vote against them.

¹¹And frequently I punished them in all the synagogues to make them blaspheme; and in my bitter fury against them, I harassed (troubled, molested, persecuted) *and* pursued them even to foreign cities.

¹²Thus engaged I proceeded to Damascus with the authority and orders of the chief priests,

¹³When on the road at midday, O king, I saw a light from heaven surpassing the brightness of the sun, flashing about me and those who were traveling with me.

¹⁴And when we had all fallen to the ground, I heard a voice in the Hebrew tongue saying to me, Saul, Saul, why do you continue to persecute Me [to harass and trouble and molest Me]? It is dangerous *and* turns out badly for you to keep kicking against the goads [to keep offering vain and perilous resistance].

¹⁵And I said, Who are You, Lord? And the Lord said, I am Jesus, Whom you are persecuting.

¹⁶But arise and stand upon your feet; for I have appeared to you for this purpose, that I might appoint you to serve as [My] minister and to bear witness both to what you have seen of Me and to that in which I will appear to you,

¹⁷ᵃChoosing you out [selecting you for Myself] *and* ᵇdelivering you from among this [Jewish] people and the Gentiles to whom I am sending you—[Ezek. 2:1, 3.]

¹⁸To open their eyes that they may turn from darkness to light and from the power of Satan to God, so that they may thus receive forgiveness *and* release from their sins and a place *and* portion among those who are consecrated *and* purified by faith in Me. [Isa. 42:7, 16.]

¹⁹Wherefore, O King Agrippa, I was not disobedient unto the heavenly vision,

²⁰But made known openly first of all to those at Damascus, then at Jerusalem and throughout the whole land of Judea, and also among the Gentiles, that they should repent and turn to God, and do works *and* live lives consistent with *and* worthy of their repentance.

²¹Because of these things the Jews seized me in the temple [ᶜenclosure] and tried to do away with me.

²²[But] to this day I have had the help which comes from God [as my ᵇally], and so I stand here testifying to small and great alike, asserting nothing beyond what the prophets and Moses declared would come to pass—

²³That the Christ (the Anointed One) must suffer and that He, by being the first to rise from the dead, would declare *and* show light both to the [Jewish] people and to the Gentiles.

²⁴And as he thus proceeded with his defense, Festus called out loudly, Paul, you are mad! Your great learning is driving you insane!

²⁵But Paul replied, I am not mad, most noble Festus, but I am uttering the straight, sound truth.

²⁶For the king understands about these things well

---

ᵃ 14 Or *Hebrew*

ᵃ Joseph Thayer, *A Greek-English Lexicon.*   ᵇ G. Abbott-Smith, *Manual Greek Lexicon.*   ᶜ Richard Trench, *Synonyms of the New Testament.*

## New International Version

I am convinced that none of this has escaped his notice, because it was not done in a corner. [27]King Agrippa, do you believe the prophets? I know you do."

[28]Then Agrippa said to Paul, "Do you think that in such a short time you can persuade me to be a Christian?"

[29]Paul replied, "Short time or long—I pray to God that not only you but all who are listening to me today may become what I am, except for these chains."

[30]The king rose, and with him the governor and Bernice and those sitting with them. [31]After they left the room, they began saying to one another, "This man is not doing anything that deserves death or imprisonment."

[32]Agrippa said to Festus, "This man could have been set free if he had not appealed to Caesar."

### Paul Sails for Rome

**27** When it was decided that we would sail for Italy, Paul and some other prisoners were handed over to a centurion named Julius, who belonged to the Imperial Regiment. [2]We boarded a ship from Adramyttium about to sail for ports along the coast of the province of Asia, and we put out to sea. Aristarchus, a Macedonian from Thessalonica, was with us.

[3]The next day we landed at Sidon; and Julius, in kindness to Paul, allowed him to go to his friends so they might provide for his needs. [4]From there we put out to sea again and passed to the lee of Cyprus because the winds were against us. [5]When we had sailed across the open sea off the coast of Cilicia and Pamphylia, we landed at Myra in Lycia. [6]There the centurion found an Alexandrian ship sailing for Italy and put us on board. [7]We made slow headway for many days and had difficulty arriving off Cnidus. When the wind did not allow us to hold our course, we sailed to the lee of Crete, opposite Salmone. [8]We moved along the coast with difficulty and came to a place called Fair Havens, near the town of Lasea.

[9]Much time had been lost, and sailing had already become dangerous because by now it was after the Day of Atonement.[a] So Paul warned them, [10]"Men, I can see that our voyage is going to be disastrous and bring great loss to ship and cargo, and to our own lives also." [11]But the centurion, instead of listening to what Paul said, followed the advice of the pilot and of the owner of the ship. [12]Since the harbor was unsuitable to winter in, the majority decided that we should sail on, hoping to reach Phoenix and winter there. This was a harbor in Crete, facing both southwest and northwest.

### The Storm

[13]When a gentle south wind began to blow, they saw their opportunity; so they weighed anchor and sailed along the shore of Crete. [14]Before very long, a wind of hurricane force, called the Northeaster, swept down from the island. [15]The ship was caught by the storm and could not head into the wind; so we gave way to it and were driven

## Amplified Bible

enough, and [therefore] to him I speak with bold frankness *and* confidence. I am convinced that not one of these things has escaped his notice, for all this did not take place in a corner [in secret].

[27]King Agrippa, do you believe the prophets? [Do you give credence to God's messengers and their words?] I perceive *and* know that you do believe.

[28]Then Agrippa said to Paul, You think it a small task to make a Christian of me [just offhand to induce me with little ado and persuasion, at very short notice].

[29]And Paul replied, Whether short or long, I would to God that not only you, but also all who are listening to me today, might become such as I am, except for these chains.

[30]Then the king arose, and the governor and Bernice and all those who were seated with them;

[31]And after they had gone out, they said to one another, This man is doing nothing deserving of death or [even] of imprisonment.

[32]And Agrippa said to Festus, This man could have been set at liberty if he had not appealed to Caesar.

**27** Now when it was determined that we [including Luke] should sail for Italy, they turned Paul and some other prisoners over to a centurion of the imperial regiment named Julius.

[2]And going aboard a ship from Adramyttium which was about to sail for the ports along the coast of [the province of] Asia, we put out to sea; and Aristarchus, a Macedonian from Thessalonica, accompanied us.

[3]The following day we landed at Sidon, and Julius treated Paul in a loving way, with much consideration (kindness and care), permitting him to go to his friends [there] and be refreshed *and* be cared for.

[4]After putting to sea from there we passed to the leeward (south side) of Cyprus [for protection], for the winds were contrary to us.

[5]And when we had sailed over [the whole length] of sea which lies off Cilicia and Pamphylia, we reached Myra in Lycia.

[6]There the centurion found an Alexandrian ship bound for Italy, and he transferred us to it.

[7]For a number of days we made slow progress and arrived with difficulty off Cnidus; then, as the wind did not permit us to proceed, we went under the lee (shelter) of Crete off Salmone,

[8]And coasting along it with difficulty, we arrived at a place called Fair Havens, near which is located the town of Lasea.

[9]But as [the season was well advanced, for] much time had been lost and navigation was already dangerous, for the time for the Fast [the Day of Atonement, about the beginning of October] had already gone by, Paul warned *and* advised them,

[10]Saying, Sirs, I perceive [after careful observation] that this voyage will be attended with disaster and much heavy loss, not only of the cargo and the ship but of our lives also.

[11]However, the centurion paid greater attention to the pilot and to the owner of the ship than to what Paul said.

[12]And as the harbor was not well situated *and* so unsuitable to winter in, the majority favored the plan of putting to sea again from there, hoping somehow to reach Phoenice, a harbor of Crete facing southwest and northwest, and winter there.

[13]So when the south wind blew softly, supposing they were gaining their object, they weighed anchor and sailed along Crete, hugging the coast.

[14]But soon afterward a violent wind [of the character of a typhoon], called a northeaster, came bursting down from the island.

[15]And when the ship was caught and was unable to head against the wind, we gave up and, letting her drift, were borne along.

---

[a] 9 That is, Yom Kippur

## New International Version

along. [16]As we passed to the lee of a small island called Cauda, we were hardly able to make the lifeboat secure, [17]so the men hoisted it aboard. Then they passed ropes under the ship itself to hold it together. Because they were afraid they would run aground on the sandbars of Syrtis, they lowered the sea anchor[a] and let the ship be driven along. [18]We took such a violent battering from the storm that the next day they began to throw the cargo overboard. [19]On the third day, they threw the ship's tackle overboard with their own hands. [20]When neither sun nor stars appeared for many days and the storm continued raging, we finally gave up all hope of being saved.

[21]After they had gone a long time without food, Paul stood up before them and said: "Men, you should have taken my advice not to sail from Crete; then you would have spared yourselves this damage and loss. [22]But now I urge you to keep up your courage, because not one of you will be lost; only the ship will be destroyed. [23]Last night an angel of the God to whom I belong and whom I serve stood beside me [24]and said, 'Do not be afraid, Paul. You must stand trial before Caesar; and God has graciously given you the lives of all who sail with you.' [25]So keep up your courage, men, for I have faith in God that it will happen just as he told me. [26]Nevertheless, we must run aground on some island."

### The Shipwreck

[27]On the fourteenth night we were still being driven across the Adriatic[b] Sea, when about midnight the sailors sensed they were approaching land. [28]They took soundings and found that the water was a hundred and twenty feet[c] deep. A short time later they took soundings again and found it was ninety feet[d] deep. [29]Fearing that we would be dashed against the rocks, they dropped four anchors from the stern and prayed for daylight. [30]In an attempt to escape from the ship, the sailors let the lifeboat down into the sea, pretending they were going to lower some anchors from the bow. [31]Then Paul said to the centurion and the soldiers, "Unless these men stay with the ship, you cannot be saved." [32]So the soldiers cut the ropes that held the lifeboat and let it drift away.

[33]Just before dawn Paul urged them all to eat. "For the last fourteen days," he said, "you have been in constant suspense and have gone without food—you haven't eaten anything. [34]Now I urge you to take some food. You need it to survive. Not one of you will lose a single hair from his head." [35]After he said this, he took some bread and gave thanks to God in front of them all. Then he broke it and began to eat. [36]They were all encouraged and ate some food themselves. [37]Altogether there were 276 of us on board. [38]When they had eaten as much as they wanted, they lightened the ship by throwing the grain into the sea.

[39]When daylight came, they did not recognize the land, but they saw a bay with a sandy beach, where they decided to run the ship aground if they could. [40]Cutting loose the

---

a 17 Or *the sails*   b 27 In ancient times the name referred to an area extending well south of Italy.   c 28 Or about 37 meters
d 28 Or about 27 meters

## Amplified Bible

[16]We ran under the shelter of a small island called Cauda, where we managed with [much] difficulty to draw the [ship's small] boat on deck *and* secure it.

[17]After hoisting it on board, they used supports with ropes to undergird *and* brace the ship; then afraid that they would be driven into the Syrtis [quicksands off the north coast of Africa], they lowered the gear (sails and ropes) and so were driven along.

[18]As we were being dangerously tossed about by the violence of the storm, the next day they began to throw the freight overboard;

[19]And the third day they threw out with their own hands the ship's equipment (the tackle and the furniture).

[20]And when neither sun nor stars were visible for many days and no small tempest kept raging about us, all hope of our being saved was finally abandoned.

[21]Then as they had eaten nothing for a long time, Paul came forward into their midst and said, Men, you should have listened to me, and should not have put to sea from Crete and brought on this disaster and harm *and* misery *and* loss.

[22]But [even] now I beg you to be in good spirits *and* take heart, for there will be no loss of life among you but only of the ship.

[23]For this [very] night there stood by my side an angel of the God to Whom I belong and Whom I serve *and* worship,

[24]And he said, Do not be frightened, Paul! It is necessary for you to stand before Caesar; and behold, God has given you all those who are sailing with you.

[25]So keep up your courage, men, for I have faith (complete confidence) in God that it will be exactly as it was told me;

[26]But we shall have to be stranded on some island.

[27]The fourteenth night had come and we were drifting *and* being driven about in the Adriatic Sea, when about midnight the sailors began to suspect that they were drawing near to some land.

[28]So they took soundings and found twenty fathoms, and a little farther on they sounded again and found fifteen fathoms.

[29]Then fearing that we might fall off [our course] onto rocks, they dropped four anchors from the stern and kept wishing for daybreak to come.

[30]And as the sailors were trying to escape [secretly] from the ship and were lowering the small boat into the sea, pretending that they were going to lay out anchors from the bow,

[31]Paul said to the centurion and the soldiers, Unless these men remain in the ship, you cannot be saved.

[32]Then the soldiers cut away the ropes that held the small boat, and let it fall *and* drift away.

[33]While they waited until it should become day, Paul entreated them all to take some food, saying, This is the fourteenth day that you have been continually in suspense *and* on the alert without food, having eaten nothing.

[34]So I urge (warn, exhort, encourage, advise) you to take some food [for your safety]—it will give you strength; for not a hair is to perish from the head of any one of you.

[35]Having said these words, he took bread and, giving thanks to God before them all, he broke it and began to eat.

[36]Then they all became more cheerful *and* were encouraged and took food themselves.

[37]All told there were 276 souls of us in the ship.

[38]And after they had eaten sufficiently, [they proceeded] to lighten the ship, throwing out the wheat into the sea.

[39]Now when it was day [and they saw the land], they did not recognize it, but they noticed a bay with a beach on which they [taking counsel] purposed to run the ship ashore if they possibly could.

# New International Version

anchors, they left them in the sea and at the same time untied the ropes that held the rudders. Then they hoisted the foresail to the wind and made for the beach. ⁴¹But the ship struck a sandbar and ran aground. The bow stuck fast and would not move, and the stern was broken to pieces by the pounding of the surf.

⁴²The soldiers planned to kill the prisoners to prevent any of them from swimming away and escaping. ⁴³But the centurion wanted to spare Paul's life and kept them from carrying out their plan. He ordered those who could swim to jump overboard first and get to land. ⁴⁴The rest were to get there on planks or on other pieces of the ship. In this way everyone reached land safely.

## Paul Ashore on Malta

**28** Once safely on shore, we found out that the island was called Malta. ²The islanders showed us unusual kindness. They built a fire and welcomed us all because it was raining and cold. ³Paul gathered a pile of brushwood and, as he put it on the fire, a viper, driven out by the heat, fastened itself on his hand. ⁴When the islanders saw the snake hanging from his hand, they said to each other, "This man must be a murderer; for though he escaped from the sea, the goddess Justice has not allowed him to live." ⁵But Paul shook the snake off into the fire and suffered no ill effects. ⁶The people expected him to swell up or suddenly fall dead; but after waiting a long time and seeing nothing unusual happen to him, they changed their minds and said he was a god.

⁷There was an estate nearby that belonged to Publius, the chief official of the island. He welcomed us to his home and showed us generous hospitality for three days. ⁸His father was sick in bed, suffering from fever and dysentery. Paul went in to see him and, after prayer, placed his hands on him and healed him. ⁹When this had happened, the rest of the sick on the island came and were cured. ¹⁰They honored us in many ways; and when we were ready to sail, they furnished us with the supplies we needed.

## Paul's Arrival at Rome

¹¹After three months we put out to sea in a ship that had wintered in the island—it was an Alexandrian ship with the figurehead of the twin gods Castor and Pollux. ¹²We put in at Syracuse and stayed there three days. ¹³From there we set sail and arrived at Rhegium. The next day the south wind came up, and on the following day we reached Puteoli. ¹⁴There we found some brothers and sisters who invited us to spend a week with them. And so we came to Rome. ¹⁵The brothers and sisters there had heard that we were coming, and they traveled as far as the Forum of Appius and the Three Taverns to meet us. At the sight of these people Paul thanked God and was encouraged. ¹⁶When we got to Rome, Paul was allowed to live by himself, with a soldier to guard him.

# Amplified Bible

⁴⁰So they cut the cables *and* severed the anchors and left them in the sea; at the same time unlashing the ropes that held the rudders and hoisting the foresail to the wind, they headed for the beach.

⁴¹But striking a crosscurrent (a place open to two seas) they ran the ship aground. The prow stuck fast and remained immovable, and the stern began to break up under the violent force of the waves.

⁴²It was the counsel of the soldiers to kill the prisoners, lest any of them should swim to land and escape;

⁴³But the centurion, wishing to save Paul, prevented their carrying out their purpose. He commanded those who could swim to throw themselves overboard first and make for the shore,

⁴⁴And the rest on heavy boards or pieces of the vessel. And so it was that all escaped safely to land.

**28** After we were safe on the island, we knew *and* recognized that it was called Malta.

²And the natives showed us unusual *and* remarkable kindness, for they kindled a fire and welcomed *and* received us all, since it had begun to rain and was cold.

³Now Paul had gathered a bundle of sticks, and he was laying them on the fire when a viper crawled out because of the heat and fastened itself on his hand.

⁴When the natives saw the little animal hanging from his hand, they said to one another, Doubtless this man is a murderer, for though he has been saved from the sea, Justice [ᵃthe goddess of avenging] has not permitted that he should live.

⁵Then [Paul simply] shook off the small creature into the fire and suffered no evil effects.

⁶However, they were waiting, expecting him to swell up or suddenly drop dead; but when they had watched him a long time and saw nothing fatal *or* harmful come to him, they changed their minds and kept saying over and over that he was a god.

⁷In the vicinity of that place there were estates belonging to the head man of the island, named Publius, who accepted *and* welcomed *and* entertained us with hearty hospitality for three days.

⁸And it happened that the father of Publius was sick in bed with recurring attacks of fever and dysentery; and Paul went to see him, and after praying and laying his hands on him, he healed him.

⁹After this had occurred, the other people on the island who had diseases also kept coming and were cured.

¹⁰They showed us every respect *and* presented many gifts to us, honoring us with many honors; and when we sailed, they provided *and* put on [board our ship] everything we needed.

¹¹It was after three months' stay there that we set sail in a ship which had wintered in the island, an Alexandrian ship with the Twin Brothers [Castor and Pollux] as its figurehead.

¹²We landed at Syracuse and remained there three days,

¹³And from there we made a circuit [following the coast] and reached Rhegium; and one day later a south wind sprang up, and the next day we arrived at Puteoli.

¹⁴There we found some [Christian] brethren and were entreated to stay with them for seven days. And so we came to Rome.

¹⁵And the [Christian] brethren there, having had news of us, came as far as the Forum of Appius and the Three Taverns to meet us. When Paul saw them, he thanked God and received new courage.

¹⁶When we arrived at Rome, *the centurion delivered the prisoners to the captain of the guard, but* Paul was permitted to live by himself with the soldier who guarded him.

---

ᵃ Alexander Souter, *Pocket Lexicon.*

## New International Version

### Paul Preaches at Rome Under Guard

[17]Three days later he called together the local Jewish leaders. When they had assembled, Paul said to them: "My brothers, although I have done nothing against our people or against the customs of our ancestors, I was arrested in Jerusalem and handed over to the Romans. [18]They examined me and wanted to release me, because I was not guilty of any crime deserving death. [19]The Jews objected, so I was compelled to make an appeal to Caesar. I certainly did not intend to bring any charge against my own people. [20]For this reason I have asked to see you and talk with you. It is because of the hope of Israel that I am bound with this chain."

[21]They replied, "We have not received any letters from Judea concerning you, and none of our people who have come from there has reported or said anything bad about you. [22]But we want to hear what your views are, for we know that people everywhere are talking against this sect."

[23]They arranged to meet Paul on a certain day, and came in even larger numbers to the place where he was staying. He witnessed to them from morning till evening, explaining about the kingdom of God, and from the Law of Moses and from the Prophets he tried to persuade them about Jesus. [24]Some were convinced by what he said, but others would not believe. [25]They disagreed among themselves and began to leave after Paul had made this final statement: "The Holy Spirit spoke the truth to your ancestors when he said through Isaiah the prophet:

[26]"'Go to this people and say,
"You will be ever hearing but never understanding;
    you will be ever seeing but never perceiving."
[27]For this people's heart has become calloused;
    they hardly hear with their ears,
    and they have closed their eyes.
Otherwise they might see with their eyes,
    hear with their ears,
    understand with their hearts
and turn, and I would heal them.'[a]

[28]"Therefore I want you to know that God's salvation has been sent to the Gentiles, and they will listen!" [29][b]

[30]For two whole years Paul stayed there in his own rented house and welcomed all who came to see him. [31]He proclaimed the kingdom of God and taught about the Lord Jesus Christ—with all boldness and without hindrance!

## Amplified Bible

[17]Three days after [our arrival], he called together the leading local Jews; and when they had gathered, he said to them, Brethren, though I have done nothing against the people or against the customs of our forefathers, yet I was turned over as a prisoner from Jerusalem into the hands of the Romans.

[18]After they had examined me, they were ready to release me because I was innocent of any offense deserving the death penalty.

[19]But when the Jews protested, I was forced to appeal to Caesar, though it was not because I had any charge to make against my nation.

[20]This is the reason therefore why I have begged to see you and to talk with you, since it is because of the Hope of Israel (the Messiah) that I am bound with this chain.

[21]And they answered him, We have not received any letters about you from Judea, and none of the [Jewish] brethren coming here has reported or spoken anything evil about you.

[22]But we think it fitting *and* are eager to hear from you what it is that you have in mind *and* believe *and* what your opinion is, for with regard to this sect it is known to all of us that it is everywhere denounced.

[23]So when they had set a day with him, they came in large numbers to his lodging. And he fully set forth *and* explained the matter to them from morning until night, testifying to the kingdom of God and trying to persuade them concerning Jesus both from the Law of Moses and from the Prophets.

[24]And some were convinced *and* believed what he said, and others did not believe.

[25]And as they disagreed among themselves, they began to leave, [but not before] Paul had added one statement [more]: The Holy Spirit was right in saying through Isaiah the prophet to your forefathers:

[26]Go to this people and say to them, You will indeed hear *and* hear with your ears but will not understand, and you will indeed look *and* look with your eyes but will not see [not perceive, have knowledge of or become acquainted with what you look at, at all].

[27]For the heart (the understanding, the soul) of this people has grown dull (stupid, hardened, and calloused), and their ears are heavy *and* hard of hearing and they have shut tight their eyes, so that they may not perceive *and* have knowledge *and* become acquainted with their eyes and hear with their ears and understand with their souls and turn [to Me and be converted], that I may heal them. [Isa. 6:9, 10.]

[28]So let it be understood by you then that [this message of] the salvation of God has been sent to the Gentiles, and they will listen [to it]! [Ps. 67:2.]

[29][a]*And when he had said these things, the Jews went away, arguing and disputing among themselves.*

[30]After this Paul lived there for two entire years [at his own expense] in his own rented lodging, and he welcomed all who came to him,

[31]Preaching to them the kingdom of God and teaching them about the Lord Jesus Christ with boldness *and* quite openly, and without being molested *or* hindered.

---

[a] 27 Isaiah 6:9,10 (see Septuagint)   [b] 29 Some manuscripts include here *After he said this, the Jews left, arguing vigorously among themselves.*

[a] Many manuscripts do not contain this verse.

# Romans

**1** Paul, a servant of Christ Jesus, called to be an apostle and set apart for the gospel of God — ²the gospel he promised beforehand through his prophets in the Holy Scriptures ³regarding his Son, who as to his earthly life*a* was a descendant of David, ⁴and who through the Spirit of holiness was appointed the Son of God in power*b* by his resurrection from the dead: Jesus Christ our Lord. ⁵Through him we received grace and apostleship to call all the Gentiles to the obedience that comes from*c* faith for his name's sake. ⁶And you also are among those Gentiles who are called to belong to Jesus Christ.

⁷To all in Rome who are loved by God and called to be his holy people:

Grace and peace to you from God our Father and from the Lord Jesus Christ.

## Paul's Longing to Visit Rome

⁸First, I thank my God through Jesus Christ for all of you, because your faith is being reported all over the world. ⁹God, whom I serve in my spirit in preaching the gospel of his Son, is my witness how constantly I remember you ¹⁰in my prayers at all times; and I pray that now at last by God's will the way may be opened for me to come to you.

¹¹I long to see you so that I may impart to you some spiritual gift to make you strong— ¹²that is, that you and I may be mutually encouraged by each other's faith. ¹³I do not want you to be unaware, brothers and sisters,*d* that I planned many times to come to you (but have been prevented from doing so until now) in order that I might have a harvest among you, just as I have had among the other Gentiles.

¹⁴I am obligated both to Greeks and non-Greeks, both to the wise and the foolish. ¹⁵That is why I am so eager to preach the gospel also to you who are in Rome.

¹⁶For I am not ashamed of the gospel, because it is the power of God that brings salvation to everyone who believes: first to the Jew, then to the Gentile. ¹⁷For in the gospel the righteousness of God is revealed—a righteousness that is by faith from first to last,*e* just as it is written: "The righteous will live by faith."*f*

## God's Wrath Against Sinful Humanity

¹⁸The wrath of God is being revealed from heaven against all the godlessness and wickedness of people, who suppress the truth by their wickedness, ¹⁹since what may be known about God is plain to them, because God has

---

*a 3* Or *who according to the flesh*    *b 4* Or *was declared with power to be the Son of God*    *c 5* Or *that is*    *d 13* The Greek word for *brothers and sisters (adelphoi)* refers here to believers, both men and women, as part of God's family; also in 7:1, 4; 8:12, 29; 10:1; 11:25; 12:1; 15:14, 30; 16:14, 17.    *e 17* Or *is from faith to faith*    *f 17* Hab. 2:4

# Romans

**1** From Paul, a bond servant of Jesus Christ (the Messiah) called to be an apostle, (a special messenger) set apart to [preach] the Gospel (good news) of *and* from God, ²Which He promised in advance [long ago] through His prophets in the sacred Scriptures— ³[The Gospel] regarding His Son, Who as to the flesh (His human nature) was descended from David, ⁴And [as to His divine nature] according to the Spirit of holiness was openly *a*designated the Son of God in power [in a striking, triumphant and miraculous manner] by His resurrection from the dead, even Jesus Christ our Lord (the Messiah, the Anointed One). ⁵It is through Him that we have received grace (God's unmerited favor) and [our] apostleship to promote obedience to the faith *and* make disciples for His name's sake among all the nations, ⁶And this includes you, called of Jesus Christ *and* invited [as you are] to belong to Him. ⁷To [you then] all God's beloved ones in Rome, called to be saints *and* designated for a consecrated life: Grace *and* spiritual blessing and peace be yours from God our Father and from the Lord Jesus Christ.

⁸First, I thank my God through Jesus Christ for all of you, because [the report of] your faith is made known to all the world *and* is *a*commended everywhere. ⁹For God is my witness, Whom I serve with my [whole] spirit [rendering priestly and spiritual service] in [preaching] the Gospel *and* [telling] the good news of His Son, how incessantly I always mention you when at my prayers. ¹⁰I keep pleading that somehow by God's will I may now at last prosper *and* come to you. ¹¹For I am yearning to see you, that I may impart *and* share with you some spiritual gift to strengthen *and* establish you; ¹²That is, that we may be mutually strengthened *and* encouraged *and* comforted by each other's faith, both yours and mine. ¹³I want you to know, brethren, that many times I have planned *and* intended to come to you, though thus far I have been hindered *and* prevented, in order that I might have some fruit (some result of my labors) among you, as I have among the rest of the Gentiles. ¹⁴Both to Greeks and to barbarians (to the cultured and to the uncultured), both to the wise and the foolish, I have an obligation to discharge *and* a duty to perform *and* a debt to pay. ¹⁵So, for my part, I am willing *and* eagerly ready to preach the Gospel to you also who are in Rome.

¹⁶For I am not ashamed of the Gospel (good news) *of Christ,* for it is God's power working unto salvation [for deliverance from eternal death] to everyone who believes *with* a personal trust *and* a confident surrender *and* firm reliance, to the Jew first and also to the Greek, ¹⁷For in the Gospel a righteousness which God ascribes is revealed, both springing from faith and leading to faith [disclosed through the way of faith that arouses to more faith]. As it is written, The man who through faith is just *and* upright shall live *and* shall live by faith. [Hab. 2:4.]

¹⁸For God's [holy] wrath *and* indignation are revealed from heaven against all ungodliness and unrighteousness of men, who in their wickedness repress *and* hinder the truth *and* make it inoperative. ¹⁹For that which is known about God is evident to them *and* made plain in their inner consciousness, because God [Himself] has shown it to them.

---

*a* Marvin Vincent, *Word Studies in the New Testament.*

## New International Version

made it plain to them. [20]For since the creation of the world God's invisible qualities—his eternal power and divine nature—have been clearly seen, being understood from what has been made, so that people are without excuse.

[21]For although they knew God, they neither glorified him as God nor gave thanks to him, but their thinking became futile and their foolish hearts were darkened. [22]Although they claimed to be wise, they became fools [23]and exchanged the glory of the immortal God for images made to look like a mortal human being and birds and animals and reptiles.

[24]Therefore God gave them over in the sinful desires of their hearts to sexual impurity for the degrading of their bodies with one another. [25]They exchanged the truth about God for a lie, and worshiped and served created things rather than the Creator—who is forever praised. Amen.

[26]Because of this, God gave them over to shameful lusts. Even their women exchanged natural sexual relations for unnatural ones. [27]In the same way the men also abandoned natural relations with women and were inflamed with lust for one another. Men committed shameful acts with other men, and received in themselves the due penalty for their error.

[28]Furthermore, just as they did not think it worthwhile to retain the knowledge of God, so God gave them over to a depraved mind, so that they do what ought not to be done. [29]They have become filled with every kind of wickedness, evil, greed and depravity. They are full of envy, murder, strife, deceit and malice. They are gossips, [30]slanderers, God-haters, insolent, arrogant and boastful; they invent ways of doing evil; they disobey their parents; [31]they have no understanding, no fidelity, no love, no mercy. [32]Although they know God's righteous decree that those who do such things deserve death, they not only continue to do these very things but also approve of those who practice them.

### God's Righteous Judgment

**2** You, therefore, have no excuse, you who pass judgment on someone else, for at whatever point you judge another, you are condemning yourself, because you who pass judgment do the same things. [2]Now we know that God's judgment against those who do such things is based on truth. [3]So when you, a mere human being, pass judgment on them and yet do the same things, do you think you will escape God's judgment? [4]Or do you show contempt for the riches of his kindness, forbearance and

## Amplified Bible

[20]For ever since the creation of the world His invisible nature *and* attributes, that is, His eternal power and divinity, have been made intelligible *and* clearly discernible in *and* through the things that have been made (His handiworks). So [men] are without excuse [altogether without any defense or justification], [Ps. 19: 1-4.]

[21]Because when they knew *and* recognized Him as God, they did not honor *and* glorify Him as God or give Him thanks. But instead they became futile *and* *a* godless in their thinking [with vain imaginings, foolish reasoning, and stupid speculations] and their senseless minds were darkened.

[22]Claiming to be wise, they became fools [professing to be smart, they made simpletons of themselves].

[23]And by them the glory and majesty *and* excellence of the immortal God were exchanged for *and* represented by images, resembling mortal man and birds and beasts and reptiles.

[24]Therefore God gave them up in the lusts of their [own] hearts to sexual impurity, to the dishonoring of their bodies among themselves [abandoning them to the degrading power of sin],

[25]Because they exchanged the truth of God for a lie and worshiped and served the creature rather than the Creator, Who is blessed forever! Amen (so be it). [Jer. 2:11.]

[26]For this reason God gave them over *and* abandoned them to vile affections *and* degrading passions. For their women exchanged their natural function for an unnatural *and* abnormal one,

[27]And the men also turned from natural relations with women and were set ablaze (burning out, consumed) with lust for one another—men committing shameful acts with men and suffering in their own *b* bodies *and* personalities the inevitable consequences *and* penalty of their wrongdoing *and* going astray, which was [their] fitting retribution.

[28]And so, since they did not see fit to acknowledge God *or* approve of Him *or* consider Him worth the knowing, God gave them over to a base *and* condemned mind to do things not proper *or* decent *but* loathsome,

[29]Until they were filled (permeated and saturated) with every kind of unrighteousness, iniquity, grasping *and* covetous greed, and malice. [They were] full of envy *and* jealousy, murder, strife, deceit *and* treachery, ill will *and* cruel ways. [They were] secret backbiters *and* gossipers,

[30]Slanderers, hateful to *and* hating God, full of insolence, arrogance, [and] boasting; inventors of new forms of evil, disobedient *and* undutiful to parents.

[31][They were] without understanding, conscienceless *and* faithless, heartless *and* loveless [and] merciless.

[32]Though they are fully aware of God's righteous decree that those who do such things deserve to die, they not only do them themselves but approve *and* applaud others who practice them.

**2** Therefore you have no excuse *or* defense *or* justification, O man, whoever you are who judges *and* condemns another. For in posing as judge *and* passing sentence on another, you condemn yourself, because you who judge are habitually practicing the very same things [that you censure and denounce].

[2][But] we know that the judgment (adverse verdict, sentence) of God falls justly *and* in accordance with truth upon those who practice such things.

[3]And do you think *or* imagine, O man, when you judge *and* condemn those who practice such things and yet do them yourself, that you will escape God's judgment *and* elude His sentence *and* adverse verdict?

[4]Or are you [so blind as to] trifle with *and* presume

---

*a* Alexander Souter, *Pocket Lexicon of the Greek New Testament.*
*b* *Webster's New International Dictionary* offers this as a definition of "selves."

## New International Version

patience, not realizing that God's kindness is intended to lead you to repentance?

5But because of your stubbornness and your unrepentant heart, you are storing up wrath against yourself for the day of God's wrath, when his righteous judgment will be revealed. 6God "will repay each person according to what they have done."a 7To those who by persistence in doing good seek glory, honor and immortality, he will give eternal life. 8But for those who are self-seeking and who reject the truth and follow evil, there will be wrath and anger. 9There will be trouble and distress for every human being who does evil: first for the Jew, then for the Gentile; 10but glory, honor and peace for everyone who does good: first for the Jew, then for the Gentile. 11For God does not show favoritism.

12All who sin apart from the law will also perish apart from the law, and all who sin under the law will be judged by the law. 13For it is not those who hear the law who are righteous in God's sight, but it is those who obey the law who will be declared righteous. 14(Indeed, when Gentiles, who do not have the law, do by nature things required by the law, they are a law for themselves, even though they do not have the law. 15They show that the requirements of the law are written on their hearts, their consciences also bearing witness, and their thoughts sometimes accusing them and at other times even defending them.) 16This will take place on the day when God judges people's secrets through Jesus Christ, as my gospel declares.

### The Jews and the Law

17Now you, if you call yourself a Jew; if you rely on the law and boast in God; 18if you know his will and approve of what is superior because you are instructed by the law; 19if you are convinced that you are a guide for the blind, a light for those who are in the dark, 20an instructor of the foolish, a teacher of little children, because you have in the law the embodiment of knowledge and truth— 21you, then, who teach others, do you not teach yourself? You who preach against stealing, do you steal? 22You who say that people should not commit adultery, do you commit adultery? You who abhor idols, do you rob temples? 23You who boast in the law, do you dishonor God by breaking the law? 24As it

## Amplified Bible

upon *and* despise *and* underestimate the wealth of His kindness and forbearance and long-suffering patience? Are you unmindful *or* actually ignorant [of the fact] that God's kindness is intended to lead you to repent (ato change your mind and inner man to accept God's will)?

5But by your callous stubbornness *and* impenitence of heart you are storing up wrath *and* indignation for yourself on the day of wrath *and* indignation, when God's righteous judgment (just doom) will be revealed.

6For He will render to every man according to his works [justly, as his deeds deserve]: [Ps. 62:12.]

7To those who by patient persistence in well-doing [bspringing from piety] seek [unseen but sure] glory and honor and [bthe eternal blessedness of] immortality, He will give eternal life.

8But for those who are self-seeking *and* self-willed *and* disobedient to the Truth but responsive to wickedness, there will be indignation and wrath.

9[And] there will be tribulation *and* anguish and calamity *and* constraint for every soul of man who [habitually] does evil, the Jew first and also the Greek (Gentile).

10But glory and honor and [heart] peace shall be awarded to everyone who [habitually] does good, the Jew first and also the Greek (Gentile).

11For God shows no partiality [cundue favor or unfairness; with Him one man is not different from another]. [Deut. 10:17; II Chron. 19:7.]

12All who have sinned without the Law will also perish without [regard to] the Law, and all who have sinned under the Law will be judged *and* condemned by the Law.

13For it is not merely hearing the Law [read] that makes one righteous before God, but it is the doers of the Law who will be held guiltless *and* acquitted *and* justified.

14When Gentiles who have not the [divine] Law do instinctively what the Law requires, they are a law to themselves, since they do not have the Law.

15They show that the essential requirements of the Law are written in their hearts *and* are operating there, with which their consciences (sense of right and wrong) also bear witness; and their [moral] bdecisions (their arguments of reason, their condemning or approving dthoughts) will accuse or perhaps defend *and* excuse [them]

16On that day when, as my Gospel proclaims, God by Jesus Christ will judge men in regard to dthe things which they conceal (their hidden thoughts). [Eccl. 12:14.]

17But if you bear the name of Jew and rely upon the Law and pride yourselves in God *and* your relationship to Him,

18And know *and* understand His will and discerningly approve the better things *and* have a sense of what is vital, because you are instructed by the Law;

19And if you are confident that you [yourself] are a guide to the blind, a light to those who are in darkness, and [that

20You are] a corrector of the foolish, a teacher of the childish, having in the Law the embodiment of knowledge and truth—

21Well then, you who teach others, do you not teach yourself? While you teach against stealing, do you steal (take what does not really belong to you)?

22You who say not to commit adultery, do you commit adultery [are you unchaste in action or in thought]? You who abhor *and* loathe idols, do you rob temples [do you appropriate to your own use what is consecrated to God, thus robbing the sanctuary and edoing sacrilege]?

23You who boast in the Law, do you dishonor God by breaking the Law [by stealthily infringing upon or carelessly neglecting or openly breaking it]?

a Alexander Souter, *Pocket Lexicon*. b Joseph Thayer, *A Greek-English Lexicon of the New Testament*. c James Moulton and George Milligan, *The Vocabulary of the Greek Testament*. d Henry Alford, *The Greek New Testament, with Notes*. e James Moulton and George Milligan, *The Vocabulary*.

a 6 Psalm 62:12; Prov. 24:12

## New International Version

is written: "God's name is blasphemed among the Gentiles because of you."[a]

²⁵Circumcision has value if you observe the law, but if you break the law, you have become as though you had not been circumcised. ²⁶So then, if those who are not circumcised keep the law's requirements, will they not be regarded as though they were circumcised? ²⁷The one who is not circumcised physically and yet obeys the law will condemn you who, even though you have the[b] written code and circumcision, are a lawbreaker.

²⁸A person is not a Jew who is one only outwardly, nor is circumcision merely outward and physical. ²⁹No, a person is a Jew who is one inwardly; and circumcision is circumcision of the heart, by the Spirit, not by the written code. Such a person's praise is not from other people, but from God.

### God's Faithfulness

**3** What advantage, then, is there in being a Jew, or what value is there in circumcision? ²Much in every way! First of all, the Jews have been entrusted with the very words of God.

³What if some were unfaithful? Will their unfaithfulness nullify God's faithfulness? ⁴Not at all! Let God be true, and every human being a liar. As it is written:

"So that you may be proved right when you speak
and prevail when you judge."[c]

⁵But if our unrighteousness brings out God's righteousness more clearly, what shall we say? That God is unjust in bringing his wrath on us? (I am using a human argument.) ⁶Certainly not! If that were so, how could God judge the world? ⁷Someone might argue, "If my falsehood enhances God's truthfulness and so increases his glory, why am I still condemned as a sinner?" ⁸Why not say—as some slanderously claim that we say—"Let us do evil that good may result"? Their condemnation is just!

### No One Is Righteous

⁹What shall we conclude then? Do we have any advantage? Not at all! For we have already made the charge that Jews and Gentiles alike are all under the power of sin. ¹⁰As it is written:

"There is no one righteous, not even one;
¹¹ there is no one who understands;
there is no one who seeks God.
¹²All have turned away,
they have together become worthless;
there is no one who does good,
not even one."[d]
¹³"Their throats are open graves;
their tongues practice deceit."[e]
"The poison of vipers is on their lips."[f]
¹⁴ "Their mouths are full of cursing and bitterness."[g]
¹⁵"Their feet are swift to shed blood;
¹⁶ ruin and misery mark their ways,
¹⁷and the way of peace they do not know."[h]
¹⁸ "There is no fear of God before their eyes."[i]

¹⁹Now we know that whatever the law says, it says to those who are under the law, so that every mouth may be silenced and the whole world held accountable to God.

## Amplified Bible

²⁴For, as it is written, The name of God is maligned *and* blasphemed among the Gentiles because of you! [The words to this effect are from your own Scriptures.] [Isa. 52:5; Ezek. 36:20.]

²⁵Circumcision does indeed profit if you keep the Law; but if you habitually transgress the Law, your circumcision is made uncircumcision.

²⁶So if a man who is uncircumcised keeps the requirements of the Law, will not his uncircumcision be credited to him as [equivalent to] circumcision?

²⁷Then those who are physically uncircumcised but keep the Law will condemn you who, although you have the code in writing and have circumcision, break the Law.

²⁸For he is not a [real] Jew who is only one outwardly *and* publicly, nor is [true] circumcision something external and physical.

²⁹But he is a Jew who is one inwardly, and [true] circumcision is of the heart, a spiritual and not a literal [matter]. His praise is not from men but from God.

**3** Then what advantage remains to the Jew? [How is he favored?] Or what is the value *or* benefit of circumcision?

²Much in every way. To begin with, to the Jews were entrusted the oracles (the brief communications, the intentions, the utterances) of God. [Ps. 147:19.]

³What if some did not believe *and* were without faith? Does their lack of faith *and* their faithlessness nullify *and* make ineffective *and* void the faithfulness of God *and* His fidelity [to His Word]?

⁴By no means! Let God be found true though every human being is false *and* a liar, as it is written, That You may be justified *and* shown to be upright in what You say, and prevail when You are judged [by sinful men]. [Ps. 51:4.]

⁵But if our unrighteousness thus establishes *and* exhibits the righteousness of God, what shall we say? That God is unjust *and* wrong to inflict His wrath upon us [Jews]? I speak in a [purely] human way.

⁶By no means! Otherwise, how could God judge the world?

⁷But [you say] if through my falsehood God's integrity is magnified *and* advertised *and* abounds to His glory, why am I still being judged as a sinner?

⁸And why should we not do evil that good may come?—as some slanderously charge us with teaching. Such [false teaching] is justly condemned by them.

⁹Well then, are we [Jews] superior *and* better off than they? No, not at all. We have already charged that all men, both Jews and Greeks (Gentiles), are under sin [held down by and subject to its power and control].

¹⁰As it is written, None is righteous, just *and* truthful *and* upright *and* conscientious, no, not one. [Ps. 14:3.]

¹¹No one understands [no one intelligently discerns *or* comprehends]; no one seeks out God. [Ps. 14:2.]

¹²All have turned aside; together they have gone wrong *and* have become unprofitable *and* worthless; no one does right, not even one!

¹³Their throat is a yawning grave; they use their tongues to deceive (to mislead and to deal treacherously). The venom of asps is beneath their lips. [Ps. 5:9; 140:3.]

¹⁴Their mouth is full of cursing and bitterness. [Ps. 10:7.]

¹⁵Their feet are swift to shed blood.

¹⁶Destruction [as it dashes them to pieces] and misery mark their ways.

¹⁷And they have no experience of the way of peace [they know nothing about peace, for a peaceful way they do not even recognize]. [Isa. 59:7, 8.]

¹⁸There is no [reverential] fear of God before their eyes. [Ps. 36:1.]

¹⁹Now we know that whatever the Law says, it speaks to those who are under the Law, so that [the murmurs and excuses of] every mouth may be hushed and all the world may be held accountable to God.

---

*a 24* Isaiah 52:5 (see Septuagint); Ezek. 36:20,22    *b 27* Or *who, by means of a*    *c 4* Psalm 51:4    *d 12* Psalms 14:1-3; 53:1-3; Eccles. 7:20
*e 13* Psalm 5:9    *f 13* Psalm 140:3    *g 14* Psalm 10:7 (see Septuagint)
*h 17* Isaiah 59:7,8    *i 18* Psalm 36:1

## New International Version

20Therefore no one will be declared righteous in God's sight by the works of the law; rather, through the law we become conscious of our sin.

### Righteousness Through Faith

21But now apart from the law the righteousness of God has been made known, to which the Law and the Prophets testify. 22This righteousness is given through faith in*a* Jesus Christ to all who believe. There is no difference between Jew and Gentile, 23for all have sinned and fall short of the glory of God, 24and all are justified freely by his grace through the redemption that came by Christ Jesus. 25God presented Christ as a sacrifice of atonement,*b* through the shedding of his blood—to be received by faith. He did this to demonstrate his righteousness, because in his forbearance he had left the sins committed beforehand unpunished— 26he did it to demonstrate his righteousness at the present time, so as to be just and the one who justifies those who have faith in Jesus.

27Where, then, is boasting? It is excluded. Because of what law? The law that requires works? No, because of the law that requires faith. 28For we maintain that a person is justified by faith apart from the works of the law. 29Or is God the God of Jews only? Is he not the God of Gentiles too? Yes, of Gentiles too, 30since there is only one God, who will justify the circumcised by faith and the uncircumcised through that same faith. 31Do we, then, nullify the law by this faith? Not at all! Rather, we uphold the law.

### Abraham Justified by Faith

4 What then shall we say that Abraham, our forefather according to the flesh, discovered in this matter? 2If, in fact, Abraham was justified by works, he had something to boast about—but not before God. 3What does Scripture say? "Abraham believed God, and it was credited to him as righteousness."*c*

4Now to the one who works, wages are not credited as a gift but as an obligation. 5However, to the one who does not work but trusts God who justifies the ungodly, their faith is credited as righteousness. 6David says the same thing when he speaks of the blessedness of the one to whom God credits righteousness apart from works:

## Amplified Bible

20For no person will be justified (made righteous, acquitted, and judged acceptable) in His sight by observing the works prescribed by the Law. For [the real function of] the Law is to make men recognize *and* be conscious of sin [*a*not mere perception, but an acquaintance with sin which works toward repentance, faith, and holy character].

21But now the righteousness of God has been revealed independently *and* altogether apart from the Law, although actually it is attested by the Law and the Prophets,

22Namely, the righteousness of God which comes by believing *with* personal trust *and* confident reliance on Jesus Christ (the Messiah). [And it is meant] for all who believe. For there is no distinction,

23Since all have sinned and are falling short of the honor *and* glory *a*which God bestows *and* receives.

24[All] are justified *and* made upright *and* in right standing with God, freely *and* gratuitously by His grace (His unmerited favor and mercy), through the redemption which is [provided] in Christ Jesus,

25Whom God put forward [*b*before the eyes of all] as a mercy seat *and* propitiation by His blood [the cleansing and life-giving sacrifice of atonement and reconciliation, to be received] through faith. This was to show God's righteousness, because in His divine forbearance He had passed over *and* ignored former sins without punishment.

26It was to demonstrate *and* prove at the present time (*c*in the now season) that He Himself is righteous and that He justifies *and* accepts as righteous him who has [true] faith in Jesus.

27Then what becomes of [our] pride *and* [our] boasting? It is excluded (banished, ruled out entirely). On what principle? [On the principle] of doing good deeds? No, but on the principle of faith.

28For we hold that a man is justified *and* made upright by faith independent of *and* distinctly apart from good deeds (works of the Law). [The observance of the Law has nothing to do with justification.]

29Or is God merely [the God] of Jews? Is He not the God of Gentiles also? Yes, of Gentiles also,

30Since it is one and the same God Who will justify the circumcised by faith [*a*which germinated from Abraham] and the uncircumcised through their [newly acquired] faith. [For it is the same trusting faith in both cases, a firmly relying faith in Jesus Christ].

31Do we then by [this] faith make the Law of no effect, overthrow it *or* make it a dead letter? Certainly not! On the contrary, we confirm *and* establish *and* uphold the Law.

4 [But] if so, what shall we say about Abraham, our forefather humanly speaking—[what did he] find out? [How does this affect his position, and what was gained by him?]

2For if Abraham was justified (*d*established as just by acquittal from guilt) by good works [that he did, then] he has grounds for boasting. But not before God!

3For what does the Scripture say? Abraham believed in (trusted in) God, and it was credited to his account as righteousness (right living and right standing with God). [Gen. 15:6.]

4Now to a laborer, his wages are not counted as a favor *or* a gift, but as an obligation (something owed to him).

5But to one who, not working [by the Law], trusts (believes fully) in Him Who justifies the ungodly, his faith is credited to him as righteousness (the standing acceptable to God).

6Thus David *c*congratulates the man *and* pronounces a blessing on him to whom God credits righteousness apart from the works he does:

*a* 22 Or *through the faithfulness of*   *b* 25 The Greek for *sacrifice of atonement* refers to the atonement cover on the ark of the covenant (see Lev. 16:15,16).   *c* 3 Gen. 15:6; also in verse 22

*a* Marvin Vincent, *Word Studies.*   *b* Johann Bengel, *Gnomon Novi Testamenti.*   *c* Literal translation.   *d* Hermann Cremer, *Biblico-Theological Lexicon of New Testament Greek.*   *e* Alexander Souter, *Pocket Lexicon.*

## New International Version

7 "Blessed are those
whose transgressions are forgiven,
whose sins are covered.
8 Blessed is the one
whose sin the Lord will never count against them."[a]

9 Is this blessedness only for the circumcised, or also for the uncircumcised? We have been saying that Abraham's faith was credited to him as righteousness. 10 Under what circumstances was it credited? Was it after he was circumcised, or before? It was not after, but before! 11 And he received circumcision as a sign, a seal of the righteousness that he had by faith while he was still uncircumcised. So then, he is the father of all who believe but have not been circumcised, in order that righteousness might be credited to them. 12 And he is then also the father of the circumcised who not only are circumcised but who also follow in the footsteps of the faith that our father Abraham had before he was circumcised.

13 It was not through the law that Abraham and his offspring received the promise that he would be heir of the world, but through the righteousness that comes by faith. 14 For if those who depend on the law are heirs, faith means nothing and the promise is worthless, 15 because the law brings wrath. And where there is no law there is no transgression.

16 Therefore, the promise comes by faith, so that it may be by grace and may be guaranteed to all Abraham's offspring—not only to those who are of the law but also to those who have the faith of Abraham. He is the father of us all. 17 As it is written: "I have made you a father of many nations."[b] He is our father in the sight of God, in whom he believed—the God who gives life to the dead and calls into being things that were not.

18 Against all hope, Abraham in hope believed and so became the father of many nations, just as it had been said to him, "So shall your offspring be."[c] 19 Without weakening in his faith, he faced the fact that his body was as good as dead—since he was about a hundred years old—and that Sarah's womb was also dead. 20 Yet he did not waver through unbelief regarding the promise of God, but was strengthened in his faith and gave glory to God, 21 being fully persuaded that God had power to do what he had promised. 22 This is why "it was credited to him as righteousness." 23 The words "it was credited to him" were written not for him alone, 24 but for us, to whom God will credit righteousness—for us who believe in him who raised Jesus our Lord from the dead. 25 He was delivered over to death for our sins and was raised to life for our justification.

## Amplified Bible

7 Blessed *and* happy *and* [a] to be envied are those whose iniquities are forgiven and whose sins are covered up *and* completely buried.
8 Blessed *and* happy *and* [a] to be envied is the person of whose sin the Lord will take no account *nor* reckon it against him. [Ps. 32:1, 2.]

9 Is this blessing (happiness) then meant only for the circumcised, or also for the uncircumcised? We say that faith was credited to Abraham as righteousness.
10 How then was it credited [to him]? Was it before or after he had been circumcised? It was not after, but before he was circumcised.
11 He received the mark of circumcision as a token *or* an evidence [and] seal of the righteousness which he had by faith while he was still uncircumcised—[faith] so that he was to be made the father of all who [truly] believe, though without circumcision, and who thus have righteousness (right standing with God) imputed to them *and* credited to their account,
12 As well as [that he be made] the father of those circumcised persons who are not merely circumcised, but also walk in the way of that faith which our father Abraham had before he was circumcised.
13 For the promise to Abraham or his posterity, that he should inherit the world, did not come through [observing the commands of] the Law but through the righteousness of faith. [Gen. 17:4-6; 22:16-18.]
14 If it is the adherents of the Law who are to be the heirs, then faith is made futile *and* empty of all meaning and the promise [of God] is made void (is annulled and has no power).
15 For the Law results in [divine] wrath, but where there is no law there is no transgression [of it either].
16 Therefore, [inheriting] the promise is the outcome of faith *and* depends [entirely] on faith, in order that it might be given as an act of grace (unmerited favor), to make it stable *and* valid *and* guaranteed to all his descendants—not only to the devotees *and* adherents of the Law, but also to those who share the faith of Abraham, who is [thus] the father of us all.
17 As it is written, I have made you the father of many nations. [He was appointed our father] in the sight of God in Whom he believed, Who gives life to the dead and speaks of the nonexistent things that [He has foretold and promised] as if they [already] existed. [Gen. 17:5.]
18 [For Abraham, human reason for] hope being gone, hoped in faith that he should become the father of many nations, as he had been promised, So [numberless] shall your descendants be. [Gen. 15:5.]
19 He did not weaken in faith when he considered the [utter] impotence of his own body, which was as good as dead because he was about a hundred years old, or [when he considered] the barrenness of Sarah's [deadened] womb. [Gen. 17:17; 18:11.]
20 No unbelief *or* distrust made him waver (doubtingly question) concerning the promise of God, but he grew strong *and* was empowered by faith as he gave praise *and* glory to God,
21 Fully satisfied *and* assured that God was able *and* mighty to keep His word *and* to do what He had promised.
22 That is why his faith was credited to him as righteousness (right standing with God).
23 But [the words], It was credited to him, were written not for his sake alone,
24 But [they were written] for our sakes too. [Righteousness, standing acceptable to God] will be granted *and* credited to us also who believe in (trust in, adhere to, and rely on) God, Who raised Jesus our Lord from the dead,
25 Who was betrayed *and* put to death because of our misdeeds and was raised to secure our justification (our [b] acquittal), [making our account balance and absolving us from all guilt before God].

---

a 8 Psalm 32:1,2   b 17 Gen. 17:5   c 18 Gen. 15:5

a Alexander Souter, *Pocket Lexicon.*   b G. Abbott-Smith, *Manual Greek Lexicon of the New Testament.*

## New International Version

### Peace and Hope

**5** Therefore, since we have been justified through faith, we[a] have peace with God through our Lord Jesus Christ, [2]through whom we have gained access by faith into this grace in which we now stand. And we[b] boast in the hope of the glory of God. [3]Not only so, but we[b] also glory in our sufferings, because we know that suffering produces perseverance; [4]perseverance, character; and character, hope. [5]And hope does not put us to shame, because God's love has been poured out into our hearts through the Holy Spirit, who has been given to us.

[6]You see, at just the right time, when we were still powerless, Christ died for the ungodly. [7]Very rarely will anyone die for a righteous person, though for a good person someone might possibly dare to die. [8]But God demonstrates his own love for us in this: While we were still sinners, Christ died for us.

[9]Since we have now been justified by his blood, how much more shall we be saved from God's wrath through him! [10]For if, while we were God's enemies, we were reconciled to him through the death of his Son, how much more, having been reconciled, shall we be saved through his life! [11]Not only is this so, but we also boast in God through our Lord Jesus Christ, through whom we have now received reconciliation.

### Death Through Adam, Life Through Christ

[12]Therefore, just as sin entered the world through one man, and death through sin, and in this way death came to all people, because all sinned—

[13]To be sure, sin was in the world before the law was given, but sin is not charged against anyone's account where there is no law. [14]Nevertheless, death reigned from the time of Adam to the time of Moses, even over those who did not sin by breaking a command, as did Adam, who is a pattern of the one to come.

[15]But the gift is not like the trespass. For if the many died by the trespass of the one man, how much more did God's grace and the gift that came by the grace of the one man, Jesus Christ, overflow to the many! [16]Nor can the gift of God be compared with the result of one man's sin:

## Amplified Bible

**5** Therefore, since we are justified ([a]acquitted, declared righteous, and given a right standing with God) through faith, let us [grasp the fact that we] have [the peace of reconciliation to hold and to [b]enjoy] peace with God through our Lord Jesus Christ (the Messiah, the Anointed One).

[2]Through Him also we have [our] access (entrance, introduction) by faith into this grace (state of God's favor) in which we [firmly and safely] stand. And let us rejoice and exult in our hope of experiencing and enjoying the glory of God.

[3]Moreover [let us also be full of joy now!] let us exult and triumph in our troubles and rejoice in our sufferings, knowing that pressure and affliction and hardship produce patient and unswerving endurance.

[4]And endurance (fortitude) develops maturity of [c]character (approved faith and [d]tried integrity). And character [of this sort] produces [the habit of] [e]joyful and confident hope of eternal salvation.

[5]Such hope never disappoints or deludes or shames us, for God's love has been poured out in our hearts through the Holy Spirit Who has been given to us.

[6]While we were yet in weakness [powerless to help ourselves], at the fitting time Christ died for (in behalf of) the ungodly.

[7]Now it is an extraordinary thing for one to give his life even for an upright man, though perhaps for a noble and lovable and generous benefactor someone might even dare to die.

[8]But God shows and clearly proves His [own] love for us by the fact that while we were still sinners, Christ (the Messiah, the Anointed One) died for us.

[9]Therefore, since we are now justified ([f]acquitted, made righteous, and brought into right relationship with God) by Christ's blood, how much more [certain is it that] we shall be saved by Him from the indignation and wrath of God.

[10]For if while we were enemies we were reconciled to God through the death of His Son, it is much more [certain], now that we are reconciled, that we shall be saved (daily delivered from sin's dominion) through His [f]resurrection] life.

[11]Not only so, but we also rejoice and exultingly glory in God [in His love and perfection] through our Lord Jesus Christ, through Whom we have now received and enjoy [our] reconciliation. [Jer. 9:24.]

[12]Therefore, as sin came into the world through one man, and death as the result of sin, so death spread to all men, [[e]no one being able to stop it or to escape its power] because all men sinned.

[13][To be sure] sin was in the world before ever the Law was given, but sin is not charged to men's account where there is no law [to transgress].

[14]Yet death held sway from Adam to Moses [the Lawgiver], even over those who did not themselves transgress [a positive command] as Adam did. Adam was a type (prefigure) of the One Who was to come [in reverse, [e]the former destructive, the Latter saving]. [Gen. 5:5; 7:22; Deut. 34:5.]

[15]But God's free gift is not at all to be compared to the trespass [His grace is out of all proportion to the fall of man]. For if many died through one man's falling away (his lapse, his offense), much more profusely did God's grace and the free gift [that comes] through the undeserved favor of the one Man Jesus Christ abound and overflow to and for [the benefit of] many.

[16]Nor is the free gift at all to be compared to the effect of that one [man's] sin. For the sentence [following the

---

[a] G. Abbott-Smith, *Manual Greek Lexicon of the New Testament.*  [b] Literal translation: "have" or "hold," so "enjoy."  [c] Alexander Souter, *Pocket Lexicon.*  [d] Marvin Vincent, *Word Studies.*  [e] Joseph Thayer, *A Greek-English Lexicon.*  [f] G. Abbott-Smith, *Manual Greek Lexicon.*

## New International Version

The judgment followed one sin and brought condemnation, but the gift followed many trespasses and brought justification. [17]For if, by the trespass of the one man, death reigned through that one man, how much more will those who receive God's abundant provision of grace and of the gift of righteousness reign in life through the one man, Jesus Christ!

[18]Consequently, just as one trespass resulted in condemnation for all people, so also one righteous act resulted in justification and life for all people. [19]For just as through the disobedience of the one man the many were made sinners, so also through the obedience of the one man the many will be made righteous.

[20]The law was brought in so that the trespass might increase. But where sin increased, grace increased all the more, [21]so that, just as sin reigned in death, so also grace might reign through righteousness to bring eternal life through Jesus Christ our Lord.

### Dead to Sin, Alive in Christ

**6** What shall we say, then? Shall we go on sinning so that grace may increase? [2]By no means! We are those who have died to sin; how can we live in it any longer? [3]Or don't you know that all of us who were baptized into Christ Jesus were baptized into his death? [4]We were therefore buried with him through baptism into death in order that, just as Christ was raised from the dead through the glory of the Father, we too may live a new life.

[5]For if we have been united with him in a death like his, we will certainly also be united with him in a resurrection like his. [6]For we know that our old self was crucified with him so that the body ruled by sin might be done away with,[a] that we should no longer be slaves to sin— [7]because anyone who has died has been set free from sin.

[8]Now if we died with Christ, we believe that we will also live with him. [9]For we know that since Christ was raised from the dead, he cannot die again; death no longer has mastery over him. [10]The death he died, he died to sin once for all; but the life he lives, he lives to God.

[11]In the same way, count yourselves dead to sin but alive to God in Christ Jesus. [12]Therefore do not let sin reign in your mortal body so that you obey its evil desires. [13]Do not offer any part of yourself to sin as an instrument of wickedness, but rather offer yourselves to God as those who have been brought from death to life; and offer every part of yourself to him as an instrument of righteousness.

## Amplified Bible

trespass] of one [man] brought condemnation, whereas the free gift [following] many transgressions brings justification ([a]an act of righteousness).

[17]For if because of one man's trespass (lapse, offense) death reigned through that one, much more surely will those who receive [God's] overflowing grace (unmerited favor) and the free gift of righteousness [putting them into right standing with Himself] reign as kings in life through the one Man Jesus Christ (the Messiah, the Anointed One).

[18]Well then, as one man's trespass [one man's false step and falling away led] to condemnation for all men, so one Man's act of righteousness [leads] to acquittal and right standing with God and life for all men.

[19]For just as by one man's disobedience (failing to hear, [b]heedlessness, and carelessness) the many were constituted sinners, so by one Man's obedience the many will be constituted righteous (made acceptable to God, brought into right standing with Him).

[20]But then Law came in, [only] to expand and increase the trespass [making it more apparent and exciting opposition]. But where sin increased and abounded, grace (God's unmerited favor) has surpassed it and increased the more and superabounded,

[21]So that, [just] as sin has reigned in death, [so] grace (His unearned and undeserved favor) might reign also through righteousness (right standing with God) which issues in eternal life through Jesus Christ (the Messiah, the Anointed One) our Lord.

**6** What shall we say [to all this]? Are we to remain in sin in order that God's grace (favor and mercy) may multiply and overflow?

[2]Certainly not! How can we who died to sin live in it any longer?

[3]Are you ignorant of the fact that all of us who have been baptized into Christ Jesus were baptized into His death?

[4]We were buried therefore with Him by the baptism into death, so that just as Christ was raised from the dead by the glorious [power] of the Father, so we too might [habitually] live and behave in newness of life.

[5]For if we have become one with Him by sharing a death like His, we shall also be [one with Him in sharing] His resurrection [by a new life lived for God].

[6]We know that our old (unrenewed) self was nailed to the cross with Him in order that [our] body [which is the instrument] of sin might be made ineffective and inactive for evil, that we might no longer be the slaves of sin.

[7]For when a man dies, he is freed (loosed, delivered) from [the power of] sin [among men].

[8]Now if we have died with Christ, we believe that we shall also live with Him,

[9]Because we know that Christ (the Anointed One), being once raised from the dead, will never die again; death no longer has power over Him.

[10]For by the death He died, He died to sin [ending His relation to it] once for all; and the life that He lives, He is living to God [in unbroken fellowship with Him].

[11]Even so consider yourselves also dead to sin and your relation to it broken, but alive to God [living in unbroken fellowship with Him] in Christ Jesus.

[12]Let not sin therefore rule as king in your mortal (short-lived, perishable) bodies, to make you yield to its cravings and be subject to its lusts and evil passions.

[13]Do not continue offering or yielding your bodily members [and [c]faculties] to sin as instruments (tools) of wickedness. But offer and yield yourselves to God as though you have been raised from the dead to [perpetual] life, and your bodily members [and [c]faculties] to God, presenting them as implements of righteousness.

[a] Literal translation. [b] Marvin Vincent, *Word Studies*. [c] Marvin Vincent, *Word Studies*: Greek *mele*—"Physical; though some commentators interpret it to include the mental faculties as well."

[a] 6 Or *be rendered powerless*

## New International Version

[14] For sin shall no longer be your master, because you are not under the law, but under grace.

### Slaves to Righteousness

[15] What then? Shall we sin because we are not under the law but under grace? By no means! [16] Don't you know that when you offer yourselves to someone as obedient slaves, you are slaves of the one you obey—whether you are slaves to sin, which leads to death, or to obedience, which leads to righteousness? [17] But thanks be to God that, though you used to be slaves to sin, you have come to obey from your heart the pattern of teaching that has now claimed your allegiance. [18] You have been set free from sin and have become slaves to righteousness.

[19] I am using an example from everyday life because of your human limitations. Just as you used to offer yourselves as slaves to impurity and to ever-increasing wickedness, so now offer yourselves as slaves to righteousness leading to holiness. [20] When you were slaves to sin, you were free from the control of righteousness. [21] What benefit did you reap at that time from the things you are now ashamed of? Those things result in death! [22] But now that you have been set free from sin and have become slaves of God, the benefit you reap leads to holiness, and the result is eternal life. [23] For the wages of sin is death, but the gift of God is eternal life in[a] Christ Jesus our Lord.

### Released From the Law, Bound to Christ

**7** Do you not know, brothers and sisters—for I am speaking to those who know the law—that the law has authority over someone only as long as that person lives? [2] For example, by law a married woman is bound to her husband as long as he is alive, but if her husband dies, she is released from the law that binds her to him. [3] So then, if she has sexual relations with another man while her husband is still alive, she is called an adulteress. But if her husband dies, she is released from that law and is not an adulteress if she marries another man.

[4] So, my brothers and sisters, you also died to the law through the body of Christ, that you might belong to another, to him who was raised from the dead, in order that we might bear fruit for God. [5] For when we were in the realm of the flesh,[b] the sinful passions aroused by the law were at work in us, so that we bore fruit for death. [6] But now, by dying to what once bound us, we have been released from the law so that we serve in the new way of the Spirit, and not in the old way of the written code.

### The Law and Sin

[7] What shall we say, then? Is the law sinful? Certainly not! Nevertheless, I would not have known what sin was

## Amplified Bible

[14] For sin shall not [any longer] exert dominion over you, since now you are not under Law [as slaves], but under grace [as subjects of God's favor and mercy].

[15] What then [are we to conclude]? Shall we sin because we live not under Law but under God's favor *and* mercy? Certainly not!

[16] Do you not know that if you continually surrender yourselves to anyone to do his will, you are the slaves of him whom you obey, whether that be to sin, which leads to death, or to obedience which leads to righteousness (right doing and right standing with God)?

[17] But thank God, though you were once slaves of sin, you have become obedient with all your heart to the standard of teaching in which you were instructed *and* to which you were committed.

[18] And having been set free from sin, you have become the servants of righteousness (of conformity to the divine will in thought, purpose, and action).

[19] I am speaking in familiar human terms because of your natural limitations. For as you yielded your bodily members [and [a] faculties] as servants to impurity and ever increasing lawlessness, so now yield your bodily members [and [a] faculties] once for all as servants to righteousness (right being and doing) [which leads] to sanctification.

[20] For when you were slaves of sin, you were free in regard to righteousness.

[21] But then what benefit (return) did you get from the things of which you are now ashamed? [None] for the end of those things is death.

[22] But now since you have been set free from sin and have become the slaves of God, you have your present reward in holiness and its end is eternal life.

[23] For the wages which sin pays is death, but the [bountiful] free gift of God is eternal life through (in union with) Jesus Christ our Lord.

**7** Do you not know, brethren—for I am speaking to men who are acquainted with the Law—that legal claims have power over a person only for as long as he is alive?

[2] For [instance] a married woman is bound by law to her husband as long as he lives; but if her husband dies, she is loosed *and* discharged from the law concerning her husband.

[3] Accordingly, she will be held an adulteress if she unites herself to another man while her husband lives. But if her husband dies, the marriage law no longer is binding on her [she is free from that law]; and if she unites herself to another man, she is not an adulteress.

[4] Likewise, my brethren, you have undergone death as to the Law through the [crucified] body of Christ, so that now you may belong to Another, to Him Who was raised from the dead in order that we may bear fruit for God.

[5] When we were living in the flesh (mere physical lives), the sinful passions that were awakened *and* aroused up by [what] the Law [makes sin] were constantly operating in our natural powers (in our bodily organs, [b] in the sensitive appetites and wills of the flesh), so that we bore fruit for death.

[6] But now we are discharged from the Law *and* have terminated all intercourse with it, having died to what once restrained *and* held us captive. So now we serve not under [obedience to] the old code of written regulations, but [under obedience to the promptings] of the Spirit in newness [of life].

[7] What then do we conclude? Is the Law identical with sin? Certainly not! Nevertheless, if it had not been for the Law, I should not have recognized sin *or* have known its meaning. [For instance] I would not have known about covetousness [would have had no consciousness of sin or

---

[a] 23 Or *through*    [b] 5 In contexts like this, the Greek word for *flesh* (*sarx*) refers to the sinful state of human beings, often presented as a power in opposition to the Spirit.

[a] Marvin Vincent, *Word Studies*: Greek *mele*—"Physical; though some commentators interpret it to include the mental faculties as well."
[b] Matthew Henry, *Commentary on the Holy Bible*.

## New International Version

had it not been for the law. For I would not have known what coveting really was if the law had not said, "You shall not covet."[a] [8]But sin, seizing the opportunity afforded by the commandment, produced in me every kind of coveting. For apart from the law, sin was dead. [9]Once I was alive apart from the law; but when the commandment came, sin sprang to life and I died. [10]I found that the very commandment that was intended to bring life actually brought death. [11]For sin, seizing the opportunity afforded by the commandment, deceived me, and through the commandment put me to death. [12]So then, the law is holy, and the commandment is holy, righteous and good.

[13]Did that which is good, then, become death to me? By no means! Nevertheless, in order that sin might be recognized as sin, it used what is good to bring about my death, so that through the commandment sin might become utterly sinful.

[14]We know that the law is spiritual; but I am unspiritual, sold as a slave to sin. [15]I do not understand what I do. For what I want to do I do not do, but what I hate I do. [16]And if I do what I do not want to do, I agree that the law is good. [17]As it is, it is no longer I myself who do it, but it is sin living in me. [18]For I know that good itself does not dwell in me, that is, in my sinful nature.[b] For I have the desire to do what is good, but I cannot carry it out. [19]For I do not do the good I want to do, but the evil I do not want to do—this I keep on doing. [20]Now if I do what I do not want to do, it is no longer I who do it, but it is sin living in me that does it.

[21]So I find this law at work: Although I want to do good, evil is right there with me. [22]For in my inner being I delight in God's law; [23]but I see another law at work in me, waging war against the law of my mind and making me a prisoner of the law of sin at work within me. [24]What a wretched man I am! Who will rescue me from this body that is subject to death? [25]Thanks be to God, who delivers me through Jesus Christ our Lord!

So then, I myself in my mind am a slave to God's law, but in my sinful nature[c] a slave to the law of sin.

## Amplified Bible

sense of guilt] if the Law had not [repeatedly] said, You shall not covet *and* have an evil desire [for one thing and another]. [Exod. 20:17; Deut. 5:21.]

[8]But sin, finding opportunity in the commandment [to express itself], got a hold on me *and* aroused *and* stimulated all kinds of forbidden desires (lust, covetousness). For without the Law sin is dead [the sense of it is inactive and a lifeless thing].

[9]Once I was alive, but quite apart from *and* unconscious of the Law. But when the commandment came, sin lived again and I died (was sentenced by the Law to death). [Ps. 73:22.]

[10]And the very legal ordinance which was designed *and* intended to bring life actually proved [to mean to me] death. [Lev. 18:5.]

[11]For sin, seizing the opportunity *and* getting a hold on me [by taking its incentive] from the commandment, beguiled *and* entrapped *and* cheated me, and using it [as a weapon], killed me.

[12]The Law therefore is holy, and [each] commandment is holy and just and good.

[13]Did that which is good then prove fatal [bringing death] to me? Certainly not! It was sin, working death in me by using this good thing [as a weapon], in order that through the commandment sin might be shown up clearly to be sin, that the extreme malignity and immeasurable sinfulness of sin might plainly appear.

[14]We know that the Law is spiritual; but I am a creature of the flesh [carnal, unspiritual], having been sold into slavery under [the control of] sin.

[15]For I do not understand my own actions [I am baffled, bewildered]. I do not practice *or* accomplish what I wish, but I do the very thing that I loathe [*a*which my moral instinct condemns].

[16]Now if I do [habitually] what is contrary to my desire, [that means that] I acknowledge *and* agree that the Law is good (morally excellent) *and* that I take sides with it.

[17]However, it is no longer I who do the deed, but the sin [principle] which is at home in me *and* has possession of me.

[18]For I know that nothing good dwells within me, that is, in my flesh. I can will what is right, but I cannot perform it. [I have the intention and urge to do what is right, but no power to carry it out.]

[19]For I fail to practice the good deeds I desire to do, but the evil deeds that I do not desire to do are what I am [ever] doing.

[20]Now if I do what I do not desire to do, it is no longer I doing it [it is not myself that acts], but the sin [principle] which dwells within me [*b*fixed and operating in my soul].

[21]So I find it to be a law (rule of action of my being) that when I want to do what is right *and* good, evil is ever present with me *and* I am subject to its insistent demands.

[22]For I endorse *and* delight in the Law of God in my inmost self [with my new nature]. [Ps. 1:2.]

[23]But I discern in my bodily members [*c*in the sensitive appetites and wills of the flesh] a different law (rule of action) at war against the law of my mind (my reason) and making me a prisoner to the law of sin that dwells in my bodily organs [*c*in the sensitive appetites and wills of the flesh].

[24]O unhappy *and* pitiable *and* wretched man that I am! Who will release *and* deliver me from [the shackles of] this body of death?

[25]O thank God! [He will!] through Jesus Christ (the Anointed One) our Lord! So then indeed I, of myself with the mind *and* heart, serve the Law of God, but with the flesh the law of sin.

---

*a* Frederic Godet, cited by Marvin Vincent, *Word Studies.*  *b* Joseph Thayer, *A Greek-English Lexicon.*  *c* Matthew Henry, *Commentary on the Holy Bible.*

## New International Version

### Life Through the Spirit

**8** Therefore, there is now no condemnation for those who are in Christ Jesus, [2]because through Christ Jesus the law of the Spirit who gives life has set you[a] free from the law of sin and death. [3]For what the law was powerless to do because it was weakened by the flesh,[b] God did by sending his own Son in the likeness of sinful flesh to be a sin offering.[c] And so he condemned sin in the flesh, [4]in order that the righteous requirement of the law might be fully met in us, who do not live according to the flesh but according to the Spirit.

[5]Those who live according to the flesh have their minds set on what the flesh desires; but those who live in accordance with the Spirit have their minds set on what the Spirit desires. [6]The mind governed by the flesh is death, but the mind governed by the Spirit is life and peace. [7]The mind governed by the flesh is hostile to God; it does not submit to God's law, nor can it do so. [8]Those who are in the realm of the flesh cannot please God.

[9]You, however, are not in the realm of the flesh but are in the realm of the Spirit, if indeed the Spirit of God lives in you. And if anyone does not have the Spirit of Christ, they do not belong to Christ. [10]But if Christ is in you, then even though your body is subject to death because of sin, the Spirit gives life[d] because of righteousness. [11]And if the Spirit of him who raised Jesus from the dead is living in you, he who raised Christ from the dead will also give life to your mortal bodies because of[e] his Spirit who lives in you.

[12]Therefore, brothers and sisters, we have an obligation—but it is not to the flesh, to live according to it. [13]For if you live according to the flesh, you will die; but if by the Spirit you put to death the misdeeds of the body, you will live.

[14]For those who are led by the Spirit of God are the children of God. [15]The Spirit you received does not make you slaves, so that you live in fear again; rather, the Spirit you received brought about your adoption to sonship.[f] And by him we cry, *"Abba,[g] Father."* [16]The Spirit himself testifies with our spirit that we are God's children. [17]Now if we are children, then we are heirs—heirs of God and co-heirs with Christ, if indeed we share in his sufferings in order that we may also share in his glory.

---

[a] 2 The Greek is singular; some manuscripts *me*  [b] 3 In contexts like this, the Greek word for *flesh (sarx)* refers to the sinful state of human beings, often presented as a power in opposition to the Spirit; also in verses 4-13.  [c] 3 Or *flesh, for sin*  [d] 10 Or *you, your body is dead because of sin, yet your spirit is alive*  [e] 11 Some manuscripts *bodies through*  [f] 15 The Greek word for *adoption to sonship* is a term referring to the full legal standing of an adopted male heir in Roman culture; also in verse 23.  [g] 15 Aramaic for *father*

## Amplified Bible

**8** Therefore, [there is] now no condemnation (no adjudging guilty of wrong) for those who are in Christ Jesus, *who live [and] walk not after the dictates of the flesh, but after the dictates of the Spirit.* [John 3:18.]

[2]For the law of the Spirit of life [which is] in Christ Jesus [the law of our new being] has freed me from the law of sin and of death.

[3]For God has done what the Law could not do, [its power] being weakened by the flesh [[a]the entire nature of man without the Holy Spirit]. Sending His own Son in the guise of sinful flesh and as an offering for sin, [God] condemned sin in the flesh [[b]subdued, overcame, [c]deprived it of its power over all who accept that sacrifice], [Lev. 7:37.]

[4]So that the righteous *and* just requirement of the Law might be fully met in us who live *and* move not in the ways of the flesh but in the ways of the Spirit [our lives governed not by the standards and according to the dictates of the flesh, but controlled by the Holy Spirit].

[5]For those who are according to the flesh *and* are controlled by its unholy desires set their minds on *and* [b]pursue those things which gratify the flesh, but those who are according to the Spirit *and* are controlled by the desires of the Spirit set their minds on *and* [b]seek those things which gratify the [Holy] Spirit.

[6]Now the mind of the flesh [which is sense and reason without the Holy Spirit] is death [death that [b]comprises all the miseries arising from sin, both here and hereafter]. But the mind of the [Holy] Spirit is life and [soul] peace [both now and forever].

[7][That is] because the mind of the flesh [with its carnal thoughts and purposes] is hostile to God, for it does not submit itself to God's Law; indeed it cannot.

[8]So then those who are living the life of the flesh [catering to the appetites and impulses of their carnal nature] cannot please *or* satisfy God, *or* be acceptable to Him.

[9]But you are not living the life of the flesh, you are living the life of the Spirit, if the [Holy] Spirit of God [really] dwells within you [directs and controls you]. But if anyone does not possess the [Holy] Spirit of Christ, he is none of His [he does not belong to Christ, is not truly a child of God]. [Rom. 8:14.]

[10]But if Christ lives in you, [then although] your [natural] body is dead by reason of sin *and* guilt, the spirit is alive because of [the] righteousness [that He imputes to you].

[11]And if the Spirit of Him Who raised up Jesus from the dead dwells in you, [then] He Who raised up Christ *Jesus* from the dead will also restore to life your mortal (short-lived, perishable) bodies through His Spirit Who dwells in you.

[12]So then, brethren, we are debtors, but not to the flesh [we are not obligated to our carnal nature], to live [a life ruled by the standards set up by the dictates of] the flesh.

[13]For if you live according to [the dictates of] the flesh, you will surely die. But if through the power of the [Holy] Spirit you are [habitually] putting to death (making extinct, deadening) the [evil] deeds prompted by the body, you shall [really and genuinely] live forever.

[14]For all who are led by the Spirit of God are sons of God.

[15]For [the Spirit which] you have now received [is] not a spirit of slavery to put you once more in bondage to fear, but you have received the Spirit of adoption [the Spirit producing sonship] in [the bliss of] which we cry, Abba (Father)! Father!

[16]The Spirit Himself [thus] testifies together with our own spirit, [assuring us] that we are children of God.

[17]And if we are [His] children, then we are [His] heirs also: heirs of God and fellow heirs with Christ [sharing His inheritance with Him]; only we must share His suffering if we are to share His glory.

---

[a] Philip Melanchthon, cited by Marvin Vincent, *Word Studies.*  [b] Joseph Thayer, *A Greek-English Lexicon.*  [c] Marvin Vincent, *Word Studies.*

## New International Version

### Present Suffering and Future Glory

<sup>18</sup>I consider that our present sufferings are not worth comparing with the glory that will be revealed in us. <sup>19</sup>For the creation waits in eager expectation for the children of God to be revealed. <sup>20</sup>For the creation was subjected to frustration, not by its own choice, but by the will of the one who subjected it, in hope <sup>21</sup>that<sup>a</sup> the creation itself will be liberated from its bondage to decay and brought into the freedom and glory of the children of God.

<sup>22</sup>We know that the whole creation has been groaning as in the pains of childbirth right up to the present time. <sup>23</sup>Not only so, but we ourselves, who have the firstfruits of the Spirit, groan inwardly as we wait eagerly for our adoption to sonship, the redemption of our bodies. <sup>24</sup>For in this hope we were saved. But hope that is seen is no hope at all. Who hopes for what they already have? <sup>25</sup>But if we hope for what we do not yet have, we wait for it patiently.

<sup>26</sup>In the same way, the Spirit helps us in our weakness. We do not know what we ought to pray for, but the Spirit himself intercedes for us through wordless groans. <sup>27</sup>And he who searches our hearts knows the mind of the Spirit, because the Spirit intercedes for God's people in accordance with the will of God.

<sup>28</sup>And we know that in all things God works for the good of those who love him, who<sup>b</sup> have been called according to his purpose. <sup>29</sup>For those God foreknew he also predestined to be conformed to the image of his Son, that he might be the firstborn among many brothers and sisters. <sup>30</sup>And those he predestined, he also called; those he called, he also justified; those he justified, he also glorified.

### More Than Conquerors

<sup>31</sup>What, then, shall we say in response to these things? If God is for us, who can be against us? <sup>32</sup>He who did not spare his own Son, but gave him up for us all—how will he not also, along with him, graciously give us all things? <sup>33</sup>Who will bring any charge against those whom God has chosen? It is God who justifies. <sup>34</sup>Who then is the one who

## Amplified Bible

<sup>18</sup>[But what of that?] For I consider that the sufferings of this present time (this present life) are not worth being compared with the glory that is about to be revealed to us and in us and <sup>a</sup>for us and <sup>b</sup>conferred on us!

<sup>19</sup>For [even the whole] creation (all nature) waits expectantly and longs earnestly for God's sons to be made known [waits for the revealing, the disclosing of their sonship].

<sup>20</sup>For the creation (nature) was subjected to <sup>b</sup>frailty (to futility, condemned to frustration), not because of some intentional fault on its part, but by the will of Him Who so subjected it—[yet] with the hope [Eccl. 1:2.]

<sup>21</sup>That nature (creation) itself will be set free from its bondage to decay and corruption [and gain an entrance] into the glorious freedom of God's children.

<sup>22</sup>We know that the whole creation [of irrational creatures] has been moaning together in the pains of labor until now. [Jer. 12:4, 11.]

<sup>23</sup>And not only the creation, but we ourselves too, who have and enjoy the firstfruits of the [Holy] Spirit [a foretaste of the blissful things to come] groan inwardly as we wait for the redemption of our bodies [from sensuality and the grave, which will reveal] our adoption (our manifestation as God's sons).

<sup>24</sup>For in [this] hope we were saved. But hope [the object of] which is seen is not hope. For how can one hope for what he already sees?

<sup>25</sup>But if we hope for what is still unseen by us, we wait for it with patience and composure.

<sup>26</sup>So too the [Holy] Spirit comes to our aid and bears us up in our weakness; for we do not know what prayer to offer nor how to offer it worthily as we ought, but the Spirit Himself goes to meet our supplication and pleads in our behalf with unspeakable yearnings and groanings too deep for utterance.

<sup>27</sup>And He Who searches the hearts of men knows what is in the mind of the [Holy] Spirit [what His intent is], because the Spirit intercedes and pleads [before God] in behalf of the saints according to and in harmony with God's will. [Ps. 139:1, 2.]

<sup>28</sup>We are assured and know that [<sup>c</sup>God being a partner in their labor] all things work together and are [fitting into a plan] for good to and for those who love God and are called according to [His] design and purpose.

<sup>29</sup>For those whom He foreknew [of whom He was <sup>d</sup>aware and <sup>e</sup>loved beforehand], He also destined from the beginning [foreordaining them] to be molded into the image of His Son [and share inwardly His likeness], that He might become the firstborn among many brethren.

<sup>30</sup>And those whom He thus foreordained, He also called; and those whom He called, He also justified (acquitted, made righteous, putting them into right standing with Himself). And those whom He justified, He also glorified [raising them to a heavenly dignity and condition or state of being].

<sup>31</sup>What then shall we say to [all] this? If God is for us, who [can be] against us? [Who can be our foe, if God is on our side?] [Ps. 118:6.]

<sup>32</sup>He who did not withhold or spare [even] His own Son but gave Him up for us all, will He not also with Him freely and graciously give us all [other] things?

<sup>33</sup>Who shall bring any charge against God's elect [when it is] God Who justifies [that is, Who puts us in right relation to Himself? Who shall come forward and accuse or impeach those whom God has chosen? Will God, Who acquits us?]

---

<sup>a</sup> 20,21 Or subjected it in hope. <sup>21</sup>For   <sup>b</sup> 28 Or that all things work together for good to those who love God, who; or that in all things God works together with those who love him to bring about what is good—with those who

---

<sup>a</sup> Charles B. Williams, The New Testament: A Translation in the Language of the People.  <sup>b</sup> Joseph Thayer, A Greek-English Lexicon.  <sup>c</sup> Some manuscripts read, "God works all things with them."  <sup>d</sup> H.A. W. Meyer, cited by Marvin Vincent, Word Studies.  <sup>e</sup> John Murray, The Sovereignty of God.

## New International Version

condemns? No one. Christ Jesus who died—more than that, who was raised to life—is at the right hand of God and is also interceding for us. [35] Who shall separate us from the love of Christ? Shall trouble or hardship or persecution or famine or nakedness or danger or sword? [36] As it is written:

"For your sake we face death all day long;
we are considered as sheep to be slaughtered."[a]

[37] No, in all these things we are more than conquerors through him who loved us. [38] For I am convinced that neither death nor life, neither angels nor demons,[b] neither the present nor the future, nor any powers, [39] neither height nor depth, nor anything else in all creation, will be able to separate us from the love of God that is in Christ Jesus our Lord.

### Paul's Anguish Over Israel

**9** I speak the truth in Christ—I am not lying, my conscience confirms it through the Holy Spirit— [2] I have great sorrow and unceasing anguish in my heart. [3] For I could wish that I myself were cursed and cut off from Christ for the sake of my people, those of my own race, [4] the people of Israel. Theirs is the adoption to sonship; theirs the divine glory, the covenants, the receiving of the law, the temple worship and the promises. [5] Theirs are the patriarchs, and from them is traced the human ancestry of the Messiah, who is God over all, forever praised![c] Amen.

### God's Sovereign Choice

[6] It is not as though God's word had failed. For not all who are descended from Israel are Israel. [7] Nor because they are his descendants are they all Abraham's children. On the contrary, "It is through Isaac that your offspring will be reckoned."[d] [8] In other words, it is not the children by physical descent who are God's children, but it is the children of the promise who are regarded as Abraham's offspring. [9] For this was how the promise was stated: "At the appointed time I will return, and Sarah will have a son."[e]

[10] Not only that, but Rebekah's children were conceived at the same time by our father Isaac. [11] Yet, before the twins were born or had done anything good or bad—in order that God's purpose in election might stand: [12] not by works but by him who calls—she was told, "The older will serve the younger."[f] [13] Just as it is written: "Jacob I loved, but Esau I hated."[g]

[14] What then shall we say? Is God unjust? Not at all! [15] For he says to Moses,

## Amplified Bible

[34] Who is there to condemn [us]? Will Christ Jesus (the Messiah), Who died, or rather Who was raised from the dead, Who is at the right hand of God actually pleading *as* He intercedes for us?

[35] Who shall ever separate us from Christ's love? Shall suffering *and* affliction *and* tribulation? Or calamity *and* distress? Or persecution or hunger or destitution or peril or sword?

[36] Even as it is written, For Thy sake we are put to death all the day long; we are regarded *and* counted as sheep for the slaughter. [Ps. 44:22.]

[37] Yet amid all these things we are more than conquerors *a and* gain a surpassing victory through Him Who loved us.

[38] For I am persuaded beyond doubt (am sure) that neither death nor life, nor angels nor principalities, nor things *b* impending *and* threatening nor things to come, nor powers,

[39] Nor height nor depth, nor anything else in all creation will be able to separate us from the love of God which is in Christ Jesus our Lord.

**9** I am speaking the truth in Christ. I am not lying; my conscience [enlightened and prompted] by the Holy Spirit bearing witness with me

[2] That I have bitter grief and incessant anguish in my heart.

[3] For I could wish that I myself were accursed *and* cut off *and* banished from Christ for the sake of my brethren *and* instead of them, my natural kinsmen *and* my fellow countrymen. [Exod. 32:32.]

[4] For they are Israelites, and to them belong God's adoption [as a nation] and the glorious Presence (Shekinah). With them were the special covenants made, to them was the Law given. To them [the temple] worship was revealed and [God's own] promises announced. [Exod. 4:22; Hos. 11:1.]

[5] To them belong the patriarchs, and as far as His natural descent was concerned, from them is the Christ, Who is exalted *and* supreme over all, God, blessed forever! Amen (so let it be).

[6] However, it is not as though God's Word had failed [coming to nothing]. For it is not everybody who is a descendant of Jacob (Israel) who belongs to [the true] Israel.

[7] And they are not all the children of Abraham because they are by blood His descendants. No, [the promise was] Your descendants will be called *and* counted through the line of Isaac [though Abraham had an older son]. [Gen. 21:9-12.]

[8] That is to say, it is not the children of the body [of Abraham] who are made God's children, but it is the offspring to whom the promise applies that shall be counted [as Abraham's true] descendants.

[9] For this is what the promise said, About this time [next year] will I return and Sarah shall have a son. [Gen. 18:10.]

[10] And not only that, but this too: Rebecca conceived [two sons under exactly the same circumstances] by our forefather Isaac,

[11] And the children were yet unborn and had so far done nothing either good or evil. Even so, in order further to carry out God's purpose of selection (election, choice), which depends not on works *or* what men can do, but on Him Who calls [them],

[12] It was said to her that the elder [son] should serve the younger [son]. [Gen. 25:21-23.]

[13] As it is written, Jacob have I loved, but Esau have I hated (held in *c* relative disregard in comparison with My feeling for Jacob). [Mal. 1:2, 3.]

[14] What shall we conclude then? Is there injustice upon God's part? Certainly not!

---

*a 36* Psalm 44:22   *b 38* Or *nor heavenly rulers*   *c 5* Or *Messiah, who is over all. God be forever praised!* Or *Messiah. God who is over all be forever praised!*   *d 7* Gen. 21:12   *e 9* Gen. 18:10,14   *f 12* Gen. 25:23   *g 13* Mal. 1:2,3

*a* Joseph Thayer, *A Greek-English Lexicon.*   *b* Marvin Vincent, *Word Studies.* The literal translation is "standing in sight."   *c* G. Abbott-Smith, *Manual Greek Lexicon.*

## New International Version

"I will have mercy on whom I have mercy,
and I will have compassion on whom I have
compassion."[a]

[16]It does not, therefore, depend on human desire or effort, but on God's mercy. [17]For Scripture says to Pharaoh: "I raised you up for this very purpose, that I might display my power in you and that my name might be proclaimed in all the earth."[b] [18]Therefore God has mercy on whom he wants to have mercy, and he hardens whom he wants to harden.

[19]One of you will say to me: "Then why does God still blame us? For who is able to resist his will?" [20]But who are you, a human being, to talk back to God? "Shall what is formed say to the one who formed it, 'Why did you make me like this?'"[c] [21]Does not the potter have the right to make out of the same lump of clay some pottery for special purposes and some for common use?

[22]What if God, although choosing to show his wrath and make his power known, bore with great patience the objects of his wrath—prepared for destruction? [23]What if he did this to make the riches of his glory known to the objects of his mercy, whom he prepared in advance for glory— [24]even us, whom he also called, not only from the Jews but also from the Gentiles? [25]As he says in Hosea:

"I will call them 'my people' who are not my people;
and I will call her 'my loved one' who is not my loved
one,"[d]

[26]and,

"In the very place where it was said to them,
'You are not my people,'
there they will be called 'children of the living
God.'"[e]

[27]Isaiah cries out concerning Israel:

"Though the number of the Israelites be like the sand
by the sea,
only the remnant will be saved.
[28]For the Lord will carry out
his sentence on earth with speed and finality."[f]

[29]It is just as Isaiah said previously:

"Unless the Lord Almighty
had left us descendants,
we would have become like Sodom,
we would have been like Gomorrah."[g]

### Israel's Unbelief

[30]What then shall we say? That the Gentiles, who did not pursue righteousness, have obtained it, a righteousness that is by faith; [31]but the people of Israel, who pursued the law as the way of righteousness, have not attained their goal. [32]Why not? Because they pursued it not by faith but as if it were by works. They stumbled over the stumbling stone. [33]As it is written:

"See, I lay in Zion a stone that causes people to
stumble
and a rock that makes them fall,
and the one who believes in him will never be put to
shame."[h]

## Amplified Bible

[15]For He says to Moses, I will have mercy on whom I will have mercy and I will have compassion (pity) on whom I will have compassion. [Exod. 33:19.]

[16]So then [God's gift] is not a question of human will and human effort, but of God's mercy. [It depends not on one's own willingness nor on his strenuous exertion as in running a race, but on God's having mercy on him.]

[17]For the Scripture says to Pharaoh, I have raised you up for this very purpose of displaying My power in [dealing with] you, so that My name may be proclaimed the whole world over.

[18]So then He has mercy on whomever He wills (chooses) and He hardens (makes stubborn and unyielding the heart of) whomever He wills.

[19]You will say to me, Why then does He still find fault and blame us [for sinning]? For who can resist and withstand His will?

[20]But who are you, a mere man, to criticize and contradict and answer back to God? Will what is formed say to him that formed it, Why have you made me thus? [Isa. 29:16; 45:9.]

[21]Has the potter no right over the clay, to make out of the same mass (lump) one vessel for beauty and distinction and honorable use, and another for menial or ignoble and dishonorable use?

[22]What if God, although fully intending to show [the awfulness of] His wrath and to make known His power and authority, has tolerated with much patience the vessels (objects) of [His] anger which are ripe for destruction? [Prov. 16:4.]

[23]And [what if] He thus purposes to make known and show the wealth of His glory in [dealing with] the vessels (objects) of His mercy which He has prepared beforehand for glory,

[24]Even including ourselves whom He has called, not only from among the Jews but also from among the Gentiles (heathen)?

[25]Just as He says in Hosea, Those who were not My people I will call My people, and her who was not beloved [I will call] My beloved. [Hos. 2:23.]

[26]And it shall be that in the very place where it was said to them, You are not My people, they shall be called sons of the living God. [Hos. 1:10.]

[27]And Isaiah calls out (solemnly cries aloud) over Israel: Though the number of the sons of Israel be like the sand of the sea, only the remnant (a small part of them) will be saved [[a]from perdition, condemnation, judgment]!

[28]For the Lord will execute His sentence upon the earth [He will conclude and close His account with men completely and without delay], rigorously cutting it short in His justice. [Isa. 10:22, 23.]

[29]It is as Isaiah predicted, If the Lord of hosts had not left us a seed [from which to propagate descendants], we [Israel] would have fared like Sodom and have been made like Gomorrah. [Isa. 1:9.]

[30]What shall we say then? That Gentiles who did not follow after righteousness [who did not seek salvation by right relationship to God] have attained it by faith [a righteousness imputed by God, based on and produced by faith],

[31]Whereas Israel, though ever in pursuit of a law [for the securing] of righteousness (right standing with God), actually did not succeed in fulfilling the Law. [Isa. 51:1.]

[32]For what reason? Because [they pursued it] not through faith, relying [instead] on the merit of their works [they did not depend on faith but on what they could do]. They have stumbled over the Stumbling Stone. [Isa. 8:14; 28:16.]

[33]As it is written, Behold I am laying in Zion a Stone that will make men stumble, a Rock that will make them fall; but he who believes in Him [who adheres to, trusts in, and relies on Him] shall not be put to shame nor be disappointed in his expectations. [Isa. 28:16.]

---

[a] 15 Exodus 33:19   [b] 17 Exodus 9:16   [c] 20 Isaiah 29:16; 45:9
[d] 25 Hosea 2:23   [e] 26 Hosea 1:10   [f] 28 Isaiah 10:22,23 (see Septuagint)   [g] 29 Isaiah 1:9   [h] 33 Isaiah 8:14; 28:16

[a] Hermann Cremer, *Biblico-Theological Lexicon.*

## New International Version

**10** Brothers and sisters, my heart's desire and prayer to God for the Israelites is that they may be saved. ²For I can testify about them that they are zealous for God, but their zeal is not based on knowledge. ³Since they did not know the righteousness of God and sought to establish their own, they did not submit to God's righteousness. ⁴Christ is the culmination of the law so that there may be righteousness for everyone who believes.

⁵Moses writes this about the righteousness that is by the law: "The person who does these things will live by them."ᵃ ⁶But the righteousness that is by faith says: "Do not say in your heart, 'Who will ascend into heaven?'"ᵇ (that is, to bring Christ down) ⁷or 'Who will descend into the deep?'"ᶜ (that is, to bring Christ up from the dead). ⁸But what does it say? "The word is near you; it is in your mouth and in your heart,"ᵈ that is, the message concerning faith that we proclaim: ⁹If you declare with your mouth, "Jesus is Lord," and believe in your heart that God raised him from the dead, you will be saved. ¹⁰For it is with your heart that you believe and are justified, and it is with your mouth that you profess your faith and are saved. ¹¹As Scripture says, "Anyone who believes in him will never be put to shame."ᵉ ¹²For there is no difference between Jew and Gentile—the same Lord is Lord of all and richly blesses all who call on him, ¹³for, "Everyone who calls on the name of the Lord will be saved."ᶠ

¹⁴How, then, can they call on the one they have not believed in? And how can they believe in the one of whom they have not heard? And how can they hear without someone preaching to them? ¹⁵And how can anyone preach unless they are sent? As it is written: "How beautiful are the feet of those who bring good news!"ᵍ

¹⁶But not all the Israelites accepted the good news. For Isaiah says, "Lord, who has believed our message?"ʰ ¹⁷Consequently, faith comes from hearing the message, and the message is heard through the word about Christ. ¹⁸But I ask: Did they not hear? Of course they did:

## Amplified Bible

**10** Brethren, [with all] my heart's desire *and* goodwill for [Israel], I long and pray to God that they may be saved.

²I bear them witness that they have a [certain] zeal *and* enthusiasm for God, but it is not enlightened *and* according to [correct and vital] knowledge.

³For being ignorant of the righteousness that God ascribes [which makes one acceptable to Him in word, thought, and deed] and seeking to establish a *righteousness (a means of salvation)* of their own, they did not obey *or* submit themselves to God's righteousness.

⁴For Christ is the end of the Law [the limit at which it ceases to be, for the Law leads up to Him Who is the fulfillment of its types, and in Him the purpose which it was designed to accomplish is fulfilled. That is, the purpose of the Law is fulfilled in Him] as the means of righteousness (right relationship to God) for everyone who trusts in *and* adheres to *and* relies on Him.

⁵For Moses writes that the man who [can] practice the righteousness (perfect conformity to God's will) which is based on the Law [with all its intricate demands] shall live by it. [Lev. 18:5.]

⁶But the righteousness based on faith [imputed by God and bringing right relationship with Him] says, Do not say in your heart, Who will ascend into Heaven? that is, to bring Christ down;

⁷Or who will descend into the abyss? that is, to bring Christ up from the dead [as if we could be saved by our own efforts]. [Deut. 30:12, 13.]

⁸But what does it say? The Word (God's message in Christ) is near you, on your lips and in your heart; that is, the Word (the message, the basis and object) of faith which we preach, [Deut. 30:14.]

⁹Because if you acknowledge *and* confess with your lips that Jesus is Lord and in your heart believe (adhere to, trust in, and rely on the truth) that God raised Him from the dead, you will be saved.

¹⁰For with the heart a person believes (adheres to, trusts in, and relies on Christ) and so is justified (declared righteous, acceptable to God), and with the mouth he confesses (declares openly and speaks out freely his faith) *and* confirms [his] salvation.

¹¹The Scripture says, No man who believes in Him [who adheres to, relies on, and trusts in Him] will [ever] be put to shame *or* be disappointed. [Ps. 34:22; Isa. 28:16; 49:23; Jer. 17:7.]

¹²[No one] for there is no distinction between Jew and Greek. The same Lord is Lord over all [of us] and He generously bestows His riches upon all who call upon Him [in faith].

¹³For everyone who calls upon the name of the Lord [invoking Him as Lord] will be saved. [Joel 2:32.]

¹⁴But how are people to call upon Him Whom they have not believed [in Whom they have no faith, on Whom they have no reliance]? And how are they to believe in Him [adhere to, trust in, and rely upon Him] of Whom they have never heard? And how are they to hear without a preacher?

¹⁵And how can men [be expected to] preach unless they are sent? As it is written, How beautiful are the feet of those who bring glad tidings! [How welcome is the coming of those who preach the good news of His good things!] [Isa. 52:7.]

¹⁶But they have not all heeded the Gospel; for Isaiah says, Lord, who has believed (had faith in) what he has heard from us? [Isa. 53:1.]

¹⁷So faith comes by hearing [what is told], and what is heard comes by the preaching [of the message that came from the lips] of Christ (the Messiah Himself).

¹⁸But I ask, Have they not heard? Indeed they have; [for

---

ᵃ 5 Lev. 18:5   ᵇ 6 Deut. 30:12   ᶜ 7 Deut. 30:13   ᵈ 8 Deut. 30:14
ᵉ 11 Isaiah 28:16 (see Septuagint)   ᶠ 13 Joel 2:32   ᵍ 15 Isaiah 52:7
ʰ 16 Isaiah 53:1

## New International Version

"Their voice has gone out into all the earth,
   their words to the ends of the world."[a]

19Again I ask: Did Israel not understand? First, Moses says,

"I will make you envious by those who are not a nation;
   I will make you angry by a nation that has no
      understanding."[b]

20And Isaiah boldly says,

"I was found by those who did not seek me;
   I revealed myself to those who did not ask for me."[c]

21But concerning Israel he says,

"All day long I have held out my hands
   to a disobedient and obstinate people."[d]

### The Remnant of Israel

**11** I ask then: Did God reject his people? By no
means! I am an Israelite myself, a descendant of
Abraham, from the tribe of Benjamin. 2God did not reject
his people, whom he foreknew. Don't you know what Scripture says in the passage about Elijah—how he appealed
to God against Israel: 3"Lord, they have killed your prophets and torn down your altars; I am the only one left, and
they are trying to kill me"[e]? 4And what was God's answer
to him? "I have reserved for myself seven thousand who
have not bowed the knee to Baal."[f] 5So too, at the present
time there is a remnant chosen by grace. 6And if by grace,
then it cannot be based on works; if it were, grace would
no longer be grace.

7What then? What the people of Israel sought so earnestly they did not obtain. The elect among them did, but
the others were hardened, 8as it is written:

"God gave them a spirit of stupor,
   eyes that could not see
   and ears that could not hear,
to this very day."[g]

9And David says:

"May their table become a snare and a trap,
   a stumbling block and a retribution for them.
10 May their eyes be darkened so they cannot see,
   and their backs be bent forever."[h]

### Ingrafted Branches

11Again I ask: Did they stumble so as to fall beyond recovery? Not at all! Rather, because of their transgression,
salvation has come to the Gentiles to make Israel envious.
12But if their transgression means riches for the world,
and their loss means riches for the Gentiles, how much
greater riches will their full inclusion bring!

13I am talking to you Gentiles. Inasmuch as I am the
apostle to the Gentiles, I take pride in my ministry 14in the

## Amplified Bible

the Scripture says] Their voice [that of nature bearing
God's message] has gone out to all the earth, and their
words to the far bounds of the world. [Ps. 19:4.]

19Again I ask, Did Israel not understand? [Did the Jews
have no warning that the Gospel was to go forth to the
Gentiles, to all the earth?] First, there is Moses who says,
I will make you jealous of those who are not a nation; with
a foolish nation I will make you angry. [Deut. 32:21.]

20Then Isaiah is so bold as to say, I have been found
by those who did not seek Me; I have shown (revealed)
Myself to those who did not [consciously] ask for Me. [Isa.
65:1.]

21But of Israel he says, All day long I have stretched
out My hands to a people unyielding *and* disobedient and
self-willed [to a faultfinding, contrary, and contradicting
people]. [Isa. 65:2.]

**11** I ask then: Has God totally rejected *and* disowned
His people? Of course not! Why, I myself am an
Israelite, a descendant of Abraham, a member of the tribe
of Benjamin! [I Sam. 12:22; Jer. 31:37; 33:24-26; Phil. 3:5.]

2No, God has not rejected *and* disowned His people
[whose destiny] He had marked out *and* appointed *and*
foreknown from the beginning. Do you not know what the
Scripture says of Elijah, how he pleads with God against
Israel? [Ps. 94:14; I Kings 19.]

3Lord, they have killed Your prophets; they have demolished Your altars, and I alone am left, and they seek
my life.

4But what is God's reply to him? I have kept for Myself
seven thousand men who have not bowed the knee to Baal!
[I Kings 19:18.]

5So too at the present time there is a remnant (a small
believing minority), selected (chosen) by grace (by God's
unmerited favor and graciousness).

6But if it is by grace (His unmerited favor and graciousness), it is no longer conditioned on works or anything
men have done. Otherwise, grace would no longer be
grace [it would be meaningless].

7What then [shall we conclude]? Israel failed to obtain
what it sought [God's favor by obedience to the Law]. Only
the elect (those chosen few) obtained it, while the rest of
them became callously indifferent (blinded, hardened,
and made insensible to it).

8As it is written, God gave them a spirit (an attitude) of
stupor, eyes that should not see and ears that should not
hear, [that has continued] down to this very day. [Deut.
29:4; Isa. 29:10.]

9And David says, Let their table (their feasting, banqueting) become a snare and a trap, a pitfall and a *a*just
retribution [*b*rebounding like a boomerang upon them];
[Ps. 69:22.]

10Let their eyes be darkened (dimmed) so that they cannot see, and make them bend their back [stooping beneath
their burden] forever. [Ps. 69:23.]

11So I ask, Have they stumbled so as to fall [to their
utter spiritual ruin, irretrievably]? By no means! But
through their false step *and* transgression salvation [has
come] to the Gentiles, so as to arouse Israel [to see and
feel what they forfeited] and so to make them jealous.

12Now if their stumbling (their lapse, their transgression) has so enriched the world [at large], and if [Israel's]
failure means such riches for the Gentiles, think what an
enrichment *and* greater advantage will follow their full
reinstatement!

13But now I am speaking to you who are Gentiles. Inasmuch then as I am an apostle to the Gentiles, I lay great
stress on my ministry *and* magnify my office,

---

*a 18* Psalm 19:4    *b 19* Deut. 32:21    *c 20* Isaiah 65:1
*d 21* Isaiah 65:2    *e 3* 1 Kings 19:10,14    *f 4* 1 Kings 19:18
*g 8* Deut. 29:4; Isaiah 29:10    *h 10* Psalm 69:22,23

*a* Marvin Vincent, *Word Studies.*  *b* Literal translation: "a return, a
recompense."

## New International Version

hope that I may somehow arouse my own people to envy and save some of them. [15]For if their rejection brought reconciliation to the world, what will their acceptance be but life from the dead? [16]If the part of the dough offered as firstfruits is holy, then the whole batch is holy; if the root is holy, so are the branches.

[17]If some of the branches have been broken off, and you, though a wild olive shoot, have been grafted in among the others and now share in the nourishing sap from the olive root, [18]do not consider yourself to be superior to those other branches. If you do, consider this: You do not support the root, but the root supports you. [19]You will say then, "Branches were broken off so that I could be grafted in." [20]Granted. But they were broken off because of unbelief, and you stand by faith. Do not be arrogant, but tremble. [21]For if God did not spare the natural branches, he will not spare you either.

[22]Consider therefore the kindness and sternness of God: sternness to those who fell, but kindness to you, provided that you continue in his kindness. Otherwise, you also will be cut off. [23]And if they do not persist in unbelief, they will be grafted in, for God is able to graft them in again. [24]After all, if you were cut out of an olive tree that is wild by nature, and contrary to nature were grafted into a cultivated olive tree, how much more readily will these, the natural branches, be grafted into their own olive tree!

### All Israel Will Be Saved

[25]I do not want you to be ignorant of this mystery, brothers and sisters, so that you may not be conceited: Israel has experienced a hardening in part until the full number of the Gentiles has come in, [26]and in this way[a] all Israel will be saved. As it is written:

"The deliverer will come from Zion;
    he will turn godlessness away from Jacob.
[27]And this is[b] my covenant with them
    when I take away their sins."[c]

[28]As far as the gospel is concerned, they are enemies for your sake; but as far as election is concerned, they are loved on account of the patriarchs, [29]for God's gifts and his call are irrevocable. [30]Just as you who were at one time disobedient to God have now received mercy as a result of their disobedience, [31]so they too have now become disobedient in order that they too may now[d] receive mercy as a result of God's mercy to you. [32]For God has bound

## Amplified Bible

[14]In the hope of making my fellow Jews jealous [in order to stir them up to imitate, copy, and appropriate], and thus managing to save some of them.

[15]For if their rejection and exclusion from the benefits of salvation were [overruled] for the reconciliation of a world to God, what will their acceptance and admission mean? [It will be nothing short of] life from the dead!

[16]Now if the first handful of dough offered as the first-fruits [Abraham and the patriarchs] is consecrated (holy), so is the whole mass [the nation of Israel]; and if the root [Abraham] is consecrated (holy), so are the branches. [Num. 15:19-21.]

[17]But if some of the branches were broken off, while you, a wild olive shoot, were grafted in among them to share the richness [of the root and sap] of the olive tree,

[18]Do not boast over the branches and pride yourself at their expense. If you do boast and feel superior, remember it is not you that support the root, but the root [that supports] you.

[19]You will say then, Branches were broken (pruned) off so that I might be grafted in!

[20]That is true. But they were broken (pruned) off because of their unbelief (their lack of real faith), and you are established through faith [because you do believe]. So do not become proud and conceited, but rather stand in awe and be reverently afraid.

[21]For if God did not spare the natural branches [because of unbelief], neither will He spare you [if you are guilty of the same offense].

[22]Then note and appreciate the gracious kindness and the severity of God: severity toward those who have fallen, but God's gracious kindness to you—provided you continue in His grace and abide in His kindness; otherwise you too will be cut off (pruned away).

[23]And even those others [the fallen branches, Jews], if they do not persist in [clinging to] their unbelief, will be grafted in, for God has the power to graft them in again.

[24]For if you have been cut from what is by nature a wild olive tree, and against nature grafted into a cultivated olive tree, how much easier will it be to graft these natural [branches] back on [the original parent stock of] their own olive tree.

[25]Lest you be self-opinionated (wise in your own conceits), I do not want you to miss this hidden truth and mystery, brethren: a hardening (insensibility) has [temporarily] befallen a part of Israel [to last] until the [a]full number of the ingathering of the Gentiles has come in,

[26]And so all Israel will be saved. As it is written, The Deliverer will come from Zion, He will banish ungodliness from Jacob. [Isa. 59:20, 21.]

[27]And this will be My covenant (My agreement) with them when I shall take away their sins. [Isa. 27:9; Jer. 31:33.]

[28]From the point of view of the Gospel (good news), they [the Jews, at present] are enemies [of God], which is for your advantage and benefit. But from the point of view of God's choice (of election, of divine selection), they are still the beloved (dear to Him) for the sake of their forefathers.

[29]For God's gifts and His call are irrevocable. [He never withdraws them when once they are given, and He does not change His mind about those to whom He gives His grace or to whom He sends His call.]

[30]Just as you were once disobedient and rebellious toward God but now have obtained [His] mercy, through their disobedience,

[31]So they also now are being disobedient [when you are receiving mercy], that they in turn may one day, through the mercy you are enjoying, also receive mercy [that they may share the mercy which has been shown to you— through you as messengers of the Gospel to them].

---

[a] 26 Or and so   [b] 27 Or will be   [c] 27 Isaiah 59:20,21; 27:9 (see Septuagint); Jer. 31:33,34   [d] 31 Some manuscripts do not have now.

[a] Joseph Thayer, A Greek-English Lexicon.

## New International Version

everyone over to disobedience so that he may have mercy on them all.

### Doxology

33 Oh, the depth of the riches of the wisdom and[a]
knowledge of God!
How unsearchable his judgments,
and his paths beyond tracing out!
34 "Who has known the mind of the Lord?
Or who has been his counselor?"[b]
35 "Who has ever given to God,
that God should repay them?"[c]
36 For from him and through him and for him are all
things.
To him be the glory forever! Amen.

### A Living Sacrifice

**12** Therefore, I urge you, brothers and sisters, in view of God's mercy, to offer your bodies as a living sacrifice, holy and pleasing to God—this is your true and proper worship. 2 Do not conform to the pattern of this world, but be transformed by the renewing of your mind. Then you will be able to test and approve what God's will is—his good, pleasing and perfect will.

### Humble Service in the Body of Christ

3 For by the grace given me I say to every one of you: Do not think of yourself more highly than you ought, but rather think of yourself with sober judgment, in accordance with the faith God has distributed to each of you. 4 For just as each of us has one body with many members, and these members do not all have the same function, 5 so in Christ we, though many, form one body, and each member belongs to all the others. 6 We have different gifts, according to the grace given to each of us. If your gift is prophesying, then prophesy in accordance with your[d] faith; 7 if it is serving, then serve; if it is teaching, then teach; 8 if it is to encourage, then give encouragement; if it is giving, then give generously; if it is to lead,[e] do it diligently; if it is to show mercy, do it cheerfully.

### Love in Action

9 Love must be sincere. Hate what is evil; cling to what is good. 10 Be devoted to one another in love. Honor one another above yourselves. 11 Never be lacking in zeal, but keep your spiritual fervor, serving the Lord. 12 Be joyful in hope, patient in affliction, faithful in prayer. 13 Share with the Lord's people who are in need. Practice hospitality.

14 Bless those who persecute you; bless and do not curse. 15 Rejoice with those who rejoice; mourn with those

## Amplified Bible

32 For God has consigned (penned up) all men to disobedience, only that He may have mercy on them all [alike].

33 Oh, the depth of the riches and wisdom and knowledge of God! How unfathomable (inscrutable, unsearchable) are His judgments (His decisions)! And how untraceable (mysterious, undiscoverable) are His ways (His methods, His paths)!

34 For who has known the mind of the Lord *and* who has understood His thoughts, or who has [ever] been His counselor? [Isa. 40:13, 14.]

35 Or who has first given God anything that he might be paid back *or* that he could claim a recompense?

36 For from Him and through Him and to Him are all things. [For all things originate with Him and come from Him; all things live through Him, and all things center in and tend to consummate and to end in Him.] To Him be glory forever! Amen (so be it).

**12** I appeal to you therefore, brethren, *and* beg of you in view of [all] the mercies of God, to make a decisive dedication of your bodies [presenting all your members and faculties] as a living sacrifice, holy (devoted, consecrated) and well pleasing to God, which is your reasonable (rational, intelligent) service *and* spiritual worship.

2 Do not be conformed to this world (this age), [fashioned after and adapted to its external, superficial customs], but be transformed (changed) by the [entire] renewal of your mind [by its new ideals and its new attitude], so that you may prove [for yourselves] what is the good and acceptable and perfect will of God, *even* the thing which is good and acceptable and perfect [in His sight for you].

3 For by the grace (unmerited favor of God) given to me I warn everyone among you not to estimate *and* think of himself more highly than he ought [not to have an exaggerated opinion of his own importance], but to rate his ability with sober judgment, each according to the degree of faith apportioned by God to him.

4 For as in one physical body we have many parts (organs, members) and all of these parts do not have the same function *or* use,

5 So we, numerous as we are, are one body in Christ (the Messiah) and individually we are parts one of another [mutually dependent on one another].

6 Having gifts (faculties, talents, qualities) that differ according to the grace given us, let us use them: [He whose gift is] prophecy, [let him prophesy] according to the proportion of his faith;

7 [He whose gift is] practical service, let him give himself to serving; he who teaches, to his teaching;

8 He who exhorts (encourages), to his exhortation; he who contributes, let him do it in simplicity *and* liberality; he who gives aid *and* superintends, with zeal *and* singleness of mind; he who does acts of mercy, with genuine cheerfulness *and* joyful eagerness.

9 [Let your] love be sincere (a real thing); hate what is evil [loathe all ungodliness, turn in horror from wickedness], but hold fast to that which is good.

10 Love one another with brotherly affection [as members of one family], giving precedence *and* showing honor to one another.

11 Never lag in zeal *and* in earnest endeavor; be aglow *and* burning with the Spirit, serving the Lord.

12 Rejoice *and* exult in hope; be steadfast and patient in suffering *and* tribulation; be constant in prayer.

13 Contribute to the needs of God's people [sharing in the necessities of the saints]; pursue the practice of hospitality.

14 Bless those who persecute you [who are cruel in their attitude toward you]; bless and do not curse them.

15 Rejoice with those who rejoice [sharing others' joy], and weep with those who weep [sharing others' grief].

---

*a* 33 Or *riches and the wisdom and the*   *b* 34 Isaiah 40:13
*c* 35 Job 41:11   *d* 6 Or *the*   *e* 8 Or *to provide for others*

## New International Version

who mourn. [16]Live in harmony with one another. Do not be proud, but be willing to associate with people of low position.[a] Do not be conceited.

[17]Do not repay anyone evil for evil. Be careful to do what is right in the eyes of everyone. [18]If it is possible, as far as it depends on you, live at peace with everyone. [19]Do not take revenge, my dear friends, but leave room for God's wrath, for it is written: "It is mine to avenge; I will repay,"[b] says the Lord. [20]On the contrary:

"If your enemy is hungry, feed him;
    if he is thirsty, give him something to drink.
In doing this, you will heap burning coals on his
    head."[c]

[21]Do not be overcome by evil, but overcome evil with good.

### Submission to Governing Authorities

**13** Let everyone be subject to the governing authorities, for there is no authority except that which God has established. The authorities that exist have been established by God. [2]Consequently, whoever rebels against the authority is rebelling against what God has instituted, and those who do so will bring judgment on themselves. [3]For rulers hold no terror for those who do right, but for those who do wrong. Do you want to be free from fear of the one in authority? Then do what is right and you will be commended. [4]For the one in authority is God's servant for your good. But if you do wrong, be afraid, for rulers do not bear the sword for no reason. They are God's servants, agents of wrath to bring punishment on the wrongdoer. [5]Therefore, it is necessary to submit to the authorities, not only because of possible punishment but also as a matter of conscience.

[6]This is also why you pay taxes, for the authorities are God's servants, who give their full time to governing. [7]Give to everyone what you owe them: If you owe taxes, pay taxes; if revenue, then revenue; if respect, then respect; if honor, then honor.

### Love Fulfills the Law

[8]Let no debt remain outstanding, except the continuing debt to love one another, for whoever loves others has fulfilled the law. [9]The commandments, "You shall not commit adultery," "You shall not murder," "You shall not steal," "You shall not covet,"[d] and whatever other command there may be, are summed up in this one command: "Love your neighbor as yourself."[e] [10]Love does no harm to a neighbor. Therefore love is the fulfillment of the law.

### The Day Is Near

[11]And do this, understanding the present time: The hour has already come for you to wake up from your slumber, because our salvation is nearer now than when we first believed. [12]The night is nearly over; the day is almost here. So let us put aside the deeds of darkness and put on the armor of light. [13]Let us behave decently, as in the daytime, not in carousing and drunkenness, not in sexual immorality and debauchery, not in dissension and jealou-

## Amplified Bible

[16]Live in harmony with one another; do not be haughty (snobbish, high-minded, exclusive), but readily adjust yourself to [people, things] and give yourselves to humble tasks. Never overestimate yourself or be wise in your own conceits. [Prov. 3:7.]

[17]Repay no one evil for evil, but take thought for what is honest and proper and noble [aiming to be above reproach] in the sight of everyone. [Prov. 20:22.]

[18]If possible, as far as it depends on you, live at peace with everyone.

[19]Beloved, never avenge yourselves, but leave the way open for [God's] wrath; for it is written, Vengeance is Mine, I will repay (requite), says the Lord. [Deut. 32:35.]

[20]But if your enemy is hungry, feed him; if he is thirsty, give him drink; for by so doing you will heap burning coals upon his head. [Prov. 25:21, 22.]

[21]Do not let yourself be overcome by evil, but overcome (master) evil with good.

**13** Let every person be loyally subject to the governing (civil) authorities. For there is no authority except from God [by His permission, His sanction], and those that exist do so by God's appointment. [Prov. 8:15.]

[2]Therefore he who resists and sets himself up against the authorities resists what God has appointed and arranged [in divine order]. And those who resist will bring down judgment upon themselves [receiving the penalty due them].

[3]For civil authorities are not a terror to [people of] good conduct, but to [those of] bad behavior. Would you have no dread of him who is in authority? Then do what is right and you will receive his approval and commendation.

[4]For he is God's servant for your good. But if you do wrong, [you should dread him and] be afraid, for he does not bear and wear the sword for nothing. He is God's servant to execute His wrath (punishment, vengeance) on the wrongdoer.

[5]Therefore one must be subject, not only to avoid God's wrath and escape punishment, but also as a matter of principle and for the sake of conscience.

[6]For this same reason you pay taxes, for [the civil authorities] are official servants under God, devoting themselves to attending to this very service.

[7]Render to all men their dues. [Pay] taxes to whom taxes are due, revenue to whom revenue is due, respect to whom respect is due, and honor to whom honor is due.

[8]Keep out of debt and owe no man anything, except to love one another; for he who loves his neighbor [who practices loving others] has fulfilled the Law [relating to one's fellowmen, meeting all its requirements].

[9]The commandments, You shall not commit adultery, You shall not kill, You shall not steal, You shall not covet (have an evil desire), and any other commandment, are summed up in the single command, You shall love your neighbor as [you do] yourself. [Exod. 20:13-17; Lev. 19:18.]

[10]Love does no wrong to one's neighbor [it never hurts anybody]. Therefore love meets all the requirements and is the fulfilling of the Law.

[11]Besides this you know what [a critical] hour this is, how it is high time now for you to wake up out of your sleep (rouse to reality). For salvation (final deliverance) is nearer to us now than when we first believed (adhered to, trusted in, and relied on Christ, the Messiah).

[12]The night is far gone and the day is almost here. Let us then drop (fling away) the works and deeds of darkness and put on the [full] armor of light.

[13]Let us live and conduct ourselves honorably and becomingly as in the [open light of] day, not in reveling (carousing) and drunkenness, not in immorality and debauchery (sensuality and licentiousness), not in quarreling and jealousy.

---

[a] 16 Or willing to do menial work    [b] 19 Deut. 32:35
[c] 20 Prov. 25:21,22    [d] 9 Exodus 20:13-15,17; Deut. 5:17-19,21
[e] 9 Lev. 19:18

## New International Version

sy. [14]Rather, clothe yourselves with the Lord Jesus Christ, and do not think about how to gratify the desires of the flesh.[a]

### The Weak and the Strong

**14** Accept the one whose faith is weak, without quarreling over disputable matters. [2]One person's faith allows them to eat anything, but another, whose faith is weak, eats only vegetables. [3]The one who eats everything must not treat with contempt the one who does not, and the one who does not eat everything must not judge the one who does, for God has accepted them. [4]Who are you to judge someone else's servant? To their own master, servants stand or fall. And they will stand, for the Lord is able to make them stand.

[5]One person considers one day more sacred than another; another considers every day alike. Each of them should be fully convinced in their own mind. [6]Whoever regards one day as special does so to the Lord. Whoever eats meat does so to the Lord, for they give thanks to God; and whoever abstains does so to the Lord and gives thanks to God. [7]For none of us lives for ourselves alone, and none of us dies for ourselves alone. [8]If we live, we live for the Lord; and if we die, we die for the Lord. So, whether we live or die, we belong to the Lord. [9]For this very reason, Christ died and returned to life so that he might be the Lord of both the dead and the living.

[10]You, then, why do you judge your brother or sister[b]? Or why do you treat them with contempt? For we will all stand before God's judgment seat. [11]It is written:

"'As surely as I live,' says the Lord,
'every knee will bow before me;
every tongue will acknowledge God.'"[c]

[12]So then, each of us will give an account of ourselves to God.

[13]Therefore let us stop passing judgment on one another. Instead, make up your mind not to put any stumbling block or obstacle in the way of a brother or sister. [14]I am convinced, being fully persuaded in the Lord Jesus, that nothing is unclean in itself. But if anyone regards something as unclean, then for that person it is unclean. [15]If your brother or sister is distressed because of what you eat, you are no longer acting in love. Do not by your eating destroy someone for whom Christ died. [16]Therefore do not let what you know is good be spoken of as evil. [17]For the kingdom of God is not a matter of eating and drinking, but of righteousness, peace and joy in the Holy Spirit, [18]because anyone who serves Christ in this way is pleasing to God and receives human approval.

[19]Let us therefore make every effort to do what leads to peace and to mutual edification. [20]Do not destroy the work

## Amplified Bible

[14]But clothe yourself with the Lord Jesus Christ (the Messiah), and make no provision for [indulging] the flesh [put a stop to thinking about the evil cravings of your physical nature] to [gratify its] desires (lusts).

**14** As for the man who is a weak believer, welcome him [into your fellowship], but not to criticize his opinions *or* pass judgment on his scruples *or* perplex him with discussions.

[2]One [man's faith permits him to] believe he may eat anything, while a weaker one [limits his] eating to vegetables.

[3]Let not him who eats look down on *or* despise him who abstains, and let not him who abstains criticize *and* pass judgment on him who eats; for God has accepted *and* welcomed him.

[4]Who are you to pass judgment on *and* censure another's household servant? It is before his own master that he stands or falls. And he shall stand *and* be upheld, for the Master (the Lord) is mighty to support him *and* make him stand.

[5]One man esteems one day as better than another, while another man esteems all days alike [sacred]. Let everyone be fully convinced (satisfied) in his own mind.

[6]He who observes the day, observes it in honor of the Lord. He also who eats, eats in honor of the Lord, since he gives thanks to God; while he who abstains, abstains in honor of the Lord and gives thanks to God.

[7]None of us lives to himself [but to the Lord], and none of us dies to himself [but to the Lord, for]

[8]If we live, we live to the Lord, and if we die, we die to the Lord. So then, whether we live or we die, we belong to the Lord.

[9]For Christ died and lived again for this very purpose, that He might be Lord both of the dead and of the living.

[10]Why do you criticize *and* pass judgment on your brother? Or you, why do you look down upon *or* despise your brother? For we shall all stand before the judgment seat of God.

[11]For it is written, As I live, says the Lord, every knee shall bow to Me, and every tongue shall confess to God [acknowledge Him to His honor and to His praise]. [Isa. 45:23.]

[12]And so each of us shall give an account of himself [give an answer in reference to judgment] to God.

[13]Then let us no more criticize *and* blame *and* pass judgment on one another, but rather decide *and* endeavor never to put a stumbling block *or* an obstacle or a hindrance in the way of a brother.

[14]I know and am convinced (persuaded) as one in the Lord Jesus, that nothing is [forbidden as] essentially unclean (defiled and unholy in itself). But [none the less] it is unclean (defiled and unholy) to anyone who thinks it is unclean.

[15]But if your brother is being pained *or* his feelings hurt *or* if he is being injured by what you eat, [then] you are no longer walking in love. [You have ceased to be living and conducting yourself by the standard of love toward him.] Do not let what you eat hurt *or* cause the ruin of one for whom Christ died!

[16]Do not therefore let what seems good to you be considered an evil thing [by someone else]. [In other words, do not give occasion for others to criticize that which is justifiable for you.]

[17][After all] the kingdom of God is not a matter of [getting the] food and drink [one likes], but instead it is righteousness (that state which makes a person acceptable to God) and [heart] peace and joy in the Holy Spirit.

[18]He who serves Christ in this way is acceptable *and* pleasing to God and is approved by men.

[19]So let us then definitely aim for *and* eagerly pursue what makes for harmony and for mutual upbuilding (edification and development) of one another.

---

[a] 14 In contexts like this, the Greek word for *flesh* (*sarx*) refers to the sinful state of human beings, often presented as a power in opposition to the Spirit.   [b] 10 The Greek word for *brother or sister* (*adelphos*) refers here to a believer, whether man or woman, as part of God's family; also in verses 13, 15 and 21.   [c] 11 Isaiah 45:23

## New International Version

of God for the sake of food. All food is clean, but it is wrong for a person to eat anything that causes someone else to stumble. [21] It is better to not eat meat or drink wine or to do anything else that will cause your brother or sister to fall.

[22] So whatever you believe about these things keep between yourself and God. Blessed is the one who does not condemn himself by what he approves. [23] But whoever has doubts is condemned if they eat, because their eating is not from faith; and everything that does not come from faith is sin.[a]

**15** We who are strong ought to bear with the failings of the weak and not to please ourselves. [2] Each of us should please our neighbors for their good, to build them up. [3] For even Christ did not please himself but, as it is written: "The insults of those who insult you have fallen on me."[b] [4] For everything that was written in the past was written to teach us, so that through the endurance taught in the Scriptures and the encouragement they provide we might have hope.

[5] May the God who gives endurance and encouragement give you the same attitude of mind toward each other that Christ Jesus had, [6] so that with one mind and one voice you may glorify the God and Father of our Lord Jesus Christ.

[7] Accept one another, then, just as Christ accepted you, in order to bring praise to God. [8] For I tell you that Christ has become a servant of the Jews[c] on behalf of God's truth, so that the promises made to the patriarchs might be confirmed [9] and, moreover, that the Gentiles might glorify God for his mercy. As it is written:

"Therefore I will praise you among the Gentiles;
    I will sing the praises of your name."[d]

[10] Again, it says,

"Rejoice, you Gentiles, with his people."[e]

[11] And again,

"Praise the Lord, all you Gentiles;
    let all the peoples extol him."[f]

[12] And again, Isaiah says,

"The Root of Jesse will spring up,
    one who will arise to rule over the nations;
    in him the Gentiles will hope."[g]

[13] May the God of hope fill you with all joy and peace as you trust in him, so that you may overflow with hope by the power of the Holy Spirit.

## Amplified Bible

[20] You must not, for the sake of food, undo *and* break down and destroy the work of God! Everything is indeed [ceremonially] clean *and* pure, but it is wrong for anyone to hurt the conscience of others *or* to make them fall by what he eats.

[21] The right thing is to eat no meat or drink no wine [at all], or [do anything else] if it makes your brother stumble *or* hurts his conscience *or* offends or weakens him.

[22] Your personal convictions [on such matters]—exercise [them] as in God's presence, keeping them to yourself [striving only to know the truth and obey His will]. Blessed (happy, [a] to be envied) is he who has no reason to judge himself for what he approves [who does not convict himself by what he chooses to do].

[23] But the man who has doubts (misgivings, an uneasy conscience) about eating, and then eats [perhaps because of you], stands condemned [before God], because he is not true to his convictions *and* he does not act from faith. For whatever does not originate *and* proceed from faith is sin [whatever is done without a conviction of its approval by God is sinful].

**15** We who are strong [in our convictions and of robust faith] ought to bear with the failings *and* the frailties *and* the tender scruples of the weak; [we ought to help carry the doubts and qualms of others] and not to please ourselves.

[2] Let each one of us make it a practice to please (make happy) his neighbor for his good *and* for his true welfare, to edify him [to strengthen him and build him up spiritually].

[3] For Christ did not please Himself [gave no thought to His own interests]; but, as it is written, The reproaches *and* abuses of those who reproached *and* abused you fell on Me. [Ps. 69:9.]

[4] For whatever was thus written in former days was written for our instruction, that by [our steadfast and patient] endurance and the encouragement [drawn] from the Scriptures we might hold fast to *and* cherish hope.

[5] Now may the God Who gives the power of patient endurance (steadfastness) and Who supplies encouragement, grant you to live in such mutual harmony *and* such full sympathy with one another, in accord with Christ Jesus,

[6] That together you may [unanimously] with united hearts *and* one voice, praise and glorify the God and Father of our Lord Jesus Christ (the Messiah).

[7] Welcome *and* receive [to your hearts] one another, then, even as Christ has welcomed *and* received you, for the glory of God.

[8] For I tell you that Christ (the Messiah) became a servant *and* a minister to the circumcised (the Jews) in order to show God's truthfulness *and* honesty by confirming (verifying) the promises [given] to our fathers,

[9] And [also in order] that the Gentiles (nations) might glorify God for His mercy [not covenanted] to them. As it is written, Therefore I will praise You among the Gentiles and sing praises to Your name. [Ps. 18:49.]

[10] Again it is said, Rejoice (exult), O Gentiles, along with His [own] people; [Deut. 32:43.]

[11] And again, Praise the Lord, all you Gentiles, and let all the peoples praise Him! [Ps. 117:1.]

[12] And further Isaiah says, There shall be a [b] Sprout from the Root of Jesse, He Who rises to rule over the Gentiles; in Him shall the Gentiles hope. [Isa. 11:1, 10; Rev. 5:5; 22:16.]

[13] May the God of your hope so fill you with all joy and peace in believing [through the experience of your faith] that by the power of the Holy Spirit you may abound *and* be overflowing (bubbling over) with hope.

---

[a] 23 Some manuscripts place 16:25-27 here; others after 15:33.
[b] 3 Psalm 69:9   [c] 8 Greek *circumcision*   [d] 9 2 Samuel 22:50;
Psalm 18:49   [e] 10 Deut. 32:43   [f] 11 Psalm 117:1   [g] 12 Isaiah 11:10
(see Septuagint)

---

[a] Alexander Souter, *Pocket Lexicon*.   [b] G. Abbott-Smith, *Manual Greek Lexicon*.

## New International Version

### Paul the Minister to the Gentiles

14 I myself am convinced, my brothers and sisters, that you yourselves are full of goodness, filled with knowledge and competent to instruct one another. 15 Yet I have written you quite boldly on some points to remind you of them again, because of the grace God gave me 16 to be a minister of Christ Jesus to the Gentiles. He gave me the priestly duty of proclaiming the gospel of God, so that the Gentiles might become an offering acceptable to God, sanctified by the Holy Spirit.

17 Therefore I glory in Christ Jesus in my service to God. 18 I will not venture to speak of anything except what Christ has accomplished through me in leading the Gentiles to obey God by what I have said and done— 19 by the power of signs and wonders, through the power of the Spirit of God. So from Jerusalem all the way around to Illyricum, I have fully proclaimed the gospel of Christ. 20 It has always been my ambition to preach the gospel where Christ was not known, so that I would not be building on someone else's foundation. 21 Rather, as it is written:

"Those who were not told about him will see,
and those who have not heard will understand."[a]

22 This is why I have often been hindered from coming to you.

### Paul's Plan to Visit Rome

23 But now that there is no more place for me to work in these regions, and since I have been longing for many years to visit you, 24 I plan to do so when I go to Spain. I hope to see you while passing through and to have you assist me on my journey there, after I have enjoyed your company for a while. 25 Now, however, I am on my way to Jerusalem in the service of the Lord's people there. 26 For Macedonia and Achaia were pleased to make a contribution for the poor among the Lord's people in Jerusalem. 27 They were pleased to do it, and indeed they owe it to them. For if the Gentiles have shared in the Jews' spiritual blessings, they owe it to the Jews to share with them their material blessings. 28 So after I have completed this task and have made sure that they have received this contribution, I will go to Spain and visit you on the way. 29 I know that when I come to you, I will come in the full measure of the blessing of Christ.

30 I urge you, brothers and sisters, by our Lord Jesus Christ and by the love of the Spirit, to join me in my struggle by praying to God for me. 31 Pray that I may be kept safe from the unbelievers in Judea and that the contribution I take to Jerusalem may be favorably received by the Lord's people there, 32 so that I may come to you with joy, by God's will, and in your company be refreshed. 33 The God of peace be with you all. Amen.

## Amplified Bible

14 Personally I am satisfied about you, my brethren, that you yourselves are rich in goodness, amply filled with all [spiritual] knowledge and competent to admonish and counsel and instruct one another also.

15 Still on some points I have written to you the more boldly and unreservedly by way of reminder. [I have done so] because of the grace (the unmerited favor) bestowed on me by God

16 In making me a minister of Christ Jesus to the Gentiles. I act in the priestly service of the Gospel (the good news) of God, in order that the sacrificial offering of the Gentiles may be acceptable [to God], consecrated and made holy by the Holy Spirit.

17 In Christ Jesus, then, I have legitimate reason to glory (exult) in my work for God [in what through Christ Jesus I have accomplished concerning the things of God].

18 For [of course] I will not venture (presume) to speak thus of any work except what Christ has actually done through me [as an instrument in His hands] to win obedience from the Gentiles, by word and deed,

19 [Even as my preaching has been accompanied] with the power of signs and wonders, [and all of it] by the power of the Holy Spirit. [The result is] that starting from Jerusalem and as far round as Illyricum, I have fully preached the Gospel [faithfully executing, accomplishing, carrying out to the full the good news] of Christ (the Messiah) in its entirety.

20 Thus my ambition has been to preach the Gospel, not where Christ's name has already been known, lest I build on another man's foundation;

21 But [instead I would act on the principle] as it is written, They shall see who have never been told of Him, and they shall understand who have never heard [of Him]. [Isa. 52:15.]

22 This [ambition] is the reason why I have so frequently been hindered from coming to visit you.

23 But now since I have no further opportunity for work in these regions, and since I have longed for a enough years to come to you,

24 I hope to see you in passing [through Rome] as I go [on my intended trip] to Spain, and to be aided on my journey there by you, after I have enjoyed your company for a little while.

25 For the present, however, I am going to Jerusalem to bring aid (relief) for the saints (God's people there).

26 For it has been the good pleasure of Macedonia and Achaia to make some contribution for the poor among the saints of Jerusalem.

27 They were pleased to do it; and surely they are in debt to them, for if these Gentiles have come to share in their [the Jerusalem Jews'] spiritual blessings, then they ought also to be of service to them in material blessings.

28 When therefore I have completed this mission and have delivered to them [at Jerusalem] what has been raised, I shall go on by way of you to Spain.

29 And I know that when I do come to you, I shall come in the abundant blessing of the Gospel of Christ.

30 I appeal to you [I entreat you], brethren, for the sake of our Lord Jesus Christ and by the love [given by] the Spirit, to unite with me in earnest wrestling in prayer to God in my behalf.

31 [Pray] that I may be delivered (rescued) from the unbelievers in Judea and that my mission of relief to Jerusalem may be acceptable and graciously received by the saints (God's people there),

32 So that by God's will I may subsequently come to you with joy (with a happy heart) and be refreshed [by the interval of rest] in your company.

33 May [our] peace-giving God be with you all! Amen (so be it).

---

a 21 Isaiah 52:15 (see Septuagint)

a Marvin Vincent, *Word Studies.*

## New International Version

### Personal Greetings

**16** I commend to you our sister Phoebe, a deacon[a,b] of the church in Cenchreae. [2] I ask you to receive her in the Lord in a way worthy of his people and to give her any help she may need from you, for she has been the benefactor of many people, including me.

[3] Greet Priscilla[c] and Aquila, my co-workers in Christ Jesus. [4] They risked their lives for me. Not only I but all the churches of the Gentiles are grateful to them.
[5] Greet also the church that meets at their house.
Greet my dear friend Epenetus, who was the first convert to Christ in the province of Asia.
[6] Greet Mary, who worked very hard for you.
[7] Greet Andronicus and Junia, my fellow Jews who have been in prison with me. They are outstanding among[d] the apostles, and they were in Christ before I was.
[8] Greet Ampliatus, my dear friend in the Lord.
[9] Greet Urbanus, our co-worker in Christ, and my dear friend Stachys.
[10] Greet Apelles, whose fidelity to Christ has stood the test.
Greet those who belong to the household of Aristobulus.
[11] Greet Herodion, my fellow Jew.
Greet those in the household of Narcissus who are in the Lord.
[12] Greet Tryphena and Tryphosa, those women who work hard in the Lord.
Greet my dear friend Persis, another woman who has worked very hard in the Lord.
[13] Greet Rufus, chosen in the Lord, and his mother, who has been a mother to me, too.
[14] Greet Asyncritus, Phlegon, Hermes, Patrobas, Hermas and the other brothers and sisters with them.
[15] Greet Philologus, Julia, Nereus and his sister, and Olympas and all the Lord's people who are with them.
[16] Greet one another with a holy kiss.
All the churches of Christ send greetings.

[17] I urge you, brothers and sisters, to watch out for those who cause divisions and put obstacles in your way that are contrary to the teaching you have learned. Keep away from them. [18] For such people are not serving our Lord Christ, but their own appetites. By smooth talk and flattery they deceive the minds of naive people. [19] Everyone has heard about your obedience, so I rejoice because of you; but I want you to be wise about what is good, and innocent about what is evil.
[20] The God of peace will soon crush Satan under your feet.
The grace of our Lord Jesus be with you.
[21] Timothy, my co-worker, sends his greetings to you, as do Lucius, Jason and Sosipater, my fellow Jews.
[22] I, Tertius, who wrote down this letter, greet you in the Lord.
[23] Gaius, whose hospitality I and the whole church here enjoy, sends you his greetings.
Erastus, who is the city's director of public works, and our brother Quartus send you their greetings. [24] e

[25] Now to him who is able to establish you in accordance with my gospel, the message I proclaim about Jesus Christ, in keeping with the revelation of the mystery

---

*a 1* Or *servant*    *b 1* The word *deacon* refers here to a Christian designated to serve with the overseers/elders of the church in a variety of ways; similarly in Phil. 1:1 and 1 Tim. 3:8,12.    *c 3* Greek *Prisca*, a variant of *Priscilla*    *d 7* Or *are esteemed by*    *e 24* Some manuscripts include here *May the grace of our Lord Jesus Christ be with all of you. Amen.*

## Amplified Bible

**16** Now I introduce *and* commend to you our sister Phoebe, a deaconess of the church at Cenchreae,
[2] That you may receive her in the Lord [with a Christian welcome], as saints (God's people) ought to receive one another. And help her in whatever matter she may require assistance from you, for she has been a helper of many including myself [shielding us from suffering].
[3] Give my greetings to Prisca and Aquila, my fellow workers in Christ Jesus,
[4] Who risked their lives [endangering their very necks] for my life. To them not only I but also all the churches among the Gentiles give thanks.
[5] [Remember me] also to the church [that meets] in their house. Greet my beloved Epaenetus, who was a firstfruit (first convert) to Christ in Asia.
[6] Greet Mary, who has worked so hard among you.
[7] Remember me to Andronicus and Junias, my tribal kinsmen and once my fellow prisoners. They are men held in high esteem among the apostles, who also were in Christ before I was.
[8] Remember me to Ampliatus, my beloved in the Lord.
[9] Salute Urbanus, our fellow worker in Christ, and my dear Stachys.
[10] Greet Apelles, that one tried *and* approved in Christ (the Messiah). Remember me to those who belong to the household of Aristobulus.
[11] Greet my tribal kinsman Herodion, and those in the Lord who belong to the household of Narcissus.
[12] Salute those workers in the Lord, Tryphaena and Tryphosa. Greet my dear Persis, who has worked so hard in the Lord.
[13] Remember me to Rufus, eminent in the Lord, also to his mother [who has been] a mother to me as well.
[14] Greet Asyncritus, Phlegon, Hermes, Patrobas, Hermas, and the brethren who are with them.
[15] Greet Philologus, Julia, Nereus and his sister, and Olympas, and all the saints who are with them.
[16] Greet one another with a holy (consecrated) kiss. All the churches of Christ (the Messiah) wish to be remembered to you.
[17] I appeal to you, brethren, to be on your guard concerning those who create dissensions and difficulties *and* cause divisions, in opposition to the doctrine (the teaching) which you have been taught. [I warn you to turn aside from them, to] avoid them.
[18] For such persons do not serve our Lord Christ but their own appetites *and* base desires, and by ingratiating and flattering speech, they beguile the hearts of the unsuspecting *and* simpleminded [people].
[19] For while your loyalty *and* obedience is known to all, so that I rejoice over you, I would have you well versed *and* wise as to what is good, and innocent *and* guileless as to what is evil.
[20] And the God of peace will soon crush Satan under your feet. The grace of our Lord Jesus Christ (the Messiah) be with you.
[21] Timothy, my fellow worker, wishes to be remembered to you, as do Lucius and Jason and Sosipater, my tribal kinsmen.
[22] I, Tertius, the writer of this letter, greet you in the Lord.
[23] Gaius, who is host to me and to the whole church here, greets you. So do Erastus, the city treasurer, and our brother Quartus.
[24] *The grace of our Lord Jesus Christ (the Messiah) be with you all. Amen (so be it).*
[25] Now to Him Who is able to strengthen you in the faith which is in accordance with my Gospel and the preaching of (concerning) Jesus Christ (the Messiah), according to the revelation (the unveiling) of the mystery of the plan of redemption which was kept in silence *and* secret for long ages,

## New International Version

hidden for long ages past, [26]but now revealed and made known through the prophetic writings by the command of the eternal God, so that all the Gentiles might come to the obedience that comes from[a] faith — [27]to the only wise God be glory forever through Jesus Christ! Amen.

## Amplified Bible

[26]But is now disclosed and through the prophetic Scriptures is made known to all nations, according to the command of the eternal God, [to win them] to obedience to the faith,

[27]To [the] only wise God be glory forevermore through Jesus Christ (the Anointed One)! Amen (so be it).

## New International Version

# 1 Corinthians

**1** Paul, called to be an apostle of Christ Jesus by the will of God, and our brother Sosthenes,

²To the church of God in Corinth, to those sanctified in Christ Jesus and called to be his holy people, together with all those everywhere who call on the name of our Lord Jesus Christ—their Lord and ours:

³Grace and peace to you from God our Father and the Lord Jesus Christ.

### Thanksgiving

⁴I always thank my God for you because of his grace given you in Christ Jesus. ⁵For in him you have been enriched in every way—with all kinds of speech and with all knowledge— ⁶God thus confirming our testimony about Christ among you. ⁷Therefore you do not lack any spiritual gift as you eagerly wait for our Lord Jesus Christ to be revealed. ⁸He will also keep you firm to the end, so that you will be blameless on the day of our Lord Jesus Christ. ⁹God is faithful, who has called you into fellowship with his Son, Jesus Christ our Lord.

### A Church Divided Over Leaders

¹⁰I appeal to you, brothers and sisters,ᵃ in the name of our Lord Jesus Christ, that all of you agree with one another in what you say and that there be no divisions among you, but that you be perfectly united in mind and thought. ¹¹My brothers and sisters, some from Chloe's household have informed me that there are quarrels among you. ¹²What I mean is this: One of you says, "I follow Paul"; another, "I follow Apollos"; another, "I follow Cephasᵇ"; still another, "I follow Christ."

¹³Is Christ divided? Was Paul crucified for you? Were you baptized in the name of Paul? ¹⁴I thank God that I did not baptize any of you except Crispus and Gaius, ¹⁵so no one can say that you were baptized in my name. ¹⁶(Yes, I also baptized the household of Stephanas; beyond that, I don't remember if I baptized anyone else.) ¹⁷For Christ did not send me to baptize, but to preach the gospel—not with wisdom and eloquence, lest the cross of Christ be emptied of its power.

ᵃ 10 The Greek word for *brothers and sisters* (*adelphoi*) refers here to believers, both men and women, as part of God's family; also in verses 11 and 26; and in 2:1; 3:1; 4:6; 6:8; 7:24, 29; 10:1; 11:33; 12:1; 14:6, 20, 26, 39; 15:1, 6, 50, 58; 16:15, 20.   ᵇ 12 That is, Peter

## Amplified Bible

### THE FIRST LETTER OF PAUL TO THE

# Corinthians

**1** Paul, summoned by the will *and* purpose of God to be an apostle (special messenger) of Christ Jesus, and our brother Sosthenes,

²To the church (assembly) of God which is in Corinth, to those consecrated *and* purified *and* made holy in Christ Jesus, [who are] selected *and* called to be saints (God's people), together with all those who in any place call upon *and* give honor to the name of our Lord Jesus Christ, both their Lord and ours:

³Grace (favor and spiritual blessing) be to you and [heart] peace from God our Father and the Lord Jesus Christ.

⁴I thank my God at all times for you because of the grace (the favor and spiritual blessing) of God which was bestowed on you in Christ Jesus,

⁵[So] that in Him in every respect you were enriched, in full power *and* readiness of speech [to speak of your faith] and complete knowledge *and* illumination [to give you full insight into its meaning].

⁶In this way [our] witnessing concerning Christ (the Messiah) was so confirmed *and* established *and* made sure in you

⁷That you are not [consciously] falling behind *or* lacking in any special spiritual endowment *or* Christian grace [ᵃthe reception of which is due to the power of divine grace operating in your souls by the Holy Spirit], while you wait *and* watch [constantly living in hope] for the coming of our Lord Jesus Christ *and* [His] being made visible to all.

⁸And He will establish you to the end [keep you steadfast, give you strength, and guarantee your vindication; He will be your warrant against all accusation or indictment so that you will be] guiltless *and* irreproachable in the day of our Lord Jesus Christ (the Messiah).

⁹God is faithful (reliable, trustworthy, and therefore ever true to His promise, and He can be depended on); by Him you were called into companionship *and* participation with His Son, Jesus Christ our Lord.

¹⁰But I urge *and* entreat you, brethren, by the name of our Lord Jesus Christ, that all of you be in perfect harmony *and* full agreement in what you say, and that there be no dissensions *or* factions *or* divisions among you, but that you be perfectly united in your common understanding and in your opinions *and* judgments.

¹¹For it has been made clear to me, my brethren, by those of Chloe's household, that there are contentions *and* wrangling *and* factions among you.

¹²What I mean is this, that each one of you [either] says, I belong to Paul, or I belong to Apollos, or I belong to Cephas (Peter), or I belong to Christ.

¹³Is Christ (the Messiah) divided into parts? Was Paul crucified on behalf of you? Or were you baptized into the name of Paul?

¹⁴I thank God that I did not baptize any of you except Crispus and Gaius,

¹⁵Lest anyone should say that I baptized in my own name.

¹⁶[Yes] I did baptize the household of Stephanas also. More than these, I do not remember that I baptized anyone.

¹⁷For Christ (the Messiah) sent me out not to baptize but [to evangelize by] preaching the glad tidings (the Gospel), and that not with verbal eloquence, lest the cross of Christ should be deprived of force *and* emptied of its power *and* rendered vain (fruitless, void of value, and of no effect).

ᵃ Joseph Thayer, *A Greek-English Lexicon of the New Testament.*

## New International Version

### Christ Crucified Is God's Power and Wisdom

[18]For the message of the cross is foolishness to those who are perishing, but to us who are being saved it is the power of God. [19]For it is written:

"I will destroy the wisdom of the wise;
the intelligence of the intelligent I will frustrate."[a]

[20]Where is the wise person? Where is the teacher of the law? Where is the philosopher of this age? Has not God made foolish the wisdom of the world? [21]For since in the wisdom of God the world through its wisdom did not know him, God was pleased through the foolishness of what was preached to save those who believe. [22]Jews demand signs and Greeks look for wisdom, [23]but we preach Christ crucified: a stumbling block to Jews and foolishness to Gentiles, [24]but to those whom God has called, both Jews and Greeks, Christ the power of God and the wisdom of God. [25]For the foolishness of God is wiser than human wisdom, and the weakness of God is stronger than human strength.

[26]Brothers and sisters, think of what you were when you were called. Not many of you were wise by human standards; not many were influential; not many were of noble birth. [27]But God chose the foolish things of the world to shame the wise; God chose the weak things of the world to shame the strong. [28]God chose the lowly things of this world and the despised things—and the things that are not—to nullify the things that are, [29]so that no one may boast before him. [30]It is because of him that you are in Christ Jesus, who has become for us wisdom from God—that is, our righteousness, holiness and redemption. [31]Therefore, as it is written: "Let the one who boasts boast in the Lord."[b]

**2** And so it was with me, brothers and sisters. When I came to you, I did not come with eloquence or human wisdom as I proclaimed to you the testimony about God.[c] [2]For I resolved to know nothing while I was with you except Jesus Christ and him crucified. [3]I came to you in weakness with great fear and trembling. [4]My message and

## Amplified Bible

[18]For the story and message of the cross is sheer absurdity and folly to those who are perishing and on their way to perdition, but to us who are being saved it is the [manifestation of] the power of God.

[19]For it is written, I will baffle and render useless and destroy the learning of the learned and the philosophy of the philosophers and the cleverness of the clever and the discernment of the discerning; I will frustrate and nullify [them] and bring [them] to nothing. [Isa. 29:14.]

[20]Where is the wise man (the philosopher)? Where is the scribe (the scholar)? Where is the investigator (the logician, the debater) of this present time and age? Has not God shown up the nonsense and the folly of this world's wisdom?

[21]For when the world with all its earthly wisdom failed to perceive and recognize and know God by means of its own philosophy, God in His wisdom was pleased through the foolishness of preaching [salvation, procured by Christ and to be had through Him], to save those who believed (who clung to and trusted in and relied on Him).

[22]For while Jews [demandingly] ask for signs and miracles and Greeks pursue philosophy and wisdom,

[23]We preach Christ (the Messiah) crucified, [preaching which] to the Jews is a scandal and an offensive stumbling block [that springs a snare or trap], and to the Gentiles it is absurd and utterly unphilosophical nonsense.

[24]But to those who are called, whether Jew or Greek (Gentile), Christ [is] the Power of God and the Wisdom of God.

[25][This is] because the foolish thing [that has its source in] God is wiser than men, and the weak thing [that springs] from God is stronger than men.

[26]For [simply] consider your own call, brethren; not many [of you were considered to be] wise according to human estimates and standards, not many influential and powerful, not many of high and noble birth.

[27][No] for God selected (deliberately chose) what in the world is foolish to put the wise to shame, and what the world calls weak to put the strong to shame.

[28]And God also selected (deliberately chose) what in the world is lowborn and insignificant and branded and treated with contempt, even the things that are nothing, that He might depose and bring to nothing the things that are,

[29]So that no mortal man should [have pretense for glorying and] boast in the presence of God.

[30]But it is from Him that you have your life in Christ Jesus, Whom God made our Wisdom from God, [revealed to us a knowledge of the divine plan of salvation previously hidden, manifesting itself as] our Righteousness [thus making us upright and putting us in right standing with God], and our Consecration [making us pure and holy], and our Redemption [providing our ransom from eternal penalty for sin].

[31]So then, as it is written, Let him who boasts and proudly rejoices and glories, boast and proudly rejoice and glory in the Lord. [Jer. 9:24.]

**2** As for myself, brethren, when I came to you, I did not come proclaiming to you the testimony and evidence or [a]mystery and secret of God [concerning what He has done through Christ for the salvation of men] in lofty words of eloquence or human philosophy and wisdom;

[2]For I resolved to know nothing (to be acquainted with nothing, to make a display of the knowledge of nothing, and to be conscious of nothing) among you except Jesus Christ (the Messiah) and Him crucified.

[3]And I was in ([b]passed into a state of) weakness and fear (dread) and great trembling [[b]after I had come] among you.

---

## New International Version

my preaching were not with wise and persuasive words, but with a demonstration of the Spirit's power, ⁵so that your faith might not rest on human wisdom, but on God's power.

### God's Wisdom Revealed by the Spirit

⁶We do, however, speak a message of wisdom among the mature, but not the wisdom of this age or of the rulers of this age, who are coming to nothing. ⁷No, we declare God's wisdom, a mystery that has been hidden and that God destined for our glory before time began. ⁸None of the rulers of this age understood it, for if they had, they would not have crucified the Lord of glory. ⁹However, as it is written:

"What no eye has seen,
    what no ear has heard,
and what no human mind has conceived"ᵃ—
    the things God has prepared for those who love
    him—

¹⁰these are the things God has revealed to us by his Spirit.

The Spirit searches all things, even the deep things of God. ¹¹For who knows a person's thoughts except their own spirit within them? In the same way no one knows the thoughts of God except the Spirit of God. ¹²What we have received is not the spirit of the world, but the Spirit who is from God, so that we may understand what God has freely given us. ¹³This is what we speak, not in words taught us by human wisdom but in words taught by the Spirit, explaining spiritual realities with Spirit-taught words.ᵇ ¹⁴The person without the Spirit does not accept the things that come from the Spirit of God but considers them foolishness, and cannot understand them because they are discerned only through the Spirit. ¹⁵The person with the Spirit makes judgments about all things, but such a person is not subject to merely human judgments, ¹⁶for,

"Who has known the mind of the Lord
    so as to instruct him?"ᶜ

But we have the mind of Christ.

## Amplified Bible

⁴And my language and my message were not set forth in persuasive (enticing and plausible) words of wisdom, but they were in demonstration of the [Holy] Spirit and power [ᵃa proof by the Spirit and power of God, operating on me and stirring in the minds of my hearers the most holy emotions and thus persuading them],

⁵So that your faith might not rest in the wisdom of men (human philosophy), but in the power of God.

⁶Yet when we are among the full-grown (spiritually mature Christians who are ripe in understanding), we do impart a [higher] wisdom (the knowledge of the divine plan previously hidden); but it is indeed not a wisdom of this present age or of this world nor of the leaders and rulers of this age, who are being brought to nothing and are doomed to pass away.

⁷But rather what we are setting forth is a wisdom of God once hidden [from the human understanding] and now revealed to us by God—[that wisdom] which God devised and decreed before the ages for our glorification [to lift us into the glory of His presence].

⁸None of the rulers of this age or world perceived and recognized and understood this, for if they had, they would never have crucified the Lord of glory.

⁹But, on the contrary, as the Scripture says, What eye has not seen and ear has not heard and has not entered into the heart of man, [all that] God has prepared (made and keeps ready) for those who love Him [ᵃwho hold Him in affectionate reverence, promptly obeying Him and gratefully recognizing the benefits He has bestowed]. [Isa. 64:4; 65:17.]

¹⁰Yet to us God has unveiled and revealed them by and through His Spirit, for the [Holy] Spirit searches diligently, exploring and examining everything, even sounding the profound and bottomless things of God [the ᵃdivine counsels and things hidden and beyond man's scrutiny].

¹¹For what person perceives (knows and understands) what passes through a man's thoughts except the man's own spirit within him? Just so no one discerns (comes to know and comprehend) the thoughts of God except the Spirit of God.

¹²Now we have not received the spirit [that belongs to] the world, but the [Holy] Spirit Who is from God, [given to us] that we might realize and comprehend and appreciate the gifts [of divine favor and blessing so freely and lavishly] bestowed on us by God.

¹³And we are setting these truths forth in words not taught by human wisdom but taught by the [Holy] Spirit, combining and interpreting spiritual truths with spiritual language [to those who possess the Holy Spirit].

¹⁴But the natural, nonspiritual man does not accept or welcome or admit into his heart the gifts and teachings and revelations of the Spirit of God, for they are folly (meaningless nonsense) to him; and he is incapable of knowing them [of progressively recognizing, understanding, and becoming better acquainted with them] because they are spiritually discerned and estimated and appreciated.

¹⁵But the spiritual man tries all things [he ᵇexamines, investigates, inquires into, questions, and discerns all things], yet is himself to be put on trial and judged by no one [he can read the meaning of everything, but no one can properly discern or appraise or get an insight into him].

¹⁶For who has known or understood the mind (the counsels and purposes) of the Lord so as to guide and instruct Him and give Him knowledge? But we have the mind of Christ (the Messiah) and do hold the thoughts (feelings and purposes) of His heart. [Isa. 40:13.]

---

ᵃ 9 Isaiah 64:4   ᵇ 13 Or Spirit, interpreting spiritual truths to those who are spiritual   ᶜ 16 Isaiah 40:13

ᵃ Joseph Thayer, A Greek-English Lexicon.   ᵇ Joseph P. Lightfoot, Notes on the Epistles of Saint Paul.

## New International Version

### The Church and Its Leaders

**3** Brothers and sisters, I could not address you as people who live by the Spirit but as people who are still worldly—mere infants in Christ. ²I gave you milk, not solid food, for you were not yet ready for it. Indeed, you are still not ready. ³You are still worldly. For since there is jealousy and quarreling among you, are you not worldly? Are you not acting like mere humans? ⁴For when one says, "I follow Paul," and another, "I follow Apollos," are you not mere human beings?

⁵What, after all, is Apollos? And what is Paul? Only servants, through whom you came to believe—as the Lord has assigned to each his task. ⁶I planted the seed, Apollos watered it, but God has been making it grow. ⁷So neither the one who plants nor the one who waters is anything, but only God, who makes things grow. ⁸The one who plants and the one who waters have one purpose, and they will each be rewarded according to their own labor. ⁹For we are co-workers in God's service; you are God's field, God's building.

¹⁰By the grace God has given me, I laid a foundation as a wise builder, and someone else is building on it. But each one should build with care. ¹¹For no one can lay any foundation other than the one already laid, which is Jesus Christ. ¹²If anyone builds on this foundation using gold, silver, costly stones, wood, hay or straw, ¹³their work will be shown for what it is, because the Day will bring it to light. It will be revealed with fire, and the fire will test the quality of each person's work. ¹⁴If what has been built survives, the builder will receive a reward. ¹⁵If it is burned up, the builder will suffer loss but yet will be saved—even though only as one escaping through the flames.

¹⁶Don't you know that you yourselves are God's temple and that God's Spirit dwells in your midst? ¹⁷If anyone destroys God's temple, God will destroy that person; for God's temple is sacred, and you together are that temple.

¹⁸Do not deceive yourselves. If any of you think you are wise by the standards of this age, you should become "fools" so that you may become wise. ¹⁹For the wisdom of

## Amplified Bible

**3** However, brethren, I could not talk to you as to spiritual [men], but as to nonspiritual [men of the flesh, in whom the carnal nature predominates], as to mere infants [in the new life] in Christ [ᵃunable to talk yet!]

²I fed you with milk, not solid food, for you were not yet strong enough [to be ready for it]; but even yet you are not strong enough [to be ready for it],

³For you are still [unspiritual, having the nature] of the flesh [under the control of ordinary impulses]. For as long as [there are] envying and jealousy ᵃnd wrangling and factions among you, are you not unspiritual ᵃnd of the flesh, behaving yourselves after a human standard ᵃnd like mere (unchanged) men?

⁴For when one says, I belong to Paul, and another, I belong to Apollos, are you not [proving yourselves] ordinary (unchanged) men?

⁵What then is Apollos? What is Paul? Ministering servants [not heads of parties] through whom you believed, even as the Lord appointed to each his task:

⁶I planted, Apollos watered, but God [all the while] was making it grow ᵃnd [He] gave the increase.

⁷So neither he who plants is anything nor he who waters, but [only] God Who makes it grow ᵃnd become greater.

⁸He who plants and he who waters are equal (one in aim, of the same importance and esteem), yet each shall receive his own reward (wages), according to his own labor.

⁹For we are fellow workmen (joint promoters, laborers together) with ᵃnd for God; *you* are God's ᵇgarden ᵃnd vineyard ᵃnd field under cultivation, [you are] God's building. [Isa. 61:3.]

¹⁰According to the grace (the special endowment for my task) of God bestowed on me, like a skillful architect ᵃnd master builder I laid [the] foundation, and now another [man] is building upon it. But let each [man] be careful how he builds upon it,

¹¹For no other foundation can anyone lay than that which is [already] laid, which is Jesus Christ (the Messiah, the Anointed One).

¹²But if anyone builds upon the Foundation, whether it be with gold, silver, precious stones, wood, hay, straw,

¹³The work of each [one] will become [plainly, openly] known (shown for what it is); for the day [of Christ] will disclose ᵃnd declare it, because it will be revealed with fire, and the fire will test ᵃnd critically appraise the character ᵃnd worth of the work each person has done.

¹⁴If the work which any person has built on this Foundation [any product of his efforts whatever] survives [this test], he will get his reward.

¹⁵But if any person's work is burned up [under the test], he will suffer the loss [of it all, losing his reward], though he himself will be saved, but only as [one who has passed] through fire. [Job 23:10.]

¹⁶Do you not discern ᵃnd understand that you [the whole church at Corinth] are God's temple (His sanctuary), and that God's Spirit has His permanent dwelling in you [to be at home in you, ᶜcollectively as a church and also individually]?

¹⁷If anyone ᵈdoes hurt to God's temple *or* corrupts it [ᶜwith false doctrines] *or* destroys it, God will ᵈdo hurt to him *and* bring him to the corruption of death *and* destroy him. For the temple of God is holy (sacred to Him) and that [temple] you [ᶜthe believing church and its individual believers] are.

¹⁸Let no person deceive himself. If anyone among you supposes that he is wise in this age, let him become a fool [let him discard his worldly discernment and recognize himself as dull, stupid, and foolish, without true learning and scholarship], that he may become [really] wise. [Isa. 5:21.]

---

ᵃ Literal translation: "non-speakers." ᵇ Johann Bengel, *Gnomon Novi Testamenti.* ᶜ Matthew Henry, *Commentary on the Holy Bible.* ᵈ The *Cambridge Bible for Schools and Colleges.*

# New International Version

this world is foolishness in God's sight. As it is written: "He catches the wise in their craftiness"[a]; [20]and again, "The Lord knows that the thoughts of the wise are futile."[b] [21]So then, no more boasting about human leaders! All things are yours, [22]whether Paul or Apollos or Cephas[c] or the world or life or death or the present or the future—all are yours, [23]and you are of Christ, and Christ is of God.

## The Nature of True Apostleship

**4** This, then, is how you ought to regard us: as servants of Christ and as those entrusted with the mysteries God has revealed. [2]Now it is required that those who have been given a trust must prove faithful. [3]I care very little if I am judged by you or by any human court; indeed, I do not even judge myself. [4]My conscience is clear, but that does not make me innocent. It is the Lord who judges me. [5]Therefore judge nothing before the appointed time; wait until the Lord comes. He will bring to light what is hidden in darkness and will expose the motives of the heart. At that time each will receive their praise from God.

[6]Now, brothers and sisters, I have applied these things to myself and Apollos for your benefit, so that you may learn from us the meaning of the saying, "Do not go beyond what is written." Then you will not be puffed up in being a follower of one of us over against the other. [7]For who makes you different from anyone else? What do you have that you did not receive? And if you did receive it, why do you boast as though you did not?

[8]Already you have all you want! Already you have become rich! You have begun to reign—and that without us! How I wish that you really had begun to reign so that we also might reign with you! [9]For it seems to me that God has put us apostles on display at the end of the procession, like those condemned to die in the arena. We have been made a spectacle to the whole universe, to angels as well as to human beings. [10]We are fools for Christ, but you are so wise in Christ! We are weak, but you are strong! You are honored, we are dishonored! [11]To this very hour we go

# Amplified Bible

[19]For this world's wisdom is foolishness (absurdity and stupidity) with God, for it is written, He lays hold of the wise in their [own] craftiness; [Job 5:13.]

[20]And again, The Lord knows the thoughts *and* reasonings of the [humanly] wise *and* recognizes how futile they are. [Ps. 94:11.]

[21]So let no one exult proudly concerning men [boasting of having this or that man as a leader], for all things are yours,

[22]Whether Paul or Apollos or Cephas (Peter), or the universe or life or death, or the immediate *and* [a]threatening present or the [subsequent and uncertain] future—all are yours,

[23]And you are Christ's, and Christ is God's.

**4** So then, let us [apostles] be looked upon as ministering servants of Christ and stewards (trustees) of the mysteries (the secret purposes) of God.

[2]Moreover, it is [essentially] required of stewards that a man should be found faithful [proving himself worthy of trust].

[3]But [as for me personally] it matters very little to me that I should be put on trial by you [on this point], *and* that you or any other human tribunal should investigate *and* question *and* cross-question me. I do not even put myself on trial *and* judge myself.

[4]I am not conscious of anything against myself, *and* I feel blameless; but I am not vindicated *and* acquitted before God on that account. It is the Lord [Himself] Who examines *and* judges me.

[5]So do not make any hasty *or* premature judgments before the time when the Lord comes [again], for He will both bring to light the secret things that are [now hidden] in darkness and disclose *and* expose the [secret] aims (motives and purposes) of hearts. Then every man will receive his [due] commendation from God.

[6]Now I have applied all this [about parties and factions] to myself and Apollos for your sakes, brethren, so that from what I have said of us [as illustrations], you may learn [to think of men in accordance with Scripture and] not to go beyond that which is written, that none of you may be puffed up *and* inflated with pride *and* boast in favor of one [minister and teacher] against another.

[7]For who separates you from the others [as a faction leader]? [Who makes you superior and sets you apart from another, giving you the preeminence?] What have you that was not given to you? If then you received it [from someone], why do you boast as if you had not received [but had gained it by your own efforts]?

[8][b]You behave as if] you are already filled *and* think you have enough [you are full and content, feeling no need of anything more]! Already you have become rich [in spiritual gifts and graces]! [Without any counsel or instruction from us, in your conceit], you have ascended your thrones *and* come into your kingdom without including us! And would that it were true *and* that you did reign, so that we might be sharing the kingdom with you!

[9]For it seems to me that God has made an exhibit of us apostles, exposing us to view last [of all, like men in a triumphal procession who are] sentenced to death [and displayed at the end of the line]. For we have become a spectacle to the world [a show in the world's amphitheater] with both men and angels [as spectators].

[10]We are [looked upon as] fools on account of Christ *and* for His sake, but you are [supposedly] so amazingly wise *and* prudent in Christ! We are weak, but you are [so very] strong! You are highly esteemed, but we are in disrepute *and* contempt!

[11]To this hour we have gone both hungry and thirsty;

---

[a] 19 Job 5:13   [b] 20 Psalm 94:11   [c] 22 That is, Peter

[a] Marvin Vincent, *Word Studies.*   [b] Henry Alford, *The Greek New Testament, with Notes.*

## New International Version

hungry and thirsty, we are in rags, we are brutally treated, we are homeless. ¹²We work hard with our own hands. When we are cursed, we bless; when we are persecuted, we endure it; ¹³when we are slandered, we answer kindly. We have become the scum of the earth, the garbage of the world—right up to this moment.

### Paul's Appeal and Warning
¹⁴I am writing this not to shame you but to warn you as my dear children. ¹⁵Even if you had ten thousand guardians in Christ, you do not have many fathers, for in Christ Jesus I became your father through the gospel. ¹⁶Therefore I urge you to imitate me. ¹⁷For this reason I have sent to you Timothy, my son whom I love, who is faithful in the Lord. He will remind you of my way of life in Christ Jesus, which agrees with what I teach everywhere in every church.

¹⁸Some of you have become arrogant, as if I were not coming to you. ¹⁹But I will come to you very soon, if the Lord is willing, and then I will find out not only how these arrogant people are talking, but what power they have. ²⁰For the kingdom of God is not a matter of talk but of power. ²¹What do you prefer? Shall I come to you with a rod of discipline, or shall I come in love and with a gentle spirit?

### Dealing With a Case of Incest
**5** It is actually reported that there is sexual immorality among you, and of a kind that even pagans do not tolerate: A man is sleeping with his father's wife. ²And you are proud! Shouldn't you rather have gone into mourning and have put out of your fellowship the man who has been doing this? ³For my part, even though I am not physically present, I am with you in spirit. As one who is present with you in this way, I have already passed judgment in the name of our Lord Jesus on the one who has been doing this. ⁴So when you are assembled and I am with you in spirit, and the power of our Lord Jesus is present, ⁵hand this man over to Satan for the destruction of the flesh,ᵃ,ᵇ so that his spirit may be saved on the day of the Lord.

⁶Your boasting is not good. Don't you know that a little yeast leavens the whole batch of dough? ⁷Get rid of the old yeast, so that you may be a new unleavened batch—as you really are. For Christ, our Passover lamb, has been sacrificed. ⁸Therefore let us keep the Festival, not with the old bread leavened with malice and wickedness, but with the unleavened bread of sincerity and truth.

⁹I wrote to you in my letter not to associate with sexually immoral people— ¹⁰not at all meaning the people of this

## Amplified Bible

we [ᵃhabitually] wear but one undergarment [and shiver in the cold]; we are roughly knocked about and wander around homeless.

¹²And we still toil unto weariness [for our living], working hard with our own hands. When men revile us [ᵇwound us with an accursed sting], we bless them. When we are persecuted, we take it patiently *and* endure it.

¹³When we are slandered *and* defamed, we [try to] answer softly *and* bring comfort. We have been made and are now the rubbish *and* filth of the world [the offscouring of all things, the scum of the earth].

¹⁴I do not write this to shame you, but to warn *and* counsel you as my beloved children.

¹⁵After all, though you should have ten thousand teachers (guides to direct you) in Christ, yet you do not have many fathers. For I became your father in Christ Jesus through the glad tidings (the Gospel).

¹⁶So I urge *and* implore you, be imitators of me.

¹⁷For this very cause I sent to you Timothy, who is my beloved and trustworthy child in the Lord, who will recall to your minds my methods of proceeding *and* course of conduct *and* way of life in Christ, such as I teach everywhere in each of the churches.

¹⁸Some of you have become conceited *and* arrogant *and* pretentious, counting on my not coming to you.

¹⁹But I will come to you [and] shortly, if the Lord is willing, and then I will perceive *and* understand not what the talk of these puffed up *and* arrogant spirits amount to, but their force (ᶜthe moral power and excellence of soul they really possess).

²⁰For the kingdom of God consists of *and* is based on not talk but power (ᶜmoral power and excellence of soul).

²¹Now which do you prefer? Shall I come to you with a rod of correction, or with love and in a spirit of gentleness?

**5** It is actually reported that there is sexual immorality among you, impurity of a sort that is condemned *and* does not occur even among the heathen; for a man has [his own] father's wife. [Deut. 22:30; 27:20.]

²And you are proud *and* arrogant! And you ought rather to mourn (bow in sorrow and in shame) until the person who has done this [shameful] thing is removed from your fellowship *and* your midst!

³As for my attitude, though I am absent [from you] in body, I am present in spirit, and I have already decided *and* passed judgment, as if actually present,

⁴In the name of the Lord Jesus *Christ,* on the man who has committed such a deed. When you and my own spirit are met together with the power of our Lord Jesus,

⁵You are to deliver this man over to Satan ᵈfor physical discipline [to destroy carnal lusts which prompted him to incest], that [his] spirit may be [yet] saved in the day of the Lord Jesus.

⁶[About the condition of your church] your boasting is not good [indeed, it is most unseemly and entirely out of place]. Do you not know that [just] a little leaven will ferment the whole lump [of dough]?

⁷Purge (clean out) the old leaven that you may be fresh (new) dough, still uncontaminated [as you are], for Christ, our Passover [Lamb], has been sacrificed.

⁸Therefore, let us keep the feast, not with old leaven, nor with leaven of vice *and* malice and wickedness, but with the unleavened [bread] of purity (nobility, honor) *and* sincerity and [unadulterated] truth. [Exod. 12:19; 13:7; Deut. 16:3.]

⁹I wrote you in my [previous] letter not to associate [closely and habitually] with unchaste (impure) people—

¹⁰Not [meaning of course that you must] altogether

---

ᵃ 5 In contexts like this, the Greek word for *flesh* (*sarx*) refers to the sinful state of human beings, often presented as a power in opposition to the Spirit.  ᵇ 5 Or *of his body*

ᵃ Alexander Souter, *Pocket Lexicon of the Greek New Testament.*
ᵇ Kenneth Wuest, *Word Studies in the Greek New Testament.*  ᶜJoseph Thayer, *A Greek-English Lexicon.*  ᵈ G. Abbott-Smith, *Manual Greek Lexicon of the New Testament.*

## New International Version

world who are immoral, or the greedy and swindlers, or idolaters. In that case you would have to leave this world. [11]But now I am writing to you that you must not associate with anyone who claims to be a brother or sister[a] but is sexually immoral or greedy, an idolater or slanderer, a drunkard or swindler. Do not even eat with such people.

[12]What business is it of mine to judge those outside the church? Are you not to judge those inside? [13]God will judge those outside. "Expel the wicked person from among you."[b]

### Lawsuits Among Believers

**6** If any of you has a dispute with another, do you dare to take it before the ungodly for judgment instead of before the Lord's people? [2]Or do you not know that the Lord's people will judge the world? And if you are to judge the world, are you not competent to judge trivial cases? [3]Do you not know that we will judge angels? How much more the things of this life! [4]Therefore, if you have disputes about such matters, do you ask for a ruling from those whose way of life is scorned in the church? [5]I say this to shame you. Is it possible that there is nobody among you wise enough to judge a dispute between believers? [6]But instead, one brother takes another to court—and this in front of unbelievers!

[7]The very fact that you have lawsuits among you means you have been completely defeated already. Why not rather be wronged? Why not rather be cheated? [8]Instead, you yourselves cheat and do wrong, and you do this to your brothers and sisters. [9]Or do you not know that wrongdoers will not inherit the kingdom of God? Do not be deceived: Neither the sexually immoral nor idolaters nor adulterers nor men who have sex with men[c] [10]nor thieves nor the greedy nor drunkards nor slanderers nor swindlers will inherit the kingdom of God. [11]And that is what some of you were. But you were washed, you were sanctified, you were justified in the name of the Lord Jesus Christ and by the Spirit of our God.

### Sexual Immorality

[12]"I have the right to do anything," you say—but not everything is beneficial. "I have the right to do anything"— but I will not be mastered by anything. [13]You say, "Food

---

[a] 11 The Greek word for *brother or sister* (*adelphos*) refers here to a believer, whether man or woman, as part of God's family; also in 8:11, 13.   [b] 13 Deut. 13:5; 17:7; 19:19; 21:21; 22:21,24; 24:7   [c] 9 The words *men who have sex with men* translate two Greek words that refer to the passive and active participants in homosexual acts.

## Amplified Bible

shun the immoral people of this world, or the greedy graspers and cheats *and* thieves or idolaters, since otherwise you would need to get out of the world *and* human society altogether!

[11]But now I write to you not to associate with anyone who bears the name of [Christian] brother if he is known to be guilty of immorality or greed, or is an idolater [whose soul is devoted to any object that usurps the place of God], or is a person with a foul tongue [railing, abusing, reviling, slandering], or is a drunkard or a swindler *or* a robber. [No] you must not so much as eat with such a person.

[12]What [business] of mine is it *and* what right have I to judge outsiders? Is it not those inside [the church] upon whom you are to pass disciplinary judgment [passing censuring sentence on them as the facts require]?

[13]God alone sits in judgment on those who are outside. Drive out that wicked one from among you [expel him from your church].

**6** Does any of you dare, when he has a matter of complaint against another [brother], to go to law before unrighteous men [men neither upright nor right with God, laying it before them] instead of before the saints (the people of God)?

[2]Do you not know that the saints (the believers) will [one day] judge *and* govern the world? And if the world [itself] is to be judged *and* ruled by you, are you unworthy *and* incompetent to try [such petty matters] of the smallest courts of justice?

[3]Do you not know also that we [Christians] are to judge the [very] angels *and* pronounce opinion between right and wrong [for them]? How much more then [as to] matters pertaining to this world *and* of this life only!

[4]If then you do have such cases of everyday life to decide, why do you appoint [as judges to lay them before] those who [from the standpoint of] the church count for least *and* are without standing?

[5]I say this to move you to shame. Can it be that there really is not one man among you who [in action is governed by piety and integrity and] is wise *and* competent enough to decide [the private grievances, disputes, and quarrels] between members of the brotherhood,

[6]But brother goes to law against brother, and that before [Gentile judges who are] unbelievers [without faith or trust in the Gospel of Christ]?

[7]Why, the very fact of your having lawsuits with one another at all is a defect (a defeat, an evidence of positive moral loss for you). Why not rather let yourselves suffer wrong *and* be deprived of what is your due? Why not rather be cheated (defrauded and robbed)?

[8]But [instead it is you] yourselves who wrong and defraud, and that even your own brethren [by so treating them]!

[9]Do you not know that the unrighteous *and* the wrongdoers will not inherit *or* have any share in the kingdom of God? Do not be deceived (misled): neither the impure *and* immoral, nor idolaters, nor adulterers, nor those who participate in homosexuality,

[10]Nor cheats (swindlers and thieves), nor greedy graspers, nor drunkards, nor foulmouthed revilers *and* slanderers, nor extortioners *and* robbers will inherit *or* have any share in the kingdom of God.

[11]And such some of you were [once]. But you were washed clean (purified by a complete atonement for sin and made free from the guilt of sin), and you were consecrated (set apart, hallowed), and you were justified [pronounced righteous, by trusting] in the name of the Lord Jesus Christ and in the [Holy] Spirit of our God.

[12]Everything is permissible (allowable and lawful) for me; but not all things are helpful (good for me to do, expedient and profitable when considered with other things). Everything is lawful for me, but I will not become the slave of anything *or* be brought under its power.

## New International Version

for the stomach and the stomach for food, and God will destroy them both." The body, however, is not meant for sexual immorality but for the Lord, and the Lord for the body. ¹⁴By his power God raised the Lord from the dead, and he will raise us also. ¹⁵Do you not know that your bodies are members of Christ himself? Shall I then take the members of Christ and unite them with a prostitute? Never! ¹⁶Do you not know that he who unites himself with a prostitute is one with her in body? For it is said, "The two will become one flesh."ᵃ ¹⁷But whoever is united with the Lord is one with him in spirit.ᵇ

¹⁸Flee from sexual immorality. All other sins a person commits are outside the body, but whoever sins sexually, sins against their own body. ¹⁹Do you not know that your bodies are temples of the Holy Spirit, who is in you, whom you have received from God? You are not your own; ²⁰you were bought at a price. Therefore honor God with your bodies.

### Concerning Married Life

**7** Now for the matters you wrote about: "It is good for a man not to have sexual relations with a woman." ²But since sexual immorality is occurring, each man should have sexual relations with his own wife, and each woman with her own husband. ³The husband should fulfill his marital duty to his wife, and likewise the wife to her husband. ⁴The wife does not have authority over her own body but yields it to her husband. In the same way, the husband does not have authority over his own body but yields it to his wife. ⁵Do not deprive each other except perhaps by mutual consent and for a time, so that you may devote yourselves to prayer. Then come together again so that Satan will not tempt you because of your lack of self-control. ⁶I say this as a concession, not as a command. ⁷I wish that all of you were as I am. But each of you has your own gift from God; one has this gift, another has that.

⁸Now to the unmarriedᶜ and the widows I say: It is good for them to stay unmarried, as I do. ⁹But if they cannot control themselves, they should marry, for it is better to marry than to burn with passion.

¹⁰To the married I give this command (not I, but the Lord): A wife must not separate from her husband. ¹¹But if she does, she must remain unmarried or else be reconciled to her husband. And a husband must not divorce his wife.

¹²To the rest I say this (I, not the Lord): If any brother

## Amplified Bible

¹³Food [is intended] for the stomach and the stomach for food, but God will finally end [the functions of] both *and* bring them to nothing. The body is not intended for sexual immorality, but [is intended] for the Lord, and the Lord [is intended] for the body [ᵃto save, sanctify, and raise it again].

¹⁴And God both raised the Lord to life and will also raise us up by His power.

¹⁵Do you not see *and* know that your bodies are members (bodily parts) of Christ (the Messiah)? Am I therefore to take the parts of Christ and make [them] parts of a prostitute? Never! Never!

¹⁶Or do you not know *and* realize that when a man joins himself to a prostitute, he becomes one body with her? The two, it is written, shall become one flesh. [Gen. 2:24.]

¹⁷But the person who is united to the Lord becomes one spirit with Him.

¹⁸Shun immorality *and* all sexual looseness [flee from impurity in thought, word, or deed]. Any other sin which a man commits is one outside the body, but he who commits sexual immorality sins against his own body.

¹⁹Do you not know that your body is the temple (the very sanctuary) of the Holy Spirit Who lives within you, Whom you have received [as a Gift] from God? You are not your own,

²⁰You were bought with a price [purchased with a ᵇpreciousness and paid for, ᵇmade His own]. So then, honor God *and* bring glory to Him in your body.

**7** Now as to the matters of which you wrote me. It is well [and by that I mean advantageous, expedient, profitable, and wholesome] for a man not to touch a woman [to cohabit with her] *but* to remain unmarried.

²But because of the temptation to impurity *and* to avoid immorality, let each [man] have his own wife and let each [woman] have her own husband.

³The husband should give to his wife her conjugal rights (goodwill, kindness, and what is due her as his wife), and likewise the wife to her husband.

⁴For the wife does not have [exclusive] authority *and* control over her own body, but the husband [has his rights]; likewise also the husband does not have [exclusive] authority *and* control over his body, but the wife [has her rights].

⁵Do not refuse *and* deprive *and* defraud each other [of your due marital rights], except perhaps by mutual consent for a time, so that you may devote yourselves unhindered to prayer. But afterwards resume marital relations, lest Satan tempt you [to sin] through your lack of restraint of sexual desire. [Exod. 19:15.]

⁶But I am saying this more as a matter of permission *and* concession, not as a command *or* regulation.

⁷I wish that all men were like I myself am [in this matter of self-control]. But each has his own special gift from God, one of this kind and one of another.

⁸But to the unmarried people and to the widows, I declare that it is well (good, advantageous, expedient, and wholesome) for them to remain [single] even as I do.

⁹But if they have not self-control (restraint of their passions), they should marry. For it is better to marry than to be aflame [with passion and tortured continually with ungratified desire].

¹⁰But to the married people I give charge—not I but the Lord—that the wife is not to separate from her husband.

¹¹But if she does [separate from and divorce him], let her remain single or else be reconciled to her husband. And [I charge] the husband [also] that he should not put away *or* divorce his wife.

¹²To the rest I declare—I, not the Lord [for Jesus did not discuss this]—that if any brother has a wife who does not

---

ᵃ 16 Gen. 2:24   ᵇ 17 Or *in the Spirit*   ᶜ 8 Or *widowers*

ᵃ *The Cambridge Bible.* See also Rom. 8:11; I Cor. 15:35-54.   ᵇ Joseph Thayer, *A Greek-English Lexicon.*

## New International Version

has a wife who is not a believer and she is willing to live with him, he must not divorce her. ¹³And if a woman has a husband who is not a believer and he is willing to live with her, she must not divorce him. ¹⁴For the unbelieving husband has been sanctified through his wife, and the unbelieving wife has been sanctified through her believing husband. Otherwise your children would be unclean, but as it is, they are holy.

¹⁵But if the unbeliever leaves, let it be so. The brother or the sister is not bound in such circumstances; God has called us to live in peace. ¹⁶How do you know, wife, whether you will save your husband? Or, how do you know, husband, whether you will save your wife?

### Concerning Change of Status

¹⁷Nevertheless, each person should live as a believer in whatever situation the Lord has assigned to them, just as God has called them. This is the rule I lay down in all the churches. ¹⁸Was a man already circumcised when he was called? He should not become uncircumcised. Was a man uncircumcised when he was called? He should not be circumcised. ¹⁹Circumcision is nothing and uncircumcision is nothing. Keeping God's commands is what counts. ²⁰Each person should remain in the situation they were in when God called them.

²¹Were you a slave when you were called? Don't let it trouble you—although if you can gain your freedom, do so. ²²For the one who was a slave when called to faith in the Lord is the Lord's freed person; similarly, the one who was free when called is Christ's slave. ²³You were bought at a price; do not become slaves of human beings. ²⁴Brothers and sisters, each person, as responsible to God, should remain in the situation they were in when God called them.

### Concerning the Unmarried

²⁵Now about virgins: I have no command from the Lord, but I give a judgment as one who by the Lord's mercy is trustworthy. ²⁶Because of the present crisis, I think that it is good for a man to remain as he is. ²⁷Are you pledged to a woman? Do not seek to be released. Are you free from such a commitment? Do not look for a wife. ²⁸But if you do marry, you have not sinned; and if a virgin marries, she has not sinned. But those who marry will face many troubles in this life, and I want to spare you this.

²⁹What I mean, brothers and sisters, is that the time is short. From now on those who have wives should live as if they do not; ³⁰those who mourn, as if they did not; those who are happy, as if they were not; those who buy something, as if it were not theirs to keep; ³¹those who use the things of the world, as if not engrossed in them. For this world in its present form is passing away.

## Amplified Bible

believe [in Christ] and she consents to live with him, he should not leave or divorce her.

¹³And if any woman has an unbelieving husband and he consents to live with her, she should not leave or divorce him.

¹⁴For the unbelieving husband is set apart (separated, withdrawn from heathen contamination, and affiliated with the Christian people) by union with his consecrated (set-apart) wife, and the unbelieving wife is set apart and separated through union with her consecrated husband. Otherwise your children would be unclean (unblessed heathen, ᵃoutside the Christian covenant), but as it is they are ᵇprepared for God [pure and clean].

¹⁵But if the unbelieving partner [actually] leaves, let him do so; in such [cases the remaining] brother or sister is not morally bound. But God has called us to peace.

¹⁶For, wife, how can you be sure of converting and saving your husband? Husband, how can you be sure of converting and saving your wife?

¹⁷Only, let each one [seek to conduct himself and regulate his affairs so as to] lead the life which the Lord has allotted and imparted to him and to which God has invited and summoned him. This is my order in all the churches.

¹⁸Was anyone at the time of his summons [from God] already circumcised? Let him not seek to remove the evidence of circumcision. Was anyone at the time [God] called him uncircumcised? Let him not be circumcised.

¹⁹For circumcision is nothing and counts for nothing, neither does uncircumcision, but [what counts is] keeping the commandments of God.

²⁰Everyone should remain after God calls him in the station or condition of life in which the summons found him.

²¹Were you a slave when you were called? Do not let that trouble you. But if you are able to gain your freedom, avail yourself of the opportunity.

²²For he who as a slave was summoned in [to union with] the Lord is a freedman of the Lord, just so he who was free when he was called is a bond servant of Christ (the Messiah).

²³You were bought with a price [purchased with a preciousness and paid for by Christ]; then do not yield yourselves up to become [in your own estimation] slaves to men [but consider yourselves slaves to Christ].

²⁴So, brethren, in whatever station or state or condition of life each one was when he was called, there let him continue with and close to God.

²⁵Now concerning the virgins (the marriageable ᶜmaidens) I have no command of the Lord, but I give my opinion and advice as one who by the Lord's mercy is rendered trustworthy and faithful.

²⁶I think then, because of the impending distress [that is even now setting in], it is well (expedient, profitable, and wholesome) for a person to remain as he or she is.

²⁷Are you bound to a wife? Do not seek to be free. Are you free from a wife? Do not seek a wife.

²⁸But if you do marry, you do not sin [in doing so], and if a virgin marries, she does not sin [in doing so]. Yet those who marry will have physical and earthly troubles, and I would like to spare you that.

²⁹I mean, brethren, the appointed time has been ᶜwinding down and it has grown very short. From now on, let even those who have wives be as if they had none,

³⁰And those who weep and mourn as though they were not weeping and mourning, and those who rejoice as though they were not rejoicing, and those who buy as though they did not possess anything,

³¹And those who deal with this world [ᶜoverusing the enjoyments of this life] as though they were not absorbed by it and as if they had no dealings with it. For the outward form of this world (the present world order) is passing away.

ᵃ Robert Jamieson, A. R. Fausset and David Brown, *A Commentary on the Old and New Testaments*. ᵇ Joseph Thayer, *A Greek-English Lexicon*. ᶜ Marvin Vincent, *Word Studies*.

## New International Version

32I would like you to be free from concern. An unmarried man is concerned about the Lord's affairs—how he can please the Lord. 33But a married man is concerned about the affairs of this world—how he can please his wife— 34and his interests are divided. An unmarried woman or virgin is concerned about the Lord's affairs: Her aim is to be devoted to the Lord in both body and spirit. But a married woman is concerned about the affairs of this world—how she can please her husband. 35I am saying this for your own good, not to restrict you, but that you may live in a right way in undivided devotion to the Lord.

36If anyone is worried that he might not be acting honorably toward the virgin he is engaged to, and if his passions are too strong[a] and he feels he ought to marry, he should do as he wants. He is not sinning. They should get married. 37But the man who has settled the matter in his own mind, who is under no compulsion but has control over his own will, and who has made up his mind not to marry the virgin—this man also does the right thing. 38So then, he who marries the virgin does right, but he who does not marry her does better.[b]

39A woman is bound to her husband as long as he lives. But if her husband dies, she is free to marry anyone she wishes, but he must belong to the Lord. 40In my judgment, she is happier if she stays as she is—and I think that I too have the Spirit of God.

### Concerning Food Sacrificed to Idols

8 Now about food sacrificed to idols: We know that "We all possess knowledge." But knowledge puffs up while love builds up. 2Those who think they know something do not yet know as they ought to know. 3But whoever loves God is known by God.[c]

4So then, about eating food sacrificed to idols: We know that "An idol is nothing at all in the world" and that "There is no God but one." 5For even if there are so-called gods, whether in heaven or on earth (as indeed there are many "gods" and many "lords"), 6yet for us there is but one God, the Father, from whom all things came and for whom we live; and there is but one Lord, Jesus Christ, through whom all things came and through whom we live.

7But not everyone possesses this knowledge. Some people are still so accustomed to idols that when they eat sacrificial food they think of it as having been sacrificed to a god, and since their conscience is weak, it is defiled. 8But

## Amplified Bible

32My desire is to have you free from all anxiety and distressing care. The unmarried man is anxious about the things of the Lord—how he may please the Lord; 33But the married man is anxious about worldly matters—how he may please his wife— 34And he is drawn in diverging directions [his interests are divided and he is distracted from his devotion to God]. And the unmarried woman or girl is concerned and anxious about the matters of the Lord, how to be wholly separated and set apart in body and spirit; but the married woman has her cares [centered] in earthly affairs—how she may please her husband.

35Now I say this for your own welfare and profit, not to put [a halter of] restraint upon you, but to promote what is seemly and in good order and to secure your undistracted and undivided devotion to the Lord.

36But if any man thinks that he is not acting properly toward and in regard to his virgin [that he is preparing disgrace for her or incurring reproach], in case she is passing the bloom of her youth and if there is need for it, let him do what to him seems right; he does not sin; let them marry.

37But whoever is firmly established in his heart [strong in mind and purpose], not being forced by necessity but having control over his own will and desire, and has resolved this in his heart to keep his own virginity, he is doing well.

38So also then, he [the father] who gives his virgin (his daughter) in marriage does well, and he [the father] who does not give [her] in marriage does better.

39A wife is bound to her husband by law as long as he lives. If the husband dies, she is free to be married to whom she will, only [provided that he too is] in the Lord.

40But in my opinion [a widow] is happier (more blessed and ato be envied) if she does not remarry. And also I think I have the Spirit of God.

8 Now about food offered to idols: of course we know that all of us possess knowledge [concerning these matters. Yet mere] knowledge causes people to be puffed up (to bear themselves loftily and be proud), but love (affection and goodwill and benevolence) edifies and builds up and encourages one to grow [to his full stature].

2If anyone imagines that he has come to know and understand much [of divine things, without love], he does not yet perceive and recognize and understand as strongly and clearly, nor has he become as intimately acquainted with anything as he ought or as is necessary.

3But if one loves God truly [bwith affectionate reverence, prompt obedience, and grateful recognition of His blessing], he is known by God [arecognized as worthy of His intimacy and love, and he is owned by Him].

4In this matter, then, of eating food offered to idols, we know that an idol is nothing (has no real existence) and that there is no God but one. [Deut. 6:4.]

5For although there may be so-called gods, whether in heaven or on earth, as indeed there are many of them, both of gods and of lords and masters,

6Yet for us there is [only] one God, the Father, Who is the Source of all things and for Whom we [have life], and one Lord, Jesus Christ, through and by Whom are all things and through and by Whom we [ourselves exist]. [Mal. 2:10.]

7Nevertheless, not all [believers] possess this knowledge. But some, through being all their lives until now accustomed to [thinking of] idols [as real and living], still consider the food [offered to an idol] as that sacrificed to an [actual] god; and their weak consciences become defiled and injured if they eat [it].

---

a 36 Or if she is getting beyond the usual age for marriage   b 36-38 Or 36If anyone thinks he is not treating his daughter properly, and if she is getting along in years (or if her passions are too strong), and he feels she ought to marry, he should do as he wants. He is not sinning. He should let her get married. 37But the man who has settled the matter in his own mind, who is under no compulsion but has control over his own will, and who has made up his mind to keep the virgin unmarried—this man also does the right thing. 38So then, he who gives his virgin in marriage does right, but he who does not give her in marriage does better.   c 2,3 An early manuscript and another ancient witness think they have knowledge do not yet know as they ought to know. 3But whoever loves truly knows.

a Alexander Souter, Pocket Lexicon.   b Joseph Thayer, A Greek-English Lexicon.

## New International Version

food does not bring us near to God; we are no worse if we do not eat, and no better if we do.

⁹Be careful, however, that the exercise of your rights does not become a stumbling block to the weak. ¹⁰For if someone with a weak conscience sees you, with all your knowledge, eating in an idol's temple, won't that person be emboldened to eat what is sacrificed to idols? ¹¹So this weak brother or sister, for whom Christ died, is destroyed by your knowledge. ¹²When you sin against them in this way and wound their weak conscience, you sin against Christ. ¹³Therefore, if what I eat causes my brother or sister to fall into sin, I will never eat meat again, so that I will not cause them to fall.

### Paul's Rights as an Apostle

**9** Am I not free? Am I not an apostle? Have I not seen Jesus our Lord? Are you not the result of my work in the Lord? ²Even though I may not be an apostle to others, surely I am to you! For you are the seal of my apostleship in the Lord.

³This is my defense to those who sit in judgment on me. ⁴Don't we have the right to food and drink? ⁵Don't we have the right to take a believing wife along with us, as do the other apostles and the Lord's brothers and Cephas*a*? ⁶Or is it only I and Barnabas who lack the right to not work for a living?

⁷Who serves as a soldier at his own expense? Who plants a vineyard and does not eat its grapes? Who tends a flock and does not drink the milk? ⁸Do I say this merely on human authority? Doesn't the Law say the same thing? ⁹For it is written in the Law of Moses: "Do not muzzle an ox while it is treading out the grain."*b* Is it about oxen that God is concerned? ¹⁰Surely he says this for us, doesn't he? Yes, this was written for us, because whoever plows and threshes should be able to do so in the hope of sharing in the harvest. ¹¹If we have sown spiritual seed among you, is it too much if we reap a material harvest from you? ¹²If others have this right of support from you, shouldn't we have it all the more?

But we did not use this right. On the contrary, we put up with anything rather than hinder the gospel of Christ.

¹³Don't you know that those who serve in the temple get their food from the temple, and that those who serve at the altar share in what is offered on the altar? ¹⁴In the same way, the Lord has commanded that those who preach the gospel should receive their living from the gospel.

## Amplified Bible

⁸Now food [itself] will not cause our acceptance by God *nor* commend us to Him. Eating [food offered to idols] gives us no advantage; neither do we come short *or* become any worse if we do not eat [it].

⁹Only be careful that this power of choice (this permission and liberty to do as you please) which is yours, does not [somehow] become a hindrance (cause of stumbling) to the weak *or* overscrupulous [giving them an impulse to sin].

¹⁰For suppose someone sees you, a man having knowledge [of God, with an intelligent view of this subject and] reclining at table in an idol's temple, might he not be encouraged *and* emboldened [to violate his own conscientious scruples] if he is weak *and* uncertain, and eat what [to him] is for the purpose of idol worship?

¹¹And so by your enlightenment (your knowledge of spiritual things), this weak man is ruined (is lost and perishes)—the brother for whom Christ (the Messiah) died!

¹²And when you sin against your brethren in this way, wounding *and* damaging their weak conscience, you sin against Christ.

¹³Therefore, if [my eating a] food is a cause of my brother's falling *or* of hindering [his spiritual advancement], I will not eat [such] flesh forever, lest I cause my brother to be tripped up *and* fall *and* to be offended.

**9** Am I not an apostle (a special messenger)? Am I not free (unrestrained and exempt from any obligation)? Have I not seen Jesus our Lord? Are you [yourselves] not [the product and proof of] my workmanship in the Lord?

²Even if I am not considered an apostle (a special messenger) by others, at least I am one to you; for you are the seal (the certificate, the living evidence) of my apostleship in the Lord [confirming and authenticating it].

³This is my [real ground of] defense (my vindication of myself) to those who would put me on trial *and* cross-examine me.

⁴Have we not the right to our food and drink [at the expense of the churches]?

⁵Have we not the right also to take along with us a Christian sister as wife, as do the other apostles and the Lord's brothers and Cephas (Peter)?

⁶Or is it only Barnabas and I who have no right to refrain from doing manual labor for a livelihood [in order to go about the work of the ministry]?

⁷[Consider this:] What soldier at any time serves at his own expense? Who plants a vineyard and does not eat any of the fruit of it? Who tends a flock and does not partake of the milk of the flock?

⁸Do I say this only on human authority *and* as a man reasons? Does not the Law endorse the same principle?

⁹For in the Law of Moses it is written, You shall not muzzle an ox when it is treading out the corn. Is it [only] for oxen that God cares? [Deut. 25:4.]

¹⁰Or does He speak certainly *and* entirely for our sakes? [Assuredly] it is written for our sakes, because the plowman ought to plow in hope, and the thresher ought to thresh in expectation of partaking of the harvest.

¹¹If we have sown [the seed of] spiritual good among you, [is it too] much if we reap from your material benefits?

¹²If others share in this rightful claim upon you, do not we [have a still better and greater claim]? However, we have never exercised this right, but we endure everything rather than put a hindrance in the way [of the spread] of the good news (the Gospel) of Christ.

¹³Do you not know that those men who are employed in the services of the temple get their food from the temple? And that those who tend the altar share with the altar [in the offerings brought]? [Deut. 18:1.]

¹⁴[On the same principle] the Lord directed that those who publish the good news (the Gospel) should live (get their maintenance) by the Gospel.

---

*a* 5 That is, Peter   *b* 9 Deut. 25:4

## New International Version

[15]But I have not used any of these rights. And I am not writing this in the hope that you will do such things for me, for I would rather die than allow anyone to deprive me of this boast. [16]For when I preach the gospel, I cannot boast, since I am compelled to preach. Woe to me if I do not preach the gospel! [17]If I preach voluntarily, I have a reward; if not voluntarily, I am simply discharging the trust committed to me. [18]What then is my reward? Just this: that in preaching the gospel I may offer it free of charge, and so not make full use of my rights as a preacher of the gospel.

### Paul's Use of His Freedom

[19]Though I am free and belong to no one, I have made myself a slave to everyone, to win as many as possible. [20]To the Jews I became like a Jew, to win the Jews. To those under the law I became like one under the law (though I myself am not under the law), so as to win those under the law. [21]To those not having the law I became like one not having the law (though I am not free from God's law but am under Christ's law), so as to win those not having the law. [22]To the weak I became weak, to win the weak. I have become all things to all people so that by all possible means I might save some. [23]I do all this for the sake of the gospel, that I may share in its blessings.

### The Need for Self-Discipline

[24]Do you not know that in a race all the runners run, but only one gets the prize? Run in such a way as to get the prize. [25]Everyone who competes in the games goes into strict training. They do it to get a crown that will not last, but we do it to get a crown that will last forever. [26]Therefore I do not run like someone running aimlessly; I do not fight like a boxer beating the air. [27]No, I strike a blow to my body and make it my slave so that after I have preached to others, I myself will not be disqualified for the prize.

### Warnings From Israel's History

**10** For I do not want you to be ignorant of the fact, brothers and sisters, that our ancestors were all under the cloud and that they all passed through the sea. [2]They were all baptized into Moses in the cloud and in the sea. [3]They all ate the same spiritual food [4]and drank the same spiritual drink; for they drank from the spiritual rock that accompanied them, and that rock was Christ.

## Amplified Bible

[15]But I have not made use of any of these privileges, nor am I writing this [to suggest] that any such provision be made for me [now]. For it would be better for me to die than to have anyone make void *and* deprive me of my [ground for] glorifying [in this matter].

[16]For if I [merely] preach the Gospel, that gives me no reason to boast, for I feel compelled of necessity to do it. Woe is me if I do not preach the glad tidings (the Gospel)!

[17]For if I do this work of my own free will, then I have my pay (my reward); but if it is not of my own will, but is done reluctantly *and* under compulsion, I am [still] entrusted with a [sacred] trusteeship *and* commission.

[18]What then is the [actual] reward that I get? Just this: that in my preaching the good news (the Gospel), I may offer it [absolutely] free of expense [to anybody], not taking advantage of my rights *and* privileges [as a preacher] of the Gospel.

[19]For although I am free in every way from anyone's control, I have made myself a bond servant to everyone, so that I might gain the more [for Christ].

[20]To the Jews I became as a Jew, that I might win Jews; to men under the Law, [I became] as one under the Law, though not myself being under the Law, that I might win those under the Law.

[21]To those without (outside) law I became as one without law, not that I am without the law of God *and* lawless toward Him, but that I am [especially keeping] within *and* committed to the law of Christ, that I might win those who are without law.

[22]To the weak (wanting in discernment) I have become weak (wanting in discernment) that I might win the weak *and* overscrupulous. I have [in short] become all things to all men, that I might by all means (at all costs and in any and every way) save some [by winning them to faith in Jesus Christ].

[23]And I do this for the sake of the good news (the Gospel), in order that I may become a participator in it *and* share in its [blessings along with you].

[24]Do you not know that in a race all the runners compete, but [only] one receives the prize? So run [your race] that you may lay hold [of the prize] *and* make it yours.

[25]Now every athlete who goes into training conducts himself temperately *and* restricts himself in all things. They do it to win a wreath that will soon wither, but we [do it to receive a crown of eternal blessedness] that cannot wither.

[26]Therefore I do not run uncertainly (without definite aim). I do not box like one beating the air *and* striking without an adversary.

[27]But [like a boxer] I buffet my body [handle it roughly, discipline it by hardships] and subdue it, for fear that after proclaiming to others the Gospel *and* things pertaining to it, I myself should become unfit [not stand the test, be unapproved and rejected as a counterfeit].

**10** For I do not want you to be ignorant, brethren, that our forefathers were all under *and* protected by the cloud [in which God's Presence went before them], and every one of them passed safely through the [Red] Sea, [Exod. 13:21; 14:22, 29.]

[2]And each one of them [allowed himself also] to be baptized into Moses in the cloud and in the sea [they were thus brought under obligation to the Law, to Moses, and to the covenant, consecrated and set apart to the service of God];

[3]And all [of them] ate the same spiritual (supernaturally given) food, [Exod. 16:4, 35.]

[4]And they all drank the same spiritual (supernaturally given) drink. For they drank from a spiritual Rock which followed them [produced by the sole power of God Himself without natural instrumentality], and the Rock was Christ. [Exod. 17:6; Num. 20:11.]

## New International Version

5Nevertheless, God was not pleased with most of them; their bodies were scattered in the wilderness.

6Now these things occurred as examples to keep us from setting our hearts on evil things as they did. 7Do not be idolaters, as some of them were; as it is written: "The people sat down to eat and drink and got up to indulge in revelry."[a] 8We should not commit sexual immorality, as some of them did—and in one day twenty-three thousand of them died. 9We should not test Christ,[b] as some of them did—and were killed by snakes. 10And do not grumble, as some of them did—and were killed by the destroying angel.

11These things happened to them as examples and were written down as warnings for us, on whom the culmination of the ages has come. 12So, if you think you are standing firm, be careful that you don't fall! 13No temptation[c] has overtaken you except what is common to mankind. And God is faithful; he will not let you be tempted[c] beyond what you can bear. But when you are tempted,[c] he will also provide a way out so that you can endure it.

### Idol Feasts and the Lord's Supper

14Therefore, my dear friends, flee from idolatry. 15I speak to sensible people; judge for yourselves what I say. 16Is not the cup of thanksgiving for which we give thanks a participation in the blood of Christ? And is not the bread that we break a participation in the body of Christ? 17Because there is one loaf, we, who are many, are one body, for we all share the one loaf.

18Consider the people of Israel: Do not those who eat the sacrifices participate in the altar? 19Do I mean then that food sacrificed to an idol is anything, or that an idol is anything? 20No, but the sacrifices of pagans are offered to demons, not to God, and I do not want you to be partici-

## Amplified Bible

5Nevertheless, God was not pleased with the great majority of them, for they were overthrown and strewn down along [the ground] in the wilderness. [Num. 14:29, 30.]

6Now these things are examples (warnings and admonitions) for us not to desire or crave or covet or lust after evil and carnal things as they did. [Num. 11:4, 34.]

7Do not be worshipers of false gods as some of them were, as it is written, The people sat down to eat and drink [the sacrifices offered to the golden calf at Horeb] and rose to sport (to dance and give way to jesting and hilarity). [Exod. 32:4, 6.]

8We must not gratify evil desire and indulge in immorality as some of them did—and twenty-three thousand [suddenly] fell dead in a single day! [Num. 25:1-18.]

9We should not tempt the Lord [try His patience, become a trial to Him, critically appraise Him, and exploit His goodness] as some of them did—and were killed by poisonous serpents; [Num. 21:5, 6.]

10Nor discontentedly complain as some of them did—and were [a]put out of the way entirely by the destroyer (death). [Num. 16:41, 49.]

11Now these things befell them by way of a figure [as an example and warning to us]; they were written to admonish and fit us for right action by good instruction, we in whose days the ages have reached their climax (their consummation and concluding period).

12Therefore let anyone who thinks he stands [who feels sure that he has a steadfast mind and is standing firm], take heed lest he fall [into sin].

13For no temptation (no trial regarded as enticing to sin), [no matter how it comes or where it leads] has overtaken you and laid hold on you that is not common to man [that is, no temptation or trial has come to you that is beyond human resistance and that is not [a]adjusted and [b]adapted and belonging to human experience, and such as man can bear]. But God is faithful [to His Word and to His compassionate nature], and He [can be trusted] not to let you be tempted and tried and assayed beyond your ability and strength of resistance and power to endure, but with the temptation He will [always] also provide the way out (the means of escape to [c]a landing place), that you may be capable and strong and powerful to bear up under it patiently.

14Therefore, my dearly beloved, shun (keep clear away from, avoid by flight if need be) any sort of idolatry (of loving or venerating anything more than God).

15I am speaking as to intelligent (sensible) men. Think over and make up your minds [for yourselves] about what I say. [I appeal to your reason and your discernment in these matters.]

16The cup of blessing [of wine at the Lord's Supper] upon which we ask [God's] blessing, does it not mean [that in drinking it] we participate in and share a fellowship (a communion) in the blood of Christ (the Messiah)? The bread which we break, does it not mean [that in eating it] we participate in and share a fellowship (a communion) in the body of Christ?

17For we [no matter how] numerous we are, are one body, because we all partake of the one Bread [the One Whom the communion bread represents].

18Consider those [physically] people of Israel. Are not those who eat the sacrifices partners of the altar [united in their worship of the same God]? [Lev. 7:6.]

19What do I imply then? That food offered to idols is [intrinsically changed by the fact and amounts to] anything or that an idol itself is a [living] thing?

20No, I am suggesting that what the pagans sacrifice they offer [in effect] to demons (to evil spiritual powers) and not to God [at all]. I do not want you to fellowship and be partners with diabolical spirits [by eating at their feasts]. [Deut. 32:17.]

---

[a] 7 Exodus 32:6   [b] 9 Some manuscripts test the Lord
[c] 13 The Greek for temptation and tempted can also mean testing and tested.

[a] Joseph Thayer, A Greek-English Lexicon.   [b] Henry Alford, The Greek New Testament.   [c] Marvin Vincent, Word Studies.

## New International Version

pants with demons. <sup>21</sup>You cannot drink the cup of the Lord and the cup of demons too; you cannot have a part in both the Lord's table and the table of demons. <sup>22</sup>Are we trying to arouse the Lord's jealousy? Are we stronger than he?

### The Believer's Freedom

<sup>23</sup>"I have the right to do anything," you say—but not everything is beneficial. "I have the right to do anything"—but not everything is constructive. <sup>24</sup>No one should seek their own good, but the good of others.

<sup>25</sup>Eat anything sold in the meat market without raising questions of conscience, <sup>26</sup>for, "The earth is the Lord's, and everything in it."ᵃ

<sup>27</sup>If an unbeliever invites you to a meal and you want to go, eat whatever is put before you without raising questions of conscience. <sup>28</sup>But if someone says to you, "This has been offered in sacrifice," then do not eat it, both for the sake of the one who told you and for the sake of conscience. <sup>29</sup>I am referring to the other person's conscience, not yours. For why is my freedom being judged by another's conscience? <sup>30</sup>If I take part in the meal with thankfulness, why am I denounced because of something I thank God for?

<sup>31</sup>So whether you eat or drink or whatever you do, do it all for the glory of God. <sup>32</sup>Do not cause anyone to stumble, whether Jews, Greeks or the church of God— <sup>33</sup>even as I try to please everyone in every way. For I am not seeking my own good but the good of many, so that they may be saved.

**11** <sup>1</sup>Follow my example, as I follow the example of Christ.

### On Covering the Head in Worship

<sup>2</sup>I praise you for remembering me in everything and for holding to the traditions just as I passed them on to you. <sup>3</sup>But I want you to realize that the head of every man is Christ, and the head of the woman is man,ᵇ and the head of Christ is God. <sup>4</sup>Every man who prays or prophesies with his head covered dishonors his head. <sup>5</sup>But every woman who prays or prophesies with her head uncovered dishonors her head—it is the same as having her head shaved. <sup>6</sup>For if a woman does not cover her head, she might as well have her hair cut off; but if it is a disgrace for a woman to have her hair cut off or her head shaved, then she should cover her head.

<sup>7</sup>A man ought not to cover his head,ᶜ since he is the image and glory of God; but woman is the glory of man. <sup>8</sup>For man did not come from woman, but woman from man;

---

ᵃ 26 Psalm 24:1   ᵇ 3 Or of the wife is her husband   ᶜ 4-7 Or ⁴Every man who prays or prophesies with long hair dishonors his head. ⁵But every woman who prays or prophesies with no covering of hair dishonors her head—she is just like one of the "shorn women." ⁶If a woman has no covering, let her be for now with short hair; but since it is a disgrace for a woman to have her hair shorn or shaved, she should grow it again. ⁷A man ought not to have long hair

## Amplified Bible

<sup>21</sup>You cannot drink the Lord's cup and the demons' cup. You cannot partake of the Lord's table and the demons' table.

<sup>22</sup>Shall we thus provoke the Lord to jealousy *and* anger *and* indignation? Are we stronger than He [that we should defy Him]? [Deut. 32:21; Eccl. 6:10; Isa. 45:9.]

<sup>23</sup>All things are legitimate [permissible—and we are free to do anything we please], but not all things are helpful (expedient, profitable, and wholesome). All things are legitimate, but not all things are constructive [to character] *and* edifying [to spiritual life].

<sup>24</sup>Let no one then seek his own good *and* advantage *and* profit, but [rather] each one of the other [let him seek the welfare of his neighbor].

<sup>25</sup>[As to meat offered to idols] eat anything that is sold in the meat market without raising any question *or* investigating on the grounds of conscientious scruples,

<sup>26</sup>For the [whole] earth is the Lord's and everything that is in it. [Ps. 24:1; 50:12.]

<sup>27</sup>In case one of the unbelievers invites you to a meal and you want to go, eat whatever is served to you without examining into its source because of conscientious scruples.

<sup>28</sup>But if someone tells you, This has been offered in sacrifice to an idol, do not eat it, out of consideration for the person who informed you, and for conscience's sake—

<sup>29</sup>I mean for the sake of his conscience, not yours, [do not eat it]. For why should another man's scruples apply to me *and* my liberty of action be determined by his conscience?

<sup>30</sup>If I partake [of my food] with thankfulness, why am I accused *and* spoken evil of because of that for which I give thanks?

<sup>31</sup>So then, whether you eat or drink, or whatever you may do, do all for the honor *and* glory of God.

<sup>32</sup>Do not let yourselves be [hindrances by giving] an offense to the Jews or to the Greeks or to the church of God [ᵃdo not lead others into sin by your mode of life];

<sup>33</sup>Just as I myself strive to please [to accommodate myself to the opinions, desires, and interests of others, adapting myself to] all men in everything I do, not aiming at *or* considering my own profit *and* advantage, but that of the many in order that they may be saved.

**11** Pattern yourselves after me [follow my example], as I imitate *and* follow Christ (the Messiah).

<sup>2</sup>I appreciate *and* commend you because you always remember me in everything and keep firm possession of the traditions (the substance of my instructions), just as I have [verbally] passed them on to you.

<sup>3</sup>But I want you to know *and* realize that Christ is the Head of every man, the head of a woman is her husband, and the Head of Christ is God.

<sup>4</sup>Any man who prays or prophesies (teaches, refutes, reproves, admonishes, and comforts) with his head covered dishonors his Head (Christ).

<sup>5</sup>And any woman who [publicly] prays or prophesies (teaches, refutes, reproves, admonishes, or comforts) when she is bareheaded dishonors her head (her husband); it is the same as [if her head were] shaved.

<sup>6</sup>For if a woman will not wear [a head] covering, then she should cut off her hair too; but if it is disgraceful for a woman to have her head shorn or shaven, let her cover [her head].

<sup>7</sup>For a man ought not to wear anything on his head [in church], for he is the image and [reflected] glory of God [ᵃhis function of government reflects the majesty of the divine Rule]; but woman is [the expression of] man's glory (majesty, preeminence). [Gen. 1:26.]

<sup>8</sup>For man was not [created] from woman, but woman from man; [Gen. 2:21-23.]

---

ᵃ Joseph Thayer, *A Greek-English Lexicon.*

## New International Version

9neither was man created for woman, but woman for man. 10It is for this reason that a woman ought to have authority over her own[a] head, because of the angels. 11Nevertheless, in the Lord woman is not independent of man, nor is man independent of woman. 12For as woman came from man, so also man is born of woman. But everything comes from God.

13Judge for yourselves: Is it proper for a woman to pray to God with her head uncovered? 14Does not the very nature of things teach you that if a man has long hair, it is a disgrace to him, 15but that if a woman has long hair, it is her glory? For long hair is given to her as a covering. 16If anyone wants to be contentious about this, we have no other practice—nor do the churches of God.

### Correcting an Abuse of the Lord's Supper

17In the following directives I have no praise for you, for your meetings do more harm than good. 18In the first place, I hear that when you come together as a church, there are divisions among you, and to some extent I believe it. 19No doubt there have to be differences among you to show which of you have God's approval. 20So then, when you come together, it is not the Lord's Supper you eat, 21for when you are eating, some of you go ahead with your own private suppers. As a result, one person remains hungry and another gets drunk. 22Don't you have homes to eat and drink in? Or do you despise the church of God by humiliating those who have nothing? What shall I say to you? Shall I praise you? Certainly not in this matter!

23For I received from the Lord what I also passed on to you: The Lord Jesus, on the night he was betrayed, took bread, 24and when he had given thanks, he broke it and said, "This is my body, which is for you; do this in remembrance of me." 25In the same way, after supper he took the cup, saying, "This cup is the new covenant in my blood; do this, whenever you drink it, in remembrance of me." 26For whenever you eat this bread and drink this cup, you proclaim the Lord's death until he comes.

27So then, whoever eats the bread or drinks the cup of the Lord in an unworthy manner will be guilty of sinning against the body and blood of the Lord. 28Everyone ought to examine themselves before they eat of the bread and

## Amplified Bible

9Neither was man created on account of or for the benefit of woman, but woman on account of and for the benefit of man. [Gen. 2:18.]

10[a]Therefore she should [be subject to his authority and should] have a covering on her head [as a token, a symbol, of her submission to authority, [b]that she may show reverence as do] the angels [and not displease them].

11Nevertheless, in [the plan of] the Lord and from His point of view woman is not apart from and independent of man, nor is man aloof from and independent of woman;

12For as woman was made from man, even so man is also born of woman; and all [whether male or female go forth] from God [as their Author].

13Consider for yourselves; is it proper and decent [according to your customs] for a woman to offer prayer to God [publicly] with her head uncovered?

14Does not [b]the native sense of propriety (experience, common sense, reason) itself teach you that for a man to wear long hair is a dishonor [humiliating and degrading] to him,

15But if a woman has long hair, it is her ornament and glory? For her hair is given to her for a covering.

16Now if anyone is disposed to be argumentative and contentious about this, we hold to and recognize no other custom [in worship] than this, nor do the churches of God generally.

17But in what I instruct [you] next I do not commend [you], because when you meet together, it is not for the better but for the worse.

18For in the first place, when you assemble as a congregation, I hear that there are cliques (divisions and factions) among you; and I in part believe it,

19For doubtless there have to be factions or parties among you in order that they who are genuine and of approved fitness may become evident and plainly recognized among you.

20So when you gather for your meetings, it is not the supper instituted by the Lord that you eat,

21For in eating each one [hurries] to get his own supper first [not waiting for the poor], and one goes hungry while another gets drunk.

22What! Do you have no houses in which to eat and drink? Or do you despise the church of God and mean to show contempt for it, while you humiliate those who are poor (have no homes and have brought no food)? What shall I say to you? Shall I commend you in this? No, [most certainly] I will not!

23For I received from the Lord Himself that which I passed on to you [it was given to me personally], that the Lord Jesus on the night when He was treacherously delivered up and while His betrayal was in progress took bread,

24And when He had given thanks, He broke [it] and said, Take, eat. This is My body, which is broken for you. Do this to call Me [affectionately] to remembrance.

25Similarly when supper was ended, He took the cup also, saying, This cup is the new covenant [ratified and established] in My blood. Do this, as often as you drink [it], to call Me [affectionately] to remembrance.

26For every time you eat this bread and drink this cup, you are representing and signifying and proclaiming the fact of the Lord's death until He comes [again].

27So then whoever eats the bread or drinks the cup of the Lord in a way that is unworthy [of Him] will be guilty of [profaning and sinning against] the body and blood of the Lord.

28Let a man [thoroughly] examine himself, and [only when he has done] so should he eat of the bread and drink of the cup.

---

[a] 10 Or have a sign of authority on her

[a] G. D. Kypke, cited by Adam Clarke, The Holy Bible with A Commentary.
[b] Joseph Thayer, A Greek-English Lexicon.

## New International Version

drink from the cup. ²⁹For those who eat and drink without discerning the body of Christ eat and drink judgment on themselves. ³⁰That is why many among you are weak and sick, and a number of you have fallen asleep. ³¹But if we were more discerning with regard to ourselves, we would not come under such judgment. ³²Nevertheless, when we are judged in this way by the Lord, we are being disciplined so that we will not be finally condemned with the world.

³³So then, my brothers and sisters, when you gather to eat, you should all eat together. ³⁴Anyone who is hungry should eat something at home, so that when you meet together it may not result in judgment.

And when I come I will give further directions.

### Concerning Spiritual Gifts

**12** Now about the gifts of the Spirit, brothers and sisters, I do not want you to be uninformed. ²You know that when you were pagans, somehow or other you were influenced and led astray to mute idols. ³Therefore I want you to know that no one who is speaking by the Spirit of God says, "Jesus be cursed," and no one can say, "Jesus is Lord," except by the Holy Spirit.

⁴There are different kinds of gifts, but the same Spirit distributes them. ⁵There are different kinds of service, but the same Lord. ⁶There are different kinds of working, but in all of them and in everyone it is the same God at work.

⁷Now to each one the manifestation of the Spirit is given for the common good. ⁸To one there is given through the Spirit a message of wisdom, to another a message of knowledge by means of the same Spirit, ⁹to another faith by the same Spirit, to another gifts of healing by that one Spirit, ¹⁰to another miraculous powers, to another prophecy, to another distinguishing between spirits, to another speaking in different kinds of tongues,ᵃ and to still another the interpretation of tongues.ᵃ ¹¹All these are the work of one and the same Spirit, and he distributes them to each one, just as he determines.

### Unity and Diversity in the Body

¹²Just as a body, though one, has many parts, but all its many parts form one body, so it is with Christ. ¹³For we were all baptized byᵇ one Spirit so as to form one body—whether Jews or Gentiles, slave or free—and we were all

## Amplified Bible

²⁹For anyone who eats and drinks without discriminating *and* recognizing with due appreciation that [it is Christ's] body, eats and drinks a sentence (a verdict of judgment) upon himself.

³⁰That [careless and unworthy participation] is the reason many of you are weak and sickly, and quite enough of you have fallen into the sleep of death.

³¹For if we searchingly examined ourselves [detecting our shortcomings and recognizing our own condition], we should not be judged *and* penalty decreed [by the divine judgment].

³²But when we [fall short and] are judged by the Lord, we are disciplined *and* chastened, so that we may not [finally] be condemned [to eternal punishment along] with the world.

³³So then, my brothers, when you gather together to eat [the Lord's Supper], wait for one another.

³⁴If anyone is hungry, let him eat at home, lest you come together to bring judgment [on yourselves]. About the other matters, I will give you directions [personally] when I come.

**12** Now about the spiritual gifts (the special endowments of supernatural energy), brethren, I do not want you to be misinformed.

²You know that when you were heathen, you were led off after idols that could not speak [habitually] as impulse directed *and* whenever the occasion might arise.

³Therefore I want you to understand that no one speaking under the power *and* influence of the [Holy] Spirit of God can [ever] say, Jesus be cursed! And no one can [really] say, Jesus is [my] Lord, except by *and* under the power *and* influence of the Holy Spirit.

⁴Now there are distinctive varieties *and* distributions of endowments (gifts, ᵃextraordinary powers distinguishing certain Christians, due to the power of divine grace operating in their souls by the Holy Spirit) and they vary, but the [Holy] Spirit remains the same.

⁵And there are distinctive varieties of service *and* ministration, but it is the same Lord [Who is served].

⁶And there are distinctive varieties of operation [of working to accomplish things], but it is the same God Who inspires *and* energizes them all in all.

⁷But to each one is given the manifestation of the [Holy] Spirit [the evidence, the spiritual illumination of the Spirit] for good *and* profit.

⁸To one is given in *and* through the [Holy] Spirit [the power to speak] a message of wisdom, and to another [the power to express] a word of knowledge *and* understanding according to the same [Holy] Spirit;

⁹To another [ᵇwonder-working] faith by the same [Holy] Spirit, to another the extraordinary powers of healing by the one Spirit;

¹⁰To another the working of miracles, to another prophetic insight (ᶜthe gift of interpreting the divine will and purpose); to another the ability to discern *and* distinguish between [the utterances of true] spirits [and false ones], to another various kinds of [unknown] tongues, to another the ability to interpret [such] tongues.

¹¹All these [gifts, achievements, abilities] are inspired *and* brought to pass by one and the same [Holy] Spirit, Who apportions to each person individually [exactly] as He chooses.

¹²For just as the body is a unity and yet has many parts, and all the parts, though many, form [only] one body, so it is with Christ (the Messiah, the Anointed One).

¹³For by [ᵈmeans of the personal agency of] one [Holy] Spirit we were all, whether Jews or Greeks, slaves or free, baptized [and ᵃby baptism united together] into one body, and all made to drink of one [Holy] Spirit.

---

ᵃ Joseph Thayer, *A Greek-English Lexicon*.   ᵇ Marvin Vincent, *Word Studies*.   ᶜ G. Abbott-Smith, *Manual Greek Lexicon*.   ᵈ Kenneth Wuest, *Word Studies*.

---

ᵃ 10 Or *languages*; also in verse 28     ᵇ 13 Or *with*; or *in*

## New International Version

given the one Spirit to drink. [14]Even so the body is not made up of one part but of many.

[15]Now if the foot should say, "Because I am not a hand, I do not belong to the body," it would not for that reason stop being part of the body. [16]And if the ear should say, "Because I am not an eye, I do not belong to the body," it would not for that reason stop being part of the body. [17]If the whole body were an eye, where would the sense of hearing be? If the whole body were an ear, where would the sense of smell be? [18]But in fact God has placed the parts in the body, every one of them, just as he wanted them to be. [19]If they were all one part, where would the body be? [20]As it is, there are many parts, but one body.

[21]The eye cannot say to the hand, "I don't need you!" And the head cannot say to the feet, "I don't need you!" [22]On the contrary, those parts of the body that seem to be weaker are indispensable, [23]and the parts that we think are less honorable we treat with special honor. And the parts that are unpresentable are treated with special modesty, [24]while our presentable parts need no special treatment. But God has put the body together, giving greater honor to the parts that lacked it, [25]so that there should be no division in the body, but that its parts should have equal concern for each other. [26]If one part suffers, every part suffers with it; if one part is honored, every part rejoices with it.

[27]Now you are the body of Christ, and each one of you is a part of it. [28]And God has placed in the church first of all apostles, second prophets, third teachers, then miracles, then gifts of healing, of helping, of guidance, and of different kinds of tongues. [29]Are all apostles? Are all prophets? Are all teachers? Do all work miracles? [30]Do all have gifts of healing? Do all speak in tongues[a]? Do all interpret? [31]Now eagerly desire the greater gifts.

### Love Is Indispensable

And yet I will show you the most excellent way.

**13** If I speak in the tongues[b] of men or of angels, but do not have love, I am only a resounding gong or a clanging cymbal. [2]If I have the gift of prophecy and can fathom all mysteries and all knowledge, and if I have a faith that can move mountains, but do not have love, I am

## Amplified Bible

[14]For the body does not consist of one limb *or* organ but of many.

[15]If the foot should say, Because I am not the hand, I do not belong to the body, would it be therefore not [a part] of the body?

[16]If the ear should say, Because I am not the eye, I do not belong to the body, would it be therefore not [a part] of the body?

[17]If the whole body were an eye, where [would be the sense of] hearing? If the whole body were an ear, where [would be the sense of] smell?

[18]But as it is, God has placed *and* arranged the limbs *and* organs in the body, each [particular one] of them, just as He wished *and* saw fit *and* with the best adaptation.

[19]But if [the whole] were all a single organ, where would the body be?

[20]And now there are [certainly] many limbs *and* organs, but a single body.

[21]And the eye is not able to say to the hand, I have no need of you, nor again the head to the feet, I have no need of you.

[22]But instead, there is [absolute] necessity for the parts of the body that are considered the more weak.

[23]And those [parts] of the body which we consider rather ignoble are [the very parts] which we invest with additional honor, and our unseemly parts *and* those unsuitable for exposure are treated with seemliness (modesty and decorum],

[24]Which our more presentable parts do not require. But God has so adjusted (mingled, harmonized, and subtly proportioned the parts of) the whole body, giving the greater honor *and* richer endowment to the inferior parts which lack [apparent importance],

[25]So that there should be no division *or* discord *or* lack of adaptation [of the parts of the body to each other], but the members all alike should have a mutual interest in *and* care for one another.

[26]And if one member suffers, all the parts [share] the suffering; if one member is honored, all the members [share in] the enjoyment of it.

[27]Now you [collectively] are Christ's body and [individually] you are members of it, each part severally *and* distinct [each with his own place and function].

[28]So God has appointed some in the church [[a]for His own use]: first apostles (special messengers); second prophets (inspired preachers and expounders); third teachers; then wonder-workers; then those with ability to heal the sick; helpers; administrators; [speakers in] different (unknown) tongues.

[29]Are all apostles (special messengers)? Are all prophets (inspired interpreters of the will and purposes of God)? Are all teachers? Do all have the power of performing miracles?

[30]Do all possess extraordinary powers of healing? Do all speak with tongues? Do all interpret?

[31]But earnestly desire *and* zealously cultivate the greatest *and* best gifts *and* graces (the higher gifts and the choicest graces). And yet I will show you a still more excellent way [one that is better by far and the highest of them all—love].

**13** If I [can] speak in the tongues of men and [even] of angels, but have not love (that reasoning, intentional, spiritual devotion such [b]as is inspired by God's love for and in us), I am only a noisy gong or a clanging cymbal.

[2]And if I have prophetic powers ([c]the gift of interpreting the divine will and purpose), and understand all the secret truths *and* mysteries and possess all knowledge, and if I have [sufficient] faith so that I can remove mountains, but have not love (God's love in me) I am nothing (a useless nobody).

---

[a] 30 Or *other languages*   [b] 1 Or *languages*

[a] Marvin Vincent, *Word Studies*.   [b] Alexander Souter, *Pocket Lexicon*.
[c] G. Abbott-Smith, *Manual Greek Lexicon*.

## New International Version

nothing. ³If I give all I possess to the poor and give over my body to hardship that I may boast,ᵃ but do not have love, I gain nothing.

⁴Love is patient, love is kind. It does not envy, it does not boast, it is not proud. ⁵It does not dishonor others, it is not self-seeking, it is not easily angered, it keeps no record of wrongs. ⁶Love does not delight in evil but rejoices with the truth. ⁷It always protects, always trusts, always hopes, always perseveres.

⁸Love never fails. But where there are prophecies, they will cease; where there are tongues, they will be stilled; where there is knowledge, it will pass away. ⁹For we know in part and we prophesy in part, ¹⁰but when completeness comes, what is in part disappears. ¹¹When I was a child, I talked like a child, I thought like a child, I reasoned like a child. When I became a man, I put the ways of childhood behind me. ¹²For now we see only a reflection as in a mirror; then we shall see face to face. Now I know in part; then I shall know fully, even as I am fully known.

¹³And now these three remain: faith, hope and love. But the greatest of these is love.

### Intelligibility in Worship

**14** Follow the way of love and eagerly desire gifts of the Spirit, especially prophecy. ²For anyone who speaks in a tongueᵇ does not speak to people but to God. Indeed, no one understands them; they utter mysteries by the Spirit. ³But the one who prophesies speaks to people for their strengthening, encouraging and comfort. ⁴Anyone who speaks in a tongue edifies themselves, but the one who prophesies edifies the church. ⁵I would like every

## Amplified Bible

³Even if I dole out all that I have [to the poor in providing] food, and if I surrender my body to be burned or ᵃin order that I may glory, but have not love (God's love in me), I gain nothing.

⁴Love endures long and is patient and kind; love never is envious nor boils over with jealousy, is not boastful or vainglorious, does not display itself haughtily.

⁵It is not conceited (arrogant and inflated with pride); it is not rude (unmannerly) and does not act unbecomingly. Love (God's love in us) does not insist on its own rights or its own way, for it is not self-seeking; it is not touchy or fretful or resentful; it takes no account of the evil done to it [it pays no attention to a suffered wrong].

⁶It does not rejoice at injustice and unrighteousness, but rejoices when right and truth prevail.

⁷Love bears up under anything and everything that comes, is ever ready to believe the best of every person, its hopes are fadeless under all circumstances, and it endures everything [without weakening].

⁸Love never fails [never fades out or becomes obsolete or comes to an end]. As for prophecy (ᵇthe gift of interpreting the divine will and purpose), it will be fulfilled and pass away; as for tongues, they will be destroyed and cease; as for knowledge, it will pass away [it will lose its value and be superseded by truth].

⁹For our knowledge is fragmentary (incomplete and imperfect), and our prophecy (our teaching) is fragmentary (incomplete and imperfect).

¹⁰But when the complete and perfect (total) comes, the incomplete and imperfect will vanish away (become antiquated, void, and superseded).

¹¹When I was a child, I talked like a child, I thought like a child, I reasoned like a child; now that I have become a man, I am done with childish ways and have put them aside.

¹²For now we are looking in a mirror that gives only a dim (blurred) reflection [of reality as ᶜin a riddle or enigma], but then [when perfection comes] we shall see in reality and face to face! Now I know in part (imperfectly), but then I shall know and understand ᶜfully and clearly, even in the same manner as I have been ᶜfully and clearly known and understood [ᵈby God].

¹³And so faith, hope, love abide [faith—conviction and belief respecting man's relation to God and divine things; hope—joyful and confident expectation of eternal salvation; love—true affection for God and man, growing out of God's love for and in us], these three; but the greatest of these is love.

**14** Eagerly pursue and seek to acquire [this] love [make it your aim, your great quest]; and earnestly desire and cultivate the spiritual endowments (gifts), especially that you may prophesy (ᵇinterpret the divine will and purpose in inspired preaching and teaching).

²For one who speaks in an [unknown] tongue speaks not to men but to God, for no one understands or catches his meaning, because in the [Holy] Spirit he utters secret truths and hidden things [not obvious to the understanding].

³But [on the other hand], the one who prophesies [who ᵇinterprets the divine will and purpose in inspired preaching and teaching] speaks to men for their upbuilding and constructive spiritual progress and encouragement and consolation.

⁴He who speaks in a [strange] tongue edifies and improves himself, but he who prophesies [ᵇinterpreting the divine will and purpose and teaching with inspiration] edifies and improves the church and promotes growth [in Christian wisdom, piety, holiness, and happiness].

---

ᵃ 3 Some manuscripts *body to the flames*    ᵇ 2 Or *in another language*; also in verses 4, 13, 14, 19, 26 and 27

ᵃ Some ancient manuscripts so read.  ᵇ G. Abbott-Smith, *Manual Greek Lexicon*.  ᶜ Marvin Vincent, *Word Studies*.  ᵈ Matthew Henry, *Commentary on the Holy Bible*.

## New International Version

one of you to speak in tongues,[a] but I would rather have you prophesy. The one who prophesies is greater than the one who speaks in tongues,[a] unless someone interprets, so that the church may be edified.

[6]Now, brothers and sisters, if I come to you and speak in tongues, what good will I be to you, unless I bring you some revelation or knowledge or prophecy or word of instruction? [7]Even in the case of lifeless things that make sounds, such as the pipe or harp, how will anyone know what tune is being played unless there is a distinction in the notes? [8]Again, if the trumpet does not sound a clear call, who will get ready for battle? [9]So it is with you. Unless you speak intelligible words with your tongue, how will anyone know what you are saying? You will just be speaking into the air. [10]Undoubtedly there are all sorts of languages in the world, yet none of them is without meaning. [11]If then I do not grasp the meaning of what someone is saying, I am a foreigner to the speaker, and the speaker is a foreigner to me. [12]So it is with you. Since you are eager for gifts of the Spirit, try to excel in those that build up the church.

[13]For this reason the one who speaks in a tongue should pray that they may interpret what they say. [14]For if I pray in a tongue, my spirit prays, but my mind is unfruitful. [15]So what shall I do? I will pray with my spirit, but I will also pray with my understanding; I will sing with my spirit, but I will also sing with my understanding. [16]Otherwise when you are praising God in the Spirit, how can someone else, who is now put in the position of an inquirer,[b] say "Amen" to your thanksgiving, since they do not know what you are saying? [17]You are giving thanks well enough, but no one else is edified.

[18]I thank God that I speak in tongues more than all of you. [19]But in the church I would rather speak five intelligible words to instruct others than ten thousand words in a tongue.

[20]Brothers and sisters, stop thinking like children. In regard to evil be infants, but in your thinking be adults. [21]In the Law it is written:

"With other tongues
    and through the lips of foreigners
I will speak to this people,
    but even then they will not listen to me,
                              says the Lord."[c]

[22]Tongues, then, are a sign, not for believers but for unbelievers; prophecy, however, is not for unbelievers but for

[a] 5 Or in other languages; also in verses 6, 18, 22, 23 and 39
[b] 16 The Greek word for inquirer is a technical term for someone not fully initiated into a religion; also in verses 23 and 24.
[c] 21 Isaiah 28:11,12

## Amplified Bible

[5]Now I wish that you might all speak in [unknown] tongues, but more especially [I want you] to prophesy (to be inspired to preach and interpret the divine will and purpose). He who prophesies [who is inspired to preach and teach] is greater (more useful and more important) than he who speaks in [unknown] tongues, unless he should interpret [what he says], so that the church may be edified and receive good [from it].

[6]Now, brethren, if I come to you speaking in [unknown] tongues, how shall I make it to your advantage unless I speak to you either in revelation (disclosure of God's will to man) in knowledge or in prophecy or in instruction?

[7]If even inanimate musical instruments, such as the flute or the harp, do not give distinct notes, how will anyone [listening] know or understand what is played?

[8]And if the war bugle gives an uncertain (indistinct) call, who will prepare for battle?

[9]Just so it is with you; if you in the [unknown] tongue speak words that are not intelligible, how will anyone understand what you are saying? For you will be talking into empty space!

[10]There are, I suppose, all these many [to us unknown] tongues in the world [somewhere], and none is destitute of [its own power of] expression and meaning.

[11]But if I do not know the force and significance of the speech (language), I shall seem to be a foreigner to the one who speaks [to me], and the speaker who addresses [me] will seem a foreigner to me.

[12]So it is with yourselves; since you are so eager and ambitious to possess spiritual endowments and manifestations of the [Holy] Spirit, [concentrate on] striving to excel and to abound [in them] in ways that will build up the church.

[13]Therefore, the person who speaks in an [unknown] tongue should pray [for the power] to interpret and explain what he says.

[14]For if I pray in an [unknown] tongue, my spirit [by the [a]Holy Spirit within me] prays, but my mind is unproductive [it bears no fruit and helps nobody].

[15]Then what am I to do? I will pray with my spirit [by the [a]Holy Spirit that is within me], but I will also pray [intelligently] with my mind and understanding; I will sing with my spirit [by the Holy Spirit that is within me], but I will sing [intelligently] with my mind and understanding also.

[16]Otherwise, if you bless and render thanks with [your] spirit [[b]thoroughly aroused by the Holy Spirit], how can anyone in the position of an outsider or he who is not gifted with [interpreting of unknown] tongues, say the Amen to your thanksgiving, since he does not know what you are saying? [I Chron. 16:36; Ps. 106:48.]

[17]To be sure, you may give thanks well (nobly), but the bystander is not edified [it does him no good].

[18]I thank God that I speak in [strange] tongues (languages) more than any of you or all of you put together;

[19]Nevertheless, in public worship, I would rather say five words with my understanding and intelligently in order to instruct others, than ten thousand words in a [strange] tongue (language).

[20]Brethren, do not be children [immature] in your thinking; continue to be babes in [matters of] evil, but in your minds be mature [men].

[21]It is written in the Law, By men of strange languages and by the lips of foreigners will I speak to this people, and not even then will they listen to Me, says the Lord. [Isa. 28:11, 12.]

[22]Thus [unknown] tongues are meant for a [supernatural] sign, not for believers but for unbelievers [on the point of believing], while prophecy (inspired preaching and teaching, interpreting the divine will and purpose) is not for unbelievers [on the point of believing] but for believers.

[a] Marvin Vincent, Word Studies.   [b] Joseph Thayer, A Greek-English Lexicon.

## New International Version

believers. 23So if the whole church comes together and everyone speaks in tongues, and inquirers or unbelievers come in, will they not say that you are out of your mind? 24But if an unbeliever or an inquirer comes in while everyone is prophesying, they are convicted of sin and are brought under judgment by all, 25as the secrets of their hearts are laid bare. So they will fall down and worship God, exclaiming, "God is really among you!"

### Good Order in Worship

26What then shall we say, brothers and sisters? When you come together, each of you has a hymn, or a word of instruction, a revelation, a tongue or an interpretation. Everything must be done so that the church may be built up. 27If anyone speaks in a tongue, two—or at the most three—should speak, one at a time, and someone must interpret. 28If there is no interpreter, the speaker should keep quiet in the church and speak to himself and to God.

29Two or three prophets should speak, and the others should weigh carefully what is said. 30And if a revelation comes to someone who is sitting down, the first speaker should stop. 31For you can all prophesy in turn so that everyone may be instructed and encouraged. 32The spirits of prophets are subject to the control of prophets. 33For God is not a God of disorder but of peace—as in all the congregations of the Lord's people.

34Women*a* should remain silent in the churches. They are not allowed to speak, but must be in submission, as the law says. 35If they want to inquire about something, they should ask their own husbands at home; for it is disgraceful for a woman to speak in the church.*b*

36Or did the word of God originate with you? Or are you the only people it has reached? 37If anyone thinks they are a prophet or otherwise gifted by the Spirit, let them acknowledge that what I am writing to you is the Lord's command. 38But if anyone ignores this, they will themselves be ignored.*c*

39Therefore, my brothers and sisters, be eager to prophesy, and do not forbid speaking in tongues. 40But everything should be done in a fitting and orderly way.

### The Resurrection of Christ

**15** Now, brothers and sisters, I want to remind you of the gospel I preached to you, which you received and on which you have taken your stand. 2By this gospel

## Amplified Bible

23Therefore, if the whole church assembles and all of you speak in [unknown] tongues, and the ungifted *and* uninitiated or unbelievers come in, will they not say that you are demented?

24But if all prophesy [giving inspired testimony and interpreting the divine will and purpose] and an unbeliever or untaught outsider comes in, he is told of his sin *and* reproved *and* convicted *and* convinced by all, and his defects *and* needs are examined (estimated, determined) *and* he is called to account by all,

25The secrets of his heart are laid bare; and so, falling on [his] face, he will worship God, declaring that God is among you in very truth.

26What then, brethren, is [the right course]? When you meet together, each one has a hymn, a teaching, a disclosure of special knowledge *or* information, an utterance in a [strange] tongue, or an interpretation of it. [But] let everything be constructive *and* edifying and for the good of all.

27If some speak in a [strange] tongue, let the number be limited to two or at the most three, and each one [taking his] turn, and let one interpret *and* explain [what is said].

28But if there is no one to do the interpreting, let each of them keep still in church and talk to himself and to God.

29So let two or three prophets speak [those inspired to preach or teach], while the rest pay attention *and* weigh *and* discern what is said.

30But if an inspired revelation comes to another who is sitting by, then let the first one be silent.

31For in this way you can give testimony [prophesying and thus interpreting the divine will and purpose] one by one, so that all may be instructed and all may be stimulated *and* encouraged;

32For the spirits of the prophets (the speakers in tongues) are under the speaker's control [and subject to being silenced as may be necessary],

33For He [Who is the source of their prophesying] is not a God of confusion *and* disorder but of peace *and* order. As [is the practice] in all the churches of the saints (God's people),

34The women should keep quiet in the churches, for they are not authorized to speak, but should take a secondary *and* subordinate place, just as the Law also says. [Gen. 3:16.]

35But if there is anything they want to learn, they should ask their own husbands at home, for it is disgraceful for a woman to talk in church [*a*for her to usurp and exercise authority over men in the church].

36What! Did the word of the Lord originate with you [Corinthians], or has it reached only you?

37If anyone thinks *and* claims that he is a prophet [filled with and governed by the Holy Spirit of God and inspired to interpret the divine will and purpose in preaching or teaching] or has any other spiritual endowment, let him understand (recognize and acknowledge) that what I am writing to you is a command of the Lord.

38But if anyone disregards *or* does not recognize [*b*that it is a command of the Lord], he is disregarded *and* not recognized [he is *c*one whom God knows not].

39So [to conclude], my brethren, earnestly desire *and* set your hearts on prophesying (on being inspired to preach and teach and to interpret God's will and purpose), and do not forbid *or* hinder speaking in [unknown] tongues.

40But all things should be done with regard to decency *and* propriety and in an orderly fashion.

**15** And now let me remind you [since it seems to have escaped you], brethren, of the Gospel (the glad tidings of salvation) which I proclaimed to you, which you welcomed *and* accepted and upon which your faith rests,

---

*a* 33,34 Or *peace. As in all the congregations of the Lord's people,* 34*women*
*b* 34,35 In a few manuscripts these verses come after verse 40.
*c* 38 Some manuscripts *But anyone who is ignorant of this will be ignorant*

*a* W. Robertson Nicoll, ed., *The Expositor's Greek New Testament.*
*b* Joseph Thayer, *A Greek-English Lexicon.* *c* Marvin Vincent, *Word Studies.* Some manuscripts read: "he is not known."

## New International Version

you are saved, if you hold firmly to the word I preached to you. Otherwise, you have believed in vain.

[3] For what I received I passed on to you as of first importance[a]: that Christ died for our sins according to the Scriptures, [4] that he was buried, that he was raised on the third day according to the Scriptures, [5] and that he appeared to Cephas,[b] and then to the Twelve. [6] After that, he appeared to more than five hundred of the brothers and sisters at the same time, most of whom are still living, though some have fallen asleep. [7] Then he appeared to James, then to all the apostles, [8] and last of all he appeared to me also, as to one abnormally born.

[9] For I am the least of the apostles and do not even deserve to be called an apostle, because I persecuted the church of God. [10] But by the grace of God I am what I am, and his grace to me was not without effect. No, I worked harder than all of them—yet not I, but the grace of God that was with me. [11] Whether, then, it is I or they, this is what we preach, and this is what you believed.

### The Resurrection of the Dead

[12] But if it is preached that Christ has been raised from the dead, how can some of you say that there is no resurrection of the dead? [13] If there is no resurrection of the dead, then not even Christ has been raised. [14] And if Christ has not been raised, our preaching is useless and so is your faith. [15] More than that, we are then found to be false witnesses about God, for we have testified about God that he raised Christ from the dead. But he did not raise him if in fact the dead are not raised. [16] For if the dead are not raised, then Christ has not been raised either. [17] And if Christ has not been raised, your faith is futile; you are still in your sins. [18] Then those also who have fallen asleep in Christ are lost. [19] If only for this life we have hope in Christ, we are of all people most to be pitied.

[20] But Christ has indeed been raised from the dead, the firstfruits of those who have fallen asleep. [21] For since death came through a man, the resurrection of the dead comes also through a man. [22] For as in Adam all die, so in Christ all will be made alive. [23] But each in turn: Christ, the firstfruits; then, when he comes, those who belong to him. [24] Then the end will come, when he hands over the kingdom to God the Father after he has destroyed all dominion, authority and power. [25] For he must reign until he

## Amplified Bible

[2] And by which you are saved, if you hold fast *and* keep firmly what I preached to you, unless you believed at first without effect *and* all for nothing.

[3] For I passed on to you first of all what I also had received, that Christ (the Messiah, the Anointed One) died for our sins in accordance with [what] the Scriptures [foretold], [Isa. 53:5-12.]

[4] That He was buried, that He arose on the third day as the Scriptures foretold, [Ps. 16:9, 10.]

[5] And [also] that He appeared to Cephas (Peter), then to the Twelve.

[6] Then later He showed Himself to more than five hundred brethren at one time, the majority of whom are still alive, but some have fallen asleep [in death].

[7] Afterward He was seen by James, then by all the apostles (the special messengers),

[8] And last of all He appeared to me also, as to one prematurely *and* born dead [[a] no better than an unperfected fetus among living men].

[9] For I am the least [worthy] of the apostles, who am not fit *or* deserving to be called an apostle, because I once wronged *and* pursued *and* molested the church of God [oppressing it with cruelty and violence].

[10] But by the grace (the unmerited favor and blessing) of God I am what I am, and His grace toward me was not [found to be] for nothing (fruitless and without effect). In fact, I worked harder than all of them [the apostles], though it was not really I, but the grace (the unmerited favor and blessing) of God which was with me.

[11] So, whether then it was I or they, this is what we preach and this is what you believed [what you adhered to, trusted in, and relied on].

[12] But now if Christ (the Messiah) is preached as raised from the dead, how is it that some of you say that there is no resurrection of the dead?

[13] But if there is no resurrection of the dead, then Christ has not risen;

[14] And if Christ has not risen, then our preaching is in vain [it amounts to nothing] and your faith is devoid of truth *and* is fruitless (without effect, empty, imaginary, and unfounded).

[15] We are even discovered to be misrepresenting God, for we testified of Him that He raised Christ, Whom He did not raise in case it is true that the dead are not raised.

[16] For if the dead are not raised, then Christ has not been raised;

[17] And if Christ has not been raised, your faith is mere delusion [futile, fruitless], and you are still in your sins [under the control and penalty of sin];

[18] And further, those who have died in [[b] spiritual fellowship and union with] Christ have perished (are lost)!

[19] If we who are [abiding] in Christ have hope only in this life *and* that is all, then we are of all people most miserable *and* to be pitied.

[20] But the fact is that Christ (the Messiah) has been raised from the dead, and He became the firstfruits of those who have fallen asleep [in death].

[21] For since [it was] through a man that death [came into the world, it is] also through a Man that the resurrection of the dead [has come].

[22] For just as [because of their [c] union of nature] in Adam all people die, so also [by virtue of their [c] union of nature] shall all in Christ be made alive.

[23] But each in his own rank *and* turn: Christ (the Messiah) [is] the firstfruits, then those who are Christ's [own will be resurrected] at His coming.

[24] After that comes the end (the completion), when He delivers over the kingdom to God the Father after rendering inoperative *and* abolishing every [other] rule and every authority and power.

[a] Marvin Vincent, *Word Studies*. [b] Joseph Thayer, *A Greek-English Lexicon*. [c] Robert Jamieson, A. R. Fausset and David Brown, *A Commentary*.

[a] 3 Or *you at the first*   [b] 5 That is, Peter

## New International Version

has put all his enemies under his feet. [26]The last enemy to be destroyed is death. [27]For he "has put everything under his feet."[a] Now when it says that "everything" has been put under him, it is clear that this does not include God himself, who put everything under Christ. [28]When he has done this, then the Son himself will be made subject to him who put everything under him, so that God may be all in all.

[29]Now if there is no resurrection, what will those do who are baptized for the dead? If the dead are not raised at all, why are people baptized for them? [30]And as for us, why do we endanger ourselves every hour? [31]I face death every day—yes, just as surely as I boast about you in Christ Jesus our Lord. [32]If I fought wild beasts in Ephesus with no more than human hopes, what have I gained? If the dead are not raised,

"Let us eat and drink,
for tomorrow we die."[b]

[33]Do not be misled: "Bad company corrupts good character."[c] [34]Come back to your senses as you ought, and stop sinning; for there are some who are ignorant of God—I say this to your shame.

### The Resurrection Body

[35]But someone will ask, "How are the dead raised? With what kind of body will they come?" [36]How foolish! What you sow does not come to life unless it dies. [37]When you sow, you do not plant the body that will be, but just a seed, perhaps of wheat or of something else. [38]But God gives it a body as he has determined, and to each kind of seed he gives its own body. [39]Not all flesh is the same: People have one kind of flesh, animals have another, birds another and fish another. [40]There are also heavenly bodies and there are earthly bodies; but the splendor of the heavenly bodies is one kind, and the splendor of the earthly bodies is another. [41]The sun has one kind of splendor, the moon another and the stars another; and star differs from star in splendor.

[42]So will it be with the resurrection of the dead. The body that is sown is perishable, it is raised imperishable; [43]it is sown in dishonor, it is raised in glory; it is sown in weakness, it is raised in power; [44]it is sown a natural body, it is raised a spiritual body.

If there is a natural body, there is also a spiritual body. [45]So it is written: "The first man Adam became a living being"[d]; the last Adam, a life-giving spirit. [46]The spiritual did

## Amplified Bible

[25]For [Christ] must be King and reign until He has put all [His] enemies under His feet. [Ps. 110:1.]

[26]The last enemy to be subdued and abolished is death.

[27]For He [the Father] has put all things in subjection under His [Christ's] feet. But when it says, All things are put in subjection [under Him], it is evident that He [Himself] is excepted Who does the subjecting of all things to Him. [Ps. 8:6.]

[28]However, when everything is subjected to Him, then the Son Himself will also subject Himself to [the Father] Who put all things under Him, so that God may be all in all [be everything to everyone, supreme, the indwelling and controlling factor of life].

[29]Otherwise, what do people mean by being [themselves] baptized in behalf of the dead? If the dead are not raised at all, why are people baptized for them?

[30][For that matter], why do I live [dangerously as I do, running such risks that I am] in peril every hour?

[31][I assure you] by the pride which I have in you in [your [a]fellowship and union with] Christ Jesus our Lord, that I die daily [I face death every day and die to self].

[32]What do I gain if, merely from the human point of view, I fought with [wild] beasts at Ephesus? If the dead are not raised [at all], let us eat and drink, for tomorrow we will be dead. [Isa. 22:13.]

[33]Do not be so deceived and misled! Evil companionships (communion, associations) corrupt and deprave good manners and morals and character.

[34]Awake [[b]from your drunken stupor and return] to sober sense and your right minds, and sin no more. For some of you have not the knowledge of God [you are utterly and willfully and disgracefully ignorant, and continue to be so, lacking the sense of God's presence and all true knowledge of Him]. I say this to your shame.

[35]But someone will say, How can the dead be raised? With what [kind of] body will they come forth?

[36]You foolish man! Every time you plant seed, you sow something that does not come to life [germinating, springing up, and growing] unless it dies first.

[37]Nor is the seed you sow then the body which it is going to have [later], but it is a naked kernel, perhaps of wheat or some of the rest of the grains.

[38]But God gives to it the body that He plans and sees fit, and to each kind of seed a body of its own. [Gen. 1:11.]

[39]For all flesh is not the same, but there is one kind for humans, another for beasts, another for birds, and another for fish.

[40]There are heavenly bodies (sun, moon, and stars) and there are earthly bodies (men, animals, and plants), but the beauty and glory of the heavenly bodies is of one kind, while the beauty and glory of earthly bodies is a different kind.

[41]The sun is glorious in one way, the moon is glorious in another way, and the stars are glorious in their own [distinctive] way; for one star differs from and surpasses another in its beauty and brilliance.

[42]So it is with the resurrection of the dead. [The body] that is sown is perishable and decays, but [the body] that is resurrected is imperishable (immune to decay, immortal). [Dan. 12:3.]

[43]It is sown in dishonor and humiliation; it is raised in honor and glory. It is sown in infirmity and weakness; it is resurrected in strength and endued with power.

[44]It is sown a natural (physical) body; it is raised a supernatural (a spiritual) body. [As surely as] there is a physical body, there is also a spiritual body.

[45]Thus it is written, The first man Adam became a living being (an individual personality); the last Adam (Christ) became a life-giving Spirit [restoring the dead to life]. [Gen. 2:7.]

---

[a] 27 Psalm 8:6　 [b] 32 Isaiah 22:13　 [c] 33 From the Greek poet Menander　 [d] 45 Gen. 2:7

[a] Joseph Thayer, *A Greek-English Lexicon.* 　 [b] Marvin Vincent, *Word Studies.*

## New International Version

not come first, but the natural, and after that the spiritual. [47]The first man was of the dust of the earth; the second man is of heaven. [48]As was the earthly man, so are those who are of the earth; and as is the heavenly man, so also are those who are of heaven. [49]And just as we have borne the image of the earthly man, so shall we[a] bear the image of the heavenly man.

[50]I declare to you, brothers and sisters, that flesh and blood cannot inherit the kingdom of God, nor does the perishable inherit the imperishable. [51]Listen, I tell you a mystery: We will not all sleep, but we will all be changed— [52]in a flash, in the twinkling of an eye, at the last trumpet. For the trumpet will sound, the dead will be raised imperishable, and we will be changed. [53]For the perishable must clothe itself with the imperishable, and the mortal with immortality. [54]When the perishable has been clothed with the imperishable, and the mortal with immortality, then the saying that is written will come true: "Death has been swallowed up in victory."[b]

[55]"Where, O death, is your victory?
    Where, O death, is your sting?"[c]

[56]The sting of death is sin, and the power of sin is the law. [57]But thanks be to God! He gives us the victory through our Lord Jesus Christ.

[58]Therefore, my dear brothers and sisters, stand firm. Let nothing move you. Always give yourselves fully to the work of the Lord, because you know that your labor in the Lord is not in vain.

### The Collection for the Lord's People

**16** Now about the collection for the Lord's people: Do what I told the Galatian churches to do. [2]On the first day of every week, each one of you should set aside a sum of money in keeping with your income, saving it up, so that when I come no collections will have to be made. [3]Then, when I arrive, I will give letters of introduction to the men you approve and send them with your gift to Jerusalem. [4]If it seems advisable for me to go also, they will accompany me.

### Personal Requests

[5]After I go through Macedonia, I will come to you—for I will be going through Macedonia. [6]Perhaps I will stay with you for a while, or even spend the winter, so that you can help me on my journey, wherever I go. [7]For I do not want to see you now and make only a passing visit; I hope to spend some time with you, if the Lord permits. [8]But I will stay on at Ephesus until Pentecost, [9]because a great

## Amplified Bible

[46]But it is not the spiritual life which came first, but the physical and then the spiritual.

[47]The first man [was] from out of earth, made of dust (earthly-minded); the second Man [is] *the Lord* from out of heaven. [Gen. 2:7.]

[48]Now those who are made of the dust are like him who was first made of the dust (earthly-minded); and as is [the Man] from heaven, so also [are those] who are of heaven (heavenly-minded).

[49]And just as we have borne the image [of the man] of dust, so shall we *and so* [a]*let us* also bear the image [of the Man] of heaven.

[50]But I tell you this, brethren, flesh and blood cannot [become partakers of eternal salvation and] inherit *or* share in the kingdom of God; nor does the perishable (that which is decaying) inherit *or* share in the imperishable (the immortal).

[51]Take notice! I tell you a mystery (a secret truth, an event decreed by the hidden purpose or counsel of God). We shall not all fall asleep [in death], but we shall all be changed (transformed)

[52]In a moment, in the twinkling of an eye, at the [sound of the] last trumpet call. For a trumpet will sound, and the dead [in Christ] will be raised imperishable (free and immune from decay), and we shall be changed (transformed).

[53]For this perishable [part of us] must put on the imperishable [nature], and this mortal [part of us, this nature that is capable of dying] must put on immortality (freedom from death).

[54]And when this perishable puts on the imperishable and this that was capable of dying puts on freedom from death, then shall be fulfilled the Scripture that says, Death is swallowed up (utterly vanquished [b]forever) in *and* unto victory. [Isa. 25:8.]

[55]O death, where is your victory? O death, where is your sting? [Hos. 13:14.]

[56]Now sin is the sting of death, and sin exercises its power [c][upon the soul] through [c][the abuse of] the Law.

[57]But thanks be to God, Who gives us the victory [making us conquerors] through our Lord Jesus Christ.

[58]Therefore, my beloved brethren, be firm (steadfast), immovable, always abounding in the work of the Lord [always being superior, excelling, doing more than enough in the service of the Lord], knowing *and* being continually aware that your labor in the Lord is not futile [it is never wasted or to no purpose].

**16** Now concerning the money contributed for [the relief of] the saints (God's people): you are to do the same as I directed the churches of Galatia to do.

[2]On the first [day] of each week, let each one of you [personally] put aside something and save it up as he has prospered [in proportion to what he is given], so that no collections will need to be taken after I come.

[3]And when I arrive, I will send on those whom you approve *and* authorize with credentials to carry your gift [of charity] to Jerusalem.

[4]If it seems worthwhile that I should go too, they will accompany me.

[5]After passing through Macedonia, I will visit you, for I intend [only] to pass through Macedonia;

[6]But it may be that I will stay with you [for a while], perhaps even spend the winter, so that you may bring me forward [on my journey] to wherever I may go.

[7]For I am unwilling to see you right now [just] in passing, but I hope later to remain for some time with you, if the Lord permits.

[8]I will remain in Ephesus [however] until Pentecost,

---

[a] 49 Some early manuscripts *so let us*    [b] 54 Isaiah 25:8
[c] 55 Hosea 13:14

[a] Many ancient manuscripts read "let us."   [b] Marvin Vincent, *Word Studies.*   [c] Joseph Thayer, *A Greek-English Lexicon.*

## New International Version

door for effective work has opened to me, and there are many who oppose me.

[10] When Timothy comes, see to it that he has nothing to fear while he is with you, for he is carrying on the work of the Lord, just as I am. [11] No one, then, should treat him with contempt. Send him on his way in peace so that he may return to me. I am expecting him along with the brothers.

[12] Now about our brother Apollos: I strongly urged him to go to you with the brothers. He was quite unwilling to go now, but he will go when he has the opportunity.

[13] Be on your guard; stand firm in the faith; be courageous; be strong. [14] Do everything in love.

[15] You know that the household of Stephanas were the first converts in Achaia, and they have devoted themselves to the service of the Lord's people. I urge you, brothers and sisters, [16] to submit to such people and to everyone who joins in the work and labors at it. [17] I was glad when Stephanas, Fortunatus and Achaicus arrived, because they have supplied what was lacking from you. [18] For they refreshed my spirit and yours also. Such men deserve recognition.

### Final Greetings

[19] The churches in the province of Asia send you greetings. Aquila and Priscilla[a] greet you warmly in the Lord, and so does the church that meets at their house. [20] All the brothers and sisters here send you greetings. Greet one another with a holy kiss.

[21] I, Paul, write this greeting in my own hand.

[22] If anyone does not love the Lord, let that person be cursed! Come, Lord[b]!

[23] The grace of the Lord Jesus be with you.

[24] My love to all of you in Christ Jesus. Amen.[c]

## Amplified Bible

[9] For a wide door of opportunity for effectual [service] has opened to me [there, a great and promising one], and [there are] many adversaries.

[10] When Timothy arrives, see to it that [you put him at ease, so that] he may be fearless among you, for he is [devotedly] doing the Lord's work, just as I am.

[11] So [see to it that] no one despises him *or* treats him as if he were of no account *or* slights him. But send him off [cordially, speed him on his way] in peace, that he may come to me, for I am expecting him [to come along] with the other brethren.

[12] As for our brother Apollos, I have urgently encouraged him to visit you with the other brethren, but it was not at all his will *or* [a] God's will that he should go now. He will come when he has opportunity.

[13] Be alert *and* on your guard; stand firm in your faith ([b] your conviction respecting man's relationship to God and divine things, keeping the trust and holy fervor born of faith and a part of it). Act like men *and* be courageous; grow in strength! [Ps. 31:24.]

[14] Let everything you do be done in love (true love to God and man as inspired by God's love for us).

[15] Now, brethren, you know that the household of Stephanas were the first converts *and* our firstfruits in Achaia (most of Greece), and how they have consecrated *and* devoted themselves to the service of the saints (God's people).

[16] I urge you to pay all deference to such leaders *and* to enlist under them *and* be subject to them, as well as to everyone who joins *and* cooperates [with you] *and* labors earnestly.

[17] I am happy because Stephanas and Fortunatus and Achaicus have come [to me], for they have made up for your absence.

[18] For they gave me [c] respite from labor *and* rested me *and* refreshed my spirit as well as yours. Deeply appreciate *and* thoroughly know *and* fully recognize such men.

[19] The churches of Asia send greetings *and* best wishes. Aquila and Prisca, together with the church [that meets] in their house, send you their hearty greetings in the Lord.

[20] All the brethren wish to be remembered to you *and* wish you well. Greet one another with a holy kiss.

[21] I, Paul, [add this final] greeting with my own hand.

[22] If anyone does not love the Lord [does not have a friendly affection for Him and is not kindly disposed toward Him], he shall be accursed! Our Lord will come! (Maranatha!)

[23] The grace (favor and spiritual blessing) of our Lord Jesus *Christ* be with you.

[24] My love (that true love growing out of sincere devotion to God) be with you all in Christ Jesus. *Amen (so be it).*

---

[a] 19 Greek *Prisca*, a variant of *Priscilla*   [b] 22 The Greek for *Come, Lord* reproduces an Aramaic expression (*Marana tha*) used by early Christians.   [c] 24 Some manuscripts do not have *Amen.*

[a] Although "his" may refer to Apollos, the probable reference here is to "God's will."   [b] Joseph Thayer, *A Greek-English Lexicon.*   [c] G. Abbott-Smith, *Manual Greek Lexicon.*

# 2 Corinthians

**1** Paul, an apostle of Christ Jesus by the will of God, and Timothy our brother,

To the church of God in Corinth, together with all his holy people throughout Achaia:

[2]Grace and peace to you from God our Father and the Lord Jesus Christ.

### Praise to the God of All Comfort

[3]Praise be to the God and Father of our Lord Jesus Christ, the Father of compassion and the God of all comfort, [4]who comforts us in all our troubles, so that we can comfort those in any trouble with the comfort we ourselves receive from God. [5]For just as we share abundantly in the sufferings of Christ, so also our comfort abounds through Christ. [6]If we are distressed, it is for your comfort and salvation; if we are comforted, it is for your comfort, which produces in you patient endurance of the same sufferings we suffer. [7]And our hope for you is firm, because we know that just as you share in our sufferings, so also you share in our comfort.

[8]We do not want you to be uninformed, brothers and sisters,[a] about the troubles we experienced in the province of Asia. We were under great pressure, far beyond our ability to endure, so that we despaired of life itself. [9]Indeed, we felt we had received the sentence of death. But this happened that we might not rely on ourselves but on God, who raises the dead. [10]He has delivered us from such a deadly peril, and he will deliver us again. On him we have set our hope that he will continue to deliver us, [11]as you help us by your prayers. Then many will give thanks on our behalf for the gracious favor granted us in answer to the prayers of many.

### Paul's Change of Plans

[12]Now this is our boast: Our conscience testifies that we have conducted ourselves in the world, and especially in our relations with you, with integrity[b] and godly sincerity. We have done so, relying not on worldly wisdom but

---

# Corinthians

**1** Paul, an apostle (a special messenger) of Christ Jesus by the will of God, and Timothy [our] brother, to the church (assembly) of God which is at Corinth, and to all the saints (the people of God) throughout Achaia (most of Greece):

[2]Grace (favor and spiritual blessing) to you and [heart] peace from God our Father and the Lord Jesus Christ (the Messiah, the Anointed One).

[3]Blessed be the God and Father of our Lord Jesus Christ, the Father of sympathy (pity and mercy) and the God [Who is the Source] of every comfort (consolation and encouragement),

[4]Who comforts (consoles and encourages) us in every trouble (calamity and affliction), so that we may also be able to comfort (console and encourage) those who are in any kind of trouble *or* distress, with the comfort (consolation and encouragement) with which we ourselves are comforted (consoled and encouraged) by God.

[5]For just as Christ's [[a]own] sufferings fall to our lot [b][as they overflow upon His disciples, and we share and experience them] abundantly, so through Christ comfort (consolation and encouragement) is also [shared and experienced] abundantly by us.

[6]But if we are troubled (afflicted and distressed), it is for your comfort (consolation and encouragement) and [for your] salvation; and if we are comforted (consoled and encouraged), it is for your comfort (consolation and encouragement), which works [in you] when you patiently endure the same evils (misfortunes and calamities) that we also suffer *and* undergo.

[7]And our hope for you [our joyful and confident expectation of good for you] is ever unwavering (assured and unshaken); for we know that just as you share *and* are partners in [our] sufferings *and* calamities, you also share *and* are partners in [our] comfort (consolation and encouragement).

[8]For we do not want you to be uninformed, brethren, about the affliction *and* oppressing distress which befell us in [the province of] Asia, how we were so utterly and unbearably weighed down *and* crushed that we despaired even of life [itself].

[9]Indeed, we felt within ourselves that we had received the [very] sentence of death, but that was to keep us from trusting in *and* depending on ourselves instead of on God Who raises the dead.

[10][For it is He] Who rescued *and* saved us from such a perilous death, and He will still rescue *and* save us; in *and* on Him we have set our hope (our joyful and confident expectation) that He will again deliver us [from danger and destruction and [c]draw us to Himself],

[11]While you also cooperate by your prayers for us [helping and laboring together with us]. Thus [the lips of] many persons [turned toward God will eventually] give thanks on our behalf for the grace (the blessing of deliverance) granted us at the request of the many who have prayed.

[12]It is a reason for pride *and* exultation to which our conscience testifies that we have conducted ourselves in the world [generally] and especially toward you, with devout *and* pure motives and godly sincerity, not in fleshly wisdom but by the grace of God (the unmerited favor and [d]merciful kindness by which God, exerting His holy influence upon souls, turns them to Christ, and keeps, strengthens, and increases them in Christian virtues).

---

*a 8* The Greek word for *brothers and sisters (adelphoi)* refers here to believers, both men and women, as part of God's family; also in 8:1; 13:11.   *b 12* Many manuscripts *holiness*

*a* Marvin Vincent, *Word Studies in the New Testament.*   *b* Marvin Vincent, *Word Studies.*   *c* Joseph Thayer, *A Greek-English Lexicon of the New Testament*: Primary meaning: "to draw to one's self."   *d* Joseph Thayer, *A Greek-English Lexicon of the New Testament.*

# New International Version

on God's grace. [13]For we do not write you anything you cannot read or understand. And I hope that, [14]as you have understood us in part, you will come to understand fully that you can boast of us just as we will boast of you in the day of the Lord Jesus.

[15]Because I was confident of this, I wanted to visit you first so that you might benefit twice. [16]I wanted to visit you on my way to Macedonia and to come back to you from Macedonia, and then to have you send me on my way to Judea. [17]Was I fickle when I intended to do this? Or do I make my plans in a worldly manner so that in the same breath I say both "Yes, yes" and "No, no"?

[18]But as surely as God is faithful, our message to you is not "Yes" and "No." [19]For the Son of God, Jesus Christ, who was preached among you by us—by me and Silas[a] and Timothy—was not "Yes" and "No," but in him it has always been "Yes." [20]For no matter how many promises God has made, they are "Yes" in Christ. And so through him the "Amen" is spoken by us to the glory of God. [21]Now it is God who makes both us and you stand firm in Christ. He anointed us, [22]set his seal of ownership on us, and put his Spirit in our hearts as a deposit, guaranteeing what is to come.

[23]I call God as my witness—and I stake my life on it— that it was in order to spare you that I did not return to Corinth. [24]Not that we lord it over your faith, but we work with you for your joy, because it is by faith you stand firm.

**2** [1]So I made up my mind that I would not make another painful visit to you. [2]For if I grieve you, who is left to make me glad but you whom I have grieved? [3]I wrote as I did, so that when I came I would not be distressed by those who should have made me rejoice. I had confidence in all of you, that you would all share my joy. [4]For I wrote you out of great distress and anguish of heart and with many tears, not to grieve you but to let you know the depth of my love for you.

### Forgiveness for the Offender

[5]If anyone has caused grief, he has not so much grieved me as he has grieved all of you to some extent—not to put it too severely. [6]The punishment inflicted on him by the

# Amplified Bible

[13]For we write you nothing else but simply what you can read and understand [there is no double meaning to what we say], and I hope that you will become thoroughly acquainted [with [a]divine things] and know and understand [them] accurately and well to the end,

[14][Just] as you have [already] partially known and understood and acknowledged and recognized that you can [honestly] be proud of us, even as we [can be proud] of you on the day of our Lord Jesus.

[15]It was with assurance of this that I wanted and planned to visit you first [of all], so that you might have a double favor and token of grace (goodwill).

[16][I wanted] to visit you on my way to Macedonia, and [then] to come again to you [on my return trip] from Macedonia and have you send me forward on my way to Judea.

[17]Now because I changed my original plan, was I being unstable and capricious? Or what I plan, do I plan according to the flesh [like a worldly man], ready to say Yes, yes, [when it may mean] No, no?

[18]As surely as God is trustworthy and faithful and means what He says, our speech and message to you have not been Yes [that might mean] No.

[19]For the Son of God, Christ Jesus (the Messiah), Who has been preached among you by us, by myself, Silvanus, and Timothy, was not Yes and No; but in Him it is [always the divine] Yes.

[20]For as many as are the promises of God, they all find their Yes [answer] in Him [Christ]. For this reason we also utter the Amen (so be it) to God through Him [in His Person and by His agency] to the glory of God.

[21]But it is God Who confirms and makes us steadfast and establishes us [in joint fellowship] with you in Christ, and has consecrated and anointed us [[b]enduing us with the gifts of the Holy Spirit];

[22][He has also appropriated and acknowledged us as His by] putting His seal upon us and giving us His [Holy] Spirit in our hearts as the security deposit and guarantee [of the fulfillment of His promise].

[23]But I call upon God as my soul's witness: it was to avoid hurting you that I refrained from coming to Corinth—

[24]Not that we have dominion [over you] and lord it over your faith, but [rather that we work with you as] fellow laborers [to promote] your joy, for in [your] faith ([c]in your strong and welcome conviction or belief that Jesus is the Messiah, through Whom we obtain eternal salvation in the kingdom of God) you stand firm.

**2** But I definitely made up my mind not to grieve you with another painful and distressing visit.

[2]For if I cause you pain [with merited rebuke], who is there to provide me enjoyment but the [very] one whom I have grieved and made sad?

[3]And I wrote the same to you so that when I came, I might not be myself pained by those who are the [very] ones who ought to make me glad, for I trusted in you all and felt confident that my joy would be shared by all of you.

[4]For I wrote you out of great sorrow and deep distress [with mental torture and anxiety] of heart, [yes, and] with many tears, not to cause you pain but in order to make you realize the overflowing love that I continue increasingly to have for you.

[5]But if someone [the one among you who committed incest] has caused [all this] grief and pain, he has caused it not to me, but in some measure, not to put it too severely, [he has distressed] all of you.

[6]For such a one this censure by the majority [which he has received is] sufficient [punishment].

[a] Joseph Thayer, *A Greek-English Lexicon of the New Testament.*
[b] Brooke F. Westcott, *The Epistles of Saint John,* has a helpful insight here in his comment on I John 2:20.   [c] Joseph Thayer, *A Greek-English Lexicon.*

[a] 19 Greek *Silvanus,* a variant of *Silas*

## New International Version

majority is sufficient. [7]Now instead, you ought to forgive and comfort him, so that he will not be overwhelmed by excessive sorrow. [8]I urge you, therefore, to reaffirm your love for him. [9]Another reason I wrote you was to see if you would stand the test and be obedient in everything. [10]Anyone you forgive, I also forgive. And what I have forgiven—if there was anything to forgive—I have forgiven in the sight of Christ for your sake, [11]in order that Satan might not outwit us. For we are not unaware of his schemes.

### Ministers of the New Covenant

[12]Now when I went to Troas to preach the gospel of Christ and found that the Lord had opened a door for me, [13]I still had no peace of mind, because I did not find my brother Titus there. So I said goodbye to them and went on to Macedonia.

[14]But thanks be to God, who always leads us as captives in Christ's triumphal procession and uses us to spread the aroma of the knowledge of him everywhere. [15]For we are to God the pleasing aroma of Christ among those who are being saved and those who are perishing. [16]To the one we are an aroma that brings death; to the other, an aroma that brings life. And who is equal to such a task? [17]Unlike so many, we do not peddle the word of God for profit. On the contrary, in Christ we speak before God with sincerity, as those sent from God.

**3** Are we beginning to commend ourselves again? Or do we need, like some people, letters of recommendation to you or from you? [2]You yourselves are our letter, written on our hearts, known and read by everyone. [3]You show that you are a letter from Christ, the result of our ministry, written not with ink but with the Spirit of the living God, not on tablets of stone but on tablets of human hearts.

[4]Such confidence we have through Christ before God. [5]Not that we are competent in ourselves to claim anything for ourselves, but our competence comes from God. [6]He has made us competent as ministers of a new covenant—not of the letter but of the Spirit; for the letter kills, but the Spirit gives life.

### The Greater Glory of the New Covenant

[7]Now if the ministry that brought death, which was engraved in letters on stone, came with glory, so that the Israelites could not look steadily at the face of Moses because of its glory, transitory though it was, [8]will not the

## Amplified Bible

[7]So [instead of further rebuke, now] you should rather turn *and* [graciously] forgive and comfort *and* encourage [him], to keep him from being overwhelmed by excessive sorrow *and* despair.

[8]I therefore beg you to reinstate him in your affections *and* assure him of your love for him;

[9]For this was my purpose in writing you, to test your attitude *and* see if you would stand the test, whether you are obedient *and* altogether agreeable [to following my orders] in everything.

[10]If you forgive anyone anything, I too forgive that one; and what I have forgiven, if I have forgiven anything, has been for your sakes in the presence [and with the approval] of Christ (the Messiah),

[11]To keep Satan from getting the advantage over us; for we are not ignorant of his wiles *and* intentions.

[12]Now when I arrived at Troas [to preach] the good news (the Gospel) of Christ, a door of opportunity was opened for me in the Lord,

[13]Yet my spirit could not rest (relax, get relief) because I did not find my brother Titus there. So I took leave from them *and* departed for Macedonia.

[14]But thanks be to God, Who in Christ always leads us in triumph [as trophies of Christ's victory] and through us spreads *and* makes evident the fragrance of the knowledge of God everywhere,

[15]For we are the sweet fragrance of Christ [which exhales] unto God, [discernible alike] among those who are being saved *and* among those who are perishing:

[16]To the latter it is an aroma [wafted] from death to death [a fatal odor, the smell of doom]; to the former it is an aroma from life to life [a vital fragrance, living and fresh]. And who is qualified (fit and sufficient) for these things? [Who is able for such a ministry? We?]

[17]For we are not, like so many, [like hucksters making a trade of] peddling God's Word [shortchanging and adulterating the divine message]; but like [men] of sincerity *and* the purest motive, as [commissioned and sent] by God, we speak [His message] in Christ (the Messiah), in the [very] sight *and* presence of God.

**3** Are we starting to commend ourselves again? Or we do not, like some [false teachers], need written credentials *or* letters of recommendation to you or from you, [do we]?

[2] [No] you yourselves are our letter of recommendation (our credentials), written in [a]your hearts, to be known (perceived, recognized) and read by everybody.

[3]You show *and* make obvious that you are a letter from Christ delivered by us, not written with ink but with [the] Spirit of [the] living God, not on tablets of stone but on tablets of human hearts. [Exod. 24:12; 31:18; 32:15, 16; Jer. 31:33.]

[4]Such is the reliance *and* confidence that we have through Christ toward *and* with reference to God.

[5]Not that we are fit (qualified and sufficient in ability) of ourselves to form personal judgments *or* to claim *or* count anything as coming from us, but our power *and* ability *and* sufficiency are from God.

[6] [It is He] Who has qualified us [making us to be fit and worthy and sufficient] as ministers *and* dispensers of a new covenant [of salvation through Christ], not [ministers] of the letter (of legally written code) but of the Spirit; for the code [of the Law] kills, but the [Holy] Spirit makes alive. [Jer. 31:31.]

[7]Now if the dispensation of death engraved in letters on stone [the ministration of the Law], was inaugurated with such glory *and* splendor that the Israelites were not able to look steadily at the face of Moses because of its brilliance, [a glory] that was to fade *and* pass away, [Exod. 34:29-35.]

[a] Many ancient manuscripts read "our."

## New International Version

ministry of the Spirit be even more glorious? [9]If the ministry that brought condemnation was glorious, how much more glorious is the ministry that brings righteousness! [10]For what was glorious has no glory now in comparison with the surpassing glory. [11]And if what was transitory came with glory, how much greater is the glory of that which lasts!

[12]Therefore, since we have such a hope, we are very bold. [13]We are not like Moses, who would put a veil over his face to prevent the Israelites from seeing the end of what was passing away. [14]But their minds were made dull, for to this day the same veil remains when the old covenant is read. It has not been removed, because only in Christ is it taken away. [15]Even to this day when Moses is read, a veil covers their hearts. [16]But whenever anyone turns to the Lord, the veil is taken away. [17]Now the Lord is the Spirit, and where the Spirit of the Lord is, there is freedom. [18]And we all, who with unveiled faces contemplate[a] the Lord's glory, are being transformed into his image with ever-increasing glory, which comes from the Lord, who is the Spirit.

### Present Weakness and Resurrection Life

**4** Therefore, since through God's mercy we have this ministry, we do not lose heart. [2]Rather, we have renounced secret and shameful ways; we do not use deception, nor do we distort the word of God. On the contrary, by setting forth the truth plainly we commend ourselves to everyone's conscience in the sight of God. [3]And even if our gospel is veiled, it is veiled to those who are perishing. [4]The god of this age has blinded the minds of unbelievers, so that they cannot see the light of the gospel that displays the glory of Christ, who is the image of God. [5]For what we preach is not ourselves, but Jesus Christ as Lord, and ourselves as your servants for Jesus' sake. [6]For God, who said, "Let light shine out of darkness,"[b] made his light

## Amplified Bible

[8]Why should not the dispensation of the Spirit [this spiritual [a]ministry whose task it is to cause men to obtain and be governed by the Holy Spirit] be attended with much greater *and* more splendid glory?

[9]For if the service that condemns [the ministration of doom] had glory, how infinitely more abounding in splendor *and* glory must be the service that makes righteous [the ministry that produces and fosters righteous living and right standing with God]!

[10]Indeed, in view of this fact, what once had splendor [[b]the glory of the Law in the face of Moses] has come to have no splendor at all, because of the overwhelming glory that exceeds *and* excels it [[b]the glory of the Gospel in the face of Jesus Christ].

[11]For if that which was but passing *and* fading away came with splendor, how much more must that which remains *and* is permanent abide in glory *and* splendor!

[12]Since we have such [glorious] hope (such joyful and confident expectation), we speak very freely *and* openly *and* fearlessly.

[13]Nor [do we act] like Moses, who put a veil over his face so that the Israelites might not gaze upon the finish of the vanishing [splendor which had been upon it].

[14]In fact, their minds were grown hard *and* calloused [they had become dull and had lost the power of understanding]; for until this present day, when the Old Testament (the old covenant) is being read, that same veil still lies [on their hearts], not being lifted [to reveal] that in Christ it is made void *and* done away.

[15]Yes, down to this [very] day whenever Moses is read, a veil lies upon their minds *and* hearts.

[16]But whenever a person turns [in repentance] to the Lord, the veil is stripped off *and* taken away.

[17]Now the Lord is the Spirit, and where the Spirit of the Lord is, there is liberty (emancipation from bondage, freedom). [Isa. 61:1, 2.]

[18]And all of us, as with unveiled face, [because we] continued to behold [in the Word of God] as in a mirror the glory of the Lord, are constantly being transfigured into His *very own* image in ever increasing splendor *and* from one degree of glory to another; [for this comes] from the Lord [Who is] the Spirit.

**4** Therefore, since we do hold *and* engage in this ministry by the mercy of God [granting us favor, benefits, opportunities, and especially salvation], we do not get discouraged (spiritless and despondent with fear) *or* become faint with weariness and exhaustion.

[2]We have renounced disgraceful ways (secret thoughts, feelings, desires and underhandedness, the methods and arts that men hide through shame); we refuse to deal craftily (to practice trickery and cunning) *or* to adulterate *or* handle dishonestly the Word of God, but we state the truth openly (clearly and candidly). And so we commend ourselves in the sight *and* presence of God to every man's conscience.

[3]But even if our Gospel (the glad tidings) also be hidden (obscured and covered up with a veil that hinders the knowledge of God), it is hidden [only] to those who are perishing *and* obscured [only] to those who are spiritually dying *and* veiled [only] to those who are lost.

[4]For the god of this world has blinded the unbelievers' minds [that they should not discern the truth], preventing them from seeing the illuminating light of the Gospel of the glory of Christ (the Messiah), Who is the Image *and* Likeness of God.

[5]For what we preach is not ourselves but Jesus Christ as Lord, and ourselves [merely] as your servants (slaves) for Jesus' sake.

[6]For God Who said, Let light shine out of darkness, has

---

[a] 18 Or *reflect*   [b] 6 Gen. 1:3

[a] Joseph Thayer, *A Greek-English Lexicon.*   [b] Marvin Vincent, *Word Studies.*

## New International Version

shine in our hearts to give us the light of the knowledge of God's glory displayed in the face of Christ.

[7]But we have this treasure in jars of clay to show that this all-surpassing power is from God and not from us. [8]We are hard pressed on every side, but not crushed; perplexed, but not in despair; [9]persecuted, but not abandoned; struck down, but not destroyed. [10]We always carry around in our body the death of Jesus, so that the life of Jesus may also be revealed in our body. [11]For we who are alive are always being given over to death for Jesus' sake, so that his life may also be revealed in our mortal body. [12]So then, death is at work in us, but life is at work in you.

[13]It is written: "I believed; therefore I have spoken."[a] Since we have that same spirit of[b] faith, we also believe and therefore speak, [14]because we know that the one who raised the Lord Jesus from the dead will also raise us with Jesus and present us with you to himself. [15]All this is for your benefit, so that the grace that is reaching more and more people may cause thanksgiving to overflow to the glory of God.

[16]Therefore we do not lose heart. Though outwardly we are wasting away, yet inwardly we are being renewed day by day. [17]For our light and momentary troubles are achieving for us an eternal glory that far outweighs them all. [18]So we fix our eyes not on what is seen, but on what is unseen, since what is seen is temporary, but what is unseen is eternal.

### Awaiting the New Body

**5** For we know that if the earthly tent we live in is destroyed, we have a building from God, an eternal house in heaven, not built by human hands. [2]Meanwhile we groan, longing to be clothed instead with our heavenly dwelling, [3]because when we are clothed, we will not be found naked. [4]For while we are in this tent, we groan and are burdened, because we do not wish to be unclothed but to be clothed instead with our heavenly dwelling, so that what is mortal may be swallowed up by life. [5]Now the one who has fashioned us for this very purpose is God, who has given us the Spirit as a deposit, guaranteeing what is to come.

## Amplified Bible

shone in our hearts so as [to beam forth] the Light for the illumination of the knowledge of the majesty *and* glory of God [as it is manifest in the Person and is revealed] in the face of *Jesus* Christ (the Messiah). [Gen. 1:3.]

[7]However, we possess this precious treasure [the divine Light of the Gospel] in [frail, human] vessels of earth, that the grandeur *and* exceeding greatness of the power may be shown to be from God and not from ourselves.

[8]We are hedged in (pressed) on every side [troubled and oppressed in every way], but not cramped *or* crushed; we suffer embarrassments *and* are perplexed *and* unable to find a way out, but not driven to despair;

[9]We are pursued (persecuted and hard driven), but not deserted [to stand alone]; we are struck down to the ground, but never struck out *and* destroyed;

[10]Always carrying about in the body the liability *and* exposure to the same putting to death that *the Lord* Jesus suffered, so that the [[a]resurrection] life of Jesus also may be shown forth by *and* in our bodies.

[11]For we who live are constantly [experiencing] being handed over to death for Jesus' sake, that the [[a]resurrection] life of Jesus also may be evidenced through our flesh which is liable to death.

[12]Thus death is actively at work in us, but [it is in order that [b]our] life [may be actively at work] in you.

[13]Yet we have the same spirit of faith as he had who wrote, I have believed, and therefore have I spoken. We too believe, and therefore we speak, [Ps. 116:10.]

[14]Assured that He Who raised up the Lord Jesus will raise us up also with Jesus and bring us [along] with you into His presence.

[15]For all [these] things are [taking place] for your sake, so that the more grace (divine favor and spiritual blessing) extends to more and more people *and* multiplies through the many, the more thanksgiving may increase [and redound] to the glory of God.

[16]Therefore we do not become discouraged (utterly spiritless, exhausted, and wearied out through fear). Though our outer man is [progressively] decaying *and* wasting away, yet our inner self is being [progressively] renewed day after day.

[17]For our light, momentary affliction (this slight distress of the passing hour) is ever more and more abundantly preparing *and* producing *and* achieving for us an everlasting weight of glory [beyond all measure, excessively surpassing all comparisons and all calculations, a vast and transcendent glory and blessedness never to cease!],

[18]Since we consider *and* look not to the things that are seen but to the things that are unseen; for the things that are visible are temporal (brief and fleeting), but the things that are invisible are deathless *and* everlasting.

**5** For we know that if the tent which is our earthly home is destroyed (dissolved), we have from God a building, a house not made with hands, eternal in the heavens.

[2]Here indeed, in this [present abode, body], we sigh *and* groan inwardly, because we yearn to be clothed over [we yearn to put on our celestial body like a garment, to be fitted out] with our heavenly dwelling,

[3]So that by putting it on we may not be found naked (without a body).

[4]For while we are still in this tent, we groan under the burden *and* sigh deeply (weighed down, depressed, oppressed)—not that we want to put off the body (the clothing of the spirit), but rather that we would be further clothed, so that what is mortal (our dying body) may be swallowed up by life [[b]after the resurrection].

[5]Now He Who has fashioned us [preparing and making us fit] for this very thing is God, Who also has given us the [Holy] Spirit as a guarantee [of the fulfillment of His promise].

---

[a] 13 Psalm 116:10 (see Septuagint)   [b] 13 Or *Spirit-given*

[a] Marvin Vincent, *Word Studies*.   [b] Joseph Thayer, *A Greek-English Lexicon*.

## New International Version

[6]Therefore we are always confident and know that as long as we are at home in the body we are away from the Lord. [7]For we live by faith, not by sight. [8]We are confident, I say, and would prefer to be away from the body and at home with the Lord. [9]So we make it our goal to please him, whether we are at home in the body or away from it. [10]For we must all appear before the judgment seat of Christ, so that each of us may receive what is due us for the things done while in the body, whether good or bad.

### The Ministry of Reconciliation
[11]Since, then, we know what it is to fear the Lord, we try to persuade others. What we are is plain to God, and I hope it is also plain to your conscience. [12]We are not trying to commend ourselves to you again, but are giving you an opportunity to take pride in us, so that you can answer those who take pride in what is seen rather than in what is in the heart. [13]If we are "out of our mind," as some say, it is for God; if we are in our right mind, it is for you. [14]For Christ's love compels us, because we are convinced that one died for all, and therefore all died. [15]And he died for all, that those who live should no longer live for themselves but for him who died for them and was raised again.

[16]So from now on we regard no one from a worldly point of view. Though we once regarded Christ in this way, we do so no longer. [17]Therefore, if anyone is in Christ, the new creation has come:[a] The old has gone, the new is here! [18]All this is from God, who reconciled us to himself through Christ and gave us the ministry of reconciliation: [19]that God was reconciling the world to himself in Christ, not counting people's sins against them. And he has committed to us the message of reconciliation. [20]We are therefore Christ's ambassadors, as though God were making his appeal through us. We implore you on Christ's behalf:

## Amplified Bible

[6]So then, we are always full of good *and* hopeful *and* confident courage; we know that while we are at home in the body, we are abroad from the home with the Lord [that is promised us].

[7]For we walk by faith [we *a*regulate our lives and conduct ourselves by our conviction or belief respecting man's relationship to God and divine things, with trust and holy fervor; thus we walk] not by sight *or* appearance.

[8][Yes] we have confident *and* hopeful courage and are pleased rather to be away from home out of the body and be at home with the Lord.

[9]Therefore, whether we are at home [on earth away from Him] or away from home [and with Him], we are constantly ambitious *and* strive earnestly to be pleasing to Him.

[10]For we must all appear *and* be revealed as we are before the judgment seat of Christ, so that each one may receive [his pay] according to what he has done in the body, whether good or evil [considering *a*what his purpose and motive have been, and what he has *b*achieved, been busy with, and given himself and his attention to accomplishing].

[11]Therefore, being conscious of fearing the Lord with respect *and* reverence, we seek to win people over [to persuade them]. But *a*what sort of persons we are is plainly recognized *and* thoroughly understood by God, and I hope that it is plainly recognized *and* thoroughly understood also by your consciences (your inborn discernment).

[12]We are not commending ourselves to you again, but we are providing you with an occasion *and* incentive to be [rightfully] proud of us, so that you may have a reply for those who pride themselves on surface appearances [*a*on the virtues they only appear to have], although their heart is devoid of them.

[13]For if we are beside ourselves [mad, as some say], it is for God *and* concerns Him; if we are in our right mind, it is for your benefit,

[14]For the love of Christ controls *and* urges *and* impels us, because we are of the opinion *and* conviction that [if] One died for all, then all died;

[15]And He died for all, so that all those who live might live no longer to *and* for themselves, but to *and* for Him Who died and was raised again for their sake.

[16]Consequently, from now on we estimate *and* regard no one from a [purely] human point of view [in terms of natural standards of value]. [No] even though we once did estimate Christ from a human viewpoint *and* as a man, yet now [we have such knowledge of Him that] we know Him no longer [in terms of the flesh].

[17]Therefore if any person is [ingrafted] in Christ (the Messiah) he is a new creation (a new creature altogether); the old [previous moral and spiritual condition] has passed away. Behold, the fresh *and* new has come!

[18]But all things are from God, Who through *Jesus* Christ reconciled us to Himself [received us into favor, brought us into harmony with Himself] and gave to us the ministry of reconciliation [that by word and deed we might aim to bring others into harmony with Him].

[19]It was God [personally present] in Christ, reconciling *and* restoring the world to favor with Himself, not counting up *and* holding against [men] their trespasses [but cancelling them], and committing to us the message of reconciliation (of the restoration to favor).

[20]So we are Christ's ambassadors, God making His appeal as it were through us. We [as Christ's personal representatives] beg you for His sake to lay hold of the divine favor [now offered you] *and* be reconciled to God.

---

*a* Joseph Thayer, *A Greek-English Lexicon.* *b* Alexander Souter, *Pocket Lexicon of the Greek New Testament.*

---

*a* 17 Or *Christ, that person is a new creation.*

## New International Version

Be reconciled to God. [21]God made him who had no sin to be sin[a] for us, so that in him we might become the righteousness of God.

**6** As God's co-workers we urge you not to receive God's grace in vain. [2]For he says,

"In the time of my favor I heard you,
and in the day of salvation I helped you."[b]

I tell you, now is the time of God's favor, now is the day of salvation.

### Paul's Hardships

[3]We put no stumbling block in anyone's path, so that our ministry will not be discredited. [4]Rather, as servants of God we commend ourselves in every way: in great endurance; in troubles, hardships and distresses; [5]in beatings, imprisonments and riots; in hard work, sleepless nights and hunger; [6]in purity, understanding, patience and kindness; in the Holy Spirit and in sincere love; [7]in truthful speech and in the power of God; with weapons of righteousness in the right hand and in the left; [8]through glory and dishonor, bad report and good report; genuine, yet regarded as impostors; [9]known, yet regarded as unknown; dying, and yet we live on; beaten, and yet not killed; [10]sorrowful, yet always rejoicing; poor, yet making many rich; having nothing, and yet possessing everything.

[11]We have spoken freely to you, Corinthians, and opened wide our hearts to you. [12]We are not withholding our affection from you, but you are withholding yours from us. [13]As a fair exchange—I speak as to my children—open wide your hearts also.

### Warning Against Idolatry

[14]Do not be yoked together with unbelievers. For what do righteousness and wickedness have in common? Or what fellowship can light have with darkness? [15]What harmony is there between Christ and Belial[c]? Or what does a believer have in common with an unbeliever? [16]What agreement is there between the temple of God and idols? For we are the temple of the living God. As God has said:

"I will live with them
and walk among them,
and I will be their God,
and they will be my people."[d]

[17]Therefore,

"Come out from them
and be separate,
says the Lord.
Touch no unclean thing,
and I will receive you."[e]

## Amplified Bible

[21]For our sake He made Christ [virtually] to be sin Who knew no sin, so that in *and* through Him we might become [[a]endued with, viewed as being in, and examples of] the righteousness of God [what we ought to be, approved and acceptable and in right relationship with Him, by His goodness].

**6** Laboring together [as God's fellow workers] with Him then, we beg of you not to receive the grace of God in vain [that [b]merciful kindness by which God exerts His holy influence on souls and turns them to Christ, keeping and strengthening them—do not receive it to no purpose].

[2]For He says, In the time of favor (of an assured welcome) I have listened to *and* heeded your call, and I have helped you on the day of deliverance (the day of salvation). Behold, now is truly the time for a gracious welcome *and* acceptance [of you from God]; behold, now is the day of salvation! [Isa. 49:8.]

[3]We put no obstruction in anybody's way [we give no offense in anything], so that no fault may be found *and* [our] ministry blamed *and* discredited.

[4]But we commend ourselves in every way as [true] servants of God: through great endurance, in tribulation *and* suffering, in hardships *and* privations, in sore straits *and* calamities;

[5]In beatings, imprisonments, riots, labors, sleepless watching, hunger;

[6]By innocence *and* purity, knowledge *and* spiritual insight, longsuffering *and* patience, kindness, in the Holy Spirit, in unfeigned love;

[7]By [speaking] the word of truth, in the power of God, with the weapons of righteousness for the right hand [to attack] and for the left hand [to defend];

[8]Amid honor and dishonor; in defaming *and* evil report and in praise *and* good report. [We are branded] as deceivers (impostors), and [yet vindicated as] truthful *and* honest.

[9][We are treated] as unknown *and* ignored [by the world], and [yet we are] well-known *and* recognized [by God and His people]; as dying, and yet here we are alive; as chastened by suffering and [yet] not killed;

[10]As grieved *and* mourning, yet [we are] always rejoicing; as poor [ourselves, yet] bestowing riches on many; as having nothing, and [yet in reality] possessing all things.

[11]Our mouth is open to you, Corinthians [we are hiding nothing, keeping nothing back], and our heart is expanded wide [for you]! [Isa. 60:5; Ezek. 33:22.]

[12]There is no lack of room for you in [our hearts], but you lack room in your own affections [for us].

[13]By way of return then, do this for me—I speak as to children—open wide your hearts also [to us].

[14]Do not be unequally yoked with unbelievers [do not make mismated alliances with them or come under a different yoke with them, inconsistent with your faith]. For what partnership have right living *and* right standing with God with iniquity *and* lawlessness? Or how can light have fellowship with darkness?

[15]What harmony can there be between Christ and Belial [the devil]? Or what has a believer in common with an unbeliever?

[16]What agreement [can there be between] a temple of God and idols? For we are the temple of the living God; even as God said, I will dwell in *and* with *and* among them and will walk in *and* with *and* among them, and I will be their God, and they shall be My people. [Exod. 25:8; 29:45; Lev. 26:12; Jer. 31:1; Ezek. 37:27.]

[17]So, come out from among [unbelievers], and separate (sever) yourselves from them, says the Lord, and touch not [any] unclean thing; then I will receive you kindly *and* treat you with favor, [Isa. 52:11.]

---

[a] 21 Or *be a sin offering*    [b] 2 Isaiah 49:8    [c] 15 Greek *Beliar*, a variant of *Belial*    [d] 16 Lev. 26:12; Jer. 32:38; Ezek. 37:27    [e] 17 Isaiah 52:11; Ezek. 20:34,41

---

[a] Henry Alford, *The Greek New Testament, with Notes.*    [b] Joseph Thayer, *A Greek-English Lexicon.*

## New International Version

18And,

"I will be a Father to you,
and you will be my sons and daughters,
says the Lord Almighty."*a*

**7** Therefore, since we have these promises, dear friends, let us purify ourselves from everything that contaminates body and spirit, perfecting holiness out of reverence for God.

### Paul's Joy Over the Church's Repentance

2Make room for us in your hearts. We have wronged no one, we have corrupted no one, we have exploited no one. 3I do not say this to condemn you; I have said before that you have such a place in our hearts that we would live or die with you. 4I have spoken to you with great frankness; I take great pride in you. I am greatly encouraged; in all our troubles my joy knows no bounds.

5For when we came into Macedonia, we had no rest, but we were harassed at every turn—conflicts on the outside, fears within. 6But God, who comforts the downcast, comforted us by the coming of Titus, 7and not only by his coming but also by the comfort you had given him. He told us about your longing for me, your deep sorrow, your ardent concern for me, so that my joy was greater than ever.

8Even if I caused you sorrow by my letter, I do not regret it. Though I did regret it—I see that my letter hurt you, but only for a little while— 9yet now I am happy, not because you were made sorry, but because your sorrow led you to repentance. For you became sorrowful as God intended and so were not harmed in any way by us. 10Godly sorrow brings repentance that leads to salvation and leaves no regret, but worldly sorrow brings death. 11See what this godly sorrow has produced in you: what earnestness, what eagerness to clear yourselves, what indignation, what alarm, what longing, what concern, what readiness to see justice done. At every point you have proved yourselves to be innocent in this matter. 12So even though I wrote to you, it was neither on account of the one who did the wrong nor on account of the injured party, but rather that before God you could see for yourselves how devoted to us you are. 13By all this we are encouraged.

In addition to our own encouragement, we were especially delighted to see how happy Titus was, because his spirit has been refreshed by all of you. 14I had boasted to

## Amplified Bible

18And I will be a Father to you, and you shall be My sons and daughters, says the Lord Almighty. [Isa. 43:6; Hos. 1:10.]

**7** Therefore, since these [great] promises are ours, beloved, let us cleanse ourselves from everything that contaminates *and* defiles body and spirit, and bring [our] consecration to completeness in the [reverential] fear of God.

2Do open your hearts to us again [enlarge them to take us in]. We have wronged no one, we have betrayed *or* corrupted no one, we have cheated *or* taken advantage of no one.

3I do not say this to reproach *or* condemn [you], for I have said before that you are [nested] in our hearts, [and you will remain there] together [with us], whether we die or live.

4I have great boldness *and* free *and* fearless confidence *and* cheerful courage toward you; my pride in you is great. I am filled [brimful] with the comfort [of it]; with all our tribulation *and* in spite of it, [I am filled with comfort] I am overflowing with joy.

5For even when we arrived in Macedonia, our bodies had no ease *or* rest, but we were oppressed in every way *and* afflicted at every turn—fighting *and* contentions without, dread *and* fears within [us].

6But God, Who comforts *and* encourages *and* refreshes *and* cheers the depressed *and* the sinking, comforted *and* encouraged *and* refreshed *and* cheered us by the arrival of Titus.

7[Yes] and not only by his coming but also by [his account of] the comfort with which he was encouraged *and* refreshed *and* cheered as to you, while he told us of your yearning affection, of how sorry you were [for me] and how eagerly you took my part, so that I rejoiced still more.

8For even though I did grieve you with my letter, I do not regret [it now], though I did regret it; for I see that that letter did pain you, though only for a little while;

9Yet I am glad now, not because you were pained, but because you were pained into repentance [and so turned back to God]; for you felt a grief such as God meant you to feel, so that in nothing you might suffer loss through us *or* harm for what we did.

10For godly grief *and* the pain God is permitted to direct, produce a repentance that leads *and* contributes to salvation *and* deliverance from evil, and it never brings regret; but worldly grief (the hopeless sorrow that is characteristic of the pagan world) is deadly [breeding and ending in death].

11For [you can look back now and] observe what this same godly sorrow has done for you *and* has produced in you: what eagerness *and* earnest care to explain *and* clear yourselves [of all *a*complicity in the condoning of incest], what indignation [at the sin], what alarm, what yearning, what zeal [to do justice to all concerned], what readiness to mete out punishment [*a*to the offender]! At every point you have proved yourselves cleared *and* guiltless in the matter. [I Cor. 5.]

12So although I did write to you [as I did], it was not for the sake *and* because of the one who did [the] wrong, nor on account of the one who suffered [the] wrong, but in order that you might realize before God [that your readiness to accept our authority revealed] how zealously you do care for us.

13Therefore we are relieved *and* comforted *and* encouraged [at the result]. And in addition to our own [personal] consolation, we were especially delighted at the joy of Titus, because you have all set his mind at rest, soothing *and* refreshing his spirit.

14For if I had boasted to him at all concerning you, I was

---

*a 18* 2 Samuel 7:14; 7:8

*a* Marvin Vincent, *Word Studies.*

## New International Version

him about you, and you have not embarrassed me. But just as everything we said to you was true, so our boasting about you to Titus has proved to be true as well. ¹⁵And his affection for you is all the greater when he remembers that you were all obedient, receiving him with fear and trembling. ¹⁶I am glad I can have complete confidence in you.

### The Collection for the Lord's People

**8** And now, brothers and sisters, we want you to know about the grace that God has given the Macedonian churches. ²In the midst of a very severe trial, their overflowing joy and their extreme poverty welled up in rich generosity. ³For I testify that they gave as much as they were able, and even beyond their ability. Entirely on their own, ⁴they urgently pleaded with us for the privilege of sharing in this service to the Lord's people. ⁵And they exceeded our expectations: They gave themselves first of all to the Lord, and then by the will of God also to us. ⁶So we urged Titus, just as he had earlier made a beginning, to bring also to completion this act of grace on your part. ⁷But since you excel in everything—in faith, in speech, in knowledge, in complete earnestness and in the love we have kindled in you*ᵃ*—see that you also excel in this grace of giving.

⁸I am not commanding you, but I want to test the sincerity of your love by comparing it with the earnestness of others. ⁹For you know the grace of our Lord Jesus Christ, that though he was rich, yet for your sake he became poor, so that you through his poverty might become rich.

¹⁰And here is my judgment about what is best for you in this matter. Last year you were the first not only to give but also to have the desire to do so. ¹¹Now finish the work, so that your eager willingness to do it may be matched by your completion of it, according to your means. ¹²For if the willingness is there, the gift is acceptable according to what one has, not according to what one does not have.

¹³Our desire is not that others might be relieved while you are hard pressed, but that there might be equality. ¹⁴At the present time your plenty will supply what they need, so that in turn their plenty will supply what you need. The goal is equality, ¹⁵as it is written: "The one who gathered much did not have too much, and the one who gathered little did not have too little."*ᵇ*

## Amplified Bible

not disappointed *or* put to shame, but just as everything we ever said to you was true, so our boasting [about you] to Titus has proved true also.

¹⁵And his heart goes out to you more abundantly than ever as he recalls the submission [to his guidance] that all of you had, and the reverence *and* anxiety [to meet all requirements] with which you accepted *and* welcomed him.

¹⁶I am very happy because I now am of good courage *and* have perfect confidence in you in all things.

**8** We want to tell you further, brethren, about the grace (the favor and spiritual blessing) of God which has been evident in the churches of Macedonia [arousing in them the desire to give alms];

²For in the midst of an ordeal of severe tribulation, their abundance of joy and their depth of poverty [together] have overflowed in wealth of lavish generosity on their part.

³For, as I can bear witness, [they gave] according to their ability, yes, and beyond their ability; and [they did it] voluntarily,

⁴Begging us most insistently for the favor *and* the fellowship of contributing in this ministration for [the relief and support of] the saints [in Jerusalem].

⁵Nor [was this gift of theirs merely the contribution] that we expected, but first they gave themselves to the Lord and to us [as His agents] by the will of God [*ᵃ*entirely disregarding their personal interests, they gave as much as they possibly could, having put themselves at our disposal to be directed by the will of God]—

⁶So much so that we have urged Titus that as he began it, he should also complete this beneficent *and* gracious contribution among you [the church at Corinth].

⁷Now as you abound *and* excel *and* are at the front in everything—in faith, in expressing yourselves, in knowledge, in all zeal, and in your love for us—[see to it that you come to the front now and] abound *and* excel in this gracious work [of almsgiving] also.

⁸I give this not as an order [to dictate to you], but to prove, by [pointing out] the zeal of others, the sincerity of your [own] love also.

⁹For you are becoming progressively acquainted with *and* recognizing more strongly *and* clearly the grace of our Lord Jesus Christ (His kindness, His gracious generosity, His undeserved favor and spiritual blessing), [in] that though He was [so very] rich, yet for your sakes He became [so very] poor, in order that by His poverty you might become enriched (abundantly supplied).

¹⁰[It is then] my counsel *and* my opinion in this matter that I give [you when I say]: It is profitable *and* fitting for you [now to complete the enterprise] which more than a year ago you not only began, but were the first to wish to do anything [about contributions for the relief of the saints at Jerusalem].

¹¹So now finish doing it, that your [enthusiastic] readiness in desiring it may be equalled by your completion of it according to your ability *and* means.

¹²For if the [eager] readiness to give is there, then it is acceptable *and* welcomed in proportion to what a person has, not according to what he does not have.

¹³For it is not [intended] that other people be eased *and* relieved [of their responsibility] and you be burdened *and* suffer [unfairly],

¹⁴But to have equality [share and share alike], your surplus over necessity at the present time going to meet their want *and* to equalize the difference created by it, so that [at some other time] their surplus in turn may be given to supply your want. Thus there may be equality,

¹⁵As it is written, He who gathered much had nothing over, and he who gathered little did not lack. [Exod. 16:18.]

---

*ᵃ* 7 Some manuscripts *and in your love for us*   *ᵇ* 15 Exodus 16:18     *ᵃ* Joseph Thayer, *A Greek-English Lexicon*.

## New International Version

### Titus Sent to Receive the Collection

[16]Thanks be to God, who put into the heart of Titus the same concern I have for you. [17]For Titus not only welcomed our appeal, but he is coming to you with much enthusiasm and on his own initiative. [18]And we are sending along with him the brother who is praised by all the churches for his service to the gospel. [19]What is more, he was chosen by the churches to accompany us as we carry the offering, which we administer in order to honor the Lord himself and to show our eagerness to help. [20]We want to avoid any criticism of the way we administer this liberal gift. [21]For we are taking pains to do what is right, not only in the eyes of the Lord but also in the eyes of man.

[22]In addition, we are sending with them our brother who has often proved to us in many ways that he is zealous, and now even more so because of his great confidence in you. [23]As for Titus, he is my partner and co-worker among you; as for our brothers, they are representatives of the churches and an honor to Christ. [24]Therefore show these men the proof of your love and the reason for our pride in you, so that the churches can see it.

**9** There is no need for me to write to you about this service to the Lord's people. [2]For I know your eagerness to help, and I have been boasting about it to the Macedonians, telling them that since last year you in Achaia were ready to give; and your enthusiasm has stirred most of them to action. [3]But I am sending the brothers in order that our boasting about you in this matter should not prove hollow, but that you may be ready, as I said you would be. [4]For if any Macedonians come with me and find you unprepared, we—not to say anything about you—would be ashamed of having been so confident. [5]So I thought it necessary to urge the brothers to visit you in advance and finish the arrangements for the generous gift you had promised. Then it will be ready as a generous gift, not as one grudgingly given.

### Generosity Encouraged

[6]Remember this: Whoever sows sparingly will also reap sparingly, and whoever sows generously will also reap generously. [7]Each of you should give what you have decided in your heart to give, not reluctantly or under compulsion, for God loves a cheerful giver. [8]And God is able to bless you abundantly, so that in all things at all times, having all that you need, you will abound in every good work. [9]As it is written:

## Amplified Bible

[16]But thanks be to God Who planted the same earnest zeal and care for you in the heart of Titus.

[17]For he not only welcomed and responded to our appeal, but was himself so keen in his enthusiasm and interest in you that he is going to you of his own accord.

[18]But we are sending along with him that brother [Luke?] whose praise in the Gospel ministry [is spread] throughout all the churches;

[19]And more than that, he has been appointed by the churches to travel as our companion in regard to this bountiful contribution which we are administering for the glory of the Lord Himself and [to show] our eager readiness [as Christians to help one another].

[20][For] we are on our guard, intending that no one should find anything for which to blame us in regard to our administration of this large contribution.

[21]For we take thought beforehand and aim to be honest and absolutely above suspicion, not only in the sight of the Lord but also in the sight of men.

[22]Moreover, along with them we are sending our brother, whom we have often put to the test and have found him zealous (devoted and earnest) in many matters, but who is now more [eagerly] earnest than ever because of [his] absolute confidence in you.

[23]As for Titus, he is my colleague and shares my work in your service; and as for the [other two] brethren, they are the [special] messengers of the churches, a credit and glory to Christ (the Messiah).

[24]Show to these men, therefore, in the sight of the churches, the reality and plain truth of your love (your affection, goodwill, and benevolence) and what [good reasons] I had for boasting about and being proud of you.

**9** Now about the offering that is [to be made] for the saints (God's people in Jerusalem), it is quite superfluous that I should write you;

[2]For I am well acquainted with your willingness (your readiness and your eagerness to promote it) and I have proudly told about you to the people of Macedonia, saying that Achaia (most of Greece) has been prepared since last year for this contribution; and [consequently] your enthusiasm has stimulated the majority of them.

[3]Still, I am sending the brethren [on to you], lest our pride in you should be made an empty boast in this particular case, and so that you may be all ready, as I told them you would be;

[4]Lest, if [any] Macedonians should come with me and find you unprepared [for this generosity], we, to say nothing of yourselves, be humiliated for our being so confident.

[5]That is why I thought it necessary to urge these brethren to go to you before I do and make arrangements in advance for this bountiful, promised gift of yours, so that it may be ready, not as an extortion [wrung out of you] but as a generous and willing gift.

[6][Remember] this: he who sows sparingly and grudgingly will also reap sparingly and grudgingly, and he who sows generously [[a]that blessings may come to someone] will also reap generously and with blessings.

[7]Let each one [give] as he has made up his own mind and purposed in his heart, not reluctantly or sorrowfully or under compulsion, for God loves (He [a]takes pleasure in, prizes above other things, and is unwilling to abandon or to do without) a cheerful (joyous, "prompt to do it") giver [whose heart is in his giving]. [Prov. 22:9.]

[8]And God is able to make all grace (every favor and [a]earthly blessing) come to you in abundance, so that you may always and under all circumstances and whatever the need [b]be self-sufficient [possessing enough to require no aid or support and furnished in abundance for every good work and charitable donation].

[a] Joseph Thayer, *A Greek-English Lexicon.*   [b] Marvin Vincent, *Word Studies.*

# New International Version

"They have freely scattered their gifts to the poor; their righteousness endures forever."[a]

[10]Now he who supplies seed to the sower and bread for food will also supply and increase your store of seed and will enlarge the harvest of your righteousness. [11]You will be enriched in every way so that you can be generous on every occasion, and through us your generosity will result in thanksgiving to God.

[12]This service that you perform is not only supplying the needs of the Lord's people but is also overflowing in many expressions of thanks to God. [13]Because of the service by which you have proved yourselves, others will praise God for the obedience that accompanies your confession of the gospel of Christ, and for your generosity in sharing with them and with everyone else. [14]And in their prayers for you their hearts will go out to you, because of the surpassing grace God has given you. [15]Thanks be to God for his indescribable gift!

### Paul's Defense of His Ministry

**10** By the humility and gentleness of Christ, I appeal to you—I, Paul, who am "timid" when face to face with you, but "bold" toward you when away! [2]I beg you that when I come I may not have to be as bold as I expect to be toward some people who think that we live by the standards of this world. [3]For though we live in the world, we do not wage war as the world does. [4]The weapons we fight with are not the weapons of the world. On the contrary, they have divine power to demolish strongholds. [5]We demolish arguments and every pretension that sets itself up against the knowledge of God, and we take captive every thought to make it obedient to Christ. [6]And we will be ready to punish every act of disobedience, once your obedience is complete.

[7]You are judging by appearances.[b] If anyone is confident that they belong to Christ, they should consider again that we belong to Christ just as much as they do. [8]So even if I boast somewhat freely about the authority the Lord gave us for building you up rather than tearing you down, I will not be ashamed of it. [9]I do not want to seem to be trying to frighten you with my letters. [10]For some say, "His letters are weighty and forceful, but in person he is unimpressive and his speaking amounts to nothing." [11]Such people should realize that what we are in our letters when we are absent, we will be in our actions when we are present.

[12]We do not dare to classify or compare ourselves with

# Amplified Bible

[9]As it is written, He [the benevolent person] scatters abroad; He gives to the poor; His deeds of justice and goodness and kindness and benevolence will go on and endure forever! [Ps. 112:9.]

[10]And [God] Who provides seed for the sower and bread for eating will also provide and multiply your [resources for] sowing and increase the fruits of your righteousness [a which manifests itself in active goodness, kindness, and charity]. [Isa. 55:10; Hos. 10:12.]

[11]Thus you will be enriched in all things and in every way, so that you can be generous, and [your generosity as it is] administered by us will bring forth thanksgiving to God.

[12]For the service that the ministering of this fund renders does not only fully supply what is lacking to the saints (God's people), but it also overflows in many [cries of] thanksgiving to God.

[13]Because at [your] standing of the test of this ministry, they will glorify God for your loyalty and obedience to the Gospel of Christ which you confess, as well as for your generous-hearted liberality to them and to all [the other needy ones].

[14]And they yearn for you while they pray for you, because of the surpassing measure of God's grace (His favor and mercy and spiritual blessing which is shown forth) in you.

[15]Now thanks be to God for His Gift, [precious] beyond telling [His indescribable, inexpressible, free Gift]!

**10** Now I myself, Paul, beseech you, by the gentleness and consideration of Christ [Himself; I] who [am] lowly enough [so they say] when among you face to face, but bold (fearless and outspoken) to you when [I am] absent from you!

[2]I entreat you when I do come [to you] that I may not [be driven to such] boldness as I intend to show toward those few who suspect us of acting according to the flesh [on the low level of worldly motives and as if invested with only human powers].

[3]For though we walk (live) in the flesh, we are not carrying on our warfare according to the flesh and using mere human weapons.

[4]For the weapons of our warfare are not physical [weapons of flesh and blood], but they are mighty before God for the overthrow and destruction of strongholds,

[5][Inasmuch as we] refute arguments and theories and reasonings and every proud and lofty thing that sets itself up against the [true] knowledge of God; and we lead every thought and purpose away captive into the obedience of Christ (the Messiah, the Anointed One),

[6]Being in readiness to punish every [insubordinate for his] disobedience, when your own submission and obedience [as a church] are fully secured and complete.

[7]Look at [this obvious fact] which is before your eyes. If anyone is confident that he is Christ's, let him reflect and remind himself that even as he is Christ's, so too are we.

[8]For even though I boast rather freely about our power and authority, which the Lord gave for your upbuilding and not for demolishing you, yet I shall not be put to shame [for exceeding the truth],

[9]Neither would I seem to be overawing or frightening you with my letters;

[10]For they say, His letters are weighty and impressive and forceful and telling, but his personality and bodily presence are weak, and his speech and delivery are utterly contemptible (of no account).

[11]Let such people realize that what we say by letters when we are absent, [we put] also into deeds when we are present—

[12]Not that we [have the audacity to] venture to class or [even to] compare ourselves with some who exalt and

---

[a] 9 Psalm 112:9    [b] 7 Or Look at the obvious facts

[a] Joseph Thayer, A Greek-English Lexicon.

## New International Version

some who commend themselves. When they measure themselves by themselves and compare themselves with themselves, they are not wise. ¹³We, however, will not boast beyond proper limits, but will confine our boasting to the sphere of service God himself has assigned to us, a sphere that also includes you. ¹⁴We are not going too far in our boasting, as would be the case if we had not come to you, for we did get as far as you with the gospel of Christ. ¹⁵Neither do we go beyond our limits by boasting of work done by others. Our hope is that, as your faith continues to grow, our sphere of activity among you will greatly expand, ¹⁶so that we can preach the gospel in the regions beyond you. For we do not want to boast about work already done in someone else's territory. ¹⁷But, "Let the one who boasts boast in the Lord."*ᵃ* ¹⁸For it is not the one who commends himself who is approved, but the one whom the Lord commends.

### Paul and the False Apostles

**11** I hope you will put up with me in a little foolishness. Yes, please put up with me! ²I am jealous for you with a godly jealousy. I promised you to one husband, to Christ, so that I might present you as a pure virgin to him. ³But I am afraid that just as Eve was deceived by the serpent's cunning, your minds may somehow be led astray from your sincere and pure devotion to Christ. ⁴For if someone comes to you and preaches a Jesus other than the Jesus we preached, or if you receive a different spirit from the Spirit you received, or a different gospel from the one you accepted, you put up with it easily enough.

⁵I do not think I am in the least inferior to those "super-apostles."*ᵇ* ⁶I may indeed be untrained as a speaker, but I do have knowledge. We have made this perfectly clear to you in every way. ⁷Was it a sin for me to lower myself in order to elevate you by preaching the gospel of God to you free of charge? ⁸I robbed other churches by receiving support from them so as to serve you. ⁹And when I was with you and needed something, I was not a burden to anyone, for the brothers who came from Macedonia supplied what I needed. I have kept myself from being a burden to you in any way, and will continue to do so. ¹⁰As surely as the truth of Christ is in me, nobody in the regions of Achaia will stop this boasting of mine. ¹¹Why? Because I do not love you? God knows I do!

¹²And I will keep on doing what I am doing in order to cut the ground from under those who want an opportunity to be considered equal with us in the things they boast

## Amplified Bible

furnish testimonials for themselves! However, when they measure themselves with themselves and compare themselves with one another, they are without understanding *and* behave unwisely.

¹³We, on the other hand, will not boast beyond our legitimate province *and* proper limit, but will keep within the limits [of our commission which] God has allotted us as our measuring line and which reaches *and* includes even you.

¹⁴For we are not overstepping the limits of our province *and* stretching beyond our ability to reach, as though we reached not (had no legitimate mission) to you, for we were [the very first] to come even as far as to you with the good news (the Gospel) of Christ.

¹⁵We do not boast therefore, beyond our proper limit, over other men's labors, but we have the hope *and* confident expectation that as your faith continues to grow, our field among you may be greatly enlarged, still within the limits of our commission,

¹⁶So that [we may even] preach the Gospel in lands [lying] beyond you, without making a boast of work already done in another [man's] sphere of activity [before we came on the scene].

¹⁷However, let him who boasts *and* glories boast *and* glory in the Lord. [Jer. 9:24.]

¹⁸For [it is] not [the man] who praises *and* commends himself who is approved *and* accepted, but [it is the person] whom the Lord accredits *and* commends.

**11** I wish you would bear with me while I indulge in a little [so-called] foolishness. Do bear with me!

²For I am ᵃzealous for you with a godly eagerness *and* a divine jealousy, for I have betrothed you to one Husband, to present you as a chaste virgin to Christ. [Hos. 2:19, 20.]

³But [now] I am fearful, lest that even as the serpent beguiled Eve by his cunning, so your minds may be corrupted *and* seduced from wholehearted *and* sincere *and* pure devotion to Christ. [Gen. 3:4.]

⁴For [you seem readily to endure it] if a man comes and preaches another Jesus than the One we preached, or if you receive a different spirit from the [Spirit] you [once] received or a different gospel from the one you [then] received *and* welcomed; you tolerate [all that] well enough!

⁵Yet I consider myself as in no way inferior to these [precious] ᵇextra-super [false] apostles.

⁶But even if [I am] unskilled in speaking, yet [I am] not [unskilled] in knowledge [I know what I am talking about]; we have made this evident to you in all things.

⁷But did I perhaps make a mistake *and* do you a wrong in debasing *and* cheapening myself so that you might be exalted *and* enriched in dignity *and* honor *and* happiness by preaching God's Gospel without expense to you?

⁸Other churches I have robbed by accepting [more than their share of] support for my ministry [from them in order] to serve you.

⁹And when I was with you and ran short financially, I did not burden any [of you], for what I lacked was abundantly made up by the brethren who came from Macedonia. So I kept myself from being burdensome to you in any way, and will continue to keep [myself from being so].

¹⁰As the truth of Christ is in me, this my boast [of independence] shall not be debarred (silenced or checked) in the regions of Achaia (most of Greece).

¹¹And why? Because I do not love you [do not have a preference for you, wish you well, and regard your welfare]? God perceives *and* knows that I do!

¹²But what I do, I will continue to do, [for I am determined to maintain this independence] in order to cut off the claim of those who would like [to find an occasion and incentive] to claim that in their boasted [mission] they work on the same terms that we do.

*ᵃ* 17 Jer. 9:24    *ᵇ* 5 Or *to the most eminent apostles*

*ᵃ* G. Abbott-Smith, *Manual Greek Lexicon of the New Testament.*
*ᵇ* Frederick W. Farrar, *The Life and Work of Saint Paul.*

## New International Version

about. ¹³For such people are false apostles, deceitful workers, masquerading as apostles of Christ. ¹⁴And no wonder, for Satan himself masquerades as an angel of light. ¹⁵It is not surprising, then, if his servants also masquerade as servants of righteousness. Their end will be what their actions deserve.

### Paul Boasts About His Sufferings

¹⁶I repeat: Let no one take me for a fool. But if you do, then tolerate me just as you would a fool, so that I may do a little boasting. ¹⁷In this self-confident boasting I am not talking as the Lord would, but as a fool. ¹⁸Since many are boasting in the way the world does, I too will boast. ¹⁹You gladly put up with fools since you are so wise! ²⁰In fact, you even put up with anyone who enslaves you or exploits you or takes advantage of you or puts on airs or slaps you in the face. ²¹To my shame I admit that we were too weak for that!

Whatever anyone else dares to boast about—I am speaking as a fool—I also dare to boast about. ²²Are they Hebrews? So am I. Are they Israelites? So am I. Are they Abraham's descendants? So am I. ²³Are they servants of Christ? (I am out of my mind to talk like this.) I am more. I have worked much harder, been in prison more frequently, been flogged more severely, and been exposed to death again and again. ²⁴Five times I received from the Jews the forty lashes minus one. ²⁵Three times I was beaten with rods, once I was pelted with stones, three times I was shipwrecked, I spent a night and a day in the open sea, ²⁶I have been constantly on the move. I have been in danger from rivers, in danger from bandits, in danger from my fellow Jews, in danger from Gentiles; in danger in the city, in danger in the country, in danger at sea; and in danger from false believers. ²⁷I have labored and toiled and have often gone without sleep; I have known hunger and thirst and have often gone without food; I have been cold and naked. ²⁸Besides everything else, I face daily the pressure of my concern for all the churches. ²⁹Who is weak, and I do not feel weak? Who is led into sin, and I do not inwardly burn?

³⁰If I must boast, I will boast of the things that show my weakness. ³¹The God and Father of the Lord Jesus, who is to be praised forever, knows that I am not lying. ³²In Damascus the governor under King Aretas had the city of the Damascenes guarded in order to arrest me. ³³But I was lowered in a basket from a window in the wall and slipped through his hands.

## Amplified Bible

¹³For such men are false apostles [spurious, counterfeits], deceitful workmen, masquerading as apostles (special messengers) of Christ (the Messiah).

¹⁴And it is no wonder, for Satan himself masquerades as an angel of light;

¹⁵So it is not surprising if his servants also masquerade as ministers of righteousness. [But] their end will correspond with their deeds.

¹⁶I repeat then, let no one think I have lost my wits; but even if you do, then bear with a witless man, so that I too may boast a little.

¹⁷What I say by way of this confident boasting, I say not with the Lord's authority [by inspiration] but, as it were, in pure witlessness.

¹⁸[For] since many boast of worldly things *and* according to the flesh, I will glory (boast) also.

¹⁹For you readily *and* gladly bear with the foolish, since you are so smart *and* wise yourselves!

²⁰For you endure it if a man assumes control of your souls *and* makes slaves of you, or devours [your substance, spends your money] *and* preys upon you, or deceives *and* takes advantage of you, or is arrogant *and* puts on airs, or strikes you in the face.

²¹To my discredit, I must say, we have shown ourselves too weak [for you to show such tolerance of us and for us to do strong, courageous things like that to you]! But in whatever any person is bold *and* dares [to boast]—mind you, I am speaking in this foolish (witless) way—I also am bold *and* dare [to boast].

²²They are Hebrews? So am I! They are Israelites? So am I! They are descendants of Abraham? So am I!

²³Are they [ministering] servants of Christ (the Messiah)? I am talking like one beside himself, [but] I am more, with far more extensive *and* abundant labors, with far more imprisonments, [beaten] with countless stripes, and frequently [at the point of] death.

²⁴Five times I received from [the hands of] the Jews forty [lashes all] but one; [Deut. 25:3.]

²⁵Three times I have been beaten with rods; once I was stoned. Three times I have been aboard a ship wrecked at sea; a [whole] night and a day I have spent [adrift] on the deep;

²⁶Many times on journeys, [exposed to] perils from rivers, perils from bandits, perils from [my own] nation, perils from the Gentiles, perils in the city, perils in the desert places, perils in the sea, perils from those posing as believers [but destitute of Christian knowledge and piety];

²⁷In toil and hardship, watching often [through sleepless nights], in hunger and thirst, frequently driven to fasting by want, in cold and exposure *and* lack of clothing.

²⁸And besides those things that are without, there is the daily [inescapable pressure] of my care *and* anxiety for all the churches!

²⁹Who is weak, and I do not feel [his] weakness? Who is made to stumble *and* fall *and* have his faith hurt, and I am not on fire [with sorrow or indignation]?

³⁰If I must boast, I will boast of the things that [show] my infirmity [of the things by which I am made weak and contemptible in the eyes of my opponents].

³¹The God and Father of the Lord Jesus *Christ* knows, He Who is blessed *and* to be praised forevermore, that I do not lie.

³²In Damascus, the city governor acting under King Aretas guarded the city of Damascus [on purpose] to arrest me,

³³And I was [actually] let down in a [rope] basket *or* hamper through a window (a small door) in the wall, and I escaped through his fingers.

## New International Version

### Paul's Vision and His Thorn

**12** I must go on boasting. Although there is nothing to be gained, I will go on to visions and revelations from the Lord. [2]I know a man in Christ who fourteen years ago was caught up to the third heaven. Whether it was in the body or out of the body I do not know—God knows. [3]And I know that this man—whether in the body or apart from the body I do not know, but God knows— [4]was caught up to paradise and heard inexpressible things, things that no one is permitted to tell. [5]I will boast about a man like that, but I will not boast about myself, except about my weaknesses. [6]Even if I should choose to boast, I would not be a fool, because I would be speaking the truth. But I refrain, so no one will think more of me than is warranted by what I do or say, [7]or because of these surpassingly great revelations. Therefore, in order to keep me from becoming conceited, I was given a thorn in my flesh, a messenger of Satan, to torment me. [8]Three times I pleaded with the Lord to take it away from me. [9]But he said to me, "My grace is sufficient for you, for my power is made perfect in weakness." Therefore I will boast all the more gladly about my weaknesses, so that Christ's power may rest on me. [10]That is why, for Christ's sake, I delight in weaknesses, in insults, in hardships, in persecutions, in difficulties. For when I am weak, then I am strong.

### Paul's Concern for the Corinthians

[11]I have made a fool of myself, but you drove me to it. I ought to have been commended by you, for I am not in the least inferior to the "super-apostles,"[a] even though I am nothing. [12]I persevered in demonstrating among you the marks of a true apostle, including signs, wonders and miracles. [13]How were you inferior to the other churches, except that I was never a burden to you? Forgive me this wrong!

[14]Now I am ready to visit you for the third time, and I will not be a burden to you, because what I want is not your possessions but you. After all, children should not have to save up for their parents, but parents for their children. [15]So I will very gladly spend for you everything I have and expend myself as well. If I love you more, will you love me less? [16]Be that as it may, I have not been a burden to you. Yet, crafty fellow that I am, I caught you by trickery! [17]Did I exploit you through any of the men I sent to you? [18]I

## Amplified Bible

**12** True, there is nothing to be gained by it, but [as I am obliged] to boast, I will go on to visions and revelations of the Lord.

[2]I know a man in Christ who fourteen years ago— whether in the body or out of the body I do not know, God knows—was caught up to the third heaven.

[3]And I know that this man—whether in the body or away from the body I do not know, God knows—

[4]Was caught up into paradise, and he heard utterances beyond the power of man to put into words, which man is not permitted to utter.

[5]Of this same [man's experiences] I will boast, but of myself (personally) I will not boast, except as regards my infirmities (my weaknesses).

[6]Should I desire to boast, I shall not be a witless braggart, for I shall be speaking the truth. But I abstain [from it] so that no one may form a higher estimate of me than [is justified by] what he sees in me or hears from me.

[7]And to keep me from being puffed up *and* too much elated by the exceeding greatness (preeminence) of these revelations, there was given me a thorn (*a* a splinter) in the flesh, a messenger of Satan, to rack *and* buffet *and* harass me, to keep me from being excessively exalted. [Job. 2:6.]

[8]Three times I called upon the Lord *and* besought [Him] about this *and* begged that it might depart from me;

[9]But He said to me, My grace (My favor and lovingkindness and mercy) is enough for you [sufficient against any danger and enables you to bear the trouble manfully]; for *My* strength *and* power are made perfect (fulfilled and completed) *and* [b]show *themselves most effective* in [your] weakness. Therefore, I will all the more gladly glory in my weaknesses *and* infirmities, that the strength *and* power of Christ (the Messiah) may rest (yes, may [c]pitch a tent over and dwell) upon me!

[10]So for the sake of Christ, I am well pleased *and* take pleasure in infirmities, insults, hardships, persecutions, perplexities *and* distresses; for when I am weak [[d]in human strength], then am I [truly] strong (able, powerful [d]in divine strength).

[11]Now I have been [speaking like] a fool! But you forced me to it, for I ought to have been [[c]saved the necessity and] commended by you. For I have not fallen short one bit *or* proved myself at all inferior to those superlative [false] apostles [of yours], even if I am nothing (a nobody).

[12]Indeed, the signs that indicate a [genuine] apostle were performed among you fully *and* most patiently in miracles and wonders and mighty works.

[13]For in what respect were you put to a disadvantage in comparison with the rest of the churches, unless [it was for the fact] that I myself did not burden you [with my financial support]? Pardon me [for doing you] this injustice!

[14]Now for the third time I am ready to come to [visit] you. And I will not burden you [financially], for it is not your [money] that I want but you; for children are not duty bound to lay up store for their parents, but parents for their children.

[15]But I will most gladly spend [myself] and be utterly spent for your souls. If I love you exceedingly, am I to be loved [by you] the less?

[16]But though granting that I did not burden you [with my support, some say that] I was crafty [and that] I cheated *and* got the better of you with my trickery.

[17]Did I [then] take advantage of you *or* make any money out of you through any of those [messengers] whom I sent to you?

*a* James Moulton and George Milligan, *The Vocabulary of the Greek Testament*. *b* Two Greek texts so read. *c* Marvin Vincent, *Word Studies*. *d* Joseph Thayer, *A Greek-English Lexicon*.

*a 11* Or *the most eminent apostles*

## New International Version

urged Titus to go to you and I sent our brother with him. Titus did not exploit you, did he? Did we not walk in the same footsteps by the same Spirit?

[19] Have you been thinking all along that we have been defending ourselves to you? We have been speaking in the sight of God as those in Christ; and everything we do, dear friends, is for your strengthening. [20] For I am afraid that when I come I may not find you as I want you to be, and you may not find me as you want me to be. I fear that there may be discord, jealousy, fits of rage, selfish ambition, slander, gossip, arrogance and disorder. [21] I am afraid that when I come again my God will humble me before you, and I will be grieved over many who have sinned earlier and have not repented of the impurity, sexual sin and debauchery in which they have indulged.

### Final Warnings

**13** This will be my third visit to you. "Every matter must be established by the testimony of two or three witnesses."[a] [2] I already gave you a warning when I was with you the second time. I now repeat it while absent: On my return I will not spare those who sinned earlier or any of the others, [3] since you are demanding proof that Christ is speaking through me. He is not weak in dealing with you, but is powerful among you. [4] For to be sure, he was crucified in weakness, yet he lives by God's power. Likewise, we are weak in him, yet by God's power we will live with him in our dealing with you.

[5] Examine yourselves to see whether you are in the faith; test yourselves. Do you not realize that Christ Jesus is in you—unless, of course, you fail the test? [6] And I trust that you will discover that we have not failed the test. [7] Now we pray to God that you will not do anything wrong—not so that people will see that we have stood the test but so that you will do what is right even though we may seem to have failed. [8] For we cannot do anything against the truth, but only for the truth. [9] We are glad whenever we are weak but you are strong; and our prayer is that you may be fully restored. [10] This is why I write these things when I am absent, that when I come I may not have to be harsh in my use of authority—the authority the Lord gave me for building you up, not for tearing you down.

### Final Greetings

[11] Finally, brothers and sisters, rejoice! Strive for full restoration, encourage one another, be of one mind, live in peace. And the God of love and peace will be with you.

## Amplified Bible

[18] [Actually] I urged Titus [to go], and I sent the brother with [him]. Did Titus overreach or take advantage of you [in anything]? Did he and I not act in the same spirit? Did we not [take the] same steps?

[19] Have you been supposing [all this time] that we have been defending ourselves and apologizing to you? [It is] in the sight and the [very] presence of God [and as one] in Christ (the Messiah) that we have been speaking, dearly beloved, and all in order to build you up [spiritually].

[20] For I am fearful that somehow or other I may come and find you not as I desire to find you, and that you may find me too not as you want to find me—that perhaps there may be factions (quarreling), jealousy, temper (wrath, intrigues, rivalry, divided loyalties), selfishness, whispering, gossip, arrogance (self-assertion), and disorder among you.

[21] [I am fearful] that when I come again, my God may humiliate and humble me in your regard, and that I may have to sorrow over many of those who sinned before and have not repented of the impurity, sexual vice, and sensuality which they formerly practiced.

**13** This is the third time that I am coming to you. By the testimony of two or three witnesses must any charge and every accusing statement be sustained and confirmed. [Deut. 19:15.]

[2] I have already warned those who sinned formerly and all the rest also, and I warn them now again while I am absent, as I did when present on my second visit, that if I come back, I will not spare [them],

[3] Since you desire and seek [perceptible] proof of the Christ Who speaks in and through me. [For He] is not weak and feeble in dealing with you, but is a mighty power within you;

[4] For though He was crucified in weakness, yet He goes on living by the power of God. And though we too are weak in Him [as He was humanly weak], yet in dealing with you [we shall show ourselves] alive and strong in [fellowship with] Him by the power of God.

[5] Examine and test and evaluate your own selves to see whether you are holding to your faith and showing the proper fruits of it. Test and prove yourselves [[a] not Christ]. Do you not yourselves realize and know [thoroughly by an ever-increasing experience] that Jesus Christ is in you—unless you are [counterfeits] disapproved on trial and rejected?

[6] But I hope you will recognize and know that we are not disapproved on trial and rejected.

[7] But I pray to God that you may do nothing wrong, not in order that we [[a] our teaching] may appear to be approved, but that you may continue doing right, [though] we may seem to have failed and be unapproved.

[8] For we can do nothing against the Truth [[b] not serve any party or personal interest], but only for the Truth [[c] which is the Gospel].

[9] For we are glad when we are weak ([a] unapproved) and you are really strong. And this we also pray for: your all-round strengthening and perfecting of soul.

[10] So I write these things while I am absent from you, that when I come to you, I may not have to deal sharply in my use of the authority which the Lord has given me [to be employed, however] for building [you] up and not for tearing [you] down.

[11] Finally, brethren, farewell (rejoice)! Be strengthened (perfected, completed, made what you ought to be); be encouraged and consoled and comforted; be of the same [agreeable] mind one with another; live in peace, and [then] the God of love [Who is the Source of affection, goodwill, love, and benevolence toward men] and the Author and Promoter of peace will be with you.

---

[a] 1 Deut. 19:15.

[a] Marvin Vincent, Word Studies. [b] James C. Gray and George M. Adams, Bible Commentary. [c] Joseph Thayer, A Greek-English Lexicon.

## New International Version

[12] Greet one another with a holy kiss. [13] All God's people here send their greetings.

[14] May the grace of the Lord Jesus Christ, and the love of God, and the fellowship of the Holy Spirit be with you all.

## Amplified Bible

[12] Greet one another with a consecrated kiss.

[13] All the saints (the people of God here) salute you.

[14] The grace (favor and spiritual blessing) of the Lord Jesus Christ and the love of God and the presence *and* fellowship (the communion and sharing together, and participation) in the Holy Spirit be with you all. *Amen (so be it).*

## New International Version

# Galatians

**1** Paul, an apostle—sent not from men nor by a man, but by Jesus Christ and God the Father, who raised him from the dead— ²and all the brothers and sisters[a] with me,

To the churches in Galatia:

³Grace and peace to you from God our Father and the Lord Jesus Christ, ⁴who gave himself for our sins to rescue us from the present evil age, according to the will of our God and Father, ⁵to whom be glory for ever and ever. Amen.

### No Other Gospel

⁶I am astonished that you are so quickly deserting the one who called you to live in the grace of Christ and are turning to a different gospel— ⁷which is really no gospel at all. Evidently some people are throwing you into confusion and are trying to pervert the gospel of Christ. ⁸But even if we or an angel from heaven should preach a gospel other than the one we preached to you, let them be under God's curse! ⁹As we have already said, so now I say again: If anybody is preaching to you a gospel other than what you accepted, let them be under God's curse!

¹⁰Am I now trying to win the approval of human beings, or of God? Or am I trying to please people? If I were still trying to please people, I would not be a servant of Christ.

### Paul Called by God

¹¹I want you to know, brothers and sisters, that the gospel I preached is not of human origin. ¹²I did not receive it from any man, nor was I taught it; rather, I received it by revelation from Jesus Christ.

¹³For you have heard of my previous way of life in Judaism, how intensely I persecuted the church of God and tried to destroy it. ¹⁴I was advancing in Judaism beyond many of my own age among my people and was extremely zealous for the traditions of my fathers. ¹⁵But when God, who set me apart from my mother's womb and called me by his grace, was pleased ¹⁶to reveal his Son in me so that

## Amplified Bible

### THE LETTER OF PAUL TO THE

# Galatians

**1** Paul, an apostle—[special messenger appointed and commissioned and sent out] not from [any body of] men nor by or through ᵃany man, but by and through Jesus Christ (the Messiah) and God the Father, Who raised Him from among the dead—

²And all the brethren who are with me, to the churches of Galatia:

³Grace and spiritual blessing be to you and [soul] peace from God the Father and our Lord Jesus Christ (the Messiah),

⁴Who gave (yielded) Himself up [ᵃto atone] for our sins [and ᵃto save and sanctify us], in order to rescue and deliver us from this present wicked age and world order, in accordance with the will and purpose and plan of our God and Father—

⁵To Him [be ascribed all] the glory through all the ages of the ages and the eternities of the eternities! Amen (so be it).

⁶I am surprised and astonished that you are so quickly ᵇturning renegade and deserting Him Who invited and called you ᵃby the grace (unmerited favor) of Christ (the Messiah) [and that you are transferring your allegiance] to a different [even an opposition] gospel.

⁷Not that there is [or could be] any other [genuine Gospel], but there are [obviously] some who are troubling and disturbing and bewildering you [ᵃwith a different kind of teaching which they offer as a gospel] and want to pervert and distort the Gospel of Christ (the Messiah) [into something which it absolutely is not].

⁸But even if we or an angel from heaven should preach to you a gospel contrary to and different from that which we preached to you, let him be accursed (anathema, devoted to destruction, doomed to eternal punishment)!

⁹As we said before, so I now say again: If anyone is preaching to you a gospel different from or contrary to that which you received [from us], let him be accursed (anathema, devoted to destruction, doomed to eternal punishment)!

¹⁰Now am I trying to win the favor of men, or of God? Do I seek to please men? If I were still seeking popularity with men, I should not be a bond servant of Christ (the Messiah).

¹¹For I want you to know, brethren, that the Gospel which was proclaimed and made known by me is not man's gospel [a human invention, according to or patterned after any human standard].

¹²For indeed I did not receive it from man, nor was I taught it, but [it came to me] through a [direct] revelation [given] by Jesus Christ (the Messiah).

¹³You have heard of my earlier career and former manner of life in the Jewish religion (Judaism), how I persecuted and abused the church of God furiously and extensively, and [with fanatical zeal did my best] to make havoc of it and destroy it.

¹⁴And [you have heard how] I outstripped many of the men of my own generation among the people of my race in [my advancement in study and observance of the laws of] Judaism, so extremely enthusiastic and zealous I was for the traditions of my ancestors.

¹⁵But when He, Who had chosen and set me apart [even] before I was born and had called me by His grace (His undeserved favor and blessing), saw fit and was pleased [Isa. 49:1; Jer. 1:5.]

¹⁶To reveal (unveil, disclose) His Son within me so that I might proclaim Him among the Gentiles (the non-Jewish

---

ᵃ 2 The Greek word for *brothers and sisters* (*adelphoi*) refers here to believers, both men and women, as part of God's family; also in verse 11; and in 3:15; 4:12, 28, 31; 5:11, 13; 6:1, 18.

ᵃ Marvin Vincent, *Word Studies in the New Testament.* ᵇ Joseph P. Lightfoot, *Notes on the Epistles of Saint Paul.*

# New International Version

I might preach him among the Gentiles, my immediate response was not to consult any human being. [17] I did not go up to Jerusalem to see those who were apostles before I was, but I went into Arabia. Later I returned to Damascus.

[18] Then after three years, I went up to Jerusalem to get acquainted with Cephas[a] and stayed with him fifteen days. [19] I saw none of the other apostles—only James, the Lord's brother. [20] I assure you before God that what I am writing you is no lie.

[21] Then I went to Syria and Cilicia. [22] I was personally unknown to the churches of Judea that are in Christ. [23] They only heard the report: "The man who formerly persecuted us is now preaching the faith he once tried to destroy." [24] And they praised God because of me.

## Paul Accepted by the Apostles

**2** Then after fourteen years, I went up again to Jerusalem, this time with Barnabas. I took Titus along also. [2] I went in response to a revelation and, meeting privately with those esteemed as leaders, I presented to them the gospel that I preach among the Gentiles. I wanted to be sure I was not running and had not been running my race in vain. [3] Yet not even Titus, who was with me, was compelled to be circumcised, even though he was a Greek. [4] This matter arose because some false believers had infiltrated our ranks to spy on the freedom we have in Christ Jesus and to make us slaves. [5] We did not give in to them for a moment, so that the truth of the gospel might be preserved for you.

[6] As for those who were held in high esteem—whatever they were makes no difference to me; God does not show favoritism—they added nothing to my message. [7] On the contrary, they recognized that I had been entrusted with the task of preaching the gospel to the uncircumcised,[b] just as Peter had been to the circumcised.[c] [8] For God, who was at work in Peter as an apostle to the circumcised, was also at work in me as an apostle to the Gentiles. [9] James, Cephas[d] and John, those esteemed as pillars, gave me and

# Amplified Bible

world) as the glad tidings (Gospel), immediately I did not confer with flesh and blood [did not consult or counsel with any frail human being or communicate with anyone].

[17] Nor did I [even] go up to Jerusalem to those who were apostles (special messengers of Christ) before I was, but I went away *and* retired into Arabia, and afterward I came back again to Damascus.

[18] Then three years later, I did go up to Jerusalem to become [personally] acquainted with Cephas (Peter), and remained with him for fifteen days.

[19] But I did not see any of the other apostles (the special messengers of Christ) except James the brother of our Lord.

[20] Now [note carefully what I am telling you, for it is the truth], I write this as if I were standing before the bar of God; I do not lie.

[21] Then I went into the districts (countries, regions) of Syria and Cilicia.

[22] And so far I was still unknown by sight to the churches of Christ in Judea (the country surrounding Jerusalem).

[23] They were only hearing it said, He who used to persecute us is now proclaiming the very faith he once reviled *and* which he set out to ruin *and* tried with all his might to destroy.

[24] And they glorified God [as the Author and Source of what had taken place] in me.

**2** Then after [an interval] of fourteen years I again went up to Jerusalem. [This time I went] with Barnabas, taking Titus along with [me] also.

[2] I went because it was specially *and* divinely revealed to me that I should go, and I put before them the Gospel [declaring to them that] which I preach among the Gentiles. However, [I presented the matter] privately before those of repute, [for I wanted to make certain, by thus at first confining my communication to this private conference] that I was not running or had not run in vain [guarding against being discredited either in what I was planning to do or had already done].

[3] But [all went well!] even Titus, who was with me, was not compelled [as some had anticipated] to be circumcised, although he was a Greek.

[4] [My precaution was] because of false brethren who had been secretly smuggled in [to the Christian brotherhood]; they had slipped in to spy on our liberty *and* the freedom which we have in Christ Jesus, that they might again bring us into bondage [under the Law of Moses].

[5] To them we did not yield submission even for a moment, that the truth of the Gospel might continue to be [preserved] for you [in its purity].

[6] Moreover, [no new requirements were made] by those who were reputed to be something—though what was their individual position *and* whether they really were of importance or not makes no difference to me; God is not impressed with the positions that men hold *and* He is not partial *and* recognizes no external distinctions—those [I say] who were of repute imposed no new requirements upon me [had nothing to add to my Gospel, and from them I received no new suggestions]. [Deut. 10:17.]

[7] But on the contrary, when they [really] saw that I had been entrusted [to carry] the Gospel to the uncircumcised [Gentiles, just as definitely] as Peter had been entrusted [to proclaim] the Gospel to the circumcised [Jews, they were agreeable];

[8] For He Who motivated *and* fitted Peter *and* worked effectively through him for the mission to the circumcised, motivated *and* fitted me *and* worked through me also for [the mission to] the Gentiles.

[9] And when they knew (perceived, recognized, understood, and acknowledged) the grace (God's unmerited favor and spiritual blessing) that had been bestowed upon me, James and Cephas (Peter) and John, who were re-

---

[a] *18* That is, Peter   [b] *7* That is, Gentiles   [c] *7* That is, Jews; also in verses 8 and 9   [d] *9* That is, Peter; also in verses 11 and 14

## New International Version

Barnabas the right hand of fellowship when they recognized the grace given to me. They agreed that we should go to the Gentiles, and they to the circumcised. [10]All they asked was that we should continue to remember the poor, the very thing I had been eager to do all along.

### Paul Opposes Cephas

[11]When Cephas came to Antioch, I opposed him to his face, because he stood condemned. [12]For before certain men came from James, he used to eat with the Gentiles. But when they arrived, he began to draw back and separate himself from the Gentiles because he was afraid of those who belonged to the circumcision group. [13]The other Jews joined him in his hypocrisy, so that by their hypocrisy even Barnabas was led astray.

[14]When I saw that they were not acting in line with the truth of the gospel, I said to Cephas in front of them all, "You are a Jew, yet you live like a Gentile and not like a Jew. How is it, then, that you force Gentiles to follow Jewish customs?

[15]"We who are Jews by birth and not sinful Gentiles [16]know that a person is not justified by the works of the law, but by faith in Jesus Christ. So we, too, have put our faith in Christ Jesus that we may be justified by faith in[a] Christ and not by the works of the law, because by the works of the law no one will be justified.

[17]"But if, in seeking to be justified in Christ, we Jews find ourselves also among the sinners, doesn't that mean that Christ promotes sin? Absolutely not! [18]If I rebuild what I destroyed, then I really would be a lawbreaker.

[19]"For through the law I died to the law so that I might live for God. [20]I have been crucified with Christ and I no longer live, but Christ lives in me. The life I now live in the body, I live by faith in the Son of God, who loved me and gave himself for me. [21]I do not set aside the grace of God, for if righteousness could be gained through the law, Christ died for nothing!"[b]

## Amplified Bible

puted to be pillars of the Jerusalem church, gave to me and Barnabas the right hand of fellowship, with the understanding that we should go to the Gentiles and they to the circumcised (Jews).

[10]They only [made one stipulation], that we were to remember the poor, which very thing I was also eager to do.

[11]But when Cephas (Peter) came to Antioch, I protested and opposed him to his face [concerning his conduct there], for he was blameable and stood condemned.

[12]For up to the time that certain persons came from James, he ate his meals with the Gentile [converts]; but when the men [from Jerusalem] arrived, he withdrew and held himself aloof from the Gentiles and [ate] separately for fear of those of the circumcision [party].

[13]And the rest of the Jews along with him also concealed their true convictions and acted insincerely, with the result that even Barnabas was carried away by their hypocrisy (their example of insincerity and pretense).

[14]But as soon as I saw that they were not straightforward and were not living up to the truth of the Gospel, I said to Cephas (Peter) before everybody present, If you, though born a Jew, can live [as you have been living] like a Gentile and not like a Jew, how do you dare now to urge and practically force the Gentiles to [comply with the ritual of Judaism] and live like Jews?

[15][I went on to say] Although we ourselves (you and I) are Jews by birth and not Gentile (heathen) sinners,

[16]Yet we know that a man is justified or reckoned righteous and in right standing with God not by works of the Law, but [only] through faith and [absolute] reliance on and adherence to and trust in Jesus Christ (the Messiah, the Anointed One). [Therefore] even we [ourselves] have believed on Christ Jesus, in order to be justified by faith in Christ and not by works of the Law [for we cannot be justified by any observance of the ritual of the Law given by Moses], because by keeping legal rituals and by works no human being can ever be justified (declared righteous and put in right standing with God). [Ps. 143:2.]

[17]But if, in our desire and endeavor to be justified in Christ [to be declared righteous and put in right standing with God wholly and solely through Christ], we have shown ourselves sinners also and convicted of sin, does that make Christ a minister (a party and contributor) to our sin? Banish the thought! [Of course not!]

[18]For if I [or any others who have taught that the observance of the Law of Moses is not essential to being justified by God should now by word or practice teach or intimate that it is essential to] build up again what I tore down, I prove myself a transgressor.

[19]For I through the Law [under the operation of the curse of the Law] have [in Christ's death for me] myself died to the Law and all the Law's demands upon me, so that I may [henceforth] live to and for God.

[20]I have been crucified with Christ [in Him I have shared His crucifixion]; it is no longer I who live, but Christ (the Messiah) lives in me; and the life I now live in the body I live by faith in (by adherence to and reliance on and complete trust in) the Son of God, Who loved me and gave Himself up for me.

[21][Therefore, I do not treat God's gracious gift as something of minor importance and defeat its very purpose]; I do not set aside and invalidate and frustrate and nullify the grace (unmerited favor) of God. For if justification (righteousness, acquittal from guilt) comes through [observing the ritual of] the Law, then Christ (the Messiah) died groundlessly and to no purpose and in vain. [His death was then wholly superfluous.]

[a] 16 Or but through the faithfulness of . . . justified on the basis of the faithfulness of    [b] 21 Some interpreters end the quotation after verse 14.

# New International Version

## Faith or Works of the Law

**3** You foolish Galatians! Who has bewitched you? Before your very eyes Jesus Christ was clearly portrayed as crucified. ²I would like to learn just one thing from you: Did you receive the Spirit by the works of the law, or by believing what you heard? ³Are you so foolish? After beginning by means of the Spirit, are you now trying to finish by means of the flesh?[a] ⁴Have you experienced[b] so much in vain—if it really was in vain? ⁵So again I ask, does God give you his Spirit and work miracles among you by the works of the law, or by your believing what you heard? ⁶So also Abraham "believed God, and it was credited to him as righteousness."[c]

⁷Understand, then, that those who have faith are children of Abraham. ⁸Scripture foresaw that God would justify the Gentiles by faith, and announced the gospel in advance to Abraham: "All nations will be blessed through you."[d] ⁹So those who rely on faith are blessed along with Abraham, the man of faith.

¹⁰For all who rely on the works of the law are under a curse, as it is written: "Cursed is everyone who does not continue to do everything written in the Book of the Law."[e] ¹¹Clearly no one who relies on the law is justified before God, because "the righteous will live by faith."[f] ¹²The law is not based on faith; on the contrary, it says, "The person who does these things will live by them."[g] ¹³Christ redeemed us from the curse of the law by becoming a curse for us, for it is written: "Cursed is everyone who is hung on a pole."[h] ¹⁴He redeemed us in order that the blessing given to Abraham might come to the Gentiles through Christ Jesus, so that by faith we might receive the promise of the Spirit.

## The Law and the Promise

¹⁵Brothers and sisters, let me take an example from everyday life. Just as no one can set aside or add to a human covenant that has been duly established, so it is in

# Amplified Bible

**3** O you poor *and* silly *and* thoughtless *and* unreflecting *and* senseless Galatians! Who has fascinated *or* bewitched *or* cast a spell over you, unto whom—right before your very eyes—Jesus Christ (the Messiah) was openly *and* graphically set forth *and* portrayed as crucified?

²Let me ask you this one question: Did you receive the [Holy] Spirit as the result of obeying the Law *and* doing its works, or was it by hearing [the message of the Gospel] and believing [it]? [Was it from observing a law of rituals or from a message of faith?]

³Are you so foolish *and* so senseless *and* so silly? Having begun [your new life spiritually] with the [Holy] Spirit, are you now reaching perfection [by dependence] on the flesh?

⁴Have you suffered so many things *and* experienced so much all for nothing (to no purpose)—if it really is to no purpose *and* in vain?

⁵Then does He Who supplies you with His marvelous [Holy] Spirit and works powerfully *and* miraculously among you do so on [the grounds of your doing] what the Law demands, or because of your believing in *and* adhering to *and* trusting in *and* relying on the message that you heard?

⁶Thus Abraham believed in *and* adhered to *and* trusted in *and* relied on God, and it was reckoned *and* placed to his account *and* credited as righteousness (as conformity to the divine will in purpose, thought, and action). [Gen. 15:6.]

⁷Know *and* understand that it is [really] the people [who live] by faith who are [the true] sons of Abraham.

⁸And the Scripture, foreseeing that God would justify (declare righteous, put in right standing with Himself) the Gentiles in consequence of faith, proclaimed the Gospel [foretelling the glad tidings of a Savior long beforehand] to Abraham in the promise, saying, In you shall all the nations [of the earth] be blessed. [Gen. 12:3.]

⁹So then, those who are people of faith are blessed *and* made happy *and* favored by God [as partners in fellowship] with the believing *and* trusting Abraham.

¹⁰And all who depend on the Law [who are seeking to be justified by obedience to the Law of rituals] are under a curse *and* doomed to disappointment *and* destruction, for it is written in the Scriptures, Cursed (accursed, devoted to destruction, doomed to eternal punishment) be everyone who does not continue to abide (live and remain) by all the precepts *and* commands written in the Book of the Law and to practice them. [Deut. 27:26.]

¹¹Now it is evident that no person is justified (declared righteous and brought into right standing with God) through the Law, for the Scripture says, The man in right standing with God [the just, the righteous] shall live by *and* out of faith *and* he who through *and* by faith is declared righteous *and* in right standing with God shall live. [Hab. 2:4.]

¹²But the Law does not rest on faith [does not require faith, has nothing to do with faith], for it itself says, He who does them [the things prescribed by the Law] shall live by them [not by faith]. [Lev. 18:5.]

¹³Christ purchased our freedom [redeeming us] from the curse (doom) of the Law [and its condemnation] by [Himself] becoming a curse for us, for it is written [in the Scriptures], Cursed is everyone who hangs on a tree (is crucified); [Deut. 21:23.]

¹⁴To the end that through [their receiving] Christ Jesus, the blessing [promised] to Abraham might come upon the Gentiles, so that we through faith might [all] receive [the realization of] the promise of the [Holy] Spirit.

¹⁵To speak in terms of human relations, brethren, [if] even a man makes a last will and testament (a merely human covenant), no one sets it aside *or* makes it void *or* adds to it when once it has been drawn up *and* signed (ratified, confirmed).

---

*a* 3 In contexts like this, the Greek word for *flesh* (*sarx*) refers to the sinful state of human beings, often presented as a power in opposition to the Spirit.  *b* 4 Or *suffered*  *c* 6 Gen. 15:6  *d* 8 Gen. 12:3; 18:18; 22:18  *e* 10 Deut. 27:26  *f* 11 Hab. 2:4  *g* 12 Lev. 18:5  *h* 13 Deut. 21:23

## New International Version

this case. ¹⁶The promises were spoken to Abraham and to his seed. Scripture does not say "and to seeds," meaning many people, but "and to your seed,"ᵃ meaning one person, who is Christ. ¹⁷What I mean is this: The law, introduced 430 years later, does not set aside the covenant previously established by God and thus do away with the promise. ¹⁸For if the inheritance depends on the law, then it no longer depends on the promise; but God in his grace gave it to Abraham through a promise.

¹⁹Why, then, was the law given at all? It was added because of transgressions until the Seed to whom the promise referred had come. The law was given through angels and entrusted to a mediator. ²⁰A mediator, however, implies more than one party; but God is one.

²¹Is the law, therefore, opposed to the promises of God? Absolutely not! For if a law had been given that could impart life, then righteousness would certainly have come by the law. ²²But Scripture has locked up everything under the control of sin, so that what was promised, being given through faith in Jesus Christ, might be given to those who believe.

### Children of God

²³Before the coming of this faith,ᵇ we were held in custody under the law, locked up until the faith that was to come would be revealed. ²⁴So the law was our guardian until Christ came that we might be justified by faith. ²⁵Now that this faith has come, we are no longer under a guardian.

²⁶So in Christ Jesus you are all children of God through faith, ²⁷for all of you who were baptized into Christ have clothed yourselves with Christ. ²⁸There is neither Jew nor Gentile, neither slave nor free, nor is there male and female, for you are all one in Christ Jesus. ²⁹If you belong to Christ, then you are Abraham's seed, and heirs according to the promise.

**4** What I am saying is that as long as an heir is underage, he is no different from a slave, although he owns the whole estate. ²The heir is subject to guardians and trustees until the time set by his father. ³So also, when

## Amplified Bible

¹⁶Now the promises (covenants, agreements) were decreed *and* made to Abraham and his Seed (his Offspring, his Heir). He [God] does not say, And to seeds (descendants, heirs), as if referring to many persons, but, And to your Seed (your Descendant, your Heir), obviously referring to one individual, Who is [none other than] Christ (the Messiah). [Gen. 13:15; 17:8.]

¹⁷This is my argument: The Law, which began 430 years after the covenant [concerning the coming Messiah], does not *and* cannot annul the covenant previously established (ratified) by God, so as to abolish the promise *and* make it void. [Exod. 12:40.]

¹⁸For if the inheritance [of the promise depends on observing] the Law [as these false teachers would like you to believe], it no longer [depends] on the promise; however, God gave it to Abraham [as a free gift solely] by virtue of His promise.

¹⁹What then was the purpose of the Law? It was added [later on, after the promise, to disclose and expose to men their guilt] because of transgressions *and* [to make men more conscious of the sinfulness] of sin; and it was intended to be in effect until the Seed (the Descendant, the Heir) should come, to *and* concerning Whom the promise had been made. And it [the Law] was arranged *and* ordained *and* appointed through the instrumentality of angels [and was given] by the hand (in the person) of a go-between [Moses, an intermediary person between God and man].

²⁰Now a go-between (intermediary) has to do with *and* implies more than one party [there can be no mediator with just one person]. Yet God is [only] one Person [and He was the sole party in giving that promise to Abraham. But the Law was a contract between two, God and Israel; its validity was dependent on both].

²¹Is the Law then contrary *and* opposed to the promises of God? Of course not! For if a Law had been given which could confer [spiritual] life, then righteousness *and* right standing with God would certainly have come by Law.

²²But the Scriptures [picture all mankind as sinners] shut up *and* imprisoned by sin, so that [the inheritance, blessing] which was promised through faith in Jesus Christ (the Messiah) might be given (released, delivered, and committed) to [all] those who believe [who adhere to and trust in and rely on Him].

²³Now before the faith came, we were perpetually guarded under the Law, kept in custody in preparation for the faith that was destined to be revealed (unveiled, disclosed),

²⁴So that the Law served ᵃ[to us Jews] as our trainer [our guardian, our guide to Christ, to lead us] until Christ [came], that we might be justified (declared righteous, put in right standing with God) by *and* through faith.

²⁵But now that the faith has come, we are no longer under a trainer (the guardian of our childhood).

²⁶For in Christ Jesus you are all sons of God through faith.

²⁷For as many [of you] as were baptized into Christ [into a spiritual union and communion with Christ, the Anointed One, the Messiah] have put on (clothed yourselves with) Christ.

²⁸There is [now no distinction] neither Jew nor Greek, there is neither slave nor free, there is not male ᵇand female; for you are all one in Christ Jesus.

²⁹And if you belong to Christ [are in Him Who is Abraham's Seed], then you are Abraham's offspring and [spiritual] heirs according to promise.

**4** Now what I mean is that as long as the inheritor (heir) is a child and under age, he does not differ from a slave, although he is the master of all the estate;

²But he is under guardians and administrators *or* trustees until the date fixed by his father.

ᵃ 16 Gen. 12:7; 13:15; 24:7   ᵇ 22,23 Or *through the faithfulness of Jesus . . . ²³Before faith came*

ᵃ Marvin Vincent, *Word Studies.* ᵇ Literal translation.

## New International Version

we were underage, we were in slavery under the elemental spiritual forces[a] of the world. [4]But when the set time had fully come, God sent his Son, born of a woman, born under the law, [5]to redeem those under the law, that we might receive adoption to sonship.[b] [6]Because you are his sons, God sent the Spirit of his Son into our hearts, the Spirit who calls out, *"Abba,[c]* Father." [7]So you are no longer a slave, but God's child; and since you are his child, God has made you also an heir.

### Paul's Concern for the Galatians

[8]Formerly, when you did not know God, you were slaves to those who by nature are not gods. [9]But now that you know God—or rather are known by God—how is it that you are turning back to those weak and miserable forces[d]? Do you wish to be enslaved by them all over again? [10]You are observing special days and months and seasons and years! [11]I fear for you, that somehow I have wasted my efforts on you.

[12]I plead with you, brothers and sisters, become like me, for I became like you. You did me no wrong. [13]As you know, it was because of an illness that I first preached the gospel to you, [14]and even though my illness was a trial to you, you did not treat me with contempt or scorn. Instead, you welcomed me as if I were an angel of God, as if I were Christ Jesus himself. [15]Where, then, is your blessing of me now? I can testify that, if you could have done so, you would have torn out your eyes and given them to me. [16]Have I now become your enemy by telling you the truth?

[17]Those people are zealous to win you over, but for no good. What they want is to alienate you from us, so that you may have zeal for them. [18]It is fine to be zealous, provided the purpose is good, and to be so always, not just when I am with you. [19]My dear children, for whom I am again in the pains of childbirth until Christ is formed in you, [20]how I wish I could be with you now and change my tone, because I am perplexed about you!

### Hagar and Sarah

[21]Tell me, you who want to be under the law, are you not aware of what the law says? [22]For it is written that Abra-

## Amplified Bible

[3]So we [Jewish Christians] also, when we were minors, were kept like slaves under [the rules of the Hebrew ritual and subject to] the elementary teachings of a system of external observations *and* regulations.

[4]But when the proper time had fully come, God sent His Son, born of a woman, born subject to [the regulations of] the Law,

[5]To purchase the freedom of (to ransom, to redeem, to *a* atone for) those who were subject to the Law, that we might be adopted *and* have sonship conferred upon us [and be recognized as God's sons].

[6]And because you [really] are [His] sons, God has sent the [*b* Holy] Spirit of His Son into our hearts, crying, Abba (Father)! Father!

[7]Therefore, you are no longer a slave (bond servant) but a son; and if a son, then [it follows that you are] an heir *c* by the aid of God, *through Christ.*

[8]But at that previous time, when you had not come to be acquainted with *and* understand *and* know the true God, you [Gentiles] were in bondage to gods who by their very nature could not be gods at all [gods that really did not exist].

[9]Now, however, that you have come to be acquainted with *and* understand *and* know [the true] God, or rather to be understood *and* known by God, how can you turn back again to the weak and beggarly *and* worthless elementary things [*c* of all religions before Christ came], whose slaves you once more want to become?

[10]You observe [particular] days and months and seasons and years!

[11]I am alarmed [about you], lest I have labored among *and* over you to no purpose *and* in vain.

[12]Brethren, I beg of you, become as I am [free from the bondage of Jewish ritualism and ordinances], for I also have become as you are [*b* a Gentile]. You did me no wrong [*b* in the days when I first came to you; do not do it now].

[13]On the contrary, you know that it was on account of a bodily ailment that [I remained and] preached the Gospel to you the first time.

[14]And [yet] although my physical condition was [such] a trial to you, you did not regard it with contempt, or scorn *and* loathe *and* reject me; but you received me as an angel of God, [even] as Christ Jesus [Himself]!

[15]What has become of that blessed enjoyment *and* satisfaction *and* self-congratulation that once was yours [in what I taught you and in your regard for me]? For I bear you witness that you would have torn out your own eyes and have given them to me [to replace mine], if that were possible.

[16]Have I then become your enemy by telling the truth to you *and* dealing sincerely with you?

[17]These men [the Judaizing teachers] are zealously trying to dazzle you [paying court to you, making much of you], but their purpose is not honorable *or* worthy *or* for any good. What they want to do is to isolate you [from us who oppose them], so that they may win you over to their side *and* get you to court their favor.

[18]It is always a fine thing [of course] to be zealously sought after [as you are, provided that it is] for a good purpose *and* done *d* by reason of purity of heart and life, and not just when I am present with you!

[19]My little children, for whom I am again suffering birth pangs until Christ is completely *and* permanently formed (molded) within you,

[20]Would that I were with you now and could coax you vocally, for I am fearful *and* perplexed about you!

[21]Tell me, you who are bent on being under the Law, will you listen to what the Law [really] says?

---

*a* 3 Or *under the basic principles*    *b* 5 The Greek word for *adoption to sonship* is a legal term referring to the full legal standing of an adopted male heir in Roman culture.    *c* 6 Aramaic for *Father*    *d* 9 Or *principles*

*a* *Webster's New International Dictionary* offers this as a definition of "redeem." *b* Marvin Vincent, *Word Studies.* *c* Joseph Thayer, *A Greek-English Lexicon of the New Testament.* *d* Joseph Thayer, *A Greek-English Lexicon.*

## New International Version

ham had two sons, one by the slave woman and the other by the free woman. [23]His son by the slave woman was born according to the flesh, but his son by the free woman was born as the result of a divine promise.

[24]These things are being taken figuratively: The women represent two covenants. One covenant is from Mount Sinai and bears children who are to be slaves: This is Hagar. [25]Now Hagar stands for Mount Sinai in Arabia and corresponds to the present city of Jerusalem, because she is in slavery with her children. [26]But the Jerusalem that is above is free, and she is our mother. [27]For it is written:

"Be glad, barren woman,
    you who never bore a child;
shout for joy and cry aloud,
    you who were never in labor;
because more are the children of the desolate woman
    than of her who has a husband."[a]

[28]Now you, brothers and sisters, like Isaac, are children of promise. [29]At that time the son born according to the flesh persecuted the son born by the power of the Spirit. It is the same now. [30]But what does Scripture say? "Get rid of the slave woman and her son, for the slave woman's son will never share in the inheritance with the free woman's son."[b] [31]Therefore, brothers and sisters, we are not children of the slave woman, but of the free woman.

### Freedom in Christ

**5** It is for freedom that Christ has set us free. Stand firm, then, and do not let yourselves be burdened again by a yoke of slavery.

[2]Mark my words! I, Paul, tell you that if you let yourselves be circumcised, Christ will be of no value to you at all. [3]Again I declare to every man who lets himself be circumcised that he is obligated to obey the whole law. [4]You who are trying to be justified by the law have been alienated from Christ; you have fallen away from grace. [5]For through the Spirit we eagerly await by faith the righteousness for which we hope. [6]For in Christ Jesus neither circumcision nor uncircumcision has any value. The only thing that counts is faith expressing itself through love.

[7]You were running a good race. Who cut in on you to keep you from obeying the truth? [8]That kind of persuasion does not come from the one who calls you. [9]"A little yeast works through the whole batch of dough." [10]I am confident

## Amplified Bible

[22]For it is written that Abraham had two sons, one by the bondmaid and one by the free woman. [Gen. 16:15; 21:2, 9.]

[23]But whereas the child of the slave woman was born according to the flesh *and* had an ordinary birth, the son of the free woman was born in fulfillment of the promise.

[24]Now all this is an allegory; these [two women] represent two covenants. One covenant originated from Mount Sinai [where the Law was given] and bears [children destined] for slavery; this is Hagar.

[25]Now Hagar is (stands for) Mount Sinai in Arabia and she corresponds to *and* belongs in the same category with the present Jerusalem, for she is in bondage together with her children.

[26]But the Jerusalem above ([a]the Messianic kingdom of Christ) is free, and she is our mother.

[27]For it is written in the Scriptures, Rejoice, O barren woman, who has not given birth to children; break forth into a joyful shout, you who are not feeling birth pangs, for the desolate woman has many more children than she who has a husband. [Isa. 54:1.]

[28]But we, brethren, are children [[a]not by physical descent, as was Ishmael, but] like Isaac, born [a]in virtue of promise.

[29]Yet [just] as at that time the child [of ordinary birth] born according to the flesh despised *and* persecuted him [who was born remarkably] according to [the promise and the working of] the [Holy] Spirit, so it is now also. [Gen. 21:9.]

[30]But what does the Scripture say? Cast out *and* send away the slave woman and her son, for never shall the son of the slave woman be heir *and* share the inheritance with the son of the free woman. [Gen. 21:10.]

[31]So, brethren, we [who are born again] are not children of a slave woman [[b]the natural], but of the free [[b]the supernatural].

**5** In [this] freedom Christ has made us free [and completely liberated us]; stand fast then, and do not be hampered *and* held ensnared *and* submit again to a yoke of slavery [which you have once put off].

[2]Notice, it is I, Paul, who tells you that if you receive circumcision, Christ will be of no profit (advantage, avail) to you [[c]for if you distrust Him, you can gain nothing from Him].

[3]I once more protest *and* testify to every man who receives circumcision that he is under obligation *and* bound to practice the whole of the Law *and* its ordinances.

[4]If you seek to be justified *and* declared righteous *and* to be given a right standing with God through the Law, you are brought to nothing *and* so separated (severed) from Christ. You have fallen away from grace (from God's gracious favor and unmerited blessing).

[5]For we, [not relying on the Law but] through the [Holy] Spirit's [help], by faith anticipate *and* wait for the blessing *and* good for which our righteousness *and* right standing with God [our [d]conformity to His will in purpose, thought, and action, causes us] to hope.

[6]For [if we are] in Christ Jesus, neither circumcision nor uncircumcision counts for anything, but only faith activated *and* energized *and* expressed *and* working through love.

[7]You were running the race nobly. Who has interfered in (hindered and stopped you from) your heeding *and* following the Truth?

[8]This [evil] persuasion is not from Him Who called you [Who invited you to freedom in Christ].

[9]A little leaven (a slight inclination to error, or a few false teachers) leavens the whole lump [it perverts the whole conception of faith or misleads the whole church].

---

[a] Marvin Vincent, *Word Studies.* [b] Joseph S. Exell, ed., *The Biblical Illustrator.* [c] John Chrysostom, one of the Doctors of the Greek Church. [d] G. Abbott-Smith, *Manual Greek Lexicon of the New Testament.*

[a] 27 Isaiah 54:1    [b] 30 Gen. 21:10

## New International Version

in the Lord that you will take no other view. The one who is throwing you into confusion, whoever that may be, will have to pay the penalty. [11] Brothers and sisters, if I am still preaching circumcision, why am I still being persecuted? In that case the offense of the cross has been abolished. [12] As for those agitators, I wish they would go the whole way and emasculate themselves!

### Life by the Spirit

[13] You, my brothers and sisters, were called to be free. But do not use your freedom to indulge the flesh[a]; rather, serve one another humbly in love. [14] For the entire law is fulfilled in keeping this one command: "Love your neighbor as yourself."[b] [15] If you bite and devour each other, watch out or you will be destroyed by each other.

[16] So I say, walk by the Spirit, and you will not gratify the desires of the flesh. [17] For the flesh desires what is contrary to the Spirit, and the Spirit what is contrary to the flesh. They are in conflict with each other, so that you are not to do whatever[c] you want. [18] But if you are led by the Spirit, you are not under the law.

[19] The acts of the flesh are obvious: sexual immorality, impurity and debauchery; [20] idolatry and witchcraft; hatred, discord, jealousy, fits of rage, selfish ambition, dissensions, factions [21] and envy; drunkenness, orgies, and the like. I warn you, as I did before, that those who live like this will not inherit the kingdom of God.

[22] But the fruit of the Spirit is love, joy, peace, forbearance, kindness, goodness, faithfulness, [23] gentleness and self-control. Against such things there is no law. [24] Those who belong to Christ Jesus have crucified the flesh with its passions and desires. [25] Since we live by the Spirit, let us keep in step with the Spirit. [26] Let us not become conceited, provoking and envying each other.

### Doing Good to All

**6** Brothers and sisters, if someone is caught in a sin, you who live by the Spirit should restore that person gently. But watch yourselves, or you also may be tempted. [2] Carry each other's burdens, and in this way you will ful-

## Amplified Bible

[10] [For my part] I have confidence [toward you] in the Lord that you will take no contrary view of the matter *but* will come to think with me. But he who is unsettling you, whoever he is, will have to bear the penalty.

[11] But, brethren, if I still preach circumcision [as some accuse me of doing, as necessary to salvation], why am I still suffering persecution? In that case the cross has ceased to be a stumbling block *and* is made meaningless (done away).

[12] I wish those who unsettle *and* confuse you would [[a] go all the way and] cut themselves off!

[13] For you, brethren, were [indeed] called to freedom; only [do not let your] freedom be an incentive to your flesh *and* an opportunity *or* excuse [for [a] selfishness], but through love you should serve one another.

[14] For the whole Law [concerning human relationships] is [a] complied with in the one precept, You shall love your neighbor as [you do] yourself. [Lev. 19:18.]

[15] But if you bite and devour one another [in partisan strife], be careful that you [and your whole fellowship] are not consumed by one another.

[16] But I say, walk *and* live [habitually] in the [Holy] Spirit [responsive to *and* controlled *and* guided by the Spirit]; then you will certainly not gratify the cravings *and* desires of the flesh (of human nature without God).

[17] For the desires of the flesh are opposed to the [Holy] Spirit, and the [desires of the] Spirit are opposed to the flesh (godless human nature); for these are antagonistic to each other [continually withstanding and in conflict with each other], so that you are not free *but* are prevented from doing what you desire to do.

[18] But if you are guided (led) by the [Holy] Spirit, you are not subject to the Law.

[19] Now the doings (practices) of the flesh are clear (obvious): they are immorality, impurity, indecency,

[20] Idolatry, sorcery, enmity, strife, jealousy, anger (ill temper), selfishness, divisions (dissensions), party spirit (factions, sects with peculiar opinions, heresies),

[21] Envy, drunkenness, carousing, and the like. I warn you beforehand, just as I did previously, that those who do such things shall not inherit the kingdom of God.

[22] But the fruit of the [Holy] Spirit [the work which His presence within accomplishes] is love, joy (gladness), peace, patience (an even temper, forbearance), kindness, goodness (benevolence), faithfulness,

[23] Gentleness (meekness, humility), self-control (self-restraint, continence). Against such things there is no law [[a] that can bring a charge].

[24] And those who belong to Christ Jesus (the Messiah) have crucified the flesh (the godless human nature) with its passions and appetites *and* desires.

[25] If we live by the [Holy] Spirit, let us also walk by the Spirit. [If by the Holy Spirit [b] we have our life in God, let us go forward [a] walking in line, our conduct controlled by the Spirit.]

[26] Let us not become vainglorious *and* self-conceited, competitive *and* challenging *and* provoking *and* irritating to one another, envying *and* being jealous of one another.

**6** Brethren, if any person is overtaken in misconduct *or* sin of any sort, you who are spiritual [who are responsive to and controlled by the Spirit] should set him right *and* restore *and* reinstate him, without any sense of superiority *and* with all gentleness, keeping an attentive eye on yourself, lest you should be tempted also.

[2] Bear (endure, carry) one another's burdens *and* [c] troublesome moral faults, and in this way fulfill *and* observe perfectly the law of Christ (the Messiah) *and* complete [a] what is lacking [in your obedience to it].

---

*a 13* In contexts like this, the Greek word for *flesh* (*sarx*) refers to the sinful state of human beings, often presented as a power in opposition to the Spirit; also in verses 16, 17, 19 and 24; and in 6:8.   *b 14* Lev. 19:18   *c 17* Or *you do not do what*

*a* Marvin Vincent, *Word Studies.*   *b* Adam Clarke, *The Holy Bible with A Commentary.*   *c* Joseph Thayer, *A Greek-English Lexicon.*

## New International Version

fill the law of Christ. ³If anyone thinks they are something when they are not, they deceive themselves. ⁴Each one should test their own actions. Then they can take pride in themselves alone, without comparing themselves to someone else, ⁵for each one should carry their own load. ⁶Nevertheless, the one who receives instruction in the word should share all good things with their instructor.

⁷Do not be deceived: God cannot be mocked. A man reaps what he sows. ⁸Whoever sows to please their flesh, from the flesh will reap destruction; whoever sows to please the Spirit, from the Spirit will reap eternal life. ⁹Let us not become weary in doing good, for at the proper time we will reap a harvest if we do not give up. ¹⁰Therefore, as we have opportunity, let us do good to all people, especially to those who belong to the family of believers.

### Not Circumcision but the New Creation

¹¹See what large letters I use as I write to you with my own hand!

¹²Those who want to impress people by means of the flesh are trying to compel you to be circumcised. The only reason they do this is to avoid being persecuted for the cross of Christ. ¹³Not even those who are circumcised keep the law, yet they want you to be circumcised that they may boast about your circumcision in the flesh. ¹⁴May I never boast except in the cross of our Lord Jesus Christ, through whichᵃ the world has been crucified to me, and I to the world. ¹⁵Neither circumcision nor uncircumcision means anything; what counts is the new creation. ¹⁶Peace and mercy to all who follow this rule—toᵇ the Israel of God.

¹⁷From now on, let no one cause me trouble, for I bear on my body the marks of Jesus.

¹⁸The grace of our Lord Jesus Christ be with your spirit, brothers and sisters. Amen.

## Amplified Bible

³For if any person thinks himself to be somebody [too important to condescend to shoulder another's load] when he is nobody [of superiority except in his own estimation], he deceives *and* deludes *and* cheats himself.

⁴But let every person carefully scrutinize *and* examine *and* test his own conduct *and* his own work. He can then have the personal satisfaction *and* joy of doing something commendable [ᵃin itself alone] without [resorting to] boastful comparison with his neighbor.

⁵For every person will have to bear (ᵇbe equal to understanding and calmly receive) his own [ᶜlittle] load ᵇ [of oppressive faults].

⁶Let him who receives instruction in the Word [of God] share all good things with his teacher [contributing to his support].

⁷Do not be deceived *and* deluded *and* misled; God will not allow Himself to be sneered at (scorned, disdained, or mocked ᵈby mere pretensions or professions, or by His precepts being set aside.) [He inevitably deludes himself who attempts to delude God.] For whatever a man sows, that *and* ᵃthat only is what he will reap.

⁸For he who sows to his own flesh (lower nature, sensuality) will from the flesh reap decay *and* ruin *and* destruction, but he who sows to the Spirit will from the Spirit reap eternal life.

⁹And let us not lose heart *and* grow weary *and* faint in acting nobly *and* doing right, for in due time *and* at the appointed season we shall reap, if we do not loosen *and* relax our courage *and* faint.

¹⁰So then, as occasion *and* opportunity open up to us, let us do good [ᵃmorally] to all people [not only ᵃbeing useful or profitable to them, but also doing what is for their spiritual good and advantage]. Be mindful to be a blessing, especially to those of the household of faith [those who belong to God's family with you, the believers].

¹¹See with what large letters I am writing with my own hand. [ᵃMark carefully these closing words of mine.]

¹²Those who want to make a good impression *and* a fine show in the flesh would try to compel you to receive circumcision, simply so that they may escape being persecuted for allegiance to the cross of Christ (the Messiah, the Anointed One).

¹³For even the circumcised [Jews] themselves do not [really] keep the Law, but they want to have you circumcised in order that they may glory in your flesh (your subjection to external rites).

¹⁴But far be it from me to glory [in anything or anyone] except in the cross of our Lord Jesus Christ (the Messiah) through Whom the world has been crucified to me, and I to the world!

¹⁵For neither is circumcision [now] of any importance, nor uncircumcision, but [only] a new creation [the result of a new birth and a new nature in Christ Jesus, the Messiah].

¹⁶Peace and mercy be upon all who walk by this rule [who discipline themselves and regulate their lives by this principle], even upon the [true] Israel of God! [Ps. 125:5.]

¹⁷From now on let no person trouble me [by ᵃmaking it necessary for me to vindicate my apostolic authority and the divine truth of my Gospel], for I bear on my body the [brand] marks of the Lord Jesus [the wounds, scars, and other outward evidence of persecutions—these testify to His ownership of me]!

¹⁸The grace (spiritual favor, blessing) of our Lord Jesus Christ (the Anointed One, the Messiah) be with your spirit, brethren. Amen (so be it).

---

ᵃ Marvin Vincent, *Word Studies*. ᵇ Joseph Thayer, *A Greek-English Lexicon*. ᶜ Diminutive (indicating small size) form of the Greek word. ᵈ Matthew Henry, *Commentary on the Holy Bible*.

---

ᵃ 14 Or *whom*    ᵇ 16 Or *rule and to*

## New International Version

# Ephesians

**1** Paul, an apostle of Christ Jesus by the will of God,

To God's holy people in Ephesus,[a] the faithful in Christ Jesus:

[2]Grace and peace to you from God our Father and the Lord Jesus Christ.

### Praise for Spiritual Blessings in Christ

[3]Praise be to the God and Father of our Lord Jesus Christ, who has blessed us in the heavenly realms with every spiritual blessing in Christ. [4]For he chose us in him before the creation of the world to be holy and blameless in his sight. In love [5]he[b] predestined us for adoption to sonship[c] through Jesus Christ, in accordance with his pleasure and will— [6]to the praise of his glorious grace, which he has freely given us in the One he loves. [7]In him we have redemption through his blood, the forgiveness of sins, in accordance with the riches of God's grace [8]that he lavished on us. With all wisdom and understanding, [9]he[d] made known to us the mystery of his will according to his good pleasure, which he purposed in Christ, [10]to be put into effect when the times reach their fulfillment— to bring unity to all things in heaven and on earth under Christ.

[11]In him we were also chosen,[e] having been predestined according to the plan of him who works out everything in conformity with the purpose of his will, [12]in order that we, who were the first to put our hope in Christ, might be for the praise of his glory. [13]And you also were included in Christ when you heard the message of truth, the gospel of your salvation. When you believed, you were marked in him with a seal, the promised Holy Spirit, [14]who is a deposit guaranteeing our inheritance until the redemption of those who are God's possession—to the praise of his glory.

### Thanksgiving and Prayer

[15]For this reason, ever since I heard about your faith in the Lord Jesus and your love for all God's people, [16]I have not stopped giving thanks for you, remembering you in my prayers. [17]I keep asking that the God of our Lord Jesus

---

## Amplified Bible

THE LETTER OF PAUL TO THE

# Ephesians

**1** Paul, an apostle (special messenger) of Christ Jesus (the Messiah), by the divine will (the purpose and the choice of God) to the saints (the consecrated, set-apart ones) [a]at Ephesus who are also faithful *and* loyal *and* steadfast in Christ Jesus:

[2]May grace (God's unmerited favor) and spiritual peace [which means peace with God and harmony, unity, and undisturbedness] be yours from God our Father and from the Lord Jesus Christ.

[3]May blessing (praise, laudation, and eulogy) be to the God and Father of our Lord Jesus Christ (the Messiah) Who has blessed us *in Christ* with every spiritual (given by the Holy Spirit) blessing in the heavenly realm!

[4]Even as [in His love] He chose us [actually picked us out for Himself as His own] in Christ before the foundation of the world, that we should be holy (consecrated and set apart for Him) and blameless in His sight, *even* above reproach, before Him in love.

[5]For He foreordained us (destined us, planned in love for us) to be adopted (revealed) as His own children through Jesus Christ, in accordance with the purpose of His will [[b]because it pleased Him and was His kind intent]—

[6][So that we might be] to the praise *and* the commendation of His glorious grace (favor and mercy), which He so freely bestowed on us in the Beloved.

[7]In Him we have redemption (deliverance and salvation) through His blood, the remission (forgiveness) of our offenses (shortcomings and trespasses), in accordance with the riches *and* the generosity of His gracious favor,

[8]Which He lavished upon us in every kind of wisdom and understanding (practical insight and prudence),

[9]Making known to us the mystery (secret) of His will (of His plan, of His purpose). [And it is this:] In accordance with His good pleasure (His merciful intention) which He had previously purposed *and* set forth in [c]Him,

[10][He planned] for the maturity of the times *and* the climax of the ages to unify all things *and* head them up *and* consummate them in Christ, [both] things in heaven and things on the earth.

[11]In Him we also were made [God's] heritage (portion) *and* we obtained an inheritance; for we had been foreordained (chosen and appointed beforehand) in accordance with His purpose, Who works out everything in agreement with the counsel *and* design of His [own] will,

[12]So that we who first hoped in Christ [who first put our confidence in Him have been destined and appointed to] live for the praise of His glory!

[13]In Him you also who have heard the Word of Truth, the glad tidings (Gospel) of your salvation, and have believed in *and* adhered to *and* relied on Him, were stamped with the seal of the long-promised Holy Spirit.

[14]That [Spirit] is the guarantee of our inheritance [the firstfruits, the pledge and foretaste, the down payment on our heritage], in anticipation of its full redemption *and* our acquiring [complete] possession of it—to the praise of His glory.

[15]For this reason, because I have heard of your faith in the Lord Jesus and your love toward all the saints (the people of God),

[16]I do not cease to give thanks for you, making mention of you in my prayers.

[17][For I always pray to] the God of our Lord Jesus Christ,

---

[a] 1 Some early manuscripts do not have *in Ephesus.*   [b] 4,5 Or *sight in love. 5He*   [c] 5 The Greek word for *adoption to sonship* is a legal term referring to the full legal standing of an adopted male heir in Roman culture.   [d] 8,9 Or *us with all wisdom and understanding. 9And he*   [e] 11 Or *were made heirs*

[a] Some manuscripts do not contain "at Ephesus."   [b] Marvin Vincent, *Word Studies in the New Testament.*   [c] Some commentators interpret "in Him" to mean "in Himself," while others see it as "in Christ."

## New International Version

Christ, the glorious Father, may give you the Spirit[a] of wisdom and revelation, so that you may know him better. [18]I pray that the eyes of your heart may be enlightened in order that you may know the hope to which he has called you, the riches of his glorious inheritance in his holy people, [19]and his incomparably great power for us who believe. That power is the same as the mighty strength [20]he exerted when he raised Christ from the dead and seated him at his right hand in the heavenly realms, [21]far above all rule and authority, power and dominion, and every name that is invoked, not only in the present age but also in the one to come. [22]And God placed all things under his feet and appointed him to be head over everything for the church, [23]which is his body, the fullness of him who fills everything in every way.

### Made Alive in Christ

**2** As for you, you were dead in your transgressions and sins, [2]in which you used to live when you followed the ways of this world and of the ruler of the kingdom of the air, the spirit who is now at work in those who are disobedient. [3]All of us also lived among them at one time, gratifying the cravings of our flesh[b] and following its desires and thoughts. Like the rest, we were by nature deserving of wrath. [4]But because of his great love for us, God, who is rich in mercy, [5]made us alive with Christ even when we were dead in transgressions—it is by grace you have been saved. [6]And God raised us up with Christ and seated us with him in the heavenly realms in Christ Jesus, [7]in order that in the coming ages he might show the incomparable riches of his grace, expressed in his kindness to us in Christ Jesus. [8]For it is by grace you have been saved, through faith—and this is not from yourselves, it is the

## Amplified Bible

the Father of glory, that He may grant you a spirit of wisdom and revelation [of insight into mysteries and secrets] in the [deep and intimate] knowledge of Him,

[18]By having the eyes of your heart flooded with light, so that you can know *and* understand the hope to which He has called you, and how rich is His glorious inheritance in the saints (His set-apart ones),

[19]And [so that you can know and understand] what is the immeasurable *and* unlimited *and* surpassing greatness of His power in *and* for us who believe, as demonstrated in the working of His mighty strength,

[20]Which He exerted in Christ when He raised Him from the dead and seated Him at His [own] right hand in the heavenly [places],

[21]Far above all rule and authority and power and dominion and every name that is named [above every title that can be conferred], not only in this age *and* in this world, but also in the age *and* the world which are to come.

[22]And He has put all things under His feet and has appointed Him the universal and supreme Head of the church [a headship exercised throughout the church], [Ps. 8:6.]

[23]Which is His body, the fullness of Him Who fills all in all [for in that body lives the full measure of Him Who makes everything complete, and Who fills everything everywhere with Himself].

**2** And you [He made alive], when you were dead (slain) by [your] trespasses and sins

[2]In which at one time you walked [habitually]. You were following the course *and* fashion of this world [were under the sway of the tendency of this present age], following the prince of the power of the air. [You were obedient to and under the control of] the [demon] spirit that still constantly works in the sons of disobedience [the careless, the rebellious, and the unbelieving, who go against the purposes of God].

[3]Among these we as well as you once lived *and* conducted ourselves in the passions of our flesh [our behavior governed by our corrupt and sensual nature], obeying the impulses of the flesh and the thoughts of the mind [our cravings dictated by our senses and our dark imaginings]. We were then by nature children of [God's] wrath *and* heirs of [His] indignation, like the rest of mankind.

[4]But God—so rich is He in His mercy! Because of *and* in order to satisfy the great *and* wonderful *and* intense love with which He loved us,

[5]Even when we were dead (slain) by [our own] shortcomings *and* trespasses, He made us alive together in fellowship *and* in union with Christ; [He gave us the very life of Christ Himself, the same new life with which He quickened Him, for] it is by grace (His favor and mercy which you did not deserve) that you are saved (ᵃdelivered from judgment and made partakers of Christ's salvation).

[6]And He raised us up together with Him and made us sit down together [giving us ᵇjoint seating with Him] in the heavenly sphere [by virtue of our being] in Christ Jesus (the Messiah, the Anointed One).

[7]He did this that He might clearly demonstrate through the ages to come the immeasurable (limitless, surpassing) riches of His free grace (His unmerited favor) in [His] kindness *and* goodness of heart toward us in Christ Jesus.

[8]For it is by free grace (God's unmerited favor) that you are saved (ᶜdelivered from judgment *and* made partakers of Christ's salvation) through [your] faith. And this [salvation] is not of yourselves [of your own doing, it came not through your own striving], but it is the gift of God;

---

[a] 17 Or *a spirit* [b] 3 In contexts like this, the Greek word for *flesh* (*sarx*) refers to the sinful state of human beings, often presented as a power in opposition to the Spirit.

[a] Joseph Thayer, *A Greek-English Lexicon of the New Testament.* [b] H.A. W. Meyer, *Commentary on the New Testament.* [c] Joseph Thayer, *A Greek-English Lexicon.*

## New International Version

gift of God— [9]not by works, so that no one can boast. [10]For we are God's handiwork, created in Christ Jesus to do good works, which God prepared in advance for us to do.

### Jew and Gentile Reconciled Through Christ

[11]Therefore, remember that formerly you who are Gentiles by birth and called "uncircumcised" by those who call themselves "the circumcision" (which is done in the body by human hands)— [12]remember that at that time you were separate from Christ, excluded from citizenship in Israel and foreigners to the covenants of the promise, without hope and without God in the world. [13]But now in Christ Jesus you who once were far away have been brought near by the blood of Christ.

[14]For he himself is our peace, who has made the two groups one and has destroyed the barrier, the dividing wall of hostility, [15]by setting aside in his flesh the law with its commands and regulations. His purpose was to create in himself one new humanity out of the two, thus making peace, [16]and in one body to reconcile both of them to God through the cross, by which he put to death their hostility. [17]He came and preached peace to you who were far away and peace to those who were near. [18]For through him we both have access to the Father by one Spirit.

[19]Consequently, you are no longer foreigners and strangers, but fellow citizens with God's people and also members of his household, [20]built on the foundation of the apostles and prophets, with Christ Jesus himself as the chief cornerstone. [21]In him the whole building is joined together and rises to become a holy temple in the Lord. [22]And in him you too are being built together to become a dwelling in which God lives by his Spirit.

### God's Marvelous Plan for the Gentiles

**3** For this reason I, Paul, the prisoner of Christ Jesus for the sake of you Gentiles—

[2]Surely you have heard about the administration of God's grace that was given to me for you, [3]that is, the mys-

## Amplified Bible

[9]Not because of works [not the fulfillment of the Law's demands], lest any man should boast. [It is not the result of what anyone can possibly do, so no one can pride himself in it or take glory to himself.]

[10]For we are God's [own] handiwork (His workmanship), [a]recreated in Christ Jesus, [born anew] that we may do those good works which God predestined (planned beforehand) for us [taking paths which He prepared ahead of time], that we should walk in them [living the good life which He prearranged and made ready for us to live].

[11]Therefore, remember that at one time you were Gentiles (heathens) in the flesh, called Uncircumcision by those who called themselves Circumcision, [itself a [b]mere mark] in the flesh made by human hands.

[12][Remember] that you were at that time separated (living apart) from Christ [excluded from all part in Him], utterly estranged *and* outlawed from the rights of Israel as a nation, and strangers with no share in the sacred compacts of the [Messianic] promise [with no knowledge of or right in God's agreements, His covenants]. And you had no hope (no promise); you were in the world without God.

[13]But now in Christ Jesus, you who once were [so] far away, through (by, in) the blood of Christ have been brought near.

[14]For He is [Himself] our peace (our bond of unity and harmony). He has made us both [Jew and Gentile] one [body], and has broken down (destroyed, abolished) the hostile dividing wall between us,

[15]By abolishing in His [own crucified] flesh the enmity [caused by] the Law with its decrees and ordinances [which He annulled]; that He from the two might create in Himself one new man [one new quality of humanity out of the two], so making peace.

[16]And [He designed] to reconcile to God both [Jew and Gentile, united] in a single body by means of His cross, thereby killing the mutual enmity *and* bringing the feud to an end.

[17]And He came and preached the glad tidings of peace to you who were afar off and [peace] to those who were near. [Isa. 57:19.]

[18]For it is through Him that we both [whether far off or near] now have an introduction (access) by one [Holy] Spirit to the Father [so that we are able to approach Him].

[19]Therefore you are no longer outsiders (exiles, migrants, and aliens, excluded from the rights of citizens), but you now share citizenship with the saints (God's own people, consecrated and set apart for Himself); and you belong to God's [own] household.

[20]You are built upon the foundation of the apostles and prophets with Christ Jesus Himself the chief Cornerstone.

[21]In Him the whole structure is joined (bound, welded) together harmoniously, and it continues to rise (grow, increase) into a holy temple in the Lord [a sanctuary dedicated, consecrated, and sacred to the presence of the Lord].

[22]In Him [and in fellowship with one another] you yourselves also are being built up [into this structure] with the rest, to form a fixed abode (dwelling place) of God in (by, through) the Spirit.

**3** For this reason [[c]because I preached that you are thus built up together], I, Paul, [am] the prisoner of Jesus the Christ [c]for the sake *and* on behalf of you Gentiles—

[2]Assuming that you have heard of the stewardship of God's grace (His unmerited favor) that was entrusted to me [to dispense to you] for your benefit,

[a] Arthur S. Way, *Way's Epistles: The Letters of St. Paul to Seven Churches and Three Friends.* [b] Arthur S. Way, *The Letters of St. Paul to Seven Churches and Three Friends.* [c] Matthew Henry, *Commentary on the Holy Bible*: The Jews persecuted and imprisoned Paul because he was an apostle to the Gentiles and preached the Gospel to them.

## New International Version

tery made known to me by revelation, as I have already written briefly. [4]In reading this, then, you will be able to understand my insight into the mystery of Christ, [5]which was not made known to people in other generations as it has now been revealed by the Spirit to God's holy apostles and prophets. [6]This mystery is that through the gospel the Gentiles are heirs together with Israel, members together of one body, and sharers together in the promise in Christ Jesus.

[7]I became a servant of this gospel by the gift of God's grace given me through the working of his power. [8]Although I am less than the least of all the Lord's people, this grace was given me: to preach to the Gentiles the boundless riches of Christ, [9]and to make plain to everyone the administration of this mystery, which for ages past was kept hidden in God, who created all things. [10]His intent was that now, through the church, the manifold wisdom of God should be made known to the rulers and authorities in the heavenly realms, [11]according to his eternal purpose that he accomplished in Christ Jesus our Lord. [12]In him and through faith in him we may approach God with freedom and confidence. [13]I ask you, therefore, not to be discouraged because of my sufferings for you, which are your glory.

### A Prayer for the Ephesians

[14]For this reason I kneel before the Father, [15]from whom every family[a] in heaven and on earth derives its name. [16]I pray that out of his glorious riches he may strengthen you with power through his Spirit in your inner being, [17]so that Christ may dwell in your hearts through faith. And I pray that you, being rooted and established in love, [18]may have power, together with all the Lord's holy people, to grasp how wide and long and high and deep is the love of Christ, [19]and to know this love that surpasses knowledge—that you may be filled to the measure of all the fullness of God.

## Amplified Bible

[3][And] that the mystery (secret) was made known to me *and* I was allowed to comprehend it by direct revelation, as I already briefly wrote you.

[4]When you read this you can understand my insight into the mystery of Christ.

[5][This mystery] was never disclosed to human beings in past generations as it has now been revealed to His holy apostles (consecrated messengers) and prophets by the [Holy] Spirit.

[6][It is this:] that the Gentiles are now to be fellow heirs [with the Jews], members of the same body and joint partakers [sharing] in the same divine promise in Christ through [their acceptance of] the glad tidings (the Gospel).

[7]Of this [Gospel] I was made a minister according to the gift of God's free grace (undeserved favor) which was bestowed on me by the exercise (the working in all its effectiveness) of His power.

[8]To me, though I am the very least of all the saints (God's consecrated people), this grace (favor, privilege) was granted *and* graciously entrusted: to proclaim to the Gentiles the unending (boundless, fathomless, incalculable, and exhaustless) riches of Christ [wealth which no human being could have searched out],

[9]Also to enlighten all men *and* make plain to them what is the plan [regarding the Gentiles and providing for the salvation of all men] of the mystery kept hidden through the ages *and* concealed until now in [the mind of] God Who created all things *by Christ Jesus.*

[10][The purpose is] that through the church the [a]complicated, many-sided wisdom of God in all its infinite variety *and* innumerable aspects might now be made known to the angelic rulers and authorities (principalities and powers) in the heavenly sphere.

[11]This is in accordance with the terms of the eternal *and* timeless purpose which He has realized *and* carried into effect in [the person of] Christ Jesus our Lord,

[12]In Whom, because of our faith in Him, we dare to have the boldness (courage and confidence) of free access (an unreserved approach to God with freedom and without fear).

[13]So I ask you not to lose heart [not to faint or become despondent through fear] at what I am suffering in your behalf. [Rather glory in it] for it is an honor to you.

[14]For this reason [[b]seeing the greatness of this plan by which you are built together in Christ], I bow my knees before the Father *of our Lord Jesus Christ,*

[15]For Whom every family in heaven and on earth is named [that Father from Whom all fatherhood takes its title and derives its name].

[16]May He grant you out of the rich treasury of His glory to be strengthened *and* reinforced with mighty power in the inner man by the [Holy] Spirit [Himself indwelling your innermost being and personality].

[17]May Christ through your faith [actually] dwell (settle down, abide, make His permanent home) in your hearts! May you be rooted deep in love *and* founded securely on love,

[18]That you may have the power *and* be strong to apprehend *and* grasp with all the saints [God's devoted people, the experience of that love] what is the breadth and length and height and depth [of it];

[19][That you may really come] to know [practically, [c]through experience for yourselves] the love of Christ, which far surpasses [c]mere knowledge [without experience]; that you may be filled [through all your being] [c]unto all the fullness of God [may have the richest measure of the divine Presence, and [d]become a body wholly filled and flooded with God Himself]!

---

[a] *Webster's New International Dictionary* offers this as a definition of "manifold" (the *King James Version's* rendering of the Greek *polupoikilos*). [b] Many manuscripts consider that Paul here resumes the thread of verse 1. [c] Marvin Vincent, *Word Studies.* [d] Joseph Thayer, *A Greek-English Lexicon.*

---

[a] 15 The Greek for *family* (*patria*) is derived from the Greek for *father* (*pater*).

## New International Version

20Now to him who is able to do immeasurably more than all we ask or imagine, according to his power that is at work within us, 21to him be glory in the church and in Christ Jesus throughout all generations, for ever and ever! Amen.

### Unity and Maturity in the Body of Christ

4 As a prisoner for the Lord, then, I urge you to live a life worthy of the calling you have received. 2Be completely humble and gentle; be patient, bearing with one another in love. 3Make every effort to keep the unity of the Spirit through the bond of peace. 4There is one body and one Spirit, just as you were called to one hope when you were called; 5one Lord, one faith, one baptism; 6one God and Father of all, who is over all and through all and in all.

7But to each one of us grace has been given as Christ apportioned it. 8This is why it*a* says:

"When he ascended on high,
he took many captives
and gave gifts to his people."*b*

9(What does "he ascended" mean except that he also descended to the lower, earthly regions*c*? 10He who descended is the very one who ascended higher than all the heavens, in order to fill the whole universe.) 11So Christ himself gave the apostles, the prophets, the evangelists, the pastors and teachers, 12to equip his people for works of service, so that the body of Christ may be built up 13until we all reach unity in the faith and in the knowledge of the Son of God and become mature, attaining to the whole measure of the fullness of Christ.

14Then we will no longer be infants, tossed back and forth by the waves, and blown here and there by every wind of teaching and by the cunning and craftiness of people in their deceitful scheming. 15Instead, speaking the truth in love, we will grow to become in every respect the mature body of him who is the head, that is, Christ. 16From him the whole body, joined and held together by

## Amplified Bible

20Now to Him Who, by (in consequence of) the [action of His] power that is at work within us, is able to [carry out His purpose and] do superabundantly, far over *and* above all that we [dare] ask or think [infinitely beyond our highest prayers, desires, thoughts, hopes, or dreams]—
21To Him be glory in the church and in Christ Jesus throughout all generations forever and ever. Amen (so be it).

4 I therefore, the prisoner for the Lord, appeal to *and* beg you to walk (lead a life) worthy of the [divine] calling to which you have been called [with behavior that is a credit to the summons to God's service,
2Living as becomes you] with complete lowliness of mind (humility) and meekness (unselfishness, gentleness, mildness), with patience, bearing with one another *and* making allowances because you love one another.
3Be eager *and* strive earnestly to guard *and* keep the harmony *and* oneness of [and produced by] the Spirit in the binding power of peace.
4[There is] one body and one Spirit—just as there is also one hope [that belongs] to the calling you received—
5[There is] one Lord, one faith, one baptism,
6One God and Father of [us] all, Who is above all [Sovereign over all], pervading all and [living] in [us] all.
7Yet grace (God's unmerited favor) was given to each of us individually [not indiscriminately, but in different ways] in proportion to the measure of Christ's [rich and bounteous] gift.
8Therefore it is said, When He ascended on high, He led captivity captive [He led a train of *a*vanquished foes] and He bestowed gifts on men. [Ps. 68:18.]
9[But He ascended?] Now what can this, He ascended, mean but that He had previously descended from [the heights of] heaven into [the depths], the lower parts of the earth?
10He Who descended is the [very] same as He Who also has ascended high above all the heavens, that He [His presence] might fill all things (the whole universe, from the lowest to the highest).
11And His gifts were [varied; He Himself appointed and gave men to us] some to be apostles (special messengers), some prophets (inspired preachers and expounders), some evangelists (preachers of the Gospel, traveling missionaries), some pastors (shepherds of His flock) and teachers.
12His intention was the perfecting *and* the full equipping of the saints (His consecrated people), [that they should do] the work of ministering toward building up Christ's body (the church),
13[That it might develop] until we all attain oneness in the faith and in the comprehension of the [*b*full and accurate] knowledge of the Son of God, that [we might arrive] at really mature manhood (the completeness of personality which is nothing less than the standard height of Christ's own perfection), the measure of the stature of the fullness of the Christ *and* the completeness found in Him.
14So then, we may no longer be children, tossed [like ships] to and fro between chance gusts of teaching *and* wavering with every changing wind of doctrine, [the prey of] the cunning *and* cleverness of *c*unscrupulous men, [gamblers engaged] in every shifting form of trickery in inventing errors to mislead.
15Rather, let our lives lovingly *b*express truth [in all things, speaking truly, dealing truly, living truly]. Enfolded in love, let us grow up in every way *and* in all things into Him Who is the Head, [even] Christ (the Messiah, the Anointed One).
16For because of Him the whole body (the church, in all its various parts), closely joined and firmly knit together by the joints *and* ligaments with which it is supplied, when

*a* Matthew Henry, *Commentary on the Holy Bible*: "He conquered those who had conquered us—such as sin, the devil, and death." *b* Marvin Vincent, *Word Studies*. *c* Literal translation: "dice-playing."

*a* 8 Or *God*   *b* 8 Psalm 68:18   *c* 9 Or *the depths of the earth*

## New International Version

every supporting ligament, grows and builds itself up in love, as each part does its work.

### Instructions for Christian Living

17So I tell you this, and insist on it in the Lord, that you must no longer live as the Gentiles do, in the futility of their thinking. 18They are darkened in their understanding and separated from the life of God because of the ignorance that is in them due to the hardening of their hearts. 19Having lost all sensitivity, they have given themselves over to sensuality so as to indulge in every kind of impurity, and they are full of greed.

20That, however, is not the way of life you learned 21when you heard about Christ and were taught in him in accordance with the truth that is in Jesus. 22You were taught, with regard to your former way of life, to put off your old self, which is being corrupted by its deceitful desires; 23to be made new in the attitude of your minds; 24and to put on the new self, created to be like God in true righteousness and holiness.

25Therefore each of you must put off falsehood and speak truthfully to your neighbor, for we are all members of one body. 26"In your anger do not sin"*a*: Do not let the sun go down while you are still angry, 27and do not give the devil a foothold. 28Anyone who has been stealing must steal no longer, but must work, doing something useful with their own hands, that they may have something to share with those in need.

29Do not let any unwholesome talk come out of your mouths, but only what is helpful for building others up according to their needs, that it may benefit those who listen. 30And do not grieve the Holy Spirit of God, with whom you were sealed for the day of redemption. 31Get rid of all bitterness, rage and anger, brawling and slander, along with every form of malice. 32Be kind and compassionate to one another, forgiving each other, just as in Christ God forgave you.

5 1Follow God's example, therefore, as dearly loved children 2and walk in the way of love, just as Christ loved

## Amplified Bible

each part [with power adapted to its need] is working properly [in all its functions], grows to full maturity, building itself up in love.

17So this I say and solemnly testify in [the name of] the Lord [as in His presence], that you must no longer live as the heathen (the Gentiles) do in their perverseness [in the folly, vanity, and emptiness of their souls and the futility] of their minds.

18Their *a*moral understanding is darkened *and* their reasoning is beclouded. [They are] alienated (estranged, self-banished) from the life of God [with no share in it; this is] because of the ignorance (the want of knowledge and perception, the willful blindness) that is *a*deep-seated in them, due to their hardness of heart [to the insensitiveness of their moral nature].

19In their spiritual apathy they have become callous *and* past feeling *and* reckless and have abandoned themselves [a prey] to unbridled sensuality, eager *and* greedy to indulge in every form of impurity [that their depraved desires may suggest and demand].

20But you did not so learn Christ!

21Assuming that you have really heard Him *and* been taught by Him, as [all] Truth is in Jesus [embodied and personified in Him],

22Strip yourselves of your former nature [put off and discard your old unrenewed self] which characterized your previous manner of life and becomes corrupt through lusts *and* desires that spring from delusion;

23And be constantly renewed in the spirit of your mind [having a fresh mental and spiritual attitude],

24And put on the new nature (the regenerate self) created in God's image, [Godlike] in true righteousness and holiness.

25Therefore, rejecting all falsity *and* being done now with it, let everyone express the truth with his neighbor, for we are all parts of one body *and* members one of another. [Zech. 8:16.]

26When angry, do not sin; do not ever let your wrath (your exasperation, your fury or indignation) last until the sun goes down.

27Leave no [such] room *or* foothold for the devil [give no opportunity to him].

28Let the thief steal no more, but rather let him be industrious, making an honest living with his own hands, so that he may be able to give to those in need.

29Let no foul *or* polluting language, *nor* evil word *nor* unwholesome *or* worthless talk [ever] come out of your mouth, but only such [speech] as is good *and* beneficial to the spiritual progress of others, as is fitting to the need *and* the occasion, that it may be a blessing *and* give grace (God's favor) to those who hear it.

30And do not grieve the Holy Spirit of God [do not offend or vex or sadden Him], by Whom you were sealed (marked, branded as God's own, secured) for the day of redemption (of final deliverance through Christ from evil and the consequences of sin).

31Let all bitterness and indignation *and* wrath (passion, rage, bad temper) and resentment (anger, animosity) and quarreling (brawling, clamor, contention) and slander (evil-speaking, abusive or blasphemous language) be banished from you, with all malice (spite, ill will, or baseness of any kind).

32And become useful *and* helpful *and* kind to one another, tenderhearted (compassionate, understanding, loving-hearted), forgiving one another [readily and freely], as God in Christ forgave you.

5 Therefore be imitators of God [copy Him *and* follow His example], as well-beloved children [imitate their father].

2And walk in love, [esteeming and delighting in one

---

*a* 26 Psalm 4:4 (see Septuagint)

*a* Marvin Vincent, *Word Studies.*

## New International Version

us and gave himself up for us as a fragrant offering and sacrifice to God.

[3] But among you there must not be even a hint of sexual immorality, or of any kind of impurity, or of greed, because these are improper for God's holy people. [4] Nor should there be obscenity, foolish talk or coarse joking, which are out of place, but rather thanksgiving. [5] For of this you can be sure: No immoral, impure or greedy person—such a person is an idolater—has any inheritance in the kingdom of Christ and of God.[a] [6] Let no one deceive you with empty words, for because of such things God's wrath comes on those who are disobedient. [7] Therefore do not be partners with them.

[8] For you were once darkness, but now you are light in the Lord. Live as children of light [9] (for the fruit of the light consists in all goodness, righteousness and truth) [10] and find out what pleases the Lord. [11] Have nothing to do with the fruitless deeds of darkness, but rather expose them. [12] It is shameful even to mention what the disobedient do in secret. [13] But everything exposed by the light becomes visible—and everything that is illuminated becomes a light. [14] This is why it is said:

"Wake up, sleeper,
rise from the dead,
and Christ will shine on you."

[15] Be very careful, then, how you live—not as unwise but as wise, [16] making the most of every opportunity, because the days are evil. [17] Therefore do not be foolish, but understand what the Lord's will is. [18] Do not get drunk on wine, which leads to debauchery. Instead, be filled with the Spirit, [19] speaking to one another with psalms, hymns, and songs from the Spirit. Sing and make music from your heart to the Lord, [20] always giving thanks to God the Father for everything, in the name of our Lord Jesus Christ.

### Instructions for Christian Households

[21] Submit to one another out of reverence for Christ.

[22] Wives, submit yourselves to your own husbands as you do to the Lord. [23] For the husband is the head of the wife as Christ is the head of the church, his body, of which he is the Savior. [24] Now as the church submits to Christ, so also wives should submit to their husbands in everything.

[25] Husbands, love your wives, just as Christ loved the church and gave himself up for her [26] to make her holy,

## Amplified Bible

another] as Christ loved us and gave Himself up for us, a [a] slain offering and sacrifice to God [for you, so that it became] a sweet fragrance. [Ezek. 20:41.]

[3] But immorality (sexual vice) and all impurity [[b] of lustful, rich, wasteful living] or greediness must not even be named among you, as is fitting *and* proper among saints (God's consecrated people).

[4] Let there be no filthiness (obscenity, indecency) nor foolish *and* sinful (silly and corrupt) talk, nor coarse jesting, which are not fitting *or* becoming; but instead voice your thankfulness [to God].

[5] For be sure of this: that no person practicing sexual vice or impurity in thought or in life, or one who is covetous [who has lustful desire for the property of others and is greedy for gain]—for he [in effect] is an idolater—has any inheritance in the kingdom of Christ and of God.

[6] Let no one delude *and* deceive you with empty excuses *and* groundless arguments [for these sins], for through these things the wrath of God comes upon the sons of rebellion *and* disobedience.

[7] So do not associate *or* be sharers with them.

[8] For once you were darkness, but now you are light in the Lord; walk as children of Light [lead the lives of those native-born to the Light].

[9] For the fruit (the effect, the product) of the Light *or* [c] *the Spirit* [consists] in every form of kindly goodness, uprightness of heart, and trueness of life.

[10] And try to learn [in your experience] what is pleasing to the Lord [let your lives be constant proofs of what is most acceptable to Him].

[11] Take no part in *and* have no fellowship with the fruitless deeds *and* enterprises of darkness, but instead [let your lives be so in contrast as to] [b] expose *and* reprove *and* convict them.

[12] For it is a shame even to speak of *or* mention the things that [such people] practice in secret.

[13] But when anything is exposed *and* reproved by the light, it is made visible *and* clear; and where everything is visible *and* clear there is light.

[14] Therefore He says, Awake, O sleeper, and arise from the dead, and Christ shall shine (make day dawn) upon you *and* give you light. [Isa. 26:19; 60:1, 2.]

[15] Look carefully then how you walk! Live purposefully *and* worthily *and* accurately, not as the unwise *and* witless, but as wise (sensible, intelligent people),

[16] Making the very most of the time [buying up each opportunity], because the days are evil.

[17] Therefore do not be vague *and* thoughtless *and* foolish, but understanding *and* firmly grasping what the will of the Lord is.

[18] And do not get drunk with wine, for that is debauchery; but ever be filled *and* stimulated with the [Holy] Spirit. [Prov. 23:20.]

[19] Speak out to one another in psalms and hymns and spiritual songs, offering praise with voices [[d] and instruments] and making melody with all your heart to the Lord,

[20] At all times and for everything giving thanks in the name of our Lord Jesus Christ to God the Father.

[21] Be subject to one another out of reverence for Christ (the Messiah, the Anointed One).

[22] Wives, be subject (be submissive and adapt yourselves) to your own husbands as [a service] to the Lord.

[23] For the husband is head of the wife as Christ is the Head of the church, Himself the Savior of [His] body.

[24] As the church is subject to Christ, so let wives also be subject in everything to their husbands.

[25] Husbands, love your wives, as Christ loved the church and gave Himself up for her,

---

[a] Marvin Vincent, *Word Studies.* [b] Joseph Thayer, *A Greek-English Lexicon.* [c] Some ancient manuscripts so read. [d] George R. Berry, *Greek-English New Testament Lexicon.*

## New International Version

cleansing[a] her by the washing with water through the word, [27]and to present her to himself as a radiant church, without stain or wrinkle or any other blemish, but holy and blameless. [28]In this same way, husbands ought to love their wives as their own bodies. He who loves his wife loves himself. [29]After all, no one ever hated their own body, but they feed and care for their body, just as Christ does the church— [30]for we are members of his body. [31]"For this reason a man will leave his father and mother and be united to his wife, and the two will become one flesh."[b] [32]This is a profound mystery—but I am talking about Christ and the church. [33]However, each one of you also must love his wife as he loves himself, and the wife must respect her husband.

**6** Children, obey your parents in the Lord, for this is right. [2]"Honor your father and mother"—which is the first commandment with a promise— [3]"so that it may go well with you and that you may enjoy long life on the earth."[c]

[4]Fathers,[d] do not exasperate your children; instead, bring them up in the training and instruction of the Lord.

[5]Slaves, obey your earthly masters with respect and fear, and with sincerity of heart, just as you would obey Christ. [6]Obey them not only to win their favor when their eye is on you, but as slaves of Christ, doing the will of God from your heart. [7]Serve wholeheartedly, as if you were serving the Lord, not people, [8]because you know that the Lord will reward each one for whatever good they do, whether they are slave or free.

[9]And masters, treat your slaves in the same way. Do not threaten them, since you know that he who is both their Master and yours is in heaven, and there is no favoritism with him.

### The Armor of God

[10]Finally, be strong in the Lord and in his mighty power. [11]Put on the full armor of God, so that you can take your stand against the devil's schemes. [12]For our struggle is not against flesh and blood, but against the rulers, against the authorities, against the powers of this dark world and against the spiritual forces of evil in the heavenly realms.

## Amplified Bible

[26]So that He might sanctify her, having cleansed her by the washing of water with the Word,

[27]That He might present the church to Himself in glorious splendor, without spot or wrinkle or any such things [that she might be holy and faultless].

[28]Even so husbands should love their wives as [being in a sense] their own bodies. He who loves his own wife loves himself.

[29]For no man ever hated his own flesh, but nourishes *and* carefully protects and cherishes it, as Christ does the church,

[30]Because we are members (parts) of His body.

[31]For this reason a man shall leave his father and his mother and shall be joined to his wife, and the two shall become one flesh. [Gen. 2:24.]

[32]This mystery is very great, but I speak concerning [the relation of] Christ and the church.

[33]However, let each man of you [without exception] love his wife as [being in a sense] his very own self; and let the wife see that she respects *and* reverences her husband [*a*that she notices him, regards him, honors him, prefers him, venerates, and esteems him; and *a*that she defers to him, praises him, and loves and admires him exceedingly]. [I Pet. 3:2.]

**6** Children, obey your parents in the Lord [as His representatives], for this is just and right.

[2]Honor (esteem and value as precious) your father and your mother—this is the first commandment with a promise—[Exod. 20:12.]

[3]That all may be well with you and that you may live long on the earth.

[4]Fathers, do not irritate *and* provoke your children to anger [do not exasperate them to resentment], but rear them [tenderly] in the training *and* discipline and the counsel *and* admonition of the Lord.

[5]Servants (slaves), be obedient to those who are your physical masters, having respect for them and eager concern to please them, in singleness of motive *and* with all your heart, as [service] to Christ [Himself]—

[6]Not in the way of eye-service [as if they were watching you] and only to please men, but as servants (slaves) of Christ, doing the will of God heartily *and* with your whole soul;

[7]Rendering service readily with goodwill, as to the Lord and not to men,

[8]Knowing that for whatever good anyone does, he will receive his reward from the Lord, whether he is slave or free.

[9]You masters, act on the same [principle] toward them and give up threatening *and* using violent *and* abusive words, knowing that He Who is both their Master and yours is in heaven, and that there is no respect of persons (no partiality) with Him.

[10]In conclusion, be strong in the Lord [be empowered through your union with Him]; draw your strength from Him [that strength which His boundless might provides].

[11]Put on God's whole armor [the armor of a heavy-armed soldier which God supplies], that you may be able successfully to stand up against [all] the strategies *and* the deceits of the devil.

[12]For we are not wrestling with flesh and blood [contending only with physical opponents], but against the despotisms, against the powers, against [the master spirits who are] the world rulers of this present darkness, against the spirit forces of wickedness in the heavenly (supernatural) sphere.

*a Webster's New International Dictionary* offers this as a list of English words with the same (or nearly the same) essential meaning as "respect" and "reverence." The latter ("reverence") includes the concept of "adore" in the sense not applied to deity.

---

*a* 26 Or *having cleansed*    *b 31* Gen. 2:24    *c 3* Deut. 5:16
*d 4* Or *Parents*

## New International Version

<sup>13</sup>Therefore put on the full armor of God, so that when the day of evil comes, you may be able to stand your ground, and after you have done everything, to stand. <sup>14</sup>Stand firm then, with the belt of truth buckled around your waist, with the breastplate of righteousness in place, <sup>15</sup>and with your feet fitted with the readiness that comes from the gospel of peace. <sup>16</sup>In addition to all this, take up the shield of faith, with which you can extinguish all the flaming arrows of the evil one. <sup>17</sup>Take the helmet of salvation and the sword of the Spirit, which is the word of God.

<sup>18</sup>And pray in the Spirit on all occasions with all kinds of prayers and requests. With this in mind, be alert and always keep on praying for all the Lord's people. <sup>19</sup>Pray also for me, that whenever I speak, words may be given me so that I will fearlessly make known the mystery of the gospel, <sup>20</sup>for which I am an ambassador in chains. Pray that I may declare it fearlessly, as I should.

### Final Greetings
<sup>21</sup>Tychicus, the dear brother and faithful servant in the Lord, will tell you everything, so that you also may know how I am and what I am doing. <sup>22</sup>I am sending him to you for this very purpose, that you may know how we are, and that he may encourage you.

<sup>23</sup>Peace to the brothers and sisters,[a] and love with faith from God the Father and the Lord Jesus Christ. <sup>24</sup>Grace to all who love our Lord Jesus Christ with an undying love.[b]

## Amplified Bible

<sup>13</sup>Therefore put on God's complete armor, that you may be able to resist *and* stand your ground on the evil day [of danger], and, having done all [the crisis demands], to stand [firmly in your place]. <sup>14</sup>Stand therefore [hold your ground], having tightened the belt of truth around your loins and having put on the breastplate of integrity *and* of moral rectitude *and* right standing with God, <sup>15</sup>And having shod your feet in preparation [to face the enemy with the *a*firm-footed stability, the promptness, and the readiness *b*produced by the good news] of the Gospel of peace. [Isa. 52:7.]

<sup>16</sup>Lift up over all the [covering] shield of *a*saving faith, upon which you can quench all the flaming missiles of the wicked [one].

<sup>17</sup>And take the helmet of salvation and the sword that the Spirit *c*wields, which is the Word of God.

<sup>18</sup>Pray at all times (on every occasion, in every season) in the Spirit, with all [manner of] prayer and entreaty. To that end keep alert and watch with strong purpose *and* perseverance, interceding in behalf of all the saints (God's consecrated people).

<sup>19</sup>And [pray] also for me, that [freedom of] utterance may be given me, that I may open my mouth to proclaim boldly the mystery of the good news (the Gospel),

<sup>20</sup>For which I am an ambassador in a coupling chain [in prison. Pray] that I may declare it boldly *and* courageously, as I ought to do.

<sup>21</sup>Now that you may know how I am and what I am doing, Tychicus, the beloved brother and faithful minister in the Lord [and His service], will tell you everything.

<sup>22</sup>I have sent him to you for this very purpose, that you may know how we are and that he may *b*console *and* cheer *and* encourage *and* strengthen your hearts.

<sup>23</sup>Peace be to the brethren, and love joined with faith, from God the Father and the Lord Jesus Christ (the Messiah, the Anointed One).

<sup>24</sup>Grace (God's undeserved favor) be with all who love our Lord Jesus Christ with undying *and* incorruptible [love]. *Amen (so let it be).*

---

*a* 23 The Greek word for *brothers and sisters* (*adelphoi*) refers here to believers, both men and women, as part of God's family.
*b* 24 Or *Grace and immortality to all who love our Lord Jesus Christ.*

*a* Marvin Vincent, *Word Studies.* *b* Joseph Thayer, *A Greek-English Lexicon.* *c* Charles B. Williams, *The New Testament: A Translation in the Language of the People*: Subjective genitive—a type of genitive of possession. Thus here the Spirit is the subject or agent of the verbal action.

# New International Version

# Philippians

**1** Paul and Timothy, servants of Christ Jesus,

To all God's holy people in Christ Jesus at Philippi, together with the overseers and deacons[a]:

[2] Grace and peace to you from God our Father and the Lord Jesus Christ.

## Thanksgiving and Prayer

[3] I thank my God every time I remember you. [4] In all my prayers for all of you, I always pray with joy [5] because of your partnership in the gospel from the first day until now, [6] being confident of this, that he who began a good work in you will carry it on to completion until the day of Christ Jesus.

[7] It is right for me to feel this way about all of you, since I have you in my heart and, whether I am in chains or defending and confirming the gospel, all of you share in God's grace with me. [8] God can testify how I long for all of you with the affection of Christ Jesus.

[9] And this is my prayer: that your love may abound more and more in knowledge and depth of insight, [10] so that you may be able to discern what is best and may be pure and blameless for the day of Christ, [11] filled with the fruit of righteousness that comes through Jesus Christ—to the glory and praise of God.

## Paul's Chains Advance the Gospel

[12] Now I want you to know, brothers and sisters,[b] that what has happened to me has actually served to advance the gospel. [13] As a result, it has become clear throughout the whole palace guard[c] and to everyone else that I am in chains for Christ. [14] And because of my chains, most of the brothers and sisters have become confident in the Lord and dare all the more to proclaim the gospel without fear.

[15] It is true that some preach Christ out of envy and rivalry, but others out of goodwill. [16] The latter do so out of love,

---

*a 1* The word *deacons* refers here to Christians designated to serve with the overseers/elders of the church in a variety of ways; similarly in Romans 16:1 and 1 Tim. 3:8,12.   *b 12* The Greek word for *brothers and sisters (adelphoi)* refers here to believers, both men and women, as part of God's family; also in verse 14; and in 3:1, 13, 17; 4:1, 8, 21.   *c 13* Or *whole palace*

# Amplified Bible

# Philippians

**1** Paul and Timothy, bond servants of Christ Jesus (the Messiah), to all the saints (God's consecrated people) in Christ Jesus who are at Philippi, with the bishops (overseers) and deacons (assistants):

[2] Grace (favor and blessing) to you and [heart] peace from God our Father and the Lord Jesus Christ (the Messiah).

[3] I thank my God in all my remembrance of you.

[4] In every prayer of mine I always make my entreaty *and* petition for you all with joy (delight).

[5] [I thank my God] for your fellowship (your *a*sympathetic cooperation and contributions and partnership) in advancing the good news (the Gospel) from the first day [you heard it] until now.

[6] And I am convinced *and* sure of this very thing, that He Who began a good work in you will continue until the day of Jesus Christ [right up to the time of His return], developing [that good work] *and* perfecting *and* bringing it to full completion in you.

[7] It is right *and* appropriate for me to have this confidence *and* feel this way about you all, because *b*you have me in your heart *and* I hold you in my heart as partakers *and* sharers, one *and* all with me, of grace (God's unmerited favor and spiritual blessing). [This is true] both when I am shut up in prison and when I am out in the defense and confirmation of the good news (the Gospel).

[8] For God is my witness how I long for *and* *c*pursue you all with love, in the tender mercy of Christ Jesus [Himself]!

[9] And this I pray: that your love may abound yet more and more *and* extend to its fullest development in knowledge and all keen insight [that your love may *a*display itself in greater depth of acquaintance and more comprehensive discernment],

[10] So that you may surely learn to sense what is vital, *and* approve *and* prize what is excellent *and* of real value [recognizing the highest and the best, and distinguishing the moral differences], and that you may be untainted *and* pure and unerring *and* blameless [so that with hearts sincere and certain and unsullied, you may approach] the day of Christ [not stumbling *nor* causing others to stumble].

[11] May you abound in *and* be filled with the fruits of righteousness (of right standing with God and right doing) which come through Jesus Christ (the Anointed One), to the honor and praise of God [*a*that His glory may be both manifested and recognized].

[12] Now I want you to know *and* continue to rest assured, brethren, that what [has happened] to me [this imprisonment] has actually only served to advance *and* give a renewed impetus to the [spreading of the] good news (the Gospel).

[13] So much is this a fact that throughout the whole imperial guard and to all the rest [here] my imprisonment has become generally known to be in Christ [that I am a prisoner in His service and for Him].

[14] And [also] most of the brethren have derived fresh confidence in the Lord because of my chains and are much more bold to speak *and* publish fearlessly the Word of God [acting with more freedom and indifference to the consequences].

[15] Some, it is true, [actually] preach Christ (the Messiah) [for no better reason than] out of envy and rivalry (party spirit), but others are doing so out of a loyal spirit *and* goodwill.

---

*a* Marvin Vincent, *Word Studies in the New Testament.*   *b* Alternate translation.   *c* Joseph Thayer, *A Greek-English Lexicon of the New Testament.*

## New International Version

knowing that I am put here for the defense of the gospel. ¹⁷The former preach Christ out of selfish ambition, not sincerely, supposing that they can stir up trouble for me while I am in chains. ¹⁸But what does it matter? The important thing is that in every way, whether from false motives or true, Christ is preached. And because of this I rejoice.

Yes, and I will continue to rejoice, ¹⁹for I know that through your prayers and God's provision of the Spirit of Jesus Christ what has happened to me will turn out for my deliverance.ᵃ ²⁰I eagerly expect and hope that I will in no way be ashamed, but will have sufficient courage so that now as always Christ will be exalted in my body, whether by life or by death. ²¹For to me, to live is Christ and to die is gain. ²²If I am to go on living in the body, this will mean fruitful labor for me. Yet what shall I choose? I do not know! ²³I am torn between the two: I desire to depart and be with Christ, which is better by far; ²⁴but it is more necessary for you that I remain in the body. ²⁵Convinced of this, I know that I will remain, and I will continue with all of you for your progress and joy in the faith, ²⁶so that through my being with you again your boasting in Christ Jesus will abound on account of me.

### Life Worthy of the Gospel

²⁷Whatever happens, conduct yourselves in a manner worthy of the gospel of Christ. Then, whether I come and see you or only hear about you in my absence, I will know that you stand firm in the one Spirit,ᵇ striving together as one for the faith of the gospel ²⁸without being frightened in any way by those who oppose you. This is a sign to them that they will be destroyed, but that you will be saved—and that by God. ²⁹For it has been granted to you on behalf of Christ not only to believe in him, but also to suffer for him, ³⁰since you are going through the same struggle you saw I had, and now hear that I still have.

### Imitating Christ's Humility

**2** Therefore if you have any encouragement from being united with Christ, if any comfort from his love, if any common sharing in the Spirit, if any tenderness and compassion, ²then make my joy complete by being like-minded, having the same love, being one in spirit and of one

## Amplified Bible

¹⁶ᵃThe latter [proclaim Christ] out of love, because they recognize and know that I am [providentially] put here for the defense of the good news (the Gospel).

¹⁷ᵃBut the former preach Christ out of a party spirit, insincerely [out of no pure motive, but thinking to annoy me], supposing they are making my bondage more bitter and my chains more galling.

¹⁸But what does it matter, so long as either way, whether in pretense [for personal ends] or in all honesty [for the furtherance of the Truth], Christ is proclaimed? And in that I [now] rejoice, yes, and I shall rejoice [hereafter] also.

¹⁹For I am well assured and indeed know that through your prayers and a ᵇbountiful supply of the Spirit of Jesus Christ (the Messiah) this will turn out for my preservation (for the spiritual health and ᵇwelfare of my own soul) and avail toward the saving work of the Gospel.

²⁰This is in keeping with my own eager desire and persistent expectation and hope, that I shall not disgrace myself nor be put to shame in anything; but that with the utmost freedom of speech and unfailing courage, now as always heretofore, Christ (the Messiah) will be magnified and get glory and praise in this body of mine and be boldly exalted in my person, whether through (by) life or through (by) death.

²¹For me to live is Christ [His life in me], and to die is gain [the gain of the glory of eternity].

²²If, however, it is to be life in the flesh and I am to live on here, that means fruitful service for me; so I can say nothing as to my personal preference [I cannot choose],

²³But I am hard pressed between the two. My yearning desire is to depart (to be free of this world, to set forth) and be with Christ, for that is far, far better;

²⁴But to remain in my body is more needful and essential for your sake.

²⁵Since I am convinced of this, I know that I shall remain and stay by you all, to promote your progress and joy in believing,

²⁶So that in me you may have abundant cause for exultation and glorying in Christ Jesus, through my coming to you again.

²⁷Only be sure as citizens so to conduct yourselves [that] your manner of life [will be] worthy of the good news (the Gospel) of Christ, so that whether I [do] come and see you or am absent, I may hear this of you: that you are standing firm in united spirit and purpose, striving side by side and contending with a single mind for the faith of the glad tidings (the Gospel).

²⁸And do not [for a moment] be frightened or intimidated in anything by your opponents and adversaries, for such [constancy and fearlessness] will be a clear sign (proof and seal) to them of [their impending] destruction, but [a sure token and evidence] of your deliverance and salvation, and that from God.

²⁹For you have been granted [the privilege] for Christ's sake not only to believe in (adhere to, rely on, and trust in) Him, but also to suffer in His behalf.

³⁰So you are engaged in the same conflict which you saw me [wage] and which you now hear to be mine [still].

**2** So by whatever [appeal to you there is in our mutual dwelling in Christ, by whatever] strengthening and consoling and encouraging [our relationship] in Him [affords], by whatever persuasive ᵇincentive there is in love, by whatever participation in the [Holy] Spirit [we share], and by whatever depth of affection and compassionate sympathy,

²Fill up and complete my joy by living in harmony and being of the same mind and one in purpose, having the same love, being in full accord and of one harmonious mind and intention.

ᵃ The order of verses 16 and 17 is that of the most ancient manuscripts; the King James Version has them reversed. ᵇ Marvin Vincent, Word Studies.

---

ᵃ 19 Or vindication; or salvation ᵇ 27 Or in one spirit

## New International Version

mind. ³Do nothing out of selfish ambition or vain conceit. Rather, in humility value others above yourselves, ⁴not looking to your own interests but each of you to the interests of the others.

⁵In your relationships with one another, have the same mindset as Christ Jesus:

⁶Who, being in very nature*ᵃ* God,
did not consider equality with God something to be used to his own advantage;
⁷rather, he made himself nothing
by taking the very nature*ᵇ* of a servant,
being made in human likeness.
⁸And being found in appearance as a man,
he humbled himself
by becoming obedient to death—
even death on a cross!

⁹Therefore God exalted him to the highest place
and gave him the name that is above every name,
¹⁰that at the name of Jesus every knee should bow,
in heaven and on earth and under the earth,
¹¹and every tongue acknowledge that Jesus Christ is Lord,
to the glory of God the Father.

### Do Everything Without Grumbling

¹²Therefore, my dear friends, as you have always obeyed—not only in my presence, but now much more in my absence—continue to work out your salvation with fear and trembling, ¹³for it is God who works in you to will and to act in order to fulfill his good purpose.

¹⁴Do everything without grumbling or arguing, ¹⁵so that you may become blameless and pure, "children of God without fault in a warped and crooked generation."*ᶜ* Then you will shine among them like stars in the sky ¹⁶as you hold firmly to the word of life. And then I will be able to boast on the day of Christ that I did not run or labor in vain. ¹⁷But even if I am being poured out like a drink offering on the sacrifice and service coming from your faith, I am glad and rejoice with all of you. ¹⁸So you too should be glad and rejoice with me.

### Timothy and Epaphroditus

¹⁹I hope in the Lord Jesus to send Timothy to you soon, that I also may be cheered when I receive news about you.

## Amplified Bible

³Do nothing from factional motives [through contentiousness, strife, selfishness, or for unworthy ends] or prompted by conceit *and* empty arrogance. Instead, in the true spirit of humility (lowliness of mind) let each regard the others as better than *and* superior to himself [thinking more highly of one another than you do of yourselves].

⁴Let each of you esteem *and* look upon *and* be concerned for not [merely] his own interests, but also each for the interests of others.

⁵Let this same attitude *and* purpose *and* [humble] mind be in you which was in Christ Jesus: [Let Him be your example in humility:]

⁶Who, although being essentially one with God *and* in the form of God [*ᵃ*possessing the fullness of the attributes which make God God], did not *ᵇ*think this equality with God was a thing to be eagerly grasped *ᵇor* retained,

⁷But stripped Himself [of all privileges and *ᶜ*rightful dignity], so as to assume the guise of a servant (slave), in that He became like men *and* was born a human being.

⁸And after He had appeared in human form, He abased *and* humbled Himself [still further] and carried His obedience to the extreme of death, even the death of the cross!

⁹Therefore [because He stooped so low] God has highly exalted Him and has *ᵈ*freely bestowed on Him the name that is above every name,

¹⁰That in (at) the name of Jesus every knee *ᵉ*should (must) bow, in heaven and on earth and under the earth,

¹¹And every tongue [*ᵈ*frankly and openly] confess *and* acknowledge that Jesus Christ is Lord, to the glory of God the Father.

¹²Therefore, my dear ones, as you have always obeyed [my suggestions], so now, not only [with the enthusiasm you would show] in my presence but much more because I am absent, work out (cultivate, carry out to the goal, and fully complete) your own salvation with reverence *and* awe and trembling (self-distrust, *ᵈ*with serious caution, tenderness of conscience, watchfulness against temptation, timidly shrinking from whatever might offend God and discredit the name of Christ).

¹³[Not in your own strength] for it is God Who is all the while *ᵈ*effectually at work in you [energizing and creating in you the power and desire], both to will and to work for His good pleasure *and* satisfaction *and ᶠ*delight.

¹⁴Do all things without grumbling *and* faultfinding *and* complaining [*ᵈ*against God] and *ᵈ*questioning *and* doubting [among yourselves],

¹⁵That you may show yourselves to be blameless *and* guileless, innocent *and* uncontaminated, children of God without blemish (faultless, unrebukable) in the midst of a crooked *and* wicked generation [spiritually perverted and perverse], among whom you are seen as bright lights (stars or beacons shining out clearly) in the [dark] world,

¹⁶Holding out [to it] *and* offering [to all men] the Word of Life, so that in the day of Christ I may have something of which exultantly to rejoice *and* glory in that I did not run my race in vain or spend my labor to no purpose.

¹⁷Even if [my lifeblood] must be poured out as a libation on the sacrificial offering of your faith [to God], still I am glad [to do it] and *ᵍ*congratulate you all on [your share in] it.

¹⁸And you also in like manner be glad and *ᵍ*congratulate me on [my share in] it.

¹⁹But I hope *and* trust in the Lord Jesus soon to send Timothy to you, so that I may also be encouraged *and* cheered by learning news of you.

---

*ᵃ* B. B. Warfield, *Biblical Doctrines*. *ᵇ* Joseph Thayer, *A Greek-English Lexicon*. *ᶜ* George R. Berry, *Greek-English New Testament Lexicon*. *ᵈ* Marvin Vincent, *Word Studies*. *ᵉ* "Should" is the past tense of "shall," implying authority or compulsion. *ᶠ* Alexander Souter, *Pocket Lexicon of the Greek New Testament*. *ᵍ* Joseph P. Lightfoot, *Saint Paul's Epistle to the Philippians* and James Moulton and George Milligan, *The Vocabulary of the Greek Testament*.

---

*ᵃ* 6 Or *in the form of*    *ᵇ* 7 Or *the form*    *ᶜ* 15 Deut. 32:5

## New International Version

[20]I have no one else like him, who will show genuine concern for your welfare. [21]For everyone looks out for their own interests, not those of Jesus Christ. [22]But you know that Timothy has proved himself, because as a son with his father he has served with me in the work of the gospel. [23]I hope, therefore, to send him as soon as I see how things go with me. [24]And I am confident in the Lord that I myself will come soon.

[25]But I think it is necessary to send back to you Epaphroditus, my brother, co-worker and fellow soldier, who is also your messenger, whom you sent to take care of my needs. [26]For he longs for all of you and is distressed because you heard he was ill. [27]Indeed he was ill, and almost died. But God had mercy on him, and not on him only but also on me, to spare me sorrow upon sorrow. [28]Therefore I am all the more eager to send him, so that when you see him again you may be glad and I may have less anxiety. [29]So then, welcome him in the Lord with great joy, and honor people like him, [30]because he almost died for the work of Christ. He risked his life to make up for the help you yourselves could not give me.

### No Confidence in the Flesh

**3** Further, my brothers and sisters, rejoice in the Lord! It is no trouble for me to write the same things to you again, and it is a safeguard for you. [2]Watch out for those dogs, those evildoers, those mutilators of the flesh. [3]For it is we who are the circumcision, we who serve God by his Spirit, who boast in Christ Jesus, and who put no confidence in the flesh— [4]though I myself have reasons for such confidence.

If someone else thinks they have reasons to put confidence in the flesh, I have more: [5]circumcised on the eighth day, of the people of Israel, of the tribe of Benjamin, a Hebrew of Hebrews; in regard to the law, a Pharisee; [6]as for zeal, persecuting the church; as for righteousness based on the law, faultless.

[7]But whatever were gains to me I now consider loss for the sake of Christ. [8]What is more, I consider everything a loss because of the surpassing worth of knowing Christ Jesus my Lord, for whose sake I have lost all things. I consider them garbage, that I may gain Christ [9]and be found

## Amplified Bible

[20]For I have no one like him [no one of so kindred a spirit] who will be so genuinely interested in your welfare *and* devoted to your interests.

[21]For the others all seek [to advance] their own interests, not those of Jesus Christ (the Messiah).

[22]But Timothy's tested worth you know, how as a son with his father he has toiled with me zealously in [serving and helping to advance] the good news (the Gospel).

[23]I hope therefore to send him promptly, just as soon as I know how my case is going to turn out.

[24]But [really] I am confident *and* fully trusting in the Lord that shortly I myself shall come to you also.

[25]However, I thought it necessary to send Epaphroditus [back] to you. [He has been] my brother and companion in labor and my fellow soldier, as well as [having come as] your special messenger (apostle) and minister to my need.

[26]For he has been [homesick] longing for you all and has been distressed because you had heard that he was ill.

[27]He certainly was ill [too], near to death. But God had compassion on him, and not only on him but also on me, lest I should have sorrow [over him] [a]coming upon sorrow.

[28]So I have sent him the more willingly *and* eagerly, that you may be gladdened at seeing him again, and that I may be the less disquieted.

[29]Welcome him [home] then in the Lord with all joy, and honor *and* highly appreciate men like him,

[30]For it was through working for Christ that he came so near death, risking his [very] life to complete the deficiencies in your service to me [which distance prevented you yourselves from rendering].

**3** For the rest, my brethren, delight yourselves in the Lord *and* continue to rejoice that you are in Him. To keep writing to you [over and over] of the same things is not irksome to me, and it is [a precaution] for your safety.

[2]Look out for those dogs [Judaizers, legalists], look out for those mischief-makers, look out for those who mutilate the flesh.

[3]For we [Christians] are the true circumcision, who worship God in spirit *and* by the Spirit of God and exult *and* glory *and* pride ourselves in Jesus Christ, and put no confidence *or* dependence [on what we are] in the flesh *and* on outward privileges *and* physical advantages *and* external appearances—

[4]Though for myself I have [at least grounds] to rely on the flesh. If any other man considers that he has *or* seems to have reason to rely on the flesh *and* his physical *and* outward advantages, I have still more!

[5]Circumcised when I was eight days old, of the race of Israel, of the tribe of Benjamin, a Hebrew [and the son] of Hebrews; as to the observance of the Law I was of [the party of] the Pharisees,

[6]As to my zeal, I was a persecutor of the church, and by the Law's standard of righteousness (supposed justice, uprightness, and right standing with God) I was proven to be blameless *and* no fault was found with me.

[7]But whatever former things I had that might have been gains to me, I have come to consider as [[b]one combined] loss for Christ's sake.

[8]Yes, furthermore, I count everything as loss compared to the possession of the priceless privilege (the overwhelming preciousness, the surpassing worth, and supreme advantage) of knowing Christ Jesus my Lord *and* of progressively becoming more deeply *and* intimately acquainted with Him [of perceiving and recognizing and understanding Him more fully and clearly]. For His sake I have lost everything and consider it all to be mere rubbish (refuse, dregs), in order that I may win (gain) Christ (the Anointed One),

---

[a] Marvin Vincent, *Word Studies*.  [b] Marvin Vincent, *Word Studies*: His "gains" are plural, but they are all counted as one combined "loss" (singular).

## New International Version

in him, not having a righteousness of my own that comes from the law, but that which is through faith in[a] Christ—the righteousness that comes from God on the basis of faith. [10]I want to know Christ—yes, to know the power of his resurrection and participation in his sufferings, becoming like him in his death, [11]and so, somehow, attaining to the resurrection from the dead.

[12]Not that I have already obtained all this, or have already arrived at my goal, but I press on to take hold of that for which Christ Jesus took hold of me. [13]Brothers and sisters, I do not consider myself yet to have taken hold of it. But one thing I do: Forgetting what is behind and straining toward what is ahead, [14]I press on toward the goal to win the prize for which God has called me heavenward in Christ Jesus.

### Following Paul's Example

[15]All of us, then, who are mature should take such a view of things. And if on some point you think differently, that too God will make clear to you. [16]Only let us live up to what we have already attained.

[17]Join together in following my example, brothers and sisters, and just as you have us as a model, keep your eyes on those who live as we do. [18]For, as I have often told you before and now tell you again even with tears, many live as enemies of the cross of Christ. [19]Their destiny is destruction, their god is their stomach, and their glory is in their shame. Their mind is set on earthly things. [20]But our citizenship is in heaven. And we eagerly await a Savior from there, the Lord Jesus Christ, [21]who, by the power that enables him to bring everything under his control, will transform our lowly bodies so that they will be like his glorious body.

### Closing Appeal for Steadfastness and Unity

4 Therefore, my brothers and sisters, you whom I love and long for, my joy and crown, stand firm in the Lord in this way, dear friends!

[2]I plead with Euodia and I plead with Syntyche to be of the same mind in the Lord. [3]Yes, and I ask you, my true companion, help these women since they have contended at my side in the cause of the gospel, along with Clement and the rest of my co-workers, whose names are in the book of life.

## Amplified Bible

[9]And that I may [actually] be found and known as in Him, not having any [self-achieved] righteousness that can be called my own, based on my obedience to the Law's demands (ritualistic uprightness and supposed right standing with God thus acquired), but possessing that [genuine righteousness] which comes through faith in Christ (the Anointed One), the [truly] right standing with God, which comes from God by [saving] faith.

[10][For my determined purpose is] that I may know Him [that I may progressively become more deeply and intimately acquainted with Him, perceiving and recognizing and understanding the wonders of His Person more strongly and more clearly], and that I may in that same way come to know the power outflowing from His resurrection [[a]which it exerts over believers], and that I may so share His sufferings as to be continually transformed [in spirit into His likeness even] to His death, [in the hope]

[11]That if possible I may attain to the [[b]spiritual and moral] resurrection [that lifts me] out from among the dead [even while in the body].

[12]Not that I have now attained [this ideal], or have already been made perfect, but I press on to lay hold of (grasp) and make my own, that for which Christ Jesus (the Messiah) has laid hold of me and made me His own.

[13]I do not consider, brethren, that I have captured and made it my own [yet]; but one thing I do [it is my one aspiration]: forgetting what lies behind and straining forward to what lies ahead,

[14]I press on toward the goal to win the [supreme and heavenly] prize to which God in Christ Jesus is calling us upward.

[15]So let those [of us] who are spiritually mature and full-grown have this mind and hold these convictions; and if in any respect you have a different attitude of mind, God will make that clear to you also.

[16]Only let us hold true to what we have already attained and walk and order our lives by that.

[17]Brethren, together follow my example and observe those who live after the pattern we have set for you.

[18]For there are many, of whom I have often told you and now tell you even with tears, who walk (live) as enemies of the cross of Christ (the Anointed One).

[19]They are doomed and their [c]fate is eternal misery (perdition); their god is their stomach (their appetites, their sensuality) and they glory in their shame, [c]siding with earthly things and being of their party.

[20]But we are citizens of the state (commonwealth, homeland) which is in heaven, and from it also we [a]earnestly and patiently await [the coming of] the Lord Jesus Christ (the Messiah) [as] Savior,

[21]Who will [a]transform and fashion anew the body of our humiliation to conform to and be like the body of His glory and majesty, by exerting that power which enables Him even to subject everything to Himself.

4 Therefore, my brethren, whom I love and yearn to see, my delight and crown (wreath of victory), thus stand firm in the Lord, my beloved.

[2]I entreat and advise Euodia and I entreat and advise Syntyche to agree and to work in harmony in the Lord.

[3]And I exhort you too, [my] genuine yokefellow, help these [two women to keep on cooperating], for they have toiled along with me in [the spreading of] the good news (the Gospel), as have Clement and the rest of my fellow workers whose names are in the Book of Life.

---

[a] Marvin Vincent, Word Studies.  [b] Charles B. Williams, The New Testament: A Translation in the Language of the People: A spiritual, moral resurrection—not the final, physical one, which will be the climax.  [c] Joseph Thayer, A Greek-English Lexicon.

## New International Version

### Final Exhortations

[4]Rejoice in the Lord always. I will say it again: Rejoice! [5]Let your gentleness be evident to all. The Lord is near. [6]Do not be anxious about anything, but in every situation, by prayer and petition, with thanksgiving, present your requests to God. [7]And the peace of God, which transcends all understanding, will guard your hearts and your minds in Christ Jesus.

[8]Finally, brothers and sisters, whatever is true, whatever is noble, whatever is right, whatever is pure, whatever is lovely, whatever is admirable—if anything is excellent or praiseworthy—think about such things. [9]Whatever you have learned or received or heard from me, or seen in me—put it into practice. And the God of peace will be with you.

### Thanks for Their Gifts

[10]I rejoiced greatly in the Lord that at last you renewed your concern for me. Indeed, you were concerned, but you had no opportunity to show it. [11]I am not saying this because I am in need, for I have learned to be content whatever the circumstances. [12]I know what it is to be in need, and I know what it is to have plenty. I have learned the secret of being content in any and every situation, whether well fed or hungry, whether living in plenty or in want. [13]I can do all this through him who gives me strength.

[14]Yet it was good of you to share in my troubles. [15]Moreover, as you Philippians know, in the early days of your acquaintance with the gospel, when I set out from Macedonia, not one church shared with me in the matter of giving and receiving, except you only; [16]for even when I was in Thessalonica, you sent me aid more than once when I was in need. [17]Not that I desire your gifts; what I desire is that more be credited to your account. [18]I have received full payment and have more than enough. I am amply supplied, now that I have received from Epaphroditus the gifts you sent. They are a fragrant offering, an acceptable sacrifice, pleasing to God. [19]And my God will meet all your needs according to the riches of his glory in Christ Jesus.

## Amplified Bible

[4]Rejoice in the Lord always [delight, gladden yourselves in Him]; again I say, Rejoice! [Ps. 37:4.]

[5]Let all men know and perceive and recognize your unselfishness (your considerateness, your forbearing spirit). The Lord is near [He is [a]coming soon].

[6]Do not fret or have any anxiety about anything, but in every circumstance and in everything, by prayer and petition ([a]definite requests), with thanksgiving, continue to make your wants known to God.

[7]And God's peace [shall be yours, that [a]tranquil state of a soul assured of its salvation through Christ, and so fearing nothing from God and being content with its earthly lot of whatever sort that is, that peace] which transcends all understanding shall [b]garrison and mount guard over your hearts and minds in Christ Jesus.

[8]For the rest, brethren, whatever is true, whatever is worthy of reverence and is honorable and seemly, whatever is just, whatever is pure, whatever is lovely and lovable, whatever is kind and winsome and gracious, if there is any virtue and excellence, if there is anything worthy of praise, think on and weigh and take account of these things [fix your minds on them].

[9]Practice what you have learned and received and heard and seen in me, and model your way of living on it, and the God of peace (of [c]untroubled, undisturbed wellbeing) will be with you.

[10]I was made very happy in the Lord that now you have revived your interest in my welfare after so long a time; you were indeed thinking of me, but you had no opportunity to show it.

[11]Not that I am implying that I was in any personal want, for I have learned how to be [d]content (satisfied to the point where I am not disturbed or disquieted) in whatever state I am.

[12]I know how to be abased and live humbly in straitened circumstances, and I know also how to enjoy plenty and live in abundance. I have learned in any and all circumstances the secret of facing every situation, whether well-fed or going hungry, having a sufficiency and enough to spare or going without and being in want.

[13]I have strength for all things in Christ Who empowers me [I am ready for anything and equal to anything through Him Who [e]infuses inner strength into me; I am [f]self-sufficient in Christ's sufficiency].

[14]But it was right and commendable and noble of you to contribute for my needs and to share my difficulties with me.

[15]And you Philippians yourselves well know that in the early days of the Gospel ministry, when I left Macedonia, no church (assembly) entered into partnership with me and opened up [a debit and credit] account in giving and receiving except you only.

[16]For even in Thessalonica you sent [me contributions] for my needs, not only once but a second time.

[17]Not that I seek or am eager for [your] gift, but I do seek and am eager for the fruit which increases to your credit [the harvest of blessing that is accumulating to your account].

[18]But I have [your full payment] and more; I have everything I need and am amply supplied, now that I have received from Epaphroditus the gifts you sent me. [They are the] fragrant odor of an offering and sacrifice which God welcomes and in which He delights.

[19]And my God will liberally supply ([a]fill to the full) your every need according to His riches in glory in Christ Jesus.

---

[a] Joseph Thayer, *A Greek-English Lexicon*. [b] William Gurnall, cited by Marvin Vincent, *Word Studies*. [c] Hermann Cremer, *Biblico-Theological Lexicon of New Testament Greek*. [d] Literal translation: "self-sufficient." [e] Marvin Vincent, *Word Studies*. [f] Note that in Phil. 4:11, the Greek *autarkas*, translated "content," is literally "self-sufficient."

## New International Version

[20]To our God and Father be glory for ever and ever. Amen.

### Final Greetings

[21]Greet all God's people in Christ Jesus. The brothers and sisters who are with me send greetings. [22]All God's people here send you greetings, especially those who belong to Caesar's household.

[23]The grace of the Lord Jesus Christ be with your spirit. Amen.[a]

## Amplified Bible

[20]To our God and Father be glory forever and ever (through the endless eternities of the eternities). *Amen (so be it).*

[21]Remember me to every saint (every born-again believer) in Christ Jesus. The brethren (my [a]associates) who are with me greet you.

[22]All the saints (God's consecrated ones here) wish to be remembered to you, especially those of Caesar's household.

[23]The grace (spiritual favor and blessing) of the Lord Jesus Christ (the Anointed One) be with your spirit. *Amen (so be it).*

---

[a] 23 Some manuscripts do not have *Amen*.

[a] Alexander Souter, *Pocket Lexicon.*

## New International Version

# Colossians

**1** Paul, an apostle of Christ Jesus by the will of God, and Timothy our brother,

[2] To God's holy people in Colossae, the faithful brothers and sisters[a] in Christ:

Grace and peace to you from God our Father.[b]

### Thanksgiving and Prayer

[3] We always thank God, the Father of our Lord Jesus Christ, when we pray for you, [4] because we have heard of your faith in Christ Jesus and of the love you have for all God's people— [5] the faith and love that spring from the hope stored up for you in heaven and about which you have already heard in the true message of the gospel [6] that has come to you. In the same way, the gospel is bearing fruit and growing throughout the whole world—just as it has been doing among you since the day you heard it and truly understood God's grace. [7] You learned it from Epaphras, our dear fellow servant,[c] who is a faithful minister of Christ on our[d] behalf, [8] and who also told us of your love in the Spirit.

[9] For this reason, since the day we heard about you, we have not stopped praying for you. We continually ask God to fill you with the knowledge of his will through all the wisdom and understanding that the Spirit gives,[e] [10] so that you may live a life worthy of the Lord and please him in every way: bearing fruit in every good work, growing in the knowledge of God, [11] being strengthened with all power according to his glorious might so that you may have great endurance and patience, [12] and giving joyful thanks to the Father, who has qualified you[f] to share in the inheritance of his holy people in the kingdom of light. [13] For he has rescued us from the dominion of darkness and brought us into the kingdom of the Son he loves, [14] in whom we have redemption, the forgiveness of sins.

### The Supremacy of the Son of God

[15] The Son is the image of the invisible God, the first-born over all creation. [16] For in him all things were created:

*a* 2 The Greek word for *brothers and sisters (adelphoi)* refers here to believers, both men and women, as part of God's family; also in 4:15.
*b* 2 Some manuscripts *Father and the Lord Jesus Christ*   *c* 7 Or *slave*
*d* 7 Some manuscripts *your*   *e* 9 Or *all spiritual wisdom and understanding*   *f* 12 Some manuscripts *us*

## Amplified Bible

### THE LETTER OF PAUL TO THE

# Colossians

**1** Paul, an apostle (special messenger) of Christ Jesus (the Messiah), by the will of God, and Timothy [our] brother,

[2] To the saints (the consecrated people of God) and [a] believing *and* faithful brethren in Christ who are at Colossae: Grace (spiritual favor and blessing) to you and [heart] peace from God our Father.

[3] We [b] continually give thanks to God the Father of our Lord Jesus Christ (the Messiah), as we are praying for you,

[4] For we have heard of your faith in Christ Jesus [[c] the leaning of your entire human personality on Him in absolute trust and confidence in His power, wisdom, and goodness] and of the love which you [have and show] for all the saints (God's consecrated ones),

[5] Because of the hope [of experiencing what is] laid up ([a] reserved and waiting) for you in heaven. Of this [hope] you heard in the past in the message of the truth of the Gospel,

[6] Which has come to you. Indeed, in the whole world [that Gospel] is bearing fruit *and* still is growing [d] [by its own inherent power], even as it has done among yourselves ever since the day you first heard and came to know *and* understand the grace of God in truth. [You came to know the grace or undeserved favor of God in reality, deeply and clearly and thoroughly, becoming accurately and intimately acquainted with it.]

[7] You so learned it from Epaphras, our beloved fellow servant. He is a faithful minister of Christ in our stead *and* as our representative *and* [e] yours.

[8] Also he has informed us of your love in the [Holy] Spirit.

[9] For this reason we also, from the day we heard of it, have not ceased to pray *and* make [[a] special] request for you, [asking] that you may be filled with the [a] full (deep and clear) knowledge of His will in all spiritual wisdom [[d] in comprehensive insight into the ways and purposes of God] and in understanding *and* discernment of spiritual things—

[10] That you may walk (live and conduct yourselves) in a manner worthy of the Lord, fully pleasing to Him *and* [f] desiring to please Him in all things, bearing fruit in every good work *and* steadily growing *and* increasing in *and* by the knowledge of God [with fuller, deeper, and clearer insight, [g] acquaintance, and recognition].

[11] [We pray] that you may be invigorated *and* strengthened with all power according to the might of His glory, [to exercise] every kind of endurance and patience (perseverance and forbearance) with joy,

[12] Giving thanks to the Father, Who has qualified *and* made us fit to share the [h] portion which is the inheritance of the saints (God's holy people) in the Light.

[13] [The Father] has delivered *and* [i] drawn us to Himself out of the control *and* the dominion of darkness and has transferred us into the kingdom of the Son [j] of His love,

[14] In Whom we have our redemption *through His blood,* [which means] the forgiveness of our sins.

[15] [Now] He is the [k] exact likeness of the unseen God [the visible representation of the invisible]; He is the Firstborn of all creation.

*a* Marvin Vincent, *Word Studies in the New Testament.*   *b* Marvin Vincent, *Word Studies in the New Testament:* "Continually" belongs with "give thanks," not elsewhere.   *c* Alexander Souter, *Pocket Lexicon of the Greek New Testament.*   *d* Alexander Souter, *Pocket Lexicon.*   *e* Many ancient manuscripts read "yours."   *f* Joseph Thayer, *A Greek-English Lexicon of the New Testament.*   *g* G. Abbott-Smith, *Manual Greek Lexicon of the New Testament.*   *h* Marvin Vincent, *Word Studies.*   *i* Joseph Thayer, *A Greek-English Lexicon.*   *j* Literal translation.   *k* Charles B. Williams, *The New Testament: A Translation in the Language of the People:* Strong terms—thus translated "exact likeness."

## New International Version

things in heaven and on earth, visible and invisible, whether thrones or powers or rulers or authorities; all things have been created through him and for him. [17]He is before all things, and in him all things hold together. [18]And he is the head of the body, the church; he is the beginning and the firstborn from among the dead, so that in everything he might have the supremacy. [19]For God was pleased to have all his fullness dwell in him, [20]and through him to reconcile to himself all things, whether things on earth or things in heaven, by making peace through his blood, shed on the cross.

[21]Once you were alienated from God and were enemies in your minds because of[a] your evil behavior. [22]But now he has reconciled you by Christ's physical body through death to present you holy in his sight, without blemish and free from accusation— [23]if you continue in your faith, established and firm, and do not move from the hope held out in the gospel. This is the gospel that you heard and that has been proclaimed to every creature under heaven, and of which I, Paul, have become a servant.

### Paul's Labor for the Church

[24]Now I rejoice in what I am suffering for you, and I fill up in my flesh what is still lacking in regard to Christ's afflictions, for the sake of his body, which is the church. [25]I have become its servant by the commission God gave me to present to you the word of God in its fullness— [26]the mystery that has been kept hidden for ages and generations, but is now disclosed to the Lord's people. [27]To them God has chosen to make known among the Gentiles the glorious riches of this mystery, which is Christ in you, the hope of glory.

[28]He is the one we proclaim, admonishing and teaching everyone with all wisdom, so that we may present everyone fully mature in Christ. [29]To this end I strenuously contend with all the energy Christ so powerfully works in me.

**2** I want you to know how hard I am contending for you and for those at Laodicea, and for all who have not met me personally. [2]My goal is that they may be encouraged

## Amplified Bible

[16]For it was in Him that all things were created, in heaven and on earth, things seen and things unseen, whether thrones, dominions, rulers, or authorities; all things were created *and* exist through Him [by His service, intervention] and in *and* for Him.

[17]And He Himself existed before all things, and in Him all things consist (cohere, are held together). [Prov. 8:22-31.]

[18]He also is the Head of [His] body, the church; seeing He is the Beginning, the Firstborn from among the dead, so that He alone in everything *and* in every respect might occupy the chief place [stand first and be preeminent].

[19]For it has pleased [the Father] that all the divine fullness (the sum total of the divine perfection, powers, and attributes) should dwell in Him [a]permanently.

[20]And God purposed that through ([b]by the service, the intervention of) Him [the Son] all things should be completely reconciled [a]back to Himself, whether on earth or in heaven, as through Him, [the Father] made peace by means of the blood of His cross.

[21]And although you at one time were estranged *and* alienated from Him and were of hostile attitude of mind in your wicked activities,

[22]Yet now has [Christ, the Messiah] reconciled [you to God] in the body of His flesh through death, in order to present you holy and faultless and irreproachable in His [the Father's] presence.

[23][And this He will do] provided that you continue to [a]stay with *and* in the faith [in Christ], well-grounded and settled *and* steadfast, not shifting *or* moving away from the hope [which rests on and is inspired by] the glad tidings (the Gospel), which you heard and which has been preached [c][as being designed for and offered without restrictions] to every person under heaven, and of which [Gospel] I, Paul, became a minister.

[24][Even] now I rejoice in [a]the midst of my sufferings on your behalf. And in my own person I am making up whatever is still lacking *and* remains to be completed [a]on our part] of Christ's afflictions, for the sake of His body, which is the church.

[25]In it I became a minister in accordance with the divine [a]stewardship which was entrusted to me for you [as its object and for your benefit], to make the Word of God fully known [among you]—

[26]The mystery of which was hidden for ages and generations [d]from angels and men], but is now revealed to His holy people (the saints),

[27]To whom God was pleased to make known how great for the Gentiles are the riches of the glory of this mystery, which is Christ within *and* among you, the Hope of [realizing the] glory.

[28]Him we preach *and* proclaim, warning *and* admonishing everyone and instructing everyone in all wisdom ([e]comprehensive insight into the ways and purposes of God), that we may present every person mature (full-grown, fully initiated, complete, and perfect) in Christ (the Anointed One).

[29]For this I labor [a]unto weariness], striving with all the [a]superhuman energy which He so mightily enkindles *and* works within me.

**2** For I want you to know how great is my solicitude for you [how severe an inward struggle I am engaged in for you] and for those [believers] at Laodicea, and for all who [a]like yourselves] have never seen my face *and* known me personally.

[2][For my concern is] that their hearts may be [a]braced (comforted, cheered, and encouraged) as they are knit to-

[a] Marvin Vincent, *Word Studies.* [b] Joseph Thayer, *A Greek-English Lexicon.* [c] Adam Clarke, *The Holy Bible with A Commentary.* [d] Johann Bengel, *Gnomon Novi Testamenti* and Henry Alford, *The Greek New Testament.* [e] Alexander Souter, *Pocket Lexicon.*

## New International Version

in heart and united in love, so that they may have the full riches of complete understanding, in order that they may know the mystery of God, namely, Christ, ³in whom are hidden all the treasures of wisdom and knowledge. ⁴I tell you this so that no one may deceive you by fine-sounding arguments. ⁵For though I am absent from you in body, I am present with you in spirit and delight to see how disciplined you are and how firm your faith in Christ is.

### Spiritual Fullness in Christ

⁶So then, just as you received Christ Jesus as Lord, continue to live your lives in him, ⁷rooted and built up in him, strengthened in the faith as you were taught, and overflowing with thankfulness.

⁸See to it that no one takes you captive through hollow and deceptive philosophy, which depends on human tradition and the elemental spiritual forces*a* of this world rather than on Christ.

⁹For in Christ all the fullness of the Deity lives in bodily form, ¹⁰and in Christ you have been brought to fullness. He is the head over every power and authority. ¹¹In him you were also circumcised with a circumcision not performed by human hands. Your whole self ruled by the flesh*b* was put off when you were circumcised by*c* Christ, ¹²having been buried with him in baptism, in which you were also raised with him through your faith in the working of God, who raised him from the dead.

¹³When you were dead in your sins and in the uncircumcision of your flesh, God made you*d* alive with Christ. He forgave us all our sins, ¹⁴having canceled the charge of our legal indebtedness, which stood against us and condemned us; he has taken it away, nailing it to the cross. ¹⁵And having disarmed the powers and authorities, he made a public spectacle of them, triumphing over them by the cross.*e*

## Amplified Bible

gether in love, that they may come to have all the abounding wealth *and* blessings of assured conviction of understanding, and that they may become progressively *a*more intimately acquainted with *and* may know more definitely *and* accurately *and* thoroughly that mystic secret of God, [which is] Christ (the Anointed One).

³In Him all the treasures of [divine] wisdom (*b*comprehensive insight into the ways and purposes of God) and [all the riches of spiritual] knowledge *and* enlightenment are stored up *and* lie hidden.

⁴I say this in order that no one may mislead *and* delude you by plausible *and* persuasive *and* attractive arguments *and* beguiling speech.

⁵For though I am away from you in body, yet I am with you in spirit, delighted at the sight of your [standing shoulder to shoulder in such] orderly array and the firmness *and* the solid front *and* steadfastness of your faith in Christ [that *b*leaning of the entire human personality on Him in absolute trust and confidence in His power, wisdom, and goodness].

⁶As you have therefore received Christ, [even] Jesus the Lord, [so] walk (regulate your lives and conduct yourselves) in union with *and* conformity to Him.

⁷Have the roots [of your being] firmly *and* deeply planted [in Him, fixed and founded in Him], being continually built up in Him, becoming increasingly more confirmed *and* established in the faith, just as you were taught, and abounding *and* overflowing in it with thanksgiving.

⁸See to it that no one carries you off as spoil *or* makes you yourselves captive by his so-called philosophy *and* intellectualism and vain deceit (idle fancies and plain nonsense), following human tradition (men's ideas of the material rather than the spiritual world), just crude notions following the rudimentary *and* elemental teachings of the universe and disregarding [the teachings of] Christ (the Messiah).

⁹For in Him the whole fullness of Deity (the Godhead) continues to dwell in bodily form [giving complete expression of the divine nature].

¹⁰And you *c*are in Him, made full *and* having come to fullness of life [in Christ you too are filled with the Godhead—Father, Son and Holy Spirit—and reach full spiritual stature]. And He is the Head of all rule and authority [of every angelic principality and power].

¹¹In Him also you were circumcised with a circumcision not made with hands, but in a [spiritual] circumcision [performed by] Christ by stripping off the body of the flesh (the whole corrupt, carnal nature with its passions and lusts).

¹²[Thus *d*you were circumcised when] you were buried with Him in [your] baptism, in which you were also raised with Him [*c*to a new life] through [your] faith in the working of God [*c*as displayed] when He raised Him up from the dead.

¹³And you who were dead in trespasses and in the uncircumcision of your flesh (your sensuality, your sinful carnal nature), [God] brought to life together with [Christ], having [freely] forgiven us all our transgressions,

¹⁴Having cancelled *and* blotted out *and* wiped away the handwriting of the note (bond) with its legal decrees *and* demands which was in force *and* stood against us (hostile to us). This [note with its regulations, decrees, and demands] He set aside *and* cleared *c*completely out of our way by nailing it to [His] cross.

¹⁵[God] disarmed the principalities and powers that were ranged against us and made a bold display *and* public example of them, in triumphing over them in Him *and* in it [the cross].

---

*a 8* Or *the basic principles*; also in verse 20      *b 11* In contexts like this, the Greek word for *flesh* (*sarx*) refers to the sinful state of human beings, often presented as a power in opposition to the Spirit; also in verse 13. 
*c 11* Or *put off in the circumcision of*      *d 13* Some manuscripts *us* 
*e 15* Or *them in him*

*a* Richard Trench, *Synonyms of the New Testament.*   *b* Alexander Souter, *Pocket Lexicon.*   *c* Marvin Vincent, *Word Studies.*   *d* Marvin Vincent, *Word Studies:* "The aorist tense puts the burial as contemporaneous with the circumcision."

## New International Version

### Freedom From Human Rules

¹⁶Therefore do not let anyone judge you by what you eat or drink, or with regard to a religious festival, a New Moon celebration or a Sabbath day. ¹⁷These are a shadow of the things that were to come; the reality, however, is found in Christ. ¹⁸Do not let anyone who delights in false humility and the worship of angels disqualify you. Such a person also goes into great detail about what they have seen; they are puffed up with idle notions by their unspiritual mind. ¹⁹They have lost connection with the head, from whom the whole body, supported and held together by its ligaments and sinews, grows as God causes it to grow.

²⁰Since you died with Christ to the elemental spiritual forces of this world, why, as though you still belonged to the world, do you submit to its rules: ²¹"Do not handle! Do not taste! Do not touch!"? ²²These rules, which have to do with things that are all destined to perish with use, are based on merely human commands and teachings. ²³Such regulations indeed have an appearance of wisdom, with their self-imposed worship, their false humility and their harsh treatment of the body, but they lack any value in restraining sensual indulgence.

### Living as Those Made Alive in Christ

**3** Since, then, you have been raised with Christ, set your hearts on things above, where Christ is, seated at the right hand of God. ²Set your minds on things above, not on earthly things. ³For you died, and your life is now hidden with Christ in God. ⁴When Christ, who is your[a] life, appears, then you also will appear with him in glory.

⁵Put to death, therefore, whatever belongs to your earthly nature: sexual immorality, impurity, lust, evil desires and greed, which is idolatry. ⁶Because of these, the wrath of God is coming.[b] ⁷You used to walk in these ways, in the life you once lived. ⁸But now you must also rid yourselves of all such things as these: anger, rage, malice, slander, and filthy language from your lips. ⁹Do not lie to each other, since you have taken off your old self with its practices ¹⁰and have put on the new self, which is being renewed in knowledge in the image of its Creator. ¹¹Here there is no Gentile or Jew, circumcised or uncircumcised,

## Amplified Bible

¹⁶Therefore let no one sit in judgment on you in matters of food and drink, or with regard to a feast day or a New Moon or a Sabbath.

¹⁷Such [things] are only the shadow of things that are to come, *and* they have only a symbolic value. But the reality (the substance, the solid fact of what is foreshadowed, the body of it) belongs to Christ.

¹⁸Let no one defraud you by acting as an umpire *and* declaring you unworthy *and* disqualifying you for the prize, insisting on self-abasement and worship of angels, taking his stand on visions [he claims] he has seen, vainly puffed up by his sensuous notions *and* inflated by his unspiritual fleshly thoughts *and* fleshly conceit,

¹⁹And not holding fast to the Head, from Whom the entire body, supplied and knit together by means of its joints and ligaments, grows with a growth that is from God.

²⁰If you have died with Christ to material ways of looking at things *and* have escaped from the world's crude *and* elemental notions *and* teachings of externalism, why do you live as if you still belong to the world? [Why do you submit to rules *and* regulations?—such as]

²¹Do not handle [this], Do not taste [that], Do not even touch [them],

²²Referring to things all of which perish with being used. To do this is to follow human precepts and doctrines. [Isa. 29:13.]

²³Such [practices] have indeed the outward appearance [that popularly passes] for wisdom, in promoting self-imposed rigor of devotion *and* delight in self-humiliation *and* severity of discipline of the body, but they are of no value in checking the indulgence of the flesh (the lower nature). [Instead, they do not honor God but serve only to indulge the flesh.]

**3** If then you have been raised with Christ [to a new life, thus sharing His resurrection from the dead], aim at *and* seek the [rich, eternal treasures] that are above, where Christ is, seated at the right hand of God. [Ps. 110:1.]

²And set your minds *and* keep them set on what is above (the higher things), not on the things that are on the earth.

³For [as far as this world is concerned] you have died, and your [new, real] life is hidden with Christ in God.

⁴When Christ, Who is our life, appears, then you also will appear with Him in [the splendor of His] glory.

⁵So kill (deaden, ᵃdeprive of power) the evil desire lurking in your members [those animal impulses and all that is earthly in you that is employed in sin]: sexual vice, impurity, sensual appetites, unholy desires, and all greed *and* covetousness, for that is idolatry (the deifying of self and other created things instead of God).

⁶It is on account of these [very sins] that the [holy] anger of God is ever coming upon the sons of disobedience (those who are obstinately opposed to the divine will),

⁷Among whom you also once walked, when you were living in *and* addicted to [such practices].

⁸But now put away *and* rid yourselves [completely] of all these things: anger, rage, bad feeling toward others, curses *and* slander, and foulmouthed abuse *and* shameful utterances from your lips!

⁹Do not lie to one another, for you have stripped off the old (unregenerate) self with its evil practices,

¹⁰And have clothed yourselves with the new [spiritual self], which is [ever in the process of being] renewed *and* remolded into [fuller and more perfect ᵇknowledge upon] knowledge after the image (the likeness) of Him Who created it. [Gen. 1:26.]

¹¹[In this new creation all distinctions vanish.] There ᶜis no room for *and* there can be neither Greek nor Jew,

---

ᵃ Joseph Thayer, *A Greek-English Lexicon.*   ᵇ Literal translation.
ᶜ Marvin Vincent, *Word Studies.*

## New International Version

barbarian, Scythian, slave or free, but Christ is all, and is in all.

¹²Therefore, as God's chosen people, holy and dearly loved, clothe yourselves with compassion, kindness, humility, gentleness and patience. ¹³Bear with each other and forgive one another if any of you has a grievance against someone. Forgive as the Lord forgave you. ¹⁴And over all these virtues put on love, which binds them all together in perfect unity.

¹⁵Let the peace of Christ rule in your hearts, since as members of one body you were called to peace. And be thankful. ¹⁶Let the message of Christ dwell among you richly as you teach and admonish one another with all wisdom through psalms, hymns, and songs from the Spirit, singing to God with gratitude in your hearts. ¹⁷And whatever you do, whether in word or deed, do it all in the name of the Lord Jesus, giving thanks to God the Father through him.

### Instructions for Christian Households

¹⁸Wives, submit yourselves to your husbands, as is fitting in the Lord.

¹⁹Husbands, love your wives and do not be harsh with them.

²⁰Children, obey your parents in everything, for this pleases the Lord.

²¹Fathers,ᵃ do not embitter your children, or they will become discouraged.

²²Slaves, obey your earthly masters in everything; and do it, not only when their eye is on you and to curry their favor, but with sincerity of heart and reverence for the Lord. ²³Whatever you do, work at it with all your heart, as working for the Lord, not for human masters, ²⁴since you know that you will receive an inheritance from the Lord as a reward. It is the Lord Christ you are serving. ²⁵Anyone who does wrong will be repaid for their wrongs, and there is no favoritism.

**4** Masters, provide your slaves with what is right and fair, because you know that you also have a Master in heaven.

### Further Instructions

²Devote yourselves to prayer, being watchful and thankful. ³And pray for us, too, that God may open a door

## Amplified Bible

circumcised nor uncircumcised, [nor difference between nations whether alien] barbarians or Scythians [ᵃwho are the most savage of all], nor slave or free man; but Christ is all and in all [ᵇeverything and everywhere, to all men, without distinction of person].

¹²Clothe yourselves therefore, as God's own chosen ones (His own picked representatives), [who are] purified and holy and well-beloved [by God Himself, by putting on behavior marked by] tenderhearted pity and mercy, kind feeling, a lowly opinion of yourselves, gentle ways, [and] patience [which is tireless and long-suffering, and has the power to endure whatever comes, with good temper].

¹³Be gentle and forbearing with one another and, if one has a difference (a grievance or complaint) against another, readily pardoning each other; even as the Lord has [freely] forgiven you, so must you also [forgive].

¹⁴And above all these [put on] love and enfold yourselves with the bond of perfectness [which binds everything together completely in ideal harmony].

¹⁵And let the peace (soul harmony which comes) from Christ rule (act as umpire continually) in your hearts [deciding and settling with finality all questions that arise in your minds, in that peaceful state] to which as [members of Christ's] one body you were also called [to live]. And be thankful (appreciative), [giving praise to God always].

¹⁶Let the word [spoken by] Christ (the Messiah) have its home [in your hearts and minds] and dwell in you in [all its] richness, as you teach and admonish and train one another in all insight and intelligence and wisdom [in spiritual things, and as you sing] psalms and hymns and spiritual songs, making melody to God with [His] grace in your hearts.

¹⁷And whatever you do [no matter what it is] in word or deed, do everything in the name of the Lord Jesus and in [dependence upon] His Person, giving praise to God the Father through Him.

¹⁸Wives, be subject to your husbands [subordinate and adapt yourselves to them], as is right and fitting and your proper duty in the Lord.

¹⁹Husbands, love your wives [be affectionate and sympathetic with them] and do not be harsh or bitter or resentful toward them.

²⁰Children, obey your parents in everything, for this is pleasing to the Lord.

²¹Fathers, do not provoke or irritate or fret your children [do not be hard on them or harass them], lest they become discouraged and sullen and morose and feel inferior and frustrated. [Do not break their spirit.]

²²Servants, obey in everything those who are your earthly masters, not only when their eyes are on you as pleasers of men, but in simplicity of purpose [with all your heart] because of your reverence for the Lord and as a sincere expression of your devotion to Him.

²³Whatever may be your task, work at it heartily (from the soul), as [something done] for the Lord and not for men,

²⁴Knowing [with all certainty] that it is from the Lord [and not from men] that you will receive the inheritance which is your [real] reward. [The One Whom] you are actually serving [is] the Lord Christ (the Messiah).

²⁵For he who deals wrongfully will [reap the fruit of his folly and] be punished for his wrongdoing. And [with God] there is no partiality [no matter what a person's position may be, whether he is the slave or the master].

**4** Masters, [on your part] deal with your slaves justly and fairly, knowing that also you have a Master in heaven. [Lev. 25:43, 53.]

²Be earnest and unwearied and steadfast in your prayer [life], being [both] alert and intent in [your praying] with thanksgiving.

³And at the same time pray for us also, that God may

ᵃ Marvin Vincent, *Word Studies.*  ᵇ James C. Gray and George M. Adams, *Bible Commentary.*

## New International Version

for our message, so that we may proclaim the mystery of Christ, for which I am in chains. 4Pray that I may proclaim it clearly, as I should. 5Be wise in the way you act toward outsiders; make the most of every opportunity. 6Let your conversation be always full of grace, seasoned with salt, so that you may know how to answer everyone.

### Final Greetings

7Tychicus will tell you all the news about me. He is a dear brother, a faithful minister and fellow servant*a* in the Lord. 8I am sending him to you for the express purpose that you may know about our*b* circumstances and that he may encourage your hearts. 9He is coming with Onesimus, our faithful and dear brother, who is one of you. They will tell you everything that is happening here.

10My fellow prisoner Aristarchus sends you his greetings, as does Mark, the cousin of Barnabas. (You have received instructions about him; if he comes to you, welcome him.) 11Jesus, who is called Justus, also sends greetings. These are the only Jews*c* among my co-workers for the kingdom of God, and they have proved a comfort to me. 12Epaphras, who is one of you and a servant of Christ Jesus, sends greetings. He is always wrestling in prayer for you, that you may stand firm in all the will of God, mature and fully assured. 13I vouch for him that he is working hard for you and for those at Laodicea and Hierapolis. 14Our dear friend Luke, the doctor, and Demas send greetings. 15Give my greetings to the brothers and sisters at Laodicea, and to Nympha and the church in her house. 16After this letter has been read to you, see that it is also read in the church of the Laodiceans and that you in turn read the letter from Laodicea.

17Tell Archippus: "See to it that you complete the ministry you have received in the Lord."

18I, Paul, write this greeting in my own hand. Remember my chains. Grace be with you.

## Amplified Bible

open a door to us for the Word (the Gospel), to proclaim the mystery concerning Christ (the Messiah) on account of which I am in prison;

4That I may proclaim it fully *and* make it clear [speak boldly and unfold that mystery], as is my duty.

5Behave yourselves wisely [living prudently and with discretion] in your relations with those of the outside world (the non-Christians), making the very most of the time *and* seizing (buying up) the opportunity.

6Let your speech at all times be gracious (pleasant and winsome), seasoned [as it were] with salt, [so that you may never be at a loss] to know how you ought to answer anyone [who puts a question to you].

7Tychicus will give you full information about my affairs; [he is] a much-loved brother and faithful ministering assistant and fellow servant [with us] in the Lord.

8I have sent him to you for this very purpose, that you may know how we are faring and that he may comfort *and* cheer *and* encourage your hearts.

9And with [him is] Onesimus, [our] faithful and beloved brother, who is [one] of yourselves. They will let you know everything that has taken place here [in Rome].

10Aristarchus my fellow prisoner wishes to be remembered to you, as does Mark the relative of Barnabas. You received instructions concerning him; if he comes to you give him a [*a*hearty] welcome.

11And [greetings also from] Jesus, who is called Justus. These [Hebrew Christians] alone of the circumcision are among my fellow workers for [the extension of] God's kingdom, and they have proved a relief *and* a comfort to me.

12Epaphras, who is one of yourselves, a servant of Christ Jesus, sends you greetings. [He is] always striving for you earnestly in his prayers, [pleading] that you may [as persons of ripe character and clear conviction] stand firm *and* mature [in spiritual growth], convinced *and* fully assured in *b*everything willed by God.

13For I bear him testimony that he has labored hard in your behalf and for [the believers] in Laodicea and those in Hierapolis.

14Luke the beloved physician and Demas salute you.

15Give my greetings to the brethren at Laodicea, and to Nympha and the assembly (the church) which meets in her house.

16And when this epistle has been read before you, [see] that it is read also in the assembly (the church) of the Laodiceans, and also [see] that you yourselves in turn read the [letter that comes to you] from Laodicea.

17And say to Archippus, See that you discharge carefully [the duties of] the ministry *and* fulfill the stewardship which you have received in the Lord.

18I, Paul, [add this final] greeting, writing with my own hand. Remember I am still in prison *and* in chains. May grace (God's unmerited favor and blessing) be with you! *Amen (so be it).*

---

*a* 7 Or *slave*; also in verse 12   *b* 8 Some manuscripts *that he may know about your*   *c* 11 Greek *only ones of the circumcision group*

*a* Charles B. Williams, *The New Testament: A Translation*: A very strong verb—thus translated "give him a hearty welcome."   *b* Marvin Vincent, *Word Studies.*

# 1 Thessalonians

**1** Paul, Silas[a] and Timothy,

To the church of the Thessalonians in God the Father and the Lord Jesus Christ:

Grace and peace to you.

### Thanksgiving for the Thessalonians' Faith

[2] We always thank God for all of you and continually mention you in our prayers. [3] We remember before our God and Father your work produced by faith, your labor prompted by love, and your endurance inspired by hope in our Lord Jesus Christ.

[4] For we know, brothers and sisters[b] loved by God, that he has chosen you, [5] because our gospel came to you not simply with words but also with power, with the Holy Spirit and deep conviction. You know how we lived among you for your sake. [6] You became imitators of us and of the Lord, for you welcomed the message in the midst of severe suffering with the joy given by the Holy Spirit. [7] And so you became a model to all the believers in Macedonia and Achaia. [8] The Lord's message rang out from you not only in Macedonia and Achaia—your faith in God has become known everywhere. Therefore we do not need to say anything about it, [9] for they themselves report what kind of reception you gave us. They tell how you turned to God from idols to serve the living and true God, [10] and to wait for his Son from heaven, whom he raised from the dead—Jesus, who rescues us from the coming wrath.

### Paul's Ministry in Thessalonica

**2** You know, brothers and sisters, that our visit to you was not without results. [2] We had previously suffered and been treated outrageously in Philippi, as you know, but with the help of our God we dared to tell you his gospel in the face of strong opposition. [3] For the appeal we make does not spring from error or impure motives, nor are we trying to trick you. [4] On the contrary, we speak as those approved by God to be entrusted with the gospel. We are not trying to please people but God, who tests our hearts. [5] You know we never used flattery, nor did we put on a mask to cover up greed—God is our witness. [6] We were not looking for praise from people, not from you or

---

# Thessalonians

**1** Paul, Silvanus (Silas), and Timothy, to the assembly (church) of the Thessalonians in God the Father and the Lord Jesus Christ (the Messiah): Grace (spiritual blessing and divine favor) to you and [heart] peace.

[2] We are ever giving thanks to God for all of you, continually mentioning [you when engaged] in our prayers,

[3] Recalling unceasingly before our God and Father your work energized by faith and service motivated by love and unwavering hope in [the return of] our Lord Jesus Christ (the Messiah). [I Thess. 1:10.]

[4] [O] brethren beloved by God, we recognize *and* know that He has selected (chosen) you;

[5] For our [preaching of the] glad tidings (the Gospel) came to you not only in word, but also in [its own inherent] power and in the Holy Spirit and with great conviction *and* absolute certainty [on our part]. You know what kind of men we proved [ourselves] to be among you for your good.

[6] And you [set yourselves to] become imitators of us and [through us] of the Lord Himself, for you welcomed our message in [spite of] much persecution, with joy [inspired] by the Holy Spirit;

[7] So that you [thus] became a pattern to all the believers (those who adhere to, trust in, and rely on Christ Jesus) in Macedonia and Achaia (most of Greece).

[8] For not only has the Word concerning *and* from the Lord resounded forth from you unmistakably in Macedonia and Achaia, but everywhere the report has gone forth of your faith in God [of your [a] leaning of your whole personality on Him in complete trust and confidence in His power, wisdom, and goodness]. So we [find that we] never need to tell people anything [further about it].

[9] For they themselves volunteer testimony concerning us, telling what an entrance we had among you, and how you turned to God from [your] idols to serve a God Who is alive and true *and* genuine,

[10] And [how you] look forward to *and* await the coming of His Son from heaven, Whom He raised from the dead—Jesus, Who personally rescues *and* delivers us out of *and* from the wrath [bringing punishment] which is coming [upon the impenitent] *and* [b] draws us to Himself [[c] investing us with all the privileges and rewards of the new life in Christ, the Messiah].

**2** For you yourselves know, brethren, that our coming among you was not useless *and* fruitless.

[2] But though we had already suffered and been outrageously treated at Philippi, as you know, yet in [the strength of] our God we summoned courage to proclaim to you unfalteringly the good news (the Gospel) with earnest contention *and* much conflict *and* great opposition.

[3] For our appeal [in preaching] does not [originate] from delusion *or* error or impure purpose *or* motive, nor in fraud *or* deceit.

[4] But just as we have been approved by God to be entrusted with the glad tidings (the Gospel), so we speak not to please men but to please God, Who tests our hearts [[d] expecting them to be approved].

[5] For as you well know, we never resorted either to words of flattery or to any cloak to conceal greedy motives *or* pretexts for gain, [as] God is our witness.

[6] Nor did we seek to extract praise *and* honor *and* glory from men, either from you or from anyone else, though we

---

[a] 1 Greek *Silvanus*, a variant of *Silas*  [b] 4 The Greek word for *brothers and sisters (adelphoi)* refers here to believers, both men and women, as part of God's family; also in 2:1, 9, 14, 17; 3:7; 4:1, 10, 13; 5:1, 4, 12, 14, 25, 27.

[a] Alexander Souter, *Pocket Lexicon of the Greek New Testament.*  [b] Literal translation of the verb "to deliver."  [c] Marvin Vincent, *Word Studies in the New Testament.*  [d] G. Abbott-Smith, *Manual Greek Lexicon of the New Testament.*

# New International Version

anyone else, even though as apostles of Christ we could have asserted our authority. [7]Instead, we were like young children[a] among you.

Just as a nursing mother cares for her children, [8]so we cared for you. Because we loved you so much, we were delighted to share with you not only the gospel of God but our lives as well. [9]Surely you remember, brothers and sisters, our toil and hardship; we worked night and day in order not to be a burden to anyone while we preached the gospel of God to you. [10]You are witnesses, and so is God, of how holy, righteous and blameless we were among you who believed. [11]For you know that we dealt with each of you as a father deals with his own children, [12]encouraging, comforting and urging you to live lives worthy of God, who calls you into his kingdom and glory.

[13]And we also thank God continually because, when you received the word of God, which you heard from us, you accepted it not as a human word, but as it actually is, the word of God, which is indeed at work in you who believe. [14]For you, brothers and sisters, became imitators of God's churches in Judea, which are in Christ Jesus: You suffered from your own people the same things those churches suffered from the Jews [15]who killed the Lord Jesus and the prophets and also drove us out. They displease God and are hostile to everyone [16]in their effort to keep us from speaking to the Gentiles so that they may be saved. In this way they always heap up their sins to the limit. The wrath of God has come upon them at last.[b]

## Paul's Longing to See the Thessalonians

[17]But, brothers and sisters, when we were orphaned by being separated from you for a short time (in person, not in thought), out of our intense longing we made every effort to see you. [18]For we wanted to come to you—certainly I, Paul, did, again and again—but Satan blocked our way. [19]For what is our hope, our joy, or the crown in which we will glory in the presence of our Lord Jesus when he comes? Is it not you? [20]Indeed, you are our glory and joy.

**3** So when we could stand it no longer, we thought it best to be left by ourselves in Athens. [2]We sent Timothy, who is our brother and co-worker in God's service in spreading the gospel of Christ, to strengthen and encourage you in your faith, [3]so that no one would be unsettled by these trials. For you know quite well that we are destined for them. [4]In fact, when we were with you, we kept telling

# Amplified Bible

might have asserted our authority [stood on our dignity and claimed honor] as apostles (special missionaries) of Christ (the Messiah).

[7]But we behaved gently when we were among you, like a devoted mother nursing *and* cherishing her own children.

[8]So, being thus tenderly *and* affectionately desirous of you, we continued to share with you not only God's good news (the Gospel) but also our own lives as well, for you had become so very dear to us.

[9]For you recall our hard toil and struggles, brethren. We worked night and day [and plied our trade] in order not to be a burden to any of you [for our support] while we proclaimed the glad tidings (the Gospel) of God to you.

[10]You are witnesses, [yes] and God [also], how unworldly and upright and blameless was our behavior toward you believers [who adhered to and trusted in and relied on our Lord Jesus Christ].

[11]For you know how, as a father [dealing with] his children, we used to exhort each of you personally, stimulating *and* encouraging and charging you

[12]To live lives worthy of God, Who calls you into His own kingdom and the glorious blessedness [[a]into which true believers will enter after Christ's return].

[13]And we also [especially] thank God continually for this, that when you received the message of God [which you heard] from us, you welcomed it not as the word of [mere] men, but as it truly is, the Word of God, which is effectually at work in you who believe [[b]exercising its superhuman power in those who adhere to and trust in and rely on it].

[14]For you, brethren, became imitators of the assemblies (churches) of God in Christ Jesus which are in Judea, for you too have suffered the same kind of treatment from your own fellow countrymen as they did [who were persecuted at the hands] of the Jews,

[15]Who killed both the Lord Jesus and the prophets, and harassed *and* drove us out, and continue to make themselves hateful *and* offensive to God and to show themselves foes of all men,

[16]Forbidding *and* hindering us from speaking to the Gentiles (the nations) that they may be saved. So as always they fill up [to the brim the measure of] their sins. But God's wrath has come upon them at last [completely and forever]! [Gen. 15:16.]

[17]But since we were bereft of you, brethren, for a little while in person, [of course] not in heart, we endeavored the more eagerly and with great longing to see you face to face,

[18]Because it was our will to come to you. [I mean that] I, Paul, again and again [wanted to come], but Satan hindered *and* impeded us.

[19]For what is our hope or happiness or our victor's wreath of exultant triumph when we stand in the presence of our Lord Jesus at His coming? Is it not you?

[20]For you are [indeed] our glory and our joy!

**3** Therefore, when [the suspense of separation and our yearning for some personal communication from you] became intolerable, we consented to being left behind alone at Athens.

[2]And we sent Timothy, our brother and God's servant in [spreading] the good news (the Gospel) of Christ, to strengthen *and* establish and to exhort *and* comfort *and* encourage you in your faith,

[3]That no one [of you] should be disturbed *and* beguiled *and* led astray by these afflictions *and* difficulties [to which I have referred]. For you yourselves know that this is [unavoidable in our position, and must be recognized as] our appointed lot.

[4]For even when we were with you, [you know] we

---

[a] Joseph Thayer, *A Greek-English Lexicon of the New Testament.*
[b] Marvin Vincent, *Word Studies.*

## New International Version

you that we would be persecuted. And it turned out that way, as you well know. ⁵For this reason, when I could stand it no longer, I sent to find out about your faith. I was afraid that in some way the tempter had tempted you and that our labors might have been in vain.

### Timothy's Encouraging Report

⁶But Timothy has just now come to us from you and has brought good news about your faith and love. He has told us that you always have pleasant memories of us and that you long to see us, just as we also long to see you. ⁷Therefore, brothers and sisters, in all our distress and persecution we were encouraged about you because of your faith. ⁸For now we really live, since you are standing firm in the Lord. ⁹How can we thank God enough for you in return for all the joy we have in the presence of our God because of you? ¹⁰Night and day we pray most earnestly that we may see you again and supply what is lacking in your faith.

¹¹Now may our God and Father himself and our Lord Jesus clear the way for us to come to you. ¹²May the Lord make your love increase and overflow for each other and for everyone else, just as ours does for you. ¹³May he strengthen your hearts so that you will be blameless and holy in the presence of our God and Father when our Lord Jesus comes with all his holy ones.

### Living to Please God

**4** As for other matters, brothers and sisters, we instructed you how to live in order to please God, as in fact you are living. Now we ask you and urge you in the Lord Jesus to do this more and more. ²For you know what instructions we gave you by the authority of the Lord Jesus.

³It is God's will that you should be sanctified: that you should avoid sexual immorality; ⁴that each of you should learn to control your own body*ᵃ* in a way that is holy and honorable, ⁵not in passionate lust like the pagans, who do not know God; ⁶and that in this matter no one should wrong or take advantage of a brother or sister.*ᵇ* The Lord will punish all those who commit such sins, as we told you and warned you before. ⁷For God did not call us to be im-

## Amplified Bible

warned you plainly beforehand that we were to be pressed with difficulties *and* made to suffer affliction, just as to your own knowledge it has [since] happened.

⁵That is the reason that, when I could bear [the suspense] no longer, I sent that I might learn [how you were standing the strain, and the endurance of] your faith, [for I was fearful] lest somehow the tempter had tempted you and our toil [among you should prove to] be fruitless *and* to no purpose.

⁶But now that Timothy has just come back to us from [his visit to] you and has brought us the good news of [the steadfastness of] your faith and [the warmth of your] love, and [reported] how kindly you cherish a constant *and* affectionate remembrance of us [and that you are] longing to see us as we [are to see] you,

⁷Brethren, for this reason, in [spite of all] our stress and crushing difficulties we have been filled with comfort *and* cheer about you [because of] your faith (*ᵃ*the leaning of your whole personality on God in complete trust and confidence).

⁸Because now we [really] live, if you stand [firm] in the Lord.

⁹For what [adequate] thanksgiving can we render to God for you for all the gladness *and* delight which we enjoy for your sakes before our God?

¹⁰[And we] continue to pray especially *and* with most intense earnestness night and day that we may see you face to face and mend *and* make good whatever may be imperfect *and* lacking in your faith.

¹¹Now may our God and Father Himself and our Lord Jesus *Christ (the Messiah)* guide our steps to you.

¹²And may the Lord make you to increase and excel *and* overflow in love for one another and for all people, just as we also do for you,

¹³So that He may strengthen *and* confirm *and* establish your hearts faultlessly pure *and* unblamable in holiness in the sight of our God and Father, at the coming of our Lord Jesus *Christ (the Messiah)* with all His saints (the *ᵇ*holy and glorified people of God)! *Amen, (so be it)!*

**4** Furthermore, *ᵇ*brethren, we beg and admonish you in [virtue of our union with] the Lord Jesus, that [you follow the instructions which] you learned from us about how you ought to walk so as to please *and* gratify God, as indeed you are doing, [and] that you do so even more and more abundantly [attaining yet greater perfection in living this life].

²For you know what charges *and* precepts we gave you [*ᶜ*on the authority and by the inspiration of] the Lord Jesus.

³For this is the will of God, that you should be consecrated (separated and set apart for pure and holy living): that you should abstain *and* shrink from all sexual vice,

⁴That each one of you should know how to *ᵈ*possess (control, manage) his own *ᵉ*body in consecration (purity, separated from things profane) and honor,

⁵Not [to be used] in the passion of lust like the heathen, who are ignorant of the true God *and* have no knowledge of His will,

⁶That no man transgress and overreach his brother *and* defraud him in this matter *or* defraud his brother in business. For the Lord is an avenger in all these things, as we have already warned you solemnly *and* *ᶜ*told you plainly.

⁷For God has not called us to impurity but to consecration [to dedicate ourselves to the most thorough purity].

---

*ᵃ* Alexander Souter, *Pocket Lexicon.* *ᵇ* Marvin Vincent, *Word Studies.* *ᶜ* G. Abbott-Smith, *Manual Greek Lexicon.* *ᵈ* *The American Standard Version* and others so read. *ᵉ* Some of the early versions of the Bible read "vessel" here. The reading "body" is supported by most lexicons, and by such translations as Ronald Knox, *The Holy Bible: A Translation from the Latin Vulgate*; J. B. Phillips, *New Testament in Modern English*; and Arthur S. Way, *Way's Epistles: The Letters of St. Paul to Seven Churches and Three Friends.*

---

*ᵃ* 4 Or *learn to live with your own wife*; or *learn to acquire a wife*
*ᵇ* 6 The Greek word for *brother or sister (adelphos)* refers here to a believer, whether man or woman, as part of God's family.

## New International Version

pure, but to live a holy life. ⁸Therefore, anyone who rejects this instruction does not reject a human being but God, the very God who gives you his Holy Spirit.

⁹Now about your love for one another we do not need to write to you, for you yourselves have been taught by God to love each other. ¹⁰And in fact, you do love all of God's family throughout Macedonia. Yet we urge you, brothers and sisters, to do so more and more, ¹¹and to make it your ambition to lead a quiet life: You should mind your own business and work with your hands, just as we told you, ¹²so that your daily life may win the respect of outsiders and so that you will not be dependent on anybody.

### Believers Who Have Died

¹³Brothers and sisters, we do not want you to be uninformed about those who sleep in death, so that you do not grieve like the rest of mankind, who have no hope. ¹⁴For we believe that Jesus died and rose again, and so we believe that God will bring with Jesus those who have fallen asleep in him. ¹⁵According to the Lord's word, we tell you that we who are still alive, who are left until the coming of the Lord, will certainly not precede those who have fallen asleep. ¹⁶For the Lord himself will come down from heaven, with a loud command, with the voice of the archangel and with the trumpet call of God, and the dead in Christ will rise first. ¹⁷After that, we who are still alive and are left will be caught up together with them in the clouds to meet the Lord in the air. And so we will be with the Lord forever. ¹⁸Therefore encourage one another with these words.

### The Day of the Lord

5 Now, brothers and sisters, about times and dates we do not need to write to you, ²for you know very well that the day of the Lord will come like a thief in the night. ³While people are saying, "Peace and safety," destruction will come on them suddenly, as labor pains on a pregnant woman, and they will not escape.

⁴But you, brothers and sisters, are not in darkness so that this day should surprise you like a thief. ⁵You are all children of the light and children of the day. We do not belong to the night or to the darkness. ⁶So then, let us not be like others, who are asleep, but let us be awake and sober. ⁷For those who sleep, sleep at night, and those who get drunk, get drunk at night. ⁸But since we belong to the day, let us be sober, putting on faith and love as a breastplate, and the hope of salvation as a helmet. ⁹For God did not appoint us to suffer wrath but to receive salvation through

## Amplified Bible

⁸Therefore whoever disregards (sets aside and rejects this) disregards not man but God, Whose [very] Spirit [Whom] He gives to you is holy (chaste, pure).

⁹But concerning brotherly love [for all other Christians], you have no need to have anyone write you, for you yourselves have been [personally] taught by God to love one another.

¹⁰And indeed you already are [extending and displaying your love] to all the brethren throughout Macedonia. But we beseech and earnestly exhort you, brethren, that you ᵃexcel [in this matter] more and more,

¹¹To make it your ambition and definitely endeavor to live quietly and peacefully, to mind your own affairs, and to work with your hands, as we charged you,

¹²So that you may bear yourselves becomingly and be correct and honorable and command the respect of the outside world, being dependent on nobody [self-supporting] and having need of nothing.

¹³Now also we would not have you ignorant, brethren, about those who fall asleep [ᵇin death], that you may not grieve [for them] as the rest do who have no hope [beyond the grave].

¹⁴For since we believe that Jesus died and rose again, even so God will also bring with Him through Jesus those who have fallen asleep [ᵇin death].

¹⁵For this we declare to you by the Lord's [own] word, that we who are alive and remain until the coming of the Lord shall in no way precede [into His presence] or have any advantage at all over those who have previously fallen asleep [in Him ᵇin death].

¹⁶For the Lord Himself will descend from heaven with a loud cry of summons, with the shout of an archangel, and with the blast of the trumpet of God. And those who have departed this life in Christ will rise first.

¹⁷Then we, the living ones who remain [on the earth], shall simultaneously be caught up along with [the resurrected dead] in the clouds to meet the Lord in the air; and so always (through the eternity of the eternities) we shall be with the Lord!

¹⁸Therefore comfort and encourage one another with these words.

5 But as to the suitable times and the precise seasons and dates, brethren, you have no necessity for anything being written to you.

²For you yourselves know perfectly well that the day of the [return of the] Lord will come [as unexpectedly and suddenly] as a thief in the night.

³When people are saying, All is well and secure, and, There is peace and safety, then in a moment unforeseen destruction (ruin and death) will come upon them as suddenly as labor pains come upon a woman with child; and they shall by no means escape, for there will be no escape.

⁴But you are not in [given up to the power of] darkness, brethren, for that day to overtake you by surprise like a thief.

⁵For you are all sons of light and sons of the day; we do not belong either to the night or to darkness.

⁶Accordingly then, let us not sleep, as the rest do, but let us keep wide awake (alert, watchful, cautious, and on our guard) and let us be sober (calm, collected, and circumspect).

⁷For those who sleep, sleep at night, and those who are drunk, get drunk at night.

⁸But we belong to the day; therefore, let us be sober and put on the breastplate (corslet) of faith and love and for a helmet the hope of salvation.

⁹For God has not appointed us to [incur His] wrath [He did not select us to condemn us], but [that we might] obtain [His] salvation through our Lord Jesus Christ (the Messiah)

---

ᵃ G. Abbott-Smith, *Manual Greek Lexicon*. ᵇ Hermann Cremer, *Biblico-Theological Lexicon of New Testament Greek*.

## New International Version

our Lord Jesus Christ. ¹⁰He died for us so that, whether we are awake or asleep, we may live together with him. ¹¹Therefore encourage one another and build each other up, just as in fact you are doing.

### Final Instructions

¹²Now we ask you, brothers and sisters, to acknowledge those who work hard among you, who care for you in the Lord and who admonish you. ¹³Hold them in the highest regard in love because of their work. Live in peace with each other. ¹⁴And we urge you, brothers and sisters, warn those who are idle and disruptive, encourage the disheartened, help the weak, be patient with everyone. ¹⁵Make sure that nobody pays back wrong for wrong, but always strive to do what is good for each other and for everyone else.

¹⁶Rejoice always, ¹⁷pray continually, ¹⁸give thanks in all circumstances; for this is God's will for you in Christ Jesus.

¹⁹Do not quench the Spirit. ²⁰Do not treat prophecies with contempt ²¹but test them all; hold on to what is good, ²²reject every kind of evil.

²³May God himself, the God of peace, sanctify you through and through. May your whole spirit, soul and body be kept blameless at the coming of our Lord Jesus Christ. ²⁴The one who calls you is faithful, and he will do it.

²⁵Brothers and sisters, pray for us. ²⁶Greet all God's people with a holy kiss. ²⁷I charge you before the Lord to have this letter read to all the brothers and sisters.

²⁸The grace of our Lord Jesus Christ be with you.

## Amplified Bible

¹⁰Who died for us so that whether we are still alive or are dead [at Christ's appearing], we might live together with Him *and* share His life.

¹¹Therefore encourage (admonish, exhort) one another and edify (strengthen and build up) one another, just as you are doing.

¹²Now also we beseech you, brethren, get to know those who labor among you [recognize them for what they are, acknowledge and appreciate and respect them all]—your leaders who are over you in the Lord and those who warn *and* kindly reprove *and* exhort you.

¹³And hold them in very high and most affectionate esteem in [intelligent and sympathetic] appreciation of their work. Be at peace among yourselves.

¹⁴And we earnestly beseech you, brethren, admonish (warn and seriously advise) those who are out of line [the loafers, the disorderly, and the unruly]; encourage the timid *and* fainthearted, help *and* give your support to the weak souls, [and] be very patient with everybody [always keeping your temper]. [Isa. 35:4.]

¹⁵See that none of you repays another with evil for evil, but always aim to show kindness *and* seek to do good to one another and to everybody.

¹⁶Be happy [in your faith] *and* rejoice *and* be glad-hearted continually (always);

¹⁷Be unceasing in prayer [praying perseveringly];

¹⁸Thank [God] in everything [no matter what the circumstances may be, be thankful and give thanks], for this is the will of God for you [who are] in Christ Jesus [the Revealer and Mediator of that will].

¹⁹Do not quench (suppress or subdue) the [Holy] Spirit;

²⁰Do not spurn the gifts *and* utterances of the prophets [do not depreciate prophetic revelations nor despise inspired instruction or exhortation or warning].

²¹But test *and* prove all things [until you can recognize] what is good; [to that] hold fast.

²²Abstain from evil [shrink from it and keep aloof from it] in whatever form *or* whatever kind it may be.

²³And may the God of peace Himself sanctify you through and through [separate you from profane things, make you pure and wholly consecrated to God]; and may your spirit and soul and body be preserved sound *and* complete [and found] blameless at the coming of our Lord Jesus Christ (the Messiah).

²⁴Faithful is He Who is calling you [to Himself] *and* utterly trustworthy, and He will also do it [fulfill His call by hallowing and keeping you].

²⁵Brethren, pray for us.

²⁶Greet all the brethren with a sacred kiss.

²⁷I solemnly charge you [in the name of] the Lord to have this letter read before all the brethren.

²⁸The grace (the unmerited favor and blessings) of our Lord Jesus Christ (the Messiah) be with you all. *Amen, (so be it).*

# 2 Thessalonians

## New International Version

**1** Paul, Silas*a* and Timothy,

To the church of the Thessalonians in God our Father and the Lord Jesus Christ:

²Grace and peace to you from God the Father and the Lord Jesus Christ.

### Thanksgiving and Prayer

³We ought always to thank God for you, brothers and sisters,*b* and rightly so, because your faith is growing more and more, and the love all of you have for one another is increasing. ⁴Therefore, among God's churches we boast about your perseverance and faith in all the persecutions and trials you are enduring.

⁵All this is evidence that God's judgment is right, and as a result you will be counted worthy of the kingdom of God, for which you are suffering. ⁶God is just: He will pay back trouble to those who trouble you ⁷and give relief to you who are troubled, and to us as well. This will happen when the Lord Jesus is revealed from heaven in blazing fire with his powerful angels. ⁸He will punish those who do not know God and do not obey the gospel of our Lord Jesus. ⁹They will be punished with everlasting destruction and shut out from the presence of the Lord and from the glory of his might ¹⁰on the day he comes to be glorified in his holy people and to be marveled at among all those who have believed. This includes you, because you believed our testimony to you.

¹¹With this in mind, we constantly pray for you, that our God may make you worthy of his calling, and that by his power he may bring to fruition your every desire for goodness and your every deed prompted by faith. ¹²We pray this so that the name of our Lord Jesus may be glorified in you, and you in him, according to the grace of our God and the Lord Jesus Christ.*c*

### The Man of Lawlessness

**2** Concerning the coming of our Lord Jesus Christ and our being gathered to him, we ask you, brothers and sisters, ²not to become easily unsettled or alarmed by the

## Amplified Bible

**1** Paul, Silvanus (Silas), and Timothy, to the church (assembly) of the Thessalonians in God our Father and the Lord Jesus Christ (the Messiah, the Anointed One):

²Grace (unmerited favor) be to you and [heart] peace from God the Father and the Lord Jesus Christ (the Messiah, the Anointed One).

³We ought *and* indeed are obligated [as those in debt] to give thanks always to God for you, brethren, as is fitting, because your faith is growing exceedingly and the love of every one of you each toward the others is increasing *and* abounds.

⁴And this is a cause of our mentioning you with pride among the churches (assemblies) of God for your steadfastness (your unflinching endurance and patience) and your firm faith in the midst of all the persecutions and crushing distresses *and* afflictions under which you are holding up.

⁵This is positive proof of the just *and* right judgment of God to the end that you may be deemed deserving of His kingdom [a plain token of His fair verdict which designs that you should be made *and* counted worthy of the kingdom of God], for the sake of which you are also suffering.

⁶[It is a fair decision] since it is a righteous thing with God to repay with distress *and* affliction those who distress *and* afflict you,

⁷And to [*a*recompense] you who are so distressed *and* afflicted [by granting you] relief *and* rest along with us [your fellow sufferers] when the Lord Jesus is revealed from heaven with His mighty angels in a flame of fire,

⁸To deal out retribution (chastisement and vengeance) upon those who do not know *or* perceive *or* become acquainted with God, and [upon those] who ignore *and* refuse to obey the Gospel of our Lord Jesus *Christ*.

⁹Such people will pay the penalty *and* suffer the punishment of everlasting ruin (destruction and perdition) *and* eternal exclusion and banishment from the presence of the Lord and from the glory of His power,

¹⁰When He comes to be glorified in His saints [on that day He will be made more glorious in His consecrated people], and [He will] be marveled at *and* admired [in His glory reflected] in all who have believed [who have adhered to, trusted in, and relied on Him], because our witnessing among you was confidently accepted *and* believed [and confirmed in your lives].

¹¹With this in view we constantly pray for you, that our God may deem *and* count you worthy of [your] calling and [His] every gracious purpose of goodness, and with power may complete in [your] every particular work of faith (faith which is that *b*leaning of the whole human personality on God in absolute trust and confidence in His power, wisdom, and goodness).

¹²Thus may the name of our Lord Jesus *Christ* be glorified *and* become more glorious through *and* in you, and may you [also be glorified] in Him according to the grace (favor and blessing) of our God and the Lord Jesus Christ (the Messiah, the Anointed One).

**2** But relative to the coming of our Lord Jesus Christ (the Messiah) and our gathering together to [meet] Him, we beg you, brethren,

²Not to allow your minds to be quickly unsettled *or* disturbed or kept excited *or* alarmed, whether it be by some

*a 1* Greek *Silvanus*, a variant of *Silas*     *b 3* The Greek word for *brothers and sisters (adelphoi)* refers here to believers, both men and women, as part of God's family; also in 2:1, 13, 15; 3:1, 6, 13.     *c 12* Or *God and Lord, Jesus Christ*

*a* Robert Jamieson, A. R. Fausset and David Brown, *A Commentary on the Old and New Testaments.*  *b* Alexander Souter, *Pocket Lexicon of the Greek New Testament.*

## New International Version

teaching allegedly from us—whether by a prophecy or by word of mouth or by letter—asserting that the day of the Lord has already come. ³Don't let anyone deceive you in any way, for that day will not come until the rebellion occurs and the man of lawlessness*ᵃ* is revealed, the man doomed to destruction. ⁴He will oppose and will exalt himself over everything that is called God or is worshiped, so that he sets himself up in God's temple, proclaiming himself to be God.

⁵Don't you remember that when I was with you I used to tell you these things? ⁶And now you know what is holding him back, so that he may be revealed at the proper time. ⁷For the secret power of lawlessness is already at work; but the one who now holds it back will continue to do so till he is taken out of the way. ⁸And then the lawless one will be revealed, whom the Lord Jesus will overthrow with the breath of his mouth and destroy by the splendor of his coming. ⁹The coming of the lawless one will be in accordance with how Satan works. He will use all sorts of displays of power through signs and wonders that serve the lie, ¹⁰and all the ways that wickedness deceives those who are perishing. They perish because they refused to love the truth and so be saved. ¹¹For this reason God sends them a powerful delusion so that they will believe the lie ¹²and so that all will be condemned who have not believed the truth but have delighted in wickedness.

### Stand Firm

¹³But we ought always to thank God for you, brothers and sisters loved by the Lord, because God chose you as firstfruits*ᵇ* to be saved through the sanctifying work of the Spirit and through belief in the truth. ¹⁴He called you to this through our gospel, that you might share in the glory of our Lord Jesus Christ.

¹⁵So then, brothers and sisters, stand firm and hold fast to the teachings*ᶜ* we passed on to you, whether by word of mouth or by letter.

¹⁶May our Lord Jesus Christ himself and God our Father, who loved us and by his grace gave us eternal encouragement and good hope, ¹⁷encourage your hearts and strengthen you in every good deed and word.

### Request for Prayer

**3** As for other matters, brothers and sisters, pray for us that the message of the Lord may spread rapidly and be honored, just as it was with you. ²And pray that we may

## Amplified Bible

[pretended] revelation of [the] Spirit or by word or by letter [alleged to be] from us, to the effect that the day of the Lord has [already] arrived *and* is here.

³Let no one deceive *or* beguile you in any way, for that day will not come except the *ᵃ*apostasy comes first [unless the predicted great *ᵃ*falling away of those who have professed to be Christians has come], and the man of lawlessness (sin) is revealed, who is the son of doom (of perdition), [Dan. 7:25; 8:25; I Tim. 4:1.]

⁴Who opposes and exalts himself so proudly *and* insolently against *and* over all that is called God or that is worshiped, [even to his actually] taking his seat in the temple of God, proclaiming that he himself is God. [Ezek. 28:2; Dan. 11:36, 37.]

⁵Do you not recollect that when I was still with you, I told you these things?

⁶And now you know what is restraining him [from being revealed at this time]; it is so that he may be manifested (revealed) in his own [appointed] time.

⁷For the mystery of lawlessness (that hidden principle of rebellion against constituted authority) is already at work in the world, [but it is] restrained only until *ᵇ*he who restrains is taken out of the way.

⁸And then the lawless one (the antichrist) will be revealed and the Lord Jesus will slay him with the breath of His mouth and bring him to an end by His appearing at His coming. [Isa. 11:4.]

⁹The coming [of the lawless one, the antichrist] is through the activity *and* working of Satan and will be attended by great power and with all sorts of [pretended] miracles and signs *and* delusive marvels—[all of them] lying wonders—

¹⁰And by unlimited seduction to evil *and* with all wicked deception for those who are perishing (going to perdition) because they did not welcome the Truth *but* refused to love it that they might be saved.

¹¹Therefore God sends upon them a misleading influence, a working of error *and* a strong delusion to make them believe what is false,

¹²In order that all may be judged *and* condemned who did not believe in [who refused to adhere to, trust in, and rely on] the Truth, but [instead] took pleasure in unrighteousness.

¹³But we, brethren beloved by the Lord, ought *and* are obligated [as those who are in debt] to give thanks always to God for you, because God chose you from the beginning *ᶜas His firstfruits (first converts)* for salvation through the sanctifying work of the [Holy] Spirit and [your] belief in (adherence to, trust in, and reliance on) the Truth.

¹⁴[It was] to this end that He called you through our Gospel, so that you may obtain *and* share in the glory of our Lord Jesus Christ (the Messiah).

¹⁵So then, brethren, stand firm and hold fast to the traditions *and* instructions which you were taught by us, whether by our word of mouth or by letter.

¹⁶Now may our Lord Jesus Christ Himself and God our Father, Who loved us and gave us everlasting consolation *and* encouragement and well-founded hope through [His] grace (unmerited favor),

¹⁷Comfort *and* encourage your hearts and strengthen them [make them steadfast and keep them unswerving] in every good work and word.

**3** Furthermore, brethren, do pray for us, that the Word of the Lord may speed on (spread rapidly and run its course) and be glorified (extolled) *and* triumph, even as [it has done] with you,

---

*ᵃ* A possible rendering of the Greek *apostasia* is "departure [of the church]." *ᵇ* Many believe this One Who restrains the antichrist to be the Holy Spirit, Who lives in all believers and will be removed with them at Christ's coming; yet a majority thinks it refers to the Roman Empire. *ᶜ* Many ancient manuscripts so read.

---

*ᵃ 3 Some manuscripts sin* *ᵇ 13 Some manuscripts because from the beginning God chose you* *ᶜ 15 Or traditions*

## New International Version

be delivered from wicked and evil people, for not everyone has faith. ³But the Lord is faithful, and he will strengthen you and protect you from the evil one. ⁴We have confidence in the Lord that you are doing and will continue to do the things we command. ⁵May the Lord direct your hearts into God's love and Christ's perseverance.

### Warning Against Idleness

⁶In the name of the Lord Jesus Christ, we command you, brothers and sisters, to keep away from every believer who is idle and disruptive and does not live according to the teaching*a* you received from us. ⁷For you yourselves know how you ought to follow our example. We were not idle when we were with you, ⁸nor did we eat anyone's food without paying for it. On the contrary, we worked night and day, laboring and toiling so that we would not be a burden to any of you. ⁹We did this, not because we do not have the right to such help, but in order to offer ourselves as a model for you to imitate. ¹⁰For even when we were with you, we gave you this rule: "The one who is unwilling to work shall not eat."

¹¹We hear that some among you are idle and disruptive. They are not busy; they are busybodies. ¹²Such people we command and urge in the Lord Jesus Christ to settle down and earn the food they eat. ¹³And as for you, brothers and sisters, never tire of doing what is good.

¹⁴Take special note of anyone who does not obey our instruction in this letter. Do not associate with them, in order that they may feel ashamed. ¹⁵Yet do not regard them as an enemy, but warn them as you would a fellow believer.

### Final Greetings

¹⁶Now may the Lord of peace himself give you peace at all times and in every way. The Lord be with all of you.

¹⁷I, Paul, write this greeting in my own hand, which is the distinguishing mark in all my letters. This is how I write.

¹⁸The grace of our Lord Jesus Christ be with you all.

## Amplified Bible

²And that we may be delivered from perverse (improper, unrighteous) and wicked (actively malicious) men, for not everybody has faith *and* is held by it.

³Yet the Lord is faithful, and He will strengthen [you] *and* set you on a firm foundation and guard you from the evil [one].

⁴And we have confidence in the Lord concerning you, that you are doing and will continue to do the things which we suggest *and* with which we charge you.

⁵May the Lord direct your hearts into [realizing and showing] the love of God and into the steadfastness *and* patience of Christ *and* *a* in waiting for His return.

⁶Now we charge you, brethren, in the name *and* on the authority of our Lord Jesus Christ (the Messiah) that you withdraw *and* keep away from every brother (fellow believer) who is slack in the performance of duty *and* is disorderly, living as a shirker *and* not walking in accord with the traditions *and* instructions that you have received from us.

⁷For you yourselves know how it is necessary to imitate our example, for we were not disorderly *or* shirking of duty when we were with you [we were not idle].

⁸Nor did we eat anyone's bread without paying for it, but with toil and struggle we worked night and day, that we might not be a burden *or* impose on any of you [for our support].

⁹[It was] not because we do not have a right [to such support], but [we wished] to make ourselves an example for you to follow.

¹⁰For while we were yet with you, we gave you this rule *and* charge: If anyone will not work, neither let him eat.

¹¹Indeed, we hear that some among you are disorderly [that they are passing their lives in idleness, neglectful of duty], being busy with other people's affairs instead of their own and doing no work.

¹²Now we charge and exhort such persons [as *b*ministers in Him exhorting those] in the Lord Jesus Christ (the Messiah) that they work in quietness and earn their own food *and* other necessities.

¹³And as for you, brethren, do not become weary *or* lose heart in doing right [but continue in well-doing without weakening].

¹⁴But if anyone [in the church] refuses to obey what we say in this letter, take note of that person and do not associate with him, so that he may be ashamed.

¹⁵Do not regard him as an enemy, but simply admonish *and* warn him as [being still] a brother.

¹⁶Now may the Lord of peace Himself grant you His peace (the peace of His kingdom) at all times and in all ways [under all circumstances and conditions, whatever comes]. The Lord [be] with you all.

¹⁷I, Paul, write you this final greeting with my own hand. This is the mark *and* sign [that it is not a forgery] in every letter of mine. It is the way I write [my handwriting and signature].

¹⁸The grace (spiritual blessing and favor) of our Lord Jesus Christ (the Messiah) be with you all. *Amen (so be it).*

---

*a* Joseph Thayer, *A Greek-English Lexicon of the New Testament.*   *b* Robert Jamieson, A. R. Fausset and David Brown, *A Commentary.*

# 1 Timothy

# Timothy

**1** Paul, an apostle of Christ Jesus by the command of God our Savior and of Christ Jesus our hope,

2 To Timothy my true son in the faith:

Grace, mercy and peace from God the Father and Christ Jesus our Lord.

### Timothy Charged to Oppose False Teachers

3 As I urged you when I went into Macedonia, stay there in Ephesus so that you may command certain people not to teach false doctrines any longer 4 or to devote themselves to myths and endless genealogies. Such things promote controversial speculations rather than advancing God's work—which is by faith. 5 The goal of this command is love, which comes from a pure heart and a good conscience and a sincere faith. 6 Some have departed from these and have turned to meaningless talk. 7 They want to be teachers of the law, but they do not know what they are talking about or what they so confidently affirm.

8 We know that the law is good if one uses it properly. 9 We also know that the law is made not for the righteous but for lawbreakers and rebels, the ungodly and sinful, the unholy and irreligious, for those who kill their fathers or mothers, for murderers, 10 for the sexually immoral, for those practicing homosexuality, for slave traders and liars and perjurers—and for whatever else is contrary to the sound doctrine 11 that conforms to the gospel concerning the glory of the blessed God, which he entrusted to me.

### The Lord's Grace to Paul

12 I thank Christ Jesus our Lord, who has given me strength, that he considered me trustworthy, appointing me to his service. 13 Even though I was once a blasphemer and a persecutor and a violent man, I was shown mercy because I acted in ignorance and unbelief. 14 The grace of our Lord was poured out on me abundantly, along with the faith and love that are in Christ Jesus.

15 Here is a trustworthy saying that deserves full acceptance: Christ Jesus came into the world to save sinners—of whom I am the worst. 16 But for that very reason I was shown mercy so that in me, the worst of sinners, Christ Jesus might display his immense patience as an example for those who would believe in him and receive eternal life.

**1** Paul, an apostle (special messenger) of Christ Jesus by appointment *and* command of God our Savior and of Christ Jesus (the Messiah), our Hope,

2 To Timothy, my true son in the faith: Grace (spiritual blessing and favor), mercy, and [heart] peace [be yours] from God the Father and Christ Jesus our Lord.

3 As I urged you when I was on my way to Macedonia, stay on where you are at Ephesus in order that you may warn *and* admonish *and* charge certain individuals not to teach any different doctrine,

4 Nor to give importance to *or* occupy themselves with legends (fables, myths) and endless genealogies, which foster *and* promote useless speculations *and* questionings rather than acceptance in faith of God's administration *and* the divine training that is in faith (*a* in that leaning of the entire human personality on God in absolute trust and confidence)—

5 Whereas the object *and* purpose of our instruction *and* charge is love, which springs from a pure heart and a good (clear) conscience and sincere (unfeigned) faith.

6 But certain individuals have missed the mark on this very matter [and] have wandered away into vain arguments *and* discussions *and* purposeless talk.

7 They are ambitious to be doctors of the Law (teachers of the Mosaic ritual), but they have no understanding either of the words *and* terms they use or of the subjects about which they make [such] dogmatic assertions.

8 Now we recognize *and* know that the Law is good if anyone uses it lawfully [for the purpose for which it was designed],

9 Knowing *and* understanding this: that the Law is not enacted for the righteous (the upright and just, who are in right standing with God), but for the lawless and unruly, for the ungodly and sinful, for the irreverent and profane, for those who strike *and* beat *and* [even] murder fathers and strike *and* beat *and* [even] murder mothers, for manslayers,

10 [For] impure *and* immoral persons, those who abuse themselves with men, kidnapers, liars, perjurers—and whatever else is opposed to wholesome teaching *and* sound doctrine

11 As laid down by the glorious Gospel of the blessed God, with which I have been entrusted.

12 I give thanks to Him Who has granted me [the needed] strength *and* made me able [for this], Christ Jesus our Lord, because He has judged *and* counted me faithful *and* trustworthy, appointing me to [this stewardship of] the ministry.

13 Though I formerly blasphemed and persecuted and was shamefully *and* outrageously *and* aggressively insulting [to Him], nevertheless, I obtained mercy because I had acted out of ignorance in unbelief.

14 And the grace (unmerited favor and blessing) of our Lord [actually] flowed out superabundantly *and* beyond measure for me, accompanied by faith and love that are [to be realized] in Christ Jesus.

15 The saying is sure *and* true and worthy of full *and* universal acceptance, that Christ Jesus (the Messiah) came into the world to save sinners, of whom I am foremost.

16 But I obtained mercy for the reason that in me, as the foremost [of sinners], Jesus Christ might show forth *and* display all His perfect long-suffering *and* patience for an example to [encourage] those who would thereafter believe on Him for [the gaining of] eternal life.

---

*a* Alexander Souter, *Pocket Lexicon of the Greek New Testament.*

## New International Version

[17]Now to the King eternal, immortal, invisible, the only God, be honor and glory for ever and ever. Amen.

### The Charge to Timothy Renewed

[18]Timothy, my son, I am giving you this command in keeping with the prophecies once made about you, so that by recalling them you may fight the battle well, [19]holding on to faith and a good conscience, which some have rejected and so have suffered shipwreck with regard to the faith. [20]Among them are Hymenaeus and Alexander, whom I have handed over to Satan to be taught not to blaspheme.

### Instructions on Worship

**2** I urge, then, first of all, that petitions, prayers, intercession and thanksgiving be made for all people— [2]for kings and all those in authority, that we may live peaceful and quiet lives in all godliness and holiness. [3]This is good, and pleases God our Savior, [4]who wants all people to be saved and to come to a knowledge of the truth. [5]For there is one God and one mediator between God and mankind, the man Christ Jesus, [6]who gave himself as a ransom for all people. This has now been witnessed to at the proper time. [7]And for this purpose I was appointed a herald and an apostle—I am telling the truth, I am not lying—and a true and faithful teacher of the Gentiles.

[8]Therefore I want the men everywhere to pray, lifting up holy hands without anger or disputing. [9]I also want the women to dress modestly, with decency and propriety, adorning themselves, not with elaborate hairstyles or gold or pearls or expensive clothes, [10]but with good deeds, appropriate for women who profess to worship God.

[11]A woman[a] should learn in quietness and full submission. [12]I do not permit a woman to teach or to assume authority over a man;[b] she must be quiet. [13]For Adam was formed first, then Eve. [14]And Adam was not the one deceived; it was the woman who was deceived and became a sinner. [15]But women[c] will be saved through childbearing—if they continue in faith, love and holiness with propriety.

### Qualifications for Overseers and Deacons

**3** Here is a trustworthy saying: Whoever aspires to be an overseer desires a noble task. [2]Now the overseer is to be above reproach, faithful to his wife, temperate,

## Amplified Bible

[17]Now to the King of eternity, incorruptible *and* immortal, invisible, the only God, be honor and glory forever and ever (to the ages of ages). Amen (so be it).

[18]This charge *and* admonition I commit in trust to you, Timothy, my son, [a]in accordance with prophetic intimations which I formerly received concerning you, so that inspired *and* aided by them you may wage the good warfare,

[19]Holding fast to faith ([b]that leaning of the entire human personality on God in absolute trust and confidence) and having a good (clear) conscience. By rejecting *and* thrusting from them [their conscience], some individuals have made shipwreck of their faith.

[20]Among them are Hymenaeus and Alexander, whom I have delivered to Satan in order that they may be disciplined [by punishment and learn] not to blaspheme.

**2** First of all, then, I admonish *and* urge that petitions, prayers, intercessions, and thanksgivings be offered on behalf of all men,

[2]For kings and all who are in positions of authority *or* high responsibility, that [outwardly] we may pass a quiet *and* undisturbed life [and inwardly] a peaceable one in all godliness *and* reverence and seriousness in every way.

[3]For such [praying] is good *and* right, and [it is] pleasing *and* acceptable to God our Savior,

[4]Who wishes all men to be saved and [increasingly] to perceive *and* recognize *and* discern *and* know precisely *and* correctly the [divine] Truth.

[5]For there [is only] one God, and [only] one Mediator between God and men, the Man Christ Jesus,

[6]Who gave Himself as a ransom for all [people, a fact that was] attested to at the right *and* proper time.

[7]And of this matter I was appointed a preacher and an apostle (special messenger)—I am speaking the truth *in Christ,* I do not falsify [when I say this]—a teacher of the Gentiles in [the realm of] faith and truth.

[8]I desire therefore that in every place men should pray, without anger *or* quarreling *or* resentment or doubt [in their minds], lifting up holy hands.

[9]Also [I desire] that women should adorn themselves modestly *and* appropriately and sensibly in seemly apparel, not with [elaborate] hair arrangement or gold or pearls or expensive clothing,

[10]But by doing good deeds (deeds in themselves good and for the good and advantage of those contacted by them), as befits women who profess reverential fear for *and* devotion to God.

[11]Let a woman learn in quietness, in entire submissiveness.

[12]I allow no woman to teach or to have authority over men; she is to remain in quietness *and* keep silence [in religious assemblies].

[13]For Adam was first formed, then Eve; [Gen. 2:7, 21, 22.]

[14]And it was not Adam who was deceived, but [the] woman who was deceived *and* deluded and fell into transgression. [Gen. 3:1-6.]

[15]Nevertheless [the sentence put upon women of pain in motherhood does not hinder their souls' salvation, and] they will be saved [eternally] if they continue in faith and love and holiness with self-control, [saved indeed] [c]through the Childbearing *or* by the birth of the divine Child.

**3** The saying is true *and* irrefutable: If any man [eagerly] seeks the office of bishop (superintendent, overseer), he desires an excellent task (work).

[2]Now a bishop (superintendent, overseer) must give no grounds for accusation *but* must be above reproach, the

---

[a] 11 Or *wife*; also in verse 12    [b] 12 Or *over her husband*
[c] 15 Greek *she*

*[a] Marvin Vincent, Word Studies in the New Testament. [b] Alexander Souter, Pocket Lexicon. [c] Marvin Vincent, Word Studies. See also Gal. 4:4.*

## New International Version

self-controlled, respectable, hospitable, able to teach, ³not given to drunkenness, not violent but gentle, not quarrelsome, not a lover of money. ⁴He must manage his own family well and see that his children obey him, and he must do so in a manner worthy of full*ᵃ* respect. ⁵(If anyone does not know how to manage his own family, how can he take care of God's church?) ⁶He must not be a recent convert, or he may become conceited and fall under the same judgment as the devil. ⁷He must also have a good reputation with outsiders, so that he will not fall into disgrace and into the devil's trap.

⁸In the same way, deacons*ᵇ* are to be worthy of respect, sincere, not indulging in much wine, and not pursuing dishonest gain. ⁹They must keep hold of the deep truths of the faith with a clear conscience. ¹⁰They must first be tested; and then if there is nothing against them, let them serve as deacons.

¹¹In the same way, the women*ᶜ* are to be worthy of respect, not malicious talkers but temperate and trustworthy in everything.

¹²A deacon must be faithful to his wife and must manage his children and his household well. ¹³Those who have served well gain an excellent standing and great assurance in their faith in Christ Jesus.

### Reasons for Paul's Instructions

¹⁴Although I hope to come to you soon, I am writing you these instructions so that, ¹⁵if I am delayed, you will know how people ought to conduct themselves in God's household, which is the church of the living God, the pillar and foundation of the truth. ¹⁶Beyond all question, the mystery from which true godliness springs is great:

He appeared in the flesh,
   was vindicated by the Spirit,*ᵈ*
was seen by angels,
   was preached among the nations,
was believed on in the world,
   was taken up in glory.

4 The Spirit clearly says that in later times some will abandon the faith and follow deceiving spirits and things taught by demons. ²Such teachings come through hypocritical liars, whose consciences have been seared as with a hot iron. ³They forbid people to marry and order them to abstain from certain foods, which God created to be received with thanksgiving by those who believe and who know the truth. ⁴For everything God created is good, and nothing is to be rejected if it is received with thanks-

---

*ᵃ 4* Or *him with proper*   *ᵇ 8* The word *deacons* refers here to Christians designated to serve with the overseers/elders of the church in a variety of ways; similarly in verse 12; and in Romans 16:1 and Phil. 1:1.   *ᶜ 11* Possibly deacons' wives or women who are deacons   *ᵈ 16* Or *vindicated in spirit*

## Amplified Bible

husband of one wife, circumspect *and* temperate *and* self-controlled; [he must be] sensible *and* well behaved *and* dignified and lead an orderly (disciplined) life; [he must be] hospitable [showing love for and being a friend to the believers, especially strangers or foreigners, and be] a capable *and* qualified teacher,

³Not given to wine, Not combative but gentle *and* considerate, not quarrelsome *but* forbearing *and* peaceable, and not a lover of money [insatiable for wealth and ready to obtain it by questionable means].

⁴He must rule his own household well, keeping his children under control, with true dignity, commanding their respect in every way *and* keeping them respectful.

⁵For if a man does not know how to rule his own household, how is he to take care of the church of God?

⁶He must not be a new convert, or he may [develop a beclouded and stupid state of mind] as the result of pride [be blinded by conceit, and] fall into the condemnation that the devil [once] did. [Isa. 14:12-14.]

⁷Furthermore, he must have a good reputation *and* be well thought of by those outside [the church], lest he become involved in slander *and* incur reproach and fall into the devil's trap.

⁸In like manner the deacons [must be] worthy of respect, not shifty *and* double-talkers *but* sincere in what they say, not given to much wine, not greedy for base gain [craving wealth and resorting to ignoble and dishonest methods of getting it].

⁹They must possess the mystic secret of the faith [Christian truth as hidden from ungodly men] with a clear conscience.

¹⁰And let them also be tried *and* investigated *and* proved first; then, if they turn out to be above reproach, let them serve [as deacons].

¹¹*ᵃ* [The] women likewise must be worthy of respect *and* serious, not gossipers, but temperate *and* self-controlled, [thoroughly] trustworthy in all things.

¹²Let deacons be the husbands of but one wife, and let them manage [their] children and their own households well.

¹³For those who perform well as deacons acquire a good standing for themselves and also gain much confidence *and* freedom *and* boldness in the faith which is [founded on and centers] in Christ Jesus.

¹⁴Although I hope to come to you before long, I am writing these instructions to you so that,

¹⁵If I am detained, you may know how people ought to conduct themselves in the household of God, which is the church of the living God, the pillar and stay (the prop and support) of the Truth.

¹⁶And great *and* important *and* weighty, we confess, is the hidden truth (the mystic secret) of godliness. He [*ᵇ*God] was made visible in human flesh, justified *and* vindicated in the [Holy] Spirit, was seen by angels, preached among the nations, believed on in the world, [and] taken up in glory.

4 But the [Holy] Spirit distinctly *and* expressly declares that in latter times some will turn away from the faith, giving attention to deluding *and* seducing spirits and doctrines that demons teach,

²Through the hypocrisy *and* pretensions of liars whose consciences are seared (cauterized),

³Who forbid people to marry and [teach them] to abstain from [certain kinds of] foods which God created to be received with thanksgiving by those who believe *and* have [an increasingly clear] knowledge of the truth.

⁴For everything God has created is good, and nothing is to be thrown away or refused if it is received with thanksgiving.

---

*ᵃ* Either their wives or the deaconesses, or both.   *ᵇ* Some manuscripts read "God."

## New International Version

giving, [5]because it is consecrated by the word of God and prayer.

[6]If you point these things out to the brothers and sisters,[a] you will be a good minister of Christ Jesus, nourished on the truths of the faith and of the good teaching that you have followed. [7]Have nothing to do with godless myths and old wives' tales; rather, train yourself to be godly. [8]For physical training is of some value, but godliness has value for all things, holding promise for both the present life and the life to come. [9]This is a trustworthy saying that deserves full acceptance. [10]That is why we labor and strive, because we have put our hope in the living God, who is the Savior of all people, and especially of those who believe.

[11]Command and teach these things. [12]Don't let anyone look down on you because you are young, but set an example for the believers in speech, in conduct, in love, in faith and in purity. [13]Until I come, devote yourself to the public reading of Scripture, to preaching and to teaching. [14]Do not neglect your gift, which was given you through prophecy when the body of elders laid their hands on you. [15]Be diligent in these matters; give yourself wholly to them, so that everyone may see your progress. [16]Watch your life and doctrine closely. Persevere in them, because if you do, you will save both yourself and your hearers.

### Widows, Elders and Slaves

**5** Do not rebuke an older man harshly, but exhort him as if he were your father. Treat younger men as brothers, [2]older women as mothers, and younger women as sisters, with absolute purity.

[3]Give proper recognition to those widows who are really in need. [4]But if a widow has children or grandchildren, these should learn first of all to put their religion into practice by caring for their own family and so repaying their parents and grandparents, for this is pleasing to God. [5]The widow who is really in need and left all alone puts her hope in God and continues night and day to pray and to ask God for help. [6]But the widow who lives for pleasure is dead even while she lives. [7]Give the people these instructions, so that no one may be open to blame. [8]Anyone who does not provide for their relatives, and especially for their own household, has denied the faith and is worse than an unbeliever.

[9]No widow may be put on the list of widows unless she is over sixty, has been faithful to her husband, [10]and is well

---

[a] 6 The Greek word for *brothers and sisters* (*adelphoi*) refers here to believers, both men and women, as part of God's family.

## Amplified Bible

[5]For it is hallowed *and* consecrated by the Word of God and by prayer.

[6]If you lay all these instructions before the brethren, you will be a worthy steward *and* a good minister of Christ Jesus, ever nourishing your own self on the truths of the faith and of the good [Christian] instruction which you have closely followed.

[7]But refuse *and* avoid irreverent legends (profane and impure and godless fictions, mere grandmothers' tales) and silly myths, *and* express your disapproval of them. Train yourself toward godliness (piety), [keeping yourself spiritually fit].

[8]For physical training is of some value (useful for a little), but godliness (spiritual training) is useful *and* of value in everything *and* in every way, for it holds promise for the present life and also for the life which is to come.

[9]This saying is reliable *and* worthy of complete acceptance by everybody.

[10]With a view to this we toil and strive, [yes and] [a]*suffer reproach*, because we have [fixed our] hope on the living God, Who is the Savior (Preserver, Maintainer, Deliverer) of all men, especially of those who believe (trust in, rely on, and adhere to Him).

[11]Continue to command these things and to teach them.

[12]Let no one despise *or* think less of you because of your youth, but be an example (pattern) for the believers in speech, in conduct, in love, in faith, and in purity.

[13]Till I come, devote yourself to [public and private] reading, to exhortation (preaching and personal appeals), and to teaching *and* instilling doctrine.

[14]Do not neglect the gift which is in you, [that special inward endowment] which was directly imparted to you [by the Holy Spirit] by prophetic utterance when the elders laid their hands upon you [at your ordination].

[15]Practice *and* cultivate *and* meditate upon these duties; throw yourself wholly into them [as your ministry], so that your progress may be evident to everybody.

[16]Look well to yourself [to your own personality] and to [your] teaching; persevere in these things [hold to them], for by so doing you will save both yourself and those who hear you.

**5** Do not sharply censure *or* rebuke an older man, but entreat *and* plead with him as [you would with] a father. Treat younger men like brothers;

[2][Treat] older women like mothers [and] younger women like sisters, in all purity.

[3][Always] treat with great consideration *and* give aid to those who are truly widowed (solitary and without support).

[4]But if a widow has children or grandchildren, see to it that these are first made to understand that it is their religious duty [to defray their natural obligation to those] at home, and make return to their parents *or* grandparents [for all their care by contributing to their maintenance], for this is acceptable in the sight of God.

[5]Now [a woman] who is a real widow and is left entirely alone *and* desolate has fixed her hope on God and perseveres in supplications and prayers night and day,

[6]Whereas she who lives in pleasure *and* self-gratification [giving herself up to luxury and self-indulgence] is dead even while she [still] lives.

[7]Charge [the people] thus, so that they may be without reproach *and* blameless.

[8]If anyone fails to provide for his relatives, and especially for those of his own family, he has disowned the faith [by failing to accompany it with fruits] and is worse than an unbeliever [who performs his obligation in these matters].

[9]Let no one be put on the roll of widows [who are to receive church support] who is under sixty years of age or who has been the wife of more than one man;

---

[a] Some manuscripts so read.

## New International Version

known for her good deeds, such as bringing up children, showing hospitality, washing the feet of the Lord's people, helping those in trouble and devoting herself to all kinds of good deeds.

[11]As for younger widows, do not put them on such a list. For when their sensual desires overcome their dedication to Christ, they want to marry. [12]Thus they bring judgment on themselves, because they have broken their first pledge. [13]Besides, they get into the habit of being idle and going about from house to house. And not only do they become idlers, but also busybodies who talk nonsense, saying things they ought not to. [14]So I counsel younger widows to marry, to have children, to manage their homes and to give the enemy no opportunity for slander. [15]Some have in fact already turned away to follow Satan.

[16]If any woman who is a believer has widows in her care, she should continue to help them and not let the church be burdened with them, so that the church can help those widows who are really in need.

[17]The elders who direct the affairs of the church well are worthy of double honor, especially those whose work is preaching and teaching. [18]For Scripture says, "Do not muzzle an ox while it is treading out the grain,"[a] and "The worker deserves his wages."[b] [19]Do not entertain an accusation against an elder unless it is brought by two or three witnesses. [20]But those elders who are sinning you are to reprove before everyone, so that the others may take warning. [21]I charge you, in the sight of God and Christ Jesus and the elect angels, to keep these instructions without partiality, and to do nothing out of favoritism.

[22]Do not be hasty in the laying on of hands, and do not share in the sins of others. Keep yourself pure.

[23]Stop drinking only water, and use a little wine because of your stomach and your frequent illnesses.

[24]The sins of some are obvious, reaching the place of judgment ahead of them; the sins of others trail behind them. [25]In the same way, good deeds are obvious, and even those that are not obvious cannot remain hidden forever.

**6** All who are under the yoke of slavery should consider their masters worthy of full respect, so that God's name and our teaching may not be slandered. [2]Those who have believing masters should not show them disrespect just because they are fellow believers. Instead, they should serve them even better because their masters are dear to them as fellow believers and are devoted to the welfare[c] of their slaves.

### False Teachers and the Love of Money

These are the things you are to teach and insist on. [3]If anyone teaches otherwise and does not agree to the sound instruction of our Lord Jesus Christ and to godly teaching,

## Amplified Bible

[10]And she must have a reputation for good deeds, as one who has brought up children, who has practiced hospitality to strangers [of the brotherhood], washed the feet of the saints, helped to relieve the distressed, [and] devoted herself diligently to doing good in every way.

[11]But refuse [to enroll on this list the] younger widows, for when they become restive *and* their natural desires grow strong, they withdraw themselves against Christ [and] wish to marry [again].

[12]And so they incur condemnation for having set aside *and* slighted their previous pledge.

[13]Moreover, as they go about from house to house, they learn to be idlers, and not only idlers, but gossips and busybodies, saying what they should not say *and* talking of things they should not mention.

[14]So I would have younger [widows] marry, bear children, guide the household, [and] not give opponents of the faith occasion for slander or reproach.

[15]For already some [widows] have turned aside after Satan.

[16]If any believing woman *or believing man* has [relatives or persons in the household who are] widows, let him relieve them; let the church not be burdened [with them], so that it may [be free to] assist those who are truly widows (those who are all alone and are dependent).

[17]Let the elders who perform the duties of their office well be considered doubly worthy of honor [and of adequate [a]financial support], especially those who labor faithfully in preaching and teaching.

[18]For the Scripture says, You shall not muzzle an ox when it is treading out the grain, and again, The laborer is worthy of his hire. [Deut. 25:4; Luke 10:7.]

[19]Listen to no accusation [presented before a judge] against an elder unless it is confirmed by the testimony of two or three witnesses. [Deut. 19:15.]

[20]As for those who are guilty *and* persist in sin, rebuke *and* admonish them in the presence of all, so that the rest may be warned *and* stand in wholesome awe *and* fear.

[21]I solemnly charge you in the presence of God and of Christ Jesus and of the chosen angels that you guard *and* keep [these rules] without personal prejudice *or* favor, doing nothing from partiality.

[22]Do not be in a hurry in the laying on of hands [giving the sanction of the church too hastily in reinstating expelled offenders or in ordination in questionable cases], nor share *or* participate in another man's sins; keep yourself pure.

[23]Drink water no longer exclusively, but use a little wine for the sake of your stomach and your frequent illnesses.

[24]The sins of some men are conspicuous (openly evident to all eyes), going before them to the judgment [seat] *and* proclaiming their sentence in advance; but the sins of others appear later [following the offender to the bar of judgment and coming into view there].

[25]So also, good deeds are evident *and* conspicuous, and even when they are not, they cannot remain hidden [indefinitely].

**6** Let all who are under the yoke as bond servants esteem their own [personal] masters worthy of honor *and* fullest respect, so that the name of God and the teaching [about Him] may not be brought into disrepute *and* blasphemed.

[2]Let those who have believing masters not be disrespectful *or* scornful [to them] on the grounds that they are brothers [in Christ]; rather, they should serve [them all the better] because those who benefit by their kindly service are believers and beloved. Teach and urge these duties.

[3]But if anyone teaches otherwise and does not [a]assent to the sound *and* wholesome messages of our Lord Jesus Christ (the Messiah) and the teaching which is in agreement with godliness (piety toward God),

[a] 18 Deut. 25:4   [b] 18 Luke 10:7   [c] 2 Or *and benefit from the service*       [a] Marvin Vincent, *Word Studies.*

## New International Version

[4]they are conceited and understand nothing. They have an unhealthy interest in controversies and quarrels about words that result in envy, strife, malicious talk, evil suspicions [5]and constant friction between people of corrupt mind, who have been robbed of the truth and who think that godliness is a means to financial gain.

[6]But godliness with contentment is great gain. [7]For we brought nothing into the world, and we can take nothing out of it. [8]But if we have food and clothing, we will be content with that. [9]Those who want to get rich fall into temptation and a trap and into many foolish and harmful desires that plunge people into ruin and destruction. [10]For the love of money is a root of all kinds of evil. Some people, eager for money, have wandered from the faith and pierced themselves with many griefs.

### Final Charge to Timothy

[11]But you, man of God, flee from all this, and pursue righteousness, godliness, faith, love, endurance and gentleness. [12]Fight the good fight of the faith. Take hold of the eternal life to which you were called when you made your good confession in the presence of many witnesses. [13]In the sight of God, who gives life to everything, and of Christ Jesus, who while testifying before Pontius Pilate made the good confession, I charge you [14]to keep this command without spot or blame until the appearing of our Lord Jesus Christ, [15]which God will bring about in his own time—God, the blessed and only Ruler, the King of kings and Lord of lords, [16]who alone is immortal and who lives in unapproachable light, whom no one has seen or can see. To him be honor and might forever. Amen.

[17]Command those who are rich in this present world not to be arrogant nor to put their hope in wealth, which is so uncertain, but to put their hope in God, who richly provides us with everything for our enjoyment. [18]Command them to do good, to be rich in good deeds, and to be generous and willing to share. [19]In this way they will lay up treasure for themselves as a firm foundation for the coming age, so that they may take hold of the life that is truly life.

[20]Timothy, guard what has been entrusted to your care. Turn away from godless chatter and the opposing ideas of what is falsely called knowledge, [21]which some have professed and in so doing have departed from the faith.

Grace be with you all.

## Amplified Bible

[4]He is puffed up with pride *and* stupefied with conceit, [although he is] woefully ignorant. He has a [a]morbid fondness for controversy and disputes *and* strife about words, which result in (produce) envy *and* jealousy, quarrels *and* dissension, abuse *and* insults *and* slander, and base suspicions,

[5]And protracted wrangling *and* wearing discussion *and* perpetual friction among men who are corrupted in mind and bereft of the truth, who imagine that godliness *or* righteousness is a [b]source of profit [a moneymaking business, a means of livelihood]. *From such withdraw.*

[6][And it is, indeed, a source of immense profit, for] godliness accompanied with contentment (that contentment which is a sense of [b]inward sufficiency) is great *and* abundant gain.

[7]For we brought nothing into the world, and *obviously* we cannot take anything out of the world;

[8]But if we have food and clothing, with these we shall be content (satisfied).

[9]But those who crave to be rich fall into temptation and a snare and into many foolish (useless, godless) and hurtful desires that plunge men into ruin *and* destruction and miserable perishing.

[10]For the love of money is a root of all evils; it is through this craving that some have been led astray *and* have wandered from the faith and pierced themselves through with many [c]acute [mental] pangs.

[11]But as for you, O man of God, flee from all these things; aim at *and* pursue righteousness (right standing with God and true goodness), godliness (which is the loving fear of God and being Christlike), faith, love, steadfastness (patience), and gentleness of heart.

[12]Fight the good fight of the faith; lay hold of the eternal life to which you were summoned and [for which] you confessed the good confession [of faith] before many witnesses.

[13]In the presence of God, Who preserves alive all living things, and of Christ Jesus, Who in His testimony before Pontius Pilate made the good confession, I [solemnly] charge you

[14]To keep all His precepts unsullied *and* flawless, irreproachable, until the appearing of our Lord Jesus Christ (the Anointed One),

[15]Which [appearing] will be shown forth in His own proper time by the blessed, only Sovereign (Ruler), the King of kings and the Lord of lords,

[16]Who alone has immortality [in the sense of exemption from every kind of death] and lives in unapproachable light, Whom no man has ever seen or can see. Unto Him be honor and everlasting power *and* dominion. Amen (so be it).

[17]As for the rich in this world, charge them not to be proud *and* arrogant *and* contemptuous of others, nor to set their hopes on uncertain riches, but on God, Who richly *and* ceaselessly provides us with everything for [our] enjoyment.

[18][Charge them] to do good, to be rich in good works, to be liberal *and* generous of heart, ready to share [with others],

[19]In this way laying up for themselves [the riches that endure forever as] a good foundation for the future, so that they may grasp that which is life indeed.

[20]O Timothy, guard *and* keep the deposit entrusted [to you]! Turn away from the irreverent babble *and* godless chatter, with the vain *and* empty *and* worldly phrases, and the subtleties *and* the contradictions in what is falsely called knowledge *and* spiritual illumination.

[21][For] by making such profession some have erred (missed the mark) as regards the faith. Grace (divine favor and blessing) be with you all! *Amen (so be it).*

[a] Joseph Thayer, *A Greek-English Lexicon of the New Testament.*
[b] Marvin Vincent, *Word Studies.* [c] Alexander Souter, *Pocket Lexicon.*

# 2 Timothy

**1** Paul, an apostle of Christ Jesus by the will of God, in keeping with the promise of life that is in Christ Jesus,

² To Timothy, my dear son:

Grace, mercy and peace from God the Father and Christ Jesus our Lord.

## Thanksgiving

³ I thank God, whom I serve, as my ancestors did, with a clear conscience, as night and day I constantly remember you in my prayers. ⁴ Recalling your tears, I long to see you, so that I may be filled with joy. ⁵ I am reminded of your sincere faith, which first lived in your grandmother Lois and in your mother Eunice and, I am persuaded, now lives in you also.

## Appeal for Loyalty to Paul and the Gospel

⁶ For this reason I remind you to fan into flame the gift of God, which is in you through the laying on of my hands. ⁷ For the Spirit God gave us does not make us timid, but gives us power, love and self-discipline. ⁸ So do not be ashamed of the testimony about our Lord or of me his prisoner. Rather, join with me in suffering for the gospel, by the power of God. ⁹ He has saved us and called us to a holy life—not because of anything we have done but because of his own purpose and grace. This grace was given us in Christ Jesus before the beginning of time, ¹⁰ but it has now been revealed through the appearing of our Savior, Christ Jesus, who has destroyed death and has brought life and immortality to light through the gospel. ¹¹ And of this gospel I was appointed a herald and an apostle and a teacher. ¹² That is why I am suffering as I am. Yet this is no cause for shame, because I know whom I have believed, and am convinced that he is able to guard what I have entrusted to him until that day.

¹³ What you heard from me, keep as the pattern of sound teaching, with faith and love in Christ Jesus. ¹⁴ Guard the good deposit that was entrusted to you—guard it with the help of the Holy Spirit who lives in us.

**1** Paul, an apostle (special messenger) of Christ Jesus by the will of God, according to the promise of life that is in Christ Jesus,

² To Timothy, [my] beloved child: Grace (favor and spiritual blessing), mercy, and [heart] peace from God the Father and Christ Jesus our Lord!

³ I thank God Whom I worship with a pure conscience, ᵃ in the spirit of my fathers, when without ceasing I remember you night and day in my prayers,

⁴ And when, as I recall your tears, I yearn to see you so that I may be filled with joy.

⁵ I am calling up memories of your sincere *and* unqualified faith (the ᵇ leaning of your entire personality on God in Christ in absolute trust and confidence in His power, wisdom, and goodness), [a faith] that first lived permanently in [the heart of] your grandmother Lois and your mother Eunice and now, I am [fully] persuaded, [dwells] in you also.

⁶ That is why I would remind you to stir up (rekindle the embers of, fan the flame of, and keep burning) the [gracious] gift of God, [the inner fire] that is in you by means of the laying on of my hands [ᵃ with those of the elders at your ordination].

⁷ For God did not give us a spirit of timidity (of cowardice, of craven and cringing and fawning fear), but [He has given us a spirit] of power and of love and of calm *and* well-balanced mind *and* discipline *and* self-control.

⁸ Do not blush *or* be ashamed then, to testify to *and* for our Lord, nor of me, a prisoner for His sake, but [ᵃ with me] take your share of the suffering [to which the preaching] of the Gospel [may expose you, and do it] in the power of God.

⁹ [For it is He] Who delivered *and* saved us and called us with a calling in itself holy *and* leading to holiness [to a life of consecration, a vocation of holiness]; [He did it] not because of anything of merit that we have done, but because of *and* to further His own purpose and grace (unmerited favor) which was given us in Christ Jesus before the world began [eternal ages ago].

¹⁰ [It is that purpose and grace] which He now has made known *and* has fully disclosed *and* made real [to us] through the appearing of our Savior Christ Jesus, Who annulled death *and* made it of no effect and brought life and immortality (immunity from eternal death) to light through the Gospel.

¹¹ For [the proclaiming of] this [Gospel] I was appointed a herald (preacher) and an apostle (special messenger) and a teacher *of the Gentiles.*

¹² And this is why I am suffering as I do. Still I am not ashamed, for I know (perceive, have knowledge of, and am acquainted with) Him Whom I have believed (adhered to and trusted in and relied on), and I am [positively] persuaded that He is able to guard *and* keep that which has been entrusted to me *and* which ᶜ I have committed [to Him] until that day.

¹³ Hold fast *and* follow the pattern of wholesome *and* sound teaching which you have heard from me, in [all] the faith and love which are [for us] in Christ Jesus.

¹⁴ Guard *and* keep [with the greatest care] the precious *and* excellently adapted [Truth] which has been entrusted [to you], by the [help of the] Holy Spirit Who makes His home in us.

ᵃ Marvin Vincent, *Word Studies in the New Testament.* ᵇ Alexander Souter, *Pocket Lexicon of the Greek New Testament.* ᶜ Alternate translation.

## New International Version

### Examples of Disloyalty and Loyalty

¹⁵You know that everyone in the province of Asia has deserted me, including Phygelus and Hermogenes. ¹⁶May the Lord show mercy to the household of Onesiphorus, because he often refreshed me and was not ashamed of my chains. ¹⁷On the contrary, when he was in Rome, he searched hard for me until he found me. ¹⁸May the Lord grant that he will find mercy from the Lord on that day! You know very well in how many ways he helped me in Ephesus.

### The Appeal Renewed

**2** You then, my son, be strong in the grace that is in Christ Jesus. ²And the things you have heard me say in the presence of many witnesses entrust to reliable people who will also be qualified to teach others. ³Join with me in suffering, like a good soldier of Christ Jesus. ⁴No one serving as a soldier gets entangled in civilian affairs, but rather tries to please his commanding officer. ⁵Similarly, anyone who competes as an athlete does not receive the victor's crown except by competing according to the rules. ⁶The hardworking farmer should be the first to receive a share of the crops. ⁷Reflect on what I am saying, for the Lord will give you insight into all this.

⁸Remember Jesus Christ, raised from the dead, descended from David. This is my gospel, ⁹for which I am suffering even to the point of being chained like a criminal. But God's word is not chained. ¹⁰Therefore I endure everything for the sake of the elect, that they too may obtain the salvation that is in Christ Jesus, with eternal glory. ¹¹Here is a trustworthy saying:

If we died with him,
  we will also live with him;
¹²if we endure,
  we will also reign with him.
If we disown him,
  he will also disown us;
¹³if we are faithless,
  he remains faithful,
  for he cannot disown himself.

### Dealing With False Teachers

¹⁴Keep reminding God's people of these things. Warn them before God against quarreling about words; it is of no value, and only ruins those who listen. ¹⁵Do your best to present yourself to God as one approved, a worker who does not need to be ashamed and who correctly handles the word of truth. ¹⁶Avoid godless chatter, because those who indulge in it will become more and more ungodly. ¹⁷Their teaching will spread like gangrene. Among them are Hymenaeus and Philetus, ¹⁸who have departed from

## Amplified Bible

¹⁵You already know that all who are in Asia turned away *and* forsook me, Phygelus and Hermogenes among them. ¹⁶May the Lord grant [His] mercy to the family of Onesiphorus, for he often showed me kindness *and* ministered to my needs [comforting and reviving and bracing me like fresh air]! He was not ashamed of my chains *and* imprisonment [for Christ's sake]. ¹⁷No, rather when he reached Rome, he searched diligently *and* eagerly for me and found me. ¹⁸May the Lord grant to him that he may find mercy from the Lord on that [great] day! And you know how many things he did for me *and* what a help he was at Ephesus [you know better than I can tell you].

**2** So you, my son, be strong (strengthened inwardly) in the grace (spiritual blessing) that is [to be found only] in Christ Jesus. ²And the [instructions] which you have heard from me along with many witnesses, transmit *and* entrust [as a deposit] to reliable *and* faithful men who will be competent *and* qualified to teach others also. ³Take [with me] your share of the hardships *and* suffering [which you are called to endure] as a good (first-class) soldier of Christ Jesus. ⁴No soldier when in service gets entangled in the enterprises of [civilian] life; his aim is to satisfy *and* please the one who enlisted him. ⁵And if anyone enters competitive games, he is not crowned unless he competes lawfully (fairly, according to the rules laid down). ⁶[It is] the hard-working farmer [who labors to produce] who must be the first partaker of the fruits. ⁷Think over these things I am saying [understand them and grasp their application], for the Lord will grant you full insight *and* understanding in everything.

⁸Constantly keep in mind Jesus Christ (the Messiah) [as] risen from the dead, [as the prophesied King] descended from David, according to the good news (the Gospel) that I preach. [Ps. 16:10.] ⁹For that [Gospel] I am suffering affliction *and* even wearing chains like a criminal. But the Word of God is not chained *or* imprisoned! ¹⁰Therefore I [am ready to] persevere *and* stand my ground with patience *and* endure everything for the sake of the elect [God's chosen], so that they too may obtain [the] salvation which is in Christ Jesus, with [the reward of] eternal glory. ¹¹The saying is sure *and* worthy of confidence: If we have died with Him, we shall also live with Him. ¹²If we endure, we shall also reign with Him. If we deny *and* disown *and* reject Him, He will also deny *and* disown *and* reject us. ¹³If we are faithless [do not believe and are untrue to Him], He remains true (faithful to His Word and His righteous character), for He cannot deny Himself.

¹⁴Remind [the people] of these facts and [solemnly] charge them in the presence of the Lord to avoid petty controversy over words, which does no good but upsets *and* undermines the faith of the hearers. ¹⁵Study *and* be eager *and* do your utmost to present yourself to God approved (tested by trial), a workman who has no cause to be ashamed, correctly analyzing *and* accurately dividing [rightly handling and skillfully teaching] the Word of Truth. ¹⁶But avoid all empty (vain, useless, idle) talk, for it will lead people into more *and* more ungodliness. ¹⁷And their teaching [will devour; it] will eat its way like cancer *or* spread like gangrene. So it is with Hymenaeus and Philetus, ¹⁸Who have missed the mark *and* swerved from the

## New International Version

the truth. They say that the resurrection has already taken place, and they destroy the faith of some. ¹⁹Nevertheless, God's solid foundation stands firm, sealed with this inscription: "The Lord knows those who are his," and, "Everyone who confesses the name of the Lord must turn away from wickedness."

²⁰In a large house there are articles not only of gold and silver, but also of wood and clay; some are for special purposes and some for common use. ²¹Those who cleanse themselves from the latter will be instruments for special purposes, made holy, useful to the Master and prepared to do any good work.

²²Flee the evil desires of youth and pursue righteousness, faith, love and peace, along with those who call on the Lord out of a pure heart. ²³Don't have anything to do with foolish and stupid arguments, because you know they produce quarrels. ²⁴And the Lord's servant must not be quarrelsome but must be kind to everyone, able to teach, not resentful. ²⁵Opponents must be gently instructed, in the hope that God will grant them repentance leading them to a knowledge of the truth, ²⁶and that they will come to their senses and escape from the trap of the devil, who has taken them captive to do his will.

**3** But mark this: There will be terrible times in the last days. ²People will be lovers of themselves, lovers of money, boastful, proud, abusive, disobedient to their parents, ungrateful, unholy, ³without love, unforgiving, slanderous, without self-control, brutal, not lovers of the good, ⁴treacherous, rash, conceited, lovers of pleasure rather than lovers of God— ⁵having a form of godliness but denying its power. Have nothing to do with such people.

⁶They are the kind who worm their way into homes and gain control over gullible women, who are loaded down with sins and are swayed by all kinds of evil desires, ⁷always learning but never able to come to a knowledge of

## Amplified Bible

truth by arguing that the resurrection has already taken place. They are undermining the faith of some.

¹⁹But the firm foundation of (laid by) God stands, sure *and* unshaken, bearing this seal (inscription): The Lord knows those who are His, and, Let everyone who names [himself by] the name of the Lord give up all iniquity *and* stand aloof from it. [Num. 16:5; Isa. 26:13.]

²⁰But in a great house there are not only vessels of gold and silver, but also [utensils] of wood and earthenware, and some for honorable *and* noble [use] and some for menial *and* ignoble [use].

²¹So whoever cleanses himself [from what is ignoble *and* unclean, who separates himself from contact with contaminating and corrupting influences] will [then himself] be a vessel set apart *and* useful for honorable *and* noble purposes, consecrated *and* profitable to the Master, fit *and* ready for any good work.

²²Shun youthful lusts *and* flee from them, and aim at *and* pursue righteousness (all that is virtuous and good, right living, conformity to the will of God in thought, word, and deed); [and aim at and pursue] faith, love, [and] peace (harmony and concord with others) in fellowship with all [Christians], who call upon the Lord out of a pure heart.

²³But refuse (shut your mind against, have nothing to do with) trifling (ill-informed, unedifying, stupid) controversies over ignorant questionings, for you know that they foster strife *and* breed quarrels.

²⁴And the servant of the Lord must not be quarrelsome (fighting and contending). Instead, he must be kindly to everyone *and* mild-tempered [preserving the bond of peace]; he must be a skilled *and* suitable teacher, patient *and* forbearing *and* willing to suffer wrong.

²⁵He must correct his opponents with courtesy *and* gentleness, in the hope that God may grant that they will repent and come to know the Truth [that they will perceive and recognize and become accurately acquainted with and acknowledge it],

²⁶And that they may come to their senses [and] escape out of the snare of the devil, having been held captive by him, [henceforth] to do His [God's] will.

**3** But understand this, that in the last days will come (set in) perilous times of great stress *and* trouble [hard to deal with and hard to bear].

²For people will be lovers of self *and* [utterly] self-centered, lovers of money *and* aroused by an inordinate [greedy] desire for wealth, proud *and* arrogant *and* contemptuous boasters. They will be abusive (blasphemous, scoffing), disobedient to parents, ungrateful, unholy *and* profane.

³[They will be] without natural [human] affection (callous and inhuman), relentless (admitting of no truce or appeasement); [they will be] slanderers (false accusers, troublemakers), intemperate *and* loose in morals *and* conduct, uncontrolled *and* fierce, haters of good.

⁴[They will be] treacherous [betrayers], rash, [and] inflated with self-conceit. [They will be] lovers of sensual pleasures *and* vain amusements more than *and* rather than lovers of God.

⁵For [although] they hold a form of piety (true religion), they deny *and* reject *and* are strangers to the power of it [their conduct belies the genuineness of their profession]. Avoid [all] such people [turn away from them].

⁶For among them are those who worm their way into homes and captivate silly *and* weak-natured *and* spiritually dwarfed women, loaded down with [the burden of their] sins [and easily] swayed *and* led away by various evil desires *and* seductive impulses.

⁷[These weak women will listen to anybody who will teach them]; they are forever inquiring *and* getting information, but are never able to arrive at a recognition *and* knowledge of the Truth.

## New International Version

the truth. [8]Just as Jannes and Jambres opposed Moses, so also these teachers oppose the truth. They are men of depraved minds, who, as far as the faith is concerned, are rejected. [9]But they will not get very far because, as in the case of those men, their folly will be clear to everyone.

### A Final Charge to Timothy

[10]You, however, know all about my teaching, my way of life, my purpose, faith, patience, love, endurance, [11]persecutions, sufferings—what kinds of things happened to me in Antioch, Iconium and Lystra, the persecutions I endured. Yet the Lord rescued me from all of them. [12]In fact, everyone who wants to live a godly life in Christ Jesus will be persecuted, [13]while evildoers and impostors will go from bad to worse, deceiving and being deceived. [14]But as for you, continue in what you have learned and have become convinced of, because you know those from whom you learned it, [15]and how from infancy you have known the Holy Scriptures, which are able to make you wise for salvation through faith in Christ Jesus. [16]All Scripture is God-breathed and is useful for teaching, rebuking, correcting and training in righteousness, [17]so that the servant of God[a] may be thoroughly equipped for every good work.

**4** In the presence of God and of Christ Jesus, who will judge the living and the dead, and in view of his appearing and his kingdom, I give you this charge: [2]Preach the word; be prepared in season and out of season; correct, rebuke and encourage—with great patience and careful instruction. [3]For the time will come when people will not put up with sound doctrine. Instead, to suit their own desires, they will gather around them a great number of teachers to say what their itching ears want to hear. [4]They will turn their ears away from the truth and turn aside to myths. [5]But you, keep your head in all situations, endure hardship, do the work of an evangelist, discharge all the duties of your ministry.

[6]For I am already being poured out like a drink offering, and the time for my departure is near. [7]I have fought the

## Amplified Bible

[8]Now just as [a]Jannes and Jambres were hostile to and resisted Moses, so these men also are hostile to and oppose the Truth. They have depraved and distorted minds, and are reprobate and counterfeit and to be rejected as far as the faith is concerned. [Exod. 7:11.]

[9]But they will not get very far, for their rash folly will become obvious to everybody, as was that of those [magicians mentioned].

[10]Now you have closely observed and diligently followed my teaching, conduct, purpose in life, faith, patience, love, steadfastness,

[11]Persecutions, sufferings—such as occurred to me at Antioch, at Iconium, and at Lystra, persecutions I endured, but out of them all the Lord delivered me.

[12]Indeed all who delight in piety and are determined to live a devoted and godly life in Christ Jesus will meet with persecution [will be made to suffer because of their religious stand].

[13]But wicked men and imposters will go on from bad to worse, deceiving and leading astray others and being deceived and led astray themselves.

[14]But as for you, continue to hold to the things that you have learned and of which you are convinced, knowing from whom you learned [them],

[15]And how from your childhood you have had a knowledge of and been acquainted with the sacred Writings, which are able to instruct you and give you the understanding for salvation which comes through faith in Christ Jesus [through the [b]leaning of the entire human personality on God in Christ Jesus in absolute trust and confidence in His power, wisdom, and goodness].

[16]Every Scripture is God-breathed (given by His inspiration) and profitable for instruction, for reproof and conviction of sin, for correction of error and discipline in obedience, [and] for training in righteousness (in holy living, in conformity to God's will in thought, purpose, and action),

[17]So that the man of God may be complete and proficient, well fitted and thoroughly equipped for every good work.

**4** I charge [you] in the presence of God and of Christ Jesus, Who is to judge the living and the dead, and by (in the light of) His coming and His kingdom:

[2]Herald and preach the Word! Keep your sense of urgency [stand by, be at hand and ready], whether the opportunity seems to be favorable or unfavorable. [Whether it is convenient or inconvenient, whether it is welcome or unwelcome, you as preacher of the Word are to show people in what way their lives are wrong.] And convince them, rebuking and correcting, warning and urging and encouraging them, being unflagging and inexhaustible in patience and teaching.

[3]For the time is coming when [people] will not tolerate (endure) sound and wholesome instruction, but, having ears itching [for something pleasing and gratifying], they will gather to themselves one teacher after another to a considerable number, chosen to satisfy their own liking and to foster the errors they hold,

[4]And will turn aside from hearing the truth and wander off into myths and man-made fictions.

[5]As for you, be calm and cool and steady, accept and suffer unflinchingly every hardship, do the work of an evangelist, fully perform all the duties of your ministry.

[6]For I am already about to be sacrificed [my life is about to be poured out as a drink offering]; the time of my [spirit's] release [from the body] is at hand and I will soon go free.

## New International Version

good fight, I have finished the race, I have kept the faith. [8]Now there is in store for me the crown of righteousness, which the Lord, the righteous Judge, will award to me on that day—and not only to me, but also to all who have longed for his appearing.

### Personal Remarks

[9]Do your best to come to me quickly, [10]for Demas, because he loved this world, has deserted me and has gone to Thessalonica. Crescens has gone to Galatia, and Titus to Dalmatia. [11]Only Luke is with me. Get Mark and bring him with you, because he is helpful to me in my ministry. [12]I sent Tychicus to Ephesus. [13]When you come, bring the cloak that I left with Carpus at Troas, and my scrolls, especially the parchments.

[14]Alexander the metalworker did me a great deal of harm. The Lord will repay him for what he has done. [15]You too should be on your guard against him, because he strongly opposed our message.

[16]At my first defense, no one came to my support, but everyone deserted me. May it not be held against them. [17]But the Lord stood at my side and gave me strength, so that through me the message might be fully proclaimed and all the Gentiles might hear it. And I was delivered from the lion's mouth. [18]The Lord will rescue me from every evil attack and will bring me safely to his heavenly kingdom. To him be glory for ever and ever. Amen.

### Final Greetings

[19]Greet Priscilla[a] and Aquila and the household of Onesiphorus. [20]Erastus stayed in Corinth, and I left Trophimus sick in Miletus. [21]Do your best to get here before winter. Eubulus greets you, and so do Pudens, Linus, Claudia and all the brothers and sisters.[b]

[22]The Lord be with your spirit. Grace be with you all.

## Amplified Bible

[7]I have fought the good (worthy, honorable, and noble) fight, I have finished the race, I have kept (firmly held) the faith.

[8][As to what remains] henceforth there is laid up for me the [victor's] crown of righteousness [for being right with God and doing right], which the Lord, the righteous Judge, will award to me *and* recompense me on that [great] day—and not to me only, but also to all those who have loved *and* yearned for *and* welcomed His appearing (His return).

[9]Make every effort to come to me soon.

[10]For Demas has deserted me for love of this present world and has gone to Thessalonica; Crescens [has gone] to Galatia, Titus to Dalmatia.

[11]Luke alone is with me. Get Mark and bring him with you, for he is very helpful to me for the ministry.

[12]Tychicus I have sent to Ephesus.

[13][When] you come, bring the cloak that I left at Troas with Carpus, also the books, especially the parchments.

[14]Alexander the coppersmith did me great wrongs. The Lord will pay him back for his actions.

[15]Beware of him yourself, for he opposed *and* resisted our message very strongly *and* exceedingly.

[16]At my first trial no one acted in my defense [as my advocate] *or* took my part *or* [even] stood with me, but all forsook me. May it not be charged against them!

[17]But the Lord stood by me and strengthened me, so that through me the [Gospel] message might be fully proclaimed and all the Gentiles might hear. So I was delivered out of the jaws of the lion.

[18][And indeed] the Lord will certainly deliver *and* [a]draw me to Himself from every assault of evil. He will preserve *and* bring me safe unto His heavenly kingdom. To Him be the glory forever and ever. Amen (so be it).

[19]Give my greetings to Prisca and Aquila and to the household of Onesiphorus.

[20]Erastus stayed on at Corinth, but Trophimus I left ill at Miletus.

[21]Do hasten *and* try your best to come to me before winter. Eubulus wishes to be remembered to you, as do Pudens and Linus and Claudia and all the brethren.

[22]The Lord *Jesus Christ* be with your spirit. Grace (God's favor and blessing) be with you. *Amen (so be it).*

---

*a* 19 Greek *Prisca*, a variant of *Priscilla*   *b* 21 The Greek word for *brothers and sisters* (*adelphoi*) refers here to believers, both men and women, as part of God's family.

*a* Joseph Thayer, *A Greek-English Lexicon of the New Testament*: A primary meaning of the Greek *ruomai*: "draw to one's self."

# Titus

# Titus

**1** Paul, a servant of God and an apostle of Jesus Christ to further the faith of God's elect and their knowledge of the truth that leads to godliness— ²in the hope of eternal life, which God, who does not lie, promised before the beginning of time, ³and which now at his appointed season he has brought to light through the preaching entrusted to me by the command of God our Savior,

⁴To Titus, my true son in our common faith:

Grace and peace from God the Father and Christ Jesus our Savior.

### Appointing Elders Who Love What Is Good

⁵The reason I left you in Crete was that you might put in order what was left unfinished and appoint*ᵃ* elders in every town, as I directed you. ⁶An elder must be blameless, faithful to his wife, a man whose children believe*ᵇ* and are not open to the charge of being wild and disobedient. ⁷Since an overseer manages God's household, he must be blameless—not overbearing, not quick-tempered, not given to drunkenness, not violent, not pursuing dishonest gain. ⁸Rather, he must be hospitable, one who loves what is good, who is self-controlled, upright, holy and disciplined. ⁹He must hold firmly to the trustworthy message as it has been taught, so that he can encourage others by sound doctrine and refute those who oppose it.

### Rebuking Those Who Fail to Do Good

¹⁰For there are many rebellious people, full of meaningless talk and deception, especially those of the circumcision group. ¹¹They must be silenced, because they are disrupting whole households by teaching things they ought not to teach—and that for the sake of dishonest gain. ¹²One of Crete's own prophets has said it: "Cretans are always liars, evil brutes, lazy gluttons."*ᶜ* ¹³This saying is true. Therefore rebuke them sharply, so that they will be sound in the faith ¹⁴and will pay no attention to Jewish myths or to the merely human commands of those who reject the truth. ¹⁵To the pure, all things are pure, but to those who are corrupted and do not believe, nothing is pure. In fact, both their minds and consciences are cor-

**1** Paul, a bond servant of God and an apostle (a special messenger) of Jesus Christ (the Messiah) to stimulate *and* promote the faith of God's chosen ones and to lead them on to accurate discernment *and* recognition of *and* acquaintance with the Truth which belongs to *and* harmonizes with *and* tends to godliness,

²[Resting] in the hope of eternal life, [life] which the ever truthful God Who cannot deceive promised before the world *or* the ages of time began.

³And [now] in His own appointed time He has made manifest (made known) His Word *and* revealed it as His message through the preaching entrusted to me by command of God our Savior;

⁴To Titus, my true child according to a common (general) faith: Grace (favor and spiritual blessing) and [heart] peace from God the Father and *the Lord* Christ Jesus our Savior.

⁵For this reason I left you [behind] in Crete, that you might set right what was defective *and* finish what was left undone, and that you might appoint elders *and* set them over the churches (assemblies) in every city as I directed you.

⁶[These elders should be] men who are of unquestionable integrity *and* are irreproachable, the husband of [but] one wife, whose children are [well trained and are] believers, not open to the accusation of being loose in morals *and* conduct or unruly *and* disorderly.

⁷For the bishop (an overseer) as God's steward must be blameless, not self-willed *or* arrogant *or* presumptuous; he must not be quick-tempered or given to drink *or* pugnacious (brawling, violent); he must not be grasping *and* greedy for filthy lucre (financial gain);

⁸But he must be hospitable (loving and a friend to believers, especially to strangers and foreigners); [he must be] a lover of goodness [of good people and good things], sober-minded (sensible, discreet), upright *and* fair-minded, a devout man *and* religiously correct, temperate *and* keeping himself in hand.

⁹He must hold fast to the sure *and* trustworthy Word of God as he was taught it, so that he may be able both to give stimulating instruction *and* encouragement in sound (wholesome) doctrine and to refute *and* convict those who contradict *and* oppose it [showing the wayward their error].

¹⁰For there are many disorderly *and* unruly men who are idle (vain, empty) *and* misleading talkers and self-deceivers *and* deceivers of others. [This is true] especially of those of the circumcision party [who have come over from Judaism].

¹¹Their mouths must be stopped, for they are mentally distressing *and* subverting whole families by teaching what they ought not to teach, for the purpose of getting base advantage *and* disreputable gain.

¹²One of their [very] number, a prophet of their own, said, Cretans are always liars, hurtful beasts, idle *and* lazy gluttons.

¹³And this account of them is [really] true. Because it is [true], rebuke them sharply [deal sternly, even severely with them], so that they may be sound in the faith *and* free from error,

¹⁴[And may show their soundness by] ceasing to give attention to Jewish myths *and* fables or to rules [laid down] by [mere] men who reject *and* turn their backs on the Truth.

¹⁵To the pure [in heart and conscience] all things are pure, but to the defiled *and* corrupt and unbelieving nothing is pure; their very minds and consciences are defiled *and* polluted.

*ᵃ 5* Or *ordain*    *ᵇ 6* Or *children are trustworthy*    *ᶜ 12* From the Cretan philosopher Epimenides

## New International Version

rupted. [16]They claim to know God, but by their actions they deny him. They are detestable, disobedient and unfit for doing anything good.

### Doing Good for the Sake of the Gospel

**2** You, however, must teach what is appropriate to sound doctrine. [2]Teach the older men to be temperate, worthy of respect, self-controlled, and sound in faith, in love and in endurance.

[3]Likewise, teach the older women to be reverent in the way they live, not to be slanderers or addicted to much wine, but to teach what is good. [4]Then they can urge the younger women to love their husbands and children, [5]to be self-controlled and pure, to be busy at home, to be kind, and to be subject to their husbands, so that no one will malign the word of God.

[6]Similarly, encourage the young men to be self-controlled. [7]In everything set them an example by doing what is good. In your teaching show integrity, seriousness [8]and soundness of speech that cannot be condemned, so that those who oppose you may be ashamed because they have nothing bad to say about us.

[9]Teach slaves to be subject to their masters in everything, to try to please them, not to talk back to them, [10]and not to steal from them, but to show that they can be fully trusted, so that in every way they will make the teaching about God our Savior attractive.

[11]For the grace of God has appeared that offers salvation to all people. [12]It teaches us to say "No" to ungodliness and worldly passions, and to live self-controlled, upright and godly lives in this present age, [13]while we wait for the blessed hope—the appearing of the glory of our great God and Savior, Jesus Christ, [14]who gave himself for us to redeem us from all wickedness and to purify for himself a people that are his very own, eager to do what is good.

[15]These, then, are the things you should teach. Encourage and rebuke with all authority. Do not let anyone despise you.

## Amplified Bible

[16]They profess to know God [to recognize, perceive, and be acquainted with Him], but deny *and* disown *and* renounce Him by what they do; they are detestable *and* loathsome, unbelieving *and* disobedient *and* disloyal *and* rebellious, and [they are] unfit *and* worthless for good work (deed or enterprise) of any kind.

**2** But [as for] you, teach what is fitting *and* becoming to sound (wholesome) doctrine [the character and right living that identify true Christians].

[2]Urge the older men to be temperate, venerable (serious), sensible, self-controlled, and sound in the faith, in the love, and in the steadfastness *and* patience [of Christ].

[3]Bid the older women similarly to be reverent *and* devout in their deportment as becomes those engaged in sacred service, not slanderers or slaves to drink. They are to give good counsel *and* be teachers of what is right *and* noble,

[4]So that they will wisely train the young women to be [a]sane and sober of mind (temperate, disciplined) and to love their husbands and their children,

[5]To be self-controlled, chaste, homemakers, good-natured (kindhearted), adapting *and* subordinating themselves to their husbands, that the word of God may not be exposed to reproach (blasphemed or discredited).

[6]In a similar way, urge the younger men to be self-restrained *and* to behave prudently [taking life seriously].

[7]And show your own self in all respects to be a pattern *and* a model of good deeds *and* works, teaching what is unadulterated, showing gravity [having the strictest regard for truth and purity of motive], with dignity *and* seriousness.

[8]And let your instruction be sound *and* fit *and* wise *and* wholesome, vigorous *and* [b]irrefutable *and* above censure, so that the opponent may be put to shame, finding nothing discrediting *or* evil to say about us.

[9][Tell] bond servants to be submissive to their masters, to be pleasing *and* give satisfaction in every way. [Warn them] not to talk back *or* contradict,

[10]Nor to steal by taking things of small value, but to prove themselves truly loyal *and* entirely reliable *and* faithful throughout, so that in everything they may be an ornament *and* do credit to the teaching [which is] from *and* about God our Savior.

[11]For the grace of God (His unmerited favor and blessing) has come forward (appeared) for the deliverance from sin *and* the eternal salvation for all mankind.

[12]It has trained us to reject *and* renounce all ungodliness (irreligion) and worldly (passionate) desires, to live discreet (temperate, self-controlled), upright, devout (spiritually whole) lives in this present world,

[13]Awaiting *and* looking for the [fulfillment, the realization of our] blessed hope, even the glorious appearing of our great God and Savior Christ Jesus (the Messiah, the Anointed One),

[14]Who gave Himself on our behalf that He might redeem us (purchase our freedom) from all iniquity and purify for Himself a people [to be peculiarly His own, people who are] eager *and* enthusiastic about [living a life that is good and filled with] beneficial deeds. [Deut. 14:2; Ps. 130:8; Ezek. 37:23.]

[15]Tell [them all] these things. Urge (advise, encourage, warn) and rebuke with full authority. Let no one despise *or* disregard *or* think little of you [conduct yourself and your teaching so as to command respect].

---

[a] Marvin Vincent, *Word Studies in the New Testament*: The Greek verb here translated "train" means "to make sane or sober of mind, to moderate, to discipline."  [b] Arthur S. Way, *Way's Epistles: The Letters of St. Paul to Seven Churches and Three Friends.*

## New International Version

### Saved in Order to Do Good

**3** Remind the people to be subject to rulers and author-ities, to be obedient, to be ready to do whatever is good, ²to slander no one, to be peaceable and considerate, and always to be gentle toward everyone.

³At one time we too were foolish, disobedient, deceived and enslaved by all kinds of passions and pleasures. We lived in malice and envy, being hated and hating one an-other. ⁴But when the kindness and love of God our Savior appeared, ⁵he saved us, not because of righteous things we had done, but because of his mercy. He saved us through the washing of rebirth and renewal by the Holy Spirit, ⁶whom he poured out on us generously through Jesus Christ our Savior, ⁷so that, having been justified by his grace, we might become heirs having the hope of eter-nal life. ⁸This is a trustworthy saying. And I want you to stress these things, so that those who have trusted in God may be careful to devote themselves to doing what is good. These things are excellent and profitable for everyone.

⁹But avoid foolish controversies and genealogies and arguments and quarrels about the law, because these are unprofitable and useless. ¹⁰Warn a divisive person once, and then warn them a second time. After that, have noth-ing to do with them. ¹¹You may be sure that such people are warped and sinful; they are self-condemned.

### Final Remarks

¹²As soon as I send Artemas or Tychicus to you, do your best to come to me at Nicopolis, because I have decided to winter there. ¹³Do everything you can to help Zenas the lawyer and Apollos on their way and see that they have everything they need. ¹⁴Our people must learn to devote themselves to doing what is good, in order to provide for urgent needs and not live unproductive lives.

¹⁵Everyone with me sends you greetings. Greet those who love us in the faith.

Grace be with you all.

## Amplified Bible

**3** Remind people to be submissive to [their] magistrates and authorities, to be obedient, to be prepared *and* willing to do any upright *and* honorable work,

²To slander *or* abuse *or* speak evil of no one, to avoid being contentious, to be forbearing (yielding, gentle, and conciliatory), and to show unqualified courtesy toward everybody.

³For we also were once thoughtless *and* senseless, ob-stinate *and* disobedient, deluded *and* misled; [we too were once] slaves to all sorts of cravings *and* pleasures, wasting our days in malice and jealousy *and* envy, hateful (hated, detestable) and hating one another.

⁴But when the goodness and loving-kindness of God our Savior to man [as man] appeared,

⁵He saved us, not because of any works of righteous-ness that we had done, but because of His own pity *and* mercy, by [the] cleansing [bath] of the new birth (regen-eration) and renewing of the Holy Spirit,

⁶Which He poured out [so] richly upon us through Jesus Christ our Savior.

⁷[And He did it in order] that we might be justified by His grace (by His favor, wholly undeserved), [that we might be acknowledged and counted as conformed to the divine will in purpose, thought, and action], and that we might become heirs of eternal life according to [our] hope.

⁸This message is most trustworthy, and concerning these things I want you to insist steadfastly, so that those who have believed in (trusted in, relied on) God may be careful to apply themselves to honorable occupations *and* to doing good, for such things are [not only] excellent *and* right [in themselves], but [they are] good *and* profitable for the people.

⁹But avoid stupid *and* foolish controversies and gene-alogies and dissensions and wrangling about the Law, for they are unprofitable and futile.

¹⁰[As for] a man who is factious [a heretical sectarian and cause of divisions], after admonishing him a first and second time, reject [him from your fellowship and have nothing more to do with him],

¹¹Well aware that such a person has utterly changed (is perverted and corrupted); he goes on sinning [though he] is convicted of guilt *and* self-condemned.

¹²When I send Artemas or [perhaps] Tychicus to you, lose no time *but* make every effort to come to me at Nicop-olis, for I have decided to spend the winter there.

¹³Do your utmost to speed Zenas the lawyer and Apol-los on their way; see that they want for (lack) nothing.

¹⁴And let our own [people really] learn to apply them-selves to good deeds (to honest labor and honorable em-ployment), so that they may be able to meet necessary demands *ᵃ*whenever the occasion may require and not be living idle *and* uncultivated *and* unfruitful lives.

¹⁵All who are with me wish to be remembered to you. Greet those who love us in the faith. Grace (God's favor and blessing) be with you all. *Amen (so be it)*.

---

*ᵃ* Marvin Vincent, *Word Studies*.

# Philemon

<sup>1</sup>Paul, a prisoner of Christ Jesus, and Timothy our brother,

To Philemon our dear friend and fellow worker— <sup>2</sup>also to Apphia our sister and Archippus our fellow soldier— and to the church that meets in your home:

<sup>3</sup>Grace and peace to you[a] from God our Father and the Lord Jesus Christ.

### Thanksgiving and Prayer

<sup>4</sup>I always thank my God as I remember you in my prayers, <sup>5</sup>because I hear about your love for all his holy people and your faith in the Lord Jesus. <sup>6</sup>I pray that your partnership with us in the faith may be effective in deepening your understanding of every good thing we share for the sake of Christ. <sup>7</sup>Your love has given me great joy and encouragement, because you, brother, have refreshed the hearts of the Lord's people.

### Paul's Plea for Onesimus

<sup>8</sup>Therefore, although in Christ I could be bold and order you to do what you ought to do, <sup>9</sup>yet I prefer to appeal to you on the basis of love. It is as none other than Paul—an old man and now also a prisoner of Christ Jesus— <sup>10</sup>that I appeal to you for my son Onesimus,[b] who became my son while I was in chains. <sup>11</sup>Formerly he was useless to you, but now he has become useful both to you and to me.

<sup>12</sup>I am sending him—who is my very heart—back to you. <sup>13</sup>I would have liked to keep him with me so that he could take your place in helping me while I am in chains for the gospel. <sup>14</sup>But I did not want to do anything without your consent, so that any favor you do would not seem forced but would be voluntary. <sup>15</sup>Perhaps the reason he was separated from you for a little while was that you might have him back forever— <sup>16</sup>no longer as a slave, but better than a slave, as a dear brother. He is very dear to me but even dearer to you, both as a fellow man and as a brother in the Lord.

<sup>17</sup>So if you consider me a partner, welcome him as you would welcome me. <sup>18</sup>If he has done you any wrong or owes you anything, charge it to me. <sup>19</sup>I, Paul, am writing this with my own hand. I will pay it back—not to mention that you owe me your very self. <sup>20</sup>I do wish, brother, that I may have some benefit from you in the Lord; refresh my heart in Christ. <sup>21</sup>Confident of your obedience, I write to you, knowing that you will do even more than I ask.

# Philemon

<sup>1</sup>Paul, a prisoner [for the sake] of Christ Jesus (the Messiah), and our brother Timothy, to Philemon our dearly beloved sharer with us in our work,

<sup>2</sup>And to Apphia our sister and Archippus our fellow soldier [in the Christian warfare], and to the church [assembly that meets] in your house:

<sup>3</sup>Grace (spiritual blessing and favor) be to all of you and [heart] peace from God our Father and the Lord Jesus Christ (the Messiah).

<sup>4</sup>I give thanks to my God for you always when I mention you in my prayers,

<sup>5</sup>Because I continue to hear of your love and of your loyal faith which you have toward the Lord Jesus and [which you show] toward all the saints (God's consecrated people).

<sup>6</sup>[And I pray] that the participation in *and* sharing of your faith may produce *and* promote full recognition *and* appreciation *and* understanding *and* precise knowledge of every good [thing] that is ours in [our identification with] Christ *Jesus* [and unto His glory].

<sup>7</sup>For I have derived great joy and comfort *and* encouragement from your love, because the hearts of the saints [who are your fellow Christians] have been cheered *and* refreshed through you, [my] brother.

<sup>8</sup>Therefore, though I have abundant boldness in Christ to charge you to do what is fitting *and* required *and* your duty to do,

<sup>9</sup>Yet for love's sake I prefer to appeal to you just for what I am—I, Paul, an ambassador [of Christ Jesus] *and* an old man and now a prisoner for His sake also—

<sup>10</sup>I appeal to you for my [own spiritual] child, Onesimus [meaning profitable], whom I have begotten [in the faith] while a captive in these chains.

<sup>11</sup>Once he was unprofitable to you, but now he is indeed profitable to you as well as to me.

<sup>12</sup>I am sending him back to you in [a]his own person, [and it is like sending] my very heart.

<sup>13</sup>I would have chosen to keep him with me, in order that he might minister to my needs in your stead during my imprisonment for the Gospel's sake.

<sup>14</sup>But it has been my wish to do nothing about it without first consulting you *and* getting your consent, in order that your benevolence might not seem to be the result of compulsion *or* of pressure but might be voluntary [on your part].

<sup>15</sup>Perhaps it was for this reason that he was separated [from you] for a while, that you might have him back as yours forever,

<sup>16</sup>Not as a slave any longer but as [something] more than a slave, as a brother [Christian], especially dear to me but how much more to you, both in the flesh [as a servant] and in the Lord [as a fellow believer].

<sup>17</sup>If then you consider me a partner *and* a [a]comrade in fellowship, welcome *and* receive him as you would [welcome and receive] me.

<sup>18</sup>And if he has done you any wrong in any way or owes anything [to you], charge that to my account.

<sup>19</sup>I, Paul, write it with my own hand, I promise to repay it [in full]—and that is to say nothing [of the fact] that you owe me your very self!

<sup>20</sup>Yes, brother, let me have some profit from you in the Lord. Cheer *and* refresh my heart in Christ.

<sup>21</sup>I write to you [perfectly] confident of your obedient compliance, knowing that you will do even more than I ask.

---

[a] 3 The Greek is plural; also in verses 22 and 25; elsewhere in this letter "you" is singular.    [b] 10 *Onesimus* means *useful.*

[a] Marvin Vincent, *Word Studies in the New Testament.*

## New International Version

<sup>22</sup>And one thing more: Prepare a guest room for me, because I hope to be restored to you in answer to your prayers.

<sup>23</sup>Epaphras, my fellow prisoner in Christ Jesus, sends you greetings. <sup>24</sup>And so do Mark, Aristarchus, Demas and Luke, my fellow workers.

<sup>25</sup>The grace of the Lord Jesus Christ be with your spirit.

## Amplified Bible

<sup>22</sup>At the same time prepare a guest room [in expectation of extending your hospitality] to me, for I am hoping through your prayers to be granted [the gracious privilege of coming] to you.

<sup>23</sup>Greetings to you from Epaphras, my fellow prisoner here in [the cause of] Christ Jesus (the Messiah),

<sup>24</sup>And [from] Mark, Aristarchus, Demas, and Luke, my fellow workers.

<sup>25</sup>The grace (blessing and favor) of the Lord Jesus Christ (the Messiah) be with your spirit. *Amen (so be it).*

## New International Version

## Hebrews

### God's Final Word: His Son

**1** In the past God spoke to our ancestors through the prophets at many times and in various ways, ²but in these last days he has spoken to us by his Son, whom he appointed heir of all things, and through whom also he made the universe. ³The Son is the radiance of God's glory and the exact representation of his being, sustaining all things by his powerful word. After he had provided purification for sins, he sat down at the right hand of the Majesty in heaven. ⁴So he became as much superior to the angels as the name he has inherited is superior to theirs.

### The Son Superior to Angels

⁵For to which of the angels did God ever say,

"You are my Son;
today I have become your Father"ᵃ?

Or again,

"I will be his Father,
and he will be my Son"ᵇ?

⁶And again, when God brings his firstborn into the world, he says,

"Let all God's angels worship him."ᶜ

⁷In speaking of the angels he says,

"He makes his angels spirits,
and his servants flames of fire."ᵈ

⁸But about the Son he says,

"Your throne, O God, will last for ever and ever;
a scepter of justice will be the scepter of your kingdom.
⁹You have loved righteousness and hated wickedness;
therefore God, your God, has set you above your companions
by anointing you with the oil of joy."ᵉ

¹⁰He also says,

"In the beginning, Lord, you laid the foundations of the earth,
and the heavens are the work of your hands.
¹¹They will perish, but you remain;
they will all wear out like a garment.
¹²You will roll them up like a robe;
like a garment they will be changed.
But you remain the same,
and your years will never end."ᶠ

¹³To which of the angels did God ever say,

"Sit at my right hand
until I make your enemies
a footstool for your feet"ᵍ?

¹⁴Are not all angels ministering spirits sent to serve those who will inherit salvation?

### Warning to Pay Attention

**2** We must pay the most careful attention, therefore, to what we have heard, so that we do not drift away. ²For since the message spoken through angels was bind-

## Amplified Bible

## Hebrews

**1** In many separate revelations [ᵃeach of which set forth a portion of the Truth] and in different ways God spoke of old to [our] forefathers in *and* by the prophets.

²[But] in ᵇthe last of these days He has spoken to us in [the person of a] Son, Whom He appointed Heir *and* lawful Owner of all things, also by *and* through Whom He created the worlds *and* the reaches of space *and* the ages of time [He made, produced, built, operated, and arranged them in order].

³He is the sole expression of the glory of God [the Light-being, the ᶜout-raying or radiance of the divine], and He is the perfect imprint *and* very image of [God's] nature, upholding *and* maintaining *and* guiding *and* propelling the universe by His mighty word of power. When He had *by offering Himself* accomplished *our* cleansing of sins *and* riddance of guilt, He sat down at the right hand of the divine Majesty on high,

⁴[Taking a place and rank by which] He Himself became as much superior to angels as the glorious Name (title) which He has inherited is different from *and* more excellent than theirs.

⁵For to which of the angels did [God] ever say, You are My Son, today I have begotten You [established You in an official Sonship relation, with kingly dignity]? And again, I will be to Him a Father, and He will be to Me a Son? [II Sam. 7:14; Ps. 2:7.]

⁶Moreover, when He brings the firstborn Son ᵈagain into the habitable world, He says, Let all the angels of God worship Him.

⁷Referring to the angels He says, [God] Who makes His angels winds and His ministering servants flames of fire; [Ps. 104:4.]

⁸But as to the Son, He says to Him, Your throne, O God, is forever and ever (to the ages of the ages), and the scepter of Your kingdom is a scepter of absolute righteousness (of justice and straightforwardness).

⁹You have loved righteousness [You have delighted in integrity, virtue, and uprightness in purpose, thought, and action] and You have hated lawlessness (injustice and iniquity). Therefore God, [even] Your God (ᵉGodhead), has anointed You with the oil of exultant joy *and* gladness above *and* beyond Your companions. [Ps. 45:6, 7.]

¹⁰And [further], You, Lord, did lay the foundation of the earth in the beginning, and the heavens are the works of Your hands.

¹¹They will perish, but You remain *and* continue permanently; they will all grow old *and* wear out like a garment.

¹²Like a mantle [thrown about one's self] You will roll them up, and they will be changed *and* replaced by others. But You remain the same, and Your years will never end *nor* come to failure. [Ps. 102:25-27.]

¹³Besides, to which of the angels has He ever said, Sit at My right hand [associated with Me in My royal dignity] till I make your enemies a stool for your feet? [Ps. 110:1.]

¹⁴Are not the angels all ministering spirits (servants) sent out in the service [of God for the assistance] of those who are to inherit salvation?

**2** Since all this is true, we ought to pay much closer attention than ever to the truths that we have heard, lest in any way we drift past [them] *and* slip away.

²For if the message given through angels [the Law spo-

---

ᵃ 5 Psalm 2:7   ᵇ 5 2 Samuel 7:14; 1 Chron. 17:13   ᶜ 6 Deut. 32:43 (see Dead Sea Scrolls and Septuagint)   ᵈ 7 Psalm 104:4   ᵉ 9 Psalm 45:6,7   ᶠ 12 Psalm 102:25-27   ᵍ 13 Psalm 110:1

ᵃ Marvin Vincent, *Word Studies in the New Testament.*   ᵇ Henry Alford, *The Greek New Testament, with Notes.*   ᶜ Literal translation.   ᵈ Henry Alford, *The Greek New Testament, with Notes* and W. Robertson Nicoll, ed., *The Expositor's Greek New Testament.*   ᵉ Arthur S. Way, *Way's Epistles: The Letters of St. Paul to Seven Churches and Three Friends.*

## New International Version

ing, and every violation and disobedience received its just punishment, [3]how shall we escape if we ignore so great a salvation? This salvation, which was first announced by the Lord, was confirmed to us by those who heard him. [4]God also testified to it by signs, wonders and various miracles, and by gifts of the Holy Spirit distributed according to his will.

### Jesus Made Fully Human

[5]It is not to angels that he has subjected the world to come, about which we are speaking. [6]But there is a place where someone has testified:

"What is mankind that you are mindful of them,
     a son of man that you care for him?
[7]You made them a little[a] lower than the angels;
     you crowned them with glory and honor
[8]     and put everything under their feet."[b,c]

In putting everything under them,[d] God left nothing that is not subject to them.[d] Yet at present we do not see everything subject to them.[d] [9]But we do see Jesus, who was made lower than the angels for a little while, now crowned with glory and honor because he suffered death, so that by the grace of God he might taste death for everyone.

[10]In bringing many sons and daughters to glory, it was fitting that God, for whom and through whom everything exists, should make the pioneer of their salvation perfect through what he suffered. [11]Both the one who makes people holy and those who are made holy are of the same family. So Jesus is not ashamed to call them brothers and sisters.[e] [12]He says,

"I will declare your name to my brothers and sisters;
     in the assembly I will sing your praises."[f]

[13]And again,

"I will put my trust in him."[g]

And again he says,

"Here am I, and the children God has given me."[h]

[14]Since the children have flesh and blood, he too shared in their humanity so that by his death he might break the power of him who holds the power of death—that is, the devil— [15]and free those who all their lives were held in slavery by their fear of death. [16]For surely it is not angels he helps, but Abraham's descendants. [17]For this reason he had to be made like them,[i] fully human in every way, in order that he might become a merciful and faithful high priest in service to God, and that he might make atonement for the sins of the people. [18]Because he himself suf-

---

[a] 7 Or *them for a little while*   [b] 6-8 Psalm 8:4-6   [c] 7,8 Or *You made him a little lower than the angels;/ you crowned him with glory and honor/ [8]and put everything under his feet."*   [d] 8 Or *him*   [e] 11 The Greek word for *brothers and sisters (adelphoi)* refers here to believers, both men and women, as part of God's family; also in verse 12; and in 3:1, 12; 10:19; 13:22.   [f] 12 Psalm 22:22   [g] 13 Isaiah 8:17   [h] 13 Isaiah 8:18   [i] 17 Or *like his brothers*

## Amplified Bible

ken by them to Moses] was authentic *and* proved sure, and every violation and disobedience received an appropriate (just and adequate) penalty,

[3]How shall we escape [appropriate retribution] if we neglect *and* refuse to pay attention to such a great salvation [as is now offered to us, letting it drift past us forever]? For it was declared at first by the Lord [Himself], and it was confirmed to us *and* proved to be real *and* genuine by those who personally heard [Him speak].

[4][Besides this evidence] it was also established *and* plainly endorsed by God, Who showed His approval of it by signs and wonders and various miraculous manifestations of [His] power and by imparting the gifts of the Holy Spirit [to the believers] according to His own will.

[5]For it was not to angels that God subjected the habitable world of the future, of which we are speaking.

[6]It has been solemnly *and* earnestly said in a certain place, What is man that You are mindful of him, or the son of man that You graciously *and* helpfully care for *and* visit *and* look after him?

[7]For some little time You have ranked him lower than *and* inferior to the angels; You have crowned him with glory and honor *and set him over the works of Your hands,* [Ps. 8:4-6.]

[8]For You have put everything in subjection under his feet. Now in putting everything in subjection to man, He left nothing outside [of man's] control. But at present we do not yet see all things subjected to him [man].

[9]But we are able to see Jesus, Who was ranked lower than the angels for a little while, crowned with glory and honor because of His having suffered death, in order that by the grace (unmerited favor) of God [to us sinners] He might experience death for every individual person.

[10]For it was an act worthy [of God] *and* fitting [to the divine nature] that He, for Whose sake and by Whom all things have their existence, in bringing many sons into glory, should make the Pioneer of their salvation perfect [should bring to maturity the human experience necessary to be perfectly equipped for His office as High Priest] through suffering.

[11]For both He Who sanctifies [making men holy] and those who are sanctified all have one [Father]. For this reason He is not ashamed to call them brethren;

[12]For He says, I will declare Your [the Father's] name to My brethren; in the midst of the [worshiping] congregation I will sing hymns of praise to You. [Ps. 22:22.]

[13]And again He says, My trust *and* assured reliance *and* confident hope shall be fixed in Him. And yet again, Here I am, I and the children whom God has given Me. [Isa. 8:17, 18.]

[14]Since, therefore, [these His] children share in flesh and blood [in the physical nature of human beings], He [Himself] in a similar manner partook of the same [nature], that by [going through] death He might bring to nought *and* make of no effect him who had the power of death—that is, the devil—

[15]And also that He might deliver *and* completely set free all those who through the [haunting] fear of death were held in bondage throughout the whole course of their lives.

[16]For, as we all know, He [Christ] did not take hold of angels [[a]the fallen angels, to give them a helping and delivering hand], but He did take hold of [[a]the fallen] descendants of Abraham [to reach out to them a helping and delivering hand]. [Isa. 41:8, 9.]

[17]So it is evident that it was essential that He be made like His brethren in every respect, in order that He might become a merciful (sympathetic) and faithful High Priest in the things related to God, to make atonement *and* propitiation for the people's sins.

---

[a] Matthew Henry, *Commentary on the Holy Bible.*

# New International Version

fered when he was tempted, he is able to help those who are being tempted.

## Jesus Greater Than Moses

**3** Therefore, holy brothers and sisters, who share in the heavenly calling, fix your thoughts on Jesus, whom we acknowledge as our apostle and high priest. ²He was faithful to the one who appointed him, just as Moses was faithful in all God's house. ³Jesus has been found worthy of greater honor than Moses, just as the builder of a house has greater honor than the house itself. ⁴For every house is built by someone, but God is the builder of everything. ⁵"Moses was faithful as a servant in all God's house,"ᵃ bearing witness to what would be spoken by God in the future. ⁶But Christ is faithful as the Son over God's house. And we are his house, if indeed we hold firmly to our confidence and the hope in which we glory.

## Warning Against Unbelief

⁷So, as the Holy Spirit says:

"Today, if you hear his voice,
⁸   do not harden your hearts
   as you did in the rebellion,
      during the time of testing in the wilderness,
⁹where your ancestors tested and tried me,
      though for forty years they saw what I did.
¹⁰That is why I was angry with that generation;
   I said, 'Their hearts are always going astray,
      and they have not known my ways.'
¹¹So I declared on oath in my anger,
   'They shall never enter my rest.'"ᵇ

¹²See to it, brothers and sisters, that none of you has a sinful, unbelieving heart that turns away from the living God. ¹³But encourage one another daily, as long as it is called "Today," so that none of you may be hardened by sin's deceitfulness. ¹⁴We have come to share in Christ, if indeed we hold our original conviction firmly to the very end. ¹⁵As has just been said:

"Today, if you hear his voice,
   do not harden your hearts
   as you did in the rebellion."ᶜ

¹⁶Who were they who heard and rebelled? Were they not all those Moses led out of Egypt? ¹⁷And with whom

# Amplified Bible

¹⁸For because He Himself [in His humanity] has suffered in being tempted (tested and tried), He is able [immediately] ᵃto run to the cry of (assist, relieve) those who are being tempted *and* tested *and* tried [and who therefore are being exposed to suffering].

**3** So then, brethren, consecrated *and* set apart for God, who share in the heavenly calling, [thoughtfully and attentively] consider Jesus, the Apostle and High Priest Whom we confessed [as ours when we embraced the Christian faith].

²[See how] faithful He was to Him Who appointed Him [Apostle and High Priest], as Moses was also faithful in the whole house [of God]. [Num. 12:7.]

³Yet Jesus has been considered worthy of much greater honor *and* glory than Moses, just as the builder of a house has more honor than the house [itself].

⁴For [of course] every house is built *and* furnished by someone, but the Builder of all things and the Furnisher [of the entire equipment of all things] is God.

⁵And Moses certainly was faithful in the administration of all God's house [but it was only] as a ministering servant. [In his entire ministry he was but] a testimony to the things which were to be spoken [the revelations to be given afterward in Christ]. [Num. 12:7.]

⁶But Christ (the Messiah) was faithful over His [own Father's] house as a Son [and Master of it]. And it is we who are [now members] of this house, if we hold *fast and firm to the end* our joyful *and* exultant confidence and sense of triumph in our hope [in Christ].

⁷Therefore, as the Holy Spirit says: Today, if you will hear His voice,

⁸Do not harden your hearts, as [happened] in the rebellion [of Israel] *and* their provocation *and* ᵇembitterment [of Me] in the day of testing in the wilderness,

⁹Where your fathers tried [My patience] *and* tested [My forbearance] *and* ᶜfound I stood their test, and they saw My works for forty years.

¹⁰And so I was provoked (displeased and sorely grieved) with that generation, and said, They always err *and* are led astray in their hearts, and they have not perceived *or* recognized My ways *and* become progressively better *and* more experimentally *and* intimately acquainted with them.

¹¹Accordingly, I swore in My wrath *and* indignation, They shall not enter into My rest. [Ps. 95:7-11.]

¹²[Therefore beware] brethren, take care, lest there be in any one of you a wicked, unbelieving heart [which refuses to cleave to, trust in, and rely on Him], leading you to turn away *and* desert *or* stand aloof from the living God.

¹³But instead warn (admonish, urge, and encourage) one another every day, as long as it is called Today, that none of you may be hardened [into settled rebellion] by the deceitfulness of sin [by the fraudulence, the stratagem, the trickery which the delusive glamor of his sin may play on him].

¹⁴For we ᵈhave become fellows with Christ (the Messiah) *and* share in all He has for us, if only we hold our first newborn confidence *and* original assured expectation [in virtue of which we are believers] firm *and* unshaken to the end.

¹⁵Then while it is [still] called Today, if you would hear His voice *and* when you hear it, do not harden your hearts as in the rebellion [in the desert, when the people provoked and irritated and embittered God against them]. [Ps. 95:7, 8.]

¹⁶For who were they who heard *and* yet were rebellious *and* provoked [Him]? Was it not all those who came out of Egypt led by Moses?

---

ᵃ Kenneth Wuest, *Word Studies in the New Testament.* ᵇ Alexander Souter, *Pocket Lexicon of the Greek New Testament.* ᶜ Charles B. Williams, *The New Testament: A Translation in the Language of the People.* ᵈ Marvin Vincent, *Word Studies.*

ᵃ 5 Num. 12:7   ᵇ 11 Psalm 95:7-11   ᶜ 15 Psalm 95:7,8

# New International Version

was he angry for forty years? Was it not with those who sinned, whose bodies perished in the wilderness? [18] And to whom did God swear that they would never enter his rest if not to those who disobeyed? [19] So we see that they were not able to enter, because of their unbelief.

## A Sabbath-Rest for the People of God

4 Therefore, since the promise of entering his rest still stands, let us be careful that none of you be found to have fallen short of it. [2] For we also have had the good news proclaimed to us, just as they did; but the message they heard was of no value to them, because they did not share the faith of those who obeyed.[a] [3] Now we who have believed enter that rest, just as God has said,

"So I declared on oath in my anger,
'They shall never enter my rest.'"[b]

And yet his works have been finished since the creation of the world. [4] For somewhere he has spoken about the seventh day in these words: "On the seventh day God rested from all his works."[c] [5] And again in the passage above he says, "They shall never enter my rest."

[6] Therefore since it still remains for some to enter that rest, and since those who formerly had the good news proclaimed to them did not go in because of their disobedience, [7] God again set a certain day, calling it "Today." This he did when a long time later he spoke through David, as in the passage already quoted:

"Today, if you hear his voice,
do not harden your hearts."[d]

[8] For if Joshua had given them rest, God would not have spoken later about another day. [9] There remains, then, a Sabbath-rest for the people of God; [10] for anyone who enters God's rest also rests from their works,[e] just as God did from his. [11] Let us, therefore, make every effort to enter that rest, so that no one will perish by following their example of disobedience.

[12] For the word of God is alive and active. Sharper than any double-edged sword, it penetrates even to dividing soul and spirit, joints and marrow; it judges the thoughts

# Amplified Bible

[17] And with whom was He irritated *and* provoked *and* grieved for forty years? Was it not with those who sinned, whose [a]dismembered bodies were strewn *and* left in the desert?

[18] And to whom did He swear that they should not enter His rest, but to those who disobeyed [who had not listened to His word and who refused to be compliant or be persuaded]?

[19] So we see that they were not able to enter [into His rest], because of their unwillingness to adhere to *and* trust in *and* rely on God [unbelief had shut them out]. [Num. 14:1-35.]

4 Therefore, while the promise of entering His rest still holds *and* is offered [today], let us be afraid [[a]to distrust it], lest any of you should [a]think he has come too late *and* has come short of [reaching] it.

[2] For indeed we have had the glad tidings [Gospel of God] proclaimed to us just as truly as they [the Israelites of old did when the good news of deliverance from bondage came to them]; but the message they heard did not benefit them, because it was not mixed with faith (with [b]the leaning of the entire personality on God in absolute trust and confidence in His power, wisdom, and goodness) by those who heard it; [c]*neither were they united in faith with the ones [Joshua and Caleb] who heard (did believe).*

[3] For we who have believed (adhered to and trusted in and relied on God) do enter that rest, [a]in accordance with His declaration that those [who did not believe] should not enter when He said, As I swore in My wrath, They shall not enter My rest; and this He said although [His] works had been completed *and* prepared [and waiting for all who would believe] from the foundation of the world. [Ps. 95:11.]

[4] For in a certain place He has said this about the seventh day: And God rested on the seventh day from all His works. [Gen. 2:2.]

[5] And [they forfeited their part in it, for] in this [passage] He said, They shall not enter My rest. [Ps. 95:11.]

[6] Seeing then that the promise remains over [from past times] for some to enter that rest, and that those who formerly were given the good news about it *and* the opportunity, failed to appropriate it *and* did not enter because of disobedience,

[7] Again He sets a definite day, [a new] Today, [and gives another opportunity of securing that rest] saying through David after so long a time in the words already quoted, Today, if you would hear His voice *and* when you hear it, do not harden your hearts. [Ps. 95:7, 8.]

[8] [This mention of a rest was not a reference to their entering into Canaan.] For if Joshua had given them rest, He [God] would not speak afterward about another day.

[9] So then, there is still awaiting a full *and* complete Sabbath-rest reserved for the [true] people of God;

[10] For he who has once entered [God's] rest also has ceased from [the weariness and pain of] human labors, just as God rested from those labors [a]peculiarly His own. [Gen. 2:2.]

[11] Let us therefore be zealous *and* exert ourselves *and* strive diligently to enter that rest [of God, to know and experience it for ourselves], that no one may fall *or* perish by the same kind of unbelief *and* disobedience [into which those in the wilderness fell].

[12] For the Word that God speaks is alive and full of power [making it active, operative, energizing, and effective]; it is sharper than any two-edged sword, penetrating to the dividing line of the [d]breath of life (soul) and [the immortal] spirit, and of joints and marrow [of the deepest parts of our nature], exposing *and* sifting *and* analyzing *and* judging the very thoughts and purposes of the heart.

---

[a] 2 Some manuscripts *because those who heard did not combine it with faith* [b] 3 Psalm 95:11; also in verse 5 [c] 4 Gen. 2:2 [d] 7 Psalm 95:7,8 [e] 10 Or *labor*

[a] Marvin Vincent, *Word Studies.* [b] Alexander Souter, *Pocket Lexicon.* [c] Many manuscripts so read. [d] Joseph Thayer, *A Greek-English Lexicon of the New Testament.*

## New International Version

and attitudes of the heart. [13]Nothing in all creation is hidden from God's sight. Everything is uncovered and laid bare before the eyes of him to whom we must give account.

### Jesus the Great High Priest

[14]Therefore, since we have a great high priest who has ascended into heaven,[a] Jesus the Son of God, let us hold firmly to the faith we profess. [15]For we do not have a high priest who is unable to empathize with our weaknesses, but we have one who has been tempted in every way, just as we are—yet he did not sin. [16]Let us then approach God's throne of grace with confidence, so that we may receive mercy and find grace to help us in our time of need.

**5** Every high priest is selected from among the people and is appointed to represent the people in matters related to God, to offer gifts and sacrifices for sins. [2]He is able to deal gently with those who are ignorant and are going astray, since he himself is subject to weakness. [3]This is why he has to offer sacrifices for his own sins, as well as for the sins of the people. [4]And no one takes this honor on himself, but he receives it when called by God, just as Aaron was.

[5]In the same way, Christ did not take on himself the glory of becoming a high priest. But God said to him,

"You are my Son;
today I have become your Father."[b]

[6]And he says in another place,

"You are a priest forever,
in the order of Melchizedek."[c]

[7]During the days of Jesus' life on earth, he offered up prayers and petitions with fervent cries and tears to the one who could save him from death, and he was heard because of his reverent submission. [8]Son though he was, he learned obedience from what he suffered [9]and, once made perfect, he became the source of eternal salvation for all who obey him [10]and was designated by God to be high priest in the order of Melchizedek.

### Warning Against Falling Away

[11]We have much to say about this, but it is hard to make it clear to you because you no longer try to understand. [12]In fact, though by this time you ought to be teachers, you need someone to teach you the elementary truths of God's word all over again. You need milk, not solid food! [13]Anyone who lives on milk, being still an infant, is not acquainted with the teaching about righteousness. [14]But sol-

## Amplified Bible

[13]And not a creature exists that is concealed from His sight, but all things are open *and* exposed, naked *and* defenseless to the eyes of Him with Whom we have to do.

[14]Inasmuch then as we have a great High Priest Who has [already] ascended *and* passed through the heavens, Jesus the Son of God, let us hold fast our confession [of faith in Him].

[15]For we do not have a High Priest Who is unable to understand *and* sympathize *and* have a shared feeling with our weaknesses *and* infirmities *and* liability to the assaults of temptation, but One Who has been tempted in every respect as we are, yet without sinning.

[16]Let us then fearlessly *and* confidently *and* boldly draw near to the throne of grace (the throne of God's unmerited favor to us sinners), that we may receive mercy [for our failures] and find grace to help in good time for every need [appropriate help and well-timed help, coming just when we need it].

**5** For every high priest chosen from among men is appointed to act on behalf of men in things relating to God, to offer both gifts and sacrifices for sins.

[2]He is able to exercise gentleness *and* forbearance toward the ignorant and erring, since he himself also is liable to moral weakness *and* physical infirmity.

[3]And because of this he is obliged to offer sacrifice for his own sins, as well as for those of the people.

[4]Besides, one does not appropriate for himself the honor [of being high priest], but he is called by God *and* receives it of Him, just as Aaron did.

[5]So too Christ (the Messiah) did not exalt Himself to be made a high priest, but was appointed *and* exalted by Him Who said to Him, You are My Son; today I have begotten You; [Ps. 2:7.]

[6]As He says also in another place, You are a Priest [appointed] forever after the order (with [a]the rank) of Melchizedek. [Ps. 110:4.]

[7]In the days of His flesh [Jesus] offered up definite, special petitions [for that which He not only wanted [b]but needed] and supplications with strong crying and tears to Him Who was [always] able to save Him [out] from death, and He was heard because of His reverence toward God [His godly fear, His piety, [c]in that He shrank from the horrors of separation from the bright presence of the Father].

[8]Although He was a Son, He learned [active, special] obedience through what He suffered

[9]And, [His completed experience] making Him perfectly [equipped], He became the Author *and* Source of eternal salvation to all those who give heed *and* obey Him, [Isa. 45:17.]

[10]Being [d]designated *and* recognized *and* saluted by God as High Priest after the order (with [a]the rank) of Melchizedek. [Ps. 110:4.]

[11]Concerning this we have much to say which is hard to explain, since you have become dull in your [spiritual] hearing *and* sluggish [even [b]slothful in achieving spiritual insight].

[12]For even though by this time you ought to be teaching others, you actually need someone to teach you over again the very first principles of God's Word. You have come to need milk, not solid food.

[13]For everyone who continues to feed on milk is obviously inexperienced *and* unskilled in the doctrine of righteousness (of conformity to the divine will in purpose, thought, and action), for he is a mere infant [not able to talk yet]!

[a] Joseph Thayer, *A Greek-English Lexicon.* [b] G. Abbott-Smith, *Manual Greek Lexicon of the New Testament.* [c] Robert Jamieson, A. R. Fausset and David Brown, *A Commentary on the Old and New Testaments.* [d] Alexander Souter, *Pocket Lexicon.*

[a] 14 Greek *has gone through the heavens*    [b] 5 Psalm 2:7
[c] 6 Psalm 110:4

## New International Version

id food is for the mature, who by constant use have trained themselves to distinguish good from evil.

**6** Therefore let us move beyond the elementary teachings about Christ and be taken forward to maturity, not laying again the foundation of repentance from acts that lead to death,[a] and of faith in God, [2]instruction about cleansing rites,[b] the laying on of hands, the resurrection of the dead, and eternal judgment. [3]And God permitting, we will do so.

[4]It is impossible for those who have once been enlightened, who have tasted the heavenly gift, who have shared in the Holy Spirit, [5]who have tasted the goodness of the word of God and the powers of the coming age [6]and who have fallen[c] away, to be brought back to repentance. To their loss they are crucifying the Son of God all over again and subjecting him to public disgrace. [7]Land that drinks in the rain often falling on it and that produces a crop useful to those for whom it is farmed receives the blessing of God. [8]But land that produces thorns and thistles is worthless and is in danger of being cursed. In the end it will be burned.

[9]Even though we speak like this, dear friends, we are convinced of better things in your case—the things that have to do with salvation. [10]God is not unjust; he will not forget your work and the love you have shown him as you have helped his people and continue to help them. [11]We want each of you to show this same diligence to the very end, so that what you hope for may be fully realized. [12]We do not want you to become lazy, but to imitate those who through faith and patience inherit what has been promised.

### The Certainty of God's Promise

[13]When God made his promise to Abraham, since there was no one greater for him to swear by, he swore by himself, [14]saying, "I will surely bless you and give you many descendants."[d] [15]And so after waiting patiently, Abraham received what was promised.

[16]People swear by someone greater than themselves, and the oath confirms what is said and puts an end to all argument. [17]Because God wanted to make the unchanging nature of his purpose very clear to the heirs of what was promised, he confirmed it with an oath. [18]God did this

## Amplified Bible

[14]But solid food is for full-grown men, for those whose senses *and* mental faculties are trained by practice to discriminate *and* distinguish between what is morally good *and* noble and what is evil *and* contrary either to divine or human law.

**6** Therefore let us go on and get past the elementary stage in the teachings *and* doctrine of Christ (the Messiah), advancing steadily toward the completeness *and* perfection that belong to spiritual maturity. Let us not again be laying the foundation of repentance *and* abandonment of dead works (dead formalism) and of the faith [by which you turned] to God,

[2]With teachings about purifying, the laying on of hands, the resurrection from the dead, and eternal judgment *and* punishment. [These are all matters of which you should have been fully aware long, long ago.]

[3]If indeed God permits, we will [now] proceed [to advanced teaching].

[4]For it is impossible [to restore and bring again to repentance] those who have been once for all enlightened, who have consciously tasted the heavenly gift and have become sharers of the Holy Spirit,

[5]And have felt how good the Word of God is and the mighty powers of the age *and* world to come,

[6]If they then deviate from the faith *and* turn away from their allegiance—[it is impossible] to bring them back to repentance, for (because, while, as long as) they nail upon the cross the Son of God afresh [as far as they are concerned] and are holding [Him] up to contempt *and* shame *and* public disgrace.

[7]For the soil which has drunk the rain that repeatedly falls upon it and produces vegetation useful to those for whose benefit it is cultivated partakes of a blessing from God.

[8]But if [that same soil] persistently bears thorns and thistles, it is considered worthless and near to being cursed, whose end is to be burned. [Gen. 3:17, 18.]

[9]Even though we speak this way, yet in your case, beloved, we are now firmly convinced of better things that are near to salvation *and* accompany it.

[10]For God is not unrighteous to forget *or* overlook your labor and the love which you have shown for His name's sake in ministering to the needs of the saints (His own consecrated people), as you still do.

[11]But we do [[a]strongly and earnestly] desire for each of you to show the same diligence *and* sincerity [all the way through] in realizing *and* enjoying the full assurance *and* development of [your] hope until the end,

[12]In order that you may not grow disinterested *and* become [spiritual] sluggards, but imitators, behaving as do those who through faith ([b]by their leaning of the entire personality on God in Christ in absolute trust and confidence in His power, wisdom, and goodness) and by practice of patient endurance *and* waiting are [now] inheriting the promises.

[13]For when God made [His] promise to Abraham, He swore by Himself, since He had no one greater by whom to swear,

[14]Saying, Blessing I certainly will bless you and multiplying I will multiply you. [Gen. 22:16, 17.]

[15]And so it was that he [Abraham], having waited long *and* endured patiently, realized *and* obtained [in the birth of Isaac as a pledge of what was to come] what God had promised him.

[16]Men indeed swear by a greater [than themselves], and with them in all disputes the oath taken for confirmation is final [ending strife].

[17]Accordingly God also, in His desire to show more convincingly *and* beyond doubt to those who were to inherit the promise the unchangeableness of His purpose *and* plan, intervened (mediated) with an oath.

---

[a] 1 Or *from useless rituals*    [b] 2 Or *about baptisms*    [c] 6 Or *age,* [6]*if they fall*    [d] 14 Gen. 22:17

[a] Marvin Vincent, *Word Studies.*    [b] Alexander Souter, *Pocket Lexicon.*

## New International Version

so that, by two unchangeable things in which it is impossible for God to lie, we who have fled to take hold of the hope set before us may be greatly encouraged. [19]We have this hope as an anchor for the soul, firm and secure. It enters the inner sanctuary behind the curtain, [20]where our forerunner, Jesus, has entered on our behalf. He has become a high priest forever, in the order of Melchizedek.

### Melchizedek the Priest

[7] This Melchizedek was king of Salem and priest of God Most High. He met Abraham returning from the defeat of the kings and blessed him, [2]and Abraham gave him a tenth of everything. First, the name Melchizedek means "king of righteousness"; then also, "king of Salem" means "king of peace." [3]Without father or mother, without genealogy, without beginning of days or end of life, resembling the Son of God, he remains a priest forever.

[4]Just think how great he was: Even the patriarch Abraham gave him a tenth of the plunder! [5]Now the law requires the descendants of Levi who become priests to collect a tenth from the people—that is, from their fellow Israelites—even though they also are descended from Abraham. [6]This man, however, did not trace his descent from Levi, yet he collected a tenth from Abraham and blessed him who had the promises. [7]And without doubt the lesser is blessed by the greater. [8]In the one case, the tenth is collected by people who die; but in the other case, by him who is declared to be living. [9]One might even say that Levi, who collects the tenth, paid the tenth through Abraham, [10]because when Melchizedek met Abraham, Levi was still in the body of his ancestor.

### Jesus Like Melchizedek

[11]If perfection could have been attained through the Levitical priesthood—and indeed the law given to the people established that priesthood—why was there still need for another priest to come, one in the order of Melchizedek, not in the order of Aaron? [12]For when the priesthood is changed, the law must be changed also. [13]He of whom these things are said belonged to a different tribe, and no one from that tribe has ever served at the altar. [14]For it is clear that our Lord descended from Judah, and in regard to that tribe Moses said nothing about priests. [15]And what we have said is even more clear if another priest like Melchizedek appears, [16]one who has become a priest not on the basis of a regulation as to his ancestry but on the basis of the power of an indestructible life. [17]For it is declared:

## Amplified Bible

[18]This was so that, by two unchangeable things [His promise and His oath] in which it is impossible for God ever to prove false or deceive us, we who have fled [to Him] for refuge might have mighty indwelling strength and strong encouragement to grasp and hold fast the hope appointed for us and set before [us].

[19][Now] we have this [hope] as a sure and steadfast anchor of the soul [it cannot slip and it cannot [a]break down under whoever steps out upon it—a hope] that reaches [a]farther and enters into [the very certainty of the Presence] within the veil, [Lev. 16:2.]

[20]Where Jesus has entered in for us [in advance], a Forerunner having become a High Priest forever after the order (with [b]the rank) of Melchizedek. [Ps. 110:4.]

[7] For this Melchizedek, king of Salem [and] priest of the Most High God, met Abraham as he returned from the slaughter of the kings and blessed him,

[2]And Abraham gave to him a tenth portion of all [the spoil]. He is primarily, as his name when translated indicates, king of righteousness, and then he is also king of Salem, which means king of peace.

[3]Without [record of] father or mother or ancestral line, neither with beginning of days nor ending of life, but, resembling the Son of God, he continues to be a priest without interruption and without successor.

[4]Now observe and consider how great [a personage] this was to whom even Abraham the patriarch gave a tenth [the topmost or the pick of the heap] of the spoils.

[5]And it is true that those descendants of Levi who are charged with the priestly office are commanded in the Law to take tithes from the people—which means, from their brethren—though these have descended from Abraham.

[6]But this person who has not their Levitical ancestry received tithes from Abraham [himself] and blessed him who possessed the promises [of God].

[7]Yet it is beyond all contradiction that it is the lesser person who is blessed by the greater one.

[8]Furthermore, here [in the Levitical priesthood] tithes are received by men who are subject to death; while there [in the case of Melchizedek], they are received by one of whom it is testified that he lives [perpetually].

[9]A person might even say that Levi [the father of the priestly tribe] himself, who received tithes (the tenth), paid tithes through Abraham,

[10]For he was still in the loins of his forefather [Abraham] when Melchizedek met him [Abraham].

[11]Now if perfection (a perfect fellowship between God and the worshiper) had been attainable by the Levitical priesthood—for under it the people were given the Law—why was it further necessary that there should arise another and different kind of Priest, one after the order of Melchizedek, rather than one appointed after the order and rank of Aaron?

[12]For when there is a change in the priesthood, there is of necessity an alteration of the law [concerning the priesthood] as well.

[13]For the One of Whom these things are said belonged [not to the priestly line but] to another tribe, no member of which has officiated at the altar.

[14]For it is obvious that our Lord sprang from the tribe of Judah, and Moses mentioned nothing about priests in connection with that tribe.

[15]And this becomes more plainly evident when another Priest arises Who bears the likeness of Melchizedek, [Ps. 110:4.]

[16]Who has been constituted a Priest, not on the basis of a bodily legal requirement [an externally imposed command concerning His physical ancestry], but on the basis of the power of an endless and indestructible Life.

[a] Marvin Vincent, *Word Studies.* [b] Joseph Thayer, *A Greek-English Lexicon.*

## New International Version

"You are a priest forever,
in the order of Melchizedek."[a]

18The former regulation is set aside because it was weak and useless 19(for the law made nothing perfect), and a better hope is introduced, by which we draw near to God.

20And it was not without an oath! Others became priests without any oath, 21but he became a priest with an oath when God said to him:

"The Lord has sworn
and will not change his mind:
'You are a priest forever.'"[a]

22Because of this oath, Jesus has become the guarantor of a better covenant.

23Now there have been many of those priests, since death prevented them from continuing in office; 24but because Jesus lives forever, he has a permanent priesthood. 25Therefore he is able to save completely[b] those who come to God through him, because he always lives to intercede for them.

26Such a high priest truly meets our need—one who is holy, blameless, pure, set apart from sinners, exalted above the heavens. 27Unlike the other high priests, he does not need to offer sacrifices day after day, first for his own sins, and then for the sins of the people. He sacrificed for their sins once for all when he offered himself. 28For the law appoints as high priests men in all their weakness; but the oath, which came after the law, appointed the Son, who has been made perfect forever.

### The High Priest of a New Covenant

**8** Now the main point of what we are saying is this: We do have such a high priest, who sat down at the right hand of the throne of the Majesty in heaven, 2and who serves in the sanctuary, the true tabernacle set up by the Lord, not by a mere human being.

3Every high priest is appointed to offer both gifts and sacrifices, and so it was necessary for this one also to have something to offer. 4If he were on earth, he would not be a priest, for there are already priests who offer the gifts prescribed by the law. 5They serve at a sanctuary that is a copy and shadow of what is in heaven. This is why Moses was warned when he was about to build the tabernacle: "See to it that you make everything according to the pattern shown you on the mountain."[c] 6But in fact the ministry Jesus has received is as superior to theirs as the covenant of which he is mediator is superior to the old one, since the new covenant is established on better promises.

## Amplified Bible

17For it is witnessed of Him, You are a Priest forever after the order (with the rank) of Melchizedek. [Ps. 110:4.]

18So a previous physical regulation *and* command is cancelled because of its weakness *and* ineffectiveness and uselessness—

19For the Law never made anything perfect—but instead a better hope is introduced through which we [now] come close to God.

20And it was not without the taking of an oath [that Christ was made Priest],

21For those who formerly became priests received their office without its being confirmed by the taking of an oath by God, but this One was designated *and* addressed *and* saluted with an oath, The Lord has sworn and will not regret it *or* change His mind, You are a Priest forever *according to the order of Melchizedek*. [Ps. 110:4.]

22In keeping with [the oath's greater strength and force], Jesus has become the Guarantee of a better (stronger) agreement [a more excellent and more advantageous covenant].

23[Again, the former successive line of priests] was made up of many, because they were each prevented by death from continuing [perpetually in office];

24But He holds His priesthood unchangeably, because He lives on forever.

25Therefore He is able also to save to the uttermost (completely, perfectly, finally, and for all time and eternity) those who come to God through Him, since He is always living to make petition to God *and* intercede with Him *and* intervene for them.

26[Here is] the High Priest [perfectly adapted] to our needs, as was fitting—holy, blameless, unstained by sin, separated from sinners, and exalted higher than the heavens.

27He has no day by day necessity, as [do each of these other] high priests, to offer sacrifice first of all for his own [personal] sins and then for those of the people, because He [met all the requirements] once for all when He brought Himself [as a sacrifice] which He offered up.

28For the Law sets up men in their weakness [frail, sinful, dying human beings] as high priests, but the word of [God's] oath, which [was spoken later] after the institution of the Law, [chooses and appoints as priest One Whose appointment is complete and permanent], a Son Who has been made perfect forever. [Ps. 110:4.]

**8** Now the main point of what we have to say is this: We have such a High Priest, One Who is seated at the right hand of the majestic [God] in heaven, [Ps. 110:1.]

2As officiating Priest, a Minister in the holy places *and* in the true tabernacle which is erected not by man but by the Lord.

3For every high priest is appointed to offer up gifts and sacrifices; so it is essential for this [High Priest] to have some offering to make also.

4If then He were still living on earth, He would not be a priest at all, for there are [already priests] who offer the gifts in accordance with the Law.

5[But these offer] service [merely] as a pattern and as a foreshadowing of [what has its true existence and reality in] the heavenly sanctuary. For when Moses was about to erect the tabernacle, he was warned by God, saying, See to it that you make it all [exactly] according to the copy (the model) which was shown to you on the mountain. [Exod. 25:40.]

6But as it now is, He [Christ] has acquired a [priestly] ministry which is as much superior *and* more excellent [than the old] as the covenant (the agreement) of which He is the Mediator (the Arbiter, Agent) is superior *and* more excellent, [because] it is enacted *and* rests upon more important (sublimer, higher, and nobler) promises.

---

[a] 17,21 Psalm 110:4    [b] 25 Or *forever*    [c] 5 Exodus 25:40

## New International Version

### Amplified Bible

**New International Version**

7For if there had been nothing wrong with that first covenant, no place would have been sought for another. 8But God found fault with the people and said*a*:

"The days are coming, declares the Lord,
    when I will make a new covenant
with the people of Israel
    and with the people of Judah.
9It will not be like the covenant
    I made with their ancestors
when I took them by the hand
    to lead them out of Egypt,
because they did not remain faithful to my covenant,
    and I turned away from them,
                                    declares the Lord.
10This is the covenant I will establish with the people of
    Israel
    after that time, declares the Lord.
I will put my laws in their minds
    and write them on their hearts.
I will be their God,
    and they will be my people.
11No longer will they teach their neighbor,
    or say to one another, 'Know the Lord,'
because they will all know me,
    from the least of them to the greatest.
12For I will forgive their wickedness
    and will remember their sins no more."*b*

13By calling this covenant "new," he has made the first one obsolete; and what is obsolete and outdated will soon disappear.

#### Worship in the Earthly Tabernacle

**9** Now the first covenant had regulations for worship and also an earthly sanctuary. 2A tabernacle was set up. In its first room were the lampstand and the table with its consecrated bread; this was called the Holy Place. 3Behind the second curtain was a room called the Most Holy Place, 4which had the golden altar of incense and the gold-covered ark of the covenant. This ark contained the gold jar of manna, Aaron's staff that had budded, and the stone tablets of the covenant. 5Above the ark were the cherubim of the Glory, overshadowing the atonement cover. But we cannot discuss these things in detail now.

6When everything had been arranged like this, the priests entered regularly into the outer room to carry on their ministry. 7But only the high priest entered the inner room, and that only once a year, and never without blood, which he offered for himself and for the sins the people had committed in ignorance. 8The Holy Spirit was showing by this that the way into the Most Holy Place had not yet been disclosed as long as the first tabernacle was still functioning. 9This is an illustration for the present time,

**Amplified Bible**

7For if that first covenant had been without defect, there would have been no room for another one *or* an attempt to institute another one.

8However, He finds fault with them [showing its inadequacy] when He says, Behold, the days will come, says the Lord, when I will make *and* ratify a new covenant *or* agreement with the house of Israel and with the house of Judah.

9It will not be like the covenant that I made with their forefathers on the day when I grasped them by the hand to help *and* relieve them *and* to lead them out from the land of Egypt, for they did not abide in My agreement with them, and so I withdrew My favor *and* disregarded them, says the Lord.

10For this is the covenant that I will make with the house of Israel after those days, says the Lord: I will imprint My laws upon their minds, even upon their innermost thoughts *and* understanding, and engrave them upon their hearts; and I will be their God, and they shall be My people.

11And it will nevermore be necessary for each one to teach his neighbor and his fellow citizen or each one his brother, saying, Know (perceive, have knowledge of, and get acquainted by experience with) the Lord, for all will know Me, from the smallest to the greatest of them.

12For I will be merciful *and* gracious toward their sins and I will remember their deeds of unrighteousness no more. [Jer. 31:31-34.]

13When God speaks of a new [covenant or agreement], He makes the first one obsolete (out of use). And what is obsolete (out of use and annulled because of age) is ripe for disappearance *and* to be dispensed with altogether.

**9** Now even the first covenant had its own rules *and* regulations for divine worship, and it had a sanctuary [but one] of this world. [Exod. 25:10-40.]

2For a tabernacle (tent) was erected, in the outer division *or* compartment of which were the lampstand and the table with [its loaves of] the showbread set forth. [This portion] is called the Holy Place. [Lev. 24:5, 6.]

3But [inside] beyond the second curtain *or* veil, [there stood another] tabernacle [division] known as the Holy of Holies. [Exod. 26:31-33.]

4It had the golden *a*altar of incense and the ark (chest) of the covenant, covered over with wrought gold. This [ark] contained a golden jar which held the manna and the rod of Aaron that sprouted and the [two stone] slabs of the covenant [bearing the Ten Commandments]. [Exod. 16:32-34; 30:1-6; Num. 17:8-10.]

5Above [the ark] and overshadowing the mercy seat were the representations of the cherubim [winged creatures which were the symbols] of glory. We cannot now go into detail about these things.

6These arrangements having thus been made, the priests enter [habitually] into the outer division of the tabernacle in performance of their ritual acts of worship.

7But into the second [division of the tabernacle] none but the high priest goes, and he only once a year, and never without taking a sacrifice of blood with him, which he offers for himself and for the errors *and* sins of ignorance *and* thoughtlessness which the people have committed. [Lev. 16:15.]

8By this the Holy Spirit points out that the way into the [true Holy of] Holies is not yet thrown open as long as the former [the outer portion of the] tabernacle remains a recognized institution *and* is still standing,

9Seeing that that first [outer portion of the] tabernacle was a parable (a visible symbol or type or picture of the

---

*a 8* Some manuscripts may be translated *fault and said to the people.*
*b 12* Jer. 31:31-34

*a* Henry Alford, *The Greek New Testament, with Notes*: Not kept permanently in the Holy of Holies, but taken in on the Day of Atonement.

## New International Version

indicating that the gifts and sacrifices being offered were not able to clear the conscience of the worshiper. [10]They are only a matter of food and drink and various ceremonial washings—external regulations applying until the time of the new order.

### The Blood of Christ

[11]But when Christ came as high priest of the good things that are now already here,[a] he went through the greater and more perfect tabernacle that is not made with human hands, that is to say, is not a part of this creation. [12]He did not enter by means of the blood of goats and calves; but he entered the Most Holy Place once for all by his own blood, thus obtaining[b] eternal redemption. [13]The blood of goats and bulls and the ashes of a heifer sprinkled on those who are ceremonially unclean sanctify them so that they are outwardly clean. [14]How much more, then, will the blood of Christ, who through the eternal Spirit offered himself unblemished to God, cleanse our consciences from acts that lead to death,[c] so that we may serve the living God!

[15]For this reason Christ is the mediator of a new covenant, that those who are called may receive the promised eternal inheritance—now that he has died as a ransom to set them free from the sins committed under the first covenant.

[16]In the case of a will,[d] it is necessary to prove the death of the one who made it, [17]because a will is in force only when somebody has died; it never takes effect while the one who made it is living. [18]This is why even the first covenant was not put into effect without blood. [19]When Moses had proclaimed every command of the law to all the people, he took the blood of calves, together with water, scarlet wool and branches of hyssop, and sprinkled the scroll and all the people. [20]He said, "This is the blood of the covenant, which God has commanded you to keep."[e] [21]In the same way, he sprinkled with the blood both the tabernacle and everything used in its ceremonies. [22]In fact, the law requires that nearly everything be cleansed with blood, and without the shedding of blood there is no forgiveness.

[23]It was necessary, then, for the copies of the heavenly things to be purified with these sacrifices, but the heavenly things themselves with better sacrifices than these. [24]For Christ did not enter a sanctuary made with human hands that was only a copy of the true one; he entered heaven itself, now to appear for us in God's presence.

## Amplified Bible

present age). In it gifts and sacrifices are offered, and yet are incapable of perfecting the conscience *or* of cleansing *and* renewing the inner man of the worshiper.

[10]For [the ceremonies] deal only with clean and unclean meats and drinks and different washings, [mere] external rules *and* regulations for the body imposed to tide the worshipers over until the time of setting things straight [of reformation, of the complete new order when Christ, the Messiah, shall establish the reality of what these things foreshadow—a better covenant].

[11]But [that appointed time came] when Christ (the Messiah) appeared as a High Priest of the better things that have come *and* are to come. [Then] through the greater and more perfect tabernacle not made with [human] hands, that is, not a part of this material creation,

[12]He went once for all into the [Holy of] Holies [of heaven], not by virtue of the blood of goats and calves [by which to make reconciliation between God and man], but His own blood, having found *and* secured a complete redemption (an everlasting release for us).

[13]For if [the mere] sprinkling of unholy *and* defiled persons with blood of goats and bulls and with the ashes of a burnt heifer is sufficient for the purification of the body, [Lev. 16:6, 16; Num. 19:9, 17, 18.]

[14]How much more surely shall the blood of Christ, Who [a]by virtue of [His] eternal Spirit [His own preexistent [b]divine personality] has offered Himself as an unblemished sacrifice to God, purify our consciences from dead works *and* lifeless observances to serve the [ever] living God?

[15][Christ, the Messiah] is therefore the Negotiator *and* Mediator of an [entirely] new agreement (testament, covenant), so that those who are called *and* offered it may receive the fulfillment of the promised everlasting inheritance—since a death has taken place which rescues *and* delivers *and* redeems them from the transgressions committed under the [old] first agreement.

[16]For where there is a [last] will *and* testament involved, the death of the one who made it must be established,

[17]For a will *and* testament is valid and takes effect only at death, since it has no force *or* legal power as long as the one who made it is alive.

[18]So even the [old] first covenant (God's will) was not inaugurated *and* ratified *and* put in force without the shedding of blood.

[19]For when every command of the Law had been read out by Moses to all the people, he took the blood of slain calves and goats, together with water and scarlet wool and with a bunch of hyssop, and sprinkled both the Book (the roll of the Law and covenant) itself and all the people,

[20]Saying these words: This is the blood that seals *and* ratifies the agreement (the testament, the covenant) which God commanded [me to deliver to] you. [Exod. 24:6-8.]

[21]And in the same way he sprinkled with the blood both the tabernacle and all the [sacred] vessels *and* appliances used in [divine] worship.

[22][In fact] under the Law almost everything is purified by means of blood, and without the shedding of blood there is neither release from sin *and* its guilt *nor* the remission of the due *and* merited punishment for sins.

[23]By such means, therefore, it was necessary for the [earthly] copies of the heavenly things to be purified, but the actual heavenly things themselves [required far] better *and* nobler sacrifices than these.

[24]For Christ (the Messiah) has not entered into a sanctuary made with [human] hands, only a copy *and* pattern *and* type of the true one, but [He has entered] into heaven itself, now to appear in the [very] presence of God on our behalf.

---

[a] 11 Some early manuscripts *are to come*     [b] 12 Or *blood, having obtained*     [c] 14 Or *from useless rituals*     [d] 16 Same Greek word as *covenant*; also in verse 17     [e] 20 Exodus 24:8

[a] Marvin Vincent, *Word Studies*.   [b] Henry Alford, cited by Kenneth Wuest, *Word Studies*.

## New International Version

25 Nor did he enter heaven to offer himself again and again, the way the high priest enters the Most Holy Place every year with blood that is not his own. 26 Otherwise Christ would have had to suffer many times since the creation of the world. But he has appeared once for all at the culmination of the ages to do away with sin by the sacrifice of himself. 27 Just as people are destined to die once, and after that to face judgment, 28 so Christ was sacrificed once to take away the sins of many; and he will appear a second time, not to bear sin, but to bring salvation to those who are waiting for him.

### Christ's Sacrifice Once for All

**10** The law is only a shadow of the good things that are coming—not the realities themselves. For this reason it can never, by the same sacrifices repeated endlessly year after year, make perfect those who draw near to worship. 2 Otherwise, would they not have stopped being offered? For the worshipers would have been cleansed once for all, and would no longer have felt guilty for their sins. 3 But those sacrifices are an annual reminder of sins. 4 It is impossible for the blood of bulls and goats to take away sins.

5 Therefore, when Christ came into the world, he said:

"Sacrifice and offering you did not desire,
    but a body you prepared for me;
6 with burnt offerings and sin offerings
    you were not pleased.
7 Then I said, 'Here I am—it is written about me in the scroll—
    I have come to do your will, my God.'"[a]

8 First he said, "Sacrifices and offerings, burnt offerings and sin offerings you did not desire, nor were you pleased with them"—though they were offered in accordance with the law. 9 Then he said, "Here I am, I have come to do your will." He sets aside the first to establish the second. 10 And by that will, we have been made holy through the sacrifice of the body of Jesus Christ once for all.

11 Day after day every priest stands and performs his religious duties; again and again he offers the same sacrifices, which can never take away sins. 12 But when this priest had offered for all time one sacrifice for sins, he sat down at the right hand of God, 13 and since that time he waits for his enemies to be made his footstool. 14 For by one sacrifice he has made perfect forever those who are being made holy.

15 The Holy Spirit also testifies to us about this. First he says:

16 "This is the covenant I will make with them
    after that time, says the Lord.
I will put my laws in their hearts,
    and I will write them on their minds."[b]

## Amplified Bible

25 Nor did He [enter into the heavenly sanctuary to] offer Himself regularly again and again, as the high priest enters the [Holy of] Holies every year with blood not his own. 26 For then would He often have had to suffer [over and over again] since the foundation of the world. But as it now is, He has once for all at the consummation *and* close of the ages appeared to put away *and* abolish sin by His sacrifice [of Himself]. 27 And just as it is appointed for [all] men once to die, and after that the [certain] judgment, 28 Even so it is that Christ, having been offered to take upon Himself *and* bear as a burden the sins of many once *and* *a* once for all, will appear a second time, not to carry any burden of sin *nor* to deal with sin, but to bring to full salvation those who are [eagerly, constantly, and patiently] waiting for *and* expecting Him.

**10** For since the Law has merely a rude outline (foreshadowing) of the good things to come—instead of fully expressing those things—it can never by offering the same sacrifices continually year after year make perfect those who approach [its altars]. 2 For if it were otherwise, would [these sacrifices] not have stopped being offered? Since the worshipers had *a* once for all been cleansed, they would no longer have any guilt *or* consciousness of sin. 3 But [as it is] these sacrifices annually bring a fresh remembrance of sins [to be atoned for], 4 Because the blood of bulls and goats is powerless to take sins away. 5 Hence, when He [Christ] entered into the world, He said, Sacrifices and offerings You have not desired, but instead You have made ready a body for Me [to offer]; 6 In burnt offerings and sin offerings You have taken no delight. 7 Then I said, Behold, here I am, coming to do Your will, O God—[to fulfill] what is written of Me in the volume of the Book. [Ps. 40:6-8.] 8 When He said just before, You have neither desired, nor have You taken delight in sacrifices and offerings and burnt offerings and sin offerings—all of which are offered according to the Law— 9 He then went on to say, Behold, [here] I am, coming to do Your will. Thus He does away with *and* annuls the first (former) order [as a means of expiating sin] so that He might inaugurate *and* establish the second (latter) order. [Ps. 40:6-8.] 10 And in accordance with this will [of God], we have been made holy (consecrated and sanctified) through the offering made once for all of the body of Jesus Christ (the Anointed One). 11 Furthermore, every [human] priest stands [at his altar of service] ministering daily, offering the same sacrifices over and over again, which never are able to strip [from every side of us] the sins [that envelop us] *and* take them away— 12 Whereas this One [Christ], after He had offered a single sacrifice for our sins [that shall avail] for all time, sat down at the right hand of God, 13 Then to wait until His enemies should be made a stool beneath His feet. [Ps. 110:1.] 14 For by a single offering He has forever completely cleansed *and* perfected those who are consecrated *and* made holy. 15 And also the Holy Spirit adds His testimony to us [in confirmation of this]. For having said, 16 This is the agreement (testament, covenant) that I will set up *and* conclude with them after those days, says the Lord: I will imprint My laws upon their hearts, and I will inscribe them on their minds (on their inmost thoughts and understanding),

---

[a] 7 Psalm 40:6-8 (see Septuagint)    [b] 16 Jer. 31:33      [a] G. Abbott-Smith, *Manual Greek Lexicon.*

## New International Version

[17]Then he adds:

"Their sins and lawless acts
I will remember no more."[a]

[18]And where these have been forgiven, sacrifice for sin is no longer necessary.

### A Call to Persevere in Faith

[19]Therefore, brothers and sisters, since we have confidence to enter the Most Holy Place by the blood of Jesus, [20]by a new and living way opened for us through the curtain, that is, his body, [21]and since we have a great priest over the house of God, [22]let us draw near to God with a sincere heart and with the full assurance that faith brings, having our hearts sprinkled to cleanse us from a guilty conscience and having our bodies washed with pure water. [23]Let us hold unswervingly to the hope we profess, for he who promised is faithful. [24]And let us consider how we may spur one another on toward love and good deeds, [25]not giving up meeting together, as some are in the habit of doing, but encouraging one another—and all the more as you see the Day approaching.

[26]If we deliberately keep on sinning after we have received the knowledge of the truth, no sacrifice for sins is left, [27]but only a fearful expectation of judgment and of raging fire that will consume the enemies of God. [28]Anyone who rejected the law of Moses died without mercy on the testimony of two or three witnesses. [29]How much more severely do you think someone deserves to be punished who has trampled the Son of God underfoot, who has treated as an unholy thing the blood of the covenant that sanctified them, and who has insulted the Spirit of grace? [30]For we know him who said, "It is mine to avenge; I will repay,"[b] and again, "The Lord will judge his people."[c] [31]It is a dreadful thing to fall into the hands of the living God.

[32]Remember those earlier days after you had received the light, when you endured in a great conflict full of suf-

## Amplified Bible

[17]He then goes on to say, And their sins and their lawbreaking I will remember no more. [Jer. 31:33, 34.]
[18]Now where there is absolute remission (forgiveness and cancellation of the penalty) of these [sins and lawbreaking], there is no longer any offering made to atone for sin.
[19]Therefore, brethren, since we have full freedom and confidence to enter into the [Holy of] Holies [by the power and virtue] in the blood of Jesus,
[20]By this fresh (new) and living way which He initiated and dedicated and opened for us through the separating curtain (veil of the Holy of Holies), that is, through His flesh,
[21]And since we have [such] a great and wonderful and noble Priest [Who rules] over the house of God,
[22]Let us all come forward and draw near with true (honest and sincere) hearts in unqualified assurance and absolute conviction engendered by faith (by [a]that leaning of the entire human personality on God in absolute trust and confidence in His power, wisdom, and goodness), having our hearts sprinkled and purified from a guilty (evil) conscience and our bodies cleansed with pure water.
[23]So let us seize and hold fast and retain without wavering the [b]hope we cherish and confess and our acknowledgement of it, for He Who promised is reliable (sure) and faithful to His word.
[24]And let us consider and give [c]attentive, continuous care to watching over one another, studying how we may stir up (stimulate and incite) to love and helpful deeds and noble activities,
[25]Not forsaking or neglecting to assemble together [as believers], as is the habit of some people, but admonishing (warning, urging, and encouraging) one another, and all the more faithfully as you see the day approaching.
[26]For if we go on deliberately and willingly sinning after once acquiring the knowledge of the Truth, there is no longer any sacrifice left to atone for [our] sins [no further offering to which to look forward].
[27][There is nothing left for us then] but a kind of awful and fearful prospect and expectation of divine judgment and the fury of burning wrath and indignation which will consume those who put themselves in opposition [to God]. [Isa. 26:11.]
[28]Any person who has violated and [thus] rejected and set at naught the Law of Moses is put to death without pity or mercy on the evidence of two or three witnesses. [Deut. 17:2-6.]
[29]How much worse (sterner and heavier) punishment do you suppose he will be judged to deserve who has spurned and [thus] trampled underfoot the Son of God, and who has considered the covenant blood by which he was consecrated common and unhallowed, thus profaning it and insulting and outraging the [Holy] Spirit [Who imparts] grace (the unmerited favor and blessing of God)? [Exod. 24:8.]
[30]For we know Him Who said, Vengeance is Mine [retribution and the meting out of full justice rest with Me]; I will repay [I will exact the compensation], *says the Lord*. And again, The Lord will judge and determine and solve and settle the cause and the cases of His people. [Deut. 32:35, 36.]
[31]It is a fearful (formidable and terrible) thing to incur the divine penalties and be cast into the hands of the living God!
[32]But be ever mindful of the days gone by in which, after you were first spiritually enlightened, you endured a great and painful struggle,

---

[a]17 Jer. 31:34    [b]30 Deut. 32:35    [c]30 Deut. 32:36; Psalm 135:14

[a] Alexander Souter, *Pocket Lexicon*.    [b] William Tyndale, *The Tyndale Bible*, Miles Coverdale, *The Coverdale Bible*, and others.    [c] Marvin Vincent, *Word Studies*.

## New International Version

fering. ³³Sometimes you were publicly exposed to insult and persecution; at other times you stood side by side with those who were so treated. ³⁴You suffered along with those in prison and joyfully accepted the confiscation of your property, because you knew that you yourselves had better and lasting possessions. ³⁵So do not throw away your confidence; it will be richly rewarded.

³⁶You need to persevere so that when you have done the will of God, you will receive what he has promised. ³⁷For,

"In just a little while,
    he who is coming will come
    and will not delay."ᵃ

³⁸And,

"But my righteousᵇ one will live by faith.
    And I take no pleasure
    in the one who shrinks back."ᶜ

³⁹But we do not belong to those who shrink back and are destroyed, but to those who have faith and are saved.

### Faith in Action

**11** Now faith is confidence in what we hope for and assurance about what we do not see. ²This is what the ancients were commended for.

³By faith we understand that the universe was formed at God's command, so that what is seen was not made out of what was visible.

⁴By faith Abel brought God a better offering than Cain did. By faith he was commended as righteous, when God spoke well of his offerings. And by faith Abel still speaks, even though he is dead.

⁵By faith Enoch was taken from this life, so that he did not experience death: "He could not be found, because God had taken him away."ᵈ For before he was taken, he was commended as one who pleased God. ⁶And without faith it is impossible to please God, because anyone who comes to him must believe that he exists and that he rewards those who earnestly seek him.

⁷By faith Noah, when warned about things not yet seen, in holy fear built an ark to save his family. By his faith he condemned the world and became heir of the righteousness that is in keeping with faith.

## Amplified Bible

³³Sometimes being yourselves a gazingstock, publicly exposed to insults *and* abuse and distress, and sometimes claiming fellowship *and* making common cause with others who were so treated.

³⁴For you did sympathize *and* suffer along with those who were imprisoned, and you bore cheerfully the plundering of your belongings *and* the confiscation of your property, in the knowledge *and* consciousness that you yourselves had a better and lasting possession.

³⁵Do not, therefore, fling away your fearless confidence, for it carries a great *and* glorious compensation of reward.

³⁶For you have need of steadfast patience *and* endurance, so that you may perform *and* fully accomplish the will of God, and thus receive *and* ᵃcarry away [and enjoy to the full] what is promised.

³⁷For still a little while (a very little while), and the Coming One will come and He will not delay.

³⁸But the just shall live by faith [My righteous servant shall live ᵇby his conviction respecting man's relationship to God and divine things, and holy fervor born of faith and conjoined with it]; and if he draws back *and* shrinks in fear, My soul has no delight *or* pleasure in him. [Hab. 2:3, 4.]

³⁹But our way is not that of those who draw back to eternal misery (perdition) and are utterly destroyed, but we are of those who believe [who cleave to and trust in and rely on God through Jesus Christ, the Messiah] *and* by faith preserve the soul.

**11** Now faith is the assurance (the confirmation, ᶜthe title deed) of the things [we] hope for, being the proof of things [we] do not see *and* the conviction of their reality [faith perceiving as real fact what is not revealed to the senses].

²For by [faith—ᵇtrust and holy fervor born of faith] the men of old had divine testimony borne to them *and* obtained a good report.

³By faith we understand that the worlds [during the successive ages] were framed (fashioned, put in order, and equipped for their intended purpose) by the word of God, so that what we see was not made out of things which are visible.

⁴[Prompted, actuated] by faith Abel brought God a better and more acceptable sacrifice than Cain, because of which it was testified of him that he was righteous [that he was upright and in right standing with God], and God bore witness by accepting *and* acknowledging his gifts. And though he died, yet [through the incident] he is still speaking. [Gen. 4:3-10.]

⁵Because of faith Enoch was caught up *and* transferred to heaven, so that he did not have a glimpse of death; and he was not found, because God had translated him. For even before he was taken to heaven, he received testimony [still on record] that he had pleased *and* been satisfactory to God. [Gen. 5:21-24.]

⁶But without faith it is impossible to please *and* be satisfactory to Him. For whoever would come near to God must [necessarily] believe that God exists and that He is the rewarder of those who earnestly *and* diligently seek Him [out].

⁷[Prompted] by faith Noah, being forewarned by God concerning events of which as yet there was no visible sign, took heed *and* diligently and reverently constructed *and* prepared an ark for the deliverance of his own family. By this [his faith which relied on God] he passed judgment *and* sentence on the world's unbelief and became an heir *and* possessor of righteousness (ᵇthat relation of being right into which God puts the person who has faith). [Gen. 6:13-22.]

---

ᵃ 37 Isaiah 26:20; Hab. 2:3    ᵇ 38 Some early manuscripts *But the righteous*    ᶜ 38 Hab. 2:4 (see Septuagint)    ᵈ 5 Gen. 5:24

ᵃ Marvin Vincent, *Word Studies.*   ᵇ Joseph Thayer, *A Greek-English Lexicon.*   ᶜ James Moulton and George Milligan, *The Vocabulary of the Greek Testament.*

## New International Version

[8]By faith Abraham, when called to go to a place he would later receive as his inheritance, obeyed and went, even though he did not know where he was going. [9]By faith he made his home in the promised land like a stranger in a foreign country; he lived in tents, as did Isaac and Jacob, who were heirs with him of the same promise. [10]For he was looking forward to the city with foundations, whose architect and builder is God. [11]And by faith even Sarah, who was past childbearing age, was enabled to bear children because she[a] considered him faithful who had made the promise. [12]And so from this one man, and he as good as dead, came descendants as numerous as the stars in the sky and as countless as the sand on the seashore.

[13]All these people were still living by faith when they died. They did not receive the things promised; they only saw them and welcomed them from a distance, admitting that they were foreigners and strangers on earth. [14]People who say such things show that they are looking for a country of their own. [15]If they had been thinking of the country they had left, they would have had opportunity to return. [16]Instead, they were longing for a better country—a heavenly one. Therefore God is not ashamed to be called their God, for he has prepared a city for them.

[17]By faith Abraham, when God tested him, offered Isaac as a sacrifice. He who had embraced the promises was about to sacrifice his one and only son, [18]even though God had said to him, "It is through Isaac that your offspring will be reckoned."[b] [19]Abraham reasoned that God could even raise the dead, and so in a manner of speaking he did receive Isaac back from death.

[20]By faith Isaac blessed Jacob and Esau in regard to their future.

[21]By faith Jacob, when he was dying, blessed each of Joseph's sons, and worshiped as he leaned on the top of his staff.

[22]By faith Joseph, when his end was near, spoke about the exodus of the Israelites from Egypt and gave instructions concerning the burial of his bones.

[23]By faith Moses' parents hid him for three months after he was born, because they saw he was no ordinary child, and they were not afraid of the king's edict.

[24]By faith Moses, when he had grown up, refused to be known as the son of Pharaoh's daughter. [25]He chose to be mistreated along with the people of God rather than to enjoy the fleeting pleasures of sin. [26]He regarded dis-

## Amplified Bible

[8][Urged on] by faith Abraham, when he was called, obeyed and went forth to a place which he was destined to receive as an inheritance; and he went, although he did not know or trouble his mind about where he was to go.

[9][Prompted] by faith he dwelt as a temporary resident in the land which was designated in the promise [of God, though he was like a stranger] in a strange country, living in tents with Isaac and Jacob, fellow heirs with him of the same promise. [Gen. 12:1-8.]

[10]For he was [waiting expectantly and confidently] looking forward to the city which has fixed and firm foundations, whose Architect and Builder is God.

[11]Because of faith also Sarah herself received physical power to conceive a child, even when she was long past the age for it, because she considered [God] Who had given her the promise to be reliable and trustworthy and true to His word. [Gen. 17:19; 18:11-14; 21:2.]

[12]So from one man, though he was physically as good as dead, there have sprung descendants whose number is as the stars of heaven and as countless as the innumerable sands on the seashore. [Gen. 15:5, 6; 22:17; 32:12.]

[13]These people all died controlled and sustained by their faith, but not having received the tangible fulfillment of [God's] promises, only having seen it and greeted it from a great distance by faith, and all the while acknowledging and confessing that they were strangers and temporary residents and exiles upon the earth. [Gen. 23:4; Ps. 39:12.]

[14]Now those people who talk as they did show plainly that they are in search of a fatherland (their own country).

[15]If they had been thinking with [homesick] remembrance of that country from which they were emigrants, they would have found constant opportunity to return to it.

[16]But the truth is that they were yearning for and aspiring to a better and more desirable country, that is, a heavenly [one]. For that reason God is not ashamed to be called their God [even to be surnamed their God—the God of Abraham, Isaac, and Jacob], for He has prepared a city for them. [Exod. 3:6, 15; 4:5.]

[17]By faith Abraham, when he was put to the test [while the testing of his faith was [a] still in progress], [a] had already brought Isaac for an offering; he who had gladly received and welcomed [God's] promises was ready to sacrifice his only son, [Gen. 22:1-10.]

[18]Of whom it was said, Through Isaac shall your descendants be reckoned. [Gen. 21:12.]

[19]For he reasoned that God was able to raise [him] up even from among the dead. Indeed in the sense that Isaac was figuratively dead [potentially sacrificed], he did [actually] receive him back from the dead.

[20][With eyes of] faith Isaac, looking far into the future, invoked blessings upon Jacob and Esau. [Gen. 27:27-29, 39, 40.]

[21][Prompted] by faith Jacob, when he was dying, blessed each of Joseph's sons and bowed in prayer over the top of his staff. [Gen. 48.]

[22][Actuated] by faith Joseph, when nearing the end of his life, referred to [the promise of God for] the departure of the Israelites out of Egypt and gave instructions concerning the burial of his own bones. [Gen. 50:24, 25; Exod. 13:19.]

[23][Prompted] by faith Moses, after his birth, was kept concealed for three months by his parents, because they saw how comely the child was; and they were not overawed and terrified by the king's decree. [Exod. 1:22; 2:2.]

[24][Aroused] by faith Moses, when he had grown to maturity and [b]become great, refused to be called the son of Pharaoh's daughter, [Exod. 2:10, 15.]

[25]Because he preferred to share the oppression [suffer the hardships] and bear the shame of the people of God rather than to have the fleeting enjoyment of a sinful life.

---

[a] 11 Or By faith Abraham, even though he was too old to have children—and Sarah herself was not able to conceive—was enabled to become a father because he   [b] 18 Gen. 21:12

[a] Marvin Vincent, Word Studies.   [b] Literal translation.

## New International Version

grace for the sake of Christ as of greater value than the treasures of Egypt, because he was looking ahead to his reward. [27]By faith he left Egypt, not fearing the king's anger; he persevered because he saw him who is invisible. [28]By faith he kept the Passover and the application of blood, so that the destroyer of the firstborn would not touch the firstborn of Israel.

[29]By faith the people passed through the Red Sea as on dry land; but when the Egyptians tried to do so, they were drowned.

[30]By faith the walls of Jericho fell, after the army had marched around them for seven days.

[31]By faith the prostitute Rahab, because she welcomed the spies, was not killed with those who were disobedient.[a]

[32]And what more shall I say? I do not have time to tell about Gideon, Barak, Samson and Jephthah, about David and Samuel and the prophets, [33]who through faith conquered kingdoms, administered justice, and gained what was promised; who shut the mouths of lions, [34]quenched the fury of the flames, and escaped the edge of the sword; whose weakness was turned to strength; and who became powerful in battle and routed foreign armies. [35]Women received back their dead, raised to life again. There were others who were tortured, refusing to be released so that they might gain an even better resurrection. [36]Some faced jeers and flogging, and even chains and imprisonment. [37]They were put to death by stoning;[b] they were sawed in two; they were killed by the sword. They went about in sheepskins and goatskins, destitute, persecuted and mistreated— [38]the world was not worthy of them. They wandered in deserts and mountains, living in caves and in holes in the ground.

[39]These were all commended for their faith, yet none of them received what had been promised, [40]since God had planned something better for us so that only together with us would they be made perfect.

**12** Therefore, since we are surrounded by such a great cloud of witnesses, let us throw off everything that hinders and the sin that so easily entangles. And let us run with perseverance the race marked out for us, [2]fixing our eyes on Jesus, the pioneer and perfecter

## Amplified Bible

[26]He considered the contempt *and* abuse *and* shame [borne for] the Christ (the Messiah Who was to come) to be greater wealth than all the treasures of Egypt, for he looked forward *and* away to the reward (recompense).

[27][Motivated] by faith he left Egypt behind him, being unawed *and* undismayed by the wrath of the king; for he never flinched *but* held staunchly to his purpose *and* endured steadfastly as one who gazed on Him Who is invisible. [Exod. 2:15.]

[28]By faith (simple trust and confidence in God) he instituted *and* carried out the Passover and the sprinkling of the blood [on the doorposts], so that the destroyer of the firstborn (the angel) might not touch those [of the children of Israel]. [Exod. 12:21-30.]

[29][Urged on] by faith the people crossed the Red Sea as [though] on dry land, but when the Egyptians tried to do the same thing they were swallowed up [by the sea]. [Exod. 14:21-31.]

[30]Because of faith the walls of Jericho fell down after they had been encompassed for seven days [by the Israelites]. [Josh. 6:12-21.]

[31][Prompted] by faith Rahab the prostitute was not destroyed along with those who refused to believe *and* obey, because she had received the spies in peace [without enmity]. [Josh. 2:1-21; 6:22-25.]

[32]And what shall I say further? For time would fail me to tell of Gideon, Barak, Samson, Jephthah, of David and Samuel and the prophets, [Judg. 4:1-5; 6:1-8, 35; 11:1-12, 15; 13:1-16; I Sam. 1-30; II Sam. 1-24; I Kings 1-2; Acts 3:24.]

[33]Who by [the help of] faith subdued kingdoms, administered justice, obtained promised blessings, closed the mouths of lions, [Dan. 6.]

[34]Extinguished the power of raging fire, escaped the devourings of the sword, out of frailty *and* weakness won strength *and* became stalwart, even mighty *and* resistless in battle, routing alien hosts. [Dan. 3.]

[35][Some] women received again their dead by a resurrection. Others were tortured [a]to death with clubs, refusing to accept release [offered on the terms of denying their faith], so that they might be resurrected to a better life. [I Kings 17:17-24; II Kings 4:25-37.]

[36]Others had to suffer the trial of mocking and scourging and even chains and imprisonment.

[37]They were stoned to death; they were lured with tempting offers [to renounce their faith]; they were sawn asunder; they were slaughtered by the sword; [while they were alive] they had to go about wrapped in the skins of sheep and goats, utterly destitute, oppressed, cruelly treated—

[38][Men] of whom the world was not worthy—roaming over the desolate places and the mountains, and [living] in caves *and* caverns and holes of the earth.

[39]And all of these, though they won divine approval by [means of] their faith, did not receive the fulfillment of what was promised,

[40]Because God had us in mind *and* had something better *and* greater in view for us, so that they [these heroes and heroines of faith] should not come to perfection apart from us [before we could join them].

**12** Therefore then, since we are surrounded by so great a cloud of witnesses [who have borne testimony to the Truth], let us strip off *and* throw aside every encumbrance (unnecessary weight) and that sin which so readily (deftly and cleverly) clings to *and* entangles us, and let us run with patient endurance *and* steady *and* active persistence the appointed course of the race that is set before us,

[2]Looking away [from all that will distract] to Jesus, Who is the Leader *and* the Source of our faith [giving the

---

*a* 31 Or *unbelieving*   *b* 37 Some early manuscripts *stoning; they were put to the test;*

*a* Marvin Vincent, *Word Studies.*

## New International Version

of faith. For the joy set before him he endured the cross, scorning its shame, and sat down at the right hand of the throne of God. ³Consider him who endured such opposition from sinners, so that you will not grow weary and lose heart.

### God Disciplines His Children

⁴In your struggle against sin, you have not yet resisted to the point of shedding your blood. ⁵And have you completely forgotten this word of encouragement that addresses you as a father addresses his son? It says,

"My son, do not make light of the Lord's discipline,
    and do not lose heart when he rebukes you,
⁶because the Lord disciplines the one he loves,
    and he chastens everyone he accepts as his son."ᵃ

⁷Endure hardship as discipline; God is treating you as his children. For what children are not disciplined by their father? ⁸If you are not disciplined—and everyone undergoes discipline—then you are not legitimate, not true sons and daughters at all. ⁹Moreover, we have all had human fathers who disciplined us and we respected them for it. How much more should we submit to the Father of spirits and live! ¹⁰They disciplined us for a little while as they thought best; but God disciplines us for our good, in order that we may share in his holiness. ¹¹No discipline seems pleasant at the time, but painful. Later on, however, it produces a harvest of righteousness and peace for those who have been trained by it.

¹²Therefore, strengthen your feeble arms and weak knees. ¹³"Make level paths for your feet,"ᵇ so that the lame may not be disabled, but rather healed.

### Warning and Encouragement

¹⁴Make every effort to live in peace with everyone and to be holy; without holiness no one will see the Lord. ¹⁵See to it that no one falls short of the grace of God and that no bitter root grows up to cause trouble and defile many. ¹⁶See that no one is sexually immoral, or is godless like Esau, who for a single meal sold his inheritance rights as the oldest son. ¹⁷Afterward, as you know, when he wanted to inherit this blessing, he was rejected. Even though he sought the blessing with tears, he could not change what he had done.

## Amplified Bible

first incentive for our belief] and is also its Finisher [bringing it to maturity and perfection]. He, for the joy [of obtaining the prize] that was set before Him, endured the cross, despising and ignoring the shame, and is now seated at the right hand of the throne of God. [Ps. 110:1.]

³Just think of Him Who endured from sinners such grievous opposition and bitter hostility against Himself [reckon up and consider it all in comparison with your trials], so that you may not grow weary or exhausted, losing heart and relaxing and fainting in your minds.

⁴You have not yet struggled and fought agonizingly against sin, nor have you yet resisted and withstood to the point of pouring out your [own] blood.

⁵And have you [completely] forgotten the divine word of appeal and encouragement in which you are reasoned with and addressed as sons? My son, do not think lightly or scorn to submit to the correction and discipline of the Lord, nor lose courage and give up and faint when you are reproved or corrected by Him;

⁶For the Lord corrects and disciplines everyone whom He loves, and He punishes, even scourges, every son whom He accepts and welcomes to His heart and cherishes.

⁷You must submit to and endure [correction] for discipline; God is dealing with you as with sons. For what son is there whom his father does not [thus] train and correct and discipline?

⁸Now if you are exempt from correction and left without discipline in which all [of God's children] share, then you are illegitimate offspring and not true sons [at all]. [Prov. 3:11, 12.]

⁹Moreover, we have had earthly fathers who disciplined us and we yielded [to them] and respected [them for training us]. Shall we not much more cheerfully submit to the Father of spirits and so [truly] live?

¹⁰For [our earthly fathers] disciplined us for only a short period of time and chastised us as seemed proper and good to them; but He disciplines us for our certain good, that we may become sharers in His own holiness.

¹¹For the time being no discipline brings joy, but seems grievous and painful; but afterwards it yields a peaceable fruit of righteousness to those who have been trained by it [a harvest of fruit which consists in righteousness—in conformity to God's will in purpose, thought, and action, resulting in right living and right standing with God].

¹²So then, brace up and reinvigorate and set right your slackened and weakened and drooping hands and strengthen your feeble and palsied and tottering knees, [Isa. 35:3.]

¹³And cut through and make firm and plain and smooth, straight paths for your feet [yes, make them safe and upright and happy paths that go in the right direction], so that the lame and halting [limbs] may not be put out of joint, but rather may be cured.

¹⁴Strive to live in peace with everybody and pursue that consecration and holiness without which no one will [ever] see the Lord.

¹⁵Exercise foresight and be on the watch to look [after one another], to see that no one falls back from and fails to secure God's grace (His unmerited favor and spiritual blessing), in order that no root of resentment (rancor, bitterness, or hatred) shoots forth and causes trouble and bitter torment, and the many become contaminated and defiled by it—

¹⁶That no one may become guilty of sexual vice, or become a profane (godless and sacrilegious) person as Esau did, who sold his own birthright for a single meal. [Gen. 25:29-34.]

¹⁷For you understand that later on, when he wanted [to regain title to] his inheritance of the blessing, he was rejected (disqualified and set aside), for he could find no opportunity to repair by repentance [what he had done, no chance to recall the choice he had made], although he sought for it carefully with [bitter] tears. [Gen. 27:30-40.]

ᵃ 5,6 Prov. 3:11,12 (see Septuagint)    ᵇ 13 Prov. 4:26

## New International Version

### The Mountain of Fear and the Mountain of Joy

18You have not come to a mountain that can be touched and that is burning with fire; to darkness, gloom and storm; 19to a trumpet blast or to such a voice speaking words that those who heard it begged that no further word be spoken to them, 20because they could not bear what was commanded: "If even an animal touches the mountain, it must be stoned to death."*a* 21The sight was so terrifying that Moses said, "I am trembling with fear."*b*

22But you have come to Mount Zion, to the city of the living God, the heavenly Jerusalem. You have come to thousands upon thousands of angels in joyful assembly, 23to the church of the firstborn, whose names are written in heaven. You have come to God, the Judge of all, to the spirits of the righteous made perfect, 24to Jesus the mediator of a new covenant, and to the sprinkled blood that speaks a better word than the blood of Abel.

25See to it that you do not refuse him who speaks. If they did not escape when they refused him who warned them on earth, how much less will we, if we turn away from him who warns us from heaven? 26At that time his voice shook the earth, but now he has promised, "Once more I will shake not only the earth but also the heavens."*c* 27The words "once more" indicate the removing of what can be shaken—that is, created things—so that what cannot be shaken may remain.

28Therefore, since we are receiving a kingdom that cannot be shaken, let us be thankful, and so worship God acceptably with reverence and awe, 29for our "God is a consuming fire."*d*

### Concluding Exhortations

**13** Keep on loving one another as brothers and sisters. 2Do not forget to show hospitality to strangers, for by so doing some people have shown hospitality to angels without knowing it. 3Continue to remember those in prison as if you were together with them in prison, and those who are mistreated as if you yourselves were suffering.

4Marriage should be honored by all, and the marriage bed kept pure, for God will judge the adulterer and all the sexually immoral. 5Keep your lives free from the love of money and be content with what you have, because God has said,

## Amplified Bible

18For you have not come [as did the Israelites in the wilderness] to a [material] mountain that can be touched, [a mountain] that is ablaze with fire, and to gloom and darkness and a raging storm,

19And to the blast of a trumpet and a voice whose words make the listeners beg that nothing more be said to them. [Exod. 19:12-22; 20:18-21; Deut. 4:11, 12; 5:22-27.]

20For they could not bear the command that was given: If even a wild animal touches the mountain, it shall be stoned to death. [Exod. 19:12, 13.]

21In fact, so awful *and* terrifying was the [phenomenal] sight that Moses said, I am terrified (aghast and trembling with fear). [Deut. 9:19.]

22But rather, you have come to Mount Zion, even to the city of the living God, the heavenly Jerusalem, and to countless multitudes of angels in festal gathering,

23And to the church (assembly) of the Firstborn who are registered [as citizens] in heaven, and to the God Who is Judge of all, and to the spirits of the righteous (the redeemed in heaven) who have been made perfect,

24And to Jesus, the Mediator (Go-between, Agent) of a new covenant, and to the sprinkled blood which speaks [of mercy], a better *and* nobler *and* more gracious message than the blood of Abel [which cried out for vengeance]. [Gen. 4:10.]

25So see to it that you do not reject Him *or* refuse to listen to *and* heed Him Who is speaking [to you now]. For if they [the Israelites] did not escape when they refused to listen *and* heed Him Who warned *and* divinely instructed them [here] on earth [revealing with heavenly warnings His will], how much less shall we escape if we reject *and* turn our backs on Him Who cautions *and* admonishes [us] from heaven?

26Then [at Mount Sinai] His voice shook the earth, but now He has given a promise: Yet once more I will shake *and* make tremble not only the earth but also the [starry] heavens. [Hag. 2:6.]

27Now this expression, Yet once more, indicates the final removal *and* transformation of all [that can be] shaken—that is, of that which has been created—in order that what cannot be shaken may remain *and* continue. [Ps. 102:26.]

28Let us therefore, receiving a kingdom that is firm *and* stable *and* cannot be shaken, offer to God pleasing service *and* acceptable worship, with modesty *and* pious care and godly fear *and* awe;

29For our God [is indeed] a consuming fire. [Deut. 4:24.]

**13** Let love for your fellow believers continue *and* be a fixed practice with you [never let it fail].

2Do not forget *or* neglect *or* refuse to extend hospitality to strangers [in the brotherhood—being friendly, cordial, and gracious, sharing the comforts of your home and doing your part generously], for through it some have entertained angels without knowing it. [Gen. 18:1-8; 19:1-3.]

3Remember those who are in prison as if you were their fellow prisoner, and those who are ill-treated, since you also are liable to bodily sufferings.

4Let marriage be held in honor (esteemed worthy, precious, of great price, and especially dear) in all things. And thus let the marriage bed be undefiled (kept undishonored); for God will judge *and* punish the unchaste [all guilty of sexual vice] and adulterous.

5Let your *a*character *or* moral disposition be free from love of money [including greed, avarice, lust, and craving for earthly possessions] and be satisfied with your present [circumstances and with what you have]; for He [God]

---

*a 20* Exodus 19:12,13   *b 21* See Deut. 9:19.   *c 26* Haggai 2:6
*d 29* Deut. 4:24.

*a* Marvin Vincent, *Word Studies.*

## New International Version

"Never will I leave you;
never will I forsake you."[a]

[6]So we say with confidence,

"The Lord is my helper; I will not be afraid.
What can mere mortals do to me?"[b]

[7]Remember your leaders, who spoke the word of God to you. Consider the outcome of their way of life and imitate their faith. [8]Jesus Christ is the same yesterday and today and forever.

[9]Do not be carried away by all kinds of strange teachings. It is good for our hearts to be strengthened by grace, not by eating ceremonial foods, which is of no benefit to those who do so. [10]We have an altar from which those who minister at the tabernacle have no right to eat.

[11]The high priest carries the blood of animals into the Most Holy Place as a sin offering, but the bodies are burned outside the camp. [12]And so Jesus also suffered outside the city gate to make the people holy through his own blood. [13]Let us, then, go to him outside the camp, bearing the disgrace he bore. [14]For here we do not have an enduring city, but we are looking for the city that is to come.

[15]Through Jesus, therefore, let us continually offer to God a sacrifice of praise—the fruit of lips that openly profess his name. [16]And do not forget to do good and to share with others, for with such sacrifices God is pleased.

[17]Have confidence in your leaders and submit to their authority, because they keep watch over you as those who must give an account. Do this so that their work will be a joy, not a burden, for that would be of no benefit to you.

[18]Pray for us. We are sure that we have a clear conscience and desire to live honorably in every way. [19]I particularly urge you to pray so that I may be restored to you soon.

### Benediction and Final Greetings

[20]Now may the God of peace, who through the blood of the eternal covenant brought back from the dead our Lord Jesus, that great Shepherd of the sheep, [21]equip you with

## Amplified Bible

[a]Himself has said, I will not in any way fail you *nor* [a]give you up *nor* leave you without support. [I will] not, [b] [I will] not, [I will] not in any degree leave you helpless *nor* forsake *nor* [b]let [you] down ([a]relax My hold on you)! [[c]Assuredly not!] [Josh. 1:5.]

[6]So we take comfort *and* are encouraged *and* confidently *and* boldly say, The Lord is my Helper; I will not be seized with alarm [I will not fear or dread or be terrified]. What can man do to me? [Ps. 27:1;118:6.]

[7]Remember your leaders *and* superiors in authority [for it was they] who brought to you the Word of God. Observe attentively *and* consider their manner of living (the outcome of their well-spent lives) and imitate their faith ([d]their conviction that God exists and is the Creator and Ruler of all things, the Provider and Bestower of eternal salvation through Christ, and their [e]leaning of the entire human personality on God in absolute trust and confidence in His power, wisdom, and goodness).

[8]Jesus Christ (the Messiah) is [always] the same, yesterday, today, [yes] and forever (to the ages).

[9]Do not be carried about by different *and* varied and alien teachings; for it is good for the heart to be established *and* ennobled *and* strengthened by means of grace (God's favor and spiritual blessing) and not [to be devoted to] foods [rules of diet and ritualistic meals], which bring no [spiritual] benefit *or* profit to those who observe them.

[10]We have an altar from which those who serve *and* [a]worship in the tabernacle have no right to eat.

[11]For when the blood of animals is brought into the sanctuary by the high priest as a sacrifice for sin, the victims' bodies are burned outside the limits of the camp. [Lev. 16:27.]

[12]Therefore Jesus also suffered *and* died outside the [city's] gate in order that He might purify *and* consecrate the people through [the shedding of] His own blood *and* set them apart as holy [for God].

[13]Let us then go forth [from all that would prevent us] to Him outside the camp [at Calvary], bearing the contempt *and* abuse *and* shame with Him. [Lev. 16:27.]

[14]For here we have no permanent city, but we are looking for the one which is to come.

[15]Through Him, therefore, let us constantly *and* at all times offer up to God a sacrifice of praise, which is the fruit of lips that thankfully acknowledge *and* confess *and* glorify His name. [Lev. 7:12; Isa. 57:19; Hos. 14:2.]

[16]Do not forget *or* neglect to do kindness *and* good, to be generous *and* distribute *and* contribute to the needy [of the church [d]as embodiment and proof of fellowship], for such sacrifices are pleasing to God.

[17]Obey your spiritual leaders and submit to them [continually recognizing their authority over you], for they are constantly keeping watch over your souls *and* guarding your spiritual welfare, as men who will have to render an account [of their trust]. [Do your part to] let them do this with gladness and not with sighing *and* groaning, for that would not be profitable to you [either].

[18]Keep praying for us, for we are convinced that we have a good (clear) conscience, that we want to walk uprightly *and* live a noble life, acting honorably *and* in complete honesty in all things.

[19]And I beg of you [to pray for us] the more earnestly, in order that I may be restored to you the sooner.

[20]Now may the God of peace [Who is the Author and the Giver of peace], Who brought again from among the dead our Lord Jesus, that great Shepherd of the sheep, by the blood [that sealed, ratified] the everlasting agreement (covenant, testament), [Isa. 55:3; 63:11; Ezek. 37:26; Zech. 9:11.]

[a] Marvin Vincent, *Word Studies*. [b] Kenneth Wuest, *Word Studies*: Three negatives precede the verb. [c] Alexander Souter, *Pocket Lexicon*. [d] Joseph Thayer, *A Greek-English Lexicon*.

[a] 5 Deut. 31:6    [b] 6 Psalm 118:6,7

## New International Version

everything good for doing his will, and may he work in us what is pleasing to him, through Jesus Christ, to whom be glory for ever and ever. Amen.

22 Brothers and sisters, I urge you to bear with my word of exhortation, for in fact I have written to you quite briefly.

23 I want you to know that our brother Timothy has been released. If he arrives soon, I will come with him to see you.

24 Greet all your leaders and all the Lord's people. Those from Italy send you their greetings.

25 Grace be with you all.

## Amplified Bible

21 Strengthen (complete, perfect) and make you what you ought to be and equip you with everything good that you may carry out His will; [while He Himself] works in you and accomplishes that which is pleasing in His sight, through Jesus Christ (the Messiah); to Whom be the glory forever and ever (to the ages of the ages). Amen (so be it).

22 I call on you, brethren, to listen patiently and bear with this message of exhortation and admonition and encouragement, for I have written to you briefly.

23 Notice that our brother Timothy has been released [from prison]. If he comes here soon, I will see you along with him.

24 Give our greetings to all of your spiritual leaders and to all of the saints (God's consecrated believers). The Italian Christians send you their greetings [also].

25 Grace (God's favor and spiritual blessing) be with you all. Amen (so be it).

# New International Version

## James

**1** James, a servant of God and of the Lord Jesus Christ,

To the twelve tribes scattered among the nations:

Greetings.

### Trials and Temptations

[2] Consider it pure joy, my brothers and sisters,[a] whenever you face trials of many kinds, [3] because you know that the testing of your faith produces perseverance. [4] Let perseverance finish its work so that you may be mature and complete, not lacking anything. [5] If any of you lacks wisdom, you should ask God, who gives generously to all without finding fault, and it will be given to you. [6] But when you ask, you must believe and not doubt, because the one who doubts is like a wave of the sea, blown and tossed by the wind. [7] That person should not expect to receive anything from the Lord. [8] Such a person is double-minded and unstable in all they do.

[9] Believers in humble circumstances ought to take pride in their high position. [10] But the rich should take pride in their humiliation—since they will pass away like a wild flower. [11] For the sun rises with scorching heat and withers the plant; its blossom falls and its beauty is destroyed. In the same way, the rich will fade away even while they go about their business.

[12] Blessed is the one who perseveres under trial because, having stood the test, that person will receive the crown of life that the Lord has promised to those who love him.

[13] When tempted, no one should say, "God is tempting me." For God cannot be tempted by evil, nor does he tempt anyone; [14] but each person is tempted when they are dragged away by their own evil desire and enticed. [15] Then, after desire has conceived, it gives birth to sin; and sin, when it is full-grown, gives birth to death.

[16] Don't be deceived, my dear brothers and sisters. [17] Every good and perfect gift is from above, coming down from the Father of the heavenly lights, who does not change like shifting shadows. [18] He chose to give us birth through the word of truth, that we might be a kind of firstfruits of all he created.

### Listening and Doing

[19] My dear brothers and sisters, take note of this: Everyone should be quick to listen, slow to speak and slow to become angry, [20] because human anger does not produce the righteousness that God desires. [21] Therefore, get rid of

*a 2* The Greek word for *brothers and sisters* (*adelphoi*) refers here to believers, both men and women, as part of God's family; also in verses 16 and 19; and in 2:1, 5, 14; 3:10, 12; 4:11; 5:7, 9, 10, 12, 19.

# Amplified Bible

## THE LETTER OF
## James

**1** James, a servant of God and of the Lord Jesus Christ, to the twelve tribes scattered abroad [among the Gentiles in the dispersion]: Greetings (*a*rejoice)!

[2] Consider it wholly joyful, my brethren, whenever you are enveloped in *or* encounter trials of any sort *or* fall into various temptations.

[3] Be assured *and* understand that the trial *and* proving of your faith bring out endurance *and* steadfastness *and* patience.

[4] But let endurance *and* steadfastness *and* patience have full play *and* do a thorough work, so that you may be [people] perfectly and fully developed [with no defects], lacking in nothing.

[5] If any of you is deficient in wisdom, let him ask of *a*the giving God [Who gives] to everyone liberally *and* ungrudgingly, without reproaching *or* faultfinding, and it will be given him.

[6] Only it must be in faith that he asks with no wavering (no hesitating, no doubting). For the one who wavers (hesitates, doubts) is like the billowing surge out at sea that is blown hither *and* thither and tossed by the wind.

[7] For truly, let not such a person imagine that he will receive anything [he asks for] from the Lord,

[8] [For being as he is] a man of two minds (hesitating, dubious, irresolute), [he is] unstable *and* unreliable *and* uncertain about everything [he thinks, feels, decides].

[9] Let the brother in humble circumstances glory in his elevation [as a Christian, called to the true riches and to be an heir of God],

[10] And the rich [person ought to glory] in being humbled [by being shown his human frailty], because like the flower of the grass he will pass away.

[11] For the sun comes up with a scorching heat and parches the grass; its flower falls off and its beauty fades away. Even so will the rich man wither *and* die in the midst of his pursuits. [Isa. 40:6, 7.]

[12] Blessed (happy, *b*to be envied) is the man who is patient under trial *and* stands up under temptation, for when he has stood the test *and* been approved, he will receive [the victor's] crown of life which God has promised to those who love Him.

[13] Let no one say when he is tempted, I am tempted from God; for God is incapable of being tempted by [what is] evil and He Himself tempts no one.

[14] But every person is tempted when he is drawn away, enticed *and* baited by his own evil desire (lust, passions).

[15] Then the evil desire, when it has conceived, gives birth to sin, and sin, when it is fully matured, brings forth death.

[16] Do not be misled, my beloved brethren.

[17] Every good gift and every perfect (*c*free, large, full) gift is from above; it comes down from the Father of all [that gives] light, in [the shining of] Whom there can be no variation [rising or setting] or shadow cast by His turning [as in an eclipse].

[18] And it was of His own [free] will that He gave us birth [as sons] by [His] Word of Truth, so that we should be a kind of firstfruits of His creatures [a sample of what He created to be consecrated to Himself].

[19] Understand [this], my beloved brethren. Let every man be quick to hear [a ready listener], slow to speak, slow to take offense *and* to get angry.

[20] For man's anger does not promote the righteousness God [wishes and requires].

*a* Literal translation. *b* Alexander Souter, *Pocket Lexicon of the Greek New Testament*. *c* Marvin Vincent, *Word Studies in the New Testament*.

## New International Version

all moral filth and the evil that is so prevalent and humbly accept the word planted in you, which can save you.

22Do not merely listen to the word, and so deceive yourselves. Do what it says. 23Anyone who listens to the word but does not do what it says is like someone who looks at his face in a mirror 24and, after looking at himself, goes away and immediately forgets what he looks like. 25But whoever looks intently into the perfect law that gives freedom, and continues in it—not forgetting what they have heard, but doing it—they will be blessed in what they do.

26Those who consider themselves religious and yet do not keep a tight rein on their tongues deceive themselves, and their religion is worthless. 27Religion that God our Father accepts as pure and faultless is this: to look after orphans and widows in their distress and to keep oneself from being polluted by the world.

### Favoritism Forbidden

**2** My brothers and sisters, believers in our glorious Lord Jesus Christ must not show favoritism. 2Suppose a man comes into your meeting wearing a gold ring and fine clothes, and a poor man in filthy old clothes also comes in. 3If you show special attention to the man wearing fine clothes and say, "Here's a good seat for you," but say to the poor man, "You stand there" or "Sit on the floor by my feet," 4have you not discriminated among yourselves and become judges with evil thoughts?

5Listen, my dear brothers and sisters: Has not God chosen those who are poor in the eyes of the world to be rich in faith and to inherit the kingdom he promised those who love him? 6But you have dishonored the poor. Is it not the rich who are exploiting you? Are they not the ones who are dragging you into court? 7Are they not the ones who are blaspheming the noble name of him to whom you belong?

8If you really keep the royal law found in Scripture, "Love your neighbor as yourself,"[a] you are doing right. 9But if you show favoritism, you sin and are convicted by the law as lawbreakers. 10For whoever keeps the whole law and yet stumbles at just one point is guilty of breaking all of it. 11For he who said, "You shall not commit adultery,"[b] also said, "You shall not murder."[c] If you do not commit adultery but do commit murder, you have become a lawbreaker.

## Amplified Bible

21So get rid of all uncleanness and the rampant outgrowth of wickedness, and in a humble (gentle, modest) spirit receive *and* welcome the Word which implanted *and* rooted [in your hearts] contains the power to save your souls.

22But be doers of the Word [obey the message], and not merely listeners to it, betraying yourselves [into deception by reasoning contrary to the Truth].

23For if anyone only listens to the Word without obeying it *and* being a doer of it, he is like a man who looks carefully at his [own] natural face in a mirror;

24For he thoughtfully observes himself, and then goes off and promptly forgets what he was like.

25But he who looks carefully into the faultless law, the [law] of liberty, and is faithful to it *and* perseveres in looking into it, being not a heedless listener who forgets but an active doer [who obeys], he shall be blessed in his doing (his life of obedience).

26If anyone thinks himself to be religious (piously observant of the external duties of his faith) and does not bridle his tongue but deludes his own heart, this person's religious service is worthless (futile, barren).

27External *a*religious worship [*b*religion as it is expressed in outward acts] that is pure and unblemished in the sight of God the Father is this: to visit *and* help *and* care for the orphans and widows in their affliction *and* need, and to keep oneself unspotted *and* uncontaminated from the world.

**2** My brethren, pay no servile regard to people [show no prejudice, no partiality]. Do not [attempt to] hold *and* practice the faith of our Lord Jesus Christ [the Lord] of glory [together with snobbery]!

2For if a person comes into your congregation whose hands are adorned with gold rings and who is wearing splendid apparel, and also a poor [man] in shabby clothes comes in,

3And you pay special attention to the one who wears the splendid clothes and say to him, Sit here in this preferable seat! while you tell the poor [man], Stand there! or, Sit there on the floor at my feet!

4Are you not discriminating among your own and becoming critics *and* judges with wrong motives?

5Listen, my beloved brethren: Has not God chosen those who are poor in the eyes of the world to be rich in faith *and* in their position as believers and to inherit the kingdom which He has promised to those who love Him?

6But you [in contrast] have insulted (humiliated, dishonored, and shown your contempt for) the poor. Is it not the rich who domineer over you? Is it not they who drag you into the law courts?

7Is it not they who slander *and* blaspheme that precious name by which you are distinguished *and* called [the name of Christ invoked in baptism]?

8If indeed you [really] fulfill the royal Law in accordance with the Scripture, You shall love your neighbor as [you love] yourself, you do well. [Lev. 19:18.]

9But if you show servile regard (prejudice, favoritism) for people, you commit sin and are rebuked *and* convicted by the Law as violators *and* offenders.

10For whosoever keeps the Law [as a] whole but stumbles *and* offends in one [single instance] has become guilty of [breaking] all of it.

11For He Who said, You shall not commit adultery, also said, You shall not kill. If you do not commit adultery but do kill, you have become guilty of transgressing the [whole] Law. [Exod. 20:13, 14; Deut. 5:17, 18.]

---

*a* Robert Jamieson, A. R. Fausset and David Brown, *A Commentary on the Old and New Testaments*: "Religion in its rise interests us about **ourselves**; in its progress, about our **fellow creatures**; in its highest stage, about the honor of **God**." *b* G. Abbott-Smith, *Manual Greek Lexicon of the New Testament*.

*a 8* Lev. 19:18    *b 11* Exodus 20:14; Deut. 5:18    *c 11* Exodus 20:13; Deut. 5:17

## New International Version

¹²Speak and act as those who are going to be judged by the law that gives freedom, ¹³because judgment without mercy will be shown to anyone who has not been merciful. Mercy triumphs over judgment.

### Faith and Deeds

¹⁴What good is it, my brothers and sisters, if someone claims to have faith but has no deeds? Can such faith save them? ¹⁵Suppose a brother or a sister is without clothes and daily food. ¹⁶If one of you says to them, "Go in peace; keep warm and well fed," but does nothing about their physical needs, what good is it? ¹⁷In the same way, faith by itself, if it is not accompanied by action, is dead.

¹⁸But someone will say, "You have faith; I have deeds."

Show me your faith without deeds, and I will show you my faith by my deeds. ¹⁹You believe that there is one God. Good! Even the demons believe that—and shudder.

²⁰You foolish person, do you want evidence that faith without deeds is useless[a]? ²¹Was not our father Abraham considered righteous for what he did when he offered his son Isaac on the altar? ²²You see that his faith and his actions were working together, and his faith was made complete by what he did. ²³And the scripture was fulfilled that says, "Abraham believed God, and it was credited to him as righteousness,"[b] and he was called God's friend. ²⁴You see that a person is considered righteous by what they do and not by faith alone.

²⁵In the same way, was not even Rahab the prostitute considered righteous for what she did when she gave lodging to the spies and sent them off in a different direction? ²⁶As the body without the spirit is dead, so faith without deeds is dead.

### Taming the Tongue

**3** Not many of you should become teachers, my fellow believers, because you know that we who teach will be judged more strictly. ²We all stumble in many ways. Anyone who is never at fault in what they say is perfect, able to keep their whole body in check.

³When we put bits into the mouths of horses to make them obey us, we can turn the whole animal. ⁴Or take ships as an example. Although they are so large and are driven by strong winds, they are steered by a very small rudder wherever the pilot wants to go. ⁵Likewise, the tongue is a

## Amplified Bible

¹²So speak and so act as [people should] who are to be judged under the law of liberty [the moral instruction given by Christ, especially about love].

¹³For to him who has shown no mercy the judgment [will be] merciless, but mercy [full of glad confidence] exults victoriously over judgment.

¹⁴What is the use (profit), my brethren, for anyone to profess to have faith if he has no [good] works [to show for it]? Can [such] faith save [his soul]?

¹⁵If a brother or sister is poorly clad and lacks food for each day,

¹⁶And one of you says to him, Good-bye! Keep [yourself] warm and well fed, without giving him the necessities for the body, what good does that do?

¹⁷So also faith, if it does not have works (deeds and actions of obedience to back it up), by itself is destitute of power (inoperative, dead).

¹⁸But someone will say [to you then], You [say you] have faith, and I have [good] works. Now you show me your [alleged] faith apart from any [good] works [if you can], and I by [good] works [of obedience] will show you my faith.

¹⁹You believe that God is one; you do well. So do the demons believe and shudder [in terror and horror such as [a]make a man's hair stand on end and contract the surface of his skin]!

²⁰Are you willing to be shown [proof], you foolish (unproductive, spiritually deficient) fellow, that faith apart from [good] works is inactive *and* ineffective *and* worthless?

²¹Was not our forefather Abraham [shown to be] justified (made acceptable to God) by [his] works when he brought to the altar as an offering his [own] son Isaac? [Gen. 22:1-14.]

²²You see that [his] faith was cooperating with his works, and [his] faith was completed *and* reached its supreme expression [when he implemented it] by [good] works.

²³And [so] the Scripture was fulfilled that says, Abraham believed in (adhered to, trusted in, and relied on) God, and this was accounted to him as righteousness (as conformity to God's will in thought and deed), and he was called God's friend. [Gen. 15:6; II Chron. 20:7; Isa. 41:8.]

²⁴You see that a man is justified (pronounced righteous before God) through what he does and not alone through faith [through works of obedience as well as by what he believes].

²⁵So also with Rahab the harlot—was she not shown to be justified (pronounced righteous before God) by [good] deeds when she took in the scouts (spies) and sent them away by a different route? [Josh. 2:1-21.]

²⁶For as the human body apart from the spirit is lifeless, so faith apart from [its] works of obedience is also dead.

**3** Not many [of you] should become teachers ([b]self-constituted censors and reprovers of others), my brethren, for you know that we [teachers] will be judged by a higher standard *and* with greater severity [than other people; thus we assume the greater accountability and the more condemnation].

²For we all often stumble *and* fall *and* offend in many things. And if anyone does not offend in speech [never says the wrong things], he is a fully developed character *and* a perfect man, able to control his whole body *and* to curb his entire nature.

³If we set bits in the horses' mouths to make them obey us, we can turn their whole bodies about.

⁴Likewise, look at the ships: though they are so great and are driven by rough winds, they are steered by a very small rudder wherever the impulse of the helmsman determines.

---

*a* Marvin Vincent, *Word Studies.*   *b* John Calvin, cited by Robert Jamieson, A. R. Fausset and David Brown, *A Commentary.*

*a* 20 Some early manuscripts *dead*   *b* 23 Gen. 15:6

## New International Version

small part of the body, but it makes great boasts. Consider what a great forest is set on fire by a small spark. [6]The tongue also is a fire, a world of evil among the parts of the body. It corrupts the whole body, sets the whole course of one's life on fire, and is itself set on fire by hell.

[7]All kinds of animals, birds, reptiles and sea creatures are being tamed and have been tamed by mankind, [8]but no human being can tame the tongue. It is a restless evil, full of deadly poison.

[9]With the tongue we praise our Lord and Father, and with it we curse human beings, who have been made in God's likeness. [10]Out of the same mouth come praise and cursing. My brothers and sisters, this should not be. [11]Can both fresh water and salt water flow from the same spring? [12]My brothers and sisters, can a fig tree bear olives, or a grapevine bear figs? Neither can a salt spring produce fresh water.

### Two Kinds of Wisdom

[13]Who is wise and understanding among you? Let them show it by their good life, by deeds done in the humility that comes from wisdom. [14]But if you harbor bitter envy and selfish ambition in your hearts, do not boast about it or deny the truth. [15]Such "wisdom" does not come down from heaven but is earthly, unspiritual, demonic. [16]For where you have envy and selfish ambition, there you find disorder and every evil practice.

[17]But the wisdom that comes from heaven is first of all pure; then peace-loving, considerate, submissive, full of mercy and good fruit, impartial and sincere. [18]Peacemakers who sow in peace reap a harvest of righteousness.

### Submit Yourselves to God

**4** What causes fights and quarrels among you? Don't they come from your desires that battle within you? [2]You desire but do not have, so you kill. You covet but you cannot get what you want, so you quarrel and fight. You do not have because you do not ask God. [3]When you ask, you do not receive, because you ask with wrong motives, that you may spend what you get on your pleasures.

[4]You adulterous people,[a] don't you know that friendship with the world means enmity against God? Therefore, anyone who chooses to be a friend of the world becomes an

## Amplified Bible

[5]Even so the tongue is a little member, and it can boast of great things. See how much wood *or* how great a forest a tiny spark can set ablaze!

[6]And the tongue is a fire. [The tongue is a] world of wickedness set among our members, contaminating *and* depraving the whole body and setting on fire the wheel of birth (the cycle of man's nature), being itself ignited by hell (Gehenna).

[7]For every kind of beast and bird, of reptile and sea animal, can be tamed and has been tamed by human genius (nature).

[8]But the human tongue can be tamed by no man. It is a restless (undisciplined, irreconcilable) evil, full of deadly poison.

[9]With it we bless the Lord and Father, and with it we curse men who were made in God's likeness!

[10]Out of the same mouth come forth blessing and cursing. These things, my brethren, ought not to be so.

[11]Does a fountain send forth [simultaneously] from the same opening fresh water and bitter?

[12]Can a fig tree, my brethren, bear olives, or a grapevine figs? Neither can a salt spring furnish fresh water.

[13]Who is there among you who is wise and intelligent? Then let him by his noble living show forth his [good] works with the [unobtrusive] humility [which is the proper attribute] of true wisdom.

[14]But if you have bitter jealousy (envy) and contention (rivalry, selfish ambition) in your hearts, do not pride yourselves on it and thus be in defiance of *and* false to the Truth.

[15]This [superficial] wisdom is not such as comes down from above, but is earthly, unspiritual (animal), even devilish (demoniacal).

[16]For wherever there is jealousy (envy) and contention (rivalry and selfish ambition), there will also be confusion (unrest, disharmony, rebellion) and all sorts of evil *and* vile practices.

[17]But the wisdom from above is first of all pure (undefiled); then it is peace-loving, courteous (considerate, gentle). [It is willing to] yield to reason, full of compassion and good fruits; it is wholehearted *and* straightforward, impartial *and* unfeigned (free from doubts, wavering, and insincerity).

[18]And the harvest of righteousness (of conformity to God's will in thought and deed) is [the fruit of the seed] sown in peace by those who work for *and* make peace [in themselves and in others, that peace which means concord, agreement, and harmony between individuals, with undisturbedness, in a peaceful mind free from fears and agitating passions and moral conflicts].

**4** What leads to strife (discord and feuds) *and* how do conflicts (quarrels and fightings) originate among you? Do they not arise from your sensual desires that are ever warring in your bodily members?

[2]You are jealous *and* covet [what others have] and your desires go unfulfilled; [so] you become murderers. [To hate is to murder as far as your hearts are concerned.] You burn with envy *and* anger and are not able to obtain [the gratification, the contentment, and the happiness that you seek], so you fight and war. You do not have, because you do not ask. [I John 3:15.]

[3][Or] you do ask [God for them] and yet fail to receive, because you ask with wrong purpose and evil, selfish motives. Your intention is [when you get what you desire] to spend it in sensual pleasures.

[4]You [are like] unfaithful wives [having illicit love affairs with the world and breaking your marriage vow to God]! Do you not know that being the world's friend is being God's enemy? So whoever chooses to be a friend of the world takes his stand as an enemy of God.

---

[a] 4 An allusion to covenant unfaithfulness; see Hosea 3:1.

## New International Version

enemy of God. ⁵Or do you think Scripture says without reason that he jealously longs for the spirit he has caused to dwell in us*ᵃ*? ⁶But he gives us more grace. That is why Scripture says:

> "God opposes the proud
> but shows favor to the humble."*ᵇ*

⁷Submit yourselves, then, to God. Resist the devil, and he will flee from you. ⁸Come near to God and he will come near to you. Wash your hands, you sinners, and purify your hearts, you double-minded. ⁹Grieve, mourn and wail. Change your laughter to mourning and your joy to gloom. ¹⁰Humble yourselves before the Lord, and he will lift you up.

¹¹Brothers and sisters, do not slander one another. Anyone who speaks against a brother or sister*ᶜ* or judges them speaks against the law and judges it. When you judge the law, you are not keeping it, but sitting in judgment on it. ¹²There is only one Lawgiver and Judge, the one who is able to save and destroy. But you—who are you to judge your neighbor?

### Boasting About Tomorrow

¹³Now listen, you who say, "Today or tomorrow we will go to this or that city, spend a year there, carry on business and make money." ¹⁴Why, you do not even know what will happen tomorrow. What is your life? You are a mist that appears for a little while and then vanishes. ¹⁵Instead, you ought to say, "If it is the Lord's will, we will live and do this or that." ¹⁶As it is, you boast in your arrogant schemes. All such boasting is evil. ¹⁷If anyone, then, knows the good they ought to do and doesn't do it, it is sin for them.

### Warning to Rich Oppressors

**5** Now listen, you rich people, weep and wail because of the misery that is coming on you. ²Your wealth has rotted, and moths have eaten your clothes. ³Your gold and silver are corroded. Their corrosion will testify against you and eat your flesh like fire. You have hoarded wealth in the last days. ⁴Look! The wages you failed to pay the workers who mowed your fields are crying out against you. The cries of the harvesters have reached the ears of the Lord Almighty. ⁵You have lived on earth in luxury and self-indulgence. You have fattened yourselves in the day of slaughter.*ᵈ* ⁶You have condemned and murdered the innocent one, who was not opposing you.

### Patience in Suffering

⁷Be patient, then, brothers and sisters, until the Lord's coming. See how the farmer waits for the land to yield its valuable crop, patiently waiting for the autumn and spring

---

*ᵃ 5 Or that the spirit he caused to dwell in us envies intensely; or that the Spirit he caused to dwell in us longs jealously    ᵇ 6 Prov. 3:34    ᶜ 11 The Greek word for brother or sister (adelphos) refers here to a believer, whether man or woman, as part of God's family.    ᵈ 5 Or yourselves as in a day of feasting*

## Amplified Bible

⁵Or do you suppose that the Scripture is speaking to no purpose that says, The Spirit Whom He has caused to dwell in us yearns over us *and* He yearns for the Spirit [to be welcome] with a jealous love? [Jer. 3:14; Hos. 2:19ff.]

⁶But He gives us more and more grace (*ᵃ*power of the Holy Spirit, to meet this evil tendency and all others fully). That is why He says, God sets Himself against the proud and haughty, but gives grace [continually] to the lowly (those who are humble enough to receive it). [Prov. 3:34.]

⁷So be subject to God. Resist the devil [stand firm against him], and he will flee from you.

⁸Come close to God and He will come close to you. [Recognize that you are] sinners, get your soiled hands clean; [realize that you have been disloyal] wavering individuals with divided interests, and purify your hearts [of your spiritual adultery].

⁹[As you draw near to God] be deeply penitent and grieve, even weep [over your disloyalty]. Let your laughter be turned to grief and your mirth to dejection *and* heartfelt shame [for your sins].

¹⁰Humble yourselves [feeling very insignificant] in the presence of the Lord, and He will exalt you [He will lift you up and make your lives significant].

¹¹[My] brethren, do not speak evil about or accuse one another. He that maligns a brother or judges his brother is maligning *and* criticizing the Law *and* judging the Law. But if you judge the Law, you are not a practicer of the Law but a censor *and* judge [of it].

¹²One only is the Lawgiver *and* Judge Who is able to save and to destroy [the One Who has the absolute power of life and death]. [But you] who are you that [you presume to] pass judgment on your neighbor?

¹³Come now, you who say, Today or tomorrow we will go into such *and* such a city and spend a year there and carry on our business and make money.

¹⁴Yet you do not know [the least thing] about what may happen tomorrow. What is the nature of your life? You are [really] but a wisp of vapor (a puff of smoke, a mist) that is visible for a little while and then disappears [into thin air].

¹⁵You ought instead to say, If the Lord is willing, we shall live and we shall do this or that [thing].

¹⁶But as it is, you boast [falsely] in your presumption *and* your self-conceit. All such boasting is wrong.

¹⁷So any person who knows what is right to do but does not do it, to him it is sin.

**5** Come now, you rich [people], weep aloud and lament over the miseries (the woes) that are surely coming upon you.

²Your abundant wealth has rotted *and* is ruined, and your [many] garments have become moth-eaten.

³Your gold and silver are completely rusted through, and their rust will be testimony against you and it will devour your flesh as if it were fire. You have heaped together treasure for the last days.

⁴[But] look! [Here are] the wages that you have withheld by fraud from the laborers who have reaped your fields, crying out [for vengeance]; and the cries of the harvesters have come to the ears of the Lord of hosts.

⁵[Here] on earth you have abandoned yourselves to soft (prodigal) living and to [the pleasures of] self-indulgence *and* self-gratification. You have fattened your hearts in a day of slaughter.

⁶You have condemned and have murdered the righteous (innocent man), [while] he offers no resistance to you.

⁷So be patient, brethren, [as you wait] till the coming of the Lord. See how the farmer waits expectantly for the precious harvest from the land. [See how] he keeps up his patient [vigil] over it until it receives the early and late rains.

---

*ᵃ Adam Clarke, The Holy Bible with A Commentary.*

## New International Version

rains. [8]You too, be patient and stand firm, because the Lord's coming is near. [9]Don't grumble against one another, brothers and sisters, or you will be judged. The Judge is standing at the door!

[10]Brothers and sisters, as an example of patience in the face of suffering, take the prophets who spoke in the name of the Lord. [11]As you know, we count as blessed those who have persevered. You have heard of Job's perseverance and have seen what the Lord finally brought about. The Lord is full of compassion and mercy.

[12]Above all, my brothers and sisters, do not swear—not by heaven or by earth or by anything else. All you need to say is a simple "Yes" or "No." Otherwise you will be condemned.

### The Prayer of Faith

[13]Is anyone among you in trouble? Let them pray. Is anyone happy? Let them sing songs of praise. [14]Is anyone among you sick? Let them call the elders of the church to pray over them and anoint them with oil in the name of the Lord. [15]And the prayer offered in faith will make the sick person well; the Lord will raise them up. If they have sinned, they will be forgiven. [16]Therefore confess your sins to each other and pray for each other so that you may be healed. The prayer of a righteous person is powerful and effective.

[17]Elijah was a human being, even as we are. He prayed earnestly that it would not rain, and it did not rain on the land for three and a half years. [18]Again he prayed, and the heavens gave rain, and the earth produced its crops.

[19]My brothers and sisters, if one of you should wander from the truth and someone should bring that person back, [20]remember this: Whoever turns a sinner from the error of their way will save them from death and cover over a multitude of sins.

## Amplified Bible

[8]So you also must be patient. Establish your hearts [strengthen and confirm them in the final certainty], for the coming of the Lord is very near.

[9]Do not complain, brethren, against one another, so that you [yourselves] may not be judged. Look! The Judge is [already] standing at the very door.

[10][As] an example of suffering and ill-treatment together with patience, brethren, take the prophets who spoke in the name of the Lord [as His messengers].

[11]You know how we call those blessed (happy) who were steadfast [who endured]. You have heard of the endurance of Job, and you have seen the Lord's [purpose and how He richly blessed him in the] end, inasmuch as the Lord is full of pity *and* compassion *and* tenderness and mercy. [Job 1:21, 22; 42:10; Ps. 111:4.]

[12]But above all [things], my brethren, do not swear, either by heaven or by earth or by any other oath; but let your yes be [a simple] yes, and your no be [a simple] no, so that you may not sin *and* fall under condemnation.

[13]Is anyone among you afflicted (ill-treated, suffering evil)? He should pray. Is anyone glad at heart? He should sing praise [to God].

[14]Is anyone among you sick? He should call in the church elders (the spiritual guides). And they should pray over him, anointing him with oil in the Lord's name.

[15]And the prayer [that is] of faith will save him who is sick, and the Lord will restore him; and if he has committed sins, he will be forgiven.

[16]Confess to one another therefore your faults (your slips, your false steps, your offenses, your sins) and pray [also] for one another, that you may be healed *and* restored [to a spiritual tone of mind and heart]. The earnest (heartfelt, continued) prayer of a righteous man makes tremendous power available [dynamic in its working].

[17]Elijah was a human being with a nature such as we have [with feelings, affections, and a constitution like ours]; and he prayed earnestly for it not to rain, and no rain fell on the earth for three years and six months. [I Kings 17:1.]

[18]And [then] he prayed again and the heavens supplied rain and the land produced its crops [as usual]. [I Kings 18:42-45.]

[19][My] brethren, if anyone among you strays from the Truth *and* falls into error and another [person] brings him back [to God],

[20]Let the [latter] one be sure that whoever turns a sinner from his evil course will save [that one's] soul from death and will cover a multitude of sins [*a*procure the pardon of the many sins committed by the convert].

---

*a* Adam Clarke, *The Holy Bible with A Commentary* and many other translators.

# 1 Peter

**1** Peter, an apostle of Jesus Christ,

To God's elect, exiles scattered throughout the provinces of Pontus, Galatia, Cappadocia, Asia and Bithynia, [2]who have been chosen according to the foreknowledge of God the Father, through the sanctifying work of the Spirit, to be obedient to Jesus Christ and sprinkled with his blood:

Grace and peace be yours in abundance.

## Praise to God for a Living Hope

[3]Praise be to the God and Father of our Lord Jesus Christ! In his great mercy he has given us new birth into a living hope through the resurrection of Jesus Christ from the dead, [4]and into an inheritance that can never perish, spoil or fade. This inheritance is kept in heaven for you, [5]who through faith are shielded by God's power until the coming of the salvation that is ready to be revealed in the last time. [6]In all this you greatly rejoice, though now for a little while you may have had to suffer grief in all kinds of trials. [7]These have come so that the proven genuineness of your faith—of greater worth than gold, which perishes even though refined by fire—may result in praise, glory and honor when Jesus Christ is revealed. [8]Though you have not seen him, you love him; and even though you do not see him now, you believe in him and are filled with an inexpressible and glorious joy, [9]for you are receiving the end result of your faith, the salvation of your souls.

[10]Concerning this salvation, the prophets, who spoke of the grace that was to come to you, searched intently and with the greatest care, [11]trying to find out the time and circumstances to which the Spirit of Christ in them was pointing when he predicted the sufferings of the Messiah and the glories that would follow. [12]It was revealed to them that they were not serving themselves but you, when they spoke of the things that have now been told you by those who have preached the gospel to you by the Holy Spirit sent from heaven. Even angels long to look into these things.

## Be Holy

[13]Therefore, with minds that are alert and fully sober, set your hope on the grace to be brought to you when Jesus Christ is revealed at his coming. [14]As obedient children, do not conform to the evil desires you had when you lived in ignorance. [15]But just as he who called you is holy, so be holy in all you do; [16]for it is written: "Be holy, because I am holy."[a]

# Peter

**1** Peter, an apostle (a special messenger) of Jesus Christ, [writing] to the elect exiles of the dispersion scattered (sowed) abroad in Pontus, Galatia, Cappadocia, Asia, and Bithynia,

[2]Who were chosen and foreknown by God the Father and consecrated (sanctified, made holy) by the Spirit to be obedient to Jesus Christ (the Messiah) and to be sprinkled with [His] blood: May grace (spiritual blessing) and peace be given you in increasing abundance [that spiritual peace to be [a]realized in and through Christ, [b]freedom from fears, agitating passions, and moral conflicts].

[3]Praised (honored, blessed) be the God and Father of our Lord Jesus Christ (the Messiah)! By His boundless mercy we have been born again to an ever-living hope through the resurrection of Jesus Christ from the dead,

[4][Born anew] into an inheritance which is beyond the reach of change and decay [imperishable], unsullied and unfading, reserved in heaven for you,

[5]Who are being guarded (garrisoned) by God's power through [your] faith [till you fully inherit that [c]final] salvation that is ready to be revealed [for you] in the last time.

[6][You should] be exceedingly glad on this account, though now for a little while you may be distressed by trials and suffer temptations,

[7]So that [the genuineness] of your faith may be tested, [your faith] which is infinitely more precious than the perishable gold which is tested and purified by fire. [This proving of your faith is intended] to redound to [your] praise and glory and honor when Jesus Christ (the Messiah, the Anointed One) is revealed.

[8]Without having seen Him, you love Him; though you do not [even] now see Him, you believe in Him and exult and thrill with inexpressible and glorious (triumphant, heavenly) joy.

[9][At the same time] you receive the result (outcome, consummation) of your faith, the salvation of your souls.

[10]The prophets, who prophesied of the grace (divine blessing) which was intended for you, searched and inquired earnestly about this salvation.

[11]They sought [to find out] to whom or when this was to come which the Spirit of Christ working within them was indicating when He predicted the sufferings of Christ and the glories that should follow [them].

[12]It was then disclosed to them that the services they were rendering were not meant for themselves and their period of time, but for you. [It is these very] things which have now already been made known plainly to you by those who preached the good news (the Gospel) to you by the [same] Holy Spirit sent from heaven. Into these things [the very] angels long to look!

[13]So brace up your minds; be sober (circumspect, morally alert); set your hope wholly and unchangeably on the grace (divine favor) that is coming to you when Jesus Christ (the Messiah) is revealed.

[14][Live] as children of obedience [to God]; do not conform yourselves to the evil desires [that governed you] in your former ignorance [when you did not know the requirements of the Gospel].

[15]But as the One Who called you is holy, you yourselves also be holy in all your conduct and manner of living.

[16]For it is written, You shall be holy, for I am holy. [Lev. 11:44, 45.]

---

[a] Hermann Cremer, *Biblico-Theological Lexicon of New Testament Greek.*
[b] *Webster's New International Dictionary* offers this as a definition of "peace." [c] Charles B. Williams, *The New Testament: A Translation in the Language of the People.*

## New International Version

[17]Since you call on a Father who judges each person's work impartially, live out your time as foreigners here in reverent fear. [18]For you know that it was not with perishable things such as silver or gold that you were redeemed from the empty way of life handed down to you from your ancestors, [19]but with the precious blood of Christ, a lamb without blemish or defect. [20]He was chosen before the creation of the world, but was revealed in these last times for your sake. [21]Through him you believe in God, who raised him from the dead and glorified him, and so your faith and hope are in God.

[22]Now that you have purified yourselves by obeying the truth so that you have sincere love for each other, love one another deeply, from the heart.[a] [23]For you have been born again, not of perishable seed, but of imperishable, through the living and enduring word of God. [24]For,

"All people are like grass,
    and all their glory is like the flowers of the field;
the grass withers and the flowers fall,
[25]    but the word of the Lord endures forever."[b]

And this is the word that was preached to you.

**2** Therefore, rid yourselves of all malice and all deceit, hypocrisy, envy, and slander of every kind. [2]Like newborn babies, crave pure spiritual milk, so that by it you may grow up in your salvation, [3]now that you have tasted that the Lord is good.

### The Living Stone and a Chosen People

[4]As you come to him, the living Stone—rejected by humans but chosen by God and precious to him— [5]you also, like living stones, are being built into a spiritual house[c] to be a holy priesthood, offering spiritual sacrifices acceptable to God through Jesus Christ. [6]For in Scripture it says:

"See, I lay a stone in Zion,
    a chosen and precious cornerstone,
and the one who trusts in him
    will never be put to shame."[d]

[7]Now to you who believe, this stone is precious. But to those who do not believe,

"The stone the builders rejected
    has become the cornerstone,"[e]

[8]and,

"A stone that causes people to stumble
    and a rock that makes them fall."[f]

They stumble because they disobey the message—which is also what they were destined for.

[9]But you are a chosen people, a royal priesthood, a holy nation, God's special possession, that you may declare the

## Amplified Bible

[17]And if you call upon Him as [your] Father Who judges each one impartially according to what he does, [then] you should conduct yourselves with true reverence throughout the time of your temporary residence [on the earth, whether long or short].

[18]You must know (recognize) that you were redeemed (ransomed) from the useless (fruitless) way of living inherited by tradition from [your] forefathers, not with corruptible things [such as] silver and gold,

[19]But [you were purchased] with the precious blood of Christ (the Messiah), like that of a [sacrificial] lamb without blemish or spot.

[20]It is true that He was chosen *and* foreordained (destined and foreknown for it) before the foundation of the world, but He was brought out to public view (made manifest) in these last days (at the end of the times) for the sake of you.

[21]Through Him you believe in (adhere to, rely on) God, Who raised Him up from the dead and gave Him honor *and* glory, so that your faith and hope are [centered and rest] in God.

[22]Since by your obedience to the Truth *through the [Holy] Spirit* you have purified your hearts for the sincere affection of the brethren, [see that you] love one another fervently from a *pure* heart.

[23]You have been regenerated (born again), not from a mortal [a]origin ([b]seed, sperm), but from one that is immortal by the *ever* living and lasting Word of God.

[24]For all flesh (mankind) is like grass, and all its glory (honor) like [the] flower of grass. The grass withers and the flower drops off,

[25]But the Word of the Lord ([c]divine instruction, the Gospel) endures forever. And this Word is the good news which was preached to you. [Isa. 40:6-9.]

**2** So be done with every trace of wickedness (depravity, malignity) and all deceit and insincerity (pretense, hypocrisy) and grudges (envy, jealousy) and slander *and* evil speaking of every kind.

[2]Like newborn babies you should crave (thirst for, earnestly desire) the pure (unadulterated) spiritual milk, that by it you may be nurtured *and* grow unto [completed] salvation,

[3]Since you have [already] tasted the goodness *and* kindness of the Lord. [Ps. 34:8.]

[4]Come to Him [then, to that] Living Stone which men [d]tried *and* threw away, but which is chosen [and] precious in God's sight. [Ps. 118:22; Isa. 28:16.]

[5][Come] and, like living stones, be yourselves built [into] a spiritual house, for a holy (dedicated, consecrated) priesthood, to offer up [those] spiritual sacrifices [that are] acceptable *and* pleasing to God through Jesus Christ.

[6]For thus it stands in Scripture: Behold, I am laying in Zion a chosen ([d]honored), precious chief Cornerstone, and he who believes in Him [who adheres to, trusts in, and relies on Him] shall never be [c]disappointed *or* put to shame. [Isa. 28:16.]

[7]To you then who believe (who adhere to, trust in, and rely on Him) is the preciousness; but for those who disbelieve [it is true], The [very] Stone which the builders rejected has become the main Cornerstone, [Ps. 118:22.]

[8]And, A Stone that will cause stumbling and a Rock that will give [men] offense; they stumble because they disobey *and* disbelieve [God's] Word, as those [who reject Him] were destined (appointed) to do.

[9]But you are a chosen race, a royal priesthood, a dedicated nation, [God's] own [e]purchased, special people, that you may set forth the wonderful deeds *and* display the vir-

[a] 22 Some early manuscripts *from a pure heart*    [b] 25 Isaiah 40:6-8 (see Septuagint)    [c] 5 Or *into a temple of the Spirit*    [d] 6 Isaiah 28:16 [e] 7 Psalm 118:22    [f] 8 Isaiah 8:14

[a] Joseph Thayer, *A Greek-English Lexicon of the New Testament.*    [b] G. Abbott-Smith, *Manual Greek Lexicon of the New Testament.*    [c] Joseph Thayer, *A Greek-English Lexicon.*    [d] Marvin Vincent, *Word Studies in the New Testament.*    [e] John Wycliffe, *The Wycliffe Bible.*

## New International Version

praises of him who called you out of darkness into his wonderful light. [10]Once you were not a people, but now you are the people of God; once you had not received mercy, but now you have received mercy.

### Living Godly Lives in a Pagan Society

[11]Dear friends, I urge you, as foreigners and exiles, to abstain from sinful desires, which wage war against your soul. [12]Live such good lives among the pagans that, though they accuse you of doing wrong, they may see your good deeds and glorify God on the day he visits us.

[13]Submit yourselves for the Lord's sake to every human authority: whether to the emperor, as the supreme authority, [14]or to governors, who are sent by him to punish those who do wrong and to commend those who do right. [15]For it is God's will that by doing good you should silence the ignorant talk of foolish people. [16]Live as free people, but do not use your freedom as a cover-up for evil; live as God's slaves. [17]Show proper respect to everyone, love the family of believers, fear God, honor the emperor.

[18]Slaves, in reverent fear of God submit yourselves to your masters, not only to those who are good and considerate, but also to those who are harsh. [19]For it is commendable if someone bears up under the pain of unjust suffering because they are conscious of God. [20]But how is it to your credit if you receive a beating for doing wrong and endure it? But if you suffer for doing good and you endure it, this is commendable before God. [21]To this you were called, because Christ suffered for you, leaving you an example, that you should follow in his steps.

[22]"He committed no sin,
    and no deceit was found in his mouth."[a]

[23]When they hurled their insults at him, he did not retaliate; when he suffered, he made no threats. Instead, he entrusted himself to him who judges justly. [24]"He himself bore our sins" in his body on the cross, so that we might die to sins and live for righteousness; "by his wounds you have been healed." [25]For "you were like sheep going astray,"[b] but now you have returned to the Shepherd and Overseer of your souls.

**3** Wives, in the same way submit yourselves to your own husbands so that, if any of them do not believe the word, they may be won over without words by the behavior

## Amplified Bible

tues and perfections of Him Who called you out of darkness into His marvelous light. [Exod. 19:5, 6.]

[10]Once you were not a people [at all], but now you are God's people; once you were unpitied, but now you are pitied *and* have received mercy. [Hos. 2:23.]

[11]Beloved, I implore you as aliens and strangers *and* exiles [in this world] to abstain from the sensual urges (the evil desires, the passions of the flesh, your lower nature) that wage war against the soul.

[12]Conduct yourselves properly (honorably, righteously) among the Gentiles, so that, although they may slander you as evildoers, [yet] they may by witnessing your good deeds [come to] glorify God in the day of inspection [[a]when God shall look upon you wanderers as a pastor or shepherd looks over his flock].

[13]Be submissive to every human institution *and* authority for the sake of the Lord, whether it be to the emperor as supreme,

[14]Or to governors as sent by him to bring vengeance (punishment, justice) to those who do wrong and to encourage those who do good service.

[15]For it is God's will *and* intention that by doing right [your good and honest lives] should silence (muzzle, gag) the ignorant charges *and* ill-informed criticisms of foolish persons.

[16][Live] as free people, [yet] without employing your freedom as a pretext for wickedness; but [live at all times] as servants of God.

[17]Show respect for all men [treat them honorably]. Love the brotherhood (the Christian fraternity of which Christ is the Head). Reverence God. Honor the emperor.

[18][You who are] household servants, be submissive to your masters with all [proper] respect, not only to those who are kind and considerate *and* reasonable, but also to those who are surly (overbearing, unjust, and crooked).

[19]For one is regarded favorably (is approved, acceptable, and thankworthy) if, as in the sight of God, he endures the pain of unjust suffering.

[20][After all] what [b]kind of glory [is there in it] if, when you do wrong and are punished for it, you take it patiently? But if you bear patiently with suffering [which results] when you do right *and* that is undeserved, it is acceptable *and* pleasing to God.

[21]For even to this were you called [it is inseparable from your vocation]. For Christ also suffered for you, leaving you [His personal] example, so that you should follow in His footsteps.

[22]He was guilty of no sin, neither was deceit (guile) ever found on His lips. [Isa. 53:9.]

[23]When He was reviled *and* insulted, He did not revile *or* offer insult in return; [when] He was abused *and* suffered, He made no threats [of vengeance]; but he trusted [Himself and everything] to Him Who judges fairly.

[24]He personally bore our sins in His [own] body on the tree [c][as on an altar and offered Himself on it], that we might die (cease to exist) to sin and live to righteousness. By His wounds you have been healed.

[25]For you were going astray like [so many] sheep, but now you have come back to the Shepherd and Guardian ([b]the Bishop) of your souls. [Isa. 53:5, 6.]

**3** In like manner, you married women, be submissive to your own husbands [subordinate yourselves as being secondary to and dependent on them, and adapt yourselves to them], so that even if any do not obey the Word [of God], they may be won over not by discussion but by the [godly] lives of their wives,

---

[a] 22 Isaiah 53:9    [b] 24,25 Isaiah 53:4,5,6 (see Septuagint)

[a] J. Rawson Lumby, cited by *Speaker's Commentary*.    [b] Literal translation.
[c] Marvin Vincent, *Word Studies*.

## New International Version

of their wives, ²when they see the purity and reverence of your lives. ³Your beauty should not come from outward adornment, such as elaborate hairstyles and the wearing of gold jewelry or fine clothes. ⁴Rather, it should be that of your inner self, the unfading beauty of a gentle and quiet spirit, which is of great worth in God's sight. ⁵For this is the way the holy women of the past who put their hope in God used to adorn themselves. They submitted themselves to their own husbands, ⁶like Sarah, who obeyed Abraham and called him her lord. You are her daughters if you do what is right and do not give way to fear.

⁷Husbands, in the same way be considerate as you live with your wives, and treat them with respect as the weaker partner and as heirs with you of the gracious gift of life, so that nothing will hinder your prayers.

### Suffering for Doing Good

⁸Finally, all of you, be like-minded, be sympathetic, love one another, be compassionate and humble. ⁹Do not repay evil with evil or insult with insult. On the contrary, repay evil with blessing, because to this you were called so that you may inherit a blessing. ¹⁰For,

"Whoever would love life
    and see good days
must keep their tongue from evil
    and their lips from deceitful speech.
¹¹They must turn from evil and do good;
    they must seek peace and pursue it.
¹²For the eyes of the Lord are on the righteous
    and his ears are attentive to their prayer,
but the face of the Lord is against those who do evil."ᵃ

¹³Who is going to harm you if you are eager to do good? ¹⁴But even if you should suffer for what is right, you are blessed. "Do not fear their threatsᵇ; do not be frightened."ᶜ ¹⁵But in your hearts revere Christ as Lord. Always be prepared to give an answer to everyone who asks you to give the reason for the hope that you have. But do this with gen-

## Amplified Bible

²When they observe the pure *and* modest way in which you conduct yourselves, together with your ᵃreverence [for your husband; you are to feel for him all that reverence includes: to respect, defer to, revere him—to honor, esteem, appreciate, prize, and, in the human sense, to adore him, that is, to admire, praise, be devoted to, deeply love, and enjoy your husband].

³Let not yours be the [merely] external adorning with [elaborate] ᵃinterweaving *and* knotting of the hair, the wearing of jewelry, or changes of clothes;

⁴But let it be the inward adorning *and* beauty of the hidden person of the heart, with the incorruptible *and* unfading charm of a gentle and peaceful spirit, which [is not anxious or wrought up, but] is very precious in the sight of God.

⁵For it was thus that the pious women of old who hoped in God were [accustomed] to beautify themselves and were submissive to their husbands [adapting themselves to them as themselves secondary and dependent upon them].

⁶It was thus that Sarah obeyed Abraham [following his guidance and acknowledging his headship over her by] calling him lord (master, leader, authority). And you are now her true daughters if you do right and let nothing terrify you [not giving way to hysterical fears or letting anxieties unnerve you].

⁷In the same way you married men should live considerately with [your wives], with an ᵇintelligent recognition [of the marriage relation], honoring the woman as [physically] the weaker, but [realizing that you] are joint heirs of the grace (God's unmerited favor) of life, in order that your prayers may not be hindered *and* cut off. [Otherwise you cannot pray effectively.]

⁸Finally, all [of you] should be of one *and* the same mind (united in spirit), sympathizing [with one another], loving [each other] as brethren [of one household], compassionate *and* courteous (tenderhearted and humble).

⁹Never return evil for evil or insult for insult (scolding, tongue-lashing, berating), but on the contrary blessing [praying for their welfare, happiness, and protection, and truly pitying and loving them]. For *know that* to this you have been called, that you may yourselves inherit a blessing [from God—that you may obtain a blessing as heirs, bringing welfare and happiness and protection].

¹⁰For let him who wants to enjoy life and see good days [good—whether apparent or not] keep his tongue free from evil and his lips from guile (treachery, deceit).

¹¹Let him turn away from wickedness *and* shun it, and let him do right. Let him search for peace (harmony; undisturbedness from fears, agitating passions, and moral conflicts) and seek it eagerly. [Do not merely desire peaceful relations with God, with your fellowmen, and with yourself, but pursue, go after them!]

¹²For the eyes of the Lord are upon the righteous (those who are upright and in right standing with God), and His ears are attentive to their prayer. But the face of the Lord is against those who practice evil [to oppose them, to frustrate, and defeat them]. [Ps. 34:12-16.]

¹³Now who is there to hurt you if you are ᶜzealous followers of that which is good?

¹⁴But even in case you should suffer for the sake of righteousness, [you are] blessed (happy, to be envied). Do not dread *or* be afraid of their threats, nor be disturbed [by their opposition].

¹⁵But in your hearts set Christ apart as holy [and acknowledge Him] as Lord. Always be ready to give a logical defense to anyone who asks you to account for the hope that is in you, but do it courteously and respectfully. [Isa. 8:12, 13.]

---

ᵃ 12 Psalm 34:12-16   ᵇ 14 Or *fear what they fear*   ᶜ 14 Isaiah 8:12

ᵃ Joseph Thayer, *A Greek-English Lexicon.*   ᵇ Marvin Vincent, *Word Studies.*   ᶜ Best manuscripts read "zealous."

## New International Version

tleness and respect, [16]keeping a clear conscience, so that those who speak maliciously against your good behavior in Christ may be ashamed of their slander. [17]For it is better, if it is God's will, to suffer for doing good than for doing evil. [18]For Christ also suffered once for sins, the righteous for the unrighteous, to bring you to God. He was put to death in the body but made alive in the Spirit. [19]After being made alive,[a] he went and made proclamation to the imprisoned spirits— [20]to those who were disobedient long ago when God waited patiently in the days of Noah while the ark was being built. In it only a few people, eight in all, were saved through water, [21]and this water symbolizes baptism that now saves you also—not the removal of dirt from the body but the pledge of a clear conscience toward God.[b] It saves you by the resurrection of Jesus Christ, [22]who has gone into heaven and is at God's right hand— with angels, authorities and powers in submission to him.

### Living for God

**4** Therefore, since Christ suffered in his body, arm yourselves also with the same attitude, because whoever suffers in the body is done with sin. [2]As a result, they do not live the rest of their earthly lives for evil human desires, but rather for the will of God. [3]For you have spent enough time in the past doing what pagans choose to do— living in debauchery, lust, drunkenness, orgies, carousing and detestable idolatry. [4]They are surprised that you do not join them in their reckless, wild living, and they heap abuse on you. [5]But they will have to give account to him who is ready to judge the living and the dead. [6]For this is the reason the gospel was preached even to those who are now dead, so that they might be judged according to human standards in regard to the body, but live according to God in regard to the spirit.

[7]The end of all things is near. Therefore be alert and of sober mind so that you may pray. [8]Above all, love each other deeply, because love covers over a multitude of sins. [9]Offer hospitality to one another without grumbling.

## Amplified Bible

[16][And see to it that] your conscience is entirely clear ([a]unimpaired), so that, when you are falsely accused as evildoers, those who threaten you abusively *and* revile your right behavior in Christ may come to be ashamed [of slandering your good lives].

[17]For [it is] better to suffer [unjustly] for doing right, if that should be God's will, than to suffer [justly] for doing wrong.

[18]For Christ [the Messiah Himself] died for sins once [b]for all, the Righteous for the unrighteous (the Just for the unjust, the Innocent for the guilty), that He might bring us to God. In His human body He was put to death, but He was made alive in the spirit,

[19]In which He went and preached to the spirits in prison,

[20][The souls of those] who long before in the days of Noah had been disobedient, when God's patience waited during the building of the ark in which a few [people], actually eight in number, were saved through water. [Gen. 6-8.]

[21]And baptism, which is a figure [of their deliverance], does now also save you [from inward questionings and fears], not by the removing of outward body filth [bathing], but by [providing you with] the answer of a good and clear conscience (inward cleanness and peace) before God [because you are demonstrating what you believe to be yours] through the resurrection of Jesus Christ.

[22][And He] has now entered into heaven and is at the right hand of God, with [all] angels and authorities and powers made subservient to Him.

**4** So, since Christ suffered in the flesh [c]for us, for you, arm yourselves with the same thought *and* [d]purpose [patiently to suffer rather than fail to please God]. For whoever has suffered in the flesh [having [e]the mind of Christ] is done with [intentional] sin [has stopped pleasing himself and the world, and pleases God],

[2]So that he can no longer spend the rest of his natural life living by [his] human appetites *and* desires, but [he lives] for what God wills.

[3]For the time that is past already suffices for doing what the Gentiles like to do—living [as you have done] in shameless, insolent wantonness, in lustful desires, drunkenness, reveling, drinking bouts *and* abominable, lawless idolatries.

[4]They are astonished *and* think it very queer that you do not now run hand in hand with them in the same excesses of dissipation, and they abuse [you].

[5]But they will have to give an account to Him Who is ready to judge *and* pass sentence on the living and the dead.

[6]For this is why the good news (the Gospel) was preached [f]in their lifetime] even to the dead, that though judged in fleshly bodies as men are, they might live in the spirit as God does.

[7]But the end *and* culmination of all things has now come near; keep sound minded *and* self-restrained and alert therefore for [the practice of] prayer.

[8]Above all things have intense *and* unfailing love for one another, for love covers a multitude of sins [forgives and [b]disregards the offenses of others]. [Prov. 10:12.]

[9]Practice hospitality to one another (those of the household of faith). [Be hospitable, be a lover of strangers, with brotherly affection for the unknown guests, the foreigners, the poor, and all others who come your way who are of Christ's body.] And [in each instance] do it ungrudgingly (cordially and graciously, without complaining but as representing Him).

---

[a] Marvin Vincent, *Word Studies.*  [b] Joseph Thayer, *A Greek-English Lexicon.*  [c] Some ancient manuscripts read "for us," while some "for you."  [d] G. Abbott-Smith, *Manual Greek Lexicon.*  [e] *The Cambridge Bible for Schools and Colleges.*  [f] Most commentators interpret this preaching to be a past event, done not after these people had died, but while they were still alive.

---

[a] 18,19 Or *but made alive in the spirit,* [19]*in which also*   [b] 21 Or *but an appeal to God for a clear conscience*

## New International Version

[10]Each of you should use whatever gift you have received to serve others, as faithful stewards of God's grace in its various forms. [11]If anyone speaks, they should do so as one who speaks the very words of God. If anyone serves, they should do so with the strength God provides, so that in all things God may be praised through Jesus Christ. To him be the glory and the power for ever and ever. Amen.

### Suffering for Being a Christian

[12]Dear friends, do not be surprised at the fiery ordeal that has come on you to test you, as though something strange were happening to you. [13]But rejoice inasmuch as you participate in the sufferings of Christ, so that you may be overjoyed when his glory is revealed. [14]If you are insulted because of the name of Christ, you are blessed, for the Spirit of glory and of God rests on you. [15]If you suffer, it should not be as a murderer or thief or any other kind of criminal, or even as a meddler. [16]However, if you suffer as a Christian, do not be ashamed, but praise God that you bear that name. [17]For it is time for judgment to begin with God's household; and if it begins with us, what will the outcome be for those who do not obey the gospel of God? [18]And,

"If it is hard for the righteous to be saved,
    what will become of the ungodly and the sinner?"[a]

[19]So then, those who suffer according to God's will should commit themselves to their faithful Creator and continue to do good.

### To the Elders and the Flock

**5** To the elders among you, I appeal as a fellow elder and a witness of Christ's sufferings who also will share in the glory to be revealed: [2]Be shepherds of God's flock that is under your care, watching over them—not because you must, but because you are willing, as God wants you to be; not pursuing dishonest gain, but eager to serve; [3]not lording it over those entrusted to you, but being examples to the flock. [4]And when the Chief Shepherd appears, you will receive the crown of glory that will never fade away.

[5]In the same way, you who are younger, submit yourselves to your elders. All of you, clothe yourselves with humility toward one another, because,

## Amplified Bible

[10]As each of you has received a gift (a particular spiritual talent, a gracious divine endowment), employ it for one another as [befits] good trustees of God's many-sided grace [faithful stewards of the [a]extremely diverse powers and gifts granted to Christians by unmerited favor].

[11]Whoever speaks, [let him do it as one who utters] oracles of God; whoever renders service, [let him do it] as with the strength which God furnishes [a]abundantly, so that in all things God may be glorified through Jesus Christ (the Messiah). To Him be the glory and dominion forever and ever (through endless ages). Amen (so be it).

[12]Beloved, do not be amazed *and* bewildered at the fiery ordeal which is taking place to test your quality, as though something strange (unusual and alien to you and your position) were befalling you.

[13]But insofar as you are sharing Christ's sufferings, rejoice, so that when His glory [full of radiance and splendor] is revealed, you may also rejoice with triumph [exultantly].

[14]If you are censured *and* suffer abuse [because you bear] the name of Christ, blessed [are you—happy, fortunate, [b]to be envied, [c]with life-joy, and satisfaction in God's favor and salvation, regardless of your outward condition], because the Spirit of glory, the Spirit of God, is resting upon you. *On their part He is blasphemed, but on your part He is glorified.* [Isa. 11:2.]

[15]But let none of you suffer as a murderer or a thief or any sort of criminal, or as a mischief-maker (a meddler) in the affairs of others [infringing on their rights].

[16]But if [one is ill-treated and suffers] as a Christian [which he is contemptuously called], let him not be ashamed, but give glory to God that he is [deemed worthy to suffer] in this name.

[17]For the time [has arrived] for judgment to begin with the household of God; and if it begins with us, what will [be] the end of those who do not respect *or* believe *or* obey the good news (the Gospel) of God?

[18]And if the righteous are barely saved, what will become of the godless and wicked? [Prov. 11:31.]

[19]Therefore, those who are ill-treated *and* suffer in accordance with God's will must do right and commit their souls [in charge as a deposit] to the One Who created [them] and will never fail [them].

**5** I warn *and* counsel the elders among you (the pastors and spiritual guides of the church) as a fellow elder and as an eyewitness [called to testify] of the sufferings of Christ, as well as a sharer in the glory (the honor and splendor) that is to be revealed (disclosed, unfolded):

[2]Tend (nurture, guard, guide, and fold) the flock of God that is [your responsibility], not by coercion *or* constraint, but willingly; not dishonorably motivated by the advantages *and* profits [belonging to the office], but eagerly *and* cheerfully;

[3]Not domineering [as arrogant, dictatorial, and overbearing persons] over those in your charge, but being examples (patterns and models of Christian living) to the flock (the congregation).

[4]And [then] when the Chief Shepherd is revealed, you will win the [d]conqueror's crown of glory.

[5]Likewise, you who are younger *and* of lesser rank, be subject to the elders (the ministers and spiritual guides of the church)—[giving them due respect and yielding to their counsel]. Clothe (apron) yourselves, all of you, with humility [as the garb of a servant, [e]so that its covering cannot possibly be stripped from you, with freedom from

---

[a] Joseph Thayer, *A Greek-English Lexicon.* [b] Alexander Souter, *Pocket Lexicon of the Greek New Testament.* [c] Hermann Cremer, *Biblico-Theological Lexicon.* [d] Marvin Vincent, *Word Studies*: When Paul uses the word translated "crown," he typically has the conqueror's crown in mind, using the imagery of the winner of an athletic contest (see I Cor. 9:25). Peter seems to have this same imagery in mind as a symbol of the heavenly reward. [e] Johann Bengel, *Gnomon Novi Testamenti.*

---

[a] 18 Prov. 11:31 (see Septuagint)

## New International Version

"God opposes the proud
    but shows favor to the humble."[a]

[6]Humble yourselves, therefore, under God's mighty hand, that he may lift you up in due time. [7]Cast all your anxiety on him because he cares for you.

[8]Be alert and of sober mind. Your enemy the devil prowls around like a roaring lion looking for someone to devour. [9]Resist him, standing firm in the faith, because you know that the family of believers throughout the world is undergoing the same kind of sufferings.

[10]And the God of all grace, who called you to his eternal glory in Christ, after you have suffered a little while, will himself restore you and make you strong, firm and steadfast. [11]To him be the power for ever and ever. Amen.

### Final Greetings

[12]With the help of Silas,[b] whom I regard as a faithful brother, I have written to you briefly, encouraging you and testifying that this is the true grace of God. Stand fast in it. [13]She who is in Babylon, chosen together with you, sends you her greetings, and so does my son Mark. [14]Greet one another with a kiss of love.

Peace to all of you who are in Christ.

## Amplified Bible

pride and arrogance] toward one another. For God sets Himself against the proud (the insolent, the overbearing, the disdainful, the presumptuous, the boastful)—[and He opposes, frustrates, and defeats them], but gives grace (favor, blessing) to the humble. [Prov. 3:34.]

[6]Therefore humble yourselves [demote, lower yourselves in your own estimation] under the mighty hand of God, that in due time He may exalt you,

[7]Casting the [a]whole of your care [all your anxieties, all your worries, all your concerns, [a]once and for all] on Him, for He cares for you affectionately and cares about you [a]watchfully. [Ps. 55:22.]

[8]Be well balanced (temperate, sober of mind), be vigilant and cautious at all times; for that enemy of yours, the devil, roams around like a lion roaring [[a]in fierce hunger], seeking someone to seize upon and devour.

[9]Withstand him; be firm in faith [against his onset—rooted, established, strong, immovable, and determined], knowing that the same ([a]identical) sufferings are appointed to your brotherhood (the whole body of Christians) throughout the world.

[10]And after you have suffered a little while, the God of all grace [Who imparts all blessing and favor], Who has called you to His [own] eternal glory in Christ Jesus, will Himself complete and make you what you ought to be, establish and ground you securely, and strengthen, and settle you.

[11]To Him be the dominion (power, authority, rule) forever and ever. Amen (so be it).

[12]By Silvanus, a true (loyal, consistent, incorruptible) brother, as I consider him, I have written briefly to you, to counsel and urge and stimulate [you] and to declare [to you] that this is the true [account of the] grace (the undeserved favor) of God. Be steadfast and persevere in it.

[13]She [your sister church here] in Babylon, [who is] elect (chosen) with [yourselves], sends you greetings, and [so does] my son (disciple) Mark.

[14]Salute one another with a kiss of love [the symbol of mutual affection]. To all of you that are in Christ Jesus (the Messiah), may there be peace ([b]every kind of peace and blessing, especially peace with God, and [c]freedom from fears, agitating passions, and moral conflicts). Amen (so be it).

[a] Marvin Vincent, Word Studies. [b] Joseph Thayer, A Greek-English Lexicon. [c] Webster's New International Dictionary offers this as a definition of "peace."

[a] 5 Prov. 3:34    [b] 12 Greek Silvanus, a variant of Silas

# 2 Peter

# Peter

**1** Simon Peter, a servant and apostle of Jesus Christ,

To those who through the righteousness of our God and Savior Jesus Christ have received a faith as precious as ours:

<sup>2</sup>Grace and peace be yours in abundance through the knowledge of God and of Jesus our Lord.

## Confirming One's Calling and Election

<sup>3</sup>His divine power has given us everything we need for a godly life through our knowledge of him who called us by his own glory and goodness. <sup>4</sup>Through these he has given us his very great and precious promises, so that through them you may participate in the divine nature, having escaped the corruption in the world caused by evil desires. <sup>5</sup>For this very reason, make every effort to add to your faith goodness; and to goodness, knowledge; <sup>6</sup>and to knowledge, self-control; and to self-control, perseverance; and to perseverance, godliness; <sup>7</sup>and to godliness, mutual affection; and to mutual affection, love. <sup>8</sup>For if you possess these qualities in increasing measure, they will keep you from being ineffective and unproductive in your knowledge of our Lord Jesus Christ. <sup>9</sup>But whoever does not have them is nearsighted and blind, forgetting that they have been cleansed from their past sins.

<sup>10</sup>Therefore, my brothers and sisters,<sup>a</sup> make every effort to confirm your calling and election. For if you do these things, you will never stumble, <sup>11</sup>and you will receive a rich welcome into the eternal kingdom of our Lord and Savior Jesus Christ.

## Prophecy of Scripture

<sup>12</sup>So I will always remind you of these things, even though you know them and are firmly established in the truth you now have. <sup>13</sup>I think it is right to refresh your memory as long as I live in the tent of this body, <sup>14</sup>because I know that I will soon put it aside, as our Lord Jesus Christ has made clear to me. <sup>15</sup>And I will make every effort to see that after my departure you will always be able to remember these things.

<sup>16</sup>For we did not follow cleverly devised stories when we told you about the coming of our Lord Jesus Christ in power, but we were eyewitnesses of his majesty. <sup>17</sup>He

**1** Simon Peter, a servant and apostle (special messenger) of Jesus Christ, to those who have received (obtained an equal privilege of) like precious faith with ourselves in *and* through the righteousness of our God and Savior Jesus Christ:

<sup>2</sup>May grace (God's favor) and peace (which is <sup>a</sup>perfect well-being, all necessary good, all spiritual prosperity, and <sup>b</sup>freedom from fears and agitating passions and moral conflicts) be multiplied to you in [the full, personal, <sup>c</sup>precise, and correct] knowledge of God and of Jesus our Lord.

<sup>3</sup>For His divine power has bestowed upon us all things that [are requisite and suited] to life and godliness, through the [<sup>d</sup>full, personal] knowledge of Him Who called us by *and* to His own glory and excellence (virtue).

<sup>4</sup>By means of these He has bestowed on us His precious and exceedingly great promises, so that through them you may escape [by flight] from the moral decay (rottenness and corruption) that is in the world because of covetousness (lust and greed), and become sharers (partakers) of the divine nature.

<sup>5</sup>For this very reason, <sup>d</sup>adding your diligence [to the divine promises], employ every effort in <sup>e</sup>exercising your faith to develop virtue (excellence, resolution, Christian energy), and in [exercising] virtue [develop] knowledge (intelligence),

<sup>6</sup>And in [exercising] knowledge [develop] self-control, and in [exercising] self-control [develop] steadfastness (patience, endurance), and in [exercising] steadfastness [develop] godliness (piety),

<sup>7</sup>And in [exercising] godliness [develop] brotherly affection, and in [exercising] brotherly affection [develop] Christian love.

<sup>8</sup>For as these qualities are yours and increasingly abound in you, they will keep [you] from being idle or unfruitful unto the [<sup>c</sup>full personal] knowledge of our Lord Jesus Christ (the Messiah, the Anointed One).

<sup>9</sup>For whoever lacks these qualities is blind, [<sup>d</sup>spiritually] shortsighted, <sup>f</sup>seeing only what is near to him, and has become oblivious [to the fact] that he was cleansed from his old sins.

<sup>10</sup>Because of this, brethren, be all the more solicitous *and* eager to make sure (to ratify, to strengthen, to make steadfast) your calling and election; for if you do this, you will never stumble *or* fall.

<sup>11</sup>Thus there will be richly *and* abundantly provided for you entry into the eternal kingdom of our Lord and Savior Jesus Christ.

<sup>12</sup>So I intend always to remind you about these things, although indeed you know them and are firm in the truth that [you] now [hold].

<sup>13</sup>I think it right, as long as I am in this tabernacle (tent, body), to stir you up by way of remembrance,

<sup>14</sup>Since I know that the laying aside of this body of mine will come speedily, as our Lord Jesus Christ made clear to me.

<sup>15</sup>Moreover, I will diligently endeavor [to see to it] that [even] after my departure (decease) you may be able at all times to call these things to mind.

<sup>16</sup>For we were not following cleverly devised stories when we made known to you the power and coming of our Lord Jesus Christ (the Messiah), but we were eyewitnesses of His majesty (grandeur, authority of sovereign power).

<sup>a</sup> Matthew Henry, *Commentary on the Holy Bible.* <sup>b</sup> *Webster's New International Dictionary* offers this as a definition of "peace." <sup>c</sup> Joseph Thayer, *A Greek-English Lexicon of the New Testament.* <sup>d</sup> Marvin Vincent, *Word Studies in the New Testament.* <sup>e</sup> Marvin Vincent, *Word Studies.* <sup>f</sup> Joseph P. Rotherham, *The Emphasized Bible.*

<sup>a</sup> 10 The Greek word for *brothers and sisters* (*adelphoi*) refers here to believers, both men and women, as part of God's family.

## New International Version

received honor and glory from God the Father when the voice came to him from the Majestic Glory, saying, "This is my Son, whom I love; with him I am well pleased."*a* [18]We ourselves heard this voice that came from heaven when we were with him on the sacred mountain.

[19]We also have the prophetic message as something completely reliable, and you will do well to pay attention to it, as to a light shining in a dark place, until the day dawns and the morning star rises in your hearts. [20]Above all, you must understand that no prophecy of Scripture came about by the prophet's own interpretation of things. [21]For prophecy never had its origin in the human will, but prophets, though human, spoke from God as they were carried along by the Holy Spirit.

### False Teachers and Their Destruction

**2** But there were also false prophets among the people, just as there will be false teachers among you. They will secretly introduce destructive heresies, even denying the sovereign Lord who bought them—bringing swift destruction on themselves. [2]Many will follow their depraved conduct and will bring the way of truth into disrepute. [3]In their greed these teachers will exploit you with fabricated stories. Their condemnation has long been hanging over them, and their destruction has not been sleeping.

[4]For if God did not spare angels when they sinned, but sent them to hell,*b* putting them in chains of darkness*c* to be held for judgment; [5]if he did not spare the ancient world when he brought the flood on its ungodly people, but protected Noah, a preacher of righteousness, and seven others; [6]if he condemned the cities of Sodom and Gomorrah by burning them to ashes, and made them an example of what is going to happen to the ungodly; [7]and if he rescued Lot, a righteous man, who was distressed by the depraved conduct of the lawless [8](for that righteous man, living among them day after day, was tormented in his righteous soul by the lawless deeds he saw and heard) — [9]if this is so, then the Lord knows how to rescue the godly from trials and to hold the unrighteous for punishment on the day of judgment. [10]This is especially true of those who follow the corrupt desire of the flesh*d* and despise authority.

Bold and arrogant, they are not afraid to heap abuse on celestial beings; [11]yet even angels, although they are stronger and more powerful, do not heap abuse on such beings when bringing judgment on them from*e* the Lord. [12]But these people blaspheme in matters they do not understand. They are like unreasoning animals, creatures of instinct, born only to be caught and destroyed, and like animals they too will perish.

[13]They will be paid back with harm for the harm they have done. Their idea of pleasure is to carouse in broad

## Amplified Bible

[17]For when He was invested with honor and glory from God the Father and a voice was borne to Him by the [splendid] Majestic Glory [in the bright cloud that overshadowed Him, saying], This is My beloved Son in Whom I am well pleased *and* delight,

[18]We [actually] heard this voice borne out of heaven, for we were together with Him on the holy mountain.

[19]And we have the prophetic word [made] firmer still. You will do well to pay close attention to it as to a lamp shining in a dismal (squalid and dark) place, until the day breaks through [the gloom] and the Morning Star rises (*a*comes into being) in your hearts.

[20][Yet] first [you must] understand this, that no prophecy of Scripture is [a matter] of any personal *or* private *or* special interpretation (loosening, solving).

[21]For no prophecy ever originated because some man willed it [to do so—it never came by human impulse], but men spoke from God who were borne along (moved and impelled) by the Holy Spirit.

**2** But also [in those days] there arose false prophets among the people, just as there will be false teachers among yourselves, who will subtly *and* stealthily introduce heretical doctrines (destructive heresies), even denying *and* disowning the Master Who bought them, bringing upon themselves swift destruction.

[2]And many will follow their immoral ways *and* lascivious doings; because of them the true Way will be maligned *and* defamed.

[3]And in their covetousness (lust, greed) they will exploit you with false (cunning) arguments. From of old the sentence [of condemnation] for them has not been idle; their destruction (eternal misery) has not been asleep.

[4]For God did not [even] spare angels that sinned, but cast them into hell, delivering them to be kept there in pits of gloom till the judgment *and* their doom.

[5]And He spared not the ancient world, but preserved Noah, a preacher of righteousness, with seven other persons, when He brought a flood upon the world of ungodly [people]. [Gen. 6-8; I Peter 3:20.]

[6]And He condemned to ruin *and* extinction the cities of Sodom and Gomorrah, reducing them to ashes [and thus] set them forth as an example to those who would be ungodly; [Gen. 19:24.]

[7]And He rescued righteous Lot, greatly worn out *and* distressed by the wanton ways of the ungodly *and* lawless—[Gen. 19:16, 29.]

[8]For that just man, living [there] among them, tortured his righteous soul every day with what he saw and heard of [their] unlawful and wicked deeds—

[9]Now if [all these things are true, then be sure] the Lord knows how to rescue the godly out of temptations *and* trials, and how to keep the ungodly under chastisement until the day of judgment *and* doom,

[10]And particularly those who walk after the flesh and indulge in the lust of polluting passion and scorn *and* despise authority. Presumptuous [and] daring [self-willed and self-loving creatures]! They scoff at *and* revile dignitaries (glorious ones) without trembling,

[11]Whereas [even] angels, though superior in might and power, do not bring a defaming charge against them before the Lord.

[12]But these [people]! Like unreasoning beasts, mere creatures of instinct, born [only] to be captured and destroyed, railing at things of which they are ignorant, they shall utterly perish in their [own] corruption [in their destroying they shall surely be destroyed],

[13]Being destined to receive [punishment as] the reward of [their] unrighteousness [suffering wrong as the hire for their wrongdoing]. They count it a delight to revel in the daytime [living luxuriously and delicately]. They are blots

---

*a 17* Matt. 17:5; Mark 9:7; Luke 9:35   *b 4* Greek *Tartarus*   *c 4* Some manuscripts *in gloomy dungeons*   *d 10* In contexts like this, the Greek word for *flesh* (*sarx*) refers to the sinful state of human beings, often presented as a power in opposition to the Spirit; also in verse 18.
*e 11* Many manuscripts *beings in the presence of*

*a* G. Abbott-Smith, *Manual Greek Lexicon of the New Testament.*

## New International Version

daylight. They are blots and blemishes, reveling in their pleasures while they feast with you.[a] [14]With eyes full of adultery, they never stop sinning; they seduce the unstable; they are experts in greed—an accursed brood! [15]They have left the straight way and wandered off to follow the way of Balaam son of Bezer,[b] who loved the wages of wickedness. [16]But he was rebuked for his wrongdoing by a donkey—an animal without speech—who spoke with a human voice and restrained the prophet's madness.

[17]These people are springs without water and mists driven by a storm. Blackest darkness is reserved for them. [18]For they mouth empty, boastful words and, by appealing to the lustful desires of the flesh, they entice people who are just escaping from those who live in error. [19]They promise them freedom, while they themselves are slaves of depravity—for "people are slaves to whatever has mastered them." [20]If they have escaped the corruption of the world by knowing our Lord and Savior Jesus Christ and are again entangled in it and are overcome, they are worse off at the end than they were at the beginning. [21]It would have been better for them not to have known the way of righteousness, than to have known it and then to turn their backs on the sacred command that was passed on to them. [22]Of them the proverbs are true: "A dog returns to its vomit,"[c] and, "A sow that is washed returns to her wallowing in the mud."

### The Day of the Lord

**3** Dear friends, this is now my second letter to you. I have written both of them as reminders to stimulate you to wholesome thinking. [2]I want you to recall the words spoken in the past by the holy prophets and the command given by our Lord and Savior through your apostles.

[3]Above all, you must understand that in the last days scoffers will come, scoffing and following their own evil desires. [4]They will say, "Where is this 'coming' he promised? Ever since our ancestors died, everything goes on as it has since the beginning of creation." [5]But they deliberately forget that long ago by God's word the heavens came into being and the earth was formed out of water and by water. [6]By these waters also the world of that time was deluged and destroyed. [7]By the same word the present heavens and earth are reserved for fire, being kept for the day of judgment and destruction of the ungodly.

[8]But do not forget this one thing, dear friends: With the Lord a day is like a thousand years, and a thousand years are like a day. [9]The Lord is not slow in keeping his promise, as some understand slowness. Instead he is patient with you, not wanting anyone to perish, but everyone to come to repentance.

[10]But the day of the Lord will come like a thief. The heavens will disappear with a roar; the elements will be

## Amplified Bible

and blemishes, reveling in their [a]deceptions and carousing together [even] as they feast with you.

[14]They have eyes full of harlotry, insatiable for sin. They beguile and bait and lure away unstable souls. Their hearts are trained in covetousness (lust, greed), [they are] children of a curse [[b]exposed to cursing]!

[15]Forsaking the straight road they have gone astray; they have followed the way of Balaam [the son] of Beor, who loved the reward of wickedness. [Num. 22:5, 7.]

[16]But he was rebuked for his own transgression when a dumb beast of burden spoke with human voice and checked the prophet's madness. [Num. 22:21-31.]

[17]These are springs without water and mists driven along before a tempest, for whom is reserved *forever* the gloom of darkness.

[18]For uttering loud boasts of folly, they beguile and lure with lustful desires of the flesh those who are barely escaping from those who are wrongdoers.

[19]They promise them liberty, when they themselves are the slaves of depravity and defilement—for by whatever anyone is made inferior or worse or is overcome, to that [person or thing] he is enslaved.

[20]For if, after they have escaped the pollutions of the world through [the full, personal] knowledge of our Lord and Savior Jesus Christ, they again become entangled in them and are overcome, their last condition is worse [for them] than the first.

[21]For never to have obtained a [full, personal] knowledge of the way of righteousness would have been better for them than, having obtained [such knowledge], to turn back from the holy commandment which was [verbally] delivered to them.

[22]There has befallen them the thing spoken of in the true proverb, The dog turns back to his own vomit, and, The sow is washed only to wallow again in the mire. [Prov. 26:11.]

**3** Beloved, I am now writing you this second letter. In [both of] them I have stirred up your unsullied (sincere) mind by way of remembrance,

[2]That you should recall the predictions of the holy (consecrated, dedicated) prophets and the commandment of the Lord and Savior [given] through your apostles (His special messengers).

[3]To begin with, you must know and understand this, that scoffers (mockers) will come in the last days with scoffing, [people who] walk after their own fleshly desires

[4]And say, Where is the promise of His coming? For since the forefathers fell asleep, all things have continued exactly as they did from the beginning of creation.

[5]For they willfully overlook and forget this [fact], that the heavens [came into] existence long ago by the word of God, and the earth also which was formed out of water and by means of water,

[6]Through which the world that then [existed] was deluged with water and perished. [Gen. 1:6-8; 7:11.]

[7]But by the same word the present heavens and earth have been stored up (reserved) for fire, being kept until the day of judgment and destruction of the ungodly people.

[8]Nevertheless, do not let this one fact escape you, beloved, that with the Lord one day is as a thousand years and a thousand years as one day. [Ps. 90:4.]

[9]The Lord does not delay and is not tardy or slow about what He promises, according to some people's conception of slowness, but He is long-suffering (extraordinarily patient) toward you, not desiring that any should perish, but that all should turn to repentance.

[10]But the day of the Lord will come like a thief, and then the heavens will vanish (pass away) with a thunderous crash, and the [c]material] elements [of the universe] will

---

*a 13 Some manuscripts in their love feasts*   *b 15 Greek Bosor*
*c 22 Prov. 26:11*

*a Some ancient manuscripts read "love feasts."*   *b Joseph Thayer, A Greek-English Lexicon.*   *c G. Abbott-Smith, Manual Greek Lexicon.*

## New International Version

destroyed by fire, and the earth and everything done in it will be laid bare.[a]

[11] Since everything will be destroyed in this way, what kind of people ought you to be? You ought to live holy and godly lives [12] as you look forward to the day of God and speed its coming.[b] That day will bring about the destruction of the heavens by fire, and the elements will melt in the heat. [13] But in keeping with his promise we are looking forward to a new heaven and a new earth, where righteousness dwells.

[14] So then, dear friends, since you are looking forward to this, make every effort to be found spotless, blameless and at peace with him. [15] Bear in mind that our Lord's patience means salvation, just as our dear brother Paul also wrote you with the wisdom that God gave him. [16] He writes the same way in all his letters, speaking in them of these matters. His letters contain some things that are hard to understand, which ignorant and unstable people distort, as they do the other Scriptures, to their own destruction.

[17] Therefore, dear friends, since you have been forewarned, be on your guard so that you may not be carried away by the error of the lawless and fall from your secure position. [18] But grow in the grace and knowledge of our Lord and Savior Jesus Christ. To him be glory both now and forever! Amen.

## Amplified Bible

be dissolved with fire, and the earth and the works that are upon it will be burned up.

[11] Since all these things are thus [a] in the process of being dissolved, what kind of person ought [each of] you to be [in the meanwhile] in consecrated and holy behavior and devout and godly qualities,

[12] While you wait and earnestly long for (expect and hasten) the coming of the day of God by reason of which the flaming heavens will be dissolved, and the [[b] material] elements [of the universe] will flare and melt with fire? [Isa. 34:4.]

[13] But we look for new heavens and a new earth according to His promise, in which righteousness (uprightness, freedom from sin, and right standing with God) is to abide. [Isa. 65:17; 66:22.]

[14] So, beloved, since you are expecting these things, be eager to be found by Him [at His coming] without spot or blemish and at peace [in serene confidence, [c] free from fears and agitating passions and moral conflicts].

[15] And consider that the long-suffering of our Lord [[d] His slowness in avenging wrongs and judging the world] is salvation ([d] that which is conducive to the soul's safety), even as our beloved brother Paul also wrote to you according to the spiritual insight given him,

[16] Speaking of this as he does in all of his letters. There are some things in those [epistles of Paul] that are difficult to understand, which the ignorant and unstable twist and misconstrue to their own [d] utter destruction, just as [they distort and misinterpret] the rest of the Scriptures.

[17] Let me warn you therefore, beloved, that knowing these things beforehand, you should be on your guard, lest you be carried away by the error of lawless and wicked [persons and] fall from your own [present] firm condition [your own steadfastness of mind].

[18] But grow in grace (undeserved favor, spiritual strength) and [e] recognition and knowledge and understanding of our Lord and Savior Jesus Christ (the Messiah). To Him [be] glory (honor, majesty, and splendor) both now and to the day of eternity. Amen (so be it)!

[a] Marvin Vincent, Word Studies.  [b] G. Abbott-Smith, Manual Greek Lexicon.  [c] Webster's New International Dictionary offers this as a definition of "peace."  [d] Joseph Thayer, A Greek-English Lexicon.
[e] Hermann Cremer, Biblico-Theological Lexicon of New Testament Greek.

# New International Version

## 1 John

### The Incarnation of the Word of Life

**1** That which was from the beginning, which we have heard, which we have seen with our eyes, which we have looked at and our hands have touched—this we proclaim concerning the Word of life. ²The life appeared; we have seen it and testify to it, and we proclaim to you the eternal life, which was with the Father and has appeared to us. ³We proclaim to you what we have seen and heard, so that you also may have fellowship with us. And our fellowship is with the Father and with his Son, Jesus Christ. ⁴We write this to make our*ᵃ* joy complete.

### Light and Darkness, Sin and Forgiveness

⁵This is the message we have heard from him and declare to you: God is light; in him there is no darkness at all. ⁶If we claim to have fellowship with him and yet walk in the darkness, we lie and do not live out the truth. ⁷But if we walk in the light, as he is in the light, we have fellowship with one another, and the blood of Jesus, his Son, purifies us from all*ᵇ* sin.

⁸If we claim to be without sin, we deceive ourselves and the truth is not in us. ⁹If we confess our sins, he is faithful and just and will forgive us our sins and purify us from all unrighteousness. ¹⁰If we claim we have not sinned, we make him out to be a liar and his word is not in us.

**2** My dear children, I write this to you so that you will not sin. But if anybody does sin, we have an advocate with the Father—Jesus Christ, the Righteous One. ²He is the atoning sacrifice for our sins, and not only for ours but also for the sins of the whole world.

### Love and Hatred for Fellow Believers

³We know that we have come to know him if we keep his commands. ⁴Whoever says, "I know him," but does not

# Amplified Bible

## John

**1** [We are writing] about the Word of Life [*ᵃ*in] Him Who existed from the beginning, Whom we have heard, Whom we have seen with our [own] eyes, Whom we have gazed upon [for ourselves] and have touched with our [own] hands.

²And the Life [*ᵃ*an aspect of His being] was revealed (made manifest, demonstrated), and we saw [as eyewitnesses] and are testifying to and declare to you the Life, the eternal Life [*ᵃ*in Him] Who already existed with the Father and Who [actually] was made visible (was revealed) to us [His followers].

³What we have seen and [ourselves] heard, we are also telling you, so that you too may *ᵃ*realize *and* enjoy fellowship as partners *and* partakers with us. And [this] fellowship that we have [which is a *ᵃ*distinguishing mark of Christians] is with the Father and with His Son Jesus Christ (the Messiah).

⁴And we are now writing these things to you so that our joy [in seeing you included] may be full [and *ᵇ*your joy may be complete].

⁵And this is the message [the message of *ᵃ*promise] which we have heard from Him and now are reporting to you: God is Light, and there is no darkness in Him at all [*ᶜ*no, not in any way].

⁶[So] if we say we are partakers together *and* enjoy fellowship with Him when we live *and* move *and* are walking about in darkness, we are [both] speaking falsely and do not live *and* practice the Truth [which the Gospel presents].

⁷But if we [really] are living *and* walking in the Light, as He [Himself] is in the Light, we have [true, unbroken] fellowship with one another, and the blood of Jesus *Christ* His Son cleanses (removes) us from all sin *and* guilt [keeps us cleansed from sin in all its forms and manifestations].

⁸If we say we have no sin [refusing to admit that we are sinners], we delude *and* lead ourselves astray, and the Truth [which the Gospel presents] is not in us [does not dwell in our hearts].

⁹If we [freely] admit that we have sinned *and* confess our sins, He is faithful and just (true to His own nature and promises) and will forgive our sins [dismiss our lawlessness] and [continuously] cleanse us from all unrighteousness [everything not in conformity to His will in purpose, thought, and action].

¹⁰If we say (claim) we have not sinned, we contradict His Word *and* make Him out to be false *and* a liar, and His Word is not in us [the divine message of the Gospel is not in our hearts].

**2** My little children, I write you these things so that you may not violate God's law *and* sin. But if anyone should sin, we have an Advocate (One Who will intercede for us) with the Father—[it is] Jesus Christ [the all] righteous [upright, just, Who conforms to the Father's will in every purpose, thought, and action].

²And He [*ᵈ*that same Jesus Himself] is the propitiation (the atoning sacrifice) for our sins, and not for ours alone but also for [the sins of] the whole world.

³And this is how we may discern [*ᵈ*daily, by experience] that we are coming to know Him [to perceive, recognize, understand, and become better acquainted with Him]: if we keep (bear in mind, observe, practice) His teachings (precepts, commandments).

---

## New International Version

do what he commands is a liar, and the truth is not in that person. [5]But if anyone obeys his word, love for God[a] is truly made complete in them. This is how we know we are in him: [6]Whoever claims to live in him must live as Jesus did.

[7]Dear friends, I am not writing you a new command but an old one, which you have had since the beginning. This old command is the message you have heard. [8]Yet I am writing you a new command; its truth is seen in him and in you, because the darkness is passing and the true light is already shining.

[9]Anyone who claims to be in the light but hates a brother or sister[b] is still in the darkness. [10]Anyone who loves their brother and sister[c] lives in the light, and there is nothing in them to make them stumble. [11]But anyone who hates a brother or sister is in the darkness and walks around in the darkness. They do not know where they are going, because the darkness has blinded them.

### Reasons for Writing

[12]I am writing to you, dear children,
  because your sins have been forgiven on account of
    his name.
[13]I am writing to you, fathers,
  because you know him who is from the beginning.
I am writing to you, young men,
  because you have overcome the evil one.

[14]I write to you, dear children,
  because you know the Father.
I write to you, fathers,
  because you know him who is from the beginning.
I write to you, young men,
  because you are strong,
  and the word of God lives in you,
  and you have overcome the evil one.

### On Not Loving the World

[15]Do not love the world or anything in the world. If anyone loves the world, love for the Father[d] is not in them. [16]For everything in the world—the lust of the flesh, the lust of the eyes, and the pride of life—comes not from the Father but from the world. [17]The world and its desires pass away, but whoever does the will of God lives forever.

### Warnings Against Denying the Son

[18]Dear children, this is the last hour; and as you have heard that the antichrist is coming, even now many antichrists have come. This is how we know it is the last hour. [19]They went out from us, but they did not really belong to us. For if they had belonged to us, they would have remained with us; but their going showed that none of them belonged to us.

---

[a] 5 Or *word, God's love*   [b] 9 The Greek word for *brother or sister* (*adelphos*) refers here to a believer, whether man or woman, as part of God's family; also in verse 11; and in 3:15, 17; 4:20; 5:16.   [c] 10 The Greek word for *brother and sister* (*adelphos*) refers here to a believer, whether man or woman, as part of God's family; also in 3:10; 4:20, 21.   [d] 15 Or *world, the Father's love*

## Amplified Bible

[4]Whoever says, I know Him [I perceive, recognize, understand, and am acquainted with Him] but fails to keep *and* obey His commandments (teachings) is a liar, and the Truth [[a]of the Gospel] is not in him.

[5]But he who keeps (treasures) His Word [who bears in mind His precepts, who observes His message in its entirety], truly in him has the love of *and* for God been perfected (completed, reached maturity). By this we may perceive (know, recognize, and be sure) that we are in Him:

[6]Whoever says he abides in Him ought [as [b]a personal debt] to walk *and* conduct himself in the same way in which He walked *and* conducted Himself.

[7]Beloved, I am writing you no new commandment, but an old commandment which you have had from the beginning; the old commandment is the message which you have heard [the [a]doctrine of salvation through Christ].

[8]Yet I am writing you a new commandment, which is true (is realized) in Him and in you, because the darkness ([b]moral blindness) is clearing away and the true Light ([b]the revelation of God in Christ) is already shining.

[9]Whoever says he is in the Light and [yet] hates his brother [Christian, [a]born-again child of God his Father] is in darkness even until now.

[10]Whoever loves his brother [believer] abides (lives) in the Light, and in It *or* in him there is no occasion for stumbling *or* cause for error *or* sin.

[11]But he who hates (detests, despises) his brother [[a]in Christ] is in darkness and walking (living) in the dark; he is straying *and* does not perceive *or* know where he is going, because the darkness has blinded his eyes.

[12]I am writing to you, little children, because for His name's sake your sins are forgiven [pardoned through His name and on account of confessing His name].

[13]I am writing to you, fathers, because you have come to know (recognize, be aware of, and understand) Him Who [has existed] from the beginning. I am writing to you, young men, because you have been victorious over the wicked [one]. I write to you, [c]boys (lads), because you have come to know (recognize and be aware) of the Father.

[14]I write to you, fathers, because you have come to know (recognize, be conscious of, and understand) Him Who [has existed] from the beginning. I write to you, young men, because you are strong *and* vigorous, and the Word of God is [always] abiding in you (in your hearts), and you have been victorious over the wicked one.

[15]Do not love *or* cherish the world or the things that are in the world. If anyone loves the world, love for the Father is not in him.

[16]For all that is in the world—the lust of the flesh [craving for sensual gratification] and the lust of the eyes [greedy longings of the mind] and the pride of life [assurance in one's own resources or in the stability of earthly things]—these do not come from the Father but are from the world [itself].

[17]And the world passes away *and* disappears, and with it the forbidden cravings (the passionate desires, the lust) of it; but he who does the will of God and carries out His purposes in his life abides (remains) forever.

[18][c]Boys (lads), it is the last time (hour, the end of this age). And as you have heard that the antichrist [he who will oppose Christ in the guise of Christ] is coming, even now many antichrists have arisen, which confirms our belief that it is the final (the end) time.

[19]They went out from our number, but they did not [really] belong to us; for if they had been of us, they would have remained with us. But [they withdrew] that it might be plain that they all are not of us.

---

[a] Joseph Thayer, *A Greek-English Lexicon of the New Testament.*
[b] Marvin Vincent, *Word Studies.*   [c] G. Abbott-Smith, *Manual Greek Lexicon of the New Testament.*

# New International Version

²⁰But you have an anointing from the Holy One, and all of you know the truth.ᵃ ²¹I do not write to you because you do not know the truth, but because you do know it and because no lie comes from the truth. ²²Who is the liar? It is whoever denies that Jesus is the Christ. Such a person is the antichrist—denying the Father and the Son. ²³No one who denies the Son has the Father; whoever acknowledges the Son has the Father also.

²⁴As for you, see that what you have heard from the beginning remains in you. If it does, you also will remain in the Son and in the Father. ²⁵And this is what he promised us—eternal life.

²⁶I am writing these things to you about those who are trying to lead you astray. ²⁷As for you, the anointing you received from him remains in you, and you do not need anyone to teach you. But as his anointing teaches you about all things and as that anointing is real, not counterfeit—just as it has taught you, remain in him.

## God's Children and Sin

²⁸And now, dear children, continue in him, so that when he appears we may be confident and unashamed before him at his coming.

²⁹If you know that he is righteous, you know that everyone who does what is right has been born of him.

**3** See what great love the Father has lavished on us, that we should be called children of God! And that is what we are! The reason the world does not know us is that it did not know him. ²Dear friends, now we are children of God, and what we will be has not yet been made known. But we know that when Christ appears,ᵇ we shall be like him, for we shall see him as he is. ³All who have this hope in him purify themselves, just as he is pure.

⁴Everyone who sins breaks the law; in fact, sin is lawlessness. ⁵But you know that he appeared so that he might take away our sins. And in him is no sin. ⁶No one who lives in him keeps on sinning. No one who continues to sin has either seen him or known him.

# Amplified Bible

²⁰But you have been anointed by [you hold a sacred appointment from, you have been given an unction from] the Holy One, and you all know [the Truth] *or you know all things.*

²¹I write to you not because you are ignorant *and* do not perceive *and* know the Truth, but because you do perceive *and* know it, and [know positively] that nothing false (no deception, no lie) is of the Truth.

²²Who is [such a] liar as he who denies that Jesus is the Christ (the Messiah)? He is the antichrist (the antagonist of Christ), who [ᵃhabitually] denies *and* refuses to acknowledge the Father and the Son.

²³No one who [ᵃhabitually] denies (disowns) the Son ᵃeven has the Father. *Whoever confesses (acknowledges and has) the Son has the Father also.*

²⁴As for you, keep in your hearts what you have heard from the beginning. If what you heard from the first dwells *and* remains in you, then you will dwell in the Son and in the Father [always].

²⁵And this is what He Himself has promised us—the life, the eternal [life].

²⁶I write this to you with reference to those who would deceive you [seduce and lead you astray].

²⁷But as for you, the anointing (the sacred appointment, the unction) which you received from Him abides [ᵇpermanently] in you; [so] then you have no need that anyone should instruct you. But just as His anointing teaches you concerning everything and is true and is no falsehood, so you must abide in (live in, never depart from) Him [being ᵇrooted in Him, knit to Him], just as [His anointing] has taught you [to do].

²⁸And now, little children, abide (live, remain ᵇpermanently) in Him, so that when He is made visible, we may have *and* enjoy perfect confidence (boldness, assurance) and not be ashamed *and* shrink from Him at His coming.

²⁹If you know (perceive and are sure) that He [Christ] is [absolutely] righteous [conforming to the Father's will in purpose, thought, and action], you may also know (be sure) that everyone who does righteously [and is therefore in like manner conformed to the divine will] is born (begotten) of Him [ᶜGod].

**3** See what [ᵃan incredible] quality of love the Father has given (shown, bestowed on) us, that we should [be permitted to] be named *and* called and counted the children of God! And so we are! The reason that the world does not know (recognize, acknowledge) us is that it does not know (recognize, acknowledge) Him.

²Beloved, we are [even here and] now God's children; it is not yet disclosed (made clear) what we shall be [hereafter], but we know that when He comes *and* is manifested, we shall [ᵈas God's children] resemble *and* be like Him, for we shall see Him ᵃjust as He [really] is.

³And everyone who has this hope [resting] on Him cleanses (purifies) himself just as He is pure (chaste, undefiled, guiltless).

⁴Everyone who commits (practices) sin is guilty of lawlessness; for [that is what] sin is, lawlessness (the breaking, violating of God's law by transgression or neglect—being unrestrained and unregulated by His commands and His will).

⁵You know that He appeared in visible form and became Man to take away [upon Himself] sins, and in Him there is no sin [ᵃessentially and forever].

⁶No one who abides in Him [who lives and remains ᵃin communion with and in obedience to Him—deliberately, knowingly, and ᵃhabitually] commits (practices) sin. No one who [habitually] sins has either seen *or* known Him [recognized, perceived, or understood Him, or has had an experiential acquaintance with Him].

ᵃ Marvin Vincent, *Word Studies.* ᵇ Joseph Thayer, *A Greek-English Lexicon.* ᶜ Brooke F. Westcott, *The Epistles of Saint John:* When John thinks of God in relation to men, he never thinks of Him apart from Christ. ᵈ Robert Jamieson, A. R. Fausset and David Brown, *A Commentary on the Old and New Testaments.*

ᵃ 20 Some manuscripts *and you know all things*    ᵇ 2 Or *when it is made known*

# New International Version

[7]Dear children, do not let anyone lead you astray. The one who does what is right is righteous, just as he is righteous. [8]The one who does what is sinful is of the devil, because the devil has been sinning from the beginning. The reason the Son of God appeared was to destroy the devil's work. [9]No one who is born of God will continue to sin, because God's seed remains in them; they cannot go on sinning, because they have been born of God. [10]This is how we know who the children of God are and who the children of the devil are: Anyone who does not do what is right is not God's child, nor is anyone who does not love their brother and sister.

## More on Love and Hatred

[11]For this is the message you heard from the beginning: We should love one another. [12]Do not be like Cain, who belonged to the evil one and murdered his brother. And why did he murder him? Because his own actions were evil and his brother's were righteous. [13]Do not be surprised, my brothers and sisters,[a] if the world hates you. [14]We know that we have passed from death to life, because we love each other. Anyone who does not love remains in death. [15]Anyone who hates a brother or sister is a murderer, and you know that no murderer has eternal life residing in him.

[16]This is how we know what love is: Jesus Christ laid down his life for us. And we ought to lay down our lives for our brothers and sisters. [17]If anyone has material possessions and sees a brother or sister in need but has no pity on them, how can the love of God be in that person? [18]Dear children, let us not love with words or speech but with actions and in truth.

[19]This is how we know that we belong to the truth and how we set our hearts at rest in his presence: [20]If our hearts condemn us, we know that God is greater than our hearts, and he knows everything. [21]Dear friends, if our hearts do not condemn us, we have confidence before God [22]and receive from him anything we ask, because we keep his commands and do what pleases him. [23]And this is his

# Amplified Bible

[7a]Boys (lads), let no one deceive *and* lead you astray. He who practices righteousness [who is upright, conforming to the divine will in purpose, thought, and action, living a consistently conscientious life] is righteous, even as He is righteous.

[8][But] he who commits sin [who practices evildoing] is of the devil [takes his character from the evil one], for the devil has sinned (violated the divine law) from the beginning. The reason the Son of God was made manifest (visible) was to undo (destroy, loosen, and dissolve) the works the devil [has done].

[9]No one born (begotten) of God [deliberately, knowingly, and [b]habitually] practices sin, for God's nature abides in him [His principle of life, the divine sperm, remains permanently within him]; and he cannot practice sinning because he is born (begotten) of God.

[10]By this it is made clear who take their nature from God *and* are His children and who take their nature from the devil *and* are his children: no one who does not practice righteousness [who does not conform to God's will in purpose, thought, and action] is of God; neither is anyone who does not love his brother (his fellow [c]believer in Christ).

[11]For this is the message (the announcement) which you have heard from the first, that we should love one another,

[12][And] not be like Cain who [took his nature and got his motivation] from the evil one and slew his brother. And why did he slay him? Because his deeds (activities, works) were wicked *and* malicious and his brother's were righteous (virtuous).

[13]Do not be surprised *and* wonder, brethren, that the world detests *and* pursues you with hatred.

[14]We know that we have passed over out of death into Life by the fact that we love the brethren (our fellow Christians). He who does not love abides (remains, is [c]held and kept continually) in [spiritual] death.

[15]Anyone who hates (abominates, detests) his brother [in Christ] is [at heart] a murderer, and you know that no murderer has eternal life abiding ([c]persevering) within him.

[16]By this we come to know (progressively to recognize, to perceive, to understand) the [essential] love: that He laid down His [own] life for us; and we ought to lay [our] lives down for [those who are our] brothers [[c]in Him].

[17]But if anyone has this world's goods (resources for sustaining life) and sees his brother *and* [c]fellow believer in need, yet closes his heart of compassion against him, how can the love of God live *and* remain in him?

[18]Little children, let us not love [merely] in theory *or* in speech but in deed and in truth (in practice and in sincerity).

[19]By this we shall come to know (perceive, recognize, and understand) that we are of the Truth, and can reassure (quiet, conciliate, and pacify) our hearts in His presence,

[20]Whenever our hearts in [[b]tormenting] self-accusation make us feel guilty *and* condemn us. [For [b]we are in God's hands.] For He is above *and* greater than our consciences (our hearts), and He knows (perceives and understands) everything [nothing is hidden from Him].

[21]And, beloved, if our consciences (our hearts) do not accuse us [if they do not make us feel guilty and condemn us], we have confidence (complete assurance and boldness) before God,

[22]And we receive from Him whatever we ask, because we [[b]watchfully] obey His orders [observe His suggestions and injunctions, follow His plan for us] *and* [[b]habitually] practice what is pleasing to Him.

---

[a] 13 The Greek word for *brothers and sisters* (*adelphoi*) refers here to believers, both men and women, as part of God's family; also in verse 16.

[a] G. Abbott-Smith, *Manual Greek Lexicon*. [b] Marvin Vincent, *Word Studies*. [c] Joseph Thayer, *A Greek-English Lexicon*.

## New International Version

command: to believe in the name of his Son, Jesus Christ, and to love one another as he commanded us. ²⁴The one who keeps God's commands lives in him, and he in them. And this is how we know that he lives in us: We know it by the Spirit he gave us.

### On Denying the Incarnation

**4** Dear friends, do not believe every spirit, but test the spirits to see whether they are from God, because many false prophets have gone out into the world. ²This is how you can recognize the Spirit of God: Every spirit that acknowledges that Jesus Christ has come in the flesh is from God, ³but every spirit that does not acknowledge Jesus is not from God. This is the spirit of the antichrist, which you have heard is coming and even now is already in the world.

⁴You, dear children, are from God and have overcome them, because the one who is in you is greater than the one who is in the world. ⁵They are from the world and therefore speak from the viewpoint of the world, and the world listens to them. ⁶We are from God, and whoever knows God listens to us; but whoever is not from God does not listen to us. This is how we recognize the Spirit*ᵃ* of truth and the spirit of falsehood.

### God's Love and Ours

⁷Dear friends, let us love one another, for love comes from God. Everyone who loves has been born of God and knows God. ⁸Whoever does not love does not know God, because God is love. ⁹This is how God showed his love among us: He sent his one and only Son into the world that we might live through him. ¹⁰This is love: not that we loved God, but that he loved us and sent his Son as an atoning sacrifice for our sins. ¹¹Dear friends, since God so loved us, we also ought to love one another. ¹²No one has ever seen God; but if we love one another, God lives in us and his love is made complete in us.

¹³This is how we know that we live in him and he in us:

## Amplified Bible

²³And this is His order (His command, His injunction): that we should believe in (put our faith and trust in and adhere to and rely on) the name of His Son Jesus Christ (the Messiah), and that we should love one another, just as He has commanded us.

²⁴All who keep His commandments [who obey His orders and follow His plan, live and continue to live, to stay and] abide in Him, and He in them. [ᵃThey let Christ be a home to them and they are the home of Christ.] And by this we know *and* understand *and* have the proof that He [really] lives *and* makes His home in us: by the [Holy] Spirit Whom He has given us.

**4** Beloved, do not put faith in every spirit, but prove (test) the spirits to discover whether they proceed from God; for many false prophets have gone forth into the world.

²By this you may know (perceive and recognize) the Spirit of God: every spirit which acknowledges *and* confesses [the fact] that Jesus Christ (the Messiah) [actually] has become man *and* has come in the flesh is of God [has God for its source];

³And every spirit which does not acknowledge *and* confess *that* Jesus *Christ has come in the flesh* [but would ᵇannul, destroy, ᶜsever, disunite Him] is not of God [does not proceed from Him]. This [ᵈnonconfession] is the [spirit] of the antichrist, [of] which you heard that it was coming, and now it is already in the world.

⁴Little children, you are of God [you belong to Him] and have [already] defeated *and* overcome them [the agents of the antichrist], because He Who lives in you is greater (mightier) than he who is in the world.

⁵They proceed from the world *and* are of the world; therefore it is out of the world [its ᵈwhole economy morally considered] that they speak, and the world listens (pays attention) to them.

⁶We are [children] of God. Whoever is learning to know God [progressively to perceive, recognize, and understand God by observation and experience, and to ᵈget an ever-clearer knowledge of Him] listens to us; and he who is not of God does not listen *or* pay attention to us. By this we know (recognize) the Spirit of Truth and the spirit of error.

⁷Beloved, let us love one another, for love is (springs) from God; and he who loves [his fellowmen] is begotten (born) of God and is coming [progressively] to know *and* understand God [to perceive and recognize and get a better and clearer knowledge of Him].

⁸He who does not love has not become acquainted with God [does not and never did know Him], for God is love.

⁹In this the love of God was made manifest (displayed) where we are concerned: in that God sent His Son, the only begotten *or* ᵉunique [Son], into the world so that we might live through Him.

¹⁰In this is love: not that we loved God, but that He loved us and sent His Son to be the propitiation (the atoning sacrifice) for our sins.

¹¹Beloved, if God loved us so [very much], we also ought to love one another.

¹²No man has at any time [yet] seen God. But if we love one another, God abides (lives and remains) in us and His love (that love which is essentially His) is brought to completion (to its full maturity, runs its full course, is perfected) in us!

¹³By this we come to know (perceive, recognize, and understand) that we abide (live and remain) in Him and He in us: because He has given (imparted) to us of His [Holy] Spirit.

ᵃ Bede, a translator of portions of the Bible from the Latin into Old English. ᵇ An ancient reading. ᶜ *The Latin Vulgate.* ᵈ Marvin Vincent, *Word Studies.* ᵉ James Moulton and George Milligan, *The Vocabulary of the Greek Testament.*

## New International Version

He has given us of his Spirit. [14]And we have seen and testify that the Father has sent his Son to be the Savior of the world. [15]If anyone acknowledges that Jesus is the Son of God, God lives in them and they in God. [16]And so we know and rely on the love God has for us.

God is love. Whoever lives in love lives in God, and God in them. [17]This is how love is made complete among us so that we will have confidence on the day of judgment: In this world we are like Jesus. [18]There is no fear in love. But perfect love drives out fear, because fear has to do with punishment. The one who fears is not made perfect in love.

[19]We love because he first loved us. [20]Whoever claims to love God yet hates a brother or sister is a liar. For whoever does not love their brother and sister, whom they have seen, cannot love God, whom they have not seen. [21]And he has given us this command: Anyone who loves God must also love their brother and sister.

### Faith in the Incarnate Son of God

**5** Everyone who believes that Jesus is the Christ is born of God, and everyone who loves the father loves his child as well. [2]This is how we know that we love the children of God: by loving God and carrying out his commands. [3]In fact, this is love for God: to keep his commands. And his commands are not burdensome, [4]for everyone born of God overcomes the world. This is the victory that has overcome the world, even our faith. [5]Who is it that overcomes the world? Only the one who believes that Jesus is the Son of God.

[6]This is the one who came by water and blood—Jesus Christ. He did not come by water only, but by water and blood. And it is the Spirit who testifies, because the Spirit is the truth. [7]For there are three that testify: [8]the[a] Spirit, the water and the blood; and the three are in agreement. [9]We accept human testimony, but God's testimony is greater because it is the testimony of God, which he has given about his Son. [10]Whoever believes in the Son of God

## Amplified Bible

[14]And [besides] we ourselves have seen (have deliberately and steadfastly contemplated) and bear witness that the Father has sent the Son [as the] Savior of the world.

[15]Anyone who confesses (acknowledges, owns) that Jesus is the Son of God, God abides (lives, makes His home) in him and he [abides, lives, makes his home] in God.

[16]And we know (understand, recognize, are conscious of, by observation and by experience) and believe (adhere to and put faith in and rely on) the love God cherishes for us. God is love, and he who dwells *and* continues in love dwells *and* continues in God, and God dwells *and* continues in him.

[17]In this [union and communion with Him] love is brought to completion *and* attains perfection with us, that we may have confidence for the day of judgment [with assurance and boldness to face Him], because as He is, so are we in this world.

[18]There is no fear in love [dread does not exist], but full-grown (complete, perfect) love [a]turns fear out of doors *and* expels every trace of terror! For fear [b]brings with it the thought of punishment, and [so] he who is afraid has not reached the full maturity of love [is not yet grown into love's complete perfection].

[19]We love *Him,* because He first loved us.

[20]If anyone says, I love God, and hates (detests, abominates) his brother [[b]in Christ], he is a liar; for he who does not love his brother, whom he has seen, cannot love God, Whom he has not seen.

[21]And this command (charge, order, injunction) we have from Him: that he who loves God shall love his brother [[b]believer] also.

**5** Everyone who believes (adheres to, trusts, and relies on the fact) that Jesus is the Christ (the Messiah) is a born-again child of God; and everyone who loves the Father also loves the one born of Him (His offspring).

[2]By this we come to know (recognize and understand) that we love the children of God: when we love God and obey His commands (orders, charges)—[when we keep His ordinances and are mindful of His precepts and His teaching].

[3]For the [true] love of God is this: that we do His commands [keep His ordinances and are mindful of His precepts and teaching]. And these orders of His are not irksome (burdensome, oppressive, or grievous).

[4]For whatever is born of God is victorious over the world; and this is the victory that conquers the world, even our faith.

[5]Who is it that is victorious over [that conquers] the world but he who believes that Jesus is the Son of God [who adheres to, trusts in, and relies on that fact]?

[6]This is He Who came by (with) water and blood [[a]His baptism and His death], Jesus Christ (the Messiah)—not by (in) the water only, but by (in) the water and the blood. And it is the [Holy] Spirit Who bears witness, because the [Holy] Spirit is the Truth.

[7]So there are three witnesses [c]*in heaven: the Father, the Word and the Holy Spirit, and these three are One;*

[8]and there are three witnesses on the earth: the Spirit, the water, and the blood; and these three agree [are in unison; their testimony coincides].

[9]If we accept [as we do] the testimony of men [if we are willing to take human authority], the testimony of God is greater (of stronger authority), for this is the testimony of God, even the witness which He has borne regarding His Son.

[10]He who believes in the Son of God [who adheres to, trusts in, and relies on Him] has the testimony [possesses this divine attestation] within himself. He who does not

---

[a] 7,8 Late manuscripts of the Vulgate *testify in heaven: the Father, the Word and the Holy Spirit, and these three are one.* 8And there are three *that testify on earth: the* (not found in any Greek manuscript before the fourteenth century)

[a] Marvin Vincent, *Word Studies.* [b] Joseph Thayer, *A Greek-English Lexicon.* [c] The italicized section is found only in late manuscripts.

## New International Version

accepts this testimony. Whoever does not believe God has made him out to be a liar, because they have not believed the testimony God has given about his Son. [11]And this is the testimony: God has given us eternal life, and this life is in his Son. [12]Whoever has the Son has life; whoever does not have the Son of God does not have life.

### Concluding Affirmations

[13]I write these things to you who believe in the name of the Son of God so that you may know that you have eternal life. [14]This is the confidence we have in approaching God: that if we ask anything according to his will, he hears us. [15]And if we know that he hears us—whatever we ask—we know that we have what we asked of him.

[16]If you see any brother or sister commit a sin that does not lead to death, you should pray and God will give them life. I refer to those whose sin does not lead to death. There is a sin that leads to death. I am not saying that you should pray about that. [17]All wrongdoing is sin, and there is sin that does not lead to death.

[18]We know that anyone born of God does not continue to sin; the One who was born of God keeps them safe, and the evil one cannot harm them. [19]We know that we are children of God, and that the whole world is under the control of the evil one. [20]We know also that the Son of God has come and has given us understanding, so that we may know him who is true. And we are in him who is true by being in his Son Jesus Christ. He is the true God and eternal life.

[21]Dear children, keep yourselves from idols.

## Amplified Bible

believe God [in this way] has made Him out to be *and* represented Him as a liar, because he has not believed (put his faith in, adhered to, and relied on) the evidence (the testimony) that God has borne regarding His Son.

[11]And this is that testimony (that evidence): God gave us eternal life, and this life is in His Son.

[12]He who possesses the Son has that life; he who does not possess the Son of God does not have that life.

[13]I write this to you who believe in (adhere to, trust in, and rely on) the name of the Son of God [in [a]the peculiar services and blessings conferred by Him on men], so that you may know [with settled and absolute knowledge] that you [already] have life, [b]yes, eternal life.

[14]And this is the confidence (the assurance, the privilege of boldness) which we have in Him: [we are sure] that if we ask anything (make any request) according to His will (in agreement with His own plan), He listens to *and* hears us.

[15]And if (since) we [positively] know that He listens to us in whatever we ask, we also know [with settled and absolute knowledge] that we have [granted us as our present possessions] the requests made of Him.

[16]If anyone sees his brother [believer] committing a sin that does not [lead to] death (the extinguishing of life), he will pray and [God] will give him life [yes, He will grant life to all those whose sin is not one leading to death]. There is a sin [that leads] to death; I do not say that one should pray for that.

[17]All wrongdoing is sin, and there is sin which does not [involve] death [that may be repented of and forgiven].

[18]We know [absolutely] that anyone born of God does not [deliberately and knowingly] practice committing sin, but the One Who was begotten of God carefully watches over *and* protects him [Christ's divine presence within him preserves him against the evil], and the wicked one does not lay hold (get a grip) on him *or* touch [him].

[19]We know [positively] that we are of God, and the whole world [around us] is under the power of the evil one.

[20]And we [have seen and] know [positively] that the Son of God has [actually] come to this world and has given us understanding *and* insight [progressively] to perceive (recognize) *and* come to know better *and* more clearly Him Who is true; and we are in Him Who is true—in His Son Jesus Christ (the Messiah). This [Man] is the true God and Life eternal.

[21]Little children, keep yourselves from idols (false gods)—[from anything and everything that would occupy the place in your heart due to God, from any sort of substitute for Him that would take first place in your life]. *Amen (so let it be).*

---

[a] Joseph Thayer, *A Greek-English Lexicon.*   [b] Brooke F. Westcott, cited by *Speaker's Commentary.*

# 2 John

# John

¹The elder,

To the lady chosen by God and to her children, whom I love in the truth—and not I only, but also all who know the truth— ²because of the truth, which lives in us and will be with us forever:

³Grace, mercy and peace from God the Father and from Jesus Christ, the Father's Son, will be with us in truth and love.

⁴It has given me great joy to find some of your children walking in the truth, just as the Father commanded us. ⁵And now, dear lady, I am not writing you a new command but one we have had from the beginning. I ask that we love one another. ⁶And this is love: that we walk in obedience to his commands. As you have heard from the beginning, his command is that you walk in love.

⁷I say this because many deceivers, who do not acknowledge Jesus Christ as coming in the flesh, have gone out into the world. Any such person is the deceiver and the antichrist. ⁸Watch out that you do not lose what we[a] have worked for, but that you may be rewarded fully. ⁹Anyone who runs ahead and does not continue in the teaching of Christ does not have God; whoever continues in the teaching has both the Father and the Son. ¹⁰If anyone comes to you and does not bring this teaching, do not take them into your house or welcome them. ¹¹Anyone who welcomes them shares in their wicked work.

¹²I have much to write to you, but I do not want to use paper and ink. Instead, I hope to visit you and talk with you face to face, so that our joy may be complete.

¹³The children of your sister, who is chosen by God, send their greetings.

---

¹The elderly elder [of the church addresses this letter] to the elect (chosen) lady (Cyria) and her children, whom I truly love—and not only I but also all who are [progressively] learning to recognize *and* know *and* understand the Truth—

²Because of the Truth which lives *and* stays on in our hearts and will be with us forever:

³Grace (spiritual blessing), mercy, and [soul] peace will be with us, from God the Father and from Jesus Christ (the Messiah), the Father's Son, in all sincerity (truth) and love.

⁴I was greatly delighted to find some of your children walking (living) in [the] Truth, just as we have been commanded by the Father [Himself].

⁵And now I beg you, lady (Cyria), not as if I were issuing a new charge (injunction or command), but [simply recalling to your mind] the one we have had from the beginning, that we love one another.

⁶And what this love consists in is this: that we live *and* walk in accordance with *and* guided by His commandments (His orders, ordinances, precepts, teaching). This is the commandment, as you have heard from the beginning, that you continue to walk in love [guided by it and following it].

⁷For many imposters (seducers, deceivers, and false leaders) have gone out into the world, men who will not acknowledge (confess, admit) the coming of Jesus Christ (the Messiah) in bodily form. Such a one is the imposter (the seducer, the deceiver, the false leader, the antagonist of Christ) and the antichrist.

⁸Look to yourselves (take care) that you may not lose (throw away or destroy) all that we *and* you have labored for, but that you may [persevere until you] win *and* receive back a perfect reward [in full].

⁹Anyone who runs on ahead [of God] and does not abide in the doctrine of Christ [who is not content with what He taught] does not have God; but he who continues to live in the doctrine (teaching) of Christ [does have God], he has both the Father and the Son.

¹⁰If anyone comes to you and does not bring this doctrine [is disloyal to what Jesus Christ taught], do not receive him [do not accept him, do not welcome or admit him] into [your] house or bid him Godspeed *or* give him any encouragement.

¹¹For he who wishes him success [who encourages him, wishing him Godspeed] is a partaker in his evil doings.

¹²I have many things to write to you, but I prefer not to do so with paper and ink; I hope to come to see you and talk with you face to face, so that our joy may be complete.

¹³The children of your elect (chosen) sister wish to be remembered to you. *Amen (so be it).*

---

*a* 8 Some manuscripts *you*

# 3 John

# John

[1]The elder,

To my dear friend Gaius, whom I love in the truth.

[2]Dear friend, I pray that you may enjoy good health and that all may go well with you, even as your soul is getting along well. [3]It gave me great joy when some believers came and testified about your faithfulness to the truth, telling how you continue to walk in it. [4]I have no greater joy than to hear that my children are walking in the truth.

[5]Dear friend, you are faithful in what you are doing for the brothers and sisters,[a] even though they are strangers to you. [6]They have told the church about your love. Please send them on their way in a manner that honors God. [7]It was for the sake of the Name that they went out, receiving no help from the pagans. [8]We ought therefore to show hospitality to such people so that we may work together for the truth.

[9]I wrote to the church, but Diotrephes, who loves to be first, will not welcome us. [10]So when I come, I will call attention to what he is doing, spreading malicious nonsense about us. Not satisfied with that, he even refuses to welcome other believers. He also stops those who want to do so and puts them out of the church.

[11]Dear friend, do not imitate what is evil but what is good. Anyone who does what is good is from God. Anyone who does what is evil has not seen God. [12]Demetrius is well spoken of by everyone—and even by the truth itself. We also speak well of him, and you know that our testimony is true.

[13]I have much to write you, but I do not want to do so with pen and ink. [14]I hope to see you soon, and we will talk face to face.

Peace to you. The friends here send their greetings. Greet the friends there by name.

[1]The elderly elder [of the church addresses this letter] to the beloved (esteemed) Gaius, whom I truly love. [2]Beloved, I pray that you may prosper in every way and [that your body] may keep well, even as [I know] your soul keeps well *and* prospers. [3]In fact, I greatly rejoiced when [some of] the brethren from time to time arrived and spoke [so highly] of the sincerity *and* fidelity of your life, as indeed you do live in the Truth [the whole Gospel presents]. [4]I have no greater joy than this, to hear that my [spiritual] children are living their lives in the Truth. [5]Beloved, it is a fine *and* faithful work that you are doing when you give any service to the [Christian] brethren, and [especially when they are] strangers. [6]They have testified before the church of your love *and* friendship. You will do well to forward them on their journey [and you will please do so] in a way worthy of God's [service]. [7]For these [traveling missionaries] have gone out for the Name's sake (for His sake) and are accepting nothing from the Gentiles (the heathen, the non-Israelites). [8]So we ourselves ought to support such people [to welcome and provide for them], in order that we may be fellow workers in the Truth (the whole Gospel) *and* cooperate with its teachers. [9]I have written briefly to the church; but Diotrephes, who likes to take the lead among them *and* put himself first, does not acknowledge my authority *and* refuses to accept my suggestions *or* to listen to me. [10]So when I arrive, I will call attention to what he is doing, his boiling over *and* casting malicious reflections upon us with insinuating language. And not satisfied with that, he refuses to receive *and* welcome the [missionary] brethren himself, and also interferes with *and* forbids those who would welcome them, and tries to expel (excommunicate) them from the church. [11]Beloved, do not imitate evil, but imitate good. He who does good is of God; he who does evil has not seen (discerned or experienced) God [has enjoyed no vision of Him and does not know Him at all]. [12]Demetrius has warm commendation from everyone—and from the Truth itself; we add our testimony also, and you know that our testimony is true. [13]I had much [to say to you when I began] to write, but I prefer not to put it down with pen (a reed) and ink; [14]I hope to see you soon, and we will talk together face to face. [15]Peace be to you! (Good-bye!) The friends here send you greetings. Remember me to the friends there [to every one of them personally] by name.

---

[a] 5 The Greek word for *brothers and sisters* (*adelphoi*) refers here to believers, both men and women, as part of God's family.

# Jude

¹Jude, a servant of Jesus Christ and a brother of James,

To those who have been called, who are loved in God the Father and kept for*a* Jesus Christ:

²Mercy, peace and love be yours in abundance.

## The Sin and Doom of Ungodly People
³Dear friends, although I was very eager to write to you about the salvation we share, I felt compelled to write and urge you to contend for the faith that was once for all entrusted to God's holy people. ⁴For certain individuals whose condemnation was written about*b* long ago have secretly slipped in among you. They are ungodly people, who pervert the grace of our God into a license for immorality and deny Jesus Christ our only Sovereign and Lord.

⁵Though you already know all this, I want to remind you that the Lord*c* at one time delivered his people out of Egypt, but later destroyed those who did not believe. ⁶And the angels who did not keep their positions of authority but abandoned their proper dwelling—these he has kept in darkness, bound with everlasting chains for judgment on the great Day. ⁷In a similar way, Sodom and Gomorrah and the surrounding towns gave themselves up to sexual immorality and perversion. They serve as an example of those who suffer the punishment of eternal fire.

⁸In the very same way, on the strength of their dreams these ungodly people pollute their own bodies, reject authority and heap abuse on celestial beings. ⁹But even the archangel Michael, when he was disputing with the devil about the body of Moses, did not himself dare to condemn him for slander but said, "The Lord rebuke you!"*d* ¹⁰Yet these people slander whatever they do not understand, and the very things they do understand by instinct—as irrational animals do—will destroy them.

¹¹Woe to them! They have taken the way of Cain; they have rushed for profit into Balaam's error; they have been destroyed in Korah's rebellion.

¹²These people are blemishes at your love feasts, eating with you without the slightest qualm—shepherds who feed only themselves. They are clouds without rain, blown along by the wind; autumn trees, without fruit and uprooted—twice dead. ¹³They are wild waves of the sea, foaming up their shame; wandering stars, for whom blackest darkness has been reserved forever.

# Jude

¹Jude, a servant of Jesus Christ (the Messiah), and brother of James, [writes this letter] to those who are called (chosen), dearly loved by God the Father *and separated (set apart)* and kept for Jesus Christ:

²May mercy, [soul] peace, and love be multiplied to you.

³Beloved, my whole concern was to write to you in regard to our common salvation. [But] I found it necessary *and* was impelled to write you and urgently appeal to *and* exhort [you] to contend for the faith which was once for all *a*handed down to the saints [the faith which is that sum of Christian belief which was delivered *a*verbally to the holy people of God].

⁴For certain men have crept in stealthily [*b*gaining entrance secretly by a side door]. Their doom was predicted long ago, ungodly (impious, profane) persons who pervert the grace (the spiritual blessing and favor) of our God into lawlessness *and* wantonness *and* immorality, and disown *and* deny our sole Master and Lord, Jesus Christ (the Messiah, the Anointed One).

⁵Now I want to remind you, though you were fully informed once for all, that though the Lord [at one time] delivered a people out of the land of Egypt, He subsequently destroyed those [of them] who did not believe [who refused to adhere to, trust in, and rely upon Him].

⁶And angels who did not keep (care for, guard, and hold to) their own first place of power but abandoned their proper dwelling place—these He has reserved in custody in eternal chains (bonds) under the thick gloom of utter darkness until the judgment *and* doom of the great day.

⁷[The wicked are sentenced to suffer] just as Sodom and Gomorrah and the adjacent towns—which likewise gave themselves over to impurity and indulged in unnatural vice *and* sensual perversity—are laid out [in plain sight] as an exhibit of perpetual punishment [to warn] of everlasting fire. [Gen. 19.]

⁸Nevertheless in like manner, these dreamers also corrupt the body, scorn *and* reject authority *and* government, and revile *and* libel *and* scoff at [heavenly] glories (the glorious ones).

⁹But when [even] the archangel Michael, contending with the devil, judicially argued (disputed) about the body of Moses, he dared not [presume to] bring an abusive condemnation against him, but [simply] said, The Lord rebuke you! [Zech. 3:2.]

¹⁰But these men revile (scoff and sneer at) anything they do not happen to be acquainted with *and* do not understand; and whatever they do understand physically [that which they know by mere instinct], like irrational beasts—by these they corrupt themselves *and* are destroyed (perish).

¹¹Woe to them! For they have run riotously in the way of Cain, and have abandoned themselves for the sake of gain [it offers them, following] the error of Balaam, and have perished in rebellion [like that] of Korah! [Gen. 4:3-8; Num. 16; 22-24.]

¹²These are hidden reefs (elements of danger) in your love feasts, where they boldly feast sumptuously [carousing together in your midst], without scruples providing for themselves [alone]. They are clouds without water, swept along by the winds; trees, without fruit at the late autumn gathering time—twice (doubly) dead, [lifeless and] plucked up by the roots;

¹³Wild waves of the sea, flinging up the foam of their own shame *and* disgrace; wandering stars, for whom the gloom of eternal darkness has been reserved forever.

---

*a 1* Or *by;* or *in*   *b 4* Or *individuals who were marked out for condemnation*   *c 5* Some early manuscripts *Jesus*   *d 9* Jude is alluding to the Jewish *Testament of Moses* (approximately the first century A.D.).

*a* G. Abbott-Smith, *Manual Greek Lexicon of the New Testament.*   *b* The use of this verb paints this kind of picture.

## New International Version

[14]Enoch, the seventh from Adam, prophesied about them: "See, the Lord is coming with thousands upon thousands of his holy ones [15]to judge everyone, and to convict all of them of all the ungodly acts they have committed in their ungodliness, and of all the defiant words ungodly sinners have spoken against him."[a] [16]These people are grumblers and faultfinders; they follow their own evil desires; they boast about themselves and flatter others for their own advantage.

### A Call to Persevere

[17]But, dear friends, remember what the apostles of our Lord Jesus Christ foretold. [18]They said to you, "In the last times there will be scoffers who will follow their own ungodly desires." [19]These are the people who divide you, who follow mere natural instincts and do not have the Spirit.

[20]But you, dear friends, by building yourselves up in your most holy faith and praying in the Holy Spirit, [21]keep yourselves in God's love as you wait for the mercy of our Lord Jesus Christ to bring you to eternal life.

[22]Be merciful to those who doubt; [23]save others by snatching them from the fire; to others show mercy, mixed with fear—hating even the clothing stained by corrupted flesh.[b]

### Doxology

[24]To him who is able to keep you from stumbling and to present you before his glorious presence without fault and with great joy— [25]to the only God our Savior be glory, majesty, power and authority, through Jesus Christ our Lord, before all ages, now and forevermore! Amen.

## Amplified Bible

[14]It was of these people, moreover, that Enoch in the seventh [generation] from Adam prophesied when he said, Behold, the Lord comes with His myriads of holy ones (ten thousands of His saints)

[15]To execute judgment upon all and to convict all the impious (unholy ones) of all their ungodly deeds which they have committed [in such an] ungodly [way], and of all the severe (abusive, jarring) things which ungodly sinners have spoken against Him.

[16]These are inveterate murmurers (grumblers) who complain [of their lot in life], going after their own desires [controlled by their passions]; their talk is boastful *and* arrogant, [and they claim to] admire men's persons *and* pay people flattering compliments to gain advantage.

[17]But you must remember, beloved, the predictions which were made by the apostles (the special messengers) of our Lord Jesus Christ (the Messiah, the Anointed One).

[18]They told you beforehand, In the last days (in the end time) there will be scoffers [who seek to gratify their own unholy desires], following after their own ungodly passions.

[19]It is these who are [agitators] setting up distinctions *and* causing divisions—merely sensual [creatures, carnal, worldly-minded people], devoid of the [Holy] Spirit *and* destitute of any higher spiritual life.

[20]But you, beloved, build yourselves up [founded] on your most holy faith [amake progress, rise like an edifice higher and higher], praying in the Holy Spirit;

[21]Guard *and* keep yourselves in the love of God; expect *and* patiently wait for the mercy of our Lord Jesus Christ (the Messiah)—[which will bring you] unto life eternal.

[22]And *refute [so as to] convict some who dispute with you, and* on some have mercy who waver *and* doubt.

[23][Strive to] save others, snatching [them] out of [the] fire; on others take pity [but] with fear, loathing even the garment spotted by the flesh *and* polluted by their sensuality. [Zech. 3:2-4.]

[24]Now to Him Who is able to keep you without stumbling *or* slipping *or* falling, and to present [you] unblemished (blameless and faultless) before the presence of His glory in triumphant joy *and* exultation [with unspeakable, ecstatic delight]—

[25]To the one only God, our Savior through Jesus Christ our Lord, be glory (splendor), majesty, might *and* dominion, and power *and* authority, before all time and now and forever (unto all the ages of eternity). Amen (so be it).

---

[a] 14,15 From the Jewish *First Book of Enoch* (approximately the first century B.C.)    [b] 22,23 The Greek manuscripts of these verses vary at several points.

[a] Joseph Thayer, *A Greek-English Lexicon of the New Testament.*

# Revelation

## Prologue

**1** The revelation from Jesus Christ, which God gave him to show his servants what must soon take place. He made it known by sending his angel to his servant John, ²who testifies to everything he saw—that is, the word of God and the testimony of Jesus Christ. ³Blessed is the one who reads aloud the words of this prophecy, and blessed are those who hear it and take to heart what is written in it, because the time is near.

## Greetings and Doxology

⁴John,

To the seven churches in the province of Asia:

Grace and peace to you from him who is, and who was, and who is to come, and from the seven spirits*a* before his throne, ⁵and from Jesus Christ, who is the faithful witness, the firstborn from the dead, and the ruler of the kings of the earth.

To him who loves us and has freed us from our sins by his blood, ⁶and has made us to be a kingdom and priests to serve his God and Father—to him be glory and power for ever and ever! Amen.

⁷"Look, he is coming with the clouds,"*b*
    and "every eye will see him,
  even those who pierced him";
    and all peoples on earth "will mourn because of him."*c*
                                      So shall it be! Amen.

⁸"I am the Alpha and the Omega," says the Lord God, "who is, and who was, and who is to come, the Almighty."

## John's Vision of Christ

⁹I, John, your brother and companion in the suffering and kingdom and patient endurance that are ours in Jesus, was on the island of Patmos because of the word of God and the testimony of Jesus. ¹⁰On the Lord's Day I was in the Spirit, and I heard behind me a loud voice like a trumpet, ¹¹which said: "Write on a scroll what you see and send it to the seven churches: to Ephesus, Smyrna, Pergamum, Thyatira, Sardis, Philadelphia and Laodicea."

¹²I turned around to see the voice that was speaking to me. And when I turned I saw seven golden lampstands,

---

# THE
# Revelation
## TO JOHN

**1** [This is] the revelation of Jesus Christ [His unveiling of the divine mysteries]. God gave it to Him to disclose *and* make known to His bond servants certain things which must shortly *and* speedily come to pass *a*in their entirety. And He sent and communicated it through His angel (messenger) to His bond servant John,

²Who has testified to *and* vouched for all that he saw [*a*in his visions], the word of God and the testimony of Jesus Christ.

³Blessed (happy, *b*to be envied) is the man who reads aloud [in the assemblies] the word of this prophecy; and blessed (happy, *b*to be envied) are those who hear [it read] and who keep themselves true to the things which are written in it [heeding them and laying them to heart], for the time [for them to be fulfilled] is near.

⁴John to the seven assemblies (churches) that are in Asia: May grace (God's unmerited favor) be granted to you and spiritual peace (*c*the peace of Christ's kingdom) from Him Who is and Who was and Who is to come, and from the seven Spirits [*d*the sevenfold Holy Spirit] before His throne, [Isa. 11:2.]

⁵And from Jesus Christ the faithful *and* trustworthy Witness, the Firstborn of the dead [first to be brought back to life] and the Prince (Ruler) of the kings of the earth. To Him Who *e*ever loves us and has *e*once [for all] loosed *and* freed us from our sins by His own blood, [Ps. 89:27.]

⁶And formed us into a kingdom (a royal race), priests to His God and Father—to Him be the glory and the power *and* the majesty and the dominion throughout the ages *and* forever and ever. Amen (so be it). [Exod. 19:6; Isa. 61:6.]

⁷Behold, He is coming with the clouds, and every eye will see Him, even those who pierced Him; and all the tribes of the earth shall gaze upon Him *and* beat their breasts *and* mourn *and* lament over Him. Even so [must it be]. Amen (so be it). [Dan. 7:13; Zech. 12:10.]

⁸I am the Alpha and the Omega, *the Beginning and the End,* says the Lord God, He Who is and Who was and Who is to come, the Almighty (the Ruler of all). [Isa. 9:6.]

⁹I, John, your brother and companion (sharer and participator) with you in the tribulation and kingdom and patient endurance [which are] in Jesus *Christ,* was on the isle called Patmos, [banished] on account of [my witnessing to] the Word of God and the testimony (the proof, the evidence) for Jesus *Christ.*

¹⁰I was in the Spirit [rapt in His power] on the Lord's Day, and I heard behind me a great voice like the calling of a *f*war trumpet,

¹¹Saying, *I am the Alpha and the Omega, the First and the Last.* Write promptly what you see (your vision) in a book and send it to the seven churches *which are in Asia*—to Ephesus and to Smyrna and to Pergamum and to Thyatira and to Sardis and to Philadelphia and to Laodicea.

¹²Then I turned to see [whose was] the voice that was speaking to me, and on turning I saw seven golden lampstands,

---

*a* Marvin Vincent, *Word Studies in the New Testament.* *b* Alexander Souter, *Pocket Lexicon of the Greek New Testament.* *c* G. Abbott-Smith, *Manual Greek Lexicon of the New Testament.* *d* Richard of St. Victor, cited by Richard Trench, *Synonyms of the New Testament.* *e* Charles B. Williams, *The New Testament: A Translation in the Language of the People:* "ever" and "once" captures the idea of ongoing and completed action contained within the Greek present and aorist (past) verb tenses used here. *f* Marvin Vincent, *Word Studies.*

---

*a* 4 That is, the sevenfold Spirit    *b* 7 Daniel 7:13    *c* 7 Zech. 12:10

## New International Version

13and among the lampstands was someone like a son of man,[a] dressed in a robe reaching down to his feet and with a golden sash around his chest. 14The hair on his head was white like wool, as white as snow, and his eyes were like blazing fire. 15His feet were like bronze glowing in a furnace, and his voice was like the sound of rushing waters. 16In his right hand he held seven stars, and coming out of his mouth was a sharp, double-edged sword. His face was like the sun shining in all its brilliance.

17When I saw him, I fell at his feet as though dead. Then he placed his right hand on me and said: "Do not be afraid. I am the First and the Last. 18I am the Living One; I was dead, and now look, I am alive for ever and ever! And I hold the keys of death and Hades.

19"Write, therefore, what you have seen, what is now and what will take place later. 20The mystery of the seven stars that you saw in my right hand and of the seven golden lampstands is this: The seven stars are the angels[b] of the seven churches, and the seven lampstands are the seven churches.

### To the Church in Ephesus

**2** "To the angel[c] of the church in Ephesus write:

These are the words of him who holds the seven stars in his right hand and walks among the seven golden lampstands. 2I know your deeds, your hard work and your perseverance. I know that you cannot tolerate wicked people, that you have tested those who claim to be apostles but are not, and have found them false. 3You have persevered and have endured hardships for my name, and have not grown weary.

4Yet I hold this against you: You have forsaken the love you had at first. 5Consider how far you have fallen! Repent and do the things you did at first. If you do not repent, I will come to you and remove your lampstand from its place. 6But you have this in your favor: You hate the practices of the Nicolaitans, which I also hate.

7Whoever has ears, let them hear what the Spirit says to the churches. To the one who is victorious, I will give the right to eat from the tree of life, which is in the paradise of God.

### To the Church in Smyrna

8"To the angel of the church in Smyrna write:

These are the words of him who is the First and the Last, who died and came to life again. 9I know your afflictions and your poverty—yet you are rich! I know about the slander of those who say they are Jews and are not, but are a synagogue of Satan. 10Do not be afraid of what you are about to suffer. I tell you, the devil will put some of you in prison to test you, and you will suffer persecution for ten days. Be faithful, even to the point of death, and I will give you life as your victor's crown.

## Amplified Bible

13And in the midst of the lampstands [One] like a Son of Man, clothed with a robe which reached to His feet and with a girdle of gold about His breast. [Dan. 7:13; 10:5.]

14His head and His hair were white like white wool, [as white] as snow, and His eyes [flashed] like a flame of fire. [Dan. 7:9.]

15His feet glowed like burnished (bright) bronze as it is refined in a furnace, and His voice was like the sound of many waters. [Dan. 10:6.]

16In His right hand He held seven stars, and from His mouth there came forth a sharp two-edged sword, and His face was like the sun shining in full power at midday. [Exod. 34:29.]

17When I saw Him, I fell at His feet as if dead. But He laid His right hand on me and said, Do not be afraid! I am the First and the Last, [Isa. 44:6.]

18And the Ever-living One [I am living in the eternity of the eternities]. I died, but see, I am alive forevermore; and I possess the keys of death and Hades (the realm of the dead).

19Write therefore the things you see, what they are [and signify] and what is to take place hereafter.

20As to the hidden meaning (the mystery) of the seven stars which you saw on My right hand and the seven lampstands of gold: the seven stars are the seven angels (messengers) of the seven assemblies (churches) and the seven lampstands are the seven churches.

**2** To the angel (messenger) of the assembly (church) in Ephesus write: These are the words of Him Who holds the seven stars [which are the messengers of the seven churches] in His right hand, Who goes about among the seven golden lampstands [which are the seven churches]:

2I know your industry and activities, laborious toil and trouble, and your patient endurance, and how you cannot tolerate wicked [men] and have tested and critically appraised those who call [themselves] apostles (special messengers of Christ) and yet are not, and have found them to be impostors and liars.

3I know you are enduring patiently and are bearing up for My name's sake, and you have not fainted or become exhausted or grown weary.

4But I have this [one charge to make] against you: that you have left (abandoned) the love that you had at first [you have deserted Me, your first love].

5Remember then from what heights you have fallen. Repent (change the inner man to meet God's will) and do the works you did previously [when first you knew the Lord], or else I will visit you and remove your lampstand from its place, unless you change your mind and repent.

6Yet you have this [in your favor and to your credit]: you hate the works of the Nicolaitans [what they are doing as corrupters of the people], which I Myself also detest.

7He who is able to hear, let him listen to and give heed to what the Spirit says to the assemblies (churches). To him who overcomes (is victorious), I will grant to eat [of the fruit] of the tree of life, which is in the paradise of God. [Gen. 2:9; 3:24.]

8And to the angel (messenger) of the assembly (church) in Smyrna write: These are the words of the First and the Last, Who died and came to life again: [Isa. 44:6.]

9I know your affliction and distress and pressing trouble and your poverty—but you are rich! and how you are abused and reviled and slandered by those who say they are Jews and are not, but are a synagogue of Satan.

10Fear nothing that you are about to suffer. [Dismiss your dread and your fears!] Behold, the devil is indeed about to throw some of you into prison, that you may be tested and proved and critically appraised, and for ten days you will have affliction. Be loyally faithful unto death [even if you must die for it], and I will give you the crown of life. [Rev. 3:10, 11.]

---

[a] 13 See Daniel 7:13.   [b] 20 Or messengers   [c] 1 Or messenger; also in verses 8, 12 and 18

## New International Version

### Amplified Bible

<sup>11</sup>Whoever has ears, let them hear what the Spirit says to the churches. The one who is victorious will not be hurt at all by the second death.

### To the Church in Pergamum

<sup>12</sup>"To the angel of the church in Pergamum write:

These are the words of him who has the sharp, double-edged sword. <sup>13</sup>I know where you live— where Satan has his throne. Yet you remain true to my name. You did not renounce your faith in me, not even in the days of Antipas, my faithful witness, who was put to death in your city—where Satan lives.

<sup>14</sup>Nevertheless, I have a few things against you: There are some among you who hold to the teaching of Balaam, who taught Balak to entice the Israelites to sin so that they ate food sacrificed to idols and committed sexual immorality. <sup>15</sup>Likewise, you also have those who hold to the teaching of the Nicolaitans. <sup>16</sup>Repent therefore! Otherwise, I will soon come to you and will fight against them with the sword of my mouth.

<sup>17</sup>Whoever has ears, let them hear what the Spirit says to the churches. To the one who is victorious, I will give some of the hidden manna. I will also give that person a white stone with a new name written on it, known only to the one who receives it.

### To the Church in Thyatira

<sup>18</sup>"To the angel of the church in Thyatira write:

These are the words of the Son of God, whose eyes are like blazing fire and whose feet are like burnished bronze. <sup>19</sup>I know your deeds, your love and faith, your service and perseverance, and that you are now doing more than you did at first.

<sup>20</sup>Nevertheless, I have this against you: You tolerate that woman Jezebel, who calls herself a prophet. By her teaching she misleads my servants into sexual immorality and the eating of food sacrificed to idols. <sup>21</sup>I have given her time to repent of her immorality, but she is unwilling. <sup>22</sup>So I will cast her on a bed of suffering, and I will make those who commit adultery with her suffer intensely, unless they repent of her ways. <sup>23</sup>I will strike her children dead. Then all the churches will know that I am he who searches hearts and minds, and I will repay each of you according to your deeds.

<sup>24</sup>Now I say to the rest of you in Thyatira, to you who do not hold to her teaching and have not learned Satan's so-called deep secrets, 'I will not impose any other burden on you, <sup>25</sup>except to hold on to what you have until I come.'

<sup>26</sup>To the one who is victorious and does my will to the end, I will give authority over the nations— <sup>27</sup>that

<sup>11</sup>He who is able to hear, let him listen to *and* heed what the Spirit says to the assemblies (churches). He who overcomes (is victorious) shall in no way be injured by the second death.

<sup>12</sup>Then to the angel (messenger) of the assembly (church) in Pergamum write: These are the words of Him Who has *and* wields the sharp two-edged sword:

<sup>13</sup>I know where you live—a place where Satan sits enthroned. [Yet] you are clinging to *and* holding fast My name, and you did not deny My faith, even in the days of Antipas, My witness, My faithful one, who was killed (martyred) in your midst—where Satan dwells.

<sup>14</sup>Nevertheless, I have a few things against you: you have some people there who are clinging to the teaching of Balaam, who taught Balak to set a trap *and* a stumbling block before the sons of Israel, [to entice them] to eat food that had been sacrificed to idols and to practice lewdness [giving themselves up to sexual vice]. [Num. 25:1, 2; 31:16.]

<sup>15</sup>You also have some who in a similar way are clinging to the teaching of the Nicolaitans [those corrupters of the people] *which thing I hate.*

<sup>16</sup>Repent [then]! Or else I will come to you quickly and fight against them with the sword of My mouth.

<sup>17</sup>He who is able to hear, let him listen to *and* heed what the Spirit says to the assemblies (churches). To him who overcomes (conquers), I will give to eat of the manna that is hidden, and I will give him a white stone with a new name engraved on the stone, which no one knows *or* understands except he who receives it. [Ps. 78:24; Isa. 62:2.]

<sup>18</sup>And to the angel (messenger) of the assembly (church) in Thyatira write: These are the words of the Son of God, Who has eyes that flash like a flame of fire, and Whose feet glow like bright *and* burnished *and* white-hot bronze: [Dan. 10:6.]

<sup>19</sup>I know your record *and* what you are doing, your love and faith and service and patient endurance, and that your recent works are more numerous *and* greater than your first ones.

<sup>20</sup>But I have this against you: that you tolerate the woman Jezebel, who calls herself a prophetess [claiming to be inspired], and who is teaching and leading astray my servants *and* beguiling them into practicing sexual vice and eating food sacrificed to idols. [I Kings 16:31; II Kings 9:22, 30.]

<sup>21</sup>I gave her time to repent, but she has no desire to repent of her immorality [symbolic of idolatry] *and* refuses to do so.

<sup>22</sup>Take note: I will throw her on a bed [<sup>a</sup>of anguish], and those who commit adultery with her [her paramours] I will bring down to <sup>b</sup>pressing distress *and* severe affliction, unless they turn away their minds from conduct [such as] hers *and* repent of <sup>c</sup>*their* doings.

<sup>23</sup>And I will strike her children (her proper followers) dead [thoroughly exterminating them]. And all the assemblies (churches) shall recognize *and* understand that I am He Who searches minds (the thoughts, feelings, and purposes) and the [inmost] hearts, and I will give to each of you [the reward for what you have done] as your work deserves. [Ps. 62:12; Jer. 17:10.]

<sup>24</sup>But to the rest of you in Thyatira, who do not hold this teaching, who have not explored *and* known the depths of Satan, as they say—I tell you that I do not lay upon you any other [fresh] burden:

<sup>25</sup>Only hold fast to what you have until I come.

<sup>26</sup>And he who overcomes (is victorious) and who obeys My commands to the [very] end [doing the works that please Me], I will give him authority *and* power over the nations;

---

<sup>a</sup> Marvin Vincent, *Word Studies.* <sup>b</sup> Literal translation. <sup>c</sup> Many ancient manuscripts so read.

## New International Version

one 'will rule them with an iron scepter and will dash them to pieces like pottery'*a*—just as I have received authority from my Father. [28]I will also give that one the morning star. [29]Whoever has ears, let them hear what the Spirit says to the churches.

### To the Church in Sardis

**3** "To the angel*b* of the church in Sardis write:

These are the words of him who holds the seven spirits*c* of God and the seven stars. I know your deeds; you have a reputation of being alive, but you are dead. [2]Wake up! Strengthen what remains and is about to die, for I have found your deeds unfinished in the sight of my God. [3]Remember, therefore, what you have received and heard; hold it fast, and repent. But if you do not wake up, I will come like a thief, and you will not know at what time I will come to you.

[4]Yet you have a few people in Sardis who have not soiled their clothes. They will walk with me, dressed in white, for they are worthy. [5]The one who is victorious will, like them, be dressed in white. I will never blot out the name of that person from the book of life, but will acknowledge that name before my Father and his angels. [6]Whoever has ears, let them hear what the Spirit says to the churches.

### To the Church in Philadelphia

[7]"To the angel of the church in Philadelphia write:

These are the words of him who is holy and true, who holds the key of David. What he opens no one can shut, and what he shuts no one can open. [8]I know your deeds. See, I have placed before you an open door that no one can shut. I know that you have little strength, yet you have kept my word and have not denied my name. [9]I will make those who are of the synagogue of Satan, who claim to be Jews though they are not, but are liars—I will make them come and fall down at your feet and acknowledge that I have loved you. [10]Since you have kept my command to endure patiently, I will also keep you from the hour of trial that is going to come on the whole world to test the inhabitants of the earth.

[11]I am coming soon. Hold on to what you have, so that no one will take your crown. [12]The one who is victorious I will make a pillar in the temple of my God. Never again will they leave it. I will write on them the name of my God and the name of the city of my God, the new Jerusalem, which is coming down out of heaven from my God; and I will also write on them my new name. [13]Whoever has ears, let them hear what the Spirit says to the churches.

### To the Church in Laodicea

[14]"To the angel of the church in Laodicea write:

These are the words of the Amen, the faithful and true witness, the ruler of God's creation. [15]I know

## Amplified Bible

[27]And he shall rule them with a sceptre (rod) of iron, as when earthen pots are broken in pieces, and [his power over them shall be] like that which I Myself have received from My Father; [Ps. 2:8, 9.]

[28]And I will give him the Morning Star.

[29]He who is able to hear, let him listen to *and* heed what the [Holy] Spirit says to the assemblies (churches).

**3** And to the angel (messenger) of the assembly (church) in Sardis write: These are the words of Him Who has the seven Spirits of God [*a*the sevenfold Holy Spirit] and the seven stars: I know your record *and* what you are doing; you are supposed to be alive, but [in reality] you are dead.

[2]Rouse yourselves *and* keep awake, and strengthen *and* invigorate what remains and is on the point of dying; for I have not found a thing that you have done [any work of yours] meeting the requirements of My God *or* perfect in His sight.

[3]So call to mind the lessons you received and heard; continually lay them to heart *and* obey them, and repent. In case you will not rouse yourselves *and* keep awake *and watch*, I will come upon you like a thief, and you will not know *or* suspect at what hour I will come.

[4]Yet you still have a few [persons'] names in Sardis who have not soiled their clothes, and they shall walk with Me in white, because they are worthy *and* deserving.

[5]Thus shall he who conquers (is victorious) be clad in white garments, and I will not erase *or* blot out his name from the Book of Life; I will acknowledge him [as Mine] *and* I will confess his name openly before My Father and before His angels. [Ps. 69:28; Dan. 12:1.]

[6]He who is able to hear, let him listen to *and* heed what the [Holy] Spirit says to the assemblies (churches).

[7]And to the angel (messenger) of the assembly (church) in Philadelphia write: These are the words of the Holy One, the True One, He Who has the key of David, Who opens and no one shall shut, Who shuts and no one shall open: [Isa. 22:22.]

[8]I know your [record of] works *and* what you are doing. See! I have set before you a door wide open which no one is able to shut; I know that you have but little power, and yet you have kept My Word *and* guarded My message and have not renounced *or* denied My name.

[9]Take note! I will make those of the synagogue of Satan who say they are Jews and are not, but lie—behold, I will make them come and bow down before your feet and learn *and* acknowledge that I have loved you. [Isa. 43:4; 49:23; 60:14.]

[10]Because you have guarded *and* kept My word of patient endurance [have held fast the *b*lesson of My patience with the *b*expectant endurance that I give you], I also will keep you [safe] from the hour of trial (testing) which is coming on the whole world to try those who dwell upon the earth.

[11]I am coming quickly; hold fast what you have, so that no one may rob you *and* deprive you of your crown.

[12]He who overcomes (is victorious), I will make him a pillar in the sanctuary of My God; he shall never be put out of it *or* go out of it, and I will write on him the name of My God and the name of the city of My God, the new Jerusalem, which descends from My God out of heaven, and My own new name. [Isa. 62:2; Ezek. 48:35.]

[13]He who can hear, let him listen to *and* heed what the Spirit says to the assemblies (churches).

[14]And to the angel (messenger) of the assembly (church) in Laodicea write: These are the words of the Amen, the trusty *and* faithful and true Witness, the Origin *and* Beginning *and* Author of God's creation: [Isa. 55:4; Prov. 8:22.]

---

*a* Richard of St. Victor, cited by Richard Trench, *Synonyms of the New Testament.* *b* Joseph Thayer, *A Greek-English Lexicon of the New Testament*: The Greek, which we translate "of patient endurance," paints a picture of "a patient, steadfast waiting" for someone or something.

---

*a 27* Psalm 2:9   *b 1* Or *messenger*; also in verses 7 and 14   *c 1* That is, the sevenfold Spirit

## New International Version

your deeds, that you are neither cold nor hot. I wish you were either one or the other! 16So, because you are lukewarm—neither hot nor cold—I am about to spit you out of my mouth. 17You say, 'I am rich; I have acquired wealth and do not need a thing.' But you do not realize that you are wretched, pitiful, poor, blind and naked. 18I counsel you to buy from me gold refined in the fire, so you can become rich; and white clothes to wear, so you can cover your shameful nakedness; and salve to put on your eyes, so you can see.

19Those whom I love I rebuke and discipline. So be earnest and repent. 20Here I am! I stand at the door and knock. If anyone hears my voice and opens the door, I will come in and eat with that person, and they with me.

21To the one who is victorious, I will give the right to sit with me on my throne, just as I was victorious and sat down with my Father on his throne. 22Whoever has ears, let them hear what the Spirit says to the churches."

### The Throne in Heaven

**4** After this I looked, and there before me was a door standing open in heaven. And the voice I had first heard speaking to me like a trumpet said, "Come up here, and I will show you what must take place after this." 2At once I was in the Spirit, and there before me was a throne in heaven with someone sitting on it. 3And the one who sat there had the appearance of jasper and ruby. A rainbow that shone like an emerald encircled the throne. 4Surrounding the throne were twenty-four other thrones, and seated on them were twenty-four elders. They were dressed in white and had crowns of gold on their heads. 5From the throne came flashes of lightning, rumblings and peals of thunder. In front of the throne, seven lamps were blazing. These are the seven spirits[a] of God. 6Also in front of the throne there was what looked like a sea of glass, clear as crystal.

In the center, around the throne, were four living creatures, and they were covered with eyes, in front and in back. 7The first living creature was like a lion, the second was like an ox, the third had a face like a man, the fourth was like a flying eagle. 8Each of the four living creatures had six wings and was covered with eyes all around, even under its wings. Day and night they never stop saying:

"'Holy, holy, holy
is the Lord God Almighty,'[b]
who was, and is, and is to come."

9Whenever the living creatures give glory, honor and thanks to him who sits on the throne and who lives for ever

## Amplified Bible

15I know your [record of] works *and* what you are doing; you are neither cold nor hot. Would that you were cold or hot!

16So, because you are lukewarm and neither cold nor hot, I will spew you out of My mouth!

17For you say, I am rich; I have prospered *and* grown wealthy, and I am in need of nothing; and you do not realize *and* understand that you are wretched, pitiable, poor, blind, and naked. [Hos. 12:8.]

18Therefore I counsel you to purchase from Me gold refined *and* tested by fire, that you may be [truly] wealthy, and white clothes to clothe you and to keep the shame of your nudity from being seen, and salve to put on your eyes, that you may see.

19Those whom I [dearly and tenderly] love, I tell their faults and convict *and* convince *and* reprove and chasten [I discipline and instruct them]. So be enthusiastic *and* in earnest *and* burning with zeal and repent [changing your mind and attitude]. [Prov. 3:12.]

20Behold, I stand at the door and knock; if anyone hears *and* listens to *and* heeds My voice and opens the door, I will come in to him and will eat with him, and he [will eat] with Me.

21He who overcomes (is victorious), I will grant him to sit beside Me on My throne, as I Myself overcame (was victorious) and sat down beside My Father on His throne.

22He who is able to hear, let him listen to *and* heed what the [Holy] Spirit says to the assemblies (churches).

**4** After this I looked, and behold, a door standing open in heaven! And the first voice which I had heard addressing me like [the calling of] a [a]war trumpet said, Come up here, and I will show you what must take place in the future.

2At once I came under the [Holy] Spirit's power, and behold, a throne stood in heaven, with One seated on the throne! [Ezek. 1:26.]

3And He Who sat there appeared like [the crystalline brightness of] jasper and [the fiery] sardius, and encircling the throne there was a halo that looked like [a rainbow of] emerald. [Ezek. 1:28.]

4Twenty-four other thrones surrounded the throne, and seated on these thrones were twenty-four elders ([b]the members of the heavenly Sanhedrin), arrayed in white clothing, with crowns of gold upon their heads.

5Out from the throne came flashes of lightning and rumblings and peals of thunder, and in front of the throne seven blazing torches burned, which are the seven Spirits of God [[c]the sevenfold Holy Spirit];

6And in front of the throne there was also what looked like a transparent glassy sea, as if of crystal. And around the throne, in the center at each side of the throne, were four living creatures (beings) who were full of eyes in front and behind [with intelligence as to what is before and at the rear of them]. [Ezek. 1:5, 18.]

7The first living creature (being) was like a lion, the second living creature like an ox, the third living creature had the face of a man, and the fourth living creature [was] like a flying eagle. [Ezek. 1:10.]

8And the four living creatures, individually having six wings, were full of eyes all over and within [underneath their wings]; and day and night they never stop saying, Holy, holy, holy is the Lord God Almighty (Omnipotent), Who was and Who is and Who is to come. [Isa. 6:1-3.]

9And whenever the living creatures offer glory and honor and thanksgiving to Him Who sits on the throne, Who lives forever and ever (through the eternities of the eternities), [Ps. 47:8.]

---

[a] Marvin Vincent, *Word Studies*.  [b] George R. Berry, *Greek-English New Testament Lexicon*.  [c] Richard of St. Victor, cited by Richard Trench, *Synonyms of the New Testament*.

[a] 5 That is, the sevenfold Spirit   [b] 8 Isaiah 6:3

## New International Version

and ever, ¹⁰the twenty-four elders fall down before him who sits on the throne and worship him who lives for ever and ever. They lay their crowns before the throne and say:

¹¹ "You are worthy, our Lord and God,
    to receive glory and honor and power,
for you created all things,
    and by your will they were created
    and have their being."

### The Scroll and the Lamb

**5** Then I saw in the right hand of him who sat on the throne a scroll with writing on both sides and sealed with seven seals. ²And I saw a mighty angel proclaiming in a loud voice, "Who is worthy to break the seals and open the scroll?" ³But no one in heaven or on earth or under the earth could open the scroll or even look inside it. ⁴I wept and wept because no one was found who was worthy to open the scroll or look inside. ⁵Then one of the elders said to me, "Do not weep! See, the Lion of the tribe of Judah, the Root of David, has triumphed. He is able to open the scroll and its seven seals."

⁶Then I saw a Lamb, looking as if it had been slain, standing at the center of the throne, encircled by the four living creatures and the elders. The Lamb had seven horns and seven eyes, which are the seven spirits⁴ of God sent out into all the earth. ⁷He went and took the scroll from the right hand of him who sat on the throne. ⁸And when he had taken it, the four living creatures and the twenty-four elders fell down before the Lamb. Each one had a harp and they were holding golden bowls full of incense, which are the prayers of God's people. ⁹And they sang a new song, saying:

"You are worthy to take the scroll
    and to open its seals,
because you were slain,
    and with your blood you purchased for God
    persons from every tribe and language and people
        and nation.
¹⁰ You have made them to be a kingdom and priests to
        serve our God,
    and they will reign⁵ on the earth."

¹¹Then I looked and heard the voice of many angels, numbering thousands upon thousands, and ten thousand times ten thousand. They encircled the throne and the living creatures and the elders. ¹²In a loud voice they were saying:

"Worthy is the Lamb, who was slain,
    to receive power and wealth and wisdom and
        strength
    and honor and glory and praise!"

¹³Then I heard every creature in heaven and on earth and under the earth and on the sea, and all that is in them, saying:

"To him who sits on the throne and to the Lamb
    be praise and honor and glory and power,
        for ever and ever!"

## Amplified Bible

¹⁰The twenty-four elders (ᵃthe members of the heavenly Sanhedrin) fall prostrate before Him Who is sitting on the throne, and they worship Him Who lives forever and ever; and they throw down their crowns before the throne, crying out,

¹¹Worthy are You, our Lord and God, to receive the glory and the honor and dominion, for You created all things; by Your will they were [brought into being] and were created. [Ps. 19:1.]

**5** And I saw lying on the ᵇopen hand of Him Who was seated on the throne a scroll (book) written within and on the back, closed *and* sealed with seven seals; [Isa. 29:11; Ezek. 2:9, 10; Dan. 12:4.]

²And I saw a strong angel announcing in a loud voice, Who is worthy to open the scroll? And [who is entitled and deserves and is morally fit] to break its seals?

³And no one in heaven or on earth or under the earth [in the realm of the dead, Hades] was able to open the scroll or to take a [single] look at its contents.

⁴And I wept audibly *and* bitterly because no one was found fit to open the scroll or to inspect it.

⁵Then one of the elders [ᵃof the heavenly Sanhedrin] said to me, Stop weeping! See, the Lion of the tribe of Judah, the Root (Source) of David, has won (has overcome and conquered)! He can open the scroll and break its seven seals! [Gen. 49:9, 10; Isa. 11:1, 10; Rev. 22:16.]

⁶And there between the throne and the four living creatures (beings) and among the elders [ᵃof the heavenly Sanhedrin] I saw a Lamb standing, as though it had been slain, with seven horns and with seven eyes, which are the seven Spirits of God [ᶜthe sevenfold Holy Spirit] Who have been sent [on duty far and wide] into all the earth. [Isa. 53:7; Zech. 3:8, 9; 4:10.]

⁷He then went and took the scroll from the right hand of Him Who sat on the throne.

⁸And when He had taken the scroll, the four living creatures and the twenty-four elders [ᵃof the heavenly Sanhedrin] prostrated themselves before the Lamb. Each was holding a harp (lute or guitar), and they had golden bowls full of incense (fragrant spices and gums for burning), which are the prayers of God's people (the saints).

⁹And [now] they sing a new song, saying, You are worthy to take the scroll and to break the seals that are on it, for You were slain (sacrificed), and with Your blood You purchased men unto God from every tribe and language and people and nation. [Ps. 33:3.]

¹⁰And You have made them a kingdom (royal race) and priests to our God, and they shall reign [as kings] over the earth! [Exod. 19:6; Isa. 61:6.]

¹¹Then I looked, and I heard the voices of many angels on every side of the throne and of the living creatures and the elders [ᵃof the heavenly Sanhedrin], and they numbered ten thousand times ten thousand and thousands of thousands, [Dan. 7:10.]

¹²Saying in a loud voice, Deserving is the Lamb, Who was sacrificed, to receive all the power and riches and wisdom and might and honor and majesty (glory, splendor) and blessing!

¹³And I heard every created thing in heaven and on earth and under the earth [in Hades, the place of departed spirits] and on the sea and all that is in it, crying out together, To Him Who is seated on the throne and to the Lamb be ascribed the blessing and the honor and the majesty (glory, splendor) and the power (might and dominion) forever and ever (through the eternities of the eternities)! [Dan. 7:13, 14.]

---

ᵃ George R. Berry, *Greek-English New Testament Lexicon.* ᵇ Marvin Vincent, *Word Studies.* ᶜ Richard of St. Victor, cited by Richard Trench, *Synonyms of the New Testament.*

---

ᵃ 6 That is, the sevenfold Spirit    ᵇ 10 Some manuscripts *they reign*

## New International Version

¹⁴The four living creatures said, "Amen," and the elders fell down and worshiped.

### The Seals

**6** I watched as the Lamb opened the first of the seven seals. Then I heard one of the four living creatures say in a voice like thunder, "Come!" ²I looked, and there before me was a white horse! Its rider held a bow, and he was given a crown, and he rode out as a conqueror bent on conquest.

³When the Lamb opened the second seal, I heard the second living creature say, "Come!" ⁴Then another horse came out, a fiery red one. Its rider was given power to take peace from the earth and to make people kill each other. To him was given a large sword.

⁵When the Lamb opened the third seal, I heard the third living creature say, "Come!" I looked, and there before me was a black horse! Its rider was holding a pair of scales in his hand. ⁶Then I heard what sounded like a voice among the four living creatures, saying, "Two pounds*a* of wheat for a day's wages,*b* and six pounds*c* of barley for a day's wages,*b* and do not damage the oil and the wine!"

⁷When the Lamb opened the fourth seal, I heard the voice of the fourth living creature say, "Come!" ⁸I looked, and there before me was a pale horse! Its rider was named Death, and Hades was following close behind him. They were given power over a fourth of the earth to kill by sword, famine and plague, and by the wild beasts of the earth.

⁹When he opened the fifth seal, I saw under the altar the souls of those who had been slain because of the word of God and the testimony they had maintained. ¹⁰They called out in a loud voice, "How long, Sovereign Lord, holy and true, until you judge the inhabitants of the earth and avenge our blood?" ¹¹Then each of them was given a white robe, and they were told to wait a little longer, until the full number of their fellow servants, their brothers and sisters,*d* were killed just as they had been.

¹²I watched as he opened the sixth seal. There was a great earthquake. The sun turned black like sackcloth made of goat hair, the whole moon turned blood red, ¹³and the stars in the sky fell to earth, as figs drop from a fig tree when shaken by a strong wind. ¹⁴The heavens receded like a scroll being rolled up, and every mountain and island was removed from its place.

¹⁵Then the kings of the earth, the princes, the generals, the rich, the mighty, and everyone else, both slave and free, hid in caves and among the rocks of the mountains. ¹⁶They called to the mountains and the rocks, "Fall on us and hide us*e* from the face of him who sits on the throne

## Amplified Bible

¹⁴Then the four living creatures (beings) said, Amen (so be it)! And the elders [*a*of the heavenly Sanhedrin] prostrated themselves and worshiped *Him Who lives for- ever and ever.*

**6** Then I saw as the Lamb broke open one of the seven seals, and as if in a voice of thunder I heard one of the four living creatures call out, Come!

²And I looked, and saw there a white horse whose rider carried a bow. And a crown was given him, and he rode forth conquering and to conquer. [Ps. 45:4, 5; Zech. 1:8; 6:1-3.]

³And when He broke the second seal, I heard the sec- ond living creature call out, Come!

⁴And another horse came out, flaming red. And its rider was empowered to take the peace from the earth, so that men slaughtered one another; and he was given a huge sword.

⁵When He broke open the third seal, I heard the third living creature call out, Come *and look*! And I saw, and behold, a black horse, and in his hand the rider had a pair of scales (a balance).

⁶And I heard what seemed to be a voice from the midst of the four living creatures, saying, A quart of wheat for a denarius [a whole day's wages], and three quarts of bar- ley for a denarius; but do not harm the oil and the wine! [II Kings 6:25.]

⁷When the Lamb broke open the fourth seal, I heard the fourth living creature call out, Come!

⁸So I looked, and behold, an ashy pale horse [*b*black and blue as if made so by bruising], and its rider's name was Death, and Hades (the realm of the dead) followed him closely. And they were given authority *and* power over a fourth part of the earth to kill with the sword and with fam- ine and with plague (pestilence, disease) and with wild beasts of the earth. [Ezek. 5:12; Hos. 13:14.]

⁹When the Lamb broke open the fifth seal, I saw at the foot of the altar the souls of those whose lives had been sacrificed for [adhering to] the Word of God and for the testimony they had borne.

¹⁰They cried in a loud voice, O [Sovereign] Lord, holy and true, how long now before You will sit in judgment and avenge our blood upon those who dwell on the earth? [Gen. 4:10; Ps. 79:5; Zech. 1:12.]

¹¹Then they were each given a *c*long *and* flowing *and* festive white robe and told to rest *and* wait patiently a little while longer, until the number should be complete of their fellow servants and their brethren who were to be killed as they themselves had been.

¹²When He [the Lamb] broke open the sixth seal, I looked, and there was a great earthquake; and the sun grew black as sackcloth of hair, [the full disc of] the moon became like blood. [Joel 2:10, 31.]

¹³And the stars of the sky dropped to the earth like a fig tree shedding its unripe fruit out of season when shaken by a strong wind. [Isa. 34:4.]

¹⁴And the *d*sky rolled up like a scroll *and* vanished, and every mountain and island was dislodged from its place.

¹⁵Then the kings of the earth and their noblemen and their magnates and their military chiefs and the wealthy and the strong and [everyone, whether] slave or free hid themselves in the caves and among the rocks of the moun- tains, [Isa. 2:10.]

¹⁶And they called to the mountains and the rocks, Fall on (before) us and hide us from the face of Him Who sits on the throne and from the *c*deep-seated indignation *and* wrath of the Lamb. [Isa. 2:19-21; Hos. 10:8.]

---

*a* 6 Or about 1 kilogram   *b* 6 Greek *a denarius*   *c* 6 Or about 3 kilograms   *d 11* The Greek word for *brothers and sisters (adelphoi)* refers here to believers, both men and women, as part of God's family; also in 12:10; 19:10.   *e 16* See Hosea 10:8.

*a* George R. Berry, *Greek-English New Testament Lexicon.*   *b* A description of the livid, ashen, discolored appearance of the dead; it symbolizes death and pestilence.   *c* Marvin Vincent, *Word Studies.*   *d* James Moulton and George Milligan, *The Vocabulary of the Greek Testament.*

## New International Version

and from the wrath of the Lamb! [17]For the great day of their[a] wrath has come, and who can withstand it?"

### 144,000 Sealed

**7** After this I saw four angels standing at the four corners of the earth, holding back the four winds of the earth to prevent any wind from blowing on the land or on the sea or on any tree. [2]Then I saw another angel coming up from the east, having the seal of the living God. He called out in a loud voice to the four angels who had been given power to harm the land and the sea: [3]"Do not harm the land or the sea or the trees until we put a seal on the foreheads of the servants of our God." [4]Then I heard the number of those who were sealed: 144,000 from all the tribes of Israel.

[5]From the tribe of Judah 12,000 were sealed,
  from the tribe of Reuben 12,000,
  from the tribe of Gad 12,000,
[6]from the tribe of Asher 12,000,
  from the tribe of Naphtali 12,000,
  from the tribe of Manasseh 12,000,
[7]from the tribe of Simeon 12,000,
  from the tribe of Levi 12,000,
  from the tribe of Issachar 12,000,
[8]from the tribe of Zebulun 12,000,
  from the tribe of Joseph 12,000,
  from the tribe of Benjamin 12,000.

### The Great Multitude in White Robes

[9]After this I looked, and there before me was a great multitude that no one could count, from every nation, tribe, people and language, standing before the throne and before the Lamb. They were wearing white robes and were holding palm branches in their hands. [10]And they cried out in a loud voice:

"Salvation belongs to our God,
  who sits on the throne,
  and to the Lamb."

[11]All the angels were standing around the throne and around the elders and the four living creatures. They fell down on their faces before the throne and worshiped God, [12]saying:

"Amen!
Praise and glory
and wisdom and thanks and honor
and power and strength
be to our God for ever and ever.
Amen!"

[13]Then one of the elders asked me, "These in white robes—who are they, and where did they come from?"

[14]I answered, "Sir, you know."

And he said, "These are they who have come out of the great tribulation; they have washed their robes and made them white in the blood of the Lamb. [15]Therefore,

"they are before the throne of God
  and serve him day and night in his temple;
and he who sits on the throne
  will shelter them with his presence.
[16]'Never again will they hunger;
  never again will they thirst.
The sun will not beat down on them,'[b]
  nor any scorching heat.
[17]For the Lamb at the center of the throne
  will be their shepherd;
'he will lead them to springs of living water.'[b]
  'And God will wipe away every tear from their
    eyes.'[c]"

## Amplified Bible

[17]For the great day of His wrath (vengeance, retribution, indignation) has come, and who is able to stand before it? [Joel 2:11; Mal. 3:2.]

**7** After this I saw four angels stationed at the four corners of the earth, [a]firmly holding back the four winds of the earth so that no wind should blow on the earth or sea or upon any tree. [Zech. 6:5.]

[2]Then I saw a second angel coming up from the east (the rising of the sun) and carrying the seal of the living God. And with a loud voice he called out to the four angels who had been given authority *and* power to injure earth and sea,

[3]Saying, Harm neither the earth nor the sea nor the trees, until we have sealed the bond servants of our God upon their foreheads. [Ezek. 9:4.]

[4]And [then] I heard how many were sealed (marked) out of every tribe of the sons of Israel: there were 144,000.

[5]Twelve thousand were sealed (marked) out of the tribe of Judah, 12,000 of the tribe of Reuben, 12,000 of the tribe of Gad,

[6]Twelve thousand of the tribe of Asher, 12,000 of the tribe of Naphtali, 12,000 of the tribe of Manasseh,

[7]Twelve thousand of the tribe of Simeon, 12,000 of the tribe of Levi, 12,000 of the tribe of Issachar,

[8]Twelve thousand of the tribe of Zebulun, 12,000 of the tribe of Joseph, 12,000 of the tribe of Benjamin.

[9]After this I looked and a vast host appeared which no one could count, [gathered out] of every nation, from all tribes and peoples and languages. These stood before the throne and before the Lamb; they were attired in white robes, with palm branches in their hands.

[10]In loud voice they cried, saying, [Our] salvation is due to our God, Who is seated on the throne, and to the Lamb [to Them we owe our deliverance]!

[11]And all the angels were standing round the throne and round the elders [b]of the heavenly Sanhedrin] and the four living creatures, and they fell prostrate before the throne and worshiped God.

[12]Amen! (So be it!) they cried. Blessing and glory *and* majesty *and* splendor and wisdom and thanks and honor and power and might [be ascribed] to our God to the ages and ages (forever and ever, throughout the eternities of the eternities)! Amen! (So be it!)

[13]Then, addressing me, one of the elders [b]of the heavenly Sanhedrin] said, Who are these [people] clothed in the long white robes? And from where have they come?

[14]I replied, Sir, you know. And he said to me, These are they who have come out of the great tribulation (persecution), and have washed their robes and made them white in the blood of the Lamb. [Gen. 49:11; Dan. 12:1.]

[15]For this reason they are [now] before the [very] throne of God and serve Him day and night in His sanctuary (temple); and He Who is sitting upon the throne will protect *and* spread His tabernacle over *and* shelter them with His presence.

[16]They shall hunger no more, neither thirst any more; neither shall the sun smite them, nor any [b]scorching heat. [Isa. 49:10; Ps. 121:6.]

[17]For the Lamb Who is in the midst of the throne will be their Shepherd, and He will guide them to the springs of the waters of life; and God will wipe away every tear from their eyes. [Ps. 23:2; Isa. 25:8; Ezek. 34:23.]

---

[a] 17 Some manuscripts *his*    [b] 16,17 Isaiah 49:10    [c] 17 Isaiah 25:8

[a] Marvin Vincent, *Word Studies.*   [b] George R. Berry, *Greek-English New Testament Lexicon.*

## New International Version

### The Seventh Seal and the Golden Censer

**8** When he opened the seventh seal, there was silence in heaven for about half an hour.

²And I saw the seven angels who stand before God, and seven trumpets were given to them.

³Another angel, who had a golden censer, came and stood at the altar. He was given much incense to offer, with the prayers of all God's people, on the golden altar in front of the throne. ⁴The smoke of the incense, together with the prayers of God's people, went up before God from the angel's hand. ⁵Then the angel took the censer, filled it with fire from the altar, and hurled it on the earth; and there came peals of thunder, rumblings, flashes of lightning and an earthquake.

### The Trumpets

⁶Then the seven angels who had the seven trumpets prepared to sound them.

⁷The first angel sounded his trumpet, and there came hail and fire mixed with blood, and it was hurled down on the earth. A third of the earth was burned up, a third of the trees were burned up, and all the green grass was burned up.

⁸The second angel sounded his trumpet, and something like a huge mountain, all ablaze, was thrown into the sea. A third of the sea turned into blood, ⁹a third of the living creatures in the sea died, and a third of the ships were destroyed.

¹⁰The third angel sounded his trumpet, and a great star, blazing like a torch, fell from the sky on a third of the rivers and on the springs of water— ¹¹the name of the star is Wormwood.ᵃ A third of the waters turned bitter, and many people died from the waters that had become bitter.

¹²The fourth angel sounded his trumpet, and a third of the sun was struck, a third of the moon, and a third of the stars, so that a third of them turned dark. A third of the day was without light, and also a third of the night.

¹³As I watched, I heard an eagle that was flying in midair call out in a loud voice: "Woe! Woe! Woe to the inhabitants of the earth, because of the trumpet blasts about to be sounded by the other three angels!"

**9** The fifth angel sounded his trumpet, and I saw a star that had fallen from the sky to the earth. The star was given the key to the shaft of the Abyss. ²When he opened the Abyss, smoke rose from it like the smoke from a gigantic furnace. The sun and sky were darkened by the smoke from the Abyss. ³And out of the smoke locusts came down on the earth and were given power like that of scorpions of the earth. ⁴They were told not to harm the grass of the earth or any plant or tree, but only those people who did not have the seal of God on their foreheads. ⁵They were not allowed to kill them but only to torture them for five months. And the agony they suffered was like that of the sting of a scorpion when it strikes. ⁶During those days

## Amplified Bible

**8** When he [the Lamb] broke open the seventh seal, there was silence for about half an hour in heaven.

²Then I saw the seven angels who stand before God, and to them were given seven trumpets.

³And another angel came and stood over the altar. He had a golden censer, and he was given very much incense (fragrant spices and gums which exhale perfume when burned), that he might mingle it with the prayers of all the people of God (the saints) upon the golden altar before the throne. [Ps. 141:2.]

⁴And the smoke of the incense (the perfume) arose in the presence of God, with the prayers of the people of God (the saints), from the hand of the angel.

⁵So the angel took the censer and filled it with fire from the altar and cast it upon the earth. Then there followed peals of thunder *and* loud rumblings and blasts *and* noises, and flashes of lightning and an earthquake. [Lev. 16:12; Ezek. 10:2.]

⁶Then the seven angels who had the seven trumpets prepared to sound them.

⁷The first angel blew [his] trumpet, and there was a storm of hail and fire mingled with blood cast upon the earth. And a third part of the earth was burned up and a third of the trees were burned up and all the green grass was burned up. [Exod. 9:23-25.]

⁸The second angel blew [his] trumpet, and something resembling a great mountain, blazing with fire, was hurled into the sea. [Jer. 51:25.]

⁹And a third of the sea was turned to blood, a third of the living creatures in the sea perished, and a third of the ships were destroyed.

¹⁰The third angel blew [his] trumpet, and a huge star fell from heaven, burning like a torch, and it dropped on a third of the rivers and on the springs of water—

¹¹And the name of the star is Wormwood. A third part of the waters was changed into wormwood, and many people died from using the water, because it had become bitter.

¹²Then the fourth angel blew [his] trumpet, and a third of the sun was smitten, and a third of the moon, and a third of the stars, so that [the light of] a third of them was darkened, and a third of the daylight [itself] was withdrawn, and likewise a third [of the light] of the night was kept from shining.

¹³Then I [looked and I] saw a solitary eagle flying in midheaven, and as it flew I heard it crying with a loud voice, Woe, woe, woe to those who dwell on the earth, because of the rest of the trumpet blasts which the three angels are about to sound!

**9** Then the fifth angel blew [his] trumpet, and I saw a star that had fallen from the sky to the earth; and to the angel was given the key ᵃ of the shaft of the Abyss (the bottomless pit).

²He opened the ᵃlong shaft of the Abyss (the bottomless pit), and smoke like the smoke of a huge furnace puffed out of the ᵃlong shaft, so that the sun and the atmosphere were darkened by the smoke from the long shaft. [Gen. 19:28; Exod. 19:18; Joel 2:10.]

³Then out of the smoke locusts came forth on the earth, and such power was granted them as the power the earth's scorpions have. [Exod. 10: 12-15.]

⁴They were told not to injure the herbage of the earth nor any green thing nor any tree, but only [to attack] such human beings as do not have the seal (mark) of God on their foreheads. [Ezek. 9:4.]

⁵They were not permitted to kill them, but to torment (distress, vex) them for five months; and the pain caused them was like the torture of a scorpion when it stings a person.

---

ᵃ 11 Wormwood is a bitter substance.

ᵃ Marvin Vincent, *Word Studies*.

| New International Version | Amplified Bible |
|---|---|

**New International Version**

people will seek death but will not find it; they will long to die, but death will elude them.

⁷The locusts looked like horses prepared for battle. On their heads they wore something like crowns of gold, and their faces resembled human faces. ⁸Their hair was like women's hair, and their teeth were like lions' teeth. ⁹They had breastplates like breastplates of iron, and the sound of their wings was like the thundering of many horses and chariots rushing into battle. ¹⁰They had tails with stingers, like scorpions, and in their tails they had power to torment people for five months. ¹¹They had as king over them the angel of the Abyss, whose name in Hebrew is Abaddon and in Greek is Apollyon (that is, Destroyer).

¹²The first woe is past; two other woes are yet to come.

¹³The sixth angel sounded his trumpet, and I heard a voice coming from the four horns of the golden altar that is before God. ¹⁴It said to the sixth angel who had the trumpet, "Release the four angels who are bound at the great river Euphrates." ¹⁵And the four angels who had been kept ready for this very hour and day and month and year were released to kill a third of mankind. ¹⁶The number of the mounted troops was twice ten thousand times ten thousand. I heard their number.

¹⁷The horses and riders I saw in my vision looked like this: Their breastplates were fiery red, dark blue, and yellow as sulfur. The heads of the horses resembled the heads of lions, and out of their mouths came fire, smoke and sulfur. ¹⁸A third of mankind was killed by the three plagues of fire, smoke and sulfur that came out of their mouths. ¹⁹The power of the horses was in their mouths and in their tails; for their tails were like snakes, having heads with which they inflict injury.

²⁰The rest of mankind who were not killed by these plagues still did not repent of the work of their hands; they did not stop worshiping demons, and idols of gold, silver, bronze, stone and wood—idols that cannot see or hear or walk. ²¹Nor did they repent of their murders, their magic arts, their sexual immorality or their thefts.

### The Angel and the Little Scroll

**10** Then I saw another mighty angel coming down from heaven. He was robed in a cloud, with a rainbow above his head; his face was like the sun, and his legs were like fiery pillars. ²He was holding a little scroll, which lay open in his hand. He planted his right foot on the sea and his left foot on the land, ³and he gave a loud shout like the roar of a lion. When he shouted, the voices of the seven thunders spoke. ⁴And when the seven thunders spoke, I was about to write; but I heard a voice from heaven say, "Seal up what the seven thunders have said and do not write it down."

⁵Then the angel I had seen standing on the sea and on the land raised his right hand to heaven. ⁶And he swore

**Amplified Bible**

⁶And in those days people will seek death and will not find it; and they will yearn to die, but death evades *and* flees from them. [Job 3:21.]

⁷The locusts resembled horses equipped for battle. On their heads was something like golden crowns. Their faces resembled the faces of people. [Joel 2:4.]

⁸They had hair like the hair of women, and their teeth were like lions' teeth. [Joel 1:6.]

⁹Their breastplates (scales) resembled breastplates made of iron, and the [whirring] noise made by their wings was like the roar of a vast number of horse-drawn chariots going at full speed into battle. [Joel 2:5.]

¹⁰They have tails like scorpions, and they have stings, and in their tails lies their ability to hurt men for [the] five months.

¹¹Over them as king they have the angel of the Abyss (of the bottomless pit). In Hebrew his name is Abaddon [destruction], but in Greek he is called Apollyon [destroyer].

¹²The first woe (calamity) has passed; behold, two others are yet to follow.

¹³Then the sixth angel blew [his] trumpet, and from the four horns of the golden altar which stands before God I heard a solitary voice,

¹⁴Saying to the sixth angel who had the trumpet, Liberate the four angels who are bound at the great river Euphrates.

¹⁵So the four angels who had been in readiness for that hour in the appointed day, month, and year were liberated to destroy a third of mankind.

¹⁶The number of their troops of cavalry was twice ten thousand times ten thousand (200,000,000); I heard what their number was.

¹⁷And in [my] vision the horses and their riders appeared to me like this: the riders wore breastplates the color of fiery red and sapphire blue and sulphur (brimstone) yellow. The heads of the horses looked like lions' heads, and from their mouths there poured fire and smoke and sulphur (brimstone).

¹⁸A third of mankind was killed by these three plagues—by the fire and the smoke and the sulphur (brimstone) that poured from the mouths of the horses.

¹⁹For the power of the horses to do harm is in their mouths and also in their tails. Their tails are like serpents, for they have heads, and it is by means of them that they wound people.

²⁰And the rest of humanity who were not killed by these plagues even then did not repent of [the worship of] the works of their [own] hands, so as to cease paying homage to the demons and idols of gold and silver and bronze and stone and wood, which can neither see nor hear nor move. [Ps. 115:4-7; 135:15-17; Isa. 17:8.]

²¹And they did not repent of their murders or their practice of magic (sorceries) or their sexual vice or their thefts.

**10** Then I saw another mighty angel coming down from heaven, robed in a cloud, with a [halo like a] rainbow over his head; his face was like the sun, and his feet (legs) were like columns of fire.

²He had a little book (scroll) open in his hand. He set his right foot on the sea and his left foot on the land,

³And he shouted with a loud voice like the roaring of a lion; and when he had shouted, the seven thunders gave voice *and* uttered their message in distinct words.

⁴And when the seven thunders had spoken (sounded), I was going to write [it down], but I heard a voice from heaven saying, Seal up what the seven thunders have said! Do not write it down!

⁵Then the [mighty] angel whom I had seen stationed on sea and land raised his right hand to heaven (the ᵃsky), [Deut. 32:40; Dan. 12:6, 7.]

---

ᵃ G. Abbott-Smith, *Manual Greek Lexicon.*

## New International Version

by him who lives for ever and ever, who created the heavens and all that is in them, the earth and all that is in it, and the sea and all that is in it, and said, "There will be no more delay! [7]But in the days when the seventh angel is about to sound his trumpet, the mystery of God will be accomplished, just as he announced to his servants the prophets."

[8]Then the voice that I had heard from heaven spoke to me once more: "Go, take the scroll that lies open in the hand of the angel who is standing on the sea and on the land."

[9]So I went to the angel and asked him to give me the little scroll. He said to me, "Take it and eat it. It will turn your stomach sour, but 'in your mouth it will be as sweet as honey.'[a] [10]I took the little scroll from the angel's hand and ate it. It tasted as sweet as honey in my mouth, but when I had eaten it, my stomach turned sour. [11]Then I was told, "You must prophesy again about many peoples, nations, languages and kings."

### The Two Witnesses

**11** I was given a reed like a measuring rod and was told, "Go and measure the temple of God and the altar, with its worshipers. [2]But exclude the outer court; do not measure it, because it has been given to the Gentiles. They will trample on the holy city for 42 months. [3]And I will appoint my two witnesses, and they will prophesy for 1,260 days, clothed in sackcloth." [4]They are "the two olive trees" and the two lampstands, and "they stand before the Lord of the earth."[b] [5]If anyone tries to harm them, fire comes from their mouths and devours their enemies. This is how anyone who wants to harm them must die. [6]They have power to shut up the heavens so that it will not rain during the time they are prophesying; and they have power to turn the waters into blood and to strike the earth with every kind of plague as often as they want.

[7]Now when they have finished their testimony, the beast that comes up from the Abyss will attack them, and overpower and kill them. [8]Their bodies will lie in the public square of the great city—which is figuratively called Sodom and Egypt—where also their Lord was crucified. [9]For three and a half days some from every people, tribe, language and nation will gaze on their bodies and refuse them burial. [10]The inhabitants of the earth will gloat over them and will celebrate by sending each other gifts, because these two prophets had tormented those who live on the earth.

## Amplified Bible

[6]And swore in the name of (by) Him Who lives forever and ever, Who created the heavens ([a]sky) and all they contain, and the earth and all that it contains, and the sea and all that it contains. [He swore] that no more time should intervene *and* there should be no more waiting *or* delay,

[7]But that when the days come when the trumpet call of the seventh angel is about to be sounded, then God's mystery (His secret design, His hidden purpose), as He had announced the glad tidings to His servants the prophets, should be fulfilled (accomplished, completed). [Dan. 12:6, 7.]

[8]Then the voice that I heard from heaven spoke again to me, saying, Go and take the little book (scroll) which is open on the hand of the angel who is standing on the sea and on the land.

[9]So I went up to the angel and asked him to give me the little book. And he said to me, Take it and eat it. It will embitter your stomach, though in your mouth it will be as sweet as honey. [Ezek. 2:8, 9; 3:1-3.]

[10]So I took the little book from the angel's hand and ate *and* swallowed it; it was as sweet as honey in my mouth, but once I had swallowed it, my stomach was embittered.

[11]Then they said to me, You are to make a fresh prophecy concerning many peoples *and* races and nations and languages and kings. [Jer. 1:10.]

**11** A reed [as a measuring rod] was then given to me, [shaped] like a staff, and I was told: Rise up and measure the sanctuary of God and the altar [of incense], and [number] those who worship there. [Ezek. 40:3.]

[2]But leave out of your measuring the court outside the sanctuary of God; omit that, for it is given over to the Gentiles (the nations), and they will trample the holy city underfoot for 42 months (three and one-half years). [Isa. 63:18; Zech. 12:3.]

[3]And I will grant the power of prophecy to My two witnesses for 1,260 (42 months; three and one-half years), dressed in sackcloth.

[4]These [witnesses] are the two olive trees and the two lampstands which stand before the Lord of the earth. [Zech. 4:3, 11-14.]

[5]And if anyone attempts to injure them, fire pours from their mouth and consumes their enemies; if anyone should attempt to harm them, thus he is doomed to be slain. [II Kings 1:10; Jer. 5:14.]

[6]These [two witnesses] have power to shut up the sky, so that no rain may fall during the days of their prophesying (their [b]prediction of events relating to Christ's kingdom and its speedy triumph); and they also have power to turn the waters into blood and to smite *and* scourge the earth with all manner of plagues as often as they choose. [Exod. 7:17, 19; I Kings 17:1.]

[7]But when they have finished their testimony *and* their evidence is all in, the beast (monster) that comes up out of the Abyss (bottomless pit) will wage war on them, and conquer them and kill them. [Dan. 7:3, 7, 21.]

[8]And their dead bodies [will lie exposed] in the open street ([c]a public square) of the great city which is in a spiritual sense called [by the mystical and allegorical names of] Sodom and Egypt, where also their Lord was crucified. [Isa. 1:9.]

[9]For three and a half days men from the races and tribes and languages and nations will gaze at their dead bodies and will not allow them to be put in a tomb.

[10]And those who dwell on the earth will gloat *and* exult over them *and* rejoice exceedingly, taking their ease and sending presents [in congratulation] to one another, because these two prophets had been such a vexation *and* trouble *and* torment to all the dwellers on the earth.

---

[a]9 Ezek. 3:3    [b]4 See Zech. 4:3,11,14.

[a]G. Abbott-Smith, *Manual Greek Lexicon*.  [b]Joseph Thayer, *A Greek-English Lexicon*.  [c]Alexander Souter, *Pocket Lexicon*.

## New International Version

11 But after the three and a half days the breath[a] of life from God entered them, and they stood on their feet, and terror struck those who saw them. 12 Then they heard a loud voice from heaven saying to them, "Come up here." And they went up to heaven in a cloud, while their enemies looked on.

13 At that very hour there was a severe earthquake and a tenth of the city collapsed. Seven thousand people were killed in the earthquake, and the survivors were terrified and gave glory to the God of heaven.

14 The second woe has passed; the third woe is coming soon.

### The Seventh Trumpet

15 The seventh angel sounded his trumpet, and there were loud voices in heaven, which said:

"The kingdom of the world has become
    the kingdom of our Lord and of his Messiah,
    and he will reign for ever and ever."

16 And the twenty-four elders, who were seated on their thrones before God, fell on their faces and worshiped God, 17 saying:

"We give thanks to you, Lord God Almighty,
    the One who is and who was,
because you have taken your great power
    and have begun to reign.
18 The nations were angry,
    and your wrath has come.
The time has come for judging the dead,
    and for rewarding your servants the prophets
and your people who revere your name,
    both great and small—
and for destroying those who destroy the earth."

19 Then God's temple in heaven was opened, and within his temple was seen the ark of his covenant. And there came flashes of lightning, rumblings, peals of thunder, an earthquake and a severe hailstorm.

### The Woman and the Dragon

**12** A great sign appeared in heaven: a woman clothed with the sun, with the moon under her feet and a crown of twelve stars on her head. 2 She was pregnant and cried out in pain as she was about to give birth. 3 Then another sign appeared in heaven: an enormous red dragon with seven heads and ten horns and seven crowns on its heads. 4 Its tail swept a third of the stars out of the sky and flung them to the earth. The dragon stood in front of the woman who was about to give birth, so that it might devour her child the moment he was born. 5 She gave birth to a son, a male child, who "will rule all the nations with an iron scepter."[b] And her child was snatched up to God and to his throne. 6 The woman fled into the wilderness to a place prepared for her by God, where she might be taken care of for 1,260 days.

7 Then war broke out in heaven. Michael and his angels fought against the dragon, and the dragon and his angels fought back. 8 But he was not strong enough, and they lost their place in heaven. 9 The great dragon was hurled

## Amplified Bible

11 But after three and a half days, by God's gift the breath of life again entered into them, and they rose up on their feet, and great dread and terror fell on those who watched them. [Ezek. 37:5, 10.]

12 Then [the two witnesses] heard a strong voice from heaven calling to them, Come up here! And before the very eyes of their enemies they ascended into heaven in a cloud. [II Kings 2:11.]

13 And at that [very] hour there was a tremendous earthquake and one tenth of the city was destroyed (fell); seven thousand people perished in the earthquake, and those who remained were filled with dread and terror and were awe-struck, and they glorified the God of heaven.

14 The second woe (calamity) has passed; now the third woe is speedily to come.

15 The seventh angel then blew [his] trumpet, and there were mighty voices in heaven, shouting, The dominion (kingdom, sovereignty, rule) of the world has now come into the possession and become the kingdom of our Lord and of His Christ (the Messiah), and He shall reign forever and ever (for the eternities of the eternities)! [Ps. 22:28; Dan. 7:13, 14, 27.]

16 Then the twenty-four elders [of a the heavenly Sanhedrin], who sit on their thrones before God, prostrated themselves before Him and worshiped,

17 Exclaiming, To You we give thanks, Lord God Omnipotent, [the One] Who is and [ever] was, for assuming the high sovereignty and the great power that are Yours and for beginning to reign.

18 And the heathen (the nations) raged, but Your wrath (retribution, indignation) came, the time when the dead will be judged and Your servants the prophets and saints rewarded—and those who revere (fear) Your name, both low and high and small and great—and [the time] for destroying the corrupters of the earth. [Ps. 2:1.]

19 Then the sanctuary of God in heaven was thrown open, and the ark of His covenant was seen standing inside in His sanctuary; and there were flashes of lightning, loud rumblings (blasts, mutterings), peals of thunder, an earthquake, and a terrific hailstorm. [I Kings 8:1-6.]

**12** And a great sign (wonder)—[warning of future events of ominous significance] appeared in heaven: a woman clothed with the sun, with the moon under her feet, and with a crownlike garland (tiara) of twelve stars on her head.

2 She was pregnant and she cried out in her birth pangs, in the anguish of her delivery.

3 Then another ominous sign (wonder) was seen in heaven: Behold, a huge, fiery-red dragon, with seven heads and ten horns, and seven kingly crowns (diadems) upon his heads. [Dan. 7:7.]

4 His tail swept [across the sky] and dragged down a third of the stars and flung them to the earth. And the dragon stationed himself in front of the woman who was about to be delivered, so that he might devour her child as soon as she brought it forth. [Dan. 8:10.]

5 And she brought forth a male Child, One Who is destined to shepherd (rule) all the nations with an iron staff (scepter), and her Child was caught up to God and to His throne. [Ps. 2:8, 9; 110:1, 2.]

6 And the woman [herself] fled into the desert (wilderness), where she has a retreat prepared [for her] by God, in which she is to be fed and kept safe for 1,260 days (42 months; three and one-half years).

7 Then war broke out in heaven; Michael and his angels went forth to battle with the dragon, and the dragon and his angels fought.

8 But they were defeated, and there was no room found for them in heaven any longer.

---

a 11 Or *Spirit* (see Ezek. 37:5,14)    b 5 Psalm 2:9

a George R. Berry, *Greek-English New Testament Lexicon.*

## New International Version

down—that ancient serpent called the devil, or Satan, who leads the whole world astray. He was hurled to the earth, and his angels with him.

[10] Then I heard a loud voice in heaven say:

"Now have come the salvation and the power
 and the kingdom of our God,
 and the authority of his Messiah.
For the accuser of our brothers and sisters,
 who accuses them before our God day and night,
 has been hurled down.
[11] They triumphed over him
 by the blood of the Lamb
 and by the word of their testimony;
they did not love their lives so much
 as to shrink from death.
[12] Therefore rejoice, you heavens
 and you who dwell in them!
But woe to the earth and the sea,
 because the devil has gone down to you!
He is filled with fury,
 because he knows that his time is short."

[13] When the dragon saw that he had been hurled to the earth, he pursued the woman who had given birth to the male child. [14] The woman was given the two wings of a great eagle, so that she might fly to the place prepared for her in the wilderness, where she would be taken care of for a time, times and half a time, out of the serpent's reach. [15] Then from his mouth the serpent spewed water like a river, to overtake the woman and sweep her away with the torrent. [16] But the earth helped the woman by opening its mouth and swallowing the river that the dragon had spewed out of his mouth. [17] Then the dragon was enraged at the woman and went off to wage war against the rest of her offspring—those who keep God's commands and hold fast their testimony about Jesus.

### The Beast out of the Sea

**13** The dragon[a] stood on the shore of the sea. And I saw a beast coming out of the sea. It had ten horns and seven heads, with ten crowns on its horns, and on each head a blasphemous name. [2] The beast I saw resembled a leopard, but had feet like those of a bear and a mouth like that of a lion. The dragon gave the beast his power and his throne and great authority. [3] One of the heads of the beast seemed to have had a fatal wound, but the fatal wound had been healed. The whole world was filled with wonder and followed the beast. [4] People worshiped the dragon because he had given authority to the beast, and they also worshiped the beast and asked, "Who is like the beast? Who can wage war against it?"

[5] The beast was given a mouth to utter proud words and blasphemies and to exercise its authority for forty-two months. [6] It opened its mouth to blaspheme God, and to slander his name and his dwelling place and those who live in heaven. [7] It was given power to wage war against God's holy people and to conquer them. And it was given authority over every tribe, people, language and nation.

## Amplified Bible

[9] And the huge dragon was cast down *and* out—that age-old serpent, who is called the Devil and Satan, he who is the seducer (deceiver) of all humanity the world over; he was forced out *and* down to the earth, and his angels were flung out along with him. [Gen. 3:1, 14, 15; Zech. 3:1.]

[10] Then I heard a strong (loud) voice in heaven, saying, Now it has come—the salvation and the power and the kingdom (the dominion, the reign) of our God, and the power (the sovereignty, the authority) of His Christ (the Messiah); for the accuser of our brethren, he who keeps bringing before our God charges against them day and night, has been cast out! [Job 1:9-11.]

[11] And they have overcome (conquered) him by means of the blood of the Lamb and by the utterance of their testimony, for they did not love *and* cling to life even when faced with death [holding their lives cheap till they had to die for their witnessing].

[12] Therefore be glad (exult), O heavens and you that dwell in them! But woe to you, O earth and sea, for the devil has come down to you in fierce anger (fury), because he knows that he has [only] a short time [left]! [Isa. 44:23; 49:13.]

[13] And when the dragon saw that he was cast down to the earth, he went in pursuit of the woman who had given birth to the male Child.

[14] But the woman was supplied with the two wings of a giant eagle, so that she might fly from the presence of the serpent into the desert (wilderness), to the retreat where she is to be kept safe *and* fed for a time, and times, and half a time (three and one-half years, or 1,260 days). [Dan. 7:25; 12:7.]

[15] Then out of his mouth the serpent spouted forth water like a flood after the woman, that she might be carried off with the torrent.

[16] But the earth came to the rescue of the woman, and the ground opened its mouth and swallowed up the stream of water which the dragon had spouted from his mouth.

[17] So then the dragon was furious (enraged) at the woman, and he went away to wage war on the remainder of her descendants—[on those] who obey God's commandments and who have the testimony of Jesus *Christ* [and adhere to it and [a] bear witness to Him].

**13** [As] [b] I stood on the sandy beach, I saw a beast coming up out of the sea with ten horns and seven heads. On his horns he had ten royal crowns (diadems) and blasphemous titles (names) on his heads.

[2] And the beast that I saw resembled a leopard, but his feet were like those of a bear and his mouth was like that of a lion. And to him the dragon gave his [own] might *and* power and his [own] throne and great dominion.

[3] And one of his heads seemed to have a deadly wound. But his death stroke was healed; and the whole earth went after the beast in amazement *and* admiration.

[4] They fell down *and* paid homage to the dragon, because he had bestowed on the beast all his dominion *and* authority; they also praised *and* worshiped the beast, exclaiming, Who is a match for the beast, and, Who can make war against him?

[5] And the beast was given the power of speech, uttering boastful and blasphemous words, and he was given freedom to exert his authority *and* to exercise his will during forty-two months (three and a half years). [Dan. 7:8.]

[6] And he opened his mouth to speak slanders against God, blaspheming His name and His abode, [even vilifying] those who live in heaven.

[7] He was further permitted to wage war on God's holy people (the saints) and to overcome them. And power was given him to extend his authority over every tribe and people and tongue and nation, [Dan. 7:21, 25.]

---

[a] 1 Some manuscripts *And I*

[a] Charles B. Williams, *The New Testament: A Translation in the Language of the People.* [b] Many ancient manuscripts read "he."

## New International Version

8All inhabitants of the earth will worship the beast—all whose names have not been written in the Lamb's book of life, the Lamb who was slain from the creation of the world.*a*

9Whoever has ears, let them hear.

10 "If anyone is to go into captivity,
  into captivity they will go.
If anyone is to be killed*b* with the sword,
  with the sword they will be killed."*c*

This calls for patient endurance and faithfulness on the part of God's people.

### The Beast out of the Earth

11Then I saw a second beast, coming out of the earth. It had two horns like a lamb, but it spoke like a dragon. 12It exercised all the authority of the first beast on its behalf, and made the earth and its inhabitants worship the first beast, whose fatal wound had been healed. 13And it performed great signs, even causing fire to come down from heaven to the earth in full view of the people. 14Because of the signs it was given power to perform on behalf of the first beast, it deceived the inhabitants of the earth. It ordered them to set up an image in honor of the beast who was wounded by the sword and yet lived. 15The second beast was given power to give breath to the image of the first beast, so that the image could speak and cause all who refused to worship the image to be killed. 16It also forced all people, great and small, rich and poor, free and slave, to receive a mark on their right hands or on their foreheads, 17so that they could not buy or sell unless they had the mark, which is the name of the beast or the number of its name.

18This calls for wisdom. Let the person who has insight calculate the number of the beast, for it is the number of a man.*d* That number is 666.

### The Lamb and the 144,000

**14** Then I looked, and there before me was the Lamb, standing on Mount Zion, and with him 144,000 who had his name and his Father's name written on their foreheads. 2And I heard a sound from heaven like the roar of rushing waters and like a loud peal of thunder. The sound I heard was like that of harpists playing their harps. 3And they sang a new song before the throne and before the four living creatures and the elders. No one could learn the song except the 144,000 who had been redeemed from the earth. 4These are those who did not defile themselves with women, for they remained virgins. They follow the Lamb wherever he goes. They were purchased from among mankind and offered as firstfruits to God and the Lamb. 5No lie was found in their mouths; they are blameless.

### The Three Angels

6Then I saw another angel flying in midair, and he had the eternal gospel to proclaim to those who live on the earth—to every nation, tribe, language and people. 7He

## Amplified Bible

8And all the inhabitants of the earth will fall down in adoration *and* pay him homage, everyone whose name has not been recorded in the Book of Life of the Lamb that was slain [in sacrifice] *a*from the foundation of the world.

9If anyone is able to hear, let him listen:

10Whoever leads into captivity will himself go into captivity; if anyone slays with the sword, with the sword must he be slain. Herein is [the call for] the patience and the faith *and* fidelity of the saints (God's people). [Jer. 15:2.]

11Then I saw another beast rising up out of the land [itself]; he had two horns like a lamb, and he spoke (roared) like a dragon.

12He exerts all the power *and* right of control of the former beast in his presence, and causes the earth and those who dwell upon it to exalt *and* deify the first beast, whose deadly wound was healed, *and* to worship him.

13He performs great signs (startling miracles), even making fire fall from the sky to the earth in men's sight.

14And because of the signs (miracles) which he is allowed to perform in the presence of the [first] beast, he deceives those who inhabit the earth, commanding them to erect a statue (an image) in the likeness of the beast who was wounded by the [small] sword and still lived. [Deut. 13:1-5.]

15And he is permitted [also] to impart the breath of life into the beast's image, so that the statue of the beast could actually talk and cause to be put to death those who would not bow down *and* worship the image of the beast. [Dan. 3:5.]

16Also he compels all [alike], both small and great, both the rich and the poor, both free and slave, to be marked with an inscription [*b*stamped] on their right hands or on their foreheads,

17So that no one will have power to buy or sell unless he bears the stamp (mark, inscription), [that is] the name of the beast or the number of his name.

18Here is [room for] discernment [a call for the wisdom *b*of interpretation]. Let anyone who has intelligence (penetration and insight enough) calculate the number of the beast, for it is a human number [the number of a certain man]; his number is 666.

**14** Then I looked, and behold, the Lamb stood on Mount Zion, and with Him 144,000 [men] who had His name and His Father's name inscribed on their foreheads.

2And I heard a voice from heaven like the sound of great waters and like the rumbling of mighty thunder; the voice I heard [seemed like the music] of harpists *c*accompanying themselves on their harps.

3And they sang a new song before the throne [of God] and before the four living creatures and before the elders [of *d*the heavenly Sanhedrin]. No one could learn [to sing] that song except the 144,000 who had been ransomed (purchased, redeemed) from the earth.

4These are they who have not defiled themselves by relations with women, for they are [*e*pure as] virgins. These are they who follow the Lamb wherever He goes. These are they who have been ransomed (purchased, redeemed) from among men as the firstfruits for God and the Lamb.

5No lie was found to be upon their lips, for they are blameless (spotless, untainted, without blemish) *before the throne of God.*

6Then I saw another angel flying in midair, with an eternal Gospel (good news) to tell to the inhabitants of the earth, to every race and tribe and language and people.

---

*a* 8 Or *written from the creation of the world in the book of life belonging to the Lamb who was slain*   *b* 10 Some manuscripts *anyone kills*   *c* 10 Jer. 15:2   *d* 18 Or *is humanity's number*

*a* Alternate translation: "recorded from the foundation of the world in the Book of Life of the Lamb that was slain [in sacrifice]."   *b* Joseph Thayer, *A Greek-English Lexicon.*   *c* Marvin Vincent, *Word Studies.*   *d* George R. Berry, *Greek-English New Testament Lexicon.*   *e* Charles B. Williams, *The New Testament: A Translation.*

## New International Version

said in a loud voice, "Fear God and give him glory, because the hour of his judgment has come. Worship him who made the heavens, the earth, the sea and the springs of water."

[8]A second angel followed and said, "'Fallen! Fallen is Babylon the Great,'[a] which made all the nations drink the maddening wine of her adulteries."

[9]A third angel followed them and said in a loud voice: "If anyone worships the beast and its image and receives its mark on their forehead or on their hand, [10]they, too, will drink the wine of God's fury, which has been poured full strength into the cup of his wrath. They will be tormented with burning sulfur in the presence of the holy angels and of the Lamb. [11]And the smoke of their torment will rise for ever and ever. There will be no rest day or night for those who worship the beast and its image, or for anyone who receives the mark of its name." [12]This calls for patient endurance on the part of the people of God who keep his commands and remain faithful to Jesus.

[13]Then I heard a voice from heaven say, "Write this: Blessed are the dead who die in the Lord from now on."

"Yes," says the Spirit, "they will rest from their labor, for their deeds will follow them."

### Harvesting the Earth and Trampling the Winepress

[14]I looked, and there before me was a white cloud, and seated on the cloud was one like a son of man[b] with a crown of gold on his head and a sharp sickle in his hand. [15]Then another angel came out of the temple and called in a loud voice to him who was sitting on the cloud, "Take your sickle and reap, because the time to reap has come, for the harvest of the earth is ripe." [16]So he who was seated on the cloud swung his sickle over the earth, and the earth was harvested.

[17]Another angel came out of the temple in heaven, and he too had a sharp sickle. [18]Still another angel, who had charge of the fire, came from the altar and called in a loud voice to him who had the sharp sickle, "Take your sharp sickle and gather the clusters of grapes from the earth's vine, because its grapes are ripe." [19]The angel swung his sickle on the earth, gathered its grapes and threw them into the great winepress of God's wrath. [20]They were trampled in the winepress outside the city, and blood flowed out of the press, rising as high as the horses' bridles for a distance of 1,600 stadia.[c]

### Seven Angels With Seven Plagues

**15** I saw in heaven another great and marvelous sign: seven angels with the seven last plagues—last, because with them God's wrath is completed. [2]And I

[a] 8 Isaiah 21:9    [b] 14 See Daniel 7:13.    [c] 20 That is, about 180 miles or about 300 kilometers

## Amplified Bible

[7]And he cried with a mighty voice, Revere God and give Him glory (honor and praise in worship), for the hour of His judgment has arrived. Fall down before Him; pay Him homage *and* adoration *and* worship Him Who created heaven and earth, the sea and the springs (fountains) of water.

[8]Then another angel, a second, followed, declaring, Fallen, fallen is Babylon the great! She who made all nations drink of the [maddening] wine of her passionate unchastity [[a]idolatry]. [Isa. 21:9.]

[9]Then another angel, a third, followed them, saying with a mighty voice, Whoever pays homage to the beast and his statue and permits the [beast's] stamp (mark, inscription) to be put on his forehead or on his hand,

[10]He too shall [have to] drink of the wine of God's indignation *and* wrath, poured undiluted into the cup of His anger; and he shall be tormented with fire and brimstone in the presence of the holy angels and in the presence of the Lamb. [Gen. 19:24.]

[11]And the smoke of their torment ascends forever and ever; and they have no respite (no pause, no intermission, no rest, no peace) day or night—these who pay homage to the beast and to his image and whoever receives the stamp of his name upon him. [Isa. 34:10.]

[12]Here [comes in a call for] the steadfastness of the saints [the patience, the endurance of the people of God], those who [habitually] keep God's commandments and [their] faith in Jesus.

[13]Then I heard further [[a]perceiving the distinct words of] a voice from heaven, saying, Write this: Blessed (happy, [b]to be envied) are the dead from now on who die in the Lord! Yes, blessed (happy, [b]to be envied indeed), says the Spirit, [in] that they may rest from their labors, for their works (deeds) do follow (attend, accompany) them!

[14]Again I looked, and behold, [I saw] a white cloud, and sitting on the cloud [c]One resembling a Son of Man, with a crown of gold on His head and a sharp scythe (sickle) in His hand. [Dan. 7:13.]

[15]And another angel came out of the temple sanctuary, calling with a mighty voice to Him Who was sitting upon the cloud, Put in Your scythe and reap, for the hour has arrived to gather the harvest, for the earth's crop is fully ripened. [Joel 3:13.]

[16]So He Who was sitting upon the cloud swung His scythe (sickle) on the earth, and the earth's crop was harvested.

[17]Then another angel came out of the temple [sanctuary] in heaven, and he also carried a sharp scythe (sickle).

[18]And another angel came forth from the altar, [the angel] who has authority *and* power over fire, and he called with a loud cry to him who had the sharp scythe (sickle), Put forth your scythe and reap the fruitage of the vine of the earth, for its grapes are entirely ripe.

[19]So the angel swung his scythe on the earth and stripped the grapes *and* gathered the vintage from the vines of the earth and cast it into the huge winepress of God's indignation *and* wrath.

[20]And [the grapes in] the winepress were trodden outside the city, and blood poured from the winepress, [reaching] as high as horses' bridles, for a distance of 1,600 stadia (about 200 miles). [Joel 3:13.]

**15** Then I saw another wonder (sign, token, symbol) in heaven, great and marvelous [warning of events of ominous significance]: There were seven angels bringing seven plagues (afflictions, calamities), which are the last, for with them God's wrath (indignation) is completely expressed [reaches its climax and is ended]. [Lev. 26:21.]

[a] Joseph Thayer, *A Greek-English Lexicon*.    [b] Alexander Souter, *Pocket Lexicon*.    [c] There is no consensus of opinion concerning the figure resembling a "son of man." Thus the capitals are tentatively presented as a possible interpretation. Many commentators question whether this refers to Christ.

## New International Version

saw what looked like a sea of glass glowing with fire and, standing beside the sea, those who had been victorious over the beast and its image and over the number of its name. They held harps given them by God ³and sang the song of God's servant Moses and of the Lamb:

"Great and marvelous are your deeds,
    Lord God Almighty.
Just and true are your ways,
    King of the nations.ᵃ
⁴Who will not fear you, Lord,
    and bring glory to your name?
For you alone are holy.
All nations will come
    and worship before you,
for your righteous acts have been revealed."ᵇ

⁵After this I looked, and I saw in heaven the temple—that is, the tabernacle of the covenant law—and it was opened. ⁶Out of the temple came the seven angels with the seven plagues. They were dressed in clean, shining linen and wore golden sashes around their chests. ⁷Then one of the four living creatures gave to the seven angels seven golden bowls filled with the wrath of God, who lives for ever and ever. ⁸And the temple was filled with smoke from the glory of God and from his power, and no one could enter the temple until the seven plagues of the seven angels were completed.

### The Seven Bowls of God's Wrath

**16** Then I heard a loud voice from the temple saying to the seven angels, "Go, pour out the seven bowls of God's wrath on the earth."

²The first angel went and poured out his bowl on the land, and ugly, festering sores broke out on the people who had the mark of the beast and worshiped its image.

³The second angel poured out his bowl on the sea, and it turned into blood like that of a dead person, and every living thing in the sea died.

⁴The third angel poured out his bowl on the rivers and springs of water, and they became blood. ⁵Then I heard the angel in charge of the waters say:

"You are just in these judgments, O Holy One,
    you who are and who were;
⁶for they have shed the blood of your holy people and
        your prophets,
    and you have given them blood to drink as they
        deserve."

⁷And I heard the altar respond:

"Yes, Lord God Almighty,
    true and just are your judgments."

⁸The fourth angel poured out his bowl on the sun, and the sun was allowed to scorch people with fire. ⁹They were seared by the intense heat and they cursed the name of God, who had control over these plagues, but they refused to repent and glorify him.

¹⁰The fifth angel poured out his bowl on the throne of the beast, and its kingdom was plunged into darkness. People gnawed their tongues in agony ¹¹and cursed the

## Amplified Bible

²Then I saw what seemed to be a glassy sea blended with fire, and those who had come off victorious from the beast and from his statue and from the number corresponding to his name were standing beside the glassy sea, with harps of God in their hands.

³And they sang the song of Moses the servant of God and the song of the Lamb, saying, Mighty and marvelous are Your works, O Lord God the Omnipotent! Righteous (just) and true are Your ways, O Sovereign of the ages (King of the ᵃnations)! [Exod. 15:1; Ps. 145:17.]

⁴Who shall not reverence and glorify Your name, O Lord [giving You honor and praise in worship]? For You only are holy. All the nations shall come and pay homage *and* adoration to You, for Your just judgments (Your righteous sentences and deeds) have been made known *and* displayed. [Ps. 86:9, 10; Jer. 10:7.]

⁵After this I looked and the sanctuary of the tent of the testimony in heaven was thrown open,

⁶And there came out of the temple sanctuary the seven angels bringing the seven plagues (afflictions, calamities). They were arrayed in pure gleaming linen, and around their breasts they wore golden girdles.

⁷And one of the four living creatures [then] gave the seven angels seven golden bowls full of the wrath *and* indignation of God, Who lives forever and ever (in the eternities of the eternities).

⁸And the sanctuary was filled with smoke from the glory (the radiance, the splendor) of God and from His might *and* power, and no one was able to go into the sanctuary until the seven plagues (afflictions, calamities) of the seven angels were ended. [I Kings 8:10; Isa. 6:4; Ezek. 44:4.]

**16** Then I heard a mighty voice from the temple sanctuary saying to the seven angels, Go and empty out on the earth the seven bowls of God's wrath *and* indignation. [Ps. 69:24; Isa. 66:6.]

²So the first [angel] went and emptied his bowl on the earth, and foul and painful ulcers (sores) came on the people who were marked with the stamp of the beast and who did homage to his image. [Exod. 9:10, 11; Deut. 28:35.]

³The second [angel] emptied his bowl into the sea, and it turned into blood like that of a corpse [thick, corrupt, ill-smelling, and disgusting], and every living thing that was in the sea perished.

⁴Then the third [angel] emptied out his bowl into the rivers and the springs of water, and they turned into (became) blood. [Exod. 7:17-21.]

⁵And I also heard the angel of the waters say, Righteous (just) are You in these Your decisions *and* judgments, You Who are and were, O Holy One!

⁶Because they have poured out the blood of Your people (the saints) and the prophets, and You have given them blood to drink. Such is their due [they deserve it]! [Ps. 79:3.]

⁷And [from] the altar I heard [the] cry, Yes, Lord God the Omnipotent, Your judgments (sentences, decisions) are true and just *and* righteous! [Ps. 119:137.]

⁸Then the fourth [angel] emptied out his bowl upon the sun, and it was permitted to burn (scorch) humanity with [fierce, glowing] heat (fire).

⁹People were severely burned (scorched) by the fiery heat, and they reviled *and* blasphemed the name of God, Who has control of these plagues, and they did not repent of their sins [felt no regret, contrition, and compunction for their waywardness, refusing to amend their ways] to give Him glory.

¹⁰Then the fifth [angel] emptied his bowl on the throne of the beast, and his kingdom was [plunged] in darkness; and people gnawed their tongues for the torment [of their excruciating distress and severe pain] [Exod. 10:21.]

---

ᵃ 3 Some manuscripts *ages*    ᵇ 3,4 Phrases in this song are drawn from Psalm 111:2,3; Deut. 32:4; Jer. 10:7; Psalms 86:9; 98:2.

ᵃ Many manuscripts read "nations."

## New International Version

God of heaven because of their pains and their sores, but they refused to repent of what they had done. [12]The sixth angel poured out his bowl on the great river Euphrates, and its water was dried up to prepare the way for the kings from the East. [13]Then I saw three impure spirits that looked like frogs; they came out of the mouth of the dragon, out of the mouth of the beast and out of the mouth of the false prophet. [14]They are demonic spirits that perform signs, and they go out to the kings of the whole world, to gather them for the battle on the great day of God Almighty.

[15]"Look, I come like a thief! Blessed is the one who stays awake and remains clothed, so as not to go naked and be shamefully exposed."

[16]Then they gathered the kings together to the place that in Hebrew is called Armageddon.

[17]The seventh angel poured out his bowl into the air, and out of the temple came a loud voice from the throne, saying, "It is done!" [18]Then there came flashes of lightning, rumblings, peals of thunder and a severe earthquake. No earthquake like it has ever occurred since mankind has been on earth, so tremendous was the quake. [19]The great city split into three parts, and the cities of the nations collapsed. God remembered Babylon the Great and gave her the cup filled with the wine of the fury of his wrath. [20]Every island fled away and the mountains could not be found. [21]From the sky huge hailstones, each weighing about a hundred pounds,[a] fell on people. And they cursed God on account of the plague of hail, because the plague was so terrible.

### Babylon, the Prostitute on the Beast

**17** One of the seven angels who had the seven bowls came and said to me, "Come, I will show you the punishment of the great prostitute, who sits by many waters. [2]With her the kings of the earth committed adultery, and the inhabitants of the earth were intoxicated with the wine of her adulteries."

[3]Then the angel carried me away in the Spirit into a wilderness. There I saw a woman sitting on a scarlet beast that was covered with blasphemous names and had seven heads and ten horns. [4]The woman was dressed in purple and scarlet, and was glittering with gold, precious stones and pearls. She held a golden cup in her hand, filled with abominable things and the filth of her adulteries. [5]The name written on her forehead was a mystery:

BABYLON THE GREAT
THE MOTHER OF PROSTITUTES
AND OF THE ABOMINATIONS OF THE EARTH.

[6]I saw that the woman was drunk with the blood of God's holy people, the blood of those who bore testimony to Jesus.

When I saw her, I was greatly astonished. [7]Then the angel said to me: "Why are you astonished? I will explain to you the mystery of the woman and of the beast she rides, which has the seven heads and ten horns. [8]The beast,

## Amplified Bible

[11]And blasphemed the God of heaven because of their anguish and their ulcers (sores), and they did not deplore their wicked deeds *or* repent [for what they had done].

[12]Then the sixth [angel] emptied his bowl on the mighty river Euphrates, and its water was dried up to make ready a road for [the coming of] the kings of the east (from the rising sun). [Isa. 11:15, 16.]

[13]And I saw three loathsome spirits like frogs, [leaping] from the mouth of the dragon and from the mouth of the beast and from the mouth of the false prophet. [Exod. 8:3; I Kings 22:21-23.]

[14]For really they are the spirits of demons that perform signs (wonders, miracles). And they go forth to the rulers *and* leaders all over the world, to gather them together for war on the great day of God the Almighty.

[15]Behold, I am going to come like a thief! Blessed (happy, [a]to be envied) is he who stays awake (alert) and who guards his clothes, so that he may not be naked and [have the shame of being] seen exposed!

[16]And they gathered them together at the place which in Hebrew is called Armageddon. [II Kings 9:27.]

[17]Then the seventh [angel] emptied his bowl into the air, and a mighty voice came out of the sanctuary *of heaven* from the throne [of God], saying, It is done! [It is all over, it is all accomplished, it has come!] [Isa. 66:6.]

[18]And there followed lightning flashes, loud rumblings, peals of thunder, and a tremendous earthquake; nothing like it has ever occurred since men dwelt on the earth, so severe *and* far-reaching was that earthquake. [Exod. 19:16; Dan. 12:1.]

[19]The mighty city was broken into three parts, and the cities of the nations fell. And God kept in mind mighty Babylon, to make her drain the cup of His furious wrath *and* indignation.

[20]And every island fled and no mountains could be found.

[21]And great (excessively oppressive) hailstones, as heavy as a talent [between fifty and sixty pounds], of immense size, fell from the sky on the people; and men blasphemed God for the plague of the hail, so very great was [the torture] of that plague. [Exod. 9:23.]

**17** One of the seven angels who had the seven bowls then came and spoke to me, saying, Come with me! I will show you the doom (sentence, judgment) of the great harlot (idolatress) who is seated on many waters, [Jer. 51:13.]

[2][She] with whom the rulers of the earth have joined in prostitution (idolatry) and with the wine of whose immorality (idolatry) the inhabitants of the earth have become intoxicated. [Jer. 25:15, 16.]

[3]And [the angel] bore me away [rapt] in the Spirit into a desert (wilderness), and I saw a woman seated on a scarlet beast that was all covered with blasphemous titles (names), and he had seven heads and ten horns.

[4]The woman was robed in purple and scarlet and bedecked with gold, precious stones, and pearls, [and she was] holding in her hand a golden cup full of the accursed offenses and the filth of her lewdness *and* vice. [Jer. 51:7.]

[5]And on her forehead there was inscribed a name of mystery [with a secret symbolic meaning]: Babylon the great, the mother of prostitutes (idolatresses) and of the filth *and* atrocities *and* abominations of the earth.

[6]I also saw that the woman was drunk, [drunk] with the blood of the saints (God's people) and the blood of the martyrs [who witnessed] for Jesus. And when I saw her, I was utterly amazed *and* wondered greatly.

[7]But the angel said to me, Why do you wonder? I will explain to you the [secret symbolic meaning of the] mystery of the woman, as well as of the beast having the seven heads and ten horns that carries her.

---

[a] 21 Or about 45 kilograms

[a] Alexander Souter, *Pocket Lexicon*.

## New International Version

which you saw, once was, now is not, and yet will come up out of the Abyss and go to its destruction. The inhabitants of the earth whose names have not been written in the book of life from the creation of the world will be astonished when they see the beast, because it once was, now is not, and yet will come.

⁹"This calls for a mind with wisdom. The seven heads are seven hills on which the woman sits. ¹⁰They are also seven kings. Five have fallen, one is, the other has not yet come; but when he does come, he must remain for only a little while. ¹¹The beast who once was, and now is not, is an eighth king. He belongs to the seven and is going to his destruction.

¹²"The ten horns you saw are ten kings who have not yet received a kingdom, but who for one hour will receive authority as kings along with the beast. ¹³They have one purpose and will give their power and authority to the beast. ¹⁴They will wage war against the Lamb, but the Lamb will triumph over them because he is Lord of lords and King of kings—and with him will be his called, chosen and faithful followers."

¹⁵Then the angel said to me, "The waters you saw, where the prostitute sits, are peoples, multitudes, nations and languages. ¹⁶The beast and the ten horns you saw will hate the prostitute. They will bring her to ruin and leave her naked; they will eat her flesh and burn her with fire. ¹⁷For God has put it into their hearts to accomplish his purpose by agreeing to hand over to the beast their royal authority, until God's words are fulfilled. ¹⁸The woman you saw is the great city that rules over the kings of the earth."

### Lament Over Fallen Babylon

**18** After this I saw another angel coming down from heaven. He had great authority, and the earth was illuminated by his splendor. ²With a mighty voice he shouted:

> "'Fallen! Fallen is Babylon the Great!'ᵃ
> She has become a dwelling for demons
> and a haunt for every impure spirit,
> a haunt for every unclean bird,
> a haunt for every unclean and detestable animal.
> ³For all the nations have drunk
> the maddening wine of her adulteries.
> The kings of the earth committed adultery with her,
> and the merchants of the earth grew rich from her
> excessive luxuries."

### Warning to Escape Babylon's Judgment

⁴Then I heard another voice from heaven say:

> "'Come out of her, my people,'ᵇ
> so that you will not share in her sins,
> so that you will not receive any of her plagues;
> ⁵for her sins are piled up to heaven,
> and God has remembered her crimes.

## Amplified Bible

⁸The beast that you saw [once] was, but [now] is no more, and he is going to come up out of the Abyss (the bottomless pit) and proceed to go to perdition. And the inhabitants of the earth whose names have not been recorded in the Book of Life from the foundation of the world will be astonished when they look at the beast, because he [once] was, but [now] is no more, and he is [yet] to come. [Dan. 7:3.]

⁹This calls for a mind [to consider that is packed] with wisdom *and* intelligence [it is something for a particular mode of thinking and judging of thoughts, feelings, and purposes]. The seven heads are seven hills upon which the woman is sitting;

¹⁰And they are also seven kings, five of whom have fallen, one still exists [and is reigning]; the other [the seventh] has not yet appeared, and when he does arrive, he must stay [but] a brief time.

¹¹And as for the beast that [once] was, but now is no more, he [himself] is an eighth ruler (king, head), but he is of the seven *and* belongs to them, and he goes to perdition.

¹²Also the ten horns that you observed are ten rulers (kings) who have as yet received no royal dominion, but together they are to receive power *and* authority as rulers for a single hour, along with the beast. [Dan. 7:20-24.]

¹³These have one common policy (opinion, purpose), and they deliver their power and authority to the beast.

¹⁴They will wage war against the Lamb, and the Lamb will triumph over them; for He is Lord of lords and King of kings—and those with Him *and* on His side are chosen and called [elected] and loyal *and* faithful followers. [Dan. 2:47.]

¹⁵And [the angel further] said to me, The waters that you observed, where the harlot is seated, are races and multitudes and nations and dialects (languages).

¹⁶And the ten horns that you saw, they and the beast will [be the very ones to] hate the harlot (the idolatrous woman); they will make her cheerless (bereaved, desolate), and they will strip her and eat up her flesh and utterly consume her with fire.

¹⁷For God has put it into their hearts to carry out His own purpose by acting in harmony in surrendering their royal power *and* authority to the beast, until the prophetic words (intentions and promises) of God shall be fulfilled.

¹⁸And the woman that you saw is herself the great city which dominates *and* controls the rulers *and* the leaders of the earth.

**18** Then I saw another angel descending from heaven, possessing great authority, and the earth was illuminated with his radiance *and* splendor.

²And he shouted with a mighty voice, She is fallen! Mighty Babylon is fallen! She has become a resort *and* dwelling place for demons, a dungeon haunted by every loathsome spirit, an abode for every filthy and detestable bird.

³For all nations have drunk the wine of her passionate unchastity, and the rulers *and* leaders of the earth have joined with her in committing fornication (idolatry), and the businessmen of the earth have become rich with the wealth of her excessive luxury *and* wantonness. [Jer. 25:15, 27.]

⁴I then heard another voice from heaven saying, Come out from her, my people, so that you may not share in her sins, neither participate in her plagues. [Isa. 48:20; Jer. 50:8.]

⁵For her iniquities (her crimes and transgressions) are piled up as high as heaven, and God has remembered her wickedness *and* [her] crimes [and calls them up for settlement]. [Jer. 51:9.]

---

ᵃ 2 Isaiah 21:9    ᵇ 4 Jer. 51:45

## New International Version

6 Give back to her as she has given;
    pay her back double for what she has done.
    Pour her a double portion from her own cup.
7 Give her as much torment and grief
    as the glory and luxury she gave herself.
In her heart she boasts,
    'I sit enthroned as queen.
I am not a widow;*a*
    I will never mourn.'
8 Therefore in one day her plagues will overtake her:
    death, mourning and famine.
She will be consumed by fire,
    for mighty is the Lord God who judges her.

### Threefold Woe Over Babylon's Fall

9 "When the kings of the earth who committed adultery with her and shared her luxury see the smoke of her burning, they will weep and mourn over her. 10 Terrified at her torment, they will stand far off and cry:

"'Woe! Woe to you, great city,
    you mighty city of Babylon!
In one hour your doom has come!'

11 "The merchants of the earth will weep and mourn over her because no one buys their cargoes anymore— 12 cargoes of gold, silver, precious stones and pearls; fine linen, purple, silk and scarlet cloth; every sort of citron wood, and articles of every kind made of ivory, costly wood, bronze, iron and marble; 13 cargoes of cinnamon and spice, of incense, myrrh and frankincense, of wine and olive oil, of fine flour and wheat; cattle and sheep; horses and carriages; and human beings sold as slaves.

14 "They will say, 'The fruit you longed for is gone from you. All your luxury and splendor have vanished, never to be recovered.' 15 The merchants who sold these things and gained their wealth from her will stand far off, terrified at her torment. They will weep and mourn 16 and cry out:

"'Woe! Woe to you, great city,
    dressed in fine linen, purple and scarlet,
    and glittering with gold, precious stones and pearls!
17 In one hour such great wealth has been brought to
    ruin!'

"Every sea captain, and all who travel by ship, the sailors, and all who earn their living from the sea, will stand far off. 18 When they see the smoke of her burning, they will exclaim, 'Was there ever a city like this great city?' 19 They will throw dust on their heads, and with weeping and mourning cry out:

"'Woe! Woe to you, great city,
    where all who had ships on the sea
    became rich through her wealth!
In one hour she has been brought to ruin!'

20 "Rejoice over her, you heavens!
    Rejoice, you people of God!
    Rejoice, apostles and prophets!
For God has judged her
    with the judgment she imposed on you."

### The Finality of Babylon's Doom

21 Then a mighty angel picked up a boulder the size of a large millstone and threw it into the sea, and said:

"With such violence
    the great city of Babylon will be thrown down,
    never to be found again.

a 7 See Isaiah 47:7,8.

## Amplified Bible

6 Repay to her what she herself has paid [to others] and double [her doom] in accordance with what she has done. Mix a double portion for her in the cup she mixed [for others]. [Ps. 137:8.]
7 To the degree that she glorified herself and reveled in her wantonness [living deliciously and luxuriously], to that measure impose on her torment *and* anguish and tears *and* mourning. Since in her heart she boasts, I am not a widow; as a queen [on a throne] I sit, and I shall never see suffering *or* experience sorrow—[Isa. 47:8, 9.]
8 So shall her plagues (afflictions, calamities) come thick upon her in a single day, pestilence and anguish *and* sorrow and famine; and she shall be utterly consumed (burned up with fire), for mighty is the Lord God Who judges her.
9 And the rulers *and* leaders of the earth who joined her in her immorality (idolatry) and luxuriated with her will weep *and* beat their breasts and lament over her when they see the smoke of her conflagration. [Ezek. 26:16, 17.]
10 They will stand a long way off, in terror of her torment, and they will cry, Woe *and* alas, the great city, the mighty city, Babylon! In one single hour how your doom (judgment) has overtaken you!
11 And earth's businessmen will weep and grieve over her because no one buys their freight (cargo) any more. [Ezek. 27:36.]
12 Their merchandise is of gold, silver, precious stones, and pearls; of fine linen, purple, silk, and scarlet [stuffs]; all kinds of scented wood, all sorts of articles of ivory, all varieties of objects of costly woods, bronze, iron, and marble; [Ezek. 27:12, 13, 22.]
13 Of cinnamon, spices, incense, ointment *and* perfume, and frankincense, of wine and olive oil, fine flour and wheat; of cattle and sheep, horses and conveyances; and of slaves (the bodies) and souls of men!
14 The ripe fruits *and* delicacies for which your soul longed have gone from you, and all your luxuries *and* dainties, your elegance *and* splendor are lost to you, never again to be recovered *or* experienced!
15 The dealers who handled these articles, who grew wealthy through their business with her, will stand a long way off, in terror of her doom *and* torment, weeping and grieving aloud, and saying,
16 Alas, alas for the great city that was robed in fine linen, in purple and scarlet, bedecked *and* glittering with gold, with precious stones, and with pearls! [Ezek. 27:31, 36.]
17 Because in one [single] hour all the vast wealth has been destroyed (wiped out). And all ship captains *and* pilots, navigators and all who live by seafaring, the crews and all who ply their trade on the sea, stood a long way off, [Isa. 23:14; Ezek. 27:26-30.]
18 And exclaimed as they watched the smoke of her burning, What city could be compared to the great city!
19 And they threw dust on their heads as they wept and grieved, exclaiming, Woe *and* alas, for the great city, where all who had ships on the sea grew rich [through her extravagance] from her great wealth! In one single hour she has been destroyed *and* has become a desert! [Ezek. 27:30-34.]
20 Rejoice (celebrate) over her, O heaven! O saints (people of God) and apostles and prophets, because God has executed vengeance for you upon her! [Isa. 44:23; Jer. 51:48.]
21 Then a single powerful angel took up a boulder like a great millstone and flung it into the sea, crying, With such violence shall Babylon the great city be hurled down to destruction and shall never again be found. [Jer. 51:63, 64; Ezek. 26:21.]

## New International Version

22 The music of harpists and musicians, pipers and
   trumpeters,
   will never be heard in you again.
No worker of any trade
   will ever be found in you again.
The sound of a millstone
   will never be heard in you again.
23 The light of a lamp
   will never shine in you again.
The voice of bridegroom and bride
   will never be heard in you again.
Your merchants were the world's important people.
   By your magic spell all the nations were led astray.
24 In her was found the blood of prophets and of God's
   holy people,
   of all who have been slaughtered on the earth."

### Threefold Hallelujah Over Babylon's Fall

**19** After this I heard what sounded like the roar of a
great multitude in heaven shouting:

"Hallelujah!
Salvation and glory and power belong to our God,
2   for true and just are his judgments.
He has condemned the great prostitute
   who corrupted the earth by her adulteries.
He has avenged on her the blood of his servants."

3 And again they shouted:

"Hallelujah!
The smoke from her goes up for ever and ever."

4 The twenty-four elders and the four living creatures
fell down and worshiped God, who was seated on the
throne. And they cried:

"Amen, Hallelujah!"

5 Then a voice came from the throne, saying:

"Praise our God,
   all you his servants,
you who fear him,
   both great and small!"

6 Then I heard what sounded like a great multitude, like
the roar of rushing waters and like loud peals of thunder,
shouting:

"Hallelujah!
   For our Lord God Almighty reigns.
7 Let us rejoice and be glad
   and give him glory!
For the wedding of the Lamb has come,
   and his bride has made herself ready.
8 Fine linen, bright and clean,
   was given her to wear."

(Fine linen stands for the righteous acts of God's holy people.)

9 Then the angel said to me, "Write this: Blessed are
those who are invited to the wedding supper of the Lamb!"
And he added, "These are the true words of God."

10 At this I fell at his feet to worship him. But he said
to me, "Don't do that! I am a fellow servant with you and
with your brothers and sisters who hold to the testimony
of Jesus. Worship God! For it is the Spirit of prophecy who
bears testimony to Jesus."

## Amplified Bible

22 And the sound of harpists and minstrels and flute
players and trumpeters shall never again be heard in
you, and no skilled artisan of any craft shall ever again be
found in you, and the sound of the millstone shall never
again be heard in you. [Isa. 24:8; Ezek. 26:13.]
23 And never again shall the light of a lamp shine in
you, and the voice of bridegroom and bride shall never be
heard in you again; for your businessmen were the great
*and* prominent men of the earth, and by your magic spells
*and* poisonous charm all nations were led astray (seduced
and deluded).
24 And in her was found the blood of prophets and of
saints, and of all those who have been slain (slaughtered)
on earth. [Jer. 51:49.]

**19** After this I heard what sounded like a mighty
shout of a great crowd in heaven, exclaiming, Hallelujah (praise the Lord)! Salvation and glory (splendor
and majesty) and power (dominion and authority) [be-
long] to our God!
2 Because His judgments (His condemnation and punishment, His sentences of doom) are true *and* sound and
just *and* upright. He has judged (convicted, pronounced
sentence, and doomed) the great *and* notorious harlot
(idolatress) who corrupted *and* demoralized *and* poisoned
the earth with her lewdness *and* adultery (idolatry). And
He has avenged (visited on her the penalty for) the blood
of His servants at her hand. [Deut. 32:43.]
3 And again they shouted, Hallelujah (praise the Lord)!
The smoke of her [burning] shall continue to ascend forever and ever (through the eternities of the eternities).
[Isa. 34:10.]
4 Then the twenty-four elders [of *a* the heavenly San-
hedrin] and the four living creatures fell prostrate and
worshiped [paying divine honors to] God, Who sits on the
throne, saying, Amen! Hallelujah (praise the Lord)!
5 Then from the throne there came a voice, saying,
Praise our God, all you servants of His, you who reverence
Him, both small and great! [Ps. 115:13.]
6 After that I heard what sounded like the shout of a vast
throng, like the boom of many pounding waves, and like
the roar of terrific *and* mighty peals of thunder, exclaiming, Hallelujah (praise the Lord)! For now the Lord our
God the Omnipotent (the All-Ruler) reigns!
7 Let us rejoice and shout for joy [exulting and trium-
phant]! Let us celebrate *and* ascribe to Him glory *and*
honor, for the marriage of the Lamb [at last] has come,
and His bride has prepared herself. [Ps. 118:24.]
8 She has been permitted to dress in fine (radiant) linen,
dazzling and white—for the fine linen is (signifies, represents) the righteousness (the upright, just, and godly
living, deeds, and conduct, and right standing with God)
of the saints (God's holy people).
9 Then [the angel] said to me, Write this down: Blessed
(happy, *b* to be envied) are those who are summoned (invited, called) to the marriage supper of the Lamb. And he
said to me [further], These are the true words (the genuine and exact declarations) of God.
10 Then I fell prostrate at his feet to worship (to pay
divine honors) to him, but he [restrained me] and said,
Refrain! [You must not do that!] I am [only] another servant with you and your brethren who have [accepted and
hold] the testimony borne by Jesus. Worship God! For the
substance (essence) of the truth revealed by Jesus is the
spirit of all prophecy [the vital breath, the inspiration of
all inspired preaching and interpretation of the divine will
and purpose, including both mine and yours].

---

*a* George R. Berry, *Greek-English New Testament Lexicon.* *b* Alexander
Souter, *Pocket Lexicon.*

## New International Version

### The Heavenly Warrior Defeats the Beast

[11]I saw heaven standing open and there before me was a white horse, whose rider is called Faithful and True. With justice he judges and wages war. [12]His eyes are like blazing fire, and on his head are many crowns. He has a name written on him that no one knows but he himself. [13]He is dressed in a robe dipped in blood, and his name is the Word of God. [14]The armies of heaven were following him, riding on white horses and dressed in fine linen, white and clean. [15]Coming out of his mouth is a sharp sword with which to strike down the nations. "He will rule them with an iron scepter."[a] He treads the winepress of the fury of the wrath of God Almighty. [16]On his robe and on his thigh he has this name written:

KING OF KINGS AND LORD OF LORDS.

[17]And I saw an angel standing in the sun, who cried in a loud voice to all the birds flying in midair, "Come, gather together for the great supper of God, [18]so that you may eat the flesh of kings, generals, and the mighty, of horses and their riders, and the flesh of all people, free and slave, great and small."

[19]Then I saw the beast and the kings of the earth and their armies gathered together to wage war against the rider on the horse and his army. [20]But the beast was captured, and with it the false prophet who had performed the signs on its behalf. With these signs he had deluded those who had received the mark of the beast and worshiped its image. The two of them were thrown alive into the fiery lake of burning sulfur. [21]The rest were killed with the sword coming out of the mouth of the rider on the horse, and all the birds gorged themselves on their flesh.

### The Thousand Years

**20** And I saw an angel coming down out of heaven, having the key to the Abyss and holding in his hand a great chain. [2]He seized the dragon, that ancient serpent, who is the devil, or Satan, and bound him for a thousand years. [3]He threw him into the Abyss, and locked and sealed it over him, to keep him from deceiving the nations anymore until the thousand years were ended. After that, he must be set free for a short time.

[4]I saw thrones on which were seated those who had been given authority to judge. And I saw the souls of those who had been beheaded because of their testimony about Jesus and because of the word of God. They[b] had not worshiped the beast or its image and had not received its mark on their foreheads or their hands. They came to life and reigned with Christ a thousand years. [5](The rest of the

## Amplified Bible

[11]After that I saw heaven opened, and behold, a white horse [appeared]! The One Who was riding it is called Faithful (Trustworthy, Loyal, Incorruptible, Steady) and True, and He passes judgment and wages war in righteousness (holiness, justice, and uprightness). [Ezek. 1:1.]

[12]His eyes [blaze] like a flame of fire, and on His head are many kingly crowns (diadems); and He has a title (name) inscribed which He alone knows or can understand. [Dan. 10:6.]

[13]He is dressed in a robe dyed by [a]dipping in blood, and the title by which He is called is The Word of God.

[14]And the troops of heaven, clothed in fine linen, dazzling and clean, followed Him on white horses.

[15]From His mouth goes forth a sharp sword with which He can smite (afflict, strike) the nations; and He will shepherd and control them with a staff (scepter, rod) of iron. He will tread the winepress of the fierceness of the wrath and indignation of God the All-Ruler (the Almighty, the Omnipotent). [Ps. 2:9.]

[16]And on His garment (robe) and on His thigh He has a name (title) inscribed, KING OF KINGS AND LORD OF LORDS. [Deut. 10:17; Dan. 2:47.]

[17]Then I saw a single angel stationed in the sun's [b]light, and with a mighty voice he shouted to all the birds that fly across the sky, Come, gather yourselves together for the great supper of God, [Ezek. 39:4, 17-20.]

[18]That you may feast on the flesh of rulers, the flesh of generals and captains, the flesh of powerful and mighty men, the flesh of horses and their riders, and the flesh of all humanity, both free and slave, both small and great!

[19]Then I saw the beast and the rulers and leaders of the earth with their troops mustered to go into battle and make war against Him Who is mounted on the horse and against His troops.

[20]And the beast was seized and overpowered, and with him the false prophet who in his presence had worked wonders and performed miracles by which he led astray those who had accepted or permitted to be placed upon them the stamp (mark) of the beast and those who paid homage and gave divine honors to his statue. Both of them were hurled alive into the fiery lake that burns and blazes with brimstone.

[21]And the rest were killed with the sword that issues from the mouth of Him Who is mounted on the horse, and all the birds fed ravenously and glutted themselves with their flesh.

**20** Then I saw an angel descending from heaven; he was holding the key of the Abyss (the bottomless pit) and a great chain was in his hand.

[2]And he gripped and overpowered the dragon, that old serpent [of primeval times], who is the devil and Satan, and [securely] bound him for a thousand years.

[3]Then he hurled him into the Abyss (the bottomless pit) and closed it and sealed it above him, so that he should no longer lead astray and deceive and seduce the nations until the thousand years were at an end. After that he must be liberated for a short time.

[4]Then I saw thrones, and sitting on them were those to whom authority to act as judges and to pass sentence was entrusted. Also I saw the souls of those who had been slain with axes [beheaded] for their witnessing to Jesus and [for preaching and testifying] for the Word of God, and who had refused to pay homage to the beast or his statue and had not accepted his mark or permitted it to be stamped on their foreheads or on their hands. And they lived again and ruled with Christ (the Messiah) a thousand years. [Dan. 7:9, 22, 27.]

---

[a] 15 Psalm 2:9    [b] 4 Or God; I also saw those who

[a] Some ancient manuscripts read "sprinkled with blood."    [b] Joseph Thayer, *A Greek-English Lexicon*.

## New International Version

dead did not come to life until the thousand years were ended.) This is the first resurrection. ⁶Blessed and holy are those who share in the first resurrection. The second death has no power over them, but they will be priests of God and of Christ and will reign with him for a thousand years.

### The Judgment of Satan

⁷When the thousand years are over, Satan will be released from his prison ⁸and will go out to deceive the nations in the four corners of the earth—Gog and Magog—and to gather them for battle. In number they are like the sand on the seashore. ⁹They marched across the breadth of the earth and surrounded the camp of God's people, the city he loves. But fire came down from heaven and devoured them. ¹⁰And the devil, who deceived them, was thrown into the lake of burning sulfur, where the beast and the false prophet had been thrown. They will be tormented day and night for ever and ever.

### The Judgment of the Dead

¹¹Then I saw a great white throne and him who was seated on it. The earth and the heavens fled from his presence, and there was no place for them. ¹²And I saw the dead, great and small, standing before the throne, and books were opened. Another book was opened, which is the book of life. The dead were judged according to what they had done as recorded in the books. ¹³The sea gave up the dead that were in it, and death and Hades gave up the dead that were in them, and each person was judged according to what they had done. ¹⁴Then death and Hades were thrown into the lake of fire. The lake of fire is the second death. ¹⁵Anyone whose name was not found written in the book of life was thrown into the lake of fire.

### A New Heaven and a New Earth

**21** Then I saw "a new heaven and a new earth,"ᵃ for the first heaven and the first earth had passed away, and there was no longer any sea. ²I saw the Holy City, the new Jerusalem, coming down out of heaven from God, prepared as a bride beautifully dressed for her husband. ³And I heard a loud voice from the throne saying, "Look! God's dwelling place is now among the people, and he will dwell with them. They will be his people, and God himself will be with them and be their God. ⁴'He will wipe every tear from their eyes. There will be no more death'ᵇ or mourning or crying or pain, for the old order of things has passed away."

⁵He who was seated on the throne said, "I am making everything new!" Then he said, "Write this down, for these words are trustworthy and true."

⁶He said to me: "It is done. I am the Alpha and the Ome-

## Amplified Bible

⁵The remainder of the dead were not restored to life again until the thousand years were completed. This is the first resurrection.

⁶Blessed (happy, ᵃto be envied) and holy (spiritually whole, of unimpaired innocence and proved virtue) is the person who takes part (shares) in the first resurrection! Over them the second death exerts no power or authority, but they shall be ministers of God and of Christ (the Messiah), and they shall rule along with Him a thousand years.

⁷And when the thousand years are completed, Satan will be released from his place of confinement,

⁸And he will go forth to deceive and seduce and lead astray the nations which are in the four quarters of the earth—Gog and Magog—to muster them for war; their number is like the sand of the sea. [Ezek. 38:2, 9, 15, 22.]

⁹And they swarmed up over the broad plain of the earth and encircled the fortress (camp) of God's people (the saints) and the beloved city; but fire descended from heaven and consumed them. [II Kings 1:10-12; Ezek. 38:2, 22.]

¹⁰Then the devil who had led them astray [deceiving and seducing them] was hurled into the fiery lake of burning brimstone, where the beast and false prophet were; and they will be tormented day and night forever and ever (through the ages of the ages).

¹¹Then I saw a great white throne and the One Who was seated upon it, from Whose presence and from the sight of Whose face earth and sky fled away, and no place was found for them.

¹²I [also] saw the dead, great and small; they stood before the throne, and books were opened. Then another book was opened, which is [the Book] of Life. And the dead were judged (sentenced) by what they had done [ᵇtheir whole way of feeling and acting, their aims and endeavors] in accordance with what was recorded in the books.

¹³And the sea delivered up the dead who were in it, death and Hades (ᶜthe state of death or disembodied existence) surrendered the dead in them, and all were tried and their cases determined by what they had done [according to their motives, aims, and works].

¹⁴Then death and Hades (ᶜthe state of death or disembodied existence) were thrown into the lake of fire. This is the second death, the lake of fire.

¹⁵And if anyone's [name] was not found recorded in the Book of Life, he was hurled into the lake of fire.

**21** Then I saw a new ᵇsky (heaven) and a new earth, for the former ᵇsky and the former earth had passed away (vanished), and there no longer existed any sea. [Isa. 65:17; 66:22.]

²And I saw the holy city, the new Jerusalem, descending out of heaven from God, all arrayed like a bride beautified and adorned for her husband;

³Then I heard a mighty voice from the throne and I perceived its distinct words, saying, See! The abode of God is with men, and He will live (encamp, tent) among them; and they shall be His people, and God shall personally be with them and be their God. [Ezek. 37:27.]

⁴God will wipe away every tear from their eyes; and death shall be no more, neither shall there be anguish (sorrow and mourning) nor grief nor pain any more, for the old conditions and the former order of things have passed away. [Isa. 25:8; 35:10.]

⁵And He Who is seated on the throne said, See! I make all things new. Also He said, Record this, for these sayings are faithful (accurate, incorruptible, and trustworthy) and true (genuine). [Isa. 43:19.]

⁶And He [further] said to me, It is done! I am the Alpha and the Omega, the Beginning and the End. To the thirsty

---

ᵃ Alexander Souter, *Pocket Lexicon.* ᵇ Joseph Thayer, *A Greek-English Lexicon.* ᶜ James Orr et al., eds., *The International Standard Bible Encyclopedia.*

ᵃ 1 Isaiah 65:17   ᵇ 4 Isaiah 25:8

## New International Version

ga, the Beginning and the End. To the thirsty I will give water without cost from the spring of the water of life. [7]Those who are victorious will inherit all this, and I will be their God and they will be my children. [8]But the cowardly, the unbelieving, the vile, the murderers, the sexually immoral, those who practice magic arts, the idolaters and all liars—they will be consigned to the fiery lake of burning sulfur. This is the second death."

### The New Jerusalem, the Bride of the Lamb

[9]One of the seven angels who had the seven bowls full of the seven last plagues came and said to me, "Come, I will show you the bride, the wife of the Lamb." [10]And he carried me away in the Spirit to a mountain great and high, and showed me the Holy City, Jerusalem, coming down out of heaven from God. [11]It shone with the glory of God, and its brilliance was like that of a very precious jewel, like a jasper, clear as crystal. [12]It had a great, high wall with twelve gates, and with twelve angels at the gates. On the gates were written the names of the twelve tribes of Israel. [13]There were three gates on the east, three on the north, three on the south and three on the west. [14]The wall of the city had twelve foundations, and on them were the names of the twelve apostles of the Lamb.

[15]The angel who talked with me had a measuring rod of gold to measure the city, its gates and its walls. [16]The city was laid out like a square, as long as it was wide. He measured the city with the rod and found it to be 12,000 stadia[a] in length, and as wide and high as it is long. [17]The angel measured the wall using human measurement, and it was 144 cubits[b] thick.[c] [18]The wall was made of jasper, and the city of pure gold, as pure as glass. [19]The foundations of the city walls were decorated with every kind of precious stone. The first foundation was jasper, the second sapphire, the third agate, the fourth emerald, [20]the fifth onyx, the sixth ruby, the seventh chrysolite, the eighth beryl, the ninth topaz, the tenth turquoise, the eleventh jacinth, and the twelfth amethyst.[d] [21]The twelve gates were twelve pearls, each gate made of a single pearl. The great street of the city was of gold, as pure as transparent glass.

[22]I did not see a temple in the city, because the Lord God Almighty and the Lamb are its temple. [23]The city does not need the sun or the moon to shine on it, for the glory of God gives it light, and the Lamb is its lamp. [24]The nations will walk by its light, and the kings of the earth will bring their splendor into it. [25]On no day will its gates ever be shut, for there will be no night there. [26]The glory

## Amplified Bible

I [Myself] will give water without price from the fountain (springs) of the water of Life. [Isa. 55:1.]

[7]He who is victorious shall inherit all these things, and I will be God to him and he shall be My son.

[8]But as for the cowards *and* the ignoble *and* the contemptible *and* the cravenly lacking in courage *and* the cowardly submissive, and as for the unbelieving and faithless, and as for the depraved and defiled with abominations, and as for murderers and the lewd *and* adulterous and the practicers of magic arts and the idolaters (those who give supreme devotion to anyone or anything other than God) and all liars (those who knowingly convey untruth by word or deed)—[all of these shall have] their part in the lake that blazes with fire and brimstone. This is the second death. [Isa. 30:33.]

[9]Then one of the seven angels who had the seven bowls filled with the seven final plagues (afflictions, calamities) came and spoke to me. He said, Come with me! I will show you the bride, the Lamb's wife.

[10]Then in the Spirit He conveyed me away to a vast and lofty mountain and exhibited to me the holy (hallowed, consecrated) city of Jerusalem descending out of heaven from God, [Ezek. 40:2.]

[11]Clothed in God's glory [in all its splendor and radiance]. The luster of it resembled a rare *and* most precious jewel, like jasper, shining clear as crystal.

[12]It had a massive and high wall with twelve [large] gates, and at the gates [there were stationed] twelve angels, and [on the gates] the names of the twelve tribes of the sons of Israel were written: [Exod. 28:21; Ezek. 48:30-35.]

[13]On the east side three gates, on the north side three gates, on the south side three gates, and on the west side three gates.

[14]And the wall of the city had twelve foundation [stones], and on them the twelve names of the twelve apostles of the Lamb.

[15]And he who spoke to me had a golden measuring reed (rod) to measure the city and its gates and its wall. [Ezek. 40:5.]

[16]The city lies in a square, its length being the same as its width. And he measured the city with his reed—12,000 stadia (about 1,500 miles); its length and width and height are the same.

[17]He measured its wall also—144 cubits (about 72 yards) by a man's measure [[a]of a cubit from his elbow to his third fingertip], which is [the measure] of the angel.

[18]The wall was built of jasper, while the city [itself was of] pure gold, clear and transparent like glass.

[19]The foundation [stones] of the wall of the city were ornamented with all of the precious stones. The first foundation [stone] was jasper, the second sapphire, the third chalcedony (or white agate), the fourth emerald, [Isa. 54:11, 12.]

[20]The fifth onyx, the sixth sardius, the seventh chrysolite, the eighth beryl, the ninth topaz, the tenth chrysoprase, the eleventh jacinth, the twelfth amethyst.

[21]And the twelve gates were twelve pearls, each separate gate being built of one solid pearl. And the main street (the broadway) of the city was of gold as pure *and* translucent as glass.

[22]I saw no temple in the city, for the Lord God Omnipotent [Himself] and the Lamb [Himself] are its temple.

[23]And the city has no need of the sun nor of the moon to give light to it, for the splendor *and* radiance (glory) of God illuminate it, and the Lamb is its lamp. [Isa. 24:23; 60:1, 19.]

[24]The nations shall walk by its light and the rulers *and* leaders of the earth shall bring into it their glory.

[25]And its gates shall never be closed by day, and there shall be no night there. [Isa. 60:11.]

---

[a] 16 That is, about 1,400 miles or about 2,200 kilometers   [b] 17 That is, about 200 feet or about 65 meters   [c] 17 Or *high*   [d] 20 The precise identification of some of these precious stones is uncertain.

[a] Adam Clarke, *The Holy Bible with A Commentary.*

## New International Version

and honor of the nations will be brought into it. ²⁷Nothing impure will ever enter it, nor will anyone who does what is shameful or deceitful, but only those whose names are written in the Lamb's book of life.

### Eden Restored

**22** Then the angel showed me the river of the water of life, as clear as crystal, flowing from the throne of God and of the Lamb ²down the middle of the great street of the city. On each side of the river stood the tree of life, bearing twelve crops of fruit, yielding its fruit every month. And the leaves of the tree are for the healing of the nations. ³No longer will there be any curse. The throne of God and of the Lamb will be in the city, and his servants will serve him. ⁴They will see his face, and his name will be on their foreheads. ⁵There will be no more night. They will not need the light of a lamp or the light of the sun, for the Lord God will give them light. And they will reign for ever and ever.

### John and the Angel

⁶The angel said to me, "These words are trustworthy and true. The Lord, the God who inspires the prophets, sent his angel to show his servants the things that must soon take place."

⁷"Look, I am coming soon! Blessed is the one who keeps the words of the prophecy written in this scroll."

⁸I, John, am the one who heard and saw these things. And when I had heard and seen them, I fell down to worship at the feet of the angel who had been showing them to me. ⁹But he said to me, "Don't do that! I am a fellow servant with you and with your fellow prophets and with all who keep the words of this scroll. Worship God!"

¹⁰Then he told me, "Do not seal up the words of the prophecy of this scroll, because the time is near. ¹¹Let the one who does wrong continue to do wrong; let the vile person continue to be vile; let the one who does right continue to do right; and let the holy person continue to be holy."

### Epilogue: Invitation and Warning

¹²"Look, I am coming soon! My reward is with me, and I will give to each person according to what they have done. ¹³I am the Alpha and the Omega, the First and the Last, the Beginning and the End.

¹⁴"Blessed are those who wash their robes, that they may have the right to the tree of life and may go through the gates into the city. ¹⁵Outside are the dogs, those who practice magic arts, the sexually immoral, the murderers, the idolaters and everyone who loves and practices falsehood.

## Amplified Bible

²⁶They shall bring the glory (the splendor and majesty) and the honor of the nations into it.

²⁷But nothing that defiles or profanes or is ᵃunwashed shall ever enter it, nor anyone who commits abominations (unclean, detestable, morally repugnant things) or practices falsehood, but only those whose names are recorded in the Lamb's Book of Life.

**22** Then he showed me the river whose waters give life, sparkling like crystal, flowing out from the throne of God and of the Lamb

²Through the middle of the broadway of the city; also, on either side of the river was the tree of life with its twelve varieties of fruit, yielding each month its fresh crop; and the leaves of the tree were for the healing and the restoration of the nations. [Gen. 2:9.]

³There shall no longer exist there anything that is accursed (detestable, foul, offensive, impure, hateful, or horrible). But the throne of God and of the Lamb shall be in it, and His servants shall worship Him [pay divine honors to Him and do Him holy service]. [Zech. 14:21.]

⁴They shall see His face, and His name shall be on their foreheads. [Ps. 17:15.]

⁵And there shall be no more night; they have no need for lamplight or sunlight, for the Lord God will illuminate them and be their light, and they shall reign [as kings] forever and ever (through the eternities of the eternities).

⁶And he [of the seven angels further] said to me, These statements are reliable (worthy of confidence) and genuine (true). And the Lord, the God of the spirits of the prophets, has sent His messenger (angel) to make known and exhibit to His servants what must soon come to pass.

⁷And behold, I am coming speedily. Blessed (happy and ᵃto be envied) is he who observes and lays to heart and keeps the truths of the prophecy (the predictions, consolations, and warnings) contained in this [little] book.

⁸And I, John, am he who heard and witnessed these things. And when I heard and saw them, I fell prostrate before the feet of the messenger (angel) who showed them to me, to worship him.

⁹But he said to me, Refrain! [You must not do that!] I am [only] a fellow servant along with yourself and with your brethren the prophets and with those who are mindful of and practice [the truths contained in] the messages of this book. Worship God!

¹⁰And he [further] told me, Do not seal up the words of the prophecy of this book and make no secret of them, for the time ᵇwhen things are brought to a crisis and the period of their fulfillment is near.

¹¹He who is unrighteous (unjust, wicked), let him be unrighteous still; and he who is filthy (vile, impure), let him be filthy still; and he who is righteous (just, upright, in right standing with God), let him do right still; and he who is holy, let him be holy still. [Dan. 12:10.]

¹²Behold, I am coming soon, and I shall bring My wages and rewards with Me, to repay and render to each one just what his own actions and his own work merit. [Isa. 40:10; Jer. 17:10.]

¹³I am the Alpha and the Omega, the First and the Last (the Before all and the End of all). [Isa. 44:6; 48:12.]

¹⁴Blessed (happy and ᵃto be envied) are those who cleanse their garments, that they may have the authority and right to [approach] the tree of life and to enter through the gates into the city. [Gen. 2:9; 3:22, 24.]

¹⁵[But] without are the dogs and those who practice sorceries (magic arts) and impurity [the lewd, adulterers] and the murderers and idolaters and everyone who loves and deals in falsehood (untruth, error, deception, cheating).

---

ᵃ Alexander Souter, *Pocket Lexicon*.  ᵇ Joseph Thayer, *A Greek-English Lexicon*.

## New International Version

[16]"I, Jesus, have sent my angel to give you[a] this testimony for the churches. I am the Root and the Offspring of David, and the bright Morning Star."

[17]The Spirit and the bride say, "Come!" And let the one who hears say, "Come!" Let the one who is thirsty come; and let the one who wishes take the free gift of the water of life.

[18]I warn everyone who hears the words of the prophecy of this scroll: If anyone adds anything to them, God will add to that person the plagues described in this scroll. [19]And if anyone takes words away from this scroll of prophecy, God will take away from that person any share in the tree of life and in the Holy City, which are described in this scroll.

[20]He who testifies to these things says, "Yes, I am coming soon."

Amen. Come, Lord Jesus.

[21]The grace of the Lord Jesus be with God's people. Amen.

## Amplified Bible

[16]I, Jesus, have sent My messenger (angel) to you to witness *and* to give you assurance of these things for the churches (assemblies). I am the Root (the Source) and the Offspring of David, the radiant *and* brilliant Morning Star. [Isa. 11:1, 10.]

[17]The [Holy] Spirit and the bride (the church, the true Christians) say, Come! And let him who is listening say, Come! And let everyone come who is thirsty [who is painfully conscious of his need [a]of those things by which the soul is refreshed, supported, and strengthened]; and whoever [earnestly] desires to do it, let him come, take, appropriate, *and* drink the water of Life without cost. [Isa. 55:1.]

[18]I [personally solemnly] warn everyone who listens to the statements of the prophecy [the [a]predictions and the consolations and admonitions pertaining to them] in this book: If anyone shall add anything to them, God will add *and* lay upon him the plagues (the afflictions and the calamities) that are recorded *and* described in this book.

[19]And if anyone cancels *or* takes away from the statements of the book of this prophecy [these [a]predictions relating to Christ's kingdom and its speedy triumph, together with the consolations and admonitions or warnings pertaining to them], God will cancel *and* take away from him his share in the tree of life and in the city of holiness (purity and hallowedness), which are described *and* promised in this book.

[20]He Who gives this warning *and* affirms *and* testifies to these things says, Yes (it is true). [Surely] I am coming quickly (swiftly, speedily). Amen (so let it be)! Yes, come, Lord Jesus!

[21]The grace (blessing and favor) of the Lord Jesus *Christ (the Messiah)* be [b]with all the saints (God's holy people, [a]those set apart for God, to be, as it were, exclusively His). Amen (so let it be)!

[a] Joseph Thayer, *A Greek-English Lexicon.*  [b] Some manuscripts have "be with all," while others have "be with the saints." .

# Table of Weights and Measures

| | Biblical Unit | Approximate American Equivalent | Approximate Metric Equivalent |
|---|---|---|---|
| **Weights** | talent (60 minas) | 75 pounds | 34 kilograms |
| | mina (50 shekels) | 1 1/4 pounds | 560 grams |
| | shekel (2 bekas) | 2/5 ounce | 11.5 grams |
| | pim (2/3 shekel) | 1/4 ounce | 7.8 grams |
| | beka (10 gerahs) | 1/5 ounce | 5.7 grams |
| | gerah | 1/50 ounce | 0.6 gram |
| | daric | 1/3 ounce | 8.4 grams |
| **Length** | cubit | 18 inches | 45 centimeters |
| | span | 9 inches | 23 centimeters |
| | handbreadth | 3 inches | 7.5 centimeters |
| | stadion (pl. stadia) | 600 feet | 183 meters |
| **Capacity** | | | |
| *Dry Measure* | cor [homer] (10 ephahs) | 6 bushels | 220 liters |
| | lethek (5 ephahs) | 3 bushels | 110 liters |
| | ephah (10 omers) | 3/5 bushel | 22 liters |
| | seah (1/3 ephah) | 7 quarts | 7.5 liters |
| | omer (1/10 ephah) | 2 quarts | 2 liters |
| | cab (1/18 ephah) | 1 quart | 1 liter |
| *Liquid Measure* | bath (1 ephah) | 6 gallons | 22 liters |
| | hin (1/6 bath) | 1 gallon | 3.8 liters |
| | log (1/72 bath) | 1/3 quart | 0.3 liter |

The figures of the table are calculated on the basis of a shekel equaling 11.5 grams, a cubit equaling 18 inches and an ephah equaling 22 liters. The quart referred to is either a dry quart (slightly larger than a liter) or a liquid quart (slightly smaller than a liter), whichever is applicable. The ton referred to in the footnotes is the American ton of 2,000 pounds. These weights are calculated relative to the particular commodity involved. Accordingly, the same measure of capacity in the text may be converted into different weights in the footnotes.

This table is based upon the best available information, but it is not intended to be mathematically precise; like the measurement equivalents in the footnotes, it merely gives approximate amounts and distances. Weights and measures differed somewhat at various times and places in the ancient world. There is uncertainty particularly about the ephah and the bath; further discoveries may shed more light on these units of capacity.